FUNDING SOURCES FOR COMMUNITY AND ECONOMIC DEVELOPMENT

14th Edition

Schoolhouse Partners LLC
West Lafayette, Indiana

Why 'Partners'? Partners work together as a team, with each person contributing different skills and expressing his or her individual interests and opinions to the unity and efficiency of the group in order to achieve common goals. Our aim is to make worthwhile resources available to you so that you and your institution or organization can and will achieve those goals.

Copyright © 2014 by Schoolhouse Partners LLC
Schoolhouse Partners, 1281 Win Hentschel Blvd, West Lafayette, IN 47906
www.schoolhousepartners.net
Published 1995, 14th edition 2014

All rights reserved. No part of this publication may be reproduced or transmitted
in any form or by any means, electronic or mechanical, including
photocopying, recording, or by any information storage and
retrieval system, without permission in writing
from Schoolhouse Partners.

Printed and bound in the United States of America

ISBN 978-0-9860357-5-3
0-9860357-5-0

Table of Contents

Introduction iv

How to Use This Directory v

Government and Organization Acronyms viii

Grant Programs 1

Subject Index 799

Program Type Index 1019

Geographic Index 1141

Introduction

For over three decades the GRANTS Database and its print complements, including the annual *Funding Sources for Community and Economic Development*, have provided the grant seeking community with funding sources to enrich or improve the lives of community residents. Funding ranges from capital construction to social service programs. Community development is based on the premise that the most effective and sustainable development is driven at the local level by residents working through governmental agencies, foundations, citizen action groups, and nonprofit organizations.

With local funding sources declining and funding amounts diminishing, the struggle to fund community-based projects is immense. For decades the GRANTS Database has provided those seeking funding for community and economic development projects, health care and humanities, research, and performing arts programs with up-to-date information.

Funding Sources for Community and Economic Development

Funding Sources for Community and Economic Development features more than 5,150 listings that support programs and projects initiated by organizations and individuals on national, state, and local levels to be implemented within communities to develop resources that enrich and improve the lives of community residents. Listings in the main section of *Funding Sources* contain annotations describing each program's focuses and goals, program requirements explaining eligibility, funding amounts, deadlines, *Catalog of Federal Domestic Assistance* program number (for U.S. government programs only), sponsor name and address, contact information, and the sponsor's Internet Web address. Grantseekers with access to the Internet can use the addresses to locate further information about the organizations and their application procedures. Internet addresses are also provided, when available, within listings. Some of the grant programs listed in the main section have geographic restrictions for applicants.

The following people have devoted a great deal of patience, hard work and thought to keep this project and the database an informative service for the user. It is especially important to mention the GrantSelect team – Louis S. Schafer, Ed.S., and Anita Schafer – for their diligent research, editorial work, development and assignment of index terms, and production – as well as all Schoolhouse Partners staff who contribute to the GRANTS effort.

Indexes. The Subject Index of this *Funding Sources* lists all program titles—with accession numbers—under their applicable subject terms. Other indexes follow, including the Grants by Program Type Index, which lists 44 program categories, such as Basic Research, Fellowships, Travel Grants, etc., with the grants that fall within their scope; and the Geographic Index, which lists programs that have state, regional, or international focus. See How to Use This Directory on pages v-vii for sample index entries.

Using *Funding Sources* for Grantseeking

By using this edition of *Funding Sources for Community and Economic Development*, grantseekers can match the needs of their particular programs with those sponsors offering funding in the grantseekers' area of interest. The information listed here is meant to eliminate the costs incurred by both grantseekers and grantmakers when inappropriate proposals are submitted for a sponsor's funding program. However, because the GRANTS Database is updated on a daily basis, with program listings continually added, deleted, and revised, grantseekers using this edition of *Funding Sources* may also search the GRANTS database online through *GrantSelect* (www.grantselect.com).

All new and revised information within *Funding Sources for Community and Economic Development* has been taken from (1) the sponsor's updated of previously published program statements included in earlier editions of GRANTS publications, (2) questionnaires sent to sponsors whose programs were not listed in previous editions, or (3) other materials published by the sponsor and furnished to Schoolhouse Partners. Updated information for U.S. government programs includes new and revised program information published in the *Federal Register*; the latest edition of the *Catalog of Federal Domestic Assistance*; the *NIH Guide*, published weekly by the National Institutes of Health; and the *NSF E-Bulletin*, a monthly publication of the National Science Foundation. Included in this edition are identifying document numbers from the NIH and NSF publications. Located at the ends of the program descriptions in certain entries, the numbers indicated the ongoing NIH program number (PA) or the request for applications number (RFA). For programs of the National Science Foundation, the *NSF Bulletin* number appears. This information will help users identify the programs when seeking additional information from program staff.

While Schoolhouse Partners has made every effort to verify that all information is both accurate and current within the confines of format and scope, the publisher does not assume and hereby disclaims any liability to any party for loss or damages caused by errors or omissions in this *Funding Sources*, whether such errors or missions result from accident, negligence, or any other cause. Anyone having questions regarding the content, format, or any other aspect of the *Funding Sources for Community and Economic Development 2014*, GrantSelect, or the GRANTS Database should contact the Editors, GRANTS, Schoolhouse Partners or editor@schoolhousepartners.net.

How to Use This Directory

The *Funding Sources for Community and Economic Development* is designed to allow the user quick and easy access to information regarding funding programs in a researcher's specific area of interest. This *Funding Sources* is composed of a main section, Grant Programs, which lists grant programs in alphabetical order, and three indexes: the Subject Index, the Grants by Program Type Index, and the Geographic Index.

GRANT PROGRAMS

Each listing in this section consists of the following elements: an annotation describing each program's focus and goals, requirements explaining eligibility, funding amounts, application and renewal dates, sponsor information, contact information, and Internet address.

GRANT TITLE — Paul G. Allen Family Foundation Grants   4298 — **ACCESSION NUMBER**

The single foundation, created through the consolidation of Allen's six previous foundations (The Allen Foundation for the Arts, The Paul G. Allen Charitable Foundation, The Paul G. Allen Foundation for Medical Research, The Paul G. Allen Forest Protection Foundation, The Allen Foundation for Music, and The Paul G. Allen Virtual Education Foundation), will continue to focus on the Allen family's philanthropic interests in the areas of arts and culture, youth engagement, community development and social change, and scientific and technological innovation. The Arts and Culture Program fosters creativity and promotes critical thinking by helping strong arts organizations become sustainable and supporting projects that feature innovative and diverse artistic forms. — **GRANT DESCRIPTION**

The Youth Engagement Program improves the way young people learn by supporting organizations that use innovative teaching strategies and provide opportunities for children to address issues relevant to their lives. The Community Development and Social Change Program promotes individual and community development by supporting initiatives and organizations that provide access to resources and opportunities. The Scientific and Technological Innovation Program advances promising scientific and technology research that has the potential to enhance understanding and stewardship of the world in which we live. Organizations may only receive one grant per year. Organizations must not have any delinquent final reports due to any of the Paul G. Allen Foundations for previous grants. Grantseekers are encouraged to apply through the online application process, where basic organizational and project information will be requested. Guidelines are available online.

REQUIREMENTS — *Requirements* 501(c)3 tax-exempt organizations, status from the Internal Revenue government entities, and IRS-recognized tribes are eligible. Eligible organizations must be located in, or serving populations of, the Pacific Northwest, which includes Alaska, Idaho, Montana, Oregon, and Washington.

RESTRICTIONS — *Restrictions* In general, the foundation will not consider requests for general fund drives, annual appeals, or federated campaigns; special events or sponsorships; direct grants, scholarships, or loans for the benefit of specific individuals; projects of organizations whose policies or practices discriminate on the basis of race, ethnic origin, sex, creed, or sexual orientation; contributions to sectarian or religious organizations whose principle activity is for the benefit of their own members or adherents; loans or debt retirement; projects that will benefit the students of a single school; general operating support for ongoing activities; or projects not aligned with the foundation's specified program areas. 509(a) private foundations are ineligible.

APPLICATION/ DUE DATE — *Date(s) Application Is Due* Mar 31; Sep 30.

Contact Grants Administrator, (206) 342-2030; fax: (206) 342-3030; email: info@pgafamilyfoundation.org — **CONTACT**

INTERNET ADDRESS — *Internet* http://www.pgafamilyfoundation.org

Sponsor Paul G. Allen Family Foundation — **SPONSOR INFORMATION**
505 Fifth Ave S, Ste 900
Seattle, WA 98104

SUBJECT INDEX

The most effective way to access specific funding programs is through the Subject Index. This index lists the subject terms with applicable grants program titles – and their accession numbers – alphabetically under each term. Terms were assigned to target the specific area of research designated in the description of each program. Cross-references are used to link subjects and assist the user in finding specific grant information.

Following are general guidelines that can make your search of this index more successful. First, check under the specific topic of interest rather than a more general term. For instance, if you are interested in chemical engineering, look under "Chemical Engineering" rather than "Engineering." Items indexed under "Engineering" indicate funding in broad areas of engineering.

Use general headings when you want grants covering broader areas or if you can't find a specific topic. For example, many grants list funding for humanities research, health programs, or science and technology. To find these grants use such headings as "Humanities," "Medical Programs," "Science," or "Technology." For additional grant information on more specific humanities research opportunities, such as in American History or Cultural Anthropology, also check under the topics "United States History" and "Anthropology, Cultural."

Many of the grant programs provide funding for research-related scholarships, faculty fellowships, dissertations, undergraduate education, conferences, or internships. If grant funds are designated for specific disciplines, you will find the items under the specific subject. Scholarships and fellowships are also listed under the terms "Native American Education," "African Americans (Student Support)," "Hispanic Education," "Minority Education," and "Women's Education."

Grants concerning study of a particular country are listed under the name of the country. Grants concerning the history, literature, art and language of a country are listed under the name of the country also, e.g., "Chinese Art" and "Chinese Language/Literature."

SUBJECT TERM ──────── **Education**
  A.L. Mailman Family Foundation Grants, 5
  AAAS Science & Technology Policy Fellowships - Health, Education & Human Services, 22
  AARP Andrus Foundation Grants, 104
  Abbott Laboratories Fund Grants, 125
  ACIE Host University Edmund S. Muskie/Freedom Support Act Graduate Fellowships, 156
  ACT Awards, 189
  Akonadi Foundation Anti-Racism Grants, 351 ──────── **PROGRAM TITLE**
  Akron Community Foundation Grants, 352
  Albert and Margaret Alkek Foundation Grants, 370
  Albuquerque Community Foundation Grants, 379
  Alcoa Foundation Grants, 380
  Alcon Foundation Grants Program, 382

GEOGRAPHIC INDEX

This index lists programs that have state, regional, or international geographic focus. The Geographic Index is arranged by state, followed by Canadian programs, then by international programs by country, and lists grant program titles and their corresponding accession numbers.

COUNTRY ──────── **United States**
  Alabama ────────────────────────────────── **STATE**
    3M Fndn Grants, 2
    Alabama Humanities Fndn Grants Program, 368
    Arkema Inc. Fndn Science Teachers Program, 705
    CDC Injury Control Research Centers Grants, 1198
PROGRAM TITLE ──── DOE Experimental Program to Stimulate Competitive Research (EPSCoR), 1653
    Hill Crest Fndn Grants, 2293
    Linn-Henley Charitable Trust Grants, 2777
    NOAA Community-Based Restoration Program (CRP) Grants, 3843
    Southern Company's Longleaf Pine Reforestation Fund, 4726

PROGRAM TYPE INDEX

This index is broken into 44 categories according to the type of program funded:

- Adult Basic Education
- Adult/Family Literacy Training
- Awards/Prizes
- Basic Research
- Building Construction and/or Renovation
- Capital Campaigns
- Centers: Research/Demonstration/Service
- Citizenship Instruction
- Community Development
- Consulting/Visiting Personnel
- Cultural Outreach
- Curriculum Development/Teacher Training
- Demonstration Grants
- Development (Institutional/Departmental)
- Dissertation/Thesis Research Support
- Educational Programs
- Emergency Programs
- Endowments
- Environmental Programs
- Exchange Programs
- Exhibitions, Collections, Performances, Video/Film Production
- Faculty/Professional Development
- Fellowships
- General Operating Support
- Graduate Assistantships
- Grants to Individuals
- International Exchange Programs
- International Grants
- Job Training/Adult Vocational Programs
- Land Acquisition
- Matching/Challenge Funds
- Materials/Equipment Acquisition (Computers, Books, Tapes, etc.)
- Preservation/Restoration
- Professorships
- Publishing/Editing/Translating
- Religious Programs
- Scholarships
- Seed Grants
- Service Delivery Programs
- Symposia, Conferences, Workshops, Seminars
- Technical Assistance
- Training Programs/Internships
- Travel Grants
- Vocational Education

Government and Organization Acronyms

AAAAI	American Academy of Allergy Asthma and Immunology	ANS	American Numismatic Society
AAAS	American Association for the Advancement of Science	AOA	American Osteopathic Association
		AOCS	American Oil Chemists' Society
AACAP	American Academy of Child and Adolescent Psychiatry	APA	American Psychological Association
		APAP	Association of Performing Arts Presenters
AACN	American Association of Critical Care Nurses	APEAL	Asian Pacific Partners for Empowerment and Leadership
AACR	American Association of Cancer Research	APS	Arizona Public Service
AAFCS	American Association of Family and Consumer Sciences	APSA	American Political Science Association
		ARIT	American Research Institute in Turkey
AAF	American Architectural Foundation	ARO	Army Research Office
AAFP	American Academy of Family Physicians Foundation	ASA	American Statistical Association
		ASCSA	American School of Classical Studies at Athens
AAFPRS	American Academy of Facial Plastic and Reconstructive Surgery	ASECS	American Society for Eighteenth-Century Studies
		ASF	American-Scandinavian Foundation
AAP	American Academy of Pediatrics	ASHA	American Speech-Language-Hearing Association
AAR	American Academy in Rome	ASHRAE	American Society of Heating, Refrigerating, and Air Conditioning Engineers
AAS	American Antiquarian Society		
AASL	American Association of School Libraries	ASME	American Society of Mechanical Engineers
AAUW	American Association of University Women	ASNS	American Society for Nutritional Sciences
ABA	American Bar Association	ASPRS	American Society of Photogrammetry and Remote Sensing
ACC	Asian Cultural Council		
ACF	Administration on Children, Youth and Families	ASTA	American String Teachers Association
ACLS	American Council of Learned Societies	ATA	Alberta Teachers Association
ACM	Association for Computing Machinery	AWHONN	Association of Women's Health, Obstetric, and Neonatal Nurses
ACE	American Council on Education		
ACMP	Amateur Chamber Music Players	AWU	Associated Western Universities
ACS	American Cancer Society	AWWA	American Water Works Association
ADA	American Diabetes Association	BA	British Academy
ADHF	American Digestive Health Foundation	BBF	Barbara Bush Foundation
AF	Arthritis Foundation	BCBS	Blue Cross Blue Shield
AFAR	American Federation for Aging Research	BCBSM	Blue Cross Blue Shield of Michigan
AFOSR	Air Force Office of Scientific Research	BCBSNC	Blue Cross Blue Shield of North Carolina
AFUD	American Foundation for Urologic Disease	BWF	Burroughs Wellcome Fund
AFUW	Australian Federation of University Women	CBIE	Canadian Bureau for International Education
AGS	American Geriatrics Society	CCF	Catholic Community Foundation
AHA	American Heart Association	CCF	Common Council Foundation
AHAF	American Health Assistance Foundation	CCFF	Canadian Cystic Fibrosis Foundation
AFHMR	Alberta Heritage Foundation for Medical Research	CCFF	Christopher Columbus Fellowship Foundation
AHRQ	Agency for Healthcare Research and Quality	CDC	Centers for Disease Control and Prevention
AICR	American Institute for Cancer Research	CDECD	Connecticut Department of Economic and Community Development
AIIS	American Institute for Indian Studies		
AJA	American Jewish Archives	CDI	Children's Discovery Institute
AJL	American Jewish Libraries	CEC	Council for Exceptional Children
ALA	American Library Association	CEF	Chemical Educational Foundation
ALISE	Association for Library and Information Science Education	CES	Council for European Studies
		CF	The Commonwealth Fund
AMNH	American Museum of Natural History	CFF	Cystic Fibrosis Foundation
AMS	American Musicological Society	CFFVR	Community Foundation for the Fox Valley Region
ANL	Argonne National Library	CFKF	Classic for Kids Foundation

CFNCR	Community Foundation for the National Capital Region	**IRC**	International Rescue Committee
CFPC	College of Family Physicians of Canada	**IREX**	International Research and Exchanges Board
CFUW	Canadian Federation of University Women	**IUCP**	Indiana University Center on Philanthropy
CHCF	California Health Care Foundation	**IYI**	Indiana Youth Institute
CHEA	Canadian Home Economics Association	**JDF**	Juvenile Diabetes Foundation International
CICF	Central Indiana Community Foundation	**JMO**	John M. Olin Foundation
CIES	Council for International Exchange of Scholars	**JSPS**	Japan Society for the Promotion of Science
CIUS	Canadian Institute of Ukrainian Studies	**KFC**	Kidney Foundation of Canada
CLA	Canadian Lung Association	**LISC**	Local Initiatives Support Corporation
CLF	Canadian Liver Foundation	**LSA**	Leukemia Society of America
CMS	Centers for Medicare and Medicaid Services	**MFRI**	Military Family Research Institute
CNCS	Corporation for National and Community Service	**MHRC**	Manitoba Health Research Council
CRI	Cancer Research Institute	**MLA**	Medical Library Association
CTCNet	Community Technology Centers Network	**MLB**	Major League Baseball
DAAD	Deutscher Akademische Austauschdienst (German Academic Exchange Service)	**MMA**	Metropolitan Museum of Art
		MMS	Massachusetts Medical Society
DHHS	Department of Health and Human Services	**MSSC**	Multiple Sclerosis Society of Canada
DOA	Department of Agriculture	**NAA**	Newspaper Association of America
DOC	Department of Commerce	**NAACP**	National Association for the Advancement of Colored People
DOD	Department of Defense		
DOE	Department of Energy	**NAGC**	National Association for Gifted Children
DOI	Department of the Interior	**NAPNAP**	National Association of Pediatric Nurse Associates and Practitioners
DOJ	Department of Justice		
DOL	Department of Labor	**NARSAD**	National Alliance for Research on Schizophrenia and Depression
DOS	Department of State		
DOT	Department of Transportation	**NASA**	National Aeronautics and Space Administration
EFA	Epilepsy Foundation of America	**NASE**	National Association for the Self-Employed
EIF	Entertainment Industry Foundation	**NASM**	National Air and Space Museum
EPA	Environmental Protection Agency	**NATO**	North Atlantic Treaty Organization
ESF	European Science Foundation	**NCCAM**	National Center for Complementary and Alternative Medicine
ETS	Educational Testing Service		
FCAR	Formation de Chercheurs et L'Aide a la Recherche	**NCFL**	National Center for Family Literacy
FCD	Foundation for Child Development	**NCI**	National Cancer Institute
FDA	Food and Drug Administration	**NCIC**	National Cancer Institute of Canada
FIC	Fogarty International Center	**NCRR**	National Center for Research Resources
GAAC	German American Academic Council	**NCSS**	National Council for the Social Studies
GCA	Garden Club of America	**NEA**	National Education Association
GEF	Green Education Foundation	**NEH**	National Endowment for the Humanities
GNOF	Greater New Orleans Foundation	**NEI**	National Eye Institute
HAF	Humboldt Area Foundation	**NFID**	National Foundation for Infectious Diseases
HBF	Herb Block Foundation	**NFL**	National Football League
HHS	Health and Human Services	**NFWF**	National Fish and Wildlife Foundation
HHMI	Howard Hughes Medical Institute	**NGA**	National Gardening Association
HRSA	Health Resources and Services Administration	**NHGRI**	National Human Genome Research Institute
HUD	Department of Housing and Urban Development	**NHLBI**	National Heart, Lung and Blood Institute
ICC	Indiana Campus Compact	**NHSCA**	New Hampshire State Council on the Arts
IIE	Institute of International Education	**NIA**	National Institute on Aging
IRA	International Reading Association	**NIAF**	National Italian American Foundation
		NIAAA	National Institute on Alcohol Abuse and Alcoholism

NIAF	National Italian American Foundation	**OREF**	Orthopaedic Research and Education Foundation
NIAID	National Institute of Allergy and Infectious Diseases	**ORISE**	Oak Ridge Institute for Science and Education
NIAMS	National Institute of Arthritis and Musculoskeletal Skin Diseases	**OSF**	Open Society Foundation
		PAS	Percussive Arts Society
NICHD	National Institute of Child Health and Human Development	**PCA**	Pennsylvania Council on the Arts
		PDF	Peace Development Fund
NIDA	National Institute on Drug Abuse	**PDF**	Parkinson's Disease Foundation
NIDCD	National Institute on Deafness and Other Communication Disorders	**PhRMA**	Pharmaceutical Research and Manufacturers of American Foundation
NIDCR	National Institute of Dental and Craniofacial Research	**PHSC**	The Photographic Historical Society of Canada
		PSEG	Public Service Enterprise Group
NIDDK	National Institute of Diabetes, and Digestive and Kidney Diseases	**RCF**	Richland County Foundation
		RCPSC	Royal College of Physicians and Surgeons of Canada
NIDRR	National Institute on Disability and Rehabilitation Research	**RSC**	Royal Society of Canada
		RWJF	Robert Wood Johnson Foundation
NIEHS	National Institute of Environmental Health Sciences	**SAMHSA**	Substance Abuse and Mental Health Services Administration
NIGMS	National Institute of General Medical Sciences	**SLA**	Special Libraries Association
NIH	National Institutes of Health	**SME**	Society of Manufacturing Engineers
NIJ	National Institute of Justice	**SOCFOC**	Sisters of Charity Foundation of Cleveland
NIMH	National Institute of Mental Health	**SORP**	Society of Biological Psychiatry
NINDS	National Institute of Neurological Disorders and Strokes	**SSHRC**	Social Sciences and Humanities Research Council of Canada
NINR	National Institute of Nursing Research	**SSRC**	Social Science Research Council
NIOSH	National Institute for Occupational Safety and Health	**STTI**	Sigma Theta Tau International
		SVP	Social Venture Partners
NIST	National Institute of Standards and Technology	**SWE**	Society of Women Engineers
NJSCA	New Jersey State Council on the Arts	**TAC**	Tennessee Arts Commission
NKF	National Kidney Foundation	**TOMF**	Tucson Osteopathic Medical Foundation
NL	Newberry Library	**TRCF**	Three Rivers Community Fund
NLM	National Library of Medicine	**TSYSF**	Teemu Selanne Youth Sports Foundation
NMF	National Medical Fellowships, Inc.	**UPS**	United Parcel Service
NMSS	National Multiple Sclerosis Society	**USHMM**	United States Holocaust Memorial Museum Research Institute
NNEDVF	National Network to End Domestic Violence Fund	**USIA**	United States Information Agency
NOAA	National Oceanic and Atmospheric Administration	**USAID**	United States Agency for International Development
NRA	National Rifle Association	**USDA**	United States Department of Agriculture
NRC	National Research Council	**USFA**	United States Fencing Association
NSERC	Natural Sciences and Engineering Research Council of Canada	**USGA**	United States Golf Association
		USIP	United States Institute of Peace
NSF	National Science Foundation	**USTA**	United States Tennis Association
NSTA	National Science Teachers Association	**UUA**	Unitarian Universalist Association
NYCH	New York Council for the Humanities	**WAWH**	Western Association of Woman Historians
NYCT	New York Community Trust	**WHO**	Women Helping Others
NYFA	New York Foundation for the Arts		
NYSCA	New York State Council on the Arts		
OAH	Organization of American Historians		
ODKF	Outrigger Duke Kahanamoku Foundation		
OJJDP	Office of Juvenile Justice and Delinquency Prevention		
ONF	Oncology Nursing Foundation		
ONR	Office of Naval Research		

Grant Programs

1st and 10 Foundation Grants   **1**
Chad and Robin Pennington created the 1st and 10 Foundation in 2003 with the mission to build stronger communities by funding programs and institutions that seek to improve quality of life throughout West Virginia, Tennessee, and South Florida. Primary fields of interest include: children and youth services; community and economic development; crime and abuse prevention; and residential/hospice care. The application can be downloaded at the website, and the annual deadline is February 15.
Requirements: 501(c)3 organizations serving Tennessee, West Virginia, and southern Florida are welcome to apply.
Restrictions: Generally, no support for fund raising or sponsorship events. Further, no grants are given to individuals, or for meeting or conference expenses, salaries, or travel.
Geographic Focus: Florida, Tennessee, West Virginia
Date(s) Application is Due: Feb 15
Contact: Jennifer Correa, (631) 384-3667; director@1stand10foundation.com
Internet: http://www.1stand10foundation.com/
Sponsor: 1st and 10 Foundation
P.O. Box 192
Guild, NH 03754-0192

1st Source Foundation Ernestine M. Raclin Community Leadership Award   **2**
The Ernestine M. Raclin Community Leadership Award has been established by 1st Source Bank to honor and encourage leadership in volunteerism through the businesses in its banking communities. The award recognizes Ernestine M. Raclin, Chairman Emeritus of 1st Source, who strongly demonstrated the spirit of volunteerism throughout her career by giving of her time and talents to help others. Nomination forms for the Award will be available in January. As many as five employees of locally owned companies who are business clients of 1st Source Bank will be selected by a blue ribbon panel of community leaders from the 1st Source market area. Additionally, up to five employees of 1st Source Bank will be selected to receive the award. Award recipients will be presented a globe of leadership, a $1,000 personal cash award and a $1,000 award donated to the local charity of their choice. The awards will be presented at a luncheon hosted by 1st Source Bank.
Requirements: Residents of Indiana communities where 1st Source Banks are located are eligible for nomination.
Geographic Focus: Indiana
Amount of Grant: 2,000 USD
Contact: Lee Morton, Vice President and Trustee; (574) 235-2790 or (574) 235-2254
Internet: https://www.1stsource.com/about-us/ernestine-raclin-community-leadership-award
Sponsor: 1st Source Foundation
100 N Michigan Street, P.O. Box 1602
South Bend, IN 46601-1630

1st Source Foundation Grants   **3**
Established in 1952 in Indiana and administered by the 1st Source Bank, the Foundation supports community foundations, youth clubs and organizations involved with television, education, health, and human services. The Foundation provides support to organizations working in the following areas: social welfare and human services; education; culture and the arts; and community, civic and neighborhood involvement. Giving is primarily centered in Indiana, and the major type of funding given is for general operating support. Since there are no specific applications forms required or deadlines with which to adhere, applicants should send a letter of request detailing the project and the amount of funding needed.
Requirements: Any 501(c)3 serving the residents of Indiana communities where 1st Source Banks are located are eligible to apply.
Geographic Focus: Indiana
Amount of Grant: 500 - 30,000 USD
Samples: South Bend Heritage Foundation, South Bend, Indiana, $3,000 - general operations support (2011); Medical Education Foundation, South Bend, Indiana, $15,000 - general operations support (2011); Independent Colleges of Indiana, Indianapolis, Indiana, $1,000 - general operations support (2011).
Contact: Lee Morton, Vice President and Trustee; (574) 235-2790 or (574) 235-2254
Internet: https://www.1stsource.com/about-us/community-involvement
Sponsor: 1st Source Foundation
100 N Michigan Street, P.O. Box 1602
South Bend, IN 46601-1630

2 Depot Square Ipswich Charitable Foundation Grants   **4**
In December of 2005, Ipswich Co-operative Bank established the 2 Depot Square Ipswich Charitable Foundation with an initial contribution of $200,000. Charitable giving has been a cornerstone of the Bank's business philosophy for many years. The Foundation plays a vital role in supporting economic development and improving the quality of life in the communities that it serves. The Foundation focuses its giving in the following areas: economic and community empowerment—includes programs which focus on the promotion and development of access to safe and affordable housing, and programs which support community revitalization efforts; youth development—initiatives that encourage youth through social, educational, athletic or cultural programs; arts and culture—programs and organizations which provide art and cultural programs that enrich communities; and health and human services—organizations which strive to enhance the health and well-being of children and families in its communities. The Grant Committee meets in April and November. Completed applications are due April 1st and November 1st.
Requirements: The Foundation awards funds to non-profit organizations based in Ipswich and the surrounding communities. Applications for grants will only be accepted from qualified 501(c)3 or 501(c)1 organizations.
Geographic Focus: Massachusetts
Date(s) Application is Due: Apr 1; Nov 1
Contact: Tammy Roeger; (978) 462-3106; fax (978) 462-1980; tammy.roeger@ifs-nbpt.com
Internet: http://www.institutionforsavings.com/site/charitable_2depot_about.html
Sponsor: 2 Depot Square Ipswich Charitable Foundation
2 Depot Square
Ipswich, MA 01938-1914

2 Life 18 Foundation Grants   **5**
2 Life 18 Help and Rescue was founded by David and Orly Perez who jumped into action in the aftermath of Hurricane Katrina by airlifting over 384 people from the Gulf States to safety. The foundation gives primarily to coordinate and provide help, rescue, and compassion during and after disasters and emergencies. Currently, the foundation is actively providing ongoing financial aid and logistical support to displaced families in San Diego, Louisiana, and Mississippi.
Restrictions: Assistance is generally restricted to Alabama, Florida, Louisiana, Mississippi, Texas.
Geographic Focus: Alabama, Florida, Louisiana, Mississippi, Texas
Contact: David Perez; (858) 704-5050; fax (858) 704-5055; david@perez18.com
Internet: http://www.2life18.org/
Sponsor: 2 Life 18 Foundation
P.O. Box 1130
Del Mar, CA 92014-1130

2COBS Private Charitable Foundation Grants   **6**
The Foundation, established in Colorado in 2005, supports a variety of causes, which include: health care; cancer services; community services; and local community foundations. Although giving is centered around the Durango, Colorado, region, it is not uncommon for support to be offered to 501(c)3 programs across the country. There are no specific application formats or deadlines with which to adhere, and applicants should send a letter of request outlining the program need and overall budget.
Geographic Focus: All States
Amount of Grant: 250 - 1,000 USD
Contact: Christopher J. O'Brien, Chairperson; (970) 247-7828 or (970) 385-1740
Sponsor: 2COBS Private Charitable Foundation
10 Town Plaza, Suite 100
Durango, CO 81301-6910

3 B's Foundation Grants   **7**
The Foundation, established by David C. Beebe, Jr., in 2005, has as its primary field of interest the funding of housing/shelter development projects and community development. With giving centered in the State of Massachusetts, the Foundation has no specific guidelines, application forms, or deadlines with which to adhere. Potential applicants should contact the office directly.
Geographic Focus: Massachusetts
Amount of Grant: 15,000 USD
Contact: Lucius L. Fowler, Executive Vice President of Fiduciary Trust Co. International; (212) 632-3000; lfowler@ftci.com
Sponsor: 3 B's Foundation
600 Fifth Avenue
New York, NY 10020-2326

3 Dog Garage Museum Tours   **8**
Established in 2007 in Pennsylvania, 3 Dog Garage offers educational tours to K-12 students and adults. Founder Ross Myers got his start in the old car hobby at an early age, and his father had antique Fords which now comprise part of his 3 Dog Garage collection. Despite its value to history, the 3 Dog Garage has deliberately kept a low profile and is not well known by the general public or even by most car enthusiasts. The collection is housed in a facility in Boyertown, Pennsylvania, that its founder has turned into a museum, open for educational tours by appointment. Those interested should contact the office directly.
Geographic Focus: All States
Contact: Teresa Hasson, (610) 222-8800; fax (610) 222-3300; 3dg@comcast.net
Internet: http://www.3dog.org/
Sponsor: 3 Dog Garage
1805 Berks Road, P.O. Box 1340
Worcester, PA 19490

GRANT PROGRAMS

3 Rivers Wet Weather Demonstration Grants 9
The organization is committed to improving the quality of Allegheny County, Pennsylvania's water resources by helping communities address the issue of untreated sewage and storm water overflowing into the region's waterways. To promote the most cost-effective, long-term, sustainable solutions, the organization benchmarks sewer technology, provides financial grants, educates the public and advocates inter-municipal partnerships. Specifically, the 3 Rivers Wet Weather Demonstration Program (3RWW) announces that it is now accepting applications for grants to fund the design and construction of Stormwater Best Management Practice (BMP) projects. This program is expected to include several aspects of interest to MS4s and other involved parties including public education, public outreach and demonstration projects that address all aspects of stormwater management starting from the point where the rain (or snow) hits the ground, buildings and streets, flows into the stormwater collection systems, and is then conveyed to the outfalls that discharge the stormwater into our local streams and rivers. Grant application guidelines are available, including forms and instructions which outline the project categories, ranking criteria, selection process, content requirements, and eligible costs.
Requirements: Municipalities, municipal authorities, universities and research institutions, professional organizations and 501(c)3 non-profit organizations are eligible to submit proposals.
Geographic Focus: Pennsylvania
Date(s) Application is Due: May 30
Contact: John Schombert, (412) 578-8375; fax (412) 578-8065; jschombert@achd.net
Internet: http://www.3riverswetweather.org/f_resources/f_stormwater_grant_intro.stm
Sponsor: 3 Rivers Wet Weather Demonstration Program
3901 Penn Avenue, Building 3
Pittsburgh, PA 15224-1318

3 Roots Foundation Grants 10
The 3 Roots Foundation, established by Dennis C. and Sally A. Von Waaden in 2002, offers funding primarily in Texas. Its major fields of interest are children and youth programs, as well as support social services agencies. Funding comes in form of project support. There are no specific guidelines, application forms, or deadlines with which to adhere, and applicants should contact the office directly for further details.
Geographic Focus: Texas
Samples: Center for Child Protection, Austin, Texas, $20,000—to assist victims of child abuse during the investigation and prosecution of their cases; Lutheran Social Services, Austin, Texas, $6,000—for New Life Treatment Center.
Contact: Monica D. Tovar-Von Waaden, Director; (512) 401-6550; fax (512) 401-6551; ContactUs@RollingDough.com
Sponsor: 3 Roots Foundation
13809 Research Boulevard, Suite 810
Austin, TX 78750-1211

3M Community Volunteer Award 11
The foundation supports employees involved with arts and culture, education, the environment, health, employment, disaster relief, youth development, human services, and minorities. The foundation annually awards the 3M Community Volunteer Award in recognition of exceptional employee and retiree volunteer contribution. The honor includes a $1,000 grant to a nonprofit organization of the winner's choice.
Geographic Focus: All States
Amount of Grant: 1,000 USD
Contact: Cynthia F. Kleven; (651) 733-0144 or (651) 736-8146; cfkleven@mmm.com
Internet: http://solutions.3m.com/wps/portal/3M/en_US/CommunityAffairs/Community Giving/US/Volunteerism/
Sponsor: 3M Company Contributions
3M Center, Building 225-01-S-23
Saint Paul, MN 55144-1000

3M Company Arts and Culture Grants 12
Parallel to its Foundation, the 3M Company makes charitable contributions to nonprofit art and cultural organizations directly. Support is given on a national basis. Most giving is initiated through a Request for Proposal process that allows the company to focus our giving and maximize results. Arts and culture programming, especially those with strong education and outreach, help build the quality of life in 3M communities. The Company supports creative expression that enriches lives and helps people to learn more about the world around them. Areas of interest for Arts and Culture include: to encourage arts organizations with strong education and community outreach; to promote artistic and cultural diversity; and to support premier arts organizations. Types of support include: building and renovation; capital campaigns; donated equipment; donated land; donated products; employee volunteer services; general operating support; in-kind gifts; internship funds; program development; seed money; technical assistance; and use of facilities.
Restrictions: No support is offered for: political, fraternal, social, veterans, or military organizations; propaganda or lobbying organizations; religious organizations not of direct benefit to the entire community; animal-related organizations; or disease-specific organizations. No grants are given to individuals, or for electronic media promotion or sponsorships, athletic events, non-3M equipment, endowments, emergency needs, conferences, seminars, workshops, symposia, fund raising or testimonial events, travel, or film or video production.
Geographic Focus: Alabama, Alaska, Arkansas, California, Connecticut, Georgia, Hawaii, Illinois, Indiana, Iowa, Kentucky, Massachusetts, Michigan, Minnesota, Missouri, Nebraska, New Jersey, New York, Ohio, South Carolina, South Dakota, Texas, Utah, Wisconsin
Contact: Cynthia F. Kleven, Secretary; (651) 733-0144 or (651) 736-8146; fax (651) 737-3061; cfkleven@mmm.com
Internet: http://solutions.3m.com/wps/portal/3M/en_US/CommunityAffairs/Community Giving/US/ArtsCulture/
Sponsor: 3M Company Contributions
3M Center, Building 225-01-S-23
Saint Paul, MN 55144-1000

3M Company Environmental Giving Grants 13
Parallel to its Foundation, the 3M Company makes charitable contributions to nonprofit environmentally-conscious organizations directly. Support is given on a national basis. Most giving is initiated through a Request for Proposal process that allows the company to focus our giving and maximize results. The Company supports programs that make meaningful contributions to the sustainability of the Earth's ecosystems. Areas of interest for the Environment include: to preserve biodiversity; to positively impact climate change; to provide access to natural areas; and to offer opportunities for local volunteer involvement. Types of support include: building and renovation; capital campaigns; donated equipment; donated land; donated products; employee volunteer services; general operating support; in-kind gifts; internship funds; program development; seed money; technical assistance; and use of facilities.
Restrictions: No support is offered for: political, fraternal, social, veterans, or military organizations; propaganda or lobbying organizations; religious organizations not of direct benefit to the entire community; animal-related organizations; or disease-specific organizations. No grants are given to individuals, or for electronic media promotion or sponsorships, athletic events, non-3M equipment, endowments, emergency needs, conferences, seminars, workshops, symposia, fund raising or testimonial events, travel, or film or video production; no cause-related marketing.
Geographic Focus: Alabama, Alaska, Arkansas, California, Connecticut, Georgia, Hawaii, Illinois, Indiana, Iowa, Kentucky, Massachusetts, Michigan, Minnesota, Missouri, Nebraska, New Jersey, New York, Ohio, South Carolina, South Dakota, Texas, Utah, Wisconsin
Amount of Grant: 500 - 10,000 USD
Samples: Clinton County Conservation, Grand Mound, Iowa, $2,500 - Educational Displays for the Mississippi River (2011); Santa Ana Watershed Association, Redlands, California, $2,500 - Traveling Naturalist (2011); Ice Age Trail Alliance, Cross Plains, Wisconsin, $1,000 - Plover River Segment Benches (2011).
Contact: Cynthia F. Kleven; (651) 733-0144; fax (651) 737-3061; cfkleven@mmm.com
Internet: http://solutions.3m.com/wps/portal/3M/en_US/CommunityAffairs/Community Giving/US/Environment/
Sponsor: 3M Company Contributions
3M Center, Building 225-01-S-23
Saint Paul, MN 55144-1000

3M Company Health and Human Services Grants 14
Parallel to its Foundation, the 3M Company makes charitable contributions to nonprofit health and human services organizations directly. Support is given on a national basis. Most giving is initiated through a Request for Proposal process that allows the company to focus our giving and maximize results. Areas of interest for Health and Human Services include: to increase resiliency in youth through prevention efforts from early childhood to 12th grade; and to build and sustain healthy communities. Types of support include: building and renovation; capital campaigns; donated equipment; donated land; donated products; employee volunteer services; general operating support; in-kind gifts; internship funds; program development; seed money; technical assistance; and use of facilities. The Company also reaches out to bring assistance and help communities prepare for disaster.
Restrictions: No support is offered for: political, fraternal, social, veterans, or military organizations; propaganda or lobbying organizations; religious organizations not of direct benefit to the entire community; animal-related organizations; or disease-specific organizations. No grants are given to individuals, or for electronic media promotion or sponsorships, athletic events, non-3M equipment, endowments, emergency needs, conferences, seminars, workshops, symposia, fund raising or testimonial events, travel, or film or video production; no cause-related marketing.
Geographic Focus: Alabama, Alaska, Arkansas, California, Connecticut, Georgia, Hawaii, Illinois, Indiana, Iowa, Kentucky, Massachusetts, Michigan, Minnesota, Missouri, Nebraska, New Jersey, New York, Ohio, South Carolina, South Dakota, Texas, Utah, Wisconsin
Samples: Community and Family Services, Hartford City, Indiana, $2,500 - Feeding our Community (2011); Habitat for Humanity of Marion County, Guin, Alabama, $35,000 - Rebuild Hackleburg Blitz (2011); Mary Rigg Neighborhood Center, Indianapolis, Indiana, $2,500 - Hunger Relief and Help Support (2011).
Contact: Cynthia F. Kleven, Secretary; (651) 733-0144 or (651) 736-8146; fax (651) 737-3061; cfkleven@mmm.com
Internet: http://solutions.3m.com/wps/portal/3M/en_US/CommunityAffairs/Community Giving/US/HHS/
Sponsor: 3M Company Contributions
3M Center, Building 225-01-S-23
Saint Paul, MN 55144-1000

3M Foundation Community Giving Grants 15
The foundation supports organizations involved with arts and culture, K-12 education, higher education, the environment, and health and human services. Special emphasis is directed toward programs designed to help prepare individuals and families for success. Fields of interest are: arts; arts education; business education; disaster relief, preparedness, and services; economics; elementary and secondary education; employment training; engineering; environmental causes; family services; federated giving programs; health care; higher education; human services; mathematics; minorities; science programs; youth development; and youth, services. Types of support include: building construction and renovation, capital campaigns, curriculum development, employee matching gifts, general operating support,

in-kind gifts, program development, and scholarship funds. The foundation utilizes an invitational Request For Proposal (RFP) process for organizations located in Minneapolis and St. Paul, Minnesota, and Austin, Texas. Application forms are not required.
Requirements: Established 501(c)3 organizations in all 3M communities are eligible.
Restrictions: The 3M Foundation does not accept unsolicited proposals in St. Paul/Minneapolis, Minnesota, and Austin, Texas. No support for religious organizations, conduit agencies, political groups, fraternal organizations, social groups, or veteran organizations. No funding for hospitals, K-12 schools, military organizations, animal-related organizations, or disease-specific organizations. No grants to individuals, or for endowments, emergency operating support, advocacy and lobbying efforts, fundraising events and associated advertising, travel, publications, start-up needs, non -equipment, debt reduction, conferences, athletic events, or film or video production; no loans or investments.
Geographic Focus: Alabama, Alaska, Arkansas, California, Connecticut, Georgia, Hawaii, Illinois, Indiana, Iowa, Kentucky, Massachusetts, Michigan, Minnesota, Missouri, Nebraska, New York, Ohio, South Carolina, South Dakota, Texas, Utah, Wisconsin
Contact: Cynthia F. Kleven, Secretary; (651) 733-0144 or (651) 736-8146; fax (651) 737-3061; cfkleven@mmm.com
Internet: http://solutions.3m.com/wps/portal/3M/en_US/3M-Sustainability/Global/Stakeholders/Giving/
Sponsor: 3M Foundation
3M Center, Building 225-01-S-23
Saint Paul, MN 55144-1000

4imprint One by One Charitable Giving   16
4imprint's one by one charitable program is based on the company's culture and our team members' belief that nonprofit organizations are important and the work they do makes this world a better place.Each business day 4imprint gives a worthy organization $500 in promotional products. Nonprofits can select any product on www.4imprint.com for a donation. Applications will be reviewed by the one by one committee. All decisions will be based on geographic location, programming diversity, charitable diversity, value and merit of cause, and audience served.
Requirements: In order to apply for a donation you must be employed by or be a member of the Board of Directors for a 501(c)3 organization, a school, a registered Canadian charity/society or a religious organization. Applicants must be at least 18 years of age. There are no deadline dates, however you should submit your application a minimum of 2 months before you need the items. Applicants can select more than one product. If your organization is chosen for a donation, you may split your donation between 2 – 3 different products. If your total amount exceeds the $500 donation, the recipient must pay the difference.
Restrictions: In order to help as many organizations as possible, 4imprint can only grant one donation per year to a particular organization. The donation must be used within 30 days of the date that you were selected.
Geographic Focus: All States, Canada
Amount of Grant: Up to 500 USD
Contact: Cheryl Sina, Giving Coordinator; (877) 446-7746; onebyone@4imprint.com
Internet: http://onebyone.4imprint.com/default.aspx
Sponsor: 4imprint Inc.
101 Commerce Street
Oshkosh, WI 54901

4S Ranch~Del Sur Community Foundation Grants   17
The purpose and vision of the Foundation is to improve the quality of life and meet emerging needs by: increasing responsibility and effective philanthropy; building a community endowment for the benefit of 4SRanch~Del Sur; providing funds annually to community organizations and causes; and giving the community a vehicle for legacy planning.
Requirements: Applying organization must provide services in the communities of 4S Ranch, Del Sur, Santa Fe Valley, Santa Luz, and any of the closely surrounding communities.
Restrictions: Generally, the Foundation does not provide grants for: annual campaigns and fund raising events; capital campaigns for building of facilities; stipends for attendance at conferences; endowments; for-profit organizations and individuals unaffiliated with a qualified fiscal sponsor; projects that promote religious or political doctrine; research; or scholarships.
Geographic Focus: California
Date(s) Application is Due: Feb 18
Amount of Grant: 1,000 - 10,000 USD
Contact: Trudy Amstrong; (619) 814-1384; trudy@sdfoundation.org
Internet: http://www.endowtheranchcommunity.org/grants.html
Sponsor: 4S Ranch~Del Sur Community Foundation
11770 Bernardo Plaza Court, Suite 206
San Diego, CA 92128

7-Eleven Coorporate Giving Grants   18
The program provides support to organizations in communities where 7-Eleven operates stores. In general, support is provided at the local level for police, school and youth sports programs and community events. It supports programs and projects in the area of education, with emphasis on workforce development, language education, and programs to assist at-risk and economically disadvantaged individuals. Other areas of interest include multicultural understanding, crime prevention, and hunger. Types of support include specific projects, programs, and events. Applicants should begin the process by contacting the office directly.
Requirements: 7-Eleven charitable contributions support: 501(c)3 not-for-profit organizations and government agencies, such as public schools, libraries or police departments; organizations and initiatives that support communities where 7-Eleven operates stores; organizations and initiatives that support its strategic focus areas (safety, education, health and wellness, and community revitalization projects).
Restrictions: 7-Eleven charitable contributions do not support: religious or political organizations; general operating, multi-year commitments or capital, building or endowment campaigns; sponsorships for individuals; or organizations that discriminate on the basis of race, religion, sex or national origin.
Geographic Focus: All States
Amount of Grant: 1,000 - 2,500 USD
Contact: Nancy Lear; (972) 828-7480; fax (972) 828-8972; nancy.lear@7-11.com
Internet: http://www.corp.7-eleven.com/InTheCommunity/HowWeGive/tabid/207/Default.aspx
Sponsor: 7-Eleven
1722 Routh Street, Local 199, P.O. Box 711
Dallas, TX 75221

18th Street Arts Complex Residency Grants   19
The complex promotes, assists and presents the work of a wide array of artists and art organizations by supporting intercultural exchange and understanding through the arts and encourages a deeper appreciation of the arts locally and internationally. The Program provides partially subsidized studio space to artists and arts organizations depending upon need and the quality of residency proposals. Residents are given access to office and audio/visual equipment, meeting and exhibition space, grant writing and financial management consultation, event posting service to the internet, full representation on Web site and fiscal receiver services. Individual artists receive a standard 1-year lease with a 2-year renewal option and organizations receive a 4-year renewal option. Download the application from the website.
Requirements: Residents of the Los Angeles area are eligible to apply for the Residency Program. Foreign artists from Australia, Eastern Europe, Taiwan and Southeast Asia may also be eligible for our International Visiting Artist Program by applying through cooperative programs with outside government agencies and private foundation.
Geographic Focus: California
Contact: Jan Williamson; (310) 453-3711, ext. 102; fax (310) 453-4347; office@18thstreet.org
Internet: http://www.18thstreet.org/resident_artists.html
Sponsor: 18th Street Arts Complex
1639 18th Street
Santa Monica, CA 90404-3807

21st Century ILGWU Heritage Fund Grants   20
The 21st Century ILGWU Heritage Fund is a grant-giving organization funded by the International Ladies Garment Workers Union (ILGWU). The Fund focuses its giving on issues such as employment, human services, and education, particularly law school. Applications and guidelines are available, and annual deadlines for receipt of applications are April 30 and October 31. Notification occurs within two to three months after submission.
Restrictions: No grants are given to individuals, or for general operating support.
Geographic Focus: New York
Date(s) Application is Due: Apr 30; Oct 31
Amount of Grant: Up to 40,000 USD
Contact: Muzaffar Chishti, Executive Director; (212) 645-2740; fax (212) 645-2761
Sponsor: International Ladies Garment Workers Union
275 Seventh Avenue, 18th Floor
New York, NY 10001-6708

21st Century Threshold Project Gifts   21
The 21st Century Threshold Project is a nontraditional, extended-day children's learning initiative situated in southwest Baltimore City's Washington Village and Pigtown community, that focuses on fostering academic remediation, enrichment social confidence, and positive values. Fields of interest include: child development; early childhood education; elementary and secondary education; and youth programs. Support comes in the form of in-kind gifts. There are no specific applications or deadlines with which to adhere, and applicants should contact the organization directly for further details.
Requirements: Applicants must serve the children and youth of Baltimore City's Washington Village and Pigtown community.
Geographic Focus: Maryland
Contact: Judith Rinaldi, Vice President; (410) 494 8085
Sponsor: 21st Century Threshold Project
116 Willow Avenue
Towson, MD 21286

41 Washington Street Foundation Grants   22
The Foundation, established in 2003 in Michigan, offers grant support primarily in Grand Rapids and Holland, Michigan. Its primary fields of interest include: Christian agencies and churches; Pre-K through 12th grade education; higher education; and community service programs. Support is given in the form of capital campaigns, general operating funds, and program grants. There are no application forms or deadlines with which to adhere, and applicants should approach the Foundation initially in writing.
Requirements: The Foundation offers grants to 501(c)3 organizations serving the Grand Rapids and Holland, Michigan, regions.
Geographic Focus: Michigan
Amount of Grant: Up to 100,000 USD
Contact: James P. Hovinga, Director; (616) 850-1330; fax (616) 850-7640
Sponsor: 41 Washington Street Foundation
914 S. Harbor Drive
Grand Haven, MI 49417-1745

4 | GRANT PROGRAMS

49ers Foundation Grants 23
The San Francisco 49ers foundation is designed to enhance the educational, health, social, and cultural needs of the San Francisco Bay Area community. The current funding priority concentrates on supporting organizations and programs that focus on tackling violence and that help establish life goals; encourage positive character building choices; teach life skills; and demonstrate respect, tolerance and appreciation of diversity. Grant proposals are accepted January through April each year. Submit proposals of three or less pages.
Requirements: 49ers Foundation grants will be awarded only to 501(c)3 organizations in the greater San Francisco Bay Area that address violence prevention.
Geographic Focus: California
Amount of Grant: Up to 5,000 USD
Contact: Shauna Standart; (408) 562-4949; 49ersfoundation@niners.nfl.com
Internet: http://www.49ers.com/community/foundation.html
Sponsor: 49ers Foundation
4949 Centennial Boulevard
Santa Clara, CA 95054-1229

100 Angels Charitable Foundation Grants 24
The Foundation, a furniture industry-based public charity, is spearheading projects to encourage all segments of the home furnishings industry to support human service programs across the country. Although grants are given throughout Florida, giving is primarily centered in and around the Pensacola area. Types of support include general support and operating support, as well as disaster relief efforts. There are no particular application formats or deadlines with which to adhere, and applicants should contact the Foundation directly via a letter of application.
Restrictions: Giving is primarily centered in and around Pensacola, Florida. Grants are not made to individuals.
Geographic Focus: Florida
Contact: Martin Libowsky, Chairman; (800) 643-0975 or (205) 368-4815; fax (850) 916-4550; mbigdaddy125@aol.com
Sponsor: 100 Angels Charitable Foundation
P.O. Box 1379
Gulf Breeze, FL 32562-1379

100 Club of Arizona Benefit Grants 25
The mission of the 100 Club of Arizona is to provide financial assistance to families of public safety officers and firefighters who are seriously injured or killed in the line-of-duty, and to provide resources to enhance their safety and welfare. The Club pays a one-time benefit or $15,000 to surviving families of public safety officers and firefighters killed while on duty. The families of officers and firefighters, who are seriously injured, receive assistance up to $18,000. $5,000 is paid to the family of a public safety officer or firefighter who dies while off duty but while employed by a qualified agency.
Requirements: Applicants must be the spouse, son, daughter or stepchild of: Arizona certified municipal, county, tribal, and state law enforcement officers; Arizona certified correctional, probation and parole officers; firefighters; federal law enforcement officers working in the state of Arizona; or military personnel called to active duty while employed by a qualified public safety agency as an officer or firefighter.
Geographic Focus: Arizona
Amount of Grant: Up to 18,000 USD
Contact: Sharon Knutson-Felix, Executive Director; (602) 485-0100 or (877) 564-6100; fax (480) 242-1715; sharon@100club.org
Internet: http://www.100club.org/HOWWEHELP/BENEFITFORMS/tabid/61/Default.aspx
Sponsor: 100 Club of Arizona
5033 N 19th Avenue, Suite 123
Phoenix, AZ 85015-3203

100 Club of Arizona Safety Enhancement Stipends 26
The overall mission of the 100 Club of Arizona is to provide financial assistance to families of public safety officers and firefighters who are seriously injured or killed in the line-of-duty, and to provide resources to enhance their safety and welfare. Safety Enhancement Stipends (SES) provide assistance to public safety agencies to purchase equipment or provide training to enhance the safety of their officers and firefighters. This program allows agencies to obtain equipment and training that is unavailable through other funding.
Requirements: Eligible applicants include: Arizona certified municipal, county, tribal, and state law enforcement officers; Arizona certified correctional, probation and parole officers; firefighters; federal law enforcement officers working in the state of Arizona; and military personnel called to active duty while employed by a qualified public safety agency as an officer or firefighter. There are no restrictions on the number of times an agency can apply for a stipend. Any agency who receives a SES award is asked to wait one quarter before they reapply.
Geographic Focus: Arizona
Date(s) Application is Due: Mar 1; Jun 1; Sep 1; Dec 1
Contact: Sharon Knutson-Felix, Executive Director; (602) 485-0100 or (877) 564-6100; fax (480) 242-1715; sharon@100club.org
Internet: http://www.100club.org/HOWWEHELP/SAFETYENHANCEDSTIPENDS/tabid/64/Default.aspx
Sponsor: 100 Club of Arizona
5033 N 19th Avenue, Suite 123
Phoenix, AZ 85015-3203

100 Mile Man Foundation Grants 27
Established in 2004 and formerly known as the Itzler Family Foundation, the 100 Mile Man Foundation currently offers support primarily to New York organizations, including: health organizations and agencies, social services groups, Jewish agencies and synagogues, and medical research groups. There are no specific guidelines, applications, or deadlines with which to adhere. Generally, grants have ranged from $100 to $160,000.
Requirements: Giving is limited to 501(c)3 organizations serving the residents of the greater New York metropolitan area.
Geographic Focus: New York
Contact: Jesse Itzler; (212) 867-0790 or (888) 843-1006; info@the100mileman.com
Internet: http://the100mileman.com/?page_id=276
Sponsor: 100 Mile Man Foundation
230 Park Avenue, Suite 850
New York, NY 10169

100 Women in Hedge Funds Foundation Grants 28
The foundation seeks to advance the hedge fund industry and the business activities of professional women within it in New York. Through the volunteer efforts led by its members, the foundation makes a difference in industry and community with unique educational programming, professional development initiatives, and philanthropy. To date 100 Women in Hedge Funds has raised over $13 million for charitable organizations focused on women's health, education and mentoring.
Requirements: Applicants must be: charitable organizations that serve woman in New York; and referred by a member of the Foundation.
Geographic Focus: New York
Contact: Anne Popkin, President; +44 (0)20 3180 3000; fax +44 (0) 20 3180 3011; apopkin@bluecrestcapital.com
Internet: http://www.100womeninhedgefunds.org/pages/foundation.php
Sponsor: 100 Women in Hedge Funds Foundation
331 W 57th Street, P.O. Box 239
New York, NY 10019-3101

118 Foundation Grants 29
The mission of The 118 Foundation is to support organizations that play a key role in making communities better in the areas of housing, education, and health care. The foundation has also expanded its outreach internationally to support organizations that also fight poverty, create jobs, and transform lives. Giving is primarily to public charities that match the foundation's mission in the areas of child and youth development, affordable housing, and micro-finance and micro-enterprise development, in disadvantaged communities in both the U.S. and abroad.
Restrictions: No support is available for organizations lacking 501(c)3 status. No grants are given to individuals, or for endowments, capital campaigns, scholarships, or medical research.
Geographic Focus: All States
Amount of Grant: Up to 135,000 USD
Contact: Diane Tollefson, Executive Director; (703) 338-5948; the118foundation@mac.com or grants@webmethods.org
Sponsor: 118 Foundation
1350 Beverly Road, #115-325
McLean, VA 22101

200 Club of Mercer County Grants 30
The 200 Club of Mercer County is one of several hundred associations nationwide dedicated to providing financial assistance to the families of public safety and rescue personnel who are killed in the line of duty. This includes the police officers (state, county, and municipal), correction officers, fire fighters, and rescue squad technicians of Mercer County, New Jersey. The 200 Club of Mercer County provides financial support to the family to take care of funeral arrangements, a mortgage payment or anything else the family needs during this time of devastating loss.
Requirements: The Organization supports the families of Police, Fire, and EMT in Mercer County, New Jersey, who have been killed.
Geographic Focus: New Jersey
Contact: Cathy Frank-White, President; (609) 895-1100, ext. 114 or (609) 712-2012; fax (609) 392-0244; cathywhite@aol.com or info@mercer200club.com
Internet: http://www.mercer200club.com/about.htm
Sponsor: 200 Club of Mercer County
P.O. Box 6755
Lawrenceville, NJ 08648-0755

300th Quincy Block Association Grants 31
In 1952, a small group of homeowners united to create what is now known as the 300 Block Association. Its members are a group that continues to grow. Now more than ever, the Association is determined to unite the community of Brooklyn, and is interested in collaborating with other block associations to develop strong community ties. Funding is offered to assist in community development. There are no specific guidelines, application formats, or deadlines. Potential applicants should contact the association directly.
Geographic Focus: New York
Contact: Curtis Felton, President; (718) 638-2376
Sponsor: 300th Quincy Block Association
378 Quincy Street
Brooklyn, NY 11216-1502

360 Degrees of Giving Grants 32
The group's mission is to bring full circle the resources and talents of young women to promote opportunities for young women, and to benefit organizations serving women and girls. The objective of this funding cycle is to impact the lives of young women by providing experience in a professional environment through a paid internship. The group hopes to encourage healthy partnerships between young women and positive adult female role models and support efforts that yield the highest payback for both the intern and the agency. Individual grants will be awarded up to $5,000.
Requirements: Applicants must be a 501(c)3 organization and: serve women and/or girls; be located in Cass, Clay, Jackson, Platte or Ray counties in Missouri; Johnson, Leavenworth or Wyandotte counties in Kansas; identify a mentor accountable for the intern's experience; and use grant funds exclusively for intern compensation.
Restrictions: 360 Degrees of Giving will not fund: government agencies; programs inconsistent with non-discrimination policies; religious organizations for religious purposes/activities; organizations which restrict choices or limit options; or political parties, candidates or political activities.
Geographic Focus: Kansas, Missouri
Date(s) Application is Due: Feb 27
Amount of Grant: Up to 5,000 USD
Contact: Emily Fish; (913) 831-0711, ext. 27; fax (913) 831-0881; women@wfgkc.org
Internet: http://www.wfgkc.org/grants_360.html
Sponsor: Women's Foundation of Greater Kansas City
6950 Squibb Road, Suite 220
Mission, KS 66202

786 Foundation Grants 33
The Foundation, established in 1990 and administered by the Marshell and Ilsley Trust Company, has the following primary fields of interest: education, the environment, natural resource development, housing and shelter for the poor, human and social service programs, and YMHA/YMCAs. Giving is designated throughout Wisconsin, and typically comes in the form of curriculum development, general operating support, matching funds, and scholarship endowments. There are no specific application forms or deadlines with which to adhere, and applicants should begin by contacting the Foundation in writing.
Requirements: (all 501(c)3 organizations either based in or serving residents of Wisconsin are eligible to apply. There is also some giving outside of Wisconsin.
Geographic Focus: Wisconsin
Amount of Grant: Up to 40,000 USD
Samples: Camp Manito-Wish, Boulder Junction, Wisconsin, $20,000; Michael Fields Agricultural Institute, East Troy, Wisconsin, $10,000.
Contact: Sharon Blank, (414) 815-3813 or (608) 232-2056
Sponsor: 786 Foundation
P.O. Box 2977
Milwaukee, WI 53201

1104 Foundation Grants 34
The Foundation gives primarily to support religious programs, health, education, children and youth, and community service organizations. Amounts range from $100 to $50,000. There are no application forms or deadlines to which applicants must adhere. Though giving is primarily restricted to the Charlotte, North Carolina, region, grants are also awarded to national organizations which are aligned with the foundation's interests.
Geographic Focus: All States
Contact: Charles V. Ricks, Treasurer; (704) 566-3349 or (704) 568-5550
Sponsor: 1104 Foundation
6000 Monroe Road, Suite 100
Charlotte, NC 28212-6119

1675 Foundation Grants 35
The foundation is a private family foundation dedicated to improving the quality of life for individuals and families through the support of non-profit organizations working in the areas of health, human services, education, the environment, and history. Priority is given to organizations serving Chester County, southeastern Pennsylvania, the Greater Boston area, and other geographic areas of interest to the Trustees. Grants are made for operating support, special projects, endowment, and capital. Grants range from $2,000 to $50,000 and are made twice a year at the discretion of the Trustees. Requests should be in writing and mailed to the executive director.
Requirements: 501(c)3 nonprofits and public charities under IRS Code 509(a) are eligible.
Restrictions: The foundation does not make grants to individuals, nor are they made for political purposes.
Geographic Focus: Massachusetts, Pennsylvania
Date(s) Application is Due: Mar 1; Oct 1
Amount of Grant: 2,000 - 50,000 USD
Contact: Marge Brennan; (610) 896-3868; mbrennan@1675foundation.org
Internet: http://www.1675foundation.org/guidelines.htm
Sponsor: 1675 Foundation
16 East Lancaster Avenue, Suite 102
Ardmore, PA 19003-2228

1772 Foundation Fellowships 36
The 1772 Foundation is a national, non-profit organization whose mission is to fund those entities that preserve and enhance America's built and natural environment. The Foundation offers paid internship and fellowship opportunities for highly qualified undergraduate seniors and graduate students pursuing a degree in historic preservation or a closely allied field such as museum studies, architectural history, history, landscape architecture and planning at an accredited college or university. Key areas of interest are: revolving funds for endangered properties; New Jersey inner-city revitalization; preservation trades and crafts schools and programs; agricultural endeavors, 5) Historic site sustainability training and conferences; and African American historic site development. Full proposals are by invitation only, upon review of initial letter of inquiry. Grants generally range from $4,000 to $50,000.
Requirements: Applicants must be 501(c)3 organizations, privately owned structures, relocation or purchase of historic structures, hospitals, or religious organizations, primarily on the East Coast, with emphasis on Connecticut, Massachusetts, Maine, New Jersey, New York, and Rhode Island.
Restrictions: No grants to individuals, or for general operating support, scholarships, professional fees, studies and reports, books, strategic planning, endowments, or sabbaticals. No support is offered for schools and universities.
Geographic Focus: Connecticut, Maine, Massachusetts, New Jersey, New York, Rhode Island
Amount of Grant: 4,000 - 50,000 USD
Contact: Mary Anthony, Executive Director; (860) 928-1772 or (860) 928-2125; maryanthony@1772Foundation.org
Internet: http://www.1772foundation.org/
Sponsor: 1772 Foundation
P.O. Box 112
Pomfret Center, CT 06259

2701 Foundation Grants 37
The Foundation's primary interest areas include: animal welfare; wildlife; the environment; housing development; and human services. The Foundation's geographic restriction is Florida, and grants are relatively small—from $50 to $150. There are no specific deadlines with which to adhere, and applicants should submit a written letter indicating 501(c)3 status, nature of charity, and financial requirements.
Requirements: The Foundation's geographic restriction is primarily Florida, though some giving takes place outside of the state.
Geographic Focus: Florida
Contact: Maurice D. Wiener, Director; (305) 854-6803; fax (305) 856-7342
Sponsor: 2701 Foundation
1870 S Bayshore Drive
Miami, FL 33133-3308

A & B Family Foundation Grants 38
The A & B Family Foundation was established in Illinois in 1999 by Kenneth D. Alpart, founder and managing partner of the 34-employee Alpart Trading Company. The foundation's activities include: youth entrepreneurship education, job and career exposure, academic enrichment, and sports. There is no specific application or deadline with which to adhere, and initial contact should be made in written form.
Geographic Focus: Illinois
Amount of Grant: 1,000 - 20,000 USD
Samples: Tatiana Kidd, South Holland, Illinois, $16,500—general assistance for an individual indigent child; Victory Outreach, Chicago, Illinois, $1,500—general operations.
Contact: Kenneth D. Alpart, Director; (312) 327-4000; fax (312) 327-4001
Sponsor: A and B Family Foundation
601 South LaSalle, 2nd Floor, Suite 200
Chicago, IL 60605

A.C. Ratshesky Foundation Grants 39
The foundation gives priority consideration to programs in education and training, and arts and culture. Support for programs that serve disadvantaged Jewish populations is also of special interest. Preference is given to small and medium-sized organizations. The foundation makes grants for operating support, start-up support/seed money, programs, and organizational capacity building or technical assistance. Contact office for application forms.
Requirements: Boston area nonprofits may apply.
Restrictions: Grants are not awarded to individuals or for continuing support, annual campaigns, general endowments, deficit financing, land acquisition, scientific or other research, publications, conferences, or loans.
Geographic Focus: Massachusetts
Date(s) Application is Due: Feb 1; Jul 1; Oct 1
Amount of Grant: 5,000 - 10,000 USD
Contact: Yasmin Shah, Program Officer; (617) 391-3094 or (617) 426-7080; fax (617) 426-7087; yshah@gmafoundations.com
Internet: http://ratsheskyfoundation.grantsmanagement08.com/?page_id=5
Sponsor: A.C. Ratshesky Foundation
77 Summer Street, 8th Floor
Boston, MA 02110-1006

A.H.K. Foundation Grants 40
The A.H.K. Foundation was established in Illinois by Jerald F. Kehe in 1994, president of the largest privately held specialty food distributor in the United States. The major purpose of the Foundation is to support Christian agencies and churches in La Mirada, California, Colorado Springs, Colorado, and throughout the State of Illinois. There are no deadlines with which to adhere. A formal application is not required, and applicants should formulate a proposal in the form of a narrative letter stating the overall purpose, population helped, and funding needed. Most recently, grants have ranged from $5,000 to $20,000.
Requirements: Applicants should be affiliated with Christian agencies and churches in the La Mirada, California, Colorado Springs, Colorado, and State of Illinois regions.
Geographic Focus: California, Colorado, Illinois
Amount of Grant: 5,000 - 20,000 USD

Samples: The Navigators, Colorado Springs, Colorado, $5,000 - general operations (2012); Bravehearts, Harvard, Illinois, $20,000 - general operations (2012).
Contact: Jerald F. Kehe, President; (815) 886-3700; fax (815) 886-8661
Sponsor: A.H.K. Foundation
900 N. Schmidt Road
Romeoville, IL 60446-4056

A.J. Fletcher Foundation Grants 41
A chief foundation objective for nearly two decades has been to help ensure the strength of North Carolina's nonprofit sector. The foundation has made grants to organizations in diverse fields to strengthen their internal operations. These grants have been used for staff salaries, administrative education and resource development, technical assistance and program development, and foundation-sponsored conferences for nonprofit boards and staff, focusing on management issues and technical tools. The foundation does not accept unsolicited grant requests.
Geographic Focus: North Carolina
Contact: Deremia Johnson; (919) 573-4647; fax (919) 573-4660; djohnson@ajf.org
Internet: http://www.ajf.org/grants.htm
Sponsor: A.J. Fletcher Foundation
220 Fayetteville Street Mall, Suite 300, P.O. Box 12800
Raleigh, NC 27601

A. J. Macdonald Foundation for Animal Welfare 42
The A. J. Macdonald Foundation for Animal Welfare provides awards in the Province of Quebec in the area of animal welfare. Its primary field of interest is community and economic development. There are no specified annual deadlines or application formats, and interested parties should begin by contacting the Foundation directly.
Geographic Focus: Canada
Contact: Lise De Carufel, Director; (450) 687-8202
Sponsor: A. J. Macdonald Foundation for Aminal Welfare
1521 Montcalm
Laval, QC H7W1X2 Canada

A.J. Muste Memorial Institute Counter Recruitment Fund Grants 43
The fund makes 30 to 50 grants annually of up to $1,500 to support grassroots efforts in the U.S. to inform young people about the realities of war and military service, help them find other options for educational funding and employment, and provide alternative points of view to those presented by military recruiters. The maximum grant amount is $1,500. Organizations of any size may apply for funding to support specific projects, but priority will be given to groups with smaller budgets and projects with less access to other funding sources.
Requirements: Groups do not need to be incorporated or to have non-profit tax-exempt 501(c)3 status or a fiscal sponsor to receive a grant from the CR Fund. However, the program does not issue checks to individuals.
Geographic Focus: All States
Date(s) Application is Due: Feb 8; Apr 11; Jul 18; Oct 3
Amount of Grant: 1,500 USD
Samples: Art for Change, New York, NY, $500—for local youth to develop and distribute original counter-recruitment posters and artwork; Community Alliance of Lane County, Eugene, OR, $1,000—for the Committee for Countering Military Recruitment; Just Don't Go, Helena, Montana, $500—for the Montana Youth Network for Resistance.
Contact: Grants Administrator; (212) 533-4335; fax (212) 228-6193; info@ajmuste.org
Internet: http://www.ajmuste.org/counter-recruit.htm
Sponsor: A.J. Muste Memorial Institute
339 Lafayette Street
New York, NY 10012

A.J. Muste Memorial Institute General Grants 44
The A.J. Muste Memorial Institute funds projects which promote the use of nonviolence to achieve social justice. The Institute makes about 25 to 35 grants annually of up to $2,000 for grassroots activist projects in the U.S. and around the world, giving priority to those with small budgets and little access to more mainstream funding sources. It is especially interested in funding efforts to: stop war and militarism; abolish the death penalty; support labor organizing; defend immigrant rights; oppose prison injustice; and expose the dangers of nuclear weapons and nuclear power.
Requirements: 501(c)3 nonprofit organizations are eligible to apply.
Restrictions: The institute does not fund: individual efforts or scholarships; schools or universities; organizations with significant access to government, corporate or mainstream charitable funding; academic or research projects; art, theater, film or video projects which are not tied to direct activism for social justice; economic development projects; capital campaigns or expenses; direct social services; legal defense or litigation; lobbying or electoral campaigns; projects geared toward participants' personal improvement or business success; and conflict resolution or violence reduction projects, unless they directly promote activism for social justice.
Geographic Focus: All States
Date(s) Application is Due: Feb 8; Apr 11; Jul 18; Oct 3
Amount of Grant: Up to 2,000 USD
Contact: Grants Administrator; (212) 533-4335; fax (212) 228-6193; info@ajmuste.org
Internet: http://www.ajmuste.org/guidelin.htm
Sponsor: A.J. Muste Memorial Institute
339 Lafayette Street
New York, NY 10012

A.J. Muste Memorial Institute International Nonviolence Training Fund Grants 45
The fund makes grants of up to $3,000 for trainings which help people learn how to collectively use the theory and practice of nonviolent action to effectively carry out struggles for social justice. Projects must be located outside the United States, or within Native nations in the US. Projects eligible for support include: those which build capacity and leadership among people engaged in nonviolent struggles; those which prepare participants for specific nonviolent actions or campaigns; those geared to training the trainers, in order to expand and multiply nonviolence training throughout a targeted community. Preference is given to: projects which involve trainers from the local area or region, where such trainers are available; and groups which are small, community-based and have less access to funding from other sources.
Requirements: Groups applying must be small, community-based, and with little likelihood of funding from other grantmaking institutions.
Restrictions: The program does not fund: trainings which are geared primarily toward resolving conflicts between individuals, building life skills or job skills, or achieving personal empowerment or economic independence; conflict resolution or violence reduction programs which do not directly promote activism for social justice; scholarships or other funding for people to travel abroad to attend courses or training sessions; or trainings with budgets over US$50,000, or organizations with annual budgets over US$500,000.
Geographic Focus: All States
Date(s) Application is Due: Mar 7; Sep 5; Dec 7
Amount of Grant: Up to 3,000 USD
Contact: Grants Administrator; (212) 533-4335; fax (212) 228-6193; info@ajmuste.org
Internet: http://www.ajmuste.org/guidintf.htm
Sponsor: A.J. Muste Memorial Institute
339 Lafayette Street
New York, NY 10012

A.O. Smith Community Grants 46
The foundation supports nonprofit organizations in communities where A.O. Smith Corporation has facilities. The foundation supports elementary and secondary school projects that focus on the quality of educational programs and curriculum development; civic, cultural, and social welfare of communities; and medical research and improved local health services. Types of support include continuing support, annual campaigns, building/renovation, scholarship funds, and employee matching gifts. Proposals should describe the project's benefits and constituency, budget information including other sources of funding, and how results will be reported. There is no deadline for applications, although proposals to be considered for the following year's foundation budget must be received by October 30.
Requirements: Nonprofit organizations in company areas may apply.
Restrictions: Grants do not support political organizations or organizations whose chief purpose is to influence legislation.
Geographic Focus: All States
Date(s) Application is Due: Oct 30
Amount of Grant: 500 - 20,000 USD
Contact: Edward J. O'Connor, (414) 359-4000; fax (414) 359-4064
Internet: http://www.aosmith.com/About/Detail.aspx?id=132
Sponsor: A.O. Smith Foundation
P.O. Box 245008
Milwaukee, WI 53224-9510

A.V. Hunter Trust Grants 47
The purpose of the foundation's grant program is to support Colorado nonprofit organizations that give direct aid, comfort, support, or assistance to children or aged persons or indigent adults. Types of support include program support and general operating support.
Requirements: Applications are considered from charitable 501(c)3 nonprofit Colorado-based organizations or projects or endeavors located in Colorado. The trust will consider only one request from an organization during any 12-month period.
Restrictions: The Foundation does not fund: new programs in their first three years of operation; grants or loans to individuals; developmental, pass-through or start-ups; research projects; publications, films or other media projects; capital campaigns or capital acquisitions, including construction and renovations; grants for education or scholarship aid; grants to cover deficits or retirement of debt; purchase of tickets for fundraising benefits, special events or sponsorships; endowments; recruiting and training; or gathering and disseminating information.
Geographic Focus: Colorado
Date(s) Application is Due: Mar 1; Jun 1; Aug 1
Amount of Grant: 10,000 - 20,000 USD
Contact: Barbara L. Howie; (303) 399-5450; barbarahowie@avhuntertrust.org
Internet: http://avhuntertrust.org
Sponsor: A.V. Hunter Trust
650 South Cherry Street, Suite 535
Glendale, CO 80246

A/H Foundation Grants 48
The A/H Foundation was established in California in 1996, and was named after the initials of its two founders, Albert Friedman and Harvey Friedman. Its primary mission is to support: cancer research, community and economic development; law enforcement and police agencies; community health organizations; public and private universities; human services; and Jewish agencies and synagogues. There are no specific deadlines with which to adhere, and initial approach should be by letter.
Requirements: Giving is primarily in the State of California to 501(c)3 organizations (although there is some giving outside of California).
Geographic Focus: California
Amount of Grant: Up to 25,000 USD

Contact: Keith J. Rosen, (818) 920-9888; fax (818)920-9388; info@wantacpa.com
Sponsor: A/H Foundation
15545 Devonshire Street, Suite 210
Mission Hills, CA 91345

AAAAI RSLAAIS Leadership Award 49
The RSLAAIS Leaderships Award recognizes an outstanding leader in a state, regional or local allergy, asthma, immunology society that is part of the Federation of Regional, State & Local Allergy, Asthma and Immunology Societies (RSLAAIS). This award was created to honor active leadership in a member society of the RSLAAIS, long-term community involvement, and clinical teaching at the local level. Additionally, contributions to the mission of the AAAAI as a speaker, volunteer or leader will also be considered as supplementary factors. Award candidates will have a demonstrated involvement in the local society directed toward building, strengthening, and contributing to that society toward the local medical and patient communities, the specialty of allergy/immunology, and the American AAAAI of Allergy, Asthma & Immunology (AAAAI).
Requirements: Award nominations will include a letter of nomination from the local society leadership, two letters of reference from society members, and the award candidate's C.V. to be submitted to the RSLAAIS Board of Governors. The Governors will review the nominations and determine the award candidates. The final roster of candidates will be presented to the Awards, Memorials and Commemorative Lectureships (AMCL) Committee who will select the award candidate. The AMCL Committee will present the candidate nomination to the AAAAI Board of Directors at their June meeting for their final approval.
Geographic Focus: All States
Date(s) Application is Due: Jan 14
Contact: Dr. Stuart L. Abramson; (414) 272-6071; fax (414) 276-3349
Internet: http://www.aaaai.org/professional-education-and-training/grants-—-awards/past-aaaaI-honorary-award-recipients.aspx#rslaais
Sponsor: American Academy of Allergy, Asthma, and Immunology
555 East Wells Street, Suite 1100
Milwaukee, WI 53202-3823

AAA Foundation for Traffic Safety Grants 50
The foundation sponsors research that not only identifies critical traffic safety problems, but also searches for underlying causes and possible solutions, as well as identifying early trends and offering solutions before the general public is aware of the problem. The foundation continues research into ways to help the growing numbers of teen drivers and older drivers evaluate and improve their driving performance. A sampling of recent research includes drunk driving, seeking additional solutions; seated for safety; headlight glare countermeasures; supplemental transportation programs for seniors; distracted driving, phase I; and longer combination vehicle safety study. Prior to submitting unsolicited proposals, applicants may email a one-page preproposal to gauge the foundation's general interest in the proposed topic.
Requirements: Research institutions and nonprofits with 501(c)3 status are eligible.
Restrictions: The foundation does not fund research to develop new devices. No grants are made for community action initiatives or other purely local traffic safety programs.
Geographic Focus: All States
Contact: Fairley Mahlum; (202) 638-5944; fax (202) 638-5943; info@aaafoundation.org
Internet: http://www.aaafoundation.org/about_us/index.cfm
Sponsor: AAA Foundation for Traffic Safety
607 14th Street NW, Suite 201
Washington, DC 20005

AAAS Early Career Award for Public Engagement with Science 51
The AAAS Early Career Award for Public Engagement with Science, established in 2010, recognizes early-career scientists and engineers who demonstrate excellence in their contribution to public engagement with science activities. A monetary prize of $5,000, a commemorative plaque, complimentary registration to the AAAS Annual Meeting, and reimbursement for reasonable hotel and travel expenses to attend the AAAS Annual Meeting to receive the prize are given to the recipient. For the purposes of this award, public engagement activities are defined as the individual's active participation in efforts to engage with the public on science- and technology-related issues and promote meaningful dialogue between science and society, as highlighted in this video. The award will be given at the AAAS Annual Meeting.
Requirements: Nominee must be an early-career scientist or engineer in academia, government or industry actively conducting research in any scientific discipline (including social sciences and medicine). Groups or institutions will not be considered for this award. AAAS employees are ineligible. One scientist or engineer will be chosen to receive the award on an annual basis. Nominee will have demonstrated excellence in his/her contribution to public engagement with science activities, with a focus on interactive dialogue between the individual and a non-scientific, public audience(s).
Geographic Focus: All States
Date(s) Application is Due: Oct 15
Amount of Grant: 5,000 USD
Contact: Linda Cendes, (202) 326-6656; fax (202) 289-4950; lcendes@aaas.org
Internet: http://www.aaas.org/aboutaaas/awards/public_engagement/
Sponsor: American Association for the Advancement of Science
1200 New York Avenue NW
Washington, DC 20005-3920

AAAS Science and Technology Policy Fellowships: Energy, Environment, and Agriculture 52
Fellows chosen for this program engage in projects, programs, policies and outreach initiatives to protect environmental and human health, tackle energy challenges and opportunities, and to safeguard our air, water, land, and natural resources. Placement opportunities are available with the national Oceanic Atmospheric Association, National Science Foundation, U.S. Department of Agriculture, USDA Forest Service, U.S. Department of Energy, and U.S. Environmental Protection Agency. Fellowships are awarded to highly qualified individuals interested in learning about the science-policy interface while applying their scientific and technical knowledge and analytical skills to the federal policy realm. Stipends range from $55,000 to more than $85,000.
Requirements: Prospective fellows must have a PhD or equivalent doctoral level degree. Persons with a master's degree in engineering and at least three years of post-degree professional experience may apply. Candidates must demonstrate exceptional competence in some area of science or engineering, and an interest in applying their expertise to the economic and technical assessment of problems relating to human health, agriculture, and the environment. Applications are invited from individuals in any physical, biological, or social science; any field of engineering; or any relevant interdisciplinary field. Persons with a DVM, MD, or a PhD in the natural sciences or economics are especially encouraged to apply. Applicants must be U.S. citizens.
Restrictions: Federal employees are ineligible.
Geographic Focus: All States
Date(s) Application is Due: Dec 5
Amount of Grant: 55,000 - 85,000 USD
Contact: Kira E. Mock; (202) 326-6700; fax (202) 289-4950; kmock@aaas.org
Internet: http://fellowships.aaas.org/02_Areas/02_index.shtml#EEA
Sponsor: American Association for the Advancement of Science
1200 New York Avenue NW
Washington, DC 20005-3920

AAAS Science and Technology Policy Fellowships: Health, Education and Human Services 53
Fellows chosen for this program focus their experience to support improved programs, policies, planning, and risk analysis for initiatives in: preventive and community health, disease identification and response, and medical research; individual, family and community social services, systems and support; food, processing and distribution safety; and science education, research, and innovation. Placement opportunities are available with the National Institutes of Health, National Science Foundation, USDA Food Safety Inspection Services and U.S. Department of Health & Human Services. Fellowships are awarded to highly qualified individuals interested in learning about the science-policy interface while applying their scientific and technical knowledge and analytical skills to the federal policy realm.
Requirements: Prospective fellows must have a PhD or equivalent doctoral level degree. Persons with a master's degree in engineering and at least three years of post-degree professional experience may apply. Candidates must demonstrate exceptional competence in some area of science or engineering, and an interest in applying their expertise to the economic and technical assessment of problems relating to human health, agriculture, and the environment. Applications are invited from individuals in any physical, biological, or social science; any field of engineering; or any relevant interdisciplinary field. Persons with a DVM, MD, or a PhD in the natural sciences or economics are especially encouraged to apply. Applicants must be U.S. citizens.
Restrictions: Federal employees are not eligible.
Geographic Focus: All States
Date(s) Application is Due: Dec 5
Amount of Grant: 55,000 - 85,000 USD
Contact: Robert Harper, Program Manager; (202) 326-6700; fax (202) 289-4950; rharper@aaas.org or fellowships@aaas.org
Internet: http://fellowships.aaas.org/02_Areas/02_index.shtml#HEHS
Sponsor: American Association for the Advancement of Science
1200 New York Avenue NW
Washington, DC 20005-3920

AACC Building Better Communities Through Regional Economic Development Partnerships 54
The initiative is a 2 year $2.5 million effort sponsored by the Wal-Mart Foundation to develop regional approaches to adult and postsecondary education, workforce, and economic development. The initiative will be managed by AACC's Center for Workforce and Economic Development and twenty community colleges will receive grants totaling $100,000 over 2 years. The Request for Applications (RFA) is available online. The deadline for applications is August 8, at Noon EDT.
Geographic Focus: All States
Date(s) Application is Due: Aug 8
Amount of Grant: 100,000 USD
Contact: Jen Hilmer Capece, (202) 728-0200; jhilmercapece@aacc.nche.edu
Internet: http://www.aacc.nche.edu/Content/NavigationMenu/ResourceCenter/Projects_Partnerships/Current/Center_for_Workforce_and_Economic_Development/Wal-Mart_Foundation_Initiative.htm
Sponsor: American Association of Community Colleges
One Dupont Circle NW, Suite 410
Washington, DC 20036-1176

AACC Plus 50 Initiative Grants 55
The AACC Plus 50 Initiative is a 3.5 year effort to identify a pilot group of two-year institutions that will create or expand campus programs to engage the 50+ population in learning; training/re-training programs; and/or volunteer, civic, service activities. The initiative is funded by a $3.2 million grant to AACC from The Atlantic Philanthropies. AACC provides sub-grants to member colleges selected through a competitive grant process. This comprises grants of up to $70,000 (total over 3 years) to 5 Mentor Colleges and grants of up to $40,000 (total over 3 years) to 10 Demonstration Colleges.

8 | Grant Programs

Geographic Focus: All States
Amount of Grant: 40,000 - 70,000 USD
Contact: Mary Sue Vickers, (202) 728-0200, ext. 248; mvickers@aacc.nche.edu
Internet: http://www.aacc.nche.edu/Content/NavigationMenu/ResourceCenter/Projects_Partnerships/Current/Plus_50_Initiative/index.htm
Sponsor: American Association of Community Colleges
One Dupont Circle NW, Suite 410
Washington, DC 20036-1176

AACC Project Reach Grants   56
AACC will fund service learning programs that involve community college students with disabilities as service learners, with a focus on their transition from school to work. Mentee colleges must complete a pilot activity that integrates service learning into one or more courses. Subsequent requirements for years two and three will be available. A service learning advisory committee (comprising at least one administrator, one disability support services staff member, one service learning coordinator or director-if applicable, one student, and one community agency or preK-12 school partner) must participate in proposal preparation and project oversight. Only electronic applications will be accepted. The complete RFP is available online. Contact sponsor for information about the next 3-year grant cycle.
Requirements: Applicants must be member institutions of AACC.
Geographic Focus: All States
Date(s) Application is Due: Nov 1
Amount of Grant: 7,000 - 47,000 USD
Contact: Quintin Doromal, Manager; (202) 728-0200, ext. 267; fax (202) 833-2467; qdoromal@aacc.nche.edu
Internet: http://www.aacc.nche.edu/Content/NavigationMenu/ResourceCenter/Projects_Partnerships/Current/Project_Reach/RFP_-_Project_Reach.htm
Sponsor: American Association of Community Colleges
One Dupont Circle NW, Suite 410
Washington, DC 20036-1176

AACC Service Learning Mini-Grants   57
The Program is intended to fund mini-grants for community colleges interested in organizing and hosting a regional service learning workshop. AACC will select up to six workshop sites based on geographical diversity, ease of transportation to the site, topics featured, need for training, and ability to present a well-run workshop. Matching funds of $2,000 (cash or in-kind) are required. The AACC is particularly interested in organizing workshops in states that have not received Horizons funding before (AK, DE, ID, MA, MO, ND, NE, NH, NV, WV) and that do not generally have statewide or regional service learning training opportunities available.
Requirements: The intended audience of the workshop may include faculty, department chairs, deans, service learning coordinators, administrators, student services staff, students, and/or community representatives at novice, intermediate, and/or advanced levels. Applicants must indicate how many participants they expect to attend.
Geographic Focus: All States
Date(s) Application is Due: Aug 1
Amount of Grant: 2,000 USD
Contact: Gail Robinson; (202) 728-0200, ext. 254; grobinson@aacc.nche.edu
Internet: http://www.aacc.nche.edu/Content/NavigationMenu/ResourceCenter/Projects_Partnerships/Current/HorizonsServiceLearningProject/GrantOpportunities1/Grant_Opportunities.htm
Sponsor: American Association of Community Colleges
One Dupont Circle NW, Suite 410
Washington, DC 20036-1176

AAF Accent on Architecture Community Grants   58
AAF's Accent on Architecture Community grants assist local, non-profit organizations in producing innovative design-education programs for children. In past years, successful grant recipients have enlisted architects and other design professionals, educators, community leaders, and government officials to enrich the public's understanding and appreciation of architecture and design. Accent on Architecture Grants have supported creative programming initiatives including television programs, symposia, design workshops, and teacher education. They enhance the visibility and public understanding of architecture and strengthen relationships between communities and local design groups.
Requirements: 501(c)3 or 501(c)6 organizations whose projects are specifically targeted to teaching children about architecture and design are eligible. Projects should illustrate an increased awareness, appreciation, and understanding of architecture and design among students in the K-12 age range.
Geographic Focus: All States
Date(s) Application is Due: Dec 17
Contact: Liz Blazevich, Program Director; (202) 787-1001; fax (202) 787-1002; eblazevich@archfoundation.org or info@archfoundation.org
Internet: http://www.archfoundation.org/2010/03/accent-on-architecture-community-grants-past-recipients/
Sponsor: American Architectural Foundation
2101 L Street NW, Suite 670
Washington, DC 20037

AAF Richard Riley Award   59
The Richard Riley Award promotes the idea of schools as centers of community. The award, carrying a $5,000 prize, recognizes schools that engage local residents and open their doors to learners of all ages. It honors both design and educational excellence with an emphasis on innovation. This initiative was part of an effort to support school districts and communities that make school facilities more conducive to learning and more accessible to the entire community. Sometimes referred to as "community learning centers," schools that fulfill this role provide a rich array of social, civic, recreational, and artistic opportunities to the broader community. Educational and municipal buildings are often clustered together, offering additional services for all. This helps to maximize local tax dollars and often improves student achievement.
Requirements: The program is open to all existing elementary and secondary public schools. The school can be recently constructed, opened or renovated; it does not have to be new.
Restrictions: The prize will be offered to the school only; individuals are not eligible to receive the award.
Geographic Focus: All States
Amount of Grant: 5,000 USD
Contact: Liz Blazevich, Program Director; (202) 787-1001; fax (202) 787-1002; eblazevich@archfoundation.org or info@archfoundation.org
Internet: http://161.58.76.77/aaf/aaf/Programs.Riley.htm
Sponsor: American Architectural Foundation
2101 L Street NW, Suite 670
Washington, DC 20037

AAG Meredith F. Burrill Award   60
The purpose of the Burrill Award is to stimulate and reward talented individuals and groups whose accomplishments parallel the intellectual traditions Burrill pursued as a geographer, particularly those concerned with fundamental geographical concepts and their practical applications, especially in local, national, and international policy arenas. The award consists of a certificate and cash honorarium, and is given at the Association's Annual Meeting. Digital submissions are encouraged.
Geographic Focus: All States
Date(s) Application is Due: Dec 31
Contact: Ehsan Khater, Coordinator; (202) 234-1450; fax (202) 234-2744; ekhater@aag.org or grantsawards@aag.org
Internet: http://www.aag.org/Grantsawards/burrill.htm
Sponsor: Association of American Geographers
1710 Sixteenth Street NW
Washington, DC 20009-3198

AAP Anne E. Dyson Child Advocacy Awards   61
The AAP Resident Section Anne E. Dyson Child Advocacy Award, supported by the Dyson Foundation, celebrates the efforts of pediatricians-in-training as they work in their communities to improve the health of children. This award seeks to showcase projects that are designed and implemented by residents, which aim to improve the lives of children. The Award includes: $300 in funds to advance the winning projects' goals; travel and lodging expenses for up to 2 residents per project to the AAP National Conference and Exhibition (NCE); and presentation of the Advocacy Award plaque during the Resident Section assembly meeting.
Requirements: Any resident-sponsored and/or resident led project that seeks to advocate on behalf of children is eligible for this award.
Geographic Focus: All States
Date(s) Application is Due: Jul 15
Amount of Grant: 300 USD
Contact: Kimberley VandenBrook, Grants Administrator; (800) 433-9016, ext. 7134; kvandenbrook@core.com
Internet: http://www.aap.org/sections/ypn/r/funding_awards/anne_dyson.html
Sponsor: American Academy of Pediatrics
141 Northwest Point Boulevard
Elk Grove Village, IL 60007-1098

AAP Community Access To Child Health (CATCH) Advocacy Training Grants   62
The Program supports five pediatric faculty-resident pairs (10 people) to attend the AAP Legislative Conference in Washington, DC each year. Each faculty-resident pair is required to implement an educational activity on child advocacy in coordination with their local AAP chapter following the conference. Local chapters will receive up to $1,000 toward completing the educational activity in conjunction with the faculty-resident pairs. The next call for applications will be available each fall.
Geographic Focus: All States
Date(s) Application is Due: Nov 9
Amount of Grant: Up to 1,000 USD
Contact: Kathy Kocvara, Program Coordinator; (847) 434-7085 or (800) 433-9016, ext. 7632; kkocvara@aap.org or catch@aap.org
Internet: http://www.aap.org/commpeds/cpti/Opportunities.htm
Sponsor: American Academy of Pediatrics
141 Northwest Point Boulevard
Elk Grove Village, IL 60007-1098

AAP Community Access To Child Health (CATCH) Implementation Grants   63
This program supports pediatricians in the initial and/or pilot stage of developing and implementing a community-based child health initiative. Grants of up to $12,000 are awarded each year on a competitive basis to pediatricians who want to address the local needs of children in the community. Priority will be given to projects serving communities with the greatest demonstrated health care access needs and health disparities. Strong collaborative community partnerships and future sustainability of the project are encouraged.
Requirements: A pediatrician must lead the project and be significantly involved in proposal development and project activities.
Restrictions: Only applicants from the United States and its territories are eligible to apply.

Geographic Focus: All States
Date(s) Application is Due: Jan 29
Amount of Grant: Up to 12,000 USD
Contact: Kathy Kocvara, Program Coordinator; (847) 434-7085 or (800) 433-9016, ext. 7632; kkocvara@aap.org or catch@aap.org
Internet: http://www.aap.org/catch/implementgrants.htm
Sponsor: American Academy of Pediatrics
141 Northwest Point Boulevard
Elk Grove Village, IL 60007-1098

AAP Community Access to Child Health (CATCH) Planning Grants   64
The program awards competitive grants to pediatricians who want to plan community-based initiatives to increase access to children's health care. Proposed initiatives must be broad-based community partnerships. Priority will be given to proposals promoting medical homes for under-served children and those with special health care needs; collaborating with SCHIP or Medicaid, and representing new initiatives within the community. Grant funds must be used for planning, not implementation. Planning activities may include needs assessments and community asset mapping, feasibility studies, community meetings, focus groups, and development of grant proposals. If an applicant is not an AAP member, a letter of support from the AAP chapter president in his/her area must be obtained. Applicants must contact their chapter CATCH facilitators for approval of applications prior to submission. Technical assistance for applicants is available from CATCH staff and facilitators. Annual deadline dates may vary; contact program staff for exact dates.
Requirements: U.S. pediatricians and those in U.S. territories are eligible. Every program must be led by, facilitated by, or have the significant involvement of a pediatrician. During the planning phase, the involvement of other community members should be secured in order to ensure local support for the program. Applicants are encouraged to demonstrate collaboration with state child health insurance programs and/or state Medicaid programs.
Restrictions: Only applicants from the United States and its territories are eligible to apply.
Geographic Focus: All States
Date(s) Application is Due: Jul 30
Amount of Grant: 2,500 - 12,000 USD
Contact: Kathy Kocvara, Program Coordinator, CATCH; (847) 434-7632; fax (847) 228-6432; kkocvara@aap.org
Internet: http://www.aap.org/catch/planninggrants.htm
Sponsor: American Academy of Pediatrics
141 Northwest Point Boulevard
Elk Grove Village, IL 60007-1098

AAP Community Access To Child Health (CATCH) Residency Training Grants   65
The Community Pediatrics Training Initiative (CPTI) partners with the Community Access to Child Health (CATCH) Program to provide this grant opportunity targeting pediatric residency training programs. The mission of the program is to provide support to residency programs to build sustainable opportunities for residents to gain experience working on community-based child health initiatives that increase access to medical homes or specific health services not otherwise available. Grants of up to $15,000 will be awarded on a competitive basis to pediatric residency programs which submit proposals to plan and implement community-based child health initiatives as part of the training curriculum over the course of 16 months. The next Call for Proposals will be available in September.
Requirements: A pediatric faculty member must oversee the project and provide mentorship for residents participating in project activities.
Geographic Focus: All States
Date(s) Application is Due: Nov 18
Amount of Grant: Up to 15,000 USD
Contact: Kathy Kocvara, Program Coordinator; (847) 434-7085 or (800) 433-9016, ext. 7632; kkocvara@aap.org or catch@aap.org
Internet: http://www.aap.org/commpeds/cpti/Opportunities.htm
Sponsor: American Academy of Pediatrics
141 Northwest Point Boulevard
Elk Grove Village, IL 60007-1098

AAP Community Access To Child Health (CATCH) Resident Grants   66
The Community Access to Child Health (CATCH) Resident Funds program supports pediatric residents in the planning of community-based child health initiatives. Grants of up to $3,000 are awarded twice each year on a competitive basis for pediatric residents to address the needs of children in their communities. CATCH Resident Funds grant projects must include planning activities and also may include some implementation activities. Resident grants are available twice a year - May to July, during the CATCH Planning Funds grant cycle, and November to January, during the CATCH Implementation Funds grant cycle.
Requirements: A pediatric resident must lead the project and be significantly involved in proposal development and project activities.
Restrictions: Only pediatric residents from the United States and its territories are eligible to apply for CATCH Resident Funds grants.
Geographic Focus: All States
Date(s) Application is Due: Jan 31; Jul 31
Amount of Grant: Up to 3,000 USD
Contact: Kathy Kocvara, Program Coordinator; (847) 434-7085 or (800) 433-9016, ext. 7632; kkocvara@aap.org or catch@aap.org
Internet: http://www.aap.org/catch/residentgrants.htm
Sponsor: American Academy of Pediatrics
141 Northwest Point Boulevard
Elk Grove Village, IL 60007-1098

AAP Leonard P. Rome Community Access to Child Health Visiting Professorships   67
The purpose of the Leonard P. Rome Community Access to Child Health (CATCH) Visiting Professorships Program is to promote advocacy for children and advance the field of community pediatrics. Beginning with the 2008 grant cycle, CATCH will be collaborating with the Community Pediatrics Training Initiative (CPTI) to implement this program. Four accredited pediatric residency programs will receive up to $4,500 each to fund a 2-or 3-day educational program focusing on the field of community pediatrics. District CATCH Facilitators (DCFs) and Chapter CATCH Facilitators (CCFs) are available to provide technical assistance.
Geographic Focus: All States
Amount of Grant: Up to 4,500 USD
Contact: Alanna Bailey Whybrew, (847) 434-7085, ext. 7397; awhybrew@aap.org
Internet: http://www.aap.org/catch/vp.htm
Sponsor: American Academy of Pediatrics
141 Northwest Point Boulevard
Elk Grove Village, IL 60007-1098

AAP Program Delegate Awards   68
The travel grants are available to residents who serve as program delegates to the AAP. This grant serves to support the program delegate's travel to the AAP Resident Section meeting at the annual National Conference and Exhibition (NCE). The travel grant is available to both categorical and combined-training pediatric residents. However, there is only one grant available per institution. The AAP Program Delegate will automatically receive the $300 travel grant.
Geographic Focus: All States
Date(s) Application is Due: Sep 14
Amount of Grant: 300 USD
Contact: Kimberley VandenBrook; (800) 433-9016, ext. 7134; kvandenbrook@core.com
Internet: http://www.aap.org/sections/ypn/r/funding_awards/nce.html
Sponsor: American Academy of Pediatrics
141 Northwest Point Boulevard
Elk Grove Village, IL 60007-1098

AAP Resident Initiative Fund Grants   69
The Program is offering twenty-five (25) grants of up to $1,000 each. The funding will enable residents to educate fellow residents and/or parents on a specific aspect of one of the Academy's national child health priorities (Special Health Care Needs, Foster Care, Oral Health, Disaster Preparedness, Mental Health, Obesity, and Immunizations). The Academy hopes that this program will: increase the number of new, creative and innovative opportunities for residents to apply their leadership and advocacy skills within the AAP structure; increase residents' knowledge of the Academy's child health priorities; and increase resident collaboration with national AAP and its chapters.
Geographic Focus: All States
Date(s) Application is Due: Mar 31
Amount of Grant: 1,000 USD
Contact: Kimberley VandenBrook; (800) 433-9016, ext. 7134; kvandenbrook@core.com
Internet: http://www.aap.org/sections/ypn/r/funding_awards/res_initiative.html
Sponsor: American Academy of Pediatrics
141 Northwest Point Boulevard
Elk Grove Village, IL 60007-1098

Aaron Catzen Foundation Grants   70
The Aaron Catzen Foundation, established in Maryland in 2001, offers support for human service agencies, Jewish agencies and synagogues, and federated giving programs in the Baltimore, Maryland, area. The maximum grant is $1,250, and is given most often in the form of general operating support. Requests should be made in narrative form explaining the specific program or programs to which the requested grant would apply, and the nature of the organization applying for the grant. There are no specific deadlines with which to adhere.
Requirements: 501(c)3 and Jewish organizations are welcome to apply.
Restrictions: No grant funding is offered to individuals.
Geographic Focus: Maryland
Amount of Grant: Up to 1,250 USD
Contact: Holly Bricken; (410) 429-4132 or (410) 598-8601; huntmeet@aol.com
Sponsor: Aaron Catzen Foundation
4 Yearling Way
Lutherville, MD 21093-4590

Aaron Copland Fund for Music Recording Program   71
The program's objectives are to document and provide wider exposure for the music of contemporary American composers, develop audiences for contemporary American music through record distribution and other retail markets, and effect the release and dissemination of recordings of previously unreleased contemporary American music and the reissuance of recordings that are no longer available. Grants for recordings of orchestral works may cover up to a maximum of 50 percent of total project costs, including musicians' recording fees, production, marketing, and distribution. Grants for recordings of other works and for reissuance of out-of-print recordings may cover greater percentages of total project costs. An award will be held for up to two years. Contact the program for the current application materials and deadlines.
Requirements: Proposals may be submitted by nonprofit professional performance ensembles, presenting institutions, and nonprofit or commercial recording companies. Performance ensembles and presenting institutions must include a letter of intent from either a nonprofit or commercial recording company. Organizations which received grants in past years are eligible only if previously funded recordings have been released or are likely to be released within acceptable time frames.

Grant Programs

Restrictions: Grants will not be made for the purpose of commissions to composers.
Geographic Focus: All States
Date(s) Application is Due: Jan 15
Amount of Grant: 2,000 - 20,000 USD
Contact: James M. Kendrick; (212) 461-6956; recording@coplandfund.org
Internet: http://www.coplandfund.org/recording.html
Sponsor: American Music Center
322 8th Avenue, Suite 1401
New York, NY 10001

Aaron Foundation Grants 72
The Aaron Foundation, established in California in 1987 by the Aaron Mortgage Corporation, supports programs for children and youth, health care facilities, and human services agencies. Giving is primarily centered in the Bakersfield, California, region. Applicants should submit: a copy of current year's organizational budget and/or project budget; a copy of IRS Determination Letter; a detailed description of project and amount of funding requested; a statement of the problem that the project will address; and a brief history of organization and description of its mission.
Requirements: The proposed project must benefit the residents of Bakersfield, California.
Geographic Focus: California
Date(s) Application is Due: Nov 30
Contact: Hal E. Aaron, Trustee; (661) 322-6353; fax (661) 322-6120
Sponsor: Aaron Foundation
651 H Street, Suite 100
Bakersfield, CA 93304-1305

Aaron Foundation Grants 73
Established in Massachusetts in 1951, the Aaron Foundation awards grants to eligible nonprofit organizations in its areas of interest, including: arts and culture; health care; higher education; Jewish services and temples; health care; social services; and youth. There are no application deadlines or forms with which to adhere. Applicants should submit: results expected from proposed grant; a copy of IRS Determination Letter; copy of most recent annual report/audited financial statement or 990; a listing of board of directors, trustees, officers and other key people and their affiliations; and a copy of current year's organizational budget and/or project budget.
Requirements: Connecticut, Massachusetts, and Rhode Island nonprofit organizations are eligible to apply.
Restrictions: Individuals are ineligible to apply.
Geographic Focus: Connecticut, Massachusetts, Rhode Island
Amount of Grant: 1,000 - 100,000 USD
Contact: Avram J. Goldberg, Trustee; (617) 695-1300 or (617) 695-1946
Sponsor: Aaron Foundation
225 Franklin Street, Suite 1450
Boston, MA 02110

AAUW Breaking through Barriers Award 74
The American Association of University Women's Breaking through Barriers Award is given annually at the AAUW National Convention in recognition outstanding programs chosen from across the U.S. Awardees receive a $3,000 cash prize in recognition of breaking down barriers for women and girls. Any branch of the AAUW may apply for the Award by completing the online application. States/branches are urged to apply for a Breaking through Barriers Award to receive recognition for their effective mission-based programming and to support the replication of exemplary programs by states/branches nationwide.
Restrictions: Faxed or mailed application are not accepted.
Geographic Focus: All States
Amount of Grant: 3,000 USD
Contact: Grants Manager; (202) 728-7602; fax (202) 872-1425; fellowships@aauw.org
Internet: http://www.aauw.org/learn/awards/btb.cfm
Sponsor: American Association of University Women
1111 16th Street NW
Washington, DC 20036

AAUW Community Action Grants 75
Community Action grants provide funds to individuals, AAUW branches and AAUW state organizations as well as local community-based nonprofit organizations for innovative programs or non-degree research projects that promote education and equality for women and girls. One-year grants from $2,000 to $7,000 provide funding for community-based projects. Two-year grants from $5,000 to $10,000 provide start-up funds for new projects that address the particular needs of the community and develop girls' sense of efficacy through leadership or advocacy opportunities. Topic areas are unrestricted, but should include a clearly defined activity that promotes education and equality for women and girls. Special consideration is given to projects focused on K-12 and community college girls' and women's achievements in science, technology, engineering, or math.
Requirements: Applicants must be women who are U.S. citizens or permanent residents. Grant projects must have direct public impact, be nonpartisan, and take place within the U.S. or its territories.
Geographic Focus: All States
Amount of Grant: 2,000 - 10,000 USD
Contact: Customer Service; (319) 337-1716, ext. 60; aauw@act.org
Internet: http://www.aauw.org/learn/fellowships_grants/community_action.cfm
Sponsor: American Association of University Women
1111 16th Street NW
Washington, DC 20036

AAUW International Project Grants 76
International Project Grants are intended to provide fellows the opportunity to develop knowledge and skills that will directly benefit their home countries. To support the continuation of fellows' work after they return home, AAUW will award a limited number of International Project Grants of $5,000 to $7,000 to those who held an AAUW International Fellowship within the last ten years. The grants provide support for community-based projects that benefit women and girls in the fellow's home country. Applications may be submitted online between August 1 and December 15, and are available at the AAUW website.
Requirements: Applicants must be citizens in a country other than the U.S. They must also have completed an AAUW International Fellowship within the last ten years. Proposed projects must be implemented in the applicant's home country, and have a direct, positive impact on women and girls. The applicant must be the primary director of the project, with controlling programmatic, administrative, fiscal, and editorial responsibility for the project's implementation. Additional requirements and guidelines are posted at the website.
Restrictions: Funds are not available for the following: salaries or stipends for primary director, project directors, or permanent positions, or to reimburse employees; tuition; higher education scholarships for students and participants; personal expenses (shelter, vehicle, insurance); building funds, construction, or renovations; previous expenditures, deficits, or loans (in existence at time of grant award); purchase of equipment; overhead or general operating expenses for any organization or nonprofit organization; creating or providing grants to other organizations; entertainment; travel expenses (unless directly related to project activities); copyright or attorney fees; or fundraising activities.
Geographic Focus: All Countries
Date(s) Application is Due: Dec 15
Amount of Grant: Up to 20,000 USD
Contact: Grant Contact; (202) 785-7700 or (800) 326-AAUW; aauw@act.org
Internet: http://www.aauw.org/learn/fellows_directory/ipg.cfm
Sponsor: American Association of University Women
1111 16th Street NW
Washington, DC 20036

ABA Labor Lawyer Student Writing Contest 77
The annual student writing competition is open to students at all accredited law schools. Papers may be written on any topic in the field of labor and employment law, and will be reviewed by The Labor Lawyer staff and a committee of ABA's editorial board. The winning paper will be published in The Labor Lawyer. Runner-up papers may also be published. Papers must not exceed forty 40 double-spaced pages (including endnotes).
Requirements: Students at all accredited law schools may submit papers.
Geographic Focus: All States
Date(s) Application is Due: Aug 31
Amount of Grant: 500 USD
Contact: Administrator; (202) 662-1000; fax (202) 662-1755; abalsd@abanet.org
Internet: http://www.abanet.org/labor/proopp.html#laborlawyer
Sponsor: American Bar Association
740 15th Street NW
Washington, DC 20005-1019

Abbey Charitable Trust Grants 78
Trust funds projects that meet one (or more) of the following three priorities to help disadvantaged people: education and training; financial advice to help people manage their money; and community regeneration. It also funds tangible items, such as equipment, workbooks, training materials, guides and other capital items. Most recently, the trust began to support salaries and worker fees, as long as this does not exceed 50% of the value of the donation and is appropriate for one-off funding. Preference is given to fund a complete element of a project rather than a partial donation to a much larger fund raising appeal.
Requirements: The Trust regrets that it can only make donations to registered, excepted or exempt charities. It can fund Industrial and Provident societies only if they are founded under charitable, not membership, rules.
Restrictions: The Trust does not make donations which: replace statutory funding; are for general running costs or major capital projects; support a specific individual (this includes Gap year funding, travel overseas to help a charity, medical treatment, holidays, etc.); support lobbying or political parties; benefit a single religious or a single ethnic group; help causes outside the UK; help to gain specialist school status; or are for commercial sponsorship or for fund raising events, conferences or advertising.
Geographic Focus: All States, United Kingdom
Amount of Grant: 500 - 20,000 GBP
Contact: Trust Administrator; 0870 608 0104; communitypartnership@abbey.com
Internet: http://www.aboutabbey.com/csgs/Satellite?c=GSInformacion&cid=282596177748070&pagename=AboutAbbey%2FGSInformacion%2FPAAI_generic
Sponsor: Abbey Charitable Trust
P.O. Box 911
Milton Keynes, MK 9 1AD England

Abbot and Dorothy H. Stevens Foundation Grants 79
The Abbot and Dorothy H. Stevens Foundation funds Massachusetts non-profits with a emphasis on the greater Lawrence/Merrimack Valley area. Giving primarily for the arts, education, conservation, and health and human services. Fields of interest include: arts; children/youth, services; crime/violence prevention, domestic violence; education; elderly; environment, natural resources; health care; health organizations, association; historic preservation/historical societies; humanities; human services; immigrants; medical school/education; museums. Types of support include: building/renovation; capital campaigns; continuing support; endowments; equipment; general/operating support; management

development/capacity building; matching/challenge support; program-related investments/ loans; program development; technical assistance.
Requirements: Massachusetts 501(c)3 tax-exempt organizations serving the greater Lawrence and Merrimack Valley are eligible. There is no deadline date when applying for funding, nor is there a application form required. The Foundation will however accept the Associated Grantmakers Common Proposal Form. Applicants should submit a copy of their IRS Determination Letter and one copy of their proposal when applying for funding. The board meets and reviews proposals monthly except for the months of July and August.
Restrictions: Grants do not support national organizations, state or federal agencies, individuals, annual campaigns, deficit financing, exchange programs, internships, professorships, scholarships, or fellowships.
Geographic Focus: Massachusetts
Amount of Grant: 1,000 - 20,000 USD
Contact: Josh Miner; (978) 688-7211; grantprocess@stevensfoundation.com
Sponsor: Abbot and Dorothy H. Suitevens Foundation
P.O. Box 111
North Andover, MA 01845-7211

Abbott Fund Access to Health Care Grants 80
Abbott's Access to Health Care programs seek innovative solutions to improve and expand access to health care services for disadvantaged populations. Specific areas of focus include cardiovascular health, diabetes, nutrition, maternal and child health and neonatal care. Many Abbott Fund programs are engaged in closing gaps in ethnic and minority communities, promoting health and nutrition education for families, training health workers, and improving delivery of health services. Complete and submit the Abbott Fund online grant application, posted when available. It should include your organization's Federal Tax ID. At times when the Abbott Fund is accepting unsolicited grant applications, it will acknowledge receipt of an online application via email. The Fund will notify an applicant of its decision on a funding request within six to eight weeks.
Requirements: Grants are made to tax-exempt organizations supporting access to health care.
Restrictions: The Abbott Fund does not accept unsolicited grant applications for projects outside the United States. Contributions will not be made to individuals; for-profit entities; purely social organizations; political parties or candidates; sectarian religious organizations; advertising; symposia, conferences, and meetings; ticket purchases; memberships; business-related purposes; volunteer efforts of non-Abbott employees; or marketing sponsorships.
Geographic Focus: Arizona, California, Illinois, Kansas, Massachusetts, Michigan, New Jersey, New York, North Carolina, Ohio, Puerto Rico, Texas, Utah, Virginia
Amount of Grant: 20,000 - 100,000 USD
Contact: Cindy Schwab; (847) 937-7075; fax (847) 935-5051; cindy.schwab@abbott.com
Internet: http://www.abbottfund.org/tags/access
Sponsor: Abbott Fund
100 Abbott Park Road, Department 379, Building 6D
Abbott Park, IL 60064-3500

Abbott Fund Community Grants 81
The Abbott Fund Community Grant program is active in communities around the world where Abbott has a significant presence. It pursues local partnerships and creative programs that address unmet needs of a community. Emphasis is placed on improving access to health care and promoting science education. The program also supports major civic, arts and other cultural institution programming, primarily in the Chicago metropolitan area where Abbott is headquartered. Complete and submit the Abbott Fund online grant application, posted when available. It should include your organization's Federal Tax ID. At times when the Abbott Fund is accepting unsolicited grant applications, it will acknowledge receipt of an online application via email. The Fund will notify an applicant of its decision on a funding request within six to eight weeks.
Requirements: Grants are made to tax-exempt organizations supporting company operating areas in Arizona, California, Illinois, Kansas, Massachusetts, Michigan, New Jersey, New York, North Carolina, Ohio, Puerto Rico, Texas, and Virginia, and Utah. It also supports the communities of: Abingdon, England; Brockville, Canada; Campoverde, Italy; Clonmel, Ireland; Cootehill, Ireland; Delkenheim, Germany; Kanata, Canada; Katsuyama, Japan; Ludwigshafen, Germany; Queenborough, England; Rio de Janeiro, Brazil; Sligo, Ireland; and Zwolle, the Netherlands.
Restrictions: Contributions will not be made to individuals; for-profit entities; purely social organizations; political parties or candidates; sectarian religious organizations; advertising; symposia, conferences, and meetings; ticket purchases; memberships; business-related purposes; volunteer efforts of non-Abbott employees; or marketing sponsorships.
Geographic Focus: Arizona, California, Illinois, Kansas, Massachusetts, Michigan, New Jersey, New York, North Carolina, Ohio, Puerto Rico, Texas, Utah, Virginia, Brazil, Canada, Germany, Great Britain, Ireland, Italy, Japan, Netherlands
Amount of Grant: 10,000 - 100,000 USD
Contact: Cindy Schwab; (847) 937-7075; fax (847) 935-5051; cindy.schwab@abbott.com
Internet: http://www.abbottfund.org/tags/community/1
Sponsor: Abbott Fund
100 Abbott Park Road, Department 379, Building 6D
Abbott Park, IL 60064-3500

Abbott Fund Global AIDS Care Grants 82
Abbott has been a significant contributor to the fight against HIV/AIDS for more than two decades. Since 2000, Abbott and the Abbott Fund have invested $225 million in grants and product donations targeted to resource poor countries most impacted by HIV/AIDS. The focus of these efforts includes expanding access to care, testing and treatment; strengthening HIV/AIDS health care systems; preventing mother-to-child transmission; and supporting children and families affected by HIV/AIDS. In addition, Abbott and the Abbott Fund have helped pioneer innovative model programs to combat the disease. For example, we helped build the Baylor International Pediatric AIDS Initiative's first pediatric outpatient clinic in Romania in 2001 that has served an average of 600 patients per year. The clinic has reduced pediatric HIV mortality rates by more than 90 percent. Today Baylor has replicated the Romania model in additional clinics throughout Africa and now serves nearly 60,000 children and young people with HIV – including those at two clinics built by and supported by the Abbott Fund in Malawi and Tanzania.
Requirements: Grants are made to tax-exempt organizations supporting global HIV/AIDS programs.
Restrictions: Contributions will not be made to individuals; for-profit entities; purely social organizations; political parties or candidates; sectarian religious organizations; advertising; symposia, conferences, and meetings; ticket purchases; memberships; business-related purposes; volunteer efforts of non-Abbott employees; or marketing sponsorships.
Geographic Focus: Arizona, California, Illinois, Kansas, Massachusetts, Michigan, New Jersey, New York, North Carolina, Ohio, Puerto Rico, Texas, Utah, Virginia
Amount of Grant: 10,000 - 100,000 USD
Contact: Cindy Schwab; (847) 937-7075; fax (847) 935-5051; cindy.schwab@abbott.com
Internet: http://www.abbottfund.org/project/20/30/Helping-Children-and-Young-People-Living-with-HIV-AIDS
Sponsor: Abbott Fund
100 Abbott Park Road, Department 379, Building 6D
Abbott Park, IL 60064-3500

Abbott Fund Science Education Grants 83
The world urgently needs people who are well-trained in science and technology, and the Abbott Fund is committed to doing its part to address this challenge. Serving as a catalyst by stimulating community investment and engagement, Abbott's investment in science education: engages and inspires students, families and teachers in scientific exploration in out-of-school informal settings; encourages young people to be more proficient in science and attracts more scientists to the field; and builds strong partnerships that are systemic, replicable and sustainable for multiple years and multiple locations. Complete and submit the Abbott Fund online grant application, posted when available. It should include your organization's Federal Tax ID. At times when the Abbott Fund is accepting unsolicited grant applications, it will acknowledge receipt of an online application via email. The Fund will notify an applicant of its decision on a funding request within six to eight weeks.
Requirements: Grants are made to tax-exempt organizations supporting company operating areas in Arizona, California, Illinois, Kansas, Massachusetts, Michigan, New Jersey, New York, North Carolina, Ohio, Puerto Rico, Texas, and Virginia, and Utah. It also supports the communities of: Abingdon, England; Brockville, Canada; Campoverde, Italy; Clonmel, Ireland; Cootehill, Ireland; Delkenheim, Germany; Kanata, Canada; Katsuyama, Japan; Ludwigshafen, Germany; Queenborough, England; Rio de Janeiro, Brazil; Sligo, Ireland; and Zwolle, the Netherlands.
Restrictions: Contributions will not be made to individuals; for-profit entities; purely social organizations; political parties or candidates; sectarian religious organizations; advertising; symposia, conferences, and meetings; ticket purchases; memberships; business-related purposes; volunteer efforts of non-Abbott employees; or marketing sponsorships.
Geographic Focus: Arizona, California, Illinois, Kansas, Massachusetts, Michigan, New Jersey, New York, North Carolina, Ohio, Puerto Rico, Texas, Utah, Virginia, Brazil, Canada, Germany, Great Britain, Ireland, Italy, Japan, Netherlands
Amount of Grant: 20,000 - 100,000 USD
Contact: Cindy Schwab; (847) 937-7075; fax (847) 935-5051; cindy.schwab@abbott.com
Internet: http://www.abbottfund.org/tags/science/1
Sponsor: Abbott Fund
100 Abbott Park Road, Department 379, Building 6D
Abbott Park, IL 60064-3500

ABC-CLIO Award for Best Book in Library Literature 84
The ABC-CLIO Award for Best Book in Library Literature is intended to recognize those who improve management principles and practice, understanding and application of new techniques, or further the education of librarians or other information specialists. This $2,500 award is given out on an annual basis. Interested parties should complete an online application by the annual deadline of December 1.
Requirements: Award title(s): must deal with topics and issues pertinent to library professionals; must be an original work; may be part of a monographic series; must be published in the United States or Canada; may be of joint authorship; and must have been published between January 1 and December 31 of the year preceding announcement of the award. Titles published by the award sponsor, Greenwood Publishing Group, are eligible for the award if they meet all eligibility requirements and criteria, and as long as no Greenwood Publishing Group employees are serving on the ALA Awards Committee.
Geographic Focus: All States
Date(s) Application is Due: Dec 1
Amount of Grant: 2,500 USD
Contact: Cheryl Malden; (312) 280-3247; fax (312) 944-3897; cmalden@ala.org
Internet: http://www.ala.org/awardsgrants/awards/33391/apply
Sponsor: American Library Association
50 East Huron Street
Chicago, IL 60611-2795

ABC Charities Grants 85
ABC Charities, formerly known as ADE Charities, is based in Indianapolis, Indiana, and primarily offers its support to organizations that maintain a home for destitute, abandoned, neglected, and dependent children, as well as to Christian organizations, including missions. Its major fields of interest include: children and youth; Christian

agencies and churches; higher education; human and social services; Protestant agencies and churches; and residential/custodial care facilities. Although ABC's geographic stated focus is in Indiana, the Foundation has also given grants in Ohio, Alabama, Florida, Arizona, Texas, and Tennessee.
Geographic Focus: Alabama, Arizona, Florida, Indiana, Ohio, Tennessee, Texas
Amount of Grant: Up to 120,000 USD
Contact: D. Michael Hockett, Director; (317) 862-7325; fax (317) 862-7325
Sponsor: ABC Charities
8250 Woodfield Crossing Boulevard, Suite 300, P.O. Box 39026
Indianapolis, IN 46239-0026

Abel and Sophia Sheng Charitable Foundation Grants   86
The Abel and Sophia Sheng Charitable Foundation awards grants to nonprofit organizations in its areas of interest, including: fine arts, secondary education, higher education, museums, hospitals, and general charitable giving. Types of support include general operating support. There are no application forms or deadlines, and applicants should begin by contacting the office directly in writing with a general description of their program.
Geographic Focus: Massachusetts, New York, Rhode Island
Contact: Abel Sheng, (201) 784-0238 or (201) 567-5991; fax (201) 567-8862
Sponsor: Abel and Sophia Sheng Charitable Foundation
52 Rio Vista Drive, P.O. Box 1042
Alpine, NJ 07620-1042

Abelard Foundation East Grants   87
The Abelard Foundation is a family foundation, with offices on both the east and west coasts, which has been making grants in support of progressive social change since 1958. The foundation is committed to social change activities that expand and protect civil liberties and civil and human rights; increase opportunities for the poor, the disenfranchised, and people of color; and enhance and expand community involvement in, and control over, economic and environmental decisions affecting members of the community. Grants support activities such as community and grassroots organizing, action research, and advocacy. Seed grants, project, and/or general support grants are awarded for new projects or organizations addressing issues that traditional philanthropic sources might avoid. By supporting model efforts that can be duplicated elsewhere and that offer the potential for broader impact, the foundation encourages grantees to use these funds as leverage in gaining additional support. The foundation accepts proposals on a year-around basis.
Requirements: Eligible applicants must represent or be associated with a nonprofit, 501(c)3 tax-exempt organization. The foundation gives priority to projects that are in their first years of development and have budgets less than $300,000. Nonprofit organizations offering services east of the Mississippi are eligible. The foundation is not able to respond to phone inquiries. Inquiries should be made by mail or email.
Restrictions: The foundation does not support social service programs offering ongoing or direct delivery of service; medical, educational, or cultural institutions; capital expenditure, construction, or renovation programs; programs undertaken at government initiative; or scholarship funds or other aid to individuals.
Geographic Focus: Alabama, Arkansas, Connecticut, Delaware, District of Columbia, Florida, Georgia, Illinois, Indiana, Kentucky, Louisiana, Maine, Maryland, Massachusetts, Michigan, Minnesota, Mississippi, Missouri, New Hampshire, New Jersey, New York, North Carolina, Ohio, Pennsylvania, Rhode Island, South Carolina, Tennessee, Vermont, Virginia, West Virginia, Wisconsin
Date(s) Application is Due: Mar 15; Sep 15
Amount of Grant: Up to 10,000 USD
Contact: Susan B. Collins, Vice President; eastabel@aol.com
Internet: http://foundationcenter.org/grantmaker/abelardeast/index.html
Sponsor: Abelard Foundation East
P.O. Box 148
Lincoln, MA 01773

Abelard Foundation West Grants   88
The Abelard Foundation West is committed to grassroots social change activities that expand and protect civil liberties and civil and human rights; increase opportunities for the poor, the disenfranchised, and people of color; and enhance and expand community involvement in, and control over, economic and environmental decisions affecting members of the community. Grants support activities such as community and grassroots organizing, action research, and advocacy. Seed grants, project, and/or general support grants are awarded for new projects or organizations addressing issues that traditional philanthropic sources might avoid. By supporting model efforts that can be duplicated elsewhere and that offer the potential for broader impact, the foundation encourages grantees to use funds as leverage in gaining additional support. Applicants located in the Northern Rockies, the Great Basin, the Northwest, the Southwest, or California should contact the office listed at the website. Deadlines for Letters of Inquiry are January 15th and June 15th (LOIs must be received by these dates) for Spring and Fall grant making meetings. Decisions usually take at least 4-6 months from the date of submittal.
Requirements: 501(c)3 organizations located in the Northern Rockies, the Great Basin, the Northwest, the Southwest, and California are eligible.
Restrictions: The foundation does not support social service programs offering ongoing or direct delivery of service; medical, educational, or cultural institutions; capital expenditure, construction, or renovation programs; programs undertaken at government initiative; or scholarship funds or other aid to individuals.
Geographic Focus: Arizona, California, Colorado, Idaho, Kansas, Montana, Nebraska, Nevada, North Dakota, Oklahoma, Oregon, South Dakota, Utah, Washington, Wyoming
Date(s) Application is Due: Jan 15; Jun 15
Amount of Grant: 6,000 - 12,000 USD
Contact: Patricia St. Onge; (510) 834-2995; fax (510) 834-2998; info@commoncounsel.org
Internet: http://www.commoncounsel.org/Abelard%20Foundation%20West
Sponsor: Abelard Foundation West
678 13th Street, Suite 100
Oakland, CA 94612

Abeles Foundation Grants   89
Established in New Mexico in 2002, the Abeles Foundation is an organization that provides general operating to the areas of elementary and secondary education, public foundations, higher education, and the performing arts in the Albuquerque and Santa Fe areas. The Foundation makes gifts to organizations based on their interactions living within the community. There is no formal application required or annual deadlines. Applicants should contact the Foundation directly. Awards range up to about $1,200.
Restrictions: No grants are made to individuals and applicant's organization must be a qualified 501(c)3 organization.
Geographic Focus: New Mexico
Amount of Grant: Up to 1,200 USD
Contact: Richard A. Abeles, (505) 988-1115; fax (505) 984-2040; rick@abeles.net
Sponsor: Abeles Foundation
3730 Old Santa Fe Trail
Santa Fe, NM 87505-4573

Abel Foundation Grants   90
The foundation awards grants to eligible Nebraska nonprofit organizations in its areas of interest, which include: environmental programs and natural resource conservation; health care; higher education; Protestant religion and churches; arts and culture; and social services. Types of support include building construction and/or renovation, capital campaigns, general operating support, and program grants. Contact the office for application forms. Application deadlines are March 31, July 15, and October 31 each year. Applications qualifying for review will be considered within 1 to 3 months of receipt.
Requirements: Nebraska nonprofit organizations are eligible. Preference is given to requests from Lincoln, Nebraska, and the state's southeastern region.
Restrictions: The Foundation does not accept applications from organizations: that have had requests approved or declined in the past 12 months; or that are currently received payments for a multi-year grant.
Geographic Focus: Nebraska
Date(s) Application is Due: Mar 31; Jul 15; Oct 31
Amount of Grant: 50 - 40,000 USD
Contact: J. Ross McCown, Vice President; (402) 434-1212; fax (402) 434-1799; rossm@nebcoinc.com or nebcoinfo@nebcoinc.com
Internet: http://www.abelfoundation.org/grant.htm
Sponsor: Abel Foundation
1815 Y Street, P.O. Box 80268
Lincoln, NE 68501-0268

Abell-Hanger Foundation Grants   91
The foundation makes grants to nonprofit Texas organizations, other than private foundations, that are involved in such undertakings for the public/society benefit including arts, cultural, and humanities; education; health; human services; and religion. Types of support include general operating support, continuing support, annual campaigns, capital campaigns, building construction/renovation, equipment acquisition, endowment funds, program development, seed funds, scholarship funds, research grants, and matching funds. Block scholarship grants are made only to institutions of higher education located in Texas. Recipient colleges and universities are free to administer the grants. Education grants are limited generally to institutions of higher education, including religious institutions (Baptist, Christian, Lutheran, Methodist, and Presbyterian). Applicants must seek funding for the same proposal from various sources because sole sponsorship of programs is rarely undertaken. Grant requests are considered and awarded throughout each year. The trustees prefer to consider only one request per applicant each fiscal year. Unsuccessful proposals may not be resubmitted for at least 12 months. Applicant organizations that have never received funding from the foundation should request a preproposal questionnaire; the trustees will review the request to determine whether it warrants a complete proposal.
Requirements: Applicant organizations must be located in Texas and be 501(c)3 tax-exempt. National organizations with significant operations in, or providing material benefits to the citizens of, Texas will be considered based on the degree of operations/benefits within the state.
Restrictions: The foundation does not fund grants, scholarships, or fellowships for individuals.
Geographic Focus: Texas
Date(s) Application is Due: Feb 28; May 31; Sep 30; Nov 11
Amount of Grant: 20,000 - 50,000 USD
Contact: David L. Smith; (432) 684-6655; fax (432) 684-4474; ahf@abell-hanger.org
Internet: http://www.abell-hanger.org/GrantCriteria.htm
Sponsor: Abell-Hanger Foundation
P.O. Box 430
Midland, TX 79702-0430

Abell Foundation Arts and Culture Grants   92
In recognition of the overall economic health of a city, the Foundation seeks funding opportunities to strengthen existing cultural arts organizations and to support emerging arts groups that are providing programming in under-served neighborhoods. The Foundation looks for initiatives that help keep artists working and living in the metropolitan area;

increase organizations' capacity to expand audiences; attract more cultural visitors; and stabilize and revitalize neighborhoods. The Foundation also supports pilot projects that seek to determine the outcomes of cultural arts curricula on overall student academic achievement while at the same time reinforcing the State's mandate to integrate the cultural arts into the K-12 educational programming.
Requirements: 501(c)3 organizations serving Maryland communities, especially in the Baltimore area, may apply. The foundation prefers grantees that show strong fiscal management, their project's benefit to the community, ability to achieve goals, unique work, and other sources of financial support.
Restrictions: The Foundation does not fund educational programs at higher education institutions, medical facilities, individual scholarships, fellowships, annual operating expenses, sponsorships, deficit financing, endowments, travel or memberships.
Geographic Focus: Maryland
Date(s) Application is Due: Jan 1; Mar 1; May 1; Aug 1; Sep 1; Nov 1
Contact: Robert C. Embry, Jr.; (410) 547-1300; embry@abell.org or abell@abell.org
Internet: http://www.abell.org/programareas/arts.html
Sponsor: Abell Foundation
111 S Calvert Street, Suite 2300
Baltimore, MD 21202-6174

Abell Foundation Community Development Grants   93
The Foundation recognizes the need to enhance the livability of neighborhoods and create desirable housing and commercial areas as a means to retain and attract both residents and jobs. By encouraging investment in redevelopment projects and housing renovations, leveraging of public and private capital, community planning and maximizing reuse of historic structures, the Foundation focuses on those initiatives that foster improvement of downtown and neighborhoods. It further seeks to promote cost-efficient delivery of municipal services, maximize Baltimore's use of competitive funding sources and increase the tax base. The Foundation also encourages efforts to tie the health of the City to the region and state, through the support of housing mobility, regional planning and growth management.
Requirements: 501(c)3 organizations serving Maryland communities, especially in the Baltimore area, may apply. The foundation prefers grantees that show strong fiscal management, their project's benefit to the community, ability to achieve goals, unique work, and other sources of financial support.
Restrictions: The Foundation does not fund educational programs at higher education institutions, medical facilities, individual scholarships, fellowships, annual operating expenses, sponsorships, deficit financing, endowments, travel or memberships.
Geographic Focus: Maryland
Date(s) Application is Due: Jan 1; Mar 1; May 1; Aug 1; Sep 1; Nov 1
Amount of Grant: 5,000 - 50,000 USD
Contact: Tracey M. Barbour-Gillett, Program Officer; (410) 547-1300; fax (410) 539-6579; tbarbour@abell.org or abell@abell.org
Internet: http://www.abell.org/programareas/community.html
Sponsor: Abell Foundation
111 S Calvert Street, Suite 2300
Baltimore, MD 21202-6174

Abell Foundation Conservation and Environment Grants   94
The Foundation supports organizations that are working to protect and preserve Maryland's natural resources. Partnering with the public and private sectors, the Foundation places special emphasis on those initiatives supporting ecosystem-wide conservation programs, including forests, wetlands, agricultural lands, watersheds and air and water quality. The Foundation also focuses attention on local projects reinforcing Maryland's Smart Growth, Rural Legacy and Green Print initiatives. Areas of interest include: environmental justice in underserved communities; advocacy for healthy air and clean water; enforcement and legal compliance initiatives; preservation of farmland and creation of effective buffer zones; preservation of parklands for recreational and educational purposes; sustainable and safe use of resources; and watershed and habitat protection.
Requirements: 501(c)3 organizations serving Maryland communities, especially in the Baltimore area, may apply. The foundation prefers grantees that show strong fiscal management, their project's benefit to the community, ability to achieve goals, unique work, and other sources of financial support.
Restrictions: Grants are not given to individuals, or for sponsorships, deficit financing, operating budgets, annual sustaining funds, travel, or loans. The foundation currently does not fund housing projects, hospitals, or medical research.
Geographic Focus: Maryland
Date(s) Application is Due: Jan 1; Mar 1; May 1; Aug 1; Sep 1; Nov 1
Amount of Grant: 5,000 - 50,000 USD
Contact: Robert C. Embry, Jr., President; (410) 547-1300; fax (410) 539-6579; embry@abell.org or abell@abell.org
Internet: http://www.abell.org/programareas/conservation.html
Sponsor: Abell Foundation
111 S Calvert Street, Suite 2300
Baltimore, MD 21202-6174

Abell Foundation Criminal Justice and Addictions Grants   95
The Foundation seeks to increase access to substance abuse treatment and supportive services such as housing and job training for the uninsured and drug addicted individuals residing in Baltimore City. The Foundation works to increase the impact and effectiveness of treatment services through cutting edge research and support of innovative service models designed to reach under-served populations. The Foundation supports programs and initiatives that increase public safety and reduce recidivism with a special focus on initiatives that address the barriers facing the returning ex-offender. Areas of interest include: substance abuse treatment, prevention, and research; supportive housing; prisoner reentry; criminal justice system reform; and juvenile justice. A particular emphasis is placed on initiatives that provide transitional housing and the necessary wraparound services to support a successful return to the community.
Requirements: 501(c)3 organizations serving Maryland communities, especially in the Baltimore area, may apply. The foundation prefers grantees that show strong fiscal management, their project's benefit to the community, ability to achieve goals, unique work, and other sources of financial support.
Restrictions: The Foundation does not fund educational programs at higher education institutions, medical facilities, individual scholarships, fellowships, annual operating expenses, sponsorships, deficit financing, endowments, travel or memberships.
Geographic Focus: Maryland
Date(s) Application is Due: Jan 1; Mar 1; May 1; Aug 1; Sep 1; Nov 1
Amount of Grant: 5,000 - 50,000 USD
Contact: Amanda Owens; (410) 547-1300; aowens@abell.org or abell@abell.org
Internet: http://www.abell.org/programareas/criminal.html
Sponsor: Abell Foundation
111 S Calvert Street, Suite 2300
Baltimore, MD 21202-6174

Abell Foundation Health and Human Services Grants   96
Through grants awarded in this area, the Foundation seeks to address societal issues associated with family disintegration, family planning, child support, teenage parenting, domestic violence, children's health and well-being, child abuse and neglect, hunger, food self-sufficiency and homelessness. The Foundation also supports advocacy programs for better health care and social services for children and youth as well as for a comprehensive system of universal health care. Of particular concern is the support of efforts to combat childhood lead paint poisoning and mental health disorders. Furthermore, the Foundation continues to provide opportunities for low-income families to live in quality housing in good neighborhoods in the region. While the Foundation's primary focus is on the development of permanent housing, it also will consider emergency and transitional housing.
Requirements: 501(c)3 organizations serving Maryland communities, especially in the Baltimore area, may apply. The foundation prefers grantees that show strong fiscal management, their project's benefit to the community, ability to achieve goals, unique work, and other sources of financial support.
Restrictions: The Foundation does not fund educational programs at higher education institutions, medical facilities, individual scholarships, fellowships, annual operating expenses, sponsorships, deficit financing, endowments, travel or memberships.
Geographic Focus: Maryland
Date(s) Application is Due: Jan 1; Mar 1; May 1; Aug 1; Sep 1; Nov 1
Amount of Grant: 5,000 - 50,000 USD
Contact: Theresa Staudenmaier; (410) 547-1300; staudenmaier@abell.org o
Internet: http://www.abell.org/programareas/health.html
Sponsor: Abell Foundation
111 S Calvert Street, Suite 2300
Baltimore, MD 21202-6174

Abell Foundation Workforce Development Grants   97
The Foundation supports job skills training that enables low-income, unemployed and underemployed job seekers to secure jobs that pay family-sustaining wages. Priority is given to programs that link hard-to-serve job seekers with employment, that promote job retention for at least one year of employment, and that enhance opportunities for low-wage workers to improve their skills and move into higher wage jobs. The Foundation works with nonprofit organizations, employers and public agencies to improve how public workforce development funding is being spent in Baltimore and to link effective programs with public funding. The Foundation also works with nonprofit organizations to increase job seekers' access to needed services, including literacy services, transportation, substance abuse treatment, and services for ex-offenders. Finally, The Foundation seeks to strengthen policy initiatives that support low-income families and enhance wages.
Requirements: 501(c)3 organizations serving Maryland communities, especially in the Baltimore area, may apply. The foundation prefers grantees that show strong fiscal management, their project's benefit to the community, ability to achieve goals, unique work, and other sources of financial support.
Restrictions: The Foundation does not fund educational programs at higher education institutions, medical facilities, individual scholarships, fellowships, annual operating expenses, sponsorships, deficit financing, endowments, travel or memberships.
Geographic Focus: Maryland
Date(s) Application is Due: Jan 1; Mar 1; May 1; Aug 1; Sep 1; Nov 1
Amount of Grant: 5,000 - 50,000 USD
Contact: Melanie Styles; (410) 547-1300; styles@abell.org or abell@abell.org
Internet: http://www.abell.org/programareas/workforce.html
Sponsor: Abell Foundation
111 S Calvert Street, Suite 2300
Baltimore, MD 21202-6174

Abernethy Family Foundation Grants   98
The Abernethy Family Foundation was established in 2000 in Florida with a mission of supporting elementary and secondary education programs, curriculum development, agricultural programs, and health care within St. Lucie and Indian River counties, Florida. General operating funding is its primary type of support. There are no deadlines with which to adhere, and applicant organizations should begin by requesting an application form directly from the Foundation.

14 | Grant Programs

Restrictions: Giving is restricted to eligible organizations within St. Lucie and Indian River counties, Florida.
Geographic Focus: Florida
Contact: Bruce R. Abernethy, Jr; (772) 489-4901; babernethy@bruceapa.com
Sponsor: Abernethy Family Foundation
500 Virginia Avenue, Suite 202
Fort Pierce, FL 34982-5882

ABIG Foundation Grants 99
The ABIG Foundation targets the South Florida community and other locations where American Bankers Insurance Group conducts its business. It supports programs in arts and culture, children and youth, education, and social services. Proposals must be submitted in typewritten form, preferable on organization letterhead. There are no application deadline dates with which to adhere.
Requirements: South Florida nonprofit organizations are eligible.
Geographic Focus: Florida
Amount of Grant: 5,000 - 200,000 USD
Contact: R. Kirk Landon; (305) 253-2244 or (800) 852-2244; fax (305) 252-6987
Sponsor: ABIG Foundation
11222 Quail Roost Drive
Miami, FL 33157-6596

Abington Foundation Grants 100
The Abington Foundation awards grants to Ohio nonprofit organizations serving Cuyahoga County in its areas of interest, including pre-primary and higher education, geriatric healthcare and nursing, the promotion or sustenance of individual and family economic independence, and cultural activities. Priority is given to funding requests for specific programs or projects that represent critical periods in a child's development from birth to age 5, and to early adolescence, ages 10-15. Requests for endowment or general operating support are discouraged. Foundation staff is available for consultation during the proposal preparation process.
Requirements: Ohio nonprofit organizations serving Cuyahoga County are eligible.
Geographic Focus: Ohio
Date(s) Application is Due: May 1; Sep 1; Dec 1
Amount of Grant: 5,000 - 50,000 USD
Contact: Janet E. Narten; (216) 621-2901 or (216) 621-2632; fax (216) 621-8198
Internet: http://www.fmscleveland.com/abington
Sponsor: Abington Foundation
1422 Euclid Avenue, Suite 627
Cleveland, OH 44115-1952

Able To Play Challenge Grants 101
The project provides challenge grants and technical assistance for the development of play environments throughout the state of Michigan. The program will work with communities to create play environments that incorporate full integration and universal accessibility with rigorous, challenging, developmentally appropriate, and sensory-rich activities to benefit children of all abilities/disabilities. Information and application are available online.
Geographic Focus: All States
Amount of Grant: 25,000 - 225,000 USD
Contact: Administrator; (860) 243-8315; fax (860) 243-5854; info@abletoplay.org
Internet: http://www.boundlessplaygrounds.org/about/index.php
Sponsor: National Center for Boundless Playgrounds
280 Trumbull Street, 23rd Floor
Hartford, CT 06103

Able To Serve Grants 102
Able to Serve Inc. is a public charity, providing services and opportunities for persons with mental and physical disabilities. Able primarily serves Wake and Johnston counties in North Carolina with some services extended to surrounding counties when resources are available. There are currently four programs that cover the services Able fund within the local community; Local Ministry Network, Community Partnerships, Van Transportation Services, and Computer Learning/Donations.
Requirements: Able to Serve provides each service and program at no charge to the individual or family receiving services within the Wake and Johnston counties of North Carolina.
Geographic Focus: North Carolina
Contact: Carlton S. McDaniel, President; (919) 779-5545; carlton@abletoserve.com
Internet: www.abletoserve.com
Sponsor: Able To Serve
P.O. Box 334
Garner, NC 27529-0334

Able Trust Vocational Rehabilitation Grants for Agencies 103
The trust supports individuals and non-profit vocational rehabilitation programs throughout Florida with fund-raising, grant making and public awareness of disability issues. The program provides grant funds to Florida not-for-profit agencies and Floridians with disabilities for a wide array of projects leading to the employment of individuals with disabilities. To be considered for funding a proposal must address the employment of individuals with disabilities and priority is given to those projects with direct employment placement outcomes during the grant time period. Grants to organizations are typically around $45,000. Historically grants have been made between $5,000 and $200,000. The amount is relative to the scale, scope and complexity of the proposed employment project.
Requirements: Agency applicants must be a 501(c)3 organization serving the disability community in Florida and interested in providing employment services for individuals with disabilities. Any employment program that will provide direct placement in competitive employment, the transition from school-to-work, transition from sheltered/work enclave settings to community-based employment, job skills training such as resume and interview assistance, computer skills, office skills and etiquette, transportation training to access work, and other research, public awareness and promotion that focuses on creating employment opportunities for individuals with disabilities. There are no deadlines. Guidelines, helpful tips and application forms can be found at the sponsor's website.
Restrictions: Grants funds may not be used to purchase: vehicles, property, building improvements, capital campaigns, endowments, fellowships, scholarships, travel grants, tuition where state and federal aid is available, lobbying, medical items, incurred debt, and program expenses prior to grant approval.
Geographic Focus: Florida
Amount of Grant: 5,000 - 200,000 USD
Contact: Guenevere Crum, Senior Vice President; (850) 224-4493; fax (850) 224-4496; guenevere@abletrust.org or info@abletrust.org
Internet: http://www.abletrust.org/grant/booklet.shtml
Sponsor: Able Trust
3320 Thomasville Road, Suite 200
Tallahassee, FL 32308

Able Trust Vocational Rehabilitation Grants for Individuals 104
The trust supports individuals and non-profit vocational rehabilitation programs throughout Florida with fund-raising, grant making and public awareness of disability issues. Created by the Florida Legislature in 1990, the Florida Endowment Foundation for Vocational Rehabilitation, parent organization of the Able Trust, is 501(c)3 non-profit public/private partnership with a goal of assisting Floridians with disabilities in achieving employment. The trust provides grant funds to Florida not-for-profit agencies and Floridians with disabilities for a wide array of projects leading to the employment of individuals with disabilities. To be considered for funding a proposal must address the employment individuals with disabilities and priority is given to those projects with direct employment placement outcomes during the grant time period. Grants to individuals are typically around $2,500. Historically grants have been made between $500-$4,000 for job accommodations.
Requirements: Individuals currently residing in the state of Florida that need emergency on-the-job accommodations to accept an employment offer, retain or receive a promotion at their current employment and are not currently open clients with a state agency provider may apply to be considered for assistance. There are no deadlines; guidelines, helpful tips and forms can be found at the sponsor's website.
Restrictions: Grants funds may not be used to purchase: vehicles, property, building improvements, capital campaigns, endowments, fellowships, scholarships, travel grants, tuition where state and federal aid is available, lobbying, medical items, incurred debt, and proposed expenses prior to grant approval.
Geographic Focus: Florida
Amount of Grant: 500 - 4,000 USD
Contact: Guenevere Crum, Senior Vice President; (850) 224-4493; fax (850) 224-4496; guenevere@abletrust.org or info@abletrust.org
Internet: http://www.abletrust.org/grant/booklet.shtml
Sponsor: Able Trust
3320 Thomasville Road, Suite 200
Tallahassee, FL 32308

Abney Foundation Grants 105
The foundation makes grants for innovative and creative projects, and to programs that are responsive to changing community needs in the areas of health, social service, education, and cultural affairs in South Carolina. The foundation's primary focus is on higher education. All requests must be in writing and in accordance with foundation guidelines, which are available upon request, and from the website. Applicants may submit a Letter of Intent (LOI) briefly describing the project before submitting a proposal in order to find out if their ideas are potentially supported by the foundation.
Requirements: Agencies applying for funds should be serving the citizens of South Carolina.
Restrictions: The foundation does not generally fund requests for operating expenses.
Geographic Focus: South Carolina
Date(s) Application is Due: Nov 15
Amount of Grant: 5,000 - 100,000 USD
Contact: David C. King, Executive Director; (864) 964-9201; fax (864) 964-9209; info@abneyfoundation.org
Internet: http://www.abneyfoundation.org/guideline.htm
Sponsor: Abney Foundation
100 Vine Street
Anderson, SC 29621-3265

Aboudane Family Foundation Grants 106
Established in Michigan in 2007, the Aboudane Family Foundation offers awards for operating support to Islamic organizations throughout the United States. Primary fields of interest are stated to be: health; education; and community services. There are no specific application forms or annual deadlines, and applicants should contact the Foundation directly before beginning the writing process. Grants generally range from $1,000 to $15,000.
Geographic Focus: All States
Amount of Grant: 1,000 - 15,000 USD
Contact: Zakwan A. Aboudane, (810) 742-8770; fax (810) 742-8772
Sponsor: Aboudane Family Foundation
5032 Parkwood Court
Flushing, MI 48433-1390

GRANT PROGRAMS | 15

ABS Foundation Grants   107
Established in California in 2003, the ABS Foundation funds programs in areas of company operations in California, Colorado, Georgia, and Hawaii. Its primary fields of interest include: the arts; education; human services; and youth development. Types of support funding include capital campaigns, endowments, and general operations. Applicants should contact the Foundation directly to request an application. There are no specified annual deadlines, and grant amounts typically range from $1,000 to $3,000.
Geographic Focus: California, Colorado, Georgia, Hawaii
Amount of Grant: 1,000 - 3,000 USD
Contact: Mark C. Ballantyne, President; (916) 503-4100
Sponsor: ABS Foundation
P.O. Box 276227
Sacramento, CA 95827-6227

Abundance Foundation International Grants   108
The Abundance Foundation makes grants to organizations aligned with its mission to improve global health through education, economic empowerment and health systems strengthening. It is focused on programs that unlock the potential of local communities particularly in Africa, Central America and Haiti. Its grantee partners train, support and empower local leaders to create new capabilities that result in lasting improvement in quality of life. In addition to direct grant funding that allows for upscaling of successful existing programs, the Foundation raise awareness about local leaders whose vision and heroism are creating positive change in their communities.
Geographic Focus: All States, Haiti
Contact: Stephen Kahn; (510) 841-4123; fax (510) 841-4093; info@abundancefound.org
Internet: http://www.abundancefound.org/grants/
Sponsor: Abundance Foundation
127 University Avenue
Berkeley, CA 94710-1616

Abundance Foundation Local Community Grants   109
The Abundance Foundation is a Non-Profit 501(c)3 Public Charity established in California in 2004. The Foundation makes grants in the San Francisco Bay Area to support youth development, the arts and education. Its current partners train, support and empower local leaders to create new capabilities and lasting improvement in quality of life. Though no specific deadlines are listed, applicants should begin by contacting the Foundation offices directly.
Geographic Focus: California
Contact: Stephen Kahn; (510) 841-4123; fax (510) 841-4093; info@abundancefound.org
Internet: http://www.abundancefound.org/grants/
Sponsor: Abundance Foundation
127 University Avenue
Berkeley, CA 94710-1616

Access Fund Climbing Preservation Grants   110
The program awards grants to projects that preserve and enhance climbing opportunities and conserve the climbing environment throughout the United States. Grants support projects that encourage access to or enhance opportunities for climbing; be supported by the climbing community; raise awareness about climber responsibilities through stewardship projects; develop or support partnerships with resource management agencies, conservation organizations, land trusts, and local climbing groups; reduce climber impacts on natural and cultural resources; develop knowledge about natural and cultural resource values where the information is used to open climbing areas or mitigate climbing impacts; include volunteer labor and/or pro bono services; use some matching funds; and be located within the United States. Requests over $10,000 are considered if the project has national significance and offers a high percentage of matching funds. Contact the office before submitting an application for a large grant.
Requirements: Applications may be submitted by local climbing groups or organizations; governmental agencies that wish to sponsor or organize a local project; and research groups, conservation organizations, and land trusts. 501(c)3 tax-exempt status is not necessary.
Restrictions: The Fund does not support: fixed anchors, bolts, bolt installation, etc; outdoor programs (e.g. taking groups climbing, at-risk programs, youth groups); climbing equipment; marketing or membership recruitment; facility construction (e.g. indoor climbing walls, artificial climbing facilities, ice parks); paid positions and travel stipends; or political campaigns.
Geographic Focus: All States
Date(s) Application is Due: Mar 1; Aug 1
Amount of Grant: 500 - 20,000 USD
Contact: Zachary Lesch-Huie, Affiliate Director; (303) 545-6772, ext. 107; fax (303) 545-6774; zachary@accessfund.org or grantapplications@accessfund.org
Internet: http://www.accessfund.org/cons/guidelines.php
Sponsor: Access Fund
207 Canyon, Suite 201, P.O. Box 17010
Boulder, CO 80308

ACE Charitable Foundation Grants   111
ACE supports the communities around the world in which its employees live and work through its established ACE Foundations and through company-sponsored volunteer initiatives. They focus their philanthropic support in the areas of education, poverty and health, and the environment. Particular consideration is given to opportunities where ACE employees' time and expertise can be utilized in addition to financial support. ACE encourages the development of local and regional initiatives, which reflect their employees' commitment to the needs of the communities in which they live and work. ACE employees direct a significant portion of the company's charitable giving.
Requirements: The mission of the ACE Charitable Foundation is to assist less fortunate individuals and communities in achieving and sustaining productive and healthy lives in geographic areas where ACE employees live and work. The ACE Charitable Foundation strives to accomplish this by focusing the majority of its funds on clearly defined projects that have measurable objectives and outcomes and solve problems in the areas of education, the environment and poverty and health. Submit a brief letter of introduction to the Executive Director for consideration.
Geographic Focus: Arizona, Arkansas, California, Colorado, Connecticut, Delaware, District of Columbia, Florida, Georgia, Hawaii, Illinois, Indiana, Kansas, Louisiana, Maryland, Massachusetts, Michigan, Minnesota, Nevada, New Jersey, New York, North Carolina, Ohio, Oregon, Pennsylvania, Puerto Rico, South Carolina, Texas, Virginia, Washington
Samples: The following is a partial list of organizations with which the ACE Charitable Foundation is associated: American Red Cross; City of Hope Cancer Center; Fairmount Park Conservancy; Kids' Chance; Need in Deed; Philadelphia Cares; Philadelphia Museum of Art; Philadelphia Academies, Inc; United Way
Contact: Eden Kratchman, Executive Director; acefoundation@acegroup.com
Internet: http://www.acelimited.com/AceLimitedRoot/About+ACE/ACE+Philanthropy+Worldwide/The+ACE+INA+Foundation+One+Column.htm
Sponsor: ACE Charitable Foundation
436 Walnut Street, WA 08G
Philadelphia, PA 19106

ACF ACYF Runaway and Homeless Youth Basic Center Grants   112
The Administration on Children, Youth and Families is a part of the Administration for Children and Families (ACF), under the Department of Health and Human Services, and is administered by a Commissioner who is a Presidential appointee. ACYF is divided into two bureaus, each of which is responsible for different issues involving children, youth and families and a cross-cutting unit responsible for research and evaluation. The purpose of the program is to support agencies that provide crisis intervention services to runaway and homeless youth outside the traditional juvenile justice and law enforcement systems. The overall goal of the program is to reunite youth with their families whenever possible, or to arrange for other suitable placements. The Family and Youth Services Bureau (FYSB) awards discretionary grants annually on a competitive basis. Deadline dates may vary; contact program staff for exact dates.
Requirements: Any State, unit of local government, public or private agency, Indian Tribe, organization, or institution is eligible to apply for these discretionary funds.
Geographic Focus: All States
Amount of Grant: 100,000 - 200,000 USD
Contact: Maiso Bryant, Acting Commissioner; (301) 608-8098
Internet: http://www.acf.hhs.gov/programs/fbci/progs/fbci_rhyouth.html
Sponsor: Administration on Children, Youth and Families
P.O. Box 13505
Silver Spring, MD 20911-3505

ACF Adoption Opportunities Project Grants   113
The Adoption Opportunities program provides discretionary funds for projects designed to eliminate barriers to adoption and help find permanent families for children who would benefit from adoption, particularly children with special needs. Some of the major program areas include: the development and implementation of a national adoption information exchange system; increasing services in support of the placement in adoptive families of minority children who are in foster care and have the goal of adoption, with a special emphasis on the recruitment of minority families; increasing post-legal adoption services for families who have adopted children with special needs; and, supporting the placement of children in kinship care arrangements, pre-adoptive, or adoptive homes.
Requirements: Eligible entities include States, local government entities, federally recognized Indian Tribes and tribal organizations, faith-based and community organizations, colleges and universities, public or private non-profit licensed child welfare or adoption agencies, and adoption exchanges.
Geographic Focus: All States
Contact: Geneva Ware-Rice, (202) 205-8354
Internet: http://www.acf.hhs.gov/programs/fbci/progs/fbci_adoption.html
Sponsor: Administration on Children, Youth and Families
P.O. Box 13505
Silver Spring, MD 20911-3505

ACF Assets for Independence Demonstration Grants   114
The goals of the AFI Program are to: create, through project activities and interventions, meaningful asset accumulation opportunities for eligible low-income individuals and families, including households eligible for Temporary Assistance for Needy Families (TANF); evaluate the effectiveness of the projects and the project designs, and determine the extent to which an asset-based program can lead to economic self-sufficiency of participants; and, determine the social, civic, psychological, and economic effects of providing to low-income individuals and families an incentive to accumulate assets, and the extent to which an asset-based policy stabilizes and improves families and communities. An AFI grantee establishes a Reserve Fund, combining Federal grant money and the required non-Federal funding, to match the project participants' investment of savings from earned income in matched savings accounts called Individual Savings Accounts (IDAs). The IDA savings may be used for acquisition of the following assets: the purchase or building of a first home; the capitalization of a business; the costs of post-secondary education; and/or transfers of IDAs to family members.
Requirements: Eligible applicants include: state governments; county governments; city or township governments; special district governments; independent school districts; public and state controlled institutions of higher education; Native American tribal governments (federally recognized); public housing authorities and/or Indian housing authorities;

Native American tribal organizations (other than federally recognized tribal governments); nonprofits having a 501(c)3 status with the IRS, other than institutions of higher education; nonprofits that do not have a 501(c)3 status with the IRS, other than institutions of higher education; private institutions of higher education; for profit organizations other than small businesses; and small businesses.
Geographic Focus: All States
Date(s) Application is Due: Jan 25; Mar 25; May 25
Contact: Jim Gatz, Program Manager; (202) 401- 5284; james.gatz@acf.hhs.gov
Internet: http://www.acf.hhs.gov/grants/open/foa/view/HHS-2011-ACF-OCS-EI-0137
Sponsor: Administration for Children and Families
370 L'Enfant Promenade SW, 5th Floor
Washington, DC 20447

ACF Assets for Independence Individual Development Account Grants 115
The Assets for Independence (AFI) program provides five-year grants to nonprofit organizations and government agencies that empower low-income families to become economically self-sufficient for the long-term. Grantees provide financial education training on money management issues, and they assist participants with saving earned income in special matched savings accounts called Individual Development Accounts (IDAs). Participants use the IDAs to accumulate funds with the goal of acquiring a first home, post-secondary education, or starting up or expanding a small business.
Requirements: Eligible applicants include: state governments; county governments; local governments; city or township governments; regional organizations; independent school districts; public and state-controlled institutions of higher education; Indian/Native American tribal governments (federally recognized); Indian/Native American tribal organizations (other than federally recognized); Indian/Native American tribally designated organizations; Public/Indian housing authorities; non-profits with 501(c)3 IRS status (other than institutions of higher education); private institutions of higher education; Hispanic-serving institutions; historically Black colleges and universities (HBCUs); tribally controlled colleges and universities (TCCUs); Alaska Native and Native Hawaiian serving institutions; and special district governments. Non-profit entities that do not have 501(c)3 status may only apply as a joint applicant with an entity that is so certified. Low-Income Credit Unions and Community Development Financial Institutions are eligible only if they demonstrate a strong collaborative relationship with one or more local community-based organization(s) that seek to address poverty and the economic needs of community residents. Such community-based organizations may be any number of types of entities such as philanthropic foundations, community foundations, for-profit organizations, or non-profit organizations. If a non-profit, they are not required to have 501(c)3 status. Faith-based and community organizations that meet the statutory eligibility requirements are eligible to apply under this announcement. As a condition of their Federal AFI grant, grantees must provide non-Federal funds to support their AFI project in an amount at least equal to the Federal AFI grant amount. A primary feature of each AFI project is that project participants are given access to special matched savings accounts called Individual Development Accounts (IDA), in which participants save earned income for the purchase of a home, for business capitalization, or to attend higher education or training. Grantees also ensure that participants have access to financial literacy education and coaching including training on money management and consumer issues. Participants receive up to $2,000 per individual or $4,000 per household from the Federal AFI grant and at least an equal amount in non-Federal funds as match funds for their IDA savings. After saving earned income in the IDA for a number of months or years, participants use their IDA savings and match funds for qualified purchases including homeownership, business capitalization or to obtain higher education or training. Participants may transfer their IDA savings to an IDA owned by their spouse or a dependent. In addition to enabling participants to save in an IDA, grantees also ensure that participants have access to financial literacy education and coaching including training on money management and consumer issues. Project and budget periods are for five years or 60 months. Applicants should submit a budget for the full five-year project period. All applicants must have a D&B Data Universal Numbering System (D-U-N-S) number.
Restrictions: Foreign entities are not eligible under this announcement.
Geographic Focus: All States
Date(s) Application is Due: Jan 15; Mar 25; Jun 25
Amount of Grant: 350,000 USD
Contact: James Gatz, Program Manager; (202) 401-5284; james.gatz@acf.hhs.gov
Internet: https://www.acf.hhs.gov/programs/ocs/resource/for-prospective-grantees
Sponsor: Administration for Children and Families
370 L'Enfant Promenade SW, 5th Floor
Washington, DC 20447

ACF Community-Based Abstinence Education Grants 116
The Community-Based Abstinence Education program supports communities across the country in delivering the message that abstinence is the surest way to avoid out-of-wedlock pregnancy and sexually-transmitted diseases (STDs). Funding through this program will also finance comprehensive evaluations of abstinence education programs. This program provides funding directly to individual organizations to support public and private entities in the development and implementation of abstinence education programs for adolescents, ages 12 through 18, in communities across the country.
Requirements: Non-profit organizations and other community-based organizations, including faith-based organizations, are eligible to apply for funding. There is no match requirement for Federal funds received under the Community-Based Abstinence Education Grant program. Applicants must indicate how proposed programs will target the prevention of teenage pregnancy, premarital sexual activity, and the incidence of sexually transmitted disease among adolescents using culturally sensitive and age-appropriate materials. For the purposes of this program, the term 'abstinence education' means an educational or motivational program which teaches: the social, psychological, and health gains to be realized by abstaining from sexual activity as its exclusive purpose; that abstinence from sexual activity is the expected standard outside marriage for all school age children; that abstinence from sexual activity is the only certain way to avoid out-of-wedlock pregnancy, sexually transmitted diseases, and other associated health problems; that a mutually faithful monogamous relationship in the context of marriage is the expected standard of human sexual activity; that sexual activity outside of the context of marriage is likely to have harmful psychological and physical effects; that bearing children out-of-wedlock is likely to have harmful consequences for the child, the child's parents, and society; young people how to reject sexual advances and how alcohol and drug use increases vulnerability to sexual advances; and, teaches the importance of attaining self-sufficiency before engaging in sexual activity.
Restrictions: Applicants must agree not to provide a participating adolescent any other education regarding sexual conduct in the same setting.
Geographic Focus: All States
Contact: Jeff Trimbath, (202) 401-9205; JTrimbath@acf.hhs.gov
Internet: http://www.acf.hhs.gov/programs/fbci/progs/fbci_cbaep.html
Sponsor: Administration on Children, Youth and Families
P.O. Box 13505
Silver Spring, MD 20911-3505

ACFEF Disaster Relief Fund Member Assistance 117
The American Culinary Federation Education Foundation (ACFEF) is the educational arm of the American Culinary Federation (ACF). ?Funds from the ACFEF Disaster Relief Fund are available to assist ACF members, schools with ACFEF programmatic accreditation and its students, communities and individuals affected by catastrophic events and natural disasters. Disaster relief can be provided in the form of a check, gift card, services and/or goods to ensure that victims have the basic necessities, such as food, clothing, housing (including repairs), transportation and medical assistance (including psychological counseling).
Requirements: Requests must be completed by an ACF members in need of basic necessities, such as food, clothing, housing (including repairs), transportation, and medical assistance (including psychological counseling) due to losses suffered as a result of a catastrophic event and/or natural disaster.
Geographic Focus: All States
Contact: Michelle Whitfield, (904) 484-0202; mwhitfield@acfchefs.net
Internet: https://www.acfchefs.org/Source/Meetings/acf_Disaster_Relief.cfm
Sponsor: American Culinary Federation Education Foundation
180 Center Place Way
St. Augustine, FL 32095

ACF Ethnic Community Self-Help Grants 118
The Office of Refugee Resettlement (ORR) invites the submission of applications for funding, on a competitive basis, to connect newcomer refugees and their communities with community resources. The objective of this program is to strengthen organized ethnic communities comprised and representative of refugee populations to ensure ongoing support and services to refugees after initial resettlement. Ethnic Community Self-Help applications are for project periods of up to three years (36 months). Awards, on a competitive basis, will be for twelve (12) month budget periods although project periods may be up to thirty-six (36) months. Applications for continuation grants funded under these awards, beyond the twelve (12)-month budget period but within the thirty-six (36) month project period, will be entertained in subsequent years on a non-competitive basis subject to availability of funds, satisfactory progress of the grantee and determination that continued funding would be in the best interest of the government.
Requirements: Public or private nonprofit agencies are eligible applicants. Faith-based and community organizations that meet the statutory eligibility requirements are also eligible to apply. ORR is interested in applications from national, regional (multi-state) or local refugee community organizations that address community building, facilitate cultural adjustment and integration of refugees, and deliver mutually supportive functions such as information exchange, civic participation, resource enhancement, orientation and support to newly arriving refugees (and other refugees that maybe in need of such assistance regardless of their resettlement date) and public education to the larger community on the background, needs and potential of refugees. Applicants to this program will be of two general types: national or multi-site ethnic organizations that propose to develop or strengthen local ethnic groups and/or a national network of ethnic entities for purposes of linking refugees to community resources and promoting and strengthening community participation; or emerging local ethnic communities that seek to function as bridges between newly arrived refugees and mainstream local resources and organizations.
Restrictions: Foreign entities are not eligible under this announcement.
Geographic Focus: All States
Date(s) Application is Due: Mar 13
Amount of Grant: 100,000 - 250,000 USD
Contact: Thomas Giossi, Program Manager, Division of Community Resettlement; (202) 401-5720; fax (202) 401-4685; thomas.giossi@acf.hhs.gov
Internet: http://www.acf.hhs.gov/grants/open/foa/view/HHS-2011-ACF-ORR-RE-0173
Sponsor: Administration for Children and Families
370 L'Enfant Promenade SW, 5th Floor
Washington, DC 20447

ACF Foundation Grants 119
The Foundation supports organizations involved with arts and culture, children and youth services, community and economic development, education, health care, higher education, and human services. Giving is limited to areas of company operations, with emphasis on St. Louis and St. Charles, Missouri. There are no specific deadlines or forms, and applicants should forward the entire proposal to the office.

Requirements: 501(c)3 nonprofit organizations, based in or serving the the communities of St. Louis or St. Charles, Missouri, are eligible to apply.
Restrictions: No grants are given to individuals.
Geographic Focus: Missouri
Contact: Nancy Collins; (636) 940-5101 or (636) 940-5000; ncollins@arleasing.com
Sponsor: ACF Foundation
101 Clark Street, Suite 201
St. Charles, MO 63301-2081

ACF Head Start and Early Head Start Grants 120

Head Start has a long tradition of delivering comprehensive services designed to foster healthy development in the most vulnerable young children, including those with disabilities. Head Start and Early Head Start grantees and delegate agencies provide a range of individualized services in the areas of education and early childhood development; medical, dental, mental health, and nutrition services; and family and community partnership development through parent involvement. In addition, all Head Start services are responsive and appropriate to each child and family's developmental, ethnic, cultural, and linguistic heritage and experience.
Requirements: Proposals are welcome for projects to support the development of innovation and improvement projects that could help improve the effectiveness and management of local Head Start and Early Head Start sites. Presidential priority areas that could be addressed include, but are not limited to, Early Literacy Development; Improving Services to Rural Areas; Positive Youth Development; Strengthening Families/Fatherhood; and Faith-Based and Community-Based Initiatives. Conceivably these projects could address improvements in transportation services, nutrition services, services to special populations, program management, and a number of other areas. Grants for the operation of Head Start and Early Head Start programs may be awarded to public or private, for profit or nonprofit organizations, including Faith based organizations or to public school systems. A currently funded grantee will continue to serve as the Head Start agency in the community until the grantee organization decides it no longer wants to be a sponsoring agency, or unless the Head Start Bureau terminates the grant for cause. If a grantee gives up or loses funding, Head Start funds will be awarded to another eligible organization in the same community through a competitive process. Grants for Head Start Innovation and Improvement Projects may be awarded to public or private nonprofit organizations, including State and local governments and universities, federally recognized Indian tribes, and faith-based and community-based organizations. Private for-profit organizations may apply provided no grant funds are to be paid as profit to grantees.
Restrictions: Grantees that operate Early Head Start programs must provide at least 20 percent of the total approved costs of the project.
Geographic Focus: All States
Contact: Jean Simpson, (202) 205-8421; jsimpson@acf.hhs.gov
Internet: http://www.acf.hhs.gov/programs/fbci/progs/fbci_headstart.html
Sponsor: Administration on Children, Youth and Families
P.O. Box 13505
Silver Spring, MD 20911-3505

ACF Mentoring Children of Prisoners Grants 121

Through the Mentoring Children of Prisoners Program, FYSB awards grants to faith-based and community organizations, along with tribes and state and local government entities, which provide children and youth of incarcerated parents with caring adult mentors. Each mentoring program is designed to ensure that mentors provide young people with safe and trusting relationships; healthy messages about life and social behavior; appropriate guidance from a positive adult role model; and opportunities for increased participation in education, civic service, and community activities. ACF solicits applications for the Mentoring Children of Prisoners Program through funding announcements on Grants.gov. Grant awards for these one to three year projects are made on a competitive basis, with funding for each one-year budget period determined annually.
Requirements: Grant recipients are required to provide services, both directly and in collaboration with other local agencies, to strengthen and support children of incarcerated parents and their families. This includes preserving families and connecting the children with their imprisoned parent when appropriate. Recipients are also required to cultivate mentors from within the child's family and community through recruitment, screening, training, and monitoring and evaluation: Recruiting—Grantees are required to recruit mentors who are committed to spending at least one hour per week with their assigned child for a period of at least one year; Screening—Grant recipients are required to screen volunteers extensively through appropriate reference checks, criminal background checks, and child and domestic abuse record checks, to ensure that they pose no safety risk to the young people; Training—Mentors must attend an orientation and training in mentoring skills and the practice of mentoring before being assigned to a young person, and grant recipients are responsible for matching each child to a suitable adult mentor; Monitoring and Evaluating—Grantees are required to provide ongoing support and oversight of the mentoring relationship to ensure that young people are receiving appropriate support and are benefiting from the mentor match. Outcomes for each participating youth are measured by such factors as academic achievement and avoidance of risky behaviors. ACF encourages grantees to incorporate elements of a positive youth development approach. That approach suggests that the best way to prevent young people's involvement in risky behavior is to help them achieve their full potential. Youth development strategies, therefore, focus on giving young people the chance to exercise leadership, build skills, and become involved in their communities.
Geographic Focus: All States
Contact: Lisa Dammar, (202) 401-5513; ACFOGME-Grants@acf.hhs.gov
Internet: http://www.acf.hhs.gov/programs/fbci/progs/fbci_mcp.html
Sponsor: Administration on Children, Youth and Families
P.O. Box 13505
Silver Spring, MD 20911-3505

ACF Native American Environmental Regulatory Enhancement Grants 122

In 1990, NAPA was amended to strengthen tribal government capacity to identify, plan, develop, and implement environmental programs that will bolster regulatory efforts in a manner that is consistent with a Tribe's cultural preservation and natural resource management priorities. Ultimate success in this program will be realized when the applicant's desired level of environmental quality is acquired and maintained. This Funding Opportunity Announcement emphasizes community-based, locally-designed projects that strengthen tribal governments' and organizations' ability to identify, plan, develop, and implement environmental regulatory programs in a manner that is consistent with the goals and priorities of native communities. ANA has identified program areas of interest and project types for this Funding Opportunity Announcement, but also emphasizes that funding is not restricted to those listed below: establishing baseline condition for regulatory purposes; developing regulations, ordinances, and laws to protect the environment; building the technical and program capability of the Tribe or organization to perform essential environmental program functions to meet tribal and Federal regulatory requirements; building the technical and program capability of personnel to monitor compliance and enforcement of tribal and Federal environmental regulations, ordinances, and laws; informing the community about regulations and environmental stewardship; and establishing demonstration projects to exhibit technologies, which can lead to compliance with environmental regulations.
Requirements: Eligible applicants include Federally recognized Indian Tribes; incorporated non-Federally and State recognized Indian Tribes; Alaska Native villages, as defined in the Alaska Native Claims Settlement Act, and/or non-profit village consortia; non-profit Alaska Native Regional Corporations/Associations in Alaska with village specific projects; other Tribal or village organizations or consortia of Indian Tribes; and tribal governing bodies (Indian Reorganization Act or Traditional Councils) as recognized by the Bureau of Indian Affairs. Grantees must provide at least 20 percent of the total approved cost of the project.
Restrictions: Individuals, foreign entities, and sole proprietorship organizations are not eligible to compete for, or receive, awards made under this announcement.
Geographic Focus: All States
Date(s) Application is Due: Jan 31
Amount of Grant: 100,000 - 300,000 USD
Contact: Sarah Schappert, (877) 922-9262; ana@acf.hhs.gov
Tim Chappelle, (202) 401-4855; tim.chappelle@acf.hhs.gov
Internet: http://www.acf.hhs.gov/grants/open/foa/view/HHS-2011-ACF-ANA-NR-0142
Sponsor: Administration for Children and Families
370 L'Enfant Promenade SW, Aerospace Center, 2nd Floor-West
Washington, DC 20447

ACF Native American Social and Economic Development Strategies Grants 123

Grant awards made under this Funding Opportunity Announcement are for projects that promote economic and social self sufficiency for American Indians, Alaska Natives, Native Hawaiians, and other Native American Pacific Islanders from American Samoa, Guam, and Commonwealth of the Northern Mariana Islands. ANA is particularly interested in projects designed to grow local economies, strengthen Native American families, and decrease the high rate of social challenges caused by the lack of community-based business, and social and economic infrastructure. ANA has identified two major program areas of interest for this funding opportunity announcement, which include social development and economic development. In the area of social development, of most interest are proposals that improve: human services; community living; early childhood development; youth development; community health; arts and culture; safety and security; nutrition and fitness; and the strengthening of families. In the area of economic development, of most interest are proposals that improve: economic stability; economic competitiveness; agriculture; infrastructure; emergency preparedness; subsistence; and commercial trade.
Requirements: Eligible applicants include Federally recognized Indian Tribes; consortia of Indian Tribes; incorporated non-Federally recognized Tribes; incorporated non-profit, multi-purpose, community-based Indian organizations; urban Indian centers; National or regional incorporated non-profit Native American organizations with Native American community-specific objectives; Alaska Native villages, as defined in the Alaska Native Claims Settlement Act and/or non-profit village consortia; incorporated non-profit Alaska Native multi-purpose, community-based organizations; non-profit Alaska Native Regional Corporations/Associations in Alaska with village-specfic projects; non-profit native organizations in Alaska with village-specific projects; public and non-profit private agencies serving Native Hawaiians; public and private non-profit agencies serving native peoples from Guam, American Samoa, or the Commonwealth of the Northern Mariana Islands (the populations served may be located on these islands or in the United States); tribally controlled community colleges, tribally controlled post-secondary vocational institutions, and colleges and universities located in Hawaii, Guam, American Samoa, or the Commonwealth of the Northern Mariana Islands which serve Native Pacific Islanders; and non-profit Alaska Native community entities or tribal governing bodies (Indian Reorganization Act or Traditional Councils) as recognized by the Bureau of Indian Affairs. Faith-based and community organizations that meet eligibility requirements are eligible to receive awards under this funding opportunity announcement. Grantees must provide at least 20 percent of the total approved cost of the project.
Restrictions: Individuals, foreign entities, and sole proprietorship organizations are not eligible to compete for, or receive, awards made under this announcement.
Geographic Focus: Alaska
Date(s) Application is Due: Jan 31
Amount of Grant: 50,000 - 400,000 USD
Contact: Sarah Schappert; (877) 922-9262; fax (202) 690-7441; ana@acf.hhs.gov
Internet: http://www.acf.hhs.gov/grants/open/foa/view/HHS-2011-ACF-ANA-NA-0143
Sponsor: Administration for Children and Families
370 L'Enfant Promenade SW, Aerospace Center, 2nd Floor-West
Washington, DC 20447

ACF Preferred Communities Grants 124

The purpose and objectives of the Preferred Communities program are to support resettlement of newly arriving refugees with the best opportunities for their self-sufficiency and integration into new communities, and to support refugees with special needs that require more intensive case management. Applicants may apply to support resettlement in new communities targeted to geographic sites or special populations agreed to in consultation with the Department of State/Bureau for Population, Refugees and Migration (BPRM) and ORR. There are two types of Preferred Communities programs for the purposes of this grant. The first type of Preferred Communities program should expect to receive a minimum of 100 new refugees annually. ORR will consider exceptions to this standard where the applicant provides substantial justification for the request and documents the community's history of arrivals, the period of time needed to reach a level of 100 new refugees and the record of outcomes for achieving self-sufficiency soon after arrival. The second type of Preferred Communities program will expect to receive a proposed number of cases that will need intensive case management. If the Preferred Community plans to focus resources on special needs cases, a history of its qualifications and experience with serving special needs cases should be provided.

Requirements: Eligible applicants are ten national voluntary agencies that currently resettle refugees under a Reception and Placement Cooperative Agreement with the Department of State or with the Department of Homeland Security. The Preferred Communities program is restricted to these agencies because placements of new arrivals occur under the terms of the cooperative agreements, and no other agencies place new arrivals or participate in determining their resettlement sites. The ten eligible applicants are the following: Church World Service, Inc; Domestic and Foreign Missionary Society; Ethiopian Community Development Council, Inc; Hebrew Immigrant Aid Society, Inc; International Rescue Committee; Lutheran Immigration and Refugee Service; State of Iowa; U.S. Conference of Catholic Bishops; U.S. Committee for Refugees and Immigrants; and World Relief Corporation. Faith-based and community organizations that meet the statutory eligibility requirements are eligible to apply under this announcement. Preferred Communities are those localities that support populations where refugees have excellent opportunities to achieve early employment and sustained economic independence without public assistance. Preferred Communities should have a history of low welfare utilization by refugees. In addition, refugees should have the potential for earned income at a favorable level relative to the cost of living and to public assistance benefits. Characteristics of these communities include: a moderate cost of living; excellent employment opportunities in a strong, entry-level labor market; affordable housing and transportation accessible for employment; low secondary out-migration rates for refugees; communities that meet the religious needs of arriving populations; local community support and positive reception for the refugees; receptive school environments; and other related community features that contribute to a favorable quality of life for arriving refugees, such as excellent medical facilities.

Restrictions: Foreign entities are not eligible under this announcement.

Geographic Focus: All States

Date(s) Application is Due: Mar 1

Amount of Grant: 100,000 - 225,000 USD

Contact: Susan S. Benjamin, (202) 401-4851; susan.benjamin@acf.hhs.gov

Internet: http://www.acf.hhs.gov/grants/open/HHS-2008-ACF-ORR-RP-0112.html

Sponsor: Administration for Children and Families
370 L'Enfant Promenade SW, 5th Floor
Washington, DC 20447

ACF Supplemental Services for Recently Arrived Refugees Grants 125

The purpose and objectives ORR seeks to achieve through Supplemental Services for Recently Arrived Refugees are to provide additional resources to communities where the refugee services are insufficient. Under these circumstances, resources are needed to provide additional service capacity to accommodate an increase of refugees. Through Supplemental Services for Recently Arrived Refugees, ORR intends to offer to communities the resources to respond to the needs of newly arrived refugees with adequate and culturally and linguistically appropriate social services. This grant program is intended to provide services to arriving refugees or sudden and unexpected large secondary migration of refugees where communities are not sufficiently prepared in terms of linguistic or culturally appropriate services. In providing services to refugees who have arrived in country less than three years, applicants should view these resources as a temporary solution to insufficient services currently available to meet emerging needs of recently arrived refugees in a specific community. ORR formula social service funds are awarded to States to provide services proportionate to the number of refugee arrivals during the previous three years. ORR invites applications that propose seventeen (17) month projects for a minimum of 100 refugees annually. Examples of situations for which applicants may request funds for grants under Supplemental Services for Recently Arrived Refugees are as follows: refugee services do not presently exist or the service capacity is not sufficient to accommodate significant increases in arrivals; and the existing service system does not have culturally and linguistically compatible staff.

Requirements: Public or private nonprofit agencies are eligible applicants. Faith-based and community organizations that meet the statutory eligibility requirements are eligible to apply. Allowable activities in the Supplemental Services for Recently Arrived Refugees program are social services for refugees that are appropriate and accessible in language and culture. Examples of allowable social or emergency services to recently arrived refugees include: information and referral services; outreach services; social adjustment services; emergency services; health-related services; home management services; day care for children; transportation; translation and interpretation; case management; citizenship and naturalization preparation services; employment services; employability assessment; on-the job training; English language instruction; vocational training; skills recertification; and any additional services approved by the Director of ORR as supporting the objectives of this program.

Restrictions: Foreign entities are not eligible under this announcement.

Geographic Focus: All States

Date(s) Application is Due: Mar 16

Amount of Grant: 75,000 - 200,000 USD

Contact: Susan S. Benjamin, (202) 401-4851; susan.benjamin@acf.hhs.gov

Internet: http://www.acf.hhs.gov/grants/open/foa/view/HHS-2011-ACF-ORR-RU-0149

Sponsor: Administration for Children and Families
370 L'Enfant Promenade SW, 5th Floor
Washington, DC 20447

A Charitable Foundation Grants 126

Funded by the Tactical Investment Management Corporation, the A Charitable Foundation offers support primarily in California, Hawaii, and New York, as well as Brazil. Its major fields of interest include: educational research; the environment; food banks; human services; and international development. Types of support include annual campaigns, building and renovation projects, emergency assistance, basic research, and grants to individuals. Applications should include a detailed description of the project, purpose of the research (if applicable), and a detailed budget. There are no annual deadlines, and grants typically range from $250 to $30,000.

Geographic Focus: California, Hawaii, New York

Amount of Grant: 250 - 30,000 USD

Contact: David S. Druz, President; (702) 248-8184

Sponsor: A Charitable Foundation
2657 Windmill Parkway, Suite 220
Henderson, NV 89014

Achelis Foundation Grants 127

Elisabeth Achelis was born in Brooklyn Heights in 1880. She used her inheritance from her father Fritz Achelis, who was President of the American Hard Rubber Company, to establish the Achelis Foundation in 1940 to aid and contribute to charitable, benevolent, educational and religious uses and purposes for the moral, ethical, physical, mental and intellectual well-being and progress of mankind; to aid and contribute to methods for the peaceful settlement of international differences; to aid and contribute to the furtherance of the objects and purposes of any charitable, benevolent, educational or religious institution or agency; and to establish and maintain charitable, benevolent and educational institutions and agencies. The Achelis Foundation shares trustees, staff, office space, and even a website with the Bodman Foundation which has a similar mission and geographic area of concentration (both foundations give in New York City, while the Bodman Foundation also gives in New Jersey). Funding is concentrated in six program areas: Arts and Culture, Education, Employment, Health, Public Policy, and Youth and Families.

Requirements: 501(c)3 organizations based in New York City that fall within the foundation's areas of interest are welcome to submit an inquiry or proposal letter by regular mail (initial inquiries by email or fax are not accepted, nor are CDs, DVDs, computer discs, or video tapes). An initial inquiry to the foundation should include only the following items: a proposal letter that briefly summarizes the history of the project, need, objectives, time period, key staff, project budget, and evaluation plan; the applicant's latest annual report and complete set of audited financial statements; and the applicant's IRS 501(c)3 tax-exemption letter. Applications may be submitted at any time during the year. Each request is reviewed by staff and will usually receive a written response within thirty days. Those requests deemed consistent with the interests and resources of the foundation will be evaluated further and more information will be requested. Foundation staff may request a site visit, conference call, or meeting. All grants are reviewed and approved by the Trustees at one of their three board meetings in May, September, or December.

Restrictions: The foundation generally does not make grants for the following purposes or program areas: nonprofit organizations outside of New York; annual appeals, dinner functions, and fundraising events; endowments and capital campaigns; loans and deficit financing; direct grants to individuals; individual day-care and after-school programs; housing; organizations or projects based outside the U.S; films or video projects; small art, dance, music, and theater groups; individual K-12 schools (except charter schools); national health and mental health organizations; and government agencies or nonprofit organizations significantly funded or reimbursed by government agencies. Limited resources prevent the foundations from funding the same organization on an ongoing annual basis.

Geographic Focus: New York

Contact: John B. Krieger; (212) 644-0322; main@achelis-bodman-fnds.org

Internet: http://www.achelis-bodman-fnds.org/guidelines.html

Sponsor: Achelis Foundation
767 Third Avenue, 4th Floor
New York, NY 10017-2023

A Child Waits Foundation Grants 128

A Child Waits Foundation's Grant program is specifically designed to help older children and children with special needs who are still living in international orphanages to become part of a family. The grant program provides assistance to families who are pursuing adoption of these special children. Giving is primarily aimed at providing financial assistance to individuals adopting foreign-born children. Support for adoption, adoption funding, international adoption and child welfare and the child must meet special needs criteria, and adoptive family must meet financial criteria.

Requirements: Selection of the recipients will be based on a combination of age and medical condition of the child, cost of the adoption and the families' financial situation. Adoptions must be in process through a 501(c)3 agency licensed to place children.

Geographic Focus: All States

Amount of Grant: Up to 5,000 USD

Samples: America-World Adoption Association, McLean, Virginia, $32,500; Kidsave International, Los Angeles, California, $22,000; Children's Home Society and Family Services, Saint Paul, Minnesota, $11,000.

Contact: Cynthia Nelson; (866) 999-2445; fax (518) 794-6243; cnelson@achildwaits.org
Internet: http://www.achildwaits.org/Grant%20Program.htm
Sponsor: A Child Waits Foundation
1136 Barker Road, #12
Pittsfield, MA 01201

Ackerman Foundation Grants 129
The foundation was established as a charitable trust in 1992 by James F. Ackerman, a local entrepreneur and philanthropist. As an Indianapolis based organization, grants are made predominately to central Indiana organizations as well as a few national medical research institutions. Specifically, the foundation focuses on Indiana cultural institutions and organizations benefiting health and human services, community development, and education. Grant requests will be considered for both operating fund purposes as well as capital campaigns. The foundation does not have grant application forms. To be considered for assistance, an organization should write a brief one or two page letter describing its proposal. The Trustees of the foundation meet semi-annually on the business day that falls on or closest to June 15 and December 15.
Requirements: Established under the laws of the State of Indiana, the foundation considers grant proposals from eligible organizations which are tax exempt under the United States Internal Revenue Service Code section 501(c)3.
Restrictions: The foundation does not make grants to individuals.
Geographic Focus: All States
Date(s) Application is Due: May 15; Nov 15
Amount of Grant: 500 - 100,000 USD
Contact: Director; (317) 663-0205; fax (317) 663-0215; jdisbro@cardinalep.com
Internet: http://ackermanfoundation.com/
Sponsor: Ackerman Foundation of Indiana
280 E. 96th Street, Suite 350
Indianapolis, IN 46240-3858

ACMP Foundation Community Music Grants 130
Awards provide funding to community arts organizations in support of ongoing programs that offer musicians of all ages the opportunity to play and be coached in chamber music. Community Music grants to organizations serving pre-college players favor programs for students of intermediate level and above. Grants averaging $1,000-$3,000 are generally made in support of scholarship aid and program staff salaries. This funding often makes it possible for students to experience chamber music for the first time. Community Music grants also support ongoing programs for adults at all levels of expertise in chamber music.
Restrictions: ACMP does not provide funding for: individual or group lessons in instrumental technique; choral, orchestral, and chamber orchestra programs; guest artist performances; activities intended for audience development; or general administration.
Geographic Focus: All States
Date(s) Application is Due: Dec 15
Amount of Grant: 3,000 USD
Contact: Administrator; (212) 645-7424; fax (212) 741-2678; acmpfoundation@acmp.net
Internet: http://www.acmp.net/grants
Sponsor: Amateur Chamber Music Players Foundation
1123 Broadway, Suite 904
New York, NY 10010-2007

Acorn Foundation Grants 131
The foundation supports projects dedicated to building a sustainable future for the planet and to restoring a healthy global environment. The foundation is particularly interested in small and innovative community-based projects that preserve and restore habitats supporting biological diversity and wildlife; advocate for environmental justice, particularly in low-income and indigenous communities; and prevent or remedy toxic pollution. Grantees are asked to submit year-end reports, and Acorn will consider renewal grants to organizations that have fulfilled its reporting requirements. Most grants are made in North America, though occasional grants are made in Latin America.
Requirements: Nonprofit organizations are eligible.
Restrictions: Grants do not support direct services; capital expenditure, construction or renovation programs; programs undertaken by tax-supported institutions or government initiative; emergency funding; scholarship funds or other aid to individuals; and educational, cultural and medical institutions.
Geographic Focus: All States
Date(s) Application is Due: Jan 15; Jun 15
Amount of Grant: 5,000 - 10,000 USD
Contact: Elizabeth Wilcox; (510) 834-2995; fax (510) 834-2998; ccounsel@igc.apc.org
Internet: http://www.commoncounsel.org/Acorn%20Foundation
Sponsor: Acorn Foundation
1221 Preservation Parkway, Suite 101
Oakland, CA 94612-1206

ACS Award for Encouraging Disadvantaged Students into Careers in the 132
Chemical Sciences
The Camille and Henry Dreyfus Foundation established the Award for Encouraging Disadvantaged Students into Careers in the Chemical Sciences in 1993 to recognize significant accomplishments by individuals in stimulating students, underrepresented in the profession, to elect careers in the chemical sciences and engineering. The award consists of $5,000 and a certificate. A grant of $10,000 will also be made to an eligible non-profit institution, designated by the recipient, to strengthen its activities in meeting the objectives of the award. The award is intended to recognize significant accomplishments in the United States by individuals in stimulating students, especially those currently underrepresented in the profession, to elect careers in the chemical sciences and engineering, and in generating a broader appreciation of chemistry as the central science.
Requirements: Nominees for the award may come from any professional setting: academia, industry, government, or other independent facility.
Geographic Focus: All States
Date(s) Application is Due: Nov 1
Amount of Grant: 15,000 USD
Contact: Mark J. Cordillo, Executive Director; (212) 753-1760; fax (212) 593-2256; mcardillo@dreyfus.org or admin@dreyfus.org
Internet: http://www.dreyfus.org/awards/acs_award_for_students.shtml
Sponsor: Camille and Henry Dreyfus Foundation
555 Madison Avenue, 20th Floor
New York, NY 10022-3301

ACS Award for Encouraging Women into Careers in the Chemical Sciences 133
The Camille and Henry Dreyfus Foundation established the Award for Encouraging Women into Careers in the Chemical Sciences in 1993 to recognize significant accomplishments by individuals who have stimulated or fostered the interest of women in chemistry, promoting their professional development as chemists or chemical engineers. The award consists of $5,000 and a certificate. A grant of $10,000 will also be made to an eligible non-profit institution, designated by the recipient, to strengthen its activities in meeting the objectives of the award. Nominees for the award may come from any professional setting: academia, industry, government, or other independent facility. The award is intended to recognize significant accomplishments by individuals in stimulating women to elect careers in the chemical sciences and engineering, and in generating a broader appreciation of chemistry as the central science.
Requirements: Nominees for the award may come from any professional setting: academia, industry, government, or other independent facility.
Geographic Focus: All States
Date(s) Application is Due: Nov 1
Amount of Grant: 15,000 USD
Contact: Mark J. Cordillo, Executive Director; (212) 753-1760; fax (212) 593-2256; mcardillo@dreyfus.org or admin@dreyfus.org
Internet: http://www.dreyfus.org/awards/acs_award_for_women.shtml
Sponsor: Camille and Henry Dreyfus Foundation
555 Madison Avenue, 20th Floor
New York, NY 10022-3301

ACTION Council of Monterey County Grants 134
The ACTION (Advocacy, Community Transformation, Incubating, Organizing, Networking) Council of Monterey County was created in 1994 to address the reduction in government funding for health and human services for low-income and vulnerable people. Its primary goals are: to create public/private partnerships to promote economic and social justice; to initiate community dialogue and action on critical issues; to provide a focal point for achieving community transformation; and to develop resources to facilitate needed change. The ACTION Council has four areas of focus: fiscal sponsorship—ACMC acts as fiscal agent for 24 coalitions of individuals who provide valuable services, which are often not available through traditional community resources; program incubation—based on periodic community assessments, the ACTION Council has initiated several programs which demonstrate success in identifying community needs, developing program plans, securing funding, implementing and sustaining programs; research, evaluation and assessment—REAP provides a full-range of research, evaluation, and assessment services to local nonprofits, foundations, public agencies, and other community-based organizations; and convening—ACMC has initiated community-wide forums on such issues as the status of women and girls and the effects of the economic downturn on non-profit organizations.
Restrictions: Giving is primarily restricted to the Monterey County, California, region
Geographic Focus: California
Contact: Ricki Mazzullo; (831) 783-1244; fax (831) 783-1276; richard@actioncouncil.org
Internet: http://www.actioncouncil.org/about.html
Sponsor: ACTION Council of Monterey County
369 Main Street, Suite 201
Salinas, CA 93901-2770

Action for Affordable Housing Grants 135
The Program is intended to assist home buyers in initial purchase of their homes. Giving is primarily directed toward home-buyers approved by the Department of Housing and Urban Development (HUD) for a down payment assistance program. A formal application is required, and can be obtained by contacting the office directly. There are no specific deadlines, and funding ranges from $1,000 to $15,000.
Requirements: Applicants must be residents of Colorado who can prove adequate need.
Geographic Focus: Colorado
Amount of Grant: 1,000 - 15,000 USD
Contact: Rod Weimer, Director; (303) 779-7979; fax (303) 731-3367
Sponsor: Action for Affordable Housing
8480 E Orchard Road, Suite 1100
Englewood, CO 80111-5015

Active Awareness Fund Grants 136
The Active Awareness Fund is a not for profit 501(c)3 community fund that engages endurance athletes from around the world in an effort to assist and sustain existing charities. This effort will ultimately create positive and enduring social change in both the athlete and the communities they serve. The vision for the Active Awareness Fund was born out of a desire to initiate an enduring spirit of giving among athletes one community at a time.

There are no particular application forms or deadlines with which to adhere, and potential applicants should contact the charitable foundation directly.
Geographic Focus: All States
Contact: Michael L. Stone, (303) 554-0230
Sponsor: Active Awareness Fund
973 Poplar Avenue
Boulder, CO 80304-0738

Actors Fund Dancers' Resource 137
Launched in the summer of 2007, The Dancers' Resource has been created in response to the unique situation dancers face due to the physically demanding nature of their work, coupled with the significant financial challenges of earning a living in dance. Founded by Actors Fund Vice President Bebe Neuwirth, The Dancers' Resource comes out of her personal experience from having hip replacement surgery after several years of physical therapy, arthroscopic surgery and excruciating pain and the emotional stress of not being able to dance and not wanting people to know about her condition. Recognizing that the situations faced by injured dancers are all-encompassing in terms of both life and career, the program was started to create a support system that addresses the needs of dancers. The program provides: emotional support for dancers dealing with injuries by providing individual and group counseling; referrals for health care and health insurance; information and advocacy with Worker Compensation and Disability Insurance; educational seminars on injury prevention, nutrition and wellness, financial planning and more; emergency financial assistance; and, connection to other dancers to share experiences, resources and advice.
Requirements: Any professional dancer is welcome to call The Dancers' Resource for direct services or referrals to community agencies. Eligibility for The Fund's financial assistance program requires an interview, application and documentation of professional earnings and financial need.
Geographic Focus: All States
Contact: Western Region; (323) 933-9244, ext. 55; intakela@actorsfund.org
Internet: http://new.actorsfund.org/services/Social_Services_and_Financial_Assistance/The_Dancers_Resource
Sponsor: Actors Fund
729 7th Avenue, 10th Floor
New York, NY 10019

Actors Fund Funeral and Burial Assistance 138
One of the earliest services The Actors Fund provided was assistance with the cost and arrangements of funerals and burials (initiated in 1886). The Fund continues to assist with the cost of funerals and provide a grave site with a head stone to those in need. In addition, The Fund offers pre-pay arrangements for those interested in purchasing a grave site.
Requirements: Eligibility for The Fund's financial assistance program requires an application, documentation of your professional earnings and an interview. In general, eligibility for financial assistance is based on: a minimum of five years of industry employment with earnings of at least $6,500 for three out of the last five years, or a minimum of 20 years of employment with earnings of at least $2,000 for 10 years; and, financial need.
Geographic Focus: All States
Contact: Western Region; (323) 933-9244, ext. 55; intakela@actorsfund.org
Internet: http://new.actorsfund.org/services/Social_Services_and_Financial_Assistance/Funerals_Burials
Sponsor: Actors Fund
729 7th Avenue, 10th Floor
New York, NY 10019

Actors Fund Social Services and Financial Assistance 139
The Actors Fund Social Services offer comprehensive programs designed to meet the critical needs of entertainment professionals throughout their lives. Social workers provide crisis intervention, individual and family needs assessments, and develop long-term plans include ongoing support, education, information and referrals. In addition, financial assistance can be provided for essential living expenses such as rent, utilities or medical costs.
Requirements: Eligibility for financial assistance varies by program. You are encouraged to call and speak with an Intake Social Worker who can best determine how the program may be of assistance. Overall eligibility for financial assistance is based on: a minimum of five years of industry employment with earnings of at least $6,500 for three out of the last five years and financial need. To apply for financial assistance, an application with supporting documentation and an interview is required. There are no specific deadlines.
Geographic Focus: All States
Contact: Western Region; (323) 933-9244, ext. 55; intakela@actorsfund.org
Internet: http://new.actorsfund.org/services/Social_Services_and_Financial_Assistance/index_html
Sponsor: Actors Fund
729 7th Avenue, 10th Floor
New York, NY 10019

Acuity Charitable Foundation Grants 140
The Acuity Charitable Foundation was established in 2003 with a major donation from the Acuity Mutual Insurance Company. The foundation primarily supports Sheboygan, Wisconsin, organizations involved with arts and culture, elementary and secondary education, engineering, health care, cancer, and youth development. Types of support include general operating support, program development, and sponsorships. Though formal application forms are not required, proposals should be submitted using the organization's letterhead. There are no deadlines, and applicants should submit the entire proposal, which should include: need for the project, group being served, evaluation process, and necessary funding.
Requirements: 501(c)3 organizations based in or serving residents of Sheboygan, Wisconsin, can apply.
Geographic Focus: Wisconsin
Contact: Lynn Yunger, (920) 458-9131
Sponsor: Acuity Charitable Foundation
2800 S. Taylor Drive, P.O. Box 58
Sheboygan, WI 53082-0058

Acumen East Africa Fellowship 141
The East Africa Fellowships are designed to develop leadership skills. The fellowship is structured like an executive MBA, so the awardee remains on the job for the fellowship period. The fellowship creates a unique opportunity for East Africans to receive world-class business training, leadership development, and mentoring. Highlights of the fellowship include: support to refine the applicant's own projects for a large social impact; leadership skills development; and continual guidance from experienced mentors and trainers in strategy and problem solving. Awardees are most likely be successful in their fellowship if they have a deep passion and commitment to the East African region; a proven track record of leadership and management responsibilities; and an unrelenting perseverance, personal integrity and critical thinking skills.
Requirements: Applicants must be at least 18 to apply. There is no educational requirement for the program. The most important requirement is that the applicant have been driving a social change project for at least three years. A "social change project" is defined as any project, initiative, or program that addresses a pressing social issue with an innovative solution that has a positive impact in the lives of the community. The fellowship includes five seminars, including one regional trip. A conference at the end of the fellowship is designed and implemented by the fellowship awardees so they may implement the skills they have learned. The selection process is rigorous and takes place over three months. Online applications are reviewed from March 16 to April 15; phone interviews are conducted from April 17 to May 7; selection conference takes place on May 21 in Nairobi; and finalists are announced on May 31.
Restrictions: Because awardees hold jobs during their fellowship, they do not receive stipends or health insurance.
Geographic Focus: Burundi, Djibouti, Eritrea, Ethiopia, Kenya, Rwanda, Somalia, Sudan, Tanzania, Uganda
Contact: Suraj Sudhakar, East Africa Fellows Manager; +254-20-386-1559 or +254-20-386-1561; ssudhakar@acumenfund.org
Internet: http://www.acumenfund.org/fellows/east-africa-fellows-program.html
Sponsor: Acumen Fund
76 Ninth Avenue, Suite 315
New York, NY 10011

Acumen Global Fellowships 142
The Global Fellowship is a full-time one-year fellowship focused on leadership development and operational experience. Fellows come from all over the world and undergo two months of leadership training in New York and are then placed in one of Acumen Fund's global investments for nine months. Applicants are encouraged to review the website videos of past fellowship recipients. Applicants should also refer to the website for current application information.
Requirements: Applicants should submit a resume/curriculum vitae; personal profile information; two professional references; a letter of recommendation; and four short essay questions. Applicants should review the website's key factors as indicators of a successful fellowship: a proven record of leadership and management responsibilities; experience working in emerging markets; unrelenting perseverance, personal integrity, and critical thinking skills; strong passion and commitment; and 3-7 years of work experience, with a graduate degree preferred.
Restrictions: Fellows are expected to travel frequently and on short notice, sometimes to difficult environments. The program is intensive, time-consuming and requires significant commitment and flexibility. When in the field, access to Internet and phone systems will be available wherever possible, but applicants should expect times when frequent communication with family and friends is not possible or affordable.
Geographic Focus: All States, All Countries
Contact: Blair Miller; (646) 747-3961; bmiller@acumenfund.org
Internet: http://www.acumenfund.org/fellows/fellows-programs.html
Sponsor: Acumen Fund
76 Ninth Avenue, Suite 315
New York, NY 10011

Acushnet Foundation Grants 143
The foundation awards one-year, renewable grants to eligible Massachusetts nonprofit organizations in its areas of interest, including community, hospitals and health care, family, and youth and at-risk youths. Types of support include capital grants (building funds and materials), seed money grants, annual campaigns, and emergency funds. Applicants should submit a letter of inquiry.
Requirements: Massachusetts 501(c)3 tax-exempt organizations serving the New Bedford area are eligible.
Restrictions: Grants are not made to individuals.
Geographic Focus: Massachusetts
Amount of Grant: 1,000 - 95,000 USD
Contact: William Blasdale, Seamark Financial Services Contact; (508) 758-6159
Sponsor: Acushnet Foundation
P.O. Box 1498
Mattapoisett, MA 02739

Adam Reineman Charitable Trust Grants   144
The Foundation, managed by PNC Advisors, offers support for a variety of programs, primarily in the Pittsburgh, Pennsylvania, region. Its primary fields of interest include: the elderly; homeless; at-risk youth; neighborhood development; and other under-served populations throughout the city. Applications forms are not required, though initial approach should be by letter of inquiry or telephone. Full proposals will not be accepted; proposals will be invited upon review of inquiry.
Restrictions: No support is offered for for fraternal, political, advocacy or labor organizations. Additionally, no grants are considered for individuals, general operating costs, or events.
Geographic Focus: Pennsylvania
Date(s) Application is Due: Feb 1; May 1; Aug 1; Oct 1
Contact: Elizabeth Gay, PNC Trust Officer; (412) 762-3576
Sponsor: Adam Reineman Charitable Trust
620 Liberty Avenue, 25th Floor
Pittsburgh, PA 15222-2705

Adam Richter Charitable Trust Grants   145
The Trust, which is administered by the Bank of America in Dallas, Texas, was established in California in 1994. Offering grants on a national basis, its primary fields of interest include: the arts; animal welfare; Christian agencies and churches; the environment; health organizations; higher education; hospitals; and human services. There are no deadlines, though a formal application is required. Interested applicants should begin by sending a letter of inquiry to the Trust office.
Restrictions: Funding is not available for grants to individuals.
Geographic Focus: California
Amount of Grant: 3,000 - 20,000 USD
Contact: Michael Schlebach, Specialty Asset Manager; (866) 461-7281
Sponsor: Adam Richter Charitable Trust
c/o Bank of America, N.A.
Dallas, TX 75201-3115

Adams-Mastrovich Family Foundation Grants   146
Mary Adams Balmat established the Adams-Mastrovich Family Foundation in 1957. Born in 1898 in Lead, South Dakota, she married William Emory Adams II in 1927. He was a prominent businessman in Deadwood, South Dakota, as well as its mayor for six terms during the 1920s. The couple maintained residences in both South Dakota and California. Their home in Deadwood now belongs to the local Historic Preservation Commission. Over the years Mary shared her resources with education, the performing arts, institutions of higher learning, Roman Catholic parishes, hospitals, museums and libraries, as well as programs for battered women and an organization serving delinquent teenage boys. The Foundation continues to support these same organizations today, primarily throughout South Dakota and Los Angeles County, California. Types of funding include: building and renovation, ongoing operating support, equipment purchase, program development, and support of scholarship funds. A formal application is available, with the annual submission deadline August 1. The Board meets in September for final decision-making.
Requirements: 501(c)3 organizations located in, or serving residents of, South Dakota or Los Angeles County, California, are eligible to apply.
Geographic Focus: California, South Dakota
Date(s) Application is Due: Aug 1
Amount of Grant: Up to 100,000 USD
Contact: Halsey H. Halls, Vice President; (612) 667-9084 or (612) 316-4112
Sponsor: Adams-Mastrovich Family Foundation
P.O. Box 53456, MAC S4101-22G
Phoenix, AZ 85072-3456

Adams and Reese LLP Corporate Giving Grants   147
At Adams and Reese, the corporation takes pride in giving back to its communities and believes success is directly related to the prosperity and the quality of life within the communities it serves. Its corporate philanthropy program, HUGS (Hope, Understanding, Giving, and Support) was founded in 1988 by Partner, Mark Surprenant. Since its inception, the firm has devoted financial resources and thousands of volunteer hours to offer assistance to those in need. A fundamental commitment to volunteerism is the deep-rooted characteristic of the corporation. Primary activities include grants in support of health, youth development, and human services. Fields of interest are: general charitable giving, operating support, health care organizations, legal services, social services, and youth programs.
Requirements: Regions of corporate operation include the states of: Alabama, Florida, Louisiana, Mississippi, Tennessee, Texas, and Washington, DC, and applicants from these areas are eligible for support.
Geographic Focus: Alabama, District of Columbia, Florida, Louisiana, Mississippi, Tennessee, Texas
Contact: Mark Surprenant; (504) 581-3234; Mark.Surprenant@arlaw.com
Internet: http://www.adamsandreese.com/community/
Sponsor: Adams and Reese LLP Corporation
701 Poydras Street, Suite 4500
New Orleans, LA 70139-7755

Adams County Community Foundation of Indiana Grants   148
The Adams County Community Foundation and supporting organization, John and Kay Boch, award numerous grants annually. Areas of primary interest include: children and youth; community and economic development; education; and parks and recreation. Money awarded from the various funds helps to enrich and enhance the quality of life throughout Adams County, Indiana. Grants awarded annually help both businesses and the communities in which it serves. Quarterly deadlines are the second Thursday of January, April, July, and October.
Requirements: Applicants must support businesses, educational programs, or residents of Adams County, Indiana.
Geographic Focus: Indiana
Amount of Grant: 200 - 2,000 USD
Contact: Coni Mayer; (260) 724-3939; fax (260) 724-2299; accfoundation@earthlink.net
Internet: http://www.adamscountyfoundation.org/grant-info.aspx
Sponsor: Adams County Community Foundation
102 N. Second Street
Decatur, IN 46733

Adams County Community Foundation of Pennsylvania Grants   149
The Adams County Community Foundation was established in October of 2007 as a Pennsylvania corporation to succeed the Adams County Foundation which for 22 years had operated as a trust-based community foundation. The Foundation is a public charity that the IRS has determined to be a 501(c)3 organization. The purpose of this foundation is to inspire people and communities to build and distribute charitable funds for good, for Adams County, forever. After one year of operation, the foundation had acquired nine funds established by individual people or families, members of the Foundation's Board of Directors, groups of business people, a local charity and by a visionary patriot from the 1700s. The Foundation's assets are managed by a professional investment company hired by the Board of Directors and overseen by the Foundation's Investment & Finance Committee. From these funds, distribution of grants is made to qualified, local charities who demonstrate that they are meeting community needs. With a 16 member Board of Directors, Adams County Community Foundation serves as a good steward of the monies of our donors and demonstrates accountability, transparency, confidentiality, compassion, inclusiveness and excellence in its work. The foundation gives to organizations that assist, promote and improve the moral, mental, social and physical well-being of area residents. Fields of interest include: arts; Christian agencies and churches; community and economic development; education; and health organizations.
Requirements: Applicants must serve residents living in Adams County, Pennsylvania.
Geographic Focus: Pennsylvania
Contact: Barbara Ernico, (717) 337-0060 or (717) 337-3353; info@adamscountycf.org
Internet: http://www.adamscountycf.org/receive.html
Sponsor: Adams County Community Foundation
101 W Middle Street, P.O. Box 4565
Gettysburg, PA 17325-2109

Adams Family Foundation I Grants   150
The Foundation, founded in 1993, offers support primarily in Tennessee and the southeastern portion of the United States. Its major fields of interest include: the arts, children and youth services, Christian agencies and churches, elementary and secondary education programs, and human services. The primary type of funding is general operating support. There are no specific deadlines with which to adhere, and applicants should forward a request by letter outlining the project and a detailed budgetary need. Most grants are in the neighborhood of $500 to $10,000, though occasionally reach as high as $100,000.
Requirements: Any 501(c)3 that is located in, or offers support to, Tennessee or the southeastern portion of the United States is eligible to apply.
Geographic Focus: Tennessee
Contact: Robert G. Adams; (615) 890-2020 or (615) 896-0374; fax (615) 890-0123
Sponsor: Adams Family Foundation I
2217 Battleground Drive
Murfreesboro, TN 37129-6006

Adams Family Foundation of Ohio Grants   151
The Adams Family Foundation was established in Muskingum County, Ohio, with the intent of providing financial awards to local organizations that have the mission of supporting the residents of Muskingum County. Its primary areas of interest include community services, human services, family, and religious organizations. Grants are typically given for general operating support. There are no specific application materials or annual deadlines identified, and interested parties should contact the Foundation directly by way of a brief letter outlining the need and budgetary requirements.
Requirements: 501(c)3 organizations serving the residents of Muskingum County, Ohio, are eligible to apply.
Geographic Focus: Ohio
Contact: Robert Gregory Adams, Presiident; (740) 826-4154
Sponsor: Adams Family Foundation
165 W. Main Street
New Concord, OH 43762

Adams Family Foundation of Tennessee Grants   152
The Adams Family Foundation, established in Tennessee in 2006, provides grants to individuals for family services, cemetery and burial needs, and for the prevention of domestic violence in the Paris, Tennessee, region. Its primary fields of interest have been identified as: agriculture and food; education; and youth development programs. There are no application forms or deadlines with which to adhere, and those in need should forward a letter of request directly to the Foundation office. Most recently, awards have ranged from $1,000 to $2,000.
Geographic Focus: Tennessee
Amount of Grant: 1,000 - 2,000 USD
Contact: David E. Sullivan, Director; (731) 642-2940 or (731) 642-2752
Sponsor: Adams Family Foundation
1101 East Wood Street, P.O. Box 909
Paris, TN 38242-0909

22 | GRANT PROGRAMS

Adams Foundation Grants 153
Established in Alabama in 1992 with a donation from Ralph W. Adams, Jr., of Adams Insurance, the Adams Foundation limits funding to the Montgomery, Alabama, area. Its primary fields of interest include: Boy Scouts, diabetes research, educational scholarship funds, higher education, performing arts, and theater. A formal application is required, though there are no specified annual deadlines. Most recent grants have ranged from $1,000 to $50,000.
Requirements: 501(c)3 organizations serving the residents of Montgomery, Alabama, are eligible to apply.
Geographic Focus: Alabama
Amount of Grant: 1,000 - 50,000 USD
Samples: Alabama Council on Economic Education, Birmingham, Alabama, $35,000 - funding for education (2011); Alabama Shakespeare Festival, Montgomery, Alabama, $5,000 - cultural education (2011).
Contact: Samuel Adams, Secretary-Treasurer; (334) 265-4359
Sponsor: Adams Foundation
P.O. Box 4562
Montgomery, AL 36103-4562

Adams Foundation Grants 154
The Adams Foundation, established in South Hadley, Massachusetts, in 2006, offers support for the arts, human services, environmental education, beautification projects, and other environmental programs throughout the State of Massachusetts. There are no specific application formats or deadlines with which to adhere, and potential applications should be directed in written letter form describing the purpose and budgetary needs of the project. Organizations that forward a letter of interest should wait for a go-ahead before submitting an entire application.
Geographic Focus: Massachusetts
Amount of Grant: 10,000 - 20,000 USD
Contact: Russell Adams, Manager; (413) 532-0787
Sponsor: Adams Foundation
349 Pearl Street
South Hadley, MA 01075-1053

Adams Foundation Grants 155
Established in 1955, the Adams Foundations was initially funded through a donation by Rolland L. Adams, who became owner of the Bethlehem Globe newspaper in 1929. The newspaper won a Pulitzer Prize for editorial writing in 1972. Abarta, which operates the Foundation, was founded by members of the Adams, Bitzer, Roehr and Taylor families - names which form the acronym of the company title. Grants are currently awarded in both Pittsburgh, Pennsylvania, and Ithaca, New York, along with the surrounding areas of these two communities. It supports food banks and civic centers, as well as organizations involved with arts and culture, education, mental health, and arthritis treatments. Funding comes in the form of general operating support. Applicants should submit letters of application detailing the project need and funding requested. Though there are no specified annual deadlines, the board meets each February and August. Most recent grant awards have ranged from $3,500 to $125,500.
Requirements: Any 501(c)3 organization serving the residents of Pittsburgh, Pennsylvania, and Ithaca, New York, are eligible to apply.
Geographic Focus: New York, Pennsylvania
Amount of Grant: 3,500 - 150,000 USD
Contact: Shelley M. Taylor, President; (412) 963-1087 or (412) 963-3163
Sponsor: Adams Foundation
1000 Gamma Drive, 5th Floor
Pittsburgh, PA 15238-2929

Adam Shikiar Foundation Grants 156
The Foundation, founded in 1989, is interested in supporting Jewish agencies and temples, as well as libraries and library science. Its geographic focus is the New York metropolitan area, northern New Jersey, and some portions of Pennsylvania. Funding is primarily used for general operating costs. There are no specific deadlines or application forms, and initial approach should be by letter of inquiry.
Restrictions: No grants are given to individuals.
Geographic Focus: New York
Contact: Stuart A. Shikiar, Treasurer; (212) 888-6565
Sponsor: Adam Shikiar Foundation
30 E 85th Street, Suite 24B
New York, NY 10028-0408

Adams Rotary Memorial Fund A Grants 157
Established in Indiana, the Adams Rotary Memorial Fund A offers funding in Howard County, Indiana, with a primary goal to support handicapped children throughout the county. With this in mind, its primary fields of interest include: children and youth services; alleviation of disabilities; and money to support families who have a family member with a disability. Money supports philanthropy and volunteerism, and is given to individual applicants. There are no application deadlines or specific formats, and those in need should begin by contacted the Fund trustee directly.
Geographic Focus: Indiana
Contact: Glenn Grundmann, Trustee; (317) 464-8212 or (574) 282-8839
Sponsor: Adams Rotary Memorial Fund
224 N. Main Street
Kokomo, IN 46901

ADC Foundation Technology Access Grants 158
The foundation awards grants in ADC locations to support nonprofit access to technology. Grants are made to organizations where the proposed project serves to promote nonprofit access to technology by providing the nonprofit sector with competitive computing or telecommunications technologies, with the end goal of using technology tools to improve service delivery and enhance sector capacity. Requests should be for one year or less in project duration, even if the project is embedded in a larger initiative. Requests for activity accomplished through collaboratives or intermediary organizations is encouraged. The foundation accepts letters of inquiry continuously throughout the year and makes funding decisions quarterly.
Requirements: The Foundation provides funding in its primary operating locations, including: Twin Cities Metro Area for Minnesota; Marietta, Georgia; Santa Teresa, New Mexico; Sidney, Nebraska; Delicias & Juarez, Mexico; Cheltenham, United Kingdom; Bangalore, India; and Berlin, Germany.
Restrictions: Requests for computers or Internet service for individual nonprofits or schools will not be accepted. The foundation will not consider requests for in-kind giving, general operating grants, capital grants, fundraisers or similar benefits, individuals, or religious purpose grants.
Geographic Focus: Georgia, Minnesota, Nebraska, New Mexico, Germany, India, Mexico, United Kingdom
Contact: Bill Linder-Scholer; (952) 917-0580; bill.linder-scholer@adc.com
Internet: http://www.adc.com/aboutadc/adcfoundation
Sponsor: ADC Foundation
P.O. Box 1101, MS 70
Minneapolis, MN 55440-1101

ADEC Agricultural Telecommunications Grants 159
Grants will be awarded competitively to encourage the development and utilization of an agricultural communications network to facilitate and to strengthen agricultural extension, resident education, and research, and domestic and international marketing of United States agricultural commodities and products through a partnership between eligible institutions and the Department of Agriculture. The network will employ satellite and other telecommunications technology to disseminate and to share academic instruction, cooperative extension programming, agricultural research, and marketing information. Proposals will be accepted from new applicants (lead institutions) and repeat applicants (lead institutions). Proposals may be submitted electronically via the Web site, or applicants may contact the office for application materials.
Requirements: Proposals are invited from accredited institutions of higher education.
Geographic Focus: All States
Date(s) Application is Due: Jul 15
Amount of Grant: Up to 50,000 USD
Contact: Dr. Janet Poley; (402) 472-7000; fax (402) 472-9060; jpoley@unl.edu
Internet: http://www.adec.edu/fed-pgms.html
Sponsor: American Distance Education Consortium
P.O. Box 830952
Lincoln, NE 68583-0952

Adelaide Benevolent Society Grants 160
Also known as Adele Koller-Knusli Foundation, the Adelaide Benevolent Society is an independent, not-for-profit organisation that has been providing affordable housing and financial assistance to disadvantaged South Australians for more than 160 years. With a portfolio of more than 175 houses and units across Adelaide that are rented out at below market rates, the Adelaide Benevolent Society continues to expand its service through a carefully planned process of development and construction. The Society is committed to increasing the amount of affordable housing in South Australia because it passionately believes that housing is the foundation on which families and individuals transform, develop and enhance their lives.
Geographic Focus: Australia
Contact: Jonathan Lardne, Chief Executive Officer; 08 8231 5321; fax 08 8231 5818; jlardner@adelaide.org.au or luisa@adelaide.org.au
Internet: http://www.adelaide.org.au/
Sponsor: Adelaide Benevolent Society
17 Morialta Street
Adelaide, SA 5000 Australia

Adelaide Breed Bayrd Foundation Grants 161
The Adelaide Breed Bayrd Foundation supports programs and projects of nonprofit organizations serving the Boston, Massachusetts, area with emphasis on the Malden community. Areas of interest include: adult and continuing education; aging centers and services; arts; children and youth services; community and economic development; education; family services; health care; health organizations; hospitals (general); human services; libraries and library science; residential and custodial care; and hospices. The Foundation funds annual campaigns, building and renovation, capital campaigns, emergency requests, equipment, program development, and scholarship funds. Grants have been awarded in the past to support public libraries, hospitals, and the Girl Scouts. The foundation accepts the Associated Grant Makers (AGM) Common Proposal Form available from the AGM website; however an application form is not required. Applicants should submit the following: a copy of their IRS Determination Letter; copies of their most recent annual report, audited financial statements, and 990; a detailed description of their project and the amount of funding requested; and a copy of their organizational or project budget for the current year. Proposals should be submitted before the second Tuesday in February. Awardees will be notified in April or May.
Requirements: 501(c)3 organizations serving the Boston, Massachusetts area are eligible. Preference will be given to organizations serving the community of Malden, Massachusetts.

Restrictions: The foundation does not support the following categories: requests from individuals; the performing arts (except for certain educational programs); matching or challenge grants; demonstration projects; conferences; publications; research or endowment funds; or loans.
Geographic Focus: Massachusetts
Amount of Grant: 1,000 - 150,000 USD
Contact: C. Henry Kezer, President; (781) 324-1231
Sponsor: Adelaide Breed Bayrd Foundation
350 Main Street, Suite 13
Malden, MA 02148-5023

Adelaide Christian Home For Children Grants 162
The Adelaide Christian Home For Children provides support to evangelical Christian organizations serving children and youth, with priority given to local California ministries. Its primary fields of interest include: Christian agencies and churches; education; human services; religion; and youth development. Target populations are children, the economically disadvantaged; and single parents. Interested parties should be aware that there is a formal application. Though there are no specified annual deadlines, the board does meet in both January and September to decide funding awards.
Geographic Focus: California
Amount of Grant: Up to 120,000 USD
Contact: Sherry Parsons, Director; (949) 361-1346
Sponsor: Adelaide Christian Home For Children
122 Avenida Del Mar
San Clemente, CA 92672

Adelaide Dawson Lynch Trust Grants 163
Robert M. Lynch established the Adelaide Dawson Lynch Trust in memory of his wife in 1993. This trust supports charitable organizations that provide food and shelter to Rhode Island citizens who are economically disadvantaged. Grants are typically between $1,000 and $5,000, and larger or multi-year grants may be made for special campaigns. The application deadline for the Adelaide Dawson Lynch Trust is 11:59 p.m. on October 1. Applicants must apply online at the grant website. Applicants are strongly encouraged to do the following before applying: review the downloadable state application procedures for additional helpful information and clarifications; review the downloadable online-application guidelines at the grant website; review the trust's funding history (link is available from the grant website); review the online application questions in advance; and review the list of required attachments. These will generally include: a list of board members, financial statements (audited, reviewed, or compiled by independent auditor); an organization summary; a list of other funding sources; an IRS Determination letter; and other required documents. All attachments must be uploaded in the online application as PDF, Word, or Excel files. Applicants will be notified of grant decisions by letter within two to three months after the proposal deadline.
Requirements: Applicant organizations must have 501(c)3 tax-exempt status and serve the people of Rhode Island.
Restrictions: The trust does not support requests from individuals, organizations attempting to influence policy through direct lobbying, or any political campaigns.
Geographic Focus: Rhode Island
Date(s) Application is Due: Oct 1
Amount of Grant: 1,000 - 5,000 USD
Contact: Emma Greene, Director; (617) 434-0329; emma.m.greene@baml.com
Internet: https://www.bankofamerica.com/philanthropic/fn_search.action
Sponsor: Adelaide Dawson Lynch Trust
225 Franklin Street, 4th Floor, MA1-225-04-02
Boston, MA 02110

Adler-Clark Electric Community Commitment Foundation Grants 164
Established in Wisconsin in 2004, the Adler-Clark Electric Community Commitment Foundation offers grants in Clark County, Wisconsin. It supports athletics and amateur leagues, fire prevention and control, education, food banks, food services, health care, human services, public libraries, and recreation programs. Types of support include: equipment purchase; general operations; and program development. A formal application is required, and the annual deadline has been identified as December 1. Funding amounts range from $500 to $3,000.
Geographic Focus: Wisconsin
Date(s) Application is Due: Dec 1
Amount of Grant: 500 - 3,000 USD
Contact: Timothy E. Stewart, Trustee; (715) 267-6188 or (800) 272-6188
Internet: http://www.cecoop.com/home
Sponsor: Adler-Clark Electric Community Commitment Foundation
P.O. Box 190
Greenwood, WI 54437-9419

Administaff Community Affairs Grants 165
Five areas qualify for Administaff corporate contribution consideration: the elderly, education, social service, environment, and health. Administaff will consider four types of requests: volunteers and grants; grants; event sponsorships; and in-kind donations—equipment such as computers, copiers and furniture. All contribution requests must be made in writing. Guidelines and sample cover letter are available online.
Requirements: Charitable organizations must have 501(c)3 status, according to IRS standards; operate in one of Administaff's district markets; and submit a written request. Qualifying organizations also must submit a financial statement to the Better Business Bureau before consideration.
Restrictions: Ineligible entities include: religious organizations (i.e., churches, temples, and other houses of worship, or those whose main purpose is to promote a particular faith or creed); political organizations; individuals; athletic groups; or school clubs.
Geographic Focus: All States
Amount of Grant: 5,000 USD
Contact: Betty Collins, Program Director, Community Involvement; (281) 358-8986; fax (281) 312-3559; community_involvement@administaff.com
Internet: http://www.administaff.com/about_asf/grants.asp
Sponsor: Administaff Corporation
19001 Crescent Springs Drive
Kingwood, TX 77339-3802

Administration on Aging Senior Medicare Patrol Project Grants 166
The goal of SMP Projects is to empower beneficiaries/consumers to prevent health care fraud through outreach and education. Program coverage must target vulnerable, hard-to-reach population beneficiaries, their families and other consumers. The purpose of this competition is to provide the opportunity to fund one (1) Project in each of 26 eligible states including the District of Columbia for a project period of up to three (3) years.
Requirements: Domestic public or private and non-profit entities including state, local and Indian tribal governments (American Indian/Alaskan Native/Native American), faith-based organizations, community-based organizations, hospitals, and institutions of higher education are eligible to apply. Through this competition, AoA plans to fund one project in each of the following 26 states and the District of Columbia: Alaska, Arizona, Arkansas, Colorado, Delaware, the District of Columbia, Florida, Georgia, Idaho, Kansas, Kentucky, Maine, Massachusetts, Michigan, Montana, New Jersey, New Mexico, Ohio, Oklahoma, Oregon, Puerto Rico, Tennessee, Texas, Virginia, Washington, and West Virginia.
Geographic Focus: All States
Date(s) Application is Due: Apr 11
Amount of Grant: Up to 345,000 USD
Contact: Barbara Lewis, Project Officer; (202) 357-3532; Barbara.Lewis@aoa.hhs.gov
Internet: http://www.aoa.dhhs.gov/doingbus/fundopp/fundopp.asp
Sponsor: Administration on Aging
1 Massachusetts Avenue NW
Washington, DC 20001

Adobe Art and Culture Grants 167
Adobe supports strategic programs and partnerships that help make its communities better, stronger, and more vibrant places to live, work and do business. Adobe's focus areas for giving and grants programs are designed to: increase Adobe's impact in the community through support of more organizations; and strengthen Adobe's role as a corporate partner by creating deeper, stronger, and richer partnerships. Specifically, the Arts and Culture grants program directs grants towards organizations with a principal focus on creation and exhibition of visual and multimedia art. This primarily includes programs that directly encourage the creation or exhibition of art with special emphasis on digital and multimedia art.
Requirements: Adobe is currently accepting grant proposals in the following communities: San Jose/Silicon Valley, California (southern San Mateo County, Santa Clara County, southern Alameda County); San Francisco, California; Seattle/King County, Washington; and Ottawa, Ontario, Canada.
Restrictions: Adobe does not support theater arts, performance arts or art education/appreciation programs.
Geographic Focus: California, Washington, Canada
Contact: Lesley Dierks, Community Relations; (408) 536-6000 or (408) 536-3993; fax (408) 537-6000; ldierks@adobe.com or community_relations@adobe.com
Internet: http://www.adobe.com/aboutadobe/philanthropy/commgivingprgrm.html#Community%20giving%20programs
Sponsor: Adobe Systems
345 Park Avenue
San Jose, CA 95110-2704

Adobe Community Investment Grants 168
Adobe supports strategic programs and partnerships that help make its communities better, stronger, and more vibrant places to live, work and do business. Adobe's focus areas for giving and grants programs are designed to: increase Adobe's impact in the community through support of more organizations; and strengthen Adobe's role as a corporate partner by creating deeper, stronger, and richer partnerships. The Adobe Community Investment Grant program provides multi-year (with annual review), comprehensive support, including cash, software, volunteers, and facilities use through an Adobe-initiated, RFP application process. Grant amounts are at least $20,000 and can be for up to three years. Organizations selected become Adobe Community Investment Partners and are required to sit out one year after the grant ends before reapplying.
Requirements: Adobe is currently accepting grant proposals in the following communities: San Jose/Silicon Valley, California (southern San Mateo County, Santa Clara County, southern Alameda County); San Francisco, California; Seattle/King County, Washington; and Ottawa, Ontario, Canada.
Geographic Focus: California, Washington, Canada
Contact: Lesley Dierks, Community Relations; (408) 536-6000 or (408) 536-3993; fax (408) 537-6000; ldierks@adobe.com or community_relations@adobe.com
Internet: http://www.adobe.com/aboutadobe/philanthropy/commgivingprgrm.html#Community%20giving%20programs
Sponsor: Adobe Systems
345 Park Avenue
San Jose, CA 95110-2704

Adobe Hunger and Homelessness Grants 169
Adobe supports strategic programs and partnerships that help make its communities better, stronger, and more vibrant places to live, work and do business. Adobe's focus areas for giving and grants programs are designed to: increase Adobe's impact in the community through support of more organizations; and strengthen Adobe's role as a corporate partner by creating deeper, stronger, and richer partnerships. Specifically, the Hunger and Homelessness grants program directs grants towards services and programs that reduce hunger and homelessness and/or provide affordable housing. This primarily includes food banks, shelters and other direct services to homeless or at-risk individuals.
Requirements: Adobe is currently accepting grant proposals in the following communities: San Jose/Silicon Valley, California (southern San Mateo County, Santa Clara County, southern Alameda County); San Francisco, California; Seattle/King County, Washington; and Ottawa, Ontario, Canada.
Restrictions: Adobe does not support indirect services or programs that focus primarily on workforce development.
Geographic Focus: California, Washington, Canada
Contact: Lesley Dierks, Community Relations; (408) 536-6000 or (408) 536-3993; fax (408) 537-6000; ldierks@adobe.com or community_relations@adobe.com
Internet: http://www.adobe.com/aboutadobe/philanthropy/commgivingprgrm.html#Community%20giving%20programs
Sponsor: Adobe Systems
345 Park Avenue
San Jose, CA 95110-2704

Adobe Youth Voices Grants 170
The Adobe Youth Voices (AYV) Grants Program supports leading youth-focused programs and organizations through a competitive grants process to engage youth in breakthrough learning experiences using digital tools to express themselves and create with purpose. Grantees develop a specific Adobe Youth Voices project and then make the completed youth produced media available for wide distribution by AYV.
Requirements: Tax-exempt 501(c)3 nonprofit organization or a public educational institution (no geographic limitations) that serves low-income, disadvantaged middle and high school youth (ages 11-18). Applicants will design a new Adobe Youth Voices project that will engage youth in expressing themselves about topics that are personally meaningful to them and relevant to the context of their communities
Geographic Focus: All States
Date(s) Application is Due: May 1
Amount of Grant: 35,000 USD
Contact: Lesley Dierks, Community Relations; (408) 536-6000 or (408) 536-3993; fax (408) 537-6000; ldierks@adobe.com or community_relations@adobe.com
Internet: http://www.adobe.com/aboutadobe/philanthropy/youthvoices/ayv_grants.html
Sponsor: Adobe Systems
345 Park Avenue
San Jose, CA 95110-2704

Adolph Coors Foundation Grants 171
The Coors Foundation supports organizations that promote the western values of self-reliance, personal responsibility, and integrity. The foundation believes these values foster an environment where entrepreneurial spirits flourish and help Coloradans reach their full potential. High priority is placed on programs that help youth to prosper, that encourage economic opportunities for adults, and that advance public policies that uphold traditional American values. Traditional areas of support include one-on-one mentoring programs, job training, and a variety of self-help initiatives. The foundation also has an interest in bringing integrative medicine into the medical mainstream. In each of its giving areas, the foundation seeks evidenced-based results. Civic and cultural programs attracting the Foundation's attention are typically those that enhance our culture and heritage, that demonstrate our creativity as a people and that are likely to be economic benefit to and broadly used by the communities they serve. Past grants have supported boys and girls clubs and inner-city health programs. Types of support include building funds, general operating budgets, seed money, and special projects. The foundation has moved to an online screening and application system which is accessible from the foundation website. Application deadlines are March 1, July 1, and November 1.
Requirements: All applicants must be classified as 501(c)3 organizations by the Internal Revenue Service and must operate within the United States.
Restrictions: The foundation does not provide support for the following expenses or entities: organizations primarily supported by tax-derived funds; conduit organizations that pass funds to non-exempt organizations; organizations with two consecutive years of operating loss; K-12 schools or the ancillary programs and projects of those schools; individuals; research projects; production of films or other media-related projects; historic renovation; churches or church projects; museums or museum projects; animals or animal-related projects; preschools, day-care centers, nursing homes, extended-care facilities, or respite care; deficit funding or retirement of debt; special events, meetings, or seminars; purchase of computer equipment; adaptive sports programs; and national health organizations. Organizations applying for start-up funding must have been in operation for at least one full year.
Geographic Focus: All States
Date(s) Application is Due: Mar 1; Jul 1; Nov 1
Contact: Jeanne Bistranin, Program Officer; (303) 388-1636; fax (303) 388-1684
Internet: http://www.coorsfoundation.org/Process/index.html
Sponsor: Adolph Coors Foundation
4100 E Mississippi Avenue, Suite 1850
Denver, CO 80246

Advanced Micro Devices Community Affairs Grants 172
AMD awards grants to nonprofit organizations and schools that serve the communities in which it operates: Sunnyvale, CA, and Austin, TX, and in Europe and Asia. AMD grants funds to agencies that serve the community's health and human service, education and civic needs. AMD K-12 initiatives target programs that increase student interest and/or proficiency in literacy, math, science, and computer technology. AMD also funds programs aimed at developing and supporting effective classroom instruction. AMD also funds basic needs programs to local health and human services organizations. In addition, AMD matches employee gifts to organizations whose activities fall within one of the approved funding areas. AMD also supports engineering education at universities throughout the United States. Generally, funds are granted for specific projects, not for general operating expenses. Requests must be submitted in writing, using appropriate forms, and must include a description of the applicant organization with a statement of its purposes and objectives, a statement regarding the need the grant will address and the geographic area and population served, the names and qualifications of the person(s) who will administer the grant, and amount requested with an explanation of how the funds will be used. Awards are made on a quarterly basis.
Requirements: IRS 501(c)3 tax-exempt organizations and schools based in Sunnyvale, CA, and Austin, TX, are eligible.
Restrictions: AMD will not fund political activities, national programs, advocacy programs, religious or fraternal organizations, individuals, fund-raising events, conferences, seminars, door prizes, registration fees, advertising, or sports leagues.
Geographic Focus: California, Texas, Albania, Andorra, Armenia, Austria, Azerbaijan, Belarus, Belgium, Bosnia & Herzegovina, Bulgaria, Croatia, Cyprus, Czech Republic, Denmark, Estonia, Finland, France, Georgia, Germany, Greece, Hungary, Iceland, Ireland, Italy, Kosovo, Latvia, Liechtenstein, Lithuania, Luxembourg, Macedonia, Malta, Moldova, Monaco, Montenegro, Norway, Poland, Portugal, Romania, Russia, San Marino, Serbia, Slovakia, Slovenia, Spain, Sweden, Switzerland, The Netherlands, Turkey, Ukraine, United Kingdom, Vatican City
Date(s) Application is Due: May 1
Contact: Community Affairs Manager; (408) 749-5373
Internet: http://www.amd.com/us-en/Corporate/AboutAMD/0,,51_52_7697_7702,00.html
Sponsor: Advanced Micro Devices
P.O. Box 3453
Sunnyvale, CA 94088-3453

Advancing Colorado's Mental Health Care Project Grants 173
This project, a joint venture of the foundation, the Colorado Trust, the Denver Foundation, and HealthOne Alliance, focuses on improving the integration and coordination of mental health services for adults with serious mental illness and children with severe emotional disturbances. The project will support the integration of mental health services in five to eight Colorado communities so that people with significant mental health needs can be treated across agencies, regardless of funding sources, organizational structures, or policy and practice differences. Applicant communities propose the target population(s), local approaches for accomplishing improved system integration, and specific strategies and structures for integrating services. Complete program information is available online.
Requirements: Applicants must have the following qualifications and characteristics: a fiscal agent that has 501(c)3 tax-exempt status or is a governmental entity; and an existing collaborative identified to oversee project policy and funding that includes members from agencies and provider organizations serving persons with mental health needs, as well as recipients of mental health services and their families.
Restrictions: Applicants may not propose the use of grant or match funds for new construction or renovation; grants to individuals; retirement of debt; institutional indirect cost recovery; lobbying or political purposes; religious purposes; activities other than charitable activities; replacement of existing or lost funds; or payment for individual services that could be covered by existing funding sources or that falls outside the intent of the grant (i.e., hospital or medication expenses).
Geographic Focus: Colorado
Date(s) Application is Due: May 31
Amount of Grant: 375,000 - 650,000 USD
Contact: Rachel Mondragon, (303) 837-1200 or (888) 847-9140; rachel@coloradotrust.org
Internet: http://www.coloradotrust.org/index.cfm?fuseAction=Grantmaking.FundingOpportunities
Sponsor: Caring for Colorado Foundation
4100 E Mississippi Avenue, #605
Denver, CO 80246

Advocate Safehouse Project Grants 174
The organization provides support to victims of domestic violence, and educates authorities and the general public on domestic violence issues. Choices might include counseling, contacting an attorney, getting a protection order, taking a break from their relationship, or relocating to a safe haven. Funding is provided for these and numerous other needs in an ongoing fashion. Those in need should contact the Safehouse directly.
Geographic Focus: Colorado
Contact: Julie Olson, Executive Director; (970) 945-2632 or (970) 945-4439
Sponsor: Advocate Safehouse Project
P.O. Box 2036
Glenwood Springs, CO 81602

AEC Trust Grants 175
The AEC Trust is a private foundation established in 1980 as a philanthropic, grantmaking organization. The trust awards grants to eligible nonprofits in Colorado, Florida, Georgia, and Massachusetts in its areas of interest, including: AIDS, arts and culture, community

development, elementary education, the environment, health care, higher education, social services, museums, and women. Types of support include building construction/renovation, capital campaigns, challenge/matching grants, equipment acquisition, general operating support, land acquisition, project support, and publications. Request guidelines in writing. There are two annual deadlines: April 1 and September 1.
Requirements: 501(c)3 nonprofit organizations in the communities of Boulder, Colorado, Gainesville, Florida, Atlanta, Georgia, and Amherst, Massachusetts, are eligible.
Restrictions: Grants do not support individuals, international organizations, political organizations, religious organizations, school districts, special events/benefit dinners, state and local government agencies, United Way agencies, national public charities, endowments, sponsorships, or annual fund campaigns.
Geographic Focus: Colorado, Florida, Georgia, Massachusetts
Date(s) Application is Due: Apr 1; Sep 1
Amount of Grant: 5,000 - 50,000 USD
Contact: Edith Dee Cofrin; (800) 839-1754; requests@foundationsource.com
Internet: https://online.foundationsource.com/public/home/aec
Sponsor: AEC Trust
501 Silverside Road, Suite 123
Wilmington, DE 19809-1377

AEGON Transamerica Foundation Arts and Culture Grants 176
The foundation will consider favorably grants to established organizations with reputations for excellence and cost-effectiveness. The Foundation's Arts and Culture Grants program is interested in supporting programs that foster creativity in the areas of music and the performing arts, including venues for artistic expression; all of which contribute to the quality of life, sustainability and growth of our communities. Types of support include continuing support, matching funds, operating budgets, employee-related scholarships, and special projects. Contributions are normally made on a year-to-year basis with no assurance of renewal of support. In certain cases, pledges may be considered for periods not exceeding three years.
Requirements: Nonprofit organizations within the Foundation's focus areas and mission, and that are designated for a community where there is a significant employee presence are eligible. Requests can be directed to the attention of the AEGON Transamerica Foundation at one of the following locations: Atlanta, Georgia; Baltimore, Maryland; Bedford, Texas; Cedar Rapids, Iowa; Exton, Pennsylvania; Harrison, New York; Little Rock, Arkansas; Los Angeles, California; Plano, Texas; and St. Petersburg, Florida.
Restrictions: Individuals, as well as the following types of organizations or programs are not eligible to receive grants from the Foundation: athletes or athletic organizations; conferences, seminars or trips; courtesy or goodwill advertising; fellowships; fraternal organizations; K-12 school fundraisers or events; political parties, campaigns or candidates; religious or denominational organizations except for specific programs broadly promoted and available to anyone and free from religious orientation; or social organizations.
Geographic Focus: Arkansas, California, Florida, Georgia, Iowa, Maryland, New York, Pennsylvania, Texas
Amount of Grant: 1,000 - 50,000 USD
Contact: David Blankenship; (319) 398-8895 or (319) 355-8511; fax (319) 398-8030; david.blankenship@transamerica.com or shaegontransfound@aegonusa.com
Internet: http://www.transamerica.com/about_us/aegon_transamerica_foundation.asp
Sponsor: AEGON Transamerica Foundation
4333 Edgewood Road, NE
Cedar Rapids, IA 52499-0010

AEGON Transamerica Foundation Civic and Community Grants 177
The foundation will consider favorably grants to established organizations with reputations for excellence and cost-effectiveness. The Foundation's Civic and Community Grants provides funding for programs that strive to promote community development, encourage civic leadership, enhance workforce and business development opportunities, and empower people and strengthen communities. Types of support include continuing support, matching funds, operating budgets, employee-related scholarships, and special projects. Contributions are normally made on a year-to-year basis with no assurance of renewal of support. In certain cases, pledges may be considered for periods not exceeding three years.
Requirements: Nonprofit organizations within the Foundation's focus areas and mission, and that are designated for a community where there is a significant employee presence are eligible. Requests can be directed to the attention of the AEGON Transamerica Foundation at one of the following locations: Atlanta, Georgia; Baltimore, Maryland; Bedford, Texas; Cedar Rapids, Iowa; Exton, Pennsylvania; Harrison, New York; Little Rock, Arkansas; Los Angeles, California; Plano, Texas; and St. Petersburg, Florida.
Restrictions: Individuals, as well as the following types of organizations or programs are not eligible to receive grants from the Foundation: athletes or athletic organizations; conferences, seminars or trips; courtesy or goodwill advertising; fellowships; fraternal organizations; K-12 school fundraisers or events; political parties, campaigns or candidates; religious or denominational organizations except for specific programs broadly promoted and available to anyone and free from religious orientation; or social organizations.
Geographic Focus: Arkansas, California, Florida, Georgia, Iowa, Maryland, New York, Pennsylvania, Texas
Amount of Grant: 1,000 - 50,000 USD
Contact: David Blankenship; (319) 398-8895 or (319) 355-8511; fax (319) 398-8030; david.blankenship@transamerica.com or shaegontransfound@aegonusa.com
Internet: http://www.transamerica.com/about_us/aegon_transamerica_foundation.asp
Sponsor: AEGON Transamerica Foundation
4333 Edgewood Road, NE
Cedar Rapids, IA 52499-0010

AEGON Transamerica Foundation Disaster Relief Grants 178
AEGON Transamerica Foundation Disaster Relief Grants are supported by a special fund established for employee donations, often matched dollar-for-dollar, and provided to a specific organization devoted to assisting in the relief effort. Such funding is available and donated wherever the need should arise. Obviously, there are no annual deadlines for this support.
Requirements: The Foundation provides disaster relief funding throughout the world, wherever it is needed.
Restrictions: Individuals, as well as the following types of organizations or programs are not eligible to receive grants from the Foundation: athletes or athletic organizations; conferences, seminars or trips; courtesy or goodwill advertising; fellowships; fraternal organizations; K-12 school fundraisers or events; political parties, campaigns or candidates; religious or denominational organizations except for specific programs broadly promoted and available to anyone and free from religious orientation; or social organizations.
Geographic Focus: All States, All Countries
Contact: David Blankenship; (319) 398-8895 or (319) 355-8511; fax (319) 398-8030; david.blankenship@transamerica.com or shaegontransfound@aegonusa.com
Internet: http://www.transamerica.com/about_us/aegon_transamerica_foundation.asp
Sponsor: AEGON Transamerica Foundation
4333 Edgewood Road, NE
Cedar Rapids, IA 52499-0010

AEGON Transamerica Foundation Health and Welfare Grants 179
The foundation will consider favorably grants to established organizations with reputations for excellence and cost-effectiveness. The Foundation's Health and Welfare Grants initiative is interested in supporting programs committed to improving the condition of the human body through nutrition, housing for the homeless, disease prevention and other support services. Types of support include continuing support, matching funds, operating budgets, employee-related scholarships, and special projects. Contributions are normally made on a year-to-year basis with no assurance of renewal of support. In certain cases, pledges may be considered for periods not exceeding three years.
Requirements: Nonprofit organizations within the Foundation's focus areas and mission, and that are designated for a community where there is a significant employee presence are eligible. Requests can be directed to the attention of the AEGON Transamerica Foundation at one of the following locations: Atlanta, Georgia; Baltimore, Maryland; Bedford, Texas; Cedar Rapids, Iowa; Exton, Pennsylvania; Harrison, New York; Little Rock, Arkansas; Los Angeles, California; Plano, Texas; and St. Petersburg, Florida.
Restrictions: Individuals, as well as the following types of organizations or programs are not eligible to receive grants from the Foundation: athletes or athletic organizations; conferences, seminars or trips; courtesy or goodwill advertising; fellowships; fraternal organizations; K-12 school fundraisers or events; political parties, campaigns or candidates; religious or denominational organizations except for specific programs broadly promoted and available to anyone and free from religious orientation; or social organizations.
Geographic Focus: Arkansas, California, Florida, Georgia, Iowa, Maryland, New York, Pennsylvania, Texas
Amount of Grant: 1,000 - 50,000 USD
Contact: David Blankenship; (319) 398-8895 or (319) 355-8511; fax (319) 398-8030; david.blankenship@transamerica.com or shaegontransfound@aegonusa.com
Internet: http://www.transamerica.com/about_us/aegon_transamerica_foundation.asp
Sponsor: AEGON Transamerica Foundation
4333 Edgewood Road, NE
Cedar Rapids, IA 52499-0010

AEP Corporate Giving Grants 180
Contributions are made principally in the areas of education, the environment, and human services (i.e., hunger, housing, health, safety). Priority is based on the perceived overall benefit to communities in the company's service area. In the area of education, preference is given to grades K-12 in the fields of science, technology, and math. Multiyear commitments to capital campaigns generally do not exceed five years. AEP and its employees provide strong support to many annual United Way campaigns within its service territory; therefore, additional support to United Way agencies is extremely limited. There is no formal application form or deadline. Requests for contributions must be made in writing and can be submitted anytime. Guidelines are available online.
Requirements: Nonprofit organizations in Arkansas, Illinois, Indiana, Kentucky, Louisiana, Michigan, Ohio, Oklahoma, Tennessee, Texas, West Virginia, and Virginia are eligible.
Restrictions: Grants do not support religious, fraternal, service and veteran organizations (except for nonsectarian social service activities available to the broader community); athletic activities; or individuals.
Geographic Focus: Arkansas, Indiana, Kentucky, Louisiana, Michigan, Ohio, Oklahoma, Tennessee, Texas, Virginia, West Virginia
Amount of Grant: Up to 4,000,000 USD
Contact: Administrator; (614) 716-1000; mkwalsh@aep.com or mkwalsh@aep.com
Internet: http://www.aep.com/about/community/corpGive/Default.htm
Sponsor: American Electric Power
1 Riverside Plaza, 19th Floor
Columbus, OH 43215

Aetna Foundation Arts Grants in Connecticut 181
The Aetna Foundation is the independent charitable and philanthropic arm of Aetna Inc. Founded in 1972, the Foundation helps build strong communities by promoting volunteerism, forming partnerships, and funding initiatives that improve the quality of life where its employees and customers live and work. With its Arts Grants in Connecticut, the Foundation supports programs designed to promote arts and culture in Hartford and Middletown, Connecticut.

26 | GRANT PROGRAMS

Requirements: 501(c)3 tax-exempt organizations serving the residents of Hartford and Middletown, Connecticut, are eligible.
Restrictions: The Foundation generally does not fund: endowment or capital costs, including construction, renovation, or equipment; direct delivery of reimbursable health care services; basic biomedical research; grants or scholarships to individuals; work for which results and impact cannot be measured; advertising; golf tournaments; advocacy, political causes or events; sacramental or theological functions of religious organizations; operational expenses; or existing deficits.
Geographic Focus: Connecticut
Contact: Melenie O. Magnotta; (860) 273-1012; aetnafoundation@aetna.com
Internet: http://www.aetna.com/about-aetna-insurance/aetna-foundation/aetna-grants/connecticut-grants-program-arts.html
Sponsor: Aetna Foundation
151 Farmington Avenue
Hartford, CT 06156-3180

Aetna Foundation Diversity Grants in Connecticut   182
The Aetna Foundation is the independent charitable and philanthropic arm of Aetna Inc. Founded in 1972, the Foundation helps build healthy communities by promoting volunteerism, forming partnerships and funding initiatives that improve the quality of life where its employees and customers live and work. With its Diversity Grants in Connecticut, the foundation awards funding to: strengthen Latino communities; focus on urban issues; and bring diverse exhibits to Hartford and beyond. Support is limited to Hartford and Middletown, Connecticut. Grants of up to $10,000 are awarded on a quarterly basis.
Requirements: 501(c)3 tax-exempt organizations serving the residents of Hartford and Middletown, Connecticut, are eligible.
Restrictions: The Foundation generally does not fund: endowment or capital costs, including construction, renovation, or equipment; direct delivery of reimbursable health care services; basic biomedical research; grants or scholarships to individuals; work for which results and impact cannot be measured; advertising; golf tournaments; advocacy, political causes or events; sacramental or theological functions of religious organizations; operational expenses; or existing deficits.
Geographic Focus: Connecticut
Amount of Grant: Up to 10,000 USD
Contact: Melenie O. Magnotta; (860) 273-1012; aetnafoundation@aetna.com
Internet: http://www.aetna.com/about-aetna-insurance/aetna-foundation/aetna-grants/diversity.html
Sponsor: Aetna Foundation
151 Farmington Avenue
Hartford, CT 06156-3180

Aetna Foundation Education Grants in Connecticut   183
The Aetna Foundation is the independent charitable and philanthropic arm of Aetna Inc. Founded in 1972, the Foundation helps build healthy communities by promoting volunteerism, forming partnerships and funding conferences/seminars that help to improve the quality of life where employees and customers live and work. With its Education Grants in Connecticut, the Foundation supports programs designed to: make Hartford a science and education destination; revitalize urban schools; and enrich academic opportunities.
Requirements: 501(c)3 tax-exempt organizations serving the residents of Hartford and Middletown, Connecticut, are eligible.
Restrictions: The Foundation generally does not fund: endowment or capital costs, including construction, renovation, or equipment; direct delivery of reimbursable health care services; basic biomedical research; grants or scholarships to individuals; work for which results and impact cannot be measured; advertising; golf tournaments; advocacy, political causes or events; sacramental or theological functions of religious organizations; operational expenses; or existing deficits.
Geographic Focus: Connecticut
Contact: Melenie O. Magnotta; (860) 273-1012; aetnafoundation@aetna.com
Internet: http://www.aetna.com/about-aetna-insurance/aetna-foundation/aetna-grants/connecticut-grants-education.html
Sponsor: Aetna Foundation
151 Farmington Avenue
Hartford, CT 06156-3180

Aetna Foundation Health Grants in Connecticut   184
The Aetna Foundation is the independent charitable and philanthropic arm of Aetna Inc. Founded in 1972, the Foundation helps build strong communities by promoting volunteerism, forming partnerships and funding initiatives that improve the quality of life where our employees and customers live and work. With its Health Grants in Connecticut program, the Foundation supports programs designed to enhance the quality of health care, and address disabilities and chronic diseases. Support is limited to Hartford and Middletown, Connecticut. Grants of up to $35,000 are awarded.
Requirements: 501(c)3 tax-exempt organizations serving the residents of Hartford and Middletown, Connecticut, are eligible.
Restrictions: The Foundation generally does not fund: endowment or capital costs, including construction, renovation, or equipment; direct delivery of reimbursable health care services; basic biomedical research; grants or scholarships to individuals; work for which results and impact cannot be measured; advertising; golf tournaments; advocacy, political causes or events; sacramental or theological functions of religious organizations; operational expenses; or existing deficits.
Geographic Focus: Connecticut
Amount of Grant: Up to 35,000 USD
Contact: Melenie O. Magnotta; (860) 273-1012; aetnafoundation@aetna.com
Internet: http://www.aetna.com/about-aetna-insurance/aetna-foundation/aetna-grants/connecticut-grants-health.html
Sponsor: Aetna Foundation
151 Farmington Avenue
Hartford, CT 06156-3180

Aetna Foundation Obesity Grants   185
With its Obesity Grants program, the Foundation wants to understand the contributors to obesity, particularly among minority populations, and what supports and sustains better choices that can stave off overeating and reduce inactivity. Grant-making in this area focuses on initiatives that create a better understanding of the root causes of the obesity epidemic. Examples of grants the Foundation would support include projects and/or studies that identify causes of obesity and potential best practices for addressing obesity, such as: domestic food policies and their impact on individual food choices' the impact of our neighborhoods and the built environment on promoting population health and weight loss; assessments of why communities with high rates of food insecurity also are more likely to experience high rates of obesity; how children use recreation time; and how school lunch and food policies impact our children.
Requirements: 501(c)3 tax-exempt organizations are eligible.
Restrictions: The Foundation generally does not fund: endowment or capital costs, including construction, renovation, or equipment; direct delivery of reimbursable health care services; basic biomedical research; grants or scholarships to individuals; work for which results and impact cannot be measured; advertising; golf tournaments; advocacy, political causes or events; sacramental or theological functions of religious organizations; operational expenses; or existing deficits.
Geographic Focus: All States
Amount of Grant: 50,000 - 300,000 USD
Contact: Melenie O. Magnotta; (860) 273-1012; aetnafoundation@aetna.com
Internet: http://www.aetna-foundation.org/foundation/aetna-foundation-programs/obesity/index.html
Sponsor: Aetna Foundation
151 Farmington Avenue
Hartford, CT 06156-3180

Aetna Foundation Racial and Ethnic Health Care Equity Grants   186
With its Racial and Ethnic Health Care Equity Grant program, the Aetna Foundation focuses philanthropic giving on understanding connections between where people live and receive health care, and the quality and equity of the care they receive. The Aetna Foundation also is interested in how to improve health and health care among the nation's Medicaid population, particularly in settings with large numbers of minority patients. Examples of grants the Foundation would support include projects and/or studies to: explore how a stronger primary care model and relationships with providers could benefit minority populations and close the persistent health care gap; help providers who treat large minority populations become leaders in delivering high-quality care; determine what can be done to reduce the numbers of low-birth weight babies born to mothers at risk; examine, through observational studies, the correlation between a mother's health, stress level, and social supports; and the likelihood of having a healthy baby who lives through its first year of life; and determine, through interventional studies, whether stress-reduction programs (including yoga and meditation) can improve health outcomes for minority patients with chronic conditions, as well as postnatal outcomes for mothers and pregnant women.
Requirements: 501(c)3 tax-exempt organizations are eligible.
Restrictions: The Foundation generally does not fund: endowment or capital costs, including construction, renovation, or equipment; direct delivery of reimbursable health care services; basic biomedical research; grants or scholarships to individuals; work for which results and impact cannot be measured; advertising; golf tournaments; advocacy, political causes or events; sacramental or theological functions of religious organizations; operational expenses; or existing deficits.
Geographic Focus: All States
Amount of Grant: 50,000 - 300,000 USD
Contact: Melenie O. Magnotta; (860) 273-1012; aetnafoundation@aetna.com
Internet: http://www.aetna-foundation.org/foundation/aetna-foundation-programs/racial-ethnic-healthcare-equity/index.html
Sponsor: Aetna Foundation
151 Farmington Avenue
Hartford, CT 06156-3180

Aetna Foundation Regional Health Grants   187
The Aetna Foundation's Regional Grants fund community wellness initiatives that serve those who are most at risk for poor health - low-income, underserved or minority populations. A healthy diet and regular exercise can help prevent obesity and many chronic conditions. Grants will target communities where healthy food can be difficult to buy, and where social and environmental factors may limit people's ability to be physically active. Types of projects the Foundation seeks to support include: school-based or after-school nutrition and fitness programs that help children learn healthy habits at an early age; community-based nutrition education programs for children and families; efforts to increase the availability or affordability of fresh fruits and vegetables in communities; and community gardening and urban farming activities for children and families. Funding ranges from $25,000 to $40,000.
Requirements: 501(c)3 tax-exempt organizations in regionally designated communities are eligible, including: Phoenix, Arizona; Los Angeles, San Diego, Fresno, and San Francisco, in California; Connecticut; Miami and Tampa, Florida; Atlanta, Georgia; Chicago, Illinois; Maine; New Jersey; New York, New York; Charlotte, North Carolina; Cleveland and Columbus, Ohio; Philadelphia and Pittsburgh, Pennsylvania; Nashville and

Memphis, Tennessee; Dallas, Houston, Austin, and San Antonio, in Texas; Washington, D.C; Baltimore, Maryland; Northern Virginia; and Washington State.
Restrictions: The Foundation generally does not fund: endowment or capital costs, including construction, renovation, or equipment; direct delivery of reimbursable health care services; basic biomedical research; grants or scholarships to individuals; work for which results and impact cannot be measured; advertising; golf tournaments; advocacy, political causes or events; sacramental or theological functions of religious organizations; operational expenses; or existing deficits.
Geographic Focus: Arizona, California, Connecticut, District of Columbia, Florida, Georgia, Illinois, Maine, Maryland, New Jersey, New York, North Carolina, Ohio, Pennsylvania, Tennessee, Texas, Virginia, Washington
Date(s) Application is Due: Sep 15
Amount of Grant: 25,000 - 50,000 USD
Contact: Melenie O. Magnotta; (860) 273-1012; aetnafoundation@aetna.com
Internet: http://www.aetna-foundation.org/foundation/apply-for-a-grant/regional-grants/index.html
Sponsor: Aetna Foundation
151 Farmington Avenue
Hartford, CT 06156-3180

Aetna Foundation Strengthening Neighborhhods Grants in Connecticut 188
The Aetna Foundation is the independent charitable and philanthropic arm of Aetna Inc. Founded in 1972, the Foundation helps build healthy communities by promoting volunteerism, forming partnerships and funding initiatives that improve the quality of life where its employees and customers live and work. With its Strengthening Neighborhoods Grants in Connecticut, the foundation supports programs designed to improve neighborhood economic strength and revitalize neighborhoods. Support is limited to Hartford and Middletown, Connecticut. Grants typically range from $2,500 to $15,000.
Requirements: 501(c)3 tax-exempt organizations serving the residents of Hartford and Middletown, Connecticut, are eligible.
Restrictions: The Foundation generally does not fund: endowment or capital costs, including construction, renovation, or equipment; direct delivery of reimbursable health care services; basic biomedical research; grants or scholarships to individuals; work for which results and impact cannot be measured; advertising; golf tournaments; advocacy, political causes or events; sacramental or theological functions of religious organizations; operational expenses; or existing deficits.
Geographic Focus: Connecticut
Amount of Grant: 2,500 - 15,000 USD
Contact: Melenie O. Magnotta; (860) 273-1012; aetnafoundation@aetna.com
Internet: http://www.aetna.com/about-aetna-insurance/aetna-foundation/aetna-grants/aetna-grants-neighborhoods.html
Sponsor: Aetna Foundation
151 Farmington Avenue
Hartford, CT 06156-3180

Aetna Foundation Summer Academic Enrichment Grants 189
Through its Summer Academic Enrichment Grants program, the Aetna Foundation provides academic and cultural enrichment opportunities to thousands of at-risk, Hartford-area students. Grants have been made to such organizations as Boys and Girls Club of Hartford, Center City Churches, ConnectiKids, Dance Connecticut, Organized Parents Make a Difference, and many others. In Hartford, a $250,000 Aetna Foundation investment is supporting a local education fund (LEF) designed to improve student retention and achievement
Requirements: 501(c)3 tax-exempt organizations in Hartford, Connecticut, are eligible.
Restrictions: The Foundation generally does not fund: endowment or capital costs, including construction, renovation, or equipment; direct delivery of reimbursable health care services; basic biomedical research; grants or scholarships to individuals; work for which results and impact cannot be measured; advertising; golf tournaments; advocacy, political causes or events; sacramental or theological functions of religious organizations; operational expenses; or existing deficits.
Geographic Focus: Connecticut
Amount of Grant: 500 - 5,000 USD
Contact: Melenie O. Magnotta; (860) 273-1012; aetnafoundation@aetna.com
Internet: http://www.aetna.com/about-aetna-insurance/aetna-foundation/aetna-grants/connecticut-grants-education.html
Sponsor: Aetna Foundation
151 Farmington Avenue
Hartford, CT 06156-3180

Aetna Foundation Volunteer Grants 190
The Aetna Foundation is the independent charitable and philanthropic arm of Aetna Inc. Founded in 1972, the Foundation helps build healthy communities by promoting volunteerism, forming partnerships and funding initiatives that improve the quality of life where its employees and customers live and work. The foundation awards Aetna Volunteers grants of up to $300 to nonprofit organizations with which employees and retirees of Aetna volunteer at least twenty hours per year.
Requirements: 501(c)3 tax-exempt organizations are eligible.
Restrictions: The Foundation generally does not fund: endowment or capital costs, including construction, renovation, or equipment; direct delivery of reimbursable health care services; basic biomedical research; grants or scholarships to individuals; work for which results and impact cannot be measured; advertising; golf tournaments; advocacy, political causes or events; sacramental or theological functions of religious organizations; operational expenses; or existing deficits.
Geographic Focus: All States
Amount of Grant: Up to 300 USD
Contact: Melenie O. Magnotta; (860) 273-1012; aetnafoundation@aetna.com
Internet: http://www.aetna-foundation.org/foundation/index.html
Sponsor: Aetna Foundation
151 Farmington Avenue
Hartford, CT 06156-3180

AFG Industries Grants 191
The corporation awards general operating grants to nonprofits in its headquarters area in the categories of arts and humanities, civic and public affairs, education at all levels, health care, and social services. There are no application deadlines. Submit a brief letter of inquiry.
Requirements: Tennessee nonprofits are eligible.
Geographic Focus: Tennessee
Amount of Grant: 100,000 - 250,000 USD
Contact: Human Resources; (800) 251-0441 or (423) 229-7200; fax (423) 229-7459
Internet: http://www.afgglass.com
Sponsor: AFG Industries
P.O. Box 929
Kingsport, TN 37662

African American Fund of New Jersey Grants 192
Since 1980 the African American Fund of New Jersey (AAFNJ) has touched the lives of more than three million people who live in New Jersey urban areas. The fund concentrates on providing significant funding to New Jersey's African-American communities to promote and enhance human-services delivery and community empowerment. Primary funding consideration is given to proposals which fall in the areas of pre-school through high-school educational initiatives, technology initiatives, environmental and health-related initiatives, community issues, and building wealth. Programs that emphasize positive family values, traditions, social customs, and family practices that have contributed to the survival of the African-American family are encouraged. Types of support include general operating grants, program development grants, and technical assistance. Proposals must demonstrate the intention to commit the necessary financial and human resources to a program that is well coordinated with related human services within the respective communities. Annual deadline dates may vary; prospective applicants should contact program staff or visit the AAFNJ website for exact dates, guidelines, and application forms.
Requirements: Any 501(c)3 agency, community-based organization, or school operating in the state of New Jersey may submit a proposal to AAFNJ for funding consideration. AAFNJ also accepts applications from organizations that are closely aligned with theirs.
Geographic Focus: New Jersey
Date(s) Application is Due: Sep 1
Amount of Grant: 500 - 5,000 USD
Contact: Sondra Clark; (973) 676-5283; fax (973) 672-5030; sclark@aafnj.org
Internet: http://www.aafnj.org/index.php/grants/grants
Sponsor: African American Fund of New Jersey
132 South Harrison Street
East Orange, NJ 07018

African American Heritage Grants 193
Grants are awarded to assist organizations in the preservation and promotion of historic African American properties and sites in Indiana. Awards are made on a four-to-one matching basis, funding 80% of the total project cost up to $2,500, whichever is less.
Requirements: Civic groups, schools, libraries, historical societies, and other nonprofit agencies are eligible to apply for grants for organizational assistance, studies assisting in or leading to the preservation of a historic African American place, and programs promoting the preservation, interpretation, and/or visitation of a historic African American place. Contact the regional community preservation specialist that serves your community (see website for list of regional offices or contact the state headquarters office) for guidelines and forms.
Restrictions: Properties must be located in Indiana.
Geographic Focus: Indiana
Amount of Grant: 500 - 2,500 USD
Contact: Carla Jones; (317) 639-4534; fax (317) 639-6734; info@historiclandmarks.org
Internet: http://www.historiclandmarks.org/help/grants.html
Sponsor: Historic Landmarks Foundation of Indiana
340 W Michigan Street
Indianapolis, IN 46202

A Friends' Foundation Trust Grants 194
The Foundation, founded as the Hubbard Foundation in 1959 by philanthropist Frank M. Hubbard, primarily serves central Florida with its support of health research and health care, education at all levels, children and youth activities, the arts, and religious agencies. Grants typically range from $5,000 to $35,000, though some higher amounts are given. There are no specific application formats or deadlines with which to adhere, and applicants should send a letter of request to the Foundation address listed.
Requirements: Applicants must be 501(c)3 organizations serving residents of central Florida.
Geographic Focus: Florida
Amount of Grant: 5,000 - 35,000 USD
Samples: Fisher House Foundation, Rockville, Maryland, $5,000 - general operations (2011); Bok Tower Gardens, Lake Wales, Florida, $22,500 - general operations (2011); Adult Literacy League, Orlando, Florida, $2,000 - general operations (2011).
Contact: L. Evans Hubbard, (407) 876-3122; ehubbard@cfl.rr.com
Sponsor: A Friends' Foundation Trust
9000 Hubbard Place
Orlando, FL 32819

28 | GRANT PROGRAMS

A Fund for Women Grants   195
A Fund For Women, a component fund of The Madison Community Foundation was established in 1993 to improve the lives of girls and women in the local community. The fund provides grants to women and girls in the community that enhance education, employment and self-esteem. All grants are driven by the overall goal of helping women and children learn self-reliance and reach self-sufficiency. Under that umbrella, the Fund focuses on the following four key areas of need: keeping elderly or disabled women in their homes, or in community settings; providing services to victims of domestic abuse; helping women achieve economic self sufficiency and increase their earning potential; and reducing homelessness for women and girls. AFFW is particularly interested in innovative programs and services that will reach women and girls from diverse backgrounds in urban, suburban or rural Dane County. Proposals should indicate how the project or program will help connect women or girls to a support network or community that will help them to overcome emotional, social, intellectual, spiritual, occupational and/or physical barriers to self-sufficiency. Applications are due annually by July 1, at 4:30 p.m.
Requirements: Applicants must be non-profit organizations (exempt from Federal income taxes under section 501(c)3 of the Internal Revenue Code), schools, governmental bodies, or under the supervision of such a group. Projects must focus on women and girls in Dane County.
Geographic Focus: Wisconsin
Date(s) Application is Due: Jul 1
Amount of Grant: 2,000 - 25,000 USD
Contact: Jan Gietzel, Executive Director; (608) 441-0630; fax (608) 232-1772; kwoit@madisoncommunityfoundation.org or affw@madisoncommunityfoundation.org
Internet: http://www.affw.org/grants/apply.php
Sponsor: A Fund for Women
2 Science Court, P.O. Box 5010
Madison, WI 53705-0010

Agape Foundation for Nonviolent Social Change Alice Hamburg Emergency Grants   196
The Agape Foundation Fund for Nonviolent Social Change is a non-profit public foundation founded in 1969 out of opposition to the war in Southeast Asia. The Alice Hamburg Emergency Grant Fund, established in 1991 by donors in opposition to the Gulf War, helps groups respond to unforeseen events. The event must be unforeseen and there must be no funds allocated for this event. The organization must show that resources are not available, warranting an Emergency Grant. Agape considers the following to be examples of an emergency: an organized response to a military mobilization and or action; an organized response to an environmental disaster; support for a protest or mobilization in response to a government or corporate action. The Board of Trustees makes competitive emergency grants throughout the year to organizations that fit the funding priorities.
Requirements: Agape Foundation considers proposals for an Emergency grants from organizations that promote peace and social justice.
Restrictions: Agape considers the following not to be an emergency: a foreseen event where fund raising fell short; travel and related expenses to a conference or planned meeting; budgetary shortfalls for operating expenses. Agape does not fund social service or direct service organizations unless they have a major advocacy component.
Geographic Focus: All States
Contact: Karen Topakian, (415) 701-8707; karen@agapefn.org or info@agapefn.org
Internet: http://www.agapefdn.org/sec/s-gr/AHEG_g.html
Sponsor: Agape Foundation for Nonviolent Social Change
1095 Market Street, Suite 304
San Francisco, CA 94103

Agape Foundation for Nonviolent Social Change Board of Trustees Grants   197
Agape will fund eligible nonprofit groups in the following areas: peace (promotion of alternatives to violence, militarism, and war, and alternatives to nuclear power, weapons and waste); human rights (defense of civil rights, lesbian/gay/bisexual/transgender rights, women's rights, or racial justice) environmental protection (defense of the environment, ecological restoration, and environmental justice); economic justice (promotion of solutions to economic inequality); grassroots organizing (support for campaigns that help local residents to call for peaceful solutions to injustice and inequity); and progressive arts and media (distribution of media projects that support grassroots organizing and promote peace and justice). An organization can receive a grant only once in a 12-month period. Proposals from organizations that have not previously received an Agape grant will have higher priority. Letters of Intent are due by August 3, with full proposals due by September 3 each year. Guidelines are available online.
Requirements: Agape will consider proposals from 501(c)3 organizations or fiscally sponsored groups that practice and promote nonviolence in their organizational relations, structure, process, and actions; demonstrate a commitment to grassroots participation; are unable to secure funding from traditional sources; integrate both peace and social justice issues; are located in, and whose work is focused in, California; are five years old or younger, with annual budgets or expenditures under $100,000; and whose staff (paid or volunteer) is representative of and emerges from the constituencies they serve.
Restrictions: Agape does not fund social or direct service organizations unless they have a major advocacy component. Individuals are not eligible. Proposals are not accepted by fax or email.
Geographic Focus: California
Date(s) Application is Due: Aug 3; Sep 1
Contact: Karen Topakian, (415) 701-8707; fax (415) 701-8706; karen@agapefn.org
Internet: http://www.agapefn.org/sec/s-gr/BOTG_g.html
Sponsor: Agape Foundation for Nonviolent Social Change
1095 Market Street, Suite 304
San Francisco, CA 94103

Agape Foundation for Nonviolent Social Change Peace Prizes   198
The goals of the prize are to bring recognition to Northern California peacemakers, organizations, and individuals; raise awareness and understanding about emerging peacemakers, their work, and accomplishments; put peace, and those working for it, on the forefront of the movement for social change and equality; and create a venue that will enable emerging and established peacemakers to network, share information, and develop strategic alliances that promote social justice and human rights. Prizes include the Long Haul Prize, and the Rising Peacemaker Prize. Prize winners receive cash; and capacity building from Bay Area experts and trainers, including, fund raising, media and public relations, event planning, financial planning and budgeting, and building and maintaining a board of directors. Guidelines and nomination form are available online.
Requirements: Northern California organizations, individuals, collectives, and other peacemakers are eligible. Nominees should support the following basic tenet of peace: opposed to all armed conflict to solve international problems.
Geographic Focus: California
Date(s) Application is Due: Jun 25
Amount of Grant: 250 - 10,000 USD
Contact: Karen Topakian, (415) 701-8707; karen@agapefn.org or info@agapefn.org
Internet: http://www.agapefdn.org/PeacePrize2009/2009_peace_prize_sponsor_benefits.jpg
Sponsor: Agape Foundation for Nonviolent Social Change
1095 Market Street, Suite 304
San Francisco, CA 94103

Agere Corporate and Community Involvement Grants   199
The corporation awards grants to nonprofit organizations in areas where Agere employees live and work. Corporate programs focus on education, specifically K-12 programs that enhance math, science, and technology; professional development for teachers, especially in the areas of math, science, and the use of technology in the classroom; programs providing educational enrichment and assistance to students before, during, and after school; and programs that encourage and support parental involvement in their children's education. Grant awards will be limited and based on projected impact, population served, collaborative efforts, and measurable results. Local Community Involvement Councils (CICs) support local educational programs and environmental and community development initiatives. Specialized employee funding programs include matching gifts and United Way Campaigns. Proposals are reviewed from October 1 through June 1. Information and application guidelines are available online.
Requirements: 501(c)3 organizations and 170 E,B educational organizations are eligible.
Restrictions: Grants do not support individuals including awards, sponsorships (e.g., walk-a-thons), or any form of personal assistance; organizations not eligible for tax-deductible support; religious programs; endowments or capital campaigns; conferences, seminars, trips, and tours; national health organizations or social services other than through United Way; political organizations/campaigns; or fraternal, athletic, social clubs/programs/events.
Geographic Focus: Pennsylvania
Date(s) Application is Due: Jun 1
Contact: Stephanie Polak, spolak@agere.com
Internet: http://www.agere.com/company/phil/regional_guidelines.html
Sponsor: Agere Systems
1110 American Parkway NE
Allentown, PA 18109

A Glimmer of Hope Foundation Grants   200
A Glimmer of Hope in Austin is committed to improving the lives of young people (up to age 25 years old) and seniors (aged 60 and above) who suffer from exclusion, social injustices, neglect, abandonment and educational disadvantages. Grants are generally awarded for one year. These grants are social seed capital for new and innovative projects and funded organizations are encouraged to seek additional funds from other sources.
Requirements: The foundation funds projects that provide services to young people and seniors residing primarily in East and South Austin. Grants are made only to qualified 501(c)3 organizations. Funds are disbursed on a quarterly basis with continuing funding contingent upon availability of funds and the recipient's ability to successfully meet the objectives outlined in their original proposal.
Restrictions: A Glimmer of Hope Foundation does not fund or support: grants to individuals; political causes; cultural exchange programs; travel or scholarship assistance; general operating funds; construction projects; hardware upgrades or labs; fundraising events; mass mailings; advertising projects; attendance of professional conferences and symposia; out-of-state performances or competition expenses; or academic or scientific research.
Geographic Focus: Texas
Date(s) Application is Due: Apr 2; Oct 2
Amount of Grant: Up to 20,000 USD
Contact: David Porter III; (512) 328-9944; austinprojects@aglimmerofhope.org
Internet: http://www.aglimmerofhopeaustin.org/grants/index.html
Sponsor: A Glimmer of Hope Foundation
3600 North Capital Texas Highway, Building. B, Suite 330
Austin, TX 78746-3314

AGMA Relief Fund Grants   201
The American Guild of Musical Artists (AGMA) Relief Fund provides support and temporary financial assistance to members who are in need. AGMA contracts with The Actors Fund to administer this program nationally as well as to provide comprehensive social services including counseling and referrals for personal, family or work-related problems. Linkage is made to community resources for legal services, elder care, entitlement benefits and childcare. Workshops are offered on how to locate affordable housing, as well as on financial education and health insurance options. Financial assistance is available for

rent, utilities, mental health and medical care, as well as other basic living expenses. Grants are made case-by-case, based on need.
Requirements: All AGMA members may call The Actors Fund for information, referrals and access to our social services. To be eligible for financial assistance from the AGMA Relief Fund a member must be in good standing or on honorable withdrawal and must be able to document the need for financial assistance.
Geographic Focus: All States
Contact: Western Region; (323) 933-9244, ext. 55; intakela@actorsfund.org
Internet: http://new.actorsfund.org/services/Partner_Programs/AGMA_Relief_Fund/index_html
Sponsor: American Guild of Musical Artists
1430 Broadway, 14th Floor
New York, NY 10018

Agnes B. Hunt Trust Grants 202
The trust awards grants to eligible Georgia nonprofit organizations in the general areas of health, welfare, and education for the poor and needy in its local community. Apply online; complete guidelines are provided.
Requirements: 501(c)3 nonprofits in Griffin and Spalding County, GA, are eligible.
Geographic Focus: Georgia
Date(s) Application is Due: Nov 1
Amount of Grant: 500 - 5,000 USD
Contact: Joseph Walker
Internet: http://www.agnesbhunttrust.org
Sponsor: Agnes B. Hunt Trust
P.O. Box 1610
Griffin, GA 30224-1610

Agnes M. Lindsay Trust Grants 203
The Trust makes grants to nonprofit organizations in the states of Maine, Massachusetts, New Hampshire and, Vermont to improve the quality of life. Areas of interest include: health & welfare organizations; recreation, camp scholarships (camperships); education; educational scholarships. The Trust awards grants for capital needs; capital campaigns, building renovations, equipment; computers, furniture , etc. Grant proposals are reviewed on a monthly basis, grants average $1,000 - $15,000. Campership applications must be submitted by March 1st and range from $1,000 - $4,000.
Requirements: 501(c)3 Maine, Massachusetts, New Hampshire, and Vermont tax-exempt organizations are eligible to apply for funding. To begin the application process, submit a letter of inquiry prior to submitting a full proposal for funding. In addition to basic information about your organization, include a brief outline of your statement of need and a project budget. You may complete this as a word document and attach it to an email addressed to: adminatlindsaytrustdotorg. Grant proposals should contain: proposal summary document (available at Trust website); narrative of the organization and description of need; financial statements for last two years or Form 990; budget for capital expenditures; estimates or quotes obtained; IRS Determination letter. Submit your proposal and all attachments electronically in either a PDF format and/or Microsoft Word and EXCEL to: proposalsatlindsaytrustdotorg. Applicants requesting a camp scholarships (camperships) provide the following: proposal summary document (available at Trust website); most recent audited financial statements (one calender year) or Form 990; and IRS Determination Letter. Submit your proposal electronically in a PDF file to: proposalsatlindsaytrustdotorg. The trust will accept Microsoft Word documents and Excel documents as attachments. If you are unable to send your proposal or any portion thereof electronically, you may submit it via U.S. mail. A status report for the grant awarded is required after the grant has been expended.
Restrictions: The Trust does not fund: endowments, public entities, awarded to individuals, municipalities, libraries, museums, sectarian organizations, or capital grants to private schools. The Trust very rarely provides funding for operating /program support. If your organization received a grant, wait one year before reapplying for additional funding.
Geographic Focus: Maine, Massachusetts, New Hampshire, Vermont
Date(s) Application is Due: Mar 1
Amount of Grant: 1,000 - 15,000 USD
Contact: Susan Bouchard, Administrative Director; (603) 669-1366 or (866) 669-1366; fax (603) 665-8114; admin@lindsaytrust.org
Internet: http://www.lindsaytrust.org/index.html
Sponsor: Agnes M. Lindsay Trust
660 Chestnut Street
Manchester, NH 03104

A Good Neighbor Foundation Grants 204
Established in Cincinnati, Ohio, in 2002, A Good Neighbor Foundation offers support primarily to individuals and families that are in need of immediate aid and services. Its major fields of interest include: cancer; children's services; human services; and emergency aid. Funding comes in the form of general operating support for residents of Cincinnati, Ohio, and northern Kentucky. There are no specific deadlines or application forms, and applicants should contact the office in writing or via telephone.
Geographic Focus: Kentucky, Ohio
Amount of Grant: Up to 400,000 USD
Samples: Redwood School and Rehabilitation Center, Fort Mitchell, Kentucky, $350,000—for capital campaign; Saint Joseph Infant and Maternity Home, Cincinnati, Ohio, $330,000—for capital campaign.
Contact: Michele Kelley, Secretary-Treasurer; (513) 651-9333
Sponsor: A Good Neighbor Foundation
414 Walnut Street, Suite 1014
Cincinnati, OH 45202-3913

Agway Foundation Grants 205
The primary goal of the foundation is to support organizations dedicated to serving the interests of farmers and rural communities in the Northeast, including health care, children and youth services, rural youth organizations, and agriculture. The foundation also supports organizations that contribute to the quality of life in the Agway headquarters area and it actively promotes employee volunteer involvement in community service.
Requirements: 501(c)3 nonprofit organizations are eligible for grant support.
Restrictions: The foundation funds are not used for individuals; political, religious, or labor organizations; scholarships; matching gift programs or capital campaigns of educational institutions; memberships in professional societies or trade associations; or the general operating funds of health care facilities.
Geographic Focus: Connecticut, Maine, Massachusetts, New Hampshire, Rhode Island, Vermont
Amount of Grant: 1,000 - 10,000 USD
Contact: Stephen Hoefer; (315) 449-6474; info@agway.com or chairman@agway.com
Internet: http://www.colebrook-nh.com/Public_Documents/ColebrookNH_BBoard/I008D1C75
Sponsor: Agway Foundation
P.O. Box 4933
Syracuse, NY 13221

Ahearn Family Foundation Grants 206
Established in Connecticut in 1994, the Ahearn Family Foundation limits its giving to the Hartford County, Connecticut, region, particularly the Hartford inner city. Its primary field of interest is urban community development in the areas of health care, children and youth, libraries, housing, families, and scholarship endowments. Application forms are required, and annual deadlines are April 15, July 15, October 15, and January 15. Grants range from $500 to $3,000.
Requirements: Any 501(c)3 organization serving the residents of Hartford County, Connecticut, can apply.
Geographic Focus: Connecticut
Date(s) Application is Due: Jan 15; Apr 15; Jul 15; Oct 15
Amount of Grant: 500 - 3,000 USD
Contact: Terrence O. Ahearn, Chairperson; (860) 249-9104
Sponsor: Ahearn Family Foundation
P.O. Box 37
Manchester, CT 06045-0037

Ahmanson Foundation Grants 207
The Foundation reviews grant requests from 501(c)3 organizations that are based in and serving Los Angeles County in the areas of education (elementary and secondary education, higher education, nursing school education, and adult literacy and basic skills), the arts and humanities (including libraries and cultural programs), disadvantaged, domestic violence, health and medicine, human services including youth, and religion (Christian, Episcopal, interdenominational, Jewish, Lutheran, Methodist, Presbyterian, Roman Catholic, and Salvation Army). Types of grant support include capital campaigns, challenge, building/renovations, equipment, endowment funds, matching funds, program development, scholarship funds, and seed money. There are no application forms; the board meets four times annually to consider requests. Full proposals will be invited. Letters of inquiry are to be sent through the postal service following the guidelines listed.
Requirements: 501(c)3 nonprofit organizations that serve or are based in Los Angeles County, California, may apply.
Restrictions: Grants are not awarded to individuals or for continuing support, annual campaigns, professorships or internships, fellowships, or film production.
Geographic Focus: California
Amount of Grant: 10,000 - 50,000 USD
Contact: Leonard Walcott Jr.; (310) 278-0770; info@theahmansonfoundation.org
Internet: http://www.theahmansonfoundation.org/fund.html
Sponsor: Ahmanson Foundation
9215 Wilshire Boulevard
Beverly Hills, CA 90210

AHS Foundation Grants 208
Established in Minnesota in 1968, the AHS Foundation offers funding primarily in California, Hawaii, Minnesota, New Jersey, and Ohio. The Foundation's main purpose is support for the relief of poverty and the advancement of education, religion, and community issues. Its primary fields of interest include: the arts; Catholic agencies and churches; Christian agencies and churches; education; human services; performing arts; Protestant agencies and churches; and federated giving programs. Types of support are building and renovations, capital campaigns, endowments, general operations, and program development. Application forms are not required, and interested groups should forward a detailed description of the project, as well as a detailed budget request. There is no specified annual deadline, although the board typically meets in July.
Restrictions: No grants are offered to individuals, and no loans are considered.
Geographic Focus: California, Hawaii, Minnesota, New Jersey, Ohio
Amount of Grant: 5,000 - 20,000 USD
Contact: Thomas Wright, Secretary Treasurer; (612) 667-1784
Sponsor: AHS Foundation
90 South 7th Street, Suite 5300
Minneapolis, MN 55402-4120

AIChE Women's Initiatives Committee Mentorship Excellence Award 209
The AIChE Women's Initiatives Committee Mentorship Excellence Award is sponsored by the Women's Initiatives Committee. The award recognizes women faculty who have contributed to the development of the next generation of chemical engineers through outstanding mentoring. Awardees will be recognized at the Annual Meeting WIC Luncheon.
Geographic Focus: All States
Date(s) Application is Due: Aug 1
Amount of Grant: 5,000 USD
Contact: Gordon Ellis, Awards Administrator; (646) 495-1348; fax (646) 495-1503; gorde@aiche.org or awards@aiche.org
Internet: http://www.aiche.org/Students/Awards/WICMentor.aspx
Sponsor: American Institute of Chemical Engineers
3 Park Avenue
New York, NY 10016

Aid for Starving Children African American Independence Single Mother's Grants 210
Aid for Starving Children, formerly known as the African American Self-Help Foundation, has been helping save the lives of children for over thirty years. The foundation belongs to a coalition of organizations on four continents which coordinate both resources and efforts in order to achieve maximum results and efficiency and to save the world - one child at a time. In the United States, Aid For Starving Children sponsors programs that meet critical needs, develop life and work skills, and strengthen relationships with church and community to help African-American single mothers and their children break free of the cycle of poverty. Organizations interested in partnering with Aid to Starving Children in programs to strengthen the economic futures of single African-American mothers and their children should call or email the foundation for more information.
Geographic Focus: All States
Contact: Jeff Baugham, U.S. Director; (937) 275—7310; RevJB@donet.com
Internet: http://www.aidforstarvingchildren.org/emergency_assistance
Sponsor: Aid for Starving Children
182 Farmers Lane, Suite 201
Santa Rosa, CA 95405

Aid for Starving Children Emergency Assistance Fund Grants 211
Aid for Starving Children, formerly known as the African American Self-Help Foundation, has been helping save the lives of children for over thirty years. The foundation belongs to a coalition of organizations on four continents which coordinate both resources and efforts in order to achieve maximum results and efficiency and to save the world - one child at a time. In the United States, Aid For Starving Children sponsors programs that meet critical needs, develop life and work skills, and strengthen relationships with church and community to help African-American single mothers and their children break free of the cycle of poverty. Additionally the organization provides a limited number of small cash grants to help qualified African-American single mothers meet emergency financial needs. Applicants for the cash grants must meet the minimum qualifications and submit a completed application with all required documentation in order to be considered for this program. Complete guidelines and the application for the cash grants are available at the Aid for Starving Children website.
Requirements: Applicants who meet all of the following requirements are eligible to apply for small cash grants: Currently-employed, African-American single mothers who live in the United States and have at least one child under the age of seventeen living with them (the employment equirement may be waived under emergency conditions); individuals who have documentation that they have sought and been unable to obtain help from family or other local sources; and individuals who have an emergency need such as an overdue rent or mortgage payment or utility bill, a critical car maintenance or repair, or a critical medical need (similar types of emergencies may also qualify).
Restrictions: Requests for help with household and personal expenses (eg. food, clothing, furniture, etc.), education and business expenses, gifts, and credit card payments will not be considered.
Geographic Focus: All States
Contact: Jeff Baugham, U.S. Director; (937) 275—7310; RevJB@donet.com
Internet: http://www.aidforstarvingchildren.org/emergency_assistance
Sponsor: Aid for Starving Children
182 Farmers Lane, Suite 201
Santa Rosa, CA 95405

Aid for Starving Children International Grants 212
Aid for Starving Children, formerly known as the African American Self-Help Foundation, has been helping save the lives of children for over thirty years. The foundation belongs to a coalition of organizations on four continents which coordinate both resources and efforts in order to achieve maximum results and efficiency and to save the world - one child at a time. In sub-Saharan Africa, the Foundation rescues orphaned and abandoned children who have lost their family members to AIDS and/or other devastation, and provides them with new lives of love and hope; provides poor children with support for a healthier and more productive future through feeding programs, medical care and education; and helps poor parents provide a better life for their own children through sustainable agriculture and clean water projects. Organizations interested in partnering with Aid to Starving Children in these programs should call or email the foundation for more information.
Geographic Focus: All States, Algeria, Angola, Benin, Botswana, Burkina Faso, Burundi, Cameroon, Cape Verde, Central African Republic, Chad, Comoros, Congo, Congo, Democratic Republic of, Cote d' Ivoire (Ivory Coast), Djibouti, Egypt, Equatorial Guinea, Eritrea, Ethiopia, Gabon, Gambia, Ghana, Guinea, Guinea-Bissau, Kenya, Lesotho, Liberia, Libya, Madagascar, Malawi, Mali, Mauritania, Mauritius, Morocco, Mozambique, Namibia, Niger, Nigeria, Rwanda, Sao Tome & Principe, Senegal, Seychelles, Sierra Leone, Somalia, South Africa, Sudan, Swaziland
Contact: Jeff Baugham, U.S. Director; (937) 275—7310; RevJB@donet.com
Internet: http://www.aidforstarvingchildren.org/africa
Sponsor: Aid for Starving Children
182 Farmers Lane, Suite 201
Santa Rosa, CA 95405

AIG Disaster Relief Fund Grants 213
American International Group (AIG) traces its root to 1919, when American Cornelius Vander Starr established a general insurance agency, American Asiatic Underwriters, in Shanghai, China. Since then, the company has become one of the world's leading insurers. AIG is committed to giving back to the communities it serves, including those affected by disasters, through programs and partnerships that leverage the skills, experience, knowledge, and enthusiasm of AIG employees. The AIG Disaster Relief Fund (DRF) was established by AIG to assist victims of natural and man-made disasters around the world. Grant-seekers should contact AIG for information on how to be considered for DRF grants.
Geographic Focus: All States, All Countries
Contact: David Herzog, Chairman; (212) 770-7000
Internet: http://www.aig.com/citizenship_3171_437858.html
Sponsor: American International Group
180 Maiden Lane
New York, NY 10038

Air Force Association Civil Air Patrol Unit Grants 214
The Air Force Association (AFA) helps provide educational opportunities for America's youth. To accomplish their educational goals, the AFA communicates directly with the American public about the importance of maintaining a sound aerospace infrastructure and the importance of maintaining a strong Air Force to ensure national security. Another important part of their educational efforts is to support the educational objectives of the Air Force and Civil Air Patrol (CAP). As part of that support, the AFA recognizes outstanding contributions in the field of aerospace education. To support CAP's aerospace education programs, the AFA provides aerospace education grants for Civil Air Patrol units.
Requirements: Grants must be used for aerospace education-related items/activities such as books, videotapes, aerospace-oriented field trips, and aerospace education events for the cadets and/or for the community. Grants cannot exceed $250 per request. Grant cycle deadlines are June 30 and December 31. Completed applications should be emailed to afa@capnhq.gov.
Restrictions: Unit grants may not be used for uniforms or honor guard/color guard activities, nor may they be used for individual member flying instruction.
Geographic Focus: All States
Date(s) Application is Due: Jun 30; Dec 31
Amount of Grant: Up to 250 USD
Contact: Lynette Cross, (800) 727-3337 ext. 4807; LCross@afa.org
Internet: http://members.gocivilairpatrol.com/aerospace_education/general/afa.cfm
Sponsor: Air Force Association
1501 Lee Highway
Arlington, VA 22209

Air Force Association Junior ROTC Grants 215
The AFJROTC Grant was established to promote aerospace education throughout classrooms and units. The grants provide units and classrooms with up to $250 every other academic year. Funds may be used for any aerospace education related activity from purchasing textbooks or videotapes, to going on a field trip to an aerospace museum, Air Force base or other aerospace facility. Funds may be divided between multiple aerospace activities. Grants are issued twice a year. Deadlines for applications are October 10 and February 10.
Requirements: Aerospace Science Instructors should complete the required form and a one-page feedback from which describes how you plan to use the grant. The business card of the principal or of the school should be attached with your application.
Restrictions: Funds may not be used for purchasing uniforms, honor guard or color guard activities, etc.
Geographic Focus: All States
Date(s) Application is Due: Feb 10; Oct 10
Amount of Grant: Up to 250 USD
Contact: Lynette Cross, 800-727-3337 ext. 4807; LCross@afa.org
Internet: http://www.afa.org/aef/aid/rotc.asp
Sponsor: Air Force Association
1501 Lee Highway
Arlington, VA 22209

Air Products and Chemicals Grants 216
The foundation supports nonprofit organizations in company-operating areas in the fields of precollege and higher education; fitness, health, and welfare; community and economic development, arts and culture; and the environment and safety. Types of support include capital grants, employee matching gifts, general operating support, multiyear-continuing grants, project grants, seed grants, fellowships, employee-related scholarships, and donated equipment. There are no application forms; requests must be in writing. Guidelines are available online.
Requirements: 501(c)3 nonprofit organizations in company-operating areas are eligible.
Restrictions: Grants are not made to/for individuals, sectarian or denominational organizations, political candidates or activities, veterans organizations, organizations receiving United Way support, labor groups, elementary or secondary schools, capital campaigns of national organizations, hospital operating expenses, national health organizations, or goodwill advertising.

Geographic Focus: All States
Contact: Kassie Hilgert, Program Manager; hilgerk@airproducts.com
Internet: http://www.airproducts.com/Responsibility/SocialResponsibility
Sponsor: Air Products and Chemicals Corporation
7201 Hamilton Boulevard
Allentown, PA 18195-1501

Akonadi Foundation Anti-Racism Grants 217
The foundation's mission is to work with others to eliminate racism, with a particular focus on structural and institutional racism. Grants have supported programmatic approaches including research, policy work, advocacy, litigation, organizing, media, arts, diversity training, education, and other tools in their anti-racism work. The foundation awards general operating grants and project grants. Grants are made to organizations in the San Francisco Bay area and to national organizations with national reach. Letters of interest will be accepted year round. Full proposals should only be submitted upon request.
Geographic Focus: California
Date(s) Application is Due: Feb 18
Amount of Grant: 10,000 - 50,000 USD
Contact: Grants Administrator; (510) 663-3867; info@akonadi.org
Internet: http://www.akonadi.org/application_guidelines.html
Sponsor: Akonadi Foundation
469 9th Street, Suite 210
Oakland, CA 94607

Akron Community Foundation Arts & Culture Grants 218
Part of the Akron Community Foundation Community Fund, the Arts and Culture fund serves to advance the interests and education of the community in performing arts (music, theater and dance) and art museums, historical societies and museums, libraries, historic preservation, media, language/literature and journalism.
Requirements: IRS 501(c)3 nonprofit Summit County, OH, organizations are eligible.
Restrictions: The foundation generally does not consider requests for general operating support, computers, office equipment, or travel expenses. Grants may not be used for endowments, scholarships, religious purposes, capital campaigns, or deficit expenses. Organizations that do not operate programs in Summit County are not eligible for grants. Grants are not made to individuals.
Geographic Focus: Ohio
Date(s) Application is Due: Apr 1
Contact: Donae Eckert; (330) 376-8522; deckert@akroncommunityfdn.org
Internet: https://www.akroncommunityfdn.org/cgi-bin/displayContent.pl?type=section&id=122
Sponsor: Akron Community Foundation
345 West Cedar Street
Akron, OH 44307-2407

Akzo Nobel Chemicals Grants 219
The company awards grants to U.S. nonprofits to support arts and humanities, civic and public affairs, education (higher education, minority education, special education, vocational and technical education, and international exchanges), and the environment. Types of support include capital grants, employee matching gifts, fellowships, scholarships, and matching funds. There are no application deadlines or formal application procedures.
Restrictions: The company does not support fraternal, political, or religious organizations.
Geographic Focus: All States
Contact: Grants Administrator; (312) 544-7000; fax (312) 544-7322
Internet: http://www.akzonobel.com/com/Social+responsibility/In_Society/Community+Program.htm
Sponsor: Akzo Nobel Chemicals
525 W Van Buren Street
Chicago, IL 60607-3823

ALA Adelaide Del Frate Conference Sponsorship Award 220
The Federal Librarians Adelaide Del Frate Conference Sponsorship Award is given to a library school student who has an interest in working in a Federal Library. One student will receive an award of $1,000 for registration fees, transportation, and other related expenses to the ALA Annual Conference. Nominations are accepted between January and mid-April of each year. The annual deadline has been identified as April 15.
Requirements: Students who are currently enrolled in any ALA-accredited library school, who do not already have an ALA accredited degree, and who have expressed an interest in Federal librarianship are eligible. Applicants must be full or part-time students at the time of the nomination.
Geographic Focus: All States
Date(s) Application is Due: Apr 15
Amount of Grant: 1,000 USD
Contact: Shirley Loo; (202) 707-6785 or (800) 941-8478; sloo@crs.loc.gov
Internet: http://www.ala.org/awardsgrants/awards/239/apply
Sponsor: American Library Association
50 East Huron Street
Chicago, IL 60611-2795

ALA Allie Beth Martin Award 221
The Martin Award provides recognition to a public librarian who has demonstrated extraordinary range and depth of knowledge about books and other library materials, with a distinguished ability to share than knowledge. The $3,000 award is given annually. The application with instructions is available at the website.
Restrictions: Members of the current Allie Beth Martin Award Jury are ineligible to receive the award. Persons who have not earned an MLS are ineligible to receive the award.
Geographic Focus: All States
Date(s) Application is Due: Dec 1
Amount of Grant: 3,000 USD
Contact: Julianna Kloeppel; (312) 280-5026; fax (312) 280-5029; jkloeppel@ala.org
Internet: http://www.ala.org/awardsgrants/awards/72/apply
Sponsor: American Library Association
50 East Huron Street
Chicago, IL 60611-2795

ALA ALSC Bookapalooza Grants 222
The core purpose of the Association for Library Service to Children (ALSC) is creating a better future for all children through libraries. The Association believes that: in every library, children come first; the importance of high quality children's service with adequate materials and resources; collections, services, resources, and staff reflect the communities they serve; the library's physical space reflects the developmental needs of children; and children and their families are served by a variety of non-traditional programs and activities in off-site locations. With this in mind, Bookapalooza Grants offer select libraries a collection of materials that will help transform their collection, and provide the opportunity for these materials to be used in their community in creative and innovative ways. Each application is judged on the following criteria: degree of need in the community and need of the library where the materials will be used; extent to which the materials will improve service to children in the community; the plan for using the materials in a creative and innovative way; and the clarity and effectiveness of the statement of need. The application is available at the ALA website.
Requirements: Applicants must be personal members of ALSC as well as ALA. Libraries must be located in the U.S.
Restrictions: Organizational members are not eligible to apply.
Geographic Focus: All States
Date(s) Application is Due: Feb 1
Contact: Courtney Jones, Staff Liaison; (312) 280-5710; cjones@ala.org
Internet: http://www.ala.org/awardsgrants/awards/247/apply
Sponsor: American Library Association
50 East Huron Street
Chicago, IL 60611-2795

ALA ALSC Distinguished Service Award 223
The $3,000 Distinguished Service Award recognizes an individual member of the library profession who has, over a significant period of time, made an outstanding national contribution to school librarianship and school library development. The nomination form is available at the website.
Requirements: Nominations are made by personal members of the American Association of School Librarians (AASL). Individuals nominated should have demonstrated achievements in one of more of the following areas: service and visionary leadership to the organized profession through AASL and related organizations; significant and influential research on school library programs; publication of a body of scholarly and/or theoretical writing contributing to school library development; and influencing the planning and development of exemplary school library programs through legislative efforts, implementation of models, establishment of guidelines, or the teaching and/or mentoring of future library professionals.
Restrictions: Current AASL Directors and Board members are not eligible.
Geographic Focus: All States
Date(s) Application is Due: Feb 1
Amount of Grant: 3,000 USD
Contact: Meg Featheringham; (800) 545-2433, ext. 1396; mfeatheringham@ala.org
Internet: http://www.ala.org/awardsgrants/awards/203/apply
Sponsor: American Library Association
50 East Huron Street
Chicago, IL 60611-2795

ALA ALTAFF/GALE Outstanding Trustee Conference Grant 224
The ALTAFF/Gale Outstanding Trustee Conference Grant enables a public library trustee to attend the ALA Annual Conference. A grant of $850 each is awarded annually to a public library Trustee who has demonstrated qualitative interests and efforts in supportive service of the local public library. The Conference Grant, made possible by an annual gift from Gale Cengage Learning, is administered by ALTAFF. A formal presentation to winners is made at the ALA Annual Conference. Applications are due in January, and winners will be notified by late March of the Annual Conference year. Applicants are required to include a brief statement of exhibited interest and activities resulting in their subsequent appointment/election as a public library trustee. They should include reasons for wishing to attend an ALA Annual Conference and how this relates to their library-related goals and philosophy. A list of all relevant library activities and experience, including professional member associations (local, state, and national) is also required.
Requirements: Applicants should be current personal members of ALA and ALTA, and current members of a local public library board. They should also have never attended an ALA Annual Conference.
Geographic Focus: All States
Date(s) Application is Due: Jan 13
Contact: Coordinator; (800) 545-2433, ext. 2161; fax (215) 545-3821; united@ala.org
Internet: http://www.ala.org/awardsgrants/awards/76/apply
Sponsor: American Library Association
50 East Huron Street
Chicago, IL 60611-2795

ALA Annual Conference Professional Development Attendance Award 225
In the spirit of ALA's New Members Round Table (NMRT), the Annual Conference Professional Development Attendance Award fosters active involvement in ALA through various special events at the Annual Conference. The Award is presented to two NMRT members each year. The award provides professional development and networking opportunities to NMRT members by providing a ticket to attend the event of their choice. The award was developed to foster professional involvement in new members, and to increase their networking opportunities. Applicants write a short essay, explaining why they want to attend one of the following events at the annual conference: Amelia Bloomer Project Breakfast; Coretta Scott King Awards Breakfast; Gala Author Tea; International Librarians Reception; Literary Tastes Breakfast; Margaret A. Edwards Luncheon; Michael L. Printz Program and Reception; Newbery Caldecott Wilder Banquet; ProQuest Scholarship Bash; Stonewall Book Awards Brunch; or any other ticketed event for which the applicant provides justification (up to $100).
Requirements: Eligibility is open to all NMRT members who are not currently serving on the Annual Conference Professional Development Attendance Award Committee. Applicants must write an essay of about 250 words, explaining why they want to attend the event of their choice, including how they would benefit personally and professionally.
Geographic Focus: All States
Date(s) Application is Due: Apr 16
Contact: Kimberly L. Redd; (312) 280-4279; fax (312) 280-3256; klredd@ala.org
Internet: http://www.ala.org/awardsgrants/awards/31672/apply
Sponsor: American Library Association
50 East Huron Street
Chicago, IL 60611-2795

ALA Arthur Curley Memorial Lecture 226
Arthur Curley was an American librarian listed as one of the 100 most important library leaders of the 20th century. The Memorial Lecture series commemorates Curley's lifelong dedication to the principles of intellectual freedom and free public access to information. Curley served as president of ALA and was director of the Boston Public Library. He was a champion of the arts and of the library's role as a center that can transform the community.
Geographic Focus: All States
Date(s) Application is Due: Feb 28
Contact: Mark R. Gould; (312) 944-5042; fax (312) 944-8520; mgould@ala.org
Internet: http://www.ala.org/awardsgrants/awards/195/apply
Sponsor: American Library Association
50 East Huron Street
Chicago, IL 60611-2795

ALA Atlas Systems Mentoring Award 227
Sponsored by Atlas Systems, Inc., the Mentoring Award offers $1,250 to fund travel expenses associated with attending ALA's annual conference. The recipient will be a library practitioner who is new to the field of inter-library loan/document delivery or electronic reserves, and who has daily, hands-on involvement in the areas of borrowing, lending, document delivery, electronic reserves, material delivery, or resource sharing. The nomination form is available at the ALA website.
Requirements: This award is intended for persons who have been in the profession for less than two years, or an individual who is newly employed in interlibrary loan, resource sharing or electronic reserves position and has little or no experience in that area. M.L.S. or ALA membership is not required for this award. Preference will be given to those with greatest demonstrated need for the purposes of professional development, networking, education, and service to their local community. The STARS/Atlas Systems Mentoring Committee will assign a mentor to the recipient for the conference to help them navigate through the conference experience. The recipient is expected to participate in STARS events throughout the conference.
Geographic Focus: All States
Date(s) Application is Due: Dec 15
Contact: Leighann Wood; (800) 545-2433; fax (574) 631-6772; lwood@ala.org
Internet: http://www.ala.org/awardsgrants/awards/429/apply
Sponsor: American Library Association
50 East Huron Street
Chicago, IL 60611-2795

ALA Baker and Taylor Conference Grants 228
The Baker and Taylor Conference Grant is awarded to librarians who work directly with young adults. Two grants of $1,000 each are awarded. One grant is given to a school librarian, and the other is given to a public librarian. The application form is available at the ALA website.
Requirements: Applicants must be personal members of the Young Adult Library Services Association (YALSA). They should have experience working with teenagers for no more than ten years, and no previous attendance at an Annual ALA Conference.
Geographic Focus: All States
Date(s) Application is Due: Dec 1
Contact: Letitia Smith; (312) 280-4390 or (800) 545-2433; lsmith@ala.org
Internet: http://www.ala.org/awardsgrants/awards/233/apply
Sponsor: American Library Association
50 East Huron Street
Chicago, IL 60611-2795

ALA Baker and Taylor Entertainment Audio Music/Video Product Award 229
The purpose of the Baker and Taylor Entertainment Audio Music/Video Product Award is to promote the development of a circulating audio music/video product collection in public libraries and increase the exposure of the format within the community. One public library will receive $2,500 worth of audio music or video products. The application is available at the ALA website.
Requirements: Any public library is eligible to apply.
Restrictions: Public libraries with employees on the current Baker and Taylor Entertainment Audio Music/Video Product Award Jury are not eligible.
Geographic Focus: All States
Date(s) Application is Due: Dec 1
Amount of Grant: 2,500 USD
Contact: Julianna Kloeppel; (312) 280-5026; fax (312) 280-5029; jkloeppel@ala.org
Internet: http://www.ala.org/awardsgrants/awards/175/apply
Sponsor: American Library Association
50 East Huron Street
Chicago, IL 60611-2795

ALA Baker and Taylor Summer Reading Program Grant 230
The Baker and Taylor Summer Reading Program Grant is designed to encourage outstanding summer reading programs by providing financial assistance, while recognizing ALSC members for outstanding program development. Each application will be judged on the plan and outline submitted for a theme-based summer reading program in a public library. The award of $3,000 is given out each year.
Requirements: The applicant must plan and present an outline for a theme-based summer reading program in a public library. The committee also encourages innovative proposals involving children with physical or mental disabilities.
Restrictions: Applicants must be personal members of ALSC as well as ALA. Organizational members are not eligible. Programs must be open to all children (birth to 14 years), and must take place at a public library.
Geographic Focus: All States
Date(s) Application is Due: Nov 30
Amount of Grant: 3,000 USD
Contact: Courtney Jones; (312) 280-5710; fax (312) 440-9374; cjones@ala.org
Internet: http://www.ala.org/awardsgrants/awards/85/apply
Sponsor: American Library Association
50 East Huron Street
Chicago, IL 60611-2795

Alabama Humanities Foundation Mini Grants 231
Designed for flexibility, Mini Grants support a wide variety of projects from workshops to radio programs and reading/discussion series. Up to $2,000 in outright and $2,000 in matching funds is available. Preliminary application can be completed anytime, with final proposals due the first working day of the following months: February, May, August, and November.
Requirements: Applications must be submitted three months prior to start date of the program. Grants are made to nonprofit public or private organizations. Funds are to be used in state only.
Restrictions: Grants are not made to individuals.
Geographic Focus: Alabama
Contact: Susan Perry; (205) 558-3980 or (205) 558-3989; sperry@ahf.net
Internet: http://www.ahf.net/programs/grantsProgram.html
Sponsor: Alabama Humanities Foundation
1100 Ireland Way, Suite 101
Birmingham, AL 35205

Alabama Humanities Foundation Planning/Consultant Grants 232
Available for planning Major Grants only, these Planning/Consultant Grants provide funds for humanities scholar honoraria and travel, as well as other planning expense. These grants are awarded in support of organizations that do not have extensive grant writing experience or expertise in planning public humanities projects. Application deadlines are the first working day of February, May, August, and November.
Requirements: Grants are made to nonprofit public or private organizations. Funds are to be used in state only.
Restrictions: Grants are not made to individuals. Colleges and universities are ineligible.
Geographic Focus: Alabama
Amount of Grant: Up to 1,000 USD
Contact: Susan Perry; (205) 558-3980 or (205) 558-3989; sperry@ahf.net
Internet: http://www.ahf.net/programs/grantsProgram.html
Sponsor: Alabama Humanities Foundation
1100 Ireland Way, Suite 101
Birmingham, AL 35205

Alabama Power Foundation Grants 233
The foundation's mission is to improve the lives and circumstances of Alabama residents and to strengthen the communities in which they live. It supports programs that will improve education (by supporting innovative programs and assisting teachers in their crucial responsibilities), strengthen communities, promote arts and culture or restore and enhance the environment. The project must meet several of the guidelines to be considered. The majority of grants are made to support targeted efforts with specific objectives. The foundation also provides general operating assistance to organizations, capital grants for endowment and building, and scholarship funds. Applications should be sent to the local Alabama Power Company office for review and recommendation to the foundation. The amount of the request determines the review frequency.
Requirements: Applications are accepted from Alabama nonprofit organizations whose programs fall within foundation guidelines.
Restrictions: Grants are not made to individuals, for sectarian religious purposes, or for political activities.
Geographic Focus: Alabama
Date(s) Application is Due: Feb 1; May 1; Aug 1; Nov 1

Amount of Grant: 1,000 - 100,000 USD
Contact: William Johnson, President; (205) 257-2508; fax (205) 257-1860
Internet: http://www.alabamapower.com/foundation/grantsandinitiatives.asp
Sponsor: Alabama Power Foundation
600 N 18th Street, P.O. Box 2641
Birmingham, AL 35291-0011

Alabama Power Plant a Tree Grants   234
The goal of this program is to provide funding to plant trees in urban areas across the state. Thus, the foundation awards grants to eligible Alabama nonprofit organizations to purchase and plant trees in community parks, along roadways, on school grounds, and at other community sites. Funding will be awarded based on the environmental benefits of the proposed project, support of local community leaders and volunteers and the needs of the applicant's local area. Grants will be awarded up to $2,000.
Requirements: Alabama local governments, public and private nonprofit groups, schools, colleges, and universities are eligible.
Restrictions: Funds will be available for the purchase of trees only. Planting, watering, and maintenance must be provided through other funding methods or volunteer involvement. All trees shall be planted according to the procedures prescribed by the International Society of Arborculture or the National Arbor Day Foundation.
Geographic Focus: Alabama
Date(s) Application is Due: Aug 31
Amount of Grant: Up to 2,000 USD
Contact: Grants Administrator; (205) 257-2508; fax (205) 257-1860; aufa@bsc.edu
Internet: http://www.aufa.com/grants.html
Sponsor: Alabama Power Foundation
600 N 18th Street, P.O. Box 2641
Birmingham, AL 35291-0011

Alabama State Council on the Arts Collaborative Ventures Grants   235
Support is provided primarily to statewide service organizations through partnership agreement grants with the State Arts Council. These agreements are characterized by broad, service-oriented efforts consistent with goals and objectives of the Council. Collaboration between the applicant and the Council on design and implementation is required. Agreements may or may not involve matching requirements. Specific outcomes will be proposed, measured and analyzed. Multi-year, long-term partnerships are possible. A program manager of the Council acts as an agency liaison in partnership ventures.
Requirements: An organization is eligible to apply for funding support of arts activities taking place in Alabama if the organization is legally domiciled in Alabama, and meets either of the following qualifications: the organization is non-profit with a determination letter from the Internal Revenue Service declaring the organization exempt from federal income tax under Section 501(c)3 of the Internal Revenue Code; or the organization is a public or private educational institution (such as an elementary or secondary school), a school board, a local or county governmental agency or a college or university. Private educational institutions must be non-profit and meet the tax-exempt requirements described above.
Restrictions: The Council does not fund: projects not available to the general public; activities and performances planned solely for fund raising purposes; food, beverages or other refreshments; interest on loans, fines, penalties, and/or litigation costs; expenses incurred prior to October 1 or after September 30 of the current grant year; investments of any kind; projects which have sectarian or religious purposes (however, such institutions may apply on behalf of the community for arts activities or programming where artistic expression is a primary focus); or indirect costs.
Geographic Focus: Alabama
Contact: Albert B. Head, Executive Director; (334) 242-4076, ext. 245; fax (334) 240-3269; al.head@arts.alabama.gov or staff@arts.alabama.gov
Internet: http://arts.state.al.us/grants/index-grants.html
Sponsor: Alabama State Council on the Arts
201 Monroe Street, Suite 110
Montgomery, AL 36130-1800

Alabama State Council on the Arts Community Collaborative Ventures Grants   236
Opportunities exist for collaborative ventures and long-term partnerships that will expand exposure to the arts. In this program, collaboration involves community-wide services and/or collaborative efforts among two or more communities. Funded projects must reflect multifaceted planning and participation as well as broad population inclusion. As a partnership venture, the Council provides funding for DesignAlabama, a statewide, non-profit, membership organization which promotes awareness and appreciation of eight design disciplines: architecture, landscape architecture, urban design, interior design, industrial design, graphic design, fashion design and engineering. Through volunteer design and planning assistance to under-served communities, the organization makes valuable contributions to the quality of life and economic well-being of the state. Communities, organizations, individual artists, schools and other interested parties are assisted through programs and direct services.
Restrictions: The Council does not fund: projects not available to the general public; activities and performances planned solely for fund raising purposes; food, beverages or other refreshments; interest on loans, fines, penalties, and/or litigation costs; expenses incurred prior to October 1 or after September 30 of the current grant year; investments of any kind; projects which have sectarian or religious purposes (however, such institutions may apply on behalf of the community for arts activities or programming where artistic expression is a primary focus); or indirect costs.
Geographic Focus: Alabama
Contact: Randy Shoults, Community Arts Program Manager; (334) 242-4076, ext. 224; fax (334) 240-3269; randy.shoults@arts.alabama.gov or staff@arts.alabama.gov

Internet: http://arts.state.al.us/grants/index-grants.html
Sponsor: Alabama State Council on the Arts
201 Monroe Street, Suite 110
Montgomery, AL 36130-1800

Alabama State Council on the Arts Community Arts Operating Support Grants   237
Larger local arts councils and arts centers that have developed a successful track record of diverse programs and services in the community and region may qualify for general operating assistance. It is expected that strong cooperation will exist with local government entities. All organizations receiving operating support from the Council will be required to match the grant with an equal amount in local government contributions of either cash or cash and in-kind support.
Requirements: To be eligible for funding under this category, organizations must have been incorporated and recognized as having non-profit tax exempt status by the Internal Revenue Service for at least three years prior to application, or have been an agency of a city or county government for that length of time. To qualify, a Local Arts Council or Arts Center must have an actual three-year average cash income of at least $300,000. Organizations receiving operating support must also have a full time administrative staff responsible for overall functions of the organization and have an annual audit conducted by an independent Certified Public Accountant.
Restrictions: The Council does not fund: projects not available to the general public; activities and performances planned solely for fund raising purposes; food, beverages or other refreshments; interest on loans, fines, penalties, and/or litigation costs; expenses incurred prior to October 1 or after September 30 of the current grant year; investments of any kind; projects which have sectarian or religious purposes (however, such institutions may apply on behalf of the community for arts activities or programming where artistic expression is a primary focus); or indirect costs.
Geographic Focus: Alabama
Date(s) Application is Due: Jun 1
Contact: Randy Shoults, Community Arts Program Manager; (334) 242-4076, ext. 224; fax (334) 240-3269; randy.shoults@arts.alabama.gov or staff@arts.alabama.gov
Internet: http://arts.state.al.us/grants/index-grants.html
Sponsor: Alabama State Council on the Arts
201 Monroe Street, Suite 110
Montgomery, AL 36130-1800

Alabama State Council on the Arts Community Arts Presenting Grants   238
This Program provides support for performing arts series or single events where an artist or group is contracted to give a public performance. Grants are reviewed by discipline, so applications for music, theatre and dance performances should be submitted separately. More than one group may be included in a single application as long as they perform in the same discipline. An example would be a series of chamber music concerts. Priorities for funding are proposals that include educational workshops and residencies, or implement a comprehensive plan for audience or community development. Performances of highly commercial or seasonal entertainment, which could be self-supporting, are unlikely to be funded. When costs are offset through grants from other public funding sources, the total combined funding from the State Arts Council and the other grants may not exceed 50 percent of the total cost of the presentation, including marketing, space rental and other costs. There is no limit on how much can be requested, however, grant amounts rarely exceed $10,000.
Requirements: The artist or group being presented must live outside the county in which the performance takes place in order to be eligible for funding, and should generally having touring experience and a reputation for quality presentations. The grants must be matched dollar-for-dollar in cash.
Restrictions: The Council does not fund: projects not available to the general public; activities and performances planned solely for fund raising purposes; food, beverages or other refreshments; interest on loans, fines, penalties, and/or litigation costs; expenses incurred prior to October 1 or after September 30 of the current grant year; investments of any kind; projects which have sectarian or religious purposes (however, such institutions may apply on behalf of the community for arts activities or programming where artistic expression is a primary focus); or indirect costs.
Geographic Focus: Alabama
Date(s) Application is Due: Jun 1; Sep 1
Amount of Grant: Up to 10,000 USD
Contact: Randy Shoults, Community Arts Program Manager; (334) 242-4076, ext. 224; fax (334) 240-3269; randy.shoults@arts.alabama.gov or staff@arts.alabama.gov
Internet: http://arts.state.al.us/grants/index-grants.html
Sponsor: Alabama State Council on the Arts
201 Monroe Street, Suite 110
Montgomery, AL 36130-1800

Alabama State Council on the Arts Community Development Grants   239
These grants help the forward-looking community arts organizations grow and adapt to change. For example, all-volunteer groups have been able to add paid staff and professional organizations have developed better functioning structures and have opened up new markets with these grants. Funds may not be received for more than three consecutive years, but subsequent applications in other categories are encouraged. Requests submitted under this category should be for a minimum of $10,000. All applications must be submitted by June 1 for the full year.
Restrictions: The Council does not fund: projects not available to the general public; activities and performances planned solely for fund raising purposes; food, beverages or other refreshments; interest on loans, fines, penalties, and/or litigation costs; expenses incurred prior to October 1 or after September 30 of the current grant year; investments of any kind; projects which have sectarian or religious purposes (however, such institutions

34 | Grant Programs

may apply on behalf of the community for arts activities or programming where artistic expression is a primary focus); or indirect costs.
Geographic Focus: Alabama
Date(s) Application is Due: Jun 1
Amount of Grant: 10,000 USD
Contact: Randy Shoults, Community Arts Program Manager; (334) 242-4076, ext. 224; fax (334) 240-3269; randy.shoults@arts.alabama.gov or staff@arts.alabama.gov
Internet: http://arts.state.al.us/grants/index-grants.html
Sponsor: Alabama State Council on the Arts
201 Monroe Street, Suite 110
Montgomery, AL 36130-1800

Alabama State Council on the Arts Community Arts Technical Assistance Grants 240
Organizations and individual artists receive funding for special, one-time needs such as purchasing materials for a small-scale project, attending a conference, or bringing in a consultant. These grants generally do not exceed $1,000; the minimum amount is $250. A match will strengthen the application, but is not required. In communities without a local arts agency, a city, county or other appropriate tax exempt group is eligible to apply for start-up costs not to exceed $2,500 for one year only. Contact program manager for funding availability.
Restrictions: Requests must not relate to any program or project already funded or applied for in another component, and must not be eligible and appropriate for funding under any other component. The Council does not fund: projects not available to the general public; activities and performances planned solely for fund raising purposes; food, beverages or other refreshments; interest on loans, fines, penalties, and/or litigation costs; expenses incurred prior to October 1 or after September 30 of the current grant year; investments of any kind; projects which have sectarian or religious purposes (however, such institutions may apply on behalf of the community for arts activities or programming where artistic expression is a primary focus); or indirect costs.
Geographic Focus: Alabama
Amount of Grant: 250 - 1,000 USD
Contact: Randy Shoults, Community Arts Program Manager; (334) 242-4076, ext. 224; fax (334) 240-3269; randy.shoults@arts.alabama.gov or staff@arts.alabama.gov
Internet: http://arts.state.al.us/grants/index-grants.html
Sponsor: Alabama State Council on the Arts
201 Monroe Street, Suite 110
Montgomery, AL 36130-1800

Alabama State Council on the Arts Community Planning & Design Grants 241
The program has been established to support projects that use design disciplines to impact the quality of life in Alabama communities. Applications may be submitted in any of the design disciplines: architecture, landscape architecture, urban design, interior design, industrial design, graphic design, fashion design, and engineering. Applications may also be submitted for community cultural planning where there is an established partnership with city or county government. There is no limit on how much can be requested, however, grant amounts rarely exceed $10,000.
Restrictions: The Council does not fund: projects not available to the general public; activities and performances planned solely for fund raising purposes; food, beverages or other refreshments; interest on loans, fines, penalties, and/or litigation costs; expenses incurred prior to October 1 or after September 30 of the current grant year; investments of any kind; projects which have sectarian or religious purposes (however, such institutions may apply on behalf of the community for arts activities or programming where artistic expression is a primary focus); or indirect costs.
Geographic Focus: Alabama
Amount of Grant: Up to 10,000 USD
Contact: Randy Shoults, Community Arts Program Manager; (334) 242-4076, ext. 224; fax (334) 240-3269; randy.shoults@arts.alabama.gov or staff@arts.alabama.gov
Internet: http://arts.state.al.us/grants/index-grants.html
Sponsor: Alabama State Council on the Arts
201 Monroe Street, Suite 110
Montgomery, AL 36130-1800

Alabama State Council on the Arts in Education Partnership Grants 242
The Program provides support to projects which advance arts education through collaborations between arts organizations and educational entities. Partnership projects should expand or enhance the arts education efforts of arts organizations, schools and/or other nonprofit entities. They should have a lasting impact on the arts education programs of all partners. Partnership projects should also be innovative and have the potential to be replicated across the state. The Council is particularly interested in projects that relate to the school curriculum and the Alabama Course of Study, that target rural areas and/or at-risk students, and that address learner outcomes in arts education and the professional development of classroom teachers. Grant funds may be used for artistic and administrative expenses related to the partnership project.
Requirements: A partnership may be made up of more than two partners, but at least one partner must be an arts organization and one must be a school or local school system. Funds cannot be used solely for salary support. Grants must be matched at least dollar-for-dollar with cash or with a combination of cash and in-kind support.
Restrictions: The Council does not fund: projects not available to the general public; activities and performances planned solely for fund raising purposes; food, beverages or other refreshments; interest on loans, fines, penalties, and/or litigation costs; expenses incurred prior to October 1 or after September 30 of the current grant year; investments of any kind; projects which have sectarian or religious purposes (however, such institutions may apply on behalf of the community for arts activities or programming where artistic expression is a primary focus); or indirect costs.

Geographic Focus: Alabama
Date(s) Application is Due: Sep 1
Contact: Diana F. Green, Program Manager; (334) 242-4076, ext. 241; fax (334) 240-3269; diana.green@arts.alabama.gov or staff@arts.alabama.gov
Internet: http://arts.state.al.us/grants/index-grants.html
Sponsor: Alabama State Council on the Arts
201 Monroe Street, Suite 110
Montgomery, AL 36130-1800

Alabama State Council on the Arts Multi-Discipline and Festival Grants 243
The Program provides support for activities that include more than one art discipline. It is intended to give audiences and communities activities that provide a broad spectrum of artistic expression. Many exciting projects have been designed to incorporate dance, music, theater, literature and visual arts. While festivals are the most common example, other innovative and unique activities are appropriate for this category. Festivals that exclusively present or have components that present Alabama traditional artists may also be eligible to apply under the Folklife Program. Organizations undertaking projects which focus exclusively on one discipline should consult most appropriate. There is no limit on how much can be requested, however, grant amounts rarely exceed $10,000.
Restrictions: The Council does not fund: projects not available to the general public; activities and performances planned solely for fund raising purposes; food, beverages or other refreshments; interest on loans, fines, penalties, and/or litigation costs; expenses incurred prior to October 1 or after September 30 of the current grant year; investments of any kind; projects which have sectarian or religious purposes (however, such institutions may apply on behalf of the community for arts activities or programming where artistic expression is a primary focus); or indirect costs.
Geographic Focus: Alabama
Amount of Grant: Up to 10,000 USD
Contact: Randy Shoults, Community Arts Program Manager; (334) 242-4076, ext. 224; fax (334) 240-3269; randy.shoults@arts.alabama.gov or staff@arts.alabama.gov
Internet: http://arts.state.al.us/grants/index-grants.html
Sponsor: Alabama State Council on the Arts
201 Monroe Street, Suite 110
Montgomery, AL 36130-1800

Alabama State Council on the Arts Operating Support Grants 244
These grants are designed to provide support and stability to large arts organizations with far-reaching cultural impact, to promote general program development and stimulate private and other public funding. Eligible groups are expected to show a high level of professionalism, both artistically and administratively, strong community service and educational outreach, and well-established, ongoing fund raising efforts.
Requirements: An organization is eligible to apply for funding support of arts activities taking place in Alabama if the organization is legally domiciled in Alabama, and meets either of the following qualifications: the organization is non-profit with a determination letter from the Internal Revenue Service declaring the organization exempt from federal income tax under Section 501(c)3 of the Internal Revenue Code; or the organization is a public or private educational institution (such as an elementary or secondary school), a school board, a local or county governmental agency or a college or university. Private educational institutions must be non-profit and meet the tax-exempt requirements described above.
Restrictions: Organizations receiving operating support may not submit more than two (2) applications per deadline or more than three (3) per year, including the operating support request. The Council does not fund: projects not available to the general public; activities and performances planned solely for fund raising purposes; food, beverages or other refreshments; interest on loans, fines, penalties, and/or litigation costs; expenses incurred prior to October 1 or after September 30 of the current grant year; investments of any kind; projects which have sectarian or religious purposes (however, such institutions may apply on behalf of the community for arts activities or programming where artistic expression is a primary focus); or indirect costs.
Geographic Focus: Alabama
Date(s) Application is Due: Jun 1
Amount of Grant: 5,000 - 7,500 USD
Contact: Albert B. Head, Executive Director; (334) 242-4076, ext. 245; fax (334) 240-3269; al.head@arts.alabama.gov or staff@arts.alabama.gov
Internet: http://arts.state.al.us/grants/index-grants.html
Sponsor: Alabama State Council on the Arts
201 Monroe Street, Suite 110
Montgomery, AL 36130-1800

Alabama State Council on the Arts Presenting Grants 245
Eligible organizations may apply for grants to offset the costs of presenting (booking) performances or exhibitions by individual artists, institutions or companies producing dance, music, theater, exhibitions and readings. Priorities for funding are proposals that include educational workshops and residencies or a comprehensive plan for audience or community development. A meaningful educational component should be engaging and well planned.
Requirements: Presenting grants must be matched dollar-for-dollar in cash. An organization is eligible to apply for funding support of arts activities taking place in Alabama if the organization is legally domiciled in Alabama, and meets either of the following qualifications: the organization is non-profit with a determination letter from the Internal Revenue Service declaring the organization exempt from federal income tax under Section 501(c)3 of the Internal Revenue Code; or the organization is a public or private educational institution (such as an elementary or secondary school), a school board, a local or county governmental agency or a college or university. Private educational institutions must be non-profit and meet the tax-exempt requirements described above.

Restrictions: Artists whose work is to be presented must be from outside of the home county of the applicant organization. No more than four (4) presentations per year will be funded. The Council does not fund: projects not available to the general public; activities and performances planned solely for fund raising purposes; food, beverages or other refreshments; interest on loans, fines, penalties, and/or litigation costs; expenses incurred prior to October 1 or after September 30 of the current grant year; investments of any kind; projects which have sectarian or religious purposes (however, such institutions may apply on behalf of the community for arts activities or programming where artistic expression is a primary focus); or indirect costs.
Geographic Focus: Alabama
Date(s) Application is Due: Jun 1; Sep 1
Contact: Albert B. Head, Executive Director; (334) 242-4076, ext. 245; fax (334) 240-3269; al.head@arts.alabama.gov or staff@arts.alabama.gov
Internet: http://arts.state.al.us/grants/index-grants.html
Sponsor: Alabama State Council on the Arts
201 Monroe Street, Suite 110
Montgomery, AL 36130-1800

Alabama State Council on the Arts Program Development Grants 246
Requests may be submitted to fund establishment of permanent staff, existing staff development, program specialists, consultants, and general operating costs. Applicants will be expected to describe how this assistance will upgrade organizational programs. Programming development support is limited to three years, based on the assumption that the organization will be strong enough to sustain more advanced operations by that time. Generally, organizations that have a proven track record of programming for three years can be considered. All applications in this category must be submitted by June 1 for the full year.
Requirements: Grants must be matched dollar-for-dollar in cash or a combination of cash and in-kind support. An organization is eligible to apply for funding support of arts activities taking place in Alabama if the organization is legally domiciled in Alabama, and meets either of the following qualifications: the organization is non-profit with a determination letter from the Internal Revenue Service declaring the organization exempt from federal income tax under Section 501(c)3 of the Internal Revenue Code; or the organization is a public or private educational institution (such as an elementary or secondary school), a school board, a local or county governmental agency or a college or university. Private educational institutions must be non-profit and meet the tax-exempt requirements described above.
Restrictions: Large cultural institutions receiving operating support and non-arts organizations such as cities, schools, universities and civic groups are not eligible to apply. The Council does not fund: projects not available to the general public; activities and performances planned solely for fund raising purposes; food, beverages or other refreshments; interest on loans, fines, penalties, and/or litigation costs; expenses incurred prior to October 1 or after September 30 of the current grant year; investments of any kind; projects which have sectarian or religious purposes (however, such institutions may apply on behalf of the community for arts activities or programming where artistic expression is a primary focus); or indirect costs.
Geographic Focus: Alabama
Date(s) Application is Due: Jun 1
Contact: Albert B. Head, Executive Director; (334) 242-4076, ext. 245; fax (334) 240-3269; al.head@arts.alabama.gov or staff@arts.alabama.gov
Internet: http://arts.state.al.us/grants/index-grants.html
Sponsor: Alabama State Council on the Arts
201 Monroe Street, Suite 110
Montgomery, AL 36130-1800

Alabama State Council on the Arts Project Assistance Grants 247
These grants provide support for specific activities and services that contribute to organizational development, increase arts activities for the community, assist artists in the creation of new work, enhance the quality of artistic productions, and contribute to the cultural enrichment of the public. Organizations are expected to work toward making projects self-supporting after a reasonable period of funding by the council.
Requirements: Project grants must be matched dollar-for-dollar in cash or a combination of cash and in-kind support. Applicants must be Alabama residents and have resided in the state at least two years prior to making an application. An organization is eligible to apply for funding support of arts activities taking place in Alabama if the organization is legally domiciled in Alabama, and meets either of the following qualifications: the organization is non-profit with a determination letter from the Internal Revenue Service declaring the organization exempt from federal income tax under Section 501(c)3 of the Internal Revenue Code; or the organization is a public or private educational institution (such as an elementary or secondary school), a school board, a local or county governmental agency or a college or university. Private educational institutions must be non-profit and meet the tax-exempt requirements described above.
Restrictions: The Council does not fund: projects not available to the general public; activities and performances planned solely for fund raising purposes; food, beverages or other refreshments; interest on loans, fines, penalties, and/or litigation costs; expenses incurred prior to October 1 or after September 30 of the current grant year; investments of any kind; projects which have sectarian or religious purposes (however, such institutions may apply on behalf of the community for arts activities or programming where artistic expression is a primary focus); or indirect costs.
Geographic Focus: Alabama
Date(s) Application is Due: Jun 1; Sep 1
Contact: Albert B. Head, Executive Director; (334) 242-4076, ext. 245; fax (334) 240-3269; al.head@arts.alabama.gov or staff@arts.alabama.gov
Internet: http://arts.state.al.us/grants/index-grants.html
Sponsor: Alabama State Council on the Arts
201 Monroe Street, Suite 110
Montgomery, AL 36130-1800

Alabama State Council on the Arts Projects of Individual Artists Grants 248
Consistent with its charge from the Legislature, the Council has adopted a number of programs to address the needs of the arts in Alabama. These programs currently consist of Arts in Education, Community Arts, Folklife, Performing Arts, Visual Arts, and Literary Arts. An arts project by an individual artist may be funded through an organization which acts as fiscal agent and administers the grant. Successful applications will show considerable planning and collaboration between the artist and supporting organization.
Requirements: Grants must be matched dollar-for-dollar in cash or a combination of cash and in-kind support. An organization is eligible to apply for funding support of arts activities taking place in Alabama if the organization is legally domiciled in Alabama, and meets either of the following qualifications: the organization is non-profit with a determination letter from the Internal Revenue Service declaring the organization exempt from federal income tax under Section 501(c)3 of the Internal Revenue Code; or the organization is a public or private educational institution (such as an elementary or secondary school), a school board, a local or county governmental agency or a college or university. Private educational institutions must be non-profit and meet the tax-exempt requirements described above.
Restrictions: The Council does not fund: projects not available to the general public; activities and performances planned solely for fund raising purposes; food, beverages or other refreshments; interest on loans, fines, penalties, and/or litigation costs; expenses incurred prior to October 1 or after September 30 of the current grant year; investments of any kind; projects which have sectarian or religious purposes (however, such institutions may apply on behalf of the community for arts activities or programming where artistic expression is a primary focus); or indirect costs.
Geographic Focus: Alabama
Date(s) Application is Due: Jun 1; Sep 1
Contact: Albert B. Head, Executive Director; (334) 242-4076, ext. 245; fax (334) 240-3269; al.head@arts.alabama.gov or staff@arts.alabama.gov
Internet: http://arts.state.al.us/grants/index-grants.html
Sponsor: Alabama State Council on the Arts
201 Monroe Street, Suite 110
Montgomery, AL 36130-1800

Alabama State Council on the Arts Technical Assistance Grants for Individuals 249
Funds may be available to provide artists with up to $1,000 for technical assistance. Applicants have used these grants for marketing, establishing a portfolio, learning tax laws and accounting basics for self-employment, resource development or perfecting a technique or style of work. Funds may be used to attend workshops or seminars, to study under another artist or participate in a special institute for artists. Performing, literary and visual artists are encouraged to apply. For funding availability at any time throughout the year, applicants should contact the appropriate program manager.
Requirements: An applicant must be a legal resident of Alabama who has lived in the state for the two years prior to the application.
Restrictions: The Council does not fund: projects not available to the general public; activities and performances planned solely for fund raising purposes; food, beverages or other refreshments; interest on loans, fines, penalties, and/or litigation costs; expenses incurred prior to October 1 or after September 30 of the current grant year; investments of any kind; projects which have sectarian or religious purposes (however, such institutions may apply on behalf of the community for arts activities or programming where artistic expression is a primary focus); or indirect costs.
Geographic Focus: Alabama
Amount of Grant: Up to 1,000 USD
Contact: Albert B. Head, Executive Director; (334) 242-4076, ext. 245; fax (334) 240-3269; al.head@arts.alabama.gov or staff@arts.alabama.gov
Internet: http://arts.state.al.us/grants/index-grants.html
Sponsor: Alabama State Council on the Arts
201 Monroe Street, Suite 110
Montgomery, AL 36130-1800

Alabama State Council on the Arts Tech Assistance Grants for Organizations 250
Organizations and schools may receive grants to meet special needs for material purchases for a small-scale project, for costs of attending a conference, bringing in a consultant, or other one-time expenses. Requests must not relate to any program or project area already funded or applied for in another category, and must not be eligible or appropriate for funding under another category. Technical assistance grants often serve to meet emergency needs or allow organizations to meet a unique opportunity. Amounts of $1,000 or less may be approved by the Council's executive director. For funding availability at any time throughout the year, please contact the appropriate program manager.
Requirements: An organization is eligible to apply for funding support of arts activities taking place in Alabama if the organization is legally domiciled in Alabama, and meets either of the following qualifications: the organization is non-profit with a determination letter from the Internal Revenue Service declaring the organization exempt from federal income tax under Section 501(c)3 of the Internal Revenue Code; or the organization is a public or private educational institution (such as an elementary or secondary school), a school board, a local or county governmental agency or a college or university. Private educational institutions must be non-profit and meet the tax-exempt requirements described above.
Restrictions: The Council does not fund: projects not available to the general public; activities and performances planned solely for fund raising purposes; food, beverages or other refreshments; interest on loans, fines, penalties, and/or litigation costs; expenses incurred prior to October 1 or after September 30 of the current grant year; investments of any kind; projects which have sectarian or religious purposes (however, such institutions may apply on behalf of the community for arts activities or programming where artistic expression is a primary focus); or indirect costs.
Geographic Focus: Alabama

Contact: Albert B. Head, Executive Director; (334) 242-4076, ext. 245; fax (334) 240-3269; al.head@arts.alabama.gov or staff@arts.alabama.gov
Internet: http://arts.state.al.us/grants/index-grants.html
Sponsor: Alabama State Council on the Arts
201 Monroe Street, Suite 110
Montgomery, AL 36130-1800

ALA Bogle Pratt International Library Travel Fund Grant 251
The Bogle Pratt International Library Travel Fund Grant is sponsored by the Bogle Memorial Fund and the Pratt Institute School of Information and Library Science. The award is in recognition of Sarah Comly Norris Bogle, a prominent U.S. librarian who made notable contributions to international library service. An award of $1,000 is given to an ALA personal member to attend their first international conference. The application is available at the ALA website.
Requirements: Applicants must be personal members of the ALA.
Geographic Focus: All States
Date(s) Application is Due: Jan 1
Amount of Grant: 1,000 USD
Contact: Delin R. Guerra; (312) 280-3201; fax (312) 280-4392; dguerra@ala.org
Internet: http://www.ala.org/awardsgrants/awards/261/apply
Sponsor: American Library Association
50 East Huron Street
Chicago, IL 60611-2795

ALA BWI Collection Development Grant 252
The BWI Collection Development Grant awards YALSA members who represent a public library and work directly with young adults ages 12 to 18. Up to two awards of $1,000 each are given every year. Applications are judged on the basis of the degree of need for additional materials for young adults; the current collection's use and the specificity of examples used; soundness of the rationale for the selection of materials; the quality of the benefits the grant will bring to young adults; and the degree to which the applicant's philosophy reflects the concepts identified in Directions for Library Service to Young Adults. Each candidate must submit a one-page report to the YALSA Office within six months of receiving the grant, detailing how the award has impacted the grant recipient's collection of materials for young adults.
Requirements: All applicants must be current personal members of ALA/YALSA at the time the application is submitted. Applicants should send their membership application with the grant application if they are in the process of joining YALSA.
Geographic Focus: All States
Date(s) Application is Due: Dec 1
Amount of Grant: Up to 1,000 USD
Contact: Letitia Smith, YALSA; (312) 280-4390 or (800) 545-2433; lsmith@ala.org
Nichole Gilbert, Application Contact; (800) 545-2433, ext 4387; ngilbert@ala.org
Internet: http://www.ala.org/awardsgrants/awards/168/apply
Sponsor: American Library Association
50 East Huron Street
Chicago, IL 60611-2795

ALA Carnegie-Whitney Awards 253
The Carnegie-Whitney Awards were established to provide grants for the preparation and publication of popular or scholarly reading lists, indexes and other guides to library resources that will be useful to users of all types of libraries. The grants are intended to cover preparation costs appropriate to the development of a useful product, including the cost of research, compilation, and production exclusive of printing. Grants may be used for print and electronic projects of varying lengths. The amount (up to $5,000) and number of grants vary from year to year. Additional information, including a list of previously funded projects, is available at the website.
Requirements: Grants are awarded to individuals; local, regional or state libraries, associations or organizations, including units, affiliates and committees of the American Library Association, or programs of information and library studies/science. International applicants are welcome.
Restrictions: The grant does not cover the purchase of equipment for production/manufacturing of the final product. Funding may be used to provide support staff with a stipend, but not the applicant. Completed works, works under contract for publication, or projects associated with the completion of academic work are not eligible for funding.
Geographic Focus: All States, All Countries
Date(s) Application is Due: Nov 7
Amount of Grant: Up to 5,000 USD
Contact: Mary Jo Bolduc; (800) 545-2433, ext. 5416; mbolduc@ala.org
Internet: http://www.ala.org/awardsgrants/awards/42/apply
Sponsor: American Library Association
50 East Huron Street
Chicago, IL 60611-2795

ALA Carnegie Corporation/New York Times I Love My Librarian Award 254
The award encourages library users to recognize the accomplishments of librarians for their efforts to improve the lives of people in their community. Up to ten winners are selected to receive a $5,000 cash award, a plaque, and a $500 travel stipend to attend the awards reception in New York City. A plaque is also given to each award winner's library. Winners are selected based on the following criteria: the extent to which the nominee has helped make the experience of a library a positive one for the nominator(s); how the nominee makes the library or community a better place; how the nominee has improved the lives of his/her users (public librarians) or had an impact on the learning process (school and college, community college, university librarians); and how the nominee makes the library a better place (public librarians) or demonstrates leadership in the school or campus community (school and college, community college, university librarians). Nominations are accepted through the online process at the website.
Requirements: Each nominee must be a librarian with a master's degree from a program accredited by the ALA in library and information studies or a master's degree with a specialty in school library media from an educational unit accredited by the National Council for the Accreditation of Teacher Education. Nominees must be currently working in the U.S. in a public library, a library at an accredited two- or four-year college or university, or at an accredited K-12 school.
Geographic Focus: All States
Date(s) Application is Due: Sep 20
Amount of Grant: 5,500 USD
Contact: Megan Humphrey; (312) 280-4020; fax (312) 440-8520; mhumphrey@ala.org
Internet: http://www.ala.org/awardsgrants/awards/134/apply
Sponsor: American Library Association
50 East Huron Street
Chicago, IL 60611-2795

ALA Carroll Preston Baber Research Grant 255
The Carroll Preston Baber Research Grant is given annually to one or more librarians or library educators who will conduct innovative research that could lead to an improvement in services to any specified group(s) of people. The project should aim to answer a question that is of vital importance to the library community and the researchers should plan to provide documentation of the results of their work. Up to $3,000 is available. Half of the amount will be paid within one month of the Annual Conference. The remaining half will be provided approximately six months later after a satisfactory progress report. The application cover sheet and information about additional materials required are available at the website.
Requirements: Any ALA member may apply. The jury would welcome projects that involve both a practicing librarian and a researcher. Applications must be clearly defined, with the potential to address a currently important issue in library service that is national in scope. Applications must also demonstrate the ability to undertake and successfully complete the project, with a reasonable dissemination plan.
Restrictions: Institutional overhead is not an acceptable budget item within the parameters of the Baber Grant, nor should overhead be listed as institutional support. If travel for dissemination of results is in the budget, it must be less than 10% of the total.
Geographic Focus: All States
Date(s) Application is Due: Jan 10
Amount of Grant: Up to 3,000 USD
Contact: Rudolph Rose, (800) 545-2433; fax (312) 280-4392; nrose@ala.org
Internet: http://www.ala.org/awardsgrants/awards/55/apply
Sponsor: American Library Association
50 East Huron Street
Chicago, IL 60611-2795

ALA Charlie Robinson Award 256
The Charlie Robinson Award honors a public library director who has been a risk taker, innovator and/or a change agent in a public library over a period of seven years. The recipient should have been active in national and other professional associations, and be known for developing and implementing programs responsive to community needs. The annual award consists of $1,000 and a gift to a librarian at the ALA Annual Conference. The nomination form is available at the website.
Restrictions: Members of the current Charlie Robinson Award Jury are not eligible.
Geographic Focus: All States
Date(s) Application is Due: Dec 1
Amount of Grant: 1,000 USD
Contact: Julianna Kloeppel; (312) 280-5026; fax (312) 280-5029; jkloeppel@ala.org
Internet: http://www.ala.org/awardsgrants/awards/83/apply
Sponsor: American Library Association
50 East Huron Street
Chicago, IL 60611-2795

ALA Citizens-Save-Libraries Grants 257
United for Libraries has secured $75,000 from the Neal-Schuman Foundation to support library advocacy at the local level for libraries with troubled budgets. The Citizens-Save-Libraries grants will send expert advocates to 20 locations over the course of two years to help friends of the library groups, library directors and trustees develop individual blueprints for advocacy campaigns to restore, increase or save threatened library budgets.
Requirements: Eligibility includes: a demonstrated need for help with a library advocacy campaign; a minimum of five volunteers committed to working on a leadership team for a campaign (each member understands that this commitment may require at least weekly meetings for up to 90 days); and a leadership team available for two days of on-site, in-person training.
Geographic Focus: All States
Date(s) Application is Due: Mar 15
Contact: Staff Liaison; (800) 545-2433, ext. 2161; united@ala.org
Internet: http://www.ala.org/awardsgrants/awards/32480/apply
Sponsor: American Library Association
50 East Huron Street
Chicago, IL 60611-2795

ALA Clarence Day Award 258
The Clarence Day Award is presented to a librarian for outstanding work in encouraging the love of reading and books. The committee recognizes distinctive productions such as a book, essay, or series of lectures or programs, which promoted a love of books and reading,

and caused attention within three years prior to the presentation. The Award includes $1,000 and a contemporary print.
Geographic Focus: All States
Amount of Grant: 1,000 USD
Contact: Cheryl Madden; (312) 280-3247; fax (312) 944-3897; cmalden@ala.org
Internet: http://www.ala.org/awardsgrants/awards/385/apply
Sponsor: American Library Association
50 East Huron Street
Chicago, IL 60611-2795

ALA Coretta Scott King-Virginia Hamilton Award for Lifetime Achievement 259
This award recognizes an African American author, illustrator, or author/illustrator for a body of his or her published books for children and/or young adults who has made a significant and lasting literary contribution. The Award pays tribute to the late Virginia Hamilton and the quality and magnitude of her exemplary contributions through her literature and advocacy for children and youth, especially in her focus on African American life, history and consciousness. A plaque and $1,500 cash award is given at the ALA Annual Conference. The recipient must attend the CSK Book Awards Breakfast and deliver an acceptance speech. In even-numbered years, the award is given to authors, illustrators, or author/illustrators. In odd-numbered years, practitioners are recognized (librarians, educators or youth advocates). Each application is available at the website.
Geographic Focus: All States
Date(s) Application is Due: Dec 1
Amount of Grant: 1,500 USD
Contact: John Amundsen; (312) 280-2140; fax (312) 280-3256; jamundsen@ala.org
Internet: http://www.ala.org/awardsgrants/awards/339/apply
Sponsor: American Library Association
50 East Huron Street
Chicago, IL 60611-2795

ALA Coretta Scott King Book Awards 260
Designed to commemorate the life and works of Dr. Martin Luther King, Jr. and to honor Coretta Scott King for her courage and determination to continue the work for peace, the Coretta Scott King Book Awards annually recognize outstanding books for young adults and children by African American authors and illustrators that reflect the African American experience. Further, the Award encourages the artistic expression of the black experience via literature and the graphic arts in biographical, social, and historical treatments by African American authors and illustrators. The winner receives $1,000 and a plaque. Winners are announced during the ALA Youth Media Awards Announcement at the ALA Midwinter Meeting in January. Previous book winners are posted on the website. Candidates may apply through the online process at the website.
Requirements: The author or illustrator must live in the U.S. or maintain dual residency/citizenship. The book must have been published in the January to December range of the year preceding the award. The book must also meet the following criteria: portray some aspect of the black experience, past, present, or future; written/illustrated by an African American; an original work; meet established standards of quality writing for youth (clear plot, well drawn characters, suitable for young adults); and written for preschool to grade 4, grades 5 through 8, or grades 9 through 12. Particular attention will be paid to titles which seek to motivate readers to develop their own attitudes and behaviors as well as comprehend their personal duty and responsibility as citizens in a pluralistic society. Awardees are expected to attend the Coretta Scott King Book Awards Breakfast during ALA Annual Conference to deliver an acceptance speech. Publishers of winning titles: produce study guide, breakfast program, and promotional materials/handouts for the breakfast; provide ten copies of each winning title to the OLOS office and ten copies to ALA Public Information Office; provide author/illustrator winner headshot; purchase tables for the breakfast; and provide copies of winning titles for fifty children in attendance at breakfast.
Geographic Focus: All States
Date(s) Application is Due: Dec 1
Amount of Grant: 1,000 USD
Contact: John Amundsen; (312) 280-2140; fax (312) 280-3256; jamundsen@ala.org
Internet: http://www.ala.org/awardsgrants/awards/24/apply
Sponsor: American Library Association
50 East Huron Street
Chicago, IL 60611-2795

ALA Coretta Scott King Book Donation Grant 261
The CSK Book Donations Grant was created to help build collections and bring books into the lives of children in latchkey, preschool programs, faith-based reading projects, homeless shelters, charter schools and underfunded libraries. Approximately 300 books by African American authors and illustrators are given out every year. Applications are judged based on the following criteria: the degree of need in the community; the demonstrated need of the institution applying for the materials; the extent to which the materials will improve service to children and youth in the community; the extent to which the materials will be used to promote positive self-image of African American children and youth and/or broaden the worldview of children and youth; the clarity and effectiveness of the statement of need; and the clarity and effectiveness of the plan to make the materials available in their community, including the demonstrated ability of the applicant agency to implement their proposal. The application is available at the website.
Requirements: Any agency that serves children or youth may apply. This includes, but is not limited to schools, libraries, social service agencies, prisons, detention centers, churches or other religious organizations, and institutions of higher education. Five copies of the application must be submitted.

Restrictions: Shipping and handling are the responsibility of the institution selected to receive the materials. Materials must be claimed within one month of notification of the donation. Recipients agree to accept all materials offered. Institutions may receive materials no more than once every five years.
Geographic Focus: All States
Date(s) Application is Due: Feb 28
Contact: Victoria Schwoebel, (800) 545-2433, ext. 4295; vschwoebel@ala.org
Internet: http://www.ala.org/awardsgrants/awards/82/apply
Sponsor: American Library Association
50 East Huron Street
Chicago, IL 60611-2795

ALA Dartmouth Medal 262
The Dartmouth Medal honors the creation of a reference work of outstanding quality and significance including writing, compiling, editing, or publishing books or electronic information. Previous winners include an international encyclopedia of political science, and a dictionary of slang. The winner receives a medal, and certificates are given to the honorable mentions. Nomination forms are available at the website.
Requirements: Works that have been published or made available for the first time during the previous year are eligible.
Geographic Focus: All States
Date(s) Application is Due: Dec 15
Contact: Andrea Hill, Staff Liaison; (312) 280-4397; fax (312) 280-5273; ahill@ala.org
Internet: http://www.ala.org/awardsgrants/awards/155/apply
Sponsor: American Library Association
50 East Huron Street
Chicago, IL 60611-2795

Aladdin Industries Foundation Grants 263
The foundation awards grants, primarily in Tennessee, in its areas of interest, including arts and culture, youth services, health and human services, education, business, drug abuse, and the elderly. Types of support include general operating support, seed grants, and employee-related scholarships. Proposals are reviewed quarterly.
Requirements: Most grants are awarded in Tennessee. Proposals are reviewed quarterly.
Geographic Focus: Tennessee
Contact: L.B. Jenkins, Secretary & Treasurer; (615) 748-3360
Sponsor: Aladdin Industries Foundation
703 Murfreesboro Road
Nashville, TN 37210-4521

ALA DEMCO New Leaders Travel Grants 264
The DEMCO New Leaders Travel Grants are designed to enhance the professional development and improve the expertise of public librarians new to the field. These grants were established to enable Public Library Association (PLA) members who are new to the profession, and who have not had the opportunity to attend a major PLA continuing education event in the last five years, to attend such an event. Eligible events are the PLA Spring Symposium workshops, PLA National Conferences, and other PLA events, such as preconferences, held in conjunction with ALA's Annual Conferences. The application is available through the ALA website.
Requirements: Applicants must be a current members of the Public Library Association and practicing librarians (with an MLS from an accredited institution) for five years or less. Grant recipients must use their award within 14 months of the announcement of the awards. Recipients must also submit a detailed report regarding the event they attended within a month of their return.
Restrictions: Applicants or their supervisors cannot be a current officer or member of the PLA Board of Directors or the New Leaders Travel Grant jury. Applicants also cannot have attended a major PLA continuing education program in the last five years due to limited or non-existent funding for professional travel at their institution.
Geographic Focus: All States
Date(s) Application is Due: Dec 1
Amount of Grant: Up to 1,500 USD
Contact: Julianna Kloeppel; (312) 280-5026; fax (312) 280-5029; jkloeppel@ala.org
Internet: http://www.ala.org/awardsgrants/awards/48/apply
Sponsor: American Library Association
50 East Huron Street
Chicago, IL 60611-2795

ALA Distinguished Education and Behavioral Sciences Librarian Award 265
This award honors a distinguished academic librarian who has made an outstanding contribution as an education and/or behavioral sciences librarian through accomplishments and service to the profession. The award, which includes $2,000 and a citation sponsored by Wiley and Sons, Inc., is given each year. The nomination form is available at the website.
Requirements: Those nominated must be ACRL EBSS members. Nominees should have demonstrated achievements in one or more of the following areas: service to the organized profession through ACRL/EBSS and related organizations; significant academic library service in the areas of education and/or behavioral sciences; significant research and publication in areas of academic library services in education and/or behavioral sciences; and planning and implementation of academic library programs in education and/or the behavioral sciences disciplines of such quality that they could serve as a model for others.
Geographic Focus: All States
Date(s) Application is Due: Dec 2
Amount of Grant: 2,000 USD
Contact: Casey Kinson; (800) 545-2433, ext. 2511; ckinson@ala.org

38 | Grant Programs

Internet: http://www.ala.org/awardsgrants/awards/196/apply
Sponsor: American Library Association
50 East Huron Street
Chicago, IL 60611-2795

ALA Distinguished School Administrator Award   266

The Distinguished School Administrators Award honors a school administrator who has made worthy contributions to the operations of an exemplary school library, and advanced the role of the school library in the educational program. The purpose of the award is to: honor those administrators outside the library profession have made worthy contributions to the operations of effective school library services; recognize the responsible and influential role of those administrators outside the school library department in developing successful school library programs; and stimulate planning, implementing and support of the library services. The nomination form is available at the website.

Requirements: State, county or district school superintendents and building principals, currently in administrative office, directly responsible for a school or group of schools at any level, who is not working in a library services department and who is not a regular ALA/AASL member are eligible for nomination. District administrators responsible for broad instructional leadership such as assistant superintendents, directors of curriculum and instruction and directors of elementary and/or secondary education are also eligible provided they are not working in a library services department or a regular ALA/AASL member.
Restrictions: Nominations must be made by personal members of the American Association of School Librarians (AASL).
Geographic Focus: All States
Date(s) Application is Due: Feb 1
Amount of Grant: 2,000 USD
Contact: Meg Featheringham, Staff Liaison; (800) 545-2433, ext. 1396 or (312) 280-4382; fax (312) 280-5276; mfeatheringham@ala.org
Internet: http://www.ala.org/awardsgrants/awards/170/apply
Sponsor: American Library Association
50 East Huron Street
Chicago, IL 60611-2795

ALA Diversity and Outreach Fair   267

Each year, the ALA Office for Literacy and Outreach Services (OLOS) invites library professionals from all kinds of institutions to submit proposals to participate in the ALA Diversity and Outreach Fair, which is held during ALA's Annual Conferences. Sponsored by DEMCO, the ALA Diversity and Outreach Fair is an opportunity for libraries and member groups to share their successful diversity and outreach initiatives with ALA Annual Conference attendees, celebrate diversity in America's libraries and exhibit diversity in action ideas. The Fair highlights library services to underserved or underrepresented communities, including people with disabilities; poor and homeless populations; people of color; English-language learners; gay, lesbian, bisexual and transgender people; new Americans, new and non-readers; older adults; people living in rural areas; incarcerated people and ex-offenders; and mobile library services and bookmobiles. Each year's fair focuses on a special theme based on service to one of these communities. Selected presenters will develop and facilitate a poster session to be held during the ALA Annual Conference in the exhibits hall. In addition, the participants are encouraged to submit, in digital format, information and resources from their program. Prizes are awarded for best displays. Winners receive a $200, $100, or $50 DEMCO gift card, respectively. The application is available at the website, in addition to samples of previous winners, include abstracts.
Geographic Focus: All States
Amount of Grant: 50 - 200 USD
Contact: Victoria Schwoebel, Staff Liaison; (800) 545-2433, ext. 4295; fax (312) 440-9374; vschwoebel@ala.org or olos@ala.org
Internet: http://www.ala.org/offices/olos/divfair/diversityfair
Sponsor: American Library Association
50 East Huron Street
Chicago, IL 60611-2795

ALA Diversity Research Grant   268

The ALA Office for Diversity began sponsorship of the Diversity Research Grant to address critical gaps in the knowledge of diversity issues within library and information science. The grant consists of a one-time $2,000 award for original research and a $500 travel grant to attend and present at the ALA Annual Conference. Proposals are evaluated on the following criteria: contributions; professional impact; sustainability; adaptability; design; management plan; budget; personnel; evaluation; and cooperation and dissemination. The annual deadline has been identified as April 30.
Requirements: Persons submitting a proposal must be current member of the American Library Association. Proposals are only accepted after the announcement of the three annual topics. Proposals must demonstrate relevance to that year's designated research topics to be considered.
Geographic Focus: All States
Date(s) Application is Due: Apr 30
Amount of Grant: 2,500 USD
Contact: Grant Coordinator; (800) 545-2433; fax (312) 440-9374; diversity@ala.org
Internet: http://www.ala.org/awardsgrants/awards/374/apply
Sponsor: American Library Association
50 East Huron Street
Chicago, IL 60611-2795

ALA Donald G. Davis Article Award   269

The Donald G. Davis Article Award is presented by the Library History Round Table of the American Library Association every second year to recognize the best article written in English in the field of United States and Canadian library history including the history of libraries, librarianship, and book culture. Entries are judged on quality of scholarship, clarity of style, depth of research, and ability to place research findings in a broad social, cultural, and political context. One award will be given every second year unless the jury does not find a suitable candidate for that biennial period. Any member of the Library History Round Table may nominate one or more articles by sending a recommendation to the Chair of the Davis Award Committee. Also, the editor of the LHRT Newsletter Library History Bibliography will submit a list of candidates. The winner will be announced in a press release on or about June 1st of the award year. Certificates honoring the author(s) and journal will be presented at a Library History Round Table awards ceremony during the American Library Association Annual Conference in the year of the award.
Requirements: Entries for each biennial award must have been published between January 1 and December 31 of the two years preceding the award year.
Restrictions: Papers that have won the Justin Winsor or Jesse Shera Awards are not eligible for consideration.
Geographic Focus: All States
Date(s) Application is Due: Jan 15
Contact: Norman Rose; (312) 280-4283; fax (312) 280-4392; nrose@ala.org
Internet: http://www.ala.org/awardsgrants/awards/138/apply
Sponsor: American Library Association
50 East Huron Street
Chicago, IL 60611-2795

ALA e-Learning Scholarships   270

The e-Learning Scholarships provide opportunities for librarians, library school students, or support staff to update their skills and knowledge by participating in an ACRL e-Learning webcast. Twenty scholarships are awarded each year. The ACRL Professional Development Coordinating Committee reviews and selects scholarship applicants based on their application and response to the written statement. The committee will strive to achieve both diversity and balance among scholarship recipients, and preference will be given to individuals who have not previously been awarded an ACRL scholarship. Scholarships can be redeemed for webcasts offered through August of the following year. The application is available at the website.
Requirements: Scholarship applicants must: be ACRL members; complete the online application form; and submit a brief written statement that describes how participation in an ACRL e-learning webcast meets their professional needs and goals.
Restrictions: Individuals may only receive one ACRL scholarship per professional development event.
Geographic Focus: All States
Date(s) Application is Due: Dec 7
Contact: Megan Griffin; (312) 280-2514; fax (312) 280-2520; mgriffin@ala.org
Margot Conahan, Professional Development Manager; (312) 280-2522; fax (312) 280-2520; mconahan@ala.org
Internet: http://www.ala.org/awardsgrants/awards/326/apply
Sponsor: American Library Association
50 East Huron Street
Chicago, IL 60611-2795

ALA EBSCO Community College Learning Resources Leadership Awards   271

This annual award recognizes significant achievement in the areas of programs and leadership. Each award winner receives $500 and a citation. Nominees for the program award should demonstrate significant achievement in development of a unique and innovative learning resources/library program. Nominees for the leadership award should demonstrate significant achievement in advocacy of learning resources/library programs or services, or leadership in professional organizations that are associated with the mission of community, junior, or technical colleges. The nomination form is available at the website.
Requirements: Individuals or groups from two-year institutions, as well as the two-year institutions themselves, are eligible to receive awards. Nominations will be kept on file for three consecutive years. Nominations should be sent to the nomination form coordinator, and should include the nomination form, a letter describing the achievements, and any supporting attachments.
Geographic Focus: All States
Date(s) Application is Due: Dec 2
Amount of Grant: 500 USD
Contact: Casey Kinson; (800) 545-2433, ext. 2511; fax (312) 440-9374; ckinson@ala.org
Amy Gonzalez Ferguson, Nomination Form Coordinator; (972) 238-6112 or (972) 238-6081; AFerguson@dcccd.edu or AmyGFerguson@gmail.com
Internet: http://www.ala.org/awardsgrants/awards/198/apply
Sponsor: American Library Association
50 East Huron Street
Chicago, IL 60611-2795

ALA EBSCO Community College Library Program Achievement Award   272

The Community College Library Program Achievement Award recognizes significant achievement in the area of programs. A citation and $500 is given annually. Nominees for the program award should demonstrate significant achievement in development of a unique and innovative learning resources/library program. The nomination form is available at the website.
Requirements: Individuals or groups from two-year institutions, as well as the two-year institutions themselves, are eligible to receive awards. Nominations are kept on file for three consecutive years.

Geographic Focus: All States
Date(s) Application is Due: Dec 2
Amount of Grant: 500 USD
Contact: Casey Kinson; (800) 545-2433, ext. 2511; fax (312) 440-9374; ckinson@ala.org
Internet: http://www.ala.org/awardsgrants/awards/285/apply
Sponsor: American Library Association
50 East Huron Street
Chicago, IL 60611-2795

ALA EBSCO Excellence in Small and/or Rural Public Library Service Award   273
This award provides recognition and a honorarium to a public library serving a population of 10,000 or less that demonstrates excellence of service to its community as exemplified by an overall service program or a special program of significant accomplishment. A public library is honored for uniqueness of service of program, impact of program or service on community, and/or how the service or program will affect the future of the library and its community. A plaque and a $1,000 cash award is given from EBSCO Information Services. Nominations are submitted for this award. The online application is available at the website. PLA will forward the nominations to the current chair of the EBSCO Excellence in Small and/or Rural Public Library Service Award Committee. The jury shall review the candidates and select a winner at the ALA Midwinter Meeting. Announcement shall be made at that time. The award shall be presented at the PLA President's Program during the ALA Annual Conference. A list of previous award winners is posted on the website.
Geographic Focus: All States
Date(s) Application is Due: Dec 1
Amount of Grant: 1,000 USD
Contact: Julianna Kloeppel, (312) 280-5026; jkloeppel@ala.org or pla@ala.org
Internet: http://www.ala.org/pla/awards/ebscoexcellencesmallruralaward
Sponsor: American Library Association
50 East Huron Street
Chicago, IL 60611-2795

ALA EBSCO Midwinter Meeting Sponsorship   274
This award allows librarians to attend the ALA's Midwinter Meeting. Recipients are reimbursed for $1,500 of expenses related to attending the meeting. The application with instructions is available at the website.
Requirements: Applicants must be ALA members currently working as librarians or paraprofessionals in a library. All applicants submit a brief curriculum vitae and an essay of no more than 250 words that addresses the following statement: how would you lead the discussion in your library to bring about meaningful change to an existing process, service, or procedure?
Geographic Focus: All States
Date(s) Application is Due: Nov 1
Amount of Grant: 1,500 USD
Contact: Cheryl Malden; (312) 280-3247; cmalden@ala.org or awards@ala.org
Internet: http://www.ala.org/awardsgrants/awards/351/apply
Sponsor: American Library Association
50 East Huron Street
Chicago, IL 60611-2795

ALA Esther J. Piercy Award   275
The Esther J. Piercy Award was established by the Resources and Technical Services Division of the American Library Association in memory of Esther J. Piercy, editor of Journal of Cataloging and Classification and of Library Resources and Technical Services. The annual award winner receives $1,500 and a citation. Selection criteria is based on the person's accomplishments, as related to technical services and resources in activities such as: leadership in local, state, regional, or national professional associations; contributions to the development, application, or utilization of new or improved methods, techniques, and routines; significant contribution to professional literature; and conduct of studies or research in the technical services.
Requirements: The nominee must have less than ten years of professional experience and be an ALCTS member. Nominations should include the following: the nominee's name; date of nominee's first professional position and a formal statement of nomination, with a brief rationale for the nomination; a resume or narrative career outline; and letters of endorsement.
Geographic Focus: All States
Date(s) Application is Due: Dec 1
Amount of Grant: 1,500 USD
Contact: Charles Wilt, Staff Liaison, (312) 280-5030; fax (312) 280-5033; cwilt@ala.org
Internet: http://www.ala.org/awardsgrants/awards/189/apply
Sponsor: American Library Association
50 East Huron Street
Chicago, IL 60611-2795

ALA Excellence in Academic Libraries Award   276
The Excellence in Academic Libraries Award recognizes academic librarians and staff who work together to develop academic libraries that are outstanding in furthering the educational missions of their insitutions. The program will support three annual awards of $3,000 each by type of academic library (community, college, and university). Awards are judged on the following criteria: how academic librarians and staff work together to develop an academic library that is outstanding in furthering the educational mission of its parent institution; creativity and innovation in meeting the needs of their academic community; leadership in developing and implementing exemplary programs that other libraries can emulate; and substantial and productive relationships with classroom faculty and students. Awards will be made by an ACRL representative at a presentation at each institution receiving the award. Further recognition of award recipients will be made at the ACRL President's Program at the annual ALA conference. Funding will cover the outright awards and provide $3,000 for travel to presentation ceremonies. Applications are kept in the award pool for three years. Applications may be updated each year, as long as they are received by the award deadline. Application forms are available at the website.
Requirements: Academic and research libraries may apply. The award winners will agree to take responsibility for organizing and funding a recognition ceremony on campus to receive the award.
Geographic Focus: All States
Date(s) Application is Due: Dec 2
Amount of Grant: 6,000 USD
Contact: Megan Griffin; (800) 545-2433, ext. 2514; fax (312) 440-9374; mgriffin@ala.org
Internet: http://www.ala.org/awardsgrants/awards/234/apply
Sponsor: American Library Association
50 East Huron Street
Chicago, IL 60611-2795

ALA Excellence in Library Programming Award   277
The ALA Excellence in Library Programming Award recognizes a library that demonstrates excellence in library programming by creating a cultural/thematic program type or program series, presented during the preceding year (September 1 - August 31), that engages the community in planning, sponsorship and/or active participation, addresses an identified community need, and has a measurable impact. The Award consists of $5,000 and a citation of achievement. It is given out on an annual basis.
Requirements: n recognition that programming is an essential part of service delivery in all types of libraries, school, public, academic, and special libraries are all eligible. The nominated program/series must have been for a public audience.
Geographic Focus: All States
Date(s) Application is Due: Dec 1
Amount of Grant: 5,000 USD
Contact: Cheryl Malden; (312) 280-3247; fax (312) 944-3897; cmalden@ala.org
Internet: http://www.ala.org/awardsgrants/awards/31960/apply
Sponsor: American Library Association
50 East Huron Street
Chicago, IL 60611-2795

ALA Exceptional Service Award   278
The Exceptional Service Award recognized exceptional service to patients, the homebound, to medical, nursing, and other professional staff in hospitals and to inmates, as well as professional leadership, effective interpretation of programs, pioneering activity, and significant research of experimental projects. The nomination form is available at the website.
Requirements: Along with the nomination application, nominators should describe how the nominee fulfills the criteria for the award. They should also include the nominee's resume and/or summary of their activities and contributions, and two letters of endorsement.
Geographic Focus: All States
Date(s) Application is Due: Feb 1
Contact: Liz Markel; (800) 545-2433, ext. 4398; fax (312) 440-9374; lmarkel@ala.org
Internet: http://www.ala.org/awardsgrants/awards/152/apply
Sponsor: American Library Association
50 East Huron Street
Chicago, IL 60611-2795

ALA First Step Award/Wiley Professional Development Grant   279
This grant provides librarians new to the continuing resources field with the opportunity to broaden their perspective, and encourage professional development in ALA Conference, in addition to participation in Continuing Resources Section activities. Selection criteria is based on: commitment to professional development in the continuing resources field as evidenced by participation in continuing education activities, workshops, previous participation in professional activities; the candidate's written justification for the grant in terms of commitment to and interest in serials related work; personal and professional development, and financial need. The cash award of $1,500 is applicable toward round trip transportation, lodging, and registration fees. The recipient will be notified just prior to the ALA Midwinter Meeting. There is no application for this award. Interested candidates should contact ALA.
Requirements: Eligibility is open to ALCTS members with five years or less of professional experience in continuing resources and those who have not attended a previous ALA Annual Conference. Eligible applicants may apply more than once.
Geographic Focus: All States
Date(s) Application is Due: Dec 1
Amount of Grant: 1,500 USD
Contact: Charles Wilt; (312) 280-5030; fax (312) 280-5033; cwilt@ala.org
Internet: http://www.ala.org/awardsgrants/awards/47/apply
Sponsor: American Library Association
50 East Huron Street
Chicago, IL 60611-2795

ALA Gale Cengage History Research and Innovation Award   280
The Gale Cengage History Research and Innovation Award consists of up to $2,500 and a citation recognizing an MLS degreed librarian to further research relating to history and history librarianship. The project will be evaluated with the following criteria: value of the project to the history librarianship community; quality, depth, comprehensiveness of the literature reviewed; feasibility of the project, with a combination of the appropriateness of the research method/research design and the reasonableness of the timeline; the applicant's

qualifications; and the raasonableness of proposed expenditures. The nomination form is available at the website.
Requirements: Librarians with an ALA accredited degree are encouraged to apply. Historical research must consist of an emphasis in an area reflected by the History Section's subject-oriented committees: American history; genealogy, local history, instruction and research services, and historical materials. Candidates must be members of the RUSA History section by the time the award is presented.
Geographic Focus: All States
Date(s) Application is Due: Dec 15
Amount of Grant: Up to 2,500 USD
Contact: Janice Schultz, Coordinator, Gale Cengage History Research and Innovation Award; (816) 252-7228; jschultz@mymcpl.org
Internet: http://www.ala.org/awardsgrants/awards/31876/apply
Sponsor: American Association of School Librarians
50 East Huron Street
Chicago, IL 60611-2795

ALA Gale Cengage Learning Award for Excellence in Reference and Adult Library Services 281
The Learning Award for Excellence in Reference and Adult Library Services is presented to a library or library system for developing an imaginative and unique resource to meet patrons' reference needs. The award includes a citation and $3,000. The nomination form is available at the website. Along with the nomination form should include a letter describing the resource in detail, the target audience for the resource, criteria used for selection material for inclusion, and an explanation of what makes the resource imaginative or unique.
Requirements: The resource can be a bibliography, a guide to the literature of a specific subject, a directory, a database, or any other project that has helped the library meet adult or children's reference needs. Tools, guides or databases that have been developed for reader's advisory or adult service questions and needs are also eligible for the award.
Geographic Focus: All States
Date(s) Application is Due: Jan 15
Contact: Anita Hill, Staff Liaison; (312) 280-4397; fax (312) 440-9374; ahill@ala.org
Internet: http://www.ala.org/awardsgrants/awards/187/apply
Sponsor: American Library Association
50 East Huron Street
Chicago, IL 60611-2795

ALA Great Books Giveaway Competition 282
Each year the Young Adult Library Services Association (YALSA) receives about 1,200 newly published books, videos, CDs, and other materials targeted toward young adults. Publishers and producers submit copies for selection committees to review and nominate. YALSA believes these materials should be passed along to schools, public libraries, or institutions in need. Selection criteria is based on: the degree of need in the community, school, public library, or institution where the library is located; how service would be improved for young adults in the community; the clarity and effectiveness of the statement of need; the age of the nonfiction collection in the application; and the currency and completeness of the institution's board approved collection development policy, including the materials selection policy, with procedures for handling challenges. Detailed application instructions are available at the website.
Requirements: Applicants must be personal members of YALSA and ALA.
Restrictions: The recipient of the materials is responsible for shipping costs. ALA organizational members and previous winners are not eligible.
Geographic Focus: All States
Date(s) Application is Due: Dec 1
Contact: Letitia Smith; (312) 280-4390; fax (312) 440-9374; lsmith@ala.org
Internet: http://www.ala.org/awardsgrants/awards/67/apply
Sponsor: American Library Association
50 East Huron Street
Chicago, IL 60611-2795

ALA H.W. Wilson Library Staff Development Grant 283
This annual H.W. Wilson Library Staff Development Grant, consisting of $3,500 and a 24k gold-framed citation, is awarded to a library organization to aid in a current or proposed program designed to further staff development objectives. Applicants must show a need for staff development and propose a plan to implement the project. The grant is based on the merit of the application and considers several criteria, including a clearly defined documentation of the organizational goals and objectives and a well-defined program that meets the needs of the organization. This program is sponsored by the H.W. Wilson Company, and administered by the ALA. Applications are available at the ALA website.
Requirements: Staff development is defined as a program of learning activities that is developed by the library organization and develops the on-the-job staff capability and improves the abilities of personnel to contribute to the overall effectiveness of the library organization. A library organization is defined as an individual library; library system; group of cooperating libraries; state governmental agency; or local, state, or regional association.
Geographic Focus: All States
Date(s) Application is Due: Dec 1
Amount of Grant: 3,500 USD
Contact: Cheryl M. Malden, Program Officer; (800) 545-2433, ext. 3247 or (312) 280-3247; fax (312) 944-3897; cmalden@ala.org or awards@ala.org
Internet: http://www.ala.org/awardsgrants/hw-wilson-library-staff-development-grant
Sponsor: American Library Association
50 East Huron Street
Chicago, IL 60611-2795

ALA Harrassowitz Award for Leadership in Library Acquisitions Award 284
The Harrassowitz Award is given to recognize the contributions and outstanding leadership of an individual to the field of acquisitions librarianship. This recognition is made for individual achievement of a high order in this area. The award may be divided among two or more individuals who have participated jointly in the achievement being granted. An annual award of $1,500 and a citation is given.
Requirements: Nominees must have demonstrated leadership and achievement related to acquisitions librarianship, which has contributed significantly to improvements in the field as evidenced by one or more of the following: professional associations; literature including research; education of acquisitions professionals; and advancement of the profession. Nominations should include relevant biographical information; statement of work and/or professional experience, professional activities, honors, and other relevant factors; and two letters of recommendation.
Restrictions: Employees of the Harrassowitz Company are not eligible to receive the award.
Geographic Focus: All States
Date(s) Application is Due: Dec 1
Amount of Grant: 1,500 USD
Contact: Charles Wilt, Staff Liaison; (312) 280-5030; fax (312) 280-5033; cwilt@ala.org
Internet: http://www.ala.org/awardsgrants/awards/103/apply
Sponsor: American Library Association
50 East Huron Street
Chicago, IL 60611-2795

ALA Highsmith Library Innovation Award 285
The Highsmith Library Innovation Award recognizes a public library's innovative and creative service program to the community. Any innovative, cutting-edge program, activity or service will be considered. Examples include: a dynamic solution to a problem; a unique program that reached a special population; or a special marketing campaign that brought dramatic, measurable results. Programs should be unique and cutting-edge and must have had measurable impact on the library's clientele. Proposals will be judged on the following: collaborative efforts of the staff and community in the planning and implementation process; measurements of success in the community based on usage, program attendance, or greater community awareness; sustainability of the program over time; program can be replicated by other public libraries; and quality and appropriateness of submitted materials (supporting documents may be included). The winner receives $2,000 and a plaque from Highsmith, Inc. The application is available through the online system at the website.
Requirements: Any public library is eligible to apply.
Restrictions: Public libraries with current employees on the Highsmith Library Innovation Award jury are not eligible. Award winners must agree to publicize their program.
Geographic Focus: All States
Date(s) Application is Due: Dec 1
Amount of Grant: 2,000 USD
Contact: Julianna Kloeppel; (312) 280-5026; fax (312) 280-5029; jkloeppel@ala.org
Internet: http://www.ala.org/awardsgrants/awards/37/apply
Sponsor: American Library Association
50 East Huron Street
Chicago, IL 60611-2795

ALA Information Technology Pathfinder Award 286
The Information Technology Pathfinder Award recognizes and honors school librarians demonstrating vision and leadership through the use of information technology to build lifelong learners. The award is divided into two divisions: division one recognizes the innovative use of information technology in elementary (K through grade 6) school libraries, while division two recognizes secondary (grades 7 through 12) school libraries. Each award gives $1,000 to the school librarian and $500 to the library. Each application is judged on the following criteria: the identification and utilization of technologies which address the needs of the school community; the integration of technology into the school curriculum; and the depth of the impact on student learning. For the purpose of this award, information technology is defined as any technology or combination of technologies that enables students and teachers to access, integrate, manage and produce information in a wide variety of formats. These technologies include, but are not limited to, computers and computer applications, databases, Internet, CD-ROM, laser technology, video, telecommunications, networking, distance learning, and other emerging technologies.
Requirements: Applicants must be personal members of the AASL.
Geographic Focus: All States
Date(s) Application is Due: Feb 1
Amount of Grant: 500 - 1,000 USD
Contact: Meg Featheringham; (312) 280-4382, ext. 1396; mfeatheringham@ala.org
Internet: http://www.ala.org/awardsgrants/awards/257/apply
Sponsor: American Association of School Librarians
50 East Huron Street
Chicago, IL 60611-2795

ALA Information Today Library of the Future Award 287
The purpose of the Information Today Library of the Future Award, consisting of $1,500 and a 24k gold-framed citation of achievement, is to honor an individual library, library consortium, group of librarians, or support organization for innovative planning for, applications of, or development of patron training programs about information technology in a library setting. Selection criteria should include the benefit to clients served; benefit to the technology information community; impact on library operations; public relations value; and impact on the perception of the library or librarian in the work setting and to the specialized and/or general public. Applicants should complete the online application by February 3 each year.

Geographic Focus: All States
Date(s) Application is Due: Feb 3
Amount of Grant: 1,500 USD
Contact: Cheryl Malden; (312) 280-3247; cmalden@ala.org or awards@ala.org
Internet: http://www.ala.org/awardsgrants/awards/213/apply
Sponsor: American Library Association
50 East Huron Street
Chicago, IL 60611-2795

ALA Innovation Award   288
This annual award recognizes a project that demonstrates creative, innovative, or unique approaches within the context of national trends to information literacy instruction or programming. The winner receives $3,000 and a certificate.
Requirements: Academic librarians or academic project teams that include an academic librarian are eligible to receive the award. Recipients must have implemented their project in an academic or research library, or through the sponsorship of a professional library organization no more than two years prior to the nomination submission deadline. Electronic submissions are required. Nominations must include a description of the innovative project, a letter supporting the project, and sufficient supporting documentation for the committee to understand its purpose, content, impact, and innovative aspects.
Geographic Focus: All States
Date(s) Application is Due: Dec 3
Amount of Grant: 3,000 USD
Contact: Casey Kinson; (800) 545-2433, ext. 2511; fax (312) 440-9374; ckinson@ala.org
Internet: http://www.ala.org/awardsgrants/awards/244/apply
Sponsor: American Library Association
50 East Huron Street
Chicago, IL 60611-2795

ALA Intellectual Freedom Award   289
The Intellectual Freedom Award is given for upholding the principles of intellectual freedom as set forth by the American Association of School Libraries and the American Library Association. The recipient is awarded $2,000 and $1,000 is awarded to the school library of the recipient's choice. The application is available at the website's online system.
Requirements: Applicants must be AASL personal members.
Geographic Focus: All States
Date(s) Application is Due: Feb 7
Amount of Grant: 3,000 USD
Contact: Meg Featheringham; (312) 280-4382, ext. 1396; mfeatheringham@ala.org
Internet: http://www.ala.org/awardsgrants/awards/62/apply
Sponsor: American Library Association
50 East Huron Street
Chicago, IL 60611-2795

ALA Isadore Gilbert Mudge Award   290
The Mudge Award recognizes an individual who has made a distinguished contribution to reference librarianship. This contribution may include an imaginative and constructive program in a particular library; authorship of a significant book or articles in the reference field; creative and inspirational teaching; active participation in professional associations devoted to reference services; or leadership in other noteworthy professional activities. The winner receives $5,000 and a citation.
Requirements: Nominations should be submitted to the award committee chair. Submitted materials should include the following: a letter of nomination explaining why the nominee is deserving of this recognition and citing specific achievements; up to five letters of recommendation; a copy of the nominee's resume or curriculum vitae; and any other appropriate documentation.
Geographic Focus: All States
Date(s) Application is Due: Dec 15
Amount of Grant: 5,000 USD
Contact: Leighann Wood; (800) 545-2433; fax (574) 631-6772; lwood@ala.org
Internet: http://www.ala.org/awardsgrants/awards/167/apply
Sponsor: American Library Association
50 East Huron Street
Chicago, IL 60611-2795

ALA Jan Merrill-Oldham Professional Development Grant   291
The Merrill-Oldham Award was established by the Preservation and Reformatting Section (PARS) of the Association for Library Collections & Technical Services (ALCTS) to honor the career and influence of Jan Merrill-Oldham, distinguished leader, author, and mentor in the field of library and archives preservation. This annual award consists of a $1,250 grant donated by the Library Binding Institute, and a citation. The grant is applicable toward airfare, lodging, and registration fees related to the ALA Annual Conference attendance. Application instructions are available at the website.
Requirements: Applicants must have no more than five years of experience in the field of library and archives preservation, and no previous attendance to an ALA Annual Conference. They should currently work as a librarian or para-professional within a library or archives preservation department, or have preservation responsibilities within their institution, or be currently enrolled in a preservation-related graduate program. They must be willing to participate in designated conference events, and submit a summary of their conference experience to the ALCTS Newsletter Online no later than 30 days after the conference.
Restrictions: Previous winners are not eligible.
Geographic Focus: All States
Date(s) Application is Due: Dec 1
Amount of Grant: 1,250 USD
Contact: Charles Wilt, Staff Liaison; (312) 280-5030; fax (312) 280-5033; cwilt@ala.org
Internet: http://www.ala.org/awardsgrants/awards/31536/apply
Sponsor: American Library Association
50 East Huron Street
Chicago, IL 60611-2795

ALA John Cotton Dana Library Public Relations Award   292
Sponsored by EBSCO Publishing, the H.W. Wilson Foundation, and the American Library Association, the John Cotton Dana Award honors outstanding effective strategic communication campaigns that show results, no matter what size or type of library. Not only does the John Cotton Dana Award bring a substantial prize, winners have the opportunity to show their successful campaign to other libraries and serve as role models for libraries nationwide. Outstanding library public relations may involve a summer reading program, a year-long centennial celebration, fund-raising for a new college library, an awareness campaign, or an innovative partnership in the community. In recognition of their achievement, award winners receive a cash development grant from the H.W. Wilson Foundation. The John Cotton Dana Awards are presented at a reception hosted by EBSCO Publishing held during the American Library Association Annual Conference. Eight grants are awarded at $10,000 each. The contest is open to libraries of all sizes, types and budgets, agencies and associations that promote library service. Selection criteria is based on needs assessment and planning (35%); implementation and creativity (35%), and evaluation (30%). The application and additional instructions are available at the website.
Requirements: Strategic library communication campaigns may be submitted by any library, Friends group, consulting agency or service provider. An application must be a public relations/strategic communication program that occurred entirely during the previous year or a multi-year project completed in the previous year.
Restrictions: Institutions represented by John Cotton Dana Award Committee members, John Cotton Dana Award Committee members from the previous year, organizational units of the American Library Association, and EBSCO Publishing are not eligible to apply. Presentation portfolios are not required.
Geographic Focus: All States
Date(s) Application is Due: Mar 15
Amount of Grant: 10,000 USD
Contact: Fred Reuland; (312) 280-5032; fax (312) 280-5033; freuland@ala.org
Internet: http://www.ala.org/awardsgrants/awards/438/apply
Sponsor: American Library Association
50 East Huron Street
Chicago, IL 60611-2795

ALA John Phillip Immroth Memorial Award   293
The Immroth Award honors intellectual freedom fighters in and outside the library profession who have demonstrated remarkable personal courage in resisting censorship. Selection criteria is based on the duration of the nominee's support of intellectual freedom, in addition to specific incidents worth noting. Relevant supportive data such as newspaper articles and recommendation letters are encouraged.
Requirements: Individuals, a group, or an organization are eligible for the award.
Geographic Focus: All States
Date(s) Application is Due: Dec 1
Amount of Grant: 500 USD
Contact: Jonathan Kelley, Staff Liaison; (312) 280-4226 or (800) 545-2433, ext. 4226; fax (312) 280-4227; jokelley@ala.org
Internet: http://www.ala.org/awardsgrants/awards/201/apply
Sponsor: American Library Association
50 East Huron Street
Chicago, IL 60611-2795

ALA Joseph W. Lippincott Award   294
The annual Lippincott Award consists of $1,000 and a 24k gold-framed citation presented to a librarian for distinguished service in the profession of librarianship. Such service is to include outstanding participation in the activities of the professional library association, notable published professional writing, or other significant activities on behalf of the profession and its aims. Applicants should submit the online application and six copies of supporting materials.
Geographic Focus: All States
Date(s) Application is Due: Dec 1
Amount of Grant: 1,000 USD
Contact: Cheryl M. Malden, Staff Liaison; (800) 545-2433, ext. 3247 or (312) 280-3247; fax (312) 944-3897; cmalden@ala.org or awards@ala.org
Internet: http://www.ala.org/awardsgrants/awards/142/apply
Sponsor: American Library Association
50 East Huron Street
Chicago, IL 60611-2795

ALA Loleta D. Fyan Grant   295
Past ALA President Loleta Fyan bequeathed funds to ALA for the development and improvement of public libraries and the services they provide. Fyan believed that every individual, regardless of residence, is entitled to high quality library service and that librarians must use the political process to acquire this right of citizenship. The application, along with additional proposal requirements, is posted on the website.
Requirements: Applicants can include but are not limited to: local, regional or state libraries, associations or organizations, including units of the American Library Association; library schools; or individuals. The project(s) must: result in the development and improvement

of public libraries and the services they provide; have the potential for broader impact and application beyond meeting a specific local need; be designed to effect changes in public library services that are innovative and responsive to the future; and be capable of completion within one year.
Geographic Focus: All States
Date(s) Application is Due: Dec 21
Amount of Grant: Up to 5,000 USD
Contact: Rudolph Rose; (800) 545-2433, ext. 4283; fax (312) 440-9374; nrose@ala.org
Internet: http://www.ala.org/awardsgrants/awards/154/apply
Sponsor: American Library Association
50 East Huron Street
Chicago, IL 60611-2795

ALA MAE Award for Best Teen Literature Program 296

This award honors a Young Adult and Library Services Association (YALSA) member for developing an outstanding reading or literature program for young adults. The MAE Award for Best Literature Program for Teens is sponsored by the Margaret A. Edwards Trust. Edwards was a well-known and innovative young adult services librarian at Enoch Pratt Free Library in Baltimore for more than 30 years. Winners receive $500 and an additional $500 for their library. The application is available at the website.
Requirements: The program must be specifically designed for and targeted to young adults to encourage life-long reading habits. All or part of the program must have taken place in the 12 months preceding the award deadline of December 1. The applicant must work directly with young adults and be a personal member of the Young Adult Library Services Association.
Geographic Focus: All States
Date(s) Application is Due: Dec 1
Amount of Grant: 1,000 USD
Contact: Letitia Smith; (312) 280-4390; fax (312) 280-5276; lsmith@ala.org
Internet: http://www.ala.org/awardsgrants/awards/147/apply
Sponsor: American Library Association
50 East Huron Street
Chicago, IL 60611-2795

ALA Margaret Mann Citation 297

This citation is awarded for outstanding professional achievement in cataloging or classification either through publication of significant professional literature, participation in professional cataloging associations, or valuable contributions to practice in individual libraries. The winner receives a citation, and a $2,000 scholarship is given to the U.S. or Canadian library school of the winner's choice. Application instructions are available at the website.
Requirements: Those eligible must be Association for Library Collections and Technical Services (ALCTS) members. Nominations made by members or friends of the profession are invited. Achievements such as notable publications, outstanding contribution to the activities of professional cataloging associations, technical improvement of cataloging and classification and/or the introduction of a new technique of recognized importance, and achievement in the area of teaching cataloging and classification will be considered.
Restrictions: Except in unusual circumstances, the achievement shall have culminated within the last five years.
Geographic Focus: All States, Canada
Date(s) Application is Due: Dec 1
Amount of Grant: 2,000 USD
Contact: Charles Wilt, Staff Liaison; (312) 280-5030; fax (312) 280-5033; cwilt@ala.org
Internet: http://www.ala.org/awardsgrants/awards/205/apply
Sponsor: American Library Association
50 East Huron Street
Chicago, IL 60611-2795

ALA Margaret T. Lane/Virginia F. Saunders Memorial Research Award 298

The award is given annually to an author or shared among collaborative authors of an outstanding research article in which government documents, either published or archival in nature, form a substantial part of the documented research. Preference may be given to articles published in library literature and those that appeal to a broader audience. A plaque and $2,000 is awarded to the recipient(s). The nomination form is available at the website. Awards are announced following the ALA Midwinter meeting and presented at the Government Documents Round Table (GODORT) reception at the ALA Annual Conference.
Requirements: The article must be published, either in print or online, no more than 18 months prior to the due date for nominations. The award is not restricted to articles in library journals.
Restrictions: Only articles are eligible for the award. Book chapters, books, and dissertations are not eligible.
Geographic Focus: All States
Date(s) Application is Due: Dec 3
Amount of Grant: 2,000 USD
Contact: Andrea Sevetson, Award Coordinator; (541) 992-5461; asevetson@hotmail.com
Internet: http://www.ala.org/awardsgrants/awards/31624/apply
Sponsor: American Library Association
50 East Huron Street
Chicago, IL 60611-2795

ALA Maureen Hayes Author/Illustrator Award 299

The $4,000 ALA ALSC Maureen Hayes Author/Illustrator Award was established with funding from Simon and Schuster Children's Publishing, in honor of Maureen Hayes, to bring together children and nationally recognized authors/illustrators by funding an author/illustrator visit to a library.
Requirements: Applicants must: be personal members of ALSC as well as ALA; organizational members are not eligible; act as host for the author/illustrator visit, the date to be arranged at the mutual convenience of the artist/illustrator and the host institution; the award covers only the honorarium and travel expense to and from the host city. The host is responsible for making travel arrangements that are mutually agreed upon by the host and the author/illustrator, and for paying the up front travel costs. Maximum award is $4,000; host institution must arrange to pay for any reception, dinner, or other hospitality honoring the speaker following the visit and to pay for all local lodging, means, etc. of the lecturer; prepare and distribute publicity; if applicable, autographing and sale of books may be arranged with the publisher by the host institution. Any other programs/events (other than those promoting the visit) must be arranged with the author/illustrator's publisher(s) or agent, and must be arranged with the author/illustrator's knowledge and permission, and must be funded separately
Geographic Focus: All States
Date(s) Application is Due: Dec 21
Amount of Grant: 4,000 USD
Contact: Nancy Baumann, Administrative Committee; (800) 545-2433, ext. 2163; fax (312) 280-5271; horsepwr2010@gmail.com or awards@ala.org
Internet: http://www.ala.org/ala/mgrps/divs/alsc/awardsgrants/profawards/hayesaward/index.cfm
Sponsor: American Library Association
50 East Huron Street
Chicago, IL 60611-2795

ALA May Hill Arbuthnot Honor Lecture Award 300

The May Hill Arbuthnot Honor Lecture Award is a unique collaboration between several groups of people—the committee, the chosen lecturer, the ALSC staff and Board of Directors, and the host site coordinators. The result is an opportunity to celebrate and add to the knowledge and scholarship in the field of children's literature. Publication in Children & Libraries: The Journal of the Association for Library Service to Children ensures the lecture will be a lasting contribution that is available to a broad audience. The winning lecturer will receive a $1,000 honorarium. Suggestions for lecturers are welcomed from both ALSC members and the ALSC award committee. The Lecturer is announced at the Youth Media Awards Press Conference at Midwinter Meeting. The host site is announced at the ALSC Membership Meeting in the summer.
Requirements: The lecturer may be an author, critic, librarian, historian, or teacher of children's literature from any country. A school library, department of education in college or university, or a children's library system may be considered as host for the lecture. Nominations should include: name; professional title/occupation; biographical sketch; justification for consideration; and major publications. Anyone may apply to host the lecture, particularly ALSC member organizations or institutions.
Restrictions: Those serving on the Arbuthnot Selection Committee may not be selected as either lecturer or host during the term of their service on the committee.
Geographic Focus: All States, All Countries
Date(s) Application is Due: May 1
Amount of Grant: 1,000 USD
Contact: Courtney Jones; (312) 280-5710; fax (312) 280-5271; cjones@ala.org
Internet: http://www.ala.org/awardsgrants/awards/197/apply
Sponsor: American Library Association
50 East Huron Street
Chicago, IL 60611-2795

ALA Melvil Dewey Medal 301

The Melvil Dewey Medal is given each year for recent creative leadership of high order, particularly in the fields of library management, library training, cataloging and classification, and the tools and techniques of librarianship. The annual award consists of $2,000, a bronzed medal, and a 24k gold-framed citation of achievement. The application is available at the website.
Requirements: Applicants must submit six copies of the application and supporting materials.
Geographic Focus: All States
Date(s) Application is Due: Feb 15
Amount of Grant: 2,000 USD
Contact: Cheryl Malden; (312) 280-3247; fax (312) 944-3897; cmalden@ala.org
Internet: http://www.ala.org/awardsgrants/awards/44/apply
Sponsor: American Library Association
50 East Huron Street
Chicago, IL 60611-2795

ALA Morningstar Public Librarian Support Award 302

This annual award offers travel funds for ALA's Annual Conference to a public librarian who has performed outstanding business reference service, and who requires financial assistance to attend the conference. The award offers $1,000 in travel funds. Applicants are evaluated on their involvement in special projects, creation of a business web site, outstanding service to the community, publications or related activities. The nomination form is available at the website.
Requirements: The winner must be a member of ALA, RUSA, and BRASS. The recipient shall have a demonstrated interest in pursuing a career as a business reference librarian and the potential to be a leader in the profession. The winner will be expected to participate in BRASS activities at the conference, and write a short statement regarding his or her experience at the conference for publication after the event.
Geographic Focus: All States
Date(s) Application is Due: Jan 15
Amount of Grant: 1,000 USD
Contact: Melissa Jeter; (419) 259-5270; melissacjeter@gmail.com

Internet: http://www.ala.org/awardsgrants/awards/274/apply
Sponsor: American Library Association
50 East Huron Street
Chicago, IL 60611-2795

ALA National Friends of Libraries Week Awards 303
The National Friends of Libraries Week Awards recognize Friends groups for activities and programming presented during National Friends of Libraries Week. Five Friends groups are awarded $250 each. Applications are judged on the following: creativity and innovation; involvement of Friends, library staff, trustees and/or advisory committees; recognition of Friends group; and promotion of Friends group to the community, school, students, and/or faculty. The application is available at the website.
Requirements: Applicants must be current members of the ALTAFF Friends section or Friends board affiliates.
Geographic Focus: All States
Date(s) Application is Due: Dec 1
Amount of Grant: 250 USD
Contact: Sally Gardner Reed; (800) 545-2433, ext. 2161; sreed@ala.org
Internet: http://www.ala.org/awardsgrants/awards/318/apply
Sponsor: American Library Association
50 East Huron Street
Chicago, IL 60611-2795

ALA NewsBank/Readex Catharine J. Reynolds Award 304
The NewsBank/Readex Catharine J. Reynolds Award provides funding for research in the field of documents librarianship or in a related area that would benefit the individual's performance as a documents librarian or make a contribution to the field. This award is named for Catharine J. Reynolds, former Head of Government Publications at the University of Colorado. It is supported by an annual contribution from the NewsBank/Readex Corporation. Up to three grants a year are awarded. Recipients are selected on the basis of proven or potential ability, promise of future usefulness and permanence in the profession, financial need, and benefit of the project to the profession as well as the individual. The application is available at the website. Award recipient(s) will be announced as soon as all recipients are informed following the ALA Midwinter meeting. Awards are presented at the Government Documents Round Table (GODORT) reception at the ALA Annual Conference.
Requirements: Any documents librarian may apply. The awards support research in all areas of government information, U.S., foreign, international, state, regional, or local. The grant can be used to finance research costs, such as computer time or travel.
Restrictions: The Awards Committee may designate the amount of each award at its discretion.
Geographic Focus: All States
Date(s) Application is Due: Dec 3
Amount of Grant: 2,000 USD
Contact: Andrea Sevetson; (541) 992-5461; asevetson@hotmail.com
Internet: http://www.ala.org/awardsgrants/awards/207/apply
Sponsor: American Library Association
50 East Huron Street
Chicago, IL 60611-2795

ALA NMRT Professional Development Grant 305
The purpose of the grant is to encourage professional development and participation by new librarians in national ALA and NMRT activities. This annual grant covers round trip airfare, lodging, registration and other expenses to attend the ALA Annual Conference. Selection is based on the following criteria: the applicant's ability or initiative to attend future national conferences if finances are provided this year; how the applicant plans to use the conference experience; their current involvement at local, state, and regional associations; the impact of winning the grant on the applicant's current position and future career options; potential contributions the applicant will make to ALA and NMRT; and the applicant's overall presentation. The application is available at the website.
Requirements: The recipients must be current members of ALA and the New Members Round Table (NMRT) working in the U.S. Eligible applicants may apply more than once and may have attended previous ALA conferences. All recipients will be asked to sign an acceptance statement agreeing to the following: confirm in writing that they will be able to attend the annual conference and their employer has approved their attendance; attend certain conference related functions as requested in advance and participate in NMRT's mentoring program; schedule a two hour appearance at the 3M book during the conference; and keep a daily log or diary in a format requested by the grant committee and submit it to the committee to be used as project evaluation and publicity after the conference.
Geographic Focus: All States
Date(s) Application is Due: Dec 1
Contact: Kimberly L. Redd; (312) 280-4279; fax (312) 280-3256; klredd@ala.org
Internet: http://www.ala.org/awardsgrants/awards/264/apply
Sponsor: American Library Association
50 East Huron Street
Chicago, IL 60611-2795

ALA Pat Carterette Professional Development Grant 306
The Pat Carterette Professional Development Grant, in honor of the passing of our past-president, Pat Carterette, is designed to honor her passion for professional development in the field of library and information sciences. A former staff development coordinator at the Cleveland Heights-University Heights Public Library and the first Continuing Education Coordinator for the State Library of Georgia, Pat's legacy focused on providing outstanding educational opportunities for her colleagues to grow and develop within their career field. Funding for this grant comes from gifts and donations made in Pat's honor and through the proceeds from LearnRT pre-conference events and sponsorship of the LearnRT Training Showcase. The grant, in the amount of $1,000, will be awarded to an individual to provide monetary support to participate in continuing education event(s) to keep current in their career field. Funds can be used to cover registration, travel, lodging or other expenses related to the event. The grant monies will be available for twelve months from date it is awarded at which time any un-used monies will be forfeited.
Geographic Focus: All States
Amount of Grant: Up to 1,000 USD
Contact: Kimberly L. Redd; (312) 280-4279; fax (312) 280-3256; klredd@ala.org
Internet: http://www.ala.org/awardsgrants/awards/33154/apply
Sponsor: American Library Association
50 East Huron Street
Chicago, IL 60611-2795

ALA Paul Howard Award for Courage 307
The Howard Award honors a librarian, library board, library group, or an individual who has exhibited unusual courage for the benefit of library programs or services. Courageous action may be, but is not limited to, successful strategies to restore and build library funding, personal struggles against professional and public opinion to support free expression or professional ethics or to combat bias and prejudice, or battles on behalf of intellectual freedom. The award consists of $1,000 and a 24k gold-framed citation of achievement. The application is available at the website, but six copies of the application and supporting materials must be submitted.
Geographic Focus: All States
Date(s) Application is Due: Feb 15
Amount of Grant: 1,000 USD
Contact: Cheryl Malden; (800) 545-2433, ext. 3247; fax (312) 944-3897; cmalden@ala.org
Internet: http://www.ala.org/awardsgrants/awards/250/apply
Sponsor: American Library Association
50 East Huron Street
Chicago, IL 60611-2795

ALA Penguin Young Readers Group Award 308
The Penguin Group Award provides a $600 stipend for up to four children's librarians to attend their first ALA Annual Conference. Each applicant is judged on the following: their involvement in ALSC, as well as any other professional or education association of which they were a member, officer, or chairman; new programs or innovations began by the applicants at the library they work; and library experience.
Requirements: Applicants must be personal members of ALSC and ALA. They must also work directly with children in any school or public library, have less than ten years of experience as a librarian, and have no previous attendance at an ALA Conference. Applicants should complete the application form, describe the library program in which they work, and provide their supervisor's supporting statement.
Restrictions: Organizational members of ALA and ALSC are not eligible.
Geographic Focus: All States
Date(s) Application is Due: Dec 1
Amount of Grant: 600 USD
Contact: Caroline Jewell; (312) 280-4274; fax (312) 440-9374; cjewell@ala.org
Internet: http://www.ala.org/awardsgrants/awards/237/apply
Sponsor: American Library Association
50 East Huron Street
Chicago, IL 60611-2795

ALA Polaris Innovation in Technology John Iliff Award 309
The Iliff Award recognizes the contributions of a library worker, librarian, or library that has used technology and innovative thinking as a tool to improve services to public library users. The purpose is to encourage innovative user-oriented thinking and practical solutions using old and new technologies. The annual award consists of $1,000 and a plaque. The nomination form is available at the website.
Restrictions: Members of the current Polaris Innovation in Technology John Iliff Award Jury are ineligible to apply for the award.
Geographic Focus: All States
Date(s) Application is Due: Dec 1
Amount of Grant: 1,000 USD
Contact: Julianna Kloeppel; (312) 280-5026; fax (312) 280-5029; jkloeppel@ala.org
Internet: http://www.ala.org/awardsgrants/awards/186/apply
Sponsor: American Library Association
50 East Huron Street
Chicago, IL 60611-2795

ALA President's Award for Advocacy 310
This ALA President's Award for Advocacy honors and recognizes statewide advocacy for libraries with a $1,000 grant for the development of a program or programs for Friends and Trustees at the state library association conference. In addition to the grant award, the recipient receives an honorable mention by the ALA President at the Annual Conference. All entries and enclosures may be used by ALTAFF in exhibits, and may be published in The Voice or other ALTAFF publications. The application and additional instructions are available at the website.
Requirements: The winning advocacy campaign must be: conducted statewide; result in either an increase in state funding for libraries, or a decrease or elimination of a proposed reduction in state funding for libraries; use Capwiz or a similar interactive database to communicate with state legislators; show significant participation by citizens in making the case for libraries; and have been conducted during the previous year.

44 | Grant Programs

Geographic Focus: All States
Date(s) Application is Due: Mar 15
Amount of Grant: 1,000 USD
Contact: ALTAFF President's Award for Advocacy Coordinator; (800) 545-2433; fax (215) 545-3821; altaff@ala.org
Internet: http://www.ala.org/awardsgrants/awards/403/apply
Sponsor: American Library Association
50 East Huron Street
Chicago, IL 60611-2795

ALA ProQuest Documents to the People Award   311
The ProQuest Documents to the People Award is a tribute to an individual, library, institution, or other non-commercial group that has most effectively encouraged the use of government documents in support of library service. A framed plaque with the individual's name and achievement plus a $3,000 monetary prize to be assigned to a project of the recipient's choice is given annually. The nomination form is available at the website.
Restrictions: The recipient is responsible for any travel expenses to attend the ALA Annual Conference.
Geographic Focus: All States
Date(s) Application is Due: Dec 3
Amount of Grant: 3,000 USD
Contact: Andrea Sevetson; (541) 992-5461; asevetson@hotmail.com
Internet: http://www.ala.org/awardsgrants/awards/435/apply
Sponsor: American Library Association
50 East Huron Street
Chicago, IL 60611-2795

ALA Reference Service Press Award   312
The Reference Service Press Award is given to recognize the most outstanding article published in the RUSQ journal during the preceding two-volume year. The winner receives $2,500 and a plaque. The article is selected on the basis of originality, timeliness, relevance to RUSA areas of interest and concern, and quality of writing. An article is defined as any submitted or invited article or any invited column written by one or more individuals or by a committee, organization, or other group. The nomination form is available at the website.
Requirements: Nominations should be sent to the committee chair. Letters must clearly state the nominee's contributions in the field of business librarianship, explaining their significance and the magnitude of their influence. Self-nominations are accepted.
Restrictions: Authors of articles published in the journal during the award period and members of the editorial board or those assisting in the referee process during the three years preceding the award year are not eligible.
Geographic Focus: All States
Date(s) Application is Due: Dec 15
Amount of Grant: 2,500 USD
Contact: Robert H. Kieft; (323) 259-2504; fax (610) 896-1102; kieft@oxy.edu
Internet: http://www.ala.org/awardsgrants/awards/45/apply
Sponsor: American Library Association
50 East Huron Street
Chicago, IL 60611-2795

ALA Robert L. Oakley Memorial Scholarship   313
The Oakley Scholarship supports research and advanced study for librarians in their early-to-mid careers who are interested and/or active in the fields that Robert Oakley was expert in-intellectual property, public policy, copyright and their impacts on libraries, and the ways libraries serve their communities. A $1,000 scholarship is given annually. Awardees may receive the Oakley Scholarship up to two times in a lifetime. Funds may be used for equipment, expendable supplies, travel necessary to conduct, attend conferences, release from library duties or other reasonable and appropriate research expenses. Detailed application instructions are available at the website.
Requirements: Highest consideration will be given to applicants who are librarian(s) in their early-to-mid-careers. They must demonstrate interest in or be professional actively in copyright and public policy and their impacts on libraries and the ways libraries serve their communities.
Geographic Focus: All States
Date(s) Application is Due: Mar 1
Amount of Grant: 1,000 USD
Contact: Carrie Russell, Staff Liaison; (800) 545-2433, ext. 8219 or (202) 628-8410; fax (202) 628-8419; crussell@alawash.org
Internet: http://www.ala.org/awardsgrants/awards/31464/apply
Sponsor: American Library Association
50 East Huron Street
Chicago, IL 60611-2795

ALA Romance Writers of America Library Grant   314
The Romance Writers of America Library Grant provides a public library the opportunity to build or expand its romance fiction collection and/or host romance fiction programming. The annual grant consists of $4,500 to be used toward the purchase of romance fiction, author honorariums and travel expenses, and other applicable program expenses. The application is available at the website.
Requirements: Any public library is eligible to apply. The library must demonstrate a plan or examples for use of the funds, such as hosting a system-wide training day on the romance genre, buying romance novels for the library collection, creating readers advisory materials on the genre and/or hosting romance fiction oriented programs. The library must show a desire to improve awareness of the romance genre in the library. Priority will be given to libraries with a financial need or in disaster recovery areas looking to rebuild their romance fiction collections.
Geographic Focus: All States
Date(s) Application is Due: Dec 1
Amount of Grant: 4,500 USD
Contact: Julianna Kloeppel; (312) 280-5026; fax (312) 280-5029; jkloeppel@ala.org
Internet: http://www.ala.org/awardsgrants/awards/441/apply
Sponsor: American Library Association
50 East Huron Street
Chicago, IL 60611-2795

ALA Routledge Distance Learning Librarianship Conference Sponsorship Award   315
This conference sponsorship award honors any individual member of the Association of College and Research Libraries (ACRL) working in the field of or contributing to the success of distance learning librarianship or related library service in higher education. The award of $1,200 helps defray the cost of travel to the ALA annual meeting. Applicants or nominators should send the online nomination form to the DLS Award Chair.
Requirements: Nominees must be ACRL members. Nominees should also have demonstrated achievements in one or more of the following areas: contribution to or support for distance learning librarianship and library services (service to students and faculty, publications, training, innovation and/or leadership); consultation services in support of higher education distance students and programs beyond the traditional library boundaries; training of faculty and staff who support library services for distance students; advocacy at decision-making levels, especially in funding and policy development as related to distance learning librarianship; work with outside agencies in support of students learning at a distance; significant research and publication in areas of distance learning librarianship; and planning and implementation of distance learning library programs of such quality that they serve as a model for others.
Geographic Focus: All States
Date(s) Application is Due: Dec 2
Amount of Grant: 1,200 USD
Contact: Casey Kinson; (312) 280-2511 or (312) 280-2523; ckinson@ala.org
Internet: http://www.ala.org/awardsgrants/awards/352/apply
Sponsor: Association of College and Research Libraries
50 East Huron Street
Chicago, IL 60611-2795

ALA Sara Jaffarian School Library Award for Exemplary Humanities Programming   316
The purpose of the Sara Jaffarian School Library Program Award is to recognize, promote and support excellence in humanities programming in elementary and middle school libraries that serve children K-8. To promote and encourage other school libraries interested in developing outstanding humanities programs, a professional development/training opportunity will be presented by the ALA Public Programs Office, in consultation with the Public and Cultural Programs Advisory Committee and the American Association of School Librarians. An annual award of $4,000 is given, in addition to the promotion of the winner as a model program and training opportunity for other school libraries. Selection of the winner is based on the following criteria: excellence, appeal and innovation of program content and presentation; impact, as evidenced by involvement and awareness of parents, administrators and community leaders (letters of support of the nomination are encouraged); evidence of collaborative relationships in developing the programming (e.g., parents, teachers, administrators, humanities scholars, community groups); relationship of the programming to the curriculum and evidence of a curriculum component for classroom treatment of the humanities theme(s) or topic(s) emphasized in the program; and replicability of the programming and the winner's willingness to participate in a conference program or online meeting to showcase the winner as a model for excellence for other school libraries. The self-nomination form is available at the website. Six copies of the form and all supporting materials must be submitted.
Requirements: Any elementary or middle school (public or private) library or any school library program in the U.S. that serves children in any combination of grades K-8 is eligible.
Geographic Focus: All States
Date(s) Application is Due: Dec 15
Amount of Grant: 4,000 USD
Contact: Ana C. Barbus, Staff Liaison; (800) 545-2433, ext. 5053; fax (312) 440-9374; cbarbus@ala.org or publicprograms@ala.org
Internet: http://www.ala.org/awardsgrants/awards/160/apply
Sponsor: American Library Association
50 East Huron Street
Chicago, IL 60611-2795

ALA Schneider Family Book Award   317
The Schneider Family Book Award is given annually in each of the following three categories: birth through grade school (age 0-10); middle school (age 11-13); and teens (age 13-18). Each award honors an author or illustrator that embodies an artistic expression of the disability experience for child and adolescent audiences. Selection is based on specific criteria for content, style, and illustration. The application and additional instructions for submission are available at the website. Winners are notified the morning of the Midwinter Conference.
Requirements: Books must portray some aspect of living with a disability, whether the disability is physical, mental, or emotional. The books must be published in English. Books may be fiction, biography, or other form of nonfiction (essay, journal, memoir, diary, textbook, etc). The disability should be part of a full life, and not something to be pitied or overcome. Characters should avoid exaggeration or stereotype. Book themes must be appropriate for the intended audience. Information on the disability should be accurate. Text and images should complement each other, with appropriate format, typeface, and layout. Awards may be given posthumously. Publications from the previous two years are eligible.

Restrictions: Books with death as the main theme are generally disqualified. Books previously discussed and voted on are not eligible in the future.
Geographic Focus: All States
Date(s) Application is Due: Dec 1
Amount of Grant: 5,000 USD
Contact: Cheryl Malden; (312) 280-3247; fax (312) 944-3897; cmalden@ala.org
Internet: http://www.ala.org/awardsgrants/awards/1/apply
Sponsor: American Library Association
50 East Huron Street
Chicago, IL 60611-2795

ALA Scholastic Library Publishing Award 318
The Scholastic Library Publishing Award is presented to a librarian in a community or in a school who has made an unusual contribution to the stimulation and guidance of reading by children and young people. The award, consisting of $1,000 and a 24k gold-framed citation, is given for outstanding work with children and young people through high school age for continued service, or in recognition of one particular contribution of lasting value. The nomination form is available at the website, but six copies, along with six copies of supporting material, must be submitted to the Governance Office at ALA.
Geographic Focus: All States
Date(s) Application is Due: Dec 1
Amount of Grant: 1,000 USD
Contact: Cheryl Malden; (312) 280-3247; fax (312) 944-3897; cmalden@ala.org
Internet: http://www.ala.org/awardsgrants/awards/69/apply
Sponsor: American Library Association
50 East Huron Street
Chicago, IL 60611-2795

ALA Scholastic Library Publishing National Library Week Grant 319
The Scholastic Library Publishing National Library Week Grant awards $3,000 to a single U.S. library for the best public awareness campaign. Funds are used to support the winner's National Library Week promotional activities. The application and descriptions of the winning proposals of previous awardees are available at the website.
Requirements: Any type of library or library organization may apply. All proposals must use the Communities matters library theme, incorporating the Campaign for America's Libraries library brand, on promotional and publicity material supporting National Library Week activities.
Restrictions: Funds cannot be used for capital expenses such as books or equipment.
Geographic Focus: All States
Date(s) Application is Due: Oct 22
Contact: Megan McFarlane, Campaign Coordinator; (800) 545-2433, ext. 2148 or (312) 280-2148; fax (312) 440-9374; mmcfarlane@ala.org
Internet: http://www.ala.org/awardsgrants/awards/192/apply
Sponsor: American Library Association
50 East Huron Street
Chicago, IL 60611-2795

Alaska Airlines Corporate Giving Grants 320
Alaska Airlines and Horizon Air Corporate Giving support health and human services, arts and cultural programs, as well as education, environmental, and civic organizations. The program focuses on communities served now or in the near future and where a significant number of its employees live or work. When considering requests, the corporation favors organizations and efforts that are most likely to enhance a community's cultural and economic vitality and improve the quality of life for its citizens. Objectives of the Corporate Giving Program are to: provide support to charitable and cultural organizations within our communities; and maintain a reasonable balance of contributions supporting a wide range of organizations.
Requirements: Giving is on a national and international basis in areas of company operations, with emphasis on Alaska and Washington; some further giving occurs in Canada and Mexico.
Restrictions: Alaska Airlines or Horizon Air do not provide support for: loans and grants to individuals or private business; groups that discriminate; endowments; religious organizations (if for sacramental purposes); pageants; capital projects; multi-year commitment or automatic renewal grants; general operating expenses; publicly or privately funded educational institutions; or organizations whose prime purpose is to influence legislation.
Geographic Focus: Alaska, Washington, Canada, Mexico
Contact: Susan Bramstedt, Director of Public Affairs (Alaska); (907) 266-7230; fax (907) 266-7229; susan.bramstedt@alaskaair.com
Internet: http://www.alaskaair.com/as/www2/company/csr/social-responsibility.asp
Sponsor: Alaska Airlines
4750 Old International Airport Road
Anchorage, AK 99502

Alaska Airlines Foundation Grants 321
A small number of cash grants ranging on average from $5,000 to $15,000 are given to 501(c)3 non-profit organizations classified as public charities in Alaska and Washington. These grants should focus on educational efforts that address a unique need or value to a community. The Foundation supports health and human services, arts and cultural programs, as well as education, environmental, and civic organizations.
Requirements: 501(c)3 organizations based in Alaska and Washington are eligible.
Restrictions: Alaska Airlines or Horizon Air do not provide support for: loans and grants to individuals or private business; groups that discriminate; endowments; religious organizations (if for sacramental purposes); pageants; capital projects; multi-year commitment or automatic renewal grants; general operating expenses; publicly or privately funded educational institutions; or organizations whose prime purpose is to influence legislation.
Geographic Focus: Alaska, Washington
Amount of Grant: 5,000 - 15,000 USD
Contact: Susan Bramstedt, Director of Public Affairs (Alaska); (907) 266-7230; fax (907) 266-7229; susan.bramstedt@alaskaair.com
Internet: http://www.alaskaair.com/as/www2/company/csr/as-foundation.asp
Sponsor: Alaska Airlines Foundation
4750 Old International Airport Road
Anchorage, AK 99502

Alaska Conservation Foundation Awards 322
The foundation supports projects and organizations whose work is consistent with ACFs mission to protect the integrity of Alaska's intact ecosystems and promote sustainable livelihoods for all Alaskan communities and peoples. Each year, ACF seeks nominations for individuals who have done outstanding environmental work, offering the following awards: the Olaus Murie Award for Outstanding Professional Contributions; the Celia Hunter Award for Outstanding Volunteer Contributions; the Denny Wilcher Award for Young Environmental Activists; the Lowell Thomas, Jr. Award for Outstanding Civil Service; the Jerry S. Dixon Award for Excellence in Environmental Education; the Daniel Housberg Wilderness Image Award for Excellence in Still Photography and Excellence in Film or Video; the Award for Alaska Native Writers or Storytellers on the Environment; and the Lifetime Achievement Award (presented every two years). Nomination guidelines and form are available online. Self-nominations are accepted.
Geographic Focus: All States
Amount of Grant: 500 - 3,000 USD
Contact: Polly Carr, Program Officer; (907) 276-1917; fax (907) 274-4145; pcarr@alaskaconservation.org or grants@akcf.org
Internet: http://alaskaconservation.org/_pages/grants_amp_awards/awards/general_information_and_awards_categories.php
Sponsor: Alaska Conservation Foundation
441 West Fifth Avenue, Suite 402
Anchorage, AK 99501-2340

Alaska Conservation Foundation Operating Support Grants 323
ACF awards operating support grants to in-state, Alaska-based conservation organizations focused on effective conservation advocacy. Operating support grants are used at the discretion of the recipients, within the limits of laws governing the use of ACF funds. These funds can be used to cover administrative and/or program costs including salaries, facilities, travel, equipment, supplies, training, membership, fundraising, and specific program activities.
Requirements: Applicant organizations must be engaged in environmental advocacy, incorporated as a nonprofit corporation, a 501(c)3 or (c)4 organization for at least three years from application date, and have a dues-paying membership of more than 300. Applicants must first send a letter of inquiry to the program officer.
Restrictions: Proposals received via fax or email will not be accepted.
Geographic Focus: Alaska
Date(s) Application is Due: Dec 1
Amount of Grant: Up to 15,000 USD
Contact: Polly Carr, Program Officer; (907) 276-1917; fax (907) 274-4145; pcarr@alaskaconservation.org or grants@akcf.org
Internet: http://alaskaconservation.org/_pages/grants_amp_awards/types_of_grants/operating_support.php
Sponsor: Alaska Conservation Foundation
441 West Fifth Avenue, Suite 402
Anchorage, AK 99501-2340

Alaska Conservation Foundation Opportunity Grants 324
ACF Opportunity Grants are for discrete, short-term projects beyond foreseeable organizational operating expenses that seek to address an emerging threat or opportunity. These projects should be completed within six months and the maximum request is $2,500. Priority areas of interest include: climate change; energy; marine conservation; mining; and rainforest conservation. There are no application deadlines; however applicants must first contact ACF program staff via email or phone prior to sending a proposal. Grant requests are on a monthly cycle.
Requirements: Although 501(c)3 nonprofit organizations are preferred, non-incorporated organizations and individuals may also apply.
Restrictions: Ineligible requests include: operating expenses, including existing staff salary and overhead; projects outside Alaska; expenses or activities that have already occurred; land acquisition; equipment purchases; capital campaigns; literary and/or film projects; endowments; scholarships; special events; or research.
Geographic Focus: Alaska
Amount of Grant: Up to 2,500 USD
Contact: Polly Carr; (907) 276-1917; fax (907) 274-4145; pcarr@alaskaconservation.org
Internet: http://alaskaconservation.org/_pages/grants_amp_awards/types_of_grants/small_grants.php
Sponsor: Alaska Conservation Foundation
441 West Fifth Avenue, Suite 402
Anchorage, AK 99501-2340

Alaska Conservation Foundation Rapid Response Grants 325
The foundation awards grants to protect Alaska's intact ecosystems and promote sustainable livelihoods for all Alaskan communities and peoples. The Rapid Response Fund allows a timely response to fast-breaking environmental issues and needs of statewide or national importance (e.g., fighting off unexpected riders in Congress). Areas of interest include ecosystem and lands protection; marine conservation; conservation advocacy; and

expanding conservation constituencies. Favored strategies include convening diverse constituencies; organizing media campaigns; encouraging compliance with environmental laws and regulations; organizing advocacy campaigns on emerging issues; promoting citizen participation in public process; and providing public forums for continuing environmental awareness. There are no application deadlines; however applicants must first contact ACF program staff via email or phone prior to sending a proposal.
Requirements: Incorporated tax-exempt organizations, non-incorporated organizations, and individuals are eligible.
Restrictions: Ineligible requests include requests for more than $15,000; projects outside the state of Alaska; land acquisition; research; capital campaigns; endowments; scholarships; or projects or activities that lead to direct action.
Geographic Focus: Alaska
Amount of Grant: 2,500 - 15,000 USD
Contact: Polly Carr; (907) 276-1917; fax (907) 274-4145; pcarr@alaskaconservation.org
Internet: http://alaskaconservation.org/_pages/grants_amp_awards/types_of_grants/rapid_response.php
Sponsor: Alaska Conservation Foundation
441 West Fifth Avenue, Suite 402
Anchorage, AK 99501-2340

Alaska Conservation Foundation Watchable Wildlife Conservation Trust Grants   326
The Watchable Wildlife Conservation Trust is a donor-advised fund developed in cooperation with the Alaska Department of Fish and Game. The purpose of the Trust is to fund those projects that emphasize non-consumptive use of wildlife, expand wildlife conservation efforts, and broaden public support for conserving Alaska's wildlife resources. Areas of interest include: interpretation (e.g., signage, viewing guides, media programming); education (e.g., curriculum development or publication development and distribution); facilities construction; applied ecosystem research; and projects involving a state wildlife sanctuary. The Trust makes grants once per calendar year. The annual deadline is October 1. Prospective grantees should contact ACF to determine if the project fits within the grant making program and when to submit their proposal. The Trust generally funds projects in the $1,000 to $4,000 range.
Requirements: As a 501(c)3 public foundation, ACF accepts requests for funding from incorporated, tax-exempt organizations, non-incorporated organizations, and individuals.
Restrictions: Ineligible requests include: projects outside the state of Alaska; general operating support; litigation or lobbying; endowments; and scholarships.
Geographic Focus: Alaska
Date(s) Application is Due: Oct 1
Amount of Grant: 1,000 - 4,000 USD
Contact: Polly Carr; (907) 276-1917; fax (907) 274-4145; pcarr@alaskaconservation.org
Internet: http://alaskaconservation.org/_pages/grants_amp_awards/types_of_grants/watchable_wildlife.php
Sponsor: Alaska Conservation Foundation
441 West Fifth Avenue, Suite 402
Anchorage, AK 99501-2340

Alaska State Council on the Arts Community Arts Development Grants   327
Community Arts Development grants are designed to stimulate grassroots arts activity, and to encourage public interest and participation in the arts throughout Alaska. Grants assist small nonprofit Alaskan organizations in developing art programs in underserved areas of the state and/or underserved disciplines. Exhibits, concerts, dance performances and festivals, workshops, readings, theater productions are examples of the kinds of arts projects funded through this grant category. Grants will also be given to assist developing organizations in the area of arts administration such as board development, accounting systems and budget development. Priority will be given to those organizations that operate on a volunteer basis with no paid staff. Grant amounts will not exceed $2,000. Applications must be made online.
Requirements: Alaskan nonprofit organizations, schools, local government agencies and tribal entities proposing arts or cultural heritage activities in the state are eligible for funds. All funded programs must be open to the public. All applicants must provide matching funds, and grants will not exceed 50 percent of the total cash costs of a project.
Restrictions: The council will not fund academic scholarships or tuition assistance, purchase of equipment, or deficits of completed projects. The primary purpose of the program may not be for academic credit.
Geographic Focus: Alaska
Date(s) Application is Due: Mar 1; Jun 1; Sep 1; Dec 1
Amount of Grant: Up to 2,000 USD
Contact: Andrea Noble; (907) 269-6605 or (888) 278-7424; andrea.noble@alaska.gov
Internet: http://www.eed.state.ak.us/aksca/grants2.htm#cad
Sponsor: Alaska State Council on the Arts
411 W Fourth Avenue, Suite 1E
Anchorage, AK 99501-2343

Alaska State Council on the Arts Operating Support Grants   328
Grants assist with a portion of an organization's ongoing artistic and administrative functions. These may include, but are not limited to, salaries, travel, promotion, and production costs of an entire program or a majority of the organization's yearly activities. The council funds applications in all areas of the arts: dance, visual arts, literature, music, theater, media arts, and traditional Native arts. Applications that promote and develop the cultural heritage of Alaska and the creation of new works by Alaskan artists are encouraged.
Requirements: The council awards funds only to Alaskan nonprofit organizations, schools, or government agencies. Eligible organizations must: be involved in producing, presenting, or undertaking a series of events or ongoing arts programs; provide proof of 501(c)3 status; be at least three years from the date of incorporation; and have a cash budget of at least $50,000. A maximum award amount is not set; however, applicants must provide matching funds, and grants will not exceed 50 percent of the total cash expenses.
Geographic Focus: Alaska
Date(s) Application is Due: Mar 1
Amount of Grant: Up to 21,000 USD
Contact: Andrea Noble; (907) 269-6605 or (888) 278-7424; andrea.noble@alaska.gov
Internet: http://www.eed.state.ak.us/aksca/grants2.htm#osla
Sponsor: Alaska State Council on the Arts
411 W Fourth Avenue, Suite 1E
Anchorage, AK 99501-2343

ALA Stonewall Book Awards - Barbara Gittings Literature Award   329
The Stonewall Book Awards are presented to English language books that have exceptional merit relating to the gay/lesbian/bisexual/transgendered experience. Each award consists of a cash stipend and commemorative plaque and is determined annually by the Gay, Lesbian, Bisexual, and Transgendered Round Table (GLBTRT) of ALA. The Barbara Gittings Literature Award is given for work that encompasses novels, short stories, poetry, and drama. Anthologies comprised of both nonfiction and literary pieces will be categorized by whichever form predominates. Awardees are expected to receive their award and give an acceptance speech during the Stonewall Book Award Brunch at the ALA Annual Conference.
Requirements: The award is given to works published in the U.S. in the previous calendar year (although works published elsewhere may be considered). A short statement describing why the book is being recommended should accompany the request, which is only accepted by email.
Restrictions: Reprints of previously published books will not be considered, unless there is substantial change in the new editions or English translation. Recommendations for nomination will not be accepted from the publisher of a proposed book, agents, the author's representatives, or anyone else who may gain directly from the book's nomination. Members of the Award Committee may not nominate a book they have contributed to, edited, or in any way been affiliated with, or a book authored or edited by a member of their immediate family or household.
Geographic Focus: All States
Date(s) Application is Due: Oct 31
Contact: John Amundsen; (312) 280-2140; fax (312) 280-3256; jamundsen@ala.org
Internet: http://www.ala.org/awardsgrants/awards/177/apply
Sponsor: American Library Association
50 East Huron Street
Chicago, IL 60611-2795

ALA Stonewall Book Awards - Israel Fishman Nonfiction Award   330
The Stonewall Book Awards are presented to English language books that have exceptional merit relating to the gay/lesbian/bisexual/transgendered experience. Each award consists of a cash stipend and commemorative plaque, and is determined annually by the Gay, Lesbian, Bisexual, and Transgendered Round Table (GLBTRT) of ALA. The Israel Fishman Nonfiction Award is given for work that encompasses biography, history, criticism, reference works, fine arts, and other traditional nonfiction genres. Anthologies comprised of both nonfiction and literary pieces will be categorized by whichever form predominates. Awardees are expected to receive their award, then give an acceptance speech during the Stonewall Book Award Brunch at the ALA Annual Conference.
Requirements: The award is given to works published in the U.S. in the previous calendar year. Works published elsewhere may be considered. A short statement describing why the book is being recommended should accompany the request, which must be emailed.
Restrictions: Reprints of previously published books are not considered, unless substantial change is made to the new edition or English translation. Recommendations for nominations will not be accepted from the publisher of a proposed book, agents, representatives, or anyone else who may gain directly from the book's nomination. Members of the Award Committee may not nominate a book they have contributed to, edited, or in any way been affiliated with, or a book authored or edited by a member of their immediately family or household.
Geographic Focus: All States
Date(s) Application is Due: Oct 31
Contact: John Amundsen; (312) 280-2140; fax (312) 280-3256; jamundsen@ala.org
Internet: http://www.ala.org/awardsgrants/awards/177/apply
Sponsor: American Library Association
50 East Huron Street
Chicago, IL 60611-2795

ALA Student Chapter of the Year Award   331
The Student Chapter of the Year Award is presented in recognition of a chapter's outstanding contributions to the American Library Association, their school, and the profession. The purpose of the award is to increase student involvement in ALA through student chapters, and to recognize future leaders in the profession. The nomination form is available at the website. Seven copies of the completed form, along with supporting documentation, may be emailed or mailed to the Committee Chair.
Requirements: All ALA Student Chapters in good standing are eligible to apply. There is no limit on the number of times a student chapter may win the award. Any ALA Student Chapter advisor, Student Chapter officer or member, or ALA member may nominate a Student Chapter for the award. Self-nominations are encouraged.
Geographic Focus: All States
Date(s) Application is Due: Feb 26
Amount of Grant: 1,000 USD
Contact: Elizabeth Downey; (662) 325-3834; edowney@library.msstate.edu
Internet: http://www.ala.org/awardsgrants/awards/111/apply
Sponsor: American Library Association
50 East Huron Street
Chicago, IL 60611-2795

Grant Programs | 47

ALA Sullivan Award for Administrators Supporting Services to Children 332
The Sullivan Award is given to an individual who has shown exceptional understanding and support of public library service to children, while having general management, supervisory, or administrative responsibility that includes public library service to children. The award consists of a commemorative gift and 24k gold framed citation. The application is available at the website.
Requirements: Six copies of the application and supporting materials must be submitted. Information must also include the nominee's brief career summary, educational background, memberships and participations in professional organizations, publications/productions/presentations, and other significant contributions.
Geographic Focus: All States
Date(s) Application is Due: Feb 15
Contact: Cheryl Malden; (312) 280-3247; fax (312) 944-3897; cmalden@ala.org
Internet: http://www.ala.org/awardsgrants/awards/172/apply
Sponsor: American Library Association
50 East Huron Street
Chicago, IL 60611-2795

ALA Supporting Diversity Stipend 333
The Supporting Diversity Stipend allows two members of the Young Adult Library Services Association (YALSA) with a diverse background to attend the ALA Annual Conference. Each member receives $1,000. Selection criteria is based on the following: the applicant's written justification in terms of diverse background and commitment to young adult services; their desired learning outcomes for attending the conference; and their financial and professional development needs. The application is available at the website.
Requirements: Applicants should be from a diverse background including, but not limited to economically, socially, culturally, geographically, or ethnically diverse.
Geographic Focus: All States
Date(s) Application is Due: Mar 31
Amount of Grant: 1,000 USD
Contact: Nichole Gilbert; (800) 545-2433, ext. 4387; ngilbert@ala.org
Internet: http://www.ala.org/awardsgrants/awards/116/apply
Sponsor: American Library Association
50 East Huron Street
Chicago, IL 60611-2795

ALA Ulrich's Serials Librarianship Award 334
This award, donated by the CSA/Ulrich Company, is given for contributions to serials librarianship in areas of professional association participation, library education, serials literature, research, or development of tools leading to better understanding of the field of serials. This annual award consists of $1,500 and a citation. The winner is notified after the Midwinter meeting.
Requirements: Applicants must be members of the Association for Library Collections and Technical Services (ALCTS). They must show a record of outstanding contributions to serials and continuing resources librarianship over the course of a professional career. Nominations should include a resume and letters of recommendation.
Restrictions: Employees of the CSA/Ulrich Company are not eligible to apply.
Geographic Focus: All States
Date(s) Application is Due: Dec 1
Contact: Charles Wilt, Staff Liaison; (312) 280-5030; fax (312) 280-5033; cwilt@ala.org
Internet: http://www.ala.org/awardsgrants/awards/216/apply
Sponsor: American Library Association
50 East Huron Street
Chicago, IL 60611-2795

Alavi Foundation Grants 335
The foundation's purposes are charitable and philanthropic with an emphasis on education and civic concerns. One of its primary aims is to promote understanding and harmony among people of different religions. Another basic aim of the foundation is to promote the study of the humanities, arts, and pure and applied sciences. The foundation gives assistance to public charitable organizations during times of hardship and deprivation caused by war or natural disasters. It also provides financial assistance to nonprofit organizations that are involved in the teaching of Islamic culture and the Persian language. The foundation seeks to support the establishment of a six-year Persian Studies program. The foundation will support an endeavor to teach the Persian language to children of all ages. There are no application forms or deadlines. Submit a letter of inquiry.
Restrictions: The foundations contributions are limited only to public charities that are tax exempt under IRS ruling.
Geographic Focus: All States
Contact: Program Contact; (212) 944-8333; fax (212) 921-0325
Internet: http://www.alavifoundation.org/index.html
Sponsor: Alavi Foundation
500 Fifth Avenue, Suite 2320
New York, NY 10110

ALA Writers Live at the Library Grants 336
Writers Live provides grant opportunities for libraries to present theme-based cultural programming for adults and family audiences to explore important issues and ideas, featuring live appearances by literary, visual, and performing artists. The project is an initiative of the ALA Public Programs Office, with major support from the National Endowment for the Arts, Wallace-Reader's Digest Funds, John S. and James L. Knight Foundation, and additional support from the National Endowment for the Humanities. Applicants may sign up for an email alert to be informed about current opportunities.
Geographic Focus: All States
Date(s) Application is Due: Feb 28
Contact: Lainie Castle, Project Director, Public Programs; (800) 545-2433, ext. 5055 or (312) 280-5055; fax (312) 280-5759; lcastle@ala.org or publicprograms@ala.org
Internet: http://www.ala.org/awardsgrants/awards/256/apply
Sponsor: American Library Association
50 East Huron Street
Chicago, IL 60611-2795

ALA Young Adult Literature Symposium Stipend 337
The Young Adult Literature Symposium Stipend enables two recipients to attend YALSA's Literature Symposium. Up to two biannual stipends of up to $1,000 each are awarded to a library worker and to a student. Individual applications are available at the website.
Requirements: Applicants must be one of the following: a library worker who works directly with young adults, with one to ten years of experience; or a student enrolled in an ALA-accredited MLS program, with a focus supplement of serving young adults in a library. All applicants must be personal members of YALSA.
Geographic Focus: All States
Date(s) Application is Due: Jan 10
Amount of Grant: 1,000 USD
Contact: Nichole Gilbert; (312) 280-4387; fax (312) 280-5276; ngilbert@ala.org
Internet: http://www.ala.org/awardsgrants/awards/174/apply
Sponsor: American Library Association
50 East Huron Street
Chicago, IL 60611-2795

Alberta Law Foundation Grants 338
The objectives of the foundation are to conduct research into and recommend reform of law and the administration of justice; establish, maintain, and operate law libraries; contribute to the legal education and knowledge of the people of Alberta and provide programs and facilities for those purposes; provide assistance to native people's legal programs, student legal aid programs, and programs of like nature; and contribute to the costs incurred by the Legal Aid Society of Alberta to administer a plan to provide legal aid. To be considered for funding, programs or projects must fall within these objectives. Operating grants and project grants are awarded. The application process begins with a discussing the program or project idea with the executive director. This will be followed by an exchange of drafts during the development of the application.
Restrictions: Grants will not be made to an individual or for the support of a commercial venture. Funds are not available for bursaries, fellowships, sabbatical leave support, endowments, building funds, etc.
Geographic Focus: All States, Canada
Contact: David Aucoin, Executive Director; (403) 264-4701; fax (403) 294-9238; contact@albertalawfoundation.org
Internet: http://www.albertalawfoundation.org/Apply/general.html
Sponsor: Alberta Law Foundation
407 8th Avenue SW, Suite 300
Calgary, AB T2P 1E5 Canada

Albert and Bessie Mae Kronkosky Charitable Foundation Grants 339
The charitable foundation supports efforts to improve the quality of life in San Antonio-area counties for the elderly and those with disabilities; programs encouraging character and leadership development of youth; efforts to free children from abuse and neglect; cultural activities and broadening public participation in museums and libraries; improvement of public parks, zoos, and wildlife sanctuaries; prevention of cruelty to animals; and assistance for victims of public disasters in Texas. The foundation also supports a computer resources program that is designed to build the capacity of nonprofit organizations. Eligible organizations may submit proposals for computer resources for administrative purposes, such as office administration, program evaluation, donor management, and client tracking. Letters of inquiry may be submitted at any time. The distribution committee will meet bi-monthly in January, March, May, July, September and November.
Requirements: Nonprofits in Texas counties Bandera, Bexar, Comal, and Kendall, are eligible to receive grant support.
Restrictions: Grants do not support economic development, annual fund and fundraising event sponsorships, political or lobbying activities, or religious organizations for sectarian purposes.
Geographic Focus: Texas
Amount of Grant: 550 - 1,000,000 USD
Contact: Grants Administrator; (888) 309-9001 or (210) 475-9000; fax (210) 354-2204; kronfndn@kronkosky.org
Internet: http://www.kronkosky.org
Sponsor: Albert and Bessie Mae Kronkosky Charitable Foundation
112 E Pecan Street, Suite 830
San Antonio, TX 78205

Albert and Margaret Alkek Foundation Grants 340
The foundation awards grants to Texas nonprofit organizations to support charitable, religious, scientific (primarily medical), literary, cultural and educational organizations and programs. Preference will be given to research and education-related projects that will pay lasting dividends in terms of new discoveries and improved quality of life. One application per 12-month period will be considered. There are no application deadlines or forms. Applicants should submit a one- to two-page letter of inquiry that includes a brief description of the organization and the project for which funds are being considered, and the amount of funding need in total as well as the amount being requested. Inquiries should be sent via U.S. postal mail; fax or email applications are not accepted.

Requirements: Texas nonprofit organizations are eligible.
Restrictions: The foundation does not make grants to individuals or loans of any type. The foundation does not make direct scholarships to students. All scholarship programs are administered through educational institutions. The foundation prefers not to fund: organizations that in turn make grants to others; grants intended to influence legislation or to support candidates for political office; fund-raising events such as luncheons, dinners, galas, advertising in programs, or other similar activities; charities operated by service clubs; memorials for individuals; student organizations; or purchase of uniforms, equipment, or trips for school-related organizations or sports teams.
Geographic Focus: Texas
Contact: Grants Administrator; (713) 951-0019; fax (713) 951-0043; info@alkek.org
Internet: http://www.alkek.org/grantguidelines.htm
Sponsor: Albert and Margaret Alkek Foundation
1221 McKinney, Suite 4525
Houston, TX 77010-2023

Albert B. Cuppage Charitable Foundation Grants 341
The Foundation has a primary focus of giving to Christian agencies and churches, human and community service organizations, youth groups, general charitable agencies, and individuals. Giving is limited to the Albert Lea, Minnesota, region. Though there are no particular deadlines to abide by, a formal application is required. For further details and guidelines, contact the Foundation directly.
Requirements: A formal application process is required.
Restrictions: Although giving is primarily open to the Albert Lea region and its surrounding area, the Foundation does give grants throughout Minnesota.
Geographic Focus: Minnesota
Amount of Grant: 1,000 - 10,000 USD
Contact: Clarence J. Schroeder, Treasurer; (507) 373-2778
Sponsor: Albert B. Cuppage Charitable Foundation
135 South Broadway
Albert Lea, MN 56007-2545

Albert E. and Birdie W. Einstein Fund Grants 342
The trust awards grants primarily in Florida for the arts and cultural programs; education; and human services, including children and youth services, churches and Jewish services, and families. Contact the office for guidelines and application.
Requirements: Florida nonprofit organizations are eligible.
Geographic Focus: Florida
Amount of Grant: 1,000 - 100,000 USD
Contact: Joyce Boyer, Grants Administrator
Sponsor: Albert E. and Birdie W. Einstein Fund
P.O. Box 246
Islamorada, FL 33036

Alberto Culver Corporate Contributions Grants 343
The company prefers to make small donations to a large number of organizations rather than substantial contributions to a few institutions. Major areas of support are civic and community programs, health and welfare, education, culture and art, and youth activities. Special consideration is given to proposals that benefit a large number of people; directly or indirectly assist women's groups or other purchasers or potential customers of Alberto-Culver products; are involved in programs that rehabilitate, train, teach skills or employ the underprivileged, handicapped or minorities; have received support from Alberto-Culver in the past; and received matching grants for donations. Grants are awarded for one year and may be renewed.
Requirements: Only 501(c)3 organizations are eligible. Requests should be in writing on organization letterhead and should state amount requested, and whether the donation will be used for operating funds, capital expansion, supplies or special projects. The objectives and programs of the organization should be clearly defined.
Restrictions: Grants are not awarded to support United Way affiliates, religious groups, preschools, K-12 schools, tax-supported colleges, projects that duplicate other efforts, and multiyear commitments.
Geographic Focus: All States
Contact: V. James Marino, Director; (708) 450-3000; fax (708) 450-3435
Internet: http://www.alberto.com
Sponsor: Alberto Culver
2525 Armitage Avenue
Melrose Park, IL 60160

Albert Pick Jr. Fund Grants 344
The fund contributes to organizations in the following categories: culture, education, health and human services, civic and community organizations. The fund will consider assistance to new and creative programs within these areas and to operating support. Support will be given to requests from organizations that conduct their programs in Chicago, IL, only. The fund functions on a calendar year; applications are considered four times a year based on dates of board meetings. The fund prefers that prospective grantees call or write for guidelines prior to sending their proposals.
Requirements: Only Illinois organizations may apply.
Restrictions: Funds will not be provided for reduction or liquidation of debts, religious purposes, endowments, long-term commitments, building programs, individuals, political purposes, or advertising/program books.
Geographic Focus: Illinois
Date(s) Application is Due: Jan 21; Apr 1; Jul 1; Oct 1
Amount of Grant: 3,000 USD
Contact: Cleopatra Alexander; (312) 236-1192; cleopatra@albertpickjrfund.org
Internet: http://www.albertpickjrfund.org
Sponsor: Albert Pick Jr. Fund
30 N Michigan Avenue, Suite 1002
Chicago, IL 60602

Albertson's Charitable Giving Grants 345
Albertson's Inc invests in its operating communities and makes corporate contributions to support nonprofits. Areas of charitable giving include health and hunger relief—food banks, churches, and other community-based relief groups; health and nutrition—medical services, flu shots, health screening for diseases such as diabetes and heart disease; and education and development of youth—academic excellence or nurturing efforts. Submit requests in writing and include information about the organization's goals, accomplishments, evaluation plans, leadership, and finances. Requests are accepted throughout the year.
Requirements: Applicants must pass an online eligibility test. Preference will be given to requests that offer volunteerism opportunities.
Restrictions: Contributions cannot be made to churches or religious organizations for purposes of religious advocacy.
Geographic Focus: Arizona, Arkansas, California, Colorado, Delaware, Florida, Georgia, Idaho, Illinois, Indiana, Iowa, Kansas, Louisiana, Maine, Maryland, Massachusetts, Michigan, Minnesota, Mississippi, Missouri, Montana, Nebraska, Nevada, New Hampshire, New Jersey, New Mexico, North Dakota, Oklahoma, Oregon, Pennsylvania, South Dakota, Tennessee, Texas, Utah, Vermont, Washington, Wisconsin, Wyoming
Contact: Community Relations Manager; (877) 932-7948 or (208) 395-6200; fax (208) 395-4382; albertsonscustomercare@albertsons.com
Internet: http://www.albertsons.com/abs_inthecommunity
Sponsor: Albertson's
250 E Parkcenter Boulevard
Boise, ID 83706

Albert W. Cherne Foundation Grants 346
The foundation awards grants to nonprofit organizations, primarily in Minnesota, for general operating support, continuing support, and annual campaigns in its areas of interest, which include adult basic education and literacy, children and youth services, services for the disabled, and human services.
Requirements: Grants support nonprofit organizations primarily in the five-county metropolitan area of Minneapolis and Saint Paul, MN.
Restrictions: Grants do not support veterans, fraternal, or labor organizations; religious purposes; conduit organizations; civil rights/social action groups; mental health counseling; specific-disease organizations; housing programs; individuals; capital improvements; or endowment funds.
Geographic Focus: Minnesota
Amount of Grant: 1,000 - 55,000 USD
Contact: Sara Ribbens; (952) 944-4378; sararibbens@awchernefoundation.org
Sponsor: Albert W. Cherne Foundation
P.O. Box 975
Minneapolis, MN 55440

Albert W. Rice Charitable Foundation Grants 347
The Albert W. Rice Charitable Foundation was established in 1959 to support and promote quality educational, human-services, and health-care programming for underserved populations. In the area of education, the foundation supports academic access, enrichment, and remedial programming for children, youth, adults, and senior citizens that focuses on preparing individuals to achieve while in school and beyond. In the area of health care, the foundation supports programming that improves access to primary care for traditionally underserved individuals, health education initiatives and programming that impact at-risk populations, and medical research. In the area of human services the foundation tries to meet evolving needs of communities. Currently the foundation's focus is on (but is not limited to) youth development, violence prevention, employment, life-skills attainment, and food programs. Grant requests for general operating support are strongly encouraged. Program support and occasional capital support will also be considered. Special consideration is given to charitable organizations that serve the people of Worcester, Massachusetts, and its surrounding communities. The majority of grants from the Rice Foundation are one year in duration; on occasion, multi-year support is awarded. Applicants must apply online at the grant website. Applicants are strongly encouraged to do the following before applying: review the downloadable state application procedures for additional helpful information and clarifications; review the downloadable online-application guidelines at the grant website; review the foundation's funding history (link is available from the grant website); review the online application questions in advance; and review the list of required attachments. These will generally include: a list of board members, financial statements (audited, reviewed, or compiled by independent auditor); an organization summary; a list of other funding sources; an IRS Determination letter; and other required documents. All attachments must be uploaded in the online application as PDF, Word, or Excel files. The application deadline for the Albert W. Rice Charitable Foundation is 11:59 p.m. on July 1. Applicants will be notified of grant decisions before September 30.
Requirements: Applicants must have 501(c)3 tax-exempt status.
Restrictions: The foundation does not support requests from individuals, organizations attempting to influence policy through direct lobbying, or any political campaigns.
Geographic Focus: Massachusetts
Date(s) Application is Due: Jul 1
Contact: Michealle Larkins; (866) 778-6859; michealle.larkins@baml.com
Internet: https://www.bankofamerica.com/philanthropic/fn_search.action
Sponsor: Albert W. Rice Charitable Foundation
225 Franklin Street, 4th Floor, MA1-225-04-02
Boston, MA 02110

Albuquerque Community Foundation Grants 348
The foundation seeks to improve the quality of life in the greater Albuquerque, New Mexico, area by providing support for projects and organizations that serve the community in arts and culture, education, environmental and historic preservation, children and youth, and health and human services. Through its grant program, the foundation supports projects that are innovative, meet the needs of underserved segments of the community, encourage matching funds or additional gifts, promote cooperation among agencies, empower the disadvantaged and disabled, and enhance the effectiveness of local charitable organizations. Types of support include continuing support, general operating support, program development, publication, seed grants, scholarships funds and scholarships to individuals, and technical assistance.
Requirements: IRS 501(c)3 organizations based in Albuquerque, NM, are eligible. Proposals are reviewed on the basis of the following priorities: impact, innovation, leverage, management, and nonduplication.
Restrictions: Grants are generally not made to or for individuals, political or religious purposes, debt retirement, payment of interest or taxes, annual campaigns, endowments, emergency funding, to influence legislation or elections, scholarships, awards, or to private foundations and other grantmaking organizations.
Geographic Focus: New Mexico
Date(s) Application is Due: Apr 16; Aug 15
Amount of Grant: Up to 10,000 USD
Contact: R. Randall Royster; (505) 883-6240; rroyster@albuquerquefoundation.org
Internet: http://www.albuquerquefoundation.org/grants/grant-home.htm
Sponsor: Albuquerque Community Foundation
P.O. Box 36960
Albuquerque, NM 87176-6960

Alcatel-Lucent Technologies Foundation Grants 349
The Alcatel-Lucent Foundation is the philanthropic arm of Alcatel-Lucent and it leads the company's charitable activities. With a focus on volunteerism, the Foundation's mission is to support the commitment of Alcatel-Lucent to social responsibility by serving and enhancing the communities where its employees and customers live and work. To accomplish its mission, the Foundation manages grants and employee volunteerism on a global level. It receives its income from the corporation - Alcatel-Lucent - whose name it bears. However, legally the Foundation is an independent, charitable, non-profit and private entity and is governed by its own board of trustees that is separate from the corporate board of directors. Global Foundation grants are dedicated to the main focus areas of the Foundation and are managed by the Foundation.
Requirements: Giving is on an international basis.
Geographic Focus: All States, All Countries
Amount of Grant: 500 - 5,000 USD
Contact: Bishalakhi Ghosh, Executive Director; +91-99-58418547 or +91-22-66798700; fax +91-22-26598542; bishalakhi.ghosh@alcatel-lucent.com
Internet: http://www.alcatel-lucent.com/wps/portal/foundation
Sponsor: Alcatel-Lucent Technologies Foundation
600 Mountain Avenue, Room 6F4
Murray Hill, NJ 07974-2008

Alcoa Foundation Grants 350
General priorities of the foundation include safe and healthy children and families—ensuring that children and their families have the tools, the knowledge and the services to remain healthy and safe at home, in the community and in the workplace; conservation and sustainability—educating young leaders on conservation issues, protecting forests, promoting sound public policy research, and understanding the linkages between business and the environment; skills today for tomorrow—providing individuals with critical skills and services to be economically connected, workplace-ready, and productive in a changing economy; business and community partnerships—strengthening the nonprofit sector and developing meaningful partnerships among nonprofits, the private sector, and local government; and global education in science, engineering, technology and business—broadening student participation in areas central to Alcoa to prepare a diverse cross-section of our communities for a global workplace. Types of support include capital grants, building funds, challenge grants, matching gifts, general support, research grants, scholarships, and seed money. Initial contact should be a letter of inquiry.
Requirements: The foundation awards grants to nonprofit public charities in communities where Alcoa has a presence. Local Alcoans work within their communities to evaluate organizations and make recommendations for funding to Alcoa Foundation. Nonprofit organizations that serve localized communities should find the Alcoa facility nearest to them and write a one-page letter describing their mission, nature of request, connection to the areas of excellence and offering contact information. If interested, the Alcoa location contact will notify the requesting organization and invite them to submit more information. Areas of operation include western Pennsylvania; Davenport, Iowa; Evansville, Indiana; Massena, New York; New Jersey; Cleveland, Ohio; Knoxville, Tennessee; and Rockdale, Texas.
Restrictions: The foundation does not make gifts to local projects other than those near Alcoa plant or office locations; endowment funds, deficit reduction, or operating reserves; hospital capital campaign programs unless the hospital presents a comprehensive area analysis that justifies, on a regional rather than an individual institutional basis, the need for the capital improvement; individuals, except for the scholarship program for children of Alcoa employees; tickets and other promotional activities; trips, tours, or student exchange programs; or documentaries and videos.
Geographic Focus: All States
Amount of Grant: 1,000 - 50,000 USD
Contact: Meg McDonald, President and Treasurer; (412) 553-2348; fax (412) 553-4498; alcoa.foundation@alcoa.com
Internet: http://www.alcoa.com/global/en/community/foundation.asp
Sponsor: Alcoa Foundation
201 Isabella Street
Pittsburgh, PA 15212-5858

Alcon Foundation Grants 351
The foundation supports organizations in the fields of health care, leadership programs, research, education and community responsibility. Programs that advance the education and skill levels of eye care professionals are given special consideration. General operating grants to organizations and institutions improving education and research in the areas of specialization of Alcon Laboratories—ophthalmology and vision care. Grants are also awarded to community activities that benefit company employees. Applications may be submitted at any time.
Requirements: Grants are not made for building programs.
Restrictions: Non 501(c)3organizations, individuals and scholarship programs, religious, veterans or fraternal organizations, political causes, capital campaigns, matching gifts, trips, tournaments and tours, and endowments are not supported.
Geographic Focus: All States
Amount of Grant: 100 - 50,000 USD
Contact: Mary Dulle, Chair; (817) 293-0450; Mary.Dulle@Alconlabs.com
Internet: http://www.alconlabs.com/corporate-responsibility/alcon-foundation.asp
Sponsor: Alcon Foundation
6201 S Freeway
Fort Worth, TX 76134

Alexander & Baldwin Foundation Hawaiian and Pacific Island Grants 352
The foundation awards grants to eligible Hawaii nonprofit organizations in its areas of interest, including health and human services, education, the community, culture and arts, the maritime arena and the environment. Grant preferences are given to organizations and projects that address significant community needs, have the active support of A&B employees, are preventive in nature, and have demonstrated support of the community. Start-up, general operating and special project needs, as well as major and minor capital requests are considered. Deadlines listed are for organizations in Hawaii and the Pacific Islands. Although the majority of grants range between $1,000 and $5,000, the Foundation considers request upward of $20,000.
Requirements: The foundation gives funding to community-based projects and organizations that qualify with 501(c)3 status.
Restrictions: Grants are not awarded to support United Way agencies for operating support, individuals, events, travel expenses, or scholarships.
Geographic Focus: Hawaii
Date(s) Application is Due: Feb 1; Apr 1; Jun 1; Aug 1; Oct 1; Dec 1
Amount of Grant: 1,000 - 5,000 USD
Contact: Nami Nielipinski, (808) 525-6641; fax (808) 525-6677; nnielipinski@abinc.com
Internet: http://www.alexanderbaldwinfoundation.org/appguide.htm
Sponsor: Alexander and Baldwin Foundation
P.O. Box 3440
Honolulu, HI 96801-3440

Alexander & Baldwin Foundation Mainland Grants 353
The foundation awards grants to eligible U.S. nonprofit organizations in its areas of interest, including health and human services, education, the community, culture and arts, the maritime arena and the environment. Grant preferences are given to organizations and projects that address significant community needs, have the active support of A&B employees, are preventive in nature, and have demonstrated support of the community. Start-up, general operating and special project needs, as well as major and minor capital requests are considered. Although the majority of grants range between $1,000 and $5,000, the Foundation considers request upward of $20,000.
Requirements: The foundation gives funding to community-based projects and organizations that qualify with 501(c)3 status.
Restrictions: Grants are not awarded to support United Way agencies for operating support, individuals, events, travel expenses, or scholarships.
Geographic Focus: All States
Date(s) Application is Due: Jan 1; Feb 1; Mar 1; Apr 1; May 1; Jun 1; Jul 1; Aug 1; Sep 1; Oct 1; Nov 1; Dec 1
Amount of Grant: 1,000 - 5,000 USD
Contact: Paul Merwin, (707) 421-8121; fax (707) 421-1835; plmifm@aol.com
Internet: http://www.alexanderbaldwinfoundation.org/appguide.htm
Sponsor: Alexander and Baldwin Foundation
555 12th Street
Oakland, CA 94607

Alexander and Margaret Stewart Trust Grants 354
The trust awards grants in the greater Washington, DC, area for cancer treatment, especially equipment used in diagnosis and treatment; and caring for children who are physically ill, mentally ill, or disabled. Grants also support research, education, and prevention of common childhood diseases, including negative societal behavioral patterns that impact children. Proposals for projects aiding the economically deprived receive preference. The trust awards start-up funding. Applications may be submitted at any time; requests received by the listed deadline date are reviewed by the end of the year.
Requirements: Nonprofits in the greater District of Columbia area are eligible.
Restrictions: Requests for support of endowments, buildings, or capital campaigns are denied.
Geographic Focus: District of Columbia
Date(s) Application is Due: Sep 15

Amount of Grant: 50,000 - 150,000 USD
Contact: William J. Bierbower, (202) 785-9892; wbierbower@stewart-trust.org
Internet: http://www.stewart-trust.org/guidelines.htm
Sponsor: Alexander and Margaret Stewart Trust
888 17th Street NW, Brawner Building, Suite 610
Washington, DC 20006-3321

Alexander Eastman Foundation Grants 355
The purposes of the Alexander Eastman Foundation are served through grant support to organizations awarded in response to proposals and special initiative commitments planned collaboratively by the Foundation with local service providers. Grants are awarded to support the capital, special projects and operations needs of qualifying organizations. In considering proposals, priority is given to funding activity which serves the Foundation's priority interests. The Alexander Eastman Foundation supports: Education - provide information and community education to improve the health and well-being of residents of the greater Derry area; address goals for healthy individuals and families through a long-term commitment to prevention, health promotion and education of consumers and providers; foster individual responsibility, independence, self-care and healthy life-style choices; Family Systems - strengthen families as the critical unit for community health and well-being; recognize the changing nature of families and provide resources and assistance to reduce stress on families and improve family function; Access - expand access to quality health care and prevention services for people with financial need. Applications are available at the Foundations website.
Requirements: Nonprofit organizations serving Derry, Londonderry, Windham, Chester, Hampstead, and Sandown, NH, are eligible.
Restrictions: Grants are made neither to individuals nor to qualifying organizations to support the cost of services to particular individuals, except through the Alexander Eastman Scholarship Program.
Geographic Focus: New Hampshire
Date(s) Application is Due: Apr 1; Oct 1
Contact: Amy Lockwood; (888) 228-1821, ext. 80; alockwood@alexandereastman.org
Internet: http://www.alexandereastman.org/02grants.html
Sponsor: Alexander Eastman Foundation
26 South Main Street, PMB 250
Concord, NH 03301

Alexander Foundation Emergency Grants 356
The program provides emergency grants to those individuals who are experiencing temporary financial difficulties. Emergency grants are intended for purposes such as rent, security deposits, medical expenses, food, clothing, utility bills and other basic living expenses. The maximum grant is $200. Emergency grants are processed once a week. Referral agencies must call or fax the Alexander Foundation office to request emergency grants for an applicant. Mailed applications will not be accepted.
Requirements: Applicants must be gay, lesbian, bisexual or transgendered, reside in Colorado and pre-approved by a recognized referral agency. Applicants must demonstrate financial need and must not have received an Alexander Foundation emergency grant within the previous 12 month period.
Geographic Focus: Colorado
Amount of Grant: 200 USD
Contact: Jack Heruska; (303) 331-7733; egrants@thealexanderfoundation.org
Internet: http://www.thealexanderfoundation.org/emergency.html
Sponsor: Alexander Foundation
P.O. Box 1995
Denver, CO 80201-1995

Alexander Foundation Holiday Grants 357
The Holiday Grant program provides grants to gay, lesbian, bisexual or transgendered people on a onetime basis during the traditional holiday season. The program is designed to assist individuals with significant chronic problems. Applications are received from potential recipients and from these requests a random sample is selected, pseudonyms assigned, and a direct solicitation to the community is made during November and December. Although many recipients deal with HIV issues, this is not just an HIV related program. The amount of the grant is based on need and the financial support and response from the community but can range generally from $100 to $500. Applications must be received by the stated deadline date, which is usually in November.
Requirements: The recipient must be gay, lesbian, bisexual or transgendered and demonstrate financial need. This program is for HIV and non-HIV persons. Additionally, recipients must reside in Colorado. A certification from a representative of the referring agency must accompany the application.
Geographic Focus: Colorado
Amount of Grant: 100 - 500 USD
Contact: Jack Heruska; (303) 331-7733; egrants@thealexanderfoundation.org
Internet: http://www.thealexanderfoundation.org/holiday.html
Sponsor: Alexander Foundation
P.O. Box 1995
Denver, CO 80201-1995

Alexander H. Bright Charitable Trust Grants 358
The trust operates in Massachusetts and awards general operating grants to nonprofit organizations in its areas of interest, including wildlife and environmental conservation, children and youth, education, and social services. There are no application forms. The board meets in March, June, September, and December.
Requirements: Northeast U.S. nonprofits are eligible. Preference is given to requests from Massachusetts.
Geographic Focus: Connecticut, Maine, Massachusetts, New Hampshire, Rhode Island, Vermont
Amount of Grant: 100 - 75,000 USD
Contact: Administrator, c/o The Boston Family Office; (617) 227-2676 or (617) 624-0800
Sponsor: Alexander H. Bright Charitable Trust
88 Broad Street
Boston, MA 02110

Alex Brown and Sons Charitable Foundation Grants 359
The foundation awards one-year renewable grants to U.S. nonprofit organizations in its areas of interest, including arts and culture, community affairs, education, medicine, and science. Types of support include annual campaigns, capital grants, endowment funds, general operating grants, program development grants, and scholarship funds. Applicants should submit a letter of intent that briefly outlines the purpose of the grant.
Requirements: 501(c)3 tax-exempt organizations in Maryland are eligible.
Restrictions: No support for private schools or churches. Grants are not made to individuals.
Geographic Focus: Maryland
Amount of Grant: 1,000 - 100,000 USD
Contact: Margaret Preston, Secretary, c/o Deutsche Bank Alex Brown Inc
Sponsor: Alex Brown and Sons Charitable Foundation
P.O. Box 2257
Baltimore, MD 21203

Alex Stern Family Foundation Grants 360
The foundation awards grants to North Dakota and Minnesota nonprofits in its areas of interest, including arts and culture, child welfare, the elderly, alcohol abuse, community funds, family and social services, education, minorities, hospices, and cancer research. Types of support include general operating support, continuing support, annual campaigns, building construction/renovation, equipment acquisition, emergency funds, program development, scholarship funds, research, and matching funds. Applications are reviewed in June and November.
Requirements: Moorhead, MN, and Fargo, ND, nonprofit organizations are eligible.
Restrictions: Grants are not awarded to individuals or for endowments.
Geographic Focus: Minnesota, North Dakota
Date(s) Application is Due: Mar 31; Aug 31
Amount of Grant: 1,000 - 50,000 USD
Contact: Donald Scott, Executive Director; (701) 237-0170
Sponsor: Alex Suitern Family Foundation
609 1/2 1st Avenue N, Suite 205
Fargo, ND 58102

ALFJ Astraea U.S. and International Movement Fund 361
Astraea's Movement Resource Fund provides grants to enhance the capacity and effectiveness of our grantee partners and ally organizations to engage in movement building work. Grants are generally provided in three areas: Technical Assistance, Travel/Peer-to-Peer Learning and Historic Convenings. Letters of inquiry are accepted year round.
Requirements: One page letters of inquiry should be sent to the program officer. Information should include information about the organization, the purpose of the request, and a budget summary of how the funds would be used.
Restrictions: Although any organization that fits the funding criteria may apply, Astraea prioritizes current Astraea grantee partners.
Geographic Focus: All States, All Countries
Contact: Namita Chad; (212) 529-8021; fax (212) 982-3321; nchad@astraeafoundation.org
Internet: http://www.astraeafoundation.org/grants/grant-applications-and-deadlines
Sponsor: Astraea Lesbian Foundation for Justice
116 E 16th Street, 7th Floor
New York, NY 10003

ALFJ Astraea U.S. General Fund 362
The Astraea Lesbian Foundation for Justice works for social, racial, and economic justice in the U.S. and internationally. The Foundation's U.S. General Fund offers grants to lesbian, gay, bisexual, transgender, and intersex (LGBTI) social change organizations and projects (including film, video, media and cultural projects) that directly address critical issues in LGBTI communities.
Requirements: Applicants submit letters of interest (accepted throughout the year) to see if their project is appropriate for the Foundation. Applicants are notified within 12 weeks if their project will be reviewed for possible funding. Their primary work must be for social change and they must address the multiple issues of oppression experienced by lesbians and the LGBTI communities (social, racial, economic, and gender). Applicants should refer to the website for current deadlines.
Restrictions: Applicants must have an annual budget of no more than $750,000. Exclusions in funding include: individual projects; organizations with strong leadership from only one individual; private business or profit-making efforts; organizations with budgets of over $750,000; projects that are based in or sponsored by university, college, or other academic institution; capital campaigns, endowments, or deficit financing; social service/research projects or one-time events; organizational projects not based in the U.S; efforts that endorse candidates for public office.
Geographic Focus: All States
Amount of Grant: 4,000 - 10,000 USD
Contact: J. Bob Alotta; (212) 529-8021; fax (212) 982-3321; jbalotta@astraeafoundation.org
Internet: http://www.astraeafoundation.org/grants/grant-applications-and-deadlines
Sponsor: Astraea Lesbian Foundation for Justice
116 E 16th Street, 7th Floor
New York, NY 10003

Grant Programs | 51

Alfred and Tillie Shemanski Testamentary Trust Grants   363
Alfred Shemanski was an immigrant from Poland with little formal education. He understood the struggles of being a stranger in a strange land and became a champion for both Jewish and secular education. His successes never blinded him to the plight of those less fortunate. Mr. Shemanski exercised philanthropy in the purest definition of the word — love of mankind. The Alfred & Tillie Shemanski Trust was established in 1974 to: improve the capacity of and cooperation among Jewish congregations in the City of Seattle, Washington; support interfaith tolerance and understanding; provide scholarship assistance, primarily to the University of Washington and Seattle University; and support and promote quality educational, human-services, and health-care programming for economically disadvantaged individuals and families. Grant requests for general operating support, start-up funding, and prizes or awards are encouraged. Grants from the Shemanski Trust are one year in duration. Application materials are available for download at the grant website. Applicants are strongly encouraged to review the state application guidelines for additional helpful information and clarifications before applying. Applicants are also encouraged to review the trust's funding history (link is available from the grant website). The application deadline for the Shemanski Trust is October 15. Applicants will be notified of grant decisions before November 30.
Requirements: Applicants must serve residents of the Seattle and Puget Sound area.
Restrictions: Requests for fundraising events or sponsorship opportunities will not be considered. The trust does not support requests from individuals, organizations attempting to influence policy through direct lobbying, or any political campaigns.
Geographic Focus: Washington
Date(s) Application is Due: Oct 15
Contact: Nancy Atkinson, Vice President; (800) 848-7177; nancy.l.atkinson@baml.com
Internet: https://www.bankofamerica.com/philanthropic/fn_search.action
Sponsor: Alfred and Tillie Shemanski Testamentary Trust
800 5th Avenue, WA1-501-33-23
Seattle, WA 98104

Alfred Bersted Foundation Grants   364
The Alfred Bersted Foundation was established in 1972 to support and promote quality educational, human services, and health care programming for underserved populations. The Foundation specifically serves the people of DeKalb, DuPage, Kane, and McHenry counties in Illinois. Application materials are available for download at the grant website. Applicants are strongly encouraged to review the state application guidelines for additional helpful information and clarifications before applying. Applicants are also encouraged to review the foundation's funding history (link is available from the grant website). The foundation has a rolling application deadline. In general, applicants will be notified of grant decisions three to four months after proposal submission.
Requirements: Applicant organizations must have 501(c)3 tax-exempt status and a physical presence in one of the following counties: DeKalb, DuPage, Kane, or McHenry.
Restrictions: The Alfred Bersted Foundation does not make grants to degree-conferring institutions of higher education, religious houses of worship, or organizations testing for public safety. In general, grant requests for endowment campaigns will not be considered.
Geographic Focus: Illinois
Contact: Debra Grand; (312) 828-4154; ilgrantmaking@bankofamerica.com
Internet: https://www.bankofamerica.com/philanthropic/fn_search.action
Sponsor: Alfred Bersted Foundation
231 South LaSalle Street, IL1-231-13-32
Chicago, IL 60604

Alfred C. and Ersa S. Arbogast Foundation Grants   365
The Alfred C. and Ersa S. Arbogast Foundation, established in Indiana, supports organizations and programs throughout the State of Indiana, as well as a few throughout the United States. The Foundation's primary fields of interest include: animal/wildlife preservation and protection; human service programs; and United Ways and federated programs. The major type of support being offered is general operations funding. There are no particular deadlines or application formats with which to adhere, and applicants should submit the following: copy of IRS determination letter; and a detailed description of the project, with the amount of funding requested.
Requirements: 501(c)3 organizations located in, or supporting the residents of, Indiana can apply, as well as non-profits whose goals are aligned with the Arbogast Foundation's.
Geographic Focus: All States
Contact: Michelle Kindler, Lake City Bank Trustee; (260) 428-5009 or (574) 267-9187
Sponsor: Alfred C. and Ersa S. Arbogast Foundation
114 E. Market Street, P.O. 1387
Warsaw, IN 46580

Alfred E. Chase Charitable Foundation Grants   366
The Alfred E. Chase Charitable Foundation was established in 1956 to support and promote quality educational, human-services, and health-care programming for underserved populations. Special consideration is given to charitable organizations that serve the people of the city of Lynn and the North Shore of Massachusetts. The foundation is a generous supporter of the Associated Grant Makers (AGM) Summer Fund which provides operating support for summer camps serving low-income urban youth from Boston, Cambridge, Chelsea, and Somerville. Excluding the grant to the AGM Summer Fund, the typical grant range is $10,000 to $30,000. In the area of education the foundation supports academic access, enrichment, and remedial programming for children, youth, adults, and senior citizens that focuses on preparing individuals to achieve while in school and beyond. In the area of human services the foundation supports organizations meeting the basic needs of all individuals to include but not limited to youth development, violence prevention, employment, life skills attainment, and food programs. In the area of health care, the foundation supports programming that improves access to primary care for traditionally underserved individuals, as well as supporting health education initiatives and programs that impact at-risk populations. Grant requests for general operating support are strongly encouraged. Program support will also be considered. Small, program-related capital expenses may be included in general operating or program requests. The majority of grants from the Chase Charitable Foundation are one year in duration. On occasion, multi-year support is awarded. Applicants must apply online at the grant website. Applicants are strongly encouraged to do the following before applying: review the downloadable Massachusetts state application procedures for additional helpful information and clarifications; review the downloadable online-application guidelines at the grant website; review the foundation's funding history (link is available from the grant website); review the online application questions in advance; and review the list of required attachments. These will generally include: a list of board members, financial statements (audited, reviewed, or compiled by independent auditor); an organization summary; a list of other funding sources; an IRS Determination letter; and other required documents. All attachments must be uploaded in the online application as PDF, Word, or Excel files. The application deadline is 11:59 p.m. on April 1. Applicants will be notified of grant decisions before June 30.
Requirements: Applicants must have 501(c)3 tax-exempt status.
Restrictions: The foundation does not support requests from individuals, organizations attempting to influence policy through direct lobbying, or any political campaigns.
Geographic Focus: Massachusetts
Date(s) Application is Due: Apr 1
Amount of Grant: 10,000 - 30,000 USD
Contact: Miki C. Akimoto, Vice President; (866) 778-6859; miki.akimoto@baml.com
Internet: https://www.bankofamerica.com/philanthropic/fn_search.action
Sponsor: Alfred E. Chase Charitable Foundation
225 Franklin Street, 4th Floor, MA1-225-04-02
Boston, MA 02110

Alfred J Mcallister and Dorothy N Mcallister Foundation Grants   367
The foundation was established in 2000 and gives primarily in the Greater Lafayette area in Indiana. Giving has been focused on animals and wildlife, educational programs and human services in the immediate community. Grants typically range up to $50,0000.
Requirements: Unsolicited requests for funds and applications are not accepted. The foundation has a preference for giving in the immediate area of Lafayette, Indiana. Send a letter of inquiry via mail to determine if the foundation will consider entertaining a request.
Geographic Focus: Indiana
Amount of Grant: Up to 50,000 USD
Contact: Charles Max Layden, (765) 742-7646; fax (765) 742-0983
Sponsor: Alfred J Mcallister and Dorothy N Mcallister Foundation
2310 N 725 E
Lafayette, IN 47905

Alfred P. Sloan Foundation Civic Initiatives Grants   368
The goal of the Program is to make a contribution to the Foundation's home area, New York City. There are two directions to the Program: to respond to special opportunities in New York City; and to fund high-leverage projects in New York City that are related to other parts of our program. Interested readers should refer to the descriptions of other program areas in the Foundation website. Grant requests can be made at any time for support of activities related to Foundation program areas and interests. The Foundation is generally limited to supporting tax-exempt organizations.
Requirements: Concise, well-organized proposals are preferred. In no case should the body of the proposal exceed 20 double-spaced pages.
Restrictions: The Foundation's activities do not normally extend to religion, the creative or performing arts, elementary or secondary education, medical research or health care, the humanities or to activities outside the United States. Grants are not made for endowments or for buildings or equipment.
Geographic Focus: New York
Contact: Paula J. Olsiewski, (212) 649-1658 or (212) 649-1649; olsiewski@sloan.org
Internet: http://www.sloan.org/major-program-areas/select-national-issues/civic-initiatives/
Sponsor: Alfred P. Sloan Foundation
630 Fifth Avenue, Suite 2550
New York, NY 10111-0242

Alfred P. Sloan Foundation Public Service Awards   369
The goal of this program is to recognize outstanding contributions by outstanding civil servants. This program annually honors six outstanding civil servants whose work performance and commitment to the public transcend not merely the ordinary but the extraordinary - day after day and year after year. In honoring these winners, the Fund also acknowledges the contributions of the many thousands of dedicated public servants who, with integrity and devotion, perform the work that keeps this complex city running.
Geographic Focus: New York
Samples: Sarah Carroll, Director of Preservation, Landmarks Preservation Commission (2012); Donna Leno Gordon. Director, Behavioral Health Nursing and Palliative Care, Coney Island Hospital, Health and Hospitals Corporation (2012); James McConnell, Assistant Commissioner for Strategic Data, Office of Emergency Management (2012).
Contact: Paula J. Olsiewski, Program Director; (212) 649-1658 or (212) 649-1649; fax (212) 757-5117; olsiewski@sloan.org
Internet: http://www.sloan.org/program/31
Sponsor: Alfred P. Sloan Foundation
630 Fifth Avenue, Suite 2550
New York, NY 10111-0242

Alfred P. Sloan Foundation Selected National Issues Grants 370
The Alfred P. Sloan Foundation recognizes that there are select opportunities outside of science, education and economics in which it can create an important benefit to society. Its National Issues program area looks for unique opportunities where Foundation funds promise to advance a significant national interest. Grants in the Select National Issues program are funding work to increase America's biosecurity and investigate how recent advances in information technology affect the spread of knowledge and the structure of scientific endeavor. The Foundation has no deadlines or standard forms. The Foundation accepts proposals sent by email. A brief letter of inquiry, rather than a fully developed proposal, is an advisable first step for an applicant, conserving his or her time and allowing for a preliminary response regarding the possibility of support.
Requirements: Concise, well-organized proposals are preferred. In no case should the body of the proposal exceed 20 double-spaced pages.
Restrictions: The Foundation does not make grants: to individuals; to for-profit institutions (except in rare instances); in religion, medical research or the humanities; to projects aimed at pre-college students; to projects in the creative or performing arts, except when those projects are related to educating the public about science, technology or economics; for endowments, buildings or equipment, or fundraising drives, including fundraising dinners; or to political campaigns, to support political activities or to lobby for or against particular pieces of legislation.
Geographic Focus: All States
Contact: Paula J. Olsiewski, (212) 649-1658 or (212) 649-1649; olsiewski@sloan.org
Internet: http://www.sloan.org/about-the-foundation/staff-directory/show-staff/show/people/paula-j-olsiewski/
Sponsor: Alfred P. Sloan Foundation
630 Fifth Avenue, Suite 2550
New York, NY 10111-0242

Alice C. A. Sibley Fund Grants 371
The purpose of the Alice C.A. Sibley Fund is to provide medical eye care to vulnerable populations of all ages in Worcester including: hospital and surgical fees; medical equipment; and eye glasses and corrective treatment. Approximately $24,000 in grants will be awarded annually to one or more organizations that directly support people's eye health.
Requirements: Applicants must be tax-exempt, nonprofit organizations as recognized by IRS code 501(c)3, and must be located in or providing services to residents of Worcester, Massachusetts.
Geographic Focus: Massachusetts
Date(s) Application is Due: Apr 15
Amount of Grant: Up to 24,000 USD
Contact: Lois Smith; (508) 755-0980, ext. 107; lsmith@greaterworcester.org
Internet: http://www.greaterworcester.org/grants/Sibley.htm
Sponsor: Greater Worcester Community Foundation
370 Main Street, Suite 650
Worcester, MA 01608-1738

Alice Tweed Tuohy Foundation Grants 372
The foundation promotes organizations that promote young people; that provide outstanding opportunities for performance, growth, and creativity; that nurture personal integrity and ambition; and that reward high achievement. The foundation assists organizations offering services to children whose choices might otherwise be unfairly restricted by need; supported are activities both academic and extracurricular that challenge young people while encouraging the growth of responsibility and personal integrity. Organizations dedicated to improving the quality of life by meeting the vital needs of the community are also supported. Types of support include building construction/ renovation, scholarship funds, and matching funds. Financing priority is accorded those organizations with the least in-house capacity to raise capital, assisting these groups to surmount critical monetary obstacles and continue productive service to the community. Proposals may be submitted annually between July 1 and September 15. However, the foundation has announced that a three-year partial moratorium period on awarding grants will commence July 1, 2009.
Requirements: Applications are considered only from Santa Barbara, CA public, tax-exempt organizations. Priority consideration is given to applications from organizations serving young people, education, health and medicine, community affairs, and the arts.
Restrictions: Excluded from consideration are applications for the benefit of specific individuals, organizations outside the Santa Barbara area, organizations in overpopulated nonprofit areas, national campaigns, fund-raising normally carried out by the organization, operating expenses, or budgetary support.
Geographic Focus: California
Date(s) Application is Due: Sep 15
Amount of Grant: 750 - 98,000 USD
Contact: Program Contact; (805) 962-6430; fax (805) 962-7135; atuohyfdn@aol.com
Sponsor: Alice Tweed Tuohy Foundation
205 E Carrillo Street, Room 219, P.O. Box 1328
Santa Barbara, CA 93102-1328

A Little Hope Grants 373
A Little Hope is a not-for-profit publicly supported charitable foundation, recognized by the IRS under 501(c)3, which grants funds to organizations that provide bereavement support services and grief counseling to children and teens who have experienced the death of a parent, sibling or loved one. Strong preference is given to applicants who demonstrate a commitment to the use of community trained volunteers, whose programs demonstrate multicultural competence in addressing children and adolescent's bereavement needs, and whose programs are likely to be replicable in other communities. Grant applications are by invitation only and are processed during the last quarter of each year. To be considered, email (no telephone calls): the name of your program, your website address, the name of your executive director, and the name of the program director, including their credentials. No other information is needed or will be processed. Do not send letters of inquiry or any other materials unless they have been requested by A Little Hope. No other organizations are authorized to solicit RFP's or information on our behalf.
Geographic Focus: All States
Contact: Tanhya Vancho; (516) 639-6727; granting@alittlehope.org
Internet: http://www.alittlehope.org/granting/applicants.aspx
Sponsor: A Little Hope
810 Seventh Avenue, 37th Floor
New York, NY 10019

Allan C. and Leila J. Garden Foundation Grants 374
The mission of the Allan C. and Leila J. Garden Foundation is to support charitable organizations that maintain, care for and educate orphan or underprivileged children. It is also the Foundation's intent to support organizations that provide medical, dental, hospital care, nursing and treatment of crippled or physically handicapped children. Grants from Allan C. and Leila J. Garden Foundation are primarily one year in duration. On occasion, multi-year support is awarded. Applicants must apply online at the grant website. Applicants are strongly encouraged to do the following before applying: review the downloadable state application procedures for additional helpful information and clarifications; review the downloadable online-application guidelines at the grant website; review the foundation's funding history (link is available from the grant website); review the online application questions in advance; and review the list of required attachments. These will generally include: a list of board members, financial statements (audited, reviewed, or compiled by independent auditor); an organization summary; a list of other funding sources; an IRS Determination letter; and other required documents. All attachments must be uploaded in the online application as PDF, Word, or Excel files. The Allan C. & Leila J. Garden Foundation application deadline is 11:59 p.m. on June 1. Applicants will be notified of grant decisions by letter within three to four months after the deadline.
Requirements: Applicants must have 501(c)3 tax-exempt status and serve residents of Ben Hill, Irwin, and Wilcox Counties in Georgia. A breakdown of number/percentage of people served by specific counties is required on the online application.
Restrictions: The foundation does not support requests from individuals, organizations attempting to influence policy through direct lobbying, or any political campaigns.
Geographic Focus: Georgia
Date(s) Application is Due: Jun 1
Contact: Quanda Allen, Vice President; (404) 264-1377; quanda.allen@baml.com
Internet: https://www.bankofamerica.com/philanthropic/fn_search.action
Sponsor: Allan C. and Leila J. Garden Foundation
3414 Peachtree Road, N.E., Suite 1475, GA7-813-14-04
Atlanta, GA 30326-1113

Allegan County Community Foundation Grants 375
The foundation awards one-year grants to eligible Michigan charitable organizations to improve the quality of life in Allegan County. Areas of interest include education, health, and social services. Types of support include youth grants, general grants, matching/challenge grants, building construction/renovation, program development, and emergency funds. A copy of the IRS tax-exemption letter must be submitted with application. Any youth group, club, school or class can apply for the T.A.G. awards but must have an adult leader who oversees the project and any funds awarded.
Requirements: 501(c)3 tax-exempt organizations serving Allegan County, Michigan, residents are eligible. All applicants are required to schedule an appointment with foundation staff prior to submitting an application.
Restrictions: Individuals are ineligible. All T.A.G. mini-grants must be handwritten by youth 18 or younger.
Geographic Focus: Michigan
Date(s) Application is Due: Dec 4
Contact: Theresa Bray, Executive Director; (269) 673-8344; fax (269) 673-8745
Internet: http://www.alleganfoundation.org/grants.htm
Sponsor: Allegan County Community Foundation
524 Marshall Street
Allegan, MI 49010

Allegheny Foundation Grants 376
The foundation awards general operating grants, seed grants, and grants for projects and programs to nonprofit organizations in western Pennsylvania in the areas of education, historic preservation, and civic development. There are no application forms or deadlines. The foundation generally considers grants at an annual meeting held in November; however, requests may be submitted at any time and will be reviewed as soon as possible.
Requirements: Initial inquiries should be in letter form signed by the organization's president, or authorized representative, and have the approval of the board of directors. The letter should include a concise description of the specific program for which funds are requested. Additional information must include a budget for the program and for the organization, the latest audited financial statement, an annual report, and a board of director's list. A copy of the organization's 501(c)3 letter is required. Only Pennsylvania residents may apply.
Restrictions: Grants are not made to individuals.
Geographic Focus: Pennsylvania
Amount of Grant: 1,000 - 100,000 USD
Contact: Matthew Groll, Executive Director; (412) 392-2900
Internet: http://www.scaife.com/alleghen.html
Sponsor: Allegheny Foundation
1 Oxford Center, 301 Grant Street, Suite 3900
Pittsburgh, PA 15219-6401

Allegheny Technologies Charitable Trust 377
The corporation awards one-year renewable grants to nonprofit organizations to enhance the quality of life for people in company operating locations. Areas of interest include arts and culture, civic and public affairs, education, health, and social services. Types of support include capital grants, general operating grants, program development grants, and employee matching gifts. Applicants should submit a letter of inquiry that describes the organization, purpose of grants, and funds sought. No particular form or information is required. Potential applicants are requested to provide proof of exempt public charity status. There are no deadlines.
Requirements: 501(c)3 tax-exempt organizations in company-operating areas are eligible.
Restrictions: Contributions are made only to public charities. Individuals and private foundations are excluded.
Geographic Focus: Pennsylvania
Amount of Grant: 1,000 - 35,000 USD
Samples: Pittsburgh Symphony Society (Pittsburgh, PA)—grant recipient, $55,000.
Contact: Jon D. Walton, Jr., Trustee; (412) 394-2800; fax (412) 394-3034
Internet: http://www.alleghenytechnologies.com
Sponsor: Allegheny Technologies
1000 Six PPG Place
Pittsburgh, PA 15222

Allen Hilles Fund Grants 378
The fund awards grants to support education, women's issues, economic development in disadvantaged communities, activities of the Religious Society of Friends, and organizations with annual budgets of less than $2 million. Types of support include project grants, seed money, and operating support for small organizations.
Requirements: Philadelphia-area and Wilmington nonprofit organizations are eligible.
Restrictions: Funding requests for endowments, scholarships, capital expenditures, political purposes, or agency promotion (i.e., marketing, development, publication of annual reports, or fundraising events) are denied.
Geographic Focus: Delaware, Pennsylvania
Date(s) Application is Due: Feb 1; May 1; Oct 1
Amount of Grant: 3,000 - 10,000 USD
Contact: Judith L. Bardes, Manager; (610) 828-8145; fax (610) 834-8175; hilles@grants-info.org or judy1@aol.com
Internet: http://www.grants-info.org/hilles
Sponsor: Allen Hilles Fund
P.O. Box 540
Plymouth Meeting, PA 19462

Allen Lane Foundation Grants 379
The foundation operates in the United Kingdom and Ireland in the field of social welfare and awards grants to institutions at the local, regional, and national levels. Areas of interest include projects in Scotland, Northern Ireland, Wales, and regions outside the London area; groups supporting refugees and asylum-seekers; advisory and information services; and the coordination of small groups. The broad areas of work which are priorities for the foundation include the provision of advice, information, and advocacy; community development; employment and training; mediation, conflict resolution, and alternatives to violence; research and education aimed at changing public attitudes or policy; and social welfare.
Requirements: Grants may be made for project costs or revenue costs. The foundation no longer has closing dates.
Restrictions: The foundation only very rarely makes grants to national organizations with an income of more than $500,000 per annum or to local organizations with an income of more than about $150,000. Grants are not made to individuals.
Geographic Focus: All States, United Kingdom
Amount of Grant: 500 - 15,000 GBP
Contact: Gill Aconley; 01-904-613-223; fax 01-904-613-133; info@allenlane.org.uk
Internet: http://www.allenlane.org.uk
Sponsor: Allen Lane Foundation
90 The Mount
York, YO24 1AR England

Allen P. and Josephine B. Green Foundation Grants 380
The mission of the foundation is to improve the quality of life in Missouri. Grants support programs to bring health care services to people; counseling and educational services for children and adults with physical, mental, or behavioral problems; innovative developmental and educational programs for children; cultural and preservation projects to safeguard our heritage and to promote broader awareness and understanding of such programs and activities on the part of Missourians; and environmental and conservation projects based in Missouri. Grants will be made for one year only. Priority will be given to new projects and to those that have not been funded for at least one year. The board meets in May and November. Guidelines are available online.
Requirements: Grants are awarded to 501(c)3 nonprofit organizations in Missouri.
Restrictions: Grants are not awarded to individuals; to projects and programs located outside of the United States; to charities that are not publicly supported; for social causes or for social activism; for lobbying, propagandizing, or for political campaigns; or to requests deemed as inappropriate for a variety of other reasons. Grant requests that probably will not be approved include projects and programs located outside of Missouri; commitment of funds for more than one year; funding to the same organization for two years in a row; grants for operating funds and annual budgets; unspecified general funds; other than to specific projects or programs; projects with a perceived small chance of success; programs that would seem unlikely to continue without further funding from the Green Foundation; large capital fund drives; large building fund drives; large endowments; to an organization whose primary mission is to raise and distribute funds; or to federated giving programs.
Geographic Focus: Missouri
Date(s) Application is Due: Mar 15; Jun 15; Sep 15; Dec 15
Contact: Walter Staley, Jr. , Secretary-Treasurer; (573) 581-5568; fax (573) 581-1714; wstaley@greenfdn.org
Internet: http://www.greenfdn.org
Sponsor: Allen P. and Josephine B. Green Foundation
P.O. Box 523
Mexico, MO 65265

All for the Earth Foundation Grants 381
Established in 1999, the All for the Earth Foundation concentrates its giving in the states of Minnesota and California. Primary areas of interest include: education, the environment, humanities, and community programs. There are no specific application forms, guidelines, or deadlines with which to adhere, and potential applicants should begin by contacting the office directly in writing.
Requirements: Applicants should be 501(c)3 organizations serving the residents of Minnesota or California.
Geographic Focus: All States
Amount of Grant: 3,000 USD
Contact: John D. Westley, (952) 891-2100
Sponsor: All for the Earth Foundation
1747 Bluebill Drive
Eagan, MN 55122

Alliance for Community Trees Home Depot Foundation NeighborWoods Grants 382
The Alliance for Community Trees manages competitive pass-through grants funded by The Home Depot Foundation. Grants go to the community coalitions with the most innovative, promising approaches for using urban forestry to grow stronger, healthier neighborhoods. The program enhances community quality of life by engaging citizens in the planting, care, and stewardship of their community trees.
Requirements: Applicants with an urban forestry mission and focus, sustained community presence, and record of tangible, on-the-ground achievements are preferred. Projects must feature a partnership between the grantee and a local KaBOOM! project, affiliate of YouthBuild USA, a community development corporation, an affordable housing organization, or other community-based group. Projects that enhance locations where Home Depot volunteers have previously built playgrounds or constructed or rehabilitated affordable housing are highly desirable.
Geographic Focus: All States
Contact: Jared Liu; (301) 220-3279; fax (301) 277-0042; jared@actrees.org
Internet: http://actrees.org/site/whatwedo/nwGrants.php
Sponsor: Alliance for Community Trees
4603 Calvert Road
College Park, MD 20740

Alliance Healthcare Foundation Grants 383
The Foundation provides a public voice for the critical health care needs of its communities. Areas of interest include: Access to Health, Mental Health, Community Health, and HIV Health Care programs. Grants to local organizations support a wide range of programs and services. Priority is given to program and financing strategies that can produce discernible outcomes. All grant applicants should start by submitting a Letter of Intent (LOI), written and addressed according to the Foundation's guidelines. The LOI is the only form of application the Foundation accepts. Letters are reviewed on a monthly basis. Each is carefully evaluated by program staff in relation to other funding requests. Applicants will be notified about the results of the review within four to six weeks.
Restrictions: The Foundation does not fund projects and programs outside San Diego and Imperial Counties. In addition, the Foundation does not fund: research; lobbying; underwriting of medical expenses; general operating expenses we deem to be excessive; construction or renovation; the purchase of costly equipment; development activities, such as fundraising events, capital campaigns or annual fund drives; projects or proposals from individuals; or organizations that do not have 501(c)3 status.
Geographic Focus: California
Contact: Karen Romero, (858) 614-4888; fax (858) 874 3656; kromero@alliancehf.org
Internet: http://www.alliancehf.org/grants_prog/what_we_fund/access_healthcare.html
Sponsor: Alliance Healthcare Foundation
9325 Sky Park Court, Suite 350
San Diego, CA 92123

Alliant Energy Foundation Community Grants 384
The Alliant Energy Foundation's community grants are directed to programs and projects that benefit the residents and communities in the four Midwestern states (Illinois, Iowa, Minnesota, Wisconsin) served by Alliant Energy's utility subsidiaries, Interstate Power and Light Company and Wisconsin Power and Light Company. Alliant Energy gives primary emphasis to organizations in communities where Alliant has a presence and where Alliant Energy employees live and work. The Foundation supports organizations and programs in the areas of human needs, education, culture and art, and civic engagement. Projects that qualify in multiple categories receive special consideration for funding. Organizations that support the physical and emotional well being of people across all age groups, educate and motivate today's youth, place an emphasis on excellence in education, promote literacy, culture and arts activities that enhance the overall quality of life in the area, civic organizations that strengthen the overall quality of life, and organizations that promote environmental initiatives are all supported. Requests are accepted on an ongoing basis throughout the year, but are considered only in the next grant making cycle.

Requirements: All applicants must be helping to improve the quality of life in Illinois, Iowa, Minnesota, and Wisconsin. Eligible organizations should be either: 501(c)3 tax-exempt organizations; fully accredited public or private schools or universities; or instruments of federal, state or local governments as provided by Section 170(c)1 of the Code.
Restrictions: The foundation does not fund contributions to individuals; energy assistance projects; ads in programs, door prizes, raffle tickets, dinner tables, golf outings, or sponsorships of organized sports teams or activities; religious, fraternal, or social clubs; endowments; fiscal agents; fraternal or social clubs; religious institutions whose main purpose is to promote a specific faith, creed or religion and/or direct resources to advocate for a specific ideology; endowments; registration or participation fees for individuals or teams for fundraising events; or books, magazines, or professional journal articles.
Geographic Focus: Illinois, Iowa, Minnesota, Wisconsin
Date(s) Application is Due: Jan 15; May 15; Sep 15
Amount of Grant: 500 - 5,000 USD
Contact: Julie Bauer; (608) 458-4483 or (866) 769-3779; foundation@alliantenergy.com
Internet: http://www.alliantenergy.com/CommunityInvolvement/CharitableFoundation/Programs/029784
Sponsor: Alliant Energy Foundation
4902 North Biltmore Lane, Suite 1000
Madison, WI 53718-2148

Alliant Energy Foundation Hometown Challenge Grants 385
Hometown Challenge Grants are designed to enhance efforts and provide assistance in meeting an important community need. Participation in the program requires commitment on behalf of an organization and the Alliant Energy Foundation. Applicants should obtain the Foundation's approval and commitment prior to the start of any fundraising efforts. Once the applicant reaches their fundraising goal and meets specific requirements, the Foundation will reward hard work by matching the dollars raised on a one-to-one basis up to $3,000.
Requirements: Applicants must hold at least two fundraising events to qualify for the program, but the more fundraisers you have, the more dollars you qualify for. The project must be a special, one-time, safety-related effort and not an ongoing fundraising event.
Geographic Focus: Illinois, Iowa, Minnesota, Wisconsin
Contact: Julie Bauer; (608) 458-4483 or (866) 769-3779; foundation@alliantenergy.com
Internet: http://www.alliantenergy.com/CommunityInvolvement/CharitableFoundation/Programs/029791
Sponsor: Alliant Energy Foundation
4902 North Biltmore Lane, Suite 1000
Madison, WI 53718-2148

Allstate Corporate Giving Grants 386
Allstate is a company of energized people with great ideas. The Corporate Giving program is committed to supporting the communities where company employees live and work by contributing to programs where its experience, partnership and leadership will have the greatest impact. The company offers financial support to a variety of programs and organizations throughout the country that help create strong and vital communities.
Requirements: The Allstate Corporation makes grants to nonprofit, tax-exempt groups under Section 501(c)3 of the Internal Revenue Code.
Geographic Focus: All States
Contact: Director; (847) 402-5000 or (847) 402-5502; allfound@allstate.com
Internet: http://www.allstate.com/social-responsibility/social-impact/corporate-contributions.aspx
Sponsor: Allstate Corporation
2775 Sanders Road, Suite F4
Northbrook, IL 60062

Allstate Corporate Hometown Commitment Grants 387
Allstate takes a special interest in the greater Chicagoland community, the company's hometown for more than 75 years. The corporation is particularly invested in this community because it recognizes that a thriving hometown is critical to Allstate's success. The company recruits local talent, relies on local infrastructure, and depends on the city's vibrancy to ensure that its associates have a rich quality of life. By supporting organizations that build strong Chicagoland communities, the company contributes to the city's position as a center of global culture, education and business.
Requirements: The Allstate Corporation makes grants to Chicago area nonprofit, tax-exempt groups under Section 501(c)3 of the Internal Revenue Code.
Geographic Focus: Illinois, Indiana
Contact: Director; (847) 402-5000 or (847) 402-5502; allfound@allstate.com
Internet: http://www.allstate.com/social-responsibility/corporate/corporate-giving.aspx
Sponsor: Allstate Corporation
2775 Sanders Road, Suite F4
Northbrook, IL 60062

Allstate Foundation Agency Hands in the Community Grants 388
Established in 1952, The Allstate Foundation is an independent, charitable organization made possible by subsidiaries of The Allstate Corporation. Allstate employees, agency owners and personal financial representatives are committed volunteers in the communities where they live and work. Collectively, they volunteer more than 200,000 hours each year. To recognize outstanding community involvement, The Allstate Foundation awards $500 and $1,000 grants to nonprofit organizations with Allstate volunteers. These grants are by invitation only from the Allstate volunteer. Awards are managed through field office grant committees, which meet regularly to review requests.
Requirements: The Allstate Foundation makes grants to nonprofit, tax-exempt organizations under Section 501(c)3 of the Internal Revenue Code, or be a municipal, state or federal government entity.
Restrictions: The Foundation does not support the following: individuals; fundraising events, sponsorships; capital and endowment campaigns; equipment purchase unless part of a community outreach program; athletic events; memorial grants; athletic teams, bands, and choirs; organizations that advocate religious beliefs or restrict participation on the basis of religion; groups or organizations that will re-grant the Foundation's gift to other organizations or individuals; scouting groups; private secondary schools; requests to support travel; grant requests for production of audio, film, or video; multiyear pledge requests; or non-domestic (international) causes.
Geographic Focus: All States
Amount of Grant: 500 - 1,000 USD
Contact: Vicky Dinges, Vice President of Corporate Social Responsibility; (847) 402-5600 or (847) 402-7893; fax (847) 326-7517; allfound@allstate.com
Internet: http://www.allstate.com/foundation/employee-agency-grants.aspx
Sponsor: Allstate Foundation
2775 Sanders Road, Suite F4
Northbrook, IL 60062-6127

Allstate Foundation Economic Empowerment Grants 389
Established in 1952, The Allstate Foundation is an independent, charitable organization made possible by subsidiaries of The Allstate Corporation. The Foundation is committed to empowering Americans with the economic resources and knowledge they need to make informed decisions about their financial future. Its Economic Empowerment funding priorities are: domestic violence - helping survivors live free and stay free from violence by building their financial security; and financial and economic literacy - building a more secure financial future for Americans. Proposals are accepted throughout the year, though the regional grant proposal deadline is May 31. The average grant amount ranges from $5,000 to $20,000.
Requirements: The Allstate Foundation makes grants to nonprofit, tax-exempt organizations under Section 501(c)3 of the Internal Revenue Code, or be a municipal, state or federal government entity.
Restrictions: The Foundation does not support the following: individuals; fundraising events, sponsorships; capital and endowment campaigns; equipment purchase unless part of a community outreach program; athletic events; memorial grants; athletic teams, bands, and choirs; organizations that advocate religious beliefs or restrict participation on the basis of religion; groups or organizations that will re-grant the Foundation's gift to other organizations or individuals; scouting groups; private secondary schools; requests to support travel; grant requests for production of audio, film, or video; multiyear pledge requests; or non-domestic (international) causes.
Geographic Focus: All States
Amount of Grant: 5,000 - 20,000 USD
Contact: Vicky Dinges, Vice President of Corporate Social Responsibility; (847) 402-5600 or (847) 402-7893; fax (847) 326-7517; allfound@allstate.com
Internet: http://www.allstatefoundation.org/grant-focus-areas
Sponsor: Allstate Foundation
2775 Sanders Road, Suite F4
Northbrook, IL 60062-6127

Allstate Foundation Safe and Vital Communities Grants 390
Established in 1952, The Allstate Foundation is an independent, charitable organization made possible by subsidiaries of The Allstate Corporation. The Foundation is dedicated to fostering safe and vital communities where people live, work and raise families. We strive to foster communities that are economically strong, crime-free, and give residents a sense of belonging and commitment. Our Safe and Vital Communities funding priorities are: teen safe driving - helping to save young lives and instill a lifetime of safe driving attitudes and behaviors; catastrophe response - rebuilding lives after a natural disaster strikes; and neighborhood revitalization - nurturing safe, strong, and healthy communities. Proposals are accepted throughout the year, though the regional grant proposal deadline is May 31. The average grant amount ranges from $5,000 to $20,000 for regional grants.
Requirements: The Allstate Foundation makes grants to nonprofit, tax-exempt organizations under Section 501(c)3 of the Internal Revenue Code, or be a municipal, state or federal government entity.
Restrictions: The Foundation does not support the following: individuals; fundraising events, sponsorships; capital and endowment campaigns; equipment purchase unless part of a community outreach program; athletic events; memorial grants; athletic teams, bands, and choirs; organizations that advocate religious beliefs or restrict participation on the basis of religion; groups or organizations that will re-grant the Foundation's gift to other organizations or individuals; scouting groups; private secondary schools; requests to support travel; grant requests for production of audio, film, or video; multiyear pledge requests; or non-domestic (international) causes.
Geographic Focus: All States
Date(s) Application is Due: May 31
Amount of Grant: 5,000 - 20,000 USD
Contact: Vicky Dinges, Vice President of Corporate Social Responsibility; (847) 402-5600 or (847) 402-7893; fax (847) 326-7517; allfound@allstate.com
Internet: http://www.allstatefoundation.org/grant-focus-areas
Sponsor: Allstate Foundation
2775 Sanders Road, Suite F4
Northbrook, IL 60062-6127

Allstate Foundation Tolerance, Inclusion, and Diversity Grants 391
Established in 1952, The Allstate Foundation is an independent, charitable organization made possible by subsidiaries of The Allstate Corporation. The Foundation believes that in order for a community to be strong, it has to recognize and value all of its members. That's why the Foundation is committed to programs that bring tolerance, inclusion, and

value to people of all backgrounds regardless of ethnicity, sexual orientation, gender, age or physical challenges. Its Tolerance, Inclusion, and Diversity funding priorities are: teaching tolerance to youth and fostering a generation free of bias and intolerance; and alleviating discrimination by encouraging communities to be free of prejudice. Proposals are accepted throughout the year, though the regional grant proposal deadline is May 31. The average grant amount ranges from $5,000 to $20,000 for regional grants.
Requirements: The Allstate Foundation makes grants to nonprofit, tax-exempt organizations under Section 501(c)3 of the Internal Revenue Code, or be a municipal, state or federal government entity.
Restrictions: The Foundation does not support the following: individuals; fundraising events, sponsorships; capital and endowment campaigns; equipment purchase unless part of a community outreach program; athletic events; memorial grants; athletic teams, bands, and choirs; organizations that advocate religious beliefs or restrict participation on the basis of religion; groups or organizations that will re-grant the Foundation's gift to other organizations or individuals; scouting groups; private secondary schools; requests to support travel; grant requests for production of audio, film, or video; multiyear pledge requests; or non-domestic (international) causes.
Geographic Focus: All States
Amount of Grant: 5,000 - 20,000 USD
Contact: Vicky Dinges, Vice President of Corporate Social Responsibility; (847) 402-5600 or (847) 402-7893; fax (847) 326-7517; allfound@allstate.com
Internet: http://www.allstatefoundation.org/grant-focus-areas
Sponsor: Allstate Foundation
2775 Sanders Road, Suite F4
Northbrook, IL 60062-6127

Allyn Foundation Grants 392
The mission of the Allyn Foundation is to improve the quality of life in Central New York. To accomplish this, the foundation focuses its grant making in the following areas: health facilities and services: promote the delivery of quality health care in our communities; higher education in the Onondaga and Cayuga counties: expand access and success in education beyond high school, particularly for students of low income or other underrepresented backgrounds; basic human services: work to ensure that all people have basic daily needs of food, clothing, and shelter and enable the means to provide for themselves; family planning medical and educational services: promote education in family planning and improved access to service; quality of life for youth: improve quality of life for children and families through organizations that are focused on at risk youth and families.
Requirements: Nonprofit organizations in Onondaga and Cayuga Counties, NY, may submit grant applications.
Restrictions: Grants are not awarded for religious purposes, endowments, loans, or to individuals.
Geographic Focus: New York
Samples: Auburn Memorial Hospital, $350,000; Frank Hiscock Legal Aid Society, $18,000; Child Care Council of the Finger Lakes, $4,000.
Contact: Margaret O'Connell; (315) 685-5059; info@allynfoundation.org
Internet: http://www.allynfoundation.org/apply.html
Sponsor: Allyn Foundation
14 West Genesee Street, P.O. Box 22
Skaneateles, NY 13152

Alpha Kappa Alpha Educational Advancement Foundation Community Assistance 393 Awards
Community Assistance Awards are awarded to assist individuals and organizations for a specific civic, educational or human service program or project. Because they support initiatives designed and implemented by individuals who know their community's needs best, Community Assistance Awards help leverage funds in a manner that does the most good.
Geographic Focus: All States
Date(s) Application is Due: Aug 15
Contact: Andrea Kerr, Program/Scholarship Coordinator; (800) 653-6528 or (773) 947-0026; fax (773) 947-0277; akerr@akaeaf.net or akaeaf@akaeaf.net
Internet: http://www.akaeaf.org/programsandinitiatives/
Sponsor: Alpha Kappa Alpha Educational Advancement Foundation
5656 South Stony Island Avenue
Chicago, IL 60637

Alpine Winter Foundation Grants 394
Established in California in 1963, the Alpine Winter Foundation's primary purpose is to support alpine safety, health programs, and education within the Tahoe-Donner, California, region. Applications should be in the form of a written request, and should include the specific purpose and history of the requesting organization. There are no specific deadlines with which to adhere.
Requirements: Giving is limited to organizations described in Section 170(b)(1)(a) and Section 501(c)3(a) that promote alpine safety, heath, and education within the Tahoe-Donner area of California.
Geographic Focus: California
Amount of Grant: Up to 40,000 USD
Samples: Donner Trail School, Soda Springs, California, $1,500—for winter survival training programs; Sugar Bowl Ski Team Foundation, Norden, California, $37,500—for need-based scholarships and a building fund *2008).
Contact: Mary S. Tilden, President; (415) 221-7762
Sponsor: Alpine Winter Foundation
3863 Jackson Street, P.O. Box 591659
San Francisco, CA 94118-1610

ALSAM Foundation Grants 395
The foundation awards grants in its areas of interest, including agriculture, Christian agencies and churches, higher education, health care and medical research, human services, minorities, and the economically disadvantaged. Types of support include building construction/renovation, general operating costs, and scholarships. The board meets in January and October. Contact the office for application forms.
Requirements: Higher education institutions, nonprofit organizations, religious organizations, and research institutions are eligible.
Restrictions: No grants to individuals.
Geographic Focus: All States
Amount of Grant: 5,000 - 50,000 USD
Contact: Ron Cutshall, Chair; (801) 266-4950
Sponsor: ALSAM Foundation
6190 Moffat Farm Lane
Salt Lake City, UT 84121

Alticor Corporation Community Contributions Grants 396
The corporation awards grants to enhance the quality of peoples' lives, especially for disadvantaged or disabled people; and to help people overcome barriers to success and fulfillment in their lives. Requests are welcome for support in the areas of health and human services, education, community/economic development, and arts and culture. Requests may be considered outside of these areas, but all requests should directly support the corporation's vision of helping people live better lives. Most grants are awarded in corporate operating areas, including Grand Rapids, MI; Buena Park, CA; Norcross, GA; Honolulu, HI; Arlington, TX; and Kent, WA. The corporation, parent company of Amway, Quixtar, and Access Business Group, may donate products and services to nonprofit organizations that are addressing a serious community need. Obtain an application form via postal mail, phone, or email.
Restrictions: Grants do not support individuals seeking personal help, travel support, scholarships, or loans; fraternal organizations; school athletic teams, bands, or choirs; school publications and advertisements; social events; religious projects; or sports events.
Geographic Focus: All States
Contact: Director; (616) 787-5219; fax (616) 787-4764; contributions@alticor.com
Internet: http://www.alticor.com/resource-center/faq/communityfaq.aspx
Sponsor: Alticor
7575 Fulton Street E, 78-2N
Ada, MI 49355

Altman Foundation Health Care Grants 397
The Altman Foundation's mission is to support programs, and institutions that enrich the quality of life in New York City, with a particular focus on initiatives that help individuals, families, and communities benefit from the services and opportunities that will enable them to achieve their full potential.
Requirements: IRS 501(c)3 organizations in New York are eligible.
Restrictions: Grants are not awarded to individuals. As a general rule, the foundation does not consider requests for bricks and mortar funds or the purchase of capital equipment.
Geographic Focus: New York
Contact: Karen L. Rosa; (212) 682-0970; krosa@altman.org
Internet: http://www.altmanfoundation.org/guide.html
Sponsor: Altman Foundation
521 Fifth Avenue, 35th Floor
New York, NY 10175

Altman Foundation Strengthening Communities Grants 398
The Foundation mission is to support programs and institutions that enrich the quality of life in New York City, with a particular focus on initiatives that help individuals, families and communities benefit from the services and opportunities that will enable them to achieve their full potential. The Foundation has an historic interest in ensuring that individuals and families living in the city have access to the services and resources they need to pursue and sustain successful lives. The Foundation has chosen to focus on efforts that: build and preserve economic security and independence among lowincome individuals and families; and promote and sustain the availability of, and equitable access to, essential community resources needed to support stable, healthy communities.
Requirements: IRS 501(c)3 organizations in New York are eligible.
Restrictions: Grants are not awarded to individuals. As a general rule, the foundation does not consider requests for bricks and mortar funds or the purchase of capital equipment.
Geographic Focus: New York
Contact: Karen L. Rosa; (212) 682-0970; krosa@altman.org
Internet: http://www.altmanfoundation.org/guide.html
Sponsor: Altman Foundation
521 Fifth Avenue, 35th Floor
New York, NY 10175

Altria Group Arts and Culture Grants 399
For more than 50 years, Altria Group has been a strong supporter of both the visual and performing arts. The Group champions organizations that inspire and reflect the qualities it values in its business operations – creativity, diversity, excellence and innovation. Altria supports arts and cultural initiatives in Richmond, Virginia, Washington, D.C., and other communities where its companies operate. The Group's arts and culture grants are focused on: innovative programs to develop new audiences and increase access to the arts; major sponsorships that bring thought-provoking, world-class cultural experiences to our communities; and arts education programs that enhance the overall performance and development of middle school students, primarily in the public schools of Greater Richmond, Virginia.

Requirements: Unsolicited applications are generally not accepted. The company utilizes an invitation process for giving, which is the result of a letter of inquiry.
Geographic Focus: District of Columbia, Virginia
Date(s) Application is Due: Jan 30
Amount of Grant: 15,000 - 1,000,000 USD
Contact: Grants Administrator; (804) 274-2200
Internet: http://www.altria.com/en/cms/Responsibility/investing-in-communities/programs/arts-and-culture/default.aspx
Sponsor: Altria Group
6601 West Broad Street
Richmond, VA 23230-1723

Altria Group Environment Grants 400
The Altria Group and its companies are committed to reducing environmental impact and promoting the sustainability of natural resources on which it depends. Altria and its companies support organizations that focus on: sustainable agriculture in tobacco-growing regions; water quality and conservation in communities where we operate; and nationwide litter prevention and cleanup. In particular, Philip Morris USA, one of Altria's subsidiaries, supports specific efforts that help reduce cigarette butt litter. This effort includes its longstanding partnership with Keep America Beautiful and the Cigarette Litter Prevention Program.
Requirements: Unsolicited applications are generally not accepted. The company utilizes an invitation process for giving, which is the result of a letter of inquiry.
Geographic Focus: All States
Date(s) Application is Due: Sep 30
Amount of Grant: 15,000 - 1,000,000 USD
Contact: Cultural Programs Manager; (804) 274-2200
Internet: http://www.altria.com/en/cms/Responsibility/investing-in-communities/programs/Environment/default.aspx
Sponsor: Altria Group
6601 West Broad Street
Richmond, VA 23230-1723

Altria Group Positive Youth Development Grants 401
Philip Morris USA has had a focus on positive youth development since the creation of its Youth Smoking Prevention department in 1998. Today that program has evolved to Underage Tobacco Prevention, and Altria's tobacco operating companies invest in a range of programs to support its goals of helping reduce underage tobacco use. As part of these efforts, the Group's tobacco operating companies have become a leading funder of positive youth development in the U.S. These investments focus on organizations and programs that emphasize kids' strengths, promote positive behaviors, connect youth with caring adults and enhance community-based resources for kids. These programs are designed to help kids develop the confidence and skills they need to avoid risky behaviors, such as underage tobacco use. The Group's tobacco companies also support adolescent tobacco cessation programs. Its tobacco operating companies' funding supports organizations that: provide evidence-based programs for kids like mentoring, life skills education and substance abuse prevention curricula; help national youth-serving organizations reach more young people, improve program quality and better measure their impact; help community leaders align youth programs and policies; and conduct research on effective positive youth development programs.
Requirements: Unsolicited applications are generally not accepted. The company utilizes an invitation process for giving, which is the result of a letter of inquiry.
Geographic Focus: All States
Date(s) Application is Due: Feb 20
Contact: Grants Administrator; (804) 274-2200
Internet: http://www.altria.com/en/cms/Responsibility/investing-in-communities/programs/positive_youth_development/default.aspx
Sponsor: Altria Group
6601 West Broad Street
Richmond, VA 23230-1723

Alvah H. and Wyline P. Chapman Foundation Grants 402
The Alvah H. and Wyline P. Chapman Foundation was created in 1967 to honor and memorialize Alvah H. and Wyline P. Chapman and to perpetuate their charity and concern for others. The trustees and members of the foundation are the direct descendants (and spouses) of Alvah H. and Wyline P. Chapman, including their children, Alvah H. Chapman, Jr. and Wyline C. Sayler. Current fields of interest include: the arts, children and youth services, Christian agencies and churches, civil rights, racial relations, education, family services, homelessness, human services, literature, medical care, rehabilitation, performing arts, orchestras, science, and substance abuse prevention. Types of support offered by the Foundation are: building and renovation, capital campaigns, continuing support, emergency funds, endowments, and general operating support. The two annual deadlines for applications are April 15 and October 15.
Requirements: Applicants should submit the following: copy of IRS Determination Letter; copy of most recent annual report/audited financial statement/990; listing of board of directors, trustees, officers and other key people and their affiliations; detailed description of project and amount of funding requested; and a copy of current year's organizational budget and/or project budget.
Geographic Focus: Florida
Date(s) Application is Due: Apr 15; Oct 15
Contact: Alan Sayler, Chairperson; (727) 580-2728; vsayler@saylerfamily.com
Sponsor: Alvah H. and Wyline P. Chapman Foundation
P.O. Box 55398
St. Petersburg, FL 33732-5398

Alvin and Fanny Blaustein Thalheimer Foundation Grants 403
The foundation makes grants that strengthen the lives of individuals, families, and communities in the Baltimore region. Program areas include economic opportunity—technical and business entrepreneurship training, and asset-building strategies; health and human services—improve quality of service, and advocacy and policy initiatives; arts and culture—strengthening education and outreach programs that link arts institutions with communities and schools; and strengthening Jewish communities—renewal and development of communities in Eastern Europe and the Former Soviet Union; and addressing threats of anti-Semitism. Guidelines are available online.
Requirements: Only Maryland organizations are eligible to apply.
Restrictions: Grants are not made to individuals.
Geographic Focus: Maryland
Contact: Betsy Ringel, (410) 347-7103; fax (410) 347-7210; info@blaufund.org
Internet: http://www.blaufund.org/foundations/alvinandfanny_f.html
Sponsor: Alvin and Fanny Blaustein Thalheimer Foundation
10 E Baltimore Street, Suite 1111
Baltimore, MD 21202

Alvin and Lucy Owsley Foundation Grants 404
The foundation gives grants in to organizations in the state of Texas in various interest areas including (but not limited to) arts, community development, education.
Requirements: There are no specific deadlines, but the board meets in March, June, September and December. Submit your proposal before the board meets. The application process is a letter no more than 2 pages in length with no attachments.
Geographic Focus: Texas
Amount of Grant: 500 - 100,000 USD
Contact: Alvin Owsley, Trustee; (713) 229-1272
Sponsor: Alvin and Lucy Owsley Foundation
65 Brair Hollow Lane
Houston, TX 77027

ALZA Corporate Contributions Grants 405
The corporation awards grants to eligible California nonprofit organizations in four areas of interest: education—K-12 after school programs, professional development for teachers, and health care workers, nonprofit educational outreach programs; health and human services—projects that particularly access to healthcare for underserved and underrepresented members of our community; arts & culture—arts programs that have an education component or art related to health and healing are of particular interest; and environment—projects that focus on sustainable solutions, stewardship, & education.
Requirements: Nonprofit organizations in ALZA's California operating areas are eligible.
Restrictions: Grants will not be made to individuals, or to organizations whose activities or policies include sectarian or denominational religious activities, political campaigns, or organizations that discriminate on the basis of religion, race, nationality, sexual preference, or gender.
Geographic Focus: California
Amount of Grant: Up to 10,000 USD
Contact: Ellen Rose, Director; (650) 564-5000; fax (650) 564-7070
Internet: http://www.alza.com/alza/community
Sponsor: ALZA Corporation
1900 Charleston Road, P.O. Box 7210
Mountain View, CA 94043

AMA-MSS Chapter Involvement Grants 406
The AMA-MSS Chapter Involvement Grant (CIG) Program provides each MSS chapter with up to $1,000 per academic year for chapter activities including recruitment and retention, chapter development, education, and community service events. A maximum of $250 or $500 is available for each event, depending on the type of event. Applications are due at least 30 days prior to the event.
Geographic Focus: All States
Amount of Grant: 250 - 500 USD
Contact: Rebecca Gierhahn, Director; (800) 262-3211, ext. 4753; rebecca.gierhahn@ama-assn.org or mss@ama-assn.org
Internet: http://www.ama-assn.org/ama/pub/about-ama/our-people/member-groups-sections/medical-student-section/opportunities/grants-awards-scholarships.shtml
Sponsor: American Medical Association
515 N State Street
Chicago, IL 60654

AMA-MSS Chapter of the Year (COTY) Award 407
The AMA-MSS Chapter of the Year (COTY) Award recognizes the true strength of the AMA-MSS organization, the local chapters. Applicant chapters are judged in a number of areas, including membership, community service, advocacy, innovation, and collaboration. The winning chapter is awarded a $500 grant to be used toward chapter activities and is recognized at the MSS Annual Meeting. All MSS chapters are encouraged to apply.
Geographic Focus: All States
Date(s) Application is Due: Apr 30
Amount of Grant: 500 USD
Contact: Rebecca Gierhahn, Director; (800) 262-3211, ext. 4753; rebecca.gierhahn@ama-assn.org or mss@ama-assn.org
Internet: http://www.ama-assn.org/ama/pub/about-ama/our-people/member-groups-sections/medical-student-section/opportunities/grants-awards-scholarships.shtml
Sponsor: American Medical Association
515 N State Street
Chicago, IL 60654

Amador Community Foundation Grants 408
The foundation supports organizations that enhance the quality of life for the people of Amador County by: encouraging private giving for the public good by providing a flexible, cost-effective and tax-exempt vehicle for donors with varied charitable interests and abilities to give; building and maintaining a permanent endowment fund in order to provide a continuing source of income for grants; making grants that are innovative, strategic and relevant in the support of nonprofit sectors; and serving as a catalyst to address changing and challenging community issues. There are no set project or program areas for funding.
Restrictions: The Foundation does not award grants for political or religious purposes, to retire long-term indebtedness, to influence legislation or elections, to private foundations and other grant-making organizations.
Geographic Focus: California
Contact: Administrator; (209) 223-2148; acf@amadorcommunityfoundation.org
Internet: http://www.amadorcommunityfoundation.org/grant.html
Sponsor: Amador Community Foundation
21-B Main Street, P.O. Box 1154
Jackson, CA 95642

AMA Foundation Fund for Better Health Grants 409
The philosophy of the AMA Foundation Fund for Better Health begins with the idea that local communities and organizations have great knowledge and insight into their community's health care issues. Based on this thought, the AMA Foundation, with support from the AMA Alliance, created the Fund for Better Health. Through this program, the AMA Foundation provides seed grants for grassroots, public health projects in communities throughout America. Over the years, the fund has provided over 200 grants totaling nearly $300,000 to projects that address healthy lifestyles, domestic violence prevention, substance abuse prevention, health literacy, patient safety and care for the uninsured. A maximum of $5,000 will be distributed to each grant recipient. The number of grant recipients will be determined by the AMA Foundation after all applications have been received. Typically, the number of grants awarded does not exceed twenty.
Requirements: Organizations are eligible to apply for grants which further the charitable and educational purposes of the AMA Foundation. Grants made in 2009 support programs addressing the issue of healthy lifestyles in the areas of nutrition and physical fitness, alcohol, substance abuse and smoking prevention (and cessation), and violence prevention. The three types of organizations eligible to apply are organizations with annual operating budgets of $1 million or less; new organizations begun in the last 5 years; or established organizations starting a new service or expanding a current service to an underserved population.
Restrictions: None of the funds awarded are to pay for staff salary or overhead expenses.
Geographic Focus: All States
Date(s) Application is Due: Jul 15
Amount of Grant: Up to 5,000 USD
Contact: Dina Lindenberg, Program Officer; (312) 464-4193; fax (312) 464-5973; dina.lindenberg@ama-assn.org or amafoundation@ama-assn.org
Internet: http://www.ama-assn.org/ama/pub/about-ama/ama-foundation/our-programs/public-health/fund-better-health.shtml
Sponsor: American Medical Association Foundation
515 N State Street
Chicago, IL 60654

AMA Foundation Healthy Communities/Healthy America Grants 410
Through the Healthy Communities/Healthy America program, the AMA Foundation awards $10,000-$25,000 grants to physician-led free clinics. Grants will be awarded to free clinics that: are requesting funds for specific projects, not for activities such as routine operations, maintenance or facility repairs; have regular and considerable operating hours; have significant physician involvement; and provide medical services. Preference will be given to applicants who demonstrate how grant dollars will be leveraged to provide the greatest amount of care.
Restrictions: Clinics that provide both medical and dental services, but are requesting funds for a project that is dental care-specific will not be considered.
Geographic Focus: All States
Contact: Steven W. Churchill, Executive Director; (312) 464-2593 or (312) 464-4200; fax (312) 464-4142; Steven.Churchill@ama-assn.org or healthliteracy@ama-assn.org
Internet: http://www.ama-assn.org/ama/pub/about-ama/ama-foundation/our-programs/public-health/healthy-communities-healthy.shtml
Sponsor: American Medical Association Foundation
515 N State Street
Chicago, IL 60654

AMA Foundation Jack B. McConnell, MD Awards for Excellence in Volunteerism 411
The Jack B. McConnell, MD, Award for Excellence in Volunteerism recognizes the work of senior physicians who provides treatment to U.S. patients who lack access to health care. After a full career of practice, these physicians remain dedicated to the future of medicine through the spirit of volunteerism. A $2,500 grant will be given to the institution or organization with which the recipient works. The recipient will also receive travel expenses and accommodations to the Excellence in Medicine Awards Banquet, and the AMA National Advocacy Conference in Washington D.C.
Requirements: To qualify, nominees must: have volunteered a significant portion of their medical services while over the age of 55; demonstrate their commitment to health care access by assisting underserved U.S. patients.
Geographic Focus: All States
Date(s) Application is Due: Nov 16
Amount of Grant: 2,500 USD
Contact: Steven W. Churchill, Executive Director; (312) 464-2593 or (312) 464-4200; fax (312) 464-4142; Steven.Churchill@ama-assn.org or amafoundation@ama-assn.org
Internet: http://www.ama-assn.org/ama/pub/about-ama/ama-foundation/our-programs/public-health/excellence-medicine-awards.shtml
Sponsor: American Medical Association Foundation
515 N State Street
Chicago, IL 60654

Amarillo Area/Harrington Foundations Grants 412
The community foundation seeks to improve the quality of life in the 26 northernmost counties of the Texas Panhandle. Grants are awarded to nonprofits in support of arts and culture, education, health care, and social services. Types of support include research, building construction/renovation, equipment acquisition, program development, seed grants, scholarship funds, and matching funds.
Requirements: Nonprofit 501(c)3 organizations located in the northernmost 26 counties of the Texas Panhandle, including Dallam, Sherman, Hansford, Ochiltree, Lipscomb, Hartley, Moore, Hutchinson, Roberts, Hemphill, Oldham, Potter, Carson, Gray, Wheeler, Deaf Smith, Randall, Armstrong, Donley, Collingsworth, Parmer, Castro, Swisher, Briscoe, Hall, and Childress, are eligible.
Restrictions: The foundation does not make grants to or for religious activities; political lobbying or legislative activities; endowments; debt retirement; deficit financing, reduction of operating deficit, etc; private or parochial schools; national, state, or local fund-raising activities; general operating expenses for United Way agencies; or umbrella funding organizations that would distribute requested funds at their own discretion.
Geographic Focus: Texas
Date(s) Application is Due: Jan 5; Jul 6
Contact: Kathy Grant, (806) 376-4521; kathie@aaf-hf.org
Internet: http://aaf-hf.org/grants/guidelines.htm
Sponsor: Amarillo Area/Harrington Foundations
801 S Fillmore Street, Suite 700
Amarillo, TX 79101

Amber Grants 413
The Amber Foundation Grants began in 1998, launched in conjunction with the entreprenuerial community for women, WomensNet.Net, to honor the memory of a young woman who died in 1981, at the age of 19. The purpose of the Amber Grants is to help other women achieve the dreams that Amber could not in her short time with us. The primary focus is assisting women who are trying to start small businesses, home-based or online. The grants are small, usually $500 to $1000, and are intended to be used to upgrade equipment, pay for a web site, etc. - the small but essential expenses that can often make the difference between getting started or being forever stalled. Grant periods vary and the current grant period will be posted on the home page of the Amber Foundation
Requirements: Applicant must be at least 18 years old and must be a member of WomensNet Online to apply. (Membership is free and can be done at the website.) There are no restrictions as to type of business, or location. Applications must be submitted with true and verifiable information.
Geographic Focus: All States
Contact: Melody Wigdahl, (513) 751-0488; netlady@womensnet.net
Internet: http://www.womensnet.net/Amber-Grants/
Sponsor: WomensNet.net
P.O. Box 310214
New Braunfels, TX 78131

Ambrose and Ida Fredrickson Foundation Grants 414
The foundation supports various human services activities with a focus on the Millburn/Short Hills, NJ area, projects for the restoration and preservation of designated historical sites used for the purpose of teaching or re-creating U.S. history, projects for conservation and restoration of woodlands, programs in the visual and the performance arts offered to general and heterogeneous population, and unique educational programs.
Requirements: The Foundation supports all grant areas consistent with its philosophy, however, consideration will be given to certain organizations listed online.
Geographic Focus: New Jersey
Date(s) Application is Due: Mar 15; Jul 15; Sep 15; Dec 15
Contact: Gale Sykes, Wachovia Bank Contact; grantinquiriesnj@wachovia.com
Internet: http://www.wachovia.com/corp_inst/charitable_services/0,,4269_6584,00.html
Sponsor: Ambrose and Ida Fredrickson Foundation
190 River Road
Summit, NJ 07901

Ambrose Monell Foundation Grants 415
The foundation's mission is to aid and contribute to religious, charitable, scientific, literary, and educational purposes in New York, the United States, and worldwide. Submit a brief inquiry letter that describes the organization and states what funds will be used for and when they are needed. If interested, the foundation will request a full proposals.
Requirements: Tax-exempt organizations are eligible.
Restrictions: Individuals are ineligible.
Geographic Focus: All States
Date(s) Application is Due: Apr 30; Oct 31
Amount of Grant: 5,000 - 500,000 USD
Contact: George Rowe Jr.; (212) 586-0700; fax (212) 245-1863; info@monellvetlesen.org
Internet: http://www.monellvetlesen.org/monell/default.htm
Sponsor: Ambrose Monell Foundation
One Rockefeller Plaza, Suite 301
New York, NY 10020-2002

AMD Corporate Contributions Grants 416
AMD has established two global focus areas: strengthening community and strengthening education. Priority is given to basic needs (food, shelter, and basic health care), education (math and science, teacher development, and college and career awareness), and university education. The k-12 initiatives target programs that increase student interest and/or proficiency in literacy, match, science, and computer technology. AMD also funds programs aimed at developing and supporting effective classroom instruction.
Requirements: Most contributions are made to accredited schools and 501(c)3 nonprofit agencies operating in Austin, Texas (Travis County) or Sunnyvale, California (Santa Clara County) with which AMD has a strong established relationship.
Restrictions: AMD does not consider unsolicited applications for programs outside of the communities in which they operate or outside their focus areas. Also excluded are individuals, medical research, religious, political, service or fraternal organizations, arts or cultural programs, advocacy groups, athletic teams, recreational programs, or individual scouting troops. Organization must be non-discriminatory.
Geographic Focus: All States
Date(s) Application is Due: May 1
Amount of Grant: Up to 25,000,000 USD
Contact: Community Affairs Manager; (800) 538-8450, ext. 45373; fax (408) 749-5373
Internet: http://www.amd.com/us-en/Corporate/AboutAMD/0,,51_52_7697_7702,00.html
Sponsor: AMD Corporation
P.O. Box 3453, M/S 42, 1 AMD Pl
Sunnyvale, CA 94088

Amelia Sillman Rockwell and Carlos Perry Rockwell Charities Fund Grants 417
The Amelia Sillman Rockwell and Carlos Perry Rockwell Charities Fund was established in 1962 to support and promote quality educational, human-services, and health-care programming for underserved populations. Special consideration is given to charitable organizations that serve children or the elderly. Grant requests for general operating support are strongly encouraged. Program support will also be considered. Small, program-related capital expenses may be included in general operating or program requests. The majority of grants from the Rockwell Charities Fund are one year in duration; on occasion, multi-year support is awarded. Applicants must apply online at the grant website. Applicants are strongly encouraged to do the following before applying: review the downloadable state application procedures for additional helpful information and clarifications; review the downloadable online-application guidelines at the grant website; review the foundation's funding history (link is available from the grant website); review the online application questions in advance; and review the list of required attachments. These will generally include: a list of board members, financial statements (audited, reviewed, or compiled by independent auditor); an organization summary; a list of other funding sources; an IRS Determination letter; and other required documents. All attachments must be uploaded in the online application as PDF, Word, or Excel files. The application deadline for the Rockwell Charities Fund is 11:59 p.m. on February 1. Applicants will be notified of grant decisions before May 31.
Requirements: Applicants must have 501(c)3 tax-exempt status.
Restrictions: The trust does not support requests from individuals, organizations attempting to influence policy through direct lobbying, or any political campaigns.
Geographic Focus: Massachusetts
Date(s) Application is Due: Feb 1
Contact: Miki C. Akimoto, Vice President; (866) 778-6859; miki.akimoto@baml.com
Internet: https://www.bankofamerica.com/philanthropic/fn_search.action
Sponsor: Amelia Sillman Rockwell and Carlos Perry Rockwell Charities Fund
225 Franklin Street, 4th Floor, MA1-225-04-02
Boston, MA 02110

Ameren Corporation Community Grants 418
The corporation awards grants in Ameren Illinois and Ameren Missouri service areas to programs in arts and culture, civic affairs, public safety, housing, higher education, services for youth and the elderly, and the environment. Types of support include annual campaigns, building construction and renovation, capital campaigns, challenge/matching grants, conferences and seminars, equipment acquisition, federated giving, general operating support, multi-year support, project development, seed money, and sponsorships. Applicants should provide the following information on the nonprofit's letterhead: organization's mission and how the project addresses its mission; program description and expected outcomes; fundraising goal and current funding status; the organization's budget and audited financial statements; tax status determination letter; roster of governing board and executive staff; and specific amount requested. Nonprofits in the Saint Louis, Missouri, metropolitan area should send applications to Ameren Corporate Contributions at the office listed. Nonprofits in the Springfield, Illinois, metropolitan area should send applications to Ameren Public Affairs, 607 E Adams Street, C1301, Springfield, Illinois 62739.
Requirements: Illinois and Missouri tax-exempt organizations in Ameren service areas are eligible.
Restrictions: Grants do not support individuals or political, religious, fraternal, veteran, social, or similar groups. Ameren cannot donate electric or natural gas service.
Geographic Focus: Illinois, Missouri
Amount of Grant: 5,000 - 75,000 USD
Contact: Otie Cowan; (314) 554-4740; fax (314) 554-2888; ocowan@ameren.com
Internet: http://www.ameren.com/CommunityMembers/CharitableTrust/Pages/Corporationcharitabletrust.aspx
Sponsor: Ameren Corporation
P.O. Box 66149, MC 100
Saint Louis, MO 63166-6149

American-Scandinavian Foundation Public Project Grants 419
The American-Scandinavian Foundation promotes the cultures of the Nordic countries in the United States and American culture in the Nordic countries by encouraging programs that will enhance public appreciation of culture, art, and thought. In establishing priorities, the Foundation considers the lasting benefits that may be achieved by any grant, and favors projects where its contribution will complement support from other sources. Requests for funding are welcome.
Requirements: Awards are given to non-profit organizations only. Proof of an organization's non-profit status (as a 501(c)3 or equivalent) is required.
Restrictions: Awards are not given to support: the underwriting of book publication; the production of commercial CDs or cassettes; individuals' conference participation; or participation in studio residencies other than those with which the Foundation already has an ongoing affiliation. Awards to Scandinavian-American cultural festivals are restricted to supporting the participation of Scandinavian performers or artists brought to the U.S. for the event. The maximum amount awarded for this type of project is $500.
Geographic Focus: All States
Date(s) Application is Due: Jan 30; Apr 15; Aug 15; Oct 15
Contact: Ellen McKey; (212) 879-9779; fax (212) 249-3444; grants@amscan.org
Internet: http://www.amscan.org/public.html
Sponsor: American-Scandinavian Foundation
58 Park Avenue
New York, NY 10016

American Academy of Dermatology Shade Structure Grants 420
The program awards grants to support the purchase of shade structures designed to provide shade and ultraviolet radiation protection for outdoor areas. Locations can include any area where children and adults gather and are exposed to the harmful rays of the sun, such as playgrounds, pools, bleachers, and eating or recreation areas.
Requirements: The program is open to non-profit organizations or educational institutions that serve children and teenagers, ages 18 and younger. Applicants will be reviewed based on the following: demonstrated commitment to sun safety within the organization and community; sponsorship of application by an academy member dermatologist; and ability to meet the build timeline outlined in grant criteria. Application and guidelines are available online.
Restrictions: Faxed nor emailed applications will not be accepted.
Geographic Focus: All States
Date(s) Application is Due: Apr 12
Amount of Grant: Up to 8,000 USD
Contact: Jennifer Allyn, Program Director; (847) 240-1730; jallyn@aad.org
Internet: http://www.aad.org/public/sun/grants.html
Sponsor: American Academy of Dermatology
930 E Woodfield Road
Schaumburg, IL 60173

American Academy of Religion Regional Development Grants 421
Grants provide funds for special projects within the regions that promise to benefit the scholarly and professional life of AAR members and the work of the regions. Workshops, special programs, training events and other innovative regional projects may be funded through this source. Where possible projects should be designed so that they may be duplicated or transported to other regions. Applications should include a narrative description of the project, not to exceed two pages, detailing how the project promises to benefit the scholarly and professional life of AAR members and the work of the region. Include comments on how these projects or activities may be adapted to other regional groups. The application should state the time period covered by the project and provide a detailed budget (office expenses, travel expenses, honoraria, stipend, and other expenses).
Restrictions: Institutional overhead costs are not covered.
Geographic Focus: All States
Date(s) Application is Due: Aug 1
Amount of Grant: Up to 4,000 USD
Contact: Jessica Davenport, (404) 727-4707; jdavenport@aarweb.org or info@aarweb.org
Internet: http://www.aarweb.org/About_AAR/Board_and_Governance/Regional_Directors/reghandbook.asp#VI2
Sponsor: American Academy of Religion
825 Houston Mill Road, Suite 300
Atlanta, GA 30329-4205

Americana Foundation Grants 422
The foundation awards grants in Michigan to support education and advocacy programs that address preservation of American agriculture, the conservation of natural resources, and the protection and presentation of expressions of America's heritage. Types of support include general operating support, endowment funds, program development, conferences and seminars, technical assistance, and matching funds.
Requirements: Michigan nonprofit organizations are eligible.
Restrictions: The program does not support private foundations, political organizations for political purposes, individuals, fund-raising events, or scholarships.
Geographic Focus: Michigan
Date(s) Application is Due: Jan 15; Apr 15; Jul 15; Oct 15
Amount of Grant: 1,500 - 50,000 USD
Contact: Marlene Fluharty; (248) 347-3863; fax (248) 347-3349; fluhart5@msu.edu
Sponsor: Americana Foundation
28115 Meadowbrook Road
Novi, MI 48377-3128

American Chemical Society Award for Team Innovation 423
This award was established to highlight the value and importance of technical teams and teamwork to the chemical and allied industries by recognizing a multidisciplinary team for successfully moving an innovative idea to a product now in commercial use. For each team member, the award consists of $3,000 and a certificate. Up to $1,000 for travel expenses to the meeting at which the award will be presented will be reimbursed to each team member. A certificate will also be provided to the employers of the team.
Requirements: The team shall be multidisciplinary in nature and consist of not fewer than two nor more than five members. The team's work leading to this award must have been carried out primarily in the United States and the technical accomplishments of the team must be documented in the technical literature as a publication(s) or a patent(s). The output of the team must also demonstrate innovation, commercialization of a product or process, be of a special value to society, and of a nature that could only be achieved by professionals working together effectively. The rate of commercialization of the team's output will also be considered in the selection of the recipients of this award.
Restrictions: Application or self-nomination is not acceptable.
Geographic Focus: All States
Date(s) Application is Due: Nov 1
Amount of Grant: 3,000 - 6,000 USD
Contact: Administrator; (202) 872-4575 or (202) 872-4408; awards@acs.org
Internet: http://webapps.acs.org/findawards/detail.jsp?ContentId=CTP_004554
Sponsor: American Chemical Society
1155 Sixteenth Street, NW
Washington, DC 20036-4801

American Chemical Society Chemical Technology Partnership Mini Grants 424
The American Chemical Society (ACS) offers mini grants to help collaboration activities among industry, academia, and the community that are essential to the education and professional development of chemical technicians. The program aims to: (1) Raise community and industry awareness of the changing needs of professional technicians; (2) Highlight opportunities for industry, academia, professional societies, and the community to collaborate on meeting those needs; (3) Increase involvement of current and future technicians in the American Chemical Society.
Requirements: Eligible programs or activities must meet the following conditions: (1) Program/activity must support technician education or career development; (2) Representatives from at least two different sectors of the chemical enterprise (academia, industry, workforce organizations, professional societies, etc.) must be involved; (3) Program/activity must take place during the year of application.
Geographic Focus: All States
Date(s) Application is Due: Feb 20
Contact: Blake J. Aronson, (800) 227-5558 or (202) 872-4600; b_aronson@acs.org
Internet: http://portal.acs.org/portal/acs/corg/content?_nfpb=true&_pageLabel=PP_TRANSITIONMAIN&node_id=1772&use_sec=false&sec_url_var=region1
Sponsor: American Chemical Society
1155 Sixteenth Street, NW
Washington, DC 20036-4801

American Chemical Society Corporate Associates Seed Grants 425
The American Chemical Society recognizes activities at the community level and provides grants to support programs that advance the public's understanding of chemistry. Awards are generally $1,000 up to a maximum of $10,000 per calendar year. CA Seed Grants should not be considered as continuous support.
Requirements: Proposals will be considered in the following areas: (a) Education in the field of chemical sciences; (b) Education of the public regarding the chemical industry; (c) Enhancement of professionalism or safety in chemistry. Specific proposal guidelines and application instructions are available at the sponsor's website.
Geographic Focus: All States
Date(s) Application is Due: Feb 15; Jul 1
Amount of Grant: Up to 10,000 USD
Contact: Nelufar Mohajeri; (202) 872-4443; n_mohajeri@acs.org
Internet: http://portal.acs.org/portal/acs/corg/content?_nfpb=true&_pageLabel=PP_TRANSITIONMAIN&node_id=1454&use_sec=false&sec_url_var=region1
Sponsor: American Chemical Society
1155 Sixteenth Street, NW
Washington, DC 20036-4801

American College of Bankruptcy Grants 426
The college awards grants for existing bankruptcy or consumer-debtor programs, programs in development, and research projects to improve the delivery of pro bono bankruptcy services. Grants also support organizations for broad educational purposes. There are no application guidelines. Guidelines and application are available online.
Geographic Focus: All States
Date(s) Application is Due: Mar 1
Amount of Grant: 1,000 - 10,000 USD
Contact: Shari Bedker, Executive Director; (703) 934-6154; fax (703) 802-0207; sbedker@amercol.org or college@amercol.org
Internet: http://www.amercol.org/acb_foundation.cfm
Sponsor: American College of Bankruptcy
PMB 626A, 11350 Random Hills Road, Suite 800
Fairfax, VA 22030-6044

American Council of the Blind Scholarships 427
The council funds scholarships to assist outstanding blind and visually impaired students to continue their education at the postsecondary level. Education may be contemplated in an academic, technical, vocational, or professional training program. These scholarships are one-time awards with no renewal. Contact office for availability.
Requirements: Applicant must be legally blind in both eyes; must be a U.S. citizen or resident alien; and must be enrolled in or under consideration for admission at the postsecondary level.
Geographic Focus: All States
Date(s) Application is Due: Mar 1
Contact: Terry Pacheco, (800) 424-8666 or (202) 467-5081, ext. 19; fax (202) 467-5085; TerryPach@aol.com or info@acb.org
Internet: http://www.acb.org/magazine/2005/bf022005-5.html
Sponsor: American Council of the Blind
1155 15th Street NW, Suite 1004
Washington, DC 20005

American Electric Power Grants 428
The corporate contributions program awards grants to nonprofit organizations in company-operating areas. Contributions are made principally in the areas of education, the environment, and human services (i.e., hunger, housing, health, safety). Priority is based on the perceived overall benefit to communities in the company's service area. In the area of education, preference is given to grades pre-K through 12 in the fields of science, technology and math. Multiyear commitments to capital campaigns generally do not exceed five years. AEP and its employees provide strong support to many annual United Way campaigns within its service territory; therefore, additional support to United Way agencies is extremely limited. There is no formal application form or deadline. Each request should include evidence of tax-exempt status; amount of funds requested; description of intended use of requested funds, who will benefit, and how they will benefit; overall budget of related program; and description of how the organization will measure results and report outcome of the use of funds being requested. Written requests for local or statewide projects may be submitted to the appropriate AEP state office. Electronic requests in MS Word format may be submitted to the corresponding email address. Guidelines are available online.
Requirements: 501(c)3 nonprofit organizations in Arkansas, Indiana, Kentucky, Louisiana, Michigan, Ohio, Oklahoma, Tennessee, Texas, Virginia and West Virginia are eligible. Grant-seekers should first approach their local AEP operating company.
Restrictions: Grants are not awarded to religious, fraternal, service, and veteran organizations, except for nonsectarian social service activities available to the broader community; organizations with a purpose that is solely athletic in nature; or to individuals.
Geographic Focus: Arkansas, Indiana, Kentucky, Louisiana, Michigan, Ohio, Oklahoma, Tennessee, Texas, Virginia, West Virginia
Contact: Administrator; (614) 716-1000; mkwalsh@aep.com or mkwalsh@aep.com
Internet: http://www.aep.com/about/community/corpGive/Default.htm
Sponsor: American Electric Power
1 Riverside Plaza, 19th Floor
Columbus, OH 43215

American Express Charitable Fund Grants 429
The American Express Charitable Fund supports community foundations and organizations involved with arts and culture, education, hunger, housing development, disaster relief, public safety, human services, community development, and civic affairs. The grantmaker has identified the following major areas of interest: employee matching gifts - fund matches contributions made by employees of American Express to nonprofit organizations on a one-for-one basis from $25 to $8,000 per employee, per year; and Global Volunteer Action Fund (GVAF) - fund awards grants of up to $1,000 to nonprofit organizations with which employees or teams of employees of American Express volunteer. Aside from these, applications are accepted from community organizations and municipal agencies for general operating support.
Requirements: Giving is primarily on a national basis in areas of company operations, with emphasis on: the State of Arizona; Los Angeles and San Francisco, California; Washington, DC; southern Florida; Atlanta, Georgia; Chicago, Illinois; Boston, Massachusetts; Greensboro, North Carolina; New York, New York; Philadelphia, Pennsylvania; Dallas and Houston, Texas; and Salt Lake City, Utah.
Restrictions: No support is available for discriminatory organizations, religious organizations not of direct benefit to the entire community, or political organizations. No grants are offered to individuals (except for employee-related scholarships), or for fundraising, goodwill advertising, souvenir journals, dinner programs, travel, books, magazines, articles in professional journals, endowments or capital campaigns, traveling exhibitions, or sports sponsorships.
Geographic Focus: Arizona, California, District of Columbia, Florida, Georgia, Illinois, Massachusetts, New York, North Carolina, Pennsylvania, Texas, Utah
Contact: Mary Ellen Craig, Director; (212) 640-5660
Internet: http://about.americanexpress.com/csr/e-driven.aspx
Sponsor: American Express Charitable Fund
200 Vesey Street, 48th Floor
New York, NY 10285-1000

American Express Foundation Community Service Grants 430
Whether it is feeding the hungry, mentoring students, building homes for the homeless or cleaning up the environment, tens of thousands of American Express employees serve their communities through volunteerism and personal financial contributions, and the Foundation views this activity as an extension of the service ethic that lies at the heart of its business. It encourages good citizenship by supporting organizations that cultivate meaningful opportunities for civic engagement by employees and members of the community. The Foundation also serves its communities by supporting immediate and long-term relief and recovery efforts to help victims of natural disasters. Funding also

goes to support preparedness programs that allow relief agencies to be better equipped in responding to emergencies as they occur.
Requirements: Eligible organizations must: certify tax-exempt status under Section 501(c)3 and 509(a)1, 2 or 3 of the U.S. Internal Revenue Code. Organizations outside the U.S. must be able to document not-for-profit status.
Restrictions: The program does not fund: individual needs, including scholarships, sponsorships and other forms of financial aid; fund-raising activities, such as galas, benefits, dinners and sporting events; goodwill advertising, souvenir journals or dinner programs; travel for individuals or groups; sectarian activities of religious organizations; political causes, candidates, organizations or campaigns; or books, magazines or articles in professional journals.
Geographic Focus: All States, All Countries
Contact: Timothy McClimon, President; (212) 640-5661; fax (212) 693-1033
Internet: http://about.americanexpress.com/csr/comm_serv.aspx
Sponsor: American Express Foundation
200 Vesey Street, 48th Floor
New York, NY 10285-4804

American Express Foundation Historic Preservation Grants 431
The funding supports organizations and projects that preserve or rediscover important cultural works and major historic sites in order to provide ongoing access and enjoyment for current and future audiences. The types of programs supported include a broad range of arts and culture: from historic landmarks and public spaces to dance, theater, music, film and the visual arts. The Foundation emphasizes preserving works that represent a range of diverse cultures. Supported programs must embrace preservation and enable ongoing public access and exposure through one or more of the following: ensuring public engagement with a restored work of art or historic site; producing or presenting a new interpretation of a work that is in danger of being lost; or preserving significant cultural traditions.
Requirements: Eligible organizations must: certify tax-exempt status under Section 501(c)3 and 509(a)1, 2 or 3 of the U.S. Internal Revenue Code. Organizations outside the U.S. must be able to document not-for-profit status.
Restrictions: The program does not fund: individual needs, including scholarships, sponsorships and other forms of financial aid; fund-raising activities, such as galas, benefits, dinners and sporting events; goodwill advertising, souvenir journals or dinner programs; travel for individuals or groups; sectarian activities of religious organizations; political causes, candidates, organizations or campaigns; or books, magazines or articles in professional journals.
Geographic Focus: All States, All Countries
Contact: Timothy McClimon, President; (212) 640-5661; fax (212) 693-1033
Internet: http://about.americanexpress.com/csr/hpc.aspx
Sponsor: American Express Foundation
200 Vesey Street, 48th Floor
New York, NY 10285-4804

American Express Foundation Leaders for Tomorrow Grants 432
Through this giving theme, the Foundation extends its commitment to leadership development to a broader community. It seeks the best methods, programs and partners that provide current and future nonprofit leaders with practical opportunities to learn and build leadership skills. The Foundation is especially interested in proposals that cultivate leadership opportunities for diverse communities within the nonprofit sector or that focus on innovative leadership development programs for emerging leaders of world-class institutions. It specifically targets programs for emerging nonprofit leaders in the arts, environment, higher education and social service sectors. It will also accept a limited number of requests for programs impacting emerging leaders of the public sector.
Requirements: Eligible organizations must: certify tax-exempt status under Section 501(c)3 and 509(a)1, 2 or 3 of the U.S. Internal Revenue Code. Organizations outside the U.S. must be able to document not-for-profit status.
Restrictions: Applications for youth leadership programs are discouraged. The program does not fund: individual needs, including scholarships, sponsorships and other forms of financial aid; fund-raising activities, such as galas, benefits, dinners and sporting events; goodwill advertising, souvenir journals or dinner programs; travel for individuals or groups; sectarian activities of religious organizations; political causes, candidates, organizations or campaigns; or books, magazines or articles in professional journals.
Geographic Focus: All States, All Countries
Contact: Timothy McClimon, President; (212) 640-5661; fax (212) 693-1033
Internet: http://about.americanexpress.com/csr/leadership.aspx
Sponsor: American Express Foundation
200 Vesey Street, 48th Floor
New York, NY 10285-4804

American Foodservice Charitable Trust Grants 433
American Foodservice Charitable Trust provides funding in the following areas of interest: Christian agencies & churches; community/economic development; higher education; hospitals (general) and; youth development. The types of support available are: general/operating support; program development; scholarship funds. Giving is primarily available in the areas of: King of Prussia, Pennsylvania; Thomasville, Georgia; and Fort Worth, Texas.
Requirements: Qualifying IRA 501(c)3 nonprofit organizations are eligible to apply. There's no application form nor is there a deadline date to adhere to when submitting a proposal to the Foundation.
Restrictions: No grants to individuals.
Geographic Focus: Georgia, Pennsylvania, Texas
Contact: Richard S. Downs, Trustee; (610) 933-9792
Sponsor: American Foodservice Charitable Trust
860 First Avenue, Suite 9A
King of Prussia, PA 19406-1404

American Forests Global ReLeaf Grants 434
Global ReLeaf Forests are reforestation projects on public lands — managed by a local, state or federal organization — or certain public-accessible projects meeting special criteria on private lands. They have been selected by the staff of American Forests as lands where additional private-sector donations can create a new forest that would not be possible under existing programs and budgets. American Forests is always looking for quality tree-planting projects to be funded — they are particularly interested in partnering with private and public sector organizations and agencies to plant trees and improve the environment in projects that would otherwise not be feasible. They support projects that plant the right trees in the right places for the right reasons.
Requirements: American Forests collaborates with a number of different agencies including (but not limited to) U.S. Forest Service; U.S. Bureau of Land Management; U.S. Fish & Wildlife Service; state parks, forests & wildlife areas; U.S. Army Corps of Engineers; Soil & Water Conservation Districts; The Nature Conservancy; Indian nations; Natural Resource & Conservation Service; nonprofit tree planting organizations; counties; communities; and schools. An advisory committee assists with the identification and selection of eligible projects, which meet the criteria: 1) Project is on land owned by a government entity, or project is on public-accessible private land meeting special criteria. 2) Plantable area is 20 acres or larger or has the potential to be 20 acres or more. 3) Forest ecosystem has been damaged by wildfire, hurricanes, tornadoes, insects, diseases, misguided treatment by humans, or other causes. 3) Funds for planting the area are not available from regular programs or sources. 5) Proposals for cost-share Global ReLeaf Forest grants are to cover costs generally associated with the planting of seedlings (i.e. site preparation, seedling purchase, contracting, transportation, shelters, etc). Due to the keen competition for grants, successful project proposals leverage local support resulting in a lower cost per tree and maximizing the number of trees planted for the funds available. 6) Proposal contains an assessment of public benefits (including water quality/quantity and communities served by the watershed) and visibility of the restored area. 7) Proposal includes a strong, multiple-use ecosystem repair component and a diversity of native species that will be planted. 8) Proposal includes efforts to build local partnerships. 9) Adequacy of the planting, care, and long-term maintenance that will be provided by or supervised by experts. 10) Proposal contains new or innovative efforts, restorative approaches, or technology that have the potential for application elsewhere. 11) Recognition and consideration given for the protection of endangered or threatened plant and animal species or ecosystems.
Geographic Focus: All States
Date(s) Application is Due: Jan 15; Jul 1
Contact: Margo Dawley, (202) 737-1944, ext. 224; fax (202) 737-2457; MDawley@amfor.org
Internet: http://www.americanforests.org/global_releaf/grants/
Sponsor: American Forests
P.O. Box 2000
Washington, DC 20013

American for the Arts Emergency Relief Fund 435
The Emergency Relief Fund was developed to provide financial assistance to areas impacted by a major disaster for the purpose of helping them rebuild the arts in their communities. Support will go directly to local arts agencies to assist with their own recovery or to provide needed services and funding to local nonprofit arts groups, individual artists, and other relief efforts dedicated to the arts. The application, which is available online, may be submitted online or by fax. There are no deadlines.
Requirements: The applicant must be a local arts agency—a locally based arts funding and/or service organization, which could be either a government arts agency or a 501(c)3 nonprofit organization; and be located in an area declared a disaster by a governmental agency.
Restrictions: Individual artists are not eligible for emergency relief funds.
Geographic Focus: All States
Amount of Grant: 1,000 - 5,000 USD
Contact: Grants Administrator; (202) 371-2830; fax (202) 371-0424
Internet: https://ww2.americansforthearts.org/secure/registration/application_disasterfund/index.asp
Sponsor: American for the Arts
1000 Vermont Avenue NW, 6th Floor
Washington, DC 20005

American Foundation Grants 436
The foundation is a public charity that helps individuals, families, and corporations create foundations that give financial support to their favorite charities. The foundation's primary focus is helping charities become more efficient and successful by supporting efforts in the following areas: governance and organization (structure)—efforts made to create, strengthen, and reinforce the mission statement of an organization; human resources—staff recruitment for competence and expertise; and operations—access to high technology and leading-edge equipment and procedures. The foundation favors organizations with the following characteristics: competent management, clearly defined missions, organizational ethos, a multiplying and continuing impact, providing needed service, and fiscally responsible. Application and guidelines are available online.
Requirements: 501(c)3, 509(a)1, and 509(a)2 public charities are eligible.
Restrictions: Funding will not be considered for the following requests: organizations without tax-exempt 501(c)3, 509(a)1 or 509(a)2 public charity status; general endowment funds; direct aid to individuals; or governmental or quasi-governmental entities or activities other than colleges or universities.
Geographic Focus: All States
Contact: Administrator; (602) 955-4770; grantinfo@americanfoundation.org
Internet: http://www.americanfoundation.org
Sponsor: American Foundation
4518 N 32nd Street
Phoenix, AZ 85018

Grant Programs | 61

American Gas Foundation Grants   437
Established by the American Gas Association in 1989, the Foundation has set its primary purpose as the advancement of education concerning the distribution and transmission of natural gas by providing training and educational programs and conferences, and conducting charitable and other activities. Giving is on a national basis. There are no specific application formats or deadlines with which to adhere, and applicants should contact the Foundation office for further details on how to proceed.
Restrictions: No support is offered for fraternal, political, labor or religious organizations, United Way-supported organizations, or for organizations whose programs are local in scope. No grants are given to individuals (except for Louis A. Sarkes Scholarship Program), capital fund drives, fund raising dinners, conferences or other special events or general operating support.
Geographic Focus: All States
Contact: Jay Copan; (202) 824-7270; fax (202) 824-9170; jcopan@gasfoundation.org
Internet: http://www.gasfoundation.org/
Sponsor: American Gas Foundation
400 N Capitol Street NW, Suite 400
Washington, DC 20001-1503

American Hiking Society National Trails Fund Grants   438
Created in 1998, American Hiking Society's National Trails Fund is the only privately supported national grants program providing funding to grassroots organizations working toward establishing, protecting and maintaining foot trails in America. Grants are available to help build and protect hiking trails. Two types of grants are available. American Hiking Society Trail Grants will range from $500 to $4,999 each; Nature Valley Trail Grants, sponsored in part by Nature Valley, will provide up to ten grants of $5,000 each. Eligible projects include: projects that have hikers as the primary constituency (though multiple human-powered train uses are eligible); projects that secure trail lands, including acquisition of trails and trail corridors and the costs associated with acquiring conservation easements; projects that will result in visible and substantial ease of access; improved hiker safety, and/or avoidance of environmental damage; and projects that promote constituency building surrounding specific trail projects, including volunteer recruitment and support.
Geographic Focus: All States
Amount of Grant: 500 - 5,000 USD
Contact: Gregory A. Miller, President; (301) 565-6704, ext. 210; fax (301) 565-6714; GMiller@AmericanHiking.org
Internet: http://www.americanhiking.org/NTF.aspx
Sponsor: American Hiking Society
1422 Fenwick Lane
Silver Spring, MD 20910

American Honda Foundation Grants   439
The American Honda Foundation (AHF) engages in grant making that reflects the basic tenets, beliefs and philosophies of Honda companies, which are characterized by the following qualities: imaginative, creative, youthful, forward-thinking, scientific, humanistic and innovative. AHF supports youth education with a specific focus on the STEM (science, technology, engineering and mathematics) subjects in addition to the environment. Funding priorities are identified as youth education, specifically in the areas of science, technology, engineering, mathematics, the environment, job training and literacy. Awards range from $20,000 to $75,000 over a one-year period.
Requirements: Nonprofit charitable organizations classified as a 501(c)3 public charity by the Internal Revenue Service, public school districts, and private/public elementary and secondary schools are eligible to apply. To be considered for funding organizations must have two years of audited financial statements examined by an independent CPA for the purpose of expressing an opinion if gross revenue is $500,000 or more. If gross revenue is less than $500,000, and the organization does not have audits, it may submit two years of financial statements accompanied by an independent CPA's review report instead. Organizations may only submit one request in a 12-month period. This includes colleges and universities with several departments/outreach programs.
Restrictions: The foundation does not consider proposals for service clubs, arts and culture, health and welfare issues, research papers, social issues, medical or educational research, trips, attempts to influence legislation, advocacy, annual funds, hospital operating funds, student exchanges, marathons, sponsorships, political activities, conferences, or fundraising events.
Geographic Focus: All States
Date(s) Application is Due: Feb 1; May 1; Aug 1; Nov 1
Amount of Grant: 20,000 - 75,000 USD
Contact: Kathryn A. Carey, Grants Manager; (310) 781-4090; fax (310) 781-4270; ahf@ahm.honda.com or kathryn_carey@ahm.honda.com
Internet: http://corporate.honda.com/america/philanthropy.aspx?id=ahf
Sponsor: American Honda Foundation
1919 Torrence Boulevard, 100-1W-5A
Torrance, CA 90501-2746

American Humane Association Second Chance Grants   440
The Second Chance Grants provide financial assistance to animal welfare organizations responsible for the temporary care of abused or neglected animals as they are prepared for adoption into permanent home, giving them a second change at life. Due to the overwhelming number of abuse cases nationwide, funding is awarded on a case-by-case basis. Funding is based on whether medical procedures will allow animals to medically recover and live a relatively pain-free life. Grants are awarded year-round as funds are available. The applications and other required forms are available at the AHA website.
Requirements: Animal sheltering agencies (public or private) and rescue groups are considered for the Second Chance Fund. Along with the application, organizations must submit a copy of their 501(c)3 letter; all veterinary receipts/estimates; a signed photo release; and before and after photos of animals.
Restrictions: Individuals, businesses, and corporations are not provided for in the guidelines of the fund. Funding may be used only to cover medical procedures for animals that have been victims of abuse or neglect and require medical treatment before being placed for adoption. Routine medical procedures — such as vaccinations, heartworm testing, spay/neuter surgery, and behavior modification and/or training are outside the scope of these grants.
Geographic Focus: All States
Amount of Grant: Up to 2,000 USD
Contact: Grants Administrator; (800) 227-4645 or (303) 792-9900; fax (303) 792-5333; info@americanhumane.org or grants@americanhumane.org
Internet: http://www.americanhumane.org/animals/professional-resources/for-shelter-professionals/grant-programs/second-chance-fund.html
Sponsor: American Humane Association
1400 16th Street NW, Suite 360
Washington, DC 20036

American Jewish World Service Grants   441
AJWS' grantmaking supports community-based organizations in the developing world that are undertaking holistic community development programs. These groups design and implement projects that creatively and effectively address economic development, education, healthcare, and sustainable agriculture. All of the initiatives also have strong components of strengthening civil society and/or promoting women's empowerment. Grantmaking links human rights and sustainable development.
Requirements: Grassroots organizations are eligible.
Restrictions: Grants are not awarded to individuals.
Geographic Focus: All States
Amount of Grant: 3,000 - 30,000 USD
Contact: Administrator; (800) 889-7146 or (212) 792-2100; grants@ajws.org
Internet: http://www.ajws.org/index.cfm?section_id=3
Sponsor: American Jewish World Service
45 W 36th Street, 10th Floor
New York, NY 10018-7904

American Legacy Foundation Small Innovative Grants   442
The program supports projects that advance creative, promising solutions based on sound principles of tobacco control to remedy the harm caused by tobacco use in America. The program was created to seed new projects or enable an organization to pilot a new idea or approach. The proposed project must demonstrate an element of creativity, ingenuity or innovation and must distinguish itself from the large number of solid programs proposed to the foundation in each grant round.
Requirements: Funding is available only to state or local political subdivisions and legally constituted tax-exempt 501(c)3 organizations based in the 46 states, the District of Columbia, and five territories (American Samoa, Guam, Northern Mariana Islands, Puerto Rico, and the Virgin Islands) identified in the MSA with tobacco product manufacturers. An Indian reservation, Indian tribe, or tribal organization located within the 46 settling states or a nongovernmental entity that serves such a reservation may also apply for funding. Successful applications submitted under the Small Innovative Grants Program must: address one or both of Legacy's goals; demonstrate innovative or new tobacco prevention or cessation efforts; demonstrate a strong likelihood for a sustainable effort after the grant period; demonstrate that the project may be replicated; address the Healthy People 2010 risk reduction objectives related to tobacco use, and; incorporate the CDC's Best Practices for Comprehensive Tobacco Control Programs as appropriate. The foundation will give special consideration to applications addressing these current areas of interest.
Restrictions: The foundation will not award a grant to any applicant that is in current receipt of any grant monies or in-kind contribution from any tobacco manufacturer, distributor, or other tobacco-related entity. In addition, the foundation expects that a grantee will not accept any grant monies or in-kind contribution from any tobacco manufacturer, distributor, or other tobacco-related entity over the duration of the grant. Additionally, will not consider applications for: Projects focusing on youth prevention, cessation, activism, or education (up to 18 years old); Nicotine replacement therapy (NRT) and pharmaceuticals (as the sole or primary focus of the grant); Conference support (as the sole or primary focus of the grant); Media & marketing campaigns (as the sole or primary focus of the grant); Research projects EXCEPT community-based participatory research, which is allowed; Projects focusing on substances other than tobacco; Replication of an existing program; Expansion of an existing program; and Replacement funds; Grants to individuals, for religious activities, to build endowments, to support operating deficits, to retire debt, for capital purchases for building improvements, for construction, for lobbying, or for real estate purchase or development.
Geographic Focus: All States
Date(s) Application is Due: Feb 27; Aug 8
Amount of Grant: 20,000 - 100,000 USD
Contact: Katherine Wilson, Assistant Vice President of Grants; (202) 454-5555; fax (202) 454-5599; grantsinfo@americanlegacy.org
Internet: http://www.americanlegacy.org/2530.aspx
Sponsor: American Legacy Foundation
1724 Massachusetts Avenue NW
Washington, DC 20036

American Psychiatric Foundation Helping Hands Grants   443
The program was established to encourage medical students to participate in community mental health service activities, particularly those focused on underserved populations. The program seeks to raise awareness of mental illness and the importance of early recognition and builds an interest among medical students in psychiatry and working in underserved

communities. The foundation makes grants up to $5,000 to medical schools for mental health service projects that are created and managed by medical students. Projects can be new initiatives conducted in partnership with community agencies or in conjunction with ongoing medical school outreach activities. Examples of fundable activities include screening in community health centers or homeless shelters; outreach and community education about mental health; and health literacy programs.
Requirements: Medical schools are eligible to apply. All projects must be conducted under the supervision of medical faculty. Medical students who participate in the program must be in their second, third, or fourth year of medical school at the time they are engaged in community service. Funds must be expended within one year. Unused funds must be returned to the foundation.
Restrictions: Grants will not fund services beyond basic mental health screenings and referrals.
Geographic Focus: All States
Date(s) Application is Due: May 26
Amount of Grant: Up to 5,000 USD
Contact: Paul T. Burke, Executive Director; (703) 907-8518 or (703) 907-8512; fax (703) 907-7851; pburke@psych.org or apf@psych.org
Internet: http://www.psychfoundation.org/GrantAndAwards/Grants/HelpingHands.aspx
Sponsor: American Psychiatric Foundation
1000 Wilson Boulevard, Suite 1825
Arlington, VA 22209

American Rivers Community-Based Restoration Program River Grants   444
The American Rivers-NOAA River Grants programs funds stream barrier removal projects in the Northeast, Mid-Atlantic, Northwest, South-Atlantic and California. Applications are being evaluated based upon four priority criteria: ecological merits of the project; technical feasibility of the project; benefits provided to the local community; and financial clarity and strength of the application. Grants are provided for three distinct project phases: construction, engineering design, and feasibility analysis. Proposals for Construction phase funding may request a maximum award of $150,000. Proposals for Engineering Design or Feasibility Analysis phases may request a maximum award of $100,000.
Requirements: Applicants must serve regions that include California, Connecticut, Delaware, District of Columbia, Idaho, Maine, Maryland, Massachusetts, New Hampshire, New Jersey, New York, Oregon, Pennsylvania, Rhode Island, Vermont, Virginia, and Washington.
Geographic Focus: California, Connecticut, Delaware, District of Columbia, Idaho, Maine, Maryland, Massachusetts, New Hampshire, New Jersey, New York, Oregon, Pennsylvania, Rhode Island, Vermont, Virginia, Washington
Date(s) Application is Due: Dec 9
Amount of Grant: Up to 150,000 USD
Contact: Serena McClain, (202) 347-7550, ext. 3004; rivergrants@AmericanRivers.org
Internet: http://www.americanrivers.org/our-work/restoring-rivers/dams/background/noaa-grants-program.html
Sponsor: American Rivers
1101 14th Street NW, Suite 1400
Washington, DC 20005

American Savings Foundation Grants   445
The foundation supports organizations and programs that improve the quality of life for residents of the communities served by the foundation, with a special emphasis on the needs of children, youth, and families. Through grants and scholarships, the foundation supports people and organizations in Connecticut. Areas of interest include human services—programs that provide direct services, including prevention and intervention programs, and economic and community development projects; arts and culture—museums, theaters, music, and art programs in our area; and education—direct service programs that enhance and enable academic achievement, tutoring programs, reading readiness, mentoring, school retention programs, and programs that support adult literacy. Types of support include program grants, capital grants, and scholarships. Proposals may be submitted at any time. Deadline listed is for scholarships. Guidelines are available online.
Requirements: Individuals applying for scholarships and 501(c)3 tax-exempt organizations in the foundation's 64-town service area in Connecticut are eligible.
Restrictions: Grants are not typically made for general operating support or endowments.
Geographic Focus: Connecticut
Date(s) Application is Due: Mar 31
Contact: Maria Sanchez, Senior Program Officer; (860) 827-2556; msanchez@asfdn.org
Internet: http://www.asfdn.org/content.cfm?page=capitalgrantsoverview
Sponsor: American Savings Foundation
185 Main Street
New Britain, CT 06051

American Schlafhorst Foundation Grants   446
The foundation awards grants to eligible North Carolina nonprofit organizations in its areas of interest, including arts, children and youth, elderly, education, health care, science, and social services delivery. Types of support include building construction/renovation, equipment acquisition, general operating grants, research grants, scholarships, and seed money grants.
Requirements: 501(c)3 organizations serving the greater Charlotte, NC, area are eligible.
Restrictions: Individuals are not eligible.
Geographic Focus: North Carolina
Amount of Grant: 1,000 - 40,000 USD
Contact: Grants Administrator; (704) 554-0800; info@schlafhorst.com
Sponsor: American Schlafhorst Foundation
8801 South Boulevard
Charlotte, NC 28224

American Society for Yad Vashem Grants   447
Established in the State of New York in 1981, the American Society for Yad Vashem gives on an international basis with emphasis on Israel. The society is the development arm of Yad Vashem, Jerusalem, which serves to remember and honor all victims of the Holocaust. Its primary fields of interest include: historical activities; genealogy; historic preservation; support of historical societies; and Jewish agencies and synagogues. There are no specified application forms or annual deadlines, and applicants should begin by forwarding a letter of application to the Society.
Geographic Focus: All States, Israel
Contact: Eli Zborowski; (212) 220-4304; fax (212) 220-4308; ezborowski@yadvashemusa.org
Internet: http://www.yadvashemusa.org/history.html
Sponsor: American Society for Yad Vashem
500 5th Avenue, 42nd Floor
New York, NY 10110-1699

American Society on Aging Hall of Fame Award   448
The ASA Hall of Fame Award is presented annually by the American Society on Aging to an individual who has made significant contributions toward improving the lives of older adults. The award is designed to: recognize an older person who, through her or his advocacy efforts, has demonstrated leadership on the national, regional or local level to improve the lives of older adults; recognize the abilities and contributions of people ages 65 and over to society as a whole; and encourage advocacy efforts among older adults. Winners receive the following: $1,000 cash prize; a program profile included in the Conference program, which will be distributed to 3,500 attendees and posted on the ASA website; and recognition by peers at an awards presentation.
Requirements: Any individual who is 65 or over may be nominated. Nominations may be made by ASA members, friends and staff.
Geographic Focus: All States
Date(s) Application is Due: Oct 1
Amount of Grant: 1,000 USD
Contact: Nancy Decia; (415) 974-9610; fax (415) 974-0300; awards@asaging.org
Internet: http://www.asaging.org/asav2/awards/description_fame.cfm?submenu1=fame#reco
Sponsor: American Society on Aging
833 Market Street, Suite 511
San Francisco, CA 94103-1824

American Society on Aging NOMA Award for Excellence in Multicultural Aging   449
Awards will be given to organizations that have demonstrated high-quality, innovative programs that enhance the lives of a multicultural aging population. Using the framework that supports the broader vision of diversity at the American Society on Aging, the NOMA Award for Excellence in Multicultural Aging seeks to identify and recognize best practices in developing and implementing programs and/or services that meet the needs of a multicultural aging population. Up to three programs will receive cash awards of $1,500, one complimentary conference registration, one night's lodging for one person at the conference and a one-year complimentary membership to ASA and the Network on Multicultural Aging (NOMA).
Requirements: Eligible applicants must: be an organization or have an affiliation with an organization that focuses on providing information and services to an aging population; have a program and/or service targeted to a multicultural aging population that has been tested, has a proven and successful track record, and has been in existence for a minimum of one year; and have a membership with ASA.
Geographic Focus: All States
Date(s) Application is Due: Dec 15
Amount of Grant: 1,500 USD
Contact: Mahi Sadeghi; (415) 974-9602; fax (415) 974-0300; awards@asaging.org
Internet: http://www.asaging.org/asav2/awards/description_noma.cfm?submenu1=noma
Sponsor: American Society on Aging
833 Market Street, Suite 511
San Francisco, CA 94103-1824

American Sociological Association Sydney S. Spivack Program in Applied Social Research and Social Policy   450
The program is intended to encourage sociologists to undertake community action projects that bring social science knowledge, methods, and expertise to bear in addressing community-identified issues and concerns. Sociologists are expected to work in relevant community organizations, local public interest groups, or community action projects doing such activities as needs assessments, empirical research relevant to community activities or action planning, the design and implementation of evaluation studies, or analytic review of the social science literature related to a policy issue or problem. Grants cover direct costs associated with the project. Approximately four awards are made annually.
Requirements: Applications are encouraged from sociologists in academic settings, research institutions, private and nonprofit organizations, and government.
Restrictions: Advanced graduate students are eligible, but the funding cannot be used to support doctoral dissertation research.
Geographic Focus: All States
Date(s) Application is Due: Feb 1
Amount of Grant: 1,000 - 2,500 USD
Contact: Margaret Weigers Vitullo, Director; (202) 383-9005, ext. 323; fax (202) 638-0882; spivack@asanet.org or apap@asanet.org
Internet: http://www.asanet.org/cs/root/leftnav/funding/community_action_research_initiative
Sponsor: American Sociological Association
1430 K Street NW, Suite 600
Washington, DC 20005

America the Beautiful Fund Operation Green Plant Grants 451
The fund is offering grants of free seeds to community groups striving to better our world through gardening. Grants of 100 to 1,000 seed packets are being offered on the basis of availability and relative need.
Requirements: To apply, write a short letter describing your project. Fill out the application form (which can be downloaded from the website). Applicants are responsible for covering the costs of shipping and handling. Mail your letter, application and check to the sponsor.
Geographic Focus: All States
Contact: Nanine Bilski; (202) 638-1649; fax (202) 638-2175; info@america-the-beautiful.org
Internet: http://america-the-beautiful.org/free_seeds/index.php
Sponsor: America the Beautiful Fund
725 15th Street NW, Suite 605
Washington, DC 02005

Amerigroup Foundation Grants 452
Helping to create healthy communities is the cornerstone of the Amerigroup Foundation's mission. The objective is to serve as a national resource that fosters an environment where there is a continuum of education, access and care, all of which improve the health and well-being of the financially vulnerable and uninsured Americans. Support is available in the states of: Delaware; District of Columbia; Florida; Georgia; Nevada; New Mexico; New York; Ohio; South Carolina; Tennessee; Texas and; Virginia. The Foundation primarily provides grants is the form of general support but program development and, sponsorships are also available to qualified non-profit organizations.
Requirements: 501(c)3 non-profits are eligible to apply from the following states: Delaware; District of Columbia; Florida; Georgia; Nevada; New Mexico; New York; Ohio; South Carolina; Tennessee; Texas and; Virginia.
Restrictions: Funding is unavailable for: projects or organizations that offer a direct benefit to the trustees of the Foundation or to employees or directors of Amerigroup; projects or organizations that might in any way pose a conflict with Amerigroup's mission, goals, programs, products or employees; projects or organizations that do not benefit a broad cross section of the community; individuals; political parties, candidates or lobbying activities; benefits, raffles, souvenir programs, trips, tours or similar events; for-profit entities, including start-up businesses.
Geographic Focus: Delaware, District of Columbia, Florida, Georgia, Nevada, New Mexico, New York, Ohio, South Carolina, Tennessee, Texas, Virginia
Amount of Grant: 500 - 10,000 USD
Contact: Amy Sheyer, Grants Manager; fax (757) 490-6900; (757) 222-2360
Internet: http://www.realsolutions.com/company/pages/Foundation.aspx
Sponsor: Amerigroup Foundation
4425 Corporation Lane
Virginia Beach, VA 23462-3103

AMERIND Community Service Project Grants 453
AMERIND Risk Management Corporation's Community Service program seeks to advance the community aspect of AMERIND's vision to Protect Tribal Families First. Funding limitations for small community service projects include: housing fairs will receive a standard $500 per event; youth activities, including graffiti paint-outs, community clean-up, meth awareness will range from $100 (less than 100 participants) to $250 (more than 100 participants); and health fairs will receive a standard $250. The AMERIND Outreach Committee meets once every month to discuss funding requests received by organizations.
Requirements: Requests for AMERIND contributions must meet of the following criteria; the project must address a demonstrated need in a Native American community in which AMERIND has a presence; the project must provide an opportunity for Native Americans to make learning about fire safety and home safety fun; or the project must support a project or program involving fire safety and/or home safety, business related or other related area to expand, improve and protect the lifestyles of Native Americans and their families.
Restrictions: Powwows and rodeos are considered advertising and are not funded. AMERIND does not contribute to: individual requests; trip expenses; organizations that charge a fee or dues; lobbying organizations; or political organizations.
Geographic Focus: All States
Contact: Mike Jennings; (505) 404-5000 or (800) 352-3496; outreach@amerind-corp.org
Internet: http://www.amerind-corp.org/index.php/about-amerind/community-outreach/community-service-projects
Sponsor: AMERIND Risk Management Corporation
502 Cedar Drive
Santa Ana Pueblo, NM 87004

AMERIND Poster Contest 454
AMERIND Risk Management Corporation's Community Outreach program seeks to advance the community aspect of AMERIND's vision to Protect Tribal Families First. In conjunction with member housing authorities and regional housing association, AMERIND conducts an annual National Safety Poster Contest. Posters are judged at a national level where the first place winners from three categories are selected. The three winners are offered a $3,000 savings bond and a trip to the upcoming AMERIND Annual Meeting. The poster contest is held to educate and instill fire safety message among school-aged children in Indian Country. The Annual deadline for submission is June 30.
Geographic Focus: All States
Date(s) Application is Due: Jun 30
Contact: Mike Jennings; (505) 404-5000 or (800) 352-3496; outreach@amerind-corp.org
Internet: http://www.amerind-corp.org/index.php/2012-contests-and-awards
Sponsor: AMERIND Risk Management Corporation
502 Cedar Drive
Santa Ana Pueblo, NM 87004

AmerUs Group Charitable Foundation 455
The foundation awards general support grants to nonprofits in the metropolitan areas of Des Moines, Indianapolis, Topeka, Boston, and Long Island; in the areas of arts and culture, civic and community, education, health and human services, United Way, and new initiatives. Guidelines and application are available online.
Requirements: Nonprofit organizations in metro Des Moines, Indianapolis, Topeka, and Boston, and Long Island, New York, are eligible to apply.
Restrictions: Grants do not support athletic organizations, conferences, goodwill advertising, endowments, fellowships, festival participation, fraternal organizations, hospital or health care facilities, individual K-12 schools, political parties, religious groups for religious programs, social organizations, and trade or professional associations.
Geographic Focus: Indiana, Iowa, Massachusetts, New York
Date(s) Application is Due: Feb 9; May 4; Aug 3
Amount of Grant: Up to 150,000 USD
Contact: D'Arcy Reinhard, (515) 557-3917
Internet: http://www.avivausa.com
Sponsor: Aviva World
699 Walnut Street, Suite 2000
Des Moines, IA 50309

Amgen Foundation Grants 456
Amgen seeks to: advance science education, improve quality of care and access for patients, and support resources that create sound communities where Amgen staff members live and work. Requests must be received at least 90 days in advance of the desired contribution date. Guidelines are available online.
Requirements: 501(c)3 tax-exempt organizations located in Amgen communities are eligible. Eligible grantees may include public elementary and secondary schools, as well as public colleges and universities, public libraries and public hospitals.
Restrictions: In general, Amgen does not consider requests for the following: support to individuals, fundraising or sports-related events, corporate sponsorship requests, religious organizations unless the program is secular in nature and benefits a broad range of the community, political organization or lobbying activity, labor unions, fraternal, service or veterans' organizations, private foundations, or organizations that are discriminatory.
Geographic Focus: All States
Contact: Program Contact; (805) 447-4056 or (805) 447-1000; fax (805) 447-1010
Internet: http://wwwext.amgen.com/citizenship/apply_for_grant.html
Sponsor: Amgen Foundation
1 Amgen Center Drive, MS 38-3-B
Thousand Oaks, CA 91320-1799

AMI Semiconductors Corporate Grants 457
The company makes grants to nonprofit organizations in support of the performing arts, economic development, business education, health cost containment, and social services for senior citizens. Types of support include conferences and seminars, general operating support, matching grants, multiyear grants, professorships, research, and scholarships. There are no application deadlines. Submit a letter of inquiry that includes a description of the organization and program, amount of funds requested, purpose of the request, recently audited financial statement, and proof of tax-exempt status. Contact office for grant availability.
Restrictions: The company does not support political or lobbying groups.
Geographic Focus: All States
Amount of Grant: 1,000 - 2,500 USD
Contact: Tamera Drake, (208) 234-6890; fax (208) 234-6795; tamera_Drake@amis.com
Internet: http://www.amis.com/about
Sponsor: AMI Semiconductors
2300 Buckskin Road
Pocatello, ID 83201

Amon G. Carter Foundation Grants 458
The foundation awards grants that support benevolent, charitable, and educational purposes with emphasis on the arts and humanities. Other areas supported include education, health and medical services, human and social services, programs benefiting the youth and elderly, civic and community endeavors that enhance quality of life, religion, and visual and performing arts. Types of support include general operating support, continuing support, annual campaigns, capital campaigns, building construction/renovation, equipment acquisition, endowment funds, emergency funds, program development, professorships, seed money, research, and matching funds. The foundation's primary focus is directed to the Fort Worth/Tarrant County area of Texas, although the directors occasionally award a grant outside the Texas area. Proposals must be in writing, briefly giving background information on the requesting organization, specifically stating the purpose of the request, and the amount being requested. A current copy of the organization's IRS determination letter must be furnished. Applications are accepted at any time for consideration during the April, September, and December board meetings.
Restrictions: Grants, loans, or scholarships are not made to individuals. Online applications are not accepted.
Geographic Focus: All States
Amount of Grant: 1,000 - 250,000 USD
Contact: Terry Woodfin; (817) 332-2783; fax (817) 332-2787; terry@agcf.org
Internet: http://www.agcf.org
Sponsor: Amon G. Carter Foundation
P.O. Box 1036
Fort Worth, TX 76101-1036

Andersen Corporate Foundation 459

The Foundation contributes to: organizations that enhance self-sufficiency for people living in poverty, senior citizens, and people with disabilities; organizations that promote safe and healthy environments, as well as organizations that seek to improve health through prevention and education programs, primarily for young people, senior citizens, and people in vulnerable situations; organizations that offer intellectual and social opportunities with a focus primarily on young people, senior citizens, and people with disabilities; and support that builds, promotes, and preserves communities. Complete guidelines are available online.
Requirements: All grant recipients must meet these giving guidelines: the organization's programs and services are consistent with Andersen Corporate Foundation's mission and values; the organization's purpose and programs fit within Andersen Corporate Foundation's defined program focus areas; the organization can demonstrate sound fiscal management and effective delivery of services; nonprofit corporation is registered under section 501(c)3 of the IRS Code in the United States or for Canadian Charities with the Canadian Revenue Agency.
Restrictions: The Foundation avoids making grants in organizations that are in competition with each other to provide the same service to the community. The Foundation does not support endowments or make grants to individuals. Funding is not granted to national research organizations.
Geographic Focus: Iowa, Minnesota, Virginia, Wisconsin, Canada
Date(s) Application is Due: Apr 15; Jul 15; Oct 15; Dec 15
Contact: Program Director; (888) 439-9508 or (651) 439-1557; fax (651) 439-9480; andersencorpfdn@srinc.biz
Internet: https://www.srinc.biz/bp/index.html
Sponsor: Andersen Corporate Foundation
342 5th Avenue N
Bayport, MN 55003

Anderson Foundation Grants 460

Established in Ohio in 1949, the Anderson Family Foundation Trust gives grants in the greater Toledo, Ohio, region, including Maumee and Columbus. Giving also to organizations located within the areas of the Anderson plants in the following states: Champaign, Illinois; Delphi, Lafayette, and Dunkirk, Indiana; and Albion, Potterville, Webberville, and White Pigeon, Michigan. The Foundation's primary fields of interest include: agriculture; arts; children and youth services; education; the environment; government and public administration; higher education; human services; religion; secondary school education; and federated giving programs. Types of support include: annual campaigns; building and renovation programs; capital campaigns; conferences and seminars; emergency funds; general operating support; matching/challenge grants; program development; publications; research; scholarship funds; and seed money. Specific application forms are not required, and board decisions are made on the 3rd Monday of the month in March, June, September, and December. Grant amounts range up to $100,000 on occasion, though most average between $5,000 and $10,000.
Requirements: Nonprofit 501(c)3 agencies in Ohio, Illinois, Indiana, and Michigan serving areas of company operation are eligible to apply.
Restrictions: No support is available for private foundations, public high schools, or elementary schools. No grants are given to individuals, or for endowment funds, travel, or building or operating funds for churches or elementary schools.
Geographic Focus: Illinois, Indiana, Michigan, Ohio
Date(s) Application is Due: Feb 28; May 30; Aug 30; Nov 30
Amount of Grant: Up to 100,000 USD
Contact: Fredi Heywood; (419) 243-1706 or (419) 893-5050; fredi@toledocf.org
Sponsor: Anderson Foundation
480 W. Dussel Drive, P.O. Box 119
Maumee, OH 43537-0119

Andre Agassi Charitable Foundation Grants 461

The foundation awards grants to at-risk youth programs targeting education and recreation in the Las Vegas area. There are no application forms or deadlines. Submitted requests will be considered for funding in the following calendar year. Detailed guidelines are available online.
Requirements: Nevada 501(c)3 nonprofits serving the Las Vegas metro area are eligible.
Restrictions: Grants do not support organizations or projects outside the Las Vegas community, organizations that discriminate, individuals, advertising, religious or sectarian organizations for religious purposes, or political organizations and programs designed to influence legislation or elect candidates to public office.
Geographic Focus: Nevada
Contact: Julie Pippenger; (702) 227-5700; fax (702) 866-2928; info@agassi.net
Internet: http://www.agassifoundation.org
Sponsor: Andre Agassi Charitable Foundation
3960 Howard Hughes Parkway, Suite 750
Las Vegas, NV 89169

Andrew Family Foundation Grants 462

The Andrew Family Foundation is a private, philanthropic organization that will consider proposals from public, non-profit organizations under IRS Section 501(c)3 to support projects and organizations that foster individual growth and enhance communities through education, humanitarian efforts, and the arts. Funding primarily in the Illinois with a special interest in the Cook County region. The types of support available include: annual campaigns; building/renovation; capital campaigns; general/operating support; scholarship funds. There is no deadline date when applying for funding. Qualified grant proposals will be reviewed by the Andrew Family Foundation Grant Making Committee prior to quarterly board meetings. The committee will make a recommendation to the Board of Directors of the Foundation.
Requirements: 501(c)3 tax-exempt organizations are eligible to apply for funding. To begin the application process, take the Eligibility Quiz to confirm that you qualify for a grant from the foundation. Upon successful completion of the Eligibility Quiz, you will be invited to complete an online Letter of Inquiry. The Board will review your Letter of Inquiry and may invite you to submit a Full Application for review. Generally, the Board meets in February, May, August and November of each year.
Restrictions: The foundation does not provide funds: to individuals; taxable corporations; religious programs; political organizations; and other private foundations.
Geographic Focus: Illinois
Contact: Connor Humphrey, Grants Administrator; (708) 460-1288 or (602) 828-8471; fax (602) 385-3267; aff@inlignwealth.com or Connor.Humphrey@GenSpring.com
Internet: https://online.foundationsource.com/andrew/board2.htm
Sponsor: Andrew Family Foundation
14628 John Humphrey Drive
Orland Park, IL 60462

Andrew Goodman Foundation Grants 463

The foundation considers proposals from projects that are working against oppression based on class, race, gender, and social issues; organizing in communities and workplaces around basic social and economic issues; limited in their access to traditional funding sources; and involving youth in community and government activities. Categories of interest include civil and human rights, constituency organizing, cultural activism, economic justice, performing arts, and youth activism. Target populations served include African American, Asian/Pacific Islander, Latino/Chicano, Native American, white, women, multiracial communities, youth, and poor or working class communities. The initial approach should be a letter of inquiry no more than two pages in length that includes a cover sheet clearly listing your organization's name and contact information.
Requirements: 501(c)3 organizations or those with 501(c)3 fiscal sponsors are eligible.
Restrictions: The foundation does not fund capital campaigns, endowments, or deficit financing; organizations with relatively large budgets and access to traditional funding sources; individual projects, such as graduate research or fellowships; conferences, sponsorships; or other foundations.
Geographic Focus: All States
Date(s) Application is Due: May 15; Nov 15
Amount of Grant: 100 - 1,000 USD
Contact: Administrator; (212) 362-7265; fax (212) 362-7175; andrewgoodmanfdn@aol.com
Internet: http://hometown.aol.com/andrewgoodmanfdn
Sponsor: Andrew Goodman Foundation
161 W 86th Street, Suite 8A
New York, NY 10024

Andy Warhol Foundation for the Visual Arts Grants 464

The Foundation's grantmaking activity is focused on serving the needs of artists by funding the institutions that support them. Grants are made for scholarly exhibitions at museums; curatorial research; visual arts programming at artist-centered organizations; artist residencies and commissions; arts writing; and efforts to promote the health, welfare and first amendment rights of artists. Grants are made on a project basis to curatorial programs at museums, artists' organizations, and other cultural institutions to originate innovative and scholarly presentations of contemporary visual arts. Projects may include exhibitions, catalogues, and other organizational activities directly related to these areas. The program also supports the creation of new work through regranting initiatives and artist-in-residence programs. The work of choreographers and performing artists occasionally is funded when the visual arts are an inherent element of a production.
Requirements: Applicants must be nonprofit cultural organizations working in the visual arts both in the United States and abroad.
Restrictions: The foundation does not fund exhibitions or other activities directly related to the art of Andy Warhol and does not encourage projects that contemplate the use of Andy Warhol's name. Grants are not made directly to individuals.
Geographic Focus: All States
Date(s) Application is Due: Mar 1; Sep 1
Amount of Grant: 1,000 - 100,000 USD
Contact: Pamela Clapp; (212) 387-7555; fax (212) 387-7560; info@warholfoundation.org
Internet: http://www.warholfoundation.org/grant/overview.html
Sponsor: Andy Warhol Foundation for the Visual Arts
65 Bleecker Street, 7th Floor
New York, NY 10012

Angels Baseball Foundation Grants 465

Since its inception in 2004, the Angels Baseball Foundation has awarded many grants to worthy organizations throughout the community, ranging from music programs to at-risk youth shelters. Currently, it focuses on initiatives aimed to create and improve education, health care, arts and sciences, and community related youth programs, in addition to providing children the opportunity to experience the game of baseball. Giving is limited to the greater Los Angeles, California, area. Fields of interest include: the arts, athletics/sports activities, children and youth, cancer detection, cancer research, community and economic development, education (at all levels), health care, and community service programs. Applicants should begin by contacting the Foundation directly.
Requirements: Applicants must serve the residents of the greater Los Angeles area.
Geographic Focus: California
Contact: Anne Bafus, Community Relations; (714) 940-2174 or (714) 940-2244
Internet: http://losangeles.angels.mlb.com/ana/community/baseball_foundation.jsp
Sponsor: Angels Baseball Foundation
2000 E Gene Autry Way
Anaheim, CA 92806-6100

Angels for Kids Foundation Grants 466
Angels For Kids is a non-profit, privately funded organization, and we are entirely focused on giving a helping hand to children in the Central Florida area, strictly on an enrichment basis. By lending assistance to children and families in need of a helping hand, Angels For Kids hopes to provide a valuable service for the community at large, and the children within. A child that is determined to be eligible before his or her 16th birthday can receive a gift. Some examples of things that the foundation might fund are summer programs, enrichment classes, field trips, music or art programs, sports equipment, and science equipment.
Requirements: Applications must be made on behalf of children under the age of 16 (upon application approval) residing in the central Florida region.
Restrictions: Angels for Kids will not fund daycare, medical supplies or medicine, food, clothing, or school supplies.
Geographic Focus: Florida
Contact: Michael J Holecek, Director; (630) 382-3310; info@angelsforkids.org
Internet: http://www.angelsforkids.org/
Sponsor: Angels for Kids Foundation
P.O. Box 784
Windermere, FL 34786-0784

Angels in Motion Foundation Grants 467
The Foundation, established in Michigan in 2003 by a CPA, tax, and financial consultant group, is primarily interested in providing direct support to indigent individuals in the greater Detroit metropolitan area. There are no specific applications or deadlines with which to adhere, and applicants should simply provide a brief letter outlining the need. Funding generally ranges from $50 up to $800.
Geographic Focus: Michigan
Contact: Stephen A. Metzler, (248) 822-9010; fax (248) 822-9030; postmaster@mlscocpa.com
Sponsor: Angels in Motion Foundation
1800 W Big Beaver, Suite 100
Troy, MI 48084-3531

Angels On Track Foundation Grants 468
The Foundation's primary mission is to support and promote the safety of highway vehicular traffic and pedestrians around railroad grade crossings in Ohio, and to develop programs designed to provide public education to increase awareness of railroad grade crossing safety and/or to improve public safety by addressing existing hazards at railroad grade crossings. At the Foundation's discretion, it is also vital to provide funding for the improvement of railroad crossings, working with local, state and federal agencies and railroad companies who are responsible for all aspects of railroad grade crossing safety.
Geographic Focus: Ohio
Contact: Dennis F. Moore; (330) 738-3197; fax (330) 738-3198; info@angelsontrack.org
Internet: http://www.angelsontrack.org/index.html
Sponsor: Angels On Track Foundation
8286 Clover Road NE
Salineville, OH 43945

Angels Wings Foundation International Grants 469
THE Foundation was founded in 2002 as a direct means to build and fund schools, orphanages, supply health care and support various issues that impact underprivileged children in Thailand. Shaped from under the wings of native Thai philanthropist, former Miss Universe, Good Will Ambassador to the United Nations and spokesperson for UNICEF and the UNFPA, Porntip Bui Simon (Porntip Nakhirunkanok), Angels Wings has built schools in rural Thailand and continues to supply funding and tuition for the students in these institutions. Application forms are not required, and applicants should contact the Foundation in writing.
Requirements: Giving is primarily restricted to Thailand.
Geographic Focus: All States
Contact: Porntip Bui Simon; bui@angelswingsfoundation.com
Internet: http://www.angelswingsfoundation.com/index.html
Sponsor: Angels Wings Foundation International
1482 East Valley Road, Suite 428
Montecito, CA 93108

Anheuser-Busch Foundation Grants 470
Support is provided almost exclusively to causes that are located in communities in which the company has manufacturing facilities. Contributions are made for education, health, social services, minorities and youth, cultural enrichment, and environmental protection programs. Types of support include capital grants, employee matching gifts, equipment and material acquisition, general support, and donated products. Full proposals are accepted throughout the year. At the Web site, click on Guidelines for Charitable Giving.
Requirements: 501(c)3 tax-exempt organizations in St. Louis, MO; Baldwinsville, N.Y; Cartersvile, Ga; Columbus, Oh; Fairfield, Ca; Fort Collins, Co; Houston, Tx; Jacksonville, Fl; Los Angeles, Ca; Merrimack, N.H; Newark, N.J; Williamsburg, Va., Orlando, Fl; Tampa, Fl; San Antonio, Tx; San Diego, Tx.
Restrictions: Grants are not made to individuals; political, social, fraternal, religious, or athletic organizations; or hospitals for operating funds.
Geographic Focus: California, Colorado, Florida, Georgia, Missouri, New Hampshire, New Jersey, New York, Ohio, Texas, Virginia
Contact: Assistant Manager; (314) 577-2453; fax (314) 557-3251
Internet: http://www.anheuser-busch.com/CharitableGivingIndex.html
Sponsor: Anheuser-Busch Foundation
One Busch Place
Saint Louis, MO 63118-1852

ANLAF International Fund for Sexual Minorities Grants 471
Astraea's primary purpose is to advance the economic, political, educational, and cultural well-being of lesbians. Astraea raises and distributes funds to organizations, individuals, and projects that promote a feminist perspective advancing the social, political, economic, educational, and cultural well-being of lesbians and all women and girls. Programs and policies will be supported that actively work to eliminate those forms of oppression based on sexual orientation, class, race, age, physical and mental ability, religious affiliation, and all other factors that affect lesbians and gay men in the United States and internationally. Organizations may apply for general support or project support. Deadlines are the beginning of June and the beginning of November; contact program staff for exact dates.
Requirements: Groups must be based in Latin America, the Caribbean, Asia, the Pacific, Eastern Europe, the former Soviet Republics, the Middle East, and Africa.
Restrictions: Astraea Foundation generally does not fund government agencies or organizations with budgets above $500,000.
Geographic Focus: All States
Date(s) Application is Due: Mar 15; Oct 15
Amount of Grant: Up to 10,000 USD
Contact: Namita Chad, Grants Administrator; (212) 529-8021; fax (212) 982-3321; namita.astraeafoundation.org or grants@astraeafoundation.org
Internet: http://www.astraea.org/PHP/Grants/Main.php4
Sponsor: Astraea Lesbian Foundation for Justice
116 E 16th Street, 7th Floor
New York, NY 10003

Anna Fitch Ardenghi Trust Grants 472
The Anna Fitch Ardenghi Trust was established in 1981 to support and promote quality educational, cultural, human services, and health care programming for underserved populations living in New Haven, Connecticut. Special preference is given to charitable organizations that focus on the arts or youth-related programming. The deadline for applications is July 1, and applicants will be notified of grant decisions by letter within 2 to 3 months after the proposal deadline. Grants from the Ardenghi Trust are 1 year in duration.
Requirements: 501(c)3 organizations serving the residents of New Haven, Connecticut, are eligible to apply.
Restrictions: Grant requests for capital projects will not be considered. Applicants will not be awarded a grant for more than 3 consecutive years.
Geographic Focus: Connecticut
Date(s) Application is Due: Jul 1
Contact: Carmen Britt; (860) 657-7019; carmen.britt@baml.com
Internet: https://www.bankofamerica.com/philanthropic/grantmaking.action
Sponsor: Anna Fitch Ardenghi Trust
200 Glastonbury Boulevard, Suite #200, CT2-545-02-05
Glastonbury, CT O6033-4056

Ann and Robert H. Lurie Family Foundation Grants 473
Founded in 1986, the foundation initially had set up six categories: medical services and research; child-related medical organizations; basic services including food and shelter; education; the arts; and so-called wild things. When Ann Lurie's husband, Robert, died in 1990, she was left with a fortune worth hundreds of millions and six kids — ages 5 to 15. She has given away well over $100-million since Robert H. Lurie died at age 48, generally spurning requests from nonprofit groups with undistinguished records and concentrating her gifts on some of the world's biggest problems, including hunger, cancer, and inadequate health care. Today, the foundation supports educating and providing resources to children so they are better prepared for the future.
Requirements: There are no specific deadlines or application forms to fill out. An organization requesting funding should have finances in good order, demonstrating that it is making good use of its resources. Note: Ann Lurie has a preference for identifying her own projects, rather than responding to solicitations.
Geographic Focus: Illinois, Michigan
Contact: Ann Lurie, President; (312) 466-3750; fax (312) 466-3700
Sponsor: Ann and Robert H. Lurie Family Foundation
2 N Riverside Plaza, Suite 1500
Chicago, IL 60606-2600

Ann Arbor Area Community Foundation Grants 474
The foundation is interested in funding projects that will improve the quality of life for citizens of the Ann Arbor, Michigan, area. Eligible projects generally fall within the categories of education, culture, social service, community development, environmental awareness, health and wellness, and youth and senior citizens. Types of support include: emergency funds, program development, conferences and seminars, publication, seed grants, scholarship funds, research, and matching funds. Higher priority is given to programs that are preventive rather than remedial, increase individual access to community resources, examine and address the underlying causes of local problems, promote independence and personal achievement, attract volunteer resources and support, strengthen the private nonprofit sector, encourage collaboration with other organizations, and build the capacity of the applying organization. Organizations interested in applying are strongly encouraged to discuss their project with the program director prior to submitting an application.
Requirements: 501(c)3 nonprofit organizations in the Ann Arbor, MI, area, which is the area that falls within the boundaries of the Ann Arbor public schools district, are eligible.
Restrictions: The foundation usually does not make grants for construction projects, annual giving campaigns or capital campaigns, normal operating expenses (except for start-up purposes), religious or sectarian purposes, computer hardware equipment, individuals, advocacy or political purposes, multiyear funding, or regranting.
Geographic Focus: Michigan

Date(s) Application is Due: Feb 11; Oct 7
Contact: Phil D'Anieri; (734) 663-0401; fax (734) 663-3514; pdanieri@aaacf.org
Internet: http://www.aaacf.org/grants.asp
Sponsor: Ann Arbor Area Community Foundation
301 N Main Street, Suite 300
Ann Arbor, MI 48104

Anne J. Caudal Foundation Grants 475
The Anne J. Caudal Foundation was established in 2007 to benefit disabled veterans of any time or of any branch of the United States armed forces and to perpetuate the recognition or memory of their accomplishments or sacrifice in time of war or otherwise. Special consideration is given to organizations that serve disabled veterans in New Jersey. Grant requests for general operating support are strongly encouraged. Program support will also be considered. Small, program-related capital expenses may be included in general operating or program requests. The majority of grants from the Caudal Foundation are one year in duration. On occasion, multi-year support is awarded. Application materials are available for download from the grant website. The application deadline for the Anne J. Caudal Foundation is July 1. Applicants are encouraged to review the state application guidelines for additional helpful information and clarification before applying. Applicants are also encouraged to view the foundation's funding history (link is available at the grant website). Applicants will be notified of grant decisions before August 15.
Requirements: Applicants must have 501(c)3 tax-exempt status.
Restrictions: The foundation does not support requests from individuals, organizations attempting to influence policy through direct lobbying, or any political campaigns.
Geographic Focus: All States
Date(s) Application is Due: Jul 1
Contact: Maryann Clemente; (646) 855-0786; maryann.clemente@baml.com
Internet: https://www.bankofamerica.com/philanthropic/fn_search.action
Sponsor: Anne J. Caudal Foundation
One Bryant Park, NY1-100-28-05
New York, NY 10036

Anne L. and George H. Clapp Charitable and Educational Trust Grants 476
The foundation awards grants to southwestern Pennsylvania nonprofit organizations in its areas of interest, including education, social services, youth and child welfare programs, aging, culture, historic preservation, and environmental conservation. Applicants may submit the common grant application form of the Grantmakers of Western Pennsylvania. Proposals should be submitted between January 1 and May 31. The board meets in August and awards grants in September.
Requirements: Southwestern Pennsylvania nonprofit organizations are eligible.
Restrictions: Grants are not made to individuals.
Geographic Focus: Pennsylvania
Date(s) Application is Due: May 31
Contact: Annette Calgaro, Vice President; (412) 234-1634; fax (412) 234-1073
Sponsor: Anne L. and George H. Clapp Charitable and Educational Trust
1 Mellon Bank Center, Room 3825
Pittsburgh, PA 15258

Annenberg Foundation Grants 477
The foundation provides support for projects within its grantmaking interests of education and youth development, arts and culture, civic, community and the environment, and health and human services. It encourages the development of more effective ways to share ideas and knowledge. Letters of inquiry may be submitted at all times during the year and there are no deadlines. Please review the grants database for additional types of grants given.
Requirements: 501(c)3 tax-exempt organizations are eligible.
Restrictions: Full proposals are not accepted unless requested by a Foundation representative. The foundation is not presently considering inquiries for: individuals, individual K-12 schools, for-profit organizations, political activities or attempts to influence specific legislation, individual scholarships, projects focused exclusively on research, or programs outside of its grant-making interests.
Geographic Focus: All States
Contact: Leonard Aube; (310) 209-4560; info@annenbergfoundation.org
Internet: http://www.annenbergfoundation.org/grants
Sponsor: Annenberg Foundation
2000 Avenue of the Stars, Suite 1000
Los Angeles, CA 90067

Anne Thorne Weaver Family Foundation Grants 478
Established in Nebraska in 1993, the Anne Thorne Weaver Family Foundation offers grants in its primary fields of interest, which include: the arts; community development; economic development; higher education; and human services. Support is offered throughout the States of Nebraska and Iowa, although giving is centered primarily around the Omaha metropolitan area. Funds are primarily offered to fund general operations. An application form is required, and can be secured through the Foundation office. Initially, applicants should send a query letter with a detailed description of the project and budgetary needs. There are no identified annual deadlines. Typical amounts range between $50 and $5,000, with amounts occasionally reaching as much as $75,000.
Requirements: Any 501(c)3 supporting residents of Nebraska are eligible to apply.
Geographic Focus: Iowa, Nebraska
Contact: Anne Thorne Weaver, President; (402) 391-1511 or (402) 551-1919
Sponsor: Anne Thorne Weaver Family Foundation
1301 S. 75th Street, No. 200
Omaha, NE 68124

Annie's Cases for Causes Product Donations 479
Annie's offers a limited number of product donations to non-profit school yard gardens, community gardens, youth agriculture programs and other educational programs that connect children directly to gardening.
Requirements: The program will donate only to schools and non-profit organizations. Annie's focuses it's giving in the areas of School and Community Gardens and Garden Education and Sustainable Agriculture. If funds permit, they may consider Environmental Education and Children's Health groups. There is no deadline, however applications must be submitted 60 days prior to your event.
Restrictions: Annie's does not make grants or donations to individuals, athletic teams or events, or health fairs.
Geographic Focus: All States
Contact: John Foraker, CEO; (800) 288-1089
Internet: http://www.annies.com/cases_for_causes
Sponsor: Annie's
564 Gateway Drive
Napa, CA 94558

Annie's Grants for Gardens 480
Annie's offers a limited number of small grants to community gardens, school gardens and other educational programs that connect children directly to gardening. These funds can be used to buy gardening tools, seeds or other needed supplies.
Requirements: Applicants must be schools and non-profit organizations located within the United States. Grants are only available to groups that focus on School and Community Gardens or Sustainable Agriculture. Organizations must apply at least 60 days prior. Annie's requests no phone calls please.
Restrictions: Annie's does not make grants or donations to individuals, athletic teams or events, or health fairs.
Geographic Focus: All States
Contact: John Foraker, CEO; (800) 288-1089
Internet: http://www.annies.com/grants_for_gardens
Sponsor: Annie's
564 Gateway Drive
Napa, CA 94558

Annie E. Casey Foundation Grants 481
In general, the grantmaking of the foundation is limited to initiatives that have significant potential to demonstrate innovative policy, service delivery, and community supports for children and families. Most grantees have been invited by the foundation to participate in these projects. Much of the foundation's current funding is targeted to its Making Connections Initiative and its 22 sites. The foundation's Baltimore Direct Services Grants Program annually funds a wide range of nonprofit community-based or community-serving organizations that work directly with disadvantaged children, youth, and families, primarily in Baltimore City. Organizations wishing to send a proposal should submit a letter of no more than three typewritten pages describing the organization, its programs, the amount of funds requested, and a brief explanation of how the proposed work fits within the mission of the foundation. There are no submission deadlines. The foundation annually declines a very high percentage of otherwise worthy proposals that do not meet these guidelines.
Restrictions: The foundation does not make grants to individuals, nor does it provide grants for capital projects, medical research, direct services (with the exception of Baltimore City), or work outside the United States.
Geographic Focus: All States
Amount of Grant: 2,000 - 20,000 USD
Contact: Grants Administrator; (410) 547-6600; fax (410) 547-6624
Internet: http://www.aecf.org/about/grantguidelines.htm
Sponsor: Annie E. Casey Foundation
701 Saint Paul Street
Baltimore, MD 21202

Annie Sinclair Knudsen Memorial Fund/Kaua'i Community Grants 482
The priorities of the Fund are projects and services that benefit the Kaua'i community including: culture and arts; education; environment; and health and human services. Priority will be given to programs that are well-defined and likely to be successful, address a community need, demonstrate an ability to deliver, and have an adequate budget. Application information is available online.
Requirements: Any nonprofit, tax-exempt 501(c)3 organization, neighborhood group or project is eligible.
Geographic Focus: Hawaii
Date(s) Application is Due: Jul 16
Amount of Grant: 2,000 - 15,000 USD
Contact: Deborah Rice, (808) 245-4585; drice@hcf-hawaii.org
Internet: http://www.hawaiicommunityfoundation.org/index.php?id=71&categoryID=22
Sponsor: Hawai'i Community Foundation
1164 Bishop Street, Suite 800
Honolulu, HI 96813

Ann L. and Carol Green Rhodes Charitable Trust Grants 483
Ann Rhodes and her mother Carol Green Rhodes were both very supportive of the local arts throughout their lives. Their charitable trust was established in 2010 to honor their love of theater and the local community. Ann was also an animal-lover who fed the wild animals that came into her backyard each night. The Ann L. and Carol Green Rhodes Charitable Trust supports charitable organizations focused on the arts, museums open to the public, theaters and other performing arts organizations, organizations whose primary purpose is to support

the arts, organizations providing human services; and occasional support for animal-related charitable organizations. Ms. Rhodes requested that preference be given to organizations that she supported in her lifetime. Applicants must apply online at the grant website. Applicants are strongly encouraged to do the following before applying: review the downloadable state application procedures for additional helpful information and clarifications; review the downloadable online-application guidelines at the grant website; review the trust's funding history (link is available from the grant website); review the online application questions in advance; and review the list of required attachments. These will generally include: a list of board members, financial statements (audited, reviewed, or compiled by independent auditor); an organization summary; a list of other funding sources; an IRS Determination letter; and other required documents. All attachments must be uploaded in the online application as PDF, Word, or Excel files. This trust has bi-annual application deadlines of March 31 and September 30. Applications must be submitted by 11:59 p.m. on the deadline dates.
Requirements: Applicants must have 501(c)3 tax-exempt status.
Restrictions: This trust is restricted to Tarrant County. The trust does not support requests from individuals, organizations attempting to influence policy through direct lobbying, or any political campaigns.
Geographic Focus: Texas
Date(s) Application is Due: Mar 31; Sep 30
Contact: Mark J. Smith; (817) 390-6028; tx.philanthropic@baml.com
Internet: https://www.bankofamerica.com/philanthropic/fn_search.action
Sponsor: Ann L. and Carol Green Rhodes Charitable Trust
500 West 7th Street, 15th Floor, TX1-497-15-08
Fort Worth, TX 76102-4700

Ann Peppers Foundation Grants 484
The foundation awards grants to eligible California nonprofit organizations in its areas of interest, including arts and cultural programs, disabled, elderly, health care, private education, and social services. Types of support include capital grants, general operating grants on a temporary basis, matching grants, scholarships, and research grants. Grants are initiated by the foundation manager. There are no application deadlines; the board meets quarterly to consider requests.
Requirements: Southern California 501(c)3 nonprofits, colleges, and universities are eligible. Preference is given to requests from Los Angeles County.
Geographic Focus: California
Amount of Grant: 2,000 - 50,000 USD
Contact: Jack Alexander, Secretary; (626) 449-0793
Sponsor: Ann Peppers Foundation
625 S Fair Oaks Avenue
South Pasadena, CA 91030

Annunziata Sanguinetti Foundation Grants 485
The foundation supports charitable organizations in San Francisco, California that are devoted wholly or partially to the care, treatment, rehabilitation, and education of children with physical or mental defects or illnesses. The distribution committee meets annually, usually in November or early December. Proposals are accepted each year between July 1 and October 31.
Requirements: Nonprofit organizations in the San Francisco, California area are eligible to apply. Initial approach should be through a letter of inquiry. There is no application form required when submitting a proposal. The Proposal should include the following items: copy of IRS Determination Letter; copy of most recent annual report/audited financial statement/990; detailed description of project and amount of funding requested; 1 copy of the proposal.
Restrictions: Restricted to organizations which benefit the children residing in San Francisco County, California.
Geographic Focus: California
Date(s) Application is Due: Oct 31
Amount of Grant: 5,000 - 50,000 USD
Contact: Eugene Ranghiasci, Vice President; (415) 396-3215; fax (415) 834-0604
Sponsor: Annunziata Sanguinetti Foundation
420 Montgomery Street, 5th Floor
San Francisco, CA 94106

Anschutz Family Foundation Grants 486
The foundation makes grants in Colorado's rural and urban communities, to assist the elderly, the young, and the economically disadvantaged. Support is given to programs and projects that strengthen families and enable individuals to become productive and responsible citizens of society. Religious organizations, including Christian, Lutheran, Presbyterian, Roman Catholic, and the Salvation Army, also are eligible for funding. Types of support include special projects, general operating budgets, continuing support, seed money, emergency funds, technical assistance, and publications.
Requirements: Nonprofit organizations in Colorado may apply.
Restrictions: Grants are not awarded to individuals, programs outside of Colorado, graduate and post-graduate research, religious organizations for religious purposes, special events, promotions or conferences, candidates for political office, endowments, debt reduction, multi-year grants, and capital campaigns.
Geographic Focus: Colorado
Date(s) Application is Due: Jan 15; Aug 1
Contact: Sue Anschutz-Rodgers, President & Executive Director; (303) 293-2338; fax (303) 299-1235; info@anschutzfamilyfoundation.org
Internet: http://www.anschutzfamilyfoundation.org/info.htm
Sponsor: Anschutz Family Foundation
555 17th Street, Suite 2400
Denver, CO 80202

Ansell, Zaro, Grimm & Aaron Foundation Grants 487
The Ansell, Zaro, Grimm and Aaron Foundation was established in New Jersey in 2007 by a leading law firm of the same name. Funding is offered primarily in the State of New Jersey to Jewish agencies and synagogues, health research, and social service agencies in support of the economically disadvantaged. There are no specific deadlines or application forms with which to adhere, and applicants should initially approach the Foundation with a letter of request detailing the purpose of the grant and verification of tax exempt status. Most recently, the maximum amount given has been $7,500.
Requirements: 501(c)3 organizations supporting the residents of New Jersey are eligible.
Geographic Focus: New Jersey
Amount of Grant: Up to 7,500 USD
Contact: Jerold L. Zaro, Trustee; (732) 922-1000; fax (732) 922-6161; jlz@ansellzaro.com
Sponsor: Ansell, Zaro, Grimm and Aaron Foundation
1500 Lawrence Avenue
Ocean, NJ 07712-4023

Anthem Blue Cross and Blue Shield Grants 488
As a multistate entity, the program supports charitable, civic, and nonprofit groups in company operating areas. Categories of giving include healthy minds (educational), healthy bodies (health oriented), and healthy communities (community projects and human services initiatives). Joint sponsorships with hospitals and providers for programs that benefit the community are encouraged. Requests must be submitted in writing. Contact the office for guidelines.
Requirements: 501(c)3 tax-exempt organizations in corporate communities are eligible.
Restrictions: Grants do not support individuals; political organizations/candidates; religious organizations; fraternal, military, or labor organizations; or providers/hospitals.
Geographic Focus: Colorado, Connecticut, Indiana, Kentucky, Maine, Missouri, Nevada, New Hampshire, Ohio, Virginia, Wisconsin
Contact: Vicki Perkins, (317) 488-6216
Internet: http://www.anthem.com/wps/portal/ahpculdesac?content_path=shared/noapplication/f4/s0/t0/pw_018991.htm&na=aboutanthem&rootLevel=3&label=Charity%20Guidelines
Sponsor: Anthem Blue Cross and Blue Shield
120 Monument Circle
Indianapolis, IN 46204

Anthony R. Abraham Foundation Grants 489
For more than 30 years, the Anthony R. Abraham Foundation mission has been to help non-profit organizations worldwide. The foundations strives to: provide programs and services to help people around the world become self-productive and give back to their communities; ensure that no child is denied medical treatment due to a lack of insurance; provide education that breaks barriers; guarantee that research into the cure of catastrophic diseases continues; help raise the quality of life. It's been a privilege for the Foundation to be able to help ease poverty, raise hospitals, build orphanages and further medical research and the Foundation looks forward to doing even more. Some of the organizations helped include: Domestic organizations -St. Jude Children's Research Hospital; Camillus House; Miami Rescue Mission; Habitat for Humanity of Greater Miami; America's Second Harvest; Miami Children's Hospital; Jackson Memorial Hospital; Florida Heart Research Institute; Big Brothers/Big Sisters; Alonzo Mourning Charities; Honey Shine Mentoring Program; Cancer Link; The Miami Lighthouse for the Blind; Overtown Youth Center. International organizations: Brothers of the Good Shepherd; School for the Blind, Lebanon; Rene Moawad Foundation; Haitian Foundation; Children's International Network; Doctors without Borders; Little Sisters of Nazareth; Maronite Order of the Holy Family.
Requirements: Non-profit 501(c)3 organization requesting funding should fill out a funds-request form and submit it at the Foundation's website. The Foundation will contact you, if your organization qualifies under the Foundation's guidelines and the law.
Restrictions: Grants are not made to individuals.
Geographic Focus: All States
Amount of Grant: 100 - 50,000 USD
Contact: Anthony R. Abraham, Chairman; (305) 665-2222
Internet: http://www.abrahamfoundation.com/about
Sponsor: Anthony R. Abraham Foundation
1320 S Dixie Highway, Suite 241
Coral Gables, FL 33146-2937

Antone & Edene Vidinha Charitable Trust Grants 490
The trust provides partial support to programs and projects of tax-exempt, public charities in Hawaii to improve the quality of life in the state, particularly the island of Kauai. Grants of one year's duration are awarded in categories of interest to the trust, including: churches on Kauai; hospitals; health organizations which benefit the people of Kauai; educational scholarships to colleges and universities in the State of Hawaii for deserving students from the Island of Kauai. Types of support include building/renovation; equipment; general/operating support; program development; scholarship funds. Grants average from $2,000 - $80,000.
Requirements: 501(c)3 nonprofit organizations in Hawaii are eligible to apply. The Trust places a special emphasis on the island of Kauai. Contact Paula Boyce to acquire the cover sheet/application forms and any additional guidelines required to begin the application process. Proposals must be submitted by December 1st.
Restrictions: No grants to/for: individuals; endowments; multi-year pledges.
Geographic Focus: Hawaii
Date(s) Application is Due: Dec 1
Contact: Paula Boyce; (808) 538-4944; fax (808) 538-4647; pboyce@boh.com
Internet: http://www.hawaiicommunityfoundation.org/index.php?id=290
Sponsor: Antone and Edene Vidinha Charitable Trust
Bank of Hawai'i, Foundation Administration Department 758
Honolulu, HI 96802-3170

AON Foundation Grants 491

AON funds community-based initiatives that focus on youths' development through health, education, the arts and cultural activities to schools, school districts and other nonprofit organizations in communities where the company operates, especially the Chicago area. Supported initiatives include community-based projects that focus on youths' development mentally, physically, and academically, and demonstrate positive intervention by including an outcome-evaluation component. The foundation supports higher and other education, social services, community funds, and hospitals and health associations. The board meets three times each year to consider requests. There is no specific application. A letter is acceptable.
Requirements: Nonprofit organizations in AON Corporation domestic and international operating communities, especially organizations in the Chicago area, may apply.
Restrictions: Awards are restricted or limited to charitable, educational (excluding the operation of a secondary educational institution or vocational school) and scientific organizations that qualify as 501(c)3 or 509(a)(1),(2), or (3).
Geographic Focus: All States
Date(s) Application is Due: Apr 1; Jul 1; Oct 1
Contact: Carolyn Labutka, VP/Executive Director; (312) 381-3549; fax (312) 701-4533
Internet: http://edreform.com/info/grant.htm
Sponsor: AON Foundation
200 East Randolph Street
Chicago, IL 60601

APAP Cultural Exchange Grants 492

The Association of Performing Arts Presenters (APAP) recognizes that cross-cultural programs are essential to fully engage audiences and communities in the breadth and diversity of performing-arts experiences, and provide an opportunity for presenting professionals to expand and deepen their knowledge of artists, traditions, and cultures from around the world. The Cultural Exchange Fund (CEF) is a travel-subsidy program to assist U.S.-based presenting professionals and their organizations and companies in building partnerships and collaborations with international touring artists and their collaborators. APAP strongly encourages but does not limit travel to the following regions: Africa, Asia, Latin America, and the Middle East. Up to $2000 may be awarded to individual organizations or artists to help cover travel costs and per diem. Group-travel subsidies are also available for groups of three or more individuals from different APAP-member presenting organizations. The maximum award for a group is $10,000, with no more than $2,000 awarded per organization in the group. Applicants must submit an online application form at the grant website by the applicable deadline date. Funds are issued once original copies of all travel and per diem receipts have been submitted with a final report (within 30 days of travel). Deadlines may vary from year to year. Interested applicants are encouraged to verify current deadline dates. APAP is a non-profit 501(c)3 national-service and advocacy organization dedicated to bringing artists and audiences together. APAP's membership roll of nearly 2,000 represents a growing number of self-presenting artists, leading performing-arts centers, municipal and university performance facilities, nonprofit performing-arts centers, and culturally-specific organizations as well as artist agencies, managers, touring companies, and national consulting practices that serve the field.
Requirements: All applicants must be members of APAP; additionally travelers must be one of the following entities: individuals from presenting organizations who are part of the decision-making process for programming and presentations; independent managers, agents, or producers who are working with one or more presenters to develop a project or tour with foreign artists and who can demonstrate a mission and history of relationship building or project development that serves the presenting field or a particular community; groups of presenters from different presenting organizations who may be collaborating on a new project or program initiative; or individual professional artists. All applicants applying for group travel must designate a lead organization. The lead organization must be a presenter or presenting organization and will be responsible for submitting the application on behalf of the group. The lead organization will serve as the point of contact for related inquiries, reporting, and reimbursements of travel funds. Successful applications must demonstrate that anticipated travel will meet at least two of the following criteria: build the presenter's schedule and programming season as informed by attendance at live performances by international artists based outside the U.S; increase the presenting professional's knowledge and understanding of foreign performing artists based outside the U.S. and the cultural context for their work; create relationships with artists, producers and presenters from around the world to advance the work of U.S.-based presenter(s) and presenting organization(s); increase relationship building, project development, and tours or performances with foreign artists to serve the presenting field or a particular community in the U.S; and advance a project, presentation (non-performance), and/or the cultural research of a U.S.-based artist that will serve the presenting field.
Restrictions: APAP welcomes new applications from previous CEF grantees. Applicants may submit only one application per round. APAP will not award travel subsidies for the following types of requests: for-profit organizations that cannot demonstrate a mission and history of relationship-building or project development that serves the presenting field or a particular community; applicants that cannot provide a three-year history of presenting artists and companies or a three-year history of developing global exchange projects; student artists; artists wishing to travel abroad to perform in a festival or tour; incomplete applications; presenters, managers, agents, producers or artists based outside of the U.S; and board members of applicant organizations.
Geographic Focus: All States
Date(s) Application is Due: May 1; Nov 16
Contact: Laura Benson, Professional Development Associate; (888) 820-2787 or (202) 207-3852; fax (202) 833-1543; lbenson@artspresenters.org or info@artspresenters.org
Internet: http://www.apap365.org/KNOWLEDGE/GrantPrograms/Pages/cef.aspx
Sponsor: Association of Performing Arts Presenters
1211 Connecticut Avenue, Northwest, Suite 200
Washington, DC 20036

Appalachian Community Fund General Fund Grants 493

The Appalachian Community Fund (ACF) makes grants on a yearly basis from the General Fund Program which is supported by a combination of unrestricted funds and monies from the Alexander Fund of the New York Community Trust. ACF's General Fund is an annual board-directed program focusing on organizing for social change and is monies organizations may use for general support as well as for programs and projects. Organizations may apply for funding in one of two categories: Emerging Group/Seed Grant—up to $5,000 for groups in earlier stages of development; and Movement Building Group—up to $10,000 for more established groups.
Requirements: Nonprofit organizations in select Appalachian counties—including Kentucky, West Virginia, Virginia, and Tennessee—are eligible.
Restrictions: ACF does not fund: profit-making organizations; electoral lobbying for initiatives or public office; individual efforts; major capital projects; or social services organizations (unless they demonstrate some analysis and strategies to challenge the systems that lead to the problem).
Geographic Focus: Kentucky, Tennessee, Virginia, West Virginia
Date(s) Application is Due: Nov 8
Amount of Grant: Up to 10,000 USD
Contact: Margo Miller, Executive Director; (865) 523-5783; fax (865) 523-1896; margo@appalachiancommunityfund.org or info@appalachiancommunityfund.org
Internet: http://www.appafund.org/html/generalfund.html
Sponsor: Appalachian Community Fund
530 South Gay Street, Suite 700
Knoxville, TN 37902

Appalachian Community Fund GLBTQ Initiative Grants 494

The GLBTQ Initiative (Gay, Lesbian, Bisexual, Transgender, Questioning Initiative) was established in 2006 by a gift from a Tennessee donor to develop and strengthen resources for GLBTQ organizing efforts in Central Appalachian communities. This Initiative is designed to support GLBTQ organizational building, strengthening Gay and Lesbian Community institutional resources, and capacity building for GLBTQ organizing efforts. ACF also seeks applications from new and emerging organizations, work with GLBTQ youth, and networking efforts to connect GLBTQ work throughout Central Appalachia. Organizations may apply for up to $2,000.
Requirements: Nonprofit organizations in select Appalachian counties—including Kentucky, West Virginia, Virginia, and Tennessee—are eligible.
Restrictions: ACF does not fund: profit-making organizations; electoral lobbying for initiatives or public office; individual efforts; major capital projects; or social services organizations (unless they demonstrate some analysis and strategies to challenge the systems that lead to the problem).
Geographic Focus: Kentucky, Tennessee, Virginia, West Virginia
Amount of Grant: Up to 2,000 USD
Contact: Margo Miller, Executive Director; (865) 523-5783; fax (865) 523-1896; margo@appalachiancommunityfund.org or info@appalachiancommunityfund.org
Internet: http://www.appafund.org/html/GLBTQInitiative.html
Sponsor: Appalachian Community Fund
530 South Gay Street, Suite 700
Knoxville, TN 37902

Appalachian Community Fund Media Justice Grants 495

The Appalachian Community Fund, as part of the Funding Exchange's Media Justice Fund, seeks proposals for Media Justice Toolkits Grants and Community Media Collaboration Grants. These grants will support organizing efforts to reform media policies, establish community media infrastructure and promote accountability by corporate media. A media justice toolkit is comprised of materials in print, audio, video, digital, web-based or PowerPoint formats that provide language and understanding around media policy and advocacy. Community Media Collaboration (CMC) grants support campaigns that change the structure of the media and a community's right to use and be fairly represented within it.
Requirements: Media Justice-Media Toolkit and Community Media Collaboration grants are open to any organization working for media and/or social justice located within Central Appalachia: East Tennessee, Eastern Kentucky, Southwest Virginia and West Virginia.
Restrictions: ACF does not fund: profit-making organizations; electoral lobbying for initiatives or public office; individual efforts; major capital projects; or social services organizations (unless they demonstrate some analysis and strategies to challenge the systems that lead to the problem).
Geographic Focus: Kentucky, Tennessee, Virginia, West Virginia
Date(s) Application is Due: Jan 15
Contact: Margo Miller, Executive Director; (865) 523-5783; fax (865) 523-1896; margo@appalachiancommunityfund.org or info@appalachiancommunityfund.org
Internet: http://www.appafund.org/html/mediajusticefund.html
Sponsor: Appalachian Community Fund
530 South Gay Street, Suite 700
Knoxville, TN 37902

Appalachian Community Fund Seize the Moment Grants 496

The Appalachian Community Fund's Seize the Moment grants were created to supplement annual General Fund grant cycle. These are small grants designed for social change groups needing to take quick action on issues that arise outside ACF's regular cycles. These issues may call for immediate organizing or action, cannot be predicted and are not budgeted. The maximum Seize the Moment grant is $200 and it is to be used within six months of receipt. Check the website, since the program is occasionally temporarily suspended.
Requirements: Nonprofit organizations in select Appalachian counties—including Kentucky, West Virginia, Virginia, and Tennessee—are eligible.

Restrictions: These grants are not for: ooperational or budget emergencies; travel, unless travel is needed by compelling circumstances; or projects that could have applied through ACF's General Fund. ACF does not fund: profit-making organizations; electoral lobbying for initiatives or public office; individual efforts; major capital projects; or social services organizations (unless they demonstrate some analysis and strategies to challenge the systems that lead to the problem).
Geographic Focus: Kentucky, Tennessee, Virginia, West Virginia
Amount of Grant: Up to 200 USD
Contact: Margo Miller, Executive Director; (865) 523-5783; fax (865) 523-1896; margo@appalachiancommunityfund.org or info@appalachiancommunityfund.org
Internet: http://www.appafund.org/html/seizethemoment.html
Sponsor: Appalachian Community Fund
530 South Gay Street, Suite 700
Knoxville, TN 37902

Appalachian Community Fund Special Opportunities Grants   497
The Appalachian Community Fund (ACF) was founded in 1987 to bring new resources for grant funding to groups working for progressive social change in Central Appalachia (East Tennessee, Eastern Kentucky, Southwest Virginia and West Virginia), and to be a sustainable resource base for community organizing and social change work in this region. From time to time, ACF is able to offer special funding opportunities and initiatives grants. Check the website for updates.
Requirements: Nonprofit organizations in select Appalachian counties—including Kentucky, West Virginia, Virginia, and Tennessee—are eligible.
Restrictions: ACF does not fund: profit-making organizations; electoral lobbying for initiatives or public office; individual efforts; major capital projects; or social services organizations (unless they demonstrate some analysis and strategies to challenge the systems that lead to the problem).
Geographic Focus: Kentucky, Tennessee, Virginia, West Virginia
Contact: Margo Miller, Executive Director; (865) 523-5783; fax (865) 523-1896; margo@appalachiancommunityfund.org or info@appalachiancommunityfund.org
Internet: http://www.appafund.org/html/grantops.html
Sponsor: Appalachian Community Fund
530 South Gay Street, Suite 700
Knoxville, TN 37902

Appalachian Community Fund Technical Assistance Grants   498
The Appalachian Community Fund's Technical Assistance Program is designed to help build strong organizations. These are small grants for specific technical assistance needs identified by the organization. By helping staff, board, and members hone their skills, ACF believes an organization's work will be stronger and more effective. Technical Assistance grants are designed to build organizational capacity and to help train board and/or staff in organization building skills such as but not limited to: leadership development; fund raising; planned giving; board responsibilities and roles; long range planning; financial management/planning; legal issues (e.g., non-profit incorporation); community organizing; informing community/media about work; and trainer's fees, materials, and travel. The maximum Technical Assistance grant is $800.
Requirements: Nonprofit organizations in select Appalachian counties—including Kentucky, West Virginia, Virginia, and Tennessee—are eligible.
Restrictions: ACF does not fund: profit-making organizations; electoral lobbying for initiatives or public office; individual efforts; major capital projects; or social services organizations (unless they demonstrate some analysis and strategies to challenge the systems that lead to the problem).
Geographic Focus: Kentucky, Tennessee, Virginia, West Virginia
Contact: Margo Miller, Executive Director; (865) 523-5783; fax (865) 523-1896; margo@appalachiancommunityfund.org or info@appalachiancommunityfund.org
Internet: http://www.appafund.org/html/ta_grant.html
Sponsor: Appalachian Community Fund
530 South Gay Street, Suite 700
Knoxville, TN 37902

Appalachian Ministries Grants   499
The program invites individual consortia members into partnership by applying for a grant to assist the member in developing and implementing a course or educational program. Grants are made for experiential/contextual educational programs, events, courses, or seminars with an Appalachian or other rural immersion component. Grant proposals must provide for ecumenical or inter-institution involvement. Proposals from single schools or agencies must provide for reasonable access by students from other schools or agencies. Priority will be given to proposals clearly demonstrating inter-institution involvement. The program also awards scholarships to students from consortium-member institutions.
Requirements: Only members of the Appalachian Ministries Educational Resource Center (AMERC) consortium are eligible to receive a grant. Membership in AMERC is open to theological schools that are members of the Association of Theological Schools (ATS), regionally accredited colleges or universities whose aim corresponds with the purpose of AMERC, oversight agencies of the church—denominational judicatories or other church organization whose purpose is overseeing the development of Christian leaders in Appalachia or similar rural or urban settings and who support AMERC's purpose, and supporting organizations that embrace AMERC's purpose and help to provide and secure resources necessary for its mission.
Restrictions: Grant proceeds may not be used for capital improvements, the purchase of equipment, or for permanent library acquisitions beyond the textbooks for the course (the library of each sponsoring school will receive a set of the text books being used for the course).
Geographic Focus: All States
Date(s) Application is Due: Mar 1
Amount of Grant: 500 - 15,000 USD
Contact: Lon D. Oliver, (859) 986-8789; fax (859) 986-2576; loliver@amerc.org
Internet: http://www.amerc.org/grants.html
Sponsor: Appalachian Ministries Educational Resource Center
300 Harrison Road
Berea, KY 40403

Appalachian Regional Commission Asset-Based Development Project Grants   500
ARC's Asset-Based Development Project grants seek to help communities identify and leverage local assets to create jobs and build prosperity while preserving the character of their community. Development strategies include: capitalizing on traditional arts, culture, and heritage; leveraging ecological assets for outdoor sports such as fishing, camping, whitewater rafting, and rock climbing; adding value to farming through specialized agricultural development, including processing specialty food items, fish farming, and organic farming; getting the most from hardwood forests by maximizing sustainable timber harvesting and value-added processing; encouraging the development of local leadership and civic entrepreneurs; and converting overlooked and underused facilities into industrial parks, business incubators, or educational facilities. The Commission has allocated $3 million annually for regional initiatives. The ARDA includes as eligible for funding under Section 205 the following types of projects: assessments of training and job skill needs for an industry; development of curricula and training methods, including electronic learning or technology-based training; identification of training providers and the development of partnerships between the industry and educational institutions, including community colleges; development of apprenticeship programs; development of training programs for workers, including dislocated workers; and development of training plans for businesses. Other types of projects, however, that meet the general eligibility criteria may also be considered for funding.
Requirements: States, and through states, public bodies and private nonprofit organizations are eligible to apply.
Restrictions: Asset-based development does not include filling gaps, addressing deficiencies, or the provision of amenities, which often occur at the expense of leveraging unique assets and community strengths. Generally, ARC grants are limited to 50% of project costs.
Geographic Focus: Alabama, Georgia, Kentucky, Maryland, Mississippi, New York, North Carolina, Ohio, Pennsylvania, South Carolina, Tennessee, Virginia, West Virginia
Contact: Jill Wilmoth, Budget and Program Specialist; (202) 884-7668 or (202) 884-7700; fax (202) 884-7691; jwilmoth@arc.gov
Internet: http://www.arc.gov/program_areas/ARCARCGuidelinesforAssetBasedDevelopmentProjectsFY2005.asp
Sponsor: Appalachian Regional Commission
1666 Connecticut Avenue NW, Suite 700
Washington, DC 20009-1068

Appalachian Regional Commission Business Development Grants   501
ARC supports a variety of activities to promote entrepreneurship and business development in the Appalachian Region. These activities help diversify the Region's economic base, develop and market strategic assets, increase the competitiveness of existing businesses, foster the development and use of innovative technologies, and enhance entrepreneurial activity. ARC entrepreneurship and business development activities include: giving entrepreneurs greater access to capital, including support for microcredit programs, revolving loan funds, and development venture capital funds; educating and training entrepreneurs through youth education programs and adult training initiatives; encouraging sector-based strategies to maximize the economic strengths of local communities; and providing strategic support for business incubators and other forms of technical assistance. Business development revolving loan funds (RLFs) in particular are pools of money used by grantees for the purpose of making loans to create and retain jobs. As loans are repaid, money is returned to the fund and made available for additional loans. ARC has long used revolving loan funds as an effective tool of economic development.
Requirements: States, and through states, public bodies and private nonprofit organizations are eligible to apply.
Restrictions: Generally, ARC grants are limited to 50% of project costs.
Geographic Focus: Alabama, Georgia, Kentucky, Maryland, Mississippi, New York, North Carolina, Ohio, Pennsylvania, South Carolina, Tennessee, Virginia, West Virginia
Contact: Jill Wilmoth, Budget and Program Specialist; (202) 884-7668 or (202) 884-7700; fax (202) 884-7691; jwilmoth@arc.gov
Internet: http://www.arc.gov/funding/BusinessDevelopmentRevolvingLoanFundGrants.asp
Sponsor: Appalachian Regional Commission
1666 Connecticut Avenue NW, Suite 700
Washington, DC 20009-1068

Appalachian Regional Commission Community Infrastructure Grants   502
ARC's community infrastructure work focuses primarily on the provision of water and wastewater services to support business and community development projects, and to alleviate public and environmental health hazards. Many Appalachian communities lack basic public services and do not have the financial capacity to fund water and wastewater improvements. More than 25 percent of the Region's population is not served by a community water system and must rely on private well water for their drinking water needs. Nearly half of all Appalachian households rely on on-site wastewater disposal. ARC's residential infrastructure program targets the Region's most economically distressed communities, and utility systems that are struggling to resolve public health and environmental emergencies. ARC also supports infrastructure investments that promote economic and employment opportunities. The provision of water, sewer, gas, fiber, and access roads are critical to attracting new development and supporting the expansion and economic health of the Region's existing business sector. ARC uses grant funds to leverage other public dollars

70 | GRANT PROGRAMS

and private-sector investment to attract commercial and industrial development. The ARDA includes as eligible for funding under Section 205 the following types of projects: assessments of training and job skill needs for an industry; development of curricula and training methods, including electronic learning or technology-based training; identification of training providers and the development of partnerships between the industry and educational institutions, including community colleges; development of apprenticeship programs; development of training programs for workers, including dislocated workers; and development of training plans for businesses. Other types of projects, however, that meet the general eligibility criteria may also be considered for funding.
Requirements: States, and through states, public bodies and private nonprofit organizations are eligible to apply.
Restrictions: Generally, ARC grants are limited to 50% of project costs.
Geographic Focus: Alabama, Georgia, Kentucky, Maryland, Mississippi, New York, North Carolina, Ohio, Pennsylvania, South Carolina, Tennessee, Virginia, West Virginia
Contact: Jill Wilmoth, Budget and Program Specialist; (202) 884-7668 or (202) 884-7700; fax (202) 884-7691; jwilmoth@arc.gov
Internet: http://www.arc.gov/infrastructure
Sponsor: Appalachian Regional Commission
1666 Connecticut Avenue NW, Suite 700
Washington, DC 20009-1068

Appalachian Regional Commission Distressed Counties Grants 503
ARC has provided special funds for the Region's poorest counties since 1983. Currently 78 counties qualify for distressed county status on the basis of low per capita income and high rates of poverty and unemployment. In the past, the distressed county program focused mainly on providing badly needed public facilities, especially systems to furnish clean drinking water and sanitary waste disposal, and human resource projects such as literacy training. In October 2000, the Commission approved the creation of a new enhanced program for distressed counties. The program has two parts: a capacity-building effort and a telecommunications and information technology initiative. Elements of the program include: a minigrant program to provide strategic planning and technical assistance so local communities can jump-start the process of economic development; workshops, knowledge sharing, and other activities to encourage community learning and leadership development; and ARC outreach efforts that give local communities access to other resources, including nonprofits, foundations, and government agencies.
Requirements: Specified counties in Alabama, Georgia, Kentucky, Maryland, Mississippi, New York, North Carolina, Ohio, Pennsylvania, South Carolina, Tennessee, Virginia, and West Virginia are eligible to apply.
Geographic Focus: Alabama, Georgia, Kentucky, Maryland, Mississippi, New York, North Carolina, Ohio, Pennsylvania, South Carolina, Tennessee, Virginia, West Virginia
Contact: Jill Wilmoth, Budget and Program Specialist; (202) 884-7668 or (202) 884-7700; fax (202) 884-7691; jwilmoth@arc.gov
Internet: http://www.arc.gov/distressedcounties
Sponsor: Appalachian Regional Commission
1666 Connecticut Avenue NW, Suite 700
Washington, DC 20009-1068

Appalachian Regional Commission Education and Training Grants 504
Education and training are driving forces behind Appalachia's economic growth, preparing students and workers to compete successfully in the world economy. ARC education and training activities focus on a range of issues including workforce skills, early childhood education, dropout prevention, and improved college attendance. Strategies include: supporting the development and expansion of workforce training and vocational education programs; supporting local and regional efforts that raise the levels of educational achievement and attainment for all students; supporting programs that increase college-going rates; supporting the development of access to early childhood education programs; and supporting dropout prevention programs. The ARDA includes as eligible for funding under Section 205 the following types of projects: assessments of training and job skill needs for an industry; development of curricula and training methods, including electronic learning or technology-based training; identification of training providers and the development of partnerships between the industry and educational institutions, including community colleges; development of apprenticeship programs; development of training programs for workers, including dislocated workers; and development of training plans for businesses. Other types of projects, however, that meet the general eligibility criteria may also be considered for funding.
Requirements: States, and through states, public bodies and private nonprofit organizations are eligible to apply.
Restrictions: Generally, ARC grants are limited to 50% of project costs.
Geographic Focus: Alabama, Georgia, Kentucky, Maryland, Mississippi, New York, North Carolina, Ohio, Pennsylvania, South Carolina, Tennessee, Virginia, West Virginia
Contact: Jill Wilmoth, Budget and Program Specialist; (202) 884-7668 or (202) 884-7700; fax (202) 884-7691; jwilmoth@arc.gov
Internet: http://www.arc.gov/funding/ARCProjectGrants.asp
Sponsor: Appalachian Regional Commission
1666 Connecticut Avenue NW, Suite 700
Washington, DC 20009-1068

Appalachian Regional Commission Energy Grants 505
ARC provides a range of assistance to help communities develop clean energy programs, as well as support to help new energy businesses expand and create local jobs. Commission-supported activities include: training and education programs focusing on energy efficiency, renewable energy, and clean fossil energy production; direct grant support for energy-efficient buildings and water facility projects, and the underwriting of programs to help clean-energy businesses expand and grow; strategic partnerships to develop new policies and programs with leaders in the new energy economy, such as industry trade associations, nonprofit organizations, utilities, and public agencies; and research into economic opportunities provided by the new energy economy. Thus far, ARC has held four energy grant competitions focusing on a range of activities, including renewable energy production, energy-efficient construction, community energy planning, and energy education programming.
Requirements: States, and through states, public bodies and private nonprofit organizations are eligible to apply.
Restrictions: Generally, ARC grants are limited to 50% of project costs.
Geographic Focus: Alabama, Georgia, Kentucky, Maryland, Mississippi, New York, North Carolina, Ohio, Pennsylvania, South Carolina, Tennessee, Virginia, West Virginia
Contact: Jill Wilmoth, Budget and Program Specialist; (202) 884-7668 or (202) 884-7700; fax (202) 884-7691; jwilmoth@arc.gov
Internet: http://www.arc.gov/energy
Sponsor: Appalachian Regional Commission
1666 Connecticut Avenue NW, Suite 700
Washington, DC 20009-1068

Appalachian Regional Commission Export and Trade Development Grants 506
Expanding export trade opportunities is an important strategy for increasing economic and employment success in the Appalachian Region. In 1995, ARC established the ARC Export Trade Advisory Council (ETAC) to advise the Commission on developing trade policy issues and to serve as an advocate for the Region within the global businesses community. Council members include trade directors and other officials from the 13 Appalachian states, international trade experts from the U.S. Commercial Service, representatives from the Development District Association of Appalachia, and members of the ARC federal staff. Through the council's Appalachia USA initiative, created in 2005, ETAC members plan and administer a variety of activities focused on promoting export opportunities for businesses across the Region. ETAC helps establish and sustain export trade partnerships and information-sharing opportunities, and focuses special attention on helping small to medium-sized Appalachian businesses become more successful in international commerce. Projects include support for conferences and events stressing trade economics and best practices, and for research on issues affecting the Region's ability to engage, compete, and succeed in the global economy of the 21st century.
Requirements: States, and through states, public bodies and private nonprofit organizations are eligible to apply.
Restrictions: Generally, ARC grants are limited to 50% of project costs.
Geographic Focus: Alabama, Georgia, Kentucky, Maryland, Mississippi, New York, North Carolina, Ohio, Pennsylvania, South Carolina, Tennessee, Virginia, West Virginia
Contact: Jill Wilmoth, Budget and Program Specialist; (202) 884-7668 or (202) 884-7700; fax (202) 884-7691; jwilmoth@arc.gov
Internet: http://www.arc.gov/export
Sponsor: Appalachian Regional Commission
1666 Connecticut Avenue NW, Suite 700
Washington, DC 20009-1068

Appalachian Regional Commission Health Care Grants 507
Access to comprehensive, affordable health care is vital to social and economic growth in the Appalachian Region. ARC's health projects focus on community-based efforts to encourage health-promotion and disease-prevention activities. Strategies include: using best practices in public health to develop targeted approaches to wellness and disease prevention; supporting partnerships that educate children and families about basic health risks; using telecommunications and other technology to reduce the high cost of health-care services; and encouraging the development and expansion of health professional education services within the Region. ARC health care grants have helped provide equipment for hospitals and rural clinics, training for health care professionals, and support for community-based health education activities. ARC also works with other organizations to address the high incidence of life-threatening diseases in the Region, as in its ongoing partnership with the Centers for Disease Control and Prevention in diabetes and cancer education, prevention, and treatment programs in the Region's distressed counties.
Requirements: States, and through states, public bodies and private nonprofit organizations are eligible to apply.
Restrictions: Generally, ARC grants are limited to 50% of project costs.
Geographic Focus: Alabama, Georgia, Kentucky, Maryland, Mississippi, New York, North Carolina, Ohio, Pennsylvania, South Carolina, Tennessee, Virginia, West Virginia
Contact: Jill Wilmoth, Budget and Program Specialist; (202) 884-7668 or (202) 884-7700; fax (202) 884-7691; jwilmoth@arc.gov
Internet: http://www.arc.gov/funding/ARCProjectGrants.asp
Sponsor: Appalachian Regional Commission
1666 Connecticut Avenue NW, Suite 700
Washington, DC 20009-1068

Appalachian Regional Commission Housing Grants 508
ARC provides funds for basic infrastructure services, including water and sewer facilities, that enhance economic development opportunities or address serious health issues for residential customers. ARC supports projects that stimulate the construction or rehabilitation of housing for low- and moderate-income residents. ARC housing grants fund plannng, technical services, and other preliminary expenses of developing housing projects, as well as demolition and necessary site improvements, including excavation, land fills, land clearing and grading; and infrastructure improvements, such as water and sewer system construction.
Requirements: States, and through states, public bodies and private nonprofit organizations are eligible to apply.
Restrictions: Generally, ARC grants are limited to 50% of project costs.

Geographic Focus: Alabama, Georgia, Kentucky, Maryland, New York, North Carolina, Ohio, Pennsylvania, South Carolina, Tennessee, Virginia, West Virginia
Contact: Jill Wilmoth, Budget and Program Specialist; (202) 884-7668 or (202) 884-7700; fax (202) 884-7691; jwilmoth@arc.gov
Internet: http://www.arc.gov/funding/ARCProjectGrants.asp
Sponsor: Appalachian Regional Commission
1666 Connecticut Avenue NW, Suite 700
Washington, DC 20009-1068

Appalachian Regional Commission Leadership Development and Capacity Building Grants 509
ARC Leadership Development and Capacity Building grants support projects that build leadership development skills; foster broad citizen involvement; support the development of strategic planning processes; and promote collaborations among business, government, nonprofit, and philanthropic organizations. Strategies include: building the capacity to collaborate among government, business, and nonprofit and philanthropic sectors; encouraging partnerships and promoting regional efforts in economic development; promoting community dialogue on economic development; and providing training and consultation services to local governments and nonprofit organizations engaged in economic development.
Requirements: States, and through states, public bodies and private nonprofit organizations are eligible to apply.
Restrictions: Generally, ARC grants are limited to 50% of project costs.
Geographic Focus: Alabama, Georgia, Kentucky, Maryland, Mississippi, New York, North Carolina, Ohio, Pennsylvania, South Carolina, Tennessee, Virginia, West Virginia
Contact: Jill Wilmoth, Budget and Program Specialist; (202) 884-7668 or (202) 884-7700; fax (202) 884-7691; jwilmoth@arc.gov
Internet: http://www.arc.gov/funding/ARCProjectGrants.asp
Sponsor: Appalachian Regional Commission
1666 Connecticut Avenue NW, Suite 700
Washington, DC 20009-1068

Appalachian Regional Commission Telecommunications Grants 510
ARC funds a number of telecommunications activities, including strategic community planning, equipment acquisition, and hardware and software for network building. ARC funds can be used for strategic telecommunications planning activities, telecommunication service inventory and assessment activities, agregation of demand projects, community awareness information technology (IT) outreach training programs, sector-specific training programs in IT/e-commerce for small and medium-sized businesses, activities related to assisting in the development of IT business development, the acquisition of telecommunications equipment and related software, general operational and administrative expenses associated with project implementation, the installation of telecommunication infrastructure necessary to implement projects or support the development of IT incubators or Smart Parks, and limited telephone line charge expenses associated with the implementation of projects.
Requirements: States, and through states, public bodies and private nonprofit organizations are eligible to apply.
Restrictions: Generally, ARC grants are limited to 50% of project costs.
Geographic Focus: Alabama, Georgia, Kentucky, Maryland, Mississippi, New York, North Carolina, Ohio, Pennsylvania, South Carolina, Tennessee, Virginia, West Virginia
Contact: Jill Wilmoth, Budget and Program Specialist; (202) 884-7668 or (202) 884-7700; fax (202) 884-7691; jwilmoth@arc.gov
Internet: http://www.arc.gov/funding/ARCProjectGrants.asp
Sponsor: Appalachian Regional Commission
1666 Connecticut Avenue NW, Suite 700
Washington, DC 20009-1068

Appalachian Regional Commission Tourist Development Grants 511
Tourism development can be an important part of a community's strategy for building a sustainable economic future. Many Appalachian communities have developed successful tourism strategies based on the Region's cultural heritage, history, and natural beauty. ARC supports a wide variety of tourism projects, including: building and rehabilitating facilities and infrastructure to make the Region more accessible and attractive to visitors; training artisans and artists to improve their business and marketing skills; developing strategic plans and feasibility studies to help communities maximize the potential of their cultural assets; and investing in new technologies that create new experiences for visitors. Each project has specific and community-based goals, but all contribute to the overall impact of tourism as a key component in building long-term economic health in the Region.
Requirements: States, and through states, public bodies and private nonprofit organizations are eligible to apply.
Restrictions: Generally, ARC grants are limited to 50% of project costs.
Geographic Focus: Alabama, Georgia, Kentucky, Maryland, Mississippi, New York, North Carolina, Ohio, Pennsylvania, South Carolina, Tennessee, Virginia, West Virginia
Contact: Jill Wilmoth, Budget and Program Specialist; (202) 884-7668 or (202) 884-7700; fax (202) 884-7691; jwilmoth@arc.gov
Internet: http://www.arc.gov/tourism
Sponsor: Appalachian Regional Commission
1666 Connecticut Avenue NW, Suite 700
Washington, DC 20009-1068

Appalachian Regional Commission Transportation and Highways Grants 512
The Appalachian Development Highway System (ADHS), a 3,090-mile system of modern highways that connects with the Interstate Highway System, is the cornerstone of ARC's transportation efforts. Now approximately 85 percent open to traffic, the ADHS has stimulated economic and employment opportunity throughout the Appalachian Region. Building on the foundation of the ADHS, ARC supports transportation activities aimed at improving travel within the Region as well as enhancing access to coastal cities and ports. Connecting Appalachia to both a domestic and a worldwide chain of suppliers and markets is essential to the economic and employment success of its businesses, communities, and people. By coordinating the ADHS with rail and inland waterway systems, Appalachia can help its existing businesses become more competitive and attract new businesses and employment to the Region. ARC's transportation development strategies include: completing the Appalachian Development Highway System; improving the capacity, efficiency, and responsiveness of Appalachia's railways, including the development of new intermodal corridors and critical short line rail links to smaller communities and rural areas; enhancing the growth and success of Appalachia's waterway navigation system, including obtaining Marine Highway Corridor designation for key inland navigation links; strengthening Appalachia's access to key coastal ports, which serve as Appalachian gateways to international commerce; and developing new intermodal terminals throughout the Region to better coordinate highway, rail, and inland navigation services and to ensure convenient access to the transportation system by Appalachia's businesses, communities, and people.
Requirements: States, and through states, public bodies and private nonprofit organizations are eligible to apply.
Restrictions: Generally, ARC grants are limited to 50% of project costs.
Geographic Focus: Alabama, Georgia, Kentucky, Maryland, Mississippi, New York, North Carolina, Ohio, Pennsylvania, South Carolina, Tennessee, Virginia, West Virginia
Contact: Jill Wilmoth, Budget and Program Specialist; (202) 884-7668 or (202) 884-7700; fax (202) 884-7691; jwilmoth@arc.gov
Internet: http://www.arc.gov/program_areas/index.asp?PROGRAM_AREA_ID=19
Sponsor: Appalachian Regional Commission
1666 Connecticut Avenue NW, Suite 700
Washington, DC 20009-1068

Apple Worldwide Developers Conference (WWDC) Student Scholarships 513
The WWDC Student Scholarship provides Apple Developers Conference (ADC) Student Members and student Team Members in the iPhone Developer University Program the opportunity to get a free pass to attend WWDC. Scholarship recipients have full access to the conference including the range of in-depth technical sessions, access to Apple engineers at the hands-on labs, and the opportunity to meet hiring managers from around the world at the Student Career Fair. Student attendees will be admitted to the regularly scheduled conference sessions, labs, and special events during the week. The WWDC Student Scholarship Program features a Welcome Session and a Career Fair. Note that all sessions are presented in English and cover highly technical content.
Requirements: Scholarship applicants must complete all required questions in the application form, and submit a resume in PDF (Portable Document Format). Applications may be submitted only through the WWDC Student Scholarship Application website. To be eligible to apply you must be an Apple Developer Connection Student Member or iPhone Developer University Program Student team member, enrolled part-time or full-time at a college or university, have a student identification number, and be at least 18 years of age. Eligibility subject to verification by Apple. Student Scholarship applicants will be judged on technical ability, creativity of ideas expressed in products or projects, prior WWDC attendance, technical and work experience. If there is a tie between applicants in the final judging process, Apple will base its final decision on the number of past WWDC events the applicant has attended.
Restrictions: Void where prohibited by law. Employees of Apple Inc., their affiliates, subsidiaries, advertising and promotion agencies and their immediate family members and/or those living in same household of each are not eligible.
Geographic Focus: All States
Date(s) Application is Due: Apr 14
Contact: Developer; (408) 974-4897 or (800) 633-2152; fax (408) 974-7683
Internet: http://developer.apple.com/wwdc/students/
Sponsor: Apple, Inc.
1 Infinite Loop
Cupertino, CA 95014

Applied Biosystems Grants 514
The company is committed to the communities where its employees live and work. Financial contributions as well as in-kind and product donations are awarded to nonprofit organizations. The focus is on education, health and human services, community outreach programs, environment, arts & culture, and civic. Precollege, college, graduate, and other unique programs that use technology to improve science, math, and engineering education are education programs supported. Organizations providing access to quality health care facilities and innovative solutions to chronic problems through disease and therapeutic research are supported. Outreach programs and civic groups that improve communities with innovative science, technology, and education are supported. Programs maintaining a healthy environment, arts and culture, and civic programs are also supported. Requests are accepted at any time.
Requirements: Nonprofit organizations in communities where Applied Biosystems has operations are eligible.
Geographic Focus: All States
Contact: Program Officer; (800) 327-3002 or (650) 638-5800; fax (650) 638-5998
Internet: http://www.appliedbiosystems.com/about/community.cfm
Sponsor: Applied Biosystems
850 Lincoln Centre Drive
Foster City, CA 94404

App

lied Materials Corporate Philanthropy Program 515

The program supports nonprofits in its areas of interest. Applied Materials has a special interest in funding arts and culture grant proposals that have broad community appeal, take arts and culture outside traditional settings to reach young people of diverse backgrounds, particularly economically disadvantaged neighborhoods, support nonprofit organizations in bringing the arts to educational programs and organizations. Education proposals must benefit students in grades K-12, focus on traditional skills such as reading, writing, math, technology, and other subjects that prepare young people for entering the workforce, address critical education needs through innovative approaches to learning, expand existing efforts in order to reach more students or a wider geographic area, actively partner with other nonprofit groups to create, implement or evaluate shared programs, and provide adult education and training in communities where unemployment or underemployment are particular challenges. Proposals for civic grants must meet basic needs such as food, housing and clothing, focus on youth-based programs, such as mentoring and leadership training, provide innovative programs that can be replicated to reach more communities, or foster environmental beautification and reclamation projects for public areas such as parks, hiking, and biking trails, restoration of greenbelts, waterways, and wetlands.Generally, Applied Materials supports programs or projects that are based in, or directed toward, a city or region where Applied Materials has operations. Locations currently accepting grant requests are listed in the Proposal Resource Kit. Applications are reviewed on a quarterly basis.
Requirements: IRS 501(c)3 organizations in company-operating areas are eligible to apply.
Restrictions: Grants are not awarded to individuals or religious organizations for religious purposes.
Geographic Focus: All States
Date(s) Application is Due: Jan 14; Apr 15; Jul 15; Oct 17
Samples: Communities In Schools (Austin, TX)—to provide counseling to approximately 175 students and their families who evacuated to Austin due to Hurricane Katrina and are suffering post-traumatic stress disorder, depression, and anxiety, $75,000.
Contact: Contribution Program Manager; community_affairs@appliedmaterials.com
Internet: http://www.appliedmaterials.com/about/grant_guidelines.html
Sponsor: Applied Materials
3050 Bowers Avenue, MS 2765
Santa Clara, CA 95054

APSAA Foundation Grants 516

The mission of the APF Committee is to raise funds and sponsor programs promoting a better understanding of psychoanalysis and encouraging effective and innovative dissemination of psychoanalytic ideas and services to the public. The APF Committee's objective is to educate the public, the community of mental health workers, and allied disciplines about the relevance of psychoanalysis as a powerful therapeutic and research instrument whose applications span a wide range of understanding of individual behavior and cultural phenomena. One or several of the following elements should be a part of the proposal in order to be considered: community outreach; national focus—not a program that is generally put on as a regular activity by a society or institute; fund raising element—seeks co-funding, matching or other sources of support for project (grant money may be used as seed money for helping Grantee to get other sources of funding); transportable—broad applicability to other psychoanalytic institutes, societies and foundations (the program can serve as a model for other programs); and creative and original.
Geographic Focus: All States
Amount of Grant: 1,000 - 5,000 USD
Samples: Washington Center for Psychoanalysis—to enable the design and implementation of a system of psychodynamic support for Jubilee JumpStart, a new child care and education facility for low-income families, $5,000; Allen Creek Preschool, Ann Arbor, Michigan—to support the Early Childhood Training Initiative, a new outreach program designed to nurture the growth of early childhood educators and day care workers through professional training, workshops, and consultations, $4,000.
Contact: Dean K. Stein, Executive Director; (212) 752-0450; fax (212) 593-0571; deankstein@apsa.org or info@apsa.org
Internet: http://www.apsa.org/AmericanPsychoanalyticbrFoundationCommittee/tabid/70/Default.aspx
Sponsor: American Psychoanalytic Association
309 East 49th Street
New York, NY 10007-1601

APSA Minority Fellowships 517

The program is designed primarily for minority students applying to enter a doctoral program in political science for the first time. The association has re-focused and increased its efforts to assist minority students in completing their doctorates by concentrating not only on the recruitment of minorities, but also on the retention of these groups within the profession. The program designates six stipend minority fellows each year. Additional applicants who do not receive funds from the association may also be recognized and recommended for admission and financial support to graduate political science programs. Fellows with stipends receive a fellowship that is disbursed in two payments - one at the end of their first graduate year and one at the end of their second - provided that they remain in good academic standing. Awards are based on students' undergraduate course work, GPA, extracurricular activities, GRE scores, and recommendations from faculty. Guidelines are available online.
Requirements: Applicants must: be members of one of the following racial/ethnic minority groups - African Americans, Latinos/as, and Native Americans (federal and state recognized tribes); demonstrate an interest in teaching and potential for research in political science; be a U.S. citizen at time of award; and demonstrate financial need.
Geographic Focus: All States
Date(s) Application is Due: Oct 2

Amount of Grant: 4,000 USD
Contact: Jeffrey R. Biggs, Program Director; (202) 483-2512, ext. 521; fax (202) 483-2657; jbiggs@apsanet.org or cfp@apsanet.org
Internet: http://www.apsanet.org/content_3284.cfm
Sponsor: American Political Science Association
1527 New Hampshire Avenue, NW
Washington, DC 20036-1206

APS Foundation Grants 518

Through its Corporate Giving and Foundation, APS continues to be the leading Arizona corporate citizen. It supports nonprofit organizations with a 501(c)3 Internal Revenue Service tax-exempt status through cash and/or in kind services. The Foundation support Arizona communities in five strategic areas: health and human services, community development, education, arts and culture, and environment.
Restrictions: APS does not fund individual requests, charter or private schools, religious, political, fraternal, legislative or lobbying efforts or organizations, travel-related or hotel expenses, private or family foundations, private non-profit organizations, salaries and/or debt reduction.
Geographic Focus: Arizona
Amount of Grant: Up to 100,000 USD
Samples: Phoenix Art Museum, Phoenix, Arizona, $100,000; Phoenix Zoo, Phoenix, Arizona, $40,000; Phoenix Indian Center, Phoenix, Arizona, $25,000.
Contact: Teresa DeValle, Contributions Coordinator; (602) 250-2259; fax (602) 250-3066; Teresa.DeValle@aps.com
Internet: http://www.aps.com/general_info/AboutAPS_14_Archive.html
Sponsor: Arizona Public Service Foundation
P.O. Box 53999, MS 8010
Phoenix, AZ 85072-3999

AptarGroup Foundation Grants 519

The foundation awards grants to Illinois nonprofit organizations in its areas of interest, including in order of priority, health and social services, cultural activities and programs, and higher education.
Requirements: Illinois nonprofit organizations are eligible.
Restrictions: Grants do not support nursing homes, animal welfare groups, national or international relief organizations, primary, secondary, or theological schools, or religious, civic, fraternal, veterans', social, or political organizations. Individuals, testimonial dinners, fundraising events, courtesy advertising, or trips or tours will not be supported.
Geographic Focus: Illinois
Date(s) Application is Due: Mar 15; Oct 15
Contact: Lawrence Lowrimore, Secretary; (815) 477-0424; fax (815) 477-0481; info@aptargroup.com
Sponsor: AptarGroup Charitable Foundation
475 W Terra Cotta Avenue, Suite E
Crystal Lake, IL 60014-9695

A Quiet Place Grants 520

With funding centered primarily in Florida, the Independent Foundation offers grant awards to individuals in support of their work in Christian missions. There are no specific applications or deadlines with which to adhere, and those in need should begin the formal application process by contacting the Foundation directly. Grants average approximately $1,500, and can be used for anything related to missionary work (transportation, supplies, food, etc.).
Requirements: Applicants must work with individuals in Florida.
Geographic Focus: Florida
Amount of Grant: 1,500 USD
Contact: Marc R. White, President; (352) 771-0071; marc@corpfl.com
Sponsor: A Quiet Place
14030 Lake Yale Road
Umatilla, FL 32784-8100

Aquila Corporate Grants 521

Aquila has identified youth development as its primary area for grant consideration. Grants in youth development support activities aimed at broad-scale outreach to area youth for the purposes of building leadership, social skills and self-esteem; enhancing business education and academic performance; and fostering the successful transition from youth to productive adulthood. Other focus areas supported include community betterment, education and literacy, human services, and safe, affordable, energy-efficient housing. Organizations that will be considered for economic development grants will aim at strengthening neighborhoods and business communities and attracting tourism. As part of its social responsibility, the corporation acknowledges the benefits of supporting the arts and culture in order to promote creative and enriched communities. Given these areas of primary concern, the corporation will respond to unique challenges, ideas, and projects that lie beyond the identified areas of focus. Letters of intent for requests may be submitted at anytime.
Requirements: 501(c)3 tax-exempt organizations in Colorado, Iowa, Kansas, Missouri, and Nebraska are eligible.
Restrictions: Exclusions include organizations that do not have current 501(c)3 tax-exempt status; organizations that practice discrimination by race, creed, color, gender, religion, sexual preference, age, or national origin; organizations not located in communities where Aquila has a business interest; organizations or events whose primary purpose is to redistribute funds to other charitable establishments; appeals for unrestricted funds; religious organizations whose primary purpose is to promote sectarian values; veterans groups and labor organizations when serving only their own membership; political or lobbying activities; or funding for a program or project that lasts longer than five years.

Geographic Focus: Colorado, Iowa, Kansas, Missouri, Nebraska
Contact: Grants Administrator; (816) 467-3617; fax (816) 467-9617; partner@aquila.com
Internet: http://www.aquila.com/about/community/contributions.shtml
Sponsor: Aquila
20 W Ninth Street, MSC 4-271
Kansas City, MO 64105

Aragona Family Foundation Grants 522
Giving primarily in Austin, Texas, the Aragona Family Foundation provides general operating support grants in the following areas of interest: animals/wildlife, preservation/protection; cancer; children/youth, services; community/economic development; education; food banks; hospitals (general); philanthropy/voluntarism; protestant agencies & churches. Grants range from $2,000 - $100,000.
Requirements: Qualifying 501(c)3 organizations are eligible to apply for funding. There is no: application form required; deadline date to adhere to.
Geographic Focus: Texas
Amount of Grant: 2,000 - 100,000 USD
Samples: St. Stephens Episcopal School, Austin, TX, $100,000—to further the organizations charitable mission; Harvard University, Cambridge, MA, $533,300—to further the organizations charitable mission.
Contact: Joseph C. Aragona, President; (512) 328-2178
Sponsor: Aragona Family Foundation
3311 Westlake Drive
Austin, TX 78746-1901

Aratani Foundation Grants 523
The foundation awards grants to nonprofits in its areas of interest, including education, health care, museums, recreation, and religion. Preference is given to Japanese-American cultural organizations. Types of support include annual campaigns, building construction/renovation, capital campaigns, conferences and seminars, continuing support, curriculum development, endowments, exchange programs, fellowships, general operating support, program development, scholarship funds, and seed grants.
Requirements: The Foundation gives primarily in the state of California but funding is also available in the states of: New York; District of Columbia; Washington; Florida; Rhode Island; Oregon. Application forms are not required, but application outlines are available. Contact the Foundation directly for additional guidelines. Applications maybe submitted in English and Japanese. There are no application deadline dates.
Restrictions: Grants are not made to individuals.
Geographic Focus: California, District of Columbia, Florida, New York, Oregon, Rhode Island, Washington
Amount of Grant: 1,000 - 150,000 USD
Contact: George Aratani, President; (310) 530-9900
Sponsor: Aratani Foundation
23505 Crenshaw Boulevard, North 230
Hollywood, CA 90505

Arbor Day Foundation Grants 524
The mission of the National Tree Trust continues through the Arbor Day Foundation, a nonprofit, environmental education organization with a mission of inspiring people to plant, nurture, and celebrate trees. The Program provides appropriate support and resources to urban and community forestry and conservation nonprofit organizations working to engage the members of their community in urban and community forestry. The programs of the Foundation are Seeds—technology, general office equipment and supplies, rent for office space, salaries and wages, general printing and postage, and professional contract services; Roots—education, involvement of underserved communities, tree planting and maintenance, community nursery, and service learning; and Branches—community outreach. Guidelines are available online.
Requirements: Eligible organizations will include qualified 501(c)3 nonprofits that have been in existence for two years, and are either an urban and community forestry organization or a conservation-focused organization working on urban and community forestry projects.
Geographic Focus: All States
Contact: Mark Derowitsch; (888) 448-7337; mderowitsch@arborday.org
Internet: http://www.arborday.org/programs/
Sponsor: Arbor Day Foundation
100 Arbor Avenue
Nebraska City, NE 68410

Arcadia Foundation Grants 525
The foundation awards grants to Pennsylvania nonprofit organizations to improve the quality of life. Areas of interest include hospitals and hospital building funds, health agencies and services, nursing, hospices, early childhood, adult and higher education, libraries, child development and welfare agencies, youth organizations, and social service and general welfare agencies, including care of the handicapped, aged, and hungry. Also supported are family services, environment and conservation, wildlife and animal welfare, religious organizations, historical preservation, and music organizations. Types of support include general operating support, continuing support, annual campaigns, capital campaigns, building construction/renovation, equipment acquisition, endowment funds, program development, scholarship funds, and research. Applications are accepted between September 1 and November 1.
Requirements: Eastern Pennsylvania organizations whose addresses have zip codes of 18000-19000 are eligible. Application form not required. The initial approach should be a letter or proposal—not exceeding two pages.
Restrictions: Grants are not awarded to support individuals, deficit financing, land acquisition, fellowships, demonstration projects, publications, or conferences.
Geographic Focus: Pennsylvania
Date(s) Application is Due: Nov 1
Contact: Marilyn Lee Steinbright, President; (610) 275-8460
Sponsor: Arcadia Foundation
105 E Logan Street
Norristown, PA 19401

Arca Foundation Grants 526
The Arca Foundation believes that access to knowledge, vigorous public education and citizen engagement are essential to democracy. However, there exist structures and private interests that serve to limit the transparency of our government, stifle public debate on critical issues, and foster an environment where government is not effectively serving the interests of its citizens. In order to promote greater social equity and justice at home and abroad, the foundation supports organizations and projects that work to advance transparent, accountable, and just policies. They support strategic initiatives that work to directly affect policies by: Developing and advocating for innovative ideas; Promoting transparency and access to information; Fostering greater public debate on critical issues; Educating key stakeholders; Engaging citizens in strategic organizing and advocacy that builds power and drives change.
Requirements: Domestically, in the current sociopolitical climate, the foundation is concerned about the promotion of a more equitable, accountable, and transparent economic recovery. They are considering proposals that work to advance more just policies on this and other critical issues. Internationally, the foundation has a long history of working to promote greater dialogue between the U.S. and Cuba. They are considering proposals that advance policies that further normalized US-Cuban relations, as well as proposals that work to foster more just policies on a range of international issues. The Arca Foundation has two deadlines annually, on March 1 and September 1 of every year, for consideration in June and December respectively. When deadline dates fall on a weekend, the deadline is effective on the next weekday. The foundation will not respond to letters of inquiry, but will accept complete proposals submitted according to the application guidelines on regular grant deadlines.
Restrictions: The foundation does not fund organizations that provide direct social services, scholarship funds or scholarly research, capital projects or endowments, individuals, or government programs. Proposals received via fax or email will not be considered. Late proposals will not be considered, and extensions are not available for any reason.
Geographic Focus: All States
Date(s) Application is Due: Mar 1; Sep 1
Amount of Grant: 50,000 USD
Contact: Emily Casteel; (202) 822-9193; fax (202) 785-1446; grants@arcafoundation.org
Internet: http://www.arcafoundation.org/howtoapply.htm
Sponsor: Arca Foundation
1308 19th Street NW
Washington, DC 20036

Archer Daniels Midland Foundation Grants 527
The foundation prefers to fund programs that will directly impact the communities where operating units are located. Nearly a third of the funding is directed toward educational institutions, including elementary, secondary, and higher education. The advocacy category covers world affairs and foreign relations groups that deal with international trade; also supported are projects stressing free enterprise and assistance for women. Support of social services goes to minority group development, cultural activities, and hospital and youth agencies. Health service funding supports hospital and disease association programs. Conservation funding supports programs for protecting the environment and beautification as well as conservation. Religion grants support Christian, Jewish, and Roman Catholic organizations, such as churches, colleges and universities, international ministries/missions, Jewish welfare, and the Salvation Army. Applications are accepted at any time; initial contact by letter of inquiry is encouraged.
Requirements: Tax-exempt organizations are eligible. Current United Way recipients and national organizations are also eligible.
Geographic Focus: Arkansas, California, Georgia, Illinois, Indiana, Iowa, Kansas, Kentucky, Massachusetts, Michigan, Minnesota, Mississippi, Missouri, Montana, Nebraska, New Jersey, New York, North Carolina, North Dakota, Ohio, Oklahoma, Pennsylvania, Puerto Rico, South Carolina, Tennessee, Texas, Washington, Wisconsin
Amount of Grant: 10,000 USD
Contact: Brian Peterson; (217) 424-5413 or (217) 424-5200; corpaffairs@admworld.com
Internet: http://www.adm.com/en-US/responsibility/social_investing/Pages/default.aspx
Sponsor: Archer Daniels Midland Foundation
4666 Faries Parkway, P.O. Box 1470
Decatur, IL 62526-5630

ARCO Foundation Education Grants 528
The foundation will concentrate its aid to education in support of the following: precollege programs to improve the quality of teaching and learning in urban public education; programs aimed at decreasing attrition rates among low-income and minority students; programs to motivate low-income and minority students to succeed in college, especially in mathematics-based careers of engineering, science, and business; support for laboratory renovation and scientific equipment in academic disciplines of interest at major research universities; programs to retain the most talented young faculty in academic careers in selected disciplines; selected liberal arts programs at colleges and universities of interest; state associations of private colleges in the states where the company has interests; academic programs relevant to energy interests at regional universities and colleges; and national education associations and organizations that seek to improve education in public high schools and at higher academic levels. Grants are awarded for operating budgets, seed money, equipment, land acquisition, matching funds, employee matching gifts, employee

related scholarships, special projects, and technical assistance. Applications are accepted at any time; annual report should be obtained prior to submitting a formal proposal.
Requirements: The foundation is a regional organization funding nonprofit organizations in states where ARCO has facilities and personnel, including Alaska, Arizona, California, Colorado, Nevada, Texas, and Washington. Requests from those states and those nearby should be addressed to the local community affairs managers.
Restrictions: The foundation discourages applications from the following: programs not focused on promoting self-sufficiency and economic development of minority populations; historic preservation or urban development projects not tied to neighborhood economic revitalization; proposals from religious organizations; or funding requests from federal, state, county, and municipal agencies, including school districts. The foundation does not generally consider support of hospital building or endowment campaigns, medical equipment, medical research programs, single-issue health organizations, or health services not directed at low-income people.
Geographic Focus: Alaska, Arizona, California, Colorado, Nevada, Texas, Washington
Amount of Grant: 1,500 - 360,000 USD
Contact: Virginia Victorin, Grants Administrator; (213) 486-3342; fax (213) 486-0113
Internet: http://www.ntlf.com/html/grants/5977.htm
Sponsor: ARCO Foundation
151 South Flower Street
Los Angeles, CA 90071

Arcus Foundation Fund Grants 529
The Arcus Foundation is a private grantmaking foundation that supports organizations around the world working in two areas - lesbian, gay, bisexual, and transgender (LGBT) human rights; and conservation of the world's great apes. In the former area, the Foundation supports organizations that are working to achieve social justice that is inclusive of sexual orientation, gender identity and race. In the latter area, it supports organizations seeking to ensure respect and survival of great apes and their natural habitat. Specifically, the Arcus Fund supports efforts within Michigan to improve the quality of life for the gay, lesbian, bisexual and transgender (GLBT) community. Areas of special interest include social equity, public awareness and understanding, health and safety, and scientific inquiry. Types of support include: annual campaigns; building/renovation; capital campaigns; conferences and seminars; consulting services; continuing support; curriculum development; employee matching gifts; endowments; general operating support; matching/challenge support; program development; program evaluation; program-related investments/loans; publication; and technical assistance.
Requirements: Nonprofit organizations are eligible.
Restrictions: No grants to are given to individuals, or for religious or political activities, medical research or film/video production.
Geographic Focus: Michigan
Amount of Grant: 1,000 - 50,000 USD
Contact: Myron Cobbs, Program Assistant; (269) 373-4373, ext. 110; fax (269) 373-0277; myron@arcusfoundation.org or info@arcusfoundation.org
Internet: http://www.arcusfoundation.org/pages_2/home.cfm
Sponsor: Arcus Foundation
402 East Michigan Avenue
Kalamazoo, MI 49007

Arcus Foundation Gay and Lesbian Fund Grants 530
The Arcus Foundation is a private grantmaking foundation that supports organizations around the world working in two areas - lesbian, gay, bisexual, and transgender (LGBT) human rights; and conservation of the world's great apes. In the former area, the Foundation supports organizations that are working to achieve social justice that is inclusive of sexual orientation, gender identity and race. In the latter area, it supports organizations seeking to ensure respect and survival of great apes and their natural habitat. Specifically, the Arcus Gay and Lesbian Fund's goals are: to improve the quality of life in Southwest Michigan, especially Kalamazoo County, by funding projects and organizations that promote social justice, youth, arts and culture and the environment; and to celebrate the gay, lesbian, bisexual and transgender (GLBT) community in Southwest Michigan and Kalamazoo County, and to make its presence better known and appreciated by highlighting the contributions and presence of the GLBT community, promoting understanding and appreciation of GLBT issues and concerns and/or inspiring philanthropy by members of the GLBT community.
Requirements: Nonprofit organizations are eligible.
Restrictions: No grants to are given to individuals, or for religious or political activities, medical research or film/video production.
Geographic Focus: Michigan
Contact: Myron Cobbs, Program Assistant; (269) 373-4373, ext. 110; fax (269) 373-0277; myron@arcusfoundation.org or info@arcusfoundation.org
Internet: http://www.arcusfoundation.org/pages_2/home.cfm
Sponsor: Arcus Foundation
402 East Michigan Avenue
Kalamazoo, MI 49007

Arcus Foundation National Fund Grants 531
The Arcus Foundation is a private grantmaking foundation that supports organizations around the world working in two areas - lesbian, gay, bisexual, and transgender (LGBT) human rights; and conservation of the world's great apes. In the former area, the Foundation supports organizations that are working to achieve social justice that is inclusive of sexual orientation, gender identity and race. In the latter area, it supports organizations seeking to ensure respect and survival of great apes and their natural habitat. Specifically, the Arcus National Fund supports efforts with national scope and impact to improve the quality of life of the GLBT community nationwide. Areas of special interest include social equity, public awareness and understanding, health, safety and scientific inquiry.

Requirements: Nonprofit organizations are eligible.
Restrictions: No grants to are given to individuals, or for religious or political activities, medical research or film/video production.
Geographic Focus: All States
Amount of Grant: 1,000 - 50,000 USD
Contact: Lucia Leandro Gimeno, Program Assistant; (212) 488-3000; fax (212) 488-3010; lucialeandro@arcusfoundation.org
Internet: http://www.arcusfoundation.org/pages_2/home.cfm
Sponsor: Arcus Foundation
402 East Michigan Avenue
Kalamazoo, MI 49007

Argyros Foundation Grants 532
The foundation annually awards grants for cultural activities, higher education, religious projects, social services, recreation, and health services. Types of support include general operating support and program development. Proposals must give a detailed outline of the project for which funds are requested.
Requirements: Giving is primarily made to organizations in Orange County, CA.
Geographic Focus: California
Date(s) Application is Due: Jun 1
Amount of Grant: 5,000 - 50,000 USD
Contact: Daniel Russo, Argyros Charitable Trusts; (714) 481-5000
Sponsor: Argyros Foundation
949 S Coast Drive, #600
Costa Mesa, CA 92626

Arie and Ida Crown Memorial Grants 533
The program supports programs that offer opportunities to the disadvantaged, strengthens the bond of families, and improves the quality of people's lives. As a general rule, the Foundation funds organizations that serve the greater Chicago area as well as organizations that serve the broader Jewish community. Most grants are awarded to organizations within the city of Chicago. Organizations are supported in the areas of arts and culture (concentrating on educational and enrichment programs for youth), civic affairs, education, health (stressing access to services, hospice and health promotion), and human service (focusing on programs which offer assistance for children and families).
Requirements: Nonprofits in Chicago and Cook County, IL, may apply for grant support.
Restrictions: Grants are not made to support individuals, conference expenses, film projects, government programs (50 percent government funded), or research projects.
Geographic Focus: Illinois
Date(s) Application is Due: Jan 31; Jul 31
Amount of Grant: 1,000 - 200,000 USD
Contact: Susan Crown; (312) 236-6300; fax (312) 984-1499; AICM@crown-Chicago.com
Internet: http://www.crownmemorial.org/
Sponsor: Arie and Ida Crown Memorial
222 N LaSalle Street, Suite 2000
Chicago, IL 60601

Arizona Cardinals Grants 534
The National Football League franchise supports programs designed to improve the quality of life and enhance opportunities for children, women, and minorities in the state of Arizona. Specific areas of interest include arts and culture, civic affairs, education, health, science, and social services. The foundation is interested in expanding its giving and looks for new charities to fund. First-time applicant organizations generally will receive grants of $5000 or less.
Requirements: Applicants must be exempt under 501(c)3 of the Internal Revenue Service.
Geographic Focus: Arizona
Date(s) Application is Due: Aug 1
Amount of Grant: 2,000 - 5,000 USD
Contact: Pat Tankersley, (602) 379-0101; fax (480) 785-7327
Internet: http://www.azcardinals.com/community/charities.php
Sponsor: Arizona Cardinals
P.O. Box 888
Phoenix, AZ 85001-0888

Arizona Commission on the Arts After-School Program Residencies 535
Projects are initiated by Schools and School Districts. The grant provides matching funds to support the fees, travel and per diem expenses for artists providing arts learning residencies for students in schools, after school, out of school or inter session programs. These programs focus on student learning and may additionally provide professional development services. Residencies are designed to facilitate and support programs that help Arizona children, families, and communities reject drugs.
Requirements: 501(c)3 Arizona nonprofit organizations or schools are eligible. An unincorporated Arizona organization may apply through a fiscal agent, providing that the fiscal agent is an Arizona 501(c)3 or governmental organization.
Restrictions: Arts organizations and art schools are not eligible to apply.
Geographic Focus: Arizona
Date(s) Application is Due: Mar 22
Amount of Grant: 500 - 5,000 USD
Contact: Mandy Buscas; (602) 771-6525; mbuscas@azarts.gov
Internet: http://www.azarts.gov/artslearning/grants.htm#
Sponsor: Arizona Commission on the Arts
417 W Roosevelt Street
Phoenix, AZ 85003

Arizona Commission on the Arts Education Projects Grants 536
The Arizona Commission on the Arts is committed to making the arts fundamental to education, particularly in programs that serve Pre-K-12 students, classroom teachers, teaching artists, arts specialists and administrators in school, after-school and summer/inter-session programs. Our goal is that applicants present a plan that creatively stimulates arts education in their school/community organizations.
Requirements: An applicant organization must be a 501(c)3 Arizona nonprofit organization or school, or a unit of government. An unincorporated Arizona organization may apply through a fiscal agent, providing that the fiscal agent is an Arizona 501(c)3 or a governmental organization. Grant applications must be submitted online.
Restrictions: No more than one Arts Learning project per individual site is funded per year. Support for staff salaries, funding for insurance or supplies are not provided through this grant.
Geographic Focus: Arizona
Date(s) Application is Due: Mar 22
Contact: Alison Marshall; (602) 771-6523; amarshall@azarts.gov
Internet: http://www.azarts.gov/index.htm
Sponsor: Arizona Commission on the Arts
417 W Roosevelt Street
Phoenix, AZ 85003

Arizona Commission on the Arts Folklorist Residencies 537
In this residency program, folklorists guide students and teachers in the process of researching, identifying, and documenting traditional art forms in their community. Students develop a new sense of community as they learn and experience the significance of family, community, and cultural traditions directly from parents and family members, employers and workers, senior citizens, public officials, and other community members. Residency lengths are variable and are built around a combination of services: training for students and teachers in research methodology; fieldwork conducted by the folklorist with participating students and teachers; classroom workshops; lecture-demonstrations on traditional art forms; interviews with local traditional artists; and presentation of traditional artists/art forms in school or community settings. A travel, lodging, and meal subsidy is provided for artists funded for out-of-town residencies in addition to their payment for services.
Requirements: 501(c)3 tax-exempt Arizona nonprofit organizations, schools, or units of government are eligible. Schools must select an individual artist, performing company, folklorists, or interdisciplinary artists from the Arizona Artist Roster.
Geographic Focus: Arizona
Amount of Grant: 500 - 3,500 USD
Contact: Robert Booker; (602) 771-6501; fax (602) 256-0282; rbooker@azarts.gov
Internet: http://www.azarts.gov/localarts/index.htm#
Sponsor: Arizona Commission on the Arts
417 W Roosevelt Street
Phoenix, AZ 85003

Arizona Commission on the Arts Individual Artist Residencies 538
In the individual artist residency, the artist works with many different teachers and students at the school. A first-year sponsor may request a 10-day residency to introduce the school to the residency program. After the school's first year in the program, a 20-day length is the minimum for this type of residency. A travel, lodging, and meals subsidy is provided for artists funded for out-of-town residencies and is in addition to their payment for services.
Requirements: 501(c)3 Arizona nonprofit organizations, schools, and units of government are eligible. Schools must select an individual artist, performing company, folklorists, or interdisciplinary artists from the Arizona Artist Roster.
Geographic Focus: Arizona
Amount of Grant: 1,500 - 3,000 USD
Contact: Robert C. Booker, (602) 771-6501; fax (602) 256-0282; rbooker@azarts.gov
Internet: http://www.azarts.gov/index.htm
Sponsor: Arizona Commission on the Arts
417 W Roosevelt Street
Phoenix, AZ 85003

Arizona Commission on the Arts Visual/Media Arts Organizations Grants 539
Visual arts and media arts organizations may apply for matching grants for artists' fees for residencies, workshops, lectures, conferences, exhibitions, catalogs, festivals, or other projects involving the visual arts, artists, or arts-related issues. In visual/media arts, grant awards are made to assist all types of organizations with providing quality arts programming to their community. Project grants are awarded, in general, to assist with the costs of connecting artists (or their artistic work) with the community. The commission gives funding priority to exhibitions that include activities such as guest artists lectures, demonstrations, and workshops designed to increase community awareness and create a dialog about the visual arts; and residencies in schools and communities which feature in-depth workshops by guest artists.
Requirements: An applicant organization must be a 501(c)3 Arizona nonprofit organization or school, or a unit of government. An unincorporated Arizona organization may apply through a fiscal agent, providing that the fiscal agent is an Arizona 501(c)3 or governmental organization. The proposal should name the guest artist(s) and consultant(s) and describe the selection process used. If artists from the Arizona Artist Roster are named, please indicate that they are roster artists. If the proposal includes bringing in an out-of-country artist(s), the application should describe how the selection of the artist benefits the arts in Arizona and relates to the mission of the organization.
Restrictions: Funding may not be requested for printing of invitations, mailings, or costs of receptions.
Geographic Focus: Arizona
Contact: Gregory Sale, Visual Arts Director; (602) 771-6530; gsale@azarts.gov
Internet: http://www.azarts.gov/index.htm
Sponsor: Arizona Commission on the Arts
417 W Roosevelt Street
Phoenix, AZ 85003

Arizona Community Foundation Grants 540
The foundation focuses on areas that bring together donor interests with community needs, best practices and respected research to influence long-term systemic change. The foundation's goal is to improve conditions, circumstances and opportunities for people across Arizona and beyond. The foundation focus areas include: arts in the schools; arts in the communities; children, youth and families; campaign for working families; community development; communities for all ages; capacity building; alliance of Arizona nonprofits; strategic partnerships; Hispanics in partnership; and the tapestry community fund. Types of support include general operating support, continuing support, building construction/renovation, equipment acquisition, emergency funds, program development, publication, seed money, scholarship funds, research, technical assistance, and matching funds. For a complete list of criteria, visit the website.
Requirements: Arizona 501(c)3 organizations are eligible as well as public schools, Native American tribes and their component agencies, and selected public programs.
Restrictions: Grants will not be made to individuals; for deficit financing; endowment funds; employee matching gifts; basic research; conferences and seminars; religious organizations for religious purposes; direct lobbying or influencing of elections; tax-supported governmental functions or programs; fund-raising campaigns and expenses; telephone and/or mail solicitation, capital campaigns; or support of veteran, fraternal, and labor organizations.
Geographic Focus: Arizona
Date(s) Application is Due: Apr 1; Oct 1
Contact: Alice McKinney, Grants Administrator; (602) 381-1400 or (800) 222-8221; fax (602) 381-1575; amckinney@azfoundation.org
Internet: http://www.azfoundation.org/File/static/grant_seekers/initiatives.shtml
Sponsor: Arizona Community Foundation
2201 E Camelback Road, Suite 202
Phoenix, AZ 85016

Arizona Community Foundation Scholarships 541
The Arizona Community Foundation sponsors the Dorrance Family Foundation scholarships to provide academic and financial support to Arizona's first generation college students. The foundation awards up to 25 scholarships annually to incoming freshmen who will attend one of three Arizona public universities. The award is renewable for up to three years for a total of eight semesters of full-time undergraduate study. Scholarships are renewed based on academic standing, participation in program events and activities, and community service projects. Any academic major is eligible.
Requirements: Applicants must be Arizona residents; seniors in good standing at an accredited Arizona high school; first generation applicants to attend college; hold a minimum cumulative 3.0 GPA; an SAT score of 1040 or composite ACT score of 22 (excluding writing score); demonstrate financial need; accepted by one of Arizona's three residential public universities (Arizona State, Northern Arizona University, or University of Arizona); and demonstrated leadership and community service. Visit the website for a current application and deadline information.
Restrictions: Applicants must be Arizona residents.
Geographic Focus: Arizona
Amount of Grant: 10,000 USD
Contact: Grant Administrator; (602) 381-1400 or (800) 222-8221; fax (602) 381-1575; nstaylor@azfoundation.org
Internet: http://www.dorrancescholarship.org/index.php?hs=1
Sponsor: Arizona Community Foundation
2201 E Camelback Road, Suite 202
Phoenix, AZ 85016

Arizona Diamondbacks Charities Grants 542
The major-league baseball franchise awards grants in Arizona to support as wide as possible a variety of charitable causes. Priority will be given to organizations that fall under the foundation's focus areas of health care for the indigent, homelessness and youth education. Types of support include general support, project grants, donated equipment, employee matching gifts, corporate sponsorships, and speakers. Organizations wishing to apply for a grant can fax a request to the community affairs department.
Requirements: Applicants must be 501(c)3 Arizona-based organizations committed to spending grant proceeds in Arizona.
Geographic Focus: Arizona
Contact: Program Contact; (602) 462-6500; fax (602) 462-6575
Internet: http://arizona.diamondbacks.mlb.com/ari/community/foundation.jsp
Sponsor: Arizona Diamondbacks
P.O. Box 2095
Phoenix, AZ 85001

Arizona Foundation for Women Deborah G. Carstens Fund Grants 543
Arizona Foundation for Women funds projects and programs that enhance the lives of Arizona women and children. They educate others about the barriers facing women and children and involve members of the community in efforts to remove those barriers. The Deborah G. Carstens Fund provides grants to not-for-profit organizations that motivate and empower girls and women to take responsibility for their economic lives by developing skills, building self-esteem and identifying challenges that impede their success.

Geographic Focus: Arizona
Contact: Nancy A. Dean; (602) 532-2800; fax (602) 532-2801
Internet: http://www.azfoundationforwomen.org/
Sponsor: Arizona Foundation for Women
2828 North Central Avenue
Phoenix, AZ 85004

Arizona Foundation for Women General Grants 544
Arizona Foundation for Women funds projects and programs that enhance the lives of Arizona women and children. They educate others about the barriers facing women and children and involve members of the community in efforts to remove those barriers. Current types of programs supported include: the Men's Anti-violence Network (M.A.N); Emergency Crisis Transportation; Medical Services for Victims of Domestic Violence; ASU Hispanic Mother-Daughter Program; and the Arizona Coalition on Adolescent Pregnancy and Parenting (ACAPP). The Foundation's General Grant program provides funding to address identified unmet needs of women and girls. Grant funding focuses upon innovative and/or model primary prevention programs.
Requirements: Programs must address social change so that women and girls may live free from fear and violence, attain self-reliance and achieve social equity.
Restrictions: Operational funding is not available.
Geographic Focus: Arizona
Contact: Nancy A. Dean; 602-532-2800; fax 602-532-2801
Internet: http://www.azfoundationforwomen.org/
Sponsor: Arizona Foundation for Women
2828 North Central Avenue
Phoenix, AZ 85004

Arizona Public Service Corporate Giving Program Grants 545
Grants are awarded to support Arizona nonprofit organizations in the areas of health and human services, community development, arts and culture, education, and environment. The foundation awards support for project grants, capital building funds, research, employee matching gifts, in-kind services, conferences and seminars, and operating support. Applications are accepted on an ongoing basis.
Requirements: Arizona 501(c)3 nonprofits are eligible.
Restrictions: APS Corporate Giving does not fund individual request, charter or private schools, religious, political fraternal, legislative or lobbying efforts to organizations, travel-related or hotel expenses, private or family foundation, private non-profit organizations, salaries and/or debt reduction.
Geographic Focus: Arizona
Contact: Cindy Slick; (602) 250-4707; fax (602) 250-2113; Cindy.Slick@aps.com
Internet: http://www.aps.com/main/community/dev/default.html
Sponsor: Arizona Public Service Corporation
P.O. Box 53999, MS 8010
Phoenix, AZ 85072-3999

Arizona Republic Foundation Grants 546
The foundation awards grants in Arizona, with emphasis on the Phoenix metropolitan area, in its focus areas, including arts and culture, children, hunger, homelessness, the elderly, neighborhoods, victims of domestic violence, literacy, and community-based education programs. Support is given for general support, operating expenses, project grants, in-kind services, and donated products. Contact office for deadlines and availability.
Requirements: Arizona nonprofits may apply.
Geographic Focus: Arizona
Contact: Gene D'Adamo, Vice President; (602) 444-8202
Internet: http://www.azcentral.com/arizonarepublic/relations/initiatives.html
Sponsor: Arizona Republic Foundation
200 E Van Buren
Phoenix, AZ 85004

Arizona Republic Newspaper Corporate Contributions Grants 547
The corporation awards grants in Arizona, primarily in the Phoenix metropolitan area, for programs in its areas of interest, including child abuse prevention, domestic violence prevention, education and literacy, arts, drowning prevention, community leadership, regional community building, diversity and cultural awareness. Initiatives focus on the basic needs of individuals, with children as a primary focus. Priority is given to agencies that serve low-income and under-served families and children. Application materials and proposal guidelines are available from the office. Annual deadline dates may vary; contact program staff for exact dates.
Requirements: Arizona nonprofits may apply.
Geographic Focus: Arizona
Amount of Grant: 10,000 - 20,000 USD
Contact: Laura McBride, Grants Manager; (602) 444-8071; fax (602) 444-8242
Internet: http://www.azcentral.com/arizonarepublic/relations
Sponsor: Arizona Republic Newspaper
200 E Van Buren
Phoenix, AZ 85004

Arizona State Library LSTA Collections Grants 548
The Arizona State Library, Archives, and Public Records Agency (State Library) offers libraries the opportunity to apply for grant funding. Collections projects support exemplary stewardship of library collections in a variety of formats; as well as facilitate access to, discovery of, and use of those collections. Collections Grant programs and activities include: access to electronic books; creating, providing, and informing about databases of periodical and reference resources; materials for the visually impaired or those with other disabilities; Arizona Memory Projects; cataloging, access to, and promotion of Arizona governmental publications; online job and career materials; historic Arizona newspapers access; and print materials for tribal and rural libraries. Collections Grants should address these LSTA priorities: establishment or enhancement of electronic and other linkages and improved coordination among and between libraries and entities for the purpose of improving the quality of and access to library and information services; and the development of library services that provide all users access to information through local, state, regional, national and international collaborations and networks.
Requirements: All public libraries recognized by the State Library, including museum libraries, are eligible to apply for LSTA funds. To be eligible to receive LSTA funds in Arizona, all libraries must meet the following criteria: be open to the public at least 750 hours per year, with regular, posted hours; provide core library services, such as borrowing privileges and computer use, free of charge to all residents within the library's service area.
Geographic Focus: Arizona
Date(s) Application is Due: Mar 1
Contact: Mary Villegas, (602) 926-3600; mvillegas@azlibrary.gov
Internet: http://www.azlibrary.gov/lsta/documents/pdf/13guidelines.pdf
Sponsor: Arizona State Library
1700 W Washington, Suite 300
Phoenix, AZ 85007-2935

Arizona State Library LSTA Community Grants 549
The Arizona State Library, Archives, and Public Records Agency (State Library) offers libraries the opportunity to apply for grant funding. Community Grant program and activities include: job assistance and training; small business development; community referral; civic engagement; and legal information. Community Grants should address these LSTA priorities: develop public and private partnerships with other agencies and community-based organizations; target library services to individuals of diverse geographic, cultural, and socioeconomic backgrounds, to individuals with disabilities, and to individuals with limited functional literacy or information skills; and target library and information services to persons having difficulty using a library and to under-served urban and rural communities including children from families with incomes below the poverty line.
Requirements: All public libraries recognized by the State Library, including museum libraries, are eligible to apply for LSTA funds. To be eligible to receive LSTA funds in Arizona, all libraries must meet the following criteria: be open to the public at least 750 hours per year, with regular, posted hours; provide core library services, such as borrowing privileges and computer use, free of charge to all residents within the library's service area.
Geographic Focus: Arizona
Date(s) Application is Due: Mar 1
Contact: Dale Savage, (602) 926-3988; dsavage@azlibrary.gov
Internet: http://www.azlibrary.gov/lsta/documents/pdf/13guidelines.pdf
Sponsor: Arizona State Library
1700 W Washington, Suite 300
Phoenix, AZ 85007-2935

Arizona State Library LSTA Learning Grants 550
The Arizona State Library, Archives, and Public Records Agency (State Library) offers libraries the opportunity to apply for grant funding. Learning Grant programs and activities include: early literacy programs; youth and adult reading programs; information literacy classes and resources; and programming for youth and adults. Learning Grants should address these LSTA priorities: expand services for learning and access to information and educational resources in a variety of formats, in all types of libraries, for individuals of all ages in order to support such individuals' needs for education, lifelong learning, workforce development, and digital literacy skills; target library services to individuals of diverse geographic, cultural, and socioeconomic backgrounds, to individuals with disabilities, and to individuals with limited functional literacy or information skills; and target library and information services to persons having difficulty using a library and to under-served urban and rural communities including children from families with incomes below the poverty line.
Requirements: All public libraries recognized by the State Library, including museum libraries, are eligible to apply for LSTA funds. To be eligible to receive LSTA funds in Arizona, all libraries must meet the following criteria: be open to the public at least 750 hours per year, with regular, posted hours; provide core library services, such as borrowing privileges and computer use, free of charge to all residents within the library's service area.
Geographic Focus: Arizona
Date(s) Application is Due: Mar 1
Contact: Holly Henley, Grants Administrator; (602) 926-3366; hhenley@azlibrary.gov
Internet: http://www.azlibrary.gov/lsta/documents/pdf/13guidelines.pdf
Sponsor: Arizona State Library
1700 W Washington, Suite 300
Phoenix, AZ 85007-2935

Arkansas Arts Council AIE After School/Summer Residency Grants 551
The AIE After-School/Summer Residency program is designed to strengthen the role of the arts in education with the understanding that the development of aesthetic awareness and participation in the arts should be an integral part of life and the basic education process. The Arkansas Arts Council will award AIE After-School/Summer Residency grants of up to $10,000 to sponsor artist residencies that provide positive alternatives for children and youth during non-school hours. Possible residency disciplines include the following art forms: crafts; dance; design arts; folk arts; literature; music; theater; opera/music theater; photography/media arts; visual arts; multi-disciplinary; and interdisciplinary. Grants are made for projects, programs, and activities that occur between July 1 and June 30. Award payments are made to accommodate the grantee's program requirements as much

as possible. Grant funds may be used to place professional artists in residencies outside of the school environment, school day or school year. The settings include after-school and summer programs, and can be located in community/neighborhood centers, low-income housing projects, juvenile facilities, social service centers, parks/recreation programs, boys and girls clubs and other community-based or governmental organizations and institutions that provide facilities and guidance during non-school hours. Additional information and guidelines are available at the website.
Requirements: Applicants must meet the following *Requirements:* be 501(c)3 tax-exempt organizations or a federal, state, or local government or governmental unit; a church or convention/association of churches; a hospital, hospital service organization, or medical research affiliate; a public school or institution of higher learning. They must also be nonprofit organizations that have been involved in youth programming for a minimum of three years, and have paid and/or volunteer staff that can devote time and effort to implement the program. A one to one cash match is required. The source for matching funds cannot be other Arts Council funds, Arkansas Arts on Tour reimbursements, subsidies for artist fees through the Mid-America Arts Alliance, or grants from the National Endowment for the Arts.
Restrictions: In-kind contributions may not be used as matching funds on applications or counted as matching funds on final reports. They may, however, be included in applications as evidence of the commitment of additional resources. Funding is not allowed for the following: deficits or start-up costs for new organizations; contingency funds or any form of scholarship or student financial aid; contributions and donations to other organizations or individuals; building renovations or capital expenditures for facilities; entertainment expenses; tuition for academic study; staff of faculty salaries; lobbying expenses; interest and other financial costs or fund raising expenses.
Geographic Focus: Arkansas
Date(s) Application is Due: Feb 1
Amount of Grant: Up to 10,000 USD
Contact: Cynthia Haas, Arts in Education Manager; (501) 324-9769 or (501) 324-9766; fax (501) 324-9207; cynthia@arkansasheritage.org or info@arkansasarts.com
Internet: http://www.arkansasarts.org/grants/aie_as.aspx
Sponsor: Arkansas Arts Council
323 Center Street, Suite 1500
Little Rock, AR 72201-2606

Arkansas Arts Council AIE Arts Curriculum Project Grants 552
The AIE Arts Curriculum Project program is designed to strengthen the role of arts in education with the understanding that the development of aesthetic awareness and participation in the arts should be an integral part of life and the basic education process. The Arts in Education Arts Curriculum Project (AIE ACP) grants of up to $10,000 are awarded to schools and nonprofit or governmental organizations and institutions to help support projects that advance the goal of arts as a basic part of education. Projects should seek to enhance current arts curricula or assist in the goal of establishing on-going arts programming and/or curricula in schools and organizations. An AIE ACP may last from one day to one year. Arts in Education Arts Curriculum Project (AIE ACP) grant awards are made for projects, programs, and activities occurring between July 1 and June 30. Grant funds may be used for workshops, technical assistance, in-service training and other projects designed to increase skills in and awareness of arts in education. Activities may serve pre K-12 students, adult and/or special constituents directly or indirectly. The application, specific guidelines, and additional instructions are available at the website.
Requirements: Applicants must meet the following *Requirements:* be 501(c)3 tax-exempt organizations; or be a federal, state or local government or governmental unit; a church or convention/association of churches; a hospital, hospital service organization or medical research affiliate; a public school or institution of higher learning. Colleges, universities, arts centers, local arts councils, museums, public schools and other such entities are encouraged to apply, but must demonstrate involvement with elementary or secondary schools. A one to one cash match is required. The source for matching funds cannot be other Arts Council funds, Arkansas Arts on Tour reimbursements, subsidies for artist fees through the Mid-America Arts Alliance or grants from the National Endowment for the Arts.
Restrictions: In-kind contributions may not be used as matching funds on applications or counted as matching funds on final reports. They may, however, be included in the application as evidence of the commitment of additional resources. Funds are not available for deficits or start-up costs for new organizations; contingency funds or any form of scholarship or student financial aid; contributions and donations to other organizations or individuals; building renovations or capital expenditures for facilities; entertainment expenses; tuition for academic study; staff or faculty salaries; lobbying expenses; interest and other financial costs; fund raising expenses.
Geographic Focus: Arkansas
Date(s) Application is Due: Feb 1
Amount of Grant: 10,000 USD
Contact: Cynthia Haas, Arts in Education Manager; (501) 324-9769 or (501) 324-9766; fax (501) 324-9207; cynthia@arkansasheritage.org or info@arkansasarts.com
Internet: http://www.arkansasarts.org/grants/aie_ac.aspx
Sponsor: Arkansas Arts Council
323 Center Street, Suite 1500
Little Rock, AR 72201-2606

Arkansas Arts Council AIE In-School Residency Program Grants 553
The AIE In-School Residency Program is designed to strengthen the role of the arts in education with the understanding that the development of aesthetic awareness and participation in the arts should be an integral part of life and the basic education process. The Arkansas Arts Council Arts in Education In-School Residency (AIE ISR) grants of up to $40,000 are awarded to place professional artists in residencies at specific school sites or in conjunction with other nonprofit community or governmental organizations and institutions. The AIE In-School Residency program provides a way for artists to demonstrate their art form, create or perform works of art so that participants may observe the creative process and relate their art form to other K-12 curriculum areas. Arts in Education In-School Residency Program grant awards are made for projects, programs, and activities occurring between July 1 and June 30. Possible residency disciplines include the following art forms: crafts; dance; design arts; folk arts; literature; music; theater; opera/music theater; photography/media arts; visual arts; multidisciplinary arts; and interdisciplinary arts. Grant award payments are scheduled to accommodate the grantee's program requirements to the extent possible. The application, along with additional information and specific guidelines are available at the website.
Requirements: Applicants must meet the following *Requirements:* be certified 501(c)3 tax-exempt organizations; or be a federal, state or local government or governmental unit; a church or convention/association of churches; a hospital, hospital service organization or medical research affiliate; a public school or institution of higher learning. A one to one cash match is required. The source cannot be other Arts Council funds, Arkansas Arts on Tour reimbursements, subsidies for artist fees through the Mid-America Arts Alliance, or grants from the National Endowment for the Arts.
Restrictions: In-kind contributions may not be used as matching funds on applications or counted as matching funds on final reports. They may, however, be included in the application as evidence of the commitment of additional resources. Funding is not available for deficits or start-up costs for new organizations; contingency funds or any form of scholarship or student financial aid; contributions and donations to other organizations or individuals; building renovations or capital expenditures for facilities; entertainment expenses; tuition for academic study; staff or faculty salaries; lobbying expenses; interest and other financial costs; or fund raising expenses.
Geographic Focus: Arkansas
Date(s) Application is Due: Feb 1
Amount of Grant: Up to 40,000 USD
Contact: Cynthia Haas, Arts in Education Manager; (501) 324-9769 or (501) 324-9766; fax (501) 324-9207; cynthia@arkansasheritage.org or info@arkansasarts.com
Internet: http://www.arkansasarts.org/grants/aie_is.aspx
Sponsor: Arkansas Arts Council
323 Center Street, Suite 1500
Little Rock, AR 72201-2606

Arkansas Arts Council AIE Mini Grants 554
The AIE Mini Grants fund pre K-12 schools for programs during school hours, and/or organizations that provide after school or summer programs. This funding helps bring quality, professional artists into the classroom or other location to present one- to five-day hands on, curriculum based arts activities. Artists must be selected from the Arkansas AIE Artist Roster included as a section in the guidelines. Applicants may receive up to $2,000 using established AIE program rates for the artist's fees, travel, lodging and supplies. The application and planning guide are available at the website. There is no specific deadline for the application, but programs must occur between October 1 and August 31.
Requirements: Applicants must be a school district recognized by the Arkansas Department of Education or have an IRS letter of determination qualifying the school, organization, or its administrative authority as a nonprofit organization. Applicants must provide a teacher or organization staff member to remain in the classroom/organization site during the mini-residency program. They must also be an organization or institution involved in youth programming for a minimum of three years, and must have paid and/or volunteer staff who will devote time and effort to implement the mini-residency program.
Restrictions: Mini-grant funding is not available for the following: scholarships; tuition for academic study; expenses including buses for field trips, tickets to performances, or refreshments; staff or faculty salaries; fundraising expenses; building renovations; or capital expenditures for facilities.
Geographic Focus: Arkansas
Amount of Grant: Up to 2,000 USD
Contact: Cynthia Haas, Arts in Education Manager; (501) 324-9769; fax (501) 324-9150; cynthia@arkansasheritage.org or info@arkansasarts.com
Internet: http://www.arkansasarts.com/grants/#10
Sponsor: Arkansas Arts Council
323 Center Street, Suite 1500
Little Rock, AR 72201-2606

Arkansas Arts Council Collaborative Project Support 555
The Arkansas Arts Council Collaborative Project Support grants assist with the cost of such arts activities as presenting or sponsoring separate individual artists or arts companies selected by the applicant collaborators for particular projects, subsidizing fees for technicians hired for the project, or underwriting special expenses for projects that involve the collaborators' own artists. Grants range from $1,000 to $10,000, with a one to one cash match. Funding is based the project overview and artists involved, community interaction and accessibility, educational outreach, and project plans and methods for evaluation. The application and additional information are available at the website.
Requirements: A Collaborative Project Support applicant must meet the following criteria: be a certified 501(c)3 tax-exempt organization that does not receive operational support from the Arkansas Arts Council; or be a federal, state, or local government or governmental unit, church or convention/association of churches, hospital, hospital service organization or medical research affiliate, public school of institution of higher learning. Applicants must also be proposing a collaborative arts project that involves some form of community outreach, involving one or more underserved community groups. A Collaborative Project Support request must be matched one to one by cash from sources other than the Arkansas Arts Council, the Mid-America Arts Alliance, or the National Endowment for the Arts.

Other portions of the proposal not involved in the specific Arts Council request and its match may be funded by government sources.
Restrictions: In-kind contributions may not be used as matching funds on an application, nor counted as matching funds on final reports. They should, however, be included in applications as evidence of the commitment of other resources to the applicant. Auxiliaries, guilds, or other groups directly affiliated with arts organizations which receive operational support from the Arkansas Arts Council are not eligible. A Collaborative Project Support grant may be used only for contracted administrative or artistic expenses related to the proposed event. It may not be used for general administrative expenses incurred by the applicant or any of the collaborators—which include administrative salaries/benefits, capital expenditures, or general marketing costs—or to cover artistic and technical staff salaries/benefits for the applicant or any collaborator.
Geographic Focus: Arkansas
Date(s) Application is Due: Jan 11
Amount of Grant: 1,000 - 10,000 USD
Contact: Jess Anthony; (501) 324-9768; fax (501) 324-9207; jess@arkansasheritage.org
Internet: http://www.arkansasarts.org/grants/cps.aspx
Sponsor: Arkansas Arts Council
323 Center Street, Suite 1500
Little Rock, AR 72201-2606

Arkansas Arts Council Expansion Arts Grants 556
The Expansion Arts grant program is designed to strengthen small and mid-sized nonprofit art organizations by providing salary assistance and technical support for an executive director for a period of three years. Positions to be funded with this program will be equivalent to part-time employment. For example, an all-volunteer applicant organization could use the grant to hire its first half-time executive director, or an applicant organization with a new, part-time executive director could use the grant amount to make that position full-time. Expansion Arts participants must commit to attend workshops and conferences, submit to organizational reviews, and meet predetermined standards for board management. By the close of this cycle, organizations can expect to have a strategic plan, grant writing skills, and fundraising and marketing objectives. The application and additional information is available at the website.
Requirements: An organization is eligible to apply if it has received an Expansion Arts grant in the current year, produced or presented community cultural programming, and is a tax-exempt, 501(c)3 organization. All Expansion Arts grant requests must indicate in their budget statements at least a two to one dollar-matching amount for year 3 in overall organizational expenditures that comes from the applicant's own resources. For example, if the request is for $15,000, the applicant's projected budget must show at least $30,000 in other operating revenue or contributed income.
Restrictions: Year 3 Expansion Arts grants are restricted to organizations that were selected to begin participation in the three-year program in the previous year. Failure to attend workshops, conferences, or complete required plans may result in loss of funding.
Geographic Focus: Arkansas
Date(s) Application is Due: Jan 25
Amount of Grant: Up to 15,000 USD
Contact: Janet Harney, Expansion Arts Program Manager; (501) 324-9782; fax (501) 324-9207; janet@arkansasheritage.org or info@arkansasarts.com
Internet: http://www.arkansasarts.org/grants/expansion.aspx
Sponsor: Arkansas Arts Council
323 Center Street, Suite 1500
Little Rock, AR 72201-2606

Arkansas Arts Council General Operating Support 557
The Arkansas Arts Council General Operating Support grants help fund administrative operating expenses of established nonprofit local arts agencies or single discipline organizations with a budget equal to or greater than $50,000. Funding may be spent only for non-programmatic, administrative expenses. These can include, but are not limited to, administrative staff salaries, general marketing and fundraising costs, facility rental, utilities, maintenance of the facility, staff travel, or other expenses associated with the general operation of the organization. Grant review criteria for the organization is based on the organization's history and program description, community interaction and accessibility, its educational outreach, and long ranging planning and evaluation. Applicants may request a percentage of the adjusted operating total income of their last completed fiscal year, with the amount based on their budget size. The deadline is January 25, with a letter of intent due by December 7. The application and detailed financial guidelines are available at the website.
Requirements: An organization is eligible for general operating support (GOS) if it received a GOS for the current year as a 501(c)3 arts organization with a total operating budget equal to or greater than $50,000, or it has been approved as a newly eligible GOS applicant after filing a letter of intent by a certain date. It may also be eligible if it meets the following criteria: employs a full-time executive director if its annual budget total ranges from $150,000 to $999,999; or employs at least a part time paid executive director, with its annual budget ranging from $50,000 to $149,999. Applicants may also be eligible if they have an independent audit of their current fiscal year on file with the Council, with a budget of $500,000 or more, or have an IRS tax form 990 on file with a budget of less than $500,000. GOS requests for administrative support must be matched two to one by the applicant's expenditures on artistic programming. The cash must be from sources other than the Arkansas Arts Council, the Mid-America Arts Alliance, or the National Endowment for the Arts. Other portions of the proposal not involved in the specific Arts Council request and its match may be funded by government sources.
Restrictions: Funding may not be used for artistic or technical staff, or for contracted administrative or artistic costs.
Geographic Focus: Arkansas
Date(s) Application is Due: Jan 25

Contact: Jess Anthony; (501) 324-9768; fax (501) 324-9207; jess@arkansasheritage.org
Internet: http://www.arkansasarts.org/grants/gos.aspx
Sponsor: Arkansas Arts Council
323 Center Street, Suite 1500
Little Rock, AR 72201-2606

Arkansas Arts Council Sally A. Williams Artist Fund Grants 558
The Arkansas Arts Council established the Sally A. Williams Artist Fund in memory of Williams, who served as the Council's Artist Services Manager for 25 years. Artist assistance grants of up to $500 are available to Arkansas artists in the literary, performing and visual arts fields. The application process is ongoing as long as funding is available. Projects may include the following: registration or travel to a conference, retreat, symposium or workshop that will enhance the professional work of the recipient; and consulting fees for establishing or growing the recipient's art-related business, such as a marketing or business plan. The application is available at the website. There is no application deadline, but funding should be used between July 1 and June 30.
Requirements: The applicant must be at least 21 years old, and an Arkansas resident for at least one year at the time of the application.
Restrictions: Applicants under the age of 21, full time students, and non-Arkansas residents are not eligible to apply. Recipients of an individual artist grant during the current year, and recipients of a S.A.W. Artist Assistance grant during the past three years are also not eligible to apply. The grant will also not support the following: fees or travel for the artist whose primary reason for attending an activity or program is to present or teach a workshop; publishing costs; supplies; capital equipment; or any expense not directly related to artist professional development.
Geographic Focus: Arkansas
Contact: Robin Muse McClea, Artist Services Program Manager; (501) 324-9348 or (501) 324-9766; fax (501) 324-9207; robinm@arkansasheritage.org
Internet: http://www.arkansasarts.org/grants/williamsfund.aspx
Sponsor: Arkansas Arts Council
323 Center Street, Suite 1500
Little Rock, AR 72201-2606

Arkansas Community Foundation Arkansas Black Hall of Fame Grants 559
Grants support programs and projects that address problems, challenges, and opportunities in black communities in Arkansas. Categories of interest include education; health and wellness; youth development; and small business and/or economic development. Priority goes to proposals that show multiple sponsoring agencies/organizations; include evidence of local financial support; demonstrate collaborative ventures among community organizations; and have promise for sustainability beyond the period of the grant.
Requirements: Tax-exempt entities such as schools, churches, or government entities are eligible. Preference is given to applications submitted by 501(c)3 nonprofit organizations.
Restrictions: Funds cannot be allocated for adult salary support in carrying out the duties of the project; used to support general operating budgets outside of the specific proposal or project; or for scholarships for formal education at any level.
Geographic Focus: Arkansas
Date(s) Application is Due: Apr 10
Contact: Cecilia Patterson; (501) 372-1116; fax (501) 372-1166; cpatterson@arcf.org
Internet: http://www.arcf.org/page27973.cfm
Sponsor: Arkansas Community Foundation
1400 West Markham, Suite 206
Little Rock, AR 72201

Arkansas Community Foundation Giving Tree Grants 560
Annually, the Foundation solicits proposals for innovative programs to correspond to that year's Board theme of community and economic development. Typically in February, the Board announces the annual theme of its Giving Tree Fund unrestricted grants initiative. The May announcement of recipients of this grant program coincides with the initial meeting more than 30 years ago of the founders of the Arkansas Community Foundation.
Geographic Focus: Arkansas
Contact: Cecilia Patterson, Program Director; (501) 372-1116; fax (501) 372-1166; cpatterson@arcf.org or arcf@arcf.org
Internet: http://www.arcf.org/page27763.cfm
Sponsor: Arkansas Community Foundation
1400 West Markham, Suite 206
Little Rock, AR 72201

Arkansas Community Foundation Grants 561
The Arkansas Community Foundation (ARCF) serves philanthropic donors and supports non-profits in Arkansas. ARCF makes grants from charitable funds established by individuals, families, corporations, and non-profit organizations. From among over 1100 funds, its donors make grants in the following areas of interest: animal welfare, arts and humanities, community development, education, environment, health, human services, and religion. While the Foundation's discretionary grant cycles are few, grants are usually modest and, generally, fund capital or building campaigns are not funded.
Requirements: 501(c)3 Arkansas nonprofit organizations are eligible.
Geographic Focus: Arkansas
Contact: Cecilia Patterson, Program Director; (501) 372-1116; fax (501) 372-1166; cpatterson@arcf.org or arcf@arcf.org
Internet: http://www.arcf.org/page12714.cfm
Sponsor: Arkansas Community Foundation
1400 West Markham, Suite 206
Little Rock, AR 72201

Arkell Hall Foundation Grants 562

The primary mission of the foundation is the operation and maintenance of a home for elderly women. Funds that may become available above the needs of the home may be distributed annually to tax-exempt organizations providing services in the target community—Western Montgomery County, NY—with preference given to those active in service to senior citizens, education (higher education, medical education, adult basic education and literacy), religion (Christian, Christian Reformed Church, Lutheran, Methodist, Roman Catholic, the Salvation Army, and United Methodist), and health care. Types of support include capital, challenge, endowment, general support, matching, and seed money grants. Grants are made on a single-year basis and are awarded annually in October or November. It is recommended that requests be submitted between July 1 and September 15. Initial review of requests is performed upon receipt. Results are forwarded to the applicant within one month.
Requirements: IRS 501(c)3 organizations directly impacting the Western Montgomery County, NY, community are eligible.
Restrictions: Requests that do not include written proof of 501(c)3 status will not be considered. Projects or organizations with large service areas, such as national or regional, will not qualify for funding, nor will projects in which the target community is not the primary area of focus.
Geographic Focus: New York
Date(s) Application is Due: Oct 1
Amount of Grant: 1,000 - 50,000 USD
Contact: Joseph Santangelo, Vice President; (518) 673-5417; fax (518) 673-5493
Sponsor: Arkell Hall Foundation
68 Front Street, P.O. Box 240
Canajoharie, NY 13317-0240

Arkema Foundation Science Teachers Program 563

This program is an intensive week-long session for elementary and secondary school teachers. Armed with innovative science experiment kits and the guidance of chemical engineers and scientists, teachers learn new and fascinating ways to illustrate scientific concepts. Scientific topics explored include life, earth and physical science and technology. School principals are asked to nominate two teachers in grades three through six, who are then chosen by the corporate committee to participate in the program. Application forms and contact information are available on the Web site.
Requirements: Teachers in the following geographic areas may participate: Alabama (Mobile county); Kentucky (Graves, Livingston, Lyon, Marshall, McCracken, Carroll, Gallatin, Trimble, Jefferson counties); Michigan (Wayne county); Minnesota (Didge, Mower, Steele counties); New Jersey (Burlington, Camden, Gloucester, and Salem counties); New York (Genesee, Livingston counties); Pennsylvania (Berks, Bucks, Chester, Delaware, Montgomery, and Philadelphia counties); Tennessee (Shelby county); Texas (Jasper, Newton, Jefferson, Orange, Harris, and Brazos counties).
Geographic Focus: Alabama, Kentucky, Michigan, Minnesota, New Jersey, New York, Pennsylvania, Tennessee, Texas
Contact: Jane Crawford, (215) 419-7614; jane.crawford@arkemagroup.com
Internet: http://www.products.arkemagroup.com/index.cfm?pag=190
Sponsor: Arkema Foundation
2000 Market Street
Philadelphia, PA 19103-3222

Arlington Community Foundation Grants 564

The foundation awards grants in Arlington to educators and nonprofit organizations for innovative projects that supplement and enrich the learning environment for preschool to adult students. The focus is curriculum enrichment, the arts (musical, dramatic, visual), pursuit of higher education, vocational education, after school and summer programs, life-long learning, environmental issues, parent involvement, and community involvement. The community enhancement grants support arts and humanities, children & families, community improvement, health, housing/homeless & hunger, legal, social services, and senior enrichment. The purpose of the Prompt Response Fund is to enable nonprofit groups in Arlington respond quickly to unanticipated opportunities or unexpected, urgent community needs. Deadlines may vary. Guidelines and applications are available online.
Requirements: Organizations and individuals with projects designed to meet educational needs of Arlington residents are encouraged to apply.
Restrictions: The foundation does not make grants for endowments, capital campaigns, religious purposes, individual debts, or political lobbying.
Geographic Focus: Virginia
Contact: Wanda L. Pierce; (703) 243-4785; fax (703) 243-4796; info@arlcf.org
Internet: http://www.arlcf.org/grants.html
Sponsor: Arlington Community Foundation
2525 Wilson Boulevard
Arlington, VA 22201

Armstrong McDonald Foundation Grants 565

The foundation awards grants to eligible nonprofit organizations in its areas of interest, including animal welfare, children and youth, education, special needs, health, and relief and social.
Requirements: 510(c)3 nonprofit organizations, colleges and universities, schools, and school districts are eligible. Application must be downloaded from website.
Restrictions: Grants do not support advocacy organizations, individuals, international organizations, political organizations, or state and local government agencies. The foundation does not fund capital campaigns, salaries/stipends, and multi-year projects. Organization must have received a grant from the foundation within the last five years unless it is located within the states of Arizona or Nebraska. No organization east of the Mississippi is eligible for a grant.
Geographic Focus: All States
Date(s) Application is Due: Sep 30
Amount of Grant: 1,000 - 80,000 USD
Contact: Laurie Bouchard; (520) 878-9627; info@ArmstrongMcDonaldFoundation.org
Internet: http://www.armstrongmcdonaldfoundation.org/
Sponsor: Armstrong McDonald Foundation
P.O. Box 70110
Tucson, AZ 85737.01

A Rocha USA Grants 566

A Rocha USA is part of an international family of conservation organizations working to show God's love for all creation through community-based efforts focused on science and research, practical conservation, environmental education, and environmental health. The organization works toward the conservation of habitats and species world-wide through environmental education, conservation activities, and scientific research; and seeks to build a sense of community among individuals, communities, and their environments through biblical faith. Fields of interest include: community and economic development, environmental health, environmental education, research, and Jewish agencies and synagogues. Giving is both national and international in scope. There are no specific application formats or deadlines with which to adhere, and potential applicants should contact the office directly.
Geographic Focus: All States
Contact: Thomas Rowley, Executive Director; (830) 992-7940; usa@arocha.org
Internet: http://www.arocha.org/int-en/index.html
Sponsor: A Rocha USA
P.O. Box 1338
Fredericksburg, TX 78624-1338

Arronson Foundation Grants 567

The foundation supports nonprofit organizations in the areas of religion, including churches (Baptist, Christian, Jewish, Roman Catholic, and Salvation Army) and religious education, higher education, health care, hospices, Jewish welfare, international ministries/missions, and youth. The foundation awards grants primarily in New York, NY; Philadelphia, PA; and Israel. Types of support include endowment funds, general operating support grants, research, scholarships, and seed money grants. Applicants should submit a brief letter of inquiry and include information on the organization and its work. There are no application deadlines.
Requirements: Nonprofit organizations in Pennsylvania, with emphasis on the Philadelphia area, are eligible to apply.
Geographic Focus: Pennsylvania
Amount of Grant: 200 - 25,000 USD
Contact: Joseph Kohn; (215) 238-1700 or (215) 238-1968; jkohn@kohnswift.com
Sponsor: Arronson Foundation
1 S Broad Street, Suite 2100
Philadelphia, PA 19107

ARS Foundation Grants 568

The mission of the foundation is to make a positive difference in the lives of others. They support human and social services, the arts, children and the elderly, and health care but will consider other organizations. Giving is focused in New York City and Fairfield County, CT, areas. Applicants should submit a cover letter containing a brief history and description of the organization, the program(s), the needs/goals to be addressed, and a description of the project; an itemized budget, current organizational annual budget, and recent audited financial statement; annual report; other funding sources; and 501(c)3 determination letter. There are no application deadlines or forms.
Requirements: Qualified 501(c)3 charitable organizations in the New York City and Fairfield County, CT, areas are eligible.
Restrictions: The foundation does not give grants to individuals, private foundations, or organizations not qualified as charitable organizations.
Geographic Focus: Connecticut, New York
Contact: Administrator; (212) 986-1533; fax (212) 972-2303; info@arsfoundation.com
Internet: http://www.arsfoundation.com
Sponsor: Adolph and Ruth Schnurmacher Foundation
551 Fifth Avenue, Suite 1210
New York, NY 10176

ARTBA Transportation Development Foundation Grants 569

Established in 1985, the ARTBA Transportation Development Foundation (ARTBA-TDF) is a 501(c)3 tax-exempt entity designed to support research, education and public awareness. The Foundation supports a variety of initiatives, including educational scholarships, awards programs, professional development courses, safety training, a national exhibition on transportation, conferences and seminars, webinars, and a facility dedicated to improving safety in roadway construction zones. The Foundation has also become the industry's primary advocate in environmental regulatory actions and litigation. See the web site for further information. Application forms are required.
Geographic Focus: All States
Contact: Matt Jeanneret, ARTBA Executive Director; (202) 289-4434, ext. 106; fax (202) 289-4435; mjeanneret@artba.org
Internet: http://www.artba.org/about/transportation-development-foundation/
Sponsor: American Road and Transportation Builders Association
1219 28th Street NW
Washington, DC 20007-3389

Arthur and Rochelle Belfer Foundation Grants 570
The foundation awards grants to nonprofit organizations of the Jewish faith, with a focus on New York. Grants are targeted toward programs supporting the elderly and women; education/higher education; institutions such as seminaries, synagogues, and temples; hospitals; Jewish welfare; and medical centers. Types of support include general support grants and fellowships. There are no application deadlines. Applicants should send a brief letter of inquiry describing the program.
Restrictions: Grants are not made to individuals.
Geographic Focus: New York
Amount of Grant: 1,000 - 100,000 USD
Contact: Robert Belfer, President; (212) 508-6020
Sponsor: Arthur and Rochelle Belfer Foundation
767 Fifth Avenue, 46th Floor
New York, NY 10153-0002

Arthur and Sara Jo Kobacker, Alfred and Ida Kobacker Foundation Grants 571
Established in 1993, the Arthur and Sara Jo Kobacker, Alfred and Ida Kobacker Foundation is committed to reducing poverty and assisting the disadvantaged, with particular attention given to African Americans, through grants awarded to educational or charitable organizations. Funding is available to the central ohio region of the United States.
Requirements: Central Ohio, tax-exempt organizations are eligible to apply. Giving primarily in the Columbus, Ohio area.
Restrictions: No grants to individuals.
Geographic Focus: Ohio
Contact: Tamera Durrence, Assistant Vice President and Director of Supporting Foundations; (614) 251-4000; fax (614) 251-4009; tdurrence@columbusfoundation.org
Internet: http://www.columbusfoundation.org/find/support/kobacker.aspx
Sponsor: Columbus Foundation
1234 E Broad Street
Columbus, OH 43205

Arthur Ashley Williams Foundation Grants 572
AAW Foundation awards grants to charitable organizations to help improve quality of life for those seeking assistance from these charitable organizations. Grant requests will be considered for program support, seed money, challenge grants, and capital improvements.
Requirements: To apply for a grant, applicants must be non-profit 501(c)3 organizations or public schools.
Restrictions: The Foundation will not fund political or sectarian activities.
Geographic Focus: All States
Amount of Grant: 1,000 - 15,000 USD
Contact: Program Contact; (508) 893-0757; clambert@rcn.com
Internet: http://www.aawfoundation.org/requests.php
Sponsor: Arthur Ashley Williams Foundation
P.O. Box 6280
Holliston, MA 01746

Arthur B. Schultz Foundation Grants 573
The foundation awards grants to eligible nonprofit organizations in its areas of interest, including environmental conservation—design proactive approaches to conservation, protect and connect diverse ecosystems, and enhance wildlife habitats; disabled access and recreational opportunity—provide greater outdoor solutions to basis mobility needs in the developing world and support recreational outlets that enable the disabled to connect with nature; international microenterprise—create socially and environmentally responsible entrepreneurial efforts in underdeveloped free market nations, help buy equipment, forge ecologically responsible initiatives, and bolster local services; and global understanding—promote progressive dialog that bridges divides caused by historical, ethnic, and cultural differences, and help people find common ground and nonviolent solutions. There are no application deadlines or forms; submit a brief letter of inquiry.
Requirements: 501(c)3 nonprofit organizations are eligible.
Geographic Focus: All States
Contact: Director; (307) 413-2273; fax (307) 353-2273; info@absfoundation.org
Internet: http://www.absfoundation.org/programs.html
Sponsor: Arthur B. Schultz Foundation
620 Table Rock West Road
Alta, WY 83414

Arthur F. and Alice E. Adams Charitable Foundation Grants 574
Established in Florida in 1987, the Arthur F. and Alice E. Adams Charitable Foundation is managed by a board of governors with the Wells Fargo Bank acting as corporate governor. The Foundation offers support in the arts, education, and human services. Primary fields of interest include: performing arts centers, opera, and medical research. Grants range from $5,000 to $250,000, with giving throughout the United States. The annual deadline is February 15, though board members meet in both May and November. Applicants should forward a letter describing their need and budget.
Requirements: 501(c)3 organizations located in, or serving the residents of, the following areas are eligible to apply: Miami, Florida; New York, New York; and Memphis, Tennessee.
Restrictions: No grants are awarded to individuals.
Geographic Focus: All States
Date(s) Application is Due: Feb 15
Contact: Paul L Guiabo, President; (336) 747-8186; grantadministration@wellsfargo.com
Sponsor: Arthur F. and Alice E. Adams Charitable Foundation
1525 W. WT Harris Boulevard
Charlotte, NC 28288-5709

Artist Trust GAP Grants 575
The mission of the trust is to support individual artists working in all disciplines in order to enrich community life throughout the state of Washington. Grants for Artist Projects (GAP) provide support for artist-generated projects, which can include but are not limited to the development, completion, or presentation of new work. Projects created in all disciplines are eligible. A multidisciplinary panel of artists and arts professionals from around Washington State select GAP recipients. Applications/guidelines are available online only to Artist Trust members. Non-members may visit Artist Trust's office to pick up guidelines or request paper guidelines by sending a self-addressed, stamped, business-sized envelope to Artist Trust Office: Attn: GAP, 1835 12th Avenue, Seattle, WA, 98122-2437
Requirements: The applicant must be a practicing artist and submit only one application per year; be 18 years of age or older by the application deadline; and be a resident of the state of Washington at the time of application and when the award is granted. Applications must be made in the name of an individual artist.
Restrictions: The applicant must not be a graduate or undergraduate matriculated student enrolled in any degree program. Applications made in the name of collectives, companies, bands, groups, and ensembles will not be accepted.
Geographic Focus: Washington
Date(s) Application is Due: Jun 25
Amount of Grant: 1,500 USD
Contact: Monica Miller; (206) 467-8734, ext. 10; fax (206) 467-9633; info@artisttrust.org
Internet: http://www.artisttrust.org/grants
Sponsor: Artist Trust
1835 12th Avenue
Seattle, WA 98122-2437

Arts and Science Council Grants 576
The council administers a number of grant programs, allocating funds to affiliate organizations, schools, artists, and arts, science, history, and heritage organizations based on a competitive application process. Types of grants offered are fellowships, basic operating grants, Community Cultural Connections grants, education grants, Grassroots Grants Program, and the Regional Artist Project Grants Program. Application forms are available on the Web site.
Requirements: Artists and organizations in North Carolina's Mecklenburg County, and the City of Charlotte are eligible.
Geographic Focus: North Carolina
Amount of Grant: Up to 13,000,000 USD
Contact: Cathy Switalski, Grants Officer; (704) 372-9667, ext. 246; fax (704) 372-8210; cathy.switalski@artsandscience.org
Internet: http://www.artsandscience.org/index.asp?fuseaction=GrantsServices.GrantPrograms
Sponsor: Arts and Science Council - Charlotte/Mecklenburg
227 W Trade Street, Suite 250
Charlotte, NC 28202

Arts Council of Winston-Salem and Forsyth County Organizational Support Grants 577
The council awards a variety of grants to area organizations and individuals. The Organizational Support Grant is an evaluative program that rewards organizations demonstrating artistic and organizational excellence with financial support for operating and administrative costs. To apply for an Grant, whether a new applicant or current Funded Partner, applicants must attend one of two mandatory information sessions scheduled each year.
Requirements: Only members of The Arts Council of Winston-Salem and Forsyth County with an individual 501(c)3 IRS designation are eligible to apply.
Geographic Focus: North Carolina
Date(s) Application is Due: May 2
Contact: Chris Koenig, Director of Partner & Grant Programs; (336) 722-2585, ext. 121; fax (336) 761-8286; ckoenig@intothearts.org
Internet: http://www.intothearts.org/grants/available.asp
Sponsor: Arts Council of Winston-Salem and Forsyth County
226 North Marshall Street
Winston-Salem, NC 27101

Arts Foundation 578
Formerly known as the Friends of the Library Charitable Trust, the Arts Foundation was initially established in 1998 in Iowa, with giving primarily centered around Davenport, Iowa. The Foundation's major fields of interest include: the arts; Christian agencies and churches; historical activities; genealogy; historic preservation; historical societies; and public libraries. There are no application forms or deadlines specified, and applicants should begin by forwarding a letter of request to the Foundation office.
Requirements: Only 501(c)3 organizations located in, or serving the residents of, Davenport, Iowa, should apply.
Geographic Focus: Iowa
Contact: L. Ted Sloane, Trustee; (563) 355-5330
Sponsor: Arts Foundation
2435 Kimberly Road, Suite 290 North
Bettendorf, IA 52722

Arts Midwest Performing Arts Grants 579
Engagement must feature a professional performing artist/ensemble from outside applicant's state. Arts Midwest prefers to support the fine arts of dance, theater, music, youth and family entertainment, and other meaningful non-commercial performing arts forms appropriate for the community. The engagement includes at least one in-depth educational activity preferable conducted by the artist/ensemble and about their art form, performance technique, their training/background, etc. with the intent of educating adult and/or student

audiences about the fine arts. Some examples of activities include workshops, masterclasses, educational lecture/demonstrations, and performances specifically for K-12 students.
Restrictions: Applicant must be a nonprofit 501(c)3 organization or a unit of a state, local, or tribal government located in the nine state area. Artists appearing as part of benefits or fundraisers are not eligible for funding. Producing arts organizations may not request fee support for guest artists appearing as part of the organization's performances. Engagements of professional performing artists/ensembles from the same state as the applicant are not supported.
Geographic Focus: Illinois, Indiana, Iowa, Michigan, Minnesota, North Dakota, Ohio, South Dakota, Wisconsin
Contact: Christy Dickinson; (612) 341-0755; fax (612) 341-0902; christy@artsmidwest.org
Internet: http://www.artsmidwest.org/programs/programs.asp
Sponsor: Arts Midwest
2908 Hennepin Avenue, Suite 200
Minneapolis, MN 55408

ArtsWave Impact Grants 580
The arts in the greater Cincinnati region — music, dance, theater, museums, festivals, and more, are happening in large and small ways in neighborhoods all over — making the area an amazing place to live, work, play and stay. They make communities more exciting and lively, and bring all different kinds of people together throughout the area. ArtsWave: supports the arts that connect people across communities, enabling them to get to know each other; creates connections between arts organizations and with people all over; advocates on behalf of the arts; provides funding and services to the arts; and promotes arts and cultural assets as a defining characteristic of the region. Impact Grants are available to provide support to arts organizations in our region whose work aligns with ArtsWave's community impact agenda. These grants range from $10,000 to over $1 million and may be one-year or two-year commitments. Letters of Interest are mandatory, and are due by November 1 each year. Invitations to apply will be extended by November 26, and final applications will be due by the following April 1.
Requirements: Organizations must: be 501(c)3 nonprofits based in the Cincinnati region; be financially stable over a three-year period; have at least three years of continuous operating history; and have arts programming with differentiated target audience.
Geographic Focus: Ohio
Amount of Grant: 10,000 - 1,500,000 USD
Contact: Tara Townsend, Director, Impact, Planning & Analysis; (513) 632-0134 or (513) 871-2787; fax (513) 871-2706; tara.townsend@theartswave.org
Internet: http://www.theartswave.org/impact/apply-for-funding
Sponsor: ArtsWave
20 East Central Parkway, Suite 200
Cincinnati, OH 45202

ArtsWave Project Grants 581
The arts in the greater Cincinnati region — music, dance, theater, museums, festivals, and more, are happening in large and small ways in neighborhoods all over — making the area an amazing place to live, work, play and stay. They make communities more exciting and lively, and bring all different kinds of people together throughout the area. ArtsWave: supports the arts that connect people across communities, enabling them to get to know each other; creates connections between arts organizations and with people all over; advocates on behalf of the arts; provides funding and services to the arts; and promotes arts and cultural assets as a defining characteristic of the region. Project Grants support special, one-time events that complement or expand upon the regular cultural programming of the applying organization. These one-year grants do not exceed $10,000. The annual deadline is January 7.
Requirements: Organizations must: be nonprofit in nature and should have or be working towards tax exempt status; be based in the Cincinnati region; have arts programming; and not be receiving impact funding from ArtsWave for the current fiscal year. First time applicants must contact Services Office to schedule interview prior to submitting application.
Geographic Focus: Ohio
Date(s) Application is Due: Jan 7
Amount of Grant: Up to 10,000 USD
Contact: Tara Townsend, Director, Impact, Planning & Analysis; (513) 632-0134 or (513) 871-2787; fax (513) 871-2706; tara.townsend@theartswave.org
Internet: http://www.theartswave.org/impact/apply-for-funding
Sponsor: ArtsWave
20 East Central Parkway, Suite 200
Cincinnati, OH 45202

ArvinMeritor Foundation Arts and Culture Grants 582
The foundation provides grants primarily in company-operating locations in the areas of education and training, civic and health, youth organizations, and arts and culture. In the area of Arts and Culture, the foundation supports cultural programs designed to enrich community life. Special emphasis is directed toward programs designed to reach out to young people and encourage them to develop their talents. Types of support include general operating budgets, building funds, continuing support, equipment, and projects. The committee foundation meets every six to eight weeks to review grant requests. Contact program staff for current guidelines.
Requirements: Nonprofit 501(c)3 organizations should submit a one- to two-page letter outlining the purpose and needs of the program, its budget, duration, goals, leadership, and amount requested.
Restrictions: Ineligibility applies to individuals; organizations that limit participation or services based on race, gender, religion, color, creed, age, or national origin; projects without ties to a community that is home to an ArvinMeritor facility; organizations that pose any conflict with the goals and mission of ArvinMeritor, its employees, communities, or products; operating expenses for United Way local agencies, except through the foundation's support of annual United Way campaigns; sponsorships of fundraising activities by individuals (i.e., walk-a-thons); requests for loans or debt retirement; religious or sectarian programs for religious purposes; labor, political, or veterans organizations; fraternal, athletic, or social clubs; or seminars, conferences, trips, and tours.
Geographic Focus: All States
Contact: Jerry Rush; (248) 435-7907; fax (248) 245-1031; jerry.rush@arvinmeritor.com
Internet: http://www.arvinmeritor.com/community/community.asp
Sponsor: ArvinMeritor Foundation
2135 W Maple Road
Troy, MI 48084

ArvinMeritor Foundation Civic Grants 583
The foundation provides grants primarily in company-operating locations in the areas of education and training, civic and health, youth organizations, and arts and culture. The Civics area supports programs designed to: promote safety; enhance neighborhoods; encourage civic pride; and build a better future for young people. Types of support include general operating budgets, building funds, continuing support, equipment, and projects. The committee foundation meets every six to eight weeks to review grant requests. Contact program staff for current guidelines.
Requirements: Nonprofit 501(c)3 organizations should submit a one- to two-page letter outlining the purpose and needs of the program, its budget, duration, goals, leadership, and amount requested.
Restrictions: Ineligibility applies to individuals; organizations that limit participation or services based on race, gender, religion, color, creed, age, or national origin; projects without ties to a community that is home to an ArvinMeritor facility; organizations that pose any conflict with the goals and mission of ArvinMeritor, its employees, communities, or products; operating expenses for United Way local agencies, except through the foundation's support of annual United Way campaigns; sponsorships of fund raising activities by individuals (i.e., walk-a-thons); requests for loans or debt retirement; religious or sectarian programs for religious purposes; labor, political, or veterans organizations; fraternal, athletic, or social clubs; or seminars, conferences, trips, and tours.
Geographic Focus: All States
Contact: Jerry Rush; (248) 435-7907; fax (248) 245-1031; jerry.rush@arvinmeritor.com
Internet: http://www.arvinmeritor.com/community/community.asp
Sponsor: ArvinMeritor Foundation
2135 W Maple Road
Troy, MI 48084

ArvinMeritor Foundation Human Services Grants 584
The foundation provides grants primarily in company-operating locations in the areas of education and training, civic and health, youth organizations, and arts and culture. In the area of Human Services, the foundation supports programs designed to provide emergency help and critical support toward promoting self-sufficiency. Types of support include general operating budgets, building funds, continuing support, equipment, and projects. The committee foundation meets every six to eight weeks to review grant requests. Contact program staff for current guidelines.
Requirements: Nonprofit 501(c)3 organizations should submit a one- to two-page letter outlining the purpose and needs of the program, its budget, duration, goals, leadership, and amount requested.
Restrictions: Ineligibility applies to individuals; organizations that limit participation or services based on race, gender, religion, color, creed, age, or national origin; projects without ties to a community that is home to an ArvinMeritor facility; organizations that pose any conflict with the goals and mission of ArvinMeritor, its employees, communities, or products; operating expenses for United Way local agencies, except through the foundation's support of annual United Way campaigns; sponsorships of fund raising activities by individuals (i.e., walk-a-thons); requests for loans or debt retirement; religious or sectarian programs for religious purposes; labor, political, or veterans organizations; fraternal, athletic, or social clubs; or seminars, conferences, trips, and tours.
Geographic Focus: All States
Contact: Jerry Rush; (248) 435-7907; fax (248) 245-1031; jerry.rush@arvinmeritor.com
Internet: http://www.arvinmeritor.com/community/community.asp
Sponsor: ArvinMeritor Foundation
2135 W Maple Road
Troy, MI 48084

ArvinMeritor Grants 585
ArvinMeritor???s philanthropic programs focus on education and the communities where its employees live and work. Grants support engineering and technical schools worldwide to increase the number of engineers and scientists in the field of automotive engineering, and to stimulate technological development and innovation in this field. The corporation also partners with local, private, and public agencies in order to improve the quality of life in the areas of education, cultural programs, civic responsibility, and health and human services. There are no application deadlines.
Requirements: Nonprofit organizations in ArvinMeritor communities are eligible.
Restrictions: Grants do not support organizations without nonprofit status; individuals; organizations that limit participation or services based on race, gender, religion, color, creed, age, or national origin; projects without ties to a community that is home to an ArvinMeritor facility; organizations that pose any conflict with the goals and mission of ArvinMeritor, its employees, communities, or products; operating expenses for United Way local agencies, except through support of annual United Way campaigns; sponsorships of fund-raising activities by individuals; requests for loans or debt retirement; religious

or sectarian programs for religious purposes; labor, political, or veterans organizations; fraternal, athletic, or social clubs; or seminars, conferences, trips, and tours.
Geographic Focus: All States
Amount of Grant: 1,000 - 100,000 USD
Contact: Jerry Rush; (248) 435-7907; fax (248) 245-1031; jerry.rush@arvinmeritor.com
Internet: http://www.arvinmeritor.com/community/guidelines.asp
Sponsor: ArvinMeritor
2135 W Maple Road
Troy, MI 48084-7186

ASA Deming Lecturer Award   586
The Deming Lecturer Award was established in 1995 to honor the accomplishments of W. Edwards Deming, recognize the accomplishments of the awardee, and enhance the awareness among the statistical community of the scope and importance of Deming's contributions. The awardee will give the Deming Lecture (an invited paper) at the Joint Statistical Meetings and receive a $1,000 honorarium, an award plaque, and travel expenses.
Requirements: The individual must have either made significant contributions in fields related to those in which Deming devoted his career-including survey sampling, statistics in the transportation industry, quality management, and quality improvement-or has made significant contributions through effective promotion of statistics and statistical thinking in business and industry.
Geographic Focus: All States
Date(s) Application is Due: Dec 31
Amount of Grant: 1,000 USD
Contact: Ronald Wasserstein; (703) 684-1221, ext. 1859; fax (703) 684-6456; ron@amstat.org
Internet: http://www.amstat.org/careers/deminglectureraward.cfm
Sponsor: American Statistical Association
732 N Washington Street
Alexandria, VA 22314-3415

Ashland Corporate Contributions Grants   587
The foundation awards grants to eligible Kentucky, Ohio, and West Virginia nonprofit organizations in its areas of interest, including education, arts, communities/civic, disaster relief, environment, and health and human services. Types of support include seed money grants, project grants, endowments, matching gifts, and employee volunteers. The foundation does not provide an application. Most giving is centered on programs that best address the needs of Ashland's employees, stockholders, customers, and other constituencies, and the communities in which they live. Funding requests are not solicited but will be considered. The primary focus is on education, with an emphasis on mentoring, literacy and/or diversity.
Requirements: 501(c)3 tax-exempt organizations in Boyd and Greenup Counties, KY, Lawrence County, OH, and Cabell and Wayne Counties, WV, are eligible. Charitable groups within church or religious organizations are eligible.
Restrictions: The foundation does not support individuals, capital campaigns for building or equipment, endowments, travel, film or video production, tickets, religious or political activities, or goodwill advertising.
Geographic Focus: Kentucky, Ohio, West Virginia
Contact: Program Contact; (859) 815-3333; community@ashland.com
Internet: http://www.ashland.com/commitments/contributions.asp
Sponsor: Ashland
50 East Rivercenter Boulevard, P.O. Box 391
Covington, KY 41012-0391

Asian American Institute Impact Fellowships   588
The program is an intensive six-week leadership program seeking to develop young civic-minded leaders interested in working in the Asian Pacific American community. Fellows will receive 96 hours of training. Workshops will address different issue and skills areas: Asian Pacific American identity; leadership training; communication, career development, networking, and team building; and, social justice issues. At the end of the training, the Fellows will be placed in four-week internships with nonprofit and government sector agencies to learn about regional issues and organizations. Fellows will also meet on a weekly basis for more leadership development such as field trips to Springfield and visits to non-profit institutions. The goal of program is to develop a pipeline of young leaders who will make an impact in the Asian Pacific American community by becoming aware of social issues, and engaged in civic participation. Fellows will receive a $500 stipend, travel, and lunch for the training phase, and during weekly training sessions.
Requirements: The application process will target youth interested in working in the Asian Pacific American community. The mix of Fellows will reflect diversity of gender, class, age, ethnicity, immigration, community service, and other interests. Additional consideration will be given to individuals with disadvantaged backgrounds and situations. Applicants must: (a) be ages 17 to 24; (b) be either currently enrolled in high school, college, or a recent graduate; (c) reside in Illinois; (d) be able to attend works and internships (no accommodations will be provide); and (e) have an understanding of or interested in the Asian American community.
Geographic Focus: Illinois
Date(s) Application is Due: May 19; Jun 2
Amount of Grant: 500 USD
Contact: Mitch Schneider; (773) 271-0899; fax (773) 271-1982; coordinator@aaichicago.org
Internet: http://www.aaichicago.org/ifp.html
Sponsor: Asian American Institute - Chicago
4753 North Broadway Street, Suite 904
Chicago, IL 60640

ASM Congressional Science Fellowships   589
The program will select a postdoctoral to mid-career microbiologist to spend one year on the staff of an individual congressman, congressional committee, or with some other appropriate organizational unit of Congress. The purpose of the program is to make practical contributions to more effective use of scientific knowledge in government, to educate the scientific communities regarding public policy, and to broaden the perspective of both the scientific and governmental communities regarding the value of such science-government interaction. The ASM Fellow will function as special legislative assistant within the congressional staff. The American Association for the Advancement of Science will arrange a carefully structured orientation program, guide the placement process, and coordinate weekly seminars throughout the year for the ASM Fellow, as well as other Congressional Fellows. The period of appointment is from September 1 and extends for one year. The award will include a $60,000 stipend plus health care benefits. The stipend is supported by the Martin Frobisher Fund.
Requirements: Prospective Fellows must be citizens of the United States, be members of ASM for at least one year and must have completed their Ph.D. by the time the fellowship begins in September. Candidates are expected to show competence in some aspect of microbiology, have a broad background in science and technology, and have interest and some experience in applying scientific knowledge toward the solution of social problems. Candidates are expected to be articulate, literate, adaptable, interested in work on a range of public policy problems, and able to work with a variety of people from diverse professional backgrounds. A Complete Application for the Fellowship must include: a letter from the candidate indicating a desire to apply and listing three references; three letters of references; a statement from the candidate about his or her qualifications and career goals.
Restrictions: Candidates selected for interviews must provide travel to and from Washington at their own expense. The candidate is responsible for soliciting the required references, providing the six guidelines for the reference response and seeing that the references are forwarded before the deadline.
Geographic Focus: All States
Date(s) Application is Due: Feb 20
Amount of Grant: 60,000 USD
Contact: Heather Garvey, (202) 942-9209; fax (202) 942-9335; hgarvey@usmusa.org
Internet: http://www.asm.org/Policy/index.asp?bid=12335
Sponsor: American Society for Microbiology
1752 N Street, N.W.
Washington, DC 20036-2904

ASME Charles T. Main Awards   590
The purpose of the ASME Charles T. Main Awards is to encourage student members and young engineers to become active in public service. The awards recognize ASME student members whose leadership and service qualities have contributed to the program and operation of a Student Section of the ASME. Award consideration is given to local, regional, and/or national levels of involvement. Candidates must have been members for more than a year. First place award winners receive a gold medal, certificate, $3,000, and travel expenses to attend the award presentation. Second place winners receive a silver medal, certificate, $2,000, and travel expenses to attend the award presentation. Up to eight $500 honorable mentions will be presented to qualified candidates. Nomination forms and instructions are available at the website.
Geographic Focus: All States, All Countries
Date(s) Application is Due: Mar 1
Amount of Grant: 500 - 3,000 USD
Contact: G.A. Anderkay, Committee Chair; (212) 591-7094; mckivorf@asme.org
Internet: http://www.asme.org/about-asme/honors-awards/achievement-awards/charles-t—main-student-section-awards
Sponsor: American Society of Mechanical Engineers
3 Park Avenue
New York, NY 10016

ASM Gen-Probe Joseph Public Health Award   591
The ASM Gen-Probe Joseph Public Health Award honors a distinguished microbiologist who has exhibited exemplary leadership and service in the field of public health. This award has been established in memory of J. Mehsen Joseph, Ph.D., who dedicated his life toward the advancement of both microbiology and public health.
Requirements: The nominee must be a microbiologist identified with public health. The recipient will be recognized for significant achievements in integrating the science of microbiology into the practice of public health and for promoting the importance of linking these two disciplines. Nominations must consist of the following: curriculum vitae, including a list of nominee's publications; letter of nomination, describe the nominee's leadership and service in the field of public health; letters of support, two letters of support must come from persons, other than the nominator, who are familiar with the nominee's qualifications and accomplishments, citing in particular the nominee's leadership and service in the field of public health. No more than one of the three letters may be from the nominee's institution or from the same institution.
Geographic Focus: All States
Date(s) Application is Due: Oct 1
Amount of Grant: 2,000 USD
Contact: Awards Committee; (202) 942-9226; fax (202) 942-9353; awards@asmusa.org
Internet: http://www.asm.org/Academy/index.asp?bid=36040
Sponsor: American Society for Microbiology
1752 N Street, N.W.
Washington, DC 20036-2904

Aspen Community Foundation Grants 592
The Aspen Community Foundation awards grants to 501(c)3 nonprofits that serve the residents of Pitkin, Garfield, and west Eagle Counties of Colorado in its areas of interest, including: health and human services (particularly with respect to children and families); education programs that develop thoughtful, self-sufficient citizens who contribute to their communities; and strengthening community to promote positive community integration, inter-ethnic understanding, citizen responsibility, volunteerism, and the capacity of communities to solve problems. Types of support include technical assistance, capital grants, general operating support, continuing support, program development, seed grants, and matching funds. Organizations applying for projects that have not previously received funds from the foundation should review their proposals with the program director in advance of submission.
Requirements: The foundation supports 501(c)3 organizations that enhance the quality of life in Pitkin, Garfield, and west Eagle counties of Colorado.
Restrictions: The foundation does not consider grants for projects that have been completed or that will be held prior to the allocations decisions; deficits, retirement of debt, or endowments; religious purposes; political campaigns or organizations that publicly take political positions; medical research; organizations primarily supported by tax-derived funding; or conduit organizations. The foundation does not give priority to applications for hospital equipment; conferences; sports/recreational groups; civic, environmental, or media projects; or arts and culture groups.
Geographic Focus: Colorado
Amount of Grant: 1,000 - 100,000 USD
Contact: Tamara Tormohlen, Executive Director; (970) 925-9300; fax (970) 920-2892; info@aspencommunityfoundation.org
Internet: http://www.aspencommunityfoundation.org/grant-making/apply-for-a-grant-through-acfs-competitive-cycle/
Sponsor: Aspen Community Foundation
110 East Hallam Street, Suite 126
Aspen, CO 81611

Assisi Foundation of Memphis Capital Project Grants 593
The foundation supports organizations in its areas of interest, including health and human services—promote the health and well-being of the Mid-South community and help the health care system respond more effectively to community needs; education and literacy—projects/programs that build organizational capacity of provider agencies, provide professional development to service providers, promote collaboration among provider agencies, and leverage resources (local, state, and federal); social justice/ethics—projects/programs that strengthen ethical values among Mid-South citizens and promote social justice leading to a better understanding of and a more effective response to economic or social threats to the community; and cultural enrichment and the arts—projects/programs that foster an appreciation of the arts in the Greater Memphis community. Religious organizations seeking funding for religious programs also are eligible. Typical capital projects include: building - new construction, addition to existing facility, or renovation; technology - Information Management System installation/upgrade, computer hardware, audio-visual equipment/systems; and furnishings/equipment. Typically, payment of capital project grants is made when the organization begins the construction/renovation. Specific terms and schedule of payments will be based upon the scope of the project, amount of award, duration of the project, and completion of required reporting at appropriate intervals.
Requirements: The Foundation makes grants only to organizations that are classified as tax-exempt under Section 501(c)3 of the Internal Revenue Code and as public charities under Section 509(a) of that Code. The Foundation uses its resources for charitable endeavors that advance the well-being of people and institutions located in Shelby, Fayette, and Tipton Counties in Tennessee; Crittenden County, Arkansas; and Desoto County, Mississippi.
Restrictions: Grants are not made for individuals, national fundraising drives, projects that address the needs of only one congregation, tickets for benefits, political organizations or candidates for public office, lobbying activities, recurring budget deficits, or tournament fees and/or travel for athletic competitions.
Geographic Focus: Arkansas, Mississippi, Tennessee
Date(s) Application is Due: Feb 15; May 17; Aug 16; Nov 15
Contact: Jan Young, Executive Director; (901) 684-1564; jyoung@assisifoundation.org
Internet: http://www.assisifoundation.org/capitalproject.html
Sponsor: Assisi Foundation of Memphis
515 Erin Drive
Memphis, TN 38117

Assisi Foundation of Memphis General Grants 594
The foundation supports organizations in its areas of interest, including health and human services—promote the health and well-being of the Mid-South community and help the health care system respond more effectively to community needs; education and literacy—projects/programs that build organizational capacity of provider agencies, provide professional development to service providers, promote collaboration among provider agencies, and leverage resources (local, state, and federal); social justice/ethics—projects/programs that strengthen ethical values among Mid-South citizens and promote social justice leading to a better understanding of and a more effective response to economic or social threats to the community; and cultural enrichment and the arts—projects/programs that foster an appreciation of the arts in the Greater Memphis community. Religious organizations seeking funding for religious programs also are eligible. Deadlines are set to coordinate with quarterly meetings of the Board of Directors of the Foundation.
Requirements: The Foundation makes grants only to organizations that are classified as tax-exempt under Section 501(c)3 of the Internal Revenue Code and as public charities under Section 509(a) of that Code. The Foundation uses its resources for charitable endeavors that advance the well-being of people and institutions located in Shelby, Fayette, and Tipton Counties in Tennessee; Crittenden County, Arkansas; and Desoto County, Mississippi.
Restrictions: Grants are not made for individuals, national fundraising drives, projects that address the needs of only one congregation, tickets for benefits, political organizations or candidates for public office, lobbying activities, recurring budget deficits, or tournament fees and/or travel for athletic competitions.
Geographic Focus: Arkansas, Mississippi, Tennessee
Date(s) Application is Due: Feb 15; May 17; Aug 16; Nov 15
Amount of Grant: Up to 20,000 USD
Contact: Jan Young, Executive Director; (901) 684-1564; jyoung@assisifoundation.org
Internet: http://www.assisifoundation.org/generalgrants.html
Sponsor: Assisi Foundation of Memphis
515 Erin Drive
Memphis, TN 38117

Assisi Foundation of Memphis Mini Grants 595
A limited number of Mini-Grants are considered annually for consulting services, training, and other items that meet specific criteria. For these grants, the benefit to the organization or to the community served should be clearly identified and easily evaluated. The proposal should increase management efficiency, program capacity or quality of services provided by the organization. All requests must be clearly related to the organization's current long-range plan or be part of an effort to develop such a plan. Projects that require continued funding or ongoing maintenance and support should have future sources of this support documented.
Requirements: The Foundation makes Mini Grants only to organizations that are classified as tax-exempt under Section 501(c)3 of the Internal Revenue Code and as public charities under Section 509(a) of that Code. The Foundation uses its resources for charitable endeavors that advance the well-being of people and institutions located in Shelby, Fayette, and Tipton Counties in Tennessee; Crittenden County, Arkansas; and Desoto County, Mississippi. Organizations should provide some matching commitment to the project through either cash or the dedication of other resources.
Restrictions: Grants are not made for individuals, national fundraising drives, projects that address the needs of only one congregation, tickets for benefits, political organizations or candidates for public office, lobbying activities, recurring budget deficits, or tournament fees and/or travel for athletic competitions. Normal overhead expenses and staff salaries are not considered as matching resources. Purchase or replacement of equipment for administrative purposes, that is part of the normal requirements for the operation of the organization and not related to the organization's long-range plan, will not be considered.
Geographic Focus: Alabama, Mississippi, Tennessee
Date(s) Application is Due: Feb 15; May 17; Aug 16; Nov 15
Amount of Grant: Up to 1,500 USD
Contact: Jan Young , Executive Director; (901) 684-1564; jyoung@assisifoundation.org
Internet: http://www.assisifoundation.org/minigrants.html
Sponsor: Assisi Foundation of Memphis
515 Erin Drive
Memphis, TN 38117

Assurant Health Foundation Grants 596
The foundation awards grants in Wisconsin in its areas of interest, including health care access and promotion, disease prevention, the arts and education, as well as the foundation's national public policy initiatives. Types of support include capital campaigns, consulting services, continuing support, employee matching gifts, employee-related scholarships, in-kind gifts, matching/challenge support, and program development.
Requirements: Wisconsin nonprofit organizations are eligible. Preference is given to requests serving southeastern Wisconsin.
Restrictions: Unsolicited requests for funds not accepted. Requests for funds only accepted after the foundation sends out requests for proposals.
Geographic Focus: Wisconsin
Contact: Grants Administrator; (414) 299-1348; megan.hindman@assurant.com
Internet: http://www.newsroom.eassuranthealth.com/corp/news/newsroom/articles/press_06092005.htm
Sponsor: Assurant Health Foundation
501 W Michigan Street
Milwaukee, WI 53203

ASTA Academic Scholarships 597
ASTA's Tourism Cares refers to its scholarships for undergraduate or graduate level students as "Academic" Scholarships. Tourism Cares is offering 59 Academic Scholarships, ranging from $1,000 from $5,000. The Academic Scholarship Program benefits undergraduate or graduate students of travel- and-tourism-related, or hospitality-related, programs of study, at accredited schools. Each undergraduate scholarship award can be used to cover expenses for tuition, books, and educational fees only. Each graduate scholarship award can be used to cover expenses for tuition, books, educational fees, and research-related expenses only. Each graduate research scholarship award can be used to cover expenses for tuition, books, educational fees, and research-related expenses only. Scholarship offerings (for Graduating High School Seniors or Undergraduate Students include: ASTA Alaska Airlines Scholarship (one at $1,000); ASTA America Express Travel Scholarship (one at $1,000); ASTA Arizona Scholarship (one at $2,000); ASTA Holland America Line Undergraduate Scholarship (one at $1,500); ASTA Northern California Chapter Richard Epping Scholarship (one at $2,000); ASTA Pacific Northwest Chapter - William Hunt Scholarship (two at $1,500); ASTA Princess Cruises Scholarship (one at $2,500); ASTA Stan and Leone Pollard Scholarship (one at $1,000). Scholarship offerings for Graduate Students or Graduate Research Students include: ASTA Arnold Rigby Scholarship (two at $2,500); ASTA Avis Budget Group Scholarship (one at $2,000); ASTA Healy Scholarship (one at $1,000); ASTA Holland America Line Graduate Research Scholarship (one at $4,000); ASTA Joseph R. Stone Scholarship (three at $2,500). Scholarship offering

for an Undergraduate or Graduate Internship (at ASTA's Research Department in the Washington, DC area fall semester): ASTA David J. Hallissey Memorial Internship (one at $2,000). Scholarships for Entering, or Presently Working, Travel Professionals include: ASTA A. J. Spielman Scholarship (one at $1,000); ASTA George Reinke Scholarship (two at $1,500). Specific ASTA Chapters also have scholarship offerings of their own, though many of these have resident requirements.
Requirements: Tourism Cares scholarship awards are merit-based, meaning applicants are evaluated on: academic performance, extracurricular and volunteer activities and experiences, motivation, and leadership potential. In general, all applicants must be enrolled in school for the upcoming fall semester or term to be eligible to receive the scholarship award. Scholarship eligibility criteria are determined by each fund donor contact. Applicants may only apply for the Academic Scholarship Program through the on-line application.
Restrictions: A student may win only one scholarship award from Tourism Cares per calendar year.
Geographic Focus: All States
Amount of Grant: 1,000 - 4,000 USD
Contact: Danielle Belanger, Student Programs Coordinator; 781-821-5990 x 215; scholarships@tourismcares.org or danielleb@tourismcares.org
Internet: http://www.asta.org/Education/content.cfm?ItemNumber=2552&navItemNumber=614
Sponsor: American Society of Travel Agents
1101 King Street, Suite 200
Alexandria, VA 22314

As You Sow 598
As You Sow was founded in 1992 and has grown into two programs that strive to increase corporate accountability. The Environmental Enforcement Program seeks to reduce and remove carcinogenic exposures by pursuing compliance with California's Safe Drinking Water and Toxic Enforcement Act. In its consideration of grant requests, As You Sow will give priority to proposals in the following areas: education of consumers about the risks of toxic exposure and their right to know what goes into consumer products; toxics education and reduction in minority communities; enforcement of local, state, or federal consumer and environment-related laws; education of youth on environmental issues; and related areas will be considered on a case-by-case basis but the proposal must generally have an environmental enforcement or education component. The grants are generally in the range of $5,000 to $10,000.
Requirements: As You Sow gives priority to proposals that will substantially benefit citizens of California through neighborhood, regional, or statewide projects. As You Sow will also give consideration to proposals from organizations outside the state if the project or organization has a California emphasis or component.
Geographic Focus: All States
Amount of Grant: 5,000 - 10,000 USD
Contact: Conrad MacKerron, Senior Program Director; (415) 391-3212; fax (415) 391-3245; mack@asyousow.org
Internet: http://www.asyousow.org/grantmaking/guidelines.shtml
Sponsor: As You Sow
311 California Street, Suite 510
San Francisco, CA 94104

AT&T Foundation Civic and Community Service Program Grants 599
The foundation supports programs that enhance education by integrating new technologies and increasing learning opportunities, improve economic development through technology and local initiatives, provide vital assistance to key community-based organizations, support cultural institutions that make a community unique, and advance the goals and meet the needs of diverse populations.
Requirements: The foundation makes 501(c)3 grants to tax-exempt, nonprofit organizations in certain states. Requirements are available online.
Geographic Focus: All States
Samples: Leader Dogs for the Blind (Rochester, Mich.) received a $25,000 grant for blind and visually impaired individuals. Communities in Schools of San Antonio - received a grant to enhance the technology infrastructure to reach more young people at risk of dropping out of school.
Contact: Marilyn Reznick, (212) 387-6555; fax (212) 387-5097; reznick@att.com
Internet: http://www.att.com/gen/corporate-citizenship?pid=7736&DCMP=att_foundation
Sponsor: AT&T Foundation
32 Avenue of the Americas, 24th Floor
New York, NY 10013

ATA Local Community Relations Grants 600
The Alberta Teachers Association offers Community Relations Grants to locals undertaking activities that profile public education and show teachers as active and concerned citizens. Locals that qualify receive a base grant of $250, plus $1 per member. Examples of activities funded are available in the community relations grants booklet at the ATA website. The Association also works with the Alberta division of the Canadian Mental Health Association (CMHA) to promote mental health, discourage the negative stigma often associated with mental illness, and provide teachers with information resources to help them support students with mental health needs. Locals are encouraged to use their CR grants for activities that promote the mental health of children and youth. Such activities would double their grant so that they are eligible for up to $500, plus $2 per member, for community relations projects relating to mental health issues. Applicants should address questions and submit proposals to the contact person.
Geographic Focus: Canada
Date(s) Application is Due: Apr 1
Contact: Philip McRae, Executive Staff Officer; (800) 232-7208; philip.mcrae@ata.ab.ca
Internet: http://www.teachers.ab.ca/For%20Members/Programs%20and%20Services/Grants%20Awards%20and%20Scholarships/Pages/Local%20Community%20Relations%20Grants.aspx
Sponsor: Alberta Teachers Association
11010 142nd Street NW
Edmonton, AB T5N 2R1 Canada

ATA Political Engagement Grant 601
The Alberta Teachers Association offers an annual political engagement grant to support the development of meaningful relationships between locals and elected officials. Locals that develop a political engagement plan may be eligible for a grant in the amount of one-half of the cost of implementing the plan to a maximum of $600. The grant may be paid in two installments, the first to a maximum of $300 on approval of a political engagement plan, and the remainder on receipt of expenses and a report of activities undertaken. The application is available at the website.
Geographic Focus: Canada
Contact: Jonathan Teghtmeyer, Associate Coordinator, Communications; (780) 447-9477 or (800) 232-7208; fax (780) 455-6481; jonathan.teghtmeyer@ata.ab.ca
Internet: http://www.teachers.ab.ca/For%20Members/Programs%20and%20Services/Grants%20Awards%20and%20Scholarships/Pages/Index.aspx
Sponsor: Alberta Teachers Association
11010 142nd Street NW
Edmonton, AB T5N 2R1 Canada

ATA School-Community Relations Awards 602
To recognize excellence, effective communications, and meaningful relationships between schools and the communities they serve, the Alberta Teachers Association presents an annual award to a teacher and to a school in the Alberta public education system for planning and executing exemplary school-community public relations programs. The School Award of Excellence is open to qualifying schools that have developed and implemented a school-community relations program or project. The School Award winner will receive an engraved plaque and a $300 honorarium. The Teacher Award for Excellence is open to teachers in Alberta who have developed and implemented a school-community or classroom-community relations program or project. Teachers may apply for this award themselves or nominate deserving colleagues. The Teacher Award winner will receive an engraved plaque and a $250 honorarium. In addition to granting awards for excellence, judges may select up to ten additional submissions in either category for merit awards. The competition entry form is available at the website, but must be mailed, along with supporting documentation, to the contact person.
Requirements: Any ATA member currently working in an Alberta public or separate school is eligible to apply. Those applying for the school award should designate a project leader to serve as a contact for the purposes of the application. Submissions should take into consideration the judging criteria and include a competition entry form; goals and objectives of the program; an outline of the activities undertaken; benefits to students; contributions to the community; samples of support materials and/or relevant photography; and letters of support/commendation.
Restrictions: The ATA reserves the right to reproduce and publish copies of project materials submitted in support of an application.
Geographic Focus: Canada
Date(s) Application is Due: Mar 2
Contact: Jonathan Teghtmeyer, Associate Coordinator, Communications; (780) 447-9477 or (800) 232-7208; fax (780) 455-6481; jonathan.teghtmeyer@ata.ab.ca
Internet: http://www.teachers.ab.ca/For%20Members/Programs%20and%20Services/Grants%20Awards%20and%20Scholarships/Pages/School-Community%20Public%20Relations%20Awards.aspx
Sponsor: Alberta Teachers Association
11010 142nd Street NW
Edmonton, AB T5N 2R1 Canada

ATF Gang Resistance Education and Training Cooperative Agreements 603
The program goals are to prevent youth crime, violence, and gang involvement among school-aged youth in all communities by reducing the precursor attitudes and behaviors associated with these behaviors. It functions as a cooperative program that utilizes the skills of BJA, federal, state, and local law enforcement personnel, as well as individuals from the community and civic groups. The program trains police officers to provide instruction to elementary- and middle school-aged children in gang prevention and anti-violence techniques. GREAT consists of three major phases: School-Based Education (Phase I), Summer Education/Intervention (Phase II), and Parent Involvement (Phase III). Although the primary focus of the program is Phase I, applicants who are selected for financial assistance will be required to develop programs tailored to their respective communities for Phases II and III. The funding opportunity number is BJA-2007-1449.
Requirements: The application must be submitted through Grants.gov.
Restrictions: Applicants are limited to state, local, or tribal jurisdictions or their respective law enforcement agencies, including school police, housing authority police, prosecution, probation and parole agencies possessing the power of arrest.
Geographic Focus: All States
Date(s) Application is Due: Dec 14
Amount of Grant: 3,500 - 500,000 USD
Contact: Linda Hammond-Deckard; (202) 616-6500; Great@atfhq.atf.treas.gov
Internet: http://www.ojp.usdoj.gov/BJA/grant/great.html
Sponsor: U.S. Department of Justice - 1
810 Seventh Street NW, 4th Floor
Washington, DC 20531

Atherton Family Foundation Grants 604
The foundation supports the establishment, maintenance, or promotion of such religious, charitable, educational, benevolent, scientific, or other like purposes in Hawaii. Types of support include general operating grants, equipment acquisition, capital fund projects, seed grants, and theology scholarships to children of ministers in the state. The grant period generally is one year, though some multiyear grants will be awarded. Applications are due one month prior to board meetings. Contact the office for application procedures.
Requirements: Hawaii nonprofit organizations are eligible.
Restrictions: Requests for annual operating support or mature programs, an organization that has already received a grant in the same calendar year (with some exceptions), individuals or for the benefit of specific individuals, loans, grants to endowment funds, private foundations, purpose of lobbying, conferences, festivals and one-time events, re-granting, or individual Department of Education schools not typically funded.
Geographic Focus: Hawaii
Date(s) Application is Due: Feb 1; Apr 1; Aug 1; Oct 1; Dec 1
Amount of Grant: 2,000 - 75,000 USD
Contact: Grant Coordinator; (808) 566-5524 or (888) 731-3863, ext. 524; fax (808) 521-6286; foundations@hcf-hawaii.org
Internet: http://www.Athertonfamilyfoundation.org
Sponsor: Atherton Family Foundation
1164 Bishop Street, Suite 800
Honolulu, HI 96813

Athwin Foundation Grants 605
Established in 1956, the Athwin Foundation serves the Minneapolis, St. Paul, Bloomington, Minnesota, Wisconsin area. Primary areas of interest include: arts and culture, church related projects, education, and social services. Providing support in the form of: capital campaigns, general/operating support and, program development. Contact the Foundation by submitting a Letter of Inquiry, if they are interested in your project, a formal request will be made & then a proposal maybe submitted.
Requirements: IRS 501(c)3 non-profit organizations are eligible to apply. The foundation prefers applicants to use the Minnesota Common Grant Application Form that can be obtained by calling the Minnesota Council on foundations (612) 338-1989 or by visiting their web site.
Restrictions: Grants do not support: individuals, scholarships, fellowships, or loans.
Geographic Focus: Minnesota, Wisconsin
Date(s) Application is Due: Mar 1
Amount of Grant: 2,000 - 100,000 USD
Contact: Bruce Bean, Trustee; (952) 915-6165
Sponsor: Athwin Foundation
5200 Wilson Road, Suite 307
Minneapolis, MN 55424-1344

Atkinson Foundation Community Grants 606
Community grants are awarded to agencies located within San Mateo County, CA, or serving residents of the county, with primary emphasis on the North County and Coastside areas. International grants are awarded to nonprofits in Latin America. The goals of the program are to provide opportunities for people to reach their highest potential and to improve the quality of their lives; and to foster the efforts of individuals and families to become socially, economically, and physically self-sufficient. Program priorities are to support nonprofit agencies that serve children, youth, and families; the elderly and the ill; immigrants; the disadvantaged, needy, and homeless; the mentally and physically disabled; and those suffering from drug, alcohol, or physical abuse. Priority also will be given to programs that provide basic human social, physical, and economic services; secondary, vocational, and higher education; adult literacy and basic skills; planning and health education; respite and child care; rehabilitation and job training; counseling; and community enrichment, including environmental conservation. Types of support include general operating support, continuing support, program development, seed grants, scholarship funds, and technical assistance. It is suggested that organizations contact the foundation by phone prior to submission of a grant request to ascertain whether or not the request is within current guidelines.
Requirements: International grants are awarded to organizations working in the Caribbean, Central America, and Mexico; domestic grants are awarded in San Mateo County, CA. 501(c)3 tax-exempt organizations are eligible but those serving residents of San Mateo County, CA, are given preference.
Restrictions: The fund does not make grants to organizations without proof of tax-exempt status; grants to organizations chartered outside the United States; grants, scholarships, or loans to individuals; grants designed to influence legislation; grants for doctoral study or research; grants for travel to conferences or events; grants for media presentations; donations to annual campaigns or special fund-raising events; sponsorship of sports groups; or grants to national or statewide umbrella organizations.
Geographic Focus: California, Antigua & Barbuda, Bahamas, Barbados, Belize, Costa Rica, Cuba, Dominica, Dominican Republic, El Salvador, Grenada, Guatemala, Haiti, Honduras, Jamaica, Mexico, Nicaragua
Date(s) Application is Due: Feb 1; May 1; Aug 1; Nov 1
Amount of Grant: 5,000 - 15,000 USD
Contact: Elizabeth Curtis, Administrator; (650) 357-1101; atkinfdn@aol.com
Internet: http://www.atkinsonfdn.org/guidelines.html
Sponsor: Atkinson Foundation
1720 South Amphlett Boulevard, Suite 100
San Mateo, CA 94402-2710

Atlanta Falcons Youth Foundation Grants 607
The foundation supports Georgia youth organizations with a focus on team building experiences; football coach or adult leader training; opportunities for youth leadership in team sports programming; academic achievement through athletics or fitness; organizational effectiveness assistance for athletics or fitness programs; and community/school athletic field renovation or development.
Requirements: Georgia 501(c)3 and 509(a) nonprofit organizations are eligible.
Restrictions: The foundation does not provide funding for events, individuals, government agencies, municipalities, or parochial or private schools.
Geographic Focus: Georgia
Contact: Kendyl Moss, Program Officer; (770) 965-3115
Internet: http://www.atlantafalcons.com/community/youthFound.jsp
Sponsor: Atlanta Falcons Youth Foundation
4400 Falcon Parkway
Flowery Branch, GA 30542

Atlanta Foundation Grants 608
Grants are awarded to assist Georgia charitable and educational institutions to improve the quality of life in Fulton and DeKalb Counties. Primary areas of interest include education, cultural programs, housing, and other charitable giving. Additional areas of support include adult basic education and literacy training; higher education; health care organizations; recreation; and youth, family, and human services. The board meets in August to consider requests.
Requirements: Nonprofit organizations in Georgia's DeKalb and Fulton Counties may apply for grant support.
Restrictions: Grants are not awarded to individuals or for scholarships, fellowships, or loans.
Geographic Focus: Georgia
Date(s) Application is Due: Mar 1; Sep 1
Amount of Grant: 2,500 - 50,000 USD
Contact: Trustee, c/o Wachovia Bank of Georgia NA; grantinquiriesga@wachovia.com
Internet: http://www.wachovia.com/corp_inst/charitable_services/0,,4269_3296,00.html
Sponsor: Atlanta Foundation
3414 Peachtree Road, 5th Floor, MC GA8023
Atlanta, GA 30326

Atlanta Women's Foundation Grants 609
The foundation awards grants to southern nonprofits to encourage projects that empower women and girls. The foundation supports efforts to promote economic justice, end all forms of violence, and develop alternatives to homelessness and other effects of poverty. Types of support include start-up and operating costs, conferences, fund-raising efforts that show a significant return, films, and small equipment.
Requirements: Southern nonprofits serving one or more of the following counties: Barrow, Bartow, Butts, Carroll, Cherokee, Clayton, Cobb, Cowetta, DeKalb, Douglas, Fayette, Forsyth, Fulton, Gwinnett, Hall, Henry, Newton, Paulding, Pickens, Rockdale, Spalding, and/or Walton are eligible.
Restrictions: Grants are not awarded for endowments, debt reduction, religious groups, building funds, or large equipment (e.g., vehicles).
Geographic Focus: Georgia
Amount of Grant: 5,000 - 25,000 USD
Contact: DiShonda Hughes, Program Contact; (404) 577-5000, ext. 104; fax (404) 589-0000; dhughes@atlantawomen.org or info@atlantawomen.org
Internet: http://awf.techbridge.org/grants/grants.asp
Sponsor: Atlanta Women's Foundation
50 Hurt Plaza, Suite 401
Atlanta, GA 30303

Atran Foundation Grants 610
The foundation supports Jewish nonprofits with a focus on New York and Israel in the areas of higher education, Jewish education, religious education, community services, Jewish welfare, temples, international ministries and missions, temples, medical centers, and women's affairs. Types of support include conferences and seminars, endowment funds, general support, matching funds, multiyear/continuing support, project support, research, scholarships, and seed money grants. The foundation requires that proposals be in writing. Proposals should include the nature of the project, its objectives and significance, time estimate, and budget.
Requirements: 501(c)3 tax-exempt Jewish organizations are eligible.
Restrictions: Grants are not made to individuals.
Geographic Focus: All States
Date(s) Application is Due: Sep 30
Amount of Grant: 250 - 100,000 USD
Contact: Diane Fischer, President; (212) 505-9677
Sponsor: Atran Foundation
23-25 E 21st Street, 3rd Floor
New York, NY 10010

Auburn Foundation Grants 611
The purpose of the Foundation is to stimulate giving and cooperative leadership among the citizens of Auburn; help improve the lives of all community residents, especially those who are most vulnerable; and enrich the cultural environment and community life. Of special interest are projects that bring together all ages and sections of the town, or that contribute to healthy, active living. Application is available online.
Requirements: Any nonprofit that serves residents of Auburn is invited to apply.
Restrictions: Grants will not be awarded to for-profit businesses or expenses already incurred by the applicant.

86 | GRANT PROGRAMS

Geographic Focus: Massachusetts
Date(s) Application is Due: Apr 15
Amount of Grant: 5,000 USD
Contact: Lois Smith; (508) 755-0980, ext. 107; lsmith@greaterworcester.org
Internet: http://www.greaterworcester.org/grants/Auburn.htm
Sponsor: Auburn Foundation
370 Main Street, Suite 650
Worcester, MA 01608-1738

Audrey and Sydney Irmas Charitable Foundation Grants 612
The foundation awards grants to eligible nonprofit organizations in its areas of interest, including arts and culture, higher education, homeless and urban issues, hospitals, and Jewish welfare. Grants support long-term, nonrenewable pledges and general operating grants. Most grants are made to Los Angeles County, CA, nonprofits.
Requirements: 501(c)3 nonprofit organizations are eligible.
Geographic Focus: California
Amount of Grant: 1,000 - 75,000 USD
Contact: Robert Irmas; (818) 382-3313; fax (818) 382-3315; robirm@aol.com
Sponsor: Audrey and Sydney Irmas Charitable Foundation
16830 Ventura Boulevard, Suite 364
Encino, CA 91436-2797

Aurora Foundation Grants 613
The foundation provides grants to eligible nonprofit organizations in the following categories: education, social services, health care, and the arts and humanities. In general, grants are made for capital purposes only, not for operating expenses. Evidence of tax-exempt status must be submitted with all applications. Preference will be given to requests that demonstrate the most urgent and immediate need for funding. Grants are ordinarily made for one year only.
Requirements: 501(c)3 and 170(b)1a nonprofit agencies located in the foundation's service area, which includes the City of Aurora, southern Kane County, and Kendall County in Illinois, are eligible.
Restrictions: The foundation rarely provides the entire support of a project. Grants are not generally available for those agencies and institutions that are funded primarily through tax support. Telephone the office prior to submitting a formal proposal.
Geographic Focus: Illinois
Date(s) Application is Due: Aug 1
Contact: Grants Administrator; (630) 896-7800; grant@aurorafdn.org
Internet: http://www.aurorafdn.org/grantmaking.html
Sponsor: Aurora Foundation
111 W Downer Place, Suite 312
Aurora, IL 60506

Austin-Bailey Health and Wellness Foundation Grants 614
The foundation awards grants to Ohio nonprofit organizations to support programs that promote the physical and mental well-being of the citizens of Holmes, Stark, Tuscarawas and Wayne Counties in the state of Ohio. The Foundation emphasizes healthcare affordability concerns of the uninsured adn underinsured, the poor, children, single parents and the aging. It also advocates programs that speak to the mental health needs of the individuals and families. Opportunities to work with other foundations and organizations to promote the principles of health and wellness are welcome.
Requirements: Applicant organizations must provide a current copy of IRS determination indicating 501(c)3 and 509(a) tax-exempt status; serve part or all of the four county area of Holmes, Stark, Tuscarawas, and Wayne; provide a description of the organization and its activities; state the need to be addressed; and provide a brief description of the project or program and how it will address the health and wellness needs of the community.
Restrictions: The foundation generally does not support annual appeals or membership drives; fund-raising events, program advertising, lobbying activities, endowment funds or organizations not classified as tax exempt by the IRS.
Geographic Focus: Ohio
Date(s) Application is Due: Jun 30; Dec 17
Amount of Grant: 1,000 - 15,000 USD
Contact: Administrator; (330) 580-2380; fax (330) 580-2381; abfdn@sbcglobal.net
Internet: http://fdncenter.org/grantmaker/austinbailey/guide.html
Sponsor: Austin-Bailey Health and Wellness Foundation
2719 Fulton Road NW, Suite D
Canton, OH 44718

Austin College Leadership Award 615
The award honors an outstanding individual who through his/her life's work has demonstrated the principles of servant leadership by: taking a courageous stand on a public policy issue that advances a humanitarian or educational purpose; serving the youth of a state, nation, or international community to improve the quality of health, educational, or community services; or creating opportunities for young people that help them enhance their educational experience and move to a new level of service to society. The recipient also will visit Austin College to speak to community leaders and interact with students and faculty. Nomination form and guidelines are available online.
Requirements: Nominees will be leaders from all levels whose leadership position will have placed him/her in a unique and special position among leaders throughout the world.
Geographic Focus: All States
Date(s) Application is Due: Jun 1
Amount of Grant: 100,000 USD
Contact: Award Administrator; (903) 813-2000 or (800) 526-4276; fax (903) 813-3199

Internet: http://www.austincollege.edu/category.asp?3523
Sponsor: Austin College
900 North Grand Avenue
Sherman, TX 75090-4400

Austin Community Foundation Grants 616
The Austin Community Foundation has a competitive grants cycle in which grant requests from organizations in Austin and surrounding areas are reviewed and may receive funding from the Foundation's unrestricted fund or from donor-advised funds. The Foundation grants funds for projects and programs that address community needs in the areas of: arts and culture; education and training; community development and community service; environment; health; human services; recreation, and animal-related services. Foundation encourages grant requests for projects or programs that: are likely to have a substantial impact on the quality of life of a significant number of people in the community; propose practical ways to address community issues and problems; leverage other sources of support (i.e., funds or volunteers); stimulate others to participate in addressing community problems; are innovative, a new initiative, or an enhancement of a program; assist non-profit organizations to maximize effective management; are cooperative efforts and minimize or eliminate duplication of services; and are sustainable over time. The Foundation accepts grant requests submitted through its online application process.
Requirements: Texas 501(c)3 and 170(b)(1)a(vi) tax-exempt organizations located in the central Texas area, including Travis County, are eligible.
Restrictions: Faxed requests will not be accepted. In general, the Foundation does not grant funds for: unrestricted general operating expenses; the use of and payment for services of a fiscal agent; endowment funds; religious organizations for religious purposes; fund raising activities or events (i.e., annual fund drives, telephone solicitations, benefit tickets); umbrella funding organizations that intend to distribute funds at their own discretion; political lobbying or legislative activities; or individuals.
Geographic Focus: Texas
Contact: Meagan Anderson Longley, Director of Grants and Scholarships; (512) 220-1412 or (512) 472-4483; fax (512) 472-4486; mlongley@austincf.org
Internet: http://www.austincommunityfoundation.org/?nd=grants_intro
Sponsor: Austin Community Foundation
4315 Guadalupe, Suite 300, P.O. Box 5159
Austin, TX 78763

Austin S. Nelson Foundation Grants 617
The primary purpose of the Austin S. Nelson Foundation is to support charitable interests throughout Alberta, Canada. Its major interest areas include: medical research; religious organizations and agencies, community services, and human services. In the area of medicine, it will provide funding for pediatrics, palliative care, cancer research, cerebral palsy, heart disease, diabetes, lung disease, kidney disorders, leukemia, multiple sclerosis, Alzheimer disease, and severe burns. It also supports Christian organizations and Anglican churches. Other areas of giving includes support for organizations that help the blind, physically disabled children, animal welfare, emergency shelters, crisis intervention services, the poor, alcohol and drug abuse, young offenders, crime prevention, mental health, domestic violence victims, abused children, and sexual assault victims. Though there are no specified annual deadlines, grant decisions are made primarily in November. Interested applicants should contact the Foundation by mail.
Geographic Focus: Canada
Contact: Director
Sponsor: Austin S. Nelson Foundation
4825 89th Street
Edmonton, AB T6E5L3 Canada

Autauga Area Community Foundation Grants 618
The Autauga Area Community Foundation (AACF) is a public foundation which links charitable resources with community needs and opportunities. Each year, the Foundation awards grants to nonprofits offering projects and programs in Autauga County that, in the opinion of AACF's Advisory Committee, will improve the quality of life in the community. While many factors are considered, priority is given to proposals that meet the following criteria: programs that address issues affecting Autauga County; seed grants to initiate promising new projects addressing underlying causes of community problems; expanding programs representing innovative and efficient approaches to serving community needs and opportunities; programs that maximize resources and leverage other monies; projects reflecting the cooperative efforts of multiple agencies within the community; and programs that can demonstrate funding plans for the continuation of the project beyond initial funding by the AACF. The maximum grant award is $2500, with the average grant ranging from $500 to $1000. Applications will be accepted online.
Requirements: Nonprofits located in, or serving the residents of, Autauga County are eligible.
Restrictions: Grants are not awarded to: individuals, fundraising events, or capital campaigns.
Geographic Focus: Alabama
Date(s) Application is Due: Mar 8
Amount of Grant: Up to 2,500 USD
Contact: Caroline Montgomery Clark, Vice President, Community Services; (334) 264-6223; fax (334) 263-6225; cacfgrants@bellsouth.net
Internet: http://www.cacfinfo.org/aacf/grants.html
Sponsor: Autauga Area Community Foundation
434 N. McDonough Street
Montgomery, AL 36104

Grant Programs | 87

Autodesk Community Relations Grants 619
Autodesk plays an active role in the communities where employees live and work. Grants are awarded to local nonprofit organizations in the program's areas of interest, including community development, arts, the disabled, education, environment, health and human services, science and technology, and civic affairs. Grants are awarded on a national basis. Preference is given to organizations where Autodesk does business. There are no application deadlines. Written proposal requirements are available online.
Requirements: 501(c)3 tax-exempt organizations are eligible.
Restrictions: Grants do not support sporting events or athletic teams, churches or religious organizations, political parties or organizations, general advertising, video, film or television productions, individuals, subscription fees or admission tickets, fraternal, veteran or sectarian groups or direct funds to Autodesk employees participating in fund-raising events.
Geographic Focus: All States
Amount of Grant: 1,000 - 3,000 USD
Contact: Community Relations Manager; (415) 507-6138
Internet: http://usa.autodesk.com/adsk/servlet/index?siteID=123112&id=1064603
Sponsor: Autodesk
111 McInnis Parkway
San Rafael, CA 94903

AutoNation Corporate Giving Program Grants 620
AutoNation (formerly Republic Industries, Inc. Corporate Giving Program) makes charitable contributions to nonprofit organizations involved with arts and culture, education, the environment, children and youth safety, families, and civic affairs. Support is given on a national basis in areas of company operations. Giving is on a national basis in areas of company operations, with some emphasis on southern Forida. Its fields of interest include: arts, education, the environment, family services, public affairs, and safety/disasters. The primary types of giving are:: charitable contributions, events, sponsorships, volunteerism, and diversity efforts. Each market is responsible for its own outreach; however, there is a corporate fund that can help address local needs.
Requirements: Giving on a national basis, with some emphasis on southern Florida.
Restrictions: No support is provided for religious or fraternal organizations not of direct benefit to the entire community, political organizations, or international organizations. No grants are available to individuals (except for scholarships), or for travel or political campaigns; no new or used vehicle donations.
Geographic Focus: All States
Contact: Marc Cannon; (954) 769-3146; cannonm@autonation.com
Internet: http://corp.autonation.com/about/philantrophy.asp
Sponsor: AutoNation Corporation
110 South East 6th Street
Fort Lauderdale, FL 33301-5005

AutoZone Community Relations Grants 621
AutoZone awards grants to support civic groups and community development projects that aim to improve the quality of life in its operating communities. Areas of interest include education, human services, and civic endeavors. Education grants support workforce development initiatives that build a skilled workforce with expertise in the areas of vehicle maintenance, technology, customer service and retail management; schools and organizations that train future drivers in vehicle maintenance and safety; organizations that develop and promote entrepreneurial skills; and literacy programs. Human services grants support community agencies that provide basic essential human needs such as food, clothing, and shelter. Civic grants support community development initiatives and projects that enhance the quality of life and provide amenities in AutoZone areas. Guidelines and application are available online.
Requirements: 501(c)3 tax-exempt organizations in AutoZone communities are eligible.
Restrictions: Grants do not support individuals, political causes, high school advertising, such as calendars or posters, yearbook advertising, general advertising, athletic organizations and teams, family reunions, beauty contests, churches or religious organizations.
Geographic Focus: All States
Date(s) Application is Due: Feb 1
Contact: Community Relations Coordinator
Internet: http://www.autozoneinc.com/about_us/community_relations/index.html
Sponsor: AutoZone
P.O. Box 2198, Department 8014
Memphis, TN 38101-9842

Autzen Foundation Grants 622
The foundation awards grants to Oregon nonprofit organizations in its areas of interest of arts, children/youth, services, environment, health care, higher education, human services, and performing arts. Types of support include building construction/renovation, continuing support, matching/challenge grants, program development, and seed grants.
Requirements: Nonprofit organizations in the Pacific Northwest are eligible with an emphasis on those in Oregon.
Restrictions: Grants do not support individuals, scholarships, fellowships, or loans.
Geographic Focus: Oregon, Washington
Date(s) Application is Due: Mar 15; Aug 15; Nov 15
Amount of Grant: 2,000 - 27,000 USD
Contact: Kim Freed, Administrator; (503) 226-6051; autzen@europa.com
Sponsor: Autzen Foundation
P.O. Box 3709
Portland, OR 97208-3709

Avery Dennison Foundation Grants 623
The vision of the Avery Dennison Foundation is to inspire human promise toward a more intelligent and sustainable world. This vision drives the Avery Dennison Foundation mission to advance the causes of education and sustainability in the communities where Avery Dennison employees live and work. In cooperation with organizations that receive grants, the Foundation also encourages corporate employees to engage in local community investment opportunities and, through volunteer work, bring the same spirit of invention and innovation found at the heart of our company's success. The Avery Dennison Foundation is expanding our global giving and community investment opportunities. In addition to communities now receiving grants, the Foundation global giving program will expand in China and to India and Brazil. All grant awards will relate to and extend its strategic focus to support education, as well as community-based sustainable environmental projects. The Avery Dennison Foundation uses an on-line application process that is user-friendly and facilitates efficient handling of applications.
Requirements: 501(c)3 nonprofits are eligible.
Restrictions: Grants do not support: organizations that discriminate against a person or a group on the basis of age, political affiliation, race, national origin, ethnicity, gender, disability, sexual orientation or religious belief; individuals(scholarships, stipends, fellowships, travel grants, etc); for-profit organizations or ventures; government agencies; sponsorships (sports teams, fundraising initiatives); religious groups for religious purposes; political organizations, candidates, ballot measure or other political activities; and institutional endowments.
Geographic Focus: All States, Brazil, China
Amount of Grant: Up to 200,000 USD
Contact: Alicia Procello Maddox; (626) 304-2000; fax (626) 304-2192
Internet: http://www.averydennison.com/avy/en_us/Sustainability/Community
Sponsor: Avery Dennison Foundation
150 N Orange Grove Boulevard
Pasadena, CA 91103

Avista Foundation Grants 624
The foundation focuses its giving on grants that strengthen communities and enhance the quality of lives of the people served by Avista Utilities. Emphasis is in the areas of education— K-12 education (particularly in the fields of science, math and technology) and higher education including scholarships; vulnerable and limited income populations—providing assistance to those on limited incomes and support for initiatives to reduce poverty; and economic and cultural vitality—supporting projects that help communities and citizens to grow and prosper. Information is available online.
Requirements: Grants support nonprofit organizations in Avista Utilities' service territory, including eastern Washington; northern Idaho and southern Oregon; Sanders County, MT; and South Lake Tahoe, CA.
Geographic Focus: California, Idaho, Montana, Oregon, Washington
Contact: Grants Administrator; (509) 495-8031; contributions@avistacorp.org
Internet: http://www.avistafoundation.org/who_are_we.asp
Sponsor: Avista Foundation
P.O. Box 3727
Spokane, WA 99220-3727

Avon Products Foundation Grants 625
The foundation's two-fold focus is to support education, community and social services, and arts organizations and programs that provide economic opportunities for women and girls; and to support breast cancer and other women's health organizations and programs. The foundation awards grants in cities and regions with a large concentration of representatives and business operations, with the majority of funds going to US-based institutions. National, international, and New York metropolitan area programs are administered through the foundation's headquarters in New York. For regional funding support, refer to the Avon Foundation website.
Requirements: Applying organizations must be tax-exempt; national and municipal organizations are eligible. Request the guidelines brochure prior to submitting a formal proposal.
Restrictions: Grants do not support individuals; memberships; lobbying organizations; political activities and organizations; religious, veteran, or fraternal organizations; fundraising events; and journal advertisements.
Geographic Focus: All States
Amount of Grant: Up to 23,000,000 USD
Contact: Grants Administrator; (866) 505-2866; info@avonfoundation.org
Internet: http://www.avoncompany.com/women/avonfoundation
Sponsor: Avon Products Foundation
1345 Avenue of the Americas
New York, NY 10105

Award for Volunteer Service to the American Chemical Society 626
The purpose of the Award is to recognize the volunteer efforts of individuals who have served the ACS, contributing significantly to the goals and objectives of the Society. The volunteerism to be recognized may comprise a variety of activities, including, but not limited to, the initiation or sponsorship of a singular endeavor or exemplary performance as a member or chair of a national level ACS committee, or as an elected division or local section officer, or outstanding service in a leadership role in regional meeting(s) or a local section. The award consists of $3,000, a certificate, and an inscription of the recipient's name on a plaque displayed at ACS Headquarters in Washington, DC.
Requirements: A nominee will have been a member of the ACS for at least 15 years, and will have made significant contributions to the ACS.
Restrictions: Past and present members of the ACS Board of Directors and staff are ineligible for the award.

Geographic Focus: All States
Date(s) Application is Due: Nov 1
Amount of Grant: 3,000 USD
Contact: Felicia Dixon, Awards Administrator; (800) 227-5558 or (202) 872-4408; fax (202) 776-8008; f_dixon@acs.org or awards@acs.org
Internet: http://portal.acs.org/portal/acs/corg/content?_nfpb=true&_pageLabel=PP_ARTICLEMAIN&node_id=1319&content_id=CTP_004556&use_sec=true&sec_url_var=region1
Sponsor: American Chemical Society
1155 Sixteenth Street, NW
Washington, DC 20036-4801

AWDF Main Grants 627
AWDF's grant-making ensures resources reach the hundreds of African women's organizations that are working in diverse ways to improve the lives of women and African society at large. The AWDF Main Grants program is pan-African and supports local, national, sub-regional and regional organizations in Africa working towards women's empowerment. AWDF will give grants for projects related to any of its thematic areas, applicants are expected to build in reasonable core costs into their project proposals. Grants can be given to support the capacity and institutional strengthening of organizations including grants for strategic planning, governance systems and fundraising/communication strategies. Typically, grants in this category range from $1,000 to $25,000.
Geographic Focus: All States, All Countries
Amount of Grant: 1,000 - 25,000 USD
Contact: Bisi Adeleye-Fayemi, Executive Director/President; 233 (0) 302 521257 or 233 (0) 302 923626; grants@awdf.org or awdf@awdf.org
Internet: http://www.awdf.org/the-process/main-grants
Sponsor: African Women's Development Fund
PMB CT 89 Cantonments
Accra, Ghana

AWDF Solidarity Fund Grants 628
AWDF's grant-making ensures resources reach the hundreds of African women's organizations that are working in diverse ways to improve the lives of women and African society at large. The Solidarity Fund has been established to create an additional source of funding for current or potential AWDF grantees, to enable them engage in activities which promote learning and the sharing of experiences on a local, national and international level. To this end, the Solidarity Fund will support African women to participate in exchange visits, conferences, seminars and workshops, thereby providing valuable opportunities for networking and information, all of which are vital to the strengthening of the African women's movement. Organizations can apply for grants ranging from $1,000 to $5,000. Applications to the Solidarity Fund can be sent in at any time, and must be received at least three months before the identified activity.
Geographic Focus: All States, All Countries
Amount of Grant: 1,000 - 5,000 USD
Contact: Bisi Adeleye-Fayemi, Executive Director/President; 233 (0) 302 521257 or 233 (0) 302 923626; grants@awdf.org or awdf@awdf.org
Internet: http://www.awdf.org/the-process/solidarity-fund
Sponsor: African Women's Development Fund
PMB CT 89 Cantonments
Accra, Ghana

AXA Foundation Scholarships 629
The foundation carries out activities to improve the quality of life in communities across the country where AXA has a presence. AXA Achievement is the foundation's innovative, long-term strategy to provide America's youth with the advice and access necessary to succeed in college and beyond. Programs include: AXA Achievement Scholarship, in association with U.S. News and World Report—52 annual scholarships to youth throughout the nation (one from each state, the District of Columbia, and Puerto Rico); AXA Achievement Community Scholarship Program—provides advice and access to young people and their parents in the local AXA communities where AXA people live and work; Families of Freedom 2—scholarships for financially impacted families in lower Manhattan who have lost businesses, jobs, or income as a result of the September 11 attacks; and AXA Family Scholarship—scholarships for children of AXA employees and associates.
Requirements: Grants support youth-service organizations targeting at-risk youth and the principal arts institutions in New York City.
Geographic Focus: New York
Contact: Grants Administrator; (212) 554-1234
Internet: http://www.axa-financial.com/axa_foundation/33a_National_Initiatives.html
Sponsor: AXA Foundation
1290 Avenue of the Americas, 13th Floor
New York, NY 10104

Ayres Foundation Grants 630
Incorporated in Indiana in 1944, the Ayres Foundation was established with donations from Theodore B. Griffith, his wife, and their company, L.S. Ayres. Though giving was initially centered around Indianapolis and central Indiana, it has spread throughout the state. Giving is primarily intended to support community services, education, and to strengthen cultural programs. The Foundation's fields of interest include: the arts; community and economic development; higher education; and secondary education programs. Population groups most often supported have been: people with disabilities; economically disadvantaged; mentally challenged; and physically disabled individuals. Types of support offered include: annual campaigns; building and renovation projects; capital campaigns; general operating funds; equipment purchase and rental; program development; and seed money. There is no application form specified, and annual deadlines are April 15 and October 15. Final notification of awards is given approximately eight weeks after each deadline. Grant amounts typically range from $200 to $25,000.
Requirements: Nonprofit 501(c)3 organizations located in, or serving the residents of, Indiana are eligible to apply.
Geographic Focus: Indiana
Date(s) Application is Due: Apr 15; Oct 15
Amount of Grant: 200 - 25,000 USD
Contact: John E.D. Peacock, President; (317) 443-1868; ayresfoundationinc@gmail.com
Sponsor: Ayres Foundation
545 West 93rd Street
Indianapolis, IN 46260-1415

Azadoutioun Foundation Grants 631
The foundation provides general operating and project support for programs and activities in its areas of interest, including adult basic education and literacy, reading, the environment, human services, and international economic development. Types of support include general operating support and program development. Application forms are not required; initial approach should be by letter. Letters of application are accepted at any time. Grants to support Ammenia's attempt to educate it's citizens in the fields of agriculture and ecology. The foundation operates a farm to assist in educating individuals in the field of agriculture to enable them to operate farms for the benefit of citizens.
Restrictions: Grants are not made to individuals.
Geographic Focus: All States
Amount of Grant: 5,000 - 50,000 USD
Contact: Laurie LeBlanc, (978) 374-5504; lleblanc9498C@aol.com
Sponsor: Azadoutioun Foundation
160 2nd Street
Cambridge, MA 02142

Babcock Charitable Trust Grants 632
The Babcock Charitable Trust was established in Pennsylvania in 1957, by way of a donation from Fred C. and Mary A. Babcock. The Trust's primary purpose has always been to support both education and health care throughout the states of Pennsylvania and Florida. With that in mind, the Trust's specified fields of interest include: children and youth services; education; health care programs; higher education; and religion. Application forms are not required, and there are no specific deadlines. Applicants should provide, in written form, a brief overview or history of their organization, a mission statement, a detailed description of the project proposed, and an amount of funding requested. The amount of funding ranges up to $25,000.
Geographic Focus: Florida, Pennsylvania
Amount of Grant: Up to 25,000 USD
Contact: Courtney B. Borntraeger, Treasurer; (412) 351-3515
Sponsor: Babcock Charitable Trust
2220 Palmer Street
Pittsburgh, PA 15218-2603

Back Home Again Foundation Grants 633
Based in Indianapolis, Indiana, the Back Home Again Foundation offers funding in the areas of: animal welfare; the arts; children's services and programs; food services; health organizations; higher education; human services; museums; performing arts; and recreational programming. Since there are no specific application forms or deadlines with which to adhere, applicants should contact the office directly with a description of their program or project, and a detailed budget. Grants range from $1,500 to $30,000.
Geographic Focus: Indiana
Amount of Grant: 1,500 - 30,000 USD
Contact: Randolph H. Deer, Secretary; (317) 844-2886
Sponsor: Back Home Again Foundation
5846 West 73rd Street
Indianapolis, IN 46268

Bacon Family Foundation Grants 634
The foundation awards grants to Colorado nonprofit organizations in its areas of interest, including arts and culture, community development, disabilities, economic development, education, food distribution, environment, health care, historic preservation, homelessness, housing, literacy, recreation/parks, religion, social services, and youth. Types of support include capital campaigns, challenge/matching grants, equipment acquisition, general operating support, project grants, and seed grants. A letter should outline the project or program in brief but sufficient detail for the Foundation to initially evaluate the proposal. There are no application deadlines. The Bacon Family Foundation meets quarterly to consider applications.
Requirements: Colorado nonprofit organizations are eligible. Preference will be given to requests from western Colorado.
Restrictions: No grants are made to individuals.
Geographic Focus: Colorado
Contact: Linda Simpson, (970) 243-3767; lsimpson@wc-cf.org
Internet: http://www.wc-cf.org/bacon.htm
Sponsor: Bacon Family Foundation
P.O. Box 4570
Grand Junction, CO 81502-4570

Bailey Foundation Grants 635
The foundation supports South Carolina nonprofits, primarily in Laurens County, its areas of interest, include: health clinics and organizations involved with theater, education, human services, business promotion, Christianity and awards college scholarships to students graduating from public high schools in Laurens County, South Carolina. Support is offered in the form of : capital campaigns; employee matching gifts; endowments; matching/challenge support; scholarship funds, including individual scholarships; annual campaigns; building/renovation grants. Initial contact may be by telephone or letter. Deadline for scholarship applications is April 15, contact Foundation to request an application form.
Requirements: Nonprofit organizations in Laurens County, South Carolina are eligible.
Restrictions: No grants to individuals, or for general operating support.
Geographic Focus: South Carolina
Date(s) Application is Due: Apr 15; Oct 1
Amount of Grant: 2,500 - 50,000 USD
Contact: Robert S. Link, Jr.; (864) 938-2632; fax (864) 938-2669
Sponsor: Bailey Foundation
P.O. Box 494
Clinton, SC 29325-0494

Balfe Family Foundation Grants 636
The Balfe Family Foundation, established in Florida in 1999, has as its primary fields of interest: education, health care and research, human services, and social services. Types of support are typically in the form of general operations, service delivery support, and seed funding. There are particular application forms or deadlines with which to adhere. Applicants should contact the Foundation in writing, outlining the program and funding need.
Geographic Focus: All States
Amount of Grant: 50 - 50,000 USD
Contact: Opal M. Balfe, President; (954) 462-6300; fax (954) 462-4607
Sponsor: Balfe Family Foundation
2731 NE 14 Street Causeway, #829
Pomano Beach, FL 33062-3562

Ball Brothers Foundation General Grants 637
Founded in the name of Edmund B. Ball and his brothers, the Foundation seeks to build and sustain a high quality of life in Indiana by awarding grants to nonprofit organizations in broad subject areas, including elementary, secondary, higher, and adult basic education and literacy skills; cultural activities; community betterment; the environment; and health and human services. Usually, Muncie and Delaware Counties receive a higher priority for funding than requests from across the state. Types of support include general operations, annual campaigns, capital campaigns, building construction/renovation, program development, conferences and seminars, professorships, publication, curriculum development, research, fellowships, matching funds, seed grants, and technical assistance. Preference will be given to catalytic grants that will stimulate others to participate in problem solving or in matching fund programs and to innovative approaches for addressing either traditional or emerging community needs. Applications are reviewed by the board of directors in January, May, and September of each calendar year. Proposals are encouraged to be submitted from February to May. Grant seekers may send a preliminary proposal, complete proposal, or ask for a personal visit to discuss a potential grant request.
Requirements: Indiana 501(c)3 nonprofit institutions and organizations are eligible.
Restrictions: The Foundation will not support: direct assistance to individuals or scholarships; applications coming from outside of Indiana; booster organizations; on-going salary requests of staff personnel to support an organization; services that the community-at-large should normally underwrite (i.e. roads, bus transportation, etc.); capital building projects; research projects (except for philanthropic studies); or unsolicited proposals (all requests must begin with a preliminary proposal).
Geographic Focus: Indiana
Date(s) Application is Due: Apr 1; Sep 1
Amount of Grant: Up to 100,000 USD
Contact: Donna Munchel, Executive Assistant; (765) 741-5500; fax (765) 741-5518; donna.munchel@ballfdn.org or info@ballfdn.org
Internet: http://www.ballfdn.org
Sponsor: Ball Brothers Foundation
222 South Mulberry Street
Muncie, IN 47305

Ball Brothers Foundation Organizational Effectiveness/Executive Mentoring Grants 638
Ball Brothers Foundation, in collaboration with the Indiana Youth Institute, is pleased to announce funding for up to two grants per year to youth-serving organizations who wish to re-energize their organization in the areas of strategic planning, evaluation and/or assessment, marketing, board training, fundraising, technology planning, and volunteer recruitment and retention. In addition each organization may apply for up to one year of assistance from an experienced executive mentor working with an organization's executive director or key staff member. In each instance, the organization will be offered up to 120 hours of Professional Nonprofit Coaching and/or 120 hours of Executive Mentoring.
Requirements: The requests are limited to nonprofit youth serving organizations in 6 counties in East Central Indiana, including: Delaware, Madison, Henry, Randolph, Jay and Blackford counties. There must be a: demonstrated need for the service and a willingness to have the request assessed by representatives to determine the focus of the consultation, coaching, and mentoring; and commitment to follow through, including timely responses to requests for information from assigned coaches, with a final product that is produced and the coaching process as the result of the service provided.
Restrictions: The Foundation will not support: direct assistance to individuals or scholarships; applications coming from outside of Indiana; booster organizations; on-going salary requests of staff personnel to support an organization; services that the community-at-large should normally underwrite (i.e. roads, bus transportation, etc.0; capital building projects; research projects (except for philanthropic studies); or unsolicited proposals (all requests must begin with a preliminary proposal).
Geographic Focus: Indiana
Date(s) Application is Due: May 1
Contact: Donna Munchel, Executive Assistant; (765) 741-5500; fax (765) 741-5518; donna.munchel@ballfdn.org or info@ballfdn.org
Internet: http://www.ballfdn.org/index/applying-for-grant/types-of-grants.asp
Sponsor: Ball Brothers Foundation
222 South Mulberry Street
Muncie, IN 47305

Ball Brothers Foundation Rapid Grants 639
Ball Brothers Foundation offers funding opportunities for a limited number of Ball Rapid Grants that are designed to provide funding to organizations requiring immediate funding for the following types of needs: to continue or complete a project; to provide professional development; to buy equipment or materials for a project; for travel to meet representatives to advance ideas for a current or future project; to formulate a project idea; to carry out a mandated law or event; or for seed money to begin a new project. Generally requests up to $5,000 are considered. Ball Rapid Grants do not fall within the normal granting period. Requests may be submitted at any time between February 1 and November 30; decisions will be made within four business days and awards sent within 7 to 10 business days.
Requirements: Ball Brothers Foundation is restricted by its charter to grants to nonprofit institutions and organizations within Indiana.
Restrictions: The Foundation will not support: direct assistance to individuals or scholarships; applications coming from outside of Indiana; booster organizations; on-going salary requests of staff personnel to support an organization; services that the community-at-large should normally underwrite (i.e. roads, bus transportation, etc.0; capital building projects; research projects (except for philanthropic studies); or unsolicited proposals (all requests must begin with a preliminary proposal).
Geographic Focus: Indiana
Date(s) Application is Due: Nov 30
Contact: Donna Munchel, Executive Assistant; (765) 741-5500; fax (765) 741-5518; donna.munchel@ballfdn.org or info@ballfdn.org
Internet: http://www.ballfdn.org/index/staff/generalinfo.asp
Sponsor: Ball Brothers Foundation
222 South Mulberry Street
Muncie, IN 47305

Bally's Total Fitness Equipment Grants 640
The program donates fitness equipment through its corporate giving program to major metropolitan areas where a Bally's Fitness Center is located. Equipment donations support at-risk youth, inner-city schools, and fundraisers. There are no application deadlines. Contact Bally for application.
Requirements: Nonprofit organizations where Bally's operates are eligible.
Restrictions: Bally Total Fitness does not deliver equipment, all equipment must be picked up by the organization. Additionally, a receipt and release must be signed on behalf of the organization.
Geographic Focus: All States
Contact: Public Relations; (773) 399-7668; fax (773) 399-0476; kpetkus@ballyfiness.com
Internet: http://www.ballyfitness.com/company/bfit_communities.asp
Sponsor: Bally's Total Fitness
8700 W Bryn Mawr Avenue, 2nd Floor
Chicago, IL 60631

Baltimore Community Foundation Arts and Culture Path Grants 641
The strength of the community depends upon participation by all residents in Baltimore's economic, social, political and cultural arenas. Therefore, BCF seeks to advance the ideals of a welcoming environment, open access and civic engagement-with all of its privileges and responsibilities-in every area of community life. The Foundation believes that a strong regional arts and culture scene enhances individual lives and creates social bonds necessary to the health of the larger community. Arts and culture grants aim to help arts organizations build audiences, increase access, strengthen operations and increase financial stability. Arts and Culture grants focus on: extending cultural experiences to all who live, work, study in or visit Baltimore; supporting cultural districts within Baltimore; encouraging the cultural sector to work together to meet collective needs; and helping arts organizations become stronger, smarter and more efficient. Applicants should submit a two-page letter of inquiry, with basic background on their organization, the identified needs the project proposes to address, an overview of the proposed project, and the amount your organization intends to request.
Requirements: 501(c)3 organizations serving the greater Baltimore region are eligible.
Restrictions: The foundation does not usually make grants for annual fund campaigns; operating support, except for start-up; religious or sectarian purposes; campaigns for capital to which the foundation can contribute no more than a small fraction of the total need; or individuals.
Geographic Focus: Maryland
Date(s) Application is Due: Mar 1; Jun 1; Dec 1
Contact: Aisha Samples, Program Contact; (410) 332-4172, ext. 145; fax (410) 837-4701; asamples@bcf.org or grants@bcf.org
Internet: http://www.bcf.org/ourgrants/ourgrantsdetail.aspx?grid=10
Sponsor: Baltimore Community Foundation
2 East Read Street, 9th Floor
Baltimore, MD 21202

Grant Programs

Baltimore Community Foundation Children's Fresh Air Society Fund Grants 642

The mission of the Children's Fresh Air Society Fund is to provide disadvantaged and disabled Metropolitan Baltimore children the benefits of a summer camp experience. Grants are made in the form of camperships; that is, scholarships equal to the amount of normal camp fees and tuition. The next application deadline is the spring, and applicants should check back for exact date.
Requirements: Organizations (or their fiscal agents) serving the Baltimore area that qualify as public charities under section 501(c)3 of the Internal Revenue Code. Charitable organizations that operate a day or residential camp program are eligible to apply for a grant.
Restrictions: Grants from the Fund are not intended to provide core operating support.
Geographic Focus: Maryland
Amount of Grant: 5,000 USD
Contact: Anne Knoeller; (410) 332-4172, ext. 171; fax (410) 837-4701; aknoeller@bcf.org
Internet: http://www.bcf.org/ourgrants/ourgrantsdetail.aspx?grid=24
Sponsor: Baltimore Community Foundation
2 East Read Street, 9th Floor
Baltimore, MD 21202

Baltimore Community Foundation Environment Path Grants 643

The strength of the community depends upon participation by all residents in Baltimore's economic, social, political and cultural arenas. Therefore, BCF seeks to advance the ideals of a welcoming environment, open access and civic engagement-with all of its privileges and responsibilities-in every area of community life. Environment grants focus on: advancing the City of Baltimore's Cleaner, Greener Baltimore Initiative; promoting community recycling, anti-litter, and neighborhood greening programs; increasing local tree canopy; supporting the goals of the Chesapeake Bay Agreement by improving water quality in local watersheds through neighborhood-led efforts; encouraging neighborhood level efforts to meet Baltimore City's sustainability goals; promoting broad use of Baltimore's green spaces; and supporting organizations advocating for healthy, well-cared-for watersheds and parks, and increasing participation in that advocacy. To apply to the Foundation for funding, applicants should submit a two-page letter of inquiry, with basic background on your organization, the identified needs your project proposes to address, an overview of the proposed project, and the amount you intend to request.
Requirements: 501(c)3 organizations serving the greater Baltimore region are eligible.
Restrictions: The foundation does not usually make grants for annual fund campaigns; operating support, except for start-up; religious or sectarian purposes; campaigns for capital to which the foundation can contribute no more than a small fraction of the total need; or individuals.
Geographic Focus: Maryland
Date(s) Application is Due: Mar 1; Jun 1; Dec 1
Amount of Grant: 3,500 USD
Contact: Aisha Samples; (410) 332-4172, ext. 145; asamples@bcf.org or grants@bcf.org
Internet: http://www.bcf.org/ourgrants/ourgrantsdetail.aspx?grid=12
Sponsor: Baltimore Community Foundation
2 East Read Street, 9th Floor
Baltimore, MD 21202

Baltimore Community Foundation Human Services Path Grants 644

BCF seeks to advance the ideals of a welcoming environment, open access and civic engagement-with all of its privileges and responsibilities-in every area of community life. Human Services grants focus on: aging—with a special emphasis on helping seniors remain in their homes and actively engaged in their communities; health—including access to health care interventions and advocacy for better access to quality health care-including dental care and mental health services-for children, low-income families, victims of violence, recovering addicts, ex-prisoners, and other disadvantaged populations; and family economic success—including a variety of related efforts to prevent and alleviate homelessness, help job seekers find, keep, and advance in careers in specified industry sectors, provide working families with access to income supports, and teach low-income families about saving, managing, and growing their assets beyond earned income. To apply to the Foundation for funding, applicants should submit a two-page letter of inquiry, with basic background on your organization, the identified needs your project proposes to address, an overview of the proposed project, and the amount you intend to request.
Requirements: The Baltimore Community Foundation (BCF) welcomes grant applications from organizations serving Baltimore City and Baltimore County that are tax exempt under section 501(c)3 of the Internal Revenue Code.
Restrictions: The foundation does not usually make grants for annual fund campaigns; operating support, except for start-up; religious or sectarian purposes; campaigns for capital to which the foundation can contribute no more than a small fraction of the total need; or individuals.
Geographic Focus: Maryland
Amount of Grant: 10,000 USD
Contact: Aisha Samples, Program Contact; (410) 332-4172, ext. 145; fax (410) 837-4701; asamples@bcf.org or grants@bcf.org
Internet: http://www.bcf.org/ourgrants/ourgrantsdetail.aspx?grid=17
Sponsor: Baltimore Community Foundation
2 East Read Street, 9th Floor
Baltimore, MD 21202

Baltimore Community Foundation Kelly People's Emergency Fund Grants 645

The Ensign C. Markland Kelly People's Emergency Fund, established by the Baltimore Community Foundation in 1985, was designed to provide short-term assistance to individuals who are in crisis in order to avoid their decline into long-term dependency. These tend to be people who fall through the cracks of our system and need short-term help. Each year, the Baltimore Community Foundation distributes grants from the Kelly People's Emergency Fund to non-profit organizations that are prepared to re-distribute these monies as emergency assistance grants to individuals in need. All monies awarded must be distributed to individuals; no part of the grant awarded to the organization may be applied to overhead or the expenses of program operation.
Requirements: Organizations (or their fiscal agents) serving the Baltimore area that qualify as public charities under section 501(c)3 of the Internal Revenue Code and do not discriminate on the basis of race, creed, national origin, color, physical handicap, gender or sexual orientation are eligible to apply.
Restrictions: The foundation does not usually make grants for annual fund campaigns; operating support, except for start-up; religious or sectarian purposes; campaigns for capital to which the foundation can contribute no more than a small fraction of the total need; or individuals.
Geographic Focus: Maryland
Date(s) Application is Due: Oct 1
Contact: Maya Smith, Program Administrative Assistant; (410) 332-4172, ext. 142; fax (410) 837-4701; msmith@bcf.org
Internet: http://www.bcf.org/ourgrants/ourgrantsdetail.aspx?grid=3
Sponsor: Baltimore Community Foundation
2 East Read Street, 9th Floor
Baltimore, MD 21202

Baltimore Community Foundation Neighborhood Grants Program (NGP) 646

The Neighborhood Grants Program (NGP), established in 2000 as an integral part of the Baltimore Community Foundation's Community Development priority area, offers funding for resident-driven and -led community-based organizations in Baltimore City and Baltimore County neighborhoods. The primary purposes of the NGP are: to support and increase residents' involvement and investment in their communities; to increase the effectiveness of community organizations by providing financial resources and other support to enable them to initiate and complete priority neighborhood projects; to help neighborhoods become supportive environments for families and businesses; and to strengthen neighborhoods so that current and potential residents and businesses are more willing to invest time, effort and money in the community. There are generally two grant cycles annually, in March and September.
Requirements: The Baltimore Community Foundation (BCF) welcomes grant applications from organizations serving Baltimore City and Baltimore County that are tax exempt under section 501(c)3 of the Internal Revenue Code.
Restrictions: The foundation does not usually make grants for annual fund campaigns; operating support, except for start-up; religious or sectarian purposes; campaigns for capital to which the foundation can contribute no more than a small fraction of the total need; or individuals.
Geographic Focus: Maryland
Amount of Grant: 7,000 USD
Contact: Dion Cartwright; (410) 332-4172, ext. 144; dcartwright@bcf.org
Internet: http://www.bcf.org/ourgrants/ourgrantsdetail.aspx?grid=5
Sponsor: Baltimore Community Foundation
2 East Read Street, 9th Floor
Baltimore, MD 21202

Baltimore Community Foundation Neighborhoods Path Grants 647

The Foundation seeks to advance the ideals of a welcoming environment, open access and civic engagement-with all of its privileges and responsibilities-in every area of community life. BCF believes in a strengthened network of neighborhoods where people choose to live due to the high quality of life and welcoming environment they offer. BCF focuses its investments in supporting informed citizen action, which is at the core of neighborhood revitalization. Neighborhoods grants focus on: increasing residents' and businesses' involvement in their communities and nurturing resident leadership; improving communication among neighbors; making communities more racially and economically diverse; improving neighborhood housing markets while preserving affordable housing; and strengthening Baltimore's network of community development organizations.
Requirements: The Baltimore Community Foundation (BCF) welcomes grant applications from organizations serving Baltimore City and Baltimore County that are tax exempt under section 501(c)3 of the Internal Revenue Code.
Restrictions: The foundation does not usually make grants for annual fund campaigns; operating support, except for start-up; religious or sectarian purposes; campaigns for capital to which the foundation can contribute no more than a small fraction of the total need; or individuals.
Geographic Focus: Maryland
Contact: Aisha Samples, Program Contact; (410) 332-4172, ext. 145; fax (410) 837-4701; asamples@bcf.org or grants@bcf.org
Internet: http://www.bcf.org/ourgrants/ourgrantsdetail.aspx?grid=19
Sponsor: Baltimore Community Foundation
2 East Read Street, 9th Floor
Baltimore, MD 21202

Baltimore Community Foundation Transportation Path Grants 648

BCF believes that the Baltimore metropolitan area needs a rapid and reliable transit system and a network of walking and biking paths that together link diverse neighborhoods, job centers, and entertainment and tourist destinations. Transportation grants focus on: building public support of and mobilizing key constituencies to advocate for better transit options; improving the quality of our public transit system and MARC commuter rail service. To apply to the Foundation for funding, applicants should submit a two-page letter of inquiry, with basic background on your organization, the identified needs your project proposes to address, an overview of the proposed project, and the amount you intend to request.
Requirements: The Baltimore Community Foundation (BCF) welcomes grant applications from organizations serving Baltimore City and Baltimore County that are tax exempt under section 501(c)3 of the Internal Revenue Code.

Restrictions: The foundation does not usually make grants for annual fund campaigns; operating support, except for start-up; religious or sectarian purposes; campaigns for capital to which the foundation can contribute no more than a small fraction of the total need; or individuals.
Geographic Focus: Maryland
Amount of Grant: 5,000 - 10,000 USD
Contact: Aisha Samples, Program Contact; (410) 332-4172, ext. 145; fax (410) 837-4701; asamples@bcf.org or grants@bcf.org
Internet: http://www.bcf.org/ourgrants/ourgrantsdetail.aspx?grid=21
Sponsor: Baltimore Community Foundation
2 East Read Street, 9th Floor
Baltimore, MD 21202

Baltimore Community Foundation Youth Path Grants 649
BCF seeks to advance the ideals of a welcoming environment, open access and civic engagement-with all of its privileges and responsibilities-in every area of community life. Youth grants focus on: making sure that children enter school ready to learn; funding high quality programs that help our region's most vulnerable young people develop skills in the areas of academics, arts, and athletics; creating opportunities for children and youth to cultivate civic responsibility and engagement in their communities; ensuring that adults serving youth are well-trained, competent and caring; connecting young people with college preparatory activities, college retention programs and workforce entry opportunities; providing opportunities for out-of-school youth and adjudicated youth to re-enter the community and re-connect with school; encouraging students, parents, and community members to speak out on issues related to children and youth; and sustaining and enhancing public funding for child and youth development. To apply to the Foundation for funding, applicants should submit a two-page letter of inquiry, with basic background on your organization, the identified needs your project proposes to address, an overview of the proposed project, and the amount you intend to request.
Requirements: The Baltimore Community Foundation (BCF) welcomes grant applications from organizations serving Baltimore City and Baltimore County that are tax exempt under section 501(c)3 of the Internal Revenue Code.
Restrictions: The foundation does not usually make grants for annual fund campaigns; operating support, except for start-up; religious or sectarian purposes; campaigns for capital to which the foundation can contribute no more than a small fraction of the total need; or individuals.
Geographic Focus: Maryland
Date(s) Application is Due: Jan 12; Jun 1; Sep 1; Dec 1
Amount of Grant: 10,000 USD
Contact: Aisha Samples, Program Contact; (410) 332-4172, ext. 145; fax (410) 837-4701; asamples@bcf.org or grants@bcf.org
Internet: http://www.bcf.org/ourgrants/ourgrantsdetail.aspx?grid=22
Sponsor: Baltimore Community Foundation
2 East Read Street, 9th Floor
Baltimore, MD 21202

Baltimore Women's Giving Circle Grants 650
Self-sufficiency is interpreted to mean assisting adult women to live productive lives either independently or within a family unit, as well as preparing younger women to achieve the confidence and competence to take care of themselves and their children, if they have them. Programs that serve women of all ages are eligible for consideration. Grants are given to nonprofit organizations whose programs and services promote self-sufficiency for women and their children, with a focus on assisting those who are economically disadvantaged. Programs addressing housing, addiction, financial counseling, education, parenting and life skills, mentoring, workforce development, legal services, and violence against women are indicative of the types of programs funded. Grants are awarded in amounts up to and including $20,000.
Requirements: BWGC welcomes grant applications from organizations that are tax exempt under section 501(c)3 of the Internal Revenue Code. Funded programs must serve women and/or children in Baltimore City or Baltimore County.
Restrictions: The following are ineligible for funding: organizational endowments; capital improvements including furniture and fixtures except for computers which will be used by clients; purchase of event tickets or event sponsorships; grants made to individuals; deficit reduction; annual drives or annual giving campaigns; political activities or political action committees; and programs requiring adherence to or acceptance of a particular religious belief, or programs requiring participation in a religious service or activity.
Geographic Focus: Maryland
Date(s) Application is Due: Dec 8
Amount of Grant: Up to 20,000 USD
Contact: Dion Cartwright, Program Officer; (410) 332-4172, ext. 144; fax (410) 837-4701; dcartwright@bcf.org
Internet: http://www.bcf.org/ourgrants/ourgrantsdetail.aspx?grid=26
Sponsor: Baltimore Women's Giving Circle
2 East Read Street, 9th Floor
Baltimore, MD 21202

BancorpSouth Foundation Grants 651
The BancorpSouth Foundation supports organizations involved with orchestras, secondary and higher education, legal aid, housing, youth development, and human services. Support is available in the form of general/operating grants in areas of operation, that include Arkansas, Mississippi and Tennessee. Applications for funding are accepted on a rolling basis and reviewed quarterly.
Requirements: Arkansas, Mississippi and Tennessee 501(c)3 non-profit organizations are eligible to apply. There is no application deadline nor is there an application form required when applying for funding. Applicants should include a detailed description of project and amount of funding requested in the proposal.
Restrictions: No grants to individuals.
Geographic Focus: Arkansas, Mississippi, Tennessee
Amount of Grant: 5,000 - 15,000 USD
Contact: Nash Allen, Grants Manager; (662) 680-2000
Sponsor: BancorpSouth Foundation
P.O. Box 789
Tupelo, MS 38802-0789

Banfield Charitable Trust Grants 652
This trust offers grants annually to nonprofit organizations and educational institutions that make life better for Pets and their families. Special considerations will be given to collaborative programs with Pet-related organizations and Banfield team members working together towards a shared goal. At this time, Banfield Charitable Trust is pursuing the following funding priorities: promotion of preventative healthcare for Pets; educating children about veterinary medicine and the Pets they love; programs based on the human-Pet bond and how this relates to longer, healthier lives for Pets and people; and veterinary education programs. The Trust does not generally fund an entire project, but expects to be one of multiple funding sources. Typically, the Trust will not fund more than 50% of the project's entire budget.
Requirements: 501(c)3 tax-exempt organizations and educational institutions are eligible.
Restrictions: Funding will not be considered for the following purposes: Spay and neuter or adoption programs; General operating expenses, deficit reduction, or general administrative overhead expenses; Fundraising campaigns, including special events; Grants to individuals, or to provide support for business enterprise.
Geographic Focus: All States
Date(s) Application is Due: Jun 30; Nov 30
Contact: Darlene Schwartz, Program Coordinator; (503) 922-5801; fax (503) 922-6801; info@banfieldcharitabletrust.org
Internet: http://www.banfieldcharitabletrust.org/Grants
Sponsor: Banfield Charitable Trust
8000 North East Tillamook Street, P.O. Box 13998
Portland, OR 97213

Banfi Vintners Foundation Grants 653
The foundation awards general operating grants to nonprofits in its areas of interest, including higher education, civic and public affairs, arts and humanities, wildlife protection, health (hospitals and disease research/prevention), religion, science, social services, and international. Grants are made nationwide, with preference given to requests from Massachusetts and the New York, NY, area.
Geographic Focus: Massachusetts, New York
Amount of Grant: 100 - 465,000 USD
Contact: Philip Calderone, Executive Director; (516) 626-9200
Sponsor: Banfi Vintners Foundation
1111 Cedar Swamp Road
Glen Head, NY 11545

BankAtlantic Foundation Grants 654
The Foundation was created in 1994 as a 501(c)3 corporate foundation. Since then, the BA Foundation and BankAtlantic have awarded more than $10 million to charitable organizations throughout the state of Florida. The Foundation supports four key areas: community and economic development; human services; education; and the arts. The Foundation considers requests for specific projects, as well as for general operations. The majority of the grants made by the Foundation fall within the $1000 to $3000 range.
Requirements: Giving is limited to Florida. Funding consideration will be given to programs where BankAtlantic has a business presence. The Foundation will fund an organization one time per calendar year, up to three consecutive years. After three consecutive years of support, an organization may reapply after a one-year non-funding period.
Restrictions: No support is offered for hospitals, K-12 schools, national health-related organizations, political or lobbying organizations, religious, veteran, or fraternal organizations, school athletic teams, cheerleading squads, bands, or choirs. No grants are given to individuals, or for capital or building campaigns, courtesy or goodwill advertising to benefit publications, endowments, fund raising events, ticket purchases, travel, medical research, social functions, or sporting events.
Geographic Focus: Florida
Date(s) Application is Due: Mar 30; Oct 31
Amount of Grant: 1,000 - 3,000 USD
Contact: Marcia Barry-Smith, Executive Director; (954) 940-5058; fax (954) 940-5030
Internet: https://www.bankatlantic.com/bafoundation/
Sponsor: BankAtlantic Foundation
2100 West Cypress Creek Road
Fort Lauderdale, FL 33309-1823

Bank of America Charitable Foundation Community Development Grants 655
Housing remains a pressing issue in communities across the country. In response, the Bank of America Charitable Foundation funds programs focused on foreclosure counseling and mitigation, real-estate owned disposition and affordable housing. In conjunction, the Foundation supports financial education and coaching as well as other financial empowerment programs that help individuals become more financially capable and that lead to long-term neighborhood stability. Recognizing that large organizations, such as arts institutions and hospitals, act as economic catalysts in communities, the Foundation funds programs that help advance overall community revitalization.
Requirements: To be considered for support, a qualifying nonprofit organizations must: have a tax-exempt status by the Internal Revenue Service and not classified as a private foundation; and be based in and serve communities in markets listed at the web site.

Restrictions: The following categories are ineligible for funding: individuals, including those seeking scholarships or fellowship assistance; political, labor, fraternal organizations, or civic clubs; religious organizations (for example, churches and synagogues); individual pre-K through 12 schools (public or private); Pre-Sixth Form/College (London, UK); sports, athletic events, or athletic programs; travel-related events, including student trips or tours; development or production of books, films, videos, or television programs; memorial campaigns; national health organizations (or their local affiliates) or research/disease advocacy groups; and colleges and universities.
Geographic Focus: All States
Date(s) Application is Due: May 10
Contact: Anne M. Finucane; (617) 434-9410; anne.m.finucane@bankofamerica.com
Internet: http://about.bankofamerica.com/en-us/global-impact/charitable-foundation-funding.html#fbid=wq9wE7VdEpC
Sponsor: Bank of America Charitable Foundation
100 North Tryon Street
Charlotte, NC 28255

Bank of America Charitable Foundation Critical Needs Grants   656
Individuals continue to struggle to provide basic necessities for their families. Bank of America Charitable Foundation Critical Needs philanthropic support is focused on helping these individuals at their point of need, from immediate human needs such as food and shelter, to addressing financial wellness and stability issues facing low-income communities such as access to benefits and resources. Primary areas of interest include: hunger relief and food access; emergency shelter and short-term housing; and transitioning individuals and families to financial stability.
Requirements: To be considered for support, a qualifying nonprofit organizations must: have a tax-exempt status by the Internal Revenue Service and not classified as a private foundation; and be based in and serve communities in markets listed at the web site.
Restrictions: The following categories are ineligible for funding: individuals, including those seeking scholarships or fellowship assistance; political, labor, fraternal organizations, or civic clubs; religious organizations (for example, churches and synagogues); individual pre-K through 12 schools (public or private); Pre-Sixth Form/College (London, UK); sports, athletic events, or athletic programs; travel-related events, including student trips or tours; development or production of books, films, videos, or television programs; memorial campaigns; national health organizations (or their local affiliates) or research/disease advocacy groups; and colleges and universities. The annual deadline for applications is August 2.
Geographic Focus: All States
Date(s) Application is Due: Aug 2
Contact: Anne M. Finucane; (617) 434-9410; anne.m.finucane@bankofamerica.com
Internet: http://about.bankofamerica.com/en-us/global-impact/charitable-foundation-funding.html#fbid=wq9wE7VdEpC
Sponsor: Bank of America Charitable Foundation
100 North Tryon Street
Charlotte, NC 28255

Bank of America Charitable Education and Workforce Development Grants   657
The Bank of America Charitable Foundation provides philanthropic support to address needs vital to the health of our communities through a focus on preserving neighborhoods, educating the workforce for 21st century jobs and addressing critical needs. Connecting individuals to employment opportunities is a key component contributing to each community's economic growth. The Foundation supports workforce development and educational opportunities that help small businesses and individuals, including youth, the unemployed, and underserved such as veterans and the disabled, obtain the training and education that lead to post-secondary completion, employment and stronger small businesses. It does this by supporting: high school graduation and post-secondary access; post-secondary completion; job readiness for unemployed and underemployed; and small business. The application period is January 22 through February 15.
Requirements: To be considered for support, a qualifying nonprofit organizations must: have a tax-exempt status by the Internal Revenue Service and not classified as a private foundation; and be based in and serve communities in markets listed at the web site.
Restrictions: The following categories are ineligible for funding: individuals, including those seeking scholarships or fellowship assistance; political, labor, fraternal organizations, or civic clubs; religious organizations (for example, churches and synagogues); individual pre-K through 12 schools (public or private); Pre-Sixth Form/College (London, UK); sports, athletic events, or athletic programs; travel-related events, including student trips or tours; development or production of books, films, videos, or television programs; memorial campaigns; national health organizations (or their local affiliates) or research/disease advocacy groups; and colleges and universities.
Geographic Focus: All States
Date(s) Application is Due: Feb 15
Contact: Anne M. Finucane; (617) 434-9410; anne.m.finucane@bankofamerica.com
Internet: http://about.bankofamerica.com/en-us/global-impact/charitable-foundation-funding.html#fbid=wq9wE7VdEpC
Sponsor: Bank of America Charitable Foundation
100 North Tryon Street
Charlotte, NC 28255

Bank of America Charitable Foundation Matching Gifts   658
The Bank of America Charitable Foundation Matching Gifts program encourages employees to contribute to qualifying charitable organizations. This program supports employee giving by offering a way to double – up to $5,000 (US) per person each calendar year – employees' cash or securities contributions to their favorite charitable organizations and thus improve their communities.
Requirements: Charitable organizations in the United States must be tax-exempt under section 501(c)3 of the Internal Revenue Code and not be classified as a private foundation. Charitable Organizations located in England or Wales must be registered with the Charity Commission. Charitable organizations outside of the United States, England or Wales must be qualified as eligible for donations from CAFAmerica.
Restrictions: The Bank of America Charitable Foundation does not: match charitable gifts to private, family or donor advised funds, or gifts to political or fraternal organizations; or match charitable gifts that benefit students directly or that result in an employee receiving a benefit, including tuition or sponsorships.
Geographic Focus: All States, District of Columbia, Guam, Marshall Islands, Northern Mariana Islands, Puerto Rico, U.S. Virgin Islands, American Samoa, Canada, United Kingdom
Contact: Anne M. Finucane; (617) 434-9410; anne.m.finucane@bankofamerica.com
Internet: http://about.bankofamerica.com/en-us/global-impact/matching-gifts-features-and-eligibility.html#fbid=wq9wE7VdEpC
Sponsor: Bank of America Charitable Foundation
100 North Tryon Street
Charlotte, NC 28255

Bank of America Charitable Foundation Student Leaders Grants   659
The Bank of America is committed to supporting the development of the next generation of neighborhood leaders by investing in and cultivating future leaders. Successful applicants will attend an eight week paid summer internship program with select community organizations for Student Leaders, so they can experience first-hand how they can help shape their communities now and in the future. To maximize the experience, Student Leaders will participate in a leadership program with local Bank of America executives. Applications for our Neighborhood Excellence Student Leaders awards are accepted beginning January 1 through February 20.
Requirements: Applicants must be: a citizen or a legal permanent resident of the United States; a junior or senior in high school; a student in good standing at his/her school located in one of the participating markets; able to commit to an 8-week (35-hours per week) internship with a nonprofit organization (to be determined) in the summer; able to participate in a series of leadership and community service activities with local Bank of America executives. Participating markets are listed online. Application is made online.
Restrictions: Bank of America associates or members of their immediate family are not eligible for nomination.
Geographic Focus: All States
Date(s) Application is Due: Feb 20
Contact: Anne M. Finucane; (617) 434-9410; anne.m.finucane@bankofamerica.com
Internet: http://www.bankofamerica.com/foundation/index.cfm?template=fd_studentleaders
Sponsor: Bank of America Charitable Foundation
100 North Tryon Street
Charlotte, NC 28255

Bank of America Charitable Foundation Volunteer Grants   660
Bank of America employees volunteer thousands of hours globally in our neighborhoods each year. In fact, more than 3,000 charitable organizations benefit from the Foundation's employees' dedication each year. To honor those who give their time and service to causes important to them, the Bank of America Charitable Foundation awards grants, which are up to $500 per employee for each calendar year and are made in the name of the employee, to eligible charitable organizations. An unrestricted grant is made to any eligible nonprofit organization for which an employee or retiree has committed substantial volunteer hours within a calendar year. For 50 hours of volunteer time within a calendar year, Bank of America Charitable Foundation will give a $250 grant; for 100 hours of volunteer time within a calendar year, the grant is $500. Employee hour registration must be completed by January 31 after the year in which the hours were volunteered. Organizations must verify hours by May 15 after the year in which the hours were volunteered.
Requirements: Charitable organizations in the United States must be tax-exempt under section 501(c)3 of the Internal Revenue Code and not be classified as a private foundation. Charitable Organizations located in England or Wales must be registered with the Charity Commission. Charitable organizations outside of the United States, England or Wales must be qualified as eligible for donations from CAFAmerica. Employees must complete an application and have the recipient organization verify the hours.
Geographic Focus: All States, District of Columbia, Guam, Marshall Islands, Northern Mariana Islands, Puerto Rico, U.S. Virgin Islands, American Samoa, Canada, United Kingdom
Date(s) Application is Due: Jan 31
Contact: Anne M. Finucane; (617) 434-9410; anne.m.finucane@bankofamerica.com
Internet: http://www.bankofamerica.com/foundation/index.cfm?template=fd_volunteergrants
Sponsor: Bank of America Charitable Foundation
100 North Tryon Street
Charlotte, NC 28255

Bank of America Corporation Sponsorships   661
Through its regional U.S. sponsorships, the Bank of America Corporation supports the economic, social and cultural life of the places where its customers live and work. The Corporation provide an extensive program of arts and sports sponsorships to help maintain vibrant, healthy communities. This includes underwriting art exhibitions, events and performances that require private funding to make them a reality. Its regional sports sponsorship investments include the Bank of America Chicago Marathon, Major League Baseball, and Bank of America 500.
Requirements: To be considered for support, a qualifying nonprofit organizations must: have a tax-exempt status by the Internal Revenue Service and not classified as a private foundation; and be based in and serve communities in markets listed at the web site.

Restrictions: The following categories are ineligible for funding: individuals, including those seeking scholarships or fellowship assistance; political, labor, fraternal organizations, or civic clubs; religious organizations (for example, churches and synagogues); individual pre-K through 12 schools (public or private); Pre-Sixth Form/College (London, UK); sports, athletic events, or athletic programs; travel-related events, including student trips or tours; development or production of books, films, videos, or television programs; memorial campaigns; national health organizations (or their local affiliates) or research/disease advocacy groups; and colleges and universities.
Geographic Focus: All States
Contact: Anne M. Finucane; (617) 434-9410; anne.m.finucane@bankofamerica.com
Internet: http://about.bankofamerica.com/en-us/global-impact/find-grants-sponsorships.html?cm_mmc=EBZ-CorpRep-_-vanity-_-EE01LT0021_Vanity_foundation-_-Enterprise#fbid=wq9wE7VdEpC
Sponsor: Bank of America Corporation
100 North Tryon Street
Charlotte, NC 28255

Banrock Station Wines Wetlands Conservation Grants 662
This fund provides seed grants to nonprofit groups and/or public agencies in the United States that are planning and implementing wetlands and waterways conservation and/or restoration projects at the local level. The goals of the program are to: Educate key audiences about the importance of wetlands; Support action-oriented wetlands conservation projects across America; Create partnerships between public, private and nonprofit organizations to leverage resources for wetlands protection in the US; Showcase Banrock Station supported success stories, bringing visibility to effective conservation; and Link Banrock Station's resources with wetland projects that address critical community issues.
Requirements: Grants will be awarded to U.S. nonprofit organizations and public agencies according to the following criteria: Significance of the project to local wetland protection efforts; Innovativeness of idea or approach; Support in the community; Opportunity for employee involvement; Likelihood of tangible results; Leverage of grant funds with matching support from other sources; Capacity of the organization to complete the funded project; Compatibility with Banrock Station's Good Earth Philosophy.
Geographic Focus: All States
Amount of Grant: 1,000 - 5,000 USD
Contact: Program Administrator; (703) 525-6300; info@conservationfund.org
Internet: http://www.conservationfund.org/?article=2831
Sponsor: Conservation Fund
1655 N Fort Myer Drive, Suite 1300
Arlington, VA 22209-2156

Baptist-Trinity Lutheran Legacy Foundation Grants 663
The Foundation provides support in the greater Kansas City area for crisis related medical assistance, neighborhood school health grants, and health education programs and services in the service area of Baptist Medical Center and Trinity Lutheran Hospital. Funding priorities include: emergency medical assistance; health education; and health education in neighborhood schools. Highest consideration will be given for funding programs or services that demonstrate diversity, have measurable outcomes and can document continued existence after grant funding. Health Education Grant requests will be reviewed in January, March, May, July, September and November.
Requirements: All applicants must be non-profit, tax exempt organizations.
Restrictions: No grants will be made to individuals, political parties, candidates or political activities. Grants will not be given for special events, annual campaigns, endowments, or construction projects.
Geographic Focus: Missouri
Contact: Becky Schaid; (816) 276-7515 or (816) 276-7555; becky@btllf.org
Internet: http://www.btllf.org/funding.html
Sponsor: Baptist-Trinity Lutheran Legacy Foundation
6601 Rockhill Road
Kansas City, MO 64131

Baptist Community Ministries Grants 664
BCM funds grants primarily in four major areas of interest: health; education; public safety; and governmental oversight. Applications not falling in these four major areas of interest are not typically considered. BCM funds transom grants and strategic grants. Transom grants are unsolicited grant proposals submitted by qualified, nonprofit organizations during our two semi-annual open transom cycles, and encourage the development of new ideas and nurture inventive solutions to community problems. Strategic grants generally target the long-range goals in each area of interest and are longer in duration. Strategic grants are usually generated through Request for Proposals or by invitation.
Requirements: Grants are made to eligible organizations in one or more of the five Louisiana parishes of Orleans, Jefferson, St. Bernard, St. Tammany and Plaquemines. Beneficiaries of grants should reside in one or more of the five parishes. It is preferred that the organization receiving a grant also be located in the same five-parish region and be overseen by unpaid volunteers living in the area.
Restrictions: Grants are not made to private foundations described in Section 509(a) of the Internal Revenue Code, private or publicly held corporations, limited liability corporations, partnerships, or sub-chapter S corporations. Funding requests not supported are: capital projects; ongoing general operating expenses; projects of national or statewide scope; single-disease charities; direct support to individuals or fraternal bodies.
Geographic Focus: Louisiana
Date(s) Application is Due: Mar 15; Sep 15
Amount of Grant: 50,000 USD
Contact: Joanne M. Schmidt, Grants Manager; (504) 593-2345 or (504) 593-2323; fax (504) 593-2301; jschmidt@bcm.org or info@bcm.org
Internet: http://www.bcm.org/grantmaking/
Sponsor: Baptist Community Ministries
400 Poydras Street, Suite 2950
New Orleans, LA 70130-3245

Barbara Meyer Elsner Foundation Grants 665
Established in Wisconsin in 1991, the Barbara Meyer Elsner Foundation offer grant funding in its primary fields of interest, which include: animals and wildlife; and the arts. Its support comes in the form of general operations funding. There are no annual deadlines or specified application forms, so potential applicants should begin the process by contacting the Foundation either via telephone or in writing. Typically, grants range from $50 to $1,000, though occasionally higher amounts are given.
Requirements: 501(c)3 organization in, or serving the residents of, Wisconsin are eligible.
Geographic Focus: Wisconsin
Amount of Grant: Up to 50,000 USD
Samples: Milwaukee Art Museum, Milwaukee, Wisconsin, $4,000 - general operations (2011); Franklin Lloyd Wright Fund, Madison, Wisconsin, $50,200 - general operations (2011); Wild Spaces, Milwaukee, Wisconsin, $1,500 - general operations (2011).
Contact: Barbara Elsner, Secretary-Treasurer; (414) 961-2496
Sponsor: Barbara Meyer Elsner Foundation
2420 N. Terrace Avenue
Milwaukee, WI 53211-4511

Barberton Community Foundation Grants 666
The foundation awards grants to improve the quality of life for the citizens of Barberton. In addition to the regular grants program quarterly deadlines, the Foundation's Small Grant Program accepts applications monthly for grants up to $1,000. Areas of interest include charitable endeavors, education, public health, and public recreation.
Requirements: The eligibility requirements for small grants and large grants differ. See the Application Guidelines for specific requirements.
Restrictions: Grants are not given to: individuals; endowments housed at institutions other than the Barberton Community Foundation; religious organizations for religious purposes; projects that do not exclusively benefit the citizens of Barberton; fund debt reductions, deficits, or previous obligations; fund annual fund raising drives; fund ongoing operating expenses; fund political projects, sabbatical leaves or scholarly research; or fund venture capital for competitive profit-making activities.
Geographic Focus: Ohio
Date(s) Application is Due: Jan 2; Apr 1; Jul 1; Oct 1
Amount of Grant: Up to 1,000 USD
Contact: Chuck Sandstrom; (330) 745-5995; fax (330) 745-3990; csandstrom@bcfcharity.org
Internet: http://www.bcfcharity.org/bcf/grant/grants.shtml
Sponsor: Barberton Community Foundation
460 W Paige Avenue
Barberton, OH 44203

Baring Foundation Grants 667
The foundation awards grants in three categories arts, international, and strengthening the voluntary sector, to eligible applicants in the United Kingdom and internationally. Grants are awarded to nongovernmental organizations and community-based groups based in the United Kingdom, Africa south of the Sahara, and Central and South America.
Requirements: Community-based groups in the United Kingdom, Africa, and Central and South America are eligible. Grants in the United Kingdom are restricted to organizations in London, Merseyside, and the northeast section of England.
Restrictions: Grants are not made to individuals.
Geographic Focus: All States, United Kingdom
Contact: Director; 020-7767-1348; baring.foundation@uk.ing.com
Internet: http://www.baringfoundation.org.uk/program.htm
Sponsor: Baring Foundation
60 London Wall
London, EC2M 5TQ England

Barker Foundation Grants 668
The foundation offers funding to New Hampshire non-profit organizations in the areas of: children/youth services; education; health organizations, association; hospitals (general); and human services. Giving primarily for health associations, social services and youth. Grants are awarded in the following types: Annual campaigns building/renovation; capital campaigns; continuing support; equipment; general/operating support and; program development.
Requirements: New Hampshire nonprofit organizations are eligible for funding. The Foundation accepts written requests only. No formal application form is required. Send a 1 page concept paper and request for guidelines to the Foundation with a SASE for response.
Restrictions: Grants are not made to individuals.
Geographic Focus: New Hampshire
Amount of Grant: 2,000 - 13,000 USD
Samples: Boys and Girls Club of Greater Nashua, Nashua, NH, $10,000; Senior Activity Center, Nashua, NH, $2,000; Nashua Soup Kitchen and Shelter, Nashua, NH, $13,000.
Contact: Allan Barker, Treasurer
Sponsor: Barker Foundation
P.O. Box 328
Nashua, NH 03061-0328

Barker Welfare Foundation Grants 669
The mission of the foundation is to make grants to qualified charitable organizations whose initiatives improve the quality of life, with an emphasis on strengthening youth and families and to reflect the philosophy of Catherine B. Hickox, the Founder. Consideration will be given to applications from institutions and agencies operating in the fields of health, welfare, education and literacy, cultural activities, and civic affairs, primarily serving the metropolitan area of New York, NY, and Michigan City, IN. The foundation board meets twice per year to consider requests.
Requirements: In advance of submitting a request, a brief letter or telephone call is suggested to determine if the organization seeking to apply for a grant falls within the current general policy of the Foundation. Before the Foundation sends out its application form, a brief 2-3 page letter describing the organization, the purpose and amount requested should be sent. A copy of the first page of the most recent 990 filed with the IRS and a current budget for the whole organization and a budget for program/project (if requesting program/project support) including income and expense should be sent with the letter of inquiry. Grants are made to tax-exempt organizations which have received a ruling by the Internal Revenue Service that they are organizations described in Section 501(c)3 and classified in Section 509(a)(1),(2), or (3) of the Internal Revenue Code (publicly supported organizations and their affiliates).
Restrictions: Appeals for the following will be declined: organizations not located in nor directly serving the defined areas; national health; welfare; or education agencies; institutions or funds; scholarships; fellowships; loans; student aid; appeals from individuals; medical and scientific research; private elementary and secondary schools; colleges; universities; professional schools; trade organizations; films; program advertising; conferences; seminars; benefits and fund raising costs; start-up organizations; emergency funds; and deficit financing; lobbying-related or legislative activities; endowment funds; and intermediary organizations.
Geographic Focus: Indiana, New York
Date(s) Application is Due: Feb 1; Aug 1
Amount of Grant: 7,500 - 15,000 USD
Contact: Sarane Ross, President; (516) 759-5592; BarkerSMD@aol.com
Internet: http://www.barkerwelfare.org
Sponsor: Barker Welfare Foundation
P.O. Box 2
Glen Head, NY 11545

Barnes and Noble Local Sponsorships and Charitable Donations 670
The Barnes & Noble Community Relations program supports pre-K-12 schools and not-for-profit arts and literacy organizations. The program offers a limited number of sponsorships and donations to organizations that meet the program's mission. There are no specific deadlines.
Requirements: Opportunities must be located in the community or communities in which we operate, and serve the greater good of the local community or region. Preference is given to partnerships that offer in-store events, visibility, and reach a wide audience.
Restrictions: For donations and sponsorships, submit your proposal to the community relations manager or store manager at your local Barnes & Noble store. Stores can be located using the store finder (found at the website). The proposal will be reviewed to see if it meets the criteria, and a limited number of proposals will be forwarded to the district manager and regional community relations manager for approval.
Geographic Focus: All States
Contact: Community Relations Manager local Barnes & Noble Store Manager
Internet: http://www.barnesandnobleinc.com/our_company/sponsorship/sponsorship_local/donations_local.html
Sponsor: Barnes and Noble
122 Fifth Avenue
New York, NY 10011

Barnes and Noble National Sponsorships and Charitable Donations 671
Barnes & Noble's corporate contributions program supports non-profit organizations that focus on literacy, the arts or education (pre-K - 12).
Requirements: The sponsor will accept requests for donations from non-profit organizations that meet the following criteria: (a) Reach a national audience; (b) Serve the greater good nationally; (c) Offer opportunities for in-store events; (d) Are able to work with Barnes & Noble and other appropriate sponsors on promotion and execution of the program. Requests will only be accepted via email (contributions@bn.com) or in writing.
Geographic Focus: All States
Contact: Mary Ellen Keating, Senior Vice President
Internet: http://www.barnesandnobleinc.com/our_company/sponsorship/sponsorships_national/donations_national.html
Sponsor: Barnes and Noble
122 Fifth Avenue
New York, NY 10011

Barnes Group Foundation Grants 672
The foundation awards grants in the following areas of interest: Education; Health and Welfare; Hospitals; Culture and Art and Civic and Youth Organizations. Highest priority is given to the support of organizations and projects in communities where the company has its executive office, group headquarters offices, plants and other facilities. There are no deadlines for submitting requests. Initial contact should be by letter.
Requirements: In order to be considered for support by the Foundation, a grant seeker must furnish a copy of its ruling from the Internal Revenue Service determining that it is an organization described in Section 501(c)3 and Section 509(a)(1), (2), (3), or (4) of the Internal Revenue Code.
Restrictions: No grants are made to organizations located outside the United States. The Foundation will consider only one grant request per organization during any one year period. The Foundation will not contribute directly or indirectly to any political activities or legislative lobbying efforts.
Geographic Focus: Connecticut, Maine, Massachusetts, New Hampshire, Rhode Island, Vermont
Contact: Secretary; (860) 973-2112; fax (860) 589-7466
Internet: http://www.barnesgroupinc.com/about/foundation.html
Sponsor: Barnes Group Foundation
123 Main Street, P.O. Box 489
Bristol, CT 06011-0489

Barra Foundation Community Fund Grants 673
Community Fund grants provide unrestricted contributions to qualified organizations primarily in the Greater Philadelphia area. These grants are generally in amounts between $1,000 and $10,000 per year. The Foundation's categories of funding for these grants are: human services; arts and culture; health; and education. These grants are made at certain times of the year, depending on the category of grant. The categories and time frames for each are as follows: human services—March 1 with grants made in the Spring of each year; arts and culture—June 1 with grants made in the Summer of each year; and health and education—September 1 with grants made in the fall of each year.
Requirements: Applications are welcome from 501(c)3 organizations serving the greater Philadelphia region.
Geographic Focus: Pennsylvania
Date(s) Application is Due: Mar 1; Jun 1; Sep 1
Amount of Grant: 2,000 - 15,000 USD
Contact: William Harral, III, President; (215) 233-5115; fax (215) 836-1033; william.harral@verizon.net
Internet: http://www.barrafoundation.org/grants/index.html
Sponsor: Barra Foundation
8200 Flourtown Avenue, Suite 12
Wyndmoor, PA 19038-7976

Barra Foundation Project Grants 674
Project grants are one-time grants generally for amounts above $10,000. The Foundation considers grants for innovative projects that aid research in advancing the frontiers of human services, arts and culture, health and education. Grants are not made for ongoing or expanding programs where substantial initial support was previously provided from other sources. Three principal criteria are strictly adhered to in judging the merits of a proposed project. They are: innovation; evaluation; and dissemination. Proposals may be submitted at any time of the year. Initial requests for project grants should be in the form of a preliminary concept paper, generally not to exceed two pages, summarizing: the principal focus and objectives of the proposed project; uniqueness of the concept; the overall methodology; estimated timetable; preliminary budget data; and other sources of support for the project.
Restrictions: The foundation does not provide grants for: ongoing operating budgets; staff salaries; budget deficits; endowments; capital campaigns and projects; international programs; environmental and religious organizations; scholarships and fellowships; or audio/video projects, publications, catalogs, and exhibitions.
Geographic Focus: Pennsylvania
Amount of Grant: 10,000 - 500,000 USD
Contact: William Harral, III; (215) 233-5115; fax (215) 836-1033; william.harral@verizon.net
Internet: http://www.barrafoundation.org/grants/index.html
Sponsor: Barra Foundation
8200 Flourtown Avenue, Suite 12
Wyndmoor, PA 19038-7976

Barrasso Usdin Kupperman Freeman and Sarver LLC Corporate Grants 675
Barrasso Usdin Kupperman Freeman and Sarver are dedicated to giving back to the community of New Orleans. Through its partnerships the Corporation makes charitable contributions to educational institutions and nonprofit organizations involved with arts and culture, health care, and youth development. Primary fields of interest include: the arts; education; health care; legal services; and youth development. Types of support are employee volunteer programs, general operations funding, pro bono services, program development, and contributions to scholarship funds. There are no no specified application materials or deadlines, and interested groups should contact the corporate giving office.
Requirements: Limited to schools and 501(c)3 organizations either in, or serving, the New Orleans region.
Geographic Focus: Louisiana
Contact: Corporate Manager; (504) 589-9700 or (504) 589-9734; fax (504) 589-9701
Internet: http://www.barrassousdin.com/community.php
Sponsor: Barrasso Usdin Kupperman Freeman and Sarver LLC
909 Poydras Street, 24th Floor
New Orleans, LA 70112-4053

Barr Foundation Grants (Massachusetts) 676
The foundation is committed to enhancing the quality of life for all of Boston's citizens. The foundation's focus areas include: providing quality education—the Boston Public School system, schools of excellence, early education, and after school programs; making a more livable city—increasing the quality and quantity of open space and water resources, developing environmental citizenship, supporting environmental justice, as well as facilitating regional development planning and urban design; and enhancing cultural vitality—cultural projects that enhance the foundation's educational or environmental goals, support major and mid-sized institutions, promote diversity, or foster civic engagement and community cohesion. In addition to these areas of strategic community engagement, the foundation supports a broad array of organizations in Boston through its annual community support program.

Requirements: Boston organizations that improve the quality of life for city residents are eligible.
Geographic Focus: Massachusetts
Amount of Grant: 1,000 - 100,000 USD
Contact: Kerri Hurley, Grants Manager; (617) 854-3500; fax (617) 854-3501; info@barrfoundation.org
Internet: http://www.barrfoundation.org/about/index.html
Sponsor: Barr Foundation (Massachusetts)
The Pilot House, Lewis Wharf
Boston, MA 02110

Barr Foundation Grants (Oklahoma) 677
The mission of the foundation is to assist in the alleviation of the poverty of body, mind, and spirit. The foundation's goals are to provide permanent shelter for homeless children; facilitate greater educational opportunities for girls and women in order to empower women to participate more fully in the future of their children and the economic and political lives of their cultures; facilitate disaster relief in Nicaragua; provide additional supplies to those in Nicaragua serving the welfare of the poor; and to facilitate donations to carry out goals and objectives consistent with those of the foundation. There are no application deadlines. Applicants should submit a detailed description of their project and amount of funding requested.
Geographic Focus: All States
Samples: Mercado Cooperative, Managua, Nicaragua, $3,550—education and health care for women; La Casita, Cancun, Mexico, $17,200— shelter and education for homeless children grant; Fundacion Superemos, Esteli, Nicaragua, $82,844—education, training, health care grant.
Contact: Robert Barr, (405) 590-7475 or (405) 828-7218; fax (405) 590-7475 or (405) 828-72; robertbarr@cox.net
Sponsor: Barr Foundation (Oklahoma)
P.O. Box 217
Dover, OK 73734-0217

Barr Fund Grants 678
The fund awards grants to Illinois nonprofits in its areas of interest, including services for children and youth, orchestras, higher education, mental health/crisis services, Jewish temples and organizations, and social services. Grants are awarded for general operating support. There are no application forms or deadlines. Submit a letter of request.
Requirements: Illinois nonprofits are eligible.
Restrictions: Individuals are not eligible.
Geographic Focus: Illinois
Amount of Grant: 100 - 75,000 USD
Contact: Donald Lubin, President; (312) 782-4710; fax (312) 876-8000
Sponsor: Barr Fund
230 West Monroe Street, Suite 330
Chicago, IL 60606-4701

Batchelor Foundation Grants 679
The foundation supports food banks and organizations involved with arts and culture, education, the environment, animals and wildlife, health, human services, and economically disadvantaged people. Special emphasis is directed toward programs designed to engage in medical research and provide care for childhood diseases; and promote study, preservation, and public awareness of the natural environment. Funding is available in the form of: capital campaigns; continuing support; endowments; general/operating support; and program development grants. There are no application forms. Initial approach should be a letter that details the grant proposal.
Requirements: Florida area nonprofits are eligible.
Restrictions: Individuals are not eligible.
Geographic Focus: Florida
Amount of Grant: 1,000 - 1,000,000 USD
Contact: Anne Batchelor-Robjohns, (305) 416-9066; jbatchelor@bellsouth.net
Sponsor: Batchelor Foundation
111 NE 1st Street, Suite 820
Miami, FL 33132

Baton Rouge Area Foundation Credit Bureau Grants 680
The Credit Bureau of Baton Rouge Foundation's purpose is to support, fund, present and participate in programs for schools, businesses and civic groups to educate the public about the consumer credit system and the wise use of consumer credit, and to address other current and emerging community needs and opportunities. There are two types of grants awarded: capital grants and program grants. Capital grants are made for new construction, major renovation, the purchase of permanent assets and endowments; these grants may also cover major equipment costs, such as phone systems, computers, and technology upgrading as well as vans or busses. Program grants support the direct and operational costs needed to run new programs or projects; allowable costs may include staff salaries and benefits, supplies, equipment, travel, office leases, utilities and training. Grant awards may range between $2,500 and $50,000. The annual deadline is March 15.
Requirements: The organization, or its fiscal agent, must be tax exempt under Section 501(c)3 of the Internal Revenue Code. A fiscal agent must submit a letter of agreement.
Restrictions: The Credit Bureau of Baton Rouge Foundation does not make grants to individuals, private business ventures or partisan political organizations. Funding will not be awarded for start up costs for new organizations. Organizations may apply each year for support for the same program for up to three years.
Geographic Focus: Louisiana

Date(s) Application is Due: Mar 15
Amount of Grant: 2,500 - 50,000 USD
Contact: John G. Davies; (225) 387-6126; fax (225) 387-6153; jdavies@braf.org
Internet: http://www.braf.org/index.cfm/page/4/n/2
Sponsor: Baton Rouge Area Foundation
402 North Fourth Street
Baton Rouge, LA 70802

Baton Rouge Area Foundation Every Kid a King Fund Grants 681
Every Kid a King Fund was established by Jim and Dana Bernhard and the Shaw Group in 2010 with the purpose of supporting non-profits in Louisiana, focusing on the Greater Baton Rouge Area, that meet the immediate needs of disadvantaged children in the areas of welfare, health, and education. The Every Kid a King Fund advisory board meets on a quarterly basis to review grant requests in the program areas of human services, healthcare, education, safety and wellness. It will provide grants that have an immediate impact on disadvantaged children. Application deadlines are January 1, April 1, July 1, and October 1. Notification of awards will be given April 1, July 1, September 1, and January 1.
Requirements: The Fund will primarily support nonprofit organizations in the greater communities of Baton Rouge, Louisiana, with future growth throughout the state of Louisiana. The organization must have a non-discriminatory policy. It must demonstrate that it manages its business wisely and that an appropriate percentage of the grant will go to programs rather than administration. Organizations eligible for funding should have values consistent with those of the original donor founders, including the following values: a top priority of everyone is to honor commitments, both personally and professionally; the workplace atmosphere is one of openness and fairness where everyone communicates directly and honestly, and is governed by the same rules; a goal of everyone is to grow, personally and professionally, and to contribute to the achievement of the organization; the importance of innovation is recognized and peak performers are rewarded; and the value of excellence in product quality, customer service and financial performance is stressed.
Geographic Focus: Louisiana
Date(s) Application is Due: Jan 1; Apr 1; Jul 1; Oct 1
Contact: John G. Davies; (225) 387-6126; fax (225) 387-6153; jdavies@braf.org
Internet: http://www.braf.org/index.cfm/page/4/n/2
Sponsor: Baton Rouge Area Foundation
402 North Fourth Street
Baton Rouge, LA 70802

Baton Rouge Area Foundation Grants 682
The Baton Rouge Area Foundation seeks to enhance the quality of life for all citizens of Baton Rouge, Louisiana. The foundation concentrates on projects and programs in the areas of community development, education, environment, health and medical, and religion. Applicants should call the office to determine if their project or program is consistent with the foundation's goals before sending an application.
Requirements: Only nonprofits that are registered as 501(c)3 organizations working in the service region of East and West Baton Rouge Parish, East and West Feliciana, Ascension, Livingston, Iberville and Pointe Coupee are eligible to apply for grants.
Geographic Focus: Louisiana
Contact: John G. Davies; (225) 387-6126; fax (225) 387-6153; jdavies@braf.org
Internet: http://www.braf.org/index.cfm/page/4/n/8
Sponsor: Baton Rouge Area Foundation
402 North Fourth Street
Baton Rouge, LA 70802

Batters Up USA Equipment Grants 683
Batters Up USA provides free baseball and/or softball equipment, primarily bats, balls, tee ball sets, helmets, catcher's gear, and bases to local organizations to support the start up of new programs or to assist existing programs to grow. The organization serves boys and girls recreational programs up to age 13. Batters Up USA will provide the safety-type baseballs and softballs so that the games may be played without gloves and to minimize the risk of ball impact injuries. Equipment will be provided on an as-available basis; first come, first served.
Requirements: A grant application form is available on the website. Grant applications may be submitted on a year-round basis. Equipment quantities are based on the size of the program and are subject to availability. Priority is given to those programs serving a high percentage of youth in need such as inner-city and after-school programs. Batters Up has contributed to many such programs run by Parks Departments, Schools, Boys and Girls Clubs, YMCA's Police Athletic Leagues, independent local leagues, Little League, and the other organized youth baseball/softball organizations. The organization also supports the American Baseball Federation Basic after-school reading/baseball program with equipment and reading materials.
Geographic Focus: All States
Contact: Jess Heald, Executive Director; playballusa@msn.com
Internet: http://www.battersupusa.org/Equipment.html
Sponsor: Batters Up USA, Inc.
1014 Paseo Bufalo
Taos, NM 87571

Battle Creek Community Foundation Grants 684
The Battle Creek Community Foundation focuses on the greater Battle community, and is most interested in projects that focus on education, health, human services, arts and culture, public affairs or community development. In general, priority is given to those grant ideas that: increases the capacity of the community to participate in identifying needs and developing and implementing solutions; encourages cooperation; demonstrates a clean and convincing need; develops self-reliance; avoids unnecessary duplication of services; targets gaps in services; Mirrors the diversity of our community; promotes equity among its various

segments; and has clean, defined goals and/or measurable outcomes. Grant applications and guidelines are available on the Web site.
Requirements: Grants will be considered only from 501(c)3 nonprofit agencies in Michigan offering services to the residents of Battle Creek.
Restrictions: Individuals are not eligible to receive grants.
Geographic Focus: Michigan
Amount of Grant: 5,000 - 10,000 USD
Contact: Kelly Boles Chapman; (269) 962-2181; fax (269) 962-2182; bccf@bccfoundation.org
Internet: http://www.bccfoundation.org/grants/
Sponsor: Battle Creek Community Foundation
1 Riverwalk Centre, 34 W Jackson Street
Battle Creek, MI 49017-3505

Battle Creek Community Foundation Mini-Grants 685
Mini-grants of up to $1,000 are also available through the Community Foundation. They are intended to be a fast, flexible, local funding opportunity for small but important community needs. Mini-grant proposals may be submitted at any time, and are reviewed on an ongoing basis.
Requirements: The Battle Creek Community Foundation welcomes grant applications from non-profit programs, organizations and community groups that are either located in the greater Battle Creek area, or that will directly benefit residents in the greater Battle Creek community.
Geographic Focus: Michigan
Amount of Grant: 1,000 USD
Contact: Kelly Boles Chapman, Vice President of Programs; (269) 962-2181; fax (269) 962-2182; bccf@bccfoundation.org
Internet: http://www.bccfoundation.org/page26819.cfm
Sponsor: Battle Creek Community Foundation
1 Riverwalk Centre, 34 W Jackson Street
Battle Creek, MI 49017-3505

Battle Creek Community Foundation Neighborhood Grants 686
The Battle Creek Community Foundation is a public foundation built by individuals, families and businesses that care about their community. Neighborhood grants are a tool that groups of residents in Battle Creek, Michigan, can utilize to help make their neighborhood or community a better place to live. The amount of funding available varies with the size of the project and its impact.
Requirements: Any group of residents who live in the city of Battle Creek and who share a vision for improving their neighborhood can receive a grant.
Geographic Focus: Michigan
Amount of Grant: 5,000 - 10,000 USD
Contact: Kathy Szenda Wilson; (269) 962-2181; kathy@bccfoundation.org
Internet: http://www.bccfoundation.org/grants/neighborhood-grants/
Sponsor: Battle Creek Community Foundation
1 Riverwalk Centre, 34 W Jackson Street
Battle Creek, MI 49017-3505

Batts Foundation Grants 687
Established in 1988, the Batts Foundation supports organizations involved with arts and culture, K-12 and higher education, disease, and human services. Types of support include: annual campaigns, building and renovation; capital campaigns; continuing support; operating support; endowments; matching grants; program development; and scholarship funding. Grants will be awarded primarily in the western Michigan area, particularly the communities of Huron, Zeeland, and Grand Rapids. There are no application forms or deadlines with which to adhere, and applicants should begin by submitting a one page letter summarizing the project.
Requirements: Michigan nonprofit organizations are eligible.
Restrictions: Individuals are ineligible.
Geographic Focus: Michigan
Amount of Grant: 250 - 25,000 USD
Contact: Robert Batts, Director; (616) 956-3053; jsand@battsgroup.com
Sponsor: Batts Foundation
3855 Sparks Drive SE, Suite 222
Grand Rapids, MI 49546-2427

Baughman Foundation Grants 688
The foundation awards grants to eligible nonprofit organizations in its areas of interest, including civic affairs, community development, higher education, and youth programs. Types of support include building construction/renovation, endowment funds, operating budgets, and special projects. Giving is primarily in southwest Kansas, the Oklahoma panhandle, and southeast Colorado. The board meets monthly; application deadlines are the first Wednesday of each month. Please contact the Foundation for guidelines.
Requirements: Grants are only available to charitable organizations as defined under IRS Code Section 501(c)3.
Geographic Focus: Colorado, Kansas, Oklahoma
Contact: Carol Feather-Francis, President; (620) 624-1371
Sponsor: Baughman Foundation
112 West 3rd Street, P.O. Box 1356
Liberal, KS 67905-1356

Baxter International Corporate Giving Grants 689
As a complement to its Foundation, the Baxter Corporation makes charitable contributions to nonprofit organizations directly. Primary fields of interest include: disaster preparedness and services; elementary and secondary education; employment services; the environment; health care and health care rights; health organizations; hemophilia; immunology; kidney diseases; mathematics; patients' rights; science; teacher training and education; and youth services. Types of support include: conferences and seminars; curriculum development; donated products; employee volunteer services; general operating support; in-kind and matching gifts; and sponsorships. Support is given primarily in areas of company operations.
Geographic Focus: All States, All Countries
Amount of Grant: Up to 500,000 USD
Contact: Department Chair; (224) 948-2000
Internet: http://www.sustainability.baxter.com/community-support/
Sponsor: Baxter International Corporation
1 Baxter Parkway
Deerfield, IL 60015-4625

Baxter International Foundation Foster G. McGaw Prize 690
Through its prize programs, the Baxter International Foundation celebrates excellence in community service and research. The Foster G. McGaw Prize honors health delivery organizations (hospitals, health systems, integrated networks, or self-defined community partnerships) that have demonstrated exceptional commitment to community service. The Baxter International Foundation takes no role in the selection of recipients or the application process. The annual deadline for applications is April 6.
Requirements: Any health delivery organization that exhibits leadership, Commitment, partnerships, breadth and depth of initiatives, and community involvement is eligible to apply for the Prize.
Geographic Focus: All States, All Countries
Date(s) Application is Due: Apr 6
Amount of Grant: 100,000 USD
Contact: Prize Coordinator; (312) 422-3932 or (847) 948-4605; fdninfo@baxter.com
Internet: http://www.baxter.com/about_baxter/sustainability/international_foundation/foster_mcgaw_prize.html
Sponsor: Baxter International Foundation
One Baxter Parkway
Deerfield, IL 60015-4633

Baxter International Foundation Grants 691
The Baxter International Foundation's grant program is focused on increasing access to healthcare worldwide. The foundation funds initiatives that improve the access, quality and cost-effectiveness of healthcare. Grants awarded most recently fulfilled local needs to increase access to dental care, mental health, and other healthcare services for children, the uninsured, veterans, and the elderly. Funding often comes in the form of salary support and general operations. Focusing on these priorities, the foundation's primary concern is on communities where Baxter has a corporate presence. In Illinois, grants are restricted to Lake, McHenry and Cook counties. The foundation also funds programs throughout the U.S., Asia, Australia, Canada, Europe, Latin America and Mexico.
Requirements: U.S. nonprofits in Lake, McHenry and Cook counties of Illinois are eligible to apply. Internationally, the following regions are eligible to apply: U.S., Asia, Australia, Canada, Europe, Latin America, and Mexico.
Restrictions: In general, The Baxter International Foundation does not make grants to: capital and endowment campaigns (includes requests for infrastructure of any kind, equipment, vehicles, etc.); disease or condition-specific organizations or programs; educational grants/continuing professional education scholarships; educational institutions, except in instances where a grant would help achieve other goals, such as increasing community-based direct health services or the skills and availability of community health-care providers, in areas where there are Baxter facilities; general operating support or maintenence of effort; hospitals; individuals, including scholarships for individuals; lobbying and political organizations; magazines, professional journals, documentary, film, video, radio or website productions; medical missions; organizations seeking travel support for individuals or groups, medical missions or conferences; organizations soliciting contributions for advertising space, tickets to dinners, benefits, social and fund-raising events, sponsorships and promotional materials; organizations with a limited constituency, such as fraternal, veterans or religious organizations; research.
Geographic Focus: All States, Illinois, All Countries
Date(s) Application is Due: Jan 21; Apr 13; Jul 13; Sep 29
Amount of Grant: Up to 100,000 USD
Contact: Foundation Contact; (847) 948-4605; fdninfo@baxter.com
Internet: http://www.baxter.com/about_baxter/sustainability/international_foundation/grants_program.html
Sponsor: Baxter International Foundation
One Baxter Parkway
Deerfield, IL 60015-4633

Bay and Paul Foundations, Inc Grants 692
General operating and project grants are awarded for support of children's services and precollege educational programs, with an emphasis on technology and enhancement of science, math, and writing curricula; preservation of cultural and natural history collections and collections care training in museums, zoos, libraries, and botanical gardens; advocacy and research programs for preserving biodiversity; and Native American cultural heritage preservation and economic development programs. There are no application forms. Proposals should be directed to the executive director and should include a brief description of the applicant organization and of the program for which funding is requested, including objectives and numbers served; a project budget or financials; other expected sources of support; qualifications of key personnel; and evidence of tax-exempt status. The foundation's directors meet three times a year, usually in January, May, and October, to consider grant proposals. Requests are not accepted via fax. Regular postal service delivery is the preferred method of proposal acceptance.

Grant Programs | 97

Requirements: Nonprofits in Connecticut, Massachusetts, Maine, New Hampshire, New Jersey, New York, Rhode Island, and Vermont are eligible.
Restrictions: Grants do not support requests for endowments, building campaigns, building construction or maintenance, sectarian religious programs, books or studies, individual scholarships or fellowships, loans, travel, film, television or video productions, programs consisting primarily of conferences, for annual fund appeals, or to other than publicly recognized charities. First time grants for K-12 arts-in-education programs and K-12 science and math programs are currently geographically restricted to the New York City metropolitan area.
Geographic Focus: Connecticut, Maine, Massachusetts, New Hampshire, New Jersey, New York, Rhode Island, Vermont
Contact: Frederick Bay, Executive Director; (212) 663-1115; fax (212) 932-0316; info@bayandpaulfoundations.org
Internet: http://www.bayandpaulfoundations.org/areas.html
Sponsor: Bay and Paul Foundations
17 West 94th Street
New York, NY 10025

Bay and Paul Foundations Grants 693
The majority of grants are now directed to professional development with an emphasis on facilitative, distributive leadership and to the intentional interruption of inequitable policies, practices, and cultural norms. Many grants support a variety of efforts to empower students and teachers by promoting the practice of democracy in schools, encouraging student voice, advancing an ethic of environmental stewardship, and integrating academic course work with meaningful community service. In addition, math and science projects and projects that seek to strengthen the developmentally critical role of the arts are supported.
Requirements: Proposals should be addressed to the Executive Director and submitted by mail. Please prepare applications with a concern for the environment. Submit only one copy of the proposal and limit the amount of supporting materials. There is no required application form.
Restrictions: Grants are not made to individuals (except Biodiversity Leadership awards), building campaigns, sectarian religious programs, or to other than publicly recognized charities.
Geographic Focus: All States
Date(s) Application is Due: Mar 1; Sep 1; Dec 1
Amount of Grant: 3,000 - 10,000 USD
Contact: Frederick Bay, Executive Director; (212) 663-1115; fax (212) 932-0316; info@bayandpaulfoundations.org
Internet: http://www.bayandpaulfoundations.org/grants.html
Sponsor: Bay and Paul Foundations
17 West 94th Street
New York, NY 10025

Bay Area Community Foundation Grants 694
The foundation serves only the Bay County area of Michigan and is interested in dynamic projects that have direct relevance to problems concerning this geographic area. Grants support charitable cultural, artistic, civic, educational, and scientific organizations. Requests must be submitted on the foundation's application form. Any agency or organization interested in discussing its funding request is encouraged to contact the foundation office.
Requirements: IRS 501(c)3 organizations serving the Bay County, Michigan, area are eligible to apply. Evidence of 501(c)3 status should be submitted with grant requests.
Restrictions: The foundation will not typically make grants for the following unless designated by a donor: capital campaigns; existing obligations, debts, or liabilities; endowments; individuals; fund raising events.
Geographic Focus: Michigan
Date(s) Application is Due: Mar 1; Oct 1
Amount of Grant: Up to 5,000 USD
Contact: Ashley Morse, Program Officer; (800) 926-3217 or (989) 893-4438; fax (517) 893-4448; ashleym@bayfoundation.org
Internet: http://www.bayfoundation.org/page19432.cfm
Sponsor: Bay Area Community Foundation
919 Boutell Place, Suite 200
Bay City, MI 48708

Bayer Advanced Grow Together with Roses School Garden Awards 695
The program will help 25 schools establish rose gardens designed to nurture peaceful relations and instill a strong sense of community. Garden programs will be selected based on plans to integrate these goals and involve members of their community. 25 school gardens will each receive a selection of 10 rose bushes from All-America Rose Selections (AARS), and educational materials, including rose planting and maintenance information from NGA, the AARS rose documentary, 'Love at First Sight,' and the book 'Roses for Dummies.'
Requirements: School and community organizations across the United States that plan to garden with at least 15 children between the ages of 3 and 18. No purchase necessary. Purchase of a product does not improve your chances of receiving an award.
Restrictions: Employees of the National Gardening Association and its sponsors are ineligible to apply.
Geographic Focus: All States
Contact: Donna Booska, (800) 538-7476, ext. 115; fax (802) 864-6889; donnab@garden.org
Internet: http://www.kidsgardening.org/grants/rosegrant.asp
Sponsor: National Gardening Association
1100 Dorset Street
South Burlington, VT 05403

Bayer Foundation Grants 696
The Bayer Foundation supports programs that enhance the quality of life, provide unique and enriching opportunities that connect diverse groups and ensure preparedness for tomorrow's leaders. The Foundation welcomes proposals from 501(c)3 organizations whose programming matches at least one of the following areas: Civic and Social Service Programs; Education and Workforce Development; Arts and Culture and Health and Human Services.
Requirements: 501(c)3 nonprofits in Bayer operating communities are eligible. Submit proposals to regional offices in California, Connecticut, Georgia, Indiana, Kansas, Massachusetts, New Jersey, New York, North Carolina, Ohio, Pennsylvania, Texas and West Virginia.
Restrictions: The Foundation will not fund: For-profit organizations or those without Internal Revenue Service code 501(c)3 nonprofit, tax-exempt status; Organizations that discriminate on the basis of race, color, creed, gender, sexual orientation or national origin; General operating support for United Way affiliated agencies. Only support for special projects will be considered; Organizations or programs designed to influence legislation or elect candidates to public office; General endowment funds; Deficit reduction or operating reserves; Religious organizations; Charitable dinners, events or sponsorships; Community or event advertising; Individuals; Student trips or exchange programs; Athletic sponsorships or scholarships; Telephone solicitations; Organizations outside of the United States or its territories
Geographic Focus: California, Connecticut, Georgia, Indiana, Kansas, Massachusetts, New Jersey, New York, North Carolina, Ohio, Pennsylvania, Texas, West Virginia
Contact: Bayer Foundation; (800) 422-9374
Internet: http://www.bayerus.com/about/community/i_foundation.html
Sponsor: Bayer Foundation
100 Bayer Road, Building 4
Pittsburgh, PA 15205-9741

BBF Florida Family Literacy Initiative Grants 697
As Governor of Florida, Jeb Bush made education and strengthening families a top priority, beginning with his initiative in family literacy. Today, Jeb Bush's commitment to families and education lives strong within the programs of the Florida Family Literacy Initiative, a program of the Volunteer USA Foundation. This Initiative supports a network of Family Literacy academies which help adults become workforce ready through classes that encompass reading, math, parenting skills, and GED instruction; helps children start school ready to excel; and perpetuates lifelong learning as a family value to be passed on through the generations. The initiative awards one-year grants to enhance existing literacy instructional programs in Florida so that a complete family literacy program can be created and will tie family literacy education to cutting-edge reforms in K-12 education. Applications and guidelines are available online.
Requirements: Florida nonprofit literacy programs are eligible.
Geographic Focus: Florida
Contact: Roxann R. Campbell, Director of Programs; (850) 562-5300; fax (850) 224-6532; Roxann.Campbell@volunteerusafund.org
Internet: http://www.barbarabushfoundation.com/site/c.jhLSK2PALmF/b.4425703/k.FC7B/The_Florida_Family_Literacy_Initiative.htm
Sponsor: Barbara Bush Foundation for Family Literacy
1201 15th Street NW, Suite 420
Washington, DC 20005

BBF Maine Family Literacy Initiative Implementation Grants 698
The program is designed to support the development and/or improvement of family literacy throughout the State of Maine. Family literacy programs must provide adult literacy, early childhood, parenting and inter-generational literacy services to families with at least one adult reading at less than a 12th grade level and at least one child between the ages of birth and eight who is at risk of being unprepared for starting school. A distinctive feature of each recipient program is the collaboration among the various groups that provide services to adults, children and families. Grants of up to $25,000 are available for the implementation or expansion of comprehensive family literacy programs in year two and three of the grant cycle. These will be awarded based on design, performance, and approval of a panel of Maine experts on literacy.
Requirements: Eligible applicants for these grants include: local education agencies, correctional agencies, community-based organizations, public or non-profit agencies or a consortium of these agencies located in Maine who have been in existence for two or more years, have demonstrated fiscal accountability, and have a literacy program that has operated for at least two years.
Geographic Focus: Maine
Date(s) Application is Due: Mar 16
Contact: Rebecca V. Dyer; (352) 365-9845; becky@mainefamilyliteracy.com
Internet: http://www.mainefamilyliteracy.com/grants/
Sponsor: Barbara Bush Foundation for Family Literacy
1201 15th Street NW, Suite 420
Washington, DC 20005

BBF Maine Family Literacy Initiative Planning Grants 699
The program is designed to support the development and/or improvement of family literacy throughout the State of Maine. Family literacy programs must provide adult literacy, early childhood, parenting and inter-generational literacy services to families with at least one adult reading at less than a 12th grade level and at least one child between the ages of birth and eight who is at risk of being unprepared for starting school. A distinctive feature of each recipient program is the collaboration among the various groups that provide services to adults, children and families. Applicants may submit a proposal for a Planning Grant of up to $5,000 for the exploration and planning of future family literacy programs for year one.
Requirements: Eligible applicants for these grants include: local education agencies, correctional agencies, community-based organizations, public or non-profit agencies or

a consortium of these agencies located in Maine who have been in existence for two or more years, have demonstrated fiscal accountability, and have a literacy program that has operated for at least two years.
Geographic Focus: Maine
Date(s) Application is Due: Mar 16
Amount of Grant: Up to 5,000 USD
Contact: Rebecca V. Dyer, Director; (352) 365-9845; fax (352) 365-9845; becky@mainefamilyliteracy.com
Internet: http://www.mainefamilyliteracy.com/grants/
Sponsor: Barbara Bush Foundation for Family Literacy
1201 15th Street NW, Suite 420
Washington, DC 20005

BBF Maryland Family Literacy Initiative Implementation Grants   700
The mission of the Barbara Bush Foundation for Family Literacy is: to establish literacy as a value in every family in America by helping every family in the nation understand that the home is the child's first school, that the parent is the child's first teacher, and that reading is the child's first subject; and to break the inter-generational cycle of illiteracy, by supporting the development of family literacy programs where parents and children can learn and read together. Founded by Doro Bush Koch and Tricia Reilly Koch in 2003, the Foundation's Maryland Family Literacy Initiative supports nonprofit organizations, public school systems, municipal agencies and educational institutions working to improve family literacy rates across the state of Maryland. Between $40,000 and $50,000 is given for up to ten programs annually for Implementation Grants. Grantees are announced each spring at the Maryland Celebration of Reading, a special event sponsored by the Maryland Family Literacy Initiative.
Requirements: Applicants must be a nonprofit or public organization in the state of Maryland.
Geographic Focus: Maryland
Amount of Grant: 40,000 - 50,000 USD
Contact: Benita Somerfield, Executive Director; (202) 955-6183; fax (202) 955-8084
Internet: http://www.barbarabushfoundation.com/site/c.jhLSK2PALmF/b.4425723/k.1021/The_Maryland_Family_Literacy_Initiative.htm
Sponsor: Barbara Bush Foundation for Family Literacy
1201 15th Street NW, Suite 420
Washington, DC 20005

BBF Maryland Family Literacy Initiative Planning Grants   701
The mission of the Barbara Bush Foundation for Family Literacy is: to establish literacy as a value in every family in America by helping every family in the nation understand that the home is the child's first school, that the parent is the child's first teacher, and that reading is the child's first subject; and to break the inter-generational cycle of illiteracy, by supporting the development of family literacy programs where parents and children can learn and read together. Founded by Doro Bush Koch and Tricia Reilly Koch in 2003, the Foundation's Maryland Family Literacy Initiative supports nonprofit organizations, public school systems, municipal agencies and educational institutions working to improve family literacy rates across the state of Maryland. Up to $5,000 is given for Planning Grants each year. Grantees are announced each spring at the Maryland Celebration of Reading, a special event sponsored by the Maryland Family Literacy Initiative.
Requirements: Applicants must be a nonprofit or public organization in Maryland.
Geographic Focus: Maryland
Amount of Grant: Up to 5,000 USD
Contact: Benita Somerfield, Executive Director; (202) 955-6183; fax (202) 955-8084
Internet: http://www.barbarabushfoundation.com/site/c.jhLSK2PALmF/b.4425723/k.1021/The_Maryland_Family_Literacy_Initiative.htm
Sponsor: Barbara Bush Foundation for Family Literacy
1201 15th Street NW, Suite 420
Washington, DC 20005

BBF National Grants for Family Literacy   702
Founded by Barbara Bush in 1989, the Barbara Bush Foundation for Family Literacy supports the development and expansion of family literacy programs across the United States. Grants are awarded on a competitive basis to nonprofit organizations, correctional institutions, homeless shelters, schools and school districts, libraries as well as community and faith-based agencies. The Foundation's grant-making program seeks to develop or expand projects designed to support the development of literacy skills for adult primary care givers and their children. A total of approximately $650,000 will be awarded; no grant request should exceed $65,000.
Requirements: Funding opportunities are available to: nonprofit organizations, public school districts, and other agencies across the United States to improve the literacy skills of parents and their children. In order to be considered eligible for a grant, an organization must meet the following criteria: must have current nonprofit or public status and have been in existence for two or more years as of the date of the application; must have maintained fiscal accountability; and must operate an instructional literacy program that has been in existence for at least 2 years, and includes one or more of the following components - literacy for adults, parent education, pre-literacy or literacy instruction for children pre-k to grade 3, and, intergenerational literacy activities.
Geographic Focus: All States
Contact: Kiev Richardson; (202) 263-4781; fax (202) 955-8084; krichardson@cfncr.org
Internet: http://www.barbarabushfoundation.com/site/c.jhLSK2PALmF/b.4425435/k.544A/Current_Funding_Opportunities.htm
Sponsor: Barbara Bush Foundation for Family Literacy
1201 15th Street NW, Suite 420
Washington, DC 20005

BBVA Compass Foundation Charitable Grants   703
BBVA Compass is a leading U.S. banking franchise located in the Sunbelt region. Headquartered in Birmingham, Alabama, it operates more than 720 branches throughout Texas, Alabama, Arizona, California, Florida, Colorado and New Mexico. The BBVA Compass Foundation works with local contributions committees in its major markets and city presidents in its community markets, ensuring a localized, focused and inclusive community giving strategy dedicated to making a meaningful, measurable impact in the communities it serves. The Foundation funds eligible 501(c)3 organizations through six focus areas: Community Development (including Financial Education), Education, Health and Human Services, Arts and Culture, Diversity and Inclusion, and Environment and Natural Resources.
Requirements: To be considered for grant funding, organizations must meet the following criteria: have a nonprofit, tax-exempt classification under section 501(c)3 of the Internal Revenue Code; be located or provide service in BBVA Compass' markets; have broad community support and address specific community needs; demonstrate fiscal and administrative stability; and align with one or more of the Foundation's six focus areas. The applicant organization should: exhibit significant support (through the contribution of time or financial resources) from a BBVA Compass employee(s); target individuals or communities with low- to moderate-income levels; help build inclusive and diverse communities; and foster collaborative efforts that leverage our community investments.
Restrictions: The BBVA Compass Foundation will not make contributions to support certain types of requests. These include, but may not be limited to, the following: sponsorships, events or projects for which BBVA Compass and/or its employees receive tangible benefits or privileges. This includes golf tournaments, tables at events and other fundraising activities that include tickets, meals or other benefits; general operating expenses for organizations that already receive substantial support through United Way or other campaigns in which BBVA Compass participates; programs of a national scope that do not specifically benefit communities in our footprint; organizations based outside of the United States political action committees, political causes or candidates; Veteran and fraternal organizations; alumni organizations; religious organizations that are not engaged in a significant project that is nonsectarian and benefits a broad base of the community; an organization or project that discriminates on the basis of age, disability, ethnicity, gender, gender identity, national origin, race, religion, sexual orientation, veteran's status, or any other status or other classification protected by federal, state or local law; private foundations; individual pre-college schools – private, parochial, charter or home schools; individual schools in public school systems (other than through efforts to benefit system-wide programs and initiatives or as a part of a BBVA Compass-sponsored partnership program).
Geographic Focus: Alabama, Arizona, California, Colorado, Florida, Georgia, New Mexico, Texas
Date(s) Application is Due: Sep 30
Contact: Office of Community Giving; (713) 831-5866; grants@bbvacompass.com or corporateresponsibility@bbvacompass.com
Internet: http://www.bbvacompass.com/compass/responsibility/foundations.jsp#grants
Sponsor: BBVA Compass Foundation
15 South 20th Street
Birmingham, AL 35233

**BCBSM Building Healthy Communities Engaging Elementary Schools and   704
Community Partners Grants**
BCBSM (Blue Cross Blue Shield of Michigan) is offering this grant program to strengthen school and community efforts to reduce the risk and prevalence of childhood obesity through prevention and partnership. With this request for proposals Blue Cross invited Michigan elementary schools to collaborate with students, parents and community partners to address childhood obesity's root causes by promoting awareness of and education about physical activity and nutrition. See BCBSM website for all required forms.
Requirements: Electronic notice of intent is to be submitted no later then April 3. The application must be postmarked by April 24 to be eligible and be submitted with three copies of the proposal.
Geographic Focus: Michigan
Date(s) Application is Due: Apr 3; Apr 24
Contact: BHC Director; (800) 658-6715; buildhealth@bcbsm.com
Internet: http://www.bcbsm.com/buildhealth/index.shtml
Sponsor: Blue Cross Blue Shield of Michigan Foundation
600 East Lafayette Boulevard
Detroit, MI 48226-2998

BCBSM Children Angel Awards   705
Blue Cross Blue Shield of Michigan and Blue Care Network sponsor the awards, which honor volunteers who have touched the lives of Michigan children. A panel of community leaders from across the state review the nominations and select five finalists. A children's category invites nominations of volunteers between 8 and 17 years of age whose efforts meet the awards nomination criteria. From among the finalists, one Grand Angel is chosen to receive a donation to his/her affiliated nonprofit organization. The other four finalists' organizations each receive a donation. The Grand Angel, four finalists, and children's finalist will be honored at a ceremony in Detroit in the fall. Each Angel also receives a trophy. Nominations are due annually by the second Friday in April. Nomination forms are available online.
Requirements: Donations must be made to 501(c)3 tax-exempt organizations.
Geographic Focus: Michigan
Date(s) Application is Due: Apr 14
Contact: Community Affairs Hotline, (800) 733-2583
Internet: http://www.bcbsm.com/home/commitment/community_recognition_awards.shtml
Sponsor: Blue Cross Blue Shield of Michigan Foundation
600 East Lafayette Boulevard
Detroit, MI 48226-2998

GRANT PROGRAMS | 99

BCBSM Corporate Contributions Grants   706
The BCBSM (Blue Cross Blue Shield of Michigan) corporate giving program supports nonprofit 501(3)(c) organizations throughout Michigan. BCBSM invests in local communities by supporting organizations that share a commitment to Michigan. BCBSM charitable contributions support programs that: address health issues specific to Michigan's youth and seniors; extend a nonprofit organization's reach through effective use of volunteers; emphasize collaboration across regions within Michigan. Contribution requests are accepted year round and are reviewed monthly by BCBSM's director of community affairs.
Requirements: To be considered for a charitable contribution from the BCBSM, an organization must be: nonprofit 501(3)(c) status; Michigan based and focused. Requests for contributions must be submitted in writing, and include: Corporate Contributions Cover Sheet (available on BCBSM website); IRS 501(c)3 tax exemption documentation; organization's annual report. Submit requests for contribution one of three ways: mail; fax and; email.
Restrictions: Contributions are not made to: individuals; political organizations, campaigns or candidates; extracurricular school activities; endowments; alumni associations; scholarship programs; research projects; multi-year pledges; operational expenses; group travel expenses; capital campaigns.
Geographic Focus: Michigan
Contact: Cathy Mozham, BCBSM Community Responsibility Director; (313) 225-0539; fax (313) 225-9693; cmozham@bcbsm.com
Internet: http://www.bcbsm.com/home/commitment/corporate_contributions.shtml
Sponsor: Blue Cross Blue Shield of Michigan Foundation
600 East Lafayette Boulevard
Detroit, MI 48226-2998

BCBSM Foundation Community Health Matching Grants   707
The program focuses on access to care for the uninsured and under insured. The program's purpose is to encourage nonprofit community based organizations to form partnerships with health care organizations, research organizations, or governmental agencies to develop and rigorously evaluate new ways of increasing access to care for the under and uninsured, in Michigan. The program offers up to $50,000 per year for two years, contingent on a 25% match.
Requirements: Nonprofit 501(c)3 organizations based in Michigan are eligible. Nonprofits do not need a firm commitment of matching support prior to the submission of the proposal [letters from potential funding partners are encouraged, indicating their support for the project and interest in possible funding partnership(s)]. Proposals must include a rigorous evaluation of the outcome of the initiative in accomplishing its objectives (preferably an independent or university-based evaluation).
Restrictions: In-kind contributions are not accepted as a match. Grants under this program do not pay for the cost of equipment (e.g., personal computers), hardware or software. The BCBSM Foundation does not provide support to for?profit organizations or individuals associated with organizations not located in Michigan.
Geographic Focus: Michigan
Amount of Grant: Up to 100,000 USD
Contact: Nora Maloy, Dr.P.H.; (313) 225-8706; fax (313) 225-7730; foundation@bcbsm.com
Internet: http://www.bcbsm.com/foundation/grant.shtml
Sponsor: Blue Cross Blue Shield of Michigan Foundation
600 East Lafayette Boulevard
Detroit, MI 48226-2998

BCBSM Foundation Investigator Initiated Research Grants   708
The program provides grants for applied research that focuses on quality, cost and appropriate access to health care in Michigan. Grants average $75,000 for one year. Multi-year grants or grants in excess of $75,000 are awarded for exemplary projects. Projects that focus on the quality and cost of health care and appropriate access are considered priority and include: Organization and delivery of health care services; Evaluation of new methods or approaches to containing health care costs; Evaluation of new methods or approaches to providing access to high quality health care; Assessment and assurance of quality care; Identification and validation of clinical protocols and evidence-based practice guidelines. Applications are accepted at any time.
Requirements: Applications will be accepted from medical- and doctoral-level researchers based in hospitals, university settings, non-profit health care organizations, health systems, medical or nursing schools, schools of public health, or other relevant academic disciplines such as psychology, sociology and urban studies.
Restrictions: This program does not support basic science or biomedical research, including drug studies or studies using animals, costs of equipment (e.g., personal computers), hardware, software or on-going operating or developmental expenses. The BCBSM Foundation does not provide support to for-profit organizations or individuals associated with organizations not located in Michigan. Blue Cross and Blue Shield of Michigan employees, members of their immediate families, and employees and immediate family members of any Blue Cross and Blue Shield of Michigan affiliate or subsidiary are not eligible to receive BCBSM Foundation grants.
Geographic Focus: Michigan
Contact: Nora Maloy, Dr. P.H.; (313) 225-8706; fax (313) 225-7730; foundation@bcbsm.com
Internet: http://www.bcbsm.com/foundation/grant.shtml
Sponsor: Blue Cross Blue Shield of Michigan Foundation
600 East Lafayette Boulevard
Detroit, MI 48226-2998

BCBSM Foundation Proposal Development Awards   709
The program is intended to help Michigan-based nonprofit community organizations develop grant proposals for new healthcare initiatives. This award of up to $3,500 is available to help nonprofits obtain grant writing resources so they may secure the funding they need to bring creative community-based healthcare programs to life. Applications are accepted at any time.
Requirements: Applicants must be Michigan-based nonprofit community organizations that deliver health services. Michigan nonprofits are encouraged to apply for all available funding, including Federal grants. Nonprofits may also use the award funds to develop proposals for private, community or corporate foundations, either through local Michigan or national foundations, or from the state of Michigan. Expenditure of award funds is restricted to proposal development costs, such as technical assistance, freelance proposal writers and related proposal development costs.
Restrictions: Award funds are not intended to support any type of project activity or to supplement operational expenses. Proposals already completed are not eligible for funding.
Geographic Focus: Michigan
Amount of Grant: Up to 3,500 USD
Contact: Nora Maloy, Dr. P.H.; (313) 225-8706; fax (313) 225-7730; foundation@bcbsm.com
Internet: http://www.bcbsm.com/foundation/grant.shtml
Sponsor: Blue Cross Blue Shield of Michigan Foundation
600 East Lafayette Boulevard
Detroit, MI 48226-2998

BCBSM Foundation Student Award Program   710
The program offers a one year stipend to fund a wide range of health care projects, including applied research, pilot programs, or demonstration and evaluation projects.
Requirements: All doctoral and medical students enrolled in Michigan universities are eligible. For consideration, the proposed project must focus geographically on the state of Michigan and address the BCBSM Foundation's objectives.
Restrictions: Completed or substantially completed dissertations or research projects are not eligible. Students who previously received this award are not eligible. Blue Cross and Blue Shield of Michigan affiliates and subsidiaries are not eligible. Investigation of pharmaceutical efficacy, basic research or research involving non-human subjects is not eligible. Grant monies are not intended to support field placements, practica or internships.
Geographic Focus: Michigan
Date(s) Application is Due: Apr 30
Amount of Grant: 3,000 USD
Contact: Ira Strumwasser; (313) 225-8706; fax (313) 225-7730; foundation@bcbsm.com
Internet: http://www.bcbsm.com/foundation/
Sponsor: Blue Cross Blue Shield of Michigan Foundation
600 East Lafayette Boulevard
Detroit, MI 48226-2998

BCBSNC Foundation Fit Together Grants   711
The program provides funding and technical assistance to rural North Carolina communities that seek to improve community health by implementing innovative and integrated strategies to increase physical activity. Up to five grantees will be chosen to develop and maintain interdisciplinary community partnerships that seek to implement programs, policies, physical projects, and promotional strategies that increase access and reduce barriers to opportunities for active living.
Requirements: North Carolina nonprofit or government organizations are eligible.
Geographic Focus: North Carolina
Date(s) Application is Due: Dec 16
Contact: Polly Leousis, (919) 765-4102
Internet: http://www.bcbsnc.com/foundation/fitogether_grants.html
Sponsor: Blue Cross Blue Shield of North Carolina Foundation
P.O. Box 2291
Durham, NC 27707-0718

BCBSNC Foundation Grants   712
The foundation's primary objective is to fund clearly defined, innovative grants that further the foundation mission of improving the health and well-being of North Carolinians. The foundation funds programs typically possessing the following characteristics: programs and/or services designed to produce measurable, long-term impact; programs that are sustainable and designed to be ongoing, rather than one-time or sporadic events; programs and/or services that are replicable. The three primary focus areas include health of vulnerable populations, healthy active communities and community impact through nonprofit excellence.
Requirements: Applicants must meet the following criteria to be eligible for funding: organization is located within North Carolina; organization is a 501(c)3 organization or an educational or governmental entity with tax-exempt status, that is not a private foundation or Type III supporting organization; organization must be able to provide its most recent IRS Form 990. Depending on the type of grant and the size of the organization, an audit may be required as part of the submitted proposal.
Restrictions: The foundation will not provide funding for annual campaigns, political campaigns, religious purposes, individuals, endowments, purchase of advertisements, or for the sole purpose of receiving goods or entitlements from a charitable organization.
Geographic Focus: North Carolina
Contact: Grant Review Committee; (919) 765-7347; foundation@bcbsnc.com
Internet: http://www.bcbsnc.com/foundation/grants.html?previouslyOver=true¤tlyOver=true
Sponsor: Blue Cross Blue Shield of North Carolina Foundation
P.O. Box 2291
Durham, NC 27707-0718

BCBS of Massachusetts Foundation Grants   713
With a mission to expand access to health care, the foundation awards grants intended to make a significant impact on the health of Massachusetts's low income and uninsured residents. Grant programs include Innovation Fund for the Uninsured; Connecting Consumers with Care; Strengthening the Voice for Access; Pathways to Culturally Competent Health Care; Catalyst Fund; Building Bridges in Children's Mental Health;

and Policy Research and Analysis. Grant awards in particular focus areas are made during specific grant cycles. Deadlines and additional information are available online.
Requirements: Massachusetts 501(c)3 nonprofit organizations or government agencies with a mission that includes improving access and removing barriers to healthcare for low-income or uninsured Massachusetts's residents are eligible.
Restrictions: The foundation will not fund individuals; for-profit organizations; capital campaigns, endowments, or building drives; fundraising drives and events; retiring debt or operating deficits; direct political or lobbying activity; projects outside of Massachusetts; or religious organizations for religious purposes (proposals for secular programs of faith-based organizations that meet funding criteria will be considered). Grants are rarely made for curriculum development, conferences, film or video production, or scholarships.
Geographic Focus: Massachusetts
Date(s) Application is Due: Jan 20; Sep 7
Contact: Coordinator; (617) 246-3744; fax (617) 246-3992; grantinfo@bcbsmafoundation.org
Internet: http://www.bcbsmafoundation.org/foundationroot/en_US/grants/focusArea.jsp#aInnovation%20Fund%20for%20the%20Uninsured
Sponsor: Blue Cross Blue Shield of Massachusetts Foundation
401 Park Drive
Boston, MA 02115-3326

Beazley Foundation Grants 714
The foundation makes grants to Virginia nonprofit organizations engaged in educational, charitable, and religious activities. The focus of support is within the South Hampton Roads cities and counties. Past awards include: music appreciation; educational outreach and mentoring programs; health and wellness; equipment and operating expenses; environmental education programs; renovations and repairs; literacy and community development. Grant applications can be found online.
Requirements: 501(c)3 nonprofit organizations in Virginia are eligible.
Restrictions: Individuals are ineligible.
Geographic Focus: Virginia
Date(s) Application is Due: Jan 4; Mar 1; Jun 1; Oct 1
Contact: Donna Russell, (757) 393-1605; fax (757) 393-4708; info@beazleyfoundation.org
Sponsor: Beazley Foundation
3720 Brighton Street
Portsmouth, VA 23707-3902

Bechtel Group Foundation Building Positive Community Relationships Grants 715
Bechtel Group Foundation was created in 1954 to respond to the needs of the communities around the world in which Bechtel has offices or major projects. These grants support educational, civic and cultural, and social service programs in the communities that host major Bechtel offices and projects. Bechtel offices are located in the following regions/countries: Australia; Brazil; Canada; Chile; Greater China; Egypt; France; India; Indonesia; Japan; Korea; Libya; Malaysia; Peru; Philippines; Poland; Qatar; Russia; Saudi Arabia; Singapore; Taiwan; Thailand; Turkey; United Arab Emirates; United Kingdom - London, England; United States - Maryland, Arizona; Texas; Virginia; New York; Tennessee; Washington; California; Washington, D.C. These grants are typically under U.S. $5,000.
Geographic Focus: Arizona, California, Maryland, Tennessee, Texas, Virginia, Washington, Australia, Brazil, Canada, China, Japan, Peru, Philippines, Poland, Russia, United Kingdom
Amount of Grant: 1,000 - 5,000 USD
Contact: Susan Grisso, Foundation Manager; (415) 768-5444; becfoun@bechtel.com
Internet: http://www.bechtel.com/foundation.html
Sponsor: Bechtel Group Foundation
50 Beale Street
San Francisco, CA 94105

Beckley Area Foundation Grants 716
The Foundation makes annual discretionary grants to charitable organizations in the areas of education, health and human services, the arts, public recreation and civic beautification. Using several general unrestricted endowments which generate income, BAF makes these grants to address the community's current most pressing needs and promising opportunities.
Requirements: To be eligible for a grant from the Beckley Area Foundation, applicants must be a non-profit organizatiion tax-exempt under section 501(c)3 of the Internal Revenue Code, or they must be a public institution. Programs funded through this annual grant must be located in Raleigh County.
Restrictions: As a Community Foundation, BAF cannot accept requests on behalf of individuals or groups that do not have official recognition as a non-profit charity or public entity. Grants are for one year only. Generally grants are not made for: annual campaigns; endowments; sectarian religious programs; political purposes or lobbying; ongoing operating expenses; expenses outside the grant period.
Geographic Focus: West Virginia
Date(s) Application is Due: Dec 15
Amount of Grant: 10,000 USD
Contact: Administrator; (304) 253-3806; funds@beckleyareafoundation.com
Internet: http://beckleyareafoundation.com/id7.html
Sponsor: Beckley Area Foundation
129 Main Street, Suite 203
Beckley, WV 25801

Beerman Foundation Grants 717
The foundation awards general support grants to nonprofits in Ohio in its areas of interest, including Christian and Jewish religion, higher education, community services, Holocaust, Israel, Jewish education, Jewish welfare, museums, religious higher education, social issues, temples, and youth groups such as YMCA/YWCA. Applicants should submit a brief letter of inquiry describing the program and organization. Specify charitable function and purpose of funds sought. There are no application deadlines.
Requirements: Nonprofit organizations in Ohio are eligible.
Geographic Focus: Ohio
Contact: Timothy D. Albro, (937) 222-1285, ext. 104; talbro@beermanrealty.com
Internet: http://www.beermanrealty.com/beerman_foundation.asp
Sponsor: Beerman Foundation
11 West Monument Building, 8th Floor
Dayton, OH 45402

Beim Foundation Grants 718
The foundation awards grants to eligible nonprofit organizations in its areas of interest, including arts and culture, environmental conservation, education, and social services. Types of support include program grants, general operating grants, capital campaigns, building construction/renovation, land acquisition, equipment acquisition, and seed grants. High priority is given to the following types of projects: capital drives and equipment purchases; innovative start-up programs that require a moderate amount of grant money; intergenerational projects that involve community service; cooperative projects that involve several agencies or volunteers; on-going programs that have proven themselves unique and essential; matching funds drives. Low priority is given to the following types of projects: medical research, debt retirement, national fundraising programs, and requests from public schools and governmental agencies due to the lack of good financial data. Deadlines are February 3 for education, and human services; and July 3 for arts, arts small capital equipment, and environment. Guidelines are available online.
Requirements: 501(c)3 tax-exempt organizations located within Minnesota, as well as the city of Denver, CO; counties of Park and Gallatin in Montana; county of Santa Fe in New Mexico; and county of Cumberland in Maine are eligible.
Restrictions: The foundation does not fund individuals; private foundations; political organizations or campaigns; religious organizations, including schools, except for secular human service activities; memberships, subscriptions, tickets for benefits, conferences, fundraising events, or annual campaigns; organizations that have as a substantial part of their purpose the influencing of legislation; endowment; multi-year commitments; or international efforts.
Geographic Focus: Colorado, Maine, Minnesota, New Mexico
Date(s) Application is Due: Jan 17; Jul 18
Amount of Grant: 2,000 - 10,000 USD
Contact: Grants Administrator; (612) 605-8192; contact@beimfoundation.org
Internet: http://www.beimfoundation.org/guide.html
Sponsor: Beim Foundation
3109 W 50th Street, Suite 120
Minneapolis, MN 55410-2102

Beirne Carter Foundation Grants 719
The Foundation places an emphasis on health, education, local history, nature, ecology and youth. Except in rare instances, grants are limited to institutions and organizations located in the Commonwealth of Virginia. Requests that are not of a recurring nature are given preference. Any organization that has been awarded a grant is encouraged to wait at least three years before submitting a new grant request. Any organization seeking grant consideration must complete a Preliminary Proposal form which is online. Its content should be limited to the two page format provided online.
Requirements: The Foundation is organized exclusively for charitable purposes. Grants are made only to institutions and organizations which qualify under IRS regulations as tax exempt and which are not private operating foundations as defined by the IRS.
Restrictions: Grants will not normally be made: to endowment funds (including scholarship funds); to organizations supported primarily by government funds (such as public secondary schools and colleges and local municipalities); to churches and related organizations; for ongoing operating expenses (such as salaries, rent, office supplies, etc.); for existing deficits; or for debt reduction. Grants are not made to individuals.
Geographic Focus: Virginia
Date(s) Application is Due: Feb 1; Aug 3
Contact: Peter C. Toms; (804) 521-0272; fax (804) 521-0274; bcarterfn@aol.com
Internet: http://www.bcarterfdn.org
Sponsor: Beirne Carter Foundation
1802 Bayberry Court, Suite 401
Richmond, VA 23226-3773

Beldon Fund Grants 720
The fund focuses project and general support grants in two programs: human health and the environment, and key states. Human health and the environment—the fund seeks proposals that engage new constituencies in exposing the connection between toxic chemicals and human health and in promoting public policies that prevent or eliminate environmental risks to people's health. The program focuses grant making in three areas: new advocates, human exposure to toxic chemicals, and environmental justice. Key states—the fund believes that states hold the key to bringing about rapid, real change on environmental issues and policy in the United States. By strengthening public support for environmental protection in several of these key states, the fund hopes to transform the nation's approach to environmental protection. The fund is currently accepting proposals from Florida, Michigan, Minnesota, Wisconsin, and North Carolina for this program. Proposals do not need to be tied to any particular issue or set of issues, but targeted issues must be those that will build active public support for the environment. From time to time, the fund will add and remove states from this program. Types of support include special projects, seed money, general operating budgets, and technical assistance. One-year and multiyear

grants are awarded. Due date applies to the letter of intent; full proposals are by invitation. By supporting effective, nonprofit advocacy organizations, the Beldon Fund seeks to build a national consensus to achieve and sustain a healthy planet. The Fund plans to invest its entire principal and earnings by 2009 to attain this goal.
Requirements: 501(c)3 tax-exempt organizations are eligible.
Restrictions: Grants do not support international efforts, academic or university efforts, school-based environmental education, land acquisition, wildlife or habitat preservation, film or video production, deficit reduction, endowments, capital campaigns, acquisitions of museums, service delivery, scholarshp, publications, or arts/culture.
Geographic Focus: Florida, Michigan, Minnesota, North Carolina, Wisconsin
Date(s) Application is Due: Feb 28; Jun 13
Amount of Grant: 5,000 - 100,000 USD
Contact: Holeri Faruolo, Grants Manager; (800) 591-9595 or (212) 616-5600; fax (212) 616-5656; info@beldon.org
Internet: http://www.beldon.org
Sponsor: Beldon Fund
99 Madison Avenue, 8th Floor
New York, NY 10016

Belk Foundation Grants 721
The Foundation makes grants to a wide variety of community-based nonprofit organizations and institutions whose missions and actions support the advancement of Christian causes and the up-building of mankind. The Foundation supports local and regional organizations by: assisting secondary schools, colleges and universities and their programs; assisting religious institutions and organizations and their programs; supporting area arts and other cultural organizations and their programs; supporting community-based human services organizations and their programs; and aiding hospitals and health care organizations and their programs.
Requirements: 501(c)3 nonprofits in communities in the 14 states where Belk stores are located. Preference is given to organizations in North Carolina.
Restrictions: Grants are not awarded to: individuals, including students; public, government or quasi-governmental programs, agencies or organizations (excluding certain public secondary schools, colleges and universities); or international programs and/or organizations. Additionally, the Foundation does not provide door prizes, gift certificates, merchandise or other giveaways.
Geographic Focus: Alabama, Arkansas, Florida, Georgia, Kentucky, Louisiana, Maryland, Mississippi, North Carolina, South Carolina, Tennessee, Texas, Virginia, West Virginia
Date(s) Application is Due: Apr 15; Oct 15
Contact: Susan C. Blount, (704) 426-8396; susan_blount@belk.com
Internet: http://www.belk.com/AST/Misc/Belk_Stores/About_Us/Belk_Community/Belk_Foundation.jsp
Sponsor: Belk Foundation
2801 W Tyvola Road
Charlotte, NC 28217-4500

Bella Vista Foundation Grants 722
The foundation has two main focus areas: early childhood—healthy emotional development in children during the first years of their lives, and parents involvement to help their children deal with the internal issues of attachment and independence; and environment restoration—restoration of land, streams, wetlands, habitat, etc., and acquisition of land for the purpose of preservation, particularly requests that include restoration efforts. Deadlines are January 30 and June 15 for environmental restoration grants, and January 15 and June 15 for early childhood grants. Guidelines are available online.
Requirements: Early childhood grants support public charities located in California's San Francisco, Marin, San Mateo, and Santa Clara counties. Environmental restoration grants support projects in California or Oregon.
Restrictions: Grants will not be made to or for the arts, sectarian religious purposes, individuals, or benefit events, and will only be made for medical research, health care, publications, or video production under special circumstances and only in the early childhood development focus area. The foundation does not make multiyear grants.
Geographic Focus: California, Oregon
Date(s) Application is Due: Jan 15; Jan 30; Jun 15
Contact: Mary Gregory; (415) 561-6540; fax (415) 561-6477; mgregory@pfs-llc.net
Internet: http://www.pfs-llc.net/bellavista/index.html
Sponsor: Bella Vista Foundation
Presidio Building 1016, Suite 300, P.O. Box 29906
San Francisco, CA 94129-0906

Bemis Company Foundation Grants 723
Funding is concentrated on those institutions, programs and organizations that encourage the development of educational, social welfare and health, cultural and civic institutions. Programs such as the Bemis Scholarship Program are designed to benefit employees. Additionally, funds are directed to organizations reflecting employees' volunteerism wherever possible, and employee matching programs such as FoodShare and the Educational and Nonprofit Gift Matching Plans are designed to enhance employees' personal donations.
Requirements: Grant proposals need not follow a specific format, but all proposals should cover the following points: name of organization and amount requested, brief description of the objectives for which the grant is sought, details regarding how the objectives are to be met, budget-including information about existing and other sources of income, and officers and Board members. Grant applications should also include a statement that the organization has tax-exempt status under Section 501(c)3 of the Internal Revenue Code and that contributions to it are tax deductible.
Restrictions: All initial inquiries should be made by mail, not by telephone or personal visit. Bemis does not make grants to individuals or organizations for religious or political purposes, either for lobbying efforts or campaigns. Bemis generally does not make grants for educational capital funds programs, endowment purposes, or for trips or tours. No grants will be made for more than three years.
Geographic Focus: All States
Contact: Grant Administrator; BemisFoundation@bemis.com
Internet: http://www.bemis.com/citizenship
Sponsor: Bemis Company Foundation
222 South Ninth Street, Suite 440
Minneapolis, MN 55402-3373

Ben & Jerry's Foundation Grants 724
The foundation funds grassroots projects that typically are initiated and run by young people, that demonstrate long-term viability, and that empower those who traditionally have been disenfranchised in society. A variety of youth-led efforts will be funded, including ones that support minority or at-risk youths in leadership skills. Additional grantmaking areas include children and families and the environment. Each quarter, the foundation also funds a small number of material grants. The foundation accepts and reviews letters of intent throughout the year. Formal proposals will be invited, and the deadlines are listed. Small awards of under $1000 require only a letter. A letter of interest cover page is available on the Web site.
Requirements: Grants are distributed to organizations with IRS 501(c)3 status or who have a sponsoring agency with this status. Generally, the foundation funds projects with budgets less than $250,000. For all correspondence, use recycled paper, and print on both sides. Avoid plastic covers, sheet protectors, and glossy photos.
Restrictions: The foundation does not fund discretionary or emergency requests, colleges or universities, individuals or scholarship programs, research projects, capital campaigns, state agencies, religious programs, international or foreign-based programs, or social service programs.
Geographic Focus: All States
Amount of Grant: 1,001 - 15,000 USD
Contact: Program Contact; (802) 846-1500; fax (802) 846-1556; info@benjerry.com
Internet: http://www.benjerry.com/foundation/index.html
Sponsor: Ben and Jerry's Foundation
30 Community Drive
South Burlington, VT 05403-6828

Ben B. Cheney Foundation Grants 725
Ben B. Cheney Foundation supports projects in communities where the Cheney Lumber Company was active. These areas include: Tacoma, Pierce, southwestern Washington, southwestern Oregon with a focus on Medford, portions of Del Norte, Humboldt, Lassen, Shasta, Siskiyou, and Trinity counties in California. The Foundation's goal is to improve the quality of life in those communities by making grants to a wide range of activities including: Charity (programs providing for basic needs such as food, shelter, and clothing); Civic (programs improving the quality of life in a community as a whole such as museums and recreation facilities); Culture (programs encompassing the arts); Education (programs supporting capital projects and scholarships, primarily for fourteen pre-selected colleges and universities in the Pacific Northwest); Elderly (programs serving the social, health, recreational, and other needs of older people); Health (programs related to providing health care); Social Services (programs serving people with physical or mental disabilities or other special needs); Youth (programs helping young people to gain the skills needed to become responsible and productive adults). Ben B. Cheney Foundation prefers to fund projects that: develop new and innovative approaches to community problem; facilitate the improvement of services or programs; invest in equipment or facilities that will have a long-lasting impact on community needs. The Foundation's application process always begins with a two to three page proposal letter. The process is the same for past grantees and new grant seekers. There are no deadlines. The Foundation accepts proposal letters throughout the year. It may take six to nine months from the receipt of a proposal letter to consideration of a grant application by the Board of Directors.
Requirements: Ben B. Cheney Foundation makes grants to private, nonprofit organizations that have received their 501(c)3 status from the IRS and that qualify as public charities. In special circumstances proposals from governmental organizations are allowed.
Restrictions: Ben B. Cheney Foundation generally does not make grants for: general operating budgets, annual campaigns, projects which are primarily or normally financed by tax funds, religious organizations for sectarian purposes, basic research, endowment funds, individuals, produce books, films, videos, conferences, seminars, attendance, individual student, or student groups raising money for school related trips.
Geographic Focus: California, Oregon, Washington
Amount of Grant: Up to 300,000 USD
Contact: Bradbury F. Cheney; (253) 572-2442; info@benbcheneyfoundation.org
Internet: http://www.benbcheneyfoundation.org
Sponsor: Ben B. Cheney Foundation
3110 Ruston Way, Suite A
Tacoma, WA 98402-5307

Bender Foundation Grants 726
The foundation supports projects for higher education, health agencies, Jewish welfare funds and organizations, Christian youth organizations, and social welfare. Emphasis is support for programs to assist the elderly and aging, children and parenting, and environmental programs. Grants are awarded for challenge/matching grants, endowments, general operations, and scholarships.
Requirements: Grants are made to organizations and institutions in Maryland and Washington, DC. An applicant should initially send a brief letter of intent. Full proposals are by invitation.
Restrictions: Grants are not made to individuals.

Geographic Focus: District of Columbia, Maryland
Date(s) Application is Due: Nov 30
Amount of Grant: 100 - 100,000 USD
Contact: Julie Bender Silver, President; (202) 828-9000; fax (202) 785-9347
Sponsor: Bender Foundation
1120 Connecticut Avenue NW, Suite 1200
Washington, DC 20036

Beneficia Foundation Grants 727

Incorporated in Pennsylvania in 1953, the foundation awards grants in support of the arts and environmental conservation, with an emphasis on tropical and marine ecosystems, natural resource conservation, animals and wildlife, and the arts. The foundation favors programs that are innovative, catalytic, address unmet needs, strive for self-sustainability, and have limited alternative sources of funding. Project grants and general operating grants are awarded. Full proposals are by invitation only. Interested applicants should send a pre-proposal concept in writing to the Foundation office. The Board meets in May to consider concept proposals, and the annual deadline for full proposal submissions is January 15.
Requirements: Nonprofit 501(c)3 tax-exempt organizations are eligible.
Restrictions: Individuals are not eligible to apply.
Geographic Focus: All States
Date(s) Application is Due: Jan 15
Amount of Grant: 10,000 - 100,000 USD
Contact: Feodor U. Pitcairn, Executive Director; (215) 887-6700
Sponsor: Beneficia Foundation
1 Pitcairn Place, Suite 3000
Jenkintown, PA 19046

Bennett Family Foundation of Texas Grants 728

The Bennett Family Foundation of Texas was established by Daniel A. Bennett, founder of Sunbelt Sportswear, in San Antonio, Texas, in 1993. Giving is concentrated in the State of Texas, though some giving has occurred in Maryland, New York, California, New Jersey, North Carolina, and Florida. The Foundation's primary interest areas include: environmental programs, the arts, medical research, and community development. Most recently, grant amounts have ranged from $500 to $25,000. Applicants should submit an outline of the purpose, a copy of their IRS determination letter, and an overall budget. The annual deadline is October 30.
Requirements: Copy of the 501(c)3 IRS determination letter from the applicant organizations.
Restrictions: No grants are given to individuals
Geographic Focus: Texas
Date(s) Application is Due: Oct 30
Amount of Grant: 500 - 25,000 USD
Contact: Daniel A. Bennett, President; (210) 824-3224 or (210) 804-0100
Sponsor: Bennett Family Foundation
3011 Nacogdoches Road, Building 2
San Antonio, TX 78217

Benton Community Foundation - The Cookie Jar Grant 729

The Benton Community Foundation - The Cookie Jar Grant was established by women in the Benton County area to fund programs that empower women. The Cookie Jar is a collaboration of women working together to create a stronger community where women and girls are empowered to reach their full potential. Priority is given to programs that improve the overall health or well-being of women and/or girls in Benton County. Priority is also given to programs that: reach as many people as possible; are run by a collaboration of non-profit organizations; and have multiple sources of funding for their project.
Requirements: Organizations should submit the grant application to the Foundation to include the following information: their organizational information and contacts; a summary of their program with amount requested; program details, such as how the program will benefit women or girls in Benton County; the program's anticipated timeline; the organization's top three goals for the project and how they plan to meet them; budget details; and a list of the organization's board of directors.
Restrictions: Foundation grant programs generally do not fund: ongoing operating expenses; individuals; special events such as parades, festivals and sporting events; debt or deficit reduction.
Geographic Focus: Indiana
Date(s) Application is Due: Sep 15
Amount of Grant: 4,000 USD
Contact: Ashley Bice; (765) 884-8022; fax (765) 884-8023; ashley@bentoncf.org
Internet: http://www.bentoncf.org/cookiejar.html
Sponsor: Benton Community Foundation
P.O. Box 351
Fowler, IN 47944

Benton Community Foundation Grants 730

The Foundation grants address the broad needs of Benton County residents. Funding is allocated in the following categories: civic affairs; cultural affairs; education; health and safety; and social services. Priority is given to programs that: reach as many people as possible; improve the ability of the organization to serve the community over the long term; serve Benton County residents; are run by a collaboration of nonprofit organizations; and have multiple sources of funding for the project.
Requirements: Grant requests are accepted year-round. Applicants are encouraged to contact the Foundation prior to submitting a request to confirm that the project is appropriate for Foundation funding. To make a request of $750 or less, organizations should submit a letter of application which includes a description of the organization, statement of the problem or need being addressed, explanation of the project, estimated expenses, timeframe for completion, and the amount being requested. Grant decisions are made within 30 days of application. Organizations requesting more than $750 are encouraged to contact the Foundation to discuss the proposed project/program prior to submitting an application. They will then complete the Community Grant Application. Grant decisions are made within 90 days of application.
Restrictions: Benton Community Foundation generally does not fund: political organizations or candidates; endowments; ongoing operating expenses; individuals; special events such as parades, festivals, and sporting events; debt or deficit reduction; or projects funding in a previous year, unless invited to resubmit.
Geographic Focus: Indiana
Date(s) Application is Due: Aug 1
Contact: Ashley Bice; (765) 884-8022; fax (765) 884-8023; ashley@bentoncf.org
Internet: http://www.bentoncf.org/grants_community.html
Sponsor: Benton Community Foundation
P.O. Box 351
Fowler, IN 47944

Benton County Foundation Grants 731

The Foundation's investment philosophy is built on the precepts of diversification, long-term strategic focus, and prudent risk management. The mission is to establish endowments, manage the funds received, and distribute a portion of the earnings each year to benefit youth and community. The Foundation focuses on funding programs that enhance youth education and/or provide positive character building and life skills experience.
Requirements: Organizations must be located in Benton County, Oregon.
Geographic Focus: Oregon
Date(s) Application is Due: Mar 13
Contact: Dick Thompson; (541) 753-1603 or (541) 231-7604; BCF@peak.org
Internet: http://www.bentoncountyfoundation.org/grants/
Sponsor: Benton County Foundation
P.O. Box 911
Corvallis, OR 97330

Benwood Foundation Community Grants 732

Funding is to provide opportunities for creativity and innovation on the part of organizations in the community. The Community Grantmaking area will also provide support for Capital Campaigns. Organizations contemplating a Capital Campaign and desiring Foundation support are encouraged to discuss the campaign with a Foundation staff prior to making application. Capital support to an organization will not exceed $250,000 for any campaign.
Requirements: Applications will only be considered from charities organized under Section 509(a)1 or 509(a)2 of the Internal Revenue Code. Programs must benefit the communities of Hamilton County, Tennessee. Grants presently are not being considered for supporting organizations organized under Section 509(a)3. Faxed or electronically submitted applications are not accepted.
Restrictions: Organizations may apply only one time in a twelve-month period. The foundation does not fund individuals; endowments; debt reduction; political organizations or causes; fundraising events; general operating expenses; multi-year grants; grants outside of Hamilton County; Allied Arts agencies (except for capital campaigns); United Way agencies (except for capital campaigns).
Geographic Focus: Tennessee
Date(s) Application is Due: Mar 1; Sep 1
Amount of Grant: Up to 50,000 USD
Contact: Lauren Boehm, Communications and Community Grant Officer; (423) 267-4311; fax (423) 267-9049; lboehm@benwood.org
Internet: http://www.benwood.org/community.htm
Sponsor: Benwood Foundation
736 Market Street, Suite 1600
Chattanooga, TN 37402

Benwood Foundation Focus Area Grants 733

The Benwood Foundation has identified four focus areas that are critical to the future of the community and are within the reach of philanthropy to affect in a positive and long-term way: Public Education; Arts and Culture; Environment; and, Neighborhood and Community Development. The Foundation will identify specific opportunities for positive, long-term change in these areas and issue Requests for Proposal. Although each area can be considered self-contained, the Foundation will explore interrelationships among them and possibilities for synergistic approaches.
Requirements: Any non-profit organization in Hamilton County, Tennessee may apply for a Community Grant. Organizations seeking support for capital campaigns are encouraged to discuss their request with the Benwood Staff prior to submitting a proposal. Benwood Foundation will not entertain unsolicited proposals for Focus Area Grants. However, the foundation seeks creative and innovative solutions, as well as effective partners, to build and strengthen the community. Focus Area Grants are made in response to specific Requests for Proposal issued by the Foundation. To be considered for a Focus Area Grant, send your ideas in a brief (less than one page) email to ideas@benwood.org. If approved, Benwood Foundation will issue a Request for Proposal.
Restrictions: Except for capital campaigns, United Way and Allied Arts agencies cannot be funded through Community Grants, since the Foundation is already supporting them through its support of United Way and Allied Arts. Organizations may apply only one time in a twelve-month period.
Geographic Focus: Tennessee
Contact: Kristy Huntley, Program Officer for Arts & Culture, Environment and Community Development Focus Areas; (423) 267-4311; fax (423) 267-9049; khuntley@benwood.org

Internet: http://www.benwood.org/focus.htm
Sponsor: Benwood Foundation
736 Market Street, Suite 1600
Chattanooga, TN 37402

Berks County Community Foundation Grants 734
The foundation supports a broad range of community projects in this Pennsylvania county, including the arts and culture, economic development, education, the environment, and health and human services. Types of support include general operating grants, capital campaigns, demonstration grants, seed grants, and program grants. Although applicants do not have to be located in Berks County, they must provide programs and services within the county.
Requirements: Tax exempt or public benefit organizations, individuals, associations and private or public agencies are eligible to apply. The grant must be used for charitable purposes only. Organizations are eligible to apply to more than one grant program in the same year.
Geographic Focus: Pennsylvania
Contact: Richard Mappin; (610) 685-2223; fax (610) 685-2240; info@bccf.org
Internet: http://www.bccf.org/pages/grants.html
Sponsor: Berks County Community Foundation
501 Washington Street, Suite 801, P.O. Box 212
Reading, PA 19603-0212

Bernard and Audre Rapoport Foundation Arts and Culture Grants 735
Bernard and Audre Rapoport Foundation supports artistic and cultural programs, especially those that encourage participation, and enrich the lives of children and disadvantaged members of the community. Education and cultivation of new and young patrons is encouraged. The primary focus of the Foundation is on programs that benefit children and youth in Waco and McLennan County, Texas. Proposals that fall outside of this geographical focus are considered as long as they offer imaginative, and when possible, long-range solutions to the problems of the most needy members of society, and ideally solutions that can be replicated in other communities.
Requirements: Program seeking funding must be a catalyst for change and promote both individual competence and social capacity.
Restrictions: Bernard and Audre Rapoport Foundation only supports organizations that are nonprofit 501(c)3 tax-exempt.
Geographic Focus: All States
Date(s) Application is Due: Jun 15; Aug 15
Amount of Grant: 4,000 - 250,000 USD
Contact: Carole Jones; (254) 741-0510; fax (254) 741-0092; carole@rapoportfdn.org
Internet: http://www.rapoport-fdn.org/
Sponsor: Bernard and Audre Rapoport Foundation
5400 Bosque Boulevard, Suite 245
Waco, TX 76710

Bernard and Audre Rapoport Foundation Community Building and Social Service Grants 736
The Foundation seeks to build communities that improve the quality of life for all citizens and foster the growth and development of children. The Foundation encourages programs that build grassroots neighborhood networks, provide job training and job opportunities for the unemployed and under-employed, or provide a comprehensive safety net of social services for the least-advantaged citizens. The primary focus of the Foundation is on programs that benefit children and youth in Waco and McLennan County, Texas. Proposals that fall outside of this geographical focus are considered as long as they offer imaginative, and when possible, long-range solutions to the problems of the most needy members of society, and ideally solutions that can be replicated in other communities.
Requirements: Program seeking funding must be a catalyst for change and promote both individual competence and social capacity.
Restrictions: Bernard and Audre Rapoport Foundation only supports organizations that are nonprofit 501(c)3 tax-exempt.
Geographic Focus: All States
Date(s) Application is Due: Jun 15; Aug 15
Amount of Grant: 4,000 - 250,000 USD
Contact: Carole Jones; (254) 741-0510; fax (254) 741-0092; carole@rapoportfdn.org
Internet: http://www.rapoport-fdn.org/
Sponsor: Bernard and Audre Rapoport Foundation
5400 Bosque Boulevard, Suite 245
Waco, TX 76710

Bernard and Audre Rapoport Foundation Democracy & Civic Participation Grants 737
Bernard and Audre Rapoport Foundation supports efforts both to make government more responsive and to encourage citizens to take an active interest and role in political life. The Foundation promotes intergovernmental cooperation as well as initiatives that broaden citizen awareness of public policy issues and alternatives, build skills necessary for political leadership, and provide opportunities for community service. The primary focus of the Foundation is on programs that benefit children and youth in Waco and McLennan County, Texas. Proposals that fall outside of this geographical focus are considered as long as they offer imaginative, and when possible, long-range solutions to the problems of the most needy members of society, and ideally solutions that can be replicated in other communities.
Requirements: Program seeking funding must be a catalyst for change and promote both individual competence and social capacity.
Restrictions: Bernard and Audre Rapoport Foundation only supports organizations that are nonprofit 501(c)3 tax-exempt.
Geographic Focus: All States
Date(s) Application is Due: Jun 15; Aug 15
Amount of Grant: 4,000 - 250,000 USD
Contact: Carole Jones; (254) 741-0510; fax (254) 741-0092; carole@rapoportfdn.org
Internet: http://www.rapoport-fdn.org/
Sponsor: Bernard and Audre Rapoport Foundation
5400 Bosque Boulevard, Suite 245
Waco, TX 76710

Bernard and Audre Rapoport Foundation Health Grants 738
Bernard and Audre Rapoport Foundation seeks to improve the quality and delivery of healthcare services to all citizens, especially to women, children, and those who do not have access to conventional medical resources. Community-based outreach initiatives such as immunization programs are of interest to the Foundation. The primary focus of the Foundation is on programs that benefit children and youth in Waco and McLennan County, Texas. Proposals that fall outside of this geographical focus are considered as long as they offer imaginative, and when possible, long-range solutions to the problems of the most needy members of society, and ideally solutions that can be replicated in other communities.
Requirements: Program seeking funding must be a catalyst for change and promote both individual competence and social capacity.
Restrictions: Bernard and Audre Rapoport Foundation only supports organizations that are nonprofit 501(c)3 tax-exempt.
Geographic Focus: All States
Date(s) Application is Due: Jun 15; Aug 15
Amount of Grant: 4,000 - 250,000 USD
Contact: Carole Jones; (254) 741-0510; fax (254) 741-0092; carole@rapoportfdn.org
Internet: http://www.rapoport-fdn.org/
Sponsor: Bernard and Audre Rapoport Foundation
5400 Bosque Boulevard, Suite 245
Waco, TX 76710

Bernard and Audre Rapoport Foundation University of Texas at Austin Scholarship 739
Bernard and Audre Rapoport Foundation funds scholarships to freshmen enrolled in The University of Texas College of Liberal Arts. The scholarship awards up to $7,500 per year for three years beginning the summer after the freshman year and includes the assignment of a laptop computer. Bernard and Audre Rapoport Foundation encourages innovation as demonstrated by The University of Texas Service Learning Scholarship. This concept bundles academic scholarship with a required community services component. More than just spending hours at a nonprofit agency, students use their community work to complement their curriculum. Time for reflection and cohort study encourages students to consider their nonprofit work as a possible career. Other UT scholars are currently supported by the Rapoport Foundation. More than $27 million has been given or pledged to the University by the Rapoport family and the Foundation. Bernard Rapoport, an alumnus and former chair of the University of Texas System Board of Regents, along with his wife Audre, are long-time supporters of the University. Applications are available on the University of Texas website or via contacting the University of Texas Liberal Arts Department.
Requirements: This program is only open to freshmen enrolled within The University of Texas College of Liberal Arts program.
Restrictions: The service scholarship is a need-based program with preference given to Waco-McLennan County area students.
Geographic Focus: All States
Date(s) Application is Due: Jun 15; Aug 15
Amount of Grant: 7,500 USD
Contact: Carole Jones; (254) 741-0510; fax (254) 741-0092; carole@rapoportfdn.org
Internet: http://www.rapoportfdn.org/priorities.php
Sponsor: Bernard and Audre Rapoport Foundation
5400 Bosque Boulevard, Suite 245
Waco, TX 76710

Bernard F. and Alva B. Gimbel Foundation Grants 740
The foundation's areas of interest are currently education, workforce and economic development, civil legal services, criminal justice, reproductive rights, and the environment. In most program areas, the Foundation seeks to fund both direct services programs and advocacy efforts. The Foundation's support for direct services programs is limited to those operating in New York City.
Requirements: Grants are made only to tax-exempt 501(c)3 organizations.
Restrictions: The Foundation does not make grants to: individuals; direct service programs outside of New York City; individual schools; short-term educational programs and workshops; mentoring programs; after-school and summer programs; youth development programs. Unsolicited proposals for the Environment program are not accepted.
Geographic Focus: New York
Contact: Leslie Gimbel, Executive Director; (212) 895-8050; fax (212) 895-8052
Internet: http://www.gimbelfoundation.org/index.html
Sponsor: Bernard F. and Alva B. Gimbel Foundation
271 Madison Avenue, Suite 605
New York, NY 10016

Bernard F. Reynolds Charitable Trust Grants 741
The independent foundation, eastablished in New York in 1999, is interested in supporting human rights programs and agencies, both in the U.S. and internationally. The brainchild of Bernard F. Reynolds, chief executive officer of ASI Solutions, the charitable group hopes to battle hunger, homelessness, and displacement of the world's most vulnerable population. There are no specific applications required or deadlines with which to adhere. Applicants should contact the charitable trust via written proposal.

Geographic Focus: All States
Amount of Grant: Up to 140,000 USD
Contact: Bernard F. Reynolds, (631) 367-9513
Sponsor: Bernard F. Reynolds Charitable Trust
6 Merry Meeting Lane
Lloyd Harbor, NY 11743-1609

Bernard Osher Foundation Grants 742

The purpose of the foundation is to improve the quality of life in San Francisco, Alameda and the State of Maine. Grantees over the years have included performing arts groups, literary programs, educational and environmental groups, and social service organizations. Growing emphasis now is on assisting arts and cultural organizations. The first step is to submit a letter or email providing a brief overview of the proposed project. There are no application deadlines.
Requirements: California 501(c)3 organizations are eligible to apply with preference given to those serving Alameda and San Francisco Counties.
Restrictions: Individuals are ineligible.
Geographic Focus: California, Maine
Contact: Jeanie Hirokane; (415) 861-5587; jhirokane@osherfoundation.org
Internet: http://www.osherfoundation.org/index.php?culture
Sponsor: Bernard Osher Foundation
One Ferry Building, Suite 255
San Francisco, CA 94111

Bernice Barbour Foundation Grants 743

The Foundation is a trust to be used for preservation and care of animals, and prevention of cruelty to animals in the United States. The Foundation primarily supports programs of IRS 501(c)3 organizations whose purpose is to benefit animals. Hands-on projects are of special interest. Applications are welcomed earlier but must be received no later than August 10. Notification of grant decisions is made in December.
Requirements: Organizations must have completed one year of actual hands-on animal care.
Restrictions: The Foundation does not fund lobbying, or indirect costs. Organizations involved in companion animal well-being should note the Foundation only funds those which spay and neuter all animals before adopting them out, before they leave the Shelter. Certificates, contracts, or deposits for sterilizing animals after they have left the Shelter are not acceptable. Funding requests for exotics, species not indigenous to the United States, or land acquisition will not be considered. The Foundation does not fund government agencies (local, county, state or federal), activism or litigation.
Geographic Focus: All States
Date(s) Application is Due: Aug 10
Contact: Eve Lloyd Thompson; (561) 791-0861; fax (561) 753-9153; eve@bernicebarbour.org
Internet: http://www.bernicebarbour.org/
Sponsor: Bernice Barbour Foundation
14434 Laurel Trail
Wellington, FL 33414

Berrien Community Foundation Grants 744

The community foundation awards grants to nonprofits in Berrien County, Michigan, that address community needs. The Foundation is very interested in providing start-up funding for programs that address our focus areas of nurturing children, building community spirit/arts and culture and youth leadership and development. Higher priority is given to requests that demonstrate community-based collaborative solutions likely to stay in place after Foundation funding concludes. Low priority is given to requests for bricks and mortar, operational funds on a repetitive basis, annual fund drives, equipment, and ongoing programs where alternative funding is not planned to carry a program/project forward following a Foundation grant. Low priority is also given to advertising and capital campaigns and grants to cover deficits or other previously incurred obligations. Applicants must first call the Foundation's program director to discuss the proposed program/project.
Requirements: Grant applications will only be accepted from nonprofit 501(c)3 and grass roots organizations serving Berrien County residents.
Restrictions: Grants are not made for sectarian religious purposes, national fundraising efforts, political organizations or campaigns. Grants are not made to individuals, and form letters/emails are neither reviewed nor acknowledged.
Geographic Focus: Michigan
Date(s) Application is Due: Sep 1
Amount of Grant: Up to 10,000 USD
Contact: Anne McCausland; (269) 983-3304; AnneMcCausland@BerrienCommunity.org
Internet: http://www.berriencommunity.org
Sponsor: Berrien Community Foundation
2900 South State Street, Suite 2 East
Saint Joseph, MI 49085

Bertha Russ Lytel Foundation Grants 745

The foundation awards grants to eligible California nonprofit organizations in its areas of interest, including civic affairs; cultural programs, libraries and museums; elementary education; higher education, including agricultural and nursing scholarships; health organizations, including hospitals and hospice; and social services for the elderly and disabled. The primary focus of the Foundation is programs for seniors. Types of support include building construction/renovation, continuing support, equipment acquisition, general operating grants, matching grants, scholarship funds, and seed grants. Contact the Foundation Manager for guidelines and application information.
Requirements: California nonprofit organizations in Humboldt County are eligible.
Geographic Focus: California

Contact: Don Hindley, Manager; (707) 786-9236
Sponsor: Bertha Russ Lytel Foundation
P.O. Box 893
Ferndale, CA 95536

Bertha Wolf-Rosenthal Foundation for Community Service Stipend 746

The Bertha Wolf-Rosenthal Foundation Fund for Community Service Stipend, a program of the Liberty Hill Foundation, will provide up to five young people (ages 18-25 as of the end of December last year) with a stipend of $5,000 each to help cover basic living costs (e.g., rent, food, utilities, transportation and childcare) while they work at a nonprofit organization anywhere in California.
Requirements: Eligible applicants must show a history of community service work (in and/or out of school), demonstrate financial need, and currently work full-time (at least 30 hours per week) for a nonprofit organization in California.
Geographic Focus: California
Date(s) Application is Due: Mar 11
Contact: James Williams, (310) 453-3611, ext. 114; fax (310) 453-7806; jwilliams@libertyhill.org or info@libertyhill.org
Internet: http://www.libertyhill.org/donor/whatwefund.html
Sponsor: Liberty Hill Foundation
2121 Cloverfield Boulevard, Suite 113
Santa Monica, CA 90404

Bert W. Martin Foundation Grants 747

The foundation awards grants to eligible nonprofit organizations in its areas of interest, including higher education, healthcare, sports, and general charitable giving. There are no application forms or deadlines. Proposal letters are accepted by postal mail only. No email proposals accepted.
Requirements: Nonprofit organizations in Florida and Arizona.
Geographic Focus: Arizona, Florida
Contact: Grants Administrator, c/o Northern Trust Co.
Sponsor: Bert W. Martin Foundation
50 S LaSalle Street, B-3
Chicago, IL 60675-0002

Besser Foundation Grants 748

The foundation limits its giving to nonprofits in the Alpena, MI area. Areas of interest include education, social services, civic affairs, arts and culture, religion, and international. Types of support include scholarship funds, matching funds, operating budgets, and continuing support. The board meets quarterly to consider requests.
Requirements: Only nonprofits in Michigan may apply.
Restrictions: Unless specifically requested by a Trustee, the Foundation will not consider grant requests from organizations outside of Alpena; nor for endowment funds, to defray meeting or conference expenses, or to pay for travel of individuals or groups. We will not relieve organizations or the public of their responsibilities, nor make grants to individuals for any purpose.
Geographic Focus: Michigan
Contact: J. Richard Wilson; (989) 354-4722; besserfoundation@verizon.net
Sponsor: Besser Foundation
123 North Second Avenue, Suite 3
Alpena, MI 49707-2801

Best Buy Children's Foundation @15 Community Grants 749

Best Buy Children's Foundation Community Grants Program selects nonprofit organizations from across the United States with initiatives to make technology opportunities more accessible to teens. In 2011, Best Buy Children's Foundation gave $2 million in Community Grants. Applications are accepted once a year in the Summer and grants are issued in the Fall.
Requirements: Best Buy will seek applications from organizations that have current 501(c)3 tax status and are serving a diverse population of teens and providing teens with access to opportunity through technology. Funding must: serve a diverse population in local or regional communities; build academic, leadership and life skills in early adolescents (primarily ages 13-17); show positive results against a demonstrated community need; reach at-risk children in working families.
Restrictions: Organization must be located and serve within the United States.
Geographic Focus: All States
Date(s) Application is Due: Jul 1
Contact: Stephanie Woods; (612) 291-6108; communityrelations@bestbuy.com
Internet: http://www.bestbuy-communityrelations.com/community_grants.htm
Sponsor: Best Buy Children's Foundation
7601 Penn Avenue S.
Richfield, MN 55423

Best Buy Children's Foundation @15 Scholarship 750

Best Buy's @15 Scholarship Program is pleased to award $1,000 scholarships to 1,099 students living in the U.S. and Puerto Rico who will be entering college in the fall after their high school graduation. Scholarships are awarded to students in grades 9-12 who demonstrate academic achievements, volunteer efforts and work experience. As part of its teen platform, Best Buy and Best Buy Children's Foundation are focused on opportunities to help teen students prepare for a brighter future with dollars for college tuition. With the inception of the scholarship program in 1999, Best Buy has now provided nearly $19.7 million in scholarship funds to help 15,438 students attend college.
Requirements: Scholarships are awarded to students in grades 9-12 who demonstrate academic achievements, volunteer efforts and work experience.

Geographic Focus: All States, Puerto Rico
Contact: Stephanie Woods; (612) 291-6108; communityrelations@bestbuy.com
Internet: http://www.bestbuy-communityrelations.com/scholarship.htm
Sponsor: Best Buy Children's Foundation
7601 Penn Avenue S.
Richfield, MN 55423

Best Buy Children's Foundation @15 Teach Awards 751
The @15 Teach Award program helps schools serving grades 7-12 meet their technology needs. Teens (ages 13-18) who are registered on www.at15.com can nominate their school to win a Teach@15 Award. Teen members can vote once a day for 15 days for one nomination. Every 15 days, Best Buy will award 3 schools with Best Buy Gift Cards based on member votes. The school with the most votes will win $1,500, second most votes wins $1,000 and third most votes wins $500.
Requirements: Must be an accredited non-profit junior or senior public, private, parochial, magnet and charter high schools (serving any grades 7-12). All schools must be 501(c)3 certified nonprofit. All schools must be located in the United States. Nominations must be made by Members of the @15 Site.
Restrictions: Home schools, pre-K schools/programs, after-school programs, colleges, universities and vocational-technical schools are not eligible
Geographic Focus: All States
Contact: Stephanie Woods; (612) 291-6108; communityrelations@bestbuy.com
Internet: http://www.bestbuy-communityrelations.com/teach_awards.htm
Sponsor: Best Buy Children's Foundation
7601 Penn Avenue S.
Richfield, MN 55423

Best Buy Children's Foundation National Grants 752
Best Buy Children's Foundation strengthens communities by supporting organizations that empower teens to thrive. Best Buy Children's Foundation National Grants Fund supports initiatives with a national focus committed to funding programs that will help teens excel in school, engage in their communities, and develop life and leadership skills.
Requirements: To receive funding organizations must be a nonprofit 501(c)3 certified organization; serve a national audience; have a national distribution plan in place; provide positive experiences that will empower early adolescents (primarily ages 12-17) to excel in school, engage in their communities, and develop life and leadership skills.
Restrictions: Best Buy Children's Foundation National Grant Fund will not support: organizations not certified as 501(c)3 by the IRS; organizations more frequently than annually (not including TagTeam Awards); individuals; schools (please refer to Teach@15 Program); general operating expenses; product requests; endowments; fraternal organizations or social clubs; units of government or quasi-governmental agencies; labor organizations or political campaigns; organizations designed primarily for lobbying; for-profit organizations or travel programs; fundraising dinners, testimonials, conferences or similar events; sole support of operating or advertising expenses; religious organizations for religious purposes; health, medical, or therapeutic programs or living subsidies; athletic teams or events; multi-year requests (grants must be reviewed/made annually).
Geographic Focus: All States
Contact: Stephanie Woods; (612) 291-6108; communityrelations@bestbuy.com
Internet: http://www.bestbuy-communityrelations.com/national_grants.htm
Sponsor: Best Buy Children's Foundation
7601 Penn Avenue S.
Richfield, MN 55423

Best Buy Children's Foundation Twin Cities Minnesota Capital Grants 753
Best Buy Children's Foundation considers proposals from nonprofit organizations that serve a 7-county metro area, provide access to opportunities for teens through technology, and add vibrancy to the Twin Cities area. Applications are reviewed on a quarterly basis. Nonprofits must submit a letter of inquiry including general description of the campaign by February 1st. Organizations will be contacted within 30 days and advised as to whether or not a full proposal will be accepted. If accepted, nonprofits should submit immediately through the on-line process. Accepted capital requests will be presented at the Q1 Foundation meeting, generally in April. Site visits may be conducted between April and June with final decisions announced after the Q2 meeting, generally in July.
Requirements: Best Buy Children's Foundation will only consider capital requests in the 7-county Metro area only. Nonprofits must have received past program support from the Foundation.
Restrictions: Best Buy Children's Foundation Twin Cities Minnesota Capital Grants will not fund: organizations not certified as 501(c)3 by the IRS; organizations more frequently than annually (not including TagTeam Awards); individuals; schools (please refer to Teach@15 Program); general operating expenses; product requests; endowments; fraternal organizations or social clubs; units of government or quasi-governmental agencies; labor organizations or political campaigns; organizations designed primarily for lobbying; for-profit organizations or travel programs; fundraising dinners, testimonials, conferences or similar events; sole support of operating or advertising expenses; religious organizations for religious purposes; health, medical, or therapeutic programs or living subsidies; athletic teams or events; multi-year requests (grants must be reviewed/made annually).
Geographic Focus: Minnesota
Date(s) Application is Due: Feb 1; May 1; Aug 1; Nov 1
Contact: Stephanie Woods; (612) 291-6108; communityrelations@bestbuy.com
Internet: http://www.bestbuy-communityrelations.com/twin_cities.htm
Sponsor: Best Buy Children's Foundation
7601 Penn Avenue S.
Richfield, MN 55423

Better Way Foundation Grants 754
Formerly Alpha Omega Foundation, the Better Way Foundation was established in Florida in 1994. Giving is centered geographically in California, Indiana, Minnesota, Washington, and Tanzania. For the most part, the Foundation supports programs designed to provide holistic and cost-effective development opportunities to young children and families. Special emphasis is directed toward programs designed to improve early childhood outcomes. Its primary fields of interest include: Catholic agencies and churches; early childhood education; family services; health care; higher education; human services; and nutrition. Types of funding support includes: capital campaigns; general operating support; program development; research; and scholarship funding. Application forms are not required, and there are no annual deadlines. Funding amounts range up to $200,000.
Requirements: Unsolicited full proposals are not accepted. Organizations interested in presenting an idea for funding must submit a brief letter of inquiry.
Geographic Focus: California, Indiana, Minnesota, Washington, Tanzania
Amount of Grant: Up to 200,000 USD
Contact: Matthew Rauenhorst, (952) 656-4597; info@betterwayfoundation.org
Sponsor: Better Way Foundation
10350 Bren Road West
Minnetonka, MN 55343-9014

Better World Books LEAP Grants for Libraries 755
LEAP (Literacy and Education in Action Program) funds literacy and educational nonprofits and libraries for specific projects — the front lines of the fight to reduce global poverty through education. At certain times of the year the sponsor invites literacy-focused organizations to apply for grants for specific, high-impact literacy projects. Nonprofit groups or libraries write up what they will do with their grant (down to the dollar), and then the sponsor funds the projects found to have the biggest bang for the buck. $30,000 in funding is available, and the maximum grant amount per project is $15,000. There will be at least two winners — one voted on by the Better World Books community of customers and fans, a second picked by Better World Books.
Requirements: Projects should address the literacy needs of underserved populations in their community. Literacy needs are defined by broadly identifying, understanding, interpreting, creating, communicating, and computing information to live a more fulfilling and productive life. Applicants may pitch only one project each, with a maximum award of $15,000. Projects that involve partnerships with local government agencies are highly encouraged. Projects that will have a measurable and long-term impact on an underserved population and will continue to operate after grant funds have been utilized will be looked upon favorably.
Geographic Focus: All States, All Countries
Date(s) Application is Due: Apr 9
Amount of Grant: 15,000 USD
Contact: Grant Coordinator; (678) 646-5100
Internet: http://www.betterworldbooks.com/go/leap-grants
Sponsor: Better World Books
11560 Great Oaks Way
Alpharetta, GA 30022

Better World Books LEAP Grants for Nonprofits 756
LEAP (Literacy and Education in Action Program) funds literacy and educational nonprofits and libraries for specific projects — the front lines of the fight to reduce global poverty through education. At certain times of the year the sponsor invites literacy-focused organizations to apply for grants for specific, high-impact literacy projects. Nonprofit groups or libraries write up what they will do with their grant (down to the dollar), and then the sponsor funds the projects found to have the biggest bang for the buck. $30,000 in funding is available, and the maximum grant amount per project is $15,000. There will be at least two winners — one voted on by the Better World Books community of customers and fans, a second picked by Better World Books.
Requirements: Projects should address the literacy needs of underserved populations in their community. Literacy needs are defined by broadly identifying, understanding, interpreting, creating, communicating, and computing information to live a more fulfilling and productive life. Applicants may pitch only one project each, with a maximum award of $15,000. Projects that involve partnerships with local government agencies are highly encouraged. Projects that will have a measurable and long-term impact on an underserved population and will continue to operate after grant funds have been utilized will be looked upon favorably.
Geographic Focus: All States, All Countries
Date(s) Application is Due: Apr 9
Amount of Grant: 15,000 USD
Contact: Grant Coordinator; (678) 646-5100
Internet: http://www.betterworldbooks.com/go/leap-grants
Sponsor: Better World Books
11560 Great Oaks Way
Alpharetta, GA 30022

Beverley Taylor Sorenson Art Works for Kids Grants 757
The program provides grants, community development assistance, and encourages networking and advocacy to promote quality, sequential arts education in Utah schools. Grants fund teaching artists in schools, equipment and materials, professional development opportunities for teachers, district and university initiatives, and community arts programs.
Requirements: Only funds Utah elementary schools, school districts, program within University Fine Arts and Education colleges or departments, and community programs with proven track records of delivering high-quality, sequential arts education to children.
Geographic Focus: Utah
Contact: Lisa Cluff, Director; (801) 455-6169; lisa@artworksforkids.org
Internet: http://www.artworksforkids.org/

Sponsor: Friends of Art Works for Kids
P.O. Box 711126
Salt Lake City, UT 84171-1126

BHHS Legacy Foundation Grants 758
BHHS Legacy Foundation funds efforts that enhance and improve the quality of life and health of children, families and senior citizens that are primarily low-income and under-served in the greater Phoenix and Tri-State regions. The Foundation places a high priority on collaborative projects and programs with other foundations, government agencies and nonprofit entities seeking to strengthen communities and support systemic change in health care access, health improvement and delivery. It also places a strong emphasis on funding nonprofit community organizations to increase their capacity to serve. These may include projects and programs offered by established nonprofit entities as well as those provided by start-up nonprofit organizations. Types of grants include: program/project; education; capacity building; capital equipment; operating; transition; and : Community Assistance Relief for Emergencies (CARE) funding. The foundation recommends discussing project or program concept and proposal with a foundation representative prior to submitting a written request for funding.
Restrictions: Giving is primarily restricted to the greater Phoenix and Bullhead/Laughlin regions, Arizona.
Geographic Focus: Arizona
Date(s) Application is Due: Apr 3; Aug 7; Dec 4
Amount of Grant: 25,000 - 75,000 USD
Contact: Karen E. Orth, Grants Manager; (602) 778-1200; fax (602) 778-1255; korth@bhhslegacy.org or info@bhhslegacy.org
Internet: http://bhhslegacy.org/access_healthcare.aspx
Sponsor: BHHS Legacy Foundation
2999 N 44th Street, Suite 530
Phoenix, AZ 85018

Bicknell Fund Grants 759
The fund awards grants to eligible Ohio nonprofit organizations in its areas of interest. In general, fifty percent of grants are made for Social and Human Services to help the needy, homeless and disadvantaged in the Cleveland area. More than one-quarter of funding is for education. Grants support only the local chapter of national institutions with broad public support. No faxed or emailed proposals will be accepted. Guidelines and questionnaire are available online.
Requirements: Applicants must be qualified non-profit organizations which are classified by the Internal Revenue Code as tax exempt 501(c)3 organizations.
Restrictions: The Fund does not provide grants for individuals, organizations located outside the Cleveland area, endowment funding or political advocacy. The Fund does not distribute multi-year pledges.
Geographic Focus: Ohio
Date(s) Application is Due: Apr 1; Sep 1
Contact: Robert Acklin, Secretary/Treasurer; (216) 363-6482
Internet: http://fdncenter.org/grantmaker/bicknellfund
Sponsor: Bicknell Fund
1422 Euclid Avenue, Suite 1010
Cleveland, OH 44115-2078

Bikes Belong Foundation Paul David Clark Bicycling Safety Grants 760
The Bikes Belong Foundation, launched in 2006, is a separate, complementary organization to the Bikes Belong Coalition, an organization sponsored by the U.S. bicycle industry. The foundation's focus is on bicycle-safety projects and children's bicycle programs. The foundation offers three distinct grant programs: the REI Grant Program; Bikes Belong Research Grants; and the Paul David Clark Bicycling Safety Fund. The latter is geared toward advocacy efforts to improve bicycling safety. The fund is named for Paul David Clark, one of more than 600 U.S. cyclists killed in motor vehicle collisions and accidents in 2005. Paul was an avid cyclist who loved the outdoors. An attorney, he provided pro bono service to nonprofit conservation groups, including the Natural Resources Defense Council and the Trust for Public Land. In the wake of the accident, Bikes Belong teamed with Paul's brother, Blair, to create a fund to support projects that increase bicycle safety, particularly in northern California. The fund's mission is two-fold: to encourage motorists to be more aware of bicyclists; and to compel motorists and cyclists to respectfully share the road. Interested applicants are encouraged to contact the foundation for information on funding availability and how to apply.
Geographic Focus: All States
Contact: Zoe Kircos; (303) 449-4893 ext. 5; fax (303) 442-2936; zoe@bikesbelong.org
Sponsor: Bikes Belong Foundation
207 Canyon Boulevard. Suite 202
Boulder, CO 80302

Bikes Belong Foundation REI Grants 761
The Bikes Belong Foundation, launched in 2006, is a separate, complementary organization to the Bikes Belong Coalition, an organization sponsored by the U.S. bicycle industry. The foundation's focus is on bicycle-safety projects and children's bicycle programs. It offers three distinct grant programs: the Paul David Clark Bicycling Safety Fund; Bikes Belong Research Grants; and the REI Grant Program, a partnership with Recreational Equipment, Inc. (REI). The latter provides grants to communities working to improve their bicycle programs, outreach, and infrastructure. In 2011 Bikes Belong was pleased to offer REI Bicycling Design Best Practices Grants. These grants provide funding to cities whose leaders particpate in the Green Lane Project and specifically support improvements to the bicycling environment based on experiences from study tours and workshops. Interested applicants are encouraged to visit the grant web for details on future funding availability.

Requirements: In the current initiative, city leaders are required to participate in the Green Lane Project tours and workshops in order for the city to be eligible.
Geographic Focus: All States
Amount of Grant: Up to 25,000 USD
Contact: Zoe Kircos; (303) 449-4893 ext. 5; fax (303) 442-2936; zoe@bikesbelong.org
Internet: http://www.bikesbelong.org/bikes-belong-foundation/foundation-grants/
Sponsor: Bikes Belong Foundation
207 Canyon Boulevard. Suite 202
Boulder, CO 80302

Bikes Belong Foundation Research Grants 762
The Bikes Belong Foundation, launched in 2006, is a separate, complementary organization to the Bikes Belong Coalition, an organization sponsored by the U.S. bicycle industry. The foundation's focus is on bicycle-safety projects and children's bicycle programs. The foundation offers three distinct grant programs: the Paul David Clark Bicycling Safety Fund; the REI Grant Program; and Bikes Belong Research Grants. The latter focuses on two priority areas of research: projects that examine the economic impact of additional or improved bicycling facilities or bike-related events; and innovative or unique research on the benefits of bicycling (special opportunities). Applicants interested in the special opportunities research area are asked to contact the Research Analyst (see contact information on this page) before submitting an application. Examples of research that has particular interest for Bikes Belong are as follows: economic benefits of bicycling facilities; economic benefits of removing parking and adding bicycle infrastructure; economic benefits of Sunday Streets/Ciclovia events; Quantitative trails to sales studies (bike businesses only); savings for businesses that promote bicycling among employees; academic performance of children who bike to school; and state, regional, or city-level studies of the economic impact of bicycling. Bikes Belong Foundation reviews research applications twice per year. Application guidelines and downloadable applications are available at the website. Organizations should submit their completed applications along with a cover letter and any required supporting materials in one pdf file via email by the deadline date. See application guidelines for more detailed information. Deadlines may vary from year to year. Prospective applicants are encouraged to verify current year deadlines at the grant website.
Requirements: Applicants are limited to U.S. colleges, universities, or other institutions of higher education and non-profit research organizations.
Restrictions: Individuals will not be considered for funding.
Geographic Focus: All States
Date(s) Application is Due: Mar 30; Sep 28
Amount of Grant: 5,000 - 10,000 USD
Contact: Kate Powlison, Research Analyst and Communications Coordinator; (303) 449-4893 ext. 7; fax (303) 442-2936; kate@bikesbelong.org or grants@bikesbelong.org
Internet: http://www.bikesbelong.org/bikes-belong-foundation/foundation-grants/research-grants
Sponsor: Bikes Belong Foundation
207 Canyon Boulevard. Suite 202
Boulder, CO 80302

Bikes Belong Grants 763
Sponsored by the U.S. bicycle industry, the Bikes Belong Coalition has the mission of putting more people on bicycles more often. Bikes Belong grants fund important and influential projects that leverage federal funding and build momentum for bicycling in communities across the U.S. These projects include bike paths, lanes, and routes, as well as bike parks, mountain-bike trails, BMX facilities, and large-scale bicycle-advocacy initiatives. Bikes Belong grants fall into two application categories: facility applications and advocacy applications. The Bikes Belong Coalition usually offers two to three grant cycles per year (see the Schedules and Deadlines section of the website for current deadline dates). Application guidelines and downloadable applications are available at the website. Organizations should submit their completed applications along with a cover letter and any required supporting materials in one pdf file via email by the deadline date. See application guidelines for more detailed instructions.
Requirements: Nonprofit organizations whose missions are bicycle- and/or trail-specific and city, state, regional, and federal agencies are eligible to apply for facility grants. Government entities are encouraged to align with a local bicycle-advocacy group that will help develop and advance the project or program. Only organizations whose primary mission is bicycle advocacy are eligible to apply for advocacy grants. New organizations who have not yet received their nonprofit status may submit an application with the assistance of another nonprofit that has agreed to serve as their fiscal sponsor. In the facility category, the coalition will consider funding construction costs and matching funds. The coalition is particularly interested in projects that serve a range of age and ability levels and that reach the "interested but concerned" riders - those who would bicycle more but don't because of safety issues. Eligible facility requests include bike paths, lanes, trails, and bridges; end-of-trip facilities such as bike racks, parking and storage; mountain-bike facilities; bike parks; and BMX facilities. Preferred advocacy projects include large-scale, innovative, replicable initiatives that significantly increase ridership and improve conditions for bicycling in big U.S. cities. Eligible projects include programs that transform city streets (such as Ciclovias), innovative pilot projects, and initiatives that have a significant political impact. Advocacy projects should demonstrate a reasonable degree of measuring success and of future sustainability.
Restrictions: Bikes Belong will not fund individuals and rarely awards grants to organizations and communities that have received Bikes Belong funding within the past three years. Bikes Belong will NOT consider facility applications for the following types of funding: feasibility studies, master plans, policy documents, or litigation; signs, maps, and travel; trailheads, information kiosks, benches, and restroom facilities; bicycles, helmets, tools, and other accessories or equipment; events, races, clinics/classes, or bicycle rodeos; bike recycling, repair, or earn-a-bike programs; or projects in which Bikes Belong is the sole

or primary funder. Bikes Belong will NOT consider advocacy project applications for the following types of funding: general operating costs; staff salaries, except where used to support a specific advocacy initiative; rides and event sponsorships; planning and retreats; or bicycles, helmets, tools, and accessories or equipment.
Geographic Focus: All States
Contact: Zoe Kircos; (303) 449-4893 ext. 5; fax (303) 442-2936; zoe@bikesbelong.org
Internet: http://www.bikesbelong.org/grants/apply-for-a-grant/grant-seekers-guide/
Sponsor: Bikes Belong Coalition
P.O. Box 2359
Boulder, CO 80306

Bill and Katie Weaver Charitable Trust Grants 764
The Bill and Katie Weaver Charitable Trust offers grants primarily in the Dallas, Texas, metro area, though funding is sometimes given outside of Texas. The Trust's primary fields of interest include: community development; economic development; fund raising; higher education; performing arts; orchestras; religion agencies; and the Salvation Army. Types of funding offered include: annual campaigns; continuing support; and general operating support. Since a formal application is not required, interested parties should forward a letter of application, which should include: current staff salaries; details of the program or project; budgetary needs; additional sources of funding; and attachments (IRS letter, organization's current budget, and list of board members). There are no specified annual deadlines.
Restrictions: No grant awards are given directly to individuals.
Geographic Focus: Colorado, District of Columbia, Texas
Contact: William R. Weaver, Trustee; (214) 999-9497 or (214) 999-9494
Sponsor: Bill and Katie Weaver Charitable Trust
1845 Woodall Rogers Freeway, Suite 1275
Dallas, TX 75201-2299

Bill and Melinda Gates Foundation Agricultural Development Grants 765
The Agricultural Development Program supports projects that enable small farmers in developing countries to break the cycle of hunger and poverty, to sell what they grow or raise, increase their incomes, and make their farms more productive and sustainable. Previously funded initiatives include projects that employ a collaborative and comprehensive approach to agricultural development; provide small farmers with the supplies and support they need to succeed; address the needs of women farmers; help small farmers profit from their crops; use science and technology to develop crops that can thrive; gather and analyze data to improve decision-making; encourage greater investment and involvement in agricultural development; and encourage policy and advocacy efforts that accelerate progress against the world's most acute poverty. Additional information on each agricultural development initiative can be found on the website. New proposals are considered, as well as expansion of existing initiatives currently funded by the Foundation.
Requirements: Proposals should aim to help the world's poorest people lift themselves out of hunger and poverty. The Foundation seeks proposals that: are able to produce measurable results; use preventive approaches; promise significant and long-lasting change; leverage support from other sources; and accelerate or are in accordance with work the Foundation already supports.
Restrictions: The majority of funding is made to organizations that are independently identified by Foundation staff. Unsolicited proposals are not accepted. Proposals must be made through 501(c)3 or other tax-exempt organizations. The Foundation is unable to make grants directly to individuals. The Foundation will not fund projects addressing health problems in developed countries; political campaigns and legislative lobbying efforts; building or capital campaigns; or projects that exclusively serve religious purposes.
Geographic Focus: All Countries
Contact: Sam Dryden; (206) 709-3400 or (206) 709-3140; info@gatesfoundation.org
Internet: http://www.gatesfoundation.org/agriculturaldevelopment/Pages/default.aspx
Sponsor: Bill and Melinda Gates Foundation
P.O. Box 23350
Seattle, WA 98102

Bill and Melinda Gates Foundation Emergency Response Grants 766
The Foundation supports effective relief agencies and local organizations that respond quickly to people's most pressing needs in challenging conditions. The Foundation is interested in proposals that deliver food and clean water; improve sanitation; provide medical attention and shelter; prevent or minimize outbreaks of disease; and support livelihoods through cash-for-work programs. The Foundation currently supports people affected by the global food crisis; people in Sri Lanka and Pakistan displaced by political unrest and violence; victims of the earthquake in Haiti; communities affected by Typhoon Ketsana in the Philippines and Vietnam; and a consortium of leading humanitarian aid organizations.
Requirements: Relief agencies must have extensive experience and local relationships and be able to deliver help within days, when needs are most crucial. The Foundation also funds organizational capacity-building and explores learning opportunities to reinforce emergency response capabilities.
Restrictions: The majority of funding is made to organizations that are independently identified by Foundation staff. Unsolicited proposals are not accepted. Proposals must be made through 501(c)3 or other tax-exempt organizations. The Foundation is unable to make grants directly to individuals. The Gates Foundation will not fund:projects addressing health problems in developed countries; political campaigns and legislative lobbying efforts; building or capital campaigns; or projects that exclusively serve religious purposes.
Geographic Focus: All Countries
Contact: Emergency Response Coordinator; (206) 709-3140; info@gatesfoundation.org
Internet: http://www.gatesfoundation.org/topics/Pages/emergency-response.aspx
Sponsor: Bill and Melinda Gates Foundation
P.O. Box 23350
Seattle, WA 98102

Bill and Melinda Gates Foundation Financial Services for the Poor Grants 767
The Gates Foundation seeks to deliver reliable access to a range of safe, affordable financial tools and services to help the world's poorest households build better, healthier lives. The Foundation currently supports distribution channels, saving products, financial systems, and complementary financial systems. To ensure these services benefit the poorest populations will require new models and innovative approaches. New proposals are considered, as well as expansion of existing initiatives currently funded under the Gates Foundation.
Requirements: New technologies and innovative partnerships make it possible to create a "next-generation" banking system. The Foundation seeks to partner with banks, governments, mobile phone companies, retail store chains, and others to make financial services and technology accessible to billions of people throughout the world. The Foundation seeks proposals that are able to produce measurable results; use preventive approaches; promise significant and long-lasting change; leverage support from other sources; and accelerate or are in accordance with work the Foundation already supports.
Restrictions: The majority of funding is made to organizations that are independently identified by Foundation staff. Unsolicited proposals are not accepted. Proposals must be made through 501(c)3 or other tax-exempt organizations. The Foundation is unable to make grants directly to individuals. The Foundation will not fund projects addressing health problems in developed countries; political campaigns and legislative lobbying efforts; building or capital campaigns; or projects that exclusively serve religious purposes.
Geographic Focus: All States, All Countries
Contact: Rodger Vorhies; (206) 709-3140; info@gatesfoundation.org
Internet: http://www.gatesfoundation.org/financialservicesforthepoor/Pages/default.aspx
Sponsor: Bill and Melinda Gates Foundation
P.O. Box 23350
Seattle, WA 98102

Bill and Melinda Gates Foundation Library Grants 768
The Foundation supports proposals that seek to improve the quality and availability of library resources, particularly information technology. The Foundation seeks proposals that make information technology more accessible and affordable; provide quality computer hardware and Internet services; provide free access to the Internet and technological training; and work towards narrowing the technological gap. For most people in developing and transitioning countries, quality Internet access is not available or affordable. Worldwide, approximately 5 billion people - nearly 90 percent of the world's population - do not have Internet access. Grants are offered to libraries in the United States and on a global basis. Detailed information is available at the Foundation website.
Requirements: Support is only given to libraries located within the United States, Chile, Mexico, Botswana, Lithuania, Latvia, Romania, Ukraine, Poland, Bulgaria, and Vietnam. The Gates Foundation seeks proposals that are able to produce measurable results; use preventive approaches; promise significant and long-lasting change; leverage support from other sources; and accelerate or are in accordance with work the Foundation already supports.
Restrictions: The majority of funding is made to organizations that are independently identified by Foundation staff. Unsolicited proposals are not accepted. Proposals must be made through 501(c)3 or other tax-exempt organizations. The Foundation is unable to make grants directly to individuals. The Foundation will not fund projects addressing health problems in developed countries; political campaigns and legislative lobbying efforts; building or capital campaigns; or projects that exclusively serve religious purposes.
Geographic Focus: All States, Botswana, Bulgaria, Chile, Latvia, Lithuania, Mexico, Poland, Romania, Ukraine, Vietnam
Contact: Deborah Jacobs, Director; (206) 709-3140; info@gatesfoundation.org
Director, U.S. Libraries Program; (206) 709-3140; info@gatesfoundation.org
Internet: http://www.gatesfoundation.org/libraries/Pages/default.aspx
Sponsor: Bill and Melinda Gates Foundation
P.O. Box 23350
Seattle, WA 98102

Bill and Melinda Gates Foundation Policy and Advocacy Grants 769
The Foundation supports proposals that do one or more of the following: promote awareness of global development issues; advocate for least-advantaged populations; draw international attention and commitment; identify and promote powerful solutions; work towards additional and more effective investments; and are capable of lasting progress against global hunger and poverty.
Requirements: The Foundation seeks proposals that are able to produce measurable results; use preventive approaches; promise significant and long-lasting change; leverage support from other sources; and accelerate or are in accordance with work the Foundation already supports.
Restrictions: The majority of funding is made to organizations that are independently identified by our staff. Unsolicited proposals are not accepted. Proposals must be made through 501(c)3 or other tax-exempt organizations. The Foundation is unable to make grants directly to individuals. The Gates Foundation will not fund: projects addressing health problems in developed countries; political campaigns and legislative lobbying efforts; building or capital campaigns; or projects that exclusively serve religious purposes.
Geographic Focus: All Countries
Contact: Geoff Lamb, President; (206) 709-3140; info@gatesfoundation.org
Internet: http://www.gatesfoundation.org/global-development/Pages/overview.aspx
Sponsor: Bill and Melinda Gates Foundation
P.O. Box 23350
Seattle, WA 98102

Bill and Melinda Gates Foundation Water, Sanitation and Hygiene Grants 770
Poor sanitation causes severe diarrhea, which kills 1.5 million children each year. Smart investments in sanitation can reduce disease, increase family incomes, keep girls in school, help preserve the environment, and enhance human dignity. The Foundation is looking

to work with partners in an effort to expand affordable access to sanitation. Detailed information is available at the Foundation website.
Requirements: The Gates Foundation seeks proposals that are able to produce measurable results; use preventive approaches; promise significant and long-lasting change; leverage support from other sources; and accelerate or are in accordance with work the foundation already supports.
Restrictions: The majority of funding is made to organizations that are independently identified by Foundation staff. Unsolicited proposals are not accepted. Proposals must be made through 501(c)3 or other tax-exempt organizations. The Foundation is unable to make grants directly to individuals. The Gates Foundation will not fund projects addressing health problems in developed countries; political campaigns and legislative lobbying efforts; building or capital campaigns; or projects that exclusively serve religious purposes.
Geographic Focus: All States, All Countries
Contact: Kellie Sloan; (206) 709-3140; info@gatesfoundation.org
Internet: http://www.gatesfoundation.org/watersanitationhygiene/Pages/home.aspx
Sponsor: Bill and Melinda Gates Foundation
P.O. Box 23350
Seattle, WA 98102

Bill Hannon Foundation Grants 771
The foundation awards grants to eligible California organizations in its areas of interest, including education, religious programs, and social services delivery.
Requirements: The Foundation limits its grants to programs primarily in the greater Los Angeles area, where Mr. Hannon lived and worked. Only IRS certified, non-profit public charities are eligible for grants. There are no application deadlines or forms. Submit a letter of interest; full proposals are by invitation.
Geographic Focus: California
Amount of Grant: Up to 27,000,000 USD
Contact: Grants Administrator; (310) 207-0303; fax (310) 207-8077; elaine@redshift.com
Internet: www.hannonfoundation.org/grantmaking.html#b
Sponsor: Bill Hannon Foundation
729 Montana Avenue, Suite 5
Santa Monica, CA 90403

Bingham McHale LLP Pro Bono Services 772
The Bingham Greenebaum Doll firm is committed to the communities it serves, including: Indianapolis, Jasper, Evansville, and Vincennes, Indiana; Louisville, Frankfort, and Lexington, Kentucky; and Cincinnati, Ohio. This commitment includes sharing legal services with those who cannot afford legal assistance on their own. As attorneys, the firm recognizes that it has a special responsibility to provide legal services to the underprivileged within the communities where its attorneys work and live. low income families
Requirements: Residents of communities that the Bingham Greenebaum Doll firm serves are eligible.
Geographic Focus: Indiana
Contact: Partners and Associates; (317) 635-8900; fax (317) 236-9907
Internet: http://www.bgdlegal.com/aboutus/xprGeneralContent2.aspx?xpST=CommunityService
Sponsor: Bingham McHale LLP Pro Bono Program
2700 Market Tower, 10 W. Market Street
Indianapolis, IN 46204-4900

Biogen Corporate Giving Grants 773
The corporate giving program gives back to Biogen communities through grants awarded to nonprofit, community-based organizations, most of which are dedicated to education, community service, healthcare, and culture and the arts. There are no application forms or deadlines; guidelines are available online. See submission information for proposal mailing instructions.
Requirements: To be eligible for funding, an organization must be: a non-profit agency with tax-exempt status under section 501(c)3 of the Internal Revenue Service code; serving residents of Cambridge or the Greater Boston area, San Diego or San Diego County, and Raleigh-Durham, NC.
Restrictions: Eligible organizations must not: advocate, support or practice discrimination based on race, religion, age, national origin, language, gender, sexual preference or physical limitation; include the promotion of any particular religious faith as an explicit and primary goal; have the nomination or election of candidates to political office as an explicit goal, be government agencies, political organizations or individuals. Grants should not cover fundraising or capital campaign activities.
Geographic Focus: California, Massachusetts, North Carolina
Amount of Grant: 500 - 2,500 USD
Contact: Kathryn Bloom, Communications; (617) 679-2000; fax (617) 679-2617
Internet: http://www.biogen.com/site/014.html
Sponsor: Biogen
14 Cambridge Center
Cambridge, MA 02142

Birmingham Foundation Grants 774
The Birmingham Foundation is a private, independent foundation, dedicated to health-related and human services grant-making in the south neighborhoods of Pittsburgh, Pennsylvania, which are part of the 15203, 15210 and 15211 zip code areas. The Board of Directors meets three times a year to act on grant proposals, in March, June and November.
Requirements: 501(c)3 nonprofits in South Pittsburgh communities including Allentown, Arlington and Arlington Heights, Beltzhoover, Bon Air, Carrick, Duquesne Heights, Knoxville, Mount Oliver, Mount Washington, Saint Clair Village, and South Side are eligible.
Restrictions: Grants are not normally made for operating budgets, deficits, fund-raising campaigns, general research, overhead costs, scholarships, political campaigns, or loans. Grants are not made to individuals, to other private foundations, for sectarian religious activities, or for the efforts to influence legislation unless grant-related.
Geographic Focus: Pennsylvania
Amount of Grant: 2,500 - 50,000 USD
Contact: Chris Mason; (412) 481-2777; fax (412) 481-2727; info@birmfoundpgh.org
Internet: http://www.birminghamfoundation.org
Sponsor: Birmingham Foundation
2005 Sarah Street, 2nd Floor
Pittsburgh, PA 15203

Bishop Robert Paddock Trust Grants 775
The Trust, managed by Ball Baker Leake of New York, is an independent foundation that supports the Episcopal religion, social welfare programs, and theological education. Its fields of interest include: Christian agencies and churches; higher education; human and social services; Protestant agencies and churches; and theological education programs. Types of support include: endowments; publications; and general research. Correspondence should be directed to the Mid-Hudson Regional Office. Written applications have no deadlines, although submissions should allow sufficient time for trustees to evaluate the request.
Geographic Focus: All States
Amount of Grant: 5,000 USD
Contact: Contact; (845) 338-1086 or (845) 331-6796; holycrosskingston@dioceseny.org
Sponsor: Bishop Robert Paddock Trust
30 Pinegrove Avenue
Kingston, NY 12401

Bitha Godfrey & Maude J. Thomas Charitable Foundation Grants 776
The Foundation, established in Arkansas, offers its supports in a number of areas, including: children and youth services; community and economic development; education; federated giving programs; and Protestant agencies and churches. Types of support include building and renovation, general operations, and scholarship funds. Grants range from approximately $500 to $7,000. There are no specific application forms or deadlines with which to adhere, and applicants should contact the Foundation in writing.
Requirements: Applicants must be 501(c)3 agencies serving the residents of Arkansas.
Geographic Focus: Arkansas
Amount of Grant: 500 - 7,000 USD
Contact: Bruce McNeill, Trustee; (479) 452-8900
Sponsor: Bitha Godfrey and Maude J. Thomas Charitable Foundation
3901 S 33rd Street
Fort Smith, AR 72903-5972

BJ's Charitable Foundation Grants 777
Established with the goal of creating a positive, long-lasting impact on the communities BJ's serves, the mission of BJ's Charitable Foundation is to enhance and enrich community programs that primarily benefit children and families. The majority of the foundation's giving is focused on organizations that: (a) Promote the safety, security and well-being of children and families; (b) Support education and health programs; (c) Provide community service opportunities; or, (d) Aid in hunger and disaster relief.
Requirements: Organizations that are tax-exempt under 501(c)3 of the Internal Revenue Code and recognized as a 'public charity' by the IRS may apply. The program must align with the foundation's mission of supporting children and families in the specific areas of safety, security and well-being, education, health, community service, hunger/homelessness and disaster relief. And, the program must positively impact communities where BJ's Clubs are located. All organizations are limited to one (1) application per 12-month period. Additional applications will not be considered.
Restrictions: The foundation does not provide funding for: (1) Organizations that discriminate on the basis of race, color, gender, sexual orientation, age, religion, national or ethnic origin or physical disability. (2) Political organizations, fraternal groups or social clubs that engage in any kind of political activity. (3) Religious organizations, unless they serve the general public in a significant non-denominational way. (4) Programs that have been in place for less than one (1) year. (5) Individuals. (6) Organizations located outside BJ's markets. (7) Capital campaigns. (8) Private foundations. (9) Sponsorships for music, film and art festivals. (10) Business expositions/conferences. (11) Journal or program advertisements.
Geographic Focus: Connecticut, Delaware, Florida, Georgia, Maine, Maryland, Massachusetts, New Hampshire, New Jersey, New York, North Carolina, Ohio, Pennsylvania, Rhode Island, South Carolina, Virginia
Date(s) Application is Due: Mar 6; Jul 10; Dec 6; Dec 30
Contact: Community Relations Manager; (508) 651-7400; fax (508) 651-6623
Internet: http://www.bjs.com/about/community/charity.shtml
Sponsor: BJ's Charitable Foundation
1 Mercer Road, P.O. Box 9614
Natick, MA 01760

BJ's Wholesale Clubs Local Charitable Giving 778
In addition to the wide range of community programs offered at the corporate level and through BJ's Charitable Foundation, BJ's also offers a structured charitable giving program administered through its local clubs. By giving each of its Clubs an annual donation budget, BJ's is able to provide local support to community nonprofit organizations that primarily benefit children and families, enabling them to have a direct and immediate impact on the communities they serve.
Requirements: This program is available to local community nonprofit organizations with a Club in the area. (See http://www.bjs.com/locations/ to find the store nearest you.)

To request an in-kind donation of product(s) or gift cards, submit a request, written on your organization's letterhead, to your local Club a minimum of 4 - 6 weeks prior to your donation deadline. Include in your request a brief description of your organization's mission and an explanation of your donation needs.
Geographic Focus: Connecticut, Delaware, Florida, Georgia, Maine, Maryland, Massachusetts, New Hampshire, New Jersey, New York, North Carolina, Ohio, Pennsylvania, Rhode Island, South Carolina, Virginia
Contact: Foundation Director; (508) 651-7400; fax (508) 651-6623
Internet: http://www.bjs.com/about/community/local.shtml
Sponsor: BJ's Wholesale Clubs
1 Mercer Road, P.O. Box 9614
Natick, MA 01760

Blackford County Community Foundation - WOW Grants   779
The Blackford County Community Foundation - WOW Grants offer funding for projects that encourage, educate, and enlighten women and/or children. Applicants may be individuals, groups, or organizations.
Requirements: Applicants should submit the following items to the Foundation: cover page; project narrative with a detailed description of the project, including timeline and results expected; and a detailed budget. All grant recipients will be required to give a brief report about their project at the spring meeting.
Restrictions: The following are not eligible for funding: operating deficits, post-event or after the fact situations; special fundraising events, including endowment campaigns; political endeavors and propaganda; and profit-making enterprises and/or projects for personal gain.
Geographic Focus: Indiana
Date(s) Application is Due: Feb 1
Contact: Patricia Poulson; (765) 348-3411; ppoulson@blackfordcounty.org
Internet: http://www.blackfordcofoundation.org/pages.asp?Page=Women%20of%20Worth&PageIndex=411
Sponsor: Blackford County Community Foundation
121 North High Street
Hartford City, IN 47348

Blackford County Community Foundation Grants   780
The Blackford County Community Foundation and its supporting organizations award numerous grants annually. Primary areas of interest include: community and economic development; education; community services planning and coordination; and human services. The Foundation has quarterly deadlines for submitting applications on January 31, March 31, June 30, and September 30.
Requirements: Applicants must contact the Executive Director to determine if their project is suitable for the funding. If the organization is asked to submit a formal proposal, it must consider the following criteria: purpose and definition of the project or program; background of the request office; officers and staff personnel of requesting organization; financial information and budgets; evaluation results; and how the project will be affected if funding is not received. The Foundation will judge the proposal on its merit, priority, and substantive quality.
Restrictions: The Blackford County Community Foundation generally does not fund: profit-making enterprises; political activities; operating budgets of organizations, except for limited experimental or demonstration periods; sectarian or religious organizations operated primarily for the benefit of their own members; endowment purposes; capital grants to building campaigns will only be made when there is evidence that such support is vital to the success of a program meeting priority needs of the community. Grants are not awarded for endowment purposes.
Geographic Focus: Indiana
Date(s) Application is Due: Jan 31; Mar 31; Jun 30; Sep 30
Contact: Patricia D. Poulson, Executive Director; (765) 348-3411; fax (765) 348-4945; ppoulson@blackfordcounty.org or foundation@blackfordcounty.org
Internet: http://blackfordcofoundation.org/Grants
Sponsor: Blackford County Community Foundation
121 North High Street
Hartford City, IN 47348

Black Hills Corporation Grants   781
The corporation is committed to improving the quality of life in the communities it serves. Through corporate contributions and employee contributions and voluntarism, the company assumes a leadership role in community-building. Major areas that have received funding in the past are human services, civic and community development, education, arts and culture, and environment. While the committee judges each request on its own merits, the following requests are less likely to be approved than others: organizations that do not serve the Black Hills Corporation service territory; organizations and programs primarily designed to influence legislation; religious organizations for religious purposes; grants to individuals or organizations that are not designated by the IRS to be 501(c)3 nonprofits; proposals for conferences, seminars, or festivals; individual or group trips, tours, or pageants; single disease research programs; endowment campaigns; requests to fund deficit operating expenses; and athletic sponsorships.
Requirements: Nonprofit organizations offering services in South Dakota where the corporation operates are eligible.
Geographic Focus: South Dakota
Contact: Barbara Zar; (605) 721-1700; bhc@bh-corp.com
Internet: http://www.blackhillscorp.com/giveguide.htm
Sponsor: Black Hills Corporation
P.O. Box 1400
Rapid City, SD 57709

Black River Falls Area Foundation Grants   782
Grant applications are evaluated with consideration to the policies, funding objectives and the mission statement of the Foundation. General categories of support include: education, health services, cultural activities, social services and civic projects. Grants to be considered are those that meet charitable needs of: a new or innovative nature to fulfill unmet needs; one-time projects; capital improvements; equipment needs; start-up expenses; special programs; and emergency funding. Applications will be accepted April 1 through May 15.
Requirements: Any non-profit organization in Jackson County, Wisconsin, may apply for a grant. A copy of the organization's tax-exempt status is required.
Restrictions: Requests to support endowments, operating expenses, debt repayment, religious purposes, individuals, and lobbying expenses are usually discouraged.
Geographic Focus: Wisconsin
Date(s) Application is Due: May 15
Contact: Beth Overlien, Administrative Assistant; (715) 284-3113
Internet: http://www.brfareafoundation.org/application
Sponsor: Black River Falls Area Foundation
P.O. Box 99
Black River Falls, WI 54615

Blade Foundation Grants   783
The foundation awards general operating grants to cultural, educational, and social service organizations in Ohio. Scholarships also are awarded to children of employees of Toledo Blade with at least three years of employment. There are no application deadlines for grants.
Requirements: Ohio nonprofits and individuals are eligible.
Geographic Focus: Ohio
Contact: Dave Huey, (419) 724-6417
Sponsor: Blade Foundation
541 N Superior Street
Toledo, OH 43660

Blanche and Irving Laurie Foundation Grants   784
The Blanche & Irving Laurie Foundation was established in 1983 by New Brunswick philanthropist Irving Laurie. The foundation makes charitable gifts to institutions and nonprofits in broad areas of interest, including the arts, especially theater and music; education; health care; social services; and needs and concerns of the Jewish community. Capital grants, operating support grants, grants for programs/projects, and scholarships are awarded. Applicants should submit seven copies of a written proposal containing the following items: copies of the most recent annual report, audited financial statement, and 990; a detailed description of the project and amount of funding requested; and a copy of the current year's organization budget and/or project budget. The foundation's board meets quarterly to evaluate proposals. Final notification occurs within three to four months from submission. An informational brochure and application guidelines are available from the foundation.
Requirements: Nonprofit organizations in New Jersey are eligible.
Restrictions: The foundation does not support medical research.
Geographic Focus: New Jersey
Contact: Gene Korf, Executive Director; (973) 993-1583
Sponsor: Blanche and Irving Laurie Foundation
P.O. Box 53
Roseland, NJ 07068-5788

Blanche and Julian Robertson Family Foundation Grants   785
The Blanche and Julian Robertson Family Foundation is totally committed to the goal of improving the quality of life in Salisbury and Rowan County. The general direction of the Foundation's interest is: programs which address social problems and nurture positive social relationships; efforts aimed at enriching lives through exposure to the cultural arts; neighborhood revitalization programs, especially when such programs encourage development of transitional housing and enable first-time homeowners to purchase homes; programs that improve opportunities for youth at risk and families in crisis; efforts to improve broad-based educational, recreational, and athletic opportunities; efforts which address health and the environment. The Foundation is also interested in programs and projects that demonstrate the attributes of leverage (where a grant will attract matching gifts or other funding), as well as innovation, thoroughness, passion, and commitment. Contact the office for application and guidelines.
Requirements: North Carolina nonprofits serving Salisbury and Rowan County.
Restrictions: Foundation does not make grants outside Salisbury and Rowan County.
Geographic Focus: North Carolina
Date(s) Application is Due: Mar 30
Contact: David Setzer, (704) 637-0511; fax (704) 637-0177; bjrfoundation@aol.com
Sponsor: Blanche and Julian Robertson Family Foundation
141 East Council Street, P.O. Box 4242
Salisbury, NC 28145-4242

Blanche M. Walsh Charity Trust Grants   786
The trust awards grants to U.S. nonprofits organizations in its areas of interest, including Roman Catholic charities, education, and social services delivery. Grants are awarded for one year, with possible renewal for a second year. All inquiries must be in writing.
Requirements: 501(c)3 tax-exempt organizations listed in the Kennedy Directory are eligible. Applicants must indicate the page numbers of their listings in the Kennedy Directory.
Geographic Focus: All States
Contact: Robert Murphy, Trustee; (978) 454-5655
Sponsor: Blanche M. Walsh Charity Trust
174 Central Street, Suite 311
Lowell, MA 01852

Blandin Foundation Expand Opportunity Grants   787

The Blandin Foundation's vision for its work is to be the premier partner for building healthy rural communities, grounded in strong economies, where burdens and benefits are widely shared. This vision drives the Foundation's priorities, including areas of focus for grant-making. Expand Opportunity Grants is an evolving area of work in which the Blandin Foundation seeks to blend educational attainment, economic opportunity and broader inclusion in rural Minnesota communities, so all residents have greater opportunities to prosper. Emphasis is on work that moves beyond traditional approaches and that increases impact through a synergistic approach. Roughly 75% of Foundation grants will be made in this focus area. Priority will be given to projects that demonstrate: a strategy involving inter-relationships between economy, education and inclusivity; and clear outcomes such as expanded enterprises and entrepreneurship, increased educational or economic success for populations that have faced historical barriers, and expanded relationships between educational systems, employers and parents.

Requirements: Grants will be made to organizations with a nonprofit 501(c)3 tax exempt status. Units of government may also apply for a grant, but only if the purpose of the grant request goes beyond the normal limits of expected government services and taxpayer responsibility. Grant proposals greater than $50,000 should be received by: March 15 for review in June, September 15 for review in December, and December 15 for review in March. Quick Response grants (less than $50,000), BCLP Quick Start grants and Itasca County Area community donations may be submitted at any time.

Restrictions: The Blandin Foundation does not make grants directly to individuals, except in the case of its Educational Awards Program. Funding does not support: grants outside the state of Minnesota; religious activities; medical research; publications, films or videos; travel grants for individuals or groups; camping and athletic programs; ordinary government services; grants to individuals; grants solely intended to influence legislation.

Geographic Focus: Minnesota
Date(s) Application is Due: Mar 15; Sep 15; Dec 15
Amount of Grant: Up to 250,000 USD
Contact: Wade Fauth, Grants Director; (218) 327-8706 or (218) 326-0523; fax (218) 327-1949; bfinfo@blandinfoundation.org
Internet: http://www.blandinfoundation.org/grants/grants-detail.php?intResourceID=5
Sponsor: Blandin Foundation
100 North Pokegama Avenue
Grand Rapids, MN 55744

Blandin Foundation Invest Early Grants   788

Invest Early, launched in the fall of 2005, seeks to reach children under the age of five who, due to income or other factors, may be at risk of entering kindergarten without those early skills which are so critical to success in school. Invest Early combines the resources of childhood educators, health and human services professionals, health care professionals, family development specialists, and others to provide a comprehensive program of early childhood care and education services. Some of the services offered through Invest Early include: infant/toddler/preschool programs; parent education; adult basic education (ABE); mental health support; wrap-around childcare; home visits; and transportation.

Requirements: The program is available to qualifying children and their families throughout Itasca County and works in partnership with local school districts, federal, state and county programs, and non-profit resources.

Geographic Focus: Minnesota
Contact: Wade Fauth; (218) 327-8706 or (218) 326-0523; bfinfo@blandinfoundation.org
Internet: http://www.blandinfoundation.org/resources/case-studies-detail.php?intResourceID=130
Sponsor: Blandin Foundation
100 North Pokegama Avenue
Grand Rapids, MN 55744

Blandin Foundation Itasca County Area Vitality Grants   789

The Blandin Foundation's vision for its work is to be the premier partner for building healthy rural communities, grounded in strong economies, where burdens and benefits are widely shared. This vision drives the Foundation's priorities, including areas of focus for grant-making. Itasca County Area Vitality Grants carry on the legacy and commitments of businessman and Blandin Foundation founder Charles K. Blandin to his adopted hometown of Grand Rapids, Minnesota, and surrounding communities. These are grants available only for cultural and social services activities that directly benefit the communities of Itasca County and the neighboring communities of Blackduck, Northome, Hill City and Remer, Minnesota. Low priority is placed on large capital grants, recreation and community amenities. Priority will be given to projects that demonstrate: clear articulation of strategies and outcomes that will strengthen the local community, with particular consideration given to proposals that build the capacity of distressed populations to live in greater dignity; cost-effective service delivery strategies, including collaboration with organizations addressing similar issues; and community support and sustainability evidenced by significant matching contributions.

Requirements: Grants will be made to organizations with a nonprofit 501(c)3 tax exempt status. Units of government may also apply for a grant, but only if the purpose of the grant request goes beyond the normal limits of expected government services and taxpayer responsibility. Grant proposals greater than $50,000 should be received by: March 15 for review in June, September 15 for review in December, and December 15 for review in March. Quick Response grants (less than $50,000), BCLP Quick Start grants and Itasca County Area community donations may be submitted at any time.

Restrictions: The Blandin Foundation does not make grants directly to individuals, except in the case of its Educational Awards Program. Funding does not support: grants outside the state of Minnesota; religious activities; medical research; publications, films or videos; travel grants for individuals or groups; camping and athletic programs; ordinary government services; grants to individuals; grants solely intended to influence legislation.

Geographic Focus: Minnesota
Date(s) Application is Due: Mar 15; Sep 15; Dec 15
Amount of Grant: Up to 250,000 USD
Contact: Wade Fauth, Grants Director; (218) 327-8706 or (218) 326-0523; fax (218) 327-1949; bfinfo@blandinfoundation.org
Internet: http://www.blandinfoundation.org/grants/grants-detail.php?intResourceID=5
Sponsor: Blandin Foundation
100 North Pokegama Avenue
Grand Rapids, MN 55744

Blandin Foundation Rural Community Leadership Grants   790

The Blandin Foundation has had a quarter-century commitment to developing and sustaining the capacity of rural residents to build healthy communities. Its primary investment in this focus area has been, and will continue to be, through its Blandin Community Leadership programs. In addition, a small number of grants will be made to support leadership development efforts that complement those of the Foundation. Priority will be given to projects that demonstrate rural leaders acting collaboratively on community strengthening efforts.

Requirements: Grants will be made to organizations with a nonprofit 501(c)3 tax exempt status. Units of government may also apply for a grant, but only if the purpose of the grant request goes beyond the normal limits of expected government services and taxpayer responsibility. Grant proposals greater than $50,000 should be received by: March 15 for review in June, September 15 for review in December, and December 15 for review in March. Quick Response grants (less than $50,000), BCLP Quick Start grants and Itasca County Area community donations may be submitted at any time.

Restrictions: The Blandin Foundation does not make grants directly to individuals, except in the case of its Educational Awards Program. Funding does not support: grants outside the state of Minnesota; religious activities; medical research; publications, films or videos; travel grants for individuals or groups; camping and athletic programs; ordinary government services; grants to individuals; grants solely intended to influence legislation.

Geographic Focus: Minnesota
Date(s) Application is Due: Mar 15; Sep 15; Dec 15
Amount of Grant: Up to 250,000 USD
Contact: Wade Fauth, Grants Director; (218) 327-8706 or (218) 326-0523; fax (218) 327-1949; bfinfo@blandinfoundation.org
Internet: http://www.blandinfoundation.org/html/scholarships.cfm
Sponsor: Blandin Foundation
100 North Pokegama Avenue
Grand Rapids, MN 55744

Bloomington Area Arts Council Grants   791

The Bloomington Area Arts Council supports public participation in the arts by developing, strengthening, and promoting the cultural resources of Bloomington and Brown, Greene, Lawrence, Monroe and Owen counties. With its Regional Arts Partnership Grant program, grants are designed to provide general public access to quality arts and cultural activities with special attention to underserved communities. The program has the following categories: Arts Organization Support (AOS) Level 1 contributes to general operating expenses for small to mid-sized arts organizations having at least one year of arts programming history, a governing body, and an annual financial audit, review, or compilation; Arts Organization Support (AOS) Level 2 contributes general operating expenses for mid to larger-sized arts organizations having more than one year history, paid staff, a strategic plan, and a biennial financial audit; Arts Project Support (APS) provides support for a one-time event, production, exhibition, residency, or series provided by a non-profit or public agency which supports a distinct aspect of the organization's arts activities; and Mini-Grants offer support for new and existing arts projects produced or presented by nonprofit organizations or public agencies. Preference will be given to organizations addressing the needs of underserved communities in Greene, Brown, Owen, and Lawrence Counties. There are no deadlines specified, and applicants should begin by submitting a letter of intent.

Requirements: Any 501(c)3 organization serving the residents of Brown, Greene, Lawrence, Monroe, or Owen counties in Indiana are eligible to apply.

Geographic Focus: Indiana
Contact: Program Director; (812) 334-3100 or (812) 334-3310; info@artlives.org
Internet: http://www.artlives.org
Sponsor: Bloomington Area Arts Council
122 S. Walnut Street
Bloomington, IN 47404-6107

Blowitz-Ridgeway Foundation Grants   792

The foundation supports nonprofit agencies that provide medical, psychiatric, and psychological care to economically disadvantaged children and adolescents. Program and capital grants are awarded, primarily in Illinois, in support of medical, psychiatric, psychological, and/or residential care; and research programs in medicine, psychology, social science, and education. The foundation supports operating budgets, and applicants may request commitments that extend beyond one year, but requests for annual funding will not be considered. Applications are accepted throughout the year and are reviewed in the order in which they are received. Guidelines and applications are available online.

Requirements: 501(c)3 nonprofit organizations that offer services to people who lack resources to provide for themselves may apply.

Restrictions: Grants will not be awarded to government agencies or to organizations that subsist mainly on third-party funding and have demonstrated no ability or expended little effort to attract private funding. Grants will not be made for religious or political purposes or for the production or writing of audio-visual materials.

Geographic Focus: Illinois
Amount of Grant: 5,000 - 30,000 USD

Contact: Serena Moy; (847) 330-1020; fax (847) 330-1028; serena@blowitzridgeway.org
Internet: http://www.blowitzridgeway.org/information/information1.html
Sponsor: Blowitz-Ridgeway Foundation
1701 E Woodfield Road, Suite 201
Schaumburg, IL 60173

Blue Cross Blue Shield of Minnesota Foundation - Health Equity: Building Health Equity Together Grants   793

The Building Health Equity Together Grant is a program focused on Minnesota local governments working in partnership with a local 501(c)3 organization to achieve health equity in their community. The partnership should address one or more of the factors that influence health in low-income communities, including education, employment, income, family and social support, and community safety. The Foundation will fund up to two grants of up to $75,000 each with the opportunity for a second year of funding at the same level based on performance; progress; and identification of practices, policies and partners that can help advance the successes of first-year work into the future. Organizations may apply through the Foundation's online application process. A detailed list of required attachments is available at the Foundation's website. A list of previously funded projects in Minnesota and other locations is also available at the website.
Requirements: Eligible applicants are local units of government (county, statutory or home rule charter city, township or school district) in partnership with a 501(c)3 community-based organization. Tribal governments in partnership with a 501(c)3 community-based organization are also eligible. Proposed projects must address one or more of the following factors: education; employment; income; family and social support; and community safety. At least two departments and a non-profit partner must commit to working jointly. A Memorandum of Understanding (MOU) is part of the application. The grant-funded work must result in a concrete initiative that has documented support from key stakeholders and can be implemented.
Geographic Focus: Minnesota
Date(s) Application is Due: Sep 28
Amount of Grant: Up to 75,000 USD
Contact: Stacey Millett, Senior Program Officer; (866) 812-1593 or (651) 662-1019; fax (651) 662-4266; Stacey_D_Millett@bluecrossmn.com
Internet: http://bcbsmnfoundation.com/pages-programs-program-Building_Health_Equity_Together?oid=19570
Sponsor: Blue Cross Blue Shield of Minnesota Foundation
1750 Yankee Doodle Road, N159
Eagan, MN 55122

Blue Cross Blue Shield of Minnesota Foundation - Healthy Children: Growing Up Healthy Grants   794

The Growing Up Healthy Grants engage community health, early childhood development, housing and environmental organizations, and other community partners to nurture the healthy growth and development of children birth to five years and their families. Through this focus area, the Blue Cross Blue Shield (BCBS) of Minnesota Foundation has improved the quality of housing, reduced children's exposure to harmful chemicals, increased readiness for kindergarten, and increased children's access to healthy foods and safe places to play. Planning grants up to $25,000 are available. Through the planning process, funded organizations and their community partners develop a shared vision of how to improve and protect the health of children through place-based projects (neighborhood, town, region) that address health and at least two of the three determinants: early childhood education, housing, and the environment. At the end of the planning period grantees that have developed a community vision, supported by a written implementation plan, may apply for implementation funding for a period of up to three years. To receive an implementation grant, projects must show broad-based community support, demonstrate innovative approaches and articulate how these approaches will result in healthier communities and children. Letter of inquiry/application instructions, previously funded projects, and an instructional webinar are available at the Foundation website.
Requirements: The Foundation encourages a wide range of organizations to apply for funding, including community- and faith-based organizations; health, environmental, housing, early childhood and civic groups; mutual assistance associations; state, county and municipal agencies; tribal governments and agencies; professional associations or collaboratives; and policy and research organizations. Applicants must be located in Minnesota or serve Minnesotans. Eligible applicants include units of government as those designated as 501(c)3 nonprofit organizations. Organizations are required contact the Foundation to discuss their project idea. Based on the outcome of the conversation, they may then be asked to submit a letter of inquiry with supporting information.
Restrictions: The Foundation is unable to provide funding for the following: individuals; lobbying, political or fraternal activities; legal services; sports events and athletic groups; religious purposes; clinical quality improvement activities; biomedical research; capital purposes (building, purchase, remodeling or furnishing of facilities); equipment or travel, except as related to requests for program support; endowments, fundraising events or development campaigns; retiring debt or covering deficits; payment of services or benefits reimbursable from other sources; supplanting funds already secured for budgeted staff and/or services; or long-term financial support.
Geographic Focus: Minnesota
Amount of Grant: Up to 25,000 USD
Contact: Jocelyn Ancheta, Program Officer; (866) 812-1593 or (651) 662-2894; fax (651) 662-4266; Jocelyn_L_Ancheta@bluecrossmn.com
Internet: http://bcbsmnfoundation.com/pages-grantmaking-initiative-Healthy_Children?oid=13827
Sponsor: Blue Cross Blue Shield of Minnesota Foundation
1750 Yankee Doodle Road, N159
Eagan, MN 55122

Blue Cross Blue Shield of Minnesota Foundation - Healthy Equity: Health Impact Assessment Demonstration Project Grants   795

The Health Impact Project: Advancing Smarter Policies for Healthier Communities, a collaboration of the Robert Wood Johnson Foundation and The Pew Charitable Trusts, encourages the use of health impact assessments (HIA) to help decision-makers identify the potential health effects of proposed policies, projects, and programs, and make recommendations that enhance their health benefits and minimize their adverse effects and any associated costs. The HI Project will support up to five HIA demonstration projects intended to inform decisions on proposed local, tribal, or state policies, projects or programs. This initiative could also fund HIAs that address federal decisions having impacts limited to a specific state, region, or local community, such as permitting a new mine or building a new highway. The HI Project seeks to produce a balanced portfolio of completed HIAs that build a compelling case to policy-makers regarding the utility and potential applications of HIA. The Foundation's call for papers seeks to demonstrate the range of useful applications across a range of sectors, levels of government, geographic regions, and types of applicant organizations. Applicants may request grants from $25,000 to $75,000 for demonstration projects to be completed within 18 months. The application and call for papers are located at the Foundation website. Applicants are also encouraged to access several informational webinars located at the website.
Requirements: Eligible applicant organizations include state, tribal, or local agencies; tax-exempt educational institutions; or tax-exempt organizations described in Section 501(c)3 of the Internal Revenue Code (including public charities and private foundations). All applicant organizations must be located in the U.S. or its territories. The Foundation encourages proposals from organizations representing a range of fields and sectors, such as transportation, education, economic and social policy, agricultural policy, energy, environmental regulation, and natural resource development. Prior experience conducting HIAs is not required. The HI Project will provide tailored training and technical assistance to all grantees throughout each grant. High priority will be giving to HIAs from geographic regions where few HIAs have been completed to date (see map located in the call for papers at the Foundation website).
Restrictions: Many demonstration project applicants will have no prior experience with the HIA process and methods. The Health Impact Project, through partnerships with experienced HIA practitioners, provides HIA training and ongoing technical assistance. Grantees who have not previously conducted an HIA will be expected to work with a technical assistance provider to organize a two-day training for HIA project staff and relevant stakeholders. Technical assistance may include, for example, help developing collaborative partnerships with other stakeholders, guidance on communications strategies, or guidance on developing an effective plan for implementing HIA recommendations. If the applicant and and partners lack the full range of technical expertise needed to complete the proposed scope of work, the HI Project may provide limited support for subject area expertise, such as epidemiological modeling, engaging stakeholders, or another sub-discipline, such as air quality analysis.
Geographic Focus: All States
Date(s) Application is Due: Sep 28
Amount of Grant: Up to 75,000 USD
Contact: Jocelyn Ancheta, Program Officer; (866) 812-1593 or (651) 662-2894; fax (651) 662-4266; Jocelyn_L_Ancheta@bluecrossmn.com
Internet: http://bcbsmnfoundation.com/pages-programs-program-Health_Impact_Assessments?oid=19532
Sponsor: Blue Cross Blue Shield of Minnesota Foundation
1750 Yankee Doodle Road, N159
Eagan, MN 55122

Blue Cross Blue Shield of Minnesota Foundation - Healthy Equity: Health Impact Assessment Program Grants   796

The Health Impact Project supports health impact assessment (HIA) initiatives to enable organizations with previous HIA experience to conduct HIAs and develop sustainable self-supporting HIA programs at the local, state, or tribal level. The project encourages the use of health impact assessments to help decision-makers identify the potential health effects of proposed policies, projects, and programs, and make recommendations that enhance their health benefits and minimize their adverse effects and any associated costs. Up to three program grants will be awarded. Grants will be up to $250,000 each and must be completed within 24 months. The program grants will support organizations that have completed at least one prior HIA to conduct at least two HIAs, and to implement a plan that establishes the relationships, systems, and funding mechanisms needed to maintain a stable HIA program that endures beyond the conclusion of the grant period. The application, how organizations will be selected, evaluated, and monitored, and several informational webinars are available at the Foundation website.
Requirements: All applicant organizations must be located in the United States or its territories. Eligible applicants include state, tribal, or local agencies; tax-exempt educational institutions; or tax-exempt organizations described in Section 501(c)3 of the Internal Revenue Code (including public charities and private foundations). All applicants must have completed at least one previously successful HIA. Recipients of these grants will be responsible for conducting at least two HIAs, and for establishing the systems, relationships, and funding mechanisms to implement a stable HIA program that endures beyond the completion of grant funding. Applicants will be asked to describe how they intend to establish a sustainable, self-supporting HIA program, what actions they will implement to bring this about, and how they will measure success. Samples of previously funded grants are discussed in the call for papers available at the Foundation website.
Restrictions: Applicants must provide $100,000 in matching funds or in-kind support. Grant funds may not be used to subsidize individuals for the costs of health care, support clinical trials of unapproved drugs or devices, construct or renovate facilities, or as a substitute for funds currently being used to support similar activities. The project limits the amount of indirect costs it will support to no more than 10% of salaries and benefits covered directly

by the grant; and limits the amount of fringe benefits it will support to no more than 33% of the total staff salaries line item. In addition, no part of the grant can be used to carry on propaganda or otherwise attempt to influence legislation, or a political campaign.
Geographic Focus: All States
Date(s) Application is Due: Dec 14
Amount of Grant: Up to 250,000 USD
Contact: Jocelyn Ancheta, Grants Administrator; (866) 812-1593 or (651) 662-2894; fax (651) 662-4266; Jocelyn_L_Ancheta@bluecrossmn.com
Internet: http://bcbsmnfoundation.com/pages-programs-program-Health_Impact_Assessments?oid=19532
Sponsor: Blue Cross Blue Shield of Minnesota Foundation
1750 Yankee Doodle Road, N159
Eagan, MN 55122

Blue Cross Blue Shield of Minnesota Foundation - Healthy Equity: Public Libraries for Health Grants 797
The Public Libraries for Health program engages public libraries as partners working collectively to improve health for low-income communities and communities of color. As trusted institutions with strong community ties, libraries can work with other organizations in their service area in creative and effective ways. The Foundation awards grants to four libraries across the state for programs or projects that advance health equity. The Foundation will fund up to four grants of up to $50,000 each. Funds may be used for an existing project or a new opportunity. Project activities may occur anywhere in the public library's local community and do not need to take place on public library premises. Organizations are encouraged to review the eligibility checklist before applying. The application and budget worksheet are available at the Foundation website.
Requirements: Organizations must meet the following requirements to apply. They must be classified at a local unit of government with city, county, or state financial support; serve low-income populations; generate library visits as a major portion of service activity beyond electronic, books-by-mail, inter-library loan and other services that do not involve a library visit; provide services that benefit local residents in their service area; retain trained staff to oversee programs and operations; and maintain a physical space for library activities and services that is accessible to the public at least 20 hour per week.
Geographic Focus: Minnesota
Amount of Grant: 50,000 USD
Contact: Jocelyn Ancheta, Program Officer; (651) 662-2894 or (866) 812-1593; fax (651) 662-4266; Jocelyn_L_Ancheta@bluecrossmn.com
Internet: http://bcbsmnfoundation.com/pages-programs-program-Public_Libraries_for_Health?oid=19529
Sponsor: Blue Cross Blue Shield of Minnesota Foundation
1750 Yankee Doodle Road, N159
Eagan, MN 55122

Blue Cross Blue Shield of Minnesota Foundation - Healthy Neighborhoods: Connect for Health Challenge Grants 798
The Foundation is expanding its focus on the health of neighborhoods and their residents. Social networks like neighborhoods help build trust, reduce isolation, and make it more likely that neighbors will work together to take action on issues affecting their neighborhood. Strong connections to friends and neighbors make people more likely to be involved in their communities, perform better in school, and live longer, healthier lives. The application is available through the Foundation's online process system. A detailed list of previously funded projects is also posted on the website.
Geographic Focus: Minnesota
Contact: Jocelyn Ancheta, Program Officer; (866) 812-1593 or (651) 662-2894; fax (651) 662-4266; Jocelyn_L_Ancheta@bluecrossmn.com
Internet: http://bcbsmnfoundation.com/pages-grantmaking-initiative-Healthy_Neighborhoods?oid=13830§ion=details
Sponsor: Blue Cross Blue Shield of Minnesota Foundation
1750 Yankee Doodle Road, N159
Eagan, MN 55122

Blue Grass Community Foundation Grants 799
The foundation awards grants to nonprofits in central Kentucky in its areas of interest, including arts and culture, housing, employment support and education. Types of support include building construction/renovation, equipment acquisition, seed grants, matching grants, and scholarships to individuals. Grants will range from approximately $5,000 to $20,000. To apply, submit a letter of inquiry of no more than three pages by 4:00 pm, August 17. Applicants will then be invited to submit full proposals, which are due by October 14.
Requirements: Central Kentucky nonprofit organizations are eligible.
Geographic Focus: Kentucky
Date(s) Application is Due: Aug 17; Oct 14
Amount of Grant: 5,000 - 20,000 USD
Contact: Barbara A. Fischer; (859) 225-3343; fax (859) 243-0770; bfischer@bgcf.org
Internet: http://www.bgcf.org/page27526.cfm
Sponsor: Blue Grass Community Foundation
250 W Main Street, Suite 1220
Lexington, KY 40507-1714

Blue Mountain Community Foundation Grants 800
The Foundation administers charitable funds to benefit people of the Blue Mountain Area. Most of the money for discretionary grants is designated by donors for use by agencies serving Walla Walla County. The Foundation's grant making policies are generally directed toward the fields of social and community services, the arts and humanities, education and health. In reviewing grant applications, careful consideration will be given to: potential impact of the program/project on the community and the number of people who will benefit; local volunteer involvement and support; commitment of the organization's Board of Directors; degree to which the applicant works with or complements the services of other community organizations; organization's fiscal responsibility and management skills; possibility of using the grant as seed money for matching funds from other sources; ability of the organization to obtain additional funding and to provide ongoing funding after the term of the grant.
Requirements: Nonprofit organizations serving the Walla Walla Valley, from Dayton to Milton-Freewater are encouraged to submit proposals.
Restrictions: Grants usually will not be made for the following: programs outside the Blue Mountain Area, operating expenses, annual fund drives, field trips, travel to or in support of conferences. No grants will be made for sectarian religious purposes nor to influence legislation or elections.
Geographic Focus: Oregon, Washington
Date(s) Application is Due: Jul 1
Amount of Grant: 125 - 4,000 USD
Contact: Lawson F. Knight; (509) 529-4371; BMCF@bluemountainfoundation.org
Internet: http://www.bluemountainfoundation.org/grant-making-programs.php
Sponsor: Blue Mountain Community Foundation
8 South Second, Suite 168, P.O. Box 603
Walla Walla, WA 99362-0015

Blue River Community Foundation Grants 801
The Blue River Community Foundation is a community-based philanthropic organization that identifies, promotes, supports, and manages programs that will enhance the quality of life in Shelby County, Indiana, for this generation and future generations. To this end, the Foundation has established five areas of interest for the competitive grant making program: community and civic—support for community programs designed to improve life in Shelby County; arts and culture—support for programs and facilities that offer wide-spread opportunities for participation and appreciation; education—support for programs at all levels of education; health—support for the promotion of health and well-being for Shelby County residents; and social services—support of human service organization programs. Organizations interested in submitting a grant request should first submit the grant interest form found on the website. If the grant request meets the Foundation's funding guidelines, the organization will be invited to submit a formal Grant Application Form. Grant applications may be submitted at any time, but will only be reviewed during the next upcoming grant cycle.
Requirements: 501(c)3 organization serving residents of Shelby County, Indiana, may apply.
Geographic Focus: Indiana
Date(s) Application is Due: Feb 1; Jun 1; Oct 1
Contact: Lynne Ensminger, Program Director; (317) 392-7955; fax (317) 392-4545; lensminger@blueriverfoundation.com or brf@blueriverfoundation.com
Internet: http://blueriverfoundation.com/main.asp?SectionID=6&TM=34321.26
Sponsor: Blue River Community Foundation
54 W Broadway Street, Suite 1, P.O. Box 808
Shelbyville, IN 46176

Blue Shield of California Grants 802
Consideration for funding will be given exclusively to organizations that pursue activities directly related to the foundation's program goals, including domestic violence prevention through service provision, education, and outreach; research and education regarding medical best practices and health technologies; and direct or indirect provision of medical insurance or health care to those populations that are uninsured or underinsured, and related policy development.
Requirements: The Foundation funds organizations that are non-profit and tax-exempt under 501(c)3 of the Internal Revenue Service Code (IRC) and defined as a public charity under 509(a)1, 2, or 3 (types I, II, or a functionally integrated type III); accredited schools; units of government/public agencies; tribal governments. The foundation will only support projects that meet the following criteria: the mission of the grantee organization is consistent with the goals and mission of the foundation; the grant is used primarily to serve Californians; the grant seeking organization has a reputation for credibility and integrity; the grant seeking organization is pursuing activities directly related to one of the Foundation's three Program Areas: Health Care and Coverage, Health and Technology and Blue Shield Against Violence.
Restrictions: The foundation does not fund award dinners, athletic events, competitions, special events, or tournaments; conferences or seminars; capital construction; television/film/media production; religious organizations for religious purposes; political causes, candidates, organizations or campaigns; capital projects over $50,000; multi-year projects (generally); grants to individuals (with the exception of the regulated Blue Shield of California Employee Scholarship Program); grants to 509(a) 3, type III supporting organizations that are not functionally integrated.
Geographic Focus: California
Contact: Grants Administrator; (415) 229-5785; fax (415) 229-6268
Internet: http://blueshieldcafoundation.org/grant-center/index.cfm
Sponsor: Blue Shield of California
50 Beale Street
San Francisco, CA 94105-1808

Blum-Kovler Foundation Grants 803
The Blum-Kovler Foundation was established in 1985 after Everett Kovler retired from his position as President of James Beam Distilling Company. The foundation awards general operating grants to eligible nonprofit organizations in its areas of interest, including social services, Jewish welfare funds, higher education, health services and medical research, and cultural programs. The foundation also supports youth- and child-welfare agencies and public-interest and civic-affairs groups. Grants are awarded primarily in the Chicago

metropolitan area and in the Washington, D.C. area. There are no application forms. Applicants should submit a one to two page written proposal with a copy of their IRS determination letter by mid-November to considered for the current year. Typical grant awarded is between $1,000-$5,000.
Requirements: Illinois and District of Columbia nonprofit organizations are eligible.
Geographic Focus: District of Columbia, Illinois
Amount of Grant: 1,000 - 1,000,000 USD
Contact: Hymen Bregar, Secretary; (312) 664-5050
Peter Kovler, Chairperson and Vice President; (312) 664-5050
Sponsor: Blum-Kovler Foundation
875 N Michigan Avenue, Suite 3400
Chicago, IL 60611-1958

Blumenthal Foundation Grants 804
In 1924 Mr. I.D. Blumenthal was a traveling salesman in need of repair to his car's radiator. A local tinsmith in Charlotte, North Carolina, repaired the radiator with a "magic powder". Impressed with the product, I.D. teamed with the tinsmith and Solder Seal became the first product of the Radiator Specialty Company. The Blumenthal Foundation was founded in 1953 and was endowed with the success of the Radiator Specialty Company. The foundation focuses the majority of its grants on programs and projects that have an impact on Charlotte, and the state of North Carolina. The philanthropic efforts of the Foundation are focused in nine areas of grant making: arts, science and culture; civic and community; education; environment; foundation affiliates; health; Jewish institutions and philanthropies; religious and interfaith; and social sciences. The foundation believes that basic operational funding for non-profits is just as important, if not more so, than support for special programs or projects; consequently, grants are provided for seed money, annual operating costs, capital campaigns, conferences and seminars, special projects, and endowments. Interested organizations may click the Grant Guidelines link at the website for detailed submission instructions. Applications must be mailed. There are no deadlines, and requests are accepted on an ongoing basis. The Board of Trustees meets quarterly to consider grant applications.
Requirements: 501(c)3 organizations and institutions that serve the city of Charlotte and the State of North Carolina in the foundation's areas of interest are eligible to apply.
Restrictions: Grants are not made to individuals for any purpose.
Geographic Focus: North Carolina
Contact: Philip Blumenthal; (704) 688-2305; fax (704) 688-2301; foundation@gunk.com
Internet: http://www.blumenthalfoundation.org/BFGrantListings.htm
Sponsor: Blumenthal Foundation
P.O. Box 34689
Charlotte, NC 28234-4689

BoatUS Foundation Grassroots Grants 805
The Foundation is looking for unique project ideas to reach recreational boaters with safety and/or clean boating messages. Information designed for boaters and delivered to boaters should be a key component of the project, not an afterthought. Projects should be planned to get wide exposure in the local community, and be replicated by others. The maximum grant request allowed is $10,000. Although applicants are free to request the maximum funding amount, the Grant Committee reserves the right to fund all or part of the proposed project. If changes are made to the funding request, the Grant Administrator will notify applicants of these changes before the application is posted online for voting. The best applications submitted will be posted for public voting in the Spring. Grant applicants will have several weeks to promote their project and encourage others to vote. After voting concludes, Foundation staff will notify the grant recipients and complete the required contracts. If a group receives a grant, they will be expected to complete all grant-related work within 12 months.
Requirements: The Grassroots Grants Program is intended for nonprofit organizations. Applicants can include boating groups, clubs and associations, student groups as well as nonprofit organizations, including local chapters of national organizations. The Foundation is looking for unique project ideas to educate boaters on safe and clean boating topics. Projects that the Foundation is most interested in funding will include several of the following elements: be unique ideas - either topic, methods or delivery mechanism; include extensive outreach efforts to boaters; use technology to educate boaters including social media and the web; have a widespread reach (not just a handful of boaters); include hands on work with the boating community; have a means to measure the success of the program. Salary requests and funding requests for equipment cannot exceed 10% of the total grant request.
Restrictions: Grants will not be awarded to government agencies, international organizations, for-profit businesses or individuals. The following types of projects are not eligible for funding: capital improvement projects or general operating funds; money to start an organization; debt repayment or reimbursement; multi-year projects unless the project will become self sufficient after the initial funding; projects that include lobbying efforts or any type of political action; promotional or membership drives for businesses or clubs; projects solely intended to benefit a group's membership; expenses for transportation, meals or lodging; specialized training or equipment for the recipient group members unless it can be shown that this training will benefit the general boating public. While the program does occasionally fund purchases of equipment for educational or display purposes, requests for electronic hardware/software, boats, motors, or other expensive boating gear is not likely to be funded.
Geographic Focus: All States
Date(s) Application is Due: Dec 17
Amount of Grant: Up to 10,000 USD
Contact: Alanna Keating, Outreach Manager; (800) 245-2628 x8354; akeating@boatus.com or BoatingSafety@BoatUS.com@boatus.com
Internet: http://www.boatus.com/foundation/grants/
Sponsor: Boat U.S. Foundation for Boating Safety and Clean Water
147 Old Solomons Island Road, Suite 513
Annapolis, MD 21401

Bodenwein Public Benevolent Foundation Grants 806
The Bodenwein Public Benevolent Foundation was established in 1938 under the will of Theodore Bodenwein, owner and publisher of The Day newspaper, to support and promote quality educational, cultural, human-services, and health-care programming for underserved populations. The Foundation specifically serves the people of Greater New London County where The Day has a substantial circulation. The majority of grants from the Bodenwein Public Benevolent Foundation are one year in duration; on occasion, multi-year support is awarded. Applicants must apply online at the grant website. Applicants are strongly encouraged to do the following before applying: review the downloadable state application procedures for additional helpful information, requirements, and restrictions; review the downloadable online-application guidelines at the grant website; review the foundation's funding history (link is available from the grant website); review the online application questions in advance; and review the list of required attachments. These will generally include: a list of board members, financial statements (audited, reviewed, or compiled by independent auditor); an organization summary; a list of other funding sources; an IRS Determination letter; and other required documents. All attachments must be uploaded in the online application as PDF, Word, or Excel files. The annual application deadline is 11:59 p.m. on November 15. Applicants will be notified of grant decisions by letter within three to four months after the proposal deadline.
Requirements: Nonprofit organizations serving Greater New London County (East Lyme, Groton, Ledyard, Lyme, Montville, Mystic, New London, North Stonington, Old Lyme, Salem, Stonington, and Waterford, Connecticut) are eligible to apply. A breakdown of number/percentage of people served by specific towns will be required in the online application.
Restrictions: The foundation does not support requests from individuals, organizations attempting to influence policy through direct lobbying, or any political campaigns.
Geographic Focus: Connecticut
Date(s) Application is Due: Nov 15
Contact: Amy Lynch; (860) 657-7015; amy.r.lynch@baml.com
Internet: https://www.bankofamerica.com/philanthropic/fn_search.action
Sponsor: Bodenwein Public Benevolent Foundation
200 Glastonbury Boulevard, Suite # 200
Glastonbury, CT 06033-4056

Bodman Foundation Grants 807
The Bodman Foundation was established by George M. Bodman and his wife Louise Clarke Bodman in 1945. George was born in Toledo, Ohio, in 1882 and died in 1950. Mrs. Bodman was born in Chicago in 1893 and died in 1955. The Bodmans lived for much of their lives in Red Bank, New Jersey, and in New York City, where George Bodman was a senior partner at the investment banking firm of Cyrus J. Lawrence and Sons. The Bodmans were generous supporters of numerous cultural, civic, and service organizations. During World War I Mr. Bodman headed the Intelligence Service of the War Trade Board. During World War II, he served as executive assistant to the Red Cross Commissioner for Great Britain and was regional director in charge of American Red Cross Club operations in England, Scotland, and Ireland. The Bodman Foundation's Certificate of Incorporation states that its funds are to be used for "the aid, support or benefit of religious, educational, charitable, and benevolent objects and purposes for the moral, ethical and physical well-being and progress of mankind." The Bodman Foundation shares trustees, staff, office space, and even a website with the Achelis Foundation which has a similar mission and geographic area of concentration (both foundations give in New York City, while the Bodman Foundation also gives in New Jersey). Funding is concentrated in six program areas: Arts and Culture, Education, Employment, Health, Public Policy, and Youth and Families.
Requirements: 501(c)3 organizations based in New York City that fall within the foundation's areas of interest are welcome to submit an inquiry or proposal letter by regular mail (initial inquiries by email or fax are not accepted, nor are CDs, DVDs, computer discs, or video tapes). An initial inquiry to the foundation should include only the following items: a proposal letter that briefly summarizes the history of the project, need, objectives, time period, key staff, project budget, and evaluation plan; the applicant's latest annual report and complete set of audited financial statements; and the applicant's IRS 501(c)3 tax-exemption letter. Applications may be submitted at any time during the year. Each request is reviewed by staff and will usually receive a written response within thirty days. Those requests deemed consistent with the interests and resources of the foundation will be evaluated further and more information will be requested. Foundation staff may request a site visit, conference call, or meeting. All grants are reviewed and approved by the Trustees at one of their three board meetings in May, September, or December.
Restrictions: The foundation generally does not make grants for the following purposes or program areas: nonprofit organizations outside of New York; annual appeals, dinner functions, and fundraising events; endowments and capital campaigns; loans and deficit financing; direct grants to individuals; individual day-care and after-school programs; housing; organizations or projects based outside the U.S; films or video projects; small art, dance, music, and theater groups; individual K-12 schools (except charter schools); national health and mental health organizations; and government agencies or nonprofit organizations significantly funded or reimbursed by government agencies. Limited resources prevent the foundations from funding the same organization on an ongoing annual basis.
Geographic Focus: New Jersey, New York
Amount of Grant: 10,000 - 100,000 USD
Contact: John B. Krieger, (212) 644-0322; main@achelis-bodman-fnds.org
Internet: http://www.achelis-bodman-fnds.org/guidelines.html
Sponsor: Bodman Foundation
767 Third Avenue, 4th Floor
New York, NY 10017-2023

Boeckmann Charitable Foundation Grants   808

The foundation awards grants to nonprofits in support of education—colleges and universities, parochial secondary education, religious education, and campus crusades; community, family, and youth services; national and international ministries and missions; religious welfare; religious broadcasting; and temples. Grants support general operations. Applicants should submit a brief letter of inquiry describing the program and the organization. There are no application deadlines.
Requirements: Christian, Evangelical, and Presbyterian nonprofits in California are eligible.
Geographic Focus: California
Amount of Grant: Up to 17,000,000 USD
Contact: Herbert Boeckmann II, Chief Executive Officer; (818) 787-3800
Sponsor: Boeckmann Charitable Foundation
15505 Roscoe Boulevard
North Hills, CA 91343

Boeing Company Contributions Grants   809

The Boeing U.S. contributions program welcomes applications in five focus areas: education; health and human services; arts and culture; civic; and the environment. Primary fields of interest include: arts; elementary and secondary education; the environment; family services, prevention of domestic violence; health care; public affairs; public safety; substance abuse programs; and general human services. The largest single block of charitable contributions goes toward supporting programs and projects related to education. Boeing also looks for innovative initiatives that promote the economic well-being of the community and neighborhood revitalization. Boeing invests in programs that promote participation in arts and cultural activities and experiences, programs that increase public understanding of and engagement in the processes and issues that affect communities and programs that protect and conserve the natural environment. Boeing accepts applications for cash grants, in-kind donations, and services.
Requirements: To apply for support you must be a U.S. based IRS 501(c)3 qualified charitable or educational organization or an accredited K-12 educational institution. U.S. grant guidelines and applications are available online.
Restrictions: Grants do not support: an individual person or families; adoption services; political candidates or organizations; religious activities, in whole or in part, for the purpose of further religious doctrine; memorials and endowments; travel expenses; nonprofit and school sponsored walk-a-thons, athletic events and athletic group sponsorships other than Special Olympics; door prizes or raffles; U.S. hospitals and medical research; school-affiliated orchestras, bands, choirs, trips, athletic teams, drama groups, yearbooks and class parties; general operating expenses for programs within the United States; organizations that do not follow our application procedures; follow-on applications from past grantees that have not met our reporting requirements or satisfactorily completed the terms of past grants; fundraising events, annual funds, galas and other special-event fundraising activities; advertising, t-shirts, giveaways and promotional items; documentary films, books, etc; debt reduction; dissertations and student research projects; loans, scholarships, fellowships and grants to individuals; for-profit businesses; gifts, honoraria, gratuities; capital improvements to rental properties.
Geographic Focus: Alabama, Arizona, California, Colorado, District of Columbia, Florida, Georgia, Hawaii, Illinois, Kansas, Maryland, Missouri, Nevada, New Mexico, Ohio, Oklahoma, Oregon, Pennsylvania, South Carolina, Texas, Utah, Washington, Australia, Canada
Contact: Antoinette Bailey, (312) 544-2000; fax (312) 544 - 2082
Internet: http://www.boeing.com/companyoffices/aboutus/community/charitable.htm
Sponsor: Boeing Company Contributions
100 North Riverside
Chicago, IL 60606-1596

Boettcher Foundation Grants   810

Grant support is given to promote the general well-being of humanity. Grants are awarded for arts and culture, community and social service, education and healthcare. Organizations seeking support from the Foundation should send a preliminary letter, describing the organization that wishes to submit a proposal and the project for which funding is being requested. The letter should be signed by the head of the applicant agency and should include a statement related to the priority of the project within the organization's overall plans. Letters of inquiry should be mailed or emailed.
Requirements: Capital grants are made in the form of challenges, conditional on an applicant agency's ability to raise the balance of the funds needed for a project. Although no absolute guidelines have been established, 50 to 75 percent of the goal should already be in hand before the grant request will be considered.
Restrictions: The Foundation does not accept proposals, or provide grants, for the following giving interests: operations; gymnasiums/athletic fields; housing; purchase of tables or tickets for dinner/events; individuals; large urban hospitals; out-of-state projects; media presentations; small business start-ups; open space/parks; conferences, seminars, workshops; organizations that primarily serve animals; debt reduction; pilot programs; endowments; religious groups or organizations for their religious purposes; scholarships; travel.
Geographic Focus: Colorado
Samples: Children's Hospital (Denver, CO)—for its fund-raising campaign to build a new hospital, $5 million; Colorado College (Colorado Springs, CO)—to renovate Palmer Hall, a classroom building, $400,000; Johnson and Wales U (Denver, CO)—for renovations and restoration at its Park Hill Campus, $100,000.
Contact: Administrator; (800) 323-9640 or (303) 534-1937; grants@boettcherfoundation.org
Internet: http://www.boettcherfoundation.org/grants/index.html
Sponsor: Boettcher Foundation
600 Seventeenth Street, Suite 2210 South
Denver, CO 80202-5422

Bohemian Foundation Pharos Fund Grants   811

The foundation awards grants to improve the quality of life in Fort Collins in its areas of interest, including youth, building the capacity of organizations working together, and citizen involvement. In the area of youth, the foundation makes grants that support youth at all social, economic, and developmental stages to achieve their greatest potential; support youth development in the areas of education and training; strengthen and align systems that affect learning and life-long opportunities; and support youth within the context of their families, communities, and the policy environment. In the area of building the capacity of organizations working together, the foundation makes grants that facilitate collaboration among community service entities to improve their effectiveness; strengthen the effectiveness of organizations working together to discover solutions to community concerns and issues; and support the development of relationships among organizations. In the area of citizen involvement, the foundation makes grants to support programs that demonstrate the need of greater public awareness; support programs that utilize existing research or information and make it more accessible to the public; and support programs, projects, or events that raise consciousness about community issues. Types of support include general operating grants, capital grants, equipment purchase, program support, and technical assistance. One request per grant cycle is permitted. Complete guidelines are available online.
Requirements: Grants are available to nonprofit, 501(c)3 organizations (other than private foundations) in Fort Collins, Colorado.
Restrictions: The program will not fund requests with the following criteria: multi-year requests; multi-program requests; fundraising events; tuition-based private schools; political campaigns or specific legislative issues; activities that have a specific religious purpose; non-501(c)3 organizations; private foundations, including private operating foundations; individual team requests; discriminatory programs; programs serving individuals; debt reduction.
Geographic Focus: Colorado
Date(s) Application is Due: Feb 1; Sep 15
Amount of Grant: Up to 30,000 USD
Contact: Administrator; (970) 482-4642; fax (970) 482-6139; info@bohemianfoundation.org
Internet: http://www.bohemianfoundation.org
Sponsor: Bohemian Foundation
103 West Mountain Avenue
Fort Collins, CO 80524

Bollinger Foundation Grants   812

The foundation provides grants in the form of scholarships to surviving members of families in which a parent worked in the fields of community development, housing, or economic development. Grants support children's education, including but not limited to grants toward special educational needs, school materials, and college tuition. The foundation invites nominations of eligible families for grants. Guidelines and nomination form are available online.
Requirements: Families must be nominated to receive grants.
Geographic Focus: All States
Date(s) Application is Due: May 20
Amount of Grant: 2,500 USD
Contact: John Dolan; (202) 223-7800; fax (202) 223-4745; jdolan@iedconline.org
Internet: http://www.bollingerfoundation.org
Sponsor: Bollinger Foundation
734 15th Street NW, Suite 900
Washington, DC 20005

Bolthouse Foundation Grants   813

The purpose of The Bolthouse Foundation is to glorify the Lord Jesus Christ by supporting charitable and religious organizations whose ministry, goals, and operating principles are consistent with evangelical Christianity as described in The Bolthouse Foundation Statement of Faith.
Requirements: 501(c)3 tax-exempt organizations are eligible. Although we fund grants on a solicited basis in a variety of areas, we welcome Unsolicited Grant Inquiries only in the areas of: Making Disciples, Ministry to the Poor, Leadership Development, and Ministry/Organizational Transformation (defined as projects that help a grantseeker reach a strategic goal without creating dependence upon The Bolthouse Foundation). Potential applicants should send a 150-maximum word paragraph or two that summarizes the project. If it is determined that the project is of interest, a full proposal will be requested. Grants are made throughout the year.
Geographic Focus: All States
Contact: Grants Administrator; (661) 334-1915
Internet: http://www.thebolthousefoundation.org
Sponsor: Bolthouse Foundation
2000 Oak Street, Suite 200
Bakersfield, CA 93301-3058

Bonfils-Stanton Foundation Grants   814

Colorado nonprofit organizations are eligible to apply, and funds must be used within the state for the benefit of Colorado citizens. The focus of the foundation is to advance excellence in the areas of arts and culture, community service, and science and medicine. Types of support include operating grants, capital campaigns, and capacity-building grants. Proposals will be reviewed at quarterly meetings. Guidelines and forms are available online.
Requirements: Colorado 501(c)3 organizations are eligible.
Restrictions: Areas generally not eligible for funding include loans, grants, or scholarships to individuals; events, media productions, seminars, conferences, or travel expenses related to meetings; activities or initiatives that have a religious purpose or objective; endowment funding, fellowships, endowed chairs; funding to retire operating debt; requests from organizations outside the State of Colorado or that are not for the benefit of Colorado citizens.
Geographic Focus: Colorado

Date(s) Application is Due: Jan 31; Apr 30; Jul 31; Oct 31
Contact: Susan France, Vice President of Programs; (303) 825-3774; fax (303) 825-0802; susan@bonfils-stanton.org
Internet: http://www.bonfils-stantonfoundation.org
Sponsor: Bonfils-Stanton Foundation
1601 Arapahoe Street, Suite 500
Denver, CO 80202

Booth-Bricker Fund Grants 815
The Foundation makes contributions for the purposes of promoting, developing and fostering religious, charitable, scientific, literary and educational programs. Requests are welcomed for capital needs, special projects and other one-time requirements. Applications should be made by letter. There are no forms or deadlines. Requests should include complete information about the applicant organization, including its history, purpose, finances, current operations, governing board and tax status. A detailed explanation of the proposed use of the funds must be provided.
Requirements: Requests are accepted for the funding of projects within the state of Louisiana. Priority is given to the New Orleans area.
Restrictions: The Foundation generally does not provide sustaining (operations and maintenance) funding. No grants are made to individuals.
Geographic Focus: Louisiana
Amount of Grant: 5,000 - 50,000 USD
Contact: Gray S. Parker, Chairperson; (504) 581-2430
Sponsor: Booth-Bricker Fund
826 Union Street, Suite 300
New Orleans, LA 70112

Booth Ferris Foundation Grants 816
The foundation awards grants in the fields of education (K-12, private higher education, theological education, smaller colleges, secondary schools, and adult basic education) and civic and urban programs for social services, environmental conservation, and cultural activities. Types of support include project, capital, and capacity- building grants. Grants are awarded nationwide, with a focus on the metropolitan New York area. There are no application forms or deadline dates. Awards are decided on a quarterly basis.
Requirements: Organizations must be classified by the Internal Revenue Service as public charities and tax-exempt under section 501(c)3 of the Internal Revenue Code of 1986.
Restrictions: A minimum of three years must elapse between grant awards. No grants are made to individuals, private foundations or for loans. Grants are not made to organizations whose primary work is conducted outside of the US, to individuals, to federated campaigns, or to work with specific diseases or disabilities. Proposals from educational institutions for scholarships, fellowships and for unrestricted endowment are discouraged, as are proposals for individual research efforts at such institutions. Proposals from social services and cultural institutions from outside the metropolitan New York area will not be considered.
Geographic Focus: New York
Amount of Grant: 50,000 - 400,000 USD
Contact: Booth Ferris Foundation, c/o JPMorgan Private Bank; (212) 464-2487
Internet: http://fdncenter.org/grantmaker/boothferris
Sponsor: Booth Ferris Foundation
NY1-N040, 345 Park Avenue, 4th Floor
New York, NY 10154

Borkee-Hagley Foundation Grants 817
The foundation awards grants in a wide range of interests, including social services to children and families, religious organizations, and environmental programs. Delaware nonprofits receive preference. The board meets in December to consider requests.
Requirements: Delaware nonprofits are eligible to apply.
Restrictions: No support for specific churches or synagogues. Grants are not made to individuals.
Geographic Focus: Delaware
Date(s) Application is Due: Nov 1
Amount of Grant: 1,000 - 25,000 USD
Contact: Henry H. Silliman Jr., President; (302) 652-8616
Sponsor: Borkee-Hagley Foundation
P.O. Box 4590
Wilmington, DE 19807-4590

Bosque Foundation Grants 818
The foundation gives primarily for higher education, human services, Baptist & Protestant agencies/churches and, medical research in Texas. Types of support include capital campaigns, building/renovation and research grants. There are no application forms or deadlines. Applicants should submit a one-page letter of intent that describes the program and request.
Requirements: Texas nonprofit and for-profit organizations are eligible.
Restrictions: Individuals are not eligible.
Geographic Focus: Texas
Amount of Grant: 5,000 - 20,000 USD
Samples: Midland Community Theater, Midland, TX, $1,000; Peoples Missionary Baptist Church, Detroit, MI, $20,000; Dallas Baptist University, Dallas, TX, $10,000.
Contact: Louis A. Beecherl Jr., Trustee; (214) 956-6732; fax (214) 956-6733
Sponsor: Bosque Foundation
5950 Cedar Springs Boulevard, Suite 210
Dallas, TX 75235-6803

Boston Foundation Grants 819
The Boston Foundation has a particular concern for low income and disenfranchised communities and residents and supports organizations and programs whose work helps advance the Foundation's high priorities in a variety of subject areas: Arts and Culture; Civic Engagement; Community Safety, Economic Development; Education/Out-of-School Time, Health and Human Services; Housing and Community Economic Development; the Nonprofit Sector, Urban Environment and Workforce Development. The Foundation generally makes the following types of grants: Project or program support for community-based efforts that improve the quality of life in the community, test new models, and promote collaborative and innovative ventures; advocacy and public policy research that is linked to specific action; support for planning to enable organizations and residents to assess community needs, respond to new challenges and opportunities, and provide for the inclusion of new populations; organizational support to develop and build the capacity of nonprofit organizations - support that helps organizations keep pace with the changing requirements and demands of their communities and broader environments; small grants awarded on a rolling basis for one-time organizational development needs through the Vision Fund. In addition, on a very limited basis, the Foundation will consider development grants and strategic alliances.
Requirements: Grants are made only to tax-exempt organizations in Massachusetts.
Restrictions: The committee does not consider more than one proposal from the same organization within a 12-month period. Discretionary grants are generally not made to the following applicants: city or state government agencies or departments; individuals; medical research; endowments; equipment; replacement of lost/expired government funding or gap funding to cover the full cost of providing services; scholarships and fellowships; video and film production; construction and renovation projects and capital campaigns; programs with religious content; travel; summer camps and lobbying. Activities that are generally lower priorities for the Foundation are conferences, lectures, one-time events, programs benefiting only a small number of participants or routine service delivery and/or operating expenses.
Geographic Focus: Massachusetts
Date(s) Application is Due: Jan 5; Jul 1
Contact: Corey Davis; (617) 338-1700; fax (617) 338-1604; info@tbf.org
Internet: http://www.tbf.org
Sponsor: Boston Foundation
75 Arlington Street, 10th Floor
Boston, MA 02116

Boston Foundation Initiative to Strengthen Arts and Cultural Service Organizations 820
The program supports Boston-area nonprofits with missions and programs that are substantially focused on serving and enhancing the capacity of individual artists and/or arts and cultural organizations. Organizations may submit proposals in either of two categories: externally focused activities that enhance or expand service delivery to artists and/or cultural organizations; or internally focused work or activities that build a service organization's own management and service capacity. Proposals that blend the two approaches are also welcomed. Evaluation criteria include management excellence, capacity to serve, and impact on and service to artists and/or small, community-based arts organizations within the greater Boston area. The listed application deadline is for letters of inquiry; full proposals are by invitation.
Requirements: 501(c)3 nonprofit agencies that provide services to artists and/or cultural nonprofits within the greater Boston service area are eligible.
Geographic Focus: Massachusetts
Date(s) Application is Due: Oct 14
Contact: Ann McQueen, (617) 338-1700; mcg@tbf.org
Internet: http://www.tbf.org/current/current-L2.asp?id=3177
Sponsor: Boston Foundation
75 Arlington Street, 10th Floor
Boston, MA 02116

Boston Globe Foundation Grants 821
The foundation concentrates on three focus areas: strengthen the reading, writing, and critical thinking of young people, while fostering their inherent love of learning; strengthen the roads that link people to culture; and strengthen the civic fabric of the city. The foundation also sponsors the Neighbor to Neighbor Initiative, which funds exceptional Dorchester focused nonprofits.
Requirements: Massachusetts nonprofits in the greater Boston area are eligible.
Restrictions: The Foundation will only review one proposal per year from any organization.
Geographic Focus: Massachusetts
Amount of Grant: 5,000 - 15,000 USD
Contact: Leah P. Bailey; (617) 929-2895; fax (617) 929-2041; foundation@globe.com
Internet: http://bostonglobe.com
Sponsor: Boston Globe Foundation
P.O. Box 55819
Boston, MA 02205-55819

Boston Jewish Community Women's Fund Grants 822
The fund, a project of Combined Jewish Philanthropies, invites letters of intent for projects that benefit women and girls. Grants are made in the areas of health, abuse, hunger, education, and empowerment. In Massachusetts, projects funded are sponsored by organizations both within the Jewish community and from the community at large. In Israel, proposals from programs that serve the Haifa community or have a documented history of funding from other North American organizations are invited to apply. Letters of intent should not be more than two pages long and must contain: your organization's mission; a statement of need for the project, how the project will address it, and how it meets BJCWF objectives; a budget narrative including the amount of funding requested, projected major expenditures, and use of BJCWF funds.

116 | GRANT PROGRAMS

Requirements: Grants are made to 501(c)3 organizations in Massachusetts or comparable organizations in Israel.
Geographic Focus: Massachusetts, Israel
Date(s) Application is Due: Oct 15
Amount of Grant: Up to 25,000 USD
Contact: Susan Ebert, (617) 457-8500; susane@cjp.org
Internet: http://www.cjp.org/section_display.html?ID=572
Sponsor: Boston Jewish Community Women's Fund
126 High Street
Boston, MA 02110

Boulder County Arts Alliance Neodata Endowment Grants 823
Boulder County Arts Alliance Neodata Endowment awards grants to eligible Boulder County nonprofit organizations in its area of interest, including arts and performing arts. Types of support include general operating support, equipment support, unrestricted fellowships, organizational projects, and grants for individual artists. The Alliance offers grants twice per year, with deadlines being the end of February and end of August. The minimum amount awarded is $1,000. Awards generally do not exceed $1,500.
Requirements: Colorado 501(c)3 nonprofits serving the Boulder area are eligible.
Geographic Focus: Colorado
Date(s) Application is Due: Feb 28; Aug 29
Amount of Grant: 500 - 1,500 USD
Contact: John Farmer, Executive Director; (303) 447-2422; info@bouldercountyarts.org
Internet: http://www.bouldercountyarts.org/grants_neodata
Sponsor: Boulder County Arts Alliance
2590 Walnut Street, Suite 9
Boulder, CO 80302

Bowling Green Community Foundation Grants 824
The mission of the foundation is to accumulate the assets needed to fund creative community plans, and to meet the ever changing needs of the citizens. The foundation enhances the health, welfare, and vitality of the Bowling Green, Ohio, community. Applications may be submitted in the range of $200 to $2,000, thereby allowing a number of organizations to benefit. As the Foundation assets grow, grant amounts will increase. The Foundation will place priority consideration on proposals which: propose creative, first-time projects or programs for the community; encourage more efficient use of community resources; promote coordination, cooperation and sharing among organizations and eliminate duplicated services; test or demonstrate new approaches and techniques in the solution of community problems; focus on the prevention of problems rather than the cure; represent an unduplicated opportunity and meet a significant community need; propose a specific program rather than a general operating support of the organization; generate matching funds, thus leveraging additional support; and include a thoughtful, reasonable plan for obtaining continuing financial support from internal and/or external sources once Foundation funds are expended.
Requirements: Applicants must be 501(c)3 organizations serving the residents of Bowling Green, Ohio, area.
Restrictions: The Foundation will not make grants from its unrestricted funds to: support the general operating budget of established organizations; annual or capital campaigns; support sectarian activities of religious organizations; or projects already completed.
Geographic Focus: Ohio
Date(s) Application is Due: Feb 20
Amount of Grant: 200 - 2,000 USD
Contact: Charlotte Scherer; (419) 728- 0290 or (419) 354-5521; bgcf@bgohcf.org
Internet: http://www.bgohcf.org/
Sponsor: Bowling Green Community Foundation
P.O. Box 1175
Bowling Green, OH 43402-1175

Boyd Gaming Corporation Contributions Program 825
From giving generously to a variety of worthy charitable organizations to continually enhancing the effectiveness of our diversity programs, Boyd Gaming Corp. has a long-standing commitment to responsible gaming, and concern for the planet, Boyd strives to make a positive differences in the communities in which it operates. The type of support offered is in: employee volunteer services; general/operating support; in-kind gifts
Requirements: All charitable requests must originate from a 501(c)3 non-profit organization and be from a state in which the company operates.
Restrictions: Boyd Gaming is not unable to act favorably on any request: for an individual, team or school-sponsored endeavor; for programs that discriminate for any reason, including race, color, creed, religion, age, sex or national origin
Geographic Focus: Hawaii, Illinois, Indiana, Louisiana, Mississippi, Nevada, New Jersey
Contact: Corporate Office; (702) 792-7200
Internet: http://www.boydgaming.com/about-boyd/corporate-responsibility
Sponsor: Boyd Gaming Corporation
3883 Howard Hughes Parkway, 9th Floor
Las Vegas, NV 89169

BP Conservation Programme Future Conservationist Awards 826
The aim of the awards is to develop leadership capacity for biodiversity conservation as a fundamental contribution to sustainable development. The program provides annual grants to passionate people developing innovative projects addressing biodiversity issues of global importance. Projects should address three key areas: development of team capabilities and skills; practical high-priority conservation projects combining research and action; and demonstrate long-term conservation benefits contributing to sustainable development. Application and guidelines are available online.
Requirements: Teams must include only members less than 35 years of age with no more than two years professional conservation and include a minimum of three people.
Restrictions: The program does not fund conference attendance, tuition fees or scholarships, salaries, costly laboratory analyses or gene storage, captive breeding projects, or high school level expeditions. Projects that are specifically for PhD research or master's dissertations will not be supported. Employees from any of the BPCP partner organizations are not eligible to apply.
Geographic Focus: All States
Date(s) Application is Due: Dec 16
Amount of Grant: Up to 12,500 USD
Contact: Marianne Dunn, Program Manager; (44 01223) 277318; fax (44 01223) 277200; bp-conservation-programme@birdlife.org
Internet: http://conservation.bp.com/applications/default.asp
Sponsor: BP Conservation Programme
Wellbrook Court, Griton Road
Cambridge, CB3 ONA England

Brad Brock Family Foundation Grants 827
Established in Texas in 2007, the Brad Brock Family Foundation offers support for education and community projects, as well Christian agencies and churches. A formal application is required, and applicants should forward the entire proposal to the office. The Foundation rarely offers funding outside of Texas. There are no deadlines for submitting a completed proposal, and grants have most recently ranged from $5,000 to $1,000,000.
Geographic Focus: Texas
Amount of Grant: 5,000 - 1,000,000 USD
Contact: Braden J. Brock, President; (409) 833-6226; fax (409) 832-3019
Sponsor: Brad Brock Family Foundation
1670 E Cardinal Drive, P.O. Box 306
Beaumont, TX 77704

Bradley-Turner Foundation Grants 828
Incorporated as the W.C. and Sarah H. Bradley Foundation in Georgia in 1943, the Bradley-Turner Foundation uses contributions from the company's success to support the community and region through many different programs and facilities funded in whole or in part by foundation donations. The foundation has a special interest in endeavors related to family and children services, education, religion (Baptist, Christian, interdenominational, Methodist, Presbyterian, Salvation Army, and United Methodist), health, and culture and the arts. Major focus is placed on the vitality and quality of life in Columbus, Georgia, though compelling programs beyond the city's boundaries will also be considered. The foundation is particularly interested in projects that have a broad base of community support. There are no application forms. Applicants are asked to submit a letter of three to five pages describing the project. Grants are reviewed quarterly, in February, May, August, and November, when the board meets.
Requirements: IRS 501(c)3 tax-exempt organizations in Georgia are eligible. Heavily focuses on the southern region of the United States, but the Foundation is not solely limited to this area. It has also donated in Massachusetts, Illinois, and Colorado.
Restrictions: Grants are not made to individuals or to for-profit businesses or corporations.
Geographic Focus: Georgia
Amount of Grant: 2,500 - 300,000 USD
Contact: Phyllis Wagner, Executive Secretary; (706) 571-6040; fax (706) 571-3408
Internet: http://www.wcbradley.com/divisions.asp
Sponsor: Bradley-Turner Foundation
1017 Front Avenue, P.O. Box 140
Columbus, GA 31902-0140

Bradley Family Foundation (California) Grants 829
Established in 2006 by Timothy M. and Linda J. Bradley, the Bradley Family Foundation supports Christian agencies and organizations, as well as educational programs. Though giving is generally centered around Westlake Village, California, just northwest of Los Angeles, the Foundation also supports national organizations across the country. Types of funding include general operating support and matching funds. Grants range from $50 to $5,000. There are no specific guidelines, application forms, or deadlines, and applicants should contact the Foundation directly prior to forwarding a full proposal.
Geographic Focus: All States
Amount of Grant: 50 - 5,000 USD
Contact: Linda J. Bradley, Secretary; (818) 889-7161
Sponsor: Bradley Family Foundation: California
5448 Island Forest Place
Westlake Village, CA 91362-5406

Bradley Family Foundation (South Carolina) Grants 830
Founded by Philip LeCroy Bradley, national board member for the Log Cabin Republicans that challenged the "Don't Ask, Don't Tell" policy of the U.S. Armed Services, the Bradley Family Foundation offers support for religion, restoration purposes, and to higher education programs. Giving is limited to the State of South Carolina, and ranges from $10,000 to $100,000. There are no specific guidelines, application forms, or deadlines, and applicants should begin by sending a brief letter outlining their program needs and a detailed budget.
Geographic Focus: South Carolina
Contact: Philip LeCroy Bradley, President; (843) 559-9810; philiplbradley@aol.com
Sponsor: Bradley Family Foundation: South Carolina
571 River Road, Boview Hall
Johns Island, SC 29455-8733

Brainerd Foundation Grants 831

The foundation is dedicated to protecting the environmental quality of the Pacific Northwest, including Washington, Oregon, Idaho, Montana, Alaska, and British Columbia. Program grants are made in the following areas: endangered ecosystems—conservation biology, conservation assessment, and mining reform and roadless areas; and communications and capacity building—organizational development, and allied voices. Program grants are awarded to cover costs associated with activities such as public education and grassroots outreach, media strategies, litigation, scientific and economic studies, computer networking, and building organizational capacity. Opportunity Fund grants are awarded to organizations for support such as outreach, litigation, applied research, and other unexpected needs. Additional types of support include general operating support, continuing support, equipment acquisition, conferences and seminars, seed money, research, technical assistance, and employee matching gifts. Applications are available online.
Requirements: Nonprofit organizations in the Pacific Northwest are eligible.
Restrictions: The foundation does not favor proposals for school education programs, land acquisition, endowments, capital campaigns, projects sponsored by government agencies, basic research, fellowships, or books or videos that are not part of a broader strategy.
Geographic Focus: Alaska, Idaho, Montana, Oregon, Washington, Canada
Amount of Grant: 250 - 25,000 USD
Contact: Ann Krumboltz; (206) 448-0676; fax (206) 448-7222; annk@brainerd.org
Internet: http://www.brainerd.org/grants/intro.php
Sponsor: Brainerd Foundation
1601 Second Avenue, Suite 610
Seattle, WA 98101-1541

Bread and Roses Community Fund Grants and Scholarships 832

The program awards grants to a broad spectrum of organizations and individuals working on social change. Programs include general fund grants—for organizations whose chief aim is to take collective action against a problem affecting the community, to work for social change, emergency/discretionary grants, Lax scholarships (graduate)—available to gay men, and the Phoebus Criminal Justice Initiative.
Requirements: Pennsylvania nonprofit organizations in the Delaware Valley (Philadelphia, Chester, Montgomery, Bucks, and Delaware Counties) and Camden County, NJ, are eligible.
Geographic Focus: New Jersey, Pennsylvania
Contact: Administrator; (215) 731-1107; fax (215) 731-0453; info@breadrosesfund.org
Internet: http://www.breadrosesfund.org/grants/grants.html
Sponsor: Bread and Roses Community Fund
1500 Walnut Street, Suite 1305
Philadelphia, PA 19102

Brett Family Foundation Grants 833

The foundation awards grants in two focus areas: Boulder County nonprofits that provide direct services and support for underserved and frequently marginalized populations; and organizations throughout the state of Colorado advocating for social, economic, gender, and racial justice. The foundation accepts proposals in two general grant cycles: March and September. The March cycle will be devoted entirely to Social Justice grants (primarily community organizing and advocacy organizations), while the September cycle will be dedicated to Direct Services in Boulder County.
Requirements: 501(c)3 nonprofits serving the communities of Boulder County are eligible.
Geographic Focus: Colorado
Date(s) Application is Due: Mar 1; Sep 1
Contact: Brian Hiatt, (303) 442-1200; fax (303) 442-1221; bhiatt@brettfoundation.org
Internet: http://www.brettfoundation.org
Sponsor: Brett Family Foundation
1123 Spruce Street
Boulder, CO 80302

Brian G. Dyson Foundation Grants 834

The Foundation, established in Atlanta in 1994 by former Coca-Cola Bottling executive, Brian G. Dyson, offers funding to community foundations, higher education, and federated programs in the Atlanta region and throughout Georgia. Grants typically range up to $20,000, and funding supports general operating costs. There are no specific guidelines, application formats, or deadlines with which to adhere, and initial contact should be made in writing.
Requirements: Applicants must be colleges, public or private schools, or other non-profit organizations located within the state of Georgia.
Geographic Focus: Georgia
Amount of Grant: Up to 20,000 USD
Contact: Brian G. Dyson, Director; (404) 364-2940
Sponsor: Brian G. Dyson Foundation
3060 Peachtree Road NW, Suite 1465
Atlanta, GA 30305-2241

Brico Fund Grants 835

The mission of the fund is to effect systemic change—to change attitudes, policies and societal patterns. Grants are made to secure full participation in society for women and girls; restore and sustain the earth's natural systems; promote a just and equitable society; and nourish the creative spirit. Types of support include general operating, program, and rarely, capital and endowment grants. Applicants should complete the fund's preliminary application form and a two-page letter of intent, describing the organization's intended project or program.
Requirements: The fund supports organizations with projects and programs within the Greater Milwaukee community. Some funding is done statewide or nationally for programs of broader scope.
Restrictions: Grants do not support conferences and meetings, disease-specific programs, educational institutions, individuals, media projects, medical institutions, religions, or organizations with a focus on animals.
Geographic Focus: Wisconsin
Date(s) Application is Due: Jan 15; Jul 15
Amount of Grant: 1,000 - 500,000 USD
Contact: Melissa Nimke, Grants Administrator; (414) 272-2747; fax (414) 272-2036; mbn@bricofund.org or bricofund@bricofund.org
Internet: http://www.bricofund.org
Sponsor: Brico Fund
205 E Wisconsin Avenue, Suite 200
Milwaukee, WI 53202

Bridgestone/Firestone Trust Fund Grants 836

The trust supports programs and projects of nonprofit organizations in the areas of education, child welfare, and environment and conservation in communities where the company has operations. While primary consideration is given to organizations and causes related to the three major focus points, the Fund recognizes the importance and value in supporting all types of civic, community and cultural activities. Assistance is regularly given for: community and neighborhood improvements; civil rights and equal opportunity; voter registration and education; job training; performing arts programs; public radio and television; cultural programs; non-academic libraries; and museums. Types of support include: annual campaigns; building/renovation; capital campaigns; continuing support; donated equipment; emergency funds; employee matching gifts; employee-related scholarships; endowments; exchange programs; fellowships; general/operating support; matching/challenge support; program development; research; scholarship funds; and sponsorships. Applications must be submitted in writing and should include a description of the organization (two-page maximum) and its record of accomplishment, objectives of the program, whom the program benefits, and proposed method to evaluate the program's success; amount sought from the trust in relation to the total need; exactly how trust fund money would be used; copy of IRS 501(c)3 confirmation letter; list of board of directors and their professional affiliations; previous year's financial report; current year's operating budget; Form 990; list of other contributors and the amount of their donations; and copy of recent audit if available. Proposals are reviewed upon receipt.
Requirements: IRS 501(c)3 nonprofit tax-exempt organizations in Alabama, Arkansas, Colorado, Connecticut, Florida, Kentucky, Illinois, Indiana, Iowa, Louisiana, Michigan, Minnesota, Mississippi, North Carolina, Ohio, Pennsylvania, South Carolina, Tennessee, Texas, Utah, and Wisconsin are eligible. Schools, governmental agencies or other nonprofit, civic organizations are included. Grant proposals should be sent directly to the management of the local Bridgestone Firestone facility.
Restrictions: It is essential that all organizations receiving grants be equal opportunity employers who will operate their programs in support of equal opportunity objectives. Contributions will not be made to groups that discriminate on the basis of race, color, religion, gender, mental or physical disabilities, sexual orientation, national origin, age, citizenship, veteran/reserve/national guard status, or other protected status; partisan political organizations; or groups limited to members of a single religious organization.
Geographic Focus: Alabama, Arkansas, Colorado, Connecticut, Florida, Illinois, Indiana, Iowa, Kentucky, Louisiana, Michigan, Minnesota, Mississippi, Nevada, North Carolina, Ohio, Pennsylvania, South Carolina, Tennessee, Texas, Utah, Wisconsin
Amount of Grant: 50 - 50,000 USD
Contact: Bernice Csaszar, Administrator; (615) 937-1415 or (615) 937-1000; fax (615) 937-1414; CsaszarBernice@bfusa.com or bfstrustfund@bfusa.com
Internet: http://www.bridgestone-firestone.com/trustfund.asp
Sponsor: Bridgestone/Firestone Trust Fund
535 Marriott Drive, P.O. Box 140990
Nashville, TN 37214-0990

Bright Family Foundation Grants 837

Established in 1986, the foundation primarily serves the Stanislaus County area of California. Areas of interest include: religion; education; medical services; medical school/education; internships; human services; children/youth services; arts & culture. The Board meets once a year in December to review proposals. Deadline date for applications is November 1.
Requirements: Stanislaus County, CA, IRS 501(c)3 tax-exempt organizations within a 20 mile radius of Modesto, CA, are eligible to apply.
Geographic Focus: California
Date(s) Application is Due: Nov 1
Amount of Grant: 5,000 - 50,000 USD
Contact: Calvin Bright, President; (209) 526-8242
Sponsor: Bright Family Foundation
1620 North Carpenter Road, Building B
Modesto, CA 95351-1155

Bright Promises Foundation Grants 838

The Bright Promises Foundation's primary activities are identifying the most pressing unmet needs of disadvantaged children in Illinois; calling for individuals, foundations, agencies, legislators, parents and the media to join the foundation in supporting these needs; soliciting grant applications and making grants that support these needs; attracting volunteers and funds to the foundation; and recognizing important role models with awards. Currently, the Bright Promises Foundation's focus is promoting better health among low-income and other at-risk children between the ages of 8-12. The Bright Promises Foundation initiated a four-year grant program called Healthy Children/Healthy Adults: Promoting Health through Better Nutritional Choices. The program responds to the escalating problem of childhood obesity in the state of Illinois. Now in its third year, the

Foundation has so far paid and pledged $481,646 to community-based multi-purpose agencies to promote better health among low-income and other at-risk children between the ages of 8-12. The foundation revisits its focus every four years to ensure relevancy.
Requirements: Grant applications are considered annually from a pool of invited applicants. Proposals are evaluated based on criteria including measurable goals and objectives, and sustainability after Bright Promises Foundation funding ends. Grantees are required to report at least twice each year on their measurable objectives, and project coordinators from the Bright Promises Foundation board of directors conduct site visits with staff during the application process and during the grant year.
Geographic Focus: Illinois
Contact: Iris Krieg, Executive Director; (312) 704-8260; info@brightpromises.org
Internet: http://www.brightpromises.org/OurPrograms/Grants/
Sponsor: Bright Promises Foundation
333 N. Michigan Avenue, Suite 510
Chicago, IL 60601

Bristol-Myers Squibb Clinical Outcomes and Research Grants 839
Bristol-Myers Squibb's mission is to extend and enhance human life. To help achieve that mission, the Company has established programs to support Investigator Sponsored Trials (ISTs). ISTs must be medically appropriate and scientifically valid. While the Company will consider requests for clinical research trials in all clinical and therapeutic areas, it currently gives priority to proposals in the following therapeutic areas: Cardiovascular/Metabolics, Infectious Diseases, Neuroscience, Oncology, Immunology, and Virology. Bristol-Myers Squibb maintains a strict policy of not exercising any influence or control over the design of any investigator initiated clinical research trial supported by BMS.
Requirements: Individuals in the following settings are eligible for support: private practice, hospitals, community health centers, cooperative groups, physician networks, and academic medical centers and universities.
Geographic Focus: All States
Contact: Amit Duggal, (212) 546-4000; fax (212) 546-9574; amit.duggal@bms.com
Internet: http://www.bms.com/responsibility/building_our_communities/Pages/default.aspx
Sponsor: Bristol-Myers Squibb Company
777 Scudders Mill Road
Plainsboro, NJ 08536

Bristol-Myers Squibb Foundation Community Initiatives Grants 840
Through its Community Initiatives Grants program, the Foundation is committed to conscientious citizenship, a helping hand for worthwhile causes and constructive action that supports a clean and healthy environment. By encouraging its own employees and its business units to support their local communities, the company and the Foundation seek to participate as responsible neighbors and members of the communities where its people live and work and where its facilities are located. Current interest area include: health and health education; women's health; science education; the environment; and other types of local community support. Nonprofit organizations in communities where Bristol-Myers Squibb maintains a facility should submit their requests for company contributions directly to that location.
Requirements: Only non-profit 501(c)3 organizations located in and around the following communities are eligible: Wallingford, Connecticut; Hopewell, New Jersey; New Brunswick, New Jersey; Plainsboro, New Jersey; Princeton, New Jersey; West Windsor, New Jersey; Devens, Massachusetts; New York, New York; Syracuse, New York.
Geographic Focus: Connecticut, Massachusetts, New Jersey, New York
Contact: John L. Damonti; (212) 546-4000 or (800) 332-2056; fax (212) 546-9574
Internet: http://www.bms.com/responsibility/building_our_communities/apply_for_community_grants/Pages/contribution_guidelines.aspx
Sponsor: Bristol-Myers Squibb Foundation
345 Park Avenue, Suite 4364
New York, NY 10154

Bristol-Myers Squibb Patient Assistance Grants 841
The Patient Assistance program was established to provide temporary assistance to qualifying patients with a financial hardship who generally have no private prescription drug insurance and are not enrolled in a prescription drug coverage plan through Medicaid or any other federal, state or local health program. The program provides free medications to indigent patients who qualify in all 50 states, Puerto Rico and the U.S. Virgin Islands. All patients and their health care providers must complete a program application to be considered for assistance. A printable version of the application is available online. Applications can also be obtained by calling the toll free telephone number.
Requirements: Applicants are required to provide information regarding household income, prescription insurance coverage, and citizenship, along with both patient and health care provider signatures.
Geographic Focus: All States
Contact: John L. Damonti; (212) 546-4000 or (800) 332-2056; fax (212) 546-9574
Internet: http://www.bms.com/responsibility/building_our_communities/people_in_need/Pages/default.aspx
Sponsor: Bristol-Myers Squibb Foundation
345 Park Avenue, Suite 4364
New York, NY 10154

British Columbia Arts Council Artists in Education Program Grants 842
The AIE program's goals and objectives include: exposing young people to performances, workshops and residencies that have artistic quality and educational merit; balancing exposure of the arts to young people in remote, rural and urban environments; establishing professional standards for arts practices and presentations in schools and expose BC's children and youth to professional quality arts programming; developing, maintaining and expanding the market for professional artists working with children and youth; facilitating communication between the arts and education communities by developing mutual awareness, respect and appreciation; and promoting the arts as an area of study and professional employment.
Requirements: The applicant organization must be a school district or the Federation of Independent School Associations in British Columbia.
Restrictions: Expenses which do not qualify for AIE funding include but are not limited to the following: non-professional artists; school assemblies with motivational speakers, magic or novelty acts; events for which tickets are purchased, or for which admission is charged; fees for artists residing outside of Canada.
Geographic Focus: All States, Canada
Contact: Cheryl Hurd; (604) 878-7144; fax (604) 683-0501; cheryl@artstarts.com
Internet: http://www.artstarts.com/funding/aie.html
Sponsor: British Columbia Arts Council
P.O. Box 9819, Station Provincial Government
Victoria, BC V8W 9W3 Canada

Broadcasting Board of Governors David Burke Distinguished Journalism Award 843
The David Burke Distinguished Journalism Award recognizes the courage, integrity, and professionalism of individuals in reporting the news within the BBG broadcast entities. Named in honor of David W. Burke, the founding chairman and leader of the BBG for its first three years, the award is presented annually to U.S. international broadcasters who demonstrate exceptional performances, including bravery and extreme hardship. The amount of the award is $2,500. David Burke had an illustrious career as a news and broadcast executive. He is the former President of CBS News and served as both Vice President and Executive Vice President of ABC News.
Geographic Focus: All States
Amount of Grant: 2,500 USD
Contact: Cheryl Peters, Grants Administrator; (202) 382-7838 or (202) 203-4400; fax (202) 203-4585; cpeters@bbg.gov or publicaffairs@bbg.gov
Internet: http://www.bbg.gov/pressroom/burke-awards/
Sponsor: Broadcasting Board of Governors
330 Independence Avenue, SW
Washington, DC 20237

Brookdale Foundation Leadership in Aging Fellowships 844
The Leadership in Aging Fellowships provide two years of support to junior academics to focus on a project that will help establish them in an area of aging research. Fellowships are open to a broad range of disciplines including, but not limited to, medical, biological and basic sciences, nursing, social sciences, and the arts and humanities. The Fellowship is paid to the candidate's sponsoring institution in support of the candidate's research project. The Fellowship amount of up to $125,000 each year is intended to cover 75% of the fellow's time, base salary and fringe benefits. The award could also be used to include the support of a graduate assistant if necessary as long as the total amount does not exceed $125,000. Additional information is available at the website.
Requirements: Fellowships are open to all professionals in the field of aging. Candidates must meet the following criteria: leadership potential; ongoing commitment to a career in aging; a mentor (or mentors); and a willingness to commit at least 75% of his or her time for career development during each of the two years of the Fellowship.
Geographic Focus: All States
Amount of Grant: Up to 125,000 USD
Contact: Anna Condegni; (212) 308-7355; fax (212) 750-0132; annaatbrookdale@aol.com
Internet: http://www.brookdalefoundation.org/Leadership/Fellows/fellows.html
Sponsor: Brookdale Foundation
950 Third Avenue, 19th Floor
New York, NY 10022-3668

Brookdale Foundation National Group Respite Grants 845
The Group Respite Grants fund community-based, social model, day service programs that provide dementia-specific group activities for participants and respite from caregiving tasks for family caregivers. Program goals include the following: to offer opportunities for persons with Alzheimer's disease or a related dementia to engage in a program of meaningful social and recreational activities in a secure and supportive setting in order to maximize their cognitive and social abilities; and to provide relief and support to family members and other primary caregivers of individuals with Alzheimer's disease or a related dementia. Additional program guidelines and examples o previously funded projects are available at the Foundation website.
Requirements: Applicants must be nonprofits with tax-exempt status under Section 501(c)3 of the Internal Revenue Code or public agencies as defined under Section 509(a).
Geographic Focus: All States
Contact: Valerie Hall; (212) 308-7355; fax (212) 750-0132; vah@brookdalefoundation.org
Internet: http://www.brookdalefoundation.org/Respite/respiteprogram2008.html
Sponsor: Brookdale Foundation
950 Third Avenue, 19th Floor
New York, NY 10022-3668

Brookdale Foundation Relatives as Parents Grants 846
The Brookdale Foundation Relatives as Parents Grants (RAPP) awards seed grants to community-based organizations to develop services for grandparents and other relatives acting as surrogate parents, in addition to state agencies planning to offer such services. Currently RAPP provides extensive services, primarily to relative caregivers caring for children outside the foster care system, in 44 states, the District of Columbia, and Puerto Rico. As part of their program, they conduct the National Orientation and Training Conference and provide

technical assistance through site bulletins, a listserv, annual newsletter, conference calls and webchats to facilitate opportunities for networking and information exchange. Programs and funding vary by state. Additional information is available at the website. Examples of previously funded programs are also available at the website.
Geographic Focus: All States, District of Columbia, Puerto Rico
Contact: Valerie Hall; (212) 308-7355; fax (212) 750-0132; vah@brookdalefoundation.org
Internet: http://www.brookdalefoundation.org/RAPP/rapp.html
Sponsor: Brookdale Foundation
950 Third Avenue, 19th Floor
New York, NY 10022-3668

Brooklyn Benevolent Society Grants 847
The society awards general support grants to nonprofits of the Christian and Roman Catholic faiths, including the Salvation Army. Youth organizations such as YMCA/YWCA and child welfare groups, community service organizations, religion (divinity schools, parochial schools, missions, religious welfare) and religious organizations, and welfare groups. Grant making is focused in the New York, NY, area. Send a brief letter of inquiry describing the program and organization descriptions.
Requirements: Nonprofit organizations of the Christian and Roman Catholic faiths in New York are eligible.
Geographic Focus: New York
Contact: Grants Administrator; (718) 624-0176
Sponsor: Brooklyn Benevolent Society
57 Willoughby Street
Brooklyn, NY 11201

Brooklyn Community Foundation Caring Neighbors Grants 848
The Caring Neighbors Fund assists vulnerable Brooklyn families and individuals with immediate need for a social safety net and seeks to provide access to health and mental health services. Its goals are to: offer paths out of poverty by supporting the work of emergency food providers and human services agencies; provide access to care for unaddressed physical or mental health needs in accessible community settings; ensure that homeless individuals and families can access safe temporary shelter and support services. The Foundation typically has two grant cycles annually, Letter of Inquiry are accepted then. Contact the Foundation directly for current grant cycles. Organizations invited to submit a complete proposal should expect a final decision from the Foundation within eight to twelve weeks of receipt.
Requirements: Organizations applying for a grant from the Brooklyn Community Foundation must be classified as tax-exempt under Section 501(c)3 of the Internal Revenue Code and as public charities under Section 509(a) of that Code. Fiscally sponsored organizations may also apply. Your organization need not be based in Brooklyn; however grants from the Brooklyn Community Foundation must directly benefit Brooklyn neighborhoods and/or Brooklyn residents. Applying for funding is a two part process: 1st step—begins with a Letter of Inquiry (LOI). This is the opportunity for an organization to provide the Foundation with an overview of the group and its proposed activities, project or program; 2nd step—applicants who have been selected to proceed to the next stage will receive an email from the Foundation's staff indicating that the organization has been approved to submit a complete proposal which best describes in detail the activities, program or project. If selected, your organization will have 30 days to submit a complete a proposal online.
Restrictions: The Foundation does not: fund individuals; support for-profit organizations; purchase tickets for dinners, golf outings or similar fundraising events; make contributions to candidates for elective office or for partisan political purposes; provide funding for religious purposes.
Geographic Focus: New York
Contact: Diane John, (718) 722-5952; info@BrooklynCommunityFoundation.org
Internet: http://www.brooklyncommunityfoundation.org/grants/caring-neighbors
Sponsor: Brooklyn Community Foundation
45 Main Street, Suite 409
Brooklyn, NY 11201

Brooklyn Community Foundation Community Arts for All Grants 849
The Arts for All Fund makes the arts a fun and essential component of life in Brooklyn, New York. Its goals are to: serve Brooklynites with diverse interests by supporting the outreach efforts of local arts and cultural organizations integrate the arts into schools and after-school programs; promote collaborations that employ the arts to address pressing community issues. Types of support available include: program, capacity building, capital, and operating support. The Foundation typically has two grant cycles annually, Letter of Inquiry are accepted then. Contact the Foundation directly for current grant cycles. Organizations invited to submit a complete proposal should expect a final decision from the Foundation within eight to twelve weeks of receipt.
Requirements: Organizations applying for a grant from the Brooklyn Community Foundation must be classified as tax-exempt under Section 501(c)3 of the Internal Revenue Code and as public charities under Section 509(a) of that Code. Fiscally sponsored organizations may also apply. Your organization need not be based in Brooklyn; however grants from the Brooklyn Community Foundation must directly benefit Brooklyn neighborhoods and/or Brooklyn residents. Applying for funding is a two part process: 1st step—begins with a Letter of Inquiry (LOI). This is the opportunity for an organization to provide the Foundation with an overview of the group and its proposed activities, project or program; 2nd step—applicants who have been selected to proceed to the next stage will receive an email from the Foundation's staff indicating that the organization has been approved to submit a complete proposal which best describes in detail the activities, program or project. If selected, your organization will have 30 days to submit a complete a proposal online.
Restrictions: The Foundation does not: fund individuals; support for-profit organizations; purchase tickets for dinners, golf outings or similar fundraising events; make contributions to candidates for elective office or for partisan political purposes; provide funding for religious purposes.
Geographic Focus: New York
Contact: Diane John, (718) 722-5952; info@BrooklynCommunityFoundation.org
Internet: http://www.brooklyncommunityfoundation.org/grants/arts-for-all
Sponsor: Brooklyn Community Foundation
45 Main Street, Suite 409
Brooklyn, NY 11201

Brooklyn Community Foundation Community Development Grants 850
The Community Development Fund supports efforts to provide affordable housing and neighborhood stability. It encourages thoughtful planning initiatives, quality urban design and sensitivity to the historic character of Brooklyn, New York neighborhoods. It also promotes family and individual economic health through support services and effective job training programs. The Fund's goals are to: strengthen and preserve access to affordable housing in Brooklyn neighborhoods; raise individual and family income by providing Brooklyn residents access to quality job training, career placement and financial support services; build the local economy by supporting neighborhood entrepreneurs and local efforts to improve our retail corridors. Types of support available include: program, capacity building, capital, and operating support. The Foundation typically has two grant cycles annually, Letter of Inquiry are accepted then. Contact the Foundation directly for current grant cycles. Organizations invited to submit a complete proposal should expect a final decision from the Foundation within eight to twelve weeks of receipt.
Requirements: Organizations applying for a grant from the Brooklyn Community Foundation must be classified as tax-exempt under Section 501(c)3 of the Internal Revenue Code and as public charities under Section 509(a) of that Code. Fiscally sponsored organizations may also apply. Your organization need not be based in Brooklyn; however grants from the Brooklyn Community Foundation must directly benefit Brooklyn neighborhoods and/or Brooklyn residents. Applying for funding is a two part process: 1st step—begins with a Letter of Inquiry (LOI). This is the opportunity for an organization to provide the Foundation with an overview of the group and its proposed activities, project or program; 2nd step—applicants who have been selected to proceed to the next stage will receive an email from the Foundation's staff indicating that the organization has been approved to submit a complete proposal which best describes in detail the activities, program or project. If selected, your organization will have 30 days to submit a complete a proposal online.
Restrictions: The Foundation does not: fund individuals; support for-profit organizations; purchase tickets for dinners, golf outings or similar fundraising events; make contributions to candidates for elective office or for partisan political purposes; provide funding for religious purposes.
Geographic Focus: New York
Contact: Diane John, (718) 722-5952; info@BrooklynCommunityFoundation.org
Internet: http://www.brooklyncommunityfoundation.org/grants/community-development
Sponsor: Brooklyn Community Foundation
45 Main Street, Suite 409
Brooklyn, NY 11201

Brooklyn Community Foundation Education and Youth Achievement Grants 851
The Education and Youth Achievement Fund promotes access to quality education and academic success for all children and adults in the Brooklyn area of New York. It also supports programs that help young people make smart life choices and nurture their social and emotional well-being. Its goals are to: combine tutoring, academic support networks, and enrichment activities to advance student achievement; encourage action-oriented, youth-led community projects that promote collaboration, leadership development, and critical thinking; build bridges between youth and trusted, responsible adult role models through effective mentoring programs. Types of support available include: program, capacity building, capital, and operating support. The Foundation typically has two grant cycles annually, Letter of Inquiry are accepted then. Contact the Foundation directly for current grant cycles. Organizations invited to submit a complete proposal should expect a final decision from the Foundation within eight to twelve weeks of receipt.
Requirements: Organizations applying for a grant from the Brooklyn Community Foundation must be classified as tax-exempt under Section 501(c)3 of the Internal Revenue Code and as public charities under Section 509(a) of that Code. Fiscally sponsored organizations may also apply. Your organization need not be based in Brooklyn; however grants from the Brooklyn Community Foundation must directly benefit Brooklyn neighborhoods and/or Brooklyn residents. Applying for funding is a two part process: 1st step—begins with a Letter of Inquiry (LOI). This is the opportunity for an organization to provide the Foundation with an overview of the group and its proposed activities, project or program; 2nd step—applicants who have been selected to proceed to the next stage will receive an email from the Foundation's staff indicating that the organization has been approved to submit a complete proposal which best describes in detail the activities, program or project. If selected, your organization will have 30 days to submit a complete a proposal online.
Restrictions: The Foundation does not: fund individuals; support for-profit organizations; purchase tickets for dinners, golf outings or similar fundraising events; make contributions to candidates for elective office or for partisan political purposes; provide funding for religious purposes.
Geographic Focus: New York
Contact: Diane John, (718) 722-5952 or (718) 722-2300; fax (718) 722-5757; info@BrooklynCommunityFoundation.org
Internet: http://www.brooklyncommunityfoundation.org/grants/education-youth
Sponsor: Brooklyn Community Foundation
45 Main Street, Suite 409
Brooklyn, NY 11201

Brooklyn Community Foundation Green Communities Grants 852
The Green Communities Fund fosters the development of green spaces, jobs, and neighborhoods. Its goals are to: encourage the protection and creation of open space, parks and community gardens; seek new ways to introduce and encourage environmental awareness in all neighborhoods through grassroots programming; train job seekers for green careers and connect them to employment opportunities. Types of support available include: program, capacity building, capital, and operating support. The Foundation typically has two grant cycles annually, Letter of Inquiry are accepted then. Contact the Foundation directly for current grant cycles. Organizations invited to submit a complete proposal should expect a final decision from the Foundation within eight to twelve weeks of receipt.
Requirements: Organizations applying for a grant from the Brooklyn Community Foundation must be classified as tax-exempt under Section 501(c)3 of the Internal Revenue Code and as public charities under Section 509(a) of that Code. Fiscally sponsored organizations may also apply. Your organization need not be based in Brooklyn; however grants from the Brooklyn Community Foundation must directly benefit Brooklyn neighborhoods and/or Brooklyn residents. Applying for funding is a two part process: 1st step—begins with a Letter of Inquiry (LOI). This is the opportunity for an organization to provide the Foundation with an overview of the group and its proposed activities, project or program; 2nd step—applicants who have been selected to proceed to the next stage will receive an email from the Foundation's staff indicating that the organization has been approved to submit a complete proposal which best describes in detail the activities, program or project. If selected, your organization will have 30 days to submit a complete a proposal online.
Restrictions: The Foundation does not: fund individuals; support for-profit organizations; purchase tickets for dinners, golf outings or similar fundraising events; make contributions to candidates for elective office or for partisan political purposes; provide funding for religious purposes.
Geographic Focus: New York
Contact: Diane John, (718) 722-5952; info@BrooklynCommunityFoundation.org
Internet: http://www.brooklyncommunityfoundation.org/grants/green-communities
Sponsor: Brooklyn Community Foundation
45 Main Street, Suite 409
Brooklyn, NY 11201

Brown County Community Foundation Grants 853
The Brown County Community Foundation strives to enhance the lives of the citizens and organizations of the community. It is a non-profit enterprise that seeks to provide the mechanism through which those who desire to help others in the community may carry out their philanthropy. By supporting charitable organizations in broad areas of community need - education, social services, health care, arts and humanities, and environment - it helps build a stronger, healthier Brown County. In general, grants shall be made for capital purposes only, not for operating expenses. Grant applications are generally available in April. Applications are due late May, with decisions announced in late June or early July.
Requirements: Evidence of nonprofit tax status must be submitted with all applications. Proposals must serve the residents of Brown County, Indiana.
Restrictions: Preference is generally given to requests that demonstrate the most urgent and immediate need for funding or satisfy an identifiable community need. Grants are ordinarily made for one year only. The Foundation rarely provides the entire support of a project. Grants are not generally available for those agencies and institutions that are funded primarily through tax support.
Geographic Focus: Indiana
Date(s) Application is Due: May 30
Contact: Larry Pejeau; (812) 988-4882; fax (812) 988-0299; larry@bccfin.org
Internet: http://bccfin.org/WhatWeDo/Grants.aspx
Sponsor: Brown County Community Foundation
91 West Mound Street, Unit 4
Nashville, IN 47448

Brown Foundation Grants 854
The foundation distributes funds for public charitable purposes, principally for support, encouragement and assistance to education, community service and the arts. The Foundation's current emphasis is in the field of public education at the primary and secondary levels with focus on supporting non-traditional and innovative approaches designed to improve public education primarily within the State of Texas. The visual and performing arts remain an area of interest. The Foundation also focuses on community service projects which serve the needs of children and families. The Foundation is interested in funding projects which fulfill one or more of the following criteria: addressing root causes of a concern rather than treating symptoms; serving as a catalyst to stimulate collaborative efforts by several sectors of the community; resulting in a long-lasting impact on the situation beyond the value of the grant itself; reflecting and encouraging sound financial planning and solid management practices in administration of the project. Proposals should be submitted a minimum of 4 months before funds are required.
Requirements: 501(c)3 organizations, public charities, and units of government are eligible.
Restrictions: Grants are not made to individuals. Only one application within a twelve month period will be considered. No proposal from an organization previously funded by the Foundation will be considered unless a full and timely report of expenditure of the previous grant has been submitted. The Foundation does not expect to support: grants to religious organizations for religious purposes; testimonial dinners, fundraising events or marketing events; grants intended directly or indirectly to support candidates for political office or to influence legislation; grants to other private foundations; grants to cover past operating deficits or debt retirements.
Geographic Focus: Texas
Contact: Nancy Pittman, Executive Director; (713) 523-6867; fax (713) 523-2917; bfi@brownfoundation.org or mbasurto@brownfoundation.org
Internet: http://www.brownfoundation.org/Guidelines.asp
Sponsor: Brown Foundation
P.O. Box 130646
Houston, TX 77219-0646

Brown Rudnick Charitable Foundation Relationship Grants 855
The Foundation has two principal grant programs, both focused on improving inner-city education for the communities of Boston, Hartford, New York and Providence. Relationship Grants are awarded annually based on proposals received in response to the foundation's request for proposal (RFP). These grants seek to create a relationship with a nonprofit grant recipient organization that ideally includes a financial contribution, pro bono legal involvement, and volunteer opportunities. Community Grants are designed to address a one-time, tangible, immediate need. Proposals must come from those on the front lines of education - the kind of need that those with funding authority don't appreciate or don't have the resources to make a priority. Grant applications and guidelines are available online.
Requirements: 501(c)3 nonprofit organizations in Boston, MA; Hartford, CT; New York, NY; and Providence, RI are eligible.
Geographic Focus: Connecticut, Massachusetts, New York, Rhode Island
Amount of Grant: 2,000 - 50,000 USD
Contact: Grants Administrator; (617) 856-8119; fax (617) 856-8201
Internet: http://www.brownrudnickcenter.com/foundation
Sponsor: Brown Rudnick Charitable Foundation
One Financial Center
Boston, MA 02111

Brunswick Foundation Dollars for Doers Grants 856
Established in 1957, the Brunswick Foundation is a 501(c)3 charitable organization that enhances the interests of its employees and the communities in which they live and work, as well as supporting causes and projects that complement the business interests of Brunswick Corporation. The Dollars for Doers program recognizes the volunteer efforts of Brunswick employees by issuing grants to 501(c)3 organizations. The foundation awards grants to nonprofit organizations for which an individual employee or group of employees has completed volunteer work, such as serving on a Board of Directors or participating in a fundraising event.
Requirements: IRS 501(c)3 organizations in Alabama, Arizona, Connecticut, Florida, Georgia, Illinois, Indiana, Kentucky, Louisiana, Maryland, Michigan, Minnesota, Mississippi, Nebraska, North Carolina, Oklahoma, Oregon, South Carolina, Tennessee, Texas, Washington, and Wisconsin are eligible.
Restrictions: Grants are not made to religious organizations for religious purposes; for any form of political activity; to veterans groups, fraternal orders, or labor groups; for loans of any kind; or for trips, tours, dinners, tickets, or advertising.
Geographic Focus: Alabama, Arizona, Connecticut, Florida, Georgia, Illinois, Indiana, Kentucky, Louisiana, Maryland, Michigan, Minnesota, Mississippi, Nebraska, North Carolina, Oklahoma, Oregon, South Carolina, Tennessee, Texas, Washington, Wisconsin
Contact: B. Russell Lockridge; (847) 735-4467 or (847) 735-4700; fax (847) 735-4765
Internet: http://www.brunswick.com/company/community/brunswickfoundation.php
Sponsor: Brunswick Foundation
1 North Field Court
Lake Forest, IL 60045-4811

Brunswick Foundation Grants 857
The Brunswick Foundation Grant Program awards direct donations to 501(c)3 organizations that enhance marine, fitness, bowling or billiards activities and related industry interests, or any other Brunswick business interest. The foundation also supports programs where Brunswick Corporation employees volunteer and efforts to provide a higher education for children of employees. Types of support include employee-matching gifts, general operating budgets, building construction and renovation, capital campaigns, special projects, research, and continuing support. Requests for guidelines must be in writing, or applicants may submit a letter describing the purpose of the organization and the request.
Requirements: IRS 501(c)3 organizations in Alabama, Arizona, Connecticut, Florida, Georgia, Illinois, Indiana, Kentucky, Louisiana, Maryland, Michigan, Minnesota, Mississippi, Nebraska, North Carolina, Oklahoma, Oregon, South Carolina, Tennessee, Texas, Washington, and Wisconsin are eligible.
Restrictions: Grants are not made to religious organizations for religious purposes; for any form of political activity; to veterans groups, fraternal orders, or labor groups; for loans of any kind; or for trips, tours, dinners, tickets, or advertising.
Geographic Focus: Alabama, Arizona, Connecticut, Florida, Georgia, Illinois, Indiana, Kentucky, Louisiana, Maryland, Michigan, Minnesota, Mississippi, Nebraska, North Carolina, Oklahoma, Oregon, South Carolina, Tennessee, Texas, Washington, Wisconsin
Date(s) Application is Due: Mar 22
Contact: B. Russell Lockridge; (847) 735-4467 or (847) 735-4700; fax (847) 735-4765
Internet: http://www.brunswickcorp.com
Sponsor: Brunswick Foundation
1 North Field Court
Lake Forest, IL 60045-4811

Bryan Adams Foundation Grants 858
The Bryan Adams Foundation was set up in 2006 by the musician and photographer Bryan Adams, in order to improve the quality of people's lives around the world. The Foundation aims to achieve this by providing financial help and support to those people who are committed to bettering the lives of other people, by providing grants to finance specific projects. The Foundation seeks to protect the most vulnerable or disadvantaged individuals in society. It aims particularly to advance education and learning opportunities for children

and young people worldwide, believing that an education is the best gift that a child can be given. The Foundation's area of support is broad and far-reaching, enabling grants to be given for projects supporting the elderly, victims of war and natural disasters, and those suffering from mental or physical illness. Applicant should send an email with the purpose of their project and budgetary needs.
Requirements: The Trustees generally do not make grants in response to unsolicited applications and do not normally make grants to individuals.
Geographic Focus: All States, All Countries
Contact: Bryan Adams, Trustee; foundation@bryanadams.com
Internet: http://www.thebryanadamsfoundation.com/index.php?target=grants
Sponsor: Bryan Adams Foundation
440 Strand
London, WC2R 0QS England

Buhl Foundation - Frick Educational Fund 859
Proposals with the following characteristics are of particular interest to the Foundation: educational programs; programs for young people; studies to produce practical applications which make a contribution to basic theory; attempts which relate specialists in a common approach to problems or which call for cooperative efforts among separate agencies; institutional, experimental, or demonstration approaches to resolving problems when they are innovative either for the institution or for institutions in general; previously supported and promising programs where time extension or new developments would afford opportunity for enhancement of values already realized. No specific application form is required. A letter of inquiry is sent to the President, to be followed by a formal proposal, if invited. Applications are reviewed three times per year.
Requirements: Giving primarily in southwestern PA, with emphasis on the Pittsburgh area. Grants are limited to organizations which are defined as tax-exempt under section 501(c)3 of the Internal Revenue Code and which are not private or operating foundations as defined in section 509(a) of the Code.
Restrictions: Grants are not normally made for building funds, overhead costs, accumulated deficits, ordinary operating budgets, general fund-raising campaigns, loans, scholarships and fellowships, other foundations, nationally funded organized groups or individuals. Grant are not made for support of propaganda, sectarian religious activities, efforts to influence legislation or for conferences or seminars, unless grant-related.
Geographic Focus: Pennsylvania
Contact: Doreen Boyce, President; (412) 566-2711; fax (412) 566-2714
Internet: http://fdncenter.org/grantmaker/buhl
Sponsor: Buhl Foundation
650 Smithfield Street, Centre City Tower, Suite 2300
Pittsburgh, PA 15222

Build-A-Bear Workshop Bear Hugs Foundation Literacy and Education Grants 860
The program provides support for children in literacy and education programs such as summer reading programs, early childhood education programs and literacy programs for children with special needs. Grants will be a one-time contribution, and generally range from $1,000 to $10,000, but the average grant tends to be $5,000. Programs that will be funded include: (1) Individual Project grants - generally for one-time purchases or to fulfill a short-term need, such as the purchase of materials or books; (2) Organization Program grants - start-up or operational costs for ongoing programs, such as a summer reading program.
Requirements: While the geographic focus of the program is broad (United States and Canada), priority is given to organizations located near Build-A-Bear Workshop stores. United States applicants must be a tax-exempt organization under Section 501(c)3 of the IRS Code, and not a private foundation, within the meaning of Code Sections 509(a)(1) or 509(a)(2), or a state college or university within the meaning of Code Section 511(a)(2)(B) (a Public Charity). In addition, grant recipients must certify that they are not a supporting organization within the meaning of Code Section 509(a)(3). Canadian applicants must be a registered Canadian charity.
Restrictions: Grant types not funded: (1) Capital Campaigns; (2) Construction or new facility expenses; (3) Fundraising or Event Sponsorships; (4) Political Activities; (5) Religious organizations for religious purposes.
Geographic Focus: All States, Canada
Date(s) Application is Due: Feb 28; May 31; Sep 30
Amount of Grant: 1,000 - 10,000 USD
Contact: Maxine Clark, President; (314) 423-8000, ext. 5366; giving@buildabear.com
Internet: http://www.buildabear.com/aboutus/community/bearhugs.aspx
Sponsor: Build-A-Bear Workshop Bear Hugs Foundation
1954 Innerbelt Business Center Drive
Saint Louis, MO 63114

Build-A-Bear Workshop Foundation Grants 861
The foundation is committed to improving communities and impacting lives through meaningful philanthropic programs that help children and families, animals and the environment. Grants range between $1,000 and $10,000 with the average grant being $2,500. Application and guidelines are available online.
Requirements: Priority is given to 501(c)3 tax-exempt organizations.
Restrictions: The foundation does not awards grants to support: capital campaigns; fundraising sponsorships or events; political activities; religious organizations for religious purposes.
Geographic Focus: All States
Contact: Maxine Clark, President; (314) 423-8000, ext. 5366; giving@buildabear.com
Internet: http://www.buildabear.com/aboutus/community/babwfoundation.aspx
Sponsor: Build-A-Bear Workshop Bear Hugs Foundation
1954 Innerbelt Business Center Drive
Saint Louis, MO 63114

Bullitt Foundation Grants 862
The foundation functions to protect and restore the environment of the Pacific Northwest, including Washington, Oregon, Idaho, western Montana, coastal rainforests in Alaska, and British Columbia, Canada. Program priorities include aquatic ecosystems; terrestrial ecosystems; conservation and stewardship in agriculture; energy and climate change; growth management and transportation; toxic and radioactive substances; training, organizational development, and unique opportunities (including education and public outreach). Areas of interest include air pollution, climate change, endangered species, energy conservation, environmental education and justice, human health, transportation, and tribal communities. The foundation supports challenge/matching, general operating, project/program, seed money, demonstration, and development grants, as well as requests for conferences/seminars and technical assistance support. Grants will be awarded for one year with possible renewal.
Requirements: Nonprofit organizations in the Pacific Northwest, including Washington, Oregon, Idaho, western Montana, coastal rainforests in Alaska, and British Columbia, Canada are eligible.
Geographic Focus: Alaska, Idaho, Montana, Oregon, Washington, Canada
Date(s) Application is Due: May 1; Nov 1
Contact: Program Officer; (206) 343-0807; fax (206) 343-0822; info@bullitt.org
Internet: http://www.bullitt.org
Sponsor: Bullitt Foundation
1212 Minor Avenue
Seattle, WA 98101-2825

Bunbury Company Grants 863
The company seeks to assist organizations primarily in Mercer County, but also in Burlington, Camden, Hunterdon, Mercer, Middlesex, Monmouth, Ocean, and Somerset with programs in the following areas: educational programs that provide opportunities for intellectual, societal or cultural growth to youth and families; environmental programs that help conserve threatened farmland, habitat or waterways and regional planning efforts that help advance these goals; community building and social service programs that empower the undeserved; cultural programs that promote local artistic initiatives. The Foundation is particularly interested in programs that are local and have the ability to positively impact the quality of life within their community. The Foundation provides basic needs support for: general operating support; building funds; challenge or matching funds; and funds for special programs.
Requirements: An applicant must have tax-exempt status under Section 501(c)3 of the Internal Revenue Service Code and be a publicly supported charity under Section 509. Nonprofit organizations additionally must be registered with the State of New Jersey as a charity unless they are schools that file their curricula with the Department of Education and are exempted from the provisions of the New Jersey Charitable Registration and Investigation Act.
Restrictions: The Foundation will not provide support for the following: endowment campaigns; sporting activities, outings or events; fraternal or religious organizations, including schools with religious affiliation; individual fellowships or scholarships; summer camps or day care facilities, unless part of a comprehensive after care program; organizations with multiple chapters if outside Mercer County; specific cultural performances; publications or surveys.
Geographic Focus: New Jersey
Date(s) Application is Due: Mar 1; May 3; Aug 2; Nov 7
Contact: Grants Manager; (609) 333-8800; fax (609) 333-8900; BunburyCo@aol.com
Internet: http://www.bunburycompany.org/grant-guidelines.html
Sponsor: Bunbury Company
2 Railroad Place
Hopewell, NJ 08525

Burden Trust Grants 864
The trust supports international nonprofit organizations in the fields of medical research and hospitals; schools and training institutions; and care of and homes for the elderly, children, and other individuals in need. Preference will be given to organizations affiliated with the Anglican Church.
Geographic Focus: All States
Date(s) Application is Due: Mar 31
Contact: Patrick O'Conor, 0117 9628611; p.oconor@netgates.co.uk
Sponsor: Burden Trust
51 Downs Park W
Bristol, BS6 7QL England

Burlington Industries Foundation Grants 865
This is a company-sponsored foundation, giving primarily in areas of company operations in North Carolina, South Carolina, and Virginia. The foundation supports organizations involved with arts and culture, education, health, youth development, community development, and civic affairs.
Requirements: 501(c)3 organizations in Burlington communities (North Carolina, South Carolina, and Virginia), are eligible for grant support. Requests for funding must be accompanied by: proof of 501(c)3 tax-exempt status; description of the organization and its objective; justification for the project; evidence that the organization is well established; information about the organization's reputation, efficiency, management ability, financial status and sources of income.
Restrictions: No support for: sectarian or denominational religious organizations, national organizations, private secondary schools, historic preservation organizations, individuals (except for employees in distress), conferences, seminars, workshops, endowments, outdoor dramas, films, documentaries, medical research, loans.
Geographic Focus: North Carolina, South Carolina, Virginia
Contact: Delores Sides; (336) 379-2903; delores.sides@itg-global.com
Sponsor: Burlington Industries Foundation
P.O. Box 26540
Greensboro, NC 27415-6540

Burlington Northern Santa Fe Foundation Grants   866
The foundation is focused on the communities where the company operates and areas where its railways pass. The foundation supports education, including scholarships for Native Americans and scholarships for children of employees in conjunction with the National Merit Scholarships program; the arts, including museums, performing arts, and libraries; and civic and public affairs. Support goes to the Nature Conservancy and for local fire departments and law enforcement. Types of support include general operating support, continuing support, annual campaigns, capital campaigns, and program development. Health and human services funding concentrates on the United Way. Awards are made for a single year and for continuing support. The company also matches employee funds given to public and private colleges and universities, cultural organizations, and hospitals in the United States. Requests for applications should describe the purpose for the grant. Requests are reviewed every six weeks.
Requirements: Any 501(c)3 organization located in Schaumburg, IL, and communities where the corporation operates, including 28 states and two Canadian provinces, are eligible to apply.
Geographic Focus: All States
Contact: Deanna Dugas; (817) 867-6407; fax (817) 352-7924; Deanna.dugas@bnsf.com
Sponsor: Burlington Northern Santa Fe Foundation
2650 Lou Menk Drive, 2nd Floor, P.O. Box 961057
Fort Worth, TX 76131-2830

Burning Foundation Grants   867
The foundation awards grants to eligible Oregon and Washington nonprofit organizations in its areas of interest, including environmental programs—to protect threatened rivers and forests, nurture native fish, and conserve land and open space for ecological and recreational purposes; conservation programs for low-income children and youth—to provide opportunities for economically disadvantaged children to learn how to protect their natural resources; and teen pregnancy protection—to address impact of overpopulation on the country's natural resources. Letters of intent must be postmarked by the third Wednesday of January and August; full proposals must be postmarked by the first Wednesday of March and October.
Requirements: Oregon and Washington nonprofit organizations are eligible.
Restrictions: Grants do not support research, video or film, private schools, computer equipment, or capital campaigns.
Geographic Focus: Oregon, Washington
Date(s) Application is Due: Jan 18; Aug 16
Amount of Grant: 5,000 - 12,000 USD
Contact: Therese Ogle; (206) 781-3472; fax (206) 784-5987; oglefounds@aol.com
Internet: http://fdncenter.org/grantmaker/burning
Sponsor: Burning Foundation
6723 Sycamore Avenue NW
Seattle, WA 98117

Burton D. Morgan Foundation Adult Entrepreneurship Grants   868
The Foundation is interested in supporting organizations that assist innovative entrepreneurs with launching their ventures and building sustainability. The Foundation believes that innovative entrepreneurship draws upon creativity, involves an element of risk, and creates value. Support is awarded to charitable organizations that provide the following kinds of entrepreneurship-related services: information, incubation, networking, continuing education, access to capital, risk management, and business planning. The Foundation is particularly interested in building entrepreneurial networks that foster a stronger entrepreneurial culture in Northeast Ohio.
Requirements: Grants are made to organizations recognized as tax-exempt under the Internal Revenue Service code section 501(c)3 which are not private foundations. The Foundation's geographic preferences complement its program and project focus by targeting: entrepreneurship-related programs in Summit County, Ohio, and surrounding counties, known collectively as the Northeast Ohio region; and Hudson, Ohio-based nonprofit organizations.
Restrictions: The Foundation does not usually make multi-year grants and does not ordinarily consider grants to annual fund drives, to units of government, or to organizations and institutions which are primarily tax supported, including state universities. The Foundation no longer makes grants to arts, mental health, and social service organizations and programs.
Geographic Focus: Ohio
Date(s) Application is Due: Mar 1; Jun 1; Oct 1
Contact: Deborah D. Hoover; (330) 665-1630 or (330) 655-1660; dhoover@bdmorganfdn.org
Internet: http://www.bdmorganfdn.org/Adult_entrepreneurship.php
Sponsor: Burton D. Morgan Foundation
22 Aurora Street
Hudson, OH 44236

Burton D. Morgan Foundation Hudson Community Grants   869
Burton D. Morgan and his family moved to Hudson in the late 1950s because Burt was starting a new business, Morgan Adhesives Co., in Stow and Mrs. Morgan's ancestors were among the early Hudson settlers. The Morgans have been dedicated to supporting projects in Hudson that contribute to the health and vibrancy of the community. The Foundation supports a wide array of Hudson projects in the fields of arts and culture, education, and the civic arena, but also seeks to work with Hudson organizations in the fields of entrepreneurship and entrepreneurship education in order to experiment with innovative ideas to advance the field.
Requirements: Grants are made to organizations recognized as tax-exempt under the Internal Revenue Service code section 501(c)3 which are not private foundations.
Restrictions: The Foundation does not usually make multi-year grants and does not ordinarily consider grants to annual fund drives, to units of government, or to organizations and institutions which are primarily tax supported, including state universities. The Foundation no longer makes grants to arts, mental health, and social service organizations and programs.
Geographic Focus: Ohio
Date(s) Application is Due: Mar 1; Jun 1; Oct 1
Contact: Deborah D. Hoover; (330) 665-1630 or (330) 655-1660; dhoover@bdmorganfdn.org
Internet: http://www.bdmorganfdn.org/hudson_community.php
Sponsor: Burton D. Morgan Foundation
22 Aurora Street
Hudson, OH 44236

Burton D. Morgan Foundation Youth Entrepreneurship Grants   870
The Burton D. Morgan Foundation supports youth education programs for elementary, middle, and high school students with a focus on the free enterprise system, financial literacy and entrepreneurship. The Foundation values programs that inspire students to become financially independent and fiscally responsible and to envision a future that includes the highest educational attainment possible. To achieve these goals, teachers must receive the necessary training to incorporate entrepreneurial thinking and economic concepts into coursework and extracurricular activities. While not every student will become an entrepreneur, every student will benefit from learning about entrepreneurship and, thereby, be better equipped to chart their own futures. The Foundation also believes that Northeast Ohio youth entrepreneurship programs will benefit from networking and collaborating and that students will be best served by the creation of educational pathways from one educational level to another.
Requirements: Grants are made to organizations recognized as tax-exempt under the Internal Revenue Service code section 501(c)3 which are not private foundations. The Foundation's geographic preferences complement its program and project focus by targeting: entrepreneurship-related programs in Summit County, Ohio, and surrounding counties, known collectively as the Northeast Ohio region; and Hudson, Ohio-based nonprofit organizations.
Restrictions: The Foundation does not usually make multi-year grants and does not ordinarily consider grants to annual fund drives, to units of government, or to organizations and institutions which are primarily tax supported, including state universities. The Foundation no longer makes grants to arts, mental health, and social service organizations and programs.
Geographic Focus: Ohio
Date(s) Application is Due: Mar 1; Jun 1; Oct 1
Contact: Deborah D. Hoover; (330) 665-1630 or (330) 655-1660; dhoover@bdmorganfdn.org
Internet: http://www.bdmorganfdn.org/youth_entrepreneurship.php
Sponsor: Burton D. Morgan Foundation
22 Aurora Street
Hudson, OH 44236

Burton G. Bettingen Grants   871
The fields of activity of the corporation are education at all levels, mental health, crime and abuse victims and public protection programs, religion (Christian, Roman Catholic, and Salvation Army), environment, and welfare. Top funding priority is children and youth. The current focus is on child prostitutes, runaways, and abandoned children. Nonprofits servicing the economically disadvantaged also may apply. The corporation provides broad types of support, including operating, capital, research, challenge/matching grants, and endowments. A letter of inquiry stating the applicant's background, goals and objectives, and the specific need for funding is welcome. Unsolicited submissions are considered but receive low priority.
Requirements: IRS 501(c)3 organizations are eligible. Giving primarily, but not limited to, Southern California.
Restrictions: The corporation does not award grants to individuals; for general fund-raising events, dinners, or mass mailings; or to grantmaking organizations.
Geographic Focus: California
Contact: Patricia Brown; (323) 938-8478; fax (323) 938-8479; burtonbet@aol.com
Sponsor: Burton G. Bettingen Corporation
134 S Mansfield Avenue
Los Angeles, CA 90036-3019

Bush Foundation Arts & Humanities Grants: Capital Projects   872
Through this program, the foundation encourages proposals from nonprofit organizations for major building construction, renovation and purchase. The capital grants usually do not exceed $1 million and are ordinarily 5%-15% of a capital project goal. Occasionally, higher percentages are approved for organizations that have limited access to other sources of capital funds. Lower percentages may be awarded for larger projects. There is no minimum request amount.
Requirements: To be eligible for consideration, your organization must: Be a 501(c)3 nonprofit, tax-exempt organization located in Minnesota, North Dakota or South Dakota; Have publicly announced the capital campaign; Have project plans completed; Have already secured at least one-third of the fundraising goal in cash or pledges from a variety of sources. The foundation has separate guidelines for capital grants for four-year private colleges - these are available by contacting the foundation directly or downloading them from the website. The application process begins with a letter of inquiry.
Restrictions: Proposals will not be accepted for: Portions of the campaign directed at general and continuing operating support; Past operating deficits, cash reserve funds or to retire mortgages or other debts; Endowment of health and human service agencies and of public colleges and universities; Small remodeling projects or the purchase of office furnishings, computers, vehicles and other equipment that are not part of a comprehensive capital campaign; Capital projects that will preserve individual historic structures; Building purchase, construction or remodeling projects for charter schools, church sanctuaries, community centers, nursing homes, hospitals, day care centers for children or adults, county historical societies, municipal and other government agencies, nature centers or public colleges and universities.

Geographic Focus: Minnesota, North Dakota, South Dakota
Date(s) Application is Due: Mar 1; Jul 1; Nov 1
Contact: Program Officer; (651) 227-0891; info@bushfoundation.org
Internet: http://www.bushfoundation.org/grants/arts_humanities.asp#Capital_Projects
Sponsor: Bush Foundation
332 Minnesota Street, Suite East 900
St. Paul, MN 55101-1315

Bush Foundation Arts & Humanities Grants: Short-Term Organizational Support   873
These grants are approved for one or more years and are intended to support particular activities for a finite period. Successful applicants typically propose activities that are part of a plan to achieve long-term organizational goals. Applicants should determine their own priorities when applying - the purposes of successful proposals are broad; however, the foundation typically approves only 10 to 15 requests each year.
Requirements: To be eligible for consideration, your organization must: Operate year-round programs based in Minnesota, North Dakota or South Dakota; Create or present performing, visual, humanities or media and/or literary arts; Have at least a three-year programming history in Minnesota or the Dakotas; Have had an average annual operating expense of more than $100,000 during the three most recently completed fiscal years; And, pay artists a reasonable salary or fee.
Restrictions: Funds are not available for sponsorship or presentation of one-time productions, events such as festivals or programs that operate only in the summer.
Geographic Focus: Minnesota, North Dakota, South Dakota, Wisconsin
Date(s) Application is Due: Mar 1; Jul 1; Nov 1
Contact: Program Officer; (651) 227-0891; info@bushfoundation.org
Internet: http://www.bushfoundation.org/grants/arts_humanities.asp#Short_Term_Support
Sponsor: Bush Foundation
332 Minnesota Street, Suite East 900
St. Paul, MN 55101-1315

Bush Foundation Ecological Health Grants   874
As part of the foundation's goal to improve the ecological health of their region, it seeks to help people and organizations develop ways to treat ecological health as an interdependent system, rather than as isolated problems to be solved. Through these efforts, the foundation hopes to help restore, preserve, and protect our resources in order to sustain the interdependent health of humans, animals, and ecosystems. This condition of interdependence is captured in the term 'ecological health.' Guidelines are available at the Bush Foundation website.
Requirements: The Foundation will make grants to benefit ecological health work in the three-state Bush region of Minnesota, North Dakota and South Dakota. Proposals that incorporate ecological health in other program areas (e.g., arts and culture) are encouraged. The preference is for initiatives that have a direct and practical bearing on humans and their communities. Specifically, the foundation will support work that: Promotes clean and renewable energy in order to improve ecological health; Protects and improves human health by reducing exposure to environmental toxins; Improves water quality by reducing pollutants in surface and ground water; Promotes decisions on land use that protect and preserve ecological health; Or, encourages farming and ranching practices that benefit the environment and the health of communities.
Restrictions: The Foundation does not make grants to environmental education programs, animal welfare organizations, humane societies, nature centers, outdoor recreation programs or day care centers. Single-issue environmental requests are unlikely to receive support.
Geographic Focus: Minnesota, North Dakota, South Dakota
Contact: Kelly Kleppe, Grants Manager, (651) 379-2222; kkleppe@bushfoundation.org
Internet: http://www.bushfoundation.org/grants/ecological_health.asp
Sponsor: Bush Foundation
332 Minnesota Street, Suite East 900
St. Paul, MN 55101-1315

Bush Foundation Health & Human Services Grants   875
The foundation responds to a broad range of human services proposals. Proposals are reviewed on a case-by-case basis; applicant organizations take the lead in identifying promising solutions to the challenges faced by people who use their programs. In recent years, most grant dollars given to human services organizations have been for programs serving children, youth, and families. The foundation also considers program proposals that will improve the quality, accessibility, and efficiency of health care services in the region.
Requirements: The foundation is most interested in proposals that: (1) Promote opportunities for individuals and communities to become fully contributing members of society by supporting organizational projects that remove barriers to effective education, economic security and good health; (2) Improve the abilities of immigrant and refugee organizations, groups and individuals to obtain basic needs and rights, promote refugee and immigrant civic engagement and enhance their contribution to economic and cultural life; (3) The foundation will also consider proposals for comprehensive capital campaigns for building purchases, major building renovations and new construction to improve physical facilities. To be eligible for consideration, your organization must be a 501(c)3 nonprofit, tax-exempt organization, located in Minnesota, North Dakota or South Dakota, and able to demonstrate that you can take the lead in identifying promising solutions to challenges faced by people who use your programs. The two-step application process begins with a letter of inquiry. Guidelines for writing the letter of inquiry are on the information sheet which is available by contacting the sponsor or by download at the website.
Restrictions: The foundation does not make grants to: Individuals; Government agencies (except in special cases dictated by foundation priorities); Projects not benefiting the three-state region of Minnesota, North Dakota and South Dakota; Or, projects outside the United States. Download the Grant Restrictions file from the website for more details.

Geographic Focus: Minnesota, North Dakota, South Dakota
Date(s) Application is Due: Mar 1; Jul 1; Nov 1
Contact: Program Officer; (651) 227-0891; grants@bushfoundation.org
Internet: http://www.bushfoundation.org/grants/human_services.asp
Sponsor: Bush Foundation
332 Minnesota Street, Suite East 900
St. Paul, MN 55101-1315

Bush Foundation Leadership Fellowships   876
The program seeks accomplished, motivated individuals who are eager to prepare themselves for greater leadership responsibilities within their communities and professions. Applicants are invited to propose academic or self-designed learning experiences that will help them attain goals that they set for themselves. The program encourages applications that will expand fellows' experiences beyond the familiar to learning environments that might be inaccessible without a fellowship. A fellowship includes a monthly stipend, as well as reimbursement for travel expenses. The program also pays for 50 percent of the first $8,000 in instructional expenses, plus 80 percent of expenses after $8,000 up to a maximum amount. Instructional expense payments do not cover the costs of books, health insurance and student activity fees. The stipends paid to fellows pursuing paid internships depend on the salary, if any, paid by the intern employer. For paid internships or sabbaticals, the total of the stipend and salary paid by the intern or sabbatical employer may not exceed the fellow's level of compensation at the time of the grant.
Requirements: Fellows are required to pursue their fellowships on a full-time basis; however, they may design their programs to include two or three segments of full-time study interrupted by periods of full-time employment. Fellowship benefits are paid only during full-time study segments. Applications are welcome from qualified individuals who: are U.S. citizens or permanent residents; are 28 years or older at the application deadline; have lived or worked at least one continuous year immediately prior to the application deadline in Minnesota, North Dakota or South Dakota; are employed full time and have at least five years experience in any field, with strong evidence of competence and leadership abilities. Some experience in a policymaking or an administrative capacity is desirable. Work experience may include part-time and volunteer work; and, are not former Bush Leadership Fellows.
Restrictions: Fellowships are unlikely to be granted for full-time study plans built on academic programs designed primarily for part-time students; programs intended to meet the continuing education requirements for professional certification; completion of basic educational requirements for entry-level jobs; segments of degree programs that cannot be completed within or near the end of a fellowship period; or projects that might be more properly the subjects of grant proposals from organizations.
Geographic Focus: Minnesota
Date(s) Application is Due: Oct 13
Contact: Martha Lee; (651) 227-0891; fax (651) 297-6485; info@bushfoundation.org
Internet: http://www.bushfellows.org/leadership
Sponsor: Bush Foundation
332 Minnesota Street, Suite East 900
St. Paul, MN 55101-1315

Bush Foundation Medical Fellowships   877
The program was established to enhance community health care in Minnesota, North Dakota, South Dakota through the professional and personal development of selected physician leaders. Each year, the program awards approximately 13 fellowships that enable physicians to take a leave of absence from their practices to pursue professional and personal goals that address the health care needs of their communities. Their programs are self designed and self managed; they may last from three to 12 months. During this time, the fellowship provides a monthly stipend, as well as other financial aid.
Requirements: Applicants to the program must be: Physicians currently practicing in Minnesota, North Dakota or South Dakota; At least 35 years old and at least 10 years out of medical or osteopathic college; Able to state clearly their needs and opportunities for application of new skills and knowledge, both for the communities they serve and their own career development; and, able to explain how their programs will benefit an underserved population or need. All applications and references should be submitted via postal or express service. emailed applications and references must be followed by hard copy.
Restrictions: Previous Bush Medical Fellows may not reapply. If a physician (or his or her spouse/partner) is an elected official or public policymaker, the applicant may receive a grant for a degree-granting program only.
Geographic Focus: Minnesota, North Dakota, South Dakota
Date(s) Application is Due: Dec 1
Contact: Michael R. Wilcox, Program Director; (952) 442-2420 or (952) 758-4144; fax (952) 442-5841; bushmed@bushfoundation.org
Internet: http://www.bushfellows.org/medical
Sponsor: Bush Foundation
332 Minnesota Street, Suite East 900
St. Paul, MN 55101-1315

Bush Foundation Regional Arts Development Program II (RADP II) Grants   878
This program is an investment in the vitality, creative potential and long-term sustainability of mid-size arts and humanities organizations throughout Minnesota, North Dakota and South Dakota as a strategy towards the foundation's goal — to maintain a diverse, vibrant and sustainable environment for the arts and humanities. Grants through this program are long-term (10 years) and non-prescriptive in the use of grant funds.
Requirements: This program is open to organizations that meet all of the following criteria: Are based in Minnesota, North Dakota or South Dakota; Create, present or serve the performing, visual, media or literary arts or humanities; Have at least a five-year programming history; Have an annual operating budget larger than $250,000 but

no greater than $5 million during the three most recently completed fiscal years; Pay artists a reasonable salary or fee; Produce, present or develop year-round arts programs for the public, rather than sponsor one-time events; Have filed a final report on all previous Foundation grants, with the exception of capital grants; Have 501(c)3 tax-exempt status. The two-step application process begins with a preliminary proposal. The Foundation will consider preliminary proposals one time per year.
Restrictions: This program is not open to organizations that exist as a government agency, local arts council, public education institution, library or public broadcasting entity, such as a nonprofit radio or television station.
Geographic Focus: Minnesota, North Dakota, South Dakota
Date(s) Application is Due: Mar 1; Jul 1
Amount of Grant: Up to 100,000 USD
Contact: Program Officer; (651) 227-0891; info@bushfoundation.org
Internet: http://www.bushfoundation.org/grants/arts_humanities.asp#RADP
Sponsor: Bush Foundation
332 Minnesota Street, Suite East 900
St. Paul, MN 55101-1315

Business Bank of Nevada Community Grants 879
Business Bank of Nevada contributes financial assistance to nonprofit institutions and organizations that enhance the quality of life and promote public interest where the company conducts its business. The four main areas of giving include education, health and human services, community development, and arts and culture.
Requirements: Nevada 501(c)3 tax-exempt organizations in communities where the Bank has a presence. Community Grants are part of Business Bank of Nevada's grants program and must comply with the Bank's overall charitable funding guidelines. Requests must include the following information: a copy of the IRS letter of nonprofit tax-exempt 501C(3) status; a statement of purpose of the organization; the purpose and amount of the grant; the geographic area served; the project budget; a list of current board members with affiliations; a list of sources and amounts of other funding obtained, pledged, or requested; a copy of the latest audited or board approved financial statement.
Geographic Focus: Nevada
Amount of Grant: 250 - 2,500 USD
Contact: Paul Stowell, Public Relations Manager; (702) 952-4415; pstowell@bbnv.com
Internet: http://www.bbnv.com/charitable_giving.php
Sponsor: Business Bank of Nevada
6085 West Twain Avenue
Las Vegas, NV 89103

Business Wire Literacy Initiative 880
The program awards a grant each year to an organization that provides adult and child literacy and education programs in the five boroughs of New York City. Grants support new, expanding, and sustaining organizational programming. At the end of the grant year, the grant recipient must submit a written report documenting program achievements, lessons learned, and a detailed list of grant expenditures. Contact the office for application and guidelines.
Requirements: New York City 501(c)3 tax-exempt organizations not classified as private foundations are eligible.
Restrictions: Organizations that discriminate in hiring staff or providing services on the basis of race, religion, ethnicity, national origin, sex, or disability; and religious, political, or fraternal organizations are ineligible.
Geographic Focus: New York
Amount of Grant: 5,000 USD
Contact: Erin Stratford; (212) 752-9600; fax (212) 752-9698; bwgrants@businesswire.com
Internet: http://fdncenter.org/pnd/rfp/rfp_item.jhtml;jsessionid=KH5UNFX25SVYCP5QALTCGXD5AAAACI2F?id=110500002
Sponsor: Business Wire
40 East 52nd Street, 14th Floor
New York, NY 10022

Butler Manufacturing Company Foundation Grants 881
The foundation's purpose is to provide sustained financial assistance to worthy charitable, educational, and health and welfare programs in the United States and to enhance the quality of life in those communities where employees of Butler Manufacturing Company reside. The focus of the support includes youth programs, minority development, job training for the disadvantaged, neighborhoods, and support of nonresidential building programs using the company's products; scholarships for children of employees, and grants to colleges and universities serving locations where employees reside; and the community's principal arts organizations. Types of support include capital grants, general operating grants, employee matching gifts, program development grants, and scholarships to children of employees. Applications are considered quarterly.
Requirements: Applicants must be nonprofit institutions meeting the human needs of society in the greater Kansas City area and other communities where employees reside.
Geographic Focus: Missouri
Amount of Grant: 500 - 50,000 USD
Samples: Missouri Repertory Theatre (MO)—for project support, $5000; Kansas City Neighborhood Alliance (MO)—for operating support, $5000.
Contact: Administrator; (816) 968-3208; fax (816) 968-3211; blfay@butlermfg.com
Internet: http://www.butlermfg.com/faq/index.asp#Ans10
Sponsor: Butler Manufacturing Company Foundation
P.O. Box 419917
Kansas City, MO 64141-0917

Bydale Foundation Grants 882
The foundation emphasizes international understanding, public policy research, environmental quality, cultural programs, the law and civil rights, social services, higher education, and economics. Funding includes support for: conference/seminars, continuing support, general operating support, matching/challenging support, program development, publication, research, and seed money. An application form is not required. Submit an initial approach in the form of a letter or proposal.
Requirements: U.S. 501(c)3 nonprofits are eligible.
Geographic Focus: All States
Date(s) Application is Due: Nov 1
Contact: Milton Solomon, Vice President; (914) 428-3232; fax (914) 428-1660
Sponsor: Bydale Foundation
11 Martine Avenue
White Plains, NY 10606

Byerly Foundation Grants 883
The Foundation intends to respond to opportunities that address the following focus areas in order of priority: education; economic development; and community life. The Foundation will concentrate on the development and awarding of grants in education. Some of these will be major in scope, requiring significant planning and execution over a period of several years. Other grants will fund educational projects/programs of less complexity. The Foundation will assign a higher priority to programs that: offer creative responses to the community's most pressing needs and concerns; demonstrate cooperation or collaboration among (two or more) agencies or program providers; maximize the impact of modest grants as well as those of significant size; leverage other funding through the use of matching grants; and projects that will become self-sustaining without requiring ongoing funding from the Foundation.
Requirements: Organizations determined as charitable under Section 501(c)3 of the Internal Revenue Code, public entities or other charitable, educational or cultural organizations may submit proposals to the Foundation. All activities funded must benefit residents of the Hartsville area.
Restrictions: The foundation does not ordinarily fund: individuals; sectarian religious programs; debts or existing obligations; lobbying or political campaigns; technical or specialized research; intermediate organizations; fundraising; teams or events; and advertising or memorials.
Geographic Focus: South Carolina
Contact: Richard Puffer, Executive Director; (843) 383-2400; fax (843) 383-0661
Internet: http://www.byerlyfoundation.org/apply.html
Sponsor: Byerly Foundation
P.O. Drawer 1925
Hartsville, SC 29551

C.F. Adams Charitable Trust Grants 884
Charles Francis Adams created the C. F. Adams Charitable Trust in 1987. He was a direct descendant of John Adams, the second President of the United States, and John Quincy Adams, the sixth President. He was an avid sailor, dedicated civic leader and respected businessman. The primary objectives of the C.F. Adams Charitable Trust are to: encourage Downeast Maine communities to work together to preserve their local cultural heritage, improve their quality of life, adapt to a changing environment, and achieve a sustainable economy; promote innovative broad-based efforts to engage families in meeting the mental health needs of children in Massachusetts and to emphasize the extraordinary therapeutic benefits of the arts; and expand public awareness of the Adams family legacy and to preserve its unique heritage. Types of support include: general operating support; income development; management development; capacity building; and program development. Applicants should begin by forwarding a brief letter containing a detailed description of the project and the amount of funding requested. Recent grants have ranged from $750 to $75,000. The Trust currently commits up to $400,000 per year in Massachusetts to children's mental health and arts therapy programs that fall within the priorities outlined above.
Requirements: Giving is primarily in eastern Massachusetts and down east Maine.
Restrictions: No grants are given to individuals.
Geographic Focus: Maine, Massachusetts
Amount of Grant: 750 - 75,000 EUR
Contact: James H, Lowell, Trustee; (617) 422-0064; info@cfadamstrust.org
Internet: http://www.cfadamstrust.org/index.html
Sponsor: C.F. Adams Charitable Trust
141 Tremont Street, Suite 200
Boston, 02111-1209

CAA Millard Meiss Publication Fund Grants 885
In general, the purpose of the grant is to support presses in the publication of projects of the highest scholarly and intellectual merit that may not generate adequate financial return. Twice a year, CAA awards grants through the Millard Meiss Publication Fund to support book-length scholarly manuscripts in the history of art and related subjects that have been accepted by a publisher on their merits, but cannot be published in the most desirable form without a subsidy. Thanks to the generous bequest of the late Prof. Millard Meiss, CAA began awarding these publishing grants in 1975. Books eligible for a Meiss grant must currently be under contract with a publisher and be on a subject in the arts or art history. The deadlines for the receipt of applications are March 15 and September 15 of each year.
Requirements: Awards are open to publishers of all nations. Commercial, university, and museum presses are all eligible. CAA urges applicant presses to become CAA institutional members, but may waive this requirement upon request. Applications for publication grants will be considered only for book-length scholarly manuscripts in the history of art, visual studies, and related subjects that have been accepted by a publisher on their merits, but cannot be published in the most desirable form without a subsidy. Applications

are judged in relation to two criteria: (1) the quality of the project; and (2) the need for financial assistance. Although the quality of the manuscript is the sine qua non for a grant, an excellent manuscript may not be funded if it is financially self-supporting. The jury is particularly sympathetic to applications that propose enhancing the visual component of the study through the inclusion of color plates or an expanded component of black-and-white illustrations. Expenses generated by exceptional design requirements (maps, line drawings, charts, and tables) are also suitable for consideration. Permission and rental fees/reproduction rights, especially in cases where they are burdensome, are also appropriate. Within a calendar year, a press may submit the same manuscript for a Meiss Grant and a Wyeth Grant, but a book that wins one CAA publishing grant is ineligible to receive another CAA-administered grant and will be removed from consideration for the other grant. Publishers are encouraged to submit no more than two or three books for consideration in any one grant period, except in extraordinary circumstances.
Restrictions: While all periods and all areas of art history and visual studies may be considered, eligibility does not embrace excavation or other technical reports, articles, previously published works (including collections of previously published essays), or congress proceedings. A project that has been rejected for a grant may not be resubmitted to the same grant, except in a rare case where substantial revision has been made to the material, and the publisher has so noted in the application. At its discretion, the jury may decline to review the resubmitted application.
Geographic Focus: All States, All Countries
Date(s) Application is Due: Mar 15; Sep 15
Contact: Alex Gershuny; (212) 392-4424; fax (212) 627-2381; agershuny@collegeart.org
Internet: http://www.collegeart.org/meiss/
Sponsor: College Art Association
50 Broadway, 21st Floor
New York, NY 10004

Cable Positive's Tony Cox Community Fund Grants 886
Cable Positive's Tony Cox Community Fund is a national grant program that exists to encourage community-based AIDS Service Organizations (ASOs) and cable outlets to partner in joint community outreach efforts, or to produce and distribute new, locally focused HIV/AIDS-related programs and Public Service Announcements (PSAs). Grants are available up to $7,000 for 501(c)3 organizations, with special consideration given to AIDS Service Organizations (ASOs) and cable systems and producers partnering with ASOs. Eligible local community outreach projects include, but are not limited to: World AIDS Day and National HIV Testing Day events, AIDS Rides/Walks, other joint efforts between AIDS organizations and local cable operators, etc. Funding is also available for production costs of HIV/AIDS-related programs and PSAs.
Requirements: In order to be considered, you must partner with a cable system. To find your local cable partner go to www.cableyellowpages.com. If you do not have an existing relationship with your local cable system, contact their Public Affairs or Community Relations department. Successful applicants usually demonstrate the following tactics: PSA or program production; Community partnering-third party participation; Local government involvement; Media outreach (press kits & promotion); and, Marketing campaign. The following three funding levels are available: 1. $3,000-Alpha Cable System (up to 150,000 television households); 2. $5,000-Beta Cable System (150,001 - 300,000 television households); 3. $7,000- Gamma Cable System more than 300,000 television households).
Geographic Focus: Oklahoma, Oregon, Pennsylvania, Rhode Island, South Carolina, South Dakota, Tennessee, Texas, Utah, Vermont, Virginia, Washington, West Virginia, Wisconsin, Wyoming
Date(s) Application is Due: Sep 12
Amount of Grant: Up to 7,000 USD
Contact: Jennifer Medina, (212) 459-1504; Jennifer@cablepositive.org
Internet: http://www.cablepositive.org/programs-tonycox.html
Sponsor: Tony Cox Community Fund
1775 Broadway, Suite 443
New York, NY 10019

Cabot Corporation Foundation Grants 887
The goal of Cabot Corporation Foundation is to support community outreach objectives, with priority given to science and technology, education, and community and civic improvement efforts in the communities where the company has major facilities or operations. Types of support include capital grants, challenge grants, employee matching gifts, fellowships, general support, professorships, project support, research, scholarships, and seed money. The board meets in January, April, July, and October to consider requests. Applications must be received at least 30 days before a board meeting.
Requirements: The Foundation supports only nonprofit 501(c)3 tax-exempt organizations in areas of company operation. Modest support is available for international organizations that qualify under U.S. tax regulations.
Restrictions: Contributions are not made to individuals; fraternal, political, athletic or veterans organizations; religious institutions; capital and endowment campaigns; sponsorships of local groups/individuals to participate in regional, national, or international competitions, conferences or events; advertising sponsorships; or Tickets or tables at fundraising events.
Geographic Focus: Georgia, Illinois, Louisiana, Massachusetts, New Mexico, Pennsylvania, Texas, West Virginia, Belgium, Canada, China, Switzerland, United Kingdom
Amount of Grant: 2,000 - 75,000 USD
Contact: Cynthia L. Gullotti, Program Manager; (617) 345-0100; fax (617) 342-6312; Cynthia_Gullotti@cabot-corp.com or cabot.corporation.foundation@cabotcorp.com
Internet: http://www.cabot-corp.com/About-Cabot/Corporate-Giving
Sponsor: Cabot Corporation Foundation
Two Seaport Lane, Suite 1300
Boston, MA 02210-2019

Caddock Foundation Grants 888
The foundation supports nonprofit national and international Evangelical Christian religious organizations including churches and religious institutions, community groups, hospitals, international missions and ministries, religious centers and facilities, and youth organizations. Types of support include conferences/seminars, fellowships, and general operating support. Application must be made in writing and include a description of the organization and its objectives and the purpose of the grant. There are no application deadlines.
Restrictions: Grants are made to Evangelical Christian organizations. Grants are not made to individuals.
Geographic Focus: All States
Amount of Grant: 1,800 - 390,000 USD
Contact: Richard E. Caddock, Jr., Treasurer; (951) 683-5361
Sponsor: Caddock Foundation
1717 Chicago Avenue
Riverside, CA 92507

Cadence Design Systems Grants 889
The corporation awards grants to support global community initiatives through various avenues: cash grants, employee matching program, the Stars and Strikes fundraising program, in-kind donations of computer and IT equipment, and volunteer time. Programs vary from region to region. There are no application deadlines; requests are reviewed quarterly.
Requirements: K-12 education institutions in the greater Santa Clara Valley, California, area are eligible.
Geographic Focus: California
Amount of Grant: 1,000 - 25,000 USD
Contact: Community Relations; (408) 943-1234; fax (408) 428-5001; kwheeler@cadence.com
Internet: http://www.cadence.com/us/pages/default.aspx
Sponsor: Cadence Design Systems
2655 Seely Avenue, MS5A1
San Jose, CA 95134

Caesar Puff Foundation Grants 890
The Caesar Puff Foundation was established in Pennsylvania by a donation from Virginia A. Campana, and serves non-profit organizations in Ohio, Pennsylvania, and West Virginia. The Foundation's primary fields of interest include: animal welfare, Christian agencies and churches, food banks, higher education, public libraries, media/communications programs, and residential/custodial care units (including hospices). There are no specific application forms or deadlines, and applicants should contact the Foundation officer before sending a full application.
Restrictions: No grant support is offered to individuals.
Geographic Focus: Ohio, Pennsylvania, West Virginia
Date(s) Application is Due: Mar 14
Amount of Grant: 4,000 - 100,000 USD
Samples: Rostraver Public Library, Belle Vernon, Pennsylvania, $90,692; Family Hospice and Palliative Care, Pittsburgh, Pennsylvania, $4,000; Franciscan University of Steubenville, Steubenville, Steubenville, Ohio, $4,000.
Contact: Beverly Suchenek, (313) 222-6297
Sponsor: Caesar Puff Foundation
P.O. Box 75000, MC 3302
Detroit, MI 48275-3302

Caesars Foundation Grants 891
Founded as Harrah's Foundation in Nevada in 2002, giving is in the area of company operations. The foundation supports programs designed to help older individuals live longer, healthier, and more fulfilling lives; promote a safe and clean environment; and improve the quality of life in communities where Caesars operates. Fields of interest include: aging centers and services; Alzheimer's disease; developmentally disabled services; the environment; food distribution programs; food services; health care; patient services; higher education; hospitals; human services; mental health services; public affairs; public safety; nutrition; and youth services. Types of support being offered include: building and renovation; capital campaigns; continuing support; general operating support; program development; research; scholarship funding; and sponsorships. There are no specific deadlines or application forms. The foundation generally funds programs and projects of $10,000 or more.
Geographic Focus: Arizona, California, Illinois, Indiana, Iowa, Louisiana, Mississippi, Missouri, Nevada, New Jersey, North Carolina, Pennsylvania
Amount of Grant: Up to 250,000 USD
Contact: Lisa Mariani; (702) 880-4728 or (702) 407-6358; caesarsfoundation@caesars.com
Internet: http://www.caesarsfoundation.com/
Sponsor: Caesars Foundation
1 Caesars Palace Drive
Las Vegas, NV 89109-8969

Cailloux Foundation Grants 892
The foundation awards grants to nonprofit organizations in its areas of interest, including civic and cultural, education and youth, family and community service, and health and rehabilitation. Requests for specific projects or programs, technical assistance, and capital projects are considered; general operations are less common and usually small; challenge grants are awarded occasionally; and endowment grants are rare. The general policy of the foundation is not to make grants to an organization more than once within any 12-month period. Applicants must submit a letter of inquiry; instructions are available online.
Requirements: 501(c)3 tax-exempt organizations are eligible. Only grant proposals originating in Kerr and the surrounding communities (Gillespie, Bandera, Edwards, Real, and Kimble Counties) will be considered.

Restrictions: In general, grants are not made for fund raising events, professional conferences, membership drives, competition expenses, or programs/projects normally funded by governmental entities. The foundation does not fund church or seminary construction, or church related entities or activities other than ecumenically oriented projects/programs that otherwise meet foundation guidelines. Grants or loans to individuals are never made.
Geographic Focus: All States
Contact: Grants Administrator; (830) 895-5222; info@cailouxfoundation.org
Internet: http://www.cailouxfoundation.org/grant_guidelines.htm
Sponsor: Cailloux Foundation
P.O. Box 291276
Kerrville, TX 78029-1276

Caleb C. and Julia W. Dula Educational and Charitable Foundation Grants 893
Grants are given in the areas of the arts and humanities (particularly museums and libraries), child welfare, the aged, community funds and appeals, health care, religion, and historical preservation. Most groups receiving foundation grants have an established reputation in their particular field. There are no set requirements. Applicants should submit a letter that describes the organization, project, and amount requested.
Requirements: Grants are given to support projects of tax-exempt organizations.
Restrictions: Support is not available to individuals.
Geographic Focus: All States
Date(s) Application is Due: Apr 1; Oct 1
Amount of Grant: 5,000 - 50,000 USD
Contact: James F. Mauze, (314) 726-2800; fax (314) 863-3821; jfmauze@msn.com
Sponsor: Caleb C. and Julia W. Dula Educational and Charitable Foundation
112 S Hanley Road
Saint Louis, MO 63105

California Arts Council Arts and Accessibility Technical Assistance Grants 894
The purpose of the California Arts and Accessibility Technical Assistance Program is to enhance opportunities for participation in the arts by people with disabilities. This is done through small, but critical grants of $500 or $1000 to artists with disabilities and arts organizations. Applicants must describe a compelling need or rationale when requesting more than $500. Applicants are only allowed to apply for one grant per calendar year (January - December). Grants for artists with disabilities are intended to support those who are committed to advancing their work and their careers. Applications are encouraged from artists in all artistic disciplines. Artist grants are for specific projects that contribute directly to their growth and development as professionals.
Requirements: California non-profit 501(c)3 arts organizations are eligible to apply.
Restrictions: This program does not fund scholarships for pursuing undergraduate or graduate education. Artists may not receive more than one grant within a 12 month period. An applicant may not apply for funding for the same activity, project or program. An applicant may not apply for projects or activities that were previously funded under this grant. The Program does not fund: programs for children; administrative or indirect costs; construction; recreational programs; underwriting an event; construction or renovations; activities or programs outside of California; or start-up costs for a small business.
Geographic Focus: California
Amount of Grant: 500 - 1,000 USD
Contact: Craig Watson; (916) 322-6335; fax (916) 322-6575; cwatson@cac.ca.gov
Internet: http://www.cac.ca.gov/programs/accessibility-ta.php
Sponsor: California Arts Council
1300 I Street, Suite 930
Sacramento, CA 95814

California Arts Council Creating Public Value Grants 895
The California Arts Council's (CAC) Creating Public Value Program (CPV) is designed to promote a framework for thinking about the intrinsic and instrumental benefits of the arts; and to recognize that the resources artists, arts organizations, and others bring to a community play a key role in making a positive contribution to the individual and collective lives of all Californians. Through CPV, the CAC will partner with small California arts organizations in rural and underserved communities to support new or expanded projects to highlight the fact that the arts are of benefit to all Californians and are worthy of state and federal investment. CPV proposals must utilize the tools of the program identified as The Three Rs: relationships (building new or expanding existing partnerships); relevance (to audiences and community by expanding public participation); and, return on investment (through public awareness, promoting your organization's public value and social/economic impact to civic and political leaders, community supporters, audiences, and participants).
Requirements: CPV supports small arts organizations based in rural or underserved communities to implement new or expanded projects. The base of operations must be located within these communities. Applicants may apply under one of two categories: rural or underserved.
Restrictions: The Council does not fund: former grantee organizations not in compliance with CAC grant requirements (as stipulated in grant agreement); continuation of current work or previously funded CPV projects; non-arts organizations not involved in arts activities; for-profit organizations; other state agencies; programs not accessible to the public; projects with religious or sectarian purposes; organizations or activities that are part of the curricula base of schools, colleges, or universities; indirect costs of schools, colleges, or universities; trust or endowment funds; purchase of equipment, land, buildings, or construction (capital outlay or expenditures); out-of-state travel activities; hospitality or food costs; and expenses incurred before the starting or after the ending date of the grant.
Geographic Focus: California
Date(s) Application is Due: Feb 10
Amount of Grant: Up to 10,000 USD
Contact: Lucero Arellano; (916) 322-6338 or (916) 322-6555; larellano@cac.ca.gov
Internet: http://www.cac.ca.gov/programs/cpv.php
Sponsor: California Arts Council
1300 I Street, Suite 930
Sacramento, CA 95814

California Arts Council State-Local Partnership Grants 896
The State-Local Partnership Program fosters cultural development on the local level through a partnership between the California Arts Council and the designated local arts agency of each county. The Partnership provides grant opportunities for general operating support and technical assistance for county-designated local arts agencies. This partnership includes funding, cooperative activities, information exchange, and leadership enabling individuals, organizations, and communities to create, present, and preserve the arts of all cultures to enrich the quality of life for all Californians. The grant application and eligibility list is available online at the California Arts Council website. May 3 is the annual deadline for submitting grant applications.
Requirements: Local arts agencies in California are eligible to apply. A local arts agency is a nonprofit organization, or agency of city or county government, officially designated to provide financial support, services, and/or other programs to a variety of arts organizations, individual artists, and the community as a whole. Matching funds, at a level of 1:1, are mandatory. The required match may be from any public or private source. In some instances, in-kind donated services for which a market value can be determined may be used for up to 50% of the required match. Applicants must: be a current grantee through the State-Local Partnership Program; be designated by resolution of their county board of supervisors to serve as the local partner; meet the legal eligibility requirements of all California Arts Council program grantees listed under Requirements; and provide a public office staffed by, at the minimum, a part-time director/professional administrator to be accessible during normal business hours.
Geographic Focus: California
Date(s) Application is Due: May 3
Contact: Rob Lautz, (916) 324-6617 or (916) 322-6555; fax (916) 322-6575; rlautz@cac.ca.gov
Internet: http://www.cac.ca.gov/programs/slp201011.php
Sponsor: California Arts Council
1300 I Street, Suite 930
Sacramento, CA 95814

California Arts Council Statewide Networks Grants 897
The Statewide Networks Program (SN) is a California Arts Council (CAC) partnership with culturally specific, multicultural, and discipline-based statewide and regional arts networks and service organizations. Its goal is to promote the public value of the arts in communities by strengthening and expanding an organization's delivery of services to its constituents through communications, professional development opportunities, networking and arts advocacy. For this purpose, SN supports new approaches or expansions to an organization's work in the areas of organizational capacity and community building through advocacy, thus fostering an environment where all California cultures are represented. SN grants will be based on a ranking system and will range between $5,000 and $20,000.
Requirements: Statewide and regional culturally specific, multicultural, and discipline-based arts networks and service organizations are eligible to apply. Applicant organizations must have at least a two-year track record of developing its field and providing services to its constituent base (individual artists and/or arts organizations). All grant recipients must provide a dollar-for-dollar (1:1) match. The cash match may be from corporate or private contributions, local or federal government, or earned income. Other State funds cannot be used as a match. A combination of cash and in-kind contributions may be used to match CAC request.
Restrictions: SN requests cannot exceed an organization's total income based on its last completed budget. The Council does dot fund: previous grantee organizations that have not completed grant requirements (progress and final reports, final invoice, etc.); continuation of current work or previously funded SN projects; for-profit organizations; non-arts service organizations; indirect costs of schools, community colleges, colleges, or universities; trust or endowment funds; programs not accessible to the public; projects with religious or sectarian purposes; organizations or activities that are part of the curricula base of schools, colleges, or universities; purchase of equipment, land, buildings, or construction (capital outlay expenditures); out of state travel activities; hospitality or food costs; or expenses incurred before the starting or after the ending date of the contract.
Geographic Focus: California
Date(s) Application is Due: Mar 16
Amount of Grant: 5,000 - 20,000 USD
Contact: Lucero Arellano, SN Program Specialist; (916) 322-6338 or (916) 322-6555; fax (916) 322-6575; larellano@cac.ca.gov
Internet: http://www.cac.ca.gov/programs/sn.php
Sponsor: California Arts Council
1300 I Street, Suite 930
Sacramento, CA 95814

California Arts Council Technical Assistance Grants 898
The California Arts Council offers technical assistance in a variety of forms. Technical assistance funds are used to support development opportunities and activities that bring the Arts to the broadest constituency. The California Arts Council partners with national services organizations, individual consultants and other technical assistance providers to conduct organizational needs assessments and cultural resource surveys to assist in strengthening the infrastructure of local arts agencies. The California Arts Council has provided scholarships and/or travel assistance to conferences.
Requirements: California non-profit 501(c)3 arts organizations are eligible to apply.
Restrictions: This program does not fund scholarships for pursuing undergraduate or graduate education. Artists may not receive more than one grant within a 12 month period. An applicant may not apply for funding for the same activity, project or program.

An applicant may not apply for projects or activities that were previously funded under this grant. The Program does not fund: programs for children; administrative or indirect costs; construction; recreational programs; underwriting an event; construction or renovations; activities or programs outside of California; or start-up costs for a small business.
Geographic Focus: California
Amount of Grant: 500 - 1,000 USD
Contact: Lucy Mochizuki, Contract and Procurement Administration; (916) 322-6337 or (916) 322-6555; fax (916) 322-6575; lmochizuki@cac.ca.gov
Internet: http://www.cac.ca.gov/programs/ta.php
Sponsor: California Arts Council
1300 I Street, Suite 930
Sacramento, CA 95814

California Coastal Art and Poetry Contest 899
Entries must have a California coastal or marine theme. Winners will be selected in each of four grade-level categories (K-3rd, 4th-6th, 7th-9th, and 10th-12th). Winners in both art and poetry categories will receive a gift certificate for $100 to an art supply store. Winners and honorable mentions will receive tickets to Aquarium of the Pacific, courtesy of the Aquarium. Each sponsoring teacher will receive a gift certificate for $40 for educational materials. Guidelines and mandatory entry form are available online.
Requirements: Artwork must be original and should be no larger than 11-inch by 17-inch. Acceptable media are paint, pencil, markers, ink, crayon, chalk or pastel (fixed), and collage. All California students, kindergarten through 12th grades, are invited to participate.
Restrictions: Three-dimensional pieces or printouts of scanned art are not acceptable. All entries must include a completed contest entry form.
Geographic Focus: California
Date(s) Application is Due: Jan 30
Amount of Grant: 40 - 100 USD
Contact: Contest Administrator; (800) 262-7848; coast4u@coastal.ca.gov
Internet: http://www.coastal.ca.gov/publiced/poster/poster.html
Sponsor: California Coastal Commission
45 Fremont Street, Suite 2000
San Francisco, CA 94105

California Community Foundation Art Grants 900
The purpose of the arts program is to strengthen individual artists, as well as arts and cultural organizations as part of a vibrant cultural community. Priorities include support of: small to mid-size community-based arts organizations, theater companies and cultural institutions with operating budgets no larger than $2 million; efforts that increase the representation and participation of people of color, immigrants and low-income individuals and communities in the arts; and the needs of local emerging and mid-career artists through the Fellowships for Visual Artists.
Requirements: IRS 501(c)3 tax-exempt organizations (not private foundations) located within or serving primarily residents of Los Angeles County are eligible.
Restrictions: Grants will not be considered for annual campaigns or special fund-raising events; building campaigns, with the exception of community development grants; endowments; existing obligations; equipment, unless it is an integral part of an eligible project; incurring a debt liability; individuals, with the exception of arts and culture grants; routine operating expenses; sectarian purposes; or programs that will in turn make grants.
Geographic Focus: California
Date(s) Application is Due: Apr 30; Aug 31; Dec 31
Amount of Grant: 50,000 - 100,000 USD
Contact: Vera de Vera; (213) 413-4130, ext. 222; fax (213) 383-2046; vdevera@ccf-la.org
Internet: http://www.calfund.org/receive/arts.php
Sponsor: California Community Foundation
445 S Figueroa Street, Suite 3400
Los Angeles, CA 90071

California Community Foundation Health Care Grants 901
The foundation strives to ensure that low-income adults and children have access to regular, sustainable, affordable and quality health care. Priorities include: efforts that serve federally designated Medically Underserved Areas or Health Professional Shortage Areas, and that deliver comprehensive health services (e.g., medical, dental, mental health, etc.) to low-income and underserved populations; efforts that enroll people in health care coverage and connect them with a source of regular care; efforts that integrate strong prevention and early intervention strategies into their health services; and requests that clearly demonstrate knowledge of the health conditions that affect the specific population to be served.
Requirements: Tax-exempt organizations (not private foundations) located within or serving primarily residents of Los Angeles County are eligible.
Restrictions: Grants will not be considered for annual campaigns or special fund-raising events; building campaigns, with the exception of community development grants; endowments; existing obligations; equipment, unless it is an integral part of an eligible project; incurring a debt liability; individuals, with the exception of arts and culture grants; routine operating expenses; sectarian purposes; or programs that will in turn make grants.
Geographic Focus: California
Date(s) Application is Due: Feb 1; Jun 1; Oct 1
Amount of Grant: 100,000 - 1,000,000 USD
Contact: Tamu Jones; (213) 413-4130, ext. 250; fax (213) 383-2046; tjones@ccf-la.org
Internet: http://www.calfund.org/receive/health_care.php
Sponsor: California Community Foundation
445 S Figueroa Street, Suite 3400
Los Angeles, CA 90071

California Community Foundation Human Development Grants 902
The human development program aims to expand support services for special populations that enable them to acquire the resources and skills that will lead to self-sufficiency. Special populations include aging adults, developmentally and/or physically disabled children and adults, at-risk youth and foster youth. Priorities include: support services for aging adults, developmentally and/or physically disabled children and adults, at-risk youth and foster youth; and efforts that promote civic dialogue and advocate for critical issues affecting aging adults, developmentally and/or physically disabled children and adults, at-risk youth and foster youth.
Requirements: IRS 501(c)3 tax-exempt organizations (not private foundations) located within or serving primarily residents of Los Angeles County are eligible.
Restrictions: Grants will not be considered for annual campaigns or special fund-raising events; building campaigns, with the exception of community development grants; endowments; existing obligations; equipment, unless it is an integral part of an eligible project; incurring a debt liability; individuals, with the exception of arts and culture grants; routine operating expenses; sectarian purposes; or programs that will in turn make grants.
Geographic Focus: California
Date(s) Application is Due: Feb 1; Jun 1; Oct 1
Amount of Grant: 50,000 - 300,000 USD
Contact: Robert Lewis; (213) 413-4130, ext. 273; fax (213) 383-2046; rlewis@ccf-la.org
Internet: http://www.calfund.org/receive/human_development.php
Sponsor: California Community Foundation
445 S Figueroa Street, Suite 3400
Los Angeles, CA 90071

California Community Foundation Neighborhood Revitalization Grants 903
The foundation focuses on solutions that promote stable living environments for low-income families and individuals by providing them with safe, affordable places to live. It is also committed to providing low-income residents with a voice in decisions that affect their quality of life and access to neighborhood services. Priorities include support for: intermediaries that provide institutional capacity building and other technical assistance to nonprofit organizations that work in affordable housing and community development; strong organizations with a proven track record in affordable housing development for low-income and special needs people (their work includes new construction, preservation of affordable units and rehabilitation of existing units for underserved populations, including disabled, elderly and homeless people; policy development and advocacy efforts that promote increased affordable housing for low-income and special needs populations; and the community-building demonstration effort (applications will be limited to nonprofit organizations located in or providing services within the demonstration site).
Requirements: Tax-exempt organizations (not private foundations) located within or serving primarily residents of Los Angeles County are eligible.
Restrictions: Grants will not be considered for annual campaigns or special fund-raising events; building campaigns, with the exception of community development grants; endowments; existing obligations; equipment, unless it is an integral part of an eligible project; incurring a debt liability; individuals, with the exception of arts and culture grants; routine operating expenses; sectarian purposes; or programs that will in turn make grants.
Geographic Focus: California
Date(s) Application is Due: Feb 1; Jun 1; Oct 1
Amount of Grant: 50,000 - 200,000 USD
Contact: Yamileth Guevara; (213) 413-4130, ext. 211; fax (213) 383-2046; yguevara@ccf-la.org
Internet: http://www.calfund.org/receive/n_revitalization.php
Sponsor: California Community Foundation
445 S Figueroa Street, Suite 3400
Los Angeles, CA 90071

California Endowment Innovative Ideas Challenge Grants 904
California Endowment was founded in 1996 as a result of Blue Cross of California's creation of its for-profit subsidiary, WellPoint Health Networks. The Endowment is a private, California-focused, grant-making foundation that advocates for health and health equity. It does this by raising awareness, by expanding access to affordable, high-quality health care for underserved communities, and by investing in fundamental improvements for the health of all Californians. The Endowment supports the statewide Health Happens Here campaign and is currently engaged in a ten-year, one-billion dollar Building Healthy Communities plan. As a part of this strategy, the Endowment's Innovative Ideas Challenge (IIC) grant-making program solicits ideas that can be classified as disruptive innovations. A disruptive innovation is one that brings to market products and services that are more affordable and, ultimately, higher in quality. It improves a product or service in ways that the market does not expect, typically by being lower priced or being designed for a different set of consumers. Proposed ideas should address either emerging or persistent health-related issues impacting underserved California communities. Interested organizations should initially submit 500-word descriptions of their idea through the Endowment's online system. These are due by 5 p.m. Pacific time on May 1st (deadline dates may vary from year to year). Applicants whose ideas are accepted will be asked to submit a full proposal. Further guidance and clarification in the form of downloadable PDFs and an FAQ are available at the Endowment website.
Requirements: California 501(c)3 nonprofits may apply. Awarded projects will demonstrate the following characteristics: be transformative and disruptively innovative; benefit California's underserved individuals and communities; demonstrate cultural and linguistic competency; build partnerships and encourage collaboration; address persistent and/or emerging health challenges; demonstrate organizational capacity to carry out work; have measurable outcomes; and align with one of the 10 Outcomes and/or 4 Big Results of the Endowment's Building Healthy Communities plan.
Restrictions: Funds may not be used for the following purposes: to carry on propaganda or otherwise attempt to influence any legislation; to influence the outcome of any public election or to carry on any voter registration drive; to make any grant which does not comply

with Internal Revenue Code Section 4945(d)3 or 4; for fees for any services resulting in substantial personal benefit including membership, alumni dues, subscriptions, or tickets to events or dinners; for capital for building acquisition or renovation; for operating deficits or retirement of debt; for scholarships, fellowships, or grants to individuals; for government and public agencies; or for direct services or core/general operating support.
Geographic Focus: California
Date(s) Application is Due: May 1
Contact: Grants Administration Team; (213) 928-8646 or (818) 703-3311; fax (213) 928-8801; tcegrantreports@calendow.org or questions@calendow.org
Internet: http://www.calendow.org/grants/
Sponsor: California Endowment
1000 North Alameda Street
Los Angeles, CA 90012

California Fertilizer Foundation School Garden Grants 905
Through the garden program, CFF provides direct funding to California schools for garden projects. The gardens provide an opportunity for students, teachers and parents to truly 'grow' together. The annual program provides 24 grants for $1,200 each to schools throughout California (12 awarded twice a year). At the end of each year, winning schools can re-apply for a progress grant of $1,500 and a free agricultural field trip.
Requirements: All public and private elementary, middle and high schools in California are eligible to apply. Applications will be accepted at any time, and reviewed twice a year after January 15 and June 15. Grantees will be notified by March 1 and August 1 each year.
Geographic Focus: California
Date(s) Application is Due: Jan 15; Jun 15
Amount of Grant: 1,200 USD
Samples: Journey School, Aliso Viejo, California, $1,500.
Contact: Pam Emery, (916) 574-9744; fax (916) 574-9484; pame@healthyplants.org
Internet: http://www.calfertilizer.org/grant.htm
Sponsor: California Fertilizer Foundation
4460 Duckhorn Drive, Suite A
Sacramento, CA 95834

California Green Trees for The Golden State Grant 906
The goal of this program is to provide funding for urban forestry tree planting projects and up to three years of initial maintenance. Preference will be given to the planting of trees that provide greater air quality benefits and to urban forestry projects that provide greater energy conservation benefits. Eligible projects include planting on public lands to shade heat islands; in public parking lots and schools; to shade public buildings; in dedicated open space within city or community jurisdiction; and in city, community, or municipal developed parks.
Requirements: California cities, counties, districts, and 501(c)3 tax-exempt organizations are eligible. Applicants must enter into an agreement with CDF to complete the project and allow for periodic inspections.
Restrictions: Ineligible projects include tree planting projects on private and federal properties; tree planting on any common private areas; tree plantings on public open space lands that have not undergone an environmental review as mandated by the California Environmental Quality Act; entities with a current tree planting grant from California Department of Forestry and Fire Protection Proposition 12; tree planting projects in new residential subdivisions or other developments where the developer has paid a tree-planting fee to the city, county, or district; projects that plant trees that will eventually conflict with overhead utilities or ground located infrastructure; or installation of elaborate and expensive irrigation systems.
Geographic Focus: California
Amount of Grant: Up to 250,000 USD
Contact: Glenn Flamik; (916) 651-6423; Glenn.Flamik@fire.ca.gov
Internet: http://www.ufei.org/files/grantinfo/Prop12Planting-Grants.html
Sponsor: California Department of Forestry and Fire Protection
P.O. Box 944246
Sacramento, CA 94244-2460

California Pizza Kitchen Foundation Grants 907
The corporation gives back to each community it serves by providing financial support and in-kind contributions to programs that better the lives of children and youth. For each new restaurant opening, the foundation donates 100 percent of pizza sales on a designated day to a local charity.
Requirements: 501(c)3 tax-exempt organizations are eligible. Preference is given to organizations located in California Pizza Kitchen communities.
Geographic Focus: All States
Contact: Restaurant Support Center; (310) 342-5000; fax (310) 342-4640
Internet: http://www.cpk.com/company_information/community_relations.aspx
Sponsor: California Pizza Kitchen
6053 W Century Boulevard, #1100
Los Angeles, CA 90045-6430

California State Parks Restoration and Cleanup Grants 908
Each year, the foundation grants financial aid to parks projects. These projects range from adding land to existing parks, helping construct visitor centers and interpretive displays, to building trails, recycling bin installations, restoring wildlife habitat, and supporting family camping programs for underserved youth.
Requirements: California state parks, community parks, environmental nonprofit organizations, and schools are eligible.
Geographic Focus: California
Contact: Erika Pringsheim-Moore, (415) 258-9975; fax (415) 258-9930; moores302@earthlink.net
Internet: http://www.calparks.org/earth_day.php
Sponsor: California State Parks Foundation
800 College Avenue, P.O. Box 548
Kentfield, CA 94914

Callaway Foundation Grants 909
The Foundation awards grants for the benefit of projects and people in LaGrange and Troup County, Georgia. Areas of interest, include: arts and entertainment; elementary, higher, and secondary education; libraries; health and hospitals; community funds; care for the aged; community development; historic preservation; and church support. Types of support include annual campaigns, building construction/renovation, capital campaigns, continuing support, equipment acquisition, general operating support, land acquisition, and matching/challenge support. Preference is given to enduring construction projects and capital equipment. The Foundation Board meets four times per year in January, April, July, and October. Grant requests and applications are due the last day of the month preceding the meetings.
Requirements: IRS 501(c)3 nonprofit organizations in LaGrange and Troup County, Georgia are eligible to apply. Letters of request should briefly cover all aspects of the project, including complete financial planning and costs involved. Copies of budgets and current financial statements should also be included. An application form is available at the Foundation's website.
Restrictions: Grants are usually not made for loans, debt retirement, endowment or operating expenses. Requests from churches located outside Troup County, Georgia, are not considered.
Geographic Focus: Georgia
Date(s) Application is Due: Mar 31; Jun 30; Sep 30; Dec 31
Amount of Grant: 1,000 - 4,000,000 USD
Contact: H. Speer Burdette; (706) 884-7348; hsburdette@callaway-foundation.org
Internet: http://www.callawayfoundation.org/grant_policies.php
Sponsor: Callaway Foundation
209 Broome Street, P.O. Box 790
La Grange, GA 30241

Callaway Golf Company Foundation Grants 910
The foundation strives to support initiatives in communities where Callaway Golf Company employees live and work. The geographic area of focus is primarily North San Diego County, California. The foundation offers support in the form of: matching funds, special projects, and general operating budgets. Areas of interest include but are not limited to: children and youth; biomedical research, with a special interest in the field of cancer; golf; education; boys & girls clubs of America; drug prevention; American Red Cross; housing; veterans; youth programs; food banks; social services; emergency programs; scholarship program for dependents of Callaway Golf employees; grants for training, competition and equipment needs. The foundation does not require the completion of a formal application document but requests a description of the organization and its history, the project at issue including goals and time lines, the qualifications of the leadership personnel involved in the project, and a detailed project budget. Grants are awarded semiannually. The Callaway Golf Company Foundation does not accept unsolicited requests for grants.
Requirements: IRS 501(c)3 nonprofit organizations in California are eligible.
Restrictions: The foundation will not fund applicants that illegally discriminate on the basis of gender, race, color, religion, national origin, ancestry, age, marital status, medical condition, or physical disability, either in the services they provide or in the hiring of staff; or promote political or particular religious doctrines.
Geographic Focus: California
Amount of Grant: 500 - 10,000 USD
Contact: Paul Thompson; (760) 930-8686; cgcfoundation@callawaygolf.com
Internet: http://www.callawaygolf.com/Global/en-US/Corporate/CallawayGolfFoundation.html
Sponsor: Callaway Golf Company Foundation
2180 Rutherford Road
Carlsbad, CA 92008-7328

Callaway Golf Company Foundation Violence Prevention Grants 911
The foundation gives primarily in San Diego, CA, to nonprofit organizations that support people in need in the areas of youth, gang, and family violence prevention. Funded projects have included counseling for families to find alternative ways to resolve debates. Applications are considered twice annually. An applicant's initial approach should be in writing.
Date(s) Application is Due: Feb 1; May 1; Aug 1
Amount of Grant: 5,000 - 10,000 USD
Contact: Paul Thompson, Executive Director; (760) 930-8686; fax (760) 930-5021; cgc_foundation@callawaygolf.com
Internet: http://www.callawaygolf.com/en/corporate.aspx?pid=community
Sponsor: Callaway Golf Company Foundation
2180 Rutherford Road
Carlsbad, CA 92008-7328

Cal Ripken Sr. Foundation Grants 912
Cal Ripken Sr. Foundation provides grants to eligible youth organizations, schools, Boys and Girls Clubs, local governments and community non-profits groups that meet our eligibility requirements, in order to support the growth of youth baseball and softball, as well as promote character education. Cal Ripken Sr. Foundation awards grants for multiple initiatives including: baseball/softball equipment grants to organizations and schools that serve disadvantaged children; public youth ball field renovation matching grants to local government departments of parks and recreation, nonprofit organizations, and/or established community baseball or softball leagues; baseball/softball league development or expansion grants in the form of cash grants to community recreation programs run by local governments,

Boys and Girls Clubs, public schools with after school and/or summer programming, and/or established community baseball for baseball/softball league development and expansion; Quickball grants to grow baseball and softball at a grassroots level through the game of Quickball; funding grants for baseball/softball programs to help Boys and Girls Clubs hire baseball/softball activity specialists, purchase baseball/softball equipment and apparel, and finance related costs such as league dues, tournament fees and playing field rental fees; camp sponsorship grants to support chosen high school student-athletes (students entering sophomore or junior years who participate on a baseball/softball team in a public school system) to attend a baseball camp to develop their skills and networks; and tournament sponsorship grants to provide selected youth teams, especially those that serve under-resourced populations, an opportunity to attend a baseball/softball tournament.
Geographic Focus: All States
Contact: Steve Salem; (410) 823-0808; fax (410) 823-0850; info@ripkenfoundation.org
Internet: http://www.ripkenfoundation.org/
Sponsor: Cal Ripken Sr. Foundation
1427 Clarkview Road, Suite 100
Baltimore, MD 21209

Cambridge Community Foundation Grants 913
Cambridge Community Foundation is dedicated to improving the quality of life for the residents of Cambridge, Massachusetts. The CCF serves Cambridge through our support of nonprofit community organizations, by making direct financial grants, providing technical assistance, and forming partnerships among organizations to coordinate services, address gaps, and highlight emerging issues. CCF primarily supports work in: early childhood services; youth service; senior services; community services; emergency outreach; arts; and the environment. See, the Foundations website http://www.cambridgecf.org/grant.html to download Proposal Summary Sheets, and additional guidelines.
Requirements: To be eligible to apply, the agency must be tax-exempt 501(c)3 under the IRS code), and the program must serve the people of Cambridge, Massachusetts.
Restrictions: Support is not provided to municipal, state, or federal agencies. Grants for individuals, scholarships, research studies, conferences, films, capital fund drives, or loans are not eligible.
Geographic Focus: Massachusetts
Date(s) Application is Due: Apr 1; Oct 1
Amount of Grant: 500 - 60,000 USD
Contact: Robert S. Hurlbut, Jr., Executive Director; (617) 576-9966; fax (617) 876-8187; RHurlbut@CambridgeCF.org or info@cambridgecf.org
Internet: http://www.cambridgecf.org
Sponsor: Cambridge Community Foundation
99 Bishop Richard Allen Drive
Cambridge, MA 02139

Camp-Younts Foundation Grants 914
The foundation supports social services, higher and secondary education, youth organizations, Protestant religion, and hospitals and other health organizations in Florida, Georgia, North Carolina, and Virginia. Applicants should submit a letter describing the program, a copy of the 501(c)3 tax-determination letter, listing of board members, and an audited budget for the previous year.
Requirements: Nonprofit organizations in Florida, Georgia, North Carolina, and Virginia may request grant support.
Geographic Focus: Florida, Georgia, North Carolina, Virginia
Date(s) Application is Due: Sep 1
Amount of Grant: 1,000 - 55,000 USD
Contact: Bobby Worrell, Executive Director; (757) 562-3439
Sponsor: Camp-Younts Foundation
P.O. Box 4655
Atlanta, GA 30302

Campbell Hoffman Foundation Grants 915
The mission of the Campbell Hoffman Foundation is to promote and fund efforts to increase access to comprehensive health care for underserved and uninsured populations in the Northern Virginia region. Northern Virginia is defined as the counties of Arlington, Fairfax, Loudoun and Prince William and the cities of Alexandria, Falls Church, Fairfax, Manassas and Manassas Park. A letter of Inquiry should be submitted, as the initial approach, when approaching the Foundation for funding. Upon review, if the letter of inquiry meets with Foundations criteria, the applicant will be asked to submit a proposal; guidelines will be provided to them when the proposal is requested.
Requirements: Eligible organizations include nonprofit 501(c)3 organizations, government agencies and faith-based organizations. Eligible organizations must be both located in and serve the target populations of Northern Virginia.
Restrictions: The Foundation will not provide funding for capital campaigns, endowment campaigns, special events and/or conferences (including travel to and participation in same), emergency funding, loans, capital projects (including but not limited to building, construction or renovation), land purchases, lawsuits, films, video or publications. The Foundation may choose to provide general operating support.
Geographic Focus: Virginia
Contact: Lyn S. Hainge; (703) 749-1794; fax (703) 442-0846; lhainge@campbellhoffman.org
Internet: http://www.campbellhoffman.org/applicants/default.aspx
Sponsor: Campbell Hoffman Foundation
1420 Spring Hill Road, Suite 600
McLean, VA 22102

Campbell Soup Foundation Grants 916
Since 1953, the Campbell Soup Foundation has provided financial support to local champions that inspire positive change in communities throughout the United States where Campbell Soup Company employees live and work. The Foundation places particular emphasis on Camden, New Jersey, birthplace of Campbell's flagship soup business and world headquarters. The Campbell Soup Foundation focuses its giving on four key areas: hunger relief-supporting food bank organizations in the communities of operation; wellness-addressing the health of consumers in the communities where they live; education-leveraging the Campbell brand portfolio to support educational programs; community revitalization-enhancing the quality of life in the communities that Campbell operates in. The Foundation only considers applications that meet the following criteria: the proposal must fit one of the key focus areas; the organization must display strong and effective leadership; the proposed plan must be clear and compelling, with measurable and sustainable commitments expressed in terms of real results; the proposed activity must be sufficiently visible to leverage additional support from other funding sources. There is no formal deadline. Proposals are accepted and reviewed on a rolling basis.
Requirements: The Foundation limits grants to nonprofit organizations which are tax-exempt under Section 501(c)3 of the Internal Revenue Code. Grants are made to institutions that serve: Camden, New Jersey; Davis, California; Sacramento, California; Stockton, California; Bloomfield, Connecticut; Norwalk, Connecticut; Lakeland, Florida; Downers Grove, Illinois; Marshall, Michigan; Maxton, North Carolina; Camden, New Jersey; South Plainfield, New Jersey; Napoleon, Ohio; Wauseon, Ohio; Willard, Ohio; Denver, Pennsylvania; Downingtown, Pennsylvania; Aiken, South Carolina; Paris, Texas; Richmond, Utah; Everett, Washington; Milwaukee, Wisconsin. Organizations do not need to be located in these communities in order to qualify for funding. However, the programs to be funded must serve these communities. Proposals must be submitted electronically via email to community_relations@campbellsoup.com. Proposals should be prepared in a concise, narrative form, without extensive documentation.
Restrictions: Grants are not made to the following: organizations that are based outside the United States and its territories; individuals; organizations that limit their services to members of one religious group or whose services propagate religious faith or creed; political organizations and those having the primary purpose of influencing legislation of/or promoting a particular ideological point of view; units of government; events and sponsorships; sports related events, activities and sponsorships. Organizations may not submit the same or similar proposals more than once in a Foundation fiscal year (July 1 - June 30). Proposals submitted via regular mail will not be reviewed.
Geographic Focus: Connecticut, Florida, Illinois, Michigan, New Jersey, North Carolina, Ohio, Pennsylvania, South Carolina, Texas, Utah, Washington, Wisconsin
Contact: Grant Administrator; (856) 342-6423 or (800) 257-8443; fax (856) 541-8185; community_relations@campbellsoup.com
Internet: http://www.campbellsoupcompany.com/community_center.asp
Sponsor: Campbell Soup Foundation
1 Campbell Place
Camden, NJ 08103-1701

Canada-U.S. Fulbright Mid-Career Professional Program Grants 917
The Fulbright Mid-Career Professional Program offers grants of up to ten months to executives of the Government of Canada to explore various aspects of the vital Canada-U.S. relationship while pursuing a graduate degree at an American university. This award, which carries a value of up to US$75,000, is intended to provide mid-career executives who have been recognized for their exceptional leadership potential with an opportunity for mid-career development and personal and professional growth.
Geographic Focus: All States, Canada
Date(s) Application is Due: Oct 30
Amount of Grant: Up to 75,000 USD
Contact: Jennifer Regan, Senior Program Officer; (613) 688-5517 or (613) 688-5540; fax (613) 237-2029; jregan@fulbright.ca
Internet: http://www.fulbright.ca/en/award.asp
Sponsor: Foundation for Educational Exchange between Canada and the USA
350 Albert Street, Suite 2015
Ottawa, ON K1R 1A4 Canada

Canadian Optometric Education Trust Fund Grants 918
Since 1980, the COETF has received applications and awarded funding to projects covering a vast and varied scope of research. The fund supports quality vision and eye care services for Canadians of all ages. Projects have been funded for improving optometrical education, professional development, and research. The Awards Committee meets annually (generally in March) to consider applications. The deadline for applications is typically in early February. Interested applicants should secure forms from the fund.
Restrictions: The fund customarily does not provide support for travel to and from sites where the results of a project are intended to be presented, i.e., a symposium or continuing education seminar.
Geographic Focus: All States, Canada
Amount of Grant: 3,000 - 5,000 CAD
Contact: Glenn Campbell, Executive Director; (888) 263-4676 or (613) 235-7924; fax (613) 235-2025; gcampbell@opto.ca or info@opto.ca
Internet: http://www.opto.ca/en/public/03_optometry/03_06_coetf.asp#apply
Sponsor: Canadian Optometric Education Trust Fund
234 Argyle Avenue
Ottawa, ON K2P 1B9 Canada

Cape Branch Foundation Grants 919
The foundation awards grants to New Jersey nonprofit organizations in its areas of interest, including education and secondary education, natural resource conservation, and museums. Types of support include general operating support, building construction/renovation, land acquisition, scholarship funds, and research grants. There are no application forms or deadlines. A letter should be submitted outlining purpose and amount of request.
Requirements: New Jersey nonprofit organization are eligible.
Geographic Focus: New Jersey
Amount of Grant: 1,000 - 329,268 USD
Contact: Dorothy Frank, (609) 987-0300; fax (609) 452-1024
Sponsor: Cape Branch Foundation
P.O. Box 86
Oldwick, NJ 08858

Capital City Bank Group Foundation Grants 920
The foundation works with organizations throughout the Capital City Bank Group service area by donating valuable funds for special projects and community needs. The foundation supports organizations involved with arts and culture, education, health, youth development, human services, and community development. A committee of Capital City Bank Group Directors and Associates review requests for funds during two application periods annually. The Foundation is managed by a board of directors who work on a voluntary, unpaid basis.
Requirements: Alabama, Florida, and Georgia 501(c)3 nonprofit organizations are eligible.
Restrictions: The foundation does not consider requests of the following nature: advertising, association memberships, athletic team or athletic event sponsorships, beauty contest sponsorships, fund-raising event sponsorships, professional telephone sales solicitations, tickets to attend community functions and fundraisers, those with religious or political affiliation, and those being located out of our market area.
Geographic Focus: Alabama, Florida, Georgia
Contact: Holli Fulmer, (850) 402-8521 or (904) 224-1171
Internet: https://www.ccbg.com/index.cfm?show=CCBG-Foundation
Sponsor: Capital City Bank Group Foundation
P.O. Box 11248
Tallahassee, FL 32302

Capital Region Community Foundation Grants 921
The foundation awards grants to eligible Michigan nonprofit organizations in its areas of interest, including education, environment, health care, human services, humanities, and public benefit. Types of support include capital grants, program development grants, and seed money grants. Grants are awarded for one year and are nonrenewable. Guidelines and application are available on-line. Application must be made on-line. Program deadlines vary: Youth Fund grant deadline is January 31; Eaton County Community Foundation grant deadline is March 1; and Capital Region Community Foundation grant deadline is April 1.
Requirements: Michigan 501(c)3 tax-exempt organizations in Clinton, Eaton, and Ingham Counties are eligible. Churches in the tri-county area are eligible for programs including food banks, after-school programs, programs assisting the needy, and charitable work benefiting the community, there grant applications are due June 1st.
Restrictions: Grants do not support sectarian or religious programs; individuals; international organizations; endowment funds; administrative costs of fund raising campaigns; annual meetings; routine operating expenses; or existing obligations, debts, or liabilities.
Geographic Focus: Michigan
Date(s) Application is Due: Jan 31; Mar 1; Apr 1
Amount of Grant: 2,000 - 25,000 USD
Contact: Brad Patterson; (517) 272-2870; fax (517) 272-2871; bpatterson@crcfoundation.org
Internet: http://crcfoundation.org/grantmaking/grants
Sponsor: Capital Region Community Foundation
6035 Executive Drive, Suite 104
Lansing, MI 48901

Captain Planet Foundation Grants 922
The foundation makes grants to nonprofits for hands-on environmental projects for children. The foundation makes small, one-year grants for projects that help kids understand environmental issues. To be eligible, projects must focus on hands-on activities; involve children and youth ages six through 18; promote group interaction and cooperation; help young people develop planning and problem-solving skills; include adult supervision; and commit to follow-up with the foundation. Types of support include matching funds, pilot projects, program development, and seed money. Proposals must include a description of the project, including the number of children involved; a line-item budget; organizational information; project start date and continuation plans; and plans for project evaluation and monitoring. Applicants must use the foundation's online application form.
Requirements: Eligible applicants must have 501 status (this includes most schools and non-profit organizations).
Restrictions: Grants do not support the purchase of real estate; endowments; general operations expenses; capital or building campaigns; t-shirts and other promotional items; expensive equipment used by only a small number of children; salaries; or transportation costs.
Geographic Focus: All States
Date(s) Application is Due: Mar 31; Jun 30; Sep 30; Dec 31
Contact: Taryn Murphy, Program Director; (404) 522-4215; tarynm@turnerfoundation.org or captain.planet.foundation@turner.com
Internet: http://www.captainplanetfdn.org/aboutUs.html
Sponsor: Captain Planet Foundation
133 Luckie Street, 2nd Floor
Atlanta, GA 30303

Cardinal Health Foundation Grants 923
The foundation's mission is to support employees' interests and to advance and fund programs that improve access to and delivery of health care services in CardinalHealth communities. Additional areas of interest include arts and culture, education, and youth development. Application forms are not required; submit a project summary of no more than three pages. Proposals are by invitation.
Requirements: 501(c)3 organizations in CardinalHealth communities are eligible.
Restrictions: Capital campaigns, endowments, religious organizations or sectarian programs for religious purposes, veteran, labor, and political organizations or campaigns, fraternal, athletic or social clubs, requests for loans or debt retirements, individual endeavors or needs, organizations that discriminate on the basis of age, disability, religion, ethnic origin, gender, or sexual orientation, or organizations with divisive or litigious public agendas will not be supported.
Geographic Focus: All States
Contact: Debra Hadley, Executive Director; (614) 757-7450; cardinalfoundation@cardinal.com or communityrelations@cardinalhealth.com
Internet: http://www.cardinal.com/us/en/community/
Sponsor: Cardinal Health Foundation
7000 Cardinal Place
Dublin, OH 43017

CarEth Foundation Grants 924
CarEth Foundation seeks to promote a compassionate world of enduring and just peace with social, economic, and political equality for all. CarEth Foundation seeks an open and cooperative working relationship with its grantees to further their mission and goals. The Foundation networks and cooperates with funders to strengthen effective and broad-based peace and justice grantmaking. Priority funding is given to civil and human rights, education, and employment issues. Types of support include general and operating support, matching and challenge support, and program development. A list of previously funded organizations is available at the Foundation website.
Requirements: Organizations must first contact the Foundation before submitting a proposal.
Geographic Focus: California, District of Columbia, New York, North Carolina
Contact: Grants Manager; (413) 256-0349; fax (413) 256-3536; careth@funder.org
Internet: http://careth.org/index.html
Sponsor: CarEth Foundation
P.O. Box 586
Warren, RI 02885

Cargill Citizenship Fund-Corporate Giving Grants 925
Cargill's purpose is to be the global leader in nourishing people. Cargill measures their performance through engaged employees, satisfied customers, profitable growth and enriched communities. Corporate giving is one important way Cargill works to enrich the 1,000 communities where they conduct business. With 149,000 employees in 63 countries, Cargill people are working everyday to nourish the lives of those around us. The Cargill Citizenship Fund provides strategic grants to organizations serving communities where Cargill has a presence. The Fund provides direct grants for regional, national and global partnerships and provides matching grants for selected local projects supported by our businesses. Cargill seeks to build sustainable communities by focusing our human and financial resources in three areas: Nutrition and Health-support for programs and projects that address long-term solutions to hunger, increase access to health education and/or basic health care in developing and emerging countries, and improve youth nutrition and wellness; Education-support for innovative programs that improve academic achievement, develop logic and thinking skills, promote leadership development, and/or increase access to education for socio-economically disadvantaged children. Cargill also supports mutually beneficial partnerships with selected higher education institutions; Environment-support for projects that protect and improve accessibility to water resources; promote biodiversity conservation in agricultural areas; and educate children about conservation and/or proper sanitation. Application and additional guidelines are available at: http://www.cargill.com/wcm/groups/public/@ccom/documents/document/doc-giving-funding-app.pdf
Requirements: Applicants must have 501(c)3 status or the equivalent; and they must be located in communities where Cargill has a business presence. Only under special circumstances will Cargill consider general operating or capital support. Organizations requesting capital or operating support should contact the Cargill Citizenship Fund staff before applying.
Restrictions: Cargill will not fund: organizations without 501(c)3 status or the equivalent; organizations that do not serve communities where Cargill has a business presence; individuals or groups seeking support for research, planning, personal needs or travel; public service or political campaigns; lobbying, political or fraternal activities; benefit dinners or tickets to the same; fundraising campaigns, walk-a-thons, or promotions to eliminate or control; specific diseases; athletic scholarships; advertising or event sponsorships; religious groups for religious purposes; publications, audio-visual productions or special broadcasts; endowments; medical equipment.
Geographic Focus: All States, Albania, Algeria, Andorra, Angola, Armenia, Austria, Azerbaijan, Belarus, Belgium, Benin, Bosnia & Herzegovina, Botswana, Bulgaria, Burkina Faso, Burundi, Cameroon, Cape Verde, Central African Republic, Chad, Comoros, Congo, Congo, Democratic Republic of, Cote d' Ivoire (Ivory Coast), Croatia, Cyprus, Czech Republic, Denmark, Djibouti, Egypt, Equatorial Guinea, Eritrea, Estonia, Ethiopia, Finland, France, Gabon, Gambia, Georgia, Germany, Ghana, Greece, Guinea, Guinea-Bissau, Hungary, Iceland, Ireland, Italy, Kenya, Kosovo, Latvia, Lesotho, Liberia, Libya, Liechtenstein, Lithuania, Luxembourg, Macedonia, Madagascar, Malawi, Mali, Malta, Mauritania, Mauritius, Moldova, Monaco, Montenegro, Morocco, Mozambique, Namibia, Niger, Nigeria, Norway, Poland, Portugal, Romania, Russia, Rwanda, San Marino, Sao Tome & Principe, Senegal, Serbia, Seychelles, Sierra Leone, Slovakia, Slovenia, Somalia, South Africa, Spain, Sudan, Swaziland, Sweden, Switzerland, The Netherlands, Turkey, Ukraine, United Kingdom, Vatican City

Amount of Grant: 500 - 100,000 USD
Contact: Stacey Smida, Grants Administrator; (952) 742-4311; stacey_smida@cargill.com
Internet: http://www.cargill.com/wcm/groups/public/@ccom/documents/document/doc-giving-funding-app.pdf
Sponsor: Cargill Corporation
P.O. Box 5650
Minneapolis, MN 55440-5650

Caring Foundation Grants 926
Blue Cross and Blue Shield of Alabama, Incorporated sponsors The Caring Foundation. The Foundation was established in 1990 in Alabama and focuses it's support primarily in the region. The foundation supports organizations involved with education, federated giving programs, health, hospitals, safety education, children and youth services. The Foundation offers support of a general/operating nature as well, as program development.
Requirements: There is no formal application form, submit a proposal containing the following: name, address and phone number of organization; brief history of organization and description of its mission; detailed description of project and amount of funding requested.
Restrictions: Grants aren't available to individuals, or for capital campaigns.
Geographic Focus: Alabama
Amount of Grant: 10,000 - 900,000 USD
Contact: James M. Brown, Senior Vice President; (205) 220-2500
Sponsor: Caring Foundation
450 Riverchase Parkway, East
Birmingham, AL 35244-2858

Carl and Eloise Pohlad Family Foundation Grants 927
The mission of the foundation is to improve the lives of economically disadvantaged children and youth and participate in projects that positively impact the quality of life in the Minneapolis/St.Paul area. The foundation awards grants to Minnesota nonprofits in its areas of interest, including arts and culture, economic development, education, environment, health care, housing, and social services. Types of support include general operating support, continuing support, capital campaigns, building construction/renovation, endowments, emergency funds, scholarship funds, and research.
Requirements: Minnesota nonprofits are eligible.
Restrictions: Individuals are not eligible. Capital request are considered only for physical plant improvements or significant technology investments. Capital requests for housing construction, endowment, program start-up or expansion or to establish operating reserves are not considered.
Geographic Focus: Minnesota
Amount of Grant: Up to 32,000,000 USD
Contact: Josette Elstad; (612) 661-3910; fax (612) 661-3715; info@pohladfamilygiving.org
Internet: http://www.pohladfamilyfoundation.org/pff/pff_default.aspx
Sponsor: Carl and Eloise Pohlad Family Foundation
60 South Sixth Street, Suite 3900
Minneapolis, MN 55402

Carl B. and Florence E. King Foundation Grants 928
The lives of Carl B. and Florence E. King were marked by warmth, compassion, and generosity. As they prospered, they believed in giving back. With gracious benevolence, they dedicated themselves to the betterment of individuals, communities, and society through informed giving. Today, the Carl B. and Florence E. King Foundation honors their memory, continues their tradition, and builds upon their vision. The Foundation is principally interested in the following areas: aging population; arts, culture, and history; children and youth; education; indigent; and to build non-profit capacity. The Foundation awards grants twice each year. Applicants must first submit a letter of inquiry, and then a full grant proposal only upon invitation.
Requirements: The King Foundation distributes grants only to entities that serve residents of Arkansas and Texas. Within Texas, the Foundation is principally interested in the Dallas-Fort Worth area and West Texas. Within Arkansas, the foundation focuses on the southern and eastern portions of the state. Applicants must also have a letter of determination from the Internal Revenue Service acknowledging tax-exempt status as described in Section 501(c)3 of the Internal Revenue Code.
Restrictions: The Foundation does not award grants: to individuals; to organizations or programs that do not serve residents of our geographic focus areas in Texas or Arkansas; to organizations that are not tax exempt; for general operating support, annual fund drives, or funds to offset operating losses (including retiring debt incurred to cover operating losses); to create endowments; toward balls, events, or galas benefiting charitable organizations; to efforts to treat or cure a single disease or condition; to church or seminary construction, or religious programs (other than social service-based initiatives); toward the cost of hosting or attending professional conferences or symposia, or participating in amateur sports competitions or similar activities.
Geographic Focus: Arkansas, Texas
Date(s) Application is Due: Jun 15; Dec 15
Amount of Grant: Up to 100,000 USD
Contact: Michelle D. Monse, President; (214) 750-1884; fax (214) 750-1651; michellemonse@kingfoundation.com
Internet: http://www.kingfoundation.com/Grants/King-Foundation-Grants.aspx
Sponsor: Carl B. and Florence E. King Foundation
2929 Carlisle Street, Suite 222
Dallas, TX 75204

Carl C. Icahn Foundation Grants 929
The foundation awards grants to New York and New Jersey nonprofits in the areas of education, arts and culture, health care, child welfare, and Jewish temples and organizations. Types of support include general operating support, annual campaigns, building construction/renovation, and matching funds. There are no application deadlines or forms.
Requirements: New York and New Jersey nonprofits are eligible to apply.
Restrictions: No grants are provided to individuals.
Geographic Focus: New Jersey, New York
Amount of Grant: 500 - 1,600,000 USD
Contact: Gail Golden-Icahn, Vice Presicent; (212) 702-4300; fax (212) 750-5815
Sponsor: Carl C. Icahn Foundation
767 5th Avenue, 47th Floor
New York, NY 10153-0023

Carl Gellert and Celia Berta Gellert Foundation Grants 930
The foundation funds religious, charitable, scientific, literary or educational purposes restricted in the nine counties of the greater San Francisco Bay Area (Alameda, Contra Costa, Marin, Napa, San Francisco, San Mateo, Santa Clara, Solano and Sonoma). No grants are made to individuals. Types of support include general operations, annual and capital campaigns, building construction/ renovation, equipment acquisition, debt reduction, program/project development, medical research, publication, and scholarships.
Requirements: California 501(c)3 tax-exempt nonprofit organizations that are not private foundations are eligible.
Restrictions: Grants are not awarded to individuals.
Geographic Focus: California
Date(s) Application is Due: Aug 15
Amount of Grant: 1,000 - 10,000 USD
Contact: Jack Fitzpatrick, Executive Director; (415) 255-2829
Internet: http://home.earthlink.net/~cgcbg
Sponsor: Carl Gellert and Celia Berta Gellert Foundation
1169 Market Street, Suite 808
San Francisco, CA 94103

Carlisle Foundation Grants 931
The foundation prefers to support proposals that are new, innovative, and/or demonstrate promise as models that might be replicated in other sites. In many instances, grants act as venture capital or seed money through which the applicant organization can demonstrate a new concept or expand its own capacity to deliver services. Although the foundation reviews a wide range of proposals, several areas receive high priority, including substance abuse; domestic and community violence; homelessness/housing; economic development; and services for children, youth, and families. The foundation prefers to make grants for restricted project support rather than general operating support. Applicant organizations should submit a one-page concept paper along with a copy of the 501(c)3 determination letter. There is no time line or deadline for concept letters.
Requirements: Connecticut, Vermont, Rhode Island, Massachusetts, New Hampshire and Maine C501(c)3 organizations are eligible. Applicant organizations should submit a one-page concept paper accompanied by a copy of the 501(c)3 determination letter.
Restrictions: Requests for capital support are rarely considered; requests for support of endowments are never considered. The foundation does not usually support programs with a primary focus on day care, disabilities, education, health services, legal services, mental retardation, or older adults. The foundation also does not provide direct support for individuals.
Geographic Focus: Connecticut, Maine, Massachusetts, New Hampshire, Rhode Island, Vermont
Contact: Richard Goldblatt, Executive Director; (401) 284-0368; fax (401) 284-0390; rag@carlislefoundation.org
Internet: http://www.carlislefoundation.org/annualgrants.htm
Sponsor: Carlisle Foundation
P.O. Box 5549
Wakefield, RI 02880-5549

Carl M. Freeman Foundation FACES Grants 932
Founded in 2000 in Delaware, FACES stands for Freeman Assists Communities with Extra Support. The FACES program is designed to find and fund the smaller, overlooked projects in it's neighborhoods. The grants are limited to Montgomery County nonprofit organizations with operating budgets of $750,000 or less and Sussex County nonprofit organizations with operating budgets of $500,000 or less. Funding applications are available in five areas of interest: arts/culture; education/environment; health & human services; housing and; other-this may include anything you feel does not fit in the above categories, for example spaying cats/dogs. Additional guidelines and applications are available at: http://www.freemanfoundation.org/carl/CarlMFreemanFoundation/Grants/GrantGuidelines/ApplyForaGrant/tabid/185/Default.aspx.
Requirements: 501(c)3 tax-exempt organizations in Montgomery & Sussex County are eligible. Nonsectarian religious programs also are eligible.
Restrictions: Grants will not be distributed to: individuals; political associations or candidates; organizations that would disperse the funding to others; organizations that discriminate by race, creed, gender, sexual orientation, age, religion, disability or national origin.
Geographic Focus: Delaware, Maryland, West Virginia
Contact: Trish Schechtman, Relationship Manager; (302) 436-3555; trish@freemanfoundation.org
Internet: http://www.freemanfoundation.org/carl/CarlMFreemanFoundation/Grants/FACES/tabid/204/Default.aspx
Sponsor: Carl M. Freeman Foundation
36097 Sand Cove Road
Selbyville, DE 19975

Carl M. Freeman Foundation Grants 933
The Carl M. Freeman Foundation has historically emphasized it's support in the following communities: Montgomery County, Maryland; Sussex County, Delaware; and the Eastern Panhandle of West Virginia . Funding is available for a wide variety of community organizations, having supported everything from arts organizations and hunger centers to educational and health related organizations. To simplify the application process, funding applications are available in five areas of interest: arts/culture; education/environment; health & human services; housing and; other-this may include anything you feel does not fit in the above categories, for example spaying cats/dogs. Additional guidelines and applications are available at: http://www.freemanfoundation.org/carl/CarlMFreemanFoundation/Grants/GrantGuidelines/ApplyForaGrant/tabid/185/Default.aspx
Requirements: 501(c)3 tax-exempt organizations in Maryland, Delaware and West Virginia are eligible. Nonsectarian religious programs also are eligible.
Restrictions: Grants will not be distributed to: individuals; political associations or candidates; organizations that would disperse the funding to others; organizations that discriminate by race, creed, gender, sexual orientation, age, religion, disability or national origin.
Geographic Focus: Delaware, Maryland, West Virginia
Amount of Grant: 5,000 - 30,000 USD
Contact: Trish Schechtman; (302) 436-3555; trish@freemanfoundation.org
Internet: http://www.freemanfoundation.org/carl/CarlMFreemanFoundation/Grants/GrantGuidelines/tabid/181/Default.aspx
Sponsor: Carl M. Freeman Foundation
36097 Sand Cove Road
Selbyville, DE 19975

Carlos and Marguerite Mason Trust Grants 934
The trust awards grants in Georgia with a focus on organ transplants. The trust's interests are patient services—needs relating to the transplantation process for the patient and the immediate family members, as well as donor family members and living donors; donation and transplantation—related education (donor education, professional education, and technical education for transplantation providers; programs to improve consent rates; and programs to promote living organ donations); and research—medical research relating to the area of transplantation. Types of support include capital improvements, start-up grants for new projects, and challenge/matching grants. Grants will be awarded for up to three years. Applicants are encouraged to contact the trustee for an appointment prior to submitting a grant request.
Requirements: Georgia nonprofit organizations are eligible.
Restrictions: Requests for general operating or administrative funds are discouraged. The trust generally does not fund endowment, nor does it fund general goodwill advertising; make grants that would replace existing sources of funding; or pay indirect overhead expenses for projects at colleges, universities, governmental units, or other established organizations.
Geographic Focus: Georgia
Date(s) Application is Due: Jun 1
Contact: Randy Karesh, (404) 332-6677; grantinquiriesga@wachovia.com
Internet: http://www.wachovia.com/corp_inst/charitable_services/0,,4269_3300,00.html
Sponsor: Carlos and Marguerite Mason Trust
3414 Peachtree Road, 5th Floor, MC GA8023
Atlanta, GA 30326

Carl R. Hendrickson Family Foundation Grants 935
The Carl R. Hendrickson Family Foundation was established in 1991 to support and promote quality educational, human-services, and health-care programming for underserved populations. Carl R. Hendrickson was a Chicago entrepreneur who, along with his father and brothers, built the Hendrickson Trucking Company. Carl and his wife, Agnes, had one child, Virginia. Virginia followed in her father's footsteps by leading the family business and by serving as President of the Hendrickson Foundation. Virginia died in 1995, leaving no heirs. The Hendricksons prided themselves on their entrepreneurial spirit, having been in the forefront of the trucking business by inventing the tandem truck. Reflecting the Hendrickson family's strong Christian faith, special consideration is given to charitable organizations that help individuals meet their basic needs while also addressing their spiritual needs. Preference is given to organizations or programs that approach their mission from an entrepreneurial perspective. The majority of grants from the Hendrickson Family Foundation are one year in duration. Application guidelines as well as a link to the downloadable application are given at the grant website. Applicants are also encouraged to review the Illinois state application guidelines and the foundation's funding history before applying (links are available from the grant website). The deadline for application to the Carl R. Hendrickson Family Foundation is July 31. Grant decisions will be made by December 31.
Requirements: Applicants must have 501(c)3 status. Applications must be mailed.
Restrictions: In general, grant requests for individuals, endowment campaigns or capital projects will not be considered. The foundation does not support requests from individuals, organizations attempting to influence policy through direct lobbying, or any political campaigns.
Geographic Focus: All States, Illinois
Date(s) Application is Due: Jul 31
Contact: Debra Grand; (312) 828-4154; ilgrantmaking@bankofamerica.com
Internet: https://www.bankofamerica.com/philanthropic/fn_search.action
Sponsor: Carl R. Hendrickson Family Foundation
231 South LaSalle Street, IL1-231-13-32
Chicago, IL 60604

Carlsbad Charitable Foundation Grants 936
The mission of the Carlsbad Charitable Foundation is to advance philanthropy in its service region in order to: build community excellence; stimulate innovation; and enhance capacity of nonprofits. Its primary purpose is to: meet emerging needs by encouraging and increasing responsible and effective philanthropy by and for the benefit of all who live, work and play in Carlsbad; build a Carlsbad community endowment; provide funding annually to Carlsbad organizations and causes; and give Carlsbad community members a vehicle for legacy planning and gifts that will benefit Carlsbad now and forever. The field of grant giving focus changes annually, so applicants should contact the office directly for specific details. Most recently, the Foundation was interested in funding Senior Health and Human Services programs managed by non-profit or government agencies.
Requirements: Any 501(c)3 organization serving the residents of Carlsbad, California, are eligible to apply. Projects must specifically target seniors over the age of 55 who live in the City of Carlsbad.
Restrictions: The Carlsbad Charitable Foundation does not make grants for: annual campaigns and fund raising events for non-specific purposes; capital campaigns for buildings or facilities; stipends for attendance at conferences; endowments or chairs; for-profit organizations or enterprises; individuals unaffiliated with a qualified fiscal sponsor; projects that promote religious or political doctrine; research projects (medical or otherwise); scholarships; or existing obligations or debt.
Geographic Focus: California
Date(s) Application is Due: Jan 12
Contact: Trudy Amstrong, Regional Manager; (619) 814-1384; trudy@sdfoundation.org
Internet: http://www.endowcarlsbad.org/grants.html
Sponsor: Carlsbad Charitable Foundation
2508 Historic Decatur Road, Suite 200
San Diego, CA 92106

Carls Foundation Grants 937
The foundation has broadly defined charitable purposes, but the principal purpose and mission of the foundation is as follows: children's welfare (primarily in Michigan), including health care facilities and programs, with special emphasis on the prevention and treatment of hearing impairment; recreational, educational, and welfare programs especially for children who are disadvantaged for economic and/or health reasons; and preservation of natural areas, open space, and historic buildings and areas having special natural beauty or significance in maintaining America's heritage and historic ideals, through assistance to land trusts and land conservancies and directly related environmental educational programs. Types of grants include capital grants, limited budget support, start up/seed money, and multi-year grants. The foundation has no formal application for grant requests. The Trustees meet minimally three times per year. Requests are accepted at all times, but organizations are encouraged to submit requests well in advance of scheduled board meetings, in January, May, and September. A letter of inquiry is not required and phone calls are welcome. Guidelines are available online.
Requirements: 501(c)3 tax-exempt organizations are eligible.
Restrictions: Grants are not awarded to individuals or for endowments, publications, conferences, seminars, film, fellowships, educational loans, travel, research, playground structures or athletic facilities, or underwriting special events.
Geographic Focus: Michigan
Date(s) Application is Due: Mar 1; Jul 1; Nov 1
Contact: Kathy Stenman, Program Officer; (313) 965-0990; fax (313) 965-0547
Internet: http://www.carlsfdn.org
Sponsor: Carls Foundation
333 W Fort Street, Suite 1940
Detroit, MI 48226

Carl W. and Carrie Mae Joslyn Trust Grants 938
Grants support activities providing services to resident children, elderly, and the disabled in El Paso County, Colorado. Areas of interest include education, medical care, rehabilitation, children and youth services, and aging centers and services. Types of support include general operating support, annual campaigns, building construction and renovation, equipment acquisition, endowment funds, and program development. Application must be in writing and must specifically describe the use of the funds. Grants are not sustaining and new applications must be submitted semiannually for renewal.
Requirements: Nonprofit organizations located in, or serving the residents of, El Paso County, Colorado, are eligible.
Restrictions: Grants are not made to individuals or for research, scholarships, fellowships, loans, or matching gifts.
Geographic Focus: Colorado
Date(s) Application is Due: Apr 30; Oct 31
Amount of Grant: 500 - 15,000 USD
Contact: Susan Bradt Laabs; (719) 227-6435 or (719) 227-6439; fax (719) 2276448
Sponsor: Carl W. and Carrie Mae Joslyn Charitable Trust
Trust Department, P.O. Box 1699
Colorado Springs, CO 80942

Carnahan-Jackson Foundation Grants 939
The foundation's areas of interest include higher and other education, libraries, hospitals, youth, the disabled, drug abuse programs, ecology, housing, community development, dance and other performing arts groups, and churches. Types of support include general operating support, continuing support, capital campaigns, building construction/renovation, equipment acquisition, programs/projects, seed grants, curriculum development, scholarship funds, and matching funds.
Requirements: IRS 501(c)3 organizations serving western New York, particularly Chautauqua County, are eligible.
Geographic Focus: New York
Contact: Stephen E. Sellstrom, (716) 483-1015
Sponsor: Carnahan-Jackson Foundation
13 East 4th Street, P.O. Box 3326
Jamestown, NY 14701-3326

Carnegie Corporation of New York Grants 940

The foundation provides research, study, and support for projects to improve government at all levels, to increase public understanding of social policy issues, to equalize opportunities for minorities and women, and to increase participation in political and civic life. Also supported are projects that promote electoral reform; education reform from early childhood through higher education; early childhood development; and urban school reform. The foundation will also fund research on the increasing availability and success of after-school and extended service programs for children and teenagers, particularly those in urban areas, that promote high academic achievement. Dissemination of best practices in teacher education will also be emphasized. There is no formal procedure for submitting a proposal. To apply under any of the corporation's grantmaking programs, applicants should submit a full proposal that describes the project's aims, duration, methods, amount of financial support required, and key personnel. The board meets four times a year, in October, February, April, and June.
Restrictions: Grants are not made for construction or maintenance of facilities or endowments. The Corporation does not generally make grants to individuals except through the Carnegie Scholars Program, that supports the work of select scholars and experts conducting research in the foundation's fields of interest.
Geographic Focus: All States
Amount of Grant: Up to 80,000,000 USD
Contact: Sarina Cipriano, Grants Manager; (212) 371-3200; fax (212) 754-4073
Internet: http://www.carnegie.org/sub/program/grant.html
Sponsor: Carnegie Corporation of New York
437 Madison Avenue
New York, NY 10022

Caroline Lawson Ivey Memorial Foundation Grants 941

The primary focus of the foundation is the Cultural Approach Workshops for Elementary Teachers, Scholarship Programs for future History Teachers, and Grant programs that support the use of the Cultural approach in teaching. The foundation awards grants to eligible Alabama and Georgia nonprofit educational organizations with an overarching goal to improve social studies and history teaching. The foundation supports K-12 projects such as curriculum planning, in-service training, and development of instructional materials for classrooms. In addition to educational grants, the foundation also offers scholarships to students pursuing a career in teaching social studies and workshops to strengthen the field.
Geographic Focus: Alabama, Georgia
Contact: Administrator; (334) 826-5760; fax (334) 826-5760; climf@mindspring.com
Internet: http://www.iveyfoundation.org/iveymain.htm
Sponsor: Caroline Lawson Ivey Memorial Foundation
P.O. Box 2028
Auburn, AL 36831-2028

Carolyn Foundation Grants 942

Priorities for funding include community and environmental grantmaking. In the community focus area needs are addressed only in the communities of interest to the foundation: Minneapolis, Minnesota and, New Haven, Connecticut. There are two community focus areas for funding: economically disadvantaged children and youth; and community and cultural vitality. The foundation works to empower economically disadvantaged children and youth by supporting their families and others to inspire, nurture, educate and guide them to achieve long-term stability and well-being. In the environmental focus area, the Carolyn Foundation environmental committee is currently most interested in funding renewable energy programs. The Foundation will consider other environmental proposals if funds allow. All proposals submitted must: address root causes and create systemic and sustainable solutions and change; address global issues with local interventions that address local needs, as well as global needs; develop and implement solutions that can be replicated in other areas; collaborate effectively with others in the community: government, non-government, foundations and private parties. The Carolyn Foundation makes grants twice a year, in June and January. Applications must be submitted by January 15 for June grants, and July 15 for January grants. This is a postmark deadline. Grant applications will be reviewed by the Executive Director and a committee of foundation volunteers. Declinations will be sent at the time a decision is made to no longer consider a proposal, typically before the end of the review cycle. Successful applicants will be notified in June and January.
Requirements: IRS 501(c)3 nonprofit organizations in Minnesota and Connecticut may apply for the environmental grants. The Community grants program is limited to the cities of Minneapolis, Minnesota and New Haven, Connecticut. The foundation encourages use of Carolyn Foundation Application Form adapted from the Minnesota Common Grant Application Form. Applicants choosing not to use the common grant form must address the same information as required by the common grant. All proposals must use the Carolyn Foundation Cover Sheet, available at the Foundation's website. It is request that summary information and description of the project be no longer than six pages, printed on one side on 8 1/2 x 11-inch paper. Supporting documents, such as financial information, list of Officers, Directors, and Executive Staff, IRS determination letter may be in addition to the six pages. Do not send bound proposals, cassettes or VCR tapes.
Restrictions: Grants are not awarded to individuals, political organizations or candidates, veterans organizations, fraternal societies or orders, annual fund drives, umbrella organizations, or to deficits already incurred. The foundation does not generally make grants to religious organizations for religious purposes or to organizations in support of operations carried on in foreign countries.
Geographic Focus: Connecticut, Minnesota
Date(s) Application is Due: Jan 15; Jul 15
Amount of Grant: 5,000 - 50,000 USD
Contact: Becky Erdahl, Executive Director; (612) 596-3279 or (612) 596-3266; fax (612) 339-1951; berdahl@carolynfoundation.org
Internet: http://www.carolynfoundation.org/guidelines.html
Sponsor: Carolyn Foundation
706 2nd Avenue South, Suite 760
Minneapolis, MN 55402

Carpenter Foundation Grants 943

The foundation's primary areas of interest include the arts, education, public interest, and human services. The foundation is deeply concerned with the well-being of children and families and their relationship to their neighborhoods and communities. Also of concern is the health of the web of agencies and organizations which serve them. Grants are awarded for general operating support, program development, capital campaigns, equipment acquisition, scholarship funds, seed money, matching funds, and technical support. Deadlines are generally about six weeks before the quarterly board meetings, held in January, March, June, and September.
Requirements: Tax exempt agencies in the Jackson and Josephine Counties of Oregon may submit proposals.
Restrictions: Grants are not made to individuals. The foundation rarely makes grants for historical applications, hospital construction or equipment, group or individual trips, or activities for religious purposes.
Geographic Focus: Oregon
Amount of Grant: 250 - 25,000 USD
Contact: Polly Williams; (541) 772-5732; fax (541) 773-3970; carpfdn@internetcds.com
Internet: http://www.carpenter-foundation.org
Sponsor: Carpenter Foundation
711 E Main Street, Suite 10
Medford, OR 97504

Carrie E. and Lena V. Glenn Foundation Grants 944

Established in 1971, the Glenn Foundation provides annual grants in the following areas of interest: arts; children/youth, services; Christian agencies & churches; Elementary/secondary education; Environment; and Human services.
Requirements: Federally tax-exempt institutions and not-for-profit agencies that serve Gaston County, NC. agencies or out-of-county agencies whose projects have an impact on Gaston County citizens are eligible to apply.
Restrictions: Funding is not available for: planning grants; grants to individuals; scholarships; capital campaigns; umbrella campaigns; and multi-year grants.
Geographic Focus: North Carolina
Date(s) Application is Due: Mar 1
Amount of Grant: 3,000 - 25,000 USD
Contact: Barbara H. Voorhees; (704) 867-0296; fax (704) 867-4496; glennfnd@bellsouth.net
Sponsor: Carrie E. and Lena V. Glenn Foundation
1552 Union Road, Suite D
Gastonia, NC 28054

Carrie Estelle Doheny Foundation Grants 945

The foundation primarily funds local, not-for profit organizations endeavoring to advance education, medicine and religion, to improve the health and welfare of the sick, aged, incapacitated, and to aid the needy. Educational funding includes support of inner city Catholic schools, and scholarship funds for Catholic high schools and universities. Adult education programs and religious education are also supported. Medical funding is focused in two areas: research and care of the disadvantaged. Religious funding is directed to support the gospel values as expressed in the Roman Catholic faith. Health and welfare funding is directed to organizations who assist individuals to lead independent satisfying lives. Specific areas of interest include adoption and foster care service groups, programs for the disabled, health education programs, and senior programs. Aiding the needy funding includes inner city youth clubs, summer camps, and food banks. Applications are accepted anytime, an application form is required for submission and may be downloaded from the foundation web site. The board meets on the last Friday of each month, except for the month of September. Requests should be submitted approximately 6 weeks in advance to allow sufficient time for processing and for distribution to the Board members prior to the meeting. Allow 2 or 3 months for notification of the Board's decision. This is done in writing following the Board of Directors Meeting each month.
Requirements: The Foundation limits its grants to programs located within the fifty states and certified as 501(c)3 non-profit public charities by the Internal Revenue Service. The vast majority of funding is done in the Greater Los Angeles area.
Restrictions: Grant requests are not considered from individuals or from tax-supported entities. Areas also excluded from consideration include support for individuals, endowment funds, publishing books, television or radio programs, travel funds, advertisement, scholarships, or political purposes in any form.
Geographic Focus: All States
Amount of Grant: 5,000 - 150,000 USD
Contact: Shirley Bernard, (213) 488-1122; fax (213) 488-1544; doheny@dohenyfoundation.org
Internet: http://www.dohenyfoundation.org/grant/grant.htm
Sponsor: Carrie Estelle Doheny Foundation
707 Wilshire Boulevard, Suite 4960
Los Angeles, CA 90017

Carrier Corporation Contributions Grants 946

Carrier donates approximately $2 million around the world to registered nonprofit organizations. In the United States, Carrier funds only qualified 501(c)3 organizations that meet its eligibility criteria and operate in locations where the company has a significant employee base. Carrier believes in helping people in the communities where they live, work and do business. To better serve those communities and to better align its corporate contributions with mission and values, it focuses giving on the following these areas:

environment and sustainability; civic & community; education; arts & culture; health & human services. All U.S. non-profits are required to complete an online grant application. Applications are accepted from March 1 through June 1 of each year, and are reviewed for funding to be paid the following year. Applicants will receive notification in the first quarter of the calendar year in which funding will occur.
Requirements: Carrier funds only qualified 501(c)3 organizations that meet eligibility criteria and operate in locations where it has a significant employee base.
Restrictions: Carrier will not fund: individuals; religious organizations; alumni groups, sororities or fraternities; booster clubs; political groups; any organization determined by Carrier to have a conflict of interest; any organization whose practices are inconsistent with the company's Code of Ethics
Geographic Focus: Alabama, Arizona, Connecticut, Georgia, Illinois, Indiana, Michigan, Nevada, New York, North Carolina, South Carolina, Tennessee, Texas
Date(s) Application is Due: Jun 1
Contact: Rajan Goel, Vice President; (860) 674-3420; fax (860) 622-0488
Internet: http://www.corp.carrier.com/vgn-ext-templating/v/index.jsp?vgnextoid=6afa80 757d7e7010VgnVCM100000cb890b80RCRD
Sponsor: Carrier Corporation
One Carrier Place
Farmington, CT 06034-4015

Carroll County Community Foundation Grants 947
The Carroll County Community Foundation funds initiatives that improve the quality of life for citizens of Carroll County, Indiana. The Foundation's grant program emphasizes change-oriented issues, with the following areas of interest: health and medical; social services; education; cultural affairs; civic affairs; and community beautification. Proposals: must strive to anticipate the changing needs of the community and be flexible in responding to them; must be change-oriented and problem-solving in nature with emphasis on "seed" money or pilot project support rather than for ongoing general operating support; support innovative efforts and projects that offer far-reaching gains and widespread community results; may coordinate with other funders and donors where possible, including using matching or challenge grant techniques; closely relate and coordinate with the programs of other sources for funding such as the government, other foundations, and associations; and achieve certain objectives such as become more efficient, increase fund-raising capabilities, and deliver better products. Grants will be made only to organizations: whose programs benefit the residents of the county, with preference given to those projects with high visibility in the community; which provide for a responsible fiscal agent and adequate accounting procedures, with preference given to those projects that generate revenue and/or have plans that sustain the project.
Requirements: A letter of inquiry to the Foundation is required as a pre-qualification. The letter should contain a brief statement of the applicant's needs for assistance, estimate of total cost of the project, and enough factual information to enable the Foundation to determine whether or not the application falls within the guidelines of its grants program. After the organization has received a response to apply for a grant, the grantee will then fill out the online application and submit ten copies of the application and all attachments to the Foundation for approval. Organizations should refer to the Foundation website for further information.
Restrictions: The Foundation typically does not award grants for: normal operating expenses and/or salaries; individuals; seminars or trips except where there are special circumstances which will benefit the larger community; sectarian religious purposes but can be made to religious organizations for general community programs; endowment purposes of recipient organizations; projects which have been proposed by individuals or organizations responsible to advisory bodies or persons; new projects and/or equipment purchased prior to the grant application being approved.
Geographic Focus: Indiana
Date(s) Application is Due: Sep 6
Contact: Ron Harper, President; (765) 454-7298 or (800) 964-0508; ron@cfhoward.org
Internet: http://cfcarroll.org/newsite/grantprogram.shtml
Sponsor: Carroll County Community Foundation
215 West Sycamore Street
Kokomo, IN 46901

Cartis Creative Services Grants 948
The corporation awards creative-services grants to an Austin-area nonprofit organization in its areas of expertise, including branding, identity development, advertising, direct marketing, graphic design, and Web site design. Service grants are awarded; no cash payments are made to grant recipients. Guidelines are available online.
Requirements: Texas 501(c)3 tax-exempt organizations in Travis, Williamson, Hays, Bastrop, Caldwell, Blanco, and Burnet counties are eligible.
Restrictions: Organizations that have completed and filed Form 1023 but not yet received an IRS determination letter are ineligible.
Geographic Focus: Texas
Date(s) Application is Due: Jun 17
Contact: Claudia Chavez, (512) 476-2600; fax (512) 476-2676; pr@cartisgroup.com
Internet: http://www.cartisgroup.com/
Sponsor: Cartis Group
3011 N Lamar
Austin, TX 77027

Carylon Foundation Grants 949
The foundation awards general support grants to nonprofits of the Christian, interdenominational, Jewish, and Presbyterian faiths. Higher education institutions, health care organizations, international missions/ministries, medical centers, religious organizations, and temples receive support. Application may be made by submitting a brief letter describing the organization and program. There are no application deadlines.
Geographic Focus: All States
Amount of Grant: 50 - 50,000 USD
Contact: Marcie Mervis, Trustee; (312) 666-7700
Sponsor: Carylon Foundation
2500 W Arthington
Chicago, IL 60612-4108

Case Foundation Grants 950
The Case Foundation, created by Steve Case and Jean Case in 1997, invests in people and ideas that can change the world. The Foundation creates and supports initiatives that leverage new technologies and entrepreneurial approaches to drive innovation in the social sector and encourage individuals to get involved with the communities and causes they care about.
Geographic Focus: All States, District of Columbia, Puerto Rico
Contact: Program Director; (202) 467-5788; fax (202) 775-8513
Internet: http://befearless.casefoundation.org/finding-fearless/grants-prizes
Sponsor: Case Foundation
1717 Rhode Island Avenue NW, 7th Floor
Washington, DC 20036

Cash 4 Clubs Sports Grants 951
Cash 4 Clubs is a sports funding scheme which gives clubs a unique chance to apply for grants to improve facilities, purchase new equipment, gain coaching qualifications, and generally invest in the sustainability of their club. The Cash 4 Clubs scheme is funded by Betfair and is supported by SportsAid, the charity for sports people. Betfair and SportsAid have worked in partnership for a number of years and both organizations understand the importance of community sport in promoting an active lifestyle and stimulating local pride. Three tiers of grants at £250, £500 and £1,000 which are awarded on a discretionary basis twice a year. There are no deadlines for submitting grant applications. Clubs are welcome to apply at any time and they will be considered at the next committee panel meeting.
Requirements: Any sports club that is registered with its sports' National Governing body or local authority can apply. No preference is given to types of sport or the age of people involved with the club, but the sponsor does look for sports clubs that play an active role in the community. Sport is a great way for the community to get together socially and get active and keep fit at the same time. Clubs can apply by filling out the required online form at the sponsor's website.
Geographic Focus: United Kingdom
Amount of Grant: 250 - 1,000 GBP
Contact: Laura Eddie, National Awards Manager; 020 7273 1975; mail@sportsaid.org.uk
Internet: http://www.cash-4-clubs.com/
Sponsor: SportsAid
3rd Floor, Victoria House
London, GLONDON WC1B 4SE United Kingdom

Cass County Community Foundation Grants 952
The Cass County Community Foundation (CCCF) assists donors in building enduring sources of charitable assets to promote education, enhance humanity, and advance community development throughout Cass County. The Foundation has the following areas of interest: education; human services; and community development. All applications are reviewed by a committee comprised of CCCF Board members and other volunteers from the community. Non-profit organizations whose projects directly impact the lives of Cass County residents are eligible to apply.
Requirements: The grant application is available online and is also available at the Foundation office. Grant seekers should include their organizational, financial, and project information, and submit seven copies of the application packet to the Foundation. Applicants are encouraged to participate in the free grant writing workshop available each spring.
Restrictions: Public schools, while non-profit, are not 501(c)3 and therefore are not eligible. The Foundation will not consider grants for: existing obligations; services supported by tax dollars; individuals or travel expenses; repeat funding; on-going operating expenses; advocacy; religious purposes or affiliations; or loans or endowments.
Geographic Focus: Indiana
Date(s) Application is Due: Jul 1
Amount of Grant: 5,000 - 14,000 USD
Contact: Deanna Crispen; (574) 722-2200; fax (574) 753-7501; dcrispen@casscountycf.org
Internet: http://casscountycf.org/page/Competitive-Grants-Cycle-id-24
Sponsor: Cass County Community Foundation
417 North Street, Suite 102, P.O. Box 441
Logansport, IN 46947

Castle and Cooke California Corporate Giving Grants 953
Castle and Cooke Real Estate makes charitable contributions to nonprofit organizations on a case by case basis. Support is given primarily in Sierra Vista, Arizona, Bakersfield, California, and Keene's Pointe, Florida. The primary type of support is for general operating expenses. Application forms are required and are sent out annually in January. Initial approach is to contact the headquarters directly to be added to application form mailing list. The deadline for applications is the end of March.
Requirements: 501(c)3 organizations serving the residents of Sierra Vista, Arizona, Bakersfield, California, and Keene's Pointe, Florida, are eligible to apply.
Geographic Focus: Arizona, California, Florida
Date(s) Application is Due: Mar 31
Contact: Renee Massey; (661) 664-4562; fax (661) 664-6500; rmassey@castlecooke.com
Sponsor: Castle and Cooke California
10000 Stockdale Highway, Suite 300, P.O. Box 11165
Bakersfield, CA 93389-1165

Caterpillar Foundation Grants 954
The foundation awards grants internationally to nonprofits in company-operating locations in support of arts, community development, environment, higher education, and health and human services. Youth health is a priority of small grants given under the civic and community activities program. Types of support include general operating support, capital campaigns, program development, and employee matching gifts. There are no application deadlines or required forms.
Requirements: Go to the Caterpillar Foundation website (above) for details about what to include in a proposal.
Restrictions: Grants do not support fraternal organizations, religious organizations for religious purposes, political activities, individuals, United Way organizations, ticket purchase, or advertising for fund-raising benefits.
Geographic Focus: All States
Contact: Grants Administrator; (309) 675-4464
Internet: http://www.cat.com/cda/layout?m=39201&x=7
Sponsor: Caterpillar Foundation
100 NE Adams Street
Peoria, IL 61629-1480

Catherine Kennedy Home Foundation Grants 955
The Catherine Kennedy Home Foundation established in 2001, supports nonprofit organizations involved with Aging, centers/services; Christian agencies & churches; developmentally disabled, centers & services; family services; domestic violence; food distribution, meals on wheels; residential/custodial care, hospices; YM/YWCAs & YM/YWHAs. Giving primarily in Wilmington, North Carolina.
Requirements: Initial approach should be made through a letter to the Foundation requesting an application form. The Foundation will provide you with additional guidelines.
Restrictions: Funding not available outside of North Carolina.
Geographic Focus: North Carolina
Date(s) Application is Due: Feb 28
Amount of Grant: 1,000 - 30,000 USD
Contact: Garry A. Garris, Director; (910) 452-0611
Sponsor: Catherine Kennedy Home
P.O. Box 4782
Wilmington, NC 28406-1782

Catherine Manley Gaylord Foundation Grants 956
The foundation awards grants to supplement the operating budgets of recognized public charities in the metropolitan Saint Louis, MO, area. Grants support general operations, materials and equipment, scholarships, symposiums and conferences, education and adult basic education, community development, and religious programs. Applications are accepted at any time.
Requirements: Saint Louis metropolitan area 501(c)3 nonprofit organizations may apply.
Geographic Focus: Missouri
Contact: Cindy Davis, Secretary; (314) 621-5757; fax (314) 621-5799
Sponsor: Catherine Manley Gaylord Foundation
1015 Locust Street, Suite 500
Saint Louis, MO 63101

Catholic Health Initiatives Healthy Communities Grants 957
The fund awards planning grants and project grants for up to three years of support to plan, develop, and implement new initiatives designed to promote healthy communities. Project grants are awarded to enable applicants to work in collaboration with others to implement an action plan that addresses a specific, documented community need. Planning grants are awarded to enable applicants to establish a broad-based coalition that involves all community stakeholders in building community capacity by creating a shared vision of what their community could be; mapping assets; setting priorities; and beginning action planning.
Requirements: Applicants must complete an application form obtained from the CEO of a Catholic Health Initiatives' facility. Application guidelines are available online. Nonprofit organizations are eligible.
Restrictions: Grants do not support overhead or indirect costs, capital needs (i.e., building construction/renovation), ongoing operations beyond the start-up phase, biomedical research, or political activities or lobbying.
Geographic Focus: All States
Amount of Grant: 20,000 - 100,000 USD
Contact: Fund Administrator; (303) 298-9100; fax (303) 298-9690
Internet: http://www.catholichealthinit.org/body.cfm?id=37924
Sponsor: Catholic Health Initiatives Mission and Ministry Fund
1999 Broadway, Suite 2600
Denver, CO 80202-4004

Cause Populi Worthy Cause Grants 958
The main purpose of the Worthy Cause marketing grant is to enhance the visibility, online presence, community engagement and fund raising aspects of qualifying nonprofit institutions. Cause Populi, LLC will provide grants of up to $50,000 per project to qualifying non-profits. Grant applications and awards will be reviewed on a monthly basis. The grant is awarded as a matching in-kind donation to the selected non-profit institution(s), and may only be applied towards services provided by Cause Populi. Typical projects funded by the grant would include website redevelopment services, event management and promotion, marketing campaign services, social networking campaigns, etc. The grant award may be applied towards a specific project, or a group of related projects. Applicants may attach documentation describing the project in detail. The deadline for grant applications is the 21st day of each month. Applications will be reviewed upon submission, and awards will be made on a first-come, first-serve basis until the monthly award funds have been allocated. Applications received after this date may be deferred to a future award cycle.
Requirements: Donated services will be distributed under this program to qualifying organizations only, not to individuals. This donation is only available to nonprofits with 501(c)3 designation. The grant award and services may not be transferred, donated or resold.
Geographic Focus: All States, All Countries
Amount of Grant: Up to 50,000 USD
Contact: Eduardo J. Alarcon, CEO; (305) 913-4604; ealarcon@causepopuli.com
Internet: http://causepopuli.com/marketing-services-grant-for-non-profits/
Sponsor: Cause Populi
201 S. Biscayne Boulevard
Miami, FL 33131

CCCF Alpha Fund Grants 959
The program is designed for worthy new Chattanooga-area Christian ministries and projects that have not yet received 501(c)3 tax-exempt status. The fund enables them to raise start-up funds and grow to a point where they are self-sustaining and no longer require the assistance of the fund. Guidelines are available online.
Requirements: Ministries eligible to receive grants include start-up ministries/programs that have been incubated by other existing tax-exempt ministries or churches. Applicant must submit a two- page letter of request, with sufficient supporting documentation, indicating that it has met all of the following criteria: be a Christian initiative, theologically and biblically conservative in character; have a clear purpose or mission statement to meet a community need; have measurable program goals and strategies; have a timeline indicating the duration of the project and/or when the organization projects when it will receive its 501(c)3 status; be governed by a well-defined board of directors, advisory board, steering committee, or accountability committee; have an identified executive director, project leader, or point person; have an established address; and has not been in existence for longer than three years.
Geographic Focus: Tennessee
Contact: Grants Administrator; (423) 266-5257; fax (423) 265-0949; info@cccfdn.org
Internet: http://www.cccfdn.org/page18301.cfm
Sponsor: Chattanooga Christian Community Foundation
736 Market Street, Suite 700
Chattanooga, TN 37402

CCCF Dora Maclellan Brown Christian Priority Grants 960
The foundation makes grants to Chattanooga-area Christian ministries and organizations, defined primarily as Cleveland, TN, to Dayton, TN, to Dalton, GA. Chattanooga residents serving in a nonlocal ministry or nonlocal ministries that are ministering to and serving within the greater Chattanooga area will also be considered. Grants are made for one year with the possibility of annual renewal. The project or work for which funds are requested must exhibit a high probability for success, a qualified staff and responsible board of directors, financial accountability with apparent planning and goal-setting skills in place, and a true need for such funds.
Requirements: Nonprofit, tax-exempt Christian ministries and institutions that are tax-exempt and agree to act as a receiving agent and fund manager are eligible.
Restrictions: No grants are made to individuals for any purpose. Grants will not be awarded to support endowment funds, capital projects, previously incurred deficit incurred from a project or operating budget, special internal projects of individual churches, equipment, supplies, fellowships, sabbaticals, study grants, or loans. Relatives of foundation board members are not eligible.
Geographic Focus: Georgia, Tennessee
Date(s) Application is Due: Feb 1; Apr 1; Jun 1; Aug 1; Oct 1; Nov 1
Contact: Grants Administrator; (423) 266-5257; fax (423) 265-0949; info@cccfdn.org
Internet: http://www.cccfdn.org/page18299.cfm
Sponsor: Chattanooga Christian Community Foundation
736 Market Street, Suite 700
Chattanooga, TN 37402

CCF Community Priorities Fund 961
Grants are awarded annually to selected Minnesota organizations. The fund will consider proposals supporting: the most vulnerable elderly age 75 and over; kids at-risk age five to 14; and young mothers with families at risk. Priority will be given to organizations that utilize volunteers for delivery of service; and programs in organizations with annual budgets less than $1 million. Proposals for larger grants may be accepted; average grant amounts vary year-to-year. Nonprofit organizations interested in being considered for one-time grants may submit a letter of inquiry at any time. Full proposals are by invitation.
Requirements: Nonprofit organizations in Minnesota's Twin Cities 12-county area (Anoka, Carver, Chisago, Dakota, Goodhue, Hennepin, LeSueur, Ramsey, Rice, Scott, Washington, and Wright) are eligible.
Restrictions: The foundation will not consider programs outside the Twin Cities 12-county area; organizations with programs/activities that are antithetical to the teachings of the Catholic Church; multiyear grants (one-year grants within multiyear programs will be considered); relieving financial deficits; funding of general administrative or development costs; or grants to individuals.
Geographic Focus: Minnesota
Amount of Grant: 1,000 - 5,000 USD
Contact: Jules Vierling, Grants Manager; (651) 389-0300; fax (651) 389-0650; vierling@ccf-mn.org or info@ccf-mn.org
Internet: http://www.catholiccommunityfoundation.org/how_to_apply.htm
Sponsor: Catholic Community Foundation
One Water Street West, Suite 200
Saint Paul, MN 55107

CCFF Community Grant 962

The $25,000 Columbus Foundation Community Grant is an additional opportunity for one finalist team to take its project to a higher level. In conjunction with a community partner, the student team uses the grant money to make part or all of its ideas a reality in the community over the course of the year following the competition. The grant is dedicated to encouraging young explorers to grow as individuals and to gain a sense of accomplishment. The grant project is designed to provide a unique opportunity for young people to see hope where there is a problem, and develop confidence in their abilities to change an unacceptable situation. Adult community leaders play an important role by administering the grant money and providing the team with guidance. The grant brings young people and adults together to create a brighter future for all of us.
Geographic Focus: All States
Amount of Grant: 25,000 USD
Contact: Judith M. Shellenberger, (315) 258-0090; judithmscolumbus@cs.com
Internet: http://www.columbusfdn.org/christophercolumbus/index.php
Sponsor: Christopher Columbus Fellowship Foundation
110 Genesee Street, Suite 390
Auburn, NY 13021

CCF Grassroots Exchange Fund Grants 963

Common Counsel Foundation partners with donors to expand philanthropic resources for progressive social movements. The Foundation's Grassroots Exchange Fund Grants provide rapid response small grants designed to support networking and collaboration between grassroots social change and environmental justice organizations throughout the United State. Funding is provided for training, travel or conference expenses. Three central goals are: to strengthen the ability of small organizations to participate in public debates; to strengthen key cross-region and cross-sector movements; and to contribute to collaborative policy victories in the realms of social, environmental and economic justice. Applications must be submitted by the first Monday of the month (February-November only). Turn around time is approximately four weeks from the deadline.
Requirements: Priority is given to: organizations that most clearly demonstrate a membership-led community organizing model that is working toward social, economic or environmental policy change; organizations based in low-income or moderate-income communities; organizations that have a strong group of leaders and board members that represent the community they serve and who are accountable to the community; organizations that have strong leadership development programs for their members; organizations that have a concrete plan to grow and to build more power by getting more people involved; organizations that organize collective action of members to bring concerns to public officials and other decision-makers; organizations with annual budgets under $1,000,000; proposed exchanges or events that promote strategy development and skills transfer between organizations and leaders; organizations working in hard to fund areas, including the southern United States and Rocky Mountain states; small organizations that do not have access to large government, corporate or private funding sources, and for whom a small grant would make a significant impact; events or exchanges that are urgent with respect to the organization's overall work; and organizations that have 501(c)3 status or a fiscal sponsor who does.
Restrictions: Organizations are only eligible for one Grant per year. The following are excluded: travel for United States-based organizations to go to a foreign country (exceptions on rare occasion for cross-border travel to Mexico or Canada);international organizations and organizations located outside of the United States; direct social services; government agencies and programs undertaken by tax-supported institutions or government initiatives; capital expenditure, endowments, construction or renovation programs; scholarship funds or other aid to individuals; schools and educational institutions, cultural institutions, or medical institutions; film, video, publications or other media projects; grant making institutions; and research or fellowships.
Geographic Focus: All States
Amount of Grant: 500 - 1,000 USD
Contact: Ronald M. Rowell; (510) 834-2995; fax (510) 834-2998; info@commoncounsel.org
Internet: http://www.commoncounsel.org/Grassroots%20Exchange%20Fund
Sponsor: Common Counsel Foundation
405 Fourteenth Street, Suite 809
Oakland, CA 94612

CCF Social and Economic Justice Fund Grants 964

Common Counsel Foundation partners with donors to expand philanthropic resources for progressive social movements. The Foundation's Social and Economic Justice Fund Grants supports organizations working on civil and human rights, youth organizing, alternative media, and economic justice for low-income immigrant communities, and communities of color in the greater San Francisco Bay Area. Support is prioritized for, but not limited to, organizations in the greater San Francisco Bay Area.
Requirements: Grants are discretionary and proposals are by invitation to apply only.
Geographic Focus: California
Contact: Ronald M. Rowell; (510) 834-2995; fax (510) 834-2998; info@commoncounsel.org
Internet: http://www.commoncounsel.org/Social%20and%20Economic%20Justice%20Fund
Sponsor: Common Counsel Foundation
405 Fourteenth Street, Suite 809
Oakland, CA 94612

CCH California Story Fund Grants 965

The California Story Fund (CSF) is a competitive grant program of the California Council for the Humanities (CCH). The purpose of CSF is to capture genuine and compelling stories from and about California's diverse communities, and to ensure that those stories can be shared widely. Telling our stories can help us make sense of our existence, give us a window into other people's lives, and make us feel part of something larger than ourselves. Sharing personal and communal narratives can enhance our understanding of where we live, with whom we live, and why we live the way we do. The Council seeks proposals for story-based projects that are informed by humanities perspectives, methods, and content; that reveal the realities of California and its cultures, peoples, and histories; and that will be of interest to local, statewide, and potentially even national and global audiences. Applicants may request up to $10,000, which must be matched by at least an equivalent contribution of non-federal funds or in-kind services and materials or any combination thereof.
Requirements: Eligible applicants must: have California tax-exempt organizational status or partner with a California tax-exempt organization that will serve as a fiscal sponsor; not have an open grant with CCH; be in good standing with CCH (e.g., without overdue reports), if a previous grantee; not submit more than one application per deadline unless acting as a CCH-approved fiscal sponsor; and have a Data Universal Numbering System (DUNS) number prior to submitting an application.
Restrictions: The Council will generally not fund CSF projects with a total budget greater than $50,000.
Geographic Focus: California
Date(s) Application is Due: Nov 15
Amount of Grant: Up to 10,000 USD
Contact: Vanessa Whang; (415) 391-1474; fax (415) 391-1312; vwhang@calhum.org
Internet: http://www.calhum.org/guidelines/guidelines_csf.htm
Sponsor: California Council for the Humanities
312 Sutter Street, Suite 601
San Francisco, CA 94108-4371

CCHD Community Development Grants 966

CCHD is committed to supporting groups of low-income individuals as they work to break the cycle of poverty and improve their communities. By helping the poor to participate in the decisions and actions that affect their lives, CCHD empowers them to move beyond poverty. The organization's efforts should directly benefit a relatively large number of people rather than a few individuals. The organization should generate cooperation among and within diverse groups in the interest of a more integrated and mutually understanding society. An applicant organization seeking seed or matching monies will also be considered. (If requesting these monies, applicants should present positive documentation that other public and/or private sources will commit their funds to support the organization's efforts.)
Requirements: Only organizations that are not now receiving an organizing grant are required to submit an Eligibility Quiz. Eligibility Quizzes are accepted on a rolling basis between September 1st and November 1st. The sponsor recommends submitting your Eligibility Quiz well in advance of the November 1st deadline, to help with processing and to give eligible applicants more time with the next step in application. To be eligible for CCHD funds, an organization must satisfy ALL the following criteria and guidelines: the activity for which funding is requested must conform to the moral and social teachings of the Catholic Church; the applicant organization must demonstrate both the intention and capacity to effectively work toward the elimination of the root causes of poverty and to enact institutional change; the organization's efforts must benefit people living in poverty. At least 50 percent of those benefiting from the organization's efforts must be people experiencing poverty; people living in poverty must have the dominant voice in the organization (at least 50 percent of those who plan, implement and make policy, hire and fire staff should be persons who are involuntarily poor; the organization should demonstrate ongoing leadership development because it is considered essential to the strength, depth and sustainability of the organization; the organization should demonstrate a clear vision for development of financial capacity that might include membership dues, grassroots fundraising, foundation and/or corporate support; and the organization must be fully nonpartisan when engaging in political activities. Organizations engaged in partisan political activity are not eligible. See the website for further explanations.
Restrictions: The following general classifications do not meet CCHD criteria and/or guidelines for community organizing grants: organizations with primary focus on direct service (e.g., daycare centers, recreation programs, community centers, scholarships, subsidies, counseling programs, referral services, cultural enrichment programs, direct clinical services, emergency shelters and other services, refugee resettlement programs, etc.); advocacy efforts where only staff, a few individuals or middle to upper-income people are speaking for a particular low income constituency without the direct involvement and leadership of low income individuals; organizations controlled by governmental (federal, state, local), educational, or ecclesiastical bodies; research projects, surveys, planning and feasibility studies, etc; individually owned, for-profit businesses; or organizations that would use CCHD money for re-granting purposes or to fund other organizations.
Geographic Focus: All States
Date(s) Application is Due: Nov 1
Amount of Grant: 25,000 - 50,000 USD
Contact: Ralph McCloud, Director; (202) 541-3367 or (202) 541-3210; fax (202) 541-3329; rmccloud@usccb.org or cchdgrants@usccb.org
Internet: http://www.usccb.org/about/catholic-campaign-for-human-development/grants/community-development-grants-program/index.cfm
Sponsor: United States Conference of Catholic Bishops
3211 Fourth Street, NE
Washington, DC 20017-1194

CCHD Economic Development Grants 967

The program focus of CCHD's Economic Development Program concentrates on Economic Development Institutions (EDIs). EDIs typically are community-based organizations and businesses. They create good jobs and just workplaces, and they develop assets for low-income people that are owned by families and communities. EDIs coincide with the CCHD mission by their commitment to the development of low income people. All EDIs have structures that promote low income leadership and ownership. CCHD funds

may be used for general operating expenses, including staff salaries/training, procurement of technical assistance, board development costs and other overhead costs. For business development, CCHD funds may be used as part of a financing package for start-up or expansion, including start-up costs or working capital. For real estate development, CCHD funds may be used for pre-development or continuing operating expenses.
Requirements: In order to be considered for funding by CCHD, an applicant organization must demonstrate that it is committed to both goals. Priority will be given to eligible applicants that address one or more of the following four priorities: to advance economic development models that enhance the scale of impact through replication or the transformation of an established model; to encourage collaboration that generates cooperation and solidarity among diverse groups in the interest of a more integrated and mutually understanding society; to link economic development with community organizing so that beneficiaries work together and with others on additional efforts to effect institutional change; or to facilitate the development of information systems in organizations that enhance planning, accountability and mutual learning by organizations and by CCHD.
Restrictions: Funds may not be used for capital expenditures (e.g. real estate, vehicles, equipment). Additionally, the following are ineligible for funding: Economic Development Institutions (EDIs) structured without opportunities for participatory control and ownership by low income people; EDIs structured without opportunities to develop community-held assets (e.g. sole proprietorships, simple partnerships or fee-simple housing projects are not eligible); EDIs owned or controlled by governmental agencies (federal, state or local), educational or ecclesiastical bodies; EDIs the primary focus of which is direct service (such services may complement an eligible EDI, but they cannot be the EDI's primary focus); EDIs that are not structured to stand on their own as sustainable institutions; or EDIs that intend to re-grant CCHD monies to other organizations.
Geographic Focus: All States
Date(s) Application is Due: Nov 1
Amount of Grant: Up to 50,000 USD
Contact: Ralph McCloud, Director; (202) 541-3367 or (202) 541-3210; fax (202) 541-3329; rmccloud@usccb.org or cchdgrants@usccb.org
Internet: http://www.usccb.org/about/catholic-campaign-for-human-development/grants/economic-development-grants-program/index.cfm
Sponsor: United States Conference of Catholic Bishops
3211 Fourth Street, NE
Washington, DC 20017-1194

CCH Documentary California Reads Grants 968
California Reads aims to bring Californians together to explore important topics through books that invite conversation. This grant and resource program of the California Council for the Humanities (CCH), in partnership with the California Center for the Book (CFB), is designed to support public libraries in developing programs that will stimulate meaningful dialogue among diverse community members by using works of fiction and non-fiction. California Reads seeks to demonstrate the power of the humanities to inspire Californians to engage with challenging issues together and showcase public libraries as active centers of community life. To coincide with CCH's two-year statewide initiative to animate a public conversation on democracy and civic values, the theme of the current round of California Reads is Searching for Democracy. CCH and CFB welcome libraries to approach their California Reads activities in a range of creative and engaging ways. Programming options (possibly in conjunction with community partners or at locations outside of the library) could include but are not limited to: story-sharing or local history activities inspired by the book or related topics; a community forum or civic engagement activities focused on a theme or topic raised by the book; participatory or interactive programming such as creating a mural, exhibit, publication, or digital media project on a topic related to the theme of democracy; live or virtual presentations or discussions involving scholars, authors or others knowledgeable of the topics to be discussed; screening and discussion programs featuring a film-adaptation or films related to the book or a topic it addresses; staged readings or other dramatizations; and relevant musical or other performing arts events. Grant awards will range from $500 to $15,000, depending on the size of the service population of the applicant organization and breadth and quality of programming plans.
Requirements: This grant opportunity is limited to California public library jurisdictions or tax-exempt library-support organizations (e.g., Friends of the Library groups) applying on behalf of CA public library jurisdictions.
Geographic Focus: California
Date(s) Application is Due: Jul 29; Aug 31; Oct 31
Amount of Grant: 500 - 15,000 USD
Contact: Vanessa Whang; (415) 391-1474; fax (415) 391-1312; vwhang@calhum.org
Internet: http://www.calhum.org/guidelines/dem_CAreads_guidelines.htm
Sponsor: California Council for the Humanities
312 Sutter Street, Suite 601
San Francisco, CA 94108-4371

CCH Documentary Project Production Grants 969
The California Documentary Project (CDP) is a competitive grant program of the California Council for the Humanities (CCH). CDP supports film, radio, and new media projects in which the humanities are used to provide context, depth, and perspective. The humanities spring from a fundamental interest in understanding the values and practices that inform our lives; the need to reflect on the past and the present to make critical choices; and the desire to be moved, delighted, and make sense of the world in which we live. Humanities disciplines include, but are not limited to: history, literature, philosophy, folklore, ethnic studies, religious studies, ethics, jurisprudence, and qualitative approaches in the social sciences. They emphasize analysis, interpretation, and the exchange of ideas. CDP Production grants are designed to strengthen the humanities content and approach of documentary media productions and help propel projects toward completion. Projects must be in the production stage, have a work-in-progress to submit, and actively involve at least two humanities advisors to help frame and contextualize subject matter at a point early enough to make meaningful contributions to the production. Eligible projects may apply for funding up to $50,000 (film and radio) or $20,000 (new media).
Requirements: Eligible applicant organizations/project directors must: have tax-exempt organizational status or a tax-exempt organization as fiscal sponsor; be in good standing with CCH (e.g., without unfulfilled reporting requirements), if a previous grantee; and not have an open grant with CCH, unless a CCH-approved sponsoring organization (see FAQ for more information).
Restrictions: The Council does not fund: institutional histories produced and/or partially funded by the institution itself; advocacy; projects that are primarily promotional in nature; projects at the research and development stage; or projects already in post-production.
Geographic Focus: California
Date(s) Application is Due: Oct 3
Amount of Grant: Up to 50,000 USD
Contact: Vanessa Whang; (415) 391-1474; fax (415) 391-1312; vwhang@calhum.org
Internet: http://www.calhum.org/guidelines/guidelines_cdp.htm
Sponsor: California Council for the Humanities
312 Sutter Street, Suite 601
San Francisco, CA 94108-4371

CCH Documentary Project Public Engagement Grants 970
The California Documentary Project (CDP) is a competitive grant program of the California Council for the Humanities (CCH). CDP supports film, radio, and new media projects in which the humanities are used to provide context, depth, and perspective. The humanities spring from a fundamental interest in understanding the values and practices that inform our lives; the need to reflect on the past and the present to make critical choices; and the desire to be moved, delighted, and make sense of the world in which we live. Humanities disciplines include, but are not limited to: history, literature, philosophy, folklore, ethnic studies, religious studies, ethics, jurisprudence, and qualitative approaches in the social sciences. They emphasize analysis, interpretation, and the exchange of ideas. CDP Public Engagement grants support the dissemination and public engagement activities of previously-supported CDP film, radio, and new media projects. The purpose of this program is to extend the reach and impact of Council-supported humanities media projects, deepen understanding and awareness of subjects and issues of relevance to California, and foster critical reflection and thoughtful analysis on the part of audiences. Sample activities may include, but are not limited to: community screenings and discussions; pre- or post-screening panel or speaker presentations; the development and distribution of public education standards-aligned lesson plans, discussion guides, or other educational materials; translation and subtitling; targeted distribution plans; design and implementation of web-based tools; and the repurposing and dissemination of collateral content. Previously-supported CDP film, radio, and new media projects that are completed or at the fine cut stage are eligible to apply.
Requirements: While there are no specific public engagement activities mandated by this grant program, proposed activities should: be clearly defined in terms of intended audience, reach, and impact; be designed to maximize use of grant funds; seek to leverage impact through strategic partnerships; and have well-defined and feasible goals. Eligible applicant organizations and project directors must: have a film, radio or new media project that is completed or at the fine cut stage that has previously received funding from the Council through the CDP Research and Development, Production, or New Media grant categories; have tax-exempt organizational status or a tax-exempt organization as a fiscal sponsor; and be in good standing with CCH (e.g., without unfulfilled reporting requirements).
Geographic Focus: California
Date(s) Application is Due: Oct 3
Amount of Grant: Up to 10,000 USD
Contact: Vanessa Whang; (415) 391-1474; fax (415) 391-1312; vwhang@calhum.org
Internet: http://www.calhum.org/guidelines/guidelines_cdp.htm
Sponsor: California Council for the Humanities
312 Sutter Street, Suite 601
San Francisco, CA 94108-4371

CCH Documentary Project Research and Development Grants 971
The California Documentary Project (CDP) is a competitive grant program of the California Council for the Humanities (CCH). CDP supports film, radio, and new media projects in which the humanities are used to provide context, depth, and perspective. The humanities spring from a fundamental interest in understanding the values and practices that inform our lives; the need to reflect on the past and the present to make critical choices; and the desire to be moved, delighted, and make sense of the world in which we live. Humanities disciplines include, but are not limited to: history, literature, philosophy, folklore, ethnic studies, religious studies, ethics, jurisprudence, and qualitative approaches in the social sciences. They emphasize analysis, interpretation, and the exchange of ideas. CDP Research and Development grants are designed to strengthen the humanities content and approach of documentary media productions in their earliest stages. Projects must actively involve at least three humanities advisors to help frame and contextualize subject matter throughout the research and development phase. Eligible projects may apply for funding up to $7,000.
Requirements: Eligible applicant organizations/project directors must: have tax-exempt organizational status or a tax-exempt organization as fiscal sponsor; be in good standing with CCH (e.g., without unfulfilled reporting requirements), if a previous grantee; and not have an open grant with CCH, unless a CCH-approved sponsoring organization (see FAQ for more information). Film, radio, and new media projects must meet all of the following criteria: be currently in the research and development stage; document the California experience and explore issues of significance to Californians; approach the subject matter from a humanities perspective—for example, making use of existing or new scholarship and research on the topic, incorporating a variety of perspectives, seeking to foster critical

reflection and thoughtful analysis on the part of the audience; actively involve at least three humanities advisors throughout the research and development phase; and be conducted by experienced film, radio, or new media producers and directors. A previously completed work sample must be submitted.
Geographic Focus: California
Date(s) Application is Due: Oct 3
Amount of Grant: Up to 7,000 USD
Contact: Vanessa Whang; (415) 391-1474; fax (415) 391-1312; vwhang@calhum.org
Internet: http://www.calhum.org/guidelines/cdp_2011_RandD_guidelines.htm
Sponsor: California Council for the Humanities
312 Sutter Street, Suite 601
San Francisco, CA 94108-4371

CDC Foundation Emergency Response Fund Grants 972
The CDC Foundation's Emergency Response Fund provides immediate, flexible resources to CDC experts addressing public health emergencies in the U.S. - whether natural disasters, emerging disease outbreaks or bioterrorist threats. Following the events of September 11, 2001, and the anthrax attacks, the CDC Foundation established the Emergency Response Fund to give CDC what it needs most in an emergency: flexibility and access to immediate resources. Federal dollars, even during emergencies, are tied to restrictions and purchasing procedures that can limit CDC's ability to act quickly. The Foundation's Emergency Response Fund gives CDC a backup source of funding to fill critical gaps and meet immediate needs. The Fund was activated for the first time in 2005 to support the public health response to Hurricane Katrina in the Gulf Coast region. Donations to the Fund from Kaiser Permanente, the Robert Wood Johnson Foundation, and other organizations and individuals enabled the CDC Foundation to immediately respond to requests for help from CDC and their public health partners in the gulf coast region. The Foundation was also able to provide new facilities for two public health agencies on the Mississippi coast, replacing buildings that had been destroyed by the storm.
Geographic Focus: All States
Contact: Verla S. Neslund, J.D., Vice President for Programs; (888) 880-4232 or (404) 653-0790; fax (404) 653-0330; vneslund@cdcfoundation.org
Internet: http://www.cdcfoundation.org/response
Sponsor: Centers for Disease Control and Prevention (CDC) Foundation
55 Park Place NE, Suite 400
Atlanta, GA 30303

CDC Foundation Global Disaster Response Fund Grants 973
Following the December 2004 tsunami disaster in southern Asia, CDC teams were called to the region to provide critical assistance to the survivors and to monitor for deadly disease outbreaks. CDC Foundation president and CEO Charles Stokes quickly met with CDC officials to find out what the Foundation could do to help. He learned that while CDC responders are well-trained and well-equipped for disaster situations, some specialized equipment – such as additional satellite phones, pocket PCs and a camera with global satellite positioning capabilities – would help them do their work more quickly and efficiently. The CDC Foundation established a new Global Disaster Response Fund to make it possible for people to contribute to CDC's tsunami response efforts and to enable CDC to instantly purchase the equipment needed. The fund was activated again in 2010 to help CDC respond to the devastating earthquake in Haiti. The fund helped address immediate needs like tarps, tents and handheld computers. Efforts are now focused on working with in-country health officials to provide public health facilities, equipment and training opportunities.
Geographic Focus: All Countries
Contact: Verla S. Neslund, J.D., Vice President for Programs; (888) 880-4232 or (404) 653-0790; fax (404) 653-0330; vneslund@cdcfoundation.org
Internet: http://www.cdcfoundation.org/globaldisaster
Sponsor: Centers for Disease Control and Prevention (CDC) Foundation
55 Park Place NE, Suite 400
Atlanta, GA 30303

CDC Grants for Violence-Related Injury Prevention Research 974
Funded projects should identify effective ways of preventing violence-related injuries and expand the use of new and current intervention methods for preventing these types of injuries. In the areas of suicide and assaultive behavior, projects may focus on understanding the factors that affect this behavior, such as the nature of suicide among gay and lesbian people as compared to the general population or how unequal access to criminal justice, health care, and education is related to violent behavior. Family and intimate violence prevention projects may examine the intervention strategies that are most effective in preventing injuries. CDC encourages projects to study the needs of mothers and children in families where intimate partner violence takes place and to use population-based research to quantify injury and disability among women as a result of partner violence. Officials are also interested in research that defines the cost of violent injuries and the cost effectiveness of prevention or intervention methods. Contact the program office for deadline dates.
Requirements: Public and private nonprofit and for-profit agencies may apply for grants. This includes state and local agencies, hospitals, and universities.
Geographic Focus: All States
Amount of Grant: Up to 300,000 USD
Contact: Paul Smutz; (770) 488-1508
Internet: http://www.cdc.gov/ncipc/res-opps/VIOLENCE_04045.htm
Sponsor: Centers for Disease Control and Prevention
1600 Clifton Road
Atlanta, GA 30333

CDC School Health Programs to Prevent the Spread of HIV Cooperative Agreements 975
The objective of the program is to support the development and implementation of effective health education for HIV and other important health problems for school-age populations (elementary- through college-age youth); parents; and relevant school, health, and education personnel. Cooperative agreement funds may be used to support personnel, their training and travel, and to purchase supplies and services for planning, organizing, and conducting activities directly related to the objectives of this program. These activities may include obtaining baseline data and establishing a system to monitor the availability and adequacy of HIV education in schools; increasing the number of schools providing HIV education; monitoring the levels of HIV-related knowledge, beliefs, and behaviors among students; collaborating with state and local health agencies in carrying out HIV education programs in the schools; establishing policies, guidelines, advisory committees, and/or standards to increase the number of schools providing HIV education; integrating HIV education within a more comprehensive program of school health education; disseminating information about accessibility, availability, and quality of educational strategies, materials, and curricula to local education agencies and schools; and providing technical assistance to local school districts and schools in implementing HIV education. The maximum project period is five years. Contact the office for deadline dates.
Requirements: Eligible state education agencies in U.S. states and territories, nonprofit organizations, and universities may apply.
Restrictions: Funds may not be spent for research activities, surveys, or questionnaires except as may be needed to collect basic evaluation requirements. In addition, funds may not be used for purchasing computer equipment, office equipment or furnishings, renting or leasing office space, or financing construction or renovation unless specifically approved.
Geographic Focus: All States
Amount of Grant: 87,000 - 650,000 USD
Contact: Mary Sue Lancaster, Program Development and Services Branch, Division of Adolescent and School Health; (770) 488-6130; fax (770) 488-6163; msl0@cdc.gov
Internet: http://www.cdc.gov
Sponsor: Centers for Disease Control and Prevention
1600 Clifton Road
Atlanta, GA 30333

CDC State and Local Childhood Lead Poisoning Prevention Grants 976
The purpose of the program is to develop, expand, and evaluate state and local childhood lead poisoning prevention programs, and to build statewide capacity to conduct surveillance of blood levels in children. Specifically, grants are intended to support screening programs and follow-up care for children potentially exposed to, or identified with, elevated blood lead level; public awareness programs regarding the dangers of lead exposure; and lead poisoning prevention programs in high-risk areas in collaboration with other government and community-based organizations. Deadlines are posted annually.
Requirements: Eligible applicants are state, territory, and tribal health departments or other state, territory, or tribal health agencies or departments deemed most appropriate by the state to direct and coordinate the childhood lead poisoning prevention program.
Restrictions: Grant funds may not be used for medical care and treatment. No more than 10 percent of any grant may be used for administrative costs.
Geographic Focus: All States
Contact: Rob Henry; (770) 488-7493; fax (770) 488-3635; zjn9@cdc.gov
Internet: http://www.cdc.gov/nceh/lead/lead.htm
Sponsor: Centers for Disease Control and Prevention
1600 Clifton Road
Atlanta, GA 30333

CDECD Arts Catalyze Placemaking in Every Community Grants 977
Arts Catalyze Placemaking's Connecticut Artist in Every Community projects promote community development, teaching, and learning through high quality arts engagement and arts integration. The program provides opportunities for residents of all ages, in every community, to interact with practicing Connecticut artists in ways that will advance Connecticut cities, towns and villages as meaningful communities in which to live, work, learn and play. ACP-1 grants provide funding for a wide range of experiences that engage Connecticut artists, through projects, performances, workshops, and short or long term school or community-based residencies. Applicants define the communities which they wish to engage and for which they seek funding. ACP-1 projects should be classified as the following: performing, which supports one time or short term projects such as performances, lectures, or master classes; connecting, with projects that are short term residences or projects with clearly defined goals and objectives, in addition to an evaluation component; or integrating, which supports long term, sequential arts learning experiences that weave ideas and concepts between and among arts and non-arts disciplines. Eligible expenses include those which are necessary to the project, activity, or program such as: insurance; artist fees; project documentation; marketing, promoting, and printing expenses; technology (hardware, software, professional services, installation, staff training, etc); or limited brick and mortar expenses associated only with the direct needs of the project. Up to 35% of funding is allowed for administrative expenses. Deadlines vary according to funding availability. Additional information and instructions, along with budget information and matching and in-kind requirements, and a list of frequently asked questions, are available at the website. Applicants are also encouraged to attend information sessions, and view the presentations on the website.
Requirements: Lead applicants to ACP-1 may be one of the following Connecticut entities: pre-k through 12 school or after school program; parent teacher organization; COA directory artist; qualified artist or arts organization; municipal department; non-profit organization; or college or university.
Restrictions: Ineligible projects include: any project, activity or program whose membership and/or participation policies do not comply with non-discrimination laws; interest expenses

paid on loans or payments to reduce or eliminate deficits; activities to eliminate or reduce existing deficits; political contributions; lobbying activities and lobbying fees; activities that have already been completed; any project, activity or program that is already funded by another COA program during the same fiscal year; religious programming, activities or paraphernalia; general brick and mortar expenses; travel and conference registration expenses; hospitality expenses; or expenses not related to the project, activity or program.
Geographic Focus: Connecticut
Date(s) Application is Due: Nov 1
Amount of Grant: 500 - 5,000 USD
Contact: John Cusano; (860) 256-2723; fax (860) 256-2811; John.Cusano@ct.gov
Internet: http://www.ct.gov/cct/cwp/view.asp?a=3933&q=507176
Sponsor: Connecticut Department of Economic and Community Development
One Constitution Plaza, 2nd Floor
Hartford, CT 06103

CDECD Arts Catalyze Placemaking Leadership Grants 978
Arts Catalyze Placemaking (ACP) Arts Leadership grants provide funding for arts-based projects, activities and programs that engage partners and advance Connecticut cities, towns, and villages as meaningful communities in which to live, work, learn and play. Funding depends on the level of the project. ACP-2 grants range from $5,000 to $25,000. ACP-3 grants provide two options: planning grants range from $2,500 to $10,000 and fund the planning of projects, activities, or program that allow applicants to identify and design a future ACP-3 implementation project; implementation grants range from $25,001 to $100,000, and fund projects, activities, or programs designed to catalyze placemaking. Eligible expenses include the following: up to 35% of administrative expenses; artist fees; project documentation; marketing, promotional, and printing expenses; technology (hardware, software, professional services; installation, staff training, etc.); limited brick and mortar expenses; and any other costs directly related to the project, activity, or program. Additional information is available at the website, including frequently asked questions,, match requirements, webinars, and information sessions.
Requirements: Lead applicants must be one of the following qualifying entities: artist (with a fiscal sponsor); arts organization; colleges and universities; municipal department (restricted level B); or arts program of a 501(c)3 non-arts organization. All Arts Leadership (ACP-2 and ACP-3) proposals must include a Connecticut artist as an integral part of the planning and/or implementation phase of the proposed project, activity or program. Applicants must supply a one-page resume and/or bio of the artist to be engaged and a brief outline of how the artist is involved in the project, activity or program. In cases where the project artist is retained for their specific discipline expertise, applicants must also submit two to four samples of the artist's work (digital materials may include photographs, video, recordings, etc.).
Restrictions: Ineligible expenses include the following: any project, activity or program whose membership and/or participation policies do not comply with non-discrimination laws; interest expenses paid on loans or payments to reduce or eliminate deficits; activities to eliminate or reduce existing deficits; political contributions; lobbying activities and lobbying fees; activities that have already been completed; any project, activity or program that is already funded by another COA program during the same fiscal year; religious programming, activities or paraphernalia; general brick and mortar expenses; travel and conference registration expenses (except as noted for ACP-3 Planning); hospitality expenses; and expenses not related to the project, activity or program.
Geographic Focus: Connecticut
Date(s) Application is Due: Nov 8
Amount of Grant: 5,000 - 100,000 USD
Contact: John Cusano; (860) 256-2723; fax (860) 256-2811; John.Cusano@ct.gov
Internet: http://www.ct.gov/cct/cwp/view.asp?a=3933&q=507176
Sponsor: Connecticut Department of Economic and Community Development
One Constitution Plaza, 2nd Floor
Hartford, CT 06103

CDECD Arts Catalyze Placemaking Sustaining Relevance Grants 979
Arts Catalyze Placemaking Sustaining Relevance Grants provide support to arts organizations whose on-going work is relevant to the community and supports COA's creative placemaking goals. Sustaining Relevance grants may be applied to any aspect of an organization's operations and/or expansion of those operations that directly support COA's creative placemaking goals. Sustaining funding is intended to advance Connecticut cities, towns and villages as meaningful communities in which to live, work, learn and play. Eligible expenses include but are not limited to: operating costs such as rent, telephone, postage and shipping, marketing, etc; documentation (photo, video, audio, collection of statistical information, etc.) and evaluation (hiring of evaluation consulting services) of organizational projects, activities and programs as described in the Activities, Goals and Outcomes Worksheet; materials and supplies, including printing; staff salaries (includes benefits) for existing or new staff; outside professional services hired to provide assistance in support of mission and/or organizational capacity; artist fees;office technologies including hardware, software, professional installation, staff training, etc; and travel and conference registration expenses for staff and/or volunteers to attend local, regional or national relevant industry conferences, workshops, retreats, and clinics that support the work of the organization (may not exceed 25% of the COA grant). Application deadlines vary according to grant levels and funding available. Additional information is available at the website, including frequently asked questions, budget instructions, matching and in-kind requirements, information sessions, and webinars.
Requirements: Lead applicants must be a Connecticut 501(c)3 nonprofit arts organization whose primary purpose is to create, perform, present, or otherwise promote the visual, performing, or literary arts. Organizations applying must have at least a three year history of arts programming.
Restrictions: Ineligible expenses include the following: any project, activity or program whose membership and/or participation policies that do not comply with non-discrimination laws; interest expenses paid on loans or payments to reduce or eliminate deficits; activities to eliminate or reduce existing deficits; political contributions; lobbying activities and lobbying fees; activities that have already been completed; any project, activity or program that is already funded by another COA program during the same fiscal year; religious programming, activities or paraphernalia; general brick and mortar expenses; and hospitality expenses.
Geographic Focus: Connecticut
Date(s) Application is Due: Oct 25
Contact: John Cusano; (860) 256-2723; fax (860) 256-2811; John.Cusano@ct.gov
Internet: http://www.ct.gov/cct/cwp/view.asp?a=3933&q=507176
Sponsor: Connecticut Department of Economic and Community Development
One Constitution Plaza, 2nd Floor
Hartford, CT 06103

CDECD Endangered Properties Grants 980
Endangered Properties Fund Grants (EPF) were created to provide financial assistance for the preservation of historic properties threatened by imminent loss or destruction. The EPF program accepts requests to apply on a rolling basis. The properties must be listed on the State or National Registers of Historic Places. Applicants must be 501(c)3 or 501(c)13 nonprofit organizations or municipalities. Grant awards range from $2,500 to $100,000, depending on funding availability. Grant awards must be matched with cash on a one-to-one basis. Additional guidelines are available at the CDECD website.
Requirements: Application to the EPF program is by invitation only. Interested parties may send a request to apply to the Construction Grants Coordinator. Project work must be consistent with the Secretary of the Interior's Standards for the Treatment of Historic Properties. A preservation restriction of limited duration must be able to be recorded on the property.
Restrictions: Connecticut state funds cannot be used as match funds.
Geographic Focus: Connecticut
Amount of Grant: 2,500 - 100,000 USD
Contact: Laura Mancuso; (860) 256-2757; fax (860) 256-2811; laura.mancuso@ct.gov
Internet: http://www.cultureandtourism.org/cct/cwp/view.asp?a=3933&q=451498
Sponsor: Connecticut Department of Economic and Community Development
One Constitution Plaza, 2nd Floor
Hartford, CT 06103

CDECD Historic Preservation Enhancement Grants 981
The Historic Preservation Enhancement Grants (HPEG) may be used by municipalities that are approved by the National Park Service (NPS), U.S. Department of the Interior as Certified Local Governments (CLG). Grants may be used to support activities sponsored by municipal historic district commissions that enhance the historic district commissions administrative capabilities, strengthen local preservation programs, and produce public education materials and activities. The Commission awards grants of up to $2,800. Grant awards do not have to be matched. A proposed program or project budget may exceed the grant request; however, additional sources of funding must be identified in the application budget. HPEG grants will be available on an annual basis to allow certified local governments and historic district commissions to develop multi-year work plans. The application and a detailed list of initiatives, projects, or programs that would qualify for funding are posted on the CDECD website.
Requirements: Eligible applicants are strictly limited to municipalities that have been formally designated as Certified Local Governments (CLG) by the National Park Service of the U.S. Department of the Interior. Those that have been designated are: Bridgeport, Brookfield, Canton, Chaplin, Colchester, Colebrook, East Hartford, Fairfield, Glastonbury, Groton, Guilford, Hamden, Harwinton, Hebron, Killingly, Ledyard, New Fairfield, New Haven, New London, New Milford, Norwich, Old Lyme, Orange, Roxbury, Salisbury, Simsbury, Southbury, Suffield, Tolland, Vernon, Waterford, Westport, Windham, Windsor, Woodbury and Woodstock.
Restrictions: Ineligible activities and costs include: capital expenses; equipment purchase; fundraising; hospitality expenses; lobbying activities; mandated expenses such as legal notices; municipal employee staff time outside of project administration; regranting; restoration or rehabilitation; scholarships; software acquisition; and travel.
Geographic Focus: Connecticut
Date(s) Application is Due: Jun 13
Amount of Grant: Up to 2,800 USD
Contact: Mary Dunne; (860) 256-2756; fax (860) 256-2811; mary.dunne@ct.gov
Internet: http://www.cultureandtourism.org/cct/cwp/view.asp?a=3933&Q=464434&PM=1#SCLG
Sponsor: Connecticut Department of Economic and Community Development
One Constitution Plaza, 2nd Floor
Hartford, CT 06103

CDECD Historic Preservation Survey and Planning Grants 982
Historic Survey and Planning Grants of up to $20,000 may be used by Connecticut non-profit organizations and municipalities for a wide range of historic preservation planning activities, including surveys, nominations to the National or State Registers of Historic Places, pre-development studies, heritage tourism, and other planning documents. Survey and Planning Grants are reimbursement grants that must be matched 50/50 by non-state funds. The grant recipient will receive a small partial payment when the state grant contract is signed. The grant recipient must expend the total project cost. Upon approval and acceptance of final products and submission of a satisfactory project completion report (which includes fiscal documentation for the total project cost), the recipient will be reimbursed for 50% of eligible project costs up to the amount of grant allocation. A grant recipient must have sufficient funds available to cover the entire cost of the project prior to reimbursement. Applications are accepted at any time as long as funding is available,

but non-profits or municipalities may have only one active S and P grant at a time. The application, along with a detailed list of examples of initiatives, projects, or programs that would qualify for funding, are posted on the website.
Requirements: Eligible applicants include Connecticut municipalities; tax-exempt 501(c)3 organizations; and other non-profit organizations applying for grant funds to survey archaeological resources on state land. Applicants must submit a letter from the state agency authorizing the application.
Restrictions: Ineligible activities and costs include: acquisition of real estate; archeological salvage; archival research not connected to historic preservation; capital expenses; construction, restoration, or rehabilitation; costs incurred prior to the date of a grant award and the execution of the state contract; court actions; curation; equipment purchase; fines or penalties; fundraising efforts; general operating expenses; hospitality expenses including alcoholic beverages, and food, meals, or entertainment; indirect costs; interest payments; lobbying activities; nonconformance with applicable Secretary of the Interior's standards; projects already underway; political contributions; regranting; scholarships; software acquisition; and travel.
Geographic Focus: Connecticut
Amount of Grant: Up to 20,000 USD
Contact: Mary Dunne; (860) 256-2756; fax (860) 256-2811; mary.dunne@ct.gov
Internet: http://www.cultureandtourism.org/cct/cwp/view.asp?a=3933&q=414860
Sponsor: Connecticut Department of Economic and Community Development
One Constitution Plaza, 2nd Floor
Hartford, CT 06103

CDECD Historic Restoration Grants 983
Historic Restoration Fund Grants provide financial assistance for the rehabilitation, restoration, stabilization, or acquisition of historic properties listed on the State or National Registers of Historic Places. Properties must be owned by a municipality or a 501(c)3 or 501(c)13 nonprofit organization. Applications are accepted once a year. Funding will range from $5,000 to $200,000. Additional guidelines, stories of previously funded projects, and a list of frequently asked questions are available at the CDEDC website.
Requirements: Grant awards must be matched on a one-to-one basis with cash. No in-kind services are allowed. Matching funds cannot be funds from the State of Connecticut, but federal funds or other non-state funds may be used. Facilities must be open to the public or work must be visible to the public. A preservation easement of limited duration must be placed on the property following completion of the project. Grant funds are paid to grantees on a single-payment reimbursement basis following the completion of the project and approval of all work by staff. Project work must be consistent with the Secretary of the Interior's Standards for Rehabilitation.
Geographic Focus: Connecticut
Date(s) Application is Due: Oct 25
Amount of Grant: 5,000 - 200,000 USD
Contact: Laura Mancuso; (860) 256-2757; fax (860) 256-2811; laura.mancuso@ct.gov
Internet: http://www.cultureandtourism.org/cct/cwp/view.asp?a=3933&q=317350
Sponsor: Connecticut Department of Economic and Community Development
One Constitution Plaza, 2nd Floor
Hartford, CT 06103

CDECD Tourism Product Development Grants 984
The Department of Economic and Community Development (DECD) Office of Tourism (COT) Tourism Product Development Grant (TPD) program provides tourism entities with matching funds for: innovative products that generate significant new visitation and spending; linking existing assets in new more powerful ways to attract greater visitation and spending; and enhancing existing assets to ensure that they stay fresh and responsive to evolving consumer demands. The intent is to fund fewer larger iconic projects rather than smaller projects. Applications are accepted twice a year for either one or two years. One year project funding ranges from $30,00 to $100,000, while two year project funding ranges from $30,000 to $75,000. The application and additional guidelines are available at the website.
Requirements: Tourism non-profit 501(c)3, 501(c)5, 501(c)6 and municipalities are eligible, with proof of non-profit status. Projects involving partners must have a lead applicant with non-profit status. Applicants shall demonstrate a fiscal accountability system that insures that the monies will be spent as indicated by the grant application. Applicants should have an initial marketing plan. Applicants without an initial marketing plan must complete the Strategic Marketing Questionnaire provided in place of the marketing plan. Applicants not incorporated in Connecticut but who are registered to do business in Connecticut must include a Certificate of Authority from the office of the Secretary of State.
Restrictions: Ineligible funding includes: organizations whose membership and participation policies do not comply with non-discrimination laws; organizations acting solely as fiscal agents for individuals or groups; state or federal agencies; brick and mortar and capital improvements; specific activities or projects that are already funded by another COT program during the same fiscal year; activities that have already been completed; activities to eliminate or reduce existing deficits; activities funded by or which generate revenue for COT; religious programming and activities; benefits, fundraisers, social events; interest expenses paid on loans or debts; scholarship assistance for academic or non-academic programs; lobbying activities; political contributions; and legal fees.
Geographic Focus: Connecticut
Date(s) Application is Due: Mar 21; Sep 21
Amount of Grant: 30,000 - 100,000 USD
Contact: Rena Calcaterra, (860) 256-2744; fax (860) 256-2811; rena.calcaterra@ct.gov
Internet: http://www.cultureandtourism.org/cct/cwp/view.asp?a=3933&q=499358
Sponsor: Connecticut Department of Economic and Community Development
One Constitution Plaza, 2nd Floor
Hartford, CT 06103

CE and S Foundation Grants 985
The foundation is interested in supporting projects that improve people's lives. Focus areas for grant making include higher education; international cooperation; urban environmental improvement, and emergency disaster relief. Preference is given to those programs that have developed methods for measuring success. Before a grant proposal is submitted, the foundation requests that organizations first call the executive director to discuss the particulars of the project and the ways in which it fits the foundation guidelines.
Requirements: Nonprofit organizations are eligible to apply.
Restrictions: The foundation does not provide support individuals or for medical research.
Geographic Focus: All States
Amount of Grant: 500 - 100,000 USD
Contact: Bruce Maza; (502) 583-0546; fax (502) 583-7648; bruce@cesfoundation.com
Internet: http://www.cesfoundation.com/grantmaking.html
Sponsor: CE and S Foundation
1650 National City Tower
Louisville, KY 40202

CECP Directors' Award 986
CECP's Excellence Awards are among the most coveted awards in the field, drawing an extraordinary pool of applications each year. Presented annually since 2000, these awards are juried by an external Selection Committee that is comprised of representatives from the corporate, nonprofit, multilateral, social investment, consulting, media, and academic communities. For nonprofit originations, the Directors' Award recognizes the partnership between their organization and a corporate partner. This award category carries with it a $25,000 cash donation from CECP's Board of Directors. The nonprofit winner is recognized at the CECP Summit in June. The winning organizations are featured in a video shown at the event, and shared through CECP's website and other communications channels. CECP works with the communications teams at the winning organizations to secure press opportunities.
Requirements: Award nominees are restricted to U.S.-based 501(c)3 nonprofit organizations working through active programs to improve the overall well-being of society at large, and/or domestic and international communities. A nominated organization must have an annual operating budget equal to or exceeding $500,000.
Restrictions: Prior award recipients are not eligible to be nominated for four years.
Geographic Focus: All States
Date(s) Application is Due: Sep 5
Amount of Grant: Up to 25,000 USD
Contact: Margaret Coady; (212) 825-1000; fax (212) 825-1251; info@corphilanthropy.org
Internet: http://www.corporatephilanthropy.org/events/excellence-awards.html
Sponsor: Committee to Encourage Corporate Philanthropy
5 Hanover Square, Suite 2102
New York, NY 10004

Ceil & Michael E. Pulitzer Foundation Grants 987
The Ceil & Michael E. Pulitzer Foundation, Inc., formerly The Michael E. Pulitzer Foundation, Inc. is a independent foundation that was established in 1993 in Missouri. Giving primarily in Missouri, California and New York, the foundation is interested in the areas of higher education, museums and human services.
Requirements: No application form exists, submit a letter of intent as a initial approach, include the following: a detailed description of project; amount of funding requested.
Geographic Focus: California, Missouri, New York
Amount of Grant: 500 - 230,000 USD
Contact: Michael E. Pulitzer, President; (314) 398-1396
Sponsor: Ceil and Michael E. Pulitzer Foundation
P.O. Box 23368
Saint Louis, MO 63156-3368

Cemala Foundation Grants 988
The Cemala Foundation is a private family foundation established in 1986 by Martha A. and Ceasar Cone II to continue the family tradition of commitment to enhancing the quality of life of the community through grants to qualified charitable organizations. Areas of interest are: arts/culture; education; health; homelessness; human services; the state of North Carolina and; public interest. Application and additional guidelines are available at the Foundation's website.
Requirements: Grants are made only to non-profit charitable organizations which are tax exempt under Section 501(c)3 of the Internal Revenue Code or to public governmental units. Generally, grants are limited to projects which benefit the citizens of Guilford County, North Carolina. Occasionally, projects which benefit the state of North Carolina as a whole are considered.
Restrictions: The Foundation does not consider support for annual campaigns, endowments, sectarian religious activities, or requests under $1,000. Grants are not made to individuals. Grants from the Cemala Foundation are usually awarded for one year only. Only one grant application may be submitted in any twelve-month period. Organizations receiving grants are required to complete an evaluation report within twelve months after receipt of the funds.
Geographic Focus: North Carolina
Date(s) Application is Due: Mar 1; Sep 1
Amount of Grant: 3,000 - 200,000 USD
Contact: Susan S. Schwartz; (336) 274-3541; fax (336) 272-8153; cemala@cemala.org
Internet: http://www.cemala.org/grant/guidelines.php
Sponsor: Cemala Foundation
330 South Greene Street, Suite 101
Greensboro, NC 27401

Center for the Study of Philanthropy International Fellowships 989
The center provides leadership training through applied research and professional mentorships for young scholar-practitioners in the nonprofit sector. The program offers leadership training to scholar-practitioners outside the U.S. as a means to help build Third-Sector capacity in the fellows' home countries. Specific topical areas are chosen each year. Special attention will also be given to diaspora philanthropy. Fellows participate in a three-month seminar on the U.S. and international voluntary sectors. Fellows are expected to produce a 30-50 page paper on their findings to be presented in the seminar. They will learn about the work of key agencies and meet with foundation and nonprofit representatives. They may also have the opportunity to attend selected conferences. Fellowship includes tuition and monthly stipend, housing, and round-trip air travel to and from the US.
Requirements: The program is open to practitioners and researchers under the age of 36 who are citizens of countries other than the US. Applicants must have a college or university degree and speak and write English fluently. Preference will be given to candidates with a strong institutional base and demonstrated research skills.
Geographic Focus: All States
Date(s) Application is Due: Sep 13
Amount of Grant: 1,300 - 15,600 USD
Contact: Dr. Kathleen McCarthy; (212) 817-2010; fax (212) 817-1572; info@philanthropy.org
Internet: http://www.philanthropy.org/programs/intnl_fellows_program.html
Sponsor: City University of New York
365 Fifth Avenue
New York, NY 10016-4309

Center for the Study of Philanthropy Senior International Fellowships 990
The center provides leadership training through applied research and professional mentorships for young scholar-practitioners in the nonprofit sector. The program offers leadership training to scholar-practitioners outside the United States as a means to help build Third-Sector capacity in the fellows' home countries. Specific topical areas are chosen each year. The current year's theme is community foundations. Fellows participate in a three-month seminar on the U.S. and international voluntary sectors. Fellows attend weekly seminars, learn about the work of key agencies and foundations, meet with nonprofit representatives, and study U.S. and international community foundation models. Fellowship includes tuition and monthly stipend, housing, and round-trip air travel to and from the United States.
Requirements: The program is open to senior-level practitioners and researchers under the age of 36 who are citizens of countries other than the United States. Applicants must have a college or university degree and speak and write English fluently. Preference will be given to candidates with a strong institutional base and demonstrated research skills.
Geographic Focus: All States
Date(s) Application is Due: Jun 15; Oct 15
Amount of Grant: 1,300 - 15,600 USD
Contact: Fellowship Coordinator, (212) 817-1572; csp@gc.cuny.edu
Internet: http://www.philanthropy.org/programs/intnl_fellows_program.html
Sponsor: City University of New York
365 Fifth Avenue
New York, NY 10016-4309

Center for Venture Philanthropy 991
The Center for Venture Philanthropy was launched in 1999 to create an environment where community donors could collaborate and drive positive change in our communities. Using a venture capital model, local investors base social venture funding on results-oriented business plans focused on specific causes. Investors work directly with the Center for Venture Philanthropy staff and nonprofit leaders to understand community and nonprofit issues, problem-solve and structure their investments.
Geographic Focus: California
Amount of Grant: 1,000 USD
Contact: Jeff Sunshine; (408) 278-2200; fax (408) 278-0280; jsunshine@cfsv.org
Internet: http://www.siliconvalleycf.org/
Sponsor: Silicon Valley Community Foundation
60 S Market Street, Suite 1000
San Jose, CA 95113-2336

Center on Philanthropy and Civil Society's Emerging Leaders International Fellows 992
The program provides leadership training through applied research and professional mentorships for young scholar-practitioners in the nonprofit sector. The program is open to scholars and practitioners interested in building Third-Sector capacity in the United States and overseas. This year???s fellows will be selected from abroad and also from communities of color under-represented in the United States grantmaking sector. Fellows are based at the Graduate Center of The City University of New York, where they design and pursue an individualized research project and participate in a seminar with Third-Sector leaders. Specific topical areas are chosen each year.
Requirements: The program is open to practitioners and researchers under the age of 36. Applicants must hold a college or university degree and speak and write English fluently. Preference will be given to candidates with strong ties to a Third-Sector institution and demonstrated research skills.
Geographic Focus: All States
Date(s) Application is Due: Dec 7
Amount of Grant: 1,300 USD
Contact: Dr. Kathleen McCarthy; (212) 817-2010; fax (212) 817-1572; csp@gc.cuny.edu
Internet: http://www.philanthropy.org/programs/ifp/application.html
Sponsor: City University of New York
365 Fifth Avenue
New York, NY 10016-4309

CenterPointEnergy Minnegasco Grants 993
CenterPoint Energy focuses on: Affordable, energy efficient housing— Support for organizations that develop, build and revitalize affordable, energy efficient housing. Priority is given to actual construction or rehabilitation of homes; Environmental programs—Support for organizations, programs and projects that promote and protect our environmental and natural resources; and Post-secondary technical education partnerships—Partnering with post-secondary technical educational institutions to influence technical curriculum development and scholarships that facilitate recruitment and retention of employees for CenterPoint Energy.
Requirements: Grants are made to Minnesota 501(c)3 tax-exempt organizations that are in compliance with applicable state charities laws and are located within the company's geographic service territory.
Restrictions: Grants do not support multiyear requests (except under extenuating circumstances); religious or political purposes; individuals; travel and related expenses; conferences; fundraising activities; national organizations; national or local fundraising campaigns, ticket sales, fundraising dinners, or similar activities; sports and athletic programs; or health or disease-related programs.
Geographic Focus: Minnesota
Amount of Grant: 1,000 - 10,000 USD
Contact: Suzanne Pierazek, (612) 321-4828 or (800) 245-2377; suzanne.pierazek@CenterPointEnergy.com
Internet: http://mn.centerpointenergy.com/global_navigation/community_relations/index.asp
Sponsor: CenterPointEnergy Minnegasco
800 LaSalle Avenue, HQ 14
Minneapolis, MN 55402

Central Carolina Community Foundation Community Impact Grants 994
The Foundation's Community Impact grants fund programmatic initiatives of nonprofit organizations. In order to support positive community change and help ensure a program's success, the Grants have a maximum request amount of $10,000. The grant making process is a bi-annual process. Proposals are accepted, April 1 - September 30, for the Fall cycle, October 1 - March 31 for the Spring cycle.
Requirements: Nonprofit organizations serving South Carolina communities are eligible.
Restrictions: Grants do not support routine operating expenses, fund raising projects, debt reduction, endowment development, medical research, conference travel, or conference underwriting or sponsorship. Letter of intent or proposal may not be submitted by email or fax.
Geographic Focus: South Carolina
Date(s) Application is Due: Mar 31; Sep 30
Amount of Grant: Up to 10,000 USD
Contact: Veronica L. Pinkett-Barber, Program Officer; (803) 254-5601 ext. 331; fax (803) 799-6663; veronica@yourfoundation.org
Internet: http://www.yourfoundation.org/nonprofits/foundationgrants/impactgrants.aspx
Sponsor: Central Carolina Community Foundation
2711 Middleburg Drive, Suite 213
Columbia, SC 29204

Central Minnesota Community Foundation Grants 995
The community foundation administers charitable funds in the form of grants to nonprofit organizations for the benefit of residents of central Minnesota. The goal of the foundation is to identify and address social and cultural needs and to foster a sense of human interdependence dedicated to building self-capacity and fullness of life for all. The board of directors gives preference to applications that address themselves to developing capacity and self-help by attempting to address the causes of problems rather than dealing only with the symptoms; enhancing human dignity by providing support for those who participate actively in determining the course of their own lives; responding to new, innovative programs of organizations by addressing opportunities and dilemmas of emerging and changing needs; preserving the historic sense of voluntarism; fostering equal opportunity and enhancement of cultural heritage and diversity; supporting programs and projects that will enable charitable agencies to reduce costs and increase efficiency; and supporting community studies, programmatic research, or other types of projects intended to help citizens understand their problems and options, foster the refinement of public policy, and encourage coordination and cooperation. Applications are accepted four times each year; contact program staff for dates. Only one grant application per year will be considered from eligible applicants.
Requirements: The primary geographic focus of the foundation includes Benton, Sherburne, and Stearns Counties, but grants also are made to organizations located in rural central Minnesota counties. IRS 501(c)3 organizations are eligible, but applicants not meeting this requirement may apply through a fiscal agent.
Restrictions: The foundation will not fund individuals, endowments, medical research, capital campaigns to which the foundation can contribute no more than a tiny fraction of the total need, debt retirement or deficit financing, dollar-for-dollar replacement of government funding that has been reduced or eliminated, religious organizations for direct religious activities, political organizations or political campaigns, fraternal organizations, societies or orders, telephone solicitations, national fundraising efforts, or grants for travel.
Geographic Focus: Minnesota
Amount of Grant: Up to 31,000,000 USD
Contact: Susan Lorenz, Program Officer; (877) 253-4380 or (320) 253-4380; fax (320) 240-9215; slorenz@communitygiving.org
Internet: http://www.communitygiving.org/about_us_cm_6.php4
Sponsor: Central Minnesota Community Foundation
101 S 7th Avenue, Suite 100
Saint Cloud, MN 56301

Central New York Community Foundation Grants 996

The foundation is looking for innovative programs that address problems to be solved or opportunities to be seized in the Central New York area, specifically Onondaga and Madison Counties. Proposals are invited that suggest practical approaches to community problems; promote cooperation among agencies without duplicating services; generate community support, both professional and volunteer; demonstrate the organization's ability to secure realistic funding; strengthen an agency's effectiveness or stability; and address prevention as well as remediation. Types of support include capital grants, program development, seed money grants, and training grants. Prospective applicants are strongly encouraged to discuss the appropriateness of their grant request with staff before beginning the application process. Applications will not be accepted by fax.
Requirements: New York 501(c)3 tax-exempt organizations in Onondaga and Madison Counties are eligible.
Restrictions: The foundation generally does not make grants for annual operating budgets, except when it is seed or bridge money; endowments; sectarian purposes; loans or assistance to individuals; or medical research.
Geographic Focus: New York
Amount of Grant: 500 - 50,000 USD
Contact: Kim Scott, (315) 422-9538; fax (315) 471-6031; kim@cnycf.org
Internet: http://www.cnycf.org/seekers/grants.cfm
Sponsor: Central New York Community Foundation
500 S Salina Street, Suite 428
Syracuse, NY 13202-3302

Central Okanagan Foundation Grants 997

The foundation seeks to enhance the quality of life in Canada and awards grants to nonprofit organizations in its areas of interest, including arts and culture, children, youth, families, education, health, community services, environmental conservation, and heritage preservation. Types of support include emergency funds, equipment acquisition, program development, scholarship funds, and seed money. Contact the foundation by phone to discuss the proposed project. Guidelines and application form will be sent if the project falls within the foundation's guidelines.
Requirements: Nonprofit British Columbia organizations in the Central Okanagan region as defined by the boundaries of BC School District 23 are eligible.
Restrictions: Grants are not awarded to individuals or religious organizations for religious purposes. Grants do not support capital campaigns, debt retirement, endowments, building construction/renovation, or operating expenses.
Geographic Focus: All States, Canada
Date(s) Application is Due: May 1; Oct 1
Contact: Cheryl Miller; (250) 861-6160; cheryl@centralokanaganfoundation.org
Internet: http://www.centralokanaganfoundation.org/pages/grants/cof-grants.php
Sponsor: Central Okanagan Foundation
217-1889 Springfield Road
Kelowna, BC V1Y 5V5 Canada

CenturyLink Clarke M. Williams Foundation Grants 998

CenturyLink's vision is to improve lives, strengthen businesses and connect communities by delivering advanced technologies and solutions with honest and personal service. CenturyLink extends this vision through the CenturyLink Clarke M. Williams Foundation, a 501(c)3 organization dedicated to contributing to endeavors that improve the well-being and overall quality of life for people throughout CenturyLink's communities. Named after CenturyLink's founder Clarke M. Williams, the Foundation is endowed by CenturyLink to support community initiatives that encourage our employees to use their time, talents and resources to strengthen the communities in which they live and work. The Foundation supports programs designed to enrich the lives of children in pre-kindergarten through 12th grade education. Special emphasis is directed toward programs designed to effectively use technology to improve pre-k through 12 public school instruction; promote innovative models to strengthen pre-k through 12 public school education; improve the skills and leadership of educators and parents; promote innovative early childhood education; and promote diversity awareness and cultural competency.
Requirements: Eligible are 501(c)3 nonprofits located in the CenturyLink service areas.
Restrictions: The Foundation does not provide support for political organizations, private foundations, pass-through organizations, or organizations that receive 3 percent or more funding from the United Way. No grants are given to individuals (except for Qwest Teacher Grants), or for scholarships, sectarian religious activities, capital campaigns, chairs, endowments, general operating support for single-disease health groups, or goodwill advertising.
Geographic Focus: Alabama, Arizona, Arkansas, California, Colorado, Connecticut, District of Columbia, Florida, Georgia, Idaho, Illinois, Indiana, Iowa, Kansas, Louisiana, Maryland, Michigan, Minnesota, Missouri, Montana, Nebraska, New Jersey, New Mexico, New York, North Carolina, North Dakota, Ohio, Pennsylvania, South Dakota, Tennessee, Texas, Utah, Virginia, Washington, Wisconsin, Wyoming
Amount of Grant: Up to 10,000 USD
Contact: David Bromberg, Manager; (800) 839-1754
Internet: http://www.centurylink.com/Pages/AboutUs/Community/Foundation/
Sponsor: CenturyLink Clarke M. Williams Foundation
100 Centurylink Drive
Monroe, LA 71203-2041

Ceres Foundation Grants 999

Grants focus on programs that aim to produce permanent improvements in peoples' lives by means of short-term interventions. Such programs address acute problems that block people's chances at critical moments in their lives. Interventions may take a few months, or even a few years, but in the end they enable beneficiaries to overcome the obstacles in their way, and to shift their lives onto promising paths. Grants are made throughout the year, and applications may be sent at any time.
Requirements: Applicants who can best demonstrate a tangible, direct connection between the services their programs provide and the positive shifts that take place in individuals' lives are favored. Also, preference is given to organizations whose chances of success can be significantly increased by Ceres' support. Applicants must use the 'Common Grant Application Format' designed by the Washington Regional Association of Grantmakers (www.washingtongrantmakers.org).
Restrictions: Applicants should be located on the West Coast or on the Eastern Seaboard of the U.S. The grants are less likely to support programs that provide educational enrichment, services for the handicapped, or activity centers for children. Also outside the scope of the foundation's mission are religious organizations that use their charitable programs to promote religious doctrines, foreign organizations that are not incorporated in the United States, and individuals who are seeking financial assistance.
Geographic Focus: California, Connecticut, Delaware, District of Columbia, Florida, Georgia, Maine, Maryland, Massachusetts, New Hampshire, New York, North Carolina, Oregon, Rhode Island, South Carolina, Vermont, Virginia, Washington, West Virginia
Amount of Grant: 20,000 - 130,000 USD
Contact: Grants Administrator; Ceresmd@comcast.net
Internet: http://foundationcenter.org/grantmaker/ceres/index.html
Sponsor: Ceres Foundation
18606 Reliant Drive
Gaithersburg, MD 20879

Cessna Foundation Grants 1000

Grants are made to organizations primarily in the areas where the company operates. Support is given for projects that take a creative approach to such fundamental issues as education, health and human services, youth enrichment, and arts and culture. The foundation values projects which take a creative approach to such fundamental issues as education, neighborhood improvement, youth development, community problem-solving, assistance to people who are disadvantaged, environmental conservation and cultural enrichment. Grants cover projects, building, equipment, capital campaigns, program development, employee matching gifts, and employee-related scholarships. All proposals must be in writing and should include the following information: needs statement and project objectives; purpose of organization; constituency; board members, community, and volunteer involvement; how results of the project will be measured; plans for continued funding of the project, if applicable; one-page project budget and an organizational chart; and primary source of funds. Proposals are accepted at any time.
Requirements: Giving limited to areas of company operations, with emphasis on Wichita.
Restrictions: Grants are not awarded to individuals; national or regional organizations, unless their programs address specific local community needs; programs or initiatives where the primary purpose is the promotion of religious doctrine or tenets; elementary or secondary schools (except to provide special initiatives or programs not provided by regular school budgets); political action or legislative advocacy groups; operational funds; medical or other research organizations; organizations located in or benefiting nations other than the United States and its territories; or fraternal groups, athletic teams, bands, veterans organizations, volunteer firefighters, or similar groups.
Geographic Focus: All States
Amount of Grant: 300 - 10,000 USD
Contact: Rhonda Fullerton, Secretary-Treasurer; (316) 517-7810; fax (316) 517-7812
Internet: http://www.cessna.com/about/corporate-citizenship.html
Sponsor: Cessna Foundation
P.O. Box 7706
Wichita, KS 67277

CFFVR Alcoholism and Drug Abuse Grants 1001

The Community Foundation for the Fox Valley Region (CFFVR) was established as a public, nonprofit organization in 1986 to enhance the quality of life for all people of the region. Since it was founded, funds within the Foundation have awarded more than $125 million in grants to nonprofit organizations, primarily in Wisconsin's Fox Valley region. The purpose of the Alcoholism and Drug Abuse Grants program is to: supports new or existing programs and projects that address the prevention and/or treatment of alcohol and other drug abuse in the Fox Valley and surrounding area.
Requirements: Organizations serving residents of Outagamie, Calumet, Waupaca, Shawano and northern Winnebago counties are eligible to apply. The grant application form is available at the CFFVR website.
Geographic Focus: Wisconsin
Amount of Grant: 2,500 USD
Contact: Todd Sutton; (920) 830-1290, ext. 28; fax (920) 830-1293; lfilapek@cffoxvalley.org
Internet: https://www.cffoxvalley.org/Page.aspx?pid=652
Sponsor: Community Foundation for the Fox Valley Region
4455 West Lawrence Street, P.O. Box 563
Appleton, WI 54912-0563

CFFVR Basic Needs Giving Partnership Grants 1002

Supported by the U.S. Oil Open Fund for Basic Needs within the Community Foundation and the J.J. Keller Foundation, the partnership assists established charitable organizations with successful programs that address root causes of poverty. Available forms of support include: capacity building; general operating support; project support; project analysis & advocacy. A single organization may request up to $15,000 per year for three years, and collaborative proposals may request up to $100,000 per year for three years. Multiple years of support will be considered only if there is a compelling case for multi-year funding and the project clearly demonstrates how progression shall occur over time.

Requirements: Eligible applicants are well-established charitable organizations that are exempt from federal income taxes under the Internal Revenue Code and have been in operation for a minimum of three years. Wisconsin organizations must serve residents in Outagamie, Calumet, Waupaca, Shawano, or northern Winnebago counties.
Restrictions: Grants from the Basic Needs Giving Partnership will not support the following: technology projects; capital campaigns or building projects; organizational set-up costs; annual fund drives or endowments; lobbying for specific legislation; activities that occur before funding is awarded; organizations with past-due or incomplete grant reports.
Geographic Focus: Wisconsin
Date(s) Application is Due: Feb 15; Sep 15
Contact: Martha Hemwall; (920) 830-1290, ext. 26; mhemwall@cffoxvalley.org
Internet: https://www.cffoxvalley.org/Page.aspx?pid=400
Sponsor: Community Foundation for the Fox Valley Region
4455 West Lawrence Street, P.O. Box 563
Appleton, WI 54912-0563

CFFVR Bridge Grants　　　　　　　　　　　　　　　　　　　　　　　　　　　1003
The Community Foundation for the Fox Valley Region (CFFVR) Bridge Program, is a temporary grant program that's to be used as a financial bridge through the economic downturn. Bridge grants will provide general operating support to charitable organizations which, due to the current economic decline, are in need of temporary funding to help maintain programs necessary to their core mission, and demonstrated prior financial health and high potential for future stability. These charitable organizations must serve residents in the Community Foundation service area, which includes Calumet, Outagamie, Shawano, Waupaca and northern Winnebago counties of Wisconsin. Applicants may request up to $25,000 for general operating support. Multiple organizations seeking to collaborate or merge for reasons of efficiency may be eligible for additional funding. Multiple organizations considering applying should contact Marti Hemwall at (920) 830-1290, before completing an application (available online).
Requirements: Eligible applicants are established Wisconsin, 501(c)3 charitable organizations that can provide compelling evidence of an urgent or impending financial need caused by the economic downturn and are able to demonstrate prior financial health and high potential for future stability. Charitable organizations must serve residents in the Community Foundation service area, which includes Calumet, Outagamie, Shawano, Waupaca and northern Winnebago counties.
Restrictions: Not eligible: educational institutions, government programs or entities, religious organizations, churches and funding for endowments. Programs and offices within an organization and organizations with a fiscal sponsor are not eligible to apply.
Geographic Focus: Wisconsin
Amount of Grant: 25,000 USD
Contact: Marti Hemwall; (920) 830-1290, ext. 26; mhemwall@cffoxvalley.org
Internet: https://www.cffoxvalley.org/Page.aspx?pid=654
Sponsor: Community Foundation for the Fox Valley Region
4455 West Lawrence Street, P.O. Box 563
Appleton, WI 54912-0563

CFFVR Capacity Building Grants　　　　　　　　　　　　　　　　　　　　　1004
Capacity Building Grants support the planning and implementation of initiatives that enable a nonprofit organization to develop a stronger infrastructure to help it fulfill its core mission more effectively. Meaningful capacity building initiatives are the result of careful planning, so two types of grants are available: planning grants and implementation grants. Planning grants support organizations interested in developing a strategic, technology, fundraising, communications or business plan, or other types of organizational assessment needs. Implementation grants support efforts to strengthen the overall functioning of an organization through strategic investments that can improve internal governance, resource and asset management, or systems for delivering services or programs, or that help the organization prepare for change due to executive succession or a new strategic alliance (such as co-location, consolidation, collaborative programming or shared administrative structures). Typically, organizations will have completed most consultation, assessment or planning activities and will be preparing to move forward with the implementation of a resulting initiative. Initiatives that build capacities in one of the following four ways will be considered: leadership capacity; adaptive capacity; management capacity; and technology capacity. Implementation grant applicants are due November 15. Planning grant applications are accepted at any time. The grant application form is available at the CFFVR website.
Requirements: Organizations serving residents of Outagamie, Calumet, Waupaca, Shawano and northern Winnebago counties are eligible. Organizations typically are eligible for Capacity Building Grants if: the organization demonstrates awareness of its strengths and weaknesses; the initiative timing is relevant for the organization's stage of development; board supports and is engaged in the capacity building effort; organization demonstrates an ability to evolve, learn and be responsive to change; the organization's financial condition is stable, or the proposal explicitly deals with improving financial management; the appropriate stakeholders are involved in the capacity building effort; the applicant has identified resources and/or consultants that are appropriate to the initiative; the initiative budget is adequate, relates to the project narrative and costs are reasonable; and the grant positions the organization for greater impact in fulfilling its mission. Capacity Building Grants typically are not more than $50,000 over two years for single organizations for implementation grants or not more than $10,000 for planning grants. Additional funding may be approved for collaborative applications.
Restrictions: The following is not funded: general operating expenses not related to the initiative; routine program development or delivery; organization start-up costs; financial audits; recurring staff training or tuition for degree programs or conferences; rent/facility expenses; and capital equipment or campaigns including feasibility studies or other planning expenses.
Geographic Focus: Wisconsin
Date(s) Application is Due: Nov 15

Contact: Marti Hemwall, Vice President, Community and Donor Engagement; (920) 830-1290, ext. 29; mhemwall@cffoxvalley.org
Internet: https://www.cffoxvalley.org/Page.aspx?pid=415
Sponsor: Community Foundation for the Fox Valley Region
4455 West Lawrence Street, P.O. Box 563
Appleton, WI 54912-0563

CFFVR Capital Credit Union Charitable Giving Grants　　　　　　　　　　1005
The Capital Credit Union Charitable Giving Fund was established to support projects and programs that provide for basic needs (food, shelter, clothing and medical care), making a positive impact on the lives of those in the communities served by Capital Credit Union. Grant applications are accepted annually with a submission deadline of December 31. The grant application is available online at the Community Foundation for the Fox Valley Region website.
Requirements: To be eligible to apply for a grant, organizations must: be a public charity, as determined by the IRS and described in 501(c)3 of the tax code (educational institutions and government programs/entities are not eligible for consideration); provide, or propose to develop, services that are focused directly on improving the availability of, or providing for, basic needs in our community; benefit specific communities served by Capital Credit Union. These include the counties of Calumet, Outagamie, and Winnebago in the state of Wisconsin.
Geographic Focus: Wisconsin
Date(s) Application is Due: Dec 31
Contact: Shelly Leadley; (920) 830-1290, ext. 34; sleadley@cffoxvalley.org
Internet: https://www.cffoxvalley.org/Page.aspx?pid=415
Sponsor: Community Foundation for the Fox Valley Region
4455 West Lawrence Street, P.O. Box 563
Appleton, WI 54912-0563

CFFVR Chilton Area Community Foundation Grants　　　　　　　　　　　　1006
The Chilton Area Community Foundation works to enhance the quality of life for the people of the greater Chilton area. Grants support specific projects or new programs for which a moderate amount of grant money can make a significant impact on an area of need. Grants are made for a broad range of purposes to a wide variety of charitable organizations in the focus areas of health, arts/culture, education and community development. Grants support projects and programs with clear goals and financial accountability, including: creative new activities or services (new programs, one-time projects, events, exhibits, studies or surveys); enhancement or strengthening of existing activities (projects to enhance, expand or strengthen the range, quantity and/or quality of an organization's programs and services); and small capital investments (items that are directly related to program delivery or service to clients, such as a refrigerator for a food pantry or equipment to comply with Americans with Disabilities Act requirements). Applications are available on the website.
Requirements: Organizations serving residents of Outagamie, Calumet, Waupaca, Shawano and northern Winnebago counties are eligible to apply. The grant application form is available at the CFFVR website.
Geographic Focus: Wisconsin
Date(s) Application is Due: Dec 31
Contact: Terry Friederichs; (920) 849-4042; tjfriederichs@charter.net
Internet: https://www.cffoxvalley.org/Page.aspx?pid=415
Sponsor: Community Foundation for the Fox Valley Region
4455 West Lawrence Street, P.O. Box 563
Appleton, WI 54912-0563

CFFVR Clintonville Area Foundation Grants　　　　　　　　　　　　　　　1007
Clintonville Area Foundation (CAF) grants are awarded from unrestricted funds to support specific projects or new programs for which a moderate amount of grant money can make an impact on an area of need. Grants are made for a broad range of purposes to a wide variety of charitable organizations in the focus areas of health, education and community development.
Requirements: Wisconsin organizations eligible to receive grants from the Community Foundation for the Fox Valley Region are those determined by the IRS to be public charities. This encompasses most charitable, scientific, social service, educational and religious organizations described as IRS 501(c)3 of the tax code, as well as government agencies. Organizations that are not public charities may apply through a fiscal sponsor. Organizations must serve residents of the Clintonville area. The grant application form is available at the CFFVR website.
Restrictions: CAF grants typically will not fund: general operating expenses not related to the proposed project; annual fund drives or fundraising events; endowment funds; programs with a sectarian or religious purpose that promote a specific journey of faith; major capital projects such as the acquisition of land or buildings; medical research; travel for individuals or groups such as bands, sports teams or classes; activities that occur before funding is awarded; organizations with past-due or incomplete grant reports.
Geographic Focus: Wisconsin
Date(s) Application is Due: Dec 15
Amount of Grant: 3,000 USD
Contact: Jenny Goldschmidt; (715) 823-7125; clintonvillefoundation@gmail.com
Todd Sutton, Grants Officer; (920) 830-1290; tsutton@cffoxvalley.org
Internet: https://www.cffoxvalley.org/Page.aspx?pid=557
Sponsor: Community Foundation for the Fox Valley Region
4455 West Lawrence Street, P.O. Box 563
Appleton, WI 54912-0563

CFFVR Clintonville Area Foundation Grants 1008

Clintonville Area Foundation (CAF) grants are awarded from unrestricted funds to support specific projects or new programs for which a moderate amount of grant money can make an impact on an area of need. Grants are made for a broad range of purposes to a wide variety of charitable organizations in the focus areas of health, education and community development. The Foundation is interesting in supporting: creative new activities or services—new programs, one-time projects, events, exhibits, studies or surveys; enhancement or strengthening of existing activities—projects to enhance, expand or strengthen the range, quantity and/or quality of an organization's programs and services; small capital investments—items that are directly related to program delivery or service to clients, such as a refrigerator for a food pantry or equipment to comply with ADA requirements. Grant applications are available online.
Requirements: Wisconsin 501(c)3 nonprofit organizations that serve the residents of the Clintonville area are eligible. General questions can also be directed to the CAF Grants Committee Chair or the Foundation.
Restrictions: The Clintonville Area Foundation will not generally fund the following: general operating expenses not related to the proposed project; annual fund drives or fundraising events; endowment funds; programs with a sectarian or religious purpose that promote a specific journey of faith; major capital projects such as the acquisition of land or buildings; medical research; travel for individuals or groups such as bands, sports teams or classes; activities that occur before funding is awarded; organizations with past-due or incomplete grant reports.
Geographic Focus: Wisconsin
Date(s) Application is Due: Dec 31
Contact: Jenny Goldschmidt, CAF Grants Committee Chair; (715) 823-7125, ext. 2603; clintonvillefoundation@gmail.com
Internet: https://www.cffoxvalley.org/Page.aspx?pid=415
Sponsor: Community Foundation for the Fox Valley Region
4455 West Lawrence Street, P.O. Box 563
Appleton, WI 54912-0563

CFFVR Doug and Carla Salmon Foundation Grants 1009

The Doug and Carla Salmon Foundation provides need-based college scholarships to highly motivated students and financial support to local charitable organizations in the Fox Valley region of Wisconsin. Grants support capital campaigns and, the development of administrative endowments. There are no deadline dates. Mail a letter of inquiry, to begin the application process to: Doug and Carla Salmon Foundation, 660 West Ridgeview Drive, Appleton, Wisconsin 54911.
Requirements: Wisconsin 501(c)3 tax-exempt organizations serving residents of Outagamie, Calumet, Waupaca, Shawano and northern Winnebago counties are eligible to apply.
Geographic Focus: Wisconsin
Contact: Sue Detienne, Executive Director; (920) 424-2228; rdetienne@new.rr.com
Internet: https://www.cffoxvalley.org/Page.aspx?pid=403
Sponsor: Community Foundation for the Fox Valley Region
4455 West Lawrence Street, P.O. Box 563
Appleton, WI 54912-0563

CFFVR Environmental Stewardship Grants 1010

The Environmental Stewardship Fund was established by the Community Foundation in 2006 to support the Wisconsin, Fox Valley-area charitable organizations and projects that further the conservation of nature and enhance education about and enjoyment of the natural world. Funding priority is given to projects that: strengthen the connection between the people and the land; further environmental values; have a wide impact; are visible and inspiring; match groups with similar aspirations.
Requirements: Wisconsin 501(c)3 tax-exempt organizations serving residents of Outagamie, Calumet, Waupaca, Shawano and northern Winnebago counties are eligible to apply. The grant application form is available at the CFFVR website.
Restrictions: Projects that will not be funded: major capital expenses; ongoing operating expenses unrelated to the proposed project; annual fund drives or fund-raising events; recurring events; endowment funds; conference fees; lobbying; activities that occur before funding is awarded; organizations with past-due or incomplete grant reports.
Geographic Focus: Wisconsin
Amount of Grant: 5,000 USD
Contact: David Horst; (920) 830-1290, ext. 24; dhorst@cffoxvalley.org
Internet: https://www.cffoxvalley.org/Page.aspx?pid=347
Sponsor: Community Foundation for the Fox Valley Region
4455 West Lawrence Street, P.O. Box 563
Appleton, WI 54912-0563

CFFVR Fox Valley Community Arts Grants 1011

Grants from the Fox Valley Community Arts Fund are designed to increase public understanding of, and access to, an array of artistic activities in Calumet, Outagamie, Shawano, Waupaca and northern Winnebago counties of Wisconsin. Grants awarded from the Fox Valley Community Arts Fund typically are for no more than $5,000, and the dollars requested cannot exceed 50% of the total project cost. Funding priority is given to projects that support quality arts organizations aiming to: bring a wider audience to understanding, experiencing, or appreciating an artistic or cultural experience; use art as a means to make connections, generate dialogue or stimulate action around a specific social issue. Grant projects must include a public service activity, such as a concert, an exhibition, etc., that is open to the entire community and occurs within one year of the grant award. Ongoing programs are eligible, although projects that received previous support through this grant program are not guaranteed future support. Preference will be given to new programs or for new additions to an established program. There is no limit to the number of organizations funded in any specific artistic discipline or the number of proposals that an organization may submit for consideration. However, the same project or program will not be funded by both the Fox Valley Community Arts Fund and a project grant from the Community Foundation unrestricted funds.
Requirements: Wisconsin 501(c)3 tax-exempt organizations serving residents of Outagamie, Calumet, Waupaca, Shawano and northern Winnebago counties are eligible to apply. The grant application form is available at the CFFVR website.
Restrictions: The Fox Valley Community Arts Fund will not typically support the following: general operating expenses of well-established organizations; annual fund drives, fundraising events or elimination of previously incurred deficits; endowment funds; major capital projects such as the acquisition of land or buildings, purchase of major equipment, or the construction or renovation of facilities; travel costs for projects or performances that occur outside of the Fox Valley region; activities that occur before funding is awarded; events and/or exhibits that occur within 90 days of the grant application deadline; activities with sectarian or religious purposes that promote a specific journey of faith; organizations with past-due or incomplete grant reports; grants to individual artists.
Geographic Focus: Wisconsin
Date(s) Application is Due: Dec 1
Amount of Grant: 5,000 USD
Contact: Todd Sutton; (920) 830-1290, ext. 28; fax (920) 830-1293; tsutton@cffoxvalley.org
Internet: https://www.cffoxvalley.org/Page.aspx?pid=484
Sponsor: Community Foundation for the Fox Valley Region
4455 West Lawrence Street, P.O. Box 563
Appleton, WI 54912-0563

CFFVR Frank C. Shattuck Community Grants 1012

The Frank C. Shattuck Community Fund supports new or supplements existing services for youth and the elderly and benefits education, the arts and health care in Winnebago and Outagamie counties of Wisconsin. Funding is available for programs, capital expenses or operating expenses of qualifying charitable organizations. Grants to projects may be either one-time payments or multi-year commitments. Application forms are available online.
Requirements: Wisconsin 501(c)3 organizations that serve residents in Outagamie or northern Winnebago counties are eligible to apply. To begin the application process, submit the following prior to the application deadline: grant application form; list of the organization's governing board members, including their professional or community affiliation; current year (board-approved) operating budget.
Restrictions: The Shattuck Fund will not typically support the following: grants for religious or political purposes; grants to support endowment funds of organizations; travel for individuals or groups such as bands, sports teams or classes; reimbursement for previously incurred expenses.
Geographic Focus: Wisconsin
Date(s) Application is Due: Mar 1; Sep 1
Contact: Shelly Leadley; (920) 830-1290, ext. 34; sleadley@cffoxvalley.org
Internet: https://www.cffoxvalley.org/Page.aspx?pid=339
Sponsor: Community Foundation for the Fox Valley Region
4455 West Lawrence Street, P.O. Box 563
Appleton, WI 54912-0563

CFFVR Infant Welfare Circle of Kings Daughters Grants 1013

Organizations submitting a grant application to the Infant Welfare Circle must serve residents in Outagamie, Calumet or Winnebago counties of Wisconsin. Preference is given to programs or projects that serve children or young adults. General operating grants are available up to $3,000.
Requirements: Wisconsin 501(c)3 non-profit organizations that serve residents in Outagamie, Calumet or Winnebago counties are eligible to apply. Grant proposal should include the following information: Submit the following prior to the application deadline: public charity name, address, phone number, email address and contact person; description of organization mission; description of program or project for which funding is requested (include timeline, people to be served, community need to be addressed, project goals/anticipated results); project budget, amount of funding requested from Infant Welfare Circle and rationale for Circle assistance, and date needed; agency revenue and expense report for previous fiscal year; revenue and expense budget for current year; list of organization's officers and directors.
Geographic Focus: Wisconsin
Date(s) Application is Due: Sep 30
Amount of Grant: 3,000 USD
Contact: Grants Officer; (920) 830-1290; fax (920) 830-1293; info@cffoxvalley.org
Internet: https://www.cffoxvalley.org/Page.aspx?pid=415
Sponsor: Community Foundation for the Fox Valley Region
4455 West Lawrence Street, P.O. Box 563
Appleton, WI 54912-0563

CFFVR Jewelers Mutual Charitable Giving Grants 1014

Through philanthropy, Jewelers Mutual Insurance Company aspires to achieve a lasting and positive impact on the Fox River Valley. Jewelers Mutual strives to be a responsible corporate citizen and a valued employer by supporting critical needs of the community. Priority areas for giving are: organizations in which Jewelers Mutual employees are actively involved; organizations that address needs in the following areas: basic needs (food, shelter, clothing), as well as programs that reduce/eliminate the root causes of poverty (such as literacy, affordable housing, job training); positive youth development and education; health and wellness, particularly diabetes, cancer, mental health, and affordable access for the disadvantaged; and the vitality of the Fox River area, including gifts to libraries, police or fire departments, parks, the arts, and preservation of the local environment. Letters of request may be sent to the Community Foundation for the Fox Valley Region.
Requirements: 501(c)3 organizations that serve residents of Fox River Valley are eligible.

Geographic Focus: Wisconsin
Contact: Shelly Leadley; (920) 830-1290; SLeadley@cffoxvalley.org
Internet: http://www.jewelersmutual.com/information.aspx?id=4305
Sponsor: Community Foundation for the Fox Valley Region
4455 West Lawrence Street, P.O. Box 563
Appleton, WI 54912-0563

CFFVR Mielke Family Foundation Grants 1015
Mielke Family Foundation grants, enhance the quality of life for residents of Appleton and, Shawano, Wisconsin. Priority areas of giving are: projects that primarily serve individuals residing within either the Appleton Area School District or the Shawano School District; special events, start-up expenses of projects expected to become self-sustaining, studies to determine future courses of action or needs, enrichment programs, or actions to meet similar objectives. Application forms are available online at the Community Foundation for the Fox Valley Region website.
Requirements: Applicants must: be a nonprofit 501(c)3 or qualifying tax-exempt organization; be able to demonstrate, to the satisfaction of the Foundation, that it has the capability to complete the proposed project.
Restrictions: The Mielke Family Foundation typically will not support: transportation costs for individuals or groups such as bands, sports teams or classes; general operating expenses not related to the proposed project; deficits incurred for past activities; programs or needs that do not serve residents in the Appleton Area School District or the Shawano Area School District. The Foundation typically prefers not to engage in long-term grant commitments.
Geographic Focus: Wisconsin
Contact: Cathy Mutschler, Community Engagement Officer; (920) 830-1290, ext. 27; fax (920) 830-1293; cmutschler@cffoxvalley.org
Internet: https://www.cffoxvalley.org/Page.aspx?pid=415
Sponsor: Community Foundation for the Fox Valley Region
4455 West Lawrence Street, P.O. Box 563
Appleton, WI 54912-0563

CFFVR Myra M. and Robert L. Vandehey Foundation Grants 1016
The Myra M. and Robert L. Vandehey Foundation's mission is support the charitable interests of the Myra and Robert Vandehey family. Areas of interest include: education; children and youth; health care and; family services. Funding opportunities are limited to nonprofit organizations that serve residents in the Fox Cities or Keshena areas of Wisconsin. Contact the Vice President for CFFVR prior to submitting a request to verify that the need aligns with current priorities. Unsolicited grant requests are not accepted from organizations not previously awarded support. Applications may be submitted at any time, and no application form is required.
Requirements: Wisconsin 501(c)3 nonprofit organizations that serve residents in the Fox Cities or Keshena are eligible for funding.
Restrictions: No grants to individuals.
Geographic Focus: Wisconsin
Contact: Cathy Mutschler; (920) 830-1290, ext. 29; cmutschler@cffoxvalley.org
Internet: https://www.cffoxvalley.org/Page.aspx?pid=415
Sponsor: Community Foundation for the Fox Valley Region
4455 West Lawrence Street, P.O. Box 563
Appleton, WI 54912-0563

CFFVR Project Grants 1017
Project grants, support specific projects or new programs for which a moderate amount of grant money can make a significant impact on an area of need. Grants are made for a broad range of purposes to a wide variety of charitable organizations in the focus areas of arts and culture, community development, education, environment, health and human services. Organizations eligible to apply must serve residents in Outagamie, Calumet, Shawano, Waupaca or northern Winnebago counties. Grants for specific projects typically are for no more than $10,000 for one year.
Requirements: Wisconsin 501(c)3 tax-exempt organizations serving residents of Outagamie, Calumet, Waupaca, Shawano and northern Winnebago counties are eligible to apply. The grant application form is available at the CFFVR website.
Restrictions: Project grants typically will not fund the following: general operating expenses not related to the proposed project; annual fund drives or fund raising events; endowment funds; programs with a sectarian or religious purpose that promote a specific journey of faith; major capital projects such as the acquisition of land or buildings; medical research; travel for individuals or groups such as bands, sports teams or classes; activities that occur before funding is awarded; health and safety equipment; playground equipment; organizations with past-due or incomplete grant reports.
Geographic Focus: Wisconsin
Date(s) Application is Due: Feb 1; Aug 1
Amount of Grant: 10,000 USD
Contact: Todd Sutton; (920) 830-1290; fax (920) 830-1293; tsutton@cffoxvalley.org
Internet: https://www.cffoxvalley.org/Page.aspx?pid=343
Sponsor: Community Foundation for the Fox Valley Region
4455 West Lawrence Street, P.O. Box 563
Appleton, WI 54912-0563

CFFVR Robert and Patricia Endries Family Foundation Grants 1018
The Robert & Patricia Endries Family Foundation was established for the benefit of people in need, primarily in the Brillion area but with some consideration to the Fox Valley, Lakeshore and Northeastern areas of Wisconsin. Priority areas of giving include: the vitality of the Brillion area; the disadvantaged, particularly the disabled, homeless, low income, single parents, troubled youth, or the chronically or mentally ill; health and human services, particularly diabetes, cancer, cerebral palsy, Alzheimer's disease, kidney disease, or mental health; religious causes or organizations with a spiritual purpose; sports or arts programming and, or sponsorships. Grants are considered for capital campaigns and, or specific capital improvements for the above priority organizations. Gifts will be directed to specific programs or opportunities, not to general operations (with exception for those organizations the foundation has had a long-established relationship with). Matching or challenge gifts are also encouraged, to motivate additional giving by others. Organizations that support needs outside of the Brillion area or that do not yet have an established relationship with the foundation should contact the foundation prior to submission of a formal request.
Requirements: Wisconsin 501(c)3 charitable organizations are eligible to apply. Contact Foundation directly be begin the application process.
Restrictions: The Foundation will not typically support the following: gifts to political organizations or causes; gifts to organizations that are not pro-life supporters or that lack sensitivity to promoting human life in any form (unborn or born); gifts to organizations affiliated with or in support of cloning or embryonic stem-cell research; grants to organizations that receive significant public/government funding; reimbursement for previously incurred expenses.
Geographic Focus: Wisconsin
Date(s) Application is Due: Jan 1; Apr 1; Oct 1
Contact: Shelly Leadley; (920) 830-1290, ext. 34; sleadley@cffoxvalley.org
Internet: https://www.cffoxvalley.org/Page.aspx?pid=415
Sponsor: Community Foundation for the Fox Valley Region
4455 West Lawrence Street, P.O. Box 563
Appleton, WI 54912-0563

CFFVR SAC Developmental Disabilities Grants 1019
The Community Foundation for the Fox Valley Region Inc. was established as a public, nonprofit organization in 1986 to enhance the quality of life for all people of the region. Since it was founded, funds within the Foundation have awarded more than $125 million in grants to nonprofit organizations, primarily in Wisconsin's Fox Valley region. The service region includes Outagamie, Calumet, Waupaca, Shawano and northern Winnebago counties. The SAC Developmental Disabilities Fund supports projects or programs that address the recreational, social and educational needs of people with developmental disabilities and other handicapping conditions.
Requirements: Wisconsin 501(c)3 tax-exempt organizations serving residents of Outagamie, Calumet, Waupaca, Shawano and northern Winnebago counties are eligible to apply. The grant application form is available at the CFFVR website.
Geographic Focus: Wisconsin
Date(s) Application is Due: Feb 1; Aug 1
Contact: Todd Sutton; (920) 830-1290, ext. 28; fax (920) 830-1293; tsutton@cffoxvalley.org
Internet: https://www.cffoxvalley.org/Page.aspx?pid=415
Sponsor: Community Foundation for the Fox Valley Region
4455 West Lawrence Street, P.O. Box 563
Appleton, WI 54912-0563

CFFVR Schmidt Family G4 Grants 1020
The Schmidt Family G4 grants provide funding to improve the quality of life of those most in need in the Fox Valley, Wisconsin region, with a focus on at-risk youth and self-sufficiency for women. This goal will be accomplished by seeking to address immediate needs and to affect meaningful change in the following areas: at-risk youth—especially those with a physical or mental illness, those who have experienced abuse or those who have significant financial need; adult self-sufficiency—with a priority on issues that affect the stability and independence of women, as well as literacy, job skills training and transitional living for all. The G4 Committee prefers: not to be the sole funder for most projects it considers, unless the amount requested is small and/or a one-time request; to support specific projects or new programs for which a moderate amount of grant money can make a significant impact on an area of need and sustainability. A broad array of requests will be considered, including capital campaigns, existing programs or recurring events as long as they fall within the other listed giving guidelines. Grant awards will typically not exceed $15,000. To assist with the educational aspect of this fund, a formal application is required (available online). Prior to submitting an application, organizations are strongly encouraged to contact Cathy Mutschlerto, discuss the potential proposal and process. Complete and submit the application prior to the March 1, October 1 deadlines.
Requirements: IRS 501(c)3 nonprofit organizations, as well as government agencies are eligible to apply for funding. Organizations that are not public charities may apply through a fiscal sponsor. Organizations must serve Fox Valley residents, particularly in Outagamie, Calumet or northern Winnebago counties of Wisconsin.
Restrictions: The G4 Fund typically will not support the following: organizations that have received funding from the G4 Committee in the most recent 20 months; multi-year requests; programs with a sectarian or religious purpose that promote a specific journey of faith; travel for individuals or groups such as bands, sports teams or classes; reimbursement for previously incurred expenses; endowment funds; fund-raising events; requests from organizations with past-due or incomplete grant reports; a program or need previously declined unless the organization is invited back by the committee; programs or needs that do not serve Fox Valley residents, particularly Outagamie, Calumet or northern Winnebago counties.
Geographic Focus: Wisconsin
Date(s) Application is Due: Mar 1; Sep 1
Amount of Grant: 15,000 USD
Contact: Cathy Mutschler; (920) 830-1290, ext. 29; cmutschler@cffoxvalley.org
Internet: https://www.cffoxvalley.org/Page.aspx?pid=340
Sponsor: Community Foundation for the Fox Valley Region
4455 West Lawrence Street, P.O. Box 563
Appleton, WI 54912-0563

CFFVR Shawano Area Community Foundation Grants 1021

Shawano Area Community Foundation works to preserve and improve the quality of life in Shawano, Wisconsin and, the surrounding area, including communities having economic, educational, cultural and recreational ties with the area. Grant applications are available online.
Requirements: Wisconsin 501(c)3 non-profits in or serving surrounding area of Shawano are eligible to apply.
Geographic Focus: Wisconsin
Date(s) Application is Due: Oct 1
Amount of Grant: 5,000 USD
Contact: Susan Hanson; (715) 253-2580; shawanofoundation@granitewave.com
Internet: https://www.cffoxvalley.org/Page.aspx?pid=412
Sponsor: Community Foundation for the Fox Valley Region
4455 West Lawrence Street, P.O. Box 563
Appleton, WI 54912-0563

CFFVR Sikora Family Memorial Grants 1022

The Sikora Family Memorial Fund supports capital or building projects within Shawano County to benefit a public chaity and to serve the entire community. Grant requests must be submitted using the application form (available online). There is no deadline and requests are reviewed as submitted.
Requirements: Wisconsin 501(c)3 non-profit organizations that serve residents in the Shawano County area are eligible to apply. Organizations that are not public charities may apply through a fiscal sponsor.
Restrictions: Grants from the fund will not support: general operations, overhead or administration; programs that serve only a limited number of community members; projects that provide only limited seasonal benefit to the community.
Geographic Focus: Wisconsin
Date(s) Application is Due: Jun 30
Amount of Grant: 500,000 USD
Contact: Todd Sutton; (920) 830-1290, ext. 28; fax (920) 830-1293; tsutton@cffoxvalley.org
Internet: https://www.cffoxvalley.org/Page.aspx?pid=415
Sponsor: Community Foundation for the Fox Valley Region
4455 West Lawrence Street, P.O. Box 563
Appleton, WI 54912-0563

CFFVR Waupaca Area Community Foundation Grants 1023

Waupaca Area Community Foundation works to preserve and improve the quality of life for the people of the greater Waupaca area of Wisconsin. The Foundation awards grants to Wisconsin non-profits, primarily in the following areas of interest: human services; arts and culture; education; community development. Grant applications are available online.
Requirements: Wisconsin 501(c)3 non-profits in or serving the residents of the Waupaca area are eligible to apply.
Restrictions: The Foundation typically will not award grants to: support routine operating expenses of established organizations, to support annual fund drives of such organizations, or to eliminate their previously incurred deficits; support new or established endowment funds; fund specific research projects; support travel for individuals or groups (such as bands, sports teams, forensics competitors, or the like); support sectarian or religious purposes or causes; reimburse anyone for previously incurred expenses.
Geographic Focus: Wisconsin
Date(s) Application is Due: Jun 30
Amount of Grant: 5,000 USD
Contact: Jack Rhodes, WACF President; (715) 256-1939
Internet: https://www.cffoxvalley.org/Page.aspx?pid=415
Sponsor: Community Foundation for the Fox Valley Region
4455 West Lawrence Street, P.O. Box 563
Appleton, WI 54912-0563

CFFVR Wisconsin King's Daughters and Sons Grants 1024

The Wisconsin Branch of the International Order of King's Daughters and Sons, in alignment with the priorities of its national parent organization, will provide grants to Fox Valley charitable organizations who provide services related to autism and literacy. Application is available online.
Requirements: Wisconsin 501(c)3 non-profit organizations in the Fox Valley region may apply. Organizations that are not public charities may apply through a fiscal sponsor.
Geographic Focus: Wisconsin
Date(s) Application is Due: Oct 15
Contact: Kathy Mutschler; (920) 830-1290, ext. 27; cmutschler@cffoxvalley.org
Internet: https://www.cffoxvalley.org/Page.aspx?pid=875
Sponsor: Community Foundation for the Fox Valley Region
4455 West Lawrence Street, P.O. Box 563
Appleton, WI 54912-0563

CFFVR Women's Fund for the Fox Valley Region Grants 1025

The Women's Fund provides grants for programs that inspire women and girls to flourish personally, economically and professionally. Grants have been distributed to programs supporting the following areas: arts & culture; physical and mental health; economic, self-sufficiency; education; parenting and child care; violence prevention. The Women's Fund believes that no project is too small or too new to be considered. Innovative approaches and projects with limited access to other funding are encouraged. Collaborative efforts are welcome. Grant applicants should address one or more of these funding priorities as they relate to women and girls: promotes economic self-sufficiency; improves safely from violence; provides opportunities to develop life skills; promotes physical and/or mental health; enhances dignity and self-worth; promotes leadership development; provides opportunities for artistic development and/or exposure to the arts; provides gender-specific solutions to problems facing women and girls; creates an environment that encourages social change. To apply submit a letter of interest by the deadline.
Requirements: To be eligible for a grant, the project must be consistent with the Women's Fund mission; benefits women and girls in the Wisconsin, Fox Valley region; organization must be a tax-exempt, not-for-profit organization under the Internal Revenue Code, section 501(c)3.
Restrictions: The Women's Fund will not fund: individuals, endowments, government agencies (however educational institutions may qualify), projects with a religious focus, and political parties, candidates or partisan activities.
Geographic Focus: Wisconsin
Date(s) Application is Due: Mar 15
Contact: Becky Boulanger; (920) 830-1290, ext. 17; bboulanger@cffoxvalley.org
Internet: https://www.cffoxvalley.org/Page.aspx?pid=415
Sponsor: Community Foundation for the Fox Valley Region
4455 West Lawrence Street, P.O. Box 563
Appleton, WI 54912-0563

CFNCR Starbucks Memorial Fund 1026

Starbucks Memorial Fund was established as a living memorial to three young Starbucks employees who were killed in a robbery at the Georgetown Starbucks store in 1997. Grants support local nonprofit organizations in the metropolitan Washington, DC region working to prevent violence, serving as advocates against violence and providing assistance to victims of violence.
Requirements: Nonprofits are eligible to apply though applications are accepted by invitation only.
Geographic Focus: District of Columbia, Maryland, Virginia
Contact: Angela Jones Hackley; (202) 955-5890; grants@cnfcr.org
Internet: http://www.cfncr.org/site/c.ihLSJ5PLKuG/b.4401615/k.44E3/Competitive_Grant_Opportunities.htm#Starbucks
Sponsor: Community Foundation for the National Capital Region
1201 15th Street NW, Suite 420
Washington, DC 20005

Chamberlain Foundation Grants 1027

The foundation awards grants to Pueblo, CO, nonprofit organizations in its areas of interest, including arts and culture, education, religion, and science. Types of support include general operating support, equipment acquisition, and program development. Submit a brief proposal that includes the purpose of the request and its relevance to the foundation; amount requested; brief history of the organization and its achievements; names, titles, and qualifications of key personnel; name of agency that conducted the last annual audit; copy of the IRS tax-exemption letter; list of other sources of financial support during the past 12 months; and names and affiliations of board members, trustees, and officers of the organization by either of the two deadlines.
Requirements: 501(c)(30 Pueblo, CO, nonprofit organizations are eligible.
Restrictions: Grants do not support individuals; conferences; political activities; religious organizations whose services are limited to members; veteran, labor, fraternal, athletic, or social clubs; national health agencies concerned with specific diseases or health issues; operating expenses for United Way-supported organizations; publications, advertising campaigns, or travel expenses.
Geographic Focus: Colorado
Amount of Grant: 1,000 - 20,000 USD
Contact: David Shaw, Foundation Chair; (719) 543-8596; fax (719) 543-8599
Sponsor: Chamberlain Foundation
501 North Main Street, Suite 222
Pueblo, CO 81003

Champ-A Champion Fur Kids Grants 1028

Grants for children's health and wellness are awarded twice each year. The program provides direct support for children in the areas of health and wellness such as childhood disease research foundations, child safety organizations and organizations that serve children with special needs. The goal is to provide grants to help many programs that are working hard to make the world a healthier and happier place for kids. Programs funded include: (a) Individual Project grants (generally for one-time purchases or to fulfill a short-term need, such as the purchase of materials or equipment); or, (b) Organization Program grants (start-up or operational costs for ongoing programs. Examples include funds for research, health and wellness educational programs, or financial assistance for children and families in-need.)
Requirements: United States applicants must be a tax-exempt organization under Section 501(c)3 of the IRS Code, and 'not a private foundation,' within the meaning of Code Sections 509(a)(1) or 509(a)(2), or a state college or university within the meaning of Code Section 511(a)(2)(B) (a 'Public Charity'). In addition, grant recipients must certify that they are not a supporting organization within the meaning of Code Section 509(a)(3). Canadian applicants must be a registered Canadian charity.
Restrictions: Programs that will not be funded include: (1) Annual Appeals or Capital Campaigns; (2) Construction or New Facility expenses; (3) Fundraising or Event Sponsorships; (4) Political Activities; (5) Religious organizations for religious purposes.
Geographic Focus: All States, Canada
Date(s) Application is Due: Feb 28; Aug 30; Nov 30
Amount of Grant: 1,000 - 10,000 USD
Contact: Maxine Clark, President; (314) 423-8000, ext. 5366; giving@buildabear.com
Internet: http://www.buildabear.com/aboutus/community/bearhugs.aspx
Sponsor: Build-A-Bear Workshop Bear Hugs Foundation
1954 Innerbelt Business Center Drive
Saint Louis, MO 63114

Champlin Foundations Grants 1029

The Champlin Foundations are comprised of three foundations, the first established in 1932 by George S. Champlin, Florence C. Hamilton and Hope C. Neaves, who also created The Second Champlin Foundation in 1947. Both of these trusts are administered by the same Distribution Committee. The Third Champlin Foundation was established by George S. Champlin in 1975 and is administered by a separate Distribution Committee. All three foundations share the same management and PNC Bank/Delaware is the trustee of each. The Champlin Foundations are private foundations as defined in Section 509(a) of the Internal Revenue Code and are exempt from Federal income tax under Section 501(c)3. The Foundations areas of interest include: Youth/Fitness; Hospitals/Healthcare; Open Space/Conservation/Environment; Education; Libraries; Social Services; Historic Preservation; Cultural/Artistic; Animal Humane Societies. The Foundations make direct grants to tax exempt organizations, substantially all in Rhode Island, mostly for capital needs. Capital needs may consist of equipment, construction, renovations, the purchase of real property and reduction of mortgage indebtedness. One important goal is to fund tax exempt organizations within Rhode Island that will have the greatest impact on the broadest possible segment of the population. Another important goal is to provide "hands on" equipment and facilities for those being served by these tax-exempt organizations. Grant applications are accepted March 1st through April 30th. No applications will be accepted via facsimile or email. Applications must be postmarked no later than April 30th, or in the case of April 30th falling on a weekend, then the first business day thereafter.
Requirements: 501(c)3 tax exempt organizations of Rhode Island are eligible to apply.
Geographic Focus: Rhode Island
Date(s) Application is Due: Apr 30
Amount of Grant: 25,000 - 65,000 USD
Contact: Keith Lang; (401) 736-0370; fax (401) 736-7248; champlinfdns@worldnet.att.net
Internet: http://www.fdncenter.org/grantmaker/champlin
Sponsor: Champlin Foundations
300 Centerville Road, Suite 300S
Warwick, RI 02886-0226

Changemakers Community-Based Grants 1030

The primary goal for Changemakers is to strengthen the field of community-based philanthropy, which is philanthropy that provides people in need with the means to solve their own problems, including the means to change unfair social structures and build vibrant communities. Changemakers makes capacity-building and collaborative grants to public foundations and fundraising organizations that are committed to the principles of community-based philanthropy. Changemakers also funds other supportive organizations that serve to strengthen this sector and help transform the wider field of philanthropy.
Requirements: There are four major categories of US-based organizations that are eligible to apply for grants: community-based public foundations; philanthropy education, research and training groups; federations/alternative workplace giving programs; and philanthropy networks and affinity groups.
Restrictions: Staff for Changemakers are located all over the world, so phone contacts are not possible. For questions or problems, email connect@changemakers.com and someone will respond promptly.
Geographic Focus: All States
Contact: Grants Administrator; connect@changemakers.com
Internet: http://www.changemakers.com/community
Sponsor: Changemakers
1700 North Moore Street, Suite 2000
Arlington, VA 22209

Changemakers Innovation Awards 1031

The Changemakers Innovation Awards recognize the best social change strategies that emerge from open competitions hosted online every two months. Each competition cycle identifies and refines solutions to a pressing global problem. Winners will be those entries that best address systemic impact, tipping point, replication, sustainability, and innovation. Awards include a cash prize for each winner chosen by vote on the online community. Entries must be submitted in English. Guidelines and nomination forms are available online. Deadlines vary for each contest.
Requirements: To be eligible to win, all project teams/organizations (with the exception of local governments and universities) must enclose a current income statement and a balance sheet. These financial statements need not be audited. Individual who are partnering with an organization to implement the work must submit a copy of the partnering organization's income financial statement. Individuals without an organizational partner are exempt from the filing requirement.
Geographic Focus: All States, All Countries
Amount of Grant: Up to 5,000 USD
Contact: Awards Director
Internet: http://www.changemakers.com/innovations
Sponsor: Changemakers
1700 North Moore Street, Suite 2000
Arlington, VA 22209

Chapin Hall International Fellowships in Children's Policy Research 1032

The program is designed to increase research and development capacity in the field of child and family policy and to develop leadership for this enterprise. Fellows will work on existing Chapin Hall projects in one of three broadly defined areas of research: developing conceptual bases for and evaluating implementation of community-based supports and services for all children; developing and using data to improve analysis, planning, and management of services for children; and developing and testing new ideas, policies, and programs for children. Some senior fellows may also work on projects of their own design that fit the Chapin Hall research agenda. The two- to 12-month appointments will provide competitive stipends and housing. A form for the fellowship letter of inquiry is available on the Web site.
Requirements: The fellowships are open to individuals from any country with any of a wide range of disciplinary interests and training, including economics, education, history, human development, law, medicine, psychology, public policy, social work, and sociology. All fellows will be expected to conduct work in English.
Geographic Focus: All States
Contact: Christin Glodek, Fellowship Coordinator; (773) 256-5151; fax (773) 256-5351; internationalprogramcoordinator@chapinhall.org
Internet: http://www.about.chapinhall.org/intprograms/intprograms.html
Sponsor: Chapin Hall Center for Children at the University of Chicago
1313 E 60th Street
Chicago, IL 60637

Chapman Charitable Foundation Grants 1033

At Chapman, the ongoing business mission includes supporting the non-profit community through innovation, service and charity. The corporation accomplishes this mission through its corporate endeavors by striving to provide non-profit agencies with comprehensive coverage at the most reasonable price. Likewise, since its inception in 2000, the Chapman Charitable Foundation has donated over $6.75 million dollars to more than 470 California based Social Service Agencies. Primarily, the foundation supports organizations involved with education, forest conservation, health, human services, and religion. Particular fields of interest include: children and youth services, foster care, Christian agencies and churches, education (all levels), the environment, health care access, health care clinics and centers, hospitals, human services, and religion. Applicants should begin by contacting the Foundation with a one-page letter of inquiry. The foundation utilizes a Recommendation Committee to select potential grantees. Application forms are not required.
Geographic Focus: California
Amount of Grant: Up to 150,000 USD
Contact: Mari Perez, Grants Coordinator; (626) 405-8031; fax (626) 405-0585; mperez@chapmanins.com or info@chapmanins.com
Internet: http://www.chapmanins.com/about/foundation
Sponsor: Chapman Charitable Foundation
265 North San Gabriel Boulevard
Pasadena, CA 91107-3423

Chapman Family Charitable Trust Grants 1034

The Chapman Family Charitable Trust was established in 1994 in Georgia, with a geographic focus in the states of South Carolina and New York. The independent foundation's primary focus is on educational programs, museum support, children and youth services, and religion. Its main fields of interest include: children and youth services, Christian agencies and churches, education (all levels), support of community foundation operation, and museums. Though there are no application forms, applicants should forward the entire proposal in letter format. There are no annual deadlines.
Geographic Focus: New York, South Carolina
Amount of Grant: Up to 30,000 USD
Contact: Laura Pease, Grants Administrator; (404) 607-5291
Sponsor: Chapman Family Charitable Trust
5033 Wittering Drive
Columbia, SC 29206-2922

Charity Incorporated Grants 1035

Grants are awarded to eligible Minnesota nonprofit organizations in support of Christian churches and organizations; elementary, secondary, and higher education; and social services for children/youth and families. Types of support include general operating grants, matching gifts, program development, and seed money grants. Submit a letter of proposal describing the organization and request, and include a copy of the IRS tax-exemption letter.
Requirements: Minnesota 501(c)3 tax-exempt organizations are eligible.
Restrictions: The foundation does not provide grants to individuals.
Geographic Focus: Minnesota
Amount of Grant: Up to 344,529 USD
Contact: Deanna Hulme, Grants Administrator; (320) 743-5466
Sponsor: Charity Incorporated
5786 118th Avenue
Clear Lake, MN 55319

CharityWorks Grants 1036

Each year, CharityWorks seeks a partner whose programs improve the quality of life for children and families in the Washington metropolitan area. CharityWorks contributes manpower and money to qualified nonprofit organizations in the Washington Metropolitan area that make a significant impact on the area's most urgent societal and educational needs. Specific focus areas are education, health, and poverty reduction. The beneficiary will receive 80 percent of the proceeds of CharityWork's fundraising efforts. The remaining 20 percent of the proceeds will be divided among the other two finalists.
Geographic Focus: District of Columbia
Date(s) Application is Due: Apr 18
Contact: Administrator; (703) 286-0758; fax (703) 286-0791; charityworks@aol.com
Internet: http://www.charityworksdc.org
Sponsor: CharityWorks
1616 Anderson Road, Suite 209
McLean, VA 22102

148 | Grant Programs

Charles A. Frueauff Foundation Grants   1037

The foundation considers proposals 501(c)3 organizations that support private four-year colleges and universities, social service agencies, and health-related agencies and institutions. Types of support include building construction/renovation, capital campaigns, equipment acquisition, general operating support, matching/challenge grants, annual campaigns, and emergency funds. Consideration will be given to programs that support persons leaving welfare, preparing students for employment in non-profit agencies, tutoring at-risk youth, and revitalizing neighborhoods. Applicants are requested to send via postal service a one-page letter of inquiry and include the following information: very brief agency mission and purpose; agency location; brief purpose of request and amount requested; and email address if you wish to receive notification via email.
Requirements: Applicants must be private nonprofit corporations with 501(c)3 status.
Restrictions: The foundation funds nationwide except: Arizona, Alaska, California, Hawaii, Idaho, Iowa, Michigan, Minnesota, Montana, Nevada, New Mexico, North Dakota, Ohio, Oregon, Utah, Washington, Wisconsin, and Wyoming. K-12 schools are ineligible. Grants are not awarded to individuals, provide emergency funds, fund research, or for loans. Multi-year grants, international projects, state supported colleges or universities, primary and secondary schools, churches, or fund raising drives and special events are not supported.
Geographic Focus: Alabama, Arkansas, Colorado, Connecticut, Delaware, District of Columbia, Florida, Georgia, Illinois, Indiana, Kansas, Kentucky, Louisiana, Maine, Maryland, Massachusetts, Mississippi, Missouri, Nebraska, New Hampshire, New Jersey, New Mexico, New York, North Carolina, Oklahoma, Pennsylvania, Rhode Island, South Carolina, South Dakota, Tennessee, Texas, Vermont, Virginia, West Virginia
Date(s) Application is Due: Mar 15; Sep 15
Contact: Sue Frueauff; (501) 324-2233; fax (501) 324-2236
Internet: http://www.frueaufffoundation.com/application/default.asp
Sponsor: Charles A. Frueauff Foundation
200 South Commerce, Suite 100
Little Rock, AR 72201

Charles and Lynn Schusterman Family Foundation Grants   1038

The foundation awards grants in Oklahoma, nationally, and internationally to nonsectarian organizations and programs focused on community service and education, with particular emphasis on children and young adults up to age 25. The foundation's primary funding interest is to support organizations that enhance Jewish life in Oklahoma, throughout the United States, and in Israel and the former Soviet Union. The foundation will consider proposals seeking support for more than one year, but discourages applicants from applying for funds for a period of more than three years. Application materials are available online.
Requirements: U.S. 501(c)3 organizations are eligible. Grants are only approved for foreign entities that meet specific charitable status requirements.
Restrictions: Grants normally do not support nonsectarian programs outside of Tulsa; local Jewish programs in communities other than Tulsa; endowments; individuals; program deficits; programs appropriately financed by a governmental agency; responsibility for permanent financing of a program; or grants that trigger expenditure responsibility by the foundation.
Geographic Focus: All States
Amount of Grant: 10,000 - 2,500,000 USD
Contact: Renee Jacobs; (918) 591-1090; fax (918) 591-1758; rjacobs@schusterman.org
Internet: http://www.schusterman.org/
Sponsor: Charles and Lynn Schusterman Family Foundation
Two West Second Street
Tulsa, OK 74103

Charles Delmar Foundation Grants   1039

Established in 1957, the Foundation supports organizations involved with inter-American studies, higher, secondary, elementary, and other education, underprivileged youth, the disadvantaged, the aged, the homeless and housing issues, general welfare organizations, and fine and performing arts. Giving primarily in the Washington, DC area in the U.S., and in Europe and South America. There are no specific deadlines with which to adhere. Contact the Foundation for further application information and guidelines.
Restrictions: No grants to individuals, or for building or endowment funds, or matching gifts; no loans.
Geographic Focus: District of Columbia, Maryland, Virginia, West Virginia, Albania, Andorra, Argentina, Armenia, Austria, Azerbaijan, Belarus, Belgium, Bolivia, Bosnia & Herzegovina, Brazil, Bulgaria, Chile, Colombia, Croatia, Cyprus, Czech Republic, Denmark, Ecuador, Estonia, Finland, France, Georgia, Germany, Greece, Guyana, Hungary, Iceland, Ireland, Italy, Kosovo, Latvia, Liechtenstein, Lithuania, Luxembourg, Macedonia, Malta, Moldova, Monaco, Montenegro, Norway, Paraguay, Peru, Poland, Portugal, Romania, Russia, San Marino, Serbia, Slovakia, Slovenia, Spain, Sweden, Switzerland, The Netherlands, Turkey, Ukraine, United Kingdom, Vatican City
Contact: Mareen D. Hughes, President; (703) 534-9109
Sponsor: Charles Delmar Foundation
5205 Leesburg Pike, Suite 209
Falls Church, VA 22041-3858

Charles F. Bacon Trust Grants   1040

The Charles F. Bacon Trust was established in 1928 to support and promote quality educational, human services, and health care programming for underserved populations. Special consideration is given to charitable organizations that serve the needs of elderly women. Grant requests for general operating support are strongly encouraged. Program support will also be considered. Small, program-related capital expenses may be included in general operating or program requests. The application deadline is April 1, and applicants will be notified of grant decisions before June 30.
Requirements: 501(c)3 organizations serving residents of Massachusetts are eligible.
Restrictions: The majority of Bacon Trust grants are 1 year in duration. On occasion, multi-year support is awarded.
Geographic Focus: Massachusetts
Date(s) Application is Due: Apr 1
Contact: Michealle Larkins; (866) 778-6859; michealle.larkins@baml.com
Internet: https://www.bankofamerica.com/philanthropic/fn_search.action
Sponsor: Charles F. Bacon Trust
225 Franklin Street, 4th Floor, MA1-225-04-02
Boston, MA 02110

Charles G. Koch Charitable Foundation Grants   1041

The foundation provides funding for academic and public policy research directed at solving social problems through voluntary action and free enterprise. In the area of research, the foundation primarily funds organizations working with doctorate-level investigators in disciplines such as economics, history, philosophy, political science, and organizational behavior. Types of support include general operating, scholarship funds, conferences and seminars, research, special projects, and seed money. There are no application deadlines. Submit preproposal letters (three-page limit).
Geographic Focus: All States
Contact: Kelly Young; (202) 393-2354; fax (202) 393-2355; email@cgkfoundation.org
Internet: http://www.cgkfoundation.org
Sponsor: Charles G. Koch Charitable Foundation
655 15th Street NW, Suite 445
Washington, DC 20005-2001

Charles H. Dater Foundation Grants   1042

The foundation makes grants to private, nonprofit organizations and public agencies in Greater Cincinnati for programs that benefit children in the region in the areas of arts/culture, education, healthcare, social services, and other community needs. Grants are usually made for one year, and subsequent grants for an extended or ongoing program are based on an evaluation of annual results. Multiple grants to an organization in the foundation's same fiscal year (September through August) are possible, but rare. The foundation looks favorably on applications that leverage a grant to seek additional funding and resources. The foundation directors/officers meet monthly to review grant applications.
Requirements: Nonprofit organizations in the greater Cincinnati area are eligible. This area is defined as the eight-county metropolitan area made up of the counties of Hamilton, Butler, Warren and Clermont in Ohio; Boone, Kenton and Campbell in Northern Kentucky; and Dearborn in Indiana.
Restrictions: The foundation does not make grants to individuals, for scholarships for individuals, for debt reduction, and, with rare exception, for capital fund projects.
Geographic Focus: Indiana, Kentucky, Ohio
Contact: Beth Broomall; (513) 241-2658; fax (513) 274-2731; bb@DaterFoundation.org
Internet: http://www.daterfoundation.org/grants.php
Sponsor: Charles H. Dater Foundation
602 Main Street, Suite 302
Cincinnati, OH 45202

Charles H. Farnsworth Trust Grants   1043

The Charles H. Farnsworth Trust was established in 1930 to assist older adults to live in dignity and with independence. In describing the purpose of his legacy, Mr. Farnsworth made clear his interest in supporting housing, particularly in developing affordable housing options, and in providing support services to older adults. Program interests include: development of housing, especially housing with support services; services for elderly persons (i.e. health care, homemaker assistance, and nutritional support to enable the elderly to continue living in the community); and research, planning, and communication to better inform individuals, institutions, and the community at large on ways to improve the quality and quantity of housing and support services for seniors. Capital grants related to construction or renovation of housing for older adults is of particular interest. While general operating grants are provided, requests for support for new or special projects/programs are preferred. Planning grants investigating strategies for the development of supportive housing for the elderly are encouraged. Capital grants generally range between $25,000 and $250,000. General operating grants are usually no more than $10,000. Applicants must apply online at the grant website. Applicants are strongly encouraged to do the following before applying: review the downloadable state application procedures for additional helpful information and clarifications; review the downloadable online-application guidelines at the grant website; review the trust's funding history (link is available from the grant website); review the online application questions in advance; and review the list of required attachments. These will generally include: a list of board members, financial statements (audited, reviewed, or compiled by independent auditor); an organization summary; a list of other funding sources; an IRS Determination letter; and other required documents. All attachments must be uploaded in the online application as PDF, Word, or Excel files. The Farnsworth Trust has biannual deadlines of February 1 and October 15. Grant applicants for the February deadline will be notified of grant decisions by May 31 and applicants for the October deadline will be notified of grant decisions by December 31.
Restrictions: Grant opportunities are restricted to the Greater Boston area.
Geographic Focus: Massachusetts
Date(s) Application is Due: Feb 1; Oct 15
Contact: Michealle Larkins; (866) 778-6859; michealle.larkins@baml.com
Internet: https://www.bankofamerica.com/philanthropic/fn_search.action
Sponsor: Charles H. Farnsworth Trust
225 Franklin Street, 4th Floor, MA1-225-04-02
Boston, MA 02110

Charles H. Hall Foundation 1044

The Charles H. Hall Foundation was established in 2007 to support and promote educational, health- and human-services, religious, and arts and cultural programming for underserved populations. Special consideration is given to programs whose purpose is the prevention of cruelty to children or animals. Grants from the Charles H. Hall Foundation are one year in duration. Applicants must apply online at the grant website. Applicants are strongly encouraged to do the following before applying: review the downloadable state application procedures for additional helpful information and clarifications; review the downloadable online-application guidelines at the grant website; review the foundation's funding history (link is available from the grant website); review the online application questions in advance; and review the list of required attachments. These will generally include: a list of board members, financial statements (audited, reviewed, or compiled by independent auditor); an organization summary; a list of other funding sources; an IRS Determination letter; and other required documents. All attachments must be uploaded in the online application as PDF, Word, or Excel files. The Charles H. Hall Foundation application deadline is 11:59 p.m. on December 1. Applicants will be notified of grant decisions by letter within three to four months of the deadline.
Requirements: The foundation specifically serves organizations based in Berkshire, Hampden, Hampshire, or Franklin Counties, Massachusetts. Grants will be considered for specific programs or projects with preference given to organizations that provide direct services.
Restrictions: Applicants will not be awarded a grant for more than 3 consecutive years. The foundation does not support requests from individuals, organizations attempting to influence policy through direct lobbying, or any political campaigns.
Geographic Focus: Massachusetts
Date(s) Application is Due: Dec 1
Contact: Amy Lynch; (860) 657-7015; amy.r.lynch@baml.com
Internet: https://www.bankofamerica.com/philanthropic/fn_search.action
Sponsor: Charles H. Hall Foundation
200 Glastonbury Boulevard, Suite # 200, CT2-545-02-05
Glastonbury, CT 06033-4056

Charles H. Pearson Foundation Grants 1045

The Charles H. Pearson Foundation Fund was established in 1922 to support and promote quality educational, human-services, and health-care programming for underserved populations. In the area of education, the fund supports academic access, enrichment, and remedial programming for children, youth, adults, and senior citizens that focuses on preparing individuals to achieve while in school and beyond. In the area of health care, the fund supports programming that improves access to primary care for traditionally underserved individuals, health education initiatives and programming that impact at-risk populations, and medical research. In the area of human services the fund tries to meet evolving needs of communities. Currently the fund's focus is on (but is not limited to) youth development, violence prevention, employment, life-skills attainment, and food programs. Grant requests for general operating support are strongly encouraged. Program support will also be considered. Small, program-related capital expenses may be included in general operating or program requests. The majority of grants from the Pearson Fund are one year in duration; on occasion, multi-year support is awarded. Applicants must apply online at the grant website. Applicants are strongly encouraged to do the following before applying: review the downloadable state application procedures for additional helpful information and clarifications; review the downloadable online-application guidelines at the grant website; review the foundation's funding history (link is available from the grant website); review the online application questions in advance; and review the list of required attachments. These will generally include: a list of board members, financial statements (audited, reviewed, or compiled by independent auditor); an organization summary; a list of other funding sources; an IRS Determination letter; and other required documents. All attachments must be uploaded in the online application as PDF, Word, or Excel files. The application deadline for the Charles H. Pearson Foundation Fund is 11:59 p.m. on July 1. Applicants will be notified of grant decisions before September 30.
Requirements: Applicants must have 501(c)3 tax-exempt status.
Restrictions: In general, capital requests are not advised. The fund does not support endowment campaigns, events such as galas or award ceremonies, and costs of fundraising events. The fund does not support requests from individuals, organizations attempting to influence policy through direct lobbying, or any political campaigns.
Geographic Focus: Massachusetts
Date(s) Application is Due: Jul 1
Contact: Michealle Larkins; (866) 778-6859; michealle.larkins@baml.com
Internet: https://www.bankofamerica.com/philanthropic/fn_search.action
Sponsor: Charles H. Pearson Foundation Fund
225 Franklin Street, 4th Floor, MA1-225-04-02
Boston, MA 02110

Charles H. Price II Family Foundation Grants 1046

The Charles H. Price II Family Foundation, established in Kansas City, Missouri, by a prominent American businessman and former Ambassador of the United States, offers support to educational programs and research primarily in Missouri and California (though funding is also occasionally provided outside of these two states). Grants are given for general operating support and scholarships. There are no specific applications or deadlines with which to adhere, and applicants should approach the Foundation in writing via a letter of application.
Geographic Focus: California, Missouri
Contact: Charles H. Price II, Director; (816) 360-6174 or (816) 360-6176
Sponsor: Charles H. Price II Family Foundation
1 W. Armour Boulevard, Suite 300
Kansas City, MO 64111-2004

Charles H. Revson Foundation Grants 1047

The foundation awards grants nationwide in its areas of interest, including urban affairs and public policy, education and higher education, biomedical research policy, and Jewish education and philanthropy. Types of support include capital campaigns, continuing support, fellowships, internship funds, program development, and research. Preference is given to requests serving New York, NY. There are no application forms or deadlines. The board meets in April, June, October, and December.
Restrictions: Grants do not support local or national health appeals or direct service programs, individuals, building construction/renovation, book projects, charity events, travel expenses, or budgetary support.
Geographic Focus: All States
Contact: Maria Marcantonio, (212) 935-3340; fax (212) 688-0633; info@revsonfoundation.org
Internet: http://www.revsonfoundation.org/guidelines.html
Sponsor: Charles H. Revson Foundation
55 E 59th Street, 23rd Floor
New York, NY 10022

Charles Hayden Foundation Grants 1048

Grants are made to institutions and organizations that serve children and youth ages three to 18, and that are located in the metropolitan New York City and Boston areas. Support is concentrated on youth development and education programs that present evidence of program impact on young people and plans for making measurable progress toward well-defined goals in a specific time frame. Program support is generally for program expansion and creation. Multiyear funding is awarded when appropriate, according to each program's specific needs and potential. Capital support is awarded for renovations to existing buildings, construction of new buildings and additions or the purchase of existing structures, and purchase of nonexpendable equipment (generally excluding computers). Youth development programs must exhibit long-term, caring relationships with youth agency staff; engaging, enriching, and safe activities during nonschool hours; and activities and counseling that help youth prepare for postsecondary education, work, and citizenship. School programs (including charter schools and ndependent and parochial schools that charge a maximum of $10,000/year for tuition) must exhibit high expectations for students' mental development, reflected in a challenging course of study that emphasizes reading, writing mathematics and other core skill and content areas; active learning within varied learning environments supportive of each child; active engagement of parents in their children's education at home and in schools; outreach to collaboration with other organizations and programs that can contribute to student's learning; and activities and counseling that help youth prepare for postsecondary education, work, and citizenship. Applications are accepted at any time. Applicants are encouraged to use the New York Area or AGM (Boston area) common grant application forms. Guidelines are available online.
Requirements: Applicant organizations must be located in the metropolitan areas of New York, NY (including New Jersey's Hudson and Essex counties and a few of the larger urban communities in Passaic and Bergen counties, such as Paterson, Hackensack, Passaic, and Clifton), and Boston, MA.
Restrictions: Capital grants are not made to those who have received capital grants in the prior two years. Grants are not awarded to individuals, hospitals, or theological institutions; or for religious organizations unless programs are community or youth oriented, endowments, or general operating support.
Geographic Focus: Massachusetts, New York
Amount of Grant: 15,000 - 400,000 USD
Contact: Maureen Fletcher; (212) 785-3677; info@charleshaydenfoundation.org
Internet: http://www.charleshaydenfoundation.org/guidelines.php
Sponsor: Charles Hayden Foundation
140 Broadway, 51st Floor
New York, NY 10005

Charles Lafitte Foundation Grants 1049

The foundation is committed to helping groups and individuals foster lasting improvement on the human condition by providing support to education, children's advocacy, medical research, and the arts. Children's advocacy grants support organizations working to improve the quality of life for children, particularly in relation to child abuse, literacy, foster housing, hunger, and after-school programs. Education grants support innovative programs that work to resolve social service issues, address the needs of students with learning disabilities, provide technology and computer-based education, offer leadership skills education, and support at-risk students. Colleges and universities also receive support for research and conferences. The foundation's medical issues and research grants support healthcare studies, with emphasis on cancer research and treatment, children's health, health education, and promoting healthy living and disease prevention. Art grants support emerging artists and educational art programs.
Requirements: 501(c)3 organizations are eligible. The Foundation does not respond to unsolicited submissions, so submit a letter of inquiry prior to preparing an application.
Restrictions: Political organizations or religious-based programs are not supported.
Geographic Focus: All States
Samples: Girl Scouts of the Jersey Shore, $200,000 (2013). Bridge of Books Foundation, $2,500 (2013). Hand in Hand, $10,000 (2013). Jersey Shore University Medical Center, $700,000 (2013).
Contact: Jennifer Vertetis, President; jennifer@charleslafitte.org
Internet: http://charleslafitte.org/grants/overview/
Sponsor: Charles Lafitte Foundation
29520 2nd Ave SW
Federal Way, WA 98023

Charles M. and Mary D. Grant Foundation Grants 1050
The Foundation awards grants primarily in the southeast United States in its areas of interest, including community and economic development, health and human services, environment, and education. The Foundation prefers project support, but considers operating support proposals from organizations with budgets of less than $1 million. Grants are made in September. A minimum of three years must elapse between grant awards. Further information is available at the website.
Requirements: Southeast U.S. 501(c)3 tax-exempt organizations are eligible. Specific grant guidelines are available online with the application, which must be filed online.
Restrictions: No grants are made to individuals or for loans. A minimum of three years must elapse between grant awards.
Geographic Focus: Alabama, Florida, Georgia, Kentucky, Mississippi, North Carolina, South Carolina, Tennessee, Virginia, West Virginia
Date(s) Application is Due: Apr 30
Amount of Grant: 20,000 - 40,000 USD
Contact: Casey Castaneda; (212) 464-2487; casey.b.castaneda@jpmchase.com
Internet: http://fdncenter.org/grantmaker/grant
Sponsor: Charles M. and Mary D. Grant Foundation
J.P. Morgan Private Bank, Philanthropic Services
Dallas, TX 75222-7237

Charles M. Bair Family Trust Grants 1051
The trust awards general support grants to Montana nonprofits in its areas of interest, including museums, performing arts, arts and culture, higher education, youth, and social services. Application forms are required.
Requirements: Montana nonprofit organizations are eligible, with emphasis on Yellowstone, Meagher and Wheatland counties.
Restrictions: Funding is not provided for: churches, conventions, or associations of churches; individuals; conferences; symposiums; or for fundraising events.
Geographic Focus: Montana
Date(s) Application is Due: Jan 15; Aug 1
Amount of Grant: 2,000 - 300,000 USD
Contact: Grants Administrator, c/o U.S. Bank, Tax Department
Sponsor: Charles M. Bair Family Trust
P.O. Box 20678
Billings, MT 59115

Charles Nelson Robinson Fund Grants 1052
The Charles Nelson Robinson Fund was established in 1970 to support and promote quality educational, human-services, and health-care programming for underserved populations in Hartford, Connecticut. Preference is given to organizations that provide human services programming to underserved adults. Grants from the Robinson Fund are one year in duration. Applicants must apply online at the grant website. Applicants are strongly encouraged to do the following before applying: review the downloadable state application procedures for additional helpful information and clarifications; review the downloadable online-application guidelines at the grant website; review the foundation's funding history (link is available from the grant website); review the online application questions in advance; and review the list of required attachments. These will generally include: a list of board members, financial statements (audited, reviewed, or compiled by independent auditor); an organization summary; a list of other funding sources; an IRS Determination letter; and other required documents. All attachments must be uploaded in the online application as PDF, Word, or Excel files. The Charles Nelson Robinson Fund has an annual deadline of 11:59 p.m. on February 15. Applicants will be notified of grant decisions by letter within two to three months of the proposal deadline.
Requirements: Applicant organizations must have 501(c)3 tax-exempt status and have a principal office located in the city of Hartford, Connecticut.
Restrictions: Grant requests for capital projects will not be considered. Applicants will not be awarded a grant for more than three consecutive years. The fund does not support requests from individuals, organizations attempting to influence policy through direct lobbying, or any political campaigns.
Geographic Focus: Connecticut
Date(s) Application is Due: Feb 15
Contact: Carmen Britt; (860) 657-7019; carmen.britt@baml.com
Internet: https://www.bankofamerica.com/philanthropic/fn_search.action
Sponsor: Charles Nelson Robinson Fund
200 Glastonbury Boulevard, Suite # 200, CT2-545-02-05
Glastonbury, CT 06033-4056

Charles Parker Trust for Public Music Fund Grants 1053
The Charles Parker Trust for Public Music Fund was established "to help in some way in furnishing good music to the public... at a nominal price or without admission price..." Applicants must apply online at the grant website. Applicants are strongly encouraged to do the following before applying: review the downloadable state application procedures for additional helpful information and clarifications; review the downloadable online-application guidelines at the grant website; review the trust's funding history (link is available from the grant website); review the online application questions in advance; and review the list of required attachments. These will generally include: a list of board members, financial statements (audited, reviewed, or compiled by independent auditor); an organization summary; a list of other funding sources; an IRS Determination letter; and other required documents. All attachments must be uploaded in the online application as PDF, Word, or Excel files. Grants from the Charles Parker Trust for Public Music Fund are one year in duration. The application deadline for the Charles Parker Trust for Public Music Fund is 11:59 p.m. on September 1. Applicants will be notified of grant decisions by letter within two to three months after the proposal deadline.
Requirements: Applicant organizations must serve the people of New Britain, Connecticut. Musical performances must be conducted in New Britain, Connecticut.
Restrictions: Grant request for capital projects will not be considered. Applicants will not be awarded a grant for more than 3 consecutive years.
Geographic Focus: Connecticut
Date(s) Application is Due: Sep 1
Contact: Carmen Britt; (860) 657-7019; carmen.britt@baml.com
Internet: https://www.bankofamerica.com/philanthropic/fn_search.action
Sponsor: Charles Parker Trust for Public Music Fund
200 Glastonbury Boulevard, Suite # 200, CT2-545-02-05
Glastonbury, CT 06033-4056

Charles Stewart Mott Foundation Anti-Poverty Program 1054
This program focuses on improving education, expanding economic opportunity, building organized communities, and special initiatives as pathways out of poverty. The overall goal is to help people vocalize and mobilize around local concerns, grow through participation in educational opportunities, and attain economic self-sufficiency by engaging more fully in the economy. Types of support include challenge/matching grants, conferences and seminars, demonstration grants, general operating grants, program grants, seed money grants, technical assistance, and training grants. The board meets in March, June, September, and December. Organizations should apply at least four months prior to the start date of the project for which they are seeking funds.
Requirements: Nonprofits and K-12 organizations are eligible to apply. A proposal may be submitted by a church-based or similar organization if the project falls clearly within program guidelines and is intended to serve as broad a segment of the population as the program of a comparable nonreligious organization.
Geographic Focus: All States
Amount of Grant: Up to 100,000,000 USD
Contact: Office of Proposal Entry; (810) 238-5651; fax (810) 766-1753; info@mott.org
Internet: http://www.mott.org/programs/poverty.asp
Sponsor: Charles Stewart Mott Foundation
503 S Saginaw Street, Suite 1200
Flint, MI 48502-1851

Charles Stewart Mott Foundation Grants 1055
The focus of the foundation's grant making is organized in four programs: civil society; environment; Flint, Michigan; and poverty. Flexibility to investigate new opportunities is maintained through an exploratory and special projects program. The civil society program promotes and supports civil society in the United States; Central/Eastern Europe and South Africa. The environment program supports efforts to achieve a healthy global environment capable of sustaining all forms of life. The Flint program seeks to strengthen the capacity of local institutions, including schools and school districts, in the foundation's home community of Flint, Michigan, to respond to economic and social needs. The poverty program addresses issues that contribute to improved life outcomes for children, youth, and families in low-income communities. Programs in low-income communities that connect schools and communities through systemic reform, improved teaching, leadership development, networking, technical assistance, and advocacy are also applicable. In all grant making, particular interest will be given to fresh approaches to solving community problems in the defined program areas; approaches that can generate long-term support from other sources and/or can be replicated in other communities; public policy development and research and development activities to further existing programs as well as to explore new fields of interest; and approaches and activities that lead to systemic change. Although proposals may be submitted at any time, applicants are strongly encouraged to submit during the first quarter of the year for which funding is requested. Grant expenditures are determined by September 1 of each year. The review process takes up to four months from the time the proposal is received. Therefore, proposals should be submitted at least four months prior to the start of the proposed grant period. Funding for unsolicited proposals is limited. It is recommended that letters of inquiry be submitted instead of a full proposal.
Requirements: Only 501(c)3 organizations are eligible, including schools and districts.
Restrictions: Grants are not made to/for individuals; religious activities or programs that serve, or appear to serve, specific religious groups or denominations; or local projects outside the Flint area unless the projects are part of a national demonstration or foundation-planned network of grants that have clear and significant implications for replication in other communities.
Geographic Focus: All States
Contact: Mary A. Gailbreath; (810) 238-5651; fax (810) 766-1753; info@mott.org
Internet: http://www.mott.org/about/programs.aspx
Sponsor: Charles Stewart Mott Foundation
503 S Saginaw Street, Suite 1200
Flint, MI 48502-1851

Charlotte County (FL) Community Foundation Grants 1056
The foundation awards grants from its unrestricted funds to support innovative solutions for the citizens of Charlotte County through the implementation of projects and programs that address specific identified needs of the community and demonstrate a wide-spread positive impact on its residents. The foundation places priority on funding requests from nonprofit organizations whose project can: Provide an unduplicated value and/or service; Leverage dollars and/or people power; Match foundation funds with funds from other sources; Establish cooperative efforts of two or more organizations where such synergy is likely to demonstrate superior results and/or lower costs; Enhance, expand and/or improve the organization's capabilities; Show visible end results within a specific timeline for completion; Demonstrate

that the Foundation grant will play an important role; Provide a meaningful outcomes evaluations process with a project completion report; Reach a large number of Charlotte County residents; and, be completed within one year with a request of less than $7,500.
Requirements: Foundation grants are made to tax exempt organizations that have been in existence for at least two years and whose focus is in one of the following areas of interest: Animal Welfare; Arts and Culture; Community Development; Education; Environment; Health, Human, and Social Services; Historic Preservation; Nonprofit Organization Capacity Building. Additionally, organizations must also show that they have: a Board of Directors composed of individuals of diverse backgrounds, at least half of whom reside in Charlotte County; Strong management and leadership qualities; Demonstrated fiscal responsibility; Submitted its prior year IRS Form 990; Benefited Charlotte County residents. To apply, submit a Letter of Intent (LOI) summarizing your request. (See instructions at the foundation's website.) If the foundation feels that the proposed project has merit, you will be asked to complete a grant proposal package to be submitted as your formal request for funding.
Restrictions: The foundation is generally not interested in requests for: General operating support; Building or capital campaigns; Deficit financing and debt reduction; Endowment funds; Fraternal organizations, societies or orders; Loans or assistance to individuals; Religious organizations for sectarian purposes; Lobbying legislators or influencing elections; Political organizations or campaigns; Fund raising events; Basic scientific research; Start up organization funding; Travel expenses for individuals or groups; or, Re-granting.
Geographic Focus: Florida
Date(s) Application is Due: Apr 5; May 5; Jul 6; Sep 16
Amount of Grant: Up to 7,500 USD
Contact: Gregory C. Bobonich; (941) 637-0077; gbobonich@charlottecommunityfoundation.org
Internet: http://www.charlottecommunityfoundation.org/index.php?subcat=20&articleid=68&page_num=1#
Sponsor: Charlotte County Community Foundation
1675 West Marion Avenue
Punta Gorda, FL 33950

Charlotte Martin Foundation Youth Grants 1057
The Charlotte Martin Foundation is a private, independent foundation dedicated to enriching the lives of youth in the areas of athletics, culture, and education and also to preserving and protecting wildlife and habitat. In the area of Youth, the foundation seeks to ensure opportunities for all youth, particularly the underserved and economically disadvantaged, to develop their skills in education, creative and cultural expression and athletics in ways that ultimately promote their habits of lifelong learning and their ability to make strong and lasting contributions to their respective communities. In regards to Youth Athletics, the foundation is interested in supporting a wide variety of sports programs and equipment for both boys and girls where youth populations are underserved (with special interest in supporting girls' sports; (limited investment in) facilities that are used primarily by youth; after school and off-hours sports programs making better use of existing facilities; and, programs that get younger children introduced to the value of sports. In regards to Youth Culture, the foundation will support projects that utilize active participation of young people in music, art, dance, literature, especially projects where youth are engaged in the production of an art form or event and projects that celebrate the heritage and cultural diversity of a community. For Youth Education grants, the foundation will support: programs in or out of the classroom, after school, weekends and summer; student-directed or inquiry-based learning where students have a clear role in designing and evaluating projects and learning activities; and, programs that promote skills for critical thinking, problem-solving and applied learning including but not limited to inquiry-based science, technology, engineering and environmental education.
Requirements: Washington, Oregon, Idaho, Montana, and Alaska nonprofit organizations are eligible. "Youth" is defined as children in kindergarten through high school, ages six to eighteen. Projects must focus on young people as the primary participants or beneficiaries.
Restrictions: The foundation does not support: large capital investment projects (e.g. track renovation, swimming pools, tennis courts, lockers, gymnasium renovation, bleachers); transportation to tournaments; fitness equipment and activities (e.g. treadmills, weight rooms); playgrounds or playground equipment; admission subsidies or purchase of tickets for events; trips to conferences; international exchange programs; passive participation by youth; artists in residence programs; children's testing or test preparation; purchase of computers or textbooks; programs whose goals are primarily social services; pre-Kindergarten programs; curriculum development; programs for college students.
Geographic Focus: Alaska, Arizona, Idaho, Montana, Oregon, Washington
Date(s) Application is Due: Apr 30; Sep 30
Amount of Grant: Up to 100,000 USD
Contact: Rebekah Wadadli, (800) 839-1821; rwadadli@foundationsource.com
Internet: http://www.charlottemartin.org/programs.htm
Sponsor: Charlotte Martin Foundation
P.O. Box 1733
Seattle, WA 98111

Charlotte R. Schmidlapp Fund Grants 1058
The fund supports programs for women and girls in Ohio that focus on math, science, and arts scholarships; research and awareness of issues affecting girls and women; and programs that strengthen the lives of all women who are self-supporting.
Requirements: 501(c)3 tax-exempt organizations in Cincinnati, Cleveland, Columbus, Dayton, and Toledo, OH are eligible.
Geographic Focus: Ohio
Contact: Dr. Lawra Baumann, Assistant Vice President; (513) 534-7001
Sponsor: Charlotte R. Schmidlapp Fund
38 Fountain Square Plaza, MD 109067
Cincinnati, OH 45263

Chase Paymentech Corporate Giving Grants 1059
The corporation awards grants to nonprofit organizations that provide needed services in the areas of education, health and human services. Preference for funding is given to organizations whose work impacts the citizens of those areas in which Paymentech offices are located, including Westerville, OH; Dallas, TX; Salem, NH; Silver Springs, MD; Tampa, FL; Tempe, AZ; and Toronto, Canada. The Corporate Giving Committee meets each quarter. Organizations are notified about funding status after each meeting.
Requirements: 501(c)3 non-profit organizations that provide needed services in the areas of education and health and human services are eligible. Applicants submit a written request on the organization's letterhead detailing the organization's mission, the amount requested and a detailed explanation of the purpose for which the funds would be used. Organizations should also submit proof of non-profit status.
Restrictions: Paymentech does not make grants to individuals; religious, fraternal, political, or veterans organizations; or colleges and universities. Nor is funding provided for the following purposes: or deficit spending or debt liquidation; annual capital campaigns of hospitals, colleges, universities, grade schools, or high schools.
Geographic Focus: Arizona, Florida, Maryland, New Hampshire, Ohio, Texas, Canada
Date(s) Application is Due: Mar 30; Jun 29; Sep 28; Dec 31
Amount of Grant: Up to 5,000 USD
Contact: Corporate Giving Director
Internet: http://www.chasepaymentech.com/portal/community/chase_paymentech/public/public_website/about_us/company_information_pages/corporate_giving_program
Sponsor: Chase Paymentech
14221 Dallas Parkway, Building Two
Dallas, TX 75254

Chatham Athletic Foundation Grants 1060
The Chatham Athletic Foundation (CAF) is a nonprofit organization created to promote youth athletics and help increase safety in youth athletics by providing funding to local non-profit organizations, schools and Chatham Township and Borough governments. Grant requests must support the mission of CAF and directly benefit youth athletics in grades K-8 in the Chathams. If awarded, the grant funding will pay for the costs of the project including, but not limited to, equipment, supplies, construction, labor, etc. The Chatham Athletic Foundation typically considers proposals from $1,000 up to $5,000.
Requirements: Single or multipurpose athletic projects in Chatham Borough and/or Chatham Township may apply. Submissions should include evidence that the project addresses a significant need with clearly defined objectives, and a cost-effective budget. Higher consideration may be given to projects that impact multiple sports and a large number of youth athletics. If your grant request project requires approval from the Borough Council, Township Committee, Board of Ed, Recreation, etc., such approval must be provided with the application.
Geographic Focus: New Jersey
Date(s) Application is Due: May 15
Amount of Grant: 1,000 - 5,000 USD
Contact: Grants Administrator, grants@chathamathleticfoundation.org
Internet: http://www.chathamathleticfoundation.org/grants.html
Sponsor: Chatham Athletic Foundation
P.O. Box 568
Chatham, NJ 07928

Chatlos Foundation Grants 1061
The Chatlos Foundation supports nonprofit organizations in the USA and around the globe. Support is provided to organizations currently exempt by the Internal Revenue Service of the United States. The Foundation's areas of interest are: Bible Colleges/Seminaries, Religious Causes, Medical Concerns, Liberal Arts Colleges and Social Concerns.
Requirements: Applicants must be U.S. tax-exempt, nonprofit organizations that provide services in the following areas: bible colleges, religious causes, medical concerns, liberal arts colleges, and social concerns. Proposals must include cover letter, specific request, tax-exemption letter, and budget. If proposal is to be considered at board level, additional information will be requested.
Restrictions: The foundation will not accept requests from individual church congregations, individuals, organizations in existence for less than two years as indicated by IRS tax-exempt letter of determination, for education below the college level, for medical research projects, or for support of the arts.
Geographic Focus: All States
Amount of Grant: 10,000 - 25,000 USD
Contact: C. J. Leff, Administrator; (407) 862-5077; cj@chatlos.org
Internet: http://www.chatlos.org/AppInfo.htm
Sponsor: Chatlos Foundation
P.O. Box 915048
Longwood, FL 32791-5048

Chautauqua Region Community Foundation Grants 1062
Grants support projects serving communities in Chautauqua County in its areas of interest, including arts and culture, libraries, education, housing and shelters, children and youth, human services and general charitable giving, and government and public administration. Types of support include general operating support, continuing support, building construction/renovation, equipment acquisition, conferences and seminars, publication, seed grants, emergency funds, and undergraduate and graduate scholarships to individuals.
Requirements: Nonprofit organizations may apply for grants in support of projects serving communities in Chautauqua County, excluding the Fredonia/Dunkirk area, which is served by the Northern Chautauqua Community Foundation.
Geographic Focus: New York

Date(s) Application is Due: Jan 31; Mar 1; Nov 1
Contact: June Diethrick; (716) 661-3392; fax (716) 488-0387; jdiethrick@crcfonline.org
Internet: http://www.crcfonline.org/
Sponsor: Chautauqua Region Community Foundation
418 Spring Street
Jamestown, NY 14701

CHCF Grants   1063
The foundation's mission is to expand access to affordable, quality health care for underserved individuals and communities in California and to promote fundamental improvements in the health status of Californians. The foundation has five funding areas: improving care delivery, business of healthcare, healthcare quality, California health policy, and California's uninsured. The one-year, renewable grants will focus on areas where the foundation's resources can initiate meaningful policy recommendations, innovative research, and the development of model programs. Philanthropic activities include foundation-initiated projects, requests for proposals, and unsolicited proposals. emailed letters of inquiry should include, in two to three pages, a brief description of the proposed project, along with an estimated time line and budget. A full proposal may be requested.
Requirements: California 501(c)3 nonprofit organizations are eligible.
Restrictions: The foundation does not generally support the cost of direct clinical care, ongoing general operating expenses, capital campaigns, annual appeals or other fund-raising events, construction, purchase or renovation of facilities, or purchase of equipment.
Geographic Focus: California
Date(s) Application is Due: Oct 14
Contact: Grants Administrator; (510) 238-1040; fax (510) 238-1388; grants@chcf.org
Internet: http://www.chcf.org/grantinfo
Sponsor: California HealthCare Foundation
1438 Webster Street, Suite 400
Oakland, CA 94612

CHCF Local Coverage Expansion Initiative   1064
This initiative supports California counties and local coalitions seeking to expand coverage to uninsured children and adults that are ineligible for public insurance programs. This solicitation will fund two types of technical assistance grants: planning grants will assist coverage expansion efforts with activities such as coalition strengthening, better defining the target population's needs, and/or developing an implementation plan; and implementation grants will provide funding for specific unmet needs associated with launching a local coverage program. Grants will be awarded for period up to one year. Application and guidelines are available online.
Requirements: Any type of organization may apply, but the program will focus on public programs seeking to expand coverage, primarily through the use of public funds. It is anticipated that successful proposals will either come from public or quasi-public agencies, or include a plan for close collaboration with public sector entities.
Geographic Focus: All States
Date(s) Application is Due: Oct 14
Amount of Grant: 100,000 - 200,000 USD
Contact: Administrator; (510) 238-1040; fax (510) 238-1388; localcoverage@chcf.org
Internet: http://www.chcf.org/grantinfo/rfps/index.cfm?itemID=21263
Sponsor: California HealthCare Foundation
1438 Webster Street, Suite 400
Oakland, CA 94612

CHC Foundation Grants   1065
The foundation awards general operating grants to southeastern Idaho nonprofit organizations in its areas of interest, including children and youth, community development, natural resource conservation and protection, and social services. Applicants should submit a letter of inquiry; the foundation will invite full proposals.
Requirements: 501(c)3 southeastern Idaho nonprofit organizations may apply.
Geographic Focus: Idaho
Date(s) Application is Due: Mar 15; Sep 1
Amount of Grant: 750 - 150,000 USD
Contact: Ralph Isom, President; (208) 522-2368
Sponsor: CHC Foundation
P.O. Box 1644
Idaho Falls, ID 83403-1644

Chefs Move to Schools Grants   1066
The Chefs Move to Schools program, founded in May 2010, is an integral part of the Let's Move! initiative and its goal of solving the childhood obesity epidemic within a generation. The program pairs chefs with interested schools in their communities to work with teachers, parents and school nutrition professionals to help educate kids about food and nutrition. The goal of the program is to promote chefs as the catalyst for creating a new nation of child food advocates and start turning the tide on unhealthy eating behaviors. Grant funds can be used to support volunteer activities such as purchasing food, equipment, supplies or giveaways for students. The ACF will have three granting opportunities for a total of 60 grants at $250 each. Grantees will be notified of their status within 30 days of the grant deadline.
Requirements: To be considered an applicant must: be currently enrolled in the Chefs Move to Schools (CMTS) program though the website (www.chefsmovetoschools.org); be officially matched with a school through the CMTS website; be currently volunteer at least twice a year with a local school through the Chefs Move to Schools program; be able to provide documentation, photos or examples of volunteer activities conducted at the school; provide a description of how funding will be used.
Geographic Focus: All States
Date(s) Application is Due: Apr 30; Aug 30; Dec 30
Amount of Grant: 250 - 250 USD
Contact: Jessica Ward; (904) 484-0226; jward@acfchefs.net
Internet: http://www.chefsmovetoschools.org/
Sponsor: American Culinary Federation
180 Center Place Way
St. Augustine, FL 32095

Chemtura Corporation Contributions Grants   1067
Chemtura makes charitable contributions to nonprofit organizations involved with education, health care, human services, economic development. Special emphasis is directed towards programs designed to provide educational and economic opportunities for disadvantaged people. Types of support include: building and renovation; general operating funding; and in-kind gifts. Support is given in areas of company operations in California, Connecticut, Georgia, Illinois, Indiana, and Pennsylvania, and on an international basis in areas of company operations.
Geographic Focus: Connecticut, Georgia, Illinois, Indiana, Pennsylvania
Contact: Grants Director; (215) 446-3911
Internet: http://www.chemtura.com/corporatev2/v/index.jsp?vgnextoid=5fe438f220d6d2 10VgnVCM1000000753810aRCRD&vgnextchannel=5fe438f220d6d210VgnVCM1000 000753810aRCRD&vgnextfmt=default
Sponsor: Chemtura Corporation
1818 Market Street, Suite 3700
Philadelphia, PA 19103-3640

Chesapeake Bay Trust Capacity Building Grants   1068
As the focus of the Chesapeake Bay restoration and protection effort shifts more and more to the local level and with the adoption of the Chesapeake Bay Total Maximum Daily Load (TMDL) that requires the development of Watershed Implementation Plans by state and local governments, watershed groups are poised to play an even greater role in the Bay's recovery. Given their growing importance in efforts to clean up the Chesapeake Bay and local rivers and streams, increased levels of financial and technical support to river and watershed organizations is imperative. The Chesapeake Bay Funders Network (CBFN) Capacity Building Initiative will provide grants and technical assistance to increase the effectiveness of organizations that protect and restore rivers and watersheds, increasing their power to advance local watershed protection priorities through collaborative strategies. Ultimately, the program seeks to establish a network of sustainable watershed organizations working collaboratively with public and private partners to make a measurable environmental difference for the Chesapeake Bay and its rivers.
Requirements: The Trust welcomes requests from the following Maryland organizations: 501(c)3 private nonprofit organizations; faith-based organizations; community associations; service, youth, and civic groups; municipal, county, regional, state, federal public agencies; soil/water conservation districts & resource conservation and development councils; forestry boards & tributary teams; public and independent higher educational institutions.
Geographic Focus: Maryland
Date(s) Application is Due: Dec 2
Contact: Jamie Baxter; (410) 974-2941, ext. 105; fax (410) 269-0387; jbaxter@cbtrust.org
Internet: http://www.cbtrust.org/site/c.miJPKXPCJnH/b.5457505/k.A038/Capacity_Building.htm
Sponsor: Chesapeake Bay Trust
60 West Street, Suite 405
Annapolis, MD 21401

Chesapeake Bay Trust Environmental Education Grants   1069
The Chesapeake Bay Trust Environmental Education Grants program is designed to engage Maryland pre-k through 12 grade students in activities that raise awareness and participation in the restoration and protection of the Chesapeake Bay and its rivers. Applicants can request funds in two different tracks: Environmental Literacy Program Track - applicants may request from $35,000 to $50,000 per year for three years ($105,000 to $150,000 total (the Trust anticipates making 1-2 awards in this track); and Meaningful Watershed Educational Experience Track - applicants may request up to $35,000 for one year (the Trust anticipates making 5 to 10 awards in this track). Letters of Intent are due by October 5, with final applications due by December 2. The Trust is piloting an online grants management system to improve ease of the application process, and if awarded, grant management.
Requirements: The Trust welcomes requests from the following organizations: municipal and county agencies and school districts; public and independent higher educational institutions; 501(c)3 private nonprofit organizations; soil/water conservation districts & resource conservation and development councils. The strongest proposals will show committed partnerships that provide funding, technical assistance, or other in-kind services to support the successful implementation of the project.
Restrictions: The Trust does not fund the following: endowments, deficit financing, individuals, building campaigns, annual giving, research, fund raising or venture capital; mitigation or capital construction activities such as structural erosion control measures; political lobbying; reimbursement for a project that has been completed or materials that have been purchased; projects and programs located outside of Maryland; budget items that are considered secondary to the project's central objective. These items include, but are not limited to, food and refreshments, t-shirts and related materials, cash prizes, cameras and video equipment, and microscopes; funding is generally restricted to projects on public property, property owned by non-profit organizations, community-owned property, and property with conservation easements, unless otherwise specified in a grant program.
Geographic Focus: Maryland
Date(s) Application is Due: Oct 16
Amount of Grant: Up to 50,000 USD

Contact: Jamie Baxter; (410) 974-2941, ext. 105; fax (410) 269-0387; jbaxter@cbtrust.org
Internet: http://www.cbtrust.org/site/c.miJPKXPCJnH/b.7634923/k.7463/Environmental_Education.htm
Sponsor: Chesapeake Bay Trust
60 West Street, Suite 405
Annapolis, MD 21401

Chesapeake Bay Trust Fisheries and Headwaters Grants **1070**

The Fisheries and Headwaters Grant Program is a partnership of the Chesapeake Bay Trust, FishAmerica Foundation, and the National Oceanic and Atmospheric Administration (NOAA) Restoration Center. The program is designed to promote the restoration of living resources of the Chesapeake Bay, its rivers, and its streams from the headwaters to the main stem of the Bay. This year, requests may be made in two tracks, the Sportfish Restoration Track (Maryland only) and the Headwaters Track (entire Bay watershed). The Sportfish Restoration Track includes but is not limited to the following projects that improve habitat for sportfish: stream restoration; fish passage; dam removal implementation; wetland creation and improvement; riparian restoration; and streambank stabilization. The Headwaters Track includes the following projects: fish passage; dam removal, riparian restoration with an in-stream component, stream restoration, or other restoration projects that improve headwaters habitat for NOAA species of interest. Proposals in both tracks must describe a significant community participation component (educational or volunteer) tied to the project and must contain both monitoring and maintenance plans. The strongest proposals will demonstrate committed partnerships (those that provide funding, technical assistance, and/or in-kind support from various organizations) and will contain staff cost requests for project-related tasks to less than 25% of the total budget request. Applicants must submit proposals using the trust's online grants system (located at the website) by 5:00 p.m. on the deadline date. To use this system, applicants must register at least 24 hours in advance of submitting an application. Applicants are strongly encouraged to submit at least a few days prior to the deadline (given the potential for high website traffic on the due date). The trust does not keep all its grant competitions open at all times. However, when a particular grant competition is open, a link will be available on the website to guidelines, deadlines and instructions. Also deadline dates may vary from year to year. The funding partners strongly encourage potential grant applicants to content them with questions about project proposals.
Requirements: Eligible applicants and partners include, but are not limited to, the following entities: private nonprofit organizations; federal, state, and local government agencies; tributary teams; community associations, civic groups, and churches; soil and water conservation districts; forestry boards; resource conservation and development councils; public and independent primary, intermediate, and secondary schools; public and independent higher educational institutions; and contractors. Chesapeake Bay Trust's Fisheries and Headwaters grant does not have a specific match requirement, but preference will be given to proposals that leverage funds and/or in-kind contributions from public, private, and nonprofit sources. While projects in both tracks are encouraged to indicate all leveraged funds for the project, applications submitted under the Headwaters Track are especially encouraged to have at least a 1:1 match (cash, in-kind, or both). Applicants are required to include an Employer Identification Number (EIN), a Dun and Bradstreet Data Universal Numbering System (DUNS) number, an organization website url, and a mission statement with their application. Projects should be completed in one year starting at the time the grant is approved. There is no commitment of additional grant funding beyond that period.
Restrictions: The following items are not eligible for funding: benefits or indirect costs; monitoring supplies and equipment greater than 10% of total project cost; incidentals such as food and T-shirts; access projects such as road construction, boat ramps or fishing piers; permit fees paid to state or local governments; endowments, individuals, loans, fundraising, advertising or publications; computer equipment; and research. Limited funds are available for travel-related requests.
Geographic Focus: Delaware, District of Columbia, Maryland, New York, Pennsylvania, Virginia, West Virginia
Contact: Kirk Mantay; (410) 974-2941, ext. 106; fax (410) 269-0387; kmantay@cbtust.org
Internet: http://www.cbtrust.org/site/c.miJPKXPCJnH/b.5587535/k.9FEC/Grant_Forms.htm
Sponsor: Chesapeake Bay Trust
60 West Street, Suite 405
Annapolis, MD 21401

Chesapeake Bay Trust Forestry Mini Grants **1071**

The Anne Arundel County Forest Conservancy District Board and the Chesapeake Bay Trust announce a new partnership to provide small community-based grants (less than $1,000) to help communities and organizations increase the number of trees and tree canopy in neighborhoods, parks, and communities throughout Anne Arundel County. Neighborhood by neighborhood, community stewardship projects are helping to raise public awareness about the health of our region's tree canopy, watersheds, air quality, streams, rivers, and the Bay, as well as the steps that can be taken to restore and protect them. There are four annual deadlines, including March 1, May 1, July 1, and September 1.
Requirements: The Trust evaluates each proposal on a case by case basis. The Trust reserves the right to fund projects and budget items that advance its mission and meet its specific funding priorities and criteria.
Restrictions: The Trust does not fund endowments, deficit financing, individuals, building campaigns, annual giving, research, fund raising or venture capital; mitigation or capital construction activities such as structural erosion control measures political lobbying; reimbursement for a project that has been completed or materials that have been purchased; projects and programs located outside of Maryland; or budget items that are considered secondary to the project's central objective. These items include, but are not limited to, cash prizes, cameras, video equipment, and microscopes. Funding is generally restricted to projects on public property, private community-owned land and conservation easements, unless otherwise specified in a grant program.
Geographic Focus: Maryland
Date(s) Application is Due: Mar 1; May 1; Jul 1; Sep 1
Amount of Grant: Up to 1,000 USD
Contact: Kacey Wetzel, (410) 974-2941, ext. 104; fax (410) 269-0387; kwetzel@cbtrust.org
Internet: http://www.cbtrust.org/site/c.miJPKXPCJnH/b.7958753/k.FEE9/Forestry_Mini_Grant.htm
Sponsor: Chesapeake Bay Trust
60 West Street, Suite 405
Annapolis, MD 21401

Chesapeake Bay Trust Mini Grants **1072**

The Chesapeake Bay Trust offers mini grants to promote public participation and awareness in the protection and restoration of the Chesapeake Bay and its tributaries in the state of Maryland. The trust seeks to fund efforts that are having a measurable impact on improving the Bay, its habitat and its water quality. The program awards up to $5,000 for projects that address one or more of the trust's grant making priorities. The majority of Mini Grant applications are submitted by schools for field experiences and on-the ground student service projects. However, organizations and agencies may also submit grants for small projects and public awareness initiatives. Groups working in Maryland's portions of the Chesapeake Bay and Youghlogheny River watersheds may apply for funding through this program. A request can be submitted at any time during the year.
Requirements: Request will not be considered when the application is submitted without sufficient time to review the application. Schools and nonprofits in the Maryland Chesapeake Bay area are eligible.
Restrictions: Grants do not support advertising campaigns, annual campaigns, capital campaigns, computer hardware/software acquisition, debt retirement, emergency funding, facilities, fellowships, general support, indirect costs, leveraging funds, loans, maintenance, membership campaigns, mortgage reduction, multiyear grants, professorships, scholarships, or travel expenses.
Geographic Focus: Maryland
Date(s) Application is Due: Jan 11; Aug 10
Amount of Grant: Up to 5,000 USD
Contact: Kacey Wetzel, (410) 974-2941, ext. 104; fax (410) 269-0387; kwetzel@cbtrust.org
Internet: http://www.cbtrust.org/site/c.miJPKXPCJnH/b.5457547/k.28ED/Mini_Grant.htm
Sponsor: Chesapeake Bay Trust
60 West Street, Suite 405
Annapolis, MD 21401

Chesapeake Bay Trust Outreach and Community Engagement Grants **1073**

The Outreach and Community Awareness Grant program seeks to increase public awareness and public involvement in the restoration and protection of the Bay and its rivers. In light of the Trust's commitment to the advancement of diversity in its grant-making and environmental work, the Trust strongly encourages grant applications for projects that increase awareness and participation of communities of color in the restoration and protection of the watershed. Available funding will range between $5,000 to $20,000. All eligible projects should be a component of a clearly defined plan to engage communities, raise awareness and ultimately change citizen behaviors. The strongest proposals will show committed partnerships that provide funding, technical assistance, or other in-kind services to support the successful implementation of the project. Applications must be received via the online grants system, available at the Chesapeake Bay Trust website.
Requirements: The Trust welcomes requests from the following Maryland organizations: 501(c)3 private nonprofit organizations; faith-based organizations; community associations; service, youth, and civic groups; municipal, county, regional, state, federal public agencies; soil/water conservation districts & resource conservation and development councils; forestry boards & tributary teams; public and independent higher educational institutions.
Restrictions: The Trust does not fund the following: endowments, deficit financing, individuals, building campaigns, annual giving, research, direct mail fund raising, or venture capital; mitigation or capital construction activities such as structural erosion control measures; political lobbying; reimbursement for a project that has been completed or materials that have been purchased; projects and programs located outside of Maryland; budget items that are considered secondary to the project's central objective. These items include, but are not limited to, cash prizes, cameras and video equipment, and microscopes. Funding is generally restricted to projects on public property, property owned by non-profit organizations, community-owned property, and property with conservation easements, unless otherwise specified in a grant program. Projects should be completed within approximately one year upon receipt of the grant award.
Geographic Focus: Maryland
Amount of Grant: 5,000 - 20,000 USD
Contact: Kacey Wetzel, (410) 974-2941, ext. 104; fax (410) 269-0387; kwetzel@cbtrust.org
Internet: http://www.cbtrust.org/site/c.miJPKXPCJnH/b.5457559/k.402C/Outreach_and_Community_Engagement.htm
Sponsor: Chesapeake Bay Trust
60 West Street, Suite 405
Annapolis, MD 21401

Chesapeake Bay Trust Pioneer Grants **1074**

The Chesapeake Bay Trust Pioneer Grant program is designed to accelerate the rate of nutrient and sediment load reduction in the Chesapeake Bay. The Program's current focused is on new techniques, new information, or new programs that will help managers, policy-makers, restoration scientists, and others achieve load reductions faster and more efficiently. The goal of the program is to encourage practitioners and user groups, including such groups as farmers, land use planners, and builders, to develop or advance ideas and projects that will result in

increased efficiency in water quality improvements in local streams, rivers, and ultimately the Chesapeake Bay. The Trust is open to various types of projects to accelerate the rates of nutrient (nitrogen and phosphorous) and sediment load reduction in the realms of agriculture, stormwater, air, and septic. Projects may be focused in the following realms: new techniques - projects that seek to evaluate nutrient/sediment reduction values or efficiencies of new Best Management Practices (BMPs) in real-world or demonstration-scale settings; new information - projects that seek to refine nutrient/sediment reduction values or efficiencies of one or more Best Management Practices (BMPs) in order to improve targeting and cost-effectiveness of existing restoration programs; new programs - projects that seek to create or contribute to new programs based on accepted Best Management Practices (BMPs). The purpose of such new programs should be to bring new, creative ideas to the implementation or financing of nutrient or sediment load reductions. The ultimate goal should be accelerated bay restoration. The strongest proposals will show committed partnerships (those that provide funding, technical assistance, or in-kind support) from various organizations, institutions, public agencies, and entities including, for example, local government planners, regulators, builders, developers, farmers, technical assistance providers, homeowners associations. Grant requests of up to $75,000 will be considered. The Trust is piloting a new online grants management system to improve ease of the application process, and if awarded, grant management.
Requirements: Applicants need not be Maryland-based organizations, but the work must be completed within the state of Maryland. Potential lead applicants include: 501(c)3 private nonprofit organizations; municipal, county, regional, state, federal public agencies; local governments; soil/water conservation districts; cooperative extensions; forestry boards; resource conservation and development councils; public and independent higher educational institutions; tributary teams.
Geographic Focus: Maryland
Date(s) Application is Due: Mar 16
Amount of Grant: Up to 100,000 USD
Contact: Jana Davis; (410) 974-2941, ext. 101; fax (410) 269-0387; jdavis@cbtrust.org
Internet: http://www.cbtrust.org/site/c.miJPKXPCJnH/b.5457589/k.C9E0/Pioneer.htm
Sponsor: Chesapeake Bay Trust
60 West Street, Suite 405
Annapolis, MD 21401

Chesapeake Bay Trust Restoration Grants 1075
The Restoration Grant program, formerly the Restoration Track of the Stewardship Grant Program, seeks to increase public awareness and public involvement in a wide array of activities that work to restore and protect the Bay and its rivers. The program was established to provide accessible funds to organizations and agencies for demonstration-scale, community-based, on-the-ground restoration projects. All projects should have three goals: accomplish on-the-ground restoration projects that will result in improvements in watershed health, either through habitat enhancement or water quality improvement; provide demonstration-scale restoration projects that can be used to showcase potential of a restoration technique; and engage the public in restoration activities and promote awareness of bay restoration, both short-term (during the project period), through volunteer or stewardship activities directly related to the project; and long-term (post-project period), through stewardship activities and/or interpretive signage. Applicants proposing projects that are specifically identified in or based on a local watershed plan, Watershed Restoration Action Strategy (WRAS), or other scientifically-based watershed planning process are permitted to request up to $50,000 for a given project. For projects that are not based on a watershed plan, the maximum request is $25,000.
Requirements: The Trust welcomes requests from the following organizations: 501(c)3 private nonprofit organizations; faith-based organizations; community associations; service, youth, and civic groups; municipal, county, regional, state, federal public agencies; soil/water conservation districts and resource conservation and development councils; forestry boards and tributary teams; and public and independent higher educational institutions.
Geographic Focus: Maryland
Date(s) Application is Due: Jul 6
Amount of Grant: 5,000 - 50,000 USD
Contact: Jen Wijetunga; (401) 974-2941, ext. 106; fax (410) 269-0387; jwijetunga@cbtrust.org
Internet: http://www.cbtrust.org/site/c.miJPKXPCJnH/b.5458129/k.93B8/Restoration.htm
Sponsor: Chesapeake Bay Trust
60 West Street, Suite 405
Annapolis, MD 21401

Chesapeake Corporation Foundation Grants 1076
The foundation supports U.S. and international nonprofits in its areas of interest, including civic affairs, community development, cultural programs, higher education, and health. Types of support include endowments, capital grants, matching gifts, and scholarships. Grants are awarded for one year with the possibility of renewal.
Requirements: Nonprofits internationally are eligible.
Restrictions: Grants do not support athletic purposes or individuals, except for employee-related scholarships.
Geographic Focus: All States
Amount of Grant: 1,000 - 10,000 USD
Contact: J.P. Causey Jr., (804) 697-1000; fax (804) 697-1199
Internet: http://www.cskcorp.com
Sponsor: Chesapeake Corporation Foundation
P.O. Box 2350
Richmond, VA 23218-2350

Chevron Hawaii Education Fund 1077
The Fund supports communities where it does business and where its employees live and work. Efforts to promote excellence in math and science, and overall quality in schools, have been a guiding factor in its focus on education. Supporting the environment in these communities, with emphasis on conservation or habitat and wildlife preservation, has also been a focus. The purpose of the Fund is to provide grants to teachers for innovative projects that will directly impact the quality of education for students in the areas of conservation, environmental stewardship and science. Preference will be given to projects that: demonstrate active learning rather than passive learning; engage students in project-based learning; are ongoing activities rather than a one time activity or field trip. Application information is available online.
Requirements: Public schools or private schools, grades K-12, statewide are eligible to apply for funding. Grants will be made payable to the school for the benefit of the teacher's project. Schools that received previous funding are eligible to reapply if all Final Report requirements are complete.
Restrictions: Teachers may only submit one application per grantmaking round.
Geographic Focus: Hawaii
Date(s) Application is Due: Oct 1
Amount of Grant: 100 - 1,000 USD
Contact: Amy Luersen, (808) 566-5550 or (888) 731-3863; aluersen@hawaiicommunityfoundation.org or aluersen@hcf-hawaii.org
Internet: http://www.hawaiicommunityfoundation.org/index.php?id=71&categoryID=20
Sponsor: Hawai'i Community Foundation
1164 Bishop Street, Suite 800
Honolulu, HI 96813

ChevronTexaco Contributions Program 1078
Chevron's primary interest is in programs that address critical issues where support can make a discernible difference. Grants target three capacity-building areas critical to economic development: providing for basic human needs—food, clean water, health, and safe shelter; supporting education and training—school-based (k-12) programs, work-based career/technical programs and training/professional development for educators; and services for entrepreneurs, business incubators, sector development support and micro credit programs.
Requirements: Grants are made to tax-exempt organizations worldwide in areas in which Chevron conducts business.
Restrictions: Unsolicited funding requests, grant applications or project proposals will not be accepted.
Geographic Focus: All States
Amount of Grant: 1,000 - 10,000 USD
Contact: Contribution Program Manager; (925) 842-1000
Internet: http://www.chevron.com/social_responsibility/community/
Sponsor: ChevronTexaco Corporation
6001 Bollinger Canyon Road, P.O. Box 6078
San Ramon, CA 94583

Chicago Board of Trade Foundation Grants 1079
The foundation provides grant support to organizations in the metropolitan Chicago, IL, area in its areas of interest: arts and culture, including libraries and museums; education, including higher education, adult basic education and literacy training, and science and technology; health care, including mental health services, cancer research, and rehabilitation; child and youth development; minorities; the economically disadvantaged; wildlife; and media and communication. Grants are awarded for general operating support, continuing support, annual campaigns, capital campaigns, and endowments. An application form is not required; the initial approach should be by letter, or via the CBOT Foundation form on the Web site. The board meets during the first quarter annually to consider requests.
Requirements: Nonprofit organizations in a 75-mile radius of the metropolitan Chicago, IL, area may apply for grant support.
Restrictions: Support is not given to hospitals or foundations. Loans and program-related investments will also be denied.
Geographic Focus: Illinois
Date(s) Application is Due: Oct 1
Contact: Grants Administrator; (312) 435-3456; fax (312) 341-3306
Internet: http://www.cbot.com/cbot/pub/page/0,3181,948,00.html
Sponsor: Chicago Board of Trade Foundation
141 W Jackson Boulevard, Suite 600-A
Chicago, IL 60604

Chicago CityArts Program Grants 1080
The CityArts Program is a triennial grant program designed to assist the not-for-profit arts and cultural community in the city of Chicago through general operating support. Since its inception in 1979, the CityArts Program has awarded over $22 million to Chicago based nonprofit organizations. The CityArts Program is divided into four categories based on an organization's adjusted income budget (total income minus government contributions/income). The adjusted income figure determines the eligible grant requested amount. CityArts also supports social service organizations with an established arts program. All social service applicants apply in the same category regardless of income budget. CityArts applicants awarded grants in year one are eligible to receive grants for two more consecutive years pending availability of funds. A modified application is required for funding in years two and three, and approval for future grants also requires a completed Final Report, proof of General Liability Insurance for each year, in addition to programming and organizational evaluations by Cultural Grants staff. Approval is contingent upon applicants meeting all prior years' reporting requirements and other related requests.
Requirements: Funding is provided for nonprofit arts organizations, cultural institutions and social service agencies that, prior to the application deadline, are: incorporated in the State of Illinois as a nonprofit corporation for at least twelve months and recognized as a 501(c)3 tax exempt organization by the U.S. Department of Treasury, Internal Revenue Service; a resident company of the City of Chicago with a Chicago street address (Post

Office Boxes are not acceptable); primarily serving the residents of the city of Chicago with (51% of the organization's annual programming occurring in Chicago with the intent to reach Chicago residents); and planning activities, including public programming, for the upcoming grant year.
Geographic Focus: Illinois
Amount of Grant: 4,000 - 10,000 USD
Contact: Meg Duguid, Cultural Grants Coordinator; (312) 744-9797 or (312) 744-5000; meg.duguid@explorechicago.org
Internet: http://www.cityofchicago.org/content/city/en/depts/dca/provdrs/grants/svcs/city_arts_applicationsummary.html
Sponsor: Chicago Department of Cultural Affairs
121 N. LaSalle Street
Chicago, IL 60602

Chicago Community Arts Assistance Grants   1081
Funding for the arts, totaling more than $1 million a year, is administered through the Chicago Department of Cultural Affairs and Special Events. Grants, issued to Chicago artists and arts organizations through a competitive, peer review process, provide funding for arts activities that reach people in every Chicago community. The Community Arts Assistance program targets new, emerging, and mid-career artists and arts organizations of all disciplines with annual operating budgets up to $150,000. Projects should address specific professional organizational and artistic development needs. The maximum request is $1,000.
Requirements: Funding is provided for nonprofit arts organizations, cultural institutions and social service agencies that, prior to the application deadline, are: incorporated in the State of Illinois as a nonprofit corporation for at least twelve months and recognized as a 501(c)3 tax exempt organization by the U.S. Department of Treasury, Internal Revenue Service; a resident company of the City of Chicago with a Chicago street address (Post Office Boxes are not acceptable); primarily serving the residents of the city of Chicago with (51% of the organization's annual programming occurring in Chicago with the intent to reach Chicago residents); and planning activities, including public programming, for the upcoming grant year.
Geographic Focus: Illinois
Amount of Grant: Up to 1,000 USD
Contact: Meg Duguid; (312) 744-9797 or (312) 744-5000; meg.duguid@explorechicago.org
Internet: http://www.cityofchicago.org/city/en/depts/dca/provdrs/grants.html
Sponsor: Chicago Department of Cultural Affairs
121 N. LaSalle Street
Chicago, IL 60602

Chicago Community Trust Arts and Culture Grants: Improving Access to Arts Learning Opportunities   1082
Arts learning grants seek to provide measurable benefits to students that have inequitable access to these essential opportunities. Elementary-age children can seldom advocate on their own behalf or vote with their feet if the programs provided are mediocre. High school students, by contrast, are quick to vote with their feet if activities are not engaging—and often pursue less constructive alternatives. This funding priority will support programs that will increase and strengthen arts opportunities for underserved children. Within this priority are two specific initiatives: Arts Infusion Initiative for High-Risk Teens and the College Pathways Initiative. The Arts Infusion Initiative currently consists of 15 grant recipients working in high-risk settings with teens who have had encounters with the criminal justice system, experienced school disciplinary action and reside in the federally-designated Comprehensive Anti-Gang Initiative (CAGI) communities. Grant recipients use resources related to the Chicago Public Schools (CPS) Guide for Teaching and Learning in the Arts and stress social/emotional learning skills associated with conflict resolution. Knowledge-sharing occurs through the Arts Infusion Initiative blog and monthly professional development sessions. Expertise is provided by the CPS Office of Arts Education and the Loyola University College of Fine and Performing Arts. Proposals will be solicited directly from specific organizations. There will be no RFP process in the Arts Infusion Initiative. For the College Pathways Initiative, Proposals in this area should provide structured opportunities for students, primarily from disadvantaged backgrounds, to explore advanced performance experience and training that will expose them to post-secondary options. The long-term goal is to build these programs in every artistic discipline for students from neighborhood CPS high schools. Proposals are due on January 5.
Requirements: The Trust funds nonprofit agencies with evidence of tax-exempt status under Section 501(c)3 of the Internal Revenue Code that are not classified as private foundations. The Trust also accepts applications from agencies that operate under a nonprofit fiscal sponsor. Organizations must be located within and/or primarily serving residents of Cook County, except for regional, statewide or national projects or research that may benefit a substantial portion of Cook County residents. Organizations must also be non-discriminatory in the hiring of staff or in providing services on the basis of race, religion, gender, sexual orientation, age, national origin or disability.
Restrictions: The Trust will not provide grants for: scholarships; individuals; sectarian purposes (programs that promote or require a religious doctrine); support of single-disease oriented research, treatment or care; the sole purpose of writing, publishing, producing or distributing audio, visual or printed material; the sole purpose of conducting conferences, festivals, exhibitions or meetings; or, reducing operating deficits or liquidating existing debt.
Geographic Focus: Illinois
Date(s) Application is Due: Jan 5
Contact: Suzanne Connor, Senior Program Officer; sconnor@cct.org
Internet: http://cct.org/apply/funding-priorities/arts#priority3
Sponsor: Chicago Community Trust
111 East Wacker Drive, Suite 1400
Chicago, IL 60601

Chicago Community Trust Arts and Culture Grants: SMART Growth   1083
The Trust believes strongly that arts offer unparalleled opportunities to engage residents and bring the community together. It is committed to enhancing access for adults, students, artists and audiences who are underserved and underrepresented, while working with colleagues to identify and fill gaps. Arts and Culture grant making also reinforces the Trust's efforts to enhance the quality of life through cultural diversity, improved public education, economic development and civic engagement, environmental sustainability and safe, healthy communities. Specific arts initiatives aim to provide resources to a select cohort of grantees to catalyze broader community impact and promote collaboration and knowledge-sharing that sparks innovation. For the Supporting the Development of Small Arts Organizations: SMART Growth funding priority, the Trust seeks to help small arts organizations develop the management capacity to effectively support their artistic mission, contribute to their communities, pay a living wage to their artists and employees, diversify sources of revenue and remain resilient in the face of economic shifts, the loss of a founder or changing demographics. The SMART Growth Initiative is a three-year capacity-building program in collaboration with the Arts & Business Council of Chicago designed to ensure that small arts organizations benefit from sound management practices that effectively support their art and ensure their resilience through economic shifts, staff transitions and evolving markets. Potential grant recipients should be deeply rooted in and reflective of a community, target population or art form that is underrepresented in the cultural spectrum of the Chicago region. For the second cohort, the Trust has already selected 31 small organizations. The Arts & Business Council of Chicago will conduct its smARTscope assessment with the Boards and staff of the selected grantees and will assist in monitoring the incremental outcomes on an annual basis. A blog has been created as a knowledge-sharing tool for SMART Growth grantees.
Requirements: The Trust funds nonprofit agencies with evidence of tax-exempt status under Section 501(c)3 of the Internal Revenue Code that are not classified as private foundations. The Trust also accepts applications from agencies that operate under a nonprofit fiscal sponsor. Organizations must be located within and/or primarily serving residents of Cook County, except for regional, statewide or national projects or research that may benefit a substantial portion of Cook County residents. Organizations must also be non-discriminatory in the hiring of staff or in providing services on the basis of race, religion, gender, sexual orientation, age, national origin or disability.
Restrictions: The Trust will not provide grants for: scholarships; individuals; sectarian purposes (programs that promote or require a religious doctrine); support of single-disease oriented research, treatment or care; the sole purpose of writing, publishing, producing or distributing audio, visual or printed material; the sole purpose of conducting conferences, festivals, exhibitions or meetings; or, reducing operating deficits or liquidating existing debt.
Geographic Focus: Illinois
Date(s) Application is Due: Sep 1
Contact: Suzanne Connor, Senior Program Officer; sconnor@cct.org
Internet: http://cct.org/apply/funding-priorities/arts#priority1
Sponsor: Chicago Community Trust
111 East Wacker Drive, Suite 1400
Chicago, IL 60601

Chicago Community Trust Arts and Culture Grants: Supporting Diverse Arts Productions and Fostering Art in Every Community   1084
During a four-year collaboration with the Wallace Foundation, the Trust explored the challenges to achieving arts participation and audience diversification that confront nonprofit arts and culture institutions everywhere. Local studies show that participation in Chicago's largest arts and cultural organizations is highest in predominantly white, high-income areas. Socioeconomic factors are more relevant predictors of arts participation than ethnicity; however, for more traditional institutions, ethnicity is still a key predictor for participation. Ethnic, diverse and small organizations successfully reach different audiences than do major institutions. Out of this work has come the realization that broadening audiences and expanding access depend less on ceaseless and creative marketing than on the relevance and authenticity of the artistic product, as well as its accessibility. Artistic collaborations have demonstrated the most measurable success by creating productions that resonate with a broader audience. The Trust has funded a series of sessions on how to structure and nurture such collaborations, in partnership with the Chicago Department of Cultural Affairs. Within this funding priority are two distinctive initiatives: the Artistic and Cultural Diversity Initiative and the Looks Like Chicago Initiative. The Artistic and Cultural Diversity Initiative is accepting Letters of Inquiry (LOI). This grant program will use a two-step application process. Arts organizations and/or presenting venues of all sizes should submit a Letter of Inquiry individually or in collaboration for support for projects that aim to achieve the following goals: showcase the talents of culturally specific artists; perform/exhibit/conduct programs in venues that are located in areas of Cook County that are culturally underserved; perform/exhibit/conduct programs in public venues (such as libraries, parks, community colleges) located in areas of Cook County that are culturally underserved; plan and implement projects with meaningful involvement by leaders/collaborators from the target community or audience; ensure affordability and accessibility for the target community or audience; include an effective means of tracking market penetration and participant response; include well-defined strategies for building on or sustaining the collaboration, cross-promotion or presence within the target market or community; and, increase the Trust's visibility within the target community. Collaborators are encouraged to work together to submit complementary proposals requesting separate grants to support the clearly defined role of each partner. This grant making area is a competitive process that will select projects/productions by different organizations each year; it is not designed to support the same organization for multiple consecutive years. For the Looks Like Chicago Initiative, the Trust envisions a regional cultural landscape that reflects the racial/ethnic make-up of its residents on its boards, staff, stages and among its audiences/patrons. Data suggests that progress toward this goal varies by genre, with classical "high" and "fine" arts lagging significantly behind media, informal and commercial arts. A request for proposal seeks demonstration projects that address this

issue, based upon the following criteria: demonstrated, sustainable commitment to achieving diversity at the board, executive staff and/or artistic leadership level; meaningful inclusion of "first-voice perspective"; and, ability and willingness to serve as a research subject, case study, role model and/or convener. Only one or two grants per year will be awarded.
Requirements: The Trust funds nonprofit agencies with evidence of tax-exempt status under Section 501(c)3 of the Internal Revenue Code that are not classified as private foundations. The Trust also accepts applications from agencies that operate under a nonprofit fiscal sponsor. Organizations must be located within and/or primarily serving residents of Cook County, except for regional, statewide or national projects or research that may benefit a substantial portion of Cook County residents. Organizations must also be non-discriminatory in the hiring of staff or in providing services on the basis of race, religion, gender, sexual orientation, age, national origin or disability.
Restrictions: The Trust will not provide grants for: scholarships; individuals; sectarian purposes (programs that promote or require a religious doctrine); support of single-disease oriented research, treatment or care; the sole purpose of writing, publishing, producing or distributing audio, visual or printed material; the sole purpose of conducting conferences, festivals, exhibitions or meetings; or, reducing operating deficits or liquidating existing debt.
Geographic Focus: Illinois
Contact: Suzanne Connor, Senior Program Officer; sconnor@cct.org
Internet: http://cct.org/apply/funding-priorities/arts#priority2
Sponsor: Chicago Community Trust
111 East Wacker Drive, Suite 1400
Chicago, IL 60601

Chicago Community Trust Education Grants Priority 2 1085
The Trust has defined the following education funding opportunity: Strengthening teacher and school leader preparation by transforming university programs to include broader resources of universities and by increasing teacher licensure standards. This grants program aims to support efforts of higher education institutions serving the Chicago metropolitan area to dramatically improve teacher and school leader education policy and practice in their institutions. One-year planning grants (up to $50,000) or one-year grants to support next steps in efforts that are already under way (up to $100,000 per institution) will be made to support work that ensures: the creation of rigorous teacher and school leader education programs in universities that access and incorporate in purposeful ways the deep and broad knowledge of the university, including that of relevant departments in Arts and Sciences as well as Centers within the university dedicated to specific disciplines; the strengthening of quality apprentice experiences that enable novice educators to become part of purposeful teaching teams in schools that are highly collaborative and supportive of teachers' learning how to teach and how to work jointly as professionals in schools; and, the alignment of high level teacher preparation programs with that of advanced professional programs in the university that are focused on preparing educators to take on specializations or endorsements that not only improve their teaching but also enable them to take on instructional leadership roles in schools and districts. In sum, the Trust seeks to enable and support higher education's commitment to creating professional preparation pathways that strengthen educators' knowledge and capacity in the core disciplines, that build their knowledge and capacity to address the varied strengths and needs of special education students and that strengthen their understanding of language development and how it needs to be supported to strengthen academic learning in every subject. Projects that aim to strengthen preparation of educators to become instructional leaders in the disciplines and that explore models for building that kind of team work and distributed leadership into systems that resembles the work of true professionals will have higher priority than traditional thinking about school leadership as limited to the principalship. While secondary education programs may be considered, high priority is given to work that focuses on the preparation of deeply knowledgeable and skilled educators for elementary levels. Grants in this arena will be considered supplemental to and supportive of financial commitments made by the universities and/or state or federal grants.
Requirements: Eligible applicants include the following: individual colleges and universities that can demonstrate they are undertaking radical transformation and improvement of teacher education that addresses the priorities and outcomes described above or that are committed to initiating a plan to do so; collaboratives or coalitions of higher education institutions with non-profit status that can demonstrate their current plans or interest in undertaking the institutional transformations described in this RFP; higher education institutions or collaboratives located within and/or primarily serving residents of Cook County, except for regional, statewide or national projects or research that may benefit a substantial portion of Cook County residents; institutions that are non-discriminatory in the hiring of staff or in providing services on the basis of race, religion, gender, sexual orientation, age, national origin or disability; institutions that provide evidence of a partnership or partnerships with districts that will support and be committed to the work, in particular supporting guided internships in schools with support for specific disciplines and the development of teacher leaders with specialized advanced degrees or credentials in specific instructional areas—applications should indicate the content of the commitments they will expect from districts. Actual letters of commitment from all partnering institutions will be required before actual grants are made.
Restrictions: The Trust will not provide grants for: scholarships; individuals; sectarian purposes (programs that promote or require a religious doctrine); support of single-disease oriented research, treatment or care; the sole purpose of writing, publishing, producing or distributing audio, visual or printed material; the sole purpose of conducting conferences, festivals, exhibitions or meetings; or, reducing operating deficits or liquidating existing debt.
Geographic Focus: Illinois
Date(s) Application is Due: May 4
Contact: Gudelia Lopez; (312) 616-8000 x 101; glopez@cct.org or education@cct.org
Internet: http://www.cct.org/apply/funding-priorities/education#priority2
Sponsor: Chicago Community Trust
111 East Wacker Drive, Suite 1400
Chicago, IL 60601

Chicago Community Trust Fellowships 1086
The Chicago Community Trust Fellowship offers professional development opportunities for both emerging and experienced leaders who are open to new learning, have a track record of accomplishments, have potential for significant community impact and demonstrate commitment to building strong nonprofit and public sectors. Fellowship applicants customize their own professional development plans. The Trust offers two fellowship tracks, one for Emerging Leaders and one for Experienced Leaders. Emerging leaders are awarded up to $30,000 and experienced leaders are awarded up to $60,000 to put these plans into practice. The award may fund salary and benefits during a leave of absence from work, costs related to academic courses, coaching or learning from other practitioners.
Requirements: Candidates for the Trust Fellowship must have a demonstrated commitment to, and passion for, their field and must be currently employed full-time in the nonprofit or public sector in the metropolitan Chicago region, which includes Cook, DuPage, Kane, Lake, McHenry and Will counties. For candidates pursuing the Emerging Leaders track, the following are required: program, budget and supervisory responsibility appropriate to the scale of the organization; at least five years of professional working experience and at least two years of management experience; track record of accomplishments which demonstrates leadership ability and potential for professional growth; and, endorsement from his/her organization's leader. For candidates pursuing the Experienced Leaders track, the following are required: membership in an organization's senior leadership team with responsibilities for organizational strategic planning, program/budget and personnel management; at least 15 years of professional working experience and 10 years of management experience; working relationship with the board of directors; and, endorsement from his/her organization's leader or board chair.
Restrictions: Past recipients of Trust Fellowships, professionals from academic institutions and employees or board members of The Chicago Community Trust and its affiliates are not eligible to apply.
Geographic Focus: Illinois
Date(s) Application is Due: Jun 13
Amount of Grant: Up to 60,000 USD
Contact: Anne Blanton, (312) 616-8000 or (312) 616-7955; fellowship@cct.org
Internet: http://www.cct.org/about/partnership-initiative/chicago-community-trust-fellowship
Sponsor: Chicago Community Trust
111 East Wacker Drive, Suite 1400
Chicago, IL 60601

Chicago Community Trust Health Grants 1087
The fragmentation and expense of the healthcare system and the lack of universal health insurance leave many low-income families and individuals who seek care frustrated, going without, or bankrupt. Chicago and Cook County have made substantial investments in publicly funded health care, but system elements could be better coordinated. The vision is that the Chicago metropolitan area would be a healthier region that would enjoy a well-coordinated, organized system of healthcare for those with and without insurance. For the first funding opportunity in this area, Improving Access to Healthcare, the Trust will support efforts led by the public sector and nonprofits to improve access to healthcare for low-income families and individuals. The healthcare accessed can be either primary care or specialty care that improves the quality of healthcare for the uninsured. Proposals are due on September 1. For the second funding opportunity, Implementing Health System Reform, the Trust will issue a request for proposals to invite national and local organizations with expertise in Medicaid policy, as well as those who understand the private insurance market as it relates to low-income populations most affected by new rules imposed by federal law, to provide support for the implementation of health care reform. The request for proposals will also seek service delivery models for low-income families and individuals for services covered under the new healthcare reform. Proposals are due on January 5. For the third funding priority, Preventing and Reducing Obesity, the Trust will support effective strategies that will include changes to public policies, school and neighborhood settings, and workplace practices in ways that make our residents healthier, with a particular focus on increasing access to healthy affordable foods and opportunities for physical activity. Community-based programs to change and sustain healthy lifestyles practices must show evidence of successful results. Funding priority will be given to work in communities with highest needs for obesity prevention efforts. Proposals must demonstrate how the work will contribute to the Trust's obesity prevention and reduction goals as outlined above. Proposals are due by May 4. The Trust will make between 10 and 12 grants under this RFP. Grants generally will be in the range of $25,000 to $150,000 for each grant awarded. Successful applicants will receive grants for a minimum of one year.
Requirements: The Trust funds nonprofit agencies with evidence of tax-exempt status under Section 501(c)3 of the Internal Revenue Code that are not classified as private foundations. The Trust also accepts applications from agencies that operate under a nonprofit fiscal sponsor. Organizations must be located within and/or primarily serving residents of Cook County, except for regional, statewide or national projects or research that may benefit a substantial portion of Cook County residents. Organizations must also be non-discriminatory in the hiring of staff or in providing services on the basis of race, religion, gender, sexual orientation, age, national origin or disability. Organizations must demonstrating a successful track record in addressing the needs of low income residents and a successful track record in system change that can work effectively with public agencies, community organization and/or the business community. The Trust requires all applicants to either adopt the Trust's Diversity Statement or have a similar policy adopted by their boards. The Trust believes that the diversity of our community is a fundamental strength of our region. Our mission to improve the quality of life for the residents of our region is best fulfilled when we embrace diversity as a value and a practice. We define diversity to include, but not limited to, age, disability status, economic circumstance, ethnicity, gender, race, religion and sexual orientation. Additionally, the Trust asks that applicants provide demographic data on board and staff as well as clients/beneficiaries of the projects. The

Trust believes that the board and staff composition of grantees should reflect the diversity and demographics of the clients/community being served, and include diversity among its leadership at the board and senior staff levels to ensure the diverse perspectives needed at the decision-making levels. For this reason, the Trust does take into consideration the demographic make-up of the board, staff and clients of a grant applicant as an important proposal evaluation criterion.
Restrictions: The Trust will not provide grants for: scholarships; individuals; sectarian purposes (programs that promote or require a religious doctrine); support of single-disease oriented research, treatment or care; the sole purpose of writing, publishing, producing or distributing audio, visual or printed material; the sole purpose of conducting conferences, festivals, exhibitions or meetings; or, reducing operating deficits or liquidating existing debt.
Geographic Focus: Illinois
Date(s) Application is Due: May 4
Amount of Grant: 25,000 - 150,000 USD
Contact: Kuliva Wilburn, Senior Program Officer; kwilburn@cct.org
Internet: http://www.cct.org/apply/funding-priorities/health
Sponsor: Chicago Community Trust
111 East Wacker Drive, Suite 1400
Chicago, IL 60601

Chicago Community Housing Grants: Advancing Affordable Rental Housing 1088
The Trust is committed to support innovation and excellence, and to fund organizations advancing research, policy, advocacy, housing development and renters' rights, making Chicago a national leader in rental solutions for the 21st century. The Trust will directly solicit proposals supporting a coordinated approach to research, policy and advocacy designed to increase resources for rental and supportive housing, remove obstacles to its preservation, rehabilitation and development, and ensure that it meets standards of quality, affordability, location and sustainability across the region; and will directly solicit proposals from groups working to provide information and resources to renters, especially those living in subsidized housing. Finally, the Trust will also issue a request for proposals from nonprofit developers that directly provide quality affordable housing and services to low- and moderate-income families in innovative, cost-effective and impactful ways.
Requirements: The Trust funds nonprofit agencies with evidence of tax-exempt status under Section 501(c)3 of the Internal Revenue Code that are not classified as private foundations. The Trust also accepts applications from agencies that operate under a nonprofit fiscal sponsor. Organizations must be located within and/or primarily serving residents of Cook County, except for regional, statewide or national projects or research that may benefit a substantial portion of Cook County residents. Organizations must also be non-discriminatory in the hiring of staff or in providing services on the basis of race, religion, gender, sexual orientation, age, national origin or disability.
Restrictions: The Trust will not provide grants for: scholarships; individuals; sectarian purposes (programs that promote or require a religious doctrine); support of single-disease oriented research, treatment or care; the sole purpose of writing, publishing, producing or distributing audio, visual or printed material; the sole purpose of conducting conferences, festivals, exhibitions or meetings; or, reducing operating deficits or liquidating existing debt.
Geographic Focus: Illinois
Date(s) Application is Due: Jan 5
Contact: Juanita Irizarry, Program Officer; juanita@cct.org
Internet: http://www.cct.org/apply/funding-priorities/housing#priority2
Sponsor: Chicago Community Trust
111 East Wacker Drive, Suite 1400
Chicago, IL 60601

Chicago Community Trust Housing Grants: Preserving Home Ownership and Preventing Foreclosure 1089
The Chicago region has suffered a tremendous impact in homeownership rates due to a foreclosure crisis of unprecedented size and complexity. The growing crisis has revealed gaps in the region's ability to respond to rising numbers of distressed homeowners, troubled renters and vacant properties. A coordinated regional response is needed to address these issues and help the region stabilize and recover from the foreclosure crisis. The Trust's response to the foreclosure crisis is guided by the Regional Home Ownership Preservation Initiative (RHOPI) Action Plan, developed in 2009 by 100+ experts from across the region, and led by several nonprofits with a region-wide footprint. The Regional HOPI has set priorities in the areas of Housing Counseling and Legal Aid, Lending and Financial Products, Vacant Properties and Research and Communications. The Trust will provide funding for RHOPI coordination and leadership, and sustainable home ownership policy/advocacy, by directly soliciting proposals from organizations participating in the initiative. Aside from addressing the current foreclosure crisis, the Trust will support efforts to establish the basis of a new financial system that encourages sustainable home ownership and focuses on quality mortgage products, financial literacy, and proper oversight. For housing counseling services for homeowners and buyers, proposals are due by the deadline date. The Trust will directly solicit proposals for technical assistance and capacity building for nonprofits and municipalities addressing the foreclosure crisis and promoting sustainable home ownership. There will be no RFP process. The Trust will make between 10 and 15 grants under this RFP. Grants generally will be in the range of $25,000 to $75,000 for each grant awarded. Successful applicants will receive grants for a minimum of one year.
Requirements: Eligible applicants include: nonprofit organizations with evidence of tax-exempt status under Section 501(c)3 of the Internal Revenue Code or those using a 501(c)3 fiscal agent; organizations located within and/or primarily serving residents of Cook County, except for regional, statewide or national projects or research that may benefit a substantial portion of Cook County residents; organizations with a commitment to diversity and inclusion for their governance, staffing, and populations served; and explicit adherence to non-discriminatory practices in the hiring of staff or in providing services on the basis of race, religion, gender, sexual orientation, age, national origin or disability; organizations with successful track records in pre-purchase home ownership counseling, home ownership-related financial literacy training and foreclosure prevention and mitigation counseling; and, organizations whose work is consistent with the Trust's response to the foreclosure crisis as guided by the Regional Home Ownership Preservation Initiative Action Plan.
Restrictions: The Trust will not provide grants for: scholarships; individuals; sectarian purposes (programs that promote or require a religious doctrine); support of single-disease oriented research, treatment or care; the sole purpose of writing, publishing, producing or distributing audio, visual or printed material; the sole purpose of conducting conferences, festivals, exhibitions or meetings; or, reducing operating deficits or liquidating existing debt.
Geographic Focus: Illinois
Date(s) Application is Due: May 4
Amount of Grant: 25,000 - 75,000 USD
Contact: Juanita Irizarry, Program Officer; juanita@cct.org
Internet: http://www.cct.org/apply/funding-priorities/housing#priority3
Sponsor: Chicago Community Trust
111 East Wacker Drive, Suite 1400
Chicago, IL 60601

Chicago Community Housing Grants: Preventing and Ending Homelessness 1090
Homelessness has been a persistent problem in all large American cities. Since Chicago's implementation of its Ten-Year Plan to End Homelessness, the number of homeless on any particular night has decreased significantly, from around 11,000 seven years ago to around 5,000 before the onset of the recession. Despite this success, maintaining a highly diffuse system and assuring that providers serve key neighborhoods and populations (including "special" populations such as teens, LGBTQ and others) is challenging. It is important to continue to improve the capabilities of the system, especially by effectively using data. Funding in this area will be developed based largely on the findings of the 2011 evaluation of the 10-Year Plan to End Homelessness conducted by the University of Chicago and Loyola University. The Trust will support two levels of work. The first is homeless service system management and support, including: local alliances to end homelessness and coordinating programs; homelessness call center; emergency funds; training in assisting clients with substance abuse or mental health disorders; and, discharge planning. Second, the Trust will support direct service provision by issuing a request for proposals from shelters that demonstrate that their work with homeless persons will eventually result in their attaining permanent housing. Allowable activities may include strengthening referral and follow-up capabilities, street outreach, housing locator, social service support, financial literacy, development of transitional housing units, or other activities clearly linked to clients finding and remaining in housing.
Requirements: The Trust funds nonprofit agencies with evidence of tax-exempt status under Section 501(c)3 of the Internal Revenue Code that are not classified as private foundations. The Trust also accepts applications from agencies that operate under a nonprofit fiscal sponsor. Organizations must be located within and/or primarily serving residents of Cook County, except for regional, statewide or national projects or research that may benefit a substantial portion of Cook County residents. Organizations must also be non-discriminatory in the hiring of staff or in providing services on the basis of race, religion, gender, sexual orientation, age, national origin or disability.
Restrictions: The Trust will not provide grants for: scholarships; individuals; sectarian purposes (programs that promote or require a religious doctrine); support of single-disease oriented research, treatment or care; the sole purpose of writing, publishing, producing or distributing audio, visual or printed material; the sole purpose of conducting conferences, festivals, exhibitions or meetings; or, reducing operating deficits or liquidating existing debt.
Geographic Focus: Illinois
Date(s) Application is Due: Sep 1
Contact: Juanita Irizarry, Program Officer; juanita@cct.org
Internet: http://www.cct.org/apply/funding-priorities/housing#priority1
Sponsor: Chicago Community Trust
111 East Wacker Drive, Suite 1400
Chicago, IL 60601

Chicago Community Trust Poverty Alleviation Grants 1091
The Trust has two priorities in the area of alleviating poverty. For the first priority, improving access to public benefits, the Trust will support the state effort to develop new benefit systems that maximize enrollment of eligible clients who desire benefits. Once the structure of the new system is determined, the Trust will issue a request for proposals from providers that can train service assistants in local community settings such as social service agencies, libraries, health care facilities, schools and religious institutions. Timing for funding of this work is subject to the roll-out of the state Framework project. For the second funding priority, effective public policy advocacy, the Trust will provide operating support for six to ten advocacy organizations, with support levels determined according to the issues facing the state and city and the types of contributions each organization is able to make. The Trust will issue a request for proposals from organizations providing advocacy on behalf of one or more of the following issues: poverty alleviation; children; seniors; homelessness and supportive housing; hunger; people with disabilities; and, immigrants. Successful applicants will need to demonstrate that: advocacy goals are likely to be achieved within the next five years or significant progress is being made; advocacy goals are important to significant numbers of persons; and, the organization's work will have a demonstrable impact on the policy process and achievement of objectives. RFPs for the public policy advocacy for the social safety net will be released on July 15 and are due on September 1.
Requirements: The Trust funds nonprofit agencies with evidence of tax-exempt status under Section 501(c)3 of the Internal Revenue Code that are not classified as private foundations. The Trust also accepts applications from agencies that operate under a nonprofit fiscal sponsor. Organizations must be located within and/or primarily serving residents of Cook County, except for regional, statewide or national projects or research that may

benefit a substantial portion of Cook County residents. Organizations must also be non-discriminatory in the hiring of staff or in providing services on the basis of race, religion, gender, sexual orientation, age, national origin or disability.
Restrictions: The Trust will not provide grants for: scholarships; individuals; sectarian purposes (programs that promote or require a religious doctrine); support of single-disease oriented research, treatment or care; the sole purpose of writing, publishing, producing or distributing audio, visual or printed material; the sole purpose of conducting conferences, festivals, exhibitions or meetings; or, reducing operating deficits or liquidating existing debt.
Geographic Focus: Illinois
Date(s) Application is Due: Sep 1
Contact: Jim Lewis, Senior Program Officer; jlewis@cct.org
Internet: http://www.cct.org/apply/funding-priorities/poverty
Sponsor: Chicago Community Trust
111 East Wacker Drive, Suite 1400
Chicago, IL 60601

Chicago Community Trust Preventing and Eliminating Hunger Grants 1092
The Chicago area has a well-developed system that delivers food to hungry persons, touching an estimated 600,000 per year. The system is highly efficient, making it rare for anyone in the Chicago area to literally starve; and it is relatively inexpensive because of the high number of volunteers who staff it. The greatest challenge facing the system is acquiring more food. Private sector food producers and retailers are becoming increasingly efficient in their production and ordering, leaving less excess food available for donation. As a result, the GCFD and other organizations seek new sources. New strategies to secure fresh food include developing direct relationships with growers, particularly in Illinois, developing collaborative purchasing, merging food banks to make processes more efficient and supporting neighborhood growers. The Trust will directly solicit proposals to support system-wide food acquisition and expanded access to food for distribution to low-income persons, and to conduct planning and support distribution of food to pantries across Cook County. The Trust will issue a request for proposals to provide support for a community-based system of food distribution networks in the areas of transportation, technical assistance, facility development or needs assessment. Successful applicants will need to demonstrate how their services are essential to maintaining anti-hunger programming in their neighborhood and how they have acted to address unmet need.
Requirements: The Trust funds nonprofit agencies with evidence of tax-exempt status under Section 501(c)3 of the Internal Revenue Code that are not classified as private foundations. The Trust also accepts applications from agencies that operate under a nonprofit fiscal sponsor. Organizations must be located within and/or primarily serving residents of Cook County, except for regional, statewide or national projects or research that may benefit a substantial portion of Cook County residents. Organizations must also be non-discriminatory in the hiring of staff or in providing services on the basis of race, religion, gender, sexual orientation, age, national origin or disability.
Restrictions: The Trust will not provide grants for: scholarships; individuals; sectarian purposes (programs that promote or require a religious doctrine); support of single-disease oriented research, treatment or care; the sole purpose of writing, publishing, producing or distributing audio, visual or printed material; the sole purpose of conducting conferences, festivals, exhibitions or meetings; or, reducing operating deficits or liquidating existing debt.
Geographic Focus: Illinois
Date(s) Application is Due: Jan 5
Contact: Juanita Irizarry, Program Officer; juanita@cct.org
Internet: http://www.cct.org/apply/funding-priorities/hunger
Sponsor: Chicago Community Trust
111 East Wacker Drive, Suite 1400
Chicago, IL 60601

Chicago Community Trust Public Safety and Justice Grants 1093
For the first funding priority in this area, Violence Prevention, the Trust will directly solicit proposals from organizations working on systemic changes and neighborhood strategies that have a proven track record of reducing or preventing violence. The definition of violence spans a large number of issues including domestic violence, inter-personal violence, gang violence and youth violence. Although the overall level of violent incidents in Chicago has decreased, the level remains unacceptable. The Trust will pursue several funding strategies, including: support for effective anti-violence programs; continued collaboration with other funders to develop an action plan to reduce youth violence; and, work with other funders to support capacity building and system change for domestic violence providers. There will be no RFP process in violence prevention. For the second funding priority, Criminal Justice System Reform, the Trust will develop a plan of action and will release a request for proposals to identify organizations that can work closely with the Trust to deliver on the specific outcomes: reduction in incarceration for nonviolent offenders; increase in community-based correctional alternatives for offenders; reduction in the number of cases heard at the criminal courts; reduction in the racial disparity of arrest and incarceration rates and recidivism rate; and, reduction in recidivism. For the second funding priority, proposals are due January 5.
Requirements: The Trust funds nonprofit agencies with evidence of tax-exempt status under Section 501(c)3 of the Internal Revenue Code that are not classified as private foundations. The Trust also accepts applications from agencies that operate under a nonprofit fiscal sponsor. Organizations must be located within and/or primarily serving residents of Cook County, except for regional, statewide or national projects or research that may benefit a substantial portion of Cook County residents. Organizations must also be non-discriminatory in the hiring of staff or in providing services on the basis of race, religion, gender, sexual orientation, age, national origin or disability.
Restrictions: The Trust will not provide grants for: scholarships; individuals; sectarian purposes (programs that promote or require a religious doctrine); support of single-disease oriented research, treatment or care; the sole purpose of writing, publishing, producing or distributing audio, visual or printed material; the sole purpose of conducting conferences, festivals, exhibitions or meetings; or, reducing operating deficits or liquidating existing debt.
Geographic Focus: Illinois
Date(s) Application is Due: Jan 5
Contact: Jim Lewis, Senior Program Officer; jlewis@cct.org
Internet: http://cct.org/apply/funding-priorities/public-safety
Sponsor: Chicago Community Trust
111 East Wacker Drive, Suite 1400
Chicago, IL 60601

Chicago Community Trust Workforce Grants 1094
Despite Chicago's strengths, the region's slow recovery from recession has meant continuing high unemployment and increased structural unemployment, which together point to the need for retraining, skill flexibility, and better labor force matching. The region's current workforce system is inefficient, allowing lags between employer needs and supply readiness. Another problem is the mismatch between job opportunities and housing. To develop a workforce that is skilled, productive and competitive in this environment, leaders in the Chicago area need to bring workforce systems and strategies to a new level. Required are regional analysis, coordination and flexibility to adapt to the ever-changing needs of employers and individuals. Also needed are accessible "on ramps" to careers as well as education for the least skilled individuals. Programs must prepare workers to contribute to the productivity of employers; evaluation must account for programs' net effect on the local economy as well as on individual clients. The Trust supports efforts to promote workforce system change and improvements through strategies that may include: working with city colleges, workforce boards and other public institutions to develop policies and practices responsive to economic needs; developing programs linking workforce development with economic development and job creation; developing benefit systems, access and policies that help make low-wage work pay sufficiently to sustain families; creating integrated data systems that facilitate evaluation and planning of workforce strategies. The Trust will support workforce development and/or employment programs that can deliver on the outcomes described. Strategies may include: programs aimed at specific underserved populations or neighborhoods; pilot programs aimed at testing innovative strategies; projects linking workforce development to specific job creation; and, pilot programs demonstrating potentially scalable solutions to workforce development challenges. For job training and placement programs, proposals are due by January 5. For improving effectiveness of public systems through public policy advocacy, proposals are due by September 1.
Requirements: The Trust funds nonprofit agencies with evidence of tax-exempt status under Section 501(c)3 of the Internal Revenue Code that are not classified as private foundations. The Trust also accepts applications from agencies that operate under a nonprofit fiscal sponsor. Organizations must be located within and/or primarily serving residents of Cook County, except for regional, statewide or national projects or research that may benefit a substantial portion of Cook County residents. Organizations must also be non-discriminatory in the hiring of staff or in providing services on the basis of race, religion, gender, sexual orientation, age, national origin or disability.
Restrictions: The Trust will not provide grants for: scholarships; individuals; sectarian purposes (programs that promote or require a religious doctrine); support of single-disease oriented research, treatment or care; the sole purpose of writing, publishing, producing or distributing audio, visual or printed material; the sole purpose of conducting conferences, festivals, exhibitions or meetings; or, reducing operating deficits or liquidating existing debt.
Geographic Focus: Illinois
Date(s) Application is Due: Jan 5; Sep 1
Contact: Jim Lewis, Senior Program Officer; jlewis@cct.org
Internet: http://www.cct.org/apply/funding-priorities/workforce
Sponsor: Chicago Community Trust
111 East Wacker Drive, Suite 1400
Chicago, IL 60601

Chicago Cultural Outreach Program Grants 1095
Funding for the arts, totaling more than $1 million a year, is administered through the Chicago Department of Cultural Affairs and Special Events. Grants, issued to Chicago artists and arts organizations through a competitive, peer review process, provide funding for arts activities that reach people in every Chicago community. Cultural Outreach is an annual grant program that supports arts organizations and social service agencies in the presentation of high quality arts classes, workshops, and performances benefiting youth, seniors, and persons with disabilities in the low-to-moderate income communities of Chicago. Organizations of all artistic disciplines with strong outreach programming may be eligible to request grants ranging on average from $7,000 to $30,000.
Requirements: Funding is provided for nonprofit arts organizations, cultural institutions and social service agencies that, prior to the application deadline, are: incorporated in the State of Illinois as a nonprofit corporation for at least twelve months and recognized as a 501(c)3 tax exempt organization by the U.S. Department of Treasury, Internal Revenue Service; a resident company of the City of Chicago with a Chicago street address (Post Office Boxes are not acceptable); primarily serving the residents of the city of Chicago with (51% of the organization's annual programming occurring in Chicago with the intent to reach Chicago residents); and planning activities, including public programming, for the upcoming grant year.
Geographic Focus: Illinois
Amount of Grant: 7,000 - 30,000 USD
Contact: Meg Duguid; (312) 744-9797 or (312) 744-5000; meg.duguid@explorechicago.org
Internet: http://www.cityofchicago.org/city/en/depts/dca/provdrs/grants.html
Sponsor: Chicago Department of Cultural Affairs
121 N. LaSalle Street
Chicago, IL 60602

Chicago Foundation for Women Grants 1096
The Chicago Foundation for Women focuses on the empowerment of women and girls in three areas: economic security; freedom from violence; and access to health information and services. The foundation remains strongly committed to increasing resources, expanding opportunities, and promoting positive social change for women and girls within the context of these broad issue areas. The following issue areas will continue to be funded: social/systems change advocacy; capacity building and organizational development; arts/culture; day care advocacy; general social services; girls; housing/homelessness; leadership development; and women's philanthropy. Issues relating to immigrant/refugee women, women of color, incarcerated women, lesbians, older women, women with disabilities will also continue to be funded. Grants are awarded in Spring and Fall cycles; submissions must be made in March or August.
Requirements: The foundation funds organizations within Chicago's six-collar county metropolitan area. These counties are: Cook, DuPage, Kane, Lake, McHenry, and Will.
Geographic Focus: Illinois
Amount of Grant: 5,000 - 50,000 USD
Contact: Monique Brunson, Senior Program Officer; (312) 577-2813 or (312) 577-2801; fax (312) 577-2802; info@cfw.org
Internet: http://www.cfw.org/page.aspx?pid=770
Sponsor: Chicago Foundation for Women
1 East Wacker Drive, Suite 1620
Chicago, IL 60601

Chicago Neighborhood Arts Program Grants 1097
The Neighborhood Arts Program is a multi-year program which encourages and supports the presentation of high quality instructional arts programs benefiting youth, senior citizens, and people with disabilities in Chicago's low-to-moderate income neighborhoods. Individual artists of all disciplines with demonstrated teaching experience are eligible to receive funding up to $4,000.
Requirements: Individual artists of all disciplines with demonstrated teaching experience are eligible to apply.
Geographic Focus: Illinois
Amount of Grant: Up to 4,000 USD
Contact: Meg Duguid; (312) 744-9797 or (312) 744-5000; meg.duguid@explorechicago.org
Internet: http://www.cityofchicago.org/city/en/depts/dca/provdrs/grants.html
Sponsor: Chicago Department of Cultural Affairs
121 N. LaSalle Street
Chicago, IL 60602

Chicago Sun Times Charity Trust Grants 1098
The trust supports nonprofit organizations serving the Chicago metropolitan area by awarding grants to support projects in the areas of arts and culture and education/literacy. Grants will be awarded primarily as seed money for new ideas or approaches to problems affecting the quality of life in the community. Although applications for general operating support and capital projects are considered, the trust prefers to fund efforts that solve specific problems. Proposals are reviewed two times each year.
Requirements: 501(c)3 organizations serving the Chicago metropolitan area are eligible.
Restrictions: The trust does not make grants to individuals, religious organizations for religious purposes, scholarships or fellowships, medical research or national health agency drives, or to political activities.
Geographic Focus: Illinois
Amount of Grant: Up to 5,000 USD
Contact: Patricia Dudek, Client and Community Services Supervisor; (312) 321-3000; fax (312) 321-2278; pdudek@hollingerintl.com
Sponsor: Chicago Sun Times Charity Trust
350 N Orleans Street
Chicago, IL 60654

Chicago Title and Trust Company Foundation Grants 1099
The company foundation supports nonprofit organizations dedicated to improving the quality of life in Chicago. Grants are awarded to support higher education; city and neighborhood cultural organizations; and community issues, such as job training, literacy, and economic development. Types of support include program development, general operating support, annual campaigns, building construction/renovation, and matching gifts.
Requirements: Nonprofit organizations serving Chicago, IL, may apply.
Geographic Focus: Illinois
Amount of Grant: 100 - 150,000 USD
Contact: Eileen Hughes, c/o Miami Corp, Treasurer; (312) 223-2911
Sponsor: Chicago Title and Trust Company Foundation
410 N Michigan Avenue
Chicago, IL 60611

Chicago Tribune Foundation Civic Grants 1100
The mission of the Chicago Tribune Foundation is to promote public knowledge and strengthen the Chicago metropolitan community by encouraging journalistic excellence, diversity and liberty; supporting diverse cultural institutions; and promoting civic efforts. Grants in the civic area support business, nonprofit or educational initiatives. Grants are accepted throughout the year, but by invitation only. Funding ranges from $2,500 to $25,00. Types of support include general operating grants, matching gifts, and program development grants. A brief summary proposal should be sent, along with a detailed list of the organization's board of directors; tax-exempt status form; audited financial statement or Form 990; organizational budget; sources of support listing which funds have been sought; and annual report or other literature on the organization's financial and strategic accomplishments.
Requirements: Grants are made to Chicago-area tax-exempt organizations.
Restrictions: The Foundation does not fund individual, capital, or international grants. If an organization previously received a Foundation grant, an updated report on that year's grant must be received before another can be considered.
Geographic Focus: Illinois
Amount of Grant: 2,500 - 5,000 USD
Contact: Jan Ellen Woelffer; (312) 222-3928; fax (312) 222-3888; jwoelffer@tribune.com
Internet: http://www.chicagotribune.com/chi-foundationspage-htmlstory,0,163555.htmlstory
Sponsor: Chicago Tribune Foundation
435 North Michigan Avenue, 2nd Floor
Chicago, IL 60611-4041

Chicago Tribune Foundation Grants for Cultural Organizations 1101
The Foundation grants funding cultural organizations in the Chicago metropolitan area. These organizations concentrate on educational programs in the arts for children from low-income communities or programs that foster diverse arts. Art education programs may be in-school or after-school. Grants range from $2,500 to $5,000. Proposals are due February 1 for a board meeting in June.
Requirements: Nonprofit organizations are eligible for funding. The Foundation accepts, but does not require, the Chicago area grant application form. Along with the narrative, organizations should include a detailed list of their board of directors; a copy of their tax-exempt form; audited financial statements or form 990; organizational budget from the current year; sources of support listing which funds have been committed; and annual report or other literature on the organization's financial and strategic accomplishments.
Restrictions: Funding is not available for individuals or capital campaigns.
Geographic Focus: Illinois
Date(s) Application is Due: Feb 1
Amount of Grant: 2,500 - 5,000 USD
Contact: Jan Ellen Woelffer; (312) 222-3920; fax (312) 222 3882; jwoelffer@tribune.com
Internet: http://www.chicagotribune.com/chi-foundationspage-htmlstory,0,163555.htmlstory
Sponsor: Chicago Tribune Foundation
435 North Michigan Avenue, 2nd Floor
Chicago, IL 60611-4041

Chicago White Metal Charitable Foundation Grants 1102
The charitable foundation awards grants to Chicago-area nonprofits in its areas of interest, including community development, government/public administration, human services, performing arts, opera, recreation, scholarships/financial aid, and youth development. Grants are awarded for one year and are renewable for a second year.
Requirements: Chicago, IL, 501(c)3 organizations are eligible.
Restrictions: Religious organizations and individuals are ineligible.
Geographic Focus: Illinois
Contact: Grants Administrator; (630) 595-4424; fax (630) 595-4474
Sponsor: Chicago White Metal Charitable Foundation
Route 38 at Eastgate Drive
Bensenville, IL 60106-9806

Chick and Sophie Major Memorial Duck Calling Contest Scholarships 1103
Honoring the memories of Stuttgart's legendary champion duck callers and duck calls makers, Chick and Sophie Major, the competition began in 1974 with a single $500 scholarship given to the winner. During its 34 year history, the renowned contest has awarded $58,500 in scholarships to young duck callers attending 32 different colleges and universities in 13 different states. The contest is associated with the World's Champion Duck Calling Contest and will take place on the Main Street Stage beside the Stuttgart Chamber of Commerce. The first-place winner will receive $2,000. Second place will receive $1,000, 3rd place will receive $750, and 4th place will receive $500.
Requirements: The contest is open to any current high school senior graduating in the current year. The only other requirement is the ability to call a duck.
Geographic Focus: All States
Date(s) Application is Due: Nov 27
Amount of Grant: 2,000 USD
Contact: Pat Peacock, (870) 673-2921; peacock38@suddenlink.net
Internet: http://stuttgartarkansas.org/index.php?fuseaction=p0004.&mod=45
Sponsor: Stuttgart Arkansas Chamber of Commerce
P.O. Box 1500
Stuttgart, AR 72160

Child's Dream Grants 1104
The organization has been brought to life by a circle of friends with one common goal to help underprivileged children in the Mekong Sub-Region, which includes: Burma, Laos, Thailand, Cambodia and Vietnam. This region is at the core of many humanitarian crises such as human trafficking, drug smuggling, child prostitution and the spread of HIV/AIDS.
Geographic Focus: All States
Contact: Coordinator; 66 0 53 201 811; fax 66 0 53 201 812; info@childsdream.org
Internet: http://www.childsdream.org/en/aboutFoundation.asp
Sponsor: Child's Dream Association
238/3 Wualai Road
T. Chang Phuak, Chiang Mai 50300 Thailand

Child Care Center Enhancement Grants 1105
Grants are awarded to child care programs for the purpose of implementing specific changes to improve the quality of care provided to children. Nonprofit, nonsectarian, individual child care facilities in Bucks, Chester, Delaware, Montgomery, and Philadelphia counties

may apply. Facilities affiliated with a religious institution/located in a religious facility must confirm that the program is a separate operation with a nonsectarian evident policy. One-year grants are awarded, unless otherwise determined by the foundation. Application and guidelines are available online.
Requirements: An applicant must be an operating, nonprofit, nonsectarian child care program that has been licensed for at least five years; have a current Child Care License from the Pennsylvania Department of Public Welfare for operating child care programs; serve preschool age children (infant to five years of age); be open for a minimum of 10 hours a day, to accommodate working families; and be open 12 months a year.
Restrictions: Kindergarten and school-age programs (i.e., before/after school) will not be considered. Ineligible uses of grants include employee salary, bonus, or benefits; operating expenses; or special events and ad books.
Geographic Focus: Pennsylvania
Date(s) Application is Due: Dec 31
Amount of Grant: Up to 4,000 USD
Contact: Grants Administrator; (610) 992-1140; tlccf@childcareabc.org
Internet: http://www.childcareabc.org/grants/ceg/ceg.asp
Sponsor: Terri Lynne Lokoff Child Care Foundation
320 S Henderson Road, 2nd Floor
King of Prussia, PA 19406

Children Affected by AIDS Foundation Camp Network Grants 1106
The mission of the CAAF Camp Network is to increase the number of children that attend camp every year by providing grants; to foster communication among agencies providing camp experiences for children and their families; and to support the development of new camps. Members of the network gain access to the competitive funding process from the CAAF's yearly financial allocation to the Camp Network.
Requirements: For consideration for membership, Camp Service Providers need to provide proof of the following: (a) Proof of 501(c)3 Not-for-Profit Status; (b) 990 IRS form if applicable; (c) Experience with children infected with or affected by HIV/AIDS and providing camp services. Camps seeking funding from CAAF need to provide proof of the following: (1) Proof of minimum Insurance Coverage's as recommended by the Camp Network; (2) Indemnity for CAAF (Camp Network) from camp agencies, including any employment related claims (Contractual provision, prior to receiving a CAAF grant award.); (3) Compliance with applicable laws such as: employment, health and safety laws and the Americans with Disabilities Act. This will be a contractual provision of the grant agreement, before receiving a CAAF grant award; (4) Release of Liability from Parent or Guardians and Children, using unique identifiers; and, (5) Evidence that the Camp has policies and procedures in place for: (a) Children's safety and emergencies; (b) Pre-screening of paid and non-paid staff; (c) Other information as needed.
Geographic Focus: All States
Date(s) Application is Due: May 16
Amount of Grant: 1,000 - 15,000 USD
Contact: Rolla Bedford, (310) 258-0850, ext. 14; rolla.bedford@caaf4kids.org
Internet: http://www.caaf4kids.org/
Sponsor: Children Affected by AIDS Foundation
6033 W Century Boulevard, Suite 603
Los Angeles, CA 90045

Children Affected by AIDS Foundation Family Assistance Emergency Grants 1107
The foundation is making available its Emergency Fund to help HIV/AIDS Service Organizations in the U.S. to meet the needs of HIV-impacted children and their families. Funds can be accessed by qualified HIV/AIDS non-profits with IRS 501(c)3 status. The Foundation will only provide grants to organizations that do not discriminate on the basis of race, color, religion, gender, gender identity, gender expression, age, sexual orientation, marital status, national origin, disability, or other characteristics protected by law. The goal of the Emergency Fund is to meet the pressing, unanticipated needs in the day-to-day life of children, up to 13 years of age, and their families. Requests may be submitted at any time, and will be reviewed shortly after being received.
Requirements: Funds requested must directly improve the well-being of children in the household. Funds can be accessed by qualified HIV/AIDS non-profits with IRS 501(c)3 status. Eligible requests include: Food; Utility assistance; School uniforms, clothing; Transportation to medical/social service appointments; Medications and medical co-pays; Transitional housing assistance; Burial expenses. Other needs not listed may be considered- please contact the Foundation Program staff prior to sending a request. To download the Emergency Fund's guidelines, go to the sponsor's site, click on 'Initiatives' on the home page, then 'Family Assistance.'
Restrictions: The emergency fund cannot be accessed by or for the following purposes: political or fraternal organizations, or for research or religious purposes.
Geographic Focus: All States
Amount of Grant: 50 - 2,000 USD
Contact: Rolla Bedford, (310) 258-0850, ext. 14; rolla.bedford@caaf4kids.org
Internet: http://www.caaf4kids.org/
Sponsor: Children Affected by AIDS Foundation
6033 W Century Boulevard, Suite 603
Los Angeles, CA 90045

Chiles Foundation Grants 1108
The foundation has a deep concern for and confidence in the future of Oregon and the Pacific Northwest. Although the foundation has made a steady commitment to the improvement of the quality of life for those who live and work in this area, it is not restricted in its grant making to the Pacific Northwest. The foundation has traditionally made grants to certain select institutions of higher education for business schools, scholarships, and athletics; supports basic research in certain select medical institutions; supports religion through divinity schools and religious education; and believes that the arts and cultural activities of a community are important and supports certain select, established institutions. Types of support include building construction/renovation, equipment acquisition, and scholarship funds. Annual deadline dates may vary; contact Foundation by a letter of Inquiry. The Foundation does not accept unsolicited proposals.
Requirements: The preferred initial method of contact is a phone call to the grants administration office to determine whether a prospective proposal is within guidelines; if so, an applicant will be invited to submit a one-page written preliminary proposal. An application form will be sent after approval of the preliminary proposal by the executive committee.
Restrictions: No support for projects involving litigation. Grants are not made to individuals, for deficit financing, mortgage retirement, or projects and conferences already completed.
Geographic Focus: California, Oregon, Germany
Amount of Grant: 1,000 - 270,000 USD
Contact: Earle M. Chiles, President; (503) 222-2143; fax (503) 228-7079; cf@uswest.net
Sponsor: Chiles Foundation
111 SW Fifth Avenue, Suite 4050
Portland, OR 97204-3643

Chingos Foundation Grants 1109
Established in Florida in 1985, the Chingos Foundation awards grants to Florida nonprofit organizations for protection of endangered wildlife and natural resource conservation. Grants support program development, general operations, land acquisition, and other purposes. There are no annual application deadlines or forms. Applicants should submit a letter detailing their proposed project and amount of funding needed. The Foundation board meets once each year in November.
Requirements: Florida nonprofit organizations are eligible.
Restrictions: Grants do not support humane societies or spay/neuter clinics.
Geographic Focus: Florida
Amount of Grant: 5,000 - 20,000 USD
Contact: William Manikas, Trustee; (561) 737-7111
Jennifer Manikas, jmanikas@bellsouth.net
Sponsor: Chingos Foundation
639 E Ocean Avenue, Suite 307
Boynton Beach, FL 33435-5016

Chiquita Brands International Grants 1110
Chiquita Brands International is based in Cincinnati, Ohio, and conducts business in more than 70 countries around the world. The majority of the company's employees work in Latin America, mostly in Costa Rica, Guatemala, Honduras and Panama. Chiquita focuses its giving in the communities where the company has a significant presence. As much as possible, we support outstanding local organizations that address local needs where our employees live and work. Chiquita gives to programs that: promote healthy living, particularly programs that educate children and help them to lead healthier lives; support environmental and social programs that advance responsible and sustainable business practices.
Requirements: Chiquita only supports not-for-profit organizations. Proof of nonprofit status is required. Applicants from the United States must be tax-exempt, nonprofit organizations as defined under Section 501(c)3 of the Internal Revenue Code. Applicants outside the United States must be charitable in purpose and identified as nongovernmental organizations (NGOs) or the equivalent of a tax-exempt nonprofit organization. All grant requests must be made through Chiquita's website to be accepted for consideration. See website for details.
Restrictions: Chiquita's charitable giving program will not support: for-profit ventures; individuals or groups seeking to raise money for personal goals. This includes scholarships, research or travel grants, stipends, fellowships, personal assistance, conferences, training or learning programs, travel for reunions/anniversaries, mission trips, travel for races, contests, or competitions, etc; development or production of books, films, videos, radio or TV programs; individual sports teams; religious groups for religious purposes; capital campaigns; lobbying, political or fraternal activities; raffles / games of chance; organizations already receiving financial support from United Way; advertising or marketing sponsorships; multi-year requests; third party requests - this includes individuals independently raising money for the nonprofit. As a general rule, we do not financially support special events (benefits, walk-a-thons, golf outings, etc.). While fund-raisers are important to the organizations hosting them, we prefer to provide support directly to programs and services. Special events are eligible for product donations.
Geographic Focus: All States
Amount of Grant: 500 - 5,000 USD
Contact: Corporate Headquarters; (513) 784-8000
Internet: http://www.chiquita.com/CompanyInfo/Guidelines.aspx
Sponsor: Chiquita Brands International
250 East Fifth Street
Cincinnati, OH 45202

Chiron Foundation Community Grants 1111
The foundation's focus areas are health and medicine, education, and community. Four imperatives guide health-care giving: accelerating progress toward the prevention and cure or successful management of cancer through research, education, early detection, and public-policy debate; combating infectious disease through prevention-related programs, educational efforts, and therapeutics targeting at-risk populations, with emphasis on the special needs of children and families; ensuring the availability and safety of the blood supply and promoting the highest standards of care for blood donors and recipients; and supporting initiatives in the international medical community to provide vaccines and immunization services to protect at-risk populations, especially children, against the devastation of crippling and lethal diseases. Four imperatives guide education giving: providing training and professional

development opportunities to enable classroom teachers to teach science and math more effectively; increasing opportunities for economically disadvantaged students to continue on to postsecondary education; supporting community-based training programs to prepare underrepresented minorities and underprivileged groups for careers in the biosciences; and encouraging and assisting promising scholars to pursue advanced research in the biosciences and medicine. Four imperatives guide community giving: providing early diagnosis, intervention, and support for children with disabilities or other special physical or emotional needs; providing essential social services such as meals and housing to those in greatest need; empowering individuals to achieve self-sufficiency through employment training and job-skill development; and enriching the character and celebrating the distinctives of local communities. Requests are accepted at anytime, and proposals are reviewed quarterly.
Requirements: 501(c)3 tax-exempt organizations in Chiron communities (San Francisco East Bay Area, including Alameda, Contra Costa, and Solano Counties; Seattle; and Philadelphia) are eligible.
Restrictions: In general, Chiron does not support organizations that do not have 501(c)3 tax status; religious, fraternal, service, or veterans' organizations; civic or cultural organizations that do not serve the areas in which Chiron is located; alumni drives and teacher organizations; memorials; municipal and for-profit hospitals; labor unions; city, municipal, or federal government departments; organizations or causes that do not support the company's commitment to non-discrimination and diversity; projects of national scope or from national organizations not related to health care; matching gifts; individuals, including scholarships (other than those awarded as part of the company-sponsored college scholarship program); travel support; fund-raising activities related to individual sponsorship; and fund-raising dinners other than those for health care or medical research organizations aligned with company research and product interests.
Geographic Focus: California, Pennsylvania, Washington
Amount of Grant: 5,000 - 75,000 USD
Contact: Community Relations; (510) 601-6952; Chiron_foundation@chiron.com
Internet: http://www.chiron.com/foundation/index.html
Sponsor: Chiron Foundation
4560 Horton Street
Emeryville, CA 94608

Christensen Fund Regional Grants 1112
The fund (TCF) focuses its grantmaking on maintaining the biological and cultural diversity of the world by focusing on four geographic regions: the greater South West (Southwest United States and Northwest Mexico); Central Asia and Turkey; the African Rift Valley (Ethiopia); and Northern Australia and Melanesia. Grants within these programs are generally directed to organizations based within those regions or, where appropriate, to internationally based organizations working in support of people and institutions on the ground. In general, grants are one year or less; currently grants up to two years are by invitation only.
Requirements: 501(c)3 nonprofit organizations and non-USA institutions with nonprofit or equivalent status in their country of origin are eligible. Partnerships or associations with USA-based nonprofit organizations are preferred.
Restrictions: The fund does not make grants directly to individuals but rather assists individuals through institutions qualified to receive nonprofit support with which such individuals are affiliated.
Geographic Focus: All States
Amount of Grant: Up to 200,000 USD
Contact: Administrator; (415) 644-1600; fax (415) 644-1601; info@christensenfund.org
Internet: http://www.christensenfund.org/index.html
Sponsor: Christensen Fund
260 Townsend Street
San Francisco, CA 94107

Christian Science Society of Boonville Irrevocable Trust 1113
The Christian Science Society of Boonville Irrevocable Trust is a Independant Foundation giving primarily to: housing; shelter; parks; recreation; and human services.
Requirements: In order to qualify, a letter of solicitation, a copy of 501(c)3, a copy of your most recent tax return and your most recent financial statement must be received by Peoples Trust & Savings Bank Trust Department.
Restrictions: Grants are not available to individuals & funds are only available in Warrick County IN.
Geographic Focus: Indiana
Contact: Sheila D. Gemlich, (812) 897-0230
Internet: http://www.ptsb-in.com/trust_services/index.html
Sponsor: Christian Science Society of Boonville
P.O. Box 307
Boonville, IN 47601-1543

Christine and Katharina Pauly Charitable Trust Grants 1114
The Christine and Katharina Pauly Charitable Trust was established in 1985 to support and promote quality educational, health, and human-services programming for underserved populations. Special consideration is given to charitable organizations that serve the needs of children or older adults. The majority of grants from the Pauly Trust are one year in duration. Applicants must apply online at the grant website. Applicants are strongly encouraged to do the following before applying: review the downloadable state application procedures for additional helpful information and clarifications; review the downloadable online-application guidelines at the grant website; review the trust's funding history (link is available from the grant website); review the online application questions in advance; and review the list of required attachments. These will generally include: a list of board members, financial statements (audited, reviewed, or compiled by independent auditor); an organization summary; a list of other funding sources; an IRS Determination letter; and other required documents. All attachments must be uploaded in the online application as PDF, Word, or Excel files. The application deadline for the Christine and Katharina Pauly Charitable Trust is 11:59 p.m. on September 1. Applicants will be notified of grant decisions by December 31. The Christine and Katharina Pauly Charitable Trust was created under the wills of Ms. Hazel Katharina Pauly and Ms. Frieda Christine Oleta Pauly.
Requirements: Applicants must have 501(c)3 tax-exempt status.
Restrictions: In general, grant requests for individuals, endowment campaigns, or capital projects will not be considered. The Fund will consider requests for general operating support only if the organization's operating budget is less than $1 million. The trust does not support requests from individuals, organizations attempting to influence policy through direct lobbying, or any political campaigns.
Geographic Focus: Missouri
Date(s) Application is Due: Sep 1
Contact: George Thorn, (312) 828-4154; ilgrantmaking@bankofamerica.com
Internet: https://www.bankofamerica.com/philanthropic/fn_search.action
Sponsor: Christine and Katharina Pauly Charitable Trust
231 South LaSalle Street, IL1-231-13-32
Chicago, IL 60604

Christy-Houston Foundation Grants 1115
The foundation awards grants to nonprofits in Rutherford County, TN, for health, education, arts and culture, and community development. Areas of interest include hospitals, nursing care, health care and health associations, nutrition, hospice care, and community development. Types of support include building construction/renovation, equipment acquisition, scholarship funds, and matching funds. Application forms are not required, and there are no application deadlines. The board meets in March, June, September, and December to consider requests.
Requirements: 501(c)3 nonprofits in Rutherford County, TN, are eligible.
Restrictions: Grants are not awarded to: religious organizations for religious purposes, veterans organizations, historical societies, individuals, operating expenses or endowments.
Geographic Focus: Tennessee
Contact: Robert B. Mifflin, Executive Director; (615) 898-1140; fax (615) 895-9524
Sponsor: Christy-Houston Foundation
1296 Dow Street
Murfreesboro, TN 37130-2413

Chula Vista Charitable Foundation Grants 1116
Community leaders throughout Chula Vista are partnering with the San Diego Foundation to create and sustain a local foundation to serve solely the community of Chula Vista. Endow Chula Vista is a community-specific effort to focus on endowment building for Chula Vista, now and for generations to come. It is part of The San Diego Foundation's region-wide initiative, Endow San Diego, to inform and inspire San Diegans regarding the benefits of endowment.
Requirements: Any 501(c)3 organization serving the residents of Chula Vista, California, are eligible to apply.
Restrictions: The Chula Vista Charitable Foundation does not make grants for: annual campaigns and fund raising events for non-specific purposes; capital campaigns for buildings or facilities; stipends for attendance at conferences; endowments or chairs; for-profit organizations or enterprises; individuals unaffiliated with a qualified fiscal sponsor; projects that promote religious or political doctrine; research projects (medical or otherwise); scholarships; or existing obligations or debt.
Geographic Focus: California
Contact: Kerry Helmer, (619) 814-1384; kerry@sdfoundation.org
Internet: http://www.endowchulavista.org/
Sponsor: Chula Vista Charitable Foundation / San Diego Foundation
2508 Historic Decatur Road, Suite 200
San Diego, CA 92106

CICF Christmas Fund 1117
The CICF - Christmas Fund was established to provide support for needy families during the holiday season. Proposals are accepted during the months of February and July, and are available at the Foundation website.
Geographic Focus: Indiana
Contact: Liz Tate; (317) 634-2423, ext. 175; fax (317) 684-0943; liz@cicf.org
Internet: http://www.cicf.org/examples-of-named-funds
Sponsor: Central Indiana Community Foundation
615 North Alabama Street, Suite 119
Indianapolis, IN 46204-1498

CICF City of Noblesville Community Grant 1118
The City of Noblesville Community Grants were established to support the charitable intentions of Noblesville. Other purposes of the grant include, but are not limited to, basic needs, economic stability, health and wellness, education, vitality of neighborhoods and communities, arts and culture, and environment. Priority is given to programs and projects most likely to have a positive effect on the city's residents. Proposals are accepted in February and July of each year. Applicants are strongly encouraged to view the Grantseeker's Guide posted on the website.
Requirements: The Foundation gives careful consideration to projects that; most benefit Noblesville residents; promote inclusiveness and diversity; respond to basic human needs; connect individuals and families to the community; complement other organizations to eliminate duplication of services; obtain additional funding and provide ongoing funding after the project. Organizations can apply through the online application.
Restrictions: The Foundation does not fund the following: organizations that are not tax exempt; multi-year grants; grants to individuals; projects aimed at promoting a particular religion

or construction projects for religious institutions; operating, program, and construction costs at schools, universities, and private academies unless there is significant opportunity for community use or collaboration; organizations or projects that discriminate based on race, ethnicity, age, gender or sexual orientation; political campaigns or direct lobbying efforts by 501(c)3 organizations; post-event, after-the-fact situations or debt retirement; medical, scientific, or academic research; publications, films, audiovisual and media materials, programs produced for artistic purposes or produced for resale; travel for bands, sports teams, classes, and similar groups; annual appeals, galas, or membership contributions; fundraising events such as golf tournaments, walk-a-thons, and fashion shows.
Geographic Focus: Indiana
Amount of Grant: 1,000 - 10,000 USD
Contact: Liz Tate; (317) 843-2479, ext. 302; fax (317) 848-5463; lizt@cicf.org
Internet: http://www.cicf.org/how-to-apply-grantmaking
Sponsor: Central Indiana Community Foundation
615 North Alabama Street, Suite 119
Indianapolis, IN 46204-1498

CICF Clare Noyes Grant 1119
The Central Indiana Community Foundation Clare Noyes Grant provides funding for high quality ballet performances for the public and ballet education programs for youth in Indianapolis and surrounding counties. Proposals are accepted in the months of February and July, and applications are available on the Foundation's website.
Geographic Focus: Indiana
Amount of Grant: 1,000 - 15,000 USD
Contact: Liz Tate; (317) 634-2423, ext. 175; fax (317) 684-0943; liz@cicf.org
Internet: http://www.cicf.org/examples-of-named-funds
Sponsor: Central Indiana Community Foundation
615 North Alabama Street, Suite 119
Indianapolis, IN 46204-1498

CICF Efroymson Grants 1120
The Central Indiana Community Foundation - Efroymson Grants are focused on providing support to not-for-profit organizations that help promote the viability of communities and provide opportunities for under-served individuals. The Foundation is specifically interested in the following areas for funding: natural environment, with efforts to preserve biological diversity with habitat preservation; welfare of the disadvantaged, with programs, initiatives, and organizations that help promote self-sufficiency; historic preservation, in order to restore and preserve Indiana's historic structures; and well-being of the Jewish people, to meet the general needs and improve relations with Indiana's Jewish community. Organizations can review the website for examples and videos of previously funded projects.
Restrictions: The Efroymson Family Fund does not accept grant applications through an open application process. Direct funding appeals to the Efroymson Family Fund Advisors is strongly discouraged unless initiated by the Advisors. All other inquiries about the Efroymson Family Fund should be directed to efroymsonfamilyfund@cicf.org.
Geographic Focus: Indiana
Amount of Grant: Up to USD
Contact: Liz Tate; (317) 634-2423, ext. 175; fax (317) 684-0943; liz@cicf.org
Internet: http://www.cicf.org/efroymson-family-fund
Sponsor: Central Indiana Community Foundation
615 North Alabama Street, Suite 119
Indianapolis, IN 46204-1498

CICF F.R. Hensel Grant for Fine Arts, Music, and Education 1121
The CICF - F.R. Hensel Grant for Fine Arts, Music, and Education funds projects for the promotion of fine arts, music, and education. Proposals are accepted in the months of February and July, and applications are available at the Foundation website.
Restrictions: Funding is limited to Marion County.
Geographic Focus: Indiana
Amount of Grant: 10,000 - 70,000 USD
Contact: Liz Tate; (317) 634-2423, ext. 175; fax (317) 684-0943; liz@cicf.org
Internet: http://www.cicf.org/examples-of-named-funds
Sponsor: Central Indiana Community Foundation
615 North Alabama Street, Suite 119
Indianapolis, IN 46204-1498

CICF Howard Intermill and Marion Intermill Fenstermaker Grants 1122
The Central Indiana Community Foundation Intermill Fenstermaker Grant exists to support programs for children and youth with disabilities. See the website's Grantseeker's Guide for a specific description of the Fenstermaker Grant. Proposal are accepted in the months of February and July, and the application is available on the Foundation's website.
Geographic Focus: Indiana
Amount of Grant: 1,000 - 15,000 USD
Contact: Liz Tate; (317) 634-2423, ext. 175; fax (317) 684-0943; liz@cicf.org
Internet: http://www.cicf.org/examples-of-named-funds
Sponsor: Central Indiana Community Foundation
615 North Alabama Street, Suite 119
Indianapolis, IN 46204-1498

CICF Indianapolis Foundation Community Grants 1123
CICF's mission is to inspire, support, and practice philanthropy, leadership, and service in the community. Proposed programs should align with any of the Foundation's Seven Elements of a Thriving Community: basic needs; economic stability; health and wellness; education; vitality and connectivity of neighborhoods and communities; arts and culture; and the environment. The application and grant request detail form are available online. Applications are accepted during the months of February and July.
Requirements: CICF welcomes grant applications from charitable organizations that are tax exempt under section 501(c)3 of the Internal Revenue Code, and from governmental agencies. New projects or organizations with pending 501(c)3 status may submit an application with the assistance of a fiscal sponsor. Grant inquiries and proposals will be prioritized using the following criteria: organizations that serve primarily Marion County residents; organizations with a demonstrable track record; programs serving populations disadvantaged due to income, age, ethnicity, language, education, disability, transportation or other adverse conditions; project/program ideas must be fully developed; and projects that strongly connect to existing community initiatives (e.g. the Blueprint to End Homelessness, Indianapolis Cultural Development Initiative, and Family Strengthening Coalition). Application information is available online.
Geographic Focus: Indiana
Contact: Liz Tate; (317) 634-2423, ext. 175; fax (317) 684-0943; liz@cicf.org
Internet: http://www.cicf.org/the-indianapolis-foundation
Sponsor: Central Indiana Community Foundation
615 North Alabama Street, Suite 119
Indianapolis, IN 46204-1498

CICF James Proctor Grant for Aged Men and Women 1124
The CICF - James Proctor Grant for Aged Men and Women funds projects that benefit elderly men and women in the fields of arts and culture, basic needs, and health and wellness. Applications are accepted in the months of February and July, and are available at the Foundation website.
Geographic Focus: Indiana
Amount of Grant: 10,000 - 60,000 USD
Contact: Liz Tate; (317) 634-2423, ext. 175; fax (317) 684-0943; liz@cicf.org
Internet: http://www.cicf.org/examples-of-named-funds
Sponsor: Central Indiana Community Foundation
615 North Alabama Street, Suite 119
Indianapolis, IN 46204-1498

CICF John Harrison Brown and Robert Burse Grant 1125
The purpose of the Central Indiana Community Foundation Brown and Burse Grant is to support academic and moral values for deserving youth in the Indianapolis area. Proposals are accepted in the months of February and July, and applications are available on the Foundation's website. Organizations are encouraged to call the Foundation before submitting their proposal to be certain it is appropriate for funding.
Geographic Focus: Indiana
Amount of Grant: 1,000 - 5,000 USD
Contact: Liz Tate; (317) 634-2423, ext. 175; fax (317) 684-0943; liz@cicf.org
Internet: http://www.cicf.org/examples-of-named-funds
Sponsor: Central Indiana Community Foundation
615 North Alabama Street, Suite 119
Indianapolis, IN 46204-1498

CICF Legacy Fund Grants 1126
The CICF - Legacy Fund Grants fund Hamilton County, Indiana nonprofits in the following areas of interest: arts and culture; basic needs; economic stability; education; environment; health and wellness; and vitality of neighborhoods and communities. Applications are accepted during the months of February and July, and are available at the Foundation's website.
Requirements: In reviewing grant applications, the Foundation gives careful consideration to projects that: impact individuals served; promote inclusiveness and diversity and are responsive to basic human needs; connect individuals and families to the community; commit to carrying out the project; complement other organizations and eliminate duplication of services; manage their fiscal responsibilities; match funds; and obtain additional funding now and in the future.
Restrictions: Limited to not-for-profit organizations and for the benefit of the people of Hamilton County, Indiana.
Geographic Focus: Indiana
Amount of Grant: 5,000 - 20,000 USD
Contact: Liz Tate; (317) 634-2423, ext. 175; fax (317) 684-0943; liz@cicf.org
Internet: http://www.cicf.org.php5-17.dfw1-1.websitetestlink.com/how-to-apply-grantmaking
Sponsor: Central Indiana Community Foundation
615 North Alabama Street, Suite 119
Indianapolis, IN 46204-1498

CICF Senior Grants 1127
The Central Indiana Community Foundation Senior Grants (formerly known as the Indianapolis Retirement Home Grant) supports programs and services that promote quality living for older adults in central Indiana. The grant is interested in supporting programs that promote overall health and wellness, ensure that the basic needs of the low-income older adults are met, enable older adults to reside in the environments of their choice, and opportunities that provide life-affirming choices. Funding is limited to central Indiana (Boone, Hamilton, Hendricks, Johnson, Marion, Morgan, and Shelby counties). Applications are available online and accepted during the months of February and July.
Requirements: Areas of interest: Health and Wellness—health promotion and intervention programs for older adults; Basic Needs—community-based efforts that provide emergency services, food, transportation, shelter, and elder violence reduction programs; Living Environment of Choice—programs that enable older adults to remain in the living environment

of their choice; and Life-Affirming Opportunities—programs that encourage older adults to utilize their talents and resources to improve the overall quality of their lives.
Restrictions: Funding is limited to central Indiana (Boone, Hamilton, Hendricks, Johnson, Marion, Morgan, and Shelby counties). Funding will not be awarded to the following: organizations not currently tax-exempt; campaigns or activities intended to influence public officials; organizations that discriminate as to age, race, religion, gender, sexual orientation, disability, or national origin; any program that promotes a particular church or religious denomination; construction projects of schools, churches, or other religious institutions; individuals; basic medical, scientific, or academic research;
Geographic Focus: Indiana
Amount of Grant: 5,000 - 50,000 USD
Contact: Brian Payne, President and CEO; (317) 634-2423; fax (317) 684-0943; brianp@cicf.org or program@cicf.org
Internet: http://www.cicf.org/how-to-apply-grantmaking
Sponsor: Central Indiana Community Foundation
615 North Alabama Street, Suite 119
Indianapolis, IN 46204-1498

CICF Summer Youth Grants 1128
The Central Indiana Community Foundation Summer Youth Grants provide grants, coordinates professional development opportunities, and disseminates community information to support summer programs serving Marion County youth. The program is designed to make the grant process easier for charitable organizations by using a single application form. Since 1995, SYPF-Indianapolis has awarded more the $29 million in grants to support summer youth programs.
Requirements: Applicants should carefully analyze their project in terms of needs assessment, program emphasis, start and end dates, budget development, recruiting of staff, length of program day, participating ages, safety, the program's site, and collaborations with other programs. Applicants are encouraged to call the Foundation to discuss their proposal in advance. They are also encouraged to review the application and the program guide at the Foundation's website.
Geographic Focus: Indiana
Contact: Mary Johnson, Grants Associate; (317) 634-2423, ext. 554
Internet: http://www.summeryouthprogramfund-indy.org/contact/
Sponsor: Central Indiana Community Foundation
615 North Alabama Street, Suite 119
Indianapolis, IN 46204-1498

Cigna Civic Affairs Sponsorships 1129
The Cigna Civic Affairs program coordinates the charitable giving and volunteer activities of Cigna and its people, with the overall goal of demonstrating Cigna's commitment to being a socially responsible and responsive corporate citizen. One of the ways Civic Affairs fulfills this mission is through the Cigna Civic Affairs Sponsorships program. These sponsorships support charitable events and activities that enhance the health of individuals and families and the well-being of communities. Its strategy for achieving healthy outcomes around the globe is driven by: promoting wellness—to help individuals and families take ownership of their own health; expanding opportunities—to make health information and services available to everyone; developing leaders—to leverage the education and hands-on life experience that promote personal and professional growth; and embracing communities—to encourage collaborative and sustainable problem-solving approaches.
Geographic Focus: All States
Amount of Grant: 5,000 - 50,000 USD
Contact: Jill Holliday; (860) 226-2094 or (866) 865-5277; jill.holliday@cigna.com
Internet: https://secure16.easymatch.com/cignagive/applications/agency/?Skip=LandingPage&ProgramID=3
Sponsor: Cigna Corporation
1601 Chestnut Street, TL06B
Philadelphia, PA 19192-1540

CIGNA Foundation Grants 1130
The Cigna Foundation has identified four areas for grant consideration: health and human services, education, community and civic affairs, and culture and the arts. Health and education are of primary concern and receive priority. Under education, priority is placed on public secondary education, higher education for minorities, and adult basic education/literacy. The foundation also considers requests from U.S. cultural, educational, and public policy organizations that have international components. Requests are accepted and reviewed throughout the year. Consideration will be given to requests for general operating support, program development, annual campaigns, conferences and seminars, fellowships, scholarship funds and employee-related scholarships, and matching gifts and funds.
Requirements: Organizations with 501(c)3 tax-exempt status are eligible.
Restrictions: The foundation will not consider applications for grants to individuals, organizations operating to influence legislation or litigation, political organizations, or religious activities. In general, the foundation will not consider applications from organizations receiving substantial support through the United Way or other CIGNA-supported federated funding agencies; hospitals' capital improvements; or research, prevention, and treatment of specific diseases.
Geographic Focus: All States
Amount of Grant: 5,000 - 50,000 USD
Contact: Jill Holliday; (860) 226-2094 or (866) 865-5277; jill.holliday@cigna.com
Internet: http://www.cigna.com/aboutus/cigna-foundation
Sponsor: Cigna Foundation
1601 Chestnut Street, TL06B
Philadelphia, PA 19192-1540

Cincinnati Bell Foundation Grants 1131
The foundation awards grants to Ohio organizations in support of elementary and secondary school programs that improve education for disadvantaged youths, such as mentoring or tutoring programs. Grants also support social services, colleges and universities, and local civic and cultural groups that make the arts accessible to everyone. Types of support include capital grants, challenge/matching grants, organizational development grants, general operating grants, and program development grants. There are no application deadlines; grant notification is made quarterly.
Requirements: 501(c)3 nonprofit organizations in the Cincinnati Bell service area are eligible. Giving primarily in northern KY, the greater Cincinnati, OH, area, and in other cities in which the company has a significant corporate presence.
Geographic Focus: Kentucky, Ohio
Contact: Robert Horine, Public Affairs Director; (513) 397-7545
Internet: http://home.cincinnatibell.com/corporate/community
Sponsor: Cincinnati Bell Foundation
201 E Fourth Street, Room 102-560
Cincinnati, OH 45202

Cincinnati Milacron Foundation Grants 1132
The Cincinnati Milacron Foundation awards grants, gifts, and loans to eligible Michigan and Ohio nonprofit organizations in its areas of interest, including the arts, community development, higher education, youth programs, and religion. Types of support include annual campaigns, building/renovations, general operations, and seed money. Grants are awarded for one year and are renewable.
Requirements: Michigan and Ohio 501(c)3 nonprofit organizations are eligible.
Restrictions: Grants are not made to individuals.
Geographic Focus: Michigan, Ohio
Amount of Grant: 5,000 - 200,000 USD
Contact: George G. Price, (513) 487-5912; fax (513) 487-5586
Sponsor: Cincinnati Milacron Foundation
2090 Florence Avenue
Cincinnati, OH 45206-2484

Cinergy Foundation Grants 1133
The Cinergy corporate contributions program was developed to reinvest in southwest Ohio, northern Kentucky, and Indiana communities. The mission of the foundation is to be a national leader in community development by creating proactive, innovative partnerships that improve the quality of life in Indiana, Ohio, and Kentucky, especially within the electric utility's 69-county service area. Grant categories include arts and culture; lifelong learning—K-12 (BASICS) and higher education; and healthy communities—environment and youth. Applicants are requested to submit grant applications to the district office closest to them; contact program staff for office locations. The board meets in April, July, October, and December to consider requests.
Requirements: The foundation supports projects and programs of 501(c)3 tax-exempt organizations located in 10 southwestern Ohio counties, six northern Kentucky counties, and sixty nine Indiana counties.
Restrictions: Grants do not support advertising; capital and endowment campaigns; competitions (scholastic or athletic); construction/renovation projects; equipment purchases of any type (playground, computers, etc.); golf events; K-12 schools outside the BASICS program; membership dues; organizations without 501(c)3 status; programs that pose a potential conflict of interest; projects/organizations benefiting an individual or a few persons; requests outside the Cinergy service territory; scholarship programs; sponsorships for athletic teams; travel expenses for individuals or groups; uniforms; or veterans, labor, religious, political, or fraternal groups.
Geographic Focus: Indiana, Kentucky, Ohio
Amount of Grant: Up to 50,000 USD
Contact: Karol King; (800) 262-3000, ext. 1251 or (513) 287-1251; kking@cinergy.com
Internet: http://www.cinergy.com/Community/Cinergy_Foundation/default.asp
Sponsor: Cinergy Foundation
139 E Fourth Street
Cincinnati, OH 45202

Cingular Wireless Charitable Contributions 1134
The company supports community-based programs and organizations that address educational, cultural, and social issues that affect the quality of life in Cingular communities. Preference is given to projects that address human needs, arts, or education; nurturing programs that inspire creativity in youth and adults or that focus specifically on teaching/developing modes of expression; proposals that are project specific, rather than requests to underwrite operating, capital, or endowment budgets; projects that stimulate partnerships among various organizations to work cooperatively and collaboratively for lasting solutions; and projects with well-defined goals and a clear picture of the need, with specific evaluation results. Contributions guidelines, regional and local office locations, and application form are available online. There are no application deadlines.
Geographic Focus: Alabama, Arkansas, California, Connecticut, District of Columbia, Florida, Georgia, Illinois, Indiana, Kentucky, Louisiana, Maryland, Michigan, Mississippi, Missouri, New York, North Carolina, Ohio, Pennsylvania, South Carolina, Tennessee, Texas, Washington
Contact: Contributions; (404) 236-6000; charitable.contributions@cingular.com
Internet: http://www.cingular.com/cingular/about_us/community_involvement
Sponsor: Cingular Wireless
5565 Glenridge Connector, Suite 1401
Atlanta, GA 30342

CIRCLE Civic Education at the High School Level Research Grants 1135

The program seeks research that will help educators and policymakers to improve civic outcomes for U.S. students of high-school age (roughly 14 to 18). Civic outcomes include, but are not limited to knowledge of politics, democracy and civil society; knowledge of social issues; values such as tolerance, trust, patriotism, concern for others' rights and well-being, and efficacy (the belief that one can make a difference); skills and habits of deliberating about public issues and participating in politics and community affairs; volunteering and membership in voluntary and/or nonprofit groups; and intentions to vote or to consider careers in public service (in the government or nonprofit sectors). CIRCLE is interested in research on interventions and reforms that may enhance civic outcomes. These interventions and reforms include, but are not limited to programs of civic education and classes on history, democracy, or law; approaches to the teaching of other disciplines that may have civic benefits; co-curricular activities, including student government and student media; service-learning; games and simulations that involve political or civic issues; student voice or participation in the governance of their schools; the basic structure of high schools (including their size, focus, requirements, climate, admissions criteria, or composition); professional development for teachers, so long as the effects on students can be assessed; and after-school or community-based programs, insofar as these have the potential to reach large numbers of adolescents or to change mainstream education. In most CIRCLE-funded research projects, the outcomes will be civic knowledge, values, skills, or behaviors. However, research that explores whether being civically engaged helps academic outcomes or positive adolescent development also will be considered. The listed application deadline is for letters of inquiry; full proposals are by invitation.
Requirements: CIRCLE welcomes proposals from academics, students (especially PhD candidates at the dissertation stage), independent scholars, practitioners, and research nonprofits and firms. CIRCLE also welcomes proposals from youth of high school age, perhaps working in partnership with adults. Such youth-led research proposals will be evaluated separately and not compared directly to proposals from adults.
Restrictions: CIRCLE funds rigorous research, not advocacy, education, or other forms of practice.
Geographic Focus: All States
Date(s) Application is Due: Dec 15
Amount of Grant: Up to 100,000 USD
Contact: Carrie Donovan, (301) 405-2790; cdonovan@umd.edu
Internet: http://www.civicyouth.org/grants/index.htm
Sponsor: University of Maryland
School of Public Policy
College Park, MD 20742

Circle K Corporation Contributions Grants 1136

Circle K strives to be a good corporate citizen by improving the quality of life in the communities in which it serves. The corporation's charitable support targets two key areas: youth-at-risk and education. Other fields of interest include: boys clubs; cerebral palsy; community and economic development; food services; girls clubs; housing; and youth development. Types of support include general operating funds, in-kind support, and sponsorships. Additionally, Circle K has been a national sponsor of United Cerebral Palsy (UCP) since 1984, giving hope and encouragement to thousands of children and adults with cerebral palsy and other disabilities. Circle K also facilitates an employee volunteer group, which lends time to company-sponsored community activities.
Geographic Focus: Alabama, Arizona, Arkansas, California, Colorado, Florida, Georgia, Illinois, Indiana, Iowa, Kentucky, Michigan, Mississippi, Nevada, New Mexico, North Carolina, Ohio, Oklahoma, Oregon, Pennsylvania, South Carolina, Tennessee, Texas, Washington
Contact: Contributions Manager; (602) 728-8000
Internet: http://www.circlek.com/CircleK/AboutUs/CommunityService.htm
Sponsor: Circle K Corporation
P.O. Box 52085
Phoenix, AZ 85072-2085

Cisco Systems Foundation San Jose Community Grants 1137

The foundation awards grants to nonprofit organizations in support of education (K-12 programs, career training for disadvantaged adults, and arts in education) and to meet basic human needs, including food, shelter, and health care.
Requirements: 501(c)3 nonprofit organizations located within 50 miles of the Cisco Systems Headquarters in San Jose, CA, are eligible to apply.
Restrictions: Grants do not support athletic events, capital building campaigns, conferences, fundraising events, sponsorships, general operating expenses, religious or political groups, scholarships, individual schools or school systems, or start-up projects.
Geographic Focus: California, Massachusetts, New York, North Carolina
Date(s) Application is Due: Apr 30; Nov 30
Amount of Grant: 10,000 - 15,000 USD
Contact: Grants Administrator; (408) 527-3040; ciscofoundation@cisco.com
Internet: http://www.cisco.com/go/foundation
Sponsor: Cisco Systems Foundation
170 W Tasman Drive
San Jose, CA 95134-1706

CIT Corporate Giving Grants 1138

The corporate giving program focuses its giving to programs that substantially strengthen the communities where CIT has a significant presence; provide services that benefit employees, their families, and communities; and support employee volunteerism. Funding priorities include organizations, institutions, or programs that work to foster excellence in education, particularly among at-risk and underprivileged youth; support local health and social welfare issues; help stabilize and improve neighborhoods by providing viable economic and educational growth opportunities to the community; and support the arts, and their accessibility, as a means of enhancing personal and social development. Proposals are reviewed on an ongoing basis and must be formally submitted by mail.
Requirements: 501(c)3 tax-exempt organizations and Canadian charities registered with the Canada Customs and Revenue Agency (CCRA) are eligible.
Restrictions: The following will not be considered for funding: political organizations, campaigns, or candidates; conferences, memberships, or sports competitions; organizations that discriminate in any way with national equal opportunity policies; organizations whose chief purpose is to influence legislation; veteran and fraternal organizations; religious organizations, unless engaged in a significant, nonsectarian project that benefits a broad base of the community; or individuals.
Geographic Focus: All States
Contact: Stacy Papas, Community Affairs Manager; stacy.papas@cit.com
Internet: http://www.cit.com/about-cit/corporate-giving/index.htm
Sponsor: CIT Group
11 West 42nd Street
New York, NY 10036

Citigroup Foundation Grants 1139

The foundation supports nonprofits worldwide in Citibank communities in the areas of financial education, educating the next generation, and building communities and entrepreneurs. Financial Education grants support efforts that help increase family stability, encourage better consumer habits, increase the individual's stake in his/her community, and deliver economic and financial education to young people. Educating the Next Generation grants support educational opportunities in low-income communities, early literacy development, technology-based curriculum resources, career and college preparation programs, teacher training and strategies that increase student achievement, student and curriculum development for graduate and undergraduate business programs, access for minorities and women within higher education and the workplace, and access to arts through curriculum and cultural institutions. Building Communities and Entrepreneurs grants reinforce community-led efforts to revitalize low-income neighborhoods through affordable housing, economic development, welfare-to-work initiatives, community infrastructure improvements, environmentally sustainable growth to local economies, community-based health and human services programs, and disaster relief efforts. Citigroup and the Citigroup Foundation prefer to solicit proposals from prospective grantees with demonstrated successes in the areas they fund. Unsolicited proposals will be accepted, but a favorable decision is less likely. Nonprofit organizations that are encouraged to submit proposals may do so at any time during a calendar year; the earlier, the better. There are no application deadlines.
Requirements: 501(c)3 nonprofit organizations in communities served by Citibank or a Citigroup company are eligible. The Citigroup Foundation receives all U.S. grant applications through an online submission system. For information on applying for a U.S. grant, contact your closest U.S. Contributions Coordinator. For information on applying for an international grant, contact the International Contributions Coordinator. Contacts are listed at the Foundation's website (given above).
Restrictions: The foundation does not to make grants to individuals for educational or other purposes; political causes or candidates; religious, veteran, or fraternal organizations, unless they are engaged in a significant project benefiting the entire community; fundraising events, telethons, marathons, races, or benefits; or courtesy advertising.
Geographic Focus: All States
Contact: Pamela P. Flaherty; (212) 559-9163; citigroupfoundation@citigroup.com
Internet: http://www.citigroup.com/citigroup/corporate/foundation/guide.htm
Sponsor: Citigroup Foundation
850 Third Avenue, 13th Floor
New York, NY 10022-6211

Citizens Bank Mid-Atlantic Charitable Foundation Grants 1140

Charitable grants are made only to qualified 501(c)3 Rhode Island-based organizations serving Rhode Island residents. Citizens look for opportunities where moderate funding can affect significant results in the community. Priority consideration is given to programs that encourage the development of innovative responses to basic human needs; promote fair housing and focus on community issues of neighborhood development and economic self-sufficiency; support the availability of quality, cost-effective, community-based health care, particularly for low-income families and children who are at risk; promote new ways to provide a quality education to populations that are underserved, including job training; promote availability and accessibility in the area of culture and the arts; and promote citizen participation in the development of new and workable solutions for improving and maintaining a healthy environment. Charitable grants are usually for capital funding (to build or renovate a facility) or implementation of a specific program.
Requirements: 501(c)3 Rhode Island-based nonprofits are eligible.
Restrictions: Grants do not support individuals, single disease/issue research organizations, religious organizations for religious purposes, labor or fraternal or veterans groups, political organizations or projects, operating deficits, underwriting of conferences and seminars, governmental public agencies, endowments, annual operating support, trips and tours, payment on bank loans, advertising, or fund-raising events.
Geographic Focus: Rhode Island
Amount of Grant: 1,000 - 100,000 USD
Contact: Jeanne Cola, Senior Vice President; (401) 456-7200; fax (401) 456-7366
Sponsor: Citizens Bank Mid-Atlantic Charitable Foundation
870 Westminster Street
Providence, RI 02903

Citizens Savings Foundation Grants 1141
In 1998, the Citizens Savings Foundation was established and funded with 300,000 shares of CFS Bancorp, Inc. stock. The primary purpose of the Foundation is to promote charitable and educational activities within the meaning of Section 501(c)3 of the Internal Revenue Code of 1986, within Lake and Porter counties in the State of Indiana and Cook, Will and DuPage counties in the State of Illinois and their neighboring communities. To that end, the Foundation: makes awards, grants or other distributions designed to expand home ownership opportunities and provide access to affordable housing; supports youth development programs to improve life options through education and work skills; and supports community organizations that contribute to the quality of life.
Geographic Focus: Illinois, Indiana
Amount of Grant: Up to 5,000 USD
Contact: Monica F. Sullivan, Vice President; (219) 836-2960 or (219) 836-5500
Internet: http://www.mybankcitizens.com/aboutcitizens/citizens_savings_foundation/
Sponsor: Citizens Savings Foundation
707 Ridge Road
Munster, IN 46321-1611

City of Oakland Cultural Arts Department Grants 1142
The arts program awards grants to Oakland-based individuals and nonprofit organizations. Organization Project Support grants support Oakland-based nonprofit organizations producing art activities in Oakland that culminate in a local public outcome for the benefit of the community. Individual Artist Project grants support Oakland resident individual artists producing art activities in Oakland that culminate in a local public outcome for the benefit of the community. Art in the Schools grants support quality, hands-on arts experiences in school settings to educate students about the process of creating and producing arts; support and enhance the classroom curriculum; and support arts residencies on the school site before, during, or after school hours. The January 6 application deadline is for organizations and individual artists; the January 13 deadline is for art in the schools. Guidelines are available online.
Requirements: Oakland-based individuals and nonprofit organizations are eligible.
Geographic Focus: All States
Date(s) Application is Due: Jan 6; Jan 13
Contact: Andrea Leal, (510) 238-6843; aleal@oaklandnet.com
Internet: http://oaklandculturalarts.org/main/programoverview.htm
Sponsor: City of Oakland Cultural Arts Department
1 Frank H Ogawa Plaza, 9th Floor
Oakland, CA 94612

Civic Change Award 1143
The award is given to an individual, organization, or community that has demonstrated extraordinary commitment to improving civic life. The award carries with it a cash prize to a nonprofit organization of the awardee's choice, a crystal momento, and an award event. Former winners include John Gardner, Paul Aicher, Alma Powell, William Winter, and the League of Women Voters of the United States. Nomination form is available online.
Geographic Focus: All States
Date(s) Application is Due: Dec 31
Contact: Dr. Suzanne Morse, (434) 971-2073; fax (434) 971-7042
Internet: http://www.pew-partnership.org/whatsnew.html
Sponsor: Pew Partnership for Civic Change
5 Boar's Head Lane, Suite 100
Charlottesville, VA 22903

Civic Education Consortium Grants 1144
The program provides seed money for innovative, collaborative civic education projects that develop effective citizenship among North Carolina's children and youth (ages five to 18). The consortium is especially interested in funding programs that foster direct application of classroom civics lessons, allowing teachers/adult leaders and students to use the community as a learning laboratory; involve youth directly in government issues, programs, processes, or services; incorporate service-learning in aspects of the curriculum that help young people learn about civic/community involvement and/or explore public policy issues; help teachers or adult leaders learn more effective ways of teaching civics, such as experience-based programs and using real life issues in the curriculum; encourage students to value democracy and exercise both rights and responsibilities of citizenship; and involve participants who are diverse in background, age, achievement level, income, ethnicity, religion, and geography. The grant is generally for a period of one year, or less. Collaborative projects are strongly encouraged. Guidelines and application are available online.
Requirements: North Carolina 501(c)3 tax-exempt organizations and government agencies, including schools, are eligible. Organizations not located in North Carolina may receive consideration for programs operated exclusively in North Carolina.
Geographic Focus: All States
Contact: Leslie Anderson, (828) 252-4913; fax (828) 232-0481; lesliea@ioa.com
Internet: http://www.civics.unc.edu/smallgrants/index.htm
Sponsor: Civic Education Consortium
10 Blackwood Road
Asheville, NC 28804

Claneil Foundation Grants 1145
The foundation awards grants to nonprofit organizations in its areas of interest, including community development, education, arts and culture, environment, health, women, domestic abuse, and social services. Types of support include capital campaigns, equipment acquisition, continuing support, building construction/renovation, exchange programs, and research. Deadlines listed are for letters of intent. Application forms are required.
Requirements: Nonprofit organizations are eligible. Preference is given to organizations serving Pennsylvania counties including Bucks, Montgomery, Chester, Delaware, and Philadelphia.
Restrictions: Grants are not awarded to governmental organizations, individuals, or religious organizations.
Geographic Focus: Pennsylvania
Date(s) Application is Due: Jun 30; Dec 15
Amount of Grant: 3,000 - 50,000 USD
Contact: Cathy Weiss, Executive Director; (610) 941-1131; cweiss@claneil.com
Internet: http://www.claneil.org
Sponsor: Claneil Foundation
630 W Germantown Pike, Suite 400
Plymouth Meeting, PA 19462

Clara Abbott Foundation Need-Based Grants 1146
To promote personal financial responsibility, the Foundation provides financial consulting, financial education classes, and monetary financial assistance for personal needs. Assistance is based on financial hardship and is provided for basic needs as a last resource. The Clara Abbott Foundation's definition of financial hardship is any situation that threatens the family's ability to provide basic living needs, such as food, utilities and rent. Additionally, the Foundation may provide financial assistance for expenses due to natural disaster, major health problems of a family member, special needs children and cases of abuse.
Requirements: To receive a financial grant to help meet basic living needs, the following criteria must be met: current employee of Abbott with at least one year of service (or one year from date of Abbott acquisition) and working a minimum of 20 hours per week; retiree of Abbott; spouse of deceased employee/retiree (until remarried); dependent child of deceased employee/retiree until age 23 for students, age 19 otherwise; special-needs children will not lose eligibility based on age; or employee who is under a disability program (sponsored by Abbott). All applicants must be enrolled in a health plan.
Geographic Focus: All States
Contact: Lisa Marie Lillge, Grant Coordinator; (847) 937-1090 or (800) 972-3859; fax (847) 938-6511; AskClara@abbott.com
Internet: http://clara.abbott.com/financial-assistance/
Sponsor: Clara Abbott Foundation
1505 S White Oak Drive
Waukegan, IL 60085

Clara Blackford Smith and W. Aubrey Smith Charitable Foundation Grants 1147
The Clara Blackford Smith & W. Aubrey Smith Charitable Foundation was established in 1978. Mrs. Smith was a well-known benefactor of health care. The foundation was established under her will to support and promote quality education, health-care, and human-services programming for underserved populations. Special consideration is given to charitable organizations that serve the people of Grayson County, Texas. The foundation makes an annual grant to Denison High School in Denison, Texas to provide college scholarship assistance for deserving graduates. The majority of grants from the Smith Charitable Foundation are one year in duration; on occasion, multi-year support is awarded. Applicants must apply online at the grant website. Applicants are strongly encouraged to do the following before applying: review the downloadable state application procedures for additional helpful information and clarifications; review the downloadable online-application guidelines at the grant website; review the foundation's funding history (link is available from the grant website); review the online application questions in advance; and review the list of required attachments. These will generally include: a list of board members, financial statements (audited, reviewed, or compiled by independent auditor); an organization summary; a list of other funding sources; an IRS Determination letter; and other required documents. All attachments must be uploaded in the online application as PDF, Word, or Excel files. The Clara Blackford Smith & W. Aubrey Smith Charitable Foundation has four deadlines annually: March 1, June 1, September 1, and December 1. Applications must be submitted by 11:59 p.m. on the deadline dates. Grant applicants are notified as follows: March deadline applicants will be notified of grant decisions by June 30; June applicants will be notified by September 30; September applicants will be notified by December 31; and December applicants will be notified by March 31 of the following year.
Requirements: Applicants must have 501(c)3 tax-exempt status.
Restrictions: The foundation does not support requests from individuals, organizations attempting to influence policy through direct lobbying, or any political campaigns.
Geographic Focus: Texas
Date(s) Application is Due: Mar 1; Jun 1; Sep 1; Dec 1
Contact: David Ross, Senior Vice President; tx.philanthropic@baml.com
Internet: https://www.bankofamerica.com/philanthropic/fn_search.action
Sponsor: Clara Blackford Smith and W. Aubrey Smith Charitable Foundation
901 Main Street, 19th Floor, TX1-492-19-11
Dallas, TX 75202-3714

Clarcor Foundation Grants 1148
Clarcor, through its foundation, seeks to improve the quality of life in the communities in which the company operates. Grants support nonprofits in the categories of health, human services, education, culture and art, and civic activities. Types of support include general operating support, annual campaigns, capital campaigns, and employee matching gifts. There are no application deadlines. The board meets in February, May, August, and November.
Requirements: Tax-exempt organizations in company-operating areas in Rockford, IL; Louisville, KY; Kearney and Gothenburg, NE; Cincinnati, OH; Oklahoma, and Lancaster, PA; are eligible.
Restrictions: Grants are not made to support individuals, endowment funds, research, scholarships, fellowships, or loans.

Geographic Focus: Illinois, Kentucky, Nebraska, North Carolina, Ohio, Oklahoma, Pennsylvania
Amount of Grant: 500 - 50,250 USD
Contact: Pete Nangel, (815) 962-8867; fax (815) 962-0417
Sponsor: Clarcor Foundation
840 Crescent Centre Drive, Suite 600
Franklin, TN 37067

Claremont Community Foundation Grants 1149
The foundation awards grants to support programs and special projects of nonprofit organizations that enrich the lives of youth and adults throughout the greater Los Angeles metropolitan area. Grants are awarded in support of the fine arts, social support services, and cultural activities. Grant proposals may be submitted for consideration through a competitive review process held in the fall and spring of each year. Interested parties should contact the office for current funding criteria, application materials, and schedules.
Requirements: Nonprofit organizations serving the greater Los Angeles, CA, metropolitan area may submit proposals.
Geographic Focus: California
Amount of Grant: 1,500 - 2,000 USD
Contact: Nickie Cleaves, Interim Executive Director; (909) 398-1060; fax (909) 624-6629; ccf-info@claremontfoundation.org
Internet: http://claremontfoundation.org
Sponsor: Claremont Community Foundation
205 Yale Avenue
Claremont, CA 91711

Clarence E. Heller Charitable Foundation Grants 1150
The charitable foundation supports nonprofit organizations, with priority given to proposals from California, in its areas of interest, including environment and health—to prevent serious risk to human health from toxic substances and other environmental hazards by supporting programs in research, education, and policy development; management of resources—to protect and preserve the earth's limited resources by assisting programs that demonstrate how natural resources can be managed on a sustainable and an ecologically sound basis, and supporting initiatives for sustainable agriculture, and for promoting the long-term viability of communities and regions; music—to encourage the playing, enjoyment, and accessibility of symphonic and chamber music by providing scholarship and program assistance at selected community music organizations and schools, and by helping community-based ensembles of demonstrated quality implement artistic initiatives, diversify and increase audiences, and improve fund-raising capacity; and education—to focus on support for programs that improve the teaching skills of educators and artists in environmental and arts education. Types of support include continuing support, general operating expenses, publications, research, seed money, and special projects. The foundation's board meets typically in March, June, and October. Letters of inquiry are accepted at any time.
Requirements: 501(c)3 tax-exempt organizations are eligible.
Restrictions: Grants are not made to individuals.
Geographic Focus: California
Contact: Bruce Hirsch; (415) 989-9839; fax (415) 989-1909; info@cehcf.org
Internet: http://cehcf.org/app_info.html
Sponsor: Clarence E. Heller Charitable Foundation
44 Montgomery Street, Suite 1970
San Francisco, CA 94104

Clarence T.C. Ching Foundation Grants 1151
The Clarence T. C. Ching Foundation provides funding opportunities to nonprofits primarily in Honolulu, Hawaii. The Foundation's areas of interest include education and health. Types of support available are: scholarship funds; general program support and; building/renovation. Grant applications are accepted year round with no application deadline date.
Requirements: Nonprofits in Honolulu, Hawaii are eligible for funding. When applying for a grant include the following in with your proposal: copy of IRS Determination Letter; detailed description of project and amount of funding requested; listing of additional sources and amount of support; five (5) copies of the proposal.
Restrictions: No grants to individuals.
Geographic Focus: Hawaii
Contact: R. Stevens Gilley, Executive Director; (808) 521-0344
Sponsor: Clarence T.C. Ching Foundation
1001 Bishop Street, Suite 960
Honolulu, HI 96813

Clark-Winchcole Foundation Grants 1152
The foundation awards grants to nonprofit organizations in the District of Columbia, with an emphasis on higher education, hospitals and health care, cultural programs, youth, the disabled, and religion. Types of support include general operating support, scholarships, and building construction/renovation. Applicants should submit a letter of inquiry that includes a description of the project, amount requested, audited financial report, budget, and proof of tax-exempt status. Further information will be requested by the foundation if interested.
Requirements: Only nonprofits in the District of Columbia are eligible to apply.
Restrictions: No support for individuals and private foundations.
Geographic Focus: District of Columbia
Amount of Grant: 5,000 - 225,000 USD
Contact: Vincent Burke, President; (301) 654-3607
Sponsor: Clark-Winchcole Foundation
3 Bethesda Metro Center, Suite 550
Bethesda, MD 20814-5358

Clark and Carolyn Adams Foundation Grants 1153
Established in 1998, the Clark and Carolyn Adams Foundation offers support primarily in Florida for education, human services, and religious groups. A formal application is required, though the initial approach should be in the form of a letter offering a detailed description of the proposed project and funding requested. Most recently, grants have ranged from $1,000 to $10,000, and comes in the form of general operating support. The annual deadline is June 30.
Geographic Focus: Florida
Amount of Grant: 1,000 - 10,000 USD
Contact: John Clark Adams, Trustee; (305) 448-9022
Sponsor: Clark and Carolyn Adams Foundation
540 Biltmore Way
Coral Gables, FL 33134

Clark and Ruby Baker Foundation Grants 1154
The Clark and Ruby Baker Foundation was established to address a number of charitable concerns. The Baker family cared deeply about the Methodist Church and founded the Foundation to support Methodist affiliated, higher educational institutions in rural or small towns; charitable organizations that serve infirm, deserving, and aged ministers; economically disadvantaged and deserving children; and orphans and orphanages. The Foundation also provides support to charitable organizations that extend financial aid to the sick and infirm receiving medical treatment in any hospital or clinic in the state of Georgia. Capital support may be considered for the following purposes: for construction of educational facilities at a college or university; for clinics and hospitals; for libraries; and for any building with a charitable use. Grants from the Clark and Ruby Baker Foundation are primarily one year in duration; on occasion, multi-year support is awarded. Applicants must apply online at the grant website. Applicants are strongly encouraged to do the following before applying: review the downloadable state application procedures for additional helpful information and clarifications; review the downloadable online-application guidelines at the grant website; review the foundation's funding history (link is available from the grant website); review the online application questions in advance; and review the list of required attachments. These will generally include: a list of board members, financial statements (audited, reviewed, or compiled by independent auditor); an organization summary; a list of other funding sources; an IRS Determination letter; and other required documents. All attachments must be uploaded in the online application as PDF, Word, or Excel files. The Clark and Ruby Baker Foundation application deadline is 11:59 p.m. on June 1. Applicants will be notified of grant decisions by letter within one to two months after the deadline.
Requirements: Applicants must have 501(c)3 tax-exempt status.
Restrictions: The foundation does not support requests from individuals, organizations attempting to influence policy through direct lobbying, or any political campaigns.
Geographic Focus: Georgia
Date(s) Application is Due: Jun 1
Contact: Quanda Allen, Vice President; (404) 264-1377; quanda.allen@baml.com
Internet: https://www.bankofamerica.com/philanthropic/fn_search.action
Sponsor: Clark and Ruby Baker Foundation
3414 Peachtree Road, N.E., Suite 1475, GA7-813-14-04
Atlanta, GA 30326-1113

Clark Charitable Trust Grants 1155
The Clark Charitable Trust awards grants to nonprofit organizations in its areas of interest, including basic human needs, environmental conservation and preservation, animal welfare, music, and higher education. Types of support include general operating support, annual campaigns, capital campaigns, building construction and renovation, equipment acquisition, endowment funds, scholarship funds, and matching funds. There are no application forms or deadlines specified. Submit a letter describing the project's purpose, an audited financial statement, and amount requested. Typical funding amounts have recently ranged from $1,000 to $10,000.
Requirements: Nonprofit organization are eligible.
Geographic Focus: All States
Amount of Grant: 1,000 - 10,000 USD
Contact: Timothy Taylor, Trustee; (781) 259-8800
Sponsor: Clark Charitable Trust
P.O. Box 681
Lincoln, MA 01773-8800

Clark County Community Foundation Grants 1156
Clark County Community Foundation will award grants to 501(c)3 charitable organizations, schools, and exempt governmental units or their subdivisions serving Clark County, Kentucky. Areas of interest include arts and culture, housing, employment support and education. Grants will range from approximately $5,000 to $10,000. To apply, submit a letter of inquiry of no more than three pages by 4:00 pm, March 15. Applicants will then be invited to submit full proposals, which are due by May 15.
Requirements: Clark County, Kentucky, nonprofit organizations are eligible.
Geographic Focus: Kentucky
Date(s) Application is Due: Mar 15; May 15
Amount of Grant: 5,000 - 10,000 USD
Contact: Barbara A. Fischer; (859) 225-3343; fax (859) 243-0770; bfischer@bgcf.org
Internet: http://www.bgcf.org/page27526.cfm
Sponsor: Clark County Community Foundation
250 W Main Street, Suite 1220
Lexington, KY 40507

Clark Foundation Grants 1157
The foundation awards grants in New York, NY, and upstate New York for charitable and educational purposes and in support of health care, youth, cultural, environmental, and community organizations. Types of support include general operating support, continuing support, annual campaigns, capital campaigns, building construction/renovation, equipment acquisition, program development, seed money, and scholarships to Cooperstown County residents.
Requirements: Nonprofits in upstate New York and New York, NY, are eligible.
Geographic Focus: New York
Date(s) Application is Due: Jan 1; Apr 1; Jul 15; Oct 1
Amount of Grant: 20,000 - 200,000 USD
Contact: Charles Hamilton, Executive Director; (212) 977-6900
Sponsor: Clark Foundation
1 Rockefeller Plaza, 31st Floor
New York, NY 10020

Claude A. and Blanche McCubbin Abbott Charitable Trust Grants 1158
The Claude A. and Blanche McCubbin Abbott Charitable Trust offers grants primarily in the states of Florida and Maryland. Its identified fields of interest include Catholic agencies and churches, as well as human services. Awards typically come in the form of general operating funds. There are no specified application forms or annual deadlines, and interested parties should begin by contacting the Trust to discuss the program and needed budget support. Grant amounts have typically ranged from $100 to $2,000.
Geographic Focus: Florida, Maryland
Amount of Grant: 100 - 2,000 USD
Contact: Christine Wells, Trustee; (410) 788-1890
Sponsor: Claude A. and Blanche McCubbin Abbott Charitable Trust
6400 Baltimore National Pike No. 105
Catonsville, MD 21228

Claude Bennett Family Foundation Grants 1159
Established in Alabama in 1993, the Claude Bennett Family Foundation has as its primary interest areas: health care, health organizations, higher education, human services, and Protestant churches and agencies. The range of funding is up to $15,000, and the Foundation has supported agencies all across the U.S. There are no specific applications or deadlines with which to adhere, and applicants should contact the Foundation in writing, stating the purpose of their request and offering a detailed budget.
Geographic Focus: All States
Contact: Harold I. Apolinsky, Trustee; (205) 930-5122 or (205) 945-4687; fax (205) 212-3888; hapolinsky@sirote.com
Sponsor: Claude Bennett Family Foundation
2311 Highland Avenue South, P.O. Box 130804
Birmingham, AL 35213-0804

Claude Pepper Foundation Grants 1160
The foundation makes grants primarily to support the work of the Claude Pepper Center and the Pepper Institute on Aging and Public Policy, both located at Florida State University, Tallahassee, FL. The foundation makes limited grants to other organizations to continue the work and vision of Claude and Mildred Pepper. The foundation also supports a visiting scholars program and an oratory competition for Florida students. Grants are usually made for a period of one year and except in rare instances no grant will be made for longer than a three-year period of time. Guidelines are available online.
Requirements: 501(c)3 tax-exempt organizations are eligible.
Geographic Focus: All States
Contact: John T. Herndon; (850) 644-9309; herndon@claudepepperfoundation.org
Internet: http://www.claudepepperfoundation.org/programs_grants.cfm
Sponsor: Claude Pepper Foundation
636 West Call Street
Tallahassee, FL 32306-1122

Claude Worthington Benedum Foundation Grants 1161
Grants are made in the areas of education, health and human services, community and economic development, environment, and the arts. Grants have been awarded to support education reform, teacher education, higher education, workforce development, rural health, professional developing in healthcare, human services, affordable housing, and economic development. Grants are awarded to organizations in West Virginia and southwestern Pennsylvania. Funds are provided for general operations for projects, sometimes including building and equipment, in West Virginia, and for projects in Pittsburgh that address regional problems and needs, that establish demonstration projects with strong potential for replication in West Virginia, or make outstanding contributions to the area. Additional types of support include matching funds, consulting services, technical assistance, capital campaigns, conferences and seminars, research, and seed grants. Organizations wishing to apply should request a copy of the annual report, which includes application guidelines. Applications may be submitted at any time; the board meets for review in March, June, September, and December.
Requirements: Southwestern Pennsylvania and West Virginia nonprofits may apply.
Restrictions: Support is not given for national health and welfare campaigns, medical research, religious activities, fellowships, scholarships, annual campaigns, or travel.
Geographic Focus: Pennsylvania, West Virginia
Contact: Margaret M. Martin, Grants Administrator; (800) 223-5948 or (412) 246-3636; fax (412) 288-0366; mmartin@benedum.org
Internet: http://www.benedum.org/pages.cfm?id=10
Sponsor: Claude Worthington Benedum Foundation
1400 Benedum-Trees Building, 223 Fourth Avenue
Pittsburgh, PA 15222

Clay Foundation Grants 1162
The primary mission of the foundation is to promote and enhance the quality of life of the citizens of West Virginia. Initially, grants will be confined to organizations or projects within the greater Kanawha Valley that significantly affect its residents. The foundation considers a broad range of organizations, though special interest is given to programs in the field of aging; health care, research, and education; vocational education; and services to disadvantaged youth and their families. Applicants are asked to submit a preliminary letter. If foundation priorities and resources permit consideration of the request, a detailed formal proposal may be requested. There are no deadline dates for the submission of preliminary letters. The board meets four times annually, generally in January, April, July, and October, at which times applications are considered and grants made.
Requirements: IRS 501(c)3 tax-exempt organizations in West Virginia are eligible.
Restrictions: Grants are not made for ongoing normal operations, debt retirement or operational deficits, contributions to endowment or scholarship funds, annual appeals or other fund-raising events, national fund-raising campaigns, religious organizations for religious purposes, or grants to conduit organizations.
Geographic Focus: West Virginia
Amount of Grant: 5,000 - 75,000 USD
Contact: Charles Avampato, President; (304) 344-8656; fax (304) 344-3805
Sponsor: Clay Foundation
1426 Kanawha Boulevard E
Charleston, WV 25301

Clayton Baker Trust Grants 1163
The trust awards grants to Maryland nonprofit organizations for programs targeting the disadvantaged, with an emphasis on the needs of children. Grants are awarded nationally in the areas of environmental protection, population control, arms control, and nuclear disarmament. Types of support include general operating support, seed grants, and special projects.
Requirements: Nonprofit organizations in Maryland are eligible to apply.
Restrictions: Grants do not support the arts, research, higher educational institutions, individuals, building construction/renovation, or endowment funding.
Geographic Focus: Maryland
Date(s) Application is Due: Apr 5; Aug 5; Dec 5
Amount of Grant: 2,000 - 100,000 USD
Contact: John Powell, Jr., Executive Director; (410) 837-3555; fax (410) 837-7711
Sponsor: Clayton Baker Trust
2 East Read Street, Suite 100
Baltimore, MD 21202

Cleo Foundation Grants 1164
The foundation supports public charities in San Francisco, San Benito, Mendocino, and southern Monterey counties, with primary interest in supporting organizations that benefit at-risk and/or low-income children, youth, and adults. The foundation is most interested in programs that can make good use of relatively small grants. Types of support include building construction/renovation, capital campaigns, continuing support, operating support, and program development. Applications are due 12 weeks before board meetings in March and September. Request guidelines in writing.
Requirements: 501(c)3 organizations in San Francisco, San Benito, Mendocino, and southern Monterey counties in California may apply.
Geographic Focus: California
Amount of Grant: 1,000 - 20,000 USD
Contact: Mary Gregory; (415) 561-6540; fax (415) 561-6477; mgregory@pfs-llc.net
Internet: http://www.pfs-llc.net/cleo.html
Sponsor: Cleo Foundation
Presidio Building 1016, Suite 300, P.O. Box 29906
San Francisco, CA 94129-0906

Cleveland-Cliffs Foundation Grants 1165
Contributions are made to nonprofit organizations to enhance the quality of life of Cleveland-Cliffs Inc employees and in recognition of a corporate responsibility toward educational, health, welfare, civic, and cultural matters within the communities where the company operates. The foundation was formed for the purpose of making contributions to groups organized and operated exclusively for religious, charitable, scientific, literary, or educational purposes and for the prevention of cruelty to children or animals. Types of support include general operating support, annual campaigns, capital campaigns, building/renovation, professorships, scholarship funds, research, and employee matching gifts. The foundation's major emphasis is on supporting education through a matching gift program and direct contributions to educational institutions. Requests for support must be in writing.
Requirements: Nonprofit organizations in the mining communities in which Cleveland-Cliffs Inc operates, including Alabama, Michigan, Minnesota, Ohio and, West Virginia are eligible.
Geographic Focus: Alabama, Michigan, Minnesota, Ohio, West Virginia
Amount of Grant: 250 - 50,000 USD
Contact: Dana W. Byrne, Vice President; (216) 694-5700; fax (216) 694-4880; publicrelations@cleveland-cliffs.com
Internet: http://www.cliffsnaturalresources.com/Development/CommunityRelations/Pages/Cleveland-CliffsFoundation.aspx
Sponsor: Cleveland-Cliffs Foundation
1100 Superior Avenue, Suite 1500
Cleveland, OH 44114-2589

Cleveland Browns Foundation Grants 1166

The foundation supports the northeast Ohio community by funding programs that improve the lives of disadvantaged children. The foundation's four focus areas are education, arts and culture, health, and career development as they relate to children. There are no application deadlines.

Requirements: Northern Ohio nonprofit organizations are eligible. Applications sold be submitted by mail

Restrictions: Organizations and causes that will not be considered for funding include fund-raising, sponsorship events, or donation requests; religious organizations for sectarian religious purposes; general or annual operation expenses; capital or building funds; or staff salaries or stipends.

Geographic Focus: Ohio

Contact: Grant Program Supervisor; (440) 891-5063; fax (440) 891-7529

Internet: http://www.clevelandbrowns.com/community/foundation

Sponsor: Cleveland Browns Foundation
Community Relations Department, 76 Lou Groza Boulevard
Berea, OH 44017

Cleveland Foundation Capital Grants 1167

The Cleveland Foundation is the community foundation serving Greater Cleveland, including Cuyahoga, Lake, and Geauga counties. It is made up of more than 1,300 funds representing individuals, families, organizations and corporations. Its mission is to enhance the lives of all residents of Greater Cleveland, now and for generations to come, by working together with our donors to build community endowment, address needs through grantmaking, and provide leadership on key community issues. Capital requests (such as those for buildings, land, or equipment), are supported when they meet certain stringent criteria. Capital projects must advance the foundation's priorities, help to meet a compelling community need, and offer a broad social benefit. When the foundation does participate in a capital project, its support is contingent on funding from other sources. Generally payment is not authorize until the organization has raised a significant amount of its total dollar goal.

Requirements: The foundation makes most of its grants to tax-exempt (private agencies classified as 501(c)3 organizations) public charities as defined by the Internal Revenue Service. Some grants are also made to government agencies. Priority is given to programs that reflect one or more of the following: improve access to services and programs for vulnerable and underserved populations; strengthen nonprofit organizations; test new ideas and partnerships; or, support policy and advocacy.

Restrictions: The foundation does not make grants to: individuals; for-profit organizations; endowment campaigns, annual appeals, or membership drives; religious organizations for religious purposes; travel for individuals or groups when travel is the proposal's primary focus; community services such as police and fire protection; staff positions for government agencies; capital projects for hospitals, nursing homes, or institutions of higher education; publications, audiovisual projects, or video productions, however, consideration may be given when they fall within a promising project.

Geographic Focus: Ohio

Date(s) Application is Due: Mar 31

Contact: Kevin McDaniel, Program Officer; (216) 615-7155; kMcDaniel@CleveFdn.org

Internet: http://www.clevelandfoundation.org/grants/apply-for-a-grant/grantmaking-guidelines/

Sponsor: Cleveland Foundation
1422 Euclid Avenue, Suite 1300
Cleveland, OH 44115

Cleveland Foundation Community Responsive Grants 1168

The Cleveland Foundation contributes one-third of its flexible grant dollars to respond to the expressed needs of the community. The Foundation's community responsive team acts as the front door to the foundation, helping organizations – large and small, relatively new and established – identify their highest priorities and guide them to funding. Applications are accepted on an ongoing basis, so you may apply for a grant at any time. Awards typically range between $50,000 and $75,000.

Requirements: The Cleveland Foundation makes most of its grants to tax-exempt (private agencies classified as 501(c)3 organizations) public charities as defined by the Internal Revenue Service. Some grants are also made to government agencies. The foundation requires all potential grant applicants to submit a grant inquiry, outlining basic information about the proposed project. Grant inquiries can be submitted at any time. If it is determined that your project fits the foundation's guidelines, you will be asked within a few weeks to submit a full application. It is recommended to submit one inquiry per proposed project. Priority is given to grant requests for programs or ideas that: improve access to services and programs for vulnerable and underserved populations; strengthen nonprofit organizations; test new ideas and different partnerships; support policy and advocacy.

Restrictions: Grants will not be awarded to/for: individuals; for-profit organizations; endowment campaigns, annual appeals, or membership drives; religious organizations for religious purposes; travel for individuals or groups when travel is the proposal's primary focus; community services such as police and fire protection; staff positions for government agencies; capital projects for hospitals, nursing homes, or institutions of higher education; publications, audiovisual projects, or video productions, however, consideration may be given when they fall within a promising project.

Geographic Focus: Ohio

Amount of Grant: Up to 75,000 USD

Contact: Kristi Andrasik, Program Officer; (216) 615-7192; kandrasik@clevefdn.org

Internet: http://www.clevelandfoundation.org/grants/responsive-grantmaking/

Sponsor: Cleveland Foundation
1422 Euclid Avenue, Suite 1300
Cleveland, OH 44115

Cleveland Foundation Fenn Educational Fund Grants 1169

The mission of the Fenn Educational Fund (Fenn) is to promote and assist cooperative education and internship programs at institutions of higher education in Greater Cleveland. Fenn is seeking proposals that create meaningful connections to local businesses and community partners and impact three key constituencies: students, faculty, and business/community partners. Research shows that many students learn better and are more prepared to enter the workforce if their course of study demonstrates how classroom learning applies in the real world. Faculty members can benefit from connections with local businesses embedding within the curriculum and can share cutting-edge research. Businesses also find that the ability to recruit talent from a pool of candidates that have real world experiences or have worked for the business itself increases the likelihood of finding the best candidate for the job and reduces the costs of recruiting, training, and retention. Fenn is seeking proposals that connect faculty members, students, and businesses in sustainable partnerships.

Requirements: Fenn grants are awarded to institutions of higher education in Greater Cleveland and tax-exempt, 501(c)3 organizations collaborating with these institutions on cooperative education or work-study programs. All proposals must come through the lead university/college's development office. The foundation encourages previous recipients of Fenn grants to apply, as well as those who have not submitted proposals in the past. Fenn has a strong interest in collaborative projects involving two or more institutions (i.e., other colleges/universities, businesses, other community partners). Priority will also be given to innovative attempts by area colleges and universities to jointly address the region's workforce needs. Successful programs will demonstrate not only written support from the highest levels of the institution, but will detail how individuals with a direct link to the president of the applicant institution will be directly engaged in the project. Projects should benefit students, employers and institutions, and will be able to adapt as necessary to ensure that the interests of all three groups are well served. It is anticipated that up to $400,000 in total will be available for high quality proposals. This represents the total amount available for all proposals. There is no upper or lower limit on the amount of funding the lead applicant may request. However, it is expected that the amount requested will be commensurate with the size and scope of the proposed program and outcomes. The Fund will consider multi-year requests for support but reserves the right to limit funding to a single year. Ordinarily, projects will not be supported for longer than three years.

Restrictions: All applicants are required to submit their request online. Hard copy applications will not be accepted.

Geographic Focus: Ohio

Date(s) Application is Due: Mar 29

Contact: Paul Putman, Program Officer; (216) 615-7254; GrantsMgmt@CleveFdn.org

Internet: http://www.clevelandfoundation.org/grants/committee-advised-funds/fenn-educational-fund/

Sponsor: Cleveland Foundation
1422 Euclid Avenue, Suite 1300
Cleveland, OH 44115

Cleveland Foundation Lake-Geauga Fund Grants 1170

The Lake-Geauga Fund of the Cleveland Foundation was established in 1986 in response to the number of key institutions in the two counties that had long-range impact on the region. The fund was developed by individuals with an interest and passion in supporting growth of the region and addressing unique needs in Lake and Geauga counties. Both are classified as rural counties with a substantial amount of open space and cultivated farmland. The fund is guided by an advisory committee of residents who have a knowledge and passion for their communities.

Requirements: The Cleveland Foundation makes most of its grants to tax-exempt (private agencies classified as 501(c)3 organizations) public charities as defined by the Internal Revenue Service. Some grants are also made to government agencies. The foundation requires all potential grant applicants to submit a grant inquiry, outlining basic information about the proposed project. Grant inquiries can be submitted at any time. If it is determined that your project fits the foundation's guidelines, you will be asked within a few weeks to submit a full application. It is recommended to submit one inquiry per proposed project. Grants are awarded on a quarterly basis.

Restrictions: Grants will not be awarded to/for: individuals; for-profit organizations; endowment campaigns, annual appeals, or membership drives; religious organizations for religious purposes; travel for individuals or groups when travel is the proposal's primary focus; community services such as police and fire protection; staff positions for government agencies; capital projects for hospitals, nursing homes, or institutions of higher education; publications, audiovisual projects, or video productions, however, consideration may be given when they fall within a promising project.

Geographic Focus: Ohio

Date(s) Application is Due: Jan 31; Apr 16; Jul 16; Sep 15

Contact: Ann Fairhurst, (440) 354-3956; aFairhurst@CleveFdn.org

Internet: http://www.clevelandfoundation.org/grants/lake-geauga-fund/

Sponsor: Cleveland Foundation
1422 Euclid Avenue, Suite 1300
Cleveland, OH 44115

Cleveland Foundation Neighborhood Connections Grants 1171

Neighborhood Connections is a small-grants and grassroots community-building program created by the Cleveland Foundation in 2003. Neighborhood Connections awards small grants of less than $5,000 to fund citizen-led neighborhood projects, events, and activities that benefit Cleveland and East Cleveland. While most foundations solely extend grants to nonprofit organizations, Neighborhood Connections grants are awarded to residents themselves to support the ideas of everyday people to make life better, right where they live. Grants may be used for a wide array of activities and projects, and groups are encouraged to think in new ways about what will work in their communities and with whom they might partner.

Requirements: Funding is available for programs or events that take place in Cleveland and in East Cleveland. Any resident-led or community group is eligible to apply, including those that aren't an official nonprofit organization. Grant applicants that do not have an official nonprofit status must identify a fiscal agent. A fiscal agent is a 501(c)3 organization that will handle the grant money on behalf of the neighborhood group. Grant recipients must secure a dollar-for-dollar match equal to the amount requested from Neighborhood Connections. The match can be in the form of cash, volunteer labor, or donated goods or services. Grant duration is up to one year. A group may only apply for one grant at a time. Grant applications will be accepted twice a year, in February and August. Groups will be notified approximately 10-12 weeks after submitting their application whether they received funding.
Restrictions: The program does not make grants to capital campaigns, endowment funds, for-profit entities, fundraising events, government agencies or departments, individuals, renovations to residential dwellings, lobbying efforts, political groups, religious organizations for religious purposes, or single businesses. No group may receive two grants within a one-year time period.
Geographic Focus: Ohio
Date(s) Application is Due: Feb 9; Aug 9
Amount of Grant: 500 - 5,000 USD
Contact: Cynthia Lewis, Grants Manager and Office Administrator; (216) 615-7582; clewis@neighborhoodgrants.org or neighborhoodconnections@clevefdn.org
Internet: http://www.neighborhoodgrants.org/
Sponsor: Cleveland Foundation
1422 Euclid Avenue, Suite 1300
Cleveland, OH 44115

Cleveland H. Dodge Foundation Grants 1172
The foundation awards grants to support projects and programs of educational and charitable nonprofit organizations concerned with the training and development of youth. Grants also are awarded to organizations for programs and projects addressing global overpopulation. Types of support include building and renovation, equipment acquisition, endowment funds, and matching funds.
Requirements: IRS 501(c)3 nonprofit organizations are eligible.
Restrictions: Individuals may not apply.
Geographic Focus: All States
Date(s) Application is Due: Jan 15; Apr 15; Oct 15
Amount of Grant: 100 - 25,000 USD
Contact: Phyllis Criscuoli; (718) 543-1221; fax (718) 543-0737; info@chdodgefoundation.org
Sponsor: Cleveland H. Dodge Foundation
670 W 247th Street
Bronx, NY 10471

CLIF Bar Family Foundation Grants 1173
The foundation's mission is to support nonprofits - grassroots organizations in particular - working to promote environmental restoration and conservation, sustainable food and agriculture, people's health, and a wide range of social concerns. It focuses on organizations whose missions support environmental restoration and conservation, sustainable food and agriculture, people's health and youth.
Requirements: The foundation funds nonprofit organizations working on projects that are well informed, have clearly defined objectives, demonstrate strong community ties, and promote values such as compassion, inclusiveness, patience, and positive development both in the program and in its implementation. Emphasis is on grassroots organizations that have the ability to engage local groups, positively impact their communities, and focus most of their resources on useful and positive actions.
Restrictions: Applications that require funding in less then 12 weeks will not be accepted. The foundation will not fund: Deficit financing; Loans or grants to individuals; Capital construction; Research projects, conferences, seminars, media events or workshops, unless they are an integral part of a broader program; State agencies; Religious groups; Individual Sponsorships; Fundraising events for your organization such as fun runs, bike rides, etc. If you are a local/regional branch of a national organization they will not fund grants to local chapters if they fund the national organization. Otherwise, they only take into consideration local offices in Northern California.
Geographic Focus: All States
Contact: Kit Crawford; (510) 859-2283; fax (510) 588-5490; familyfoundation@clifbar.com
Internet: http://clifbarfamilyfoundation.org/subtemplate.php?s=1
Sponsor: CLIF Bar Family Foundation
1610 5th Street
Berkeley, CA 94710

Clinton County Community Foundation Grants 1174
The Clinton County Community Foundation is a catalyst for stimulating and funding initiatives that improve the quality of life for citizens of Clinton County. The Foundation Grants address needs that generally fall into the following categories: health and medical; social services; education; cultural affairs; civic affairs; and community beautification.
Requirements: All applicants must receive pre-qualification prior to submitting an application by submitting a letter of inquiry to the Program Director. The letter should contain a brief statement of the applicant's needs for assistance, estimate of total cost of project, and enough information to enable the Foundation to determine if the application falls within the guidelines of its grants program. If the grant application is decided, organizations must submit one original application, plus ten copies required for review by the grantmaking committee with the following information included: grant application with the cover page; project budget; board list; evidence of board approval; 501(c)3 letter; year-end audit or financial statement; current month and year-to-date financial statement; and when applicable, three estimates must be included, one from a Clinton County business. The organization may be contacted for additional information, an interview with the grant making committee, or a possible site visit, and the time period which a grant decision will likely be made.
Geographic Focus: Indiana
Date(s) Application is Due: May 6; Sep 7
Contact: Kim Abney; (765) 454-7298 or (800) 964-0508; kim@cfhoward.org
Internet: http://www.cfclinton.org/grant_seekers_cl.html
Sponsor: Clinton County Community Foundation
215 West Sycamore Street
Kokomo, IN 46901

Clipper Ship Foundation Grants 1175
The foundation awards grants to eligible Massachusetts nonprofit organizations devoted to helping people in their community, especially those with great need, such as children, elderly, homeless, destitute, disabled, and new immigrants. The foundation favors grants for the construction or renovation of physical facilities or other capital projects over operating grants.
Requirements: Massachusetts nonprofit organizations in Greater Boston community and the cities of Brockton and Lawrence are eligible.
Geographic Focus: Massachusetts
Date(s) Application is Due: Feb 13; May 8; Aug 7; Nov 2
Amount of Grant: 5,000 - 25,000 USD
Contact: Kirstie David; (617) 426-7080, ext. 302; kdavid@grantsmanagement.com
Internet: http://www.agmconnect.org/clipper1.html
Sponsor: Clipper Ship Foundation
77 Summer Street, 8th Floor
Boston, MA 02110

Clorox Company Foundation Grants 1176
The Foundation makes grants primarily in its headquarters community of Oakland, California. Clorox manufacturing plants operate small giving programs in their local communities. These programs are administered independently and serve a three- to five-mile radius of the facility. The Foundation concentrates on two focus areas: education/youth development and culture/civic programs. The Foundation may shift funding priorities from year to year.
Requirements: Must be a 501(c)3 nonprofit organization located in Oakland, California.
Restrictions: In general, the Foundation does not fund the following: fund-raising events; athletic events or league sponsorships; field trips, tours and travel expenses; advertising or promotional sponsorships; benefit or raffle tickets; conferences, conventions, meetings; media productions; projects of a national scope; direct assistance to individuals or individual sponsorships; religious-based activities for the purpose of furthering religious doctrine; political parties, organizations, candidates or activities; exclusive membership organizations; association or membership dues; deficits or retroactive funding; capital projects; individual school projects.
Geographic Focus: California
Date(s) Application is Due: Jan 1; Apr 1; Jul 1; Oct 1
Contact: Victoria Jones; (510) 836-3223; cloroxfndt@eastbaycf.org
Internet: http://www.thecloroxcompany.com/community/guidelines.html
Sponsor: Clorox Company Foundation
De Domenico Building, 200 Frank Ogawa Plaza
Oakland, CA 94612

Clowes Fund Grants 1177
Funding is concentrated in the states of Indiana, Washington, Massachusetts, and parts of northern New England. Program interest areas and priorities vary among the different geographic areas: Washington—the arts and art education in the greater Seattle area; Indiana—social services and education in greater Indianapolis (Marion County and the seven surrounding counties), education focus is on primary and secondary schools with an emphasis on classroom instruction; Massachusetts (greater Boston area)—arts, education, and social services. In the area of social services (applicable in Indiana, Massachusetts, and northern New England) the current priority is for projects or programs that address the needs of immigrant and refugee populations, and/or workforce development. Types of support include capacity building, capital, challenge, matching operating, project/program, and seed grants. Requests for funding are limited to one request per organization per calendar year. Organizations that have no prior or recent (within the past five years) grant relationship with the fund must submit a Preliminary Proposal to be considered for funding. Guidelines and application are available online.
Requirements: Nonprofit organizations in northern New England and the metropolitan Indianapolis, IN; Boston, MA; and metropolitan Seattle, WA, areas are eligible.
Restrictions: The fund does not make grants to individuals or for publications, conferences, videos, or seminars. No grants are made to organizations in foreign countries. No grants are made for programs promoting specific religious doctrine. The fund will not accept unsolicited proposals from any organization for operating support. The fund will not accept unsolicited proposals of any sort from colleges and universities.
Geographic Focus: Connecticut, Indiana, Maine, Massachusetts, New Hampshire, Rhode Island, Vermont, Washington
Date(s) Application is Due: Jan 31; Nov 1
Amount of Grant: 10,000 - 50,000 USD
Contact: Elizabeth Casselman, Program Manager; (800) 943-7209 or (317) 833-0144; fax (317) 833-0145; staff@clowesfund.org
Internet: http://www.clowesfund.org/index.asp?p=3
Sponsor: Clowes Fund
320 N Meridian, Suite 316
Indianapolis, IN 46204

CMA Foundation Grants 1178

The foundation seeks to improve the quality of life for central Ohio residents through the promotion of wellness, prevention of disease, and delivery of services and research. The foundation will review funding requests for matching or challenge grants, multiyear commitments, and capital expenditures on a project-by-project basis. The foundation is the leading local source of funding for health care projects benefiting the local community. Application may be made online.
Requirements: Nonprofit organizations in central Ohio, including Franklin, Delaware, Fairfield, Licking, Madison, Pickaway, and Union Counties, are eligible.
Geographic Focus: Ohio
Contact: Program Contact; (614) 240-7410; yourthoughts@goodhealthcolumbus.org
Internet: http://www.cmaf-ohio.org/cmaf/grants.html
Sponsor: Columbus Medical Association Foundation
431 E Broad Street
Columbus, OH 43215

CNA Foundation Grants 1179

The CNA Foundation concentrates its support primarily in programs designed to: meet the education needs of children, assist and support children, youth and adults in developing vocational skills. Support economically disadvantaged children and families. Requests for funding are accepted year-round. However, grants will be made only in accordance with the Foundation's budgetary guidelines. Proposals must be clear and brief. The Foundation will contact the organization if more information is needed.
Requirements: IRS 501(c)3 tax-exempt organizations are eligible.
Restrictions: Grants are not made to/for individuals; political causes, candidates, or organizations; veterans, labor, alumni, military, athletic clubs, or social clubs; sectarian organizations or denominational religious organizations; capital improvement or building projects; endowed chairs or professorships; United Way-affiliated agencies; or national groups whose local chapters have already received support.
Geographic Focus: All States
Amount of Grant: 10,000 - 250,000 USD
Samples: Chicago 2016 Exploratory Committee, Chicago, IL, $250,000; National Chamber Foundation, Washington, DC, $100,000; Starlight Starbright Childrens Foundation Midwest, Chicago, IL, $50,000.
Contact: Marlene Rotstein, Director; (312) 822-7065; marlene.rotstein@cna.com or cna_foundation@cna.com
Internet: http://www.cna.com/portal/site/cna/menuitem.7204aaf0316757e8715f09f6556631a0/?vgnextoid=b1e940fa11056010VgnVCM1000005566130aRCRD
Sponsor: CNA Foundation
333 South Wabash Avenue
Chicago, IL 60604

CNCS AmeriCorps Indian Tribes Planning Grants 1180

AmeriCorps planning grants provide up to $75,000 for a one-year period to provide support to an Indian Tribe for the development of an AmeriCorps program that will engage AmeriCorps members in order to address pressing community problems. Planning grant recipients are expected to be better prepared to compete for an AmeriCorps program grant in the following grant cycle. Planning grants may not be used to support AmeriCorps members. An AmeriCorps member is an individual (recruited by an AmeriCorps grant program) who is enrolled in an approved national service position and engages in community service. Members may receive a living allowance and other benefits while serving. Upon successful completion of their service members receive a Segal AmeriCorps Education Award from the National Service Trust. CNCS is targeting AmeriCorps funding in the Education, Disaster Services, Economic Opportunity and Veterans and Military Families Focus Areas. Applications are due May 30.
Requirements: Applicants must be a federally recognized Indian Tribe, band, nation, or other organized group or community, including any Native village, Regional Corporation, or Village Corporation.
Restrictions: Planning grants may not be used to support AmeriCorps members. Project start dates may not occur prior to the date of award. Organizations that have been convicted of a Federal crime are not eligible to apply. Indian Tribe applicants must not have previously received an AmeriCorps grant.
Geographic Focus: All States
Date(s) Application is Due: May 30
Amount of Grant: Up to 75,000 USD
Contact: Vielka Garibaldi, Director for Grants Review Operations; (202) 606-7508 or (202) 606-6886; americorpsgrants@cns.gov
Internet: http://www.nationalservice.gov/build-your-capacity/grants/funding-opportunities/2013/americorps-indian-tribes-planning-grants
Sponsor: Corporation for National and Community Service
1201 New York Avenue, NW
Washington, DC 20525

CNCS AmeriCorps NCCC Project Grants 1181

Modeled after the Civilian Conservation Corps of the 1930s and the U.S. military, AmeriCorps NCCC (National Civilian Community Corps) was enacted in 1993 as a demonstration program and is currently a full-time, team-based, ten-month residential program for men and women ages 18–24. While NCCC teams resemble their CCC predecessors, who also functioned under rugged conditions for prolonged periods and engaged in strenuous conservation, wildfire-fighting, flood-control, and disaster-relief projects, the NCCC was not created to be a public-work-relief program, but rather was designed to help communities meet self-identified needs through service projects. The stated mission of AmeriCorps NCCC is "to strengthen communities and develop leaders through direct team-based national and community service." NCCC service projects normally last six to eight weeks and address community needs in the following program areas: natural and other disasters; infrastructure improvement; environmental stewardship and conservation; energy conservation; and urban and rural development. AmeriCorps NCCC has five regional campuses located in Perry Point, Maryland; Denver, Colorado; Sacramento, California; Vicksburg, Mississippi; and Vinton, Iowa. These campuses are the hubs from which AmeriCorps NCCC operates and deploys corps members in teams of eight to twelve to service projects around the country. Each campus serves as a headquarters for its multi-state region and can lodge and feed its entire regional corps, which ranges in size from 150 to 500 members. The staffs at the campuses support both the corps members and project sponsors as they engage in service activities. Members are given a living allowance of approximately $4,000 for 10 months of service; housing; meals; limited medical benefits; up to $400 a month for childcare if eligible; member uniforms; and become eligible for the Segal AmeriCorps Education Award upon successful completion of the program.
Requirements: The following organizations are eligible to apply for NCCC resources: non-profits, secular and faith based; local municipalities; state governments; federal government; national or state parks; Indian tribes; and schools. Projects must be capable of using at least one full team of eight to twelve members effectively. Transportation and some basic tools will be provided by the NCCC; however, project sponsors are required to provide materials, specialized tools, orientation, training, and technical supervision.
Geographic Focus: All States
Contact: Kate Raftery, Director, Office of AmeriCorps NCCC; (202) 606-6706
Erma Hodge, Executive Assistant
Internet: http://www.nationalservice.gov/programs/americorps/americorps-nccc
Sponsor: Corporation for National and Community Service
1201 New York Avenue, NW
Washington, DC 20525

CNCS AmeriCorps State and National Grants 1182

AmeriCorps State and National is the broadest of the AmeriCorps programs and, like other programs administered by the Corporation for National and Community Service (the Corporation), has recently been expanded under the Edward Kennedy Serve America Act (SAA). The SAA increases the annual number of persons volunteering in the Corporations's programs from 75,000 to 250,000 by 2017 and incorporates five new service corps into AmeriCorps State and National: a Clean Energy Corps to encourage energy efficiency and conservation; an Education Corps to help increase student engagement, achievement and graduation; a Healthy Futures Corps to improve health care access; a Veterans Service Corps to enhance services for veterans; and a Opportunity Corps. AmeriCorps State and National engages its volunteers (members) with local sponsors in direct service and capacity-building to address critical community needs, usually under the arrangement that AmeriCorps covers expenses of the volunteers and the sponsor covers costs of the program. Sponsors are expected to design service activities for AmeriCorps teams of eight to twelve members serving full- or part-time for one year or during the summer. Sample service activities include tutoring and mentoring youth, providing job-placement assistance to unemployed individuals, addressing childhood obesity through in-school and after-school physical activities, and weatherizing and retrofitting housing units for low-income households. AmeriCorps State and National Grants cover a wide range of grants. National opportunities are announced through Notices at the AmeriCorps website or at www.grants.gov. Regional funding opportunites are announced through the various AmeriCorps State Commissions, which are governor-appointed agencies that have direct accountability for local AmeriCorps programs in each state. Types of grants may include the following: Competitive State Grants, Professional Corps Grants, EAP (Educational Award Program) Fixed grants and Non-EAP Full-Time Fixed grants. A brief breakdown of these follows. Competitive State Grants are awarded to fund a portion of program costs and members' living allowance. Professional Corps Grants are awarded to pay a portion of program costs to place AmeriCorps members as teachers, health care providers, police officers, engineers, or other professionals in communities where there is a documented shortage of such professionals. EAP Fixed Grants are awarded to applicants that apply for a small fixed-amount grant and use their own or other resources for the majority of members' living allowance and program costs. (EAPs may enroll less-than-full-time members.) Non-EAP Full-time Fixed-amount Grant are awarded to applicants who apply for a fixed amount per Member Service Year (MSY) and use their own or other resources for the remaining cost of the program. Additionally, AmeriCorps State and National offers a "fit-finder" tool at their website which will help organizations match their program or project to the right State and National grant and will then take them directly to the latest applicable Notice for that grant. The fit-finder lists available types of State and National grants as follows: State Grants; National Direct Grants; EAP Grants; and Indian Tribe Grants. (The fit finder is located at http://www.americorps.gov/fitfinder/index.html.) As with types of grants offered, methods of applying may also vary, depending on the sponsor's program or project scope. Single-state applicants must contact their State Commission for instructions and deadlines (contact information for all the State Commissions is available at the AmeriCorps website). Single state applicants must apply directly to their State Commission. State Commissions then forward the projects they select to the Corporation to compete for funding. Organizations proposing to operate in more than one state or organizations operating in states and territories without Commissions must apply directly to the Corporation. (Multi-state applicants are also required to consult with the State Commission of each state in which they plan to operate prior to application submission.) Indian Tribes may apply through their State Commissions, or directly to the Corporation (the Corporation sets aside one percent of grant funds to support programs operated by Indian Tribes). State commissions, multi-state applicants, and Indian Tribes are encouraged to send an email to americorpsgrants@cns.gov, stating intent to apply. Commission sub-applicants should not provide this information. The Corporation requires applicants to submit applications electronically via the Corporation's web-based application system, eGrants. Applicants should draft the application as a word processing document, then copy and paste the document into eGrants no later than 10 days before the deadline. The Corporation may consider an application after the deadline, but only if the applicant submits a letter explaining the extenuating circumstance which caused the delay. The letter must be sent to LateApplications@cns.gov within the 24-hour period following the deadline. Late applications are evaluated on a case-by-case basis. If extenuating circumstances make the use of eGrants impossible, applicants may send a hard copy of the application to the contact information given in the Notice. Hard copy applications must include a cover letter detailing the circumstances that make it impossible to submit via e-Grants. Grant awards are typically awarded for three years, with funding in annual increments. Grantees will be eligible for non-competitive continuation funding in the second and third year contingent on satisfactory performance, compliance, and availability of appropriations. In awarding funds, CNCS considers continuation grants first, followed by new and re-competing grants.

Requirements: Eligible organizations are as follows: public or private nonprofit organizations, including faith-based and other community organizations; institutions of higher education; government entities within states or territories (e.g., cities, counties); Indian Tribes; labor organizations; partnerships and consortia; and intermediaries planning to subgrant funds awarded. Applicants must register with the Central Contractor's Registry (CCR) and include a Dun and Bradstreet Data Universal Numbering System (DUNS) number on their application. These may be obtained at no cost by calling the DUNS number request line at (866) 705-5711 or by applying online. The website indicates a 24-hour email turnaround time on requests for DUNS numbers; however, the Corporation suggests registering at least 30 days in advance of the application due date. AmeriCorps State and National Grants have varying match requirements. There is no match requirement for fixed-amount grants. Cost reimbursement grants (non-fixed-amount) are required to match at 24 percent for the first three-year funding period. Starting with year four, the match requirement gradually increases every year to 50 percent by year ten. (Living allowances or salaries provided to Professional Corps AmeriCorps members do not count toward the matching requirement.) Indian Tribal Government programs are subject to the same matching requirements for fixed-amount and cost reimbursement grants. However, Tribal governments may under some circumstances apply for a Tribal waiver. Under certain circumstances, applicants may qualify to meet alternative matching requirements that increase over the years to 35 percent instead of 50 percent. To qualify, applicants must demonstrate that the proposed program is either located in a rural county or in a severely economically distressed community as defined in the Application Instructions. Applicants that plan to request an alternative match schedule must submit a request at least 60 days prior to the application deadline.

Restrictions: The Corporation will encourage organizations that have never received funding from them or AmeriCorps to apply for the grants described in their Notices. The general practice is to award no more than 50 member slots for new grantees. Organizations that have been convicted of a Federal crime are disqualified from receiving these grants. Grants under this program, except for fixed-amount and EAP grants, are subject to the applicable

Geographic Focus: All States
Date(s) Application is Due: Jan 18
Amount of Grant: 6,400 - 159,600 USD
Contact: Vielka Garibaldi; (202) 606-7508 or (202) 606-6886; americorpsgrants@cns.gov
Internet: http://www.nationalservice.gov/programs/americorps/americorps-state-and-national
Sponsor: Corporation for National and Community Service
1201 New York Avenue, NW
Washington, DC 20525

CNCS AmeriCorps State and National Planning Grants 1183

AmeriCorps is a funding stream of the Corporation for National and Community Service (the Corporation) and includes the national-service programs AmeriCorps Vista, AmeriCorps NCCC, and AmeriCorps State and National. The latter is the broadest of the AmeriCorps programs and, like the rest, has recently been expanded under the Edward Kennedy Serve America Act of 2009 (SAA), which proposes an increase from 75,000 to 250,000 annual volunteers. The SAA incorporates five new service corps into the AmeriCorps State and National program: a Clean Energy Corps to encourage energy efficiency and conservation; an Education Corps to help increase student engagement, achievement and graduation; a Healthy Futures Corps to improve health care access; a Veterans Service Corps to enhance services for veterans; and an Opportunity Corps. The ultimate purpose of the AmeriCorps State and National program is to engage AmeriCorps volunteers (members) with local sponsors in direct service and capacity building to address critical community needs, usually under a cost-sharing arrangement where AmeriCorps covers expenses of the volunteers and the sponsor covers costs of the program. AmeriCorps planning grants support sponsors in developing candidate programs to engage AmeriCorps members in evidence-based interventions to solve community problems. Planning-grant recipients are expected to be better prepared to compete for an AmeriCorps program grant in the following grant cycle. Planning grants may not be used to support AmeriCorps members. Planning-grant project periods last up to one year in duration. The process of competing for federal funding in general is as follows. Types of funding offered by federal programs are set forth in the program's enabling legislation. Grant competitions for a program's funding tend to follow congressional budget and appropriations cycles (as well as multi-year funding cycles in some cases) and are announced through various Notices which provide details, guidelines, and deadlines for the competition. Notices are posted at AmeriCorp's and www.grants.gov websites. A subscription link is also provided at these sites for prospective applicants to be notified via email of upcoming grant competitions. In addition to statutory priorities, the Corporation determines priorities to focus each grant competition. Priorities are drawn from among the Corporation's strategic service areas which include education, healthy futures, environmental stewardship, veterans and military families, economic opportunity, and disaster preparedness (with special consideration given to activities that support and engage veterans and military families). Additionally Congress has set a goal that 10% of AmeriCorps funding should support encore service programs. To meet this target, the Corporation encourages programs that plan to engage a significant number of participants age fifty-five and older to apply. Sponsors that propose to operate an AmeriCorps program in one state only must contact the appropriate State Commission for application materials and must submit their application through that Commission. (State Commissions are organizations appointed by state governors to assume accountability for all AmeriCorps projects within their state.) Contact information for all the State Commissions is available at the AmeriCorps and Corporation websites. Sponsors that propose to operate in more than one state should apply directly to the Corporation. However, multi-state planning applicants must consult with the State Commission of each state in which the organization plans to operate an AmeriCorps program prior to application submission. Grant applications are submitted via eGrants, the Corporation's web-based system for grant application and management. Generally a series of technical assistance calls or workshops will be offered before the application is due. The dates of these will be posted at the Corporation's website. Applications are due no later than 5 p.m. eastern time on the deadline date. Prospective applicants must create an account at the eGrant website (link available at the Corporation website). Applicants are advised to do this at least three weeks prior to the application-submission deadline. Applicants are advised to draft the application as a word-processing document, then copy and paste the document into eGrants no later than ten days before the deadline. If extenuating circumstances make electronic submission impossible, applicants should send a hard copy of their application via overnight carrier (non-U.S. Postal Service because of security–related delays in receiving mail from the U.S. Postal Service). Hard-copy applications must include a cover letter detailing the circumstances that make it impossible to submit via e-Grants. Late applications may be accepted only if the applicant submits a letter via email to LateApplications@cns.gov within the 24-hour period following the deadline explaining the extenuating circumstance which caused the delay. Late applications are evaluated on a case-by-case basis. Application and other deadlines may vary from competition to competition. Prospective applicants are encouraged to verify current deadline dates. Notices of Intent are generally requested rather than required and are used to help the Corporation plan the review process.

Requirements: Eligible applicants include public or private nonprofit organizations (including faith-based and other community organizations); institutions of higher education; government entities within states or territories (e.g., cities, counties); Indian Tribes; labor organizations; partnerships and consortia; and intermediaries planning to subgrant funds awarded. Applicants must provide 24% of the total project cost in cash or in-kind. Indian Tribal Government programs are subject to the same matching requirements but may submit a waiver request. This must be done at least 60 days before the AmeriCorps application is due. Instructions are available by emailing TribalMatchWaiver@cns.gov. Applicants must include a Dun and Bradstreet Data Universal Numbering System (DUNS) number on their applications and register with the Central Contractor's Registry (CCR). The DUNS number does not replace an Employer Identification Number (EIN). DUNS numbers may be obtained at no cost by calling the DUNS number request line at (866) 705-5711 or by applying online: http://fedgov.dnb.com/webform. The website indicates a 24-hour email turnaround time; however, the Corporation suggests registering at least 30 days in advance of the application due date.

Restrictions: Project start dates may not occur prior to the date of award. Organizations that have been convicted of a Federal crime are not eligible to apply. Single-state planning applicants must not have previously received an AmeriCorps State grant. Multi-state planning applicants must not have previously received a multi-state AmeriCorps grant.

Geographic Focus: All States
Date(s) Application is Due: Jan 18
Amount of Grant: Up to 50,000 USD
Contact: Vielka Garibaldi; (202) 606-7508 or (202) 606-6886; americorpsgrants@cns.gov
John Gomperts, Director, AmeriCorps State and National; (202) 606-6790 or (202) 606-5000; americorpsgrants@cns.gov
Internet: http://www.nationalservice.gov/programs/americorps/americorps-state-and-national
Sponsor: Corporation for National and Community Service
1201 New York Avenue, NW
Washington, DC 20525

CNCS AmeriCorps VISTA Project Grants 1184

AmeriCorps VISTA is a national-service program of the Corporation for National and Community Service (the Corporation) which oversees a variety of programs including other AmeriCorps programs, SeniorCorps programs, and Learn and Serve America programs. Designed specifically to fight poverty, VISTA was authorized in 1964 as Volunteers in Service to America. The program was incorporated into the AmeriCorps network of programs in 1993. VISTA supports efforts to alleviate poverty by encouraging volunteers (members), ages 18 years and older, from all walks of life, to engage in a year of full-time service with a sponsoring organization (sponsor) to create or expand programs designed to bring individuals and communities out of poverty. Under this arrangement, the Corporation places a team of VISTA members with a sponsor; the sponsor funds local operating and logistics costs of the project while the Corporation covers member and certain sponsor costs as follows: a biweekly living allowance for members; a Segal AmeriCorps Education Award or post-service stipend for members; health coverage for members; a moving allowance for members relocating to serve; liability coverage for members under the Federal Employees Compensation Act and the Federal Torts Claims Act; childcare (for income-eligible members); FICA; payroll services (members receive their paychecks directly from AmeriCorps VISTA); training in project management and leadership for VISTA members and project supervisors; and assistance for sponsors to recruit VISTA members. Applications for VISTA resources are handled by Corporation State Offices which are federal offices staffed by federal employees in the states. (A list of the offices along with their contact information is available at the AmeriCorps website.) Applying for VISTA resources is a two-step process. As step one, the organization must submit a VISTA Concept Paper. If the concept paper is accepted, the organization must, as step two, submit a VISTA Project Application. Applicants will receive their project-application materials when their concept paper has been approved. The length of the application process varies, but the average length of time from the initial contact to a final decision is three to five months. Both concept papers and project applications are usually

submitted using eGrants, the Corporation's web-based system for applications. Organizations must visit the eGrant website (link available at the AmeriCorps website) to create an account prior to submitting concept papers. Organizations that cannot submit using eGrants may submit a paper copy. The forms are included in the downloadable Concept-Paper Instructions document at the AmeriCorps website. As of this writing, VISTA is giving priority to new projects that focus on the areas of housing, financial literacy, and employment.
Requirements: Public organizations such as nonprofit private organizations, Indian Tribes, state and local government organizations, and institutions of higher education can apply to be VISTA sponsors. Eligible nonprofit private organizations are not limited to those with IRS 501(c)3 status, but rather all organizations with IRS 501(c) status that focus on anti-poverty community development. Project sponsors are encouraged (but not required) to provide a financial match; however they must be able to direct the project, supervise the volunteers, and provide necessary administrative support to complete the goals and objectives of the project. Projects must be developed in accordance with all four of the VISTA Core Principles: Anti-Poverty Focus, Community Empowerment, Sustainable Solutions, and Capacity Building. All VISTA resources must be used to create, expand, or enhance projects that lift people out of poverty. Additionally, the Corporation has identified, in its strategic plan, six focus areas for funding: Economic Opportunity; Education; Healthy Futures; Veterans and Military Families; Disaster Services; and Environmental Stewardship. All new VISTA project development must fall within these six focus areas. As of this writing, the Corporation will direct most VISTA resources to the Economic Opportunity and Education focus areas; however, the Corporation will also address the other focus areas, according to the ability of Corporation State Offices to identify opportunities in those areas that can have a direct impact on breaking the cycle of poverty.
Geographic Focus: All States
Contact: Mary Strasser; (202) 606-6943 or (202) 606-5000
Kathy Little, Program Assistant; (202) 606-6852 or (202) 606-5000
Internet: http://www.nationalservice.gov/programs/americorps/americorps-vista
Sponsor: Corporation for National and Community Service
1201 New York Avenue, NW
Washington, DC 20525

CNCS Foster Grandparent Projects Grants 1185
The Foster Grandparent Program (FGP) began in 1965 as a national demonstration effort to show how low-income persons aged sixty or over have the maturity and experience to establish a personal relationship with children having either exceptional or special needs. Originally established under the Economic Opportunity Act of 1964 the FGP was operated first as an employment program and eventually as a stipended volunteer program under various federal offices and agencies. Currently RSVP is administered through the Corporation for National and Community Service (the Corporation)'s Senior Corps program. Dual purposes of the RSVP are to provide part-time volunteer service opportunities for income-eligible persons ages fifty-five and over and to give supportive person-to-person assistance in health, education, human-services, and related settings to help address the physical, mental, and emotional needs of special/exceptional-needs infants, children, or youth. The Corporation accepts FGP grant applications only when new funding is available or when it is necessary to replace an existing sponsor. In addition, eligible agencies or organizations may, under a Memorandum of Agreement with the Corporation, receive technical assistance and materials to aid in establishing and operating a non-federally-funded FGP project using local funds. Notices for nationwide competitions for new FGP grants are posted at www.grants.gov and at the Corporation and Senior Corps websites. (Subscription links for receiving RSS feeds on new funding opportunities are also available at the websites.) Notices for applicants to replace a sponsor are advertised locally through Corporation State Offices. (A list of the offices along with their contact information is available at the Corporation website.) Grant applications are submitted through the Corporation's eGrants system. For more information, interested applicants may download the FGP Handbook from the Senior Corps and Corporation websites or contact their Corporation State Office.
Requirements: The Corporation awards grants to public agencies, Indian tribes, and secular or faith-based private non-profit organizations in the United States that have authority to accept and the capacity to administer a Foster Grandparent project. The FGP requires a non-federal share of 10% of the total project cost. FGP projects are generally expected and required to be on-going. FGP sponsors may apply for continued funding from the Corporation.
Geographic Focus: All States
Amount of Grant: 250,000 USD
Contact: Wanda Carney; (202) 606-6934 or (202) 606-5000
Internet: http://www.nationalservice.gov/build-your-capacity/grants/managing-senior-corps-grants
Sponsor: Corporation for National and Community Service
1201 New York Avenue, NW
Washington, DC 20525

CNCS School Turnaround AmeriCorps Grants 1186
The School Turnaround AmeriCorps program supports the placement of a dedicated cadre of AmeriCorps members from the Corporation for National and Community Service (CNCS) in persistently underachieving schools across the country. These AmeriCorps members will be serving in schools implementing school turnaround interventions as required by Department of Education's (ED) School Improvement Grant (SIG) program or as required through Elementary and Secondary Education Act (ESEA) flexibility. Members will help keep students on track to graduate by working to increase student academic achievement, attendance and high school graduation rates; improve college and career readiness; and provide college enrollment assistance and advisement. School Turnaround AmeriCorps will be supported by an initial investment of $15 million in public funds from both agencies and leverage an anticipated $18 million in grantee match funding during a three-year cycle. In addition, AmeriCorps members who complete their service in the program will qualify for a Segal AmeriCorps Education Award, which could total $1.5 million a year for all participants.
Requirements: The program supports organizations that serve low-performing schools around the country, including those in rural areas, and expands on the efforts of Together for Tomorrow, an initiative between ED, CNCS, and the White House Office of Faith-based and Neighborhood Partnerships.
Geographic Focus: All States
Contact: School Turnaround Coordinator; (202) 606-5000 or (800) 942-2677
Internet: http://www.nationalservice.gov/programs/americorps/school-turnaround-americorps
Sponsor: Corporation for National and Community Service
1201 New York Avenue, NW
Washington, DC 20525

CNCS Senior Companion Program Grants 1187
The Senior Companions Program (SCP) was established in 1973 under Title II of the Domestic Volunteer Services Act (DVSA) to provide opportunities for older adult volunteers to assist other older adults and persons with disabilities, who, without support, might not be able to live independently. Eighteen model Senior Companion projects were funded initially. Today that number has grown to 223 projects with more than 15,000 volunteers who serve through nonprofit and public organizations (local sponsors) to help home-bound clients with chores such as light housekeeping, paying bills, buying groceries, and finding transportation to medical appointments. SCP volunteers serve from fifteen to forty hours a week and receive hourly stipends. They must be fifty-five or older and meet established income eligibility guidelines. In addition to the stipend, they receive accident, personal-liability, and excess-automobile insurance coverage; assistance with the cost of transportation; an annual physical examination; recognition; and, as feasible, meals during their assignments. Volunteers receive training in how to assist persons diagnosed with Alzheimer's disease, stroke, diabetes, mental illness, etc., as well as when to alert doctors and family members to potential health problems. Currently SCP is administered through the Corporation for National and Community Service (the Corporation)'s Senior Corps Program. The Corporation accepts SCP grant applications only when new funding is available or when it is necessary to replace an existing sponsor. In addition, eligible agencies or organizations may, under a Memorandum of Agreement with the Corporation, receive technical assistance and materials to aid in establishing and operating a non-federally-funded SCP project using local funds. Notices for nationwide competitions for new SCP grants are posted at www.grants.gov and at the Corporation and Senior Corps websites. (Subscription links for receiving RSS feeds on new funding opportunities are also available at the websites.) Notices to apply to replace a sponsor are advertised locally through Corporation State Offices. (A list of the offices along with their contact information is available at the Corporation website.) Grant applications are submitted through the Corporation's eGrants system. For more information, interested applicants may download the SCP Handbook from the Senior Corps and Corporation websites or contact their Corporation State Office.
Requirements: The Corporation awards grants to public agencies, Indian tribes, and secular or faith-based private non-profit organizations in the United States that have authority to accept and the capacity to administer an SCP project. The SCP requires a non-federal share of 10% of the total project cost. SCP projects are generally expected and required to be on-going. SCP Sponsors may apply for continued funding from the Corporation.
Restrictions: The total of cost reimbursements for Senior Companions, including stipends, insurance, transportation, meals, physical examinations, uniforms if appropriate, and recognition must be equal to at least 80 percent of the Corporation's Federal share of the grant. (Federal and non-Federal resources, including excess non-Corporation resources, can be used to make up this sum.) Key legislative pieces enabling and regulating the SCP have been the Domestic Volunteer Service Act (DVSA) of 1973, the National and Community Service Trust Act (1993), 45 C.F.R. § 1216 (non-displacement of contracts and employed workers), the Edward Kennedy Serve America Act, and 45 C.F.R. § 2551. SCP funding generally requires an Office of Management and Budget (OMB) audit.
Geographic Focus: All States
Amount of Grant: 100,000 - 300,000 USD
Contact: Wanda Carney; (202) 606-6934 or (202) 606-5000
Internet: http://www.nationalservice.gov/build-your-capacity/grants/managing-senior-corps-grants
Sponsor: Corporation for National and Community Service
1201 New York Avenue, NW
Washington, DC 20525

CNCS Senior Corps Retired and Senior Volunteer Program Grants 1188
The Retired and Senior Volunteer Program (RSVP), one of the largest volunteer efforts in the nation, has matched local problems with older adults who are willing to help since 1971. Each year nearly 430,000 older adults (ages fifty-five and over) provide community service through more than 740 locally-sponsored RSVP projects. RSVP volunteers serve through nonprofit and public organizations (local sponsors) to organize neighborhood watch programs, tutor children and teenagers, renovate homes, teach English to immigrants, teach computer software applications, help people recover from natural disasters, serve as museum docents—and do whatever else their skills and interests lead them to do to meet the needs of their community. While RSVP volunteers do not receive any monetary incentive or stipend, they may be reimbursed for certain out-of-pocket costs associated with their service activities. In addition, RSVP volunteers receive accident, personal-liability, and excess-automobile insurance, as well as community recognition. Currently RSVP is administered through the Corporation for National and Community Service (the Corporation)'s Senior Corps program. The Corporation solicits applications for new Senior Corps grants (new projects or new sponsors) only when funding is available. The Corporation will notify the public when new grants are being accepted by posting Notices of Funding Availability (NOFA) or Notices of Funding Opportunity (NOFO) at the Senior Corps and Corporation websites and at www.

grants.gov. (Subscription links for receiving RSS feeds on new funding opportunities are also available at these websites.) The application process for an RSVP grant begins with submission of a concept paper which will be used to select applicants who will then be invited to submit a full application. Applicants apply through the Corporation's online eGrants system, the link to which is available at the website. Use of eGrants requires setting up an account; the Corporation strongly recommends that applicants create their accounts at least three weeks prior to the submission deadline. Concept papers and full applications must be received by the Corporation by 5:00 p.m. (eastern standard time) on the applicable deadline in order to be considered. (Exceptions may apply under special circumstances; documentation is required.) Deadline dates may vary from funding opportunity to funding opportunity; organizations are encouraged to always verify current deadline dates. For more information, interested applicants may download the RSVP Handbook from the Corporation and Senior Corps websites or contact their Corporation State Office (a list of the state offices along with their contact information is available at the Corporation website).
Requirements: Eligible applicants include public agencies (e.g. state and local agencies and other units of government), non-profit organizations (both faith-based and secular), institutions of higher education, and Indian Tribes. New applicants may propose only to establish a new RSVP project in a geographic area unserved by a current RSVP grantee. Matching is required as follows: new RSVP applicants must budget and raise ten percent of their total project budget in year one, twenty percent in year two, and thirty percent in year three and subsequent years (if the grant is renewed beyond three years). All applications must include a Dun and Bradstreet Data Universal Numbering System (DUNS) number. The DUNS number does not replace the Employer Identification Number. DUNS numbers may be obtained at no cost by calling the DUNS number request line at (866) 705-5711 or by applying online. Either way, the Corporation suggests registering at least 30 days in advance of the application due date. Key programmatic requirements to consider are as follows. At a minimum, 20 percent of a sponsor's or project's RSVP volunteers must be placed in assignments to recruit other community volunteers, thus expanding the capacity of local non-profits to meet their missions. Additionally, all RSVP volunteers must be placed in assignments that address one or more of the 16 categories of community needs identified in the Domestic Volunteer Service Act as "Programs of National Significance (PNS)." In particular the Corporation is interested in supporting the following volunteer activities: providing in-home, non-medical independent-living support to those in need of extra help, including frail seniors, veterans of recent conflicts, and their caregivers; assisting children and youth to succeed academically through provision of mentoring, tutoring, and other assistance to remain in school; and enhancing energy efficiency at home through weatherization of homes, energy audits, or connecting people to related resources and information.
Geographic Focus: All States
Date(s) Application is Due: Feb 22
Amount of Grant: 60,000 - 80,000 USD
Contact: Dr. Erwin Tan; (202) 606-6867 or (800) 424-8867; PNS@cns.gov
Internet: http://www.nationalservice.gov/build-your-capacity/grants/managing-senior-corps-grants
Sponsor: Corporation for National and Community Service
1201 New York Avenue, NW
Washington, DC 20525

CNCS Social Innovation Grants 1189
The CNCS Social Innovation Fund is authorized by the Edward M. Kennedy Serve America Act and is administered by the Corporation for National and Community Service (the Corporation), a federal agency that engages more than five million Americans as volunteers through well-known national-service programs like Senior Corps, AmeriCorps, and Learn and Serve America. The Social Innovation Fund is primarily concerned with advancing social innovation as a key strategy for solving critical social challenges. The program's goal is to identify and help spread those innovative and potentially transformative approaches that have been developed at the local level to solve community problems. An approach is considered transformative if it not only produces strong impact, but also if it: has the potential to affect how the same challenge is addressed in other communities; addresses more than one critical community challenge concurrently; or produces significant cost savings through gains in efficiency. The operating model of the Social Innovation Fund is distinguished by four key elements: reliance on intermediaries with strong skills and track records of success in selecting, validating, and growing high-impact nonprofit organizations; assuring participation from the non-federal stake-holders by requiring each federal dollar be matched 1:1 with money from non-federal sources not only by the intermediaries but also by their subgrantees; requiring that all intermediaries engage each of their subgrantees in formal evaluations of program performance and impact; and requiring each grantee to commit to knowledge sharing and other initiatives that advance social innovation more generally in the nonprofit sector. The SIF makes grant awards of between $1 million and $10 million per year for up to five years to grantmaking intermediaries, selected through a rigorous, open competition. Intermediaries match their federal grants dollar-for-dollar and with those combined funds they then: host open, evidence-based competitions to select nonprofits implementing innovative program models; invest in expanding the capabilities and impact of the nonprofits they select; and support those nonprofits through rigorous evaluation of their programs.
Requirements: Applicants must be an eligible grantmaking institution or partnership in existence at the time of the application. Providing grants to nonprofit community organizations should be central to the applicant's mission and should be clearly reflected in the organization's promotional materials and annual operating budget. Core operations must include conducting open competitive grant competitions, negotiating specific grant requirements with grant recipients; and overseeing and monitoring performance of grant recipients. By statute Social Innovation Fund intermediaries must operate either as geographically-based or as issue-based grantmakers. A geographically-based intermediary will address one or more priority issues withing a single geographic location. An issue-based intermediary will address a single priority issue in multiple geographic locations. At the time of submission, applicants must demonstrate through a letter or other form of documentation that they have either cash-on-hand or commitments (or a combination thereof) toward meeting 50 percent of their first year matching funds.
Restrictions: Intermediaries must distribute at least 80 percent of awarded federal funds to subgrantees, run an open competition that is available to eligible nonprofit organizations beyond the intermediary's own existing grant portfolio or network, and provide sufficient public notice of the availability of Social Innovation Fund subgrants to eligible nonprofit community organizations. Given that innovation funds currently exist in the Departments of Education and Labor to invest specifically in evidence-based programs in education and job training, the Corporation does not intend to make Social Innovation Fund awards to programs in these areas unless they clearly propose a solution to an unmet need as identified in consultation with both Departments. The funding mechanism for Social Innovation Fund awards is a cooperative agreement that provides for substantial involvement by the Corporation with the intermediaries as they carry out approved activities. The assigned Corporation program officer will confer with the grantee on a regular and frequent basis to develop and/or review service delivery and project status, including work plans, budgets, periodic reports, evaluations, etc. In particular the Corporation anticipates having substantial involvement in developing and approving subgrantee selection plans; developing and approving subgrantee evaluation plans; documenting subgrantee growth plans; and documenting and sharing lessons learned through a Corporation-sponsored learning community. Grants under the Social Innovation program are subject to the Cost Principles and Uniform Administration Requirements under the applicable Office of Management and Budget (OMB) Circulars.
Geographic Focus: All States
Date(s) Application is Due: Mar 27
Amount of Grant: 1,000,000 - 5,000,000 USD
Contact: Vielka Garibaldi; (202) 606-5000 or (202) 606-3223; info@cns.gov
Internet: http://www.nationalservice.gov/about/programs/innovation.asp
Sponsor: Corporation for National and Community Service
1201 New York Avenue NW
Washington, DC 20525

CNL Corporate Giving Arts & Culture Grants 1190
The Corporation believes success of any company is closely tied to the accomplishments of the community in which it resides. Each community has its own specific requirements for success. In Central Florida, CNL is not only committed to investing in those needs, but also relying on its business experience and resources to help ensure the area's growth and prosperity. Preference is given to organizations and programs that support arts and culture, such as the Orlando Performing Arts Center and United Arts of Central Florida. Organizations wishing to be considered for a grant may access the grant application online. All applications must be submitted via standard mail. Telephone solicitations will not be considered. Applications are accepted at any time and reviewed quarterly.
Requirements: CNL awards grants to organizations that have been approved by the IRS as 501(c)3 charities and government institutions, such as schools and libraries. Applicant schools should be located in central Florida, with giving emphasis on Orlando.
Geographic Focus: Florida
Contact: Mark W. Amerman, Charitable Grants Manager; (407) 650-1262
Internet: http://www.cnl.com/givesBack/Arts.aspx
Sponsor: CNL Corporation
P.O. Box 4920
Orlando, FL 32802-4920

CNL Corporate Giving Entrepreneurship & Leadership Grants 1191
The Corporation believes it is important to invest in the citizens of today and tomorrow by supporting programs that focus on leadership and entrepreneurship, in school and in the workplace. Organizations wishing to be considered for a grant may access the grant application online. All applications must be submitted via standard mail. Telephone solicitations will not be considered. Applications are accepted at any time and reviewed quarterly.
Requirements: CNL awards grants to organizations that have been approved by the IRS as 501(c)3 charities and government institutions, such as schools and libraries. Applicant schools should be located in central Florida, with giving emphasis on Orlando.
Geographic Focus: Florida
Contact: Mark W. Amerman, Charitable Grants Manager; (407) 650-1262
Internet: http://www.cnl.com/givesBack/Entrepreneurship.aspx
Sponsor: CNL Corporation
P.O. Box 4920
Orlando, FL 32802-4920

Coastal Bend Community Foundation Grants 1192
The community foundation awards grants to nonprofit organizations in the Aransas, Bee, Jim Wells, Kleberg, Nueces, Refugio and San Patricio counties of Texas. Grants are usually made to provide seed money for innovative and start-up programs that will generate additional future funding or revenues. Capital projects will also receive favorable consideration. The board of directors approves grant recipients in early November after considering recommendations presented by the Grants Committee. Areas of interest include alcohol and drug abuse, libraries and literacy, arts and culture, higher and other education, adult basic education, child welfare, hospitals, community development, animal welfare, human services, and general charitable giving. Grants are awarded for general operating support, program and project development, equipment, seed money, scholarship funds, and fellowships. Application forms are not required.
Requirements: Nonprofit organizations in Texas in Aransas, Bee, Jim Wells, Kleberg, Nueces, Refugio, and San Patricio counties, may submit grant proposals.
Geographic Focus: Texas
Date(s) Application is Due: Sep 1

Amount of Grant: 250 - 50,000 USD
Contact: Jim Moloney; (361) 882-9745; fax (361) 882-2865; jmoloney@cbcfoundation.org
Internet: http://www.cbcfoundation.org/grant.html
Sponsor: Coastal Bend Community Foundation
600 Building, Suite 1716
Corpus Christi, TX 78473

Coastal Community Foundation of South Carolina Grants   1193

The foundation awards grants to South Carolina nonprofit organizations in its areas of interest, including arts and culture, education, environment, health, religion, justice and equity, and social services. Types of support include general operating support, emergency funds, program development, publication, seed money, scholarship funds, and technical assistance. Deadlines vary per program; check website for exact dates.
Requirements: 501(c)3 South Carolina nonprofits located in the following coastal counties are eligible to apply: Beaufort, Berkeley, Charleston, Colleton, Dorchester, Georgetown, Hampton and Jasper.
Restrictions: Grants do not support individuals (except for designated scholarship funds), endowments, deficit financing, dinners, and rarely building funds.
Geographic Focus: South Carolina
Date(s) Application is Due: Jun 1
Amount of Grant: 500 - 10,000 USD
Contact: George C. Stevens; (843) 723-3635; fax (843) 577-3671; gstevens@tcfgives.org
Internet: http://www.ccfgives.org
Sponsor: Coastal Community Foundation of South Carolina
90 Mary Street
Charleston, SC 29403

Cobb Family Foundation Grants   1194

The foundation awards grants to Florida nonprofits in its areas of interest, including community development, higher and secondary education, libraries, Protestant religion, recreation, and zoos. Grants are awarded primarily in Dade County.
Requirements: Nonprofit organizations in Florida are eligible to apply.
Geographic Focus: Florida
Amount of Grant: Up to 525,319 USD
Contact: Charles Cobb Jr., (305) 441-1700; fax (305) 445-5674
Sponsor: Cobb Family Foundation
355 Alhambra Circle, Suite 1500
Coral Gables, FL 33134

Coca-Cola Foundation Grants   1195

The foundation has established education as its philanthropic focus and set aside most of its funds to support educational initiatives that address pressing needs. To help prepare youth for life, the foundation gives in three areas: higher education—pipeline programs that connect various levels of education and help students stay in school, scholarships, and minority advancement; classroom teaching and learning—innovative K-12 projects, teacher development, and small projects that deal with classroom activities; and global education—projects that encourage international studies, global understanding, and student exchange. Grants are awarded to both public and private institutions at all levels of education: universities, colleges, and secondary and elementary schools. International educational institutions and health care organizations also receive consideration. Types of support include annual campaigns, donated equipment, employee matching gifts, operating budgets, special projects, capital campaigns, continuing support, fellowships, internships, endowment funds, matching funds, and scholarship funds. Proposals may be submitted at any time.
Requirements: The following are eligible to apply: IRS 501(c)3 non-profits; a foreign organization that has received a ruling from the IRS that it is a section 501(c)3 tax exempt organization; or a foreign organization that is the equivalent of a U.S. charity.
Restrictions: The foundation does not make grants to individuals, religious endeavors, political or fraternal organizations, or organizations without 501(c)3 status.
Geographic Focus: All States
Amount of Grant: 10,000 - 6,000,000 USD
Contact: Helen Smith Price, Executive Director; (404) 676-2568; fax (404) 676-8804
Internet: http://www.thecoca-colacompany.com/citizenship/our_communities.html
Sponsor: Coca-Cola Foundation
P.O. Box 1734
Atlanta, GA 30301

Cockrell Foundation Grants   1196

The Cockrell Trust was established in 1957 with funds donated by Ernest and Virginia Cockrell. The Foundation's special emphasis is The University of Texas at Austin. Other fields of interest are: youth services, arts, health care, cultural programs, civic, religious and social services. The Foundation awards grants to support: annual campaigns, building funds, capital campaigns, endowment funds, general purposes, matching funds, and special projects. There are no deadlines for making a request to The Cockrell Foundation. The Foundation meetings are in the late spring and late Fall. An application form is not required. See website for recommended guidelines in making a proposal: http://www.cockrell/foundation/grant_guidelines.asp .
Requirements: Texas 501(c)3 nonprofit organizations in Houston are eligible.
Restrictions: The Foundation generally makes grants for only one-year periods. An organization should apply only once during any calendar year. If a grant request is denied, the applicant must wait until the following year before submitting a new request. The Foundation does not participate in feasibility studies and generally does not make grants for the following: individuals; mass appeal solicitations; medical or scientific research projects; organizations outside of Houston, Texas and the United States. Grant requests sent via email or fax will not be accepted.

Geographic Focus: Texas
Contact: M. Nancy Williams; (713) 209-7500; foundation@cockrell.com
Internet: http://www.cockrell.com/foundation/grant_guidelines.asp
Sponsor: Cockrell Foundation
1000 Main Street, Suite 3250
Houston, TX 77002

Coeta and Donald Barker Foundation Grants   1197

The foundation awards grants to California and Oregon nonprofit organizations in its areas of interest, including arts, children and youth, community development, disabled, environmental conservation, family services, federated giving, health care and health organizations, heart and circulatory research, higher education, hospitals, mental health, and secondary school education. Types of support include building construction/renovation, equipment acquisition, general operating support, program development, and scholarship funds.
Requirements: California and Oregon nonprofit organizations are eligible.
Restrictions: Grants do not support sectarian religious purposes, federal and tax-dependent organizations, individuals, or endowment funds.
Geographic Focus: California, Oregon
Date(s) Application is Due: Mar 1; Aug 1
Amount of Grant: 100 - 20,450 USD
Samples: Santa Barbara Zoological Gardens (Santa Barbara, CA), $5000.
Contact: Nancy Harris, Executive Administrator; (760) 324-2656; fax (760) 321-8662
Sponsor: Coeta and Donald Barker Foundation
P.O. Box 936
Rancho Mirage, CA 92270

Cogswell Benevolent Trust Grants   1198

The trust assists charitable, religious, and educational organizations primarily in New Hampshire. Usually, the program must be located within the state. However, limited funds may be available for out-of-state projects. Requests to fund general operating expenses or conferences or to eliminate deficits are rarely considered. The goal of the trust is not to become a permanent source of support for particular programs. There are no deadlines or funding dates; proposals may be submitted at any time.
Restrictions: Grants are not awarded to individuals or for endowment funds, operating budgets, or deficit financing,
Geographic Focus: New Hampshire
Amount of Grant: 1,000 - 15,000 USD
Contact: Theodore Wadleigh, (603) 622-4013
Sponsor: Cogswell Benevolent Trust
95 Market Street
Manchester, NH 03101

Coleman Foundation Cancer Care Grants   1199

The Foundation has been an advocate for raising the standards of cancer care in the Midwest region and assuring that direct cancer services are available to cancer patients in the Chicago Metro area. Recently, the Foundation has employed an impact framework which provides a basic outline of the goals for the Foundation's grantmaking. For the Cancer program area, the Foundation has identified strategies that can enable health care providers to gain effective tools and resources in providing supportive oncology (care from diagnosis through end of life). The Cancer Impact Plan (see website) is intended to inform potential grantees as to the particular strategies the Foundation seeks to fund. The Foundation welcomes potential grantees to review the Cancer Impact Plan to assess and determine the best possible strategy to meet the Foundation's intended impact.
Requirements: Grants are made only to 501(c)3 or 509(a)1 nonprofit organizations that are not private foundations. The Foundation's primary geographic focus is the Midwest region, particularly the State of Illinois and the Chicago metropolitan area. Only programs within the United States will be considered, which excludes all international programs. Applicants should submit a letter of inquiry first; LOIs are accepted throughout the calendar year. The Foundation will advise you if a full proposal should be submitted for further review. Proposals are presented by Foundation staff and approved by the Board at quarterly meetings, usually in February, May, August and November.
Restrictions: The program does not fund for-profit businesses, individuals, individual scholarships, advertising books, tickets, equipment purchases (including computer hardware or software), or advertising. General solicitations and annual appeals will not be considered.
Geographic Focus: Illinois, Indiana, Iowa, Michigan, Ohio, Wisconsin
Contact: Rosa Berardi; (312) 902-7120; rberardi@colemanfoundation.org
Internet: http://www.colemanfoundation.org/what_we_fund/cancer/
Sponsor: Coleman Foundation
651 West Washington Boulevard, Suite 306
Chicago, IL 60661

Coleman Foundation Developmental Disabilities Grants   1200

The Foundation supports an array of programs that historically has supported housing, life skills and supportive employment programs. The intended impact of the Foundation's funding is for individuals in the Chicago metropolitan area with developmental disabilities to experience a higher quality of life and increased self-determination through success in their work, comfort in their home and satisfaction across the varied stages of their lives. As vocational and residential outcomes are central to achieving this vision, Foundation funding concentrates in these areas. The Foundation welcomes potential grantees to review the Developmental Disabilities Impact Plan (see website) to determine the best possible strategy to meet the Foundation's intended impact.

Requirements: Grants are made only to 501(c)3 or 509(a)1 nonprofit organizations that are not private foundations. The Foundation's primary geographic focus is the Midwest region, particularly the State of Illinois and the Chicago metropolitan area. Only programs within the United States will be considered, which excludes all international programs. Applicants should submit a letter of inquiry first; LOIs are accepted throughout the calendar year. The Foundation will advise you if a full proposal should be submitted for further review. Proposals are presented by Foundation staff and approved by the Board at quarterly meetings, usually in February, May, August and November.
Restrictions: The program does not fund for-profit businesses, individuals, individual scholarships, advertising books, tickets, equipment purchases (including computer hardware or software), or advertising. General solicitations and annual appeals will not be considered.
Geographic Focus: Illinois, Indiana, Iowa, Michigan, Ohio, Wisconsin
Contact: Clark McCain; (312) 902-7120; fax (312) 902-7124; cmccain@colemanfoundation.org
Internet: http://www.colemanfoundation.org/what_we_fund/developmental_disabilities/
Sponsor: Coleman Foundation
651 West Washington Boulevard, Suite 306
Chicago, IL 60661

Coleman Foundation Entrepreneurship Education Grants 1201
Business ownership and the creation of for-profit business ventures are central to the Coleman Foundation definition of entrepreneurship. This perspective inherently involves accepting and managing risk, exercising significant personal control and contains the potential for personal reward. It is a narrower perspective than free enterprise and does not focus on intrapreneurship or social entrepreneurship. The Foundation believes that the principles of self-determination, independence and individual initiative are characteristics essential to the development of entrepreneurs and their pursuit of self-employment. It promotes entrepreneurship as a career option and field of study for individuals of all ages and strives to improve the relevance impact of entrepreneurship education programs. The Foundation has recently established a more focused impact framework for grantmaking in its entrepreneurship program area. The Entrepreneurship Education Impact Plan (see website) has curricular and co-curricular components. Within the curriculum, strategies aim to foster development of core skills and the promotion of entrepreneurship as interdisciplinary learning. The Plan also seeks to improve the quality and quantity of experiential activities across disciplines that develop applied knowledge and experiences in self-employment. Potential grantees should look to this Entrepreneurship Impact Plan for the type of strategies the Foundation is looking to fund. The Foundation has also been promoting the concept of a Pathway for entrepreneurship exploration and education.
Requirements: Grants are made only to 501(c)3 or 509(a)1 nonprofit organizations that are not private foundations. The Foundation's primary geographic focus is the Midwest region, particularly the State of Illinois and the Chicago metropolitan area. Entrepreneurship education, one of the foundation's core initiatives, has been funded nationally. Other program initiatives are only occasionally considered outside of the primary geographic area. Only programs within the United States will be considered, which excludes all international programs. Applicants should submit a letter of inquiry first; LOIs are accepted throughout the calendar year. The Foundation will advise you if a full proposal should be submitted for further review. Proposals are presented by Foundation staff and approved by the Board at quarterly meetings, usually in February, May, August and November.
Restrictions: The program does not fund for-profit businesses, individuals, individual scholarships, advertising books, tickets, equipment purchases (including computer hardware or software), or advertising. General solicitations and annual appeals will not be considered.
Geographic Focus: Illinois, Indiana, Iowa, Michigan, Ohio, Wisconsin
Contact: Rosa Berardi; (312) 902-7120; fax (312) 902-7124; rberardi@colemanfoundation.org
Internet: http://www.colemanfoundation.org/what_we_fund/entrepreneurship/
Sponsor: Coleman Foundation
651 West Washington Boulevard, Suite 306
Chicago, IL 60661

Colgate-Palmolive Company Grants 1202
Nonprofit organizations with IRS tax-exempt status located primarily in the U.S. tristate area of New York, New Jersey, and Connecticut and in locations of foreign subsidiaries may apply for support of programs that are directed toward youth, women, minorities, education, health and welfare, culture and arts, and civic and community activities. Priority will be given to programs that address the educational needs of youth and minorities. Types of support include program grants, scholarships, general support grants, multiyear support, and employee matching gifts. Proposals are accepted at any time and should include information on the organization, purpose of request, proof of tax-exempt status, and current operating budget.
Geographic Focus: All States
Contact: Sally Phills; (212) 310-2000; fax (212) 310-2873; sally_phipps@colpal.com
Internet: http://www.colgate.com/app/Colgate/US/Corp/CommunityPrograms/HomePage.cvsp
Sponsor: Colgate-Palmolive Company
300 Park Avenue
New York, NY 10022

Colin Higgins Foundation Courage Awards 1203
Each year, the foundation salutes, celebrates, and fosters courage in the face of adversity and discrimination by awarding grants to individuals who are either: lesbian, gay, bisexual, transgender, and questioning (LGBTQ) youth (through age 21) who have bravely stood up to hostility and intolerance based on their sexual orientation and triumphed over bigotry; lesbian, gay, bisexual, and transgender (LGBT) adults who have made strong impact in the lives of LGBTQ youth or the overall LGBT movement; and allies of any age working to end homophobia and discrimination against the LGBTQ communities. Honorees will also receive an expense-paid trip to the National Gay and Lesbian Task Force Creating Change Conference. Two or three awards will be made each year. Nomination form and guidelines are available at: http://www.colinhiggins.org/courageawards/nomin_mat.cfm.
Restrictions: Self-nominations are not accepted. Awards are open to U.S. citizens only.
Geographic Focus: All States
Date(s) Application is Due: Mar 1
Amount of Grant: 10,000 USD
Contact: Administrator; (212) 509-4975; fax (212) 509-1059; info@colinhiggins.org
Internet: http://www.colinhiggins.org/courageawards/index.cfm
Sponsor: Colin Higgins Foundation
55 Exchange Place, Suite 402
New York, NY 10005

Colin Higgins Foundation Grants 1204
The foundation supports organizations that help people respond to a variety of life challenges, with a focus on responding to the AIDS pandemic by supporting innovative programs in the areas of education, service, and advocacy for people infected, affected, and at risk for HIV; and empowering lesbian, gay, bisexual, and transgender peoples by supporting community-based organizations that combat homophobia and foster leadership. The foundation is particularly interested in organizations that have a significant impact working in underserved, rural areas with traditionally underserved constituencies. The process of applying consists of two stages: submission of a letter of inquiry, and, if requested, a full proposal.
Requirements: The foundation only considers organizations with overall budgets under $2 million, or project budgets under $500,000.
Restrictions: Grants do not support projects that had previously fallen within its funding priorities, including any organizations or programs based in urban areas (population over 1 million); film and video projects; or organizations with overall budgets of over $2 million, or project budgets over $500,000. The one exception to the exclusion of programs in urban areas is those organizations and projects working with underserved communities (i.e., communities of color, low-income communities, transgender people, etc.). The foundation does not accept letters of inquiry from universities, schools, individuals, or corporations. It does not support political or legislative activities, endowments, or deficit budgets. Additionally, the foundation does not support capital campaigns, although it will consider requests for capital improvements, and does not award grants to organizations outside the United States.
Geographic Focus: All States
Date(s) Application is Due: Jul 1
Amount of Grant: 5,000 - 15,000 USD
Contact: Administrator; (212) 509-4975; fax (212) 509-1059; info@colinhiggins.org
Internet: http://www.colinhiggins.org/grantmaking/index.cfm
Sponsor: Colin Higgins Foundation
55 Exchange Place, Suite 402
New York, NY 10005

Collaboration Prize 1205
The Lodestar Foundation, an organization dedicated to maximizing the impact of philanthropy by leveraging philanthropic resources, has announced its Collaboration Prize, a $250,000 award to recognize nonprofit collaborations that achieve exceptional impact and significantly eliminate duplication of efforts. Nominations for the annual prize begin June 1 and will be accepted through July 21. The prize, which is designed to inspire cooperation among nonprofits, will be awarded to one collaboration that demonstrates that it has achieved exceptional impact and significantly eliminated the duplication of efforts through programmatic collaborations, administrative consolidation or other joint activities.
Requirements: The collaboration must be composed of two or more organizations that otherwise would compete for clients, financial resources and staff.
Geographic Focus: All States
Date(s) Application is Due: Jul 21
Amount of Grant: 250,000 USD
Contact: Amy Cox OHara, (602) 496-0185; amy.ohara@asu.edu
Internet: http://www.thecollaborationprize.org/Home.aspx
Sponsor: Lodestar Foundation / Arizona-Indiana-Michigan Alliance
6400 Hollis Street, Suite 15
Emeryville, CA 94608

Collective Brands Foundation Grants 1206
The Collective Brands Foundation invests financially in non-profit organizations that align with the Foundation's focus areas. Priority is given to organizations that provide involvement opportunities for team members and employees of Collective Brands, Inc. The Foundation may also consider sponsorships from charitable organizations in the following areas: Eastern Kansas, including Topeka, Lawrence and the Kansas City metropolitan area; New York City; Lexington, Massachusetts and the Greater Boston area; Denver, Colorado; Redlands, California; and Brookville, Ohio.
Requirements: The Collective Brands Foundation will consider requests for monetary grants from 501(c)3 non-profit organizations that manage programs in at least one of the following areas: women's preventative health; children's physical activity and fitness; improving the lives of children and youth in need; preserving the environment; and supporting industry in the United States. Applications must be submitted online at the Foundation's website.
Restrictions: Grants will not be awarded to religious organizations for projects that are sectarian and do not benefit a broad community base. Also, the Foundation will not award grants to: individuals; political causes, candidates or legislative lobbying efforts; or for capital campaigns, debt reduction, travel or conferences.
Geographic Focus: All States

Date(s) Application is Due: Aug 15
Amount of Grant: Up to 3,000 USD
Contact: Michele Gray; (877) 902-4437; grants@greaterhorizons.org
Internet: http://www.collectivebrands.com/foundation
Sponsor: Collective Brands Foundation
3231 SE 6th Avenue
Topeka, KS 66607

Collective Brands Foundation Payless Gives Shoes 4 Kids Grants   1207

The Payless Gives 4 Kids grant supports non-profit organizations serving children with coupons for free, new shoes at Payless. Payless Gives 4 Kids supports organizations in the United States, Canada, Puerto Rico, and Latin America. Applications are accepted every fall and are available at the program's website.
Requirements: 501(c)3 non-profit organizations that serve children within 100 miles of a Payless store are eligible to apply. Applicants must participate in an eligibility quiz and are required to supply the following information: organization information and mission; services and description of services provided to children, as well as an example of a child applicant organization has helped; number of coupons organization can deliver, the process for determining who receives coupons and transportation assistance to be provided; Payless or Collective Brands affiliation; and any additional tax information.
Restrictions: Organizations without a 501(c)3 status or who are more than 100 miles from a Payless ShoeSource are not eligible to apply.
Geographic Focus: All States
Samples: Covenant House Alaska, Anchorage, Alaska - coupons for new shoes for children in need; Catholic Charities of Fairfield County, Inc., Bridgeport, Connecticut - coupons for new shoes for children in need.
Contact: Michele Gray; (877) 902-4437; grants@greaterhorizons.org
Internet: http://www.paylessgives.com/about.php?page=about_the_program-what_its_about
Sponsor: Collective Brands Foundation
3231 SE 6th Avenue
Topeka, KS 66607

Collins C. Diboll Private Foundation Grants   1208

The foundation awards grants to Louisiana nonprofit organizations in the areas of higher education, human services, and youth. Field of interest include: Catholic churches and agencies; education; higher education; human services; museums (art); and protestant agencies and churches. Types of support include building construction/renovation, capital campaigns, endowment funds, and general operating support. Applicants should submit a detailed description of the project and the amount of funding requested, along with a copy of an IRS determination letter.
Requirements: Louisiana nonprofit organizations are eligible.
Restrictions: Individuals are not eligible to apply.
Geographic Focus: Louisiana
Amount of Grant: 500 - 200,000 USD
Contact: Donald W. Diboll, Chair; (504) 582-8103
Sponsor: Collins C. Diboll Private Foundation
201 Saint Charles Avenue, 50th Floor
New Orleans, LA 70170-5100

Collins Foundation Grants   1209

Grants are awarded to organizations in Oregon with emphasis on higher education, youth and health agencies, social welfare, natural resource and wildlife conservation, religion, and arts and cultural programs. A special area of support includes building and medical equipment, and programs for those who are physically or mentally disabled. Challenge/matching grants, general operating support, scholarships, and internships also are awarded. Applications may be submitted at any time, additional guidelines are available at the Foundation's website.
Requirements: Grants are made to 501(c)3 nonprofit agencies domiciled in Oregon. The proposed project must directly benefit the citizens of Oregon.
Restrictions: Grants are not made to individuals or to organizations sponsoring requests intended to be used by or for the benefit of an individual. Grants normally are not made to elementary, secondary, or public higher education institutions; or to individual religious congregations. Grants normally are not made for development office personnel, annual fundraising activities, endowments, operational deficits, financial emergencies, or debt retirement.
Geographic Focus: Oregon
Contact: Cynthia Knowles; (503) 227-7171; information@collinsfoundation.org
Internet: http://www.collinsfoundation.org/submission-guidelines
Sponsor: Collins Foundation
1618 South West First Avenue, Suite 505
Portland, OR 97201

Colonel Stanley R. McNeil Foundation Grants   1210

Colonel Stanley R. McNeil and his wife Merna created the Colonel Stanley R. McNeil Foundation in 1993 to support and promote quality educational, human-services, and health-care programming for underserved populations. Special consideration is given to charitable organizations that serve the needs of children. During their lifetimes, the McNeils were actively involved in their local church and community. Colonel McNeil also served on a number of boards, including Lake Bluff Children's Home and Ravenswood Hospital. Although the McNeils had no children, they were strong supporters of children's causes. The foundation is particularly interested in funding programs or organizations that focus on children's causes, start-up initiatives within the human-services or arts and culture arenas, and healthcare. To better support the capacity of nonprofit organizations, multi-year funding requests are considered. Grant requests for naming opportunities that honor the donors are strongly encouraged. Applicants must apply online at the grant website. Applicants are strongly encouraged to do the following before applying: review the downloadable state application procedures for additional helpful information and clarifications; review the downloadable online-application guidelines at the grant website; review the foundation's funding history (link is available from the grant website); review the online application questions in advance; and review the list of required attachments. These will generally include: a list of board members, financial statements (audited, reviewed, or compiled by independent auditor); an organization summary; a list of other funding sources; an IRS Determination letter; and other required documents. All attachments must be uploaded in the online application as PDF, Word, or Excel files. The Colonel Stanley R. McNeil Foundation has biannual deadlines of February 1 and June 1. Applications must be submitted by 11:59 p.m. on the deadline dates. Applicants for the February deadline will be notified of grant decisions by June 30. Applicants for the June deadline will be notified by November 30.
Requirements: Illinois nonprofits serving the Chicago metropolitan area are eligible.
Restrictions: Because requests for support usually exceed available resources, organizations can only apply to either the Lang Burk Fund or the Colonel Stanley McNeil Foundation in the same calendar year. Grant requests to both foundations during the same calendar year will no longer be accepted. The Foundation will consider requests for general operations only if the organization's operating budget is less than $1 million. In general, grant request for individuals, endowment campaigns or capital projects will not be considered.
Geographic Focus: Illinois
Date(s) Application is Due: Feb 1; Jun 1
Contact: George Thorn; (312) 828-4154; ilgrantmaking@bankofamerica.com
Internet: https://www.bankofamerica.com/philanthropic/fn_search.action
Sponsor: Colonel Stanley R. McNeil Foundation
231 South LaSalle Street, IL1-231-13-32
Chicago, IL 60604

Colorado Bioscience Discovery Evaluation Grants   1211

The program was first created by the Colorado legislature in 2006 with the purpose being to improve and expand the evaluation of new bioscience discoveries at research institutions with the intent of accelerating the development of new products and services - essentially a proof of concept program. 2007 legislation modified the original program by providing additional funding and targeting the new funding to SBIR/STTR recipients and biofuels research. Proof-of-Concept projects can receive a maximum grant of $150,000. SBIR/STTR projects can receive a maximum grant of $100,000.
Requirements: Eligible applicants include any institution located and operating in Colorado that is a public or private, nonprofit institution of higher education, a nonprofit teaching hospital, or a private, nonprofit medical and research center. For-profit entities are not eligible for the program. However, an Office of Technology Transfer must be affiliated with one of these research institutions in order for the Office of Technology Transfer to be eligible to apply under the Program. Application forms and guidelines are available for download at the sponsor's website.
Restrictions: For-profit entities are not eligible for the program.
Geographic Focus: Colorado
Date(s) Application is Due: Jun 30
Contact: Sonya Guram; (303) 892-3840; fax (303) 892-3848; sonya.guram@state.co.us
Internet: http://www.colorado.gov/cs/Satellite?c=Page&childpagename=OEDIT%2FOEDITLayout&cid=1167928017742&p=1167928017742&pagename=OEDITWrapper
Sponsor: Colorado Office of Economic Development and International Trade
1625 Broadway, Suite 2700
Denver, CO 80202

Colorado Clean Energy Fund Solar Innovation Grants (SIG)   1212

The program was established to support innovative programs that can demonstrate a strategy and implementation plan for breaking down financial, educational, political, and technical barriers to greater penetration of solar electric and solar thermal technologies in the residential and commercial sectors. Approximately three hundred and fifty thousand dollars ($350,000) is available during the current competitive cycle. Individual awards will not exceed $50,000.
Requirements: Funding requests will be considered for the following purposes: (a) Education - Applicants will provide educational resources to targeted sectors with the goal of expanding the quantity and quality of solar installations in Colorado. (b) Integrated Design - Applicants will address opportunities to incorporate solar technology into the commercial and production home sectors in both new and existing infrastructure. (c) Utility Programs - Applicants in this category will work to improve the viability of solar technology as a means to offset energy and power demands at the utility level. GEO is soliciting innovative solutions to promoting solar technology at the utility level. (d) Market Analysis & Policy Recommendations - Applicants will identify policy barriers to the wider implementation of solar technology in Colorado and present solutions in the form of a comprehensive policy report. (e) Financing - Applicants will present innovative financing models that will increase the affordability of integrating solar technology in the residential and commercial sectors. Potential recipients include, but are not limited to: Utilities; Home Builders; Installers / System Integrators; Lenders / Financial Institutions; Non-Profits; Trade Associations. Preference will be given to proposals that demonstrate the ability to generate substantial matching funds, however matching funding is not required should the applicant demonstrate sufficient need.
Restrictions: Grant dollars will not be used to buy down the cost of solar systems. Only electronic applications will be accepted.
Geographic Focus: Colorado
Date(s) Application is Due: Apr 20
Amount of Grant: Up to 50,000 USD
Contact: Jeff Lyng, Solar Programs Manager; (303) 866-2264; jeff.lyng@state.co.us

Internet: http://www.colorado.gov/energy/resources/SolarInnovationGrantProgram GovernorsEnergyOfficeColorado.asp
Sponsor: Colorado Governor's Energy Office
1580 Logan Street, Suite 100
Denver, CO 80203

Colorado Interstate Gas Grants 1213
Nonprofits in communities served by the company are eligible to apply for grants in the categories of education, including early child development, K-12, and higher education; civic; health and welfare; minorities; cultural programs; environmental programs, particularly those focusing on air quality; and youth groups that concentrate on improving areas where CIG employees live and work. The company also supports special event sponsorships, corporate memberships, joint projects with other organizations, and employee participation in volunteer activities.
Requirements: Colorado, Wyoming, Texas, Utah, and Kansas 501(c)3 tax-exempt organizations where the company has pipelines are eligible.
Geographic Focus: Colorado
Date(s) Application is Due: Aug 1
Amount of Grant: 200 - 20,000 USD
Contact: Richard Wheatley, Media Relations; (713) 420-6828
Internet: http://www.cigco.com
Sponsor: Colorado Interstate Gas Company
P.O. Box 1087
Colorado Springs, CO 80944

Colorado Renewables in Performance Contracting Grants 1214
The purpose of the program is to reduce the cost of incorporating renewable energy into a performance contract to the extent that the system fits within an acceptable payback period for the entire project. Additionally, this incentive is designed to promote renewable technology after, or in conjunction with, energy efficiency upgrades. The funding for this grant will be allocated on a first come, first serve basis and is a 100% matching grant.
Requirements: Organizations that are in the process of executing a performance contract, or have completed one within the last 5 years may be eligible to receive up to $25,000 in matching grant funds from the Governor's Energy Office (GEO) to add renewable energy technology to its facility. The organization's energy service company or a professional solar installer must complete the application and submit it electronically. The application form can be downloaded at the program website.
Geographic Focus: Colorado
Amount of Grant: Up to 25,000 USD
Contact: Sean Mandel; (303) 866-2407; fax (303) 866-2930; Sean.mandel@state.co.us
Internet: http://www.colorado.gov/energy/resources/funding-opportunities.asp#RenewPC
Sponsor: Colorado Governor's Energy Office
1580 Logan Street, Suite 100
Denver, CO 80203

Colorado Springs Community Trust Fund Grants 1215
Grants are awarded to El Paso and Teller Counties in Colorado. The community trust supports Colorado nonprofits with an emphasis on community funds, youth agencies, health, and child welfare. Fields of interest include the arts and cultural programs (visual arts, performing arts, museums), education (elementary education, higher education, adult basic education, literacy, and reading), health care and health organizations, substance abuse and mental health services, crime and law enforcement, human services, and community development. Continuing support for programs/projects will be awarded, as well as support for annual campaigns, building/renovations, equipment, emergency funds, and seed money. There are no application forms; initial approach should be by letter. The board meets four times each year to consider requests.
Requirements: Colorado nonprofits, with an emphasis on El Paso and Teller Counties, are eligible for grant support.
Restrictions: Grants are not awarded to individuals or for operating budgets, deficit financing, endowment funds, matching gifts, scholarships, fellowships, research, demonstration projects, publications, conferences, or loans.
Geographic Focus: Colorado
Date(s) Application is Due: Mar 1; Aug 1; Nov 1
Contact: Michael Hannigan; (719) 389-1251; fax (719) 389-1252; mhannigan@PPCF.org
Sponsor: Colorado Springs Community Trust Fund
P.O. Box 1443
Colorado Springs, CO 80901

Colorado Trust Grants 1216
The Trust's strategic grantmaking supports the development of a coordinated system of policies, programs and services that, expand health coverage, improve and expand health care. The Trust issues Requests for Proposals (RFP) and welcomes responses from nonprofit organizations and governmental entities across Colorado. When a competitive funding opportunity is available, a detailed RFP with related instructions and specific application deadlines is posted to the Funds website. On occasion, The Trust also asks organizations that are focused on strategies specific to achieving access to health to submit individual, non-competitive proposals.
Requirements: The following types of organizations are eligible to apply for grants: nonprofit organizations that are exempt under Section 501(c)3 of the Internal Revenue Code and are classified as not a private foundation under Section 509(a); independent sponsored projects of a nonprofit 501(c)3 organization acting as a fiscal agent; government and public agencies.
Restrictions: The Trust asks for proposals through a Request for Proposal process, rather than accepting unsolicited proposals. Announcements of Requests for Proposals are posted at the website. Grant seekers also may register with the Trust to receive notification of new funding opportunities. The Colorado Trust does not make grants for the following: political campaigns or voter registration drives; capital funding for the purchase, construction or renovation of any facilities or other physical infrastructure; operating deficits or retirement of debt; indirect allocations (excluding fiscal agent fees); religious purposes.
Geographic Focus: Colorado
Contact: Ed Lucero, Senior Program Officer; (888) 847-9140 or (303) 837-1200; fax (303) 839-9034; ed@coloradotrust.org
Internet: http://www.coloradotrust.org
Sponsor: Colorado Trust
1600 Sherman Street
Denver, CO 80203-1200

Colorado Trust Partnerships for Health Initiative 1217
The trust supports this statewide initiative to improve the coordination of health services at the community level. The program will support new or existing community health partnerships, consisting of local health departments, county nursing services, community-based organizations, and other interested organizations, businesses, and community members. Each partnership will identify a Healthy People 2010 focus area important to its community and will develop and implement a coordinated plan to address that health issues. Grants will be awarded to help partnerships build, strengthen, and sustain the public health infrastructure of Colorado communities by proactively addressing public health issues. The complete RFP is available online.
Requirements: Partnerships must have a 501(c)3 fiscal agent or be a governmental entity; strong community support including representatives from the public, private, and nonprofit sectors; ability to develop strategic partnerships; knowledge of the the public health system and health promotion/disease prevention issues; ability to design a service approach to meet targeted Health People 2010 needs; cultural competency and a demonstrated commitment to diversity; sound fiscal management; and willingness to work in partnership with the Colorado Trust in the planning and implementation phases of the initiative.
Geographic Focus: Colorado
Date(s) Application is Due: Nov 17
Amount of Grant: 10,000 - 15,000 USD
Contact: Susan Downs-Karkos; (888) 847-9140 or (303) 837-1200; susan@coloradotrust.org
Internet: http://www.coloradotrust.org
Sponsor: Colorado Trust
1600 Sherman Street
Denver, CO 80203-1200

Columbia Gas of Virginia Grants 1218
The company makes charitable contributions for projects and programs that meet essential needs in its operating communities. Priority consideration is directed toward specific projects that improve or enhance delivery of the following needs: energy—groups directly linked to effective use of natural gas in the community; education—schools joining in a partnership program to pay for programs such as energy-related field trips or to bring computers into the classroom; and environmental stewardship—promote efficient energy delivery and protect land, air, and water resources in the region. Requests are accepted year-round and are reviewed continuously. Proposals should be as clear and precise as possible.
Geographic Focus: Virginia
Contact: Grants Administrator; (800) 543-8911
Internet: http://www.columbiagasva.com/community/grant_process.htm
Sponsor: Columbia Gas of Virginia
1809 Coyote Drive
Chester, VA 23836

Columbus Foundation Allen Eiry Fund Grants 1219
The Fund provides support to organizations that serve older adults in Seneca County. Projects supported by the fund include transportation, recreation, homemaker services, hot meals, court ordered guardianships, information and referral programs, library programs for nursing homes, support for capital projects, and other projects that enhance the lives of needy elderly.
Requirements: The Fund welcomes requests from organizations having recognition under Section 501(c)3 of the Internal Revenue Code that serve older adults in Seneca County.
Restrictions: The Fund makes no grants to individuals. Requests for religious purposes, budget deficits, endowments, conferences, scholarly research, or projects that are normally the responsibility of a public agency are generally not funded.
Geographic Focus: Ohio
Date(s) Application is Due: Nov 5
Contact: Dottie Henderson, Executive Assistant; (614) 251-4000; fax (614) 251-4009; dhenderson@columbusfoundation.org
Internet: http://www.columbusfoundation.org/gogrants/targeted_needs/specialized_grants.aspx
Sponsor: Columbus Foundation
1234 E Broad Street
Columbus, OH 43205

Columbus Foundation Competitive Grants 1220
The foundation's competitive grants are made in the following fields: advancing philanthropy, arts and humanities, conservation, education, health, social services, and urban affairs. The Governing Committee approves distributions from unrestricted and field of interest funds through competitive grants. Competitive grants are the most common way nonprofit organizations request funding from the Foundation. Submit a Letter of Intent or a Full Proposal by accessing our online grant application system.

Requirements: Central Ohio, tax-exempt public charities under Section 501(c)3 of the Internal Revenue Service Code may submit grant requests.
Restrictions: Individuals are ineligible. Requests for religious purposes, budget deficits, endowments, conferences, scholarly research, or projects that are normally the responsibility of a public agency are generally not funded. Funding is not available for projects when funds are available elsewhere.
Geographic Focus: Ohio
Contact: Emily Savors; (614) 251-4000; fax (614) 251-4009; esavors@columbusfoundation.org
Internet: http://www.columbusfoundation.org/gogrants/index.aspx
Sponsor: Columbus Foundation
1234 E Broad Street
Columbus, OH 43205

Columbus Foundation Dorothy E. Ann Fund (D.E.A.F.) Traditional Grants — 1221

The Program encourages and supports programming that provides opportunities to strengthen the potential of youth in central Ohio who are deaf or hard-of-hearing, and is helps to initiate projects that address priorities consistent with the mission. Organizations or programs striving to fulfill the following goals are eligible to apply for a traditional grant: promoting hands on experience where youth who are deaf or hard-of-hearing can develop skills and values necessary for successful careers; encouraging organizations to provide youth who are deaf or hard-of-hearing with personal development opportunities, such as leadership training, goal setting, self-esteem building, and interpersonal/communication skills; achieving a better understanding between deaf and hard-of-hearing youth and the community at large; supporting projects that will advocate for deaf and hard-of-hearing children's full participation in their education, family, and community; and fostering collaborative relationships among agencies that serve youth who are deaf or hard-of-hearing. Projects may include seminars, workshops, camps, scholarship, equipment, special programming, or projects promoting positive growth opportunities or which advocate for equal opportunities.
Requirements: Central Ohio, tax-exempt public charities under Section 501(c)3 of the Internal Revenue Service Code may submit grant requests.
Restrictions: Individuals are ineligible. Requests for religious purposes, budget deficits, endowments, conferences, scholarly research, or projects that are normally the responsibility of a public agency are generally not funded. Funding is not available for projects when funds are available elsewhere.
Geographic Focus: Ohio
Date(s) Application is Due: Dec 15
Contact: Emily Savors; (614) 251-4000; fax (614) 251-4009; esavors@columbusfoundation.org
Internet: http://www.columbusfoundation.org/gogrants/targeted_needs/specialized_grants.aspx
Sponsor: Columbus Foundation
1234 E Broad Street
Columbus, OH 43205

Columbus Foundation J. Floyd Dixon Memorial Fund Grants — 1222

The purpose of the Fund is to provide educational programs for children, health programs for the elderly, and social services programs in Jackson County. An individual grant seldom exceeds $10,000. Applications must be received by May 28, and decisions will be announced three to four months after the application deadline.
Requirements: The fund welcomes requests from organizations having recognition under Section 501(c)3 of the Internal Revenue Code that services residents of Jackson County.
Restrictions: The Fund makes no grants to individuals, and generally does not fund governmental agencies. Requests for religious purposes, budget deficits, endowments, conferences, scholarly research, or projects that are normally the responsibility of a public agency are generally not funded.
Geographic Focus: Ohio
Date(s) Application is Due: May 28
Amount of Grant: Up to 10,000 USD
Contact: Dottie Henderson, Executive Assistant; (614) 251-4000; fax (614) 251-4009; dhenderson@columbusfoundation.org
Internet: http://www.columbusfoundation.org/gogrants/targeted_needs/specialized_grants.aspx
Sponsor: Columbus Foundation
1234 E Broad Street
Columbus, OH 43205

Columbus Foundation John W. and Edna McManus Shepard Fund Grants — 1223

The purpose of the Fund is to provide cultural and/or economic programs that benefit the residents of Cambridge and/or Guernsey County. Requests may not exceed $5,000 annually.
Requirements: The fund welcomes requests from organizations having recognition under Section 501(c)3 of the Internal Revenue Code that serves the residents of Cambridge and/or Guernsey County.
Restrictions: The fund makes no grants to individuals.
Geographic Focus: Ohio
Date(s) Application is Due: May 28
Amount of Grant: Up to 5,000 USD
Contact: Dottie Henderson, Executive Assistant; (614) 251-4000; fax (614) 251-4009; dhenderson@columbusfoundation.org
Internet: http://www.columbusfoundation.org/gogrants/targeted_needs/specialized_grants.aspx
Sponsor: Columbus Foundation
1234 E Broad Street
Columbus, OH 43205

Columbus Foundation Joseph A. Jeffrey Endowment Fund Grants — 1224

The Fund provides support for benevolent, philanthropic, charitable, and allied projects, especially those that beautify and/or improve the city of Columbus and or Franklin County. Applicants for the Small Grants Program must complete a two-page online grant application. (No other attachments will be accepted.)
Requirements: Central Ohio, tax-exempt public charities under Section 501(c)3 of the Internal Revenue Service Code may submit grant requests.
Restrictions: Requests for religious purposes, budget deficits, endowments, conferences, scholarly research, or projects that are normally the responsibility of a public agency are generally not funded.
Geographic Focus: Ohio
Date(s) Application is Due: Apr 2
Contact: Emily Savors; (614) 251-4000; fax (614) 251-4009; esavors@columbusfoundation.org
Internet: http://www.columbusfoundation.org/gogrants/targeted_needs/small_grants.aspx
Sponsor: Columbus Foundation
1234 E Broad Street
Columbus, OH 43205

Columbus Foundation Mary Eleanor Morris Fund Grants — 1225

The Fund supports quality-of-life projects, with a focus on the arts, civic affairs, conservation, education, health, and social services that benefits the residents of Logan County. Application deadlines are the first Friday in January and the first Friday in July.
Requirements: The fund welcomes requests from organizations having recognition under Section 501(c)3 of the Internal Revenue Code that services the residents of Logan County, as well as public and private schools.
Restrictions: The Fund makes no grants to individuals. Requests for religious purposes, budget deficits, endowments, conferences, scholarly research, or projects that are normally the responsibility of a public agency are generally not funded.
Geographic Focus: Ohio
Date(s) Application is Due: Jan 1; Jul 2
Contact: Emily Savors; (614) 251-4000; fax (614) 251-4009; esavors@columbusfoundation.org
Internet: http://www.columbusfoundation.org/gogrants/targeted_needs/small_grants.aspx
Sponsor: Columbus Foundation
1234 E Broad Street
Columbus, OH 43205

Columbus Foundation Neighborhood Partnership Grants (NPG) — 1226

The Program is aimed at improving neighborhhods within the central Ohio region. Proposed projects should focus on one of following three areas: economic development, which might include gateway signage, beautification, newsletters and websites, festivals and public events, or identity building projects; education, which might include youth service, leadership development, health and fitness, or community public relations; and crime prevention and safety, which might include block watches, awareness programs, anti-litter, clean and safe, anti-graffiti, or personal safety.
Requirements: Submitting organizations are required to be a 501(c)3 organization or must have a fiscal agent to receive funds.
Geographic Focus: Ohio
Date(s) Application is Due: Jan 29
Amount of Grant: 15,000 USD
Contact: Dottie Henderson, Executive Assistant; (614) 251-4000; fax (614) 251-4009; dhenderson@columbusfoundation.org
Internet: http://www.columbusfoundation.org/gogrants/targeted_needs/specialized_grants.aspx
Sponsor: Columbus Foundation
1234 E Broad Street
Columbus, OH 43205

Columbus Foundation Paul G. Duke Grants — 1227

The Foundation is primarily interested in supporting projects for children, young adults, and the family. Grants are generally made in the fields of the arts, education, health, and social services. The Foundation will also consider making challenge grants for worthwhile projects to encourage matching gifts or additional funding from other donors. Requests may be for general, capital, or specific project support, including seed money for innovative programs. The Foundation accepts proposals twice per year, and support is generally given for one year.
Requirements: Nonprofit organizations having recognition under Section 501(c)3 of the Internal Revenue Code are eligible for grants.
Restrictions: The Foundation generally does not make grants for transportation, computer hardware or software, and research or treatment for specific diseases. The Foundation does not award grants to individuals. Generally, grants are not made for religious purposes, budget deficits, or projects that are normally the responsibility of a public agency.
Geographic Focus: Ohio
Date(s) Application is Due: Apr 1; Aug 1
Contact: Tami Durrence, (614) 251-4000; mail@supportingfoundations.org
Internet: http://www.columbusfoundation.org/paul_g_duke.aspx
Sponsor: Paul G. Duke Foundation
1234 East Broad Street
Columbus, OH 43205-1453

Columbus Foundation R. Alvin Stevenson Fund Grants — 1228

The Fund provides support for the needy in Fairfield and Hocking counties, Ohio. The primary focus of funding is for social service organizations rather than performing arts. Application deadlines are the first Friday in January and the first Friday in July. Decisions will be announced three to four months after the application deadline.

Requirements: The fund welcomes requests from organizations having recognition under Section 501(c)3 of the Internal Revenue Code that serves the residents of Fairfield and/or Hocking County.
Restrictions: The Fund makes no grants to individuals. Requests for religious purposes, budget deficits, endowments, conferences, scholarly research, or projects that are normally the responsibility of a public agency are generally not funded.
Geographic Focus: Ohio
Date(s) Application is Due: Jan 1; Jul 2
Contact: Emily Savors; (614) 251-4000; fax (614) 251-4009; esavors@columbusfoundation.org
Internet: http://www.columbusfoundation.org/gogrants/targeted_needs/small_grants.aspx
Sponsor: Columbus Foundation
1234 E Broad Street
Columbus, OH 43205

Columbus Foundation Robert E. and Genevieve B. Schaefer Fund Grants   1229
The purpose of the Fund is to benefit the residents of Chillicothe and/or Ross County. The funding supports programs that enhance the community in three broad areas: cultural development, health and human welfare, and economic development.
Requirements: The Fund welcomes applications from organizations recognized under Section 501(c)3 of the Internal Revenue Code that serves the residents of Chillicothe and/or Ross County. All organizations with budgets over $75,000 must provide an audit, and those with budgets less than $75,000 must provide their most recent form 990 and compiled financial statements.
Restrictions: The Fund makes no grants to individuals, churches, governmental agencies, or school districts.
Geographic Focus: Ohio
Date(s) Application is Due: Oct 29
Contact: Dottie Henderson, Executive Assistant; (614) 251-4000; fax (614) 251-4009; dhenderson@columbusfoundation.org
Internet: http://www.columbusfoundation.org/gogrants/targeted_needs/specialized_grants.aspx
Sponsor: Columbus Foundation
1234 E Broad Street
Columbus, OH 43205

Columbus Foundation Scotts Miracle-Gro Community Garden Academy Grants   1230
Grant requests provide community gardeners in central Ohio with the training and grant money needed to begin and maintain a thriving community garden. Grants of up to $4,000 are available for qualified projects in low- and moderate-income neighborhoods. Classes are held at the Franklin Park Conservatory in Ohio during early spring where grant recipients - and any interested local gardeners - learn about soil testing, garden design, community building, and sustainability.
Requirements: Central Ohio, tax-exempt public charities under Section 501(c)3 of the Internal Revenue Service Code may submit grant requests.
Restrictions: Individuals are ineligible. Requests for religious purposes, budget deficits, endowments, conferences, scholarly research, or projects that are normally the responsibility of a public agency are generally not funded.
Geographic Focus: Ohio
Date(s) Application is Due: Oct 16
Amount of Grant: 4,000 USD
Contact: Dottie Henderson, Executive Assistant; (614) 251-4000; fax (614) 251-4009; dhenderson@columbusfoundation.org
Internet: http://www.columbusfoundation.org/gogrants/targeted_needs/specialized_grants.aspx
Sponsor: Columbus Foundation
1234 E Broad Street
Columbus, OH 43205

Columbus Foundation Siemer Family Grants   1231
The purpose of the Siemer Family Foundation is to provide funding for those institutions and organizations whose purpose is to affect continuing and long-term benefits for societal, educational, and cultural needs of the community. The Foundation's goal is to support those organizations which provide solutions for social problems, education and/or training to enable young people to be self-supporting, and support for civic and cultural organizations which enhance the quality of life in this or other communities.
Requirements: 501(c)3 organizations are eligible to apply.
Geographic Focus: All States
Contact: Tami Durrence, Foundation Contact; (614) 251-4000; fax (614) 251-4009; infosupporting@columbusfoundation.org
Internet: http://www.columbusfoundation.org/find/support/siemer.aspx
Sponsor: Siemer Family Foundation
1234 East Broad Street
Columbus, OH 43205

Columbus Foundation Small Grants   1232
The Small Grants provides support for several areas including: animals; arts; camber music; conservation; community improvement; education; health, special populations; Logan County; Hocking/Fairfield counties of Ohio. Applicants may apply for up to $25,000; however, the majority of the grants awarded will be $1,000 to $10,000. Applications must be submitted by the first Friday of April, July, and October.
Requirements: Central Ohio, tax-exempt public charities under Section 501(c)3 of the Internal Revenue Service Code may submit grant requests.
Geographic Focus: Ohio

Amount of Grant: 1,000 - 25,000 USD
Contact: Emily Savors; (614) 251-4000; fax (614) 251-4009; esavors@columbusfoundation.org
Internet: http://www.columbusfoundation.org/gogrants/targeted_needs/small_grants.aspx
Sponsor: Columbus Foundation
1234 E Broad Street
Columbus, OH 43205

Columbus Foundation Traditional Grants   1233
The Traditional Grants Program creates quality opportunities and meets community need by focusing on three areas: Basic Needs funds programs and projects that provide food, shelter, and clothing. Priority will be given to programs and projects that meet current needs and simultaneously integrate services designed to support long-term stability; Disadvantaged Children funds programs and projects that meet the diverse needs of at-risk children. Priority will be given to programs and projects that are in the home, build relationships with the family, and create a support network around and for the families of disadvantaged children; Developmental Disabilities funds programs and projects that address the needs of children and adults with physical or cognitive disabilities that impair functions or behavior and that occurred before a person reaches the age of 22. (Blindness/visual impairments and deafness/hearing impairments are not considered within this category.) If you are implementing your project in a Columbus City School building, or collaborating with the district on a project, and asked to submit a full application, you must request a letter of endorsement from the Office of Development.
Requirements: Central Ohio, tax-exempt public charities under Section 501(c)3 of the Internal Revenue Service Code may submit grant requests .If you are implementing your project in a Columbus City School building, or collaborating with the district on a project, and asked to submit a full application, you must request a letter of endorsement from the Office of Development. Letter of Intent deadlines are twice a year on the first Friday in February and September. See Foundations website for further guidelines.
Restrictions: Operating support will only be considered when the applicant demonstrates continuous innovation that enhances services.
Geographic Focus: Ohio
Date(s) Application is Due: Feb 5; Sep 3
Contact: Emily Savors; (614) 251-4000; fax (614) 251-4009; esavors@columbusfoundation.org
Internet: http://www.columbusfoundation.org/gogrants/targeted_needs/traditional_grants.aspx
Sponsor: Columbus Foundation
1234 E Broad Street
Columbus, OH 43205

Columbus Jewish Foundation Grants   1234
The foundation awards grants to support nonprofit organizations that serve to strengthen the Jewish community and establish a secure and vital future for the integrity of the Jewish family and Jewish life worldwide, with emphasis in Central Ohio. Types of grants include challenge/matching, demonstration, and seed money. Applications are accepted four times each year; guidelines are available upon request.
Requirements: U.S. and international IRS 501(c)3 organizations are eligible. Preference will be given to nonprofit organizations in central Ohio.
Restrictions: Individuals are ineligible. Grants are not awarded for operating support.
Geographic Focus: All States
Contact: Program Director; (614) 338-2365; fax (614) 338-2361; cjfndn@tcjf.org
Internet: http://www.columbusjewishfoundation.org/page10672.cfm
Sponsor: Columbus Jewish Foundation
1175 College Avenue
Columbus, OH 43209

Comcast Foundation Grants   1235
The foundation provides financial support to the organizations that make its communities stronger with particular focus on literacy, volunteerism, and youth leadership programs via the Diversity Fund and the Literacy Fund. Most of the organizations funded have been proactively identified by local Comcast sytems or are part of their existing national programs.
Requirements: 501(c)3 tax-exempt organizations are eligible. The foundation does not accept unsolicited request or proposals. If sending information, verify that your organization is located in a Comcase service area. Only organizations operating within Comcast communities will be considered. (Check service areas online at http://www.comcast.com/corporate/about/inthecommunity/foundation/serviceareas.html.
Restrictions: The foundation does not fund: Organizations without 501(c)3 status; organizations that practice discrimination by race, gender, religion, age, sexual orientation or national origin; marketing sponsorships; sporting events; trips or tours; capital campaigns; endowments; private foundations; individuals; or political candidates or organizations.
Geographic Focus: Alabama, Arizona, Arkansas, California, Colorado, Connecticut, Delaware, District of Columbia, Florida, Georgia, Idaho, Illinois, Indiana, Kansas, Kentucky, Louisiana, Maine, Maryland, Massachusetts, Michigan, Minnesota, Mississippi, Missouri, New Hampshire, New Jersey, New Mexico, Ohio, Oregon, Pennsylvania, South Carolina, Tennessee, Texas, Utah, Vermont, Virginia, Washington, West Virginia, Wisconsin
Amount of Grant: 5,000 - 50,000 USD
Contact: Allen Gomez, Executive Director; (215) 665-1700; fax (215) 981-7712
Internet: http://www.comcast.com/corporate/about/inthecommunity/foundation/comcastfoundation.html
Sponsor: Comcast Foundation
1500 Market Street, East Tower, 33rd Floor
Philadelphia, PA 19102

Comer Foundation Grants — 1236
The foundation awards grants to U.S. nonprofits in its areas of interest, including needle-exchange programs grounded in harm-reduction practice and programs providing direct services addressing health related to drug use; education—AIDS education, job training, and career guidance for low-income groups; health, with an emphasis on AIDS; social services—temporary shelters for homeless people and organizations offering diverse child, youth, and family services; and arts, culture, and humanities—to make programs of established organizations accessible to the public at large. Types of support include operating budgets, special projects, and staff development. There are no application deadlines.
Restrictions: Individuals are ineligible for grant support.
Geographic Focus: Illinois
Date(s) Application is Due: Mar 1; Jul 1; Nov 1
Amount of Grant: 5,000 - 30,000 USD
Contact: Stephanie Comer, (415) 256-9917; fax (415) 256-9918; scomer@comer-foundation.org
Internet: http://www.comer-foundation.com/home.html
Sponsor: Comer Foundation
P.O. Box 78154
San Francisco, CA 94107

Comerica Charitable Foundation Grants — 1237
The Comerica Charitable Foundation funding priorities support community needs in it's primary markets within Texas, Michigan, California, Arizona, and Florida. Applications are accepted for program support and capital expense of those non-profit organizations that support the foundation's priorities. Economic self-sufficiency for low and moderate income individuals and families will be supported in the areas of financial literacy, job readiness, job creation and retention, small business training and development, and transitional and supportive housing. Neighborhood revitalization areas to be supported are affordable housing and neighborhood business development. Financial literacy programs (K-12 and adult) and scholarships for students with income needs for studies in business, finance and growth industries will be supported. Also a priority is access to health care to include preventive care for the uninsured and under-insured. Also a priority are programs that support diversity and inclusion. Funding deadlines vary according to region. See the Foundation's website for regional offices.
Requirements: 501(c)3 nonprofits are eligible.
Restrictions: Grants are not awarded for United Way organizations, religious and fraternal groups, political parties, charitable golf events, athletic programs, multiyear pledges, or endowment funds.
Geographic Focus: Arizona, California, Florida, Michigan, Texas
Date(s) Application is Due: Mar 15; Jun 15; Sep 15; Nov 15
Contact: Program Contact; (313) 222-7356
Internet: http://www.comerica.com/vgn-ext-templating/v/index.jsp?vgnextoid=374970d75d994010VgnVCM1000004502a8c0RCRD
Sponsor: Comerica Charitable Foundation
P.O. Box 75000, MC 3390
Detroit, MI 48275-3390

Commission on Religion in Appalachia Grants — 1238
The commission supports Christian and interdenominational nonprofits in U.S. Appalachian regions. Churches and ministries and nonprofits in the areas of parochial education, religious welfare, civil rights, health care, and social services (domestic violence, housing, women's affairs, and food distribution) are awarded grants. The commission strongly encourages applicants to obtain guidelines prior to submitting proposals.
Requirements: Nonprofits in the Appalachian regions of Mississippi, Alabama, Georgia, South Carolina, North Carolina, Tennessee, Kentucky, Virginia, West Virginia, Ohio, Pennsylvania, Maryland, and New York are eligible.
Geographic Focus: Mississippi
Date(s) Application is Due: Jan 31
Amount of Grant: 5,000 - 15,000 USD
Contact: Grant Administrator; (304) 720-2672; fax (304) 720-2673; corainappa@aol.com
Internet: http://www.geocities.com/appalcora/About.html
Sponsor: Commission on Religion in Appalachia
P.O. Box 11908
Charleston, WV 25339-1908

Commonweal Foundation Community Assistance Grants — 1239
The foundation supports educational programs and projects assisting disadvantaged, at-risk youth. The foundation focuses on secondary and, to a lesser extent, elementary education. The foundation also considers grants for educational research and, to a limited extent, health care. Guidelines are available online.
Requirements: 501(c)3 tax-exempt organizations located in the District of Columbia, Maryland, or Northern Virginia are eligible. Applicant organizations should have an annual budget not exceeding $1 million.
Geographic Focus: District of Columbia, Maryland, Virginia
Date(s) Application is Due: Mar 1; Aug 1
Amount of Grant: Up to 25,000 USD
Contact: Gloria Dairsow, (240) 450-0000; fax (240) 450-4115; gdairsow@cweal.org
Internet: http://www.cweal.org/cag.htm
Sponsor: Commonweal Foundation
10770 Columbia Pike, Suite 150
Silver Spring, MD 20901

Commonwealth Edison Grants — 1240
The company recognizes its social responsibility to the area it serves, comprising Chicago and 25 northern Illinois counties, and makes grants and contributions to nonprofit organizations that address the diverse needs of this region and that can most enhance the economic, cultural, educational, and social health of its communities. Financial support is given for general operations as well as for specific projects or purposes that are in the general interest of the company or support general community needs. Contributions to hospitals are generally limited to capital fund drives. Building endowment funds or requests to relieve operating deficits are not supported. Each of the company's six commercial divisions (addresses and phone numbers available upon request) maintains a small philanthropic budget to address local needs. The corporate budget addresses needs of a wider ranging nature, such as support to United Way programs, education, and employee volunteer programs. Applications are accepted at any time. The executive review committee meets and addresses proposals quarterly, normally in February, May, August, and November.
Requirements: Nonprofits serving Chicago and 25 northern Illinois counties are eligible.
Restrictions: Support is not provided for individuals; fraternal or veteran organizations; sectarian religious organizations; non-tax-exempt organizations; municipal, state, or federal agencies; political organizations or campaigns; most United Way agencies; specific elementary or secondary schools or school systems; organizations requesting purchase of ads or sponsorship programs; or national or international organizations that do not have specific business relating to Commonwealth Edison and/or its customers.
Geographic Focus: Illinois
Amount of Grant: 1,000 - 5,000 USD
Contact: Steve Solomon, (312) 394-4321; fax (312) 394-2231
Sponsor: Commonwealth Edison Company
440 S. Lasalle Street, P.O. Box 805379
Chicago, IL 60680-5379

Commonwealth Fund Australian-American Health Policy Fellowships — 1241
The Australian Government Department of Health and Aging hopes to enrich health policy thinking as Australian-American Health Policy Fellows study how Australia approaches health policy issues, share lessons learned from the United States, and develop an international perspective and network of contacts to facilitate policy exchange and collaboration that extends beyond the fellowship experience. Australian-American Health Policy Fellowships are open to accomplished, mid-career health policy researchers and practitioners, including, academics, physicians, decision makers in managed care and other private sector health care organizations, federal and state health officials, and journalists. The Fellowship provides up to $55,000 (AUD) for terms of six to ten months, with a minimum stay of six months in Australia required. Focused on issues of common concern to Australian and U.S. policymakers, the fellowships are structured around areas of mutual policy interest, for example: health care quality and safety, the private/public mix of insurance and providers, the fiscal sustainability of health systems, the health care workforce, management and efficiency of health care delivery, and investment in preventive care strategies.
Requirements: All applicants must also meet the following criteria: be a citizen of the United States; be a mid-career health services researcher or practitioner (e.g., a physician, decision maker in a managed care organization or other private health care organization, government official or policy analyst, or journalist); have a demonstrated expertise in health policy issues and track record of informing health policy through research, policy analysis, health services, or clinical leadership; have completed a master's degree or doctorate (or the equivalent thereof) in health services research, health administration, health policy, or a related discipline, such as economics or political science; and if academically based, be at a mid-career level (e.g., research fellow to associate professor).
Restrictions: Fellowships are not awarded to support basic research or study for an academic degree.
Geographic Focus: All States
Date(s) Application is Due: Aug 15
Amount of Grant: Up to 55,000 USD
Contact: Robin Osborn; (212) 606-3809 or (212) 606-3800; ro@cmwf.org
Internet: http://www.commonwealthfund.org/Fellowships/Australian-American-Health-Policy-Fellowships.aspx
Sponsor: Commonwealth Fund
1 E 75th Street
New York, NY 10021-2692

Commonwealth Fund Harkness Fellowships in Health Care Policy and Practice — 1242
The Harkness Fellowships in Health Care Policy and Practice provide an opportunity for professionals from the Australia, Germany, the Netherlands, New Zealand, Norway, Switzerland, and the United Kingdom to spend four to 12 months in the United States conducting a research study that is relevant to health care policy and practice in both the United States and the fellow's home country, and that is focused on the issues of greatest concern to the fund. Fellowship awards provide up to $107,000, which covers round trip airfare to the United States, a living allowance, funds for project-related travel, research, and conferences, travel to attend the Commonwealth Fund program of fellowship seminars, health insurance, and U.S. and state taxes. A family supplement - including airfare, living allowance, and health insurance - is also provided to Fellows accompanied by a partner and/or children up to age 18.
Requirements: Applicants must be citizens of Australia, Germany, the Netherlands, New Zealand, Norway, Switzerland, and the United Kingdom in their late 20s to early 40s with broad educational backgrounds, not just those in research or academic careers. In order to apply, applicants must be nominated by their institution and submit a formal application, which is available from The Commonwealth Fund in New York City or its representatives in their home country.
Geographic Focus: All States, United Kingdom

Date(s) Application is Due: Sep 15
Amount of Grant: Up to 107,000 USD
Contact: Robin Osborn; (212) 606-3809 or (212) 606-3800; ro@cmwf.org
Internet: http://www.commonwealthfund.org/Fellowships/Minority-Health-Policy-Fellowship.aspx
Sponsor: Commonwealth Fund
1 E 75th Street
New York, NY 10021-2692

Communities Foundation of Texas Grants 1243
The unrestricted funds of the foundation support programs and projects intended to improve the quality of life for the citizens of the Dallas, TX, area. The funds support education, health and hospitals, social services, youth, and cultural programs. The foundation encourages projects developed in consultation with other agencies and planning groups and that promote coordination, cooperation, and sharing among organizations. Types of support include seed grants, emergency funds, building funds, equipment acquisition, matching funds, technical assistance, research, capital campaigns, and operating budgets. Requests for operating funds generally are not granted.
Requirements: 501(c)3 organizations in the Dallas, TX, area may apply.
Restrictions: Grants are not made to or for individuals, endowments, sectarian religious purposes, political or lobbying efforts, deficit financing, media projects, or for operational expenses of established organizations.
Geographic Focus: Texas
Contact: Brent Christopher; (214) 750-4222; fax (214) 750-4210; bchristopher@cftexas.org
Internet: http://www.cftexas.org
Sponsor: Communities Foundation of Texas
5500 Caruth Haven Lane
Dallas, TX 75225-8146

Community Development Financial Institution Bank Enterprise Awards 1244
Through the Bank Enterprise Award (BEA) Program, the Community Development Financial Institution (CDFI) Fund supports financial institutions around the country that are dedicated to financing and supporting community and economic development activities. The BEA Program complements the community development activities of insured depository institutions (i.e., banks and thrifts) by providing financial incentives to expand investments in CDFIs and to increase lending, investment, and service activities within economically distressed communities. Providing monetary awards for increasing community development activities leverages the Funds dollars and puts more capital to work in distressed communities throughout the nation.
Requirements: All depository institutions insured by the Federal Deposit Insurance Corporation (FDIC) are eligible to apply for a BEA Program award. Detailed guidelines and application forms can be found at the website.
Geographic Focus: All States
Date(s) Application is Due: Mar 15
Amount of Grant: 500,000 USD
Contact: Ruth Jaure, Acting Program Manager; (202) 622-9156
Internet: http://www.cdfifund.gov/what_we_do/programs_id.asp?programID=1
Sponsor: U.S. Department of the Treasury
601 13th Street NW, Suite 200 South
Washington, DC 20005

Community Foundation AIDS Endowment Awards 1245
The foundation administers an annual special grants program called the AIDS Endowment Awards. Grants of $1,000 will be awarded to one or two organizations that demonstrate a commitment to working towards the prevention, education and treatment of AIDS so that they may continue their efforts. Services provided could include education programs for the prevention of HIV/AIDS, medical and social services for those living with HIV/AIDS, housing services for those living with HIV/AIDS and medical research for the treatment and prevention of HIV/AIDS.
Requirements: Selected organizations in the metropolitan Richmond area interested in the field of AIDS education, research or community service and care are encouraged to apply. Organizations interested in applying should submit a brief proposal to foundation which should be no more than two single-spaced pages and include: [1] a description of the organization's mission; and [2] a description of the agency's work in the field of AIDS. Include a list of Board of Governors, a copy of the most recent IRS Form 990, an audited financial statement if available, and an IRS Tax Exempt Letter designating your organization a 501(c)3 non-profit.
Geographic Focus: Virginia
Date(s) Application is Due: Feb 15
Amount of Grant: 1,000 USD
Contact: Susan Hallett; (804) 330-7400; fax (804) 330-5992; shallett@tcfrichmond.org
Internet: http://www.tcfrichmond.org/Page2954.cfm
Sponsor: Community Foundation Serving Richmond and Central Virginia
7501 Boulders View Drive, Suite 110
Richmond, VA 23225

Community Foundation Alliance City of Evansville Endowment Fund Grants 1246
The City of Evansville Endowment Fund originated in 1994, when former Mayor Frank McDonald II proposed that $5 million of revenue from the gaming boat be invested in a way that would serve the City of Evansville, Indiana, forever. The City of Evansville Endowment Fund's earnings allow for grant making year after year. During its most recent grant cycle, the Fund allowed for grants totaling more than $180,000 to 21 nonprofit organizations serving the City of Evansville. The Foundation's grant cycle runs from May through October each year. Funding requests are accepted only during the grant cycle. The CEEF grants committee will consider funding requests of any amount. Requests of at least $1,000 are preferred.
Requirements: CEEF serves to provide funds to organizations that qualify as tax-exempt organizations under sections 501(c)3 and 509(a) of the Internal Revenue Code. The organization must serve within the city limits of Evansville, Indiana. At least sixty percent (60%) of grant funding will be distributed for activities that will support or benefit the 4th and 6th wards of the City of Evansville.
Restrictions: Not more than thirty percent (30%) of any grant request may be for personnel costs, travel costs, office supplies and other program operating costs.
Geographic Focus: Indiana
Date(s) Application is Due: Oct 31
Contact: Melinda Waldroup, Program Director; (812) 429-1191 or (877) 429-1191; fax (812) 429-0840; mwaldroup@alliance9.org
Internet: http://www.alliance9.org/city-of-evansville-endowment-fund
Sponsor: Community Foundation Alliance
123 NW Fourth Street, Suite 322
Evansville, IN 47708-1712

Community Foundation for Greater Buffalo Grants 1247
The Community Foundation for Greater Buffalo (CFGB) is a public charity holding more than 800 different charitable funds, large and small, established by individuals, families, nonprofit agencies and businesses to benefit Western New York. Since 1919, the foundation has served the needs of it's community and the wishes of it's donors through personalized service, financial stewardship, local expertise, and community leadership. The Foundation focuse's on four main areas of interest: strengthen the region as a center for arts and culture; natural, historic, and architectural resources; reduce racial and ethnic disparities; increase economic self-sufficiency for low-income individuals and families. Special funding will also be available to support the following: AIDS research and its cure ($5,000); programs that serve the visual, speech or hearing impaired ($5,000). Preference will be given to requests that align with one or more of the four focus areas.
Requirements: Applicants must be 501(c)3 not-for-profit organizations located within the eight counties of Western New York: Allegany, Cattaraugus, Chautauqua, Erie, Genesee, Niagara, Orleans, and Wyoming.
Restrictions: The Foundation will not consider competitive funding for: endowments; religious purposes; schools not registered with the New York State Education Department; attendance at or sponsorship of fundraising events for organizations; annual events or festivals; any partisan political activity. Funds from the foundation cannot be used to support or oppose a candidate for political office. Projects and activities that have occurred. The Foundation will not, except in extraordinary cases, provide payment or reimbursement for expenses incurred prior to the funding decision being communicated to the applicant.
Geographic Focus: New York
Date(s) Application is Due: Mar 1
Amount of Grant: 1,000 - 25,000 USD
Contact: Jean McKeown, Senior Program Officer; (716) 852-2857, ext. 204; fax (716) 852-2861; jeanm@cfgb.org
Internet: http://www.cfgb.org/page17000.cfm
Sponsor: Community Foundation for Greater Buffalo
712 Main Street
Buffalo, NY 14202

Community Foundation for Greater New Haven $5,000 and Under Grants 1248
The Community Foundation for Greater New Haven (CFFGNH) is a philanthropic institution that was established in 1928. The foundation's mission is to create positive and sustainable change in Connecticut's Greater New Haven region by increasing the amount of and enhancing the impact of community philanthropy. Funding through the CFFGNH $5,000 and Under Grants process are available to any organization with an operating budget of $2 million or less.
Requirements: IRS 501(c)3 nonprofit organizations are eligible to apply in the greater New Haven area, which includes: Ansonia; Bethany; Branford; Cheshire; Derby; East Haven; Guilford; Hamden; Madison; Milford; New Haven; North Branford; North Haven; Orange; Oxford; Seymour; Shelton; Wallingford; West Haven and; Woodbridge.
Restrictions: No organization shall be eligible to receive a grant under this process more often than once in any period of two calendar years. Grants are not made to support religious activities, lobbying, or travel.
Geographic Focus: Connecticut
Amount of Grant: 5,000 USD
Contact: Denise Canning, (203) 777-2386 or (203) 777-7076; dcanning@cfgnh.org
Internet: http://www.cfgnh.org/GrantsScholarships/TypesofGrants/tabid/199/Default.aspx
Sponsor: Community Foundation for Greater New Haven
70 Audubon Street
New Haven, CT 06510

Community Foundation for Greater New Haven Neighborhood Small Grants 1249
The Community Foundation for Greater New Haven (CFFGNH) is a philanthropic institution that was established in 1928. The foundation's mission is to create positive and sustainable change in Connecticut's Greater New Haven region by increasing the amount of and enhancing the impact of community philanthropy. The Neighborhood Program provides funding (in the range of $100 to $3,000), for technical assistance and training to civic groups to enable them to carryout their civic agenda and supports the development and implementation of projects that will have an effect on the quality of life in New Haven's neighborhoods. The Neighborhood Program seeks to help neighborhood residents to enhance their leadership and organizing skills.

Requirements: The following groups are eligible to apply: Agencies & groups that serve the elderly; Art Groups; Blockwatches; Business Associations; Faith-based Organizations; Individuals; Neighborhood Groups & Associations; Parent Groups; Tenant Associations; Service Clubs; Youth Groups; Partnerships between groups listed above are welcomed; Non-profits that are all-volunteer or have a staff of 2 or less.
Restrictions: Municipalities, agencies with three or more employees, and for-profit organizations are not eligible to apply for a grant under the New Haven Neighborhood Small Grants Program.
Geographic Focus: Connecticut
Date(s) Application is Due: Feb 12
Amount of Grant: 100 - 3,000 USD
Contact: Stephanie Sutherland, Associate Philanthropic Officer; (203) 777-2386 or (203) 777-7077; fax (203) 787-6584; ssutherland@cfgnh.org
Internet: http://www.cfgnh.org/Grantmaking/TypesofGrants/tabid/199/Default.aspx
Sponsor: Community Foundation for Greater New Haven
70 Audubon Street
New Haven, CT 06510

Community Foundation for Greater New Haven Quinnipiac River Fund Grants 1250
The Community Foundation for Greater New Haven (CFFGNH) is a philanthropic institution that was established in 1928. The foundation's mission is to create positive and sustainable change in Connecticut's Greater New Haven region by increasing the amount of and enhancing the impact of community philanthropy. The Quinnipiac River Fund established in 1990 was a result of a settlement between the National Resources Defense Council, Connecticut Fund for the Environment, and the Upjohn Corporation to improve the environmental quality of Quinnipiac River, the New Haven Harbor, and their watersheds, and otherwise benefit the environment of these resources. Consideration given to grant proposals that: research methods of reducing pollution, or otherwise improving the Quinnipiac River's environmental health; address means of reducing both non-point and point sources of pollution to the River; research the permitting process and look at the permits themselves; entail environmental advocacy, except litigation; study the ecology of the Quinnipiac River and the New Haven Harbor; provide public education about the Quinnipiac River and its watershed; purchase land on the Quinnipiac River for conservation purposes, or to reduce pollution and improve public access to the River.
Requirements: IRS 501(c)3 nonprofit organizations are eligible to apply in the greater New Haven area, which includes: Ansonia; Bethany; Branford; Cheshire; Derby; East Haven; Guilford; Hamden; Madison; Milford; New Haven; North Branford; North Haven; Orange; Oxford; Seymour; Shelton; Wallingford; West Haven and; Woodbridge.
Restrictions: Grants are not made to support religious activities, lobbying, or travel.
Geographic Focus: Connecticut
Date(s) Application is Due: Jan 15
Amount of Grant: 5,000 - 18,000 USD
Contact: Sarah Fabish, Grant/Scholarship Director; (203) 777-2386 or (203) 777-7075; fax (203) 787-6584; sfabish@cfgnh.org
Internet: http://qrwgis.newhaven.edu/QRFprojects.htm
Sponsor: Community Foundation for Greater New Haven
70 Audubon Street
New Haven, CT 06510

Community Foundation for Greater New Haven Responsive New Grants 1251
The Community Foundation for Greater New Haven is a philanthropic institution that was established in 1928. The foundation's mission is to create positive and sustainable change in Connecticut's Greater New Haven region by increasing the amount of and enhancing the impact of community philanthropy. The Responsive New Grants Program is generally awarded to address an agency's general operating, programmatic, capital or technical assistance needs. This funding source is open to all requests for projects and organizational support.
Requirements: IRS 501(c)3 nonprofit organizations are eligible to apply in the greater New Haven area, which includes: Ansonia; Bethany; Branford; Cheshire; Derby; East Haven; Guilford; Hamden; Madison; Milford; New Haven; North Branford; North Haven; Orange; Oxford; Seymour; Shelton; Wallingford; West Haven and; Woodbridge.
Restrictions: Grants are not made to support religious activities, lobbying, or travel.
Geographic Focus: Connecticut
Date(s) Application is Due: Mar 5
Amount of Grant: 10,000 - 185,000 USD
Contact: Denise Canning, Grants Manager; (203) 777-2386 or (203) 777-7076; fax (203) 787-6584; dcanning@cfgnh.org
Internet: http://www.cfgnh.org/GrantsScholarships/TypesofGrants/tabid/199/Default.aspx
Sponsor: Community Foundation for Greater New Haven
70 Audubon Street
New Haven, CT 06510

Community Foundation for Greater New Haven Sponsorship Grants 1252
The Community Foundation for Greater New Haven (CFFGNH) is a philanthropic institution that was established in 1928. The foundation's mission is to create positive and sustainable change in Connecticut's Greater New Haven region by increasing the amount of and enhancing the impact of community philanthropy. The available sponsorships are awarded throughout a calendar year, only for events and may not exceed $2,500 per event. It is recommended that nonprofits submit a sponsorship request at least 60 days in advance of their event. Applications are accepted year-round, application available online at: http://www.cfgnh.org/Grantmaking/TypesofGrants/tabid/199/Default.aspx.
Requirements: IRS 501(c)3 nonprofit organizations are eligible to apply in the greater New Haven area, which includes: Ansonia; Bethany; Branford; Cheshire; Derby; East Haven; Guilford; Hamden; Madison; Milford; New Haven; North Branford; North Haven; Orange; Oxford; Seymour; Shelton; Wallingford; West Haven and; Woodbridge.
Restrictions: Grants are not made to support religious activities, lobbying, or travel.
Geographic Focus: Connecticut
Amount of Grant: 2,500 USD
Contact: Leigh Higgins, Assistant to CEO; (203) 777-2386 or (203) 777-7092; fax (203) 787-6584; lhiggins@cfgnh.org
Internet: http://www.cfgnh.org/Grantmaking/TypesofGrants/tabid/199/Default.aspx
Sponsor: Community Foundation for Greater New Haven
70 Audubon Street
New Haven, CT 06510

Community Foundation for Greater New Haven Valley Neighborhood Grants 1253
The Valley Community Foundation (VCF), a supporting organization of The Community Foundation for Greater New Haven (CFGNH), promotes investment in it's community leaders. The Valley Neighborhood Grant Program is rooted in CFGNH's Valley Neighborhood Small Grants Program but has the purpose of encouraging, identifying, engaging and supporting neighborhood leadership. It provides funding ($100 to $3,000), technical assistance and training to civic groups to assist them in carrying out their civic agenda, and to support development and implementation of projects that will improve the quality of Valley life.
Requirements: The following groups are eligible to apply: Art Groups; Blockwatches; Business Associations; Faith-based Organizations; Groups that serve the elderly; Individuals in partnership with a non-profit; Neighborhood Groups & Associations; Parent Groups; Tenant Associations; Service Clubs; Youth Groups; Partnerships between groups listed above are welcomed; Non-profits that are all-volunteer or have a staff of 4 or less are eligible to apply. If your group does not have legal nonprofit status, establish a relationship with a 501(c)3 organization to serve as your fiduciary agent. Please Note: If you choose to work with a 501(c)3, they must submit a letter of support.
Restrictions: The Neighborhood Program will not fund requests for: salaries or stipends; recreational trips; gas grills or coolers.
Geographic Focus: Connecticut
Date(s) Application is Due: Feb 1
Amount of Grant: 100 - 3,000 USD
Contact: Stephanie Sutherland, Associate Philanthropic Officer; (203) 777-2386 or (203) 777-7077; fax (203) 787-6584; ssutherland@cfgnh.org
Internet: http://www.cfgnh.org/Grantmaking/TypesofGrants/tabid/199/Default.aspx
Sponsor: Community Foundation for Greater New Haven
70 Audubon Street
New Haven, CT 06510

Community Foundation for Greater New Haven Women & Girls Grants 1254
The Community Foundation for Greater New Haven (CFFGNH) is a philanthropic institution that was established in 1928. The foundation's mission is to create positive and sustainable change in Connecticut's Greater New Haven region by increasing the amount of and enhancing the impact of community philanthropy. The Community Fund for Women & Girls was created in 1995 by an anonymous woman to provide ongoing support for services important to women and girls in the Greater New Haven and Lower Naugatuck Valley area. Favorable grant proposals would: create and support opportunities for the economic, educational, physical, emotional, social, artistic, and personal growth of women and girls; meet special needs of women and girls and the diverse populations of women in our region; encourage the advancement and full participation of women and girls in the community and in philanthropy; advance the status of women and girls in the core areas of economic security, health, violence, education and political participation.
Requirements: IRS 501(c)3 nonprofit organizations are eligible to apply in the greater New Haven area, which includes: Ansonia; Bethany; Branford; Cheshire; Derby; East Haven; Guilford; Hamden; Madison; Milford; New Haven; North Branford; North Haven; Orange; Oxford; Seymour; Shelton; Wallingford; West Haven and; Woodbridge.
Geographic Focus: Connecticut
Date(s) Application is Due: Jan 15
Amount of Grant: 1,000 - 10,000 USD
Contact: Denise Canning, Grants Manager; (203) 777-2386 or (203) 777-7076; fax (203) 787-6584; dcanning@cfgnh.org
Internet: http://www.cfgnh.org/Grantmaking/TypesofGrants/tabid/199/Default.aspx
Sponsor: Community Foundation for Greater New Haven
70 Audubon Street
New Haven, CT 06510

Community Foundation for Monterey County Grants 1255
The community foundation supports nonprofits in Monterey, CA, in the areas of social services, education, environment, arts, health, historic preservation, and general charitable giving. Collaboratives are highly encouraged. The foundation awards grants through its General Endowment. Technical Assistance grants and Neighborhood Grants also are awarded. Types of support include seed money, emergency funds, general operating support, building funds, equipment acquisition, land acquisition, matching funds, projects, consulting services, and technical assistance. Information on how to apply for each type of grant can be accessed online.
Requirements: 501(c)3 organizations in Monterey, CA, may submit applications.
Restrictions: The foundation does not support individuals, religious activities, scholarships, fellowships, travel, research, salaries and other operating expenses of schools and public agencies, annual campaigns, or special events; create or add to endowment funds; or pay off debt.
Geographic Focus: California
Date(s) Application is Due: Jan 3; May 2; Aug 1
Amount of Grant: 5,000 - 40,000 USD

Contact: Jackie Wendland, Grants Administrator; (831) 375-9712, ext. 11; fax (831) 375-4731; jackie@cfmco.org
Internet: http://www.cfmco.org/grantsOverview.php
Sponsor: Community Foundation for Monterey County
2354 Garden Road
Monterey, CA 93940

Community Foundation for Muskegon County Grants   1256
The community foundation was established to serve the needs of the people of Muskegon County and nearby western Michigan. The foundation's strategic plan for grant making focuses on the prevention of problems rather than the cure; encourages programs that are collaborative, comprehensive, and have the potential to be continuous; encourages leveraging and matching grant opportunities from multiple funders; and supports seed money opportunities for innovative projects. Major grant interest areas include the arts, community development and urban revitalization, education, environment, health/human services, and needs of young children (ages 0-3). Types of support include seed money grants, special projects, matching funds, equipment, scholarship funds, loans, research, publications, conferences and seminars, endowment funds, consulting services, continuing support, emergency funds, internships, professorships, and renovation projects. Although the foundation generally makes one-year grant commitments, it will consider making longer term commitments for new efforts that show strong promise for positive impact. Applications are accepted on specific dates each year; it is recommended that the applicant contact the foundation to discuss their interests and to obtain the next grant application deadline.
Requirements: IRS 501(c)3 organizations and institutions in Muskegon County and nearby western Michigan are eligible.
Restrictions: Support will not be provided for routine operating expenses; capital equipment, computer hardware and software, and motor vehicles; conferences, publications, videos, films, television, or radio programs; endowment campaigns; special fund-raising events; religious programs that serve specific denominations; existing obligations or debts; individual schools or districts; or individuals.
Geographic Focus: Michigan
Amount of Grant: 250 - 50,000 USD
Contact: Marcy Joy, Program Officer; (231) 722-4538 or (231) 332-4124; fax (231) 722-4616; mjoy@cffmc.org
Internet: http://www.cffmc.org/grantapply.php
Sponsor: Community Foundation for Muskegon County
425 West Western Avenue, Suite 200
Muskegon, MI 49440

Community Foundation for Northeast Michigan Grants   1257
Grants are made to tax-exempt, northeast Michigan charitable agencies and organizations. The foundation looks for projects that prevent community problems, benefit the greatest number of people, help deliver new services or make existing services more efficient, enhance collaboration among organizations, promote youth development, address emerging community needs, try a new approach to a persistent problem, or encourage people to develop new skills and help themselves. Grant mechanisms include the general unrestricted (common) grant; the Youth Advisory Council (YAC) Grant, which may be used for projects that benefit youth; and the tobacco settlement fund grant, which is available to programs that improve the physical, mental, and emotional health of youth and seniors, with priority given to projects that address issues related to smoking. Applications are available on the Web site, or applicants may request forms by phoning the office.
Requirements: IRS 501(c)3 nonprofit organizations, schools, churches (for non-sectarian purposes), cities, townships, and other governmental units serving the four-county area of Alcona, Alpena, Montmorency, and Presque Isle in northeast Michigan are eligible to apply.
Restrictions: Grants are not given to individuals, except for awards or scholarships from designated donor funds.
Geographic Focus: Michigan
Date(s) Application is Due: Feb 1; May 1; Aug 1; Nov 1
Amount of Grant: Up to 3,500 USD
Contact: Barbara Willyard, Executive Director; (877) 354-6881 or (989) 354-6881; fax (989) 356-3319; bwillyard@cfnem.org
Internet: http://www.cfnem.org/grants/grantinfo.htm
Sponsor: Community Foundation for Northeast Michigan
111 Water Street, P.O. Box 495
Alpena, MI 49707-0495

Community Foundation for San Benito County Grants   1258
The Foundation serves donors, advances philanthropy and achieves impact by supporting the work of nonprofit organizations. The Foundation continuously monitors the San Benito County community to understand the nature of need, the forces of change, available resources and the capacity for growth. The Foundation provides funding to support impactful programs within and across the following areas of interest: arts and culture; education and youth; health and social services; agriculture and environment; community enhancement; economic development. Application deadlines are announced on the Foundation's website.
Requirements: Selection criteria and priorities are as follows: projects or services which respond to a demonstrated need within San Benito County; effective use and greatest impact of grant funds; initiatives to solve significant community issues; collaboration and coordination of service delivery; demonstrate a level of cooperation with other organizations, including leveraging financial and in-kind support from other groups and individuals; strengthening organizational capacity; addressing diverse community interests; organizational or program sustainability; organizations with demonstrated financial need; and unduplicated services. Awards are generally up to $40,000. Major projects or initiatives over $40,000 must be preliminarily discussed with Foundation staff.
Restrictions: In general the following are not funded: organizations that discriminate on the basis of age, disability, ethnic origin, gender, race or religion; grants to individuals; fraternal or service organizations, unless in support of specific programs open to or benefiting the entire community; salaries and other operating expenses of schools and public agencies; fundraising events such as annual campaigns, walk-a-thons, tournaments, fashion shows, dinners and auctions; organizations and programs designed to support political activities; organizations located outside San Benito County unless for a specific program benefiting residents within San Benito County; pay off existing obligations or enable funding of reserve accounts; endowment funds; and scholarships, fellowships, travel grants and academic, technical or specialized research.
Geographic Focus: California
Contact: Grants Manager; (831) 630-1924; fax (831) 630-1934; info@cffsbc.org
Internet: http://www.cffsbc.org/grantoverview.php
Sponsor: Community Foundation for San Benito County
829 San Benio Street, Suite 200
Hollister, CA 95023

Community Foundation for Southeast Michigan Grants   1259
The Community Foundation for Southeast Michigan is always looking for effective program and project ideas that can improve life in southeast Michigan, specifically in the seven-county service area of Wayne, Oakland, Macomb, Monroe, Washtenaw, St. Clair and Livingston. Grants are provided considering various local needs and identifying those projects which promise the strongest long-term impact on the region. In general support is provided for projects and programs in the areas of arts and culture, civic affairs, health, human services, neighborhood and regional economic development, work force development, environment and land use. Interested applicants are encouraged to review the grantmaking guidelines at the website and call the Program Officer to discuss proposals. Grants range from $5,000 to $1 million, with the majority ranging from $35,000 to $100,000. Application may be made at any time. Proposals submitted prior to February 15, May 15, August 15 and November 15 will typically receive a response within three or four months.
Requirements: Eligible organizations: are a 501(c)3 tax-exempt organization, a government entity, a school district or a university; have headquarters (or a local partner) located in the seven-county service area; serve residents in the seven-county service area; have Board and/or the CEO approval to submit a proposal; and have a current certified financial audit.
Restrictions: All final reports due to the Foundation for previous grants must be submitted before applying. Requests for sectarian religious programs, individuals, and funding for deficits or other previously incurred obligations are not eligible.
Geographic Focus: Michigan
Contact: Katie Brisson, Senior Program Officer; (888) 933-6369 or (313) 961-6675; fax (313) 961-2886; kbrisson@cfsem.org
Internet: http://cfsem.org/apply-grant
Sponsor: Community Foundation for Southeast Michigan
333 W Fort Street, Suite 2010
Detroit, MI 48226-3134

Community Foundation for Southeast Michigan HOPE Fund Grants   1260
The HOPE Fund is a permanent community endowment, established at the Community Foundation for Southeast Michigan in 1994. HOPE Fund Grants provide funding to nonprofit organizations serving the local lesbian, gay, bisexual and transgender (LGBT) communities. Grants are made to LGBT organizations and to mainstream organizations. LGBT organizations are those whose mission expressly states a primary purpose of working in the LGBT community. LGBT organizations may apply for up to $25,000 for: support for capacity building for LGBT agencies which leads to increased efficiency internally (for example, board development, software training, strategic planning, etc.); or support for efforts for two or more LGBT agencies to collaborate in meaningful ways, which leads to more efficiency and impact in the community (for example, joint fundraising endeavors, coordinated youth programming, etc.). Mainstream organizations may apply for up to $10,000 to support: expanding the services of the organization to better serve LGBT people and their families; promote tolerance or inclusion of LGBT people and their families within the larger community; or avoid duplication of services by spurring collaborative services or programs between the mainstream organization and LGBT-specific organizations in the southeast Michigan region. Typically grants to mainstream organizations are one-time only in nature, intended to spur the growth of new activity which supports LGBT people that is eventually folded into the ongoing activities of an agency.
Requirements: Eligible organizations: are a 501(c)3 tax-exempt organization, a government entity, a school district or a university; have headquarters (or a local partner) located in the seven-county service area; serve residents in the seven-county service area; have board and/or the CEO approval to submit a proposal; and have a current certified financial audit. Priority is given to requests for support of non-HIV/AIDS-related programs.
Restrictions: All final reports due to the Foundation for previous grants must be submitted before applying. Requests for sectarian religious programs, individuals, and funding for deficits or other previously incurred obligations are not eligible. A portion of funding each year is awarded to capacity-building efforts that specifically target the LGBT people-of-color communities.
Geographic Focus: Michigan
Date(s) Application is Due: Feb 15; Aug 15
Contact: Katie Brisson, Senior Program Officer; (888) 933-6369 or (313) 961-6675; fax (313) 961-2886; kbrisson@cfsem.org
Internet: http://cfsem.org/apply-grant
Sponsor: Community Foundation for Southeast Michigan
333 W Fort Street, Suite 2010
Detroit, MI 48226-3134

184 | GRANT PROGRAMS

Community Foundation for Southern Arizona Grants   1261

The foundation awards grants in southern Arizona for a broad array of charitable purposes in the areas of arts and humanities, education, the environment, health, social services. Types of support include challenge/matching grants, conferences and seminars, scholarships, equipment acquisition, fellowships, general support, multiyear support, project development, publications, research, seed funding, and technical assistance. Priority is given to proposals that promote collaboration and build on the strengths of individuals and communities. Deadlines are determined on a yearly basis.

Requirements: Nonprofit and grassroots organizations in southern Arizona communities are eligible. Southern Arizona communities include all of Cochise, Santa Cruz, and Pima Counties; and the areas of Yuma, Mariposa, Pinal, Graham, and Greenlee Counties that lie south of the Gila River.

Restrictions: Funds are generally not available for ongoing operating or capital campaigns, debt retirement, endowments, individuals, individual schools, sectarian activities, or underwriting of fund-raising events.

Geographic Focus: Arizona
Amount of Grant: 1,000 - 10,000 USD
Contact: Barbara Brown; (520) 770-0800, ext. 107; bbrown@CFSoAZ.org
Internet: http://www.cfsoaz.org/page17480.cfm
Sponsor: Community Foundation for Southern Arizona
2250 E Broadway Boulevard
Tucson, AZ 85719

Community Foundation in Jacksonville Art Ventures Small Arts Organizations Professional Assistance Grants   1262

The goals and guiding principles for the Art Ventures-Small Arts Organizations program are to: recognize and build on strengths and assets rather than needs and deficiencies; improve the ability of organizations and individuals to help themselves over the long term; foster cooperative approaches to community issues based on shared visions and mutual responsibility; include people served in the process of planning, implementation and evaluation; recognize and strengthen local leadership; anticipate and take a preventive approach to emerging community issues; serve as a catalyst for attracting other funding resources; create innovative approaches to dealing with long-standing issues; and, build a stronger sense of community. Up to six small arts organizations will be selected to receive training in governance, organizational development, and other core components to improve efficiencies and build their capacity as a nonprofit organization. Selected nonprofit small arts organizations will participate in four half-day educational sessions during September – November. Subsequently, up to three of the six organizations participating in these sessions will be selected to participate in intensive strategic planning. January – March of the following year. Organizations that have successfully completed both programs will receive preference in the next year's Art Ventures grant process, which will offer artistic and administrative development grants ranging from $3,000 - $10,000 per organization.

Requirements: Eligible organizations must be small arts organizations in Baker, Clay, Nassau, St. Johns or Duval counties. Applicants must be qualified as tax-exempt under Section 501(c)3 of the Internal Revenue Service code. Applicants must commit to participating in four half-day trainings, each one attended by two leaders of your organization, preferably the executive staff member/volunteer and a board member. It would be most beneficial if the same people attended all four sessions. Workshops will cover organizational development topics including governance, grant writing, planning and more. Applications must be received by 5:00 pm of the deadline date.

Geographic Focus: Florida
Date(s) Application is Due: Jun 13
Amount of Grant: 3,000 - 10,000 USD
Contact: Katie Patterson, (904) 356-4483; fax (904) 356-7910; kpatterson@jaxcf.org
Internet: http://www.jaxcf.org/page.aspx?pid=624
Sponsor: Community Foundation for Northeast Florida
245 Riverside Avenue, Suite 310
Jacksonville, FL 32202

Community Foundation in Jacksonville Senior Roundtable Aging Adults Grants   1263

The 65-and-older population spiked 15.1% from 2000 to 2010, and many experts expect that trend to continue over the next ten years as baby boomers continue to reach retirement age and live longer lives. To better respond to the needs of this growing aging population, The Community Foundation is investing to strengthen the sector of senior-serving organizations. The Community Foundation also partners with senior serving organizations to strengthen its collaborations with one another by continuing to provide support for The Senior Roundtable. In 2008, The Community Foundation helped to launch and continues to support this groups efforts. Membership includes organizations working directly with seniors and caregivers, institutes of higher learning and individuals working and supporting senior citizens. The Community Foundation offers competitive grants, $1,000 to $2,500, through this membership to improve the quality of life for aging adults.

Requirements: Applicants must be qualified as tax-exempt under Section 501(c)3 of the IRS or classified as a unit of local government. Organizations must serve aging adults in Duval County and must be verified members of The Senior Roundtable. Nonprofit organizations serving aging adults are encouraged to consider membership in the Nonprofit Center of Northeast Florida which provide resources for agency capacity-building and avenues for collaboration. Grants are non-renewable.

Restrictions: In general, funds are not awarded for: capital and endowment campaigns; fundraising events; or, projects that promote religious or political views.

Geographic Focus: Florida
Date(s) Application is Due: Jun 6
Amount of Grant: 1,000 - 2,500 USD
Contact: Mark LeMaire, (904) 356-4483; fax (904) 356-7910; mlemaire@jaxcf.org
Internet: http://www.seniorroundtable.org
Sponsor: Community Foundation for Northeast Florida
245 Riverside Avenue, Suite 310
Jacksonville, FL 32202

Community Foundation of Abilene Community Grants   1264

The Community Foundation of Abilene (CFA) funds projects to benefit the Abilene community. The CFA will consider funding for special projects, innovative programs, and equipment and building needs. Most grants are in the $1,000 to $25,000 range. Priority funding includes programs or projects that: propose practical solutions to community problems; respond to changing or emerging community needs; address prevention as well as assistance for a problem; promote cooperation among nonprofit agencies without duplicating efforts; leverage or generate other funding or resources; promote volunteer participation and citizen involvement in the community; or enhance and encourage sustainability. Consideration is also given to the capability of the agency and its personnel to achieve expected results, past stewardship of the agency, the adequacy and professionalism of the budget, and the support and cooperation of the agencies involved in similar projects. The application and its tutorial is available at the Foundation website.

Requirements: The Community Foundation welcomes proposals from nonprofit organizations in the Abilene, Texas area with an IRS tax exempt status. To be eligible to submit a grant proposal, an organization must be in compliance with any previous grant reporting requirements or conditions. The organization must also first submit a letter of intent. The Grant Distribution Committee will review letters of intent and determine which organizations will be requested to submit a proposal. Submitting organizations will be notified by letter and email. Priority is given to agencies located in and serving Abilene. Consideration will be given to awarding grants to agencies serving Abilene and outlying areas. An agency is not required to have a location in Abilene, but it is preferred that there is a chapter or representative in Abilene.

Restrictions: The Foundation does not make grants for activities which do not benefit the citizens of Abilene; maintenance expenses; medical or scholarly research; membership fees; ticket sales for charitable fundraising efforts; church related activities unless they involve the community as a whole; travel for groups, such as school classes, clubs or sports teams; deficit budget expenses or retroactive funding for current projects, programs or equipment; capital debt reduction; individuals, except through scholarships; or political projects. The Foundation usually does not approve multi-year grants.

Geographic Focus: Texas
Date(s) Application is Due: Feb 1; Sep 7
Contact: Courtney Vletas; (325) 676-3883, ext 102; cvletas@cfabilene.org
Internet: http://cfabilene.org/grant-information-applications
Sponsor: Community Foundation of Abilene
500 Chestnut, Suite 1634, P.O. Box 1001
Abilene, TX 79604

Community Foundation of Abilene Future Fund Grants   1265

The Future Fund Grants focus on the needs of children and youth. Future Fund awards a minimum of $15,000 in grants each year. Most grants are in the $5,000 range, although smaller and larger grants will be considered. Chances of funding increase if the project: proposes a practical solution to a youth or children's issue; promotes volunteer participation in the community; is responsive to changing or emerging community needs; leverages or generates other funding or resources; promotes cooperation among nonprofit agencies without duplicating efforts; or addresses prevention as well as assistance for a problem. Consideration is also given to the capability of the agency and its staff and volunteers to achieve expected results, the adequacy and professionalism of the budget, and the support and cooperation of agencies involved in similar projects. Applications are available at the Foundation website, and are accepted at any time.

Requirements: Future Fund will consider funding for special projects and equipment needs for programs that directly serve children and/or youth in the community. Future Fund welcomes proposals from any nonprofit organization in Abilene with an IRS tax-exempt status.

Restrictions: Funding is not available for the following: medical or scholarly research; maintenance expenses; membership fees; ticket sales for charitable fundraising events; church related activities unless they involve children in the entire community; travel for groups, such as school classes, clubs or sports teams; participation in out of town camps; projects, programs or events that have been completed or items that have already been purchased; capital debt reduction; individuals; political projects.

Geographic Focus: Texas
Amount of Grant: 1,000 - 10,000 USD
Contact: Courtney Vletas; (325) 676-3883, ext 102; cvletas@cfabilene.org
Internet: http://cfabilene.org/future-fund
Sponsor: Community Foundation of Abilene
500 Chestnut, Suite 1634, P.O. Box 1001
Abilene, TX 79604

Community Foundation of Abilene Humane Treatment of Animals Grants   1266

The Humane Treatment of Animals Grant is awarded to a nonprofit organization whose mission provides services to aid and assist in the care of homeless dogs, cats and other animals; spay and neuter programs; and educational programs on importance of humane treatment of animals. The application form and video tutorial are available at the Foundation website.

Requirements: Applicant must have an IRS 501(c)3 designation and provide services in Abilene, Texas. Organizations must submit, in narrative form, a brief history of their organization and its mission, along with a description of their programs and services. They must also identify critical challenges or deficiencies, key areas of funding needed, and measurable outcomes. Fifteen copies of the proposal must be submitted in person or by mail. Faxed proposals are not accepted.

Restrictions: The grant will not fund endowments, deficit financing and debt retirement, or fundraising events.
Geographic Focus: Texas
Date(s) Application is Due: Aug 3
Amount of Grant: 5,000 - 15,000 USD
Contact: Courtney Vletas; (325) 676-3883, ext 102; cvletas@cfabilene.org
Internet: http://cfabilene.org/grant-information-applications
Sponsor: Community Foundation of Abilene
500 Chestnut, Suite 1634, P.O. Box 1001
Abilene, TX 79604

Community Foundation of Bartholomew County Heritage Fund Grants   1267
The goal of the Heritage Fund's grant program is to achieve the maximum impact with the available resources. The Fund will consider grant applications that: are change-orientated and problem-solving in nature; strive to anticipate the changing needs of the community and to be flexible in responding to them; address the needs of a significant number of community residents and provide the greatest benefit per dollar granted; encourage support from the community by using matching, challenge and other grant techniques; have a broad funding base, with additional support being sought from the government, foundations, associations and other funders; enable grant recipients to achieve certain objectives such as capacity building, and/or increasing efficiency, effectiveness and fundraising capabilities; request technical assistance or specialized help with projects that respond to community needs; or positively impact the Heritage Fund's Areas of Initiative.
Requirements: Grants are made to not-for-profit organizations whose programs benefit the residents of Bartholomew County, Indiana.
Restrictions: Funding is not available for the following: individuals; events, performances, seminars or trips unless there are special circumstances which will benefit the community; individual school needs; faith based organizations unless the project in question is not religious in nature, is not restricted based on faith, and involves no faith based proselytizing; or agency endowments.
Geographic Focus: Indiana
Date(s) Application is Due: Mar 1; Jun 1; Sep 1; Dec 1
Amount of Grant: Up to 3,000 USD
Contact: Lynda J. Morgan; (812) 376-7772; fax (812) 376-0051; lmorgan@heritagefundbc.org
Internet: http://www.heritagefundbc.org/grants/process_guidelines_deadlines.php
Sponsor: Community Foundation of Bartholomew County
538 Franklin Street, P.O. Box 1547
Columbus, IN 47202-1547

Community Foundation of Bartholomew County James A. Henderson Award for Fundraising   1268
The Henderson Award recognizes the invaluable role volunteer fundraisers play in advancing the quality of life within Bartholomew County, Indiana. Not-for-profit organizations in the county are invited to nominate volunteers who have performed outstanding fundraising for their organizations. A committee will review the nominations and select the person to be honored. The committee will consider such criteria as innovation, sustainability, creativity, effectiveness, effort, ability to engage others, outreach to new donors, etc. Generally the amount raised will not be a major factor in the scoring. Efforts will be made to recognize unsung heroes in fundraising. The successful nominee will be recognized at the Heritage Fund's Annual Report to the Community. He/she will receive a small gift and the nominating organization will receive a $2,500 grant in honor of the winner. The nomination form is available at the website.
Geographic Focus: Indiana
Date(s) Application is Due: Mar 23
Amount of Grant: 2,500 USD
Contact: Lynda J. Morgan; (812) 376-7772; fax (812) 376-0051; lmorgan@heritagefundbc.org
Internet: http://www.heritagefundbc.com/grants/award_james_henderson.php
Sponsor: Community Foundation of Bartholomew County
538 Franklin Street, P.O. Box 1547
Columbus, IN 47202-1547

Community Foundation of Bartholomew County Women's Giving Circle   1269
The Women's Giving Circle of Bartholomew County (WGCBC) seeks to empower women givers and make a positive change in the lives of women and families in Bartholomew County. The WGCBC is a participating membership fund managed by Heritage Fund – the Community Foundation of Bartholomew County. Each year the membership of the WGCBC will vote at the spring Annual Meeting on grant proposals submitted to the membership, following guidelines set out by the Guiding Circle. These grant recommendations will be made to the Heritage Fund Board of Directors for final approval. The application is available at the website.
Requirements: The WGCBC seeks to support programs that make a significant impact on women and their families. The Circle encourage submission of requests for new, emerging and diverse programs with goals to improve the lives of women and families. In addition, it also recognizes the value of existing programs which could be enhanced, updated or broadened for increased impact. All requests must be for programs which address the following focus areas: self sufficiency for women - providing women and their families with the tools necessary to become self-sufficient. Including but not limited to, providing access to opportunities for education and mentoring; job application and interview skills; health issues; developing the knowledge and skills to make informed effective financial decisions; early childhood education - providing young learners with an opportunity to begin school ready to learn; parental support - including but not limited to helping parents and caregivers create a healthy, supportive family environment, providing for the needs of families who are caring for children with physical, mental, emotional or other types of challenges, and families dealing with the challenges of raising teens; and women in crisis - including but not limited to, providing women in unsafe situations the support to establish a productive life; dealing with homeless causes; women who are faced with the challenges of providing support for elderly parents and ill spouses. Grants are made to Bartholomew County nonprofit organizations, or to qualifying organizations that provide a responsible fiscal agent.
Restrictions: Grants will not be made for any of the following: individuals; general operating costs; scholarships; individual school needs; agency endowments; events, performances, seminars or trips unless there are special circumstances which will benefit the community; faith-based organizations unless the project in question is not religious in nature, is not restricted based on faith, and involves no faith-based proselytizing.
Geographic Focus: Indiana
Date(s) Application is Due: Feb 17
Amount of Grant: Up to 5,000 USD
Contact: Lisa Shafran, Grant Contact; (812) 376-7772; lshafran@heritagefundbc.org
Internet: http://www.heritagefundbc.org/donors/campaigns/womensgivingcircle/womensgivingcircle.php
Sponsor: Community Foundation of Bartholomew County
538 Franklin Street, P.O. Box 1547
Columbus, IN 47202-1547

Community Foundation of Bloomington and Monroe County - Precision Health Network Cycle Grants   1270
The Precision Health Network Grants are designed to develop and enhance community health education and outcomes. The Grants are available to applicants serving Monroe, Lawrence, Brown, Greene, Morgan, Owen, Orange, Martin, and Daviess counties in Indiana. Detailed guidelines and application are available at the website.
Requirements: Projects selected to receive grants must meet at least one of the following criteria: promotion of health and healthy lifestyles; prevention of disease; and self-management of chronic disease. Projects must target schools, community centers, or work sites in the defined geographic areas. Grants will be made only to non-profit, 501(c)3 organizations and programs. Programs developed through individual initiative or by the for-profit sector will need to have a not-for-profit serve as the "fiscal sponsor" for the program. The following entities may apply: community service organizations with health-related missions; public entities; employee groups; and employers.
Geographic Focus: Indiana
Date(s) Application is Due: Apr 20
Contact: Renee Chambers, Program Director; (812) 333-9016; renee@cfbmc.org
Internet: http://www.cfbmc.org/page21250.cfm
Sponsor: Community Foundation of Bloomington and Monroe County
101 W Kirkwood Avenue, Suite 321
Bloomington, IN 47404

Community Foundation of Bloomington and Monroe County Grants   1271
Grants will be made for a wide variety of programs and purposes in support of the arts and cultural activities, social and health concerns, educational activities, beautification projects, and for other community development needs that will benefit the citizens of Bloomington and Monroe County, Indiana. Start-up funds for special projects reflecting incremental growth possibilities will be given particular attention. Additional types of support include building construction and renovation, equipment acquisition, program development, seed grants, and scholarship funds. Projects that provide leverage for generating other funds and community resources or are seed money for new programs will also receive special attention. The majority of grants are made for one time only, but multi-year grants are considered in unusual circumstances. Applications are reviewed in March, June, September, and December.
Restrictions: Grants are made only to nonprofit organizations and programs in the city of Bloomington or in Monroe County, Indiana. Grants will not be made for general operating support purposes; endowment campaigns or for previously incurred debts; or for political purposes.
Geographic Focus: Indiana
Contact: Renee M. Chambers, (812) 333-9016; fax (812) 333-1153; renee@cfbmc.org
Internet: http://www.communityfoundation.ws
Sponsor: Community Foundation of Bloomington and Monroe County
101 W Kirkwood Avenue, Suite 321
Bloomington, IN 47404

Community Foundation of Boone County - Adult Literacy Initiative Grants   1272
The Community Foundation of Boone County - Adult Literacy Initiative Grants fund programs that address literacy in Boone County. The purpose of all awards is the improvement of the quality of life for Boone County residents through adult literacy. Collaboration among organizations is highly encouraged. Applicants should consider the needs of younger adults, older adults, and those with special needs and/or those who are disabled. Awards are normally made to nonprofits, but other organizations are considered if there is documented activity benefiting or serving Boone County residents or if the Foundation is acting as fiscal agent for the project or program.
Requirements: Proposals should include the following topics, addressing each briefly within the following format: the proposal cover sheet; abstract or executive summary; organization's description; statement of problem or need; objectives; proposed solution; materials/equipment; staff; facilities; evaluation; budget and its explanation; and appendices. Organizations should refer to the Foundation website for specific instructions on submitting the complete proposal. Applicants also need to provide an addendum detailing what specific group or demographic population they will be targeting, how they have identified or intend to identify their target population, how they expect to be affected, and exactly what they propose to do. Measuring outcomes and tracking results will also be a key determinant.

Results showing positive impact in the community will determine eligibility for additional grant money in future years.
Geographic Focus: Indiana
Date(s) Application is Due: Oct 31
Amount of Grant: Up to 60,000 USD
Contact: Barb Schroeder, Program Director; (317) 873-0210 or (765) 482-0024; fax (317) 873-0219; Barb@communityfoundationbc.org
Internet: http://communityfoundationbc.org/literacy.html
Sponsor: Community Foundation of Boone County
60 East Cedar Street
Zionsville, IN 46077

Community Foundation of Boone County - Women's Grants 1273
The mission of the Community Foundation of Boone County - Women's Grants is to support the Helping Hands Emergency Women's Shelter and to provide grants to Boone County organizations that promote intellectual, physical, emotional, social, economic, and spiritual growth for women of all ages.
Requirements: Organizations should fill out the online application with specific information including the organization and its nonprofit status, a description of the project and amount requested, with a timeline, equipment needed, and the organization's board of directors.
Geographic Focus: Indiana
Amount of Grant: Up to 10,000 USD
Contact: Barb Schroeder, Program Director; (317) 873-0210 or (765) 482-0024; fax (317) 873-0219; barb@communityfoundationbc.org
Internet: http://communityfoundationbc.org/womens_fund.html
Sponsor: Community Foundation of Boone County
60 East Cedar Street
Zionsville, IN 46077

Community Foundation of Boone County Grants 1274
The Community Foundation of Boone County Grants provides funding in the following areas: arts/culture; community development; education; elderly; health; human services; youth; environment; and recreation. Applications for grants of $10,000 or less should be submitted on the Short Form located on the website, while applications for more than $10,000 should follow instructions in the Content and Format section of the website. Awards will be made to nonprofit organizations exempt from federal taxation under section 501(c)3 of the Internal Revenue Code. Grants may be allowed to individuals and to non-501(c)3 organizations if there is documented charitable activity benefiting or serving the residents of Boone County, or if the Community Foundation is acting as fiscal agent for the project or program.
Requirements: Grant proposals for over $10,000 must include the following format: abstract or executive summary; description of organization; statement of problem or need; objectives; proposed solution; materials/equipment; staff; facilities; evaluation; budget and its explanation; and appendices. Organizations should review the Foundation website for specific proposal submission instructions.
Restrictions: Non-allowable expenses include support of pre-award costs (i.e., project costs generated during the preparation of a proposal for the same project); existing general fund operating expenses; regular salaries of pre-award permanent staff (unless overload compensation is justified during the life of the funded project); international travel; first-class air fare; luxury accommodations; hospitality for purposes other than those directly related to meeting program objectives as defined in the proposal; alcohol; and indirect or regular existing administrative costs (e.g., telephone, utilities, general maintenance, etc.) of the applicant organization.
Geographic Focus: Indiana
Date(s) Application is Due: Jan 24; Mar 28; May 30; Aug 1; Oct 3; Nov 21
Contact: Barbara J. Schroeder, Program Director; (317) 873-0210 or (765) 482-0024; fax (317) 873-0219; barb@communityfoundationbc.org
Internet: http://www.communityfoundationbc.org/grants.html
Sponsor: Community Foundation of Boone County
60 East Cedar Street
Zionsville, IN 46077

Community Foundation of Broward Grants 1275
Through its competitive grantmaking process, the foundation supports programs that strengthen families within low socioeconomic communities in Florida's Broward County. Grantmaking priorities include the arts, foster care, out-of-school time, and technology. Proposals also are accepted in specific areas of interest, including animal welfare—protect and educate; cancer and arthritis research—finding a cure; patient care—relief and assistance to individuals with cancer or other terminal diseases; literacy—opening worlds through language, an AIDS/HIV—through issued RFP. Proposals are accepted anytime throughout the year. Application and guidelines are available online.
Requirements: 501(c)3 organizations, public charities as defined by the IRS code, and governmental agencies located in Broward County or directly benefiting the residents of Broward County are eligible.
Restrictions: Grants are not awarded in the following areas: annual fundraising, capital campaign/improvements, deficit financing, endowment efforts, grants to individuals, religious purposes, or routine operating needs.
Geographic Focus: Florida
Contact: Sheri Brown, Vice President of Strategic Community Initiatives; (954) 761-9503, ext. 103; fax (954) 761-7102; jbull@cfbroward.org
Internet: http://www.cfbroward.org/new/grant.html
Sponsor: Community Foundation of Broward
1401 E Broward Boulevard, Suite 100
Fort Lauderdale, FL 33301

Community Foundation of Central Illinois Grants 1276
The foundation funds programs in the fields of education, arts, human services, community service, or community development, and that advance one or more of the following objectives: address and help resolve important existing or emerging community issues; support new and creative projects and organizations offering the greatest opportunity for positive and significant change; promote cooperation and collaboration among organizations; identify, enhance, and develop leadership in the community through creative and innovative activities that empower individuals; and improve the quality or scope of charitable works in our community. Application guidelines are available online.
Requirements: Nonprofit organizations within a 50-mile radius of Peoria, IL, are eligible.
Restrictions: The foundation will not fund annual campaigns, individuals, or endowments, or make grants for sectarian religious purposes.
Geographic Focus: Illinois
Date(s) Application is Due: Apr 15; Sep 15
Amount of Grant: 2,500 - 3,000 USD
Contact: Kristan Creek, Program Officer; (309) 674-8730; fax (309) 674-8754; Kristan@communityfoundationci.org
Internet: http://www.communityfoundationci.org/grant_guidelines.asp
Sponsor: Community Foundation of Central Illinois
331 Fulton Street, Suite 310
Peoria, IL 61602

Community Foundation of Collier County Capacity Building Grants 1277
The Community Foundation believes that all nonprofits can benefit from the best practices developed over time in excellent organizations. The Foundation wishes to help nonprofits become successful and sustainable, long term businesses. Capacity Building Grants are given to support best practices and sustainability for a variety of nonprofit organizational needs. The Foundation's focus is on substantial projects that: encourage and facilitate collaborations; improve communications between nonprofits with similar missions; engage in public-private partnerships; facilitate the development of strategic plans, business plans, plans for marketing & communications, fund raising plans; encourage program evaluation that focuses on results for participants; fund updated technology systems; and other projects that improve the sustainability of the organization. This grant program includes a Letter of Intent, an interview and donor briefings. The Letter of Intent must be submitted by 5:00 on September 18th. The most common grant will be between $5,000-$8,000 per/applicant. The grant award from the Foundation will require a 50% match by the organization.
Requirements: 501(c)3 tax-exempt organizations serving Collier County and are not deemed as not a private foundation under Section 509(a) are eligible to apply.
Restrictions: The Foundation does not fund the following through this grant program: grants to individuals; endowments; private schools; political campaigns/lobby activities; scholarly research; annual campaigns; organizations which exclude individuals based on the Foundation statement of diversity; reimbursement of funds spent; projects that present a clear or perceived conflict of interest.
Geographic Focus: Florida
Date(s) Application is Due: Sep 18
Amount of Grant: 5,000 - 8,000 USD
Contact: Mary Barrett; (239) 649-5000; fax (941) 649-5337; mbarrett@cfcollier.org
Internet: http://www.cfcollier.org/new_grant_program.php
Sponsor: Community Foundation of Collier County
2400 Tamiami Trail N, Suite 300
Naples, FL 34103

Community Foundation of East Central Illinois Grants 1278
The community foundation awards grants from its unrestricted funds to Champaign County, IL, nonprofit organizations to use for charitable purposes. Representative categories include arts and humanities, environmental concerns, education, health, human services, research, urban affairs, church, and youth programs. Types of support include continuing support, annual campaigns, building/renovation, equipment, publication, consulting services, and scholarships.
Requirements: Champaign County, IL, nonprofit organizations are eligible.
Geographic Focus: Illinois
Date(s) Application is Due: Aug 31
Contact: Joan Dixon, President & CEO; (217) 359-0125; fax (217) 352-6494; joandixon@cfeci.org or info@cfeci.org
Internet: http://www.cfeci.org/non-profit/grant-application
Sponsor: Community Foundation of East Central Illinois
404 West Church Street
Champaign, IL 61820-3411

Community Foundation of Grant County Grants 1279
The Community Foundation of Grant County Grants address the needs of Grant County in the fields of community development, education, and health and human services. Nonprofit organizations, coalitions, community associations, and other civic groups may apply if they provide services within the county. The project must be located in or directly serve the people in Grant County, and meet all other criteria in the guidelines and application. All proposals must be received by the Foundation on the last Friday in April, July, October, and January, with committee reviews in May, August, November, and February.
Requirements: The Board will only accept written proposals for consideration after an applicant has first consulted with the Foundation's staff to find if the project is suitable for funding. The organization should keep the following guidelines in mind when preparing their written proposal: the project's purpose; whether the Foundation will be the sole funder; how many will be served or affected by the project, if there is a broad base of support for it, or if services are duplicated by another source; if an important need has been shown; whether the objectives are realistic and measurable; is there a viable plan for future support;

who the key people are and if they are available for the long-term; and if all financial information is included and makes sense.
Restrictions: To be eligible for a grant, the project must be located in or directly serve the people and natural resources in Grant County, Indiana. Funding is not available for: profit making enterprises; political activity; operating budgets, except for limited experimental or demonstration periods; salaries; sectarian or religious purposes; endowment purposes unless for special promotions and/or matching challenges; multi-year funding requests; or capital improvements to church owned facilities or properties.
Geographic Focus: Indiana
Contact: Sherrie Stahl, Office and Program Director; (765) 662-0065; fax (765) 662-1438; sstahl@comfdn.org
Internet: http://www.comfdn.org/grants.htm
Sponsor: Community Foundation of Grant County
505 West Third Street
Marion, IN 46952

Community Foundation of Greater Birmingham Grants   1280
The community foundation serving the greater Birmingham, AL, area awards grants in arts and culture, education, environment, health, and welfare. Types of support include capital campaigns, operating support, building/renovation, equipment, program development, publication, seed money, curriculum development, and matching funds. Grant requests are considered twice a year at distribution committee meetings. The foundation requires that grant requests be submitted in writing. There is no application form. Applicants are asked to submit a cover letter and a complete statement of the purpose of the grant, including the need for the project and population and number of people to be served, project budget, other funding sources, length of time for which foundation aid is needed, a method to evaluate the project's success, description of applicant organization including annual budget, copy of IRS determination letter, and names of the board of directors or trustees.
Requirements: IRS 501(c)3 organizations that provide services in the greater Birmingham metropolitan area (Jefferson, Shelby, St. Clair, Blount and Walker counties) are eligible.
Restrictions: Grants are not made to or for individuals, operating expenses of organizations, religious organizations for religious purposes, national fund-raising drives, conference or seminar expenses, tickets for benefits, political organizations or candidates for public office, organizations with IRS 501(h) status, budget deficits, replacement of government funding cuts, or scholarships or endowment funds.
Geographic Focus: Alabama
Date(s) Application is Due: Mar 15; Sep 15
Contact: James McCrary, Senior Program Officer; (205) 327-3812 or (205) 327-3800; fax (205) 328-6576; jmccrary@foundationbirmingham.org
Internet: http://www.foundationbirmingham.org/page30508.cfm
Sponsor: Community Foundation of Greater Birmingham
2100 First Avenue N, Suite 700
Birmingham, AL 35203-4223

Community Foundation of Greater Chattanooga Grants   1281
The foundation encourages and invests in creative and long-term solutions to improve Hamilton County, Tennessee, and the lives of its citizens. The foundation supports programs and projects that target root causes of problems, foster individual and family self-sufficiency, work to combat discrimination, benefit larger rather than smaller numbers of people, create long-term impact, recognize that prevention is more cost-efficient than treatment, commit venture capital to promising but untried ideas that have a reasonable chance of success. The foundation is committed to earmarking 60 percent of its earnings to grants that address good beginnings for children with a strong interest in race relations and literacy. The grants committee meets quarterly to consider grant requests.
Requirements: IRS 501(c)3 or 501(c)4 organizations in Tennessee providing services to Hamilton County or to Hamilton County residents are eligible.
Restrictions: The foundation will not make grants to or for religious activities; private schools; operating support for existing programs; multiyear commitments; individuals; endowment campaigns; conference expenses, memberships, or tickets to events; state, regional, or national organizations; political candidates or organizations; veterans and fraternal organizations; advertising and telephone solicitations; feasibility studies; or fund-raising expenses. Low priority will be given to requests from or to public agencies for mandated services; replacement of government funding; unnecessary duplication of services already provided by other agencies; multiyear grants for unsolicited requests; federated fund drives; or capital campaign requests in excess of $25,000.
Geographic Focus: Tennessee
Date(s) Application is Due: Jan 28; May 27; Sep 23
Contact: Pamela Blass Bracher, Program Officer; (423) 265-0586; fax (423) 265-0587; pbracher@cfgc.org or info@cfgc.org
Internet: http://www.cfgc.org
Sponsor: Community Foundation of Greater Chattanooga
1270 Market Street
Chattanooga, TN 37402

Community Foundation of Greater Flint Grants   1282
The community foundation is interested in funding charitable organizations that are able to demonstrate they have planned their projects with respect to the community's needs in the areas of arts and humanities, community services, education, environment and conservation, ethics, health, human and social services, and philanthropy. The foundation's current objectives for the allocation of discretionary funds give top priority to programs that: advance the health and well-being of children; and/or improve the capacity of public education. Types of support include general operating support, program development, seed money, scholarship funds, and technical assistance. Applications are available on the Web site.
Requirements: IRS 501(c)3 organizations with programs of direct relevance to the residents of Genesee County, Michigan are eligible. Types of support include general operating support.
Restrictions: Grants will not be made to individuals. In general, requests for sectarian religious purposes, budget deficits, routine operating expenses of existing organizations, litigation, endowments, and other capital fund drives or projects are not funded.
Geographic Focus: Michigan
Samples: Greater Flint Health Coalition, $40,000—towards the Flint Healthcare Employment Opportunities (FHEO) program, which helps unemployed or low-income individuals in Genesee County to obtain employment opportunities or to advance in the healthcare industry; Genesee Chamber Foundation,$30,000— towards the Summer Youth Initiative, a summer employment and leadership development program for Genesee County youth ages 14-18; United Way of Genesee County, $66,000- in support of the BEST Project (Building Excellence, Sustainability and Trust) BEST provides technical assistance and resources designed to build the capacity of area nonprofit organizations.
Contact: Lynn Larkin; (810) 767-8270; fax (810) 767-0496; llarkin@cfgf.org
Internet: http://www.cfgf.org/page32610.cfm
Sponsor: Community Foundation of Greater Flint
500 South Saginaw Street
Flint, MI 48502-1206

Community Foundation of Greater Fort Wayne - Barbara Burt Leadership Development Grants   1283
The Community Foundation of Greater Fort Wayne administers the Barbara Burt Leadership Development Grants. These grants are designed to provide funding to Allen County nonprofit organizations for leadership development training of their officers and executive committees to enhance the effectiveness of area nonprofit agencies. Each grant awarded may not consist of more than 50% of the total cost of the leadership development program. Concept letters are due on the dates posted, then the Foundation will contact the applicant with further information.
Requirements: Grantees should consult the website for detailed information about the application process.
Geographic Focus: Indiana
Date(s) Application is Due: Jan 9; Apr 9; Jul 9; Oct 3
Contact: Annette Smith, (260) 426-4083; fax (260) 424-0114; asmith@cfgfw.org
Internet: http://www.cfgfw.org/grants/grant_acctapp.html
Sponsor: Community Foundation of Greater Fort Wayne
555 East Wayne Street
Fort Wayne, IN 46802

Community Foundation of Greater Fort Wayne - Collaborative Efforts Grants   1284
The Community Foundation of Greater Fort Wayne believes in alternative approaches to grow and stabilize area nonprofits. These approaches can be innovative strategic tools for organizations focused on providing quality, cost effective services to the constituents. This strategic restructuring includes joint ventures, informal partnerships, administrative or back office consolidations, joint programming, fiscal sponsorships, and mergers. Qualifying organizations must be federal tax-exempt status as a section 501(c)3 public charity, and serve the Allen County area. Receiving a Collaborative Efforts grant will not affect an organization's funding eligibility for other Foundation funds. Application review is ongoing. Financial support will be awarded based on a competitive review of the applications. The Foundation particularly encourages applications from organizations that: are in transition (e.g., significant growth, changes in staff or board leadership, reorganization, reduction in funding or other similar circumstances); and are providing the same or similar services as other local organizations.
Requirements: Applicants should contact the Foundation to discuss its general eligibility for grant consideration. If they are eligible to apply, they should then submit a brief proposal to the Foundation containing the following information: a cover letter summarizing the funding request; a detailed narrative discussing the background and leadership of the project and what it hopes to accomplish; a list of the board of directors, including their affiliations; a copy of the board's support of the proposal; a work plan, timeline, and budget for the project; the organization's operating budget; and its current audited financial statement. A funding decision will be made within 30 days of submitting the proposal.
Restrictions: Grant funds are limited. Funding decisions will be influenced by whether: the proposed initiative has strong board and staff buy-in and participation; the proposal clearly identifies current organizational conditions and the organizational change that is sought; the proposal is clear in its description of how the initiative will lead to stronger organizational impact.
Geographic Focus: Indiana
Contact: Christine Meek; (260) 426-4083; fax (260) 424-0114; cmeek@cfgfw.org
Internet: http://www.cfgfw.org/nonprof_res/nonprof_collab_grant.html
Sponsor: Community Foundation of Greater Fort Wayne
555 East Wayne Street
Fort Wayne, IN 46802

Community Foundation of Greater Fort Wayne - Community Endowment and Clarke Endowment Grants   1285
The Foundation encourages projects or programs that are developed in consultation with other agencies and planning groups that increase coordination and cooperation among agencies and reduce unnecessary duplication of services. Preference is given to projects or programs that: address priority community concerns; encourage more effective use of community resources; test or demonstrate new approaches and techniques in the solution of community problems; are intended to strengthen the management capabilities of agencies; promote volunteer participation and citizen involvement in community affairs. Contact program staff for current guidelines and deadlines. The deadlines listed are for concept letters, with final invited proposals due by dates provided by the Foundation.

Requirements: Nonprofit organizations in Allen County, Indiana, are eligible to apply. Applicants should mail hardcopies of the application package including the following: concept letter fact sheet; the original concept letter; a detailed program budget or agency budget; current financial statements; a copy of the organization's 501(c)3 IRS determination letter; and a list of the board of directors and their principal affiliations.
Restrictions: Grants do not support: annual fund drives; operating deficits or after-the-fact support; endowment funds, except for endowment-building matching grants for funds held at the Community Foundation; direct or grassroots lobbying; religious purposes; hospitals, medical research, or academic research; public, private, or parochial educational institutions except in special situations when support is essential to projects/programs that meet critical community needs; governmental agencies, including public school systems, except in special situations when support is essential to projects/programs that meet critical community needs; limited, special interest organizations except when such support significantly benefits the disadvantaged; and funding for sponsorships, special events, commercial advertising, films or videos, television programs, conferences, group uniforms, or group trips.
Geographic Focus: Indiana
Date(s) Application is Due: Jan 9; Apr 9; Jul 9
Contact: Annette Smith; (260) 426-4083; fax (260) 424-0114; asmith@cfgfw.org
Internet: http://www.cfgfw.org/
Sponsor: Community Foundation of Greater Fort Wayne
555 East Wayne Street
Fort Wayne, IN 46802

Community Foundation of Greater Fort Wayne - Edna Foundation Grants   1286
The Edna Foundation Fund was established to help financially support agencies in Allen County that are dedicated to promoting human services, child development, and the arts. This fund typically awards four to five grants a year, ranging from $1,000 to $5,000. The deadlines listed are for concept letters, with final invited proposals due by dates provided by the Foundation.
Requirements: Nonprofit organizations in Allen County, Indiana area are eligible to apply. To apply for funding, complete the Grant Guidelines and Procedures Concept Letter. The Concept Letter should include a cover letter indicating the grant request is for The Edna Foundation Grant.
Restrictions: Grants do not support: annual fund drives; operating deficits or after-the-fact support; endowment funds, except for endowment-building matching grants for funds held at the Community Foundation; direct or grassroots lobbying; religious purposes; hospitals, medical research, or academic research; public, private, or parochial educational institutions except in special situations when support is essential to projects/programs that meet critical community needs; governmental agencies, including public school systems, except in special situations when support is essential to projects/programs that meet critical community needs; limited, special interest organizations except when such support significantly benefits the disadvantaged; and funding for sponsorships, special events, commercial advertising, films or videos, television programs, conferences, group uniforms, or group trips.
Geographic Focus: Indiana
Date(s) Application is Due: Jan 9; Apr 9; Jul 9; Oct 3
Amount of Grant: 1,000 - 5,000 USD
Contact: Annette Smith; (260) 426-4083; fax (260) 424-0114; asmith@cfgfw.org
Internet: http://www.cfgfw.org/grants/grant_acctapp.html
Sponsor: Community Foundation of Greater Fort Wayne
555 East Wayne Street
Fort Wayne, IN 46802

Community Foundation of Greater Fort Wayne - John S. and James L. Knight Foundation Donor-Advised Grants   1287
The Community Foundation of Greater Fort Wayne administers the Knight Foundation Donor-Advised Grants. The Knight Foundation invests in communities where the Knight brothers owned newspapers to add focus on fostering informed, engaged communities. Knight believed approaches that put residents at the center of their communities are powerful ways to achieve social change, and engaged communities are better places to live, work, and play. Grant requests should address one of the following four focus areas: creating new opportunities for community participation; supporting and developing community leadership; creating spaces for engagement; and providing leadership in understanding engagement in communities. Possible examples include: provide leadership skills to youth and young professionals; support virtual and physical spaces where social interacting, public deliberation, and community action thrive; and enhance the role of citizens in local problem solving.
Requirements: Applicants should submit the online grant proposal form to the Community Foundation, along with the following information: the grantee's name and contact information; a proposal summary; a detailed proposal narrative that describes the name of the project and the organization, why it is a good fit for the Knight Foundation, and how the organization will measure and communicate the results of their work; a project budget; list of the board of directors; and the IRS letter of determination letter.
Geographic Focus: Indiana
Contact: Annette Smith; (260) 426-4083; fax (260) 424-0114; asmith@cfgfw.org
Internet: http://www.cfgfw.org/grants/grant_acctapp.html
Sponsor: Community Foundation of Greater Fort Wayne
555 East Wayne Street
Fort Wayne, IN 46802

Community Foundation of Greater Greensboro Grants   1288
The foundation supports community projects that strengthen the community, embrace the diversity of the community, demonstrate community support and in-kind investment, outline well-established proposed plans, and focus on collaborative efforts. Grants are awarded in the areas of community building, cultural and civic programs, arts, community development, health, environment, and social services. Types of support include general support, program development, seed grants, and emergency community funding. Annual deadline dates may vary; contact program staff for exact dates.
Requirements: Nonprofit organizations in Greensboro, NC, are eligible.
Restrictions: The Foundation does not award grants from the Community Grants Program for individuals, debt retirement, political organizations or campaigns, for-profit entities, capital campaigns, programming that promotes religious instruction or doctrine, or endowments.
Geographic Focus: North Carolina
Date(s) Application is Due: Feb 15; Jun 15; Oct 15
Amount of Grant: 10,000 USD
Contact: Melissa Johnson; (336) 379-9100, ext. 124; mjohnson@cfgg.org
Internet: http://www.cfgg.org/guidelines-new.htm
Sponsor: Community Foundation of Greater Greensboro
P.O. Box 20444
Greensboro, NC 27420

Community Foundation Of Greater Lafayette Grants   1289
The Community Foundation of Greater Lafayette Grants help meet the ever-changing needs of the community. Funding priorities include education, children/youth, health, diversity, physical environment, and arts and culture. Charitable organizations that serve Tippecanoe and the surrounding counties are eligible to apply. Most grants are awarded to nonprofit organizations that are located in and serve Tippecanoe County. Priority is given to projects that reach as many people as possible; improve the ability of organizations to serve the community over the long-term; serve the Greater Lafayette area; and are run by non-profit organizations. Grant seekers are encouraged to contact the Foundation office to be certain their proposal is appropriate for consideration. Proposal deadlines are listed according to dollar amount request, so grant seekers should carefully review the website to judge when to submit their proposal.
Requirements: Organizations should submit the following information along with the online application: contact and background information for the organization; a concise narrative about the project; amount requested from the foundation; and a project budget. Also included is a board of directors list; project estimates/bids; and financial statements. Applicants may be asked for further information or a site visit to clarify the request.
Restrictions: The Foundation does not fund: programs that are sectarian or religious in nature; political organizations or candidates; endowments; ongoing operating expenses; government agencies or public institutions; programs that taxpayers would normally support; individuals; special events (i.e. parades, festivals, sporting activities, fundraisers); programs already completed; multi-year grants; debt or deficit reduction; and projects funded in a previous year (unless invited to resubmit).
Geographic Focus: Indiana
Date(s) Application is Due: Apr 1; Sep 1; Dec 1
Contact: Cheryl Ubelhor, Program Director; (765) 742-9078; fax (765) 742-2428; info@cfglaf.org or cheryl@cfglaf.org
Internet: http://www.glcfonline.org/grantseekers/index.htm
Sponsor: Community Foundation of Greater Lafayette
1114 East State Street
Lafayette, IN 47905-1219

Community Foundation of Greater Memphis Grants   1290
The community foundation enters into partnerships with nonprofit organizations in the greater Memphis, TN, area that are actively involved in community-building initiatives to improve the quality of life in the area. Seed grants are awarded to support organizations in the foundation's areas of interest, which include the environment, children and youth, community development, and neighborhood development. Organizations that have not been recognized as tax-exempt by the IRS may apply if they have a fiscal agent relationship with a 501(c)3 nonprofit organization. Applications for $2500 or less will be considered on an ongoing basis and can be submitted at any time. Applications for more than $2500 will be reviewed twice a year, according to the listed application deadlines. Application materials are available upon request. Deadlines for programs are posted on the Web site
Requirements: IRS 501(c)3 nonprofit organizations involved in enhancing the quality of life for citizens in metropolitan Memphis, west Tennessee, and northwest Mississippi are eligible.
Geographic Focus: Tennessee
Contact: Melissa Wolowicz, (901) 722-0054; fax (901) 722-0010; mwolowicz@cfgm.org
Internet: http://www.cfgm.org/grant.html
Sponsor: Community Foundation of Greater Memphis
1900 Union Avenue
Memphis, TN 38104

Community Foundation of Greater New Britain Grants   1291
Grants from the Community Foundation of Greater New Britain support organizations and programs benefiting the residents of Berlin, New Britain, Plainville and Southington, Connecticut. The foundation supports organizations involved with arts, culture and heritage; community and economic development; early childhood development; education; health and human services.
Requirements: Grants are available to non-profit organizations that have tax-exempt status under Section 501(c)3 of the IRS Code or that are a qualified entity eligible to receive grants from community foundations under the IRS Code. The foundation will also consider funding a grassroots group if it consists of at least five people, has a governing body and a fiscal agent with the appropriate tax status. All grant applications must begin with a one or two page Letter of Intent summarizing the program or project for which funding is being sought. Submitted Letters of Intent will be reviewed by staff. Applicants selected by staff to submit complete, formal applications will be contacted directly to begin the proposal.

Restrictions: The Foundation does not make grants for: sectarian or religious activities; previously incurred expenses; annual or endowment campaigns; sponsorships or fundraisers; political activities; direct support of individuals, corporations, private foundations, and campership or scholarships for academic and/or enrichment programs. In addition, the Foundation generally does not make grants for performances or one-time events, conferences or advertising.
Geographic Focus: Connecticut
Date(s) Application is Due: Feb 15; Jun 15; Oct 15
Amount of Grant: 5,000 - 25,000 USD
Contact: Joeline Wruck, Program Director; (860) 229-6018, ext. 307; jwruck@cfgnb.org
Internet: http://www.cfgnb.org/GrantsScholarships/tabid/68/Default.aspx
Sponsor: Community Foundation of Greater New Britain
74A Vine Street
New Britain, CT 06052

Community Foundation of Greater Tampa Grants   1292
The Community Foundation of Tampa Bay is a nonprofit, tax-exempt organization which administers funds established by individuals, corporations, private foundations, and nonprofit organizations to support the charitable needs of the Tampa Bay area. Program interests of the Foundation include: arts and culture, community development, education, environment, animals, health and, human services.
Requirements: Florida 501(c)3 organizations based in and serving communities in Hillsborough, Pasco, Pinellas and/or Hernando counties are eligible.
Restrictions: The Foundation is generally not interested in requests for: funding of ongoing operating costs; grants for capital campaigns or expenditures; tickets for any fundraising event, conference, or advertising space in programs or other publications; legislative lobbying or political campaigns; medical research; religious or sectarian purposes; loans or assistance to individuals; a multiple year funding commitment.
Geographic Focus: Florida
Date(s) Application is Due: Mar 1; Sep 1
Amount of Grant: Up to 7,500 USD
Contact: Ann Berg, (813) 282-1975; fax (813) 282-3119; aberg@cftampabay.org
Internet: http://www.cftampabay.org/nonprofit_resources/grant_app_guidelines.html
Sponsor: Community Foundation of Greater Tampa
550 North Reo Street, Suite 301
Tampa, FL 33609

Community Foundation of Greenville-Greenville Women Giving Grants   1293
Greenville Women Giving (GWG) is a special initiative of Community Foundation of Greenville. GWG is a philanthropic organization, founded on the idea that women, informed about philanthropy and the needs in their community, collectively can make a real difference. GWG is committed to strengthening the community through the collective resources of it's members by awarding high-impact grants in five areas: arts and culture, education, health, human services, and environment. GWG will award grants ranging from a minimum of $40,000 to $100,000 to community organizations in Greenville County, South Carolina. Consideration will be given to applications requesting that funding be spent over a two year period. Additional guidelines and application are available on the GWG website: http://greenvillewomengiving.org/faq.aspx. The completed application should be mailed or delivered to Greenville Women Giving, c/o Community Foundation of Greenville on or before January 15, at 4 p.m.
Requirements: Applicants must qualify as tax-exempt under Section 501(c)3 of the Internal Revenue Code or be classified as a unit of government, located and providing services in Greenville County, South Carolina. Organizations must not discriminate on the basis of age, race, national origin, ethnicity, gender, physical ability, sexual orientation, political affiliation or religious belief.
Restrictions: Support is not available for the following: endowment campaigns; travel expenses and conferences; individuals; projects or programs that promote religious or political views; organizations for re-granting purpose.
Geographic Focus: South Carolina
Date(s) Application is Due: Jan 15
Amount of Grant: 40,000 - 100,000 USD
Contact: Debbie Cooper, Director of Donor Services; (864) 233-5925 or (864) 331-8414; fax (864) 242-9292; dcooper@cfgg.com or Cfgg@cfgg.com
Internet: http://greenvillewomengiving.org/guidelines.aspx
Sponsor: Greenville Women Giving
27 Cleveland Street, Suite 101
Greenville, SC 29601

Community Foundation of Greenville Community Enrichment Grants   1294
The Community Foundation of Greenville supports qualified nonprofit organizations in the areas of the arts and humanities, education, early childhood education, religion, and environmental programs. The Foundation is committed to the responsible allocation of the Foundation's unrestricted funds. As an organization, the Foundation seeks ways to make meaningful, sustained differences in the quality of life for the citizens of Greenville County. The goal is to seek out community-based projects where a modest grant can make a significant impact. The Foundation encourages proposals that: propose practical solutions to community problems; promote cooperation among agencies without duplicating services; use modest funds to make a significant impact; address prevention as well as remediation; make use of matching funds; strengthen an agency's effectiveness and stability; generate community support, both professional and volunteer; state project objectives in measurable terms. The application deadline is 4:00 pm on Friday, March 5.
Requirements: All 501(c)3 non-profit groups can apply for Community Foundation grants to fund innovative projects that have a direct relevance to the Greenville County, South Carolina area. An agency can receive one community enrichment grant per year.
Restrictions: The Foundation will: not make grants to individuals; not fund capacity building; will give low grant making priority to capital fund projects.
Geographic Focus: South Carolina
Date(s) Application is Due: Mar 5
Contact: Debbie Cooper, Director of Donor Services; (864) 233-5925 or (864) 331-8414; fax (864) 242-9292; dcooper@cfgg.com or Cfgg@cfgg.com
Internet: http://www.cfgreenville.org/page18740.cfm
Sponsor: Community Foundation of Greenville
27 Cleveland Street, Suite 101
Greenville, SC 29601

Community Foundation of Greenville Hollingsworth Funds Capital Grants   1295
The Hollingsworth Funds, Inc. has a competitive grant process that is administered by the Community Foundation. Consistent with the purposes established by its benefactor, John D. Hollingsworth, Jr., an astute textile executive and real estate investor. The Hollingsworth Funds will serve a broad range of charitable, educational, religious, literary and cultural purposes. For the purpose of this funding opportunity, the Hollingsworth Funds defines a capital request as a proposal that seeks funding to purchase or construct a new facility, renovate or add to a current facility, or purchase equipment with an expected useful life of at least five years. As a general rule, capital grant requests should not exceed 20% of the total capital campaign goal or $250,000. The Hollingsworth Fund will consider requests that can be awarded over a maximum period of three years. The Hollingsworth Funds will make grants: for capital projects that provide a public benefit on a nondiscriminatory basis to interdenominational faith-based organizations that benefit a broad cross-section of the community; to public/private partnerships; to projects that have a well thought out facilities use policy that evaluates the financial impact on the organization and resulting need for increased operating revenue. To submit a request for funding, a charitable organization must deliver or mail two (2) complete application packets to the Community Foundation of Greenville by 4:00 pm on September 3. All applicants will be notified of their status by December 31.
Requirements: A 501(c)3 charitable organization can submit one grant application per year for an amount not to exceed $250,000 to fund innovative capital projects/capital campaigns for the benefit of charitable uses within Greenville County, South Carolina, or for the benefit of residents of Greenville County.
Restrictions: The Hollingsworth Funds will not: make grants for special purpose district and other governmental facilities; make grants that primarily benefit the religious activities of a church, seminary, synagogue, mosque or other house of worship.
Geographic Focus: South Carolina
Date(s) Application is Due: Sep 3
Amount of Grant: Up to 250,000 USD
Contact: Debbie Cooper, Director of Donor Services; (864) 233-5925 or (864) 331-8414; fax (864) 242-9292; dcooper@cfgg.com or Cfgg@cfgg.com
Internet: http://www.cfgreenville.org/page18741.cfm
Sponsor: Community Foundation of Greenville
27 Cleveland Street, Suite 101
Greenville, SC 29601

Community Foundation of Greenville Hollingsworth Funds Grants   1296
The Hollingsworth Funds, Inc. has a competitive grant process that is administered by the Community Foundation. Consistent with the purposes established by its benefactor, John D. Hollingsworth, Jr., an astute textile executive and real estate investor. The Hollingsworth Funds will serve a broad range of charitable, educational, religious, literary and cultural purposes. The Hollingsworth Funds has adopted initial guidelines in order to assist its evaluation of charitable organizations for funding. The Hollingsworth Funds will make grants: to health and human service agencies dedicated to improving quality of life for residents of Greenville County and particularly for those which deliver services to the poor, homeless, and illiterate; to interdenominational faith-based programs that benefit a broad cross-section of the community; to a wide variety of arts and education related initiatives including high quality preschool and after school programs; for grants for capital projects that provide a public benefit on a nondiscriminatory basis; to increase the organizational capacity of a non-profit organization; to public/private partnerships. The Hollingsworth Funds will give priority to new and innovative projects that are outside of the scope of an organization's ongoing operating budget. To submit a request for funding, a charitable organization must deliver or mail two (2) complete application packets to the Community Foundation of Greenville by 4:00 pm on September 3. All applicants will be notified of their status by December 31.
Requirements: A 501(c)3 charitable organization can submit one grant application per year for an amount not to exceed $50,000 to fund innovative projects for the benefit of charitable uses within Greenville County, South Carolina, or for the benefit of residents of Greenville County.
Restrictions: The Hollingsworth Funds will not make grants: to sponsor special fundraising events, celebration functions, dinners or annual meetings; for areas that are traditionally the primary responsibility of local, state or federal governments; for core operating expenses of public, private or parochial schools; that primarily benefit the religious activities of a church, synagogue, mosque or other house of worship; to pay off existing debts; scholarship awards or grants to individuals.
Geographic Focus: South Carolina
Date(s) Application is Due: Sep 3
Amount of Grant: Up to 50,000 USD
Contact: Debbie Cooper, Director of Donor Services; (864) 233-5925 or (864) 331-8414; fax (864) 242-9292; dcooper@cfgg.com or Cfgg@cfgg.com
Internet: http://www.cfgreenville.org/page18741.cfm
Sponsor: Community Foundation of Greenville
27 Cleveland Street, Suite 101
Greenville, SC 29601

Community Foundation of Howard County Grants 1297

The Community Foundation of Howard County Grants fund initiatives that improve the quality of life for citizens of Howard County. The Foundation addresses needs that generally fall into the following categories: health and medical; social services; education; cultural affairs; civic affairs; and community beautification. The Foundation uses the following evaluation criteria: does the project fit the purpose of the organization; is there an established need for the project; how well the project's purpose has been defined; does it fit with the Foundation's guidelines; and what kind of impact the project will have on the community.
Requirements: All applicants must receive pre-qualification prior to submitting an application. A letter of inquiry addressed to the Program Director should contain a brief statement of the applicant's need for assistance, estimate of total cost of project, and enough information so that the Foundation can determine whether the application falls within the guidelines of its grants program. The organization may then submit the online application with the following information: the grant application and cover page; project budget; copy of IRS determination 501(c)3 letter; current month and year-to-date financial statement; year-end financial statements; itemized list of board members; and evidence of board approval.
Restrictions: The Foundation does not award grants for: normal operating expenses and/or salaries; individuals; seminars or trips; sectarian religious purposes; endowment purposes of recipient organizations; projects which have been proposed by individuals or organizations responsible to advisory bodies or persons; and new projects and/or equipment which were purchased prior to the grant application being approved.
Geographic Focus: Indiana
Date(s) Application is Due: Mar 5; May 7; Sep 3; Nov 5
Contact: Kim Abney; (765) 454-7298 or (800) 964-0508; kim@cfhoward.org
Internet: http://www.cfhoward.org/grants.html
Sponsor: Community Foundation of Howard County
215 West Sycamore Street
Kokomo, IN 46901

Community Foundation of Jackson County Grants 1298

The Community Foundation of Jackson County is a community focused organization dedicated to: building a visionary partnership with donors and local service organizations; trustworthy stewardship of gifts; providing funds to enhance the quality of life across Jackson County; and being a catalyst for change in the community. Areas of funding interest include: education - projects that support and enhance educational programs serving a broad spectrum of Jackson County residents; economic development - projects that explore new ways to improve the lives of Jackson County residents through development of the county's economic strength; human services - programs that support human service organizations programs and services for all ages; and arts and culture - programs designed to establish diversified cultural programs that offer widespread opportunities for participation and appreciation of the arts throughout the county. The grant proposal form is available at the website or at the Foundation office.
Requirements: Nonprofit organizations may apply with programs that serve the residents of Jackson County.
Restrictions: Funding is not available for the following: individuals or groups of individuals to attend seminars or take trips except where there are special circumstances with a clear benefit to the larger community; political organizations or campaigns; state or national fundraising efforts; programs and/or equipment that were committed to prior to the grant proposal being submitted; endowment purposes of recipient organizations; and programs specifically for sectarian religious purposes. Programs that include both religious components and social needs will be carefully reviewed.
Geographic Focus: Indiana
Date(s) Application is Due: Jul 31
Contact: Lori Miller, Development Associate; (812) 523-4483; fax (812) 523-1433
Internet: http://www.cfjacksoncounty.org/policies.php
Sponsor: Community Foundation of Jackson County
107 Community Drive
Seymour, IN 47274

Community Foundation of Louisville Grants 1299

The mission of the community foundation is to enrich the quality of life for all citizens in the Louisville area by being a leader in attracting, mobilizing, and focusing philanthropic resources to meet community needs for generations to come. The foundation's focus is the four areas of community, arts and humanities, historic preservation, and the Lee Look Fund for Spinal Injury. Community grants supportsprojects designed to help prevent poverty by better preparing children and youth to achieve economic self-sufficiency through educational, leadership, mentoring, recreational, cultural, and other activities. Arts and humanities grants supports visual arts, crafts, theater, and the Louisville Free Public Library. The historic preservation fund supports the preservation of prehistoric and historic resources in Louisville and Jefferson County. The Lee Look Fund for Spinal Injury supports public charities that help people with spinal injuries or that develop new therapies and cures for disabilities resulting from spinal injuries. Scholarships in a wide array of areas are also available. The foundation does not accept unsolicited grant proposals for any grant programs. All potential applicants should review a grant program's guidelines for more detailed information.
Requirements: Only Kentucky non-profit organizations are eligible to apply. For the community grants, programs must serve populations in Algonquin, California, Chickasaw, Limerick, Old Louisville, Park DuValle, Park Hill, Parkland, Phoenix Hill, Portland, Russell, Shawnee, Shelby Park, Smoketown, or South Louisville neighborhoods.
Geographic Focus: Kentucky
Contact: Alexandra Spoelker; (502) 585-4649, ext. 1005; alexs@cflouisville.org
Internet: http://www.cflouisville.org/page13464.cfm
Sponsor: Community Foundation of Louisville
325 W Main Street, Suite 1110, Waterfront Plaza
Louisville, KY 40202

Community Foundation of Middle Tennessee Grants 1300

The community foundation has identified several broad categories in which needs exist and in which grant requests are encouraged, including arts and humanities, civic affairs and community planning, conservation and environment, education, employment and training, health, historic preservation, housing and community development, and human services for citizens of all ages. The foundation is particularly interested in ideas that shed new light on Middle Tennessee's needs and aspirations, with an emphasis on providing long-term solutions. Types of support include program development, seed money, and in-kind gifts. Applications may not exceed three typewritten pages and should contain a summary statement, amount and purpose of funds requests, need for the project, background and purpose of the agency, a realistic line item estimate of projects costs, and project time frame and duration.
Requirements: Middle Tennessee 501(c)3 nonprofit organizations in Cannon, Cheatham, Clay, Cumberland, DeKalb, Dickson, Fentress, Houston, Humphreys, Jackson, Macon, Montgomery, Overton, Pickett, Putnam, Robertson, Rutherford, Smith, Stewart, Sumner, Trousdale, Van Buren, Warren, White, Williamson, and Wilson Counties are eligible.
Restrictions: The foundation is not likely to support fund-raising events, annual campaigns, capital campaigns, general operating funds, private schools, religious/sectarian causes, private foundations, debt retirement or restructuring, fund-raising feasibility studies, biomedical or clinical studies, political activities, lobbying activities, trips and/or conference attendance, and organizations or for purposes outside the service area.
Geographic Focus: Tennessee
Date(s) Application is Due: May 2; Sep 2
Contact: Laundrea Lewis, Grants and Scholarship Coordinator; (888) 540-5200 or (615) 321-4939; fax (615) 327-2746; mail@cfmt.org
Internet: http://www.cfmt.org
Sponsor: Community Foundation of Middle Tennessee
3833 Cleghorn Avenue, Suite 400
Nashville, TN 37215-2519

Community Foundation of Mount Vernon and Knox County Grants 1301

The Community Foundation of Mount Vernon/Knox County, awards grants and scholarships from a variety of funds. The Foundations mission is to improve the quality of life in Mount Vernon and, Knox County through charitable giving. To assess and respond to emerging and changing community needs in the fields of: education, youth services, recreation, arts and culture, social services, and civic and community development. All grant applications are considered by the Foundation board at regularly scheduled meetings in the months of February, April, June, August, October and December. Applicants should be aware grants are awarded on a competitive basis, and that deadlines for submission of requests must be strictly observed. See the Foundations website for additional guidelines, deadline dates and two different grant applications (small and major.)
Requirements: Most grants are made to tax-exempt, private agencies classified as 501(c)3 organizations, and to public charities as defined by the U.S. Internal Revenue Service. Public schools, governmental entities and Knox County colleges and universities are also eligible to apply for Foundation grants.
Restrictions: Certain projects and organizations are not eligible for funding, including but not limited to: grants to individuals; endowment campaigns; ongoing operating expenses; religious organizations (for religious purposes); purchase of computers or other equipment (that is not part of a broader project); existing obligations, debts or liabilities; police and fire protection; staff positions for government agencies travel (when it is the proposal's primary focus) organizations that do not operate programs in Knox County, or for the benefit of Knox County residents; political campaigns.
Geographic Focus: Ohio
Contact: Sam Barone, Executive Director; (740) 392-3270; fax (740) 399-5296; thefoundation@firstknox.com or sbarone@mvkcfoundation.org
Internet: http://www.mvkcfoundation.org/Grant/index.html
Sponsor: Community Foundation of Mount Vernon and Knox County
1 S Main Street, P.O. Box 1270
Mount Vernon, OH 43050

Community Foundation of Muncie and Delaware County Grants 1302

The Community Foundation of Muncie and Delaware County Grants provide funding in the following areas of interest: arts and culture, human services, economic development, education, and community betterment. The Foundation focus on: new and innovative projects and programs for which there is a demonstrable need or community benefit; capital needs of community institutions and organizations; emerging needs of Muncie and Delaware County; establishment of community priorities; monitoring of community services to avoid duplication and ineffective programs; acting as a catalyst for action and community participation. Applications are encouraged for types of projects that address one or more of the following: yield substantial benefits to the community for the resources invested; promote cooperation among agencies without duplicating services; enhance or improve institutional or organizational self-sufficiency; provide "seed money" for innovative community programs; encourage matching gifts or additional funding from other donors; and reach a broad segment of the community with needed services which are presently not provided. The Board of Directors review applications on a quarterly basis in the months of February, May, August, and November.
Requirements: First-time applicants must contact the Foundation to discuss their proposal prior to submission. Organizations are required to submit 18 copies of the application packet, but must submit different items depending on the type of funding requested. See website for submission details.
Restrictions: Requests of $25,000 or more are preferred during the first cycle of each year. The Foundation does not make grants to individuals or grants for religious purposes, budget deficits, for travel, fundraising events, endowments or projects normally the responsibility of a government agency.

Geographic Focus: Indiana
Amount of Grant: Up to USD
Contact: Suzanne Kadinger; (765) 747-7181; skadinger@cfmdin.org or info@cfmdin.org
Internet: http://www.cfmdin.org/main/grant-seekers/
Sponsor: Community Foundation of Muncie and Delaware County
201 East Jackson Street
Muncie, IN 47305

Community Foundation of Muncie and Delaware County Maxon Grants 1303
The Community Foundation of Muncie and Delaware County Maxon Grants give back to the community by supporting worthy causes in Delaware County. Organizations are notified within eight weeks whether they have been funded.
Requirements: In addition to the online application, organizations must submit the following: the grant application cover sheet; the organization's mission statement; a list of the board of directors with their affiliations; a copy of the organization's Federal IRS tax exemption letter; and a letter of endorsement from the Board President, Principal or Chief Executive Officer. They must also submit a brief proposal that provides; project goals and objectives; implementation plan; project budget including expected revenue, in-kind contributions and other grants; staff involved in project; community benefits; and the organization's method of evaluation.
Geographic Focus: Indiana
Date(s) Application is Due: Jul 30
Amount of Grant: 5,000 - 15,000 USD
Contact: Suzanne Kadinger, Program Officer; (765) 747-7181; fax (765) 289-7770; skadinger@cfmdin.org or info@cfmdin.org
Internet: http://www.cfmdin.org/main/grant-seekers/
Sponsor: Community Foundation of Muncie and Delaware County
201 East Jackson Street
Muncie, IN 47305

Community Foundation of Riverside County Grants 1304
The foundation's areas of interest include human services, arts and culture, and education. A special two-year emphasis focuses on children and families. Types of support include equipment, seed grants, scholarship funds, and matching funds. Grants are made for one year and require progress evaluations and appropriate recognition of the foundation. A conference with the program officer, by phone or in person, is highly recommended before a proposal is submitted. Grants are awarded mainly to support projects/activities in Riverside County.
Requirements: Nonprofit organizations within the county of Riverside, CA, are eligible. The Community Foundation will only accept applications from 501(c)3 organizations that can document on-going operations and nonprofit status for at least three years. The foundation will accept only one application every 12 months from each agency. (Not applicable in 2003 since there will only be one grant cycle).
Restrictions: The foundation does not make grants for operating expenses; deficits; endowment; capital or annual fund appeals; or to individuals, religious organizations, or congregations.
Geographic Focus: California
Amount of Grant: Up to 10,000 USD
Contact: Celia Cudiamat, Vice President of Grant Programs; (909) 684-4194; fax (909) 684-1911; ccudiamat@thecommunityfoundation.net
Internet: http://www.thecommunityfoundation.net/grants/current.html
Sponsor: Community Foundation of Riverside County
3880 Lemon Street, Suite 300
Riverside, CA 92501

Community Foundation of Santa Cruz County Grants 1305
The foundation promotes philanthropy to make greater Santa Cruz County a better place to live, now and in the future. Grants are designed to develop and strengthen services delivered by the nonprofit sector. Fields of interest include arts and humanities; community development; education; environment; health; historic preservation; human services; youth-led projects (11 to 14 years olds); lesbian, gay, bisexual, transgender community; and Vecinos project, to support residents' capacity to improve their neighborhoods. Management assistance grants are available for projects that strengthen the ability of an organization to fulfill its mission through improved governance and management practices. The listed application deadlines are for program grants; management assistance grants have no deadline. Complete guidelines are available online.
Requirements: To be eligible, an organization must be a nonprofit 501(c)3 organization or public agency, not classified as a private foundation; have a board-approved policy regarding staff employment, electing a governing board, and providing services without discrimination on the basis of race, religion, gender, sexual orientation, age, disability, or national origin; provide direct benefits to residents of Santa Cruz County, the Summit, or the Pajaro Valley and include representation of Santa Cruz County residents on its board of directors; and be current on all reports due to the community foundation for any previous grants.
Geographic Focus: California
Date(s) Application is Due: Feb 18; Apr 29
Amount of Grant: 1,000 - 15,000 USD
Contact: Christina Cuevas, (831) 477-0800, ext. 213; fax (831) 477-0991; christina@cfsscc.org
Internet: http://www.cfscc.org/page17117.cfm
Sponsor: Community Foundation of Santa Cruz County
2425 Porter Street, Suite 17
Soquel, CA 95073

Community Foundation of Sarasota County Grants 1306
The Foundation supports programs and projects of Sarasota County, Florida, by funding nonprofit organizations that seek to improve the quality of life for residents of the county. Grants are awarded to meet the needs of the community in the fields of music, art, and drama; social and health services; education and youth; civic improvements and historical preservation; and rehabilitation. Types of support include equipment acquisition, emergency funds, program development, seed money, and scholarship funds. Grants decisions are made once each year.
Requirements: 501(c)3 organizations in Sarasota County, FL, may apply for grant support.
Restrictions: Grants ordinarily are not made to support fraternal organizations, societies or orders, or religious organizations for sectarian purposes. No grants to individuals (except for selected scholarships), or for annual campaigns, building campaigns, endowment funds, deficit financing, debt retirement, publications, operating expenses, travel, fund raising events, scientific research, or conferences.
Geographic Focus: Florida
Amount of Grant: 500 - 6,000 USD
Contact: Wendy Hopkins; (941) 556-7152; fax (941) 556-7153; wendy@cfsarasota.org
Internet: http://www.cfsarasota.org/
Sponsor: Community Foundation of Sarasota County
2635 Fruitville Road, P.O. Box 49587
Sarasota, FL 34230-0267

Community Foundation of Shreveport-Bossier Grants 1307
The community foundation awards grants to nonprofit organizations that benefit people, activities, and institutions of Caddo and Bossier Parishes, LA. Areas of interest include arts and culture; higher education and adult basic education/literacy; health care and health organizations; human services; programs serving children, the elderly, and disabled. Types of support include capital campaigns, building/renovation, equipment, program development, seed money, scholarship funds, and matching funds. Grants are generally awarded for one year but organizations may receive up to three years of support. Grants for scholarships are given to educational institutions, which select recipients. The foundation encourages the participation of others in funding projects and sometimes provides matching funds or challenge grants. Contact the office for application forms. Before submitting a proposal it may be helpful to speak with a staff member at The Community Foundation of Shreveport-Bossier, (318) 221-0582.
Requirements: IRS 501(c)3 nonprofit organizations in Caddo and Bossier Parishes, LA, are eligible.
Restrictions: Grants are not made for political or religious purposes or to retire indebtedness, establish or add to endowment funds, support general operating expenses or annual sustaining fund drives, or to capital campaigns.
Geographic Focus: Louisiana
Date(s) Application is Due: Feb 28; Jul 31
Contact: Susan Adams; (318) 221-0582; fax (318) 221-7463; adams@comfoundsb.org
Internet: http://www.comfoundsb.org
Sponsor: Community Foundation of Shreveport-Bossier
401 Edward Street, Suite 105
Shreveport, LA 71101

Community Foundation of South Alabama Grants 1308
The Community Foundation of South Alabama is the platform for building community in Baldwin, Clarke, Conecuh, Choctaw, Escambia, Mobile, Monroe and Washington counties. The Foundation provides grant support to South Alabama nonprofit organizations in four major program areas: community and civic affairs, education, arts and recreation, and social services (health and human services). Priority consideration is given to projects that clearly provide innovative responses to community needs, are collaborative in nature when appropriate, and potentially affect broad segments of the community. Types of support include general operating support, capital campaigns, endowment funds, program development, and scholarship funds. The board of directors meets annually to consider grant requests. Application forms may be obtained from the office.
Requirements: Nonprofit organizations that have a 501(c)3, government entities and religious organizations that are located in Mobile, Baldwin, Clarke, Conecuh, Washington, Choctaw, Escambia and Monroe counties are eligible.
Restrictions: Grants generally are not provided for or to individuals, recurring requests for the same purpose for which foundation grant funds have already been awarded, research that is noncommunity-related or that does not have short-range results, films, conferences and workshops, lobbying activities, and tickets to fund-raising events.
Geographic Focus: Alabama
Amount of Grant: 2,500 - 28,000 USD
Contact: Janine Phillips, Director and Program Officer; (334) 438-5591; fax (334) 438-5592; info@communityendowment.com or program@communityendowment.com
Internet: http://communityendowment.com/grants/grants.htm
Sponsor: Community Foundation of South Alabama
212 St. Joseph Street, P.O. Box 990
Mobile, AL 36601-0990

Community Foundation of Southeastern Connecticut Grants 1309
Within its geographic area, comprising the 11 towns of southeastern Connecticut, the community foundation awards grants to assist charitable, educational, and civic institutions; promote health and general welfare; support environmental programs; provide human care services for the needy; secure the care of children and families; encourage artistic and cultural endeavors; and initiate planning of appropriate projects within these areas. High-priority programs include those that strengthen families; improve access to area resources, especially for underserved populations; encourage residents to participate in the cultural

life of the community; demonstrate collaborative efforts and inclusive practices; reinforce best practices or show innovative approaches; and add to the general well being of the community. Types of support include building/renovation, equipment, emergency funds, program development, conferences and seminars, publication, seed grants, scholarship funds, technical support, and scholarships to individuals. Applications requesting support of normal operating expenses will not be considered. Proposals may be submitted between April 1 and November 15 each year.
Requirements: IRS tax-exempt organizations serving the towns of East Lyme, Groton, Ledyard, Lyme, Montville, New London, North Stonington, Old Lyme, Salem, Stonington, and Waterford, CT, including inner-city, suburban, and rural areas, are eligible.
Restrictions: The foundation does not consider requests for direct financial assistance to individuals; religious or sectarian programs; political or lobbying purposes; fundraising events; or debt retirement.
Geographic Focus: Connecticut
Date(s) Application is Due: Nov 15
Amount of Grant: 2,000 - 10,000 USD
Contact: Jennifer O'Brien; (860) 442-3572; fax (860) 442-0584; jennob@cfsect.org
Internet: http://www.cfsect.org/grant.html
Sponsor: Community Foundation of Southeastern Connecticut
P.O. Box 769
New London, CT 06320

Community Foundation of Southern Indiana Grants 1310
The Community Foundation supports a wide variety of educational opportunities, civic projects and provided equipment and activities that benefit all ages in Floyd and Clark County. Areas of funding interest include arts and culture; community development; education; environment; health; human services; recreation; and youth development. Funding will encourage programs that enhance cooperation and collaboration among organizations in Floyd and Clark County. The application and supporting materials are available at the Foundation website.
Requirements: Organizations with 501(c)3 status in or serving Floyd and Clark counties may apply.
Restrictions: The Foundation does not typically fund any of the following: annual appeals, endowment funds, membership contributions or fundraising events; existing obligations, loans or debt retirement; long-term operating support; multi-year grants or repeat funding; medical, scientific or academic research; operating and construction costs at schools, universities and private academies unless there is significant opportunity for community use or collaboration; projects that promote a particular religion or construction projects of churches and other religious institutions; political campaigns, advocacy or direct lobbying efforts by 501(c)3 organizations; services commonly regarded as the responsibility of governmental agencies, such as fire and police protection; and travel for individuals, bands, sports teams, classes and similar groups.
Geographic Focus: Indiana
Date(s) Application is Due: Sep 1
Amount of Grant: Up to 5,000 USD
Contact: Crystal Gunther, Grants and Programs Officer; (812) 948-4662; fax (812) 948-4678; cgunther@cfsouthernindiana.com
Internet: http://www.cfsouthernindiana.com/Default.aspx?sitemapid=40
Sponsor: Community Foundation of Southern Indiana - Floyd and Clark County
4104 Charlestown Road
New Albany, IN 47150

Community Foundation of South Puget Sound Grants 1311
The foundation awards grants to a variety of charitable, cultural, education, health, and welfare organizations. Grants from the unrestricted funds are considered for general operational or program support. Typical grants range from $1,000 to $7,500. Emergency grants may be considered on a case-by-case basis. Application and guidelines for grants and scholarships are available online.
Requirements: The foundation awards grants to Washington tax-exempt organizations primarily for use in Thurston, Mason, and Lewis Counties, except on instructions of the donor at the time of the gift or bequest.
Restrictions: Grants do not support religious organizations for religious purposes; individuals; annual campaigns of organizations (direct mail or special events); political or lobbying activities; organizations that discriminate based on race, creed, or ethnic group; capital campaigns for bricks and mortar or endowment funds; or for multiple year commitments.
Geographic Focus: Washington
Date(s) Application is Due: Apr 3; Oct 2
Amount of Grant: 1,000 - 7,500 USD
Contact: Norma Schuiteman; (360) 705-3340; legacy@thecommunityfoundation.com
Internet: http://www.thecommunityfoundation.com/grants.php
Sponsor: Community Foundation of South Puget
111 Market Street NE, Suite 375
Olympia, WA 98501

Community Foundation of St. Joseph County African American Community Grants 1312
The purpose of the African American Community Grant is to enhance the lives of African Americans in St. Joseph County by providing funds for initiatives that build capacity, influence whole system improvements, and achieve tangible long-term progress. Primary consideration will be given to programs addressing these priorities: education; arts; leadership development; and the special challenges facing African American males. Up to $25,000 may be requested. Multi-year funding for exceptional programs and projects may be considered.
Requirements: Ideally, AACF grants will go to 501(c)3 organizations for projects that pursue clearly defined outcomes, and have potential for high impact. In addition to the online application, all candidates must submit the following: up to a two page proposed narrative; a detailed project budget; current board roster with officers identified; and proof of nonprofit status. See the grant website for detailed information.
Restrictions: Grants are not made to fund: routine operating expenses for established programs; conference attendance/training (unless presented as a necessary component of a larger program or objective); development and fundraising-related expenses or events; annual appeals or membership contributions; travel for bands, sports teams, classes, and similar groups; computers (unless presented as a necessary component of larger program or objective); endowments; individuals, directly; debt retirement and back taxes; post-event or after-the-fact situations; political activity.
Geographic Focus: Indiana
Date(s) Application is Due: Mar 1; Oct 1
Amount of Grant: 25,000 USD
Contact: Angela Butiste; (574) 232-0041; fax (574) 233-1906; angela@cfsjc.org
Internet: http://www.cfsjc.org/initiatives/aacf/aacf_grants.html
Sponsor: Community Foundation of St. Joseph County
205 W Jefferson Boulevard, P.O. Box 837
South Bend, IN 46624

Community Foundation of St. Joseph County ArtsEverywhere Grants 1313
The ArtsEverywhere Fund seeks to raise artistic quality, strengthen volunteer and staff leadership, enhance the capacity of arts organizations and the arts community, foster and support local talent, and inspire community pride. Grants will be competitively awarded in the following categories: capacity building (matching grants of up to $5,000); program or project support (matching grants of up to $5,000); and major venture funding (matching grants of up to $50,000, potentially renewable for up to three years, for a maximum commitment of $150,000). Applicants may apply for any or all types of funding.
Requirements: St. Joseph County nonprofit or public agencies with a demonstrated, substantial (though not necessarily exclusive) commitment to the arts as part of its overall mission and appropriate participation in the ArtsEverywhere initiative are eligible to apply for grant funding. Detailed guidelines and application information for each grant category are available at the website.
Restrictions: Grants are not made to fund: operational phases of established programs; endowment campaigns; religious organizations for religious purposes; individuals directly; development or public relations activities (e.g. literature, videos, etc.); retirement of debts; camperships; annual appeals or membership contributions; travel for bands, sports teams, classes, etc; computers (unless presented as a necessary component of larger program or objective); and post-event or after-the-fact situations.
Geographic Focus: Indiana
Date(s) Application is Due: May 1; Nov 1
Amount of Grant: Up to 50,000 USD
Contact: Angela Butiste; (574) 232-0041; fax (574) 233-1906; angela@cfsjc.org
Internet: http://www.cfsjc.org/initiatives/artseverywhere/artseverywhere_grants.html
Sponsor: Community Foundation of St. Joseph County
205 W Jefferson Boulevard, P.O. Box 837
South Bend, IN 46624

Community Foundation of St. Joseph County Special Project Challenge Grants 1314
The Special Project Challenge Grants assist public and other 501(c)3 agencies in their efforts to serve community needs. For every $1 raised by the chosen agency, the Community Foundation will match $1. The foundation encourages projects in the following areas: community development and urban affairs; health and human services; parks, recreation, and environment; and youth and education.
Requirements: In additional to the online application, all applicants must submit the following materials online: up to a two page proposal narrative; a detailed project budget; current board roster with officers identified; fiscal year income statement; proof of nonprofit status. Application materials must be submitted via email to grants@cfsjc.org in word processing format (narrative or budget) or Microsoft Excel (budget). Hard copy applications are no longer accepted.
Restrictions: Grants are not made to fund: operational phases of established programs; endowment campaigns; religious organizations for religious purposes; individuals directly; development or public relations activities (e.g. literature, videos, etc.); retirement of debts; camperships; annual appeals or membership contributions; travel for bands, sports teams, classes, etc; j) computers (unless presented as a necessary component of larger program or objective); and post-event or after-the-fact situations.
Geographic Focus: Indiana
Date(s) Application is Due: Mar 1; Oct 1
Contact: Angela Butiste; (574) 232-0041; fax (574) 233-1906; angela@cfsjc.org
Internet: http://www.cfsjc.org/grants/sproj/special_project_grants.html
Sponsor: Community Foundation of St. Joseph County
205 W Jefferson Boulevard, P.O. Box 837
South Bend, IN 46624

Community Foundation of Switzerland County Grants 1315
The Community Foundation of Switzerland County is a nonprofit organization created to make Switzerland County a better place to live for present and future generations. The Foundation gives priority to applications that focus on the basic needs of the community (food, housing, shelter, health care, clothing, personal care, and transportation). The Foundation also welcomes applications for other programs and projects that benefit Switzerland County. Organizations may request up to $5,000. Applications are reviewed monthly; there are no deadlines. The application and additional guidelines are available at the website.

Requirements: Any organization with a 501(c)3 or any organization that provides a program with charitable intent or has a fiscal agent is eligible to apply.
Geographic Focus: Indiana
Amount of Grant: Up to 5,000 USD
Contact: Pam Acton; (812) 427-9160; fax (812) 427-4033; pacton@cfsci.org
Internet: http://www.cfsci.org/
Sponsor: Community Foundation of Switzerland County
303 Ferry Street, P.O. Box 46
Vevay, IN 47043

Community Foundation of Tampa Bay Grants 1316

The Community Foundation of Tampa Bay awards creative grants from its community fund with the goal of fostering positive changes in the lives of their citizens. The areas of interest include: arts and culture, community development, education, environment and animals, and health and human services. See the Foundations website for the Grant Application Form and guidelines: http://www.cftampabay.org/nonprofit_resources/grant_app_guidelines.html
Requirements: Non-profit organizations based in and serving communities in Hillsborough, Pasco, Pinellas and Hernando counties, with a 501(c)3 status in good standing from the IRS are eligible to apply.
Restrictions: The Foundation is generally not interested in requests for: funding of ongoing operating costs; grants for capital campaigns or expenditures; tickets for any fundraising event or advertising space in programs or other publications; legislative lobbying or political campaigns; medical research; religious or sectarian purposes; loans or assistance to individuals; a multiple year funding commitment, although in exceptional cases, such funding will be considered not to exceed three years.
Geographic Focus: Florida
Date(s) Application is Due: Mar 1; Sep 1
Amount of Grant: Up to 7,500 USD
Contact: Ann Berg; (813) 282-1975; fax (813) 282-3119; aberg@cftampabay.org
Internet: http://www.cftampabay.org/nonprofit_resources/grant_app_guidelines.html
Sponsor: Community Foundation of Tampa Bay
550 North Reo Street, Suite 301
Tampa, FL 33609

Community Foundation of the Eastern Shore Community Needs Grants 1317

The Community Foundation of the Eastern Shore awards grants from its discretionary fund, known as the Lower Shore Fund for Community Needs. Monetary grants are awarded to a wide range of tax exempt organizations in Somerset, Wicomico and Worcester Counties of Maryland, whose programs benefit: health; human services; arts and culture; community affairs; environmental conservation; and historic preservation. Through this grant program, the Foundation identifies high priority needs and seeks opportunities where a relatively modest amount of grant money can make a significant difference in the community. Often the grants provide start-up or short-term funding for innovative, potentially replicable projects that meet newly identified needs or demonstrate new solutions for previously identified needs.
Requirements: To be eligible for a grant from this program, an organization must meet two fundamental criteria: it must be a governmental unit, a religious organization engaged in a non-sectarian activity, or a non-profit, tax exempt public charity, as defined in Section 501(c)3 of the Internal Revenue Code; and it must provide services to benefit the residents of the lower three counties of Maryland's Eastern Shore: Worcester, Wicomico, and Somerset. Programs are not required to serve all three counties, but regional projects are encouraged.
Restrictions: The Community Needs Grant Program does not fund: endowment funds; ongoing/operating expenses; fundraising campaigns; sectarian religious programs; playground equipment; building campaigns; operational deficits; debt retirement; capital requests; political/lobbying programs; office equipment/staff training; and school-based programs. Grants through this program are made to organizations, not individuals.
Geographic Focus: Maryland
Date(s) Application is Due: Feb 1; Aug 1
Amount of Grant: 500 - 7,500 USD
Contact: Erica N. Joseph; (410) 742-9911; fax (410) 742-6638; joseph@cfes.org
Internet: http://www.cfes.org/grants_community_needs.php
Sponsor: Community Foundation of the Eastern Shore
1324 Belmont Avenue, Suite 401
Salisbury, MD 21804

Community Foundation of the Eastern Shore Field of Interest Grants 1318

The Community Foundation of the Eastern Shore, as part of its core mission, has supported local nonprofit organizations since 1984. Field of Interest Funds are established by donors to support a particular area of interest. Within that subject area, the Foundation makes grants to the most appropriate organizations and local projects serving that interest. Selection is guided by the Foundation's Community Initiative Committee. Through this grant program, the Foundation identifies high priority needs and seeks opportunities where a relatively modest amount of grant money can make a significant difference in the community. Monetary grants are awarded to a wide range of tax exempt organizations in Somerset, Wicomico and Worcester Counties, Maryland. Most awards are in the $500 - $1,500 range, although consideration may be given to larger requests. All applicants must submit a Letter of Inquiry, following an initial review, eligible projects will be encouraged to submit a full application (format will be provided). All Letters of Inquiry will receive a written response.
Requirements: Tax exempt organizations in Somerset, Wicomico and Worcester Counties, of Maryland are eligible.
Restrictions: Grants through this program are made to charitable organizations, not individuals. The eligibility requirements will vary depending on the specific fund criteria, but Field of Interest Funds will not provide grants for: endowment funds; general operating expenses; fundraising campaigns; sectarian religious programs; playground equipment; building campaigns; operational deficits; debt retirement; capital requests and; political/lobbying programs.
Geographic Focus: Maryland
Amount of Grant: 500 - 1,500 USD
Contact: Erica N. Joseph; (410) 742-9911; fax (410) 742-6638; joseph@cfes.org
Internet: http://www.cfes.org/grants_field_of_interest.php
Sponsor: Community Foundation of the Eastern Shore
1324 Belmont Avenue, Suite 401
Salisbury, MD 21804

Community Foundation of the Eastern Shore Youth Foundation Grants 1319

The mission of the Youth Foundation Fund is to help children in the Maryland counties of Somerset, Wicomico, and Worcester by creating awareness of giving and by establishing and supporting programs that promote youth betterment. In order to carry out the mission of the Fund, students from high schools in the tri-county area have been selected to serve on the Youth Foundation Fund Advisory Committee. The Advisory Committee is responsible for overseeing fundraising and grant making activities for the Youth Foundation Fund. The Fund will be used to address the following goals: to help improve the mental and physical health of area youth; to encourage and reward academic excellence by youth; to provide additional educational opportunities for youth; to build strong citizenship in youth; to foster good character in youth. The Youth Foundation Fund will award one or more grants totaling up to $4000.00 The grant(s) will be awarded to eligible organizations that exemplify one or more of the goals set forth by the Fund. It can be used towards a program previously established by an organization or serve to establish a new program.
Requirements: Grant applicants must be within the following guidelines: must be a non-profit 501(c)3 charitable organization; the organization must be within the tri-county area. The program doesn't necessarily have to serve all three counties but those that do will be looked upon more favorably; the program must be aimed at, and benefit, youth; the organization must provide a budget that gives a breakdown of how funds received through the grant will be used. Additionally, the organization must agree to report on the use of said funds within a designated time period; the organization must be willing to undergo both a site visit and interview with one or more Youth Foundation Fund grant committee members.
Geographic Focus: Maryland
Date(s) Application is Due: Mar 5
Amount of Grant: Up to 4,000 USD
Contact: Erica N. Joseph; (410) 742-9911; fax (410) 742-6638; joseph@cfes.org
Internet: http://cfes.org/programs_youth_foundation.php
Sponsor: Community Foundation of the Eastern Shore
1324 Belmont Avenue, Suite 401
Salisbury, MD 21804

Community Foundation of the Ozarks Grants 1320

Grants from unrestricted funds of the community foundation are made to qualified nonprofit organizations that serve the Greene County area of Missouri. Areas of interest include arts, community betterment, education, and social justice. Preference will be given to projects that are exclusive of the ongoing operation of the organization; provide seed money for new programs; open the possibility of receiving matching funds; and offer the community foundation the opportunity to meet needs in full in diverse problem areas. Agencies are encouraged to ask for funding amounts that reflect their true needs. Submittal of a one-page concept letter is the first step in applying. Concept letters must be received by the August deadline for grants awarded in November, by the December deadline for grants awarded in March, and by the March deadline for grants awarded in June. Concept letters may be submitted to dmyers@cfozarks.org.
Requirements: 501(c)3 organizations that serve the Greene County area in Missouri are eligible.
Restrictions: Capital campaigns and grants to individuals are not allowed.
Geographic Focus: Missouri
Date(s) Application is Due: Mar 1; Aug 1; Dec 1
Contact: Gary Funk, President; (417) 864-6199; fax (417) 864-8344; gfunk@cfozarks.org
Internet: http://www.cfozarks.org/grantseekers.html
Sponsor: Community Foundation of the Ozarks
901 St. Louis Street, Suite 701
Springfield, MO 65806

Community Foundation of the Verdugos Educational Endowment Fund Grants 1321

The Educational Endowment Fund provides financial support to innovative as well as traditional educational programs and projects in public and private schools and community organizations in the Crescenta Valley, California region. The goal is to enrich educational opportunities by supporting building, equipment, instruction, guidance, coaching, practical application, classroom activities, in-service, training and/or practice programs. Grants will support: equipment purchase, replacement & modernization; improvement to facilities including athletic facilities; printed materials; fundraising events or capital campaigns; classroom materials; public/private schools and colleges; child day care/development centers; libraries; hospitals; community enrichment projects; salaries. All qualified organizations are invited to submit grant applications once a year for grants that will be awarded at the Crescenta Valley Chamber of Commerce Installation Luncheon in early January. Average grant sizes are from $500 to $3,000. The grant application is available at the Community Foundation of the Verdugos website. The application must be submitted by October 9th.
Requirements: 501(c)3 IRS nonprofit public charities in the Crescenta Valley region of California (includes La Crescenta, Montrose, Tujunga and La Canada) and, organizations located outside the Crescenta Valley but delivering educational programs in the Crescenta Valley are eligible to apply. Please indicate the number of Crescenta Valley residents who will be served by your program. An organization may apply for no more than two grants

during a grant cycle. Note, the president, school principal or leader must indicate awareness of multiple requests and each application must be for different types of support.
Restrictions: Grants will not support: uniforms or clothing; travel expenses; fiscal agents; individuals and individual scholarships; endowment funds; feasibility studies or consulting fees; advertising; research; political lobbying, voter registration or political campaigns; insurance or maintenance contracts; faith-based projects.
Geographic Focus: California
Date(s) Application is Due: Oct 9
Amount of Grant: 500 - 3,000 USD
Contact: Edna Karinski, Executive Director; (818) 241-8040; fax (818) 241-8045; info@communityfoundationoftheverdugos.org
Internet: http://www.glendalecommunityfoundation.org/grants_endowment.php
Sponsor: Community Foundation of the Verdugos
330 Arden Avenue, Suite 130
Glendale, CA 91203

Community Foundation of the Verdugos Grants 1322
The Community Foundation of the Verdugos welcomes grant requests from public agencies and nonprofit organizations that serve the Verdugo region including Burbank, Glendale, La Canada Flintridge, La Crescenta, Montrose, and Verdugo City of California. Grant recipients must have appropriate fiscal and program accountability. Average grant amounts range from $2,500 to $10,000. Grants are provided in the following areas of interest: arts and culture; civic; health and human services (examples include projects and services for the disabled/handicapped, general community health, or homeless services); education programs; senior services; student aid (scholarships); youth services; environment and; community. Grant application and, application guidelines are available at the Foundation's website. Grants are made three times a year. Deadline for grant applications are February 1, June 1, and September 1. Scholarship deadline is March 5. Only one proposal from an organization is permitted per grant cycle. Approval or denial of your request will be provided to you in writing.
Requirements: The Foundation funds nonprofit organizations that: have IRS nonprofit status; predominantly serve the Verdugo region of California (Glendale, La Canada Flintridge, La Crescenta, Montrose, Verdugo City) and adjacent areas; capital equipment that helps to increase your organization's long-term sustainability or services to increase impact in the Verdugo region; programs (including related overhead, supplies and administrative expenses) responsive to changing community needs and which increase impact in the Verdugo region. Requests that provide significance and impact for the Verdugo region in the areas of arts and culture, children/youth, education and literacy, health and human services, civic activities, senior services, and environmental/animal related programs.
Restrictions: The Foundation does not make grants or loans to individuals unless they are students receiving scholarships. The Foundation also does not provide funds for religious or political purposes, for budget deficits, or projects that are usually the responsibility of a public agency.
Geographic Focus: California
Date(s) Application is Due: Feb 1; Mar 5; Jun 1; Sep 1
Amount of Grant: 25,000 - 10,000 USD
Contact: Edna Karinski; (818) 241-8040; info@communityfoundationoftheverdugos.org
Internet: http://www.glendalecommunityfoundation.org/grants.php
Sponsor: Community Foundation of the Verdugos
330 Arden Avenue, Suite 130
Glendale, CA 91203

Community Foundation Of The Virgin Islands Anderson Family Teacher Grants 1323
Anderson Family Teacher Grants are provided through the Anderson Family Fund for Education at CFVI. This annual program provides grants on a competitive basis to teachers, assistant teachers, and guidance counselors for projects that seek to improve student achievement. The Anderson Family Fund was established in 2002, as a donor advised fund, to improve public education for economically disadvantaged children in the USVI by supporting educational enrichment programs unavailable as part of the regular school curriculum. Individuals may request up to $1,000 to implement an innovative project in their classrooms and schools.
Requirements: Grant awards must supplement school resources, not replace local or federal funding. Priority will be given to proposals where students are directly involved in the project, creative strategies and activities are used to improve student learning, and outcomes are measurable and substantive.
Geographic Focus: U.S. Virgin Islands
Contact: Dee Baecher-Brown; (340) 774-6031; fax (340) 774-3852; dbrown@cfvi.net
Internet: http://www.cfvi.net/subpages/grants.html
Sponsor: Community Foundation of the Virgin Islands
P.O. Box 11790
St. Thomas, VI 00801-4790

Community Foundation Of The Virgin Islands Kimelman Grants 1324
The Community Foundation of the Virgin Islands is committed to using resources from unrestricted sources to fund innovative programs and projects that show promise of developing into longer-term responses to the needs of children and families in the Virgin Islands. Established in 1990, CFVI is a growing collection of permanent endowment funds set up by donors for the long-term benefit of the USVI. Kimelman grants are established to provide quality improvements in early childhood education in non-government supported child care centers. Grants are offered to licensed child care centers for child care teachers, directors and others directly involved in the delivery of services to children. Individuals may request up to $2,500 for activities such as purchasing supplies to improve the physical appearance of the center; books or developmentally appropriate toys; training and materials for parents, staff, etc.
Requirements: Funding will be awarded on a competitive basis for initiatives that seek to improve the quality of early child care in the U.S. Virgin Islands. See the Foundation's website for application form.
Geographic Focus: U.S. Virgin Islands
Date(s) Application is Due: May 29
Amount of Grant: Up to 2,500 USD
Contact: Dee Baecher-Brown; (340) 774-6031; fax (340) 774-3852; dbrown@cfvi.net
Internet: http://www.cfvi.net/subpages/grants.html
Sponsor: Community Foundation of the Virgin Islands
P.O. Box 11790
St. Thomas, VI 00801-4790

Community Foundation Of The Virgin Islands Mini Grants 1325
The Community Foundation of the Virgin Islands is committed to using resources from unrestricted sources to fund innovative programs and projects that show promise of developing into longer-term responses to the needs of children and families in the Virgin Islands. Established in 1990, CFVI is a growing collection of permanent endowment funds set up by donors for the long-term benefit of the USVI. The Mini-Grants Program promotes the initiation of new and creative programs and projects that are of direct benefit to the children, youth or families of the Virgin Islands and demonstrate the promise of continuing after the expiration of the grant. CFVI will give priority to proposals not already being met by established programs.
Requirements: Any private group (i.e. school class or club, sports team, alumni group, etc.) or individual in the U.S. Virgin Islands may submit an application. Proposals will also be accepted from established non-profit organizations. Any applicant who was a recipient of a CFVI Mini-Grant must submit a brief written report and documentation on the use of the grant in order to be eligible for a CFVI Mini-Grant for the next yea
Restrictions: Grants cannot be used to assist with the underwriting of operating budgets.
Geographic Focus: U.S. Virgin Islands
Amount of Grant: 250 - 1,000 USD
Samples: Fishing for Families by the Salvation Army of St. Croix, USVI - to provide quality time, recreation, and community relations between parents/guardians and their children; Making Waves on St. Thomas, USVI - students will be taught not only swimming and water safety, but will also become certified to administer CPR/first aid; Sprauve School, St. John, USVI - students from the special education class will enjoy learning gardening skills as a part of the Green Thumb Gardening project;
Contact: Dee Baecher-Brown; (340) 774-6031; fax (340) 774-3852; dbrown@cfvi.net
Internet: http://www.cfvi.net/subpages/grants.html
Sponsor: Community Foundation of the Virgin Islands
P.O. Box 11790
St. Thomas, VI 00801-4790

Community Foundation of Wabash County Grants 1326
The goal of the Community Foundation of Wabash County Grants is to enrich the quality of life in Wabash County, Indiana, by responding to emerging and changing needs of the community. It also seeks to support existing organizations and institutions through grants in support of the following categories: arts and culture; community and civic development; education; environment; health and human services; and recreation. Types of support include: building or renovation; continuing support; curriculum development; endowments; equipment; general operating support; matching/challenge support; program development; program evaluation; scholarship funds; scholarships to individuals; seed money; and technical assistance.
Requirements: Proposals are accepted from organizations serving Wabash County that are defined as tax exempt under Section 501(c)3 of the IRS code or have comparable status and charitable causes. Grant selection is judged on program focus; program design; benefits; reach; and organizational profile. In addition to the online application, organizations must submit the completed cover sheet, proposal budget, a list of member of the organization's current staff and governing board; current year-end financial statement; and copy of the tax exempt IRS letter. Eight copies of the application and attached documentation are then submitted to the Foundation office for review.
Restrictions: The following are not eligible for funding: national organizations (except for local chapters serving Wabash County); annual fund campaigns; or programs or products produced for resale. Faith-based organizations may apply for program funding, provided there is not a requirement to participate in religious instruction and/or take part in religious activities.
Geographic Focus: Indiana
Date(s) Application is Due: Mar 15; Jul 15; Nov 15
Amount of Grant: Up to USD
Contact: Cathy McCarty; (260) 982-4824; fax (260) 982-8644; cathy@cfwabash.org
Internet: http://www.cfwabash.org/nonprofits-grant-information/guidelines.html
Sponsor: Community Foundation of Wabash County
218 East Main Street
North Manchester, IN 46962-0098

Community Foundation of Western North Carolina Grants 1327
The foundation serves an 18-county area, including Cherokee, Graham, Clay, Swain, Macon, Jackson, Haywood, Transylvania, Madison, Buncombe, Henderson, Yancey, McDowell, Rutherford, Polk, Burke, Mitchell, and Avery Counties. The community foundation awards grants for projects in the areas of arts and culture, children and youth, community development, education, environment, health, human services, and social justice. The foundation awards seed money grants to new or existing programs and technical assistance grants to strengthen nonprofit organizations. A workshop for grant applicants is held one month prior to the deadline at which time the guidelines are reviewed and questions are addressed; contact the foundation for date and times.

Requirements: Nonprofit 501(c)3 organizations serving areas within the 18-county region are eligible. Applicants must obtain foundation approval in order to apply for signature grants.
Restrictions: Grants are not made for the following: operating support (except for start-up); activities taking place before grant decisions are made; capital requests (except for modest budget items, such as equipment); endowments; sectarian purposes; private schools and clubs; political purposes; veteran affairs; deficit funding or debt retirement; and individuals except through scholarships. Multiple-year grants are not made. The foundation is only occasionally able to fund the second phase of a project. Organizations may not submit more than one application at a time; it is suggested that no more than one request be submitted during a 12-month period.
Geographic Focus: North Carolina
Date(s) Application is Due: Feb 1; Sep 1
Amount of Grant: Up to 10,000 USD
Contact: Tara Scholtz; (828) 254-4960; fax (828) 251-2258; scholtz@cfwnc.org
Internet: http://www.cfwnc.org/grants.html
Sponsor: Community Foundation of Western North Carolina
P.O. Box 1888
Asheville, NC 28802

Community Foundation Partnerships - Lawrence County Grants 1328
The Lawrence County Community Foundation funds charitable programs and projects that serve Lawrence County. Funding priorities include education, health and human services, civic and historical affairs, recreation, and arts and culture. Previously funded projects include nutritional programs, park revitalization, programs for children of domestic violence and literacy program. The application is available at the website.
Requirements: Nonprofits organizations such as educational institutions and governmental entities are invited to apply. Priority is given to the following projects or programs: those that reach as many people as possible; are preventative rather than remedial; increase individual access to community resources; promote independence and personal achievement; examine and address the underlying causes of local problems; attract volunteer resources and support; strengthen the private, nonprofit sector; encourage collaboration with other organizations; building the capacity of the applying organizations; and offer services not already provided in the community.
Restrictions: Grants are awarded for short term projects and are not renewable. In order to maximize funding, the Foundation gives lower priority to construction projects, normal operating expenses, computer hardware, multi-year funding, re-granting, or to organizations with an existing tax-base of support.
Geographic Focus: Indiana
Date(s) Application is Due: Apr 23
Contact: Hope Flores; (812) 279-2215; fax (812) 279-1984; hope@cfpartner.org
Internet: http://cfpartner.org/lccfgrantshowtoapply.htm
Sponsor: Community Foundation Partnership - Lawrence County
1324 K. Street, Suite 150
Bedford, IN 47421

Community Foundation Partnerships - Martin County Grants 1329
Community Foundation Partnership grants are award for programs that address emerging needs in Martin County. Awards are for short-term projects, usually one year, and are not renewable. Priority funding includes education, health and human services, civic and historical affairs, arts and culture, and recreation. Funding is given to projects or programs that provide the following priorities: reach as many people as possible; are preventative rather than remedial; increase individual access to community resources; promote independence and personal achievement; examine and address the underlying causes of local programs; attract volunteer resources and support; strengthen the private, nonprofit sector; encourage collaboration with other organizations; build the capacity of the applying organizations; and offer services not already provided in the community. The application is available at the website.
Requirements: The Foundation welcomes grant requests from nonprofit organizations recognized as 501(c)3 or that are affiliated with another tax exempt organization; educational institutions; government entities; and those located in or provide service to Martin County residents.
Restrictions: In order to maximize the use of funds, the Foundation gives low priority to construction projects; normal operating expenses; computer hardware; multi-year funding; re-granting; and organizations with an existing tax-base of support. The Foundation does not award grants to individuals; debt retirement; political organizations or campaigns; for-profit entities; capital campaigns; programing that promotes religious instruction or doctrine; or endowments.
Geographic Focus: Indiana
Date(s) Application is Due: Sep 14
Contact: Jason T. Jones; (812) 295-1022; fax (812) 295-1042; mccf@rtccom.net
Internet: http://cfpartner.org/mccfgrantshowtoapply.htm
Sponsor: Community Foundation Partnership - Martin County
P.O. Box 28
Loogootee, IN 47553

Community Foundation Silicon Valley Advancing the Arts Initiative 1330
The initiative is designed to strengthen and connect local arts organizations to one another and with the community. The primary focus of the grants program is to advance the work of individual organizations and the sector by providing one-year general support grants and technical support to small and mid-sized arts organizations with budgets between $50,000 and $2 million. The foundation will select 15 to 20 participants that represent diverse geographies, budget sizes, and disciplines. Grantees may apply for a technical assistance grant, and will meet at least twice during the year to attend workshops and network with one another. Complete guidelines are available online.

Requirements: California 501(c)3 nonprofit organizations located in Santa Clara County or Southern San Mateo County and that provide arts activities in Santa Clara County and/or Southern San Mateo County are eligible.
Restrictions: For-profit organizations; elementary schools, high schools, and colleges; and government entities are not eligible. Grants may not be applied toward support for political or religious purposes, debt retirement, or costs already incurred. Applicant organization may not be a current grantee of both The David and Lucile Packard Foundation and the James Irvine Foundation.
Geographic Focus: California
Date(s) Application is Due: Jan 9
Amount of Grant: 5,000 - 15,000 USD
Contact: Melissa Downey, (408) 278-2255; fax (408) 278-0280; mdowney@cfsv.org
Internet: http://www.cfsv.org/grants_advancingarts.html
Sponsor: Community Foundation Silicon Valley
60 S Market Street, Suite 1000
San Jose, CA 95113

Community Foundation Silicon Valley Grants 1331
The foundation supports California nonprofits in its areas of interest, including arts and cultural participation, education and lifelong learning, self-reliant individuals and family, and neighborhood and civic projects. The foundation also supports the Youth in Philanthropy program and early literacy grants. Preference is given to proposals that focus on the prevention of problems rather than the cure, equip people to become self-sufficient, encourage programs that take a comprehensive approach to addressing interrelated problems, promote cooperation and collaboration among agencies, encourage leveraging and matching grant opportunities, and provide seed funding for innovative projects. Additional types of support include program development, technical assistance, consulting services, and general operating grants. Grants generally are made for one year of support; long-term commitments are contingent upon annual review of progress and available funds. Guidelines and application are available online.
Requirements: Nonprofit organizations benefiting Santa Clara County and southern San Mateo County, CA, are eligible.
Restrictions: In general, the foundation does not consider fundraising events, capital equipment and endowment campaigns, on-going operating expenses, existing debts/obligations, for-profit schools, or individuals.
Geographic Focus: California
Amount of Grant: Up to 25,000 USD
Contact: Jeff Sunshine, Director of Programs; (408) 278-2200; fax (408) 278-0280; jsunshine@cfsv.org or info@cfsv.org
Internet: http://www.cfsv.org/grants_focusareas.html
Sponsor: Community Foundation Silicon Valley
60 S Market Street, Suite 1000
San Jose, CA 95113

Community Impact Fund 1332
The foundation awards grants aimed at meeting the needs and enhancing the lives of individuals in California's Riverside and San Bernardino Counties. Funding categories include health and human services—promoting access to healthcare for all residents and helping individuals and families obtain basic services to promote an improved quality of life; youth and families—enhancing opportunities that promote academic achievement and positive youth development and developing family support services that foster learning and growth; arts and culture—encouraging creative expression and providing opportunities for enjoyment of cultural activities and art forms; civic and public benefit—building a sense of community and promoting civic participation. Preference is given to projects that are perceived as a high need in the community being served; fill a gap in service; benefit a large number of residents; enhance collaboration and/or make the delivery of services more effective and efficient; have clear objectives and can document successful outcomes; expand successful programs to serve additional residents or new geographic areas within the two counties; serve remote areas or areas that have received little funding from the foundation. Contact the office for application deadlines and forms.
Requirements: The foundation will only accept applications from 501(c)3 organizations that can document on-going operations and nonprofit status for at least three years. Organizations may only apply once very 12 months.
Restrictions: Grants are generally not made for on-going operating expenses; retroactive funding for cost already incurred; paying off deficits or existing obligations; endowment, capital fund, or annual fund appeals; capital projects, i.e. construction of new buildings; direct support of individuals; sectarian programs or fraternal organizations; event sponsorships; research or development activities; school or college-based extracurricular activities; partisan activities; or re-granting purposes.
Geographic Focus: All States
Amount of Grant: Up to 10,000 USD
Contact: Celia Cudiamat, Vice President of Grant Programs; (951) 684-4194; fax (909) 684-1911; ccudiamat@thecommunityfoundation.net
Internet: http://www.thecommunityfoundation.net/grants/grant_commImpact_04.html
Sponsor: Community Foundation Serving Riverside and San Bernardino Counties
3880 Lemon Street, Suite 300
Riverside, CA 92501

Community in the Connecting AAPIs To Advocate and Lead Grants 1333
The program serves to support advocacy by local Asian American, Pacific Islanders (AAPI) community-based organizations and increase their participation in the national policy making process. Staff, boards, and constituents of AAPI CBOs have limited opportunities to come to Washington DC to learn about policies and resources specifically for AAPI

organizations. Components of the program include: a 'Government 101' briefing, meetings with key federal agencies, elected officials and national community development organizations, dialogue with other national AAPI organizations and training on advocacy for non-profits. The sponsor will arrange visits with key elected officials, federal agency staff, community development intermediaries, and national advocacy organizations for members visiting Washington DC.
Requirements: This is a service provided free of charge for member organizations. Membership forms are available the sponsor's website at www.nationalcapacd.org. Guidelines and the required application form can also be downloaded at the website.
Restrictions: Participants must cover their own expenses for travel and lodging.
Geographic Focus: All States
Contact: TC Duong, Community Resources Program Manager; (202) 223-2442; fax (202) 223-4144; tcduong@nationalcapacd.org
Internet: http://www.nationalcapacd.org/what.html#caapital
Sponsor: National Coalition for Asian Pacific American Community Development
1001 Connecticut Avenue NW, Suite 730
Washington, DC 20036

Community Memorial Foundation Grants 1334
The foundation encourages public/private endeavors in Illinois by nurturing the formation of creative initiatives and innovative funding strategies. Collaborative efforts may include participation with nonprofit organizations, governments, schools, and the business sector. In general, the foundation gives preference to organizations that reach underserved segments of the population. A broad range of funding includes service delivery programs for vulnerable populations, start-up funds, building construction/renovation, project support, general operating support, and educational programs. Generally, the foundation does not consider more than one proposal from any one institution and favors funding noncapital programs.
Requirements: 501(c)3 organizations located in the Illinois communities of Argo, Bridgeview, Broadview, Brookfield, Burr Ridge, Clarendon Hills, Countryside, Darien, Downers Grove, Hickory Hills, Hinsdale, Hodgkins, Indian Head Park, Justice, La Grange, La Grange Park, Lyons, McCook, North Riverside, Oak Brook, Riverside, Stickney, Summit, Westchester, Western Springs, Westmont, Willow Springs, and Willowbrooks may apply.
Restrictions: Grants are not awarded to individuals, sectarian or religious organizations, or for purposes to influence legislation or other political activities.
Geographic Focus: Illinois
Date(s) Application is Due: Mar 31; Sep 30
Amount of Grant: Up to 250,000 USD
Contact: Deborah Kustra; (630) 654-4729; fax (630) 654-3402; info@cmfdn.org
Internet: http://www.cmfdn.org/guidelines.html
Sponsor: Community Memorial Foundation
15 Spinning Wheel Road, Suite 326
Hinsdale, IL 60521

Community P.O.WER (Partners On Waste Education and Reduction) 1335
The intent of the program is to partner with community groups such as neighborhood organizations, schools, churches, senior citizen groups, youth organizations, and civic groups to reach individuals who are not currently aware of waste reduction practices. Through the program, a community group can access free resources (materials, technical assistance) as well as grants to support community waste reduction projects. Grants are distributed through a competitive process. All groups - those that require grant funds and those that don't - are invited to participate in quarterly meetings to network with other groups and learn more about important waste issues and resources. Past grantees include coalitions of churches, arts organizations, block nurse programs, neighborhood associations, and study circles.
Requirements: Grant applicants must be schools or 501(c)3 non-profit organizations. Organizations whose primary mission is NOT environmental education or environmental advocacy are strongly encouraged to apply. Environmental organizations are encouraged to partner with other organizations. Grant applicants must serve communities in Anoka, Carver, Dakota, Hennepin, Ramsey and Washington Counties of Minnesota. Projects must focus on waste and/or toxicity reduction and must contain sustainable and replicable elements. Letters of interest are due by the March 17 deadline. For complete guidelines, timeline, attachments, and application procedures, see the sponsor's website.
Restrictions: Groups that are not eligible include: (a) City, county, and state agencies (aside from school districts); or cities, townships, and counties; (b) For-profit businesses, and projects that focus on for-profit businesses or business waste; (c) Anti-littering projects; (d) Projects focused on improving water quality or water conservation; (e) Projects focused on improving a business', organization's, or school's own internal waste systems; (f) Projects that include collection of hazardous materials; (g) Projects focused on energy or energy conservation.
Geographic Focus: Minnesota
Amount of Grant: Up to 12,000 USD
Contact: Laurie Gustafson; (651) 252-1487; CommunityP.O.WER@rethinkrecycling.com
Internet: http://www.greenguardian.com/grants
Sponsor: Solid Waste Management Coordinating Board
477 Selby Avenue
St. Paul, MN 55102-1726

Community Technology Foundation of California Building Communities Through Technology Grants 1336
The foundation awards grants to eligible California nonprofit organizations in support of programs that bring communications technologies to traditionally underserved populations, including low-income, inner-city, minority, disabled, limited-English speaking, and low-income senior communities. Areas of support include community building, community economic development, education, and health. Current grantmaking focuses on the development and maintenance of—as well as the removal of barriers to—digital media, communications, and outreach for underserved Californians. Successful grantees will be those who effectively utilize ICT in a manner that enables their target communities to become more active and engaged participants in civic action. Types of support include fellowships, matching/challenge grants, and leveraged gifts. Applications for proposals are accepted on a rolling basis, with funding decisions made at quarterly meetings (usually held in January, April, July, and October). Guidelines are available online.
Requirements: California nonprofit organizations are eligible.
Restrictions: CTFC will specifically not fund projects in the following areas: general operating expenses (unless an applicant organization's sole mission and purpose is to conduct work that falls within the grantmaking guidelines); grants to individuals; grants to non-501(c)3 organizations (unless such organizations have a commitment in writing from a 501(c)3 sponsoring fiscal agent); requests for only distribution or dissemination of completed media projects; media projects used solely for distribution at agency special events, memorials, annual fundraisers, anniversary celebrations, etc; requests that are solely for equipment or software purchases without a corresponding content-based component; ICT projects that are only for organizational internal infrastructure upgrades or administrative/operational support; or any project that does not have a media, information, or communications technology component.
Geographic Focus: California
Amount of Grant: 10,000 - 50,000 USD
Contact: Grants Administrator; (415) 371-8808; fax (415) 371-8818; info@zerodivide.org
Internet: http://www.zerodivide.org
Sponsor: Community Technology Foundation of California
101 Spear Street, Suite 218
San Francisco, CA 94105

Comprehensive Health Education Foundation Grants 1337
The foundation awards grants to support programs that address health inequities. The initial grantmaking effort will focus on Clark, Pierce, and Spokane Counties in Washington State. One-year grants of up to $20,000 each will be awarded to culturally appropriate, community-led collaborations to test their best idea on how to make it easier for people who suffer from health inequities to move more and eat healthier. Health inequities are defined as differences in the incidence, prevalence, mortality, and burden of diseases that exist for specific populations in the United States. Low-income individuals and people of color within the United States generally have higher rates of poor health and injury than those who are in higher-income groups and are Caucasian.
Requirements: 501(c)3 tax-exempt organizations located in Clark, Pierce, and Spokane Counties in Washington State and units of government that are nondiscriminatory in policy and practice regarding disabilities, age, sex, sexual orientation, race, ethnic origin, or creed are eligible.
Restrictions: Support will not be provided for building or land acquisitions; equipment or furniture purchases; endowment funds; emergency funds; grants to individuals; fellowships/scholarships; research; debt retirement; fundraising activities; general fund drives; indirect overhead; or CHEF programs or products.
Geographic Focus: Washington
Amount of Grant: 500 - 20,000 USD
Contact: Kari L. Lewis; (800) 323-2433, ext. 1899; fax (206) 824-3072; KariL@chef.org
Internet: http://www.chef.org/about/grants.php
Sponsor: Comprehensive Health Education Foundation
159 S Jackson Street, Suite 510
Seattle, WA 98104

Compton Foundation Grants 1338
The foundation was founded to address community, national, and international concerns in the fields of peace and world order, population, and the environment. Other concerns of the foundation include equal educational opportunity, community welfare and social justice, and culture and the arts. The foundation makes three kinds of grants. Project grants generally are made to national organizations for projects that fall within the primary areas of peace and world order, population, and the environment. These grants may be for regional (Pacific Coastal states), national, or international activities and are usually for projects of limited duration. Project grants are considered by the board two times a year. Discretionary grants are made at the discretion, and usually at the initiation, of individual board members. Most grants in this area are made for community welfare and social justice, and culture and the arts. Renewal grants provide general support to organizations whose activities have been funded by the foundation for many years and whose work continues to be considered particularly effective by the board. Many of the foundation's grants in the area of equal educational opportunity, and some grants in peace and world order and population, are renewal grants.
Requirements: The foundation makes grants only to tax-exempt organizations and institutions.
Restrictions: Grants will not be made to individuals.
Geographic Focus: All States
Date(s) Application is Due: Mar 7; Sep 7
Amount of Grant: 5,000 - 50,000 USD
Contact: Edith T. Eddy; (650) 508-1181; fax (650) 508-1191; info@comptonfoundation.org
Internet: http://www.comptonfoundation.org/application_procedures.html
Sponsor: Compton Foundation
255 Shoreline Drive, Suite 540
Redwood City, CA 94065

Compton Foundation International Fellowships 1339
The goal of the Compton Foundation's International Fellowship Program is to contribute to the capacity of developing countries, especially in Central America and Sub-Saharan Africa, as well as Mexico, to improve policies and programs relating to Peace and Security, Population and Reproductive Health and Environment and Sustainable Development. The Foundation strives to accomplish this goal by supporting outstanding graduate students who are committed to careers in the program areas of interest to the Foundation within the developing world. Compton Fellows are chosen by selected university-based programs working in partnership with the Foundation.
Geographic Focus: All States
Contact: Edith T. Eddy; (650) 508-1181; fax (650) 508-1191; info@comptonfoundation.org
Internet: http://www.comptonfoundation.org/fellows.html
Sponsor: Compton Foundation
255 Shoreline Drive, Suite 540
Redwood City, CA 94065

Compton Foundation Mentor Fellowships 1340
The fellowship program focuses on graduating college students from the United States. This program is designed to promote creativity and support the commitment of graduating seniors as they move beyond academic preparation to real-world application and contribution. Each year ten fellows are selected from participating universities and awarded a one-year, fellowship. The stipend is to implement a self-directed project, contributing their talents and energy to real-world situations. At the core of the fellowship is the partnership between a fellow and a mentor, who provides guidance, encouragement, and impetus for continued learning and service.
Geographic Focus: All States
Amount of Grant: 36,000 USD
Contact: Edith T. Eddy; (650) 508-1181; fax (650) 508-1191; info@comptonfoundation.org
Internet: http://www.comptonfoundation.org/fellowships.html
Sponsor: Compton Foundation
255 Shoreline Drive, Suite 540
Redwood City, CA 94065

Computer Associates Community Grants 1341
CA makes grants at three geographic levels: the global level, which covers major nonprofits with a national or multinational scope of operation; the regional level, which covers more locally focused nonprofits operating in the vicinity of a philanthropically active CA office; and the Long Island level, which covers community-based nonprofits operating on Long Island. Region disaster relief grants can be made in response to acute need. Following is a summary of the criteria used to evaluate a grant proposal: addresses significant social problem; offers an innovative, sustainable approach with potential for broad, impact; outstanding leadership; fits with CA goals and values; and provides measurable results. The majority of grants are initiated by CA and do not stem from unsolicited proposals; unsolicited proposals are reviewed on an ongoing basis. Application and guidelines are available online.
Requirements: 501(c)3 nonprofit, public charities are eligible. Organizations outside of the United States must have equivalent nonprofit, charity status. Applicant organizations must serve the community at large, leveraging whenever possible existing resources.
Restrictions: Grants do not support individuals; academic or research projects; civic, religious, sectarian, or political institutions; school fundraisers (booster clubs, colleges/university, school foundations, field trips, and scholarships); capital campaigns or endowments; sponsorships, marketing opportunities, or event fundraisers; sports/athletic events and organizations (benefit dinners, walks/run, tournaments, and sports teams); research projects/programs; grantmaking organizations; or conferences/one-day seminars. CA rarely funds organizations or projects whose overhead expenses exceed 25 percent.
Geographic Focus: All States, Australia, Canada, United Kingdom
Contact: Community Relations Manager; (631) 342-3048; fax (631) 342-5737
Internet: http://www.ca.com/community/grants.htm
Sponsor: Computer Associates International
1 Computer Associates Plaza
Islandia, NY 11749

ConAgra Foods Foundation Community Impact Grants 1342
The Community Impact Grants (CIG) program will award grants between $10,000 and $100,000 to impactful, grassroots organizations that leverage innovation and creativity to address childhood hunger and nutrition needs in communities where ConAgra Foods' employees live and work or states where 20% or more of children are food insecure. Organizations that demonstrate a strong alignment with the Foundation's giving strategies (i.e., direct service, capacity building, and advocacy) and core funding priorities have the greatest chance of receiving a grant. The CIG program is a two-step, competitive process that first requires the submission of an Letter of Inquiry (LOI) and then the subsequent completion of a full application if invited to apply for a grant. For more detailed program information and guidelines see: http://www.nourishkidstoday.org/downloads/pdf/CIGGuidelines.pdf.
Requirements: The preference of ConAgra Foods Foundation is to award Community Impact Grants to organizations located in states with a child food insecurity rate of 20% or more according to Feeding America's Child Hunger Study as well as those communities where ConAgra Foods has a significant employee presence.
Restrictions: ConAgra Foods Foundation does not fund: professional or amateur sports organizations and teams, or athletic events and programs; political organizations; terrorist organizations or those not compliant with the USA Patriot Act; fundraising events; emergency funding; loans, debt reduction or operating deficits; individuals; endowments; capital campaigns (unless solicited at the founder's discretion); memorial campaigns; elementary and secondary education.
Geographic Focus: Arizona, Arkansas, California, Colorado, District of Columbia, Florida, Georgia, Idaho, Illinois, Indiana, Iowa, Louisiana, Massachusetts, Michigan, Minnesota, Mississippi, Missouri, New Mexico, North Carolina, Ohio, Oregon, Pennsylvania, South Carolina, Tennessee, Texas, Washington, Wisconsin
Date(s) Application is Due: Jan 29
Contact: Program Contact; foundation@conagrafoods.com
Internet: http://www.nourishkidstoday.org/about-us/application-guidelines.jsp
Sponsor: ConAgra Foods Foundation
One ConAgra Drive, CC-304
Omaha, NE 68102-5001

ConAgra Foods Foundation Nourish Our Community Grants 1343
The Foundation awards Nourish Our Community Grants to non-profit organizations based on recommendations from employees. While any organization that is working to address community needs is eligible for funding, preference will be given to those that seek to provide children and their families with access to food and nutrition education. Organizations must be located in the communities where ConAgra Foods employees live and work in order to be considered for a Nourish Our Community grant. Nourish Our Community grants typically range from $5,000 to $25,000, with an average grant of $10,000. The grant requests are reviewed by a committee representative of a cross-section of employees within the company. Organizations can receive funding for up to three consecutive years and then must postpone applying for support for one grant making cycle. Applications for Nourish Our Community grant requests are reviewed annually. The application process for the current fiscal year is June 1-May 31. Additional guidelines are available at: http://www.nourishkidstoday.org/about-us/application-guidelines.jsp
Restrictions: ConAgra Foods Foundation does not fund: professional or amateur sports organizations and teams, or athletic events and programs; political organizations; terrorist organizations or those not compliant with the USA Patriot Act; fundraising events; emergency funding; loans, debt reduction or operating deficits; individuals; endowments; capital campaigns (unless solicited at the founder's discretion); memorial campaigns; elementary and secondary education.
Geographic Focus: Arizona, Arkansas, California, Colorado, Connecticut, District of Columbia, Florida, Georgia, Idaho, Illinois, Indiana, Iowa, Louisiana, Maine, Massachusetts, Michigan, Minnesota, Mississippi, Missouri, New Hampshire, New Mexico, North Carolina, Ohio, Oregon, Pennsylvania, Rhode Island, South Carolina, Tennessee, Texas, Vermont, Washington, Wisconsin
Date(s) Application is Due: May 31
Contact: Program Contact; foundation@conagrafoods.com
Internet: http://www.nourishkidstoday.org/about-us/application-guidelines.jsp
Sponsor: ConAgra Foods Foundation
One ConAgra Drive, CC-304
Omaha, NE 68102-5001

Con Edison Corporate Giving Arts and Culture Grants 1344
Con Edison understands that an exposure to arts and culture cultivates success. The Corporation promotes self-directed learning, helps to sharpen critical and creative skills, and develops programs that promote openness to diversity. Con Edison supports organizations and programs throughout its service territory that contribute to arts and culture in a variety of ways, from presenting visual and performing arts to the public, to providing arts-in-education opportunities. It awards grants for specific projects rather than for general operating support. The corporate giving application process is open from March 1 to October 1. Requests for support are accepted at any time during this time period, and grants are made on a rotating basis.
Requirements: Con Edison makes grants to tax-exempt nonprofit organizations as defined under Section 501(c)3 of the U.S. Internal Revenue Code that serve the residents within its areas of operation. Organizations must be nonsectarian and nondenominational to receive support.
Restrictions: Con Edison does not award grants for reducing debts or past operating deficits. Con Edison does not reduce or donate costs of gas and electric services. Further, Con Edison does not award grants to: private foundations; individuals; labor groups; organizations with programs operating principally outside Con Edison's service area; media and literacy projects not connected to an institution or organization; houses of worship, although requests will be considered from religion-affiliated organizations whose activities benefit the overall community and do not support any religious doctrine; or public schools.
Geographic Focus: New York
Date(s) Application is Due: Oct 1
Contact: Alton Murray; (212) 460-6917; fax (212) 460-3730; MurrayA@coned.com
Internet: http://www.coned.com/Partnerships/arts_culture.asp
Sponsor: Con Edison Corporation
4 Irving Place, Room 1650-S
New York, NY 10003-3502

Con Edison Corporate Giving Civic Grants 1345
Con Edison is committed to supporting programs that offer youth, ages 8-18 years old, the skills and opportunities for lifelong civic engagement. The Corporation seeks to create interest in the democratic process by providing young people with the skills necessary to voice their opinions, affect policy changes, and remain civically engaged throughout their lives. It awards grants for specific projects rather than for general operating support. The corporate giving application process is open from March 1 to October 1. Requests for support are accepted at any time during this time period, and grants are made on a rotating basis.
Requirements: Con Edison makes grants to tax-exempt nonprofit organizations as defined under Section 501(c)3 of the U.S. Internal Revenue Code that serve the residents within its areas of operation. Organizations must be nonsectarian and nondenominational to receive support.

Restrictions: Con Edison does not award grants for reducing debts or past operating deficits. Con Edison does not reduce or donate costs of gas and electric services. Further, Con Edison does not award grants to: private foundations; individuals; labor groups; organizations with programs operating principally outside Con Edison's service area; media and literacy projects not connected to an institution or organization; houses of worship, although requests will be considered from religion-affiliated organizations whose activities benefit the overall community and do not support any religious doctrine; or public schools.
Geographic Focus: New York
Date(s) Application is Due: Oct 1
Contact: Walter Shay; (212) 460-2188; fax (212) 460-3730; ShayW@coned.com
Internet: http://www.coned.com/Partnerships/civics.asp
Sponsor: Con Edison Corporation
4 Irving Place, Room 1650-S
New York, NY 10003-3502

Con Edison Corporate Giving Community Grants 1346
As a civic-minded corporate citizen, Con Edison lends its support to community and civic based organizations that strive to build and maintain vibrant neighborhoods. These include youth and law-enforcement agencies, housing services, landmarks conservancies, educational institutions and community groups that celebrate diversity. The Corporate Giving program awards grants for specific projects rather than for general operating support. The application process is open from March 1 to October 1. Requests for support are accepted at any time during this time period, and grants are made on a rotating basis.
Requirements: Con Edison makes grants to tax-exempt nonprofit organizations as defined under Section 501(c)3 of the U.S. Internal Revenue Code that serve the residents within its areas of operation. Organizations must be nonsectarian and nondenominational to receive support.
Restrictions: Con Edison does not award grants for reducing debts or past operating deficits. Con Edison does not reduce or donate costs of gas and electric services. Further, Con Edison does not award grants to: private foundations; individuals; labor groups; organizations with programs operating principally outside Con Edison's service area; media and literacy projects not connected to an institution or organization; houses of worship, although requests will be considered from religion-affiliated organizations whose activities benefit the overall community and do not support any religious doctrine; or public schools.
Geographic Focus: New York
Date(s) Application is Due: Oct 1
Contact: Walter Shay; (212) 460-2188; fax (212) 460-3730; ShayW@coned.com
Internet: http://www.coned.com/Partnerships/community_partnerships.asp
Sponsor: Con Edison Corporation
4 Irving Place, Room 1650-S
New York, NY 10003-3502

Con Edison Corporate Giving Environmental Grants 1347
Con Edison is committed to responsible stewardship of the environment - a commitment that includes helping customers and the general public gain a greater understanding of what they can do to sustain and nurture our planet. The Corporation supports a wide array of community-based organizations, with special focus on energy efficiency, preservation of natural resources and park lands, environmental education, and green careers. Con Edison awards grants for specific projects rather than for general operating support. The corporate giving application process is open from March 1 to October 1. Requests for support are accepted at any time during this time period, and grants are made on a rotating basis.
Requirements: Con Edison makes grants to tax-exempt nonprofit organizations as defined under Section 501(c)3 of the U.S. Internal Revenue Code that serve the residents within its areas of operation. Organizations must be nonsectarian and nondenominational to receive support.
Restrictions: Con Edison does not award grants for reducing debts or past operating deficits. Con Edison does not reduce or donate costs of gas and electric services. Further, Con Edison does not award grants to: private foundations; individuals; labor groups; organizations with programs operating principally outside Con Edison's service area; media and literacy projects not connected to an institution or organization; houses of worship, although requests will be considered from religion-affiliated organizations whose activities benefit the overall community and do not support any religious doctrine; or public schools.
Geographic Focus: California
Date(s) Application is Due: Oct 1
Contact: Alton Murray; (212) 460-6917; fax (212) 460-3730; MurrayA@coned.com
Internet: http://www.coned.com/Partnerships/environment.asp
Sponsor: Con Edison Corporation
4 Irving Place, Room 1650-S
New York, NY 10003-3502

Cone Health Foundation Grants 1348
The Cone Health Foundation invests in the development and support of activities, programs, and organizations that measurably improve the health of those in the greater Greensboro, North Carolina area. The Foundation awards grants to eligible not-for-profit organizations, government agencies, public schools and academic and/or research institutions, directing resources to four funding priorities: access to necessary health services with particular emphasis on eliminating the barriers often encountered by people in need; adolescent pregnancy prevention; HIV/AIDS and other sexually transmitted infections; and mental health and substance abuse. Current applications and guidelines are available online.
Requirements: In addition to meeting our funding priorities, your organization must serve people in the greater Greensboro area and fall into one of the following categories: not-for-profit organization; government agency; public school; or academic and/or research institution.
Restrictions: The Foundation does not support: activities that exclusively benefit the members of sectarian or religious organizations; annual fund drives; political campaigns or other partisan political activity; direct financial assistance to meet the immediate needs of individuals; endowments; or retirement of debt.
Geographic Focus: North Carolina
Contact: Antonia Monk Reaves, (336) 832-9555; antonia.reaves@conehealth.com
Internet: http://www.conehealthfoundation.com/home/for-grantseekers/
Sponsor: Cone Health Foundation
721 Green Valley Road, Suite 102
Greensboro, NC 27408

Connecticut Commission on the Arts Art in Public Spaces 1349
The purpose of this program is to provide the citizens of Connecticut with an improved public environment by investing our public buildings with creative work of high quality. The program adds visibility to the cultural heritage of this state and its people.
Requirements: Local arts agencies (community, municipal, or regional organizations or agencies that provide services, programming, and/or financial support to arts organizations, individual artists, and the community in general) that have been in existence for at least one year and are registered with the state of Connecticut as nonprofit organizations may apply.
Geographic Focus: Connecticut
Amount of Grant: 1,000 - 5,000 USD
Contact: Jennifer Aniskovich, Executive Director; (860) 256-2800; fax (860) 256-2811; janiskovich@ctarts.org or artsinfo@ctarts.org
Internet: http://www.ctarts.org/artpub.htm
Sponsor: Connecticut Commission on the Arts
755 Main Street, 1 Financial Plaza
Hartford, CT 06103

Connecticut Community Foundation Grants 1350
The Connecticut Community Foundation serves the people of Greater Waterbury and Northwest Connecticut by supporting public and nonprofit organizations providing programs and services including those for the arts, human services, health care, environment, youth development and education. The Foundation gives priority to efforts that prevent problems, encourage community solutions or improve the organizational capability and financial stability of nonprofit agencies.
Requirements: Nonprofit organizations in Beacon Falls, Bethlehem, Bridgewater, Cheshire, Goshen, Litchfield, Middlebury, Morris, Naugatuck, New Milford, Oxford, Prospect, Roxbury, Southbury, Thomaston, Warren, Watertown, Washington, Wolcott, and Woodbury, CT, may submit applications.
Restrictions: Grants are not awarded for religious purposes, political activities, deficit financing, continuing support, fund-raising events, annual campaigns, newly established arts organizations, commissioning of new works of art, general operating support, or endowments.
Geographic Focus: Connecticut
Date(s) Application is Due: Jan 9; Mar 27; Aug 28
Amount of Grant: 8,000 - 10,000 USD
Contact: Carol O'Donnell; (203) 753-1315; fax (203) 756-3054; info@conncf.org
Internet: http://www.conncf.org/grants/grants.htm
Sponsor: Connecticut Community Foundation
43 Field Street
Waterbury, CT 06702

Connecticut Health Foundation Health Initiative Grants 1351
The foundation awards grants to organizations and institutions that directly respond to its current priority areas and result in improving the health status of Connecticut's underserved and unserved populations. Program priorities include children???s mental health—projects related to children???s mental health, including research, community grants, creating resources for clinical effective practices, and parent advocacy groups; oral health—improving oral health care access, quality, and utilization; and racial and ethnic health disparities—improving the diversity of the health care workforce, and increasing cultural competency in the existing workforce. The foundation awards two major types of grants: strategic and responsive. Application and guidelines are available online.
Requirements: Connecticut state and local units of government, community health centers, health advocacy organizations, community-based organizations, community and cultural groups, schools, and faith-based organizations are eligible. Applicants must have IRS 501(c)3 tax-exempt status or be public entities. Unincorporated organizations may apply through 501(c)3 fiscal agents.
Restrictions: Foundation grants do not support awards to individuals; construction of buildings; capital projects, endowments, or chairs associated with universities, and medical schools; conferences (unless part of a greater project or program); projects that do not benefit Connecticut residents; lobbying or influencing the outcomes of a proposed piece of legislation or election; and indirect cost for discretionary grants.
Geographic Focus: Connecticut
Date(s) Application is Due: Mar 15; Jun 15; Sep 15; Dec 15
Amount of Grant: 50,000 - 200,000 USD
Contact: Onell Jesus Calderas; (860) 224-2200; fax (860) 224-2230; onell@cthealth.org
Internet: http://www.cthealth.org/matriarch
Sponsor: Connecticut Health Foundation
74A Vine Street
New Britain, CT 06052

Connecticut Light and Power Corporate Contributions 1352
The program awards grants to Connecticut nonprofit organizations in its areas of interest, including economic and community development—to promote the economy and create jobs with special emphasis on small business development, entrepreneurship, new job creation and retention, and smart growth; environmental leadership and stewardship—programs

that promote environmental education, energy conservation, alternative and renewable energy, environmental conservation and those that protect or improve the environment; education and workforce development—to develop technical skills for existing and potential jobs and higher education programs targeted to meet workforce needs. For requests of $1000 or less, submit a letter detailing the activity/project, action plan, and goals. Complete the online application for requests of more than $1000.
Requirements: Nonprofits in the Connecticut Light and Power service territory are eligible.
Restrictions: Grants do not support individuals; corporations that do not qualify as IRS charitable organizations; private foundations; projects benefiting limited groups (religious, fraternal, political); athletic outings; preexisting debt reduction or elimination; healthcare issues or organizations; permanent endowment funds; advertising; or activities such as scouting, band and little leagues.
Geographic Focus: Connecticut
Contact: Theresa Hopkins-Staten, (860) 721-4063; fax (860) 721-4331; hopkit@nu.com
Internet: http://www.cl-p.com/community/partners/cinvest.asp
Sponsor: Connecticut Light and Power Company
P.O. Box 5563
Hartford, CT 06102-5563

Connelly Foundation Grants 1353
To achieve its mission to foster learning and improve the quality of life, Connelly Foundation provides grants toward costs associated with programs, direct services, general operations and capital projects to non-profit organizations and institutions working in the following fields: education; health and human services; arts and culture and civic enterprise. The Foundation supports non-profits with strong leadership, sound ideas, future viability, and attainable and well defined goals. It directs its philanthropy toward 501(c)3 organizations and institutions based in and serving Philadelphia and the counties of Bucks, Chester, Delaware, Montgomery and the City of Camden. The Foundation values the proposal process. Given its preference to review a comprehensive package as a primer for discussion, letters of inquiry or requests for pre-proposal discussions are not deemed necessary. Written proposals from nonprofit organizations are accepted and reviewed by the Connelly Foundation throughout the year, there are no deadlines.
Requirements: 501(c)3 organizations and institutions based in and serving in Philadelphia and its surrounding counties of Bucks, Chester, Delaware, and Montgomery in Pennsylvania and in the City of Camden, New Jersey are eligible to apply. There are determined parameters to the Foundation's financial support. It provides non-profit organizations only one grant within a twelve month period. As a general practice, it does not fund advocacy, annual appeals, charter schools, conferences, environmental projects, feasability or planning studies, general solicitations, historic preservation projects, national organizations, organizations focused on a single disease, public schools or research.
Restrictions: The foundation does not award grants to individuals, or political or national organizations; Nor does it respond to annual appeals or general letters of solicitation.
Geographic Focus: Pennsylvania
Contact: Emily C. Riley; (610) 834-3222; fax (610) 834-0866; info@connellyfdn.org
Sponsor: Connelly Foundation
1 Tower Bridge, Suite 1450
West Conshohocken, PA 19428

ConocoPhillips Foundation Grants 1354
The foundation makes charitable grants (primarily in the communities where it has operations) in support of education, medical programs, human services, civic, cultural, youth, and other services. Contributions will be considered for organizations such as: federated organizations; educational institutions, both public and private, primarily at the college level; youth organizations; hospital and medical facilities and programs such as hospital buildings and equipment, improvement campaigns and other medical facilities; cultural organizations; civic services; and human service organizations. Applicants may download the application form from the Web site. There are no application deadlines.
Requirements: 501(c)3 tax-exempt organizations and, where appropriate 170(c) organizations, and international nonprofit organizations are eligible. Proof of the exemption must be submitted with grant applications.
Restrictions: Grants do not support religious organizations for religious purposes; war veterans and fraternal service organizations; endowment funds; national health organizations and programs; grants or loans to individuals; fund-raising events; corporate memberships or contributions to chambers of commerce, taxpayer associations and other bodies whose activities are expected to directly benefit the company; or political organizations, campaigns and candidates.
Geographic Focus: Alaska, California, Illinois, Louisiana, Montana, New Jersey, Oklahoma, Pennsylvania, Texas, Washington
Date(s) Application is Due: Aug 1
Amount of Grant: Up to 46,000,000 USD
Contact: Community Relations Manager
Internet: http://www.conocophillips.com/about/Contribution+Guidelines/index.htm
Sponsor: ConocoPhillips Foundation Grants
600 N Dairy Ashford
Houston, TX 77079

ConocoPhillips Grants 1355
ConocoPhillips maintains a philanthropic contributions budget for nonprofit, charitable programs closely tied to its corporate goals and focused primarily in locations of strong business interests. Submit an executive summary outlining the purpose of the program or project, how it will be accomplished, expected results, a budget (noting administrative expenses such as: salaries and fees, program expenses and total income), other sources of financial support and a copy of the IRS tax determination letter that confirms 501(c)3 status. The grant must be used in the United States. Requests for grants in non-U.S. locations should be made directly to the ConocoPhillips international office doing business in that part of the world. Education and youth, civic and arts, employee volunteerism, safety and social services, and the environment are focus areas.
Requirements: Applications are accepted from areas where ConocoPhillips has a strong business presence, e.g., Texas and Oklahoma. All contributions are to be used within the United States.
Restrictions: ConocoPhillips does not award funds to individuals, sectarian or religious organization, promotional sponsorship and advertising (marketing related) or an endowment.
Geographic Focus: Alaska, California, Illinois, Louisiana, Montana, New Jersey, Oklahoma, Pennsylvania, Texas
Contact: Program Contact; (281) 293-2685
Internet: http://www.conocophillips.com/about/Contribution+Guidelines/index.htm
Sponsor: ConocoPhillips Corporation
600 N Dairy Ashford, MA 3144
Houston, TX 77079

Conrad N. Hilton Humanitarian Prize 1356
The prize is awarded to a nonprofit, nongovernmental organization that has performed with the greatest merit in alleviating human suffering in the current year. The international prize was created to draw attention to humanitarian achievements everywhere and recognizes efforts to combat the causes or effects of famine, war, disease, extreme human affliction, or human-to-human injustices. An international jury will judge on established criteria, including alleviation of suffering, extraordinary achievement, cooperation with others, and long-term impact. Application materials are available upon request. Annual deadline dates may vary; contact the foundation for specific dates.
Requirements: Eligible for nomination are established, nonprofit, charitable, and nongovernmental organizations in the United States and around the world. The nominator should have direct knowledge of the nominated organization's work.
Restrictions: The nominator may not be an officer, employee, or any other individual receiving remuneration for their services from the nominated organization; or a family member of an officer or employee of the nominated organization.
Geographic Focus: All States
Date(s) Application is Due: Nov 7
Amount of Grant: 15,000,000 USD
Contact: Leslie Shopay, (310) 556-4694; fax (310) 556-8130; Leslie@hiltonfoundation.org
Internet: http://www.hiltonfoundation.org/main.asp?id=38
Sponsor: Conrad N. Hilton Foundation
10100 Santa Monica Boulevard, Suite 1000
Los Angeles, CA 90067-4011

Conseil des arts de Montreal Diversity Award 1357
The Annual Diversity Award honors a promising group of musicians in order to increase their exposure in the artistic community and general public. Over the course of a year, the winner will benefit from creative residences and concerts presented with Vision Diversite at MAI and Place des Arts, as well as a tour of various Montreal neighborhoods with Conseil des arts de Montreal en tournee. In addition, the public will be able to listen to the winning group's music on a podcast by CBC Montreal. With an estimated value of $25,000 (including close to $15,000 in cash fees), this prize was established by the Conseil and its partners to showcase world music and foster the professional careers of Montreal's culturally diverse musicians.
Requirements: All artistic groups composed of two to six musicians from the diversity sector who are Canadian citizens or landed immigrants may apply, as long as they are pursuing a professional career in world music in Montreal. All members of the group must be residents of the Greater Montreal area at least one year. In addition to the online application, signed by the project director, candidates must submit: a recent CD of a live concert or studio demo recording; curriculum vitae of all band members; and other relevant documents such as letters or a press kit. Applications should refer to the website for further information.
Geographic Focus: Canada
Date(s) Application is Due: Apr 15
Amount of Grant: 25,000 CAD
Contact: Iulia-Anamaria Salagor; (514) 280-3586; iasalagor.p@ville.montreal.qc.ca
Claire Metras, Cultural Advisor; (514) 280-3586; cmetras.p@ville.montreal.qc.ca
Internet: http://www.artsmontreal.org/en/prizes/prix-diversite
Sponsor: Conseil des arts de Montreal
1210 Sherbrooke Street East
Montreal, QC H2L 1L9 Canada

Conseil des arts de Montreal Touring Grants 1358
The Conseil des arts de Montreal Touring Grants are mainly for professional non-profit arts organizations. Funding enables the best recent works to be presented within the following categories: circus arts, dance, music, and theatre; visual arts; media arts, film and new artistic practices; and literature. The program encourages works that reflect cultural diversity, creativity, and emerging artists. Collectives formed by professional artists working in the disciplines of circus arts, digital arts and world music can also submit an application. Cultural organizations cannot submit more than one touring project per year. In exceptional cases, service organizations may submit two different projects for the tour per year. The application, tour documents, and technical documents are available at the website.
Requirements: All organizations requesting financial assistance must be recognized as a professional organization, based in the City of Montreal, presenting artistic events on a regular basis and concerned primarily with the creation, production, and presentation of artistic activities.
Restrictions: Funding is not available for individuals.

Geographic Focus: Canada
Date(s) Application is Due: Sep 30
Contact: Michel Niquette; (514) 280-3585; mniquette.p@ville.montreal.qc.ca
Internet: http://www.artsmontreal.org/en/programs/conseil-des-arts-de-montreal-en-tournee
Sponsor: Conseil des arts de Montreal
1210 Sherbrooke Street East
Montreal, QC H2L 1L9 Canada

Conservation, Food, and Health Foundation Grants for Developing Countries 1359
The Conservation, Food, and Health Foundation's geographic focus is the developing world. Through grants to support research and through targeted grants to help solve specific problems, the foundation helps build capacity within developing countries in three areas of interest: conservation, food, and health. The foundation concentrates its grant-making on research, technical assistance, and training projects of benefit to the Third World; favors grants for pilot projects and special programs that have a potential for replication; prefers to support projects that employ and/or train personnel from the developing world; and favors research concerning problems of importance to the developing world. The foundation has two 4-month funding cycles each year. Concept papers received by January 1 will be considered for eligibility for the March 1 full proposal deadline; concept papers received by July 1 will be considered for eligibility for the September 1 full proposal deadline. Full proposals are by invitation. Concept applications must be submitted through the foundation's online application system. Detailed guidelines, instructions, and faqs are provided at the website.
Requirements: The following organizations are eligible to apply: 501(c)3 organizations that are not private foundations under section 509(a) of the United State Internal Revenue Code; "501(c)3 equivalent" foreign or domestic government units; and nongovernmental foreign organizations which can provide secure evidence of their nongovernmental status and charitable purpose.
Restrictions: The foundation does not provide support for buildings, land purchases, or vehicles; quantity purchases of durable medical equipment; endowments or fundraising activities; famine or emergency relief; direct medical care or treatment; feeding or food distribution programs; films, videos, or web-site production; scholarships, fellowships, or travel grants; conferences; re-granting through intermediaries; general operating support; or individuals (however, the foundation may support an individual engaged in research on a problem of significance to the developing world where the research is sponsored by an established, nonprofit organization such as an educational institution and conducted in close partnership with a local nongovernmental organization). The foundation does not consider the states of the former Soviet Union or former Eastern Bloc countries as within its geographic focus.
Geographic Focus: All States, All Countries
Date(s) Application is Due: Jan 1; Jul 1
Amount of Grant: Up to 25,000 USD
Contact: Prentice Zinn; (617) 391-3091 or skype: prentice.zinn; pzinn@gmafoundations.com
Internet: http://cfhfoundation.grantsmanagement08.com/?page_id=5
Sponsor: Conservation, Food, and Health Foundation
77 Summer Street, 8th Floor
Boston, MA 02110-1006

CONSOL Coal Group Grants 1360
The coal company targets the majority of its donations to universities with mining engineering programs. The remaining funding is allotted to three categories: infrastructure, or services the company relies on; headquarters, activities including such groups as symphony, ballet, and opera in Pittsburgh; and community improvement, grants focused on activities and organizations, such as Little League and arts fairs in the communities where company mines are located. Although the company's funding areas will change from time to time, CONSOL looks to fund projects that serve a number of people in the community and, when possible, promote employee participation. Contact the office for application deadlines.
Geographic Focus: All States
Contact: Thomas Hoffman, Public Relations; (412) 831-4060; fax (412) 831-4103; tomhoffman@consolenergy.com
Internet: http://www.consolenergy.com
Sponsor: CONSOL Coal Group
1800 Washington Road
Pittsburgh, PA 15241

Constance Saltonstall Foundation for the Arts Grants 1361
The foundation annually awards grants to writers and visual artists who live in the central and western counties of New York state. Grantees have used these grants in a variety of ways, including buying materials, preparing works for exhibit, and taking time to create new work. Grant categories change annually. Current categories include works on paper—printmaking, drawing, painting, collage, and other two-dimensional media on paper (excludes computer generated images); photography—digital and traditional; poetry; and creative nonfiction—a prose form that depends on the imaginative abilities of the writer. Do not use Express Mail, FedEx, Airborne, or UPS. Send the complete application by regular or priority post to the listed address. Application and guidelines are available online.
Requirements: Grant applicants must be at least 21 years of age; and reside in one of the following counties in New York: Allegany, Broome, Cattaraugus, Cayuga, Chautauqua, Chenango, Chemung, Cortland, Erie, Genesee, Jefferson, Lewis, Livingston, Madison, Monroe, Niagara, Oneida, Onondaga, Ontario, Orleans, Oswego, Schuyler, Seneca, Steuben, Tioga, Tompkins, Wayne, Wyoming, and Yates.
Geographic Focus: New York
Date(s) Application is Due: Jan 15
Amount of Grant: Up to 5,000 USD
Contact: Grants Administrator; (607) 539-3146; fax (607) 539-3147
Internet: http://www.saltonstall.org/index.php
Sponsor: Constance Saltonstall Foundation
P.O. Box 6607
Ithaca, NY 14851-6607

Constantin Foundation Grants 1362
The foundation awards grants to nonprofit organizations in Texas, with an emphasis on higher and other education, including secondary school education, vocational education, and adult continuing education. Grants also support human, family, and social service agencies; hospitals and health organizations, including substance abuse; community development; and arts and culture. Grants are awarded for continuing support, capital campaigns, building construction/renovation, equipment acquisition, challenge/matching funds, and to develop programs. Request guidelines prior to applying.
Requirements: Nonprofit organizations in Dallas County, TX, may submit applications.
Restrictions: No support for tax-supported institutions, theater groups, churches, debt retirement, political organizations or second party requesters. No grants to individuals, or for endowments, research, debt retirement, operations, research, special events, fundraisers, or second party requests; no loans.
Geographic Focus: Texas
Date(s) Application is Due: Sep 15
Amount of Grant: 1,000 - 100,000 USD
Contact: Cathy Doyle; (214) 522-9300 or (214) 522-9305; constantinfdn@sbcglobal.net
Sponsor: Constantin Foundation
4809 Cole Avenue, LB 127
Dallas, TX 75205-3578

Constellation Energy Corporate EcoStar Grants 1363
Environmental stewardship is one of Constellation Energy's core foundational values. Because of this commitment to use natural resources responsibly, prevent pollution, improve energy efficiency and enhance it's stewardship efforts, EcoStar Grants are now being offered to local communities where Constellation Energy does business. See, Constellation Energy's website for: listing of funding locations; on-line application; additional guidelines. Project should fit at least one of five environmental focus areas: Pollution Prevention; Education; Energy Efficiency; Conservation; Community Activism.
Requirements: Organization must be a 501(c)3 nonprofit with a Board of Directors.
Restrictions: Grant funds limited to maximum of 20% administration and office expenses (i.e., salaries, phone and postage).
Geographic Focus: All States
Date(s) Application is Due: Mar 16
Amount of Grant: 5,000 USD
Contact: Larry McDonnell, Director; (401) 470-7433; media@constellation.com
Internet: http://www.constellation.com/portal/site/constellation/menuitem.999b6fed85785a2399084010016176a0
Sponsor: Constellation Energy Corporate
100 Constellation Way, Suite 1000C
Baltimore, MD 21202

Constellation Energy Corporate Grants 1364
Constellation Energy provides its philanthropic resources to non-profit organizations that make an impact in these key focus areas: energy Initiatives; environment; education; economic development. Applications are accepted at various times throughout the year. Grant, Sponsorship, Banner Hanging, and In-Kind requests under $10,000 are reviewed on a rolling basis. The Corporate Contributions Committee meets bi-annually, in May and October, to review significant financial grant requests of $10,000 or more. Grant requests should be submitted by April 1 and September 1 respectively. Additional guidelines and the online applications are available at the companies website.
Requirements: The company makes charitable donations to 501(c)3 tax-exempt, nonprofit organizations.
Restrictions: Constellation Energy does not make grants to: individuals; churches or religious causes; individual schools; athletic teams or events; programs located outside Constellation Energy communities.
Geographic Focus: All States
Date(s) Application is Due: Apr 1; Sep 1
Contact: Larry McDonnell, Director; (401) 470-7433; media@constellation.com
Internet: http://www.constellation.com/portal/site/constellation/menuitem.94939662e40191875fb60610025166a0/
Sponsor: Constellation Energy Corporate
100 Constellation Way, Suite 1000C
Baltimore, MD 21202

Consumers Energy Foundation 1365
Since its creation in 1990, the Consumers Energy Foundation has touched countless lives and communities through it's grant programs, corporate giving and employee volunteers. The Foundation accepts grant applications from nonprofit organizations for innovative projects and activities creating measurable impact in five areas: Social Welfare, Michigan Growth and Environmental Enhancement, Education, Community and Civic, and Culture/Arts. The Foundation's areas of support include, operating budgets and capital funds.
Requirements: The Consumers Energy Foundation provides financial support primarily to Michigan organizations classified by the Internal Revenue Service as tax-exempt under section 501(c)3 of the Internal Revenue Code.
Restrictions: The following are ineligible for funding: individuals; individual scholarships; individual sponsorship related to fund-raising; organizations that do not qualify as charitable organizations as defined by the Internal Revenue Service; organizations that

practice discrimination on the basis of sex, age, height, weight, marital status, race, religion, sexual orientation, creed, color, national origin, ancestry, disability, handicap, or veteran status; organizations whose operating activities are already supported by the United Way (except when the request is approved by the appropriate community United Way organization); political organizations and political campaigns; religious organizations when the contribution will be used for denominational or sectarian purposes; labor or veterans organizations; fraternal orders; social clubs; sports tournaments; talent or beauty contests; loans for small business; debt reduction campaigns.
Geographic Focus: Michigan
Amount of Grant: 500 - 10,000 USD
Contact: Carolyn Bloodworth, Secretary/Treasurer; (517) 788-0432; fax (517) 788-2281; foundation@consumersenergy.com
Internet: http://www.consumersenergy.com/welcome.htm
Sponsor: Consumers Energy
1 Energy Place, Room EP8-210
Jackson, MI 49201-2276

Conwood Charitable Trust Grants 1366
The Conwood Charitable Trust was established to make a positive impact upon the communities where Conwood employees live and work by financially supporting organizations with a demonstrated ability to assist individuals in need. The elderly, underprivileged, youth, educational institutions and the arts are supported through the Conwood Charitable Trust. Funds from the Trust are donated primarily in the company's hometown of Memphis and in the surrounding Mid-South area. Additionally, contributions are made to organizations in other areas of Tennessee (Tennessee Independent Colleges and Universities Association) and in North Carolina (Independent College Fund of North Carolina).
Requirements: Eligible applicants include any 501(c)3 organization that supports the people of Tennessee.
Geographic Focus: Tennessee
Amount of Grant: 2,500 - 30,000 USD
Contact: Ed Roberson, Vice-President; (901) 761-2050; fax (901) 767-1302
Internet: http://www.reynoldsamerican.com/Responsibility/Community8.aspx
Sponsor: Conwood Charitable Trust
813 Ridge Lake Boulevard
Memphis, TN 38119

Cooke-Hay Foundation Grants 1367
Established in North Carolina in 2000, the Cooke-Hay Foundation's primary fields of interest include: animal welfare, federated giving programs, and Protestant agencies and churches. The Foundation's geographic focus is Colorado, Florida, and North Carolina. There are no specific deadlines or application forms, and potential applicants should begin by forwarding a query letter to the Foundation office.
Requirements: 501(c)3 organizations serving the residents of Colorado, Florida, and North Carolina are eligible to apply.
Geographic Focus: Colorado, Florida, North Carolina
Samples: Lift Up Food Bank, Steamboat Springs, Colorado, $4,500; Cat Tails Cat Adopt, Ocean Isle Beach, North Carolina, $1,500.
Contact: Chauncey Cooke, President; (970) 871-1240; chauncey@chaunceycooke.com
Sponsor: Cooke-Hay Foundation
43700 Old Elk Trail
Steamboat Springs, CO 80487-8428

Cooke Foundation Grants 1368
Grants are awarded primarily for culture and the arts, social services, education, programs for youth and the elderly, humanities, health, and the environment. Organizations receiving grants must be located in Hawaii or serve the people of Hawaii. Preference will be given to requests from Ohau. Types of support include general operating support, capital campaigns, building and renovations, program development, seed money, and matching funds.
Requirements: Grant making is limited to the state of Hawaii.
Restrictions: Grants are not made to individuals, churches, or religious organizations, or for endowment funds, scholarships, or fellowships.
Geographic Focus: Hawaii
Date(s) Application is Due: Mar 2; Sep 1
Amount of Grant: 5,000 - 25,000 USD
Contact: Carrie Shoda-Sutherland, Senior Program Officer; (808) 566-5524 or (888) 731-3863, ext. 524; fax (808) 521-6286; csutherland@hcf-hawaii.org
Internet: http://www.cookefdn.org/
Sponsor: Cooke Foundation, Limited
1164 Bishop Street, Suite 800
Honolulu, HI 96813

Cooper Foundation Grants 1369
The objectives of the foundation are to fund innovative ideas that promise substantial impact in Nebraska and that encourage others to make similar or larger grants for the same purpose. All grants are made in Nebraska, with the majority in Lincoln and Lancaster County. The foundation's highest priorities are education, including projects to improve teaching and learning and parent education at pre-school and K-12 levels as well as educational solutions to human service issues; human services; the arts, especially in the area of non-traditional areas of curriculum to increase accessibility by under-served audiences; the humanities; and the environment. Types of support include seed money, technical assistance, matching funds, and programs and projects. Requests for general operating funds and capital campaigns for physical facilities receive less priority.
Requirements: Nebraska 501(c)3 organizations are eligible.
Restrictions: Grants will not be made to support individuals, endowments, private foundations, businesses, proposals devoted to health issues, or proposals of a religious nature.
Geographic Focus: Nebraska
Date(s) Application is Due: Jan 15; Apr 1; Aug 1; Oct 1
Amount of Grant: Up to 10,000 USD
Contact: Administrator; (402) 476-7571; fax (402) 476-2356; info@cooperfoundation.org
Internet: http://www.cooperfoundation.org
Sponsor: Cooper Foundation
870 Wells Fargo Center, 1248 O Street
Lincoln, NE 68508

Cooper Industries Foundation Grants 1370
Cooper and the Cooper Industries Foundation annually donate more then $3 Million to nonprofit organizations serving the communities where their employees live and work. The Cooper Industries Foundation accepts and reviews grant requests throughout the year. There is no deadline; however, budgets are compiled annually each fall for the following year. Applicants must submit a brief letter explaining the purpose of the request with: concise description of organization and its mission; purpose and amount of request; budget information and other funding sources; evidence of 501(c)3 tax-exempt status; current listing of board members.
Requirements: Only 501(c)3 tax-exempt-status organizations are eligible. Programs must: benefit a community where Cooper is a significant employer; be endorsed by local Cooper management when applicable; not duplicate the efforts of the four Cooper-created programs; fulfill an important community need. Program objectives must coincide with that of the company.
Restrictions: The following types of organizations are generally ineligible for funding: United Way-funded organizations; national and state organizations; religious organizations; veterans organizations; political candidates, labor and lobbying organizations; hospitals; primary and secondary schools; scholarship organizations (except National Merit).
Geographic Focus: Alabama, Georgia, Illinois, Missouri, New York, North Carolina, South Carolina, Texas, Wisconsin, United Kingdom
Contact: Victoria B. Guennewig, VP Public Affairs; (713) 209-8800; fax (713) 209-8982; info@cooperindustries.com
Internet: http://www.cooperindustries.com/common/aboutCooper/corporateGiving.cfm?CFID=160327&CFTOKEN=61243618
Sponsor: Cooper Industries Foundation
P.O. Box 4446
Houston, TX 77210

Coors Brewing Corporate Contributions Grants 1371
The company has a firm commitment to giving back to its home-market communities—including Denver, CO; Memphis, TN; and Elkton, VA—and supports grassroots, nonprofit organizations that address community, civic and industry issues. The primary focus is on programs that enhance the quality of life. Vehicles of support include cash grants, Coors products for events, Coors logo items for fund-raisers, volunteer hours by Coors employees or retirees, or used equipment or in-kind services. Preference will be given to groups that focus on issues of national scope. Corporate Contributions usually reviews requests the first Wednesday of every month. A minimum of two months lead time is required before the event or funding need.
Requirements: IRS 501(c)3 nonprofit organizations located in Denver, CO; Memphis, TN; and Elkton, VA; are eligible.
Restrictions: Requests will not be considered for individuals in personal programs; individual scholarships; teams, groups, or races; travel expenses; third-party fund-raisers or sales promotions; political activities; or requests by telephone.
Geographic Focus: Colorado, Tennessee, Virginia
Contact: Buck Boze; (800) 642-6116 or (303) 277-5953; fax (303) 277-6132
Internet: http://www.coors.com
Sponsor: Coors Brewing Company
P.O. Box 4030, Department NH420
Golden, CO 80401

Cord Foundation Grants 1372
The foundation makes grants to a variety of groups in three broad areas: education, social services, and the arts. Grant recipients have included higher education institutions, research groups, youth organizations, community service agencies, religious organizations, and performing and visual arts centers. Types of support include general operating support, building construction/renovation, equipment acquisition, emergency funds, program development, scholarship funds, research, and matching funds. Grants are awarded nationwide, with preference given to requests from northern Nevada. Application forms are not required.
Requirements: Nonprofits are eligible but giving is primarily in the northern NV area.
Restrictions: The foundation does not support general fund-raising events, memorial campaigns, deficit fundings, conferences, dinners, or mass mailings.
Geographic Focus: Nevada
Contact: William Bradley, Trustee; (775) 323-0373
Sponsor: Cord Foundation
418 Flint Street
Reno, NV 89501-2008

Corina Higginson Trust Grants 1373
The Corina Higginson Trust makes grants to organizations based in or benefiting the greater Washington Metropolitan area. The Trust's goals are: to increase opportunities for individuals for the purpose of improvement and development of their capabilities; to provide relief of the poor, distressed, and underprivileged; to promote social welfare by organizations designed to accomplish any of the above purposes or to lessen neighborhood

tensions; to enhance opportunities for education about the arts and about the environment; and to eliminate prejudice and discrimination; or to defend civil rights secured by law.
Requirements: 501(c)3 District of Columbia, Maryland, and Virginia nonprofits are eligible.
Restrictions: Grants do not support individuals, fixed assets, religious organizations, medical or health-related programs, endowment funds to individual schools, or scholarship funds.
Geographic Focus: District of Columbia, Maryland, Virginia
Date(s) Application is Due: Mar 1; Sep 1
Amount of Grant: 5,000 - 10,000 USD
Contact: Wilton C. Corkern, Jr. , (301) 283-2113; fax (301) 283-2049
Internet: http://www.corinahigginsontrust.org/instructionsforloi.html
Sponsor: Corina Higginson Trust
3400 Bryan Point Road
Accokeek, MD 20607

Cornell Lab of Ornithology Mini-Grants 1374
Celebrate Urban Birds at the Cornell Lab of Ornithology invites organizations and educators to apply for mini-grants to help fund neighborhood events in communities everywhere. All applicants (even if they do not win funds to carry out their events) will receive free materials and training. Winning applicants will: hold a Celebrate Urban Birds event; introduce the public/youth to birds; do the 10-minute Celebrate Urban Bird observation with the people in their group, at their event, and report back to the Lab of Ornithology, either by paper forms or on-line; distribute Celebrate Urban Birds kits (with posters, seeds for planting, and more); integrate the arts; integrate gardening/habitat creation; and get people outside. Mini-grants average $100 to $500. Organizations working with underserved communities are strongly encouraged to apply.
Geographic Focus: All States
Date(s) Application is Due: Dec 15
Amount of Grant: 100 - 500 USD
Contact: Coordinator; (607) 254-2455; fax (607) 254-2111; urbanbirds@cornell.edu
Internet: http://www.birds.cornell.edu/celebration/community/minigrants/mini-grants-2012
Sponsor: Cornell Lab of Ornithology
159 Sapsucker Woods Road
Ithaca, NY 14850

Cornerstone Foundation of Northeastern Wisconsin Grants 1375
The community foundation supports nonprofit organizations primarily in Brown County, Wisconsin. The foundations area of interest are: education, cultural programs, social service and, youth agencies. With an additional interest in supporting healthcare facilities. The foundation offers the following types of support: annual campaigns; building/renovation; capital campaigns; continuing support; debt reduction; emergency funds; endowments; equipment; general/operating support; matching/challenge support; program; development. Contact the foundation by telephone for guidelines before submitting a proposal, no application form is required.
Requirements: Nonprofit organizations in Green Bay and northeastern Wisconsin may submit applications for grant support. The primary focus is Brown County.
Restrictions: No grants are available to: individuals, religious, or political organizations.
Geographic Focus: Wisconsin
Date(s) Application is Due: Jan 15; Sep 15
Amount of Grant: 10,000 - 400,000 USD
Contact: Sheri Prosser; (920) 490-8290; fax (920) 490-8620; cornerstone@cfnew.org
Sponsor: Cornerstone Foundation of Northeastern Wisconsin
111 North Washington Street, Suite 450
Green Bay, WI 54301-4208

Corning Foundation Cultural Grants 1376
Each year, the foundation provides assistance to institutions such as arts organizations, libraries, museums, and public broadcasting stations for a wide range of activities. Specific projects may include educational and cultural outreach, festivals and exhibitions, public radio music series, and partial underwriting support for the broadcast of selected public television programs. Support is given toward initiatives that improve the quality of live in and near communities where Corning is located.
Requirements: All requests to the foundation for support must be made in writing. Grant seekers are advised to submit a two- to three-page letter of inquiry, signed by the senior administrative officer of the organization.
Restrictions: Grants are not made to or for individuals; political parties, campaigns, or causes; labor or veterans organizations; religious or fraternal groups; volunteer emergency squads; athletic activities; courtesy advertising; or fund-raising events.
Geographic Focus: All States
Contact: Karen Martin; (607) 974-8722; fax (607) 974-4756; martinkc@corning.com
Internet: http://www.corning.com/inside_corning/our_commitment/community.aspx
Sponsor: Corning Foundation
1 Riverfront Plaza, MP-BH-07
Corning, NY 14831

Coughlin-Saunders Foundation Grants 1377
The foundation awards grants to nonprofit organizations in its areas of interest, including arts and arts education, higher education, religion, social services, and youth organizations. Types of support include general operating support, capital campaigns, building construction/renovation, equipment acquisition, emergency funds, program development, professorships, and scholarship funds. Proposals are preferred in January or February. Grants are made primarily for projects which benefit Alexandria, Louisiana, and the surrounding area. New Orleans and the surrounding area will be considered.
Requirements: 501(c)3 tax-exempt organizations in central Louisiana may apply.
Restrictions: Grants are not made to individuals or for fund raisers. Endowments will not be funded.
Geographic Focus: Louisiana
Contact: Ed Crump Jr.; (318) 561-4070; fax (318) 487-7339; csfoundation@kricket.net
Sponsor: Coughlin-Saunders Foundation
2010 Gus Kaplan Drive
Alexandria, LA 71301

Council on Foundations Emerging Philanthropic Leaders Fellowships 1378
The program is designed to help future foundation leaders become more effective within their communities and the larger field of organized philanthropy. Each year, two two-year fellowships are awarded. Each fellow is matched with a mentor who is a recognized leader in philanthropy. The fellows are asked to identify their professional growth goals and organizational development needs that they would like to address as part of their fellowship. The mentors, drawn from the council's membership, are asked to help develop two-year plans for providing information, advice, and referrals. Applications may be sent by mail, fax, or email.
Requirements: The nominee or applicant must have at least two years experience in the philanthropic area, with at least one year in a leadership position. The nominee or applicant's organization must have a focus on increasing and expanding philanthropic programs within communities that are historically underrepresented in institutional philanthropy. All applicants must submit a simple application letter. The chief executive of the organization also must write a brief letter of support or co-sign the applicant's submission. Nominees or applicants must be associated with a Council on Foundations member or member-eligible organization.
Geographic Focus: All States
Date(s) Application is Due: Dec 31
Contact: Evelyn Gibson, (703) 879-0691 or (703) 879-0600; Evelyn.Gibson@cof.org
Internet: http://www.cof.org/files/Documents/Diversity/diversitybrochure.pdf
Sponsor: Council on Foundations
2121 Crystal Drive, Suite 700
Arlington, VA 22202

Council on Foundations Paul Ylvisaker Award for Public Policy Engagement 1379
The Award for Public Policy Engagement celebrates grantmakers who embrace their prescribed role to help set the agenda for public consideration and debate. The award was named for Paul Ylvisaker, a courageous, often lone voice on a range of issues. Areas of interest include urban affairs, civil rights, community engagement, the environment, and philanthropy. The award is presented at the Council on Foundations Annual Conference.
Requirements: Foundations, not individuals, are eligible for the award.
Geographic Focus: All States
Date(s) Application is Due: Dec 17
Contact: Evelyn Gibson, (703) 879-0691 or (703) 879-0600; Evelyn.Gibson@cof.org
Internet: http://www.cof.org/Council/content.cfm?ItemNumber=797
Sponsor: Council on Foundations
2121 Crystal Drive, Suite 700
Arlington, VA 22202

Council on Foundations Robert W. Scrivner Award for Creative Grantmaking 1380
This award is a memorial to the creative legacy left by Robert W. Scrivner, long-time director of the Rockefeller Family Fund. The criteria for this award correspond closely to Robert Scrivner's belief that philanthropy should address emerging societal issues and retain the flexibility to change directions as conditions warrant. The award is designed to honor a creative response to a particularly important problem in society rather than commemorating lifetime achievement. In selecting the recipient, some additional criteria are considered. The achievement should be sufficiently developed so that its use as a paradigm is possible, demonstrate an entrepreneurial spirit, build on and take full advantage of existing networks, demonstrate ability and willingness to take risks, be a creative departure from past grantmaking, and ensure that the sum is greater than the parts. Nomination form and guidelines are available online.
Requirements: Individuals, not institutions, are eligible for the award. Nominees may be either a staff person or a trustee who is not the original donor of the organization. Individuals must be currently practicing grantmakers. Individuals from private, community or corporate foundations, corporate giving programs, and operating foundations that are members of the Council on Foundations or a regional association of grantmakers will be considered. Only members of the Council on Foundations are eligible to nominate individuals for the award. Nonmembers may submit or suggest nominations through a Council member. Council members, nonmembers, and nongrantmakers may submit statement of Reference forms. All requirements must be met at the time of nomination.
Geographic Focus: All States
Date(s) Application is Due: Dec 3
Contact: Evelyn Gibson, (703) 879-0691 or (703) 879-0600; Evelyn.Gibson@cof.org
Internet: http://www.cof.org/Council/content.cfm?ItemNumber=791
Sponsor: Council on Foundations
2121 Crystal Drive, Suite 700
Arlington, VA 22202

Countess Moira Charitable Foundation Grants 1381
The Countess Moira Charitable Foundation was established in 2000 with its mission being "to aid the well-being of youth anywhere in the World" by supporting charitable organizations that focus on the betterment of youth. Qualified organizations may submit inquiries for operating program, endowment and capital funding needs that support the mission of the foundation. There are no deadlines; inquiries will be accepted throughout the year.
Requirements: The foundation will only consider unsolicited inquiries from organizations in the New York tri-state area, or national organizations that may also utilize funds in the

broader international arena. Grants will only be made to 501(c)3 nonprofit organizations. Initial contact should be made via email (see below) before making a formal grant proposal.
Restrictions: Do not send unsolicited inquiries or grant proposals via paper mail to the foundation's mailing address as these will not be considered at all. Grants will not be given for events or fundraisers nor to individuals.
Geographic Focus: Connecticut, New Jersey, New York
Contact: Carolyn Gray, President/Chairperson; inquiries@countessmoirafdn.org
Internet: https://sites.google.com/a/countessmoirafdn.org/countessmoirafoundation/
Sponsor: Countess Moira Charitable Foundation
P.O. Box 8078
Pelham, NY 10803

Courage Center Judd Jacobson Memorial Award   1382
Established in 1992, the Judd Jacobson Memorial Award recognizes pursuit or achievement of a business entrepreneurial endeavor by a person with a physical disability or sensory impairment. The award recipient receives a special plaque, a $5,000 cash award to advance their entrepreneurial business endeavor and is honored at an event in November.
Requirements: Applicants must be 18 years of age and reside in Minnesota, Wisconsin, Iowa, North Dakota, or South Dakota. Applicants must also demonstrate entrepreneurial skill, financial need, exceptional personal commitment, and have received little or no public recognition for their business endeavor.
Geographic Focus: Iowa, Minnesota, North Dakota, South Dakota, Wisconsin
Date(s) Application is Due: Sep 4
Amount of Grant: 5,000 USD
Contact: Sue Warner, (763) 520-0263; fax (763) 520-0562; Sue.Warner@CourageCenter.org
Internet: http://www.couragecenter.org/contentpages/judd_jacobson.aspx
Sponsor: Courage Center
3915 Golden Valley Road
Minneapolis, MN 55422

Covenant Educational Foundation Grants   1383
The Covenant Educational Foundation offers funding for projects or programs in the arts, health organizations, or human services. Giving is primarily in the North Carolina area. There is no application, but organizations may send a summary of the project in essay form as an initial approach.
Requirements: Applicants must be from the North Carolina area.
Geographic Focus: North Carolina
Date(s) Application is Due: Apr 30
Amount of Grant: 250 - 5,500 USD
Contact: Gardner H. Altman, Sr., President; (910) 484-0041 or (910) 323-5717
Sponsor: Covenant Educational Foundation
P.O. Box 234
White Oak, NC 28399

Covenant Foundation of Atlanta Grants   1384
The Covenant Foundation of Atlanta offers funding primarily for Jewish welfare programs and temple support in the Atlanta, Georgia region. Funding is also available for culture, education, and health care programs. Applicants should submit a detailed description of the project and the amount of funding requested. There is no application form or deadline, with a full proposal as the initial approach.
Restrictions: Giving is restricted to the Atlanta, Georgia, area.
Geographic Focus: Georgia
Amount of Grant: 100 - 250,000 USD
Contact: Jay M. Davis, President; (404) 696-9440; fax (404) 505-1013
Sponsor: Covenant Foundation (Atlanta)
1 National Drive SW
Atlanta, GA 30336-1680

Covenant Foundation of New York Ignition Grants   1385
The Covenant Foundation of New York invites applications for one-year Ignition Grants of up to $20,000. Ignition Grants are designed to explore new, untested ideas or to determine how established practices can become even more effective. An Ignition Grant is appropriate for an exciting idea that is not yet ready for a multi-year Signature Grant, because it is still in the planning stage or the organization needs time to develop necessary capacity and expertise. Any organization that receives an Ignition Grant may apply for a Covenant Signature Grant after submission of the final report. Letters of Inquiry are due on February 28, with full applications due on June 26 (if invited).
Requirements: Any institutions, agencies, or organizations involved in the field of Jewish education (i.e. day schools, congregational schools, central agencies of Jewish education, Jewish community centers, summer camps, or museums) are eligible. Only a tax-exempt, non-profit organization may serve as the sponsoring organization of a Covenant Grant.
Restrictions: Grants will not be made to support feasibility studies, assessment studies, or basic research in Jewish education. The Foundation cannot fund capital expansion projects, student scholarships, ongoing operating support, or staff salary and benefit packages.
Geographic Focus: All States
Date(s) Application is Due: Jun 27
Amount of Grant: Up to 20,000 USD
Contact: Sarah Brilleman, Grants Administrator; (212) 245-3500; fax (212) 245-0619; sarah@covenantfn.org or info@covenantfn.org
Internet: http://www.covenantfn.org/grants/apply-for-a-grant/apply-for-a-grant-1/#1
Sponsor: Covenant Foundation of New York
1270 Avenue of the Americas, Suite 304
New York, NY 10020-1700

Covenant Foundation of New York Signature Grants   1386
The Covenant Foundation invites applications for innovative programs in Jewish schools, community organizations, and other institutional settings. These grants will provide funding to help creative Jewish educators develop and implement significant and financially responsible approaches to Jewish education that are potentially replicable in other settings. Covenant Grants may also be awarded for projects whose purpose is to disseminate particularly effective existing programs. Typical grants do not exceed $150,000, with generally no more than $50,000 per year. There is no minimum dollar amount associated with a Signature Grant. All proposals will be assessed by the Foundation Selection Committee for the significance of the issues addressed, potential contribution to the field, the importance and clarity of their educational objectives, the quality of the proposed program, and the feasibility of its implementation. The Committee will also discuss expected short and long-term outcomes of the project. Additionally, the Committee will consider the extent to which the program will benefit other groups beyond those immediately served and whether there are any plans for dissemination. The Committee seeks to know how the program will be funded after the grant period ends, if it is to continue. The application and additional information are available at the website.
Requirements: Any institutions, agencies, or organizations involved in the field of Jewish education (i.e. day schools, congregational schools, central agencies of Jewish education, Jewish community centers, summer camps, or museums) are eligible. Only a tax-exempt, non-profit organization may serve as the sponsoring organization of a Covenant Grant. Each proposal must identify a single Project Director who will supervise all aspects of the project throughout the grant period. Signature Grant Project Directors should be prepared to attend a two-day meeting of Project Directors each February for the duration of the grant, and communicate with the Foundation throughout the grant period.
Restrictions: Grants will not be made to support feasibility studies, assessment studies, or basic research in Jewish education. Funding is also not available for capital expansion projects, student scholarships, ongoing operating support, or staff salary and benefit packages.
Geographic Focus: All States
Date(s) Application is Due: Jun 27
Amount of Grant: Up to 50,000 USD
Contact: Sarah Brilleman, Grants Administrator; (212) 245-3500; fax (212) 245-0619; sarah@covenantfn.org or info@covenantfn.org
Internet: http://www.covenantfn.org/grants/apply-for-a-grant/apply-for-a-grant-1/#1
Sponsor: Covenant Foundation of New York
1270 Avenue of the Americas, Suite 304
New York, NY 10020-1700

Covenant Mountain Ministries Grants   1387
The program, established in 1995, is a non-profit foundation dedicated to spreading the gospel through the establishment of churches and assisting in the creation of new ministries. Grants are given primarily to West Virginia organizations (Christian agencies, churches, and family service offices) that give aid to abused spouses and children. Funding comes in the form of general operations support. Though there are no deadlines, an application form can be secured by contacting the Ministries directly.
Geographic Focus: West Virginia
Amount of Grant: 500 - 1,500 USD
Contact: Marilyn L. Perkins, (304) 487-1680; Marilyn@Marilynperkins.com
Sponsor: Covenant Mountain Ministries
573 Pigeon Roost Trail
Princeton, WV 24740-4246

Covenant to Care for Children Critical Goods Grants   1388
Covenant to Care for Children (CCC) works to mobilize and channel the generosity of caring and faithful people to advocate for, mentor, and provide direct assistance to Connecticut's children and youth who are neglected, abused, or at-risk. The organization's vision is to create a future where all Connecticut children have caring families and safe places to live. The Program facilitates family preservation and reunification through the placement of required goods in the homes of client families. Where possible, CCC also aids efforts to place children and youth in foster care and independent living through the placement of required goods. In order to accomplish this, the Program collects high quality new and used furniture, appliances, clothing and infant items from individuals and corporate donors and redistributes it to families in need.
Requirements: By appointment, the Critical Goods Coordinator picks up furniture, toys, clothing, and other goods from donor homes and businesses.
Restrictions: The Program does not accept drop-side cribs, and will dispose of them if they are included with additional furniture.
Geographic Focus: Connecticut
Contact: Charles Mulholland, Program Coordinator; (860) 243-1806, ext. 17; fax (860) 243-0100; cmulholland@covenanttocare.org
Internet: http://www.covenanttocare.org/criticalgoods/index.shtml
Sponsor: Covenant to Care for Children
120 Mountain Avenue, Suite 212
Bloomfield, CT 06002

Covenant to Care for Children Enrichment Fund Grants   1389
The Covenant to Care for Children's (CCC) Enrichment Fund is a children's advocacy program that helps respond to the less ordinary requests to meet special needs for the support, care and nurturing of youth and children in crisis. This program provides a fund designed to accept designated donations for those special expense needs of children. Social workers can request these funds for the needs of children that are not met by State Government departments, other agencies, or CCC's Adopt a Social Worker Program.

Funding examples include summer camp, haircuts, lessons, art, music, sports, tutoring, bikes, or special books. Additional information is available at the website.
Geographic Focus: Connecticut
Contact: Dave Santis; (860) 243-1806, ext. 13; fax (860) 243-0100; dsantis@covenanttocare.org
Internet: http://www.covenanttocare.org/childrens_enrichment_fund.shtml
Sponsor: Covenant to Care for Children
120 Mountain Avenue, Suite 212
Bloomfield, CT 06002

Covidien Medical Product Donations   1390
The wide variety of the Covidien product line has great appeal to many charitable organizations. Covidien annually donates millions of dollars in important healthcare products such as wound dressings, endotracheal tubes, generators, and surgical supplies to support global health and humanitarian needs. Covidien's authorized partners, AmeriCares, Direct Relief International and MedShare distribute products to nonprofit organizations and in-country clinics around the world in response to disasters, and also to support specific programs for under-served populations. Some products are made available to advance ongoing global medical missions through AmeriCares. AmeriCares offers a medical outreach program that donates the medical products of Covidien and other companies to qualified U.S. health care professionals who will use them to provide charitable medical care to those in developing countries.
Requirements: Applicants seeking aid for their mission should contact the health organizations posted on the Covidien website to see if they meet the qualifications for a donation of medical products.
Restrictions: Personal requests for products are not accepted.
Geographic Focus: All States, All Countries
Contact: Brian Skahan; (508) 261-8000; Brian.Skahan@covidien.com
Internet: http://www.covidien.com/covidien/pages.aspx?page=AboutUs/socialresponsibility/Donations
Sponsor: Covidien Healthcare Products
15 Hampshire Street
Mansfield, MA 02048

Covidien Partnership for Neighborhood Wellness Grants   1391
Covidien Partnership for Neighborhood Wellness Grants support community projects that increase access to quality, affordable healthcare; benefit people suffering from a specific disease for which treatment options are not affordable or readily available; provides assistance that has a significant impact on the health of the community; or support development of new treatments or new approaches to prevention. Funding requests may vary in range and depth, and should aim to: increase access to quality, affordable healthcare; build capacity to increase services; provide education and awareness, with an emphasis on prevention; provide medical professionals with additional tools to address specific health needs; raise money for capital campaigns for building clinics or healthcare facilities in impoverished communities; fund local community health centers or clinics to augment their medical staff, diagnostic tests and treatments or disease prevention and education initiatives; and fund consumer education related to specific diseases or medical conditions. Grants are made twice a year. Additional information about grant submission and deadlines is available at the Covidien website.
Requirements: Applicants are required to take an online eligibility quiz before submitting a grant request.
Restrictions: The following grant requests are excluded from funding: partisan political organizations, committees or candidates for public office or public office holders; religious organizations in support of their sacramental or theological functions; labor unions; endowments; capital campaigns (although capital campaigns for building clinics or healthcare facilities in impoverished communities are considered); requests for multi-year support; organizations whose prime purpose is to influence legislation; testimonial dinners; for-profit publications or organizations seeking advertisements for promotional support; individuals; fraternities, sororities, etc; or gala dinners, golf fundraisers and other special events.
Geographic Focus: All States
Contact: Teresa Hacunda; (508) 261-8000; Teresa.Hacunda@covidien.com
Internet: http://www.covidien.com/covidien/pages.aspx?page=AboutUs/socialresponsibility/Giving
Sponsor: Covidien Healthcare Products
15 Hampshire Street
Mansfield, MA 02048

Cowles Charitable Trust Grants   1392
The foundation awards grants, primarily in New York, Florida, and on the East Coast, for the arts and culture, including museums and the performing arts; environment; education, including early childhood education, secondary and higher education, medical school education, adult basic education and literacy, and adult continuing education; hospitals and AIDS programs, including research; social services, including family planning, human services, and federated giving; and community funds, including leadership development, civil rights, and race relations. Types of support include general operating support, capital campaigns, annual campaigns, equipment acquisition, endowment funds, continuing support, seed money, building construction/renovation, matching funds, professorships, and program development. Application forms are required; initial approach should be by letter. The board meets in January, April, July, and October.
Requirements: Nonprofit organizations may apply for grant support. Grants are awarded primarily along the Eastern Seaboard.
Geographic Focus: Florida, New York
Date(s) Application is Due: Mar 1; Jun 1; Sep 1; Dec 1
Amount of Grant: 1,000 - 40,000 USD
Contact: Mary Croft, Treasurer; (732) 936-9826
Sponsor: Cowles Charitable Trust
P.O. Box 219
Rumson, NJ 07760

Crail-Johnson Foundation Grants   1393
The Crail-Johnson Foundation (CJF) has defined itself as a children's charity, and the vast majority of grant-making is directed toward programs benefiting children, youth and families in the greater Los Angeles area. Proposals, which are not relevant to the foundation's mission and funding priorities, will not be considered. CJF provides grants for program initiatives and enhancements, general operating support and capital projects as well as selected endowments. CJF provides technical assistance to selected community-based initiatives benefiting children and families. The majority of Crail-Johnson Foundation funding supports organizations located in the greater Los Angeles area and projects that directly benefit Los Angeles area residents. National organizations providing services in Los Angeles are also considered. Occasionally, grants are made to programs and projects that are regional or national in scope, where potential benefits to children and families in Los Angeles can be clearly demonstrated. Initial contact with the Crail-Johnson Foundation should be in the form of a letter of inquiry, letters are accepted October through December each year for the following year's grant cycle and are generally considered in the order in which they are received. Organizations selected to submit proposals will be asked to complete a Grant Application Form provided by the Foundation.
Requirements: The foundation provides financial support primarily through grants to public non-profit organizations that are exempt under Section 501(c)3 of the Internal Revenue code and are not a private foundation under Section 509(a).
Restrictions: Support is not granted for programs and projects benefiting religious purposes, university level education, research, events recognizing individuals or organizations, political causes or programs attempting to influence legislation. No grants are made directly to individuals.
Geographic Focus: California
Amount of Grant: 5,000 - 50,000 USD
Contact: Pat Christopher, Program Officer; (310) 519-7413; fax (310) 519-7221; pat-christopher@crail-johnson.org
Internet: http://www.crail-johnson.org/grants-application.htm
Sponsor: Crail-Johnson Foundation
222 W Sixth Street, Suite 1010
San Pedro, CA 90731

Cralle Foundation Grants   1394
The foundation awards grants in the areas of education and higher education, children and youth services, community development, human services, and museums to Kentucky nonprofits. Emphasis is given to nonprofits serving residents of Louisville. Types of support include: building and renovation; capital campaigns; continuing support; endowments; equipment; operating support; matching and challenge support; program development; scholarship funds; and seed money. Interested organizations should initially send a letter requesting an application form. Applicants should submit four copies of their application. Application deadlines are March 1 and September 1. The foundation's board meets in April and October.
Requirements: Nonprofit organizations in Kentucky are eligible.
Restrictions: No grants to individuals.
Geographic Focus: Kentucky
Date(s) Application is Due: Mar 1; Sep 1
Amount of Grant: 5,000 - 50,000 USD
Contact: James Crain, Jr.; (502) 581-1148; fax (502) 581-1937; jcrain37@bellsouth.net
Sponsor: Cralle Foundation, Inc.
614 West Main Sreet, Suite 2500
Louisville, KY 40202-4252

Cranston Foundation Grants   1395
The foundation directs most of its grants to the geographic areas where Cranston Print Works Company has operations and a large number of employees, including Rhode Island, Massachusetts, Louisiana, and New York. Targeted priority areas are education, health and welfare, culture and the arts, and civic and community programs. Types of support include general operating support, employee matching gifts, and employee-related scholarships. All requests should be made in writing and should contain details and funding requirements pertaining to the project. The February deadline is for scholarships; the August deadline is for grants.
Requirements: IRS 501(c)3 organizations serving Rhode Island, Massachusetts, Louisiana, and New York are eligible.
Geographic Focus: Massachusetts, New York, Rhode Island
Date(s) Application is Due: Feb 15; Aug 31
Amount of Grant: 200 - 5,000 USD
Contact: Trustee; (401) 943-4800
Sponsor: Cranston Foundation
1381 Cranston Street
Cranston, RI 02920

Creative Work Fund Grants   1396
For the current year, interested media artists and performing artists and collaborating organizations are invited to submit three-page letters of inquiry. A media arts or performing arts project may culminate in any form, but must feature a lead artist with a strong track record as a media or performing artist. Media artists create works for film, video, video or sound installations, radio, or computer-based media. Performing artists may be creators—such as playwrights, choreographers, and composers—or may be performers. The performing arts encompass dance, opera, performance art, theater, and vocal and instrumental music.

(Spoken word poets should apply in the literary arts category in a future year.) In either discipline, artists and organizations should plan projects and prepare and sign letters of inquiry together. If the applicant uses a fiscal sponsor, that sponsor also should review and sign the letter. Artists and organizations may submit one proposal per art form per deadline and may receive only one Creative Work Fund grant every three years. Past Creative Work Fund grant recipients also must have finished their projects and completed their final reports before submitting new letters of inquiry. The listed application deadline is for letters of inquiry.
Requirements: Projects that feature one or more artists who are collaborating with a nonprofit 501(c)3 organization are eligible. The principal collaborating artists must live in San Francisco and California's Alameda, Contra Costa, and Solano Counties; and applicant organizations also must be based in those counties.
Restrictions: The fund will not consider commissions of new works by artists in which the applicant organization and artists are not collaboratively engaged in the making of that work; projects in which the lead artist and collaborating organization are not based in the eligible counties or those with multiple artists, most of whom are based outside of the four counties; projects that do not feature the artist(s) centrally as demonstrated by project descriptions and budget allocations; projects from lead artists or organizations that were awarded Creative Work Fund grants in the last two years; or projects from artists or organizations that have not completed projects and final reports for previously awarded Creative Work Fund projects.
Geographic Focus: California
Date(s) Application is Due: Nov 4
Amount of Grant: 10,000 - 35,000 USD
Contact: Fund Administrator; (415) 398-4474
Internet: http://www.creativeworkfund.org
Sponsor: Creative Work Fund
1 Lombard Street, Suite 305
San Francisco, CA 94111

Credit Suisse First Boston Foundation Grants 1397
The foundation supports educational initiatives and programs for inner-city youth, primarily in New York City. Grant requests from nonprofit organizations are received year-round, and those that meet the foundation's mission are submitted quarterly to the trustees for review. Requests must contain a description of the organization and project; the amount requested; a letter from the IRS confirming nonprofit status of the organization; and information documenting the level of employee involvement, if any.
Requirements: The majority of support goes to New York City, but the foundation also makes grants to areas where branches operate in Atlanta, GA; Baltimore, MD; Boston, MA; Chicago, IL; Dallas, and Houston, TX; Los Angeles, San Francisco, and Palo Alto, CA; Miami, FL; Washington, DC, and Philadelphia, PA.
Geographic Focus: California, Florida, Georgia, Illinois, Maryland, Massachusetts, New York, Pennsylvania, Texas
Contact: Alison Johnson; (212) 325-2000 or (212) 325-2389; alison.johnson@csfb.com
Internet: http://www.csfb.com/about_csfb/company_information/foundation/index.shtml
Sponsor: Credit Suisse First Boston Foundation
11 Madison Avenue, 9th Floor
New York, NY 10010-3629

Crescent Porter Hale Foundation Grants 1398
The foundation places emphasis on organizations engaged in Catholic endeavors, with preference given to organizations in the San Francisco Bay area counties of Alameda, Contra Costa, Marin, San Francisco, and San Mateo. Areas of concern considered desirable for funding include organizations devoted to Catholic elementary and high school, education in the fields of art and music, agencies serving disadvantaged and at-risk youth, families and elderly. Applications for capital funds, scholarship funds, requests for special projects, as well as for general operating program support will be considered. The foundation will consider other worthwhile programs that can be demonstrated as serving broad community purposes, leading toward the improvement of the quality of life. Agencies serving disadvantaged youth, the disabled, or the elderly are of particular interest. Organizations wishing to apply should address a brief letter of intent to the foundation indicating the nature of the program and/or the specific project for which funding is sought. The board meets in April, September, and December to consider requests.
Requirements: To be eligible for consideration, organizations must meet the following criteria: be a corporate non-profit organization; qualify for tax exemption by the State in which said organization or institution is incorporated; be a organization to which contributions are deductible by donors for income tax purposes, generally of the type described in Section 501(c)3 of the Internal Revenue Code of 1954 and the corresponding Sections of the 1939 Code and prior Revenue Acts; be classified as a non-private foundation pursuant to the 1969 Tax Reform Acts; have and annual financial audit in accordance with approved accounting practices.
Restrictions: Individuals are ineligible. Healthcare-related, research, or postgraduate education programs are ineligible.
Geographic Focus: California
Contact: Ulla Davis, Executive Director; (415) 388-2333; fax (415) 381-4799
Internet: http://www.crescentporterhale.org/policy/policy.htm
Sponsor: Crescent Porter Hale Foundation
655 Redwood Highway, Suite 301
Mill Valley, CA 94941

Crestlea Foundation Grants 1399
The foundation supports Delaware nonprofits in its areas of interest, including secondary education, higher education, natural resource conservation, health care, housing development, community development, social services, and public affairs. Types of support include annual campaigns, general operating support, capital campaigns, building construction/renovation, and equipment acquisition. There are no application forms.
Requirements: Delaware nonprofits are eligible.
Geographic Focus: Delaware
Date(s) Application is Due: Nov 1
Amount of Grant: 5,000 - 50,000 USD
Contact: Stephen Martinenza, Secretary-Treasurer; (302) 654-2477
Sponsor: Crestlea Foundation
100 W 10th Street, Suite 1109
Wilmington, DE 19801

Crossroads Fund Seed Grants 1400
The fund supports organizations working on issues of social and economic justice in the Chicago metropolitan area. This grants program supports new, emerging, and small community based organizations that are actively engaged in social change work. Types of support include general operating grants, start-up costs, and project development. The maximum grant in this program is $10,000.
Requirements: Community organizations rooted in the Chicago metropolitan area, including northwestern Indiana, with annual expenses under $300,000 in the last completed fiscal year are eligible. Additionally, organizations must meet the Fund's general funding criteria: Working for Social Change—organizing community members to examine and challenge the underlying causes of their problems and conditions; Cross-Issue Organizing—working with an understanding of the connectedness among the various people and issues that make up the whole community; Grassroots Leadership—involving the people who are directly affected at all levels of the organization in planning, organizing and leading, and working to continue building leadership within the grassroots community; Solid Plan—having a clear purpose to the project with well-planned goals, objectives, activities and a tool to measure outcomes and impact; a timeline and budget that reflects the proposed objectives and activities; a realistic fundraising plan.
Restrictions: The fund does not support organizations that are involved in electoral campaigns; contribute substantially to support lobbying at the federal, state, or local levels; or support private, in contrast to public, interest.
Geographic Focus: Illinois, Indiana
Amount of Grant: Up to 10,000 USD
Contact: Jane Kimondo; (773) 227-7676; fax (773) 227-7790; jane@crossroadsfund.org
Internet: http://www.crossroadsfund.org/seedfund.html
Sponsor: Crossroads Fund
3411 W Diversey Avenue, #20
Chicago, IL 60647

Crowell Trust Grants 1401
The Trustees of the Trust continue to follow the directives for grantmaking which Henry Parsons Crowell established in his original indenture. Crowell identified candidates for grants from among agencies whose purpose is: Evangelism and discipleship; international cross-cultural missions; U.S. focused missions; Christian higher education; and Christian leadership development. Types of support include matching funds, operating budgets, building funds, equipment, and scholarship funds. There are no application deadlines.
Restrictions: As a general rule grants are not made to individuals, local churches, pre-kindergarten through high school education, endowment funds, land acquisition, or building construction.
Geographic Focus: All States
Contact: Executive Director; (719) 272-8300; fax (719) 272-8305; grantadmin@crowelltrust.org or info@crowelltrust.org
Internet: http://www.crowelltrust.org/page.php?id=8
Sponsor: Crowell Trust
1880 Office Club Pointe, Suite 2200
Colorado Springs, CO 80920

Crown Point Community Foundation Grants 1402
The Crown Point Community Foundation is interested in funding projects which improve the quality of life for citizens in the Crown Point area. The foundation utilizes matching funds programs and challenge grants to stimulate the fundraising efforts of local organizations. The Crown Point Community Foundation considers grant applications for projects in the following areas: education; health and human services; civic affairs; arts and culture; and preservation/conservation. Grants are awarded in February, June, and September of each year. Applications received after the deadline will be held for consideration during the next cycle.
Requirements: The Foundation considers the following guidelines when reviewing grant applications: projects are limited within the territorial boundaries of the Crown Point Community School Corporation and the city of Crown Point; only one grant application per organization is eligible within a 12 month period, January through December; the potential community impact of the grant and the number of people who will benefit; the extent of local volunteers involvement and support for the project; the composition and level of commitment of the organization's directors/trustees; the organization's fiscal responsibility and management qualifications; the ability of the organization to obtain additional funding to implement the project; and the organization's ability to provide funding after a long-term grant has expired. Grants are usually made to 501(c)3 non-profit organizations. Grants are primarily awarded to underwrite program expenses or to fund capital expenditures. All applicants must submit the application form; a detailed three page narrative of the proposal; a proposed budget including revenue and expenses for the project; a recent financial audit or statement; a copy of the 501(c)3 tax exempt form; and a list of the organization's officers and board of directors.
Restrictions: Grants are not made for endowment purposes. No grants may be used for any political campaign, or to support attempts to influence the legislature of any governmental

body. The Foundation funds only grant seekers who do not unlawfully discriminate as to age, race, religion, sex, disability, or national origin.
Geographic Focus: Indiana
Date(s) Application is Due: Feb 1; Jun 1; Sep 1
Contact: Patricia Huber; (219) 662-7252; fax (219) 662-9493; cpcf@sbcglobal.net
Internet: http://crownpointcommunityfoundation.org/grants/guidelines/
Sponsor: Crown Point Community Foundation
115 South Court Street
Crown Point, IN 46308-0522

Crown Point Community Foundation Scholarships 1403
The Crown Point Community Foundation Scholarships are made available through donations and endowment fund distributions. A donor committee helps review and score the applications, interview the students and award the scholarships. The website lists specific scholarships available from area schools, churches, country clubs, and individuals.
Requirements: Applicants should contact the foundation for applications and more information.
Restrictions: Several scholarships have specific requirements, such as the applicant must have attended the school, studying a particular major, or the applicant must be the child of a local steelworker.
Geographic Focus: Indiana
Amount of Grant: 500 - 1,500 USD
Contact: Patricia Huber; (219) 662-7252; fax (219) 662-9493
Internet: http://crownpointcommunityfoundation.org/scholarships/available/
Sponsor: Crown Point Community Foundation
115 South Court Street
Crown Point, IN 46308-0522

Cruise Industry Charitable Foundation Grants 1404
The foundation awards grants to improve the quality of life in U.S. cities and towns where the cruise industry maintains vessel operations, employs a significant number of individuals, and purchases products and services. Areas of interest include civic and community development, educational assistance and training programs, public health programs, and environmental initiatives. There are no application deadlines, see Foundation's website for application guidelines.
Requirements: U.S. 501(c)3 organizations are eligible to apply.
Restrictions: Requests will not be considered from individuals, fraternal organizations, religious organizations, political organizations, or organizations that conduct lobbying activity.
Geographic Focus: All States
Contact: Cynthia Colenda; (703) 522-3160; fax (703) 522-3161; cicf@iccl.org
Internet: http://www.cruisefoundation.org/requirements-and-guidelines.php
Sponsor: Cruise Industry Charitable Foundation
2111 Wilson Boulevard, 8th Floor
Arlington, VA 22201

Crystelle Waggoner Charitable Trust Grants 1405
Born to a ranching family, Crystelle Waggoner raised cattle and thoroughbred horses. A patron of the arts and supporter of medical charities during her lifetime, she established a 50-year trust to benefit charitable organizations in the arts and social services. Applicants must apply online at the grant website. Applicants are strongly encouraged to do the following before applying: review the downloadable state application procedures for additional helpful information and clarifications; review the downloadable online-application guidelines at the grant website; review the trust's funding history (link is available from the grant website); review the online application questions in advance; and review the list of required attachments. These will generally include: a list of board members, financial statements (audited, reviewed, or compiled by independent auditor); an organization summary; a list of other funding sources; an IRS Determination letter; and other required documents. All attachments must be uploaded in the online application as PDF, Word, or Excel files. The Crystelle Waggoner Charitable Trust has bi-annual application deadlines of March 31 and September 30. Applications must be submitted by 11:59 p.m. on the deadline dates.
Requirements: Applicants must have 501(c)3 tax-exempt status.
Restrictions: Preference is given to charitable organizations in existence before January 24, 1982. The trust does not support requests from individuals, organizations attempting to influence policy through direct lobbying, or any political campaigns.
Geographic Focus: Texas
Date(s) Application is Due: Mar 31; Sep 30
Amount of Grant: 5,000 - 35,000 USD
Contact: Mark J. Smith; (817) 390-6028; tx.philanthropic@baml.com
Internet: https://www.bankofamerica.com/philanthropic/fn_search.action
Sponsor: Crystelle Waggoner Charitable Trust
500 West 7th Street, 15th Floor, TX1-497-15-08
Fort Worth, TX 76102-4700

CSL Behring Local Empowerment for Advocacy Development (LEAD) Grants 1406
CSL Behring Local Empowerment for Advocacy Development (LEAD) Grants are community-based grants of approximately $10,000. These grants are intended to help local patient organizations achieve their advocacy objectives. CSL Behring will award LEAD Grants to organizations that submit proposals demonstrating that financial assistance would help them address important local and state advocacy issues and initiatives. Local patient organizations have already demonstrated significant leadership in tackling complex legislative and regulatory public policy issues. Advocacy can, however, be costly. CSL Behring LEAD Grants will help defray these costs. Moreover, CSL Behring will work with the grant recipients to advance their objectives in order to obtain success.
Requirements: In order to qualify for a LEAD Grant, a local organization must be: a recognized patient advocacy organization representing individuals who use plasma/recombinant therapies to treat bleeding disorders, immune disorders, Alpha-1 deficiency or other conditions; a non-profit organization with 501(c)3 tax status; and an organization currently addressing a specific advocacy issue or intending to address such an issue.
Geographic Focus: All States
Date(s) Application is Due: Apr 30; Oct 31
Amount of Grant: Up to 10,000 USD
Contact: Patrick Collins, (610) 878-4311; Patrick.Collins@cslbehring.com
Internet: http://www.cslbehring.com/s1/cs/enco/1199979063088/content/1199979062780/content.htm
Sponsor: CSL Behring
1020 First Avenue, P.O. Box 61501
King of Prussia, PA 19406-0901

CSRA Community Foundation Grants 1407
The foundation awards grants to organizations that provide programs and services to the Greater Augusta area, including Richmond, Columbia, McDuffie, Burke, Aiken and Edgefield counties. Areas of interest include arts and cultural; children, youth, and family services; civic affairs; community development; economic development; education; environmental; health; and human services. Types of support include annual campaigns, capital campaigns, seed grants, scholarship funds, and matching funds. The board meets quarterly to consider requests. Applications are due by 11:00 am on the listed application deadline.
Requirements: Georgia 501(c)3 organizations, providing programs and services to the Greater Augusta area, including one or more of the following counties : Richmond, Columbia, McDuffie, Burke, Aiken and Edgefield are eligible to apply.
Restrictions: The Community Foundation discourages applicants from submitting applications in support of the following: computer/word processing hardware not directly related to project or services; grants for individuals; building campaigns; deficit financing and debt retirement; endowments; fraternal organizations, societies or orders; professional/association conferences or seminars (support for or attendance at); political organization or campaigns; lobbying legislators or influencing elections; special fundraising events/celebration functions; surveys, feasibility studies, marketing endeavors and personal research; travel for individuals or groups such as bands, sports teams, and classes; core operating expenses for public and private elementary and secondary schools and public and private colleges and universities; projects that are typically the funding responsibility of federal, state or local governments; fifteen passenger vans.
Geographic Focus: Georgia
Date(s) Application is Due: Jul 31
Amount of Grant: Up to 15,000 USD
Contact: Cindy Arrant; (706) 724-1314; fax (706) 724-1315; info@csracf.com
Internet: http://www.cfcsra.org/common/content.asp?PAGE=336
Sponsor: CSRA Community Foundation
P.O. Box 31358
Augusta, GA 30903

CSX Corporate Contributions Grants 1408
The program is focusing its support on personal safety education and community safety. In an effort to keep kids safe, CSX will support nonprofit organizations and school programs which help educate children and their parents on issues of personal safety, help keep children safe on the internet, teach railroad saety to children, teens and adults, and provide safe havens that keep children and adults safe from abuse. First responders are the key to a timely and effective manner of keeping a community safe. Safety, disaster, high alert and Hazmat training, equipment requirements of first responders, and projects and activities that keep communities safe, such as a fence around a neighborhood playground are supported. Programs that protect air, land and water resources in the communities in which CSX operates, preserve natural resources, and teach environmental stewardship to children and adults. A limited number of grants to local social service agencies and arts and culture organizations will be supported. Organizations in the targeted cities must submit an on-line application for sponsorship.
Requirements: 501(c)3 charities and government institutions, such as schools and libraries in their areas of operations are eligible.
Restrictions: Grants do not support individuals; galas, concerts, sports tournaments, auctions, lunches, banquets or dinners; film and video projects; churches or faith-based organizations whose projects benefit wholly their members or adherents; or organizations geographically falling outside of CSX's targeted giving areas. Operating costs or capital improvements are seldom supported.
Geographic Focus: Alabama, Connecticut, Delaware, Florida, Georgia, Illinois, Indiana, Kentucky, Louisiana, Maryland, Massachusetts, Michigan, Mississippi, New Jersey, New York, North Carolina, Ohio, Pennsylvania, South Carolina, Tennessee, Virginia, West Virginia
Contact: Ellen M. Fitzsimmons; (904) 359-3200; corporatecontributionsd@csx.com
Internet: http://www.csx.com/?fuseaction=general.csxog_giving
Sponsor: CSX Corporation
Office of the Corporate Secretary, 500 Water Street, C160
Jacksonville, FL 32202

CTCNet/Youth Visions for Stronger Neighborhoods Grants 1409
Youth Visions Grants are designed to give youth and community technology programs the opportunity to use multimedia tools and training to engage in community decision-making to strengthen their neighborhoods. Through the grants, organizations with substantial experience training youth in low-income communities will be funded to implement new or expanded community technology programs that focus on engaging youth in civic participation. Expected outcomes of the program are: a change in the

attitudes of participating youth as they realize their role in community problem-solving; an increased number of community members who perceive youth as vital assets to their neighborhoods' long-term health and success; and a robust curriculum and evaluation that can be distributed to CTCs throughout the United States. Grantees must be willing to take part in a participatory process aimed at building a strong curriculum and evaluation methodology that may be used by future sites engaged in the program. Application and guidelines are available online.
Requirements: 501(c)3 nonprofit organizations that serve at-risk youth (ages four to 18) and who have experience providing video and other multimedia training are eligible.
Geographic Focus: All States
Date(s) Application is Due: Sep 30
Amount of Grant: 20,000 USD
Contact: Tara Kumar, Program Associate; (617) 256-9226; tkumar@ctcnet.org
Internet: http://www.ctcnet.org/youthvisions
Sponsor: Community Technology Centers Network
1436 U Street NW, Suite 104
Washington, DC 20009

Cudd Foundation Grants 1410
The foundation awards grants to eligible nonprofit organizations in its areas of interest, including arts, culture, performing arts, children and youth, education, environment, health care, historic preservation, and social services. Types of support include annual campaigns, building construction/renovation, capital campaigns, continuing support, curriculum development, emergency grants, endowments, program development, research, and scholarship funds. The listed application deadline is for letters of intent; full proposals are by invitation.
Requirements: Louisiana and New Mexico nonprofit organizations are eligible.
Geographic Focus: Louisiana, New Mexico
Amount of Grant: 250 - 222,088 USD
Contact: Amanda Stuermer, (505) 986-8416; fax (505) 986-8427; cuddfdn@aol.com
Sponsor: Cudd Foundation
P.O. Box 2322
Santa Fe, NM 87504

Cullen Foundation Grants 1411
The foundation awards grants to eligible Texas nonprofit organizations in its areas of interest, including arts and culture, education, health, and public service programs. There are no application deadlines or forms. Proposals should detail the purpose and scope of the grant; the amount requested; other sources of anticipated funding; a list of trustees, directors, and staff; financial statements and tax returns of the last two years; and anticipated project budgets. Preference is given to requests from Houston.
Requirements: Texas 501(c)3 or 170(c) nonprofit organizations are eligible.
Restrictions: The board prefers not to consider galas, testimonials, and various other types of fundraising events; organizations that in turn make grants to others; activities whose sole purpose is the promotion or support of a specific religion, denomination, or church; purchase of uniforms, equipment, or trips for school-related organizations or amateur sports teams; applications from an organization more frequently than once every 12 months, whether the previous application was approved or denied; applications from an organization that has received a multi-year grant from the foundation, until all payments of that grant have been made; or oral presentations from potential applicants.
Geographic Focus: Texas
Amount of Grant: Up to 100,000,000 USD
Contact: Sue Alexander, Grant Administrator; (713) 651-8837; salexander@cullenfdn.org
Internet: http://www.cullenfdn.org
Sponsor: Cullen Foundation
601 Jefferson, 40th Floor
Houston, TX 77002

Cultural Society of Filipino Americans Grants 1412
The CSFA is a non-profit organization dedicated to the promotion and preservation of Filipino culture. Grants are made to local, regional, foreign or international organizations engaged in non-profit activities designed to improve the economic, social, emotional, physical, educational and mental well-being of members of stated organizations in fulfillment of the prescribed responsibility of CSFA.
Requirements: Grants will be made only to organizations that have evidence of 501(c)3 tax-exempt status or to organizations with the endorsement and support of a fiscal agent. In general, the Charitable Committee will look for projects or programs that: (1) fill a real need; (2) have clear, attainable, measurable objectives; (3) are likely to produce results which can be replicated or marketed; (4) are likely to reduce costs, increase revenues or otherwise pay for themselves over time; (5) propose activities which will continue after the grant period without additional funding; and, (6) contain a simple, workable, evaluation plan. The committee will give special consideration to project/programs which propose collaboration with other community organization.
Restrictions: Funds will not be given to individuals; organizations whose primary function is to influence legislation or the local, state or federal levels of government; political parties or candidates; churches or sectarian organizations; however, funds may be given to provide humanitarian aid/services on completely non-sectarian reasons.
Geographic Focus: All States
Amount of Grant: 500 - 1,000 USD
Contact: Jose Rivera, President; webmaster@csfamn.org
Internet: http://www.csfamn.org
Sponsor: Cultural Society of Filipino Americans
P.O. Box 2773
St. Paul, MN 55102

Cumberland Community Foundation Grants 1413
Cumberland Community Foundation is a nonprofit 501(c)3 charitable foundation established in 1980 by Dr. Lucile Hutaff. The Foundation has defined the following as areas of interest: arts, culture, & recreation; civic engagement; economic development & community advancement; education; environment; health & human services. Proposals accepted on a rolling basis and by request only. Contact the Grants Manager at (910) 483-4449 to discuss the proposed project. If project meets the foundation's criteria and is being considered for funding, a Data Form and Letter of Intent may then be submitted.
Requirements: The foundation will normally make grants only to 501(c)3 organizations in Cumberland County and surrounding counties in North Carolina. However, the Community Foundation remains open to proposals that identify emerging needs, even where needs assessment indicators have not yet been identified.
Restrictions: No grants are made from the Community Funds to or for: individuals; national fundraising drives; tickets for benefits or fundraising events; political organizations or candidates for public office; lobbying activities; endowment funds; scholarships; budget deficits / failure to raise adequate annual operating support; membership dues; religious organizations for religious purposes (community grants do not support programs/projects with religious content or purpose or buildings owned by religious organizations).
Geographic Focus: North Carolina
Contact: Rachel Stack Anderson; (910) 483-4449; rachel@cumberlandcf.org
Internet: http://www.cumberlandcf.org/grant_seekers.php
Sponsor: Cumberland Community Foundation
308 Green Street, P.O. Box 2345
Fayetteville, NC 28302-2171

Cumberland Community Foundation Summertime Kids Grants 1414
Cumberland Community Foundation is a nonprofit 501(c)3 charitable foundation established in 1980 by Dr. Lucile Hutaff. The Foundation has defined the following as areas of interest: arts, culture, & recreation; civic engagement; economic development & community advancement; education; environment; health & human services. The purpose of the Summertime Kids Grants is to provide nonprofit organizations, churches, or neighborhood associations funds so they may offer recreational and enrichment activities for children who otherwise would not have special summer opportunities. Programs funded through Summertime Kids generally serve children in Cumberland County, NC, who are from low-income families, live in remote areas, have disabilities, belong to a special population, or have been neglected or abused. Grants are awarded for activities and projects that serve the target population and are not covered by other funding sources. Requests should be for safe, rewarding activities for children and youth to be offered between June 1 and August 31 in Cumberland County, NC. Additional guidelines are available at: http://www.cumberlandcf.org/summer_kids_grants.php
Requirements: The foundation will normally make grants only to 501(c)3 organizations in Cumberland County and surrounding counties in North Carolina. However, the Community Foundation remains open to proposals that identify emerging needs, even where needs assessment indicators have not yet been identified.
Geographic Focus: North Carolina
Amount of Grant: 2,000 USD
Contact: Rachel Stack Anderson; (910) 483-4449; rachel@cumberlandcf.org
Internet: http://www.cumberlandcf.org/summer_kids_grants.php
Sponsor: Cumberland Community Foundation
308 Green Street, P.O. Box 2345
Fayetteville, NC 28302-2171

Cummins Foundation Grants 1415
The Foundation's areas of interest include: children and youth; education; elementary and secondary schools; civil rights; women; minorities; leadership development; increasing minority economic participation. Inquiries and proposals may be submitted in writing at any time during the year. A preliminary proposal should include a brief description of the problem being addressed, specifically what the program hopes to achieve, operating plan and cost, description of key leadership and how one will be able to tell whether or not the program worked. Upon receipt of the proposal, the Foundation staff will respond regarding the possibility of funding.
Requirements: The Foundation makes virtually all its local grants in communities where Cummins and its subsidiaries have manufacturing plants or affiliate businesses. These communities are: Columbus and Seymour, Indiana and their environs; Charleston, South Carolina; Jamestown, New York; Findlay, Ohio; Cookeville, Nashville and Memphis, Tennessee; Lake Mills, Iowa; Rocky Mount, North Carolina; El Paso, Texas; Fridley, Minnesota; Stoughton, Wisconsin. International grants are also reviewed by the Foundation Board. Proposals from the non-Indiana plant communities should be submitted first to the local plant manager or business leader.
Restrictions: The Foundation does not support political causes or candidates, or sectarian religious activities. No grants are made to individuals.
Geographic Focus: Indiana, Iowa, Minnesota, New York, North Carolina, Ohio, South Carolina, Tennessee, Texas, Wisconsin, Brazil, Japan, Mexico
Amount of Grant: 2,500 - 100,000 USD
Contact: Gayle Dudley Nay, (812) 377-3114; Cummins.Foundation@cummins.com
Internet: http://www.cummins.com/cmi/content.jsp?siteId=1&langId=1033&menuId=82&overviewId=5&menuIndex=0
Sponsor: Cummins Foundation
500 Jackson Street
Columbus, IN 47201

CUNA Mutual Group Foundation 1416

The corporation makes grants to programs and organizations that are of benefit to its subsidiaries; communities in which associates reside; and programs that are of benefit to Waverly, Bremer/Butler Counties, and Iowa (in that order). Priority areas include education, urban/civic services, human services, and the arts. Some multiyear grants will be awarded. The committee gives preference to programs in which associates and their families are involved and those involving more than just monetary funding.
Requirements: Iowa 501(c)3 organizations are eligible.
Restrictions: The committee will not consider grants for individuals; political parties, candidates, and partisan political campaigns; professional associations; operating expenses for organizations receiving United Way funding; or religious groups for religious purposes.
Geographic Focus: Iowa
Amount of Grant: 2,500 USD
Contact: Executive Director; (608) 231-7908
Internet: http://www.cunamutual.com/cmg/freeFormDetail/0,1248,888,00.html
Sponsor: CUNA Mutual Group Foundation
P.O. Box 391
Madison, WI 53701-0391

CUNA Mutual Group Foundation Grants 1417

The foundation awards focused grants to nonprofits in company operating locations in its areas of interest, including early childhood development, job training, affordable housing, and personal money management. Preference will be given to programs that involve CUNA employees, provide direct services, leverage funds, have measurable outcomes, and meet other criteria described on the application form. There are no application deadlines for grants up to $5000. For larger grants, allow at least six weeks before board meetings in February, May, and September. The foundation also offers Credit Union Movement Grants. Funding requests are accepted from credit union organizations to support their charitable causes. Preference is given to those activities or projects that are regional or national in scope. The foundation also offers Employee Involvement Grants. The Dollars for Doers program provides cash grants to 501(c)3 nonprofit organizations in which current and retired employees, and current board members, make a significant volunteer investment and a financial donation.
Requirements: Nonprofit organizations located in Iowa and Wisconsin are eligible.
Geographic Focus: Iowa, Wisconsin
Amount of Grant: 50 - 230,000 USD
Contact: Steven Goldberg, Executive Director; (800) 356-2644, ext. 7755; fax (608) 236-7755; steven.goldberg@cunamutual.com
Internet: http://www.cunamutual.com/cmg/freeFormDetail/0%2C1248%2C8174%2C00.html
Sponsor: CUNA Mutual Group Foundation
P.O. Box 391
Madison, WI 53701-0391

Curtis and Edith Munson Foundation Grants 1418

The Curtis and Edith Munson Foundation began making grants in 1987-88 with an emphasis on partnerships, collaborations and seed funding for new projects. Over 85% of the grant program is dedicated to the conservation of natural resources in North America and the Caribbean Basin with emphasis on the United States. Main programs areas are: Marine resource conservation and management with particular interest in fisheries; South Florida Ecosystems; Alabama environmental issues, Washington D.C. Metro area environmental issues; population and environmental issues.
Requirements: Non-profits with a IRS 501(c)3 letter and EIN number are eligible. No unsolicited grant proposals excepted, send a 1 - 2 page letter of inquiry and a project summary (form available on the Foundations website) to the Foundation before sending any additional materials. Letter of inquiry deadline dates are April 10th and September 11th. email inquires to info@munsonfdn.org. If invited, send in a proposal by May 15th and October 16, see Foundations website for guidelines.
Restrictions: Site specific grants are limited to South Florida and Alabama. No grants to individuals or endowment funds. Most grants are restricted and require a 1:1 match.
Geographic Focus: All States
Date(s) Application is Due: Apr 10; Sep 11
Amount of Grant: 10,000 - 80,000 USD
Contact: Angel Braestrup, (202) 887-8992; fax (202) 887-8987; info@munsonfdn.org
Internet: http://www.munsonfdn.org/guide.htm
Sponsor: Curtis and Edith Munson Foundation
1990 M Street NW, Suite 250
Washington, DC 20036

Curtis Foundation Grants 1419

The Curtis Foundation provides funding primarily in the Longview, Texas region of the United States. The Foundation's fields of interest include: arts; community/economic development; education; health care; health organizations; human services.
Requirements: Texas 501(c)3 nonprofit organizations are eligible for funding. There are no deadline dates, nor application form required, when submitting a proposal to the Foundation.
Restrictions: No grants to individuals.
Geographic Focus: Texas
Amount of Grant: 200 - 5,000 USD
Contact: Sue Curtis, President; (903) 757-2408
Sponsor: Curtis Foundation
P.O. Box 3188
Longview, TX 75606-3188

CVS All Kids Can Grants 1420

CVS Caremark and the CVS Caremark Charitable Trust will support nonprofit organizations that provide innovative programs and services that are focused on helping children with disabilities learn, play and succeed in life. The goals of CVS Caremark All Kids Can are to provide medical rehabilitation and related services to children with disabilities, to build barrier-free playgrounds so children of all abilities can play side-by-side; and to raise awareness in school and in local communities about the importance of inclusion.
Geographic Focus: All States
Date(s) Application is Due: Nov 30
Amount of Grant: 1,000 USD
Contact: Jennifer Veilleux, Director; (401) 770-4517 or (401) 770-4209; jhveilleux@cvs.com or CommunityMailbox@cvs.com
Internet: http://info.cvscaremark.com/community/our-impact/all-kids-can
Sponsor: CVS Caremark Charitable Trust
One CVS Drive
Woonsocket, RI 02895

CVS Caremark Charitable Trust Grants 1421

The trust has a goal of positively impacting the culturally diverse populations in the communities where CVS stores are located. Health programs that serve children (under the age of 18) with disabilities and address awareness, accessibility, early intervention, health and rehabilitative services are funded. Public schools (grades pre-K through 12) that are expanding programs promoting inclusion of children with disabilities in all aspects of school functions, including: student academic activities, extracurricular programs, and physical activity/play will be considered. Disabilities are impairments that limit one or more routine activities of daily living. Physical, developmental, and sensory disabilities are supported. The primary focus is on children with disabilities and health care for the uninsured. Application must be submitted online.
Requirements: 501(c)3 public charities as determined by the IRS are eligible. Organizations must benefit the customers and communities in the areas where the corporation operates, and demonstrate the specific ways that the organization benefits the community. Religious organizations are eligible for nonsectarian, nondenominational programs.
Restrictions: The trust does not provide funding for sectarian and religious organizations that do not serve the general public on a nondenominational basis; organizations that discriminate on the basis of race, color, gender, sexual orientation, age, religion, national or ethnic origin or physical disability; political or fraternal groups, social clubs, or any other organization that engages in any kind of political activity; sponsorship of sports teams; journal or program advertisements; organizations geographically located outside of CVS markets; sponsorships for music, film, and art festivals; or business expositions/conferences.
Geographic Focus: All States
Date(s) Application is Due: Jun 15
Contact: Jennifer Veilleux, Director; (401) 770-4517 or (401) 770-4209; jhveilleux@cvs.com or CommunityMailbox@cvs.com
Internet: http://info.cvscaremark.com/community/our-impact/charitable-trust
Sponsor: CVS Caremark Pharmacy Corporation
One CVS Drive
Woonsocket, RI 02895

CVS Community Grants 1422

CVS Caremark Pharmacy Community Grants target effective and innovative programs. Grants support programs that promote independence among children with disabilities including physical and occupational therapies, speech and hearing therapies, technology that will assist and recreational therapies. They also support public schools that promote inclusive programs in student activities and extracurricular programs and enrich the lives of children with disabilities. The Community Grants Program works to ensure that students are not left behind in school. Proposed programs must be fully inclusive where children with disabilities are full participants in early childhood, adolescent, or teenage programs along side their typically developing peers. CVS is also devoted to the principle of free play. The unstructured, spontaneous, voluntary activity that is so engaging for children's long been recognized as the most beneficial form. Proposed programs may include either physical activities or play opportunities and should address the specific needs of the population served. The CVS/pharmacy Community Grants Program assures that more uninsured people receive needed care that the care received is of higher quality, and that the uninsured are served by providers who participate in accountable community health care programs. There is no age limit on proposed programs that create greater access to health care services.
Requirements: All applicants must answer a number of questions before gaining access to the application. These questions help to determine if the program falls within the guidelines.
Restrictions: An EIN number must be provided before beginning the eligibility quiz for all non-profit organizations applying for a Community Grant for children under age 18 with disabilities. All public schools applying for a Community Grant for this type of program are not required to provide an EIN number. An EIN number must be provided before beginning the eligibility quiz for all non-profit organizations applying for a Community Grant for health care for uninsured people.
Geographic Focus: All States
Date(s) Application is Due: Oct 31
Amount of Grant: 5,000 USD
Contact: Jennifer Veilleux, Director; (401) 770-4517 or (401) 770-4209; jhveilleux@cvs.com or CommunityMailbox@cvs.com
Internet: http://info.cvscaremark.com/community/our-impact/community-grants
Sponsor: CVS Caremark Pharmacy Corporation
One CVS Drive
Woonsocket, RI 02895

Cyrus Eaton Foundation Grants 1423

The Cyrus Eaton Foundation is committed to providing financial support to qualifying non-profit organizations in Cleveland and northeast Ohio, whose programs enhance the quality of life in this area, and whose aims are in accord with those of our founder, the late Cyrus Eaton. The Foundation limits its funding to these priority areas: the arts; education; science; public affairs; conservation and restoration; health and social welfare. The Foundation's Board meets twice yearly to review grant applications: in June and in November. Submissions may be accepted by email, fax, or postal mail.
Requirements: Cleveland and northeast Ohio nonprofit organizations are eligible.
Restrictions: The foundation does not consider more than one proposal from the same organization within a twelve-month period, unless that organization is applying for an Impact Grant. Tickets or tables for events, municipalities or individuals will not be funded.
Geographic Focus: Ohio
Date(s) Application is Due: May 1; Oct 1
Amount of Grant: 1,000 - 15,000 USD
Contact: Raymond Szabo; (216) 320-2285; cyrus.eaton.foundation@deepcove.org
Internet: http://www.deepcove.org/Grants/guidelines.html
Sponsor: Cyrus Eaton Foundation
2475 Lee Boulevard, Suite 2B
Cleveland Heights, OH 44118

D.F. Halton Foundation Grants 1424

The foundation awards grants to nonprofit organizations in Charlotte, NC, and San Miguel County, CO, primarily in the areas of youth, education, social services, and the performing arts. Additional areas of interest include historical preservation, education, vocational education, business school education, substance abuse, cancer research, heart/circulatory diseases and research, human and family services, and community development. Grants are awarded for general operating support, annual campaigns, capital campaigns, and scholarship funds. There are no application deadlines or forms.
Requirements: Nonprofit organizations in North Carolina counties, including Mecklenburg, Union, Cleveland, Cabarrus, Stanly, Lincoln, and Gaston, may submit proposals. Nonprofit organizations in San Miguel county, CO. may also submit proposals.
Restrictions: No grants will be awarded to individuals.
Geographic Focus: Colorado, North Carolina
Contact: Dale Halton, President
Sponsor: D.F. Halton Foundation
P.O. Box 834
Ophir, CO 81426

D.V. and Ida J. McEachern Charitable Trust Grants 1425

The Trust was established to give a better start in life to all children, both educationally and physically. Most grants are made to social service agencies addressing basic human needs for children and youth. The Trust is also interested in providing creative and positive opportunities to enhance the lives of the region's children through a variety of artistic and cultural programs. The Advisory Committee prefers proposals from groups that clearly describe how their program makes a positive difference in the lives of children, provides a unique service, or addresses problems that are not being met by other agencies in the area. Grants will be made solely for capital projects and items of immediate and direct service to children. There is no letter of inquiry process. If your project fits the guidelines, submit a proposal letter with a narrative no longer than four pages.
Requirements: Grant organizations should: request capital support only (McEachern grants will generally not exceed 5% of a capital campaign budget); provide services to a broad cross-section of the population up to age 18; be established for at least five years (exceptions may be made for groups with strong community leadership and reputation, offering unique enrichment programs for children); serve Puget Sound region (particularly King, Pierce, and Snohomish Counties); have a secure and diverse funding base, with a majority of budget income derived from non-governmental sources.
Restrictions: Grants will generally not be made to endowment campaigns, individuals, private schools, public schools, day-care programs, political candidates, or religious institutions.
Geographic Focus: Washington
Date(s) Application is Due: Mar 8; Sep 8; Dec 8
Amount of Grant: 15,000 - 25,000 USD
Contact: Therese Ogle; (206) 781-3472; fax (206) 784-5987; oglefounds@aol.com
Internet: http://fdncenter.org/grantmaker/mceachern/guide.html
Sponsor: D.V. and Ida J. McEachern Charitable Trust
P.O. Box 3123
Seattle, WA 98114

D. W. McMillan Foundation Grants 1426

The D.W. McMillan Foundation, established in Alabama in 1956, supports organizations involved with children and youth services, health care, health organizations, homelessness, hospitals, human services, mental health and crisis services, residential and custodial care, hospices, people with disabilities, and the economically disadvantaged population. Giving is primarily centered in the states of Alabama and Florida. There are no specific deadlines, though applicants should submit proposals well before the annual board meeting on December 1. Applicants should begin by contacting the Foundation with a letter of inquiry. Final notification of awards are given by December 31 each year.
Geographic Focus: Alabama, Florida
Date(s) Application is Due: Nov 1
Contact: Ed Leigh McMillan II, Treasurer; (251) 867-4881
Sponsor: D.W. McMillan Foundation
329 Belleville Avenue
Brewton, AL 36426-2039

DAAD Research Grants for Doctoral Candidates and Young Academics and Scientists 1427

The Program provides young foreign academics and scientists with an opportunity to carry out a research project or a course of continuing education and training at a German state (public) or state-recognized higher education institution or non-university research institute. Research grants can be used to carry out; research projects at a German higher education institution for the purpose of gaining a doctorate in the home country; research projects at a German university for the purpose of gaining a doctorate in Germany; or research projects or continuing education and training, but without aiming at a formal degree/qualification. Depending on the project in question and on the applicant's work schedule, grants can be paid generally for between one and ten months, in the case of full doctoral programs in Germany for up to three years, and in exceptions for up to a maximum of four years. Applications for research grants to run for more than six months are decided once a year, and must be submitted by November 15. Applications by musicians, architects and visual artists must be submitted by November 1. Applications for research grants to run for up to six months are decided twice a year, and must be submitted by August 1 or November 15. At the earliest, the grant can begin 6 months after the date of application. Support can only be provided for the completion of a full doctoral program in Germany when special support policy reasons exist. Depending on the award holder's academic level, the program will pay a monthly award of 715 Euros (graduates holding a first degree) or 975 Euros (doctoral candidates). As a rule, the scholarship additionally includes certain payments towards health insurance coverage in Germany. Furthermore, the program generally will pay an appropriate flat-rate travel allowance, unless these costs are covered by the home country or by another funding source.
Requirements: Applications for DAAD research grants are open to excellently-qualified university graduates who hold a Diplom or Master's degree at the time they commence the grant-supported research and, in exceptional cases, graduates holding a Bachelor's degree or already holding a doctorate/PhD (post-docs). It is required that doctoral candidates wishing to take a doctorate/PhD in their home country will already have been admitted to an appropriate course at their home university. Besides previous study achievements, the most important selection criterion is a convincing and well-planned research or continuing education and training project to be completed during the stay in Germany and which has been coordinated and agreed with an academic supervisor at the chosen German host institute. German language skills are generally required, although the required level also depends on the applicant's project and topic, as well as on the available opportunities for learning German in the applicant's home country.
Restrictions: The award of grants is subject to an age limit of 32 years at the time of starting the grant.
Geographic Focus: All States
Date(s) Application is Due: Aug 1; Nov 1; Nov 15
Amount of Grant: 715 - 9,750 EUR
Contact: Administrator; (212) 758-3223; fax (212) 755-5780; kim@daad.org
Internet: http://www.daad.de/deutschland/foerderung/stipendiendatenbank/00462.en.html?detailid=7&fachrichtung=4&land=44&status=3&seite=1&daad=1
Sponsor: German Academic Exchange Service (DAAD)
871 United Nations Plaza
New York, NY 10017

Dade Community Foundation Community AIDS Partnership Grants 1428

The Community AIDS Partnership, is a special funding initiative established in 1990 through the National AIDS Fund and local funders to increase the availability of private funds to address gaps in the local HIV/AIDS service system, particularly in the area of prevention. The Community AIDS Partnership represents one of the major sources of private philanthropic funds for HIV prevention in Miami-Dade County. As the result of a public/private partnership with Miami-Dade County, the Foundation also awards $350,000 in county funds, which represents a significant increase in the local public sector's commitment to funding HIV prevention. Through the Community AIDS Partnership, the Foundation supports quality programs that respond to the local population risk profile and that incorporate strategies with the greatest potential to effectively address the priority populations, communities and service needs related to HIV prevention in Miami-Dade County. Grant Size: $30,000 Single Organization, $60,000 for Collaborations.
Requirements: Eligible applicants include nonprofit tax-exempt organizations, as defined by the Internal Revenue Code, which are serving the residents of Miami-Dade County. Preference will be given to or- ganizations based in Miami-Dade County or if located outside the county, are working in partnership with an organization based in Miami-Dade.
Geographic Focus: Florida
Amount of Grant: 30,000 - 60,000 USD
Contact: Gianne Ewing-Chow, Senior Program Officer; (305) 371-2711; fax (305) 371-5342; gianne.ewingchow@dadecommunityfoundation.org
Internet: http://www.dadecommunityfoundation.org/Site/wc/wc145.jsp
Sponsor: Dade Community Foundation
200 S Biscayne Boulevard, Suite 505
Miami, FL 33131-5330

Dade Community Foundation GLBT Community Projects Grants 1429

In collaboration with the National Gay and Lesbian Task Force in Washington, D. C. , Dade Community Foundation serves as a bridge to the Miami-Dade community, providing a vehicle for local grant making to gay and lesbian organizations. The GLBT Community Project Fund was created through an agreement between the NGLTF and the Gay and Lesbian Foundation of South Florida. The Fund's purpose is to advance education and public awareness with respect to GLBT issues and to support the local GLBT community. The Foundation annually considers proposals for GLBT Community Projects Fund Programs & Projects Grants that build community and address current and emerging needs within

the current funding priorities for the initiative, which are outlined in each year's guidelines. An organization may submit one proposal for which it would be the sole recipient of funding and also one proposal that represents a collaboration with other organizations in which the partners share responsibility for implementing the proposed activities and share grant funds on each partner's role.
Requirements: Applicant groups should be nonprofit organizations which: propose projects and programs that benefit Miami-Dade County residents; can clearly demonstrate involvement in addressing GLBT issues; have received IRS 502(c)(3) tax-exempt status; have a fiscal agent that is a tax-exempt organization; are a nonprofit, community group or assocation engaged in specific activities with a charitable purpose.
Geographic Focus: Florida
Date(s) Application is Due: Jul 17
Amount of Grant: 2,500 - 20,000 USD
Contact: Charisse Grant, Vice President for Programs; (305) 371-2711; fax (305) 371-5342; charisse.grant@dadecommunityfoundation.org
Internet: http://www.dadecommunityfoundation.org/Site/wc/wc205.jsp
Sponsor: Dade Community Foundation
200 S Biscayne Boulevard, Suite 505
Miami, FL 33131-5330

Dade Community Foundation Grants 1430
The funding for this program is made available through the Foundation's unrestricted and field of interest funds. This program is designed to honor both the donors interests and address significant community issues such as: education; health; human services; arts and culture; environment; economic development; at-risk youth; abused and neglected children; living with HIV/AIDS; homelessness; social justice; care of animals; heart disease and more.
Requirements: Eligible applicants include nonprofit tax-exempt organizations, as defined by the Internal Revenue Code, which are serving the residents of Miami-Dade County. Preference will be given to organizations based in Miami-Dade County or if located outside the county, are working in partnership with an organization based in Miami-Dade.
Restrictions: The Foundation does not provide grants to individuals, for memberships, fundraising events or memorials. Grants to government agencies are made on a very restricted basis.
Geographic Focus: Florida
Date(s) Application is Due: Nov 15
Amount of Grant: 7,500 USD
Contact: Charisse Grant, Vice President for Programs; (305) 371-2711; fax (305) 371-5342; charisse.grant@dadecommunityfoundation.org
Internet: http://www.dadecommunityfoundation.org/Site/programs/overview.jsp
Sponsor: Dade Community Foundation
200 S Biscayne Boulevard, Suite 505
Miami, FL 33131-5330

Dade Community Foundation Safe Passage Grants 1431
The Safe Passage Initiative represents a funding effort by Dade Community Foundation to make strategic investments toward improving the lives, opportunities and successful outcomes for youth transitioning from foster care to living independently. This includes focusing on foster care youth during the years they need to and should be receiving comprehensive preparation and the years after they have aged out of the system and must sustain themselves on their own. The primary goal is to help build the community's capacity to provide foster care youth with the preparation, support and permanent relationships they need to succeed in life on their own. Through this Request for Proposals the Foundation seeks to strengthen the array of community-based programs and resources that are not directly part of - but are working with - the state-funded child welfare system of care (i.e. Our Kids/contracted Full Case Management Agencies) that are available to serve and support youth in the target population. The initiative will award a limited number of grants up to $30,000 for a grant period of one year. This opportunity is made possible by the Foundation's DadeFund- a supporting organization of the Foundation.
Requirements: Applicant organizations must be able to demonstrate: current engagement in and a track record of success around programming with the target youth population and around any of the areas critical to success; a formal relationship (referral agreements, service contract, memorandum of understanding, etc.) that connects them with the state-funded child welfare system, or Our Kids/Full Case Management Agencies that allows applicants to consistently access youth in the target population; and/or defined relationships with other local entities that provide them strategic access to former foster care youth 18 to 23 who may or may not be receiving Independent Living services from the child-welfare system; a strategic position within the community- based on their role around this issue, the nature of their work, their ties to youth, etc. - to complement and enhance the current system of care and support; eligible applicants include tax-exempt organizations based in Miami-Dade County or if based outside the County are working in formal partnership with an eligible organization in Greater Miami.
Restrictions: The Foundation will be working directly with Our Kids of Miami-Dade, around strategies to strengthen the state-funded community-based system of care. Therefore, Full Case Management Agencies of the Our Kids network will not be eligible to apply for direct funding through this request for proposals.
Geographic Focus: Florida
Amount of Grant: Up to 30,000 USD
Contact: Charisse Grant, Vice President for Programs; (305) 371-2711; fax (305) 371-5342; charisse.grant@dadecommunityfoundation.org
Internet: http://www.dadecommunityfoundation.org/Site/wc/wc224.jsp
Sponsor: Dade Community Foundation
200 S Biscayne Boulevard, Suite 505
Miami, FL 33131-5330

DaimlerChrysler Corporation Fund Grants 1432
The fund contributes to organizations grouped under the general categories of education, health and human services, civic and community, religion, and culture and the arts. Within these categories, grants are made available for public welfare or for charitable, scientific, educational, environmental, safety, building, and affirmative action purposes. Higher education grants largely support science and engineering education and business management. A major interest of the corporation is the establishment of national certification standards for elementary and secondary teachers. Another area of concern is the encouragement of early reading skills, and a pilot project has been funded for research in this area. The fund earmarks funds for its future workforce initiatives, which support business and engineering departments, community-based job-skill training, and entry-level work preparation. Types of support include matching gifts, program grants, scholarships, annual campaigns, building construction/renovation, general support, and employee matching gifts. In considering requests, the fund evaluates each applicant organization on its own merits; considered are the programs in which it is engaged, constituencies served, operation procedures, services offered, quality of management, its accountability, finances, and fund-raising practices. Applications are accepted at any time.
Requirements: Eligible for support are nonprofit, tax-exempt educational, health, civic, and cultural organizations primarily in locations where the greatest number of employees of Chrysler and its US-based subsidiaries live and work (Alabama, Delaware, Illinois, Indiana, Michigan, Missouri, New York, Ohio, and Wisconsin). Some support is targeted for national organizations as well.
Restrictions: Grants are not awarded to support endowments, conferences, trips, direct health care delivery, multiyear pledges, capital campaigns, fund-raising activities related to sponsorships, advertising, or debt retirement.
Geographic Focus: All States
Contact: Brian Glowiak; (248) 512-2502; fax (248) 512-2503; mek@dcx.com
Internet: http://www.fund.daimlerchrysler.com
Sponsor: DaimlerChrysler Corporation Fund
1000 Chrysler Drive
Auburn Hills, MI 48326-2766

Dairy Queen Corporate Contributions Grants 1433
The Foundation's philosophy toward awarding contribution grants is to assist those organizations which have an impact on the company's home state of Minnesota and its communities and have programs geared toward children. Foundation focus is on: culture and the performing arts, education, health care and hospitals, and social welfare and community services. Application information is available online.
Requirements: U.S. nonprofits are eligible. Priority is given to Minnesota organizations.
Restrictions: Funds are not available for: strictly sectarian or denominational religious organizations; direct or indirect use for political purposes; lobbying activities; benefits and fund-raisers; commemorative, courtesy, institutional or any other form of advertising; organizations that tend to be for the benefit of the individual members, rather than the general public, such as fraternities, sororities, social clubs, labor organizations, parties and banquets; conferences, seminars or meetings; individuals or scholarships to individuals.
Geographic Focus: Minnesota
Date(s) Application is Due: Sep 1
Contact: Janelle Ianfolla; (952) 830-0207; fax (952) 830-0480; janelle.ianfolla@idq.com
Internet: http://www.dairyqueen.com/us-en/community/
Sponsor: Dairy Queen Corporation
7505 Metro Boulevard
Minneapolis, MN 55439-0286

Daisy Marquis Jones Foundation Grants 1434
The mission of the Foundation is to improve the well being of residents in Yates and Monroe counties, New York in particular, the City of Rochester. A central concern is disadvantaged children and families and the neighborhoods in which they live. The Foundation believes it can best serve those in need by granting time-limited support with programs or projects that provide access to health care, attend to the needs of young children, assist senior citizens, or help families develop economic security. The Foundation also looks for programs that: give people the tools they need to help themselves; encourage collaboration among agencies and between individuals and agencies; have measurable outcomes; and make long-term commitments to specific neighborhoods. A letter of inquiry is the first step to application and is available on line. The board reviews letters of inquiry once a month except July and August.
Requirements: Grants are awarded to qualified 501(c)3 nonprofit organizations that are located in Monroe and Yates Counties, NY.
Restrictions: Grants are not awarded to fund the arts, endowments, local chapters of national health-related organizations, private schools, religious projects, research, scholarships, projects by individuals, or organizations, projects not in Yates or Monroe Counties, or non 501(c)3 organizations.
Geographic Focus: New York
Contact: Roger Gardner, President; (585) 461-4950; fax (585) 461-9752; mail@dmjf.org
Internet: http://www.dmjf.org/funding.asp
Sponsor: Daisy Marquis Jones Foundation
1600 South Avenue, Suite 250
Rochester, NY 14620

Dale and Edna Walsh Foundation Grants 1435
The foundation joins hands with effective charitable organizations to meet human need and promote the common good worldwide. Grants support ministries, religious activities, health, relief efforts, education, community services, and arts organizations. Guidelines are available online.
Requirements: Tax-exempt, nonprofit charities are eligible.

Restrictions: The foundation does not contribute toward normal church operation; culturally liberal activist causes or organizations that primarily seek to influence legislation or government spending; or political parties or associated political organizations.
Geographic Focus: All States
Contact: Administrator; (847) 230-0056; fax (847) 901-9193; Info@dewfoundation.org
Internet: http://dewfoundation.org
Sponsor: Dale and Edna Walsh Foundation
6461 Valley Wood Drive
Reno, NV 89523

Dallas Foundation Grants 1436
The Foundation awards grants for a broad array of charitable purposes in the areas of the arts, education, health, social services, and general community that improve the well-being of the residents of the City and County of Dallas, Texas. The Foundation considers grant proposals for tax-exempt nonprofit organizations. Grants may be awarded for programs, which may include the salaries of program staff, or capital projects. Priority is given to proposals that: are likely to make a clear difference in the quality of life for a substantial number of people within Dallas County; and promote cooperation and collaboration among agencies in meeting critical needs.
Requirements: Non-profit organizations that benefit the citizens of Dallas County, TX area are eligible to apply.
Restrictions: Field of interest and Unrestricted funds are generally not available for: organizations that have received grants from Field of Interest or Unrestricted funds from the Foundation within the preceding three to five years; operating support, annual fund campaigns, and underwriting of fundraising events; religious purposes (although we do support educational and social service programs offered by faith-based organizations); organizations located outside Dallas County, unless at least 50 percent of the clients served are residents of Dallas County; debt retirement; research; scholarships; endowments; individuals. The Foundation cannot pledge future income, so multi-year grants will generally not be considered. Generally, awards are not granted for projects that are planned to begin more than one year from approval.
Geographic Focus: Texas
Contact: Shelley Fuld Nasso, Director of Community Philanthropy; (214) 741-9898, ext. 20; fax (214) 741-9848; sfuldnasso@dallasfoundation.org
Internet: http://www.dallasfoundation.org/gs_grantGuidelines.cfm
Sponsor: Dallas Foundation
900 Jackson Street, Suite 150
Dallas, TX 75202

Dallas Mavericks Foundation Grants 1437
The foundation of this National Basketball Association franchise makes grants in the Dallas, Texas, area for projects that provide education, good health, and leadership skills for kids. The foundation supports the programs and organizations in the Dallas-Fort Worth Metroplex that address the community's most pressing problems involving youth, specifically education, good health, and community service activity.
Requirements: To apply for an award, complete a grant application form which can be obtained on line. Include the supporting data: copy of IRS 501(c)3 final determination letter; fact sheet; current board roster; project timeline; project line-item detail budget; general operating budget. There is one grant cycle annually.
Restrictions: Grants will not be made to individuals, churches, public/private schools, or national organizations that do not have locally, financially independent chapters. Grants also will not be made for medical research, travel, salaries, operational phases of established programs, political campaigns or fundraising events, including the purchase of tables, tickets or advertisements. The Foundation would prefer not to commit funds for continued support of long-term programs lasting more than one year, endowment campaigns, administrative costs, advertising/fund raising drives, salaries for staff/individuals, intermediary funding agencies and/or research. The Foundation does not fund multi-year-grants.
Geographic Focus: Texas
Date(s) Application is Due: Jun 30
Contact: Dawn Holgate, (214) 658-7170
Internet: http://www.nba.com/mavericks/news/00405573.html
Sponsor: Dallas Mavericks Foundation
2909 Taylor Street
Dallas, TX 75226

Dallas Women's Foundation Grants 1438
The Foundation promotes women's philanthropy and raises money to support community programs that help women and girls realize their full potential. Priority will be given to funding programs that include elements of the following: effect long-term, positive changes to help women succeed in reaching their full potential; expanded choices and opportunities for women and girls; evaluation tools that include measurement for effectiveness with clean definition of program success; and programs specifically designed to take into consideration the gender-specific needs and differences of women and girls. The Foundation also encourages projects developed in consultation and collaboration with other agencies, and which promote coordination, cooperation and sharing among organizations. Effective use of volunteers, as well as Board diversity and involvement, are equally encouraged.
Requirements: To be eligible to receive a grant from the Foundation, applicants must meet all of the following criteria: be in receipt of a current 501(c)3 tax-exempt designation from the Internal Revenue Service (dated within the last 10 years); at least 50% of the population served must be residents of Dallas, Denton, or Collin County, with priority given to organizations serving residents of Dallas County; 75% of the clients benefiting from the grant funding must be women and/or girls.
Geographic Focus: Texas
Contact: Pat Alexander, (214) 965-9977; palexander@dallaswomensfoundation.org
Internet: http://www.dallaswomensfoundation.org/grants/highlights.html
Sponsor: Dallas Women's Foundation
4300 MacArthur Avenue, Suite 255
Dallas, TX 75209

Dammann Fund Grants 1439
The fund is committed to using its resources for the support of qualified charitable organizations operating programs in New York City, Southwestern Connecticut and Charlottesville, VA with a focus in any one or more of two areas: mental health - programs that foster living or independent living for the mentally ill; teen parenthood - programs that enable development of parenting skills in young parents. Grant recipients are eligible to receive funding for a single program for up to three consecutive years.
Requirements: Nonprofits in the greater New York City, Southwestern Connecticut and Charlottesville, VA.
Restrictions: Grants are not made to individuals and they are not made for capital or annual campaigns, endowments, loans, conferences or travel.
Geographic Focus: Connecticut, New York, Virginia
Date(s) Application is Due: Jun 30
Contact: Administrator; (212) 956-4118; fax (212) 262-9321; df@engelanddavis.com
Internet: http://www.thedammannfund.com/
Sponsor: Dammann Fund
521 Fifth Avenue, 31st Floor
New York, NY 10175

Dana Corporation Foundation Grants 1440
The foundation gives to communities throughout the country. Social services and education are top priorities. Most education grants are awarded to colleges and universities through a matching gifts program. Other grants go to civic affairs, environmental, youth, and health organizations with the smallest percentage awarded in the areas of culture and arts. Types of support include annual campaigns, building construction/renovation, continuing support, equipment acquisition, land acquisition, operating budgets, seed grants, and capital campaigns.
Requirements: 501(c)3 organizations in communities where Dana Corporation facilities are located are eligible.
Restrictions: The foundation does not make grants to individuals or to organizations that practice discrimination, religious groups for denominational purposes, political activities, or United Way-supported organizations for operating expenses. The foundation does not purchase tickets to charitable or fund-raising events or support goodwill advertising.
Geographic Focus: All States
Amount of Grant: 1,000 - 20,000 USD
Contact: Ed McNeal, (419) 535-4500
Internet: http://www.dana.com
Sponsor: Dana Corporation Foundation
P.O. Box 1000
Toledo, OH 43697

Dance Advance Grants 1441
The program, which supports dance projects in Pennsylvania's five-county region surrounding and including Philadelphia, is designed to cultivate artistic excellence, strengthen creative capacity, and promote professional standards in the area. One-year grants are awarded to individual choreographers and dance artists and dance organizations. Grants are awarded on a project basis (research and development, rehearsal and creation, production and presentation, and capacity-building projects) and not for unrestricted or general operating support. Complete guidelines and application are available online. Letters of intent are due September 21; full applications are due November 9.
Requirements: Grants are awarded to Philadelphia individual dance artists and 501(c)3 dance organizations in Bucks, Chester, Delaware, Montgomery, and Philadelphia counties. Individual applicants who are full-time employees of a university, college, or institution of higher learning may be considered.
Geographic Focus: Pennsylvania
Date(s) Application is Due: Sep 21; Nov 9
Amount of Grant: 10,000 - 20,000 USD
Contact: Administrator; (215) 732-9060; fax (215) 732-9057; info@danceadvance.org
Internet: http://www.danceadvance.org/02guidelines/index.html
Sponsor: Dance Advance
1500 Walnut Street, Suite 305
Philadelphia, PA 19102

Danellie Foundation Grants 1442
The foundation's primary areas of interest include services for the financially disadvantaged, including housing and social services. The types of support offered are: building/renovation; capital campaigns; continuing support; general/operating support; program development; scholarship funds and; sponsorships. Contact foundation for application guidelines. New York/New Jersey Area Common Application Form and New York/New Jersey Common Report Form accepted. Application form required.
Requirements: Nonprofit organizations in Southern New Jersey, (including Mercer and portions of Monmouth counties), the Greater Philadelphia, Pennsylvania area and, the Balimore, Maryland region are eligible to apply. The foundation also has an international interest in Guatemala and Haiti.
Restrictions: No support for political organizations or professional sports, libraries or museums. No grants to individuals, or for endowments or radio and television.
Geographic Focus: Maryland, New Jersey

Amount of Grant: 4,000 - 180,000 USD
Contact: Nancy Dinsmore, (856) 810-8320; danelliefoundation@verizon.net
Sponsor: Danellie Foundation
P.O. Box 376
Marlton, NJ 08053

Daniels Fund Grants 1443
The fund focuses its efforts on providing a better life and greater opportunities to thousands of individuals in Colorado, New Mexico, Utah, and Wyoming. The fund also supports national programs. The grants program addresses the following areas of need: aging, alcoholism and substance abuse, amateur sports, disabilities, education, homeless and disadvantaged, and youth development. Generally, national grants are reserved for projects with national impact, rather than projects in a single state. Grant applications are accepted at any time throughout the year, however, decisions are made quarterly.
Requirements: 501(c)3 nonprofit organizations in Colorado, New Mexico, Utah, and Wyoming—as well as nationwide—are eligible.
Restrictions: The fund generally will not support medical or scientific research; arts and cultural programs; candidates for public office; endowments; special events or fundraising events; or debt elimination.
Geographic Focus: Colorado, New Mexico, Utah, Wyoming
Contact: Program Officer; (303) 393-7220; fax (303) 393-7339; grantsinfo@danielsfund.org
Internet: http://www.danielsfund.org/Grants/index.asp
Sponsor: Daniels Fund
101 Monroe Street
Denver, CO 80206

Dan Murphy Foundation Grants 1444
The foundation awards grants to eligible nonprofit organizations in its areas of interest: support of activities and charities of Roman Catholic Church Archdiocese of Los Angeles, including education, health care, and social service programs. Types of support include building construction/renovation, capital support, continuing support, general operating support, matching grants, and program development. The majority of grants are awarded to Los Angeles, CA, nonprofits. There are no application forms or deadlines.
Geographic Focus: California
Contact: Daniel J. Donohue, President; (213) 623-3120
Sponsor: Dan Murphy Foundation
P.O. Box 711267
Los Angeles, CA 90071

Daphne Seybolt Culpeper Memorial Foundation Grants 1445
The Foundation, established in 1983, supports organizations involved with education, health care and human services. Giving is limited to Fairfield County, Connecticut and Palm Beach County, Florida. There are no specific deadlines with which to adhere. Contact the Foundation for further application information and guidelines.
Requirements: Nonprofits in Connecticut and Florida are eligible.
Restrictions: No grants to individuals, or for endowments, forums, conferences, seminars, gratuities, honorariums, travel, meals or lodging.
Geographic Focus: Connecticut, Florida
Contact: Nicholas Nardi, Secretary; (203) 762-3984
Sponsor: Daphne Seybolt Culpeper Memorial Foundation
129 Musket Ridge Road, P.O. Box 206
Norwalk, CT 06852-0206

Darden Restaurants Foundation Grants 1446
The Foundation only supports organizations that fit within its funding focus areas of arts & culture, social services & nutrition, education, and preservation of natural resources. Organizations must also align with the Foundation's core values: Integrity and Fairness; Respect and Caring: Diversity: Always Learning - Always Teaching; Being of Service; Teamwork; and Excellence. Grant applications are available online.
Requirements: Organizations located in the Central Florida area and Darden's Community Alliance Project (CAP) cities are eligible: Atlanta, Cincinnati, Chicago, Dallas, Detroit, Houston, Los Angeles, Miami, and Oklahoma City.
Geographic Focus: California, Florida, Georgia, Illinois, Michigan, Ohio, Oklahoma, Texas
Contact: Patty DeYoung; (407) 245-5213; fax (407) 245-4462; pdeyoung@darden.com
Internet: http://www.dardenrestaurants.com/com_gs_funding.asp
Sponsor: Darden Restaurants Foundation
P.O. Box 593330
Orlando, FL 32859-3330

Dave Coy Foundation Grants 1447
The foundation awards grants to Texas nonprofits in the areas of children and youth, social services for the economically disadvantaged, and religion (religious organizations, religious education, and religious welfare). Types of support include general operating support, capital campaigns, building construction/renovation, equipment acquisition, and emergency funds. Application forms are required.
Requirements: Nonprofits in Bexar County, TX, are eligible.
Restrictions: Grants are not made to individuals.
Geographic Focus: Texas
Date(s) Application is Due: Jun 1
Contact: Gregg Muenster, (210) 270-5371
Sponsor: Dave Coy Foundation
P.O. Box 121
San Antonio, TX 78291-0121

Davenport-Hatch Foundation Grants 1448
The general purpose of the foundation is to make grants to aid and support charitable, religious, educational, literary, or scientific nonprofit organizations in the Greater Rochester, NY, area. The foundation assists projects seeking funds for seed money or capital purposes. Any organization seeking funds must submit an explanation of the purpose for such requests, financial statements or budgets, and proof of tax-exempt status. The foundation generally meets during the second week of April, June, September, and December. Annual requests for funds are not encouraged.
Requirements: New York 501(c)3 organizations are eligible.
Restrictions: Local affiliates of national organizations are not eligible.
Geographic Focus: New York
Amount of Grant: 5,000 - 75,000 USD
Contact: Bill McKee, (716) 238-3340; fax (716) 232-2890
Sponsor: Davenport-Hatch Foundation
2200 Chase Square
Rochester, NY 14604

Dave Thomas Foundation for Adoption Grants 1449
The foundation supports advocacy and social service organizations working in the field of adoption. The primary goal of the foundation is to raise public awareness about children in the public welfare system awaiting adoption and to form public and private partnerships to make the adoption process easier and more affordable. Types of support include challenge/matching grants, conferences and seminars, demonstration grants, professorships, program development grants, research grants, seed money grants, and technical assistance. National, regional, or statewide projects will be considered. Priority will be given to projects that request seed money; include matching or other material support from other organizations, government agencies, or funders; coordinate service providers; include a measurement component to evaluate the project's success; and are easily replicable. Proposals are accepted throughout the year. Funding decisions are made four times per year. In order to receive serious consideration, proposals must be received by the submission deadline date for each quarter. Guidelines are available online.
Requirements: Eligible applicants are nonprofit 501(c)3 organizations.
Restrictions: The foundation will not consider funding individual adoption expenses; operating budgets or budget deficits; endowments or capital campaigns; adoption searches or reunions; scholarships; special events; institutions that discriminate on the basis of race, creed, gender, national origin, age, disability, or sexual orientation; or organizations engaged in sectarian religious activities. Unless solicited by the foundation, the following will not be considered: research, educational or promotional videos, publications, television productions, conferences, or public service announcements.
Geographic Focus: All States, Canada
Amount of Grant: 35,000 - 50,000 USD
Contact: Connie Ackert, Grants Director; (800) 275-3832; fax (614) 766-3871; connie_ackert@davethomasfoundation.org
Internet: http://www.davethomasfoundationforadoption.org
Sponsor: Dave Thomas Foundation for Adoption
525 Metro Place North, Suite 220
Dublin, OH 43017

David and Barbara B. Hirschhorn Foundation Grants 1450
Seeking to improve the lives of families and children and cultivate a level playing field, the David and Barbara B. Hirschhorn Foundation supports Jewish and secular initiatives that expand educational opportunity, address human service needs, and promote intergroup tolerance and understanding. Support is primarily given within the state of Maryland, providing grants of annual campaigns, capital campaigns, endowments, general/operating support. Letters of inquiry and proposals are accepted on a rolling basis. Your application will be acknowledged by postcard within two weeks.
Requirements: 501(c)3 non-profit organizations are eligible to apply. To begin the application process submit a letter of inquiry to the Foundation, no longer then 3 pages long. The initial application should include the following: information about the programs(s) for which funding is requested; need, purpose, activities, and evaluation plan of the proposed program(s); program budget (including sources of anticipated income as well as expenditure) and timeline; dollar amount of funding requested. Information about your organization: history, mission, and key accomplishments; information on Board members and key staff; current institutional operating budget (including major sources of revenue as well as expenditures); copy of IRS tax status determination letter or information about your fiscal agent. The Foundation will also accept initial applications that conform to the Association of Baltimore Area Grantmakers [ABAG] Common Grant Application.
Restrictions: No support available for: scholarships to individuals; unsolicited proposals for academic, scientific, or medical research; direct mail, annual giving, membership campaigns, fundraising and commemorative events.
Geographic Focus: All States
Amount of Grant: 2,500 - 350,000 USD
Samples: American Committee for Shaare Zedek Medical Center in Jerusalem, Baltimore, MD, $20,000; AMIT Women, Inc. New York, NY, $10,000; Institute for Christian and Jewish Studies, Inc., Baltimore, MD, $100,000;
Contact: Betsy Ringel, Executive Director; (410) 347-7103; fax (410) 347-7210; info@blaufund.org
Internet: http://www.blaufund.org/foundations/davidandbarbara_f.html
Sponsor: David and Barbara B. Hirschhorn Foundation
10 E Baltimore Street, Suite 1111
Baltimore, MD 21202

David Bohnett Foundation Grants 1451
The foundation's mission is to improve society through social activism. Focus areas include the promotion of the positive portrayal of lesbians and gay men in the media; voter registration activities; animal language research, animal companions, and eliminating rare animal trade; environmental conservation; the reduction and elimination of the manufacture and sale of handguns in the United States; community-based social services that benefit gays and lesbians; and the development of mass transit and non-fossil fuel transportation. Types of support include general operating support, program specific grants, seed money, and multiyear grants. Applicants should email a letter of inquiry to the program officer.
Requirements: Nonprofit organizations are eligible.
Restrictions: Grants do not support individuals, videos or other film productions, or organizations outside the United States.
Geographic Focus: All States
Date(s) Application is Due: Jan 27; Jul 28
Amount of Grant: 5,000 - 50,000 USD
Contact: Michael Fleming; (310) 277-4611; fax (310) 203-8111; mfpfleming@yahoo.com
Internet: http://www.bohnettfoundation.org/grants/grantapplication.htm
Sponsor: David Bohnett Foundation
2049 Century Park E, Suite 2151
Los Angeles, CA 90067-3123

David Geffen Foundation Grants 1452
The foundation supports nonprofits in Los Angeles, California, and New York, New York, with some giving in Israel as well. The Foundation offers support in its five principal funding areas: AIDS/HIV, civil liberties, the arts, issues of concern to the Jewish community, and health care. Support is provided for general operations and special projects. There are no application deadlines. Applicants are asked to submit a letter of request.
Requirements: 501(c)3 tax-exempt organizations in Los Angeles, CA, and New York, NY, may submit a proposal letter (without folder or binder) including description of the project, objectives, constituents served, evaluation criteria; background on the organization including key staff, volunteers, and board; copy of IRS letter confirming tax-exempt status; financial information including line-item budget for the project; and copy of non-discrimination policy from the organization's hiring guidelines.
Restrictions: The Foundation does not fund individuals, or organizations based outside of the United States. The foundation generally does not support documentaries or other types of audio-publication of books or magazines.
Geographic Focus: California, New York, Israel
Contact: J. Dallas Dishman; (310) 581-5955; fax (310) 581-5949; ddishman@geffenco.com
Sponsor: David Geffen Foundation
12011 San Vicente Boulevard, Suite 606
Los Angeles, CA 90049-4926

David N. Lane Trust Grants for Aged and Indigent Women 1453
The David N. Lane Trust for Aged & Indigent Women was established in 1964 to support and promote quality human services and health care programming for underserved older women living in Fairfield and New Haven Counties, Connecticut. Grants from the Lane Trust are one year in duration. Applicants must apply online at the grant website. Applicants are strongly encouraged to do the following before applying: review the downloadable state application procedures for additional helpful information and clarifications; review the downloadable online-application guidelines at the grant website; review the trust's funding history (link is available from the grant website); review the online application questions in advance; and review the list of required attachments. These will generally include: a list of board members, financial statements (audited, reviewed, or compiled by independent auditor); an organization summary; a list of other funding sources; an IRS Determination letter; and other required documents. All attachments must be uploaded in the online application as PDF, Word, or Excel files. The deadline for application to the David N. Lane Trust for Aged & Indigent Women is July 1. Applications must be submitted by 11:59 p.m. on the deadline date. Applicants will be notified of grant decisions by letter within two to three months after the proposal deadline.
Requirements: Applicant organizations must have 501(c)3 tax-exempt status and serve senior women in the counties of Fairfield or New Haven, Connecticut. A breakdown of number/percentage of individuals served by specific towns will be required in the online application.
Restrictions: Grant requests for capital projects will not be considered. The trust does not support requests from individuals, organizations attempting to influence policy through direct lobbying, or any political campaigns.
Geographic Focus: Connecticut
Date(s) Application is Due: Jul 1
Samples: TEAM, Derby, Connecticut, $10,000; Wesley Heights, Shelton, Connecticut, $9,000; VNA Health at Home, Watertown, Connecticut $3,000.
Contact: Kate Kerchaert; (860) 657-7016; kate.kerchaert@baml.com
Internet: https://www.bankofamerica.com/philanthropic/fn_search.action
Sponsor: David N. Lane Trust for Aged and Indigent Women
200 Glastonbury Boulevard, Suite # 200, CT2-545-02-05
Glastonbury, CT 06033-4056

David Robinson Foundation Grants 1454
Founded by David Robinson, a former National Basketball Association center who played his entire career for the San Antonio Spurs. The foundation awards grants to Texas nonprofit organizations in its areas of interest, including agriculture, family services, single parents, social services, and spirituality. The majority of grants will be awarded in the San Antonio area.
Requirements: Texas nonprofit organizations are eligible. Contributes only to pre-selected organizations.
Geographic Focus: Texas
Contact: Administrator; (210) 696-8061; drfoundation@express-news.net
Sponsor: David Robinson Foundation
24165 IH-10 West, Suite 217-628
San Antonio, TX 78257

Daviess County Community Foundation Arts and Culture Grants 1455
The Foundation considers proposals for grants on a yearly cycle, which begins each May. At the start of each cycle, a notice is mailed to nonprofit organizations that have applied for grants in the past, have received grants in the past, or have otherwise requested notification of the start of each cycle. Grants in the area of arts and culture include activities that strengthen the stability of arts organizations, make the arts accessible to low-income populations, enhance the understanding of all types of arts and humanities, and promote the appreciation or understanding of historical events. Samples of previously funded projects are posted on the website.
Requirements: The letter of inquiry is the required first step in submitting funding requests. Nonprofits that have submitted a letter of inquiry and been invited to submit a full proposal must attend one of the orientation sessions. The Foundation welcomes proposals from nonprofit organizations that are deemed tax-exempt under sections 501(c)3 and 509(a) of the Internal Revenue Code and from governmental agencies serving the County of Daviess, Indiana. Proposals from nonprofit organizations not classified as a 501(c)3 public charity may be considered provided the project is charitable and supports a community need.
Restrictions: Funding is not available for the following: religious organizations for strictly religious purposes; political parties or campaigns; endowment creation or debt reduction; operating costs (not directly related to the proposed project or program); capital campaigns; annual appeals or membership contributions; travel requests for groups or individuals such as bands, sports teams, or classes. Not more than 20% of any grant request may be for personnel costs, office supplies, or other operating costs. Operating costs for any organization must be directly related to the project or program for which funding is being requested.
Geographic Focus: Indiana
Contact: Jeanne Fields; (812) 254-9354; jeanne@daviesscommunityfoundation.org
Internet: http://www.daviesscommunityfoundation.org/program-areas
Sponsor: Daviess County Community Foundation
320 East Main Street, P.O. Box 302
Washington, IN 47501

Daviess County Community Foundation Environment Grants 1456
The Foundation considers proposals for grants on a yearly cycle, which begins each May. At the start of each cycle, a notice is mailed to nonprofit organizations that have applied for grants in the past, have received grants in the past, or have otherwise requested notification of the start of each cycle. Grants in the area of Environment include activities that: foster pollution control and abatement; protect and conserve natural resources; support botanic and horticulture programs; provide environmental beautification; provide for the preservation of open spaces; offer environmental education and outdoor survival skills; support protection and welfare of animals; help fund humane societies; support wildlife preservation and protection; enhance veterinary services; fund zoos and aquariums; and support specialty animal services. Samples of previously funded projects are available at the website.
Requirements: The letter of inquiry is the required first step in submitting funding requests. Nonprofits that have submitted a letter of inquiry and been invited to submit a full proposal must attend one of the orientation sessions. The Foundation welcomes proposals from nonprofit organizations that are deemed tax-exempt under sections 501(c)3 and 509(a) of the Internal Revenue Code and from governmental agencies serving the County of Daviess, Indiana. Proposals from nonprofit organizations not classified as a 501(c)3 public charity may be considered provided the project is charitable and supports a community need.
Restrictions: Funding is not available for the following: religious organizations for strictly religious purposes; political parties or campaigns; endowment creation or debt reduction; operating costs (not directly related to the proposed project or program); capital campaigns; annual appeals or membership contributions; travel requests for groups or individuals such as bands, sports teams, or classes. Not more than 20% of any grant request may be for personnel costs, office supplies, or other operating costs. Operating costs for any organization must be directly related to the project or program for which funding is being requested.
Geographic Focus: Indiana
Contact: Jeanne Fields; (812) 254-9354; jeanne@daviesscommunityfoundation.org
Internet: http://www.daviesscommunityfoundation.org/program-areas
Sponsor: Daviess County Community Foundation
320 East Main Street, P.O. Box 302
Washington, IN 47501

Daviess County Community Foundation Health Grants 1457
The Foundation considers proposals for grants on a yearly cycle, which begins each May. At the start of each cycle, a notice is mailed to nonprofit organizations that have applied for grants in the past, have received grants in the past, or have otherwise requested notification of the start of each cycle. Grants in the area of health include activities that: improve and promote health outcomes; provide general and rehabilitative health services; offer mental health services; provide crisis intervention programs; strengthen associations or services associated with specific diseases, disorders, and medical disciplines; and support medical research. Samples of previously funded projects are posted on the website.
Requirements: The Foundation welcomes proposals from nonprofit organizations that are deemed tax-exempt under sections 501(c)3 and 509(a) of the Internal Revenue Code and from governmental agencies serving the County of Daviess, Indiana. Proposals from nonprofit organizations not classified as a 501(c)3 public charity may be considered provided the project is charitable and supports a community need.
Restrictions: Funding is not available for the following: religious organizations for strictly religious purposes; political parties or campaigns; endowment creation or debt reduction;

operating costs (not directly related to the proposed project or program); capital campaigns; annual appeals or membership contributions; travel requests for groups or individuals such as bands, sports teams, or classes. Not more than 20% of any grant request may be for personnel costs, office supplies, or other operating costs. Operating costs for any organization must be directly related to the project or program for which funding is being requested.
Geographic Focus: Indiana
Contact: Jeanne Fields; (812) 254-9354; jeanne@daviesscommunityfoundation.org
Internet: http://www.daviesscommunityfoundation.org/program-areas
Sponsor: Daviess County Community Foundation
320 East Main Street, P.O. Box 302
Washington, IN 47501

Daviess County Community Foundation Human Services Grants   1458
The Foundation considers proposals for grants on a yearly cycle, which begins each May. At the start of each cycle, a notice is mailed to nonprofit organizations that have applied for grants in the past, have received grants in the past, or have otherwise requested notification of the start of each cycle. Grants in the area of Human Services include activities that: maximize the functioning of special needs populations in mainstream society; protect the public (crime and delinquency prevention, legal administration, legal services); promote and support employment and jobs, food and nutrition, agriculture, housing and shelter, public safety, and disaster preparedness and relief; and support the United Way, firefighting activities, and Future Farmers of America. Samples of previously funded projects are available at the website.
Requirements: The letter of inquiry is the required first step in submitting funding requests. Nonprofits that have submitted a letter of inquiry and have been invited to submit a full proposal must attend one of the orientation sessions. The Foundation welcomes proposals from nonprofit organizations that are deemed tax-exempt under sections 501(c)3 and 509(a) of the Internal Revenue Code and from governmental agencies serving the County of Daviess, Indiana. Proposals from nonprofit organizations not classified as a 501(c)3 public charity may be considered provided the project is charitable and supports a community need.
Restrictions: Funding is not available for the following: religious organizations for strictly religious purposes; political parties or campaigns; endowment creation or debt reduction; operating costs (not directly related to the proposed project or program); capital campaigns; annual appeals or membership contributions; travel requests for groups or individuals such as bands, sports teams, or classes. Not more than 20% of any grant request may be for personnel costs, office supplies, or other operating costs. Operating costs for any organization must be directly related to the project or program for which funding is being requested.
Geographic Focus: Indiana
Contact: Jeanne Fields; (812) 254-9354; jeanne@daviesscommunityfoundation.org
Internet: http://www.daviesscommunityfoundation.org/program-areas
Sponsor: Daviess County Community Foundation
320 East Main Street, P.O. Box 302
Washington, IN 47501

Daviess County Community Foundation Recreation Grants   1459
The Foundation considers proposals for grants on a yearly cycle, which begins each May. At the start of each cycle, a notice is mailed to nonprofit organizations that have applied for grants in the past, have received grants in the past, or have otherwise requested notification of the start of each cycle. Grants in the area of Recreation includes projects aimed at improving and promoting recreational and leisure activities, parks, and community sporting events and activities. Samples of previously funded projects are available at the website.
Requirements: The letter of inquiry is the required first step in submitting funding requests. Nonprofits that have submitted a letter of inquiry and been invited to submit a full proposal must attend one of the orientation sessions. The Foundation welcomes proposals from nonprofit organizations that are deemed tax-exempt under sections 501(c)3 and 509(a) of the Internal Revenue Code and from governmental agencies serving the County of Daviess, Indiana. Proposals from nonprofit organizations not classified as a 501(c)3 public charity may be considered provided the project is charitable and supports a community need.
Restrictions: Funding is not available for the following: religious organizations for strictly religious purposes; political parties or campaigns; endowment creation or debt reduction; operating costs (not directly related to the proposed project or program); capital campaigns; annual appeals or membership contributions; travel requests for groups or individuals such as bands, sports teams, or classes. Not more than 20% of any grant request may be for personnel costs, office supplies, or other operating costs. Operating costs for any organization must be directly related to the project or program for which funding is being requested.
Geographic Focus: Indiana
Contact: Jeanne Fields; (812) 254-9354; jeanne@daviesscommunityfoundation.org
Internet: http://www.daviesscommunityfoundation.org/program-areas
Sponsor: Daviess County Community Foundation
320 East Main Street, P.O. Box 302
Washington, IN 47501

Daviess County Community Foundation Youth Development Grants   1460
The Foundation considers proposals for grants on a yearly cycle, which begins each May. At the start of each cycle, a notice is mailed to nonprofit organizations that have applied for grants in the past, have received grants in the past, or have otherwise requested notification of the start of each cycle. Grants in the area of Youth Development include activities that strengthen the family unit, help children grow and develop, foster youth sports and athletics, support the YMCA, and support daycare-related issues. Samples of previously funded projects are available at the website.
Requirements: The letter of inquiry is the required first step in submitting funding requests. Nonprofits that have submitted a letter of inquiry and been invited to submit a full proposal must attend one of the orientation sessions. The Foundation welcomes proposals from nonprofit organizations that are deemed tax-exempt under sections 501(c)3 and 509(a) of the Internal Revenue Code and from governmental agencies serving the County of Daviess, Indiana. Proposals from nonprofit organizations not classified as a 501(c)3 public charity may be considered provided the project is charitable and supports a community need.
Restrictions: Funding is not available for the following: religious organizations for strictly religious purposes; political parties or campaigns; endowment creation or debt reduction; operating costs (not directly related to the proposed project or program); capital campaigns; annual appeals or membership contributions; travel requests for groups or individuals such as bands, sports teams, or classes. Not more than 20% of any grant request may be for personnel costs, office supplies, or other operating costs. Operating costs for any organization must be directly related to the project or program for which funding is being requested.
Geographic Focus: Indiana
Contact: Jeanne Fields; (812) 254-9354; jeanne@daviesscommunityfoundation.org
Internet: http://www.daviesscommunityfoundation.org/program-areas
Sponsor: Daviess County Community Foundation
320 East Main Street, P.O. Box 302
Washington, IN 47501

Davis Conservation Foundation Grants   1461
The foundation's broad purpose is to support the wise utilization, protection, and advancement of the physical environment and the different natural forms of life that inhabit it, including wildlife, sea life, and mankind as they are impacted by the environment. The foundation is primarily interested in projects related to wildlife, wildlife habitat, environmental protection, and outdoor recreation; projects that strengthen volunteer activity and outreach/community involvement in the stated areas; and projects related to the Northern Forest and the Gulf of Maine. Application and guidelines are available online.
Requirements: The foundation supports charitable organizations located primarily in northern New England (Maine, New Hampshire, Vermont and Massachusetts).
Restrictions: The foundation infrequently makes grants to organizations located in other parts of New England and rarely to organizations located outside of New England.
Geographic Focus: Connecticut, Maine, Massachusetts, New Hampshire, Rhode Island, Vermont
Date(s) Application is Due: Apr 10; Oct 10
Samples: Acadia Partners for Science and Learning, Winter Harbor, Maine, $10,000; Cape Nordic, Cape Elizabeth, Maine, $5,000; Friends of Silvio Conte National Fish and Wildlife Refuge, Harrisville, New Hampshire, $5,000.
Contact: Anne Vaillancourt; (207) 781-5504; info@davisfoundations.org
Internet: http://www.davisfoundations.org/site/conservation.asp
Sponsor: Davis Conservation Foundation
4 Fundy Road
Falmouth, ME 04105

Davis Family Foundation Grants   1462
The foundation provides grants primarily to Maine-based educational, medical, and cultural/arts charitable organizations in support of a wide variety of worthwhile projects. Eligible educational organizations include: colleges, universities, and other educational institutions. Eligible medical organizations include: hospitals, clinics and medical research organizations (grant requests will also be considered from other similar health organizations for programs designed to increase the effectiveness or decrease the cost of medical care). Eligible cultural and arts organizations include: those agencies whose customary and primary activity is to promote music, theater, drama, history, literature, the arts or other similar cultural activities. Further guidelines are available online.
Requirements: Eligible educational organizations include colleges, universities, and other educational institutions (grants are not made to public elementary and secondary schools, nor to schools whose financial support is derived primarily from a church or other religious organization. Trustees will consider grant requests from other educational organizations whose purpose is to promote systemic change in education or to provide innovative programs whose objectives are to improve education). Medical organizations eligible for support include hospitals, clinics, and medical research organizations. Grant requests will also be considered from other similar health organizations for programs designed to increase the effectiveness or decrease the cost of medical care. Eligible cultural/arts organizations include organizations whose customary and primary activity is to promote music, theater, drama, history, literature, the arts, or other similar cultural activities.
Restrictions: The Foundation does not make grants to individuals, religious programs, fellowships, or in the form of loans. The Foundation does not normally provide support for annual giving campaigns or general operating needs. Grants to endowment campaigns have a low priority.
Geographic Focus: Maine
Date(s) Application is Due: Feb 10; May 10; Aug 10; Nov 10
Contact: Anne Vaillancourt; (207) 781-5504; info@davisfoundations.org
Internet: http://www.davisfoundations.org/site/family.asp
Sponsor: Davis Family Foundation
4 Fundy Road
Falmouth, ME 04105

Dayton Foundation Grants   1463
The community foundation awards grants to a full spectrum of 501(c)3 tax-exempt nonprofit organizations - from social service to the arts to health and the environment - based upon worthy community efforts and the greatest community need. Generally grants are awarded to help launch new projects not addressed by existing organizations or to support special efforts of already-established not-for-profit organizations in the Miami Valley. The Foundation gives priority to projects that meet one or more of the following criteria: provides for more efficient use of community resources, promotes coordination, cooperation and sharing among organizations and reduces the duplication of services in the community;

tests or demonstrates new approaches and techniques for solving important community problems; promotes volunteer participation and citizen involvement in community affairs; and strengthens not-for-profit agencies and institutions by reducing operating costs, increasing public financial support and/or improving internal management. Letters of Intent are to be submitted through the LOI online system. Information is available online.
Requirements: Programs considered for discretionary support are located primarily in Montgomery, Miami, Greene, Darke and Preble counties. Eligible organizations must be: recognized as a 501(c)3 tax-exempt nonprofit organization, according to the Internal Revenue Code; benefit the citizens in the Dayton/Greater Miami Valley region; have a diversity/inclusion policy, and; address needs that are not met fully by existing organizational or community resources.
Restrictions: Generally, discretionary grants are not awarded for: general organizational operations; individuals; scientific, medical or academic research; operational deficits; religious/sectarian causes; scholarships or travel; fundraising drives; special events; political activities; public or private schools, endowment funds. Also, multi-year commitments rarely are considered.
Geographic Focus: Ohio
Date(s) Application is Due: Mar 30; Jun 27; Jul 13; Sep 28; Nov 27
Contact: Jo Dech, (937) 225-9976; jdech@daytonfoundation.org
Internet: http://www.daytonfoundation.org
Sponsor: Dayton Foundation
2300 Kettering Tower
Dayton, OH 45423-1395

Dayton Power and Light Foundation Grants 1464
The foundation contributes general operating grants to nonprofit organizations in the greater Dayton, OH, area in support of education and charitable activities and programs. Education grants are made to support adult basic education/literacy-skills development and engineering school education. Direct donations are made to civic, cultural, and health and welfare organizations that do not participate in community funds, such as United Way or community chests, but serve a real need. There is no official application form. Requests should be made in writing and must include a description of the history, structure, purpose, and program of the organization and a summary of the support needed and how it will be used. Contributions are planned a year in advance and based on a calendar-year budget. The distribution committee normally meets quarterly.
Requirements: 501(c)3 organizations in the greater Dayton, OH, area are eligible.
Restrictions: The foundation prefers not to support capital campaigns; college fund-raising associations; conduit organizations; endowment or development funds; fraternal, labor, or veterans organizations; hospital operating budgets; individual members of federated campaigns; individuals; national organizations outside the DP&L service territory; religious organizations; sports leagues; or telephone or mass-mail solicitations. Grants are rarely made to tax-supported institutions.
Geographic Focus: Ohio
Amount of Grant: 1,000 - 20,000 USD
Contact: Ginny Strausburg, Executive Director; (937) 259-7925; fax (937) 259-7923
Internet: http://www.waytogo.com/cc/cc.phtml
Sponsor: Dayton Power and Light Company Foundation
1065 Woodman Drive
Dayton, OH 45432

Daywood Foundation Grants 1465
The Foundation distributes available funds primarily to community service organizations focusing on the arts, and health and human services. Grants are available in the following types: annual campaigns; building/renovation; capital campaigns; continuing support; debt reduction; emergency funds; equipment; general/operating support; matching/challenge support; seed money.
Requirements: Nonprofit 501(c)3 organizations situated in, and benefiting Charleston, Lewisburg, Barbour, Greenbrier and Kanawha counties Of West Virginia are eligible to apply. There is no standardized grant application form. Send proposal to: William W. Booker, 1500 Chase Tower, Charleston, WV 25301.
Restrictions: Grants do not support endowment funds, research, individuals, or individual scholarships or fellowships.
Geographic Focus: West Virginia
Date(s) Application is Due: Sep 15
Contact: William W. Booker, Treasurer; (304) 343-4841
Sponsor: Daywood Foundation
707 Virginia Street E, Suite 1600
Charleston, WV 25301

DB Americas Foundation Grants 1466
Based in New York City, where the majority of grants are awarded, the foundation supports nonprofit organizations that concentrate on community development, education, and the arts. Areas of focus include: affordable housing; housing the homeless; supporting the creation of new businesses; teacher training and development; financial literacy; opportunities for disadvantaged youth; jobs in the arts; and increasing the visibility of a community as a cultural destination.
Requirements: To be considered for a grant, U.S. applicants must be nonprofit, tax-exempt organizations serving locations in which Deutsche Bank conducts business and has a grant-making program. Applicants from Canada and Latin America being considered for funding will be asked to submit a signed and sworn affidavit verifying equivalency eligibility.
Restrictions: The Foundation does not provide grants in support of endowment and capital campaigns; individuals (e.g., scholarships, expeditions); legal advocacy; political parties or their candidates; religious work of churches or sectarian organizations; United Way and pass through-funded agencies, unless they provide a fund-raising waiver from the United Way or pass through organization; veterans' and fraternal organizations; military organizations; professional and trade associations; individual artists, films, and the performing arts; and organizations that are not in full compliance with the anti-terrorism laws legislated by the USA PATRIOT Act.
Geographic Focus: All States
Contact: Grants Administrator; (212) 250-7065
Internet: http://www.community.db.com/
Sponsor: Deutsche Bank Americas Foundation
60 Wall Street, NYC60-2110
New York, NY 10005

Deaconess Community Foundation Grants 1467
The foundation awards grants to eligible Ohio nonprofit organizations in its areas of interest, including health, education, welfare, community, and social service activities. Proposals that are of greatest interest to the Foundation are those that have the strongest fit to the mission statement and that have some or all of the following characteristics: projects that have specific measurable outcomes and a tangible ability to evaluate results and measure success; projects that are supported by other funding sources; and projects that have identified potential for ongoing support beyond the life of the grant. Application information is available online.
Requirements: Only qualified non-profit organizations located in Cuyahoga County which are classified by the Internal Revenue Code as tax-exempt 501(c)3 organizations are eligible for funding consideration.
Restrictions: Grant requests for the following will not be considered: individuals, governmental agencies or any other organization that is not a tax exempt 501(c)3 organization; internal operations and capital campaigns of churches; research projects; or endowments. Grant funds may not be used to carry on propaganda or otherwise attempt to influence legislation, participate in, or intervene in, any political campaign on behalf of or in opposition to any candidate for public office, or to conduct, directly or indirectly, any voter registration drive (within the meaning of Section 4945(d)2 of the Internal Revenue Code).
Geographic Focus: Ohio
Date(s) Application is Due: Jan 15; May 15; Sep 15
Contact: Deborah Vesy; (216) 741-4077; fax (216) 741-6042; dvesy@deacomfdn.org
Internet: http://www.deacomfdn.org/guidelines.html
Sponsor: Deaconess Community Foundation
7575 Northcliff Avenue, Suite 203
Brooklyn, OH 44144

Deaconess Foundation Advocacy Grants 1468
The Deaconess Foundation's community capacity building initiative will include a series of investments designed to make the well-being of low-income children a civic priority. In its initial year, the Foundation will allocate nearly $400,000 to build the region's capacity for aligned work. The advocacy grants are part of Deaconess' evolving community capacity building strategy, which builds on the Foundation's work in recent years to assist individual child-focused organizations to become stronger and more effective agents of positive change for children. Deaconess Foundation intends to award approximately 10 organizations with grants of up to $15,000. This first round of advocacy grants is meant to spark much-needed advocacy on behalf of children, and to help the Foundation learn more about agencies pursuing this important work.
Requirements: Organizations that are eligible to apply for Deaconess Foundation's advocacy grants include: nonprofits whose primary mission is related to health/well-being of children and youth; nonprofits whose primary mission is related to impacting policy through advocacy, community organizing and/or convening; and networks with a designated nonprofit fiscal agent. Organizations from outside the St. Louis metropolitan area may propose a project; however, projects must have primary impact within Deaconess Foundation's giving area: St. Louis City and St. Louis County in Missouri, and St. Clair and Madison Counties in Illinois.
Geographic Focus: Illinois, Missouri
Date(s) Application is Due: Jun 3
Amount of Grant: Up to 15,000 USD
Contact: Rev. Starsky D. Wilson, President; (314) 436-8001; fax (314) 436-5352; starskyw@deaconess.org or info@deaconess.org
Internet: http://www.deaconess.org/CongregationalHealthGrants_17.aspx
Sponsor: Deaconess Foundation
211 N Broadway, Suite 1260
Saint Louis, MO 63102

Dean Foods Community Involvement Grants 1469
The company's community support efforts are focused in three main areas: health/nutrition (including hunger); education/arts; and environmental stewardship/conservation. It supports worthy organizations both at the corporate level and locally through its network of processing facilities nationwide. Preference is given to supporting and participating in a meaningful way with a limited number of organizations that support these three focus areas, rather than spreading limited resources more broadly. Specifically, funding goes to programs that provide direct service to individuals and communities in need. The corporation places special emphasis on supporting organizations that assist children, particularly at-risk children or children with disabilities, or that are dedicated to serving their needs. As a point of contact, the corporate headquarters requests that no phone calls be made regarding its giving programs.
Requirements: 501(3)3 tax-exempt organizations are eligible. Applications must provide background information on the organization as well as how it relates to the mission of Dean Foods. The corporation supports initiatives only in the communities in which they operate and where employees live and work.

Geographic Focus: Alabama, California, Colorado, Connecticut, Florida, Georgia, Hawaii, Idaho, Illinois, Indiana, Kentucky, Louisiana, Maine, Maryland, Massachusetts, Michigan, Minnesota, Montana, Nebraska, Nevada, New Jersey, New Mexico, New York, North Carolina, North Dakota, Ohio, Oklahoma, Pennsylvania, South Carolina, South Dakota, Tennessee, Texas, Utah, Virginia, Wisconsin
Contact: Gregg Engles, Chief Executive Officer; (214) 303-3400; fax (214) 303-3499
Internet: http://www.deanfoods.com/our-company/about-us/corporate-responsibility.aspx
Sponsor: Dean Foods
2515 McKinney Avenue, Suite 1200
Dallas, TX 75201

Dearborn Community Foundation City of Aurora Grants 1470
The City of Aurora Grant Program awards grants to not-for-profit organizations for projects that directly benefit the residents of the City of Aurora. Grants from organizations such as fire departments and emergency units may take priority over other grant requests. Entities that provide specific services for the City of Aurora are also eligible to apply. Examples of the types of services include: economic development, EMS, historic preservation, housing, technical assistance, transportation and youth services.
Requirements: Grants are awarded only to organizations whose programs benefit the residents of Dearborn County, Indiana and which provide for a responsible fiscal agent and adequate accounting procedures. All questions relating to available scholarship/educational grant opportunities should be directed to the DCF Program Director.
Restrictions: The grant review process for some grant programs takes up to three months from the grant application due date. Applicants should plan accordingly when considering the date of the project and the date of the grant submission. It is strongly suggested that all applicants consult the Foundation before submitting a grant application to ensure eligibility. Grants are not made to the following: individuals; endowment creation; travel expenses; sustain ongoing programs or projects; salaried/contracted positions; support political parties, campaigns, or issues; sectarian religious purposes; debt reduction of recipient organizations; programs, expenses and/or equipment committed to prior to the grant award date.
Geographic Focus: Indiana
Date(s) Application is Due: Mar 1
Contact: Denise Sedler; (812) 539-4115; fax (812) 539-4119; dsedler@dearborncf.org
Internet: http://www.dearborncf.org/grants/G_Aurora.aspx
Sponsor: Dearborn Community Foundation
322 Walnut Street
Lawrenceburg, IN 47025

Dearborn Community Foundation City of Lawrenceburg Community Grants 1471
The City of Lawrenceburg has allocated grant funds specifically for not-for-profit organizations that provide a benefit, direct or indirect, to the Lawrenceburg community and Dearborn County. The Dearborn Community Foundation will administer this program. The program consists of two phases, Phase I: applications requesting $5,000 or less will be accepted and considered as long as funds are available. Phase II: applications requesting $5,001 - $100,000 will be accepted to the grant application deadlines. Applications will be considered as long as funds are available. The application and specific guidelines are available at the website.
Restrictions: Funding is not available for the following: individuals; endowment creation; travel expenses; sustain ongoing programs or projects; salaried/contracted positions; political parties, campaigns, or issues; sectarian religious purposes; debt reduction of recipient organizations and programs, expenses and/or equipment committed to prior to the grant award date.
Geographic Focus: Indiana
Date(s) Application is Due: Mar 6; Jun 5; Sep 11
Amount of Grant: 5,000 - 100,000 USD
Contact: Denise Sedler; (812) 539-4115; fax (812) 539-4119; dsedler@dearborncf.org
Internet: http://www.dearborncf.org/grants/G_Lawrence.aspx
Sponsor: Dearborn Community Foundation
322 Walnut Street
Lawrenceburg, IN 47025

Dearborn Community Foundation City of Lawrenceburg Youth Grants 1472
The City of Lawrenceburg Youth Grants are made to not-for-profit organizations for programs that directly benefit youth from birth to the age of 18. Half of the total funding available is allocated to benefit youth programs where 75% of the youth reside in the Lawrenceburg School Corporation area, while the other half is allocated for programs that benefit 95% of the youth residing in Dearborn County. Applicants must provide the percentage of youth residing in Lawrenceburg and Dearborn County for their program participants. The application and additional guidelines are available at the website.
Requirements: Grants are awarded only to nonprofit organizations whose programs benefit Dearborn County residents. If they are not nonprofits, organizations must provide for a responsible fiscal agent and adequate accounting procedures. Submitted grant applications shall contain one original application and ten copies.
Restrictions: Any school corporation or school sponsored organization wishing to apply for City of Lawrenceburg Youth Grant funds must first apply for funding through the school's respective Endowment Corporation or Education Foundation. Documentation verifying the Endowment Corporation/Education Foundation's decision must accompany the completed City of Lawrenceburg Youth Grant Program application materials. Select programs/teams, those that allow participation of a few children when other organizations are available to offer the same recreational opportunities, are not eligible to apply. Funding is not provided to support political parties, campaigns, or issues; sectarian religious purposes that do not support the general public; debt reduction of recipient organizations; and programs, expenses and/or equipment committed to prior to the grant award date.
Geographic Focus: Indiana
Date(s) Application is Due: Mar 6; Jun 5; Sep 11
Amount of Grant: 10,000 USD
Contact: Denise Sedler; (812) 539-4115; fax (812) 539-4119; dsedler@dearborncf.org
Internet: http://www.dearborncf.org/grants/G_Youth.aspx
Sponsor: Dearborn Community Foundation
322 Walnut Street
Lawrenceburg, IN 47025

Dearborn Community Foundation County Progress Grants 1473
The Dearborn Community Foundation County Progress Grant supports the interests of the community from non-profit organizations for charitable purposes in the fields of community service, social service, education, health, environment, and the arts. The application is available at the website.
Geographic Focus: Indiana
Date(s) Application is Due: Mar 6; Jun 5; Sep 11
Amount of Grant: 10,000 USD
Contact: Denise Sedler; (812) 539-4115; fax (812) 539-4119; dsedler@dearborncf.org
Internet: http://www.dearborncf.org/grants/G_Progress.aspx
Sponsor: Dearborn Community Foundation
322 Walnut Street
Lawrenceburg, IN 47025

Dearborn Community Foundation Sprint Educational Excellence Grants 1474
The Sprint Educational Excellence Grant gives funding to innovative programs that improve learning opportunities in the community. Grants are awarded based on the creativity of the project. The maximum grant award allotted is $1,000 per organization per calendar year. Grants are accepted throughout the year until funds are depleted. The application and additional guidelines are available at the website.
Requirements: Grants are awarded only to organizations whose programs benefit the residents of Dearborn County, Indiana, and which provide for a responsible fiscal agent and adequate accounting procedures.
Restrictions: Organizations need to allow up to three months from the time they turn in their application before a decision is made.
Geographic Focus: Indiana
Amount of Grant: 1,000 USD
Contact: Denise Sedler; (812) 539-4115; fax (812) 539-4119; dsedler@dearborncf.org
Internet: http://www.dearborncf.org/grants/G_Sprint.aspx
Sponsor: Dearborn Community Foundation
322 Walnut Street
Lawrenceburg, IN 47025

Deborah Munroe Noonan Memorial Fund Grants 1475
The Deborah Munroe Noonan Memorial Fund was established in 1949 by her son, Walter Noonan, to support and promote quality educational, human-services, and health-care programming for underserved populations. Grant requests for general operating support are strongly encouraged. Program support will also be considered. Small, program-related capital expenses may be included in general operating or program requests. To better support the capacity of nonprofit organizations, multi-year funding requests are strongly encouraged. Applicants must apply online at the grant website. Applicants are strongly encouraged to do the following before applying: review the downloadable state application procedures for additional helpful information and clarifications; review the downloadable online-application guidelines at the grant website; review the foundation's funding history (link is available from the grant website); review the online application questions in advance; and review the list of required attachments. These will generally include: a list of board members, financial statements (audited, reviewed, or compiled by independent auditor); an organization summary; a list of other funding sources; an IRS Determination letter; and other required documents. All attachments must be uploaded in the online application as PDF, Word, or Excel files. The application deadline for the Deborah Munroe Noonan Memorial Fund is 11:59 p.m. on July 1. Applicants will be notified of grant decisions before September 30.
Requirements: Applicants must have 501(c)3 tax-exempt status and serve the people of Greater Boston.
Restrictions: The fund does not support requests from individuals, organizations attempting to influence policy through direct lobbying, or any political campaigns.
Geographic Focus: Massachusetts
Date(s) Application is Due: Jul 1
Contact: Miki C. Akimoto, Vice President; (866) 778-6859; miki.akimoto@baml.com
Internet: https://www.bankofamerica.com/philanthropic/fn_search.action
Sponsor: Deborah Munroe Noonan Memorial Fund
225 Franklin Street, 4th Floor, MA1-225-04-02
Boston, MA 02110

Decatur County Community Foundation Large Project Grants 1476
The Decatur County Community Foundation (DCCF) encourages, manages, and distributes charitable contributions to improve the quality of life of Decatur County, Indiana residents, now and in the future. The Foundation places high priority to funding projects which are: new and innovative projects or programs, including start-ups; projects which Foundation funds can be used as match, seed money or challenge grant funding from other donors; projects which will make a significant impact in the community; projects which act as a catalyst for action and community participation. The Large Project Community Grants are reviewed twice a year.
Requirements: Each applicant is required to submit a letter of intent to see if the project complies with general guidelines. No application will be sent without a letter of intent. Form letters will neither be reviewed nor acknowledged. Upon acceptance, the applicant will

receive a grant application packet. The grant committee will review the completed packet. A member of that committee may contact the applicant or request a site visit. The committee's recommendations are forwarded to the Foundation's Board of Directors, who will make final funding decisions. The Board may choose to fund the grant as written, fund part of the grant or provide no funding at all. All applicants are notified in writing regarding funding decisions.
Restrictions: The Foundation will not fund: individual and team travel expenses; multi-year or long term funding; the creation of an endowment; programs that fall appropriately under government funding; annual appeals; projects considered part of the school curriculum; attendance to conferences or seminars; annual campaigns; projects where the Foundation is the sole funder; or advertising. The Foundation will also not fund: political activities; make-up operating deficits; post event or after the fact situations; ongoing operating expenses; debt reduction; or religious organizations strictly for religious purposes.
Geographic Focus: Indiana
Date(s) Application is Due: Feb 15; Sep 15
Contact: Sharon Hollowell; (812) 662-6364; fax (812) 662-8704; sharon@dccfound.org
Internet: http://www.dccfound.org/grants.html
Sponsor: Decatur County Community Foundation
101 E Main Street, Suite 1, P.O. Box 72
Greensburg, IN 47240

Decatur County Community Foundation Small Project Grants   1477
The Decatur Foundation Small Project Grants fund organizations seeking a grant of $1,500 or less. The grant must demonstrate that it meets one or more of the following categories and criteria: youth and family enrichment - promote or provide for positive growth and development of young people or strengthen families; community development/civic engagement - promote the development of an increased quality of life within the community and foster stronger relationships among individuals or groups; cultural life - add to or enhance the variety of artistic and cultural opportunities available to all; education - demonstrate an ability to help residents gain knowledge and the skills necessary to better themselves either economically or socially, or focus on ways to allow citizens to develop skills; and health and recreation - demonstrate the ability to help residents develop healthy lifestyles. Highest priority will be given to innovative programs or projects that: include start-up costs, publicity, or specialized equipment; provide direct services to individuals or groups; enhance or enable participation by individuals or groups. Grant applications are accepted at any time. Applications received by the 10th of the month will be reviewed in the following month by the Board of Directors. The application and additional guidelines are available at the website.
Requirements: Organizations seeking grants should be a 501(c)3 nonprofit entity, an educational institution or a governmental entity. If they are not, the organization must find a qualified agency or entity to act as the fiscal agent.
Restrictions: Funding will not be considered for the following: political activities; make-up operating deficits; post-event or after the fact situations; debt reduction; or religious organizations for strictly religious purposes.
Geographic Focus: Indiana
Contact: Sharon Hollowell, Executive Director; (812) 662-6364; sharon@dccfound.org
Internet: http://www.dccfound.org/grants.html
Sponsor: Decatur County Community Foundation
101 E Main Street, Suite 1, P.O. Box 72
Greensburg, IN 47240

DeKalb County Community Foundation Garrett Hospital Aid Foundation Grants   1478
The DeKalb County Community Foundation administers the Garrett Hospital Aid Foundation Grants, which award funding to nonprofit organizations that serve residents of Garrett, Indiana. Grant proposals are accepted in January of each year and grants are awarded at the recommendation of the Garrett Hospital Aid Foundation board of directors.
Requirements: Organization should submit the online application to the DeKalb Foundation for consideration. They should include the organization's name and contact information, a description of their project and why they need it, in addition to a first and second priority they would consider.
Restrictions: The Foundation only funds projects in Garrett, Indiana.
Geographic Focus: Indiana
Date(s) Application is Due: Jan 1
Contact: Rosie Shinkel; (260) 925-0311; rshinkel@dekalbfoundation.org
Internet: http://www.dekalbfoundation.org/g_garrett.php
Sponsor: DeKalb County Community Foundation
650 West North Street
Auburn, IN 46706

DeKalb County Community Foundation - Immediate Response Grant   1479
The DeKalb County Community Foundation Immediate Response Grant awards emergency funding to DeKalb County nonprofit organizations. Examples include food programs for children and heating units for community service organizations. There are no deadlines and proposals may be accepted year round.
Requirements: Organizations should contact the Foundation office to discuss their unexpected need, and the Foundation office will help them determine if a proposal form should be submitted.
Restrictions: Organizations must first contact the Foundation office before submitting a proposal.
Geographic Focus: Indiana
Contact: Rosie Shinkel; (260) 925-0311; rshinkel@dekalbfoundation.org
Internet: http://www.dekalbfoundation.org/g_response.php
Sponsor: DeKalb County Community Foundation
650 West North Street
Auburn, IN 46706

DeKalb County Community Foundation - Literacy Grant   1480
The DeKalb County Literacy Grant was created to support adult and children's literacy opportunities in DeKalb County, Indiana. The Grant also advocates the importance of literacy to the community and encourages community members to become involved by committing resources to address literacy needs. Grants are awarded based on how a program addresses literacy needs and the ability of grantees to deliver their service in a cost-effective manner.
Requirements: Nonprofit organizations that provide literacy programs are encouraged to: submit a one-page letter of intent describing your program(s) and who you serve; include a specific dollar request; and specify that your request is for the DeKalb County Literacy Fund. Submit the letter between August 1 and August 31, with grants awarded in September. Applicants are also encouraged to call the Foundation office to discuss their ideas for a request.
Geographic Focus: Indiana
Samples: Butler Public Library, Auburn, IN: literacy program aimed at preschool children which provides bags of books that can be taken home, $300; J.E. Ober Elementary, Auburn, IN: new program "Tool Time" that will work with students in the Response to Intervention groups which are struggling with reading and are below grade level, $500; Eckhart Public Library, Auburn, IN: Book Buddies summer sessions in 2011 for parents and children participating in the Friends Mission Table at Auburn Presbyterian, $500 (2011).
Contact: Rosie Shinkel; (260) 925-0311; rshinkel@dekalbfoundation.org
Internet: http://www.dekalbfoundation.org/g_literacy.php
Sponsor: DeKalb County Community Foundation
650 West North Street
Auburn, IN 46706

DeKalb County Community Foundation Grants   1481
The DeKalb County Community Foundation Grants support programs for DeKalb County, Indiana citizens that address today's needs and prepare for tomorrow's challenges. Grant guidelines are intentionally broad in order to meet the community's ever-changing charitable needs. Grants are awarded for charitable programs and projects in the following areas of interest: art and culture; community development; education; environment; health and human services; and youth development. Grants are also available for the general operating expenses of organizations that address local charitable needs. Applicants are encouraged to contact the Foundation before submitting a proposal to be certain it follows the grant guidelines. They are also encouraged to attend a free one hour workshop to help them understand the Foundation's grant process and learn basic proposal writing tips. The Foundation gives priority to grant proposals for programs/projects that: will be completed within one year of receiving a grant; strengthen the grant seeking organization; directly relate to the grant seeker's mission; project a high degree of community impact; benefit many local people; and are proactive rather than reactive.
Requirements: After reviewing the grant guidelines, applicants will fill out the online proposal form. Applicants should include their contact information, financial information, a brief summary of the request, their organization's mission statement, and a detailed explanation of the benefits they'll receive from the grant. They should also include their operating expenses, total budget, and their source of funds. Applicants will then email the proposal form to the Foundation contact person or mail a printed copy to the Foundation address.
Restrictions: Grants are less likely to be awarded for: repeat funding for a program/project that has received a Foundation grant within the last two years; or a funding debt. The Foundation grants to religious organizations for charitable purposes but does not award grants for religious purposes.
Geographic Focus: Indiana
Date(s) Application is Due: Jul 1
Amount of Grant: 500 - 7,000 USD
Contact: Rosie Shinkel; (260) 925-0311; rshinkel@dekalbfoundation.org
Internet: http://www.dekalbfoundation.org/g_grantmaking.php
Sponsor: DeKalb County Community Foundation
650 West North Street
Auburn, IN 46706

Dekko Foundation Grants   1482
The Foundation is focused on projects that support the development of children ages birth through 18 years. Grant proposals are considered in the following three categories: early childhood development; child-centered education and sustainability for youth-serving organizations.
Requirements: Non-profit organizations in the following geographic areas will be considered for grant proposals: Limestone County, Alabama; Collier County, Florida; DeKalb, LaGrange, Kosciusko, Noble, Steuben, and Whitley Counties, Indiana; Clarke, Decatur, Lucas, Ringgold, and Union Counties, Iowa; and the Community of Ada in Minnesota. A one- to two-page summary is required.
Geographic Focus: Alabama, Florida, Indiana, Iowa, Minnesota
Contact: Manager; (260) 347-1278; fax (260) 347-7103; dekko@dekkofoundation.org
Internet: http://www.dekkofoundation.org
Sponsor: Dekko Foundation
P.O. Box 548
Kendallville, IN 46755

Delaware Community Foundation-Youth Philanthropy Board for Kent County   1483
The Youth Philanthropy Board (YPB) for Kent County of the Delaware Community Foundation is composed of 19 students from public, independent and diocesan high schools in Kent County. The Board is studying youth issues in their neighborhoods and schools, learning about community service and grant making, and will award a total of $10,000 to schools and qualified 501(c)3 organizations to carry out youth programs for residents of Kent County. This year, the Youth Philanthropy Board for Kent County will consider programs that provide support for minors who are affected by abusive situations. Additional

consideration will be given to programs that encompass reinforcement of academic achievement and/or extracurricular activities.
Requirements: 501(c)3 organizations in Kent County, Delaware are eligible to apply.
Restrictions: Programs completed prior to May 1, are ineligible for funding.
Geographic Focus: Delaware
Date(s) Application is Due: Jan 7
Contact: Ann Frazier; (302) 856-4393; fax (302) 856-4367; frazier@delcf.org
Internet: http://www.delcf.org/Apply_4_1.htm
Sponsor: Youth Philanthropy Board for Kent County c/o Delaware Community Foundation
Southern Delaware Office, 36 The Circle
Georgetown, DE 19947

Delaware Community Foundation Fund For Women Grants   1484

The Fund For Women at the Delaware Community Foundation is a charitable fund established to support special projects benefiting women and girls in the state of Delaware. Each year, since 1994, the FFW has awarded several one-year grants to nonprofit agencies with quality programs that help to meet the needs of women and girls in Delaware. The fund remains committed to supporting proposals which prepare women and girls to lead productive, self-sufficient lives, develop leadership skills and promote the value of giving and sharing. Additional guidelines and application are available at: http://www.delcf.org/Apply_4_1.htm. Send completed applications, with attachments to: thefundforwomen@yahoo.com, no later than January 31.
Requirements: IRS 501(c)3 non-profit organizations in Delaware are eligible to apply.
Restrictions: The Fund For Women does not support funding for: individuals; capital projects; debt reduction; endowment campaigns; requests over $15,000.
Geographic Focus: Delaware
Date(s) Application is Due: Jan 31
Contact: Marilyn K. Hyte, Grants Committee Chair; (302) 239-5241; hyte1@comcast.net
Internet: http://www.delcf.org/Apply_4_1.htm
Sponsor: Fund For Women
Attn: Grants Committee, P.O. Box 1636
Wilmington, DE 19899

Delaware Community Foundation Next Generation Grants   1485

The Next Generation (TNG) is a philanthropic organization that was created and is directed by young professionals living and working in Delaware. TNG leverages many of the Delaware Community Foundation's resources, but members have established their own structure to raise funds and support the community. TNG supports programs for 10 to 14-year-olds that address the underlying social factors that contribute to low graduation rates, teen pregnancy and drug abuse. Specifically, TNG will help fund out-of-school programs that incorporate other family members, role models or peers to help address these factors. All applications that meet TNG's guidelines are given thorough study by the Committee. Because the TNG receives many more grant requests than it is able to support, nonprofit organizations are encouraged to seek funding from multiple sources for a particular program or project. TNG is interested in initiatives that: demonstrate vision, effectiveness, good management and action for positive change; encourage collaboration between agencies and reduce duplication of services; leverage funds from other sources; create a sense of community through neighborhood involvement and outreach; include an evaluation component. The Fund has one competitive Program Grant cycle each year. Grant applications will be available on September 14, and are due on October 14. Grants will be awarded in January.
Requirements: Nonprofit organizations within the state of Delaware that have a 501(c)3 designation by the Internal Revenue Service are eligible to apply. Agencies receiving TNG grants must serve the state of Delaware and its residents without discrimination based on race, religion, gender, age, disability, or national origin.
Restrictions: Ineligible for support: endowment; debt reduction; religious organizations for sectarian purposes; annual fundraising campaigns or general operating expenses; projects completed before the date of grant approval by the TNG membership; sports clubs or leagues; individuals.
Geographic Focus: Delaware
Date(s) Application is Due: Oct 14
Contact: Beth Bouchelle, Director of Grants; (302) 504-5239; bbouchelle@delcf.org
Internet: http://www.delcf.org/Download/2010%20TNG%20Grant%20Guidelines.pdf
Sponsor: Next Generation c/o Delaware Community Foundation
P.O. Box 1636
Wilmington, DE 19899

Delaware Community Foundation Youth Philanthropy Board for New Castle County Grants   1486

The Delaware Community Foundation's Youth Philanthropy Board for New Castle County (YPB) is composed of 25 students from public, independent and diocesan high schools in New Castle County. The Board is studying youth issues in their neighborhoods and schools, learning about community service and grantmaking, and will award a total of $15,000 in grants to schools and qualified non-profit organizations in New Castle County. Requests for up to $2,500 will be accepted. This year, the Youth Philanthropy Board will consider funding requests for the following: programs that provide basic necessities such as clothing, school supplies and food for children grade 5 and under; programs that provide physical, athletic or other leisure activities for children with mental or physical disabilities ages 12 and under.
Requirements: Schools and qualified non-profit 501(c)3 organizations in New Castle County, Delaware are eligible to apply.
Geographic Focus: Delaware
Date(s) Application is Due: Dec 15
Amount of Grant: Up to 2,500 USD
Contact: Beth Bouchelle, Director of Grants; (302) 504-5239; bbouchelle@delcf.org
Internet: http://www.delcf.org/Apply_4_1.htm
Sponsor: Delaware Community Foundation's Youth Philanthropy Board for New Castle County
P.O. Box 1636
Wilmington, DE 19899

Delaware Division of the Arts Community-Based Organizations Grants   1487

The Delaware Division of the Arts is dedicated to nurturing and supporting the arts to enhance the quality of life for all Delawareans. Together with its advisory body, the Delaware State Arts Council, the Division administers grants and programs that support arts programming, educate the public, increase awareness of the arts, and integrate the arts into all facets of Delaware life. Opportunity grants support the presentation of performing, visual, literary, media, and folk arts in communities throughout the state. Opportunity grants of up to $1,000 are intended to increase opportunities, particularly in underserved communities, for residents who do not routinely have access to diverse types of arts activities. Projects in this category typically involve artists from outside the immediately community. Applications are evaluated on the following criteria: quality of artistic product, process, or service; increased access to diverse and quality arts programs, particularly in underserved communities; financial feasibility and need as demonstrated in the budget submitted; potential ability to attract the target audience or participants; and immediacy and uniqueness of the opportunity. Applicants may request up to 80% of the cost of artist fees and travel expenses or other performance/exhibit/workshop-related costs, with requests not to exceed $1,000. Opportunity grant applications are accepted on an ongoing basis, but must be received at least six weeks prior to the project begin date. Earlier applications are recommended, whenever possible. Applications are submitted through the egrant online process. Organizations are notified of the review committee decision within four weeks.
Requirements: To be eligible to apply for a Community-Based Organization Opportunity Grant, applicants must be a Delaware-based nonprofit organization whose primary purpose is not the arts. This includes libraries, civic groups, community/senior centers, festivals, parks/recreation programs, units of government, and university/college non-credit programs intended to serve the community. Public, private, and parochial schools are eligible only if the proposed arts project is taking place after school hours, and is open and promoted to the public.
Geographic Focus: Delaware
Amount of Grant: Up to 1,000 USD
Contact: Terry Plummer, Community Arts Development Coordinator; (302) 577-8280; terry.plummer@state.de.us
Internet: http://www.artsdel.org/grants/CBOOverview.pdf
Sponsor: Delaware Division of the Arts
820 North French Street, Carvel State Office Building
Wilmington, DE 19801

Delaware Division of the Arts Opportunity Grants—Arts Organizations   1488

Arts organizations may apply for funding for staff and/or board members to attend conferences, workshops, or mentoring sessions that will enable the organization to further develop administrative and/or artistic skills. Arts organizations with unique and unanticipated opportunities to present the literary, performing, visual, media, or folk arts in ways that will reach new audiences may apply for funding. Arts organizations may apply for funding to enable them to take advantage of unique opportunities to present their programs at events of regional, national, or international significance outside Delaware. Applicants may request up to 80 percent of the cost of the project with requests not to exceed $750. New arts organizations, including those who have not yet received their IRS nonprofit status, may apply for funding to support their early programming and organizational development efforts. Arts organizations may apply for funding to help make their programs more accessible to people with disabilities. Note: Organizations will be eligible to receive only one grant award in this category per calendar year. Annual deadline dates may vary; contact the council for exact dates.
Requirements: To be eligible to apply applicants must: Have the promotion, presentation, production, and/or teaching of the arts as their primary purpose as outlined in their charter, incorporation papers, bylaws, and IRS nonprofit determination letter; Have a stable, functioning board of directors that meets at least quarterly; Be based and chartered in Delaware as a nonprofit organization; exempt from federal income tax under Section 501(c)3 or 501(c)(4) or 509(a) of the Internal Revenue Code; and eligible to receive donations allowable as charitable contributions under Section 170(c) of the Internal Revenue Code of 1954.
Restrictions: No individual may compile or submit an application on behalf of an organization if that individual is a member or relative of a member of the Delaware State Arts Council (DSAC) or DDOA staff.
Geographic Focus: Delaware
Date(s) Application is Due: Feb 1; Apr 1; Jun 1; Aug 1; Oct 1; Dec 1
Amount of Grant: Up to 750 USD
Contact: Kent and Sussex Grants Administrator; (302) 739-5304
Internet: http://www.artsdel.org/grants/artistgrants.shtml
Sponsor: Delaware Division of the Arts
820 North French Street, Carvel State Office Building
Wilmington, DE 19801

Delaware Division of the Arts Opportunity Grants-Artists   1489

The Individual Artist Opportunity Grants support professional and artistic development and presentation opportunities for artists. Artists may apply for funding for unique, short-term opportunities that will significantly advance their professional and artistic development, such as study with a significant master available for a limited time, or participation in a residency or exchange program. An individual or collaboration may request up to 80% of the cost of the opportunity with requests not to exceed $750. Travel costs are not covered

but should be included in the budget. Artists may also apply for funding for unique, short-term presentation opportunities that will significantly advance their work or careers such as: materials to complete work committed to an exhibition, performance, or publication; contracting of professional services; or rental of equipment, instruments, or work space for a specific performance, exhibition, or publication opportunity. An individual or collaboration may request up to 80% of the cost of the opportunity with requests not to exceed $750. Applications are evaluated on the anticipated impact of the artist's work or career; the proposal's financial feasibility and need as demonstrated in the budget; plans for marketing the project to attract an audience or participants; and the immediacy and uniqueness of the opportunity. Applications are accepted on the first Monday of February, April, June, August, October, or December. Applications are notified within four weeks of the review committee's decision. Projects should begin no earlier than six weeks after the application deadline.
Requirements: Applicants must be at least 18 years of age; Delaware residents for at least one year at the time of application; not enrolled in a degree-granting program; and not a current Delaware Division of the Arts Individual Artist Fellowship recipient.
Geographic Focus: Delaware
Date(s) Application is Due: Feb 1; Apr 1; Jun 1; Aug 1; Oct 1; Dec 1
Contact: Kristin Pleasanton, (302) 577-8284; kristin.pleasanton@state.de.us
Internet: http://www.artsdel.org/grants/artistgrants.shtml
Sponsor: Delaware Division of the Arts
820 North French Street, Carvel State Office Building
Wilmington, DE 19801

Dell Foundation Open Grants 1490
The foundation, the giving arm of Dell Computer, seeks to fund collaborative and innovative solutions to community and children's issues addressing youth (ages newborn to high-school seniors) in Texas, Tennessee, Idaho, and Oregon. Through these efforts, Dell strives to effect change in its local community, while providing lessons and best practices for communities everywhere. Funded areas include arts, education, social services, and health. The foundation supports specific, preventative, and measurable programs with cash, in-kind, and volunteer contributions. Grants are awarded quarterly. An online application form is available on the Web site.
Requirements: Eligibility is open to 501(c)3 nonprofit organizations in Texas—Travis, Williamson County, and McLennan County; Tennessee—Wilson, Davidson County; Idaho—Twin Falls County; and Oregon—Roseburg, Douglas County.
Restrictions: Grants do not support individuals; academic or research projects; civic, religious, or political institutions; school fundraisers; marketing opportunities; or sports events and organizations.
Geographic Focus: Idaho, Oregon, Tennessee, Texas
Date(s) Application is Due: Jan 15; Apr 15; Jul 15; Oct 15
Contact: Grants Administrator; (512) 338-4400; the_dell_foundation@dell.com
Internet: http://www1.us.dell.com/content/topics/global.aspx/corp/foundation/en/open_grants?c=us&l=en&s=corp
Sponsor: Dell Foundation
1 Dell Way
Round Rock, TX 78682

Dell Scholars Program Scholarships 1491
Dell Scholars demonstrate their desire and ability to overcome barriers and to achieve their goals. Applicants will be evaluated on their individual determination to succeed; future goals and plans to achieve them; ability to communicate the hardships they have overcome or currently face; self motivation in completing challenging coursework; and demonstrated need for financial assistance. Students may apply directly through the Scholar website.
Requirements: To be eligible to apply for the Dell Scholarship, applicants must: participate in a Michael and Susan Dell Foundation approved college readiness program for a minimum of two of the last three years; graduate from an accredited high school this academic year; earn a minimum of a 2.4 GPA; demonstrate need for financial assistance; plan to enter a bachelor's degree program at an accredited higher education institution in the fall directly after their graduation from high school; and be a citizen or permanent resident of the U.S.
Restrictions: Applications faxed, mailed, or emailed to the Michael and Susan Dell Foundation will not be considered. The official Dell Scholars Application can only be found at this web site and must be submitted on-line during the specified application period. email attachments will not be opened.
Geographic Focus: All States
Date(s) Application is Due: Jan 15
Contact: Dell Scholar Contact; 800-294-2039; apply@dellscholars.org
Internet: http://www.dellscholars.org/Criteria.aspx
Sponsor: Michael and Susan Dell Foundation
P.O. Box 163867
Austin, TX 78716-3867

Delonne Anderson Family Foundation 1492
Founder of the Delonne Anderson Family Foundation, Margaret F. Anderson, gives to a number of university programs, including scholarships for students in the College of Humanities, Arts, and Social Sciences and College of Business. The foundation also supports religion, theater, and K-12 education programs. The foundation, named for her late husband, is also working with the Star Valley Medical Center Foundation Board.
Restrictions: Giving primarily in the State of Utah.
Geographic Focus: Utah
Contact: Robert G. Steed, Secretary, Treasurer
Sponsor: Delonne Anderson Family
559 W 500th Street South
Bountiful, UT 84010

Delta Air Lines Foundation Arts and Culture Grants 1493
Established in 1968 as Delta's company-managed giving system, the Delta Air Lines Foundation contributes more than $1 million annually in endowed funds to deserving organizations and programs. The arts and cultural activities, whether they are fine art, theatre, music, or other creative endeavors, enhance a community's quality of life. Through the Arts and Culture program the Foundation is able to understand new perspectives and better understand the world around us. Delta supports organizations that help bring the wonder and richness of human creativity to the communities it serves. Promoting understanding and appreciation for arts and cultural diversity is a top priority. Once an application is received, applicants should allow up to three months before review.
Requirements: For proposals which meet the foundation's area of focus, priority will be given to: programs meeting compelling needs in communities where Delta has a presence; proposals that exhibit clear, reasonable goals, and measurable outcomes; distinctive projects where the foundation's involvement will leave a legacy; projects that include collaboration or cooperation with other nonprofit organizations; projects that offer opportunities for Delta employee involvement. The foundation Board of Trustees reviews and approves funding in March, June, September, and November. The deadline for receiving completed proposals is the first day of each of these months.
Restrictions: The foundation will generally not consider: individual applicant's request for support of personal needs; religious activities; political organizations or campaigns; specialized single-issue health organizations; annual or automatic renewal grants; general operating expenses; endowment campaigns; capital campaigns; multiyear commitments; fraternal organizations, professional associations, or membership groups; fundraising events such as benefits; charitable dinners, or sporting events.
Geographic Focus: All States
Date(s) Application is Due: Jun 1; Sep 1; Nov 1
Contact: Administrator; (404) 715-5487 or (404) 715-2554; fax (404) 715-3267
Internet: http://www.delta.com/about_delta/community_involvement/delta_foundation/
Sponsor: Delta Air Lines Foundation
P.O. Box 20706, Department 979
Atlanta, GA 30320-6001

Delta Air Lines Foundation Community Enrichment Grants 1494
Established in 1968 as Delta's company-managed giving system, the Delta Air Lines Foundation contributes more than $1 million annually in endowed funds to deserving organizations and programs. Community Enrichment focuses on promoting Delta's presence in the community through involvement and participation in volunteer, civic, and social activities. It also encourages consciousness, awareness, and consideration for community needs and focuses on developing a higher level of sensitivity towards supporting an improved quality of life for others in the communities where we live and work. Supporting Community Enrichment helps Delta establish its position as a corporate citizen and confirms our license to operate in our communities. Once an application is received, applicants should allow up to three months before review.
Requirements: For proposals which meet the foundation's area of focus, priority will be given to: programs meeting compelling needs in communities where Delta has a presence; proposals that exhibit clear, reasonable goals, and measurable outcomes; distinctive projects where the foundation's involvement will leave a legacy; projects that include collaboration or cooperation with other nonprofit organizations; projects that offer opportunities for Delta employee involvement. The foundation Board of Trustees reviews and approves funding in March, June, September, and November. The deadline for receiving completed proposals is the first day of each of these months.
Restrictions: The foundation will generally not consider: individual applicant's request for support of personal needs; religious activities; political organizations or campaigns; specialized single-issue health organizations; annual or automatic renewal grants; general operating expenses; endowment campaigns; capital campaigns; multi-year commitments; fraternal organizations, professional associations, or membership groups; fundraising events such as benefits; charitable dinners, or sporting events.
Geographic Focus: All States
Date(s) Application is Due: Mar 1; Jun 1; Sep 1; Nov 1
Contact: Administrator; (404) 715-5487 or (404) 715-2554; fax (404) 715-3267
Internet: http://www.delta.com/about_delta/community_involvement/delta_foundation/
Sponsor: Delta Air Lines Foundation
P.O. Box 20706, Department 979
Atlanta, GA 30320-6001

Delta Air Lines Foundation Prize for Global Understanding 1495
The Delta Prize for Global Understanding, established at the University of Georgia through an endowment from The Delta Air Lines Foundation, honors individuals or groups who, by their own initiatives, have provided opportunities for greater understanding among cultures and nations. Awarded annually, The Delta Prize calls attention to a variety of contributions to peace and cooperation, such as grassroots projects that diminish hostilities in a particular region of the world, international programs that facilitate communication or commerce among different peoples and leadership in the solution of global problems.
Geographic Focus: All States, All Countries
Contact: Administrator; (404) 715-5487 or (404) 715-2554; fax (404) 715-3267
Internet: http://www.delta.com/about_delta/community_involvement/delta_foundation/
Sponsor: Delta Air Lines Foundation
P.O. Box 20706, Department 979
Atlanta, GA 30320-6001

Deluxe Corporation Foundation Grants　　　　　　　　　　　1496

The Deluxe Corporation Foundation partners with nonprofit organizations to strengthen the lives of people and communities through philanthropy and volunteerism. The foundation supports nonprofits near corporate facilities in its areas of interest, including culture, education and human services.
Requirements: Nonprofit organizations in Deluxe Corporation communities are eligible. To qualify for consideration, nonprofits must: have primary missions that meet the Foundation's grant focus areas; be tax-exempt under section 501(c)3 or 509(a)(1),(2) or (3); have been in operation at least two years; have secured support from other corporate funders; be located in and serve communities with a Deluxe facility.
Restrictions: The following categories are not eligible for Foundation grants: individuals; national organizations; religious organizations; organizations designed primarily for lobbying; seminars, conferences, workshops, fund-raisers, and other events; endowments; research projects; tours and travel expenses; start-up organizations; athletic events; sponsorships; long-term housing (focus is on emergency and transitional housing programs); community theater and music groups; civic organizations; libraries; and zoos.
Geographic Focus: Arizona, California, Colorado, Georgia, Illinois, Indiana, Kansas, Massachusetts, Minnesota, Missouri, New Jersey, New York, North Carolina, Ohio, Pennsylvania, Texas, Utah
Date(s) Application is Due: Nov 1
Amount of Grant: 2,000 - 5,000 USD
Contact: Jennifer Anderson, Director; (651) 787-5124
Internet: http://www.deluxe.com/dlxab/deluxe-foundation-guidelines.jsp
Sponsor: Deluxe Corporation Foundation
P.O. Box 64235
Saint Paul, MN 55164-0235

DeMatteis Family Foundation Grants　　　　　　　　　　　　1497

The foundation makes grants in the New York metropolitan area to eligible institutions whose mission involves education, health and human services, medical research, social services, and the arts. Types of support include facilities construction, expansion, renovation; acquisition of capital equipment; scientific/medical research; projects and programs that enable the applicant to expand its mission through new or expanded programs to reach a greater segment of the community served; project-oriented capital campaigns. In general, most grants are made to cover projects that can be accomplished within one year. For construction and longer duration projects, grants may be structured to conform to identified milestones. For major projects, the payment of the grant may be over a number of years.
Requirements: Metropolitan New York 501(c)3 tax-exempt agencies, institutions, and organizations are eligible.
Restrictions: In general, the foundation does not support grants for operating deficits; general operating support; endowments; loans, or financing of any kind; annual appeals, dinner functions, and other special fund raising events; or unrestricted funds.
Geographic Focus: New York
Contact: Grants Administrator; (516) 705-4974
Internet: http://fdncenter.org/grantmaker/dematteis/about.html
Sponsor: DeMatteis Family Foundation
P.O. Box 25
Glen Head, NY 11545

Dennis and Phyllis Washington Foundation Grants　　　　　1498

The foundation supports a broad spectrum of worthy causes benefiting people of all ages primarily serving the State of Montana and surrounding states where the Washington Companies are located. Priorities for funding are direct service, youth oriented programs and the advancement of educational opportunities through scholarships to units of higher education in Montana. The Foundation also focuses on the needs of economical and socially disadvantaged people, troubled or at-risk youth and individuals with special needs.
Requirements: Eligible applicants must be a charitable, nonprofit entity with tax exempt status under Section 501(c)3. Organizations applying for support must be categorized in one of the four giving areas of education, health and human services, community service and arts and culture. The Foundation places particular emphasis on those organizations and programs that provide a direct service to economically and socially disadvantaged youth and their families, at-risk or troubled youth, and individuals with special needs. Preference is given to applicants who are able to demonstrate that a majority, if not all, of Foundation funds will be used for direct services. The Foundation prefers giving to organizations with no or low administrative costs. Organizations may apply for funding only in the year in which funds will be used. The Foundation prefers that organizations show evidence of substantial financial support from their community, constituency groups or other funding sources prior to applying.
Restrictions: Applications will not be considered for the following organizations or purposes: organizations that, in policy or practice, unfairly discriminate against race, ethnic origin, sex, creed, or religion; to fund loans, debt retirement or operational deficits; to fund ongoing, general operations; to individuals, unless under an approved educational scholarship program; to sectarian or religious organizations for religious purposes where the principal activity is for the benefit of their own members or adherents; to veterans or fraternal organizations, unless their programs are available to members of the community as a whole; for travel expenses or trips; to general endowment funds, private or public foundations and most capital campaigns; for operation expenses of tax-supported groups; for sponsorships including auctions, dinners, tickets, advertising, or annual fundraising events; for political action or legislative advocacy groups or influencing legislation or elections; for operational costs or curriculum development at educational institutions; the purchase of motor vehicles or other forms of transportation; to organizations acting on behalf of, but without the authority of, qualified tax exempt organizations.
Geographic Focus: Montana
Contact: Mike Halligan, Executive Director; (406) 523-1325
Internet: http://www.dpwfoundation.org/home.htm
Sponsor: Dennis and Phyllis Washington Foundation
P.O. Box 16630
Missoula, MT 59808-6630

DENSO North America Foundation Grants　　　　　　　　　1499

The Foundation is committed to supporting higher education in engineering and business programs. Priority is given to programs that advance automotive engineering and supply-side business practices. Capital funding is available for equipment, lab development, technological advancements and/or installations, building campaigns and expansion projects. Student projects are supported for university-sanctioned student projects and training competitions. Funding is available for tooling and equipment offering a major, sustaining investment.
Requirements: 501(c)3 nonprofits, educational institutions, and universities located throughout North America are eligible. Proposals should contain: details on how funding will advance student development and training; demonstrate principle(s) of innovation and/or training for efficiency gains in the workplace; contain a clearly articulated desired result.
Restrictions: Grants are not awarded for administrative costs, stipends or trips, conferences and travel expenses.
Geographic Focus: All States
Amount of Grant: 2,000 USD
Contact: Administrator; (248) 372-8233; DENSOfoundation@denso-diam.com
Internet: http://www.densofoundation.org/foundation/foundation.html
Sponsor: DENSO North America Foundation
24777 Denso Drive, MC 4610
Southfield, MI 48086-5047

Denton A. Cooley Foundation Grants　　　　　　　　　　　　1500

The foundation awards grants in Texas in support of health care, health education, hospitals, and medical research. Types of support include endowments, general operating grants, program grants, and research grants. There are no application forms or deadlines. The board meets quarterly to consider requests.
Restrictions: Grants do not support conferences, loans, individuals, scholarships, fellowships, or publication.
Geographic Focus: Texas
Amount of Grant: 100 - 250,000 USD
Contact: Grants Administrator; (713) 799-2700
Sponsor: Denton A. Cooley Foundation
6624 Fannin, Suite 1640
Houston, TX 77030

Denver Broncos Charities Fund Grants　　　　　　　　　　　1501

The fund supports qualified non-profit organizations that work to impact the quality of life for youth, health and the hungry and homeless. The emphasis of the fund is on programs designed to assist young people in the areas of education and youth football with a particular emphasis on programs aimed at disadvantaged and at-risk youth. The fund will also consider programs devoted to health and hunger issues. Grants may be stand-alone grants or magnet grants that attract other corporate dollars.
Requirements: Nonprofit organizations in the state of Colorado are eligible.
Geographic Focus: Colorado
Date(s) Application is Due: Jun 1
Contact: Charities Fund Manager; (720) 258-3000
Internet: http://www.denverbroncos.com/page.php?id=1157
Sponsor: Denver Broncos Charities Fund
1701 Bryant Street, Suite 1400
Denver, CO 80204

Denver Foundation Community Grants　　　　　　　　　　　1502

The Denver Foundation carries out its mission of improving life in Metro Denver by investing in the vision, passion and expertise of hundreds of nonprofit organizations. The Community grants program awards hundreds of grants annually to nonprofit organizations in the seven-county Metro Denver area, which includes: Adams, Arapahoe, Boulder, Broomfield, Denver, Douglas, and Jefferson counties. Grants are awarded in the four major focus areas of arts and culture, health, human services and civics and education.
Requirements: To qualify for a grant an organization must be a 501(c)3 tax-exempt nonprofit organization, serve residents in seven specific Denver counties, and provide a service that falls under one of the four funding areas.
Restrictions: The Foundation will not consider requests to fund the following: requests from organizations that have received funding from the program for the three previous consecutive calendar years; organizations with fund balance deficits in their most recently completed fiscal year; organizations that discriminate on the basis of race, color, religion, gender, age, national origin; disability, marital status, sexual orientation, or military status; debt retirement; endowments or other reserve funds; membership or affiliation campaigns, dinners, or special events; conferences and symposia and related travel; grants that further political doctrine; grants that further religious doctrine; grants to individuals; scholarships or sponsorships; individual medical procedures; medical, scientific, or academic research; grants to parochial or religious schools; grants to governmental agencies, except public schools; requests from individual public schools that have not coordinated the request with their central school district administration; requests from foundations/organizations that raise money for individual public schools; creation or installation of art objects; development, production, or distribution of books, newspapers, or video productions; grants for re-granting programs; requests for capital campaigns that have not met 75% of their goal; activities, projects, or programs that will have been completed before funding becomes available; and multi-year funding requests.

Geographic Focus: Colorado
Date(s) Application is Due: Feb 2; Jun 1; Oct 1
Contact: Jeff Hirota, Vice President; (303) 300-1790, ext. 129; fax (303) 300-6547; jhirota@denverfoundation.org
Internet: http://www.denverfoundation.org/page17823.cfm
Sponsor: Denver Foundation
55 Madison, 8th Floor
Denver, CO 80206

Denver Foundation Social Venture Partners Grants 1503

Social Venture Partners Denver's mission is to catalyze positive social change by strengthening local nonprofit organizations through targeted investments of our partners' time, expertise and money. Through a rigorous grant selection process, SVP works with nonprofits that are interested in the combination of expertise and financial resources SVP and our partners can provide. All of our grantees have a clear vision, strong leadership, a commitment to measuring outcomes and a desire to collaborate with high-level volunteers. SVP Denver supports organizations whose missions include early childhood education, K-12 education and youth development programs.
Requirements: Agencies eligible for SVP Denver funding must: be a nonprofit agency with 501(c)3 status; be located and provide services within the seven county metro Denver area; be willing to work with SVP Partners to build the capacity of their organization; be entrepreneurial in spirit; be open to SVP partnering with the organization's staff and board to evaluate and implement programs, and measure results; be willing to work with other nonprofits; have strong and passionate leadership; and be willing to work with SVP for up to 3 years.
Geographic Focus: Colorado
Contact: Lisa Fasolo Frishman, Executive Director; (720) 974-2602; fax (720) 974-2603; lfrishman@denverfoundation.org
Internet: http://www.denverfoundation.org/frameviewer.cfm?sitename=http://www.svpdenver.org&pageId=17843&location=bot
Sponsor: Denver Foundation
55 Madison, 8th Floor
Denver, CO 80206

Denver Foundation Strengthening Neighborhoods Grants 1504

The Denver Foundation's Strengthening Neighborhoods Program (SNP) works with residents of partner neighborhoods to help them make their communities better places to live. Its grants program provides grants of up to $5,000 to support neighborhood projects that are as diverse as the ideas and imagination of the residents who create them. The only requirement is that projects be done by residents for the benefit of their community. SNP projects have included literacy and after-school recreation programs, block parties, neighborhood fairs and carnivals, education reform campaigns, block clean-ups, community gardening activities, sports leagues, neighborhood-wide art showcases, development of neighborhood plans, large-scale community organizing efforts, publication of neighborhood newsletters, and many other activities and events.
Requirements: To qualify for a grant an organization must be a 501(c)3 tax-exempt nonprofit organization, serve residents in seven specific Denver counties, and provide a service that falls under one of the four funding areas.
Restrictions: The Foundation will not consider requests to fund the following: requests from organizations that have received funding from the program for the three previous consecutive calendar years; organizations with fund balance deficits in their most recently completed fiscal year; organizations that discriminate on the basis of race, color, religion, gender, age, national origin; disability, marital status, sexual orientation, or military status; debt retirement; endowments or other reserve funds; membership or affiliation campaigns, dinners, or special events; conferences and symposia and related travel; grants that further political doctrine; grants that further religious doctrine; grants to individuals; scholarships or sponsorships; individual medical procedures; medical, scientific, or academic research; grants to parochial or religious schools; grants to governmental agencies, except public schools; requests from individual public schools that have not coordinated the request with their central school district administration; requests from foundations/organizations that raise money for individual public schools; creation or installation of art objects; development, production, or distribution of books, newspapers, or video productions; grants for re-granting programs; requests for capital campaigns that have not met 75% of their goal; activities, projects, or programs that will have been completed before funding becomes available; and multi-year funding requests.
Geographic Focus: Colorado
Date(s) Application is Due: Feb 2; Jun 1; Oct 1
Contact: Jeff Hirota; (303) 300-1790, ext. 129; jhirota@denverfoundation.org
Internet: http://www.denverfoundation.org/page17824.cfm
Sponsor: Denver Foundation
55 Madison, 8th Floor
Denver, CO 80206

Denver Foundation Technical Assistance Grants 1505

All nonprofit organizations need help from time to time in order to function more effectively and efficiently. This is especially true of new or emerging nonprofit organizations or those with smaller budgets. The Denver Foundation has set aside funds specifically to provide grants for nonprofit organizations to get this kind of help, usually called technical assistance. Technical Assistance (TA) can be many things, and what is most important is that TA helps the staff and/or board of the organization learn something new and increase its capacity to lead, manage and direct the organization. Examples of Technical Assistance include: obtaining training on a specific topic, such as marketing, volunteer management, financial management or fund raising; hiring a facilitator for a board retreat; or working with a consultant to develop a fund raising plan or a strategic plan for the organization.
Requirements: To qualify for a grant an organization must be a 501(c)3 tax-exempt nonprofit organization, serve residents in seven specific Denver counties, and provide a service that falls under one of the four funding areas.
Restrictions: The Foundation will not consider requests to fund the following: requests from organizations that have received funding from the program for the three previous consecutive calendar years; organizations with fund balance deficits in their most recently completed fiscal year; organizations that discriminate on the basis of race, color, religion, gender, age, national origin; disability, marital status, sexual orientation, or military status; debt retirement; endowments or other reserve funds; membership or affiliation campaigns, dinners, or special events; conferences and symposia and related travel; grants that further political doctrine; grants that further religious doctrine; grants to individuals; scholarships or sponsorships; individual medical procedures; medical, scientific, or academic research; grants to parochial or religious schools; grants to governmental agencies, except public schools; requests from individual public schools that have not coordinated the request with their central school district administration; requests from foundations/organizations that raise money for individual public schools; creation or installation of art objects; development, production, or distribution of books, newspapers, or video productions; grants for re-granting programs; requests for capital campaigns that have not met 75% of their goal; activities, projects, or programs that will have been completed before funding becomes available; and multi-year funding requests.
Geographic Focus: Colorado
Date(s) Application is Due: Feb 2; Jun 1; Oct 1
Contact: Jeff Hirota; (303) 300-1790, ext. 129; jhirota@denverfoundation.org
Internet: http://www.denverfoundation.org/page16399.cfm
Sponsor: Denver Foundation
55 Madison, 8th Floor
Denver, CO 80206

Dept of Ed Alaska Native Educational Programs 1506

The overall purpose of the program is to meet the unique education needs of Alaska Natives and to support supplemental education programs to benefit Alaska Natives. Allowable activities include, but are not limited to, the development of curricula and education programs that address the education needs of Alaska Native students, and the development and operation of student enrichment programs in science and mathematics. Eligible activities also include professional development for educators, activities carried out through Even Start programs and Head Start programs, family literacy services, and dropout prevention programs.
Requirements: Alaska Native organizations, education entities with experience in developing or operating Alaska Native programs or programs of instruction conducted in Alaska Native languages, cultural and community-based organizations with experience in developing or operating programs to benefit Alaska Natives, and consortia of organizations may apply. A state education agency (SEA) or local education agency (LEA) may apply as part of a consortium involving an Alaska Native organization. The consortium may include other eligible applicants.
Geographic Focus: All States
Contact: Alexis Fisher, (202) 401-0281; alexis.fisher@ed.gov
Internet: http://www.ed.gov/programs/alaskanative/index.html
Sponsor: U.S. Department of Education
400 Maryland Avenue SW, Room 3W217, FB-6
Washington, DC 20202-6140

Dept of Ed Child Care Access Means Parents in School Program Grants 1507

The program supports the participation of low-income parents in postsecondary education through the provision of campus-based child care services. Funds are used to support or establish campus-based child care programs primarily serving the needs of low-income students enrolled in IHEs. Grants may be used for before and after-school services. In addition, grants may be used to serve the child care needs of the community served by the institution.
Requirements: An institution of higher education is eligible to receive a grant under this program if the total amount of all Federal Pell grant funds awarded to students enrolled at the institution of higher education for the preceding fiscal year equals or exceeds $350,000.
Geographic Focus: All States
Contact: Dorothy Marshall; (202) 502-7734; dorothy.marshall@ed.gov
Internet: http://www.ed.gov/programs/campisp/index.html
Sponsor: U.S. Department of Education
1990 K Street NW, Room 7051
Washington, DC 20006-8510

Dept of Ed Even Start Grants 1508

This program offers grants to support local family literacy projects that integrate early childhood education, adult literacy (adult basic and secondary-level education and instruction for English language learners), parenting education, and interactive parent and child literacy activities for low-income families with parents who are eligible for services under the Adult Education and Family Literacy Act and their children from birth through age 7. Teen parents and their children from birth through age 7 also are eligible. All participating families must be those most in need of program services.
Requirements: Awards are made to SEAs, which in turn make competitive subgrants to partnerships of local education agencies (LEAs) and nonprofit community-based organizations.
Geographic Focus: All States
Contact: Patricia McKee; (202) 260-0991; patricia.mckee@ed.gov
Internet: http://www.ed.gov/programs/evenstartformula/index.html
Sponsor: U.S. Department of Education
400 Maryland Avenue SW
Washington, DC 20202-5960

Dept of Ed Magnet Schools Assistance Grants　　1509
These grants assist in the desegregation of public schools by supporting the elimination, reduction, and prevention of minority group isolation in elementary and secondary schools with substantial numbers of minority group students. In order to meet the statutory purposes of the program, projects also must support the development and implementation of magnet schools that assist in the achievement of systemic reforms and provide all students with the opportunity to meet challenging academic content and student academic achievement standards. Projects support the development and design of innovative education methods and practices that promote diversity and increase choices in public education programs. The program supports capacity development, the ability of a school to help all its students meet more challenging standards through professional development and other activities that will enable the continued operation of the magnet schools at a high performance level after funding ends. Finally, the program supports the implementation of courses of instruction in magnet schools that strengthen students' knowledge of academic subjects and their grasp of tangible and marketable vocational skills. Application and deadline information is available online.
Requirements: Only LEAs or consortia of LEAs that are implementing court-ordered or federally approved voluntary desegregation plans that include magnet schools are eligible to apply.
Restrictions: Private schools are not eligible to participate in this program.
Geographic Focus: All States
Contact: Steve Brockhouse; (202) 260-2476; Steve.Brockhouse@ed.gov
Internet: http://www.ed.gov/programs/magnet/index.html
Sponsor: U.S. Department of Education
400 Maryland Avenue SW, Room 4W229, FB-6
Washington, DC 20202-5961

Dept of Ed Parental Information and Resource Centers　　1510
Parent Information and Resource Centers (PIRCs) help implement successful and effective parental involvement policies, programs, and activities that lead to improvements in student academic achievement and that strengthen partnerships among parents, teachers, principals, administrators, and other school personnel in meeting the education needs of children. Sec. 5563 of the Elementary and Secondary Education Act (ESEA) requires the recipients of PIRC grants to: serve both rural and urban areas; use at least half their funds to serve areas with high concentrations of low-income children; and use at least 30 percent of the funds they receive for early childhood parent programs.
Requirements: Nonprofit organizations or a consortium of a nonprofit organization and a local education agency (LEA) may apply. In the case of an application submitted by a consortium that includes an LEA, the nonprofit organization must serve as the applicant agency. Faith-based and community organizations are eligible to apply for funding provided that they are nonprofit organizations.
Geographic Focus: All States
Contact: Steven Brockhouse, Parental Options and Information Office; (202) 260-2476; fax (202) 205-5630; steve.brockhouse@ed.gov
Internet: http://www.ed.gov/programs/pirc/index.html
Sponsor: U.S. Department of Education
400 Maryland Avenue SW, Room 4W229, FB-6
Washington, DC 20202-5961

Dept of Ed Projects with Industry Grants　　1511
The purpose of this program is to create and expand job and career opportunities for individuals with disabilities in the competitive labor market. This is accomplished by involving private industry partners to help identify competitive job and career opportunities and the skills needed to perform these jobs to create practical job and career readiness and training programs and to provide job placement and career advancement.
Requirements: Applicants may include: employers (for-profit and nonprofit); nonprofit agencies or organizations; labor organizations; trade associations; community rehabilitation program providers. Indian tribes or tribal organizations, state vocational rehabilitation (VR) agencies, and any other agencies or organizations with the capacity to create and expand job and career opportunities for individuals with disabilities..
Geographic Focus: All States
Contact: Lavanna Kia Weems; (202) 245-7569; lavanna.weems@ed.gov
Internet: http://www.ed.gov/programs/rsapwi/index.html
Sponsor: U.S. Department of Education
400 Maryland Avenue SW, Room 5006, PCP
Washington, DC 20202-2647

Dept of Ed Recreational Services for Individuals with Disabilities　　1512
The purpose of this program is to provide individuals with disabilities inclusive recreational activities and experiences that can be expected to aid them in their employment, mobility, socialization, independence, and community integration. Recreation projects may include vocational skills development, leisure education, leisure networking, leisure resource development, physical education and sports, scouting and camping, 4-H activities, music, dancing, handicrafts, art, and homemaking.
Requirements: Institutions of Higher Education (IHEs), Local Education Agencies (LEAs), Nonprofit Organizations, Other Organizations and/or Agencies, State Education Agencies (SEAs), federally recognized Indian tribal governments, YMCAs, recreation department programs, and state vocational rehabilitation (VR) agencies may apply.
Geographic Focus: All States
Contact: Dianne Hardy; (202) 245-7370; fax (202) 245-7593; dianne.hardy@ed.gov
Internet: http://www.ed.gov/programs/rsarecreation/index.html
Sponsor: U.S. Department of Education
400 Maryland Avenue SW, Room 5125, PCP
Washington, DC 20202-2800

Dept of Ed Safe and Drug-Free Schools and Communities State Grants　　1513
This program provides support to SEAs for a variety of drug and violence prevention activities focused primarily on school-age youths. Activities may include: developing instructional materials; providing counseling services and professional development programs for school personnel; implementing community service projects and conflict resolution, peer mediation, mentoring and character education programs; establishing safe zones of passage for students to and from school; acquiring and installing metal detectors; and hiring security personnel.
Requirements: State Education Agencies may apply. Local Education Agencies or intermediate education agencies or consortia must apply to the State Education Agency.
Geographic Focus: All States
Contact: Paul Kesner; (202) 205-8134; fax (202) 260-7767; paul.kesner@ed.gov
Internet: http://www.ed.gov/programs/dvpformula/index.html
Sponsor: U.S. Department of Education
400 Maryland Avenue SW, Room 3E230, FB-6
Washington, DC 20202-6450

Dept of Ed Upward Bound Program　　1514
This program provides fundamental support to participants in their preparation for college entrance. The program provides opportunities for participants to succeed in their precollege performance and ultimately in their higher education pursuits. Upward Bound serves: high school students from low-income families; high school students from families in which neither parent holds a bachelor's degree; and low-income, first-generation military veterans who are preparing to enter postsecondary education. The goal of Upward Bound is to increase the rate at which participants complete secondary education and enroll in and graduate from institutions of postsecondary education.
Requirements: Institutions of higher education, public and private agencies and organizations, or a combination of these, and in exceptional circumstances, secondary schools, are eligible to apply.
Geographic Focus: All States
Contact: Program Specialists; (202) 502-7600; fax (202) 502-7857; OPE_TRIO@ed.gov
Internet: http://www.ed.gov/programs/trioupbound/index.html
Sponsor: U.S. Department of Education
1990 K Street NW, 7th Floor
Washington, DC 20006-8510

Dept of Ed Workplace and Community Transition Training for Incarcerated Youth Offenders Program　　1515
This program provides grants to state correctional education agencies to assist and encourage incarcerated youths to acquire functional literacy, life, and job skills through the pursuit of postsecondary education certificates, associate of arts degrees, and bachelor's degrees. These youths may be assisted with this program's support while in prison. They also may receive employment counseling and other related services that start during incarceration and continue through prerelease and while on parole.
Requirements: Only designated State Correctional Education Agencies designated by the governor of the state may apply for these funds. For purposes of this grant, an eligible youth offender is defined as an individual, age 25 or younger, who is incarcerated in a State prison and is within 5 years of release or parole eligibility.
Geographic Focus: All States
Contact: Carlette Huntley, (202) 205-7943; Carlette.Huntley@ed.gov
Internet: http://www.ed.gov/programs/transitiontraining/index.html?exp=0
Sponsor: U.S. Department of Education
400 Maryland Avenue SW, Room 3E216, FB-6
Washington, DC 20202-6450

Dermody Properties Foundation Capstone Award　　1516
The Capstone gift began in 2007 as a way to say thank you to a community that helps our business thrive. Each year during the Thanksgiving season, Dermody Properties makes a substantial donation to one or more nonprofit organizations to help them continue their good works throughout the holiday season. The donation is aimed at organizations situated in northern Nevada.
Geographic Focus: Nevada
Contact: Maggie Atwood, Foundation Coordinator; (775) 741-8411 or (775) 858-8080; fax (775) 856-0831; matwood@partnerwithdp.com
Internet: http://www.partnerwithdp.com/Dermody/foundation.cfm
Sponsor: Dermody Properties Foundation
5500 Equity Avenue
Reno, NV 89502

Dermody Properties Foundation Grants　　1517
The Dermody Properties Foundation was founded in 1988, funded by the profits generated by the hard work and dedication of all the employees at Dermody Properties/DP Partners. The foundation supports nonprofits in Dermody Properties operating communities in its areas of interest, including: family and children, education, services for seniors, and the arts. Organizations and projects that have been supported include Community Child Care Services, the Children's Cabinet, Washoe County School District Educator Scholarships and the Food Bank of Northern Nevada. Grants typically range from $500 to $3,000.
Requirements: Nonprofits in Reno and Las Vegas, Nevada; Chicago, Illinois; Atlanta, Georgia; and Harrisburg, Pennsylvania, are eligible.
Geographic Focus: Georgia, Illinois, Nevada, Pennsylvania
Date(s) Application is Due: Aug 15
Amount of Grant: 500 - 3,000 USD
Contact: Maggie Atwood, Foundation Coordinator; (775) 741-8411 or (775) 858-8080; fax (775) 856-0831; matwood@dermody.com

Internet: http://www.dermody.com/dp_foundation
Sponsor: Dermody Properties Foundation
5500 Equity Avenue
Reno, NV 89502

DeRoy Testamentary Foundation Grants   1518
Established in 1979, the Foundation gives primarily in the state of Michigan. Giving primarily for youth development and services, education, human services, health care, and the arts. The Foundation offers support in the form of: scholarship funds; annual campaigns; building/renovation; continuing support; general/operating support; program development grants. There are no application deadlines. The board meets monthly.
Requirements: Michigan nonprofit organizations are eligible.
Restrictions: Grants are not made to individuals.
Geographic Focus: Michigan
Amount of Grant: 10,000 - 300,000 USD
Contact: Julie Rodecker Holly; (248) 827-0920; fax (248) 827-0922; deroyfdtn@aol.com
Sponsor: DeRoy Testamentary Foundation
26999 Central Park Boulevard, Suite 160N
Southfield, MI 48076

Detlef Schrempf Foundation Grants   1519
The focus of the foundation is on children, youth and families in the Pacific Northwest. This foundation seeks supporting organizations that can help underwrite the costs of events, enabling the maximum amount of proceeds to go directly to the benefiting charity.
Requirements: Typically, a qualifying charity partner will have a $5-million, or smaller, operating budget.
Geographic Focus: Idaho, Oregon, Washington
Contact: Nicole Morrison; (206) 464-0826; fax (206) 464-8020; info@detlef.com
Internet: http://www.detlef.com
Sponsor: Detlef Schrempf Foundation
1904 Third Avenue, Suite 339
Seattle, WA 98101

Detroit Lions Charities Grants   1520
The organization supports charitable and community causes in Michigan. Funding interests include child abuse and domestic violence prevention, youth recreation, and spinal cord injury research. Grants have been awarded to support the Never, Never Shake a Baby billboard campaign; Pigskin Geography, a learning initiative for youth; Big Brothers/Big Sisters; Grand Rapids Metropolitan YMCA—for swimming lessons for inner-city youth; and Saint Joseph Mercy Hospital—for a domestic violence education program. Requests are accepted between October 1 and December 31.
Geographic Focus: Michigan
Date(s) Application is Due: Dec 31
Contact: Detroit Lions Community Affairs Information Hotline; (313) 216-4056
Internet: http://detroitlions.com/community/index.cfm?cont_id=49715
Sponsor: Detroit Lions Charities
222 Republic Drive
Allen Park, MI 48101

Deuce McAllister Catch 22 Foundation Grants   1521
McAllister was born in Lena, Mississippi, who went on to attend the University of Mississippi. As an Ole Miss Rebel, McAllister broke and set many records as a running back. In college, during his down time, McAllister could be found visiting with children in the community establishing himself as a positive role model on and off the field. In 2001, he was drafted in the first round as the 23rd overall selection by the New Orleans Saints. After one year of orientation in the NFL, McAllister decided he wanted to start a foundation to maximize his giving in the communities he knows best; New Orleans area and Jackson area. Today, Deuce McAllister's Catch 22 Foundation is dedicated to enhancing the lives of under-privileged youth and adolescents in the Gulf South Region primarily through the establishment of positive role models in their lives, providing unique opportunities for them to experience, and a financial commitment to making a difference.
Geographic Focus: Louisiana, Mississippi
Contact: De'Shundra McAllister, Director; (601) 665-3147 or (601) 957-5050; info@catch22foundation.com or deucemcallister?@dmcallister26.com
Internet: http://www.catch22foundation.com/
Sponsor: Deuce McAllister Catch 22 Foundation
6360 I-55 North, Suite 101
Jackson, MS 39211

DFN Hurricane Katrina and Disability Rapid Response Grants   1522
The program helps nonprofit organizations meet the immediate and long-term needs of people with disabilities in the Gulf region as a result of hurricanes, storms, and other severe weather conditions. Mini grants are awarded to nonprofit organizations to meet specific needs that include, but are not limited to, transportation, shelter, medication, medical equipment and assistive technology. Grants will continue to be awarded until funds are depleted. Multiple requests from a single organization are not encouraged. Application is available online.
Requirements: Eligibility is limited to 501(c)3 nonprofit organizations. Requests from grassroots organizations will be given priority during the review process.
Restrictions: No grants will be awarded to individuals or for general operating purposes.
Geographic Focus: All States
Amount of Grant: Up to 5,000 USD
Contact: Tracey Murray, (770) 232-9001; disabilityfundersnetwork@cox.net

Internet: http://www.disabilityfunders.org/kat-rrf.html
Sponsor: Disability Funders Network
8568 Spring Breeze Terrace
Suwanee, GA 30024

DHHS Abandoned Infants Assistance Grants   1523
Funds are provided to prevent the abandonment of infants and young children including the provision of services; to identify and address their needs, especially those who have been infected with the human immunodeficiency virus or who have been prenatally exposed to the virus or a dangerous drug; to assist such children to reside with their natural families or in foster care, as appropriate; to conduct residential programs for abandoned infants and young children who are unable to reside with their families; to provide respite care for families and caregivers; to recruit, train, and obtain foster families; and to recruit and train health and social services personnel to work with families. Contact the office for deadline dates.
Requirements: Eligible applicants are state or local governments, federally recognized Native American tribal governments, U.S. territories and possessions, and nonprofit organizations.
Geographic Focus: All States
Date(s) Application is Due: Aug 12
Amount of Grant: Up to 475,000 USD
Contact: Patricia Campiglia, Program Officer; (202) 205-8060; pcampiglia@acf.hhs.gov
Internet: http://a257.g.akamaitech.net/7/257/2422/01jan20051800/edocket.access.gpo.gov/2005/05-11592.htm
Sponsor: U.S. Department of Health and Human Services
330 C Street SW, Room 2428
Washington, DC 20447

DHHS Adolescent Family Life Demonstration Projects   1524
This program has multiple components of prevention, care and research. The prevention component focuses on development and testing of abstinence based programs designed to delay the onset of sexual activity reducing the incidence of adolescent pregnancy, STD transmission and HIV/AIDS. The care component is focused on providing comprehensive health, education and social services to pregnant adolescents, adolescent parents, their infants, male partners and their families. The primary focus of research is to improve understanding of the issues surrounding sexuality, pregnancy and parenting by examining the factors that influence adolescent sexual, contraceptive and fertility behaviors, the nature and effectiveness of care services for pregnant and parenting adolescents and why adoption is a little-used alternative among pregnant adolescents. Deadlines are announced in the Federal Register and on the Office of Population Affairs Web site (http://opa.osophs.dhhs.gov).
Requirements: Public and private non-profit organizations may apply.
Geographic Focus: All States
Contact: Andrea Brandon, Chief Grants Management Officer; (301) 594-6554
Internet: http://aspe.hhs.gov/SelfGovernance/inventory/OPA/111.htm
Sponsor: U.S. Department of Health and Human Services
4350 East-West Highway
Bethesda, MD 20814

DHHS AIDS Project Grants   1525
The grants are intended to fund programs that develop and implement surveillance, epidemiological research, health education, school health, and risk reduction activities of AIDS in states and major cities. The program also gives support for cooperative agreements for AIDS activities. The funding period will be from one to five years, renewable. Applicants should contact the CDC for deadline information.
Requirements: Public and private organizations, both nonprofit and for profit, state and local governments, U.S. territories and possessions, small and minority businesses, and businesses owned by women are encouraged to apply.
Geographic Focus: All States
Amount of Grant: 45,000 - 2,000,000 USD
Contact: Cheryl Maddux, Grants Manager; (770) 498-1911
Internet: http://www.dhhs.gov
Sponsor: U.S. Department of Health and Human Services
2920 Brandywine Road
Atlanta, GA 30341

DHHS American Recovery and Reinvestment Act of 2009 Head Start Expansion   1526
The Administration for Children and Families (ACF) announces the availability of approximately $102 million to be competitively awarded to current Head Start grantees for the purpose of expanding enrollment by approximately 14,100 low-income children and their families. This expansion is only to increase the number of pre-school age children served in Head Start. ACF solicits applications from existing federally funded Head Start agencies to compete for funds that are available to provide services to unserved children and families residing in the defined federally approved service areas. Each grantee currently has a defined, approved service area and may apply to serve additional low-income children in that area. In addition, grantees may propose to serve areas that are currently unserved as long as they can demonstrate they meet the statutory requirement to be a Head Start provider in that community; i.e. an agency that would be understood by the community as a local agency, 'within a community'; i.e. an agency that has some presence in that community or the community is contiguous to its current service area and the community demonstrates its support for the applicant to be a Head Start provider in the community. Applicants proposing to both expand within their current service area and to establish a new program in an unserved area must submit separate applications. The average project award amount is $500,000 per budget period.
Requirements: Head Start serves children from the age of three to the age when children enter kindergarten. Programs serve those families who have incomes below the poverty line or are

eligible for public assistance. In addition, homeless children and children in foster care are categorically eligible for Head Start. The law permits up to 10 percent of enrolled Head Start children to be from families that do not meet these low-income criteria. A new provision in the Head Start Act, as discussed in Section 645(a)(1)(B), allows grantees that can ensure that all eligible children including homeless children are served, to enroll up to 35 percent of its participants from families with incomes greater than or equal to 100 but less than 130 percent of the poverty line. However, this expansion announcement is only for areas with children from families with incomes below the poverty line that are currently not served by Head Start. Programs may still propose that up to 10% of their enrollment be children from families not meeting Head Start income eligibility requirements. Head Start also requires that a minimum of 10 percent of children actually enrolled by the Head Start agency and delegates be children with disabilities unless a waiver is granted. Eligible applicants are limited only to current Federally-funded Head Start agencies. Delegate agencies are not eligible to apply. Applicants will compete against other applicants from the same competitive area. In other words, all applicants within a state will compete for the funds available for that area. All applicants must have a D&B Data Universal Numbering System (D-U-N-S) number.
Restrictions: Foreign entities are not eligible under this announcement.
Geographic Focus: All States
Date(s) Application is Due: Jun 23
Contact: Colleen Rathgeb, (866) 796-1591; OHS@dixon-group.com
Internet: http://www.acf.hhs.gov/grants/open/HHS-2009-ACF-OHS-SH-0089.html
Sponsor: U.S. Department of Health and Human Services
370 L'Enfant Promenade SW
Washington, DC 20447

DHHS ARRA Strengthening Communities Fund - Nonprofit Capacity Building Grants   1527

The Federal Government recognizes the important work carried out by nonprofit organizations to address the needs of those suffering economic hardships. Under this program, the Government will partner with lead organizations working in distressed communities to sustain and build the capacity of each project's selected local grassroots organizations to better serve individuals in need. Lead organizations awarded funds under this announcement will serve their selected local nonprofit organizations in order to increase those project partners' sustainability and improve their effectiveness. Helping meet the social service needs of individuals, workers, and their families will not only encourage a stronger, healthier workforce but will build vital, enduring communities. Nonprofit organizations need capacity building assistance now to continue to serve those in need in their communities. Through the Strengthening Communities Fund (SCF) Nonprofit Capacity Building program, ACF will award funds to experienced lead organizations to provide nonprofit organizations capacity building training, technical assistance, and competitive financial assistance to participating nonprofit organizations, which serve as the partners in their projects. Lead organizations will collaborate with their selected grassroots organizations in distressed communities offering capacity building activities in five critical areas: 1) organizational development, 2) program development, 3) collaboration and community engagement, 4) leadership development, and 5) evaluation of effectiveness. Capacity building activities are designed to increase an project partners' sustainability and effectiveness, enhance their ability to provide social services, and create collaborations to better serve those most in need.
Requirements: Eligible applicants are as follows: State governments; County governments; City or township governments; Public and State-controlled institutions of higher education; Indian/Native American Tribal governments (Federally recognized); Indian/Native American Tribal governments (other than Federally recognized tribal governments); Nonprofits with 501(c)3 IRS status (other than institutions of higher education); Nonprofits without 501(c)3 IRS status (other than institutions of higher education); For-profit organizations (other than small businesses); Small businesses; Special district governments, ACF encourages applications from organizations that propose to work with and have experience working with grassroots organizations that historically have not been supported by Federal funds. Lead organizations must be established organizations with well-developed connections and working relationships with the nonprofit community in the well-defined geographic area they propose to serve. In all but rare cases, lead organizations will be physically located in the geographic area they propose to serve. In addition, for a lead organization to provide effective training and technical assistance in capacity building, it should demonstrate a cultural sensitivity that establishes credibility with its target audience of nonprofit organizations in the geographic area it selects. Approved applicants must be willing to work closely with ACF, and any entities funded by ACF, to coordinate, assist, or evaluate the activities of the lead organizations providing technical assistance and issuing competitive financial assistance. Grantees must provide at least 20 percent of the total approved cost of the project. The total approved cost of the project is the sum of the ACF (Federal) share and the non-Federal share. The non-Federal share may be met by cash or in-kind contributions, although applicants are encouraged to meet their match requirements through cash contributions.
Restrictions: Funding cannot be used to enhance or expand the capacity of lead organizations beyond what is necessary to accomplish the purpose of the project. Foreign entities are not eligible under this announcement. Applications with requests that exceed the ceiling on the amount of individual awards will be deemed non-responsive and will not be considered for funding under this announcement.
Geographic Focus: All States
Date(s) Application is Due: Jul 7
Contact: Thom Campbell; (800) 281-9519; ocs@lcgnet.com
Internet: http://www.acf.hhs.gov/grants/open/HHS-2009-ACF-OCS-SI-0091.html
Sponsor: U.S. Department of Health and Human Services
370 L'Enfant Promenade SW
Washington, DC 20447

DHHS ARRA Strengthening Communities Fund - State, Local, and Tribal Government Capacity Building Grants   1528

The purpose of this grant program is to build the capacity of government offices (or their authorized designee) that provide outreach to faith-based and community-based organizations and to assist nonprofit organizations in addressing the broad economic recovery issues present in their communities, including helping low-income individuals secure and retain employment, earn higher wages, obtain better-quality jobs, and gain greater access to State and Federal benefits and tax credits. The Administration for Children and Families (ACF) will award funds to State, city, county, and Indian/Native American Tribal government offices (e.g., offices responsible for outreach to faith-based and community organizations or those interested in initiating such an effort), or their designees, to build their own capacity to partner with community-based and faith-based non-profits and to provide training and technical assistance to help nonprofit faith-based and community organizations better serve those in need and to increase nonprofit organizations' involvement in the economic recovery. Grantees will use program funds to provide free capacity building services to nonprofit organizations, such as a beneficiary benefits clearinghouse, outreach and education, facilitation of partnerships between and among nonprofits and other government agencies, and training and technical assistance to improve awareness of and access to ARRA efforts/benefits and to improve organizational capacity to be active participants in ARRA efforts/benefits. Grantees will also use program funds to build their own capacity to provide these services to nonprofits. The average projected award amount is $250,000 per project period.
Requirements: An applicant must be a State, city, county, or Indian/Native American Tribal government office or a designated private nonprofit organization authorized by such an office. All applicants, whether a government office or a private nonprofit organization, must be authorized by the State, city, county, or Indian/Native American Tribal government to apply for a SCF State, Local, and Tribal Government Capacity Building program grant through a statute, resolution, or executive order. Applicants must include a copy of the authorizing document in the application. If the document is not signed or approved prior to the application due date, a letter from the executive officer of the governing body may be submitted, with an approved statute, resolution, or executive order to be submitted by the start of the grant. This authorizing document must specify the role of the Authorized Entity as well as detail the support, access, and authority to be provided by the State, city, county, and Indian/Native American Tribal government with regard to the activities to be conducted under the grant. A State, city, county, or Indian/Native American Tribal government may designate only one authorized entity to apply for this program. All applicants must have a D&B Data Universal Numbering System (D-U-N-S) number.
Restrictions: Applications with requests that exceed the ceiling on the amount of individual awards will be deemed non-responsive and will not be considered for funding. These grants cannot be used to provide direct client services. Under the SCF State, Local, and Tribal Government Capacity Building program, organizations shall not use direct Federal grants or contracts to support inherently religious activities, such as religious instruction, worship, or proselytization. Therefore, any organization receiving funds must take steps to separate, in time or location, their inherently religious activities from the grant-funded activities. Some of the ways organizations may accomplish this include, but are not limited to, promoting only the Federally funded program in materials or websites created with any portion of the Federal funds. Further, participation in such inherently religious activity by individuals receiving services must be voluntary. Any criteria for selecting nonprofit organizations to receive training and technical assistance must be neutral to whether the nonprofits are religious or secular groups.
Geographic Focus: All States
Date(s) Application is Due: Jul 7
Contact: Thom Campbell; (800) 281-9519; ocs@lcgnet.com
Internet: http://www.acf.hhs.gov/grants/open/HHS-2009-ACF-OCS-SN-0092.html
Sponsor: U.S. Department of Health and Human Services
370 L'Enfant Promenade SW
Washington, DC 20447

DHHS Community Services Block Grant Training and Technical Assistance: Capacity-Building for Ongoing CSBG Programs and Strategic Planning and   1529

This program is intended to support Statewide capacity development projects for technical assistance in the Community Services Block Grant program. In addition, it supports Statewide strategic planning efforts related to the American Recovery and Reinvestment Act of 2009. The Recovery Act projects supported through this announcement are a part of the Federal government's overall support for training and technical assistance activities. As specified in the CSBG Act, training and technical assistance activities may support improved financial management practices, program performance measurement, information and reporting systems, coordination between fragmented State and local programs, and ensure responsiveness to locally identified community needs. The focus of strategic planning efforts supported through this grant will be on informing communities of available services supported under the Recovery Act, documenting community results, and preparing communities to sustain the impact of Recovery Act funds after additional Federal support received through the Recovery Act ends.
Requirements: Eligible applicants include Non-profits with 501(c)3 IRS status (other than institutions of higher education); Non-profits without 501(c)3 IRS status (other than institutions of higher education); or statewide or local organizations or associations, with demonstrated expertise in providing training to individuals and organizations on methods of effectively addressing the needs of low-income families and communities. Faith-based and community organizations are eligible to apply under this announcement. Organizations that applied for and received funding under funding opportunity HHS-2008-ACF-OCS-ET-0041 are eligible for funding under this announcement. However, applicants that received funding under HHS-2008-ACF-OCS-ET-0041 must describe new proposed capacity-building projects proposed in Part 1 of the grant project (Capacity-Building for Ongoing CSBG Programs) that do not duplicate those supported under the previous

application. Applicants for funding under this announcement must be recognized by the State CSBG Lead Agency as a technical assistance provider for eligible entities within the State and must include a letter of endorsement from the State CSBG Lead Agency. All applicants must have a D&B Data Universal Numbering System (D-U-N-S) number. A D-U-N-S number is required whether an applicant is submitting a paper application or using the government-wide electronic portal, Grants.gov.
Restrictions: Applications with requests that exceed the ceiling on the amount of individual awards will be deemed ineligible. Applications that do not include a letter of endorsement from the State CSBG Lead Agency will not be considered for funding. Foreign entities are not eligible under this announcement.
Geographic Focus: All States
Date(s) Application is Due: Jun 12
Amount of Grant: 105,000 USD
Contact: Seth Hassett; (800) 281-9519; OCS@lcgnet.com
Internet: http://www.acf.hhs.gov/grants/open/HHS-2009-ACF-OCS-EQ-0037.html
Sponsor: U.S. Department of Health and Human Services
370 L'Enfant Promenade SW
Washington, DC 20447

DHHS Comprehensive Community Mental Health Services Grants for Children with Serious Emotional Disturbances   1530
This program provides community-based systems of care for children and adolescents with serious emotional disturbances and their families. The program will ensure that services are provided collaboratively across child-serving systems; that each child or adolescent served through the program receives an individualized service plan developed with the participation of the family; that each individualized plan designates a case manager to assist the child and family; and that funding is provided for mental health services required to meet the needs of youngsters in these systems.
Requirements: States; political subdivisions of a state, such as county or local governments; and federally recognized Native American tribal governments are eligible to apply.
Geographic Focus: All States
Amount of Grant: 200,064 - 35,000,000 USD
Contact: Gary Blau, Chief, Child Adolescent and Family Branch; (301) 443-1333
Internet: http://mentalhealth.samhsa.gov/publications/allpubs/CA-0013/default.asp
Sponsor: U.S. Department of Health and Human Services
5600 Fishers Lane, Parklawn Building
Rockville, MD 20857

DHHS Emergency Medical Services for Children (EMSC) Program   1531
The purpose of this program is to support demonstration projects for the expansion and improvement of emergency medical services for children who need treatment for trauma or critical care. It is expected that maximum distribution of projects among the states will be made and that priority will be given to projects targeted toward populations with special needs, including Native Americans, minorities, and the disabled. Annual deadline dates may vary; contact program staff for exact dates.
Requirements: States and accredited schools of medicine are eligible to apply.
Geographic Focus: All States
Amount of Grant: 200,000 USD
Contact: Dan Kavanaugh, (301) 443-1321; dkavanaugh@hrsa.gov
Internet: http://mchb.hrsa.gov/programs/emsc
Sponsor: U.S. Department of Health and Human Services
5600 Fishers Lane, Parklawn Building
Rockville, MD 20857

DHHS Emerging Leaders Program Internships   1532
The Emerging Leaders Program (ELP) is a competitive, two-year paid, federal internship with the U.S. Department of Health and Human Services (HHS). The Program provides a unique opportunity to develop enhanced leadership skills in one of the largest federal agencies in the nation. Upon successful completion of the ELP, participants will be eligible for non-competitive conversion to a permanent appointment. The ELP offers participants the following: formal competency-based leadership training and professional development; challenging developmental rotational assignments; mentorship; fast-paced and diverse work environment; and promotion to a permanent career track that targets the following mission-critical occupation specialties: scientific, social science, human resources, administrative, information technology, public health, and law enforcement. To begin the application process, applicants apply to one or more career track(s) that match their education and/or experience specialty. Later applicants may apply to the specific positions under their chosen career track(s). At the date of this writing, the website states that the ELP is not currently accepting applications, but encourages those interested to check back for future updates.
Requirements: Applicants must qualify for a minimum of one career track to move on to the next phase of the selection process.
Geographic Focus: All States
Contact: Grants Coordinator; (877) 696-6775; ELP@hhs.gov
Internet: http://hhsu.learning.hhs.gov/elp/howtoapply.asp
Sponsor: U.S. Department of Health and Human Services
200 Independence Avenue SW
Washington, DC 20201

DHHS Health Centers Grants for Residents of Public Housing   1533
Grants are awarded to improve minority access to primary care services and reduce infant mortality by enabling grantees, directly or through contracts, to provide to public housing residents, especially pregnant residents and their infants, primary health services, including health screening, education, and counseling. Applications should be designed to improve the availability, accessibility, and provision of primary health care services, including comprehensive perinatal care, to residents of public housing. Contact the office for deadline dates.
Requirements: Eligible applicants are public and nonprofit private entities that have the capacity to administer a grant and are located in a high infant mortality area as determined by the Healthy Start Initiative criteria. Preference is given to community health centers, health care for the homeless programs, and resident management corporations.
Geographic Focus: All States
Amount of Grant: 140,000 - 400,000 USD
Contact: Office of Grants Management, Bureau of Primary Health Care; (301) 594-4235
Internet: http://www.federalgrantswire.com/health_centers_grants_for_residents_of_public_housing.html
Sponsor: U.S. Department of Health and Human Services
4350 East-West Highway
Bethesda, MD 20814

DHHS Healthy Tomorrows Partnership for Children   1534
This program encourages community-based partnerships to coordinate health resources for pregnant women, infants, and children. Grantees are encouraged to seek additional support from the private sector and foundations. Applicants must provide a dollar for dollar cash match after the end of the first year of the grant.
Requirements: Eligible applicants include public and private entities, community-based organizations, Indian tribes, and tribal organizations. Priority is given to projects in all U.S. territories and in Alabama, Delaware, Florida, Georgia, Hawaii, Idaho, Indiana, Iowa, Kansas, Louisiana, Maine, Maryland, Massachusetts, Mississippi, Missouri, Montana, Nevada, New Hampshire, New Jersey, North Carolina, North Dakota, South Carolina, Texas, West Virginia, Wisconsin, and Wyoming.
Geographic Focus: Alabama, Delaware, Florida, Georgia, Hawaii, Idaho, Indiana, Iowa, Kansas, Louisiana, Maine, Maryland, Massachusetts, Mississippi, Missouri, Montana, Nevada, New Hampshire, New Jersey, North Carolina, North Dakota, South Carolina, Texas, West Virginia, Wisconsin, Wyoming
Amount of Grant: Up to 50,000 USD
Contact: Lawrence Poole, Director, Division of Grants Management; (301) 443-2385
Internet: http://mchb.hrsa.gov/programs/training/healthytomorrows.htm
Sponsor: U.S. Department of Health and Human Services
200 Independence Avenue SW
Washington, DC 20201

DHHS Independence Demonstration Program   1535
The objective of the program is to provide for the establishment of demonstration projects designed to determine the social, civic, psychological, and economic effects of providing to individuals and families with limited means an incentive to accumulate assets by saving a portion of their earned income; the extent to which an asset-based policy that promotes saving for postsecondary education, homeownership, and microenterprise development may be used to enable individuals and families with limited means to increase their economic self-sufficiency; and the extent to which an asset-based policy stabilizes and improves families and the community in which the families live. Deadlines are announced in the Federal Register.
Requirements: Nonprofit 501(c)3 tax-exempt organizations and state or local government agencies or tribal governments submitting an application jointly with such a nonprofit organization are eligible to apply.
Geographic Focus: All States
Amount of Grant: 360,000 USD
Contact: James Gatz, (202) 401-4626; AFIProgram@acf.hhs.gov
Internet: http://www.acf.hhs.gov/grants/open/HHS-2004-ACF-OCS-EI-0027.html
Sponsor: U.S. Department of Health and Human Services
370 L'Enfant Promenade SW, Suite 500 W
Washington, DC 20447

DHHS Maternal and Child Health Projects Grants   1536
The goal of the program is to improve the quality and use of genetic services in maternal and child health care, integrate services for children with special health care needs, support state fetal and infant mortality review centers, and enhance the use of data in problem solving for maternal and child health. The four grant programs currently accepting applications are genetic services, integrated services for children with special health care needs, state fetal/infant mortality review support centers, and data utilization and enhancement for state/community infrastructure building and managed care. Genetic services projects should improve the quality, availability, accessibility, and use of genetic services as an integral part of comprehensive maternal and child health care. Integrated services for children with special health care needs should demonstrate innovative and replicable models of community-based services. State fetal/infant mortality review support centers should provide training and technical assistance to state maternal and child health agencies on their particular needs. Data utilization and enhancement for state/community infrastructure building and managed care projects should enhance the use of qualitative and quantitative analytic methods in solving health problems for women and children. Contact the office for deadlines.
Requirements: Eligible applicants are public and private nonprofit agencies, including hospitals, Native American tribes, and social service agencies. The bureau will give extra attention to applications from historically black colleges and universities and Hispanic-serving institutions.
Geographic Focus: All States
Contact: Program Contact; (301) 443-2170; fax (301) 443-1797
Internet: http://mchb.hrsa.gov/programs/default.htm
Sponsor: U.S. Department of Health and Human Services
5600 Fishers Lane, Parklawn Building
Rockville, MD 20857

DHHS Promoting Safe and Stable Families Grants 1537
The National Center on Child Abuse and Neglect is interested in research on the impact of community-based family support and family preservation programs on child abuse and neglect. Research should focus on expanding the current knowledge base, build on previous research, and provide insights into new approaches to preventing child maltreatment and preserving families through support and preservation services. The center is particularly interested in projects that address specific populations and outcomes. The populations are families who receive family support services but have had no previous contact with child protective services; families who have been referred to child protective services whose cases were unsubstantiated but were found to need services and were referred to family support programs; families who have been in the system whose child abuse or neglect cases were substantiated, who received family preservation or support services, and whose cases are now closed; and families who have open cases whose children have not been removed and who are receiving family preservation services. Outcomes of interest are case finding, which involves families who were not referred to child protective services, and the impact of family support and/or preservation services on prevention, recidivism, and removal of children. Applicants should plan and design the proposed research in collaboration with state and local CPS and Title IV-B agencies as well as community-based entities providing family support services, such as family resource centers. Contact the office for deadline dates.
Requirements: Agencies of state and local governments, public and private nonprofit agencies, and institutions engaged in child and family welfare activities and research are eligible for these grants.
Geographic Focus: All States
Amount of Grant: 194,000 - 48,000,000 USD
Contact: Joseph Bock, Program Supervisor; (202) 205-8618
Internet: http://www.acf.hhs.gov/programs/cb/programs/fpfs.htm
Sponsor: U.S. Department of Health and Human Services
330 C Street SW, Room 2428
Washington, DC 20447

DHHS Special Programs for the Aging Training, Research, and Discretionary Projects and Programs Grants 1538
Funds are given to provide adequately trained personnel in the field of aging, improve knowledge of the problems and needs of the elderly, and to demonstrate better ways of improving the quality of life for the elderly. Funds may be used to train persons to work in the field of aging, to increase the availability and accessibility of training and education programs in the field of aging, and to conduct activities for the development of knowledge to improve the circumstances of older people. Deadlines are posted in the Federal Register.
Requirements: Grants may be made to any public or nonprofit private agency, organization, or institution.
Restrictions: Grants are not available to individuals.
Geographic Focus: All States
Amount of Grant: 250,000 USD
Contact: Center for Planning and Policy Development, Administration on Aging; (202) 619-0724
Internet: http://aspe.hhs.gov/SelfGovernance/inventory/Aoa/048.htm
Sponsor: U.S. Department of Health and Human Services
330 Independence Avenue SW
Washington, DC 20201

DHHS Technical and Non-Financial Assistance to Health Centers 1539
The grants assist community health centers in the areas of collaborative activities on state or regional issues; promotion of support and involvement of state agencies in primary care; provision of, or arrangement for, training and technical assistance; and development of shared services and joint purchasing arrangements—for purposes including, but not limited to, primary care provider retention and recruitment, clinical development, assessment of community health needs, expertise in dealing with maternal and child health and other special populations, and management and maximization of nonfederal sources. Recipients will be expected to provide certain technical and nonfinancial assistance to community health centers. Support is recommended for a specified project period, not in excess of five years. Deadlines are specified in application instructions.
Requirements: Grants will be made to private nonprofit entities, including state and regional primary care associations.
Geographic Focus: All States
Amount of Grant: 580,000 USD
Contact: Cicely Nelson, (301) 594-4300; cnelson@hrsa.gov
Internet: http://www.hrsa.gov/grants/preview/primary.htm
Sponsor: U.S. Department of Health and Human Services
4350 East-West Highway
Bethesda, MD 20814

DHHS Welfare Reform Research, Evaluations, and National Studies Grants 1540
The objectives of the funding are to support research on the benefits, effects, and costs of different welfare reform interventions; and studies such as on the effects of different programs on welfare dependency, illegitimacy, teen pregnancy, employment rates, child well-being, and related areas; and to assist in the development and evaluation of innovative approaches for reducing welfare dependency and increasing the well-being of minority children in welfare families. Grants, cooperative agreements, and contracts are awarded for innovative research, demonstrations, and evaluations that are responsive to the Administration for Children and Families program priorities. Deadlines for grants are announced in the Federal Register.
Requirements: Grants and cooperative agreements may be made to or with governmental entities, colleges, universities, nonprofit, and for-profit organizations (if fee is waived). Contracts may be awarded to nonprofit or for-profit organizations. Grants or cooperative agreements cannot be made directly to individuals.
Geographic Focus: All States
Contact: Karl Koerper, Office of Planning, Research, and Evaluation, Administration for Children and Families; (202) 401-4535; fax (202) 205-3598; KKoerper@acf.dhhf.gov
Internet: http://www.acf.hhs.gov/programs/opre
Sponsor: U.S. Department of Health and Human Services
370 L'Enfant Promenade SW
Washington, DC 20447

DHL Charitable Shipment Support 1541
The corporation provides free shipment of materials supporting charitable programs. Applicants must submit a complete web questionnaire.
Requirements: Application by internet only.
Restrictions: Religious organizations are ineligible for religious sectarian activities, and political organizations are not eligible for political purposes.
Geographic Focus: All States
Contact: Technical Support; (800) 527-7298
Internet: http://www.dhl-usa.com
Sponsor: DHL International, Ltd.
1220 South Pine Island Road, Suite 600
Plantation, FL 33324

DHS ARRA Fire Station Construction Grants (SCG) 1542
The Department of Homeland Security's Assistance to Firefighters Fire Station Construction Grants (SCG) will provide financial assistance directly to fire departments on a competitive basis to build new or modify existing fire stations in order for departments to enhance their response capability and protect the community they serve from fire and fire-related hazards.
Requirements: Non-Federal Fire Departments and state and local governments that fund/operate fire departments are eligible to apply. SCG seeks to support organizations lacking the tools and resources necessary to effectively protect the health and safety of the public and their emergency response personnel with respect to fire and all other hazards.
Geographic Focus: All States
Date(s) Application is Due: Jul 10
Contact: Help Desk; (866) 274-0960; firegrants@dhs.gov
Internet: http://www.firegrantsupport.com/afscg/
Sponsor: U.S. Department of Homeland Security
500 C Street SW
Washington, DC 20472

DHS ARRA Port Security Grant Program (PSGP) 1543
The purpose of the FY 2009 ARRA PSGP is to create a sustainable, risk-based effort to protect critical port infrastructure from terrorism, particularly attacks using explosives and non-conventional threats that could cause major disruption to commerce. Funds will support increased port-wide risk management; enhanced domain awareness; and further capabilities to prevent, detect, respond to and recover from attacks involving improvised explosive devices (IEDs) and other non-conventional weapons. It is expected that about 200 awards will be granted from the estimated total program funding of $150,000,000.
Requirements: All entities covered by an Area Maritime Security Plans (AMSP) may submit an application for consideration of funding. A facility that is not expressly identified in an AMSP will be considered covered under an AMSP if the facility in question has had a risk analysis completed by the USCG utilizing the MSRAM tool. Congress has specifically directed DHS to apply these funds to the highest risk ports. In support of this, the ARRA PSGP includes a total of 147 specifically identified critical ports, representing approximately 95% of the foreign waterborne commerce of the United States. Applicants must provide a Dun and Bradstreet Data Universal Numbering System (DUNS) number with their application.
Geographic Focus: All States
Date(s) Application is Due: Jun 29
Contact: Program Director; (866) 927-5646; ASK-GMD@dhs.gov
Internet: http://www.fema.gov/government/grant/arra/index.shtm#2
Sponsor: U.S. Department of Homeland Security
500 C Street SW
Washington, DC 20472

DHS ARRA Transit Security Grant Program (TSGP) 1544
The ARRA is an economic stimulus package that was designed to jumpstart the U.S. economy, create or save millions of jobs, and put a down payment on addressing long-neglected challenges nationally. Funds received under this Act are intended to support these goals, and unprecedented levels of transparency, oversight, and accountability are required of the expenditure of Act dollars. ARRA TSGP specifically will focus on the use of visible, unpredictable deterrence through the funding of Operational Packages for canine teams, mobile explosives detection screening teams, and Anti-Terrorism Teams both due to their effectiveness in reducing risk to transit systems and their potential for job creation. In addition, funding will be provided for capital projects including Multi-User High-Density Key Infrastructure Protection, Single-User High-Density Key Infrastructure Protection, Key Operating Asset Protection, and Other Mitigation Activities. These funds are intended to preserve and create jobs across the nation through projects that can be implemented quickly. Based on those considerations, the following project types are eligible: Priority 1a Operational Packages - Hiring of transit law enforcement officers to enhance visible, unpredictable deterrence efforts in transit (e.g., K-9 teams, mobile screening teams, and Anti-Terrorism teams); Priority 1b Support and Equipment for Operational Packages - Related support

and equipment costs for new officers/capability; Priority 2 Shovel Ready Capital Projects for Asset Hardening - Capital Projects including Multi-User High-Density Key Infrastructure Protection, Single- User High-Density Key Infrastructure Protection, Key Operating Asset Protection, and Other Mitigation Activities that can certifiably begin within 90 days of release of funds and will be completed within 24 months from the release of funds date. Failure to meet the 90 day requirement may result in a loss of ARRA TSGP funding for the specific project; Priority 3 Other Security Projects - Capital Projects including Multi-User High-Density Key Infrastructure Protection, Single-User High-Density Key Infrastructure Protection, Key Operating Asset Protection, and Other Mitigation Activities.
Requirements: With the exception of ferry systems, those eligible under the FY 2009 TSGP, as well as Amtrak are eligible for FY 2009 ARRA TSGP funds. Transit agencies eligible for FY 2009 TSGP funding were identified using a comprehensive, empirically-grounded risk analysis model. The risk methodology for the TSGP is consistent across modes and is linked to the risk methodology used to determine eligibility for the core DHS State and local grant programs. TSGP basic eligibility is derived from the Urban Areas Security Initiative (UASI). Eligibility for Operational Packages (Priority 1) is determined based on the number of authorized sworn positions for transit agency police departments and law enforcement agencies with dedicated transit bureaus. Eligible transit agencies and request thresholds were determined by the following transit police force or law enforcement provider characteristics: Transit police forces or law enforcement provider must have at least 100 authorized sworn positions dedicated to transit security; Funding requests are limited to no more than five percent (5%) of the force's current authorized sworn positions and the associated support equipment requests are based on number of officers requested. Law enforcement agencies with dedicated transit bureaus are eligible through the transit agency they provide security for; the transit agency itself is the grantee, and as such must apply on behalf of the law enforcement agency. To qualify for a Priority 2 Project, Shovel Ready Capital Projects for Asset Hardening, applicants must certify that the project can begin within 90 days of the release of funds. Applicants must also certify that the project will be completed within 24 months of the release of funds date.
Restrictions: Security service providers with unsworn law enforcement officers or guards are not eligible.
Geographic Focus: All States
Date(s) Application is Due: Jun 15
Contact: Program Director; (866) 927-5646; ASK-GMD@dhs.gov
Internet: http://www.fema.gov/government/grant/arra/index.shtm#1
Sponsor: U.S. Department of Homeland Security
500 C Street SW
Washington, DC 20472

DHS FY 2009 Transit Security Grant Program (TSGP) **1545**
The Transit Security Grant Program (TSGP) is one of six grant programs that constitute the Department of Homeland Security (DHS) Fiscal Year (FY) 2009 transportation infrastructure security activities. These grant programs are part of a comprehensive set of measures authorized by Congress and implemented by the Administration to help strengthen the nation's critical infrastructure against risks associated with potential terrorist attacks. The TSGP is an important component of the Department's effort to enhance the security of the Nation's critical infrastructure. The program provides funds to owners and operators of transit systems (which include intra-city bus, commuter bus, and all forms of passenger rail) to protect critical surface transportation infrastructure and the traveling public from acts of terrorism, major disasters, and other emergencies.
Requirements: Transit agencies eligible for FY 2009 TSGP funding were identified using a comprehensive, empirically-grounded risk analysis model. The risk methodology for the TSGP is consistent across modes and is linked to the risk methodology used to determine eligibility for the core DHS State and local grant programs. TSGP basic eligibility is derived from the Urban Areas Security Initiative (UASI). Certain ferry systems are eligible to participate in the FY 2009 TSGP, and receive funds under the Tier I cooperative agreement process. However, any ferry system electing to participate and receive funds under the FY 2009 TSGP cannot participate in the FY 2009 Port Security Grant Program (PSGP), and will not be considered for funding under the FY 2009 PSGP. Likewise, any ferry system that participates in PSGP cannot be considered for funding under TSGP.
Restrictions: Eligibility does not guarantee grant funding.
Geographic Focus: All States
Date(s) Application is Due: Jun 29
Contact: Program Director; (866) 927-5646; ASK-GMD@dhs.gov
Internet: http://www.fema.gov/government/grant/tsgp/index.shtm
Sponsor: U.S. Department of Homeland Security
500 C Street SW
Washington, DC 20472

Diageo Foundation Grants **1546**
The foundation supports focuses on areas of humanitarian need, primarily in developing countries in Africa, Latin America, Asia and Eastern Europe, where it can make the most difference. The foundation provides kick-start funding and expertise in establishing local projects, some of which are run in partnership with local businesses. Grants and donations made from the Diageo Foundation must be for charitable purposes, i.e. the relief of poverty, or the advancement of education. The maximum funding available for any one project is CAD50,000. There are no deadlines. If you wish to apply, please write to the foundation providing details of the project, how it relates to the foundation's focus areas and the amount of funding required on no more than two sides of a sheet of A4 paper. The foundation will contact you if further details are required. You will normally receive written notification of whether your application has been successful or not within 6-8 weeks.
Requirements: To be eligible for funding, projects must fall within one of the four key focus areas: Skills for Life, Water of Life, Local Communities or Disaster Relief. They must also demonstrate the following: (a) addressing a community/social need, in particular excluded and disadvantaged people who, with support, can help themselves to transform their own lives; (b) building partnerships with community groups and NGOs; (c) helping build the skills-base of individuals or communities; (d) maximizing grants to make them as effective as possible; (e) building the economic prosperity of a community; (f) planning a clear exit strategy and appropriate mechanisms to ensure that the benefits derived from the project are sustainable; (g) having clear, well-defined objectives in place, including planned outcomes, desired impact, measurement and evaluation; (h) enhancing the project, if appropriate, by working in partnerhsip with a local Diageo business. There is normally a three-year limit to any funding commitment.
Restrictions: The main areas normally considered to be outside the foundation's guidelines are: organizations which are not registered charities; individuals; loans, business finance or endowment funds; medical charities or hospitals; promotion of religion; animal welfare; expeditions or overseas travel; political organizations; advertising; product donations; or, capital projects (e.g. buildings).
Geographic Focus: All States
Amount of Grant: Up to 50,000 GBP
Contact: Nicole Lovett; +44(0) 20 7927 5200; nicole.lovett@diageo.com
Internet: http://www.diageo.com/en-row/CorporateCitizenship/Communityand environment/DiageoFoundation/
Sponsor: Diageo Foundation
8 Henrietta Place
London, W1G 0NB England

DIFFA/Chicago Grants **1547**
DIFFA/Chicago (The Design Industries Foundation Fighting AIDS) is a not-for-profit fundraising and grant making foundation that distributes funds to Chicago area HIV/AIDS service agencies that provide direct service, preventative education and outreach to people who are HIV positive, living with AIDS or at risk for infection. Founded by volunteers from the fashion industry, interior design, furnishings and architecture, supporters of DIFFA now come from every field associated with fine design. DIFFA has also been an innovative agent in drawing local and national corporations into the fight against the epidemic, and enjoys tremendous support from the business community. The Foundation issues grants annually. In some cases, a special grant may be awarded during the year to meet specific funder, community or emergency needs. Grants fall under two categories: Chapter Grants and Foundation Grants. In both instances, DIFFA does not accept unsolicited grant proposals. Invitations are sent out in the fall of each year to apply. Grants are then approved by the Foundation's trustees at their January Board meeting.
Requirements: Grass-root community based agencies with a 501(c)3 that provide outstanding services, preventive education and outreach to people in the Chicago area who are HIV positive, living with AIDS or at risk of infection are welcome to submit an application. The DIFFA/Chicago granting process selects agencies providing the best care possible in Chicago, and the ability to put dollars where they have the most impact to help the men, women, and children living with HIV/AIDS. A team consisting of a professional in that field and a DIFFA/Chicago board member review each agency applying for funding. Review of proposals is followed by site visits and interviews with the organizations' staff. DIFFA/Chicago funds in the categories of advocacy and education, health and clinical services, meals and nutrition, housing, and support and counseling. The agencies shown to provide the best care receive an unrestricted grant.
Geographic Focus: Illinois
Contact: Todd Baisch; (312) 577-7147; todd_baisch@gensler.com
Internet: http://www.diffachicago.org/grants.html
Sponsor: Design Industries Foundation Fighting AIDS
222 Merchandise Mart Plaza, Suite 1647A
Chicago, IL 60654

Dining for Women Grants **1548**
Dining for Women funding is available for programs and/or projects that contribute to the empowerment of women and girls in less developed countries. Program and/or projects should be grassroots organizations that work with women and girls in the areas of health, education, environmental sustainability, and business development. Grants support one featured program each month that contributes to the mission to impact the lives, health and welfare of women and girls in developing countries. Awards are for one-to-two years, and total between $35,000 and $45,000.
Requirements: To be eligible, an applicant program must: support women and/or girls who face extreme challenges in developing countries; promote self-sufficiency, economic independence and/or good health for women and girls being supported; tie funding to direct impact on individuals' lives; provide evidence of long-term sustainability and program success; manage a DFW grant ranging between $35,000 and $45,000, which may be distributed over a two-year period; direct a minimum of 75% of expenses to programs; be a 501(c)3 U.S. nonprofit organization; operate independent of religious or political affiliation; provide informative organization website in English; and be able to provide educational materials, including a short video, that are relevant to the funded project/program.
Restrictions: Dining for Women does not fund: group trusts, foundations or other consolidated funding activity; governmental, political or religiously affiliated organizations; or major building projects, large capital expenditures, U.S. administrative fees or expenses and office costs.
Geographic Focus: All States
Date(s) Application is Due: Dec 31
Contact: Dr. Maggie Aziz; (864) 335-8401; grants@diningforwomen.org
Internet: http://www.diningforwomen.org/Programs/grants
Sponsor: Dining for Women
P.O. Box 25633
Greenville, SC 29616

District of Columbia Commission on the Arts Education Teacher Mini-Grants 1549

The purpose of the grant is to encourage creative arts education projects in D.C. Public Schools and Public Charter Schools and to support the development and implementation of innovative teaching strategies to support DCPS Arts Content Standards. The mini-grant is divided into two categories: arts curriculum development and the artist residency program.
Requirements: This grant is available to full-time art teachers (visual arts, music, dance, creative writing and theater), grades pre-K-12. Non-arts teachers may only apply to the program if partnering with an arts teacher. Teachers may receive up to two professional development/curriculum development grants per school year, schools may receive up to two residencies per year. Schools may apply for an artist residency only as part of their arts program.
Restrictions: Funds may not be used to: augment teacher salaries during the normal school day; purchase computers or other equipment with a value of $500 or over per unit and with a life expectancy of more than two years; pay for food; pay for stipends (other than artist residency honorariums); pay for materials not directly related to the proposed project; pay for programs already supported by the Commission's other grant programs.
Geographic Focus: District of Columbia
Amount of Grant: 1,000 - 2,000 USD
Contact: Mary Liniger, (202) 724-5613; fax (202) 727-4135; mary.liniger@dc.gov
Internet: http://dcarts.dc.gov/dcarts/cwp/view,a,3,q,528104,dcartsNav,|31624|.asp
Sponsor: District of Columbia Commission on the Arts and Humanities
410 Eighth Street NW, 5th Floor
Washington, DC 20004

Diversity Leadership Academy Grants 1550

The AIMD Leadership Academy is a workshop for a cross-section of leaders from government, education, religion, nonprofit and business. The Fellows Program focuses on bringing together a diverse set of community leaders in a metropolitan area. The original and flagship program is The Diversity Leadership Program of Atlanta (DLAA). Currently, the Academy offers courses in Atlanta, Indianapolis, and Greenville, and is pursuing opportunities to expand the program into other communities, including New York, Washington, D.C., Minneapolis, Des Moines, and Phoenix. What is the program design? Twice each year (Spring & Fall), a class of 30-40 leaders embark on a five-day curriculum that is spread across approximately five months. Participants are organized into learning circles and work in varied groups throughout the program, with classroom instruction, case studies, group assignments, videos, experiential learning, and practical application. Each group selects a practical issue in the community to which they apply the frameworks, processes, tools and skills to develop recommended solutions. Tuition is $3,500, however, participants may attend on fellowship provided by a sponsoring organization such as the case with the Atlanta program sponsored by The Coca-Cola Company.
Requirements: The program is designed for senior leaders of organizations that exert significant influence in the local community. The program was created to help leaders of institutions that often lack the funds for such developmental programs, such as educational institutions, religious organizations, governmental units and non-profit organizations. A small number of business representatives are also included to ensure true diversity in each class.
Geographic Focus: All States
Date(s) Application is Due: Jun 11
Contact: Beth Cole; (404) 575-2131; fax (404) 575-2139; bcole@aimd.org
Internet: http://dlagi.org
Sponsor: American Institute for Managing Diversity
1155 Peachtree Street, Suite 6B
Atlanta, GA 30303

DOE Initial H-Prize Competition for Breakthrough Advances in Materials for Hydrogen Storage 1551

The H-Prize, enacted by Congress, authorized the Secretary of Energy to create a program to competitively award cash prizes that will advance the commercial application of hydrogen energy technologies by dramatizing and incentivizing accelerated research. The H-Prize was originally established by the Energy Independence and Security Act of 2007, in Sec. 654. There are several H-Prize categories, including production, storage, distribution, utilization, and prototypes and transformational technologies. The 2009-11 prize will be awarded in the area of storage materials in mobile systems for light-duty vehicles. The Hydrogen Education Foundation, the charitable, education-focused arm of the National Hydrogen Association, has been chosen to administer the H-Prize. The competition will be a single award for $1 million in the subject area of advanced materials for hydrogen storage—a critical challenge to enable widespread commercialization of hydrogen and fuel cell technologies. (FR Doc. E9-20552)
Requirements: The competition is open to participants, defined as individuals, entities or teams, that are organized or incorporated in the United States, and maintain for the duration of the H-Prize Competition a primary place of business in the United States. Teams may be comprised of any combination of individuals or entities. All individuals (whether participating singly or as part of an entity or team) must be a citizen of, or an alien lawfully admitted for permanent residence into, the United States as of the date of registration in the competition and maintain that status for the duration of the competition. The winner must be present at the award presentation in order to win the H-Prize. If a team or entity is the winner, only the team leader must be present.
Restrictions: The participant, or any member of a participant, shall not be a Federal entity, a Federal employee acting within the scope of his or her employment, or an employee of a National Laboratory acting within the scope of his or her employment. The participant, or any member of a participant, cannot have received Federal funding for research and development of hydrogen storage materials since October 2008. An individual cannot participate on more than one team or compete with multiple entries. Participants cannot be on more than one team or compete with multiple entries.
Geographic Focus: All States
Date(s) Application is Due: Feb 15
Contact: Jeffrey Serfass, Project Director
Internet: http://www.hydrogenprize.org/
Sponsor: U.S. Department of Energy
1000 Independence Avenue SW, Forrestal Building
Washington, DC 20585-1290

DogTime Annual Grant 1552

DogTime Media actively supports the efforts of rescue groups and shelters nationwide to significantly reduce the number of homeless and neglected pets in the country by providing authoritative advice to both novice and experienced pet guardians. DogTime Media donates to pet related causes through monthly grants and a variety of other programs. This grant will provide organizations dedicated to the rescue cause with access to technology solutions to help achieve their goals.
Requirements: In order to apply, organizations must show that their focus is in preventing or rescuing homeless animals and have 501(c)3 status or be in the process of applying for 501(c)3 status. Organizations must not be proponents of the sale of animals through "puppy mills", irresponsible breeding, or pet stores. Grants will be reviewed and then distributed on an annual schedule. Once selected, the grant recipient is to place the "DogTime Rescue Grant Recipient" button on their site.
Geographic Focus: All States
Amount of Grant: 500 - 500 USD
Contact: Grants Officer; 415-830-9300; info@dogtime.com
Internet: http://dogtime.com/dog-shelter-grants/new/annual
Sponsor: DogTime Media
27 Maiden Lane, Suite 700
San Francisco, CA 94108

DogTime Technology Grant 1553

DogTime Media actively supports the efforts of rescue groups and shelters nationwide to significantly reduce the number of homeless and neglected pets in the country by providing authoritative advice to both novice and experienced pet guardians. DogTime Media donates to pet related causes through monthly grants and a variety of other programs. This grant will provide organizations dedicated to the rescue cause with access to essential technology services to help achieve their goals. Some of the basic web site services that the grant will cover include domain name setup, quick website setup, email service setup (forwarders or mailboxes), and easy access to site updates or content management. The grant will pay for one year of service. Rescues can reapply for grants in subsequent years.
Requirements: In order to apply, organizations must show that their focus is in preventing or rescuing homeless animals and have 501(c)3 status or be in the process of applying for 501(c)3 status. Organizations must not be proponents of the sale of animals through "puppy mills", irresponsible breeding, or pet stores. Organizations must be ready to prove the need for the $140 service.
Geographic Focus: All States
Contact: Grants Officer; 415-830-9300; info@dogtime.com
Internet: http://dogtime.com/dog-shelter-grants/new/technology
Sponsor: DogTime Media
27 Maiden Lane, Suite 700
San Francisco, CA 94108

DOI Urban Park and Recreation Recovery (UPARR) Program 1554

The purpose of the program is to provide federal grants to local governments for the rehabilitation of recreation areas and facilities, demonstration of innovative approaches to improve park system management and recreation opportunities, and development of improved recreation planning. Deadlines are available from regional offices.
Requirements: Eligible applicants are cities and counties meeting the eligibility requirements as listed in the October 9, 1979, Federal Register and in 36 CFR Part 72, Appendix A. Eligibility is based on need, economic and physical distress, and the relative quality and condition of urban recreation facilities and systems. Jurisdictions which are located within standard metropolitan areas that are not on the eligibility listing may apply for discretionary funds provided that these grants are in accord with the intent of the program. These discretionary funds are limited to 15 percent of the funds available annually for rehabilitation, innovation and recovery action program grants.
Geographic Focus: All States
Amount of Grant: 2,750 - 5,250,000 USD
Contact: National Center for Rec and Conservation; (202) 354-6900; fax (202) 371-5179
Internet: http://www.nps.gov/ncrc/programs/uprr/program_inbrief.html
Sponsor: U.S. Department of the Interior
1849 C Street NW
Washington, DC 20240

DOJ Children's Justice Act Partnership for Indian Communities 1555

Grants are awarded to Native American Indian tribes in developing, establishing, and operating programs designed to improve the handling of child abuse cases, particularly cases of child sexual abuse, in a manner which limits additional trauma to the child victim and improves the investigation and prosecution of cases of child abuse.
Geographic Focus: All States
Contact: Cathy Sanders, Deputy Director, Federal Crime Victims Division, Office for Victims of Crime; (202) 616-3578; Catherine.P.Sanders@usdoj.gov
Internet: http://www.usdoj.gov
Sponsor: U.S. Department of Justice
810 7th Street NW
Washington, DC 20531

DOJ Community-Based Delinquency Prevention Grants 1556
Grants are provided to increase the capacity of state and local governments to support the development of more effective education, training, research, prevention, diversion, treatment, and rehabilitation programs in the area of juvenile delinquency and programs to improve the juvenile justice system. Grants may be awarded for project periods of 36 months. Examples of funded projects include a broad range of prevention activities, from early child development strategies such as nurse home visitation and preschool/parent training programs to youth development initiatives involving the use of mentoring, after-school activities, tutoring, truancy and dropout reduction, substance abuse prevention, gang prevention outreach, and police/probation teams.
Requirements: All State agencies designated by the Chief Executive under Section 223(a)(1) of the 2002 JJDP Act are eligible to apply for Title V funds. States will invite units of local government that meet the statutorily mandated eligibility requirements to apply for funding and competitively select for funding those jurisdictions that meet the minimum selection criteria specified in the guidelines as published in the Federal Register, and other such criteria as the State shall adopt.
Geographic Focus: All States
Contact: Heidi Hsia, Office of Juvenile Justice and Delinquency Prevention; (202) 307-5924; hsiah@ojp.usdoj.gov
Internet: http://www.ojjdp.ncjrs.org/titleV
Sponsor: U.S. Department of Justice
633 Indiana Avenue NW
Washington, DC 20531

DOJ Gang-Free Schools and Communities Intervention Grants 1557
The objectives of the program include support to prevent and reduce the participation of juveniles in the activities of gangs that commit crimes. Such programs and activities may include individual, peer, family, and group counseling, including provision of life skills training and preparation for living independently, which shall include cooperation with social services, welfare, and health care programs; education and social services designed to address the social and developmental needs of juveniles; crisis intervention and counseling to juveniles, who are particularly at risk of gang involvement, and their families; the organization of the neighborhood and community groups to work closely with parents, schools, law enforcement, and other public and private agencies in the community; and training and assistance to adults who have significant relationships with juveniles who are or may become members of gangs, to assist such adults in providing constructive alternatives to participating in the activities of gangs. Deadlines are published in program announcements.
Requirements: Public or private nonprofits, organizations, or individuals may apply.
Geographic Focus: All States
Contact: Heidi Hsia, Office of Juvenile Justice and Delinquency Prevention; (202) 307-5924; hsiah@ojp.usdoj.gov
Internet: http://www.ojp.usdoj.gov/FinGuide/part4chap2.htm#ojjdp
Sponsor: U.S. Department of Justice
633 Indiana Avenue NW
Washington, DC 20531

DOJ Internet Crimes against Children Task Force Program Grants 1558
The purpose of this program is to assist state and local law enforcement agencies to enhance their investigative response to sexual exploitation of children by offenders using the Internet, online communication systems, or other computer technology. For purposes of this program announcement, Internet crimes against children (ICAC) refers to sexual exploitation of children that is facilitated by computers and includes crimes of child pornography and online solicitation for sexual purposes.
Requirements: Applicants must be state and/or local law enforcement agencies. Joint applications from two or more eligible applicants are welcome; however, one applicant must be clearly indicated as the primary applicant. Applications should include evidence of multidisciplinary, multijurisdictional partnerships among public agencies, private organizations, community-based groups, and prosecutors' offices. Applications should also include prevention activities.
Geographic Focus: All States
Contact: Program Contact; (202) 307-5911
Internet: http://www.usdoj.gov
Sponsor: U.S. Department of Justice
1100 Vermont Avenue NW
Washington, DC 20530

DOJ Juvenile Justice and Delinquency Prevention Special Emphasis Grants 1559
Grants support investigative research into and the development and implementation of programs that design, test, and demonstrate effective approaches, techniques, and methods for preventing and controlling juvenile delinquency, such as community-based alternatives to institutional confinement; developing and implementing effective means of diverting juveniles from the traditional juvenile justice and correctional system; developing and supporting programs stressing advocacy activities aimed at improving services to youth impacted by the juvenile justice system; developing model programs to strengthen and maintain the family unit, including self-help programs; developing and implementing special emphasis prevention and treatment programs relating to juveniles who commit serious crimes; developing programs to prevent hate crimes; and developing and implementing further a coordinated, national law-related education program of delinquency prevention. Deadlines are published in program announcements.
Requirements: Public and private nonprofit agencies, organizations, individuals, state and local units of government, and combinations of state and local units are eligible to apply.
Geographic Focus: All States
Contact: Program Contact; (202) 307-5914; AskDOJ@usdoj.gov
Internet: http://www.usdoj.gov
Sponsor: U.S. Department of Justice
950 Pennsylvania Avenue NW
Washington, DC 20530-0001

DOJ Juvenile Mentoring Program (JUMP) Grants 1560
Grants are provided to reduce juvenile delinquency and gang participation, improve academic performance, and reduce the dropout rate through the use of mentors for at-risk youth. Mentors must be adults who are 21 years or older. Funds may be used for activities such as mentor training, reimbursement of mentor expenses, recruitment and screening of mentors and youth, and salaries of project administrators. Contact the program office or visit the Web site for current solicitations and deadlines.
Requirements: All States, Territories, the District of Columbia, Guam, America Samoa, the Commonwealths of Puerto Rico, the Virgin Islands, and the Northern Mariana Islands in partnership with mentoring organizations and/or other public/private nonprofit organizations may apply.
Geographic Focus: All States
Contact: JUMP Coordinator; (202) 307-5914; fax (202) 514-6382; askjj@ncjrs.org
Internet: http://ojjdp.ncjrs.org/pubs/96kit/jump.htm
Sponsor: U.S. Department of Justice
810 7th Street NW
Washington, DC 20531

DOJ National Institute of Justice Visiting Fellowships 1561
Fellowships provide opportunities for experienced criminal justice practitioners and researchers to pursue projects aimed at improved understanding of crime, delinquency, and criminal justice administration by sponsoring research projects of their own creation and design. Funds may be used to conduct research on crime causation, crime measurements, crime prevention, law enforcement, criminal justice administration, and the effectiveness and efficiency of anti-crime programs. Juvenile delinquency research projects also are eligible for support under this program. Fellows conduct their studies while based at NIJ. Concept papers may be submitted at any time. Applicants should anticipate a decision time frame of six to nine months from concept paper to award. Fellowship guidelines are available at no charge by sending a self-addressed mailing label to Announcement-Visiting Fellowship Program, NCJRS, Box 6000, Rockville, MD 20849-6000, or by phone (800) 851-3420.
Requirements: Fellowships are awarded to individuals or to their parent agencies or organizations. Generally, professionals working in the criminal justice field, including university- or college-based academic researchers and upper-level managers in criminal justice agencies are eligible.
Geographic Focus: All States
Contact: National Institute of Justice Office, Department of Justice; (202) 307-2942
Internet: http://www.usdoj.gov/nij
Sponsor: U.S. Department of Justice
810 7th Street NW
Washington, DC 20531

DOJ Rural Domestic Violence and Child Victimization Enforcement Grants 1562
The objective of this program is to implement, expand, and establish cooperative efforts and projects between law enforcement officers, prosecutors, victim advocacy groups, and other related parties to investigate and prosecute incidents of domestic violence and child abuse; provide treatment and counseling to victims of domestic violence and child victimization; and work in cooperation with the community to develop education and prevention strategies directed toward such issues. Annual deadline dates may vary; deadlines and program announcements are posted on the VAWO Web site.
Requirements: State agencies in rural states may apply for assistance for statewide projects. Local units of government in rural states and public and private entities in rural states also may apply directly for assistance. The following states qualify as rural for the purposes of this program: Alaska, Arkansas, Arizona, Colorado, Idaho, Iowa, Kansas, Maine, Montana, Nebraska, Nevada, New Mexico, North Dakota, Oklahoma, Oregon, South Dakota, Utah, Vermont, and Wyoming. Only state agencies in nonrural states may apply for funding assistance; these agencies may apply on behalf of one or more of their rural jurisdictions. Rural and/or nonrural states also may submit joint applications for projects that would be implemented in more than one state. American Indian tribal governments may make individual applications or apply as a consortium. A tribal government also may apply for assistance on behalf of a nontribal government organization.
Geographic Focus: Alaska, Arizona, Arkansas, Colorado, Idaho, Iowa, Kansas, Maine, Montana, Nebraska, Nevada, New Mexico, North Dakota, Oklahoma, Oregon, South Dakota, Utah, Vermont, Wyoming
Amount of Grant: 50,000 - 900,000 USD
Contact: Program Contact, Violence Against Women Grants Office; (202) 307-6026
Internet: http://www.ojp.usdoj.gov/vawo
Sponsor: U.S. Department of Justice
810 7th Street NW
Washington, DC 20531

Dolan Foundation Grants 1563
The foundation awards community service grants with a focus on Long Island, NY. Areas of support include human services, disability services, mental health, schools, rehabilitation, hospitals, and health facilities. Grants provide program support. There are no application deadlines.
Requirements: Schools and other nonprofits in New York are eligible. Applicants outside New York should call or write prior to submitting proposals.
Geographic Focus: New York

Date(s) Application is Due: Mar 1; Jun 1; Sep 1; Nov 1
Amount of Grant: 25,000 - 375,000 USD
Contact: Robert Vizza, President; (516) 629-2103; fax (516) 629-2183
Sponsor: Dolan Foundations
1 Media Crossways
Woodbury, NY 11797

Dole Food Company Charitable Contributions 1564

Dole's charitable program is dedicated to bringing about positive change in the area of nutrition education for children. The goal of the program is to help the next generation of adults prevent many diseases by teaching the value of good nutrition to children through improved and interactive teaching curriculum for schools nationwide. Please contact Corporate Contributions for application process.
Requirements: Dole's program makes grants based on the following guidelines: the program is restricted to funding 501(c)3 charitable organizations only; documentation from the I.R.S. confirming 501(c)3 status must be provided; and the organization should provide nutrition education programs that benefit schools on a nationwide basis as opposed to assisting an individual school.
Restrictions: Grants are restricted for the following: individuals; religious, fraternal, sports or political groups; legislative or lobbying efforts or groups who have a primary focus of changing laws; and sporting events and sponsorships.
Geographic Focus: All States
Contact: Contribution Program Manager; (818) 879-6600; fax (818) 879-6615
Internet: http://dolecsr.com/Principles/CharitableGiving/tabid/410/Default.aspx
Sponsor: Dole Food Company
P.O. Box 5132
Westlake Village, CA 91361

Dolfinger-McMahon Foundation Grants 1565

The Foundation makes grants for the initiation or support of: experimental or demonstrational projects; seed money projects; projects which can reasonably be expected to be accomplished by a single grant in a relatively brief period of time; or an emergency grant to an agency or particular project of an agency. No application forms are provided.
Requirements: Nonprofit, charitable organizations serving the greater Philadelphia, PA area are eligible.
Restrictions: The Foundation does not, except in the rarest instances, make grants for: projects beyond the limits of the Greater Philadelphia area; ordinary operating expenses; creation of or additions to endowment; medical or scientific research; projects for the construction, renovation or acquisition of physical facilities (real estate or building; or equipment or supplies, except in cases where the equipment or supplies are merely incidental to the primary purposes of the project); projects which will likely entail grants from the Foundation beyond a period of three years or which may not reasonably be expected to be self-supporting thereafter; to applicants respectively year after year; to individuals for scholarship or research purposes; and for special interest advocacy through legislative lobbying, focused litigation or solicitation of governmental agencies.
Geographic Focus: Pennsylvania
Date(s) Application is Due: Apr 1; Oct 1
Contact: Sharon Renz, Executive Secretary, c/o Duane Morris, LLP; (215) 979-1768
Sponsor: Dolfinger-McMahon Foundation
30 South 17th Street
Philadelphia, PA 19103-4196

DOL Homeless Veterans Reintegration Program Grants 1566

The objective of the program is to fund projects designed to expedite the reintegration of homeless veterans into the labor force. Funded projects shall provide for employment and training and support services directly or through linkages with other service providers to assist homeless veterans to reenter the workforce. Outreach as necessary is to be performed by formerly homeless veterans. Annual deadline dates may vary; contact the program office for exact dates.
Requirements: Applications will be accepted from State and local Workforce Investment Boards, local public agencies, for-profit/commercial entities, and nonprofit organizations, including faith-based and community organizations. Applicants must have a familiarity with the area and population to be served and the ability to administer an effective and timely program.
Restrictions: Entities organized under Section 501(c)(4) of the Internal Revenue Code that engage in lobbying activities are not eligible to receive funds.
Geographic Focus: All States
Contact: Cassandra Mitchell, (202) 693-4570
Internet: http://www.dol.gov/vets/grants/main.htm
Sponsor: U.S. Department of Labor
200 Constitution Avenue NW
Washington, DC 20210

Dollar Energy Fund Grants 1567

The Dollar Energy Fund provides assistance and tangible aid to families and individuals experiencing difficulty in affording adequate and safe utility supplies in order to maintain basic living standards. Fields of interest include: economically disadvantaged; housing/shelter; and expense aid. Programs include: Hardship Program—provides grants directly to utility accounts; Customer Assistance Program (CAP)—payment is based on income and household size, not usage; and the Job Training and Career Guidance Program; Low Income Home Energy Assistance Program (LIHEAP)—federally funded program that provides assistance for heating bills.
Requirements: Each program has different eligibility guidelines, so individuals may be eligible for one or more programs. Individuals from Louisiana, Maryland, Ohio, Pennsylvania, Tennessee, Texas. Virginia, and West Virginia are eligible to apply.
Geographic Focus: Louisiana, Maryland, Ohio, Pennsylvania, Tennessee, Texas, Virginia, West Virginia
Contact: Danielle Snidow, Director; (412) 431-2800 or (800) 683-7036; fax (412) 431-2084; info@dollarenergy.org or pr@dollarenergy.org
Internet: http://www.dollarenergy.org
Sponsor: Dollar Energy Fund
P.O. Box 42329
Pittsburgh, PA 15203-0329

Dollar General Adult Literacy Grants 1568

The corporation awards community grants to direct adult literacy service providers. . Please note that the Dollar General Literacy Foundation uses the federal government's definition of literacy when reviewing grant applications. Adult literacy programs applying for funding must have one of the following three areas: Adult Basic Education, GED preparation, or English for speakers of other languages.
Requirements: U.S. nonprofits in company operating areas in the 35-state market areas are eligible. In addition, to be eligible for consideration, an organization must be located within 20 miles of a Dollar General store, must not have received funding from the Dollar General Literacy Foundation for the past two consecutive years, and must have met all reporting requirements from previous Dollar General Literacy Foundation grants.
Restrictions: The giving program does not support individuals, general fundraising events or celebration functions, attendance at professional/association conferences or seminars, film and video projects, endowments or capital campaigns, private charities or foundations, purchase of vehicles, advertising, or construction or building costs.
Geographic Focus: Alabama, Arizona, Arkansas, Colorado, Delaware, Florida, Georgia, Illinois, Indiana, Iowa, Kansas, Kentucky, Louisiana, Maryland, Michigan, Minnesota, Mississippi, Missouri, Nebraska, New Jersey, New Mexico, New York, North Carolina, Ohio, Oklahoma, Pennsylvania, South Carolina, South Dakota, Tennessee, Texas, Utah, Vermont, Virginia, West Virginia, Wisconsin
Date(s) Application is Due: Feb 25
Amount of Grant: 20,000 USD
Contact: Adult Literacy Grant Committee, (615) 855-5201
Internet: http://www.dollargeneral.com/community/communityinvestments.aspx
Sponsor: Dollar General Corporation
100 Mission Ridge
Goodlettsville, TN 37072

Dollar General Family Literacy Grants 1569

The corporation awards community grants to direct family literacy service providers. . Please note that the Dollar General Literacy Foundation uses the federal government's definition of family literacy when reviewing grant applications. Family literacy programs applying for funding must have the following four components: (1) Adult education instruction (Adult Basic Education, GED preparation, or English for speakers of other languages; (2) Children's education; (3) Parent and child together time (PACT), and; (4) Parenting classes that teach parents to be the primary teacher for their child.
Requirements: U.S. nonprofits in company operating areas in the 35-state market areas are eligible. In addition, to be eligible for consideration, an organization must be located within 20 miles of a Dollar General store, must not have received funding from the Dollar General Literacy Foundation for the past two consecutive years, and must have met all reporting requirements from previous Dollar General Literacy Foundation grants.
Restrictions: The giving program does not support individuals, general fundraising events or celebration functions, attendance at professional/association conferences or seminars, film and video projects, endowments or capital campaigns, private charities or foundations, purchase of vehicles, advertising, or construction or building costs.
Geographic Focus: Alabama, Arizona, Arkansas, Colorado, Delaware, Florida, Georgia, Illinois, Indiana, Iowa, Kansas, Kentucky, Louisiana, Maryland, Michigan, Minnesota, Mississippi, Missouri, Nebraska, New Jersey, New Mexico, New York, North Carolina, Ohio, Oklahoma, Pennsylvania, South Carolina, South Dakota, Tennessee, Texas, Utah, Vermont, Virginia, West Virginia, Wisconsin
Date(s) Application is Due: Feb 25
Contact: Family Literacy Program Coordinator; (615) 855-5201
Internet: http://www.dgliteracy.com/grant-program/family-grants.aspx
Sponsor: Dollar General Corporation
100 Mission Ridge
Goodlettsville, TN 37072

Dollar General Youth Literacy Grants 1570

Youth Literacy Grants provide funding to schools and local nonprofit organizations to help with the implementation or expansion of literacy programs for new readers, below grade level readers and readers with learning disabilities. Organizations requesting funds must provide direct services to one of the groups of readers defined above, and instruction must be designed to meet the varying learning preferences and needs of the defined target population.
Requirements: U.S. nonprofits or schools in company operating areas in the 35-state market areas are eligible. In addition, to be eligible for consideration, an organization must be located within 20 miles of a Dollar General store, must not have received funding from the Dollar General Literacy Foundation for the past two consecutive years, and must have met all reporting requirements from previous Dollar General Literacy Foundation grants.
Restrictions: The giving program does not support individuals, general fundraising events or celebration functions, attendance at professional/association conferences or seminars, film and video projects, endowments or capital campaigns, private charities or foundations, purchase of vehicles, advertising, or construction or building costs.
Geographic Focus: Alabama, Arizona, Arkansas, Colorado, Delaware, Florida, Georgia, Illinois, Indiana, Iowa, Kansas, Kentucky, Louisiana, Maryland, Michigan, Minnesota,

Mississippi, Missouri, Nebraska, New Jersey, New Mexico, New York, North Carolina, Ohio, Oklahoma, Pennsylvania, South Carolina, South Dakota, Tennessee, Texas, Utah, Vermont, Virginia, West Virginia, Wisconsin
Contact: Youth Literacy Grant Committee; (615) 855-5201
Internet: http://www.dgliteracy.com/grant-program/youth-grants.aspx
Sponsor: Dollar General Corporation
100 Mission Ridge
Goodlettsville, TN 37072

DOL Youthbuild Grants 1571
YouthBuild is a community-based alternative education program for youth between the ages of 16 and 24 who are high school dropouts, adjudicated youth, youth aging out of foster care, youth with disabilities, and other at-risk youth populations. The YouthBuild program simultaneously addresses several core issues facing low-income communities: affordable housing, education, employment, crime prevention, and leadership development. DOL will award grants to organizations to oversee the provision of education, occupational skills training, and employment services to disadvantaged youth in their communities while performing meaningful work and service to their communities. Based on the most recent estimate of funding, DOL hopes to serve approximately 5,200 participants during the grant period of performance, with projects operating in approximately 75 communities across the country. The period of performance for these grant awards will be three (3) years and four (4) months from the effective date of the grant. This includes an up to four-month planning period, two years of core program operations (education, occupational skills training, and youth leadership development activities) for one or more cohorts of youth, plus an additional nine-to-twelve months of follow-up support services and tracking of participant outcomes for each cohort of youth. This grant period of performance includes time for all necessary implementation and start-up activities.
Requirements: Eligible applicants for these grants are public or private non-profit agencies or organizations including agencies that have previously served at-risk youth in a YouthBuild or other similar program. These agencies include, but are not limited to: faith-based and community organizations; an entity carrying out activities under Workforce Investment Act (WIA), such as a local workforce investment board, American Job Center (formerly known as One-Stop Career Center), or local school board; community action agency; state or local housing development agency; Indian tribe or other agency primarily serving American Indians; community development corporation; state or local youth service conservation corps; consortium of such agencies or organizations with a designated lead applicant; or, any other public or private non-profit entity that is eligible to provide education or employment training under a Federal program. Applicants must provide new cash or in-kind resources equivalent to exactly 25 percent of the grant award amount as "matching" funds while additional cost sharing above 25 percent may be committed towards the grant as "leveraged" funds. In order to preserve one of the core aspects of the YouthBuild program as a construction skills training program, all grant programs must offer construction skills training. New applicants for DOL funding must demonstrate success with core construction skills training and are not eligible to offer other vocational training as first-time YouthBuild grantees. Construction skills training is central to the overall philosophy of the YouthBuild program and can provide a visible transformational experience for young people who have rarely had opportunities to see tangible and positive results of their efforts.
Geographic Focus: All States
Date(s) Application is Due: Mar 19
Contact: Kia Mason; (202) 693-2606; mason.kia@dol.gov
Internet: http://www.doleta.gov/grants/find_grants.cfm
Sponsor: U.S. Department of Labor
200 Constitution Avenue, NW
Washington, DC 20210

Dominion Foundation Human Needs Grants 1572
Dominion Foundation grants are made in four focus areas, and they support a variety of programs: food banks, homeless shelters, land and habitat preservation, STEM (science, technology, engineering, math) education, and neighborhood revitalization, to name a few. Special consideration is given to programs with an energy conservation or energy efficiency component. In the area of Human Needs, the Foundation focus is on: providing warmth and cooling; alleviating hunger; ensuring energy-efficient shelter; providing access to medicine and basic health care; supporting communities through the united way; and disaster assistance. Since the Dominion Foundation supports a wide range of charitable programs, most grants are in the $1,000 to $15,000 range. Higher amounts may be awarded when a program is an exceptional fit with corporate business or giving priorities, or when there is significant employee involvement in the effort. Requests are considered quarterly by the Foundation's Community Investment Boards – statewide and regional committees comprised of Dominion employees representing key geographic, business and functional areas.
Requirements: Foundation grants are limited to organizations defined as tax-exempt under Section 501(c)3 of the IRS code. Additional grants occasionally may be made directly from the corporation to sponsor special events that benefit a non-profit organization.
Restrictions: Awards are throughout a 10-state area to include: Connecticut, Maryland, Massachusetts, North Carolina, Ohio, Pennsylvania, Rhode Island, Texas, Virginia and West Virginia. Information pertaining to the specific counties served in each state is on the website.
Geographic Focus: Connecticut, Illinois, Indiana, Maryland, Massachusetts, North Carolina, Ohio, Pennsylvania, Rhode Island, Texas, Virginia, West Virginia
Amount of Grant: 1,000 - 250,000 USD
Contact: James C. Mesloh; (800) 730-7217; Educational_Grants@dom.com
Internet: http://www.dom.com/about/education/grants/index.jsp
Sponsor: Dominion Foundation
501 Martindale Street, Suite 400
Pittsburgh, PA 15222-3199

Donald and Sylvia Robinson Family Foundation Grants 1573
The foundation awards grants to U.S. nonprofit organizations in its areas of interest, including animal and wildlife protection, arms control, arts (general, performing arts, and visual arts), environmental conservation and protection, eye diseases and eye research, family planning and human reproductive health, food distribution, international affairs, Israel, Jewish social services, and social service delivery programs. Types of support include annual campaigns, building construction/renovation, capital campaigns, and general operating support. There are no application deadlines or forms.
Requirements: National nonprofit organizations are eligible to apply.
Restrictions: Individuals are ineligible.
Geographic Focus: Pennsylvania
Amount of Grant: 500 - 5,000 USD
Contact: Donald Robinson, Treasurer; (412) 661-1200; fax (412) 661-4645
Sponsor: Donald and Sylvia Robinson Family Foundation
6507 Wilkins Avenue
Pittsburgh, PA 15217

Donaldson Foundation Grants 1574
The Foundation's two key areas are education at all levels and organizations focused on assisting the transition towards economic self-sufficiency. Only applications in the focus areas described will be considered. The Foundation limits its support to local or regional agencies and programs in the communities where Donaldson employees live and work.
Requirements: All recipients must qualify for tax exemption by the IRS. Submit a brief letter of introduction to your organization and how your program fits into the Foundation's focus.
Geographic Focus: Illinois, Indiana, Iowa, Kentucky, Minnesota, Missouri, Wisconsin
Samples: U of Minnesota, Carlson School of Management (Minneapolis, MN)—to expand computer-based and online family literacy services provided at 32 organizational affiliates nationwide, $290,000.
Contact: Norm Linnell; (952) 703-4999; donaldsonfoundation@mail.donaldson.com
Internet: http://www.donaldson.com/en/about/community/foundation.html
Sponsor: Donaldson Foundation
P.O. Box 1299, MS 100
Minneapolis, MN 55440

Donald W. Reynolds Foundation Charitable Food Distribution Grants 1575
The Charitable Food Distribution Initiative builds on the success of the Foundation's previous capital support of the Regional Food Bank of Oklahoma in Oklahoma City. This initiative awards planning grants and capital grants directly to qualified food banks. However, an additional high priority under the Charitable Food Distribution Initiative is to improve the broader and more collaborative work food banks can undertake to improve efficiency and effectiveness. Application to the Charitable Food Distribution Initiative is by invitation only. Unsolicited requests will not be accepted, and applicants should begin by discussing needs with the Foundation.
Requirements: Organizations must first contact the Foundation to discuss their project before submitting a proposal.
Geographic Focus: Arkansas, Nevada, Oklahoma
Contact: Craig Willis, Program Director; (702) 804-6000; fax (702) 804-6099; craig.willis@dwrf.org or GeneralQuestions@dwrf.org
Internet: http://www.dwreynolds.org/Programs/Regional/Food.htm
Sponsor: Donald W. Reynolds Foundation
1701 Village Center Circle
Las Vegas, NV 89134-6303

Donald W. Reynolds Foundation Children's Discovery Initiative Grants 1576
The Foundation's trustees recognize that a growing number of children's discovery museums and science centers have an opportunity to play a special role in supporting the formal education system. The trustees have launched an initiative aimed at improving and expanding the discovery experiences at hands-on museums in Arkansas, Nevada, and Oklahoma. The critical component of the Foundation's initiative has been the establishment of statewide networks of museums working together to strengthen each museum's capacity and provide shared exhibits and new programs to better reach rural children, their teachers, and families. The networks provide new rotating exhibits, a mobile outreach vehicle – or museum-on-wheels, capacity-building programs, and new interactive discovery experiences to impact children even in the most rural areas of Arkansas and Oklahoma. The networks also provide classroom teachers with new hands-on resources. In addition to establishing collaborative networks of museums, the initiative has supported capital projects and awarded capital planning grants for individual museum projects in Arkansas, Oklahoma, and Nevada.
Requirements: Organizations must first contact the Foundation to discuss their project before submitting a proposal.
Geographic Focus: Arkansas, Nevada, Oklahoma
Contact: Courtney Latta Knoblock, Program Director; (702) 804-6000; fax (702) 804-6099; courtney.latta@dwrf.org or GeneralQuestions@dwrf.org
Internet: http://www.dwreynolds.org/Programs/Regional/Discovery.htm
Sponsor: Donald W. Reynolds Foundation
1701 Village Center Circle
Las Vegas, NV 89134-6303

Donald W. Reynolds Foundation Special Projects Grants 1577
Special Projects of the Foundation are awarded at the discretion of the board and encompass areas outside of the established programs of the Foundation. While these grants might result in the construction of a facility, provide for the acquisition of equipment or fund a specific program, they are unique and considered for funding based upon their individual merits. Often, Special Projects present a unique opportunity to advance patriotism,

entrepreneurship, or another special lifetime interest held by Donald W. Reynolds. Proposal invitations are usually generated directly by our Trustees. There is no application and no designated staff contact. Unsolicited proposals are rarely approved. Brief proposals may be sent to the Foundation, addressed to the attention of Special Projects.
Geographic Focus: All States
Contact: Courtney Latta Knoblock, Program Director; (702) 804-6000; fax (702) 804-6099; capitalquestions@dwrf.org or GeneralQuestions@dwrf.org
Internet: http://www.dwreynolds.org/Programs/Special/Special.htm
Sponsor: Donald W. Reynolds Foundation
1701 Village Center Circle
Las Vegas, NV 89134-6303

Donnie Avery Catches for Kids Foundation 1578
The mission of Donnie Avery's Catches for Kids Foundation is to provide opportunities, support and resources to children and families who are in need. Established in 2010, the primary focus of the Catches for Kids Foundation is to improve the lives of low-income children by providing daily support and life changing experiences. Through its signature programs: "Holiday Celebration", "Just Show Up!" and "Back to School", Catches for Kids will have impacted the lives of more than 45,000 children and their family members by the end of 2012. The Foundation will prioritize donation requests based on date submitted, need and location, and will respond to the request two weeks prior to the event.
Restrictions: Donnie Avery's Catches for Kids Foundation will only assist organizations once per calendar year.
Geographic Focus: Missouri
Internet: http://www.donnieavery.org/programs.php
Sponsor: Donnie Avery Catches for Kids Foundation
4579 Laclede Avenue #317
St. Louis, MO 63108

Dora Roberts Foundation Grants 1579
The foundation awards general operating grants to eligible Texas organizations in its areas of interest, Arts, Social Services, Health and Education. Most grants are awarded in Big Spring, TX. There are no application forms. Trustees meet annually in the Fall to review all requests received prior to the deadline.
Requirements: The Foundation can distribute grants only to qualified charitable organizations in the State of Texas. Persons who represent an organization which they believe might qualify for our support are welcome to submit an application in letter form containing: a brief narrative history of the organization's purpose and work; a specific description of the program or project for which support is asked; a statement of the amount of funds requested; proof of tax exempt status; a list of Trustees or Directors and principal staff; and budgetary information pertaining to the requested grant.
Geographic Focus: Rhode Island
Date(s) Application is Due: Sep 30
Contact: Konnie Darrow, c/o JP Morgan Chase Bank, N.A., (817) 884-4772
Sponsor: Dora Roberts Foundation
P.O. Box 2050
Fort Worth, TX 76113

Doree Taylor Charitable Foundation 1580
The mission of the Doree Taylor Charitable Foundation is to support charitable organizations that: provide relief to people the form of basic needs (including the provision of food, housing, shelter); promote the humane care of animals; provide health-care services for the underserved; and conduct Public radio or television. Occasional support will also be provided to colleges and universities as well as to environmental charitable organizations in Maine. The foundation will make grants throughout Maine, but has a priority for charitable organizations or projects located in the areas of Boothbay Harbor, Southport, and Brunswick. From time to time, the foundation may support organizations with a national scope. Grant requests for general operating support or program support are strongly encouraged and preferred; however, small capital requests may also be considered. The majority of grants from the Taylor Foundation are one year in duration; on occasion, multi-year support is awarded. Applicants must apply online at the grant website. Applicants are strongly encouraged to do the following before applying: review the downloadable state application procedures for additional helpful information and clarifications; review the downloadable online-application guidelines at the grant website; review the foundation's funding history (link is available from the grant website); review the online application questions in advance; and review the list of required attachments. These will generally include: a list of board members, financial statements (audited, reviewed, or compiled by independent auditor); an organization summary; a list of other funding sources; an IRS Determination letter; and other required documents. All attachments must be uploaded in the online application as PDF, Word, or Excel files. The application deadline for the Doree Taylor Charitable Foundation is 11:59 p.m. on April 1. Applicants will be notified of grant decisions before August 31.
Requirements: 501(c)3 charitable organizations and municipalities which meet the mission criteria are eligible to apply.
Restrictions: The foundation will not contribute to endowments or consider grant requests from individuals, organizations attempting to influence policy through direct lobbying, or political campaigns.
Geographic Focus: All States, Maine
Date(s) Application is Due: Apr 1
Contact: Miki C. Akimoto, Vice President; (866) 778-6859; miki.akimoto@baml.com
Internet: https://www.bankofamerica.com/philanthropic/fn_search.action
Sponsor: Doree Taylor Charitable Foundation
225 Franklin Street, 4th Floor, MA1-225-04-02
Boston, MA 02110

Do Right Foundation Grants 1581
The foundation's grant-making interests include the reduction of violent crime, efforts to combat joblessness, increasing productivity of the U.S. legal system, helping people with the basic transition from welfare to work, parenting education, and the improvement of integrity and efficiencies of government. Funding targets small, controlled pilot programs. The foundation has a formal grant application that is available on its Web site or by contacting the foundation. Preliminary inquiry letters are not accepted. Preliminary inquiries are mandatory.
Requirements: Nonprofit 501(c)3 organizations in the United States are eligible.
Restrictions: Support is not granted to individuals, schools, or police departments.
Geographic Focus: All States
Amount of Grant: Up to 190,000 USD
Contact: James McCrink, President; (619) 233-5634; dorightfdn@aol.com
Internet: http://www.doright.org
Sponsor: Do Right Foundation
991-C Lomas Santa Fe, #413
Solana Beach, CA 92075

Doris and Victor Day Foundation Grants 1582
The foundation supports local community organizations providing food, shelter, clothing, medical care, and education in Illinois/Iowa Quad Cities region. Preference will be given to preventive programs and projects that foster pride in the local community. Types of support include general operating support, building/renovation, equipment, emergency funds, seed grants, and scholarship funds.
Requirements: Illinois/Iowa Quad Cities region nonprofit organizations may apply.
Restrictions: The Foundation is committed to programs that are non-sectarian, and therefore, will not contribute toward programs and capital projects for religious purposes, except for modest contributions to the churches in which the Days held membership. However, clearly non-sectarian, community serving programs of religious organizations will be considered for funding.
Geographic Focus: Illinois, Iowa
Date(s) Application is Due: May 1
Samples: Transitions Mental Health Rehabilitation, $4,000—Client Home Renovation; Rock Island Economic Growth Corporation, $50,000—Neighborhood Stabilization Program; Martin Luther King Center, $175,000 — expansion and renovation.
Contact: Program Contact; (309) 788-2300; info@dayfoundation.org
Internet: http://www.dayfoundation.org/guide.htm
Sponsor: Doris and Victor Day Foundation Grants
1800 3rd Avenue, Suite 302
Rock Island, IL 61201-8019

Doris Day Animal Foundation Grants 1583
Established in 1978, the Foundation became independent from the Doris Day Animal League in 2007, when the DDAL merged with The Humane Society of the United States. The foundation is dedicated to improving the health and welfare of the community, it addresses the problems of pet overpopulation and homeless pets and the foundation supports prevention of cruelty towards animals. The programs range from providing senior citizens with food for their pets to providing information for people caring for horses, supporting in-school humane educational and reading programs, training an assistance dog, rescuing greyhounds, and establishing scholarships for veterinary students specializing in shelter medicine. Giving is on a national and international basis.
Requirements: 501(c)3 nonprofit organizations are eligible.
Geographic Focus: All States
Contact: Bill Glynn, Director; (202) 452-1100; fax (202) 546-2193; info@ddaf.org
Internet: http://www.ddaf.org/
Sponsor: Doris Day Animal Foundation (formerly Doris Day Pet Foundation)
8033 Sunset Boulevard, Suite 845
Los Angeles, CA 90046-2401

Doris Duke Charitable Foundation Arts Program Grants 1584
The mission of the Arts Program is to support performing artists with the creation and public performance of their work. The Foundation supports artists and presenters in dance, jazz, theater and multi-disciplinary performing arts. Grants are awarded in a variety of ways, including foundation-initiated invitations to apply, re-granting competitions that are administered by service organizations, and competitions that are run using request-for-proposal processes. Occasionally, the foundation also supports opportunistic grants that are more broadly related to the program missions. Most recently, the Arts Program identified three priorities that will guide its grant making over the next five years: investing in leadership, innovation, and strengthening the national sector.
Requirements: U.S. nonprofits are eligible.
Restrictions: In general, the Arts Program does not fund: visual arts, museums or galleries; literary arts; symphonies, opera companies, classical chamber music or musical forms beyond jazz; classical ballet companies; avocational arts activities; arts programs for rehabilitative or therapeutic purposes; training and conservatory programs; capital projects; research or publications.
Geographic Focus: All States
Amount of Grant: 125,000 - 3,000,000 USD
Contact: Ben Cameron, Director for the Arts; (212) 974-7000; fax (212) 974-7590
Internet: http://www.ddcf.org/page.asp?pageId=10
Sponsor: Doris Duke Charitable Foundation
650 Fifth Avenue, 19th Floor
New York, NY 10019

Doris Duke Charitable Foundation Child Abuse Prevention Grants   1585
The mission of the Program is to protect children from abuse and neglect in order to promote their healthy development. The program's primary goal is to improve parent-child interactions and to increase parental access to information and services that help prevent child maltreatment before it occurs. The foundation supports early intervention initiatives that seek to integrate child abuse prevention strategies into national systems that serve large numbers of young children (ages 0 to 6) and their families. A majority of the Program's grants are awarded to organizations that are invited to submit proposals by the foundation's staff. In addition, a small percentage of grants result from unsolicited proposals to staff that fall within the foundation's early intervention strategy. Unsolicited requests should be summarized in a two-page letter of inquiry.
Requirements: Grants are limited to the nonprofit organizations in the United States.
Restrictions: The foundation does not directly support local organizations, nor does it support treatment programs or trauma services for victims; projects related to childhood sexual abuse; documentary films; child advocacy centers; prevention of bullying at schools; self-protection or conflict resolution programs for children; or legal reform, foster care or adoption issues.
Geographic Focus: All States
Amount of Grant: 125,000 - 3,000,000 USD
Contact: Betsy Fader; (212) 974-7000; fax (212) 974-7590
Internet: http://www.ddcf.org/page.asp?pageId=13
Sponsor: Doris Duke Charitable Foundation
650 Fifth Avenue, 19th Floor
New York, NY 10019

Dorot Foundation Grants   1586
The foundation is concerned with the transmission of Jewish heritage through the generations. The foundation's grantmaking demonstrates a commitment to the Jewish past, present, and future by supporting activities in the following areas: higher education—Dorot Fellowship in Israel (a one-year, postcollegiate program designed for future American Jewish lay leaders) and Dorot Travel Grants (block grants to selected public and private colleges and universities in North America to support mainly undergraduates—up to 20 percent of funds may be spent on graduate students—in travel to and study in Israel); cultural institutions and libraries in the United States and Israel; the environment in Israel; religious pluralism in Israel; preservation of Jewish antiquity with a special emphasis on the Dead Sea Scrolls; and board-initiated grants. Letters of inquiry are accepted at any time. The board meets in February and October to consider grants. Guidelines are available online.
Requirements: U.S. and international nonprofit organizations are eligible.
Restrictions: The foundation does not consider requests for museum acquisition, capital campaigns, debt reduction, endowments, equipment purchases, events, or excavation phases of archaeological work.
Geographic Focus: All States
Contact: Michael Hill; (401) 351-8866, ext. 12; fax (401) 351-4975; michaelh@dorot.org
Internet: http://www.dorot.org/Grants
Sponsor: Dorot Foundation
439 Benefit Street
Providence, RI 02903

Dorothea Haus Ross Foundation Grants   1587
The foundation awards grants to eligible nonprofit organizations that work to relieve suffering among children who are sick, handicapped, injured, disfigured, orphaned, or otherwise vulnerable. Types of support include direct services, medical research, equipment and supplies, and small renovation projects. There are no application deadlines. The foundation has a preference for small grassroots projects that it can fully fund or nearly fully fund with the small grants that it makes. The Ross Foundation is less interested in larger projects or capital campaigns that are better left to larger foundations and organizations.
Requirements: U.S. Charities may apply if: they have 501(c)3 status; they are listed in the current edition of the Cumulative List of Charities published by the U.S. Department of the Treasury; they are a Catholic organization listed in the current edition of the Catholic Director; or they are listed in the Free Methodist Yearbook, or other Protestant Denomination Directory that has a group ruling for tax exemption from the IRS. Although grants are made internationally, Foundation by-laws prohibit sending money directly to foreign charities. Applicants from foreign countries (outside the United States) are encouraged to call or email the foundation prior to submitting any applications.
Restrictions: The Foundation does not fund day-to-day operations, individuals, conferences, day care, or public education. Although the Foundation makes international grants, there are restrictions in some countries for the following reasons: war, widespread violence, or breakdown of law and order; or countries where grants are restricted by the U.S. Government due to a boycott or other reason.
Geographic Focus: All States
Contact: Wayne S. Cook; (585) 473-6006; Rossfoundation@frontiernet.net
Internet: http://www.dhrossfoundation.org/index.php?option=com_content&view=article&id=3&catid=1
Sponsor: Dorothea Haus Ross Foundation
1036 Monroe Avenue
Rochester, NY 14620

Dorothy G. Griffin Charitable Foundation Grants   1588
The Foundation, established in 1995, is dedicated to supporting programs in Rome, New York, and surrounding communities. Its primary fields of interest include: community and economic development, education, and family and human services. The major type of support is general operations. a formal application is not required, and there are no specific deadlines with which to adhere.
Restrictions: Giving restricted to Rome, New York, and neighboring communities. There are no grants given to individuals.
Geographic Focus: New York
Amount of Grant: 500 - 10,000 USD
Contact: Charles J. Schoff, Treasurer; (315) 336-4400; fax (315) 336-0005
Sponsor: Dorothy G. Griffin Charitable Foundation
512 W Court Street
Rome, NY 13440-4010

Dorothy Rider Pool Health Care Grants   1589
The Foundation's intent is to serve as a means to improve the quality of life in the Lehigh Valley community, to build on community strengths and add to its vitality, and to increase the capacity of the community to serve the needs of all its citizens. Within this objective the Foundation's funding program is focused on education, health and welfare, culture and art and community development. Interested applicants should submit a letter of intent of five pages or less.
Requirements: Allentown, PA, nonprofit organizations are eligible.
Restrictions: The Foundation is restricted from providing funds to individuals, legislative or lobbying efforts, political or fraternal organizations or organizations outside the United States and its territories. The Foundation as a policy does not provide operating or capital funds to Sectarian institutions, organizations or programs in which funds will be used primarily for the propagation of religion, hospitals or United Way member agencies. Further, the Foundation does not underwrite charitable or testimonial dinners, fund-raising events or related advertising or the subsidization of books, mailings or articles in professional journals.
Geographic Focus: Pennsylvania
Date(s) Application is Due: Apr 1; Aug 15
Amount of Grant: 100,000 USD
Contact: Ronald Dendas; (610) 770-9346; fax (610) 770-9361; drpool@ptd.net
Internet: http://www.pooltrust.com
Sponsor: Dorothy Rider Pool Health Care Trust
1050 S Cedar Crest Boulevard, Suite 202
Allentown, PA 18103

Dorrance Family Foundation Grants   1590
The Dorrance Family Foundation was founded by Bennett Dorrance, co-owner of the Campbell Soup Company. The Foundation gives primarily in the state of Arizona, offering support in the areas of education and natural resource conservation.
Requirements: No formal application form is required, non-profits operating in Arizona are eligible to apply for these grants. Applicants should submit a proposal consisting of a detailed description of project and amount of funding requested.
Restrictions: No funding available to individuals.
Geographic Focus: Arizona
Contact: Carolyn O'Malley, Executive Director; (480) 367-7000
Sponsor: Dorrance Family Foundation
7600 East Doubletree Ranch Road, Suite 300
Scottsdale, AZ 85258

Dorr Foundation Grants   1591
Dorr Foundation grants are made primarily for programs designed to develop new science curricula from sixth-12th grade. Support is also given to special education projects for youth relating to conservation and the environment if such projects involve the school's curriculum, equipment purchase, program development, emergency funding, and seed money. In addition, some grants are made available to promote research and disseminate information on chemical, metallurgical, and sanitation engineering. Grants are awarded on a national basis, with emphasis in the Northeast states. Types of support include equipment, emergency funds, program development, seed money, curriculum development, scholarship funds, and research. Initial contact should be a phone call. There is no deadline. No response can be expected unless there is interest on the part of the trustees. Applications are accepted at any time.
Requirements: 501(c)3 tax-exempt organizations are eligible.
Restrictions: Grants are not made to individuals or for operation budgets, continuing support, annual campaigns, deficit financing, endowment funds, or conferences and seminars.
Geographic Focus: Connecticut, Maine, Massachusetts, New Hampshire, New York, Vermont
Amount of Grant: 1,000 - 40,000 USD
Contact: Barbara McMillan, Chairperson; (603) 433-6438
Sponsor: Dorr Foundation
84 Hillside Drive
Portsmouth, NH 03801-5328

Do Something BR!CK Awards   1592
The awards honor dynamic young people for service in the areas of community building, health, and the environment. BR!CK winners are leaders who identify and realize solutions to problems facing local communities across America. Nine winners will receive a minimum of $10,000 in community grants and scholarships (if applicable). Of those nine winners, 1 will be selected by a national, online vote as a Golden BR!CK Award winner. That Golden BR!CK Award winner receives a total of $100,000 in community grants. Winners are announced and recognized at an annual gala in New York City. Application and guidelines are available online.
Requirements: Applicants must be 25 years old or younger. Only winners who are age 18 and under are eligible for a scholarship of $5,000 and a $5,000 community grant (total= $10,000 BR!CK Award). Winners age 19-25 receive their entire award in the form of a community grant.
Geographic Focus: All States

Date(s) Application is Due: Dec 15
Amount of Grant: 10,000 - 100,000 USD
Contact: Jordyn Wells, (212) 254-2390, ext. 238; jwells@dosomething.org
Internet: http://www.dosomething.org/programs/awards
Sponsor: Do Something
32 Union Square E, Suite 4L
New York, NY 10003-3209

Do Something Plum Youth Grants 1593

The program awards grants to change-makers and potential community leaders age 25 and under who identify problems in their communities, and then create game plans to do something to change their world. The grants are to be used to further the growth and success of a recently created sustainable community action project, program or organization. Applications are accepted on a rolling basis and stay active for consideration for three months after submission; grants are given out weekly. Application and guidelines are available online.
Requirements: Applicants must be 25 or under and must be a U.S. or Canadian citizen. Key criteria for a successful application include: (a) Youth led and driven - The applicant is in charge of or plays a very active role in designing, leading and implementing the proposed project. (b) Measurable change - recipients strive toward tangible results. They target quantifiable situations and aim to improve that rate by a specific amount. (c) Community focus - recipients focus on problems in their communities. How an applicant defines his or her community is up to him or her. (d) Long-term problem-solving action - recipient's project can be a one-time event or an ongoing program; either way, it should strive to make lasting change in his or her community. (e) Creativity - recipients have creative, original ideas for solving problems and creating change in their local communities. (f) Diversity - projects that bring different kinds of people together are encouraged.
Restrictions: Grants cannot be used to fund: Travel Costs; Individual Sponsorships; Shipping Costs; Individual School Fees; Fundraisers.
Geographic Focus: All States, Canada
Amount of Grant: 500 USD
Contact: Jordyn Wells, (212) 254-2390, ext. 238; jwells@dosomething.org
Internet: http://www.dosomething.org/sharesomething/fund-your-project/plum-guidelines
Sponsor: Do Something
32 Union Square E, Suite 4L
New York, NY 10003-3209

Doug and Carla Salmon Foundation Grants 1594

The Salmons moved to Appleton in 1972 to work in the medical field and raise their two children. In the late 1990s, Doug and Carla began to explore ways to give back to the community that had been so good to them. The Salmons also had a strong desire to help charitable organizations in the Fox Valley — particularly through capital campaigns and the development of administrative endowments. In 2002, Doug and Carla formed the Doug & Carla Salmon Foundation, a supporting organization within the Community Foundation for the Fox Valley Region. Through this partnership, they are able to fulfill their passion for sharing with others for generations to come. There are no specific deadlines or application forms. Applicants should begin by contacted the director via email or telephone.
Requirements: All 501(c)3 organizations serving the Fox Valley Region of Wisconsin are eligible to apply.
Geographic Focus: Wisconsin
Contact: Sue Detienne, Executive Director; (920) 832-0348; rdetienne@new.rr.com
Internet: https://www.cffoxvalley.org/Page.aspx?pid=403
Sponsor: Doug and Carla Salmon Foundation
660 W. Ridgeview Drive
Appleton, 54911

Douty Foundation Grants 1595

The Foundation, established in 1968, supports projects in the fields of elementary and other education, youth, and community welfare, with special emphasis on services to disadvantaged people. Grants are sometimes made to small organizations for general operations. Preference is given to organizations that operate in Philadelphia and Montgomery counties, Pennsylvania.
Requirements: Organizations with annual budgets greater than $2 million are discouraged from applying for grants.
Restrictions: Grants for capital expenditures or endowments are not a priority for the Foundation, nor are grants for agency promotion, such as marketing, development, publication of annual reports or sponsorship of fund-raising events. Grants are not made for religious or political purposes.
Geographic Focus: Pennsylvania
Date(s) Application is Due: Feb 15; Mar 15; May 15; Oct 15
Amount of Grant: Up to 5,000 USD
Contact: Judith L. Bardes, Manager; (610) 828-8145; fax (610) 834-8175; judy1@aol.com
Internet: http://www.grants-info.org/douty/index.htm
Sponsor: Douty Foundation
P.O. Box 540
Plymouth Meeting, PA 19462-0540

Dow Chemical Company Grants 1596

The company awards grants to nonprofits in operating locations in 30 countries. The company seeks to partner with in-country organizations on projects where their support will have an impact. Dow contributions must meet at least one of the following criteria: address a demonstrated need in a city/community in which the company has a presence; provide an opportunity for hands-on science experience for students below the college level to engender a more enjoyable learning atmosphere for them to discover the values of science; support a postsecondary project or program involving science, engineering, business, or other related area to also expand and improve the pool of talented students from which to choose future employees; and enhance the environment. In-country managers and site leaders identify organizations to support through charitable contributions, as well as other community relations programs. Employee involvement is encouraged and support of programs in which employees are involved is a priority.
Restrictions: Dow does not contribute to religious organizations, individual requests, trip expenses, non-501(c)3 organizations, organizations that charge fees or dues, or lobbying organizations.
Geographic Focus: All States
Contact: Global Contributions and Community Programs Office; (988) 636-1000
Internet: http://www.dow.com/about/corp/social/guide.htm
Sponsor: Dow Chemical Company
2030 Dow Center
Midland, MI 48674

Dow Corning Corporate Contributions Grants 1597

The programs goal is to increase access to science, math and technology education, especially for children with limited access to these subjects. Some areas of interest include: teacher training and skill enhancement; hands-on learning opportunities for students that are fully integrated into the curriculum, so the experience is more than an isolated event; equipment acquisition that is fully integrated into the curriculum; and projects that enhance the interface and understanding between business and education. Colleges and universities that focus programs around these issues may be considered for funding. Inquiries about possible support may be emailed to community@dowcorning.com. The request will be forwarded to the appropriate contact for follow up.
Requirements: 501(c)3 tax-exempt organizations in Kendallville, Indiana; Carrollton and Elizabethtown, Kentucky; Bay, Midland and Saginaw counties in Michigan; and Greensboro, North Carolina are eligible to apply. Projects that increase access for those who currently have little or none will receive priority consideration. Projects that impact communities where Dow Corning employees work and live will receive priority consideration. The requesting organization must be able to define, measure and report on the progress and results of the project they propose.
Restrictions: No grants are funded for: individuals, veterans or political groups; religious groups for sectarian purposes; conferences, travel costs of groups, dinners, fund-raising events or public advertisements; and no scholarship support is available. Support is not provided for research grants nor to finance the building or maintenance of university infrastructure. Projects that are normally funded by government taxation will not be considered.
Geographic Focus: Indiana, Kentucky, Michigan, North Carolina
Contact: Contribution Program Manager; (989) 496-4400; fax (989) 496-6731; community@dowcorning.com
Internet: http://www.dowcorning.com/content/about/aboutcomm/default.asp
Sponsor: Dow Corning Corporation
P.O. Box 994
Midland, MI 48686-0994

DPA Promoting Policy Change Advocacy Grants 1598

The Drug Policy Alliance Advocacy Grants seek to broaden public and political support for drug policy reform and will fund strategic and innovative approaches to increase such support. Proposals should be designed to: educate the public and policymakers about the negative consequences of current local, state or national drug policies; promote better awareness and understanding of alternatives to current drug policies; and broaden awareness and understanding of the extent to which punitive prohibitionist policies are responsible for most drug-related problems around the country. Strategic, geographic or thematic collaborations are strongly encouraged. The Alliance prioritizes organizations focused on one or more of the following: public education campaigns and litigation to raise awareness of the negative consequences of current local, state, and national drug policies; and organizing and mobilizing constituencies that raise awareness about the negative consequences of local, state, and national drug policies. The Alliance also favors public education efforts that speak to: the failures and consequences of drug polices in the U.S. and the potential benefits of alternatives to prohibition; reducing over-reliance on the criminal justice system by raising awareness of the need for alternatives to incarceration and/or health-based approaches to drug use; discrimination in employment, housing, student loans and other benefits against those who use drugs or who have been convicted of drug law violations; the negative consequences of current drug policies on human rights; and efforts that mobilize people around the disproportionate impact of the drug war on communities of color and youth.
Requirements: Tax-exempt 501(c)3 organizations and organizations with 501(c)3 fiscal sponsors are eligible. The program provides both general support and project-specific grants. All grantmaking will be directed to organizations working within the United States, and possibly Canada, with particular emphasis on state-based activity. The Alliance will make grants to organizations that have been invited to apply and who demonstrate a clear ability and commitment to educate the public about the need for broad drug policy reform.
Geographic Focus: All States, Canada
Date(s) Application is Due: Jun 18
Amount of Grant: 15,000 - 25,000 USD
Contact: Asha Bandele, Grants Contact; (212) 613-8020; fax (212) 613-8021; abandele@drugpolicy.org or grants@drugpolicy.org
Internet: http://www.drugpolicy.org/about/jobsfunding/grants/index.cfm
Sponsor: Drug Policy Alliance
131 West 33rd Street, 15th Floor
New York, NY 10001

Dr. and Mrs. Paul Pierce Memorial Foundation Grants 1599
The Dr. and Mrs. Paul Pierce Memorial Foundation was established in 1963 to support and promote quality education, human-services, and health-care programming for underserved populations. Special consideration is given to charitable organizations that serve the people of Grayson County, Texas. Grants from the Pierce Memorial Foundation are one year in duration. Applicants must apply online at the grant website. Applicants are strongly encouraged to do the following before applying: review the downloadable state application procedures for additional helpful information and clarifications; review the downloadable online-application guidelines at the grant website; review the foundation's funding history (link is available from the grant website); review the online application questions in advance; and review the list of required attachments. These will generally include: a list of board members, financial statements (audited, reviewed, or compiled by independent auditor); an organization summary; a list of other funding sources; an IRS Determination letter; and other required documents. All attachments must be uploaded in the online application as PDF, Word, or Excel files. The Dr. and Mrs. Paul Pierce Memorial Foundation has four deadlines annually: March 1, June 1, September 1, and December 1. Applications must be submitted by 11:59 p.m. on the deadline dates. Grant applicants are notified as follows: March deadline applicants will be notified of grant decisions by June 30; June applicants will be notified by September 30; September applicants will be notified by December 31; December applicants will be notified by March 31 of the following year.
Requirements: Applicants must have 501(c) tax-exempt status.
Restrictions: The foundation does not support requests from individuals, organizations attempting to influence policy through direct lobbying, or any political campaigns.
Geographic Focus: Texas
Date(s) Application is Due: Mar 1; Jun 1; Sep 1; Dec 1
Contact: David Ross, Senior Vice President; tx.philanthropic@baml.com
Internet: https://www.bankofamerica.com/philanthropic/fn_search.action
Sponsor: Dr. and Mrs. Paul Pierce Memorial Foundation
901 Main Street, 19th Floor, TX1-492-19-11
Dallas, TX 75202-3714

Dr. John T. Macdonald Foundation Grants 1600
The Dr. John T. Macdonald Foundation awards grants to eligible Florida nonprofit organizations in Miami-Dade County for medical and health-related programs to community-based programs, with priority given to those serving children, youth, and economically disadvantaged individuals. The foundation supports medical rehabilitation, disease prevention, and health education. Types of support include capital grants, matching/challenge grants, program development grants, seed money grants, and training grants. Deadline listed is for letters of intent; full proposals are by request. Annual deadline dates may vary; contact program staff for exact dates.
Requirements: Florida nonprofit organizations serving the health care needs of people in Miami-Dade County are eligible. Priority will be given to projects in the Coral Gables community.
Restrictions: Grants do not support national projects, multiyear funding requests, for-profit organizations, political candidates or campaigns, religious projects, individuals, or other grantmaking foundations.
Geographic Focus: Florida
Amount of Grant: Up to 550,000 USD
Contact: Kim Greene; (305) 667-6017; fax (305) 667-9135; kgreene@jtmacdonaldfdn.org
Internet: http://jtmacdonaldfdn.org/grants/grants-scholarships/
Sponsor: Dr. John T. Macdonald Foundation
1550 Madruga Avenue, Suite 215
Coral Gables, FL 33146

Dr. P. Phillips Foundation Grants 1601
The primary focus of the Foundation is to respond to needs in Orange and Osceola counties. Funding for organizations outside of this geographic area will generally not be considered. Proposals that address established areas of interest are given the highest priority. These areas include: educational programs; children and youth services; social services; cultural organizations and health or rehabilitative programs. Faxed or emailed applications will not be accepted.
Requirements: Foundation awards are granted only to organizations and institutions exempt from federal taxation under Section 501(c)3 of the Internal Revenue Code.
Restrictions: The Foundation does not make grants to: individuals or private foundations; private schools for projects other than scholarships to increase total enrollment using a nationally accepted screening criteria to determine financial need; projects of social, religious, fraternal or veterans groups that primarily benefit their own members or adherents; retire accumulated debt; or for legislative lobbying or other political purposes. Requests are not encouraged for endowments, research, trips or tours, scholarships and multi-year grants, newsletters or other promotional materials, magazines or books, and television or video production. Requests for vans or other vehicles will generally not be considered.
Geographic Focus: Florida
Date(s) Application is Due: Jan 11; May 11; Sep 14
Contact: Grants Administrator; (407) 422-6105; fax (407) 422-4952
Internet: http://www.drphillips.org/grants/
Sponsor: Dr. P. Phillips Foundation
60 West Robinson Street, P.O. Box 3753
Orlando, FL 32802

Dr. Scholl Foundation Grants 1602
Applications are considered in the following areas: private education, including elementary, secondary, college and university level; programs for children, developmentally disabled, senior citizens, civic and cultural institutions, social service agencies, hospitals and health care, environmental organizations and religious institutions. The general areas of interest are not intended to limit the interest of the foundation from considering other worthwhile projects. An application form is required and may be obtained from the foundation office. All grant applications must be requested in writing. Telephone, email or fax requests will not be accepted.
Requirements: Grants are awarded on an annual basis to valid IRS 501(c)3 organizations. Non-U.S. applicants without a 501(c)3 must complete a notarized affidavit.
Restrictions: Funding is not available for: organizations that do not have a valid IRS 501(c)3 determination letter; political organizations, political action committees, or individual campaigns whose primary purpose is to influence legislation; foundations that are themselves grantmaking bodies; grants to individuals, endowments or capital campaigns; grants for loans, operating deficit reduction, the liquidation of a debt, or general support; event sponsorships including the purchase of tables, tickets or advertisements; or more than one request from the same organization in the same year.
Geographic Focus: All States
Date(s) Application is Due: Mar 1
Contact: Pamela Scholl, President; (847) 559-7430
Internet: http://www.drschollfoundation.com/procedures.htm
Sponsor: Dr. Scholl Foundation
1033 Skokie Boulevard, Suite 230
Northbrook, IL 60062

Draper Richards Kaplan Foundation Grants 1603
The Draper Richards Kaplan Foundation awards three-year grants to selected social entrepreneurs to start new nonprofit organizations that are based in the U.S. but national or global in scope with broad social impact. Selected projects will demonstrate innovative ways to solve existing social problems. The Foundation offers financial support as well as strategic and organizational assistance. Proposals are accepted at any time. Examples of previously funded projects are located on the website.
Requirements: Experienced, dedicated social entrepreneurs with a developed idea for a U.S. nonprofit organization are invited to apply. Proposals are accepted for organizations at the beginning of their development. Organizations are usually 0-3 years old and the entrepreneur is prepared to execute an ambitious plan.
Restrictions: The Foundation does not fund local community-based organizations; research; scholarships; think tanks; conferences or one-time events; organizations planning to influence policy through lobbying; or programs promoting religious doctrine.
Geographic Focus: All States
Amount of Grant: 300,000 USD
Contact: Jenny Shilling Stein; (650) 319-7808; info@draperrichards.org
Internet: http://www.drkfoundation.org/what-we-fund.html
Sponsor: Draper Richards Kaplan Foundation
1600 El Camino Road
Menlo Park, CA 94025

Dream Weaver Foundation 1604
Established in 2000 in Georgia, the Dream Weaver Foundation offers grant funding primarily in Georgia and Florida. Its major fields of interest include: animals and wildlife; education (all levels); and human services. Funding is either directed at general operating costs or specific programs. There is no formal application requires, so interested parties should offer a proposal in the form of a two- or three-page letter. This format should be comprised of a general project description, the needed budgetary allowance, and copies of tax-free status letters. There are no specified annual deadlines. Most recently, grants have typically ranged from $1,000 to $5,000.
Requirements: 501(c)3 organizations from Georgia and Florida, or those supporting residents of these two states, are eligible to apply.
Restrictions: No grants are given to individuals
Geographic Focus: Florida, Georgia
Amount of Grant: 1,000 - 5,000 USD
Contact: Charles E. Weaver, President; (770) 781-2823 or (770) 889-2599
Sponsor: Dream Weaver Foundation
6315 Holland Drive
Cumming, GA 30041-4639

Dresher Foundation Grants 1605
The foundation awards grants to eligible Maryland nonprofit organizations in its areas of interest, including capital campaigns, endowments, new or ongoing programs, operating support and scholarships. Summer camp and after-school program letters of inquiry are accepted for review only for the January and March deadlines. Letters of inquiry are accepted; full proposals are by request.
Requirements: Fund requests are generally limited to the Maryland jurisdictions of Baltimore City and Baltimore and Harford Counties. The Foundation will only make grants to organizations that are exempt from federal tax under section 501(c)3 of the IRS Code and that are not classified as private foundations under section 509(a) of the Code.
Restrictions: Support is not provided for: agencies that redistribute grant funds to nonprofits; annual giving; charter schools; public elementary or high schools; galas, special events, or golf tournaments; literacy programs; national or local chapters for specific diseases; one-time only events, seminars, or workshops; or political activities. The Foundation will not consider inquiries or proposals from any organization more than once every twelve months.
Geographic Focus: Maryland
Date(s) Application is Due: Jan 12; Mar 9; May 4; Aug 10; Oct 5
Contact: Robin Platts, Executive Director; (410) 933-0384; robin@dresherfoundation.org
Internet: http://www.dresherfoundation.org
Sponsor: Dresher Foundation
4940 Campbell Boulevard, Suite 110
Baltimore, MD 21236

Dreyer's Foundation Large Grants 1606

This grant focuses on young people from preschool to grade 12, primarily in Oakland and the East Bay. Grants will be awarded to K-12 public education and programs that help students to succeed in core academic subjects and graduate to post secondary education and/or vocational training. Priority will be given to programs, either in-school or after school, which are provided in sequential, consistent basis to students throughout the year. Organizations may request support for capital items, program expenses, operating expenses, start-up costs, materials, and/or supplies. Priority will be given to those programs/projects that support low and middle income youth and minority youth.
Requirements: Grants are awarded to nonprofit youth-serving organizations and K-12 public education organizations.
Restrictions: The Foundation does not fund basic health, clothing or shelter needs. An organization may submit only one proposal annually.
Geographic Focus: All States
Date(s) Application is Due: Jan 15
Amount of Grant: 3,000 USD
Contact: Large Grants Program Coordinator; (510) 450-4586
Internet: http://www.dreyersinc.com/dreyersfoundation/large_grants.asp
Sponsor: Dreyer's Foundation
5929 College Avenue
Oakland, CA 94618

Drs. Bruce and Lee Foundation Grants 1607

The Foundation's goal is to advance the general welfare and the quality of all life in the Florence, S.C. area by providing economic support to qualified programs and non-profit organizations. The Foundation will support a broad range of charitable purposes including, but not limited to: medical; health; human services; education; arts; religion; civic affairs; and the conservation, preservation and promotion of cultural, historical and environmental resources. There are no application deadlines. Contact the office for application materials and guidelines.
Requirements: Florence, SC, nonprofit organizations are eligible.
Restrictions: The Foundation does not purchase tickets for fundraising events. Grants to individuals will not be considered.
Geographic Focus: South Carolina
Samples: Francis Marion U (Florence, SC)—to construct a facility for the new bachelor's-degree nursing program, $5 million.
Contact: L. Bradley Callicott; (843) 664-2870; blfound@bellsouth.net
Sponsor: Drs. Bruce and Lee Foundation
181 East Evans Street, BTC Box 022
Florence, SC 29506

Drug Free Communities Support Program 1608

The grants support coalitions of youth; parents; media; law enforcement; school officials; faith-based organizations; fraternal organizations; State, local, and tribal government agencies; healthcare professionals; and other community representatives. The Drug Free Communities Support Program enables the coalitions to strengthen their coordination and prevention efforts, encourage citizen participation in substance abuse reduction efforts, and disseminate information about effective programs. While the program does not prescribe the size, shape, borders, demographics, or geographic locations of DFC grantees, some priority may be given to rural, Native American, and economically disadvantaged communities, as well as the overall geographic distribution of the grantee pool.
Requirements: The coalition must be a legally eligible entity; must have the goal of reducing substance abuse among youth as part of its principal mission; must target multiple drugs and address the two major DFC goals; must demonstrate that coalition members have worked together on substance abuse prevention for a period of at least six months prior to the date of submission of the application; must demonstrate that it has substantial participation from volunteer leaders in the community; must demonstrate that it addresses substance abuse prevention in the community in a comprehensive and long-term fashion and works to develop consensus regarding the priorities of the community to combat substance abuse among youth. Download the full RFA (pdf file) from http://www.ondcp.gov/dfc/potentialgrantees.html.
Restrictions: A coalition must fall into one of the following three categories: a) A coalition that has never received a DFC grant; b) A coalition that previously received a DFC grant but experienced a lapse in funding; c) A coalition that has concluded the first five-year funding cycle and is applying for a second five-year funding cycle.
Geographic Focus: All States
Date(s) Application is Due: Mar 19
Amount of Grant: Up to 125,000 USD
Contact: Christine Chen, Director; (240) 276-1401; Christine.chen@samhsa.hhs.gov
Internet: http://www.ondcp.gov/dfc/
Sponsor: Office of National Drug Control Policy
1 Choke Cherry Road
Rockville, MD 20857

DTE Energy Foundation Community Development Grants 1609

The foundation supports the principle that locally directed physical and economic development is a uniquely powerful tool for community and neighborhood revitalization. The foundation lends support to nonprofit organizations that spur commercial development or collaborate to develop affordable housing transforming distressed neighborhoods into healthy communities. Examples of projects include: nonprofit commercial development within core utility service areas or in support of DTE Energy Resources development projects; pre-development costs associated with environmental assessment and cleanup; and collaborative funding efforts in support of affordable housing initiatives. Grant amounts generally range from $500 to $150,000, and the application process is distinct for each of the following ranges: $500 to $2,000; $2,001 to $10,000; and any amount greater than $10,000. Applications must be submitted electronically by the stated deadlines.
Requirements: Eligible applicants must meet all of the following criteria: be located in or provide services to a community in which DTE Energy does business; and be a nonprofit (i.e. be exempt for federal income tax under section 501(c)3 of the Internal Revenue Code and not a private foundation, as defined in Section 509(a) of the Code).
Restrictions: The Foundation does not provide support to: individuals; political parties, organizations or activities; religious organizations for religious purposes; organizations that are not able to demonstrate commitment to equality and diversity; student group trips; national or international organizations, unless they are providing benefits directly to our service-area residents; projects that may result in undue personal benefit to a member of the DTE Energy Foundation board, or to any DTE Energy employee; conferences unless they are aligned with DTE Energy's business interests; single purpose health organizations; and hospitals, for building or equipment needs.
Geographic Focus: Michigan
Date(s) Application is Due: Apr 13; Jul 13; Oct 12; Dec 28
Contact: Karla D. Hall; (313) 235-9271 or (313) 235-9416; foundation@dteenergy.com
Internet: http://www.dteenergy.com/dteEnergyCompany/community/foundation/whatWeSupport.html
Sponsor: DTE Energy Foundation
One Energy Plaza, 1046 WBC
Detroit, MI 48226-1279

DTE Energy Foundation Cultural Grants 1610

The DTE Energy Foundation is at the core of DTE Energy's commitment to the communities and customers it is privileged to serve. The DTE Energy Foundation is dedicated to strengthening the cultural fabric of these communities and its connection to customers. Grant amounts generally range from $500 to $300,000, and the application process is distinct for each of the following ranges: $500 to $2,000; $2,001 to $10,000; and any amount greater than $10,000. Applications must be submitted electronically by the stated deadlines.
Requirements: Eligible applicants must meet all of the following criteria: be located in or provide services to a community in which DTE Energy does business; and be a nonprofit (i.e. be exempt for federal income tax under section 501(c)3 of the Internal Revenue Code and not a private foundation, as defined in Section 509(a) of the Code).
Restrictions: The Foundation does not provide support to: individuals; political parties, organizations or activities; religious organizations for religious purposes; organizations that are not able to demonstrate commitment to equality and diversity; student group trips; national or international organizations, unless they are providing benefits directly to our service-area residents; projects that may result in undue personal benefit to a member of the DTE Energy Foundation board, or to any DTE Energy employee; conferences unless they are aligned with DTE Energy's business interests; single purpose health organizations; hospitals, for building or equipment needs.
Geographic Focus: Michigan
Contact: Karla D. Hall; (313) 235-9271 or (313) 235-9416; foundation@dteenergy.com
Internet: http://www.dteenergy.com/dteEnergyCompany/community/foundation/whatWeSupport.html
Sponsor: DTE Energy Foundation
One Energy Plaza, 1046 WBC
Detroit, MI 48226-1279

DTE Energy Foundation Diversity Grants 1611

The foundation recognizes that the workplace, the community and the DTE Energy region encompasses a broad mix of individuals with diverse backgrounds, cultures and experiences. Learning to embrace these differences, recognizing their inherent strengths and working together are essential to building strong communities. Diversity grants focus on programs and organizations that promote personal understanding and inclusiveness. The Foundation focus is on programs and organizations that: enhance and promote understanding and inclusiveness by individuals; encourage and advocate for effective, positive change; and celebrate and enhance awareness of different cultures. Grant amounts generally range from $500 to $150,000, and the application process is distinct for each of the following ranges: $500 to $2,000; $2,001 to $10,000; and any amount greater than $10,000. Applications must be submitted electronically by the stated deadlines.
Requirements: Eligible applicants must meet all of the following criteria: be located in or provide services to a community in which DTE Energy does business; and be a nonprofit (i.e. be exempt for federal income tax under section 501(c)3 of the Internal Revenue Code and not a private foundation, as defined in Section 509(a) of the Code).
Restrictions: The foundation does not support: individuals; political parties, organizations or activities; religious organizations for religious purposes; organizations that are not able to demonstrate commitment to equality and diversity; student group trips; national or international organizations, unless they are providing benefits directly to our service-area residents; projects that may result in undue personal benefit to a member of the DTE Energy Foundation board, or to any DTE Energy employee; conferences unless they are aligned with DTE Energy's business interests; single purpose health organizations; and hospitals, for building or equipment needs.
Geographic Focus: Michigan
Date(s) Application is Due: Apr 13; Jul 13; Oct 12; Dec 28
Contact: Karla D. Hall; (313) 235-9271 or (313) 235-9416; foundation@dteenergy.com
Internet: http://www.dteenergy.com/dteEnergyCompany/community/foundation/whatWeSupport.html
Sponsor: DTE Energy Foundation
One Energy Plaza, 1046 WBC
Detroit, MI 48226-1279

DTE Energy Foundation Environmental Grants 1612
The DTE Energy Foundation believes economic development and environmental protection are not mutually exclusive. Environmental grants focus on organizations and programs that: protect and restore the environment and enhance the quality of life in the communities that we serve or are home to our facilities; and build understanding of the environment and promote an understanding of the links between environmental stewardship and sustainable development, including education about renewable energy and energy efficiency, that reaches a broad audience. Grant amounts range from $500 to $100,000, and the application process is distinct for each of the following ranges: $500 to $2,000; $2,001 to $10,000; and any amount greater than $10,000. Applications must be submitted electronically by the stated deadlines.
Requirements: Eligible applicants must meet all of the following criteria: be located in or provide services to a community in which DTE Energy does business; and be a nonprofit (i.e. be exempt for federal income tax under section 501(c)3 of the Internal Revenue Code and not a private foundation, as defined in Section 509(a) of the Code).
Restrictions: The foundation does not provide support to: individuals; political parties, organizations or activities; religious organizations for religious purposes; organizations that are not able to demonstrate commitment to equality and diversity; student group trips; national or international organizations, unless they are providing benefits directly to our service-area residents; projects that may result in undue personal benefit to a member of the DTE Energy Foundation board, or to any DTE Energy employee; conferences unless they are aligned with DTE Energy's business interests; single purpose health organizations; or hospitals, for building or equipment needs.
Geographic Focus: Michigan
Date(s) Application is Due: Apr 13; Jul 13; Oct 12; Dec 28
Amount of Grant: 500 - 100,000 USD
Contact: Karla D. Hall; (313) 235-9271 or (313) 235-9416; foundation@dteenergy.com
Internet: http://www.dteenergy.com/dteEnergyCompany/community/foundation/whatWeSupport.html
Sponsor: DTE Energy Foundation
One Energy Plaza, 1046 WBC
Detroit, MI 48226-1279

DTE Energy Foundation Health and Human Services Grants 1613
The DTE Energy Foundation is at the core of DTE Energy's commitment to the communities and customers it is privileged to serve. The DTE Energy Foundation is dedicated to strengthening the health and human services sector of these communities. Priority will be given to supporting organizations that are in the forefront of addressing the critical, acute human needs brought on by the economic downturn. Grant amounts generally range from $500 to $100,000, and the application process is distinct for each of the following ranges: $500 to $2,000; $2,001 to $10,000; and any amount greater than $10,000. Applications must be submitted electronically by the stated deadlines.
Requirements: Eligible applicants must meet all of the following criteria: be located in or provide services to a community in which DTE Energy does business; and be a nonprofit (i.e. be exempt for federal income tax under section 501(c)3 of the Internal Revenue Code and not a private foundation, as defined in Section 509(a) of the Code).
Restrictions: The Foundation does not provide support to: individuals; political parties, organizations or activities; religious organizations for religious purposes; organizations that are not able to demonstrate commitment to equality and diversity; student group trips; national or international organizations, unless they are providing benefits directly to our service-area residents; projects that may result in undue personal benefit to a member of the DTE Energy Foundation board, or to any DTE Energy employee; conferences unless they are aligned with DTE Energy's business interests; single purpose health organizations; hospitals, for building or equipment needs.
Geographic Focus: Michigan
Date(s) Application is Due: Apr 13; Jul 13; Oct 12; Dec 28
Amount of Grant: 500 - 100,000 USD
Contact: Karla D. Hall; (313) 235-9271 or (313) 235-9416; foundation@dteenergy.com
Sponsor: DTE Energy Foundation
One Energy Plaza, 1046 WBC
Detroit, MI 48226-1279

DTE Energy Foundation Leadership Grants 1614
The foundation believes that leadership encompasses activity on two planes; personal and institutional. In the interest of building thriving communities, the foundation will place special emphasis on programs that promote and nurture leadership traits in young people. In addition, vibrant communities also benefit from the efforts of a core group of institutions dedicated to improving the community's way of life. Foundation focus is on: programs that provide unique experiences to equip individuals with leadership skills; initiatives that improve the strength, stability, sustainability and leadership of the nonprofit sector; and core institutions important to the quality of life in DTE Energy communities. Grant amounts generally range from $500 to $75,000, and the application process is distinct for each of the following ranges: $500 to $2,000; $2,001 to $10,000; and any amount greater than $10,000. Applications must be submitted electronically by the stated deadlines.
Requirements: Eligible applicants must meet all of the following criteria: be located in or provide services to a community in which DTE Energy does business; and be a nonprofit (i.e. be exempt for federal income tax under section 501(c)3 of the Internal Revenue Code and not a private foundation, as defined in Section 509(a) of the Code).
Restrictions: The foundation does not provide support to: individuals; political parties, organizations or activities; religious organizations for religious purposes; organizations that are not able to demonstrate commitment to equality and diversity; student group trips; national or international organizations, unless they are providing benefits directly to our service-area residents; projects that may result in undue personal benefit to a member of the DTE Energy Foundation board, or to any DTE Energy employee; conferences unless they are aligned with DTE Energy's business interests; single purpose health organizations; and hospitals, for building or equipment needs.
Geographic Focus: Michigan
Date(s) Application is Due: Apr 13; Jul 13; Oct 12; Dec 28
Contact: Karla D. Hall; (313) 235-9271 or (313) 235-9416; foundation@dteenergy.com
Internet: http://www.dteenergy.com/dteEnergyCompany/community/foundation/whatWeSupport.html
Sponsor: DTE Energy Foundation
One Energy Plaza, 1046 WBC
Detroit, MI 48226-1279

Dubois County Community Foundation Grants 1615
The central purpose of the community foundation is to serve the needs of Dubois County, Indiana, and the philanthropic aims of donors who wish to better their community. The Foundation's fields of interest are: arts, education, environment, beautification programs, health care, human services, recreation, and youth development. Evaluation is based on the project's feasibility, soundness of its implementation plan, viability of subsequent long-term financing, and fulfillment of community need.
Requirements: Organizations should complete the applicant form, agreement, and certification available at the website. Notification of the Board's decision is made approximately four months after the submission deadline.
Restrictions: Giving is concentrated to Dubois County, Indiana. No support is available for the operational expenses of government units or agencies. No grants for operating expenses of nonprofits, funding after the fact, annual fund raising, sponsorship of events, debt retirement, or loans.
Geographic Focus: Indiana
Date(s) Application is Due: Sep 15
Contact: Brad Ward, Chief Executive Officer; (812) 482-5295; fax (812) 482-7461
Internet: http://www.dccommunityfoundation.org/funds/
Sponsor: Dubois County Community Foundation
600 McCrillus Street, P.O. Box 269
Jasper, IN 47547-0269

Duchossois Family Foundation Grants 1616
The foundation focuses its efforts in the Chicago metropolitan area and gives primary consideration to nonprofit organizations that contribute to the community in the area of health. The foundation supports organizations involved with mental health/crisis services, cancer, HIV/AIDS, cancer research, AIDS research and, human services. A one-page summary-request letter should include a description of the organization and its specific needs and purposes, the amount requested, and a list of members of the board of directors and their business/professional affiliations.
Requirements: 501(c)3 tax-exempt charities serving the Chicago metro area are eligible.
Geographic Focus: Illinois
Contact: Iris Krieg, Executive Director; (312) 641-5765; iriskrieg1@aol.com
Sponsor: Duchossois Family Foundation (Chicago)
203 N Wabash Avenue, Suite 1800
Chicago, IL 60601

Duke Endowment Child Care Grants 1617
This grant is designed to enhance the welfare of children in North Carolina and South Carolina. The goal of the grant is to assist selected organizations to serve children in the Carolinas who are without the benefit of being supported by family or who might be at risk for losing such support through abuse, neglect, unstable housing or domestic violence. Grants are made for programs and for capital projects. Applications are accepted year-round. Application forms are not required. A written proposal should be submitted after consultation with the Child Care Division.
Requirements: Grants are awarded in North Carolina and South Carolina to: accredited, licensed residential children's homes; accredited adoption placement agencies; Prevent Child Abuse of North Carolina and South Carolina and their local affiliates; Big Brothers Big Sisters agencies; accredited child advocacy centers; and public sector child welfare agencies (under certain circumstances).
Geographic Focus: North Carolina, South Carolina
Date(s) Application is Due: Jan 15; Jul 15
Contact: Rhett Mabry; (704) 376-0291; fax (704) 376-9336; rmabry@tde.org
Internet: http://www.dukeendowment.org/program-areas/child-care
Sponsor: Duke Endowment
100 N Tryon Street, Suite 3500
Charlotte, NC 28202-4012

Duke Energy Foundation Community Vitality Grants 1618
The Duke Energy Foundation, along with employee and retiree volunteers, actively works to improve the quality of life in its communities, lending expertise in the form of leadership and financial support through grants to charitable organizations. The Foundation gives primarily in areas of company operations in Indiana, Kentucky, North Carolina, Ohio and South Carolina. In the area of community vitality, the Foundation funds: human services, arts, cultural activities, community safety, and leadership development. Grants typically range from $1,000 to $1,250,000. A formal application is required, though there are no specified annual deadlines.
Requirements: Organizations with a 501(c)3 verification from the IRS or are a part of a governmental entity are eligible. All organizations applying for a grant must have: completed the Online Grant Application; a clear reason for making the contribution that relates to the areas of focus; and regular reports on the measurable results of the project.

Restrictions: Foundation funds are not provided for: organizations that discriminate by race, creed, gender, age or national origin; political activities and organizations; grants to individual agencies of the United Way or the Charlotte Arts and Science Council; capital campaigns and endowments, except in extremely rare and specialized situations that relate directly to our areas of expertise in business; individuals; athletics, including individual sports teams and all-star teams; underwriting of films, video and television productions; reducing the cost of utility service; sectarian or religious activities; conferences, trips or tours; fraternal, veteran or labor groups serving only their members; advertising; membership fees or association fees, either personal or corporate; dinners or tables at fundraisers are rarely considered; family foundations.
Geographic Focus: Indiana, Kentucky, North Carolina, Ohio, South Carolina
Amount of Grant: 1,000 - 1,250,000 USD
Contact: Alisa McDonald, Vice President; (704) 382-7200; fax (704) 382-7600
Internet: http://www.duke-energy.com/community/foundation/areas-of-focus.asp
Sponsor: Duke Energy Foundation
400 South Tryon Street, P.O. Box 1007
Charlotte, NC 28201-1007

Duke Energy Foundation Economic Development Grants — 1619
The Duke Energy Foundation, along with employee and retiree volunteers, actively works to improve the quality of life in its communities, lending expertise in the form of leadership and financial support through grants to charitable organizations. The Foundation gives primarily in areas of company operations in Indiana, Kentucky, North Carolina, Ohio and South Carolina. In the area of economic development, the Foundation funds initiatives that support the company's economic development strategies and necessary skills to strengthen the workforce. Grants range from $1,000 to $1,250,000. A formal application is required, though there are no specified annual deadlines.
Requirements: Organizations with a 501(c)3 verification from the IRS or are a part of a governmental entity are eligible. All organizations applying for a grant must have: completed the Online Grant Application; a clear reason for making the contribution that relates to the areas of focus; and regular reports on the measurable results of the project.
Restrictions: Foundation funds are not provided for: organizations that discriminate by race, creed, gender, age or national origin; political activities and organizations; grants to individual agencies of the United Way or the Charlotte Arts and Science Council; capital campaigns and endowments, except in extremely rare and specialized situations that relate directly to our areas of expertise in business; individuals; athletics, including individual sports teams and all-star teams; underwriting of films, video and television productions; reducing the cost of utility service; sectarian or religious activities; conferences, trips or tours; fraternal, veteran or labor groups serving only their members; advertising; membership fees or association fees, either personal or corporate; dinners or tables at fundraisers are rarely considered; family foundations.
Geographic Focus: Indiana, Kentucky, North Carolina, Ohio, South Carolina
Amount of Grant: 1,000 - 1,250,000 USD
Contact: Alisa McDonald, Vice President; (704) 382-7200; fax (704) 382-7600
Internet: http://www.duke-energy.com/community/foundation/areas-of-focus.asp
Sponsor: Duke Energy Foundation
400 South Tryon Street, P.O. Box 1007
Charlotte, NC 28201-1007

Duluth-Superior Area Community Foundation Grants — 1620
The foundation supports a wide variety of activities in five interest areas: Arts, Community and Economic Development, Education, Environment, and Human Services. Consideration is given to regional needs, the availability of other funding sources, and level of foundation resources. The foundation concentrates its funding support towards new projects and organizational start-up for a limited time; however, some field of interest and donor advised funds consider requests for ongoing project or organizational support, and capital and equipment support.
Requirements: Eligible organizations include: those classified as charitable organizations under Section 501(c)3 of the Internal Revenue Code; or classified as an organization under Section 170(c)(1) of the Internal Revenue Code; located in or that provide services to residents within the seven counties of northeast Minnesota (Aitkin, Carlton, Cook, Itasca, Koochiching, Lake, and St. Louis) and/or the two counties in northwest Wisconsin (Bayfield, Douglas). Some funds have a specific geographic focus area.
Restrictions: The foundation does not make grants to/for: individuals (aside from scholarships initiated or managed by the Community Foundation), fundraising activities, requests from re-granting organizations for its own grant making activities, tickets for benefits, telephone solicitations, endowments, religious organizations for religious activities, medical research, debt retirement, political organizations or campaigns, organizations with significant activity considered influencing of legislation.
Geographic Focus: Minnesota, Wisconsin
Date(s) Application is Due: Feb 1; Apr 1; Aug 1; Oct 1
Contact: Katie Gellatly, (218) 726-0232; KGellatly@dsacommunityfoundation.com
Internet: http://www.dsacommunityfoundation.com/grants
Sponsor: Duluth-Superior Area Community Foundation
324 West Superior Street, Suite 212
Duluth, MN 55802

Duneland Health Council Incorporated Grants — 1621
The Duneland Health Council, Inc. is a private foundation focused on improving the health and general welfare of the greater Michigan City, Indiana community.
Restrictions: Funding limited primarily in the metropolitan Michigan City, IN area. No support for religious organizations. No grants to individuals, or for fund-raising, endowments or advertising.
Geographic Focus: Indiana
Contact: Norm Steider; (219) 874-4193; fax (219) 873-2416; normsteider@yahoo.com
Sponsor: Duneland Health Council Incorporated
P.O. Box 9327
Michigan City, IN 46361-9327

Dunn Foundation K-12 Grants — 1622
The Foundation is particularly concerned with the impacts sprawl is having on community character and the visual quality of our communities, landscapes, streets, and neighborhoods. Therefore, the grants program is intended to foster education on the value of visually distinctive, attractive communities with a strong sense of place. The Foundation's current highest priority is to fund education programs that support ViewFinders Too use in the school classroom or in after school programs. More information on ViewFinders Too is available on the website.
Requirements: Non institutions and schools are eligible to submit letters of interest. These may be made via-email (viewfinders@dunnfoundation.org) and should include information relative to the grant seeking organization, preliminary project scope and budget estimates.
Restrictions: The Foundation will not accept nor will it acknowledge unsolicited formal applications. The Foundation cannot support capital improvement projects and individuals.
Geographic Focus: All States
Contact: Richard Youngken, (401) 367-0026; fax (401) 367-0020; dunnfndn@tiac.net
Internet: http://www.dunnfoundation.org/grants1.htm
Sponsor: Dunn Foundation
320 Thames Street, Room 274
Newport, RI 02840

Dunspaugh-Dalton Foundation Grants — 1623
The foundation awards grants to eligible nonprofit organizations in the areas of higher, secondary, and elementary education; social services; youth; health associations and hospitals; cultural programs; and civic affairs. Types of support include capital campaigns, continuing support, endowment funds, matching funds, operating support, professorships, and special projects. The board meets monthly to consider requests.
Requirements: U.S. nonprofit organizations are eligible. The foundation primarily supports programs in California, Florida, and North Carolina.
Restrictions: Individuals are not eligible.
Geographic Focus: California, Florida, North Carolina
Amount of Grant: 5,000 - 50,000 USD
Contact: William Lane Jr, (305) 668-4192; fax (305) 668-4247
Sponsor: Dunspaugh-Dalton Foundation
1533 Sunset Drive, Suite 150
Coral Gables, FL 33143-5700

DuPage Community Foundation Grants — 1624
The DuPage Community Foundation is a community-based philanthropic organization that identifies, promotes, and supports programs that raise the quality of life in DuPage County for this generation and future generations. To this end, the Foundation seeks to address the broad needs of DuPage County through grants in support of the following program categories: Arts and Culture, Education, Environmental, Health, and Human Services.
Requirements: Grant applications will be accepted from non-profit charitable organizations that: are classified as exempt from federal income taxes under section 501(c)3 of the Internal Revenue Code; and are located in DuPage County. Previous grantees must have complied with all reporting requirements and be in good standing before submitting another grant request.
Restrictions: The Foundation does not generally award grants to: organizations located outside of DuPage County (exceptions, if any, will be made by the director of grants); individuals; governmental agencies, including supporting foundations; programs for religious purposes; endowments; disease-specific organizations; private foundations and private operating foundations; or public, parochial, private or charter schools (pre-K through 12th grade).
Geographic Focus: Illinois
Date(s) Application is Due: Feb 2; Aug 3
Contact: Bonnie Heydorn, (630) 665-5556; fax (630) 665-9571; bheydorn@dcfdn.org
Internet: http://www.dcfdn.org
Sponsor: DuPage Community Foundation
2100 Manchester Road, Building A, Suite 303
Wheaton, IL 60187-4584

Durfee Foundation Sabbatical Grants — 1625
The Durfee Foundation makes grants in Southern California for projects in arts and culture, education, history, and community development. The Foundation believes that institutions are driven by creative people. The Sabbatical grants program recognizes that creative leaders need time to think and reflect if they are to keep their organizations ahead of the curve. Developed in 1997, the program seeks to replenish the stores of energy and inspiration for the community's most gifted leaders. Up to six sabbatical stipends are provided annually. Expenses up to $35,000 for travel, reflection, or otherwise renewal of themselves in whatever manner they propose. Additional support of up to $5,000 is made available to successful applicants employing organizations willing to establish a permanent, revolving fund for professional staff development. The Sabbatical program is offered biannually.
Requirements: Individual candidates for this program should: be outstanding leaders who have demonstrated a track record of contribution to the community; work for a nonprofit organization; have worked a minimum of ten years in the nonprofit sector; hold primary or significant responsibility for management of the organization's funds; be willing to participate in a peer network of program alumni; be employed full-time at the applicant organization;

and have financial need. The candidate's employing organization should: be located in Los Angeles County; have at least three full-time staff; need financial assistance to underwrite the candidate's leave; and be able to sustain regular operations during the candidate's absence.
Geographic Focus: California
Amount of Grant: Up to 40,000 USD
Contact: Executive Director; (310) 899-5120; fax (310) 899-5121; admin@durfee.org
Internet: http://durfee.org/what-we-support/sabbatical/
Sponsor: Durfee Foundation
1453 Third Street, Suite 312
Santa Monica, CA 90401

Durfee Foundation Stanton Fellowship 1626
The Durfee Foundation Stanton Fellowship provides up to six fellows with $75,000 each over a two-year period to think deeply about the intractable problems in their sector, and to tease out solutions that will improve life for the people of Los Angeles. Possible uses for the funds may include: travel to sister organizations in the U.S. or abroad; apprenticing to experts; writing policy papers; enrollment in training programs; or supplementing salaries of co-workers to allow release time for the fellow to concentrate on the project.
Requirements: Individual candidates for this program should: be outstanding leaders who have demonstrated a track record of contribution to the community; work for a nonprofit organization; have worked a minimum of ten years in the nonprofit sector; hold primary or significant responsibility for management of the organization's funds; be willing to participate in a peer network of program alumni; be employed full-time at the applicant organization; and have financial need. The candidate's employing organization should: be located in Los Angeles County; have at least three full-time staff; need financial assistance to underwrite the candidate's leave; and be able to sustain regular operations during the candidate's absence.
Geographic Focus: California
Contact: Executive Director; (310) 899-5120; fax (310) 899-5121; admin@durfee.org
Internet: http://durfee.org/what-we-support/stanton-fellowship/
Sponsor: Durfee Foundation
1453 Third Street, Suite 312
Santa Monica, CA 90401

Dwight Stuart Youth Foundation Capacity-Building Initiative Grants 1627
The Dwight Stuart Youth Foundation was endowed by Dwight L. Stuart (1924 - 1998). As a philanthropist, Mr. Stuart was honored for his work and generosity on behalf of underserved and disadvantaged children and youth. The foundation looks for projects and programs that provide direct services to underserved children and youth within Los Angeles County. The foundation's Capacity-Building Initiative builds on its regular grantmaking, which already has provided support for capacity building to a number of grantees. The Initiative's objective is to increase the foundation's commitment to strengthening youth-serving nonprofits in Los Angeles County, helping them achieve their missions by offering grant support for such purposes as staff training, creation of new staff positions such as development director, board training, facilities development and technology purchases. In addition, the Capacity-Building Initiative includes a Cornerstone Grants Program, which is by invitation only - you cannot apply for a Cornerstone grant and only current or past DSYF grantees are eligible to be invited. The purpose of these special grants is to provide up to three years of operating support (support for specific capacity-building activities also can be included) to a select group of youth-serving nonprofits in Southern California, based upon their demonstrated excellence and growth potential. Those invited to apply will be contacted by the Foundation.
Requirements: Nonprofit organizations with 501(c)3 status and in the Los Angeles County area are eligible to apply. The application process starts with a letter of inquiry. Letters of inquiry are accepted year round and are reviewed in the order they are received. If it is determined from your letter of inquiry that your request is consistent with the foundation's funding priorities and interests, you may be asked to participate in a conference call with foundation staff to further refine your request and clarify questions. During the conference call, if it is decided that your organization's objectives and activities match the foundation's criteria, you will be asked to submit a full proposal and application materials will be mailed to you at that time. Unsolicited full proposals are not accepted. Youth-serving nonprofits can apply for grant funds to support capacity-building activities of their own choosing; these requests will be considered independent of any program requests, and you may ask for both program and capacity building support at the same time. If you are seeking capacity-building support, use the Quick Assessment Tool in the Resources section (see website) to help define your needs, and include brief responses to its five questions in your Letter of Inquiry. The maximum grant amount that can be requested for capacity building is $25,000. Submit your capacity building request separately from any program requests.
Restrictions: Funding is not available for individuals; private foundations; annual giving campaigns; buildings or capital campaigns; unrestricted endowments or deficit reduction; political parties, candidates, campaigns, or lobbying activities; fundraising activities, benefit sponsorship, advertisements, or tables; medical or health programs (this includes hospitals, clinics, and mental or physical trauma recovery programs). The foundation also does not fund programs for children and youth who are diagnosed as emotionally and/or developmentally disabled, or chronically and terminally ill; organizations which, in their constitution or practice, discriminate against a person or group on the basis of age, political affiliation, race, national origin, ethnicity, gender, disability, sexual orientation, or religious belief; programs outside Los Angeles County; institutions outside the United States of America.
Geographic Focus: California
Contact: Wendy Chang, Program Director; (310) 777-5050; fax (310) 777-5060
Internet: http://www.dsyf.org/grantmaking_capacitybuilding.asp
Sponsor: Dwight Stuart Youth Foundation
9595 Wilshire Boulevard, Suite 212
Beverly Hills, CA 90212

Dwight Stuart Youth Foundation Grants 1628
The Dwight Stuart Youth Foundation was endowed by Dwight L. Stuart (1924 - 1998). As a philanthropist, Mr. Stuart was honored for his work and generosity on behalf of underserved and disadvantaged children and youth. The foundation looks for projects and programs that provide direct services to underserved children and youth within Los Angeles County. The four funding areas that are of interest are education enrichment, mentoring, leadership and school readiness.
Requirements: Nonprofit organizations with 501(c)3 status and in the Los Angeles County area are eligible to apply. The application process starts with a letter of inquiry. Letters of inquiry are accepted year round and are reviewed in the order they are received. If it is determined from your letter of inquiry that your request is consistent with the foundation's funding priorities and interests, you may be asked to participate in a conference call with foundation staff to further refine your request and clarify questions. During the conference call, if it is decided that your organization's objectives and activities match the foundation's criteria, you will be asked to submit a full proposal and application materials will be mailed to you at that time. Unsolicited full proposals are not accepted.
Restrictions: Funding is not available for individuals; private foundations; annual giving campaigns; buildings or capital campaigns; unrestricted endowments or deficit reduction; political parties, candidates, campaigns, or lobbying activities; fundraising activities, benefit sponsorship, advertisements, or tables; medical or health programs (this includes hospitals, clinics, and mental or physical trauma recovery programs). The foundation also does not fund programs for children and youth who are diagnosed as emotionally and/or developmentally disabled, or chronically and terminally ill; organizations which, in their constitution or practice, discriminate against a person or group on the basis of age, political affiliation, race, national origin, ethnicity, gender, disability, sexual orientation, or religious belief; programs outside Los Angeles County; institutions outside the United States of America.
Geographic Focus: California
Contact: Wendy Chang, Program Director; (310) 777-5050; fax (310) 777-5060
Internet: http://www.dsyf.org/grantmaking_areas.asp
Sponsor: Dwight Stuart Youth Foundation
9595 Wilshire Boulevard, Suite 212
Beverly Hills, CA 90212

Dyer-Ives Foundation Small Grants 1629
This is a competitive grants program allowing the Foundation the opportunity to react to needs expressed by the community it serves. Features of this program are: the proposals originate from the community; the ideas reflect new, innovative initiatives for which other funds are not readily available; and the funding is used for self-contained program components. The Foundation does not operate on a grantmaking cycle. A letter of proposal is accepted after contacting the Executive Director to discuss the request.
Requirements: 501(c)3 tax-exempt organizations are eligible.
Geographic Focus: All States
Amount of Grant: 2,000 - 5,000 USD
Contact: Linda Patterson, (616) 454-4502; fax (616) 454-8545; linda@dyer-ives.org
Internet: http://www.dyer-ives.org/index.php
Sponsor: Dyer-Ives Foundation
161 Ottawa NW
Grand Rapids, MI 49503-2750

Dynegy Foundation Grants 1630
The foundation supports, with both time and money, a diverse group of charitable causes in the communities where it operates. Dynegy evaluates its philanthropic activities on an annual basis, assessing proposals to determine if they align with the company's interests and financial realities. Organizations seeking a grant should submit a letter on the organization's letterhead. The letter must be signed by the President or Executive Director of the organization.
Requirements: Grants are made to organizations outside the State of Texas; however, no grants are made outside of the United States of America. Applications are not considered from any organization more than once every 12 months, whether a previous request was approved or denied. A grant agreement must be signed before any grant funds are released.
Restrictions: Request via telephone or email cannot be accepted. Dynegy does not support: organizations or programs in promotion or support of a specific religion, denomination, or church; any organizations or activities of a political nature; athletic organizations for the purchase of uniforms and/or equipment; organizations operated by fraternal or service groups; honoraria for guest speakers or panelists; memorials for individuals; activities that are typically the responsibility of government, including public elementary and secondary schools; and scholarships for individuals.
Geographic Focus: All States
Contact: David W. Byford; (713) 507-6400; david.byford@dynegy.com
Internet: http://www.dynegy.com/Community/Our_Support/Grants.shtml
Sponsor: Dynegy Foundation
1000 Louisiana, Suite 5800
Houston, TX 77002

Dyson Foundation Emergency Fund Grants 1631
The Dyson Foundation has created two emergency grant programs for nonprofit organizations in Columbia, Dutchess, Greene, Orange, Putnam, and Ulster counties in the aftermath of Hurricane Irene. The Dyson Foundation will expedite reviews of all requests for emergency funding. The Dyson Foundation will also make grants to nonprofit organizations providing direct services to residents of the Mid-Hudson Valley. These funds are to provide emergency financial assistance to help people impacted by disaster. The Foundation will accept applications from organizations with well-established emergency financial assistance programs. These funds are available for distribution to Mid-Hudson Valley residents to cover

a broad range of needs. To apply, nonprofit organizations can submit a one page narrative description of the expected use of the funds and a supporting budget.
Requirements: Nonprofit organizations can apply for emergency funds to help the organization recover from uninsured damages or losses.
Geographic Focus: New York
Contact: Diana M. Gurieva, Executive Vice President; (845) 790-6312 or (845) 677-0644; fax (845) 677-0650; dgurieva@dyson.org or submissions@dyson.org
Michell Speight, (845) 790-6315 or (845) 677-0644; fax (845) 677-0650; mspeight@dyson.org or submissions@dyson.org
Sponsor: Dyson Foundation
25 Halcyon Road
Millbrook, NY 12545-9611

Dyson Foundation Management Assistance Program Mini-Grants 1632
The purpose of the Dyson Foundation's Management Assistance Program (MAP) mini-grants is to help Mid-Hudson Valley nonprofits improve their internal operations, program development, administration, and management to better achieve their missions. Mini-grants enable nonprofit board, staff, and volunteer leaders to develop new skills by providing organizations with financial support to hire consultants to lead specific capacity building activities. Mini-grants may also be used to defray the cost of conferences, seminars, and other training opportunities for staff and board. Examples of how funds might be used include: facilitation of a strategic planning process; resource development planning; training for board members; developing a marketing and communication plan; establishing or improving fiscal systems; developing personnel policies or personnel management training; attending a relevant conference or seminar; and technology planning.
Requirements: 501(c)3 nonprofit organization or libraries based in the Mid-Hudson Valley (Columbia, Dutchess, Greene, Orange, Putnam, and Ulster counties) are eligible. Preference is given to organizations with operating budgets of less than $1 million.
Restrictions: MAP mini grants are not available for individuals, government entities, or public school systems. Consultancies and training opportunities already in progress or completed are not eligible for funding. Note that the Dyson Foundation does not generally provide management assistance funding to faith-based organizations.
Geographic Focus: New York
Amount of Grant: Up to 10,000 USD
Contact: Diana M. Gurieva, Executive Vice President; (845) 790-6312 or (845) 677-0644; fax (845) 677-0650; dgurieva@dyson.org or info@dyson.org
Internet: http://www.dysonfoundation.org/mini-grant-program
Sponsor: Dyson Foundation
25 Halcyon Road
Millbrook, NY 12545-9611

Dyson Foundation Mid-Hudson Philanthropy Grants 1633
The Dyson Foundation works toward improving people's lives through grant funding, promoting philanthropy, and strengthening the capacity of nonprofit organizations. The Dyson Foundation awards grants in several different program areas that each have specific guidelines. The Foundation makes a limited number of grants to support nonprofit organizations that work to encourage philanthropic endeavors, educate the public on the importance of charitable giving, and provide services to philanthropic organizations and individuals.
Requirements: 501(c)3 nonprofit organization or libraries based in the Mid-Hudson Valley (Columbia, Dutchess, Greene, Orange, Putnam, and Ulster counties) are eligible. Preference is given to organizations with operating budgets of less than $1 million.
Restrictions: Grants are not available for individuals, government entities, or public school systems. Consultancies and training opportunities already in progress or completed are not eligible for funding.
Geographic Focus: New York
Amount of Grant: 1,000 - 1,000,000 USD
Contact: Diana M. Gurieva, Executive Vice President; (845) 790-6312 or (845) 677-0644; fax (845) 677-0650; dgurieva@dyson.org or info@dyson.org
Internet: http://www.dysonfoundation.org/grantmaking
Sponsor: Dyson Foundation
25 Halcyon Road
Millbrook, NY 12545-9611

Dyson Foundation Mid-Hudson Valley Faith-Based Organization Grants 1634
The Foundation will consider grants for community-based service programs run by faithed-based agencies that meet certain criteria, including: services must be available to all regardless of their religion or belief in God and must not be rooted in a particular religious doctrine or belief system; there is a formal structure for provision of services (e.g., mission, staff, program policies and procedures); services go beyond religious charitable work to include activities that make a real impact on the lives of people living in their communities; and the organization or institution agrees to abide by the Foundation's policy on nondiscrimination. These guidelines apply to faith-based organizations located in any of the six counties of the Mid-Hudson Valley that the Foundation funds.
Requirements: IRS 501(c)3 nonprofits that support Hudson Valley, New York, and are not classified as foundations under section 509(a)of the code are eligible. Occasionally the foundation awards grants to fiscal sponsors of non-qualifying organizations.
Restrictions: The Foundation will not generally consider management assistance mini-grant applications or general operating support requests from faith-based organizations. Grants do not support: individuals for any purpose; dinners, fund raising events, tickets, or benefit advertising; direct mail campaigns; service clubs and similar organizations; debt or deficit reduction; governmental units; or international projects or to organizations outside of the United States.
Geographic Focus: New York

Amount of Grant: 1,000 - 1,000,000 USD
Contact: Diana M. Gurieva, Executive Vice President; (845) 790-6312 or (845) 677-0644; fax (845) 677-0650; dgurieva@dyson.org or info@dyson.org
Internet: http://www.dysonfoundation.org/funding-restrictions-for-faith-based-organizations-or-programs
Sponsor: Dyson Foundation
25 Halcyon Road
Millbrook, NY 12545-9611

Dyson Foundation Mid-Hudson Valley General Operating Support Grants 1635
General operating support grants are sometimes referred to as core support or unrestricted grants. Many organizations use general operating support grants to cover day-to-day activities or ongoing expenses such as administrative salaries, utilities, office supplies, technology maintenance, etc. Other organizations use this type of funding to cover project costs, capital, technology purchases, and professional development. The use of these funds is totally at the discretion of the organization's board and/or executive staff, although the Foundation expects all organizational expenditures to be part of a board-approved annual budget. The first step in applying for a general operating support grant is to submit a letter of inquiry.
Requirements: 501(c)3 nonprofit organization or libraries based in the Mid-Hudson Valley (Columbia, Dutchess, Greene, Orange, Putnam, and Ulster counties) are eligible. To apply for a general operating support grant, an organization must: review the principles of best practice relative to nonprofit governance, finance, public disclosure, and programming; have been a recipient of a Dyson Foundation project grant within the past three years of their general operating support request; have a mission and programs that are consistent with core funding interests of the Dyson Foundation; and have demonstrated at least three years of stable executive leadership.
Restrictions: The Foundation places no restrictions on the use of these funds, unlike project or management technical assistance grants that are restricted by the Foundation to a particular project or activity. Colleges and universities, hospitals, faith-based institutions, and organizations with annual budgets in excess of $15 million dollars are not eligible to apply for general operating support grants.
Geographic Focus: New York
Amount of Grant: 1,000 - 1,000,000 USD
Contact: Diana M. Gurieva, Executive Vice President; (845) 790-6312 or (845) 677-0644; fax (845) 677-0650; dgurieva@dyson.org or info@dyson.org
Internet: http://www.dysonfoundation.org/grantmaking/general-operating-support-grants
Sponsor: Dyson Foundation
25 Halcyon Road
Millbrook, NY 12545-9611

Dyson Foundation Mid-Hudson Valley Project Support Grants 1636
In 2009 the Dyson Foundation changed its grantmaking priorities to best support the people and communities in its region most vulnerable to the economic downturn. The Foundation's funding now focuses on organizations and activities that address basic needs such as food, housing, health care, and other human services. In limited circumstances, it will also make grants to faith-based organizations, government entities and libraries. The Foundation will also consider limited funding to arts organizations or projects that provide management support or training to other arts organizations, and to arts organizations or projects that can demonstrate the potential to increase local tourism and employment and/or other local economic development as a result of their efforts. Note that there are separate guidelines for Dutchess County and for the other Mid-Hudson Valley counties.
Requirements: IRS 501(c)3 nonprofits that support Hudson Valley, New York, and are not classified as foundations under section 509(a)of the code are eligible. The region is defined as Columbia, Dutchess, Greene, Orange, Putnam, and Ulster counties. Occasionally the foundation awards grants to fiscal sponsors of non-qualifying organizations.
Restrictions: The Foundation is not currently funding certain areas including: the environment, historic preservation, and capital projects. Grants do not support: individuals for any purpose; dinners, fund raising events, tickets, or benefit advertising; direct mail campaigns; service clubs and similar organizations; debt or deficit reduction; governmental units; or international projects or to organizations outside of the United States.
Geographic Focus: New York
Amount of Grant: 1,000 - 1,000,000 USD
Contact: Diana M. Gurieva, Executive Vice President; (845) 790-6312 or (845) 677-0644; fax (845) 677-0650; dgurieva@dyson.org or info@dyson.org
Internet: http://www.dysonfoundation.org/grantmaking/project-grants
Sponsor: Dyson Foundation
25 Halcyon Road
Millbrook, NY 12545-9611

Dyson Foundation Nonprofit Strategic Restructuring Initiative Grants 1637
Strategic restructuring is the establishment of an ongoing relationship between two or more independent organizations to increase administrative efficiency and/or further programmatic missions through shared, transferred, or combined services, resources, or programs. The results can range from jointly managed programs and consolidated administrative functions to full-scale mergers. The benefits can include reductions in duplicated services, improved efficiencies, and increased financial stability. The Dyson Foundation's Nonprofit Strategic Restructuring Initiative provides funding to help organizations through this process. Grants are made in the following four categories: preliminary exploration, planning, implementation, and post restructuring support.
Requirements: To be eligible for funding, one or more of the collaborating organizations must be a 501(c)3 nonprofit organization, a library or unit of government based in the Mid-Hudson Valley. The region includes: Columbia, Dutchess, Greene, Orange, Putnam, and Ulster counties.

Restrictions: Funding from the Strategic Restructuring Initiative is not available for individuals or private/independent schools. Grants do not support: dinners, fund raising events, tickets, or benefit advertising; direct mail campaigns; service clubs and similar organizations; debt or deficit reduction; governmental units; or international projects or to organizations outside of the United States.
Geographic Focus: New York
Amount of Grant: 10,000 - 35,000 USD
Contact: Diana M. Gurieva, Executive Vice President; (845) 790-6312 or (845) 677-0644; fax (845) 677-0650; dgurieva@dyson.org or info@dyson.org
Internet: http://www.dysonfoundation.org/nonprofit-strategic-restructuring-initiative
Sponsor: Dyson Foundation
25 Halcyon Road
Millbrook, NY 12545-9611

E.J. Grassmann Trust Grants 1638
The E.J. Grassmann Trust awards grants in central Georgia and Union County, New Jersey, in support of higher and secondary education, hospitals and health organizations, historical associations, environmental conservation, and social welfare. Primary fields of interest include: arts; Catholic agencies and churches; elementary and secondary education; the environment; natural resources; health care; higher education; historic preservation; historical societies; hospitals; and human services. Types of support include capital campaigns, building construction and/or renovation, equipment acquisition, and endowment funds. Groups with low administrative costs, that have outside funding, and that encourage self-help are preferred. Grants are awarded in May and November. Written proposals should not be longer than four pages.
Restrictions: Grants are not awarded to individuals or for operating expenses, current scholarship funds, conferences, or workshops.
Geographic Focus: Georgia, New Jersey
Date(s) Application is Due: Apr 20; Oct 15
Amount of Grant: 5,000 - 20,000 USD
Contact: William V. Engel, Executive Director; (908) 753-2440
Sponsor: E.J. Grassmann Trust
P.O. Box 4470
Warren, NJ 07059-0470

E.L. Wiegand Foundation Grants 1639
The foundation provides grants to develop and strengthen programs and projects at Arizona, California, the District of Columbia, Idaho, Nevada, New York, Oregon, Utah, and Washington educational institutions in the academic areas of science, business, fine arts, and law; and medicine and health organizations in the areas of heart, eye, and cancer surgery, treatment, and research. The foundation also considers requests for projects that enrich children, communities, public policy, and art. Grants for education, including funds for computers and scientific equipment, are awarded. The board of trustees meets in February, June, and October to choose recipients, but applications may be submitted at any time. Application guidelines are available upon request.
Requirements: Nonprofit organizations in Arizona, California, District of Columbia, Idaho, Nevada, New York, Oregon, Utah, and Washington State are eligible.
Geographic Focus: Arizona, California, District of Columbia, Idaho, Nevada, New York, Oregon, Utah, Washington
Amount of Grant: 10,000 - 200,000 USD
Contact: Kristen Avansino, Executive Director; (775) 333-0310; fax (775) 333-0314
Sponsor: E.L. Wiegand Foundation
165 W Liberty Street, Suite 200
Reno, NV 89501

E. Rhodes and Leona B. Carpenter Foundation Grants 1640
The Foundation considers grant requests from: public charities which had direct relationships with Leona or Rhodes Carpenter during their lifetime; requests in support of graduate theological education from U.S. and Canadian organizations which are public charities; public charities in communities where Carpenter Co. has had long-time manufacturing facilities; museums which have a permanent collection for the purchase, restoration and conservation of Asian art; charities involved in providing hospice care; and projects (e.g., programs, conferences, resources, etc.) offering support to lesbian, gay, bisexual and transgender persons of faith, or endeavoring to insure faith communities' understanding, affirmation, and inclusion of such persons.
Requirements: IRS 501(c)3 organizations are eligible.
Restrictions: Generally, the Foundation will not consider grant requests to support private secondary education, individuals or large public charities and will not transfer funds from its endowment to the endowment of another organization.
Geographic Focus: All States
Date(s) Application is Due: Jan 31; Jul 31
Contact: Grants Administrator; (215) 979-3221
Sponsor: E. Rhodes and Leona B. Carpenter Foundation
1735 Marker Street, Suite 3420
Philadelphia, PA 19103

Earth Island Institute Brower Youth Awards 1641
Earth Island Institute established The Brower Youth Award for Environmental Leadership in 2000 to honor renowned environmental advocate David Brower. David Brower was quoted as saying, "I love to see what young people can do, before someone old tells them it's impossible." It is with this spirit that the Earth Island Institute recognizes the outstanding leadership efforts of young people who are working for the protection of our shared planet. The Institute elevates the accomplishments of these new leaders and invests in their continued success by providing ongoing access to resources, mentors, and opportunities to develop leadership skills. Completed applications must be submitted online by May 13.
Requirements: Eligibility includes anyone aged 13-22 who is a resident of the United States or Puerto Rico and has shown leadership and produced results in at least one of the following areas: conservation—reducing the negative impacts of the use of natural resources; preservation—saving places, plants, animals, cultures, and Earth-friendly traditions that cannot be replaced if they are destroyed; and restoration—repairing damaged land and water so that it can function ecologically and support the health of human communities and/or native wildlife populations.
Geographic Focus: All States
Date(s) Application is Due: May 13
Amount of Grant: 3,000 USD
Contact: Sanjay Gupta; (510) 859-9100; fax (510) 859-9091; sanjay@earthisland.org
Internet: http://www.broweryouthawards.org/article.php?list=type&type=54
Sponsor: Earth Island Institute
2150 Allston Way, Suite 460
Berkley, CA 94704-1375

Earth Island Institute Community Wetland Restoration Grants 1642
The Earth Island Institute's Restoration Initiatives Fund provides funding to the Community Wetland Restoration Grant Program of the Southern California Wetlands Recovery project. Grants are given to projects that are located in Southern California, Santa Barbara, California to Tijuana, Mexico. The Program provides grants of $1,000 to $30,000 for community-based restoration projects in coastal wetlands and watersheds in the southern California region. The purpose of the Program is to further the goals of the WRP Regional Strategy; build local capacity to plan and implement wetland restoration projects; promote community involvement in wetland restoration activities; and foster education about wetland ecosystems.
Requirements: IRS 501(c)3 organizations located in, or serving the residents of, Southern California, Santa Barbara, California to Tijuana, Mexico, are eligible to apply
Geographic Focus: California
Date(s) Application is Due: Mar 26
Amount of Grant: 1,000 - 30,000 USD
Contact: Ariana Katovich; (510) 859.9154; fax (510) 859-9091; ariana@earthisland.org
Internet: http://www.earthisland.org/index.php/restoration/apply-for-grant
Sponsor: Earth Island Institute
2150 Allston Way, Suite 460
Berkley, CA 94704-1375

Eastman Chemical Company Foundation Grants 1643
The Foundation supports organizations and programs that help to promote its efforts of enhancing the quality of life in Eastman communities. Contributions are concentrated on the following areas: education, health and human services, civic and community, and culture and the arts. Grants may be considered outside of these areas.
Requirements: Contributions are generally restricted to organizations which have been granted 501(c)3 tax exempt status and are usually directed toward the communities in which the company has operating units.
Restrictions: Contributions will not be made to the following: individuals, athletic teams or sports related events, choirs, bands, drill teams, labor, veteran, fraternal, social or political organizations; individual agencies supported by the area United Way organization, except capital fund drives which are normally supported by the community, not the United Way; organizations that discriminate on the basis of race, color, sex or national origin; national organizations whose programs do not directly serve the region's needs; places of worship and institutions devoted solely to religious instruction; travel related, including student trips or tours.
Geographic Focus: Pennsylvania, South Carolina, Tennessee, Texas
Contact: CeeGee McCord, Contributions Manager; (423) 229-2000; fax (423) 229-6974; CeeGeeMcCord@kingsporthousing.org
Internet: http://www.eastman.com/Company/Sustainability/communities/Philanthropy/Pages/Philanthropy.aspx
Sponsor: Eastman Chemical Company
P.O. Box 431
Kingsport, TN 37662

Easton Foundations Archery Facility Grants 1644
The Easton Foundations support the development of four levels of archery facilities depending on the level of the planned archery programs and the financial commitment of the applicants: Archery Center of Excellence, Archery Center, Community Archery Facility, or Local Club or Recreation Department Facility. The Foundations' plan is to fund facilities at diversified geographic regional locations to create a strong national archery education and training program. The goal is to develop a large national pool of top archers from which to select future Olympic and World Championship teams.
Requirements: Eligible applicants include 501(c)3 organizations, universities, schools, and state/local governments with a proven record of financial stability. The Foundation will favor applicants with an existing base of local archery activities near a major population center (with several universities within one hour drive) with the potential to expand youth, interscholastic, and collegiate archery participation. Applicants must also have strong community support, financial commitments, and in-kind and/or financial contributions to the project. The Foundation does not fix the percentage that it will provide toward project costs, but the range of contribution has been 10-50% of project cost. The amount of support from the Foundation will vary depending on the capabilities of the proposed facility, quality of the planned high performance archery programs, and the local support all focused to achieve the Foundation goal of developing Olympic-style archery.
Geographic Focus: All States

Contact: Doug Engh, Outreach Director; (818) 787-2800; dengh@esdf.org
Internet: http://www.esdf.org/archery-facilities/
Sponsor: Easton Foundations
7855 Haskell Avenue, Suite 360
Van Nuys, CA 91406

East Tennessee Foundation Affordable Housing Trust Fund 1645
Founded in 1986, East Tennessee Foundation (ETF) is a public, nonprofit, community foundation created for the purpose of building charitable resources to make communities stronger and lives better through thoughtful giving. The Affordable Housing Trust Fund was established at the East Tennessee Foundation with contributions from Knoxville's Community Development Corporation (KCDC), the City of Knoxville and the Cornerstone Foundation. The Fund is intended to support the production, preservation, and rehabilitation of housing for low-income households located within the city of Knoxville. The Fund makes resources available through grants, loans and forgivable loans to nonprofit organizations determined to be a 501(c)3 by the Internal Revenue Service (IRS) and to for-profit corporations.
Requirements: 501(c)3 nonprofit organizations and to for-profit corporations are eligible to apply. The selection process for funding projects is competitive and proposals must be received 30 days in advance. See Foundation's website for application form and additional guidelines.
Restrictions: Individuals are ineligible applicants.
Geographic Focus: Tennessee
Contact: Jeanette Kelleher, Housing and Financial Officer; (865) 524-1223 or (877) 524-1223; fax (865) 637-6039; jkelleher@etf.org
Internet: http://www.easttennesseefoundation.org/grants/housing.html
Sponsor: East Tennessee Foundation
625 Market Street, Suite 1400
Knoxville, TN 37902

East Tennessee Foundation Grants 1646
East Tennessee Foundation's field-of-interest and affiliate funds support a competitive grantmaking process in broad charitable areas including arts and culture, community development, youth-at-risk or a particular East Tennessee county (Affiliate Funds) within the Foundation's 25-county service area. Field-of-interest and affiliate fund grants are offered annually or bi-annually and made through a competitive application and review process.
Requirements: Any organization determined to be a 501(c)3 by the Internal Revenue Service (IRS) that is located within the 25-county service area (unless otherwise stipulated) may apply. Grants will also be made to other tax-exempt entities such as schools, universities, units of government, or, in some instances, churches and other religious institutions. Organizations that have not received 501(c)3 status from the IRS must be fiscally sponsored by a tax-exempt 501(c)3 organization. See Foundation's website for additonal guidelines and application form.
Restrictions: No support for religious organizations which limit their services to any one religious group. No grants for annual campaigns, capital fund drives, endowment or general fundraising campaigns, research projects, or general operating budgets.
Geographic Focus: Tennessee
Amount of Grant: 1,000 - 1,850,000 USD
Contact: Beth Heller, Scholarship and Program Associate; (865) 524-1223 or (877) 524-1223; fax (865) 637-6039; bheller@etf.org
Internet: http://www.easttennesseefoundation.org/grants/competitive.html
Sponsor: East Tennessee Foundation
625 Market Street, Suite 1400
Knoxville, TN 37902

Eaton Charitable Fund Grants 1647
The Fund is dedicated to supporting programs that improve the quality of life in communities where the company operates. The Fund gives primary consideration to requests for programs located in an Eaton community, recommended by an Eaton manager and where employees demonstrate leadership involvement. Programs selected for funding will have clearly defined objectives, measurable end results, and provide a positive return on the Funds investment. The Fund's primary interests are in support of community improvement, education, and arts and cultural programs. Program, project and capital grants are awarded. Capital grants are made for special purposes that meet specific community needs within the company's funding focus. On occasion, operating grants are awarded. Proposals should be sent to the manager of the Eaton facility located in an Eaton community.
Requirements: Applicant organizations must be 501(c)3 tax exempt charities and be located in communities where the company has operations.
Restrictions: Eaton does not make contributions to: annual operating budgets of United Way agencies or hospitals; medical research; endowment funds; debt retirement; religious organizations unless they are engaged in a significant program benefiting the entire community; fraternal or labor organizations; individuals or individual endeavors; fund raising benefits, sponsorships or other events.
Geographic Focus: Arkansas, Colorado, Florida, Georgia, Kansas, Kentucky, Louisiana, Maine, Maryland, Michigan, Minnesota, New Jersey, New York, North Carolina, Ohio, Pennsylvania, South Carolina, Texas, Wisconsin
Samples: 81,640 Eaton Multicultural Scholars Program, Cleveland, OH; $15,000 Habitat for Humanity, Sumter, SC; $7,500 United Performing Arts Fund, Milwaukee, WI; and $5,000 YMCA of North Oakland County, Rochester Hills, MI.
Contact: Grants Administrator; (216) 523-4944; fax (216) 479-5013
Internet: http://www.eaton.com/EatonCom/OurCompany/AboutUs/CorporateResponsibility/SocialCommitment/CorporateGiving/index.htm
Sponsor: Eaton Charitable Fund
1111 Superior Avenue
Cleveland, OH 44114-2584

eBay Foundation Community Grants 1648
The mission of the Foundation is to make investments that improve the economic and social well-being of local communities. The Foundation works to fulfill its mission by collaborating with non-profit organizations and funding innovative programs primarily in microenterprise development. The Foundation also provides support to community organizations in areas where employees are located.
Requirements: 501(c)3 nonprofit organizations in communities where eBay has a major employment base, which includes San Jose, CA, and Salt Lake City, UT, are eligible.
Geographic Focus: California, Utah
Amount of Grant: 1,000 - 15,000 USD
Contact: Grants Administrator; ebayfdn@cfsv.org
Internet: http://pages.ebay.com/community/aboutebay/foundation/grantapp.html
Sponsor: eBay Foundation
60 South Market Street, Suite 1000
San Jose, CA 95113

Eberly Foundation Grants 1649
The foundation awards grants to eligible nonprofit organizations in the areas of: undergraduate educational opportunities; arts programming and institutions; health and human services projects; primary and secondary supplemental educational programming; and economic development activities and organizations that benefit the residents of Fayette County. The initial approach should be submittal of a letter of request.
Requirements: Nonprofit organizations in Pennsylvania are eligible.
Geographic Focus: Pennsylvania
Contact: Carolyn Blaney, President; (724) 438-3789; fax (724) 438-3856
Sponsor: Eberly Foundation
2 West Main Street, Suite 101
Uniontown, PA 15401-3448

Echoing Green Fellowships 1650
The program awards full-time fellowships to emerging entrepreneurs to create innovative domestic or international public service projects that seek to catalyze positive social change. The proposed project may be in any public service area, including but not limited to, the environment, arts, education, health, youth service and development, civil and human rights, and community and economic development. The fellowship provides a two-year stipend, health care benefits, online connectivity, access to Echoing Green's network of social entrepreneurs, training, and technical assistance.
Requirements: Applicants must be at least 18 years old and commit to leading the project for at least two years. Partnerships of up to two individuals also are eligible.
Restrictions: Faith-based, research projects, and lobbying activities are not eligible.
Geographic Focus: All States
Date(s) Application is Due: Dec 2
Amount of Grant: 60,000 - 90,000 USD
Contact: Rich Leimsider, Director of Fellow and Alumni Programs; (212) 689-1165; fax (212) 689-9010; Rich@echoinggreen.org or apply@echoinggreen.org
Internet: http://www.echoinggreen.org/fellowship
Sponsor: Echoing Green Foundation
494 Eighth Avenue, Second Floor
New York, NY 10001

Eckerd Family Foundation Grants 1651
The foundation is committed to promoting meaningful and lasting change to transform the lives of vulnerable youth and their families. Vulnerable youth are youth who face a questionable and uncertain future because they are ill prepared or incapable in their present circumstances of reaching their full potential. Successful proposals will enable vulnerable youth to meet the challenges of growing up—leading to meaningful choices regarding their education and vocation—and will help prepare them to assume the responsibilities of adulthood and good citizenship. Grant applications are invited throughout the year. Upon being invited to submit a proposal, a specific time schedule will be assigned to an applicant. Guidelines are available online.
Requirements: Nonprofit organizations are eligible. Geographic preference is given to the communities in which the directors of the foundation reside.
Restrictions: The foundation does not fund the purchase of tickets for any event or the purchase of advertising space in programs or publications; ordinarily consider applications that only address the regular operational expenses of an organization; or provide grants to an organization that, as a substantial part of its activities, engages in legislative lobbying or other activity that directly or indirectly participates or intervenes in political campaigns on behalf of any candidate for public office.
Geographic Focus: All States
Contact: Grants Administrator; (727) 446-2996; grants@eckerdfamilyfoundation.org
Internet: http://www.eckerdfamilyfoundation.org
Sponsor: Eckerd Family Foundation
P.O. Box 5165
Clearwater, FL 33758-5165

Ed and Carole Abel Foundation Grants 1652
The Ed and Carole Abel Foundation was established in Oklahoma in 1990 by the Abel Law Firm, with funding centered in the states of Colorado, Missouri, and Oklahoma. The Foundations primary interest areas of support are for religion, human services, and community services. The type of funding provided typically supports general operations. There are no specified deadlines or application formats, and interested organization should begin by contacted the Foundation representatives directly. Most recent awards have ranged from $200 to $10,000.

Geographic Focus: Colorado, Missouri, Oklahoma
Amount of Grant: 200 - 10,000 USD
Contact: Carol Abel, (405) 239-7046 or (800) 739-2235
Sponsor: Ed and Carole Abel Foundation
5917 N. Ann Arbor Avenue
Oklahoma City, OK 73122-7526

Eddie C. and Sylvia Brown Family Foundation Grants 1653
The Brown Family Foundation will focus its grant making in three general areas: the arts, education, and health (HIV/AIDS and cancer). The foundation's grant making will support programs that: provide opportunities for youth involvement in meaningful art experiences—this can include support for arts organizations or youth serving organizations that have developed programs which expose young people to the arts (programs that infuse the arts as a tool for leadership development, academic enrichment, and are built on strong youth development principles are encouraged to apply); provide access to educational opportunities for disadvantaged children and youth—this can include local organizations that work to improve PreK-12 public education and to offer enhancement and enrichment opportunities to Baltimore City students (educational opportunities are defined in the broadest sense to include, but are not limited to afterschool programs, mentoring, alternative education, computer technology, scholarship support, as well as traditional in-school K-12 programs); address the impact of HIV/AIDS on the African American community—programs that provide direct services and intervention including testing and counseling, case management strategies, and access to treatment will be considered; and address the prevention and treatment of cancer—this can include local organizations that provide cancer screening, prevention education, and treatment modalities.
Requirements: Organizations (or their fiscal agents) serving the Baltimore area that qualify as public charities under section 501(c)3 of the Internal Revenue Code and do not discriminate on the basis of race, creed, national origin, color, physical handicap, gender or sexual orientation can apply.
Restrictions: The Foundation does not make grants for: start-up programs; capital campaigns; individuals; multiple years; institutions of higher education; and organizations outside the Baltimore region.
Geographic Focus: Maryland
Date(s) Application is Due: Sep 26
Contact: Maya Smith, Program Administrative Assistant; (410) 332-4172, ext. 142; fax (410) 837-4701; msmith@bcf.org
Internet: http://www.bcf.org/ourgrants/ourgrantsdetail.aspx?grid=2
Sponsor: Eddie C. and Sylvia Brown Family Foundation
2 East Read Street, 9th Floor
Baltimore, MD 21202

Eddy Knight Family Foundation Grants 1654
The Foundation, established in 2000, honors the legacy of Eddy Knight, founder of Knight Oil Tools in Lafayette, Louisiana. Its primary fields of interest include community development, education, and youth development programs, with a particular emphasis on higher education opportunities for all employees and their families. Aside from its continued tuition assistance program for the children of all Knight employees, the Foundation provides general operating support to a number of community organizations in both Lafayette and Houston, Texas. There are no specific deadlines, and initial approach should be by letter of intent.
Geographic Focus: Louisiana
Amount of Grant: 1,000 - 10,000 USD
Contact: Kelley Sobiesk, Director; (337) 233-0464; fax (337) 233-0438
Sponsor: Eddy Knight Family Foundation
P.O. Box 52688
Lafayette, LA 70505-2688

Eden Hall Foundation Grants 1655
Eden Hall Foundation is a private foundation established pursuant to the will of Sebastian Mueller, a Pittsburgh philanthropist and vice president and director of the H. J. Heinz Company. During his lifetime, Mr. Mueller gave substantial support to improve conditions of the poor and disadvantaged, the promotion of sound education, and the support of health facilities and projects. Today, the trustees of Eden Hall Foundation continue his stewardship in the areas of social welfare, health, education and the arts. Eden Hall Foundation seeks to improve the quality of life in Pittsburgh and western Pennsylvania through support of organizations whose missions address the needs and concerns of the area. Proposals and projects of primary interest to the Foundation are: educational programs dedicated to the advancement and dissemination of useful knowledge. Support of schools is generally confined to four-year privately funded and controlled colleges, universities and other educational institutions; social welfare, women's issues, and the improvement of conditions of the poor and disadvantaged; and the advancement of better health through support of organizations dedicated to health issues. Eden Hall Foundation will entertain grant proposals for capital projects, scholarship funds, research projects, programming and, in limited cases, endowments directed toward these objectives. A specific application form is not required. Therefore, grant requests should be submitted by letter proposal to the Foundation. Acknowledgements will be made promptly, advising applicants whether or not their requests meet Eden Hall Foundation's criteria.
Requirements: Requests for grants should include: a brief statement of the background and purpose of the requesting organization; a copy of that organization's most recent financial statements, as prepared by its certified public accountants; the specific purpose for which the requested grant is to be used, including a detailed budget, timetable for implementation and proposed method of evaluation; IRA certification of tax-exempt and charitable status under sections 501(c)3 and 509(c) of the Internal Revenue Code; information concerning the status of grants solicited from other foundations in the past twelve-month period (indicating the name of each foundation and amount requested); and a listing of the organization's officers and directors, their primary occupations and the responsibilities to the organization.
Restrictions: Grants cannot be made to individuals or private foundations. Not eligible for funding are sectarian or denominational religious organizations, except those providing direct educational or health care services to the public, tax-supported organizations, political parties and fraternal organizations. Requests to cover operating expenses, endowments or accumulated deficits are discouraged.
Geographic Focus: Pennsylvania
Contact: Sylvia Fields, Executive Director; (412) 642-6697; fax (412) 642-6698
Internet: http://www.edenhallfdn.org
Sponsor: Eden Hall Foundation
600 Grant Street, Suite 3232
Pittsburgh, PA 15219

Edina Realty Foundation Grants 1656
The Foundation extends financial support to organizations primarily in Minnesota, which provide housing and related services such as counseling and medical care to homeless children, families and individuals. Application forms may be submitted at anytime, see Foundations website for Grant Application forms: http://www.edinarealty.com/Content/Content.aspx?ContentID=148855
Requirements: Nonprofits 501(C)(03) operating in Minnesota are eligible.
Geographic Focus: Minnesota
Amount of Grant: 500 - 2,000 USD
Contact: Susan Cowsert, Director; (952) 928-5900; susancowsert@edinarealty.com
Internet: http://www.edinarealty.com/Content/Content.aspx?ContentID=187015
Sponsor: Edina Realty Foundation
6800 France Avenue South, Suite 670
Edina, MN 55435-2017

Edith and Francis Mulhall Achilles Memorial Fund Grants 1657
Established in 1996, the Fund supports New York City nonprofits with an educational purpose, such as schools, libraries, and museums. There are no application forms or deadlines with which to adhere, and initial contact should be made in writing. The Fund does nor accept applications that have not been solicited.
Geographic Focus: New York, North Carolina
Amount of Grant: 7,361 - 175,000 USD
Contact: Edward Jones, Vice President, c/o JPMorgan Chase Bank; (212) 464-2441; fax (212) 464-2305; jones_ed_l@jpmorgan.com or jpmorgan.chase.grants@jpmchase.com
Sponsor: Edith and F.M. Achilles Memorial Fund
345 Park Avenue, 4th Floor
New York, NY 10154

Edna Haddad Welfare Trust Fund Scholarships 1658
The Edna Haddad Welfare Trust Fund, established in Missouri in 1988, offers scholarships to individuals living in the St. Louis, Missouri, region. An application form is required, and can be secured by sending a self-addressed stamped envelop of request to the Trust office. There is no specific deadline to apply, and scholarships range from $1,000 to $3,200 per individual annually.
Requirements: Applicants must reside in the general St. Louis, Missouri, area.
Geographic Focus: Missouri
Samples: Chiquita Rogers, St. Louis, Missouri, $1,100; Nicole Andrews, St. Louis, Missouri, $3,000; Tina Hennings, Wildwood, Missouri, $3,200.
Contact: Evelyn Goldberg, Treasurer; (314) 721-2195
Sponsor: Edna Haddad Welfare Trust Fund
7215 Creveling Drive
St. Louis, MO 63130-4124

Edna McConnell Clark Foundation Grants 1659
The foundation limits its support to direct-service nonprofits located in the Northeast corridor (Boston to Washington, DC) conducting programs during out-of-school time for low-income youth aged nine to 24. The program seeks to help youth by improving education skills or achievement, preparing for the working world, and making the transition to employment and self-sufficiency; and avoiding high-risk behaviors. All potential grantees undergo a rigorous screening process. Applicants must complete an online survey form before submitting a full proposal.
Requirements: Tax-exempt organizations are eligible.
Geographic Focus: Connecticut, Maine, Massachusetts, New Hampshire, Rhode Island, Vermont
Samples: Children's Aid Society (New York, NY)—to expand its Adolescent Pregnancy Prevention and Human Sexuality program, $500,000.
Contact: Grants Administrator; (212) 551-9100; fax (212) 421-9325; info@emcf.org
Internet: http://www.emcf.org/grants/index.htm
Sponsor: Edna McConnell Clark Foundation
415 Madison Avenue, 10th Floor
New York, NY 10077

Edna Wardlaw Charitable Trust Grants 1660
The Edna Wardlaw Charitable Trust awards general operating grants nationwide to nonprofit organizations in its areas of interest, including: children and youth services; community funds; cultural programs; human services; environmental and natural resources; conservation; health and hospitals; homelessness; international peace; and reproductive health. A formal application is not required, and the annual deadline is June 15. Grants typically range from $1,000 to $20,000.

Geographic Focus: All States
Date(s) Application is Due: Jun 15
Amount of Grant: 1,000 - 20,000 USD
Contact: Gregorie Guthrie, Secretary; (404) 419-3260 or (404) 827-6529
Sponsor: Edna Wardlaw Charitable Trust
One Riverside Building
Atlanta, GA 30327

EDS Foundation Grants — 1661
The Foundation wishes to ensure information technology champions cultural and civic change which will enrich the education of current and future generations, while enhancing the communities they serve. The Foundation is interested in supporting comprehensive technology solutions that increase performance and productivity in educational institutions and community organizations globally. Grant seekers must complete the EDS Foundation Application for Funding and have a current EDS employee volunteer partnership.
Requirements: Eligible applicants must be verified as a non-profit charitable organization (or equivalent) according to each country's rules and regulations. For the U.S., the organization must have a 501(c)3 IRS tax-exempt code.
Restrictions: Funding will not be provided for: individuals; operating deficits; foundations that are grant-making institutions; sponsorships; trips or tours; local athletic teams or events; fraternal, social or labor organizations; political or partisan organizations; journal or program advertising; private foundations; or organizations that do not comply with all applicable laws prohibiting discrimination and EDS Equal Opportunity policy.
Geographic Focus: California, Colorado, Georgia, Illinois, Michigan, Texas, Virginia
Contact: Diane Spradlin; (972) 605-8429; diane.spradlin-eds@eds.com
Internet: http://www.eds.com
Sponsor: EDS Foundation
5400 Legacy Drive, H3-6F-47
Plano, TX 75024

EDS Technology Grants — 1662
This program helps teachers of children ages 6 through 18 and school librarians purchase information technology products and services that will improve their students' ability to learn. Grants must be used to pay for technology products, training and services not provided to the teacher by the school or the school district. Applications must be obtained from a sponsoring EDS team. It is important to contact a current EDS grant sponsor before submitting a grant proposal.
Requirements: Eligible applicants: can only apply to one EDS grant sponsor; can only submit one proposal; must be a current full-time teacher of children ages 6 through 18; must teach at a public, private or charter school; must teach at a school located within 50 miles of an EDS office sponsoring a grant; and applicants can apply individually or in teams of two.
Restrictions: Ineligible applicants include the following: home school or co-op home school providers where parent is the primary teacher; after school or weekend programs managed by non-profit organizations, churches and other groups; junior colleges, state or private universities.
Geographic Focus: California, Colorado, Georgia, Illinois, Michigan, Texas, Virginia
Contact: Barbara McCann; (972) 605-1876; barbara.w.mccann@eds.com
Internet: http://www.eds.com/about/community/grants
Sponsor: Electronic Data Systems
5400 Legacy Drive
Plano, TX 75024

Edward and Ellen Roche Relief Foundation Grants — 1663
The Edward & Ellen Roche Relief Foundation was established in 1953 to support organizations serving disadvantaged women and children. Recognizing the diverse array of programs that serve these populations, the Roche Relief Foundation has chosen to focus its limited resources on programs that address one or more of the following: housing needs of women and families; economic security of low-income women; violence against women; and child welfare. Grant requests for general operating support or program/project support are strongly encouraged. Applicants must apply online at the grant website. Applicants are strongly encouraged to do the following before applying: review the downloadable state application procedures for additional helpful information and clarifications; review the downloadable online-application guidelines at the grant website; review the foundation's funding history (link is available from the grant website); review the online application questions in advance; and review the list of required attachments. These will generally include: a list of board members, financial statements (audited, reviewed, or compiled by independent auditor); an organization summary; a list of other funding sources; an IRS Determination letter; and other required documents. All attachments must be uploaded in the online application as PDF, Word, or Excel files. The application deadline for the Edward & Ellen Roche Relief Foundation is 11:59 p.m. on July 31. Grant decisions will be made by December 31.
Requirements: Applicants must have 501(c)3 status and serve residents of New York City.
Restrictions: The Roche Relief Foundation generally does not provide funding for projects in the areas of health care or disabilities, to individual schools or child care centers; or to organizations with annual budgets in excess of $10 million. In general, grant requests for endowment campaigns, capital projects, or research will not be considered. The foundation does not support requests from individuals, organizations attempting to influence policy through direct lobbying, or any political campaigns.
Geographic Focus: All States, New York, All Countries
Date(s) Application is Due: Jul 31
Contact: Sara Rosen, Assistant Vice President; (646) 743-0425; sara.rosen@baml.com
Internet: https://www.bankofamerica.com/philanthropic/fn_search.action
Sponsor: Edward and Ellen Roche Relief Foundation
One Bryant Park, NY1-100-28-05
New York, NY 10036

Edward and Helen Bartlett Foundation Grants — 1664
Established by a single donor, Edward E, Bartlett, in Oklahoma in 1961, the Foundation primarily offers grant support for: education, particularly public schools; community programs and services; health care; children and youth; and social services. There are no specific application forms or deadlines with which to adhere, and applicants should begin by forwarding a letter of application to the contact listed. In the recent past, grant amounts have ranged between $5,000 to $150,000.
Requirements: Preference id given to non-profit 501(c)3 organizations located in, or serving the residents of, Oklahoma.
Restrictions: No grants are to individuals directly.
Geographic Focus: Oklahoma
Amount of Grant: 5,000 - 150,000 USD
Contact: Bruce A. Currie, (918) 586-5273
Sponsor: Edward and Helen Bartlett Foundation
P.O. Box 3038
Milwaukee, WI 53201-3038

Edward Bangs Kelley and Elza Kelley Foundation Grants — 1665
The Foundation's interest is primarily in Barnstable County, Massachusetts. The Foundation has been the leader in improving the health and welfare of the community. Grants are made to a great variety of health, social and human service agencies, as well as to cultural and environmental organizations. Town libraries, theatre and art groups, and musical organizations have been supported. Grants are sometimes utilized as seed money by young organizations.
Requirements: Grant applicants must be tax-exempt organizations which are not private foundations and must be located in Barnstable County. The proposed project/program must have a direct benefit to the inhabitants of Barnstable County. If the tax-exempt organization is located outside of Barnstable, but the proposed project/program will have a direct and substantial benefit to the inhabitants of Barnstable, the grant application may be eligible for funding.
Restrictions: Applicants must be residents of Barnstable County, Massachusetts, or must demonstrate very significant ties to Barnstable County.
Geographic Focus: Massachusetts
Contact: Henry Murphy Jr.; (508) 775-3117; contact@kelleyfoundation.org
Internet: http://www.kelleyfoundation.org
Sponsor: Edward Bangs Kelley and Elza Kelley Foundation
243 South Street, P.O. Drawer M
Hyannis, MA 02601

Edward N. and Della L. Thome Memorial Foundation Direct Services Grants — 1666
The Edward N. and Della L. Thome Memorial Foundation was established in 2002 by Robert P. Thome to honor the memory of his parents, Edward and Della Thome. The mission of the foundation is twofold: to advance the health of older adults through (1) the support of direct service projects and (2) medical research on diseases and disorders affecting older adults. The goal of the foundation's direct services program is to support organizations in Maryland and Michigan that provide direct services addressing one or more of the following critical issues facing older adults: health care, housing, family services, neighborhood involvement, workforce opportunities, and aging with dignity at home. Grant requests for general operating support are strongly encouraged. Program support will also be considered. Program-related capital expenses may be included in general operating or program requests. To better support the capacity of nonprofit organizations, multi-year funding requests are encouraged. Applicants must apply online at the direct-services grant website above. Applicants are strongly encouraged to do the following before applying: review the downloadable state application procedures for additional helpful information and clarifications; review the downloadable online-application guidelines at the grant website; review the foundation's funding history (link is available from the grant website); review the online application questions in advance; and review the list of required attachments. These will generally include: a list of board members, financial statements (audited, reviewed, or compiled by independent auditor); an organization summary; a list of other funding sources; an IRS Determination letter; and other required documents. All attachments must be uploaded in the online application as PDF, Word, or Excel files. There is a rolling deadline for organizations applying for a direct services grant from the Thome Foundation. Applicants will generally be notified of grant decisions within six months of proposal submission. The research aspect of the foundation's mission is managed by the Medical Foundation, a Division of Health Resources in Action (HRIA). Applicants interested in applying for research funding through the Edward N. and Della L. Thome Memorial Foundation's research program will find application information at the Medical Foundation's website.
Requirements: The Thome Foundation direct services program is most interested in expanding services for older adults. Requests should clearly state how many previously-unserved older adults will now be served as a result of funding from the Thome Foundation. Applicants must have 501(c)3 tax-exempt status.
Restrictions: The foundation does not support requests from individuals, organizations attempting to influence policy through direct lobbying, or any political campaigns.
Geographic Focus: Maryland, Michigan
Contact: George Thorn; (312) 828-4154; ilgrantmaking@bankofamerica.com
Internet: https://www.bankofamerica.com/philanthropic/fn_search.action
Sponsor: Edward N. and Della L. Thome Memorial Foundation - BAML
231 South LaSalle Street, IL1-231-13-32
Chicago, IL 60604

Edward R. Godfrey Foundation Grants — 1667
The Foundation, established in 1953 in Ohio, supports the environment, natural resource programs, higher education, and the performing arts. Its giving is primarily restricted to California, Florida, and Texas. Though there are no specific application forms or mandatory deadlines with which to adhere, the Foundation prefers to be contacted in writing at the

listed contact address by September of each year. The Board meets once annually, on the 1st Monday in February.
Restrictions: No loans or scholarships are given to individuals.
Geographic Focus: California, Florida, Texas
Amount of Grant: 1,000 - 7,000 USD
Contact: Joseph E. Godfrey; (312) 630-6000
Sponsor: Edward R. Godfrey Foundation
1301 Little Blue Heron Court
Naples, FL 33963-3311

Edward S. Moore Foundation Grants 1668
The foundation awards grants to nonprofits in Connecticut and New York in its areas of interest, including youth, hospitals, education, cultural programs, museums, and Christian religion. Types of support include operating budgets, continuing support, annual campaigns, seed money, emergency funds, building funds, equipment, land acquisition, endowment funds, matching funds, internships, scholarship funds, special projects, and research. There are no application deadlines. The board meets in January, April, July, and October to consider proposals.
Requirements: Nonprofits in Connecticut and New York may submit proposals.
Restrictions: Grants are not awarded to individuals or for deficit financing, publications, or conferences.
Geographic Focus: Connecticut, New York
Amount of Grant: 10,000 - 50,000 USD
Contact: John W. Cross III, President; (203) 629-4591
Sponsor: Edward S. Moore Foundation
30 Lismore Lane
Greenwich, CT 06831

Edwards Memorial Trust Grants 1669
The trust awards grants to eligible Minnesota nonprofit organizations in support of health care for people without health insurance or who are underinsured, preventive health care for children, and programs for the disabled. Areas of support include health care and hospitals, mental health crisis services, social services, children and youth, and the disabled. Types of support include building construction/renovation, equipment acquisition, general operating grants, and program development. A copy of the tax determination letter and most recent audited financial statements must accompany applications.
Requirements: Minnesota 501(c)3 organizations in the greater Saint Paul area are eligible.
Geographic Focus: Minnesota
Date(s) Application is Due: May 1; Nov 1
Amount of Grant: 2,000 - 50,000 USD
Contact: Cheryl Nelson, c/o U.S. Bank; (651) 466-8441; fax (651) 244-4267
Sponsor: Edwards Memorial Trust
P.O. Box 64713
Saint Paul, MN 55164-0713

Edward W. and Stella C. Van Houten Memorial Fund Grants 1670
Stella C. Van Houten resided in Bergen County, New Jersey. This foundation, providing funding for health and human services, education, education of medical professionals, and the care of children, was established in 1978 in memory of her husband and herself. The Van Houten's had a particular fondness for the Valley Hospital of Ridgewood, New Jersey and for the Rollins College in Florida. The Foundation continues to honor their preferences with grants to these two organizations in addition to grants to other organizations. The Foundation's mission is to: supports agencies, institutions and services in Passaic and Bergen Counties, New Jersey, having to do with the care or cure of sick or disabled persons or for the care of orphaned children or aged persons; educates students in the medical profession; support for educational purposes; support for the care of children. A target of 10% of the grants each year is for medical scholarships.
Requirements: Passaic and Bergen Counties, New Jersey non-profits are eligible to apply. The application form & guidelines are available online at the Wachovia website. The applications must be submitted by January 31 for a March meeting & August 1 for an October meeting.
Geographic Focus: New Jersey
Date(s) Application is Due: Jan 31; Aug 1
Amount of Grant: 6,000 - 100,000 USD
Contact: Trustee, c/o Wachovia Bank; grantinquiries2@wachovia.com
Internet: https://www.wachovia.com/foundation/v/index.jsp?vgnextoid=00c78689fb0aa110VgnVCM1000004b0d1872RCRD&vgnextfmt=default
Sponsor: Edward W. and Suitella C. Van Houten Memorial Fund
190 River Road, NJ3132
Summit, NJ 07901

Edwin S. Webster Foundation Grants 1671
The policy of the foundation is to support charitable organizations that are well known to the trustees, with emphasis on special projects and capital programs, or operating income for hospitals, medical research, education, youth agencies, cultural activities, and programs addressing the needs of minorities. Types of support include operating budgets, continuing support, annual campaigns, building funds, equipment, land acquisition, endowment funds, matching funds, scholarship funds, professorships, internships, fellowships, special projects, and research.
Requirements: The Foundation confines its grants primarily to the New England area. Grantees must provide evidence of their tax-exempt status. The AGM common proposal format, available on the Internet at http://agmconnect.org is suitable for submission of proposals but not required. There are no set deadlines, but for consideration at the spring meeting, proposals should arrive by May 1 and by November 1 for consideration at the fall meeting. Proposals received after the trustees meet will be held for consideration at the next meeting.
Restrictions: Grants are not made to organizations outside the United States or to individuals.
Geographic Focus: Massachusetts
Date(s) Application is Due: May 1; Nov 1
Amount of Grant: 15,000 - 50,000 USD
Contact: Michelle Jenney; (617) 391-3087; mjenney@gmafoundations.com
Sponsor: Edwin S. Webster Foundation
GMA Foundations, 77 Summer Street, 8th Floor
Boston, MA 02110-1006

Edwin W. and Catherine M. Davis Foundation Grants 1672
The foundation awards grants to U.S. nonprofit organizations in its areas of interest, including arts, elderly, environment, higher education, housing, mental health, religion, social services, and youth. Types of support include annual campaigns, endowment funds, fellowships, operating grants, research grants, and scholarship funds. There are no application deadlines. The board meets in May or June; submit a proposal that is three pages or less in length.
Requirements: U.S. nonprofit organizations are eligible.
Geographic Focus: Washington
Amount of Grant: 1,000 - 10,000 USD
Samples: Fulfillment Fund, Los Angeles, CA, $150,000; Childrens Health Council, Palo Alto, CA, $21,000; Trust for Public Land, Seattle, WA, $88,000.
Contact: Gayle Roth, Grants Administrator; (651) 215-4408; fax (651) 228-0776
Sponsor: Edwin W. and Catherine M. Davis Foundation
30 East 7th Street, Suite 2000
Saint Paul, MN 55101-1394

Edyth Bush Charitable Foundation Grants 1673
The Foundation is operated exclusively for charitable, religious, literary, and other exempt purposes. Grants are available for challenge and development purposes, construction and renovation, equipment and expansion of functions, pilot projects and seed start-up of new programs, and study or planning grants. The Foundation has broad interests in human service, education, health care and a limited interest in the arts. Requests for grants or other funds should be submitted in writing. Contact the Program Officer before beginning any proposals or applications.
Requirements: The Foundation welcomes grant requests from otherwise eligible tax-exempt organizations under IRS Sections 501(c)3 and Section 509(a) headquartered within the Orlando MSA of Orange, Seminole, and Osceola Counties, Florida. Other grant requests should have special interest or support from one or more of our Directors.
Restrictions: The Foundation will ordinarily deny grant requests: from chiefly tax-supported institutions, or their support foundations; for individual scholarships or for individual research grants even if through an exempt or otherwise qualified educational organization; for alcoholism or drug abuse programs or facilities; for routine operating expenses; to pay off deficits or pre-existing debt; for foreign organizations or for foreign expenditure; for travel projects or fellowships; for chiefly church, sacramental, denominational or inter-denominational purposes, except outreach projects for elderly, indigents, needy, youth, or homeless regardless of belief, race, color, creed, or sex; for endowment funds or other purely revenue generating funds; advocacy organizations or advocacy component funding; for cultural or arts organizations unless their collections, exhibits, projects or performances are of demonstrated nationally recognized quality; from organizations having receipts of revenues from memberships and/or contributions of less than $25,000 in the previous year, or from any organization whose IRS Sec. 509(a) publicly supported status will need renewal in the next six (6) months.
Geographic Focus: Florida
Amount of Grant: 5,000 - 50,000 USD
Contact: Deborah Hessler; (888) 647-4322 or (407) 647-4322; dhessler@edythbush.org
Internet: http://www.edythbush.org
Sponsor: Edyth Bush Charitable Foundation
P.O. Box 1967
Winter Park, FL 32790-1967

Effie and Wofford Cain Foundation Grants 1674
The foundation gives primarily for higher and secondary education, medical research, and public service organizations. Grants also are awarded to religious organizations (Baptist, Christian, Episcopal, Presbyterian, Salvation Army, and United Methodist), and for aid for the handicapped. Additional fields of interest include elementary and secondary education, early childhood development and education, medical school education, nursing school education, hospitals and general health care and health organizations, religious federated giving programs, government and public administration, African Americans, Latinos, the disabled, the aging, and economically disadvantaged and homeless. Types of support include general operating support, continuing support, annual campaigns, capital campaigns, building/renovations, equipment acquisition, endowment funds, program development, seed money, curriculum development, fellowships, internships, scholarship funds, research, and matching funds. Organizations may reapply for funding every other fiscal year.
Requirements: The foundation only makes grants to 501(c)3 organizations in Texas.
Restrictions: Individuals are ineligible.
Geographic Focus: Texas
Amount of Grant: 1,000 - 100,000 USD
Contact: Lynn Fowler, Executive Director; (512) 346-7490; fax (512) 346-7491
Sponsor: Effie and Wofford Cain Foundation
4131 Spicewood Springs Road, Suite A-1
Austin, TX 78759

246 | Grant Programs

EIF Community Grants 1675
Grants are made in the greater Los Angeles area for education and prevention programs, creative and performing arts, environmental programs, literacy and education, family care and welfare, substance abuse prevention, and youth welfare. Applicants must apply annually and an organization may submit only one application per year. Grants fund only specific programs or special projects of an organization. Applicants must call the foundation to have an application sent to their organization.
Requirements: Grants are made to nonprofit 501(c)3 organizations in the greater Los Angeles area. Organizations must be responsive to the changing needs of the constituents served and the local community.
Restrictions: The foundation does not give funds for political organizations, capital campaigns, public or private schools, fund-raising events, or religious or sectarian purposes.
Geographic Focus: California
Amount of Grant: 3,000 - 15,000 USD
Contact: Administrator; (818) 760-7722; fax (818) 760-7898; info@eifoundation.org
Internet: http://www.eifoundation.org/grants/wp_grants/how_to_apply.asp
Sponsor: Entertainment Industry Foundation
1201 West 5th Street, Suite T-700
Los Angeles, CA 90017

Eileen Fisher Activating Leadership Grants for Women and Girls 1676
As a socially conscious company, Eileen Fisher is dedicated to supporting women through social initiatives that address their well-being, to guiding our product and process towards sustaining the environment and to practicing business responsibly with absolute regard for human rights. For the current grant cycle, Eileen Fisher will fund programs that activate leadership qualities in women and girls. We are particularly interested in programs that: bring about self-discovery and personal transformation; help women and/or girls find their inner strength and trust their intuition; address any phase of a woman's and/or girl's life. Each year, grants of $5,000 or more are awarded, including grants for general support and seed funding for grassroots organizations. The application process opens on June 3, and all applications must be received no later than 12:00 noon EST of the deadline date.
Requirements: Applications will be accepted from 501(c)3 nonprofits with preference to organizations that: show an innovative, holistic, effective and direct approach to activating leadership among women and/or girls; form partnerships with other community organizations for deeper impact; demonstrate the long-term sustainability and viability of the organization; show a clear need for the funds and a plan for their use; demonstrate a long-term commitment to their work; establish resonance with the Eileen Fisher company mission and leadership practices; and, are located near the Eileen Fisher offices, retail stores or showrooms or, if outside the United States, via U.S.-based charities only. Grants are open to any applying organization, not just those who have received a grant previously.
Geographic Focus: All States
Date(s) Application is Due: Jul 18
Amount of Grant: 5,000 USD
Contact: Cheryl Campbell; (914) 721-4153; ccampbell@eileenfisher.com
Internet: http://www.eileenfisher.com/EileenFisherCompany/CompanyGeneralContent Pages/SocialConciousness/Self_Image.jsp
Sponsor: Eileen Fisher Community Foundation
2 Bridge Street, Suite 230
Irvington, NY 10533

Eileen Fisher Women-Owned Business Grants 1677
The Eileen Fisher Business Grant Program for Women Entrepreneurs was launched in 2004 with a single grant to commemorate the company's twentieth anniversary. The grant program seeks applicants from wholly women-owned businesses that combine the principles of social consciousness, sustainability and innovation to take their established businesses to the next stage of their business plan. In addition to the key social principles, each applicant is required to have a solid business plan and a strategy for long-term growth. Each of the five grant recipients receives a $12,500 grant plus mentoring from internal Eileen Fisher teams and a trip to New York City for a three-day workshop with Eileen Fisher committee members and past grant recipients.
Requirements: The guidelines for the annual Women-Owned Business Program are continuing to evolve, and the grant applications are typically open annually from early March through May. To apply, your business must be: innovative; 100 percent women-owned; producing products or services that foster environmental and economic health in the community; a for-profit business or a for-profit/nonprofit hybrid (social enterprise); and, in operation for at least three years and ready to move to the next stage of its business plan.
Geographic Focus: All States
Date(s) Application is Due: Jul 18
Amount of Grant: 12,500 - 12,500 USD
Contact: Cheryl Campbell; (914) 721-4153; ccampbell@eileenfisher.com
Internet: http://www.eileenfisher.com/EileenFisherCompany/CompanyGeneralContent Pages/SocialConciousness/Women_Owned.jsp
Sponsor: Eileen Fisher Community Foundation
2 Bridge Street, Suite 230
Irvington, NY 10533

Eisner Foundation Grants 1678
The Eisner Foundation exists to provide access and opportunity for disadvantaged children and the aging of Los Angeles County. The Eisner Foundation has been funding innovative and effective non-profit organizations that improve and enrich the lives of underserved children in Southern California since 1996. In 2008, the Foundation recognized that many of the same attributes that the children unfortunately possess physical and emotional vulnerability, extreme poverty, lack of advocacy on their behalf, minimal access to the arts, and general powerlessness also applied to many members of our rapidly aging population in the community. The Foundation elected to broaden the funding focus to include those at both ends of the spectrum of life, the young and the old. The Foundation's now dedicated to bringing about lasting changes in the lives of disadvantaged and vulnerable people starting and ending their lives in Los Angeles County.
Requirements: California nonprofit organizations serving Los Angeles and Orange Counties are eligible to apply. Applicants can apply at any time, but should know that these proposals will be reviewed and approved at the June or December board meetings. Applying to the Foundation is a two step process. The first step is to submit a Letter of Inquiry (see Eisner Foundation website for guidelines). If Letter of Inquiry meets the Foundation's criteria, a full application will be sent to the applicant for completion and submission, completing the second step.
Restrictions: Proposals for endowments are rarely excepted.
Geographic Focus: California
Amount of Grant: 5,000 - 100,000 USD
Contact: Trent Stamp; (310) 228-6808; trent.stamp@eisnerfoundation.org
Internet: http://www.eisnerfoundation.org/what_we_do/
Sponsor: Eisner Foundation
233 South Beverly Drive
Beverly Hills, CA 90212

Elden and Mary Lee Gutwein Family Foundation Grants 1679
Established in Indiana in 2005, the Elden and Mary Lee Gutwein Family Foundation's primary fields of interest include: Christian agencies and churches; human services; and international relief efforts. Currently, there are no specific application forms (though forms are in the process of being developed), so applicants should submit a letter of request with budgetary needs. There are no annual deadlines, and recent awards have ranged from $100 to $7,000.
Geographic Focus: All States
Amount of Grant: 100 - 7,000 USD
Contact: Elden Gutwein, President; (765) 583-7796
Sponsor: Elden and Mary Lee Gutwein Family Foundation
P.O. Box 1038
Lafayette, IN 47902-1038

Elizabeth & Avola W. Callaway Foundation Grants 1680
The Elizabeth & Avola W. Callaway Foundation supports non-profit organizations primarily in the state of Georgia. General/operating support is available in the areas of : education; human services; Protestant agencies and; churches.
Requirements: Georgia 501(c)3 non-profits are eligible to apply, begin the application process by submitting a letter of inquiry to the Foundation. Letters of inquiry are accepted year round and should contain a detailed description of project and amount of funding requested.
Restrictions: No grants to individuals.
Geographic Focus: Georgia
Amount of Grant: 100 - 5,000 USD
Contact: Michael Benson, Grants Director; (706) 274-3392
Sponsor: Elizabeth and Avola W. Callaway Foundation
869 Callaway Road
Rayle, GA 30660-1421

Elizabeth Carse Foundation Grants 1681
The Elizabeth Carse Foundation was established in 1970 to promote education and child welfare in Connecticut. Special consideration is given to organizations that provide training to elementary and secondary school teachers in "assisting children to achieve better standards of living." Consideration is also given to organizations that have a direct impact on improving the welfare of others or which provide a social service to the community. Grants from the Carse Foundation are one year in duration. The Elizabeth Carse Foundation has an annual deadline of August 15. Applications should be submitted through the online application system by 11:59 p.m. on the deadline date. The link to the online application system is available at the grant website. Applicants are strongly encouraged to do the following before applying: review the downloadable Connecticut state application procedures for additional helpful information, requirements, and restrictions; review the downloadable online-application guidelines at the grant website; review the foundation's funding history (link is available from the grant website); review the online application questions in advance; and review the list of required attachments. These will generally include: a list of board members, financial statements (audited, reviewed, or compiled by independent auditor); an organization summary; a list of other funding sources; an IRS Determination letter; and other required documents. All attachments must be uploaded in the online application as PDF, Word, or Excel files. Applicants will be notified of grant decisions letter within two to three months after the deadline.
Requirements: Applicants must have 501(c)3 tax-exempt status.
Restrictions: Applicants will not be awarded a grant for more than 3 consecutive years. Grant requests for capital projects will not be considered. The foundation does not support requests from individuals, organizations attempting to influence policy through direct lobbying, or any political campaigns.
Geographic Focus: Connecticut
Date(s) Application is Due: Aug 15
Contact: Carmen Britt; (860) 657-7019; carmen.britt@baml.com
Internet: https://www.bankofamerica.com/philanthropic/fn_search.action
Sponsor: Elizabeth Carse Foundation
200 Glastonbury Boulevard, Suite # 200, CT2-545-02-05
Glastonbury, CT 06033-4056

Elizabeth Morse Genius Charitable Trust Grants 1682

Established in 1992, the Elizabeth Morse Genius Charitable Trust honors the memory of Elizabeth Morse Genius, the daughter of Charles Hosmer Morse, a nineteenth century Chicago financier, industrialist, and land developer. The trust supports and promotes charitable organizations that: encourage the principles of individual self-reliance, self-sacrifice, thrift, industry, and humility; relieve human suffering through scientific research and education regarding disease; provide assistance to youths with troubled childhoods and emotional disorders; attend to the care of the elderly; provide assistance to humankind during times of natural and man-made disasters; foster individual self-worth and dignity, with a broad emphasis on the classical fine arts; develop physical health and spiritual well-being through vigorous athletic activity; and promote world peace and understanding through the improvement of national and international means of travel by air, rail, and sea. The majority of grants from the Genius Charitable Trust are one year in duration; on occasion, multi-year support is awarded. Applicants must first submit a letter of inquiry. Downloadable application guidelines are available at the Sponsor's website by clicking on the "Grant Application Process Button", or prospective applicants may also call the second phone number given to obtain application information. A synopsis of the grant, contact information, and a link to the trust's giving history is available at the grant website. The Elizabeth Morse Genius Charitable Trust has a rolling application deadline. In general, applicants will be notified of grant decisions three to four months after proposal submission.
Requirements: Nonprofit organizations serving Chicago and Cook County are eligible.
Restrictions: The trust generally does not fund individuals; organizations outside the metropolitan Chicago city area; organizations attempting to influence policy through direct lobbying; capital campaigns; endowment campaigns; or political campaigns.
Geographic Focus: Illinois
Contact: Kristin Carlson Vogen, Senior Vice President; (312) 828-5554 or (312) 828-1029; ilgrantmaking@bankofamerica.com
Internet: https://www.bankofamerica.com/philanthropic/fn_search.action
Sponsor: Elizabeth Morse Genius Charitable Trust
231 South LaSalle Street, IL1-231-13-32
Chicago, IL 60604

Elkhart County Community Foundation Fund for Elkhart County 1683

The Fund for Elkhart County is the county's core grant making program and has the broadest guidelines designed to meet the Foundation's mission to produce a brighter future for all people in Elkhart County in Indiana. Grants are awarded from the fund's earnings on a quarterly basis. More than $550,000 has been awarded from this fund to assist non-profits in Elkhart County.
Requirements: The Fund for Elkhart County grants funding to after-school programs, temporary help for abused women and children, and services for the mentally and physically challenged. Other programs include health and dental care for the underprivileged, services for senior citizens, support of local arts and cultural events, environmental and wildlife services, historical preservations, and capacity building. Applicants should carefully review the website's grant guidelines before applying.
Geographic Focus: Indiana
Date(s) Application is Due: Nov 1
Contact: Fund for Elkhart County Contact; (574) 295-8761
Internet: http://www.elkhartccf.org/File/static/grant_seekers/FundForElkhartCounty.shtml
Sponsor: Elkhart County Community Foundation
101 S Main Street, P.O. Box 2932
Elkhart, IN 46615

Elkhart County Community Foundation Grants 1684

The foundation is looking for innovative programs or projects that address community issues in Indiana's Elkhart County. Community collaboration is encouraged, where organizations work together toward a shared goal with shared responsibility, accountability, and resources. Grants are awarded in the areas of arts and culture, community development, education, youth development, board development and succession planning, and health and human services in addition to continuing support, technical assistance, and matching funds. Most grants are single-year awards, although multi-year grants also will be considered. The staff is available for advice in the preparation of a proposal. Applicants are encouraged to read the Foundation website's "Helpful Tips for Grant Writers." Letters of interest are due to the Foundation by January 1, April 1, June 1, and August 1.
Requirements: Elkhart County non-profit organizations, or those seeking such status, and some governmental agencies, such as the public library or public school system, are eligible.
Restrictions: Support generally will not be given for continuing operating costs of established programs, projects, and agencies. The foundation does not offer support for religious or sectarian purposes. No grants are awarded to individuals (other than scholarships), or for operating budgets or budget deficits, annual fund, conferences, scholarly research, endowments, personal travel, or films.
Geographic Focus: Indiana
Date(s) Application is Due: Mar 1; Jun 1; Sep 1; Nov 1
Contact: Jim Siegmann; (574) 295-8761; fax (574) 389-7497; jim@elkhartccf.org
Internet: http://www.elkhartccf.org/File/static/grant_seekers/WhatWeFund.shtml
Sponsor: Elkhart County Community Foundation
101 S Main Street, P.O. Box 2932
Elkhart, IN 46615

Ellen Abbott Gilman Trust Grants 1685

The Ellen Abbott Gilman Trust, established in Massachusetts, has specified a number of fields of interest, including: aging centers and services; multipurpose art centers; children and youth services; education; human and community services; and museums. Support is restricted to the State of Massachusetts, and most often comes in the form of general operations. There are no specified application form or deadlines with which to adhere, and applicants should inquire directly to the Trust for more information.
Requirements: Applicants must be 501(c)3 organizations supporting the residents of Massachusetts.
Geographic Focus: Massachusetts
Amount of Grant: 1,000 - 3,000 USD
Contact: Walter G. Van Dorn, Trustee c/o Kirkpatrick & Lockhart Nicholson Graham; (617) 261-3100; fax (617) 261-3175; walter.vandorn@klgates.com
Sponsor: Ellen Abbott Gilman Trust
KL Gates 1 Lincoln Street
Boston, MA 02111-2905

Elliot Foundation Inc Grants 1686

The Elliot Foundation Inc. formerly known as Elliot Foundation for Medical Research and Education, Inc. is a independent foundation, operating primarily in the state of Indiana. The foundation offers funding in the form of general/operating support. The fields of interest include: Christian agencies & churches; crime/violence prevention; environment; natural resources; child abuses; education.
Requirements: Contact Foundation for more information.
Geographic Focus: Indiana
Contact: Richard E. Bond, Secretary; (575) 293-1165
Sponsor: Elliot Foundation
2210 East Jackson Boulevard
Elkhart, IN 46516-1165

Elmer L. and Eleanor J. Andersen Foundation Grants 1687

The foundation exists to enhance the quality of the civic, cultural, educational, environmental, and social aspects of life in Minnesota, primarily in the metropolitan area of Saint Paul and Minneapolis. Types of support include general operating support, continuing support, annual campaigns, capital campaigns, building construction/renovation, endowment funds, program development, deficit reduction, publication, seed money, curriculum development, research, technical assistance, and matching funds. The board meets four times annually.
Requirements: Minnesota nonprofit organizations are eligible.
Geographic Focus: Minnesota
Date(s) Application is Due: Feb 1; May 1; Aug 1; Nov 1
Amount of Grant: 500 - 75,000 USD
Contact: Mari Oyanagi Eggum; (651) 642-0127; fax (651) 645-4684; eandefdn@mtn.org
Sponsor: Elmer L. and Eleanor J. Andersen Foundation
2424 Territorial Road
Saint Paul, MN 55114

El Paso Community Foundation Grants 1688

The Foundation is a facilitator linking the generosity of the region's donors to local non-profit organizations to meet the charitable needs of the El Paso area. In this capacity, the Foundation helps to provide funding for programs and initiatives of these organizations for the broader good of the El Paso Community. Major areas of interest are: arts and humanities; education; public benefit; health and disabilities; environment;animals and; human services. Types of support offered include: equipment acquisition; general/operating support; management development/capacity building; matching/challenge support; program development; scholarship funds; seed money; technical assistance. Priority is given to: more effective ways of doing things; projects where a moderate amount of grant money can have an impact; and projects that show collaboration with other organizations. Application deadlines are February 1 and August 1.
Requirements: Grant requests will be considered only from agencies located within or offering services to the citizens of our community, which includes far west Texas, southern New Mexico and northern Chihuahua, Mexico. Applicants must be exempt from income taxes under Section 501(c)3 of the Internal Revenue Service Code. Application form is available on the El Paso Community Foundation website.
Restrictions: Funding is not available for/to: individuals; capital campaigns; fundraising events or projects; religious organizations for religious purposes; annual appeals and membership contributions; organizations that are political or partisan in purpose; travel for individuals or groups; organizations outside the El Paso geographic area; endowment funds; past operating deficits.
Geographic Focus: Texas
Date(s) Application is Due: Feb 1; Aug 1
Amount of Grant: 3,000 - 10,000 USD
Contact: Bonita Johnson; (915) 533-4020; fax (915) 532-0716; info@epcf.org
Internet: http://www.epcf.org/grant_guidelines
Sponsor: El Paso Community Foundation
P.O. Box 272
El Paso, TX 79943

El Paso Corporate Foundation Grants 1689

El Paso Corporate Foundation funds initiatives that strengthen the communities where employees live, work, and volunteer. The primary focus areas of the foundation are education, health and human services and the community. The Foundation's secondary focus areas are the environment and arts and culture. Organizations must be invited by the Foundation to submit a letter of inquiry for funding consideration.
Requirements: Giving is limited to nonprofits in Alabama, Colorado and Texas.
Restrictions: The following are ineligible requests for funding: organizations without 501(c)3 status; organizations that already have an active El Paso Corporate Foundation grant; capital campaigns; multi-year commitments; religious organizations for religious purposes; individuals; hospitals and medical research; athletics or youth sports organizations; national

or state-wide initiatives; war veterans and fraternal service organizations; endowment funds; pass-through grants; fundraising events, such as dinners, luncheons, and golf tournaments; political organizations, campaigns, and candidates; and technology grants, i.e. computers, software, or related hardware.
Geographic Focus: Alabama, Colorado, Texas
Date(s) Application is Due: Jan 31; May 31; Sep 30
Contact: Community Relations; (713) 420-2878; foundation@elpaso.com
Internet: http://www.elpaso.com/community/default.shtm
Sponsor: El Paso Corporate Foundation
P.O. Box 2511
Houston, TX 77252-2511

El Pomar Foundation Awards and Grants 1690
The Foundation is one of the largest and oldest private foundations in the Rocky Mountain West and contributes annually through direct grants and Community Stewardship Programs to support Colorado nonprofit organizations. The Foundation's primary focus is in health, human services, education, arts and humanities, and civic and community initiatives.
Requirements: The foundation makes grants to 501(c)3 nonprofit Colorado organizations and for activities that take place within the state.
Restrictions: The Foundation does not accept grant applications for: other foundations or nonprofits that distribute money to recipients of its own selection; endowments; individuals; organizations that practice discrimination of any kind; organizations that do not have fiscal responsibility for the proposed project; organizations that do not have an active 501(c)3 nonprofit IRS determination letter; camps, camp programs, or other seasonal activities; religious organizations for support of religious programs; cover deficits or debt elimination; cover travel, conferences, conventions, group meetings, or seminars; influence legislation or support candidates for political office; produce videos or other media projects; fund research projects or studies; primary or secondary schools (K-12).
Geographic Focus: Colorado
Amount of Grant: 500 - 500,000 USD
Contact: Executive Office; (719) 633-7733 or (800) 554-7711; grants@elpomar.org
Internet: http://www.elpomar.org/grant2.html
Sponsor: El Pomar Foundation
10 Lake Circle
Colorado Springs, CO 80906

Elsie H. Wilcox Foundation Grants 1691
The Foundation provides partial support to programs and projects of tax-exempt, public charities in Hawaii to improve the quality of life in the state, particularly the island of Kauai. Areas of interest to the Foundation, include: education, health organizations, people with disabilities; human services, performing arts, theater, religion, YM/YMCAs & YM/YWHAs. Types of support include building/renovation; equipment; general/operating support. Grants average from $5,000 - $15,000.
Requirements: 501(c)3 nonprofit organizations in Hawaii are eligible to apply. The Foundation places a special emphasis on the island of Kauai. Contact Paula Boyce to acquire the cover sheet/application forms and any additional guidelines required to begin the application process. Proposals must be submitted by October 1st.
Restrictions: No grants to individuals, or for endowments.
Geographic Focus: Hawaii
Date(s) Application is Due: Oct 1
Amount of Grant: 5,000 - 15,000 USD
Contact: Paula Boyce; (808) 538-4944; fax (808) 538-4647; pboyce@boh.com
Internet: http://www.hawaiicommunityfoundation.org/index.php?id=290
Sponsor: Elsie H. Wilcox Foundation
Bank of Hawai'i, Foundation Administration Department 758
Honolulu, HI 96802-3170

Elsie Lee Garthwaite Memorial Foundation Grants 1692
Established in 1943, the Foundation supports organizations primarily in Philadelphia, Chester, Montgomery and Delaware counties of Pennsylvania. Giving to organizations that: provide for the physical and emotional well-being of children and young people; seek to enable young people, particularly the needy, to reach their fullest potential through education, empowerment, and exposure to the arts; are smaller organizations, with budgets under $1 million per year.
Requirements: Non-profits are eligible in the Philadelphia, Chester, Montgomery and Delaware counties, PA. Contact the Foundation at least 30 days prior to deadlines with a Letter of Intent. An application form can be obtained from the Foundation after reviewing the Letter of Intent, unsolicited applications will not be excepted. Contact the Foundation for further guidelines.
Restrictions: No grants to public, private, or parochial schools, colleges and universities.
Geographic Focus: Pennsylvania
Date(s) Application is Due: Mar 31; Aug 31
Amount of Grant: 3,000 - 16,000 USD
Contact: Thomas Kaneda, Secretary; (610) 527-8101; fax (610) 527-7808
Sponsor: Elsie Lee Garthwaite Memorial Foundation
1234 Lancaster Avenue, P.O. Box 709
Rosemont, PA 19010-0709

EMC Corporation Grants 1693
The Foundation's major focus area is improving the quality of education. The Foundation supports programs that encourage students to pursue careers in math and science at the elementary, middle and high school levels. The Foundation donates and encourages the use of computer technology to augment classroom teaching, sponsor intensive teacher training and development, and support regional and national math, science, and engineering competitions. In addition, the Foundation invests in its local communities, especially to strengthen public safety, improve the lives of disadvantaged children and their families, and fund the arts. EMC considers proposals bi-monthly. All proposals should be emailed to CorporateCommunityInvolvement@emc.com. Application forms are available online.
Requirements: To be eligible for funding, organizations must meet the following criteria: must be a nonprofit and tax-exempt organization; must support an EMC site community; and overhead expenses must not exceed 25% of total operating budget.
Restrictions: The following organizations are not eligible for funding: organizations without 501(c)3 status with the exception of publicly funded academic institutions and municipalities; individuals; religious, veteran or fraternal organizations; political causes or candidates; organizations that promote or practice discrimination; direct mail solicitations; courtesy advertising; endowments; tickets for contests; and reduction of debt.
Geographic Focus: All States
Contact: Grants Administrator; CorporateCommunityInvolvement@emc.com
Internet: http://www.emc.com/about/emc_philanthropy/funding
Sponsor: EMC Corporation
35 Parkwood Drive
Hopkinton, MA 01748

Emerson Charitable Trust Grants 1694
Established in 1944 in Missouri as the Emerson Electric Manufacturing Company Charitable Trust, the Foundation supports: arts and culture—fine arts and cultural institutions to enrich the diversity, creativity, and liveliness of the community; education—programs designed to promote educational systems at all levels; health and human services—programs designed to help individuals and families in times of need, including sickness, old age, family crisis, and natural disasters; civic affairs—programs designed to protect citizenry; further economic health of the community; and build and maintain assets such as parks and zoos; and youth—programs designed to give young people the opportunity to recognize their potential, confidence, and skills to achieve their dreams. The foundation awards college scholarships to children and step-children of employees of Emerson Electric. No specific application form is required, and initial approach should be the complete proposal,
Geographic Focus: All States
Amount of Grant: 5,000 - 300,000 USD
Contact: Jo Ann Harmon, Senior Vice President; (314) 553-3722; fax (314) 553-1605
Internet: http://www.emerson.com/en-us/about_emerson/company_overview/pages/our_approach_to_corporate_philanthropy.aspx
Sponsor: Emerson Charitable Trust
8000 W Florissant Avenue, P.O. Box 4100
Saint Louis, MO 63136

Emerson Electric Company Contributions Grants 1695
Emerson believes it is important to help support organizations and institutions that play significant roles in enhancing the quality of life in the communities where its facilities are located and where its employees and their families live and work. As a complement to its foundation, Emerson makes charitable contributions to nonprofit organizations directly. Support is given on a national basis in areas of company operations, with emphasis on St. Louis, Missouri. Its primary fields of interest include the arts, education, health care, and public affairs. An application form should be obtained from the nearest company facility.
Geographic Focus: All States
Contact: Robert M. Cox, Senior Vice President; (314) 553-2000; fax (314) 553-1605
Internet: http://www.emerson.com/en-us/about_emerson/company_overview/pages/our_approach_to_corporate_philanthropy.aspx
Sponsor: Emerson Electric Company
8000 W Florissant Avenue, P.O. Box 4100
Saint Louis, MO 63136

Emerson Kampen Foundation Grants 1696
Established in Indiana in 1986, the Emerson Kampen Foundation offers grants primarily in Indiana, though awards have also been given in Illinois and New Jersey. The Foundation's primary fields of interest include: youth groups; Christian agencies and churches; higher education; and YMCAs and YWCAs. Unsolicited applications are not accepted, and interested parties should contact the Foundation in writing prior to forwarding any detailed requests. Grants range from $20,000 to $200,000.
Geographic Focus: Illinois, Indiana, New Jersey
Amount of Grant: 20,000 - 200,000 USD
Contact: Joanie Kampen Dunham, Co-Trustee; (856) 223-2872
Sponsor: Emerson Kampen Foundation
101 Cromwell Drive
Mullica Hill, NJ 08062-1807

Emily Davie and Joseph S. Kornfeld Foundation Grants 1697
The Foundation's selection criteria for all programs are: evidence of strong and visionary leadership; development of new initiatives that are replicable and sustainable; creation of new ways to address existing critical issues; interest in building connections and creative partnerships; desire to improve and enrich lives of individuals (rather than capital improvements); and original, unusual, dynamic and focused proposals. Proposal letters should include a background on the organization, a detailed description of the proposed project and financial information.
Requirements: Eligible applicants must provide a copy of a 501(c)3 determination letter.
Geographic Focus: All States
Date(s) Application is Due: Mar 1; Jul 15; Nov 15
Contact: Bobye List; (718) 624-7969; fax (718) 834-1204; office@kornfeldfdn.org

Internet: http://fdncenter.org/grantmaker/kornfeld
Sponsor: Emily Davie and Joseph S. Kornfeld Foundation
41 Schermerhorn Street, Suite 208
Brooklyn, NY 11021

Emily Hall Tremaine Foundation Grants 1698

The foundation seeks to fund innovative projects that advance solutions to basic problems within society. Emphasis is placed on U.S. elementary and secondary education. The foundation also supports programs in the arts, environmental conservation, and learning disabilities. There are no application forms or deadlines. Unsolicited proposals rarely develop into a grant; submit informative letters of inquiry that highlight the organization's mission, goals, history, strategies, and programmatic scope.
Requirements: Education-related nonprofits may apply for grant support.
Geographic Focus: All States
Amount of Grant: 1,000 - 50,000 USD
Contact: Stewart Hudson; (203) 639-5544; chevalier@tremainefoundation.org
Internet: http://www.tremainefoundation.org
Sponsor: Emily Hall Tremaine Foundation
290 Pratt Street
Meriden, CT 06450

Emma A. Sheafer Charitable Trust Grants 1699

The trust awards grants to nonprofit performing arts institutions in the New York City area for projects/programs, matching/challenge grants, and capital campaigns. Requests are reviewed twice annually. Proposal should include information about the organization and problem to be addressed, most recent annual report, list of board of directors and their affiliations, most recent financial audit, current operating budget, list of additional support with amounts, copy of the 501(c)3 letter, and detailed project description.
Requirements: 501(c)3 organizations serving the metro New York City area may apply.
Restrictions: A minimum of three years must elapse between grant awards. No grants are made to individuals, private foundations, governmental organizations, or for matching gifts or loans.
Geographic Focus: New York
Date(s) Application is Due: May 1; Nov 1
Amount of Grant: 15,000 - 25,000 USD
Contact: Edward Jones; (212) 464-2441; jpmorgan.chase.grants@jpmchase.com
Internet: http://fdncenter.org/grantmaker/sheafer
Sponsor: Emma A. Sheafer Charitable Trust
345 Park Avenue, 4th Floor
New York, NY 10154

Emma B. Howe Memorial Foundation Grants 1700

The Emma B. Howe Memorial Foundation makes grants through the Minneapolis Foundation. The focus of all grants is to improve: the health and well-being of children, youth and families; opportunities for educational achievement; access to quality affordable housing; and economic vitality throughout the region. Information on the application process is available online.
Requirements: Eligible organizations include 501(c)3 nonprofits, public institutions; and emerging groups organized for nonprofit purposes.
Restrictions: Funds are not available for: individuals; organizations/activities outside of Minnesota; conference registration fees; memberships; direct religious activities; political organizations or candidates; direct fundraising efforts; telephone solicitations; courtesy advertising; financial deficits.
Geographic Focus: Minnesota
Contact: Grants Manager; (612) 672-3836; grants@mplsfoundation.org
Internet: http://www.mplsfoundation.org/partners/emma.htm
Sponsor: Emma B. Howe Memorial Foundation
80 S Eighth Street
Minneapolis, MN 55402

Emma G. Harris Foundation Grants 1701

The Emma G. Harris Foundation was established in 1965 to support technical, industrial, household, and domestic training programs for young adults. Preference is given to community-based organizations that provide technical training programs. The majority of grants from the Harris Foundation are one year in duration; on occasion, multi-year support is awarded. Application to the Harris Foundation is a two-step process. Applicants must first submit their proposals for approval to the Rhode Island Board of Education before August 1. Approved proposals must then be submitted to Emma G. Harris Foundation by September 1. Applicants will be notified of grant decisions before December 31. Interested organizations may call the second phone number given for information on how to apply.
Requirements: The Harris Foundation supports established technical, industrial, household, and domestic training programs for young adults.
Restrictions: The foundation does not make grants to start-up programs. Grant requests for capital projects will not be considered. The foundation does not support requests from individuals, organizations attempting to influence policy through direct lobbying, or any political campaigns.
Geographic Focus: Rhode Island
Date(s) Application is Due: Jul 31; Sep 1
Contact: Emma Greene; (617) 434-0329 or (617) 434-8237; emma.m.greene@baml.com
Internet: https://www.bankofamerica.com/philanthropic/fn_search.action
Sponsor: Emma G. Harris Foundation
225 Franklin Street, 4th Floor, MA1-225-04-02
Boston, MA 02110

Emma J. Adams Memorial Fund Grants 1702

The Emma J. Adams Memorial Fund was established in New York in 1932, and giving is centered around New York City to aid the indigent elderly through a church-sponsored meals program and ecumenical medical care. Limited giving is also available for nonrecurring grants to elderly individuals who are agency, medically, or professionally-sponsored. Primary fields of interest include adults, aging, and the economically disadvantaged. Grants range from $800 to $30,000.
Restrictions: No grants are offered for operating budgets, annual campaigns, administrative expenses, building funds, special projects, endowments, or scholarships; no loans. There is no support for programs, or brick and mortar grants.
Geographic Focus: New York
Amount of Grant: 800 - 30,000 USD
Contact: Edward R. Finch, Jr., President; (212) 327-0493
Sponsor: Emma J. Adams Memorial Fund
860 Park Avenue
New York, NY 10075-1831

Emy-Lou Biedenharn Foundation Grants 1703

The Foundation awards grants to eligible Louisiana nonprofit organizations in the areas of the arts and human services. Nonprofit organizations in Quachita Parrish, Louisiana, with emphasis on Monroe, are eligible. Applicants should submit the following: statement of problem project will address; detailed contact information; copy of IRS determination letter; brief history of organization and description of its mission; detailed description of project and amount of money requested; and any additional materials/documentation.
Geographic Focus: Louisiana
Date(s) Application is Due: Dec 31
Contact: Dollie Atkins, Foundation Contact; (318) 387-5281 or (800) 362-0983
Sponsor: Emy-Lou Biedenharn Foundation
2006 Riverside Drive
Monroe, LA 71201

Encore Purpose Prize 1704

The Purpose Prize provides five $100,000 and five $50,000 awards to social innovators over 60 in encore careers. An independent national selection panel of recognized leaders in social innovation selects 10 of the top-scoring candidates to become finalists for The Purpose Prize. All 10 finalists will become Purpose Prize winners, receiving either $100,000 prizes or $50,000 prizes.
Requirements: Nominations are welcome from any organization or individual with knowledge of a potential candidate. Self-nominations are acceptable. To be eligible the nominee must be at least 60 years old by the deadline date; be a legal resident of the United States (including U.S. territories); be someone who has initiated important innovations (in a new or ongoing organization) in an encore career. Encore careers combine personal meaning and social impact with continued work in the second half of life; be currently working in a leadership capacity in an organization or institution (public, private, nonprofit, or for-profit) to address a major social problem in the United States or abroad; have initiated important innovations (in a new or ongoing organization), and have demonstrated recent creativity and leadership with the promise of more to come. Individuals working in faith-based service organizations that have a broader social mission are eligible and encouraged to apply, but the purpose of their project cannot be strictly religious or sectarian—in that it is confined exclusively to individuals within a denomination or for the sole purpose of expanding the religious mission of the denomination or faith.
Restrictions: Elected officials are not eligible for The Prize for work they conduct in their official capacity.
Geographic Focus: All States
Date(s) Application is Due: Mar 5
Amount of Grant: 50,000 - 100,000 USD
Contact: Alexandra Cespedes Kent, Director; (415) 222-7486; akent@civicventures.org
Internet: http://www.encore.org/prize
Sponsor: Civic Ventures
114 Sansome Street, Suite 850
San Francisco, CA 94104

Energy Foundation Buildings Grants 1705

The Energy Foundation's mission is to assist the United States and China in the transition to a sustainable energy future by promoting energy efficiency and renewable energy. To this end, grants in the buildings sector hope to: promote the adoption of increasingly stringent building codes, with effective local enforcement; establish stringent appliance standards and complementary consumer labels; create programs to benchmark and rate the energy consumed by buildings and encourage retrofitting the large stock of existing buildings; and develop financial incentives to buy and lease energy-efficient buildings. The Foundation has no fixed format for proposals. Applicants are urged to use the form that best conveys the strengths of their project.
Requirements: The foundation makes grants to nonprofit 501(c)3 charitable organizations. In general, a complete proposal includes the following: the attached application form as a cover sheet; a clear statement of the need(s) or problem(s) to be addressed; strategy; timeline; results you expect from your project; project budget—including a brief explanation of the budget, a list of other sources of actual and potential funding for the project, and a description of plans to secure additional funding; how you will determine whether your project is successful; and a history of organization, including mission and goals.
Restrictions: The Foundation is unable to fund: grants directly to individuals; local projects, unless they have been consciously designed for further replication or have broad regional or national implications; candidates for political office, to influence legislation, or to support sectarian or religious purposes; the research and development of technology (e.g., funds to

develop hybrid automobiles or commercialization of an invention); demonstration projects (e.g., model solar homes); community energy projects; endowments or debt reduction; annual fund-raising campaigns or capital construction; the planning, renovation, maintenance, retrofit, or purchase of buildings; the purchase of equipment; or the acquisition of land, even if the intent is to save energy; or unsolicited general operating support.
Geographic Focus: All States
Amount of Grant: 2,000 - 850,000 USD
Contact: Todd Foland; (415) 561-6700; fax (415) 561-6709; energyfund@ef.org
Internet: http://www.ef.org/programs.cfm?program=buildings
Sponsor: Energy Foundation
301 Battery Street, 5th Floor
San Francisco, 94111

Energy Foundation Climate Grants 1706
The Energy Foundation's mission is to assist the United States and China in the transition to a sustainable energy future by promoting energy efficiency and renewable energy. To this end, grants in the climate sector support work in the following areas: building support for climate protection among diverse allies, such as business associations, veterans' groups, religious organizations, and agricultural interests, among others; policy analysis (such as assessing the effects of climate policy on consumers, business, jobs, and Gross Domestic Product; modeling state-by-state impacts; or evaluating policy design options on issues such as offsets, allowance allocation, or integrating carbon controls with complementary policies for energy efficiency and renewable energy); targeted efforts to educate opinion leaders and stakeholders—nationally or in key states-about climate change and climate policy; supporting implementation of state and regional climate laws and agreements (such as California's AB 32, the Regional Greenhouse Gas Initiative in the Northeast, and the Western Climate Initiative); and improving understanding of the role of the U.S. in an international climate agreement. The Foundation has no fixed deadlines or format for proposals. Applicants are urged to use the form that best conveys the strengths of their project.
Requirements: The foundation makes grants to nonprofit 501(c)3 charitable organizations. In general, a complete proposal includes the following: the attached application form as a cover sheet; a clear statement of the need(s) or problem(s) to be addressed; strategy; timeline; results you expect from your project; project budget—including a brief explanation of the budget, a list of other sources of actual and potential funding for the project, and a description of plans to secure additional funding; how you will determine whether your project is successful; and a history of organization, including mission and goals.
Restrictions: The Foundation is unable to fund: grants directly to individuals; local projects, unless they have been consciously designed for further replication or have broad regional or national implications; candidates for political office, to influence legislation, or to support sectarian or religious purposes; the research and development of technology (e.g., funds to develop hybrid automobiles or commercialization of an invention); demonstration projects (e.g., model solar homes); community energy projects; endowments or debt reduction; annual fund-raising campaigns or capital construction; the planning, renovation, maintenance, retrofit, or purchase of buildings; the purchase of equipment; or the acquisition of land, even if the intent is to save energy; or unsolicited general operating support.
Geographic Focus: All States
Contact: Todd Foland; (415) 561-6700; fax (415) 561-6709; energyfund@ef.org
Internet: http://www.ef.org/programs.cfm?program=climate
Sponsor: Energy Foundation
301 Battery Street, 5th Floor
San Francisco, 94111

Energy Foundation Power Grants 1707
The Energy Foundation's mission is to assist the United States and China in the transition to a sustainable energy future by promoting energy efficiency and renewable energy. To this end, grants in the power sector support work in the following areas: policies that yield large-scale purchases of renewable energy; policies that open the electric system to renewable power and associated transmission while supporting resource conservation; policies that yield substantial investments to improve energy efficiency by consumers of electric power and natural gas; policies that remove market and regulatory barriers to renewables, efficiency, and clean distributed generation; resistance to permitting and regulatory approvals for new conventional coal-fired power plants; campaigns to reduce greenhouse gases by directing new utility investments toward clean energy resources; to secure stricter performance standards for emissions from new and existing coal plants, including greenhouse gases; and regulatory controls for carbon capture and sequestration systems. The Foundation has no fixed format for proposals. Applicants are urged to use the form that best conveys the strengths of their project.
Requirements: The foundation makes grants to nonprofit 501(c)3 charitable organizations. In general, a complete proposal includes the following: the attached application form as a cover sheet; a clear statement of the need(s) or problem(s) to be addressed; strategy; timeline; results you expect from your project; project budget—including a brief explanation of the budget, a list of other sources of actual and potential funding for the project, and a description of plans to secure additional funding; how you will determine whether your project is successful; and a history of organization, including mission and goals.
Restrictions: The Foundation is unable to fund: grants directly to individuals; local projects, unless they have been consciously designed for further replication or have broad regional or national implications; candidates for political office, to influence legislation, or to support sectarian or religious purposes; the research and development of technology (e.g., funds to develop hybrid automobiles or commercialization of an invention); demonstration projects (e.g., model solar homes); community energy projects; endowments or debt reduction; annual fund-raising campaigns or capital construction; the planning, renovation, maintenance, retrofit, or purchase of buildings; the purchase of equipment; or the acquisition of land, even if the intent is to save energy; or unsolicited general operating support.
Geographic Focus: All States
Amount of Grant: 2,000 - 850,000 USD
Contact: Todd Foland; (415) 561-6700; fax (415) 561-6709; energyfund@ef.org
Internet: http://www.ef.org/programs.cfm?program=power
Sponsor: Energy Foundation
301 Battery Street, 5th Floor
San Francisco, 94111

Energy Foundation Transportation Grants 1708
The Energy Foundation's mission is to assist the United States and China in the transition to a sustainable energy future by promoting energy efficiency and renewable energy. To this end, the transportation sector makes grants to promote innovative federal and state policies that reduce global warming pollution from vehicles, encourage low-carbon fuels, and discourage high-carbon fuels. The Foundation focuses on performance-based standards and incentives that guide markets toward cleaner solutions. The Foundation has no fixed deadlines or format for proposals. Applicants are urged to use the form that best conveys the strengths of their project.
Requirements: The foundation makes grants to nonprofit 501(c)3 charitable organizations. In general, a complete proposal includes the following: the attached application form as a cover sheet; a clear statement of the need(s) or problem(s) to be addressed; strategy; timeline; results you expect from your project; project budget-including a brief explanation of the budget, a list of other sources of actual and potential funding for the project, and a description of plans to secure additional funding; how you will determine whether your project is successful; and a history of organization, including mission and goals.
Restrictions: The Foundation is unable to fund: grants directly to individuals; local projects, unless they have been consciously designed for further replication or have broad regional or national implications; candidates for political office, to influence legislation, or to support sectarian or religious purposes; the research and development of technology (e.g., funds to develop hybrid automobiles or commercialization of an invention); demonstration projects (e.g., model solar homes); community energy projects; endowments or debt reduction; annual fund-raising campaigns or capital construction; the planning, renovation, maintenance, retrofit, or purchase of buildings; the purchase of equipment; or the acquisition of land, even if the intent is to save energy; or unsolicited general operating support.
Geographic Focus: All States
Amount of Grant: 2,000 - 850,000 USD
Contact: Todd Foland; (415) 561-6700; fax (415) 561-6709; energyfund@ef.org
Internet: http://www.ef.org/programs.cfm?program=transportation
Sponsor: Energy Foundation
301 Battery Street, 5th Floor
San Francisco, 94111

Ensign-Bickford Foundation Grants 1709
The corporate foundation gives primarily in areas of company operations, with emphasis on the Simsbury and Avon, CT, areas. Grants are awarded to nonprofit organizations for welfare, education, cultural programs, employee-related scholarships, and community development activities. Types of support include continuing support, annual campaigns, building/renovation, equipment acquisition, land acquisition, programs and projects, conferences and seminars, publication, seed money, internships, scholarships, research, and employee matching gifts. Applications are accepted throughout the year.
Requirements: Nonprofits in company operating areas of Connecticut are eligible to apply.
Restrictions: Grants are not awarded to individuals (except for employee-related scholarships) or for operating budgets, endowment funds, emergency funds, deficit financing, or loans.
Geographic Focus: Connecticut
Amount of Grant: 50 - 50,000 USD
Contact: Jan Delissio, (860) 843-2388
Internet: http://www.ensign-bickfordind.com/community.html
Sponsor: Ensign-Bickford Foundation
100 Grist Mill Road, P.O. Box 7
Simsbury, CT 06070-0007

Ensworth Charitable Foundation Grants 1710
The Ensworth Charitable Foundation was established in 1948 to support and promote educational, cultural, human services, religious, and health care programming for underserved populations. The foundation specifically serves the people of Hartford, Connecticut, and its surrounding communities. Grants from the Ensworth Charitable Foundation are primarily one year in duration. On occasion, multi-year support is awarded. Applicants must apply online at the grant website. Applicants are strongly encouraged to do the following before applying: review the downloadable state application procedures for additional helpful information and clarifications; review the downloadable online-application guidelines at the grant website; review the foundation's funding history (link is available from the grant website); review the online application questions in advance; and review the list of required attachments. These will generally include: a list of board members, financial statements (audited, reviewed, or compiled by independent auditor); an organization summary; a list of other funding sources; an IRS Determination letter; and other required documents. All attachments must be uploaded in the online application as PDF, Word, or Excel files. The Ensworth Charitable Foundation application deadline is January 15 at 11:59 p.m. Applicants will be notified of grant decisions by letter within three to four months after the deadline.
Requirements: Applicants must have 501(c)3 tax-exempt status and serve the people of Hartford, Connecticut, and its surrounding communities.
Restrictions: Applicants will not be awarded a grant for more than 3 consecutive years. The foundation does not support requests from individuals, organizations attempting to influence policy through direct lobbying, or any political campaigns.
Geographic Focus: Connecticut

Date(s) Application is Due: Jan 15
Amount of Grant: 1,000 - 25,000 USD
Contact: Amy R. Lynch; (860) 657-7015; amy.r.lynch@baml.com
Internet: https://www.bankofamerica.com/philanthropic/fn_search.action
Sponsor: Ensworth Charitable Foundation
200 Glastonbury Boulevard, Suite # 200
Glastonbury, CT 06033-4056

Entergy Charitable Foundation Low-Income Initiatives and Solutions Grants 1711

The primary goal of the Entergy Charitable Foundation is to support initiatives that help create and sustain thriving communities, with a special focus on low-income initiatives. Such programs may include, but are not limited to: sustaining families and self-sufficiency; technical assistance and training for non-profits; housing; home-ownership preparation; energy management and awareness; and innovative use and promotion of alternative sources of energy. In considering requests, priority is placed on programs in specific counties or parishes, including areas of: Arkansas, Louisiana, Massachusetts, Michigan, Mississippi, New Hampshire, New York, Texas, and Vermont. Contact the contributions coordinator in your state with any questions regarding your project. Each applicant must complete and submit an online application form. Annual deadlines are February 1, May 1, and July 1.
Requirements: Grants from the Entergy Corporation will only be made to the following types of organizations: non-profit organizations that are tax exempt under section 501(c)3 of the Internal Revenue Code; or schools, hospitals, governmental units and religious institutions that hold nonprofit status similar to that of 501(c)3 organizations.
Restrictions: Entergy will not fund: groups without 501(c)3 or similar non-profit status; administrative expenses (e.g., salaries, office equipment) or recurring expenses that exceed 15% of the requested amount; capital project funding (i.e., building campaigns); political candidates or groups; purchase of uniforms or trips for school-related organizations; amateur sports teams; activities whose sole purpose is promotion or support of a specific religion, denomination, or religious institution; grants to individuals or loans of any type; or any organization owned or operated by an employee of Entergy.
Geographic Focus: Arkansas, Louisiana, Massachusetts, Michigan, Mississippi, New Hampshire, New York, Texas
Date(s) Application is Due: Feb 1; May 1; Jul 1
Contact: Jennifer Quezergue, (504) 576-2674 or (504) 576-6980; jquezer@entergy.com
Internet: http://www.entergy.com/our_community/ECF_grant_guidelines.aspx
Sponsor: Entergy Charitable Foundation
639 Loyola Avenue
New Orleans, LA 70161-1000

Entergy Corporation Micro Grants 1712

The Foundation will bestow a monetary award for projects that effectively impact arts and culture, community improvement and enrichment, education and literacy, and healthy families. Organizations should be located within Entergy's service territory in Arkansas, Louisiana, Mississippi, Massachusetts, Michigan, New Hampshire, New York, Texas, or Vermont. Micro Grant applications are accepted on an ongoing basis. Applicants should allow at least 6 (six) to 8 (eight) weeks for review and notification of the result of a request.
Requirements: 501(c)3 organizations, schools, hospitals, governmental units and religious institutions are eligible. Each organization may submit only one application per year.
Restrictions: Entergy will not fund: groups without 501(c)3 or similar non-profit status; administrative expenses (e.g., salaries, office equipment) or recurring expenses that exceed 15% of the requested amount; capital project funding (i.e., building campaigns); political candidates or groups; purchase of uniforms or trips for school-related organizations; amateur sports teams; activities whose sole purpose is promotion or support of a specific religion, denomination, or religious institution; grants to individuals or loans of any type; or any organization owned or operated by an employee of Entergy.
Geographic Focus: Arkansas, Louisiana, Massachusetts, Michigan, Mississippi, New Hampshire, New York, Texas, Vermont
Amount of Grant: Up to 1,000 USD
Contact: Jennifer Quezergue, (504) 576-2674 or (504) 576-6980; jquezer@entergy.com
Internet: http://www.entergy.com/our_community/micro_grant_guidelines.aspx
Sponsor: Entergy Corporation
639 Loyola Avenue
New Orleans, LA 70161-1000

Entergy Corporation Open Grants for Arts and Culture 1713

Entergy's Open Grants Program focuses on improving communities as a whole. The arts are expressions of ourselves heritage, feelings and ideas. To cultivate that, the Corporation supports a diverse range of locally based visual arts, theater, dance and music institutions. The long-term goal is to increase the access to contemporary art for a wider public, including children and the financially disadvantaged. In considering requests for grants, priority is placed on programs in specific counties/parishes, including areas of: Arkansas, Louisiana, Massachusetts, Michigan, Mississippi, New Hampshire, New York, Texas, and Vermont. Applicants should contact the contributions coordinator in their region, which are listed on the web site. Open grant applications are accepted on an ongoing basis. Applications should be submitted at least three months prior to the time the funding is needed.
Requirements: Grants from the Entergy Corporation will only be made to the following types of organizations: non-profit organizations that are tax exempt under section 501(c)3 of the Internal Revenue Code; or schools, hospitals, governmental units and religious institutions that hold nonprofit status similar to that of 501(c)3 organizations.
Restrictions: Entergy will not fund: groups without 501(c)3 or similar non-profit status; administrative expenses (e.g., salaries, office equipment) or recurring expenses that exceed 15% of the requested amount; capital project funding (i.e., building campaigns); political candidates or groups; purchase of uniforms or trips for school-related organizations; amateur sports teams; activities whose sole purpose is promotion or support of a specific religion, denomination, or religious institution; grants to individuals or loans of any type; or any organization owned or operated by an employee of Entergy.
Geographic Focus: Arkansas, Louisiana, Massachusetts, Michigan, Mississippi, New Hampshire, New York, Texas, Vermont
Amount of Grant: Up to 1,000 USD
Contact: Jennifer Quezergue, (504) 576-2674 or (504) 576-6980; jquezer@entergy.com
Internet: http://www.entergy.com/our_community/Grant_Guidelines.aspx
Sponsor: Entergy Corporation
639 Loyola Avenue
New Orleans, LA 70161-1000

Entergy Corporation Open Grants for Community Improvement & Enrichment 1714

Entergy Corporation's Open Grants program focuses on improving communities as a whole. Entergy supports community-based projects that focus on community enrichment and improvement. A few examples include civic affairs, blighted housing improvements, and neighborhood safety. By giving to communities in this way, the Corporation helps them become more self-sufficient. In considering requests for grants, priority is placed on programs in specific counties/parishes, including areas of: Arkansas, Louisiana, Massachusetts, Michigan, Mississippi, New Hampshire, New York, Texas, and Vermont. Applicants should contact the contributions coordinator in their region, which are listed on the web site. Open grant applications are accepted on an ongoing basis. Applications should be submitted at least three months prior to the time the funding is needed.
Requirements: Grants from the Entergy Corporation will only be made to the following types of organizations: non-profit organizations that are tax exempt under section 501(c)3 of the Internal Revenue Code; or schools, hospitals, governmental units and religious institutions that hold nonprofit status similar to that of 501(c)3 organizations.
Restrictions: Entergy will not fund: groups without 501(c)3 or similar non-profit status; administrative expenses (e.g., salaries, office equipment) or recurring expenses that exceed 15% of the requested amount; capital project funding (i.e., building campaigns); political candidates or groups; purchase of uniforms or trips for school-related organizations; amateur sports teams; activities whose sole purpose is promotion or support of a specific religion, denomination, or religious institution; grants to individuals or loans of any type; or any organization owned or operated by an employee of Entergy.
Geographic Focus: Arkansas, Louisiana, Massachusetts, Michigan, Mississippi, New Hampshire, New York, Texas, Vermont
Amount of Grant: Up to 1,000 USD
Contact: Jennifer Quezergue, (504) 576-2674 or (504) 576-6980; jquezer@entergy.com
Internet: http://www.entergy.com/our_community/Grant_Guidelines.aspx
Sponsor: Entergy Corporation
639 Loyola Avenue
New Orleans, LA 70161-1000

Entergy Corporation Open Grants for Healthy Families 1715

Entergy Corporation's Open Grants program focuses on improving communities as a whole. The Corporation believes that children need a good start to grow into healthy, well-adjusted adults. With that in mind, it gives to programs that have a direct impact on children educationally and emotionally. The Corporation is also interested in family programs, like those that better prepare parents to balance the demands of work and home. In considering requests for grants, priority is placed on programs in specific counties/parishes, including areas of: Arkansas, Louisiana, Massachusetts, Michigan, Mississippi, New Hampshire, New York, Texas, and Vermont. Applicants should contact the contributions coordinator in their region, which are listed on the web site. Open grant applications are accepted on an ongoing basis. Applications should be submitted at least three months prior to the time the funding is needed.
Requirements: Grants from the Entergy Corporation will only be made to the following types of organizations: non-profit organizations that are tax exempt under section 501(c)3 of the Internal Revenue Code; or schools, hospitals, governmental units and religious institutions that hold nonprofit status similar to that of 501(c)3 organizations.
Restrictions: Entergy will not fund: groups without 501(c)3 or similar non-profit status; administrative expenses (e.g., salaries, office equipment) or recurring expenses that exceed 15% of the requested amount; capital project funding (i.e., building campaigns); political candidates or groups; purchase of uniforms or trips for school-related organizations; amateur sports teams; activities whose sole purpose is promotion or support of a specific religion, denomination, or religious institution; grants to individuals or loans of any type; or any organization owned or operated by an employee of Entergy.
Geographic Focus: Arkansas, Louisiana, Massachusetts, Michigan, Mississippi, New Hampshire, New York, Texas, Vermont
Contact: Jennifer Quezergue, (504) 576-2674 or (504) 576-6980; jquezer@entergy.com
Internet: http://www.entergy.com/our_community/Grant_Guidelines.aspx
Sponsor: Entergy Corporation
639 Loyola Avenue
New Orleans, LA 70161-1000

Enterprise Community Partners Green Charrette Grants 1716

This is a planning grant awarded to affordable housing developers to coordinate a green design charrette. Up to $5,000 to assist housing developers with integrating green building systems in their developments and engage in a serious discussion of green design possibilities. Charrettes take into consideration the existing community context by using a holistic and total-systems approach to the development process to promote health and livability throughout the life cycle of the development. The charrette is an intense working session that aims to integrate sustainable green design principles by bringing together housing development professionals, residents, technical experts, funders, policymakers, and community stakeholders.

Requirements: The grant is open to: 501(c)3 nonprofits; tribally designated housing entities; and, for-profit entities participating through joint ventures with qualified organizations. The applicant and the development team must demonstrate their qualifications to successfully carry out the proposed development. Projects must be subject to firm site control or evidence that site control is imminent. Applicant must identify whether proposed project site is an occupied or unoccupied property. Projects must also involve new construction of residential units or rehab at an estimated cost of $3,000 or more per unit. Grantees will be required to provide a match of 3:1 in private dollars. Match must be achieved at the beginning of the grant period of performance. Back up documentation must also be submitted to provide confirmation of these sources.
Geographic Focus: All States
Amount of Grant: Up to 5,000 USD
Contact: Dana L. Bourland, Vice President, Green Initiatives; (410) 772-2516 or (410) 715-7533; dbourland@enterprisecommunity.org or green@enterprisecommunity.org
Internet: http://www.enterprisecommunity.com/solutions-and-innovation/enterprise-green-communities/resources/charrette-toolkit
Sponsor: Enterprise Community Partners
70 Corporate Center
Columbia, MD 21044

Enterprise Community Partners MetLife Foundation Awards for Excellence in Affordable Housing 1717

In partnership with the MetLife Foundation, Enterprise offers the MetLife Foundation Awards for Excellence in Affordable Housing. The awards program recognizes 501(c)3 community-based or regional nonprofit organizations and Tribes or Tribally Designated Housing Entities that excel in property and asset management or provide housing to people with special needs. Awards are presented in two categories: Supportive Housing and Property and Asset Management, and the prize money may be used to cover any of the needs of the winning organizations. For each category, first place winners receive $50,000.
Requirements: Applicants must be 501(c)3 community-based or regional nonprofit organizations or Tribes/Tribally Designated Housing Entities (THDEs) and members of the Enterprise Network (membership is free - see the website for more details). The project submitted can be single-site or scattered-site, and must have a minimum of 10 dwelling units. The project submitted can be rental, cooperatively owned or condominium units, transitional or permanent housing. It cannot be emergency housing. A majority of residents of the project must have incomes at or below 60 percent of area median income. Awards will be made for individual projects only. Special consideration will be given to projects with unique characteristics. Applicants must satisfy one of the following criteria for the project: Own; Lease and operate; Act as general partner of the ownership entity; Sponsor a section 202/811 project.
Restrictions: Applicants may enter either the supportive housing category or the property and asset management category, but cannot apply for both categories.
Geographic Focus: All States
Date(s) Application is Due: May 31
Amount of Grant: 50,000 USD
Contact: Program Officer; metlifeawards@enterprisecommunity.org
Internet: http://www.enterprisecommunity.com/solutions-and-innovation/senior-housing/metlife-foundation-awards
Sponsor: Enterprise Community Partners
70 Corporate Center
Columbia, MD 21044

Enterprise Community Partners Pre-Development Design Grants 1718

Enterprise's Pre-Development Design Grant provides funding for design exploration during the early stages of affordable housing development. Designed to precede and complement Enterprise's Green Communities Charrette Grant, the grant seeks to raise the standard of design excellence in affordable housing by following a model executed by two community development corporations. The grant will support organizations that have identified a particular site, existing project or community need related to affordable housing who would like to strengthen partnerships, expand their architectural networks and set clear project goals. The $20,000 grant will cover the following reimbursable costs: a fixed fee for each of the four architects to develop and present an approach and design ideas related to the development project; a consultant fee and travel costs for the facilitator to collaborate with the grantee on the pre-development design process–this includes developing a design brief, reaching out to architecture firms, moderating the presentation day and completing progress reporting; and, program support costs incurred by the CDC for to the pre-development design process and the progress reporting.
Requirements: 501(c)3 community development corporations (CDC's), community housing development corporation (CHDO's), tribally designated housing entities, as well as for-profit entities participating through joint ventures with qualified organizations are eligible to apply. The applicant must demonstrate the development team's qualifications to successfully carry out the proposed project. Grantees will be required to provide a match of 3:1 in private dollars. Match must be achieved at the beginning of the grant period of performance.
Restrictions: The grant cannot be used to cover technical feasibility studies or full schematic design.
Geographic Focus: All States
Date(s) Application is Due: Jul 10
Amount of Grant: 20,000 USD
Contact: Dana L. Bourland, Vice President, Green Initiatives; (410) 772-2516 or (410) 715-7533; dbourland@enterprisecommunity.org or green@enterprisecommunity.org
Internet: http://www.enterprisecommunity.com/solutions-and-innovation/design-leadership/design-grant
Sponsor: Enterprise Community Partners
70 Corporate Center
Columbia, MD 21044

Enterprise Community Partners Rose Architectural Fellowships 1719

The Fellowship honors the late Frederick P. Rose, a prominent developer and philanthropist who believed strongly in the value of quality design and the spirit of public service. Under the program's innovative structure, the Enterprise Rose Architectural Fellows work deeply in communities for three years, forging community ties, developing leadership skills, and expanding the capacity of their local host organizations to execute projects with the best possible designs, meaningful community engagement, and the most advanced green building features. Fellows and host organizations promote the principles and best practices of community architecture in a variety of venues, including teaching, conference presentations, and publications. They have initiated the adoption of improved design standards and best practices by their state and local governments and industry organizations. The annual stipend paid to fellows in most communities is $45,000 ($52,000 in high-cost cities, including Los Angeles) an amount that will remain the same for the three years of the fellowship. High cost area may merit a salary adjustment. Adjustments, if any, are described in the application kit for a specific fellowship.
Requirements: Applicants must have a Social Security number or a United States Tax Identification number and must possess a professional degree in architecture from an accredited college or university, or expect to graduate from an accredited school of architecture before the fellowship begins. A professional graduate degree in architecture is preferred. The expected minimum grade point average is "B" or 3.0 on a 4.0 scale for all undergraduate and graduate work. Preference will be given to candidates who have approximately three years professional experience, have completed their Intern Development Program (IDP) requirements, and can work independently within a non-profit environment. However, recent graduates will also be considered, as will candidates who have not yet completed their IDP requirements. Fellows must make a full-time commitment of three years to the fellowship and to the host organization. Applicants with diverse educational, professional, and personal backgrounds, and individuals from disadvantaged communities, as well as minorities are encouraged to apply.
Restrictions: A Fellow may not have any other paid employment or independent consulting work, unless prior written permission is given by the director of the fellowship and an authorized representative of the partner organization. Individuals currently employed by their partner organization are not eligible to apply.
Geographic Focus: All States
Date(s) Application is Due: May 1
Amount of Grant: 45,000 - 52,000 USD
Contact: Trinity Simons, Program Officer; (781) 235-2006 or (781) 235-4011; tsimons@enterprisecommunity.org or rosefellowship@enterprisecommunity.org
Internet: http://www.enterprisecommunity.com/solutions-and-innovation/design-leadership/rose-architectural-fellowship
Sponsor: Enterprise Community Partners
70 Corporate Center
Columbia, MD 21044

Enterprise Community Partners Terwilliger Fellowship 1720

This fellowship is named for Enterprise Trustee J. Ronald Terwilliger, chairman and CEO of Trammel Crow Residential. This one-year Fellowship plays a leadership role in launching the new Enterprise Innovation Unit, which has primary responsibility for innovation: research, development and planning of potential new Enterprise programs, products and partnerships. The fellow works with the Enterprise executive management team and key partners to develop new solutions to advance Enterprise's mission.
Geographic Focus: All States
Contact: Dave Epley, (410) 772-2411; depley@enterprisecommunity.org
Internet: http://www.enterprisecommunity.com/about/fellowships-and-awards
Sponsor: Enterprise Community Partners
70 Corporate Center
Columbia, MD 21044

Enterprise Rent-A-Car Foundation Grants 1721

The Foundation's mission is to give back to and to strengthen the thousands of communities where employees and customers work and live. The Foundation supports four key focus areas: local causes by joining employees and providing a fifty percent match of contributions to United Way through the community; provides financial resources to worthwhile nonprofit initiatives that are actively supported by employees and customers; provides more sizable special grants to nonprofit groups or causes of significant strategic or social importance; and supports relief projects or causes the company deems important as they arise, such as natural disasters. A brief written proposal is requested. The Foundation Board meets three times each year.
Requirements: The Foundation provides grants only to qualified tax exempt 501(c)3 organizations in the United States.
Restrictions: Neither the Foundation nor the company donates vehicles or rentals. The Foundation considers the support of schools, churches, and sports teams a personal responsibility, and therefore discourages requests for Foundation support of these types of organizations.
Geographic Focus: All States
Date(s) Application is Due: Jan 19; Apr 6; Sep 7
Amount of Grant: 2,500 - 5,000 USD
Contact: Jo Ann Kindle, President; (314) 512-2754
Internet: http://206.196.101.205/what_we_believe/our_foundation.html
Sponsor: Enterprise Rent-A-Car Foundation
600 Corporate Park Drive
Saint Louis, MO 63105

EPA Air Pollution Control Program Support Grants 1722
The objectives of the Air Pollution Control Support program are to assist State, Tribal, Municipal, Intermunicipal, and Interstate agencies in planning, developing, establishing, improving, and maintaining adequate programs for the continuing prevention and control of air pollution and/or in the implementation of national primary and secondary air quality standards. Projects should also focus on addressing environmental justice (EJ) concerns in communities. EJ is the fair treatment and meaningful involvement of all people regardless of race, color, national origin, or income with respect to the development, implementation, and enforcement of environmental laws, regulations, and policies. Grant funds may be used for costs specifically incurred in the conduct of a State/Local/Tribal Air Pollution Control Program in accordance with the purposes enumerated in the approved application. These include personnel costs, supplies, equipment, training of personnel, travel, and other necessary expenditures during the approved project period. The range of funding is approximately $71,471 to $6,689,317 per recipient; average awards will be approximately $1,545,000. Contact the headquarters or regional office, as appropriate, for application deadlines.
Requirements: Municipal, Intermunicipal, State, Federally Recognized Indian Tribe, or Interstate or Intertribal with legal responsibility for appropriate air pollution planning, development, establishment, implementation, and maintenance of Clean Air Act air pollution control activities, including management of grant support for those activities, provided such organization furnishes funds for the current year that are equal to or in excess of its recurrent expenditures for the previous year for its approved section 105 air pollution program.
Restrictions: Funds may not be used for construction of facilities, nor for expenses incurred other than during each approved award period. Grant funds may not be used to subsidize the costs of Title V operating permit programs or to supplant otherwise available recipient resources.
Geographic Focus: All States
Amount of Grant: 71,471 - 6,689,317 USD
Contact: Jeff Whitlow, (919) 541-5523; whitlow.jeff@epa.gov
Internet: https://www.cfda.gov/?s=program&mode=form&tab=step1&id=67996d 79410 4121fd4f6b2460147c8b3
Sponsor: Environmental Protection Agency
Ariel Rios North Building
Washington, DC 20460

EPA Brownfields Area-Wide Planning Grants 1723
Brownfields Area-Wide Planning is an EPA grant program which provides funding to recipients to conduct research, technical assistance and training that will result in an area-wide plan and implementation strategy for key brownfield sites, which will help inform the assessment, cleanup and reuse of brownfields properties and promote area-wide revitalization. Funding is directed to specific areas, such as a neighborhood, downtown district, local commercial corridor, or city block, affected by a single large or multiple brownfield sites.
Requirements: Eligible governmental entities include a general purpose local unit of government; a land clearance authority or other quasi-governmental entity that operates under the supervision and control of, or as an agent of, a general purpose unit of government; a governmental entity created by a state legislature; a regional council or group of general purpose units of local government; a redevelopment agency that is chartered or otherwise sanctioned by a state; a state; an Indian Tribe (other than in Alaska), or an Alaskan Native Regional Corporation and an Alaska Native Village Corporation as those terms are defined in the Alaska Native Claims Settlement Act (43 U.S.C. 1601 and following); and the Metlakatla Indian Community. Eligible nonprofit organizations include any corporation, trust, association, cooperative, or other organization that is operated mainly for scientific, educational, service, charitable, or similar purpose in the public interest; is not organized primarily for profit; and uses net proceeds to maintain, improve, or expand the operation of the organization.
Geographic Focus: All States
Amount of Grant: Up to 200,000 USD
Contact: Director; (202) 566-2777; fax (202) 566-2757
Internet: http://www.epa.gov/brownfields/areawide_grants.htm
Sponsor: Environmental Protection Agency
1301 Constitution Avenue, NW
Washington, DC 20004

EPA Brownfields Assessment Pilot Grants 1724
Assessment grants provide funding for a grant recipient to inventory, characterize, assess, and conduct planning and community involvement related to brownfields sites. An eligible entity may apply for up to $200,000 to assess a site contaminated by hazardous substances, pollutants, or contaminants (including hazardous substances co-mingled with petroleum) and up to $200,000 to address a site contaminated by petroleum. Applicants may seek a waiver of the $200,00 limit and request up to $350,000 for a site contaminated by hazardous substances, pollutants, or contaminants and up to $350,000 to assess a site contaminated by petroleum. Such waivers must be based on the anticipated level of hazardous substances, pollutants, or contaminants (including hazardous substances co-mingled with petroleum) at a single site. A coalition of three or more eligible applicants can submit one grant proposal under the name of one of the coalition members for up to $ 1,000,000. The performance period for these grants is three years.
Requirements: Eligible governmental entities include a general purpose local unit of government; a land clearance authority or other quasi-governmental entity that operates under the supervision and control of, or as an agent of, a general purpose unit of government; a governmental entity created by a state legislature; a regional council or group of general purpose units of local government; a redevelopment agency that is chartered or otherwise sanctioned by a state; a state; an Indian Tribe (other than in Alaska), or an Alaskan Native Regional Corporation and an Alaska Native Village Corporation as those terms are defined in the Alaska Native Claims Settlement Act (43 U.S.C. 1601 and following); and the Metlakatla Indian Community. Eligible nonprofit organizations include any corporation, trust, association, cooperative, or other organization that is operated mainly for scientific, educational, service, charitable, or similar purpose in the public interest; is not organized primarily for profit; and uses net proceeds to maintain, improve, or expand the operation of the organization.
Geographic Focus: All States
Amount of Grant: 200,000 - 1,000,000 USD
Contact: Director; (202) 566-2777; fax (202) 566-2757
Internet: http://www.epa.gov/brownfields/assessment_grants.htm
Sponsor: Environmental Protection Agency
1301 Constitution Avenue, NW
Washington, DC 20004

EPA Brownfields Cleanup Grants 1725
Cleanup grants provide funding for a grant recipient to carry out cleanup activities at brownfield sites. An eligible entity may apply for up to $200,000 per site. Due to budget limitations, no entity can apply for funding cleanup activities at more than three sites. These funds may be used to address sites contaminated by petroleum and hazardous substances, pollutants, or contaminants (including hazardous substances co-mingled with petroleum). Cleanup grants require a 20 percent cost share, which may be in the form of a contribution of money, labor, material, or services, and must be for eligible and allowable costs (the match must equal 20 percent of the amount of funding provided by EPA and cannot include administrative costs). A cleanup grant applicant may request a waiver of the 20 percent cost share requirement based on hardship. An applicant must own the site for which it is requesting funding at time of application. The performance period for these grants is three years.
Requirements: Eligible governmental entities include a general purpose local unit of government; a land clearance authority or other quasi-governmental entity that operates under the supervision and control of, or as an agent of, a general purpose unit of government; a governmental entity created by a state legislature; a regional council or group of general purpose units of local government; a redevelopment agency that is chartered or otherwise sanctioned by a state; a state; an Indian Tribe (other than in Alaska), or an Alaskan Native Regional Corporation and an Alaska Native Village Corporation as those terms are defined in the Alaska Native Claims Settlement Act (43 U.S.C. 1601 and following); and the Metlakatla Indian Community. Eligible nonprofit organizations include any corporation, trust, association, cooperative, or other organization that is operated mainly for scientific, educational, service, charitable, or similar purpose in the public interest; is not organized primarily for profit; and uses net proceeds to maintain, improve, or expand the operation of the organization.
Geographic Focus: All States
Contact: Director; (202) 566-2777; fax (202) 566-2757
Internet: http://www.epa.gov/brownfields/cleanup_grants.htm
Sponsor: Environmental Protection Agency
1301 Constitution Avenue, NW
Washington, DC 20004

EPA Brownfields Environmental Workforce Development & Job Training Grants 1726
Annual Environmental Workforce Development and Job Training grants allow nonprofit and other organizations to recruit, train, and place predominantly low-income and minority, unemployed and under-employed people living in areas affected by solid and hazardous waste. Residents learn the skills needed to secure full-time, sustainable employment in the environmental field, including assessment and cleanup. These green jobs reduce environmental contamination and build more sustainable futures for communities.
Requirements: Eligible governmental entities include a general purpose local unit of government; a land clearance authority or other quasi-governmental entity that operates under the supervision and control of, or as an agent of, a general purpose unit of government; a governmental entity created by a state legislature; a regional council or group of general purpose units of local government; a redevelopment agency that is chartered or otherwise sanctioned by a state; a state; an Indian Tribe (other than in Alaska), or an Alaskan Native Regional Corporation and an Alaska Native Village Corporation as those terms are defined in the Alaska Native Claims Settlement Act (43 U.S.C. 1601 and following); and the Metlakatla Indian Community. Eligible nonprofit organizations include any corporation, trust, association, cooperative, or other organization that is operated mainly for scientific, educational, service, charitable, or similar purpose in the public interest; is not organized primarily for profit; and uses net proceeds to maintain, improve, or expand the operation of the organization.
Geographic Focus: All States
Contact: Director; (202) 566-2777; fax (202) 566-2757
Internet: http://www.epa.gov/brownfields/job.htm
Sponsor: Environmental Protection Agency
1301 Constitution Avenue, NW
Washington, DC 20004

EPA Brownfields Training, Research, and Technical Assistance Grants 1727
Funding for the brownfields training, research, and technical assistance grants and cooperative agreements is authorized under §104(k)(6) of the Comprehensive Environmental Response, Compensation, and Liability Act of 1980, as amended, (CERCLA or Superfund), 42 U.S.C. 9604(k)(6). This statute authorizes EPA to provide, or fund eligible entities or nonprofit organizations to provide brownfields training, research, and technical assistance to individuals and organizations. EPA awards grants and cooperative agreements authorized by 104(k) under a statutory ranking system that includes factors relating to community need, impact on human health and the environment, stimulation or leveraging of other funds, eligibility for funding from other sources, effective use of existing infrastructure. In addition to the statutory factors, EPA also evaluates applicants based on their ability to manage grants and other policy based factors intended to promote effective stewardship of Federal funds
Requirements: Eligible governmental entities include a general purpose local unit of government; a land clearance authority or other quasi-governmental entity that operates under the supervision

and control of, or as an agent of, a general purpose unit of government; a governmental entity created by a state legislature; a regional council or group of general purpose units of local government; a redevelopment agency that is chartered or otherwise sanctioned by a state; a state; an Indian Tribe (other than in Alaska), or an Alaskan Native Regional Corporation and an Alaska Native Village Corporation as those terms are defined in the Alaska Native Claims Settlement Act (43 U.S.C. 1601 and following); and the Metlakatla Indian Community. Eligible nonprofit organizations include any corporation, trust, association, cooperative, or other organization that is operated mainly for scientific, educational, service, charitable, or similar purpose in the public interest; is not organized primarily for profit; and uses net proceeds to maintain, improve, or expand the operation of the organization.
Geographic Focus: All States
Contact: Director; (202) 566-2777; fax (202) 566-2757
Internet: http://www.epa.gov/brownfields/trta_k6/index.htm
Sponsor: Environmental Protection Agency
1301 Constitution Avenue, NW
Washington, DC 20004

EPA Children's Health Protection Grants 1728

The objectives of this program are to catalyze community-based and regional projects and other actions that enhance public outreach and communication; assist families in evaluating risks to children and in making informed consumer choices; build partnerships that increase a community's long-term capacity to advance the protection of children's environmental health and safety; leverage private and public investments to enhance environmental quality by enabling community efforts to continue past EPA's ability to provide assistance to communities; and promote protection of children from environmental threats through lessons learned. There are no deadline dates.
Requirements: Eligible applicants include community groups, public nonprofit institutions/organizations, tribal governments, specialized groups, profit organizations, private nonprofit institutions/organizations, and municipal and local governments. Potential applicants are strongly encouraged to discuss proposed projects with or submit preapplications to program staff prior to the completion of a full proposal.
Geographic Focus: All States
Amount of Grant: 5,000 - 250,000 USD
Contact: Office of Children's Health Protection; (202) 564-2188; fax (202) 564-2733; fletcher.bettina@epa.gov
Internet: http://yosemite.epa.gov/ochp/ochpweb.nsf/content/grants.htm
Sponsor: Environmental Protection Agency
1200 Pennsylvania Avenue, NW
Washington, DC 20460

EPA Environmental Education Grants 1729

The grants support environmental education projects that promote environmental stewardship and help develop aware and responsible students, teachers, and citizens. This grant provides financial support for projects which design, demonstrate, or disseminate environmental education practices, methods, or techniques. Matching funds of at least 25% of the total cost of the grant project is required.
Requirements: Local education agencies, colleges or universities, nonprofit organizations, and noncommercial educational broadcasting entities are eligible.
Restrictions: Funds cannot be used for: technical training of environmental management professionals; environmental information projects that have no educational component; lobbying or political activities; advocacy promoting a particular point of view or course of action; non-educational research and development; or construction projects.
Geographic Focus: All States
Amount of Grant: 10,000 - 15,000 USD
Contact: Sheri Jojokian, (202) 564-0451; jojokian.sheri@epa.gov
Internet: http://www.epa.gov/enviroed/grants.html
Sponsor: Environmental Protection Agency
1200 Pennsylvania Avenue, NW
Washington, DC 20460

EPA Environmental Justice Collaborative Problem-Solving Cooperative Agreements Program 1730

This program requires selected applicants, or recipients, to use the EJ Collaborative Program-Solving Model as part of their projects. The purpose of the model is to assist affected communities so they can develop proactive, strategic, and visionary approaches to address their environmental justice issues and to achieve community health and sustainability. The key elements of the model are: issues identification, visioning, and strategic goal-setting; community capacity-building and leadership development; development of multi-stakeholder partnerships and leveraging of resources; consensus building and dispute resolution; construction engagement with other stakeholders; sound management and implementation; and evaluation.
Requirements: Eligible applicants must be an affected local community based organization defined for this program as an entity/organization that is: at the most basic level of the organizational hierarchy; located in the same area as the environmental and/or public health program that is described in the application and where the residents of the affected community reside; focused primarily on addressing the environmental and/or public health problems of the residents of the affected community; and comprised primarily of members of the affected community.
Restrictions: Ineligible applicants are: colleges and universities; hospitals; state and local governments and federally recognized Indian tribal governments; quasi-governmental entities; national, multi-state, or state-wide organizations with chapters; and non-profit organizations that engage in lobbying activities.
Geographic Focus: All States

Amount of Grant: 100,000 USD
Contact: Office of Environmental Justice; (800) 962-6215
Internet: http://www.epa.gov/compliance/environmentaljustice/grants/ej-cps-grants.html
Sponsor: Environmental Protection Agency
1200 Pennsylvania Avenue, NW
Washington, DC 20460

EPA Environmental Justice Small Grants 1731

The primary purpose of proposed projects should be to develop a comprehensive understanding of environmental and public health issues, identify ways to address these issues at the local level, and educate and empower the community. The long-term goals of the program are to help build the capacity of the affected community and create self-sustaining, community-based partnerships that will continue to improve local environments in the future. An estimated $1,250,000 will be used to support non-profit organizations with activities that address environmental justice concerns, including but not limited to: increase awareness of and lessen impacts from stormwater; actively address harmful air particles that affect the health and well being of residence; build capacity of community leaders, adults and youth through health data collection activities and watershed education; promote the connection of health issues to environmental quality through comprehensive outreach and education; reduce pesticide exposure and improve health of farm-workers by training health care providers about pesticide exposure; monitoring farm-workers' working conditions; and encourage healthy, environmentally friendly alternatives to industrially produced agriculture. The range of awards is $20,000 to $50,000 per fiscal year, with an average award being $25,000.
Requirements: Grants and cooperative agreements are available to support recipients' allowable direct costs incident to approved surveys, studies, and investigations plus allowable direct costs in accordance with established EPA policies and procedures. Assistance agreement awards under this program may involve or relate to geospatial information. An eligible applicant must be: an incorporated non-profit organization or a Native American tribal government (Federally recognized) located within the same state(s), territory, commonwealth, or tribe that the proposed project will be located. In addition, an eligible applicant must be able to demonstrate that it has worked directly with the affected community.
Geographic Focus: All States, District of Columbia, Guam, Marshall Islands, Northern Mariana Islands, Puerto Rico, U.S. Virgin Islands, American Samoa
Amount of Grant: 20,000 - 50,000 USD
Contact: Sheila Lewis, (202) 564-0152; lewis.sheila@epa.gov
Internet: https://www.cfda.gov/?s=program&mode=form&tab=step1&id=4240ebf8cadda0fedacaabdfa7ed319f
Sponsor: Environmental Protection Agency
1200 Pennsylvania Avenue, NW
Washington, DC 20460

EPA Environmental Justice Small Grants 1732

The purpose of this grant program is to support and empower communities that are working on local solutions to local environmental and/or public health issues. The program is designed to assist recipients in building collaborative partnerships that will help them understand and address the environmental and/or public health issues in their communities. Successful collaborative partnerships with other stakeholders involve well-designed strategic plans to build, maintain and sustain the partnerships, and to work towards addressing the local environmental and/or public health issues.
Requirements: An eligible applicant must be either a non-profit organization as designated by the IRS, or a non-profit organization, recognized by the state, territory, commonwealth, or tribe in which it is located.
Restrictions: Ineligible recipients include: colleges and universities; hospitals; state and local governments and federally recognized Indian tribal governments; quasi-governmental entities; national, multi-state, or state-wide organizations with chapters; and non-profit organizations that engage in lobbying activities.
Geographic Focus: All States
Contact: Director, Office of Environmental Justice; (800) 962-6215
Internet: http://www.epa.gov/compliance/environmentaljustice/index.html
Sponsor: Environmental Protection Agency
1200 Pennsylvania Avenue, NW
Washington, DC 20460

EPA Hazardous Waste Management Grants for Tribes 1733

The Hazardous Waste Management Grant program for Tribes provides capacity building grants to federally recognized tribes and tribal organizations. Its goal is to encourage comprehensive integrated hazardous waste management practices that are protective of human health and the environment by: building tribal capacity for developing and implementing hazardous waste activities; developing tribal organizational infrastructure; achieving economic sustainability of tribal hazardous waste programs; and building partnerships among tribes, federal agencies, states and local communities.
Requirements: Eligible to apply are nonprofit entities including public authorities (federal, state, interstate, and local); public agencies and institutions; private agencies, institutions; and Indian tribes.
Restrictions: For-profit organizations are not eligible to apply.
Geographic Focus: All States
Contact: Tonya Hawkins, Tribal Co-Lead; (703) 308-8278; hawkins.tonya@epa.gov
Internet: http://www.epa.gov/wastes/wyl/tribal/finance.htm
Sponsor: Environmental Protection Agency
1200 Pennsylvania Avenue, NW
Washington, DC 20460

EPA Pestwise Registration Improvement Act Partnership Grants 1734
Each year PestWise programs form dozens of new partnerships by awarding more than $3.1 million in grants to growers and researchers across the country. These grants fund projects that are exploring innovative practices, technologies and regulatory solutions to promote Integrated Pest Management (IPM) adoption. Established in 2008, the Pesticide Registration Improvement Act Partnership (PRIA) funds grant projects that advance public-private partnerships focusing on pesticide stewardship efforts, especially the use of Integrated Pest Management (IPM). Projects utilize demonstration, outreach, and/or education to increase the adoption of reduced-risk/IPM approaches. The PRIA partnership seeks to achieve the following goals: promote partnerships between stakeholders, producers, commodity groups, scientists, extension, and government agencies to demonstrate, promote, and expand reduced-risk/IPM practices; measure and document the effects and impacts of using the reduced risk/IPM programs on the environment, human health, and community; and promote the economic benefits of implementing IPM approaches and provide pesticide users data and analysis on costs associated with adopting IPM.
Requirements: Funding has historically been available to: states; U.S. territories or possessions; federally recognized Indian Tribal Governments; Native American organizations; public and private universities; hospitals and laboratories; commodity organizations, farmer groups, and other public or private nonprofit institutions; and individuals.
Geographic Focus: All States, District of Columbia, Guam, Marshall Islands, Northern Mariana Islands, Puerto Rico, U.S. Virgin Islands, American Samoa
Contact: Grants Administrator; (800) 972-7717; pesp.info@epa.gov
Internet: http://www.epa.gov/pestwise/pria2/index.html
Sponsor: Environmental Protection Agency
1200 Pennsylvania Avenue, NW
Washington, DC 20460

EPA Regional Agricultural IPM Grants 1735
The objective of the EPA Regional Agricultural IPM Grants program is to support Integrated Pest Management (IPM) implementation and approaches that reduce the risks associated with pesticide use in agriculture in the United States. This program is a competitive grant and funding is awarded by EPA's Regional grant offices. Grants may be used to fund projects that further the implementation of Integrated Pest Management (IPM) in agriculture. The type of projects that will be considered include research, monitoring, demonstration, and related activities. Projects must include efforts to implement IPM practices which lead to pest and pesticide risk reduction. Grants will range from $20,000 to $50,500, with the average being $50,000.
Requirements: Eligible applicants include the 50 States, the District of Columbia, the U.S. Virgin Islands, the Commonwealth of Puerto Rico, any Territory or Possession of the United States, any agency or instrumentality of a State including State Universities, and all Federally recognized Native American Tribes.
Restrictions: Local governments, private universities, private nonprofit entities, private businesses, and individuals are not eligible.
Geographic Focus: All States, District of Columbia, Marshall Islands, Northern Mariana Islands, Puerto Rico, U.S. Virgin Islands, American Samoa
Amount of Grant: 20,000 - 50,500 USD
Contact: Frank Ellis, (703) 308-8107; ellis.frank@epa.gov
Internet: https://www.cfda.gov/?s=program&mode=form&tab=step1&id=f381af076a712bcf95e545ba8053a8f4
Sponsor: Environmental Protection Agency
1200 Pennsylvania Avenue, NW
Washington, DC 20460

EPA Senior Environmental Employment Grants 1736
The objective of the program is to use the talents of Americans 55 years of age or older to provide technical assistance to federal, state, and local environmental agencies for projects of pollution research, prevention, abatement, and control. The Environmental Programs Assistance Act of 1984 (Pub. L. 98-313) authorized the Administrator of the EPA "to make grants to, or enter into cooperative agreements with private, nonprofit organizations designated by the Secretary of Labor under Title V of the Older Americans Act of 1965." These cooperative agreements are to utilize the talents of older Americans in temporary, full time or part time positions "providing technical assistance to Federal, State, and local environmental agencies for projects of pollution prevention, abatement, and control." "Technical assistance" may include any activity performed for the EPA in support of its projects ranging from inspections of underground storage tanks, to support for a Headquarters staff office. This allows for the coverage of all types of SEE program positions from professional to clerical. Annual funding priorities are not established at the SEE program level. Rather, Senior Resource Officials from the participating 65 program offices establish priorities requiring SEE program support. Applications are accepted at any time. The range is estimated to be $6,000 to $621,400, with the average grant funding being $137,000.
Requirements: Private, nonprofit organizations designated by the Secretary of Labor under Title V of the Older Americans Act are eligible to apply. Preapplication coordination is required.
Geographic Focus: All States
Amount of Grant: 6,000 - 621,400 USD
Contact: Susan Street; (202) 564-0410; fax (202) 564-0735; street.susan@epa.gov
Internet: https://www.cfda.gov/?s=program&mode=form&tab=step1&id=e2ef498a4772f0fc0eb25619aa62c7fa
Sponsor: Environmental Protection Agency
1200 Pennsylvania Avenue, NW
Washington, DC 20460

EPA Source Reduction Assistance Grants 1737
The goal of the EPA Source Reduction Assistance program is to provide grants to support pollution prevention (P2, source reduction and/or resource conservation activities). The goal of the RP2INC program is to fund an organization which will serve as the national coordinator of the regional P2 Resource Exchange Centers. The national coordinator will provide leadership in: framing national P2 initiatives, strengthening collaboration among the regional centers, evaluating P2 information, tools and products, and marketing the centers' services nationally. EPA is interested in supporting pollution prevention, source reduction and resource conservation projects that will provide an overall benefit to the environment by preventing pollutants at the source. Source reduction projects can include but are not limited to: improving facility and institutional operations that reduce pollutant use and exposure; reformulating and procuring products to reduce toxic constituents; providing direct technical assistance to businesses and other organizations; encouraging green product design and manufacturing; conducting outreach; collecting and analyzing data; and integrating pollution prevention concepts into state, regional and tribal environmental multimedia programs.
Requirements: Assistance under this program is available to the fifty States, the District of Columbia, the United States Virgin Islands, the Commonwealth of Puerto Rico, any territory or possession of the United States, local governments, city or township governments, independent school district governments, state controlled institutions of higher education, federally-recognized tribal governments, non-profits other than institutions of higher education, private institutions of higher education, and community-based grassroots organizations. Nonprofit organizations must be able to demonstrate that they are eligible through documentation of nonprofit status provided the U.S. Internal Revenue Service or their state of incorporation.
Geographic Focus: All States, District of Columbia, Guam, Marshall Islands, Puerto Rico, U.S. Virgin Islands, American Samoa
Amount of Grant: 20,000 - 130,000 USD
Contact: Beth Anderson, (202) 564-8833; fax (202) 564-8901; anderson.beth@epa.gov
Internet: https://www.cfda.gov/?s=program&mode=form&tab=step1&id=5e18c42c08081b24587fb3704d83b3a4
Sponsor: Environmental Protection Agency
1200 Pennsylvania Avenue, NW
Washington, DC 20460

EPA State Indoor Radon Grants 1738
Title III of the Toxic Substances Control Act (TSCA), the Indoor Radon Abatement Act (IRAA), Section 306, authorizes EPA to assist States and Federally Recognized Indian Tribes to develop and implement programs to assess and mitigate radon-related lung cancer risk. The EPA will encourage state and tribal grant recipients to work collaboratively with their (non-EPA) Federal Departments and Agencies participating in the Federal Radon Action Plan (FRAP). Projects should also focus on addressing environmental justice (EJ) concerns in communities. EJ is the fair treatment and meaningful involvement of all people regardless of race, color, national origin, or income with respect to the development, implementation, and enforcement of environmental laws, regulations, and policies. Projects funded by SIRG should focus on achieving the following outcomes: building homes to include radon-reducing features, especially in high-radon potential areas; reducing the radon level in existing homes to below 4pCi/L; and building new schools to include radon-reducing features, and reducing radon in existing schools to below 4pCi/L. To achieve these outcomes and increase results, the SIRG program aims to: improve the effectiveness of state-local/tribal radon programs; focus on high radon potential areas, especially for new home building, building code adoption, and green and healthy homes programs; encourage testing and mitigation within residential property transfers; and encourage SIRG recipients to be strategic in their risk reduction efforts and results reporting, e.g., by institutionalizing risk reduction practices and policies, utilizing best practices, and developing better sources of data and information. The following activities are eligible for funding under SIRG: radon surveys, public information and educational materials, radon control programs, purchase of radon measurement equipment or devices, purchase and maintenance of analytic equipment, training, program overhead and administration, data storage and management, mitigation demonstrations, and toll-free hotlines. The award range is $10,000 to $807,400, with the average grant being $180,000.
Requirements: Eligible entities include States (including District of Columbia), Puerto Rico, the Virgin Islands, Guam, the Canal Zone, American Samoa, the Northern Mariana Islands, Federally recognized Indian Tribes and Tribal consortia, or any other U.S. Territory or possession.
Restrictions: The statute places the following restrictions on the use of Federal funds: SIRG recipients must perform satisfactorily in the preceding budget period to be eligible to receive additional funding; State expenditures for measurement equipment/devices and mitigation demonstrations cannot exceed 50 percent of the grant amount in a budget period; State expenditures for general overhead and program administration cannot exceed 25 percent in a budget period; and SIRG applicants may use grant funds for financial assistance to persons only to the extent that such assistance is related to approved demonstration projects or the purchase and analysis of radon measurement devices.
Geographic Focus: All States, District of Columbia, Guam, Marshall Islands, Northern Mariana Islands, Puerto Rico, U.S. Virgin Islands, American Samoa
Amount of Grant: 10,000 - 807,400 USD
Contact: Philip Jalbert, (202) 343-9431; jalbert.philip@epa.gov
Internet: https://www.cfda.gov/?s=program&mode=form&tab=step1&id=0395d4c36729eaf64cb93d4020aa662c
Sponsor: Environmental Protection Agency
Ariel Rios North Building
Washington, DC 20460

EPA State Senior Environmental Employment Grants 1739

The objective of the program is to use the talents of Americans 55 years of age or older to provide technical assistance to State environmental agencies for projects of pollution prevention, abatement, and control to achieve the Agency's goals of Clean Air; Clean and Safe Water; Land Preservation and Restoration; Healthy Communities and Ecosystems; and Compliance and Environmental Stewardship. The Environmental Programs Assistance Act of 1984 (Pub. L. 98-313) authorized the Administrator of the EPA "to make grants to, or enter into cooperative agreements with private, nonprofit organizations designated by the Secretary of Labor under Title V of the Older Americans Act of 1965." These cooperative agreements are to utilize the talents of older Americans in temporary, full time or part time positions "providing technical assistance to Federal, State, and local environmental agencies for projects of pollution prevention, abatement, and control." Technical assistance may include any activity performed for the State in support of its projects ranging from inspections of large capacity cesspools, to support for a State Environmental staff office. This allows for coverage of all types of SEE program positions from professional to clerical. Awards are estimated to range from $50,000 to $250,000, with the average being $185,000.
Requirements: Private, nonprofit organizations designated by the Secretary of Labor under Title V of the Older Americans Act are eligible to apply. Pre-application coordination is required. Environmental impact information is not required for this program.
Geographic Focus: All States
Amount of Grant: 50,000 - 250,000 USD
Contact: Susan Street; (202) 564-0410; fax (202) 564-0735; street.susan@epa.gov
Internet: https://www.cfda.gov/?s=program&mode=form&tab=step1&id=56ce19745ac87bf4293b2eaff9c26bd0
Sponsor: Environmental Protection Agency
1200 Pennsylvania Avenue, NW
Washington, DC 20460

EPA Surveys, Studies, Research, Investigations, Demonstrations, and Special Purpose Activities Relating to the Clean Air Act 1740

The primary objective of the program is to support Surveys, Studies, Research, Investigations, Demonstrations and Special Purpose assistance relating to the causes, effects (including health and welfare effects), extent, prevention, and control of air pollution to include such topics as air quality, acid deposition, climate change, global programs, indoor environments, radiation, mobile source technology and community-driven approaches to transportation and emissions reduction. Projects should also focus on addressing environmental justice (EJ) concerns in communities. EJ is the fair treatment and meaningful involvement of all people regardless of race, color, national origin, or income with respect to the development, implementation, and enforcement of environmental laws, regulations, and policies. Grants and cooperative agreements are available to support recipients' allowable direct costs incident to approved Surveys, Studies, Research, Investigations, Demonstrations and Special Purpose plus allowable indirect costs, in accordance with established EPA policies and regulations. Assistance agreement awards under this program may involve or relate to geospatial information. A detailed list of acceptable activities is provided at the grant website. EPA generally award grants ranging in value from $5,000 to $750,000 per fiscal year. The average value of each grant is $150,000 per fiscal year. Contact the headquarters or regional office, as appropriate, for application deadlines.
Requirements: Assistance under this program is generally available to States, local governments, territories, Indian Tribes, and possessions of the U.S., including the District of Columbia, international organizations, public and private universities and colleges, hospitals, laboratories, other public or private nonprofit institutions, which submit applications proposing projects with significant technical merit and relevance to EPA's Office of Air and Radiation's mission.
Geographic Focus: All States
Amount of Grant: 5,000 - 750,000 USD
Contact: Maureen Hingeley, (202) 564-1306; hingeley.maureen@epa.gov
Internet: https://www.cfda.gov/?s=program&mode=form&tab=step1&id=1d601ed2ad50dabb4dd11eaa76bb7764
Sponsor: Environmental Protection Agency
Ariel Rios North Building
Washington, DC 20460

EPA Tribal Solid Waste Management Assistance Grants 1741

The Tribal Solid Waste Management Assistance Project is a mechanism by which the participating agencies provide financial assistance to tribes. Through this EPA lead initiative tribes can apply for funding under the following categories: Category 1 - characterize and assess open dumps; Category 2 - develop integrated solid waste management plans; Category 3 - establish alternative solid waste management options (i.e., transfer station, enforcement codes); and Category 4 - close, clean-up or upgrade an open dump. In additional, Tribal Solid Waste Interagency Workgroups were created to provide federal assistance to tribes in complying with the municipal solid waste landfill criteria, establish integrated solid waste management programs, and to close open dumps.
Requirements: Eligible to apply are nonprofit entities including public authorities (federal, state, interstate, and local); public agencies and institutions; private agencies, institutions; and Indian tribes.
Restrictions: For-profit organizations are not eligible to apply.
Geographic Focus: All States
Contact: Tonya Hawkins, Tribal Co-Lead; (703) 308-8278; hawkins.tonya@epa.gov
Internet: http://www.epa.gov/wastes/wyl/tribal/finance.htm
Sponsor: Environmental Protection Agency
1200 Pennsylvania Avenue, NW
Washington, DC 20460

EPA Tribal Support for the National Environmental Info Exchange Network 1742

EPA, states, tribes, and territories, are working together to implement the Exchange Network, a secure, Internet- and standards-based mechanism for electronic data reporting, sharing, and integration of both regulatory and non-regulatory environmental data. Exchange Network partners exchanging data with each other or with EPA should make the Exchange Network the standard way they exchange data and should phase out any legacy methods they have been using. The Plan's objectives include completing infrastructure, exchanging environmental data, and expanding use of the Network to support environmental decision-making. The estimated amount of the award is $160,000. The application deadline is August 30.
Requirements: Federally recognized tribes and multitribe 501(c)3 organizations whose membership consists of federally recognized tribes are eligible to apply.
Geographic Focus: All States, District of Columbia, Guam, Marshall Islands, Northern Mariana Islands, U.S. Virgin Islands, American Samoa
Date(s) Application is Due: Aug 30
Amount of Grant: 160,000 USD
Contact: Salena Reynolds; (202) 566-0466; fax (202) 566-1684; reynolds.salena@epa.gov
Internet: http://www.grants.gov/search-grants.html?agencies%3DEPA|Environmental%20Protection%20Agency
Sponsor: Environmental Protection Agency
1301 Constitution Avenue, NW
Washington, DC 20004

EQT Foundation Art and Culture Grants 1743

The Foundation focuses its resources on areas that have a direct effect on the stability of communities and in turn, contribute to the success of its business operations in those areas. Art and Culture Grants support local initiatives that are designed to give economically disadvantaged youth more exposure to artistic programming, or that promote expanded awareness, understanding and appreciation of the diverse culture and heritage of the regions where EQT operates. Recent examples include: the funding of museums and cultural centers; academic programs exposing students to the history and culture of indigenous people; and multi-cultural/diversity fairs.
Requirements: Nonprofit 501(c)3 organizations in service communities, including Pittsburgh and portions of West Virginia and Kentucky, are eligible.
Restrictions: The Foundation will not consider proposals for the following: institutions, organizations or groups that are not tax exempt under IRS Section 501(c)3; capital campaigns (includes endowments, new construction and building renovations, mortgage/rent/insurance/utility/moving costs, infrastructure improvements, etc.); churches or other organizations whose purpose promotes a particular religious faith or creed; political parties, candidates, or public policy advocates; for-profit activities, businesses, associations or organizations; tax-supported entities; fraternal, social, union or hobby/recreational clubs or organizations; individuals; sporting events, including charity golf outings; emergency or stop-gap funding; or organizations whose mission, operating philosophy or activities conflict with company policy and could potentially damage the company's reputation or could result in negative publicity for the company.
Geographic Focus: Kentucky, Pennsylvania, West Virginia
Date(s) Application is Due: Feb 1; May 1; Aug 1; Nov 1
Contact: Bruce Bickel; (412) 762-3502; fax (412) 762-5439; bruce.bickel@pncadvisors.com
Internet: http://www.eqt.com/ourcommunities/funding-priorities.aspx
Sponsor: EQT Foundation
249 Fifth Avenue, 3rd Floor, One PNC Plaza
Pittsburgh, PA 15222

EQT Foundation Community Grants 1744

The Foundation focuses its resources on areas that have a direct effect on the stability of communities and in turn, contribute to the success of its business operations in those areas. Through its Community Grants program, the Foundation encourages the development of safe, healthy, diverse, livable communities and bordering regions that can attract and retain residential, commercial and industrial growth and sustain a healthy local economy. Recent examples include: the Main Street programs for commercial business districts; community fairs, festivals and other local traditions; programs that promote awareness, acceptance, empowerment and inclusion of diverse populations, including women, seniors, minorities, veterans and the disabled; and volunteerism and community service programs.
Requirements: Nonprofit 501(c)3 organizations in service communities, including Pittsburgh and portions of West Virginia and Kentucky, are eligible.
Restrictions: The Foundation will not consider proposals for the following: institutions, organizations or groups that are not tax exempt under IRS Section 501(c)3; capital campaigns (includes endowments, new construction and building renovations, mortgage/rent/insurance/utility/moving costs, infrastructure improvements, etc.); churches or other organizations whose purpose promotes a particular religious faith or creed; political parties, candidates, or public policy advocates; for-profit activities, businesses, associations or organizations; tax-supported entities; fraternal, social, union or hobby/recreational clubs or organizations; individuals; sporting events, including charity golf outings; emergency or stop-gap funding; or organizations whose mission, operating philosophy or activities conflict with company policy and could potentially damage the company's reputation or could result in negative publicity for the company.
Geographic Focus: Kentucky, Pennsylvania, West Virginia
Date(s) Application is Due: May 1; Aug 1; Nov 1
Contact: Bruce Bickel; (412) 762-3502; fax (412) 762-5439; bruce.bickel@pncadvisors.com
Internet: http://www.eqt.com/ourcommunities/funding-priorities.aspx
Sponsor: EQT Foundation
249 Fifth Avenue, 3rd Floor, One PNC Plaza
Pittsburgh, PA 15222

EQT Foundation Education Grants 1745
The EQT Foundation focuses its resources on areas that have a direct effect on the stability of communities and in turn, contribute to the success of its business operations in those areas. The Foundation's Education Grants provide economically disadvantaged students with greater access to programs that promote proficiency in core academic skills, including reading, writing, math, science, communications and technology. This includes programming that helps these students effectively prepare to compete in the workforce, and have greater choices regarding the routes available to actively support themselves and make positive social and economic contributions to their communities. Examples include: adult literacy programming; computer camps: science fairs; writing competitions; tutors; scholarships; libraries; career planning and preparation; internships; and mentoring.
Requirements: Nonprofit 501(c)3 organizations in service communities, including Pittsburgh and portions of West Virginia and Kentucky, are eligible.
Restrictions: The Foundation will not consider proposals for the following: institutions, organizations or groups that are not tax exempt under IRS Section 501(c)3; capital campaigns (includes endowments, new construction and building renovations, mortgage/rent/insurance/utility/moving costs, infrastructure improvements, etc.); churches or other organizations whose purpose promotes a particular religious faith or creed; political parties, candidates, or public policy advocates; for-profit activities, businesses, associations or organizations; tax-supported entities; fraternal, social, union or hobby/recreational clubs or organizations; individuals; sporting events, including charity golf outings; emergency or stop-gap funding; or organizations whose mission, operating philosophy or activities conflict with company policy and could potentially damage the company's reputation or could result in negative publicity for the company.
Geographic Focus: Kentucky, Pennsylvania, West Virginia
Date(s) Application is Due: Feb 1; May 1; Aug 1; Nov 1
Contact: Bruce Bickel; (412) 762-3502; fax (412) 762-5439; bruce.bickel@pncadvisors.com
Internet: http://www.eqt.com/ourcommunities/funding-priorities.aspx
Sponsor: EQT Foundation
249 Fifth Avenue, 3rd Floor, One PNC Plaza
Pittsburgh, PA 15222

EQT Foundation Environment Grants 1746
The Foundation focuses its resources on areas that have a direct effect on the stability of communities and in turn, contribute to the success of its business operations in those areas. Environment Grants support the preservation of local natural resources and encourage residents and businesses to employ accepted conservation techniques and activities to minimize adverse impacts on the environment. Some recent examples include: community gardens; wildlife and watershed conservation; recycling and energy conservation; environmental education; and preservation and restoration of green spaces.
Requirements: Nonprofit 501(c)3 organizations in service communities, including Pittsburgh and portions of West Virginia and Kentucky, are eligible.
Restrictions: The Foundation will not consider proposals for the following: institutions, organizations or groups that are not tax exempt under IRS Section 501(c)3; capital campaigns (includes endowments, new construction and building renovations, mortgage/rent/insurance/utility/moving costs, infrastructure improvements, etc.); churches or other organizations whose purpose promotes a particular religious faith or creed; political parties, candidates, or public policy advocates; for-profit activities, businesses, associations or organizations; tax-supported entities; fraternal, social, union or hobby/recreational clubs or organizations; individuals; sporting events, including charity golf outings; emergency or stop-gap funding; or organizations whose mission, operating philosophy or activities conflict with company policy and could potentially damage the company's reputation or could result in negative publicity for the company.
Geographic Focus: Kentucky, Pennsylvania, West Virginia
Date(s) Application is Due: May 1; Aug 1; Nov 1
Contact: Bruce Bickel; (412) 762-3502; fax (412) 762-5439; bruce.bickel@pncadvisors.com
Internet: http://www.eqt.com/ourcommunities/funding-priorities.aspx
Sponsor: EQT Foundation
249 Fifth Avenue, 3rd Floor, One PNC Plaza
Pittsburgh, PA 15222

EREF Solid Waste Research Grants 1747
The Environmental Research and Education Foundation is the only private, grant making institution with a national and international scope whose sole mission is to support solid waste research. Its research grants program is led by a Research Council, a body of volunteers consisting of technical experts in industry, academia and consulting. The work of the Council is guided by a long range strategic plan with the goal to achieve greater sustainability, good environmental stewardship, higher process efficiency and increased knowledge. Council recommended projects are then reviewed by the Board's Projects Committee for a final review and funding allocation. EREF awards several grants each year for research or education in topics pertaining to any aspect of solid waste management. There are two annual deadlines for solicited proposal submissions, including January 5 and July 15. There is no formal application, and submissions should include a description of proposed activity, project timeline, budget, and resumes of principal investigators. Previously awarded grants have ranged from $15,000 to over $500,000 with the average grant being amount being $100,000.
Restrictions: Grants will not be provided for capital campaigns; political contributions; religious causes; operating funds; loans; or support of lobbying activities. The Foundation will not pay overhead in excess of 25%. Proposals submitted in response to this RFP that do not address a specific topic in the research agenda will not be reviewed.
Geographic Focus: All States
Date(s) Application is Due: Jan 5; Jul 15
Amount of Grant: 15,000 - 500,000 USD
Contact: Bryan F. Staley; (919) 861-6876, ext. 102; fax (919) 861-6878; bstaley@erefdn.org
Internet: http://erefdn.org/index.php/grants/
Sponsor: Environmental Research and Education Foundation
3301 Benson Drive, Suite 301
Raleigh, NC 27609

EREF Sustainability Research Grants 1748
The Environmental Research and Education Foundation is the only private, grant making institution with a national and international scope whose sole mission is to support solid waste research. Submissions of scientific research proposals related to sustainable solid waste management practices are invited in the following areas: waste minimization; recycling; waste conversion to energy, bio-fuels, chemicals or other useful products, including (but not limited to) the technologies of waste-to-energy, pyrolysis and gasification, oxidation, anaerobic digestion, and composting; and strategies to promote diversion from landfills (e.g. separating organics, market analysis, optimized material management, logistics, etc.). EREF awards several grants each year for research or education in topics pertaining to any aspect of solid waste management. There are two annual deadlines for solicited proposal submissions, including January 5 and July 15. There is no formal application, and submissions should include a description of proposed activity, project timeline, budget, and resumes of principal investigators. Previously awarded grants have ranged from $15,000 to over $500,000 with the average grant being amount being $100,000.
Restrictions: Grants will not be provided for capital campaigns; political contributions; religious causes; operating funds; loans; or support of lobbying activities. The Foundation will not pay overhead in excess of 25%. Proposals submitted in response to this RFP that do not address a specific topic in the research agenda will not be reviewed.
Geographic Focus: All States
Date(s) Application is Due: Jan 5; Jul 15
Amount of Grant: 15,000 - 500,000 USD
Contact: Bryan F. Staley; (919) 861-6876, ext. 102; fax (919) 861-6878; bstaley@erefdn.org
Internet: http://erefdn.org/index.php/grants/proposal
Sponsor: Environmental Research and Education Foundation
3301 Benson Drive, Suite 301
Raleigh, NC 27609

EREF Unsolicited Proposal Grants 1749
Unsolicited proposals consist of research projects or educational initiatives that fit within the EREF's mission statement but may not fit within EREF's Strategic Research Plan. Any proposals for educational initiatives must be used to develop tools (e.g. software, websites, curricula, webinars, seminars, etc.) that specifically promote awareness or increase knowledge of the solid waste industry. The development of tools to be used for commercial purposes, or that will be considered proprietary, will generally not be considered unless approved by the EREF a priori. EREF has two submittal deadlines per year for unsolicited pre-proposals, including October 1 and May 21.
Requirements: ALL unsolicited proposals must complete a pre-proposal application to be considered for funding. Successful pre-proposals will then be invited to submit a full proposal. Pre-proposal applications are not required for solicited proposals.
Restrictions: Grants will not be provided for capital campaigns; political contributions; religious causes; operating funds; loans; or support of lobbying activities. The Foundation will not pay overhead in excess of 25%. Proposals submitted in response to this RFP that do not address a specific topic in the research agenda will not be reviewed.
Geographic Focus: All States
Date(s) Application is Due: May 21; Oct 1
Amount of Grant: 15,000 - 500,000 USD
Contact: Bryan F. Staley; (919) 861-6876, ext. 102; fax (919) 861-6878; bstaley@erefdn.org
Internet: http://erefdn.org/index.php/grants/proposal
Sponsor: Environmental Research and Education Foundation
3301 Benson Drive, Suite 301
Raleigh, NC 27609

Erie Community Foundation Grants 1750
The Erie Community Foundation is a collection of charitable endowments operating under the administrative umbrella of a single public charity. Grants will be awarded in four program areas: quality of life; human services; health; and education. The Foundation's goal is to help local charities more effectively and efficiently accomplish their missions. Application information is available online. Applicants are strongly encouraged to contact the Foundation's program officer prior to submitting an application.
Requirements: Erie, PA, 501(c)3 tax-exempt organizations are eligible.
Restrictions: The Foundation does not fund: program ads; fund raising events/sponsorships; more than 50 percent of the cost of a vehicle; deficit reduction; sectarian religious activities; government funding cuts; start-up organizations; school playgrounds; fire departments or nursing homes.
Geographic Focus: Pennsylvania
Date(s) Application is Due: Feb 2; Aug 3; Oct 16
Amount of Grant: 2,000 - 15,000 USD
Contact: David Gonzalez, Program Officer; (814) 454-0843; fax (814) 456-4965; mbatchelor@eriecommunityfoundation.org
Internet: http://www.eriecommunityfoundation.org/for-grant-seekers/
Sponsor: Erie Community Foundation
459 West 6th Street
Erie, PA 16507

ESRI Conservation Program Grants 1751

The conservation grants program provides donations and discounts of GIS software, data, books, and training. There are no application deadlines. The program does not grant hardware or cash, but partners with many other groups who do (list available online). General grants and basic grants are available. Grants are awarded to organizations that can demonstrate a strong commitment to conservation; compelling reasons to use GIS in obtaining their objectives; and the organizational capacity to use GIS effectively over a long period of time. All applicants must present a credible case for how GIS and the support from ESRI will advance their cause of conservation and environmental protection, broadly defined. Successful applicants will effectively make their case about how they propose to integrate and analyze disparate spatial data to accomplish their goals. To request application materials, send a blank email message (no subject, no content) to ecpgrant@esri.com, or visit the Web site.
Requirements: Eligible applicants are US-based 501c(3) nonprofit organizations that actively engage the public in resource conservation and environmental protection. This includes, but is not limited to, grassroots conservation and environmental organizations, community action groups, economic development organizations, sustainable development groups, community-based conservation groups, growth management organizations, environmental justice groups, and tribal conservation organizations. International groups must have a US-based tax-exempt organization as their sponsor.
Restrictions: The following types of organizations are not eligible to apply: colleges and universities; public schools or school districts; local, state, and federal government agencies or natural resource conservation districts; association and coalitions organized to fund-raise for or to benefit local, state, and federal government agencies; natural resource conservation districts; and CTSP's nonprofit sponsors and their associated members.
Geographic Focus: All States
Contact: Charles Convis; (909) 793-2853, ext. 2488; fax (909) 307-3025; ecp@esri.com
Internet: http://www.conservationgis.org/aaesrigrants.html
Sponsor: Environmental Systems Research Institute
380 New York Street
Redlands, CA 92373-8100

Essex County Community Foundation Discretionary Fund Grants 1752

The grant awards funds across the broad areas of nonprofit activity, including arts and culture, education, environment, health, social and community services and youth services. The Trustees will award Discretionary Fund grants to assist nonprofits with projects which strengthen the capacity of the organization to perform its work more effectively. ECCF is interested in helping organizations improve their infrastructure so that they can better serve their communities and clients. ECCF will consider projects which address capacity building such as: strengthening Board leadership; managing organizational change and growth; providing for strategic organizational planning; supporting leadership transition; strengthening fiscal management; and improving staff skills or other organizational functions which will improve the organization's long-term capacity.
Requirements: Eligible organizations must be Massachusetts 501(c)3 agencies that serve Essex County citizens with operating budgets of less than $500,000.
Restrictions: Funds are not available for: individuals; costs associated with programs or services provided to citizens outside of Essex County; sectarian or religious purposes; political purposes; debt or deficit reduction; capital campaigns for buildings, land acquisition or endowment; or to support academic research. Funding for equipment is limited to purchases that resolve a specific problem, are part of an overall capacity building project and will strengthen the operation of the organization. Equipment for programmatic purposes will not be granted. In general, staff salaries will not be eligible for funding unless the salary is directly tied to developing the capacity of the organization.
Geographic Focus: Massachusetts
Date(s) Application is Due: Feb 10
Amount of Grant: 1,000 - 5,000 USD
Contact: Julie Bishop, Vice President of Grants and Nonprofit Services; (978) 777-8876, ext. 28; fax (978) 777-9454; j.bishop@eccf.org or info@eccf.org
Internet: http://eccf.org/discretionary-fund-42.html
Sponsor: Essex County Community Foundation
175 Andover Street, Suite 101
Danvers, MA 01923

Essex County Community Foundation Emergency Fund Grants 1753

This fund offers assistance, on a one-time basis, to non-profit organizations located within Essex County. The grants are for modest sums based on times of critical need. The fund assists non-profits with a short-term urgent funding need created by an unforeseen event that has or will significantly interrupt essential services such as natural disasters or emergency needs. Requests can be made at any time. Examples of unforeseen events include: natural disasters (e.g. fire, flood, tornado, storm damage, loss of utilities); and emergency needs (e.g. phase-out costs associated with closing a program due to a sudden loss of funding, equipment failure, civil disturbance).
Requirements: Requests may be submitted at any time by Massachusetts 501(c)3 agencies located in and serving Essex County citizens. To initiate a request an agency representative calls or emails the grants coordinator and provides an initial explanation of the emergency situation.
Restrictions: Generally, grants are not awarded: to bail out agencies because of mismanagement or poor planning; budget shortfalls; to assist individuals; for costs associated with programs or services provided to citizens outside of Essex County; for sectarian or religious purposes; for political purposes; to support ongoing program work; or to pay expenses which a group should have anticipated.
Geographic Focus: Massachusetts
Amount of Grant: Up to 5,000 USD
Contact: Julie Bishop, Vice President of Grants and Nonprofit Services; (978) 777-8876, ext. 28; fax (978) 777-9454; j.bishop@eccf.org or info@eccf.org
Internet: http://eccf.org/emergency-fund-43.html
Sponsor: Essex County Community Foundation
175 Andover Street, Suite 101
Danvers, MA 01923

Essex County Community Foundation First Jobs Grant 1754

This initiative promotes summer employment for North Shore teens 14 to 19. Local businesses are encouraged to hire teens directly within their companies. Local businesses, philanthropies and individuals are asked to contribute to a fund at the Essex County Community Foundation so that teens can be hired by local public and non-profit agencies.
Requirements: Eligible applicants are public agencies of local or state government and non-profit organizations interested in providing quality summer employment opportunities for North Shore teens. Non-profit organizations must be recognized as tax exempt under section 501(c)3.
Restrictions: This program is intended for teens from the North Shore area which is defined as 19 cities and towns including: Beverly, Danvers, Essex, Ipswich, Gloucester, Hamilton, Lynn, Lynnfield, Manchester By the Sea, Marblehead, Middleton, Nahant, Peabody, Rockport, Salem, Saugus, Swampscott, Topsfield and Wenham. Funding is limited to non-sectarian programs and positions. Programs or positions sponsored by religious organizations are eligible, provided enrollment is open to individuals of all religious and ethnic backgrounds and the program or position responsibilities are free of mandatory religious instruction, worship, or other sectarian activities.
Geographic Focus: Massachusetts
Date(s) Application is Due: Mar 10
Contact: David McDonald, (978) 741-3805; mcdonald@northshorewib.com
Internet: http://eccf.org/firstjobs63.html
Sponsor: North Shore Workforce Investment Board
70 Washington Street, Suite 314
Salem, MA 01970

Essex County Community Foundation Greater Lawrence Summer Fund Grants 1755

This fund connects donors seeking to support enriching summer opportunities for inner-city youth with agencies in need of funds for their programs. The following describe the desired impact of the funds: to respond to community needs for quality summer programs for as many school age youth as possible; to provide youth with opportunities for skill development, personal growth and exposure to new experiences; to promote and encourage interaction and communication among youth and staff from different ethnic and racial backgrounds and from different neighborhoods; and to gain maximum impact of philanthropic dollars for summer programs. Proposals must be postmarked and in electronic format no later than March 1st.
Requirements: The private non-profit agency serving as the fiscal agent for the program must have been determined to be tax exempt under section 501(c)3 of the Internal Revenue Code, and not a private foundation under Section 509(a). This fund is limited to non-sectarian programming for youth of all religious and ethnic backgrounds. Programs sponsored by religious organizations are eligible, provided the enrollment is open to all youth and the program is free of mandatory religious instruction, worship, or other sectarian activities.
Restrictions: This fund is intended for summer programs serving inner-city school-age youth from Greater Lawrence (Lawrence, Methuen, Andover, and North Andover). Programs serving youth from a diverse geographic area should reserve the funds received through the Summer Fund for youth from these cities.
Geographic Focus: Massachusetts
Date(s) Application is Due: Mar 1
Amount of Grant: 1,000 - 15,000 USD
Contact: Julie Bishop, Vice President of Grants and Nonprofit Services; (978) 777-8876, ext. 28; fax (978) 777-9454; j.bishop@eccf.org or info@eccf.org
Internet: http://eccf.org/greater-lawrence-summer-fund-62.html
Sponsor: Essex County Community Foundation
175 Andover Street, Suite 101
Danvers, MA 01923

Essex County Community Foundation Merrimack Valley General Fund Grants 1756

The fund responds to new and important community needs as they arise. The Merrimack Valley General Fund (MVGF) considers requests from agencies serving Eastern Merrimack Valley communities in most fields of interest including: arts and culture, education, social and community services, and youth service. Particular interest is in programs which: benefit children, particularly those fostering youth development; provide health care services to those without health care coverage and address the need for affordable housing. Other areas of interest include: early childhood education; adult literacy; homelessness; elder care; job development; and food, arts and culture.
Requirements: Only non-profit organizations, recognized as tax exempt under section 501(c)3 are eligible for consideration. The MVGF provides grants to the communities of: Lawrence, Methuen, Haverhill, Andover, North Andover, Boxford, Georgetown, Groveland, W. Newbury, Merrimac, Amesbury, Newburyport, Newbury and Salisbury.
Restrictions: Funds are not available for: individuals; state or local government agencies; political purposes; and sectarian or religious purposes. Generally grants are not awarded for: debt or deficit reduction; replacing public funding, or for purposes which are generally a public sector responsibility; supporting academic research; and traveling outside the region.
Geographic Focus: Massachusetts
Date(s) Application is Due: Oct 1
Amount of Grant: 1,000 - 5,000 USD
Contact: Julie Bishop, Vice President of Grants and Nonprofit Services; (978) 777-8876, ext. 28; fax (978) 777-9454; j.bishop@eccf.org or info@eccf.org
Internet: http://eccf.org/merrimack-valley-general-fund-44.html

Sponsor: Essex County Community Foundation
175 Andover Street, Suite 101
Danvers, MA 01923

Esther M. and Freeman E. Everett Charitable Foundation Grants 1757

Established in Colorado in 2001, the Esther M. and Freeman E. Everett Charitable Foundation gives primarily in Colorado and Wisconsin. Its primary fields of interest include: the arts; children and youth services; education; community foundations; and human services. Since there are no specified application forms, applicants should submit a copy of their IRS determination letter, along with a brief overview of the program, program need, outcomes, and budget. There are no annual deadlines, and grant amounts typically range between $1,000 and $10,000.
Geographic Focus: Colorado, Wisconsin
Amount of Grant: 1,000 - 10,000 USD
Contact: Grant Administrator; (719) 227-6442
Sponsor: Esther M. and Freeman E. Everett Charitable Foundation
30 E. Pikes Peak Avenue
Colorado Springs, CO 80903

Ethel and Raymond F. Rice Foundation Grants 1758

The foundation awards grants to eligible Kansas nonprofit organizations in its areas of interest, including arts and culture; elementary, secondary, and higher education; environmental programs; elderly and youth; and social services. Types of support include capital campaigns, equipment, general support, land acquisition, scholarship funds, and federated giving funds. An application form is required.
Requirements: 501(c)3 nonprofit organizations and colleges and universities, school districts, and schools in Kansas are eligible. The foundation focuses on the areas of Lawrence and Douglas counties.
Geographic Focus: Kansas
Amount of Grant: 1,000 - 150,000 USD
Contact: James Paddock, President; (785) 841-9961
Sponsor: Ethel and Raymond F. Rice Foundation
1617 St. Andrews Drive, 200A
Lawrence, KS 66047

Ethel Frends Foundation Grants 1759

The Ethel Frends Foundation was established in 1997 to support and promote canine care and/or canine education. The Frends Foundation specifically supports organizations that serve the following California counties: Los Angeles, Ventura, Santa Barbara, San Luis Obispo, Orange, Riverside, San Bernardino, and San Diego. Grant requests for general operating support are strongly encouraged. Program support will also be considered. Small, program-related capital expenses may be included in general operating or program requests. Grants from the Frends Foundation are one year in duration. Application materials are available for download at the grant website. Applicants are strongly encouraged to review the state application guidelines for additional helpful information and clarifications before applying. Applicants are also encouraged to review the foundation's funding history (link is available from the grant website). The application deadline for the Ethel Frends Foundation is January 15. Applicants will be notified of grant decisions before February 28.
Geographic Focus: California
Date(s) Application is Due: Jan 15
Contact: Hector Santillan, Vice President; (213) 861-5228; hector.m.santillan@baml.com
Internet: https://www.bankofamerica.com/philanthropic/fn_search.action
Sponsor: Ethel Frends Foundation
515 S. Flower Street, CA9-512-27-01
Los Angeles, CA 90071

Ethel S. Abbott Charitable Foundation Grants 1760

The Ethel S. Abbott Charitable Foundation, established in 1972, offers support for art and culture, education, health, federated giving, and human service programs. The Board of Trustees will generally consider grant requests for capital projects and endowment projects more favorably than grant requests for operating funds. However, the Board will occasionally make an operating grant for the start up of a new 501(c)3 or a program which will become self-sustaining after the start up period. Typically, grants range from $200,000 up to over $2 million. The application and its guidelines can be downloaded from the web site.
Requirements: The primary grant areas are: Lincoln, Nebraska and the surrounding 50 mile radius; Omaha, Nebraska and the surrounding 50 mile radius up to the Missouri River; and Western, Nebraska, which is defined as all parts of the state in the Mountain Time Zone.
Geographic Focus: Nebraska
Amount of Grant: 200,000 - 2,000,000 USD
Contact: Del Lienemann, Sr.; (402) 435-4369; fax (402) 435-4371; info@abbottfoundation.org
Internet: http://www.abbottfoundation.org/request_a_grant/index.html
Sponsor: Ethel S. Abbott Charitable Foundation
P.O. Box 81407
Lincoln, NE 68501-1407

Ethel Sergeant Clark Smith Foundation Grants 1761

The activities of the Ethel Sergeant Clark Smith (ESCS) Memorial Fund focuses on grants to organizations located in Southeastern Pennsylvania, with primary emphasis on those serving community needs in Delaware County. Grants will be made for capital projects, operating expenses and special programs in amounts that are meaningful to the success of the individual endeavors of the organizations. However, operating expense grants are typically awarded for charities without capital requirement and under circumstances where continuing funding is not expected. Grants will be made in areas of medical, educational, cultural, arts, health and welfare, and such other areas as the trustee shall identify and determine from time to time, to be responsive to changes in community needs. Application forms are available online and must be submitted by March 1 or September 1 annually.
Requirements: Southeastern Pennsylvania 501(c)3 non-profit organizations with primary emphasis on those serving community needs in Delaware County, Pennsylvania are eligible to apply. Complete applications should include the following: one original copy of the Proposal which includes the purpose and general activities of the organization should be included as well as a description of the proposed project and its justification, a budget and timetable for the project are also required; one copy of audited financial statements for the last fiscal year (or if not audited, Internal Revenue Service form 990) plus an operating budget for the current period and budgets for future period if appropriate; copy of the Internal Revenue Service tax determination letter which shows the organization is tax-exempt under Section 501(c)3 and that it is not a private foundation under section 509 (a) of the Internal Revenue Code. Any organization that is awarded a grant will be required to sign a Grant Agreement Form prior to the distribution of funds. Approximately one year after a grant has been awarded, a Progress Report should be completed by the organization. This information must be submitted prior to the consideration of any new proposals.
Restrictions: Grants will not be considered for the following: deficit financing; construction or renovations to real estate not owned by the charitable entity; salaries; professional fund raiser fees; multi-year grants over three years; to any organization more than once in a given year; to any organization more than three years in succession; any organization receiving a grant over a three year period or in three successive years will not be eligible for a future grant until two years transpire after the three year period.
Geographic Focus: Pennsylvania
Date(s) Application is Due: Mar 1; Sep 1
Contact: Wachovia Bank, N.A., Trustee; grantinquiries4@wachovia.com
Internet: https://www.wachovia.com/foundation/v/index.jsp?vgnextoid=3b3852199c0aa110VgnVCM1000004b0d1872RCRD&vgnextfmt=default
Sponsor: Ethel Sergeant Clark Smith Foundation
620 Brandywine Parkway, Mail Code PA 5042
West Chester, PA 19380

Eugene B. Casey Foundation Grants 1762

The foundation awards grants to nonprofit organizations in the District of Columbia and Maryland. Nonprofit organizations of the Christian and Roman Catholic faiths also are eligible. Organizations receiving grants include colleges and universities, community service organizations, government agencies, medical centers, parochial schools, and religious groups. Types of support include capital grants and general support grants. There are no application forms or deadlines. Applicants should submit written proposals that include an annual report, the purpose for which the funds are requested, and the amount requested compared with the total sought.
Requirements: Nonprofits in Maryland or the District of Columbia are eligible to apply.
Geographic Focus: District of Columbia, Maryland
Amount of Grant: 10,000 - 100,000 USD
Contact: Betty Brown Casey, Treasurer; (301) 948-4595
Sponsor: Eugene B. Casey Foundation
800 South Frederick Avenue, Suite 100
Gaithersburg, MD 20877-1701

Eugene G. & Margaret M. Blackford Memorial Fund Grants 1763

The Eugene G. & Margaret M. Blackford Memorial Fund was established in 1981 to support and promote quality educational, human-services, and health-care programming for the blind or visually impaired. The deadline for application is October 1. Application materials are available for download at the grant website. Applicants will be notified of the grant decision by letter within 2 to 3 months after the proposal deadline. Applicants are strongly encouraged to review the downloadable state application guidelines before applying. Applicants are also encouraged to view the fund's funding history (link is available at the grant website).
Requirements: Applicant organizations must have 501(c)3 tax-exempt status and serve blind or visually impaired individuals living in Connecticut.
Restrictions: Applicants will not be awarded a grant for more than 3 consecutive years. The fund does not support requests from individuals, organizations attempting to influence policy through direct lobbying, or any political campaigns.
Geographic Focus: Connecticut
Date(s) Application is Due: Oct 1
Contact: Carmen Britt; (860) 657-7019; carmen.britt@baml.com
Internet: https://www.bankofamerica.com/philanthropic/fn_search.action
Sponsor: Eugene G. & Margaret M. Blackford Memorial Fund
200 Glastonbury Boulevard, Suite # 200, CT2-545-02-05
Glastonbury, CT 06033-4056

Eugene M. Lang Foundation Grants 1764

The foundation awards grants in New York and Pennsylvania in its areas of interest, including education (early childhood education and higher education), medical and health programs, arts, health organizations, medical research, minorities, and performing arts. Types of support include annual campaigns, conferences and seminars, continuing support, fellowships, general operating support, internship funds, professorships, program development, scholarship funds, and seed money. The foundation favors social services such as those helping homeless or single mothers. Locally based groups wanting support must involve a Lang family member. There are no application deadlines; initial approach should be by letter.
Requirements: Organizations in New York and Pennsylvania are eligible to apply.
Restrictions: Grants are not made to individuals, or for building funds, equipment and materials, capital or endowment funds, deficit financing, publications, or matching gifts.
Geographic Focus: New York, Pennsylvania

Amount of Grant: 500 - 50,000 USD
Contact: Program Contact; (212) 949-4100
Sponsor: Eugene M. Lang Foundation
535 5th Avenue, Suite 906
New York, NY 10017

Eugene McDermott Foundation Grants 1765
The foundation awards grants to Texas nonprofit organizations in its areas of interest, including children and youth, community development, education (early childhood through higher education), health care/organizations, international human rights, medical research, minorities, and social service delivery programs. Types of support include annual campaigns, building construction/renovation, capital campaigns, equipment/land acquisition, general operating grants, matching/challenge grants, professorships, programs/project support, research grants, scholarship funds, and seed grants. There are no application deadlines or forms. The board meets quarterly to consider requests.
Requirements: Texas nonprofit organizations are eligible.
Geographic Focus: Texas
Amount of Grant: 1,000 - 25,000 USD
Contact: Grants Administrator; (214) 521-2924
Sponsor: Eugene McDermott Foundation
3808 Euclid Avenue
Dallas, TX 75205

Eugene Straus Charitable Trust 1766
The Eugene Straus Charitable Trust was established in 1974. Eugene Straus was born to a pioneer Dallas family who settled in Dallas County in the 1840's. Mr. Straus was a successful homebuilder and real estate developer. He created this trust under his will for Dallas County charitable institutions to erect and maintain permanent building improvements. The majority of grants from the Straus Charitable Trust are one year in duration; on occasion, multi-year support is awarded. Applicants must apply online at the grant website. Applicants are strongly encouraged to do the following before applying: review the downloadable state application procedures for additional helpful information and clarifications; review the downloadable online-application guidelines at the grant website; review the trust's funding history (link is available from the grant website); review the online application questions in advance; and review the list of required attachments. These will generally include: a list of board members, financial statements (audited, reviewed, or compiled by independent auditor); an organization summary; a list of other funding sources; an IRS Determination letter; and other required documents. All attachments must be uploaded in the online application as PDF, Word, or Excel files. The application deadline for the Eugene Straus Charitable Trust is 11:59 p.m. on July 31. Applicants will be notified of grant decisions before November 30.
Requirements: Applicants must have 501(c)3 tax-exempt status.
Restrictions: Grants are only awarded to organizations for the purpose of erecting and maintaining permanent building improvements in Dallas County. Requests for general operating or program-related grants will not be considered.
Geographic Focus: Texas
Date(s) Application is Due: Jul 31
Contact: David Ross, Senior Vice President; tx.philanthropic@baml.com
Internet: https://www.bankofamerica.com/philanthropic/fn_search.action
Sponsor: Eugene Straus Charitable Trust
901 Main Street, 19th Floor, TX1-492-19-11
Dallas, TX 75202-3714

Eulalie Bloedel Schneider Foundation Grants 1767
The Foundation's mission is to support secular grassroots programs that enhance individual and family self-sufficiency and economic stability. Areas of interest are skill-building and training programs that empower at-risk youth, women and families to develop skills that would bring them towards economic self-sufficiency. The Foundation supports programs that provide job-related educational and skill building opportunities, and those seeking to build character and develop self-reliance and accountability. Artistic and cultural skill-building programs for youth and families that enhance educational and future career opportunities are also of interest.
Requirements: Washington 501(c)3 groups in the Puget Sound area are eligible.
Restrictions: The Foundation will not support: groups outside the Puget Sound area; national organizations, even those with projects in the Pacific Northwest; human services or low-income services projects or organizations that are not specifically providing skill-building or training opportunities; programs with a religious or proselytizing approach or mission; educational and outreach programs of large artistic or cultural institutions; museum exhibits or related outreach programs for schools or communities; traditional academic-oriented literacy, tutoring, and mentorship programs; individual requests for research or scholarships; childcare centers, schools, or classroom projects; book, video, film, or home-page productions, unless the expenses occur within the context of a project that fits the foundation's major areas of interest; computer, software, or office equipment purchases unless clearly a component of a project that fits foundation areas of interest; and capital campaigns for building construction or renovations.
Geographic Focus: All States
Date(s) Application is Due: Feb 1; Aug 1
Amount of Grant: 1,000 - 3,500 USD
Contact: Therese Ogle; (206) 781-3472; fax (206) 784-5987; oglefounds@aol.com
Internet: http://fdncenter.org/grantmaker/schneider
Sponsor: Eulalie Bloedel Schneider Foundation
6723 Sycamore Avenue NW
Seattle, WA 98117

Eva L. and Joseph M. Bruening Foundation Grants 1768
The Foundation gives priority to grant requests that address one of the four program areas: services for vulnerable older adults; services for physically and mentally impaired individuals; secondary/higher education; and social services for the economically disadvantaged. There is no application or proposal form. Information regarding the application process is available online. Applicants are encouraged to contact the office for further clarification of the Foundation's grantmaking policies.
Requirements: Grants are awarded only to tax-exempt, nonprofit organizations located within Cuyahoga County, OH, usually for program, capital, and start-up operating support.
Restrictions: Grants are not awarded for endowment, general operating support, research, symposia or seminars. No grants are awarded to individuals, nor does the Foundation respond to mass mailings or annual campaign solicitations.
Geographic Focus: Ohio
Date(s) Application is Due: Mar 1; Jul 1; Oct 1
Contact: Janet Narten, Executive Director; (216) 621-2632; fax (216) 621-8198
Internet: http://www.fmscleveland.com/bruening
Sponsor: Eva L. and Joseph M. Bruening Foundation
1422 Euclid Avenue, Suite 627
Cleveland, OH 44115-1952

Evan and Susan Bayh Foundation Grants 1769
Established in 2002 by Senator Evan Bayh and his wife Susan, the foundation gives to various education and human services programs mostly in Indiana.
Requirements: There are no deadlines and no specific forms to use. It is suggested that you contact the foundation prior to submitting an application.
Geographic Focus: Indiana
Amount of Grant: 2,500 - 5,000 USD
Contact: G. Frederick Glass, (317) 237-0300; fred.glass@bakerd.com
Sponsor: Evan and Susan Bayh Foundation
300 N Meridian Street, Suite 2700
Indianapolis, IN 46204-1750

Evan Frankel Foundation Grants 1770
The foundation awards grants in its areas of interest, including higher education in the humanities and the environment. Giving is primarily in Manhattan and Suffolk County, NY and Los Angeles, CA. Submit a letter to request guidelines and deadline dates.
Restrictions: Individuals are not eligible.
Geographic Focus: All States
Amount of Grant: 500 - 100,000 USD
Contact: Nancy Wendell, (631) 329-2833; fax (631) 329-7102; frankelfound@hamptons.com
Sponsor: Evan Frankel Foundation
P.O. Box 5072
East Hampton, NY 11937

Evanston Community Foundation Grants 1771
Grants awarded by the Foundation: encourage and support new initiatives and innovative approaches to addressing community needs; build the capacity of local nonprofit organizations to fulfill their missions more effectively; encourage collaborative ventures that will strengthen the community; provide initial support of projects that will have impact beyond the scope and timeline of the proposed project; build community partnerships and resources; and strengthen the area's nonprofit community. Grants typically provide initial seed money to launch new projects, capstone dollars for a larger project that will grow over a longer period, and support a one-time activity or initial phase of a new program. The Foundation's area of interests include: arts and culture; basic human needs; community development; education; environment; health; women and girls and youth and families. The Foundation's RFP and application instructions are available online.
Requirements: 501(c)3 organizations serving the Evanston, IL, community are eligible.
Geographic Focus: Illinois
Date(s) Application is Due: Feb 26
Contact: Sara Schastok, Executive Director; (847) 492-0990; fax (847) 492-0904; schastok@evcommfdn.org or info@evcommfdn.org
Internet: http://evcommfdn.org/grant_making.htm
Sponsor: Evanston Community Foundation
1007 Church Street, Suite 108
Evanston, IL 60201

Evelyn and Walter Haas, Jr. Fund Gay and Lesbian Rights Grants 1772
When Evelyn and Walter Haas, Jr. created this foundation in 1953, they were motivated by a set of values that still guide the organization today. With their vision of a just and caring society as its touchstone, the Fund supports initiatives and organizations that advance and protect fundamental rights and opportunities for all. The Fund is a leading supporter of gay and lesbian equality, based on our founders' vision of a just and caring society where all people are able to live, work and raise their families with dignity. There are three funding priorities in this area: achieving marriage equality in more states; advancing nondiscrimination protections at all levels of government; and building support for gay equality in communities of faith. Applicants should begin by contacting the fund with a two- to three-page letter of inquiry, outlining the proposal and an overall project budget.
Requirements: IRS 501(c)3 organizations in California not classified as private foundations under section 509(a) are eligible. Matching funds are required.
Restrictions: The fund generally does not make grants for capital campaigns, major equipment, basic research, conferences, publications, films or videos, deficit or emergency funding, scholarships, direct mail campaigns, fundraising events, annual appeals, or endowment contributions. Exceptions may be made for requests that form part of a larger

effort in which the fund is engaged or for requests from organizations with which the fund has a long-term funding relationship. No exceptions will be made for aid to individuals.
Geographic Focus: All States
Contact: Clayton Juan; (415) 856-1400; fax (415) 856-1500; siteinfo@haasjr.org
Internet: http://www.haasjr.org/programs-and-initiatives/gays-and-lesbians
Sponsor: Evelyn and Walter Haas, Jr. Fund
114 Sansome Street, Suite 600
San Francisco, CA 94104

Evelyn and Walter Haas, Jr. Fund Immigrant Rights Grants 1773
When Evelyn and Walter Haas, Jr. created this foundation in 1953, they were motivated by a set of values that still guide the organization today. With their vision of a just and caring society as its touchstone, the Fund supports initiatives and organizations that advance and protect fundamental rights and opportunities for all. The Fund has a long history of working to lift up the voice, leadership, and civic and political participation of immigrant communities. Building on this commitment, the Fund is joining with an array of partners to help build a diverse and powerful movement for immigrant rights and integration. There are three funding priorities in this area: strengthening public understanding about the need for comprehensive immigration reform at the national level; increasing civic participation among immigrants in California; and supporting public education about the need for immigrant-friendly state and local policies in California. Applicants should begin by contacting the fund with a two- to three-page letter of inquiry, outlining the proposal and an overall project budget.
Requirements: IRS 501(c)3 organizations in California not classified as private foundations under section 509(a) are eligible. Matching funds are required.
Restrictions: The fund generally does not make grants for capital campaigns, major equipment, basic research, conferences, publications, films or videos, deficit or emergency funding, scholarships, direct mail campaigns, fundraising events, annual appeals, or endowment contributions. Exceptions may be made for requests that form part of a larger effort in which the fund is engaged or for requests from organizations with which the fund has a long-term funding relationship. No exceptions will be made for aid to individuals.
Geographic Focus: California
Contact: Clayton Juan; (415) 856-1400; fax (415) 856-1500; siteinfo@haasjr.org
Internet: http://www.haasjr.org/programs-and-initiatives/immigrants
Sponsor: Evelyn and Walter Haas, Jr. Fund
114 Sansome Street, Suite 600
San Francisco, CA 94104

Evelyn and Walter Haas, Jr. Fund Nonprofit Leadership Grants 1774
When Evelyn and Walter Haas, Jr. created this foundation in 1953, they were motivated by a set of values that still guide the organization today. With their vision of a just and caring society as its touchstone, the Fund supports initiatives and organizations that advance and protect fundamental rights and opportunities for all. Strengthening nonprofit leadership is a key grantmaking priority for the Fund. There are two funding priorities in this area: investing in the leadership of grantees so they can more effectively achieve their social change goals; and advancing knowledge and learning about nonprofit leadership. Applicants should begin by contacting the Fund with a two- to three-page letter of inquiry, outlining the proposal and an overall project budget.
Requirements: IRS 501(c)3 organizations in California not classified as private foundations under section 509(a) are eligible. Matching funds are required.
Restrictions: The fund generally does not make grants for capital campaigns, major equipment, basic research, conferences, publications, films or videos, deficit or emergency funding, scholarships, direct mail campaigns, fundraising events, annual appeals, or endowment contributions. Exceptions may be made for requests that form part of a larger effort in which the fund is engaged or for requests from organizations with which the fund has a long-term funding relationship. No exceptions will be made for aid to individuals.
Geographic Focus: California
Contact: Clayton Juan; (415) 856-1400; fax (415) 856-1500; siteinfo@haasjr.org
Internet: http://www.haasjr.org/programs-and-initiatives/helping-nonprofit-leaders-and-their-organizations-succeed
Sponsor: Evelyn and Walter Haas, Jr. Fund
114 Sansome Street, Suite 600
San Francisco, CA 94104

Ewa Beach Community Trust Fund 1775
The Fund was created to support activities and projects of charitable agencies that work to improve the quality of life of the residents of the Ewa area. Preference will be given to: organizations that are based in the Ewa area, have a history of involvement in the community, or are partnering with an Ewa organization; projects that involve or serve youth or the elderly; projects that promote positive community identity and relationships; projects that show the ability to obtain other sources of financial support (including donations); projects that result in a measurable or tangible outcome; projects that benefit a greater number of people; and projects that have not been funded within the year.
Requirements: Any nonprofit, tax exempt 501(c)3 organization, neighborhood group or project is eligible if the goal is to improve the quality of life in the Ewa area, and is not political, commercial or self-serving.
Geographic Focus: Hawaii
Date(s) Application is Due: Apr 16
Amount of Grant: 1,000 - 2,000 USD
Contact: Georgianna DeCosta; (808) 537-6333 or (888) 731-3863; gdecosta@hcf-hawaii.org
Internet: http://www.hawaiicommunityfoundation.org/index.php?id=71&categoryID=22
Sponsor: Hawai'i Community Foundation
1164 Bishop Street, Suite 800
Honolulu, HI 96813

Ewing Halsell Foundation Grants 1776
The foundation awards grants to eligible Texas nonprofit organizations in its areas of interest, including education, environment, health care and health organizations, medical research, social services, and youth services. Types of support include annual campaigns, building construction/renovation, equipment acquisition, land acquisition, publication, research, seed grants, and technical assistance. There are no application deadlines or forms.
Requirements: Texas nonprofit organizations are eligible. Preference is given to requests from southwestern Texas, particularly San Antonio.
Restrictions: The foundation's grants do not support individuals or requests for deficit financing, emergency funds, general endowments, matching gifts, scholarships, fellowships, demonstration projects, general purposes, conferences, or loans.
Geographic Focus: Texas
Contact: Grants Administrator; (210) 223-2640
Sponsor: Ewing Halsell Foundation
711 Navarro Street, Suite 537
San Antonio, TX 78205

Ewing Marion Kauffman Foundation Grants and Initiatives 1777
The vision of the Foundation is to foster a society of economically independent individuals who are engaged citizens, contributing to the improvement of their communities. The Foundation focuses its grant making and operations on two areas: advancing entrepreneurship and improving the education of children and youth. In entrepreneurship, the Foundation works nationwide to catalyze an entrepreneurial society in which job creation, innovation, and the economy flourish. In education, the Foundation works to improve the academic achievement of disadvantaged children and works with partners to support programs that directly impact a child's academic achievement, with a concentrated focus on math, science, and technology skills. The Foundation does not use a grant application form or formal application process. There are no proposal deadlines or established funding limits. Information regarding submission of a letter of inquiry is available online.
Requirements: The foundation only funds programs within the United States. The majority of education grants go to organizations within the Kansas City metropolitan area. The foundation's entrepreneurship efforts fund programs and activities nationally and within the Kansas City area.
Restrictions: The Foundation does not fund: requests from individuals, political, social, or fraternal organizations; endowments, special events, arts, or international programs; provide loans, start-up expenses or seed capital funding for private businesses or scholarships requested by individuals; proposals submitted via audiotape or videotape; institutions that discriminate on the basis of race, creed, gender, national origin, age, disability or sexual orientation in policy or in practice; programs in furtherance of sectarian religious activities, impermissible lobbying, legislative or political activities; programs targeted for people with a specific physical, medical or psychological condition; or medical research or profit-making enterprises.
Geographic Focus: All States
Contact: Grants Administrator; (816) 932-1000; fax (816) 932-1100; info@emkf.org
Internet: http://www.kauffman.org/grants.cfm
Sponsor: Ewing Marion Kauffman Foundation
4801 Rockhill Road
Kansas City, MO 64110-2046

ExxonMobil Foundation Women's Economic Opportunity Grants 1778
The ExxonMobil Women's Economic Opportunity Initiative is a global effort launched in 2005 that helps women fulfill their economic potential and drive economic and social change in their communities. The Foundation has chosen this focus area because of its enormous positive economic and social impacts — more stable, healthy, well-educated and thriving communities. The Foundation is focused on three program areas: develop women entrepreneurs and business leaders through skills development training, mentoring programs and business women's networks; create opportunities for women's economic participation through advocacy and research programs; and identify and deploy technologies that accelerate women's economic advancement through support of high-impact and sustainable innovations, research and sharing best practices. To date, ExxonMobil and the ExxonMobil Foundation have invested $47 million on programs reaching tens of thousands of women in almost 100 countries.
Requirements: The foundation makes grants only to tax-exempt organizations. A two-page letter of inquiry is requested.
Restrictions: Grants are not made to individuals for scholarships, fellowships, research, or travel. Organizations that are primarily religious in nature are ineligible.
Geographic Focus: All States, All Countries
Contact: Suzanne McCarron, President; (972) 444-1100 or (972) 444-1007; fax (972) 444-1405; contributions@exxonmobil.com
Internet: http://www.exxonmobil.com/Corporate/community_women_invest.aspx
Sponsor: ExxonMobil Foundation
5959 Las Colinas Boulevard
Irving, TX 75039-2298

Ezra M. Cutting Trust Grants 1779
The Ezra M. Cutting Trust was established in 1965 under the will of Ezra Cutting, who was born in Marlborough, Massachusetts. The Trust supports charitable organizations serving residents of Marlborough. Areas of special interest include agencies serving youth as well as those with programs fostering economic growth and the general quality of life in the City of Marlborough. Applicants must apply online at the grant website. Applicants are strongly encouraged to do the following before applying: review the downloadable state application procedures for additional helpful information and clarifications; review the downloadable online-application guidelines at the grant website; review the trust's funding history (link is available from the grant website); review the online application questions in advance;

and review the list of required attachments. These will generally include: a list of board members, financial statements (audited, reviewed, or compiled by independent auditor); an organization summary; a list of other funding sources; an IRS Determination letter; and other required documents. All attachments must be uploaded in the online application as PDF, Word, or Excel files. The Ezra M. Cutting Trust's deadline is 11:59 p.m. on January 15. Applicants will be notified of decisions by mid-March.
Requirements: Applicants must have 501(c)3 tax-exempt status.
Restrictions: Grants are restricted to organizations located in Marlborough, Massachusetts (and to other organizations which serve Marlborough residents) and are generally made for special projects and programs, with a limited number of capital gifts made each year. The trust does not support requests from individuals, organizations attempting to influence policy through direct lobbying, or any political campaigns.
Geographic Focus: Massachusetts
Date(s) Application is Due: Jan 15
Amount of Grant: 2,500 - 10,000 USD
Contact: Michealle Larkins; (866) 778-6859; michealle.larkins@baml.com
Internet: https://www.bankofamerica.com/philanthropic/fn_search.action
Sponsor: Ezra M. Cutting Trust
225 Franklin Street, 4th Floor, MA1-225-04-02
Boston, MA 02110

F.M. Kirby Foundation Grants 1780
Foundation grants are made to a wide range of nonprofit organizations in education, health and medicine, the arts and humanities, civic and public affairs, as well as religious, welfare and youth organizations. Grantees are largely in geographic areas of particular interest to the Kirby family. The Foundation has no required application format and applications will be accepted throughout the year. No solicitations by fax or email are accepted.
Requirements: North Carolina, New Jersey, and Pennsylvania tax-exempt organizations are eligible.
Restrictions: Grants are not made to individuals, public foundations or to underwrite fundraising activities such as benefits, dinners, theater or sporting events.
Geographic Focus: New Jersey, North Carolina, Pennsylvania
Date(s) Application is Due: Oct 31
Contact: S. Dillard Kirby, Executive Director; (973) 538-4800
Internet: http://www.fdncenter.org/grantmaker/kirby
Sponsor: F.M. Kirby Foundation
17 DeHart Street, P.O. Box 151
Morristown, NJ 07963-0151

F.R. Bigelow Foundation Grants 1781
The F.R. Bigelow Foundation supports the civic, educational, religious, and other needs of the community. The Foundation funds program and helps shape initiatives that strengthen and enhance the quality of life in the Saint Paul area. The Foundation will consider grant applications in the following areas of interest: human services; community and economic development; education; health care; and the arts. The Foundation's primary geographic focus is the greater St. Paul metropolitan area, which includes Ramsey, Washington, and Dakota counties with a particular emphasis on serving people who live or work in St. Paul. The Foundation will consider applications for: capital projects, program expansion, or special projects of a time-limited nature; start-up costs for promising new programs that demonstrate sound management and clear goals relevant to community needs; support for established agencies which have temporary or transitional needs; and funds to match contributions received from other sources or to provide a challenge to help raise new contributions. Grant application packets and informational videos are available online. Applicants may wish to submit a letter of inquiry describing the proposed project prior to the preparation of a full proposal.
Requirements: Nonprofit 501(c)3 organizations in the greater St. Paul, Minnesota, metropolitan area are eligible, including Ramsey, Wahington, and Dakota counties.
Restrictions: The Foundation will not consider grant applications for: annual operating expenses; sectarian religious programs; grants to individuals; medical research; and ongoing, open-ended needs.
Geographic Focus: Minnesota
Date(s) Application is Due: May 1; Aug 1; Dec 31
Amount of Grant: 10,000 - 125,000 USD
Contact: Lisa Hansen, Grants Administration Manager; (651) 325-4261 or (800) 875-6167; fax (651) 224-8123; lisa.hansen@mnpartners.org or info@frbigelow.org
Internet: http://www.frbigelow.org
Sponsor: F.R. Bigelow Foundation
55 Fifth Street, Suite 600
St. Paul, MN 55101-1797

Fairfield County Community Foundation Grants 1782
As a community foundation, FCCF makes discretionary grants to nonprofits in the broad program areas of economic opportunity (including affordable housing, neighborhood development, and workforce development); children, youth and families; health and human services; the environment; arts and culture; and nonprofit organizational effectiveness. The Foundation is particularly interested in proposals focused on: economic opportunity; education and youth development; advancing school readiness in Fairfield County; organizational effectiveness; and regionalism. Applicants must first submit a letter of inquiry. Application information is available online.
Requirements: Nonprofit organizations in Fairfield County, CT, are eligible.
Restrictions: Funds are not used to provide support for religious or political purposes, deficit financing, annual appeals, fundraising events, open space purchases, for-profit, parochial, charter or private schools, or nonprofit endowments. Grants are not given to individuals.
Geographic Focus: Connecticut

Contact: Karen Brown, Vice President of Programs; (203) 750-3200; fax (203) 750-3232; kbrown@fccfoundation.org
Internet: http://www.fccfoundation.org/cm/grantseekers/what_we_fund.html
Sponsor: Fairfield County Community Foundation
383 Main Avenue
Norwalk, CT 06851-1543

Fallon OrNda Community Health Fund Grants 1783
The purpose of the health fund is to advance projects that increase access to health care or health promotion services that improve the health status of vulnerable populations. Of particular interest are projects that result in: the support or creation of primary care outreach services to vulnerable populations; the development of continuing managed care services rather than episodic or uncoordinated care; and the removal of barriers that prevent people from receiving services such as lack of transportation, cultural competency of providers, language differences, or others. Grants may be for operational expenditures such as personnel costs, or for construction, renovation, equipment purchase or other physical improvements. Past grants have ranged from $6,500 to $30,000.
Requirements: Funding will not be provided for long-term underwriting of operational costs for any one program.
Geographic Focus: Massachusetts
Date(s) Application is Due: Feb 15
Amount of Grant: 6,500 - 30,000 USD
Contact: Lois Smith; (508) 755-0980, ext. 107; lsmith@greaterworcester.org
Internet: http://www.greaterworcester.org/grants/Fallon.htm
Sponsor: Greater Worcester Community Foundation
370 Main Street, Suite 650
Worcester, MA 01608-1738

Families Count: The National Honors Program 1784
The foundation gives support to programs that strengthen families by helping them to find and keep jobs, increase earnings, build savings and establish credit; connect with formal and informal networks that provide help, solace, support, and information and advocate for, get access to, and effectively use high-quality education, health care, and social services.
Geographic Focus: All States
Amount of Grant: 500,000 USD
Contact: Program Contact; (410) 547-6600; fax (410) 547-6624; aecf.org
Internet: http://www.aecf.org/familiescount/about_national.htm
Sponsor: Annie E. Casey Foundation
701 Saint Paul Street
Baltimore, MD 21202

Family Literacy and Hawaii Pizza Hut Literacy Fund 1785
The purpose of the fund is to increase the literacy of Hawaii residents. English literacy is the primary focus of these funds. Preference will be given to projects that: improve access to programs for low-income, immigrant/refugee and rural communities by utilizing community-based partnerships, adapting programs to be responsive to diverse cultures, and utilizing technology to increase access; improve quality of programs by utilizing research documented best practices, including nationally documented programs adapted to reflect Hawaii's diverse cultures, including an evaluation component, and/or providing teacher training through workshops or conferences to implement quality literacy programs; for family literacy programs, focus on families with young children (ages 0-8). Application information is available online.
Requirements: Hawaii organizations that are tax-exempt, including nonprofits, 501(c)3, and units of government, such as Hawaii's public schools and libraries, are eligible to apply.
Restrictions: Projects are not likely to be funded for: programs that take place as part of a school curriculum; programs that replace DOE funding; major capital projects, although some small facility improvements to improve the ability to deliver a literacy program may be considered.
Geographic Focus: Hawaii
Date(s) Application is Due: Mar 15; Aug 1
Contact: Program Contact; (808) 537-6333 or (888) 731-3863; gdecosta@hcf-hawaii.org
Internet: http://www.hawaiicommunityfoundation.org/index.php?id=71&categoryID=20
Sponsor: Hawai'i Community Foundation
1164 Bishop Street, Suite 800
Honolulu, HI 96813

Fan Fox and Leslie R. Samuels Foundation Grants 1786
The foundation's areas of funding are the performing arts and healthcare. Healthcare funding supports patient-based and social service activities that directly help the elderly of New York City. The foundation supports performing arts organizations in the City of New York, principally, but not exclusively, in the borough of Manhattan. The foundation's primary mission is to support major performing arts institutions of national or international eminence. In addition to providing direct support, the foundation also assists presenting entities that have the requisite expertise, knowledge, and artistic judgment to present groups or individuals, new works, varied repertoire, and arts-in-education projects that will be contributions to the aesthetic and intellectual life of New York. Application guidelines are available on the Web site or upon request.
Requirements: The foundation funds organizations in the New York City area only. Only 501(c)3 tax-exempt organizations are invited to apply.
Restrictions: The foundation does not give grants to individuals or for scholarships, and does not support research, film, or video, nor does it fund education or social services. The foundation no longer actively solicits applications for support of arts-in-education programs at the primary and secondary level.

Geographic Focus: New York
Date(s) Application is Due: Mar 1; Jun 1; Dec 1
Contact: Joseph Mitchell; (212) 239-3030; fax (212) 239-3039; info@samuels.org
Internet: http://www.samuels.org
Sponsor: Fan Fox and Leslie R. Samuels Foundation
350 Fifth Avenue, Suite 4301
New York, NY 10118

FAR Fund Grants 1787
The FAR Fund Project is a New Orleans-based program exploring Hurricane Katrina's effects on New Orleans therapists and therapeutic practice. It was designed by and for clinicians. The project's mission is two fold: to offer support and concrete help to local clinicians, and to develop a model for better understanding how shared trauma affects therapists and therapy. Through this project, the FAR Fund wishes to unite and revitalize clinician communities following large-scale disasters wherever they occur, starting in New Orleans.
Requirements: The FAR Fund Project is open to New Orleans psychotherapists of all disciplines and theoretical orientations. Their mission is two-fold: to offer support and concrete help to local mental health clinicians, and to develop a psychodynamic model to better understand how shared trauma affects therapists and therapy.
Geographic Focus: Louisiana
Contact: Shirlee Taylor; (212) 982-8400; fax (212) 982-8477; FARFund@mac.com
Sponsor: Far Fund
928 Broadway, Suite 902
New York, NY 10010

Fargo-Moorhead Area Foundation Grants 1788
The Foundation awards grants each year according to current and emerging community needs. The Board also prioritizes grants that: effect a broad segment of our community; leverage support from other sources; promote collaboration, without duplicating services; strengthen organization, self-sufficiency and long term stability; focus on problem solving; and show realistic planning and management. The Foundation's focus is on arts and culture, education, environment and animals, health, human services and public/society benefit. Applicants are required to use the FMAF grant application forms available online.
Requirements: The foundation welcomes grant requests from 501(c)3 organizations in Cass and Clay Counties in North Dakota and Minnesota or those serving residents of these counties.
Restrictions: Grants are not normally funded for: annual appeals or membership drives; capital debt reduction; capital campaigns; individuals or for-profit organizations; organizations with outstanding final reports from previous FMAF grants; organizations with outstanding due diligence reports from FMAF; political projects; religious groups for religious purposes; travel for groups and retroactive funding for any project expenses incurred before the decision date.
Geographic Focus: Minnesota, North Dakota
Date(s) Application is Due: Apr 20; Jun 1
Contact: Cher Hersrud; (701) 234-0756; fax (701) 234-9724; cher@areafoundation.org
Internet: http://www.areafoundation.org/page5345.cfm
Sponsor: Fargo-Moorhead Area Foundation
502 First Avenue N, Suite 202
Fargo, ND 58102

Fargo-Moorhead Area Foundation Woman's Fund Grants 1789
The Women's Fund, of the Fargo-Moorhead (FM) Area Foundation, is an endowment that will fund projects and programs that will improve the lives of women and girls in the FM area. The Fund's top three funding priorities are: children in need of care—i.e, significant percent of high risk behavior in high school girls, 13,000 children in need of after school care (Cass and Clay); 11,000 children between 0 and 5 needing child care (Cass and Clay); economic & physical well-being of women— i.e, the poverty rate and homelessness of women and households of lead by women, abuse stats; women in leadership to positively impact civic and business policy— i.e., exec roles in business, representation on boards, etc. lack of women in elected positions. The Women's Fund generally gives priority to projects that: seek to meet identified new or emerging women's or girl's issues identified by research; leverage additional support from other sources; promote cooperation among organizations without duplicating services; use a preventative approach to solving problems; show evidence of realistic organizational planning and management; will be completed within a year's time.
Requirements: The foundation welcomes grant requests from 501(c)3 tax-exempt organizations in Cass County, North Dakota or Clay County, Minnesota. Once an announcement has been made indicating that grant applications are being accepted, the Women's Fund staff will have grant applications packets available to be picked up at the Women's Fund office, accessed electronically at www.areafoundation.org, or can be emailed upon request.
Restrictions: The Women's Fund does not make grants to individuals & ordinarily doe's not support: ongoing operation expenses; annual appeals in membership drives and capital campaigns; religious groups for religious purposes; capital debt reduction; political projects; travel for groups; organizations with outstanding reports or requests; organizations outside Cass County in North Dakota and Clay County in Minnesota. Organizations are not encouraged to submit more than one request, but for those that choose to do so, they must prioritize. Grants in successive years are also discouraged. A narrative and fiscal report will be required upon completion of the project.
Geographic Focus: Minnesota, North Dakota
Amount of Grant: 300 - 2,500 USD
Contact: Cher Hersrud, (701) 234-0756; fax (701) 234-9724; cher@areafoundation.org
Internet: http://www.areafoundation.org/page24016.cfm
Sponsor: Fargo-Moorhead Area Foundation
502 First Avenue N, Suite 202
Fargo, ND 58102

Farm Aid Grants 1790
Farm Aid has granted over $17 million to farm organizations since 1985. Grants are awarded to groups building a family farm system of agriculture. Farm Aid supports projects that help farm families stay on their land and find solutions to the challenges rural communities face. Grants are awarded in the following general categories: farm resources; farm action; food systems; and farm policy. Application information is available online.
Requirements: Nonprofit groups that provide services or assistance to U.S. farmers are eligible to apply.
Restrictions: Farm Aid does not fund: grants or loans to individuals; grants or loans to support commercial operation of a farming enterprise; production of book, film, television, or radio projects; projects outside the United States; projects directed or substantially funded by government bodies (federal, state, local); legal defense funds; capital campaigns, equipment purchases, endowments or deficit funding; historic preservation of farmland or buildings; lobbying to influence elections or legislation; conferences, publications, or research projects unless they are directly connected to ongoing program activities.
Geographic Focus: All States
Date(s) Application is Due: Aug 31
Amount of Grant: 1,000 - 50,000 USD
Contact: Laura Freden, Program Director; (800) 327-6243; laura@farmaid.org
Internet: http://www.farmaid.org/site/PageServer?pagename=grants_guidelines
Sponsor: Farm Aid
11 Ward Street, Suite 200
Somerville, MA 02143

Farmers Insurance Corporate Giving Grants 1791
The corporate community relations program awards grants in the areas of education, public safety, arts and culture, civic improvement, and health and human services. Education giving focuses on literacy programs, mentoring programs, adopt-a-school programs, employee matching grants, and aid-to-education undergraduate scholarships. Public safety awards support tougher laws against drunk driving, drug- and alcohol-free graduation night parties, neighborhood crime prevention, highway safety, and earthquake relief. Arts and culture funding supports children's programs and public television. Civic improvement focuses on recognizing exemplary youth, voter registration drives, adopt-a-highway programs, and community paint-a-thons. Health and human services giving supports March of Dimes, United Way, aid for families with cancer, aid to migrant farmworkers, and feeding the hungry. There are no application deadlines. Requests for contributions should be in the form of a letter outlining the purpose of the organization or program. The letter also should include the amount requested, its intended use, and a description of how Farmers' support will be recognized. Additional information should include a budget, annual report, proof of tax-exempt status, and a roster of the board of directors.
Requirements: 501(c)3 tax-exempt organizations are eligible.
Restrictions: Farmers does not make charitable contributions to individuals, political candidates, or religious groups or for sports events, advertising or raffle tickets, construction projects, or international programs.
Geographic Focus: All States
Contact: Doris Dunn, Director of Community Relations; (888) 327-6335
Internet: http://www.farmers.com/corporate_giving.html
Sponsor: Farmers Insurance Group of Companies
4680 Wilshire Boulevard
Los Angeles, CA 90010

FAS Project Schools Grants 1792
The FAS Schools project has four primary goals: to create a nationwide network of schools committed to providing students and all members of the school community with meaningful opportunities to practice democratic freedom; develop guidelines and resources for all schools-K-12, public and private-interested in applying the First Amendment and other democratic principles throughout the school culture; encourage and develop reforms across the curriculum that deepen teaching and learning about freedom and democracy; and educating key stakeholders-including school leaders, teachers, parents, students, school board members, and other community leaders-about the vital role of First Amendment rights and responsibilities in sustaining and expanding American democracy. Grant applications are available online.
Requirements: Eligible applicants are public and independent schools in the United States, including elementary, middle, and high schools.
Geographic Focus: All States
Date(s) Application is Due: Apr 29
Amount of Grant: 10,000 USD
Contact: Emily Nicholson; (703) 284-3931; enicholson@freedomforum.org
Internet: http://www.firstamendmentschools.org/involve/involveindex.aspx
Sponsor: Association for Supervision and Curriculum Development
1703 N Beauregard Street
Alexandria, VA 22311-1714

Fassino Foundation Grants 1793
Established in 1992, the foundation awards grants to community-based organizations in the greater Boston area for programs intended to make a measurable difference in the lives of homeless, abused, and disabled children and women. Fields of interest include: children and youth services, education, family services, and hospitals. Funding comes in the form of general operating support. Preference is given to programs that have defined and measurable goals and can demonstrate a history of success in dealing with family issues. Grant ranges fall in two brackets, and require using the Associated Grant Makers application form.
Requirements: Massachusetts nonprofits serving the greater Boston area are eligible.
Geographic Focus: Massachusetts

Amount of Grant: 10,000 - 50,000 USD
Contact: Edward G. Fassino, President; (508) 653-4554; efassino@attbi.com
Sponsor: Fassino Foundation
42 Eliot Hill Road
Natick, MA 01760

Faye McBeath Foundation Grants 1794

The Faye McBeath Foundation is a private, independent foundation providing grants to tax-exempt nonprofit 501(c)3 organizations in the metropolitan Milwaukee, Wisconsin area, including Milwaukee, Waukesha, Ozaukee and Washington counties. The major areas of interest are: children; aging and elders; health; health education; civic and governmental affairs. The Foundation's Trustees are primarily interested in promising or established programs, operated by well-managed organizations. Benchmarks that will be applied to projects and organizations in all five interest areas are the following: strength of proposal - Foundation guidelines match; quality and creativity in project design, implementation and evaluation; quality of the applicant nonprofit's leadership and organizational capacity; potential to stretch or leverage McBeath funds; specific interests of Trustees and/or staff. The majority of grants support specific programs. On occasion, operating and capacity-building grants are awarded. Capital grants are limited to projects with community-wide impact that reflect the program interests of the Foundation. Any invited requests for operating or capacity-building support must include an organization's results-oriented annual plan, covering both programs and management. The trustees meet four times each year to consider grant proposals. Written notification of the Trustees' decision regarding a grant proposal will be sent within ten days of the meeting. Organizations awarded grants will receive written notification of grant conditions, payment dates and reporting requirements
Requirements: 501(c)3 nonprofit organizations in the metropolitan Milwaukee area are eligible. To begin the application process, submittal of a letter of intent, 1-2 pages long that includes: a brief description of the applicant organization, the program to be funded, the corresponding match between the Foundation's guidelines and the request, the amount requested and the estimated total project budget. Include the name and address of the organization, and the name, phone number and email address of a contact person. There are no deadlines for letters of intent. Upon receipt of a letter of intent, Foundation staff will formally acknowledge by email or letter. If the request is clearly outside the current program or geographical focus of the Foundation, a decline letter will be sent informing you of this determination. If you are formally invited by McBeath staff to submit a full proposal, you will be asked to use the Wisconsin Common Grant Application Form. The Foundation requires that a volunteer serving on the Board sign the application.
Restrictions: The Foundation does not award grants for annual fund drives, scholarships, support of individuals, sponsorship of fundraising events, or emergency funds. The Foundation does not consider or acknowledge general solicitation letters. Basic health sciences research is not funded by the Foundation. Single disease or condition organizations are typically not funded by the Foundation. An exception may be made for a creative project involving one or more of the following: service to multiple populations, collaboration and/or creation of a replicable model. There are no published deadlines for letters of intent or grant proposals. Proposal deadlines are established based upon discussion with Foundation staff. Organizations serving the disabled will be considered only if the project targets children or older adults. Any discussion of the availability of funding in a subsequent year should be initiated by the grantee and discussed with staff at least 60 days in advance of a project anniversary.
Geographic Focus: Wisconsin
Contact: Scott Gelzer; (414) 272-2626; fax (414) 272-6235; info@fayemcbeath.org
Internet: http://www.fayemcbeath.org/ProgramPriorities/index.html
Sponsor: Faye McBeath Foundation
101 West Pleasant Street, Suite 210
Milwaukee, WI 53212

Fayette County Foundation Grants 1795

The Fayette County Foundation is the community's resource for charitable giving. The Foundation serves the entire Fayette County by assisting donors and meeting community needs. To be eligible to receive funding from the Fayette County Foundation a letter of intent must be submitted by March 1, July 1 or October 1 and followed by a completed grant application by the appropriate grant deadline. All grant seekers must have prior governing board approval for the project seeking funding. The approval of signed minutes and a signed letter from governing board must be available to the Fayette County Foundation. Faith-based organizations may apply as long as the project does not mandate participation in a religious activity as a condition for receiving services. Samples of previously funded projects are available at the website.
Requirements: Projects must have public access for all Fayette County citizens. Completed grant application (original plus eight copies) must be received by the Foundation by the last Friday in March, the last Friday in July or the last Friday in October at Noon to be considered for funding.
Restrictions: Legal requirements forbid staff, trustees, directors, committee members and their families from profiting financially from any philanthropic grant. All persons actively connected with the Foundation will consistently strive to avoid self-interest in the processing and disposition of grant request. Only one successful application per 12 months will be considered. Repeat funding for the same project may be considered five years after the initial project on a case by case basis.
Geographic Focus: Indiana
Date(s) Application is Due: Mar 1; Jul 1; Oct 1
Contact: Loree Crowe; (765) 827-9966; fax (765) 827-5836; info@fayettefoundation.com
Internet: http://www.fayettefoundation.com/default.asp?Page=Grant+Policy&PageIndex=128
Sponsor: Fayette County Foundation
521 N Central Avenue, Suite A, P.O. Box 844
Connersville, IN 47331

FCD Child Development Grants 1796

The foundation awards grants to support programs for children, particularly the disadvantaged, and promote their well-being through basic and policy-relevant research about the factors that promote optimal development of children and adolescents; policy analysis, advocacy, services, and public education to enhance the discussion and adoption of social policies that support families in their important child-rearing responsibilities; and leadership development activities linked to the programmatic focus of the foundation. Grants focus on the integration of research, policy, and advocacy in two areas: the availability of and access to early childhood education programs and health care for children. Most grants support research, but a small number of direct service grants are made for New York City-based projects that advance the foundation's research and policy analysis efforts. There are no application deadlines; submit a brief letter of inquiry. Full proposals are by invitation, following a strict preproposal process.
Requirements: Nonprofit organizations are eligible.
Restrictions: The foundation does not consider requests for scholarships or support for individuals, capital campaigns, building purchase or renovation, or equipment purchase. The foundation does not make grants outside the United States.
Geographic Focus: All States
Amount of Grant: Up to 200,000 USD
Contact: Mark Bogosian, Communications and Grants Officer; (212) 867-5777; fax (212) 867-5844; mark@fcd-us.org or info@fcd-us.org
Internet: http://fcd-us.org/grants
Sponsor: Foundation for Child Development
295 Madison Avenue, 40th Floor
New York, NY 10017

FCYO Youth Organizing Grants 1797

Since its inception, FCYO has been focused on increasing philanthropic, intellectual and social capital necessary to strengthen, grow and sustain the field of youth organizing. To strategically resource, build and sustain youth organizing efforts, FCYO aims to: regrant nationally through pooled funds and a fully supported, cost-effective, collaborative learning process; promote networking and infrastructure development to connect and strengthen youth organizing efforts, and support peer exchange and relationship-building; build the capacity of youth organizing groups through convenings, research and documentation, and the development of materials and resources; and strategically partner with key youth organizing intermediaries and youth-serving professionals to strengthen and support grassroots groups at all stages of development. Interested applicants are advised to contact the organization prior to submitting application.
Requirements: Eligible applicants include independent organizations, networks, projects within adult-led organizations, intergenerational organizations, and coalitions. Preference is given to organizations with a significant history of youth organizing and budgets under $1 million. A limited percentage of funds have been set aside for emerging groups.
Geographic Focus: All States
Amount of Grant: 15,000 - 30,000 USD
Contact: Lorraine Marasigan, Program Officer; (212) 725-3386; info@fcyo.org
Internet: http://www.fcyo.org/grantmaking
Sponsor: Funders Collaborative on Youth Organizing
20 Jay Street, 210B
Brooklyn, NY 11201

FEDCO Charitable Foundation Education Grants 1798

The Foundation provides grants each year to full-time public school teachers serving students in grades kindergarten through 12 in Cerritos, Culver City, Norwalk-La Mirada, Pasadena and Los Angeles Unified school district. Grants support hands-on, classroom or real-world field trip projects that bring learning to life and increase student academic achievement. Grants are designed to encourage experiential learning, enhance student understanding and boost student achievement with respect to the curriculum standards in one of the core subject areas. There are three ways to apply. Choose only one method to submit your application. Online applications are encouraged. Application information is available online.
Requirements: Eligible teachers must currently teach full time in a public school. The school principal or administrator must understand and fully support the project. The teacher(s) must propose a class project that is aligned with and supports the curriculum standards and includes all students in the class.
Restrictions: Grant funds may not be used for the following: computer hardware, salaries, substitute teachers, video cameras, trips to theme parks, third party payments, sectarian purposes, or for substituting existing funds that are available to support similar services.
Geographic Focus: California
Amount of Grant: 500 - 1,000 USD
Contact: Cathy Choi, (213) 452-6206; fax (213) 388-2046; cchoi@ccf-la.org
Internet: http://www.calfund.org/receive/fedco.php?PHPSESSID=cb4bf58103d002581aebd716d5f008ea
Sponsor: FEDCO Charitable Foundation
445 S Figueroa Street, Suite 3400
Los Angeles, CA 90071-1638

Federal Express Corporate Contributions Program 1799

The mission of the FedEx Social Responsibility department is to actively support the communities served and to strengthen global reputation through strategic investment of people, resources, and network. The foundation directs its philanthropic efforts to health and welfare programs, education, cultural/arts and civic assistance. Charitable shipping is limited to emergency, disaster or life-threatening situations coordinated through a nonprofit organization, disaster relief agency, or agency of the federal, state, or local government. FedEx is especially interested in supporting nonprofit organizations that

request 5 percent or less of a total project budget; contingency grants; or seed monies with the thought that other sources will contribute matching amounts. Organizations must show evidence of competent management, low administrative/fundraising expense ratios, and a nondiscriminatory program benefiting broad segments of the community. FedEx Community Relations responds to all requests in writing. Requests are accepted year-round and generally are reviewed within three weeks of receipt.
Requirements: Charities must be registered 501(c)3 organizations in good financial and public standing.
Geographic Focus: All States
Contact: Grants Administrator, Community Relations; (901) 369-3600
Internet: http://www.fedex.com/us/about/responsibility/community/guidelines.html?link=4
Sponsor: Fedex Corporation
3610 Hacks Cross Road, Building A, 1st Floor
Memphis, TN 38125

Fel-Pro Mecklenburger Foundation Grants 1800
The Foundation will give priority to those proposals that address: new and innovative programs developed by Jewish organizations serving low-income Jews, immigrants and indigent populations, including employment and economic development activities; advocacy efforts to benefit low-income Jews, immigrants and indigent populations; efforts that strengthen inter-group relationships between the Jewish community and minority groups; and promoting peace in the Middle East. The Foundation does approve multi-year grants.
Requirements: Nonprofit organizations in the Chicago, IL, area are eligible.
Geographic Focus: Illinois
Amount of Grant: 20,000 - 25,000 USD
Contact: Rose Jagust; (312) 357-4954; fax (312) 855-3284; RoseJagust@juf.org
Sponsor: Fel-Pro Mecklenburger Foundation
30 South Wells Street
Chicago, IL 60606

Feldman Foundation Grants 1801
Giving is concentrated in the areas of community development, social welfare, and Jewish causes. Types of support include annual campaigns, building construction/renovation, general operating support, program development, research, and scholarship funds. Initial contact should be by proposal letter. Foundation trustees meet in the spring and fall to review proposals under serious consideration. Applications are accepted at any time.
Requirements: Organizations based in New York and Texas are eligible to apply.
Restrictions: Grants will not be awarded to individuals.
Geographic Focus: New York, Texas
Amount of Grant: 10,000 - 50,000 USD
Contact: Robert Feldman, Trustee; (214) 689-4337
Sponsor: Feldman Foundation
P.O. Box 1046
Dallas, TX 75221

FEMA Assistance to Firefighters Grants (AFG) 1802
The program provides financial assistance directly to fire departments and nonaffiliated EMS organizations to enhance their abilities with respect to fire and fire-related hazards. The primary goal is to help fire departments and nonaffiliated EMS organizations meet their firefighting and emergency response needs. AFG seeks to support organizations that lack the tools and resources necessary to more effectively protect the health and safety of the public and their emergency response personnel with respect to fire and all other hazards. The project period for any award under AFG will be twelve months from the date of the award.
Requirements: The application will be accessible from the AFG website (www.firegrantsupport.com), the U.S. Fire Administration's (USFA) website (www.usfa.fema.gov), and grants.gov website (www.grants.gov). Paper applications will be accepted, but are discouraged due to the inherent delays associated with processing them. Fire departments or nonaffiliated EMS organizations operating in any of the 50 States plus the District of Columbia, the Commonwealth of the Northern Mariana Islands, the Virgin Islands, Guam, American Samoa, and Puerto Rico are eligible for funding. A fire department is defined as an agency or organization that has a formally recognized arrangement with a State, territory, local, or tribal authority (city, county, parish, fire district, township, town, or other governing body) to provide fire suppression to a population within a fixed geographical area on a first-due basis. A nonaffiliated EMS organization is defined as a public or private nonprofit emergency medical services organization that provides direct emergency medical services, including medical transport, to a specific geographic area on a first-due basis but is not affiliated with a hospital and does not serve a geographic area where emergency medical services are adequately provided by a fire department. Fire departments may submit applications for either or both of the following program areas: Firefighter Operations and Safety; Firefighter Vehicle Acquisition. EMS applicants may apply for assistance under either the Operations and Safety program area or the Vehicle Acquisition program area, or both using separate applications. Any eligible applicant, whether a fire department or a nonaffiliated EMS organization, may act as a host applicant and apply for large-scale or regional projects on behalf of itself and any number of organizations in neighboring jurisdictions. The only activities available for application under a regional project are training and equipment acquisition that positively affect interoperability.
Restrictions: Fire departments that are Federal, or contracted by the Federal Government, and are solely responsible under a formally recognized agreement for suppression of fires on Federal installations or land are ineligible for funding. Fire stations that are not independent entities, but are part of, controlled by, or under the day-to-day operational direction of a larger fire department or agency are not eligible for funding. Fire departments that are for-profit departments (i.e., do not have specific nonprofit status or are not municipally based) are not eligible for funding. Auxiliaries, fire service organizations or associations,
and State/local agencies such as a forest service, fire marshals, hospitals, and training offices are not eligible for funding. Dive teams and search and rescue teams, or any similar organizations that do not provide medical transport, are not eligible for assistance as nonaffiliated EMS organizations.
Geographic Focus: All States
Date(s) Application is Due: May 4
Contact: Help Desk; (866) 274-0960; firegrants@dhs.gov
Internet: http://www.firegrantsupport.com/afg/
Sponsor: U.S. Department of Homeland Security
245 Murray Lane - Building 410, SW
Washington, DC 20528-7000

FEMA Staffing for Adequate Fire and Emergency Response Grants 1803
The program was created to provide funding directly to fire departments and volunteer firefighter interest organizations in order to help them increase the number of trained, front-line firefighters available in their communities. Awarded funds will assist local fire departments to increase their staffing and deployment capabilities in order to respond to emergencies whenever they may occur. Eligible activities for this grant: (1) Hiring of Firefighters; and, (2) Recruitment and Retention of Volunteer Firefighters.
Requirements: Only fire departments and volunteer firefighter interest organizations are eligible for SAFER grants. All volunteer or combination volunteer fire departments may apply for either or both of the two SAFER activities. Volunteer firefighter interest organizations are eligible for funding only in the Recruitment and Retention of Volunteer Firefighters Activity. Career fire departments are eligible for funding only in the Hiring of Firefighters Activity.
Restrictions: The limited funding available for SAFER activities precludes the award of funds for operational activities, such as the equipment and training of newly hired or recruited firefighters. Therefore, personal protective clothing, firefighting equipment, and costs for providing training to the firefighter minimum-staffing level, as offered in the Assistance to Firefighters (AFG) grant program, are not eligible.
Geographic Focus: All States
Date(s) Application is Due: Jun 27
Contact: Grant Programs Directorate Help Desk; (866) 274-0960; firegrants@dhs.gov
Internet: http://firegrantsupport.com/safer/
Sponsor: U.S. Department of Homeland Security
Tech World Building, 500 C Street SW, South Tower, 5th Floor
Washington, DC 20472

Ferree Foundation Grants 1804
The foundation is a private family foundation dedicated to promoting and supporting excellence in the arts, culture and history, education, youth engagement, health, human services, and local economic and community development. Paul W. Ware is the Chairman of Ferree Foundation and continues the Ware family tradition of using philanthropy to enhance the lives of families and institutions primarily throughout Lancaster County and, occasionally, Southeastern Pennsylvania and beyond. Grant requests should be in writing and mailed to the executive director. Guidelines are available online.
Requirements: 501(c)3 nonprofit organizations are eligible. Preference is given to organizations serving Pennsylvania's Chester and Lancaster Counties.
Restrictions: The foundation does not make grants to individuals, nor does it make loans.
Geographic Focus: Pennsylvania
Date(s) Application is Due: Sep 15
Contact: Deb Arrive; (717) 735-8288; darrive@Ferree-Foundation.org
Internet: http://www.Ferree-Foundation.org/apply.html
Sponsor: Ferree Foundation
229 North Duke Street
Lancaster, PA 17602

Fidelity Foundation Grants 1805
Fidelity Investments Chairman Edward C. Johnson 3d and his father, the founder of the company, established the Fidelity Foundation in 1965 with several operating principles in mind. These principles, still current today, guide the Foundation's decisions and grantmaking. The Foundation grant program was designed to strengthen the long-term effectiveness of nonprofit institutions. The types of projects it funds, and the way in which it funds them, are specifically intended to help nonprofits build the organizational capabilities they need to better fulfill their missions and serve their constituencies. The Fidelity Foundation considers Letters of Inquiry from organizations with current IRS 501(c)3 public charity status only. Grants are made to fund only significant, transformative projects usually budgeted at $50,000 or more. The Foundation's primary philanthropic investments are allocated to the following sectors: arts and culture; community development and social services; health; and education.
Requirements: Grants are generally made only to organizations with operating budgets of $500,000 or more. The Fidelity Foundation considers projects from organizations of regional or national importance throughout the United States.
Restrictions: Grants are not awarded to support sectarian organizations, disease-specific associations, or public school systems. Support does not go to individuals or for scholarships, civic or start-up organizations, corporate memberships, operating support, or participation in benefit events, film, or video projects.
Geographic Focus: All States
Amount of Grant: 50,000 - 1,000,000 USD
Contact: Kathleen Ward, Grant Director; (617) 563-6806; info@FidelityFoundation.org
Internet: http://www.fidelityfoundation.org/index.html
Sponsor: Fidelity Foundation
82 Devonshire Street, S2
Boston, MA 02109

Field Foundation of Illinois Grants — 1806
The Foundation awards grants only to institutions and agencies operating in the fields of urban and community affairs, culture, education, community welfare, health, and environment, primarily serving the people of Chicago with extremely limited grant making in the metropolitan area. Preference will be given to funding innovative approaches for addressing program areas.
Requirements: Applicants must reside in Illinois. Grant applications are not provided; however, a formal proposal is required. The Foundation does not accept grant requests via email or fax.
Restrictions: No grants will be made to support: endowments; individuals; medical research or national health agency appeals; propaganda organizations or committees whose efforts are aimed at influencing legislation; printed materials, video or computer equipment; fund-raising events or advertising; appeals for religious purposes; other granting agencies or foundations for ultimate distribution to agencies or programs of its own choosing; custodian afterschool programs or tutoring; most disease specific programs, research or activities; or operating support of established neighborhood health centers or clinics, day care centers for children, or small cultural groups. Requests for computer equipment will not be considered.
Geographic Focus: Illinois
Date(s) Application is Due: Jan 15; May 15; Sep 15
Amount of Grant: 50,000 USD
Contact: Joann Ross, (312) 831-0910; fax (312) 831-0961; jross@fieldfoundation.org
Internet: http://www.fieldfoundation.org
Sponsor: Field Foundation of Illinois
200 S Wacker Drive, Suite 3860
Chicago, IL 60606

Fields Pond Foundation Grants — 1807
The primary mission of the foundation is to provide financial assistance to nature and land conservation organizations that are community-based and that serve to increase environmental awareness by involving local residents in conservation issues. Types of support include project grants for trailmaking and other enhancement of public access to conservation lands, rivers, coastlines, and other natural resources; land acquisition for conservation; assistance in establishment of endowments as a means of funding stewardship of conservation areas; and related education programs and publications.
Requirements: Grantmaking programs presently are limited to organizations in New England and New York State.
Restrictions: As a normal practice, the Foundation is unlikely to make the following kinds of grants: support for deficits, for routine operating budgets or general appeals, or where the Foundation may become the predominant source of an organization's funding; for funding efforts usually supported by public subscription or through national appeals, or for purposes which are generally understood to be the responsibility of government; support sectarian religious activities; or to individuals, such as for personal needs, welfare, travel, or research.
Geographic Focus: Connecticut, Maine, Massachusetts, New Hampshire, New York, Rhode Island, Vermont
Amount of Grant: 2,000 - 10,000 USD
Contact: Grants Administrator; (781) 899-9990; fax (781) 899-2819; info@fieldspond.org
Internet: http://www.fieldspond.org
Sponsor: Fields Pond Foundation
5 Turner Street, Box 540667
Waltham, MA 02454-0667

Fieldstone Foundation Grants — 1808
The Foundation was created to provide grants, leadership and development and service to nonprofit organizations working to support individuals in the communities where the company does business. The Foundation gives emphasis to programs that serve children and families and allocates its resources in four general areas: Humanitarian, Community and Education, Cultural Arts and Christian Ministries. Faxed and emailed proposals will not be accepted. Application information is available online.
Requirements: Funding is limited to non-profit organizations serving the communities where the company is currently operating: Orange, Riverside, and San Diego counties in Southern California and Salt Lake City in Utah.
Restrictions: Support will not be provided for individuals; political parties, candidates and partisan political organizations; veteran, labor, fraternal or athletic organizations except for specific projects that benefit the broad community; advertising; or individual churches. The Foundation does not make multi-year commitments or fund capital campaigns.
Geographic Focus: California, Utah
Date(s) Application is Due: Jun 30
Contact: Janine Mason, Executive Director; janinem@fieldstone-homes.com
Internet: http://www.fieldstone-homes.com/foundation
Sponsor: Fieldstone Foundation
14 Corporate Plaza Drive
Newport Beach, CA 92660

Fifth Third Bank Corporate Giving — 1809
The concept of corporate social responsibility (CSR) is growing in visibility and importance in today's business environment. Fifth Third Bank has a long-standing desire to be a positive, contributing member of the communities it serves. It's a commitment that grew out of the Bank's history—Jacob G. Schmidlapp, one of the Bank's early leaders, was a well-known philanthropist. In 1948, the Bank was the first financial institution in the United States to establish a charitable foundation. In 2010, the Bank framed all of its community support into a Corporate Social Responsibility Report titled, "Responsibility Begins Here." The report, which is viewable as an interactive web presentation, details the Bank's commitment to being a good corporate citizen. The Bank's approach to CSR originated from its belief that the Company is only as strong as the community it serves. The report outlines the Bank's focus on five key initiatives: financial literacy; youth education; community development; diversity and inclusion; and environmental stewardship.
Requirements: Giving is limited in to communities in which Fifth Third Bank has a presence.
Geographic Focus: Florida, Illinois, Indiana, Kentucky, Michigan, Ohio, Tennessee, West Virginia
Contact: Mark Walton, CRA Manager; (513) 534-7037
Internet: https://www.53.com/site/about/in-the-community/corporate-social-responsibility.html?
Sponsor: Fifth Third Bank Corporation
38 Fountain Square Plaza, MD 10906E
Cincinnati, OH 45263

Fifth Third Foundation Grants — 1810
The Fifth Third Foundation awards grants to eligible nonprofit organizations in its areas of interest, including community development, education, health and human services, and arts and culture. Proposals are favored that are likely to make a substantial difference in the quality of community life; strengthen families and communities; expand meaningful civic engagement and build social capital; use volunteers; help nonprofit organizations build capacity and become more effective; include financial and other strategic commitments from other funding organizations; and leverage change in the capacity of community-wide systems rather than individual organizations. Interested applicants should initially contact the Foundation via a brief letter detailing the organization, its mission, the project it seeks funding for, and an approximate grant amount to be requested.
Requirements: 501(c)3 nonprofit, tax-exempt organizations operating in Fifth Third's geographic regions of Ohio, Kentucky, Indiana, Michigan, Illinois, Tennessee, West Virginia, and Florida are eligible to apply.
Restrictions: The following types of support are ineligible: capital campaigns for individual churches; publicly supported entities, such as public schools or government agencies; elementary schools; and individuals.
Geographic Focus: Florida, Illinois, Indiana, Kentucky, Michigan, Ohio, Tennessee, West Virginia
Contact: Heidi B. Jark; (513) 534-7001 or (513) 534-4397; heidi.jark@@53.com
Internet: https://www.53.com/site/about/in-the-community/foundation-office-at-fifth-third-bank.html?
Sponsor: Fifth Third Foundation
38 Fountain Square Plaza, MD 1090CA
Cincinnati, OH 45263

Financial Capability Innovation Fund II Grants — 1811
This fund will provide a powerful combination of financial and technical assistance to innovative and promising nonprofit-led projects designed to promote the financial capability of low-income and underserved consumers. Through the Fund, CFSI will award approximately $2.5 million in total to 7-10 grantees with an average award size of $250,000 - $350,000. Organizations that apply to the FCIF II have an opportunity to play an integral role in the further development of the financial capability field by exploring the effectiveness and viability of innovative programs designed to affect positive financial behavior change. Selected grantees will begin a long-term relationship with CFSI and receive strategic guidance, heightened visibility, and access to an unparalleled network in the underserved financial services industry.
Requirements: Only nonprofit organizations with 501(c)3 status are eligible to apply. Applicants must themselves possess 501(c)3 status and may not use a fiscal agent with 501(c)3 status. CFSI encourages and will accept applications from partnerships between nonprofits and for-profit service providers if the lead organization (who will receive funding) possesses 501(c)3 status. CFSI intends to fund projects that accomplish three critical objectives: 1) Aim to promote the financial capability of low-income and underserved consumers; 2) Result in positive financial behavior change; and 3) Demonstrate improved financial outcomes. Such outcomes include, but are not limited to, a greater ability to select and manage financial products and services, increased emergency and long-term savings, and improved credit scores.
Restrictions: CFSI will not consider requests for: projects without a clear and close link to financial products or services; general operating support; projects with international (non-US) focus; follow-on funding for existing projects (only new projects or significant modifications to existing projects will be considered); new financial education curriculum development; loan capital; matching funds for Individual Development Accounts (IDAs); projects that only involve research. In order for a research project to be considered, it must be part of a broader programmatic effort.
Geographic Focus: All States
Date(s) Application is Due: Nov 2
Amount of Grant: 250,000 - 350,000 USD
Contact: Sarah E. Gordon, Vice President, Advisory Services and Nonprofit Investments; (312) 881-5828; fax (312) 881-5802; questions@cfsinnovation.com
Internet: http://cfsinnovation.com/content/financial-capability-innovation-fund-ii
Sponsor: Center for Financial Services Innovation
20 N. Clark, Suite 1950
Chicago, IL 60602

Finish Line Youth Foundation Founder's Grants — 1812
Finish Line Youth Foundation focuses funding on organizations that provide opportunities for youth participation in the following areas: Youth athletic programs - Community-based programs addressing active lifestyle and team building skills; Camps - Established camps with an emphasis on sports and active lifestyle, especially programs serving disadvantaged and special needs kids. These emergency funds grants would be awarded to qualifying organizations that have an emergency need that would somehow be keeping the organization from providing

current services. Examples would be natural disasters or other unforeseen circumstances that require special funding to help build or develop facilities or equipment needs.
Requirements: Organizations operating near a Finish Line store with 501(c)3 tax-exempt status that provide opportunities for participation for children and young adults age 18 and under are eligible to apply. Preference is given to organizations whose activities provide direct services to individuals and produce tangible results, rather than those that are policy oriented. The foundation has a particular interest in the potential impact of the program/project and the number of people who will benefit; the organization's fiscal responsibility and management qualifications; and, the ability of an organization to obtain the necessary additional funding to implement a program or project and to provide ongoing funding after the term of the grant has expired.
Restrictions: The Foundation will not make grants to: Organizations not currently exempt from federal taxation under section 501(c)3 of the Internal Revenue Code or created for eligible public purposes (such as public and private schools and state-funded universities and colleges); Political campaigns, or attempts to influence public officials; Organizations that unlawfully discriminate as to race, religion, income, gender, disability or national origin; Projects or programs aimed at promoting the teachings of a particular church or religious denomination, or construction projects of churches and other religious institutions; Fraternal, veterans or labor organizations; Foundations affiliated with a for-profit entity; Endowments; Organizations for on-going operating support; Start up organizations or programs; Reduce debt; Beauty or talent contests; Individuals; Sponsor teams, special events or fundraising activities; Medical, scientific or academic research; Pay for travel or trips.
Geographic Focus: All States
Amount of Grant: 5,000 - 25,000 USD
Contact: Roger Underwood; (317) 899-1022 x6741; Youthfoundation@finishline.com
Internet: http://www.finishline.com/store/youthfoundation/special-grants.jsp
Sponsor: Finish Line Youth Foundation
3308 N Mitthoeffer Road
Indianapolis, IN 46235

Finish Line Youth Foundation Grants 1813
Finish Line Youth Foundation focuses funding on organizations that provide opportunities for youth participation in the following areas: Youth athletic programs - Community-based programs addressing active lifestyle and team building skills; Camps - Established camps with an emphasis on sports and active lifestyle, especially programs serving disadvantaged and special needs kids. The foundation may provide financial support for Programs and Projects (direct costs of youth programming for requests in their areas of interest) or Scholarships (full or partial scholarship funding for camps or youth athletic programs). In general grants range from $1,000 - $5,000.
Requirements: The foundation is particularly interested in: Organizations providing opportunities for participation for children and young adults age 18 and under; Organizations whose activities provide direct services to individuals and produce tangible results, rather than those that are policy oriented; The potential impact of the program/project and the number of people who will benefit; The organization's fiscal responsibility and management qualifications; The ability of an organization to obtain the necessary additional funding to implement a program or project and to provide ongoing funding after the term of the grant has expired; Programs operating near Finish Line stores.
Restrictions: The Foundation will not make grants to: Organizations not currently exempt from federal taxation under section 501(c)3 of the Internal Revenue Code or created for eligible public purposes (such as public and private schools and state-funded universities and colleges); Political campaigns, or attempts to influence public officials; Organizations that unlawfully discriminate as to race, religion, income, gender, disability or national origin; Projects or programs aimed at promoting the teachings of a particular church or religious denomination, or construction projects of churches and other religious institutions; Fraternal, veterans or labor organizations; Foundations affiliated with a for-profit entity; Endowments; Organizations for on-going operating support; Start up organizations or programs; Reduce debt; Beauty or talent contests; Individuals; Sponsor teams, special events or fundraising activities; Medical, scientific or academic research; Pay for travel or trips.
Geographic Focus: All States
Amount of Grant: 1,000 - 5,000 USD
Contact: Roger Underwood; (317) 899-1022 x6741; Youthfoundation@finishline.com
Internet: http://www.finishline.com/store/youthfoundation/guidelines.jsp
Sponsor: Finish Line Youth Foundation
3308 N Mitthoeffer Road
Indianapolis, IN 46235

Finish Line Youth Foundation Legacy Grants 1814
Finish Line Youth Foundation focuses funding on organizations that provide opportunities for youth participation in the following areas: Youth athletic programs - Community-based programs addressing active lifestyle and team building skills; Camps - Established camps with an emphasis on sports and active lifestyle, especially programs serving disadvantaged and special needs kids. The Legacy Grants will be awarded to qualifying organizations in need of improvements and/or renovations to existing buildings, grounds, and property or for new facilities and/or grounds.
Requirements: Organizations operating near a Finish Line store with 501(c)3 tax-exempt status that provide opportunities for participation for children and young adults age 18 and under are eligible to apply. Preference is given to organizations whose activities provide direct services to individuals and produce tangible results, rather than those that are policy oriented. The foundation has a particular interest in the potential impact of the program/project and the number of people who will benefit; the organization's fiscal responsibility and management qualifications; and, the ability of an organization to obtain the necessary additional funding to implement a program or project and to provide ongoing funding after the term of the grant has expired.
Restrictions: The Foundation will not make grants to: Organizations not currently exempt from federal taxation under section 501(c)3 of the Internal Revenue Code or created for eligible public purposes (such as public and private schools and state-funded universities and colleges); Political campaigns, or attempts to influence public officials; Organizations that unlawfully discriminate as to race, religion, income, gender, disability or national origin; Projects or programs aimed at promoting the teachings of a particular church or religious denomination, or construction projects of churches and other religious institutions; Fraternal, veterans or labor organizations; Foundations affiliated with a for-profit entity; Endowments; Organizations for on-going operating support; Start up organizations or programs; Reduce debt; Beauty or talent contests; Individuals; Sponsor teams, special events or fundraising activities; Medical, scientific or academic research; Pay for travel or trips.
Geographic Focus: All States
Contact: Roger Underwood; (317) 899-1022 x6741; Youthfoundation@finishline.com
Internet: http://www.finishline.com/store/youthfoundation/special-grants.jsp
Sponsor: Finish Line Youth Foundation
3308 N Mitthoeffer Road
Indianapolis, IN 46235

FINRA Investor Education Foundation Financial Education in Your Community Grants 1815
The FINRA Investor Education Foundation, in partnership with the United Way of America, launched this new grant program in 2009 to help community-based organizations provide effective and unbiased financial education. As part of this grant program, the FINRA Foundation and United Way provide resources and technical assistance to grantees throughout the term. Community and non-profit organizations are integral to neighborhood social networks. They can craft programs relevant to local needs and preferences. They also offer education and services in venues that are neutral, non-threatening and convenient. Financial Education in Your Community grants are awarded to community-based organizations that have demonstrated the ability to reach and engage working individuals and families through effective social marketing techniques. Successful projects build or sustain community partnerships and address local needs by introducing new and creative approaches that significantly improve participant outcomes.
Requirements: 501(c)3 tax-exempt organizations are eligible.
Restrictions: The foundation will not award grants to individuals; organizations affiliated with a current member of the foundation board of directors or FINRA board of governors; securities firms regulated by FINRA; organizations affiliated with a securities firm or individual regulated by FINRA, such as a foundation established by a securities firm; securities regulators, self-regulatory organizations, or securities industry trade associations; organizations that are termed disqualified persons pursuant to Article III, Section 3(d) of the FINRA by-laws; foreign organizations; or entities that discriminate on the basis of age, color, disability, marital status, national origin, race, religion, sex, sexual orientation, or veteran status. The Foundation will generally not consider proposals to fund: international programs or projects; expenses that are not directly related to the project for which funding is sought; salaries of permanent staff (for example, prorated salaries of administrative and executive personnel, or oversight and coordination activities of a project principal); capital costs, such as building and construction or equipment such as computer hardware and office furniture; pass-through funding (for example, if the 501(c)3 organization plans to turn over the funding to a proprietary organization or consultant); projects with a potential conflict of interest (for example where funded technical support or expertise might be provided by a board member of the 501(c)3 organization); conferences and similar activities that fail to provide a long-term solution or sufficiently broad outreach; distribution methodologies that require ongoing maintenance when the ability to perform upkeep without continued funding is questionable (for example, materials with a short "shelf life" that would require ongoing funding for frequent updating); projects with proprietary elements, such as for-profit activities, use or purchase of copyrighted or trademarked materials, and proprietary research; lobbying, political contributions, fund-raising events, or other similar activities designed to influence legislation or intervene in political campaigns; donations, endowments, challenge grants, matching funds, and other similar programs; or direct or matching payments to members of the public, such as scholarships, assistance with personal and family financial difficulties, registration fees for conferences and training, or similar activities.
Geographic Focus: All States
Contact: Susan M. Sarver, (202) 728-6948; susan.sarver@finra.com
Internet: http://www.finrafoundation.org/grants/community/
Sponsor: FINRA Investor Education Foundation
1735 K Street, NW
Washington, DC 20006-1506

FINRA Smart Investing@Your Library Grants 1816
The Smart Investing@Your Library Grant program is administered jointly by the FINRA Investor Education Foundation and the American Library Association. This special grant program funds public library efforts to provide library patrons with access to effective, unbiased financial education resources. Grant recipients—public libraries and public library networks across the country—use a variety of technologies and outreach strategies to bring quality financial and investor education opportunities within easy reach of diverse groups of library patrons at no cost to them. The grantees partner with an array of organizations, including schools, universities and local agencies, to expand the impact of the services and resources enabled by the grants. Through the program, library patrons are empowered to make smart financial decisions, both for long-term investing and day-to-day money matters. The program is especially concerned with helping those who might otherwise have limited access to important information relevant to their financial well-being.
Requirements: Public libraries and library networks throughout the United States are eligible.
Restrictions: The foundation will not award grants to individuals; organizations affiliated with a current member of the foundation board of directors or FINRA board of governors;

securities firms regulated by FINRA; organizations affiliated with a securities firm or individual regulated by FINRA, such as a foundation established by a securities firm; securities regulators, self-regulatory organizations, or securities industry trade associations; organizations that are termed disqualified persons pursuant to Article III, Section 3(d) of the FINRA by-laws; foreign organizations; or entities that discriminate on the basis of age, color, disability, marital status, national origin, race, religion, sex, sexual orientation, or veteran status. The Foundation will generally not consider proposals to fund: international programs or projects; expenses that are not directly related to the project for which funding is sought; salaries of permanent staff (for example, prorated salaries of administrative and executive personnel, or oversight and coordination activities of a project principal); capital costs, such as building and construction or equipment such as computer hardware and office furniture; pass-through funding (for example, if the 501(c)3 organization plans to turn over the funding to a proprietary organization or consultant); projects with a potential conflict of interest (for example where funded technical support or expertise might be provided by a board member of the 501(c)3 organization); conferences and similar activities that fail to provide a long-term solution or sufficiently broad outreach; distribution methodologies that require ongoing maintenance when the ability to perform upkeep without continued funding is questionable (for example, materials with a short "shelf life" that would require ongoing funding for frequent updating); projects with proprietary elements, such as for-profit activities, use or purchase of copyrighted or trademarked materials, and proprietary research; lobbying, political contributions, fund-raising events, or other similar activities designed to influence legislation or intervene in political campaigns; donations, endowments, challenge grants, matching funds, and other similar programs; or direct or matching payments to members of the public, such as scholarships, assistance with personal and family financial difficulties, registration fees for conferences and training, or similar activities.
Geographic Focus: All States
Amount of Grant: Up to 100,000 USD
Contact: Robert Ganem, (202) 728-8362; robert.ganem@finra.com
Internet: http://www.finrafoundation.org/grants/library/
Sponsor: FINRA Investor Education Foundation
1735 K Street, NW
Washington, DC 20006-1506

Firelight Foundation Grants 1817
Firelight provides small grants to community-based organizations selected for their vision and resourcefulness. The Foundation is often the first funder to an organization. Its grantmaking model is framed by a seven-year partnership model, which is divided into three phases. Firelight grantee-partners develop programs unique to the needs of their community. By working across multiple focus areas, our partners are able to address the needs of traumatized or vulnerable children and families effected by poverty, HIV and AIDS. Its primary goals include: providing basic necessities, including clothing, bedding, personal hygiene and shelter; supporting food production, feeding programs and household food assistance for vulnerable children and families; providing materials, skills and knowledge to caregivers to help them generate income and strengthen household resiliency; enhancing the caring relationships that meet the emotional, social, and recreational needs of children and help build life and coping skills; building a supportive and protective environment that prevents and responds to violence, abuse, and the exploitation of children; offering building a supportive and protective environment that prevents and responds to violence, abuse, and the exploitation of children; and extending primary health care, preventive care and HIV and AIDS-related preventive and palliative care.
Requirements: The Foundation accepts unsolicited proposals from seven countries in sub-Saharan Africa: Lesotho, Malawi, Rwanda, South Africa, Tanzania, Zambia, and Zimbabwe. In addition, Firelight awards grants to CBOs in Ethiopia, Kenya, and Uganda through solicited proposals.
Restrictions: The foundation does not fund: individuals; organizations or programs designed to influence legislation or elect public officials; programs that limit participation based on race, creed, or nationality; academic or medical research; or fundraising drives or endowments.
Geographic Focus: Ethiopia, Kenya, Lesotho, Malawi, Rwanda, South Africa, Tanzania, Uganda, Zambia, Zimbabwe
Amount of Grant: 500 - 10,000 USD
Contact: Evelyn Brown; (831) 429-8750; fax (831) 429-2036; evelyn@firelightfoundation.org
Internet: http://www.firelightfoundation.org/programs/grantmaking/
Sponsor: Firelight Foundation
740 Front Street, Suite 380
Santa Cruz, CA 95060

Fireman's Fund Insurance Company Heritage Grants 1818
Fireman's Fund Insurance Company was founded in 1863 with a mission to donate a portion of its profits to support the fire service. The program continues that tradition today through its Heritage Grants program by awarding grants to fire service organizations for needed equipment, firefighter training and communication education programs. Funding is allocated in partnership with its employees and independent insurance agents, who assist in the direction of the grants.
Requirements: To apply, a nonprofit, tax-exempt organization should send a letter to the director setting forth the request for funding and the amount desired, enclosing a financial statement, IRS letter, and a list of board members.
Restrictions: The fund does not make grants for capital campaigns; endowment funds; general operating expenses; individuals; religious organizations; fraternal, veteran, or sectarian groups; medical research and health organizations; trips or tours; advertising; video, television, or film productions; fundraising events; sporting events; political organizations; subscription fees or admission tickets; or public sector services (with the exception of some school district programs).
Geographic Focus: All States
Amount of Grant: 5,000 - 25,000 USD
Contact: Executive Director; (866) 440-8716 or (415) 899-2000; fax (415) 899-3600; heritage@ffic.com
Internet: http://www.firemansfund.com/heritage/Pages/heritage.aspx
Sponsor: Fireman's Fund Insurance Company
777 San Marin Drive
Novato, CA 94998-1406

FirstEnergy Foundation Community Grants 1819
The FirstEnergy Foundation's contributions to local nonprofit organizations help strengthen the social and economic fabric of our communities. Funded solely by FirstEnergy, the Foundation extends the corporate philosophy of providing community support. The Foundation traditionally funds these priorities: help improve the vitality of our communities and support key safety initiatives; promotion of local and regional economic development and revitalization efforts; and support of FirstEnergy employee community leadership and volunteer interests.
Requirements: 501(c)3 organizations within the FirstEnergy Corporation operating companies' service areas - Ohio Edison Company, the Cleveland Electric Illuminating Company, the Toledo Edison Company, Pennsylvania Power Company, Metropolitan Edison Company, Pennsylvania Electric Company, Jersey Central Power & Light Company, Monongahela Power Company, the Potomac Edison Company, West Penn Power Company, FirstEnergy Solutions Corporation, FirstEnergy Generation, and FirstEnergy Nuclear Operations - are eligible to apply.
Restrictions: Funding is not considered for: direct grants to individuals, political or legislative activities; organizations that receive sizable public tax funding; fraternal, religious, labor, athletic, social or veterans organizations - unless the contribution is earmarked for an eligible program or campaign open to all beneficiaries, including those not affiliated with the host organization; national or international organizations; organizations supported by federated campaigns, such as United Way; research; equipment purchases; loans or second party giving, such as endowments, debt retirement, or foundations; or public or private schools.
Geographic Focus: New Jersey, Ohio, Pennsylvania
Contact: Dee Lowery, President; (330) 761-4246; fax (330) 761-4302
Internet: http://www.firstenergycorp.com/community
Sponsor: FirstEnergy Foundation
76 South Main Street
Akron, OH 44308-1890

FirstEnergy Foundation Math, Science, and Technology Education Grants 1820
The foundation awards grants to eligible Ohio, Pennsylvania, New Jersey, Maryland, and West Virginia educators (pre-K-12) and youth group leaders for classroom projects and local teacher professional development initiatives dealing with mathematics, science, and technology. Projects that involve students directly, incorporate matching funds, are supported by community resources, have interdisciplinary or team-teaching, and involve various age groups are preferred. Teacher training and professional development projects are highly favored. Grants may be used to compensate experts who come to work with students, but not to pay teachers or staff. Equipment and trips must be shown to be just one component of a well-planned project, integrated with other curriculum materials and activities. Projects must be completed during the academic year.
Requirements: Pre-K-12 educators and youth group leaders in Ohio, Pennsylvania, New Jersey, Maryland, and West Virginia communities served by FirstEnergy are eligible.
Restrictions: Funding is generally not made to individuals, political, or legislative activities. Grants cannot be used to support: school laboratory supplies or equipment for general school use; purchase of equipment like computers, digital cameras, DVD players, display cases, etc; continuation of projects previously funded; routine responsibilities of the educator submitting the proposal; stipends for attending teacher development events; or funding for student participation in the project.
Geographic Focus: Maryland, New Jersey, Ohio, Pennsylvania, West Virginia
Amount of Grant: 500 USD
Contact: Dee Lowery, President; (330) 384-5022 or (330) 761-4246; fax (330) 761-4302
Internet: https://www.firstenergycorp.com/community/education/grants/index.html
Sponsor: FirstEnergy Foundation
76 South Main Street
Akron, OH 44308-1890

First Lady's Family Literacy Initiative for Texas Family Literacy Trailblazer Grants 1821
The First Lady's Family Literacy Initiative for Texas is a program of the Barbara Bush Texas Fund for Family Literacy. Launched at the Governor's Mansion in Austin in 1996 by Honorary Chair Laura Bush, The First Lady's Family Literacy Initiative for Texas supports family literacy programs that: increase literacy skills and educational levels of under-educated parents; implement a management and accountability system to measure program effectiveness and outcomes on a regular basis; provide a path to post-secondary education (beyond the GED) and employment; improve the quality of parent/child interaction, and adults' parenting skills in support of their children's learning; employ well-trained and dedicated staff who establish learning environments that positively affect recruitment and retention of adult learners; and encourage families to develop a love for books and reading, and prepare children for the school experience Introduce parents to the services of the library. The new Trailblazer Grant of up to $50,000 per year for three consecutive years will be awarded to no more than three organizations. Their term of funding will extend for a total of three years, pending an annual review by leadership of The First Lady's Family Literacy Initiative for Texas.
Requirements: Eligible applicants for both Planning Grants must: be a local educational agency; non-profit 501(c)3 organization; community-based organization; public institution; correctional agency; or a consortium of these agencies. Further, applicants must be based with an established organization that has maintained current non-profit or public status

for at least two years as of the date of the application be prepared to document fiscal accountability if requested by The Barbara Bush Texas Fund (i.e., provide copy of most recent annual audit report or IRS return).
Geographic Focus: Texas
Date(s) Application is Due: Mar 5
Amount of Grant: Up to 50,000 USD
Contact: Ken Appelt; (979) 845-6615; fax (979) 845-0952; kappelt@tamu.edu
Internet: http://www-tcall.tamu.edu/bbush/firstladyAnnounce.html
Sponsor: Barbara Bush Texas Fund for Family Literacy
Riverside Campus, Texas A&M University
College Station, TX 77843-4477

First Lady's Family Literacy Initiative for Texas Grants 1822
The Barbara Bush Texas Fund for Family Literacy was created in 1999 in response to the enormous success of A Celebration of Reading and the generous support so many Texans have given to help promote literacy across the nation. These grants, of up to $50,000 each, are given to help create family literacy programs by building on existing literacy programs that work with only one generation, such as children or adults, so that complete family literacy programs can be created. The grant program also funds innovative projects within existing family literacy programs, as well as replication of successful family literacy programs with new populations or in new locations.
Requirements: Awards are granted to public and private non-profit organizations that work within the family unit. Past grantees include community-based organizations, libraries, school districts, community colleges, universities, charter schools, pediatric medical clinics, prison programs, Head Start and Even Start programs, as well as other organizations.
Geographic Focus: Texas
Date(s) Application is Due: Mar 5
Amount of Grant: 50,000 USD
Contact: Pat Peebler, Grants Administrator; (800) 441-7323 or (979) 845-6615; fax (979) 845-0952; ppeebler@mcnairgrp.com or tcall@tamu.edu
Internet: http://www.barbarabushfoundation.com/site/c.jhLSK2PALmF/b.4425713/k.F15B/The_Barbara_Bush_Texas_Fund_for_Family_Literacy.htm
Sponsor: Texas Center for the Advancement of Literacy and Learning
4477 TAMU
College Station, TX 77843-4477

First Lady's Family Literacy Initiative for Texas Implementation Grants 1823
The First Lady's Family Literacy Initiative for Texas is a program of the Barbara Bush Texas Fund for Family Literacy. Launched at the Governor's Mansion in Austin in 1996 by Honorary Chair Laura Bush, The First Lady's Family Literacy Initiative for Texas supports family literacy programs that: increase literacy skills and educational levels of under-educated parents; implement a management and accountability system to measure program effectiveness and outcomes on a regular basis; provide a path to post-secondary education (beyond the GED) and employment; improve the quality of parent/child interaction, and adults' parenting skills in support of their children's learning; employ well-trained and dedicated staff who establish learning environments that positively affect recruitment and retention of adult learners; and encourage families to develop a love for books and reading, and prepare children for the school experience Introduce parents to the services of the library. Up to ten Implementation Grants of up to $50,000 will be awarded to Texas organizations. They are intended to: help create a family literacy program that offers three integrated components of adult literacy education (basic literacy, GED Test preparation, or English as a Second Language), pre-literacy or literacy instruction for young children (ages birth through grade 3) of those adults, and interactive literacy activities for the young children together with their parents or primary caregivers; expand an existing literacy program that works with only one generation so that a complete family literacy program (including the required components named above) can be created; allow for an innovative project within an existing family literacy program; or replicate a successful family literacy program with a new population or in a new location.
Requirements: Eligible applicants for both Planning Grants must: be a local educational agency; non-profit 501(c)3 organization; community-based organization; public institution; correctional agency; or a consortium of these agencies. Further, applicants must be based with an established organization that has maintained current non-profit or public status for at least two years as of the date of the application be prepared to document fiscal accountability if requested by The Barbara Bush Texas Fund (i.e., provide copy of most recent annual audit report or IRS return).
Geographic Focus: Texas
Date(s) Application is Due: Mar 5
Amount of Grant: Up to 50,000 USD
Contact: Ken Appelt; (979) 845-6615; fax (979) 845-0952; kappelt@tamu.edu
Internet: http://www-tcall.tamu.edu/bbush/firstladyAnnounce.html
Sponsor: Barbara Bush Texas Fund for Family Literacy
Riverside Campus, Texas A&M University
College Station, TX 77843-4477

First Lady's Family Literacy Initiative for Texas Planning Grants 1824
The First Lady's Family Literacy Initiative for Texas is a program of the Barbara Bush Texas Fund for Family Literacy. Launched at the Governor's Mansion in Austin in 1996 by Honorary Chair Laura Bush, The First Lady's Family Literacy Initiative for Texas supports family literacy programs that: increase literacy skills and educational levels of under-educated parents; implement a management and accountability system to measure program effectiveness and outcomes on a regular basis; provide a path to post-secondary education (beyond the GED) and employment; improve the quality of parent/child interaction, and adults' parenting skills in support of their children's learning; employ well-trained and dedicated staff who establish learning environments that positively affect recruitment and retention of adult learners; and encourage families to develop a love for books and reading, and prepare children for the school experience Introduce parents to the services of the library. Up to five Planning Grants of $5,000 will be awarded to Texas organizations to support a 9-month planning and development process (from June through February), intended to enable an organization to more effectively compete in the next annual First Lady's Family Literacy Initiative for Texas Program Implementation Grant of up to $50,000.
Requirements: Eligible applicants for both Planning Grants must: be a local educational agency; non-profit 501(c)3 organization; community-based organization; public institution; correctional agency; or a consortium of these agencies. Further, applicants must be based with an established organization that has maintained current non-profit or public status for at least two years as of the date of the application be prepared to document fiscal accountability if requested by The Barbara Bush Texas Fund (i.e., provide copy of most recent annual audit report or IRS return).
Geographic Focus: Texas
Date(s) Application is Due: Mar 5
Amount of Grant: Up to 5,000 USD
Contact: Ken Appelt; (979) 845-6615; fax (979) 845-0952; kappelt@tamu.edu
Internet: http://www-tcall.tamu.edu/bbush/firstladyAnnounce.html
Sponsor: Barbara Bush Texas Fund for Family Literacy
Riverside Campus, Texas A&M University
College Station, TX 77843-4477

First People's Fund Community Spirit Awards 1825
Nominations are accepted for the annual award, which recognizes American Indians who have made substantial contributions to their communities. The fund seeks to honor artists who are deeply rooted and maintain direct ties to their tribal community; have a commitment to building the strength of native communities by sharing their skills and talents with others in their respective communities; and have artistic practices that pass on the traditions and the life ways of the people. Four individuals will be honored with a fellowship and will be recognized at a ceremony in December. Nomination may be made online, or send a postcard to the office. Complete guidelines and nomination form are available online.
Requirements: Nominated artists must be: practicing artists of demonstrated maturity in their field, continually practicing artists for a minimum of 10 years, and be a documented affiliate of a United States tribe.
Geographic Focus: All States
Date(s) Application is Due: Apr 16
Amount of Grant: 5,000 USD
Contact: Miranne Walker; (605) 348-0324; miranne@firstpeoplesfund.org
Internet: http://www.firstpeoplesfund.org/Grant%20Programs/CommSpirit/community%20spirit%20awards.htm
Sponsor: First People's Fund
P.O. Box 2977
Rapid City, SD 57709-2977

Fisa Foundation Grants 1826
The foundation's mission is to build a culture of respect and improve the quality of life for three populations in southwestern Pennsylvania: women, girls, and people with disabilities. Emphasis is given to addressing gaps and unmet needs in the community. The foundation will consider support for new and ongoing programs and projects, operating needs, capacity building, equipment, and capital expenditures. Applicants are encouraged to submit a letter of inquiry outlining the needs to be addressed, a brief description of the proposed project or program, and the amount of the request. Letters of inquiry are reviewed on a monthly basis; full proposals are by invitation. Application and guidelines are available online.
Requirements: 501(c)3 and 509(a) nonprofit organizations in the 10-county southwestern Pennsylvania area, including Allegheny, Armstrong, Beaver, Butler, Fayette, Greene, Indiana, Lawrence, Washington and Westmoreland Counties, are eligible.
Restrictions: The foundation does not make grants in support of individuals; political campaigns or lobbying; religious organizations for religious purposes; travel, study and scholarships; services for people with disabilities that result from the aging process; renovations to improve physical accessibility of buildings; programs with the primary mission of serving individuals with mental illness; clinical research; or parenting programs, unless they specifically relate to parents with disabilities.
Geographic Focus: Pennsylvania
Contact: Mary Delaney, (412) 456-5550; fax (412) 456-5551; info@fisafoundation.org
Internet: http://www.fisafoundation.org/grtmk.ivnu
Sponsor: Fisa Foundation
1001 Liberty Avenue, Suite 650
Pittsburgh, PA 15222

FishAmerica Foundation Chesapeake Bay Grants 1827
In partnership with the Chesapeake Bay Trust, the Foundation offers grants to non-profit organizations in Maryland for projects benefiting sportfish and their habitat in the Chesapeake Bay watershed of Maryland. The CBT and FAF seek hands-on, grassroots projects that involve community groups, students, or other volunteers. Projects should have a clear and identifiable benefit to fish populations and the sport of fishing. Applicants may apply for funding for materials directly related to restoration and enhancement activities. Types of projects that will be considered include: riparian restoration; stream bank stabilization and stream restoration; fish passage improvement; wetland creation and improvement; submerged aquatic vegetation plantings; and oyster reef creation/restoration. The strongest proposals will show committed partnerships (those that provide funding, technical assistance, and/or in-kind support) from various organizations/institutions/government agencies. All projects must be completed one year from the date of the grant award.

Requirements: Maryland non-profit and not-for-profit organizations are eligible for funding. Only projects in areas of the Maryland portion of the Chesapeake Bay and its tributaries in Maryland are eligible for funding under this partnership. Applicants are encouraged to pursue projects that have been identified as part of an implementation strategy of a watershed management plan or assessment.
Restrictions: The following items are not eligible for funding: benefits or indirect costs; monitoring supplies and equipment greater than 10% of total project cost; incidentals such as food and T-shirts; access projects such as road construction, boat ramps or fishing piers; permits; endowments, individuals, loans, fund raising, advertising or publications; computer equipment; and research.
Geographic Focus: Maryland
Date(s) Application is Due: Dec 7
Amount of Grant: Up to 35,000 USD
Contact: Patrick Egan, Grants Manager; (703) 519-9691, ext. 247; fax (703) 519-1872; pegan@asafishing.org or fishamerica@asafishing.org
Internet: http://www.fishamerica.org/grants.html
Sponsor: FishAmerica Foundation
1001 North Fairfax Street, Suite 501
Alexandria, VA 22314

FishAmerica Foundation Conservation Grants 1828
The FishAmerica Foundation Conservation Grants provide funding to non-profit organizations such as sporting clubs, civic associations, conservation groups, and state agencies, in the United States and Canada. The program offers grants for stock enhancement, freshwater fisheries habitat restoration, non-habitat marine and estuarine enhancements, and family fishing waters improvement projects. Applications are accepted year-round. The review period is nine to twelve months, and the average award is $7,500.
Requirements: 501(c)3 nonprofit organizations, such as local sporting clubs and conservation associations and local and state governments, are eligible. Local and state agencies, educational institutions, and other government entities should provide their EIN number. Applicants also may have nonprofit fiscal sponsors.
Geographic Focus: All States
Amount of Grant: Up to 10,000 USD
Contact: Patrick Egan; (703) 519-9691, ext. 247; fax (703) 519-1872; pegan@asafishing.org
Internet: http://www.fishamerica.org/grants.html
Sponsor: FishAmerica Foundation
1001 North Fairfax Street, Suite 501
Alexandria, VA 22314

FishAmerica Foundation Marine and Anadromous Fish Habitat Restoration Grants 1829
The FishAmerica Foundation Marine and Anadromous Fish Habitat Restoration program requests proposals for local efforts to accomplish meaningful on-the-ground restoration of marine, estuarine and riparian habitats, including salt marshes, seagrass beds, mangrove forests, and freshwater habitats important to anadromous fish species (fish like salmon and striped bass that spawn in freshwater and migrate to the sea). Emphasis is on using a hands-on, grassroots approach to restore fisheries habitat across coastal America and the Great Lakes.
Requirements: Projects must result in the implementation of locally-driven habitat restoration projects that emphasize stewardship and yield ecological and socioeconomic benefits. These projects must clearly demonstrate significant benefits to marine, estuarine or anadromous fisheries resources, particularly sportfish, and should involve community participation through an educational or volunteer component tied to the restoration activities. Nonprofit organizations such as sporting clubs, civic organizations, conservation groups, and to a lesser extent state agencies, in the United States and Canada are eligible. Projects must result in on-the-ground habitat restoration, clearly demonstrate significant benefits to marine, estuarine or anadromous fisheries resources, particularly sportfish, and must involve community participation through an educational or volunteer component tied to the restoration activities.
Geographic Focus: All States
Date(s) Application is Due: Apr 30
Amount of Grant: 10,000 - 75,000 USD
Contact: Patrick Egan, Grants Manager; (703) 519-9691, ext. 247; fax (703) 519-1872; pegan@asafishing.org or fishamerica@asafishing.org
Internet: http://www.fishamerica.org/grants.html
Sponsor: FishAmerica Foundation
1001 North Fairfax Street, Suite 501
Alexandria, VA 22314

FishAmerica Foundation Research Grants 1830
Overall, the FishAmerica Foundation will fund research projects that further the National Fish Habitat Plan. Specifically, the program funds research projects that have regional or national implication, not local. Grants support research in the following areas: fisheries management, water quality, habitat studies, stock enhancement, economic impact studies related to sport fishing, and tagging.
Requirements: Nonprofits such as sporting clubs, civic organizations, conservation groups, and to a lesser extent state agencies, in the United States and Canada are eligible.
Restrictions: Grants do not support the following projects or purposes: donations of fishing tackle; salaries, administration, overhead, or travel for conservation projects; individuals; local stream monitoring programs; political activities that attempt to influence political campaigns or legislation; access projects such as road construction, boat ramps, or fishing piers; loans, endowments, trips, tours, tickets, advertising, or publications; or permitting and related costs.
Geographic Focus: All States
Date(s) Application is Due: Jul 31
Amount of Grant: Up to 25,000 USD
Contact: Patrick Egan, Grants Manager; (703) 519-9691, ext. 247; fax (703) 519-1872; pegan@asafishing.org or fishamerica@asafishing.org
Internet: http://www.fishamerica.org/grants.html
Sponsor: FishAmerica Foundation
1001 North Fairfax Street, Suite 501
Alexandria, VA 22314

Fisher Foundation Grants 1831
The foundation awards grants to Connecticut nonprofits that benefit education, health and human services, housing, community needs, and arts and culture. The majority of grants are single year awards. Before submitting an application, a letter of inquiry or conversation with staff to discuss the specific purpose for which the funds are being requested is strongly recommended. Application information and guidelines are available online. Do not submit applications by fax or email.
Requirements: Nonprofits located in, and/or serving the residents of the Greater Hartford area, including: Andover, Avon, Bloomfield, Bolton, Canton, East Hartford, East Granby, East Windsor, Ellington, Enfield, Farmington, Glastonbury, Granby, Hartford, Hebron, Manchester, Marlborough, Newington, Rocky Hill, Simsbury, Somers, South Windsor, Suffield, Tolland, Vernon, West Hartford, Wethersfield, Windsor, and Windsor Locks are eligible.
Restrictions: Foundation policy does not allow funding for: organizations which are not tax-exempt under IRS Code section 501(c)3; organizations which have the IRS private foundation designation; individuals; performances, conferences, retreats, one-time events, trips; annual campaigns.
Geographic Focus: Connecticut
Date(s) Application is Due: Jan 15; Apr 15; Sep 15
Contact: Beverly Boyle; (860) 570-0221; fax (860) 570-0225; bboyle@fisherfdn.org
Internet: http://www.fisherfdn.org/application/instructions.htm
Sponsor: Fisher Foundation
36 Brookside Boulevard
West Hartford, CT 06107

Fisher House Foundation Hero Miles Program 1832
The Foundation administers the Hero Miles program for the Department of Defense in accordance with Public Law 108-110, the FY 05 Defense Authorization Act. The program is comprised of individual airlines whose passengers donate their frequent flyer miles to assist service members and their families. Specifically, the Foundation provides free airline tickets to military men and women who are undergoing treatment at a military or VA medical center incident to their service in Iraq or Afghanistan, and their families. There are two categories of eligible recipients: service men and women with an approved leave of five or more days may be given a free round trip airline ticket for a trip from the medical center to their home and return if they are not eligible for government funded airfare; and qualifying service men and women may be given free round trip airline tickets to enable their family or close friends to visit them while they are being treated at the medical center. The Foundation normally uses the social work staff or service casualty offices to verify eligibility.
Restrictions: These tickets can not be used for R&R travel, ordinary leave, emergency leave, or other travel not related to a medical condition.
Geographic Focus: All States
Amount of Grant: 1,300 USD
Contact: James D. Weiskopf, Executive Vice President; (888) 294-8560 or (301) 294-8560; fax (301) 294-8562; info@fisherhouse.org
Internet: http://www.fisherhouse.org/programs/heroMiles.shtml
Sponsor: Fisher House Foundation
1401 Rockville Pike, Suite 600
Rockville, MD 20852-1402

Fisher House Foundation Newman's Own Awards 1833
Grants are made to implement innovative programs to improve the quality of life for military families and their communities. This program is administered by Fisher House, a charitable organization that provides a home-like place to stay for United States military families while a family member is receiving treatment at a major military or Veterans Administration medical facility. One award will be given to an organization supporting the Army, Navy, Air Force, Marines, or Coast Guard The organization with the most innovative project submitted will receive up to $15,000. The other four organizations will receive lesser amounts, as determined by the judges. Annual deadline dates may vary; contact program staff for exact dates.
Requirements: Eligible applicants must support an Active Duty, National Guard, or Reserve unit or installation, and be tax-exempt, a private organization, or a volunteer organization. Private, nonprofit organizations as defined in Department of Defense (DoD) Instruction 1000.15 and approved for operation on a DoD installation by the installation commander are eligible.
Geographic Focus: All States
Date(s) Application is Due: Apr 30
Amount of Grant: 1,000 - 15,000 USD
Contact: James D. Weiskopf; (888) 294-8560 or (301) 294-8560; fax (301) 294-8562; info@fisherhouse.org
Internet: http://www.fisherhouse.org/programs/newmans.shtml
Sponsor: Fisher House Foundation
1401 Rockville Pike, Suite 600
Rockville, MD 20852-1402

Fisheries and Habitat Partnership Grants 1834
Ocean Trust and the National Oceanic and Atmospheric Administration Restoration Center announce the availability of funds to support cooperative projects with America's food fishing industry to restore habitat and enhance living marine resources of the United States. Projects may include restoration, enhancement, or educational efforts directed at coastal marine or estuarine habitat, or living marine resources that provide a renewable source of food or assist in the restoration of marine species linked to the use and productivity of fishery resources. The program seeks partners and invites the submission of project proposals. Matching funds are required. Guidelines are available online.
Requirements: Individuals, associations, or companies in fish and seafood production, processing, distribution, retail, foodservice, support, or advisory services with the industry may apply.
Geographic Focus: All States
Date(s) Application is Due: Jul 31; Nov 30
Amount of Grant: 5,000 - 20,000 USD
Contact: Administrator; (703) 450-9852; fax (703) 450-9853; tjlassen@oceantrust.org
Internet: http://www.oceantrust.org/restoration.htm
Sponsor: Ocean Trust
11921 Freedom Drive, Suite 550-PMB 5580
Reston, VA 20190

Fishman Family Foundation Grants 1835
The Foundation considers grants for: research, education, and cultural development of and for the community; scholarships related to Jewish services, education, social, and community activities; medical and scientific research; providing resources to meet critical needs in Israel; and educational grants and scholarships. Proposals are reviewed in April and October. Application information is available online.
Requirements: 501(c)3 nonprofits are eligible.
Geographic Focus: All States
Date(s) Application is Due: Mar 31; Sep 30
Contact: Betty Fishman, President; info@fishman.org
Internet: http://www.fishman.org/apply.html
Sponsor: Fishman Family Foundation
730 E Cypress Avenue
Monrovia, CA 91016

Fitzpatrick, Cella, Harper & Scinto Pro Bono Services 1836
Recognizing the ever-growing need in the community for the provision of legal services to those of limited means, Fitzpatrick has instituted a firm-wide pro bono program that encourages each lawyer in the firm to devote time to pro bono service. The firm's Pro Bono Committee has a representative from each of our three offices: Donald Curry (New York), Brian Klock (Washington, D.C.) and Edward Kmett (Costa Mesa). The firm's pro bono practice has been structured around several "practice areas" focused on particular substantive areas of law. These practice areas include branches of intellectual property law, as well as areas outside intellectual property where there is a particular need for the provision of legal services to people lacking the means to afford them.
Requirements: Pro bono services are provided to needy residents of New York City, Washington, DC, and Costa Mesa, California, and the surrounding regions where the firm provides legal services.
Geographic Focus: California, District of Columbia, New York
Contact: Donald J. Curry, Pro Bono Coordinator; (212) 218-2100; fax (212) 218-2200
Internet: http://www.fitzpatrickcella.com/?p=2534
Sponsor: Fitzpatrick, Cella, Harper & Scinto
1290 Avenue of the Americas
New York, NY 10104-3800

Fitzpatrick and Francis Family Business Continuity Foundation Grants 1837
The Family Business Continuity Foundation is dedicated to providing financial support for the training and education of family business advisors either through grants directly to individuals or to institutions that provide education and training to individuals. The Foundation wants to ensure that family businesses receive the best possible advice as they create Family Councils, select a competent board of directors, and plan to successfully transfer ownership and leadership of their enterprise from one generation to the next. Primary fields of interest include: the arts, community and economic development, and education. A formal application is required, though there are no specified annual deadlines. Funding is primarily offered in Kansas, Missouri, and Vancouver, British Columbia, though the Foundation does provide grants outside of its geographic designated areas. Grants range from $500 to $10,000.
Geographic Focus: All States, Canada
Amount of Grant: 500 - 10,000 USD
Contact: John J. Fitzpatrick; (785) 273-8596 or (785) 273-8500; fax (785) 273-8768
Internet: http://familybizfoundation.org/
Sponsor: Fitzpatrick and Francis Family Business Continuity Foundation
P.O. Box 4815
Topeka, KS 66604-0815

Fleishhacker Foundation Education Grants 1838
The Foundation funds precollegiate education, K-12, with an emphasis on the K-8 level. The Foundation's general interest is in programs and projects which: take place at the school site, preferably during the school day; are innovative; involve coordination of programs and services which support the educational process; connect in-school learning to the student's home, community, and cultural life; are cost effective; and show potential for longevity. Application information is available online.
Requirements: Nonprofits in the San Francisco Bay area are eligible.
Restrictions: The foundation does not support: deficit financing; annual funds; endowment campaigns; capital campaigns over $10 million; youth who have dropped out of school; adult education; fundraising events; and travel.
Geographic Focus: California
Date(s) Application is Due: Jan 15; Jul 15
Amount of Grant: 5,000 - 10,000 USD
Contact: Christine Elbel; (415) 561-5350; info@fleishhackerfoundation.org
Internet: http://www.fleishhackerfoundation.org/education.html
Sponsor: Fleishhacker Foundation
P.O. Box 29918
San Francisco, CA 94129-0918

Fleishhacker Foundation Small Grants in the Arts 1839
The particular emphasis of the Program is to support the development and presentation of the work of living Bay Area artists. New work is the first priority, however retrospectives and classical repertory of non-living artists will be considered. Grants may be awarded for: artists' fees for creative time; production costs for performances or film/video projects; exhibition/installation costs for visual, media, or interdisciplinary arts projects; activities that contribute to overall artistic development; and efforts to strengthen an organization's artistic impact within the community.
Requirements: Applicants must be: arts and cultural organizations incorporated as not-for-profit [501(c)3]; organizations residing and offering programming in the greater San Francisco Bay Area; able to demonstrate a consistent artistic presence in the Bay Area for at least 3 years; and of budget size between $100,000 and $750,000.
Restrictions: Not eligible for funding are: programs/projects whose fundamental purpose or benefit falls within the social services, health, youth, or community development fields; individuals (unless conducting a project under the sponsorship of an eligible nonprofit organization; organizations based outside the greater San Francisco Bay Area; or deficit financing, endowment campaigns, major capital campaign requests (campaigns over $10 million).
Geographic Focus: California
Date(s) Application is Due: Jan 15; Jul 15
Amount of Grant: 1,000 - 10,000 USD
Contact: Christine Elbel; (415) 561-5350; info@fleishhackerfoundation.org
Internet: http://www.fleishhackerfoundation.org/small.html
Sponsor: Fleishhacker Foundation
P.O. Box 29918
San Francisco, CA 94129-0918

Fleishhacker Foundation Special Arts Grants 1840
Periodically grants which exceed the scope of the Small Grants Program are made to groups with budgets greater than $750,000. The project must clearly demonstrate potential for broad and long-term impact on the local community and the art form involved. This might involve: facility access or use, community-wide program initiatives, or exceptional artistic projects. Grants normally do not exceed $25,000.
Requirements: Applicants must be: arts and cultural organizations incorporated as not-for-profit [501(c)3]; organizations residing and offering programming in the greater San Francisco Bay Area; and able to demonstrate a consistent artistic presence in the Bay Area for at least 3 years.
Restrictions: Not eligible are capital campaigns over $1 million and endowment campaigns.
Geographic Focus: California
Date(s) Application is Due: Jan 15; Jul 15
Amount of Grant: Up to 25,000 USD
Contact: Christine Elbel; (415) 561-5350; info@fleishhackerfoundation.org
Internet: http://www.fleishhackerfoundation.org/special.html
Sponsor: Fleishhacker Foundation
P.O. Box 29918
San Francisco, CA 94129-0918

Flextronics Foundation Disaster Relief Grants 1841
The Flextronics Foundation seeks to aid, enrich, engage, educate and empower the communities where its company, suppliers and customers have a business presence. The Disaster Relief program provides aid to relieve human suffering that may be caused by a natural or civil disaster, or an emergency hardship. These disasters may be floods, fires, storms, earthquakes or similar large-scale adversities. Applications are evaluated on a quarterly basis at the end of March, June, September and November annually.
Requirements: Applicants must qualify as a 501(c)3 nonprofit organization or exclusively public institution or comparable charitable organization. Grants are provided for services and programs that match The Flextronics Foundation's priorities and are within the areas in which Flextronics' personnel live and work and/or where Flextronics' suppliers and customers live and work. Preference is given to those charitable organizations whose services and programs resonate with Flextronics employees (e.g., Flextronics employees donate their time and are actively involved). Grants are generally to be expended within one year, without expectation of further support.
Restrictions: The following are not eligible: Organizations that are not a 501(c)3 nonprofit or exclusively public institutions or comparable charitable organization; Religious (sectarian) and political groups; Stand-alone activities that are not an integrated part of a service or program (advertising, athletic events or league sponsorships, conventions, conferences, meetings or seminars, clubs, contests, field trips, film and/or video projects, fundraising activities such as walk-a-thons, marketing, sponsorships, travel and/or travel expenses and other stand alone or isolated activities); For-profit organizations or ventures; Organizations that discriminate based on race, creed, color, religion, gender, ethnicity, national origin, sexual orientation, age, disability or veteran status.

Geographic Focus: All States
Contact: Lori Kenepp, (408) 576-7528; lori.kenepp@flextronics.com
Internet: http://www.flextronics.com/social_resp/Flextronics_Foundation/Pages/Grants.aspx
Sponsor: Flextronics International
6201 America Center Drive
San Jose, CA 95002

Flinn Foundation Grants 1842
The foundation's grantmaking programs, limited to Arizona, include enhancing community-based solutions to local health care needs, especially those for children and youth; strengthening medical education and biomedical research programs in Arizona; strengthening Arizona's universities through an undergraduate scholarship program for outstanding Arizona high school students; and enhancing the visibility and long-term artistic mission of Arizona's principal visual and performing arts organizations. Types of support include program development, seed money, scholarship funds, and research grants.
Requirements: Arizona-based institutions or organizations whose programs are operated for the benefit of Arizona institutions and individuals are eligible to apply. Applications are accepted at any time. There is no application form, but a preliminary letter of inquiry or phone call is requested to determine the appropriateness of a full submission.
Restrictions: The foundation rarely provides grants to individuals, building projects (capital campaigns), purchase of equipment, endowment projects, annual fund-raising campaigns, ongoing operating expenses, or deficit needs. Requests to support conferences and workshops, publications, or the production of films and video are considered only when these activities are an integral component of a larger foundation initiative.
Geographic Focus: Arizona
Amount of Grant: 2,500 - 150,000 USD
Contact: JoAnn Fazio; (602) 744-6800; fax (602) 744-6815; info@flinn.org
Internet: http://www.flinn.org/about/grants.cms
Sponsor: Flinn Foundation
1802 N Central Avenue
Phoenix, AZ 85004-1506

Flinn Foundation Scholarships 1843
The Flinn Foundation scholarships, in partnership with Arizona's three state universities, provide enriched educational offerings that expand a recipient's life and career options. Students receive a financial package for their entire undergraduate study that includes free tuition, room, and board, funding for study abroad, mentorship from faculty, exposure to world leaders, and fellowship in a community of current and alumni Scholars. Total dollar value exceeds $50,000, in addition to the cash value of tuition provided by the universities. Scholars begin as a group, with a three-week seminar in Central Europe. Each Scholar also receives a stipend for at least one international summer seminar, or a semester or year at a foreign university.
Requirements: Recipients must rank in the top 5 percent of their high school graduating class with at least a 3.5 grade point average; score a minimum of 29 on the ACT or 1300 on the SAT (critical reading and math sections only); demonstrate leadership in a variety of extracurricular activities; and hold U.S. citizenship and residency in Arizona for the two years prior to application. All majors may apply.
Restrictions: Applicants must apply to one of three Arizona universities: Arizona State University, Northern Arizona University, or University of Arizona.
Geographic Focus: Arizona
Date(s) Application is Due: Oct 21
Contact: Flinn Scholarship Contact; (602) 744-6800; fscholars@flinn.org
Internet: http://www.flinnscholars.org/news/977
Sponsor: Flinn Foundation
1802 N Central Avenue
Phoenix, AZ 85004-1506

Florence Hunt Maxwell Foundation Grants 1844
The mission of the Florence Hunt Maxwell Foundation is to support charitable organizations that provide for the underserved and indigent community. Grants from the Florence Hunt Maxwell Foundation are primarily one year in duration; on occasion, multi-year support is awarded. Applicants must apply online at the grant website. Applicants are strongly encouraged to do the following before applying: review the downloadable state application procedures for additional helpful information and clarifications; review the downloadable online-application guidelines at the grant website; review the foundation's funding history (link is available from the grant website); review the online application questions in advance; and review the list of required attachments. These will generally include: a list of board members, financial statements (audited, reviewed, or compiled by independent auditor); an organization summary; a list of other funding sources; an IRS Determination letter; and other required documents. All attachments must be uploaded in the online application as PDF, Word, or Excel files. The Florence Hunt Maxwell Foundation application deadline is 11:59 p.m. on April 1. Applicants will be notified of grant decisions by letter within one to two months after the deadline.
Requirements: Applicants must have 501(c)3 tax-exempt status and serve residents of the Metro Atlanta area.
Restrictions: The foundation does not support requests from individuals, organizations attempting to influence policy through direct lobbying, or any political campaigns.
Geographic Focus: Georgia
Date(s) Application is Due: Apr 1
Contact: Quanda Allen, Vice President; (404) 264-1377; quanda.allen@baml.com
Internet: https://www.bankofamerica.com/philanthropic/fn_search.action
Sponsor: Florence Hunt Maxwell Foundation
3414 Peachtree Road, N.E., Suite 1475, GA7-813-14-04
Atlanta, GA 30326-1113

Florian O. Bartlett Trust Grants 1845
The Florian O. Bartlett Trust was established in 1937 to support and promote quality educational, human services, and health care programming for underserved populations. The application deadline for the Florian O. Bartlett Trust is April 1. Applicants will be notified of grant decisions before June 30. Grant requests for general operating support are strongly encouraged. Program support will also be considered. Small, program-related capital expenses may be included in general operating or program requests. The majority of grants from the Bartlett Trust are 1 year in duration. On occasion, multi-year support is awarded.
Geographic Focus: Massachusetts
Date(s) Application is Due: Apr 1
Contact: Michealle Larkins, (866) 778-6859; michealle.larkins@baml.com
Internet: https://www.bankofamerica.com/philanthropic/fn_search.action
Sponsor: Florian O. Bartlett Trust
225 Franklin Street, 4th Floor, MA1-225-04-02
Boston, MA 02110

Florida BRAIve Fund of Dade Community Foundation 1846
The Florida BrAIve Fund at Dade Community Foundation will award grants to non-profits to assist eligible military personnel and family members residing in Miami-Dade, Monroe, Broward, Palm Beach and Martin counties. BRAIVE Fund grants will address needs of military personnel and their families in the target population related to pre-deployment, during deployment, and their return from duty. To obtain more information and the application forms, go to http://www.dadecommunityfoundation.org/Site/wc/wc143.jsp.
Requirements: General criteria for evaluating applications to The Florida BrAIve Fund of Dade Community Foundation: applicant is a 501(c)3 organization; applicant organization has a proven record of effective service to its clientele; applicant organization demonstrates the management and financial capacity to efficiently achieve the grant purpose; grants will be made to nonprofit organizations, not individuals; programs or services can only benefit current and former military personnel serving in Iraq or Afghanistan and their families; program services must be provided in the area of Florida to be covered by Dade Community Foundation as indicated in The Florida BrAIve Fund map; successful organizations will demonstrate that the agency is currently serving military personnel and their families in Florida or has the experience to address an unmet need.
Geographic Focus: Florida
Date(s) Application is Due: Jun 8
Contact: Claudianna Williams, Administrative Assistant; (305) 371-2711; fax (305) 371-5342; claudianna.williams@dadecommunityfoundation.org
Internet: http://www.dadecommunityfoundation.org/Site/wc/wc143.jsp
Sponsor: Dade Community Foundation
200 S Biscayne Boulevard, Suite 505
Miami, FL 33131-5330

Florida Division of Cultural Affairs Community Theatre Grants 1847
Florida Division of Cultural Affairs theatre disciplines support projects that promote excellence in theatre performance. The Community Theatre discipline is for applicants producing a community theatre project. Most of the artistic staff participating in community theatre projects are not compensated. However personnel may be hired as needed to perform administrative, artistic, or production duties. Community theatre applicants should be very specific when describing how artists are compensated. Although it is assumed that most community theatre applicants will not be compensating most actors, applicants should address whether or not technical staff (directors, designers) are compensated and if any actors receive financial compensation. If a community theatre is in the process of becoming a professional house, the application should describe where the applicant is in the transition and when the applicant expects to be offering full compensation to artistic staff. The grant period start date is July 1 or the date the award agreement is executed, whichever is later. The grant period end date is June 30 unless an end date extension is approved by the Division. Community Theatre projects have a maximum request of $25,000.
Requirements: To meet the legal status requirement, an applicant organization must be either a public entity (Florida local government, entity of state government, school district, community college, college, or university) or a Florida nonprofit, tax exempt corporation as of the application deadline. Private schools, private community colleges, private colleges, and private universities are not public entities and must be nonprofit and tax exempt to meet the legal status requirement. Applicants must provide at least one dollar in cash and in-kind (donated goods or services) for every dollar requested from the division. Allowable expenses must be: directly related to the proposal; specifically and clearly detailed in the proposal budget; and incurred and paid within the grant start and end dates.
Restrictions: The following are non-allowable expenses for grant and matching funds: state funds from any source; funds used as match for other Department of State grants; expenses incurred or obligated before July 1 or after the grant period; lobbying or attempting to influence federal, state, or local legislation; building, renovation, or remodeling of facilities; capital expenditures (includes acquisitions, building projects, and renovations); costs associated with bad debts, contingencies (money set aside for possible expenses), fines and penalties, interest, taxes, and other financial costs; private entertainment, food, and beverages; plaques, awards, and scholarships; re-granting; contributions and donations; mortgage payments; or payments to current Department of State employees. No state funds may be used towards operational costs such as: phone; utilities; office supplies; equipment costing over $1,000; property improvements; fixtures; building maintenance; space rental; or other overhead or indirect costs.
Geographic Focus: Florida
Amount of Grant: Up to 25,000 USD
Contact: Laura Lewis Blischke; (850) 245-6475; llblischke@dos.state.fl.us
Internet: http://www.florida-arts.org/documents/guidelines/2012-2013.scp.guidelines.cfm#theatre

Sponsor: Florida Division of Cultural Affairs
500 South Bronough Street, 3rd Floor
Tallahassee, FL 32399-0250

Florida Division of Cultural Affairs Culture Builds Florida Expansion Funding 1848
Culture Builds Florida project grants are designed to support and encourage projects throughout the state in the four vision areas of the Division's Strategic Plan, Culture Builds Florida's Future. The Plan is a statewide cultural plan designed to redefine the role of the arts and culture in Florida. Its four vision areas include: strengthening the economy; promoting learning and wellness; building leadership; and advancing design and development. The Expansion Funding category is for applicants that already have project activity in one or more of the key areas of the Division's Strategic Plan, but are applying for a new component of an existing project. Applications in this funding category may be for a specific effort to: reach a new audience; bring a new component to an existing project (by adding new technology, new disciplines, etc.); or other expansion or enhancement to an existing project. With this information, the Division can demonstrate to the legislature and the public how our grantees are implementing a unified message and strategy for arts and culture. The grant period start date is July 1 or the date the award agreement is executed, whichever is later. The grant period end date is June 30 unless an end date extension is approved by the Division.
Requirements: An organization must qualify as a political subdivision of a municipal, county, or state government in Florida; or be a nonprofit, tax-exempt Florida corporation. A dollar-for-dollar state to local match is required, with 25 percent in kind allowed.
Restrictions: This category will only fund that portion of an existing project that represents a expansion of at least one (1) vision area of the Division's Strategic Plan.
Geographic Focus: Florida
Amount of Grant: Up to 25,000 USD
Contact: Sarah T. Stage, Program Manager; (850) 245-6459; sstage@dos.state.fl.us
Internet: http://www.florida-arts.org/documents/guidelines/2012-2013.scp.guidelines.cfm#cbf
Sponsor: Florida Division of Cultural Affairs
500 South Bronough Street, 3rd Floor
Tallahassee, FL 32399-0250

Florida Division of Cultural Affairs Culture Builds Florida Seed Funding 1849
Culture Builds Florida project grants are designed to support and encourage projects throughout the state in the four vision areas of the Division's Strategic Plan, Culture Builds Florida's Future. The Seed Funding category is designed for applicants to start a new project that fits within at least one of the designated areas of the Division's Strategic Plan. The Plan is a statewide cultural plan designed to redefine the role of the arts and culture in Florida. Its four vision areas include: strengthening the economy; promoting learning and wellness; building leadership; and advancing design and development. With this information, the Division can demonstrate to the legislature and the public how our grantees are implementing a unified message and strategy for arts and culture. The grant period start date is July 1 or the date the award agreement is executed, whichever is later. The grant period end date is June 30 unless an end date extension is approved by the Division.
Requirements: An organization must qualify as a political subdivision of a municipal, county, or state government in Florida; or be a nonprofit, tax-exempt Florida corporation. A dollar-for-dollar state to local match is required, with 25 percent in kind allowed.
Geographic Focus: Florida
Amount of Grant: Up to 25,000 USD
Contact: Sarah Thomas Stage, Arts Administrator; (850) 245-6459; sstage@dos.state.fl.us
Internet: http://www.florida-arts.org/documents/guidelines/2012-2013.scp.guidelines.cfm#cbf
Sponsor: Florida Division of Cultural Affairs
500 South Bronough Street, 3rd Floor
Tallahassee, FL 32399-0250

Florida Division of Cultural Affairs Dance Grants 1850
Florida Division of Cultural Affairs discipline-based projects are discipline specific for organizations conducting cultural projects, realizing their stated mission, and furthering the state's cultural objectives. The Dance discipline is for projects that promote excellence in dance. The grant period start date is July 1 or the date the award agreement is executed, whichever is later. The grant period end date is June 30 unless an end date extension is approved by the Division. Dance projects have a maximum request of $25,000.
Requirements: To meet the legal status requirement, an applicant organization must be either a public entity (Florida local government, entity of state government, school district, community college, college, or university) or a Florida nonprofit, tax exempt corporation as of the application deadline. Private schools, private community colleges, private colleges, and private universities are not public entities and must be nonprofit and tax exempt to meet the legal status requirement. Applicants must provide at least one dollar in cash and in-kind (donated goods or services) for every dollar requested from the division. Allowable expenses must be: directly related to the proposal; specifically and clearly detailed in the proposal budget; and incurred and paid within the grant start and end dates.
Restrictions: The following are non-allowable expenses for grant and matching funds: state funds from any source; funds used as match for other Department of State grants; expenses incurred or obligated before July 1 or after the grant period; lobbying or attempting to influence federal, state, or local legislation; building, renovation, or remodeling of facilities; capital expenditures (includes acquisitions, building projects, and renovations); costs associated with bad debts, contingencies (money set aside for possible expenses), fines and penalties, interest, taxes, and other financial costs; private entertainment, food, and beverages; plaques, awards, and scholarships; re-granting; contributions and donations; mortgage payments; or payments to current Department of State employees. No state funds may be used towards operational costs such as: phone; utilities; office supplies; equipment costing over $1,000; property improvements; fixtures; building maintenance; space rental; or other overhead or indirect costs.
Geographic Focus: Florida
Amount of Grant: Up to 25,000 USD
Contact: Laura Lewis Blischke; (850) 245-6475; llblischke@dos.state.fl.us
Internet: http://www.florida-arts.org/documents/guidelines/2012-2013.scp.guidelines.cfm#dance
Sponsor: Florida Division of Cultural Affairs
500 South Bronough Street, 3rd Floor
Tallahassee, FL 32399-0250

Florida Division of Cultural Affairs Endowment Grants 1851
The purpose of Cultural Endowment grants is to create an endowment matching funds program that will provide operating resources to participating cultural organizations. The Cultural Endowment program is comprised of two components: cultural sponsoring organization (CSO) designation; and receipt of a $240,000 State Matching Share (SMS). Although both parts require the submission of application material, each contains eligibility criteria that are unique to the components. An organization may be designated as a CSO without submitting an application for an SMS. However, CSO designation is an eligibility criterion for the receipt of an SMS.
Requirements: Eligible organizations must be a not-for-profit, tax exempt Florida corporation or a tax exempt organization as defined in Section 501(c)3 or 501(c)4 of the Internal Revenue Code of 1954. Eligible organizations must be able to provide a description and documentation of a program that qualifies it as a sponsoring organization within a cultural discipline. The description and documentation shall include printed performance or printed exhibition material such as brochures, programs, or catalogs. Applications for designation as a Cultural Sponsoring Organization may be submitted at any time. However, Cultural Sponsoring Organization designation is a criterion for eligibility to receive a State Matching Share. Designation must be recommended by the Florida Arts Council and approved by the Secretary of State before an organization can be considered eligible to receive a State Matching Share. Potential applicants are encouraged to contact the Division to inquire about the Florida Arts Council meeting schedule. An application must be received at least 30 days prior to a regular meeting of the council in order to be included on the agenda. Meetings are held four times a year; generally in March, June, September, and November. Applications for a State Matching Share must be received in the Office of the Division of Cultural Affairs (or the Department of State) by 5:00 p.m. of the deadline date. However, any application postmarked by the United States Postal Service no later than midnight of the deadline date, shall be deemed to have been timely received.
Restrictions: Ineligible programs and organizations are: Programs within the State University System and eligible for support under Section 240.257, Florida Statutes, the Florida Endowment Trust Fund for Eminent Scholars; Community colleges; Direct Support Organizations (i.e., Friends, Foundations, or Trusts) which is not primarily and directly responsible for conducting, creating, producing, presenting, staging, or sponsoring a cultural exhibit, performance, or event; federal, state, county, or city governments.
Geographic Focus: Florida
Amount of Grant: Up to 240,000 USD
Contact: Donald R. Blancett; (850) 245-6483; don.blancett@dos.myflorida.com
Internet: http://www.florida-arts.org/programs/endowment/
Sponsor: Florida Division of Cultural Affairs
500 South Bronough Street, 3rd Floor
Tallahassee, FL 32399-0250

Florida Division of Cultural Affairs Facilities Grants 1852
The purpose of the Regional Cultural Facilities (RCF) program is to coordinate and guide the State of Florida's support and funding of renovation, construction, or acquisition of regional cultural facilities. A cultural facility is a building which shall be used primarily for the programming, production, presentation, exhibition or any combination of the above functions of any of the arts and cultural disciplines. These disciplines include, but are not limited to music, dance, theater, creative writing, literature, architecture, painting, sculpture, folk arts, photography, crafts, media arts, visual arts, programs of museums, and other such allied, major art forms. The maximum grant amount that may be requested is $500,000. There is no minimum amount.
Requirements: All applicant organizations must: Be a public entity governed by either a municipality or county or be a not-for-profit, tax-exempt Florida corporation; Designated as a tax-exempt organization as defined in Section 501(c)3 or 501(c)4, of the Internal Revenue Code of 1954; and, allowed to receive contributions pursuant to the provisions of s. 170 of the Internal Revenue Code of 1954. Applicants that are not public entities must provide the organization's IRS determination letter documenting not-for-profit, tax-exempt status with each application. Additionally, applicants must have ownership of the land and building, and must retain ownership of all improvements made under the grant. The Division will not accept two (2) or more Cultural Facilities applications under a single application deadline, for the same facility, project, site, or phase. City or county governments may submit Cultural Facilities applications for their divisions or departments that are separate and distinct budgetary units, provided the applications do not address the same facility, project, site, or phase. Organizations with a Total Support and Revenue of less than $500,000 must have at least 1 dollar of match ($1) for every dollar requested from the state or a 1:1 match. Organizations with a Total Support and Revenue of $500,000 or more must have at least 2 dollars ($2) of match for every dollar requested from the state or a 2:1 match. Organizations in a Rural Economic Development Initiative (REDI) designated area may request a 1:1 match regardless of Total Support and Revenue.
Restrictions: The Cultural Facilities Program does not fund project planning, such as feasibility studies and architectural drawings, or operational support. A project funded by the Legislature outside of the review of the Florida Council on Arts and Culture or Secretary of State shall not be eligible to receive grant support for its project from the Division of Cultural Affairs within the same fiscal year in which legislative funding is appropriated.

Applicants for projects that are intended to preserve an historic structure should apply to the historic preservation grants-in-aid program administered by the Division of Historical Resources, Bureau of Historic Preservation. No project, whether it is a single-phase or multiphase project, may receive more than $1.5 million during a 5 consecutive state fiscal year period. Receive means measured from July 1 through June 30 of the fiscal year in which grant funds were awarded. Organizations seeking state support for the renovation, acquisition, or new construction of a cultural facility that will not be open and accessible to all members of the public, regardless of sex, race, color, national origin, religion, disability, age, or marital status are not eligible for this publicly funded grant.
Geographic Focus: Florida
Date(s) Application is Due: Jun 1
Amount of Grant: Up to 500,000 USD
Contact: Donald R. Blancett; (850) 245-6483; don.blancett@dos.myflorida.com
Internet: http://www.florida-arts.org/programs/facilities/
Sponsor: Florida Division of Cultural Affairs
500 South Bronough Street, 3rd Floor
Tallahassee, FL 32399-0250

Florida Division of Cultural Affairs Folk Arts Grants 1853
Florida Division of Cultural Affairs discipline-based projects are discipline specific for organizations conducting cultural projects, realizing their stated mission, and furthering the state's cultural objectives. The Folk Arts discipline is for projects that preserve and present traditional arts. This includes performances, exhibitions, festivals, and other projects featuring traditional artists and their work. Folk arts are traditional cultural expressions through which a community maintains and passes on a shared way of life. These communities can be job-related, ethnic, religious, age-related, or based on location. Folk art expresses a sense of the community's values and aesthetics. Folk art expressions are usually learned informally through a relative or the community and are maintained without formal teaching. The Folk Arts discipline includes many forms and processes of expression, including but not limited to: performing traditions in music, dance, and drama; traditional storytelling and other verbal arts; traditional crafts; visual arts; and architecture.
Requirements: To meet the legal status requirement, an applicant organization must be either a public entity (Florida local government, entity of state government, school district, community college, college, or university) or a Florida nonprofit, tax exempt corporation as of the application deadline. Private schools, private community colleges, private colleges, and private universities are not public entities and must be nonprofit and tax exempt to meet the legal status requirement. Applicants must provide at least one dollar in cash and in-kind (donated goods or services) for every dollar requested from the division. Allowable expenses must be: directly related to the proposal; specifically and clearly detailed in the proposal budget; and incurred and paid within the grant start and end dates.
Restrictions: The Folk Arts discipline is not intended for projects that focus primarily on the following activities: research for scholarly purposes only; historical presentations or re-creations; exhibits limited to historical objects; highly choreographed or orchestrated interpretations of traditional folk or ethnic dance or music; contemporary studio crafts or reproductions; or competitive events such as powwows or fiddle contests. The following are non-allowable expenses for grant and matching funds: state funds from any source; funds used as match for other Department of State grants; expenses incurred or obligated before July 1 or after the grant period; lobbying or attempting to influence federal, state, or local legislation; building, renovation, or remodeling of facilities; capital expenditures (includes acquisitions, building projects, and renovations); costs associated with bad debts, contingencies (money set aside for possible expenses), fines and penalties, interest, taxes, and other financial costs; private entertainment, food, and beverages; plaques, awards, and scholarships; re-granting; contributions and donations; mortgage payments; or payments to current Department of State employees. No state funds may be used towards operational costs such as: phone; utilities; office supplies; equipment costing over $1,000; property improvements; fixtures; building maintenance; space rental; or other overhead or indirect costs.
Geographic Focus: Florida
Amount of Grant: Up to 25,000 USD
Contact: Laura Lewis Blischke; (850) 245-6475; llblischke@dos.state.fl.us
Internet: http://www.florida-arts.org/documents/guidelines/2012-2013.scp.guidelines.cfm#folk-arts
Sponsor: Florida Division of Cultural Affairs
500 South Bronough Street, 3rd Floor
Tallahassee, FL 32399-0250

Florida Division of Cultural Affairs General Program Support Grants 1854
General Program Support (GPS) funding is designed to support the general program activities of an organization that is realizing its stated mission and furthering the state's cultural objectives by: conducting, creating, producing, presenting, staging, or sponsoring cultural exhibits, performances, educational programs, or events or providing professional services as a State Service Organization or Local Arts Agency. The Division offers three types of General Program Support: discipline-based program support for cultural and artistic programming; local arts agency program support for designated local arts agencies; and state service organization program support for cultural organizations that meet the definition of state service organization.
Requirements: Applicant organizations must be either a public entity or a Florida nonprofit, tax exempt corporation as of the application deadline. Grant request amounts must be matched at least 1:1 ($1 provided by the applicant for every $1 requested from the Division) with cash and in-kind (donated goods or services). Matching funds may be anticipated at the time of application, but must be received by the grant period end date (June 30). All expenses (both state grant and match) must be paid out (not merely encumbered) by the grant period end date.
Restrictions: Applicants must have submitted no other applications for the General Program Support or Specific Cultural Project programs in the current application cycle. No more than 25% of the Total Proposal Expenses may be in-kind. The following may not be used as match: state funds from any source (this includes any income that comes from an appropriation of state funds or grants from the State of Florida); or funds used as match for other Department of State grants.
Geographic Focus: Florida
Date(s) Application is Due: Jun 1
Amount of Grant: Up to 150,000 USD
Contact: Laura Lewis Blischke; (850) 245-6475; llblischke@dos.state.fl.us
Internet: http://www.florida-arts.org/programs/gps/
Sponsor: Florida Division of Cultural Affairs
500 South Bronough Street, 3rd Floor
Tallahassee, FL 32399-0250

Florida Division of Cultural Affairs Literature Grants 1855
Florida Division of Cultural Affairs discipline-based projects are discipline specific for organizations conducting cultural projects, realizing their stated mission, and furthering the state's cultural objectives. The Literature discipline is for projects that promote excellence in the literary arts. The grant period start date is July 1 or the date the award agreement is executed, whichever is later. The grant period end date is June 30 unless an end date extension is approved by the Division. Literature projects have a maximum request of $25,000.
Requirements: To meet the legal status requirement, an applicant organization must be either a public entity (Florida local government, entity of state government, school district, community college, college, or university) or a Florida nonprofit, tax exempt corporation as of the application deadline. Private schools, private community colleges, private colleges, and private universities are not public entities and must be nonprofit and tax exempt to meet the legal status requirement. Applicants must provide at least one dollar in cash and in-kind (donated goods or services) for every dollar requested from the division. Allowable expenses must be: directly related to the proposal; specifically and clearly detailed in the proposal budget; and incurred and paid within the grant start and end dates.
Restrictions: The following are non-allowable expenses for grant and matching funds: state funds from any source; funds used as match for other Department of State grants; expenses incurred or obligated before July 1 or after the grant period; lobbying or attempting to influence federal, state, or local legislation; building, renovation, or remodeling of facilities; capital expenditures (includes acquisitions, building projects, and renovations); costs associated with bad debts, contingencies (money set aside for possible expenses), fines and penalties, interest, taxes, and other financial costs; private entertainment, food, and beverages; plaques, awards, and scholarships; re-granting; contributions and donations; mortgage payments; or payments to current Department of State employees. No state funds may be used towards operational costs such as: phone; utilities; office supplies; equipment costing over $1,000; property improvements; fixtures; building maintenance; space rental; or other overhead or indirect costs.
Geographic Focus: Florida
Amount of Grant: Up to 25,000 USD
Contact: Laura Lewis Blischke; (850) 245-6475; llblischke@dos.state.fl.us
Internet: http://www.florida-arts.org/documents/guidelines/2012-2013.scp.guidelines.cfm#literature
Sponsor: Florida Division of Cultural Affairs
500 South Bronough Street, 3rd Floor
Tallahassee, FL 32399-0250

Florida Division of Cultural Affairs Media Arts Grants 1856
Florida Division of Cultural Affairs discipline-based projects are discipline specific for organizations conducting cultural projects, realizing their stated mission, and furthering the state's cultural objectives. The Media Arts discipline is for projects that promote excellence in film, video, radio, and television. This includes film and video festivals, and media art exhibitions, conferences, and seminars. The grant period start date is July 1 or the date the award agreement is executed, whichever is later. The grant period end date is June 30 unless an end date extension is approved by the Division. Media Arts projects have a maximum request of $25,000.
Requirements: To meet the legal status requirement, an applicant organization must be either a public entity (Florida local government, entity of state government, school district, community college, college, or university) or a Florida nonprofit, tax exempt corporation as of the application deadline. Private schools, private community colleges, private colleges, and private universities are not public entities and must be nonprofit and tax exempt to meet the legal status requirement. Applicants must provide at least one dollar in cash and in-kind (donated goods or services) for every dollar requested from the division. Allowable expenses must be: directly related to the proposal; specifically and clearly detailed in the proposal budget; and incurred and paid within the grant start and end dates.
Restrictions: The following are non-allowable expenses for grant and matching funds: state funds from any source; funds used as match for other Department of State grants; expenses incurred or obligated before July 1 or after the grant period; lobbying or attempting to influence federal, state, or local legislation; building, renovation, or remodeling of facilities; capital expenditures (includes acquisitions, building projects, and renovations); costs associated with bad debts, contingencies (money set aside for possible expenses), fines and penalties, interest, taxes, and other financial costs; private entertainment, food, and beverages; plaques, awards, and scholarships; re-granting; contributions and donations; mortgage payments; or payments to current Department of State employees. No state funds may be used towards operational costs such as: phone; utilities; office supplies; equipment costing over $1,000; property improvements; fixtures; building maintenance; space rental; or other overhead or indirect costs.

Geographic Focus: Florida
Amount of Grant: Up to 25,000 USD
Contact: Megan Burke, Program Manager; (850) 245-6458; mcburke@dos.state.fl.us
Internet: http://www.florida-arts.org/documents/guidelines/2012-2013.scp.guidelines.cfm#media-arts
Sponsor: Florida Division of Cultural Affairs
500 South Bronough Street, 3rd Floor
Tallahassee, FL 32399-0250

Florida Division of Cultural Affairs Multidisciplinary Grants   1857
Florida Division of Cultural Affairs discipline-based projects are discipline specific for organizations conducting cultural projects, realizing their stated mission, and furthering the state's cultural objectives. The Multidisciplinary discipline is for projects with programming that presents two or more separate artistic or cultural disciplines. Artistic and cultural disciplines include, but are not limited to: music; dance; theatre; creative writing; literature; architecture; painting; sculpture; folk arts; photography; crafts; media arts; and visual arts. The grant period start date is July 1 or the date the award agreement is executed, whichever is later. The grant period end date is June 30 unless an end date extension is approved by the Division. Multidisciplinary projects have a maximum request of $25,000.
Requirements: To meet the legal status requirement, an applicant organization must be either a public entity (Florida local government, entity of state government, school district, community college, college, or university) or a Florida nonprofit, tax exempt corporation as of the application deadline. Private schools, private community colleges, private colleges, and private universities are not public entities and must be nonprofit and tax exempt to meet the legal status requirement. Applicants must provide at least one dollar in cash and in-kind (donated goods or services) for every dollar requested from the division. Allowable expenses must be: directly related to the proposal; specifically and clearly detailed in the proposal budget; and incurred and paid within the grant start and end dates.
Restrictions: The following are non-allowable expenses for grant and matching funds: state funds from any source; funds used as match for other Department of State grants; expenses incurred or obligated before July 1 or after the grant period; lobbying or attempting to influence federal, state, or local legislation; building, renovation, or remodeling of facilities; capital expenditures (includes acquisitions, building projects, and renovations); costs associated with bad debts, contingencies (money set aside for possible expenses), fines and penalties, interest, taxes, and other financial costs; private entertainment, food, and beverages; plaques, awards, and scholarships; re-granting; contributions and donations; mortgage payments; or payments to current Department of State employees. No state funds may be used towards operational costs such as: phone; utilities; office supplies; equipment costing over $1,000; property improvements; fixtures; building maintenance; space rental; or other overhead or indirect costs.
Geographic Focus: Florida
Amount of Grant: Up to 25,000 USD
Contact: Laura Lewis Blischke; (850) 245-6475; llblischke@dos.state.fl.us
Internet: http://www.florida-arts.org/documents/guidelines/2012-2013.scp.guidelines.cfm#multidisciplinary
Sponsor: Florida Division of Cultural Affairs
500 South Bronough Street, 3rd Floor
Tallahassee, FL 32399-0250

Florida Division of Cultural Affairs Museum Grants   1858
Florida Division of Cultural Affairs discipline-based projects are discipline specific for organizations conducting cultural projects, realizing their stated mission, and furthering the state's cultural objectives. The Museum discipline is for projects focused on the applicant's collections and/or exhibits. Applicants may include zoos, botanical gardens, arboretums, nature centers and aquariums. Museums are encouraged but not required to participate in the American Association of Museums' Museum Assessment Program (MAP) and to pursue or maintain national accreditation through American Association of Museums (AAM), American Zoological Association (AZA), or Zoological Association of America (ZAA). Museums may include, but are not limited to, the following types: Art Museums; Historical Museums; Multidisciplinary Museums; Science Museums; and Youth and Children's Museums
Requirements: To be eligible to apply to this discipline, a museum must: be open to the public for at least 180 days each year; own or utilize works of art, historical artifacts, or other tangible objects, whether animate or inanimate; care for these works of art, historical artifacts, or other tangible objects; and exhibit these works of art, historical artifacts, or other tangible objects to the public on a regular schedule. To meet the legal status requirement, an applicant organization must be either a public entity (Florida local government, entity of state government, school district, community college, college, or university) or a Florida nonprofit, tax exempt corporation as of the application deadline. Private schools, private community colleges, private colleges, and private universities are not public entities and must be nonprofit and tax exempt to meet the legal status requirement. Applicants must provide at least one dollar in cash and in-kind (donated goods or services) for every dollar requested from the division. Allowable expenses must be: directly related to the proposal; specifically and clearly detailed in the proposal budget; and incurred and paid within the grant start and end dates.
Restrictions: The following are non-allowable expenses for grant and matching funds: state funds from any source; funds used as match for other Department of State grants; expenses incurred or obligated before July 1 or after the grant period; lobbying or attempting to influence federal, state, or local legislation; building, renovation, or remodeling of facilities; capital expenditures (includes acquisitions, building projects, and renovations); costs associated with bad debts, contingencies (money set aside for possible expenses), fines and penalties, interest, taxes, and other financial costs; private entertainment, food, and beverages; plaques, awards, and scholarships; re-granting; contributions and donations; mortgage payments; or payments to current Department of State employees. No state funds may be used towards operational costs such as: phone; utilities; office supplies; equipment costing over $1,000; property improvements; fixtures; building maintenance; space rental; or other overhead or indirect costs.
Geographic Focus: Florida
Amount of Grant: Up to 25,000 USD
Contact: Sarah T. Stage, Program Manager; (850) 245-6459; sstage@dos.state.fl.us
Internet: http://www.florida-arts.org/documents/guidelines/2012-2013.scp.guidelines.cfm#museum
Sponsor: Florida Division of Cultural Affairs
500 South Bronough Street, 3rd Floor
Tallahassee, FL 32399-0250

Florida Division of Cultural Affairs Music Grants   1859
Florida Division of Cultural Affairs discipline-based projects are discipline specific for organizations conducting cultural projects, realizing their stated mission, and furthering the state's cultural objectives. The Music discipline is for both vocal and instrumental music projects that promote excellence in music performance and creation. Applicants to the Music discipline may include chamber or jazz ensembles, choral groups, community bands, orchestras, opera, and world music ensembles. The grant period start date is July 1 or the date the award agreement is executed, whichever is later. The grant period end date is June 30 unless an end date extension is approved by the Division. Music projects have a maximum request of $25,000.
Requirements: To meet the legal status requirement, an applicant organization must be either a public entity (Florida local government, entity of state government, school district, community college, college, or university) or a Florida nonprofit, tax exempt corporation as of the application deadline. Private schools, private community colleges, private colleges, and private universities are not public entities and must be nonprofit and tax exempt to meet the legal status requirement. Applicants must provide at least one dollar in cash and in-kind (donated goods or services) for every dollar requested from the division. Allowable expenses must be: directly related to the proposal; specifically and clearly detailed in the proposal budget; and incurred and paid within the grant start and end dates.
Restrictions: The following are non-allowable expenses for grant and matching funds: state funds from any source; funds used as match for other Department of State grants; expenses incurred or obligated before July 1 or after the grant period; lobbying or attempting to influence federal, state, or local legislation; building, renovation, or remodeling of facilities; capital expenditures (includes acquisitions, building projects, and renovations); costs associated with bad debts, contingencies (money set aside for possible expenses), fines and penalties, interest, taxes, and other financial costs; private entertainment, food, and beverages; plaques, awards, and scholarships; re-granting; contributions and donations; mortgage payments; or payments to current Department of State employees. No state funds may be used towards operational costs such as: phone; utilities; office supplies; equipment costing over $1,000; property improvements; fixtures; building maintenance; space rental; or other overhead or indirect costs.
Geographic Focus: Florida
Amount of Grant: Up to 25,000 USD
Contact: Megan Burke, Program Manager; (850) 245-6458; mcburke@dos.state.fl.us
Internet: http://www.florida-arts.org/documents/guidelines/2012-2013.scp.guidelines.cfm#music
Sponsor: Florida Division of Cultural Affairs
500 South Bronough Street, 3rd Floor
Tallahassee, FL 32399-0250

Florida Division of Cultural Affairs Presenter Grants   1860
Florida Division of Cultural Affairs discipline-based projects are discipline specific for organizations conducting cultural projects, realizing their stated mission, and furthering the state's cultural objectives. The Presenter discipline supports the presentation of performing arts groups, individual artists, or other cultural providers. A Presenter is an organization that enters into agreements to provide performances or other cultural activities. The organization generally does not create, rehearse, cast, or have artistic control over the performance or activity. The grant period start date is July 1 or the date the award agreement is executed, whichever is later. The grant period end date is June 30 unless an end date extension is approved by the Division. Presenter projects have a maximum request of $25,000.
Requirements: To meet the legal status requirement, an applicant organization must be either a public entity (Florida local government, entity of state government, school district, community college, college, or university) or a Florida nonprofit, tax exempt corporation as of the application deadline. Private schools, private community colleges, private colleges, and private universities are not public entities and must be nonprofit and tax exempt to meet the legal status requirement. Applicants must provide at least one dollar in cash and in-kind (donated goods or services) for every dollar requested from the division. Allowable expenses must be: directly related to the proposal; specifically and clearly detailed in the proposal budget; and incurred and paid within the grant start and end dates.
Restrictions: The following are non-allowable expenses for grant and matching funds: state funds from any source; funds used as match for other Department of State grants; expenses incurred or obligated before July 1 or after the grant period; lobbying or attempting to influence federal, state, or local legislation; building, renovation, or remodeling of facilities; capital expenditures (includes acquisitions, building projects, and renovations); costs associated with bad debts, contingencies (money set aside for possible expenses), fines and penalties, interest, taxes, and other financial costs; private entertainment, food, and beverages; plaques, awards, and scholarships; re-granting; contributions and donations; mortgage payments; or payments to current Department of State employees. No state funds may be used towards operational costs such as: phone; utilities; office supplies; equipment costing over $1,000; property improvements; fixtures; building maintenance; space rental; or other overhead or indirect costs.
Geographic Focus: Florida

Amount of Grant: Up to 25,000 USD
Contact: Sarah T. Stage, Program Manager; (850) 245-6459; sstage@dos.state.fl.us
Internet: http://www.florida-arts.org/documents/guidelines/2012-2013.scp.guidelines.cfm#presenter
Sponsor: Florida Division of Cultural Affairs
500 South Bronough Street, 3rd Floor
Tallahassee, FL 32399-0250

Florida Division of Cultural Affairs Professional Theatre Grants 1861
Florida Division of Cultural Affairs theatre disciplines support projects that promote excellence in theatre performance. The Professional Theatre discipline is for producing professional theatres. Organizations applying to the Professional Theatre discipline must compensate their artistic staff and actors. Professional Theatre panelists strongly emphasize the importance of payment to actors. Companies should be very specific when describing the financial compensation and/or benefits that are offered to artistic staff and actors. For information on minimum pay rates for actors and staff contact a theatrical union such as Actors Equity. The grant period start date is July 1 or the date the award agreement is executed, whichever is later. The grant period end date is June 30 unless an end date extension is approved by the Division. Projects have a maximum request of $25,000.
Requirements: To meet the legal status requirement, an applicant organization must be either a public entity (Florida local government, entity of state government, school district, community college, college, or university) or a Florida nonprofit, tax exempt corporation as of the application deadline. Private schools, private community colleges, private colleges, and private universities are not public entities and must be nonprofit and tax exempt to meet the legal status requirement. Applicants must provide at least one dollar in cash and in-kind (donated goods or services) for every dollar requested from the division. Allowable expenses must be: directly related to the proposal; specifically and clearly detailed in the proposal budget; and incurred and paid within the grant start and end dates.
Restrictions: The following are non-allowable expenses for grant and matching funds: state funds from any source; funds used as match for other Department of State grants; expenses incurred or obligated before July 1 or after the grant period; lobbying or attempting to influence federal, state, or local legislation; building, renovation, or remodeling of facilities; capital expenditures (includes acquisitions, building projects, and renovations); costs associated with bad debts, contingencies (money set aside for possible expenses), fines and penalties, interest, taxes, and other financial costs; private entertainment, food, and beverages; plaques, awards, and scholarships; re-granting; contributions and donations; mortgage payments; or payments to current Department of State employees. No state funds may be used towards operational costs such as: phone; utilities; office supplies; equipment costing over $1,000; property improvements; fixtures; building maintenance; space rental; or other overhead or indirect costs.
Geographic Focus: Florida
Amount of Grant: Up to 25,000 USD
Contact: Sarah T. Stage, Arts Administrator; (850) 245-6459; sstage@dos.state.fl.us
Internet: http://www.florida-arts.org/documents/guidelines/2012-2013.scp.guidelines.cfm#theatre
Sponsor: Florida Division of Cultural Affairs
500 South Bronough Street, 3rd Floor
Tallahassee, FL 32399-0250

Florida Division of Cultural Affairs Specific Cultural Project Grants 1862
The Specific Cultural Project (SCP) grant is designed to fund a cultural project, program, exhibition, or series taking place within the grant period (July 1 through June 30). The grant activities must support the mission of the organization and further the state's cultural objectives. The Division offers four project types: Arts In Education projects (promote arts and culture in education); Discipline-Based cultural or artistic projects; Culture Builds Florida projects (directly promote one or more elements of the state's cultural strategic plan); and, Underserved Cultural Community Development projects (assist with the development of underserved cultural organizations).
Requirements: An applicant organization must be either a public entity or a Florida nonprofit, tax exempt corporation as of the application deadline. Specific Cultural Projects have a maximum request of $25,000, except for Underserved Cultural Community Development projects. Grant request amounts must be matched at least 1:1 ($1 provided by the applicant for every $1 requested from the Division) with cash and in-kind (donated goods or services). No more than 25% of the Total Proposal Expenses may be in-kind. Matching funds may be anticipated at the time of application, but must be received by the grant period end date (June 30). All expenses (both state grant and match) must be paid out (not merely encumbered) by the grant period end date.
Restrictions: An organization may only submit one Specific Cultural Project or one General Program Support application for each annual grant cycle (July 1 to June 30). Grant funds may not be used for indirect or overhead expenses. All expenses must be directly related to the project detailed in the application. State funds from any source may not be used as match. This includes any income that comes from an appropriation or grant from the State of Florida. Funds used as match for other Department of State grants may not be used as match.
Geographic Focus: Florida
Date(s) Application is Due: Jun 1
Amount of Grant: Up to 25,000 USD
Contact: Sarah Stage; (850) 245-6459; fax (850) 245-6497; sarah.stage@dos.myflorida.com
Internet: http://www.florida-arts.org/programs/scp/
Sponsor: Florida Division of Cultural Affairs
500 South Bronough Street, 3rd Floor
Tallahassee, FL 32399-0250

Florida Division of Cultural Affairs State Touring Grants 1863
The State Touring Program's purpose is to provide performances, activities, and exhibits, all by Florida artists, to as many Florida communities as possible. This is accomplished through two steps: the selection of a roster of artists who have been through a peer review process; and the provision of funding to presenters to assist in subsidizing the fees of the roster artists. Presenters may receive one-third of the artists' total fee for their venue or, if the presenter is located in an underpopulated county (population of 75,000 or less), two-thirds of the fee. The annual deadline for receipt of applications is May 1.
Requirements: Presenters are either tax-exempt, not-for-profit Florida organizations or a public entity governed by a county, municipality, school district, community college, university, or an agency of state government. Tour is defined as a production or exhibit that takes place outside the home county of the artist. There must be at least a distance of 25 miles between the artists' base and the presenting venue in order to qualify as a tour under this program.
Geographic Focus: Florida
Date(s) Application is Due: May 1
Contact: Gaylen Phillips, Associate Director of Arts Resources and Services; (850) 245-6482; gaylen.phillips@dos.myflorida.com
Internet: http://www.florida-arts.org/programs/touring/
Sponsor: Florida Division of Cultural Affairs
500 South Bronough Street, 3rd Floor
Tallahassee, FL 32399-0250

Florida Division of Cultural Affairs Underserved Cultural Community Development Grants 1864
Underserved Cultural Community Development projects support the organizational development of underserved cultural organizations. There are three funding categories for Underserved Cultural Community Development projects: capacity building; consultant; and salary assistance. Capacity building funding provides up to $2,000 for projects that increase administrative or artistic capacity. Eligible projects include but are not limited to: staff and/or volunteer exchange; professional development opportunities such as attendance at seminars and workshops; plan development opportunities such as fundraising, marketing, and arts education; and equipment and technology needs. Consultant funding category provides up to $5,000 for retaining consultants that can provide specific administrative or artistic needs. The Salary Assistance funding category allows applicants to request up to $20,000 for the full or partial salary support for one or more positions.
Requirements: All applicants to this proposal type must meet the following criteria: meet basic eligibility requirements; be an underserved (rural, minority, or lacking in resources) cultural organization; have a Total Cash Income (from the applicant's most recently completed fiscal year) of $150,000 or less; and have at least one year of completed programming.
Restrictions: The following are non-allowable expenses for grant and matching funds: state funds from any source; funds used as match for other Department of State grants; expenses incurred or obligated before July 1 or after the grant period; lobbying or attempting to influence federal, state, or local legislation; building, renovation, or remodeling of facilities; capital expenditures (includes acquisitions, building projects, and renovations); costs associated with bad debts, contingencies (money set aside for possible expenses), fines and penalties, interest, taxes, and other financial costs; private entertainment, food, and beverages; plaques, awards, and scholarships; re-granting; contributions and donations; mortgage payments; or payments to current Department of State employees. No state funds may be used towards operational costs such as: phone; utilities; office supplies; equipment costing over $1,000; property improvements; fixtures; building maintenance; space rental; or other overhead or indirect costs.
Geographic Focus: Florida
Amount of Grant: Up to 20,000 USD
Contact: Laura Lewis Blischke; (850) 245-6475; llblischke@dos.state.fl.us
Internet: http://www.florida-arts.org/documents/guidelines/2012-2013.scp.guidelines.cfm#ucd
Sponsor: Florida Division of Cultural Affairs
500 South Bronough Street, 3rd Floor
Tallahassee, FL 32399-0250

Florida Division of Cultural Affairs Visual Arts Grants 1865
Florida Division of Cultural Affairs discipline-based projects are discipline specific for organizations conducting cultural projects, realizing their stated mission, and furthering the state's cultural objectives. The Visual Arts discipline is for projects that promote excellence in the visual arts through activities such as: lectures; publications; exhibitions; educational programs; artist workshops; and professional development for visual artists. The grant period start date is July 1 or the date the award agreement is executed, whichever is later. The grant period end date is June 30 unless an end date extension is approved by the Division. Visual Arts projects have a maximum request of $25,000.
Requirements: To meet the legal status requirement, an applicant organization must be either a public entity (Florida local government, entity of state government, school district, community college, college, or university) or a Florida nonprofit, tax exempt corporation as of the application deadline. Private schools, private community colleges, private colleges, and private universities are not public entities and must be nonprofit and tax exempt to meet the legal status requirement. Applicants must provide at least one dollar in cash and in-kind (donated goods or services) for every dollar requested from the division. Allowable expenses must be: directly related to the proposal; specifically and clearly detailed in the proposal budget; and incurred and paid within the grant start and end dates.
Restrictions: The following are non-allowable expenses for grant and matching funds: state funds from any source; funds used as match for other Department of State grants; expenses incurred or obligated before July 1 or after the grant period; lobbying or attempting to influence federal, state, or local legislation; building, renovation, or remodeling of

facilities; capital expenditures (includes acquisitions, building projects, and renovations); costs associated with bad debts, contingencies (money set aside for possible expenses), fines and penalties, interest, taxes, and other financial costs; private entertainment, food, and beverages; plaques, awards, and scholarships; re-granting; contributions and donations; mortgage payments; or payments to current Department of State employees. No state funds may be used towards operational costs such as: phone; utilities; office supplies; equipment costing over $1,000; property improvements; fixtures; building maintenance; space rental; or other overhead or indirect costs.
Geographic Focus: Florida
Amount of Grant: Up to 25,000 USD
Contact: Sarah T. Stage, Program Manager; (850) 245-6459; sstage@dos.state.fl.us
Internet: http://www.florida-arts.org/documents/guidelines/2012-2013.scp.guidelines.cfm#visual-arts
Sponsor: Florida Division of Cultural Affairs
500 South Bronough Street, 3rd Floor
Tallahassee, FL 32399-0250

Florida High School/High Tech Project Grants 1866
Florida High School/High Tech (HS/HT) is designed to provide high school students with all types of disabilities the opportunity to explore jobs or postsecondary education leading to technology- related careers. HS/HT links youth to a broad range of academic, career development and experiential resources and experiences that will enable them to meet the demands of the 21st century workforce. HS/HT is a community-based partnership made up of students, parents and caregivers, businesses, educators and rehabilitation professionals. It has been shown to reduce the high school dropout rate and increase the overall self-esteem of participating students. If you are interested in participating, there is a role for you. The program provides step-down funding while the program is gaining independent funding for the future of their program.
Requirements: Any established, Florida nonprofit corporation, agency, organization or association that has been granted exemption from federal income tax under Section 501(c)3 of the IRS Tax Code is eligible to submit a proposal for review.
Geographic Focus: Florida
Contact: Guenevere Crum, Senior Vice President; (850) 224-4493; fax (850) 224-4496; guenevere@abletrust.org or info@abletrust.org
Internet: http://www.abletrust.org/hsht/
Sponsor: Able Trust
3320 Thomasville Road, Suite 200
Tallahassee, FL 32308

Florida Humanities Council Civic Reflection Grants 1867
The Florida Humanities Council seeks to partner with community organizations interested in convening meaningful conversations among citizens about the challenges we face in trying to improve our public life through community service. These grants offer those who work with nonprofit organizations and other groups involved in civic life a chance to reflect on their work using facilitated discussions of short texts drawn from literature, history, and philosophy. Many brief but provocative readings that open up fundamental questions of 1) giving, 2) serving, 3) leadership, and 4) community building provide the basis for participants to think about the importance of their work to the community. This project works as a partnership between the Florida Humanities Council and your organization. The Florida Humanities Council will provide funds and guidance to help you host a conversation for a group of your choosing. You in turn identify and recruit participants, choose a location and mail out meeting materials. Funds up to $1,500 are available to defray the costs of the facilitator, texts, and basic recruitment materials. Other costs for administration, facilities, and refreshments will be the cost share contribution of the sponsoring organization.
Requirements: There are no deadlines. No formal application is necessary. Merely write a letter of intent on your agency stationery explaining why the Civic Reflection project is appropriate for your organization.
Geographic Focus: Florida
Amount of Grant: Up to 1,500 USD
Contact: Susan Lockwood; (727) 873-2011; fax (727) 873-2014; slockwood@flahum.org
Internet: http://www.flahum.org/index.cfm/fuseaction/Grants.Appl_Civic
Sponsor: Florida Humanities Council
599 Second Street S
St. Petersburg, FL 33701

Florida Humanities Council Major Grants 1868
This program funds projects that may employ a variety of formats: workshops, lecture/discussion series, symposia, reading/discussion groups, historical dramatizations, interpretive exhibits, multi-media, etc. Media projects (exhibits, digital projects, radio) include additional guidelines. In the past, grants have been awarded to libraries, civic groups, universities, colleges, museums, historical societies, theaters, churches, and ad hoc groups such as Friends of the Library.
Requirements: Organizations must be a Florida-based, not-for-profit organization or public agency. Proposals will be required to supply 100% sponsor match, in cash and/or in-kind.
Restrictions: Individuals are not eligible. Additionally, the following are not eligible: Programs of advocacy or partisan objectives; Programs not open to the public; Profit-making or fund-raising activities; Operating costs, construction, capital improvements, or acquisition of equipment; Professional meetings, scholarships, fellowships, or international travel; Book-length publications; Museum or library acquisitions, archival preservation; Refreshments or entertainment; Programs designed primarily for children; Creative arts, performances, or ceremonies unless focused on analysis and interpretation.
Geographic Focus: Florida
Date(s) Application is Due: Feb 20; Jul 15; Nov 10
Amount of Grant: 2,000 - 25,000 USD
Contact: Susan Lockwood; (727) 873-2011; fax (727) 873-2014; slockwood@flahum.org
Internet: http://www.flahum.org/index.cfm/fuseaction/Grants.Appl_Major
Sponsor: Florida Humanities Council
599 Second Street S
St. Petersburg, FL 33701

Florida Humanities Council Mini Grants 1869
The mini grant program offers community and civic organizations that are interested in sponsoring a humanities program a way to access the FHC grant program. Proposed projects may explore any number of topics but must engage a humanities scholar and result in a public program for the adult general public. The format may vary (lecture with question-and-answer period, mini-exhibit, workshop, book or film discussion, panel discussion, etc.).
Requirements: Any nonprofit organization is eligible to apply. All FHC-funded programs must be free and open to the public. Organizations are discouraged from requesting funding from more than one FHC program related to the same project. Guidelines and application formats are available at the sponsor's website.
Restrictions: No organization will be eligible for a second grant if they already have an open grant. No organization may receive more than two grants in any twelve-month period.
Geographic Focus: Florida
Date(s) Application is Due: Jan 20; Apr 20; Oct 20
Amount of Grant: Up to 2,000 USD
Contact: Susan Lockwood; (727) 873-2011; fax (727) 873-2014; slockwood@flahum.org
Internet: http://www.flahum.org/index.cfm/fuseaction/Grants.Appl_Mini_Inst
Sponsor: Florida Humanities Council
599 Second Street S
St. Petersburg, FL 33701

Florida Humanities Council Partnership Grants 1870
This program was designed for organizations in Florida that conduct an annual series of humanities programs. Grants will be awarded to organizations that: (a) Have demonstrated a commitment to and track record for developing public humanities programs. (b) Conduct an annual series of public humanities programs. (c) Hold free programs, open to the public, that serve a broad community interest. (d) Agree to credit FHC on all organizational and promotional materials. (e) Provide sponsor cost share (cash or in-kind) equal to the requested amount. Organizations that apply for these grants may be eligible to receive these grants for three consecutive years.
Requirements: Organizations must be Florida-based, not-for-profits or public agencies.
Restrictions: During the period of the Partnership Grant, participating organizations will not be eligible to apply for either Mini or Major grants from FHC. Individuals are not eligible. Additionally, the following are not eligible: Programs of advocacy or partisan objectives; Programs not open to the public; Profit-making or fund-raising activities; Operating costs, construction, capital improvements, or acquisition of equipment; Professional meetings, scholarships, fellowships, or international travel; Book-length publications; Museum or library acquisitions, archival preservation; Refreshments or entertainment; Programs designed primarily for children; Creative arts, performances, or ceremonies unless focused on analysis and interpretation.
Geographic Focus: Florida
Date(s) Application is Due: Jul 1
Amount of Grant: 3,000 USD
Contact: Susan Lockwood; (727) 873-2011; fax (727) 873-2014; slockwood@flahum.org
Internet: http://www.flahum.org/index.cfm/fuseaction/Grants.Appl_Partner
Sponsor: Florida Humanities Council
599 Second Street S
St. Petersburg, FL 33701

Florida Sea Turtle Grants 1871
Funded by a portion of revenues from Florida's Sea Turtle Specialty License Plate, the grants program distributes funds each year to support sea turtle research, conservation, and education programs throughout Florida. Types of grants include competitive grants, funding for ongoing activities, and emergency grants.
Requirements: Florida coastal local governments, Florida-based nonprofit organizations, and education and research institutions that actively participate in marine turtle research, conservation, and educational activities within the state of Florida are eligible to apply.
Geographic Focus: Florida
Contact: Administrator; (352) 373-6441; fax (352) 375-2449; stgp@helpingseaturtles.org
Internet: http://www.helpingseaturtles.org/stgp.htm
Sponsor: Caribbean Conservation Corporation
4424 NW 13th Street, Suite B11
Gainesville, FL 32609

Florida Sports Foundation Junior Golf Grants 1872
The program is designed to assist organizations in the State of Florida for the benefit of youth, introduce young people to golf, instruct young people in golf, teach the values of golf, and stress life skills, fair play, courtesy, and self-discipline. Additionally, the grant program is intended to help organizations that provide junior golf programs that serve economically disadvantaged youth, children with special needs and the general population. Allowable use of grant funds includes: Golf instruction; Course access and/or practice range facility access; Life skills training/curriculum; Golf Equipment (bags, balls, tees, etc.); Transportation provided for participants to attend program; Snacks; Clothing; Insurance; Travel Expenses; Tuition based on sliding scale (free or reduced tuition) per combined family income (W-2).

Requirements: A major emphasis will be on an introduction element at various levels, with a life skill module and those programs servicing populations with inclusion components. Applicants should demonstrate in their proposal how certain required outcomes will be achieved, and all applicants should maintain non-profit status in the State of Florida. Programs should demonstrate the following to be eligible for funding: (1) Not-for-profit-status as defined under Section 501(c)3 of the U.S. Internal Revenue Code or government entities such as schools or municipalities. (2) For service to children through the 12th grade. Programs should provide provisions for an introduction component from beginners level to course play, and throughout various levels of competition (i.e., local, regional and national). (3) Incorporation of lessons in life skills, core values (i.e., fair play, courtesy and self-discipline), with a time certain and demonstration of effective application. (4) Affordable golf course access to the program for participants during the scheduled program and after the program is concluded.
Restrictions: Grant funds shall not be used for: Golf swing evaluation equipment; Donation for fundraising tournaments; Course and practice facility construction; Tournament entry fees, awards and trophies; Vehicle purchases; Research studies; Administrative costs, including salaries; Video and computer equipment; Lobbyist/consultant fees; or, supplanting funds.
Geographic Focus: Florida
Contact: Christy Peacock; (850) 488-8347; fax (850) 922-0482; cpeacock@flasports.com
Internet: http://www.flasports.com/page_sportsindustry_golfgrants.shtml
Sponsor: Florida Sports Foundation
2930 Kerry Forest Parkway, Suite 101
Tallahassee, FL 32309

Florida Sports Foundation Major and Regional Programs Grants 1873
The grants program is designed to to assist communities and host organizations in attracting sports events, which will generate significant out-of-state economic impact for the state of Florida. The applicant must demonstrate that 'but for' the grant award, the event will not be successful. Events that will be considered include amateur, professional, and other athletic events. Review criteria is based on economic impact, local community support, image value to the state, and financial need. When awarding grants, the foundation places emphasis on out-of-state economic impact, community support and image value to the state.
Requirements: Grant applications are only accepted through a regional Sports Commission in the State of Florida. (See the website, listed at www.flasports.com under Sports Industry, to find the Regional Sports Commission in your area.) If there is not a Sports Commission in the area where your event takes place you may apply under a local Convention & Visitor's Bureau (CVB) or a Tourist Development Council (TDC) per the direction of the Florida Sports Foundation. If there is not a local CVB or TDC in your area contact the foundation. The event must take place a minimum of 120 days from the application deadline. Download the application form at http://www.flasports.com/page_sportsindustry_grantprogram.shtml.
Restrictions: Mature events (in the same location for more than three years) currently based in Florida are not eligible for the grant program unless proof can be provided that it was secured through a bid.
Geographic Focus: Florida
Date(s) Application is Due: Jan 10; Apr 10; Jul 10; Oct 10
Contact: Christy Peacock, Director of Grants; (850) 488-8347; fax (850) 922-0482; cpeacock@flasports.com
Internet: http://www.flasports.com/page_sportsindustry_grantprogram.shtml
Sponsor: Florida Sports Foundation
2930 Kerry Forest Parkway, Suite 101
Tallahassee, FL 32309

Floyd A. and Kathleen C. Cailloux Foundation Grants 1874
The foundation awards grants in the areas of civic and cultural, education and youth, family and community service, and health and rehabilitation. Grants support specific projects or programs, technical assistance, and capital projects. Grants for general operations are less common and usually small. Endowment grants are rare. The foundation only reviews grant proposals from applicants whose letters of inquiry have been approved. Applications are taken online.
Requirements: Grants support 501(c)3 nonprofit organizations. Preference is given to requests from Texas Hill Country.
Restrictions: The Foundation does not fund church or seminary construction, or church related entities or activities other than ecumenically oriented projects/programs that otherwise meet Foundation guidelines. The general policy of the Foundation is not to make grants to an organization more than once within any 12-month period. Grants or loans to individuals are never made.
Geographic Focus: All States
Contact: Grants Administrator; (830) 895-5222; info@caillouxfoundation.org
Internet: http://www.caillouxfoundation.org/grant_guidelines.htm
Sponsor: Floyd A. and Kathleen C. Cailloux Foundation
P.O. Box 291276
Kerrville, TX 78029-1276

Fluor Foundation Grants 1875
The Fluor Corporation achieves its contribution objectives through the Fluor Foundation and corporate giving. The Foundation's areas of interest are: education; human services; cultural outreach; and public/civic affairs. The Foundation considers requests for operating, program, capital or endowment support. Priority is given to funding organizations with employee volunteer participation. Application information is available online.
Requirements: Fluor's giving programs focus on community organizations in those locations around the world where the company has a presence. See website for local contact information: http://www.fluor.com/sustainability/community/fluor_giving/Pages/applying_for_fluor_foundation_grants.aspx

Restrictions: Funding is not available for: film production/publishing activities; individuals; sports organizations/programs; veterans, fraternal, labor or religious organizations; or lobbying/political organizations or campaigns.
Geographic Focus: Alaska, California, Louisiana, New Jersey, New York, North Carolina, Pennsylvania, South Carolina, Tennessee, Texas, Virginia, Washington, Albania, Andorra, Armenia, Australia, Austria, Azerbaijan, Belarus, Belgium, Bosnia & Herzegovina, Bulgaria, Canada, Caribbean, China, Croatia, Cyprus, Czech Republic, Denmark, Estonia, Finland, France, Georgia, Germany, Greece, Hungary, Iceland, Ireland, Italy, Japan, Kosovo, Latvia, Liechtenstein, Lithuania, Luxembourg, Macedonia, Malta, Mexico, Moldova, Monaco, Montenegro, New Zealand, Norway, Peru, Philippines, Poland, Poland, Portugal, Romania, Russia, Russia, San Marino, Serbia, Slovakia, Slovenia, Spain, Sweden, Switzerland, The Netherlands, Turkey, Ukraine, United Kingdom, Vatican City, Venezuela
Contact: Suzanne Esber, Executive Director of Community Relations; (949) 349-7847; fax (949) 349-7694; suzanne.esber@fluor.com
Internet: http://www.fluor.com/sustainability/community/fluor_giving/Pages/applying_for_fluor_foundation_grants.aspx
Sponsor: Fluor Foundation
3 Polaris Way
Aliso Viejo, CA 92698

FMC Foundation Grants 1876
The foundation supports education, community improvement, urban affairs, health and human services, and public issues/economic education. Higher education is supported through scholarships and employee matching gifts. Education support tends to be in business, engineering, chemistry, and some minority education programs. Eligible applicants need to contact the FMC in their geograhic area. Each individual FMC location determines how their contributions will be given.
Requirements: Grants are awarded to 501(c)3 organizations in FMC-plant communities. US-based organizations with an international focus are also eligible.
Restrictions: Grants are not made to individuals.
Geographic Focus: Arizona, California, Delaware, Florida, Illinois, Louisiana, Maine, Maryland, Missouri, New Jersey, New York, North Carolina, Pennsylvania, Tennessee, Texas, West Virginia, Wyoming, Canada
Contact: Program Contact; (215) 299-6000; fax (215) 299-6140
Internet: http://www.fmc.com
Sponsor: FMC Foundation
1735 Market Street
Philadelphia, PA 19103

Foellinger Foundation Grants 1877
The foundation awards grants primarily in Fort Wayne and Allen County, IN, to improve the quality of life in the areas of early child development, youth development, strengthening family services, strengthening organizations, and community concerns. Special emphasis is given to projects/programs that help children and their families, particularly those with the greatest economic need and least opportunity. By doing so, the Foundation hopes to help children and their families move from dependence to independence. In addition to programs and projects, the foundation also awards grants for general operating, capital, seed money, renovation projects, conferences and seminars, consulting services, equipment, challenge/matching, and planning purposes.
Requirements: Indiana organizations are eligible to apply.
Restrictions: The foundation does not fund scholarships, travel assistance, conference fees, religious groups, public or private elementary or secondary schools, sponsorships, special events, advertising, or endowments.
Geographic Focus: Indiana
Date(s) Application is Due: Feb 1; May 1; Nov 1
Amount of Grant: 10,000 - 100,000 USD
Contact: Cheryl Taylor; (219) 422-2900; fax (219) 422-9436; info@foellinger.org
Internet: http://www.foellinger.org
Sponsor: Foellinger Foundation
520 E Berry Street
Fort Wayne, IN 46802

Fondren Foundation Grants 1878
The foundation awards grants to Texas-based programs in the areas of education, youth services, health care, and human services. The board meets quarterly to consider requests.
Requirements: Texas nonprofit organizations, with an emphasis on Houston and the Southwest are eligible to apply.
Restrictions: The Foundation does not allow funding to individuals, or for operating or annual fund drives.
Geographic Focus: Texas
Amount of Grant: 10,000 - 100,000 USD
Contact: Melanie Scioneaux, Assistant Secretary
Internet: http://www.tcc.state.tx.us/cancerfunding/regional/05.html
Sponsor: Fondren Foundation
7 TCT 37, P.O. Box 2558
Houston, TX 77252-8037

Ford Family Foundation Grants - Critical Needs 1879
The Ford Family Foundation provides small grants to organizations in response to critical needs or emergencies. These grants are highly competitive and limited. Priority is given to short term grant requests to address unforeseen emergencies that interrupt programming and/or services, such as a broken boiler. Priority is not given to requests supporting programs that do not have enough funding; general capacity building; small critical needs that fall into

the other categories funded by the Foundation (positive youth development; access to health and dental services for children; child abuse prevention and intervention; public convening spaces; or technical assistance). The application is available at the Foundation website.
Requirements: Grant requests must meet all of the following requirements before consideration will be given: applicant organizations must have current 501(c)3 public charity status from the IRS, or be a governmental entity, or be an IRS-recognized tribe. It may not be a private foundation as defined in Section 509(a) of the Internal Revenue Code; geographical focus of project must be predominately (60% or more) for the benefit of residents of rural Oregon and Siskiyou County, California. Rural is defined as communities with populations of 30,000 or less and not adjacent to or part of an urban or metropolitan area; must include significant collaboration and community buy-in (as evidenced by in-kind and cash contributions from local and regional sources); must have at least 50% of funding (may include in-kind) for the total project budget committed before applying; the organization must not be delinquent in filing final reports for previous grants from the Foundation; and the organization may not be currently receiving other responsive grant funds from the Foundation. If the organization has received prior funding from the Foundation, they must wait 12 months after the completion of the prior grant before applying again for support.
Restrictions: The Foundation will usually not consider requests for projects or programs that are indirectly funded by a fiscal agent; endowments or reserve funds; general fund drives, such as United Way; debt retirement or operating deficits; indirect expenses unrelated to the project or program being funded; sponsorship of fundraising events; or propagandizing or influencing elections or legislation.
Geographic Focus: California, Oregon
Amount of Grant: 1,000 - 10,000 USD
Contact: Grant Contact; (541) 957-5574; fax (541) 957-5720; info@tfff.org
Internet: http://www.tfff.org/Grants/GeneralInformation/tabid/81/Default.aspx
Sponsor: Ford Family Foundation
1600 NW Stewart Parkway
Roseburg, OR 97401

Ford Family Foundation Grants - Positive Youth Development 1880
Positive Youth Development Grants support programs and facilities that encourage the development of skills, instill values of a successful citizen, and create structure for kids in their free time. Priority is given to structured "out-of-school" programs including youth leadership programs, mentorship programs, and evidence-based programs that show a clear connection between the types of programming and the development of successful citizen values and behaviors. Types of funding include programmatic, operational, and capital. Funds will be released in less than 60 days, but may take six months to a year, depending on the project scope and review process. The application is available at the Foundation website.
Requirements: Grant requests must meet all of the following *Requirements:* applicant organizations must have current 501(c)3 public charity status from the IRS, or be a governmental entity, or be an IRS-recognized tribe. It may not be a private foundation as defined in Section 509(a) of the Internal Revenue Code; geographical focus of project must be predominately (60% or more) for the benefit of residents of rural Oregon and Siskiyou County, California. Rural is defined as communities with populations of 30,000 or less and not adjacent to or part of an urban or metropolitan area; must include significant collaboration and community buy-in (as evidenced by in-kind and cash contributions from local and regional sources); must have at least 50% of funding (may include in-kind) for the total project budget committed before applying; and the organization must not be delinquent in filing final reports for previous grants from the Foundation. The organization may not be currently receiving other responsive grants funds from the Foundation. If the organization has received prior funding from the Foundation, they must wait 12 months after the completion of the prior grant before applying again for support.
Restrictions: The Foundation will not consider stand-alone, unsupervised athletics facilities. In the case of positive youth development through organized sports and related facilities, the Foundation will only consider under-served communities where there is evidence of strong local support and project prioritization. The Foundation will usually not consider requests for projects or programs that are indirectly funded through a fiscal agent; endowments or reserve funds; general fund drives, such as United Way; debt retirement or operating deficits; indirect expenses unrelated to the project or program being funded; sponsorship of fundraising events; or propagandizing or influencing elections or legislation.
Geographic Focus: California, Oregon
Amount of Grant: 25,000 - 150,000 USD
Contact: Grant Contact; (541) 957-5574; fax (541) 957-5720; info@tfff.org
Internet: http://www.tfff.org/Grants/GeneralInformation/tabid/81/Default.aspx
Sponsor: Ford Family Foundation
1600 NW Stewart Parkway
Roseburg, OR 97401

Ford Family Foundation Grants - Public Convening Spaces 1881
The Public Convening Spaces Grants strive to encourage civic participation and community collaboration through the development of places that bring the community together, have substantial and broad uses, are open to the public, and serve populations. Convening spaces include libraries, community and resource centers, amphitheaters, fairgrounds, arenas, pavilions, and auditoriums. In some cases, sports related facilities that double as convening space in small communities will be considered. Priority is given to smaller communities with demonstrated need. The application is available at the Foundation website.
Requirements: Along with the online application, applicants should be prepared to provide an inventory of public meeting spaces that currently exist in the community and a list of organizations that plan to use the proposed space and for what purposes.
Restrictions: Funds requested may not exceed one-third of the project's total budget. Lower priority is given to government projects (e.g. city halls) unless there is a specific component (e.g. conference room open for broad public use) that fits the Foundation's objectives. Also, outdoor spaces that serve as passive areas for convening such as playgrounds or green space, lacking programming designed specifically to convene.
Geographic Focus: California, Oregon
Amount of Grant: 50,000 - 250,000 USD
Contact: Grant Contact; (541) 957-5574; fax (541) 957-5720; info@tfff.org
Internet: http://www.tfff.org/Grants/GeneralInformation/tabid/81/Default.aspx
Sponsor: Ford Family Foundation
1600 NW Stewart Parkway
Roseburg, OR 97401

Ford Family Foundation Grants - Technical Assistance 1882
The Ford Family Foundation Technical Assistance Grants help develop community leaders, effective organizations, and collaborations. Funding categories include: leadership development - supports leadership training for community groups,particularly youth groups; effective organizations - support technical assistance for non-profits to improve their performance; and community collaborations - supports collaborations by organizations or communities in addressing shares issues or opportunities. Priority is given to requests clearly linked to a broad, compelling community need; established organizations with evidence of past success; built on existing investments of the Ford Institute which provide a more advanced level of training; and assistance to a network or cluster of people, organizations, or communities. Funds requested may not exceed 80% of the total project budget, and a minimum of 20% cash match toward the project is required. The application is available at the Foundation website.
Requirements: Grant requests must meet all of the following requirements for consideration: applicant organizations must have current 501(c)3 public charity status from the IRS, or be a governmental entity, or be an IRS-recognized tribe. It may not be a private foundation as defined in Section 509(a) of the Internal Revenue Code; geographical focus of project must be predominately (60% or more) for the benefit of residents of rural Oregon and Siskiyou County, California. Rural is defined as communities with populations of 30,000 or less and not adjacent to or part of an urban or metropolitan area; must include significant collaboration and community buy-in (as evidenced by in-kind and cash contributions from local and regional sources); must have at least 50% of funding (may include in-kind) for the total project budget committed before applying; and the organization must not be delinquent in filing final reports for previous grants from the Foundation.
Restrictions: The Foundation usually will not consider funding for projects or programs that are indirectly funded through a fiscal agent; endowments or reserve funds; general fund drives, such as United Way; debt retirement or operating deficits; indirect expenses unrelated to the project or program being funded; sponsorship of fundraising events; or propagandizing or influencing elections or legislation. Organizations may not be currently receiving other responsive grants funds from the Foundation. If the organization has received prior funding from the Foundation, they must wait 12 months after the completion of the prior grant before applying again for support.
Geographic Focus: California, Oregon
Contact: Grant Contact; (541) 957-5574; fax (541) 957-5720; info@tfff.org
Internet: http://www.tfff.org/Grants/GeneralInformation/tabid/81/Default.aspx
Sponsor: Ford Family Foundation
1600 NW Stewart Parkway
Roseburg, OR 97401

Ford Foundation Diversity Fellowships 1883
The Ford Foundation Diversity Fellowships seek to increase the diversity of the nation's college and university faculties by increasing their ethnic and racial diversity, to maximize the educational benefits of diversity, and to increase the number of professors who can and will use diversity as a resource for enriching the education of all students. The Fellowship grants awards at the predoctoral, dissertation, and postdoctoral levels to students whom demonstrate excellence, a commitment to diversity and, a desire to enter the professoriate.
Requirements: Eligible applicants must be: citizens or nationals of the United States regardless of race, national origin, religion or sexual orientation; individuals with evidence of superior academic achievement; individuals committed to a career in teaching and research at the college or university level; individuals enrolled in or planning to enroll in an eligible research-based program leading to a Ph.D. or Sc.D. degree at a U.S. educational institution; and individuals who have not earned a doctoral degree at any time, in any field.
Geographic Focus: All States
Contact: Fellowships Office; (202) 334-2872; fax (202) 334-3419; infofell@nas.ed
Internet: http://sites.nationalacademies.org/pga/fordfellowships/
Sponsor: Ford Foundation
500 5th Street, NW
Washington, DC 20001

Ford Foundation Peace and Social Justice Grants 1884
This program area supports two categories: human rights and international cooperation, and governance and civil society. Grants under human rights and international cooperation support projects involving women's rights and civil rights in the United States, international human rights, international law, multilateral conflict prevention, and U.S. foreign policy. Governance and civil society grants support projects concerning civic participation, electoral reform, and innovations in state and local government. Most grants are given to organizations. The foundation also makes grants to individuals, though they are few in number relative to demand and are limited to research, training, and other activities related to the foundation's program interests. Support for graduate fellowships is generally provided through grants to universities and other organizations, which select recipients. Applications are considered throughout the year; a letter of inquiry is the first step of the application process.
Requirements: The letter of inquiry should include the purpose of the project, problems and issues addressed, information about the applicant organization, estimated overall budget, time period for which funds are requested, and qualifications of those engaged in the project.

Restrictions: Support is not normally given for routine operating costs of institutions or for religious activities. Except in rare cases, funding is not available for the construction or maintenance of buildings. The foundation does not award undergraduate scholarships or make grants for purely personal or local needs.
Geographic Focus: All States
Amount of Grant: 75,000 - 250,000 USD
Contact: Luis Antonio Ubinas, President; (212) 573-5000; fax (212) 599-4584; office-secretary@fordfound.org
Internet: http://www.fordfound.org/grants
Sponsor: Ford Foundation
320 E 43rd Street
New York, NY 10017

Ford Motor Company Fund Grants 1885
The fund supports not-for-profit organizations in three major areas: innovation and education; community development and American legacy, and auto-related safety education. The fund seeks to build partnerships with organizations that have a well-defined sense of purpose, a demonstrated commitment to maximizing available resources, and a reputation for meeting objectives and delivering quality programs and services. Priority is placed on the support and development of organizations that promote diversity and inclusion. Requests for support are accepted and reviewed throughout the year. The fund now implements an online application system. Details are available online.
Restrictions: Ford does not fund: advocacy-directed programs; animal-rights organizations; beauty or talent contests; day-to-day business operations; debt reduction; donation of vehicles; efforts to influence legislation, or the outcome of any elections or any specific election of candidates to public office or to carry on any voter registration drive; endowments; fraternal organizations; general operating support to hospitals and health care institutions; individual sponsorship related to fundraising activities; individuals; labor groups; loans for small businesses; loans to program-related investments; organizations that do not have 501(c)3 status; organizations that unlawfully discriminate in their provision of goods and services based on race, color, religion, gender, gender identity or expression, ethnicity, sexual orientation, national origin, physical challenge, age, or status as a protected veteran; political contributions; private K-12 schools; profit-making enterprises; religious programs or sectarian programs for religious purposes; species-specific organizations; sports teams.
Geographic Focus: All States
Contact: Ford Fund Coordinator; (888) 313-0102; Fordfund@ford.com
Internet: http://www.ford.com/en/goodWorks/fundingAndGrants/fordMotorCompanyFund/default.htm
Sponsor: Ford Motor Company Fund
P.O. Box 1899
Dearborn, MI 48121-1899

Forest Foundation Grants 1886
The Foundation awards grants to eligible Washington nonprofit organizations in its areas of interest, including community and economic development; environment; and youth development. The Foundation gives primarily to southwestern Washington counties, with emphasis on Pierce, Clallum, Cowlitz; Clark, Grays Harbor, Jefferson, Kitsap, Lewis, Mason, Pacific, Skamania; Thurston; and Wahkiakum. The Foundation Board meets six times per year. Organizations receive notification of funding in within 90 days.
Requirements: The Foundation should be initially approached with an email request for guidelines and instructions. Full proposals are by invitation only. Organizations should submit the following: copy of IRS Determination Letter; a brief history of organization and description of its mission; a listing of board of directors, trustees, officers and other key people and their affiliations; detailed description of project and amount of funding requested; a copy of the organization's current budget and/or project budget.
Restrictions: Grants do not funding for buildings or renovation projects.
Geographic Focus: Washington
Amount of Grant: 15,000 - 150,000 USD
Contact: Angela Baptiste, Grants Administrator; (253) 627-1634; fax (253) 627-6249
Sponsor: Forest Foundation
820 A Street, Suite 345
Tacoma, WA 98402

Forrest C. Lattner Foundation Grants 1887
The Foundation's primary objectives are in six areas of interest: arts and humanities; education; environment; health and social services; historic preservation; and medical research. The Foundation also wishes to encourage the development of innovative model programs. Application guidelines are available online.
Restrictions: The foundation is unable to fulfill grant requests to individuals, or to support programs that are the primary responsibility of the public sector.
Geographic Focus: Florida, Georgia, Kansas, Rhode Island, Texas
Date(s) Application is Due: Mar 1; Sep 1
Contact: Susan Lattner Lloyd; (561) 278-3781; fax (561) 278-3167; lattner@bellsouth.net
Internet: http://www.lattnerfoundation.org
Sponsor: Forrest C. Lattner Foundation
777 E Atlantic Avenue, Suite 317
Delray Beach, FL 33483

Foster Foundation Grants 1888
The Foundation funds effective, nonprofit organizations that can provide tangible benefits and ongoing support to improve the quality of life for individuals, families and communities within the Pacific Northwest. The Foundation's primary field of interests are: basic human welfare issues, education, medical research, treatment and care and cultural activities. The Foundation places special emphasis on meeting the needs of the underserved and disadvantaged segments of the population, especially children, women and seniors.
Requirements: Eligible applicants must: be a nonprofit located in or serving the populations of the Pacific Northwest; address as their mission or project intent one of the Foundation's priority issues for funding; not have any delinquent final reports due to the Foundation from previous grant cycles.
Restrictions: The Foundation will not consider requests for: direct grants, scholarships or loans for the benefit of specific individuals; projects of organizations whose policies or practices discriminate on the basis of race, ethnic origin, sex, creed or sexual orientation; contributions or program support for sectarian or religious organizations whose activities benefit only their members; or loans.
Geographic Focus: Alaska, Idaho, Montana, Oregon, Washington
Contact: Jill Goodsell; (206) 726-1815; fax (206) 903-0628; info@thefosterfoundation.org
Internet: http://thefosterfoundation.org/Grants_Guide.asp
Sponsor: Foster Foundation
601 Union Street, Suite 3707
Seattle, WA 98101

Foster G. McGaw Prize 1889
This prize, established by the Baxter Foundation and administered by the Hospital Research and Educational Trust, the research and development affiliate of the American Hospital Association, is awarded to a community hospital that has undertaken an identifiable program or project that improves the status or enhances the quality of life of community members, particularly the poor. The winner will receive a monetary prize; trophy; recognition at a special awards ceremony at the AHA annual meeting; and coverage in AHA News, Hospitals and Health Networks, and other health care publications. Up to three finalists will each receive a monetary prize and mention in AHA News, Hospitals and Health Networks, and other health care publications. Application and guidelines are available online.
Requirements: Nominations can be made by either the hospitals themselves or by other community organizations.
Geographic Focus: All States
Date(s) Application is Due: Apr 8
Amount of Grant: Up to 10,000 USD
Contact: AHA Member Relations; (312) 422-3932
Internet: http://www.aha.org/aha/awards-events/foster/application/application.html#o
Sponsor: Hospital Research and Educational Trust
1 N Franklin, 32nd Floor
Chicago, IL 60606

Foundation for a Drug-Free World Classroom Tools 1890
The foundation makes available its Truth About Drugs Education Package. The package includes everything needed to launch its classroom-tested drug-free education program in any school or community center. It features a series of 10 drug education booklets that present the facts about the most commonly abused drugs - marijuana, alcohol, inhalants, ecstasy, cocaine, crack, crystal meth, heroin, LSD, painkillers and Ritalin abuse. It also features an Educator's Guide, with a complete set of corresponding lesson plans. The Guide further offers suggested activities anyone can initiate to help start a drug-free movement in your community. Completing the package is a DVD which features a series of award-winning public service announcements. These videos compel youth to get the facts they need to make informed decisions to be drug-free.
Requirements: The Truth About Drugs Education Package is available free of charge. The foundation will further provide as many sets of booklets as required to accommodate your needs. To request the free publications, go to http://www.drugfreeworld.org/#/publications/drugs/truth-about-drugs-information-set-english or call the sponsor directly.
Geographic Focus: All States
Contact: Materials Consultant; (888) 668-6378 or (818) 952-5260
Internet: http://www.drugfreeworld.org/#/educators/educators-tools-classroom
Sponsor: Foundation for a Drug-Free World
1626 N Wilcox Avenue, Suite 1297
Los Angeles, CA 90028

Foundation for a Healthy Kentucky Grants 1891
The Foundation seeks to address the unmet health care needs of the people of Kentucky through strategic grants designed to improve health status and access to care. Funding is concentrated in the following areas: fitness and nutrition for children and families; youth smoking prevention; and youth substance abuse prevention. The Foundation also hopes to enhance access to health care for low-income and uninsured populations; health care for rural populations; and integrated mental health and medical services.
Requirements: The Foundation accepts proposals for funding only in direct response to a specific Request for Proposals (RFP) or Request for Quotes (RFQ) or grant solicitation issued by the Foundation. Organizations should familiarize themselves with the Foundation's What We Fund page, and the Grant Guidelines to determine whether they are eligible to receive funding. They should sign up for the Foundation's mail/email list to receive grant opportunities and free educational forums. Once the organization receives an RFP announcement, they should review it carefully to see that the goals of the RFP fit with their particular project. If it is acceptable, applicants should submit their proposal according to the guidelines and RFP due dates.
Restrictions: The Foundation will not review unsolicited grant requests except for requests for Matching Grant and Conference Support funds. Grants do not support direct patient care, except as part of demonstration or replication projects; capital campaigns or requests for bricks and mortar (although project related equipment may be included in requests); overhead expenses except in limited amounts for specific projects; organizations that discriminate on the basis of race, gender, age, religion, national origin, sexual orientation,

disability, military, or marital status in hiring; multi-year commitments; expenses related to registered legislative agents for the purpose of lobbying; endowment funds; individuals; private, for-profit entities; religious organizations for religious purposes; political causes; or retroactive expenses, deficit reduction, or forgiveness.
Geographic Focus: Kentucky
Contact: Susan Zepeda, President/Chief Executive Officer; (502) 326-2583 or (877) 326-2583; fax (502) 326-5748; szepeda@healthyky.org or info@healthy-ky.org
Internet: http://www.healthyky.org
Sponsor: Foundation for a Healthy Kentucky
9300 Shelbyville Road, Suite 1305
Louisville, KY 40222

Foundation for Appalachian Ohio Access to Environmental Education Mini-Grants 1892

The Foundation for Appalachian Ohio Access to Environmental Education Mini-Grants encourage and support creative, local environmental education and stewardship activities for youth that build on the unique assets and strengths of the region's individual communities. Grants ranging from $250 to $1,500 are available to public schools and 501(c)3 community youth organizations. Those who might find interest in applying include public school science and vocational agriculture classes, and youth service clubs such as 4-H, Future Farmers of America, Girl Scouts, Boy Scouts, Big Brothers Big Sisters or Key Clubs. As appropriate, applications to support youth-focused efforts of local government, civic clubs and nonprofits working with youth, including county farm bureaus, city parks and recreation departments, soil and water conservation districts, community colleges, rotary international, and others, may also wish to apply.
Requirements: Applications are available online. The following counties serving Ohio nonprofits are eligible to apply: Adams, Ashtabula, Athens, Belmont, Brown, Carroll, Clermont, Columbiana, Coshocton, Gallia, Guernsey, Harrison, Highland, Hocking, Holmes, Jackson, Jefferson, Lawrence, Mahoning, Meigs, Monroe, Morgan, Muskingum, Noble, Perry, Pike, Ross, Scioto, Trumbull, Tuscarawas, Vinton, and Washington.
Restrictions: Only certain Ohio counties are eligible to apply.
Geographic Focus: Ohio
Date(s) Application is Due: Oct 14
Amount of Grant: 250 - 1,500 USD
Contact: Cara Dingus Brook; (740) 753-1111; fax (740) 753-3333; cbrook@ffao.org
Internet: http://www.appalachianohio.org/grantees/index.php?page=248
Sponsor: Foundation for Appalachian Ohio
36 Public Square, P.O. Box 456
Nelsonville, OH 45764

Foundation for Enhancing Communities Grants 1893

The Foundation awards grants to Pennsylvania nonprofit organizations in the greater Harrisburg area. Areas of interest include art/cultural programs, education, health care and health organizations, human services, and community development. Types of support include program development, publication, seed money, and scholarships. Deadlines vary according to funding availability.
Requirements: Tax exempt 501(c)3 organizations in Pennsylvania's Dauphin, Cumberland, Franklin, and Perry Counties are eligible.
Restrictions: Grants do not support individuals, operating budgets, or capital expenses.
Geographic Focus: Pennsylvania
Contact: Jennifer Kuntch; (717) 236-5040; fax (717) 231-4463; jkuntch@tfec.org
Internet: http://www.ghf.org
Sponsor: Foundation for Enhancing Communities
200 North 3rd Street, P.O. Box 678
Harrisburg, PA 17108-0678

Foundation for Health Enhancement Grants 1894

The purpose of the Foundation for Health Enhancement is to improve care in the United States by the development of the science of delivery of all kinds of health care, including medical, surgical, dental, nursing, health education, and other curative and preventive health services. The majority of grants from the Foundation for Health Enhancement are one year in duration. Applicants must apply online at the grant website. Applicants are strongly encouraged to do the following before applying: review the downloadable state application procedures for additional helpful information and clarifications; review the downloadable online-application guidelines at the grant website; review the foundation's funding history (link is available from the grant website); review the online application questions in advance; and review the list of required attachments. These will generally include: a list of board members, financial statements (audited, reviewed, or compiled by independent auditor); an organization summary; a list of other funding sources; an IRS Determination letter; and other required documents. All attachments must be uploaded in the online application as PDF, Word, or Excel files. The Foundation for Health Enhancement has biannual deadlines of April 1 and September 1. Applications should be submitted by 11:59 p.m. on the deadline dates. In general, applicants will be notified of grant decisions 3 to 4 months after proposal submission.
Requirements: The Foundation places special emphasis on: preventive health services; smaller qualifying applicants in an area geographically proximate to Chicago and/or the Midwest; and service organizations as opposed to research organizations.
Geographic Focus: Illinois
Date(s) Application is Due: Apr 1; Sep 1
Contact: George Thorn; (312) 828-4154; ilgrantmaking@bankofamerica.com
Internet: https://www.bankofamerica.com/philanthropic/fn_search.action
Sponsor: Foundation for Health Enhancement
231 South LaSalle Street, IL1-231-13-32
Chicago, IL 60604

Foundation for Seacoast Health Grants 1895

The mission of the foundation is to invest its resources to improve the health and well being of Seacoast residents. The foundation considers a very limited number of new grant initiatives which address one or more of the following prioritized health needs; access to affordable mental health services; access to preventative and restorative dental services; access to affordable child care and after school care; access to affordable primary medical care; and coordination and dissemination of health information related to identified priority needs. The deadline for the submission of the letter of intent is March 1 for Infants, Children and Adolescence and June 1 for Promoting Health and Preventing Disease. Annual deadline dates may vary; contact program staff for exact dates.
Requirements: Nonprofit organizations in cities and towns in the New Hampshire/Maine Seacoast area, including Greenland, New Castle, Newington, North Hampton, Portsmouth, and Rye, NH; and Eliot, Kittery, and York, ME, may submit applications.
Restrictions: Grants do not support ongoing general operating expenses, deficit elimination, political activities, travel, conferences, or lodging.
Geographic Focus: Maine, New Hampshire
Date(s) Application is Due: Mar 1; Jun 1
Contact: Susan Bunting, President; (603) 422-8200; ffsh@communitycampus.org
Internet: http://www.ffsh.org/grants.cfm
Sponsor: Foundation for Seacoast Health
100 Campus Drive, Suite 1
Portsmouth, NH 03801

Foundation for the Carolinas Grants 1896

The foundation supports nonprofit organizations in North and South Carolina, especially in the greater Charlotte, NC, area. The foundation awards grants in the following program areas: education, religion, human services, the environment, historic preservation, public and civic affairs, health, the arts, youths, and senior citizens. Building Youth grants help school-age children make the transition from youth to adulthood.
Requirements: The foundation awards grants to nonprofit organizations serving the following areas in North Carolina: Cebarrus, Cleveland, Iredell, Lincoln, Mecklenburg, Richmond, Stanley, and Union Counties and the cities of Lexiington and Salisbury; and Cherokee, Lancaster, and York Counties in South Carolina.
Restrictions: Grants are not awarded for capital campaigns, operating budgets, endowments, publications, equipment, videos, or conferences, nor to individuals.
Geographic Focus: North Carolina, South Carolina
Contact: Dr. Don Jonas, Senior Vice President of Community Philanthropy; (704) 973-4500 or (800) 973-7244; fax (704) 973-4599; djonas@fftc.org
Internet: http://www.fftc.org/grants
Sponsor: Foundation for the Carolinas
P.O. Box 34769
Charlotte, NC 28234-4769

Foundation for the Mid South Community Development Grants 1897

The Foundation for the Mid South was established to bring together the public and private sectors and focus their resources on increasing social and economic opportunity. The foundation's community development work includes five key focuses that, together, enable communities to grow and prosper: Community Enrichment, Economic Development, Leadership Development, Education, and Health and Wellness. Each focus area addresses an essential community element.
Requirements: Contact a program officer to discuss your project prior to submitting a proposal To be eligible for a grant, the applying organization must possess tax-exempt status under section 501(c)3 of the Internal Revenue Code and a certificate from the Mississippi Secretary of State that designates it as a public charity or exempt for the state of Mississippi. Mississippi organizations must register and receive a certificate that designates it as a public charity or exempt for the state of Mississippi when submitting a full proposal. The application, Form URS, and instructions are available at the sponsor's website. All other organizations must apply and receive a notice of exemption, Form CE, from the Mississippi Secretary of State's office, also available from the website. If the proposed work aligns with the Foundation's priorities and goals, eligible organizations may submit the Grant Inquiry Form found on the website.
Restrictions: The Foundation does not award grants to individuals or make grants for personal needs or business assistance. Additionally, funds are not awarded for lobbying activities; ongoing general operating expenses or existing deficits; endowments; capital costs including construction, renovation, or equipment; or international programs.
Geographic Focus: Arkansas, Louisiana, Mississippi
Contact: Justin A. Burch; (601) 355-8167; fax (601) 355-6499
Internet: http://www.fndmidsouth.org/priorities/community-development
Sponsor: Foundation for the Mid South
134 East Amite Street
Jackson, MS 39201

Foundation for the Mid South Education Grants 1898

The Foundation for the Mid South was established to bring together the public and private sectors and focus their resources on increasing social and economic opportunity. The foundation supports efforts that strengthen education systems, by building the capacity of teachers and administrators to better serve student needs and advance learning. It also focuses on enrichment opportunities that provide effective and innovative ways to help students learn.
Requirements: Contact a program officer to discuss your project prior to submitting a proposal To be eligible for a grant, the applying organization must possess tax-exempt status under section 501(c)3 of the Internal Revenue Code and a certificate from the Mississippi Secretary of State that designates it as a public charity or exempt for the state of Mississippi. Mississippi organizations must register and receive a certificate that designates it as a

public charity or exempt for the state of Mississippi when submitting a full proposal. The application, Form URS, and instructions are available at the sponsor's website. All other organizations must apply and receive a notice of exemption, Form CE, from the Mississippi Secretary of State's office, also available from the website. If the proposed work aligns with the Foundation's priorities and goals, eligible organizations may submit the Grant Inquiry Form found on the website.
Restrictions: The Foundation does not award grants to individuals or make grants for personal needs or business assistance. Additionally, funds are not awarded for lobbying activities; ongoing general operating expenses or existing deficits; endowments; capital costs including construction, renovation, or equipment; or international programs.
Geographic Focus: Arkansas, Louisiana, Mississippi
Contact: Denise Ellis; (601) 355-8167; fax (601) 355-6499; bdellis@fndmidsouth.org
Internet: http://www.fndmidsouth.org/priorities/education
Sponsor: Foundation for the Mid South
134 East Amite Street
Jackson, MS 39201

Foundation for the Mid South Health and Wellness Grants   1899
The Foundation for the Mid South was established to bring together the public and private sectors and focus their resources on increasing social and economic opportunity. The Health and Wellness program supports activities that promote healthy behaviors leading to the reduction of obesity and diabetes and projects that increase mental health awareness and access to services. The program also seeks to expand access to health services, emphasizing the use of technology to serve rural communities.
Requirements: Contact a program officer to discuss your project prior to submitting a proposal To be eligible for a grant, the applying organization must possess tax-exempt status under section 501(c)3 of the Internal Revenue Code and a certificate from the Mississippi Secretary of State that designates it as a public charity or exempt for the state of Mississippi. Mississippi organizations must register and receive a certificate that designates it as a public charity or exempt for the state of Mississippi when submitting a full proposal. The application, Form URS, and instructions are available at the sponsor's website. All other organizations must apply and receive a notice of exemption, Form CE, from the Mississippi Secretary of State's office, also available from the website. If the proposed work aligns with the Foundation's priorities and goals, eligible organizations may submit the Grant Inquiry Form found on the website.
Restrictions: The Foundation does not award grants to individuals or make grants for personal needs or business assistance. Additionally, funds are not awarded for lobbying activities; ongoing general operating expenses or existing deficits; endowments; capital costs including construction, renovation, or equipment; or international programs.
Geographic Focus: Arkansas, Louisiana, Mississippi
Contact: Dwanda Moore; (601) 355-8167; fax (601) 355-6499
Internet: http://www.fndmidsouth.org/priorities/health-wellness/#theoverview
Sponsor: Foundation for the Mid South
134 East Amite Street
Jackson, MS 39201

Foundation for the Mid South Wealth Building Grants   1900
The Foundation for the Mid South was established to bring together the public and private sectors and focus their resources on increasing social and economic opportunity. The foundation supports activities that expand access to knowledge and resources to strengthen adult and youth financial competency and efforts that help families acquire assets. The foundation also seeks to increase the use of the Earned Income Tax Credit (EITC) among eligible low-wealth tax filers, as a means to increase annual income.
Requirements: Contact a program officer to discuss your project prior to submitting a proposal To be eligible for a grant, the applying organization must possess tax-exempt status under section 501(c)3 of the Internal Revenue Code and a certificate from the Mississippi Secretary of State that designates it as a public charity or exempt for the state of Mississippi. Mississippi organizations must register and receive a certificate that designates it as a public charity or exempt for the state of Mississippi when submitting a full proposal. The application, Form URS, and instructions are available at the sponsor's website. All other organizations must apply and receive a notice of exemption, Form CE, from the Mississippi Secretary of State's office, also available from the website. If the proposed work aligns with the Foundation's priorities and goals, eligible organizations may submit the Grant Inquiry Form found on the website.
Restrictions: The Foundation does not award grants to individuals or make grants for personal needs or business assistance. Additionally, funds are not awarded for lobbying activities; ongoing general operating expenses or existing deficits; endowments; capital costs including construction, renovation, or equipment; or international programs.
Geographic Focus: Arkansas, Louisiana, Mississippi
Contact: Denise Ellis; (601) 355-8167; fax (601) 355-6499; bdellis@fndmidsouth.org
Internet: http://www.fndmidsouth.org/priorities/wealth-building
Sponsor: Foundation for the Mid South
134 East Amite Street
Jackson, MS 39201

Foundation for Young Australians Indigenous Small Grants   1901
The Foundation provides an opportunity for Indigenous organizations and organizations that work with Indigenous people and communities to obtain support funding for new initiatives or to support innovation and the expansion of existing successful initiatives. Funds are available for initiatives that enhance youth participation or create opportunities for the development of young people aged 12-25 years. The Foundation's focus is on initiatives that result in meaningful change for young people. Applications and information on submission are available online.
Requirements: Applications will be accepted from non-profit organizations (including local government and schools) which are either an Indigenous organization or can provide information regarding experience in working with Indigenous people and organizations.
Restrictions: This program is unable to fund: on-going organizational infrastructure; initiatives which duplicate existing available services to an identical target group within the same geographic location; retrospective funding; medical treatment; undergraduate study; an overseas course of study or training which does not offer any special advantage over those available in Australia; or donations for unspecified initiatives.
Geographic Focus: All States, Australia
Date(s) Application is Due: May 12; Oct 14
Amount of Grant: Up to 5,000 USD
Contact: Josephine Bourne, Coordinator; 03 9670 5436; fax 03 9670 2272; fya@youngaustralians.org
Internet: http://www.youngaustralians.org/
Sponsor: Foundation for Young Australians
G.P.O. Box 239
Melbourne, VIC 3001 Australia

Foundation for Young Australians Spark Fund Grants   1902
The Spark Fund provides funding support for young people aged 12-25 years to ignite an innovative idea which makes a positive contribution to the community and enhances their skills and experiences for themselves, other young people and their communities. Applications for the Fund can be made all year, with the Selection Committee meeting three times during the year to decide on applications received.
Restrictions: This program is unable to fund: on-going organizational infrastructure; initiatives which duplicate existing available services to an identical target group within the same geographic location; retrospective funding; medical treatment; undergraduate study; an overseas course of study or training which does not offer any special advantage over those available in Australia; or donations for unspecified initiatives.
Geographic Focus: All States, Australia
Date(s) Application is Due: Mar 26; Jun 30; Sep 22
Amount of Grant: Up to 5,000 USD
Contact: Sarah Hardy, 03 9670 5436; fax 03 9670 2272; fya@youngaustralians.org
Internet: http://www.youngaustralians.org/
Sponsor: Foundation for Young Australians
G.P.O. Box 239
Melbourne, VIC 3001 Australia

Foundation for Young Australians Your Eyes Only Awards   1903
Your Eyes Only is a creative grant opportunity for young people 12 to 15 years to celebrate the strengths of their community by submitting a creative image celebrating their community through their eyes. Successful applicants will nominate a community group working with young people in their community (for example a school, youth group or sporting group) to receive a donation. This donation would then be used by the community group to further its work by either purchasing much needed equipment or adding funds to an existing program. Entries are accepted from February 12 through September 2.
Requirements: An can enter if he/she is aged between 12 and 15 years. Applicants must nominate an organization that supports young people in their community to receive the award.
Geographic Focus: All States, Australia
Date(s) Application is Due: Sep 2
Contact: Sarah Hardy, 03 9670 5436; fax 03 9670 2272; fya@youngaustralians.org
Internet: http://www.youngaustralians.org/
Sponsor: Foundation for Young Australians
G.P.O. Box 239
Melbourne, VIC 3001 Australia

Foundation for Young Australians Youth Change Makers Grants   1904
Youth Change Makers is a funding opportunity that responds to the right of young people to participate as advocates for change in their communities. It will support individuals and small groups of young people who have identified an issue in their communities and have developed an advocacy response which aims to take action that creates a positive impact and/or change in relation to that issue. Youth Change Makers grants will support initiatives up to $10,000 per applicant group.
Restrictions: This program is unable to fund: on-going organizational infrastructure; initiatives which duplicate existing available services to an identical target group within the same geographic location; retrospective funding; medical treatment; undergraduate study; an overseas course of study or training which does not offer any special advantage over those available in Australia; or donations for unspecified initiatives.
Geographic Focus: All States, Australia
Amount of Grant: Up to 10,000 USD
Contact: Sarah Hardy, 03 9670 5436; fax 03 9670 2272; fya@youngaustralians.org
Internet: http://www.youngaustralians.org/
Sponsor: Foundation for Young Australians
G.P.O. Box 239
Melbourne, VIC 3001 Australia

Foundation for Young Australians Youth Led Futures Grants   1905
Youth Led Futures grants are available to Indigenous organizations for the development and implementation of innovative projects to address issues of importance to Indigenous young people and their communities, utilizing the shared resources and expertise of young people, the supporting organization and the Foundation. The aim of the partnership is to work together to develop and implement a creative idea that results in meaningful change with young people aged 12-25 years. Grants are made in two stages. In the first stage, a small

number of partners are selected and funded to identify a priority area for young people and create an initiative proposal for funding over a number of years. In Stage 2 some proposals will be supported by the Foundation with multi-year funding and non-financial assistance.
Requirements: Applications will be accepted from non-profit organizations (including local government and schools) which are either a youth-oriented organization or can provide information regarding experience in working with young people and youth organizations.
Restrictions: This program is unable to fund: on-going organizational infrastructure; initiatives which duplicate existing available services to an identical target group within the same geographic location; retrospective funding; medical treatment; undergraduate study; an overseas course of study or training which does not offer any special advantage over those available in Australia; or donations for unspecified initiatives.
Geographic Focus: All States, Australia
Contact: Sarah Hardy, 03 9670 5436; fax 03 9670 2272; fya@youngaustralians.org
Internet: http://www.youngaustralians.org/
Sponsor: Foundation for Young Australians
G.P.O. Box 239
Melbourne, VIC 3001 Australia

Foundation Northwest Grants 1906
Grants are awarded to organizations in the Inland Northwest—eastern Washington and northern Idaho—for charitable and educational purposes in the fields of music and drama; education; civic categories which include culture, education, civic and community development; and human services. The foundation has five distinct grant programs and types of support include matching funds, special projects, seed money, and occasional operating support and capital funding. Deadlines vary according to area and contributing sponsorship; contact program support for exact dates.
Requirements: Grant applications are accepted for projects that will enrich the quality of life in the communities of eastern Washington and northern Idaho. Eligible Washington counties include Adams, Asotin, Columbia, Ferry, Garfield, Lincoln, Pend Oreille, Spokane, Steven, and Whitman. Eligible Idaho counties include Benewah, Bonner, Boundary, Clearwater, Idaho, Kootenai, Latah, Lewis, Nez Perce, and Shoshone.
Restrictions: Grants do not support endowments, debt retirement, lobbying, sectarian religious purposes, individuals, travel, sports teams and classes, projects that taxpayers or commercial interests normally support, fundraising campaigns, publications or films (unless an integral part of a foundation-supported program), or nondonor-supported research.
Geographic Focus: Idaho, Washington
Amount of Grant: 2,500 - 7,500 USD
Contact: Contact; (509) 624-2606; fax (509) 624-2608; admin@foundationnw.org
Internet: http://www.foundationnw.org
Sponsor: Foundation Northwest
221 Wall Street N, Suite 624
Spokane, WA 99201-0826

Foundations of East Chicago Community Economic Development Grants 1907
The Foundations of East Chicago are committed to improving the lives of every resident of its city. Conceived by the citizens of East Chicago to be independent, citizen-run, private foundations, it derives funding from East Chicago's local casino, and uses this money to support local churches, schools, and nonprofit organizations who know the community best and put in the money in action where it can do the most good. Community Economic Development grants are specifically focused on programs or projects designed to help East Chicago improve its communities and neighborhoods.
Requirements: Applicants must be registered 501(c)3 organizations located in East Chicago, Indiana. If an applicant is not located in East Chicago, it may still qualify if it complies with at least one of the following *Requirements:* the program that an applicant is applying for operates in East Chicago; the funding that an applicant is applying for will go toward assisting East Chicago residents.
Restrictions: All applications must be submitted via Foundations of East Chicago website. The Foundations will not accept any applications in person.
Geographic Focus: Indiana
Amount of Grant: Up to 25,000 USD
Contact: Russell G. Taylor, (219) 392-4225; grantinfo@foundationsofeastchicago.org
Internet: http://foundationsofeastchicago.org/apply-now
Sponsor: Foundations of East Chicago
100 W Chicago Avenue
East Chicago, IN 46312

Foundations of East Chicago Family Support Grants 1908
The Foundations of East Chicago are committed to improving the lives of every resident of its city. Conceived by the citizens of East Chicago to be independent, citizen-run, private foundations, it derives funding from East Chicago's local casino, and uses this money to support local churches, schools, and nonprofit organizations who know the community best and put in the money in action where it can do the most good. Family Support grants are specifically focused on programs or projects designed to help strengthen the East Chicago Family unit.
Requirements: Applicants must be registered 501(c)3 organizations located in East Chicago, Indiana. If an applicant is not located in East Chicago, it may still qualify if it complies with at least one of the following *Requirements:* the program that an applicant is applying for operates in East Chicago; the funding that an applicant is applying for will go toward assisting East Chicago residents.
Restrictions: All applications must be submitted via Foundations of East Chicago website. The Foundations will not accept any applications in person.
Geographic Focus: Indiana
Amount of Grant: Up to 15,000 USD
Contact: Russell G. Taylor, (219) 392-4225; grantinfo@foundationsofeastchicago.org
Internet: http://foundationsofeastchicago.org/apply-now
Sponsor: Foundations of East Chicago
100 W Chicago Avenue
East Chicago, IN 46312

Foundations of East Chicago Financial Independence Grants 1909
The Foundations of East Chicago are committed to improving the lives of every resident of its city. Conceived by the citizens of East Chicago to be independent, citizen-run, private foundations, it derives funding from East Chicago's local casino, and uses this money to support local churches, schools, and nonprofit organizations who know the community best and put in the money in action where it can do the most good. Financial Independence grants are specifically focused on programs or projects designed to assist East Chicagoans to become financially independent through job training, job creation or money management skills.
Requirements: Applicants must be registered 501(c)3 organizations or schools located in East Chicago, Indiana. If an applicant is not located in East Chicago, it may still qualify if it complies with at least one of the following *Requirements:* the program that an applicant is applying for operates in East Chicago; the funding that an applicant is applying for will go toward assisting East Chicago residents.
Restrictions: All applications must be submitted via Foundations of East Chicago website. The Foundations will not accept any applications in person.
Geographic Focus: Indiana
Amount of Grant: Up to 15,000 USD
Contact: Russell G. Taylor, (219) 392-4225; grantinfo@foundationsofeastchicago.org
Internet: http://foundationsofeastchicago.org/apply-now
Sponsor: Foundations of East Chicago
100 W Chicago Avenue
East Chicago, IN 46312

Foundations of East Chicago Health Grants 1910
The Foundations of East Chicago are committed to improving the lives of every resident of its city. Conceived by the citizens of East Chicago to be independent, citizen-run, private foundations, it derives funding from East Chicago's local casino, and uses this money to support local churches, schools, and nonprofit organizations who know the community best and put in the money in action where it can do the most good. Health grants are specifically focused on programs or projects which improve the quality of health education, practices and/or services for East Chicagoans.
Requirements: Applicants must be registered 501(c)3 organizations located in East Chicago, Indiana. If an applicant is not located in East Chicago, it may still qualify if it complies with at least one of the following *Requirements:* the program that an applicant is applying for operates in East Chicago; the funding that an applicant is applying for will go toward assisting East Chicago residents.
Restrictions: All applications must be submitted via Foundations of East Chicago website. The Foundations will not accept any applications in person.
Geographic Focus: Indiana
Amount of Grant: Up to 15,000 USD
Contact: Russell G. Taylor, (219) 392-4225; grantinfo@foundationsofeastchicago.org
Internet: http://foundationsofeastchicago.org/apply-now
Sponsor: Foundations of East Chicago
100 W Chicago Avenue
East Chicago, IN 46312

Foundations of East Chicago Public Safety Grants 1911
The Foundations of East Chicago are committed to improving the lives of every resident of its city. Conceived by the citizens of East Chicago to be independent, citizen-run, private foundations, it derives funding from East Chicago's local casino, and uses this money to support local churches, schools, and nonprofit organizations who know the community best and put in the money in action where it can do the most good. Public Safety grants are specifically focused on programs or projects which address crime or public safety issues in East Chicago.
Requirements: Applicants must be registered 501(c)3 organizations or schools located in East Chicago, Indiana. If an applicant is not located in East Chicago, it may still qualify if it complies with at least one of the following *Requirements:* the program that an applicant is applying for operates in East Chicago; the funding that an applicant is applying for will go toward assisting East Chicago residents.
Restrictions: All applications must be submitted via Foundations of East Chicago website. The Foundations will not accept any applications in person.
Geographic Focus: Indiana
Contact: Russell G. Taylor, (219) 392-4225; grantinfo@foundationsofeastchicago.org
Internet: http://foundationsofeastchicago.org/apply-now
Sponsor: Foundations of East Chicago
100 W Chicago Avenue
East Chicago, IN 46312

Foundations of East Chicago Youth Development Grants 1912
The Foundations of East Chicago are committed to improving the lives of every resident of its city. Conceived by the citizens of East Chicago to be independent, citizen-run, private foundations, it derives funding from East Chicago's local casino, and uses this money to support local churches, schools, and nonprofit organizations who know the community best and put in the money in action where it can do the most good. Youth Development grants are specifically focused on programs or projects whose purpose is to improve the social, physical and emotional skills of East Chicago's youth.
Requirements: Applicants must be registered 501(c)3 organizations or schools located in East Chicago, Indiana. If an applicant is not located in East Chicago, it may still qualify if

it complies with at least one of the following *Requirements:* the program that an applicant is applying for operates in East Chicago; the funding that an applicant is applying for will go toward assisting East Chicago residents.
Restrictions: All applications must be submitted via Foundations of East Chicago website. The Foundations will not accept any applications in person.
Geographic Focus: Indiana
Amount of Grant: Up to 15,000 USD
Contact: Russell G. Taylor, (219) 392-4225; grantinfo@foundationsofeastchicago.org
Internet: http://foundationsofeastchicago.org/apply-now
Sponsor: Foundations of East Chicago
100 W Chicago Avenue
East Chicago, IN 46312

Fourjay Foundation Grants 1913
The Foundation supports only those organizations whose chief purpose is to improve health and/or promote education, within Philadelphia, Montgomery, and Bucks counties in southeastern Pennsylvania. The Fourjay Foundation requires no specific application form. It will consider proposals that address a well-defined need, offer a concrete plan of action, and request a specific amount, from organizations whose staff has the ingenuity, commitment, and motivation to carry out the proposal's objectives. Requests may be for operating support, project specific funds, or capital funds.
Requirements: Organizations serving Philadelphia, Montgomery, and Bucks Counties in southeastern Pennsylvania are eligible.
Restrictions: Funding is not available for: charities operating outside Montgomery, Bucks, or Philadelphia counties; individuals; elementary or secondary educational institutions; museums, musical groups, theaters, or cultural organizations; religious organizations in support of their sacramental or theological functions; political groups or related think tanks; athletic organizations or alumni associations; libraries; public radio or television; United Way or the YMCA; civic organizations; organizations that have applied or been funded within the last 12 month period.
Geographic Focus: Pennsylvania
Date(s) Application is Due: Mar 1; Jun 1; Sep 1; Dec 1
Amount of Grant: 1,000 - 10,000 USD
Contact: Ann T. Bucci; (215) 830-1437; fax (215) 830-0157; abucci@fourjay.org
Internet: http://www.fourjay.org/grantGuidelines.asp
Sponsor: Fourjay Foundation
2300 Computer Avenue, Building G, Suite 1
Willow Grove, PA 19090-1753

Four Times Foundation Grants 1914
The foundation awards grants to eligible Native American nonprofit organizations in the areas of social and economic development. Grants are awarded to individuals pursuing a business venture or starting a nonprofit organization in one of four tribal reservations. Preference will be given to projects benefiting children. Grantees should provide a return to their tribe that is four times the original investment.
Requirements: Individuals pursuing business ventures or starting nonprofit organizations in the following reservations are eligible: Blackfeet Nation in Montana, Rosebud Lakota in South Dakota, White Earth Ojibewa in Minnesota, and the Zuni Pueblo in New Mexico.
Geographic Focus: Minnesota, Montana, New Mexico, South Dakota
Amount of Grant: 500 - 10,000 USD
Contact: Jael Kampfe, Owner; (406) 446-1870; fax (406) 446-1013; info@fourtimes.org
Sponsor: Four Times Foundation
16 1/2 North Broadway, P.O. Box 309
Red Lodge, MT 59068

France-Merrick Foundations Grants 1915
The Foundation currently awards grants in the areas of: education; community development; historic preservation and conservation; and civic and culture. The Foundation favors one-time, project-type requests which have a clear beginning and end, as opposed to annual giving or on-going operational support. Interested applicants should submit a letter of proposal. Instructions for submission are available online.
Requirements: Grants are made to Maryland nonprofit 501(c)3 organizations and institutions primarily located in the Baltimore metropolitan area.
Geographic Focus: Maryland
Contact: Robert Schaefer, Executive Director; (410) 832-5700; fax (410) 832-5704
Sponsor: France-Merrick Foundations
1122 Kenilworth Drive, Suite 118
Baltimore, MD 21204

Frances and Benjamin Benenson Foundation Grants 1916
The foundation awards grants to nonprofit organizations in support of community services, international ministries and missions, Jewish education, Jewish welfare, and religious welfare. Types of support include general operating support and scholarships. There are no application deadlines. Applications must be made in writing, stating the purpose of the grant and the amount requested.
Requirements: Nonprofits of the Jewish and Roman Catholic faiths are eligible.
Restrictions: Grants are not made to individuals.
Geographic Focus: All States
Contact: Bruce W. Benenson; (212) 867-0990; bbenenson@benensoncapital.com
Sponsor: Frances and Benjamin Benenson Foundation
708 Third Avenue, 28th Floor
New York, NY 10017

Frances and John L. Loeb Family Fund Grants 1917
The fund is committed to improving the quality of American life. To that end, its grant-making program seeks to address significant issues of society. The fund has chosen as its initial priorities the fields of education, health and family planning, including the public policy questions relating to them. In making grants, the fund favors proposals that offer new knowledge of and innovative approaches to problems rather than palliative measures. It also prefers applications that call for challenge grants and provide evaluation of results. There is no formal application form. Interested applicants should submit a preliminary request in letter form.
Requirements: Funding is directed primarily to organizations and institutions operating in the New York City metropolitan area that are tax exempt under the provisions of Section 501(c)3 of the Internal Revenue Code. Exceptions to this geographical limitation will be made for proposals that have the promise of national implication or extensive replication.
Restrictions: The fund will not consider proposals for annual or capital campaigns, building or renovation projects or loan or emergency funds. Neither will it make grants to individuals or for sectarian or religious purposes or political activities such as lobbying or propaganda. It will not fund any organization that discriminates on the basis of race, sex, religion, national origin or sexual preference.
Geographic Focus: All States
Contact: John L. Loeb, President; (212) 588-9052; fax (212) 838-6470; loebff@aol.com
Internet: http://www.geocities.com/CapitolHill/5601/family_fund_brochure.html
Sponsor: Frances and John L. Loeb Family Fund
375 Park Avenue, Suite 801
New York, NY 10152

Frances C. and William P. Smallwood Foundation Grants 1918
The foundation awards grants in support of education, higher education, and social services. Applications will be received from the following organizations; educational institutions, both public and private, primarily at the college or university level, as well as other non-profit organizations involved in American education and is confined to the area within a 100 mile radius of the Dallas/Fort Worth Metroplex, the area within a 100 mile radius of the city of Gainesville, FL, and the area within a 100 mile radius of Minden, Nevada. Potential applicants should request guidelines prior to applying.
Requirements: Contributions are limited to non-profit, tax-exempt organizations which have obtained IRS status under Section 501(c)3 of the IRS code, and, where appropriate, under Section 170(c).
Restrictions: Funding will not be considered for: general endowment funds of an organization; fund-raising events, i.e. tickets, dinner, telethons; corporate memberships or contributions to Chambers of Commerce, taxpayer associations, and other similar bodies; and contributions to political organizations, campaigns and candidates.
Geographic Focus: Florida, Nevada, Texas
Date(s) Application is Due: Feb 28
Contact: Suzanne Stockdale, (775) 782-3678
Sponsor: Frances C. and William P. Smallwood Foundation
P.O. Box 2050
Fort Worth, TX 76113

Frances L. and Edwin L. Cummings Memorial Fund Grants 1919
The foundation supports nonprofits in New York City and northern New Jersey in the areas of education, especially programs that serve public school children from disadvantaged backgrounds; social welfare concerns; and campaigns to build endowments through establishment of challenge grants. Other areas of interest include elementary education, secondary education, vocational education, adult basic education and literacy, and higher education; hospitals, medical care, AIDS, and cancer; children, youth, and human services; and community development. Support is provided for endowment funds, seed money, consulting services, matching funds, technical assistance, professorships, and program development. The board meets in June and December. Application forms are not required.
Requirements: Grants are awarded to nonprofit organizations in the metropolitan New York, NY, area, with emphasis on New York City, southern Westchester County, and northern New Jersey.
Restrictions: Grants are not awarded to individuals or for capital building campaigns, general operating support, moving expenses, conferences, surveys, annual fund-raising campaigns, or research conducted by individuals or private institutions.
Geographic Focus: New Jersey, New York
Amount of Grant: 10,000 USD
Contact: Elizabeth Costas, Administrative Director; (212) 286-1778; fax (212) 682-9458
Sponsor: Frances L. and Edwin L. Cummings Memorial Fund
501 Fifth Avenue, Suite 708
New York, NY 10017-6103

Frances W. Emerson Foundation Grants 1920
The Foundation, in the care of Goldman Tax Service of Bellingham, Massachusetts, offers grants throughout Massachusetts and Vinalhaven, Maine. Its primary fields of interest include community development, economic development, education, and health care. There is no application form required or deadlines to adhere to, and applicants should send a letter or the full proposal to Eaton Vance management in Boston.
Geographic Focus: Maine, Massachusetts
Contact: Thomas Huggins, Vice President, Eaton Vance Management; (617) 482-8260
Sponsor: Frances W. Emerson Foundation
255 State Street
Boston, MA 02109

Francis Beidler Foundation Grants 1921
Established in Illinois in 1997, the Francis Beidler Foundation offers support for human service programs in Chicago, Illinois. Its primary fields of interest include: children and youth services; education; health organizations; higher education; children's museums; public affairs; and public safety. There are no established deadlines or application formats. Applicants should begin the process by submitting a letter describing the organization, a detailed overview of the project, and amount of funding requested. Organizational literature should accompany the application letter. Grants range up to $60,000.
Requirements: Organizations serving the Chicago area are eligible to apply.
Geographic Focus: Illinois
Amount of Grant: Up to 60,000 USD
Contact: Thomas B. Dorris, Trustee; (312) 922-3792
Sponsor: Francis Beidler Foundation
53 W. Jackson Boulevard, Suite 530
Chicago, IL 60604-3422

Francis L. Abreu Charitable Trust Grants 1922
The Francis L. Abreu Charitable Trust was established under the will of May Patterson Abreu in honor of her husband, Francis, who died in 1969. The trust supports Atlanta-area nonprofit organizations in its areas of interest, including arts and cultural programs, secondary education, higher education, health associations, human services, and children and youth services. Types of support include capital campaigns, seed money, program development, and matching funds. Requests are reviewed at April and October trustee meetings. Application forms are available online.
Requirements: Georgia nonprofits serving the greater Atlanta area are eligible to apply.
Restrictions: The foundation does not approve requests for operating costs or to individuals.
Geographic Focus: Georgia
Date(s) Application is Due: Mar 31; Sep 30
Contact: Peter Abreu, Chairman; (404) 549-6743; fax (404) 549-6752
Internet: http://www.abreufoundation.org
Sponsor: Francis L. Abreu Charitable Trust
P.O. Box 502407
Atlanta, GA 31150

Francis T. & Louise T. Nichols Foundation Grants 1923
The Foundation gives primarily in the areas of education, health care, and human services. Its major fields of interest include: children and youth services; disaster relief; fire prevention and control; elementary and secondary education programs; health care; hospital support; and human/community service programs. There are no deadlines.
Requirements: Applicants should approach the Foundation initially by letter.
Restrictions: Giving primarily in Hancock County, Maine. There are no grants made to individuals.
Geographic Focus: Maine
Amount of Grant: Up to 80,000 USD
Contact: Calvin E. True, Treasurer; (207) 947-0111
Sponsor: Francis T. and Louise T. Nichols Foundation
P.O. Box 1210
Bangor, ME 04402-1210

Frank & Larue Reynolds Charitable Trust Grants 1924
The Charitable Trust, established in Missouri 2001, supports human service programs, food banks, and other community service agencies located in Buchanan County, Missouri. There are no specific application forms required. Instead, a letter stating the amount of the request, anticipated use, and any other pertinent information about the applicant's non-profit organization (history, background, mission statement) should be forwarded to the committee for review.
Requirements: Applicants must be 501(c)3 organizations operating for the benefit of the residents of Buchanan County or any county adjacent thereto, including: Dekalb, Andrew, Clinton, Platte, Doniphan, and Atchison.
Geographic Focus: Missouri
Contact: Country Club Trust Company; (816) 279-6000
Sponsor: Frank and Larue Reynolds Charitable Trust
3702 Faraon Street, P.O. Box 8305
St. Joseph, MO 64506

Frank and Lydia Bergen Foundation Grants 1925
The mission and goals of the Frank and Lydia Bergen Foundation are: to arrange for musical entertainments, concerts and recitals of a character appropriate for the education and instruction of the public in the musical arts. Paramount consideration is given to traditional classical music programs; to aid worthy students of music in securing a complete and adequate musical education; to aid organizations in their efforts to present fine music to the public, provided that such organizations are operated exclusively for educational purposes. Support is offered in the form of: scholarships; program development; capital campaigns; financial aid; community outreach programs; community programs; artist-in-residency programs and; general operating support. Applications are due April 10, for the June meeting & August 15, for the October meeting. Grant applications forms are available online. Applicants will receive notice acknowledging receipt of the grant request, and subsequently be notified of the grant declination or approval.
Requirements: Qualifying tax-exempt 501(c)3 organizations are eligible to apply. There is no geographic restriction but applying organizations must be operating exclusively for educational purposes. Proposals should be submitted in the following format: completed Common Grant Application Form; an original Proposal Statement; an audited financial report and a current year operating budget; a copy of your official IRS Letter with your tax determination; a listing of your Board of Directors. Proposal Statements (second item in the above Format) should answer these questions: what are the objectives and expected outcomes of this program/project/request; what strategies will be used to accomplish your objective; what is the timeline for completion; if this is part of an on-going program, how long has it been in operation; what criteria will you use to measure success; if the request is not fully funded, what other sources can you engage; an Itemized budget should be included; please describe any collaborative ventures. Prior to the distribution of funds, all approved grantees must sign and return a Grant Agreement Form, stating that the funds will be used for the purpose intended. Progress reports and Completion reports must also be filed as required for your specific grant. All current grantees must be in good standing with required documentation prior to submitting new proposals to any foundation.
Restrictions: Grants are not made for political purposes, nor to organizations which discriminate on the basis of race, ethnic origin, sexual or religious preference, age or gender.
Geographic Focus: All States
Date(s) Application is Due: Apr 10; Aug 15
Contact: Gale Y. Sykes; (908) 598-3576; grantinquiries2@wachovia.com
Internet: https://www.wachovia.com/foundation/v/index.jsp?vgnextoid=990852199c0aa110VgnVCM1000004b0d1872RCRD&vgnextfmt=default
Sponsor: Frank and Lydia Bergen Foundation
190 River Road, NJ3132
Summit, NJ 07901

Frank B. Hazard General Charity Fund Grants 1926
The Frank B. Hazard General Charity Fund was established in 1924 to support charitable organizations that work to improve the lives of "the poor, or the poor sick." Organizations receiving support from the fund must be managed and/or governed by individuals a majority of whom are of the Protestant religious faith. Grant requests for general operating support or program support are strongly encouraged. The majority of grants from the Hazard General Charity Fund are one year in duration. Applicants must apply online at the grant website. Applicants are strongly encouraged to do the following before applying: review the downloadable state application procedures for additional helpful information and clarifications; review the downloadable online-application guidelines at the grant website; review the trust's funding history (link is available from the grant website); review the online application questions in advance; and review the list of required attachments. These will generally include: a list of board members, financial statements (audited, reviewed, or compiled by independent auditor); an organization summary; a list of other funding sources; an IRS Determination letter; and other required documents. All attachments must be uploaded in the online application as PDF, Word, or Excel files. The application deadline for the Frank B. Hazard General Charity Fund is 11:59 p.m. on December 1. Applicants will be notified of grant decisions before January 31 of the following year.
Requirements: Applicants must have 501(c)3 tax-exempt status.
Restrictions: The Hazard General Charity Fund specifically supports charitable organizations that serve the people of Providence, Rhode Island. The fund does not support requests from individuals, organizations attempting to influence policy through direct lobbying, or any political campaigns.
Geographic Focus: Rhode Island
Date(s) Application is Due: Dec 1
Contact: Emma Greene, Director; (617) 434-0329; emma.m.greene@baml.com
Internet: https://www.bankofamerica.com/philanthropic/fn_search.action
Sponsor: Frank B. Hazard General Charity Fund
225 Franklin Street, 4th Floor, MA1-225-04-02
Boston, MA 02110

Frank E. and Seba B. Payne Foundation Grants 1927
The foundation awards grants in the Chicago, IL, area and in Pennsylvania in its areas of interest, including AIDS prevention, children and youth, cultural activities, education, and hospitals. Types of support include building construction/renovation, equipment acquisition, and general operating support.
Requirements: Nonprofit organizations in the greater Chicago, IL, metropolitan area and in Pennsylvania are eligible.
Restrictions: Grants are not made to individuals.
Geographic Focus: Illinois, Pennsylvania
Contact: M. Catherine Ryan, c/o Bank of America, (312) 828-1785
Sponsor: Frank E. Payne and Seba B. Payne Foundation
231 S LaSalle Street
Chicago, IL 60697

Frank G. and Freida K. Brotz Family Foundation Grants 1928
The Foundation supports Wisconsin nonprofits of the Christian, Lutheran, and Roman Catholic faiths, including Salvation Army. Types of support include capital support and general support. Organizations eligible to receive support include colleges and universities, community service groups, hospitals, ministries, parochial schools and religious education organizations, religious welfare organizations, and youth organizations. There are no application forms or deadlines. Applicants should submit a brief letter of inquiry that contains a description of the organization, its purpose, purpose of grant, and proof of tax-exempt status.
Requirements: Grants are awarded to publicly supported, Section 170(c) IRS qualified organizations, primarily in the State of Wisconsin.
Restrictions: No grants are awarded to individuals or organizations that require expenditure responsibility under Treasury Regulations.
Geographic Focus: Wisconsin
Contact: Stuart W. Brotz, (920) 458-2121; fax (920) 458-1923
Sponsor: Frank G. and Freida K. Brotz Family Foundation
3518 Lakeshore Road, P.O. Box 551
Sheboygan, WI 53082-0551

Franklin County Community Foundation Grants — 1929

The Franklin County Foundation's mission is simple - build substantial endowment of funds for a community through contributions large and small. These contributions are endowed, permanently invested to produce income, and never spent. The income earned is used to help meet the community's charitable needs - from social work to art and culture. The FCCF Grant Cycle begins late summer when Letters of Intent are due in the office. After these letters are reviewed, the Grants Selection Committee will send applications to the groups or organizations who meet our grant guidelines.
Requirements: To be eligible to receive funding from the Foundation, a letter of intent must be submitted followed by a completed grant application by the appropriate grant deadline. All grant seekers must have prior governing board approval for the project seeking funding. The approval of signed minutes and a signed letter from governing board must be available to the Franklin County Community Foundation.
Restrictions: Funding will not be considered for the following: operating deficits; operation budgets (salaries); annual fund campaigns: religious or sectarian purposes; propaganda, political or otherwise, attempting to influence litigation or intervene in any political affairs or campaigns on behalf of any candidate for public office so as to endanger the charitable nature of the community trust; public school services required by state law; standard instructional or regular operation costs of non-public schools; repeat funding of projects previously supported by the Foundation; individuals; travel purposes; any purpose that is not in conformity with the constraints placed upon the Foundation by the IRS.
Geographic Focus: Indiana
Date(s) Application is Due: Oct 2
Contact: Shelly Lunsford; (765) 647-6810 or (765) 265-1427; fcfoundation@yahoo.com
Internet: http://www.franklincountyindiana.com/Grants%20page.htm
Sponsor: Franklin County Community Foundation
527 Main Street
Brookville, IN 47012-1284

Franklin H. Wells and Ruth L. Wells Foundation Grants — 1930

The Foundation awards grants to support the arts, community and economic development, education, health care, and human services. Funding is also available for emergency funds, equipment, program development, and seed money. The Foundation board meets in April and October, with funding notification in May and November.
Requirements: Applications are not required. Organizations should initially submit a letter of inquiry, and if accepted, one copy of their proposal.
Restrictions: The Foundation gives primarily to Dauphin, Cumberland, and Perry counties in Pennsylvania. Funding is not available for religious activities, individuals, endowments, debts, and capital campaigns.
Geographic Focus: Pennsylvania
Date(s) Application is Due: Mar 15; Sep 15
Contact: Miles Gibbons Jr.; (866) 398-9023; mgibbons989@earthlink.net
Sponsor: Franklin H. Wells and Ruth L. Wells Foundation
One M and T Plaza, 8th Floor
Buffalo, NY 14203-2309

Frank Loomis Palmer Fund Grants — 1931

The Frank Loomis Palmer Fund was established in 1936 to support and promote quality educational, cultural, human-services, and health-care programming for underserved populations. The Palmer Fund specifically serves the people of New London, Connecticut. Grants from the Palmer Fund are primarily one year in duration; on occasion, multi-year support is awarded. Applicants must apply online at the grant website. Applicants are strongly encouraged to do the following before applying: review the downloadable state application procedures for additional helpful information and clarifications; review the downloadable online-application guidelines at the grant website; review the fund's funding history (link is available from the grant website); review the online application questions in advance; and review the list of required attachments. These will generally include: a list of board members, financial statements (audited, reviewed, or compiled by independent auditor); an organization summary; a list of other funding sources; an IRS Determination letter; and other required documents. All attachments must be uploaded in the online application as PDF, Word, or Excel files. The application deadline for the Frank Loomis Palmer Fund is 11:59 p.m. on November 15. Applicants will be notified of grant decisions by letter within three to four months after the proposal deadline.
Requirements: Applicants must have 501(c)3 tax-exempt status and serve the people of New London, Connecticut.
Restrictions: Applicants will not be awarded a grant for more than three consecutive years. The fund does not support requests from individuals, organizations attempting to influence policy through direct lobbying, or any political campaigns.
Geographic Focus: Connecticut
Date(s) Application is Due: Nov 15
Contact: Amy Lynch; (860) 657-7015; amy.r.lynch@baml.com
Internet: https://www.bankofamerica.com/philanthropic/fn_search.action
Sponsor: Frank Loomis Palmer Fund
200 Glastonbury Boulevard, Suite # 200, CT2-545-02-05
Glastonbury, CT 06033-4056

Frank M. Tait Foundation Grants — 1932

The Foundation makes grants to nonprofit organizations operating in Montgomery County, OH, for projects focusing on youth activities and culture. Fields of interest include the arts, child development services, education, historical activities, science, YW/YMCAs and YW/YMHAs. Types of support include annual campaigns, building renovation, equipment, matching and challenge support, program development, and seed money. Grants are usually for one year with possible renewal.
Requirements: An application form is not required. After contacting the foundation for a current deadline, organizations should mail a letter of inquiry along with the following: copy of IRS determination letter; copy of most current annual report/audited financial statement/990; and a copy of the current organizational budget and/or project budget. The Foundation Board meets quarterly and notifies organizations of possible funding within two months of submission.
Restrictions: Faxed or emailed proposals are not accepted. Giving is limited to Montgomery County, Ohio. Funding is not available for religious purposes; individuals; endowment funds; operating budgets; continuing support; emergency funds; deficit financing; research; publications; conferences; scholarships; fellowships; selective capital campaigns; or loans.
Geographic Focus: Ohio
Amount of Grant: 5,000 - 100,000 USD
Contact: Jennifer A. Roer, Executive Director; (937) 222-2401; fax (937) 224-6015
Sponsor: Frank M. Tait Foundation
40 North Main Street
Dayton, OH 45423

Frank Reed and Margaret Jane Peters Memorial Fund I Grants — 1933

The Frank Reed & Margaret Jane Peters Memorial Fund I was established in 1935 to support and promote quality educational, human-services, and health-care programming for underserved populations. Special consideration is given to charitable organizations that serve youth and children. The Peters Memorial Fund I is a generous supporter of the Associated Grant Makers (AGM) Summer Fund. The AGM Summer Fund is a collaborative group of donors that provides operating support for summer camps serving low-income urban youth from Boston, Cambridge, Chelsea, and Somerville. Excluding the grant made to the AGM Summer Fund, the typical grant range is $10,000 to $40,000. Grant requests for general operating support are strongly encouraged. Program support will also be considered. Small, program-related capital expenses may be included in general operating or program requests. The majority of grants from the Peters Memorial Fund I are one year in duration; on occasion, multi-year support is awarded. Applicants must apply online at the grant website. Applicants are strongly encouraged to do the following before applying: review the downloadable state application procedures for additional helpful information and clarifications; review the downloadable online-application guidelines at the grant website; review the foundation's funding history (link is available from the grant website); review the online application questions in advance; and review the list of required attachments. These will generally include: a list of board members, financial statements (audited, reviewed, or compiled by independent auditor); an organization summary; a list of other funding sources; an IRS Determination letter; and other required documents. All attachments must be uploaded in the online application as PDF, Word, or Excel files. The application deadline for the Frank Reed & Margaret Jane Peters Memorial Fund I is 11:59 p.m. on September 1. Applicants will be notified of grant decisions before November 30.
Requirements: Applicants must have 501(c)3 tax-exempt status.
Restrictions: The fund does not support requests from individuals, organizations attempting to influence policy through direct lobbying, or any political campaigns.
Geographic Focus: Massachusetts
Date(s) Application is Due: Sep 1
Contact: Miki C. Akimoto, Vice; (866) 778-6859; miki.akimoto@baml.com
Internet: https://www.bankofamerica.com/philanthropic/fn_search.action
Sponsor: Frank Reed and Margaret Jane Peters Memorial Fund I
225 Franklin Street, 4th Floor, MA1-225-04-02
Boston, MA 02110

Frank Reed and Margaret Jane Peters Memorial Fund II Grants — 1934

The Frank Reed & Margaret Jane Peters Memorial Fund II was established in 1935 to support and promote quality educational, human-services, and health-care programming for underserved populations. In the area of education, the fund supports academic access, enrichment, and remedial programming for children, youth, adults, and senior citizens that focuses on preparing individuals to achieve while in school and beyond. In the area of health care, the fund supports programming that improves access to primary care for traditionally underserved individuals, health education initiatives and programming that impact at-risk populations, and medical research. In the area of human services the fund tries to meet evolving needs of communities. Currently the fund's focus is on (but is not limited to) youth development, violence prevention, employment, life-skills attainment, and food programs. Grant requests for general operating support are strongly encouraged. Program support will also be considered. Small, program-related capital expenses may be included in general operating or program requests. The majority of grants from the Peters Memorial Fund II are one year in duration; on occasion, multi-year support is awarded. Applicants must apply online at the grant website. Applicants are strongly encouraged to do the following before applying: review the downloadable state application procedures for additional helpful information and clarifications; review the downloadable online-application guidelines at the grant website; review the foundation's funding history (link is available from the grant website); review the online application questions in advance; and review the list of required attachments. These will generally include: a list of board members, financial statements (audited, reviewed, or compiled by independent auditor); an organization summary; a list of other funding sources; an IRS Determination letter; and other required documents. All attachments must be uploaded in the online application as PDF, Word, or Excel files. The application deadline for the Frank Reed & Margaret Jane Peters Memorial Fund II is 11:59 p.m. on July 1. Applicants will be notified of grant decisions before September 30.
Requirements: Applicants must have 501(c)3 tax-exempt status.
Restrictions: In general, capital requests are not advised. The fund does not support endowment campaigns, events such as galas or award ceremonies, and costs of fundraising events. The fund does not support requests from individuals, organizations attempting to influence policy through direct lobbying, or any political campaigns.

Geographic Focus: Massachusetts
Date(s) Application is Due: Jul 1
Contact: Michealle Larkins; (866) 778-6859; michealle.larkins@baml.com
Internet: https://www.bankofamerica.com/philanthropic/fn_search.action
Sponsor: Frank Reed and Margaret Jane Peters Memorial Fund II
225 Franklin Street, 4th Floor, MA1-225-04-02
Boston, MA 02110

Frank S. Flowers Foundation Grants 1935
The Frank S. Flowers Foundation primarily serves the Gloucester County, New Jersey area. The Foundation's area of interest include: Education—supporting public high schools of Gloucester County, New Jersey, to provide scholarships for college or graduate study, vocational or technical training; Youth—supporting chapters or councils or branches of Y.M.C.A. and Boys Scouts of America located in Gloucester and/or Salem Counties, grants are also considered for organizations having branches or offices in Gloucester County, New Jersey which treat and educate children with special needs; Health-Related—support to non-profit Gloucester County hospitals; Religious organizations—support to churches in the boroughs of Paulsboro and Wenonah, New Jersey. The Foundation also has a specific interest in The Shriner's Hospital for Crippled Children in Philadelphia, Pennsylvania and the Masonic Home Charity Foundation of New Jersey. Grants range from $1,000 - $8,000. Application deadline date is February 15th, application available online. Requestors will receive a letter acknowledging the receipt of their request.
Requirements: Qualifying tax-exempt 501(c)3 organizations are eligible for grants if they meet the purpose of the foundation. Proposals should be submitted in the following format: completed Common Grant Application Form; an original Proposal Statement*; an audited financial report and a current year operating budget; a copy of your official IRS Letter with your tax determination; a listing of your Board of Directors. *Proposal Statement should answer these questions: what are the objectives and expected outcomes of this program/project/request; what strategies will be used to accomplish your objective; what is the timeline for completion; if this is part of an on-going program, how long has it been in operation; what criteria will you use to determine your success; if the request is not fully funded, what other sources can you engage. A Proposal budget should be included if this is for a specific program within your annual budget. Please describe any collaborative ventures.
Restrictions: Grants are not made for political purpose, nor to organizations which discriminate on the basis of race, ethnic origin, sexual or religious preference, age or gender.
Geographic Focus: New Jersey, Pennsylvania
Date(s) Application is Due: Feb 15
Amount of Grant: 1,000 - 8,000 USD
Contact: Gale Y. Sykes; (908) 598-3576; grantinquiries2@wachovia.com
Internet: https://www.wachovia.com/foundation/v/index.jsp?vgnextoid=68d78689fb0aa110VgnVCM1000004b0d1872RCRD&vgnextfmt=default
Sponsor: Frank S. Flowers Foundation
190 River Road
Summit, NJ 07901

Frank Stanley Beveridge Foundation Grants 1936
The foundation welcomes proposals in the areas of: animal care; arts, culture and humanities; civil rights, social action, advocacy; education; employment/jobs; environmental quality, protection and beautification; food, nutrition and agriculture; health; housing; human services; medical research; mental health; philanthropy; safety; recreation; religion; science; social services; and youth development. The board meets in October and April to consider requests. Multiyear grants are rare. Contact the foundation via the Web site only. No phone or written inquiries will be accepted.
Requirements: Applicants must be 501(c)3 nonprofit organizations or foundations in Massachusetts's Hampden and Hampshire Counties.
Restrictions: The Foundation prefers not to support: awards or prizes; commissioning of new artistic work; conferences/seminars; curriculum development; debt reduction; employee matching gifts; employee-related scholarships; endowment funds; exhibitions; faculty/staff development; fellowship funds; fellowships to individuals; film/video/radio production; foundation administered programs; general operating support; grants to individuals; income development; internship funds; management development; performance/production costs; professorships; program-related investment/loans; publications; scholarships to individuals; student aid; technical assistance.
Geographic Focus: Massachusetts
Date(s) Application is Due: Feb 1; Aug 1
Amount of Grant: 50,000 USD
Contact: Philip Caswell, President; (800) 229-9667; fax (561) 748-0644; administrator@beveridge.org or caswell@beveridge.org
Internet: http://www.beveridge.org/
Sponsor: Frank Stanley Beveridge Foundation
1340 U.S. Highway 1, Suite 102
Jupiter, FL 33469

Frank W. and Carl S. Adams Memorial Fund Grants 1937
The Frank W. and Carl S. Adams Memorial Fund was established in 1925 to support and promote quality educational, human services, and health care programming for underserved populations. Annual gifts are also awarded to the Harvard University Medical School and the Massachusetts Institute of Technology for student scholarships. Grant requests for general operating support are strongly encouraged. Program support will also be considered. Small, program-related capital expenses may be included in general operating or program requests. To better support the capacity of nonprofit organizations, multi-year funding requests are strongly encouraged. The application deadline is December 1. Applicants will be notified of grant decisions before March 31.
Requirements: 501(c)3 organizations serving residents of Massachusetts are eligible.
Geographic Focus: Massachusetts
Date(s) Application is Due: Dec 1
Contact: Miki C. Akimoto, Vice President; (866) 778-6859; miki.akimoto@baml.com
Internet: https://www.bankofamerica.com/philanthropic/fn_search.action
Sponsor: Frank W. and Carl S. Adams Memorial Fund
225 Franklin Street, 4th Floor, MA1-225-04-02
Boston, MA 02110

Fraser-Parker Foundation Grants 1938
The Foundation awards funds in its areas of interest, including Christian religion organizations, education and higher education, and hospitals. There are no application forms and no deadlines.
Geographic Focus: All States
Amount of Grant: 5,000 - 50,000 USD
Contact: John Stephenson, Executive Director; (404) 827-6529
Sponsor: Fraser-Parker Foundation
3050 Peachtree Road NW, Suie 270
Atlanta, GA 30305

Fred & Gretel Biel Charitable Trust Grants 1939
The Fred & Gretel Biel Charitable Trust was established in 2004 to support and promote quality educational, human-services, and health-care programming for underserved populations. Special consideration is given to organizations that provide food and clothing to low-income individuals and families. Consideration is also given to organizations that serve the economically disadvantaged through the provision of housing, legal assistance, or day-care services. Grant requests for general operating and capital support are encouraged. Grants from the Biel Charitable Trust are one year in duration. Application materials are available for download at the grant website. Applicants are strongly encouraged to review the state application guidelines for additional helpful information and clarifications before applying. Applicants are also encouraged to review the trust's funding history (link is available from the grant website). The application deadline for the Biel Charitable Trust is May 1. Applicants will be notified of grant decisions by June 30.
Requirements: The Biel Charitable Trust typically supports organizations serving the people of King and Snohomish Counties in the Puget Sound region of Washington. Occasionally grants will be made outside of the Puget Sound area. Applicant organizations must have 501(c)3 tax-exempt status.
Restrictions: Requests to assist with debt retirement or to correct an operating deficit will not be considered. Applicants who have received a grant for three consecutive years must wait two years before reapplying to the trust. The trust does not support requests from individuals, organizations attempting to influence policy through direct lobbying, or any political campaigns.
Geographic Focus: Washington
Date(s) Application is Due: May 1
Contact: Nancy Atkinson; (800) 848-7177 or (206) 358-0912; nancy.l.atkinson@baml.com
Internet: https://www.bankofamerica.com/philanthropic/fn_search.action
Sponsor: Fred and Gretel Biel Charitable Trust
800 5th Avenue
Seattle, WA 98104

Fred and Sherry Abernethy Foundation Grants 1940
Established in North Carolina in 2003, the Fred and Sherry Abernethy Foundation gives support primarily in North Carolina to the economically disadvantaged. Its primary fields of interest currently include Christian agencies and churches, as well as community educational programs. There are no specific application formats or deadlines with which to adhere, and applicants should approach the foundation with a letter of inquiry outlining the need and estimated budget.
Requirements: 501(c)3 organizations either located in, or serving the people of, North Carolina are eligible to apply.
Geographic Focus: North Carolina
Contact: Fred Abernethy, President; (910) 579-9177; fax (910) 579-9179
Sponsor: Fred and Sherry Abernethy Foundation
P.O. Box 6505
Shallotte, NC 28469-0505

Fred Baldwin Memorial Foundation Grants 1941
The Foundation supports programs and projects that benefit the people of Maui County. Projects in the arts, education, environment, health, and human services are of greatest interest. Funding is available for capital improvement projects. There are two annual deadlines, which fall on the first business day in February and August. Application information is available online.
Requirements: Eligible applicants must have 501(c)3 status, or must apply through a fiscal sponsor with 501(c)3 status.
Restrictions: The Foundation does not fund loans or debt service, endowments, funds for re-granting, scholarships, grants to individuals or units of government, or activities that have already occurred.
Geographic Focus: Hawaii
Date(s) Application is Due: Feb 1; Aug 1
Contact: Carrie Shoda-Sutherland, Senior Program Officer; (808) 566-5524 or (888) 731-3863, ext. 524; fax (808) 521-6286; csutherland@hcf-hawaii.org
Internet: http://www.fredbaldwinfoundation.org/
Sponsor: Fred Baldwin Memorial Foundation
1164 Bishop Street, Suite 800
Honolulu, HI 96813

Fred C. and Katherine B. Andersen Foundation Grants   1942
Fred C. and Katherine B. Andersen Foundation, formerly known as the Andersen Foundation gives on a national basis for higher education. The foundation provides funds locally in Minnesota and western Wisconsin for all areas of interest, which include: arts; health care; higher education; hospitals; and youth development. Funding is available in the forms of: capital campaigns; general/operating support and; program development.
Requirements: 501(c)3 tax-exempt organizations are eligible. Giving is on a national basis although preference is given to requests from Minnesota.
Restrictions: The foundation does not make grants to institutions that receive federal funding.
Geographic Focus: All States
Date(s) Application is Due: Mar 18; Jul 22; Oct 21
Amount of Grant: 5,000 - 12,000,000 USD
Contact: Mary Gillstrom, Director; (651) 264-5150
Sponsor: Fred C. and Katherine B. Andersen Foundation
P.O. Box 8000
Bayport, MN 55003-0080

Fred C. and Mary R. Koch Foundation Grants   1943
The foundation mainly supports organizations in its geographic area of interest. Particular interest is given to education (programs that promote the application of economic and scientific principles to problem-solving); environmental stewardship (projects that apply innovative solutions to solve local environmental problems); and human services (projects that promote self-sufficiency, individual responsibility, tolerance, and respect for others) The foundation prefers to support specific projects with clearly defined parameters and measurable results rather than fund-raising events, endowments, capital campaigns, or general operating support.
Requirements: The foundation supports nonprofit, tax-exempt organizations and institutions in communities that have Koch employees and facilities: Kansas, Minnesota, Texas, Oklahoma, Louisiana, and Alberta, Canada.
Restrictions: Grants are not made to individuals.
Geographic Focus: All States, Canada
Contact: Susan Addington; (316) 828-2646; philanthropy@kochind.com
Internet: http://www.kochind.com/community/default.asp
Sponsor: Fred C. and Mary R. Koch Foundation
4111 E 37th Street N
Wichita, KS 67220

Freddie Mac Foundation Grants   1944
The Foundation focus is on children whose families have limited resources and who are vulnerable to poor outcomes. The Foundation emphasizes the integration of services that focus on family strengthening and youth development in order to maximize the benefit to children and their families. Grants will be made for direct service projects, general operating support, capacity building, public awareness, planning and capital projects. The following funding priorities will be considered: the early years; elementary school years; junior high and high school years; children and families in crisis; and public awareness education. Proposals must be submitted online.
Requirements: Eligible organizations must be tax exempt under IRS code 501(c)3 and defined as a public charity. The Foundation's grantmaking program services the following metropolitan Washington, DC areas: District of Columbia; Virginia - the counties of Arlington, Fairfax, Loudoun and Prince William and the cities of Alexandria, Falls Church, Manassas Park, and Leesburg; Maryland - the counties of Charles, Frederick, Howard, Montgomery, and Prince George's.
Restrictions: The Foundation will not fund organizations that discriminate in the provision of services or in employment practices based on race, color, religion, ethnicity, sex, age, national origin, disability, sexual orientation, marital status, and any other characteristics protected by applicable law. Unless approved by the board, the Foundation does not fund: individuals; training in/promotion of religious doctrine; incurring a debt liability; endowment campaigns.
Geographic Focus: District of Columbia, Maryland, Virginia
Date(s) Application is Due: Sep 9
Amount of Grant: 5,000 - 50,000 USD
Contact: Ralph F. Boyd; fax (703) 918-8888; freddie_mac_foundation@freddiemac.com
Internet: http://www.freddiemacfoundation.org
Sponsor: Freddie Mac Foundation
8250 Jones Branch Drive, MS A40
McLean, VA 22102-3110

FRED Educational Ethyl Grants   1945
The Foundation for Rural Education and Development (FRED) created the Ethyl Matching Grant Program to help provide funding for rural communities and schools. The program provides matching grants ranging from $500-$2,500 to OPASTCO member telephone companies that are involved with projects aimed at bettering their schools and communities. An estimated $10,000 worth of grants will be available each year through this program. These funds have been made available through donations by Bennet and Bennet, Nortel Networks and FRED's Annual Giving Campaign.
Requirements: Applications will be accepted on a rolling basis throughout the year and will be reviewed approximately 3 months after receipt. The two focus areas for this program are Education and Community Development. To receive a grant, schools must be public and located in the service area of an OPASTCO member telephone company that is in good standing. Applications for Community Development Ethyl Grants may include projects that eliminate an eyesore, create jobs, beautify downtown, and renovate a historical building, park, monument or other public area. Preferred projects include those that can be completed with the Ethyl Grant and matched funding rather than larger projects that require multiple sources of funding. More information about the program and a downloadable application form can be found at the website.
Restrictions: Only three applications per company may be submitted every 6 months.
Geographic Focus: All States
Amount of Grant: 500 - 2,500 USD
Contact: Haley Smit; (202) 659-5990; fax (202) 659-4619; fred@opastco.org
Internet: http://www.fred.org/ethyl.html
Sponsor: Foundation for Rural Education and Development
21 Dupont Circle NW, Suite 700
Washington, DC 20036

Frederick McDonald Trust Grants   1946
The Frederick McDonald Trust was established in 1950 to support and promote quality educational, human-services, and health-care programming for underserved populations. Grant requests for general operating support, program, project and capital support will be considered. The majority of grants from the McDonald Trust are one year in duration. On occasion, multi-year support is awarded. Applicants must apply online at the grant website. Applicants are strongly encouraged to do the following before applying: review the downloadable state application procedures for additional helpful information and clarifications; review the downloadable online-application guidelines at the grant website; review the trust's funding history (link is available from the grant website); review the online application questions in advance; and review the list of required attachments. These will generally include: a list of board members, financial statements (audited, reviewed, or compiled by independent auditor); an organization summary; a list of other funding sources; an IRS Determination letter; and other required documents. All attachments must be uploaded in the online application as PDF, Word, or Excel files. The application deadline for the Frederick McDonald Trust is 11:59 p.m. on May 1. Applicants will be notified of grant decisions before August 31.
Requirements: Applicants must have 501(c)3 tax-exempt status.
Restrictions: Grants are made only to those organizations located in, or serving the people of Albany City. The trust does not support requests from individuals, organizations attempting to influence policy through direct lobbying, or any political campaigns.
Geographic Focus: New York
Date(s) Application is Due: May 1
Contact: Christine O'Donnell; (646) 855-1011; christine.l.o'donnell@baml.com
Internet: https://www.bankofamerica.com/philanthropic/fn_search.action
Sponsor: Frederick McDonald Trust
One Bryant Park, NY1-100-28-05
New York, NY 10036

Frederick S. Upton Foundation Grants   1947
The foundation awards grants, primarily in southwestern Michigan. Areas of interest include arts, child welfare, education, youth programs, and religion. Types of support include annual campaigns building construction/renovation, capital campaigns, general operating support, and special projects. The application deadline is in mid-March, and there are no specific application forms.
Geographic Focus: Michigan
Date(s) Application is Due: Mar 15; Jun 15; Oct 15
Contact: Stephen E. Upton, President; (312) 732-4260; fax (269) 982-0323; fsuptonfdn@opexonline.com or uptonfoundation@comcast.net
Sponsor: Frederick S. Upton Foundation
100 Ridgeway Street
St. Joseph, MI 49085

Frederick W. Marzahl Memorial Fund Grants   1948
The Frederick W. Marzahl Memorial Fund was established in 1974 to support and promote quality educational, human-services, and health-care programming for underserved populations in Woodbury, Connecticut. Grants from the Marzahl Memorial Fund are one year in duration. Application materials are available for download at the grant website. Applicants are strongly encouraged to review the state application guidelines for additional helpful information and clarifications before applying. Applicants are also encouraged to review the foundation's funding history (link is available from the grant website). The deadline for application to the Frederick W. Marzahl Memorial Fund is November 1. Applicants will be notified of grant decisions by letter within two to three months after the proposal deadline.
Requirements: Applicants must have 501(c)3 tax-exempt status.
Restrictions: Applicants will not be awarded a grant for more than three consecutive years. The fund does not support requests from individuals, organizations attempting to influence policy through direct lobbying, or any political campaigns.
Geographic Focus: Connecticut
Date(s) Application is Due: Nov 1
Contact: Carmen Britt; (860) 657-7019; carmen.britt@baml.com
Internet: https://www.bankofamerica.com/philanthropic/fn_search.action
Sponsor: Frederick W. Marzahl Memorial Fund
200 Glastonbury Boulevard, Suite # 200, CT2-545-02-05
Glastonbury, CT 06033-4056

Fred L. Emerson Foundation Grants   1949
The foundation gives grants to nonprofits in Auburn, Cayuga County, and upstate New York to improve the quality of life in the areas of education (primarily private, higher education), hospital and health programs, community agencies, churches, cultural institutions, youth and community service programs and social welfare agencies. An application form is not required. Proposals may be submitted in letter form detailing the project for which support is being sought.
Requirements: New York nonprofit organizations in Auburn, Cayuga County, and the upstate area are eligible.

Restrictions: Grants do not support individuals, operating budgets, or loans.
Geographic Focus: New York
Amount of Grant: 200 - 250,000 USD
Contact: Daniel J. Fessenden; (315) 253-9621; dan@emersonfoundation.com
Sponsor: Fred L. Emerson Foundation
5654 South Street Road, P.O. Box 276
Auburn, NY 13021-9602

Fred Meyer Foundation Grants   1950
The Foundation is dedicated to enriching the quality of life in the communities where stores operate and where customers and associates live and work. The Foundation focuses grants on organizations that work toward youth development or hunger reduction. Grant recipients must be invited to apply by a Fred Meyer associate.
Requirements: Grants will be awarded to nonprofits in areas served by Fred Meyer Stores.
Restrictions: The Foundation does not accept unsolicited letters of inquiry.
Geographic Focus: Alaska, Idaho, Oregon, Washington
Contact: Community Affairs Manager; (503) 232-8844; foundation@fredmeyer.com
Internet: http://www.thekrogerco.com/corpnews/corpnewsinfo_charitablegiving_fredmeyer.htm
Sponsor: Fred Meyer Foundation
3800 SE 22nd Avenue
Portland, OR 97202

FRED Technology Grants for Rural Schools   1951
The Foundation for Rural Education and Development (FRED) in cooperation with the Rural Telephone Finance Cooperative (RTFC) created the Technology Grants for Rural Schools program to help meet the growing need for innovative technology in the classroom. This grant program provides funding for projects that advance technology and foster cooperation among the telco, school and community. This includes adding new programs and curriculum for technology education and purchasing new equipment. Examples of possible grant requests include, but are not limited to: Computer-assisted learning (CAL) programs; Computer-equipment and programs, including word processors, spreadsheets and database managers; Subject-specific tools; Electronic access to information, including CD-ROMs and Internet access in each classroom. FRED, in cooperation with RTFC, will award grants on an annual basis in the range of $1,000-$10,000, depending on the scope of the grant-funding request.
Requirements: Any public K-12 school located in the service area of an OPASTCO telephone company may apply. A letter of nomination and support from the local telephone company must accompany all applications. Projects and purchases must directly benefit the rural school requesting the grant.
Restrictions: Limit 4 applications per telephone company.
Geographic Focus: All States
Date(s) Application is Due: Sep 14
Amount of Grant: 1,000 - 10,000 USD
Contact: Haley Smit; (202) 659-5990; fax (202) 659-4619; fred@opastco.org
Internet: http://www.fred.org/tech.html
Sponsor: Foundation for Rural Education and Development
21 Dupont Circle NW, Suite 700
Washington, DC 20036

Freeman Foundation Grants   1952
The foundation's major objectives include strengthening the bonds between the United States and the Far East; preservation and protection of the forests, lands, and natural resources of the United States and land conservation and farmland preservation in Vermont; and development of a vibrant, international, free enterprise system. Giving primarily in VT for conservation and environment grants; Asian studies grants are awarded nationally. Grants are awarded four times annually.
Restrictions: Grants are not made to individuals.
Geographic Focus: All States
Contact: George S. Tsandikos, (212) 649-5853; gtsandikos@rockco.com
Sponsor: Freeman Foundation
30 Rockefeller Plaza
New York, NY 10012

Fremont Area Community Foundation Amazing X Grants   1953
The Amazing X Charitable Trust, a supporting organizaton of the Fremont Area Community Foundation (FACF), was established in the late 1970s by members of the Gerber family to benefit people with disabilites and address general charitable needs in Newaygo County, Michigan. Grant requests are accepted for: projects or programs that serve people with disabilities; projects or programs that address general charitable needs. Preferred programs are innovative, collaborative, and have a significant impact on the residents of Newaygo County. Grants range from $1,000 - $60,000 range. Grant applications are due each year by July 15.
Requirements: Michigan 501(c)3 organizations located in or supporting Newaygo County are eligible for funding. When submitting your proposal, include your organizations: mission, history, description of current programs, activities, and accomplishments; purpose of the grant (describe in detail and include supporting evidence); grant proposal budget form/narrative (form available at the Foundation's website). The following list of attachments must also be included: a copy of the current IRS 501(c)3 determination letter; roster of current governing board, including addresses and affiliations; finances: organization's current annual operating budget, including all expenses and revenues, audited financial statement (most recently completed), IRS Form 990 (most recently filed), annual report, if available; resumes and job descriptions of the key project personnel; organizational chart; letters of support (up to five).
Restrictions: The foundation typically does not fund requests for projects that have previously been denied, grants to individuals, programs that advocate specific religions, or services which are government or school obligations.
Geographic Focus: Michigan
Date(s) Application is Due: Jul 15
Amount of Grant: 1,000 - 60,000 USD
Contact: Jeff Jahr; (231) 924-5350; fax (231) 924-5391; jjahr@tfacf.org
Internet: http://www.tfaf.org/grants/amazingx.html
Sponsor: Fremont Area Community Foundation
P.O. Box B
Fremont, MI 49412

Fremont Area Community Foundation Elderly Needs Grants   1954
The Foundation is focusing its grantmaking resources primarily on expanding opportunities that enhance the well being of residents from the Newaygo County, Michigan area. The purpose of the Elderly Needs Fund is to make grants to support health and enrich aging for the elderly of Newaygo County. The strategies of the Elderly Needs Fund include: promote the physical health of the elderly; promote the mental/emotional well being of the elderly and their caregivers; promote the social enrichment and prevent the social isolation of the elderly; promote the provision of basic human services for the elderly. Application deadlines are February 15 and October 15 each year.
Requirements: Michigan 501(c)3 organizations located in or supporting Newaygo County are eligible for funding. When submitting your proposal, include your organizations: mission, history, description of current programs, activities, and accomplishments; purpose of the grant (describe in detail and include supporting evidence); grant proposal budget form/narrative (form available at the Foundation's website). The following list of attachments must also be included: a copy of the current IRS 501(c)3 determination letter; roster of current governing board, including addresses and affiliations; finances: organization's current annual operating budget, including all expenses and revenues, audited financial statement (most recently completed), IRS Form 990 (most recently filed), annual report, if available; resumes and job descriptions of the key project personnel; organizational chart; letters of support (up to five).
Geographic Focus: Michigan
Date(s) Application is Due: Feb 15; Oct 15
Contact: Jeff Jahr; (231) 924-5350; fax (231) 924-5391; jjahr@tfacf.org
Internet: http://www.tfaf.org/grants/elderlyneeds.html
Sponsor: Fremont Area Community Foundation
P.O. Box B
Fremont, MI 49412

Fremont Area Community Foundation Grants   1955
The Foundation is focusing its grantmaking resources primarily on expanding opportunities that enhance the well being of children, youth and families in Newaygo County. The Foundation's areas of interest include: arts and culture, community development, education, the environment, and human services. Type of support offered include: building/renovation; capital campaigns; conferences/seminars; consulting services; continuing support; curriculum development; emergency funds; employee matching gifts; endowments; equipment; general/operating support; management development/capacity building; matching/challenge support; program-related investments/loans; program development; program evaluation; scholarship funds; scholarships-to individuals; seed money; technical assistance. Grant applications have a deadline date of February 15, May 15 and, September 15. Scholarship applications are due on March 15th.
Requirements: Michigan 501(c)3 organizations located in or supporting Newaygo County are eligible for funding. When submitting your proposal, include your organizations: mission, history, description of current programs, activities, and accomplishments; purpose of the grant (describe in detail and include supporting evidence); grant proposal budget form/narrative (form available at the Foundation's website). The following list of attachments must also be included: a copy of the current IRS 501(c)3 determination letter; roster of current governing board, including addresses and affiliations; finances: organization's current annual operating budget, including all expenses and revenues, audited financial statement (most recently completed), IRS Form 990 (most recently filed), annual report, if available; resumes and job descriptions of the key project personnel; organizational chart; letters of support (up to five).
Restrictions: The foundation typically does not fund requests for projects that have previously been denied, grants to individuals, programs that advocate specific religions, or services which are government or school obligations.
Geographic Focus: Michigan
Date(s) Application is Due: Feb 15; Mar 15; May 15; Sep 15
Contact: Jeff Jahr; (231) 924-5350; fax (231) 924-5391; jjahr@tfacf.org
Internet: http://www.tfaf.org/grants.html
Sponsor: Fremont Area Community Foundation
P.O. Box B
Fremont, MI 49412

Fremont Area Community Foundation Summer Youth Grants   1956
The Summer Youth Initiative is a special grantmaking program of the Fremont Area Community Foundation which awards grants of up to $8,000 to provide summer programs for Michigan youth residing in Newaygo County. Priority will be given to Summer Youth Initiative programs that: involve a minimum of ten youth; last for a minimum of one week; provide education and recreation; be open and accessible to all interested youth; enhance participants' self-esteem; challenge participants' creativity; involve participants in some physical exercise and teach healthy lifestyle. Grant application and proper materials are due by February 15 each year.

Requirements: Organizations applying for a Summer Youth Initiative grant must: be designated as a 501(c)3 non-profit organization or utilize a 501(c)3 organization as a fiscal sponsor; conduct programs to benefit Newaygo County residents; be experienced youth program providers; have oversight of the program by personnel with appropriate credentials; have appropriate youth/staff ratio; provide a positive and safe environment; provide nutritious snack/meal if time warrants; not discriminate on the basis of race, sex, or religious preference; include a plan for evaluation with clearly stated goals and objectives; partner with colleagues and collaborate with other organizations when possible to avoid duplication of services and overlapping of projects. When submitting your proposal, include your organizations: mission, history, description of current programs, activities, and accomplishments; purpose of the grant (describe in detail and include supporting evidence); grant proposal budget form/narrative (form available at the Foundation's website). The following list of attachments must also be included: a copy of the current IRS 501(c)3 determination letter; roster of current governing board, including addresses and affiliations; finances: organization's current annual operating budget, including all expenses and revenues, audited financial statement (most recently completed), IRS Form 990 (most recently filed), annual report, if available; resumes and job descriptions of the key project personnel; organizational chart; letters of support (up to five).
Restrictions: Fremont Area Community Foundation will not fund: t-shirts; vacation bible schools; camps whose purpose is primarily athletics; traditional or mandated summer school.
Geographic Focus: Michigan
Date(s) Application is Due: Feb 15
Amount of Grant: 8,000 USD
Contact: Jeff Jahr, Senior; (231) 924-5350; fax (231) 924-5391; jjahr@tfacf.org
Internet: http://www.tfaf.org/grants/summeryouth.html
Sponsor: Fremont Area Community Foundation
P.O. Box B
Fremont, MI 49412

Freshwater Future Advocate Mentor Program 1957
Freshwater Future announces the launch of our Advocate Mentor program in conjunction with its Grants program. The Advocate Mentor program will be a unique opportunity for new and experienced advocates to share strategies, approaches and past experiences on an ongoing basis. Each year, Freshwater Future will connect each of its grant recipients with an experienced grassroots advocate who will serve as a mentor. The Mentors and Mentees will communicate regularly to discuss topics related to their projects as well as subjects common to grassroots efforts in the Great Lakes basin. The program will have a particular focus on sharpening the participants' advocacy, technology, fundraising, and organizational management skills.
Geographic Focus: All States
Contact: Jill Ryan; (231) 348-8200; jill@freshwaterfuture.org or info@freshwaterfuture.org
Internet: http://www.freshwaterfuture.org/grant-programs/advocate-mentor-program.html
Sponsor: Freshwater Future
P.O. Box 2479
Petoskey, MI 49770

Freshwater Future Climate Grants 1958
The Climate Grants Program provides grant awards ranging from $500 to $5,000 (USD) for projects that engage communities in preparing for and responding to climate change impacts, including engagement in decision-making that takes climate change impacts into account. Projects to protect and restore shorelines, inland lakes, rivers, and wetlands in the Great Lakes Basin under the following strategic program areas will be considered: projects to protect and restore wetlands; on-the-ground restoration activities that incorporate climate adaption and include an action component to create permanent change (a small amount of funding for this area); advocating for low-impact solutions to community storm water issues; participation in land use planning and zoning that engages climate related considerations; participation in watershed planning to introduce climate related components; watch-dogging and participating in the development, implementation, and enforcement of local, state, provincial, and federal aquatic habitat protection regulations as they relate to climate; non-partisan voter education, voter registration, and candidate forums; advocating for naturally functioning river and coastal ecosystems; reducing polluted runoff; and launching special initiatives or creating unique opportunities to strengthen citizen involvement in aquatic habitat protection and restoration related to climate adaptation. Before submitting a Climate Grant Application it is mandatory to contact a Freshwater Future staff member to talk through your proposal. Climate Grant applications are due on June 1 each year.
Geographic Focus: All States
Date(s) Application is Due: Jun 1
Amount of Grant: 500 - 5,000 USD
Contact: Jill Ryan; (231) 348-8200; jill@freshwaterfuture.org or info@freshwaterfuture.org
Internet: http://www.freshwaterfuture.org/grant-programs/climate-grant-program.html
Sponsor: Freshwater Future
P.O. Box 2479
Petoskey, MI 49770

Freshwater Future Healing Our Waters Grants 1959
The Freshwater Future Healing Our Waters (HOW) grants program, with awards up to $15,000, provides financial support to aid in the development and implementation of Great Lakes Restoration Initiative and other federal proposals or projects by organizations working in or impacting the Healing Our Waters Priority Areas. Additionally, there is a second, new program for application preparation with awards up to $5,000 to be used for technical grant writing assistance to develop GLRI applications. There is no annual application deadline.
Geographic Focus: All States
Amount of Grant: Up to 15,000 USD
Contact: Jill Ryan; (231) 348-8200; jill@freshwaterfuture.org or info@freshwaterfuture.org
Internet: http://www.freshwaterfuture.org/grant-programs/healing-our-waters-grants.html
Sponsor: Freshwater Future
P.O. Box 2479
Petoskey, MI 49770

Freshwater Future Insight Services Grants 1960
The Insight Services Grants Growing Success program provides grant awards ranging from $500 to $2,500 (USD) to be used for assistance from Freshwater Future to build capacity of grassroots organizations, which could include training, board development, membership expansion, fundraising, and strategic planning. Grant funds will be used for Freshwater Future staff time to provide professional assistance to your project or organization, no monetary award will be made to your organization. A 25% match by your organization is required for this program. There is no cycle deadline.
Geographic Focus: All States
Amount of Grant: 500 - 2,500 USD
Contact: Jill Ryan; (231) 348-8200; jill@freshwaterfuture.org or info@freshwaterfuture.org
Internet: http://www.freshwaterfuture.org/grant-programs/insight-services-grant-program.html
Sponsor: Freshwater Future
P.O. Box 2479
Petoskey, MI 49770

Freshwater Future Project Grants 1961
The Project Grants program provides grant awards ranging from $500 to $5,000 (USD) to be used for specific project expenses. Projects to protect aquatic habitats in the following strategic program areas will be considered: projects to protect and restore wetlands that will result in ongoing or positive permanent change in the habitat; on-the-ground restoration activities that include an action component to create permanent change (a small amount of funding for this area); advocating for low-impact solutions to community storm water issues; participation in land use planning and zoning; participation in watershed planning; watch-dogging and participating in the development, implementation, and enforcement of local, state, provincial, and federal aquatic habitat protection regulations; non-partisan voter education, voter registration, and candidate forums; advocating for naturally functioning river and coastal ecosystems; reducing polluted runoff; launching special initiatives or creating unique opportunities to strengthen citizen involvement in aquatic habitat protection and restoration; and communicating how local wetlands, lakes and rivers are interconnected in the Great Lakes Basin. The spring cycle deadline for project grants is March 31, while the fall cycle deadline is September 30.
Geographic Focus: All States
Date(s) Application is Due: Mar 31; Sep 30
Amount of Grant: 500 - 5,000 USD
Contact: Jill Ryan; (231) 348-8200; jill@freshwaterfuture.org or info@freshwaterfuture.org
Internet: http://www.freshwaterfuture.org/grant-programs/project-grant-program.html
Sponsor: Freshwater Future
P.O. Box 2479
Petoskey, MI 49770

Freshwater Future Special Opportunity Grants 1962
The Special Opportunity Grant Program (Emergency Grants) is for river, lake, wetland, and groundwater protection efforts that may not coincide with the application timeline or funding period of Freshwater Future's other grant programs. Freshwater Future realizes that many grassroots projects can be completed for under $500 (USD), therefore it maintains a reserve to support urgent projects or those that present special, time-limited opportunities. No application deadlines or qualifying applications are funded until funds are depleted for the year.
Geographic Focus: All States
Contact: Jill Ryan; (231) 348-8200; jill@freshwaterfuture.org or info@freshwaterfuture.org
Internet: http://www.freshwaterfuture.org/grant-programs/special-opportunity-grant-program.html
Sponsor: Freshwater Future
P.O. Box 2479
Petoskey, MI 49770

Frey Foundation Grants 1963
The foundation is committed to excellence and accountability in its role as a catalyst for productive social change and makes grants to nonprofit organizations based in and serving residents of Kent, Emmet, and Charlevoix Counties in Michigan. Primary areas of interest include enhancing the lives of children and families, protecting natural resources, encouraging civic progress, nurturing community art, capital projects, and philanthropy. Community-based projects receive priority consideration. Types of support include program development, seed money, technical assistance, program evaluation, and employee matching gifts. Send a one- to two-page letter of inquiry. Requests for less than $30,000 are reviewed monthly; requests over $30,000 must be approved by the board. Guidelines are available online.
Requirements: Nonprofit organizations based in and serving residents of Kent, Emmet, and Charlevoix Counties in Michigan are eligible.
Restrictions: Individuals are not eligible to apply.
Geographic Focus: Michigan
Date(s) Application is Due: Feb 15; May 15; Aug 15; Nov 15
Contact: Teresa Crawford; (616) 451-4565; fax (616) 451-8481; freyfdn@freyfdn.org
Internet: http://www.freyfdn.org
Sponsor: Frey Foundation
40 Pearl Street NW, Suite 1100
Grand Rapids, MI 49503

Frist Foundation Grants 1964
The foundation supports a variety of organizations in the fields of health, human services, civic affairs, education, and the arts. Grants support building the capacity of nonprofit organizations by strengthening their management structure and systems. Types of support include capital, management, operating, project, and technology grants. Deadline listed is for technology grants.
Requirements: 501(c)3 nonprofits in Davidson County, TN, area may apply.
Restrictions: The foundation does not support: individuals or their projects, private foundations, political activities, or advertising or sponsorships. The foundation does not ordinarily support: projects, programs, or organizations that serve a limited audience or a relatively small number of people; organizations during their first three years of operation; disease-specific organizations seeking support for national projects and programs; biomedical or clinical research; hospitals; organizations whose principal impact is outside of Middle Tennessee; endowments; social events or similar fund-raising activities; or religious organizations for religious purposes.
Geographic Focus: Tennessee
Date(s) Application is Due: Apr 1
Amount of Grant: 500 - 10,000 USD
Contact: Peter Bird, (615) 292-3868; fax (615) 292-5843; askfrist@fristfoundation.org
Internet: http://www.fristfoundation.org/grants/general.asp
Sponsor: Frist Foundation
3100 W End Avenue, Suite 1200
Nashville, TN 37203

Fritz B. Burns Foundation Grants 1965
The foundation supports nonprofit organizations primarily in southern California by awarding grants for education, with an emphasis on buildings, equipment, endowments (except for ordinary operating expenses), student scholarship and loan funds, and faculty fellowships; to/for hospitals, hospital equipment, and medical research; and religious organizations (Christian, Jewish, Latter-day Saints, nondenominational, Presbyterian, Protestant, Roman Catholic, and Salvation Army). Proposals should be concise, containing a brief description of what is planned, with a clear statement of the objective sought; IRS letter certifying tax exemption; financial statements; and a list of officers and directors. No formalized application or proposal format is required. Proposals are considered on a quarterly basis.
Requirements: Nonprofits in southern California may apply.
Restrictions: Grant requests are not considered from individuals nor from tax-supported entities.
Geographic Focus: California
Date(s) Application is Due: Sep 30
Amount of Grant: 10,000 - 250,000 USD
Contact: Joseph Rawlinson, President; (818) 840-8802
Sponsor: Fritz B. Burns Foundation
4001 West Alameda Avenue, Suite 203
Burbank, CA 91505-4338

Frost Foundation Grants 1966
The foundation awards grants in the areas of human service needs, environmental programs, and education programs in New Mexico and Louisiana. Preference will be given to programs that have potential for wider service or educational exposure than an individual community. The foundation encourages collaborations, mergers, and the formation of alliances among agencies within the community to reduce duplication of effort and to promote a maximum effective use of funds. Applicants are urged to call the foundation for guidelines before sending a proposal. Application information is available online.
Requirements: 501(c)3 nonprofits in Louisiana and New Mexico are eligible.
Geographic Focus: Louisiana, New Mexico
Date(s) Application is Due: Jun 1; Dec 1
Contact: Mary Amelia Whited-Howell, President; (505) 986-0208; info@frostfound.org
Internet: http://www.frostfound.org
Sponsor: Frost Foundation
511 Armijo, Suite A
Santa Fe, NM 87501

Fruit Tree 101 1967
Fruit Tree 101 orchards can serve as outdoor edible classrooms, where students meet to learn about botany, ecology, and how to protect the planet's health. The program brings fruit tree orchards to schoolyards so students can improve the quality of the air and water while creating a source of tasty snacks for decades to come.
Requirements: Public schools can have their school nominated for the program by having an interested school official send an email to info@ftpf.org. The foundation is particularly interested in schools in or near the following cities: Albany, Boston, Buffalo, Hartford, Minneapolis, Pittsburgh, Providence, San Antonio, and Seattle. There are no deadlines to nominate your school.
Geographic Focus: All States
Contact: Cem Akin, Director; (831) 621-8096; fax (831) 621-7978; cem@ftpf.org
Internet: http://www.ftpf.org/fruittree101.htm
Sponsor: Fruit Tree Planting Foundation
P.O. Box 900113
San Diego, CA 92190

Fulbright/Garcia Robles Grants 1968
The program is especially interested in attracting students pursuing fieldwork or internships in public administration or public policy. Other fields of interest are projects on Mexican culture, society and politics to deepen the understanding of Mexico in the United States. Areas of collaboration go far beyond border issues, which are also of relevance, and can include projects on migration, ecological issues, public health, education, public policy, environmental protection, human rights, and trade policy. The program will also support projects in the arts that further dialogue and contact between U.S. and Mexican arts communities.
Requirements: Applicants must: be U.S. citizens at the time of application (permanent residents are not eligible); be in good health (grantees will be required to submit a satisfactory Medical Certificate of Health from a physician); and hold a B.A. degree or the equivalent before the start of the grant (applicants who have not earned a B.A. degree or the equivalent, but who have extensive professional study and/or experience in business, may be considered). Excellent spoken and written Spanish is required at the time of application.
Restrictions: Fields of study not recommended include medicine and dentistry.
Geographic Focus: All States
Contact: Jody Dudderar; (212) 984-5565; fax (212) 984-5325; jdudderar@iie.org
Internet: http://us.fulbrightonline.org/program_country.html?id=70#full
Sponsor: Institute of International Education
1400 K Street, NW, 7th Floor
Washington, DC 20005-2403

Fulbright Binational Business Grants in Mexico 1969
This program is designed to enhance the knowledge, expertise, and understanding of business in Mexico for U.S. students in business, law, or engineering. It combines graduate courses (a minimum of 3 and a maximum of 6) in the pertinent academic area (e.g., business, finance, international trade, or comparative law among others) with an internship with a Mexico-based company, firm, or NGO dedicated to international business. Candidates with a BA degree and recent M.B.A., J.D. or master's degree in business administration, finance, economics, international relations, engineering, or accounting, and some work experience are preferred. A Master's degree is recommended but not required. Significant work experience in a business environment is strongly recommended for these candidates and for candidates who do not have a business-related degree.
Requirements: Applicants must: be U.S. citizens at the time of application (permanent residents are not eligible); be in good health (grantees will be required to submit a satisfactory Medical Certificate of Health from a physician); and hold a B.A. degree or the equivalent before the start of the grant (applicants who have not earned a B.A. degree or the equivalent, but who have extensive professional study and/or experience in business, may be considered). Excellent spoken and written Spanish is required at the time of application.
Geographic Focus: All States, Mexico
Contact: Jody Dudderar; (212) 984-5565; fax (212) 984-5325; jdudderar@iie.org
Internet: http://us.fulbrightonline.org/program_country.html?id=70#binational
Sponsor: Institute of International Education
1400 K Street, NW, 7th Floor
Washington, DC 20005-2403

Fulbright Business Grants in Spain 1970
These awards are co-sponsored by the Instituto de Empresa Foundation in Madrid. Instituto de Empresa is one of Europe's leading business schools and has hosted nearly 28,000 students, representing 71 different nationalities. Awards are for full-time study in the bilingual English/Spanish International MBA program which offers the basic MBA core, two components of elective courses, and a Global Affairs Seminar in which students analyze business problems focusing on five different geographic areas.
Requirements: Applicants must: be U.S. citizens at the time of application (permanent residents are not eligible); be in good health (grantees will be required to submit a satisfactory Medical Certificate of Health from a physician); and hold a B.A. degree or the equivalent before the start of the grant (applicants who have not earned a B.A. degree or the equivalent, but who have extensive professional study and/or experience in business, may be considered). Excellent spoken and written Spanish is required at the time of application.
Geographic Focus: All States, Albania, Andorra, Armenia, Austria, Azerbaijan, Belarus, Belgium, Bosnia & Herzegovina, Bulgaria, Croatia, Cyprus, Czech Republic, Denmark, Estonia, Finland, France, Georgia, Germany, Greece, Hungary, Iceland, Ireland, Italy, Kosovo, Latvia, Liechtenstein, Lithuania, Luxembourg, Macedonia, Malta, Moldova, Monaco, Montenegro, Norway, Poland, Portugal, Romania, Russia, San Marino, Serbia, Slovakia, Slovenia, Spain, Sweden, Switzerland, The Netherlands, Turkey, Ukraine, United Kingdom, Vatican City
Contact: Jon Adler, Program Manager; (212) 984-5326; jadler@iie.org
Internet: http://us.fulbrightonline.org/program_country.html?id=98#MBA
Sponsor: Institute of International Education
1400 K Street, NW, 7th Floor
Washington, DC 20005-2403

Fulbright Graduate Degree Program Grants in Mexico 1971
This award provides candidates with the opportunity to complete a Master's or Doctorate degree at a Mexican university or qualified academic institution. Applications will be accepted in all fields of study. Of particular interest are projects conducted on Mexican culture, society, and politics to deepen the understanding of Mexico in the United States. Areas of collaboration go far beyond border issues, which are also of relevance to the Commission, and can include projects on migration, ecological issues, public health, education, public policy, environmental protection, human rights, and trade policy. The program will support up to four academic semesters in Master's and six academic semesters in Doctoral programs. Selected candidates will receive an initial two semesters of funding. Approval of subsequent financial support will be subject to academic performance and availability of funds. Benefits include monthly maintenance (up to ten months per calendar year) and one round-trip ticket.
Requirements: Applicants must: be U.S. citizens at the time of application (permanent residents are not eligible); be in good health (grantees will be required to submit a satisfactory Medical Certificate of Health from a physician); and hold a B.A. degree or the equivalent before the start of the grant (applicants who have not earned a B.A. degree or the

equivalent, but who have extensive professional study and/or experience in business, may be considered). Excellent spoken and written Spanish is required at the time of application.
Geographic Focus: All States
Contact: Jody Dudderar; (212) 984-5565; fax (212) 984-5325; jdudderar@iie.org
Internet: http://us.fulbrightonline.org/program_country.html?id=70#deg
Sponsor: Institute of International Education
1400 K Street, NW, 7th Floor
Washington, DC 20005-2403

Fulbright Public Policy Initiative Program Grants in Mexico   1972
This program is designed to enhance the knowledge, expertise, and understanding of public policy in Mexico for U.S. students in business, law, or engineering. Pursuant to this interest in public policy, the Fulbright Commission will fund three grants specifically for students conducting fieldwork or research in the areas of public administration or public policy.
Requirements: Applicants must: be U.S. citizens at the time of application (permanent residents are not eligible); be in good health (grantees will be required to submit a satisfactory Medical Certificate of Health from a physician); and hold a B.A. degree or the equivalent before the start of the grant (applicants who have not earned a B.A. degree or the equivalent, but who have extensive professional study and/or experience in business, may be considered). Excellent spoken and written Spanish is required at the time of application.
Geographic Focus: All States
Contact: Jody Dudderar; (212) 984-5565; fax (212) 984-5325; jdudderar@iie.org
Internet: http://us.fulbrightonline.org/program_country.html?id=70#public
Sponsor: Institute of International Education
1400 K Street, NW, 7th Floor
Washington, DC 20005-2403

Fuller E. Callaway Foundation Grants   1973
The foundation awards grants to nonprofit organizations and individuals in LaGrange and Troup County, GA. Grants are awarded in the areas of religion, higher and other education, social services, youth, and health. Types of support include general operating budgets, annual campaigns, building funds, equipment, matching funds, and student aid. Letters of application from organizations are accepted and have deadlines at the end of December, March, June, and September. Application forms are required for the scholarship program. Scholarship deadlines are February 15 and June 30 for law school scholarships. The board meets in January, April, July, and October to consider scholarship requests.
Requirements: Nonprofit organizations and individuals in LaGrange and Troup County, GA, are eligible for support.
Geographic Focus: Georgia
Amount of Grant: 500 - 25,000 USD
Contact: H. Speer Burdette, President; (706) 884-7348; fax (706) 884-0201; hsburdette@callaway-foundation.org
Sponsor: Fuller E. Callaway Foundation
P.O. Box 790
LaGrange, GA 30241

Fuller Foundation Grants   1974
The Fuller Foundation is a family foundation, inspired by its forward-thinking founder, Alvan T. Fuller. It's purpose is to support non-profit agencies which improve the quality of life for people, animals and the environment. The Foundation also funds the Fuller Foundation of New Hampshire which supports horticultural and educational programs for the public at Fuller Gardens. The geographic focus area is predominately the Boston area and the immediate seacoast area of New Hampshire. Through these grants the foundation strives to effect change, make an impact on the community, and inspire good deeds. Application information is available online. Faxed or emailed grant requests will not be accepted.
Requirements: Nonprofits in the Boston, MA, area and the immediate seacoast region of New Hampshire are eligible.
Restrictions: Funding is not available for: capital projects (unless in the opinion of the Trustees, the Foundation gift will have significant impact); individuals; or multi-year grants. Incomplete grants are not considered.
Geographic Focus: Massachusetts, New Hampshire
Date(s) Application is Due: Jan 15; Jun 15
Amount of Grant: 3,500 - 7,500 USD
Contact: John Bottomley; (603) 964-6998; fax (603) 964-8901; atfuller@aol.com
Internet: http://www.fullerfoundation.org/FullerFoundation/HomePage.cfm?page=appprocedures
Sponsor: Fuller Foundation
P.O. Box 479
Rye Beach, NH 03871

Fulton County Community Foundation Grants   1975
Fulton County Community Foundation is part of the Northern Indiana Community Foundation (NICF). Grant making areas of interest are: education; health; human services; arts and culture; environment; and civic and recreation. The Foundation favors activities that: reach a broad segment of the community, especially those citizens whose needs are not being met by existing services; request seed money to meet innovative opportunities in the community; stimulate and encourage additional funding; promote cooperation and avoid duplication of effort; help make charitable organizations more effective, efficient and self-sustaining; and one time projects or needs. Applications are available online. Applicants are encouraged to contact the Program Coordinator to discuss their project before applying.
Restrictions: The foundation will not consider grants for: religious organizations for the sole purpose of furthering that religion; political activities or those designated to influence legislation; national organizations (unless the monies are to be used solely to benefit citizens of Fulton County); grant that directly benefit the donor or the donor's family; fundraising projects; contributions to endowments
Geographic Focus: Indiana
Date(s) Application is Due: Sep 30
Contact: Corinne Becknell Lucas, Program Coordinator; (574) 223-2227 or (877) 432-6423; fax (574) 224-3709; corinne@nicf.org
Internet: http://www.nicf.org/fulton/grants.html
Sponsor: Fulton County Community Foundation
715 Main Street, P.O. Box 807
Rochester, IN 46975

Fulton County Community Foundation Women's Giving Circle Grants   1976
The Women's Giving Circle Grants help fund non-profit organizations in Fulton County. Organizations receiving their funds include Camp-We-Can, the County Council on Aging, and the County Cancer Fund.
Requirements: Applicants may contact Brian Johnson, the director of development at the Fulton County Community Foundation, for information about whether their project qualifies for application.
Geographic Focus: Indiana
Contact: Brian Johnson, Development Director; (574) 224-3223; fulton@nicf.org
Internet: http://www.nicf.org/fulton/grants.html
Sponsor: Fulton County Community Foundation
715 Main Street, P.O. Box 807
Rochester, IN 46975

Fund for Southern Communities Grants   1977
The fund offers grants and technical assistance to grassroots social change organizations. The fund prefers to support projects that work for an equitable distribution of economic and political power and that are unlikely to be funded by traditional funding sources. Support goes to organizations fighting discrimination, working for the rights of workers, promoting self-determination in low-income and disenfranchised communities, protecting the environment, creating alternative arts and media, or promoting peace and responsible U.S. foreign policy. The fund supports direct services only when they are tied to social change programs or when they are empowering communities. Applicants should submit 13 copies of the national Network of Grantmakers Common Application Form and attachments.
Requirements: Grassroots social change organizations in Georgia, North Carolina, and South Carolina, with organizational budgets of $150,000 or less are eligible.
Restrictions: The Fund does not fund direct services, social services, or special events.
Geographic Focus: Georgia, North Carolina, South Carolina
Date(s) Application is Due: Mar 1; Sep 1
Contact: Alice Eason Jenkins, Executive Director; (404) 371-8404; fax (404) 371-8496; alice@fundforsouth.org or fsc@fundforsouth.org
Internet: http://www.fundforsouth.org
Sponsor: Fund for Southern Communities
315 W Ponce De Leon, Suite 1061
Decatur, GA 30030

Fund for the City of New York Grants   1978
The Fund is dedicated to improving the quality of life in the city by supporting efforts to increase the efficiency and effectiveness of government agencies and the nonprofit organizations that are instrumental in promoting a healthy civic environment. The fund's programs concentrate on children and youth and community development and the urban environment. The grants provide project or general support for nonprofit organizations, including a number of watchdog and advocacy organizations. Short-term consultancy grants also are awarded to enable organizations to hire an additional person to help projects through difficult periods. Proposals must be received by April 15 to be considered for the spring cycle and August 15 to be considered for the fall cycle.
Requirements: Applicants are encouraged to contact the Foundation before submitting a letter of inquiry. Unsolicited proposals are not accepted.
Restrictions: Individuals, endowments, and capital campaigns are not eligible to apply.
Geographic Focus: New York
Date(s) Application is Due: Apr 15; Aug 15
Contact: Barbara Cohn Berman, (212) 925-6675; fax (212) 925-5675; bcohn@fcny.org
Internet: http://www.fcny.org/fcny/core/grants/
Sponsor: Fund for the City of New York
121 Avenue of the Americas, 6th Floor
New York, NY 10013

Funding Exchange Martin-Baro Fund Grants   1979
The Funding Exchange (FEX) is a network of 16 community funds across the country and the national office in New York City, all of which administer independent grantmaking programs. The Martin-Baro Fund was established to honor the memory of Father Ignacio Martin-Baro, a Jesuit priest, activist, and social psychologist who was murdered in El Salvador in 1989, and to further the goals to which he dedicated his life. Through grant-making and education, the Fund supports progressive, grassroots groups throughout the world who are challenging institutional repression and confronting the mental health consequences of violence and injustice in their communities.
Requirements: The Funding Exchange supports activities by organizations that are tax-exempt under the Internal Revenue Code Section 501(c)3, or have established a relationship with a fiscal sponsor with IRS tax-exempt status of this Code Section.
Geographic Focus: All States
Contact: Aleah Bacquie Vaughn, Program Officer; (212) 529-5356, ext. 317 or (212) 529-5300; fax (212) 982-9272; aleah.bacquievaughn@fex.org or info@fex.org

Internet: http://www.martinbarofund.org/index.html
Sponsor: Funding Exchange
666 Broadway, Suite 500
New York, NY 10012

Furth Family Foundation Grants 1980
The foundation supports children's charity programs in San Francisco and Sonoma County, California. The Foundation gives to the the following fields of interest: arts, education, human services; and public affairs. There are no application deadlines. Applicants should submit a letter describing the organization, proposed budget, and amount requested.
Restrictions: Grants are not made to individuals.
Geographic Focus: California
Amount of Grant: 1,000 - 25,000 USD
Contact: Frederick Furth, Manager; (415) 433-2070; fax (415) 982-1409
Sponsor: Furth Family Foundation
10300 Chalk Hill Road
Healdsburg, CA 95448

G.A. Ackermann Memorial Fund Grants 1981
The G. A. Ackermann Memorial Fund was established under the will of Mrs. Mary A. Ackermann in 1937 to support quality health care and human services programming for underserved populations. According to Mrs. Ackermann's wishes, the Ackermann Memorial Fund supports charitable organizations operated or controlled by the Roman Catholic church and/or members of the Roman Catholic Church, and charitable organizations operated or controlled by a Protestant Church and/or its members. Special consideration is given to hospitals. The Memorial Fund has biannual application deadlines of January 15 and June 1. Applicants for the January 15 deadline will be notified of grant decisions by June 30, and applicants for the June 1 deadline will be notified by December 31. To better support the capacity of nonprofit organizations, multi-year funding requests are considered.
Requirements: Organizations must be geographically located within the city limits of New York City or Chicago.
Restrictions: The Foundation will consider requests for general operating support only if the organization's operating budget is less than $1 million. In general, grant requests for individuals, endowment campaigns, capital projects, or research will not be considered.
Geographic Focus: Illinois, New York
Date(s) Application is Due: Jan 15; Jun 1
Contact: George Thorn; (312) 828-4154; ilgrantmaking@bankofamerica.com
Internet: https://www.bankofamerica.com/philanthropic/fn_search.action
Sponsor: G.A. Ackermann Memorial Fund
231 South LaSalle Street, IL1-231-13-32
Chicago, IL 60604

G.N. Wilcox Trust Grants 1982
The trust provides partial support to programs and projects of tax-exempt, public charities in Hawaii to improve the quality of life in the state, particularly the island of Kauai. Grants of one year's duration are awarded in categories of interest to the trust, including education, literacy programs and adult basic education, health, Protestant religion, delinquency and crime prevention, social services, youth services, and culture and the performing arts. Types of support include general operating grants, capital grants, equipment acquisition, seed grants, scholarship funds, and challenge/matching grants. Deadlines dates for general grants are: January 1; April 1; July 1; October 1. The deadline date for scholarships is February 15th.
Requirements: Giving is limited to Hawaii, with emphasis on the island of Kauai. To begin application process, contact Paula Boyce for additional guidelines.
Restrictions: Grants are not awarded to support government agencies (or organizations substantially supported by government funds), individuals, or for endowment funds, research, deficit financing, or student aid in scholarships or loans.
Geographic Focus: Hawaii
Date(s) Application is Due: Jan 1; Feb 15; Apr 1; Jul 1; Oct 1
Contact: Paula Boyce, c/o Bank of Hawaii; (808) 538-4944; fax (808) 538-4647; pboyce@boh.com or emoniz@boh.com
Sponsor: G.N. Wilcox Trust
Bank of Hawai'i, Foundation Administration Department 758
Honolulu, HI 96802-3170

Gamble Foundation Grants 1983
Founded in 1968, The Gamble Foundation is primarily interested in supporting organizations that serve disadvantaged children and youth in San Francisco, Marin and Napa counties. Within the field of youth development, the Foundation focuses on literacy, educational and personal enrichment programs designed to open doors of opportunity for at-risk youth in order to help them succeed in school and become productive, self-sufficient members of society. The Foundation is particularly interested in agricultural/environmental education, financial & computer literacy, vocational training and programs that prevent substance abuse and teen violence. To a lesser degree, the Foundation supports environmental organizations that focus on land preservation and sustainability, animal welfare and management, and pollution control. The foundation is interested in promoting green concepts that increase awareness of science based solutions that help reduce consumption of finite resources. The Foundation prefers to fund specific projects rather than annual appeals. Grants range from $5,000 to $20,000.
Requirements: Northern California 501(c)3 nonprofit organizations, with an emphasis on San Francisco, Marin, and Napa Counties, are eligible to apply. The Board meets in the spring each year and makes grants in late summer. The Foundation will accept proposals for the April meeting from January 25 - February 10. The Foundation encourages submission of proposals and attachments by email. For those submitting by email, the proposal and required attachments should be emailed in PDF format only. Send your proposals to Fiona Barrett at fbarrett@pfs-llc.net. If you do not receive an email within 24 hours confirming that your proposal has been received, please contact Fiona at (415) 561-6540, ext. 221. The Foundation will also accept a proposal submitted by mail as long as it is postmarked on or before February 10th. Proposals must include the following in the order listed: cover letter, on organization letterhead with address and phone number, including a brief summary of the request and a list of attachments (not more than one page); proposal narrative (not to exceed 5 pages); concise description of the organization (not more than two pages) including: relevant history, mission, geography and populations served, overview of programs; description of the project (not more than three pages) including: need, purpose, goals, timeline, project budget, including secured and projected sources of funding; financial statement, including actual revenue and expenses for the organization's most recently completed fiscal year; organizational budget for the present year, detailing proposed expenditures and projected sources of funding (not more than two pages); list of major public and private funders, identifying both secured and planned for funds; list of the Board of Directors, with affiliations; copy of the agency's IRS 501(c)3 tax-exempt determination letter. When submitting proposal, clasp the proposal materials with a single binder clip; do not use staples. Do not send audio-visual materials, binders, folders, or pamphlets unless requested. Receipt of proposals will be acknowledged with a written response within a reasonable period of time. Should additional information be required, applicants will be contacted.
Restrictions: In general, the Foundation does not support medical research, individuals, endowments, or capital improvements.
Geographic Focus: California
Date(s) Application is Due: Feb 10
Amount of Grant: 5,000 - 20,000 USD
Contact: Eric Sloan; (415) 561-6540, ext. 205; fax (415) 561-6477; esloan@pfs-llc.net
Internet: http://www.pfs-llc.net/gamble/gamble.html
Sponsor: Gamble Foundation
1660 Bush Street, Suite 300
San Francisco, CA 94109

Gannett Foundation Community Action Grants 1984
The Foundation awards grants to organizations in the communities in which Gannett owns a daily newspaper or television station. These communities include: Montgomery, Alabama; Phoenix & Flagstaff, Arizona; Little Rock & Mountain Home Arkansas; Palm Springs, Sacramento, Salinas & Visalia, California; Denver & Fort Collins, Colorado; Wilmington, Delaware; Montgomery, Salisbury & PG County, Maryland; Alexandria, Falls Church, Arlington & Fairfax County, Prince Wm County, Loudoun County, Virginia; Brevard County, Fort Myers, Jacksonville, Pensacola, St. Petersburg, Tallahassee, Florida; Atlanta, Macon, Georgia; Guam; Hawaii; Indianapolis, Lafayette, Muncie, Richmond, Indiana; Des Moines, Iowa City, Iowa; Louisville, Kentucky; Alexandria, Lafayette, Monroe, Opelousas, Shreveport, Louisiana; Bangor, Portland, Maine; Battle Creek, Detroit, Grand Rapids, Howell, Lansing, Port Huron, Michigan; Minneapolis & St. Cloud, Minnesota; Hattiesburg & Jackson, Mississippi; St. Louis & Springfield, Missouri; Great Falls, Montana; Reno, Nevada; Asbury Park, Bridgewater, Cherry Hill, East Brunswick, Parsippany/Morristown, Vineland, New Jersey; Binghamton, Buffalo, Elmira, Ithaca, Poughkeepsie, Rochester, White Plains, New York, New York; Asheville & Greensboro, North Carolina; Bucyrus, Chillicothe, Cincinnati, Coshocton, Cleveland, Fremont, Lancaster, Mansfield, Marion, Newark, Port Clinton, Zanesville, Ohio; Salem, Oregon; Columbia and Greenville, South Carolina; Sioux Falls, South Dakota; Clarksville, Jackson, Knoxville, Murfreesboro, Nashville, Tennessee; St. George, Utah; Burlington, Vermont; Staunton, Virginia; Appleton, Fond du Lac, Green Bay, Manitowoc, Marshfield, Oshkosh, Sheboygan, Stevens Point, Wausau, Wisconsin Rapids, Wisconsin; and the United Kingdom. The community action grant priorities include: education; neighborhood improvement; economic development; youth development; community problem-solving; assistance to disadvantaged people; environmental conservation and; cultural enrichment. The average grant amount is in the $1,000 to $5,000 range. Grant applications are accepted twice a year. Submit proposal to the contact at the daily newspaper or television station in your area by February 16th or August 17th. Some locations have earlier deadlines, and they are listed in the Grant Contact list on the Gannett Foundation website. A committee of employees reviews all proposals within one month after each deadline. Applicants are notified of final decisions about 90â€"120 days after deadlines. Please no phone or email inquiries.
Requirements: 501(c)3 nonprofit organizations in Gannett-operating areas are eligible. Each local Gannett operation establishes its own priorities, depending upon local needs, and may have additional guidelines and restrictions. Contact the local Gannett organization to learn about its priorities, restrictions, and deadlines. If unsure about an organization's eligibility, an email (or one-page letter) of inquiry to the local community contact is welcome. When applying send one copy of the application form and your proposal to the local newspaper publisher or TV station general manager. Your grant proposal must contain the following information: completed Gannett Foundation Grant Application Form (available at the Foundation's website); IRS letter of determination for 501(c)3 tax exemption; one-page project budget, and an organizational budget; project proposal of no more than five pages that includes: needs statement, objectives of the project to be funded, whether the project is new or ongoing, constituency to be served, community and volunteer involvement; sustainability statement which includes: your organization's qualifications to carry out the project, how the project will be evaluated, plans for continued funding of the project, if applicable, list of other funding sources, committed and applied for; pertinent recent publications may also be included.
Restrictions: Grants will not be considered for the following purposes: individuals; private foundations; organizations not determined by the IRS to be a tax-exempt public charity under 501(c)3; organizations classified by the IRS as 509(a)3; national or regional organizations unless their programs address specific local community needs; programs or initiatives where the primary purpose is the promotion of religious doctrine or tenets; elementary or secondary schools (except to provide special initiatives or programs not provided by regular school budgets); political action or legislative advocacy groups; endowment funds; multiple-

year pledge campaigns; medical or research organizations, including organizations funding single disease research; organizations located in or benefiting nations other than the U.S. and its territories; fraternal groups, athletic teams, bands, volunteer firefighters or similar groups. Do not send a proposal to the foundation offices in McLean, VA, unless it addresses local needs in the Washington, DC metropolitan area.
Geographic Focus: Alabama, Arizona, Arkansas, California, Colorado, Delaware, District of Columbia, Florida, Georgia, Guam, Hawaii, Indiana, Iowa, Kentucky, Louisiana, Maine, Maryland, Michigan, Minnesota, Mississippi, Missouri, Montana, Nevada, New Jersey, New York, North Carolina, Ohio, Oregon, South Carolina, South Dakota, Tennessee, Utah, Vermont, Virginia, Wisconsin, United Kingdom
Date(s) Application is Due: Feb 16; Aug 17
Amount of Grant: 1,000 - 5,000 USD
Contact: Pat Lyle, Grants Director; (703) 854-6047 or (703) 854-6000; fax (703) 854-2167; gannettfoundation@gannett.com
Internet: http://www.gannettfoundation.org/index.htm
Sponsor: Gannett Foundation
7950 Jones Branch Drive
McLean, VA 22107

Garden Crusader Award 1985
The Garden Crusader Award recognizes individuals who are using their love of gardening to improve the world. Award categories include education, beautification, feeding the hungry, and urban renewal. A nominee may be someone who is gardening to provide spiritual comfort or to teach about the environment, has beautified a forgotten piece of land, or is feeding the hungry with their produce. Gardeners throughout the country will be selected and will receive cash and merchandise. Nomination forms are available online.
Geographic Focus: All States
Contact: Coordinator; (888) 239-1553; fax (802) 660-3501; crusader@gardeners.com
Internet: http://www.gardeners.com/Garden-Crusader-Awards/5549,default,pg.html
Sponsor: Gardener's Supply Company
128 Intervale Road
Burlington, VT 05401

Gardiner Howland Shaw Foundation Grants 1986
The Foundation is committed to awarding grants that can make a real difference in the way the justice system operates. The following are funding priorities: research, analysis, and journalism, that examine important criminal and juvenile justice issues and offer ways to improve the administrations of justice in Massachusetts; initiatives that demonstrate innovative approaches to the reintegration of adult and juvenile offenders leaving correctional and detention facilities; programs that demonstrate effective inter-agency and community collaboration models for crime prevention; initiatives that address the legal, social and rehabilitative needs of juvenile and adult offenders through advocacy, public education and training. Potential applicants are encouraged to telephone the office to discuss ideas prior to submitting a proposal.
Requirements: Nonprofit Massachusetts organizations are eligible.
Restrictions: The foundation does not support capital requests, the arts, endowments, grants to individuals, or scholarships.
Geographic Focus: Massachusetts
Date(s) Application is Due: Feb 1
Amount of Grant: 15,000 - 25,000 USD
Contact: Thomas Coury; (781) 455-8303; fax (781) 433-0980; admin@shawfoundation.org
Internet: http://www.shawfoundation.org/guidelines.php
Sponsor: Gardiner Howland Shaw Foundation
355 Boylston Street
Boston, MA 02116

Gardiner Savings Institution Charitable Foundation Grants 1987
The Foundation is primarily interested in supporting and promoting human service organization, family support agencies, educational services, and community outreach programs. Generally, funding is limited to the central Maine, particularly the Gardiner, Augusta, and Boothbay areas.
Requirements: Must be a 501(c)3 organization in the State of Maine.
Geographic Focus: Maine
Contact: Arthur C. Markos, President; (207) 582-5550, ext. 2234; fax (207) 588-2145; info@savingsbankofmaine.com
Internet: http://www.gardinersavings.com/
Sponsor: Gardiner Savings Institution Charitable Foundation
190 Water Street
Gardiner, ME 04345

Garland and Agnes Taylor Gray Foundation Grants 1988
The foundation is interested principally in supporting cultural, historical and educational institutions that have a significant impact on the quality of life in the Commonwealth of Virginia. The foundation also supports organizations in any field of charitable endeavor, with emphasis on education and human services, which substantially benefit the quality of life in southside communities of Petersburg, Waverly and surrounding areas.
Requirements: Proposals will be accepted from charitable organizations that serve the residents of metropolitan Richmond and Central Virginia. In addition, the foundation will consider organizations serving the southside communities of Petersburg, Waverly, and surrounding areas.
Restrictions: Organizations that receive competitive grant support equal or greater than $25,000 from the Garland and Agnes Taylor Gray Foundation normally shall be excluded from consideration by the Gray Foundation in the calendar year (CY) immediately following the year in which the approved grant is paid in full.
Geographic Focus: Virginia
Date(s) Application is Due: May 5
Amount of Grant: 5,000 - 100,000 USD
Contact: Susan Hallett; (804) 330-7400; fax (804) 330-5992; shallett@tcfrichmond.org
Internet: http://www.tcfrichmond.org/page2954.cfm#Gray
Sponsor: Garland and Agnes Taylor Gray Foundation
7501 Boulders View Drive, Suite 110
Richmond, VA 23225

Gates Family Foundation Children, Youth & Family Grants 1989
The mission of the Foundation is to invest in Colorado-based projects and organizations primarily through capital grants which have meaningful impact and enhance the quality of life for those who live, work and visit the state. Funding goals in the area of well-being of Children, Youth and Families include: strengthening and support organizations that encourage individuals to maintain good health and well-being rather than cure disease; supporting projects that encourage individuals to develop greater self-sufficiency, including the well-being and independence of disadvantaged families and the elderly; supporting organizations that increase access for more people to health, life skills and leadership education and services; and supporting programs that provide indoor and outdoor recreational opportunities and physical challenge for youth and adults, address obesity issues, and have a strong impact on those populations.
Requirements: The Foundation: generally makes grants only to organizations in the state of Colorado; expects strong support for the project from the community; will grant funds only to properly documented tax-exempt organizations; and generally confines its grants to campaigns for capital improvement or projects.
Restrictions: The Foundation does not: provide loans, grants, or scholarships to individuals, or loans to organizations; make grants for projects that have been completed prior to the next trustees' meeting; make grants for conferences, meetings, or studies that are not initiated by the trustees; consider more than one proposal from an organization in a calendar year; make grants to other foundations or organizations engaged in grant making; grant funds for general operating support or to retire operating debt; make grants for the purchase of vehicles or office equipment; make grants directly to individual public schools or public school districts; make grants for the construction of medical facilities or for medical research; schedule interviews with the Foundation trustees unless the trustees initiate the meeting. The Foundation will not purchase tickets for fundraising dinners, parties, benefits, balls, or other social fundraising events.
Geographic Focus: Colorado
Date(s) Application is Due: Jan 15; Apr 1; Jul 15; Oct 1
Contact: Karen White Mather; (303) 722-1881; info@gatesfamilyfoundation.org
Internet: http://www.gatesfamilyfoundation.org/www/gates.php?section=grant_applications&p=funding_priorities&fp=well_being
Sponsor: Gates Family Foundation
3575 Cherry Creek North Drive, Suite 100
Denver, CO 80209-3600

Gates Family Foundation Community Development & Revitalization Grants 1990
The mission of the Foundation is to invest in Colorado-based projects and organizations primarily through capital grants which have meaningful impact and enhance the quality of life for those who live, work and visit the state. Funding goals in the area of Community Development and Revitalization include: investing in organizations that have the potential to reinforce and enhance the economic vitality of a community; supporting organizations that further the broad education of the population in the maintenance of the free enterprise system; supports educational programs that effectively teach the principles of entrepreneurship and business ethics; and supporting projects that involve partnerships between public and private sector organizations that seek to improve the economic and cultural health of communities.
Requirements: The Foundation: generally makes grants only to organizations in the state of Colorado; expects strong support for the project from the community; will grant funds only to properly documented tax-exempt organizations; and generally confines its grants to campaigns for capital improvement or projects.
Restrictions: The Foundation does not: provide loans, grants, or scholarships to individuals, or loans to organizations; make grants for projects that have been completed prior to the next trustees' meeting; make grants for conferences, meetings, or studies that are not initiated by the trustees; consider more than one proposal from an organization in a calendar year; make grants to other foundations or organizations engaged in grant making; grant funds for general operating support or to retire operating debt; make grants for the purchase of vehicles or office equipment; make grants directly to individual public schools or public school districts; make grants for the construction of medical facilities or for medical research; schedule interviews with the Foundation trustees unless the trustees initiate the meeting. The Foundation will not purchase tickets for fundraising dinners, parties, benefits, balls, or other social fundraising events.
Geographic Focus: Colorado
Date(s) Application is Due: Jan 15; Apr 1; Jul 15; Oct 1
Contact: Karen White Mather; (303) 722-1881; info@gatesfamilyfoundation.org
Internet: http://www.gatesfamilyfoundation.org/www/gates.php?section=grant_applications&p=funding_priorities&fp=community
Sponsor: Gates Family Foundation
3575 Cherry Creek North Drive, Suite 100
Denver, CO 80209-3600

Gates Family Foundation Parks, Conservation & Recreation Grants 1991
The mission of the Foundation is to invest in Colorado-based projects and organizations primarily through capital grants which have meaningful impact and enhance the quality of life for those who live, work and visit the state. Funding goals in the area of Parks, Conservation and Recreation include support for: projects that protect natural areas from over development, including a special interest in the preservation of ranch/agricultural lands through easements; projects to construct and improve urban and mountain parks and open space for public recreation and access; the state's urban and mountain trail system; programs for young people that provide recreation, environmental education and leadership opportunities; and projects that encourage the spirit of scientific inquiry as well as the preservation of natural habitat.
Requirements: The Foundation: generally makes grants only to organizations in the state of Colorado; expects strong support for the project from the community; will grant funds only to properly documented tax-exempt organizations; and generally confines its grants to campaigns for capital improvement or projects.
Restrictions: The Foundation does not: provide loans, grants, or scholarships to individuals, or loans to organizations; make grants for projects that have been completed prior to the next trustees' meeting; make grants for conferences, meetings, or studies that are not initiated by the trustees; consider more than one proposal from an organization in a calendar year; make grants to other foundations or organizations engaged in grant making; grant funds for general operating support or to retire operating debt; make grants for the purchase of vehicles or office equipment; make grants directly to individual public schools or public school districts; make grants for the construction of medical facilities or for medical research; schedule interviews with the Foundation trustees unless the trustees initiate the meeting. The Foundation will not purchase tickets for fundraising dinners, parties, benefits, balls, or other social fundraising events.
Geographic Focus: Colorado
Date(s) Application is Due: Jan 15; Apr 1; Jul 15; Oct 1
Contact: Karen White Mather; (303) 722-1881; info@gatesfamilyfoundation.org
Internet: http://www.gatesfamilyfoundation.org/www/gates.php?section=grant_applications&p=funding_priorities&fp=natural_areas
Sponsor: Gates Family Foundation
3575 Cherry Creek North Drive, Suite 100
Denver, CO 80209-3600

Gateway Foundation Grants 1992
The Foundation strives to enrich St. Louis life and culture by supporting efforts to acquire, create or improve tangible and durable art and urban design. The Foundation's focus is to foster and support cultural and artistic activities and, on occasion, related educational activities devoted to improving the quality of life in the St. Louis Metropolitan Area. The Foundation gives priority to projects involving the acquisition, creation, or improvement of items of a durable, physical nature. A letter of inquiry is a form of initial contact. Organizations considering a funding request of the Foundation are encouraged to call the office before submission.
Requirements: Non-profit organizations in the St. Louis area are eligible to apply.
Restrictions: The foundation does not award grants to organizations that knowingly discriminate on the basis of race, color, religion, gender, national origin, sexual orientation, age, disability, marital status, or status as a veteran. Except under special circumstances, the Foundation does not fund: promotional projects such as publications or videos; travel or conferences; fund raising events or advertising; endowment funds; purchase of office equipment; general operations; social service programming; or capital campaigns.
Geographic Focus: Missouri
Date(s) Application is Due: Feb 1; May 1; Aug 1; Nov 1
Contact: Administrator; (314) 241-3337; tsmith-gwfnd@sbcglobal.net
Internet: http://www.gateway-foundation.org
Sponsor: Gateway Foundation
720 Olive Street, Suite 1977
Saint Louis, MO 63101

Gaylord and Dorothy Donnelley Foundation Grants 1993
The foundation accepts unsolicited proposals for projects under the environment/conservation and arts/culture areas of interest. Applicants must be located in the Chicago Region or the Lowcountry of South Carolina. Types of support include general operating support, program development grants, building construction/renovation, and capital campaigns. Proposals are accepted on an ongoing basis for review at board meetings in March, June and November. Applications are due three months prior to board meetings. Obtain required application forms from the office.
Requirements: IRS 501(c)3 organizations serving the Chicago region or the South Carolina low country are eligible. The Chicago region includes 13 counties in three states: Illinois—Lake, McHenry, Kane, Cook, DuPage, Kendall, Grundy, and Will; Wisconsin—Kenosha, and Walworth; and Indiana—Lake, Porter, and LaPorte. Lowcountry of South Carolina counties include Beaufort, Colleton, Charleston, Berkeley, Georgetown, Dorchester, Jasper, Horry, and Hampton.
Restrictions: The foundation usually will not support requests for individuals; endowments or capital campaigns; fund-raising events; publications, films, or videos; eradication of deficits or loans; conferences; or religious purposes.
Geographic Focus: Illinois, Indiana, South Carolina, Wisconsin
Date(s) Application is Due: Dec 2
Contact: Grants Manager; (312) 977-2700; fax (312) 977-1686; gddf@gddf.org
Internet: http://www.gddf.org/grant/process.asp
Sponsor: Gaylord and Dorothy Donnelley Foundation
35 E Wacker Drive, Suite 2600
Chicago, IL 60601-2102

GCI Corporate Contributions Grants 1994
GCI's corporate contribution program awards grants to qualified, not-for-profit organizations and charities in Alaska that contribute to the quality of life in the state. Awards are given for proposals that encourage individual growth and positive decision-making. Of special interest are opportunities afforded to Alaska's youth. Emphasis is given to programs where GCI employees have chosen to invest their time and energies. Proposals can be submitted throughout the year, but will only be reviewed the first week of every month. Notification will be mailed within 10 days following award determinations.
Requirements: Proposals should include a cover sheet and no more than two typed pages of narrative. Attachments should be limited to three pages. Only written proposals in the following format will be considered: a cover sheet to include a 50-word abstract of the proposal and appropriate contact information; a description of the proposed project; amount and type of contribution requested (specify exact dollar amount and whether the request is for cash or for in-kind services such as cellular, local, long-distance, cable television or Internet); how the funds will be used; how the proposal aligns with CGI's criteria; mission and history of the program/organization; names of CGI employees involved in the proposed project/program and to what extent; and whether CGI has awarded grants to the organization in the past.
Restrictions: Support is not generally given for travel or travel-related expenses; to individuals; to religious or political organizations; to organizations based outside of Alaska; or, to organizations that discriminate on the basis of age, sex, race, color, national origin, religion, creed, marital status, sexual preference, veteran status, or disability.
Geographic Focus: Alaska
Amount of Grant: Up to 500 USD
Contact: Pebbles Harris, Grant Contact; (907) 868-5553; fax (907) 265-5676
Internet: http://www.gci.com/about/corporate-giving
Sponsor: GCI Corporation
2550 Denali Street, Suite 1000
Anchorage, AK 99503

Gebbie Foundation Grants 1995
The Foundation's mission is to support appropriate charitable and humanitarian programs to improve the quality of life, primarily in Chautauqua County, New York by focusing on: children, youth and education; arts; human services; and community development. The foundation's strategic focus is to rejuvenate downtown Jamestown, New York, through economic development. Types of funding include: annual campaigns; building/renovation; capital campaigns; continuing support; endowments; equipment; general/operating support; matching/challenge support; program-related investments/loans; scholarship funds and; seed money.
Requirements: Organizations requesting funding must be approved as (or sponsored by) a 501(c)3 organization. The Board meets quarterly and proposals are accepted throughout the year. Before preparing a complete proposal, applicants are urged to submit a letter of inquiry addressed to the Executive Director. The letter should contain a descriptive title for the project, the project's intent, objectives, outcome measures, short and long term funding needs, and other relevant factual information. After reviewing the letter of inquiry, a detailed proposal may be requested. It should not be assumed that such a request is an indication of funding. The full proposal should include a detailed narrative, budgets, a board list, an IRS determination letter, other funding sources and financial documentation. In addition, the proposal should describe expected future funding sources and should indicate whether and to what extent additional funding by the Foundation will be necessary for the proposed project to be successful. The Foundation will respond to all inquiries from eligible organizations.
Restrictions: Grants are not made to individuals or sectarian or religious organizations. Because the Foundation makes annual contributions to the United Way of Southern Chautauqua County, applications for assistance from United Way-funded agencies will not be considered unless there is a strong link to the strategic focus.
Geographic Focus: New York
Contact: John C. Merino, Executive Director; (716) 487-1062; fax (716) 484-6401; jmerino@gebbie.org or info@gebbie.org
Internet: http://www.gebbie.org
Sponsor: Gebbie Foundation
111 West Second Street, Suite 1100
Jamestown, NY 14701

GEF Green Thumb Challenge 1996
Between Feb. 1 and Aug. 31, GEF is calling on schools and youth groups nationwide to plant 10,000 classroom and outdoor gardens. The Green Thumb Challenge aims to connect kids across the country with the joys and healthy benefits of gardening, providing participants with beginner-friendly resources to plant gardens of any size. All participants receive a $10 off a $50 purchase at Lowe's, and the opportunity to be awarded a $5,000 grant in recognition of their garden project. GEF offers free Pre K-8 standards-based lessons, fun activities, songs, and book recommendations that link gardening to science, math, language arts and art.
Requirements: Any youth garden, of any size, can be a part of the Green Thumb Challenge—participants are not limited to schools. Register at the website and follow the steps for a garden project.
Geographic Focus: All States
Date(s) Application is Due: Aug 31
Amount of Grant: 5,000 USD
Contact: Victoria Waters; (508) 668-2278; vwaters@greeneducationfoundation.org
Internet: http://www.greeneducationfoundation.org/index.php?option=com_content&view=section&layout=blog&id=22&Itemid=289
Sponsor: Green Education Foundation
1412 North Street
Walpole, MA 02081

GEICO Public Service Awards 1997
This program observes the many accomplishments of federal employees. These employees are making tremendous differences in the quality and efficiency of services and are responsible for the success of many scientific, medical, and technical programs. The foundation recognizes four active and one retired federal employee who have made outstanding achievements in one of the four fields of endeavor: Substance Abuse Prevention and Treatment, Fire Prevention and Safety, Physical Rehabilitation, and Traffic Safety and Accident Prevention. Nomination information is available online.
Requirements: All career civil service employees are eligible, including employees of the Library of Congress, the General Accounting Office, the Office of the Architect of the Capital, the Government Printing Office, the Administrative Office of the U.S. Courts, the Smithsonian Institution, the Botanic Garden, and the Office of Homeland Security.
Geographic Focus: All States
Amount of Grant: 2,500 USD
Contact: Program Contact; (877) 206-0215; federal@geico.com
Internet: http://www.geico.com/insproducts/fedpsa.html
Sponsor: GEICO Philanthropic Foundation
One GEICO Plaza
Washington, DC 20076

GenCorp Foundation Grants 1998
The Foundation is dedicated to supporting the communities where our employees live, work and volunteer. While the Foundation's primary focus is education, it also supports human services, civic and arts organizations. Emphasis is on science education. Funding preference is given to projects that involve issues important to employees and requests that are recommended by Foundation coordinators at company facilities. Interested applicants should submit a letter of inquiry.
Requirements: Non-profit organizations are eligible to apply. Priority is given to organizations that are in the GenCorp communities: Huntsville, AL; Camden, AR; Sacramento, CA; Socorro, NM; Jonesborough, TN; Clearfield, UT; Gainesville and Orange, VA; or Redmond, WA.
Geographic Focus: Alabama, Arkansas, California, New Mexico, Tennessee, Utah, Virginia, Washington
Contact: Program Contact; (916) 355-3600; gencorp.foundation@gencorp.com
Internet: http://www.gencorp.com/pages/gcfound.html
Sponsor: GenCorp Foundation
P.O. Box 15619
Sacramento, CA 95852-0619

Gene Haas Foundation 1999
The Gene Haas Foundation was formed in 1999 to fund the needs of the local community and other deserving charities, at the discretion of its founder, Gene Haas. Of special importance to the Foundation are children's charities and organizations that feed the poor, especially within the local community of Ventura County. In addition, the Foundation provides scholarship funds to community colleges and vocational schools for students entering technical training programs, especially machinist-based certificate and degree programs. Giving is primarily in California.
Requirements: The Gene Haas Foundation provides grants to organizations that are exempt under Internal Revenue Code Section 501(c)3 and currently are classified as a public charity pursuant to Internal Revenue Code Section 509(a)1, 2 or 3 (an "Exempt Public Charity"). Funds from the Gene Haas Foundation must be fully utilized within 2 years of date of grant. Funds that are not expended must be returned unless other arrangements are approved by the Gene Haas Foundation.
Restrictions: Grants provided by the Gene Haas Foundation, or the interest generated from those grants, may not be used to influence any legislation or the outcome of any election, to conduct a voter registration drive or to satisfy a charitable pledge or obligation of any person or organization.
Geographic Focus: California
Amount of Grant: Up to 100,000 USD
Contact: Gene F. Haas, President; (805) 278-1800; info@ghaasfoundation.org
Internet: http://ghaasfoundation.org/
Sponsor: Gene Haas Foundation
2800 Sturgis Road
Oxnard, CA 93030-8901

Genentech Corporate Charitable Contributions Grants 2000
The Foundation's primary focus areas are health science education, patient education/advocacy, and community. The Foundation supports nonprofits through its contributions in two primary ways: project-specific or general support funding to organizations whose mission aligns with the Foundation's focus areas; and sponsorships of selected events that fall into the Foundation's focus areas. Interested applicant's are encouraged to submit applications online.
Requirements: Nonprofit organizations recognized by the IRS as tax exempt, public charities, located in the United States are eligible to apply. Eligible grantees may include public elementary and secondary schools, as well as public colleges and universities and public hospitals.
Restrictions: The Foundation does not provide funding to organizations that discriminate on the basis of age, political affiliation, race, national origin, ethnicity, gender, disability, sexual orientation or religious beliefs. Funding is not provided for: advertising journals or booklets; alumni drives; capital campaigns/building funds; continuing medical education; infrastructural requests (e.g. salaries, equipment); memorial funds; memberships; organizations based outside of the United States; political or sectarian organizations; professional sports events or athletes; religious organizations; scholarships; yearbooks.
Geographic Focus: California
Contact: Program Manager; (650) 467-9494; give@gene.com
Internet: http://www.gene.com/gene/about/community/overview.jsp
Sponsor: Genentech
1 DNA Way
South San Francisco, CA 94080-4990

General Dynamics Corporation Grants 2001
Corporate contributions funding goes to education, civic and public affairs, health and welfare, and arts and culture. Types of support include capital campaigns, general support, and operating funds. Grants are made nationally and communities where the company has operations. There is no formal application process. Interested applicants may submit a letter of application.
Geographic Focus: All States
Contact: Arlene Nestle, (703) 876-3305; fax (703) 876-3600
Internet: http://www.generaldynamics.com
Sponsor: General Dynamics Corporation
2941 Fairview Park Drive, Suite 100
Falls Church, VA 22042-4513

General Mills Foundation Celebrating Communities of Color Grants 2002
One-time project grants are awarded to nonprofit organizations in the greater Twin Cities area serving communities of color. The grants will focus mainly on social service—supporting programs that strengthen families and promote a safe, nurturing environment for children and youth; youth nutrition and fitness—supporting innovative programs that help improve nutrition and fitness behaviors; education—supporting efforts that emphasize student academic achievement, particularly at the K-12 level; and arts and culture—supporting organizations that are leaders in their field as evidenced by their innovation, program quality, and contribution to their community. Guidelines and application are available online.
Requirements: Organizations must be located in and serving diverse populations in the Twin Cities 7-county metro area; Anoka, Carver, Dakota, Hennepin, Ramsey, Scott and Washington.
Restrictions: As a standard practice, the Foundation does not fund: organizations without 501(c)3; organizations with 509(a)(3) Type III status; organizations that do not comply with the Foundation's Non-Discrimination Policy; annual appeals, federated campaigns, fund drives; recreational, sporting events or athletic associations; religious organizations for religious purposes; individuals; basic research; social, labor, veterans, alumni or fraternal organizations serving a limited constituency; organizations seeking underwriting for advertising; political causes, candidates or legislative lobbying efforts; travel by groups; emergency funding; or loans, debt reduction or operating deficits. Generally, the Foundation does not support the following: conferences, seminars or workshops; publications, films or television programs; campaigns to eliminate or control specific diseases; underwriting for program sponsorship; or special events.
Geographic Focus: Minnesota
Date(s) Application is Due: Jul 15
Amount of Grant: 10,000 USD
Contact: Coordinator; (763) 764-2211; CommunityActionQA@genmills.com
Internet: http://www.generalmills.com/corporate/commitment/communities_color.aspx
Sponsor: General Mills Foundation
1 General Mills Boulevard, P.O. Box 1113
Minneapolis, MN 55440

General Mills Foundation Grants 2003
The Foundation was created to focus its philanthropic resources on community needs. Strategic objectives are to: demonstrably improve the quality of life in communities with GM facilities and employees; initiate innovative solutions and approaches to improve youth nutrition and fitness; and to support GM employees and retirees giving to United Way, education, and arts and culture organizations through gift matching. Funding priorities include: social services; youth nutrition and fitness; education; and arts and culture. Priority is given to organizations meeting the following criteria: their mission is closely related to the Foundation's priorities; programs or activities are based in communities with GM operations and employees; programs or activities involve GM employees and retirees; and services create sustainable community improvement. Applications are accepted at any time.
Requirements: U.S. and Canadian charitable 501(c)3 and 509(a) nonprofits in communities where General Mills operates (California, Georgia, Illinois, Indiana, Iowa, Maryland, Massachusetts, Missouri, Minnesota, Missouri, Montana, New Jersey, New York, Ohio, Oklahoma, Pennsylvania, Tennessee and Wisconsin) are eligible.
Restrictions: The Foundation does not support: organizations without 501(c)3 and 509(a) status; organizations that do not comply with the Foundation's non-discrimination policy; individuals; social, labor, veterans, alumni or fraternal organizations serving a limited constituency; travel by groups; recreational, sporting events or athletic associations; religious organizations for religious purposes; basic research; organizations seeking underwriting for advertising; political causes, candidates or legislative lobbying efforts; conferences, seminars and workshops; campaigns to eliminate or control specific diseases; publications, films or television programs; underwriting for program sponsorship.
Geographic Focus: Arizona, Arkansas, California, Georgia, Illinois, Indiana, Iowa, Maryland, Massachusetts, Michigan, Minnesota, Missouri, Montana, New Jersey, New Mexico, New York, Ohio, Oklahoma, Pennsylvania, Tennessee, Wisconsin
Contact: Christina L. Shea, President; (763) 764-2211; fax (763) 764-4114
Internet: http://www.generalmills.com/corporate/commitment/foundation.aspx
Sponsor: General Mills Foundation
1 General Mills Boulevard, P.O. Box 1113
Minneapolis, MN 55440

General Motors Foundation Grants Support Program 2004
With a strong commitment to diversity in all areas, the targeted areas of focus for the Foundation are: education; health and human services; civic and community; public policy; arts and culture; and environment and energy. Primary consideration is given to requests that meet the following criteria: exhibit a clear purpose and defined need in one of the foundation's areas of focus; recognize innovative approaches in addressing the defined need; demonstrate an efficient organization and detail the organization's ability to follow through on the proposal; and, explain clearly the benefits to the foundation and the plant city communities. Paper applications are no longer accepted. Completion of an online eligibility quiz is the first step in the application process.
Requirements: Nonprofit, tax-exempt organizations and institutions are eligible to apply. Applications must be made online.
Restrictions: The Foundation not not support organizations that discriminate on the basis of race, religion, creed, gender, age, veteran status, physical challenge or national origin. Contributions are generally not provided for: individuals; religious organizations; political parties or candidates; U.S. hospitals and health care institutions (general operating support); capital campaigns; endowment funds; conferences, workshops or seminars not directly related to GM's business interests.
Geographic Focus: All States
Contact: Grant Coordinator; (313) 556-5000
Internet: http://www.gm.com/company/gmability/community/guidelines/index.html
Sponsor: General Motors Foundation
300 Renaissance Center, P.O. Box 300
Detroit, MI 48265-3000

General Service Foundation Colorado Program Grants 2005
The goal of the General Service Foundation Colorado Program Grants is to a) build the capacity of key base-building organizations committed to justice and equality in the state, and b) facilitate collaboration among grantees and also between grantees and other sectors (including media, research, leadership, policy, and issue advocacy groups) to create a permanent infrastructure capable of affecting state-wide policy change over the long term. Any base-building group with the capacity to affect policy in Colorado by working in partnership with others in the state may apply. Grants are usually within the range of $25,000 to $35,000 each year, with possible additional funds for technical support. Applications are due February 1 and September 1. Previously funded projects are posted on the Foundation website.
Requirements: All applications must be submitted through the Foundation's online process. Paper proposals are not accepted. In assessing potential grantees, the Foundation will place a priority on those organizations and projects that both fit the definition of a base-building group and meet the following criteria: the applicant works to address needs identified by the underrepresented communities that are directly impacted; the organization focuses on developing, strengthening, and empowering local community leaders or, if it is a coalition, the coalition facilitates this activity through its partners; the organization works throughout the year to engage community members in campaigns that create real change and build permanent power for their community. All proposals should answer: what is the organization's membership or community engagement philosophy; and how does it define membership and activist engagement within the organization. Please list number of members, including any classifications it places on the overall membership. Applicants should refer to the website for additional information on what the proposal should include.
Restrictions: The Foundation places top priority on Colorado organizations that are rooted in the state. It only rarely supports national organizations to work in Colorado and they must show a strong and ongoing commitment to work in partnership with in-state groups, including prioritizing locally-led campaigns rather than working off a national agenda.
Geographic Focus: Colorado
Date(s) Application is Due: Feb 1; Sep 1
Contact: Renee Fazzari; (970) 920-6834; fax (970) 920-4578; renee@generalservice.org
Internet: http://www.generalservice.org/Colorado%20Program.htm
Sponsor: General Service Foundation
557 North Mill Street, Suite 201
Aspen, CO 81611

General Service Foundation Human Rights and Economic Justice Grants 2006
The goal of the General Service Foundation's Human Rights and Economic Justice program is to support efforts that protect, promote and create good jobs with living wages for workers, including low-wage workers in the United States and Mexico. The Foundation seeks to: strengthen worker voices; promote public policies that protect labor rights; and democratize corporate power and promote corporate accountability. In assessing potential grantees, the Foundation will apply the following criteria: supporting organizations that work to address needs identified by the underrepresented and low-income communities that area directly impacted, connecting at the local and national level; and concentrating on organizations that take risks and try new ideas to enhance their skills, and reflect the diversity of their constituency. Samples of previously funded projects are posted on the Foundation website.
Requirements: All applicants, regardless of their prior grant history with the Foundation, start their application process by submitting a letter of inquiry in the spring and fall. Organizations should determine if their project is an appropriate fit for the Foundation, then send a letter of inquiry via the Foundation's online application. Letters of inquiry should include: a political and situational analysis, statement of the issues to be addressed under the proposed project, the history and goals of the organization, and an explanation of why the organization or coalition is the entity that is most likely to achieve success; a brief summary of the project, short and long term goals and anticipated outcomes; the approximate starting date and duration of the proposed activities; the total amount of funding needed, the amount requested from the Foundation, a budget, and information about other sources of support; and a copy of IRS tax exempt 501(c)3 letter. If the project is judged appropriate, the organization will be offered an application to submit to the Foundation.
Restrictions: The Foundation does not fund: organizations based outside the United States or Mexico; projects without significant promise of impact beyond a local or state level; research and publications not directly linked to policy outcomes; direct service delivery; and development or relief projects.
Geographic Focus: All States, Mexico
Date(s) Application is Due: Feb 1; Sep 1
Amount of Grant: 5,000 - 35,000 USD
Contact: Holly Bartling, Program Contact-Mexico grants; (202) 232-1005 or (970) 920-6834, ext 4; fax (970) 920-4578; holly@generalservice.org
Internet: http://www.generalservice.org/International%20Peace.htm
Sponsor: General Service Foundation
557 North Mill Street, Suite 201
Aspen, CO 81611

General Service Foundation Reproductive Justice Grants 2007
The General Service Foundation believes that in order to be effective, the reproductive health and rights movement must address the needs of all women, including women of color, low-income women, and young women. The Reproductive Justice Grants are interested in supporting organizations that work on a broad range of reproductive health and rights issues that includes, but is not limited to, abortion. The Foundation supports organizations and projects engaged in leadership development, organizing, education, policy research and advocacy. In assessing potential grantees, the Foundation places priority on organizations and projects that have a broad approach to reproductive health, try new ideas and strategies, reflect the diversity of its constituency, and address needs identified by people directly impacted by the issues and policies. A list of previously funded projects is available at the Foundation website.
Requirements: All applicants, regardless of their prior grant history with the Foundation, start their application process by submitting a letter of inquiry in the spring and fall. Organizations should determine if their project is an appropriate fit for the Foundation, then send a letter of inquiry via the Foundation's online application. Letters of inquiry should include: a political and situational analysis, statement of the issues to be addressed under the proposed project, the history and goals of the organization, and an explanation of why the organization or coalition is the entity that is most likely to achieve success; a brief summary of the project, short and long term goals and anticipated outcomes; the approximate starting date and duration of the proposed activities; the total amount of funding needed, the amount requested from the Foundation, a budget, and information about other sources of support; and a copy of IRS tax exempt 501(c)3 letter. If the project is judged appropriate, the organization will be offered an application to submit to the Foundation.
Restrictions: The Foundation does not fund direct service delivery, unless it is linked to policy and advocacy; projects without significant promise of impact beyond a local or state level; research and publications not directly linked to policy outcomes; projects outside the United States; and NARAL or Planned Parenthood affiliates.
Geographic Focus: All States
Date(s) Application is Due: Feb 1; Sep 1
Amount of Grant: 3,000 - 35,000 USD
Contact: Holly Bartling; (970) 920-6834; fax (970) 920-4578; holly@generalservice.org
Internet: http://www.generalservice.org/Reproductive%20Health.htm
Sponsor: General Service Foundation
557 North Mill Street, Suite 201
Aspen, CO 81611

George A. and Grace L. Long Foundation Grants 2008
The George A. and Grace L. Long Foundation was established in 1960 to support and promote quality educational, cultural, human-services, and health-care programming for underserved populations in Connecticut. Grants from the Long Foundation are one year in duration. Applicants must apply online at the grant website. Applicants are strongly encouraged to do the following before applying: review the downloadable state application procedures for additional helpful information and clarifications; review the downloadable online-application guidelines at the grant website; review the foundation's funding history (link is available from the grant website); review the online application questions in advance; and review the list of required attachments. These will generally include: a list of board members, financial statements (audited, reviewed, or compiled by independent auditor); an organization summary; a list of other funding sources; an IRS Determination letter; and other required documents. All attachments must be uploaded in the online application as PDF, Word, or Excel files. The George A. and Grace L. Long Foundation has biannual deadlines of March 15 and September 15. Applications must be submitted by 11:59 p.m. on the deadline dates. Applicants will be notified of grant decisions by letter within two to three months after each respective proposal deadline.
Requirements: Applicant organizations must have 501(c)3 tax-exempt status and serve the people of Connecticut.
Restrictions: Applicants will not be awarded a grant for more than three consecutive years. The foundation does not support requests from individuals, organizations attempting to influence policy through direct lobbying, or any political campaigns.
Geographic Focus: Connecticut
Date(s) Application is Due: Mar 15; Sep 15
Contact: Carmen Britt; (860) 657-7019; carmen.britt@baml.com
Internet: https://www.bankofamerica.com/philanthropic/fn_search.action
Sponsor: George A. And Grace L. Long Foundation
200 Glastonbury Boulevard, Suite # 200, CT2-545-02-05
Glastonbury, CT 06033-4056

George A. Hormel Testamentary Trust Grants 2009
The Trust, established in 1946, honors the memory of George A. Hormel, founder of the famed meat packing firm. The primary purpose of the fund is to provide financial support for capital and program budgets of local Austin, Minnesota, organizations, with a primary emphasis on youth programs and local economic development. Types of support include: building renovation; curriculum development; equipment acquisition; general operating support; and program development. An application form is required, and initial support should be made by letter of inquiry.
Restrictions: Giving is limited to Mower County, Minnesota. No grants are given to individuals, or for endowment funds, research, fellowships, deficit financing, land acquisition, publications, or conferences; no loans.
Geographic Focus: Minnesota
Date(s) Application is Due: Sep 1
Amount of Grant: Up to 20,000 USD
Contact: J.J. Gray, Director; (507) 437-9800; fax (507) 437-5129
Sponsor: George A. Hormel Testamentary Trust
301 North Main Street
Austin, MN 55912-3498

George and Ruth Bradford Foundation Grants 2010
The foundation awards grants to local nonprofit organizations in the San Francisco Bay Area and Mendocino, California region. Areas of interest include: children and youth; families; education/higher education; environmental/wildlife conservation; housing and; social services. Types of support include general operating support and scholarship funds. T
Requirements: California nonprofit organizations in the San Francisco peninsula and Mendocino, California region are eligible to apply. There is no deadline date to adhere to. The Board meets monthly, letters of inquiry may be submitted throughout the year for review.
Restrictions: No grants to individuals.
Geographic Focus: California
Contact: Myrna Oglesby, Director; (707) 462-0141; fax (707) 462-0160
Sponsor: George and Ruth Bradford Foundation
P.O. Box 720
Ukiah, CA 95482-0720

George and Sarah Buchanan Foundation Grants 2011
Established in 2006, the George and Sarah Buchanan Foundation offers funding throughout the state of Virginia. Its primary fields of interest include: health care, health organizations, and religion. Support typically is given for general operations. There are no specified application formats or annual deadlines, and applicants should proceed by forwarding a proposal to the Foundation office. Recent grants have ranged from $250 to $20,000.
Requirements: Applicants should be 501(c)3 organizations either located in, or serving residents of, Virginia. Preference is given to the general Danville, Virginia, region.
Geographic Focus: Virginia
Amount of Grant: 250 - 20,000 USD
Contact: George Buchanan, Jr., (434) 797-3543
Sponsor: George and Sarah Buchanan Foundation
400 Bridge Street
Danville, VA 24541-1404

George A Ohl Jr. Foundation Grants 2012
The purpose of the George A Ohl Jr. Foundation is to improve the well-being of the citizens of the State of New Jersey through science, health, recreation, education and increased good citizenship. Grants are made to organizations engaged in such work whether through research, publications, health, school or college activities. The Foundation's mission is the relief of the poor; the improvement of living conditions; the care of the sick, the young, the aged, the homeless, the incompetent and the helpless. The foundation will target: 35% of its grants to Community Redevelopment; 35% to Health and Human Services organizations; 15% for Arts and culture; 15% for Educational requests. Application deadlines are: January 22 for a March meeting and, June 15 for an August meeting. Application forms are available online. Applicants will receive notice acknowledging receipt of the grant request, and subsequently be notified of the grant declination or approval.
Requirements: New Jersey 501(c)3 nonprofit organizations are eligible to apply. Proposals should be submitted in the following format: completed Common Grant Application Form; an original Proposal Statement; an audited financial report and a current year operating budget; a copy of your official IRS Letter with your tax determination; a listing of your Board of Directors. Proposal Statements (second item in the above Format) should answer these questions: what are the objectives and expected outcomes of this program/project/request; what strategies will be used to accomplish your objective; what is the timeline for completion; if this is part of an on-going program, how long has it been in operation; what criteria will you use to measure success; if the request is not fully funded, what other sources can you engage; an Itemized budget should be included; please describe any collaborative ventures. Prior to the distribution of funds, all approved grantees must sign and return a Grant Agreement Form, stating that the funds will be used for the purpose intended. Progress reports and Completion reports must also be filed as required for your specific grant. All current grantees must be in good standing with required documentation prior to submitting new proposals to any foundation.
Restrictions: Grants are not made for political purposes, nor to organizations which discriminate on the basis of race, ethnic origin, sexual or religious preference, age or gender
Geographic Focus: New Jersey
Date(s) Application is Due: Jan 22; Jun 15
Amount of Grant: 3,000 - 35,000 USD
Contact: Wachovia Bank, N.A., Trustee; grantinquiries2@wachovia.com
Internet: https://www.wachovia.com/foundation/v/index.jsp?vgnextoid=e0f78689fb0aa110VgnVCM1000004b0d1872RCRD&vgnextfmt=default
Sponsor: George A Ohl Jr. Foundation
190 River Road, NJ3132
Summit, NJ 07901

George B. Page Foundation Grants 2013
The foundation awards grants to Santa Barbara, CA, nonprofit organizations in support of programs for children and youth, youth development, clubs, and centers; athletics/sports, Special Olympics; community and economic development; education; human services; YM/YWCAs and YM/YWHAs. Types of support include annual campaigns; continuing support; debt reduction; emergency funds; general/operating support; program development; and seed money.
Requirements: Application forms are required, but organizations should initially call or write the Foundation to discuss the project, and request an application.
Restrictions: Funding is not available for individuals, endowments, or matching gifts.
Geographic Focus: California
Date(s) Application is Due: Oct 1
Amount of Grant: 2,000 - 50,000 USD
Contact: Sara Sorensen, Trustee; (805) 730-3634
Sponsor: George B. Page Foundation
P.O. Box 1299
Santa Barbara, CA 93102-1299

George B. Storer Foundation Grants 2014
The foundation awards grants, primarily in Florida, in its areas of interest, including higher education, social services—particularly for the blind, youth organizations, conservation, hospitals, and cultural programs. Types of support include building construction/renovation, capital campaigns, general operating support, matching/challenge grants, and research grants. There are no application forms. Applications should be submitted between October 15 and the listed deadline.
Geographic Focus: All States
Date(s) Application is Due: Nov 15
Contact: Grants Administrator, c/o Thomas McDonald
Sponsor: George B. Storer Foundation
P.O. Box 1040
Tavernier, FL 33070

George E. Hatcher, Jr. and Ann Williams Hatcher Foundation Grants 2015
The George E. Hatcher and Ann Williams Hatcher Foundation was created to support charitable organizations that provide for the relief of diseased people and the relief of human suffering which is due to disease, ill health, physical weakness, physical disability and/or physical injury. In addition, the foundation supports organizations that aid in the promotion and prolongation of life and that support the principle of dying with dignity. Grants from George E. Hatcher and Ann Williams Hatcher Foundation are primarily one year in duration; on occasion, multi-year support is awarded. Applicants must apply online at the grant website. Applicants are strongly encouraged to do the following before applying: review the downloadable state application procedures for additional helpful information and clarifications; review the downloadable online-application guidelines at the grant website; review the foundation's funding history (link is available from the grant website); review the online application questions in advance; and review the list of required attachments. These will generally include: a list of board members, financial statements (audited, reviewed, or compiled by independent auditor); an organization summary; a list of other funding sources; an IRS Determination letter; and other required documents. All attachments must be uploaded in the online application as PDF, Word, or Excel files. The George E. Hatcher and Ann Williams Hatcher Foundation application deadline is 11:59 p.m. on May 31. Applicants will be notified of grant decisions by letter within one to two months after the deadline.
Requirements: Disbursements are authorized to institutions or organizations located in the Middle Georgia area (Bibb County & surrounding communities) which provide health care and/or shelter for individuals (especially children) who cannot otherwise obtain such services due to circumstances beyond their control. A breakdown of number/percentage of people served by specific counties is required on the online application.
Restrictions: The foundation does not support requests from individuals, organizations attempting to influence policy through direct lobbying, or any political campaigns.
Geographic Focus: Georgia
Date(s) Application is Due: May 31
Contact: Quanda Allen, Vice President; (404) 264-1377; quanda.allen@baml.com
Internet: https://www.bankofamerica.com/philanthropic/fn_search.action
Sponsor: George E. Hatcher, Jr. and Ann Williams Hatcher Foundation
3414 Peachtree Road, N.E., Suite 1475, GA7-813-14-04
Atlanta, GA 30326-1113

George F. Baker Trust Grants 2016
Grants are awarded nationwide, with preference given to nonprofits in the eastern United States, primarily for K-12, higher, and secondary education; hospitals; social services; private foundations; and zoos/zoological societies. Types of support include general operating support and matching funds. There are no application forms or deadlines. The board meets in June and November to consider requests.
Requirements: An application form is not required. Along with a letter of inquiry and brief outline of a proposal, applicants should submit the following: signature and title of chief executive officer; a copy of the organization's IRS determination letter; a detailed description of the project and amount of funding requested; and a listing of additional

sources and amount of support. As a result of the enormous number of applications received and limited number of grants, only those applicants who receive a grant will be notified.
Restrictions: Funding is given primarily in Connecticut, Florida, Massachusetts, and New York. Grants are not made to individuals for scholarships or loans.
Geographic Focus: Connecticut, Florida, Massachusetts, New York
Amount of Grant: 1,000 - 50,000 USD
Contact: Rocio Suarez; (212) 755-1890; fax (212) 319-6316; rocio@bakernye.com
Sponsor: George F. Baker Trust
477 Madison Avenue, Suite 1650
New York, NY 10022

George Family Foundation Grants 2017
The mission of the Foundation is to foster wholeness in mind, body, spirit, and community in order to enhance the development of human potential. The Foundation's areas of interest are: integrative medicine, leadership development, educational opportunities, social justice and spirituality. Non- solicited proposals will not be accepted. Invited applicants are encouraged to submit a letter of inquiry or to discuss their request with staff before submitting an application.
Requirements: 501(c)3 tax-exempt organizations are eligible. Primary giving is restricted to the Twin Cities metropolitan area.
Restrictions: Grants do not support endowment or capital campaigns, programs in which the family has no active interest or involvement; individuals; memberships, special events, or other fundraisers; or programs that address debt retirement or recovery of operating losses.
Geographic Focus: Minnesota
Date(s) Application is Due: May 30; Oct 30
Amount of Grant: 1,000 - 200,000 USD
Contact: Grants Administrator; (612) 377-8400; fax (612) 377-8407
Internet: http://www.georgefamilyfoundation.org/
Sponsor: George Family Foundation
1818 Oliver Avenue South
Minneapolis, MN 55405

George Foundation Grants 2018
The George Foundation strive to support organizations and programs that assist in developing strong, stable families across Fort Bend County region of Texas. The Foundation's areas of interest include: family stability; scholarships; foundation initiated programs, current programs include, Youth in Philanthropy (YIP), Leadership Excellence for Non-Profits, Integrated Mental Health Care, and Transportation. The Foundation prefers to fund the following types of grants to support Fort Bend organizations in their delivery of services to the community (listed in order of priority): program/project support; foundation initiated; general operating; capital. Proposal deadlines for making grant applications to the Foundation are January 15, April 15, July 15 and October 15 of each year. All proposals for capital support will be grouped together for review. The deadline for capital proposals will be October 15 of each year.
Requirements: Non-profits in Fort Bend County, Texas may submit grant proposals.
Restrictions: The Foundation does not fund: grants to organizations that do not have a current 501(c)3 determination letter; churches or other organized religious bodies; grants to another organization that distributes money to recipients of its own selection, i.e., a regranting organization; regional, national or international programs; grants for research or studies; grants for travel, conferences, conventions, group meetings, or seminars; the purchase of event tickets, tables, ads or sponsorships; support to fairs and festivals; religious or private schools; request for funds to develop films, videos, books or other media projects; direct mail campaigns; loans of any kind; grants to individuals; grants to fraternal organizations; political interests of any kind; and institutions that discriminate on the basis of race, creed, gender, national origin, age, disability or sexual orientation in policy or in practice.
Geographic Focus: Texas
Date(s) Application is Due: Jan 15; Apr 15; Jul 15; Oct 15
Amount of Grant: 1,000 - 4,000,000 USD
Contact: Dee Koch; (281) 342-6109; fax (281) 341-7635; dkoch@thegeorgefoundation.org
Internet: http://www.thegeorgefoundation.org
Sponsor: George Foundation
310 Morton Street, PMB Suite C
Richmond, TX 77469

George Frederick Jewett Foundation Grants 2019
The foundation is concerned primarily with people and values. The grants program focuses on the future and on stimulating and supporting activities and projects of established, voluntary, nonprofit organizations that are of importance to human welfare. Grants are made in the fields of arts and humanities, conservation and preservation, education, health care and medical services, population, religion, and social welfare. The foundation may support research on and studies of important problems of public concern solely for the purpose of aiding in the gathering and presenting of facts that may assist the public to better understand such problems and to arrive at realistic and effective solutions to them. From time to time, support may be given to the scholarship, fellowship, and research programs of established institutions when sufficient evidence is available to establish clearly that the applicant organization is awarding such grants in accordance with the regulations established by the IRS. Grants are awarded to support activities in progress, research into potential projects, building and equipment, general operations, program development, seed funding, research, technical assistance, and matching funds. Inquiries for clarification of the foundation's policy and program emphasis are encouraged.
Requirements: Preference is given to public charities or nonprivate foundations. The foundation confines its grants largely to requests from eastern Washington and the San Francisco Bay area.
Restrictions: Grants do not support advertising; advocacy, athletic, international, religious, political, or veterans organizations; or individuals.
Geographic Focus: California, Washington
Amount of Grant: 5,000 - 50,000 USD
Contact: Ann Gralnek, (415) 421-1351; fax (415) 421-0721; ADGjewettf@aol.com
Sponsor: George Frederick Jewett Foundation
235 Montgomery Street, Suite 612
San Francisco, CA 94104

George Gund Foundation Grants 2020
The Foundation's long-standing interests include: arts; economic development; community revitalization; education; environment; and human services. The Foundation considers global climate change an urgent issue that cuts across all of the Foundation's programs. The Foundation takes seriously it's own responsibility and wants to hear from grant applicants what they are doing or considering to reduce or to eliminate their organizational impact on climate change. The Foundation also supports special projects grants, which currently include: Retinal Degenerative Diseases research grants, making an annual commitment for research on the causes, nature and prevention of inherited retinal degenerative diseases and; philanthropic services grants, offering support to organizations that strengthen the infrastructure of the nonprofit and philanthropic communities. The George Gund Foundation also supports capital requests but only for projects that are clearly aligned with their program priorities and that meet Green Building Council LEED (Leadership in Energy and Environmental Design) certification. The Foundation's green building policy covers both planning and construction grants. In addition, the Foundation supports opportunities that cross program boundaries and that integrate elements of the Foundation's interests. Although the Foundation's focus is centered in the Greater Cleveland, Ohio region, a portion of their grantmaking will continue to support state and national policy making that bolsters their work. Proposals should be mailed directly to the George Gund Foundation. All proposals are screened and evaluated by the staff before presentation at Trustee Meetings. Receipt of proposals will be acknowledged by mail.
Requirements: 501(c)3 nonprofit organizations are eligible to apply for funding, with a special interest in Greater Cleveland, Ohio region. Proposals are accepted three times: March 15, July 15 and November 15. Proposals are due the next business day if a deadline falls on a weekend. The grant application form is available on the George Gund Foundation website. All proposals must include a climate change statement, the Foundation's website includes resources to assist grantees with this task. Applicants also must include a completed Grant Application Cover Sheet, which is signed by the organization's board chair and executive director. Proposals should also include: organizational background; history; mission; types of programs offered; constituencies served; project description; justification of need; specific goals and objectives; activities planned to meet goals and objectives; project time line; qualifications of key personnel; methods of evaluation; project budget; anticipated expenses, including details about how Foundation funds would be used; anticipated income, including information about other sources approached for funding; organizational budget; previous and current year budget and proposed budget for project year(s) showing both income and expenses; the organization's most recent audited financial statement, do not include IRS 990 forms; supporting documents; list of current trustees; letters of support; readily available printed material about organization such as annual reports and brochures; IRS letter confirming Internal Revenue Code 501(c)3 status and classification as a public charity or information confirming status as a government unit or agency. The Foundation also will accept the Ohio Common Grant Form, available at www.ohiograntmakers.org, if organizations are using it to apply to multiple funders. Faxed or electronic proposals are not accepted.
Restrictions: Do not submit proposals in notebooks, binders or plastic folders and print proposals on both sides of each sheet of paper. The Foundation normally does not consider grants for endowments. Capital requests must meet the Foundation's program goals and also adhere to green building standards of environmental sustainability. Details on these requirements are available from the Foundation. Grants are not made for debt reduction or to fund benefit events. The Foundation does not make grants to individuals, nor does it administer programs it supports. Grants are limited to organizations located in the United States.
Geographic Focus: All States
Date(s) Application is Due: Mar 15; Jul 15; Nov 15
Contact: David Abbott; (216) 241-3114; fax (216) 241-6560; info@gundfdn.org
Internet: http://www.gundfdn.org/what.asp
Sponsor: George Gund Foundation
1845 Guildhall Building, 45 Prospect Avenue, West
Cleveland, OH 44115

George H. and Jane A. Mifflin Memorial Fund Grants 2021
The foundation awards grants to Massachusetts nonprofit organizations in its areas of interest, including crime and law enforcement, disadvantaged (economically), education, environment, legal services, and social services. Types of support include capital campaigns, land acquisition, and scholarship funds. There are no application deadlines or forms. The board meets in May and September.
Requirements: Massachusetts nonprofit organizations are eligible.
Geographic Focus: Massachusetts
Date(s) Application is Due: Apr 15; Aug 15
Samples: New England Forestry Foundation (Groton, MA)—to purchase the largest forestland easement in U.S. history, which will protect 762,192 acres in Maine from development, $100,000.
Contact: Barbara Carr, (617) 523-6531; bcarr@lwcotrust.com
Sponsor: George H. and Jane A. Mifflin Memorial Fund
230 Congress Street
Boston, MA 02110

George H.C. Ensworth Memorial Fund Grants — 2022

The George H.C. Ensworth Memorial Fund was established in 1949 to support charitable organizations that focus on health and human services, youth services, enjoyment of the natural environment, education, religion, and the arts. Applicants must apply online at the grant website. Applicants are strongly encouraged to do the following before applying: review the downloadable state application procedures for additional helpful information and clarifications; review the downloadable online-application guidelines at the grant website; review the fund's funding history (link is available from the grant website); review the online application questions in advance; and review the list of required attachments. These will generally include: a list of board members, financial statements (audited, reviewed, or compiled by independent auditor); an organization summary; a list of other funding sources; an IRS Determination letter; and other required documents. All attachments must be uploaded in the online application as PDF, Word, or Excel files. The George H. C. Ensworth Memorial Fund has an annual deadline of May 15 at 11:59 p.m. Applicants will be notified of the grant decisions by letter within two months after the proposal deadline.
Requirements: Applicants must have 501(c)3 status and serve the people of Glastonbury, Connecticut. A breakdown of number/percentage of people served will be required in the online application.
Restrictions: Grant requests for capital projects will not be considered. Applicants will not be awarded a grant for more than 3 consecutive years. The fund does not support requests from individuals, organizations attempting to influence policy through direct lobbying, or any political campaigns.
Geographic Focus: Connecticut
Date(s) Application is Due: May 15
Contact: Kate Kerchaert, (860) 657-7016; kate.kerchaert@baml.com
Internet: https://www.bankofamerica.com/philanthropic/fn_search.action
Sponsor: George H. C. Ensworth Memorial Fund
200 Glastonbury Boulevard, Suite # 200, CT2-545-02-05
Glastonbury, CT 06033-4056

George I. Alden Trust Grants — 2023

The Alden Trust supports independent colleges and universities in New Jersey, New York, Pennsylvania and the six New England states having fulltime traditional undergraduate enrollments of at least 1,000 students and with a total undergraduate and graduate student population (full time equivalents) of under 5,000. Furthermore, the Trust supports YMCAs in Massachusetts and educationally related organizations in the Worcester, Massachusetts area. In addition, it supports independent secondary schools in the immediate Worcester area. With respect to institutions of higher education, the Trust typically supports capital projects for academic purposes and less frequently supports restricted endowment initiatives for need-based scholarship aid, faculty development, or technology enhancement. The Trust currently favors capital projects related to teaching and learning technology in general and to the sciences in particular. Support given to YMCAs is usually for capital projects. Grants provided for educationally related organizations in the Worcester area focus on occasional capital project support.
Requirements: The Trust supports only tax-exempt IRS 501(c)3 non-profit organizations in New Jersey, New York, Pennsylvania, Connecticut, Maine, Massachusetts, New Hampshire, Rhode Island and Vermont. Application guidelines are available at the Foundation's website. Colleges and universities that are first time applicants should not expect grants in excess of $100,000. Applications may be submitted prior to the first day of each of the following months: February, May, August, October, and December. It is advisable to submit applications well in advance of the deadline, in case the Trustees desire additional information.
Restrictions: Grants are not made to individuals.
Geographic Focus: Connecticut, Maine, Massachusetts, New Hampshire, New Jersey, New York, Pennsylvania, Rhode Island, Vermont
Date(s) Application is Due: Feb 15; May 15; Aug 15; Nov 15
Contact: Warner S. Fletcher; (508) 459-8005; fax (508) 459-8305; trustees@aldentrust.org
Internet: http://www.aldentrust.org/applicationguidelines.html
Sponsor: George I. Alden Trust
370 Main Street, 11th Floor
Worcester, MA 01608

George J. and Effie L. Seay Foundation Grants — 2024

The George J. & Effie L. Seay Foundation was established in 1957 to support and promote programs and services provided by qualifying charitable organizations in the Commonwealth of Virginia. Grants from the Seay Foundation are one year in duration. Application materials are available for download at the grant website. Applicants are strongly encouraged to review the state application guidelines for additional helpful information and clarifications before applying. Applicants are also encouraged to review the trust's funding history (link is available from the grant website). The George J. & Effie L. Seay Foundation has biannual deadlines of May 1 and November 1. Applicants for the May deadline will be notified of grant decisions by June 30. Applicants for the November deadline will be notified by February 28 of the following year.
Requirements: Applications must be mailed. Applicants must be classified by the Internal Revenue Service (IRS) as a 501(c)3 public charity.
Restrictions: Because requests for support usually exceed available resources, organizations are advised to apply to either the Morgan Trust or the Seay Foundation. An organization normally will not be considered for a subsequent grant from either the Morgan Trust or the Seay Foundation until at least 3 years after the date of the last grant payment. The Seay Foundation makes grants primarily for programs and projects designed to provide specific services or training. Requests for general operating grants will not be considered. The foundation does not support requests from individuals, organizations attempting to influence policy through direct lobbying, or any political campaigns.
Geographic Focus: Virginia
Date(s) Application is Due: May 1; Nov 1
Contact: Sarah Kay, Vice President; (804) 788-2673; sarah.kay@baml.com
Internet: https://www.bankofamerica.com/philanthropic/fn_search.action
Sponsor: George J. and Effie L. Seay Foundation
1111 E. Main Street, VA2-300-12-92
Richmond, VA 23219

George Kress Foundation Grants — 2025

The foundation awards grants to eligible Wisconsin nonprofit organizations in its areas of interest, including arts and culture; boys and girls clubs; children and youth services; Christian agencies and churches; community/economic development; education; family services; health organizations; higher education; historic preservation/historical societies; hospitals; human services; libraries; recreation; United Ways and Federated Giving Programs; and YM/YWCAs and YM/YWHAs. Types of support include annual campaigns; building/renovation; capital campaigns; continuing support; professorships; program development; and research. Preference is given to nonprofit organizations that benefit Green Bay and Madison.
Requirements: There are no application forms or deadlines. Interested applicants should submit a letter of inquiry describing their proposed project.
Geographic Focus: Wisconsin
Contact: John Kress, President; (920) 433-3109
Sponsor: George Kress Foundation
c/o Green Bay Packaging Company
Green Bay, WI 54301

George P. Davenport Trust Fund Grants — 2026

Established in Maine in 1927, the Trust awards grants for education, religion, temperance and needy children. The focus of the Trust is on the economically disadvantaged. Types of support include: building and renovation, emergency funding, general operating funds, capacity building, matching/challenge funds, and seed money. It is recommended that applicants contact the Trust office to make an initial inquiry regarding projects before beginning the application process. Interested applicants should use the standard Maine Philanthropy Center common grant application which is available at mainephilanthropy.org. Grant applications are accepted all year, with no deadlines.
Requirements: Only nonprofit organizations serving the residents of Bath, Maine, and its surrounding area are eligible to apply.
Geographic Focus: Maine
Amount of Grant: 125 - 10,000 USD
Contact: Barry M. Sturgeon; (270) 443-3431; davenporttrust@verizon.net
Sponsor: George P. Davenport Trust Fund
65 Front Street
Bath, ME 04530-2508

George S. and Dolores Dore Eccles Foundation Grants — 2027

The foundation awards grants to eligible Utah organizations in its areas of interest, including arts, children and youth, economics, higher education, hospitals, medical research, performing arts, visual arts, and social services. Types of support include building construction/renovation, capital campaigns, equipment acquisition, general operating grants, matching/challenge grants, professorships, program development, research grants, and scholarship funds. A request for application is available online.
Requirements: Giving primarily in Utah.
Restrictions: Funding requests will not be considered from the following types of organizations: those that have not received a tax exemption letter establishing 501(c)3 status from the Internal Revenue Service, unless they are a unit of government, in which case such a letter is not required; other private foundations; those of a political nature that attempt to influence legislation and/or candidacy of persons for elected public office; conduit organizations, unified funds, or those that use funds to make grants to support other organizations; those that do not have fiscal responsibility for the proposed project. Funds will also not be considered for: contingencies, deficits, or debt reduction; general endowment funds; direct aid to individuals; conferences, seminars, or medical research; requests which do not fall within the Foundation's specified areas of interest.
Geographic Focus: Utah
Contact: Director; (801) 246-5340; fax (801) 350-3510; gseg@gseccles.org
Internet: http://www.gsecclesfoundation.org
Sponsor: George S. and Dolores Dore Eccles Foundation
79 South Main Street, 12th Floor
Salt Lake City, UT 84111

George W. Brackenridge Foundation Grants — 2028

The foundation awards grants in Texas to nonprofit colleges and universities, religious education organizations, accredited K-12 schools, and youth organizations such as YMCA/YWCA. Types of support include endowment funds, project grants, research grants, and scholarships. The foundation's Areas of Interest include: arts; arts education; biomedicine research; children/youth, services; christian agencies & churches; education; elementary/secondary education; higher education; human services and; the performing arts.
Requirements: Texas nonprofit organizations in the San Antonio and the surrounding area are eligible to apply. When applying for funding, submit a letter of request on the organization's letterhead. Upon review of letter of request, you may be invited to submit a proposal. Proposal should include: signature and title of chief executive officer; copy of IRS Determination Letter; copy of most recent annual report/audited financial statement/990; detailed description of project and amount of funding requested; organization's charter and by-laws; four copies of the proposal. There are no application deadlines. The board meets in March, June, September, and December each year.

Restrictions: Grants are not made to or for: individuals; general purposes; continuing support; seed money; emergency funds; land acquisition; renovation projects; building funds; operating budgets; annual campaigns; deficit financing; matching gifts; loans.
Geographic Focus: Texas
Contact: Emily D. Thuss, Treasurer; (210) 224-1011
Sponsor: George W. Brackenridge Foundation
711 Navarro Street, Suite 535
San Antonio, TX 78205-1746

George W. Codrington Charitable Foundation Grants 2029

The George W. Codrington Charitable Foundation gives primarily to nonprofit organizations in Ohio, but may consider other areas. The Foundation funds higher education, hospitals, museums, arts groups and performing arts, and youth programs. Types of support include annual and capital campaigns, continuing support, equipment, general/operating support, program development, and research.
Requirements: Application forms are not required. Applicants should submit three copies of the following: their IRS determination letter; a brief history of the organization and description of its mission; the geographic area to be served; a list of the board of directors, trustees, officers, and other key individuals with their affiliations; and a detailed description of the project and amount of funding requested. Proposals should be submitted one month before the board meets in April, June, September, and December. Organizations are notified of funding promptly after the board meeting.
Restrictions: Funding is not available for individuals, endowment funds, or loans.
Geographic Focus: Ohio
Contact: Craig Martahus; (216) 566-8674; tommie.robertston@thomasonhine.com
Sponsor: George W. Codrington Charitable Foundation
127 Public Square, 39th Floor
Cleveland, OH 44114-1216

George W. Wells Foundation Grants 2030

The George W. Wells Foundation was established in 1934 to support and promote quality educational, human-services, and health-care programming for underserved populations. In the area of education, the fund supports academic access, enrichment, and remedial programming for children, youth, adults, and senior citizens that focuses on preparing individuals to achieve while in school and beyond. In the area of health care, the fund supports programming that improves access to primary care for traditionally underserved individuals, health education initiatives and programming that impact at-risk populations, and medical research. In the area of human services the fund tries to meet evolving needs of communities. Currently the foundation's focus is on (but is not limited to) youth development, violence prevention, employment, life-skills attainment, and food programs. Special consideration is given to charitable organizations that serve the people of Southbridge, Massachusetts, and its surrounding communities. Grant requests for general operating support are strongly encouraged. Program support will also be considered. Small, program-related capital expenses may be included in general operating or program requests. The majority of grants from the Wells Foundation are one year in duration; on occasion, multi-year support is awarded. Applicants must apply online at the grant website. Applicants are strongly encouraged to do the following before applying: review the downloadable state application procedures for additional helpful information and clarifications; review the downloadable online-application guidelines at the grant website; review the foundation's funding history (link is available from the grant website); review the online application questions in advance; and review the list of required attachments. These will generally include: a list of board members, financial statements (audited, reviewed, or compiled by independent auditor); an organization summary; a list of other funding sources; an IRS Determination letter; and other required documents. All attachments must be uploaded in the online application as PDF, Word, or Excel files. The application deadline for the George W. Wells Foundation is 11:59 p.m. on October 15. Applicants will be notified of grant decisions before December 31.
Requirements: Applicants must have 501(c)3 tax-exempt status.
Restrictions: The foundation does not support requests from individuals, organizations attempting to influence policy through direct lobbying, or any political campaigns.
Geographic Focus: Massachusetts
Date(s) Application is Due: Oct 15
Contact: Miki C. Akimoto, Vice President; (866) 778-6859; miki.akimoto@baml.com
Internet: https://www.bankofamerica.com/philanthropic/fn_search.action
Sponsor: George W. Wells Foundation
225 Franklin Street, 4th Floor, MA1-225-04-02
Boston, MA 02110

Georgia-Pacific Foundation Education Grants 2031

Since its inception, the Georgia-Pacific Foundation has recognized the value of education as one of the most important and essential building blocks of a strong, thriving community. It believes that creating, supporting and nurturing worthy educational projects are paramount to achieving its philosophical goals. The Foundation continually seeks to invest in innovative and results-driven educational initiatives that it feels will make a measurable difference in communities. The Foundation is an integral part of a wide array of community-based educational programs around the world. It helps youth transition from school to the workforce, as well as provide employees with job readiness training. The scholarships and technical programs that it funds give students and workers the skills necessary to succeed in today's workplace.
Requirements: Nonprofit organizations in Georgia-Pacific communities are eligible to apply for funding. To find out whether a program qualifies for consideration for a Georgia-Pacific Foundation grant, applicants should complete the Eligibility Survey available online. The Georgia-Pacific Foundation will accept proposals for grants and in-kind donations from January 1 through October 31. It is recommended that applicants submit proposals early in the grant cycle.
Restrictions: No support is given for discriminatory organizations, political candidates, churches or religious denominations, religious or theological schools, social, labor, veteran, alumni, or fraternal organizations not of direct benefit to the entire community, athletic associations, national organizations with local chapters already receiving support, medical or nursing schools, or pass-through organizations. No grants to individuals (except for scholarships), or for emergency needs for general operating support, political causes, legislative lobbying, or advocacy efforts, goodwill advertising, sporting events, general operating support for United Way member agencies, tickets or tables for testimonials or similar benefit events, named academic chairs, social sciences or health science programs, fundraising events, or trips or tours.
Geographic Focus: Alabama, Arkansas, California, Florida, Georgia, Illinois, Indiana, Iowa, Kentucky, Louisiana, Massachusetts, Michigan, Mississippi, New Jersey, New York, North Carolina, Ohio, Oklahoma, Oregon, Pennsylvania, South Carolina, Tennessee, Texas, Virginia, Washington, West Virginia, Wisconsin
Date(s) Application is Due: Oct 31
Contact: Curley M. Dossman, Jr.; (404) 652-4182; cmdossma@gapac.com
Internet: http://gp.com/gpfoundation/education.html
Sponsor: Georgia-Pacific Foundation
133 Peachtree Street, NE, 39th Floor
Atlanta, GA 30303

Georgia-Pacific Foundation Enrichment Grants 2032

Improving the quality of life in the communities where our employees live and where we operate is of vital importance to Georgia-Pacific. One significant way the Foundation does this is by funding those initiatives that will enrich communities in long-term, measurable ways. The Foundation has consistently nurtured and supported results-driven programs that primarily deal with community safety and affordable housing. Through donations of money and building materials, the foundation has helped foster self-reliance and economic stability in many communities.
Requirements: Nonprofit organizations in Georgia-Pacific communities are eligible to apply for funding. To find out whether a program qualifies for consideration for a Georgia-Pacific Foundation grant, applicants should complete the Eligibility Survey available online. The Georgia-Pacific Foundation will accept proposals for grants and in-kind donations from January 1 through October 31. It is recommended that applicants submit proposals early in the grant cycle.
Restrictions: No support is given for discriminatory organizations, political candidates, churches or religious denominations, religious or theological schools, social, labor, veterans', alumni, or fraternal organizations not of direct benefit to the entire community, athletic associations, national organizations with local chapters already receiving support, medical or nursing schools, or pass-through organizations. No grants to individuals (except for scholarships), or for emergency needs for general operating support, political causes, legislative lobbying, or advocacy efforts, goodwill advertising, sporting events, general operating support for United Way member agencies, tickets or tables for testimonials or similar benefit events, named academic chairs, social sciences or health science programs, fundraising events, or trips or tours.
Geographic Focus: Alabama, Arkansas, California, Florida, Georgia, Illinois, Indiana, Iowa, Kentucky, Louisiana, Massachusetts, Michigan, Mississippi, New Jersey, New York, North Carolina, Ohio, Oklahoma, Oregon, Pennsylvania, South Carolina, Tennessee, Texas, Virginia, Washington, West Virginia, Wisconsin
Date(s) Application is Due: Oct 31
Contact: Curley M. Dossman, Jr.; (404) 652-4182; cmdossma@gapac.com
Internet: http://gp.com/gpfoundation/enrichment.html
Sponsor: Georgia-Pacific Foundation
133 Peachtree Street, NE, 39th Floor
Atlanta, GA 30303

Georgia-Pacific Foundation Entrepreneurship Grants 2033

Georgia-Pacific believes that self-sufficiency and economic empowerment are two indispensable elements of every strong community. Entrepreneurs are often the catalysts of these essential components. That is why the Foundation believes that to create long-term value in GP communities, it must identify and nurture the entrepreneurial spirit, especially among youth. The Foundation partners with local elementary schools, high schools and universities that encourage and inspire a student's entrepreneurial spirit and offer incentives such as accreditation and/or certificate programs. It is particularly interested in programs that help a student transition from a classroom environment to a real working business model. The Foundation has supported programs that teach practical economic principles, the benefits of a free enterprise system, and real-world business skills to workers of any age. It realizes that student entrepreneurs, when nurtured and developed, become adult entrepreneurs, creating value and free markets. So, in addition to supporting educational programs for youth, it also supports organizations that help build capacity in small, minority or women owned businesses. There is no specific dollar amount for a request for grants. The dollar amount varies based on the budget requested, program value and Georgia-Pacific funds available. Types of support available include: annual campaigns; building and renovation; capital campaigns; conferences and seminars; continuing support; employee-related scholarships; employee volunteer services; equipment; general operating support; in-kind gifts; program development; scholarship funds; sponsorships; scholarships for individuals.
Requirements: Nonprofit organizations in Georgia-Pacific communities are eligible to apply for funding. To find out whether a program qualifies for consideration for a Georgia-Pacific Foundation grant, applicants should complete the Eligibility Survey available online. The Georgia-Pacific Foundation will accept proposals for grants and in-kind donations from January 1 through October 31. It is recommended that applicants submit proposals early in the grant cycle.
Restrictions: No support is given for discriminatory organizations, political candidates, churches or religious denominations, religious or theological schools, social, labor, veterans',

alumni, or fraternal organizations not of direct benefit to the entire community, athletic associations, national organizations with local chapters already receiving support, medical or nursing schools, or pass-through organizations. No grants to individuals (except for scholarships), or for emergency needs for general operating support, political causes, legislative lobbying, or advocacy efforts, goodwill advertising, sporting events, general operating support for United Way member agencies, tickets or tables for testimonials or similar benefit events, named academic chairs, social sciences or health science programs, fundraising events, or trips or tours.
Geographic Focus: Alabama, Arkansas, California, Florida, Georgia, Illinois, Indiana, Iowa, Kentucky, Louisiana, Massachusetts, Michigan, Mississippi, New Jersey, New York, North Carolina, Ohio, Oklahoma, Oregon, Pennsylvania, South Carolina, Tennessee, Texas, Virginia, Washington, West Virginia, Wisconsin
Date(s) Application is Due: Oct 31
Contact: Curley M. Dossman, Jr.; (404) 652-4182; cmdossma@gapac.com
Internet: http://gp.com/gpfoundation/entrepreneurship.html
Sponsor: Georgia-Pacific Foundation
133 Peachtree Street, NE, 39th Floor
Atlanta, GA 30303

Georgia-Pacific Foundation Environment Grants — 2034

Since a healthy environment is crucial to any town, city or neighborhood, nowhere is Georgia-Pacific's commitment to building strong communities better exemplified than in its stewardship of natural resources and the environment. The Foundation believes that adhering to sound science is the best way to keep and protect our natural resources. Consequently, it works with scientific institutions to develop the solutions, expertise and scientific data necessary to sustain our natural resources and help resolve environmental concerns. To support these efforts, the Georgia-Pacific Foundation funds environmental programs, such as the Keystone Institute Science School, Keep America Beautiful, and The Nature Conservancy.
Requirements: Nonprofit organizations in Georgia-Pacific communities are eligible to apply for funding. To find out whether a program qualifies for consideration for a Georgia-Pacific Foundation grant, applicants should complete the Eligibility Survey available online. The Georgia-Pacific Foundation will accept proposals for grants and in-kind donations from January 1 through October 31. It is recommended that applicants submit proposals early in the grant cycle.
Restrictions: No support is given for discriminatory organizations, political candidates, churches or religious denominations, religious or theological schools, social, labor, veterans', alumni, or fraternal organizations not of direct benefit to the entire community, athletic associations, national organizations with local chapters already receiving support, medical or nursing schools, or pass-through organizations. No grants to individuals (except for scholarships), or for emergency needs for general operating support, political causes, legislative lobbying, or advocacy efforts, goodwill advertising, sporting events, general operating support for United Way member agencies, tickets or tables for testimonials or similar benefit events, named academic chairs, social sciences or health science programs, fundraising events, or trips or tours.
Geographic Focus: Alabama, Arkansas, California, Florida, Georgia, Illinois, Indiana, Iowa, Kentucky, Louisiana, Massachusetts, Michigan, Mississippi, New Jersey, New York, North Carolina, Ohio, Oklahoma, Oregon, Pennsylvania, South Carolina, Tennessee, Texas, Virginia, Washington, West Virginia, Wisconsin
Date(s) Application is Due: Oct 31
Contact: Curley M. Dossman, Jr.; (404) 652-4182; cmdossma@gapac.com
Internet: http://gp.com/gpfoundation/environment.html
Sponsor: Georgia-Pacific Foundation
133 Peachtree Street, NE, 39th Floor
Atlanta, GA 30303

Georgia Council for the Arts Partner Grants for Organizations — 2035

The mission of Georgia Council for the Arts is to cultivate the growth of vibrant, thriving Georgia communities through the arts. Georgia Council for the Arts believes that the arts can transform communities; and that grants will go to organizations that prove it. Successful applicants will have a deep understanding of their role in their community and clear, measurable goals that will demonstrate. Partner Grants provide operating support for non-profit arts organizations located in Georgia. Applicants may apply for a maximum of $25,000.
Requirements: An eligible applicant must: be an arts organization, which GCA defines as organizations with arts-based mission statements; be registered with the office of the Secretary of State; be a 501(c)3 non-profit located in Georgia; and have completed all requirements for any previous GCA grant. Eligible applications must: include arts programming that takes place between July 1 and June 30; include a one-to-one cash match in the budget; include a public component in the programming; not include programming that is exclusively by or for students that is part of a school or college class or activity (school/college applicants must demonstrate that their proposed projects will benefit the wider community outside of the school itself; not include programming that promotes a specific religious doctrine or political party or candidate; be submitted with no missing components by the deadline of 4:45 p.m., February 12.
Geographic Focus: Georgia
Date(s) Application is Due: Feb 12
Amount of Grant: Up to 25,000 USD
Contact: Tina Lilly, Grants Program Manager; (404) 962-4827; tlilly@gaarts.org
Internet: http://www.gaarts.org/images/FY14Guidelines/fy14%20partner%20grant%20arts%20organizations_121712.pdf
Sponsor: Georgia Council for the Arts
75 Fifth Street, NW, Suite 1200
Atlanta, GA 30308

Georgia Council for the Arts Partner Grants for Service Organizations — 2036

The mission of Georgia Council for the Arts is to cultivate the growth of vibrant, thriving Georgia communities through the arts. Partner Grants provide operating support for arts organizations located in Georgia. Applicants may apply for a maximum of $25,000.
Requirements: An eligible applicant must: be an arts service organization, which GCA defines as organizations with an arts-based mission statement that provide support and services to artists and/or arts organizations. Eligible applications must: include arts programming that takes place between July 1 and June 30; include a one-to-one cash match in the budget; include a public component in the programming; not include programming that is exclusively by or for students that is part of a school or college class or activity (school/college applicants must demonstrate that their proposed projects will benefit the wider community outside of the school itself; not include programming that promotes a specific religious doctrine or political party or candidate; be submitted with no missing components by the deadline of 4:45 p.m., February 12.
Restrictions: Grant awards may not be used to fund the following expenditures, though they may be funded through cash, donations or discretionary funds: payment to parents for their participation in the project; teacher per session compensation; teacher per diem reimbursements; artist residencies during the school day.
Geographic Focus: Georgia
Date(s) Application is Due: Feb 12
Amount of Grant: Up to 25,000,000 USD
Contact: Tina Lilly, Grants Program Manager; (404) 962-4827; tlilly@gaarts.org
Internet: http://www.gaarts.org/images/fy14%20partner%20grant%20arts%20service%20organizations_final_121712.pdf
Sponsor: Georgia Council for the Arts
75 Fifth Street, NW, Suite 1200
Atlanta, GA 30308

Georgia Council for the Arts Project Grants — 2037

Project Grants provide support for arts projects in Georgia that help GCA achieve the Council's goal of Community Impact. Projects may be one-time events, such as a festival or exhibit; or a series of events, such as a roster of classes or a series of productions. Projects with multiple components must show that there is a cohesive thread and singular goal that ties the elements together. Grants will go to programs that fill needs in a community and have a deep, lasting and significant impact. Applicants may apply for a maximum of $5,000, and the annual application deadline is February 12.
Requirements: An eligible applicant must be one of the following: a non-profit organization located within Georgia and registered with the Georgia Secretary of State; a school or college/university, or a department or entity within a college/university; or a government entity. A one-to-one cash match in the budget is required.
Restrictions: Funds are not awarded for: projects limited to an historical focus, such as re-enactments or re-creations of the past; research conducted for the sole purpose of scholarly pursuit; projects dealing with dramatic or theatrical reproduction of traditional materials, such as interpretations of the traditional arts performed by non-traditional artists; productions or presentations by contemporary artists who have learned a traditional art through non-traditional means, other than the process as traditionally taught by traditional artisans and artists; projects that have been or will be in operation for more than two years, unless project funds are being applied for to overhaul and significantly change the current project design.
Geographic Focus: Georgia
Date(s) Application is Due: Feb 12
Amount of Grant: Up to 5,000 USD
Contact: Tina Lilly, Grants Program Manager; (404) 962-4827; tlilly@gaarts.org
Internet: http://www.gaarts.org/images/FY14Guidelines/fy14%20project%20grant_final_v3.pdf
Sponsor: Georgia Council for the Arts
75 Fifth Street, NW, Suite 1200
Atlanta, GA 30308

Georgiana Goddard Eaton Memorial Fund Grants — 2038

Established in 1917, the Trust supports organizations involved with improving the lives of low-income individuals of Boston, Massachusetts. The fields of interest are: education; employment; family services; homelessness; housing/shelter; human services; legal services; urban/community development. Contact the Foundation for further application information and guidelines.
Requirements: Non-profits in the Boston, MA area are eligible. Applications should be addressed to: c/o Grants Mgmt. Assocs., 77 Summer Street, 8th Floor, Boston, MA 02110-1006
Restrictions: No grants to individuals (except former employees of Community Workshops, Inc.), or for endowment funds, or matching gifts; no loans.
Geographic Focus: Massachusetts
Date(s) Application is Due: Mar 1; Sep 1
Contact: Philip Hall; (617) 426-7080; fax (617) 426-7087; phall@grantsmanagement.com
Sponsor: Georgiana Goddard Eaton Memorial Fund
45 School Street
Boston, MA 0002108-3206

Georgia Power Foundation Grants — 2039

Giving is focused on issues that directly affect customers, employees, business and shareholders. These include: improving the quality of education by partnering with organizations to assist students with personal development, mentoring and career exploration; protecting the environment by promoting programs to improve air and water quality, preserve natural resources and protect endangered species; preventing cancer; and promoting diversity. The Foundation gives strong preference to Georgia-based organizations and programs that seek to improve the quality of life for the state's residents. Applicants may apply online or with a written proposal.

Requirements: The foundation makes grants to tax-exempt organizations that seek to improve the quality of life for Georgia's residents.
Restrictions: The Foundation does not provide grants to individuals, private elementary or secondary schools, and religious organizations, nor political campaigns or causes. The Foundation does not provide multi-year funding commitments.
Geographic Focus: Georgia
Date(s) Application is Due: Feb 15; May 15; Aug 15; Nov 15
Amount of Grant: 10,000 USD
Contact: Grants Administrator; (404) 506-6784; gpfoundation@southernco.com
Internet: http://www.georgiapower.com/community/apply.asp
Sponsor: Georgia Power Foundation
241 Ralph McGill Boulevard NE, Bin 10131
Atlanta, GA 30308-3374

Geraldine R. Dodge Foundation Arts Grants 2040
The Dodge Foundation invites proposals for general operating or project-specific support from organizations that: enhance the cultural richness of the community in which they reside and contribute to New Jersey's creative economy. Priority will be given to those that: pursue and demonstrate the highest standards of artistic excellence; provide opportunities for meaningful connections between people and art within their communities, and partner with others to expand the inclusiveness and the impact of the arts; contribute to the diverse human narrative by creating new work and/or re-imagining the classics; provide creative opportunities and living wages for New Jersey artists; use the arts to revitalize public places and natural spaces and/or help citizens engage in and advocate for the environmental well-being of their communities. Letters of inquiry should be received by August 1, with full proposals due by August 30.
Requirements: In order to be eligible for funding, an applicant must: be a 501(c)3 organization that makes its home in or has a significant impact on New Jersey; demonstrate that it has the administrative and financial capacity to achieve and assess the stated goals of the proposal; be led by an effective and professional, paid staff; have a high-functioning board, with an expectation of 100% of its trustees making an annual personal contribution; and strive to make connections with other organizations, especially Dodge grantees, working in the same community or on the same issues.
Restrictions: Funding is not provided for: higher education; health; religion; capital programs; equipment purchases; indirect costs; endowment funds; and deficit reduction. The Foundation does not make direct awards to individuals or support lobbying efforts.
Geographic Focus: New Jersey
Date(s) Application is Due: Mar 1; Aug 30; Dec 3
Amount of Grant: 15,000 - 75,000 USD
Contact: Laura Aden Packer, Program Director; (973) 540-8442, ext. 105; fax (973) 540-1211; lpacker@grdodge.org or info@grdodge.org
Internet: http://www.grdodge.org/what-we-fund/arts/
Sponsor: Geraldine R. Dodge Foundation
14 Maple Avenue, Suite 400
Morristown, NJ 07960

Geraldine R. Dodge Foundation Environment Grants 2041
The Geraldine R. Dodge Foundation Environmental Grants program encourages comprehensive thinking about how to safeguard water and reinforce natural systems in order to promote more sustainable communities. The Foundation also supports ongoing, careful stewardship of the land, which includes efforts to support sustainable agriculture and develop regional food systems that offer plentiful access to fresh, local foods. It is particularly interested in empowering communities to identify their own unique challenges and opportunities, and to take ownership of thoughtful planning and decision-making. Furthermore, the Foundation believes that protecting limited resources must fundamentally include efforts to connect people to their natural environment. In particular, the Foundation strives to fulfill this vision for the Environment in New Jersey by funding organizations that: increase the quality, function and public accessibility of watersheds through land preservation, resource management, and stewardship; focus on urban greening, particularly through community-led design and decision making; and help develop regional food systems, including rural-to-urban farming connections and urban food market development. Letters of inquiry should be received by August 1, with full proposals due by August 30.
Requirements: In order to be eligible for funding, an applicant must: be a 501(c)3 organization that makes its home in or has a significant impact on New Jersey; demonstrate that it has the administrative and financial capacity to achieve and assess the stated goals of the proposal; be led by an effective and professional, paid staff; have a high-functioning board, with an expectation of 100% of its trustees making an annual personal contribution; and strive to make connections with other organizations, especially Dodge grantees, working in the same community or on the same issues.
Restrictions: Funding is not provided for: higher education; health; religion; capital programs; equipment purchases; indirect costs; endowment funds; and deficit reduction. The Foundation does not make direct awards to individuals or support lobbying efforts.
Geographic Focus: New Jersey
Date(s) Application is Due: Mar 1; Aug 30; Dec 3
Amount of Grant: 10,000 - 150,000 USD
Contact: Margaret Waldock, Program Director; (973) 540-8442, ext. 117; fax (973) 540-1211; mwaldock@grdodge.org or info@grdodge.org
Internet: http://www.grdodge.org/what-we-fund/environment/
Sponsor: Geraldine R. Dodge Foundation
14 Maple Avenue, Suite 400
Morristown, NJ 07960

Geraldine R. Dodge Foundation Media Grants 2042
The Dodge Foundation supports traditional and innovative uses of media to educate and engage the public around issues of importance to New Jersey and its citizens, as well as efforts to uncover abuses of power by the institutions the public trusts. The Foundation also believe that youth must be given a voice if they are to actively participate in civic affairs, and that communities thrive when their members are well-informed and seek to improve their lives as well as those of their neighbors. The Foundation strives to fulfill this vision for Media in New Jersey by funding organizations that: broaden and make more available New Jersey-centric news and programming; focus on investigative reporting of government, businesses and institutions; inform the public about issues related to the Foundation's priority funding areas; and empower youth and promote leadership through media production. Letters of inquiry should be received by August 30, with full proposals due by August 30.
Requirements: In order to be eligible for funding, an applicant must: be a 501(c)3 organization that makes its home in or has a significant impact on New Jersey; demonstrate that it has the administrative and financial capacity to achieve and assess the stated goals of the proposal; be led by an effective and professional, paid staff; have a high-functioning board, with an expectation of 100% of its trustees making an annual personal contribution; and strive to make connections with other organizations, especially Dodge grantees, working in the same community or on the same issues.
Restrictions: Funding is not provided for: higher education; health; religion; capital programs; equipment purchases; indirect costs; endowment funds; and deficit reduction. The Foundation does not make direct awards to individuals or support lobbying efforts.
Geographic Focus: New Jersey
Date(s) Application is Due: Mar 1; Aug 30; Dec 3
Amount of Grant: 7,500 - 125,000 USD
Contact: Molly de Aguiar, Director of Communications; (973) 540-8442, ext. 156; fax (973) 540-1211; mdeaguiar@grdodge.org or info@grdodge.org
Internet: http://www.grdodge.org/what-we-fund/media/
Sponsor: Geraldine R. Dodge Foundation
14 Maple Avenue, Suite 400
Morristown, NJ 07960

Germanistic Society of America Fellowships 2043
Usually up to six fellowships are awarded annually to enable prospective specialists to study for an academic year in Germany, primarily in art history; economics and banking; German language and literature; history; international law; philosophy; political science; and public affairs. Candidates selected for these awards, administered in the United States by the IIE, will be considered for Fulbright travel grants.
Requirements: A master's degree is desirable, but candidates must have a bachelor's degree and be U.S. citizens by November 1 of the year preceding the award.
Geographic Focus: All States
Amount of Grant: 12,000 USD
Contact: U.S. Student Division; (212) 984-5330; fax (212) 984-5325; info@iie.org
Internet: http://www.iie.org/Content/NavigationMenu/Fulbright_Demo_Site/U_S__Student_Program/Fulbright_Grant_Opportunities/Germany.htm
Sponsor: Institute of International Education
1400 K Street, NW, 7th Floor
Washington, DC 20005-2403

German Protestant Orphan Asylum Foundation Grants 2044
The German Protestant Orphan Asylum (GP.O.A) Foundation Grants funding to support programs that serve children in Louisiana. The majority of those funded offer programs in the areas of education (tutoring, literacy, LEAP remediation, after school and summer programs, GED prep, early childhood education, child abuse prevention); enrichment (arts/music, mentoring, summer camps); life skills/pre-vocational training (parenting skills, work skills); and school-based health (mental health, vision screenings, immunizations, speech pathology). The Foundation makes grant decisions in May, August, November, and February. The Foundation's average grant award is $10,000 within a range of $1,000 to $40,000.
Requirements: A concept paper is required before submitting a proposal. Applicants should download, complete, then mail one original plus 12 copies of the one-page concept paper at least four months prior to their need for funds. The concept paper will be reviewed, and the organization will be notified whether a full proposal is invited. If a full proposal is invited, the organization should then download and fill out the GP.O.A Grant Proposal Form, and mail one original plus 12 copies to the Foundation by the deadline.
Restrictions: The Foundation does not fund building or renovation expenses, sponsorship of special events, individual scholarships, or programs which do not serve children in Louisiana. Equipment is rarely funded.
Geographic Focus: Louisiana
Amount of Grant: 4,000 - 40,000 USD
Contact: Lisa Kaichen, Foundation Manager; (985) 674-5328 or (504) 895-2361; fax (504) 674-0490; gpoafoundation@aol.com
Internet: http://www.gpoafoundation.org/amenities.html
Sponsor: German Protestant Orphan Asylum Association
P.O. Box 158
Mandeville, LA 70470

Gertrude and William C. Wardlaw Fund Grants 2045
Established in 1936 in Georgia, the Gertrude and William C. Wardlaw Fund awards general operating grants to Georgia nonprofit organizations in its areas of interest, including: cultural activities; the arts; community development; education and higher education; and health care and hospitals. Specific application forms are not required, and there are no specified annual deadlines. Grants typically range from $2,500 to $50,000.
Requirements: Georgia nonprofit organizations are eligible to apply.

Geographic Focus: Georgia
Amount of Grant: 2,500 - 50,000 USD
Samples: Metro Atlant Task Force, Atlanta, Georgia, $50,000 - operating costs (2011); Wardlaw School, Atlanta, Georgia, $20,000 - general operating costs (2011); Viola White Water Foundation, Atlanta, Georgia, $2,500 - general operations (2011).
Contact: Gregorie Guthrie, Secretary; (404) 419-3260 or (404) 827-6529
Sponsor: Gertrude and William C. Wardlaw Fund
One Riverside Building
Atlanta, GA 30327

Gertrude E. Skelly Charitable Foundation Grants 2046
The primary mission of the Foundation is to provide educational opportunities, primarily at colleges and universities, and needed medical care for those who cannot afford them. The advisory committee will meet in October to review applications. There is no formal application. Interested applicants will contact the Foundation to receive application instructions and guidelines.
Requirements: 501(c)3 organizations, including colleges and universities, are eligible.
Restrictions: Funding is not available for endowments or capital projects. Multi-year commitments are generally not favored. Grants will not be made to private foundations, non-charitable organizations or directly to individuals.
Geographic Focus: All States
Date(s) Application is Due: Jul 31
Amount of Grant: Up to 50,000 USD
Contact: Bettee M. Collister; (561) 276-1008; fax (561) 272-2793; skelly@erikjoh.com
Sponsor: Gertrude E. Skelly Charitable Foundation
4600 North Ocean Boulevard, Suite 206
Boynton Beach, FL 33435-7365

Gertrude M. Conduff Foundation Grants 2047
During her lifetime, Gertrude M. Conduff supported many causes, but a specific area of interest was for the care and well-being of the elderly and those with special needs. The Gertrude M. Conduff Foundation was established in 2003 to support organizations that promote independent living for the elderly and those with special needs. Requests for general operating funds are rarely awarded. Requests for endowment funds are considered, however they are subordinate to program-related requests. Applicants must apply online at the grant website. Applicants are strongly encouraged to do the following before applying: review the downloadable state-specific application procedures at the grant website; review the downloadable online-application guidelines at the grant website; review the foundation's funding history (link is available from the grant website); review the online application questions in advance; and review the list of required attachments. These will generally include: a list of board members, financial statements (audited, reviewed, or compiled by independent auditor); an organization summary; a list of other funding sources; an IRS Determination letter; and other required documents. All attachments must be uploaded in the online application as PDF, Word, or Excel files. Grants from the Conduff Foundation are one year in duration. The Conduff Foundation has a deadline of March 15 at 11:59 p.m. Applicants will generally be notified by May 30.
Restrictions: The foundation does not support requests from individuals, organizations attempting to influence policy through direct lobbying, or any political campaigns.
Geographic Focus: Virginia
Date(s) Application is Due: Mar 15
Contact: Sarah Kay, Vice President; (804) 788-2673; sarah.kay@baml.com
Internet: https://www.bankofamerica.com/philanthropic/fn_search.action
Sponsor: Gertrude M. Conduff Foundation
1111 E. Main Street, VA2-300-12-92
Richmond, VA 23219

Gheens Foundation Grants 2048
The Foundation makes grants in Metro Louisville, Kentucky and LaFourche and Terrebonne Parishes in Louisiana. The Foundation supports a wide variety of endeavors at all levels, including education, economic development, medical, arts, social/health services, handicapped, and mental health programs. Foundation focus is on education and Christian works. There are no deadlines for applications. Guidelines and application information are available online.
Requirements: The Foundation contributes only to 501(c)3 organizations that are not private foundations.
Restrictions: The Foundation does not give to individuals.
Geographic Focus: Kentucky, Louisiana
Contact: Carl Thomas; (502) 584-4650; fax (502) 584-4652; carl@gheensfoundation.org
Internet: http://gheensfoundation.org/grant_application
Sponsor: Gheens Foundation
705 One Riverfont Plaza, 401 West Main Street
Louisville, KY 40202

Giant Eagle Foundation Grants 2049
The foundation awards grants in Pennsylvania in its areas of interest, including community development; health and human services; Jewish agencies, charitable organizations, and temples; performing arts; and philanthropy. Types of support include project grants and employee-related scholarship. There are no application deadlines. The board meets four times each year to review requests.
Requirements: Pennsylvania nonprofit organizations are eligible. Preference will be given to requests from Pittsburgh.
Geographic Focus: Ohio, Pennsylvania
Amount of Grant: 1,000 - 2,000 USD
Contact: David Shapira, Coordinator; (412) 963-6200
Sponsor: Giant Eagle Foundation
101 Kappa Drive
Pittsburgh, PA 15238

Giant Food Charitable Grants 2050
The Giant Food Charitable Grants provide funding and in-kind assistance to hundreds of charitable events and causes in schools, churches, synagogues, and civic community groups. Giant's focus is hunger relief programs, education, and wellness initiatives. Grant amounts vary, and there are no application deadlines. Submit requests by mail only.
Requirements: Organizations must send requests in writing on their letterhead, along with proof of their 501(c)3 status, and a description of the project.
Restrictions: Funding is available only in areas where Giant Food operates: District of Columbia, Maryland, Virginia, and Delaware.
Geographic Focus: Delaware, District of Columbia, Maryland, Virginia
Contact: Jamie Miller; (301) 341-8776; jmiller@giantofmaryland.com
Internet: http://www.giantfood.com/about_us/community/index.htm
Sponsor: Giant Food Corporation
8301 Professional Place, Suite 115
Landover, MD 20785

Gibson County Community Foundation Women's Fund 2051
The Gibson County Women's Fund will award a grant once a year to a single project serving women in Gibson County. Grant applications are considered on a yearly cycle which runs from June through September. Grant applications are accepted during this time period. email notices are sent to organizations that have signed up to receive information about the grant cycle. Project areas considered for funding must meet at least one of the following criteria: community development - activities that benefit women in the community or address gender equity issues within all segments of the population; education - activities that promote or strengthen the educational attainment of women, both in and out of the classroom; health - activities that improve the health outcomes for women; human services - activities that support public protection, employment/jobs, food and nutrition, agriculture, housing and shelter, public safety, disaster preparedness, and relief for women; other civic endeavors - activities that will improve the quality of life for women in Gibson County. A $5,000 grant is awarded to a single organization identified at the Women's Fund membership annual meeting. The remaining four finalists will each received $500. The application is available at the website.
Requirements: The Women's Fund welcomes applications from nonprofit organizations that are tax exempt under sections 501(c)3 and 509(a) of the Internal Revenue Code and from governmental agencies serving all women of Gibson County. Applications are also accepted from other nonprofit organizations carrying out charitable projects or activities that address issues facing women in Gibson County. In some cases, organizations without the 501(c)3 designation may be required to obtain a fiscal sponsor. Prospective applicants are invited to attend a meeting with the director to receive an overview of the funding opportunity and to ask specific questions.
Restrictions: Funding will not be considered for: requests for funding to reduce or retire debt of the organization; projects that focus solely on the spiritual needs and growth of a church congregation or members of other religious organizations; political parties or campaigns; operating costs not directly related to the proposed project (the organization's general operating expenses including equipment, staff salary, rent, and utilities); event sponsorships, annual appeals, and membership contributions; travel expenses for groups or individuals such as bands, sports teams, or classes; and scholarships or other grants to individuals.
Geographic Focus: Indiana
Date(s) Application is Due: Sep 1
Amount of Grant: 500 - 5,000 USD
Contact: Tami Muckerheide; (812) 386-8082; tami@gibsoncountyfoundation.org
Internet: http://www.gibsoncountyfoundation.org/gibson-womens-fund-grantmaking
Sponsor: Gibson County Community Foundation
109 North Hart Street, P.O. Box 180
Princeton, IN 47670

Gibson Foundation Grants 2052
The Foundation is committed to making the world a better place for children by creating, developing and supporting programs and other non-profit organizations in their efforts to advance education, music and the arts, the environment and health & welfare causes. The Foundation actively seeks out programs that will be a direct mission-fit and further its goals.
Requirements: Applicants must be 501(c)3 organizations.
Restrictions: The Foundation does not support religious or political affiliations, and does not award individual scholarships.
Geographic Focus: All States
Contact: Nina Miller; (615) 871-4500, ext. 2114; fax (615) 884-9597; nina.miller@gibson.com
Internet: http://www.gibson.com/en-us/Lifestyle/GibsonFoundation/
Sponsor: Gibson Foundation
309 Plus Park Boulevard
Nashville, TN 37217

Gil and Dody Weaver Foundation Grants 2053
Established in Texas in 1980, the Gil and Dody Weaver Foundation offers support throughout the States of Texas, Oklahoma, and Louisiana, with some emphasis on the Dallas-Fort worth area. The Foundation's primary fields of interest include: cancer; children and youth services; education; health organizations; human services; social services; and recreational camps. Major types of support come in the form of: annual campaigns; general operating/continual support; and scholarship funds. Although no formal application is required, the Foundation does provide specific application guidelines. These guidelines require a history

of the organization, detailed information about the proposed project, and budgetary needs. The annual deadline is May 31, with final notifications by September 30. Recent grants have ranged from $1,000 to $20,000, with occasional higher amounts for special circumstances.
Requirements: 501(c)3 organization serving the residents of Texas, Oklahoma, and Louisiana, are welcome to apply.
Restrictions: No grants are given to individuals. No applications are accepted from organizations located in states other than Texas, Oklahoma, or Louisiana.
Geographic Focus: California, Louisiana, Mississippi, New Mexico, Oklahoma, Texas
Date(s) Application is Due: May 31
Amount of Grant: 1,000 - 20,000 USD
Contact: William R. Weaver, (214) 999-9497; fax (214) 999-9496
Sponsor: Gil and Dody Weaver Foundation
1845 Woodall Rodgers Freeway, Suite 1275
Dallas, TX 75201-2299

Gill Foundation - Gay and Lesbian Fund Grants 2054
In partnership with grantees, the Fund works to create a vibrant, healthy Colorado, where all families can thrive, while being a vehicle for cultural change toward equality for all. Programs of interest are: arts and culture; civic leadership; healthy families; and public broadcasting. Grantmaking is carried out in three ways: events sponsorship; invitation only; and opportunity grants. Requests may not exceed 15% of an organization's total budget, or for event sponsorships, may not exceed 50% of the event budget. Application information is available online.
Requirements: Eligible recipients must: be a 501(c)3 public charity organization; have a board-approved employment nondiscrimination policy in the organization's by-laws, employee manual or other official source stating explicitly that employees will not be discriminated against based on sexual orientation; provide services or programming within the state of Colorado.
Restrictions: Funding is not available for: organizations that are not a 501(c)3 public charity; lesbian, gay, bisexual, and transgender, or HIV/AIDS organizations; housing developments; emergency requests; endowments; individuals; major capital campaigns or projects; golf tournaments; film production or promotion.
Geographic Focus: Colorado
Contact: Manager; (800) 964-5643 or (719) 473-4455; info@gayandlesbianfund.org
Internet: http://www.gillfoundation.org/glfc_grants/glfc_grants_show.htm?doc_id=408610&cat_id=1394
Sponsor: Gill Foundation
315 East Costilla Street
Colorado Springs, CO 80903

Ginger and Barry Ackerley Foundation Grants 2055
The Ginger & Barry Ackerley Foundation makes grants to public and private organizations that sponsor programs enhancing the education of young learners under the age of five, in the greater Puget Sound region. The Foundation focuses on organizations involved in skills support, literacy development, mentoring relationships and programs that connect school and home in order to produce specific and measurable results in early learning. Grants are usually made for capital drives, endowments and specific program objectives, not operating budgets. Grants are generally to be expended within one year, without expectation of further support. Priority will be given to requests that show specific plans for funding beyond the present.
Requirements: Washington State 501(c)3 tax-exempt organizations, with an active board of directors, with policy-making authority are eligible to apply. The board should demonstrate competence in the sound financial management of the organization. Organizations seeking grant support must receive an invitation from the Ackerley Foundation prior to submitting an application. To initiate the process, organizations that fit within the Foundation's mission and guidelines should submit a letter of inquiry describing the organization, the program the request is for, and the amount of funding sought. The process continues as follows: the Foundation arranges visits and meetings to learn more about the organization; suitable organizations are invited to apply for funding (Grant Request Summary form available online at the Foundation's website); all organizations must fulfill the written application requirements. The Foundation evaluates funding requests twice annually, typically in March and October. Application deadlines will be established according to funding needs and program timing.
Restrictions: Funding is not available for: organizations that discriminate on the basis of race, color, creed, sex, marital status, or handicap; individuals, except scholarship recipients chosen by educational institutions; political candidates, organizations, or committees; religious organizations whose mission, policies or practices declare a purely denominational intent; debt retirement or operating deficits, loans, or investments; team sponsorships, individual athletic endeavors, or travel expenses; annual fund drives; administrative salaries.
Geographic Focus: Washington
Amount of Grant: 100 - 500,000 USD
Contact: Twyla McFarlane, (206) 624-2888; info@ackerleyfoundation.com
Internet: http://www.ackerleyfoundation.org/apply/guidelines.html
Sponsor: Ginger and Barry Ackerley Foundation
4105 East Madison Street, Suite 210
Seattle, WA 98112

Ginn Foundation Grants 2056
The foundation's mission is to address educational and community-based health care needs through supporting effective programs and services that bring about long-term solutions for individuals and the community, principally in Cuyahoga County, OH. The Foundation will consider not only grants to academic institutions, but also to organizations that meet non-academic educational needs, such as, programs that address issues of disease avoidance, child and family counseling, after-school training, arts, housing, and employment. Preference in all of these areas will be given to organizations and programs that serve low-income recipients. Faxed applications will not be considered. Application information is available online.
Requirements: Nonprofit organizations in Cuyahoga County, OH, may apply. Consideration will also be given to trustee-sponsored grants to similar types of organizations in the Chicago, Washington, DC, and Minneapolis-St. Paul metropolitan areas.
Restrictions: The foundation will not fund requests for support of advocacy activities. Nor will it make grants to endowment, capital, or annual fund campaigns. The foundation will not fund special events or attendance at conferences or symposia.
Geographic Focus: District of Columbia, Illinois, Minnesota, Ohio
Date(s) Application is Due: Mar 15; Sep 15
Amount of Grant: 5,000 - 30,000 USD
Contact: Walter Pope Ginn, Trustee; info@ginnfoundation.org
Internet: http://www.ginnfoundation.org/index.html
Sponsor: Ginn Foundation
13938 A Cedar Road, P.O. Box 239
Cleveland Heights, OH 44118

Girl's Best Friend Foundation Grants 2057
The foundation supports and promotes programs by and for girls and young women in Illinois (ages eight through 21). The foundation is dedicated to effecting change at the grassroots level by funding community-based organizations statewide. Types of grants made include general operating support, project specific support, planning or start-up support, technical assistance, and collaborative action research (research that lays the groundwork for policy changes conducted by a partnership between two nonprofits or a nonprofit contracting with a researcher or academic institution). When multiyear funding is requested, the foundation will consider making two-year grants if the requesting organization has received at least two previous grants from GBF, is seeking two years of funding for the same purpose, and has clearly demonstrated the need for a two-year grant. Applications are due the first Monday in August.
Requirements: Letters of intent will be accepted from 501(c)3 nonprofits for projects that serve or have a direct impact on girls living in the Chicago metropolitan area including Cook, DuPage, Kane, Lake, McHenry, and Will counties.
Restrictions: Organizations with budgets that exceed $650,000 may apply only for technical assistance and/or collaborative action research grants. The foundation generally does not fund individuals, capital campaigns, debt reduction, scholarships, or government or religious organizations.
Geographic Focus: Illinois
Amount of Grant: 5,000 - 20,000 USD
Contact: Robin Dixon, Senior Program Officer; (312) 266-2842; fax (312) 266-2972; robin@girlsbestfriend.org or contact@girlsbestfriend.org
Internet: http://www.girlsbestfriend.org/apply/index.html
Sponsor: Girl's Best Friend Foundation
900 N Franklin, Suite 210
Chicago, IL 60610

Giving Sum Annual Grant 2058
Giving Sum is an organization of next generation givers working together to identify challenges in the community and to address them through education, engagement, inspiration and grants. Giving Sum is a charitable giving vehicle pooling resources raised through memberships, sponsorships, and fundraisers to establish annual grants for recipients selected by the organization and its members. Each year Giving Sum will grant 100 percent of its membership contributions to a nonprofit organization in Indianapolis working towards change. Members will be proactive in searching out these organizations in the greater Indianapolis area and having them apply.
Requirements: To be eligible, organizations must be recognized by the Internal Revenue Service as a public charity under sections 501(c)3 and 509(a)(1), (2), or (3) of the Internal Revenue Code, and provide a copy of their determination letter from the Internal Revenue Service. Organizations or the proposed project must serve audiences within the greater Indianapolis area, including the counties of: Boone, Hamilton, Hancock, Hendricks, Johnson, Marion, Morgan and Shelby. Eligible nonprofit organizations may submit only one application to request a grant of $50,000 (Money), volunteer hours (Time) and advocacy efforts (Voice) from Giving Sum to support general operations or special projects in one of Giving Sum's five Focus Areas (Arts, Culture & Humanities, Civic & Community Development, Education, Environment, and Health & Human Services). Each organization must select one of the above focus areas in which to apply. Applicants should select the focus area which best describes the primary operations or mission of their organization. If your organization and/or request is multi-disciplinary, select the category which best describes the activities that will be carried out using the Giving Sum grant. Preliminary review of the applications occurs within each of the five focus areas. Preference will be given to applications that meaningfully and creatively engage Giving Sum members in innovative, high-impact initiatives.
Restrictions: Grant funds may not be used to lobby or otherwise attempt to influence legislation, to influence the outcome of any public election, or to carry on any voter registration drive.
Geographic Focus: Indiana
Amount of Grant: 50,000 USD
Contact: Ryan Brady, Program Director; (317) 634-2423; grants@givingsum.org
Internet: http://givingsum.org/grants.asp
Sponsor: Giving Sum
615 N Alabama Street, Suite 119
Indianapolis, IN 46204-1498

Gladys Brooks Foundation Grants 2059
At the beginning of each year, the Foundation Board determines a limited scope of activities for which it will consider grant applications. Current giving will be in the fields of libraries, education, hospitals, and clinics. Applications will be considered where: outside funding (including governmental) is not available; the project will be largely funded by the grant unless the grant request covers a discrete component of a larger project; and the funds will be used for capital projects including equipment or endowments. The Foundation's application form must be used and is available online. Electronic submissions are not acceptable.
Requirements: The foundation makes grants to nonprofit, private, publicly supported, tax-exempt organizations located in Connecticut, Delaware, Florida, Illinois, Indiana, Louisiana, Maine, Maryland, Massachusetts, New Hampshire, New Jersey, New York, Ohio, Pennsylvania, Rhode Island, Tennessee, and Vermont.
Restrictions: Applications for direct salary support will not be accepted. No portion of grants shall be appropriated as an administrative or processing fee, for overseeing the project or for its general overhead.
Geographic Focus: Connecticut, Delaware, Florida, Illinois, Indiana, Louisiana, Maine, Maryland, Massachusetts, New Hampshire, New Jersey, New York, Ohio, Pennsylvania, Rhode Island, Tennessee, Vermont
Date(s) Application is Due: Jun 1
Amount of Grant: 50,000 - 100,000 USD
Contact: Jessica Rutledge, (516) 746-6103
Internet: http://www.gladysbrooksfoundation.org
Sponsor: Gladys Brooks Foundation
1055 Franklin Avenue, Suite 208
Garden City, NY 11530

GlaxoSmithKline Corporate Grants 2060
In the United States, GlaxoSmithKline Corporate makes charitable contributions through its U.S. Contributions Committee. Requests for US-based community partnerships with nonprofit organizations should address issues in one of four general areas: education—science education, K-12 literacy, teacher professional development; health and human services—child health or prevention and access to health care for women related to breast or gynecologic cancers, targeting the needs of underserved and diverse populations; arts and culture—local organizations in the Greater Philadelphia and the Research Triangle Park areas, based on local needs, focusing on public school educational outreach; and civic and community—local organizations in the Greater Philadelphia and the Research Triangle Park areas, based on local needs.
Requirements: Organizations based in the United States that have a 501(c)3 IRS designation and that meet GSK's corporate criteria for funding may complete an application. Funding for the arts and civic programs is concentrated exclusively in the Greater Philadelphia and Research Triangle Park areas where employees live and work.
Restrictions: As a matter of policy, grants are not provided for general operating expenses or capital building costs, and they are not made to individuals. Grants are not given to political, religious, fraternal, profit-making, discriminatory, hobby-oriented, or tax-subsidized organizations.
Geographic Focus: Pennsylvania
Amount of Grant: Up to 100,000,000 USD
Contact: Mary Anne Rhyne; (919) 483-2319; community.partnership@gsk.com
Internet: http://us.gsk.com/html/community/community-grants-corporate.html
Sponsor: GlaxoSmithKline Corporation
1 Franklin Plaza, FP2130, P.O. Box 7929
Philadelphia, PA 19101-7929

GlaxoSmithKline Foundation IMPACT Awards 2061
The awards reward excellence in the delivery of nonprofit community health care. Awards are made to small and mid-size community-based health care organizations in the greater Philadelphia area and, the Research Triangle Park, North Carolina area. Selection criteria include: commitment to serving people in need; facilitating access to health care delivery, education, creative partnerships, and policy development; and demonstration of a solid record of achievement, management, and leadership. The application process for the GlaxoSmithKline 1st Annual IMPACT Awards in the Research Triangle Park, North Carolina region closed on May 15. July 15 is the deadline date for the greater Philadelphia region.
Requirements: Nominees in the following Philadelphia counties are eligible: Berks, Bucks, Chester, Delaware, Lancaster, Montgomery, or Philadelphia or in the City of Camden, NJ. Nominees in the following Research Triangle Park, North Carolina counties are: Chatham, Durham, Orange and Wake Counties. Organizations must have an operating or program budget of under $2 million and have been in existence at least five years. Nonprofit healthcare organizations must be nominated by individuals knowledgeable of the complexities and challenges of healthcare delivery in their communities.
Geographic Focus: Pennsylvania
Date(s) Application is Due: May 15; Jul 15
Contact: Mary Anne Rhyne; (919) 483-2319; community.partnership@gsk.com
Internet: http://www.gsk-us.com/html/community/community-healthcare-awards.html
Sponsor: GlaxoSmithKline Foundation
1 Franklin Plaza, FP2130, P.O. Box 7929
Philadelphia, PA 19101-7929

Glazer Family Foundation Grants 2062
The foundation awards grants to eligible Florida nonprofit organizations for programs focused on youth and families in the areas of general health, safety, education, and recreation. Types of support include grants, contributions, tickets, and special programs. Proposals are accepted May 1 through July 1 and September 1 through November 1. Annual deadline dates may vary; contact program staff for exact dates.
Requirements: Florida nonprofit organizations serving the greater Tampa Bay and West Central areas are eligible.
Restrictions: Grants do not support general fundraising drives, celebrations, administrative/training costs, capital expenditures, sponsorships, individual medical needs, scholarships, research, political activities, conferences, and university capital campaigns.
Geographic Focus: Florida
Date(s) Application is Due: Jul 1; Nov 1
Amount of Grant: Up to 5,000 USD
Contact: Grants Administrator; (813) 870-2700, ext. 275; fax (813) 554-1324
Internet: http://www.glazerfamilyfoundation.com/GuidelinesforGrants.aspx
Sponsor: Glazer Family Foundation
One Buccaneer Pl
Tampa, FL 33607

Gleitsman Foundation Activist Awards 2063
The foundation accepts nominations for the Citizen Activist award, which is designed to encourage individual commitment and leadership in the United States by recognizing the exceptional achievement of people who have initiated social change. The award recognizes activist efforts in the United States to confront, challenge, and correct social injustice. The International Activist Award honors individuals in the international community who have inspired change and motivated others in the realm of social activism. Awards are made every two years. Applications are accepted in even-numbered years for the citizen award and in odd-numbered years for the international award. Nomination form and guidelines are available online.
Geographic Focus: All States
Date(s) Application is Due: Nov 4
Amount of Grant: 100,000 USD
Contact: Awards Coordinator; (810) 995-0090
Internet: http://www.gleitsman.org
Sponsor: Gleitsman Foundation
P.O. Box 6888
Malibu, CA 90264

Gloria Barron Prize for Young Heroes 2064
The Gloria Barron Prize for Young Heroes honors 25 outstanding young leaders who have made a significant positive difference to people and the planet. Candidates have focused on helping their communities and fellow human beings, in addition to protecting the health and sustainability of the environment. Nominees, who may range in age from 8 to 18 years old, must have been the prime mover of a service activity, and demonstrated positive spirit and high moral purpose in accomplishing their goals. Each winner of the Barron Prize receives: $2,500 to be applied to their higher education or to their service project; a recognition plaque; a certificate of recognition; a signed copy of The Hero's Trail, by Barron Prize founder T.A. Barron; a copy of Dream Big, a documentary film featuring several Barron Prize winners; a heroes study guide, curriculum, and bibliography; the opportunity to be paired with an adult mentor who is passionate about working in the winner's area of interest; the opportunity to connect with other Barron Prize winners through the Young Heroes Listserv; and numerous media opportunities – print, television, and radio. By submitting an entry in the Gloria Barron Prize for Young Heroes, each entrant acknowledges reading and understanding all the eligibility requirements and selection criteria published on the Prize's website and agrees to observe them. Further, each entrant acknowledges and agrees that as a condition of receiving the Prize, the selected individuals will cooperate in publicizing the Barron Prize and will grant rights of the entrant's nomination materials to the Barron Prize.
Requirements: Candidates must be nominated by responsible adults who have solid knowledge of the young person's heroic activities, and who are not related to the nominee. To nominate a young person, the adult nominator must submit a fully-completed nomination packet and reference form located at the prize website. Nominees must have organized and led a service activity which has clearly benefited other people, animals, or the planet. The nominee's service activity must have been initiated and motivated primarily by the nominee. While outside help may have been obtained, the activity must be primarily the nominee's own creation. Nominees must have done more than survive a difficult personal challenge. Their heroism must have made an impact on the world beyond themselves. Nominees must have clearly demonstrated positive spirit, courage, intelligence, generosity, and high moral purpose. Nominees must have shown initiative, tenacity, and unselfishness in pursuit of their goals.
Restrictions: The Prize committee cannot accept nominations for groups of young people, or nominations for projects done solely to complete an assignment for school or work.
Geographic Focus: All States, Canada
Date(s) Application is Due: Apr 30
Amount of Grant: 2,500 USD
Contact: Barbara Ann Richman; (970) 875-1448; ba_richman@barronprize.org
Internet: http://www.barronprize.org/about-prize
Sponsor: Barron Prize
545 Pearl Street
Boulder, CO 80302

GMFUS Black Sea Trust for Regional Corporation Grants 2065
The Black Sea Trust (BST) for Regional Cooperation invites proposals from organizations and institutions in the countries of the Wider Black Sea Region on the Trust's three programs: civic participation, cross-border initiatives, and Eastern Links. The Trust promotes regional cooperation and good governance in the Wider Black Sea region; accountable, transparent, and open governments; strong, effective civic sectors; and independent and professional media. To respond to the rapid shifts in the region, BST staff regularly consult with regional experts and aim to sharpen the program's grantmaking strategy in order to more effectively achieve the Trust's goals. With the complexity and diversity of the region, BST priorities are revised regularly to respond to the region's changing needs. Adjustments are made

in consultation with the BST Advisory Board, the German Marshall Fund's network of offices and internal expertise, and in coordination with other donors active in the region. The maximum duration of projects is 12 months. As an exception, outstanding projects of a longer duration may be considered. Grants generally range from $5,000 and $75,000, with most grants falling between $15,000 and $25,000. BST can support exceptional multi-year projects, renewable on an annual basis contingent upon satisfactory interim reports and performance. There are no application deadlines, and grant decisions are made monthly.
Requirements: Non-governmental organizations, governmental entities, community groups, policy institutes, other associations legally registered in Armenia, Azerbaijan, Bulgaria, Georgia, Moldova, Romania, Turkey, Ukraine and Russia. The projects have to be implemented in one or more of the countries mentioned. An online application and budget form are required, and must be completed in English.
Restrictions: Individuals and political parties may not apply. Non-indigenous organizations may not apply. Cooperative projects between indigenous and non-indigenous organizations are considered under the Eastern Links component, yet non-indigenous administrative costs will not receive BST support. The BST does not support scholarly research, academic fellowships and scholarships, one-off events, humanitarian aid, refugee or IDP return, religious activities, or the arts or sciences. BST only supports travel and website creation/maintenance as components of larger activities.
Geographic Focus: Armenia, Azerbaijan, Bulgaria, Moldova, Romania, Russia, Turkey, Ukraine
Amount of Grant: 15,000 - 25,000 USD
Contact: Program Contact; (202) 683-2650; fax (202) 265-1662; info@gmfus.org
Internet: http://www.gmfus.org/grants-fellowships/grantmaking-programs/black-sea-trust
Sponsor: German Marshall Fund of the United States
1744 R Street NW
Washington, DC 20009

GMFUS Marshall Memorial Fellowships 2066
The Marshall Memorial Fellowships seek to engage potential American leaders in international affairs and to strengthen ties between American and European policymakers and leaders. Fellows, who are emerging leaders chosen from business, the news media, nonprofit groups, and politics, participate in a three-week program in Europe designed to acquaint them with European economic, political, and social institutions. Deadlines vary according to each country; please contact MMF staff or your local partner organization for further information.
Requirements: Nomination is open to Americans between the ages of 28 and 40 who demonstrate clear leadership, intellectual curiosity, independence, and maturity, and who have an outstanding record of achievement in their professions, with a record of civic involvement. Candidates must be well-positioned to be influential in American society in the future and must be nominated by recognized leaders in their profession.
Restrictions: The fund generally does not offer support for building and operating funds, graduate or undergraduate education, research, or the arts.
Geographic Focus: All States
Contact: John Paul Diego; (202) 745-6674; fax (202) 265-1662; jpdiego@gmfus.org
Internet: http://www.gmfus.org/fellowships/index.cfm
Sponsor: German Marshall Fund of the United States
1744 R Street NW
Washington, DC 20009

GMFUS Urban and Regional Policy Fellowships 2067
The German Marshall Fund of the United States (GMF) grants a number of fellowships each year through the Urban and Regional Policy program. Urban and Regional Policy fellowships are intended to provide opportunities for practitioners and policy-makers working on economic and social issues at the urban and regional policy levels to meet with their counterparts across the Atlantic and discuss policies and measures that have been implemented. Fellows have the opportunity to conduct research projects (of varying length and depth) designed to shed new light on an urban or regional policy challenge by exploring how it has been addressed on the other side of the Atlantic. Fellows can then return from their time overseas equipped with the ideas and insights necessary to effect significant and lasting positive change in their own communities. GMF offers two types of fellowships that vary in length, intensity, and expected outcomes. Short-term travel grants of up to $9,000 are available for individuals seeking to gather information that pertains to a specific, social, economic, or physical challenge or obstacle in their home communities. Over three to four weeks, these fellows visit a maximum of two cities for a series of site visits and meetings with relevant individuals and institutions. Longer-term research grants of up to $10,000 per month are available for individuals interested in completing more in-depth policy analysis. These fellows are based abroad for three months and examine how three case study cities approached a discrete policy challenge through site visits and interviews. Long-term fellows are expected to review available literature in advance of their travel and adhere to a well-developed research methodology. Additional information and guidelines, along with the application, are available at the website.
Requirements: GMF welcomes applications from mid-career professionals with an interest in gaining an understanding of how similar urban and regional challenges are approached in a policy context other than their own and an ability to translate lessons learned into policy action in their own communities. Applicants should be policymakers or practitioners in state/local government, leaders from the private sector, or representatives of non-profit and policy organizations. GMF welcomes fellowship proposals that cover a wide array of topics, including urban sustainability, transportation, environmental policy, education and workforce development, and affordable housing and social inclusion.
Restrictions: Fellowships are not intended for academic research.
Geographic Focus: All States
Date(s) Application is Due: Jan 31
Contact: Brent Riddle; (202) 683-2650; fax (202) 265-1662; briddle@gmfus.org
Internet: http://www.gmfus.org/fellowships/index.cfm
Sponsor: German Marshall Fund of the United States
1744 R Street NW
Washington, DC 20009

GNOF Albert N. & Hattie M. McClure Grants 2068
The Albert N. & Hattie M. McClure Fund was established in 1963 and is a donor-advised fund of the Greater New Orleans Foundation (GNOF). The fund supports the emergency bricks and mortar projects (e.g. repairs, replacements, and additions to facilities) of eligible United Way partner agencies. The intent of the McClure Fund is to fill the funding gap between major capital expenses requiring a capital fund drive and minor capital needs which can be planned for and included in an agency's operating budget. Priority consideration will be given to those requests of a capital nature that stem from a crisis and/or emergency. GNOF will consider requests up to $15,000. The application process has no deadline date. Organizations will be notified of funding decisions within sixty days. Organizations can find a downloadable application form at the website and should contact GNOF for mailing instructions.
Requirements: Applicants must be partner agencies of United Way and should contact GNOF for further eligibility requirements.
Geographic Focus: Louisiana
Amount of Grant: Up to 15,000 USD
Contact: Ellen M. Lee, Sr. Vice President, Programs, Community Revitalization Program Director; (504) 598-4663; fax (504) 598-4676; ellen@gnof.org
Internet: http://www.gnof.org/albert-n-hattie-m-mcclure-fund/
Sponsor: Greater New Orleans Foundation
1055 St. Charles Avenue, Suite 100
New Orleans, LA 70130

GNOF Bayou Communities Grants 2069
In 2012 the Greater New Orleans Foundation (GNOF) established the Bayou Communities Foundation (BCF) that has, as its initial focus, the mission to improve life in the Louisiana parishes of Terrebonne and Lafourche, and that will work to strengthen local nonprofit capacity in compassionate and sustainable coastal communities in Louisiana for generations to come. The impetus to form BCF came from parish residents, who first organized among themselves and then approached GNOF, who had set up similar and successful foundations in St. Bernard, Plaquemines, and Jefferson Parishes after Hurricanes Katrina and Rita and the Gulf Oil Spill. BCF is set up as a GNOF donor-advised fund, an affiliate under GNOF's nonprofit umbrella. The new foundation will receive $500,000 in seed money for the next five years from the Gheens Foundation in Lafourche and has committed to raising $1 million in matching dollars. BCF has also commited to putting at least 90% of its first $100,000 from the Gheens Foundation back into the community through grants. As an affiliate foundation, BCF has access to the expertise of GNOF but makes independent decisions about BCF projects. Organizations interested in obtaining grants through BCF can contact GNOF for more information.
Geographic Focus: Louisiana
Contact: Josephine Everly; (504) 598-4663; fax (504) 598-4676; josephine@gnof.org
Internet: http://www.gnof.org/
Sponsor: Greater New Orleans Foundation
1055 St. Charles Avenue, Suite 100
New Orleans, LA 70130

GNOF Coastal 5 + 1 Grants 2070
The need for a coordinated strategy to protect and to strengthen Louisiana's coastal communities became painfully obvious to all those who survived Hurricane Katrina, the Gulf Oil Spill and other recent disasters in the Greater New Orleans metropolitan area. Coastal citizens long marginalized by or oblivious to the environmental impacts stemming from decades of poor planning and environmental degradation have been awakened to new realities and possibilities, including a newly-found voice with which to address common challenges in the region's environment, economy, and community leadership. In response to this new physical, political, and economic landscape, the Greater New Orleans Foundation launched the Coastal 5+1 Initiative in 2011. The initiative benefits the five coastal parishes of Jefferson, Lafourche, Plaquemines, St. Bernard, and Terrebonne, along with the coastal-dependent parish of New Orleans. The initiative's goal is to empower local communities to confront pressing coastal issues such as failing ecosystems and global climate change and to connect emerging leaders with immediate, concrete solutions to long-term problems. The initiative will make grants in three program areas: civic engagement and leadership; environment and sustainable communities; and sustainable economic development. The goal of the civic engagement and leadership program is to join Orleans Parish with its southern neighbors in advocating for the coast at the state and federal levels. The goal of the environment and sustainable communities program is to encourage resilience, adaptation, sustainability, and ecological, economic, and cultural vitality through support for equitable, environmentally-focused policies and programs. The sustainable economic development program will support economic opportunities that are unique to the region's resources, such as traditionally viable industries in agriculture, fisheries, and energy production. Workforce development programs specifically tailored to emerging careers in such fields as wetlands restoration and innovative surface-water management, planning, and engineering will also be supported, as well as non-traditional youth outreach and training (including after-school education efforts geared toward empowerment, self-esteem and self-discipline, wealth creation, and asset-building). GNOF accepts Coastal 5+1 applications only through its Request for Proposal (RFP) process. Interested organizations are encouraged to subscribe to GNOF's email newsletter for announcements of future funding opportunities. The subscription link is available from GNOF's Apply-for-a-Grant web page which contains a comprehensive listing of GNOF's current and past funding opportunities. Interested organizations are also encouraged to visit the GNOF website to obtain detailed background

information on the initiative, an explanation of its major goals and strategies, and examples of the types of programs it will fund.
Geographic Focus: All States
Amount of Grant: 90,000 - 200,000 USD
Contact: Dr. Marco Cocito-Monoc; (504) 598-4663; fax (504) 598-4676; marco@gnof.org
Internet: http://www.gnof.org/coastal-51-initiative/
Sponsor: Greater New Orleans Foundation
1055 St. Charles Avenue, Suite 100
New Orleans, LA 70130

GNOF Community Revitalization Grants **2071**

134,000 housing units were damaged or destroyed by Hurricane Katrina and the subsequent levee failures, creating over $100 billion in damage in the greater New Orleans region. In 2007, leading local and national foundations created the $25-million Community Revitalization Fund at the Greater New Orleans Foundation (GNOF) which has since used the fund to support the development of nearly 9,000 housing units to help with the region's recovery. The aim of the fund is two-fold: to fill gaps in public spending with private philanthropy; and to leverage public resources such as Low-Income Housing Tax Credits, Community Development Block Grants, and HOME funds. The Revitalization Fund has a mandate to support activities that create or are a component of a working system that generates equitable and affordable housing and community development at scale for the greater New Orleans region. A working system functions in the following ways: it produces high-quality, diverse, mixed-income and mixed-use development that is architecturally, culturally, and ecologically appropriate, as well as environmentally sustainable; it engages a diversity of citizens in the community revitalization process and formalizes or sustains citizen engagement in community development; it promotes accountability in government and the effectiveness of public systems; it results in the creation of a number of housing units that is commensurate with the scale of the crisis at hand and at a pace that dignifies all displaced New Orleanians; and it increases the capacity of the locally-based housing productions systems, including nonprofit and for-profit developers. The ultimate goal of the Revitalization Fund is a city of mixed-income and mixed-race neighborhoods of choice, each anchored by community facilities, schools, hospitals, pedestrian-friendly streets, and dynamic public open spaces available to and accessible by all residents. GNOF considers the efforts of New Orleanians who became "citizen planners" during post-Katrina planning processes an essential component of the working system and supports their move into leadership roles and into becoming effective stewards of the implementation process. The Community Revitalization Fund accepts Letters of Interest (LOIs) on a rolling basis. These should be submitted along with required supporting documentation via email to the address provided in the guidelines. Within one month of receiving an LOI, GNOF staff will respond in one of three ways: by requesting a full proposal; by requesting a meeting to discuss the project; or by declining the request. GNOF considers full proposals on a quarterly basis. Interested organizations are also encouraged to visit the GNOF website to obtain detailed guidelines on how to apply, background information on the Community Revitalization Fund, an explanation of its changing goals and strategies, and examples of the types of programs it will fund. A link to subscribe to the GNOF newsletter is available from GNOF's Apply-for-a-Grant web page. The newsletter keeps subscribers informed on all GNOF's upcoming funding opportunities.
Requirements: Requests for funding must do one or more of the following: address a specific need or barrier to housing development; contribute to the capacity of government, nonprofit, and/or for-profit developers to produce equitable, high-quality, mixed-income housing at scale (at least 50 units per year); increase expertise and/or capacity within the housing development industry; deliver important information and/or technical expertise on best practices in housing and community development; and collaborate across the public and private sectors to create innovative financing programs or housing policy that will increase the pace of the city's repopulation.
Geographic Focus: All States
Contact: Ellen M. Lee, Sr. Vice President, Programs, Community Revitalization Program Director; (504) 598-4663; fax (504) 598-4676; ellen@gnof.org or crfund@gnof.org
Internet: http://www.gnof.org/community-revitalization-fund-grant/
Sponsor: Greater New Orleans Foundation
1055 St. Charles Avenue, Suite 100
New Orleans, LA 70130

GNOF Cox Charities of New Orleans Grants **2072**

Cox Cable, a grant-making partner of the Greater New Orleans Foundation (GNOF), has established the Cox Charities of New Orleans Fund to improve the quality of life for people in Orleans, Jefferson, St. Charles, and St. Bernard parishes. The fund provides grants from $500 - $2,500 for new, creative, or beneficial programs in the area of youth (target ages, seven through eighteen) and education. Additionally Cox Cable will showcase projects and programs of its grantees on cable television. Grant requests and supporting materials must be emailed to the address provided on this page and must be received by 5:00 p.m. on the annual deadline date which usually occurs in May. Successful applicants are then notified in July. Requests are reviewed by an advisory committee of business and civic leaders. Exact deadlines may vary from year to year. Prospective applicants should verify the current deadline at the GNOF website where they can also obtain complete guidelines and requirements as well as a downloadable application form. Prospective applicants can also subscribe to GNOF's email newsletter for announcements of future funding opportunities. The subscription link is available from GNOF's Apply-for-a-Grant web page which contains a comprehensive listing of GNOF's current and past funding opportunities.
Requirements: Nonprofits in the parishes of Orleans, Jefferson, St. Charles, and St. Bernard are eligible to apply. Applicants must have 501(c)3 status or apply through a fiscal agent who has 501(c)3 status.
Restrictions: Only one application per organization will be accepted.
Geographic Focus: Louisiana
Date(s) Application is Due: May 16
Contact: Ellen M. Lee, Sr. Vice President, Programs, Community Revitalization Program Director; (504) 598-4663; fax (504) 598-4676; grants@gnof.org or ellen@gnof.org
Internet: http://www.gnof.org/cox-charities-of-new-orleans/
Sponsor: Greater New Orleans Foundation
1055 St. Charles Avenue, Suite 100
New Orleans, LA 70130

GNOF Environmental Fund Grants **2073**

The Environmental Fund was established in 1994 using the settlement money from a legal dispute involving a phenol spill that tainted drinking water in the Mississippi River. The original gift of $6 million was invested and has grown to $10 million. It is currently administered by the Greater New Orleans Foundation (GNOF). The endowed fund's goal is to encourage ecological, economic, and cultural vitality, resilience and sustainability in the greater New Orleans region through environmentally focused policies, programs, and projects. People in greater New Orleans have been left to grapple with the environmental consequences of policies wrought by privileged groups with limited interests, many of whom left the area in the wake of Hurricanes Katrina and Rita. As the region's wetlands continue to disappear at a rate of 25 square miles per year, the impact of future storm surges will continue to rise; if it is to survive, the greater New Orleans community must rebuild itself with an emphasis on maximum resiliency and adapt itself in a sustainable way to the uniquely fluid environment that nourishes the region's neighborhoods, culture, economy and identity. The greater New Orleans community has come to understand that real solutions can only come about through decision-making processes that are open and deliberately inclusive. In fact GNOF believes that the foundation of community sustainability is community empowerment. From time to time GNOF will make available through a request for proposal (RFP), a certain sum that will promote a set of five regionally significant and relevant transformations: make the region a national leader in the protection and beneficial use of its water resources; turn the region into the most storm-resistent and resilient area in America; make the region the most innovative and progressive energy center in America; make the region a place that is attractive, affordable, viable, and safe for businesses, workers, and their families; and keep the region as a place that celebrates its heritage but that is not captive to its past. GNOF accepts Environmental Fund applications only through its RFP process. Interested organizations are encouraged to subscribe to GNOF's email newsletter so they can be notified of future RFPs. The subscription link is available from GNOF's Apply-for-a-Grant web page which contains a comprehensive listing of GNOF's current and past funding opportunities. Interested organizations are also encouraged to visit the GNOF website to obtain detailed background information on the Environmental Fund, an explanation of its major goals and strategies, and examples of the types of programs it will fund.
Requirements: GNOF gives preference to locally-based nonprofits.
Geographic Focus: All States
Contact: Dr. Marco Cocito-Monoc; (504) 598-4663; fax (504) 598-4676; marco@gnof.org
Internet: http://www.gnof.org/the-environmental-fund-3/
Sponsor: Greater New Orleans Foundation
1055 St. Charles Avenue, Suite 100
New Orleans, LA 70130

GNOF Exxon-Mobil Grants **2074**

Exxon-Mobil, a grant-making partner of the Greater New Orleans Foundation (GNOF) has established the Exxon-Mobil fund to improve the quality of lives for people in the St. Bernard parish and a portion of Algiers. The fund provides the following types of grants: capital-fund grants for new construction or major renovation; seed-money grants to help start new organizations that respond to an important opportunity in the community; bridge grants to sustain organizations experiencing financial hardships; and grants that support new, creative, or beneficial programs. Amounts up to $4,000 are given in Algiers; amounts up to $10,000 are given in St. Bernard Parish and in extraordinary circumstances may exceed this maximum. Grant requests are reviewed by an advisory committee of business and civic leaders that meets annually. Application materials must be emailed to the address provided on this page and received by the foundation by 5:00 p.m. on August 15. Exact deadlines may vary from year to year. Prospective applicants should verify the current deadline at the GNOF website where they can also obtain complete guidelines and requirements as well as a downloadable application form. Prospective applicants can also subscribe to GNOF's email newsletter for announcements of future funding opportunities. The subscription link is available from GNOF's Apply-for-a-Grant web page which contains a comprehensive listing of GNOF's current and past funding opportunities.
Requirements: While priority is given to nonprofit organizations based in St. Bernard Parish or Algiers, nonprofit organizations servicing these areas will be given consideration. Applicants must have 501(c)3 status or apply through a fiscal agent who has such status.
Geographic Focus: Louisiana
Date(s) Application is Due: Aug 15
Contact: Dr. Marco Cocito-Monoc, Sr. Vice President, Programs, Community Revitalization Program Director; (504) 598-4663; fax (504) 598-4676; marco@gnof.org
Internet: http://www.gnof.org/exxon-mobile-fund/
Sponsor: Greater New Orleans Foundation
1055 St. Charles Avenue, Suite 100
New Orleans, LA 70130

GNOF Freeman Challenge Grants **2075**

The Freeman Challenge, a donor-advised fund of the Greater New Orleans Foundation (GNOF), is a memorial tribute to one of New Orleans' leading citizens and philanthropists Richard West Freeman who will be remembered as one of the founders of The United Fund in 1952 (now The United Way). The purpose of The Freeman Challenge is to create long-term financial stability for nonprofit organizations serving the Greater New Orleans thirteen-parish

region; the Challenge will match one dollar for every two dollars raised by nonprofits to build their own endowments. Nonprofits can elect to receive one of three matching amounts: $5,000, $10,000, or $15,000. Freeman Challenge grant applications are reviewed by a selection committee of volunteers and GNOF staff that meets annually. The committee looks for nonprofits that represent varying areas of service, e.g. education, the arts, human services, etc. Application materials are due no later 5 p.m. on September 14 and must be emailed to the email address given under the Contact Information section. Exact deadlines may vary from year to year. Prospective applicants should verify the current deadline at the GNOF website where they can also obtain a downloadable brochure about the the program as well as a downloadable application form with guidelines and requirements. Prospective applicants can also subscribe to GNOF's email newsletter for announcements of future funding opportunities. The subscription link is available from GNOF's Apply-for-a-Grant web page which contains a comprehensive listing of GNOF's current and past funding opportunities.
Requirements: To be eligible nonprofit organizations must meet the following *Requirements:* have 501(c)3 status; have been in operation for a minimum of five years; be headquartered in one of Greater New Orleans' thirteen parishes (Assumption, Jefferson, Lafourche, Orleans, Plaquemines, St. Bernard, St. Charles, St. James, St. Johns, St. Tammany, Tangipahoa, Terrebonne, or Washington); presently have no endowment with a market value that exceeds $500,000; show evidence of previous fund-raising success; conduct an annual independent audit; have a volunteer board; and have their board's approval to take part in the Freeman Challenge.
Geographic Focus: Louisiana
Date(s) Application is Due: Jun 25
Amount of Grant: 5,000 - 15,000 USD
Contact: Ellen M. Lee, Sr; (504) 598-4663; fax (504) 598-4676; grants@gnof.org
Internet: http://www.gnof.org/the-freeman-challenge/
Sponsor: Greater New Orleans Foundation
1055 St. Charles Avenue, Suite 100
New Orleans, LA 70130

GNOF Gert Community Fund Grants 2076
The Gert Community Fund, a donor-advised fund of the Greater New Orleans Foundation (GNOF), was established to enhance the quality of life for people in the Gert Town Community. Program areas include education, housing, generational services, and economic development. In addition, the committee is interested in community-beautification projects (e.g. tree planting, green-space maintenance, and neighborhood cleanup). Requests are reviewed annually by an advisory committee of business and civic leaders; grants for up to $50,000 per year will be considered. Requests must be received via mail by 5:00 p.m. on August 31. Prospective applicants should verify whether the grant is currently open for submission at the GNOF website where they can also obtain complete guidelines and requirements as well as a downloadable application form. Interested organizations can also subscribe to GNOF's email newsletter for announcements of future funding opportunities. The subscription link is available from GNOF's Apply-for-a-Grant web page which contains a comprehensive listing of GNOF's current and past funding opportunities.
Requirements: Nonprofit organizations that serve the Gert Town Community are eligible to apply but are requested to first contact GNOF for more details on the geographical boundaries for the fund. Applicants must have 501(c)3 status or apply through a fiscal agent who has such status.
Restrictions: Only one application per organization will be accepted.
Geographic Focus: All States
Date(s) Application is Due: Aug 31
Amount of Grant: Up to 50,000 USD
Contact: Amy Forsyth, Grant Coordinator; (504) 598-4663; fax (504) 598-4676
Internet: http://www.gnof.org/the-gert-town-community-fund/
Sponsor: Greater New Orleans Foundation
1055 St. Charles Avenue, Suite 100
New Orleans, LA 70130

GNOF Gulf Coast Oil Spill Grants 2077
Shortly after the tragic explosion of BP's Deepwater Horizon drilling rig in 2010, the Greater New Orleans Foundation (GNOF) responded to the crisis by establishing the Gulf Coast Oil Spill Fund to serve as a conduit between the donor community and GNOF's nonprofit partners. The Gulf Coast Oil Spill Fund (GCOS) supports work that helps fisherman and their families in the parishes most affected by the oil spill: Plaquemines, St. Bernard, lower Jefferson, Terrebonne, and Lafourche parishes. The long-term goal of GCOS is to help strengthen coastal communities against future environmental catastrophes such as the Deepwater spill. Specifically GCOS embraces the following objectives: the creation of a more resilient commercial fishing industry that is better able to respond to future crises (whether natural or man-made) through the introduction of new technologies and practices; the development and implementation of job training opportunities for fishers and charter-boat workers temporarily or permanently displaced from their chosen vocation because of the spill; the development of innovative marketing and distribution plans for local seafood; the development of a more comprehensive and accessible system for monitoring both water quality and seafood quality; a mechanism for more effectively organizing the region's commercial fishers which focuses on transcending geographic, racial, ethnic, and linguistic barriers that have traditionally divided commercial fishing populations; the development of laws and/or policies that will be of direct benefit to commercial fishers and others who derive the majority of their income from water-related activities; the provision of free or reduced-cost legal advice and mental-health services to commercial fishers and individuals whose income has been curtailed or interrupted by the oil disaster; and a mechanism for better coordinating the provision of emergency assistance to aquatic and other wildlife affected by "mini-landfalls" or other contact with lingering oil from the Deep Water Horizon spill. GNOF accepts GCOS applications through its RFP process. Interested organizations are encouraged to subscribe to GNOF's email newsletter so they can be notified of future RFPs. The subscription link is available from GNOF's Apply-for-a-Grant web page which contains a comprehensive listing of GNOF's current and past funding opportunities. Interested organizations are also encouraged to contact the GNOF Director for Regional Initiatives with any questions.
Requirements: Applicant organizations must meet all of the following criteria: be classified by the Internal Revenue Sercie as 501(c)3 nonprofit entities or make use of a fiscal agent that has a 501(c)3 designation; be based within GNOF's thirteen-parish service area (Assumption, Jefferson, Lafourche, Orleans, Plaquemines, St. Bernard, St. Charles, St. James, St. John the Baptist, St. Tammany, Tangipahoa, Terrebonne, and Washington); and demonstrate close collaboration with commercial fishing organizations or populations in affected communities in the GNOF service area.
Restrictions: The GCOS fund will not support film or documentary projects, art projects, or academic research (except in the case of developing a more comprehensive and accessible system for monitoring both water quality and seafood quality).
Geographic Focus: Louisiana
Contact: Dr. Marco Cocito-Monoc; (504) 598-4663; fax (504) 598-4676; marco@gnof.org
Internet: http://www.gnof.org/gnof-oil-spill-fund/
Sponsor: Greater New Orleans Foundation
1055 St. Charles Avenue, Suite 100
New Orleans, LA 70130

GNOF IMPACT Grants for Arts and Culture 2078
Through the IMPACT Program, the Greater New Orleans Foundation (GNOF) makes grants to organizations serving the Greater New Orleans region. The ultimate goal of the IMPACT Program is to create a resilient, sustainable, vibrant, and equitable region in which individuals and families flourish and in which the special character of the New Orleans region and its people is preserved, celebrated, and given the means to develop. Specifically GNOF hopes to accomplish the following objectives through its IMPACT grants: provide a much needed source of financial and other support to nonprofit organizations that are struggling in the current financial environment and that are important to the health and vibrancy of the region; develop a better sense of the nonprofit organizations serving the region so GNOF can more effectively match donor desires with effective charitable work; identify and nurture promising new leaders and initiatives, especially in those communities that are in greatest need; and gain knowledge that will help nonprofit leaders and GNOF staff develop better long-term strategies for addressing regional needs and taking best advantage of important opportunities. IMPACT grants are awarded in four categories: Arts and Culture, Youth Development, Education, and Health and Human Services. In the category of Arts and Culture GNOF supports organizations and programs that help preserve and grow the rich cultural heritage of the Greater New Orleans region and ensure that the originators and producers of creative goods and services can continue to enhance community life. Priority will be given to work that has the following goals: to improve the quality of life for artists and performers in the region; to demonstrate the importance of the arts and make the case for increased public support for the arts; and to form alliances and connections between grassroots-based organizations and the business community to expand income-producing opportunities for artists. Interested organizations must submit a letter of intent along with all attachments via one email by 5 p.m. on July 30. GNOF program staff will review all letters of intent and will contact those organizations that are invited to submit a full application for funding. Awards are announced in November. Deadlines may vary from year to year. Interested organizations should verify the current deadline at the GNOF website where they can also obtain complete guidelines and requirements as well as a downloadable application form and cover sheet. Prospective applicants can also subscribe to GNOF's email newsletter for announcements of future funding opportunities. The subscription link is available from GNOF's Apply-for-a-Grant web page which contains a comprehensive listing of GNOF's current and past funding opportunities.
Requirements: Nonprofit, tax-exempt organizations that serve the Greater New Orleans region are eligible to apply for funding. Organizations that are not tax-exempt but have a fiscal agent relationship with a 501(c)3 organization are also eligible.
Restrictions: Through its IMPACT program, the Greater New Orleans Foundation is unable to fund the following types of requests: requests for individual support, either through scholarships or other forms of financial assistance; special events or conferences; programs that promote religious doctrine; endowments; and scientific or medical research.
Geographic Focus: All States
Date(s) Application is Due: Jul 30
Amount of Grant: Up to 20,000 USD
Contact: Roy Williams; (504) 598-4663; grants@gnof.org or roy@gnof.org
Internet: http://www.gnof.org/programs/impact/
Sponsor: Greater New Orleans Foundation
1055 St. Charles Avenue, Suite 100
New Orleans, LA 70130

GNOF IMPACT Grants for Education 2079
Through the IMPACT Program, the Greater New Orleans Foundation (GNOF) makes grants to organizations serving the Greater New Orleans region. The ultimate goal of the IMPACT program is to create a resilient, sustainable, vibrant, and equitable region in which individuals and families flourish and in which the special character of the New Orleans region and its people is preserved, celebrated, and given the means to develop. Specifically GNOF hopes to accomplish the following objectives through its IMPACT grants: provide a much needed source of financial and other support to nonprofit organizations that are struggling in the current financial environment and that are important to the health and vibrancy of the region; develop a better sense of the nonprofit organizations serving the region so GNOF can more effectively match donor desires with effective charitable work; identify and nurture promising new leaders and initiatives, especially in those communities

that are in greatest need; and gain knowledge that will help nonprofit leaders and GNOF staff develop better long-term strategies for addressing regional needs and taking best advantage of important opportunities. IMPACT grants are awarded in four categories: Arts and Culture, Youth Development, Education, and Health and Human Services. In the category of Education support is available to organizations that seek to ensure that all young people in public K-12 schools in GNOF's 13-parish service area attend high-performing schools. Priority will be given to work that has the following goals: to advance public education reforms in Orleans parish and other under served areas in GNOF's service area; to hold public agencies accountable for the success of our public schools; to improve student achievement by training and engaging key stakeholders in education (parents, school leaders, etc.) in the skills of organizing, policy research and analysis, policy advocacy, and the use of data in making policy recommendations; and conduct research and/or work with school leaders and other financial decision makers to address the financial sustainability issues within the charter school system. Interested organizations must submit a letter of intent along with all attachments via one email by 5 p.m. on July 30. GNOF program staff will review all letters of intent and will contact those organizations that are invited to submit a full application for funding. Awards are announced in November. Deadlines may vary from year to year. Interested organizations should verify the current deadline at the GNOF website where they can also obtain complete guidelines and requirements as well as a downloadable application form and cover sheet. Prospective applicants can also subscribe to GNOF's email newsletter for announcements of future funding opportunities. The subscription link is available from GNOF's Apply-for-a-Grant web page which contains a comprehensive listing of GNOF's current and past funding opportunities.
Requirements: Nonprofit, tax-exempt organizations that serve the thirteen parishes of Greater New Orleans are eligible to apply for funding. Organizations that are not tax-exempt but have a fiscal agent relationship with a 501(c)3 organization are also eligible.
Restrictions: Through its IMPACT program, the Greater New Orleans Foundation is unable to fund the following types of requests: requests for individual support, either through scholarships or other forms of financial assistance; special events or conferences; programs that promote religious doctrine; endowments; and scientific or medical research.
Geographic Focus: All States
Date(s) Application is Due: Jul 30
Amount of Grant: Up to 20,000 USD
Contact: Roy Williams; (504) 598-4663; fax (504) 598-4676; grants@gnof.org
Internet: http://www.gnof.org/programs/impact/
Sponsor: Greater New Orleans Foundation
1055 St. Charles Avenue, Suite 100
New Orleans, LA 70130

GNOF IMPACT Grants for Health and Human Services 2080
Through the IMPACT Program, the Greater New Orleans Foundation (GNOF) makes grants to organizations serving the Greater New Orleans region. The ultimate goal of the IMPACT program is to create a resilient, sustainable, vibrant, and equitable region in which individuals and families flourish and in which the special character of the New Orleans region and its people is preserved, celebrated, and given the means to develop. Specifically GNOF hopes to accomplish the following objectives through its IMPACT grants: provide a much needed source of financial and other support to nonprofit organizations that are struggling in the current financial environment and that are important to the health and vibrancy of the region; develop a better sense of the nonprofit organizations serving the region so GNOF can more effectively match donor desires with effective charitable work; identify and nurture promising new leaders and initiatives, especially in those communities that are in greatest need; and gain knowledge that will help nonprofit leaders and GNOF staff develop better long-term strategies for addressing regional needs and taking best advantage of important opportunities. IMPACT grants are awarded in four categories: Arts and Culture, Youth Development, Education, and Health and Human Services. In the category of Health and Human Services, support is available to organizations that work to improve the health and living conditions of low-income families and their children, the disabled, the elderly, and other under served populations and help move them toward self-sufficiency. Priority will be given to work that increases Medicaid/LaCHIP or Medicare enrollment for indigent consumers of health-care services; advocates to preserve access to health care, to provide consumer protections, and/or to expand Medicaid coverage to increase access to comprehensive, quality primary care, mental health care, and preventive care for all; implements health education and outreach efforts to increase use of health-care services by the most under-served populations, African-American males in particular; uses health education to improve health literacy, influence attitudes, and improve health awareness so that indigent consumers of health care services can make better decisions and take preventive actions that will improve personal, family, and community health; and improve communication, coordination and collaboration between social-services providers to serve comprehensively the needs of low-income families, improving their chances of success in achieving self sufficiency. Interested organizations must submit a letter of intent along with all attachments via one email by 5 p.m. on July 30. GNOF program staff will review all letters of intent and will contact those organizations that are invited to submit a full application for funding. Awards are announced in November. Deadlines may vary from year to year. Interested organizations should verify the current deadline at the GNOF website where they can also obtain complete guidelines and requirements as well as a downloadable application form and cover sheet. Prospective applicants can also subscribe to GNOF's email newsletter for announcements of future funding opportunities. The subscription link is available from GNOF's Apply-for-a-Grant web page which contains a comprehensive listing of GNOF's current and past funding opportunities.
Requirements: Nonprofit, tax-exempt organizations that serve the thirteen parishes of Greater New Orleans are eligible to apply for funding. Organizations that are not tax-exempt but have a fiscal agent relationship with a 501(c)3 organization are also eligible.
Restrictions: Through its IMPACT program, the Greater New Orleans Foundation is unable to fund the following types of requests: requests for individual support, either through scholarships or other forms of financial assistance; special events or conferences; programs that promote religious doctrine; endowments; and scientific or medical research.
Geographic Focus: All States
Date(s) Application is Due: Jul 30
Amount of Grant: Up to 20,000 USD
Contact: Roy Williams; (504) 598-4663; fax (504) 598-4676; grants@gnof.org
Internet: http://www.gnof.org/programs/impact/
Sponsor: Greater New Orleans Foundation
1055 St. Charles Avenue, Suite 100
New Orleans, LA 70130

GNOF IMPACT Grants for Youth Development 2081
Through the IMPACT Program, the Greater New Orleans Foundation (GNOF) makes grants to organizations serving the Greater New Orleans region. The ultimate goal of the IMPACT Program is to create a resilient, sustainable, vibrant, and equitable region in which individuals and families flourish and in which the special character of the New Orleans region and its people is preserved, celebrated, and given the means to develop. Specifically GNOF hopes to accomplish the following objectives through its IMPACT grants: provide a much needed source of financial and other support to nonprofit organizations that are struggling in the current financial environment and that are important to the health and vibrancy of the region; develop a better sense of the nonprofit organizations serving the region so GNOF can more effectively match donor desires with effective charitable work; identify and nurture promising new leaders and initiatives, especially in those communities that are in greatest need; and gain knowledge that will help nonprofit leaders and GNOF staff develop better long-term strategies for addressing regional needs and taking best advantage of important opportunities. IMPACT grants are awarded in four categories: Arts and Culture, Youth Development, Education, and Health and Human Services. In the category of Youth Development GNOF supports organizations that undertake the following types of projects: they facilitate access to high quality programs, activities, opportunities, and services for Greater New Orleans youth that will enhance their formal education, providing the cognitive, social, and emotional skills and abilities they need to become productive members of society; they provide professional development in the form of training, education, or tools to youth-development workers that will improve their knowledge, skills, and attitudes in the areas of case management, mentoring services, tutoring, and other remediation services or programs; they provide technical assistance and training to multiple youth-serving organizations to help them define and measure program outcomes and collect and track outcome and other data on participants and participation; they organize and/or increase the advocacy power of youth-serving organizations; and they develop a coordinated, comprehensive plan and strategies to address youth needs by engaging key stakeholders, promoting partnerships and strategic alliances, and identifying a diversified funding base. Interested organizations must submit a letter of intent along with all attachments via one email by 5 p.m. on July 30. GNOF program staff will review all letters of intent and will contact those organizations that are invited to submit a full application for funding. Awards are announced in November. Deadlines may vary from year to year. Interested organizations should verify the current deadline at the GNOF website where they can also obtain complete guidelines and requirements as well as a downloadable application form and cover sheet. Prospective applicants can also subscribe to GNOF's email newsletter for announcements of future funding opportunities. The subscription link is available from GNOF's Apply-for-a-Grant web page which contains a comprehensive listing of GNOF's current and past funding opportunities.
Requirements: Nonprofit, tax-exempt organizations that serve the thirteen parishes of Greater New Orleans are eligible to apply for funding. Organizations that are not tax-exempt but have a fiscal agent relationship with a 501(c)3 organization are also eligible.
Restrictions: Through its IMPACT program, the Greater New Orleans Foundation is unable to fund the following types of requests: requests for individual support, either through scholarships or other forms of financial assistance; special events or conferences; programs that promote religious doctrine; endowments; and scientific or medical research.
Geographic Focus: All States
Date(s) Application is Due: Jul 30
Amount of Grant: Up to 20,000 USD
Contact: Roy Williams; (504) 598-4663; fax (504) 598-4676; grants@gnof.org
Internet: http://www.gnof.org/programs/impact/
Sponsor: Greater New Orleans Foundation
1055 St. Charles Avenue, Suite 100
New Orleans, LA 70130

GNOF IMPACT Gulf States Eye Surgery Fund 2082
Through the IMPACT Program, the Greater New Orleans Foundation (GNOF) makes grants to organizations serving the Greater New Orleans region. The ultimate goal of the IMPACT program is to create a resilient, sustainable, vibrant, and equitable region in which individuals and families flourish and in which the special character of the New Orleans region and its people is preserved, celebrated, and given the means to develop. Specifically GNOF hopes to accomplish the following objectives through its IMPACT grants: provide a much needed source of financial and other support to nonprofit organizations that are struggling in the current financial environment and that are important to the health and vibrancy of the region; develop a better sense of the nonprofit organizations serving the region so GNOF can more effectively match donor desires with effective charitable work; identify and nurture promising new leaders and initiatives, especially in those communities that are in greatest need; and gain knowledge that will help nonprofit leaders and GNOF staff develop better long-term strategies for addressing regional needs and taking best advantage of important opportunities. IMPACT grants are awarded in four categories: Arts and

Culture, Youth Development, Education, and Health and Human Services. In the category of Health and Human Services, special funding is available for organizations that defray the expenses of poor or indigent patients requiring or receiving eye surgery, care, or treatment. Interested organizations must submit a letter of intent along with all attachments via one email by 5 p.m. on July 30 and should indicate on the IMPACT application cover sheet that they are applying for funding from the Gulf States Eye Surgery Fund. GNOF program staff will review all letters of intent and will contact those organizations that are invited to submit a full application for funding. Awards are announced in November. Deadlines may vary from year to year. Interested organizations should verify the current deadline at the GNOF website where they can also obtain complete guidelines and requirements as well as a downloadable application form and cover sheet. Prospective applicants can also subscribe to GNOF's email newsletter for announcements of future funding opportunities. The subscription link is available from GNOF's Apply-for-a-Grant web page which contains a comprehensive listing of GNOF's current and past funding opportunities.
Requirements: Nonprofit, tax-exempt organizations that serve the thirteen parishes of Greater New Orleans are eligible to apply for funding. Organizations that are not tax-exempt but have a fiscal agent relationship with a 501(c)3 organization are also eligible.
Restrictions: Through its IMPACT program, the Greater New Orleans Foundation is unable to fund the following types of requests: requests for support from individuals, either through scholarships or other forms of financial assistance; special events or conferences; programs that promote religious doctrine; endowments; and scientific or medical research.
Geographic Focus: All States
Date(s) Application is Due: Jul 30
Amount of Grant: Up to 20,000 USD
Contact: Roy Williams; (504) 598-4663; fax (504) 598-4676; grants@gnof.org
Internet: http://www.gnof.org/programs/impact/
Sponsor: Greater New Orleans Foundation
1055 St. Charles Avenue, Suite 100
New Orleans, LA 70130

GNOF IMPACT Harold W. Newman, Jr. Charitable Trust Grants **2083**
Through the IMPACT Program, the Greater New Orleans Foundation (GNOF) makes grants to organizations serving the Greater New Orleans region. The ultimate goal of the IMPACT program is to create a resilient, sustainable, vibrant, and equitable region in which individuals and families flourish and in which the special character of the New Orleans region and its people is preserved, celebrated, and given the means to develop. Specifically GNOF hopes to accomplish the following objectives through its IMPACT grants: provide a much needed source of financial and other support to nonprofit organizations that are struggling in the current financial environment and that are important to the health and vibrancy of the region; develop a better sense of the nonprofit organizations serving the region so GNOF can more effectively match donor desires with effective charitable work; identify and nurture promising new leaders and initiatives, especially in those communities that are in greatest need; and gain knowledge that will help nonprofit leaders and GNOF staff develop better long-term strategies for addressing regional needs and taking best advantage of important opportunities. IMPACT grants are awarded in four categories: Arts and Culture, Youth Development, Education, and Health and Human Services. In the category of Health and Human Services, special funding is available for organizations that provide health-care assistance to residents of New Orleans whose U.S. adjusted gross income for the preceding tax year, when added to any tax-exempt income and income from a spouse for that same year, is at least $75,000 but not more than $200,000. The health-care assistance must be for cancer, heart disease, or Alzheimer's. Interested organizations must submit a letter of intent along with all attachments via one email by 5 p.m. on July 30 and should indicate on the IMPACT application cover sheet that they are applying for funding from the Harold W. Newman, Jr. Charitable Trust. GNOF program staff will review all letters of intent and will contact those organizations that are invited to submit a full application for funding. Awards are announced in November. Deadlines may vary from year to year. Interested organizations should verify the current deadline at the GNOF website where they can also obtain complete guidelines and requirements as well as a downloadable application form and cover sheet. Prospective applicants can also subscribe to GNOF's email newsletter for announcements of future funding opportunities. The subscription link is available from GNOF's Apply-for-a-Grant web page which contains a comprehensive listing of GNOF's current and past funding opportunities.
Requirements: Nonprofit, tax-exempt organizations that serve the thirteen parishes of Greater New Orleans are eligible to apply for funding. Organizations that are not tax-exempt but have a fiscal agent relationship with a 501(c)3 organization are also eligible.
Restrictions: Through its IMPACT program, the Greater New Orleans Foundation is unable to fund the following types of requests: requests for support from individuals, either through scholarships or other forms of financial assistance; special events or conferences; programs that promote religious doctrine; endowments; and scientific or medical research.
Geographic Focus: All States
Date(s) Application is Due: Jul 30
Amount of Grant: Up to 20,000 USD
Contact: Roy Williams; (504) 598-4663; fax (504) 598-4676; grants@gnof.org
Internet: http://www.gnof.org/programs/impact/
Sponsor: Greater New Orleans Foundation
1055 St. Charles Avenue, Suite 100
New Orleans, LA 70130

GNOF IMPACT Kahn-Oppenheim Trust Grants **2084**
Through the IMPACT Program, the Greater New Orleans Foundation (GNOF) makes grants to organizations serving the Greater New Orleans region. The ultimate goal of the IMPACT program is to create a resilient, sustainable, vibrant, and equitable region in which individuals and families flourish and in which the special character of the New Orleans region and its people is preserved, celebrated, and given the means to develop. Specifically GNOF hopes to accomplish the following objectives through its IMPACT grants: provide a much needed source of financial and other support to nonprofit organizations that are struggling in the current financial environment and that are important to the health and vibrancy of the region; develop a better sense of the nonprofit organizations serving the region so GNOF can more effectively match donor desires with effective charitable work; identify and nurture promising new leaders and initiatives, especially in those communities that are in greatest need; and gain knowledge that will help nonprofit leaders and GNOF staff develop better long-term strategies for addressing regional needs and taking best advantage of important opportunities. IMPACT grants are awarded in four categories: Arts and Culture, Youth Development, Education, and Health and Human Services. In the category of Health and Human Services, special funding is available for the development and/or improvement of public-health outreach and education programs to inform people about ways to prevent diseases like asthma, diabetes, heart disease, obesity, HIV/AIDS, and others, insofar as these programs involve physical, nutritional, or dietary regimens. Interested organizations must submit a letter of intent along with all attachments via one email by 5 p.m. on July 30 and should indicate on the IMPACT application cover sheet that they are applying for funding from the Kahn-Oppenheim Trust. GNOF program staff will review all letters of intent and will contact those organizations that are invited to submit a full application for funding. Awards are announced in November. Deadlines may vary from year to year. Interested organizations should verify the current deadline at the GNOF website where they can also obtain complete guidelines and requirements as well as a downloadable application form and cover sheet. Prospective applicants can also subscribe to GNOF's email newsletter for announcements of future funding opportunities. The subscription link is available from GNOF's Apply-for-a-Grant web page which contains a comprehensive listing of GNOF's current and past funding opportunities.
Requirements: Nonprofit, tax-exempt organizations that serve the thirteen parishes of Greater New Orleans are eligible to apply for funding. Organizations that are not tax-exempt but have a fiscal agent relationship with a 501(c)3 organization are also eligible.
Restrictions: Through its IMPACT program, the Greater New Orleans Foundation is unable to fund the following types of requests: requests for support from individuals, either through scholarships or other forms of financial assistance; special events or conferences; programs that promote religious doctrine; endowments; and scientific or medical research.
Geographic Focus: All States
Date(s) Application is Due: Jul 30
Amount of Grant: Up to 20,000 USD
Contact: Roy Williams; (504) 598-4663; fax (504) 598-4676; grants@gnof.org
Internet: http://www.gnof.org/programs/impact/
Sponsor: Greater New Orleans Foundation
1055 St. Charles Avenue, Suite 100
New Orleans, LA 70130

GNOF Jefferson Community Grants **2085**
Hurricane Katrina's landfall in 2005 only exacerbated the challenges faced by Jefferson Parish (Louisiana's most populous parish) which has begun in recent years to exhibit the typical symptoms of many traditional American "inner-ring" suburban communities: decay of public and private infrastructure; a rapid rate of diversification that outpaces the rate of integration; under-performing public schools; and exodus of families with sufficient economic resources (in this case to the more "pristine pastures north of Lake Pontchartrain"). In 2008 the Greater New Orleans Foundation (GNOF) established an affiliate community foundation in Jefferson Parish to help the parish remain a community of choice within the greater New Orleans region. GNOF seeded the Jefferson Community Foundation (JCF) with $500,000, to be distributed over a period of five years, with the agreement that JCF would set aside 10% of the seed money as an endowment. Since its inception, JCF has worked to strengthen resident-led organizations and to stabilize areas in varying states of decline through such strategies as employer-assisted housing initiatives, facade improvement programs, and direct grants to community groups wishing to beautify targeted neighborhoods. The foundation has also worked to match available housing stock with financially stable first-time homeowners whose presence can solidify the market in those areas most in need of it. Organizations interested in obtaining grants through JCF can contact GNOF for more information.
Geographic Focus: Louisiana
Contact: Dr. Marco Cocito-Monoc, Director for Regional Initiatives; (504) 598-4663; fax (504) 598-4676; marco@gnof.org
Reginald H. Smith, Chair, Board of Directors of Jefferson Parish Community Foundation; (504) 598-4663; fax (504) 598-4676
Internet: http://www.gnof.org/overview-7/
Sponsor: Greater New Orleans Foundation
1055 St. Charles Avenue, Suite 100
New Orleans, LA 70130

GNOF Maison Hospitaliere Grants **2086**
In 1879 Coralie Correjolles organized 30 women into "La Société Hospitaliere des Dames Louisianaises" to provide food and medicine to the needy of New Orleans, many of whom had lost everything during the Civil War. The group became especially concerned by the plight of elderly ladies, who, due to the loss of their husbands in the war, were destitute and living in squalid conditions. Through its collection of ten-cent monthly dues over 14 years, the Socíeté was able to raise the money for its first building, 822 Barracks Street, to provide residence for 20 women. Over the next 113 years Maison Hospitaliere evolved into a skilled nursing facility for both men and women. Hurricane Katrina scattered both residents and staff across the country, and in November 2006 the board decided to close the facility. When the Maison Hospitaliere sold its French Quarter complex for more than $4 million, the proceeds were incorporated in 2009 into a Supporting Organization of the Greater New

Orleans Foundation (GNOF) so that the Maison's mission could continue by making grants to organizations serving women and their families. These grants support direct services to women in the form of either general operating support or program support and range up to $20,000. Grant requests and supporting materials must be received via email by 5:00 p.m. on August 31. Prospective applicants can obtain complete guidelines and requirements as well as a downloadable application form at the GNOF website. Interested organizations can also subscribe to GNOF's email newsletter for announcements of future funding opportunities. The subscription link is available from GNOF's Apply-for-a-Grant web page which contains a comprehensive listing of GNOF's current and past funding opportunities.
Requirements: Grants will be made available to 501(c)3 organizations that provide living assistance and care to indigent women in the Greater New Orleans area.
Restrictions: Maison Hospitaliere will not consider capital projects, event sponsorship, or research requests. Faith-based organizations are welcome to apply for support for programs that do not include religious activities, such as religious worship, instruction, or proselytization.
Geographic Focus: All States
Date(s) Application is Due: Aug 31
Amount of Grant: Up to 20,000 USD
Contact: Ellen M. Lee, Sr. Vice President, Programs, Community Revitalization Program Director; (504) 598-4663; fax (504) 598-4676; grants@gnof.org
Internet: http://www.gnof.org/maison-hospitaliere/
Sponsor: Greater New Orleans Foundation
1055 St. Charles Avenue, Suite 100
New Orleans, LA 70130

GNOF Metropolitan Opportunities Grants 2087
In 2011, the Ford Foundation and the Greater New Orleans Foundation (GNOF) formed a partnership called the Metropolitan Opportunities Initiative. As part of a national initiative of the Ford Foundation, Metropolitan Opportunities enables GNOF to adopt and encourage a holistic approach to community revitalization on a regional scale—in this case, the entire thirteen-parish area that comprises Greater New Orleans—rather than on just one neighborhood or one block. The Metropolitan Opportunities Initiative is focused on three core areas: access to affordable housing, metropolitan land-use innovation, and access to economic opportunity. The specific goals of the Initiative are to connect people to opportunities for safe, affordable housing and efficient, effective transit, and to promote economic and workforce development. Interested organizations can contact GNOF with any questions about Metropolitan Opportunities and visit the GNOF website to obtain more detailed information about the initiative as well as its past grantees. Organizations can also subscribe to GNOF's email newsletter for announcements of future funding opportunities. The subscription link is available from GNOF's Apply-for-a-Grant web page which contains a comprehensive listing of GNOF's current and past funding opportunities.
Geographic Focus: All States
Amount of Grant: 10,000 - 300,000 USD
Contact: Ryan Albright; (504) 598-4663; fax (504) 598-4676; albright@gnof.org
Internet: http://www.gnof.org/programs/metropolitan-opportunities-initiative/
Sponsor: Greater New Orleans Foundation
1055 St. Charles Avenue, Suite 100
New Orleans, LA 70130

GNOF New Orleans Works Grants 2088
New Orleans Works (NOW) is a public-private partnership initiative housed at the Greater New Orleans Foundation (GNOF) and funded by a grant from the National Fund for Workforce Solutions (NFWS), a $31-million, five-year effort to fuel high-impact workforce partnerships and to advance 30,000 workers in 32 regions in the U.S., including the Greater New Orleans area. Led by foundations and regional public workforce systems, NOW pools funding, develops strategy, supports economic-sector-based programs and develops workforce partnerships that meet both the career-advancement needs of workers and the workforce needs of employers. Although the people of the Greater New Orleans area are creative, hardworking, and dedicated, the region's economic performance has persistently fallen below its potential. Too often residents are held back by failures in public education, the legacy of racism, and underinvestment in workforce development. Devastating hurricanes in recent years have battered the economy, inflicting costly damage to businesses and infrastructure and spurring the relocation of major corporations and large employers. Furthermore, the economic turmoil caused by the 2010 oil disaster in the Gulf of Mexico demonstrated the perils of the region's over-reliance on too few industries. To attract jobs that provide sustainable family incomes to the area, NOW takes a two-tiered approach, working both with employers and with education and training providers to create a skilled workforce that is aligned with employers' needs, sector by sector. NOW promotes individual, institutional, and system-wide change in order to achieve the following goals: connecting residents with existing and emerging career opportunities; building long-term relationships between employees, employers, and training providers; expanding the minority middle class; creating an enhanced public workforce system; providing a larger pool of skilled workers; and transforming the many lessons learned in community and environmental resilience into economic opportunities and new industries that can bring the region to the forefront of innovation. GNOF accepts NOW applications through its Request for Proposal (RFP) process. Interested organizations are encouraged to subscribe to GNOF's email newsletter for announcements of future funding opportunities. The subscription link is available from GNOF's Apply-for-a-Grant web page which contains a comprehensive listing of GNOF's current and past funding opportunities. NOW's RFP deadlines and economic-sector focus may vary from offering to offering. Interested organizations are encouraged to visit the GNOF website to obtain more detailed and up todate information on the initiative and its RFP process and to contact the NOW Site Director with any questions.
Requirements: Non-profit, not-for-profit, and for-profit organizations are eligible to apply. Job providers should select a training partner that has the sector knowledge and capacity to execute a training intervention that addresses their workforce-development needs. The funding must be awarded to an entity with the financial management system capability to accept federal funding.
Restrictions: Programs and partnerships funded by the NOW initiative must benefit the Greater New Orleans area.
Geographic Focus: All States
Date(s) Application is Due: Oct 12
Amount of Grant: Up to 250,000 USD
Contact: Bonita Robertson, New Orleans Works Interim Site Director; (504) 598-4663 ext. 40; fax (504) 598-4676; bonita@gnof.org
Danny Murphy, (504) 598-4663; fax (504) 598-4676; danny@gnof.org
Internet: http://www.gnof.org/new-orleans-works/
Sponsor: Greater New Orleans Foundation
1055 St. Charles Avenue, Suite 100
New Orleans, LA 70130

GNOF Norco Community Grants 2089
Shell Chemicals and Motiva Enterprises, grant-making partners of the Greater New Orleans Foundation (GNOF), have established the Norco Community fund to improve the quality of lives for people in Norco, Louisiana. The fund provides the following types of grants: capital-fund grants for new construction or major renovation; seed-money grants to help start new organizations which respond to an important opportunity in the community; bridge grants to sustain organizations experiencing financial hardships; program grants that support new, creative, or beneficial programs; and grants to organizations with a positive track record. Areas of interest include arts and humanities, community development, education, environment, human services, health care, community building, and youth development. Grant requests are reviewed by an advisory committee of business and civic leaders that meets annually. Application materials must be postmarked no later than September 14 and mailed to the Norco address given under the Contact Information section. If the deadline falls on a weekend or holiday, then the materials must be postmarked by the weekday immediately following; grant requests received after the deadline will be reviewed in the next year's grant cycle. Exact deadlines may vary from year to year. Prospective applicants should verify the current deadline at the GNOF website where they can also obtain complete guidelines and requirements as well as a downloadable application form. Prospective applicants can also subscribe to GNOF's email newsletter for announcements of future funding opportunities. The subscription link is available from GNOF's Apply-for-a-Grant web page which contains a comprehensive listing of GNOF's current and past funding opportunities.
Requirements: Applicants must have 501(c)3 status or apply through a fiscal agent who has such status.
Restrictions: The fund will only consider support for programs that serve the Norco community and its residents.
Geographic Focus: Louisiana
Date(s) Application is Due: Sep 14
Contact: Program Coordinator
Ellen M. Lee, Sr. Vice President, Programs, Community Revitalization Program Director; (504) 598-4663; fax (504) 598-4676; ellen@gnof.org
Internet: http://www.gnof.org/norco-community-fund/
Sponsor: Greater New Orleans Foundation
1055 St. Charles Avenue, Suite 100
New Orleans, LA 70130

GNOF Organizational Effectiveness Grants and Workshops 2090
In the wake of Hurricane Katrina and the levee failures, many new organizations have sprung up in the greater New Orleans region to address the immediate and pressing needs of recovery at the neighborhood level and up. This surge in activism and engagement holds great promise for the region, but significant issues must be addressed to give this work the greatest impact. Often, dedicated nonprofit leaders and professionals struggle with inexperienced boards, overwhelming fundraising responsibilities, and a lack of resources to develop their own infrastructure and talent. In response, the Greater New Orleans Foundation (GNOF) supports emerging leaders and organizations, empowers organizations in the region to be more competitive in their bids for state and federal funding, and serves as a convener to build connections and relationships within the greater New Orleans nonprofit sector. In partnership with the Marguerite Casey Foundation, GNOF provides training programs for staff and board members of nonprofits in the region to learn new ways of conducting fundraising, working with boards, and managing communications. In partnership with the Kellogg Foundation, GNOF provides technical-assistance grants of up to $4,000 to help nonprofit staff and/or board members increase their capacity to lead, manage, and govern their organizations. Following are examples of ways in which these technical-assistance grants can be used: working with a consultant to assist staff and board in development of fundraising or strategic plans for the organization; hiring a facilitator for a board retreat to grow governance abilities; covering expenses for attendance at a workshop or training session on a specific topic, such as evaluation, strategic communications, financial management, or fundraising; or completing an organizational assessment. All of these forms of technical assistance share the outcome that the grantee organizaqtion's staff and/or board members will be actively involved and will acquire new skills or information that will help the organization to grow and improve. GNOF accepts technical-assistance grant requests on a first-come, first-serve basis until the funding runs out. Priority will be given to requests pertaining to GNOF's current area of focus (advocacy, board governance, evaluation, financial management, fundraising, succession planning, partnering and collaboration, or fundraising). To apply for a GNOF technical-assistance grant, applicants should submit a two-page request along with required supporting documents via email to GNOF's Program Officer for Organizational Effectiveness. A decision will be made on the request approximately four weeks from the date that the request letter is received.

Complete guidelines for submission are available at the GNOF website as well as links to capacity-building resources. Prospective applicants are welcome to contact the GNOF Program Officer with any additional questions. To receive further information about GNOF's workshops for nonprofits, interested organizations in the region should check the GNOF website or contact GNOF's Vice-President of Organizational Effectiveness.
Requirements: To be eligible to apply for GNOF's technical-assistance grants, organizations must be current or former (within the last two years) recipients of GNOF discretionary grants and have a primary office located within GNOF's 13-parish service area (Assumption, Jefferson, Lafourche, Orleans, Plaquemines, St. Bernard, St. Charles, St. James, St. John the Baptist, St. Tammany, Tangipahoa, Terrebonne, and Washington). Organizations that have previously received a GNOF technical-assistance grant may apply for additional grants in subsequent years (given funding availability); successful recurring requests will show that the applicant has built upon previous strategies.
Restrictions: Technical-assistance grants may not be used to pay a board member or any party whose direct affiliation with the applicant organization could be construed as or would create a conflict of interest. While prospective applicants may have highly competent professional resources on their boards, GNOF would expect these resources to be provided as an in-kind donation. Technical-assistance grants will not be made for activities that have already occurred or are underway at the time the grant is awarded.
Geographic Focus: Louisiana
Amount of Grant: Up to 4,000 USD
Contact: Kellie Chavez Greene, Program Officer, Organizational Effectiveness; (504) 598-4663; fax (504) 598-4676; kellie@gnof.org
Internet: http://www.gnof.org/organizational-effectiveness-technical-assistance-grants/
Sponsor: Greater New Orleans Foundation
1055 St. Charles Avenue, Suite 100
New Orleans, LA 70130

GNOF Plaquemines Community Grants 2091
Plaquemines Parish is the "big toe of Louisiana's boot" protruding into the Gulf of Mexico. On August 29, 2005, Hurricane Katrina struck on the west bank of Plaquemines Parish. The 20-foot storm surge hit the southern coastline and gradually inundated the entire parish as it moved northward. A month later, Hurricane Rita's three-foot storm surge caused more damage to the already weakened parish levees, resulting in more flooding. In 2006 the Greater New Orleans Foundation (GNOF) established an affiliate community foundation in Plaquemines Parish, because GNOF believed that the rebuilding process in devastated areas should be led by those who live and work in them. GNOF seeded the Plaquemines Community Foundation (PCF) with $500,000, distributed over a period of five years, with the agreement that PCF would set aside 10% of the seed money as an endowment. The mission of PCF is to improve the quality of life for all citizens of the Plaquemine parish. PCF's board identifies current and emerging needs and addresses those needs through grants, and also fosters relationships with donors to build permanent endowments. Since its inception, the PCF has awarded grants to support education programs and agricultural initiatives. It has also partnered with the Saint Bernard Community Foundation to create the Southeast Louisiana Fisheries Assistance Center, which currently serves as a clearing house for local fishermen to receive free business planning, financial assistance (in the form of grants and low-interest loans), fishing licenses, and industry-specific training services. Plaquemine organizations interested in obtaining grants through PCF can contact GNOF for more information.
Geographic Focus: Louisiana
Contact: Dr. Marco Cocito-Monoc; (504) 598-4663; marco@gnof.org
Internet: http://www.gnof.org/overview-6/
Sponsor: Greater New Orleans Foundation
1055 St. Charles Avenue, Suite 100
New Orleans, LA 70130

GNOF St. Bernard Community Grants 2092
When Hurricane Katrina hit the Louisiana coast in 2005, a forty-two-mile swath of St. Bernard Parish was flooded, and the majority of homes in that area were destroyed; St. Bernard suffered more flooding damage from Hurricane Katrina than any other Lousiana parish. In 2006 the Greater New Orleans Foundation (GNOF) established an affiliate community foundation in St. Bernard Parish, because GNOF believed that the rebuilding process in devastated areas should be led by those who live and work in them. GNOF seeded the St. Bernard Community Foundation (SBCF) with $500,000, distributed over a period of five years, with the agreement that SBCF would set aside 10% of the seed money as an endowment. The mission of SBCF is to improve the quality of life for all citizens of the St. Bernard parish. SBCF's board identifies current and emerging needs and addresses those needs through grants, and also fosters relationships with donors to build permanent endowments. Since its inception, the SBCF has played an important role in the rebuilding of the St. Bernard community. It has also partnered with the Plaquemines Community Foundation to create the Southeast Louisiana Fisheries Assistance Center, a clearing house for local fishermen to receive free business planning, financial assistance (in the form of grants and low-interest loans), fishing licenses, and industry-specific training services. St. Bernard organizations interested in obtaining grants through SBCF can contact GNOF for more information.
Geographic Focus: Louisiana
Samples: Hannan Complex, Meraux, Louisiana—to provide a new scoreboard for the Hannan All-Sports Complex; David Boehlke, Washington, D.C.—to perform an assessment of St. Bernard Parish using the "Healthy Neighborhoods" assets-based approach for building vibrant communities; St. Bernard Parish Government, Chalmette, Louisiana—to hire a national leader in planning and public policy to rewrite the parish's zoning regulations in order to simplify the rebuilding process for both officials and private developers.
Contact: Dr. Marco Cocito-Monoc, Director for Regional Initiatives; (504) 598-4663; fax (504) 598-4676; marco@gnof.org
Internet: http://www.gnof.org/overview-5/
Sponsor: Greater New Orleans Foundation
1055 St. Charles Avenue, Suite 100
New Orleans, LA 70130

GNOF Stand Up For Our Children Grants 2093
In New Orleans almost one in two children under the age of five lives at or below the federal poverty level. The Greater New Orleans Foundation (GNOF) believes that parental involvement is the best change agent for improving conditions for children. To help address the issue, GNOF, in partnership and with assistance from the W.K. Kellogg Foundation, formed an initiative called Stand Up for Our Children. It identifies and invests in nonprofit organizations that train parents to develop leadership skills that enable them to become more effective advocates, essentially helping their voices to be heard. In 2012 a total of $575,366 was awarded to ten organizations for their success working with parents and advocating for families. In addition to receiving grants, all grantees participated in a learning community designed to share knowledge, foster coalitions and alliances, and document lessons learned. The second round of grants from the Stand Up for Our Children Initiative will take place in 2013. These grants are by invitation only. Interested organizations should contact the GNOF Program Officer (see Contact Information Section) and check the GNOF website for updates. Prospective applicants can also subscribe to GNOF's email newsletter for announcements of future funding opportunities. The subscription link is available from GNOF's Apply-for-a-Grant web page which contains a comprehensive listing of GNOF's current and past funding opportunities.
Geographic Focus: Louisiana
Amount of Grant: 40,000 - 130,000 USD
Contact: Flint D. Mitchell; (504) 598-4663; fax (504) 598-4676; flint@gnof.org
Internet: http://www.gnof.org/stand-up-for-our-children-initiative/
Sponsor: Greater New Orleans Foundation
1055 St. Charles Avenue, Suite 100
New Orleans, LA 70130

Go Daddy Cares Charitable Contributions 2094
Go Daddy has a long history of philanthropic work in support of a variety of charitable, community-wide and global organizations. Go Daddy Cares has dedicated manpower and dollars to raise awareness toward the causes of domestic violence, child abuse, and animal shelters. The corporate philanthropy program contributes to nonprofit organizations that focus on causes which are meaningful to its business, customers, employees and the communities in which it operates. In addition to making monetary contributions, Go Daddy encourages its employees to become involved in community organizations.
Requirements: Go Daddy focuses support on the communities where it resides. This includes: Greater Phoenix area; Hiawatha, IA; Denver, CO & Silicon Valley, CA. Nonprofit charitable organizations classified as a 501(c)3 public charity by the Internal Revenue Service and with a current Form 990 are eligible to apply. Charities relating to children, women's causes, animal welfare or technology related initiatives are given priority for financial allocations. All submissions for support must be made online through the Go Daddy Cares Charity Application Form. There are no deadlines, however, advance notice of 3-6 months is required for all sponsorship requests. Only one application per cause, per year will be considered.
Restrictions: Go Daddy does not consider requests for golf tournaments or walks.
Geographic Focus: Arizona, California, Colorado, Iowa
Contact: Nick Fuller, (623) 203-7744; Nick@GoDaddy.com
Internet: http://godaddycares.com/
Sponsor: Go Daddy
14455 N. Hayden Road, Suite 226
Scottsdale, AZ 85260

Godfrey Foundation Grants 2095
The Foundation, established in Wisconsin in 1945 and supported by a donation from the Fleming Companies, Inc., offers grants primarily in the Milwaukee and Waukesha, Wisconsin, region. Its major field of interest include: education; health care; human services; community development and services; and youth development programs. The major type of support comes in the form of general operations funding. An application form is required, and interested organizations should contact the Foundation for a copy. There are no particular deadlines with which to adhere, and grant amounts have ranged from $500 to $30,000.
Requirements: Applicants must be 501(c)3 organizations serving residents of Wisconsin.
Geographic Focus: Wisconsin
Amount of Grant: 500 - 30,000 USD
Contact: Terry L. Daniels, Director; (262) 275-0458
Sponsor: Godfrey Foundation
680 Kenosha Street, P.O. Box 810
Walworth, WI 53184-0810

Goizueta Foundation Grants 2096
The Foundation strives to use their resources for programs which will have the greatest possible long-term impact and sustainable change. Therefore, the Foundation is focused on the following areas: early childhood education; primary and secondary education; higher education; pre-selected youth and family homes; youth and family development; immigrant/refugee services; services for people with disabilities; and pre-selected arts and culture. Interested applicants must submit an organizational overview form. Forms are accepted on an ongoing basis.
Requirements: To be eligible, your organization must: be classified as a public charity and tax exempt under 501(c)3 of the Internal Revenue Code; benefit Georgia; not receive significant funding support from the government.

Restrictions: The Foundation does not fund: annual fund drives; events/conference sponsorships; grants to individuals; awards/prizes/competitions; capital campaigns; capital investment, construction/renovation, equipment purchase; general operating expenses; operating deficits or retirement of debt; political campaigns; legislative lobbying to influence elections; government agencies or agencies directly benefiting public entities; projects that do not fit within our current program area priorities.
Geographic Focus: Georgia
Amount of Grant: 15,000 - 10,000,000 USD
Contact: Maria Retter, Executive Director; (404) 239-0390; fax (404) 239-0018; info@goizuetafoundation.org
Internet: http://www.goizuetafoundation.org/grantseekers.htm
Sponsor: Goizueta Foundation
4401 Northside Parkway, Suite 520
Atlanta, GA 30327

Golden LEAF Foundation Grants 2097
The mission of the foundation is to support organizations that promote the social welfare of North Carolina's citizens and to receive and distribute funds to lessen the economic impact of changes in the state's tobacco economy. The Foundation looks for projects with the following characteristics: serving unmet needs in communities; supporting new technology, crops, and applications to increase the areas advantage in agriculture; job creation and retention in rural tobacco-dependent counties; creation, expansion and improvement of business activity in rural tobacco-dependent counties; training/workforce preparedness initiatives; and public infrastructure improvement projects. Applicants seeking funding are encouraged to contact the Foundation for more information regarding the grants application process and funding priorities.
Requirements: Government and 501(c)3 tax-exempt organizations in North Carolina are eligible to apply.
Restrictions: Grants will not be awarded to: endowments; capital campaigns; construction projects - except as noted; infrastructure - except as noted; debt relief; revolving loan funds; purchase of land; after-school or day care programs; general employability training programs; general use community centers/facilities.
Geographic Focus: North Carolina
Date(s) Application is Due: Aug 1
Contact: Grants Administrator; (888) 684-8404 or (252) 442-7474; fax (252) 442-7404; info@goldenleaf.org
Internet: http://www.goldenleaf.org
Sponsor: Golden LEAF (Long-term Economic Advancement Foundation) Foundation
107 SE Main Street, Suite 500
Rocky Mount, NC 27801

Golden Rule Foundation Grants 2098
The Foundation is dedicated to the American dream of Self Help. Giving is primarily made for the arts, education and social services. Unsolicited requests for funds are not considered. Application information is available online.
Requirements: Nonprofit organizations are eligible to apply. Applicants must demonstrate a successful history of financial management. Applicants should not contact the administrator unless authorized to do so.
Restrictions: Grants are not made to individuals.
Geographic Focus: All States
Date(s) Application is Due: Jun 1
Contact: Laurel Frye, Administrator; (207) 236-4104; goldenrule@prexar.com
Internet: http://www.goldrule.org
Sponsor: Golden Rule Foundation
P.O. Box 658
Camden, ME 04843

Golden State Warriors Foundation Grants 2099
The foundation committed to positively impacting the communities of Oakland and the greater San Francisco Bay Area by providing financial assistance and opportunities to other non-profit civic and community organizations that benefit and enrich the lives of children, youth and those in need. By providing financial support and unique resources, the Foundation endeavors to meet the social, educational and cultural needs of the community. Although the Warriors Foundation will not be accepting grant applications until the beginning of the 2007-08 fiscal year, it remains committed to providing assistance and in-kind support to Bay Area nonprofit organizations through the donation of tickets, autographed memorabilia, promotional items, sponsorships, and player and talent appearances. Application information and forms are available on the Web site.
Requirements: 501(c)3 nonprofit organizations that provide programs and services in the greater San Francisco Bay area are eligible.
Restrictions: Grants do not support individuals; schools; political, labor, religious, or fraternal activities; endowments; fundraising events; government agencies; or organizations with discriminatory or unlawful practices.
Geographic Focus: California
Amount of Grant: Up to 375,000 USD
Contact: Angela Cohan, President; (510) 986-5307; community_web@gs-warriors.com
Internet: http://www.nba.com/warriors/community/Warriors_Foundation-011024.html
Sponsor: Golden State Warriors Foundation
1011 Broadway
Oakland, CA 94607-4019

Goldseker Foundation Community Affairs Grants 2100
The Goldseker Foundation maintains a two-track grantmaking program that designates three priority areas but retains the ability to initiate and respond to new ideas and opportunities within our established program areas. In each of the priority grant areas, the Foundation is a directly engaged and active partner. Grants include a mix of Foundation initiatives and projects submitted independently by potential grantees. Community affairs grants cut across a number of areas, including foreclosure prevention, economic development, and improving and strengthening organizations that make living and working in Baltimore City and its metropolitan region attractive to long term residents, businesses, and talented newcomers.
Requirements: To be considered for funding, an organization must meet all of the following
Requirements: must be nonprofit organizations as defined in Section 501(c)3 and Section 509(a) of the Internal Revenue Code; must carry on their work principally in metropolitan Baltimore; and, applicants may not discriminate on the basis of race, creed, color, physical handicap, or gender. Because the Foundation is not normally a long-term source of funds, applicants are encouraged to demonstrate how proposed activities will be sustained. Applicants are expected to demonstrate adequate administrative capacity and financial stability and to describe evaluation criteria and methods in their requests.
Restrictions: The Foundation does not provide funds for endowments; individuals; building campaigns; deficit financing; annual giving; publications; arts and culture; religious programs or purposes; political action groups; specific disabilities or diseases; or, projects normally financed by government.
Geographic Focus: Maryland
Contact: Laurie Latuda Kinkel; (410) 837-6115; lmlatuda@goldsekerfoundation.org
Internet: http://www.goldsekerfoundation.org/_grants?program_area_id=5
Sponsor: Morris Goldseker Foundation
1040 Park Avenue, Suite 310
Baltimore, MD 21201

Goldseker Foundation Community Grants 2101
The Goldseker Foundation maintains a two-track grantmaking program that designates three priority areas but retains the ability to initiate and respond to new ideas and opportunities within our established program areas. In each of the priority grant areas, the Foundation is a directly engaged and active partner. Grants include a mix of Foundation initiatives and projects submitted independently by potential grantees. Baltimore's ultimate success as a city will be largely determined by its success in reviving and sustaining safe, clean, economically vibrant and welcoming neighborhoods. To help do this, the Foundation invests money and talent over an extended period of time in a market-based community development strategy that focuses on a limited number of communities, which the Foundation selects, to identify, build upon, and promote their neighborhood assets.
Requirements: To be considered for funding, an organization must meet all of the following
Requirements: must be nonprofit organizations as defined in Section 501(c)3 and Section 509(a) of the Internal Revenue Code; must carry on their work principally in metropolitan Baltimore; and, applicants may not discriminate on the basis of race, creed, color, physical handicap, or gender. Because the Foundation is not normally a long-term source of funds, applicants are encouraged to demonstrate how proposed activities will be sustained. Applicants are expected to demonstrate adequate administrative capacity and financial stability and to describe evaluation criteria and methods in their requests.
Restrictions: The Foundation does not provide funds for endowments; individuals; building campaigns; deficit financing; annual giving; publications; arts and culture; religious programs or purposes; political action groups; specific disabilities or diseases; or, projects normally financed by government.
Geographic Focus: Maryland
Contact: Laurie Latuda Kinkel; (410) 837-6115; lmlatuda@goldsekerfoundation.org
Internet: http://www.goldsekerfoundation.org/_grants?program_area_id=3
Sponsor: Morris Goldseker Foundation
1040 Park Avenue, Suite 310
Baltimore, MD 21201

Goldseker Foundation Human Services Grants 2102
The Goldseker Foundation maintains a two-track grantmaking program that designates three priority areas but retains the ability to initiate and respond to new ideas and opportunities within our established program areas. In each of the priority grant areas, the Foundation is a directly engaged and active partner. Grants include a mix of Foundation initiatives and projects submitted independently by potential grantees. Human services grants focus on those projects and organizations which have a broad reach and work to improve systems of service delivery, rather than those which provide direct services themselves.
Requirements: To be considered for funding, an organization must meet all of the following
Requirements: must be nonprofit organizations as defined in Section 501(c)3 and Section 509(a) of the Internal Revenue Code; must carry on their work principally in metropolitan Baltimore; and, applicants may not discriminate on the basis of race, creed, color, physical handicap, or gender. Because the Foundation is not normally a long-term source of funds, applicants are encouraged to demonstrate how proposed activities will be sustained. Applicants are expected to demonstrate adequate administrative capacity and financial stability and to describe evaluation criteria and methods in their requests.
Restrictions: The Foundation does not fund endowments; individuals; building campaigns; deficit financing; annual giving; publications; arts and culture; religious programs or purposes; political action groups; specific disabilities or diseases; or, projects financed by government.
Geographic Focus: Maryland
Contact: Laurie Latuda Kinkel; (410) 837-6115; lmlatuda@goldsekerfoundation.org
Internet: http://www.goldsekerfoundation.org/_grants?program_area_id=6
Sponsor: Morris Goldseker Foundation
1040 Park Avenue, Suite 310
Baltimore, MD 21201

Goldseker Foundation Non-Profit Management Assistance Grants 2103
Management assistance grants are intended to help smaller, well-established nonprofits make investments in timely organizational development activities that would not otherwise be possible because of limited budget resources. Most management assistance grant recipients have operating budgets of less than $2 million. These grants principally fund the engagement of qualified consulting expertise to conduct the following: strategic planning; fund development and sustainability; financial management systems; improvement; program evaluation; IT assessment and planning (not hardware or software purchases); board development, executive coaching, and succession planning; improving systems of service delivery; mergers, strategic alliances, and partnerships. Applications are accepted throughout the year. The board makes funding decisions approximately once per quarter.
Requirements: Non-profit 501(c)3 organizations that carry out their work principally in metropolitan Baltimore, primarily Baltimore City, are eligible to apply. Preference will be given to those organizations whose programs fit within the Foundation's published areas of interest (community development, education, and human services) but will be considered from any organization that does not conflict with the foundation's grant making policies. Organizations must call the Foundation's Program Officer to review the proposal concept before submitting an application. Applications that arrive without prior approval to submit will not be considered. Organizations with a budget of $250,000 or greater are must pledge a cash match equal to at least 50% of the requested grant amount. Organizations with budgets under $250,000 must pledge a cash match equal to at least 25% of the requested grant amount.
Restrictions: Management Assistance Grants are not intended to be a form of start-up support for new nonprofits. Organizations need to be able to demonstrate program outcomes already achieved and have completed at least two full budget years.
Geographic Focus: Maryland
Contact: Laurie Latuda Kinkel, Program Officer; (410) 837-6115; fax (410) 837-7927; lmlatuda@goldsekerfoundation.org
Internet: http://www.goldsekerfoundation.org/_grants?program_area_id=2
Sponsor: Morris Goldseker Foundation
1040 Park Avenue, Suite 310
Baltimore, MD 21201

Goodrich Corporation Foundation Grants 2104
The Foundation makes charitable grants in four categories: education; arts and culture; civic and community; and health and human services. Preference shall be given to requests for projects or programs in areas having a significant number of employees, employees serving on boards of charitable organizations or other noticeable corporate presence. The Foundation staff accepts and reviews grant requests quarterly. To request funding, applicants will need to complete the application form which is available online. Telephone and email requests or inquiries are not accepted.
Requirements: 501(c)3 tax-exempt organizations are eligible.
Restrictions: The foundation generally will not support: multiyear grants in excess of five years; individuals, private foundations, endowments, churches or religious programs, fraternal/social/ labor/veterans organizations; groups with unusually high fundraising or administrative expenses; political parties, candidates, or lobbying activities; travel funds for tours, exhibitions, or trips by individuals or special interest groups; organizations that discriminate because of race, color, religion, national origin, or areas covered by applicable federal, state, or local laws; local athletic/sports programs or equipment, courtesy advertising benefits, raffle tickets and other fundraising events; organizations that receive sizable portions of their support through municipal, county, state, or federal dollars; individual United Way agencies that already benefit from Goodrich contributions to the United Way; or international organizations.
Geographic Focus: All States
Date(s) Application is Due: Feb 1; Aug 1
Contact: Foundation Contact, Foundation Contact; (704) 423-7011
Internet: http://www.goodrich.com/CDA/GeneralContent/0,1136,59,00.html
Sponsor: Goodrich Foundation
Four Coliseum Center, 2730 West Tyvola Road
Charlotte, NC 28217-4578

Good Works Foundation Grants 2105
The Foundation was established to support good works wherever they are found and encourage innovative programs which involve collaboration in education, the arts, and the environment. In particular, the Foundation focuses on initiatives and programs that impact children, especially the culture and environment in which they learn and grow. The Foundation generally meets quarterly to evaluate requests for funding programs. Guidelines and application information is available online.
Requirements: 501(c)3 organizations in the Santa Monica and West Los Angeles area are eligible.
Restrictions: No fax or email proposals are accepted. You may not apply for fellowships, capital expenditures, construction, or endowment.
Geographic Focus: California
Contact: Laura Donnelley-Morton, (310) 828-1288; info@goodworks.org
Internet: http://www.goodworks.org/pages/guidelines
Sponsor: Good Works Foundation
2101 Wilshire Boulevard, Suite 225
Santa Monica, CA 90403

Goodyear Tire Grants 2106
Requests for charitable gifts are required to meet guidelines of strategic giving based on safety by focusing on safety programs plus at least one additional category (civic and community; culture and the arts, education, or health and human services) of giving and/or provide volunteer opportunities for company associates which are appropriately aligned with the company's strategy.
Requirements: 501(c)3 tax-exempt organizations in Goodyear communities are eligible. Organizations in the greater Akron, OH area should send requests to: Faith Stewart, Director, Goodyear Tire and Rubber Company, 1144 East Market Street, D/798, Akron, OH, 44316. Organizations in U.S. communities where Goodyear has plants and major facilities should contact the local plant manager's office for mailing instructions.
Restrictions: Grants cannot be made to: organizations outside of communities in which plants or principal offices are located; individuals or to organizations on behalf of an individual; national, political, labor, fraternal, social, veterans organizations; individual schools within public or private school systems; athletic programs/extracurricular activities, travel or exchange programs; endowments or for debt reduction; religious organizations or endeavors; major hospitals or medical center; second parties except specialized organizations.
Geographic Focus: All States
Contact: Faith Stewart, Director
Internet: http://www.goodyear.com/corporate/about/about_community.html
Sponsor: Goodyear Tire and Rubber Company
1144 East Market Street D/798
Akron, OH 44316

Google Grants Beta 2107
The Google Grants program supports organizations sharing their philosophy of community service to help the world in areas such as science and technology, education, global public health, the environment, youth advocacy, and the arts. Google Grants has awarded AdWords advertising to non-profit groups whose missions range from animal welfare to literacy, from supporting homeless children to promoting HIV education. Recipients use their award of free AdWords advertising on Google.com to raise awareness and increase traffic. Application available online only.
Requirements: In the United States - Organizations must have current 501(c)3 status, as assigned by the Internal Revenue Service to be considered for a Google Grant. Outside the U.S - currently accepting applications from eligible charitable organizations based in Australia, Brazil, Canada, Denmark, France, Germany, India, Ireland, Italy, Japan, the Netherlands, Spain, Sweden, Switzerland and the UK.
Restrictions: Organizations already participating in the Google AdSense program are not eligible for Google Grants consideration. In addition, organizations that are either religious or political in nature are not eligible, including those groups focused primarily on lobbying for political or policy change.
Geographic Focus: All States
Contact: Google Grants Team Contact; googlegrants@google.com
Internet: http://www.google.com/grants/
Sponsor: Google
1600 Amphitheatre Parkway
Mountain View, CA 94043

Grable Foundation Grants 2108
The foundation awards grants to nonprofits in the nine counties that make up southwestern Pennsylvania for programs in three areas: improving educational opportunities so children can reach their potential; supporting community efforts that create an environment in which children can succeed; and strengthening families so they serve as the core support of children and society. The foundation supports activities such as after-school programs, out-of-school efforts, early childhood education, and child care initiatives. Organizations applying for the first time should submit a one-two page letter of inquiry describing the project prior to submitting a formal proposal. Guidelines are available online.
Requirements: Nonprofits in the nine counties comprising southwest Pennsylvania are eligible.
Restrictions: The foundation does not accept unsolicited proposals for programs outside of southwestern Pennsylvania; consider requests from individuals for scholarships or other assistance; or requests for fundraising requests.
Geographic Focus: Pennsylvania
Date(s) Application is Due: Feb 1; Jun 1; Oct 1
Amount of Grant: 10,000 - 100,000 USD
Contact: Program Contact; (412) 471-4550; fax (412) 471-2267; grable@grablefdn.org
Internet: http://www.grablefdn.org/grants.htm
Sponsor: Grable Foundation
650 Smithfield Street, Suite 240
Pittsburgh, PA 15222

Grace and Franklin Bernsen Foundation Grants 2109
The Grace and Franklin Bernsen Foundation provide grants primarily within the metropolitan Tulsa, Oklahoma area. Areas of interest supported are: religious; charitable; scientific; literary and; educational purposes. Grant applications for programs and projects that will provide a defined benefit such as capital projects, building programs, specific program needs or ongoing operations from time to time are all considered. Grant applications from elementary or secondary education institutions will be considered if they involve programs for at-risk, handicapped or learning-disabled children; or if they are innovative and apply to all schools in the system.
Requirements: Applicant should submit a narrative summary no more than three pages in length. This letter should be addressed to the Trustees of the Foundation, see website for detailed description of narrative requirements. IRS 501(c)3 non-profit organizations in the metropolitan Tulsa, Oklahoma area are eligible to apply. Application may be made at any time for support of activities consistent with the Foundation's guidelines. The Foundation's Board meets monthly to review grant applications. Applications received on or before the 12th day of the month (unless the 12th falls on a Saturday, Sunday, or a holiday, in which event applications are due on the preceding business day) preceding a next regularly scheduled Board meeting are normally considered at such meeting.

Restrictions: Grant applications for individuals are not considered. The Foundation discourages applications for general support or reduction of debt, or for continuing or additional support for the same programs. The Foundation will only review one grant request per agency during our fiscal year
Geographic Focus: Oklahoma
Amount of Grant: 2,000 - 1,000,000 USD
Contact: Margaret Skyles, Administrator; (918) 584-4711; fax (918) 584-4713; mskyles@bernsen.org or info@bernsen.org
Internet: http://www.bernsen.org/grant.html
Sponsor: Grace and Franklin Bernsen Foundation
15 West Sixth Street, Suite 1308
Tulsa, OK 74119-5407

Grace Bersted Foundation Grants 2110
The Grace Bersted Foundation was established in 1986 to support and promote quality educational, human services, and health care programming for underserved populations. Special consideration is given to charitable organizations that serve the needs of children or the disabled. Applicants must apply online at the grant website. Applicants are strongly encouraged to do the following before applying: review the downloadable state application procedures for additional helpful information and clarifications; review the downloadable online-application guidelines at the grant website; review the foundation's funding history (link is available from the grant website); review the online application questions in advance; and review the list of required attachments. These will generally include: a list of board members, financial statements (audited, reviewed, or compiled by independent auditor); an organization summary; a list of other funding sources; an IRS Determination letter; and other required documents. All attachments must be uploaded in the online application as PDF, Word, or Excel files. The deadline for application to the Foundation is 11:59 p.m. on September 1, and grant decisions will be made by December 31.
Requirements: Applicant organizations must have 501(c)3 tax-exempt status and an office located in one of the following counties: DuPage, Kane, Lake, or McHenry.
Restrictions: The foundation does not support requests from individuals, organizations attempting to influence policy through direct lobbying, or any political campaigns.
Geographic Focus: Illinois
Date(s) Application is Due: Sep 1
Contact: Debra Grand; (312) 828-4154; ilgrantmaking@bankofamerica.com
Internet: https://www.bankofamerica.com/philanthropic/fn_search.action
Sponsor: Grace Bersted Foundation
231 South LaSalle Street, IL1-231-13-32
Chicago, IL 60604

Graco Foundation Grants 2111
The Foundation's goal is to help organizations grow their ability to serve community needs through grants specifically aimed at expanding or enhancing services to clients, with particular focus on capital projects and technology needs. The Foundation addresses the needs of the community in the following areas: self-sufficiency - emphasizing educational programs, human service programs that promote self-sufficiency, and sports/youth development programs; and civic projects - focusing on healthy communities. Projects that improve the community will be given special consideration. Application information is available online.
Requirements: IRS 501(c)3 organizations in company-operating areas may apply.
Restrictions: Grants are not awarded for: organizations or causes that do not directly impact Graco communities; political campaigns; individuals; religious organizations for religious purposes; fund-raising; travel; special events, dinners, courtesy advertising; fraternal organizations; national or local campaigns for disease research; first time general operating grants; or product donations.
Geographic Focus: Minnesota, Ohio, South Dakota
Date(s) Application is Due: Feb 1; May 1; Aug 1; Nov 1
Contact: Kristin R. Ridley; (612) 623-6684; kridley@graco.com
Internet: http://www.graco.com/Internet/T_Corp.nsf/SearchView/Foundation2006
Sponsor: Graco Foundation
P.O. Box 1441
Minneapolis, MN 55440-1441

Grand Circle Foundation Associates Grants 2112
The Grand Circle Foundation Associates Grants fund youth education and discovery by supporting organizations that work with Boston youth. The Foundation invites projects dedicated to improving the future for at-risk children and youth. The Foundation is interested in projects that expand horizons for young people and build confidence in their abilities and future. Projects that improve global literacy and promote global citizenship will be given strong consideration.
Requirements: Funds requested must be for a specific project. Organizations must hold an active 501(c)3 status and their operating budgets must not exceed $3 million. Applicants should submit proposals of no more than two pages to the Project Manager with the following information: detailed description of the organization, and the proposed project; how the project would help others, how much it will cost, its timeline, and how it will be evaluated; and the organization's contact person with phone number and email. Organizations should also attach the following information: a board of directors list; total agency budget; annual report, if available; and evidence of their tax-exempt status.
Restrictions: Grants are awarded only to nonprofit organizations that focus on youth in the Boston neighborhoods of Roxbury, Dorchester, Mattapan, and Allston. The Foundation does not fund individuals, political organizations, advertising, dinner-table sponsorship, religious organizations, general operating expenses, or administrative costs, which includes salaries.
Geographic Focus: Massachusetts
Date(s) Application is Due: Oct 14
Amount of Grant: 500 - 5,000 USD
Contact: Jan Byrnes, Project Manager; (617) 346-6398; fax (617) 346-6030; GCFProjectsandGrants@grandcirclefoundation.org
Internet: http://www.grandcirclefoundation.org/get-involved/2010-grand-circle-associates-fund.aspx
Sponsor: Grand Circle Foundation
347 Congress Street
Boston, MA 02210

Grand Haven Area Community Foundation Grants 2113
The community Foundation awards grants to meet the changing and emerging needs of residents of the tri-cities area in such fields as arts, education, health, the environment, youth, social services and other human needs. The Foundation encourages programs which: are collaborative, comprehensive and have potential for continuity; encourage leveraging and matching grant opportunities involving multiple funding sources; support seed money requests to assist innovative projects; encourages programs and projects focused on problem prevention rather than cure. Applicants are encouraged to call and talk with a staff member before beginning a proposal. Application information is available online.
Requirements: IRS 501(c)3 organizations working to enhance the quality of life for residents in the Tri-Cities area of Grand Haven, Spring Lake and Ferrysburg in West Michigan.
Restrictions: The Foundation does not generally fund: general operating expenses; private individuals; profit making organizations; elimination of existing financial obligations/debts/liabilities; religious programs that serve, or appear to serve, specific religious denominations; fund raising events.
Geographic Focus: Michigan
Date(s) Application is Due: Jan 7; Mar 13; Jun 26; Oct 10
Contact: Carol Bedient; (616) 842-6378; fax (616) 842-9518; cbedient@ghacf.org
Internet: http://www.ghacf.org/grants.htm
Sponsor: Grand Haven Area Community Foundation
1 South Harbor Drive
Grand Haven, MI 49417

Grand Rapids Area Community Foundation Grants 2114
The Foundation enables donors to make a difference in the community through grants, scholarships and programs. The deadline for applications is September 15th, and grants are distributed during the month of October. Specific funds include: Alzheimer's Family Support Fund; Fund for the Arts; Fund for the Community; Betty Kauppi Music Fund; Streufert Peace and Safety Fund; Warren Youngdahl Memorial Fund; and the Fund for Women. Amount of funding ranges from $500 to $3,000.
Restrictions: No funding is available for individuals.
Geographic Focus: Minnesota
Date(s) Application is Due: Sep 15
Amount of Grant: Up to 3,000 USD
Contact: Wendy Roy; (218) 999-9100; fax (218) 999-7430; wroy@gracf.org
Internet: http://www.gracf.org/index.php/grants-and-programs
Sponsor: Grand Rapids Area Community Foundation
350 NW First Avenue, Suite E
Grand Rapids, MN 55744

Grand Rapids Area Community Foundation Nashwauk Area Endowment Fund Grants 2115
The Fund is interested in supporting innovative and effective ideas that support the greater Nashwauk, Minnesota area. This area includes the areas of: Nashwauk, Nashwauk Township, Buck Lake and Pengilly. The main cycle offers grants of up to $15,000, with a deadline for application November 15th. The Mini-Grant cycle offers grants of up to $5,000, with the deadline for applications being September 15th. Nonprofit organizations that serve or benefit these areas are encouraged to submit a Letter of Inquiry.
Restrictions: Grants can only be made to charitable organizations, and cannot be made to individuals.
Geographic Focus: Minnesota
Date(s) Application is Due: Sep 15
Amount of Grant: 5,000 - 15,000 USD
Contact: Wendy Roy; (218) 999-9100; fax (218) 999-7430; wroy@gracf.org
Internet: http://www.gracf.org/index.php/grants-and-programs
Sponsor: Nashwauk Area Endowment Fund
350 NW First Avenue, Suite E
Grand Rapids, MN 55744

Grand Rapids Area Community Foundation Wyoming Grants 2116
The Wyoming Community Foundation gives priority to projects that address the areas of art & culture, community development, education, environment, health, or social needs and that: represent an innovative, start-up effort or are capital in nature (e.g., construction, renovation, equipment); promote cooperation among agencies without duplicating services; obtain the necessary additional funding to implement and maintain the project; serve the greater city of the Wyoming. Michigan area; strengthen or improve agency self-sufficiency or efficiency; yield substantial community benefits for the resources invested; serve a broad segment of the community; encourage additional and permanent funding or matching gifts from other donors; have non-profit, 501(c)3 status. The Foundation will consider proposals for the following only if they are highly unique, collaborative, and community-oriented, have limited access to other resources, demonstrate substantial impact, or will address the needs of a substantial or underserved portion of the community: hospitals; nursing or retirement facilities; K-12 schools; computers; child care centers; motorized vehicles; commonly accepted community services already supported by tax dollars.

Requirements: Michigan IRS 501(c)3 non-profit organizations in or serving the Wyoming, Michigan area are eligible to apply. General applications will be requested in Fall. For more information on how to request funding for projects in the City of Wyoming Michigan, please contact Lillian VanderVeen, Board Chair, at (616) 534-9625.
Restrictions: The Foundation generally does not support: annual fund-raising drives; films, videos or television projects; endowments or debt reduction; capital projects without site control; medical research; individuals; ongoing operating expenses of established institutions; organizations located outside greater Wyoming; political projects, or those that are primarily cause-related; religious organizations for religious purposes; sabbatical leaves; scholarly research; travel, tours or trips; underwriting of conferences; venture capital for competitive profit-making activities.
Geographic Focus: All States
Contact: Lillian VanderVeen, Board Chair; (616) 534-9625; lillian@lengertravel.com
Internet: http://www.grfoundation.org/wyoming
Sponsor: Grand Rapids Area Community Foundation-Wyoming Community Foundation
185 Oakes Street SW
Grand Rapids, MI 49503

Grand Rapids Area Community Foundation Wyoming Youth Fund Grants   2117
The Wyoming Community Foundation Youth Advisory Committee seeks to improve the community by teaching about the giving of time, talent, and treasure while funding programs that help youth gain advantages and build character. The Wyoming Community Foundation Youth Advisory Committee is offering student groups and local non-profit organizations (including schools, churches, and community groups with 501(c)3 non-profit status), an opportunity to apply for grants. These grants will be made with income derived from the Wyoming Community Foundation Youth Fund. Primary consideration will be given to projects that address drug and/or alcohol use, teen pregnancy, stress, smoking, and sexual abuse. Suggested projects or activities include: real life learning experiences, or experiential learning activities; competitive sports; arts, writing, or music-focused activities; programs that explore jobs, career options or job preparation; programs that teach self-defense strategies or martial arts; outdoor experiences, camps, or challenge courses; classes or groups to help quit smoking or using drugs. Typically, the Request for Proposals is available late December of the year and the proposals are due mid-February. Grant awards are announced the following May.
Requirements: Student groups and local non-profit organizations (including schools, churches, and community groups with 501(c)3 non-profit status), are eligible to apply for these funding opportunities.
Geographic Focus: Michigan
Date(s) Application is Due: Dec 31
Contact: Cris Kooyer; (616) 454-1751, ext. 118; ckooyer@grfoundation.org
Internet: http://www.grfoundation.org/wyoming-yac.php
Sponsor: Grand Rapids Area Community Foundation-Wyoming Community Foundation Youth Fund
185 Oakes Street SW
Grand Rapids, MI 49503

Grand Rapids Community Foundation Grants   2118
The Foundation impacts a wide range of nonprofit organizations in the communities they serve. Funding is in six broad categories: academic achievement; high quality of life; healthy people; economic prosperity; vibrant neighborhoods; and environmental integrity.
Requirements: IRS 501(c)3 organizations supporting residents of Kent County are eligible to apply, applications are available at the Foundation's website.
Restrictions: The Foundation does not fund one-time, special or annual events, annual operating funds, political or religious causes, or endowments.
Geographic Focus: Michigan
Contact: Marcia Rapp, Vice President, Programs; (616) 454-1751, ext. 104; fax (616) 454-6455; mrapp@grfoundation.org or grfound@grfoundation.org
Internet: http://www.grfoundation.org/grants.php
Sponsor: Grand Rapids Community Foundation
185 Oakes Street SW
Grand Rapids, MI 49503

Grand Rapids Community Foundation Ionia County Grants   2119
The Ionia County Community Foundation gives priority to projects that address the areas of art & culture, community development, education, environment, health, or social needs and that: represent an innovative, start-up effort or are capital in nature (e.g., construction, renovation, equipment); promote cooperation among agencies without duplicating services; obtain the necessary additional funding to implement and maintain the project; are located in Ionia County, Michigan; strengthen or improve agency self-sufficiency or efficiency; yield substantial community benefits for the resources invested; serve a broad segment of the community; encourage additional and permanent funding or matching gifts from other donors; have non-profit, 501(c)3 status. The Foundation will consider proposals for the following only if they are highly unique, collaborative, and community-oriented, have limited access to other resources; demonstrate substantial impact; or will address the needs of a substantial or underserved portion of the community: hospitals; nursing or retirement facilities; K-12 schools; computers; child care centers; motorized vehicles; commonly accepted community services already supported by tax dollars.
Requirements: Non-profit, IRS 501(c)3 status organizations, located in Ionia County, Michigan may apply.
Restrictions: The Foundation generally does not support: annual fundraising drives; film, video or television projects; endowments or debt reduction; capital projects without site control; medical research; individuals; ongoing operating expenses of established institutions; organizations located outside Ionia County; political projects, or those that are primarily cause-related; religious organizations for religious purposes; sabbatical leaves; scholarly research; travel, tours or trips; underwriting of conferences; venture capital for competitive profit-making activities.
Geographic Focus: Michigan
Date(s) Application is Due: Dec 31
Contact: Kate Luckert Schmid; (616) 454-1751, ext. 117; kluckert@grfoundation.org
Internet: http://www.grfoundation.org/ionia-general.php
Sponsor: Grand Rapids Community Foundation
185 Oakes Street SW
Grand Rapids, MI 49503

Grand Rapids Community Foundation Ionia County Youth Fund Grants   2120
The Ionia County Community Foundation's Youth Advisory Committee is committed to addressing and improving problems concerning young people, by funding programs directed toward youth. The Youth Advisory Committee is affiliated with the Ionia County Community Foundation. Current funding priorities are: Drug, alcohol, tobacco use; Teen pregnancy; Depression/suicide; Parent education; Service-learning; Guest speakers that address youth issues; Literacy; Obesity; Teen driver safety. The Youth Advisory Committee is especially interested in youth projects that assist students in bridging the achievement gap. Grant proposals should assist the applying organization to implement a project or program that benefits youth. Proposals developed by youth or with youth involvement in planning are encouraged. The proposed project or program should: have clear goals that are specific, measurable, attainable, realistic, and timely; impact a significant number of Ionia County youth from birth to age 18; avoid duplication with other projects and programs in the community; address an issue and make a significant difference for youth. In addition, the applying organization and its participants will not be discriminated against on the basis of, but not limited to, gender, religion, physical disability, sexual orientation, or ethnicity. Grants will be made with income derived from the Ionia County Community Foundation Youth Fund.
Requirements: Student groups and local IRS 501(c)3 nonprofit organizations are eligible apply for grants.
Geographic Focus: Michigan
Date(s) Application is Due: Dec 31
Contact: Cris Kooyer; (616) 454-1751, ext. 118; ckooyer@grfoundation.org
Internet: http://www.grfoundation.org/ionia-yac.php
Sponsor: Grand Rapids Community Foundation
185 Oakes Street SW
Grand Rapids, MI 49503

Grand Rapids Community Foundation Lowell Area Fund Grants   2121
The Lowell Area Community Fund gives grants to organizations that assist in fulfilling its mission: to assure community cooperation and participation that supports a healthy, dynamic community. The fund places an emphasis on broad educational initiatives, but also supports initiatives in the areas of: Arts & Culture, Community Development, Environment, Health, Human Services, and Recreation. The Lowell area is currently defined as the City of Lowell, Michigan, the Township of Lowell, and the Township of Vergennes. Grant applications are accepted three times a year on the third Friday of April, August, and December. Additional guidelines and grant application are available at the Foundation's website.
Requirements: 501(c)3 tax-exempt organizations are in the Lowell area are eligible.
Restrictions: The fund generally does not support: political projects, or those that are primarily cause-related; individuals; religious organizations for religious purposes; or profit-making activities.
Geographic Focus: Michigan
Amount of Grant: 2,000 - 75,000 USD
Contact: Kate Luckert Schmid; (616) 454-1751, ext. 117; kluckert@grfoundation.org
Internet: http://www.grfoundation.org/lowell.php
Sponsor: Grand Rapids Community Foundation
185 Oakes Street SW
Grand Rapids, MI 49503

Grand Rapids Community Foundation Southeast Ottawa Grants   2122
The Southeast Ottawa Community Foundation gives priority to projects that address the areas of art & culture, community development, education, environment, health, or social needs and that: represent an innovative, start-up effort or are capital in nature (e.g., construction, renovation, equipment); promote cooperation among agencies without duplicating services; obtain the necessary additional funding to implement and maintain the project; are located in the greater Georgetown Township, Hudsonville and Jamestown Township area of Michigan; strengthen or improve agency self-sufficiency or efficiency; yield substantial community benefits for the resources invested; serve a broad segment of the community; encourage additional and permanent funding or matching gifts from other donors; have non-profit, 501(c)3 status. The Foundation will consider proposals for the following only if they are highly unique, collaborative, and community-oriented, have limited access to other resources, demonstrate substantial impact, or will address the needs of a substantial or underserved portion of the community: hospitals; nursing or retirement facilities; K-12 schools; computers; child care centers; motorized vehicles; commonly accepted community services already supported by tax dollars.
Requirements: Michigan IRS 501(c)3 non-profit organizations that are located in the greater Georgetown Township, Hudsonville and Jamestown Township area are eligible to apply. General applications are due August 31st. For more information on how to request funding for projects, contact Larry Bergman at (616) 896-8769.
Restrictions: The Foundation generally does not support: annual fund-raising drives; films, videos or television projects; endowments or debt reduction; capital projects without site control; medical research; individuals; ongoing operating expenses of established institutions;

organizations located outside greater Georgetown Township, Hudsonville and Jamestown Township area; political projects, or those that are primarily cause-related; religious organizations for religious purposes; sabbatical leaves; scholarly research; travel, tours or trips; underwriting of conferences; venture capital for competitive profit-making activities.
Geographic Focus: Michigan
Date(s) Application is Due: Aug 31
Contact: Larry Bergman, (616) 896-8769; lbergman@charter.net
Internet: http://www.grfoundation.org/seottawa
Sponsor: Grand Rapids Area Community Foundation-Southeast Ottawa Community Foundation
185 Oakes Street SW
Grand Rapids, MI 49503

Grand Rapids Community Foundation Southeast Ottawa Youth Fund Grants   2123
The Southeast Ottawa Community Foundation's Youth Advisory Committee is seeking to fund projects or programs that positively impact youth within Georgetown, Hudsonville, and Jamestown Townships. Groups or organizations made up of (or serving) youth ages 12 - 20 are invited to apply. The committee is particularly interested in programs or activities that address youth issues, particularly: alcohol and drug use (including smoking); impaired driving; coping with external pressures from and conflicting expectations of family and peers; sexual activity, teen pregnancy, and harassment; time management related to academics, employment, and other activities; depression, self-esteem, and body image. Typically, the Request for Proposals is available late December of the year and the proposals are due mid-February. Grant awards are announced the following May.
Requirements: Any non-profit organization with 501(c)3 status located within Georgetown, Hudsonville, and Jamestown Townships of Michigan, that is in need of funding for programs that benefit youth in this area are eligible to apply.
Restrictions: Grants proposals from religious organizations for a religious purpose will not be considered.
Geographic Focus: Michigan
Date(s) Application is Due: Dec 31
Contact: Cris Kooyer, Education & Youth Program Officer; (616) 454-1751, ext. 118; ckooyer@grfoundation.org
Internet: http://www.grfoundation.org/seottawa-yac.php
Sponsor: Grand Rapids Community Foundation
185 Oakes Street SW
Grand Rapids, MI 49503

Grand Rapids Community Foundation Sparta Grants   2124
The Sparta Community Foundation gives priority to projects that address the areas of art & culture, community development, education, environment, health, or social needs and that: represent an innovative, start-up effort or are capital in nature (e.g., construction, renovation, equipment); promote cooperation among agencies without duplicating services; obtain the necessary additional funding to implement and maintain the project; are located in Sparta and its surrounding areas of Michigan; strengthen or improve agency self-sufficiency or efficiency; yield substantial community benefits for the resources invested; serve a broad segment of the community; encourage additional and permanent funding or matching gifts from other donors; have non-profit, 501(c)3 status. The Foundation will consider proposals for the following only if they are highly unique, collaborative, and community-oriented, have limited access to other resources, demonstrate substantial impact, or will address the needs of a substantial or underserved portion of the community: hospitals; nursing or retirement facilities; K-12 schools; computers; child care centers; motorized vehicles; commonly accepted community services already supported by tax dollars.
Requirements: Michigan IRS 501(c)3 non-profit organizations that are located in Sparta and its surrounding areas are eligible to apply. General applications are due September 4th. For more information on how to request funding for projects, contact Becky Cumings, Grant Committee Chair, at (616) 887-8428.
Restrictions: The Foundation generally does not support: annual fund-raising drives; films, videos or television projects; endowments or debt reduction; capital projects without site control; medical research; individuals; ongoing operating expenses of established institutions; organizations located outside greater Georgetown Township, Hudsonville and Jamestown Township area; political projects, or those that are primarily cause-related; religious organizations for religious purposes; sabbatical leaves; scholarly research; travel, tours or trips; underwriting of conferences; venture capital for competitive profit-making activities.
Geographic Focus: Michigan
Date(s) Application is Due: Sep 4
Contact: Becky Cumings, Chair; (616) 887-8428; cumingst@hotmail.com
Internet: http://www.grfoundation.org/sparta
Sponsor: Grand Rapids Area Community Foundation-Sparta Community Foundation
185 Oakes Street SW
Grand Rapids, MI 49503

Grand Rapids Community Foundation Sparta Youth Fund Grants   2125
The Sparta Community Foundation's Youth Advisory Committee is seeking to fund projects or programs that positively impact youth in the Sparta community. Groups or organizations made up of (or serving) youth ages 12 - 20 are invited to apply. The committee is particularly interested in programs or activities that address the following issues: alcohol and drug use (including smoking); impaired driving; coping with external pressures from and conflicting expectations of family and peers; sexual activity, teen pregnancy, and harassment; time management related to academics, employment, and other activities; depression, self-esteem, and body image. The projects should be youth initiated and youth driven.
Requirements: Any non-profit organization with 501(c)3 status located in or serving the Sparta area that is in need of funding for programs that benefit youth in the Sparta community.
Restrictions: Grants proposals from religious organizations for a religious purpose will not be considered.
Geographic Focus: Michigan
Date(s) Application is Due: Dec 31
Contact: Cris Kooyer, Education & Youth Program Officer; (616) 454-1751, ext. 118; ckooyer@grfoundation.org
Internet: http://www.grfoundation.org/sparta-yac.php
Sponsor: Grand Rapids Community Foundation
185 Oakes Street SW
Grand Rapids, MI 49503

Grand Victoria Foundation (GVF) Illinois Core Program Grants   2126
The mission of Grand Victoria Foundation is to assist communities in their efforts to pursue systemic solutions to problems in specific areas of education, economic development and the environment. Within the program area of Education, the Foundation is particularly interested in projects that: strengthen the profession of teaching, including pre-service training, new teacher induction, on-the-job training and continuing professional development; improve the quality, content, and process of teaching and learning from early childhood through adult education; enhance and expand youth development programs; pursue educational parity for all-aged students; increase access to quality, affordable child care and early childhood education. In the program area of Economic Development, the Foundation's interested in projects that: link workforce development efforts to jobs, job creation, transportation, and/or housing; provide greater access to capital and other resources; expand housing options and improve home ownership opportunities; implement regional growth management and land use strategies that promote economic vitality and environmental health. Projects of interest, in the area of Environment: prevent pollution; preserve and restore natural lands and waterways; implement best land use practices; expand and connect preserved natural lands; develop and implement use of clean, renewable energy and other natural resources; educate the public to increase participation in the above issues. Types of support include project support, technical assistance, capacity building, scholarship funds, challenge grants for capital projects, qualified loan funds, and land acquisition (for preservation of quality natural areas). Highest priority is placed on projects that are regional in scope, employ best practices, pursue long-term positive results, and leverage additional investment. There are no deadline dates for this grant.
Requirements: IRA 501(c)3 non-profit organizations operating in the Illinois counties of Kane, DuPage, Lake, McHenry, Kendall, Will, Winnebago, DeKalb or suburban Cook counties are eligible to apply. Regional applicants must be operating in the Chicago Metropolitan area and be collaboratively engaged in one or more of the activities that the Foundation supports to address issues that are regional in scope (air quality, transportation, and growth management). State applicants must be operating in Illinois and engaged in child care, land use and protection, and/or workforce development efforts that impact a substantial portion of Illinois. To begin application process, submit a letter of Inquiry summarizing the project. The Foundation will send a written response, notifying the applicant, whether a full proposal is invited. Organizations invited to proceed will also receive an application packet with instructions for preparing a proposal. The Foundation considers only those proposals that are invited in response to a letter of inquiry.
Restrictions: Efforts directed solely to Chicago neighborhoods typically are not supported. Funding is not available for: endowments; fund-raising events; debt or deficit reduction; political campaigns; religious purposes; individuals; taxing bodies to accomplish programs that fall within the normal scope of their responsibilities; research or planning projects unless they are a well-integrated step to program implementation.
Geographic Focus: Illinois
Contact: Laquieta Golliday; (312) 609-0200; laquieta@grandvictoriafdn.org
Internet: http://www.grandvictoriafdn.org/index.php?option=com_content&task=view&id=41§ionid=4
Sponsor: Grand Victoria Foundation
230 W Monroe Street, Suite 2530
Chicago, IL 60606

Granger Foundation Grants   2127
The primary purpose of the foundation is to enhance the quality of life within the Greater Lansing Area. The foundation's primary mission is to support Christ-centered activities. It also supports efforts that enhance the lives of community youth. The foundation trustees consider organizations and funding areas that are significant and have far-reaching value. Grants are awarded generally in Michigan's tri-county area (Ingham, Eaton, and Clinton Counties). The application is available online.
Restrictions: Grants do not support endowments, fund raising, social events, conferences, exhibits, church capital funds or improvements, public schools capital funds or improvements, individual clubs (PTO, PTA, etc.), or individuals.
Geographic Focus: Michigan
Date(s) Application is Due: Apr 15; Oct 15
Contact: Alton Granger, (517) 393-1670; elee@grangerconstruction.com
Internet: http://www.grangerfoundation.org/Guidelines.htm
Sponsor: Granger Foundation
P.O. Box 22187
Lansing, MI 48909

Grassroots Exchange Fund Grants   2128
The fund typically makes grants to grassroots community-based organizations working on economic, environmental, and social justice initiatives that give voice to the needs of low-income people, women, youth, and people of color. Priority is given to small, membership-based organizations that do not have access to large government, corporate, or private funding sources and to those organizations whose leadership reflects the low-income and/or

people of color communities in which they are based. Further priorities include to help small organizations participate in key national policy movements; train and develop new leaders; assist grassroots groups with strategy development and skills transfer between organizations and leaders; and ensure funds are well-distributed among issues and geographical areas. Grants are distributed on a monthly cycle February through November. Applications must be submitted by the first Monday of the month (February-November).
Restrictions: Grants do not support travel for US-based organizations to go to a foreign country (rare exceptions are made for cross-border organizing work between groups in the United States and Mexico or Canada); international organizations and organizations located outside of the United States; direct social services; government agencies and programs undertaken by tax-supported institutions or government initiatives; capital expenditure, endowments, construction, or renovation programs; scholarship funds or other aid to individuals; schools and educational institutions; cultural institutions; medical institutions; film, video, publications, or other media projects; grantmaking institutions; research or fellowships; or organizations with budgets larger than $1 million per year.
Geographic Focus: All States
Amount of Grant: 300 - 800 USD
Contact: Elizabeth Wilcox; (510) 834-2995; fax (510) 834-2998; ccounsel@igc.apc.org
Internet: http://www.commoncounsel.org/Grassroots%20Exchange%20Fund
Sponsor: Grassroots Exchange Fund
1221 Preservation Parkway, Suite 101
Oakland, CA 94612

Grassroots Government Leadership Award 2129
The award, sponsored by the National Association of Towns and Townships (NATaT), recognizes one outstanding township official annually. Elected officials who serve small communities (less than 10,000 population) and have a demonstrated record in promoting local entrepreneurship are encouraged to apply. Applications can be submitted by local government leaders or by representatives of organizations and agencies that have partnered with local government to advance rural entrepreneurship.
Geographic Focus: All States
Date(s) Application is Due: Jul 1
Amount of Grant: 5,000 USD
Contact: Andrew Seth; (202) 454-3954 or (866) 830-0008; aseth@tfgnet.com
Internet: http://www.natat.org/ncsc/Kauffman/entrepdefault.htm
Sponsor: National Association of Towns and Townships
444 N Capitol Street NW, Suite 397
Washington, DC 20001-1202

Great-West Life Grants 2130
The program's objectives are to support organizations that meet the most vital needs in the greater Denver metro community, including access to affordable health care, shelter, nutrition and education, and to support our employees' involvement in their communities. Funding priorities are on preventive and ongoing health services, homeless shelters, food services, and keeping children in school. Support is limited to organizations providing direct services, free or charge or on a sliding scale basis, that demonstrate effectiveness in addressing the communities vital issues. There is no formal application process. Interested applicants should submit a brief concept paper.
Requirements: To be eligible for support an organization: must be a U.S. based, charity and tax-exempt under 501(c)3 of the Internal Revenue Code; must not discriminate on the basis of race, religion, gender, age, national origin, disability, or sexual orientation; must show demonstrated success in meeting the program's objectives and fall within the program's focus areas; must serve residents in areas with a Great-West presence.
Restrictions: Funding is not provided for: capital campaigns; debt financing; endowments; advertising; grant-making foundations; individuals; political organizations; exclusively religious organizations; veterans organizations; fraternal organizations.
Geographic Focus: All States
Contact: Human Resources; (800) 537-2033; greatwestcomments@gwl.com
Internet: http://www.greatwest.com/about/community_supp.htm
Sponsor: Great-West Life and Annuity Insurance Company
8515 East Orchard Road
Greenwood Village, CO 80111

Great Clips Corporate Giving 2131
Each month, Great Clips selects one independent charity and rewards their dedication to greatness in their community with a $1,500 donation. Charities entered will also have the chance to get even more funds at the end of the year. Each charity will receive an additional donation from Great Clips based on the number of votes they receive on EverythingGreat.com.
Requirements: Nonprofit organizations in the United States and Canada may enter the monthly contests. Organizations must include their 501(c)3 number or registration document with the Charities Directorate of the Canada Revenue Agency (in Canada) within the application. The program nominated must align with Great Clips' mission of supporting organizations that inspire us with their creativity, passion and greatness and must positively impact communities where Great Clips salons are located.
Restrictions: The Great Clips Great Giving Program does not provide funding for: political organizations, fraternal groups or social clubs that engage in any kind of political activity; religious organizations, unless they serve the general public in a significant non-denominational way; individuals or individual families; organizations located outside Great Clips markets; capital campaigns; private foundations; sponsorships for music, film and art festivals; support for business expositions/conferences; scholarships; charities that are already supported from government organizations or national charities (e.g. Red Cross, United Way, Children's Miracle Network, etc.); organizations that discriminate on the basis of race, color, gender, sexual orientation, age, religion, physical disability, or national or ethnic origin; or, 501(c)3 organizations or programs/projects that have been in place for less than one year.
Geographic Focus: All States
Amount of Grant: 1,500 USD
Contact: Corporate Giving Manager; (800) 999-5959; fax (952) 844-3444
Internet: http://everythinggreat.greatclips.com/great-giving/
Sponsor: Great Clips, Inc.
4400 West 78th Street, Suite 700
Minneapolis, MN 55435

Greater Cincinnati Foundation Priority and Small Projects/Capacity-Building Grants 2132
Grants are awarded on a quarterly basis and support projects addressing community needs and priorities in six areas: arts and culture; community progress; education; environment; health; and human services. The Foundation looks for applicants that are established and fiscally sound with strong governance and a demonstrated organizational capacity/track record. Application information is available online. Nonprofits seeking grants of up to $20,000 can get a decision in eight weeks or less; all other grants above $20,000 will be awarded twice a year.
Requirements: The Foundation awards grants to qualified 501(c)3 nonprofit organizations in eight counties: Butler, Clermont, Hamilton, and Warren, Ohio; Boone, Kenton and Campbell, Kentucky; and Dearborn, Indiana.
Restrictions: Funds are not available for: individuals; units of government or government agencies; religious organizations for religious purposes; ongoing operating expenses of nonprofit organizations; annual fund raising drives, event sponsorship or underwriting; stand-alone books, films or videos unless part of a more comprehensive program activity; stand-alone travel expenses for conferences or educational purposes unless part of a more comprehensive program activity; regular operating costs or capital projects for individual public, private or parochial schools, universities, hospitals, nursing or retirement homes; endowments; scholarships; loans; scholarly or medical research; partisan political advocacy; debt retirement or funding of an activity after it is completed.
Geographic Focus: Indiana, Kentucky, Ohio
Amount of Grant: 10,000 - 100,000 USD
Contact: Kay Pennington, Community Investment Coordinator; (513) 241-2880; fax (513) 852-6886; penningtonk@greatercincinnatifdn.org
Internet: http://www.greatercincinnatifdn.org/page10004265.cfm
Sponsor: Greater Cincinnati Foundation
200 West Fourth Street
Cincinnati, OH 45202

Greater Columbus Arts Council Operating Grants 2133
GCAC grants fund the operation of arts organizations that demonstrate high-quality artistic programming, stable artistic and administrative staffing, healthy financial structures, and significant impact on the city's economy and tourism. Operating support grants allow the organization to develop and maintain managerial and artistic capacity through methods the organization deems most valuable. Operating support grants are unrestricted as to use.
Requirements: Applicant organizations must have had 501(c)3 status for at least three consecutive years prior to the date of application, demonstrate that the organization's primary focus and actual operation are artistic in nature, provide cultural programming of the highest caliber, employ professional management staff, demonstrate a wide-ranging impact on the city of Columbus, operate with a community-based board of trustees, operate with a clearly articulated artistic plan, and demonstrate fiscal accountability.
Geographic Focus: Ohio
Date(s) Application is Due: Feb 1
Contact: Program Officer; (614) 224-2606; fax (614) 224-7461; grants@gcac.org
Internet: http://www.gcac.org/org/guidelines_operating_support.php
Sponsor: Greater Columbus Arts Council
100 E Broad Street, Suite 2250
Columbus, OH 43215

Greater Des Moines Foundation Grants 2134
The Foundation's purpose is to improve the quality of life in Greater Des Moines and to work with the community toward accomplishing this mission. Proposals that address one or more of the long-range community outcomes are given the highest priority. The targeted outcomes include: encouraging the community to be inclusive, welcoming, and understanding of diverse cultures; supporting strong and stable families that provide solid beginnings for children and youth; promoting the effectiveness and long-term viability of arts and cultural organizations and/or provide access to the arts for new and underserved audiences; strengthening the nonprofit sector; and serving as a catalyst in collaborative efforts for community betterment. Application information is available online.
Requirements: 501(c)3 organizations in the greater Des Moines, IA, area are eligible.
Restrictions: The Foundation will not consider: ongoing annual operating expenses; grants to individuals; sectarian religious programs; projects not serving residents of the Greater Des Moines community.
Geographic Focus: Iowa
Contact: Kristi Knous; (515) 883-2703; knous@desmoinesfoundation.org
Internet: http://www.desmoinesfoundation.org/page30358.cfm
Sponsor: Greater Des Moines Foundation
1915 Grand Avenue, P.O. Box 7271
Des Moines, IA 50309

Greater Green Bay Community Foundation Grants — 2135

The Foundation provides assistance to worthy charities serving the people of Brown, Kewaunee, and Oconto counties, Wisconsin. The Foundation's areas of interest are: arts and culture; community development; cultural and ethnic diversity; health and human services; historic preservation; education; and the environment. The Foundation also awards special funds to projects that address issues involved with Alzheimer's Disease, Diabetes, and Hospice. Applicants should share their ideas with the Foundation before completing a formal application. Application information is available online.

Requirements: Eligible recipients meet the following criteria: are tax exempt and have 501(c)3 status; primarily serve residents of Brown, Oconto, and Kewaunee counties; and operate, choose a governing board, and provide services without discrimination.

Restrictions: Funding is not available for: annual or capital campaigns; projects that promote any religious belief; individuals; debt retirement; lobbying; activities that occur prior to the awarding of the grant; efforts substantially serving people outside of Brown, Kewaunee, and Oconto counties.

Geographic Focus: Wisconsin
Date(s) Application is Due: Jan 15; Apr 15; Jul 15; Oct 15
Amount of Grant: 1,000 - 10,000 USD
Contact: Lora Warner; (920) 432-0800; fax (920) 432-5577; lora@ggbcf.org
Internet: http://www.ggbcf.org
Sponsor: Greater Green Bay Community Foundation
301 W Walnut Street, Suite 350
Green Bay, WI 54303

Greater Kanawha Valley Foundation Grants — 2136

The Greater Kanawha Valley Foundation awards grants to projects and programs that enhance the quality of life in the Greater Kanawha Valley. The Foundation awards grants to non-profit and other charitable organizations under the broad category of community development (defined as improving quality of life, promoting economic development, and reducing poverty) in the categories of education, arts and culture, health, human services, public recreation, and land use. Priority is given to proposals that: encourage "bridging," community bonding, and connectedness; generate matching funds, thus leveraging additional support; exhibit coordination and collaboration among organizations; implement new approaches and innovative techniques to solve community problems; and focus on proactive, preventive measures. The application, specific deadlines for each field of interest, and samples of previously funded projects are available at the Foundation website. Applicants are strongly encouraged to attend the workshop for their field of interest.

Requirements: To be eligible for funding, an applicant must be a 501(c)3 as determined by the IRS, a faith-based organization, or a government entity (i.e., libraries, schools, etc.); provide services within the counties of Boone, Clay, Fayette, Kanawha, Lincoln, and Putnam; and be current on all final reports from the Foundation.

Restrictions: Funding is not available for the following: national or statewide proposals that do not focus on the Foundation's six county service area; general operating budgets established for organizations; annual campaigns or membership drives; travel expenses or school uniform purchases; ongoing support for the same project; staff costs only; consultants, consultant fees, conferences or workshop speakers; individuals, student aid or fellowships; endowments; or religious activities of religious organizations. Each organization may apply for only one grant per year.

Geographic Focus: West Virginia
Date(s) Application is Due: Feb 1; May 1; Aug 1
Contact: Sheri Ryder; (304) 346-3620; fax (304) 346-3640; sryder@tgkvf.org
Internet: http://www.tgkvf.org/page.aspx?pid=384
Sponsor: Greater Kanawha Valley Foundation
One Huntington Square
Charleston, WV 25301

Greater Milwaukee Foundation Grants — 2137

The Foundation places its highest funding priority on supporting creative efforts to address issues of poverty in the community, particularly grants focused on education, employment, and strengthening children, youth and families. Lower priority is given to projects that do not meet the above criteria and/or do not address issues of persistent poverty. In addition, the Foundation places special emphasis on programs that accomplish the following: improving understanding among people of different backgrounds through support of efforts addressing issues of racial, cultural and economic diversity; and strengthening the voluntary sector by supporting efforts to enhance the management capacities of nonprofit organizations, promote philanthropy, and encourage civic involvement and community service. Additional application information is available online.

Requirements: Grants are made only to 501(c)3 nonprofit organizations and, on occasion, to governmental agencies. Geographically, funding for the discretionary grantmaking program is limited to projects that will significantly improve the lives of people living in Milwaukee, Waukesha, Ozaukee and Washington counties.

Restrictions: Grants for ongoing operational costs or to individuals are not eligible for support from the Foundation's discretionary funds. The Foundation does not provide support for debt reduction, sectarian religious purposes, medical or scientific research, fund drives for sustaining support or organizations that are discriminatory in their practices.

Geographic Focus: Wisconsin
Contact: Fran Kowalkiewicz, Grants Manager; (414) 272-5805; fax (414) 272-6235; fkowalkiewicz@greatermilwaukeefoundation.org Internet: http://www.greatermilwaukeefoundation.org/grant_seekers/
Sponsor: Greater Milwaukee Foundation
101 West Pleasant Street, Suite 210
Milwaukee, WI 53212

Greater Saint Louis Community Foundation Grants — 2138

The Greater Saint Louis Community Foundation (GSLCF) was founded in 1915, one year after the first community foundation was established in Cleveland, Ohio. Currently GSLCF administers over 400 individual charitable funds that total $170 million in assets. These funds annually make over $17 million in grants that shape the greater Saint Louis region, touch communities across the nation, and reach across the globe. Historically, the mission of GSLCF has been two-fold: to serve donors and ensure that their dollars work in line with the goals that are important to them; and to promote charitable giving through community investment in nonprofit organizations capable of addressing community issues in measurable ways. To this end GSLCF maintains an online database YOURGivingLink to help donors find deserving nonprofit organizations that match their giving interests. Nonprofits are encouraged to register their organizations with the database; the link is available at the GSLCF website.

Requirements: While the Foundation predominately supports St. Louis area nonprofits, grants are also made to national and international charities.

Geographic Focus: Illinois, Missouri
Contact: Amy Basore Murphy, Director of Scholarships and Donor Services; (314) 588-8200, ext. 139 or (314) 880-4965; fax (314) 588-8088; amurphy@stlouisgives.org
Internet: http://www.stlouisgives.org/charities/
Sponsor: Greater Saint Louis Community Foundation
319 North Fourth Street, Suite 300
Saint Louis, MO 63102-1906

Greater Tacoma Community Foundation Grants — 2139

The Foundation invests in the community through grants to vital nonprofit agencies in Pierce County. While grants are made across all fields, principal funding areas include: arts and culture; civics; education; the environment; health; and human services. The Foundation also makes capital, equipment, project and operating support grants. Application information is available online.

Requirements: Eligible applicants must meet the following criteria: attest to non-discrimination on the basis of race, sex, age, national origin, religion, physical or mental handicap, veteran status or sexual orientation; provide a service primarily for residents of Pierce County; qualify as tax-exempt under section 501(c)3 of the IRS Code; and apply no more than once a year for any one governing or umbrella organization.

Restrictions: Grants will not be made for: fundraising events or fundraising feasibility projects; individuals; religious organizations for sacramental/theological purposes; production of books, videos, films, or other publications; annual campaign appeals; travel; political or lobbying activities; endowments; debt reduction; events or programs that occur prior to the board of directors decision/notification dates.

Geographic Focus: Washington
Contact: Rose Lincoln Hamilton; (253) 383-5622; fax (253) 272-8099; rlincoln@gtcf.org
Internet: http://www.tacomafoundation.org
Sponsor: Greater Tacoma Community Foundation
950 Pacific Avenue, Suite 1220, P.O. Box 1995
Tacoma, WA 98402

Greater Worcester Community Foundation Discretionary Grants — 2140

Grants are made to nonprofit organizations to build healthy and vibrant communities. Several large field-of-interest funds are also included in this process, providing support for culture and the arts, academic achievement for disadvantaged youth, progressive education, conservation, homelessness and affordable housing, and health and wellness for women and children. These grants enable us to be responsive to community needs and priorities.

Requirements: The Foundation considers applications only from nonprofit, tax-exempt organizations for activities serving the people of the Central Massachusetts region. Organizations not incorporated as tax-exempt may apply through an established organization that agrees to provide fiscal oversight.

Geographic Focus: Massachusetts
Date(s) Application is Due: Mar 15; Sep 15
Contact: Pamela B. Kane, (508) 755-0980; pkane@greaterworcester.org
Internet: http://www.greaterworcester.org/grants/disc-grants.htm
Sponsor: Greater Worcester Community Foundation
370 Main Street, Suite 650
Worcester, MA 01608-1738

Greater Worcester Community Foundation Jeppson Fund for Brookfield Grants — 2141

The Fund provides money to civic and community projects that help improve the lives of residents and enrich the cultural environment. The Fund provides support for: cultural or artistic performances; public seminars; festivals or exhibitions; services that help frail or vulnerable citizens, or that contribute to public health and safety; opportunities for educational enrichment; youth involvement in recreation, sports and the arts; and projects that foster community awareness and connections among different groups. Application information is available online.

Requirements: Any nonprofit or civic organization that serves the residents of Brookfield may apply.

Restrictions: Grant funds may not be used for expenses already incurred by the applicant. Fund awards are not intended to replace municipal funds.

Geographic Focus: Massachusetts
Date(s) Application is Due: Jul 15
Contact: Pamela B. Kane, (508) 755-0980; pkane@greaterworcester.org
Internet: http://www.greaterworcester.org/grants/Jeppson.htm
Sponsor: Greater Worcester Community Foundation
370 Main Street, Suite 650
Worcester, MA 01608-1738

Greater Worcester Community Foundation Mini-Grants 2142
The Foundation awards mini-grants to quickly fund low-cost projects that have an impact on the people or organizations in the community. Receiving a mini-grant does not preclude an applicant from receiving other grants from the Foundation. Areas of interest are: organizational improvement (training and conferences for staff or board members, collaborative planning efforts with other organizations, research, program evaluation, technology enhancement, or equipment purchases); events and gatherings; seminars, exhibitions, lectures, conferences; and pilot projects. Application information is available online. There are no deadlines to apply.
Requirements: Nonprofits in the Central Massachusetts region are eligible to apply.
Restrictions: A request may not exceed $2,500. Total expenses for the project should be under $10,000. Mini-grants may not be used for expenses already incurred by the applicant. Public schools or other public agencies will typically not receive mini-grants, although may be involved as partners in funded efforts. Mini-grants are not awarded to individuals.
Geographic Focus: Massachusetts
Contact: Pam Kane, Program Officer; (508) 755-0980; pkane@greaterworcester.org
Internet: http://www.greaterworcester.org/grants/Mini.htm
Sponsor: Greater Worcester Community Foundation
370 Main Street, Suite 650
Worcester, MA 01608-1738

Greater Worcester Community Foundation Ministries Grants 2143
The Community Ministries Fund welcomes applications from Worcester-based congregations - of any faith tradition that sponsor or plan to sponsor social ministries to improve the lives of neighborhood residents. Committed to values and aspirations that are shared by the world's religions, the Fund does not support programs that advance a sectarian agenda. Areas of interest include (but are not limited to): tutoring and mentoring; English as a Second Language classes (ESL); music and art enrichment; after-school programs designed to enhance academic and social skills; job training; gang intervention; urban gardening; and community organizing and public advocacy. Grant requests are limited to a maximum of $3,000 per program.
Requirements: The Foundation considers applications only from nonprofit, tax-exempt religious agencies for activities serving the people of the Central Massachusetts region.
Geographic Focus: Massachusetts
Date(s) Application is Due: Mar 15
Contact: Pam Kane, Program Officer; (508) 755-0980; pkane@greaterworcester.org
Internet: http://www.greaterworcester.org/grants/Community-Ministries.htm
Sponsor: Greater Worcester Community Foundation
370 Main Street, Suite 650
Worcester, MA 01608-1738

Greater Worcester Community Foundation Youth for Comm Improvement Grants 2144
Youth for Community Improvement (YCI), an advisory committee of the Greater Worcester Community Foundation comprised of area high school students, requests proposals from Worcester County nonprofit organizations. Areas of interest include: youth opportunities (especially college/career preparation; drug abuse prevention; and child abuse/ neglect prevention; and sports/ recreational activities, including educational field trips); hunger/ food issues (both access to and quality of food); homelessness (both affordable housing and shelter programs); financial services (for low-middle class families); citizens with disabilities and/or senior citizens; and environmental issues (including parks/ green space, beautification projects, conservation, helping animals, global warming, etc.). The award maximum is $5,000, and total project budgets may not exceed $25,000. * Arts/ Culture
Geographic Focus: Massachusetts
Date(s) Application is Due: Feb 25
Amount of Grant: Up to 5,000 USD
Contact: Amy Mosher, (508) 755-0980, ext. 111; yci@greaterworcester.org
Internet: http://www.greaterworcester.org/grants/YCIrfp.htm
Sponsor: Greater Worcester Community Foundation
370 Main Street, Suite 650
Worcester, MA 01608-1738

Great Lakes Fishery Trust Access Grants 2145
The Great Lakes Fishery Trust's (GLFT) Access to the Great Lakes Fishery grant category focuses on significantly increasing access to the Great Lakes fishery for shore-based angling and tribal fishing. The goal of this funding category is to improve or create opportunities for shore-based access to fishing for Great Lakes species for use by tribal and/or recreational users. The GLFT supports its access goals through a combination of competitive and funder-directed grantmaking. Supported activities may include: new construction of access sites; upgrades and renovations to existing access sites; engineering and feasibility studies for proposed access sites; land acquisition to support subsequent access site development; and communication and outreach efforts regarding existing shore-based angling opportunities. Fishery Access proposals are due on August 23 each year.
Requirements: Organizations that are eligible to apply for GLFT grants include nonprofit organizations with a 501(c)3 designation from the IRS (or nongovernmental organizations that hold charitable status in their country), as well as educational and governmental (including tribal) organizations.
Geographic Focus: Illinois, Indiana, Iowa, Michigan, Ohio, Wisconsin
Date(s) Application is Due: Jan 25
Contact: Jonathon Beard; (517) 371-7468; fax (517) 484-6549; jbeard@glft.org
Internet: http://www.glft.org/site/fishing_access_grant.shtml
Sponsor: Great Lakes Fishery Trust
600 W. Saint Joseph, Suite 10
Lansing, MI 48933-2265

Great Lakes Fishery Trust Habitat Protection and Restoration Grants 2146
The Great Lakes Fishery Trust pursues its efforts in habitat protection and restoration through direct investment in specific places with degraded or vulnerable habitat, as well as through collaborative efforts to develop next-generation systems for classifying and documenting the status of fish habitat in the Great Lakes. Funding is distributed through a combination of funder-directed and competitive grants. Each year the GLFT determines priorities for funding to further its mission though targeted requests for proposals that focus on different focal themes. The main theme areas for the GLFT's investments in habitat protection and restoration are: targeted land and capital efforts; and habitat information initiative. Habitat Protection and Restoration (for fish passage and other dam management projects) proposals are due by March 6. The online application will be available by January.
Requirements: Organizations that are eligible to apply for GLFT grants include nonprofit organizations with a 501(c)3 designation from the IRS (or nongovernmental organizations that hold charitable status in their country), as well as educational and governmental (including tribal) organizations.
Geographic Focus: Illinois, Indiana, Iowa, Michigan, Ohio, Wisconsin
Date(s) Application is Due: Mar 6
Contact: Jonathon Beard; (517) 371-7468; fax (517) 484-6549; jbeard@glft.org
Internet: http://www.glft.org/site/habitat_restoration.shtml
Sponsor: Great Lakes Fishery Trust
600 W. Saint Joseph, Suite 10
Lansing, MI 48933-2265

Great Lakes Protection Fund Grants 2147
The Great Lakes Protection Fund welcomes preproposals for projects that enhance the health of the Great Lakes ecosystem. Applicants should propose projects that will return the greatest ecosystem benefits. Current funding interests include preventing biological pollution, restoring natural flow regimes; and using market mechanisms for environmental improvement. Additional projects are sought to add to, and expand fund-supported work in these areas. The fund also welcomes projects that are designed to identify and explore other master variables that if acted upon, will result in tangible improvements to the health of the Great Lakes ecosystem. Proposals may be submitted at any time. The board makes grant decisions at its March, June, September, and December meetings.
Requirements: Nonprofit organizations (including environmental organizations, trade associations, and universities), for-profit businesses, government agencies, and individuals are eligible for fund support.
Restrictions: The fund does not give to general operating funds, environmental education, and groups from Indiana.
Geographic Focus: All States
Amount of Grant: 25,000 - 420,000 USD
Contact: J. David Rankin, Program Director; (847) 425-8150; fax (847) 424-9832; drankin@glpf.org or preproposals@glpf.org
Internet: http://www.glpf.org/about-the-fund
Sponsor: Great Lakes Protection Fund
1560 Sherman Avenue, Suite 880
Evanston, IL 60201

Green Bay Packers Foundation Grants 2148
The Green Bay Packers organization has enjoyed tremendous fan support through its long and storied history. To give back to the community, the team created the Green Bay Packers Foundation in December 1986. The Foundation assists in a wide variety of activities and programs that benefit education, civic affairs, health services, human services and youth-related programs.
Requirements: 501(c)3 nonprofit organizations in Wisconsin may apply for grant support.
Restrictions: No substantial part of the activities of the organization shall involve carrying on propaganda, or otherwise intervening in any political campaign on behalf of any candidate for public office.
Geographic Focus: Wisconsin
Contact: Margaret Meyers, (920) 569-7315; fax (920) 569-7309; meyersm@packers.com
Internet: http://www.packers.com/community/packers_foundation
Sponsor: Green Bay Packers Foundation
P.O. Box 10628
Green Bay, WI 54307-0628

Green Diamond Charitable Contributions 2149
Green Diamond Resource Company is a fifth-generation, family-owned forest-products company that has operations in the states of California and Washington. The mission of Green Diamond's contributions program is to improve the quality of life in communities where the company has a significant number of employees living and working; and to serve as a catalyst for employees to become involved and to provide leadership in their communities. The company has supported a broad range of organizations in its operating communities that address key community needs such as education, health services, economic development, the arts, and more. The company also provides support to environmental and conservation projects, such as environmental education, habitat restoration, and research relevant to the timber industry, as well as other projects that impact the timber business. Contributions are generally made in locations where the company has operations. To the extent possible, contributions will support organizations of interest to, or recommended by, Green Diamond employees. Green Diamond prefers to make capital contributions that will benefit the operating communities for the long term as opposed to contributing operating funds. Generally, support is committed for one year at a time and in amounts less than $5,000. The company supports the United Way in all of its operating communities. The company accepts applications twice a year, generally in May and in late summer/early

fall. Interested applicants should call or mail the contact person given for their state to request application materials. More detailed information about application deadlines will be communicated at that time.
Requirements: Organizations that serve Pierce, Mason, Thurston, and Grays Harbor counties in Washington or Del Norte and Humboldt counties in California are eligible to apply. Criteria taken into account in determining the amount of any contributions are as follows: degree of support from company employees; relative size and importance of company operations in the community (balance among Green Diamond communities); needs of organization or program for which funding is requested; amount of previous company contributions to the organization; amount committed by other companies, foundations, and/or governments (projects should demonstrate broad-based community support); and proximity of the requesting organization to Green Diamond operations or administrative offices.
Geographic Focus: California, Washington
Amount of Grant: Up to 5,000 USD
Contact: Jacki Deuschle; (707) 668-4488; fax (707) 668-4402; jdeuschle@greendiamond.com
Internet: http://www.greendiamond.com/charitable-giving/
Sponsor: Green Diamond Resource Company
1301 Fifth Avenue, Suite 2700
Seattle, WA 98101-2613

Greene County Foundation Grants — 2150
The Greene County Foundations mission is to work with charitably minded individuals and organizations to strengthen Greene County, Indiana, now and for generations to come. The Foundation administers several funding opportunities. Eligibility, criteria, and supplemental requirements are different for each grant. Contact the Foundation directly to begin application process.
Geographic Focus: Indiana
Contact: Cam Trampke, Executive Director; (812) 659-3142 or (812) 659-3144; fax (812) 659-3142; ctrampke@greenecountyfoundation.org
Internet: http://www.greenecountyfoundation.org/funds_available.php
Sponsor: Greene County Foundation
4513 West State Road 54
Bloomfield, IN 47424

Greenfield Foundation of Florida Grants — 2151
This family Foundation, established in 1991, offers funding primarily in the forms of ongoing support and capital campaigns. Focus areas include: the arts; community development; education of children and youth; environmental issues; human/social service programs that support families and seniors; and science. Of particular interest are the performing arts, including dance, music, and theater. The geographic focus is national in scope, with each of the trustees sponsoring applications for non-profit organization throughout the country. Following an initial Letter of Interest, an organization must be invited by a trustee to apply. The annual deadlines for applications are February 10, May 10, August 10, and November 10.
Requirements: Grantees must be 501(c)3 organizations with a sound track record.
Restrictions: Generally the Foundation will not provide grants for: endowments, deficit financing, debt reduction, or ordinary operating expenses; conferences, seminars, workshops, travel, surveys, advertising, fund-raising costs or research; annual giving campaigns; individuals; or projects that have already been completed.
Geographic Focus: Florida
Amount of Grant: 16,000 USD
Contact: Debra M. Jacobs, (941) 957-0442; fax (941) 957-3135; djacobs@selbyfdn.org
Internet: http://www.selbyfdn.org/
Sponsor: Greenfield Foundation
1800 Second Street, Suite 750
Sarasota, FL 34236

Green Foundation Arts Grants — 2152
The Foundation's mission is to uncover new opportunities, encourage growth and ultimately effect positive change within those institutions that best reflect the core focus areas and the communities it serves. Leonard I. Green was committed to arts programming in Los Angeles. He believed in the positive impact arts education and outreach in schools, colleges and artistic institutions had (and have) on the city's youth and adult population. The Foundation is dedicated to supporting institutions that focus on arts outreach and education and we continue to encourage growth in all areas of the arts. Priority is given to those institutions that promote the expansion of community arts programs and/or support youth and adult creativity in their regular schedules.
Requirements: 501(c)3 nonprofits (as per the IRS Service Code of 1986) are eligible. Most grant making is limited to institutions that serve the Los Angeles community; however the Foundation will consider requests beyond this geographic boundary for those institutions with the potential to impact communities statewide or nationally.
Restrictions: The Foundation does not provide funds for: those with net assets or fund balances of less than $100,000; multi-year commitments; annual meetings, conferences, and/or seminars; religious programs; capital campaigns; direct mail campaigns; conduit institutions, unified funds, fiscal agents, or institutions using grant funds from donors to support other institutions or individuals; private foundations; or individuals.
Geographic Focus: All States
Amount of Grant: 1,000 - 150,000 USD
Contact: Kylie Wright; (626) 793-6200, ext. 1; fax (626) 793-6201; kylies@ligf.org
Internet: http://www.ligf.org/arts.php
Sponsor: Green Foundation
225 South Lake Avenue, Suite 1410
Pasadena, CA 91101

Green Foundation Education Grants — 2153
The Foundation's mission is to uncover new opportunities, encourage growth and ultimately effect positive change within those institutions that best reflect the core focus areas and the communities it serves. The Foundation believes that communities whose educational systems are solid will thrive and continue to flourish. With this in mind, it supports a variety of educational programs in both public and private schools and after-school facilities in an effort to effect positive change in communities throughout Los Angeles. Priority is given to those institutions that engage in one or more of the following: strive to solve existing problems of juvenile delinquency, gang life and drugs; work to expand educational programs for youth and/or adults; encourage the use of technology in youth and/or adult learning; and promote artistic endeavors including the visual and performing arts.
Requirements: 501(c)3 nonprofits (as per the IRS Service Code of 1986) are eligible. Most grant making is limited to institutions that serve the Los Angeles community; however the Foundation will consider requests beyond this geographic boundary for those institutions with the potential to impact communities statewide or nationally.
Restrictions: The Foundation does not provide funds for: those with net assets or fund balances of less than $100,000; multi-year commitments; annual meetings, conferences, and/or seminars; religious programs; capital campaigns; direct mail campaigns; conduit institutions, unified funds, fiscal agents, or institutions using grant funds from donors to support other institutions or individuals; private foundations; individuals.
Geographic Focus: All States
Amount of Grant: 1,000 - 150,000 USD
Contact: Kylie Wright; (626) 793-6200, ext. 1; fax (626) 793-6201; kylies@ligf.org
Internet: http://www.ligf.org/education.php
Sponsor: Green Foundation
225 South Lake Avenue, Suite 1410
Pasadena, CA 91101

Green Foundation Human Services Grants — 2154
The Foundation's mission is to uncover new opportunities, encourage growth and ultimately effect positive change within those institutions that best reflect the core focus areas and the communities it serves. Within the human services area, the Foundation focuses on institutions that provide hope and support to those least able to help themselves as well as the general community; including children, adolescents, the elderly, the homeless, and families who struggle with domestic abuse.
Requirements: 501(c)3 nonprofits (as per the IRS Service Code of 1986) are eligible. Most grant making is limited to institutions that serve the Los Angeles community; however the Foundation will consider requests beyond this geographic boundary for those institutions with the potential to impact communities statewide or nationally.
Restrictions: The Foundation does not provide funds for: those with net assets or fund balances of less than $100,000; multi-year commitments; annual meetings, conferences, and/or seminars; religious programs; capital campaigns; direct mail campaigns; conduit institutions, unified funds, fiscal agents, or institutions using grant funds from donors to support other institutions or individuals; private foundations; or individuals.
Geographic Focus: All States
Amount of Grant: 1,000 - 150,000 USD
Contact: Kylie Wright; (626) 793-6200, ext. 1; fax (626) 793-6201; kylies@ligf.org
Internet: http://www.ligf.org/humanservices.php
Sponsor: Green Foundation
225 South Lake Avenue, Suite 1410
Pasadena, CA 91101

Green Foundation Special Project Grants — 2155
The Foundation's mission is to uncover new opportunities, encourage growth and ultimately effect positive change within those institutions that best reflect the core focus areas and the communities it serves. The Foundation does award grants to those institutions that fall outside of its established areas of focus. Each request is considered on an individual basis and grant-seekers should follow the application process outlined on the Foundation web site.
Requirements: 501(c)3 nonprofits (as per the IRS Service Code of 1986) are eligible. Most grant making is limited to institutions that serve the Los Angeles community; however the Foundation will consider requests beyond this geographic boundary for those institutions with the potential to impact communities statewide or nationally.
Restrictions: The Foundation does not provide funds for: those with net assets or fund balances of less than $100,000; multi-year commitments; annual meetings, conferences, and/or seminars; religious programs; capital campaigns; direct mail campaigns; conduit institutions, unified funds, fiscal agents, or institutions using grant funds from donors to support other institutions or individuals; private foundations; or individuals.
Geographic Focus: All States
Amount of Grant: 1,000 - 150,000 USD
Contact: Kylie Wright; (626) 793-6200, ext. 1; fax (626) 793-6201; kylies@ligf.org
Internet: http://www.ligf.org/specialprojects.php
Sponsor: Green Foundation
225 South Lake Avenue, Suite 1410
Pasadena, CA 91101

Greenspun Family Foundation Grants — 2156
The Greenspun Family Foundation supports many causes with an emphasis on education, health, children, Jewish issues, and the greater Las Vegas community. Preference is given to requests from the Las Vegas area. There are no application forms or deadlines. Applicants should submit a letter of inquiry. Information about current programs supported is available at the Foundation website.
Geographic Focus: Nevada
Amount of Grant: 50,000 - 2,000,000 USD

Contact: Dr. Brian Cram, Director; (702) 259-2323 or (702) 259-4023; fax (702) 259-4019; brian.cram@lasvegassun.com
Internet: http://www.thegreenspuncorp.com/philanthropy.php
Sponsor: Greenspun Family Foundation
901 North Green Valley Parkway, Suite 210
Henderson, NV 89074

Greenwall Foundation Arts and Humanities Grants 2157
Innovation and creativity in the visual, performing, literary, and media arts receive special Foundation attention. The Foundation is interested in supporting New York City's cultural life and encourages requests from local arts groups and institutions. The Foundation's grant giving focuses on emerging artists and the development of new artistic work.
Restrictions: The Foundation is not normally interested in proposals to support equipment purchase, facility construction or renovation, or general operating expenses, and will not normally consider grants to private foundations, endowment funds, or individual applicants. Grants are not made for arts education projects.
Geographic Focus: New York
Date(s) Application is Due: Feb 1; Aug 1
Amount of Grant: 5,000 - 50,000 USD
Contact: Sam Teigen; (212) 679-7266; fax (212) 679-7269; steigen@greenwall.org
Internet: http://www.greenwall.org/guidearts.htm
Sponsor: Greenwall Foundation
420 Lexington Avenue, Suite 2500
New York, NY 10170

Greenwall Foundation Bioethics Grants 2158
The Foundation provides funding for physicians, lawyers, philosophers, theologians and other professionals to address micro and macro issues in bioethics, providing guidance for those engaged in decision-making at the bedside as well as those responsible for shaping institutional and public policy. The Foundation is especially interested in the work of junior investigators and pilot projects that may lead to NIH support, and it is prepared to address issues regarded by some as sensitive or potentially controversial.
Restrictions: The Foundation is not normally interested in proposals to support equipment purchase, facility construction or renovation, or general operating expenses, and will not normally consider grants to private foundations, endowment funds, or individual applicants.
Geographic Focus: All States
Date(s) Application is Due: Feb 1; Aug 1
Amount of Grant: 5,000 - 50,000 USD
Contact: Sam Teigen; (212) 679-7266; fax (212) 679-7269; steigen@greenwall.org
Internet: http://www.greenwall.org/guidebio.htm
Sponsor: Greenwall Foundation
420 Lexington Avenue, Suite 2500
New York, NY 10170

GreenWorks! Butterfly Garden Grants 2159
Project Learning Tree (PLT), a program of the American Forest Foundation, is an award winning, multi-disciplinary environmental education program for educators and students in PreK-grade 12. Through PLT, students learn environmental content that correlates to national and state standards in science, social studies, language arts, math, and other subjects - and strengthen their critical thinking, team building, and problem solving skills. PLT is providing GreenWorks! funding for participating teachers. Grants of up to $1,000 are available for schools to create butterfly gardens in their schoolyard or community.
Requirements: To receive a GreenWorks! Butterfly Garden Grant: 1) Applicant must be trained in PLT; 2) Applicant must be registered for and participate in MonarchLIVE!: A Distance Learning Adventure; 3) A main component of the project must include the creation of a butterfly habitat garden on school grounds or in the community; 4) Youth must implement the project; 5) Project must integrate student learning and community service; 6) Project must include at least one community partner; and, 7) Project must acquire 50% matching funds (may be in-kind).
Geographic Focus: All States
Date(s) Application is Due: Dec 1
Amount of Grant: Up to 1,000 USD
Contact: Imad Aoun, (202) 463-2754; iaoun@forestfoundation.org
Internet: http://www.plt.org/cms/pages/21_22_235.html
Sponsor: American Forest Foundation
1111 19th Street NW, Suite 780
Washington, DC 20036

GreenWorks! Grants 2160
GreenWorks! grants engage Project Learning Tree (PLT) educators and their students with their local community in learning-by-doing environmental projects. Student leadership, service-learning, and community participation are the cornerstones to GreenWorks! projects. These grassroots action projects enable schools and youth organizations across the country to make a positive impact on their communities. GreenWorks! grants are awarded in the spring and fall of each year in the following two funding categories: $250 to $1,000 grants and $1,001 - $5,000 grants. Deadlines are in the spring and fall of each year.
Requirements: $250 to $1,000 GreenWorks! Grants proposal requirements include: (1) Applicant must have received training in PLT; (2) Youth must plan and implement the project; (3) The project must integrate student learning and community service; (4) The project must include at least one community partner, such as a local organization or business; (5) The project must acquire 50% matching funds. $250 - $1000 projects must be completed in one years' time. To qualify for $1,001 - $5,000 grants, applicants must meet all the above requirements, as well as: (6) Involve increased numbers of students, classes, youth organizations, and community partners; and, (7) Include a plan to administer a Project Learning Tree professional development workshop for the staff of the school(s) or organization(s) sponsoring the proposal. $1,001 - $5,000 projects must be completed within two years' time.
Geographic Focus: All States
Date(s) Application is Due: Apr 30; Oct 31
Amount of Grant: 250 - 5,000 USD
Contact: Jackie Stallard, (202) 463-2457; jstallard@forestfoundation.org
Internet: http://www.plt.org/cms/pages/21_22_21.html
Sponsor: American Forest Foundation
1111 19th Street NW, Suite 780
Washington, DC 20036

Gregory C. Carr Foundation Grants 2161
The Foundation is a non-profit organization founded in 1999 whose program activities are dedicated to the environment, human rights and the arts. The current focus is to further public education in the area of human rights, particularly in Southern Africa. There are no specific submission deadlines and no application forms. Potential applicants should contact the office by letter, and then forward eight (8) copies of the full proposal
Geographic Focus: Massachusetts, Algeria, Angola, Benin, Botswana, Burkina Faso, Burundi, Cameroon, Cape Verde, Central African Republic, Chad, Comoros, Congo, Congo, Democratic Republic of, Cote d' Ivoire (Ivory Coast), Djibouti, Egypt, Equatorial Guinea, Eritrea, Ethiopia, Gabon, Gambia, Ghana, Guinea, Guinea-Bissau, Kenya, Lesotho, Liberia, Libya, Madagascar, Malawi, Mali, Mauritania, Mauritius, Morocco, Mozambique, Namibia, Niger, Nigeria, Rwanda, Sao Tome & Principe, Senegal, Seychelles, Sierra Leone, Somalia, South Africa, Sudan, Swaziland
Amount of Grant: Up to 500,000 USD
Contact: Gregory C. Carr, President; (617) 576-9192 or (617) 301-4000; MLgray@prodigy.net or info@carrfoundation.org
Internet: http://www.carrfoundation.org/
Sponsor: Gregory C. Carr Foundation
2 Arrow Street, Suite 400
Cambridge, MA 02138

Gregory Family Foundation Grants (Massachusetts) 2162
The Foundation, established in 1989 in New York, is directed by a one-time chairman and CEO of NATCO Group, Nat Gregory. Its primary areas of funding include general operating support for secondary education, higher education, and human/social service programs. The application should include: a resume; identification of the purpose; and specific use of funding. There are no specific deadlines with which to adhere.
Requirements: Applicants must include a statement confirming that they have no family or financial ties to the foundation or its directors or officers.
Geographic Focus: Connecticut
Amount of Grant: 1,000 - 25,000 USD
Contact: Nathaniel Gregory, President; (773) 834-8781; ngregory@chicagogsb.edu
Sponsor: Gregory Family Foundation
428 Wianno Avenue, P.O. Box 237
Osterville, MA 02655-1943

Gregory L. Gibson Charitable Foundation Grants 2163
The Foundation, established in Terre Haute, Indiana, in 2005, is interested in programs that support children, youth, and families. Its primary areas of interest include: community service programs; education; health care and health care access; hospice care; technology; and youth sports. The specific type of support is for general operations. There are no specific deadlines with which to adhere, and applicants should forward a submission letter.
Requirements: 501(c)3 organizations situated in, or serving the community of, Terre Haute, Indiana, are eligible to apply.
Geographic Focus: Indiana
Amount of Grant: Up to 30,000 USD
Contact: Gregory L. Gibson, President; (812) 466-1233
Sponsor: Gregory L. Gibson Charitable Foundation
3200 E Haythorne Avenue
Terre Haute, IN 47805-002108

Greygates Foundation Grants 2164
The Greygates Foundation was created in 2001 by J. Ronald Gibbs to provide grants to organizations that serve the needs of children, the elderly, the disabled, or the disadvantaged, and to organizations that promote animal welfare or wildlife preservation. The grant award limit is $3,000, and grants are paid in Canadian dollars. The foundation funds the following types of requests: general operating support, capacity building, program support, equipment, and tuition assistance. Proposals are accepted on a rolling basis. Organizations are asked to take an online eligibility quiz before they apply. Application must be made by email. Guidelines are available for download from the trust's website. Applicants are notified promptly when their proposals are received but should expect to wait three to six months for notification of a decision. Questions may be directed to the foundation's administrator.
Requirements: Though funding may be provided for projects in any country, recipient organizations must be Canadian-registered charities. If an organization does not have such status, the foundation will consider making a grant to a Canadian-registered charity acting as a sponsor for the non-recognized organization. The Greygates Foundation grants are generally awarded to smaller nonprofit organizations, but are not limited to such organizations.
Restrictions: The Foundation does not provide funding to individuals or to organizations operated by or receiving significant support from government sources.
Geographic Focus: All States, All Countries

Amount of Grant: Up to 3,000 CAD
Contact: J. Ronald Gibbs, Administrator; (604) 896-1619; beron@telus.net
Janet Ferriaolo, Grants Manager; (415) 332-0166; jferraiolo@adminitrustllc.com
Internet: http://www.adminitrustllc.com/the-greygates-foundation/
Sponsor: Greygates Foundation
c/o Adminitrust LLC
Sausalito, CA 94965

Griffin Foundation Grants 2165
The Foundation, established in 1991, serves non-profit organizations in Fort Collins, Colorado, and Laramie, Wyoming. Its major fields of interest include: the arts; health care; higher education; performing arts; orchestras; and substance abuse service programs. Funding most often comes in the forms of building construction, renovation, and scholarships. Applicants should request an application form, and submit a detailed description of the project and budget needed.
Geographic Focus: Colorado, Wyoming
Contact: David L. Wood; (970) 482-3030; carol.wood@thegriffinfoundation.org
Internet: http://www.thegriffinfoundation.org/index.shtml
Sponsor: Griffin Foundation
303 W Prospect Road
Fort Collins, CO 80526-2003

Grotto Foundation Project Grants 2166
The Grotto Foundation works to improve the education and economic, physical and social well-being of citizens, with a special focus on families and culturally diverse groups. The Foundation funds support agencies and institutions dedicated to improving the quality of parenting and well-being of infants and children from birth to six years of age. The Foundation is further interested in increasing public understanding of American cultural heritage, the cultures of nations and the individual's responsibility to fellow human beings.
Requirements: Detailed applications for Native American grants are available online. Applicants are encouraged to contact the Foundation and discuss their early childhood development to be certain it is appropriate for funding.
Restrictions: Policy precludes grants being awarded for capital fund projects, travel, publication of books or manuscripts, undergraduate research projects, or grants to individuals.
Geographic Focus: Minnesota
Date(s) Application is Due: Jan 15; Mar 15; Jul 15; Nov 15
Amount of Grant: Up to 10,000 USD
Contact: Jennifer Kolde; (651) 209-8010; fax (651) 209-8014; jkolde@grottofoundation.org
Internet: http://www.grottofoundation.org
Sponsor: Grotto Foundation
1315 Red Fox Road, Suite 100
Arden Hills, MN 55112

Group 70 Foundation Fund 2167
The focus of the Fund is creating strong, compassionate and resilient communities in Hawaii embraced with people who are prepared, safe and secure. The Fund is designed to support projects that contribute to a better living environment in Hawaii. Selected projects must address one or more of the following categories: education, housing, culture, environment and/or design elements. Preference will be given to projects that: primarily benefit Hawaii communities; demonstrate broad reach within the community; involve active community participation in the development and implementation of the project. Application information is available online.
Requirements: The project must be carried out or fiscally sponsored by a nonprofit, tax exempt 501(c)3 organization, school or unit of government.
Geographic Focus: Hawaii
Date(s) Application is Due: Apr 20
Amount of Grant: 2,000 - 10,000 USD
Contact: Amy Luersen, (808) 566-5550 or (888) 731-3863; aluersen@hawaiicommunityfoundation.org or aluersen@hcf-hawaii.org
Internet: http://www.hawaiicommunityfoundation.org/index.php?id=71&categoryID=20
Sponsor: Hawai'i Community Foundation
1164 Bishop Street, Suite 800
Honolulu, HI 96813

Grover Hermann Foundation Grants 2168
The Grover Hermann Foundation Grants provide funding in the Chicago, Illonois and Monterrey County, California. Funding is largely in the following areas: community - local development and organizations established for youth, the elderly, or the disadvantaged, and for cultural and other community-related activities. In these categories, only organizations from the Chicago area are considered; education - although pre-college programs are eligible for grants, higher education will receive the greatest consideration. Scholarships, fellowships, challenge grants, and grants for capital expenditures are considered. Tax-supported colleges and universities receive less consideration than private institutions; health - medical facilities, basic medical research, disease-specific organizations, and other health programs; public policy - organizations dedicated to the strengthening and improvement of governmental, economic, and social systems that recognize and promote the values of individual liberty, a strong work ethic, free-market competition, and limited government; religious - established religious organizations for assistance in furthering well-defined secular causes, in the Chicago area only. Proposals are accepted at any time. The Board of Directors meets in March, June, September, and December, with funding decisions made within two weeks of board meetings.
Requirements: An application form is not required. Applicants should submit the following: results expected from proposed grant; qualifications of key personnel; statement of problem the project will address; copy of IRS Determination Letter; brief history of organization and description of its mission; copy of most recent annual report/audited financial statement/990; how project's results will be evaluated or measured; listing of board of directors, trustees, officers and other key people and their affiliations; detailed description of project and amount of funding requested; copy of current year's organizational budget and/or project budget; and a listing of additional sources and amount of support. Organizations should also submit a separate letter stating that no change in 501(c)3 status has occurred since it was issued, or is currently anticipated.
Restrictions: Funding is not available for fraternal, athletic, foreign organizations, or private foundation. Funding is also not available for individuals or operating budgets (except for national health organizations). The Foundation discourages the submission of brochures, marketing materials, newspaper or magazine clippings or booklets containing the same.
Geographic Focus: California, Illinois
Amount of Grant: 3,000 - 17,500 USD
Contact: Paul K. Rhoads, President; (630) 908-7800
Sponsor: Grover Hermann Foundation
908 Kenmare Drive
Burr Ridge, IL 60527-7091

Grundy Foundation Grants 2169
The Grundy Foundation's endowment, which sustains the operations of both the museum and library, also provides grantmaking. Grant support is given to projects that benefit the people and institutions of Pennsylvania. Upon availability, the Board of Trustees generally restricts grantmaking to Bucks County public charities, with special consideration to those of Bristol Borough. Grant applications are awarded primarily for capital projects to serve a wide area rather than a single neighborhood. Grantmaking activities include community development, arts and culture, education, environment, health, and human services. The average grant is $2,500.
Requirements: There are no applications or specific deadlines. The Foundation accepts and reviews written requests for funding throughout the year. In general, organizations having other support for core operating expenses and long-term costs of new projects are given priority. Organizations are encouraged to contact the Foundation prior to submission of a grant application. Prospective grantees may use the forms developed by the Delaware Valley Grant makers, if preferred. At a minimum, each proposal must include: One-page summary with contact name, executive director's name, organization name, address, telephone, email, and fax; project summary; amount requested; and total project budget amount; detailed proposal with mission and history of the organization; complete description of the proposed project; project budget, including other sources of support, with indication of whether support is in hand, pledged, requested, or to be requested; expected sources of support for this project in the future; and expected arrangements for future maintenance and repairs; the organization's financial report of IRS 990 filing for the most recent fiscal year (audited reports are preferred); copy of IRS 501(c)3 letter of determination or proof that the organization is a government agency; a list of officers and directors; a copy of report of the organization's activities over the most recent fiscal year. Proposals can be mailed, faxed or sent electronically (faxes and email versions require prior Foundation approval). Videotaped proposals will not be accepted.
Restrictions: The Foundation does not make grants to nonpublic schools, individuals, religious organizations, or for endowments, loans, research, or political activities.
Geographic Focus: Pennsylvania
Contact: Eugene Williams; (215) 788-5460; fax (215) 788-0915; info@grundyfoundation.com
Internet: http://www.grundymuseum.org/
Sponsor: Grundy Foundation
680 Radcliffe Street, P.O. Box 701
Bristol, PA 19007

GTECH After School Advantage Grants 2170
The GTECH After School Advantage Program is a national community investment program, which provides non-profit community agencies and public schools with state-of-the-art computer labs. These computer centers are designed to provide inner-city children aged five to 15 with a meaningful, yet fun, learning experience during the critical after-school hours, in a safe environment. This initiative is meant to provide an otherwise unavailable educational experience and bridge the digital divide among at-risk children. By applying its knowledge and expertise to this type of program GTECH hopes to increase children's interest in careers in computers and provide them with the necessary tools to help them become more competitive in school and in today's job market.
Requirements: GTECH donates up to $15,000 in state-of-the-art computers, on-line technology, computer software and volunteer hours to each after-school program in inner-city communities where the Company's offices are located nationwide (see states listed below). Applicants must be a non-profit 501(c)3 community agency or public school. Organizations must serve disadvantaged youth aged five to 15, of diverse backgrounds; must have an existing after-school program in need of a computer lab; and must have staffing and monetary support systems in place to sustain the lab.
Geographic Focus: All States
Amount of Grant: Up to 15,000 USD
Samples: Boys and Girls Club of Lynchburg, Lynchburg, VA (2013); SAFE BASE, Iola, KS (2013); Rochambeau Community Library, Providence, RI (2012).
Contact: Elena Chiaradio, (401) 392-7705; Elena.Chiaradio@gtech.com
Internet: http://gtechlottery.com/our-commitment/community-involvement/
Sponsor: GTECH Corporation
10 Memorial Boulevard
Providence, RI 02903

GTECH Community Involvement Grants 2171
GTECH strives to enrich and strengthen the communities in which its operates through a variety of programs, sponsorships, and donations. The focus of GTECH's charitable efforts can be divided into three broad areas: creating educational opportunities; fostering community initiatives; and empowering employee involvement.
Requirements: 501(c)3 nonprofit organizations in a state where GTECH does business are eligible to apply. All requests must be made in writing and must align with GTECH's corporate social responsibility strategy and business goals.
Restrictions: GTECH does not support organizations that discriminate based on age, race, color, sex, religion, disability, or sexual orientation. In general, GTECH does not support capital campaigns, golf tournaments, or other local sporting events.
Geographic Focus: Arizona, California, Colorado, Florida, Georgia, Illinois, Indiana, Kansas, Kentucky, Minnesota, Missouri, Nebraska, New Hampshire, New Jersey, New Mexico, New York, Oklahoma, Oregon, South Dakota, Tennessee, Texas, Washington, Wisconsin
Contact: Alethea Johnson; (401) 392-1000; fax (401) 392-1234; publicaffairs@gtech.com
Internet: http://gtechlottery.com/our-commitment/community-involvement/
Sponsor: GTECH Corporation
10 Memorial Boulevard
Providence, RI 02903

Guido A. and Elizabeth H. Binda Foundation Grants 2172
The Foundation supports nonprofit organizations in Southwest Michigan. Areas of interest are educational projects, culture and arts, and human services. Capital campaigns and endowments are considered on a very limited basis. Initial contact may be made by letter describing the project for which funds are sought.
Requirements: Nonprofit organizations in Battle Creek and southwestern Michigan may request grant support.
Geographic Focus: Michigan
Date(s) Application is Due: May 1; Dec 1
Contact: Nancy Taber; (269) 968-6171; fax (269) 968-5126; grants@bindafoundation.org
Internet: http://www.bindafoundation.org/grants.html
Sponsor: Guido A. and Elizabeth H. Binda Foundation
15 Capital Avenue NE, Suite 205
Battle Creek, MI 49017

GUITS Library Acquisitions Grants 2173
The Institute of Turkish Studies (ITS) is the only non-profit, private educational foundation in the United States exclusively dedicated to the support and development of Turkish Studies in American higher education. Library Acquisitions Grants are intended to enable libraries in the U.S. to purchase books and materials related to Turkish Studies. The maximum award is $2,500 per institution.
Requirements: To be eligible for a grant, applicants should be: faculty in any field of the social sciences and/or humanities; and U.S. citizens or permanent residents at the time of the application.
Geographic Focus: All States
Date(s) Application is Due: Mar 7
Contact: David C. Cuthell; (202) 687-0295; fax (202) 687-3780; dcc@turkishstudies.org
Internet: http://www.turkishstudies.org/grantinfo.html
Sponsor: Georgetown University Institute of Turkish Studies
Intercultural Center, Box 571033, Room 305R
Washington, DC 20057-1033

Gulf Coast Community Foundation Grants 2174
The Foundation is a public charity dedicated to the progressive development of the Mississippi Gulf Coast. Its primary mission is to increase philanthropy to worthy causes by providing donor services, grants and leadership for problem solving. The Foundation carries out donor wishes by making grants in the areas of health and human services, education, arts and culture, historic preservation, and neighborhood enrichment. Grant application and additional guidelines are available online at: http://www.gulfcoastfoundation.org/guidelines.html.
Requirements: Applicants must be non-profit, tax-exempt organizations that are involved in enhancing the quality of life for citizens of South Mississippi. Organizations that have not been recognized as tax-exempt by the IRS may apply if they have a fiscal agent relationship with a 501(c)3 nonprofit organization.
Restrictions: Grants do not support: capital, operating endowment fund drives; political activities; individuals; or religious activities.
Geographic Focus: Mississippi
Contact: Rose Dellenger; (228) 897-4841; fax (228) 897-4843; rdellenger@mgccf.org
Internet: http://www.gulfcoastfoundation.org/grants.html
Sponsor: Gulf Coast Community Foundation
P.O. Box 984
Gulfport, MS 39503

Gulf Coast Foundation of Community Capacity Building Grants 2175
The Capacity Building Grants program offers Grant Writer Assistance funding, which helps local nonprofits that are unable to compete for grant opportunities because of complex, lengthy grant applications. Funds may be used to hire an experienced grant writer with the capabilities to attract dollars from regional or national funders and private or government programs. Requests for grant writing assistance will be judged on the following criteria: amount is significant enough to warrant the use of grant funds to hire a grant writer; the source of the grant is non-local; the expertise of the selected grant writer is appropriate; the agency has a reasonable chance of receiving the grant; the cost to hire a grant writer would have been prohibitive to the agency if these funds were not available; and all fund requests will require a minimum 50 percent cash match by the agency.
Requirements: The Foundation will make grants to qualified organizations classified as 501(c)3 tax-exempt public charities by the Internal Revenue Service in the counties of Brevard, Charlotte, Citrus, Collier, DeSoto, Glades, Hardee, Hendry, Hernando, Highlands, Hillsborough, Indian River, Lake, Lee, Manatee, Okeechobee, Orange, Osceola, Pasco, Pinellas, Polk, Sarasota, Seminole, Sumter, and St. Lucie.
Geographic Focus: Florida
Contact: Kirstin Fulkerson; (941) 486-4600; fax (941) 486-4699; info@gulfcoastcf.org
Internet: http://www.gulfcoastcf.org/resources.php
Sponsor: Gulf Coast Foundation of Community
601 Tamiami Trail South
Venice, FL 34285

Gulf Coast Foundation of Community Operating Grants 2176
Through grants and strategic community initiatives, Gulf Coast invests in the work of effective nonprofit organizations that improve quality of life in our region. The Foundation will award operating grants over $10,000, with grant funds to be expended within one year of approval. Currently, the Foundation has four grant cycles for operating grants, which fund the core operating needs of nonprofits and help make them stronger. This includes staff and training, database and accounting systems, marketing and fundraising operations. Organizations that want to diversify income streams and generate new revenue sources may apply for an operating – earned revenue grant. Examples of successful proposals in this category include using existing facilities to generate rental income or marketing and selling a packaged program/service to other organizations. Groups that want to reduce operating costs may apply for an operating – efficiency grant. Examples of successful proposals in this category include consolidating services with other nonprofits, implementing new or improved technologies such as databases or financial systems, or "greening" offices.
Requirements: The Foundation will make grants to qualified organizations classified as 501(c)3 tax-exempt public charities by the Internal Revenue Service in the counties of Brevard, Charlotte, Citrus, Collier, DeSoto, Glades, Hardee, Hendry, Hernando, Highlands, Hillsborough, Indian River, Lake, Lee, Manatee, Okeechobee, Orange, Osceola, Pasco, Pinellas, Polk, Sarasota, Seminole, Sumter, and St. Lucie. All operating – earned revenue grant applications must provide realistic revenue estimates that result in a return on investment that exceeds the grant amount. Operating – efficiency grant applications must provide a cost?benefit analysis showing how proposed funding approaches will produce cost savings.
Geographic Focus: Florida
Contact: Kirstin Fulkerson; (941) 486-4600; fax (941) 486-4699; info@gulfcoastcf.org
Internet: http://www.gulfcoastcf.org/resources.php
Sponsor: Gulf Coast Foundation of Community
601 Tamiami Trail South
Venice, FL 34285

Gulf Coast Foundation of Community Program Grants 2177
Gulf Coast Foundation of Community Program Grants address regional priorities identified through its Environmental Scan. The environmental scanning process looked broadly at trends and conditions in its region through interviews with community leaders and analysis of available data. The findings help Gulf Coast identify the best ways to lift the regional economy and sustain community through our grantmaking. Successful program grant applicants will clearly target important regional challenges or opportunities, provide measurable data that will be the basis for assessing their impact, and share stories of transformation through a variety of social and traditional media. Organizations must have strong leadership and competent staff to execute their program and will significantly leverage their own program dollars so that they have "skin in the game" to maximize their program's impact.
Requirements: The Foundation will make grants to qualified organizations classified as 501(c)3 tax-exempt public charities by the Internal Revenue Service in the counties of Brevard, Charlotte, Citrus, Collier, DeSoto, Glades, Hardee, Hendry, Hernando, Highlands, Hillsborough, Indian River, Lake, Lee, Manatee, Okeechobee, Orange, Osceola, Pasco, Pinellas, Polk, Sarasota, Seminole, Sumter, and St. Lucie.
Geographic Focus: Florida
Contact: Kirstin Fulkerson; (941) 486-4600; fax (941) 486-4699; info@gulfcoastcf.org
Internet: http://www.gulfcoastcf.org/resources.php
Sponsor: Gulf Coast Foundation of Community
601 Tamiami Trail South
Venice, FL 34285

Gulf Coast Foundation of Community Scholarships 2178
Gulf Coast gives scholarships from dozens of scholarship funds to help local students of all ages pursue meaningful postsecondary education. Students must be accepted to or attending an accredited vocational school, college or university, or graduate institution to apply. Scholarships are available to high school seniors as well as current undergraduate and graduate students. Applicants can complete a single online application in order to be considered for all available scholarships. The annual deadline for making application is March 16th.
Requirements: Permanent legal residents of Venice or its surrounding communities (Sarasota County, Charlotte County or Boca Grande) are eligible to apply. Scholarships are need-based provided that the student meets the minimum GPA (2.5) and other required criteria for the scholarship for which he/she is applying.
Geographic Focus: Florida
Date(s) Application is Due: Mar 16
Contact: Kirstin Fulkerson, Philanthropic Advisor; (941) 486-4600 or (941) 486-4569; fax (941) 486-4699; scholarships@gulfcoastcf.org
Internet: http://www.gulfcoastcf.org/scholarships.php
Sponsor: Gulf Coast Foundation of Community
601 Tamiami Trail South
Venice, FL 34285

Gumdrop Books Librarian Scholarships 2179

Through the Fitzgerald Family Trust, Gumdrop Books offers twenty (20) $1,000 librarian scholarships. Two scholarships will be awarded in each of the states of Alabama, Arizona, Colorado, Illinois, New York, North Carolina, Pennsylvania, South Carolina, Tennessee and Virginia, to assist librarians/teachers to achieve their master's degree in Library Science. Each award will be paid directly to any university of the winner's choice that offers a master's degree in Library Science. Each scholarship can be used to cover tuition, books, on-campus room and board, or similar expenses.

Requirements: All Alabama, Arizona, Colorado, Illinois, New York, North Carolina, Pennsylvania, South Carolina, Tennessee, and Virginia librarians and teachers are eligible. Applicants must: (1) be eligible to enroll or currently enrolled in a master's degree for Library Science in the state of recommendation; (2) be recommended by a librarian who has purchased books from Gumdrop Books between July 1 through December 31; (3) submit the required scholarship application form and copies of transcripts. Preference will be given to librarians. Consideration will be given to financial need and the applicant's work and community service record. Final selections will be approved by The Greater Kansas City Community Foundation.

Geographic Focus: Alabama, Arizona, Colorado, Illinois, New York, North Carolina, Pennsylvania, South Carolina, Tennessee, Virginia

Date(s) Application is Due: Jan 15

Amount of Grant: 1,000 USD

Contact: Pat Macdonald; (816) 842-0944; macdonald@gkccf.org

Internet: http://www.gumdropbooks.com/library/Scholarship08-09.pdf

Sponsor: Gumdrop Books
802 N 41st Street
Bethany, MO 64424

Guy I. Bromley Trust Grants 2180

The Guy I. Bromley Trust was established in 1964 to support and promote quality educational, cultural, human-services, and health-care programming. In the area of education the trust supports programming that: promotes effective teaching; improves the academic achievement of, or expands educational opportunities for disadvantaged students; improves governance and management; strengthens nonprofit organizations, school leadership, and teaching; and bolsters strategic initiatives of area colleges and universities. In the area of culture the trust supports programming that: fosters the enjoyment and appreciation of the visual and performing arts; strengthens humanities and arts-related education programs; provides affordable access; enhances artistic elements in communities; and nurtures a new generation of artists. In the area of human services, the trust supports programming that: strengthens agencies that deliver critical human services and maintains the community's safety net; and helps agencies respond to federal, state, and local public policy changes. In the area of health the trust supports programming that: improves the delivery of health care to the indigent, uninsured, and other vulnerable populations; and addresses health and health-care problems that intersect with social factors. Grant requests for general operating support and program support will be considered. Grants from the trust are one year in duration. There are no application deadlines for the Bromley Trust. Proposals are reviewed on an ongoing basis. Downloadable application materials are available at the grant website. Applicants are encouraged to review the downloadable state guidelines at the grant website for further information and clarification before applying. Applicants are also encouraged to view the trust's funding history (link is available at the grant website).

Requirements: Applicants must have 501(c)3 status and serve the residents of Atchison, Kansas and the Greater Kansas City Metropolitan area. Applications must be mailed.

Restrictions: Grant requests for capital support will not be considered. The trust does not support requests from individuals, organizations attempting to influence policy through direct lobbying, or any political campaigns.

Geographic Focus: All States

Contact: Spence Heddens; (816) 292-4301; Spence.heddens@baml.com

Internet: https://www.bankofamerica.com/philanthropic/fn_search.action

Sponsor: Guy I. Bromley Trust
1200 Main Street, 14th Floor, P.O. Box 219119
Kansas City, MO 64121-9119

H & R Foundation Grants 2181

The Foundation prefers to support projects and programs that strive for excellence, improve service for clients and strengthen the organization. A major emphasis is placed on support of activities that serve underserved, low-income persons living in Jackson, Clay, and Platte counties in Missouri, and Wyandotte and Johnson counties in Kansas.

Requirements: Grants are made only to organizations that are tax-exempt from federal income taxation pursuant to Section 501(c)3 and that are not classified as private foundations within the code.

Restrictions: Except in the most unusual circumstances, the Foundation does not make grants to: organizations that knowingly discriminate on the basis of race, color, religion, gender, national origin, sexual orientation, age, disability, marital status, or status as a veteran; organizations that are not in compliance with laws and regulations that govern them; individuals or businesses; publications; projects for which the Foundation must exercise expenditure responsibility; single-disease causes; travel or conferences; historic preservation; telethons, dinners, advertising, sponsorships, or other special events; animal-related causes; sports-related causes.

Geographic Focus: Kansas, Missouri

Date(s) Application is Due: Feb 26; Apr 30; Jul 30; Oct 15

Contact: David Miles, ; (816) 854-4372 or (816) 854-4361; davmiles@hrblock.com

Internet: http://www.blockfoundation.org/nonprofit_organizations/faqs.html

Sponsor: H and R Foundation
One H&R Bloack Way
Kansas City, MO 64105

H.A. and Mary K. Chapman Charitable Trust Grants 2182

H. Allen Chapman was born in Colorado in 1919. In 1976, he established the H.A. and Mary K. Chapman Charitable Trust, a perpetual charitable private foundation that maintains endowments to fund charitable grants to public charities. The trustees and staff that administer the foundation also provide public stewardship through service to charitable organizations and causes. A major charitable focus of H. A. Chapman during his life, and the lives of his philanthropic parents, James A. and Leta Chapman, was education and medical research. Though not limited geographically, most grants and public service are within Oklahoma. Grants to human services and civic and community programs and projects are primarily focused in the area of Tulsa. There are two steps in the process of applying for a grant. The first is a Letter of Inquiry from the applicant. This letter is used to determine if the applicant will be invited to take the second step of submitting a formal Grant Proposal.

Requirements: IRS 501(c)3 non-profits are eligible to apply.

Restrictions: Grant requests for the following purposes are not favored: endowments, except as a limited part of a capital project reserved for maintenance of the facility being constructed; deficit financing and debt retirement; projects or programs for which the Chapman Trusts would be the sole source of financial support; travel, conferences, conventions, group meetings, or seminars; camp programs and other seasonal activities; religious programs of religious organizations; project or program planning; start-up ventures are not excluded, but organizations with a proven strategy and results are preferred; purposes normally funded by taxation or governmental agencies; requests made less than nine months from the declination of a previous request by an applicant, or within nine months of the last payment made on a grant made to an applicant; requests for more than one project.

Geographic Focus: Oklahoma

Amount of Grant: Up to 300,000 USD

Contact: Andrea Doyle; (918) 496-7882; fax (918) 496-7887; andie@chapmantrusts.com

Internet: http://www.chapmantrusts.org/grants_programs.html

Sponsor: H.A. and Mary K. Chapman Charitable Trust
6100 South Yale, Suite 1816
Tulsa, OK 74136

H.B. Fuller Company Foundation Grants 2183

The Foundation makes grants within the corporate headquarters community, and other key H.B. Fuller communities throughout the world. Within Minnesota, the Foundation recently served as a catalyst in drawing attention to and support for early family literacy programs, and now focuses on science, technology, engineering, and math education. In other communities and cultures, the foundation provides critical grants in education, arts/culture, and health/human services. As an international company, the foundation's commitments extend well beyond the Minnesota state borders. Making significant community grants to schools and non-governmental agencies (NGOs) in locations across Latin America, as well as key community investments in six North American cities where the H.B. Fuller Company has manufacturing operations. Most recently, expanding philanthropic giving into Asia.

Requirements: 501(c)3 organizations serving the communities where the company has operations are eligible. Organizations incorporated in countries other than the United States must qualify for tax-exempt status according to U.S. tax regulations and comply with national and/or state charity laws.

Restrictions: Funding is not available for: individuals, including scholarships for individuals; fraternal or veterans' organizations except for programs which are of direct benefit to the broader community; religious groups for religious purposes; political/lobbying organizations; travel; basic or applied research; disease specific organizations; courtesy, goodwill or public service advertisements; fundraiser events or sponsorships; general support education institutions.

Geographic Focus: California, Florida, Georgia, Illinois, Indiana, Kentucky, Michigan, Minnesota, Ohio, Texas, Washington, Abkhazia, Afghanistan, Armenia, Azerbaijan, Bahrain, Bangladesh, Bhutan, British Indian Ocean Territory, Brunei, Burma (Myanmar), Cambodia, China, Christmas Island, Cocos, Cyprus, Georgia, Hong Kong, India, Indonesia, Iran, Iraq, Israel, Japan, Jordan, Kazakhstan, Kuwait, Kyrgyzstan, Laos, Lebanon, Macau, Malaysia, Maldives, Mongolia, Nagorno-Karabakh, Nepal, North Korea, Northern Cyprus, Oman, Pakistan, Palestinian Authority, Philippines, Qatar, Russia, Saudi Arabia, Singapore, South Korea, South Ossetia, Sri Lanka, Syria, Taiwan, Tajikistan, Thailand, Timor-Lester, Turkey, Turkmenistan, United Arab Emirates, Uzbekistan, Vietnam, Yemen

Date(s) Application is Due: Feb 2; Jun 4; Oct 5

Contact: Keralyn Groff, Director; (651) 236-5104; keralyn.groff@hbfuller.com

Internet: http://www.hbfuller.com/About_Us/Community/000110.shtml#P0_0

Sponsor: H.B. Fuller Co
1200 Willow Lake Boulevard, P.O. Box 64683
Saint Paul, MN 55164-0683

H.J. Heinz Company Foundation Grants 2184

The Foundation is committed to promoting the health and nutritional needs of children and families. Priority is given to programs in communities where Heinz operates with a special focus given to southwestern Pennsylvania. The Foundation proactively donates funds to develop and strengthen organizations that are dedicated to nutrition and nutritional education, youth services and education, diversity, healthy children and families, and quality of life. Application information is available online.

Requirements: Only organizations that have 501(c)3 tax status under the U.S. Internal Revenue Code are eligible for support domestically. International organizations are encouraged to submit a letter of inquiry prior to preparing a full proposal to determine eligibility. International organizations will need to provide a 501(c)3 determination letter from the United States Internal Revenue Service or sufficient documentation to demonstrate that the non-U.S. grantee is the equivalent of a U.S. public charity. Documentation should

be provided in English. The Foundation will also accept proposals in the Common Grant Application Format. All proposals must be submitted in writing. Electronic submissions are not accepted at this time.
Restrictions: The Foundation will not provide grants to individuals nor make multi-year pledges except for major capital or grant campaigns. Generally, the Foundation does not make loans and does not provide grants for individuals, equipment, conferences, travel, general scholarships, religious programs, political campaigns, and unsolicited research projects.
Geographic Focus: All States
Contact: Tammy B. Aupperle; (412) 456-5773; heinz.foundation@hjheinz.com
Internet: http://www.heinz.com/sustainability.aspx/social/heinz-foundation.aspx
Sponsor: H.J. Heinz Company Foundation
P.O. Box 57
Pittsburgh, PA 15230-0057

H. Leslie Hoffman and Elaine S. Hoffman Foundation Grants 2185
The foundation awards general operating grants to California non-profits, primarily focusing on education. Additional funding is also available in the following areas of interest: arts; social services; hospitals; health organizations; children/youth services, including children's hospitals and, social services. There are no application forms or deadlines.
Requirements: California IRS 501(c)3 non-profits are eligible to apply. The majority of grants are funded in the Los Angeles area with a special emphasis on Pasadena.
Restrictions: Individuals are ineligible.
Geographic Focus: California
Amount of Grant: 1,000 - 200,000 USD
Contact: J. Kristoffer Popovich, Treasurer; (626) 793-0043
Sponsor: H. Leslie Hoffman and Elaine S. Hoffman Foundation
225 S Lake Avenue, Suite 1150
Pasadena, CA 91101-3005

H. Reimers Bechtel Charitable Remainder Uni-Trust Grants 2186
Established in Iowa in 1987, the H. Reimers Bechtel Charitable Remainder Uni-Trust offers support in both Iowa and Illinois. Its current fields of interest include: arts; botanical gardens; Christian agencies and churches; community and economic development; family services; higher education; and media (particularly television). There are no specific deadlines, and applicants should contact the office to secure application materials.
Requirements: 501(c)3 organizations serving the residents of Davenport, Iowa, Rock Island, Illinois, and Moline, Illinois, are eligible to apply.
Restrictions: No grants are given to individuals, or for endowment funds, debt retirement, past operating deficit, general or continuing support, or for scholarly research in an established discipline.
Geographic Focus: Illinois, Iowa
Amount of Grant: 25,000 USD
Contact: R. Richard Bittner; (563) 328-3333; fax (563) 328-3352; loseband@blwlaw.com
Sponsor: H. Reimers Bechtel Charitable Remainder Uni-Trust
201 West 2nd Street, Suite 1000
Davenport, IA 52801-1817

H. Schaffer Foundation Grants 2187
The foundation awards grants to nonprofit organizations in New York in the fields of higher education, hospitals and health care, human services, international relief, theater, aging centers and services, federated giving programs, and Jewish agencies and temples. Eligible activites include recreation, children and youth, services, and general charitable giving. There are no application forms or deadlines.
Requirements: Nonprofits in New York, with an emphasis on Schenectady, are eligible.
Geographic Focus: New York
Amount of Grant: 1,000 - 250,000 USD
Contact: Sonya Stall, President; (518) 580-0188
Sponsor: H. Schaffer Foundation
2 Claire Pass
Saratoga Springs, NY 12307

Hackett Foundation Grants 2188
The Foundation is limited by its giving to the funding of grants for supplies and equipment. Grants are primarily given, but not limited to, Catholic Missions. The primary focus of the Foundation is to provide assistance to those Catholic Organizations which promote the Health, Welfare, Education and Independence of individuals. Application information is available online.
Restrictions: Grants to individuals, scholarships, endowments and fellowships will not be considered. Grants will not be given to supporting organizations having a 509(a)(3) status. Grants will not be used as reimbursement for previously purchased items. Grants are not given for salaries, administrative expenses or matching funds. Grants will not be considered for demonstration projects and/or capital campaigns. Grants will not be provided for non-U.S. based organizations or for taxes or shipping and handling charges.
Geographic Focus: New Jersey, New York, Pennsylvania
Amount of Grant: 1,000 - 20,000 USD
Contact: Maggie Hackett, Grants Manager; (908) 238-9444
Internet: http://fdncenter.org/grantmaker/hackett
Sponsor: Hackett Foundation
P.O. Box 693
Pittstown, NJ 08867

Haddad Foundation Grants 2189
The Haddad Foundation, established in West Virginia in 2003, offers grant support primarily in Boone and Kanawha counties of West Virginia. Its identified fields of interest include: children and youth services; higher education; and human services. Funding comes in the form of general operations support. There are no specific application forms or deadlines with which to adhere, and initial approach should be with a letter of application. Amounts range up to $10,000.
Requirements: Applicants must be a 501(c)3 organization that serves the residents of either Boone or Kanawha counties, West Virginia.
Geographic Focus: West Virginia
Amount of Grant: Up to 10,000 USD
Samples: Smile Train, New York, New York, $10,000 - general operating support; University of South Florida, Tampa, Florida, $6,400 - general operating support.
Contact: Susan L. Haddad, Director; (304) 925-5418
Sponsor: Haddad Foundation
707 Virginia Street East, Suite 900
Charleston, WV 25301-2716

HAF Arts and Culture: Lynne and Bob Wells Grant for Performing Artists 2190
The Lynne and Bob Wells Fund for the Performing Arts provides encouragement and support to adult actors, singers, dancers, comedians, and other performing artists in Humboldt County. The application and additional attachments needed are available at the website.
Requirements: Applicants must be performing artists from Humboldt County. The selection committee is looking for originality, honesty, talent, passion, and inspiration.
Restrictions: Grants are not made for religious activities or projects that exclusively benefit the members of sectarian or religious organizations. Grants cannot pay for expenses that incurred before the grant award start date.
Geographic Focus: California
Date(s) Application is Due: Nov 1
Amount of Grant: 500 USD
Contact: Cassandra Wagner, Grants Program Coordinator; (707) 442-2993, ext. 323; fax (707) 442-3811; cassandraw@hafoundation.org
Internet: http://www.hafoundation.org/haf/grants/haf-grants.html
Sponsor: Humboldt Area Foundation
373 Indianola Road
Bayside, CA 95524

HAF Arts and Culture: Project Grants to Artists 2191
Project Grants to Artists support all artists and crafts people from the performing, visual, textile, literary, and media arts in the counties of Humboldt, Del Norte, and Trinity. Priorities will be given to projects of outstanding artistic merit which actively engage their communities in the process and/or product of the creation of art. Awards are given for up to $5,000. The application and additional information are available at the website.
Requirements: Applicants must be from the county of Humboldt, Del Norte, or Trinity. Artists and crafts people and organizations from the performing, visual, textile, literary, or media arts are eligible.
Restrictions: Grants will not be made for religious activities or projects that exclusively benefit the members of sectarian or religious organizations. Grants cannot pay for expenses that have already been incurred. Schools, government agencies, or Indian tribal governments can only apply if funding is used to support individual artists and not overhead expenses.
Geographic Focus: California
Date(s) Application is Due: Nov 1
Amount of Grant: Up to 5,000 USD
Contact: Cassandra Wagner; (707) 442-2993, ext. 323; cassandraw@hafoundation.org
Internet: http://www.hafoundation.org/haf/grants/haf-grants.html
Sponsor: Humboldt Area Foundation
373 Indianola Road
Bayside, CA 95524

HAF Co-op Community Fund Grants 2192
The Co-op Community Fund (CCF) is a collection of sources where the fund's appreciation/ earnings are gifted to local non-profit organizations annually through a granting process. Co-op employees, members, and shoppers have given donations directly to CCF over the years to build the endowment, which enables the fund to underwrite local projects. The funds are distributed as grant awards for special community projects each year. As part of the Co-op's commitment to the North Coast community, income from this fund is used to support sustainable agriculture, food security (defined as the access to a safe supply of quality food to all aspects of a community), or food nutrition and education. Preference is given to small to mid-sized organizations operating in Humboldt County. Grants range from $500 to $2,000 with exceptions possible on a case-by-case basis. The application and a list of previously funded projects are available at the website.
Requirements: The Co-op Fund makes grants to nonprofit tax-exempt organizations and/or public schools on an annual basis. The current focus for CCF grants are projects that address at least one of the three following areas: sustainable agriculture; food security (defined as the access to a safe supply of quality food to all aspects of a community); and food nutrition and education.
Geographic Focus: California
Date(s) Application is Due: Oct 1
Amount of Grant: 500 - 2,000 USD
Contact: Melanie Bettenhausen, (707) 826-8670, ext. 132; melanieb@northcoastco-op.com
Internet: http://www.hafoundation.org/haf/grants/affiliated-grants.html
Sponsor: Humboldt Area Foundation
373 Indianola Road
Bayside, CA 95524

HAF Community Grants 2193

The Humboldt Area Foundation's Community Grants support a broad spectrum of projects that help build strong communities and foster prosperity in the Redwood, Trinity, and Wild Rivers regions. The Community Grant Program accepts submissions from non-profit charitable or public benefit (federal tax-exempt) organizations, public schools, government agencies, and Native American tribal governments. Applicants whose proposals meet the following criteria will be given funding priority: addresses a pressing community issue; supports a project or issue that is clearly important to the community; involves those who are directly impacted by the effort; and makes use of collaborative relationships and partnerships. If the proposal meets one or more of the following criteria, it is considered even stronger: it includes and supports the interests of historically excluded people and groups; makes a lasting impact; develops a plan for sustainability; integrates and promotes youth leadership skills; and develops the leadership skills and abilities of residents to address issues of importance to them. Applications are accepted on a quarterly basis, and must arrive by the given deadline to be considered for the current grant round. Applicants are notified of their status within ten weeks. The application and a list of previously funded projects are available at the website.
Requirements: Applicants must be nonprofit charitable or public benefit organizations, public schools, government agencies, Indian tribal governments or have a qualified fiscal sponsor. Applicants must be located within Humboldt, Del Norte or Trinity counties.
Restrictions: Funding is not available for expenses outside the service area such as travel expenses or schools or groups for trips out of the area, cultural groups going on tour, good will ambassadors, or scholarships and fellowships to other countries. Grants cannot be made for the deferred maintenance or annual operating costs of public institutions, churches, services of special tax districts, government or cemeteries. Grants cannot be made for religious activities or projects that exclusively benefit the members of sectarian or religious organizations. Grants cannot pay for expenses that have already been incurred.
Geographic Focus: California
Date(s) Application is Due: Jan 14; Apr 1; Jul 1; Oct 1
Amount of Grant: 250 - 120,000 USD
Contact: Chris Witt; (707) 442-2993, ext. 302; fax (707) 442-3811; admin@hafoundation.org
Internet: http://www.hafoundation.org/haf/grants/haf-grants.html
Sponsor: Humboldt Area Foundation
373 Indianola Road
Bayside, CA 95524

HAF Community Partnerships with Native Artists (CPNA) Grants 2194

The Community Partnerships with Native Artists (CPNA) Grants, funded in partnership with the Ford Foundation, support community partnerships with native artists that produce art of outstanding quality and cultural significance while engaging communities in a process of healing. The Native Cultures Fund defines healing as the renewal of traditional relationships with a tribe, across tribes, across cultures and with the land. It is not therapy nor designed to achieve the health goal of the individual but rather builds community relationships in a social ceremony addressing areas of community healing in a meaningful way. Some examples of art that is supported includes: theater productions; contemporary visual arts; multi-media productions; storytelling workshops; radio or video productions; and sacred sites. Applicants may contact the Foundation for additional information.
Requirements: Eligible areas include urban and rural communities of California from the Tolowa peoples near the Oregon border, inland to the western Nevada border, and south to the Chumash peoples of the Santa Barbara area.
Geographic Focus: California
Contact: Chag Lowry, Program Manager of Native Cultures Fund; (707) 442-2993, ext. 321; fax (707) 442-9072; chagl@hafoundation.org
Internet: http://www.hafoundation.org/haf/grants/haf-grants.html
Sponsor: Humboldt Area Foundation
373 Indianola Road
Bayside, CA 95524

HAF Companion Animal Welfare and Rescue Grants 2195

Humboldt Area Foundation's Field of Interest Grant Program was created to connect donors with community projects in their specific areas of interest. The program brings together a collection of funds that focus on specific populations, geographical areas and/or causes. Field of Interest grants are available September 1 through November 1. The Companion Animal Welfare and Rescue Grants offers several funding sources for those wishing to support animal welfare issues, including spaying and neutering, care and feeding of dogs and cats, and the care and training of dog guides. Applicants should apply specifically for the fund that best meets the needs of their project, and may apply individually to each fund. The application and a list of previously funded projects are available at the website.
Requirements: Applicants to all funds must be nonprofit charitable or public benefit (federal tax exempt) organizations, public schools, government agencies, Indian tribal governments, or have a qualified fiscal sponsor.
Restrictions: Funding is not available for deferred maintenance or annual operating costs of public institutions, churches, and services of special tax districts, government, or cemeteries. Grants will not be made for religious activities or projects that exclusively benefit the members of sectarian or religious organizations. Expenses that have already been incurred are not eligible.
Geographic Focus: California
Date(s) Application is Due: Nov 1
Amount of Grant: 2,000 - 12,000 USD
Contact: Cassandra Wagner; (707) 442-2993, ext. 323; cassandraw@hafoundation.org
Internet: http://www.hafoundation.org/haf/grants/haf-grants.html
Sponsor: Humboldt Area Foundation
373 Indianola Road
Bayside, CA 95524

HAF Education Grants 2196

The Humboldt Area Foundation has several field of interest and donor advised funds that make grants within several interest areas. The Program brings together a collection of funds that focus on specific populations, geographic areas, and/or causes. Grant sizes and priorities vary for each fund. The Education Grants offer several funds that support Arcata public schools, educational career planning and placement services, environmental education for children, education and local maritime affairs, and local history education. Applicants will apply to the fund that is most appropriate for their project. The application and sample budget sheets are available at the website.
Requirements: Applications to all funds must be nonprofit charitable or public benefits (federal tax exempt) organizations, public schools, government agencies, Indian tribal governments, or have a qualified fiscal sponsor.
Restrictions: Funding is not available for the following: deferred maintenance or annual operating costs of public institutions, churches, and services of special tax districts, government, or cemeteries; religious activities or projects that exclusively benefit the members of sectarian or religious organizations; or expenses that have already been incurred.
Geographic Focus: California
Date(s) Application is Due: Nov 1
Amount of Grant: 400 - 1,500 USD
Contact: Chris Witt, Director of Donor Services and Planned Giving; (707) 442-2993, ext. 302; fax (707) 442-3811; admin@hafoundation.org
Internet: http://www.hafoundation.org/haf/grants/haf-grants.html
Sponsor: Humboldt Area Foundation
373 Indianola Road
Bayside, CA 95524

HAF Hansen Family Trust Christian Endowment Fund Grants 2197

To memorialize his family, Chris Hansen created this fund to benefit local Christian ministries of Humboldt County, with an emphasis on the Lutheran Church. Youth and senior activities are emphasized. The fund is also intended to help missionary activities abroad, including ELCA missions, World Hunger and World Vision. Grant requests for capital investment, administrative funds, and annual funds will be considered on a limited basis. Applications are due on January 15, April 15, July 15 and October 15, with notification within two months of the deadline. The application and additional information are available at the website.
Requirements: Along with the applicants, organizations should include a single page that describes their request with a purpose statement, needs to be met, total budget, other funding sources, partners, number of volunteers, and the population to be served.
Geographic Focus: California
Date(s) Application is Due: Jan 15; Apr 15; Jul 15; Oct 15
Contact: Cassandra Wagner, Grants Program Coordinator; (707) 422-2993, ext. 323; fax (707) 422-3811; cassandraw@hafoundation.org
Internet: http://www.hafoundation.org/haf/grants/affiliated-grants.html
Sponsor: Humboldt Area Foundation
373 Indianola Road
Bayside, CA 95524

HAF Justin Keele Make a Difference Award 2198

The Justin Keele Grant is for high school students who want to lend a helping hand. This assistance is meant to supply individuals with tools, equipment, supplies, tuition, fees, fines or other necessities to achieve their goal or reduce their hardship. The grant ranges from $200 to $2,000, with deadlines of April 1 and December 1. The application is available at the website.
Requirements: Applicants should be students from Eureka High School or Zoe Barnum High School. The applicant should have an individual, group, or cause in mind, along with a clear plan to assist a particular need. The applicant should explain why this individual, group, or cause deserves a helping hand and how the grant will help.
Geographic Focus: California
Date(s) Application is Due: Apr 1; Dec 1
Amount of Grant: 200 - 2,000 USD
Contact: Cassandra Wagner, Program Coordinator; (707) 442-2993, ext. 323; fax (707) 442-3811; cassandraw@hafoundation.org
Internet: http://www.hafoundation.org/index.php?option=content&task=view&id=61
Sponsor: Humboldt Area Foundation
373 Indianola Road
Bayside, CA 95524

HAF Kayla Wood Girls Memorial Fund Grants 2199

Soccer coaches and teachers may nominate female soccer players under the age of 14 for grants from the Kayla Wood Girls Soccer Memorial Fund. Awards are given to assist with annual soccer camps and/or league sign up fees for girls displaying a financial need. The application is available at the website.
Requirements: Applicants must be nominated by a league coach, school coach, or teacher. Candidates should be girls under the age of 14 who may not be able to play soccer because of a financial need. Letters should explain the nature of the financial hardship.
Geographic Focus: California
Date(s) Application is Due: Apr 15
Contact: Jill Moore, Program Coordinator, Community Strategies; (707) 442-2993, ext. 314; fax (707) 442-9072; jillm@hafoundation.org
Internet: http://www.hafoundation.org/haf/grants/haf-grants.html
Sponsor: Humboldt Area Foundation
373 Indianola Road
Bayside, CA 95524

HAF Mada Huggins Caldwell Fund Grants 2200
The Mada Huggins Caldwell Fund Grants were established to assist youth between the ages of 10 and 18 who have been affected by violent crime. The Fund is to be used to help youth attend Christian activities, including summer camps and other healing activities. The Fund was created by JoAnn Caldwell Sapper for her mother, Mada Huggins Caldwell. The application and additional information are available at the website.
Requirements: Applicants must be nonprofit charitable or public benefit (federal tax exempt) organizations, public schools, government agencies, Indian tribal governments in Humboldt County, or have a qualified fiscal sponsor.
Restrictions: Grants are not made for the deferred maintenance or annual operating costs of public institutions, churches, and services of special tax districts, government or cemeteries. Funding is not available for expenses that have already been incurred.
Geographic Focus: California
Date(s) Application is Due: Apr 13
Amount of Grant: 400 USD
Contact: Cassandra Wagner, Grants Program Coordinator; (707) 442-2993, ext. 323; fax (707) 442-3811; cassandraw@hafoundation.org
Internet: http://www.hafoundation.org/haf/grants/affiliated-grants.html
Sponsor: Humboldt Area Foundation
373 Indianola Road
Bayside, CA 95524

HAF Native Cultures Fund Grants 2201
Initiated and led by Native Peoples, the Native Culture Fund supports Native arts, cultural revitalization and cultural transmission between generations. The Fund has awarded nearly $1 million to California Native American artists and cultural stewards in support of over 190 community projects. Grants and regional gatherings focus on methods of building greater cultural participation in communities. The service area includes northern and central California. Eligible counties with specific areas are located on a map at the website. Applicants may contact the Foundation for additional information.
Requirements: Eligible areas include urban and rural communities of California from the Tolowa peoples near the Oregon border, inland to the western Nevada border, and south to the Chumash peoples of the Santa Barbara area.
Geographic Focus: California
Contact: Chag Lowry; (707) 442-2993, ext. 321; chagl@hafoundation.org
Internet: http://www.hafoundation.org/haf/grants/haf-grants.html
Sponsor: Humboldt Area Foundation
373 Indianola Road
Bayside, CA 95524

HAF Natural Environment Grants 2202
Humboldt Area Foundation's Field of Interest Grant Program was created to connect donors with community projects in their specific areas of interest. The program brings together a collection of funds that focus on specific populations, geographical areas and/or causes. Field of Interest grants are available September 1 through November 1. Natural Environment Grants offer several funding sources for those wishing to support environmental issues, including the following: wildlife conservation; nature exhibits; cleaning contaminated wetland areas; public access for marine or aquatic recreation; environmental education for youth; river basin restoration; and wildlife protection projects. Applicants should apply specifically for the fund that best meets their project's needs, and may apply individually to each fund. The application and a list of previously funded projects are available at the website.
Requirements: Applicants to all funds must be nonprofit charitable or public benefit (federal tax exempt) organizations, public schools, government agencies, Indian tribal governments, or have a qualified fiscal sponsor.
Restrictions: Funding is not available for deferred maintenance or annual operating costs of public institutions, churches, and services of special tax districts, government, or cemeteries. Grants will not be made for religious activities or projects that exclusively benefit the members of sectarian or religious organizations. Expenses that have already been incurred are not eligible.
Geographic Focus: California
Date(s) Application is Due: Nov 1
Amount of Grant: 750 - 10,000 USD
Contact: Cassandra Wagner; (707) 442-2993, ext. 323; cassandraw@hafoundation.org
Internet: http://www.hafoundation.org/haf/grants/haf-grants.html
Sponsor: Humboldt Area Foundation
373 Indianola Road
Bayside, CA 95524

HAF Senior Opportunities Grants 2203
Humboldt Area Foundation's Field of Interest Grant Program was created to connect donors with community projects in their specific areas of interest. The program brings together a collection of funds that focus on specific populations, geographical areas and/or causes. Field of Interest grants in the Senior Opportunity category are available September 1 through November 1 for up to $2,000. Senior Opportunities Grants offer several funding sources for those wishing to support projects such as seniors living in their own homes who need meal programs and transportation, or other programs that enhance their quality of life. Applicants should apply specifically to the fund that best meets their project's needs, and may apply individually to each fund. The application and a list of previously funded projects are available at the website.
Requirements: Applicants for any fund must be nonprofit charitable or public benefit (federal tax exempt) organizations, public schools, government agencies, Indian tribal governments, or have a qualified fiscal sponsor.
Restrictions: Funding is not available for deferred maintenance or annual operating costs of public institutions, churches, and services of special tax districts, government, or cemeteries. Grants will not be made for religious activities or projects that exclusively benefit the members of sectarian or religious organizations. Expenses that have already been incurred are not eligible.
Geographic Focus: California
Date(s) Application is Due: Nov 1
Amount of Grant: Up to 2,000 USD
Contact: Cassandra Wagner, Grants Program Coordinator; (707) 422-2993, ext. 323; fax (707) 422-3811; cassandraw@hafoundation.org
Internet: http://www.hafoundation.org/haf/grants/haf-grants.html
Sponsor: Humboldt Area Foundation
373 Indianola Road
Bayside, CA 95524

HAF Southern Humboldt Grants 2204
Humboldt Area Foundation's Field of Interest Grant Program was created to connect donors with community projects in their specific areas of interest. The program brings together a collection of funds that focus on specific populations, geographical areas and/or causes. Field of Interest grants are available September 1 through November 1, with notification by December 17. Southern Humboldt Grants may be used for charitable purposes in the Southern Humboldt area. This area is defined as the area that spans from the confluence of the South Fork and Main Fork of the Eel River, to the Mendocino county line at the south, to the Trinity county line on the east, and to the ocean, including Honeydew and Pretola to the west. Funding varies by the particular source. Applicants should apply specifically to the source that best meets their project needs, and may apply individually to each fund. The application and a list of previously funded projects are available at the website.
Requirements: Applicants to all funds must be nonprofit charitable or public benefit (federal tax exempt) organizations, public schools, government agencies, Indian tribal governments, or have a qualified fiscal sponsor.
Restrictions: Funding is not available for deferred maintenance or annual operating costs of public institutions, churches, or services of special tax districts, government, or cemeteries. Grant will not be made for religious activities or projects that exclusively benefit the members of sectarian or religious organizations. Expenses already incurred are not eligible.
Geographic Focus: California
Date(s) Application is Due: Nov 1
Amount of Grant: 1,000 - 15,000 USD
Contact: Cassandra Wagner, Grants Program Coordinator; (707) 442-2993, ext. 323; fax (707) 442-3811; cassandraw@hafoundation.org
Internet: http://www.hafoundation.org/haf/grants/haf-grants.html
Sponsor: Humboldt Area Foundation
373 Indianola Road
Bayside, CA 95524

HAF Summer Youth Funding Partnership Grants 2205
The Foundation provides Summer Youth Program funding in response to the need to provide positive opportunities for children and youth while school is not in session. Small grants are awarded to agencies to expand and enrich summer recreation programs operating between June and September. Grants are normally made for expenses such as sports and recreational equipment, arts and craft supplies, special events and field trips within HAF's service area and camperships for low-income participants. The average grant awarded is $500, although larger grants may be considered. The application deadline is April 15, with grants awarded by May 17. The application and additional guidelines are available at the website.
Requirements: Organizations that serve youth and children in Humboldt county are eligible.
Geographic Focus: California
Date(s) Application is Due: Apr 15
Amount of Grant: 500 USD
Contact: Jill Moore; (707) 442-2993, ext. 314; fax (707) 442-9072; Jillm@hafoundation.org
Internet: http://www.hafoundation.org/haf/grants/haf-grants.html#field
Sponsor: Humboldt Area Foundation
373 Indianola Road
Bayside, CA 95524

HAF Technical Assistance Program (TAP) Grants 2206
The Technical Assistance Program is a small award program which provides nonprofits with one-on-one technical assistance in a variety of forms, such as consultants, training workshops, self-pace manuals, software, or any other form identified by applicants. Awards typically range from $500 to $2,000. Funds must be used to improve the organization, its leadership or operations. Areas of assistance may include the following: strategic planning; board development; community organizing training; increasing organizational diversity; financial management, operational assessments, board development; program assessments; personnel issues; collaboration building; executive coaching; succession planning; exit strategy planning; fundraising planning; and involving those who serve in program planning, development and evaluation. Applications and information are confidential, and will not affect other potential Humboldt Area Foundation grant funding. Grant applications are accepted on the first of each month, with grants paid directly to a consultant to cover the costs of their consulting services. Additional information is available at the website.
Requirements: Funding is available to organizations and community groups in Humboldt, Del Norte, and Trinity counties.
Restrictions: TAP will not pay for grant writing, programmatic development or for duties that are typically handled by staff (e.g. data entry). Organizations less than a year old and government entities are not eligible to apply.
Geographic Focus: California

Date(s) Application is Due: Jan 1; Feb 1; Mar 1; Apr 1; May 1; Jun 1; Jul 1; Aug 1; Sep 1; Oct 1; Nov 1; Dec 1
Amount of Grant: 500 - 2,000 USD
Contact: Amy Jester, Program Manager, Health and Nonprofit Resources; (707) 442-2993, ext. 374; fax (707) 442-9072; amyj@hafoundation.org
Internet: http://www.hafoundation.org/index.php?option=content&task=view&id=74
Sponsor: Humboldt Area Foundation
373 Indianola Road
Bayside, CA 95524

Hagedorn Fund Grants 2207
William Hagedorn directed that the remainder of his estate be dedicated to this fund, in memory of his late wife, Tillie Hagedorn, that would support religious or charitable organizations in the New York City region. Funding interests include: health (including cancer, HIV/AIDS, blindness), gardens, social services, youth, education, senior services and housing and community development. All applications to the Hagedorn Fund must be submitted online, additional information is available at the Hagedorn Fund website.
Requirements: New York nonprofit organizations are eligible to apply.
Restrictions: No grants are made to individuals or private foundations or for matching gifts or loans.
Geographic Focus: New York
Date(s) Application is Due: Sep 1
Amount of Grant: 5,000 - 45,000 USD
Contact: Erin K. Hogan; (212) 464-2476; fax (212) 464-2305; erin.k.hogan@jpmorgan.com
Internet: http://fdncenter.org/grantmaker/hagedorn
Sponsor: Hagedorn Fund
270 Park Avenue, 16th Floor
New York, NY 10017

Hahl Proctor Charitable Trust Grants 2208
Before moving to Midland, Hahl Proctor studied voice in a Chicago school of music. Although very active in the ranching industry, she continued to pursue her music interests through her church and other civic organizations. In addition to her vocation and avocation, Hahl was an attractive, popular, and generous woman who loved to entertain. She established a trust in her will to provide a continuous source of financial assistance to worthwhile charities. The trust focuses on charitable organizations dedicated to children and families, the arts, and education. Applicants must apply online at the grant website. Applicants are strongly encouraged to do the following before applying: review the downloadable state application procedures for additional helpful information and clarifications; review the downloadable online-application guidelines at the grant website; review the trust's funding history (link is available from the grant website); review the online application questions in advance; and review the list of required attachments. These will generally include: a list of board members, financial statements (audited, reviewed, or compiled by independent auditor); an organization summary; a list of other funding sources; an IRS Determination letter; and other required documents. All attachments must be uploaded in the online application as PDF, Word, or Excel files. The application deadline is 11:59 p.m. on May 15.
Requirements: Applicants must have 501(c)3 tax-exempt status and serve residents of the Permian Basin Area.
Restrictions: The trust does not support requests from individuals, organizations attempting to influence policy through direct lobbying, or any political campaigns.
Geographic Focus: Texas
Date(s) Application is Due: May 15
Amount of Grant: 2,000 - 20,000 USD
Contact: Mark J. Smith; (817) 390-6028; tx.philanthropic@baml.com
Internet: https://www.bankofamerica.com/philanthropic/fn_search.action
Sponsor: Hahl Proctor Charitable Trust
500 West 7th Street, 15th Floor, TX1-497-15-08
Fort Worth, TX 76102-4700

Hall-Perrine Foundation Grants 2209
The Hall-Perrine Foundation Grants funds charitable projects for nonprofit tax-exempt organizations that benefit the Linn County, Iowa community. The Foundation screens grant applications, and those meeting the established criteria are presented to the Board of Directors. The Board reviews proposals approximately four times a year. After a decision has been reached, the organization is notified in writing of whether they have been approved for funding.
Requirements: Potential grantees should first make a preliminary inquiry to determine the Foundation's interest in their request. This communication should briefly describe the background and purposes of the organization and outline the proposed project and its goals. If the Foundation is interested, a grant application will be given to the applicant to be completed in order that the proposal may be properly evaluated. Information requested includes: a description of the organization, including its legal name, history, purposes, and activities; a list of members of the governing board; a clear and detailed description of the purpose for which the grant is requested and the goals to be achieved; the total cost of the project and amount requested with a detailed budget; a list of current and potential sources of financial support; a copy of the organization's most recent audited financial statement or the last IRS Form 990 (income tax return of organization exempt from income tax); and a copy of the IRS determination letter indicating 501(x)3 tax-exempt status.
Geographic Focus: Iowa
Contact: Kristin Novak; (319) 362-9079; fax (319) 362-7220; kristin@hallperrine.org
Internet: http://www.hallperrine.org/
Sponsor: Hall-Perrine Foundation
115 Third Street SE, Suite 803
Cedar Rapids, IA 52401-1222

Hall Family Foundation Grants 2210
The Foundation concentrates its philanthropic efforts on five areas of interest: education; children, youth and families; the arts; community development; and support of community-wide efforts that seek to provide long-term solutions to local issues of high priority. Ideas of unique merit, even though outside the boundaries of the Foundation's interests, can be considered. In considering support, preference is given to programs which: create long term solutions; are responsive to and have a positive impact on the community; promote excellence; have the capacity, through leadership, management and financial resources, to achieve the desired results; are innovative and catalytic; have the likelihood of future support for-on-going operating costs; are non-competing with government programs; and are cooperative with other community resources/agencies.
Requirements: Grants are made to charitable organizations in the Greater Kansas City area which qualify as tax exempt under Section 501(c)3 of the Interval Revenue Code.
Restrictions: The Foundation seldom makes grants to or for the following: organizations outside of the greater Kansas City area; political parties, candidates or political activities; individuals; international organizations; religious organizations where the primary purpose is promotion of specific religious doctrine; endowments; scholarly or medical research; event promotion; past operating deficits, travel or conference expenses.
Geographic Focus: Missouri
Contact: Donald J. Hall, Chairman of the Board; (816) 274-8516; fax (816) 274-8547
Internet: http://www.hallfamilyfoundation.org/grantGuidlines/apProcess.html
Sponsor: Hall Family Foundation
P.O. Box 419850, Department 323
Kansas City, MO 64141-6580

Halliburton Foundation Grants 2211
The foundation supports education at all levels and charitable organizations in the following ways: matching US- based employee donations on a two-for-one basis up to $20,000 annually per employee for accredited junior colleges, colleges, and universities; matching US-based employee donations to accredited elementary and secondary schools on a two-for-one basis up to $500 annually per employee; making direct donations to US-based elementary and secondary schools and colleges and universities; and recognizing and supporting active US-based employee volunteerism with direct donations through the Halliburton Volunteer Incentive Program. The corporate giving program makes donations to tax-exempt nonprofit organizations dedicated to education, health/welfare, civic issues, and arts and culture. The board meets quarterly. There are no application deadlines or forms.
Geographic Focus: Arizona, Texas
Amount of Grant: 250 - 20,000 USD
Contact: Margaret Carriere, (713) 676-3717; fhoufoundation@halliburton.com
Internet: http://www.halliburton.com/about/community.jsp
Sponsor: Halliburton Foundation
4100 Clinton Drive, Building 1, 7th Floor
Houston, TX 77020

Hallmark Corporate Foundation Grants 2212
The mission of the Foundation is to help create communities where: all children have the chance to grow up as healthy, productive and caring persons; vibrant arts and cultural experiences enrich the lives of all citizens; there is a strong infrastructure of basic institutions and services, especially for persons in need; and all citizens feel a responsibility to serve their community. Proposals are accepted and reviewed throughout the year. There are no deadlines. The application process can be completed online using the Hallmark General Grant Application, which is available on the Hallmark website.
Requirements: IRS Non-profit 501(c)3 organizations are eligible to apply in the following areas: Kansas City metropolitan area; Center, Texas; Columbus, Georgia; Enfield, Connecticut; Lawrence, Kansas; Leavenworth, Kansas; Liberty, Missouri; Metamora, Illinois and; Topeka, Kansas.
Restrictions: Funding is not available for: individuals for any purpose, including travel, starting a business or paying back loans; religious organizations unless they can demonstrate that services are provided to the community-at-large and separated from religious purposes; fraternal, international and veterans organizations; sports teams and athletic organizations; individual youth clubs, troops, groups or school classrooms; social clubs; disease-specific organizations whose local chapters primarily raise funds for national research; past operating deficits; endowment or foundation funds; conferences; scholarly or health-related research; scholarship funds.
Geographic Focus: Connecticut, Georgia, Illinois, Kansas, Missouri, Texas
Contact: Development Manager; (816) 545-6906; contributions@hallmark.com.
Internet: http://corporate.hallmark.com/Community/Community-Involvement-Program-Guidelines
Sponsor: Hallmark Corporate Foundation
Mail Drop 323, P.O. Box 419580
Kansas City, MO 64141-6580

Hamilton Family Foundation Grants 2213
The Foundation provides financial support primarily in the area of education, grades K-12 with a particular emphasis on literacy projects in underserved Philadelphia area schools. The Foundation considers applications for high school enrichment projects, as well as academically based after-school, arts and culture, and summer programs. Colleges and universities are not generally considered. The grant application is available online.
Requirements: Nonprofit organizations in Pennsylvania's Chester, Camden, Montgomery, and Delaware Counties are eligible.
Restrictions: Grant requests for individuals, bricks and mortar projects, endowments, and other foundations are not processed.
Geographic Focus: Pennsylvania
Date(s) Application is Due: Feb 1; May 1; Aug 1; Nov 1

Amount of Grant: 3,000 - 15,000 USD
Contact: Nancy Wingo, (610) 975-0517; nwingo@HamiltonFamilyFoundation.org
Internet: http://www.hamiltonfamilyfoundation.org/guidelines.html
Sponsor: Hamilton Family Foundation
200 Eagle Road, Suite 316
Wayne, PA 19087

Hampton Roads Community Foundation Beach Fund Grants 2214
The Foundation's mission is to inspire philanthropy and transform the quality of life in southeastern Virginia. The Beach Fund is a motivated group of young professionals who care about Hampton Roads. Members join together to learn about community needs, to pool their resources to fund grants, and to network. In 2011 the Fund awarded $15,000 in grants to nonprofits working with children in Lake Edward, an economically disadvantaged neighborhood of Virginia Beach. Grant applications are accepted annually (usually in the spring) from nonprofits working in the focus area selected by Beach Fund members. The focus of the grants varies each year. Applications usually are available by spring. Check the website for announcements including the grant focus, guidelines, and application details.
Requirements: Nonprofit organizations serving residents of south Hampton Roads (Chesapeake, Franklin, Norfolk, Portsmouth, Suffolk, Virginia Beach and Isle of Wight County) and the Eastern Shore of Virginia are eligible.
Geographic Focus: Virginia
Contact: Program Officer; (757) 622-7951; grants@hamptonroadscf.org
Internet: http://www.hamptonroadscf.org/donors/beachfund.html
Sponsor: Hampton Roads Community Foundation
One Commercial Plaza, Suite 1410
Norfolk, VA 23510

Hampton Roads Community Foundation Leadership Partners Grants 2215
The Foundation's mission is to inspire philanthropy and transform the quality of life in southeastern Virginia. Community Leadership Partners are a group of regional community leaders who pools their resources and set grant priorities each year. In 2011 the focus was nonprofits working with children, and $200,000 was awarded to 25 organizations working with school-aged children while they are not in school. The focus of the grants varies each year. Applications usually are available by spring. Check the website for announcements including the grant focus, guidelines, and application details.
Requirements: Nonprofit organizations serving residents of south Hampton Roads (Chesapeake, Franklin, Norfolk, Portsmouth, Suffolk, Virginia Beach and Isle of Wight County) and the Eastern Shore of Virginia are eligible.
Geographic Focus: Virginia
Contact: Program Officer; (757) 622-7951; grants@hamptonroadscf.org
Internet: http://www.hamptonroadscf.org/donors/communityleadershippartners.html
Sponsor: Hampton Roads Community Foundation
One Commercial Plaza, Suite 1410
Norfolk, VA 23510

Hampton Roads Community Foundation Health and Human Service Grants 2216
The Foundation's mission is to inspire philanthropy and transform the quality of life in southeastern Virginia. The Foundation believes the region will thrive only when its most vulnerable residents have the opportunities and support needed to succeed. Health and Human Services Grants focus on providing opportunities for disadvantaged people to become self-sufficient and support innovative programs that: prevent and alleviate homelessness; improve delivery of basic human services to those in need; improve access to medical care, including dental care and mental health; develop job skills and employment opportunities; and develop sound financial education and savings programs to help low income people build financial assets for long-term economic well-being. Applications are available on the website. Applicants from the Eastern Shore of Virginia should speak with a Program Officer before submitting a proposal.
Requirements: Nonprofit organizations serving residents of south Hampton Roads (Chesapeake, Franklin, Norfolk, Portsmouth, Suffolk, Virginia Beach and Isle of Wight County) and the Eastern Shore of Virginia are eligible. Proposals must articulate the program's desired outcomes and the measurement of effectiveness in reaching those outcomes.
Restrictions: Funding is generally not available for: individuals; fundraising events (such as tickets, raffles, auctions or tournaments), annual fundraising appeals or agency celebrations; ongoing operating support; capital projects and facilities and equipment upgrades that can be considered routine maintenance or replacements; houses of worship unless applying for the Nightingale Fund for faith community nursing or the E.K. Sloane Piano Fund; religious activities (organizations and activities that require religious participation by those receiving services); political or fraternal organizations; endowment building; existing obligations, debts/liabilities or costs that the agency has already incurred; scholarly research; scholarships, camper fees, fellowships or travel; passenger vans for transporting youth; national or international organizations or purposes; hospitals and similar health-care facilities unless applying for a Special Interest Grant; projects or services normally considered the responsibility of government; private primary or secondary schools, daycare facilities or academies other than those whose primary purpose is for students with special needs; and capital campaign requests exceeding 5% of campaigns valued at $1 million or more.
Geographic Focus: Virginia
Date(s) Application is Due: Jul 15
Contact: Program Officer; (757) 622-7951; grants@hamptonroadscf.org
Internet: http://www.hamptonroadscf.org/nonprofits/communityGrants-Health.html
Sponsor: Hampton Roads Community Foundation
One Commercial Plaza, Suite 1410
Norfolk, VA 23510

Hampton Roads Community Foundation Horticulture Education Grants 2217
The Foundation's mission is to inspire philanthropy and transform the quality of life in southeastern Virginia. The Julian Haden Gary and Margaret Savage Gary Fund provides Horticulture Education Grants to organizations that promote horticulture education with a preference for the work of the Fred Heutte Center, Norfolk Botanical Garden and the Virginia Zoo. Applications are available on the website. Applicants from the Eastern Shore of Virginia should speak with a Program Officer before submitting a proposal.
Requirements: Nonprofit organizations serving residents of south Hampton Roads (Chesapeake, Franklin, Norfolk, Portsmouth, Suffolk, Virginia Beach and Isle of Wight County) and the Eastern Shore of Virginia are eligible.
Geographic Focus: Virginia
Date(s) Application is Due: Oct 15
Contact: Program Officer; (757) 622-7951; grants@hamptonroadscf.org
Internet: http://www.hamptonroadscf/nonprofits/specialInterestGrants.html
Sponsor: Hampton Roads Community Foundation
One Commercial Plaza, Suite 1410
Norfolk, VA 23510

Hampton Roads Community Foundation Nonprofit Facilities Improvement Grants 2218
The Foundation's mission is to inspire philanthropy and transform the quality of life in southeastern Virginia. Nonprofit Facilities Improvement Grants focus on supporting major capital projects and capital campaigns that are transformative for the organization and the communities served. The Foundation seeks projects that will reduce building operating costs over the long term and minimize the negative environmental impacts associated with construction and operation. "Green" building practices that can reduce heating and cooling costs, save water, and reduce pollution are encouraged. Strong preference is given to proposals that incorporate these building practices. Applications are available on the website. Applicants from the Eastern Shore of Virginia should speak with a Program Officer before submitting a proposal.
Requirements: Nonprofit organizations serving residents of south Hampton Roads (Chesapeake, Franklin, Norfolk, Portsmouth, Suffolk, Virginia Beach and Isle of Wight County) and the Eastern Shore of Virginia are eligible. Applicant organizations should support one of the areas of Foundation work: arts and culture; education; environment; and health and human services.
Restrictions: Funding is generally not available for: individuals; fundraising events (such as tickets, raffles, auctions or tournaments), annual fundraising appeals or agency celebrations; ongoing operating support; capital projects and facilities and equipment upgrades that can be considered routine maintenance or replacements; houses of worship unless applying for the Nightingale Fund for faith community nursing or the E.K. Sloane Piano Fund; religious activities (organizations and activities that require religious participation by those receiving services); political or fraternal organizations; endowment building; existing obligations, debts/liabilities or costs that the agency has already incurred; scholarly research; scholarships, camper fees, fellowships or travel; passenger vans for transporting youth; national or international organizations or purposes; hospitals and similar health-care facilities unless applying for a Special Interest Grant; projects or services normally considered the responsibility of government; private primary or secondary schools, daycare facilities or academies other than those whose primary purpose is for students with special needs; and capital campaign requests exceeding 5% of campaigns valued at $1 million or more.
Geographic Focus: Virginia
Date(s) Application is Due: Jan 15
Contact: Program Officer; (757) 622-7951; grants@hamptonroadscf.org
Internet: http://www.hamptonroadscf.org/nonprofits/communityGrants-NonprofitFac.html
Sponsor: Hampton Roads Community Foundation
One Commercial Plaza, Suite 1410
Norfolk, VA 23510

Hancock County Community Foundation - Field of Interest Grants 2219
Field of Interest Grants are offered to organizations in Hancock County that present programs in one of the following areas: addictions and/or substance abuse education and treatment; arts and culture; Hanson Family Endowment Fund; Kingery Friends of Domestic Animals; Lifelong Learning; and Prevent Child Abuse. Successful applications will: document the program's relevance to the organization's mission, as well as the need in Hancock County for the program; show that the organization has a past record of being financially stable, viable, and able to sustain past the grant's time frame; operate effective programs that benefit Hancock County and its residents; show strong management by organization's Board of Directors and executive staff. Detailed guidelines and the application are available at the website.
Requirements: Organizations must be a certified nonprofit with a physical location in Hancock County in order to apply for any grants. Organizations may apply for funding up to the amount available, but must be in good standing with HCCF.
Restrictions: Organizations are only eligible to receive one Field of Interest Grant. Religious organizations may apply, but only for general community programs. No grants will be made specifically for religious purposes.
Geographic Focus: Indiana
Date(s) Application is Due: Aug 3
Amount of Grant: Up to 25,000 USD
Contact: Alyse Vail; (317) 462-8870, ext. 226; fax (317) 467-3330; avail@hccf.cc
Internet: http://www.hccf.cc/GrantTypes.aspx
Sponsor: Hancock County Community Foundation
312 Main Street
Greenfield, IN 46140

Hancock County Community Foundation - Programming Mini-Grants — 2220
Programming Mini-Grants allow nonprofit organizations to apply for up to $1,000 to be used for a particular program or project. The application process is simplified for these grants, not requiring a letter of intent or site visit, so that applications can be reviewed and funds made available more quickly. These grant requests will be reviewed and awarded monthly as long as funding is still available. Organizations need not be 501(c) organizations, but the program seeking funding must be charitable in nature. Detailed guidelines and the application are available at the website.
Geographic Focus: Indiana
Amount of Grant: Up to 1,000 USD
Contact: Alyse Vail; (317) 462-8870, ext. 226; fax (317) 467-3330; avail@hccf.cc
Internet: http://www.hccf.cc/GrantTypes.aspx
Sponsor: Hancock County Community Foundation
312 Main Street
Greenfield, IN 46140

Handsel Foundation Grants — 2221
The Handsel Foundation provides grants to organizations working to end companion animal cruelty, neglect, and overpopulation. It is most interested in supporting organizations with effective plans to reduce animal suffering through targeted spay/neuter programs to address companion animal overpopulation. These projects will be given special consideration, particularly for larger grants. The foundation occasionally provides grants for adoption and/or education programs relating to companion animals. However, these grants are rare and typically small relative to our spay/neuter grants.
Requirements: Prospective grant recipients must meet the following criteria: only 501(c)3 nonprofit organizations will be considered, as defined by the IRS; organization must have been in operation for at least one year; total expenses of less than $1 million for latest fiscal year; and must be seeking funds for programs in Oregon, Washington, or California.
Geographic Focus: All States
Date(s) Application is Due: Mar 31; Jun 30; Sep 30; Dec 31
Amount of Grant: 3,000 - 25,000 USD
Contact: Grants Coordinator; (206) 905-9887; inquiries@handselfdn.org
Internet: http://www.handselfdn.org/howtoapply.htm
Sponsor: Handsel Foundation
P.O. Box 6476
Olympia, WA 98507-6476

Hannaford Charitable Foundation Grants — 2222
The Foundation awards grants to nonprofit organizations in its areas of interest, including health and welfare, educational institutions, civic and cultural organizations, and other local charitable organizations. Types of support include capital campaigns, scholarship funds, and exchange programs. There are no application forms or deadlines. Preference for funding is given to organizations or programs that involve Hannaford associates, are located in Hannaford's marketing area, and have the potential to provide ongoing services for their customers. Small to medium requests are reviewed monthly. Allow three to four months for a response to larger requests ($50,00 or more), as these are reviewed quarterly. Large grants are usually reserved for capital drives by organizations with strong community-impact potential.
Requirements: To apply, the organization or program must: have an active and responsible board of trustees; exhibit ethical publicity methods and solicitation of funds; provide for an appropriate audit to reveal income and disbursements in reasonable detail; demonstrate long-term financial viability; be tax-exempt as described in both sections 501(c)3 and 509(a)1, 509(a)3, or 509(a)3 of the Internal Revenue Code. In addition to a letter of inquiry sent to the Foundation, organizations should also send ten copies of the following information: name, address and telephone number of your organization; contact person and title; amount requested; population and geographic area served; a two- or three-sentence mission statement of your organization, with a brief description of its history; a two- or three-page description of the specific project or program for which you are seeking funding; a list of current and potential funding sources; and a recent statement of revenues and expenses. They should also send one set of the following information: a copy of the organization's tax exemption letter, indicating both sections 501(c)3 and 509(1) status; most recent Form 990 return; and a letter attesting that the organization's tax-exempt status is current.
Restrictions: The Foundation does not offer support for the following: individuals; tax-supported institutions; institutions that, by virtue of their charters, programs or policies, are open to a relatively small or restricted segment of the public; operations of veterans, fraternal or religious organizations, except those that make their services fully available to the community on a nonsectarian basis; program advertising; operating expenses; scholarship programs outside of the Foundation's own; and organizations or events outside of the Foundation's marketing area.
Geographic Focus: Maine, Massachusetts, New Hampshire, New York, Vermont
Contact: Grants Administrator; (507) 931-1682
Internet: http://www.hannaford.com/content.jsp?pageName=charitableFoundation&leftNavArea=AboutLeftNav
Sponsor: Hannaford Charitable Foundation
P.O. Box 1000
Portland, ME 04104

Harbus Foundation Grants — 2223
The Foundation currently has three areas of support: Education - including after school programs, charter schools, continuing education/adult education and literacy, arts education, and multimedia education; Literacy - with a focus on general literacy and continuing education/adult education and literacy; and Journalism - with a focus on after school programs/youth programs in journalism and multimedia education. The Foundation is currently not accepting any unsolicited applications but interested applicants are encouraged to check the website for RFP's.
Requirements: Massachusetts 501(c)3 tax-exempt organizations serving the greater Boston area are eligible. Priority will be given to the communities of Allston and Brighton.
Restrictions: Grants do not support scholarships, fellowships, religious organizations for secular purposes, city or state governments, capital campaigns, for-profit organizations, or individual personal needs.
Geographic Focus: Massachusetts
Contact: Grants Administrator, c/o Harvard Business School; (617) 495-6528; fax (617) 495-8619; info@HarbusFoundation.org
Internet: http://www.harbusfoundation.org/grants.html
Sponsor: Harbus Foundation
Gallatin Hall E
Boston, MA 02163

Harley Davidson Foundation Grants — 2224
The mission of the Foundation is to support communities with funding and employee volunteerism. The Foundation reaches out to build healthy, thriving communities by placing an emphasis on education, community revitalization, arts and culture, health, and the environment. The Foundation targets areas of greatest need among under-served populations to enhance the quality of life in their communities. The Foundation also supports selected national causes, including veterans initiatives. In making granting decisions, the Foundation looks closely for the following detail: the proposal's relevance to the Foundation's areas of interest; the proposal's clarity in stating the expected project or program outcomes and the strategy for achieving them; the extent to which the strategy involves a collaborative approach to solving a problem or issue affecting the targeted groups or organizations. The program you are nominating should focus on one of the Foundation's funding priorities: education (core curriculum, academic enhancers), community revitalization, job enablers, neighborhood, social services, arts & culture, health, environment. The Common Application Form is located on the company website.
Requirements: 501(c)3 or 170(c) organizations serving metro Milwaukee, Wauwatosa, Franklin, Menomonee Falls or Tomahawk, Wisconsin; York, Pennsylvania; Talladega, Alabama; or Kansas City, Missouri, are eligible.
Restrictions: The Foundation does not make grants to individuals, political causes or candidates, operating or endowment funds; athletic teams, or religious organizations (unless engaged in a major project benefiting the greater community). The Foundation does not fund conferences or capital campaigns.
Geographic Focus: Alabama, Missouri, Pennsylvania, Wisconsin
Date(s) Application is Due: Jan 23; May 22; Oct 24
Contact: Mary Anne Martiny; (414) 343-4001; ma.martiny@harley-davidson.com
Internet: http://www.harley-davidson.com/CO/FOU/en/foundation.asp?locale=en_US&bmLocale=en_US
Sponsor: Harley Davidson Foundation
P.O. Box 653
Milwaukee, WI 53201

Harold Alfond Foundation Grants — 2225
The foundation awards grants to eligible organizations in its areas of interest, including secondary education, higher education, medical research, health care, and general charities. Grants support: education—public and private colleges and universities, as well as private secondary schools, to fund athletically oriented capital projects and scholarship endowments; medical research—individual research projects are considered when sponsored by a recognized medical research center; health—community support for capital campaigns and endowment funds; and general charities—community organizations that support youth, the arts, persons with disabilities, underprivileged, substance abuse rehabilitation, and annual fund drives of national organizations focusing on the above areas. There are no application deadlines or forms.
Restrictions: Grants are not made to individuals.
Geographic Focus: Florida, Maine
Contact: Gregory Powell, (207) 828-7999
Sponsor: Harold Alfond Foundation
Two Monument Square
Portland, ME 04101-4093

Harold and Arlene Schnitzer CARE Foundation Grants — 2226
The Foundation's principal purpose is to assist with Jewish, cultural, youth, education, medical, social service, and community activities. Foundation focus is on proposals for projects that enhance the quality of life in Oregon and Southwest Washington. The Foundation funds grant requests for operating expenses, special projects, matching grants, multiple-year grants and capital campaigns as well as for purchase of specific items. There is no formal application form. Interested applicants may contact the Foundation for guidelines.
Requirements: Nonprofit organizations in Oregon and Washington are eligible. Organizations located in Portland are given first funding priority. Approximately 90% of grant funds stay in the Portland metropolitan area.
Restrictions: The Foundation does not provide funds for individuals, non tax-exempt organizations, other private foundations or political groups.
Geographic Focus: Oregon, Washington
Date(s) Application is Due: Feb 28; May 31; Aug 31; Nov 30
Amount of Grant: 1,000 - 5,000,000 USD
Contact: Barbara Hall, Vice President; (503) 973-0286; fax (503) 450-0810
Sponsor: Harold and Arlene Schnitzer Foundation
P.O. Box 2708
Portland, OR 97208-2708

Harold Brooks Foundation Grants 2227
Harold Brooks, of Braintree, Massachusetts, was a successful business executive and entrepreneur who manufactured and sold prefabricated structures and underground bomb shelters during the Cold War. Mr. Brooks died in 1963 and the Foundation that bears his name was established in 1984. The Harold Brooks Foundation provides assistance to causes/organizations that help the largest possible number of residents of Massachusetts' South Shore communities, especially those that support the basic human needs of South Shore residents. The foundation supports nonprofit organizations that have the greatest impact on improving the human condition and/or that provide the neediest South Shore residents with "tools" that will help them restore their lives. The foundation focuses on five key areas: Education; Food, Agriculture, & Nutrition; Health; Housing & Shelter; and Mental Health. Multi-year (two-three years maximum) requests are welcome. Applicants must apply online at the grant website. Applicants are strongly encouraged to do the following before applying: review the downloadable Massachusetts state application procedures for additional helpful information and clarifications; review the downloadable online-application guidelines at the grant website; review the foundation's funding history (link is available from the grant website); review the online application questions in advance; and review the list of required attachments. These will generally include: a list of board members, financial statements (audited, reviewed, or compiled by independent auditor); an organization summary; a list of other funding sources; an IRS Determination letter; and other required documents. All attachments must be uploaded in the online application as PDF, Word, or Excel files. The Harold Brooks Foundation has biannual deadlines of April 1 and October 1. Applications must be submitted by 11:59 p.m. on the deadline date. Applicants for the April deadline will be notified of grant decisions before June 30. Applicants for the October deadline will be notified before December 31.
Requirements: Grants are made to 501(c)3 tax-exempt organizations that serve the following South Shore residents: Abington, Braintree, Bridgewater, Brockton, Carver, Cohasset, Duxbury, Hanover, Hanson, Hingham, Holbrook, Hull, Marshfield, Norwell, Pembroke, Plymouth, Quincy, Randolph, Rockland, Scituate, Weymouth, and Whitman.
Restrictions: Grants are made to support program/project expenses. General operating support and support for endowment campaigns are not provided. Only one request will be accepted from an organization during a twelve-month period. The foundation does not support requests from individuals, organizations attempting to influence policy through direct lobbying, or any political campaigns.
Geographic Focus: Massachusetts
Date(s) Application is Due: Apr 1; Oct 1
Contact: Miki C. Akimoto, Vice President; (866) 778-6859; miki.akimoto@baml.com
Internet: https://www.bankofamerica.com/philanthropic/fn_search.action
Sponsor: Harold Brooks Foundation
225 Franklin Street, 4th Floor, MA1-225-04-02
Boston, MA 02110

Harold K. L. Castle Foundation Grants 2228
The Foundation makes grants to organizations working in one or more of three strategic priority areas: public education redesign and enhancement (pre-K-12); nearshore Marine Resource Conservation; and strengthening the communities of Windward Oahu. The Foundation occasionally chooses to fund outside these areas, at its discretion. Such grants are increasingly rare, limited, and always initiated by the Foundation. Average grant size is approximately $110,000, but grants range from $100 to $4 million.
Requirements: Nonprofit organizations serving Hawaii and public schools are eligible to apply. Interested applicants must submit an Online Inquiry Form, which is the first step in requesting funds from the foundation. Online Inquiry Forms will be reviewed by foundation staff on a rolling basis, so they may be submitted at any time during the year. Within one month of receipt of your Online Inquiry Form, the foundation will contact you to request more information, invite you to submit a full proposal, or to inform you that the Foundation will be unable to consider a full proposal due to limited resources and/or a mismatch with Foundation priorities. The Foundation generally prefers not to be the only funder of a given project.
Restrictions: Proposals are not considered for: individuals or businesses; ongoing operating expenses (unless it is a new project or organization needing start-up funding); vehicles; computers; endowments; annual fund drives; sponsorships, special events, dinners, galas; organizations based outside of Hawaii; projects taking place outside Hawaii that do not benefit Hawaii. Each organization is limited to one active grant at a time.
Geographic Focus: Hawaii
Date(s) Application is Due: Oct 1
Contact: Elizabeth Naholowa'a Murph; (808) 263-7073; bmurph@castlefoundation.org
Internet: http://www.castlefoundation.org/eligibility-guidelines.htm
Sponsor: Harold K. L. Castle Foundation
1197 Auloa Road
Kailua, HI 96734

Harold R. Bechtel Charitable Remainder Uni-Trust Grants 2229
Established in Davenport, Iowa, in 1987, the Harold R. Bechtel Charitable Remainder Uni-Trust supports programs in Scott County, Iowa, with giving primarily for health associations, education, and for children, youth, and social services. The Foundation's primary interest areas include: children and youth services; community and economic development; education; family services; health organizations and associations; heart and circulatory research; higher education; human services; museums, music; and performing arts. Types of support building construction and renovation, as well as program-related funding. There are no specific deadlines, and applicants should contact the office in writing or via telephone to request application forms.
Requirements: 501(c)3 organizations serving residents of Rock County, Iowa, are eligible.
Restrictions: No grants are given to individuals, or for endowments, debt retirement, past operating deficit, continuing support, or scholarly research in an established discipline.
Geographic Focus: Iowa
Amount of Grant: Up to 150,000 USD
Contact: R. Richard Bittner; (563) 328-3333; fax (563) 328-3352; loseband@blwlaw.com
Sponsor: Harold R. Bechtel Charitable Remainder Uni-Trust
201 West 2nd Street, Suite 1000
Davenport, IA 52801-1817

Harold Simmons Foundation Grants 2230
The foundation awards grants to Texas nonprofit organizations, with emphasis on social services, religion, health, the arts, and youth. Grants also support community programs and projects, child development, and adult basic education/literacy programs. The foundation also supports international development and relief efforts in Third World countries. Grants are awarded for general operating support, annual campaigns, capital campaigns, building construction/renovation, continuing support, seed money, and program development. Application forms are not required, and there are no deadline dates.
Requirements: Dallas, TX, nonprofits are eligible.
Restrictions: Grants are not awarded to support individuals or for endowment funds or loans.
Geographic Focus: Texas
Contact: Lisa Simmons Epstein, President; (972) 233-2134
Sponsor: Harold Simmons Foundation
5430 LBJ Freeway, Suite 1700
Dallas, TX 75240-2697

Harris and Eliza Kempner Fund Grants 2231
The foundation provides grants primarily in the Galveston, TX, area to qualifying organizations in the broad areas of the arts, historic preservation, community development, education, health, and human services. The foundation gives preference to requests for seed money, operating funds, small capital needs, and special projects partnering with other funding sources. Application information is available online.
Requirements: Grants are made primarily to Texas qualifying organizations in the greater Galveston area.
Restrictions: Funding is not available for: fund-raising benefits; direct mail solicitations; grants to individuals; and grants to non-USA based organizations.
Geographic Focus: Texas
Date(s) Application is Due: Mar 15; Oct 15
Contact: Harrette N. Howard; (409) 762-1603; information@kempnerfund.org
Internet: http://www.kempnerfund.org/app/programs.html
Sponsor: Harris and Eliza Kempner Fund
2201 Market Street, Suite 601
Galveston, TX 77550-1529

Harris Graduate School of Public Policy Studies Research Development Grants 2232
The Harris School supports this program for social science scholars interested in food assistance research. Awards will be made to scholars who propose research including, but not limited to interactions between food assistance programs and other welfare programs with respect to participation, administration, budget exposure, and the role of food assistance as a personal and fiscal stabilizer; the effects of the macroeconomic environment on the need for food assistance, level of participation, and food assistance program costs; and the well-being of current and former food assistance recipients. Other topics related to welfare reform and macroeconomic interactions with food assistance will be considered. This program is designed to encourage experienced researchers in other areas to start projects in the area of food assistance; research on food assistance using innovative approaches and research methods; smaller, start-up projects with the potential to make a significant contribution to food assistance research; and younger and junior scholars to develop research agendas in the area of food assistance. Funding may include compensation for the principal investigator's time; research assistance; travel; and purchase of data, computers, or other research related items. Application guidelines are available online.
Requirements: Applicants must hold a PhD degree.
Geographic Focus: All States
Date(s) Application is Due: May 1
Amount of Grant: Up to 40,000 USD
Contact: USDA Research Development Grants; (773) 702-2028; spopa@uchicago.edu
Internet: http://harrisschool.uchicago.edu/Research/funding.asp
Sponsor: University of Chicago
1155 E 60th Street
Chicago, IL 60637

Harrison County Community Foundation Grants 2233
The Harrison County Community Foundation (HCCF) awards grants to eligible Indiana nonprofit organizations in its areas of interest, including arts and culture; human services; recreation; government; historical preservation; community projects; education; health and safety; and environment. The HCCF staff will provide training to all eligible not-for-profits serving the community on the proper completion of our grant application. All applicants are strongly encouraged to attend formal training sessions as announced, typically in May and November.
Requirements: Nonprofit agencies providing services to residents of Harrison County, Indiana, are eligible to apply. Tax-exempt 501(c)3 organizations and schools, religious organizations, and local governmental units are eligible.
Restrictions: The Foundation does not award grants to purchase real estate that has not been identified and an offer accepted; political activities or those designed to influence legislation; individuals; travel associated with a school-sponsored event; or religious organizations for projects that do not serve the general public. Traditional equipment, routine maintenance, or facility improvements will not be funded. Unused funding cannot be carried over into the following year.

Geographic Focus: Indiana
Date(s) Application is Due: Jan 15; Jul 15
Contact: Anna Curts; (812) 738-6668; fax (812) 738-6864; annac@hccfindiana.org
Internet: http://www.hccfindiana.org/grants/
Sponsor: Harrison County Community Foundation
1523 Foundation Way, P.O. Box 279
Corydon, IN 47112

Harrison County Community Foundation Signature Grants   2234
Grant requests from the Harrison County Community Foundation (HCCF) in the amount of $200,000 and over are considered Signature Grants. These applications will be reviewed by all members of the Grants Committee. Decisions for Signature Grants may be announced anytime during the year. A vast majority of grant applications should be planned ahead and submitted during our Spring or Fall Grant Cycles, however, the HCCF is aware that some state or federal grants requiring local matching funds are announced on short notice. To support Harrison County serving not-for-profits with local matching funds, we will consider certain grant requests anytime. Emergency grants are awarded to respond to true emergency needs of our community or those that prevent an agency or program from carrying out primary functions or services.
Requirements: Nonprofit agencies providing services to residents of Harrison County, Indiana, are eligible to apply. Tax-exempt 501(c)3 organizations and schools, religious organizations, and local governmental units are eligible.
Restrictions: The Foundation does not award grants to purchase real estate that has not been identified and an offer accepted; political activities or those designed to influence legislation; individuals; travel associated with a school-sponsored event; or religious organizations for projects that do not serve the general public. Traditional equipment, routine maintenance, or facility improvements will not be funded. Unused funding cannot be carried over into the following year.
Geographic Focus: Indiana
Amount of Grant: 200,000 - 500,000 USD
Contact: Anna Curts; (812) 738-6668; fax (812) 738-6864; annac@hccfindiana.org
Internet: http://www.hccfindiana.org/grants/
Sponsor: Harrison County Community Foundation
1523 Foundation Way, P.O. Box 279
Corydon, IN 47112

Harris Teeter Corporate Contributions Grants   2235
The Harris Teeter Program makes financial contributions to organizations to create a better quality of life in the neighborhoods where they do business. The company has focused their giving into three main areas: eliminating hunger, educating children, and serving specific community needs. To submit a request for contributions, interested applicants must submit a letter of proposal. Proposals are reviewed annually. The company prefers to give directly to an organization and a specific project rather than fundraising efforts. Instructions for submitting a proposal are available online.
Requirements: 501(c)3 tax-exempt organizations are eligible.
Restrictions: The foundation does not contribute to individuals, deficit reduction or operating reserves; trips, tours, or student exchange programs; fund drives conducted by religious or political organizations; or scholarship funds outside of Harris Teeter's own programs.
Geographic Focus: All States
Date(s) Application is Due: Aug 1
Contact: Jennifer Panetta, (800) 432-6111, ext. 3; customerrelations@harristeeter.com
Internet: http://www.harristeeter.com/Default.aspx?pageId=229
Sponsor: Harris Teeter Corporation
701 Crestdale Road
Matthews, NC 28105

Harry A. and Margaret D. Towsley Foundation Grants   2236
In 1959, Margaret Towsley created the Harry A. and Margaret D. Towsley Foundation with an initial gift of $4 Million in Dow Chemical Company stock. While the Foundation's initial goals were typical of general family foundations, its mission later became focused on programs promoting education, health care, shelter, and nutrition for children. As its assets grew, its areas of concentration expanded into college and university education, medical education, planned parenthood, and interdisciplinary programs with the schools of law and social work. These areas reflected Dr. and Mrs. Towsley's common interest in teaching. The foundation currently awards grants to Michigan organizations in its areas of interest, including environment, medical and preschool education, social services, continuing education, and research in the health sciences. Types of support include annual campaigns, building construction and renovation, capital campaigns, continuing support, employee matching gifts, endowments, general operating support, matching/challenge support, professorships, program development, research, and seed grants. There are no application forms; submit a letter of inquiry between January and the listed application deadline.
Restrictions: Grants are not awarded to individuals or for travel, scholarships, fellowships, conferences, books, publications, films, tapes, audio-visual or communication media, or loans.
Geographic Focus: Michigan
Date(s) Application is Due: Mar 31
Contact: Lynn Towsley White, President; (989) 837-1100; fax (989) 837-3240
Sponsor: Harry A. and Margaret D. Towsley Foundation
140 Ashman Street, P.O. Box 349
Midland, MI 48640

Harry B. and Jane H. Brock Foundation Grants   2237
The Harry B. and Jane H. Brock Foundation honors a former Fort Payne, Alabama, native who changed the structure of the banking industry in Alabama. Today, the Foundation awards grants to eligible Alabama organizations to support community development and higher education. Primary areas of interest include community service, community funds, education, the environment, higher education, volunteerism, women's services, social services, and cancer treatment and research. Types of support include: annual campaigns, capital campaigns, endowments, general operating support, program development, and research. Written proposals should describe the project and organization and include a copy of the IRS tax-determination letter. The annual deadline is November 1.
Requirements: 501(c)3 organizations serving the residents of Alabama are eligible.
Restrictions: No grants to individuals are awarded. Giving primarily in Birmingham and Huntsville, Alabama.
Geographic Focus: Alabama
Date(s) Application is Due: Nov 1
Amount of Grant: 1,000 - 25,000 USD
Contact: Harry B. Brock, Jr.; (205) 939-0236 or (205) 918-0833; fax (205) 939-0806
Sponsor: Harry B. and Jane H. Brock Foundation
2101 Highland Avenue, Suite 250, P.O. Box 11643
Birmingham, AL 35202-1643

Harry Bramhall Gilbert Charitable Trust Grants   2238
The Harry Bramhall Gilbert Charitable Trust supports tax-exempt organizations that contribute to the health, education, and cultural life of the Tidewater, Virginia region. The Trust currently and substantially funds nonprofits based in the cities of Norfolk, Chesapeake, and Virginia Beach, Virginia. To apply, submit a letter to the Trust (no application form is required) containing the following information: copy of IRS Determination Letter; copy of most recent annual report/audited financial statement/990; listing of board of directors, trustees, officers and other key people and their affiliations; detailed description of project and amount of funding requested. Include two copies.
Requirements: Virginia nonprofit organizations based in the cities of Norfolk, Chesapeake, and Virginia Beach are eligible.
Restrictions: No support for religious or political organizations. No grants to individuals.
Geographic Focus: Virginia
Date(s) Application is Due: Sep 30
Contact: Stuart D. Glasser, Treasurer; (757) 204-4858; sdglasser@cox.net
Internet: http://fdncenter.org/grantmaker/gilbert
Sponsor: Harry Bramhall Gilbert Charitable Trust
316 Scone Castle Loop
Chesapeake, VA 23322

Harry C. Trexler Trust Grants   2239
The trust supports charitable organizations located in the city of Allentown or in Lehigh County, Pennsylvania. The trust provides that one-fourth of the income shall be added to the corpus, one-fourth paid to the city of Allentown for park purposes, and the remainder distributed to such charitable organizations and objects as shall be of the most benefit to humanity, but limited to Allentown and Lehigh County, Pennsylvania, particularly for hospitals, churches, institutions for the care of the crippled and orphans, youth agencies, social services, cultural programs, and support of ministerial students at two named Pennsylvania institutions. Types of support include: building construction/renovation, capital campaigns, continuing support, land acquisition, equipment acquisition, program development, general operating support, and matching/challenge grants.
Requirements: Potential grantees are nonprofit organizations located in Allentown or Lehigh County, PA, and rendering exclusive or substantial services to the people residing therein.
Restrictions: Grants are not made to individuals or for endowment funds, research, scholarships, or fellowships.
Geographic Focus: Pennsylvania
Date(s) Application is Due: Dec 1
Contact: Janet Roth, Executive Director; (610) 434-9645; fax (610) 437-5721
Internet: http://www.TrexlerTrust.org/
Sponsor: Harry C. Trexler Trust
33 South 7th Street, Suite 205
Allentown, PA 18101

Harry Chapin Foundation Grants   2240
The mission of the Harry Chapin Foundation is to support organizations that have demonstrated their ability to dramatically improve the lives and livelihood of people by helping them to become self-sufficient. The Foundation's funding focuses on: community education programs that identify community needs and mobilize resources to meet them, fostering social and economic justice; arts in education programs and other approaches to educating young people. To create a healthier and more peaceful world; agricultural and environmental programs that support the preservation of individually-owned farms; support for citizen organizations that promote equitable food production and distribution; and promote a safe and sustainable environment. One year grants range from a few hundred dollars to a maximum of $10,000. An application should be made in a brief written proposal to Executive Director, Leslie Ramme. Additional guidelines and application are available at: http://www.harrychapinfoundation.org/Guidelines.html. The Foundation Board meets three times a year on an, as needed basis. To insure a timely consideration of your proposal, the sooner the request is received, the better your chances are for meeting the next Board review.
Requirements: 501(c)3 organizations operating in the United States are eligible to apply.
Restrictions: Funding is only available for programs that operate in the United States.
Geographic Focus: All States
Contact: Leslie Ramme; (631) 423-7558; fax (631) 423-7596; harrychapinfound@aol.com
Internet: http://fdncenter.org/grantmaker/harrychapin
Sponsor: Harry Chapin Foundation
16 Gerard Street
Huntington, NY 11743

Harry Edison Foundation 2241
Harry Edison Foundation was incorporated in Missouri in 2003 by one of the founders of Edison Brothers Stores, among five sons of a Latvian immigrant who had peddled shoes off a pack mule in southern Georgia. Giving is primarily centered around the Saint Louis, Missouri, region in the areas of education, hospitals, human services, Jewish organizations, and medical research. Major types of support include: annual campaigns, building and renovation costs, capital campaigns, professorships, research, and scholarship endowments. There are no specific application forms or annual deadlines, and applicants should begin by contacting the Foundation directly. Most recently, support has ranged from $100 to $120,000.
Requirements: Applicants should be 501(c)3 organizations that support the residents of St. Louis, Missouri, and its surrounding region.
Geographic Focus: Missouri
Amount of Grant: 100 - 120,000 USD
Contact: Bernard A. Edison, President; (314) 331-6504 or (314) 331-6505
Sponsor: Harry Edison Foundation
220 N. 4th Street, Suite A
St. Louis, MO 63102-1905

Harry Kramer Memorial Fund Grants 2242
The Harry Kramer Memorial Fund, established in 1982, supports Jewish organizations in the United States and Israel, involved with the care of the sick or aged, education, and religious organizations. Giving primarily in the southern Florida area. Areas of interest include: aging, centers/services; arts; disasters, 9/11/01; higher education; human services; international terrorism; Jewish federated giving programs; disabled individuals.
Requirements: There are no specific deadlines with which to adhere. Contact the Foundation for further application information and guidelines.
Restrictions: No grants to individuals, or for operating budgets or continuing support.
Geographic Focus: All States, Israel
Amount of Grant: 1,800 - 15,000 USD
Contact: Leslie J. August, Wachovia Bank Trustee; (305) 789-4645
Sponsor: Harry Kramer Memorial Fund c/o Wachovia Bank, N.A.
100 North Main Street, 13th Floor
Winston-Salem, NC 27150-0001

Harry S. Black and Allon Fuller Fund Grants 2243
The Harry S. Black and Allon Fuller Fund was established in 1930 to support quality healthcare and human-services programming for underserved populations. The grantmaking focus is in the areas of health care and physical disabilities. The fund supports access to health care; health education; health/wellness promotion and disease prevention; health policy analysis and advocacy; access programs for physically disabled individuals; disability policy analysis and advocacy; workforce development programs; and programs that improve quality of life for the disabled. Emphasis will be placed on programs serving low-income communities. Grant requests for general operating support or program/project support are strongly encouraged. Applicants must apply online at the grant website. Applicants are strongly encouraged to do the following before applying: review the downloadable state application procedures at the grant website; review the downloadable online-application guidelines at the grant website; review the foundation's funding history (link is available from the grant website); review the online application questions in advance; and review the list of required attachments. These will generally include: a list of board members, financial statements (audited, reviewed, or compiled by independent auditor); an organization summary; a list of other funding sources; an IRS Determination letter; and other required documents. All attachments must be uploaded in the online application as PDF, Word, or Excel files. The Harry S. Black and Allon Fuller Fund has a deadline of July 31. Grant decisions will be made by December 31.
Requirements: Nonprofit organizations must be geographically located within the city limits of New York City or Chicago to be eligible to apply.
Restrictions: The fund generally does not support the following: projects in the areas of health care specific to medical/academic research; organizations or programs that primarily provide mental health services; programs that primarily provide services to either the mentally or developmentally disabled; endowment campaigns; and capital projects. The fund does not support requests from individuals, organizations attempting to influence policy through direct lobbying, or any political campaigns.
Geographic Focus: Illinois, New York
Date(s) Application is Due: Jul 31
Contact: Christine O'Donnell; (646) 855-1011; christine.l.o'donnell@baml.com
Internet: https://www.bankofamerica.com/philanthropic/fn_search.action
Sponsor: Harry S. Black and Allon Fuller Fund
One Bryant Park, NY1-100-28-05
New York, NY 10036

Harry S. Truman Scholarships 2244
The scholarship is a merit-based grant awarded to undergraduate students who wish financial support to attend graduate or professional school in preparation of careers in government. The foundation seeks candidates who have extensive records of public and community service, are committed to careers in government or elsewhere in public service, and have outstanding leadership potential and communication skills.
Requirements: Candidates must attend an accredited U.S. college or university and be nominated by the institution's Truman Faculty Representative (candidates may not apply directly), be U.S. citizens or U.S. nationals, complete an application and write a policy recommendation, be in the upper quarter of their junior class, except for residents of Puerto Rico, the Virgin Islands, or a Pacific Island who must be in their senior class.
Geographic Focus: All States
Amount of Grant: 30,000 USD
Contact: Administrator; (202) 395-4831; fax (202) 395-6995; office@truman.gov
Internet: http://www.truman.gov
Sponsor: Harry S. Truman Scholarship Foundation
712 Jackson Place NW
Washington, DC 20006

Harry Sudakoff Foundation Grants 2245
The Foundation, established in 1956, offers funding primarily in the forms of ongoing support and capital campaigns. Focus areas include: federated giving programs; higher education; and human/social services. Of particular interest are the performing arts, including dance, music, and theater. The geographic focus is Sarasota, Florida, with an initial approach by Letter of Interest (LOI). Though there are no specific application forms, the annual deadline for application is August 15, with final notification by November 1st.
Requirements: Grantees must be 501(c)3 organizations with a sound track record.
Restrictions: Generally the Foundation will not provide grants for: endowments, deficit financing, debt reduction, or ordinary operating expenses; conferences, seminars, workshops, travel, surveys, advertising, fund-raising costs or research; annual giving campaigns; individuals; or projects that have already been completed.
Geographic Focus: Florida
Date(s) Application is Due: Aug 15
Amount of Grant: 46,875 USD
Contact: Janet L Dickens; (941) 952-2826; fax (941) 952-2768; janet.dickens@ustrust.com
Sponsor: Harry Sudakoff Foundation
Bank of America, 1605 Main Street
Sarasota, FL 34236-5840

Harry W. Bass, Jr. Foundation Grants 2246
The Dallas-based Harry W. Bass, Jr. Foundation seeks to enrich the lives of the citizens of Texas by providing support to qualified organizations in the areas of education, health, human services, civic & community, science, research, arts and culture. Grant applications for specific programs or projects, capital projects or, less often, general operations are considered. Endowment gifts are rare. The Harry W. Bass, Jr. Foundation also considers program-related investments as part of its grant-making activities. The foundation strives to be responsive to the needs of all eligible organizations and considers requests of any amount. There is no formal application form. Grant requests are accepted at any time throughout the year. Each organization is limited to one application within a twelve-month period. Requests are usually processed within three to four months. Electronic grant applications should be submitted to dcalhoun@hbrf.org (no file attachments, please). For more information, contact the Harry W. Bass, Jr. Foundation.
Requirements: Texas 501(c)3 tax-exempt organizations are eligible.
Restrictions: In general, grants are not made for purposes of: church or seminary construction; annual fundraising events or general sustentation drives; professional conferences and symposia; out-of-state performances or competition expenses; to other private foundations. Unsolicited grant requests are restricted to organizations based in the Greater Dallas area. In the event a grant is approved, the recipient organization will be unable to submit another grant request for two years due to the foundation policy of not providing subsequent year grants.
Geographic Focus: Texas
Contact: F. David Calhoun; (214) 599-0300; fax (214) 599-0405; dcalhoun@hbrf.org
Internet: http://www.harrybassfoundation.org/about.asp
Sponsor: Harry Bass Foundation
4809 Cole Avenue, Suite 252
Dallas, TX 75205

Hartford Aging and Health Program Awards 2247
The foundation's two principal programs are Health Care Cost and Quality and Aging and Health. The Health Care Cost and Quality program supports the community health management initiative, health care quality measures, and reducing inappropriate health care services. The Aging and Health program supports strengthening physicians' knowledge of geriatrics, reducing medication problems of the elderly, and demonstrating integrated financing and service delivery for comprehensive geriatric services. Types of support include operating budgets, continuing support, projects/programs, research, publications, and conferences and seminars. The foundation also welcomes inquiries regarding projects that may not fit these specific interests but would further its broad goal of improving health care in America. Types of support include general operations, continuing support, projects/programs, research, publications, and conferences and seminars. Applications are accepted at any time and are reviewed four times each year when the board meets.
Requirements: U.S. health, education, and social service organizations may apply.
Restrictions: Requests will be denied for general research or for projects lasting more than three years.
Geographic Focus: All States
Contact: Corinne Rieder; (212) 832-7788; fax (212) 593-4913; mail@jhartfound.com
Internet: http://www.jhartfound.org
Sponsor: John A. Hartford Foundation
55 E 59th Street, 16th Floor
New York, NY 10022-1178

Hartford Courant Foundation Grants 2248
The Foundation established in 1950, supports organizations involved with education, the arts, community development, health and social services, with an emphasis on programs benefiting children, youth and families. Grants in the area of the arts will be made only for outreach or education programs for children or families. Grants may be awarded in support of program, capital and operating expenses, for seed money and as challenge or matching grants. The Hartford Courant Foundation serves: Andover, Avon, Bloomfield, Bolton, Canton, East Granby, East Hartford, East Windsor, Ellington, Enfield, Farmington,

Glastonbury, Granby, Hartford, Hebron, Manchester, Marlborough, Middletown, New Britain, Newington, Rocky Hill, Simsbury, Somers, South Windsor, Suffield, Tolland, Vernon, West Hartford, Wethersfield, Windsor, and Windsor Locks.
Requirements: An organization wishing to apply for a grant from The Hartford Courant Foundation must be: within the Foundations service areas; a non-profit organization; submit its request using a Hartford Courant Foundation application form, available on the Foundations website; include supporting documentation.
Restrictions: The Hartford Courant Foundation's policies do not allow funding of: organizations which are not tax exempt under IRS Code section 501(c)3; organizations which have the IRS Private Foundation designation; individuals; endowment funds; religious institutions, other than for their provision of non-sectarian community services; capital projects related to the arts; performances, conferences, trips, one-time events; annual campaigns.
Geographic Focus: Connecticut
Date(s) Application is Due: Mar 15; Jun 15; Sep 15; Dec 15
Contact: Kate Miller; (860) 241-6472; fax (860) 520-6988; kmiller@hcfdn.org
Internet: http://www.hcfdn.org/application/guidelines.htm
Sponsor: Hartford Courant Foundation
285 Broad Street
Hartford, CT 06115

Hartford Foundation Application Planning Grants 2249
The purpose of this grant is to produce a strong application based on a carefully developed work plan with measurable outcomes that demonstrate community benefit. Criteria for an application planning grant: seeks help to implement a promising strategy to address a priority issue/need; generates innovative local approaches to priority community issues/needs; encourages best practice research and effective implementation in the community; promotes collaboration among two or more agencies or community groups on priority issue/need; demonstrates the capacity and the commitment of the agency to undertake complex planning and implementation of a theoretical framework and work plan; has compelling reason why quality planning cannot be carried out without a grant; enables a good proposal to become an excellent proposal.
Requirements: Nonprofit organizations in the following Connecticut towns are eligible to apply for funding: Andover, Avon, Bloomfield, Bolton, Canton, East Granby, East Hartford, East Windsor, Ellington, Enfield, Farmington, Glastonbury, Granby, Hartford, Hebron, Manchester, Marlborough, Newington, Rocky Hill, Simsbury, Somers, South Windsor, Suffield, West Hartford, Wethersfield, Windsor, Windsor Locks, Tolland, and Vernon. Proposals for statewide programs may be considered when there is a substantial benefit to residents of these communities.
Restrictions: The Foundation does not make grants from its unrestricted funds for: sectarian or religious activities; grants directly to individuals; grants to private foundations; endowments or memorials; direct or grass-roots lobbying efforts; conferences; research; or informational activities on topics that are primarily national or international in perspective. In addition, the Foundation generally does not make grants for: federal, state, or municipal agencies or departments supported by taxation; sponsorship of or support for one-time events; liquidation of obligations incurred at a previous date; or sustaining support for recurring operating expenses.
Geographic Focus: Connecticut
Amount of Grant: 7,500 USD
Contact: Cheryl L. Gerrish; (860) 548-1888; gerrish@hfpg.org or hfpg@hfpg.org
Internet: http://www.hfpg.org/GrantmakingPrograms/AboutOurGrantmaking/Typesof Grants/tabid/168/Default.aspx
Sponsor: Hartford Foundation
10 Columbus Boulevard, 8th Floor
Hartford, CT 06106

Hartford Foundation Evaluation Grants 2250
Evaluation may occur either throughout the project, to continuously assess progress and identify possible changes in implementation strategy in order to meet the intended grant outcomes, or at the end of the project, to document grant outcomes and lessons learned. Decisions regarding grants for evaluation will normally be made when the project grant is made, but will also be made early in the project for which the original grant request was funded. Criteria for an evaluation grant: implements a promising strategy addressing a priority issue/need; highlights an important challenge or issue in the community; measurable and significant community benefit is anticipated; project possesses a good theoretical framework and work plan, but implementation is untested; proposal is considered by the agency and the Foundation to involve risk, but may provide promising outcomes; Foundation's contribution is significant part of overall project budget; evaluation strategy proposed can appropriately measure project outcomes; agency demonstrates the capacity and commitment to support the evaluation. Interested applicants are encouraged to contact the Foundation and speak with a program officer.
Requirements: Nonprofit organizations in the following Connecticut towns are eligible to apply for funding: Andover, Avon, Bloomfield, Bolton, Canton, East Granby, East Hartford, East Windsor, Ellington, Enfield, Farmington, Glastonbury, Granby, Hartford, Hebron, Manchester, Marlborough, Newington, Rocky Hill, Simsbury, Somers, South Windsor, Suffield, West Hartford, Wethersfield, Windsor, Windsor Locks, Tolland, and Vernon. Proposals for statewide programs may be considered when there is a substantial benefit to residents of these communities.
Restrictions: The Foundation does not make grants from its unrestricted funds for: sectarian or religious activities; grants directly to individuals; grants to private foundations; endowments or memorials; direct or grass-roots lobbying efforts; conferences; research; or informational activities on topics that are primarily national or international in perspective. In addition, the Foundation generally does not make grants for: federal, state, or municipal agencies or departments supported by taxation; sponsorship of or support for one-time events; liquidation of obligations incurred at a previous date; or sustaining support for recurring operating expenses.
Geographic Focus: Connecticut
Contact: Cheryl L. Gerrish; (860) 548-1888; gerrish@hfpg.org or hfpg@hfpg.org
Internet: http://www.hfpg.org/GrantmakingPrograms/AboutOurGrantmaking/Typesof Grants/tabid/168/Default.aspx
Sponsor: Hartford Foundation
10 Columbus Boulevard, 8th Floor
Hartford, CT 06106

Hartford Foundation Implementation Support Grants 2251
These grants are to help strengthen implementation of a larger, existing grant. They are awarded when a program officer, with the help of the grantee, identifies an appropriate intervention that can remedy problems or respond to needs that arise during implementation of the grant project that could not have been anticipated. A request may be initiated by the grantee or may be the result of site visits or other communication by the program officer on a grant that has already been made. Criteria for this grant: initial grant addresses high priority of the Foundation and is of sufficient size and scope; need is identified early enough in project implementation to allow sufficient time for intervention to make a difference in the outcome; the grantee initiates the formal request, identifying the need and providing substantial input into the solution/remedy; the grantee demonstrates that it is dong all it can within its resources to remedy the situation before seeking the additional discretionary grant; in the judgment of the program officer, the proposed intervention can make a real difference in the outcome of the initial grant project.
Requirements: Nonprofit organizations in the following Connecticut towns are eligible to apply for funding: Andover, Avon, Bloomfield, Bolton, Canton, East Granby, East Hartford, East Windsor, Ellington, Enfield, Farmington, Glastonbury, Granby, Hartford, Hebron, Manchester, Marlborough, Newington, Rocky Hill, Simsbury, Somers, South Windsor, Suffield, West Hartford, Wethersfield, Windsor, Windsor Locks, Tolland, and Vernon. Proposals for statewide programs may be considered when there is a substantial benefit to residents of these communities.
Restrictions: The Foundation does not make grants from its unrestricted funds for: sectarian or religious activities; grants directly to individuals; grants to private foundations; endowments or memorials; direct or grass-roots lobbying efforts; conferences; research; or informational activities on topics that are primarily national or international in perspective. In addition, the Foundation generally does not make grants for: federal, state, or municipal agencies or departments supported by taxation; sponsorship of or support for one-time events; liquidation of obligations incurred at a previous date; or sustaining support for recurring operating expenses.
Geographic Focus: Connecticut
Amount of Grant: Up to 7,500 USD
Contact: Cheryl L. Gerrish; (860) 548-1888; gerrish@hfpg.org or hfpg@hfpg.org
Internet: http://www.hfpg.org/GrantmakingPrograms/AboutOurGrantmaking/Typesof Grants/tabid/168/Default.aspx#transitionaloperating
Sponsor: Hartford Foundation
10 Columbus Boulevard, 8th Floor
Hartford, CT 06106

Hartford Foundation Nonprofit Support Program Grants 2252
This program helps small to mid-sized nonprofits improve their organizational performance through an array of grants and services. These include assessments and grants in three key areas: planning, technology, and financial management. This program also provides loans to finance cash-flow, working capital, and equipment needs; workshops and multi-session training programs for agency board members and staff, access to free legal advice, and a newsletter featuring resources available to nonprofits.
Requirements: Nonprofit organizations in the following Connecticut towns are eligible to apply for funding: Andover, Avon, Bloomfield, Bolton, Canton, East Granby, East Hartford, East Windsor, Ellington, Enfield, Farmington, Glastonbury, Granby, Hartford, Hebron, Manchester, Marlborough, Newington, Rocky Hill, Simsbury, Somers, South Windsor, Suffield, West Hartford, Wethersfield, Windsor, Windsor Locks, Tolland, and Vernon. Proposals for statewide programs may be considered when there is a substantial benefit to residents of these communities.
Restrictions: The Foundation does not make grants from its unrestricted funds for: sectarian or religious activities; grants directly to individuals; grants to private foundations; endowments or memorials; direct or grass-roots lobbying efforts; conferences; research; or informational activities on topics that are primarily national or international in perspective. In addition, the Foundation generally does not make grants for: federal, state, or municipal agencies or departments supported by taxation; sponsorship of or support for one-time events; liquidation of obligations incurred at a previous date; or sustaining support for recurring operating expenses.
Geographic Focus: Connecticut
Contact: Cheryl L. Gerrish; (860) 548-1888; gerrish@hfpg.org or hfpg@hfpg.org
Internet: http://www.hfpg.org/GrantmakingPrograms/AboutOurGrantmaking/Typesof Grants/tabid/168/Default.aspx#transitionaloperating
Sponsor: Hartford Foundation
10 Columbus Boulevard, 8th Floor
Hartford, CT 06106

Hartford Foundation Regular Grants 2253
The Foundation awards grants for a broad range of purposes to a wide variety of nonprofit organizations in social services, health, education, early childhood and youth services, arts and culture, housing and neighborhood development, and other charitable fields. These grants: enhance or strengthen existing activities; provide start-up for organizations and new programs; provide support for capital improvements. Interested applicants are encouraged to phone a program contact to discuss their project before beginning the application process.

Requirements: Nonprofit organizations in the following Connecticut towns are eligible to apply for funding: Andover, Avon, Bloomfield, Bolton, Canton, East Granby, East Hartford, East Windsor, Ellington, Enfield, Farmington, Glastonbury, Granby, Hartford, Hebron, Manchester, Marlborough, Newington, Rocky Hill, Simsbury, Somers, South Windsor, Suffield, West Hartford, Wethersfield, Windsor, Windsor Locks, Tolland, and Vernon. Proposals for statewide programs may be considered when there is a substantial benefit to residents of these communities.
Restrictions: The Foundation does not make grants from its unrestricted funds for: sectarian or religious activities; grants directly to individuals; grants to private foundations; endowments or memorials; direct or grass-roots lobbying efforts; conferences; research; or informational activities on topics that are primarily national or international in perspective. In addition, the Foundation generally does not make grants for: federal, state, or municipal agencies or departments supported by taxation; sponsorship of or support for one-time events; liquidation of obligations incurred at a previous date; or sustaining support for recurring operating expenses.
Geographic Focus: Connecticut
Amount of Grant: Up to 500,000 USD
Contact: Cheryl L. Gerrish; (860) 548-1888; gerrish@hfpg.org or hfpg@hfpg.org
Internet: http://www.hfpg.org/GrantmakingPrograms/Overview/tabid/163/Default.aspx
Sponsor: Hartford Foundation
10 Columbus Boulevard, 8th Floor
Hartford, CT 06106

Harvest Foundation Grants 2254
Formed by the sale of Memorial Health Systems, the foundation is managing an endowment to invest in programs and initiatives that will address local challenges in the areas of health, education, and welfare in Martinsville/Henry County. The foundation is committed to honoring the legacy of Memorial Hospital by emphasizing prevention, safety and access to health care; by facilitating opportunities for local citizens to help their community reach its potential; and by improving the learning environment for citizenship, academic, and vocational preparedness. Application and guidelines are available online.
Requirements: To be eligible for consideration, an organization must: be located within, or have its program focused within Martinsville and/or Henry County; have a letter from the IRS stating its 501c3 status; and propose a project within one of the Foundation's three interest areas of health, education or welfare.
Restrictions: The foundation does not fund organizations that discriminate based upon race, creed, gender, or sexual orientation; scholarships, fellowships, or grants to individuals; sectarian religious activities, political lobbying, or legislative activities; profit-making businesses; emergency needs or extremely time sensitive requests; or direct replacement of discontinued government support.
Geographic Focus: Virginia
Contact: Allyson Rothrock, (276) 632-3329; arothrock@theharvestfoundation.org
Internet: http://www.theharvestfoundation.org/page.cfm/topic/strategic-map
Sponsor: Harvest Foundation
1 Ellsworth Street, P.O. Box 5183
Martinsville, VA 24115

Harvey Randall Wickes Foundation Grants 2255
The Foundation awards grants to eligible Michigan nonprofit organizations in its areas of interest, including the arts; children/youth services; education; hospitals; human services; libraries; and recreation. Types of support include annual campaigns, building/renovation, equipment, and seed money. There are no application deadline dates. Applications must be received two weeks prior to board meetings in March, June, September, and December. Award notification is given within two weeks of the board meeting.
Requirements: Michigan 501(c)3 organizations in Saginaw County are eligible.
Restrictions: Funding is not available for government where support is forthcoming from tax dollars, individuals, endowments, travel, conferences, loans, or film or video projects.
Geographic Focus: Michigan
Amount of Grant: 2,500 - 30,000 USD
Contact: Hugo Braun, Jr.; (989) 799-1850; fax (989) 799-3327; hrwickes@att.net
Sponsor: Harvey Randall Wickes Foundation
4800 Fashion Square Boulevard, Plaza N., Suite 472
Saginaw, MI 48604-2677

Hasbro Children's Fund 2256
The mission of the Fund is to assist children triumphing over critical life obstacles as well as bringing the joy of play into their lives. Through the Fund's initiatives, the mission is achieved by supporting programs which provide terminal and seriously ill children respite and access to play, educational programs for children at risk, and basics for children in need. Interested applicants are asked to submit a letter of inquiry through the online system.
Requirements: Applications are accepted from nonprofit organizations around the world.
Restrictions: Funding is not available for: religious organizations; individuals; cash free grants; research; political organizations; scholarships; travel stipends; loans; endowments; goodwill advertising; sponsorship of recreational activities; fundraisers; auctions; and schools.
Geographic Focus: Massachusetts, Rhode Island, Washington
Date(s) Application is Due: Jun 1
Amount of Grant: 1,000 - 10,000 USD
Contact: Grants Administrator; HCFinfo@hasbro.com
Internet: http://www.hasbro.com/default.cfm?page=grantmaking
Sponsor: Hasbro Children's Fund
1027 Newport Avenue
Pawtucket, RI 02862-1059

Hatton W. Sumners for the Study and Teaching of Self Government Grants 2257
The Foundation's purpose is to encourage the study, teaching and research in the science and art of self-government so that citizens understand the fundamental principles of democracy in shaping governmental policies. Working through qualified, tax-exempt organizations, the Foundation seeks to reach, educate, and motivate the general public and the current and future leaders of American society. The Foundation gives to youth organizations and higher education. Types of support include: conferences and seminars; continuing support; curriculum development; endowments; fellowships; general operating support; internship funds; matching and challenge support; and research. Application information is available at the Foundation website. Grant applications will be accepted from January 1st through August 1st of each year. Final decisions on grant proposals are made by the Trustees in October of each year.
Requirements: Grants are made only to 501(c)3 tax-exempt organizations in Texas, New Mexico, Oklahoma, Louisiana, Arkansas, Kansas, Nebraska and Missouri.
Restrictions: The Foundation does not fund religious organizations or individual grants.
Geographic Focus: Arkansas, Kansas, Louisiana, Missouri, Nebraska, New Mexico, Oklahoma, Texas
Date(s) Application is Due: Aug 1
Contact: Hugh Akin; (214) 220-2128; fax (214) 953-0737; hugh@hattonsumners.org
Internet: http://www.hattonsumners.org
Sponsor: Hatton W. Sumners Foundation for the Study and Teaching of Self Government
325 North St. Paul Street, Suite 3920
Dallas, TX 75201

Hawai'i Children's Trust Fund Community Awareness Events Grants 2258
The purpose of the Fund is to increase community awareness of strategies and activities to prevent child abuse and neglect and strengthen families in communities throughout the state. Events may focus on primary prevention, which targets the general population, or secondary prevention, which targets those who may be at risk for child abuse or neglect or training for service providers working with at risk populations. Preference will be given to proposals that: demonstrate a community partnership or collaborates in developing the event; increases access by providing an event in underserved communities; demonstrates potential for sustainability by demonstrating a match with other resources. Island-based events-events occurring on one island and serving that island population are eligible to request up to $10,000. Multiple Island or statewide events-events occurring on multiple islands or targeting participants statewide are eligible to request up to $20,000. Proposal submission instructions are available online.
Requirements: Organizations classified by the IRS as 501(c)3 and government agencies are eligible. Organizations may only receive one award for community awareness annually.
Geographic Focus: Hawaii
Date(s) Application is Due: Jan 15; Jul 15
Contact: Jennifer Murphy; (808) 566-5562 or (888) 731-3863; jmurphy@hcf-hawaii.org
Internet: http://www.hawaiicommunityfoundation.org/index.php?id=71&categoryID=24
Sponsor: Hawai'i Community Foundation
1164 Bishop Street, Suite 800
Honolulu, HI 96813

Hawaiian Electric Industries Charitable Foundation Grants 2259
To fulfill its mission of good corporate citizenship, the Foundation funds programs in the categories of: community development; education; the environment; and family services. Particular consideration will be given to organizations or programs which: demonstrate cost-effectiveness; has or will have a significant presence in company communities; provide recognition and goodwill for the company and further the well-being of the company's employees and their interests. Instructions for application submission are available online.
Requirements: Hawaii 501(c)3 tax-exempt organizations may apply.
Restrictions: Funds are not available for: activities to replace government support; programs outside the areas served by HEI companies; religious activities of a particular denomination; veterans, fraternal or labor organizations, unless the purpose benefits all the people in the community; political funds; program advertising; special events, e.g., golf tournaments, dinners or functions; direct support for specific individuals.
Geographic Focus: Hawaii
Contact: Community Relations; (808) 543-7601; fax (808) 543-7602; heicf@hei.com
Internet: http://www.hei.com/heicf/heicf.html
Sponsor: Hawaiian Electric Industries Charitable Foundation
P.O. Box 730
Honolulu, HI 96808-0730

Hawaii Community Foundation Community Capacity Building Grants 2260
The Foundation's Capacity Building program currently has two distinct funds: the Group 70 Foundation Fund—supports projects that contribute to a better living environment in Hawaii; and the Richard Smart Fund—supports organizations, community projects and collaborative efforts in Waimea that strengthen existing and build new connections between the people of Waimea. The deadline for the Group 70 Fund is April 11, while there are three deadlines for the Richard Smart Fund: January 15, May 19, and September 22.
Requirements: Nonprofit, tax-exempt 501(c)3 organizations, public schools, or units of government are eligible to apply. The Richard Smart Fund program supports projects that benefit the Waimea community.
Geographic Focus: Hawaii
Date(s) Application is Due: Jan 15; Apr 10; Jun 15
Contact: Marlene Hochuli; (808) 537-6333 or (888) 731-3863; mhochuli@hcf-hawaii.org
Internet: http://hawaiicommunityfoundation.org/index.php?id=71&categoryID=30
Sponsor: Hawai'i Community Foundation
1164 Bishop Street, Suite 800
Honolulu, HI 96813

Hawaii Community Foundation Geographic-Specific Fund Grants   2261
With its Geographic-Specific program, the Foundation supports grant making in Ewa Beach, Kamuela, Kauai, Lanai, Maui, and West Hawaii via eleven distinct funds. Generally, these funds hope to improve the lives of residents living within these distinct geographic regions of Hawaii. Funding levels and deadlines vary throughout the course of year by fund, and applicants should visit the website for specific details.
Requirements: Nonprofit, tax-exempt 501(c)3 organizations, public schools, or units of government are eligible to apply. The Richard Smart Fund program supports projects that benefit the Waimea community.
Geographic Focus: Hawaii
Contact: Georgianna deCosta; (808) 537-6333 or (888) 731-3863; gdecosta@hcf-hawaii.org
Internet: http://hawaiicommunityfoundation.org/index.php?id=71&categoryID=22
Sponsor: Hawai'i Community Foundation
1164 Bishop Street, Suite 800
Honolulu, HI 96813

Hawaii Community Foundation Human Services Grants   2262
The purpose of the Foundation's Human Services program is to support children and youth, and family strengthening. Six distinct funds have been established to support various facets of the program, including: the Hawaii Children's Trust Fund (awareness & prevention); the Oscar and Rosetta Fish Fund for Speech Therapy; the Persons In Need (PIN) Program; the Reverend Takie Okumura Family Fund for Children and Youth; the Theodore A. Vierra Fund and Kitaro Watanabe Fund; and the Victoria S. and Bradley L. Geist Foundation Supporting Enhancements for Foster Children. Deadlines and funding levels of each program vary, and applicants should contact the Foundation for further details.
Requirements: Nonprofit, tax-exempt 501(c)3 organizations, public schools, or units of government are eligible to apply.
Geographic Focus: Hawaii
Amount of Grant: 3,000 - 10,000 USD
Contact: Jennifer Murphy; (808) 537-6333 or (888) 731-3863; csutherland@hcf-hawaii.org
Internet: http://hawaiicommunityfoundation.org/index.php?id=71&categoryID=24
Sponsor: Hawai'i Community Foundation
1164 Bishop Street, Suite 800
Honolulu, HI 96813

Hawaii Community Foundation Organizational Capacity Building Grants   2263
The purpose of the Foundation's Organizational Capacity Building grant program is to support projects that strengthen organizational infrastructure, internal management and board governance. Six distinct funds have been established to support various facets of the program, including: Executive Transitions—to help nonprofits plan for a smooth transition from one Executive Director (ED) to the next, prior to hiring the new Executive Director; Intermediary Grant Program—to support coordinating entities, capacity builders, advocates, technical assistance providers, and brokers of information and knowledge; Implementation—to improve the management or governance of an organization; Planning—to develop a strategic, fund raising, communications, marketing, business or technology plan, or for an organizational assessment; Strategic Partnerships—support the planning and negotiation phase of a merger, or strategic partnership between 2 nonprofits; and the Victoria S. and Bradley L. Geist Foundation—to increase the capacity of organizations and programs to deliver and grow quality services to foster children and their families. Deadlines and funding limits for each of these funds vary, and applicants should contact the Foundation for specific details.
Requirements: Nonprofit 501(c)3 organizations or units of government are eligible to apply.
Geographic Focus: Hawaii
Contact: Pi'ikea Miller, (808) 537-6333 or (888) 731-3863; pmiller@hcf-hawaii.org
Internet: http://hawaiicommunityfoundation.org/index.php?id=71&categoryID=26
Sponsor: Hawai'i Community Foundation
1164 Bishop Street, Suite 800
Honolulu, HI 96813

Hawaii Community Foundation Reverend Takie Okumura Family Grants   2264
The Fund was established by members of the Okumura family to continue the charitable work of Reverend Okumura focusing on the healthy development of Hawaii's young children and youth. Proposals will be accepted in the following areas of focus: youth (ages 6-20 years old) and young children (ages birth to 5 years old). Priorities will be given to programs which: develop the ability to think critically; understand and appreciate one's own culture and those of others; develop the ability to settle differences peacefully; strengthen the early care and education community system. Proposal submission information is available online.
Requirements: Hawai'i organizations that are tax exempt, including nonprofit organizations, 501(c)3 organizations, religious organizations that are exempt from taxation, or units of government are eligible to apply.
Restrictions: Funding is not available for: major capitol projects; endowments; or on-going or general operating costs.
Geographic Focus: Hawaii
Date(s) Application is Due: Aug 5
Amount of Grant: 5,000 - 15,000 USD
Contact: Christel Wuerfel; (808) 537-6333 or (888) 731-3863; cwuerfel@hcf-hawaii.org
Internet: http://hawaiicommunityfoundation.org/index.php?id=71&categoryID=24
Sponsor: Hawai'i Community Foundation
1164 Bishop Street, Suite 800
Honolulu, HI 96813

Hawaii Community Foundation Social Change Grants   2265
The Hawaii Community Foundation has recently created a funding partnership to fund projects that support progressive social change. Two distinct funds exist to support this program: Funding Partnership with the Hawaii People's Fund; and Richard Smart Fund - Hoohui O Waimea. Deadlines vary for each program, and applicants should visit the web site for specific details.
Requirements: Nonprofit, tax-exempt 501(c)3 organizations, or units of government are eligible to apply. The Richard Smart Fund program supports projects that benefit the Waimea community.
Geographic Focus: Hawaii
Date(s) Application is Due: Jan 15; Mar 1; Jun 15; Sep 1
Amount of Grant: 2,000 USD
Contact: Diane U. Chadwick; (808) 537-6333 or (888) 731-3863; dchadwick@hcf-hawaii.org
Internet: http://hawaiicommunityfoundation.org/index.php?id=71&categoryID=35
Sponsor: Hawai'i Community Foundation
1164 Bishop Street, Suite 800
Honolulu, HI 96813

Hawaii Community Foundation West Hawaii Fund Grants   2266
The West Hawaii Fund was established at the Hawaii Community Foundation in 1992 by a group of concerned citizens for the purpose of accepting charitable gifts for the benefit of the people and communities of West Hawaii, from North Kohala to Hawaiian Ocean View Estates. Today, the Fund continues to grow through additional contributions and planned gifts from donors in the community to respond to current and emerging needs and improve the quality of life for the residents of West Hawaii. The strongest proposals will be those that meet the following criteria: proposal articulates how the proposed project will benefit the West Hawaii community; proposal clearly describes how the project will be implemented and how these particular activities will address critical issues in the West Hawaii community; there are clearly stated outcomes and a plan for measuring and reporting results; project demonstrates collaboration among different sectors of the community; project budget is realistic, relates to project narrative and is reasonable in cost.
Requirements: 501(c)3 organizations - Grant awards will range up to $10,000. Community organizations not designated as 501(c)3 organizations -Grant awards will range up to $2,000. To be eligible for grants of more than $2,000, organization must be designated 501(c)3 or have a 501(c)3 fiscal sponsor.
Restrictions: Projects not likely to be funded: projects that do not benefit the residents of West Hawaii; funds for endowments or for the benefit of specific individuals; out-of-state travel expenses; start-up costs of a new organization.
Geographic Focus: Hawaii
Date(s) Application is Due: Oct 1
Amount of Grant: 2,000 - 10,000 USD
Contact: Diane Chadwick; (808) 885-2174; fax (808) 885-1857; dchadwick@hcf-hawaii.org
Internet: http://www.hawaiicommunityfoundation.org/index.php?id=71&categoryID=22
Sponsor: Hawai'i Community Foundation
1164 Bishop Street, Suite 800
Honolulu, HI 96813

Haymarket People's Fund Sustaining Grants   2267
Haymarket People's Fund is an anti-racist and multi-cultural foundation committed to strengthening the movement for social justice in New England. Through grant making, fundraising, and capacity building, it supports grassroots organizations that address the root causes of injustice. Haymarket also organizes to increase sustainable community philanthropy throughout the region. Applications are evaluated according to the following criteria: self-determination and accountability; leadership development; anti-racism and anti-oppression values and practices; organizing for systemic change; movement building; diversified funding base; and limited access to traditional funding. Sustaining grants range up to $10,000 for grassroots, social change organizations (start-ups or established) that meet funding criteria. Organizations must request an application from Haymarket, and return it and all supporting materials through regular mail.
Requirements: Both incorporated organizations (with or without established 501(c)3 status) and unincorporated organizations may apply. Applicants must conduct work within New England (Connecticut, Maine, Massachusetts, New Hampshire, Rhode Island, and Vermont).
Restrictions: Haymarket does not fund: organizations providing direct services that focus on meeting people's basic needs or that focus on individual empowerment or self-help; publications, reports, workshops, classes, conferences, media events, arts or theater productions unless they are part of an ongoing community organizing effort or are accountable to social change movements; groups or work focused outside of New England; legal or research expenses; capital campaigns or endowment drives; individuals or individual projects; projects sponsored by a government agency; organizations with budgets over $350,000; small businesses, alternative business, or business associations; other foundations; elections; union organizing work, unless it benefits a wider community; and civil disobedience or other actions that involve breaking the law.
Geographic Focus: Connecticut, Maine, Massachusetts, New Hampshire, Rhode Island, Vermont
Date(s) Application is Due: Dec 5
Amount of Grant: Up to 10,000 USD
Contact: Jaime Smith; (617) 522-7676, ext. 115; fax (617) 522-9580; jaime@haymarket.org
Internet: http://www.haymarket.org/grantmaking/grants-process
Sponsor: Haymarket People's Fund
42 Seaverns Avenue
Boston, MA 02130

Haymarket Urgent Response Grants   2268

Haymarket People's Fund is an anti-racist and multi-cultural foundation committed to strengthening the movement for social justice in New England. Through grant making, fundraising, and capacity building, it supports grassroots organizations that address the root causes of injustice. Haymarket also organizes to increase sustainable community philanthropy throughout the region. Applications are evaluated according to the following criteria: self-determination and accountability; leadership development; anti-racism and anti-oppression values and practices; organizing for systemic change; movement building; diversified funding base; and limited access to traditional funding. Haymarket makes Urgent Response grants of up to $1,000/year to help grassroots, social change organizations respond quickly to unforeseen crises or opportunities that critically affect their organization and constituency. This includes unexpected events, political crises, or organizing opportunities. Grants are not to be used for ongoing program work (including expenses the organization should have anticipated), for financial crises or a shortfall in projected funding, or because the group missed a funding deadline. Organizations must call to discuss their project and request an application. Haymarket will send an application if they feel the project meets their criteria. The application and all supporting materials must be returned through regular mail.
Requirements: Organizations are not required to have tax-exempt status if their work falls within what the IRS defines as charitable or educational tax exempt activities.
Restrictions: Haymarket does not fund: organizations providing direct services that focus on meeting people's basic needs or that focus on individual empowerment or self-help; legal or research expenses; capital campaigns or endowment drives; individuals or individual projects; projects sponsored by a government agency; organizations with budgets over $350,000; small or alternative businesses or business associations; other foundations; elections; union organizing work, unless it benefits a wider community; and civil disobedience or other actions that involve breaking the law.
Geographic Focus: Connecticut, Maine, Massachusetts, New Hampshire, Rhode Island, Vermont
Date(s) Application is Due: Dec 5
Amount of Grant: Up to 1,000 USD
Contact: Jaime Smith; (617) 522-7676, ext. 115; fax (617) 522-9580; jaime@haymarket.org
Internet: http://www.haymarket.org/grantmaking/grants-process
Sponsor: Haymarket People's Fund
42 Seaverns Avenue
Boston, MA 02130

Hazen Foundation Public Education Grants   2269

The foundation seeks to assist young people, particularly minorities and those disadvantaged by poverty, to achieve their full potential as individuals and as active participants in a democratic society. The goal of the Foundation's public education program is to foster effective schools for all children, and full partnership for parents and communities in school reform. Hazen will no longer accept unsolicited letters of inquiry but rather will periodically issue Requests for Proposals and Calls for Letters of Inquiry. Organizations that wish to receive a RFP should call the Foundation and leave a message on voicemail extension #7 or submit a request with organizational contact information at the contact us page of the website or send email to hazen@hazenfoundation.org.
Requirements: Grants are awarded only to federally tax-exempt 501(c)3 organizations. The Foundation favors requests from community-based and grassroots organizations in four (4) geographic sites: Los Angeles, Miami/Dade County, the Delta of Mississippi and New York City. Organizations are invited to apply for funding through the RFP process at the discretion of the Foundation. All inquiries will be reviewed by staff, although not all inquiries will receive a response. The Foundation will endeavor to determine whether each inquiring organization meets the criteria for each program area.
Restrictions: The Foundation does not make grants to individuals, schools or school districts, or government agencies. The Foundation does not fund scholarships or fellowships; nor provides funds toward ongoing operational expenses, deficit funding, building construction or maintenance. The Foundation does not make grants to individuals, schools or school districts. In addition, the Foundation does not support organizations in U.S. territories.
Geographic Focus: California, Florida, Louisiana, Mississippi, New York
Amount of Grant: Up to 30,000 USD
Contact: Phillip E. Giles; (212) 889-3034; fax (212) 889-3039; hazen@hazenfoundation.org
Internet: http://www.hazenfoundation.org/public-education
Sponsor: Edward R. Hazen Foundation
333 Seventh Avenue, 14th Floor
New York, NY 10001

Hazen Foundation Youth Organizing Grants   2270

The Edward W. Hazen Foundation seeks to assist young people, particularly young people of color and those disadvantaged by poverty, to achieve their full potential as individuals and as active participants in a democratic society. By focusing on youth organizing as a strategy for youth development and social change, the Foundation seeks to contribute to the development of young people as leaders for social change so that they can help create policies, social systems, and public institutions that are supportive, responsible, and accountable to youth and their communities. Hazen will no longer accept unsolicited letters of inquiry but rather will periodically issue Requests for Proposals and Calls for Letters of Inquiry. Organizations that wish to receive a RFP should call the Foundation and leave a message on voicemail extension #7 or submit a request with organizational contact information at the contact us page of the website or send email to hazen@hazenfoundation.org.
Requirements: Grants are awarded only to federally tax-exempt 501(c)3 organizations. The Foundation will consider requests from community-based and grassroots organizations throughout the United States. The groups selected for funding will be primarily from parts of the country where there are cluster of youth organizing groups, youth organizing intermediaries and current or potential base of funders to support this work. A few grants will also be made to youth organizing intermediaries to enhance the capacity of Hazen grantees, and to new networks or coalitions of youth organizing groups. Organizations are invited to apply for funding through the RFP process at the discretion of the Foundation. All inquiries will be reviewed by staff, although not all inquiries will receive a response. The Foundation will endeavor to determine whether each inquiring organization meets the criteria for each program area.
Restrictions: The Foundation does not make grants to individuals, schools or school districts, or government agencies. The Foundation does not fund scholarships or fellowships; nor provides funds toward ongoing operational expenses, deficit funding, building construction or maintenance. The Foundation does not make grants to individuals, schools or school districts. In addition, the Foundation does not support organizations in U.S. territories.
Geographic Focus: All States
Contact: Phillip E. Giles; (212) 889-3034; fax (212) 889-3039; hazen@hazenfoundation.org
Internet: http://www.hazenfoundation.org/youth-development
Sponsor: Edward R. Hazen Foundation
333 Seventh Avenue, 14th Floor
New York, NY 10001

HBF Defending Freedoms Grants   2271

The Herb Block Foundation seeks proposals to safeguard the basic freedoms guaranteed in the U.S. Bill of Rights, and to help eliminate all forms of prejudice and discrimination. Anti-discrimination projects that involve joint efforts of two or more organizations are encouraged. The Foundation also will consider contemporary societal issues that may arise. Most grants will be approved for one year, but a small number will receive up to three years of funding, depending on demonstrated need.
Requirements: Applicants must be nonprofit 501(c)3 organizations. The Foundation uses a two-step, proposal-evaluation process. Applicant organizations are required to submit a letter of inquiry that briefly describes the proposed project's purpose, operation, target audience, timeline, costs, and anticipated impacts. If after reviewing the letter of Inquiry, the Foundation selects the project for further consideration, then a full proposal will be invited. A request for a full proposal does not guarantee the project will be funded, and only full proposals which have been invited by the Foundation will be considered.
Restrictions: Grants will not be made for capital or endowment programs, nor for sectarian religious purposes. Grants cannot be used for lobbying or other partisan purposes. No more than 10% of a grant may go to indirect costs (outside of those for general operating support).
Geographic Focus: All States
Date(s) Application is Due: Oct 4
Amount of Grant: 5,000 - 25,000 USD
Contact: Marcela Brane; (202) 223-8801; fax (202) 223-8804; info@herbblock.org
Internet: http://www.herbblockfoundation.org/programs/defending-freedoms
Sponsor: Herb Block Foundation
1730 M Street NW, Suite 901
Washington, DC 20036

HBF Encouraging Citizen Involvement Grants   2272

The Foundation seeks to help ensure a responsible, responsive democratic government through citizen involvement. Proposals may focus on citizen education or greater voter participation in the electoral process. All projects must be nonpartisan and may not involve lobbying for specific legislation or candidates.
Requirements: Non-profit 501(c)3 tax-exempt organizations are eligible. Applicant organizations are required to submit a letter of inquiry that briefly describes the proposed project's purpose, operation, target audience, timeline, costs, and anticipated impacts. The Foundation uses a two-step, proposal-evaluation process. Full proposals are by invitation only.
Restrictions: Grants will not be made for capital or endowment programs, nor for sectarian religious purposes. Grants cannot be used for lobbying or other partisan purposes.
Geographic Focus: All States
Date(s) Application is Due: Jun 5
Amount of Grant: 5,000 - 25,000 USD
Contact: Marcela Brane; (202) 223-8801; fax (202) 223-8804; info@herbblock.org
Internet: http://www.herbblockfoundation.org/programs/citizen-involvement
Sponsor: Herb Block Foundation
1730 M Street NW, Suite 901
Washington, DC 20036

HBF Pathways Out of Poverty Grants   2273

The Pathways Out of Poverty Program focuses on helping needy young people and adults gain a quality education. Proposals are sought that focus on improving student achievement and healthy development of young people of middle school age and above. Projects may include in-school and community-based educational programs, after-school activities, and mentoring programs. Programs designed to increase high school graduation rates are encouraged to apply. For projects serving adults, the Foundation seeks proposals to provide literacy education and GED preparation, and to offer vocational training and job placement. Most grants will be approved for one year, but a small number will receive up to three years of funding, depending on demonstrated need.
Requirements: Non-profit 501(c)3 tax-exempt organizations located in and/or provide services in the greater Washington, DC, region (defined as the District of Columbia, the counties of Arlington, Fairfax, and the city of Alexandria in Virginia, and Montgomery, and Prince George's counties in Maryland) are eligible. The Foundation uses a two-step, proposal-evaluation process. Applicant organizations are required to submit a letter of inquiry that briefly describes the proposed project's purpose, operation, target audience, timeline, costs, and anticipated impacts. Full proposals are by invitation.

Restrictions: Grants will not be made for capital or endowment programs, nor for sectarian religious purposes. Grants cannot be used for lobbying or other partisan purposes.
Geographic Focus: District of Columbia, Maryland, Virginia
Date(s) Application is Due: Feb 8
Amount of Grant: 5,000 - 25,000 USD
Contact: Marcela Brane; (202) 223-8801; fax (202) 223-8804; info@herbblock.org
Internet: http://www.herbblockfoundation.org/programs/pathways-poverty
Sponsor: Herb Block Foundation
1730 M Street NW, Suite 901
Washington, DC 20036

HCA Foundation Grants 2274
The Foundation is committed to the care and improvement of human life. Grants are made in the areas of health and well being, childhood and youth development, and the arts. Preference will be given to requests from organizations where an HCA employee volunteers or serves on the board. New applicants are asked to send a one-or two-page letter of inquiry to the Foundation, describing the proposed project, its goals and objectives and the approximate level of funding required. Foundation staff will review each request and will notify the organization as to whether the project coincides with funding priorities.
Requirements: 501(c)3 nonprofit organizations are eligible. Because the foundation focuses its giving in Middle Tennessee, all requests outside of the Nashville area should be submitted to the closest HCA facility location or division office. Organizations must have a full updated GivingMatters.com profile to be considered for funding. For more information please go to www.givingmatters.com.
Restrictions: Funding is not available for: individuals or their projects; private foundations; political activities; advertising or sponsorships of events; social events or similar fund-raising activities. The Foundation does not ordinarily support: organizations in their first three years of operation and organizations involved in research, sports, environmental, wildlife, civic and international affairs. The Foundation does not accept proposals from individual churches or schools, but will support broad faith-based initiatives consistent with it's mission and guidelines.
Geographic Focus: Tennessee
Date(s) Application is Due: Mar 12; Jun 11; Sep 10; Dec 12
Amount of Grant: 20,000 - 100,000 USD
Contact: Lois Abrams; (615) 344-2390; fax (615) 344-5722; lois.abrams@hcahealthcare.com
Internet: http://www.hcacaring.org/CustomPage.asp?guidCustomContentID=BBB7D8F2-B906-4302-A164-07643DB2582E
Sponsor: HCA Foundation
1 Park Plaza, Building 1, 4th Floor East
Nashville, TN 37203

Head Start Replacement Grantee: Colorado 2275
The Administration for Children and Families solicits applications from local public or private non-profit organizations, including faith-based organizations or local for-profit organizations, that wish to compete for funds that are available to provide Head Start services to children and families residing in the City of Alamosa, Colorado. The intent of this announcement is to provide for the continuation of services as previously provided by the former grantee, Alamosa Head Start, Inc. Funds in the amount of $987,663 annually will be available to provide Head Start program services to eligible children and their families. The former grantee was funded for a total enrollment of 161 children and families. Interested applicants should call the ACYF Operations Center at (866) 796-1591 to receive pre-application materials and additional information.
Requirements: Eligibility is limited to local public or private non-profit organizations, including faith-based organizations or local for-profit organizations, that can provide Head Start services to children and families residing in the City of Alamosa, Colorado.
Restrictions: Grantees are required to meet a non-Federal share of the project costs, in accordance with section 640(b) of the Head Start Act. Grantees must provide at least 20 percent of the total approved cost of the project.
Geographic Focus: Colorado
Date(s) Application is Due: Mar 28
Contact: Karen McKinney; (866) 796-1591; OHS@dixongroup.com
Internet: http://www.acf.hhs.gov/grants/open/HHS-2007-ACF-OHS-CH-0801.html
Sponsor: Administration for Children and Families
ACYF Operations Center, 118 Q Street NE
Washington, DC 20002

Head Start Replacement Grantee: Florida 2276
The Administration for Children and Families solicits applications from local public or private non-profit organizations, including faith-based organizations or local for-profit organizations, that wish to compete for funds that are available to provide Head Start services to children and families residing in Polk County, Florida. The intent of this announcement is to provide for the continuation of services as previously provided by the former grantee, the Polk County Opportunity Council, Inc. Funds in the amount of $6,896,580 annually will be available to provide Head Start program services to eligible children and their families. The former grantee was funded for a total enrollment of 942 children and families. Interested applicants should call the ACYF Operations Center at (866) 796-1591 to receive pre-application materials and additional information.
Requirements: Applicants should propose a design or designs that best address the needs of the proposed service area. Applicants have flexibility in determining the appropriate number of children to be served by the various program options (center-based, home-based, or combination) and program designs (hours per day, days per week, weeks per year). Preference will be given to applicants who can demonstrate efficient management of several or all of the service areas.
Restrictions: Grantees are required to meet a non-Federal share of the project costs, in accordance with section 640(b) of the Head Start Act. Grantees must provide at least 20 percent of the total approved cost of the project.
Geographic Focus: Florida
Date(s) Application is Due: Apr 13
Amount of Grant: 69,000,000 USD
Contact: Karen McKinney; (866) 796-1591; OHS@dixongroup.com
Internet: http://www.acf.hhs.gov/grants/open/HHS-2007-ACF-OHS-CH-0402.html
Sponsor: Administration for Children and Families
ACYF Operations Center, 118 Q Street NE
Washington, DC 20002

Head Start Replacement Grantee: West Virginia 2277
The Administration for Children and Families solicits applications from local public or private non-profit organizations, including faith-based organizations or local for-profit organizations, that wish to compete for funds that are available to provide Head Start services to children and families residing in Calhoun, Doddridge, Pleasants, Tyler, Wirt and/or Wood Counties, West Virginia. The intent of this announcement is to provide for the continuation of services as previously provided by the former grantee, Family Development, Inc. Applicants may apply to operate a Head Start program for one or more of the listed areas. Interested applicants should call the ACYF Operations Center at (866) 796-1591 to receive pre-application materials and additional information.
Requirements: Applicants should propose a design or designs that best address the needs of the proposed service area. Applicants have flexibility in determining the appropriate number of children to be served by the various program options (center-based, home-based, or combination) and program designs (hours per day, days per week, weeks per year). Preference will be given to applicants who can demonstrate efficient management of several or all of the service areas.
Restrictions: Grantees are required to meet a non-Federal share of the project costs, in accordance with section 640(b) of the Head Start Act. Grantees must provide at least 20 percent of the total approved cost of the project.
Geographic Focus: West Virginia
Date(s) Application is Due: Apr 23
Amount of Grant: Up to 23,000,000 USD
Contact: Karen McKinney; (866) 796-1591; OHS@dixongroup.com
Internet: http://www.acf.hhs.gov/grants/open/HHS-2007-ACF-OHS-CH-0303.html
Sponsor: Administration for Children and Families
ACYF Operations Center, 118 Q Street NE
Washington, DC 20002

Health Canada National Seniors Independence Program Grants 2278
The program is intended to provide financial assistance to Canadian seniors for projects that contribute to improving their health, well-being, and independence and to enhancing their quality of life. Particular attention will be given to projects that address the needs of women seniors, seniors living in rural and remote areas, and seniors who are less advantaged due to life circumstances. The program will provide funds for projects that support action leading to a new or improved resource or organization; test the value or feasibility of new program models; improve the quality and availability of information on particular subjects; and/or develop and strengthen the knowledge, skills, and abilities of seniors or people working with seniors. Groups and organizations interested in submitting an application should contact the appropriate regional office where program representatives are available to meet with groups to discuss their ideas and assist in the preparation of an application. Lists of regional offices are available from the national office.
Requirements: Proposals may be submitted by voluntary, nongovernmental, nonprofit groups and organizations; these may include health or social service agencies, higher educational institutions, professional associations, and other parapublic organizations.
Restrictions: Individuals, for-profit groups, and government departments are not eligible for funding.
Geographic Focus: All States, Canada
Contact: Stephanie Wilson, (613) 954-8549; Stephanie_Wilson@hc-sc.gc.ca
Internet: http://www.hc-sc.gc.ca
Sponsor: Health Canada
Postal Locator 1912
Ottawa, ON K1A 1B4 Canada

Healthcare Foundation for Orange County Grants 2279
The foundation's mission is to improve the health of the neediest and most underserved residents of Orange County, with particular emphasis on central Orange County. The foundation will address ways of improving the health of residents by advancing access to health information, prevention, and basic health care. Grantmaking is divided among initiatives that support nonprofit hospital working with community-based organizations (Partners for Health); grants directly to community-based organizations (Healthy Orange County); and increased understanding of community needs, and collaborative granting strategies (coalition projects.)
Requirements: California 501(c)3 nonprofit organizations in Orange County that administer health services consistent with the foundation's goals of providing aid to uninsured, poor families are eligible. Eighty-two percent of support goes to or through qualified nonprofit hospitals. Government agencies also are eligible.
Restrictions: Grants generally are not awarded for annual fund drives, building campaigns, major equipment, or biomedical research. Activities that exclusively benefit the members of a religious or fraternal organization are not funded.
Geographic Focus: California
Amount of Grant: Up to 10,000 USD

Contact: William B. Stannard; (714) 245-1650; fax (714) 245-1653; dflander@hfoc.org
Internet: http://www.hfoc.org/giving/
Sponsor: Healthcare Foundation for Orange County
1450 N Tustin Avenue, Suite 103
Santa Ana, CA 92705-8641

Healthcare Foundation of New Jersey Grants 2280

The Foundation's funding priorities are the vulnerable populations of the greater Newark New Jersey community; the emergent health needs of serving at-risk individuals and families in the MetroWest Jewish community; and clinical research/medical education initiatives that significantly and directly impact these populations. The Foundation seeks grant proposals that promise innovation and change or a significant enhancement of services. Proposals are accepted on a rolling basis throughout the calendar year. Proposal submission instructions are available online.
Requirements: Nonprofit organizations in the Greater Newark area are eligible to apply. The Foundation strongly suggests that application documents be submitted electronically.
Restrictions: Grants are made only to private nonprofit organizations that have tax-exempt status under Section 501(c)3 of the Internal Revenue Code and that are not private foundations. The Foundation does not make grants to individuals or government agencies. The Foundation does not typically fund the following: organizations outside of Essex, Morris or Union County, New Jersey; programs not related to health care; direct support of an individual's healthcare needs; fundraising events or endowment campaigns; advertising campaigns; lobbying; or scholarships.
Geographic Focus: New Jersey
Contact: Program Contact; (973) 921-1210; fax (973) 921-1274; info@hfnj.org
Internet: http://www.hfnj.org
Sponsor: Healthcare Foundation of New Jersey
60 East Willow Street, 2nd Floor
Millburn, NJ 07041

Health Foundation of Greater Cincinnati Grants 2281

The foundation awards grants to programs and activities that improve health in Cincinnati and 20 surrounding counties in Ohio, Kentucky, and Indiana. Health is broadly defined to include social, behavioral, environmental, and other dimensions beyond the absence of illness. Grant making is focused on strengthening primary care providers to the poor; school-based child health interventions in K-8 school settings; substance abuse; and severe mental illness. Grants also are awarded in response to requests from organizations seeking funds to support a broad range of health-related needs in the community. The Health Foundation of Greater Cincinnati considers projects for funding in three ways: through Requests for Proposals (RFPs), through invitations to submit proposals, and through grantee-initiated requests. In any case, proposals are considered using the same eligibility requirements and proposal evaluation criteria. For more information about the types of proposals, see the Foundations website or call the Grant Manager.
Requirements: 501(c)3 nonprofits in Adams, Brown, Butler, Clermont, Clington, Hamilton, Highland, and Warren Counties in Ohio; Boone, Bracken, Campbell, Gallatin, Grant, Kenton, and Pendleton Counties in Kentucky; and Dearborn, Franklin, Ohio, Ripley, and Switzerland Counties in Indiana are eligible.
Restrictions: The foundation does not normally fund capital campaigns, annual fundraising campaigns, endowments, event sponsorships, clinical research, scholarships, routine operational costs, or direct financial subsidy of health services to individuals or groups.
Geographic Focus: Indiana, Kentucky, Ohio
Contact: Shelly Stolarczyk-George; (513) 458-6619; sstolarczyk@healthfoundation.org
Internet: http://www.healthfoundation.org/grants
Sponsor: Health Foundation of Greater Cincinnati
3805 Edwards Road, Suite 500
Cincinnati, OH 45209-1948

Health Foundation of Greater Indianapolis Grants 2282

The foundation promotes health care for children, youth, and families in Marion County, IN, and seven contiguous Indiana counties. Programs of interest include school-based health, adolescent health, and HIV/AIDS Grants also are awarded to support the development of health careers and to promote cooperative effort between health professionals. Types of support include general operations, building/renovations, equipment, program/project development, conferences and seminars, seed money, technical assistance, and matching funds. Prior to submitting a proposal, contact Stephen L. Everett, Vice President of Programs, to determine if your program and proposal matches The Health Foundation of Greater Indianapolis' funding priorities and application guidelines.
Requirements: Grants are awarded to neighborhood-based service centers in Indiana's Marion County and the seven contiguous counties of Boone, Hamilton, Hancock, Hendricks, Johnson, Morgan and Shelby. Applicants must be a 501(c)3 group, organization or agency that provides health-related programs or services.
Restrictions: Grants will not be provided for: individuals; sectarian religious organizations; research projects; purchase of advertising or tickets to events; production and design of educational materials already available; endowments; short or long term loans or payment of financial obligations.
Geographic Focus: Indiana
Amount of Grant: 10,000 - 100,000 USD
Contact: Stephen Everett; (317) 630-1805; fax (317) 630-1806; severett@thfgi.org
Internet: http://www.thfgi.org
Sponsor: Health Foundation of Greater Indianapolis
429 East Vermont Street, Suite 300
Indianapolis, IN 46202

Health Foundation of Southern Florida Responsive Grants 2283

The foundation awards Responsive Grants through two grant cycles per year. With exceptions, the foundation focuses on providing one to three year grants that do not exceed $300,000 annually. The majority of grants are funded in the $50,000 to $150,000 range over one or two years. Funding is provided in four categories: Project Planning; Health Services; Organizational Capacity Building and Health System/Health Policy Development.
Requirements: Though the foundation welcomes proposal applications anytime, the applications are reviewed on a semi-annual basis. Applicant organizations must be tax-exempt nonprofit under section 501(c)3 of the Internal Revenue Code or a local or state governmental agency. The project must serve exclusively the residents of Broward, Miami-Dade and/or Monroe counties. Initially, a preliminary proposal is required (see the sponsor's website for specific details). If approved, the sponsor will then invite a full proposal. Download the sponsor's grant guide from the website.
Restrictions: The foundation does not fund: Biomedical research or other research that will not impact local residents within the immediate future (1-3 years) or that does not have a direct application to implementing a community-driven health intervention; Capital campaigns of over $1 million (versus grants toward specific health-related equipment or the 'build out' of a specific health-focused space); Secondary and tertiary services (versus preventive and primary medical, oral and behavioral health care services); Health promotion and/or health care with a high per capita cost (this figure will vary depending upon the type of intervention, but over $1,000 per person/year cost may be a rule of thumb); Service expansion or new projects without viable sustainability (unable to reach sustainability without the foundation's resources within a four-year period).
Geographic Focus: Florida
Date(s) Application is Due: Mar 13; Apr 24
Contact: Eliane Morales, (305) 374-7200; fax (305) 374-7003; emorales@hfsf.org
Internet: http://www.hfsf.org/ORIGHTML/responsive.html
Sponsor: Health Foundation of South Florida
2 South Biscayne Boulevard
Miami, FL 33131

Hearst Foundations Culture Grants 2284

The Hearst Foundations fund non-profit organizations working in the fields of culture, education, health, and social services. The Foundations have two offices, one in New York which manages funding for non-profits headquartered east of the Mississippi River and one in San Francisco which manages funding for non-profits to the west. About 80% of the Foundations' total funding goes to prior grantees; the Foundations receive approximately 1,200 grant requests annually. The Foundations' cultural funding comprises 25% of their total giving; 60% of the Foundations' cultural funding goes to organizations having budgets over ten-million dollars. In the area of culture, the Foundations look for institutions that offer meaningful programs in the arts and sciences. Preference is given to artist development and training, arts-education programs that address the lack of arts programming in K-12 curricula, and science-education programs that focus on developing academic pathways in science, technology, engineering, and math. Requests which enable engagement by young people and which create a lasting impression are given higher priority. The Foundations provide program, capital, and, on a limited basis, general and endowment support. Requests are accepted year round. These must be submitted via the Foundations' online application portal. Each request goes through an evaluation process that generally spans four to six weeks. The Foundations conduct a site visit of semi-finalists and may also consult with experts in a given field. Applicants will receive an email confirmation of receipt of submission and can follow the status of their request through the online system. Instructions for using the system, guidelines (in the form of an FAQ), and the link to the Foundations' online portal are at the Foundations' website.
Requirements: Grants are made only to 501(c)3 organizations. Well-established nonprofits that primarily serve large demographic and/or geographic constituencies are preferred. Within those, the Foundations identify organizations which achieve truly differentiated results relative to other organizations making similar efforts for similar populations. The Foundations also look for evidence of sustainability beyond their support.
Restrictions: Organizations must wait one year from the date of their notice of decline before the Foundations will consider another request. Grantees must wait a minimum of three years from their grant award date before the Foundations will consider another request. The Foundations do not fund individuals or the following types of requests: those from organizations operating outside the United States; those from organizations with operating budgets under one million dollars; those from organizations involved in publishing, radio, film, or television; those from local chapters of organizations; those from organizations lacking demonstrable long-term impact on populations served; requests to fund tours, conferences, workshops, or seminars; requests to fund advocacy or public-policy research; requests to fund special events, tickets, tables, or advertising for fundraising events; requests for seed money or to fund start-up projects; and request to fund program-related investments.
Geographic Focus: All States
Contact: Mason Granger; (212) 649-3750; fax (212) 586-1917; hearst.ny@hearstfdn.org
Internet: http://www.hearstfdn.org/funding-priorities/
Sponsor: Hearst Foundations
300 West 57th Street, 26th Floor
New York, NY 10019-3741

Hearst Foundations Social Service Grants 2285

The Hearst Foundations fund non-profit organizations working in the fields of culture, education, health, and social service. The Foundations have two offices, one in New York which manages funding for non-profits headquartered east of the Mississippi River and one in San Francisco which manages funding for non-profits to the west. About 80% of the Foundations' total funding goes to prior grantees; the Foundations receive approximately 1,200 grant requests annually. The Foundations' social-service funding comprises 15% of

their total giving; 60% of the Foundations' social-service giving goes to organizations having budgets over five-million dollars. In the area of social service, the Foundations fund direct-service organizations that tackle the roots of chronic poverty by applying effective solutions to the most challenging social and economic problems. Preference is given to affordable-housing, job-creation and job-training, literacy, and youth-development programs. In limited cases, the Foundations fund organizations focusing on domestic abuse, food delivery and food banks, sexual abuse, and substance abuse. The Foundations fund requests for program, capital, and general support. Requests are accepted year round. These must be submitted via the Foundations' online application portal. Each request goes through an evaluation process that generally spans four to six weeks. The Foundations conduct a site visit of semi-finalists and may also consult with experts in a given field. Applicants will receive an email confirmation of receipt of submission and can follow the status of their request through the online system. Instructions for using the system, guidelines (in the form of an FAQ), and the link to the Foundations' online portal are at the Foundations' website.
Requirements: Grants are made only to 501(c)3 organizations. Initiatives of an organization's national headquarters are preferred over those of local chapters. The Foundations give high priority to programs that have proven successful in facilitating economic independence and in strengthening families and that have the potential to scale productive practices in order to reach more people in need.
Restrictions: Organizations must wait one year from the date of their notice of decline before the Foundations will consider another request. Grantees must wait a minimum of three years from their grant award date before the Foundations will consider another request. The Foundations do not fund individuals or the following types of requests: those from organizations operating outside the United States; those from organizations with operating budgets under one million dollars; those from organizations involved in publishing, radio, film, or television; those from organizations lacking demonstrable long-term impact on populations served; requests to fund tours, conferences, workshops, or seminars; requests to fund advocacy or public-policy research; requests to fund special events, tickets, tables, or advertising for fundraising events; requests for seed money or to fund start-up projects; and request to fund program-related investments.
Geographic Focus: All States
Amount of Grant: Up to 100,000 USD
Contact: Mason Granger; (212) 649-3750; fax (212) 586-1917; hearst.ny@hearstfdn.org
Internet: http://www.hearstfdn.org/funding-priorities/
Sponsor: Hearst Foundations
300 West 57th Street, 26th Floor
New York, NY 10019-3741

Heartland Arts Fund 2286
The Fund supports the touring of professional performing artists specializing in the fine arts of dance, theater, music, youth and family entertainment, and other meaningful performing arts forms appropriate for communities throughout Arts Midwest's nine-state region. These engagements include public performances and in-depth educational activities reaching audiences that lack access to the performing arts. Performing Arts Fund grants are applied for by and made directly to presenting organizations in the Fund's nine-state region. Application information is available online.
Requirements: Eligible applicants must be a nonprofit 501(c)3 organization or a unit of a state, local, or tribal government located in Illinois, Indiana, Iowa, Michigan, Minnesota, North Dakota, Ohio, South Dakota, or Wisconsin.
Restrictions: Artists appearing as part of benefits or fundraisers are not eligible for funding. Producing arts organizations, such as orchestras and theater and opera companies, may not request fee support for guest artists appearing as part of the organization's performances. Engagements of professional performing artists/ensembles from the same state as the applicant are not supported.
Geographic Focus: Illinois, Indiana, Iowa, Michigan, Minnesota, North Dakota, Ohio, South Dakota, Wisconsin
Date(s) Application is Due: Mar 24
Contact: Christy Dickinson; (612) 238-8019; performingartsfund@artsmidwest.org
Internet: http://www.artsmidwest.org/programs/performing_arts.asp
Sponsor: Arts Midwest
2908 Hennepin Avenue, Suite 200
Minneapolis, MN 55408

Hedco Foundation Grants 2287
Incorporated in 1972 in California, the Hedco Foundation gives predominantly to qualified educational and health institutions, support is also available for social services. Types of support including: building/renovation; equipment; land acquisition and; matching/challenge grants.
Requirements: 501(c)3 nonprofit organizations are eligible.
Restrictions: No grants to: individuals, or for general support, operating budgets, endowment funds, scholarships, fellowships, special projects, research, publications, or conferences; no loans.
Geographic Focus: California
Contact: Mary Goriup, Manager; (925) 743-0257
Sponsor: Hedco Foundation
P.O. Box 339
Danville, CA 94526-0339

Heifer Educational Fund Grants for Principals 2288
The Strolling of the Heifer Foundation funds start up grants to underwrite school-wide projects pilot that educate the public about how to 'Live Green!' Such projects will be showcased in the Strolling of the Heifers Annual Parade or at the Dairy Fest following the parade. The $1,000 in grant money will cover the school's development of a pilot project that involves the entire school in creating a parade float, educational exhibit or theatrical performance that educates the public about the environmental imperative of our time how essential it is for all us to 'Live Green!' Funding also can be used to create a float or 'act' for the parade that encourages the public to live in harmony with Mother Earth. In addition, schools may opt to stage a performance at the Children's Entertainment Tent during the Dairy Fest. Schools selected to receive funding for pilot projects in February will be eligible to receive up to $2,000 in additional funding in the fall. This second round of grant funding will enable schools to delve more deeply in to the green theme they opt to explore.
Requirements: All projects should involve a local farmer in the development of a year-long exploration or analysis on how to sustain local agriculture or to 'Live Green!', 'Eat Green!' and/or 'Live Clean!'. Projects should raise awareness about how the community can reduce waste, save energy and/or serve as an example to stimulate the public to do so. To apply, principals should submit a letter of intent by February 22. The letter should describe the school's project, a description of how the school plans to visually render the project as part of the Annual Strolling of the Heifers Parade or at the Dairy Fest following the parade. Specifics regarding how the $1,000 in grant money for the pilot project will be spent must be included in the letter. (Money can be spent on materials, honoraria to farmers and teachers, and any other costs that are essential to the project.) Proposals for additional funding will be due by September 1.
Restrictions: Honoraria not to exceed $50 per farmer or teacher. Grant money will only be awarded to non-profit organizations or schools.
Geographic Focus: Vermont
Date(s) Application is Due: Sep 1
Amount of Grant: Up to 2,000 USD
Contact: Orly Munzing, Executive Director; (802) 258-9177; orly@svcable.net
Internet: http://www.strollingoftheheifers.org
Sponsor: Strolling of the Heifers Foundation
105 Partridge Road
East Dummerston, VT 05346

Heifer Educational Fund Grants for Teachers 2289
The Strolling of the Heifers Foundation funds opportunities for school children in the Windham County area (VT) to learn more about agriculture and the many ways that small farms contribute to the quality of life. Grants enable schools to partners with a farmer on school projects that raise awareness about the role that farming and agriculture play in the community.
Requirements: Proposed projects that will be considered should have the following: 1) Include farmers as partners by making visits to farms, inviting farmers into the classroom, etc; 2) Raise students' agricultural awareness about what farmers do, the challenges they face, and their role in the community; 3) Are achievable without undue strain on either teachers or farmers and naturally fit into participants' educational and agricultural circumstances.
Restrictions: Limited to the schools located in the Windham County area of Vermont.
Geographic Focus: Vermont
Date(s) Application is Due: Mar 5
Amount of Grant: Up to 1,000 USD
Contact: Orly Munzing, Executive Director; (802) 258-9177; orly@svcable.net
Internet: http://www.strollingoftheheifers.org
Sponsor: Strolling of the Heifers Foundation
105 Partridge Road
East Dummerston, VT 05346

Heineman Foundation for Research, Educ, Charitable and Scientific Purposes 2290
The purpose of the Heineman Foundation is to provide seed money to start-up projects and new projects within existing organizations for a maximum of three to five years. Preference will be given to organizations that we have not previously funded. The average range of our donations is $20,000.00 to $50,000.00, per annum. An organization must have 501(c)3 status and upload copies of corresponding IRS documents to the online application form in order for the application to be considered. The Foundation's general areas of interest are the following (in no particular order): programs that enable economically challenged women to enter and remain in the workplace; on site day care centers for women in the workplace; job training programs for women; language and leadership skills for women; environmental research that will help prevent, reduce and/or eliminate water degradation; music as education and preserver of culture; research into prevention of and treatment for childhood illnesses; programs that enable youth to think, create and communicate effectively; and programs that support and promote high achievement in music, science, and literature. Applications/proposals must be submitted online no later than September 1st.
Geographic Focus: All States
Date(s) Application is Due: Sep 1
Contact: Simon Rose, President; (212) 493-8000; info@heinemanfoundation.org
Internet: http://www.heinemanfoundation.org/guidelines
Sponsor: Heineman Foundation
140 Broadway
New York, NY 10005-1108

Heinz Endowments Grants 2291
The endowments support efforts to make southwestern Pennsylvania a premier place to live and work, a center of learning and educational excellence, and a home to diversity and inclusion. Committed to helping its region thrive as a whole community—economically, ecologically, educationally and culturally—the foundation works within Pennsylvania and elsewhere in the nation to develop solutions to challenges that are national and even international in scope. Fields of emphasis include arts and culture; children, youth and families; economic opportunity; education; the environment; and innovation economy. The two-step application process begins with submitting an online letter of inquiry (LoI) available at the Heinz website. The second step is a formal application process for those requests that are determined to meet the endowments' basic funding criteria. Information for submission of an LOI is available online.

Requirements: Grants are limited to 501(c)3 nonprofit organizations and 509(a) public charities in Pennsylvania and generally to the southwestern Pennsylvania region.
Restrictions: Individuals and for-profit organizations are not eligible.
Geographic Focus: Pennsylvania
Date(s) Application is Due: Feb 1; Aug 1
Contact: Program Contact; (412) 281-5777; fax (412) 281-5788
Internet: http://www.heinz.org/programs.aspx
Sponsor: Heinz Endowments
30 Dominion Tower, 625 Liberty Avenue
Pittsburgh, PA 15222-3115

Helena Rubinstein Foundation Grants 2292

The Foundation supports programs in education, community services, arts/arts in education, and health with emphasis on projects which benefit women and children. Grants are primarily targeted to organizations in New York City. Although general operating grants are made, the Foundation prefers to support specific programs. Grant proposals are accepted throughout the year. There is no formal application form; however, the New York Common Application Form may be used. Organizations seeking funds are asked not to make telephone inquiries, but to submit a brief letter outlining the project.
Requirements: U.S. nonprofit organizations are eligible.
Restrictions: Support is not offered to individuals, or for film or video projects. Grants are rarely made to endowment funds and capital campaigns. The foundation does not make loans and cannot provide emergency funds. Funding of new proposals is limited by ongoing commitments and fiscal constraints.
Geographic Focus: New York
Contact: Diane Moss, President; (212) 750-7310
Internet: http://www.helenarubinsteinfdn.org/guide.html
Sponsor: Helena Rubinstein Foundation
477 Madison Avenue, 7th Floor
New York, NY 10022-5802

Helen Bader Foundation Grants 2293

Throughout her life, Helen Bader sought to help others. She played many roles - student, mother, businesswoman, and social worker - believing that everyone should have the opportunity to reach their fullest potential. Growing up in the railroad town of Aberdeen, South Dakota, Helen learned the value of hard work and self-reliance. The Great Depression and the sacrifices of World War II also taught her the importance of reaching out to those in need. Helen attended Downer College in Milwaukee, earning a degree in botany. She married Alfred Bader, a chemist from Austria, and together they started a family and created a business, the Aldrich Chemical Company. From the 1950s to the 1970s, their hard work helped build one of Wisconsin's most successful start-up enterprises of the era. The Baders' eventual divorce led Helen to again become self-reliant. She subsequently finished her Master of Social Work at the University of Wisconsin-Milwaukee. While doing her field work with the Legal Aid Society of Milwaukee, Helen met and helped many people in need, including single mothers and adults with mental illness. In the process, she gained a deeper appreciation for their everyday struggles. After graduation, she worked at the Milwaukee Jewish Home, where working with older adults brought home the many issues of aging. At a time when Alzheimer's disease was almost a complete mystery, she helped open the resident' minds and hearts through dance and music. Helen felt that the residents' quality of life depended upon the small details, so she was happy to run errands or escort them to the symphony. She found herself touched by the arts and studied the violin and guitar at the Wisconsin Conservatory of Music. Helen eventually faced cancer. As the illness began to sap her physical strength, she shared a wish with her family: to continue to aid those in need. She died in 1989. After her death, patterns of Helen's quiet style of philanthropy became more apparent. When she had come across an organization that impressed her, she would just pull out her checkbook without a lot of fanfare. In her name, the Helen Bader Foundation (HBF) supports worthy organizations working in key areas affecting the quality of life in Milwaukee, the state of Wisconsin, and Israel. The foundation also seeks to inspire the generosity in others, as every individual can make a difference through gifts of time, talent, and resources. The foundation will consider multiple-year requests with 24 or 36 month terms. Multi-year grants are subject to annual review before funds for subsequent years are released. The application deadline for the online preliminary proposal is January 5. The application deadline for organizations invited to complete a full proposal is February 2. The link to the online application system is available at the grant website. Application deadlines may vary from year to year. Prospective applicants are encouraged to visit the grant website to verify current deadline dates.
Requirements: Grants are awarded for projects consistent with one or more of the Helen Bader Foundation's program areas: Alzheimer's and aging (national in scope, with priority given to Wisconsin); economic development (restricted to the city of Milwaukee); community partnerships for youth (restricted to the city of Milwaukee); community initiatives (restricted to greater Milwaukee); arts (restricted to the city of Milwaukee); and directed grants and initiatives such as aid and support to Israel (for which proposals must be staff-solicited). Grants are given only to U.S. organizations which are tax exempt under Section 501(c)3 of the Internal Revenue Code or to government entities; grants will only be approved for foreign entities which meet specific charitable status requirements.
Restrictions: The Foundation does not provide direct support for individuals, such as individual scholarships.
Geographic Focus: All States, All Countries
Date(s) Application is Due: Jan 5; Feb 25
Contact: Tamara Hogans; (414) 224-6464; fax (414) 224-1441; tammy@hbf.org
Internet: http://www.hbf.org/apply.htm
Sponsor: Helen Bader Foundation
233 North Water Street, Fourth Floor
Milwaukee, WI 53202

Helen Gertrude Sparks Charitable Trust Grants 2294

Helen Sparks was born in Fort Worth, TX but went to college in the East. After graduation she returned to Fort Worth where she worked with the Fort Worth Little Theater. A cultured woman, she was interested in local artists and supported them by commissioning works. She also enjoyed literature and needlepoint. The Helen Gertrude Sparks Charitable Trust made its first distributions in 1971, and was created to benefit charitable organizations focused on: the elderly; those who are disabled in any way; children who are disabled, orphaned or disadvantaged; the arts, including performing and nonperforming arts; and education. This trust makes approximately 2-3 awards each year and grants are typically between $5,000 and $15,000. Applicants must apply online at the grant website. Applicants are strongly encouraged to do the following before applying: review the downloadable state application procedures for additional helpful information and clarifications; review the downloadable online-application guidelines at the grant website; review the trust's funding history (link is available from the grant website); review the online application questions in advance; and review the list of required attachments. These will generally include: a list of board members, financial statements (audited, reviewed, or compiled by independent auditor); an organization summary; a list of other funding sources; an IRS Determination letter; and other required documents. All attachments must be uploaded in the online application as PDF, Word, or Excel files. The Helen Gertrude Sparks Charitable Trust application deadline is 11:59 p.m. on September 30.
Requirements: Applicants must have 501(c)3 tax-exempt status.
Restrictions: A preference will be shown for organizations which do not receive the predominate portion of their funds from government sources. The trust does not support requests from individuals, organizations attempting to influence policy through direct lobbying, or any political campaigns.
Geographic Focus: Texas
Date(s) Application is Due: Sep 30
Amount of Grant: 5,000 - 15,000 USD
Contact: Mark J. Smith; (817) 390-6028; tx.philanthropic@baml.com
Internet: https://www.bankofamerica.com/philanthropic/fn_search.action
Sponsor: Helen Gertrude Sparks Charitable Trust
500 West 7th Street, 15th Floor, TX1-497-15-08
Fort Worth, TX 76102-4700

Helen Irwin Littauer Educational Trust Grants 2295

Mrs. Littauer was born in Fort Worth, Texas and was a descendant of the Cetti family, a prominent family in Fort Worth, Texas. She earned a degree in journalism and worked in New York as an editor. In 1952, she moved to Connecticut and became an active community volunteer and was involved in city government. As a result of her passion for teaching, she also worked with troubled youth. She was honored with numerous awards for her civic endeavors. Mrs. Littauer established the Educational Trust in 1969 and remained involved in grant decisions until her death in 1989. The trust is particularly interested in, but not limited to charitable organizations that focus on: scholarships that enable needy, but worthy boys and girls and young adults to attend school, college, or university, with a particular emphasis on making scholarships available for attending schools of journalism; promotion of art, education, and good citizenship; alleviating human suffering; medical care and treatment for all needy persons, including hospitals and clinics; providing care, education, recreation and/or physical training for needy, orphaned or disabled children; providing care of needy persons who are sick, aged or disabled; and improvement of living and working conditions of all persons. Applicants must apply online at the grant website. Applicants are strongly encouraged to do the following before applying: review the downloadable state application procedures for additional helpful information and clarifications; review the downloadable online-application guidelines at the grant website; review the trust's funding history (link is available from the grant website); review the online application questions in advance; and review the list of required attachments. These will generally include: a list of board members, financial statements (audited, reviewed, or compiled by independent auditor); an organization summary; a list of other funding sources; an IRS Determination letter; and other required documents. All attachments must be uploaded in the online application as PDF, Word, or Excel files. The Helen Irwin Littauer Educational Trust has bi-annual application deadlines of March 31 and September 30. Applications must be submitted by 11:59 p.m. on the deadline dates.
Requirements: Applicants must have 501(c)3 tax-exempt status.
Restrictions: The trust considers requests primarily from charitable organizations that provide services to Tarrant County. The trust does not support requests from individuals, organizations attempting to influence policy through direct lobbying, or any political campaigns.
Geographic Focus: All States
Date(s) Application is Due: Mar 31; Sep 30
Amount of Grant: 1,000 - 25,000 USD
Contact: Mark J. Smith; (817) 390-6028; tx.philanthropic@baml.com
Internet: https://www.bankofamerica.com/philanthropic/fn_search.action
Sponsor: Helen Irwin Littauer Educational Trust
500 West 7th Street, 15th Floor, TX1-497-15-08
Fort Worth, TX 76012-4700

Helen K. and Arthur E. Johnson Foundation Grants 2296

The foundation makes grants to a wide variety of nonprofit organizations in an attempt to solve community problems and enrich the quality of life in Colorado in the following areas: education, youth, health, community and social services, civic and cultural, and senior citizens. Requests are welcomed throughout the year. However, to be considered at the next board meeting, complete written proposals must be received by the listed application deadline dates. Proposal submission information is available online.
Requirements: IRS 501(c)3 organizations serving Colorado residents may apply.
Restrictions: Funding is not available for: loans or fund endowments; individuals; conferences; scholarships to individuals; multiple year grants; fundraising dinners or special events. The

Foundation does not support organizations whose primary purpose is to influence (directly or indirectly) the legislative or judicial process in any manner or for any cause. In addition, the Foundation will not consider grant requests that pass through the nominal grant recipient to another organization.
Geographic Focus: Colorado
Date(s) Application is Due: Jan 1; Apr 1; Jul 1; Oct 1
Contact: John H. Alexander; (800) 232-9931 or (303) 861-4127; info@johnsonfoundation.org
Internet: http://www.johnsonfoundation.org
Sponsor: Helen K. and Arthur E. Johnson Foundation
1700 Broadway, Suite 1100
Denver, CO 80290-1718

Helen Pumphrey Denit Charitable Trust Grants 2297

The Helen Pumphrey Denit Trust for Charitable and Educational Purposes was established in 1988 to support charitable organizations that promote quality education, culture, human service, health service and arts opportunities. The grants are primarily made to organizations in the Baltimore region. Special consideration is given to the following three organizations: Montgomery General Hospital in Onley, Maryland; The George Washington University in Washington, D.C; and The Wesley Theological Seminary in Washington, D.C. Grants for capital and program support are encouraged. Requests for general operating support will be received, but they will be given lower priority than other grants that have more specific purposes. Grants are primarily one year in duration. On occasion, multi-year grants will be awarded. Applicants must apply online at the grant website. Applicants are strongly encouraged to do the following before applying: review the downloadable state application procedures for additional helpful information and clarifications; review the downloadable online-application guidelines at the grant website; review the trust's funding history (link is available from the grant website); review the online application questions in advance; and review the list of required attachments. These will generally include: a list of board members, financial statements (audited, reviewed, or compiled by independent auditor); an organization summary; a list of other funding sources; an IRS Determination letter; and other required documents. All attachments must be uploaded in the online application as PDF, Word, or Excel files. The Helen Pumphrey Denit Trust has an application deadline of 11:59 p.m. on February 1. The applicants will be notified of grant decisions by June 30.
Requirements: Applicants must have 501(c)3 tax-exempt status and serve residents of Baltimore and surrounding communities.
Restrictions: The trust does not support requests from individuals, organizations attempting to influence policy through direct lobbying, or any political campaigns.
Geographic Focus: Maryland
Date(s) Application is Due: Feb 1
Contact: Sarah Kay, Vice President; (804) 788-2673; sarah.kay@baml.com
Internet: https://www.bankofamerica.com/philanthropic/fn_search.action
Sponsor: Helen Pumphrey Denit Charitable Trust
1111 E. Main Street, VA2-300-12-92
Richmond, VA 23219

Helen S. Boylan Foundation Grants 2298

The Helen S Boylan Foundation is a private family foundation established in 1982 to continue the family tradition of commitment to enhancing the quality of life of the community through grants to qualified charitable organizations. In carrying out its mission, the Foundation considers a wide range of proposals within the following areas: arts, education, health, human services, environment, and public interest. Generally, grants are limited to projects that benefit the citizens of Jasper County, Missouri, Smith County, Texas and, Kansas City, Metropolitan area. Occasionally, projects that benefit the state of Missouri as a whole may be considered as well. The Foundation prefers to support proposals for new initiatives, special projects, expansion of current programs, capital improvements or building renovations. Grants from the Foundation are usually awarded for one year only. For projects in those areas in which the Foundation has a special interest, requests for multi-year funding and general operating support may be considered. The Board of Directors meet four times a year to consider grant requests. Applications must be received by March 31, June 30, September 30 or December 31 to be acted upon at the following meeting.
Requirements: IRS 501(c)3 nonprofit organizations operating in the Carthage, Kansas City Metro and Lindale Texas area are eligible to apply for funding. Application form is available online at the Foundation's website.
Restrictions: No support for political organizations or religious activities. No grants to individuals, or for annual campaigns or endowments.
Geographic Focus: Missouri, Texas
Date(s) Application is Due: Mar 31; Jun 30; Sep 30; Dec 31
Contact: James R. Spradling; (417) 358-4033; fax (417) 358-5937; spradlinglaw@hotmail.com
Internet: http://www.boylanfoundation.org/
Sponsor: Helen S. Boylan Foundation
320 Grant Street, P.O. Box 731
Carthage, MO 64836

Helen Steiner Rice Foundation Grants 2299

The Foundation awards grants to worthy charitable programs that assist the needy and the elderly. Essential objectives for grant consideration are: basic necessities and human needs for the poor and elderly; preference for meeting the immediate needs of the poor; and innovative approaches. Organizations in the Greater Cincinnati area should use the contact information for Cincinnati. Organizations in Lorain County should *Contact:* Linda Weaver, Community Foundation Center of Lorain County, (440) 277-0142, Ext. 23. Application forms and instructions are available online.
Requirements: Nonprofit organizations in the greater Cincinnati area and Lorain, OH, may submit grant applications.
Restrictions: Funding is not available for building or endowment programs, direct gifts to individuals, or capital fund drives.
Geographic Focus: Ohio
Date(s) Application is Due: Jul 1
Contact: James D. Huizenga, Director; (513) 241-2880; fax (513) 768-6122; huizengai@greatercincinnatifdn.org or hrice@cincymuseum.org
Internet: http://www.helensteinerrice.com/grants.html
Sponsor: Helen Suiteiner Rice Foundation
200 West Fourth Street
Cincinnati, OH 45202-2602

Helen V. Brach Foundation Grants 2300

Established in 1974 in Illinois by the wife of Frank Brach, principal owner of the E.J. Brach and Sons Candy Company of Chicago, the foundation operates to prevent cruelty to animals or to children; for religious, charitable, scientific, literary, and education purposes; and for public safety testing through support of Midwest 501(c)3 tax-exempt organizations carrying out programs and activities in these areas. Brach provides grants nationally and has wide-ranging interests. For example, it supports homeless and women's emergency shelters, teen pregnancy prevention programs, parenting education, summer school for disadvantaged children, job training for welfare mothers, orphanages, and scholarships for economically disadvantaged students. Types of support include annual campaigns, building construction and renovation, equipment, general operating support, publications, research, and special projects. The foundation ordinarily does not make multi-year grants or commitments. Applicants are required to complete in full a brief application form, which may be obtained from the office. The board of directors gives final consideration to all applications received in a given year at the board's meeting, which is usually held in March.
Requirements: Although 501(c)3 nonprofits from across the nation are eligible, giving is primarily made in the Midwest, as well as California, Massachusetts, Ohio, Pennsylvania, and South Carolina.
Restrictions: Grants are not made to individuals or to organizations outside the United States. Typically grants are not made in excess of 10 percent of a group's operating budget, which automatically excludes start-up grants.
Geographic Focus: All States
Date(s) Application is Due: Dec 31
Contact: John P. Hagnell, Associate Director; (312) 372-4417; fax (312) 372-0290
Sponsor: Helen V. Brach Foundation
55 W Wacker Drive, Suite 701
Chicago, IL 60601-1609

Help America Foundation Grants 2301

The Foundation provides volunteers and financial aid to organizations that support the poor and underpriviledged, needy and/or homeless Americans including men, women, children, and veterans of war. The Foundation also supports the families of active military personnel called to duty. The application is available at the Foundation website.
Requirements: To qualify for funds, the organization must be a Section 501(c)3 charitable organization, and complete the online general purpose application with detailed information, including, but not limited to: organizational business detail including contact information; description of plans for fund usage; amount requested; geographic area to be served; potential beneficiaries; organization purpose; tax-exempt status; and applicable financial information.
Geographic Focus: All States
Contact: Linda Curry; (708) 597-1085; fax (708) 597-1435; dccurry@athome.com
Internet: http://www.helpamericafoundation.org/howtoapply/index.htm
Sponsor: Help America Foundation
5625 West 115th Street
Alsip, IL 60803

Hendricks County Community Foundation Grants 2302

The Hendricks County Community Foundation Grants provide funding for organizations or charitable projects that serve in the following program areas: arts and culture; community development; education; environment; health and human services; and youth. These grants enable organizations to provide effective programs and respond to needs of people in the Hendricks County community.
Requirements: A letter of intent should be submitted to the organization between December 1 and January 11. The Foundation uses the following criteria when reviewing applications: sustainability; effective operations; proven success; strong leadership; innovation and creativity; accessibility; collaboration; and engagement.
Restrictions: The Foundation will not fund: bands, sports teams, or other groups without a philanthropic project; annual appeals, galas or membership contributions; fundraising events such as golf tournaments, walk-a-thons, and fashion shows; grants to individuals; projects aimed at promoting a particular religion or construction projects for religious institutions; operating, program and construction costs at schools, universities and private academies unless there is a significant opportunity for community use or collaboration; organizations or projects that discriminate based upon race, ethnicity, age, gender, sexual orientation; political campaigns or direct lobbying efforts by 501(c)3 organizations; post-event, after-the-fact situations or debt retirement; medical, scientific or academic research; publications, films, audiovisual and media materials, programs produced for artistic purposes or produced for resale.
Geographic Focus: Indiana
Contact: Susan Rozzi; (317) 718-1200; fax (317) 718-1033; janet@hendrickscountycf.org
Internet: http://www.hendrickscountycf.org/grants/oppfund_grants/index.shtml
Sponsor: Hendricks County Community Foundation
5055 East Main Street, Suite A
Avon, IN 46123

Henrietta Lange Burk Fund Grants — 2303

The Henrietta Lange Burk Fund is a private foundation created by Mrs. Henrietta Lange Burk in 1994 to support and promote quality arts, cultural, educational, health-care, and human-services programming for underserved populations. Special consideration is given to charitable organizations that address the health concerns of older adults, through either direct programming or research. Mrs. Burk created the Foundation as a memorial to her parents, Mr. and Mrs. Henry G. Lange, as well as to her husband, William Burk, and herself. Mrs. Burk was particularly interested in the performing and cultural arts; age-related health problems, research and care; as well as human services organizations, especially those that were connected to her Protestant background. The foundation will consider requests for general operating support only if the organization's operating budget is less than $1 million. The majority of grants from the Lange Burk Fund are one year in duration. Applicants must apply online at the grant website. Applicants are strongly encouraged to do the following before applying: review the downloadable state application procedures for additional helpful information and clarifications; review the downloadable online-application guidelines at the grant website; review the foundation's funding history (link is available from the grant website); review the online application questions in advance; and review the list of required attachments. These will generally include: a list of board members, financial statements (audited, reviewed, or compiled by independent auditor); an organization summary; a list of other funding sources; an IRS Determination letter; and other required documents. All attachments must be uploaded in the online application as PDF, Word, or Excel files. The Henrietta Lange Burk Fund has biannual deadlines of June 1 and November 1. Applications must be submitted by 11:59 p.m. on the deadline dates. Applicants for the June deadline will be notified of grant decisions by September 30. Applicants for the November deadline will be notified by March 31.
Requirements: Applicants must have 501(c)3 tax-exempt status and serve residents of the Chicago Metropolitan area.
Restrictions: In general, grant requests for individuals, endowment campaigns or capital projects will not be considered. Because requests for support usually exceed available resources, organizations can only apply to either the Lang Burk Fund or the Colonel Stanley NcNeil Foundation in the same calendar year. Grant requests to both foundations during the same calendar year will no longer be accepted. The foundation does not support requests from individuals, organizations attempting to influence policy through direct lobbying, or any political campaigns.
Geographic Focus: Illinois
Date(s) Application is Due: Jun 1; Nov 1
Contact: George Thorn; (312) 828-4154; ilgrantmaking@bankofamerica.com
Internet: https://www.bankofamerica.com/philanthropic/fn_search.action
Sponsor: Henrietta Lange Burk Fund
231 South LaSalle Street, IL1-231-13-32
Chicago, IL 60604

Henrietta Tower Wurts Memorial Foundation Grants — 2304

The Foundation supports organizations which are engaged in helping or caring for people in need, or alleviating the conditions under which they live, primarily for the elderly, women, family and child welfare services. Giving is limited to Philadelphia, Pennsylvania.
Requirements: Non-profits in Philadelphia, Pennsylvania are eligible. The initial approach should be a letter requesting an application form from the Foundation.
Restrictions: No grants to individuals, or for endowment funds, scholarships, fellowships, or matching gifts; no loans. Organizations or programs serving disadvantaged youth and the elderly in Philadelphia, Pennsylvania must have an annual budget of less than 3 million.
Geographic Focus: Pennsylvania
Date(s) Application is Due: Feb 1; May 1; Sep 1
Amount of Grant: 1,000 - 7,000 USD
Contact: Andrew Swinney, President; (215) 563-6417
Sponsor: Henrietta Tower Wurts Memorial Foundation
1234 Market Street, Suite 1800
Philadelphia, PA 19107-3704

Henry A. and Mary J. MacDonald Foundation — 2305

Established in 1998 in Pennsylvania, the Henry A. and Mary J. MacDonald Foundation offers funding in its primary field of interest, health care. A formal application is required, though there are no annual deadlines. Applicants should begin by contacting the Foundation directly. Most recently, grants have averaged about $3,000, though there are no limitations on award ceilings other than availability of funds.
Restrictions: No grants are given to individuals.
Geographic Focus: All States
Amount of Grant: 2,000 - 5,000 USD
Contact: James D. Cullen, President; (814) 870-7705
Sponsor: Henry A. and Mary J. MacDonald Foundation
100 State Street, Suite 700
Erie, PA 16507-1498

Henry and Ruth Blaustein Rosenberg Foundation Grants — 2306

The Henry and Ruth Blaustein Rosenberg Foundation provides support primarily in the Baltimore, Maryland region. Areas of interest are: arts and culture; youth development; health; and adult self-sufficiency. The goal of the arts and culture program is to enable cultural institutions in the Baltimore metropolitan area to reach underserved youth and to diversify audiences. Youth Development funding is provided to promote recreation, learning, and leadership development through after-school programs; prevent teen pregnancy; and advocate for policies and practices that improve outcomes for youth. Health funding is available to improve the prevention and treatment of breast cancer, diabetes, multiple sclerosis, and kidney disease. Adult Self-Sufficiency funding is provided to promote adult literacy; provide job training; improve parenting skills, especially for parents of children under age three; and eliminate domestic violence. The foundation meets three or four times a year to consider proposals. Letters of intent and proposals are accepted on a rolling basis. Applications that conform to the Association of Baltimore Area Grantmakers (ABAG) Common Grant Application are accepted and this form is available at the Henry and Ruth Blaustein Rosenberg Foundation website.
Requirements: 501(c)3 tax-exempt charitable organizations located in and/or primarily serving the metropolitan Baltimore area are eligible to apply. The initial application should include the following: information about the program(s) for which funding is requested; need, purpose, activities, and evaluation plan of the proposed program(s); program budget (including sources of anticipated income as well as expenditures) and timeline; dollar amount of funding requested; history, mission, and key accomplishments of your organization; information on Board members and key staff; current institutional operating budget (including major sources of revenue as well as expenditures); copy of your IRS tax status determination letter or information about your fiscal agent.
Restrictions: The foundation does not: make grants or scholarships to individuals; accept unsolicited proposals for academic, scientific, or medical research; support direct mail, annual giving, membership campaigns, fundraising and commemorative events. The foundations rarely make capital grants unless there is a prior relationship with the applicant organization.
Geographic Focus: Maryland
Amount of Grant: 1,000 - 40,000 USD
Contact: Michael J. Hirschhorn; (410) 347-7201; fax (410) 347-7210; info@blaufund.org
Internet: http://www.blaufund.org/foundations/henryandruth_f.html
Sponsor: Henry and Ruth Blaustein Rosenberg Foundation
10 E Baltimore Street, Suite 1111
Baltimore, MD 21202

Henry County Community Foundation - TASC Youth Grants — 2307

The TASC (Teens About Serving the County) Youth Grants Committee meets four times each school year. The TASC Committee includes one 8th grader, one freshman, one sophomore, one junior, and one senior from each of the five school districts in Henry County. The TASC Committee assignment is to evaluate grant submissions relating to youth and educational programs. These students critically evaluate each grant submission for purpose, scope, need, and viability. They then determine whether each grant will be accepted as is, partially funded, denied, or accepted with conditions. The TASC Committee grant recommendations are then taken to the Henry County Community Foundation Board of Directors for final approval. Guidelines and the application are available at the website.
Requirements: Eligibility for Youth Grants include the following categories: youth organization or club; not for profit 501(c)3; community organization; school (public or private). Grant preferences must directly relate to the foundation's mission statement; address a need for youth of Henry County; provide a time line for completion of project; and benefit the most people. Grants under $2,500 are preferred.
Restrictions: Grant money may not be used for overhead costs, salaries or wages, or direct donations to other organizations.
Geographic Focus: Indiana
Date(s) Application is Due: Feb 24; May 4; Oct 7; Dec 2
Amount of Grant: Up to 2,500 USD
Contact: Beverly Matthews; (765) 529-2235; beverly@henrycountycf.org
Internet: http://www.henrycountycf.org/index.php?submenu=TASC&src=gendocs&ref=Grant%20Guidelines&category=TASC
Sponsor: Henry County Community Foundation
700 S Memorial Drive, P.O. Box 6006
New Castle, IN 47362

Henry County Community Foundation Grants — 2308

As a community foundation, the Henry County Community Foundation addresses the broad needs in Henry County, Indiana which include, but are not limited to, the following five categories: health and medical; social services; education; cultural affairs and civic affairs. All requests for grants are reviewed by the Foundation's Grants Committee, which is made up of members of the Board of Directors and several outside advisers. Reviews and recommendations are then presented to the full Board of Directors at its regularly scheduled meetings in April and October. However, the Board reserves the right to consider individual requests at any regularly scheduled meeting, if deemed necessary. The Foundation's grant program emphasizes change-oriented and focused types of grants to achieve certain objectives such as becoming more efficient, increasing fundraising capabilities, delivering better products, etc. The guidelines and application are available at the website.
Requirements: Applications from organizations whose programs benefit the residents of Henry County are accepted only from organizations who attend the spring or fall grant workshops held at the Foundation office. Organizations must be a 501(c)3 tax-exempt or be sponsored by a 501(c) tax-exempt organization. Grants will also be accepted from school and government entities.
Restrictions: The following are not eligible for funding: operating cost; individuals; individuals or groups of individuals to attend seminars or take trips except where there are special circumstances which will benefit the community; sectarian religious purposes. No grants will be made exclusively for endowment purposes of recipient organizations; individuals or organizations that are not charitable organizations; and programs and/or equipment which were committed to prior to the submission of grant application.
Geographic Focus: Indiana
Date(s) Application is Due: Mar 30; Aug 31
Contact: Beverly Matthews; (765) 529-2235; beverly@henrycountycf.org
Internet: http://www.henrycountycf.org/index.php?submenu=Grants&src=gendocs&ref=Grants&category=Grants
Sponsor: Henry County Community Foundation
700 S Memorial Drive, P.O. Box 6006
New Castle, IN 47362

Henry E. Niles Foundation Grants 2309

The mission of the Henry E. Niles Foundation is to help in the nurturing and uplifting of people in need. The Foundation strives to support humanitarian efforts, including faith-based endeavors, that: strengthen education including special education, literacy and others; fight economic hardships through self-help opportunities; enhance public health and sanitation on a global basis. The Foundation has a particular interest in organizations that promote collaborative efforts among groups and organizations. The Board is currently highlighting the following areas: Education – Included in this interest area are primary, secondary and higher education for those motivated individuals who are unable to obtain the benefits of quality education without assistance; Economic Self-Sufficiency – This program area includes but is not limited to: job training, the encouragement and support of entrepreneurialism, mentoring, and micro-credit initiatives; Health & Independence – Special interests here include medical and public health assistance for the elderly, the poor, the disadvantaged and the disabled. Additionally, the Foundation encourages pilot initiatives that test new program models. There are no deadlines; applications are accepted throughout the year.
Requirements: The majority of the Foundation's grantmaking is focused in the northeastern United States and abroad, although, occasionally, grants may be made in other regions of the country as well. All applicants must have tax-exempt 501(c)3 status as a non-profit organization as defined by the Internal Revenue Service. Grants may range from a few thousand dollars up to $100,000. In unique circumstances, the Foundation does consider a more significant grant for a program having a major impact in one or more of its areas of interest.
Restrictions: The Foundation will generally not provide grants to the following: organizations not determined to be tax-exempt under section 501(c)3 of the Internal Revenue Code; general fundraising drives; individuals; government agencies; or organizations that subsist mainly on third party funding and have demonstrated no ability or expended little effort to attract private funding.
Geographic Focus: All States
Contact: Ashley C. Lantz, (203) 661-1000; fax (203) 629-7300; alantz@fcsn.com
Internet: http://www.heniles.org/Guidlines.htm
Sponsor: Henry E. Niles Foundation
c/o Fogarty, Cohen, Selby & Nemiroff
Greenwich, CT 06830

Henry J. Kaiser Family Foundation Grants 2310

The foundation concentrates giving in the following areas: U.S. government's role in health, health of low-income and minority groups with major emphasis on HIV/AIDS policy, reproductive health policy, and health system innovation and reform in California. The foundation also operates a major program to improve health and health care and promote social justice in South Africa. Grants are awarded for one to three years and support a range of activities, including policy analysis, applied research to define and measure public health problems, demonstration and pilot projects, and communications activities that help sharpen health care debates and improve quality of health information. Prospective applicants should submit a preliminary letter (two to three pages in length) that briefly describes the proposed project, along with an estimate of the total budget and the amount requested from the foundation. There are no deadlines and no application forms. Inquiries for projects in South Africa may be addressed to Dr. Michael Sinclair, Senior Vice President, The Henry J. Kaiser Family Foundation, 1450 G St NW, Suite 250, Washington, DC 20005, (202) 347-5270, fax: (202) 347-5274.
Requirements: Grants in response to unsolicited proposals are made only to governmental agencies and to private organizations with IRS 501(c)3 tax-exempt status.
Restrictions: The foundation does not award grants to individuals. Support is not given to ongoing general operating expenses, indirect costs, capital campaigns, annual appeals or other fundraising events, construction, purchase or renovation of facilities, or equipment purchases.
Geographic Focus: All States
Contact: Renee Wells; (415) 854-9400; fax (415) 854-4800; rwells@kff.org
Internet: http://www.kff.org
Sponsor: Henry J. Kaiser Family Foundation
2400 Sand Hill Road
Menlo Park, CA 94025

Henry M. Jackson Foundation Grants 2311

The Foundation focuses on four critical issues: international affairs education; environment and natural resources management; public service; and human rights. The Foundation is guided by the principles, values and interests of the late Senator Henry Jackson and seeks to promote dialogue and build consensus between the academic and policy worlds, between the public and private sectors, and between citizens and their government. Application information is available online.
Requirements: Nonprofit organizations in the United States and abroad are eligible.
Restrictions: The foundation does not award grants to cover unrestricted operating expenses, operating deficits, or capital expenditures.
Geographic Focus: All States
Contact: Lara Iglitzin; (206) 682-8565; fax (206) 682-8961; foundation@hmjackson.org
Internet: http://www.hmjackson.org
Sponsor: Henry M. Jackson Foundation
1501 Fourth Avenue, Suite 1580
Seattle, WA 98101

Henry W. Bull Foundation Grants 2312

Established in 1960 in California, the foundation was established by Maud Bull in memory of her husband, Henry W. Bull. The foundation grants awards on a nationwide basis, giving primarily in the areas of: arts/performing arts; education; health and; human services. Types of support include annual campaigns, building construction/renovation, capital campaigns; program development, equipment acquisition, matching/challenge grants; general operating support, continuing support, and research. There is no formal grant application form. Submit a simple, concise statement of needs and objectives with pertinent supportive data.
Requirements: 501(c)()3 nonprofits are eligible.
Restrictions: No grants to individuals or private foundations.
Geographic Focus: All States
Date(s) Application is Due: Apr 1; Sep 1
Contact: Janice Gibson; (805) 899-8405; fax (805) 884-1404
Sponsor: Henry W. Bull Foundation
P.O. Box 2340
Santa Barbara, CA 93120-2340

Herbert A. and Adrian W. Woods Foundation Grants 2313

The Herbert A. and Adrian W. Woods Foundation was established on June 9, 1999 upon the death of Mrs. Adrian W. Woods. Mrs. Woods had a long history of charitable giving in the St. Louis community and wanted to establish this foundation to continue that legacy of giving. The Foundation supports charitable organizations primarily in the greater St. Louis, Missouri area. The Trustees will consider the donor's past giving history and any special needs of any of the charities she has given to in the past. The Trustees will also consider requests from charitable organizations that fall into one or more of the following categories: abused, neglected, or troubled children; the poor; the Episcopal Church and affiliates, including outreach programs; arts and culture in the Metropolitan St. Louis area; animal welfare (in Missouri); and victims of illness or disability, including research in this area. The following types of requests may be submitted: special projects; capital campaign requests (capital grants are awarded only as a source of support among a broad community of funders); challenge or matching grants; and general operation funding. Applicants must apply online at the grant website. Applicants are strongly encouraged to do the following before applying: review the downloadable state application procedures for additional helpful information and clarifications; review the downloadable online-application guidelines at the grant website; review the foundation's funding history (link is available from the grant website); review the online application questions in advance; and review the list of required attachments. These will generally include: a list of board members, financial statements (audited, reviewed, or compiled by independent auditor); an organization summary; a list of other funding sources; an IRS Determination letter; and other required documents. All attachments must be uploaded in the online application as PDF, Word, or Excel files. The application deadline for this foundation is 11:59 p.m. on September 1. Final decisions about grant rewards will be made by November 30.
Requirements: Applicants must have 501(c)3 tax-exempt status.
Restrictions: The fund will not consider requests for multi-year grants (pledges) or endowment creation and funding. The fund does not support requests from individuals, organizations attempting to influence policy through direct lobbying, or any political campaigns.
Geographic Focus: Missouri
Date(s) Application is Due: Sep 1
Contact: Shanise Evans, Vice President; (314) 466-8027; shanise.evans@baml.com
Internet: https://www.bankofamerica.com/philanthropic/fn_search.action
Sponsor: Herbert A. and Adrian W. Woods Foundation
100 North Broadway MO2-100-07-15
Saint Louis, MO 63102-2728

Herbert B. Jones Foundation Grants 2314

The foundation believes that entrepreneurism and small business are the backbone for the strength of the nation's economic system. The foundation provides initial and temporary support of new business programs managed by postsecondary educational entities in the state of Washington. Grant requests are due by the first Monday in April.
Restrictions: Grants will not be awarded for equipment, capital projects, gifts, endowments, or food costs.
Geographic Focus: Washington
Date(s) Application is Due: Apr 5
Contact: Grants Administrator, (206) 464-3043; fax (206) 464-4683
Internet: http://www.hbjfoundation.com
Sponsor: Herbert B. Jones Foundation
505 Fifth Avenue S, Suite 170
Seattle, WA 98104

Herbert H. and Grace A. Dow Foundation Grants 2315

The Foundation has charter goals to improve the educational, religious, economic and cultural lives of Michigan's people. Priority is given to organizations that: have clearly stated objectives, strong and purposeful management and are publicly accountable; have needs which are in areas not normally funded by governmental or public financing; are not hesitant to explore, initiate, volunteer, or execute original ideas or concepts; are willing to collaborate with other persons or organizations to give synergy to a common objective or goal; have purposes which tend to advance private enterprise and the preservation of a free, open and self-resourceful society. Application information is available online.
Requirements: Only organizations in Michigan are eligible to apply.
Restrictions: The Foundation does not make grants directly to individuals. It cannot legally support: organizations to which contributions are not tax deductible, according to Internal Revenue Service regulations; organizations that practice discrimination by race, sex, creed, age or national origin; political organizations or organizations whose purposes are to influence legislation.
Geographic Focus: Michigan
Contact: Margaret Ann Riecker; (989) 631-3699; info@hhdowfoundation.org
Internet: http://www.hhdowfdn.org
Sponsor: Herbert H. and Grace A. Dow Foundation
1018 West Main Street
Midland, MI 48640-4292

Herman Abbott Family Foundation Grants 2316
The Foundation, established in 1996 in New York, supports the arts, performing arts, and Jewish agencies and temples. Grant funding most often comes in the form of general operating support. There are no specified application formats or deadlines with which to adhere, and applicants should approach the foundation initially in writing. Awards average about $25,000.
Geographic Focus: All States
Amount of Grant: Up to 35,000 USD
Contact: David Y. Bailey, Treasurer; (203) 481-1120; fax (203) 488-3027
Sponsor: Herman Abbott Family Foundation
1224 Main Street, Lockworks Square
Branford, CT 06405-3778

Herman Goldman Foundation Grants 2317
The Herman Goldman Foundation strives to enhance the quality of life through innovative grants in four main areas: 1) health — to achieve effective delivery of physical and mental health care services; 2) social justice — to develop organizational, social, and legal approaches to those who are aid deprived or handicapped; 3) education — for new or improved counseling for effective preschool, vocational and paraprofessional training; and 4) the arts — to increase opportunities for talented youth to receive training and for less affluent individuals to attend quality presentations. Grantmaking is primarily to 501(c)3 organizations in the metropolitan New York area. Types of support include: annual campaigns; building and renovation; capital campaigns; continuing support; endowments; general operating support; program development; internship funds; research; and seed money.
Requirements: Applicants should submit a proposal along with a copy of the organization's IRS determination letter. There are no deadlines. The board meets monthly, with grants considered in April, July, and November. Organizations are notified within two to three months of submission.
Restrictions: The Foundation does not fund religious organizations, individuals, or emergency funds.
Geographic Focus: New York
Contact: Richard Baron, Executive Director; (212) 797-9090; goldfound@aol.com
Sponsor: Herman Goldman Foundation
44 Wall Street, Suite 1212
New York, NY 10005-2401

Hershey Company Grants 2318
The Hershey Company remains committed to supporting the communities in which it operates and to society in general. Cash and product contributions are made to support a variety of worthy causes and non-profit organizations which support Education, Health & Human Services, Civic & Community initiatives, Arts & Culture and the Environment. Particular emphasis is placed upon causes that support kids and kids at risk. The Hershey Company has plants in the following areas: Hilo, HI; Robinson, IL; Hazleton, PA; Hershey, PA; Lancaster, PA; Memphis, TN; Stuarts Draft, VA; Sao Roque, Brazil; Guadalajara, Mexico; Monterrey, Mexico; Mumbai, India; Shanghai, China. Organizations located in communities in which The Hershey Company has manufacturing operations should direct requests for funding to the management of The Hershey Company facility in their area, see the Hershey website for additional guidelines and contact information.
Requirements: Nonprofit organizations are eligible. Preference is given to nonprofits in corporate-operating locations. All requests must be submitted in writing.
Restrictions: The following are ineligible for funding: organizations without an Internal Revenue Code 501(c)3 non-profit, tax-exempt status; individuals; organizations outside the immediate areas of The Hershey Company's manufacturing facilities, with the exception of national and state-wide organizations whose programs complement Hershey's funding priorities; political campaigns, political or lobbying organizations, or those supporting the candidacy of a particular individual; churches or religious organizations, including seminaries, Bible colleges and theological institutions; fraternal organizations; labor organizations; member agencies of United Way. Exception: requests for capital campaign funding will be considered; affiliate organizations of the Cultural Enrichment Fund in Central Pennsylvania. Exception: requests for capital campaign funding will be considered.
Geographic Focus: Hawaii, Illinois, Pennsylvania, Tennessee, Virginia, Brazil, China, Mexico
Contact: Grants Administrator; (800) 468-1714; fax (717) 534-6550
Internet: http://www.thehersheycompany.com/about/responsibility.asp
Sponsor: Hershey Company
Community Relations, 100 Crystal A Drive, P.O. Box 810
Hershey, PA 17033-0810

Highmark Corporate Giving Grants 2319
The Foundation awards grants in the following categories: health; human services; community; education; and arts and culture. Support is expressed in cash grants, sponsorships and in-kind gifts to non-profit organizations. There are no maximum or minimum limits; however, awards to programs and services are granted based on importance to the Foundation's business, social mission and corporate citizen objectives, as well as the initiative's proposed impact. Interested applicants should submit a brief proposal. For additional information or proposal submission, applicants should contact the Community Affairs department in their county of residence. Contact information by county is available online.
Requirements: The Foundation awards grants to nonprofit organizations that are defined as tax exempt under section 501(c)3 of the Internal Revenue Code and as public charities under section 509(a) of that code.
Restrictions: Proposals are not accepted for: multiple-year grants; capital campaigns; individual causes; seed money or start-up organizations; endowment funds; political causes or campaigns; fraternal or civic groups; religious programming; organizations that discriminate on the basis of race, religion, sex, disability or national origin.
Geographic Focus: Pennsylvania
Contact: Mary Ann Papale, (412) 544-4032; mary.papale@highmark.com
Internet: https://www.highmark.com/hmk2/community/corpgiving/index.shtml
Sponsor: Highmark
120 5th Avenue, Suite 2112
Pittsburgh, PA 15222-3099

Highmark Physician eHealth Collaborative Grants 2320
The program was created to encourage the adoption of health information technology used at the point of care to improve patient safety, quality of care, and cost efficiency for people in western and central Pennsylvania. Physicians may apply to receive grants, which must be used to acquire and use electronic technology systems such as a personal computer, a PDA, or electronic tablet or digital pen to generate and transmit electronically prescriptions to pharmacies. The collaborative will pay up to 75 percent of the cost for a physician's office to acquire, install, and implement the electronic technology system, with the physician's practice to pay the remaining balance. Physicians must apply online.
Requirements: Physicians must be licensed to practice medicine in Pennsylvania and must be a licensed prescriber.
Geographic Focus: Pennsylvania
Amount of Grant: Up to 7,000 USD
Contact: Grants Administrator; info@highmarkehealth.org
Internet: http://www.highmarkehealth.org
Sponsor: Pittsburgh Foundation
1 PPG Place, 30th Floor
Pittsburgh, PA 15222-5401

High Meadow Foundation Grants 2321
The foundation grants funds in support of the performing arts, especially theater and music, and other cultural organizations. Organizations supported are usually located in Berkshire County, MA. Types of support include continuing support, annual campaigns, capital campaigns, building construction/renovation, equipment acquisition, emergency funds, program development, employee-related scholarships, and matching funds. Applications are accepted at any time. Forms are not necessary; a letter outlining the proposed project should include budget and administrative information.
Requirements: Western Massachusetts 501(c)3 tax-exempt organizations in Berkshire County are eligible.
Geographic Focus: Massachusetts
Contact: Jane Fitzpatrick; (413) 298-5565 or (413) 243-1474; fax (413) 298-4058
Sponsor: High Meadow Foundation
30 Main Street
Stockbridge, MA 01262

Hilda and Preston Davis Foundation Grants 2322
The Foundation provides funds to charitable organizations whose programs advance the development of all areas of the lives of children and young adults. The Foundation places special emphasis on, and channels most of its financial resources toward, those organizations whose attention is concentrated on eating disorders and education for the underprivileged. Grants may range from $10,000 up to $100,000. In unique circumstances, the Foundation does consider a more significant grant for a program having a major impact in one or more of its areas of interest. The Foundation encourages pilot initiatives that test new program models. Of particular interest to the Foundation are organizations that promote partnerships and collaborative efforts among multiple groups and organizations. The Foundation almost always limits grant durations to three years or less. Applications are accepted throughout the year.
Requirements: ll applicants must be an approved tax-exempt non-profit organization as defined by the Internal Revenue Service. Areas of greatest importance to the Foundation are funded on a national basis. However, a good deal of the Foundation's grant making in other program areas is focused in areas of geographic importance to the donors–the northeastern United States (southern New England & the middle Atlantic states), as well as California. Priority will be given to requests that show specific plans for funding beyond the present.
Restrictions: The Foundation will not allow any funds to be earmarked for indirect costs or institutional overhead in cases where the grant relationship was developed independent of that institution's direct involvement. The Foundation generally will not provide grants to the following: organizations not determined to be tax-exempt under section 501(c)3 of the Internal Revenue Code; individuals; general fundraising drives; endowments; government agencies; or organizations that subsist mainly on third party funding and have demonstrated no ability or expended little effort to attract private funding.
Geographic Focus: California, Connecticut, Delaware, District of Columbia, Maryland, Massachusetts, New Hampshire, New Jersey, New York, Pennsylvania, Rhode Island, Vermont, Virginia, West Virginia
Contact: Grants Administrator; (203) 629-8552; fax (203) 547-6112; davis@fsllc.net
Internet: http://www.hpdavis.org/application.htm
Sponsor: Hilda and Preston Davis Foundation
640 West Putnam Avenue, 3rd Floor
Greenwich, CT 06830

Hilfiger Family Foundation Grants 2323
The Hilfiger Family Foundation was established in 1999 by Tommy Hilfiger, Principal Designer of the Tommy Hilfiger Group, a globally recognized designer brand offering American-inspired apparel and accessories. Hilfiger is actively involved in a number of charities and causes, including the Washington D.C. Martin Luther King Jr. National Memorial Project Foundation and the Anti-Defamation League. The Foundation's primary interest areas are children and youth services, the environment, federated giving programs, and human services.

Requirements: 501(c)3 organizations serving residents of New York state are eligible.
Geographic Focus: New York
Amount of Grant: 1 - 100,000 USD
Contact: Thomas R. Curtin, President; (212) 275-1500; fax (212) 275-1510
Sponsor: Hilfiger Family Foundation
75 Rockefeller Plaza, 9th Floor
New York, NY 10019-6908

Hill Crest Foundation Grants   2324
The Hill Crest Foundation awards grants to Alabama nonprofits, primarily health associations and human services and education, with some funding for the arts. Types of support include: building and renovation; capital campaigns; endowments; equipment; matching and challenge support; professorships; program development; publication; research; scholarship funds; seed money; and technical assistance. There are no deadlines or applications. The Board of Directors meets quarterly.
Requirements: Application forms are not required. Before submitting a proposal, organizations should submit a letter, detailing the project and the amount requested, along with descriptive literature about their organization.
Restrictions: Grantmaking is limited to Alabama. The Foundation does not fund individuals.
Geographic Focus: Alabama
Amount of Grant: 20,000 - 150,000 USD
Contact: Charles Terry, Chairperson; (205) 425-5800
Sponsor: Hill Crest Foundation
P.O. Box 530507
Mountain Brook, AL 35253-0507

Hillcrest Foundation Grants   2325
The Hillcrest Foundation was created by Mrs. W.W. Caruth, Sr. (Mrs. Earle Clark Caruth) in 1958 to provide financial support to qualified Texas charitable organizations for the advancement of education, the promotion of health, and the relief of poverty. Mrs. W.W. Caruth, Sr. was from a pioneer family who settled in the Dallas area in 1848. Several Caruth family generations owned and managed farms and ranches, which the family later developed into real estate properties as Dallas became a major metropolitan area. Each succeeding generation has been characterized by a pioneering spirit, vision, courage, hard work and generosity. The Hillcrest Foundation was created to carry the Caruth family's generosity to the people of Texas. Approximately 90% of grant funds are paid to organizations in North Texas, with emphasis on charitable services in the Dallas area. The trustees will give priority consideration to the following types of grant requests: construction/improvements of permanent buildings; programs and special projects for education, health and poverty relief; capital campaigns; and buildings, facilities and equipment. Grant requests for capital and program support are strongly encouraged. Grant amounts range from $10,000 to $300,000 (multi-year payment) with an average grant of $35,000. The Trustees favorably consider proposals which are unique, necessary, and of high priority for the charitable organizations, and which do not duplicate other services which are available; proposals for which funding may not be readily available from other sources; and essential projects which are sufficiently described as worthwhile, important and of a substantive nature. Grants to meet challenges or matching funds have a special appeal. The majority of grants from the Hillcrest Foundation are one year in duration. On occasion, multi-year support is awarded. Applicants must apply online at the grant website. Applicants are strongly encouraged to do the following before applying: review the downloadable state application procedures for additional helpful information and clarifications; review the downloadable online-application guidelines at the grant website; review the foundation's funding history (link is available from the grant website); review the online application questions in advance; and review the list of required attachments. These will generally include: a list of board members, financial statements (audited, reviewed, or compiled by independent auditor); an organization summary; a list of other funding sources; an IRS Determination letter; and other required documents. All attachments must be uploaded in the online application as PDF, Word, or Excel files. The Hillcrest Foundation has three deadlines annually: February 28, July 31, and November 30. Applications must be submitted by 11:59 p.m. on the deadline dates. Grant applicants are notified as follows: February deadline applicants will be notified of grant decisions by June 30; July applicants will be notified by November 30; and November applicants will be notified by March 31 of the following year.
Requirements: 501(c)3 organizations in Texas may apply.
Restrictions: Grant requests for general operating support will not be considered. Organizations that receive a one-year grant from the foundation must skip a year before submitting a subsequent application. Organizations that receive a multi-year grant are not eligible to apply until one year after the close of their grant cycle. Organizations whose last request was declined must wait one year before applying again. The foundation does not support requests from individuals, organizations attempting to influence policy through direct lobbying, or any political campaigns.
Geographic Focus: Texas
Date(s) Application is Due: Feb 28; Jul 31; Nov 30
Contact: David Ross, Senior Vice President; tx.philanthropic@baml.com
Internet: https://www.bankofamerica.com/philanthropic/fn_search.action
Sponsor: Hillcrest Foundation
901 Main Street, 19th Floor, TX1-492-19-11
Dallas, TX 75202-3714

Hill Foundation Grants   2326
The foundation awards grants mainly for special health care projects, higher education, equipment funds, and services for the elderly, disabled children, and cultural programs, primarily in Colorado. Some support is provided to social service agencies. Types of support include program development, scholarship funds, and matching funds. There are no application deadlines.
Requirements: Giving primarily in CO and WY.
Restrictions: Grants are not made to individuals nor for capital improvements. The foundation does not make multiyear commitments.
Geographic Focus: Colorado, Wyoming
Amount of Grant: 1,000 - 45,000 USD
Contact: Grants Administrator, c/o Wells Fargo Bank; (720) 947-6820
Sponsor: Hill Foundation
1740 Broadway, MC 7300-483
Denver, CO 80274

Hillman Foundation Grants   2327
The foundation provides grants to nonprofit organizations in the city of Pittsburgh and the southwestern Pennsylvania region for programs and projects designed to improve the quality of life in the area. The foundation's areas of interest include community affairs, social services, culture and the arts, education at all levels, and youth services including medical and health. Grants range widely in size and are allocated for large and small capital projects, endowment, new and expanding programs, and on a limited basis, operating support. Applications should include an annual budget of the organization, project information, and evidence of tax-exempt status. Application information is available online.
Requirements: The Foundation considers requests only from organizations classified as tax-exempt under Section 501(c)3 of the U.S. Internal Revenue Code and designated as public charities under Section 509(a).
Restrictions: Grants are not made to individuals, organizations located outside of the United States, for travel expenses for groups, or in support of events, sponsorships and meetings such as conferences, institutes and seminars.
Geographic Focus: Pennsylvania
Contact: David K. Roger; (412) 338-3466; fax (412) 338-3463; foundation@hillmanfo.com
Internet: http://www.hillmanfdn.org/grantprograms.html
Sponsor: Hillman Foundation
330 Grant Street, Suite 2000
Pittsburgh, PA 15219

Hillsdale County Community General Adult Foundation Grants   2328
General Adult Foundation grant making is made from the Foundation's named unrestricted endowment funds. These grants focus on improving the quality of life for the citizens of Hillsdale County. Eligible projects generally fall within these categories: education, fine arts, social services, community development, recreation, environmental issues, health and wellness, and improvement in the physical, mental, and moral conditions of Hillsdale County residents. The Foundation aims to support creative approaches to community needs and problems that benefit the widest possible range of people.
Requirements: The Foundation requires applicants to call and discuss their project with the Executive Director prior to submitting the application. Applications from the Hillsdale County area or outside Hillsdale County, Michigan are welcome, if a significant number of the people to be served reside within Hillsdale County. Applicants shall be tax exempt according to Section 501(c)3 of the Internal Revenue Code.
Restrictions: The current objectives of the Foundation do not allow grants for: religious or sectarian purposes; individuals; legislative or political purposes; loans; capital campaigns; routine maintenance, including office equipment; administrative costs for maintaining the present operation of an organization, including, but not limited to, staff salaries, wages, and benefits; basic education materials including state mandated/benchmark core curriculum supplies and resources.
Geographic Focus: Michigan
Date(s) Application is Due: May 1; Nov 1
Contact: Sharon Bisher, (517) 439-5101; fax (517) 439-5109; s.bisher@abouthccf.org
Internet: http://www.abouthccf.org/grants.asp
Sponsor: Hillsdale County Community Foundation
2 S Howell Street, P.O. Box 276
Hillsdale, MI 49242

Hillsdale Fund Grants   2329
The fund awards grants to nonprofit organizations in its areas of interest, including arts and culture, education, health care, social services delivery, and religion. Call for meeting dates and application materials.
Requirements: Tax-exempt organizations are eligible.
Restrictions: Grants do not support indirect costs or overhead; routine, recurring operating expenses; conferences and seminars; travel and study; or individuals.
Geographic Focus: North Carolina
Amount of Grant: 3,000 - 50,000 USD
Contact: Edward Doolan, Grants Administrator; (336) 274-5471
Sponsor: Hillsdale Fund
P.O. Box 20124
Greensboro, NC 27420-0124

Hilton Head Island Foundation Grants   2330
The Foundation exists to enhance the quality of life for individuals living and/or working in Southern Beaufort County (Hilton Head Island, Daufuskie Island, Bluffton, Okatie). Grantmaking is in the broad areas of: arts, education, and community development. The Board meets three times per year. Application information is available online.
Requirements: To be eligible for funding, an applicant must be: a nonprofit agency with a tax-exempt status under section 501(c)3 of the Internal Revenue code, or eligible to be classified as such, but are not classified as a private foundation; serve the people who live and/or work in the Hilton Head Island area community.

Restrictions: Funding is not available for: sectarian or religious activities; political activities or organizations; grants directly to individuals; endowments; annual fundraising campaigns; special events or fundraisers; scholarships for students in grades K-12.
Geographic Focus: South Carolina
Date(s) Application is Due: Apr 1; Aug 1; Dec 1
Contact: Cynthia Smith; (843) 681-9100; fax (843) 681-9101; csmith@cf-lowcountry.org
Internet: http://www.cf-lowcountry.org/receive/grants
Sponsor: Community Foundation of the Lowcountry
4 Northridge Drive, Suite A, P.O. Box 23019
Hilton Head Island, SC 29925

Hilton Hotels Corporate Giving Program Grants 2331
Hilton makes charitable contributions to nonprofit organizations involved with K-12 education, youth development, public policy, homelessness, and civic affairs. Support is given primarily in areas of company operations, with emphasis on California, including Los Angeles and San Francisco, and Tennessee, including Memphis; giving also to national organizations. Contact Ellen Gonda for additional information at: corporate_communications@hilton.com.
Requirements: 501(c)3 tax-exempt organizations are eligible.
Restrictions: No support for sport teams, religious organizations not of direct benefit to the entire community, government-supported organizations (over 20 percent of budget), hospitals, private schools, pre-schools, or day care facilities, film and video production, or promotional materials. No grants to individuals (except for employee-related scholarships), or for fellowships, sports activities, debt reduction, capital campaigns or endowments, film or video projects, or promotional merchandise.
Geographic Focus: California, Tennessee
Contact: Ellen Gonda; (310) 278-4321; corporate_communications@hilton.com
Internet: http://www.hiltonworldwide.com
Sponsor: Hilton Hotels Corporation
9336 Civic Center Drive
Beverly Hills, CA 90210-3604

Hirtzel Memorial Foundation Grants 2332
The foundation awards grants to eligible organizations in New York and Pennsylvania in its areas of interest, including medical research and health care; community and neighborhood improvement; higher education; and social and human services. Types of support include building construction and renovation, capital campaigns, scholarships, equipment acquisition, general operating support, research, and scholarships. There are no application deadlines; contact the office for appropriate forms.
Requirements: New York nonprofit organizations in Ripley, Chautauqua County, and Pennsylvania nonprofit organizations in North East, Erie County, are eligible.
Geographic Focus: New York, Pennsylvania
Amount of Grant: 750 - 250,000 USD
Contact: Laurie Moritz, c/o Mellon Financial Corporation; (412) 234-0023
Sponsor: Orris C. Hirtzel and Beatrice Dewey Hirtzel Memorial Foundation
P.O. Box 185
Pittsburgh, PA 15230

Historic Landmarks Foundation of Indiana African American Heritage Grants 2333
Historic Landmarks African American Landmarks Committee awards grants ranging from $500 to $2,500 to assist organizations in the preservation and promotion of historic African American properties and sites in Indiana. Civic groups, schools, libraries, historical societies, and other nonprofit agencies are eligible to apply for grants for organizational assistance, studies assisting in or leading to the preservation of a historic African American place, and programs promoting the preservation, interpretation, and/or visitation of a historic African American place. We make the grants on a four-to-one matching basis, funding 80% of the total project cost up to $2,500, whichever is less.
Requirements: To qualify for Historic Landmarks Foundation of Indiana's grants and loans, an organization generally must: be registered as a nonprofit corporation in the state of Indiana; be classified by or have applied to the Internal Revenue Service for status as a 501(c)3 public charity; be enrolled as a nonprofit or affiliate organizational member of Historic Landmarks Foundation; possess a charter that identifies preservation of the built environment as a primary organizational purpose; have a clearly defined organizational structure that includes regular meetings and an ongoing program; have been in existence for three years and/or have demonstrated responsible fiscal management.
Geographic Focus: Indiana
Amount of Grant: 500 - 2,500 USD
Contact: Jerry J. Fuhs, Chairman; (800) 450-4534 or (317) 639-4534; fax (317) 639-6734; info@historiclandmarks.org.
Internet: http://www.historiclandmarks.org/Resources/Pages/GrantsLoans.aspx
Sponsor: Historic Landmarks Foundation of Indiana
340 W Michigan Street
Indianapolis, IN 46202

Historic Landmarks Foundation of Indiana Historic Preservation Educ Grants 2334
Historic Landmarks Foundation and the Indiana Humanities Council make grants of up to $2,000 for educational projects related to historic properties in Indiana. Eligible projects include lectures, workshops, conferences, production of audiovisual materials, heritage and cultural tourism programs, and educational publications. Proposals for Heritage Preservation Education Grants are due in early March each year. Completed applications are due in April, and grant awards are announced in May. Online applications are available at http://www.indianahumanities.org/Grants/HistPresGrantGuidelines.html.
Requirements: To qualify for Historic Landmarks Foundation of Indiana's grants and loans, an organization generally must: be registered as a nonprofit corporation in the state of Indiana; be classified by or have applied to the Internal Revenue Service for status as a 501(c)3 public charity; be enrolled as a nonprofit or affiliate organizational member of Historic Landmarks Foundation; possess a charter that identifies preservation of the built environment as a primary organizational purpose; have a clearly defined organizational structure that includes regular meetings and an ongoing program; have been in existence for three years and/or have demonstrated responsible fiscal management.
Geographic Focus: Indiana
Date(s) Application is Due: Apr 1
Amount of Grant: 2,000 USD
Contact: Suzanne Rollins Stanis, Director of Heritage Education & Information; (800) 450-4534 or (317) 639-4534; fax (317) 639-6734; stanis@historiclandmarks.org
Internet: http://www.historiclandmarks.org/Resources/Pages/GrantsLoans.aspx#eligibilityrequirements
Sponsor: Historic Landmarks Foundation of Indiana
340 W Michigan Street
Indianapolis, IN 46202

Historic Landmarks Foundation of Indiana Legal Defense Grants 2335
The Historic Landmarks Foundation of Indiana provides grant dollars to help local preservation organizations save and restore historic places. While Historic Landmarks regards legal action as a last resort, it recognizes that it is sometimes required to save endangered structures and support preservation processes. Nonprofit preservation organizations may request grants of up to $2,000 for legal fees to defend or compel conformance with a local preservation ordinance, enforce protective covenants, or seek an injunction to prevent the demolition of a historic building. Historic Landmarks' Legal Defense Grants cover 80% of the total cost of legal counsel up to $2,000.
Requirements: To qualify for Historic Landmarks Foundation of Indiana's grants and loans, an organization generally must: be registered as a nonprofit corporation in the state of Indiana; be classified by or have applied to the Internal Revenue Service for status as a 501(c)3 public charity; be enrolled as a nonprofit or affiliate organizational member of Historic Landmarks Foundation; possess a charter that identifies preservation of the built environment as a primary organizational purpose; have a clearly defined organizational structure that includes regular meetings and an ongoing program; have been in existence for three years and/or have demonstrated responsible fiscal management.
Geographic Focus: Indiana
Amount of Grant: 2,000 USD
Contact: Jerry J. Fuhs; (800) 450-4534 or (317) 639-4534; info@historiclandmarks.org.
Internet: http://www.historiclandmarks.org/Resources/Pages/GrantsLoans.aspx
Sponsor: Historic Landmarks Foundation of Indiana
340 W Michigan Street
Indianapolis, IN 46202

Historic Landmarks Foundation of Indiana Marion County Historic Preservation Funds 2336
The Marion County Historic Preservation Fund makes grants to support nonprofit organizations working to preserve historic buildings and neighborhoods in Marion County. The program is a partnership between Historic Landmarks Foundation and The Indianapolis Foundation, an affiliate of the Central Indiana Community Foundation. Applications are accepted on an ongoing bases, and grants are awarded monthly.
Requirements: To qualify for Historic Landmarks Foundation of Indiana's grants and loans, an organization generally must: be registered as a nonprofit corporation in the state of Indiana; be classified by or have applied to the Internal Revenue Service for status as a 501(c)3 public charity; be enrolled as a nonprofit or affiliate organizational member of Historic Landmarks Foundation; possess a charter that identifies preservation of the built environment as a primary organizational purpose; have a clearly defined organizational structure that includes regular meetings and an ongoing program; have been in existence for three years and/or have demonstrated responsible fiscal management.
Restrictions: Project must be within Marion County, Indiana.
Geographic Focus: Indiana
Contact: Mark Dollase; (800) 450-4534 or (317) 639-4534; mdollase@historiclandmarks.org.
Internet: http://www.historiclandmarks.org/Resources/Pages/GrantsLoans.aspx
Sponsor: Historic Landmarks Foundation of Indiana
340 W Michigan Street
Indianapolis, IN 46202

Historic Landmarks Foundation of Indiana Preservation Grants 2337
Historic Landmarks' Indiana Preservation Grants are available to nonprofit organizations for professional architectural and engineering feasibility studies and other preservation consulting services, as well as organizational development and fund raising projects. Historic Landmarks Foundation makes Indiana Preservation Grants on a four-to-one matching basis, with four dollars from us matching each local cash dollar. We will fund 80% of the total project cost up to $2,500.
Requirements: To qualify for Historic Landmarks Foundation of Indiana's grants and loans, an organization generally must: be registered as a nonprofit corporation in the state of Indiana; be classified by or have applied to the Internal Revenue Service for status as a 501(c)3 public charity; be enrolled as a nonprofit or affiliate organizational member of Historic Landmarks Foundation; possess a charter that identifies preservation of the built environment as a primary organizational purpose; have a clearly defined organizational structure that includes regular meetings and an ongoing program; have been in existence for three years and/or have demonstrated responsible fiscal management.
Restrictions: The grants may not be used for physical restoration work.

Geographic Focus: Indiana
Amount of Grant: Up to 2,500 USD
Contact: Jerry J. Fuhs, Chairman; (800) 450-4534 or (317) 639-4534; fax (317) 639-6734; info@historiclandmarks.org.
Internet: http://www.historiclandmarks.org/Resources/Pages/GrantsLoans.aspx
Sponsor: Historic Landmarks Foundation of Indiana
340 W Michigan Street
Indianapolis, IN 46202

Historic Landmarks Legal Defense Grants 2338
While the foundation regards legal action as a last resort, it is recognized that it is sometimes required to save endangered structures and support preservation processes. The defense grants cover 80% of the total cost of legal counsel up to $2,000.
Requirements: Nonprofit preservation organizations may request grants of up to $2,000 for legal fees to defend or compel conformance with a local preservation ordinance, enforce protective covenants, or seek an injunction to prevent the demolition of a historic building.
Restrictions: Limited to Indiana only.
Geographic Focus: Indiana
Amount of Grant: Up to 2,000 USD
Contact: Carla Jones, (317) 639-4534; fax (317) 639-6734; info@historiclandmarks.org
Internet: http://www.historiclandmarks.org/help/grants.html
Sponsor: Historic Landmarks Foundation of Indiana
340 W Michigan Street
Indianapolis, IN 46202

Hitachi Foundation Business and Work Grants 2339
The Foundation's strategy focuses on discovering and expanding business practices that create tangible and enduring economic opportunities for low-wealth Americans, their families, and their communities. Their approach to advancing the fields of corporate social responsibility, or CSR, and corporate citizenship is to discover business policies and practices that both strengthen the business bottom-line and support low-income workers. This learning takes a three-pronged approach: identifying and working closely with business trailblazers; establishing sustained relationships with a few carefully selected communities ready and able to drive change; and developing standards or benchmarks that help define and reward their efforts. This program focuses on building an authentic integration of business actions and societal wellbeing in North America. The Foundation will identify suitable candidates for grants and invite proposals. Due to limited resources, the Foundation will not issue Requests for Proposals. However, it does have a web-based system for inquiries from nonprofit organizations. Visit the website for details.
Requirements: 501(c)3 tax-exempt organizations are eligible.
Restrictions: The foundation does not make grants to individuals; for-profit businesses; or to individuals for business start-ups or expansions. The foundation does not support capital drives or fund raising efforts. Funding for conferences and seminars is considered only when there is an exceptionally strong match with the foundation's mission and strategic objectives.
Geographic Focus: All States
Contact: Grants Administrator; (202) 457-0588; fax (202) 296-1098
Internet: http://www.hitachifoundation.org/grants/index.html
Sponsor: Hitachi Foundation
1509 22nd Street NW, P.O. Box 19247
Washington, DC 20037-1073

Hitachi Foundation Yoshiyama Awards 2340
Twenty-one years of experience honoring high school seniors for what they have done in their communities has proven to the Foundation that young people are remarkably creative and capable of initiating sustainable change. So the Foundation is planning to move beyond honoring young people for the changes they have made and, instead, invest directly in the changes they are making, now and into the future. The next phase for this program will invest in these young social entrepreneurs and learn from their endeavors. This change will further our objective of identifying, supporting, and learning from innovative approaches to addressing poverty. The new Yoshiyama Program will invest in young people who direct their creativity, commitment, and idealism into social ventures that help people who are economically stuck in place or losing ground.
Requirements: Graduating high school seniors in the United States and U.S. territories are eligible. (Nominees need not be college bound.) Individuals may be nominated by someone familiar with their service (clergy, school official, teacher, service agency representative, etc.).
Restrictions: Family members may not nominate their relatives and students may not nominate themselves.
Geographic Focus: All States
Contact: Awards Administrator; (202) 457-0588; fax (202) 296-1098
Internet: http://www.hitachifoundation.org/yoshiyama/index.html
Sponsor: Hitachi Foundation
1509 22nd Street NW, P.O. Box 19247
Washington, DC 20037-1073

Hoblitzelle Foundation Grants 2341
The Hoblitzelle Foundation was established by Karl and Esther Hoblitzelle in 1942. Grants made by the Directors are usually focused on specific, non-recurring needs of the educational, social service, medical, cultural, and civic organizations in Texas, particularly in the Dallas area. The Board meets three times per year. It is preferred that the initial approach be through a brief narrative letter describing the project for which funds are asked. Guidelines are available online.
Requirements: Nonprofit organizations in the State of Texas, primarily within the Dallas Metroplex, are eligible to apply.
Restrictions: No grants are made for religious purposes or to individuals. No grants are made outside the State of Texas. Contributions are not made toward operating budgets, debt retirement, research, media productions or publications, scholarships or endowments. The Foundation makes no loans.
Geographic Focus: Texas
Date(s) Application is Due: Apr 15; Aug 15; Dec 15
Contact: Paul W. Harris, President & CEO; (214) 373-0462; pharris@hoblitzelle.org
Internet: http://www.hoblitzelle.org/
Sponsor: Hoblitzelle Foundation
5956 Sherry Lane, Suite 901
Dallas, TX 75225

Hoffberger Foundation Grants 2342
The Foundation's highest priority is given to funding opportunities within the Jewish community and the general Baltimore community. The Foundation recognizes that the issues of hunger, homelessness, family instability, teen pregnancy, substance abuse and poor mental and physical health are often interrelated and interconnected to poverty, unemployment and access to adequate education. Preference will be given to proposals which meet the following criteria: enhancing and supporting self-reliance; addressing an unmet need; have measurable goals and objectives; have long-term funding strategy; have an evaluation component. A brief letter of inquiry should be submitted. LOI's are accepted on a rolling basis. Proposal instructions are available online.
Requirements: Tax-exempt organizations are eligible.
Geographic Focus: Maryland
Contact: Heller Zaiman; (410) 369-9336; fax (410) 369-9337; info@hoffbergerfoundation.org
Internet: http://www.hoffbergerfoundation.org
Sponsor: Hoffberger Foundation
101 West Mount Royal Avenue
Baltimore, MD 21201-5781

Hogg Foundation for Mental Health Grants 2343
The Foundation accomplishes its mission through the funding of external and internal projects in strategically selected areas. The Foundation operates major initiatives in three priority areas: integrated health care, cultural competence, and workforce development. Funds available through the Foundation's major initiatives and projects are distributed through a Request for Proposals (RFP) process. The Foundation does not accept unsolicited grant proposals on any topic. To be notified of future RFP opportunities, send an email message including your name, affiliation, and mailing address to: HoggCommunications@austin.utexas.edu
Geographic Focus: Texas
Contact: Program Contact; (888) 404-4336 or (512) 471-5041; fax (512) 471-9608; Hogg-Grants@austin.utexas.edu
Internet: http://www.hogg.utexas.edu/funding_grantmaking.html
Sponsor: Hogg Foundation for Mental Health
University of Texas at Austin, P.O. Box 7998
Austin, TX 78713-7998

Hoglund Foundation Grants 2344
The foundation supports nonprofits working in the areas of education, health science and services, social services, and children's health and development. Grants are made primarily in Dallas, and Houston, Texas, with a limited number of grants awarded outside of this area. Types of support include project support, capital support, and general operating support. Application guidelines are available on the foundation's Web site.
Requirements: To be eligible for consideration, an organization must provide proof that they have received a determination letter from the Internal Revenue Service indicating that it is a tax exempt organization as described in Section 501(c)3 of the Internal Revenue Code of 1986 and is treated as other than a private foundation as within the meaning of Section 509(a) of the Code. An organization may also qualify under Section 170(c)(1) if the grant requested is to be used exclusively for public purposes as described in the Code.
Restrictions: Grants are not made to individuals.
Geographic Focus: Texas
Date(s) Application is Due: Mar 15; Jul 15; Nov 15
Amount of Grant: 1,000 - 200,000 USD
Contact: Kelly Compton; (214) 987-3605; fax (214) 363-6507; info@hoglundfoundation.org
Internet: http://www.hoglundfoundation.org/grants.html
Sponsor: Hoglund Foundation
5910 North Central Expressway, Suite 255
Dallas, TX 75206

Holland/Zeeland Community Foundation Grants 2345
This Foundation funds programs and projects that focus on the arts and culture, education, environmental issues, health and human services, youth, seniors, community and economic development, affordable housing, and others that enhance the well-being of all citizens in the community. Proposals that help organizations deliver services more effectively, enhance cooperation and collaboration, address emerging needs or try new approaches, positively impact a large number of people for the resources invested, or focus on prevention receive priority consideration. The Foundation generally awards grants one-time only for a specific program or project. To apply, first call to discuss the project and confirm it meets the Foundation guidelines.
Requirements: Qualifying organizations include nonprofits that are tax-exempt under Section 501(c)3 of the Internal Revenue Code, schools, municipalities, and other governmental entities that serve a charitable purpose in the greater Holland and Zeeland area.
Restrictions: Funding is not available for the following: requests in excess of $15,000; annual fund-raising drives; services which are commonly recognized as government or school obligations (however the foundation does consider applications from schools for pilot

projects and innovative programs); endowments, loans, taxes or debt reduction; conference speakers, fieldtrips, travel or tours, for individuals or groups; religious programs that advocate specific religious doctrines or do not serve the broader community.
Geographic Focus: Michigan
Date(s) Application is Due: Jan 18; Jun 7; Sep 20
Contact: Janet DeYoung; (616) 396-6590; janet@cfhz.org or nfo@cfhz.org
Internet: http://cfhz.org/files/2010Funding_Guidelines.pdf
Sponsor: Community Foundation of the Holland/Zeeland Area
70 West 8th Street, Suite 100
Holland, MI 49423

Hollie and Anna Oakley Foundation Grants 2346
The Hollie and Anna Oakley Foundation is a private foundation organized in 1954. The Oakley Foundation was formed to promote religious, educational and charitable purposes, particularly in the states of Indiana, Illinois, Florida.
Requirements: To apply for a grant, contact the Oakley Foundation in writing via traditional mail or email. Include information about your organization, list of directors names, purpose, annual budget, mission statement, and those who benefit from the services you offer. In addition, please include your 501(C)3 number. The Oakley Foundation can only consider grants to organizations that have a valid 501(C)3 status.
Restrictions: The Oakley foundation can not grant money to any individual.
Geographic Focus: Florida, Illinois, Indiana
Date(s) Application is Due: Jan 10; Apr 10; Jul 10; Oct 10; Dec 10
Contact: Eston L. Perry; (812) 232-4437; information@oakleyfoundation.org
Internet: http://www.oakleyfoundation.org/home.asp
Sponsor: Hollie and Anna Oakley Foundation
18 South 16th Street
Terre Haute, IN 47807-4192

HomeBanc Foundation Grants 2347
Giving primarily in Florida and Georgia, the HomeBanc Foundation also, gives to national organizations. The Foundation has three main goals: provide support to cancer related causes through funding education, advocacy, and research; support the American dream of homeownership for those who might not reach it on their own; and provide college funding to students who strive to achieve their goals through education beyond high school. Scholarship forms are available online. Send a Letter of Inquiry to the Foundation, unsolicited applications are not excepted. The Foundation will contact you if your proposal fits their criteria.
Requirements: Nonprofits providing services in Georgia and Florida are eligible.
Geographic Focus: Florida, Georgia
Contact: Amanda Albertelli; (404) 497-1000; aalbertelli@homebanc.com
Sponsor: HomeBanc Foundation
2002 Summit Boulevard, Suite 100
Atlanta, GA 30319-1497

Home Building Industry Disaster Relief Fund 2348
The Home Building Industry Disaster Relief Fund (HBIDRF) makes funds available for direct contribution to other recognized charities aiming to meet similar primary needs as the HBIDRF - shelter, health care, education. The board welcomes recommendations of charitable organizations that are actively working in your region to rebuild communities. Guidelines and application form are available at the website.
Requirements: Charities can include corporations, funds, or foundations organized and operated exclusively for charitable, scientific, or educational purposes. These charitable organizations may be involved in making direct contributions to adversely impacted individuals through established process, or with coordinated building projects such as one-day builds, blitzes, etc. Other entities that could be eligible to receive funds might include vocational training programs, temporary shelters or clinics and educational ventures intended to help the local home building industry recover from disastrous events. To apply for funding, contact your local home builders association to determine if any partnering opportunities are available at this time.
Restrictions: The fund does not make assistance available directly to individuals.
Geographic Focus: All States
Contact: Jerry Howard, Executive Officer; (800) 368-5242; fax (202) 266-8400
Internet: http://www.nahb.org/generic.aspx?sectionID=842
Sponsor: Home Building Industry Disaster Relief Fund
1201 15th Street NW
Washington, DC 20005-2800

Home Ownership Participation for Everyone (HOPE) Awards 2349
The awards recognize organizations and individuals who are making outstanding contributions to the cause of increasing minority homeownership. Up to seven awards will be made, one in each of the following categories: education—organizations and individuals that have made an extraordinary contribution to educating minority homeowners; finance—organizations, programs, and individuals that have helped minorities overcome barriers to finance the purchase of a home; project of the year—the housing development or project that increases the supply of single-family homes or condominiums built and marketed to meet minority needs in minority communities; brokerage—an organization that provides a full range of real estate transaction services to minority communities; public policy—an organization or individual who has brought about changes in public policy or public programs to help increase minority home ownership; media—outstanding print or broadcast media coverage of minority homeownership; and leadership—the individual who has made a significant difference in the cause of minority homeownership during the year, or whose life work merits recognition and celebration for dedication to this issue. A partnership of real estate associations (California Association of Real Estate Brokers, Chinese American Real Estate Professionals Association of Southern California, Chinese Real Estate Association of America, National Association of Hispanic Real Estate Professionals, National Association of Real Estate Brokers, and National Association of Realtors) support the awards. Awards will be determined by a panel of distinguished judges based on the impact of the nominee's work, use of innovative ideas and applications, acceptance in the minority community, focus on minority homeownership, and affordability. Information and entry forms are available online.
Geographic Focus: All States
Date(s) Application is Due: Dec 1
Amount of Grant: 10,000 USD
Contact: Wendy Harper, (202) 383-1192; wharper@realtors.org
Internet: http://www.hopeawards.org
Sponsor: Home Ownership Participation for Everyone
700 11th Street NW
Washington, DC 20001

Homer A. Scott and Mildred S. Scott Foundation Grants 2350
The foundation awards grants to Wyoming nonprofit organizations in its areas of interest, including children and youth, higher education, and social services. Types of support include employee matching gifts and matching funds. Preference is given to requests that intervene in and prevent the problems of young people, build public awareness of youth issues, promote coordination and communication among programs serving young people, develop leadership skills, build self-esteem, and can become sustainable. Application deadlines vary; contact program staff for exact dates. Application forms must be obtained from the office. The board meets quarterly to consider requests.
Requirements: Sheridan, WY, nonprofit organizations are eligible.
Restrictions: No grants to individuals.
Geographic Focus: Montana, Wyoming
Contact: Lynn Mavrakis; (307) 672-1448; fax (307) 672-1443; lynn.mavrakis@fib.com
Sponsor: Homer A. Scott and Mildred S. Scott Foundation
P.O. Box 2007
Sheridan, WY 82801-2007

Homer C. and Martha W. Gutchess Foundation Grants 2351
Established in Cortland, New York, in 1998, the Homer C. and Martha W. Gutchess Foundation primarily offers support for cemeteries and burial services, as well as historical preservation. There are no applications or deadlines with which to adhere, and applicants should contact the Foundation directly in writing.
Geographic Focus: New York
Samples: Lime Hollow Center for Environment and Culture, Cortland, New York, $4,500; Cortland County Cemetery Foundation, Cortland, New York, $25,000.
Contact: Edmund J. Hoffman, (607) 756-5685
Sponsor: Homer C. and Martha W. Gutchess Foundation
41 Church Street
Cortland, NY 13045-2743

Homer Foundation Grants 2352
The Foundation seeks to fund innovative, creative projects that have a high likelihood of success and will have a long-term, positive impact on the community. Funding is available for arts and culture, community development, youth programs, education, health care, scholarships and the environment. Application information is available online.
Requirements: 501(c)3 nonprofit organizations and other qualified nonprofit entities located in the southwestern portion of the Kenai Peninsula, from Ninilchik south and including the communities across Kachemak Bay, are eligible. An individual who applies must be a resident of the region as described above, who will spend the funds on projects completed within this region. Projects taking place outside of this region, but by a resident, will be considered on the merit of the project and how it could benefit the community.
Geographic Focus: Alaska
Contact: Joy Steward; (907) 235-0541; fax (907) 235-0542; jsteward@homerfund.org
Internet: http://www.homerfund.org/grantmaking.html
Sponsor: Homer Foundation
P.O. Box 2600
Homer, AK 99603

Hometown Indiana Grants 2353
The Hometown Indiana matching grants program was designed to assist communities with projects in parkland acquisition and development, urban forestry, and historic preservation and archaeology. By statute, appropriated Hometown funds are divided according to the following ratios: 70% for park projects, 10% for forestry projects, and 20% for preservation projects. DNR's Division of Outdoor Recreation administers the parkland component of the program, while the Division of Forestry administers the urban forestry component. The intention of the preservation component of Hometown Indiana is to save significant historic and cultural resources that are seriously threatened or endangered. Depending on the State financial resources available, this program operates on a biannual basis. All funds distributed through the HPF grants program are awarded in the form of matching grants, which require the grant recipients or sponsoring organizations to supply a certain percentage of the total project costs. Survey projects, either architectural and historical or archaeological, are eligible for grant funding in the amount of 70% of the total project costs; the remaining 30% of the total project costs must be paid for by the grant recipient. All other types of projects are eligible for grant funding in the amount of 50% of the total project costs; the remaining 50% of the total project costs must be paid for by the grant recipient.
Requirements: Eligible applicants include (a) private, non-profit organizations with 501(c)3 tax exempt status (including local historical societies and preservation organizations), (b)

educational institutions (including public and private schools, colleges, and universities), and (c) local governmental units (including city and county agencies and commissions funded by a consortium of local governments). A subject property must be, at a minimum, listed in the Indiana Register of Historic Sites and Structures. Note that properties listed in the National Register are automatically included in the State Register.
Restrictions: Individuals and private, for-profit entities are not eligible to receive grant funds because federal regulations prohibit grant recipients from making a financial profit as a direct result of the grant-assisted project. Federal regulations do not allow grant funds to be awarded to active religious organizations, or to be used to assist buildings that are used primarily for religious functions. Note also that state and federal auditing and income tax regulations prevent the DHPA from making a grant award to an organization which is not incorporated, or which does not otherwise exist as a legal entity.
Geographic Focus: Indiana
Amount of Grant: Up to 100,000 USD
Contact: James A. Glass, Division Director; (317) 232-3492; jglass@dnr.in.gov
Internet: http://www.in.gov/dnr/historic/11816.htm#hometown
Sponsor: Indiana Department of Natural Resources
402 West Washington Street, Room W274
Indianapolis, IN 46204

Honda of America Manufacturing Foundation Grants 2354
The Foundation supports community outreach in Ohio. Each year, the Foundation funds various community projects throughout the state. This involvement helps build the community where it does business and where its associates live. The Foundation supports programs and organizations in the areas of education, arts and culture, civic and community, health and human services, and the environment. It places its priorities on the development of programs, and not supporting annual operating budgets.
Requirements: Priority consideration will be given for projects within the West Central Ohio area, including: Allen, Auglaize, Champaign, Clark, Darke, Delaware, Franklin, Hardin, Logan, Madison, Marion, Mercer, Miami, Shelby and Union counties. In addition, Honda considers projects on a case-by-case basis outside this area if the projects are Ohio-based and reflect its priorities of interest.
Restrictions: Honda of America does not make grants to: individuals; religious or political groups; organizations which are not tax-exempt under the U.S. Internal Revenue Code paragraph 501(c)3; or programs outside the state of Ohio. Generally, the Foundation does not provide contributions in support of: conferences or workshops; seminars or pageants; field trips, extra-curricular school activities or sports teams; fraternal or veterans organizations; national health organizations; courtesy advertisements, lobbying organizations, memberships or legal advocacy; staff salaries; or pilot programs.
Geographic Focus: Ohio
Date(s) Application is Due: Mar 31; Jun 30; Sep 30; Dec 31
Contact: Ginny Milburn; (937) 645-8792; ginny_milburn@ham.honda.com
Internet: http://www.ohio.honda.com/community/giving.cfm
Sponsor: Honda of America Manufacturing Foundation
24000 Honda Parkway
Marysville, OH 43040

Honeybee Health Improvement Project Grants 2355
The mysterious disappearance of bees, called Colony Collapse Disorder (CCD), is a growing threat to Honey Bees, the mainstay of pollination services in agriculture. The North American Pollinator Protection Campaign (NAPPC), a tri-national coalition dedicated to promoting the health of all pollinators partners with different organizations to perform research for improving the health of honey bees and reversing the threats they face. In partnership with Burt's Bees, the Honeybee Health Improvement Project was created. It awards annual research grants to scientists seeking solutions to improve honeybee health—including genetic stock improvements, commercial beekeeping practices, and forage opportunities on public and private land. NAPPC will fund multiple projects up to $8,000 each.
Requirements: Review and selection of proposals will be conducted by members of the Honey Bee Health Improvement Task Force (HBH). Funds must be used within a one-year period. Focused, targeted projects with a high likelihood of providing tangible results that can be applied to improving honey bee health are preferred. Proposals providing valuable extensions of previously funded projects will be considered. The HBH Task Force has identified six priority areas for funding, though other areas will be considered as well: (1) Effects of nutrition on honey bee behavior, physiology and/or colony health; (2) Effects of pesticides on honey bee behavior, physiology and/or colony health; (3) Effects of pathogens and pests on honey bee behavior, physiology and/or colony health; including the development of novel methods to mitigate these effects, such as RNAi technology; (4) Development of methods to improve genetic stocks of managed honey bee populations; (5) Effects of climate or environmental variables on: a) plants, especially nectar and pollen quantity and quality; and/or b) honey bee physiology and/or colony health; (6) The development of diagnostics or indicators for the presence of stressors that effect honey bee health, particularly those that can be used by beekeepers. Proposals that address multiple priority areas or have implications for the health of other managed or native bee species are encouraged.
Restrictions: As a nonprofit organization, the Pollinator Partnership/NAPPC does not pay overhead on funded research grants.
Geographic Focus: All States
Date(s) Application is Due: Dec 19
Amount of Grant: Up to 8,000 USD
Contact: Jennifer Tsang, (510) 643-7430; jt@pollinator.org
Internet: http://www.pollinator.org/honeybee_health.htm
Sponsor: North American Pollinator Protection Campaign
423 Washington Street, 5th Floor
San Francisco, CA 94111

Honeywell Corporation Family Safety and Security Grants 2356
Safety and security are top concerns for families everywhere. When it comes to safety and security, Honeywell believes that nothing is more important than protecting our most precious and vulnerable asset - children. At Honeywell, the Corporation has decades of experience developing and applying technologies that keep families safe and secure where they live, work and travel. Giving in this area is on a national basis within areas of company operations, with emphasis on New Jersey and New York. Applications are required, and potential applicants should begin by contacting the office by email. There are no specific deadlines.
Geographic Focus: All States
Contact: Michael Holland, Hometown Solutions Media Contact; (973) 455-2728 or (973) 727-6891; michael.holland@honeywell.com
Internet: http://honeywell.com/Citizenship/Pages/family-safety-security.aspx
Sponsor: Honeywell Corporation
101 Columbia Road
Morristown, NJ 07962

Honeywell Corporation Housing and Shelter Grants 2357
Through employee volunteer efforts and grant contributions, Hometown Solutions reaches out to help those who need home revitalization and critical infrastructure support for the communities around the world. The Corporation believes that safe, secure, comfortable housing is a basic human need. It's also a key Honeywell strength dating back more than 100 years. As a leading national corporate sponsor of the Rebuilding Together program, for example, the Corporation combines financial support with the hard work of thousands of its volunteers. This partnership is making life safer and more comfortable for low-income homeowners and communities across the U.S., Canada, and Mexico. Since 2004, more than 7,900 employee volunteers have helped renovate 289 homes and shelters in 42 Honeywell communities. Applications are required, and potential applicants should begin by contacting the office by email. There are no specific deadlines.
Geographic Focus: All States, Canada, Mexico
Contact: Michael Holland; (973) 455-2728; michael.holland@honeywell.com
Internet: http://honeywell.com/Citizenship/Pages/housing-shelter.aspx
Sponsor: Honeywell Corporation
101 Columbia Road
Morristown, NJ 07962

Honeywell Corporation Humanitarian Relief Grants 2358
Do the right work and do it right now, are the principles that guide the actions of the Honeywell Humanitarian Relief Fund (HHRF). Since the fund's creation, Honeywell has been on the forefront of relief efforts worldwide, working in partnership with key organizations like Operation USA and Rebuilding Together. Funded in part by donations from Honeywell employees, the HHRF strives to address both the immediate and long-term needs of those communities affected by natural disasters around the world. Recently, the Honeywell Corporation has been involved in a wide array of relief efforts including: the Indonesian tsunami, Hurricanes Rita and Katrina, the Sichuan earthquake, Hurricanes Ike and Gustav, and the Haiti earthquake.
Geographic Focus: All States, All Countries
Contact: Michael Holland, Hometown Solutions Media Contact; (973) 455-2728 or (973) 727-6891; michael.holland@honeywell.com
Internet: http://honeywell.com/Citizenship/Pages/our-values-and-work.aspx
Sponsor: Honeywell Corporation
101 Columbia Road
Morristown, NJ 07962

Honeywell Corporation Leadership Challenge Academy 2359
The Honeywell Leadership Challenge Academy (HCLA) is a week-long, experiential learning program exclusive to children ages 15-18 of full-time Honeywell employees around the world. Financial contributions from Honeywell Hometown Solutions and Honeywell employees help fund the scholarships, which include tuition, meals, accommodation and all materials for the program. Working in small groups, the students are presented with "Challenges" and are encouraged to explore problem-solving scenarios using hands-on science, mathematics, and engineering skills. Many of the activities require students to present their findings or opinions to a panel of experts in the field. Participants learn teamwork and communication in ways that are not easily replicated in the formal classroom. By participating in HCLA, students learn how to work through scientific problems through incremental tests and experiments.
Requirements: Students must have above average grades and an interest in math, science and technology. Participants for the program are selected through a rigorous process based on academic achievement and community involvement. No other special preparation is necessary for the program. The registration form and current program dates are available online.
Geographic Focus: All States
Contact: Coordinator; (800) 637-7223 or (256) 721-7150
Internet: http://leadership.honeywell.com/
Sponsor: Honeywell Corporation
101 Columbia Road
Morristown, NJ 07962

Honeywell Corporation Sustainable Opportunities Grants 2360
The Honeywell Corporation is dedicated to protecting the environment with a comprehensive and contemporary commitment to address some of the world's toughest challenges. Giving in this area is on a national basis within areas of company operations, with emphasis on New Jersey and New York. Types of support include: education, program development, sponsorships, and environmental protection programs. Applications are required, and potential applicants should begin by contacting the office by email. There are no specific deadlines.

Geographic Focus: All States
Contact: Michael Holland; (973) 455-2728; michael.holland@honeywell.com
Internet: http://honeywell.com/Citizenship/Pages/our-commitments.aspx
Sponsor: Honeywell Corporation
101 Columbia Road
Morristown, NJ 07962

Honor the Earth Grants 2361
As a unique national Native initiative, Honor the Earth works to raise public awareness, and raise and direct funds to grassroots Native environmental groups. Honor the Earth's Board encourages proposals on Native environmental justice, sustainable development, and cultural preservation, with a grant limit of $5,000. The organization's focus will remain on sustainable Indigenous communities support. Their work also focuses on opposition to fossil fuels extraction and destructive mining practices. Additional information, guidelines, and information on previously funded projects is available at the website. Applicants are encouraged to check back periodically for grant funding through the Building Resilience program. Proposals may be submitted in hard copy or by email. Faxed proposals cannot be accepted.
Requirements: Grants are awarded solely to organizations that are led and managed by Native peoples. Priority is given to grassroots, community-based organizations and groups with a lack of access to federal and/or tribal funding resources.
Restrictions: Funding is not available for individuals.
Geographic Focus: All States, Canada
Date(s) Application is Due: Nov 9
Amount of Grant: 1,000 - 5,000 USD
Contact: Winona LaDuke; (218) 375-3200; HonorGrants@honorearth.org
Internet: http://www.honorearth.org/grantmaking
Sponsor: Honor the Earth
607 Main Avenue
Callaway, MN 56521

Horace A. Kimball and S. Ella Kimball Foundation Grants 2362
The Kimball Foundation makes grants almost exclusively to Rhode Island operatives (charities) or those benefitting Rhode Island residents and causes. Although, the Foundation considers gifts to all areas in the state, greater emphasis is placed on South County. Areas of interest for the Foundation are: human services, the environment, and health care.
Requirements: The Foundation will consider any organization which has proper 501(c)3 and 509(a) I.R.S. tax classification status. Application form and guidelines available on foundation Web site. Application form required. Applicants should submit the following: copy of IRS Determination Letter; brief history of organization and description of its mission; copy of most recent annual report/audited financial statement/990.
Restrictions: No support for religious organizations. No grants to individuals, or for feasibility studies, capital projects or multi-year commitments.
Geographic Focus: Rhode Island
Date(s) Application is Due: Jul 15
Amount of Grant: 1,000 - 50,000 USD
Contact: Thomas F. Black III, President; (401) 364-3565
Internet: http://www.hkimballfoundation.org/index2.htm
Sponsor: Horace A. Kimball and S. Ella Kimball Foundation
130 Woodville Road
Hope Valley, RI 02832

Horace Moses Charitable Foundation Grants 2363
The Horace Moses Charitable Foundation was established in 1923 to support and promote quality educational, human-services, and health-care programming for underserved populations. Special consideration is given to charitable organizations that serve the community of Springfield and its surrounding communities. Grant requests for general operating support are strongly encouraged. Program support will also be considered. Small, program-related capital expenses may be included in general operating or program requests. The majority of grants from the Moses Charitable Foundation are one year in duration; on occasion, multi-year support is awarded. Applicants must apply online at the grant website. Applicants are strongly encouraged to do the following before applying: review the downloadable state application procedures for additional helpful information and clarifications; review the downloadable online-application guidelines at the grant website; review the foundation's funding history (link is available from the grant website); review the online application questions in advance; and review the list of required attachments. These will generally include: a list of board members, financial statements (audited, reviewed, or compiled by independent auditor); an organization summary; a list of other funding sources; an IRS Determination letter; and other required documents. All attachments must be uploaded in the online application as PDF, Word, or Excel files. The application deadline for the Horace Moses Charitable Foundation is 11:59 p.m. on April 1. Applicants will be notified of grant decisions before June 30.
Requirements: Applicants must have 501(c)3 tax-exempt status.
Restrictions: The foundation does not support requests from individuals, organizations attempting to influence policy through direct lobbying, or any political campaigns.
Geographic Focus: Massachusetts
Date(s) Application is Due: Apr 1
Contact: Michealle Larkins; (866) 778-6859; michealle.larkins@baml.com
Internet: https://www.bankofamerica.com/philanthropic/fn_search.action
Sponsor: Horace Moses Charitable Foundation
225 Franklin Street, 4th Floor, MA1-225-04-02
Boston, MA 02110

Horizon Foundation for New Jersey Grants 2364
The Foundation's purpose is to promote health, well-being, and quality of life in New Jersey communities. Foundation goals are to improve health by promoting quality health care programs and access and to enhance arts and cultural opportunities. Application information is available online. Only electronic grant applications will be accepted. Application are accepted between January 1 and September 31.
Requirements: 501(c)3 tax-exempt organizations in New Jersey communities located in and served by Horizon Blue Cross Blue Shield of New Jersey are eligible.
Restrictions: Funding is not available for: capital campaigns; endowments; hospitals or hospital foundations; individuals; political causes; political candidates; political organizations; political campaigns.
Geographic Focus: New Jersey
Amount of Grant: 10,000 - 50,000 USD
Contact: Michele Berry, Grants Coordinator; Foundation_Info@horizonblue.com
Internet: http://www.horizon-bcbsnj.com/foundation/about/funding.html?WT.svl=leftnav
Sponsor: Horizon Foundation for New Jersey
Three Penn Plaza East, PP-15V
Newark, NJ 07105-2200

Horizon Foundation Grants 2365
The Foundation supports programs and organizations that aspire to create and maintain sustainable and livable communities by: protecting and conserving land and water resources; educating children and adults about being good stewards of the environment; promoting vibrant, child-oriented arts; teaching respect for and preservation of historic assets; enabling children and adults to lead their communities in thoughtful and healthy ways; and encouraging service to others.
Requirements: 501(c)3 nonprofit organizations in Cumberland, Franklin, Lincoln and York Counties in Maine; Barnstable County in Massachusetts; Mercer County in New Jersey; and Fairfield County, Connecticut are eligible.
Restrictions: The foundation does not fund annual, building, capital, or endowment fund drives; colleges and universities; emergency requests; health/mental health; individuals; international or foreign programs; public and private schools; religious projects; or state agencies.
Geographic Focus: Connecticut, Maine, Massachusetts, New Jersey
Date(s) Application is Due: Jan 13; Jul 13
Amount of Grant: 5,000 - 20,000 USD
Contact: Administrator; (207) 773-5101; fax (207) 773-5201; info@horizonfoundation.org
Internet: http://www.horizonfoundation.org
Sponsor: Horizon Foundation
1 Monument Way, Second Floor
Portland, ME 04101

Horizons Community Issues Grants 2366
Grants support program activities or projects serving lesbian, gay, bisexual, and transgender (LGBT) people of all ages in designated California counties focusing on the following issue areas: arts and culture; advocacy, awareness, and civil rights; children, youth, and families; and community and social services. Application information is available online.
Requirements: To be eligible, an organization must: be a nonprofit, 501(c)3 organization, or provide documentation that the organization is sponsored under a fiscal agent umbrella that has 501(c)3 status. Organizations or programs must request support for one or more of the following counties: Alameda; Contra; Costa; Marin; Napa; San Francisco; San Mateo; Santa Clara; Solano; Sonoma.
Restrictions: The following are not eligible for support: costs incurred prior to the date of the grant award; government agencies; capital support, including construction and renovation; fundraising or event sponsorship; individuals; Non-LGBT organizations with budget over $1 million.
Geographic Focus: California
Contact: Jewelle Gomez; (415) 398-2333, ext. 116; jgomez@horizonsfoundation.org
Internet: http://www.horizonsfoundation.org/page/organizations/ci
Sponsor: Horizons Foundation
870 Market Street, Suite 728
San Francisco, CA 94102

Hormel Family Foundation Business Plan Award 2367
The purpose of this competition is to stimulate entrepreneurship and economic development in McCook, Nebraska. Competition is different from many other business plan competitions in the sense that the prize is not a simple cash award, but an actual investment by which the Hormel Family Foundation becomes a shareholder in the winning business. In addition to the $25,000 investment, the winner will receive business, legal and advertising services valued at $10,000. The Foundation views this competition not only as an investment in an individual or team, but primarily in the community of McCook.
Requirements: The proposed business must be located in or near McCook, Nebraska. Business owners located outside McCook city limits must be willing to relocate their business to McCook, or within a proximity acceptable to the Foundation. The business plan must be an original idea, and must be written by the applicant(s). Any copyright or intellectual property infringement will result in immediate disqualification and possible legal action. While the operations of the business must be based in the McCook area, and any tax dollars earned by the business must benefit McCook, sales of proposed products or services are not limited to McCook. This is important to note, especially in the case of internet-based businesses and businesses that might distribute products throughout the United States.
Restrictions: Applicants must be: local business owners interested in expanding or improving their existing business; any individual or team with a brand new business idea, willing to launch their business in McCook; or business owners elsewhere who are willing to relocate their business to McCook.

Geographic Focus: Nebraska
Amount of Grant: 35,000 USD
Contact: Susan Harris-Broomfield; (308) 340-0856; susan@hormelfamilyfoundation.com
Internet: http://www.hormelfamilyfoundation.com/businessplancompetition.html
Sponsor: Hormel Family Foundation
1 Prairie Hills Road
McCook, NE 69001

Hormel Foods Charitable Trust Grants 2368
The Charitable Trust was established to benefit various organizations and projects that emphasize education, hunger and quality-of-life initiatives in and around Hormel Foods plant communities. The Program operates as a compliment to its foundation, making charitable contributions to nonprofit organizations directly. Support is given primarily in areas of company operations. Fields of interest include: disaster and preparedness services; education; general charitable giving; and health care. Types of support include: scholarships; matching gifts; general operations; and sponsorships. The Public Relations Department handles giving. Annual donations to a single organization typically do not exceed $15,000. A contributions committee reviews all written requests. Applicants should submit a detailed description of the project and amount of funding requested. The board meets once each month.
Requirements: Only organizations classified as 501(c)3 are eligible for support. Applicants should be located in or serve the communities of: Aurora, Illinois; Austin, Minnesota; Algona, Iowa; Alma, Kansas; Atlanta, Georgia; Beloit, Wisconsin; Chino, California; Fort Dodge, Iowa; Fremont, Nebraska; Knoxville, Iowa; Lathrop, California; Mendota Heights, Minnesota; New Berlin, Wisconsin; Osceola, Iowa; Rochelle, Illinois; Stockton, California; Turlock, California; and Wichita, Kansas.
Restrictions: Giving is primarily limited to areas of company operations.
Geographic Focus: California, Georgia, Illinois, Iowa, Kansas, Minnesota, Nebraska, Wisconsin
Contact: Julie H. Craven; fax (507) 437-5345; media@hormel.com
Internet: http://www.hormelfoods.com/responsibility/philanthropy/default.aspx
Sponsor: Hormel Foods Charitable Trust
1 Hormel Place
Austin, MN 55912-3680

Hormel Foundation Grants 2369
The Foundation, established in 1941, is a non-profit organization dedicated to supporting higher education, health care and research, social services, and community programs located in or serving the city of Austin, Minnesota. Applications for grants must be presented to the Foundation in writing. They should be as brief as appropriate to present the necessary facts about the applying organization and the project for which the grant is being sought. An application form is required, and must be received by the Foundation office by September 1st of each year.
Requirements: Only 501(c)3 organizations in Minnesota should apply.
Geographic Focus: Minnesota
Date(s) Application is Due: Sep 1
Contact: R.L. Knowlton, Chairperson; (507) 437-9800; fax (507) 434-6731
Internet: http://www.thehormelfoundation.com/requirements.asp
Sponsor: Hormel Foundation
301 North Main Street
Austin, MN 55912-3498

Horowitz Foundation for Social Policy Grants 2370
The Horowitz Foundation approves approximately fifteen grants each year, in the amount of $7,500 per grant - $5,000 initially and an additional $2,500 upon receipt of a final report or a copy of the product of the research. The foundation supports and advances research and understanding in the major fields of the social sciences, specifically in the fields of psychology, anthropology, sociology, economics, urban affairs, area studies, political science, and other disciplines. Grants provide direct assistance to individual scholars worldwide who require small grants to further their research with emphasis on policy-oriented studies. Preference will be given to projects that deal with contemporary issues in the social sciences or issues of policy relevance, as well as to scholars in the initial stages of work. The annual deadline is January 31.
Geographic Focus: All States
Date(s) Application is Due: Jan 31
Amount of Grant: 3,000 - 7,500 USD
Contact: Mary E. Curtis, Chairman; (732) 445-2280; fax (732) 445-3138; applications@horowitz-foundation.org or info@horowitz-foundation.org
Internet: http://www.horowitz-foundation.org
Sponsor: Horowitz Foundation for Social Policy
P.O. Box 7
Rocky Hill, NJ 08553-0007

Horowitz Foundation for Social Policy Special Awards 2371
The Horowitz Foundation provides seven special awards that may be granted for certain projects. These often carry an additional modest stipend beyond the customary amounts of a grant. The eight areas are as follows: the Donald R. Cressey Award for work done at the empirical level that has direct implication for changes in criminal justice and penology practices; the Joshua Feigenbaum Award for empirical research on policy aspects of the arts and popular culture, with special reference to mass communication; the Eli Ginzberg Award for a project involving solutions to major health and welfare problems in urban settings; the Irving Louis Horowitz Higher Education Award for research that supports the development of organizational leadership in higher education (specific to Rutgers University doctoral students); the Harold D. Lasswell Award for policy related projects in international relations and foreign affairs; the Robert K. Merton Award for studies in the relation between social theory and public policy; the Martinus Nijhoff Award for policy implications of scientific, technological and medical research; and the John L. Stanley Award for a work that seeks to expand our understanding of the political and ethical foundations of policy research.
Geographic Focus: All States
Date(s) Application is Due: Jan 31
Contact: Mary E. Curtis, Chairman; (732) 445-2280; fax (732) 445-3138; applications@horowitz-foundation.org or info@horowitz-foundation.org
Internet: http://www.horowitz-foundation.org/special-awards.html
Sponsor: Horowitz Foundation for Social Policy
P.O. Box 7
Rocky Hill, NJ 08553-0007

Household International Corporate Giving Grants 2372
Household International Corporate Giving Grants (HSBC) focus on education for students ages 3 to 25. It also focuses on the environment, specifically climate change, freshwater, and terrestrial biodiversity. Special attention is given to requests from nonprofits that address issues related to financial and credit education, economic development, housing, youth development, and education, particularly for low-income and minority populations. Types of support include annual campaigns, capital campaigns, challenge/matching grants, equipment, general operating support, continuing support, research grants, and technical assistance. Grants are made at three levels: company-wide grants, local-facility grants, and the Help for Communities program administered through local branch offices. Each level has its own deadline. Guidelines and applications are posted on the website.
Requirements: Eligible non-profits applying to HSBC Bank USA, N.A., must complete the HSBC On-line Contribution Application and submit it with all required attachments.
Restrictions: The corporation generally does not support the following: organizations outside of the United States and/or organizations that do not hold 501(c)3 tax deductible status under the Internal Revenue Code; fraternal, veteran, labor, or athletic organizations; for-profit student aid or scholarship programs, aside from those already established by the company; political, lobbying or voter registration programs, or those supporting the candidacy of a particular individual; funds to support travel - group or individual; organizations that might in any way pose a conflict with our corporate values, products, customers or employees; advertising; or individuals. HSBC will not review unsolicited applications from hospitals, single disease research organizations, and religious organizations that serve a limited constituency. Only organizations receiving funding will receive a response in writing.
Geographic Focus: All States
Date(s) Application is Due: Nov 1
Contact: Administrator; (847) 564-6010; bankfoundationandgrants@us.hsbc.com
Internet: http://www.hsbcusa.com/corporateresponsibility
Sponsor: Household International Corporate Giving Program
2700 Sanders Road
Prospect Heights, IL 60070

Houston Endowment Grants 2373
The Endowment supports nonprofit organizations and educational institutions that improve life for the people of the greater Houston area. The Foundation funds programs in the arts, community enhancement, education, health, human services, the environment and neighborhood development. Requests for funding are accepted throughout the year. Further application information is available online.
Requirements: Nonprofit organizations that are recognized as charitable organizations by the Internal Revenue Code are eligible to apply. Funds are provided primarily to Harris County and contiguous counties. Grants seldom are given outside of Texas and never are made outside of the United States.
Restrictions: The Endowment does not select scholarship recipients or make direct scholarship awards to individuals. Inquiries about scholarship assistance should be made to financial aid offices at colleges and universities. Funding is not available for other grant-making organizations or to charities operated by service clubs. Funds are not available for religious activities; the purchase of uniform, equipment or trips for school-related organizations or sports teams; honoraria for speakers and panelists; fund-raising activities and galas; and memorials for individuals. The Foundation does not make loans or grants to individuals.
Geographic Focus: Texas
Amount of Grant: 2,500 - 1,000,000 USD
Contact: Harriet W. Garland; (713) 238-8100; info@houstonendowment.org
Internet: http://www.houstonendowment.org/grants/grants_apply.htm
Sponsor: Houston Endowment
600 Travis, Suite 6400
Houston, TX 77002-3000

Howard and Bush Foundation Grants 2374
The foundation's funding is limited to Rensselaer County, NY. with an emphasis on arts and culture, education, civic and urban affairs, legal services, including a women's bar association, and social service and health programs that benefit the areas resident. Requests for equipment acquisition, programs development, matching funds, building/renovation and seed money will receive consideration. There are no deadline dates, funding guidelines are sent upon request. Contact staff prior to submitting a proposal. The board meets twice a year, in April and October. Notification of proposal acceptance will be within 14 days, following the board meeting.
Requirements: Nonprofit organizations benefiting Rensselaer County, NY, and its residents may request grant support.
Restrictions: Grants are not awarded to colleges, schools, churches, or individuals or for endowment purposes, operating budgets, or deficit financing. Generally no support for government or largely tax-supported agencies, or churches not connected with the founders.
Geographic Focus: New York

Amount of Grant: 750 - 75,000 USD
Contact: Deborah Byers, Program Contact; (518) 271-1134; dogclover@aol.com
Sponsor: Howard and Bush Foundation
2 Belle Avenue
Troy, NY 12180

Howard County Community Foundation Grants 2375
The foundation awards grants to Maryland nonprofit organizations in its areas of interest, including human services, arts and culture, and education and community affairs. The board meets monthly. Project grants are reviewed in March, and operating grants are reviewed in November. Contingency grants are available year-round. Contact the office for application forms and deadlines.
Requirements: Howard County, MD, nonprofit organizations are eligible.
Restrictions: Grants do not support individuals, sectarian religious purposes, or medical research.
Geographic Focus: Maryland
Contact: Contact; (410) 730-7840; fax (410) 997-6021; info@columbiafoundation.org
Internet: http://www.columbiafoundation.org/nonprofits/index.html
Sponsor: Columbia Foundation/Howard County Community Foundation
10227 Wincopin Circle, Suite G-15
Columbia, MD 21044

Howard H. Callaway Foundation Grants 2376
The Howard H. Callaway Foundation offers support in the form of general operation grants primarily in the state of Georgia. The Foundations areas of interest include: athletics/sports; baseball; federated giving programs; higher education; human services and; public affairs. Applications are accepted year round, submit a letter of inquiry to the Foundation to begin the application process.
Requirements: Georgia 501(c)3 non-profit organizations are eligible for funding. There is neither a deadline date to adhere to nor, is there a specific application form to submit. Begin the application process by submitting a letter of inquiry to the Foundation containing: copy of IRS Determination Letter; descriptive literature about organization; detailed description of project and amount of funding requested.
Restrictions: No grants to individuals.
Geographic Focus: Georgia
Amount of Grant: 5,000 - 25,000 USD
Contact: Howard H. Callaway, President; (706) 663-5075
Sponsor: Howard H. Callaway Foundation
P.O. Box 1326
Pine Mountain, GA 31822-1326

Howe Foundation of North Carolina Grants 2377
The Howe Foundation, established in 1966, supports organizations involved with arts and culture, education, human services, Christianity, and mentally disabled individuals. Giving limited to the Belmont, North Carolina area.
Requirements: No application form required, submit your proposal to: P.O. Box 749, Belmont, NC 28012.
Restrictions: No grants to individuals.
Geographic Focus: North Carolina
Amount of Grant: 200 - 144,000 USD
Contact: Henry Howe, Treasure; (704) 825-5372
Sponsor: Howe Foundation
P.O. Box 227
Belmont, NC 28012-0227

HRF Hudson River Improvement Grants 2378
The HRF Improvement Grants were created to support projects that promote the enhancement of public use and enjoyment of the natural, scenic and cultural resources of the Hudson River and its shores, with an emphasis on physical projects that require capital construction, development or improvement. Examples of projects that may be considered for funding include: development or improvement of facilities that increase public physical or visual access to the Hudson River, including but not limited to docks, boats, piers and shore front access points; repair, restoration or creation of habitat; development or improvement and equipping of facilities suitable for Hudson River education programs, such as interpretive centers, marsh boardwalks or waterfront classrooms. The Improvement Fund encourages proposals that focus on environmentally beneficial shoreline enhancement and education projects. Samples of previously funded projects are available at the website. Application guidelines and a the application form are available at the website. Proposals should be assembled electronically and emailed. Additionally, applicants must mail six complete hard copies (one signed) to the contact person.
Requirements: Applicants must include a copy of the organization's tax exemption certificate under Section 501(c)3 of the Internal Revenue Code or an indication that the applicant is a subdivision of a government unit.
Geographic Focus: New York
Date(s) Application is Due: Nov 19
Amount of Grant: Up to 10,000 USD
Contact: Dr. Dennis Suszkowski, Science Director; (212) 483-7667; fax (212) 924-8325; dennis@hudsonriver.org or info@hudsonriver.org
Internet: http://www.hudsonriver.org/hrif/
Sponsor: Hudson River Foundation
17 Battery Place, Suite 915
New York, NY 10004

HRF New York City Environmental Grants for Newton Creek 2379
The New York City Environmental Fund (NYCEF) was formed to encourage active community stewardship of the waterways, shorelines, parklands and open spaces of the City of New York. NYCEF was created to support projects that (a) protect, preserve, improve or restore the environment; (b) facilitate the public's enjoyment of natural resources; or (c) enhance the public's awareness, knowledge, and understanding of ecological principles, natural resources and other environmental issues. The NYCEF Newtown Creek Fund requests proposals for environmental education, public access and stewardship projects that will benefit communities along Newtown Creek, one of New York City's six designated Maritime and Industrial Zones. In accordance with the settlement agreement creating the Fund, priority will be given to projects in and around Greenpoint, Brooklyn, and along Newtown Creek and the East River (both Brooklyn and Queens). NYCEF will provide financial support for qualifying projects that promote the environmental health and revitalization of natural resources and that increase public understanding of, access to and enjoyment of the environment. The NYCEF Newtown Creek Environmental Benefits Program seeks proposals for projects that protect and improve the environmental health of natural areas and the environment; educate people about the value of natural resources, biodiversity, conservation, and environmental protection; enhance access to natural areas and encourage stewardship activities to protect them; promote community involvement and encourage stewardship (personal and community responsibility and guardianship) for natural areas within the Newton Creek target area; and provide a framework for community stewardship and programming related to broader capital projects and improvements. The typical grant size will be between $5,000 and $25,000.
Requirements: Any nonprofit group or organization that qualifies as tax-exempt under Section 501(c)3 of the Internal Revenue Code is eligible to apply for support from the NYCEF Newtown Creek Environmental Benefits Program. Additionally, schools and government agencies with qualifying projects may apply. Groups without 501(c)3 certification may, for the purposes of administration of a grant, associate with an organization that does qualify.
Geographic Focus: New York
Amount of Grant: 5,000 - 25,000 USD
Contact: Dr. Dennis Suszkowski, Science Director; (212) 483-7667; fax (212) 924-8325; dennis@hudsonriver.org or info@hudsonriver.org
Internet: http://www.hudsonriver.org/nycef/ncf.html
Sponsor: Hudson River Foundation
17 Battery Place, Suite 915
New York, NY 10004

HRF Tibor T. Polgar Fellowships 2380
The Polgar Fellowships are conducted jointly by the Hudson River Foundation and the New York State Department of Environmental Conservation. The Fellowship provides summer funding, and funds for up to eight undergraduate and graduate students to conduct research on the Hudson River. Researchers gather important information on all aspects of the river, and train students in conducting estuarine studies and public policy research. Polgar Fellowships may be awarded for studies anywhere within the tidal Hudson estuary from New York Harbor to the Federal Dam at Troy, New York, including the four marshes of the National Estuarine Research Reserve (Stockport Flats, the Tivoli Bays, Iona Island Marsh, and Piermont Marsh).
Requirements: Graduate and undergraduate students are eligible. Because of the training and educational aspects of this program, each potential Fellow must be sponsored by a primary advisor. The advisor must be willing to commit sufficient time for supervision of the research, and to attend two meetings (orientation and final reports) with their students. Advisors will receive a $500 stipend.
Geographic Focus: All States
Date(s) Application is Due: Feb 20
Amount of Grant: 3,800 - 4,800 USD
Contact: Dr. Dennis Suszkowski, Science Director; (212) 483-7667; fax (212) 924-8325; dennis@hudsonriver.org or info@hudsonriver.org
Internet: http://www.hudsonriver.org/polgar.htm
Sponsor: Hudson River Foundation
17 Battery Place, Suite 915
New York, NY 10004

HRSA Nurse Education, Practice, Quality and Retention (NEPQR) Grants 2381
Through its Nurse Education, Practice, Quality and Retention grants program, the Division of Nursing will solicit three-year cooperative agreements that propose to develop and implement innovative career ladder programs that will increase the enrollment, progression, and graduation of Veterans in Bachelor of Science in Nursing programs. This VBSN program supports HRSA's strategic plan to improve access to quality health care and services; strengthen, the nation's healthcare workforce; build healthy communities; and improve health equity. Awarded VBSN applications will complement the collaborative efforts of the Health Resources and Services Administration (HRSA), the Department of Defense (DoD), and the Department of Veteran¿s Affairs (VA) that seek to: reduce barriers that prevent veterans from transitioning into nursing careers; develop BSN career ladder programs targeted to the unique needs of veterans; explore innovative educational models to award academic credit for prior health career experience/training or other relevant military training; improve employment opportunities for veterans through high demand careers training, and address the growing national demand for BSN prepared Registered Nurses. The intermediate program goals are to facilitate the transition of veterans into the field of professional nursing, while building upon skills, knowledge, and training acquired during their military service in order to increase employment opportunities. Sub-goals include increasing and diversifying the health workforce, and ensuring that healthcare providers are trained to provide high quality care that is culturally and linguistically aligned with the communities they will serve. The VBSN project will: provide program

participants with the opportunity to receive academic credit for prior military medical training and experience; provide participants with knowledge, skills, and support(s) needed to successfully matriculate through innovative BSN career ladder training programs; and prepare program participants for the National Council Licensing Examination for Registered Nurses (NCLEX- RN).
Requirements: Eligible applicants include accredited schools of nursing as defined in section 801(2), of the Public Health Service Act, a health care facility as defined in section 801(11) of the Public Health Service Act, or partnership of such a school and facility.
Geographic Focus: All States
Date(s) Application is Due: Feb 18
Contact: Rebecca Spitzgo; (301) 443-5794 or (888) 275-4772; fax (301) 443-8586
Internet: http://www.grants.gov/view-opportunity.html?oppId=249594
Sponsor: Health Resources and Services Administration
5600 Fishers Lane
Rockville, MD 20857

Huber Foundation Grants 2382
The Foundation focuses its grants program on three specific aspects of reproductive rights: keeping abortion safe, legal, and preferably increasingly rare; contraceptive choice and availability; and relevant education. The Foundation's major interest lies in funding organizations that will impact these issues on a national level. There is no formal application procedure. A letter describing the project, a budget for the project, and proof of tax-exempt status is required. Though the Foundation board meets four times annually, there are no fixed deadline dates.
Requirements: U.S. nonprofits, including advocacy groups, hospitals, legal defense groups, family planning agencies, educational organizations, universities, and women's groups may submit grant applications.
Restrictions: The foundation does not encourage proposals for projects that are local or regional in scope. It will not consider grants to individuals, foreign organizations, capital campaigns, scholarships, endowment funds, research, international projects, or film productions.
Geographic Focus: All States
Contact: Lorraine Barnhart, Executive Director; (732) 933-7700
Sponsor: Huber Foundation
P.O. Box 277
Rumson, NJ 07760-0277

Hudson Webber Foundation Grants 2383
The purpose of the Foundation is to improve the vitality and quality of life of the metropolitan Detroit community. The Foundation concentrates its giving primarily within the City of Detroit and has a particular interest in the revitalization of the urban core because this area is a focus for community activity and pride and is of critical importance to the vitality of the entire metropolitan community. The Foundation presently concentrates its efforts and resources in support of projects within five program missions: Detroit Physical Revitalization; Economic Development; The Arts; Safe Community; and the Detroit Medical Center. A brief letter signed by a senior officer of the requesting organization is the preferred form of application. Information for completing the letter of request are available online.
Requirements: The foundation concentrates its giving within Detroit.
Geographic Focus: Michigan
Contact: Katy Locker; (313) 963-7777; fax (313) 963-2818; HWF@hudson-webber.org
Internet: http://www.hudson-webber.org/HowToApply_Instructions.html
Sponsor: Hudson Webber Foundation
333 West Fort Street, Suite 1310
Detroit, MI 48226-3134

Huffy Foundation Grants 2384
The Huffy Foundation gives primarily to areas in which the company has operations in California, Ohio, Pennsylvania, and Wisconsin. These areas include: the visual arts; museums; performing arts; theater; arts/cultural programs; all levels of education; hospitals (general); health care and associations; recreation; children and youth services; and federated giving (United Way). Types of support include general and operating support; continuing support; annual campaigns; capital campaigns; building/renovation programs; emergency funds; program development; seed money; consulting services; employee matching gifts; and matching funds. Requests should include a description of the organization, its history and purpose, a description of the people it serves, and a summary of total budget and funding.
Requirements: The Foundation provides a brochure which delineates the application and grant guidelines. There is no application form. The Foundation recommends that the initial approach be in the form of a letter or a proposal. One copy of the letter/proposal should be submitted. There are no deadlines. The Board meets in February, May, August and November.
Restrictions: Grants are not made to individuals, in support of political activities or of religious organizations for religious purposes, or organizations that are not tax exempt. Grants are seldom made for medical research; to endowments; or for operating funds for organizations located outside the corporation communities.
Geographic Focus: California, Ohio, Pennsylvania, Wisconsin
Contact: Pam Booher, Secretary; (937) 866-6251
Sponsor: Huffy Foundation
225 Byers Road
Miamisburg, OH 45342

Hugh J. Andersen Foundation Grants 2385
The mission of the Hugh J. Andersen Foundation is to give back to our community through focused efforts that foster inclusivity, promote equality, and lead to increased human independence, self sufficiency and dignity. To fulfill this mission, the Foundation acts as a grantmaker, innovator, and convener. The Foundation's primary geographic area of focus is the St. Croix Valley: Washington County in Minnesota and Pierce, Polk and St. Croix Counties in Wisconsin. Secondarily, there is an interest in St. Paul, Minnesota. From time to time the Foundation may consider programs in other parts of the Metro Area and Greater Minnesota. Please contact the Program Director prior to submitting a proposal to determine if the program might be of interest to the Foundation. The Board generally considers requests in June, September, December and February. Faxed or emailed applications will not be considered.
Requirements: The Hugh J. Andersen Foundation awards grants only to qualified charitable organizations that are designated as tax exempt under Internal Revenue Service Code 501(c)3 and are not classified as private foundations.
Restrictions: The Hugh J. Andersen Foundation: does not make loans, and does not provide grants or scholarships to individuals; does not provide grants for lobbying activities, fundraising dinners and events, or travel; will generally not consider the following types of organizations and programs for funding: agencies/divisions/councils/programs that have counterparts in St. Paul or the St. Croix Valley; arts organizations exclusively focused on music, dance or visual arts; athletic teams; business/economics education; child care centers; civic action groups; debt or after the fact situations; immigration/refugee issues and programs; independent media productions; political/voter education; private or alternative schools; religious institutions. In addition, the Foundation: will generally not fund the entire project budget, but prefers to be part of an effort supported by a number of sources; considers major endowment and capital requests for funding to be a low priority; does not provide funding through fiscal agents; considers letters of inquiry. Letters of inquiry are reviewed at the Foundation's next board meeting. If the board determines that the request falls within its guidelines and interests, a full proposal will be requested from the applicant for review at the following board meeting.
Geographic Focus: Minnesota, Wisconsin
Date(s) Application is Due: Mar 15; Jun 15; Aug 15; Nov 15
Contact: Brad Kruse; (651) 275-4489 or (888) 439-9508; hjafdn@srinc.biz
Internet: https://www.srinc.biz/hja/documents/HJAGuidelines09-10.pdf
Sponsor: Hugh J. Andersen Foundation
White Pine Building, 342 Fifth Avenue North
Bayport, MN 55003

Huie-Dellmon Trust Grants 2386
The trust awards grants to Louisiana nonprofits in its areas of interest, including hospitals, higher and secondary education, libraries, and Protestant churches and organizations. Types of support include general operating support, capital campaigns, building construction/renovation, equipment acquisition, program development, scholarship funds, research, and matching funds. There are no application forms or deadlines.
Requirements: Central Louisiana nonprofit organizations are eligible.
Geographic Focus: Louisiana
Amount of Grant: 1,000 - 100,000 USD
Contact: Richard Crowell Jr., Trustee; (318) 748-8141
Sponsor: Huie-Dellmon Trust
P.O. Box 330
Alexandria, LA 71309-0330

Hulman & Company Foundation Grants 2387
The Hulman & Company Foundation was established in 1998 in the state of Indiana. The Foundation giving primarily in Indianapolis and the Terre Haute area. The Foundation supports community foundations and organizations involved with engineering education, animal welfare, and youth services.
Requirements: Contact the Foundations office with a proposal for initial approach, no application form required.
Restrictions: NO grants available to individuals.
Geographic Focus: Indiana
Amount of Grant: 5,000 - 95,000 USD
Contact: Jeffrey G. Belskus, Treasurer; (812) 232-9446
Sponsor: Hulman and Company Foundation
P.O. Box 150
Terre Haute, IN 47808-0150

Humana Foundation Grants 2388
The foundation was established to promote worthwhile organizations that improve the health and welfare of communities in its headquarters region of Louisville, KY. It supports nonprofit institutions primarily in the areas of domestic and international health, education, and civic and cultural development. Religious organizations are eligible for project-specific support (e.g., social services outreach) or funds for an accredited, church-affiliated educational institution. Grants also are awarded in Humana market areas outside of the headquarters region. Application information is available online.
Requirements: Applicant organizations must be 501(c)3 tax-exempt located in communities where Humana has a meaningful presence.
Restrictions: Grants are not given to organizations for seed money. The foundation does not contribute to social, labor, political, veterans, or fraternal organizations. Funds cannot be used solely to support an organization's salary expenses or other administrative costs. The foundation does not support lobbying efforts or political action committees.
Geographic Focus: Arizona, Colorado, Florida, Georgia, Illinois, Indiana, Kansas, Kentucky, Louisiana, Michigan, Ohio, Tennessee, Texas, Utah, Wisconsin
Date(s) Application is Due: Jan 15; Jun 15
Contact: Office; (502) 580-4140; fax (502) 580-1256; HumanaFoundation@humana.com
Internet: http://www.humanafoundation.org/philanthropy/
Sponsor: Humana Foundation
500 West Main Street, Suite 208
Louisville, KY 40202

Humane Society of the United States Foreclosure Pets Grants   2389
The Humane Society of the United States (HSUS) offers grants of up to $2,000 to animal shelters, non-sheltered rescue/adoption groups and animal care and control agencies to help establish, expand, or publicize services or programs that assist individuals in caring for their pets during the current economic downturn. Preference will be given to organizations that have or create a formal Plan of Cooperation with a local community partner such as the American Red Cross, a food bank, or other community service agency. These applications must be for programs specifically designed to help people and pets during this current economic downturn. There are no deadlines.
Requirements: Any program designed with the primary goal of assisting families or individuals whose main challenge with keeping their pet(s) is eligible to apply. HSU.S. also welcomes creative program ideas as long as the program assists families and their pets. Applicants can fill out the web form online or print the form and mail it in along with the required documents: your organization's W-9, 501(c)3 Determination Letter (or letter stating your organization can receive restricted funds if you are a municipal agency), and information related to your Plan of Cooperation (if your organization has one) as part of this application. Applications will be considered for six months upon receipt. If your organization applied over six months ago and has not received a grant, you can reapply.
Restrictions: Applications for normal funding, donations, or programs that are not related to the economic downturn will not be considered.
Geographic Focus: All States
Amount of Grant: Up to 2,000 USD
Contact: Program Coordinator; (202) 452-1100; fax (202) 778-6132
Internet: http://www.animalsheltering.org
Sponsor: Humane Society of the United States
2100 L Street NW
Washington, DC 20037

Humanitas Foundation Grants   2390
The Foundation considers proposals from Catholic organizations in the U.S. in the areas of church renewal, education and relief work. Areas of interest are: projects that promote the spirituality of the laity, high quality religious and lay leadership, vital parish life, Hispanic ministry, pastoral research, quality religious education, and direct service to the needy within disadvantaged populations. Proposal information is available online.
Requirements: Proposals for funding are accepted from Roman Catholic organizations, dioceses, groups of parishes, social agencies, religious orders, associations and other groups in the U.S. that are listed in The Official Catholic Director. Roman Catholic organizations with individual, federal tax-exempt status may also apply.
Restrictions: The Foundation does not fund capital campaigns, endowments, debt repayment, building construction, major renovations, scholarships, community organizing, or political lobbying efforts, nor does it fund already completed projects. It does not provide general support for well established programs. The Foundation does not accept proposals from individual parishes, schools, colleges, universities, seminaries or retreat houses for projects serving the ongoing functions of a particular institution. It does not make grants to support individuals. The Foundation does not accept applications from organizations outside of the U.S., or from U.S.-based organizations seeking funds for international projects.
Geographic Focus: All States
Date(s) Application is Due: Feb 1; Jul 1
Amount of Grant: 15,000 - 25,000 USD
Contact: Program Contact; (212) 704-2300; humanitas@humanitasfoundation.org
Internet: http://www.humanitasfoundation.org/infograntseekers.html
Sponsor: Humanitas Foundation
1114 Avenue of the Americas, 28th Floor
New York, NY 10036

Hundred Club of Colorado Springs Grants   2391
The Club was established in 1994 for the following purposes: to offer financial assistance to the surviving spouses and families of law enforcement officers and firefighters from the community who lose their lives in the performance of their duties through immediate and direct cash payments to the surviving family members to meet the press of expenses during a time of crisis; and to demonstrate community caring that can help provide a sense of security to spouses and family members. A $5,000 to $7,500 lump sum is typical, for payment of bills, credit card balances, housing expenses, funeral costs, etc. Annual valor awards are also given to one police officer, one firefighter and one deputy sheriff.
Requirements: Spouses and children of law enforcement officers and firefighters of Colorado Springs and El Paso County who lose their lives in the line of duty are eligible.
Geographic Focus: Colorado
Amount of Grant: Up to 7,500 USD
Contact: William J. Hybl, (719) 577-5712 or (719) 577-5763; wjhybl@elpomar.org
Sponsor: Hundred Club of Colorado Springs
P.O. Box 64
Colorado Springs, CO 80901

Hundred Club of Connecticut Grants   2392
The Club was established in 1967 for the purpose of offering financial assistance to the surviving spouses and families of law enforcement officers and firefighters from the State of Connecticut who lose their lives in the performance of their duties. This is accomplished through: $10,000 lump sum; educational scholarship assistance of up to $25,000 per year; computer and internet charges; summer camp for children 5 to 16 years old; $200 U.S. bond at birthday to 18-year-olds; $750 plus $250 per child to spouse at Christmas; Turkey for Thanksgiving and candy at Valentines day, Easter and Mother's day. A lump sum is typical within a 24-hour period, intended for payment of bills, credit card balances, housing expenses, funeral costs, etc.
Requirements: Spouses and children of law enforcement officers and firefighters of Connecticut who lose their lives in the line of duty are eligible.
Geographic Focus: Connecticut
Contact: William E. Sydenham, Jr., Executive Director; (203) 633-8357; fax (203) 633-8350; ct100@hundredclubofct.org
Internet: http://www.hundredclubofct.org/information.php
Sponsor: Hundred Club of Connecticut
119 Oakwood Drive, P.O. Box 419
Glastonbury, CT 06033

Hundred Club of Contra Costa County Survivor Benefits Grants   2393
The mission of the Club is to provide immediate financial assistance to the families of police officers and firefighters killed in the line of duty in Contra Costa County, California. To that end, the lump sum of $15,000 is available to family members of any Contra Costa County peace officer or fire fighter who is killed in the line of duty within 48 hours of his/her death to help with burial and other immediate expenses.
Requirements: Recipients must be widows, widowers, and/or dependents of police officers and firefighters who have lost their lives in the line of duty in Contra Costa County, California.
Geographic Focus: California
Amount of Grant: 15,000 USD
Contact: Marvin A. Remmich, (925) 837-0199; Marvin@MarvinRemmich.com
Internet: http://www.100clubcontracostacounty.org/index.php?option=com_content&task=view&id=6&Itemid=27
Sponsor: Hundred Club of Contra Costa County
P.O. Box 773
Danville, CA 94526

Hundred Club of Denver Grants   2394
The program provides a one-time $5,000 contribution to the surviving spouses and families of law enforcement officers and firefighters from the community who lose their lives in the performance of their duties through immediate and direct cash payments to the surviving family members to meet the press of expenses during a time of crisis. Will assess family needs and could offer financial assistance ranging up to $100,000 based on that assessment. Trust funds also provide scholarships to children.
Restrictions: The fund is inteded only for residents of the Denver metropolitan area.
Geographic Focus: Colorado
Amount of Grant: 5,000 - 100,000 USD
Contact: John Freyer, President; (303) 331-6248; fax (303) 321-5794; jefreyer@ltgc.com
Sponsor: Hundred Club of Denver
P.O. Box 5611
Denver, CO 80217-5611

Hundred Club of Durango Grants   2395
The Club was established in 1974 for the purpose of offering financial assistance to the surviving spouses and families of public safety officials, including law enforcement officers and fire fighters, who lose their lives in the performance of their duties. The mission states that it will act to free the surviving spouse from financial worry and leave the family with cash in the bank and social security benefits. This is accomplished through immediate and direct cash payments to the surviving family members to meet the press of expenses during a time of crisis and to demonstrate community caring that can help provide a sense of security to spouses and family members. A $7,000 lump sum is typical, to be utilized for payment of bills, credit card balances, housing expenses, funeral costs, etc.
Requirements: Spouses and children of public safety officials of Durango, Colorado, who lose their lives in the line of duty are eligible.
Geographic Focus: Colorado
Contact: Jasper Welch, President; (970) 247-1834; deanelk@aol.com
Sponsor: Hundred Club of Durango
P.O. Box 3146
Durango, CO 81302

Hundred Club of Los Angeles Grants   2396
The primary mission of the Club is to provide immediate financial assistance to the families of police officers and firefighters killed in the line of duty in the greater Los Angeles, California, region. To that end, a lump sum of up to $15,000 is available to family members of any Los Angeles area peace officer or fire fighter who is killed in the line of duty. Funding is intended to help with burial and other immediate expenses following a sudden death.
Requirements: Recipients must be widows, widowers, and/or dependents of police officers and firefighters who have lost their lives in the line of duty in the Los Angeles, California, area.
Geographic Focus: California
Contact: Ronald Stackler; (310) 589-0902; fax (310) 589-0628; res@pixelgate.net
Sponsor: Hundred Club of Los Angeles
Hatton, Petrie & Stackler, LLP, 6786 Shearwater Lane
Malibu, CA 90265

Hundred Club of Palm Springs Grants   2397
The mission of the Hundred Club of Palm Springs is to provide financial assistance to families of public safety officers and firefighters who are seriously injured or killed in the line-of-duty, and to provide resources to enhance their safety and welfare. A $5,000 lump sum is typical, plus more if needed. The Club matches dollar for dollar donations to purchase vests and biohazard jackets.
Requirements: Applicants must: be located or reside in Palm Springs, California, region; be a surviving spouse of a public safety officer or firefighter seriously injured or killed in the line-of-duty; and/or be an organization of firefighters or other public safety officials.

Geographic Focus: California
Amount of Grant: 5,000 USD
Contact: Mr. Michael R. McCulloch, (760) 327-1417; fax (760) 322-6343; mcculloch_Michael@email.msn.com
Sponsor: Hundred Club of Palm Springs
255 North El Cielo Road, #300
Palm Springs, CA 92264

Hundred Club of Pueblo Grants 2398
The Club was established in 1996 for the purpose of offering financial assistance to the surviving spouses and families of law enforcement officers and firefighters from the community of Pueblo who lose their lives in the performance of their duties. This is accomplished through immediate and direct cash payments to the surviving family members to meet the press of expenses during a time of crisis. A $5,000 to $7,000 lump sum is typical, intended for payment of bills, credit card balances, housing expenses, funeral costs, etc.
Requirements: Spouses and children of law enforcement officers and firefighters of Pueblo who lose their lives in the line of duty are eligible.
Geographic Focus: Colorado
Contact: Ken West, (719) 544-2791 or (719) 545-3125; fax (719) 545-2788
Sponsor: Hundred Club of Pueblo
210 South Victoria Avenue
Pueblo, CO 81003

Hundred Club of Santa Clara County Grants 2399
The mission of the 100 Club of Santa Clara County is to provide financial assistance to families of public safety officers and firefighters who are seriously injured or killed in the line-of-duty, and to provide resources to enhance their safety and welfare. The Club provides a $5,000 lump sum benefit to the surviving spouse of a firefighter or public safety official residing in Santa Clara County, California.
Requirements: Recipients must: reside in Santa Clara County, California; and be a surviving spouse of a public safety officer or firefighter seriously injured or killed in the line-of-duty.
Geographic Focus: California
Amount of Grant: 5,000 USD
Contact: Ronald W. Minnis, President; (408) 262-0656; fax (408) 262-2144
Sponsor: 100 Club of Santa Clara County
P.O. Box 36003
Miliptas, CA 95035

Huntington Arts Council Arts-in-Education Programs 2400
The Council provides many diverse programs and services to more than 600 individual and cultural organization members. The council is also the official arts coordinating agency for the Town of Huntington, and it serves as the primary regranting agency in Suffolk County for the New York State Council on the Arts. As part of the Huntington Arts Council's mission of Bringing Art to Life, the Council coordinate's and participate's in a number of Arts-in-Education programs, including: The Journey Program - Founded by Sandy Chapin over twenty years ago, the Huntington Arts Council's Journey Program is a Cultural Arts-in-Education program that joins the Huntington Arts Council as a means of integrating cultural arts into the school curriculum; Tulip Festival Art Contest - In partnership with the Town of Huntington and Astoria Federal Savings, the Huntington Arts Council administers this annual student art contest for children in grades 3-8; Scholarship Programs - The Arts-in-Education program has administered a number of privately funded scholarship programs, including the Aboff-Usdan Scholarship for talented arts students; Internship Programs - The Huntington Arts Council offers internship programs for both high school and college students. These internships offer participants a well balanced look at careers in arts administration. To apply for an internship, please send a resume, cover letter, and writing sample to Caitlin Apostoli, Arts-in-Education Coordinator; Guitar Program - With support from the D'Addario Foundation and New York State Assemblyman James Conte, the Huntington Arts Council coordinates a guitar program with the Tri-Community Youth Agency. This program provides students in Tri-CYA programs with guitars and a full summer of free guitar lessons; Discovery Nights - In partnership with the Heckscher Museum, the Arts-in-Education program participates in three nights of family fun over the course of the Summer Arts Festival.
Requirements: Applicants must be residents of Suffolk County, New York area.
Geographic Focus: New York
Contact: Caitlin Apostoli, Arts-in-Education Coordinator; (631) 271-8423, ext. 14; fax (631) 271-8428; capostoli@huntingtonarts.org
Internet: http://www.huntingtonarts.org/
Sponsor: Huntington Arts Council
213 Main Street
Huntington, NY 11743

Huntington Arts Council Decentralization Community Arts Grants 2401
Through this program, non-profit organizations and individual artists may apply annually for grants to help strengthen the arts and cultural programs in their communities. It is the intention of the New York State Council on the Arts that these funds, regranted through Decentralization, provide developmental support to those organizations exhibiting quality programming, community support, and professionalism. The request can be no great than $5,000.
Requirements: Applicants must be non-profit organizations serving the residents of Suffolk County, New York.
Geographic Focus: New York
Date(s) Application is Due: Nov 6
Amount of Grant: Up to 5,000 USD
Contact: Linda Furey, Grants Coordinator; (631) 271-8423, ext. 16; fax (631) 271-8428; lfurey@huntingtonarts.org or info@huntingtonarts.org
Internet: http://www.huntingtonarts.org/content/programs/grants/grants.cfm
Sponsor: Huntington Arts Council
213 Main Street
Huntington, NY 11743

Huntington Arts Council JP Morgan Chase Artist Reach Out Grants 2402
These grants are intended to support artist's projects, which directly involve the community as part of the creative process Community participation is required. Community involvement means people in the community connect with the artist at some point in the creative process. The program provides grants up to $2,000. This grant does not require a monetary match or additional income. Applications must be postmarked by March 13, or hand-delivered by 5:00 p.m. on March 13.
Restrictions: The following are not eligible for a grant: requests for support of programs and/or events; fellowships or projects that are primarily commercial or promotional; school systems, college or university departments, libraries, and social service agencies; religious institutions; government agencies; individuals that receive direct support from JPMorgan Chase; activities currently supported by other Huntington Arts Council Grants; prize money or awards; benefits, projects, and staff primarily used for fund raising purposes; refreshment costs; or previous grantees of Capacity Building or other Huntington Arts Council Grants who have failed to comply with grant contracts.
Geographic Focus: New York
Date(s) Application is Due: Mar 13
Amount of Grant: 2,000 USD
Contact: Linda Furey, Grants Coordinator; (631) 271-8423, ext. 16; fax (631) 271-8428; lfurey@huntingtonarts.org or info@huntingtonarts.org
Internet: http://www.huntingtonarts.org/content/programs/grants/grants.cfm
Sponsor: Huntington Arts Council
213 Main Street
Huntington, NY 11743

Huntington Arts Council JP Morgan Chase Organization/Stabilization Regrants 2403
Organization/Stabilization Grants, made possible through the JPMorgan Chase Regrant Program, help small and mid-sized arts organizations to plan more effectively and operate more efficiently. These grants support activities that build an organization's capacity to provide services to the community and are not directly tied to any specific public programs. Organizations may request support for a capacity building project that will increase the organization's ability to provide services to the Long Island Community. Specific projects eligible for support include, but are not limited to, these examples: development of a strategic or business plan; consultant fees for activities such as strategic planning, board development, or marketing; staff training; and computer software, hardware or other equipment. Grants provide grants between $2,000 and $3,000. This grant does not require a monetary match or additional income. Applications must be postmarked by March 13, or hand-delivered by 5:00 p.m. on March 13.
Requirements: Priority is given to organizations with an annual operating budget of less than $300,000 (both income and expense). Applicants must: demonstrate tax exempt status as a private, not for profit organization incorporated in Suffolk or Nassau Counties with 501(c)3 IRS tax-exempt status or NYS Charities Registration; have a mission statement that clearly delineates the arts as primary, both in focus and in actual operation; and present exhibitions, programs, or cultural activities that are accessible to the public.
Geographic Focus: New York
Date(s) Application is Due: Mar 13
Amount of Grant: Up to 3,000 USD
Contact: Linda Furey, Grants Coordinator; (631) 271-8423, ext. 16; fax (631) 271-8428; lfurey@huntingtonarts.org or info@huntingtonarts.org
Internet: http://www.huntingtonarts.org/content/programs/grants/grants.cfm
Sponsor: Huntington Arts Council
213 Main Street
Huntington, NY 11743

Huntington Clinical Foundation Grants 2404
The Foundation, established in 1986, supports health care programs and access, higher education, and medical research. Grant amounts range from approximately $4,000 to $8,000, with some larger amounts available. There are no specific applications or deadlines with which to adhere. The Board meets quarterly, and applicants should forward a detailed description of the project and amount of funding requested.
Requirements: Giving is limited to the Huntington, West Virginia, region.
Geographic Focus: West Virginia
Amount of Grant: 4,000 - 8,000 USD
Contact: Dr. J. David Daniels, President; (304) 529-4217; fax (304) 523-6051
Sponsor: Huntington Clinical Foundation
P.O. Box 117
Huntington, WV 25706-0117

Huntington County Community Foundation - Hiner Family Grant 2405
The Huntington County Community Foundation - Hiner Family Grant awards funding to projects that preserve and promote culture in Huntington County, Indiana. Applicants must be a tax exempt charitable or nonprofit entity or have a nonprofit as a fiscal agent. Completeness, merit, and quality of the application are material considerations in making grant funding decisions. Other important factors include: the beneficial impact on the Huntington County community, immediate and/or ongoing; competing known and anticipated community needs which may be eligible for and seek funding; number of persons

benefited/affected by the proposal; and a clear, complete, and comprehensible statement of purpose. Applicants are encouraged to discuss their project with the Foundation on whether it is appropriate for funding consideration.
Requirements: Organizations must submit one original set and five additional paper clipped sets of the following for funding consideration: grant proposal form; detailed project budget and organizational budget; current year-end financial statement; strategic or long-range plan; and roster of board members with titles and affiliations. They should also submit one copy of the IRS tax exempt letter and one copy of the articles of incorporation.
Restrictions: Grants will not be awarded to fund: operational or ongoing recurring (within 60 months) cost of the program; or political projects or campaigns.
Geographic Focus: Indiana
Date(s) Application is Due: Apr 15; Oct 15
Contact: Michael Howell; (260) 356-8878; fax (260) 356-0921; michael@huntingtonccf.org
Internet: http://www.huntingtonccf.org/hccf_grant_opportunities.html
Sponsor: Huntington County Community Foundation
356 West Park Drive
Huntington, IN 46750

Huntington County Community Foundation - Make a Difference Grants   2406
The Huntington County Community Foundation - Make a Difference Grants fund charitable projects that make a positive impact on the residents of Huntington County. Grant areas to be considered include: arts and culture; community development; health and human services; education; and other charitable services. These grants are awarded in spring and fall cycles. Grant decisions on based on the following criteria: the project's beneficial impact on Huntington County, immediate and ongoing; known and anticipated community needs; number of persons benefitted/affected by the project; and a clear, complete, and comprehensible statement of particulars.
Requirements: Applicants should submit one original and five additional paper clipped sets of the online application packet to include the following: grant proposal form; detailed project and organizational budget; current year-end financial statement; strategic or long-range plan; roster of board members; IRS tax exempt status; and articles of incorporation.
Restrictions: Grants will not be awarded to fund: operational or ongoing recurring (within 60 months) cost of the program; political projects or campaigns; or projects of applicants, or project owners, with taxing authority (e.g. school corporations; units of government).
Geographic Focus: Indiana
Date(s) Application is Due: Apr 15; Oct 15
Contact: Michael Howell, Executive Director; (260) 356-8878; fax (260) 356-0921; michael@huntingtonccf.org
Internet: http://www.huntingtonccf.org/hccf_grant_opportunities.html
Sponsor: Huntington County Community Foundation
356 West Park Drive
Huntington, IN 46750

Huntington County Community Foundation - Stephanie Pyle Grant   2407
The Huntington County Community Foundation - Stephanie Pyle "Spirit of the Community" Grant funds projects that keep Pyle's passion for volunteerism and community service alive in Huntington County, Indiana. Qualifying projects include those that exemplify and advance community development, embrace leadership and youth in the community (individuals or groups), or involve collaborations between two or more groups.
Requirements: Applicants are required to submit the online application and following information (six complete sets) to include: the grant proposal form; detailed organizational budget and project budget; most recent year-end financial statement; strategic or long-range plan; and a roster of the board members, their titles, and affiliations. Organizations should also submit one copy of the IRS tax exempt letter and articles of incorporation.
Restrictions: Grants will not be awarded to fund: operational or ongoing recurring (within 60 months) cost of the program; or political projects or campaigns. Applicants must be residents of Huntington County.
Geographic Focus: Indiana
Contact: Michael Howell; (260) 356-8878; fax (260) 356-0921; michael@huntingtonccf.org
Internet: http://www.huntingtonccf.org/hccf_grant_opportunities.html
Sponsor: Huntington County Community Foundation
356 West Park Drive
Huntington, IN 46750

Huntington Foundation Grants   2408
The Foundation, established in 1986, offers grants that support institutional change or assists grant recipients in making more effective use of resources they generate from other sources. The Foundation also promotes strong public-private collaborative efforts to meet community needs and foster volunteer efforts wherever possible. A formal application is required, and applicants should contact the Foundation directly by letter or telephone. The Board meets quarterly, and there are no specific deadlines with which to adhere.
Requirements: Applicants must be 501(c)3 organizations that support those living in the Huntington, West Virginia, region and across the State of West Virginia.
Geographic Focus: West Virginia
Amount of Grant: Up to 75,000 USD
Samples: Greater Huntington Park and Recreation District, Huntington, West Virginia, $68,484—for improvement and enhancement of parks; Huntington Museum of Art, Huntington, West Virginia, $33,000—for children's outreach program.
Contact: Glenna J. Smoot, Executive Secretary; (304) 522-0611
Sponsor: Huntington Foundation
401 Eleventh Street, Suite 306
Huntington, WV 25701-2218

Huntington National Bank Community Affairs Grants   2409
The corporation supports a variety of community focused initiatives that benefit children, education, economic development, health, social service housing, and the arts in each community of its banking offices. A letter of request (one to two pages) can serve as an initial application for both single- and multi-year contributions. The letter should include a brief statement about the organization, its history, objectives, and goals; purpose of the project; visibility for Huntington as a participant in the project; list of officers and directors; target population(s) to be served by contribution; and annual organization budget, total project budget, amount requested, list of other contributors, and amounts of funds anticipated or committed.
Requirements: Tax-exempt organizations in Ohio, Kentucky, Indiana, Michigan, and West Virginia may apply.
Restrictions: Community donations may not be used for political campaigns involving individuals or issues; religious, ethnic, military, fraternal, or labor groups; individuals; organizations outside of the corporate market area; or organizations without IRS 501(c)3 tax-exempt status.
Geographic Focus: Indiana, Kentucky, Michigan, Ohio, West Virginia
Amount of Grant: 1,000 - 10,000 USD
Contact: Elfi Di Bella; (614) 480-4483; fax (614) 480-4973; elfi.dibella@huntington.com
Internet: http://www.huntington.com/us/HNB3150.htm
Sponsor: Huntington Bancshares
41 South High Street, Huntington Center 3413
Columbus, OH 43215

Hutchinson Community Foundation Grants   2410
The Hutchinson Community Foundation provides funding in the counties of Hutchinson and, Reno, Kansas, inluding the immediate area surrounding area. Areas of interest include, but are not, limited to: community needs in areas such as early childhood, youth, education, arts and culutre, and neighborhood development.
Requirements: Nonprofit organizations in Kansas are eligible to apply. Special purpose units of government can apply for support of innovative projects located in Reno County.
Restrictions: Grant proposals from individuals or non-qualifying organizations will not be considered.
Geographic Focus: Kansas
Contact: Audrey Abbott Patterson; (620) 663-5293; fax (620) 663-9277; aubrey@hutchcf.org
Internet: http://www.hutchcf.org/default.asp?sm=2&si=1
Sponsor: Hutchinson Community Foundation
One North Main, Suite 501, P.O. Box 298
Hutchinson, KS 67504-0298

Hut Foundation Grants   2411
Since 1998, the Hut Foundation has been funding nonprofits primarily in the states of California and Virginia, in the following areas of interest: arts; children/youth services; community/economic development; education; health care; youth development. Unsolicited requests for funds are not accepted, therefore initial contact should be through a Letter of Inquiry. If the proposal follows the Foundations guidelines, the applicant will be invited to submit an application.
Requirements: Must be a 501(c)3 nonprofit.
Restrictions: No grants to individuals.
Geographic Focus: California, Virginia
Contact: Marcus Guerrero; (415) 834-2464; hutfoundation@gmail.com
Sponsor: Hut Foundation
19 Sutter Street
San Francisco, CA 94104

Hutton Foundation Grants   2412
The foundation awards grants throughout Santa Barbara County, California to nonprofit organizations in its areas of interest, including education, arts and culture, health and human services, and civic and community development. Preference is given to efforts that promise to bring about major change, build leadership and institutional capacity, and achieve lasting results. Types of support include standard, program related investments, marketing, media, and endowment grants. An application form is available online.
Requirements: California nonprofit organizations headquartered in Santa Barbara county are eligible to apply.
Restrictions: Funding is not available to individuals or organizations that discriminate on the basis of age, gender, race, ethnicity, sexual orientation, disability, national origin, political affiliation or religious belief.
Geographic Focus: California
Contact: Arlene R. Craig; (805) 957-4740; fax (805) 957-4743; info@huttonfoundation.org
Internet: Arlene R. Craig, Vice President;
Sponsor: Hutton Foundation
26 West Anapamu Street, 4th Floor
Santa Barbara, CA 93101

Hyams Foundation Grants   2413
The Foundation's mission is to increase economic and social justice and power within low-income communities in Boston and Chelsea, Massachusetts. The Foundation's focus is on four community priorities or outcomes: increased civic engagement, with a special focus on immigrant communities; more affordable housing, especially for very low-income families; increased family economic self-sufficiency; and expanded opportunities for low-income, older teens. Application information is available online.
Requirements: Massachusetts 501(c)3 charitable organizations are eligible. The foundation will give priority to programs that have a substantial impact on low-income neighborhoods/populations in Boston, and Chelsea.

Geographic Focus: Massachusetts
Date(s) Application is Due: Mar 1; Sep 1; Dec 1
Amount of Grant: 20,000 - 50,000 USD
Contact: Susan Perry, (617) 426-5600, ext. 307; sperry@hyamsfoundation.org
Internet: http://www.hyamsfoundation.org
Sponsor: Hyams Foundation
50 Federal Street, 9th Floor
Boston, MA 02110

Hyde Family Foundations Grants 2414

The grantmaking of the Foundation is directed primarily to initiatives that support efforts to improve the quality of life in Memphis and enhance prosperity for all its citizens. Interest is in promoting improved educational opportunities for children and their families, encouraging and empowering new community leadership, and reinforcing a vision of Memphis as a progressive city. Special interest is in helping stimulate innovation in systems that directly affect the lives of Memphians and impact the community's current well-being and future vitality. Application information is available online.
Requirements: Eligible applicants have received the 501(c)3 designation from the Internal Revenue Service and serve the city of Memphis, Tennessee or influence policy change at the statewide level.
Restrictions: Grants are not made to individuals or political organizations.
Geographic Focus: Tennessee
Date(s) Application is Due: Feb 1; Jul 15
Amount of Grant: 50,000 - 1,000,000 USD
Contact: Courtney Leon; (901) 685-3400; fax (901) 683-7478; cleon@hydefoundation.org
Internet: http://www.hydefoundation.org/grant_information/grantGuidelines
Sponsor: Hyde Family Foundations
17 West Pontotoc Avenue, Suite 200
Memphis, TN 38103

Hydrogen Student Design Contest 2415

The annual Hydrogen Student Design Contest challenges university students to design hydrogen energy applications for real-world use. Established in 2004 by the Hydrogen Education Foundation, the Contest showcases the talents of students in many disciplines, including engineering, architecture, marketing, and entrepreneurship. Although the formal rules and guidelines are still under development, this Contest plans to address three key areas: 1) Hydrogen Production—Students will develop a strategy for supplying hydrogen for the community. At least 33% of the community's hydrogen must be produced from renewable sources. In their plans, students must include at least one hydrogen energy station that co-produces power, heat, and hydrogen (also known as a CHHP system). 2) Early Markets—Students will conduct a market analysis to determine near-term customers in the community for their hydrogen supply. Early markets for hydrogen include back-up power, portable power, and materials handling vehicles. Students will identify at least five businesses or other organizations in the community that could be customers for hydrogen in these early markets. 3) Fueling Stations—Students will plan and design a cluster of hydrogen fueling stations for vehicles in the community. Teams will be required to create a plan for the cluster that identifies the number of fueling stations needed to meet passenger vehicle demand; the approximate locations for each station; the station type (retail, private fleet, mixed use, etc.); and total cost estimates for deploying the plan. Students will be required to design the main components of three fueling stations. The Grand Prize Winner will receive the opportunity to present their design in a Keynote Presentation slot in the NHA Annual Hydrogen Conference and Expo, a stipend of up to $5,000 to cover airfare, meals, hotel accommodations, NHA conference registrations, and incidental trip expenses for up to eight team members and their faculty representative, and extensive media recognition. Honorable Mentions will receive the opportunity to give poster presentations of their design at the NHA Annual Hydrogen Conference and Expo, complimentary hotel rooms and registrations to the NHA Conference for up to four team members and their faculty representative.
Requirements: The contest is open to current college and university undergraduate and graduate students in the U.S. or abroad. Team members must be enrolled in a college or university at the time of the Contest but do not have to be enrolled full-time. Given the multi-disciplinary nature of the competition, teams are encouraged to include members from any field of study relevant to the team's design. Common disciplines include: engineering, architecture/planning, industrial design, economics, business, environmental science, policy, chemistry, marketing, and education. Registration must be completed by January 22; Entries are due March 24.
Geographic Focus: All States
Date(s) Application is Due: Jan 22; Mar 24
Amount of Grant: 5,000 USD
Contact: Kyle Gibeault; (202) 223-5547; gibeaultk@hydrogenassociation.org
Internet: http://www.hydrogencontest.org/contest.asp
Sponsor: Hydrogen Education Foundation
1211 Connecticut Avenue NW, Suite 600
Washington, DC 20036-2701

I.A. O'Shaughnessy Foundation Grants 2416

The Foundation is concerned that too many schools lack sufficient resources; that students in high-poverty areas have lower achievement scores, higher drop-out rates, and lower rates of college graduation; that low-income families lack the resources to choose better schools; and that the gap between the rich and the poor is increasing. The Foundation has set its current funding interest to help address these critical matters of public concern. The Foundation is currently interested in making grants to support high quality education that prepares students in disadvantaged communities for educational and life success. Priority is given to organizations that provide support networks; remove impediments to student success; are broadly supported by the community, and have a record of demonstrated success. Additional guidelines and application forms are available at the foundation's website.
Requirements: Eligible applicant must be: nonprofit organizations; mission-consistent; fiscally sound; demonstrate a need; and capable and accountable.
Restrictions: The Foundation will not fund: grants that are not consistent with Foundation values; national or umbrella organizations that raise funds through broad-based solicitations to the general public; organizations that become overly dependent on the Foundation for on-going operational support; capital campaign gifts exceeding 20% of the campaign goal; political campaigns, events, or organizations whose purpose is to promote political candidates; lobbying; individuals.
Geographic Focus: Illinois, Kansas, Minnesota, Texas
Contact: Eileen A. O'Shaughnessy, Secretary; (952) 698-0959; fax (952) 698-0958; info@iaoshaughnessyfdn.org
Internet: http://www.iaoshaughnessyfdn.org/guidelines.htm
Sponsor: I.A. O'Shaughnessy Foundation
2001 Killebrew Drive, Suite 120
Bloomington, MN 55425

IAFF Harvard University Trade Union Scholarships 2417

This scholarship is awarded to IAFF members in good standing with an IAFF local affiliate to attend the Harvard University Trade Union Program. Awards are given to members who have demonstrated active participation within their IAFF local affiliate as an officer, committee member, etc. Two scholarships are awarded annually for the upcoming six-week session. Winners will be notified by September 30.
Requirements: Applicants must be an active member of the IAFF local affiliate and have demonstrated active participation within the IAFF local affiliate as an officer, committee member, etc. Applicants must also prepare a short statement (about 500 words) on one of the following questions: (1) Your personal interest in attending the Harvard University Trade Union Program. (2) What do you consider to be the major problems facing the labor movement in the United States today? (3) What do you consider to be the major problems facing the Fire Fighter in the Labor Union movement today?
Geographic Focus: Massachusetts
Date(s) Application is Due: Jul 1
Amount of Grant: 1,000 USD
Contact: Kevin Rader; (202) 737-8484; fax (202) 737-8418; krader@iaff.org
Internet: http://www.iaff.org/et/scholarships/harvard.html
Sponsor: International Association of Fire Fighters
1750 New York Avenue NW
Washington, DC 20006

IAFF Labour College of Canada Residential Scholarship 2418

This scholarship is awarded to IAFF members in good standing with an IAFF local affiliate to attend the LCC Residential Program in Ottawa. One scholarship is awarded annually for the upcoming four-week session. Winners will be notified in January.
Requirements: Awards are given to members who have demonstrated active participation within their IAFF local affiliate as an officer, committee member, etc. Applicants must also prepare a short statement (about 500 words) on one of the following questions: (1) Your personal interest in attending the Labour College of Canada Residential Program. (2) What do you consider to be the major problems facing the labour movement in Canada today? (3) What do you consider to be the major problems facing the Fire Fighter in the Labour Union movement today? A separate application for admission must be completed and sent directly to the LCC. For more information, go to www.labourcollege.ca. IAFF scholarship applicants are encouraged to prepare their LCC application in advance so it can be submitted before the College's deadline of December 9th. To obtain an application form contact the Labour College by telephone at 613-733-9967 or by fax at 613-733-1178.
Geographic Focus: All States, Canada
Date(s) Application is Due: Jun 30
Contact: Kevin Rader; (202) 737-8484; fax (202) 737-8418; krader@iaff.org
Internet: http://www.iaff.org/et/scholarships/canadian.html
Sponsor: International Association of Fire Fighters
1750 New York Avenue NW
Washington, DC 20006

IAFF National Labor College Scholarships 2419

The International Association of Fire Fighters annually awards scholarship funds for three (3) IAFF members to attend the National Labor College. The awards will cover tuition for one semester program consisting of up to three courses (for a total of nine academic credits), room and board, and provide $1,000 for travel and incidental expenses.
Requirements: Any IAFF member in good standing with an IAFF local affiliate is eligible to apply. Applicants must be an active member of the IAFF local affiliate and have demonstrated active participation within the IAFF local affiliate as an officer, committee member, etc. Applicants must also prepare a short statement (about 500 words) on one of the following: (1) Your personal interest in attending the National Labor College. (2) What do you consider to be the major problems facing the labor movement in the United States today? (3) What do you consider to be the major problems facing the fire fighter in the labor union movement today?
Geographic Focus: All States, Canada
Date(s) Application is Due: Jul 1
Contact: Kevin Rader, (202) 737-8484; fax (202) 737-8418; krader@iaff.org
Internet: http://www.iaff.org/et/scholarships/NLC_scholarship.htm
Sponsor: International Association of Fire Fighters
1750 New York Avenue NW
Washington, DC 20006

IAFF W. H. (Howie) McClennan Scholarship 2420
The scholarship provides financial assistance for sons, daughters or legally adopted children of fire fighters killed in the line of duty planning to attend a university, accredited college or other institution of higher learning. Scholarships are awarded annually, on or before August 1 for the proceeding academic year. They may be renewed (if approved) up to four consecutive years. Awards are based on financial need, aptitude promise and demonstrated academic achievement.
Requirements: Students eligible include sons, daughters or legally adopted children of Fire Fighters who died in the line of duty. The applicant's parent must have been a member in good standing of the International Association of Fire Fighters, AFL-CIO-CLC at the time of death. Applicants must indicate financial need, aptitude promise and demonstrate academic achievement. Applicants must provide a transcript of grades along with recommendations from two teachers; and a brief statement (about 200 words) indicating their reasons for wanting to continue their education. The required application, rules and regulations can be found at the sponsor's website.
Geographic Focus: All States
Date(s) Application is Due: Feb 1
Amount of Grant: 2,500 USD
Contact: Kevin Rader, Director, Department of Education; (202) 737-8484; fax (202) 737-8418; krader@iaff.org
Internet: http://www.iaff.org/et/scholarships/mcclennan.html
Sponsor: International Association of Fire Fighters
1750 New York Avenue NW
Washington, DC 20006

Ian Hague Perl 6 Development Grants 2421
In May 2008 The Perl Foundation (TPF) received an unprecedented gift from Ian Hague, a finance executive in New York. The amount of the gift was $200,000 and was given to TPF to support Perl 6 development. Roughly half of the donation would be used to develop TPF's own capabilities to further search for Perl 6 support, and the balance would be used to directly and indirectly support developers working on Perl 6. The nominal maximum monthly payment is $5,000 for full-time work on the grant. This amount is not changed based on changes to the schedule of the grant once the grant is in process. Payments for varying levels of part-time work will be pro-rated against this nominal amount.
Requirements: Grants will be made to projects which obviously and concretely advance the completion of a Perl 6 implementation. Other Perl 6 projects, while potentially very worthwhile, are not the focus of Hague grants. The main goal is the release of a Perl 6 implementation, so critical path elements have preference. In order to demonstrate the criticality of your grant, supporting documentation of a complete project milestone list for your implementation will be very useful. Obviously, grants that support well-documented and well planned implementations have preference.
Restrictions: Residents and nationals of countries that are prohibited by U.S. law from engaging in commerce, are ineligible to participate.
Geographic Focus: All States
Amount of Grant: Up to 15,000 USD
Contact: Richard Dice, President; rdice@perlfoundation.org
Internet: http://www.perlfoundation.org/ian_hague_perl_6_development_grants
Sponsor: Perl Foundation
6832 Mulderstraat
Grand Ledge, MI 48837

IBCAT Screening Mammography Grants 2422
The mission of the Indiana Breast Cancer Awareness Trust, Inc. (IBCAT) is to increase awareness and improve access to breast cancer screening and diagnosis throughout Indiana. IBCAT receives funds through sales of breast cancer awareness specialty license plate. Through these sales, monies are available for grants deemed to best address the unmet screening needs of the people of Indiana. Grants are intended to provide funding for Screening Mammograms programs serving low income, medically under-served women living in Indiana. Funding for this project will be for one calendar year, January 1 to December 31. Applications are accepted during the months of September and October, and announcement of awards will be made no later than December 15.
Requirements: Applicants must be a federally tax-exempt entity such as nonprofit organization, government agency, educational institution or Indian tribe. Grant applications must e postmarked no later than the first Friday of October. Organizations may only apply for one (1) grant annually. Grant requests for new programs may request up to $5,000; established screening programs may request up to $15,000. Services are to be within the State of Indiana, and all patients must be Indiana residents. American Cancer Society (ACS) guidelines for screening mammography should be followed.
Geographic Focus: Indiana
Date(s) Application is Due: Oct 4
Amount of Grant: 5,000 - 15,000 USD
Contact: Jalana Eash; (866) 724-2228; fax (812) 868-8773; ibcat@insightbb.com
Internet: http://www.breastcancerplate.org/programsgrants/grant-programs/
Sponsor: Indiana Breast Awareness Trust, Inc.
P.O. Box 8212
Evansville, IN

IBM Adult Training and Workforce Development Grants 2423
IBM's philanthropic resources are allocated to specific projects and programs that fit within our targeted areas of interest. IBM realizes the power and importance of education. IBM understands that technology can be a powerful tool in education and job training programs for adults, helping broaden opportunities and strengthening programs available to adults in need of new skills and employment. It also can help simulate real job conditions, make the acquisition of education and skills more effective and help people get the network of support they need to obtain and retain employment. Nonprofit organizations or educational institutions wishing to submit unsolicited proposals to IBM should make an initial inquiry in the form of a two-page letter. In the event that the proposal is of interest to IBM, additional information will be requested. The letter should include the following information: a brief statement fully describing the mission of the organization, the amount of money requested, and the purpose of the contribution; a description of the problem you wish to address, the solution you propose, and how IBM technology, and IBM volunteers, if appropriate, will be incorporated; proposed project budget with all other anticipated sources of income; plans to measure and evaluate program results; and the name, address and telephone number of the project contact person.
Requirements: IBM only considers requests submitted by organizations which have a tax-exempt classification under Sections 170(c) or 501(c)3 of the U.S. Internal Revenue Code. Priority is assigned to requests involving IBM technology or the volunteer efforts of its employees. In making a grant decision, they also consider what other types of IBM support (Matching Grants, Fund for Community Service, United Way) an organization may already be receiving. Videotapes and other supplemental materials are strongly discouraged at the initial stage of application.
Restrictions: IBM does not make equipment donations or grants from corporate philanthropic funds to: individuals, political, labor, religious, or fraternal organizations or sports groups; fund raising events such as raffles, telethons, walk-a-thons or auctions; capital campaigns, construction and renovation projects; chairs, endowments or scholarships sponsored by academic or nonprofit institutions; special events such as conferences, symposia or sports competitions; or, organizations that advocate, support, or practice activities inconsistent with IBM's non-discrimination policies, whether based on race, color, religion, gender, gender identity or expression, sexual orientation, national origin, disability, age or status as a protected veteran.
Geographic Focus: All States
Contact: Ann Cramer; (404) 238-6660; fax (404) 238-6138; acramer@us.ibm.com
Internet: http://www.ibm.com/ibm/ibmgives/grant/index.shtml
Sponsor: IBM Corporation
4111 Northside Parkway NW
Atlanta, GA 30327-3098

IBM Arts and Culture Grants 2424
IBM's philanthropic resources are allocated to specific projects and programs that fit within our targeted areas of interest. IBM realizes the power and importance of education. IBM's support of the arts stems from a strong tradition of bettering its communities. The Corporation feels a deep sense of responsibility both inside and outside the company — a focused determination to enhance the communities in which it does business and in which its customers and employees live. By joining with libraries, museums, and other cultural institutions in exciting partnerships that leverage IBM expertise, the Corporation also demonstrates the critical role technology plays in enhancing the arts. Nonprofit organizations or educational institutions wishing to submit unsolicited proposals to IBM should make an initial inquiry in the form of a two-page letter. In the event that the proposal is of interest to IBM, additional information will be requested. The letter should include the following information: a brief statement fully describing the mission of the organization, the amount of money requested, and the purpose of the contribution; a description of the problem you wish to address, the solution you propose, and how IBM technology, and IBM volunteers, if appropriate, will be incorporated; proposed project budget with all other anticipated sources of income; plans to measure and evaluate program results; and the name, address and telephone number of the project contact person.
Requirements: IBM only considers requests submitted by organizations which have a tax-exempt classification under Sections 170(c) or 501(c)3 of the U.S. Internal Revenue Code. Priority is assigned to requests involving IBM technology or the volunteer efforts of its employees. In making a grant decision, they also consider what other types of IBM support (Matching Grants, Fund for Community Service, United Way) an organization may already be receiving. Videotapes and other supplemental materials are strongly discouraged at the initial stage of application.
Restrictions: IBM does not make equipment donations or grants from corporate philanthropic funds to: individuals, political, labor, religious, or fraternal organizations or sports groups; fund raising events such as raffles, telethons, walk-a-thons or auctions; capital campaigns, construction and renovation projects; chairs, endowments or scholarships sponsored by academic or nonprofit institutions; special events such as conferences, symposia or sports competitions; or, organizations that advocate, support, or practice activities inconsistent with IBM's non-discrimination policies, whether based on race, color, religion, gender, gender identity or expression, sexual orientation, national origin, disability, age or status as a protected veteran.
Geographic Focus: All States
Contact: Ann Cramer; (404) 238-6660; fax (404) 238-6138; acramer@us.ibm.com
Internet: http://www.ibm.com/ibm/ibmgives/grant/index.shtml
Sponsor: IBM Corporation
4111 Northside Parkway NW
Atlanta, GA 30327-3098

IBM Community Development Grants 2425
IBM's philanthropic resources are allocated to specific projects and programs that fit within our targeted areas of interest. IBM realizes the power and importance of education. Wherever IBM does business around the globe, the Corporation forms connections to communities and supports a range of civic and nonprofit activities that help those in need through its Community Development grants. In all of its efforts, the Corporation demonstrates how technology can enrich and expand access to services and assistance. Nonprofit organizations wishing to submit unsolicited proposals to IBM should make an initial inquiry in the form of a two-page letter. In the event that the proposal is of interest to IBM, additional information will be requested. The letter should include the following

information: a brief statement fully describing the mission of the organization, the amount of money requested, and the purpose of the contribution; a description of the problem you wish to address, the solution you propose, and how IBM technology, and IBM volunteers, if appropriate, will be incorporated; proposed project budget with all other anticipated sources of income; plans to measure and evaluate program results; and the name, address and telephone number of the project contact person.
Requirements: IBM only considers requests submitted by organizations which have a tax-exempt classification under Sections 170(c) or 501(c)3 of the U.S. Internal Revenue Code. Priority is assigned to requests involving IBM technology or the volunteer efforts of its employees. In making a grant decision, they also consider what other types of IBM support (Matching Grants, Fund for Community Service, United Way) an organization may already be receiving. Videotapes and other supplemental materials are strongly discouraged at the initial stage of application.
Restrictions: IBM does not make equipment donations or grants from corporate philanthropic funds to: individuals, political, labor, religious, or fraternal organizations or sports groups; fund raising events such as raffles, telethons, walk-a-thons or auctions; capital campaigns, construction and renovation projects; chairs, endowments or scholarships sponsored by academic or nonprofit institutions; special events such as conferences, symposia or sports competitions; or, organizations that advocate, support, or practice activities inconsistent with IBM's non-discrimination policies, whether based on race, color, religion, gender, gender identity or expression, sexual orientation, national origin, disability, age or status as a protected veteran.
Geographic Focus: All States
Contact: Ann Cramer; (404) 238-6660; fax (404) 238-6138; acramer@us.ibm.com
Internet: http://www.ibm.com/ibm/ibmgives/grant/index.shtml
Sponsor: IBM Corporation
4111 Northside Parkway NW
Atlanta, GA 30327-3098

ICC Community Service Mini-Grant (CSMG) 2426
Community Service Mini-Grants are available for students interested in designing and implementing quality, direct service projects that address community needs or problems. Projects may last one day or span the length of the academic year. Common elements for projects include 1) addressing real community needs and 2) offering some long-term benefit for the collaborating community organization. Awards range from $100 to $1,000. However, ICC requires that the institution applying must cash match at least 25% of the amount requested. Mini-grant money can be spent on supplies and materials needed to implement your project, as well as transportation and food costs. The funds may not be used to buy gifts or make donations, to pay salary or wages, or to purchase capital items.
Requirements: Students and/or student groups enrolled at any Indiana Campus Compact (ICC) member institution may apply. The student(s) listed on the title page must complete all components of the grant application and will be responsible for all follow-up reporting requirements. All applications require a faculty or staff member on campus to serve as the project oversight director. If you are having difficulty identifying a project oversight director you can contact Liza Newman, eldnewma@iupui.edu for information on the designated faculty and staff representatives on your campus. Projects must involve direct service to communities outside of the campus. Applications are due on the 15th of each month throughout the academic year. Notification of awards will be made by the last day of each month. Applications must be received BEFORE the start date of the project, e.g. an application to support a community project scheduled for November 21st would need to be submitted by October 15th. Grantees would be notified by October 31. Faxes are accepted.
Restrictions: Faculty and staff members are not eligible to apply, though they are encouraged to act as a project oversight director on student-led initiatives. Projects that aim to convert others to a particular religious belief will not receive funding.
Geographic Focus: Indiana
Amount of Grant: 100 - 1,000 USD
Contact: Lindsay Doucette, Program Director; (317) 274-6500; lgdoucet@iupui.edu
Internet: http://www.indianacampuscompact.org/Default.aspx?tabid=85
Sponsor: Indiana Campus Compact
620 Union Drive, Suite 203
Indianapolis, IN 46202

ICC Day of Service Action Grants 2427
Indiana Campus Compact (ICC) is helping colleges and universities across the state mobilize thousands of students to get involved in the national movement of Days of Service. This program encourages students to utilize Earth Day; Martin Luther King, Jr. Day; Cesar Chavez Day, and 9/11 as days to serve and make a positive impact on their communities. ICC will offer a limited number of mini-grants, up to $250 each, to campuses to help defray costs of their events and programs. The following application deadlines will be utilized: 9/11 Day of Service, August 15; MLK Day, December 15; Cesar Chavez Day, February 15; Earth Day, March 15.
Requirements: Students from all ICC member institutions are eligible for this grant. Preference will be given to groups who have a clear plan for their Day of Service efforts and who demonstrate financial need. Preference will also be given to programs that have the greatest potential impact on student civic engagement.
Restrictions: The money may be used to defray costs of projects and programs (posters, speakers, food, supplies, and travel expenses). The money may not be used for capital goods, donations, or staffing costs. A 25% cash match will be required for all grant winners. For example, if a student is awarded $250, they will be required to match $62.50 for a total project cost of $312.50. Funds are on a reimbursement basis only.
Geographic Focus: Indiana
Date(s) Application is Due: Feb 15; Mar 15; Aug 15; Dec 15
Amount of Grant: Up to 250 USD
Contact: Katy Kaesebier; (317) 274-6500; katykaes@iupui.edu
Internet: http://www.indianacampuscompact.org/Default.aspx?tabid=85
Sponsor: Indiana Campus Compact
620 Union Drive, Suite 203
Indianapolis, IN 46202

ICC Faculty Fellowships 2428
Based on Ernest Boyer's concept that community engagement provides an excellent means by which the three components of faculty professional development of teaching, research, and professional service can support and strengthen each other, Indiana Campus Compact awards Faculty Fellowships as a model for faculty professional development through the scholarship of engagement. Up to 7 fellowships are competitively awarded in each academic year, in addition to one Senior Fellow. The fellowship amount is $3,750. Institutions must match at least $1,250. The fellowship fiscal period is twelve months, from June 1 to May 31.
Requirements: Faculty from all disciplines and professional schools at Indiana Campus Compact (ICC) member campuses are eligible to apply. Former Fellows are eligible to apply; however, preference is given to new applicants. Fellows are expected to model the integration of community engagement into all three aspects of their professional development in the following ways: (1) Teaching - Each Fellow will teach a service-learning course within the program period; (2) Research - Each Fellow will design a research, scholarly, or artistic project relating to the service performed with a community organization or to the practice of service-learning, to be initiated during the program period; (3) Professional Service - Each Fellow will provide direct service to a nonprofit organization during the program year to assist in addressing a particular community issue that is related to his/her academic discipline or expertise as an educator. Note: ALL proposals must be properly routed through the fiscal routing system at an applicant's institution prior to electronic submission to Indiana Campus Compact. However, if the institution is an Indiana University campus, routing through Research & Sponsored Programs or Sponsored Research Services is not required.
Geographic Focus: Indiana
Amount of Grant: 3,750 USD
Contact: J.R. Jamison; (317) 274-6500; fax (317) 274-6510; jrjamiso@iupui.edu
Internet: http://www.indianacampuscompact.org/Default.aspx?tabid=86
Sponsor: Indiana Campus Compact
620 Union Drive, Suite 203
Indianapolis, IN 46202

ICC Listening to Communities Grants 2429
Campus community service, service-learning, community service work study, and other campus community engagement activities are not possible without community partners who create and coordinate opportunities for students to serve and learn. The quality of both service and learning is largely dependent on the quality of these partnerships and to develop high quality partnerships requires a great deal of time, communication, and commitment to a reciprocal relationship in which the needs of all partners are met. Indiana Campus Compact will provide up to $400 for food, space, facilitation, and materials, and stipends for community partner organizations of $56 per participant for up to 25 total participants (limit of three (3) participants from each organization). Institutions must cash match 25% of each ($100 for food, space, facilitation, and materials, and $19 per participant for community partner stipends - for a total project amount equaling $500 for food, space, facilitation, and materials, and $75 for community partner stipends). Community partner representatives will be encouraged to share their views on what role colleges and universities should play in the community and in a democracy, what is being done well, and what can be done better, in fulfilling their civic mission.
Requirements: Indiana Campus Compact (ICC) member campuses are eligible to apply to host a Listening to Communities Meeting (LTC) funded by ICC. Any staff or faculty member who coordinates campus-community service or service-learning may serve as the Project Director. Award preference is given to campuses that previously have not been awarded an LTC Program grant. Applications will be accepted at any time, but must be submitted at least two (2) months prior to the proposed meeting date for ICC scheduling purposes. Note: ALL proposals must be properly routed through the fiscal routing system at an applicant's institution prior to electronic submission to Indiana Campus Compact. However, if the institution is an Indiana University campus, routing through Research & Sponsored Programs or Sponsored Research Services is not required.
Restrictions: The Listening to Communities program is funded on a reimbursement basis.
Geographic Focus: Indiana
Amount of Grant: Up to 1,800 USD
Contact: Lindsay Doucette, Program Director; (317) 274-6500; lgdoucet@iupui.edu
Internet: http://www.indianacampuscompact.org/Default.aspx?tabid=86
Sponsor: Indiana Campus Compact
620 Union Drive, Suite 203
Indianapolis, IN 46202

ICC Scholarship of Engagement Faculty Grants 2430
Eighteen faculty per year will be selected to choose one of three options related to the Scholarship of Engagement: develop or revise a service-learning course to be taught by the recipient, provide scholarly research on service-engagement, or provide a professional service to a local community agency. The selected faculty members will also encourage the development of service-engagement infrastructure on their respective campuses through trainings and workshops of other faculty. Award amounts are $2,250. Institutions are required to cash match at least $750.
Requirements: Adjunct or full-time faculty from all disciplines and professional schools at Indiana Campus Compact (ICC) member campuses are eligible to apply. An adjunct or full-time faculty member applicant must propose a project that focuses on one of three areas: (1) Teaching - Design a new course or revise an existing course to include a service-learning component; (2) Research - Develop and initiate a research project related to his/her discipline that addresses a community issue and advances the field of engagement

through service-learning. Preference will be given to projects that are participatory action research; (3) Professional Service - Provide direct service to a nonprofit organization to assist in addressing a particular community issue. This professional service must be related to the faculty member's academic discipline or his/her expertise as an educator. Note: ALL proposals must be properly routed through the fiscal routing system at an applicant's institution prior to electronic submission to Indiana Campus Compact. However, if the institution is an Indiana University campus, routing through Research & Sponsored Programs or Sponsored Research Services is not required.
Restrictions: Grants are awarded on a reimbursement basis. Grant funds cannot be used for indirect costs, items of durable equipment costing more than $100 (unless approved in writing by ICC), payment for participants to do service, fundraising activities, entertainment costs, tickets to recreational events, ball games, zoos, etc., clothing such as T-shirts or hats, or cash incentives.
Geographic Focus: Indiana
Date(s) Application is Due: Nov 6
Amount of Grant: 2,250 USD
Contact: Lindsay Doucette, Program Director; (317) 274-6500; lgdoucet@iupui.edu
Internet: http://www.indianacampuscompact.org/Default.aspx?tabid=86
Sponsor: Indiana Campus Compact
620 Union Drive, Suite 203
Indianapolis, IN 46202

Ida Alice Ryan Charitable Trust Grants 2431
The trust awards single-year grants for capital projects to eligible Georgia nonprofit organizations. Grants support programs of the Catholic Church and a wide variety of community causes including health organizations, legal aid societies, youth groups, educational programs, museums, and social services. Application and guidelines are available online.
Requirements: 501(c)3 tax-exempt organizations in the Atlanta area are eligible.
Geographic Focus: Georgia
Date(s) Application is Due: Feb 1; Aug 1
Contact: NA Trustee, c/o Wachovia Bank; grantinquiries8@wachovia.com
Internet: https://www.wachovia.com/foundation/v/index.jsp?vgnextoid=cf578689fb0aa110VgnVCM1000004b0d1872RCRD&vgnextfmt=default
Sponsor: Ida Alice Ryan Charitable Trust
3280 Peachtree Road NE, Suite 400, MC G0141-041
Atlanta, GA 30305

Idaho Community Foundation Eastern Region Competitive Grants 2432
The mission of the Foundation is to enrich life's quality throughout Idaho. Grants are awarded through the regional grant cycle for a wide range of organizations and for a wide range of projects consistent with that mission. Grants are made to fund activities, services, and projects of established organizations, as well as to provide assistance for new organizations to fill unmet and/or emerging community needs. Grant areas include: arts and culture; education; emergency services; libraries; natural sciences; health; recreation; social services; and public projects. Application information is available online.
Requirements: Nonprofit entities in Idaho are eligible to apply.
Restrictions: Funding is not available for: projects which replace school district responsibilities to students or that fund state or federally mandated programs; projects which are considered operating expenses or salaries normally paid by a school district; computer hardware used solely for pre-K through 12th grade educational purposes; religious organizations for the sole purpose of furthering that religion; political activities or those designed to influence legislation; national organizations; or grants that directly benefit a donor to ICF or a donor's family.
Geographic Focus: Idaho
Date(s) Application is Due: Apr 1
Amount of Grant: 5,000 USD
Contact: Administrator; (208) 342-3535; fax (208) 342-3577; grants@idcomfdn.org
Internet: http://www.idcomfdn.org/pages/grant_regional_guidelines.htm
Sponsor: Idaho Community Foundation
P.O. Box 8143
Boise, ID 83707

Idaho Power Company Corporate Contributions 2433
The company awards grants in company operating territories in its areas of interest, including arts and culture, civic and community, education, and health and human services. Types of support include building construction/renovation, capital campaigns, continuing support, equipment, general operating support, matching gifts, scholarships, and sponsorships. The corporate contribution request form is available online. There are no application deadlines.
Requirements: Nonprofit organizations in southern Idaho and eastern Oregon are eligible.
Restrictions: Grants do not support: individuals; loans or investments; churches or religious organizations for purposes of religious advocacy; tickets for contests, raffles, or other prize-oriented activities; organizations that discriminate for any reason, including race, color, religion, creed, age, sex, or national origin; individual school programs or projects with limited participation; fraternal or labor organizations; unrestricted operating funds; special occasion good-will advertising.
Geographic Focus: Idaho, Oregon
Contact: Contribution Program Manager; (208) 388-2200
Internet: http://www.idahopower.com/aboutus/community/corporateContributions.htm
Sponsor: Idaho Power Company
P.O. Box 70
Boise, ID 83707

IDEM Section 205(j) Water Quality Management Planning Grants 2434
Section 205(j) funding is for water quality management planning projects, focusing on watershed management planning and protection or restoration of critical ecosystems. Funds are to be used to determine the nature, extent and causes of point and nonpoint source pollution problems and to develop plans to resolve these problems. Funds can be requested for up to $100,000. No match is required for 205(j) projects.
Requirements: Organizations eligible for funding include municipal governments, county governments, regional planning commissions, and other public organizations. Program guidance, application instructions and application forms are available for download at the website.
Restrictions: For-profit entities, nonprofit organizations, private associations and individuals are not eligible to receive this assistance. Funds received cannot be used for any of the following: dredging; drainage or flood control; permit fees; or compliance with NPDES permits or enforcement actions.
Geographic Focus: Indiana
Amount of Grant: Up to 100,000 USD
Contact: Laura Bieberich, (317) 233-1863
Internet: http://www.in.gov/idem/resources/grants_loans/205j/index.html
Sponsor: Indiana Department of Environmental Management
Indiana Government Center North, 100 N Senate Avenue, Mail Code 50-01
Indianapolis, IN 46204-2251

IDEM Section 319(h) Nonpoint Source Program Grants 2435
This program funds projects that will work on a watershed level to reduce nonpoint source pollution in Indiana's lakes, rivers, and streams. Nonpoint source pollution does not come from a pipe. It results when water (rain or snowmelt) moves across land, such as city streets, agricultural fields and residential backyards, and picks up dirt, fertilizers, pesticides, animal wastes, road salt, motor oil and other pollutants. Nonpoint source pollution is also caused by wind, which like rain, can pick up soil particles and deposit them in lakes and streams. These pollutants have harmful effects on drinking water supplies, recreation, fisheries and wildlife. Nonpoint source pollution is the leading cause of water quality problems in Indiana and is responsible for many of the impairments identified on the 303(d) List of Impaired Waterbodies. Funding for selected projects will be provided by Clean Water Act Section 319 grant funds and match is provided by grant recipients and partners.
Requirements: To be considered for funding, the project sponsor (the entity responsible for the project and its overall success), must be one of the following: 1) Municipality; 2) County Government; 3) State Government; 4) Federal Government; 5) College/University; 6) Nonprofit 501(c)3. The program provides funding and technical assistance to groups that work on the watershed level with citizens to develop locally-based solutions to nonpoint source pollution. Specific ways to address nonpoint source water pollution include education/outreach on watershed management, information gathering activities such as conducting watershed inventories and water quality assessments for the purpose of developing comprehensive watershed management plans and implementing those plans, including implementation of best management practices that directly reduce sources of nonpoint source pollution. IDEM provides sixty percent (60%) of an approved project's total cost with Section 319 funds. A grant recipient must provide the remaining forty percent (40%) of the total project cost as match. Match may be in-kind services or cash. Match cannot come from any federal funding sources. Guidelines and application forms are available for download at the website. Do not use forms from previous years - they will not be accepted by IDEM.
Restrictions: The following is a list of activities that cannot be funded with Section 319 funds and cannot be counted as matching funds for a Section 319 grant: Permit fees; Food for meetings or other events; Purchase of agricultural equipment, or other large pieces of equipment (equipment modifications and leasing are allowable); Purchase of land or land easements (these activities can be counted as matching funds in some cases); Any project which is directed at water quantity rather than water quality, such as dredging, drainage, or flood control; Any practices, equipment, or supplies used to fulfill the requirements of any federal permit (NPDES permit, Section 401 Water Quality Certification, permits from the U.S. Army Corps of Engineers, as examples) or to comply with IDEM's Confined Feeding Operation rule or permit requirements, or to meet enforcement requirements; Wetland mitigation sites; Incentive payments or yield losses; Nonpoint source best management practices not sanctioned by IDEM or not sanctioned by a partner agency of IDEM; Practices not installed in accordance with standards and specifications developed by NRCS, IDNR or other recognized standards; Office furniture; Sales tax. Additionally, the following will not be funded by this grant program: Septic system pump outs, repairs, rehabilitations, or demonstrations of alternative septic systems; Projects whose sole purpose is data collection, research, demonstration of best management practices, or education/outreach. However, these activities may be incorporated as elements into a proposal that meets one of the three priorities.
Geographic Focus: Indiana
Date(s) Application is Due: Sep 1
Contact: Laura Bieberich, Team Leader; (317) 233-1863
Internet: http://www.in.gov/idem/resources/grants_loans/319h/index.html
Sponsor: Indiana Department of Environmental Management
Indiana Government Center North, 100 N Senate Avenue, Mail Code 50-01
Indianapolis, IN 46204-2251

IDOT Economic Development Program (EDP) Grants 2436
The purpose of the Economic Development Program (EDP) is to provide state assistance in improving highway access to new or expanding industrial distribution or tourism developments. The focus of the program is on the retention and creation of permanent full-time jobs. Funding will be available to construct highway facilities that provide direct access to industrial, distribution or tourism developments. The program is designed to assist in those situations where development of these types of facilities is imminent. The EDP program is designed to provide up to 50 percent state funding for eligible locally owned roadways, and 100 percent state funding for roadway improvements on state owned routes. The remaining 50 percent match will

be provided by local government entities or private sources. However, IDOT can only enter into an agreement with a local body of government (i.e. township, city, village or county). Although it is a requirement of the program for the sponsor to contribute local money to the project, as of January 1, 2012, IDOT will allow grants from other state agencies as an allowable funding source for the sponsor's 50 percent match if the local agency has participated in the project in some fashion such as preliminary engineering, donation of land, etc).
Requirements: The cost-effectiveness of each investment of EDP dollars is a major factor in the evaluation of proposed projects. Priority considerations are: need for the highway improvement and imminence of development; compatibility of the proposed roadway with the design of the existing roadway system; primary jobs created or retained in Illinois and total developer site cost estimate; annual and peak day attendance at tourist developments; commitment of the industrial/ distribution/tourist development to the site to be served by facility; and, willingness of the sponsoring local government to participate in the local share of the improvement cost. The local sponsor should apply for funding as soon as possible after the project site and an appropriate range of access needs are identified. Notification of the Bureau of Statewide Program Planning will trigger a site evaluation process which must occur before review of the funding application can begin.
Restrictions: Projects which only improve opportunities for development or are speculative in nature are not eligible for EDP funding. Projects providing access to retail establishments, office parks, government facilities or school/universities are not eligible for EDP funding. Examples of non-eligible items include (but are not limited to): land acquisition; building demolition; landscaping; sidewalks; street lighting; utility adjustments. Note: Due to the nature of construction practices, some items not typically eligible for EDP funding may be considered. These would have to be reviewed on a case by case basis and approved by the Central Office.
Geographic Focus: Illinois
Amount of Grant: Up to 2,000,000 USD
Contact: Jeff South, Bureau Chief; (217) 782-2755
Internet: http://www.dot.state.il.us/edp/edp.html
Sponsor: Illinois Department of Transportation
2300 South Dirksen Parkway
Springfield, IL 62764

IDOT Rail Freight Program (RFP) Loans and Grants 2437
The purpose of the RFP is to provide capital assistance to communities, railroads and shippers to preserve and improve rail freight service in Illinois. The primary role of the program is to facilitate investments in rail service by serving as a link between interested parties and channeling government funds to projects that achieve statewide economic development. IDOT will generally provide low interest loans to finance rail improvements and, in some cases, provide grants. The focus is on projects with the greatest potential for improving access to markets and maintaining transportation cost savings, and where state participation will leverage private investments to foster permanent solutions to rail service problems. A benefit/cost ratio is used to evaluate potential rail freight projects.
Requirements: Requests for RFP funds should be sent to the Bureau of Railroads, and should include the following information: a general description of the project and a location map depicting the beginning and ending points; benefits expected from the project (e.g., job creation and retention, transportation savings, etc.); the name of the industries involved, and the name title, address and telephone number of the principal contract for the project; an engineer's cost estimate, if available.
Geographic Focus: Illinois
Contact: Steve McClarty, Bureau Chief; (312) 793-3940
Internet: http://www.dot.il.gov/rfp.html
Sponsor: Illinois Department of Transportation
2300 South Dirksen Parkway
Springfield, IL 62764

IDOT Truck Access Route Program (TARP) Grants 2438
The purpose of the TARP is to help local governments upgrade roads to accommodate 80,000 pound truck loads. The department has a set aside amount of TARP funding that coincides with funding for Economic Development Program projects. When a local sponsor applies for EDP funding, they can also request TARP funding for the same route provided the roadway connects to an already existing truck route and ends at another truck route or truck generator. The department will provide up to $45,000 per lane mile and $22,000 per intersection for an eligible roadway. Please note that when requesting TARP funding in conjunction with an EDP application, the TARP funding is capped at $150,000 for the overall project.
Requirements: Every fall IDOT solicits local projects that can be constructed during the upcoming fiscal year. Submit your inquiries and requests for assistance to the Deputy Director, Regional Engineer's office that serves your county. The state participation will not exceed 50% of the total construction costs or $600,000 whichever is less. Please contact your local district office with details of how to apply for the TARP annual program.
Geographic Focus: Illinois
Contact: Darrell Lewis, Acting Bureau Chief; (217) 782-3827
Internet: http://www.dot.state.il.us/tarp.html
Sponsor: Illinois Department of Transportation
2300 South Dirksen Parkway
Springfield, IL 62764

IDPH Carolyn Adams Ticket for the Cure Community Grants 2439
On July 6, 2005, PA 92-0120 was signed into law, creating the Illinois Carolyn Adams Ticket for the Cure Lottery instant ticket. Net revenue from the sale of this ticket will go to the Illinois Department of Public Health (IDPH), Office of Women's Health, which will award grants to public and private entities in Illinois for the purpose of funding breast cancer research, and supportive services for breast cancer survivors and those impacted by breast cancer and breast cancer education. The OWH and the Ticket for the Cure Advisory Board recognize that breast cancer is the most commonly diagnosed cancer in women and sometimes affects men, as well. Awareness and education regarding early detection needs to be increased in every community, especially for low income, underserved and uninsured women with special emphasis on reaching those who are geographically or culturally isolated, older and/or members of racial/ethnic minorities. The Community Grant Program is designed to address this need.
Geographic Focus: Illinois
Contact: Grant Coordinator; 217-524-6088; fax 217-557-3326; dph.owhline@illinois.gov
Internet: http://www.idph.state.il.us/about/womenshealth/grants/tfc.htm
Sponsor: Illinois Department of Public Health
535 W. Jefferson Street, First Floor
Springfield, IL 62761-0001

IDPH Emergency Medical Services Assistance Fund Grants 2440
This project provides for distribution of moneys in the EMS Assistance Fund to each of the eleven Regions in the State in accordance with protocols established in each Region's EMS Region Plan. Objectives of this grant will be to purchase any equipment requested and complete any education as requested. Expected outcomes and goals of this grant are to help improve EMS services and increase education to EMS personal. Measurements and outcomes of this grant will be met by showing timely response to EMS calls, proper use of equipment, education of new equipment, educational objectives completed. Funds might not be equally divided among the eleven regions; consequently, award decisions will not be made based on financial parity among regions.
Requirements: Any Illinois licensed/designated EMS participant that provides EMS service within the State of Illinois may apply for funds through their Regional EMS Advisory Committee. Programs, services, and equipment funded by the EMS Assistance Fund must comply with the Emergency Medical Services (EMS) Systems Act and the Regional EMS Plan in which the applicant participates. The grant cycle runs from July 1-June 30 of each year. All funds remaining at the end of the period of time grant funds are available for expenditure (June 30 of the fiscal year the grant was awarded) shall be returned to the State within 45 days. All applications from providers must be submitted to their respective Regional EMS Advisory Committee by the deadline required by each Regional Committee. No applications will be accepted by the Department directly from an applicant.
Restrictions: Due to limited amount of grant funds available, the Department will not consider applications for new vehicles, vehicle re-chassis, building projects or grant requests over $5000.
Geographic Focus: Illinois
Date(s) Application is Due: Jan 29
Amount of Grant: Up to 5,000 USD
Contact: Mark Vassmer, PHEP Grant Coordinator; 217-558-0560
Internet: http://www.idph.state.il.us/fundop.htm
Sponsor: Illinois Department of Public Health
525-535 W. Jefferson Street
Springfield, IL 62761-0001

IDPH Hosptial Capital Investment Grants 2441
The program allows qualifying hospitals to apply for grants to fund projects to improve or renovate a hospital's physical plant, or to improve, replace or acquire equipment or technology. Projects can include activities to satisfy building code, safety standards, or life safety code; maintain, improve, renovate, expand, or construct buildings or structures; maintain, establish, or improve health information technology; or maintain or improve safety, quality of care, or access to care. Two types of awards are available: Safety Net Grants ($4,600,000 to $7,000,000) and Community Hospital Grants (approximately $350,000 to $1,000,000).
Requirements: Prior to submitting a grant application, hospitals need to submit a letter of intent to the Department which must be received at least 10 calendar days prior to the submission of a grant application. The letter will help determine if a hospital qualifies to apply and will notify the Department of an impending application. The letter must contain the following information: name of the applicant; name of the hospital where grant funds will be used; site of the proposed project, including the address of the hospital where grant funds will be used; county where the hospital is located; description of the project; hospital's Medicaid inpatient utilization rate for the rate year beginning October 1, 2008; signature and contact information of an authorized official from the hospital; and, information on whether the project requires a CON or COE from the Health Facilities and Services Review Board. (The CON/COE Assessment of Applicability Internet site can assist in this determination: http://www.hfsrb.illinois.gov/pdf/checklist-revised.doc.) A hospital that applies for this grant shall be licensed by the Illinois Department of Public Health in accordance with the Hospital Licensing Act. The license shall be valid and the hospital shall be in operation when the grant application is submitted, when the grant agreement is executed and when the project is complete. Applications must be received by the Department within 120 calendar days of the date of the notice's publication. Applications received after this deadline will not be accepted.
Geographic Focus: Illinois
Date(s) Application is Due: Nov 12
Contact: Grant Coordinator; 217-782-1624; dph.crh@illinois.gov
Internet: http://www.idph.state.il.us/fundop.htm
Sponsor: Illinois Department of Public Health
535 West Jefferson Street, Ground Floor
Springfield, IL 62761-0001

IDPH Local Health Department Public Health Emergency Response Grants 2442
The Illinois Department of Public Health, Office of Preparedness and Response, Division of Disaster Planning and Readiness, is making available approximately $5 million in unspent CDC Public Health Emergency Response (PHER) grant funding to Illinois local health departments. The purpose of the funding is to continue previously approved

PHER-funded activities, or conduct new activities that address or retest identified gaps in local health department pandemic flu response. Many local health departments have indicated that they could not use the original PHER funding for CDC's intended purpose. Therefore, grants will be awarded on a first-come, first-served basis to applicants that can best justify activities that will advance pandemic planning and preparedness based on the Grant Application Review Criteria. IDPH anticipates making about 20 to 40 awards based on the number and type of applicants. The maximum award for either single or multi-jurisdictional will be $300,000, or $1.70 per capita, per participating local health department, whichever is less.
Requirements: Applicant must be a single Illinois Certified Local Health Department. Regional partnerships may select either one certified local health department or an agent to receive the funding from IDPH and issue subgrants to other participating certified local health departments. Application must clearly describe reasonable and significant programmatic and financial participation by all partners. Funds may be used for the continuation of previously approved PHER-funded activities, or new activities that address or retest identified gaps in pandemic flu response, or new activities that directly advance pandemic planning and preparedness.
Geographic Focus: Illinois
Date(s) Application is Due: Jan 31
Contact: Mark Vassmer, PHEP Grant Coordinator; 217-558-0560
Internet: http://www.idph.state.il.us/fundop.htm
Sponsor: Illinois Department of Public Health
525-535 W. Jefferson Street
Springfield, IL 62761-0001

IEDC Industrial Development Grant Fund (IDGF) 2443
The IEDC provides financial support for infrastructure improvements in conjunction with projects creating jobs and generating capital investment in Indiana. This grant provides money to local governments for off-site infrastructure projects associated with an expansion of an existing Indiana company or the location of a new facility in Indiana. State funding through the IDGF program must be matched by a combination of local government and company financial support. The grant may be awarded to communities or other eligible applicants who have a commitment letter from representatives of the affected industry/industries indicating their plans to locate or expand a facility. Applicants will be reviewed based on the number and quality of jobs being created, the community's economic need, a local match of funding and capital investment being made by the company. Typically this grant does not exceed 50% of the total project costs.
Requirements: Eligible applicants include the following entities: City; Town; County; Special taxing district; An economic development commission; Nonprofit corporation; Corporation established under I.C. 23-17 for the purpose of distributing water for domestic and industrial use; Regional water, sewage, or solid waste district; Conservancy district that includes in its purpose the distribution of domestic water or the collection and treatment of waste. Projects which may qualify include: (1) Construction of airports, airport facilities, and tourist attractions; (2) Construction, extension, or completion of: (a) Sanitary sewer lines, storm sewers, and other related drainage facilities; (b) Waterlines; (c) Roads and storms; (d) Sidewalks; (e) Rail spurs and sidings; and (f) Information and high technology infrastructure; (3) Leasing, purchase, construction, repair, and rehabilitation of property, both real and personal; and (4) Preparation of surveys, plans, and specifications for the construction of publicly owned and operated facilities, utilities, and services.
Restrictions: Funds are limited to existing Indiana companies or the location of a new facility in Indiana.
Geographic Focus: Indiana
Contact: Charlie Sparks; (317) 233-5122; fax (317) 232-4146; csparks@iedc.in.gov
Internet: http://www.in.gov/iedc/incentives/idgf.html
Sponsor: Indiana Economic Development Corporation
1 North Capitol Avenue, Suite 700
Indianapolis, IN 46204

IEDC International Trade Show Assistance Program 2444
The program provides financial assistance for small Indiana businesses to participate in international trade shows. TSAP is designed to promote Indiana exports by encouraging companies to explore overseas markets. The maximum amount of funding is $5,000, or 100% of exhibit space rental fees, whichever is less. The State Fiscal Year runs from July 1 through June 30.
Requirements: Small businesses eligible for this program are to be defined as a manufacturing concern with worldwide employment of 500 employees or less within the preceding 12 months (this includes parent companies, subsidiaries, divisions of, etc.). Firms must be prequalified with the IEDC in order to receive reimbursement. To receive this assistance, firms must: promote their company's products at an applicable trade show, exposition or fair; have an official company representative attend the show; have less than 500 employees worldwide; manufacture at least 51% of their product in Indiana; provide market research for applicable market. NOTE: Full stay at the show is required. Those companies not exhibiting ALL days of the show are disqualified from receiving funding from TSAP. See the website for detailed guidelines and application instruction.
Restrictions: Funding for trade shows is limited to one (1) show per company per fiscal year. Also, companies may not receive funding to attend the same show every year and may not exhibit by catalog only.
Geographic Focus: Indiana
Amount of Grant: Up to 5,000 USD
Contact: Steve Akard; (317) 234-2083; fax (317) 232-4146; sakard@iedc.in.gov
Internet: http://www.in.gov/iedc/incentives/tradeShow.html
Sponsor: Indiana Economic Development Corporation
1 North Capitol Avenue, Suite 700
Indianapolis, IN 46204

IEDC Skills Enhancement Fund (SEF) 2445
The fund is a tool to encourage companies to invest in their existing workforce and train new employees. SEF provides reimbursement for eligible training expenses over a two year term. Companies may reapply for additional SEF Funds after their initial two year term. The maximum amount awarded through the SEF program typically does not exceed 50% of a company's training budget.
Requirements: Companies may claim reimbursement for training expenses that result in improved basic or transferable skills. Company specific and quality assurance training expenses are also eligible.
Restrictions: IEDC typically does not provide reimbursement for training that is required by law. Those businesses that receive SEF training assistance must commit to continue their operations at the location where the SEF training assistance is provided for at least five years after the date that the training grant is completed.
Geographic Focus: Indiana
Contact: Karen Northrop; (317) 232-0160; fax (317) 232-4146; knorthrop@iedc.in.gov
Internet: http://www.in.gov/iedc/incentives/sef.html
Sponsor: Indiana Economic Development Corporation
1 North Capitol Avenue, Suite 700
Indianapolis, IN 46204

IFP Chicago Production Fund In-Kind Grant 2446
The purpose of the Production Fund is to provide necessary in-kind production assistance to a filmmaker producing a short narrative film; to stimulate and encourage the independent film spirit in the Midwest; and to build relationships between film industry professionals in the Midwestern region. The recipient of the Fund will gain valuable experience working with quality motion-picture industry equipment and resources. The Fund provides $100,000 worth of in-kind goods and services, including film from Kodak, a Panavision camera package and editing with Black Cat Productions.
Requirements: The applicant must be: an IFP/Chicago member in good standing; a current resident of the IFP/Chicago region (Illinois, Indiana, Iowa, Kansas, Kentucky, Michigan, Missouri, Nebraska, Ohio, and Wisconsin); and one of the key creative personnel (writer, director, producer, or director of photography).
Restrictions: Only narrative works with a running time of 15 minutes or less are eligible. Since this is a production fund and not a completion grant, the principal photography on the project must not begin prior to the award being granted.
Geographic Focus: Illinois, Indiana, Iowa, Kansas, Kentucky, Michigan, Missouri, Nebraska, Ohio, Wisconsin
Date(s) Application is Due: Sep 1
Amount of Grant: Up to 100,000 USD
Contact: Production Fund Director; (312) 235-0161; fax (312) 235-0162; chicago@ifp.org
Internet: http://chi.ifp.org/htdocs/opportunities.htm
Sponsor: Independent Feature Project Chicago
1104 South Wabash, Suite 403
Chicago, IL 60605

IFP Minnesota Fresh Filmmakers Production Grants 2447
The Grant will facilitate the production of one short narrative film (ten minutes or less) directed by a filmmaker who is working in fully professional environments for the first time. It is for first-time narrative filmmakers in Minnesota and Western Wisconsin. The winner will receive $1000 in cash, along with mentors, cinematography assistance, equipment use, and a variety of additional support. The annual deadline is in August.
Requirements: Applicants must be first-time narrative filmmakers from Minnesota or Western Wisconsin.
Geographic Focus: Minnesota, Wisconsin
Date(s) Application is Due: Aug 1
Amount of Grant: 1,000 USD
Contact: Lu Lippold, (651) 644-1912, ext.106; fax (651) 644-5708; llippold@ifpmn.org
Internet: http://www.ifpmn.org/grants.html
Sponsor: Independent Feature Project Minnesota
2446 University Avenue West, Suite 100
St. Paul, MN 55114

IFP Minnesota McKnight Filmmaking Fellowships 2448
IFP Minnesota in partnership with the McKnight Foundation awards $25,000 fellowships to two Minnesota filmmakers annually. These fellowships recognize Minnesota artists for talent in working with film/video as demonstrated by two examples of completed, original works in any of the genres and formats of narrative, documentary, experimental, or animation in feature or short lengths. The program is intended to support mid-career artists by providing financial assistance, professional encouragement, and industry recognition. Work examples and application material are judged by a panel of industry professionals from outside the state of Minnesota. Judges look for consistent artistic excellence and merit, clarity and uniqueness of vision, professional quality in the technical aspects of production, and demonstrable, sustained growth in the artist's career. Additionally, judges assess the ability of the artist to present their application in an articulate and professional manner.
Geographic Focus: Minnesota
Date(s) Application is Due: Mar 3
Amount of Grant: 25,000 USD
Contact: Lu Lippold, (651) 644-1912, ext.106; fax (651) 644-5708; llippold@ifpmn.org
Internet: http://www.ifpmn.org/mcknight.html
Sponsor: Independent Feature Project Minnesota
2446 University Avenue West, Suite 100
St. Paul, MN 55114

IFP Minnesota McKnight Screenwriters Fellowships 2449

IFP Minnesota in partnership with the McKnight Foundation awards fellowships to two Minnesota screenwriters annually. These fellowships recognize Minnesota artists for talent in writing for the screen as demonstrated by one completed feature-length screenplay. The program is intended to support mid-career writers by providing financial assistance, professional encouragement, and industry recognition. Screenplays and application material are judged by two panels of industry professionals from outside the state of Minnesota. In addition to the monetary award, the winners receive entrance into the IFP Market in New York, as well as a live reading on stage at the Jungle Theater in Minneapolis with professional actors. Screenplays and applicants are judged on originality of ideas and uniqueness of writer's voice, skillful story structure, talent with creating dialog, and talent with character development.
Restrictions: The following are ineligible: organizations and companies; full-time and part-time students in any film-, video- or screenwriting-related degree program; screenplays associated with a degree-granting program; and employees of IFP/MSP or the McKnight Foundation. Fellows cannot attend school full time during the fellowship year. The screenplay may not be an adaptation of any previously written performed or filmed work by another artist; or have been submitted to the fellowship more than three times previously, under any title.
Geographic Focus: Minnesota
Date(s) Application is Due: Feb 4
Amount of Grant: 25,000 USD
Contact: Lu Lippold, (651) 644-1912, ext.106; fax (651) 644-5708; llippold@ifpmn.org
Internet: http://www.ifpmn.org/mcknight.html
Sponsor: Independent Feature Project Minnesota
2446 University Avenue West, Suite 100
St. Paul, MN 55114

IFP Minnesota TV (MNTV) Grants 2450

MNTV is seeking Minnesota-produced short films for inclusion in its annual MNTV broadcast. Programming staff from IFP Minnesota, Walker Art Center, and Intermedia Arts will select the winning entries for the program. Entries will be judged on their production quality, craft, originality, concept, diversity, and suitability for television. A licensing fee for limited television broadcast ranging from $500 to $1,000 will be paid to the winning artists.
Requirements: Works must have a running time of no longer than 40 minutes. There is no minimum length. Artists must have created the work since January 1, 2006, and resided in the state of Minnesota at the time the submitted work was produced.
Restrictions: Music videos are eligible if they were not produced as a work for hire. Applicants may not submit trailers, industrial, corporate and commercial films and videos, films and videos produced as works for hire, works in progress, and personal demo reels. If an applicant is a full-time student at the time of the submission deadline, he/she is not eligible to apply. Submitted works that were completed through a film program may be submitted; however, at the time of submission, the filmmaker cannot be a full-time student.
Geographic Focus: Minnesota
Date(s) Application is Due: Jun 19
Contact: Lu Lippold, (651) 644-1912, ext.106; fax (651) 644-5708; llippold@ifpmn.org
Internet: http://www.ifpmn.org/mntv.html
Sponsor: Independent Feature Project Minnesota
2446 University Avenue West, Suite 100
St. Paul, MN 55114

IFP New York State Council on the Arts Electronic Media and Film Grants 2451

Funding is available from IFP via a regrant from the NYSCA Electronic Media and Film Program to support the distribution of recently completed work by independent media artists residing in New York State. Grants are given for audio/radio, film, and video productions, computer based work, and installations incorporating these media. Artists may request funding support up to a maximum amount of $10,000, with the typical grant amount awarded generally lower. The funds can be used for most elements relating to distribution needs such as the production of dubbing masters, dubs, and release prints, or for the creation of other formats used for distribution purposes such as DVDs or CD-roms. The grants can also be used for expenses related to marketing and promotion and for other needs which further the opportunity for the project to reach a wider audience, such as the preparation of subtitles or closed captioning, or the payment of festival or screening fees. In addition to self-distribution efforts, strategies to supplement an existing distribution agreement with a commercial or non-profit distributor may also be supported.
Requirements: The grants are available only to New York State artists. The work proposed for support must have been completed between January 1 and November 30. The applicant should have all rights to distribute the work as proposed.
Restrictions: Works-in-progress (including works in post-production); students and student works; and any work previously considered for this category in any year, whether or not it received NYSCA support in the past, are ineligible. The grants may not be used for production or post-production costs or production deficits.
Geographic Focus: New York
Date(s) Application is Due: Jan 18
Contact: Coordinator; (212) 465-8200, ext. 207; fax (212) 465-8525; nysca-grant@ifp.org
Internet: http://market.ifp.org/newyork/nysca/index.html
Sponsor: Independent Feature Project New York
104 W 29th Street, 12th Floor
New York, NY 10001

IIE Adell and Hancock Scholarships 2452

The Institute of International Education (IIE) sponsors the Adell and Hancock Scholarship. The purpose of the Adell & Hancock Fund is to provide supplemental support to U.S. and international students who are in need of additional funds to carry out their international educational plans. The amount awarded will depend on individual need as determined by IIE/RMRC scholarship committee to not exceed $2,400 per candidate. Applicants should refer to the IIE website for further information and current application information.
Geographic Focus: All States, All Countries
Date(s) Application is Due: Oct 15
Amount of Grant: Up to 2,400 USD
Contact: Lauren Granstrom, Administrative Assistant; (303) 837-0788, ext. 27 or (303) 837-1409; rockymountainscholarships@iie.org or lgranstrom@iie.org
Internet: http://www.rockymountainiie.org/scholarships
Sponsor: Institute of International Education
1400 K Street, NW, 7th Floor
Washington, DC 20005-2403

IIE AmCham Charitable Foundation U.S. Studies Scholarship 2453

The Institute of International Education sponsors the AmCham Charitable Foundation U.S. Studies Scholarship. The scholarship funds undergraduate study at a U.S. university for high school students from Hong Kong.
Requirements: Applicants must be permanent residents of Hong Kong; they must have received at least five years of continuous education in a Hong Kong high school where they are currently enrolled; and they must have gained admission to an undergraduate degree program in a U.S. college or university for the coming year. Current applications and deadlines are found on the website.
Restrictions: Only current residents of Hong Kong may apply.
Geographic Focus: Hong Kong
Date(s) Application is Due: Apr 15
Amount of Grant: 16,000 HKD
Contact: Linda Pham, Scholarship Contact; (852) 2530-6917; fax (852) 2810-1289; lpham@amcham.org.hk or amcham@amcham.org.hk
Internet: http://www.amcham.org.hk/index.php/U.S.-Studies-Scholarship.html
Sponsor: Institute of International Education
1400 K Street, NW, 7th Floor
Washington, DC 20005-2403

IIE David L. Boren Fellowships 2454

Boren Fellowships provide up to $30,000 funding to U.S. graduate students to add an international and language component to their graduate education through specialization in area study, language study, or increased language proficiency. Boren Fellowships support study and research in areas of the world that are critical to U.S. interests, including Africa, Asia, Central & Eastern Europe, Eurasia, Latin America, and the Middle East. Boren Fellowships are funded by the National Security Education Program (NSEP), which focuses on geographic areas, languages, and fields of study that are critical to U.S. national security. Applicants should identify how their projects, as well as their future academic and career goals, will contribute to U.S. national security.
Requirements: Boren Fellowships promote long term linguistic and cultural immersion. Therefore, applicant preference will be given to those proposing overseas programs of 6 months or longer. However, applicants proposing overseas programs of 3-6 months, especially those in the STEM (science, technology, engineering, and mathematics) fields are encouraged to apply. Boren Fellowships are awarded with preference for countries, languages, and fields of study critical to U.S. national security. Preference is also given to students who will study abroad for longer periods of time, and who are highly motivated by the opportunity to work in the federal government. Applicants should refer to the website for current deadlines and detailed criteria for application.
Restrictions: Applicants must commit to a length of study of at last 12 weeks.
Geographic Focus: All States
Date(s) Application is Due: Jan 31
Amount of Grant: Up to 30,000 USD
Contact: Michael Saffle; (800) 618-6737; fax (202) 326-7672; boren@iie.org
Internet: http://www.borenawards.org/boren_fellowship
Sponsor: Institute of International Education
1400 K Street, NW, 7th Floor
Washington, DC 20005-2403

IIE Eurobank EFG Scholarships 2455

The Eurobank EFG Scholarship Program aims to identify and honor the best undergraduate students of Serbian state universities. An independent selection committee of experts evaluate all applications. Semi-finalists are invited to a personal interview conducted in English. The winners are publicly recognized at an award ceremony, with their names published in daily newspapers.
Requirements: The ideal candidate has high academic standing, leadership potential, and an interest in community development. Participation in extracurricular activities, good communication skills, and proficiency in foreign languages are also essential qualities. All applicants must have: a grade point average higher than 9.5; extracurricular activities; a demonstrated interest in community development with leadership potential; good communication skills; and proficiency in foreign languages.
Geographic Focus: Serbia
Amount of Grant: 1,000 EUR
Contact: Eurobank EFG Scholarship Team; (+36-1) 472-2283; fax (+36-1) 472-2255; eurobankefg-scholarship@iie.eu
Internet: http://www.iie.org/en/Programs/Eurobank-EFG-Scholarships
Sponsor: Institute of International Education
1400 K Street, NW, 7th Floor
Washington, DC 20005-2403

IIE Freeman Foundation Indonesia Internships 2456

The Freeman Indonesia Nonprofit Internship (FINIP) addresses the limited knowledge among Indonesian students about the nonprofit sector. It also addresses the limited understanding and exposure of U.S. students to Indonesia, despite the increasing importance of the country globally. The Freeman Indonesia Nonprofit Internship Program is an opportunity to strengthen the leadership of Indonesia's future nonprofits and deepen ties between America and Indonesia. The shared experience of collaborating to assist a local Indonesian nonprofit is a learning experience and a vehicle for cross-cultural understanding, building ongoing friendships and shared interests in the nonprofit sector in the U.S. and Indonesia.
Requirements: Applicants must meet all of the following eligibility *Requirements:* they must be a U.S. or Indonesian citizen; currently enrolled as a full time sophomore or junior pursuing their first bachelor's degree at a U.S. university; and be in good academic standing at their university. Potential applicants should refer to the website for specific instructions about the application process.
Geographic Focus: All States, Indonesia
Date(s) Application is Due: Mar 1
Contact: FINIP Contact; (212) 984-5542; fax (212) 984-5325; finip@iie.org
Internet: http://www.iie.org/Programs/FINIP
Sponsor: Institute of International Education
1400 K Street, NW, 7th Floor
Washington, DC 20005-2403

IIE Japan-U.S. Teacher Exchange for Education for Sustainable Development 2457

The Japan-U.S. Teacher Exchange Program for Education for Sustainable Development (ESD) will provide up to 48 U.S. teachers and administrators with the opportunity to travel to Japan on this fully-funded program. Up to 48 teachers from Japan will travel to the U.S., and up to 48 teachers from the U.S. will travel to Japan to learn about ESD efforts and strengthen ESD curricula in both countries. At the end of the program in each country, all 96 teachers will gather for a few days of joint collaboration. The Japan-U.S. Teacher Exchange Program for ESD is fully-funded with the exception of some meals. Travel to/from the Joint Conference in the U.S., roundtrip travel to Japan, lodging, insurance, official excursions, local transportation, and most meals are paid for by Fulbright Japan. Participants in the program will be responsible for certain additional costs, such as a few meals, pre-departure expenses (i.e. passports or travel supplies), any costs associated with being away from their jobs during the program, and any personal expenses. Participants are recommended to bring approximately $200 to Japan to cover meals not paid for by the program.
Requirements: Applicants for the Japan-U.S. Teacher Exchange Program for ESD must be U.S. citizens at the time of application, must hold teaching certificates and/or have the equivalent credentials to teach at their schools, and must be employed full-time as teachers or administrators in grades 1-12. Teachers should refer to the website for current deadlines and applications.
Restrictions: Only full time educators are eligible for the program. There are no special health requirements to apply to the program. However, applicants should be aware that the program is intensive and physically rigorous, including long days with demanding schedules (applicants who are pregnant or have walking difficulties should give these factors careful consideration). Applicants are expected to carry their own belongings. If accepted as a participant, applicants will have to complete a medical form which requires an examination conducted by a physician certifying sound physical and mental health.
Geographic Focus: All States
Date(s) Application is Due: Jan 6
Contact: ESD Contact; (888) 527-2636; esdteacher@iie.org
Internet: http://www.iie.org/Programs/ESD
Sponsor: Institute of International Education
1400 K Street NW, 7th Floor
Washington, DC 20005-2403

IIE Leonora Lindsley Memorial Fellowships 2458

The Lindsley Scholarship was established for Leonora Lindsley, an American member of an international all-female combat unit on the Western Front during World War II, who was killed the day before the war officially ended. The scholarship was created in her honor by French citizens who are descendants from Resistance fighters to fund those pursuing educational studies in the United States. An award is granted to one or two students for graduate study for a twelve month period, and is renewable for a second year. The winner(s) are chosen every other year. The amount of the award varies from year to year, but ranges from $10,000 to $12,000.
Requirements: The Fulbright Commission in Paris gathers applications and sends them to IIE where they are reviewed for completeness and eligibility. Once this is done, a selection panel is convened and finalists chosen. Any major is eligible.
Restrictions: Only descendants of French Resistance fighters are eligible. Grantees must be at an accredited U.S. university.
Geographic Focus: All States, France
Amount of Grant: Up to 12,000 USD
Contact: Leonara Lindsley Fellowship Contact; (212) 984-5552
Internet: http://www.iie.org/Programs/Leonora-Lindsley-Memorial-Fellowship
Sponsor: Institute of International Education
1400 K Street, NW, 7th Floor
Washington, DC 20005-2403

IIE Nancy Petry Scholarship 2459

The Institute of International Education sponsors the Nancy Petry Scholarship. The Nancy Petry Scholarship for Study Abroad provides financial support for students enrolled in graduate programs at universities in Colorado. Students should demonstrate some proficiency with the language of their chosen country if the program proposed is for a non-English speaking country.
Requirements: Applicants should refer to the website for current deadlines.
Restrictions: Students are not restricted to certain countries or fields of study, but the committee encourages applicants in the fields of environmental studies, international business, or economics.
Geographic Focus: Colorado
Date(s) Application is Due: Oct 21
Amount of Grant: 5,000 USD
Contact: Lauren Granstrom; (303) 837-0788, ext. 27 or (303) 837-1409; lgranstrom@iie.org
Internet: http://www.rockymountainiie.org/scholarships
Sponsor: Institute of International Education
1400 K Street, NW, 7th Floor
Washington, DC 20005-2403

IIE New Leaders Group Award for Mutual Understanding 2460

The Institute of International Education (IIE) sponsors the IIE New Leaders Group Award for Mutual Understanding to recognize the outstanding work of one current Fulbright grantee who actively promotes mutual understanding between the U.S. and another country. The individual whose work is judged to have the most impact will receive the Award to continue an ongoing project. The $5,000 Award can be for work in any field. The intent of this Award is to encourage and recognize bright young professionals for their innovative ideas, valuable knowledge, and dedication to the cause of mutual understanding. The recipient will be honored and asked to speak about the impact of this Award on their project at an IIE New Leaders Group event in the spring.
Requirements: There are no limits on the disciplines or fields supported. Individuals from any academic field or disciplines are eligible. Applicants should send a project description, resume, two references, a news article or brochure about their project (if available), along with the application available online. Current information and deadlines are found on the website.
Restrictions: The project being recognized must be an ongoing activity that is currently underway; it cannot be a proposal for a project to be done in the future. The Award is limited to current Foreign and U.S. Fulbright Scholar grantees.
Geographic Focus: All States, All Countries
Amount of Grant: 5,000 USD
Contact: Award Contact; (212) 984-5456; fax (212) 984-5566; byi@iie.org
Internet: http://www.iie.org/Who-We-Are/Awards/New-Leaders-Group-Award
Sponsor: Institute of International Education
1400 K Street, NW, 7th Floor
Washington, DC 20005-2403

IIE Toyota International Teacher Professional Development Grants 2461

The Toyota International Teacher Professional Development grant provides international, professional-development opportunities to U.S. secondary school teachers to advance environmental stewardship and global connectedness in U.S. schools and communities. Each year, the program sends educators overseas for short-term (2-3 week) study tours to countries that are at the forefront of innovative solutions to environmental challenges. Participating teachers explore social and environmental issues through hands-on activities, and apply what they learn to create interdisciplinary and solution-focused lesson plans. The objectives of this professional development are: to increase global awareness and understanding; to enhance environmental knowledge, awareness, and sensitivity; to instill a sense of responsibility in teachers to empower their students and community leaders to do the same; to facilitate and creative hands-on approach to environmental and global issues; and to strengthen ties and facilitate collaboration among local and international teachers, community members, and organizations. Toyota covers all costs of program materials, transportation, meals, and lodging. Toyota will also issue each participant's school a $500 stipend to help defray the costs of participation during the school year.
Requirements: Applicants must be U.S. educators and teacher-librarians (grades 7-12) who work in the U.S. and District of Columbia. Applicants must hold a U.S. citizenship; hold a position as a full time classroom teacher or teacher-librarian for grades 7-12; and have at least three years of full time teaching experience. Teachers of diverse backgrounds and experience are strongly encouraged to apply. All programs focus on ways in which U.S. teachers can incorporate global and environmental education into their classrooms and communities.
Geographic Focus: All States
Amount of Grant: 500 USD
Contact: Toyota International Teacher Contact; (877) 832-2457; toyotateach@iie.org
Internet: http://www.iie.org/Programs/Toyota-International-Teacher-Program
Sponsor: Institute of International Education
1400 K Street, NW, 7th Floor
Washington, DC 20005-2403

IIE Western Union Family Scholarships 2462

The Western Union Family Scholarships are intended to help two members of the same family move up the economic development ladder through education. Scholarships may be used for tuition for college/university education, language acquisition classes, technical/skill training, and/or financial literacy. Families must have overcome barriers to pursue their educational goals and demonstrate financial need, with specific plans to utilize the scholarship. Recipients are eligible to receive scholarships from $1,000 to $5,000. For example, one recipient may receive $3,500 for college tuition, while the other may receive $1,500 for an ESL course.
Requirements: Requirements for the scholarship include the following criteria: applicants must be at least 18 years of age and living in the U.S. for seven years or less; both applicants must have been born outside the U.S. and be currently living in the U.S; application must include educational providers for primary and secondary award recipients (must be two family members); and applicants must reside in one of the following U.S. locations - Los Angeles, California; San Francisco, California; Denver, Colorado; Chicago, Illinois; New York, New York; Washington, D.C., or Miami, Florida.
Restrictions: Western Union employees, agents and dependents are not eligible to apply.

Geographic Focus: California, Colorado, District of Columbia, Florida, Illinois, New York
Amount of Grant: Up to 5,000 USD
Contact: Scholarship Contact; (303) 837-0788; fax (303) 837-1409; wufamily@iie.org
Internet: http://corporate.westernunion.com/scholarship.html
Sponsor: Institute of International Education
1400 K Street, NW, 7th Floor
Washington, DC 20005-2403

Illinois Arts Council Arts-in-Education Residency Program Grants 2463
The Arts-in-Education Residency program provides support to Illinois not-for-profit organizations for professional artist residencies lasting from two weeks to six months in one fiscal year. Grant requests for any fiscal year are for activities occurring between November 1 and August 31 of the following year. The deadline to apply is May 1. Past grants have supported residencies sponsored by libraries, park districts, churches, schools, school districts, colleges, universities, local arts agencies, municipalities, hospitals, community centers, youth organizations, and senior centers. Program goals are to: create a focus around which the educational and civic community can work together to develop or strengthen programs in arts education; increase the understanding of, and appreciation for, the arts and artists in the schools and community; provide opportunities for the professional artist to work in a community context; increase public recognition and support for the arts and arts education; support arts programming that reflects the diversity and cultural richness of Illinois and encourages active participation from all residents; assist educators in the initiation of innovative strategies in arts curriculum development and implementation; and collaborate with organizations, educators, and artists throughout Illinois to better meet the arts education needs of the citizens of the state.
Requirements: Applicant must be a not-for-profit organization currently registered with the Illinois Secretary of State or an agent of a governmental body (i.e., school, school district, park district, college, or university).
Restrictions: Applicants cannot be enrolled in a degree- or certificate-granting program.
Geographic Focus: Illinois
Date(s) Application is Due: May 1
Contact: Tatiana Gant; (312) 814-6765; fax (312) 814-1471; tatiana.gant@illinois.gov
Internet: http://www.arts.illinois.gov./grants-programs/iac-grants/arts-education-residency
Sponsor: Illinois Arts Council
100 W Randolph Street, Suite 10-500
Chicago, IL 60601-3230

Illinois Arts Council Arts Service Organizations Grants 2464
Organizations whose primary mission is to provide services to the arts community have a separate guidelines and application process. An arts service organization is defined as an organization that provides specialized services to the arts and cultural community. These organizations can be discipline, geographical, or culture-based, or can serve the entire arts community. Services offered can include, but are not limited to, professional development and technical assistance such as marketing, legal and financial assistance, networking opportunities, educational forums and workshops, and printed materials including calendars, newsletters, and other publications.
Geographic Focus: Illinois
Date(s) Application is Due: Mar 15
Contact: Jennifer Armstrong; (312) 814-4993; fax (312) 814-1471; j.armstrong@illinois.gov
Internet: http://www.arts.illinois.gov./grants-programs/funding-programs/arts-service-organizations
Sponsor: Illinois Arts Council
100 W Randolph Street, Suite 10-500
Chicago, IL 60601-3230

Illinois Arts Council Artstour Grants 2465
The intent of this program is to encourage the presenter or potential presenter to initiate, expand, and/or diversify a presenting program, through the use of quality arts programming. The Artstour program has been responsive to the needs of libraries, park districts, school organizations, traditional presenters, senior citizen centers, hospitals, festivals, local arts agencies, and community organizations. Applicants may request up to a maximum of 50 percent of the roster artist's or exhibit package's contracted fee. Applications must be received at the IAC office at least eight weeks prior to the project date.
Requirements: Applicant must be a not-for-profit organization currently registered with the Illinois Secretary of State or an agent of a governmental body (i.e., school, school district, park district, college, or university).
Restrictions: The Illinois Arts Council will not fund an Artstour presentation through both the Artstour Program and the Presenters Development Program.
Geographic Focus: Illinois
Amount of Grant: Up to 30,000 USD
Contact: Walter Buford, Director, Performing Arts, Partners in Excellence; (313) 814-4992; fax (312) 814-1471; walter.buford@illinois.gov
Internet: http://www.arts.illinois.gov./grants-programs/funding-programs/artstour
Sponsor: Illinois Arts Council
100 W Randolph Street, Suite 10-500
Chicago, IL 60601-3230

Illinois Arts Council Community Arts Access Grants 2466
The Illinois Arts Council Community Arts Access provides the opportunity for local arts agencies to distribute state funds in their own service areas according to their assessment of local needs. The Illinois Arts Council provides technical assistance and consultation to organizations seeking assistance in ADA Compliance.
Geographic Focus: Illinois
Contact: Jennifer Armstrong; (312) 814-4993; fax (312) 814-1471; j.armstrong@illinois.gov
Internet: http://www.arts.illinois.gov./grants-programs/funding-programs/community-arts-access
Sponsor: Illinois Arts Council
100 W Randolph Street, Suite 10-500
Chicago, IL 60601-3230

Illinois Arts Council Dance Program Grants 2467
Program Grant funds provide artistic and operational support to established organizations that make a significant local, regional, or statewide impact on the quality of life in Illinois. Dance Program Grants are designed to support professional, regional, and community companies, including ballet, modern, avant-garde, jazz, tap, and historical dance companies and mime. As part of the narrative the applicant should describe the organization's artistic goals and programming selection process. Available funding ranges from $500 to $30,000, depending upon the applicant organization's overall past operating budget.
Requirements: Nonprofits that apply must be chartered in the state of Illinois.
Geographic Focus: Illinois
Date(s) Application is Due: Mar 15
Amount of Grant: 500 - 30,000 USD
Contact: Walter Buford; (312) 814-4991; fax (312) 814-4992; walter.buford@illinois.gov
Internet: http://www.arts.illinois.gov/Program%20Grant%3A%20Dance
Sponsor: Illinois Arts Council
100 W Randolph Street, Suite 10-500
Chicago, IL 60601-3230

Illinois Arts Council Ethnic and Folk Arts Master Apprentice Program Grants 2468
The Ethnic and Folk Arts Master Apprentice Program recognizes the vital role of the master artist/apprentice relationship in the preservation of the state's cultural heritage. The program helps communities preserve their own culture by providing an opportunity for master traditional artists to pass on their skills to a qualified apprentice in a time-honored method. Suspended since 2009 as the result of state budget cuts, the IAC is pleased to be able to reinstate the Master Apprentice Program. The Master Apprentice award is a fixed amount of $3,000, awarded to the master artist, and is to be considered as compensation for teaching the apprentice and to cover the cost of any required supplies, materials, or travel by the master artist or the apprentice artist to the teaching sessions. A portion of the budget for the apprenticeship plan should also be set aside for expenses related to documenting the apprenticeship.
Requirements: Both the master artist and the apprentice must present proof that they are U.S. citizens or have permanent resident alien status and have resided in Illinois for at least one year prior to applying. Applicant organizations must have been in operation for at least one year prior to the deadline date, be chartered in Illinois, and have nonprofit status.
Geographic Focus: Illinois
Date(s) Application is Due: Mar 30
Amount of Grant: 3,000 USD
Contact: Susan Dickson; (312) 814-6740 or (800) 237-6994; susan.dickson@illinois.gov
Internet: http://www.arts.illinois.gov./MAP
Sponsor: Illinois Arts Council
100 W Randolph Street, Suite 10-500
Chicago, IL 60601-3230

Illinois Arts Council Ethnic and Folk Arts Program Grants 2469
Ethnic and Folk Arts Program Grants are designed to support organizations, programs, and projects which create, present, perform, exhibit, or document the traditional arts of Illinois. Ethnic and Folk Arts are defined as those artistic practices that have a community or family base; express that community's aesthetic, heritage, and tradition; and have endured through several generations. These artistic practices should express the particular culture of the language, regional, tribal, or nationality group from which they originate. Types of organizations supported by Ethnic and Folk Arts Program Grants include but are not limited to museums, park districts, historical societies, schools, traditional choral groups, traditional dance groups, traditional arts publications, social service organizations, refugee and immigrant settlement associations, and traditional arts presenters. Available funding ranges from $500 to $30,000, depending upon the applicant organization's overall past operating budget.
Requirements: Nonprofit organizations must be chartered in the state of Illinois.
Restrictions: Public and private K-12 schools and community colleges are ineligible.
Geographic Focus: Illinois
Date(s) Application is Due: Mar 15
Contact: Susan Dickson, (312) 814-6740; fax (312) 814-1471; susan.dickson@illinois.gov
Internet: http://www.arts.illinois.gov/Program%20Grant%3A%20Ethnic%20and%20Folk%20Arts
Sponsor: Illinois Arts Council
100 W Randolph Street, Suite 10-500
Chicago, IL 60601-3230

Illinois Arts Council Literature Program Grants 2470
Program Grant funds provide artistic and operational support to established organizations that make a significant local, regional, or statewide impact on the quality of life in Illinois. Literature Program Grants support organizations that promote the creation, publication, and distribution of creative writing, including fiction, poetry, and creative writing (fiction, poetry, and creative non-fiction). Creative non-fiction is distinguished from non-fiction by its strong narrative and literary quality, as found in personal essays or memoirs. This does not include works that are primarily analytical, scholarly, or journalistic. Grants often support the publication of books and literary magazines, literary centers, distribution projects, readings, workshops, book fairs, festivals, and conferences. Available funding ranges from $500 to $30,000, depending upon the applicant organization's overall past operating budget.

Requirements: Organizations incorporated in Illinois and writers resident in the state for at least one year are eligible to apply.
Restrictions: Student publications are not eligible. IAC funds cannot be used to pay literary agents' fees.
Geographic Focus: Illinois
Date(s) Application is Due: Mar 15
Amount of Grant: 500 - 30,000 USD
Contact: Susan Dickson; (312) 814-6740; fax (312) 814-1471; susan.dickson@illinois.gov
Internet: http://www.arts.illinois.gov/Program%20Grant%3A%20Literature
Sponsor: Illinois Arts Council
100 W Randolph Street, Suite 10-500
Chicago, IL 60601-3230

Illinois Arts Council Local Arts Agencies Program Grants 2471
Program Grant funds provide artistic and operational support to established organizations that make a significant local, regional, or statewide impact on the quality of life in Illinois. Local Arts Agencies Program Grants are designed to provide project and/or operational support to Illinois local arts agencies (defined as a community-based organization or an agency of city or county government that supports the growth and development of all of the arts in the identified area of service). Available funding ranges from $500 to $30,000, depending upon the applicant organization's overall past operating budget.
Requirements: Nonprofits applying for funding must be chartered in the state of Illinois.
Geographic Focus: Illinois
Date(s) Application is Due: Mar 15
Amount of Grant: 500 - 30,000 USD
Contact: Jennifer Armstrong; (312) 814-4993; fax (312) 814-1471; j.armstrong@illinois.gov
Internet: http://www.arts.illinois.gov/Program%20Grant%3A%20Local%20Arts%20Agencies
Sponsor: Illinois Arts Council
100 W Randolph Street, Suite 10-500
Chicago, IL 60601-3230

Illinois Arts Council Media Arts Program Grants 2472
Media Arts Program Grants are designed to support organizations that promote the production, exhibition, and distribution of film/video and audio art. This includes documentary, experimental, animated, and narrative works; audio art consists of recorded work on cassette, compact disc, or digital audiotape (DAT) created for radio broadcast, audio installation, independent distribution or online real-time audio via the World Wide Web, experimental narratives, spoken work compositions, radio drama, documentaries, sound compositions, audio collages and montages, and radio artworks; and radio programming of and about the arts, which includes documentaries, drama, literature, and music, as well as arts reporting. Grants in media arts often support production, exhibition/broadcast, distribution, classes, seminars, publications, and publicity. These grants also support organizations that produce, broadcast, and distribute radio programming of and about the arts. A higher priority will be given to locally-produced programs and applicants who have a commitment to advancing the field of under-represented art forms. Grants are available for single radio productions or for a series. Projects may include documentaries, drama, literature, and music as well as arts reporting. Proposals should emphasize the creative use of the medium. Available funding ranges from $500 to $30,000, depending upon the applicant organization's overall past operating budget.
Requirements: Nonprofits applying for funding must be chartered in the state of Illinois.
Restrictions: This program does not fund work that is primarily instructional, journalistic, archival, or promotional.
Geographic Focus: Illinois
Date(s) Application is Due: Mar 15
Amount of Grant: 500 - 30,000 USD
Contact: Encarnacion Teruel; (312) 814-6753; encarnacion.teruel@illinois.gov
Internet: http://www.arts.illinois.gov/Program%20Grant%3A%20Media%20Arts
Sponsor: Illinois Arts Council
100 W Randolph Street, Suite 10-500
Chicago, IL 60601-3230

Illinois Arts Council Multidisciplinary Program Grants 2473
Program Grant funds provide artistic and operational support to established organizations that make a significant local, regional, or statewide impact on the quality of life in Illinois. Multidisciplinary Program Grants are designed to support organizations offering programming that involves or fuses two or more distinct artistic disciplines. Programs should be distinct, not supplemental in nature, and must integrally involve each of the participating art forms rather than be in service to a single art form. Grants are available for ongoing programming, new projects, staff, production costs, marketing, and audience development. Available funding ranges from $500 to $30,000, depending upon the applicant organization's overall past operating budget.
Requirements: Nonprofits applying for funding must be chartered in the state of Illinois.
Geographic Focus: Illinois
Date(s) Application is Due: Mar 15
Amount of Grant: 500 - 30,000 USD
Contact: Encarnacion Teruel; (312) 814-6753; encarnacion.teruel@illinois.gov
Internet: http://www.arts.illinois.gov/Program%20Grant%3A%20Multi-Disciplinary
Sponsor: Illinois Arts Council
100 W Randolph Street, Suite 10-500
Chicago, IL 60601-3230

Illinois Arts Council Music Program Grants 2474
Program Grant funds provide artistic and operational support to established organizations that make a significant local, regional, or statewide impact on the quality of life in Illinois. Music Program Grants are designed to support professional, regional, and community companies including opera, vocal ensembles, orchestras, chamber music, jazz ensembles, contemporary and early music groups, and concert and wind bands. Available funding ranges from $500 to $30,000, depending upon the applicant organization's overall past operating budget.
Requirements: Nonprofits applying for funding must be chartered in the state of Illinois.
Geographic Focus: Illinois
Date(s) Application is Due: Mar 15
Amount of Grant: 500 - 30,000 USD
Contact: Walter Buford; (312) 814-4992; fax (312) 814-1471; walter.buford@illinois.gov
Internet: http://www.arts.illinois.gov/Program%20Grant%3A%20Music
Sponsor: Illinois Arts Council
100 W Randolph Street, Suite 10-500
Chicago, IL 60601-3230

Illinois Arts Council Partners in Excellence Grants 2475
Recognizing that Illinois is the home of creative arts institutions of regional and national significance; the Illinois Arts Council has implemented the Partners in Excellence Program (PIE). The PIE Program provides general operating support to designated organizations of scale and significance in all regions of the state. Check the listing of designated organizations at the website before making application.
Requirements: Only designated organizations in Illinois can apply.
Geographic Focus: Illinois
Date(s) Application is Due: Mar 15
Contact: Walter Buford, (312) 814-4992; fax (312) 814-1471; walter.buford@illinois.gov
Internet: http://www.arts.illinois.gov./grants-programs/funding-programs/partners-excellence
Sponsor: Illinois Arts Council
100 W Randolph Street, Suite 10-500
Chicago, IL 60601-3230

Illinois Arts Council Presenters Development Program Grants 2476
Program Grant funds provide artistic and operational support to established organizations that make a significant local, regional, or statewide impact on the quality of life in Illinois. Presenters Development Program Grants are designed to provide programming or operational support to Illinois presenters. A presenter is an organization that has a distinct program which: contracts for the presentation of professional performing arts programs which have been prepared or created under some other organization's auspices; and exercises full fiscal and managerial responsibility over an ongoing schedule of three or more such events in each fiscal year. Generally the work presented has been prepared or created outside the presenting organization. Available funding ranges from $500 to $30,000, depending upon the applicant organization's overall past operating budget.
Requirements: Nonprofits applying for funding must be chartered in the state of Illinois.
Geographic Focus: Illinois
Date(s) Application is Due: Mar 15
Amount of Grant: 500 - 30,000 USD
Contact: Susan Dickson; (312) 814-6740; fax (312) 814-1471; susan.dickson@illinois.gov
Internet: http://www.arts.illinois.gov/Program%20Grant%3A%20Presenters%20Development
Sponsor: Illinois Arts Council
100 W Randolph Street, Suite 10-500
Chicago, IL 60601-3230

Illinois Arts Council Theater Program Grants 2477
Program Grant funds provide artistic and operational support to established organizations that make a significant local, regional, or statewide impact on the quality of life in Illinois. Theatre Program grants are designed to support professional, regional, and community companies, including experimental, street, and children's theater. This includes experimental, musical theatre, street performance, and theatre for young audiences. Available funding ranges from $500 to $30,000, depending upon the applicant organization's overall past operating budget.
Requirements: Nonprofits applying for funding must be chartered in the state of Illinois.
Geographic Focus: Illinois
Date(s) Application is Due: Mar 15
Amount of Grant: 500 - 30,000 USD
Contact: Walter Buford; (312) 814-4992; fax (312) 814-1471; walter.buford@illinois.gov
Internet: http://www.arts.illinois.gov/Program%20Grant%3A%20Theater
Sponsor: Illinois Arts Council
100 W Randolph Street, Suite 10-500
Chicago, IL 60601-3230

Illinois Arts Council Visual Arts Program Grants 2478
Program Grant funds provide artistic and operational support to established organizations that make a significant local, regional, or statewide impact on the quality of life in Illinois. Visual Arts Program Grants are designed to support organizations such as museums, non-commercial galleries, art centers, guilds, leagues, and other not-for-profit organizations doing visual arts programming or other activities which further the public interest in the visual arts. Grants in the visual arts often support exhibitions, performance art events, promotional activities, publications, seminars, workshops, and projects that support discourse among visual artists and other programs in the service of visual arts. Available funding ranges from $500 to $30,000, depending upon the applicant organization's overall past operating budget.

Requirements: Nonprofit organizations must be chartered in the state of Illinois, and individual artists must be residents of Illinois for at least a year before applying.
Geographic Focus: Illinois
Date(s) Application is Due: Mar 15
Amount of Grant: 500 - 30,000 USD
Contact: Encarnacion Teruel; (312) 814-6753; encarnacion.teruel@illinois.gov
Internet: http://www.arts.illinois.gov/Program%20Grant%3A%20Visual%20Arts
Sponsor: Illinois Arts Council
100 W Randolph Street, Suite 10-500
Chicago, IL 60601-3230

Illinois Clean Energy Community Foundation Energy Efficiency Grants 2479

Through its Energy Efficiency program, the Foundation supports nonprofit organizations and local governments in their efforts to reduce energy consumption in buildings. By reducing energy consumption, nonprofits and local governments help the environment and save money. The program focus is on improvements to lighting and space conditioning in existing buildings and the greening of new construction. In 2012, the Foundation will continue to support lighting upgrades in select non-profit sectors: community centers, community care providers, as well as EEPS ineligible applicants (public and non-profit customers served by rural electric cooperatives and municipal electric utilities). The Government Buildings program is open to most all types of government owned and operated buildings. The Existing Buildings Energy Efficiency Improvements program will continue to provide incentives for comprehensive upgrades in buildings owned and operated by community centers and community care providers. Geothermal, innovative HVAC and other energy reducing systems will continue to be of interest to the Foundation.
Requirements: 501(c)3 tax-exempt organizations, educational institutions, and state and local government agencies serving Illinois residents are eligible.
Restrictions: The foundation will not provide funding for remediation of environmentally impaired properties; technology research; promotion of proprietary products; reoccurring operating costs; political campaigns or lobbying; capital campaigns or support for an organization's endowment; or projects undertaken by individuals.
Geographic Focus: Illinois
Date(s) Application is Due: Jan 15; Jul 15
Contact: Bob Romo; (312) 372-5191; fax (312) 372-5190; info@illinoiscleanenergy.org
Internet: http://www.illinoiscleanenergy.org/energy-efficiency/
Sponsor: Illinois Clean Energy Community Foundation
2 N LaSalle Street, Suite 1140
Chicago, IL 60602

Illinois Clean Energy Community Foundation K-12 Wind Schools Pilot Grants 2480

The Foundation is currently conducting a pilot program to test the feasibility of a full-scale Illinois Wind Schools initiative to make funding for educational small-scale (1-5kW) wind turbines more accessible. The pilot will be conducted during 2012 on a very limited basis and will award no more than five grants to K-12 schools that have demonstrated exceptional performance as recipients of Illinois Solar Schools grants. The program offers up to $40,000 or 90% of the system and its installation costs, whichever is less.
Requirements: The project must be wholly owned by an eligible applicant and cannot include ownership by private investors or commercial interests. To be eligible for consideration under the Wind K-12 Schools Pilot, the applicant organization must: be a recipient of an Illinois Solar Schools grant; be a K-12 educational institution; have a completed and operating system under the Solar Schools program; be willing to conduct and pay for a Wind Site Assessment carried out by a Midwest Renewable Energy Association Certified Wind Site Assessor; have a suitable site for proper wind turbine installation and operation, based on the Wind Site Assessment; co-fund a minimum of 10% of the turbine system installation costs; hold a "Wind Celebration" and make a commitment to teach about wind and solar energy in the classroom; and commit to educate the community about wind and solar energy.
Geographic Focus: Illinois
Date(s) Application is Due: Feb 21
Contact: Bob Romo; (312) 372-5191; fax (312) 372-5190; info@illinoiscleanenergy.org
Internet: http://www.illinoiscleanenergy.org/k-12-wind/
Sponsor: Illinois Clean Energy Community Foundation
2 N LaSalle Street, Suite 1140
Chicago, IL 60602

Illinois Clean Energy Community Foundation Renewable Energy Grants 2481

The Illinois Clean Energy Community Foundation helps non-profit groups and local government organizations to purchase and install renewable energy technologies, including photovoltaic panels, solar thermal systems, wind turbines and biomass systems. Renewable energy provides heating, cooling, hot water, steam or electricity, in an environmentally sound manner while also lowering or stabilizing utility costs. Before considering renewable energy, make the building as energy efficient as possible so that the installed renewable energy system can be smaller, less costly and able to offset a larger percentage of the energy consumed. The Foundation's goal, through its support of renewable energy technologies, is to improve the environment, help grow the renewable energy sector in Illinois, create jobs and lower energy costs. We also work with colleges and universities, as well as K-12 schools and teachers around the state to help educate and train Illinois' next generation about the benefits and potential of renewable energy.
Requirements: 501(c)3 tax-exempt organizations, educational institutions, and state and local government agencies serving Illinois residents are eligible.
Restrictions: The foundation will not provide funding for remediation of environmentally impaired properties; technology research; promotion of proprietary products; reoccurring operating costs; political campaigns or lobbying; capital campaigns or support for an organization's endowment; or projects undertaken by individuals.

Geographic Focus: Illinois
Date(s) Application is Due: Jan 15; Jul 15
Contact: Bob Romo; (312) 372-5191; fax (312) 372-5190; info@illinoiscleanenergy.org
Internet: http://www.illinoiscleanenergy.org/renewable-energy/
Sponsor: Illinois Clean Energy Community Foundation
2 N LaSalle Street, Suite 1140
Chicago, IL 60602

Illinois Clean Energy Community Foundation Solar Thermal Installation Grants 2482

Current solar thermal technology allows us to generate electricity, heat and cool building space and provide hot water using the abundant resources of the sun. Illinois Clean Energy has supported many solar thermal installations, providing clean energy to schools, museums, community centers, public buildings, affordable housing developments, and other facilities. Current solar thermal technology allows us to generate electricity, heat and cool building space and provide hot water using the abundant resources of the sun. Illinois Clean Energy has supported many solar thermal installations, providing clean energy to schools, museums, community centers, public buildings, affordable housing developments, and other facilities. The Foundation evaluates full proposals against the funding criteria. The Foundation especially encourages the following sectors to apply for solar thermal grants: fire stations; police stations; correctional facilities; recreation centers; civic centers; arts and cultural centers; museums; youth service centers; fraternal organizations; ethnic/national cultural centers; skilled intermediate and long-term nursing care facilities; primary care community health providers; and special needs service providers. The Foundation gives priority to solar thermal projects that: have secured all additional funding; feature a strong education and outreach component; and complement the implementation of significant energy efficiency measures at the facility planning to install the solar thermal system.
Requirements: Eligible applicants from all types of sectors can apply. Eligible buildings must have steady year-round hot water/heating/cooling load. All proposal must include plan ensuring current and future facilities staff is trained to operate and maintain the solar thermal system. Grantees must monitor system performance and submit annual performance reports for the first three years of operation.
Geographic Focus: Illinois
Date(s) Application is Due: Mar 13; Sep 13
Contact: Bob Romo; (312) 372-5191; fax (312) 372-5190; info@illinoiscleanenergy.org
Internet: http://www.illinoiscleanenergy.org/solar-thermal/
Sponsor: Illinois Clean Energy Community Foundation
2 N LaSalle Street, Suite 1140
Chicago, IL 60602

Illinois DCEO Business Development Public Infrastructure Program Grants 2483

The BDPIP program is designed to provide grants to units of local government for public improvements on behalf of businesses undertaking a major expansion or relocation project that will result in substantial private investment and the creation and/or retention of a large amount of Illinois jobs. The program also provides funds for infrastructure improvements in support of economic development in the Illinois, and helps local governments finance public infrastructure needed to support economic development and private sector job creation and retention. There is no maximum amount of infrastructure funds which may be invested in any one project. However, the amounts must be commensurate with the number of jobs created or retained. For this program, at least one private sector job must be created or retained for every $10,000 awarded by the department. Typically, the department will limit its assistance to $500,000 or less. Applications will be accepted on an ongoing basis.
Requirements: Any general purpose local government (as defined by Article 7, Section 1 of the Illinois Constitution) may apply to the department for funding under the Business Development Public Infrastructure Program. Funding is available only for infrastructure projects which lead directly to private sector expansion or retention activities. General infrastructure construction and renovation activities — those which lead only indirectly to job creation and retention — are not eligible for consideration. Program funds may be used for a wide variety of public infrastructure improvements needed to induce job creation and retention. These include local roads and streets, access roads, bridges, sidewalks, waste disposal systems, water and sewer line extensions, water distribution and purification facilities, sewage treatment facilities, rail and air or water port improvements, gas and electric utility extensions, public transit systems, and the development and improvement of publicly owned industrial and commercial sites. Potential local government applicants should carefully review the application package and program requirements and are encouraged to contact department staff to discuss project ideas and fund availability. These discussions can help in determining the appropriateness of this program and whether other public or private sources may better meet community needs.
Geographic Focus: Illinois
Contact: John Casey, Deputy Director; (217) 785-6193
Internet: http://www.ildceo.net/dceo/Bureaus/Business_Development/Grants/bdpip.htm
Sponsor: Illinois Department of Commerce and Economic Opportunity
500 East Monroe
Springfield, IL 62701

Illinois DCEO Coal Competitiveness Grants 2484

The program provides partial funding to improve coal extraction, preparation and transportation systems within Illinois, and encourages communities and businesses to improve miner safety and the coal extraction, preparation and transportation systems within Illinois. The Department of Commerce and Economic Opportunity issues an annual solicitation each fiscal year. Following proposal review and selection, grants are awarded in late winter or spring. Unsolicited proposals may be submitted at any time during the year.
Requirements: Any entity may apply. Projects may require a host site, private and public cost-sharing partners, etc., prior to proposal consideration and must have significant economic

benefits for Illinois. Grants are typically between $50,000 and $1,500,000 and are issued by DCEO. DCEO typically provides up to 20 percent of the total project cost. Grants are restricted to the state fiscal period.
Geographic Focus: Illinois
Amount of Grant: 50,000 - 1,500,000 USD
Contact: John McCarthy, (217) 785-1671; fax (217) 558-2647; John.McCarthy@illinois.gov
Internet: http://ildceo.net/dceo/Bureaus/Coal/Grants/
Sponsor: Illinois Department of Commerce and Economic Opportunity
500 East Monroe Street
Springfield, IL 62701-1643

Illinois DCEO Coal Demonstration Grants   2485
The program provides partial funding to bring state-of-the-art, advanced coal-use technologies to commercial readiness. Not only are these efforts bringing a new generation of clean coal techniques to the commercial marketplace, but also each project provides near-term benefits to the state and local communities through increased employment, personal income and tax revenues. Grants are typically between $1 million and $30 million and are issued by the Department of Commerce and Economic Opportunity. Grant periods and appropriations may cross fiscal years. Unsolicited proposals may be submitted at any time during the year. However, funding of selected proposals may be substantially delayed due to the need for legislative action to establish a funding appropriation.
Requirements: Any entity may apply. Funds are intended for capital projects located in Illinois that have significant economic benefits for the state. Projects typically require a host site, power purchase agreements, private and public cost-sharing partners, etc., prior to proposal consideration.
Geographic Focus: Illinois
Amount of Grant: 1,000,000 - 30,000,000 USD
Contact: Dan Wheeler, (217) 785-1671; fax (217) 558-2647; Dan.Wheeler@illinois.gov
Internet: http://ildceo.net/dceo/Bureaus/Coal/Grants/
Sponsor: Illinois Department of Commerce and Economic Opportunity
500 East Monroe Street
Springfield, IL 62701-1643

Illinois DCEO Coal Development Grants   2486
The Coal Development Program seeks to advance promising clean coal technologies beyond the research stage towards commercialization. The program provides a 50/50 match with private industry dollars to support market-driven needs of the industry. Development processes include technology maturation, technology transfer and related studies. Grants are issued by the Illinois Clean Coal Institute (ICCI) and are typically $250,000 to $600,000. Grant periods are limited to 24 months. The annual program cycle begins in April of each year with a Request for Proposals issued by the ICCI. Proposal review and project selection is typically completed by the end of August. Unsolicited proposals may be submitted at any time.
Requirements: Any entity may apply; preference is given to Illinois applicants. These projects must be past the R&D stage and must have a significant amount of cost-sharing. Typically the development proposal is submitted by an organization with special commercial technical expertise in the area proposed, but the program benefits Illinois coal producers and electric utilities.
Geographic Focus: Illinois
Amount of Grant: 250,000 - 600,000 USD
Contact: Dr. Francois Botha, (618) 985-3500
Paul Pierre-Louis, (312) 814-3630; fax (312) 814-5247; Paul.Pierre-Louis@illinois.gov
Internet: http://www.icci.org/
Sponsor: Illinois Department of Commerce and Economic Opportunity
500 East Monroe Street
Springfield, IL 62701-1643

Illinois DCEO Coal Revival Grants   2487
The Illinois Coal Revival Program provides financial assistance in the form of grants to assist with the development of new, coal-fired electric generation capacity or coal gasification facilities in Illinois. Financial assistance through the program will be provided in the form of a grant based on State Retail Occupation Taxes that will be paid on Illinois coal purchases for new facilities. Qualifying facilities may be eligible for grants roughly equal to the present value of future sales taxes paid on Illinois-mined coal over a 25-year period, up to a maximum amount of $100 million. Unsolicited proposals may be submitted at any time during the year. Funding of selected proposals may be substantially delayed due to the need for legislative action to establish a funding appropriation.
Requirements: Businesses must propose to construct a new electric generating or expand at an existing electric generating facility, including transmission lines and associated equipment to provide baseload electric power or to construct a coal gasification facility. The proposed new facility or facility expansion must: 1) have an aggregate nameplate generating capacity of 400 megawatts or more for all units at one site, will use coal or gases derived from coal as its primary fuel source at the proposed facility, and will support the creation of at least 150 new Illinois coal-mining jobs, or 2) use coal gasification or IGCC to generate chemical feedstocks, transportation fuels or electricity.
Geographic Focus: Illinois
Amount of Grant: Up to 100,000,000 USD
Contact: Dan Wheeler, (217) 785-1671; fax (217) 558-2647; Dan.Wheeler@illinois.gov
Internet: http://www.illinoisbiz.biz/dceo/Bureaus/Coal/Grants/
Sponsor: Illinois Department of Commerce and Economic Opportunity
500 East Monroe Street
Springfield, IL 62701-1643

Illinois DCEO Community Development Assistance Program for Economic Development (CDAP-ED) Grants   2488
The CDAP-ED program is a federally funded program that is designed to provide grants to units of local government for economic development activities related to business retention and or expansion opportunities. The program is targeted to assist low-to-moderate income people by creating job opportunities and improving the quality of their living environment. Local governments qualifying to receive grant funds can then make these funds available in the form of loans to businesses locating or expanding in their community. A local government may request grant funds of up to $750,000. Funds may be used for machinery and equipment, working capital, and building construction and renovation. The local government may also use the grant funds for improvements to public infrastructure that directly support a specific economic development project. Applications may be submitted at any time. Local government entities located in heavily populated metropolitan areas of the state may receive funding directly from the federal government and therefore, are ineligible for participation through this program.
Requirements: Only units of general local government (i.e., cities, villages, townships and counties) may apply for funding. Municipalities must be 50,000 or less in population and must not be located in an urban county that receives "entitlement" funds. County and township applicants should not include areas that are incorporated within a city or village. Incorporated areas should apply on their own behalf, regardless of whether a water district or sanitary district is involved. funds may be used to assist for-profit and not-for-profit firms to carry out economic development projects. Generally, CDAP grant funds will be provided by the unit of local government to the profit or not-for-profit business under a financial assistance agreement. "Financial assistance" means the provision of funds to an eligible economic development project through the purchase of any note, stock, convertible security, treasury stock, bond, debenture, evidence of indebtedness, certificate of interest or participation in any profit-sharing agreement, preorganization certificate of subscription, transferable share, investment contract, certificate of deposit for a security, certificate of interest or participation in a patent or application therefor, or in royalty or other payments under such a patent or application, or in general, any interest or instrument commonly known as a "security" or any certificate for, receipt for, guarantee of, or option, warrant or right to subscribe to or purchase any of the foregoing, but not including any instrument which contains voting rights in the possession of the Grantee, or other means whereby financial aid is made to or on behalf of an Illinois company as appropriate to the form of agreement, for working capital, the purchase or lease of machinery and equipment, or the lease or purchase of real estate, but does not include refinancing debt. Loans, investments and lines of credit may be extended in participation with other financial institutions. By providing expanded application for CDAP funds, the unit of local government will have enhanced capacity to pool public and private resources in support of a community project. The business may use the funds for land acquisition; construction, reconstruction, installation or rehabilitation of commercial or industrial buildings, structures and other real property; equipment and improvements; and working capital expenses. Working capital is defined as inventory, employee salaries, general operational expenses and advertising/ marketing expenses. CDAP funds may not be used as grants or loans to help service or refinance existing debt. Alternatively, CDAP funds may be used to finance public facilities and improvements in support of economic development (e.g., water system upgrade to serve an expanding business).
Restrictions: The following activities are considered ineligible: construction of buildings, or portions thereof, used predominantly for the general conduct of government (e.g., city halls, courthouses, jails, police stations, etc.); general government expenses; costs of operating and maintaining public facilities and services (e.g., mowing parks and replacing street light bulbs); servicing or refinancing of existing debt. Costs incurred in preparation of applications are not reimbursable under this grant program.
Geographic Focus: Illinois
Amount of Grant: 25,000 - 750,000 USD
Contact: Maureen Palmer; (217) 785-6174 or (312) 814-5854; maureen.palmer@Illinois.gov
Internet: http://ildceo.net/dceo/Bureaus/Community_Development/Grants/Economic Development_1.htm
Sponsor: Illinois Department of Commerce and Economic Opportunity
500 East Monroe
Springfield, IL 62701-1643

Illinois DCEO Eliminate the Digital Divide Grants   2489
The Eliminate the Digital Divide grant program seeks to provide access to computers, telecommunications technologies and related training to disadvantaged communities. Under this program, the Illinois Department of Commerce and Economic Opportunity (DCEO) is authorized to award grants of up to $75,000 to plan, establish, administer and expand Community Technology Centers (CTC's) and to support basic computer literacy training programs. The following entities are eligible to apply for a grant: public hospitals; libraries; park districts; senior citizen homes; State educational agencies; local educational agencies; institutions of higher education; public and private nonprofit or for-profit educational organizations; and entities that received a Community Technology Center grant under the federal Community Technology Centers Program. The following technology access activities are allowed: training on basic computer skills and office suite computer applications; vocational skills training related to IT occupations; access to career related information, employment opportunities and Internet search capabilities; computerized instruction in: basic literacy skills, GED preparation, or English as a second language instruction; before and after school programs for academic enrichment and reinforcement; classes offered through distance learning; computer skills training and support for entrepreneurs and small businesses; access to assistive technology for disabled persons; professional development opportunities for teachers; and promotion of home access to computers.
Requirements: To be eligible, an applicant must have the capacity to expand access to computers and telecommunications technology for disadvantaged residents of economically distressed urban and rural communities who would otherwise be denied such access. To be eligible for a grant, an applicant must serve a community in which at least 40 percent of

the students are eligible for a free or reduced price lunch under the national school lunch program, or in which at least 30 percent of the students are eligible for a free lunch under the national school lunch program.
Geographic Focus: Illinois
Date(s) Application is Due: Mar 16
Contact: Pam Giroux , (312) 814-5362; pam.giroux@illinois.gov
Internet: http://www.ildceo.net/dceo/Bureaus/Technology/Technology+Grants+Programs/
Sponsor: Illinois Department of Commerce and Economic Opportunity
100 West Randolph, Suite 3-400
Chicago, IL 60601

Illinois DCEO Emerging Technological Enterprises Grants   2490
Governor Pat Quinn signed into law bills that create the $31 billion Illinois Jobs Now plan, which will revive the state's ailing economy by creating and retaining over 439,000 jobs over the next six years. Illinois Jobs Now is a capital bill that provides many long-awaited improvements to our bridges and roads, transportation networks, schools and communities. Part of this plan includes $15 million for the Emerging Technological Enterprises program. The goal of the Emerging Technological Enterprises Program is to provide grants, loans, and other investments to emerging technology enterprises to support and encourage: commercialization of technology based products and services; technology transfer projects involving the promotion of new or innovative technologies; or research and development projects to respond to unique, advanced technology projects and which foster the development of Illinois' economy through the advancement of the State's economic, scientific, and technological assets. Eligible activities include: acquiring real properties for industrial or commercial site development; acquiring, rehabilitating and reconveying industrial and commercial properties for the purpose of expanding employment and encouraging private and other public sector investment in the economy of Illinois.
Requirements: To be considered eligible under this RFA, the applicant must have the capacity for commercialization of technology based products and services; technology transfer projects involving the promotion of new or innovative technologies; or research and development projects to respond to unique, advanced technology projects and which foster the development of Illinois' economy through the advancement of the state's economic, scientific, and technological assets. Eligible organizations can be for profit or not for profit. Allowable costs must be consistent with and classified into one of the following line items: land, buildings/structures, rights of way, appraisals; relocation expenses; architectural/engineering/professional services; other architectural and engineering fees; project inspection fees; site work/preparation; demolition and removal; construction; equipment; or miscellaneous/other.
Geographic Focus: Illinois
Contact: Pam Giroux , (312) 814-5362; pam.giroux@illinois.gov
Internet: http://www.ildceo.net/dceo/Bureaus/Technology/Technology+Grants+Programs/1-EmergingTechnology.htm
Sponsor: Illinois Department of Commerce and Economic Opportunity
100 West Randolph, Suite 3-400
Chicago, IL 60601

Illinois DCEO Employer Training Investment Grants - Competitive Component   2491
The Employer Training Investment Program (ETIP) is a competitive application program for Illinois based manufactures and service companies to facilitate upgrading the skills of their workers in order to remain current in new technologies and business practices. Participation in the program will enable companies to remain competitive, expand into new markets and introduce more efficient technologies into their operations. ETIP grants may reimburse Illinois companies for up to 50 percent of the eligible cost of training their employees. Grants may be awarded to individual businesses, intermediary organizations operating multi-company training projects and original equipment manufacturers sponsoring multi-company training projects for employees of their Illinois supplier companies.
Requirements: Illinois companies that are retraining/upgrading the skills of their existing workforce may be eligible for ETIP grants. Grants may be awarded to individual companies, as well as to intermediary organizations offering training to meet the common training needs of multiple companies.
Geographic Focus: Illinois
Contact: John Glazier; (217) 524-8145; fax (217) 558-4860; John.Glazier@illinois.gov
Internet: http://www.ildceo.net/dceo/Bureaus/Business_Development/Grants/ETIP.htm
Sponsor: Illinois Department of Commerce and Economic Opportunity
500 East Monroe
Springfield, IL 62701

Illinois DCEO Employer Training Investment Grants - Incentive Component   2492
The ETIP Incentive Program is eligible to Pre- Qualified Illinois businesses applying for training funds as part of an Economic Development Incentive Project. Companies located in Illinois who are expanding, relocating, or are in jeopardy of closing may be eligible for pre-qualification in the program. Participation requires companies to meet certain capital investment and Job creation/retention goals and provide a dollar for dollar match of the grant award.
Requirements: Illinois companies that are retraining/upgrading the skills of their existing workforce may be eligible for ETIP grants. Grants may be awarded to individual companies, as well as to intermediary organizations offering training to meet the common training needs of multiple companies.
Geographic Focus: Illinois
Contact: John Glazier; (217) 524-8145; fax (217) 558-4860; John.Glazier@illinois.gov
Internet: http://www.ildceo.net/dceo/Bureaus/Business_Development/Grants/ETIP-IncentiveComponent.htm
Sponsor: Illinois Department of Commerce and Economic Opportunity
500 East Monroe
Springfield, IL 62701

Illinois DCEO Employer Training Investment Multi-Company Training Grants   2493
The Employer Training Investment Program (ETIP) is a competitive application program for Illinois based manufactures and service companies to facilitate upgrading the skills of their workers in order to remain current in new technologies and business practices. Participation in the program will enable companies to remain competitive, expand into new markets and introduce more efficient technologies into their operations. The Illinois Department of Commerce and economic Opportunity is soliciting applications from interested and qualified intermediary organizations to implement eligible training programs on behalf of companies participating in the project. The intermediary organization will conduct or sponsor the employee training programs, coordinate all grant administrative and training evaluation reporting functions on behalf of the companies in the project. Multi-company applicants can include all of the following: Illinois based business and industry associations; institutions of secondary and higher education; strategic business partnerships; and large manufacturers for supplier network companies and labor organizations.
Requirements: Illinois companies that are retraining/upgrading the skills of their existing workforce may be eligible for ETIP grants. Grants may be awarded to individual companies, as well as to intermediary organizations offering training to meet the common training needs of multiple companies.
Geographic Focus: Illinois
Contact: John Glazier; (217) 524-8145; fax (217) 558-4860; John.Glazier@illinois.gov
Internet: http://www.ildceo.net/dceo/Bureaus/Business_Development/Grants/ETIP.htm
Sponsor: Illinois Department of Commerce and Economic Opportunity
500 East Monroe
Springfield, IL 62701

Illinois DCEO Employer Training Investment Single Company Training Grants   2494
The Employer Training Investment Program (ETIP) is a competitive application program for Illinois based manufactures and service companies to facilitate upgrading the skills of their workers in order to remain current in new technologies and business practices. Participation in the program will enable companies to remain competitive, expand into new markets and introduce more efficient technologies into their operations. ETIP grants may reimburse Illinois companies for up to 50 percent of the eligible cost of training their employees. Individual companies undertaking customized on-site training programs may apply for an ETIP grant if they are: expanding the business enterprise in Illinois, expanding into new markets, introducing more efficient technologies or continuous improvement systems, expanding exports from Illinois, and providing additional training to employees who will be threatened with layoff.
Requirements: Illinois companies that are retraining/upgrading the skills of their existing workforce may be eligible for ETIP grants. Grants may be awarded to individual companies, as well as to intermediary organizations offering training to meet the common training needs of multiple companies.
Geographic Focus: Illinois
Contact: John Glazier; (217) 524-8145; fax (217) 558-4860; John.Glazier@illinois.gov
Internet: http://www.ildceo.net/dceo/Bureaus/Business_Development/Grants/ETIP.htm
Sponsor: Illinois Department of Commerce and Economic Opportunity
500 East Monroe
Springfield, IL 62701

Illinois DCEO Large Business Development Program (LBDP) Grants   2495
Large Business Development program (LBDP) is designed to provide grants to businesses undertaking a major expansion or relocation project that will result in substantial private investment and the creation and/or retention of a large number of Illinois jobs. Funds available through the program may be used by large businesses for bondable business activities, including financing the purchase of land or buildings, building construction or renovation, and certain types of machinery and equipment. Grant eligibility and amounts are determined by the amount of investment and job creation or retention involved.
Geographic Focus: All States
Contact: John Casey, Deputy Director; (217) 785-6193 or (217) 524-8449
Internet: http://www.ildceo.net/dceo/Bureaus/Business_Development/Grants/lbdp.htm
Sponsor: Illinois Department of Commerce and Economic Opportunity
500 East Monroe
Springfield, IL 62701

Illinois DNR Biodiversity Field Trip Grants   2496
Teachers in Illinois, including home-schooling teachers, may apply to the Illinois Department of Natural Resources through the ENTICE (Environment and Nature Training Institute for Conservation Education) program to receive funding for natural resources-related field trips. The field trip can include: state parks; natural areas; natural history museums; and nature centers. Items eligible for funding include transportation and substitute teachers for those instructors participating in the field trip. There is a $500 limit per teacher
Requirements: Any Illinois teacher is eligible to apply.
Restrictions: The field trip must be in Illinois.
Geographic Focus: Illinois
Date(s) Application is Due: Jan 31
Contact: Valerie Keener, Administrator; (217) 524-4126 or (217) 782-7481; fax (217) 782-9599; valerie.keener@illinois.gov or dnr.teachkids@illinois.gov
Internet: http://www.dnr.illinois.gov/grants/Pages/default.aspx
Sponsor: Illinois Department of Natural Resources
One Natural Resources Way
Springfield, IL 62702-1271

Illinois DNR Habitat Fund Grants　2497
The Office of Resource Conservation's Division of Wildlife Resources administers four special grant programs that are funded by Illinois sportsmen through the purchase of Habitat Stamps and Migratory Waterfowl Stamps. For the Illinois Habitat Fund Grant Program, eligible projects are limited to those seeking to preserve, protect, acquire or manage habitat (all wetlands, woodlands, grasslands, and agricultural lands, natural or altered) in Illinois that have the potential to support populations of wildlife in any or all phases of their life cycles. Project applications are to be received at the DNR Headquarters office no later than 5:00 p.m. on August 1.
Requirements: Eligible recipients are limited to any appropriate not-for-profit organization or government agency that has the expertise, equipment, adequate staff/workforce and permission from the landowner (if applicable) to develop and/or manage habitat.
Restrictions: Projects that are ineligible for grants include education projects and the purchase or lease of a vehicle such as a truck. All Terrain Vehicles (ATV's) are also ineligible to receive funding.
Geographic Focus: Illinois
Date(s) Application is Due: Aug 1
Contact: Valerie Keener, Administrator; (217) 524-4126 or (217) 782-2602; fax (217) 782-9599; valerie.keener@illinois.gov or dnr.specialfunds@illinois.gov
Internet: http://www.dnr.state.il.us/grants/Special_Funds/WildGrant.htm
Sponsor: Illinois Department of Natural Resources
One Natural Resources Way
Springfield, IL 62702-1271

Illinois DNR Migratory Waterfowl Stamp Fund Grants　2498
The Office of Resource Conservation's Division of Wildlife Resources administers four special grant programs that are funded by Illinois sportsmen through the purchase of Habitat Stamps and Migratory Waterfowl Stamps. The Migratory Waterfowl Stamp Fund Grant Program is dedicated to the conservation of waterfowl that pass through Illinois during their migrations. Eligible projects are limited to development of waterfowl propagation areas within the Dominion of Canada or the United States that specifically provide waterfowl for the Mississippi Flyway, and projects to implement the North American Waterfowl Management Plan for the development of waterfowl areas within the Dominion of Canada or the United States that specifically provide waterfowl for the Mississippi Flyway. Project applications are to be received at the DNR Headquarters office no later than 5:00 p.m. on August 1.
Requirements: Eligible recipients are limited to appropriate not-for-profit organizations.
Geographic Focus: Illinois
Date(s) Application is Due: Aug 1
Contact: Valerie Keener, Administrator; (217) 524-4126 or (217) 782-2602; fax (217) 782-9599; valerie.keener@illinois.gov or dnr.specialfunds@illinois.gov
Internet: http://www.dnr.state.il.us/grants/Special_Funds/WildGrant.htm
Sponsor: Illinois Department of Natural Resources
One Natural Resources Way
Springfield, IL 62702-1271

Illinois DNR Park and Recreational Facility Construction Grants　2499
The Park and Recreational Facility Construction Act (PARC) was created by Public Act 096-0820 effective November 18, 2009 to provide grants to be disbursed by the DNR to eligible local governments for park and recreation unit construction projects. Park or recreation unit construction project means the acquisition, development, construction, reconstruction, rehabilitation, improvements, architectural planning, and installation of capital facilities consisting, but not limited to, buildings, structures, and land for park and recreation purposes and open spaces and natural areas. Bondable or brick and mortar projects for capital expenditures may include, but are not limited to: demolition in preparation for additional indoor/outdoor recreation purposes; site preparation and improvements for indoor/outdoor recreation purposes; utility work for indoor/outdoor recreation purposes; reconstruction or improvement of existing buildings or facilities for indoor/outdoor recreation purposes; expansion of buildings/facilities for indoor/outdoor recreation purposes; and new construction of buildings and structures. Land acquisition projects for public park recreation and conservation purposes include, but are not limited to acquisition of land for the following: to construct new public indoor/outdoor recreation buildings, structures and facilities; to expand existing public indoor/outdoor recreation buildings, structures and facilities; general park purposes such as regional, community and neighborhood parks and playfields; frontage on public surface waters for recreation use; and open space or conservation purposes to protect floodplains, wetlands, natural areas, wildlife habitat and unique geologic and biologic features, and additions to such areas.
Requirements: Units of local government that are authorized by Illinois law to expend public funds for the acquisition and development of land for public indoor/outdoor park, recreation or conservation purposes are eligible to apply for funding assistance.
Geographic Focus: Illinois
Date(s) Application is Due: Nov 29
Contact: Valerie Keener, Administrator; (217) 524-4126 or (217) 782-7481; fax (217) 782-9599; valerie.keener@illinois.gov or dnr.grants@illinois.gov
Internet: http://dnr.state.il.us/ocd/newPARC1.htm
Sponsor: Illinois Department of Natural Resources
One Natural Resources Way
Springfield, IL 62702-1271

Illinois DNR Schoolyard Habitat Action Grants　2500
The program is a means of funding for teachers and students who are interested in creating or enhancing schoolyard habitat areas. Projects should emphasize student/youth involvement with planning, development, and maintenance, as well as increase the educational and wildlife values of the site. Project examples include: trail development; vegetation planting; designing, establishing and maintaining a schoolyard prairie plot; butterfly garden; watering station; designing and building a bird feeder or feeding station. Guidelines are available online.
Requirements: Teachers, youth group leaders and non-formal educators in Illinois are eligible to apply.
Restrictions: Funding cannot be used for consultant fees, bird seed, fuel, equipment (shovels, rakes, trowels), labor, books, web site development, or land acquisition.
Geographic Focus: Illinois
Date(s) Application is Due: Nov 30
Amount of Grant: Up to 600 USD
Contact: Valerie Keener, Administrator; (217) 524-4126 or (217) 782-7481; fax (217) 782-9552; valerie.keener@illinois.gov or dnr.teachkids@illinois.gov
Internet: http://www.dnr.illinois.gov/grants/Pages/default.aspx
Sponsor: Illinois Department of Natural Resources
One Natural Resources Way
Springfield, IL 62702-1271

Illinois DNR State Furbearer Fund Grants　2501
The Office of Resource Conservation's Division of Wildlife Resources administers four special grant programs that are funded by Illinois sportsmen through the purchase of Habitat Stamps and Migratory Waterfowl Stamps. The State Furbearer Fund Grant Program is dedicated to the conservation of fur-bearing mammals. Eligible projects are limited to those that educate hunters and trappers of fur-bearing mammals within the State and the general public concerning the role that hunting and trapping has upon fur-bearing mammal management; the laws associated with the harvesting of fur-bearing mammals; the techniques used in the hunting and trapping of fur-bearing mammals; the conservation, management, and ecology of fur-bearing mammals; and the promotion of products made from wild fur-bearing mammals. Project applications are to be received at the DNR Headquarters office no later than 5:00 p.m. on August 1.
Requirements: Eligible recipients are limited to appropriate not-for-profit organization, governmental entities, educational institutions, or corporations.
Restrictions: Projects that are ineligible for grants include the purchase or lease of a vehicle such as a truck as well as All Terrain Vehicles (ATV's).
Geographic Focus: Illinois
Date(s) Application is Due: Aug 1
Contact: Valerie Keener, Administrator; (217) 524-4126 or (217) 782-2602; fax (217) 782-9599; valerie.keener@illinois.gov or dnr.specialfunds@illinois.gov
Internet: http://www.dnr.state.il.us/grants/Special_Funds/WildGrant.htm#pheasant
Sponsor: Illinois Department of Natural Resources
One Natural Resources Way
Springfield, IL 62702-1271

Illinois DNR State Pheasant Fund Grants　2502
The Office of Resource Conservation's Division of Wildlife Resources administers four special grant programs that are funded by Illinois sportsmen through the purchase of Habitat Stamps and Migratory Waterfowl Stamps. The State Pheasant Fund Grant Program is dedicated to the conservation of wild pheasants. Eligible projects may include land acquisition, pheasant habitat improvement on public or private land, pheasant research, or education of the public regarding pheasants and pheasant hunting. Eligible projects are limited to those with the purpose of wild pheasant conservation. Examples of past funded projects include native grass and forbs seed, herbicide, and management equipment such as controlled burn tools, seeders, sprayers, native grass drills, land purchases, pheasant research, and education of the public regarding pheasants and pheasant hunting. Project applications are to be received at the DNR Headquarters office no later than 5:00 p.m. on August 1.
Requirements: Eligible recipients are limited to appropriate not-for-profit organizations.
Restrictions: Projects that are ineligible for grants include the purchase or lease of a vehicle such as a truck as well as All Terrain Vehicles (ATV's).
Geographic Focus: Illinois
Date(s) Application is Due: Aug 1
Contact: Valerie Keener, Administrator; (217) 524-4126 or (217) 782-2602; fax (217) 782-9599; valerie.keener@illinois.gov or dnr.specialfunds@illinois.gov
Internet: http://www.dnr.state.il.us/grants/Special_Funds/WildGrant.htm
Sponsor: Illinois Department of Natural Resources
One Natural Resources Way
Springfield, IL 62702-1271

Illinois DNR Urban and Community Forestry Grants　2503
The purpose of the Urban and Community Forestry Assistance Grant is to provide financial assistance to local units of government for the development of local urban and community forestry programs. These activities must help to establish, manage, conserve and preserve the urban and community forests from inner city to associated public lands. Eligible Core Local Urban Forestry Program Projects include: tree care ordinances; tree board establishment; tree inventories; tree preservation ordinances; comprehensive urban forestry management plans; forest insect and disease mitigation plans; residual wood utilization; public education on urban forestry; training of city staff on tree care; tree planting or beatification; tree care demonstrations beyond routine maintenance; Tree and Utility Conflict Resolution; and Tree preservation or tree protection demonstration sites.
Requirements: Any local unit of government or a co-application between a local unit of government and a not-for-profit defined by the General Not-For-Profit Corporation Act of 1986 is eligible. The applicant must have an approved tree care ordinance or equivalent, or must use Application A to ask for funding to create a tree care ordinance. The ordinance must accomplish the following: establish tree authority; specify duties and responsibilities of Tree Authority; specify the number of members and their qualifications; identify the

need and importance of local urban forestry programs; identify tree planting and tree care standards; and contain the provisions for hazard and diseased trees from private property.
Restrictions: By law, the program is set up as a 50/50 cost share reimbursement, with no more than 5% of the total funds available to one unit of government.
Geographic Focus: Illinois
Contact: Valerie Keener, Administrator; (217) 524-4126 or (217) 782-7481; fax (217) 782-9599; valerie.keener@illinois.gov or dnr.grants@illinois.gov
Internet: http://www.dnr.state.il.us/orc/Urbanforestry/financialasst.html
Sponsor: Illinois Department of Natural Resources
One Natural Resources Way
Springfield, IL 62702-1271

Illinois DNR Volunteer Fire Assistance Grants 2504
The key objective of the Volunteer Fire Assistance Grant program is saving lives and protecting property from fires in unprotected or inadequately protected rural areas. Each Fiscal Year the U.S. Department of Agriculture Forest Service awards the Illinois Department of Natural Resources federal funds for the Volunteer Fire Assistance Grant program. These funds will be distributed to fire fighting agencies as a 50-50 reimbursement type grant with a maximum award of $15,000. The fire agency must spend $30,000 in order to qualify for the maximum award of $15,000. This money is a part of a national allotment for rural fire protection under the Cooperative Forestry Assistance Act of 1978, as amended by the Forest Stewardship Act of 1990. Items eligible for the VFA Grant program include: self-contained breathing apparatus (SCBA); protective clothing; training and necessary equipment; installation of Dry Hydrants to improve water supplies for fire suppression; communication equipment; new motorized vehicles, such as ATV; used fire truck or other used motorized vehicles; skid or slide in units; conversion of Federal Excess Personal Property vehicles to water tenders and engines; and implementation of Class A foam technology to improve the fire suppression effectiveness of water.
Requirements: Eligibility for the VFA Grant program: only Fire Agencies defined as Fire Department, Fire District, or Fire Protection District; total population of the community protected must be under 10,000 people; must have a current Memorandum forms section of Understanding with IDNR; and local funds must be available at the time of application.
Restrictions: Items not eligible for the VFA Grant program include: new fire trucks; construction expenses for fire stations or training facilities; emergency medical equipment; or rescue equipment.
Geographic Focus: Illinois
Amount of Grant: Up to 15,000 USD
Contact: Valerie Keener, Administrator; (217) 524-4126 or (217) 782-7481; fax (217) 782-9599; valerie.keener@illinois.gov or dnr.teachkids@illinois.gov
Tom Wilson, Forest Protection Program Manager; (618) 498-1627 or (217) 785-8772; tom.wilson@illinois.gov
Internet: http://www.dnr.state.il.us/orc/habitat_resources/forestry/vfa/Program_Info.htm
Sponsor: Illinois Department of Natural Resources
One Natural Resources Way
Springfield, IL 62702-1271

Illinois DNR Wildlife Preservation Fund Large Project Grants 2505
The Illinois Wildlife Preservation Fund Grant Program is designed to preserve, protect, perpetuate and enhance non-game wildlife and native plant resources of Illinois through preservation of a satisfactory environment and an ecological balance. Projects must focus on at least one of the following categories: management - activities related to the stewardship of land and/or water which are of direct benefit to nongame wildlife, native plants and natural communities (priority will be given to projects which are on areas held in the public trust, use volunteers and occur on biologically important areas; site inventories and surveys - activities which inventory species, taxa (birds, mammals, reptiles, amphibians, fishes, plants, invertebrates, etc.), vegetation, habitats, etc. on an area of land (site, county, region); research - activities related to the Department's current concerns regarding the status, protection, and stewardship of Illinois non-game resources; education - activities which teach Illinoisans about the natural world around them and hopefully have lasting effects (types of projects might include: interpretive trails, curricula, displays, workshops, development of ongoing outdoor education activities, instructional packets and materials, and publications). The Funding Request for a proposal must exceed $2,000. Project applications are to be received at the DNR Headquarters office no later than 5:00 p.m. on April 1.
Requirements: Eligible recipients are limited to any individual, group, organization or entity seeking to preserve, protect, perpetuate or enhance non-game wildlife and/or native plant resources in Illinois through research, management or education.
Geographic Focus: Illinois
Date(s) Application is Due: Apr 1
Amount of Grant: 2,000 - 300,000 USD
Contact: Valerie Keener, Administrator; (217) 524-4126 or (217) 782-2602; fax (217) 782-9599; valerie.keener@illinois.gov or dnr.specialfunds@illinois.gov
Internet: http://www.dnr.state.il.us/grants/Special_Funds/WildGrant.htm
Sponsor: Illinois Department of Natural Resources
One Natural Resources Way
Springfield, IL 62702-1271

Illinois DNR Wildlife Preservation Fund Small Project Grants 2506
The Illinois Wildlife Preservation Fund Grant Program is designed to preserve, protect, perpetuate and enhance non-game wildlife and native plant resources of Illinois through preservation of a satisfactory environment and an ecological balance. Projects proposed for grant funding must focus on management, site inventories or education and cannot exceed $2,000.00. Management projects are those activities related to stewardship of land and/or water which are of direct benefit to non-game wildlife, native plants and natural communities. Examples of this type of project include exotic species removal, brush cutting, nest structures, and vegetation management. Site inventory projects are those activities which inventory species, taxa (birds, mammals, reptiles, amphibians, fishes, plants, invertebrates, etc.), vegetation, habitats, etc. on an area of land. Education projects are those activities that teach Illinoisans about the natural world around them and hopefully have lasting effects. Examples of this type of project include interpretive trails, trail signs, curricula, displays, workshops, development of ongoing outdoor education activities, instructional packets and materials. Project applications are to be received at the DNR Headquarters office no later than 5:00 p.m. on April 1.
Requirements: Eligible recipients are limited to any individual, group, organization or entity seeking to preserve, protect, perpetuate or enhance non-game wildlife and/or native plant resources in Illinois through research, management or education.
Geographic Focus: Illinois
Date(s) Application is Due: Apr 1
Amount of Grant: Up to 2,000 USD
Contact: Valerie Keener, Administrator; (217) 524-4126 or (217) 782-2602; fax (217) 782-9599; valerie.keener@illinois.gov or dnr.specialfunds@illinois.gov
Internet: http://www.dnr.state.il.us/grants/Special_Funds/WildGrant.htm
Sponsor: Illinois Department of Natural Resources
One Natural Resources Way
Springfield, IL 62702-1271

Illinois DNR Wildlife Preservation Maintenance of Rehabilitation Facilities 2507
The program title is Illinois Wildlife Preservation Fund – Maintenance of Wildlife Rehabilitation Facilities That Take Care of Threatened or Endangered Species. This portion of the Special Wildlife Funds Grant Program is designed to keep wildlife rehabilitation facilities that take care of threatened or endangered species in a state of good repair necessary to provide safe and sanitary conditions for threatened or endangered wildlife species being cared for in the facility and for facility staff. Individual proposals are eligible for up to $2,000 from the Wildlife Preservation Fund. Eligible projects are limited to those designed to keep wildlife rehabilitation facilities that take care of threatened or endangered species in a state of good repair necessary to provide safe and sanitary conditions for threatened or endangered wildlife species being cared for in the facility and for facility staff. Types of projects which would fall into this category include structural repair and maintenance of existing buildings, pens, cages and appurtenant facilities used to take care of threatened or endangered wildlife species; repair and maintenance of equipment used in the diagnosis and treatment of injury to or illness of threatened or endangered wildlife species. Ineligible uses of grant funds include, but may not be limited to; salaries or benefits paid to staff; costs of veterinary services for the threatened or endangered wildlife species; construction of new facilities; expansion of existing facilities, and fund-raising or promotional activities. Project applications are to be received at the DNR Headquarters office no later than 5:00 p.m. on April 1.
Requirements: Eligible recipients are limited to those persons who possess a current wildlife rehabilitation license/permit issued by the Department and who have provided care for threatened or endangered wildlife species during the 3-year period preceding the date of their application for grant funds. Those applicants who intend to use any portion of grant funds received from the Department to take care of migratory birds must also possess a current wildlife rehabilitation license/permit issued by the U.S. Fish and Wildlife Service allowing such activity.
Geographic Focus: Illinois
Date(s) Application is Due: Apr 1
Amount of Grant: Up to 2,000 USD
Contact: Valerie Keener, Administrator; (217) 524-4126 or (217) 782-2602; fax (217) 782-9599; valerie.keener@illinois.gov or dnr.specialfunds@illinois.gov
Internet: http://www.dnr.state.il.us/grants/Special_Funds/WildGrant.htm
Sponsor: Illinois Department of Natural Resources
One Natural Resources Way
Springfield, IL 62702-1271

Illinois DNR Youth Recreation Corps Grants 2508
The Illinois Youth Recreation Corps was established for making grants to local sponsors to provide wages to youth operating and instructing in recreational and conservation programs for the benefit of other youth. Such programs shall provide recreational opportunities for children of all age levels and shall include, but not be limited to, the coordination and teaching of physical activities, arts and handicrafts, and learning activities.
Requirements: Potential applicants include local sponsors who can provide necessary facilities, materials and management for summer recreational and conservation activities for youth within the community and who desire a grant for hiring eligible youth as supervisors, instructors, instructional aides or management personnel. Local sponsors must be units of local government or not?for?profit entities. Enrollment (hiring) is limited to citizens of the State of Illinois who, at the time of hiring, are 16, 17, 18 or 19 years of age, and who have skills that can be used in the summer recreation or conservation program.
Restrictions: Youth currently employed in any manner by the local sponsor are not eligible for inclusion in the program.
Geographic Focus: Illinois
Date(s) Application is Due: Jun 30
Contact: Valerie Keener, Administrator; (217) 524-4126 or (217) 782-7481; fax (217) 782-9599; valerie.keener@illinois.gov or dnr.grants@illinois.gov
Internet: http://www.dnr.illinois.gov/grants/Pages/default.aspx
Sponsor: Illinois Department of Natural Resources
One Natural Resources Way
Springfield, IL 62702-1271

Illinois Humanities Council Community General Support Grants 2509
The Illinois Humanities Council (IHC) funds public humanities programs for Illinois audiences that are shaped by and significantly involve humanities scholars and/or other community experts. The IHC's priority is to support programs developed by, for, or aimed at reaching new or historically neglected audiences. Applications are invited from organizations that serve these communities and strongly encourage other applicants to extend their proposed programs to include such audiences. General Support Grants have a maximum of $5,000 and can support programming and activities in general, as opposed to targeting funds only for a specific project.
Requirements: All nonprofit organizations serving Illinois audiences are eligible. Organizations need to demonstrate that they are primarily a humanities organization; engagement with the humanities must be evident in their mission and in their programs and activities. All project grant applications must: be rooted in one or more of the humanities disciplines; integrally feature humanities experts in all phases or the project; be public; be sponsored by a nonprofit organization; and comply with federal debarment and nondiscrimination statutes. Applications for any of the grant categories are welcome at each deadline. If you plan to apply for a grant, contact a program officer at least one month ahead of the application deadline to discuss your project. Additionally, the IHC conducts grant and resource workshops several times a year throughout the state. Workshops are held at the offices in Chicago on the third Fridays of May and November and in the fall and spring in central, eastern, western and southern Illinois communities. Notifications will be sent approximately 8 weeks after the deadline.
Restrictions: Organizations that have run humanities projects but whose primary purpose involves something other than the public humanities are not eligible for general support grants. General Support grants are not intended for new start-up organizations. The council does not fund: advocacy or social action; projects for fund raising purposes; construction or restoration costs; purchase of permanent equipment; library or museum acquisitions; individuals, research, or other endeavors intended primarily for the scholarly community; curriculum development or revisions; academic courses for credit; performing arts as ends in themselves; projects directed primarily to children or students in formal school settings; more than 50 percent of total project costs; indirect costs of sponsoring organizations; food and beverage costs for audiences or alcoholic beverages; or expenses incurred or paid out before an IHC grant award is made.
Geographic Focus: Illinois
Date(s) Application is Due: Jan 15; Apr 15; Jul 15; Oct 15
Amount of Grant: Up to 5,000 USD
Contact: Ryan M. Lewis, Senior Program Officer; rml@prairie.org or ihc@prairie.org
Internet: http://www.prairie.org/programs/community-grants-program
Sponsor: Illinois Humanities Council
17 North State Street, Suite 1400
Chicago, IL 60602-3298

Illinois Humanities Council Community Project Grants 2510
The Illinois Humanities Council (IHC) funds public humanities programs for Illinois audiences that are shaped by and significantly involve humanities scholars and/or other community experts. The IHC's priority is to support programs developed by, for, or aimed at reaching new or historically neglected audiences. Applications are invited from organizations that serve these communities and strongly encourage other applicants to extend their proposed programs to include such audiences. Project Grants have a maximum of $5,000 and are designed for the development and implementation of a public humanities project.
Requirements: All nonprofit organizations serving Illinois audiences are eligible. All project grant applications must: be rooted in one or more of the humanities disciplines; integrally feature humanities experts in all phases or the project; be public; be sponsored by a nonprofit organization; and comply with federal debarment and nondiscrimination statutes. Applications for any of the grant categories are welcome at each deadline. If you plan to apply for a grant, contact a program officer at least one month ahead of the application deadline to discuss your project. Additionally, the IHC conducts grant and resource workshops several times a year throughout the state. Workshops are held at the offices in Chicago on the third Fridays of May and November and in the fall and spring in central, eastern, western and southern Illinois communities. Notifications will be sent approximately 8 weeks after the deadline.
Restrictions: The council does not fund: advocacy or social action; projects for fund raising purposes; construction or restoration costs; purchase of permanent equipment; library or museum acquisitions; individuals, research, or other endeavors intended primarily for the scholarly community; curriculum development or revisions; academic courses for credit; performing arts as ends in themselves; projects directed primarily to children or students in formal school settings; more than 50 percent of total project costs; indirect costs of sponsoring organizations; food and beverage costs for audiences or alcoholic beverages; or expenses incurred or paid out before an IHC grant award is made.
Geographic Focus: Illinois
Date(s) Application is Due: Jan 15; Apr 15; Jul 15; Oct 15
Amount of Grant: Up to 5,000 USD
Contact: Ryan M. Lewis; (312) 422-5580; fax (312) 422-5588; rml@prairie.org
Internet: http://www.prairie.org/programs/community-grants-program
Sponsor: Illinois Humanities Council
17 North State Street, Suite 1400
Chicago, IL 60602-3298

Illinois Tool Works Foundation Grants 2511
The corporate foundation awards grants in areas of company operations, with emphasis on Chicago, Ilinoise. Grants support organizations that focus on: education, the arts, health and human services, social welfare, housing, environmental and youth issues. The Foundation contributes financial support to not-for-profit organizations through two major giving programs: a direct-giving program and a three-for-one matching gift program for employees.
Requirements: Not-for-profit organizations are eligible to apply.
Geographic Focus: All States
Amount of Grant: 5,000 - 1,000,000 USD
Contact: Mary Ann Mallahan; (847) 724-7500; fax (847) 657-4261; mmallahan@itw.com
Internet: http://www.itwinc.com/itw/corporate_citizenship/itw_foundation
Sponsor: Illinois Tool Works Foundation
3600 West Lake Avenue
Glenview, IL 60026

IMLS 21st Century Museum Professionals Grants 2512
The 21st Century Museum Professionals program supports a range of activities, including professional training in all areas of museum operations and leadership development. This program provides the museum community with support for a variety of training and personnel development activities for museum staff members across all types of museums, as well as the collection and dissemination of information to museum professionals and the public. Project design could include direct dissemination of information through workshops, seminars, and courses, or indirect communication through publications and Web sites. Projects should benefit multiple institutions or diverse constituencies.
Requirements: Museums that fulfill the Eligibility Criteria for Museums may apply. Private not-for-profit museum services organizations or associations that engage in activities designed to advance the well-being of museums and the museum profession also may apply. In addition, institutions of higher education, including public and not-for-profit universities, are eligible. Please see Program Guidelines for specific eligibility criteria.
Geographic Focus: All States
Date(s) Application is Due: Mar 15
Amount of Grant: 15,000 - 500,000 USD
Contact: Twinet G. Kimbrough; (202) 653-4703; tkimbrough@imls.gov
Internet: http://www.imls.gov/applicants/grants/21centuryMuseums.shtm
Sponsor: Institute of Museum and Library Services
1800 M Street NW, 9th Floor
Washington, DC 20036-5802

IMLS American Heritage Preservation Grants 2513
Bank of America is partnering with the Institute to provide grants to small museums, libraries, and archives. The grants will raise awareness and fund preservation of treasures held in small museums, libraries and archives. Grants will help to preserve specific items, including works of art, artifacts and historical documents that are in need of conservation. Applicants will build on completed conservation assessments of their collections to ensure that the grants are used in accordance with best practices in the field, and underscore the importance of assessment planning. Grant programs that provide assistance with conservation planning and assessment include the Institute's Conservation Assessment Program and the National Endowment for the Humanities' Preservation Assistance Grants.
Requirements: All types of museums are eligible to apply. Eligible museums include aquariums, arboretums and botanical gardens, art museums, youth museums, general museums, historic houses and sites, history museums, nature centers, natural history and anthropology museums, planetariums, science and technology centers, specialized museums and zoological parks. An eligible library applicant must be: either a unit of state or local government or private nonprofit organization that has tax-exempt status under the Internal Revenue Code; located in one of the fifty states of the United States, the District of Columbia, the Commonwealth of Puerto Rico, Guam, American Samoa, the Virgin Islands, the Commonwealth of the Northern Mariana Islands, the Republic of the Marshall Islands, the Federated States of Micronesia, or the Republic of Palau; and one of the six types of organizations listed at the web site.
Geographic Focus: All States
Date(s) Application is Due: Sep 15
Amount of Grant: 1 - 3,000 USD
Contact: Kevin Cherry, Senior Program Officer; (202) 653-4662; kcherry@imls.gov
Internet: http://www.imls.gov/collections/grants/boa.htm
Sponsor: Institute of Museum and Library Services
1800 M Street NW, 9th Floor
Washington, DC 20036-5802

IMLS Grants to State Library Administrative Agencies 2514
Through the program, the Institute of Museum and Library Services provides funds to State Library Administrative Agencies (SLAAs) using a population-based formula. State libraries may use the appropriation to support statewide initiatives and services. They also may distribute the funds through subgrant competitions or cooperative agreements to public, academic, research, school, and special libraries in their state.
Requirements: State library administrative agencies located in one of the 50 states of the United States, the District of Columbia, the Commonwealth of Puerto Rico, Guam, American Samoa, the U.S. Virgin Islands, the Commonwealth of the Northern Mariana Islands, the Republic of the Marshall Islands, the Federated States of Micronesia, and the Republic of Palau are eligible to submit five-year plans.
Geographic Focus: All States
Date(s) Application is Due: Apr 1
Amount of Grant: 1 - 2,000,000 USD
Contact: Laurie C. Brooks; (202) 653-4650; stateprograms@imls.gov
Internet: http://www.imls.gov/programs/programs.shtm
Sponsor: Institute of Museum and Library Services
1800 M Street NW, 9th Floor
Washington, DC 20036-5802

IMLS National Leadership Grants (NLG) 2515

National Leadership Grants enable libraries and museums to help people gain the knowledge, skills, attitudes, behaviors, and resources that enhance their engagement in community, work, family, and society. Projects should enable libraries and museums to address current problems in creative ways, develop and test innovative solutions, and expand the boundaries within which cultural heritage institutions operate. The results of these projects will help equip tomorrow's libraries and museums to better meet the needs of a Nation of Learners. Successful proposals will show evidence that they will have national impact and generate results - new tools, research, models, services, practices, or alliances - that can be widely adapted or replicated to extend the benefit of federal support. Proposals will reflect an understanding of current issues and needs, showing the potential for far-reaching impact throughout the museum and/or library community. Projects will provide creative solutions to issues of national importance and provide leadership for other organizations.

Requirements: All types of libraries, except federal and for-profit libraries, may apply. Eligible libraries include public, school, academic, special, private (not-for-profit), archives, library agencies, library consortia, and library associations. Research libraries and archives that give the public access to services and materials suitable for scholarly research not otherwise available and that are not part of a university or college also are eligible. Digital libraries that make library materials publicly available and provide services including selection, organization, description, reference, and preservation under the supervision of at least one permanent professional staff librarian are eligible to apply. Institutions of higher education, including public and not-for-profit universities and colleges, also are eligible. An academic unit, such as a graduate school of library and information science, may apply as part of an institution of higher education. Library applicants may apply individually or as partners. Additionally, all types of museums, large and small, are eligible for funding. Eligible museums include aquariums, arboreta and botanical gardens, art museums, youth museums, general museums, historic houses and sites, history museums, nature centers, natural history and anthropology museums, planetariums, science and technology centers, specialized museums, and zoological parks. Private nonprofit museum services organizations or associations that engage in activities designed to advance the well-being of museums and the museum profession also may apply. In addition, institutions of higher education, including public and nonprofit universities, are eligible.
Geographic Focus: All States
Date(s) Application is Due: Feb 1
Amount of Grant: 50,000 - 1,000,000 USD
Contact: Rachel Frick, Program Officer, Libraries; (202) 653-4667; rfrick@imls.gov
Internet: http://www.imls.gov/applicants/grants/nationalLeadership.shtm
Sponsor: Institute of Museum and Library Services
1800 M Street NW, 9th Floor
Washington, DC 20036-5802

IMLS National Medal for Museum and Library Service 2516

The award is made each year to a museum that demonstrate an institutional commitment to public service with innovative programs that address social, economic, or environmental issues. Winning organizations will receive a monetary award and will be honored at a special ceremony in Washington, DC. Nominations should describe the museum's goal in serving its community, the target population served, the community partnerships and efforts undertaken to achieve the goal, the outcome of these efforts during the last two to three years, and projections for future efforts in this area. Contact the office or visit the Web site for nomination forms.
Requirements: Any individual may submit a nomination, and nominations of museums of all sizes are encouraged. Public or private nonprofit institutions are eligible to receive this award. Nominated institutions must be open to the general public for at least 120 days per year and be located in the United States, the Commonwealth of Puerto Rico, the Virgin Islands, Guam, American Samoa, the Commonwealth of Northern Mariana Islands, or the Freely Associated States in the Pacific.
Restrictions: Federally operated institutions are not eligible for this award.
Geographic Focus: All States
Date(s) Application is Due: Feb 16
Amount of Grant: 10,000 USD
Contact: Michele Farrell, Libraries; (202) 653-4656; mfarrell@imls.gov
Internet: http://www.imls.gov/about/medals.shtm
Sponsor: Institute of Museum and Library Services
1800 M Street NW, 9th Floor
Washington, DC 20036-5802

IMLS Native American Library Services Basic Grants 2517

The Native American Library Services Basic Grant is noncompetitive and distributed in equal amounts among eligible applicants. Basic Grants are available to support existing library operations and to maintain core library services. The Education/Assessment Option is supplemental to the Basic Grant. It also is noncompetitive and must be requested. The purpose of the Education/Assessment Option is to provide funding for library staff to attend continuing education courses and training workshops on- or off-site, for library staff to attend or give presentations at conferences related to library services, and to hire a consultant for an on-site professional library assessment.
Requirements: Indian tribes, Alaska Native villages, regional corporations, and village corporations are eligible to apply.
Restrictions: Entities such as libraries, schools, tribal colleges, or departments of education are not eligible applicants, although they may be involved in the administration of this program and their staff may serve as project directors, in partnership with an eligible applicant.
Geographic Focus: All States
Date(s) Application is Due: Mar 1
Amount of Grant: 1 - 5,000 USD
Contact: Alison Freese, Senior Program Officer; (202) 653-4665; afreese@imls.gov
Internet: http://www.imls.gov/applicants/grants/nativeAmerican.shtm
Sponsor: Institute of Museum and Library Services
1800 M Street NW, 9th Floor
Washington, DC 20036-5802

IMLS Native American Library Services Enhancement Grants 2518

Enhancement Grants support projects to enhance existing library services or implement new library services, particularly as they relate to the goals of the Library Services and Technology Act (LSTA) listed here: to expand services for learning and access to information and educational resources in a variety of formats, in all types of libraries, for individuals of all ages; to develop library services that provide all users with access to information through local, state, regional, national, and international electronic networks; to provide electronic and other linkages between and among all types of libraries; to develop public and private partnerships with other agencies and community-based organizations; to target library services to help increase access and ability to use information resources for individuals of diverse geographic, cultural, and socioeconomic backgrounds, individuals with disabilities, and individuals with limited functional literacy or information skills; and to target library and information services to help increase access and ability to use information resources for persons having difficulty using a library and for under-served urban and rural communities, including children from birth to age 17 from families with incomes below the poverty line (as defined by the Office of Management and Budget).
Requirements: Indian tribes, Alaska Native villages, regional corporations, and village corporations are eligible to apply.
Restrictions: Entities such as libraries, schools, tribal colleges, or departments of education are not eligible applicants, although they may be involved in the administration of this program and their staff may serve as project directors, in partnership with an eligible applicant.
Geographic Focus: All States
Date(s) Application is Due: May 3
Amount of Grant: 1 - 150,000 USD
Contact: Alison Freese, Senior Program Officer; (202) 653-4665; afreese@imls.gov
Internet: http://www.imls.gov/applicants/grants/nativeEnhance.shtm
Sponsor: Institute of Museum and Library Services
1800 M Street NW, 9th Floor
Washington, DC 20036-5802

IMLS Native Hawaiian Library Services Grants 2519

The Native Hawaiian Library Services program provides new opportunities for improved library services for an important part of the nation's community of library users. Funds may be used to: expand services for learning and access to information and educational resources in a variety of formats, in all types of libraries, for people of all ages; develop library services that provide all users with access to information through local, state, regional, national, and international electronic networks; provide electronic and other links between and among all types of libraries; develop public and private partnerships with other agencies and community-based organizations; target library services to help increase access and ability to use information resources for persons of diverse geographic, cultural, and socioeconomic backgrounds; persons with disabilities; and persons with limited functional literacy or information skills; and target library and information services to help increase access and ability to use information resources for persons who have difficulty using a library and for underserved urban and rural communities, including children, from birth to age 17, from families with incomes below the poverty line (as defined by the Office of Management and Budget).
Requirements: Grants are available to private, nonprofit organizations that primarily serve and represent Native Hawaiians.
Geographic Focus: Hawaii
Date(s) Application is Due: May 17
Contact: Alison Freese, Senior Program Specialist; (202) 653-4665; afreese@imls.gov
Internet: http://www.imls.gov/applicants/grants/nativeHawaiian.shtm
Sponsor: Institute of Museum and Library Services
1800 M Street NW, 9th Floor
Washington, DC 20036-5802

IMLS Partnership for a Nation of Learners Community Collaboration Grants 2520

The purpose of these grants is to encourage effective collaborations among museums, libraries, and public broadcasting licensees in service of educational and community goals. Each project should show how such collaboration and shared resources enable partners to meet clearly defined needs for one or more audience segments within their local communities. The term of the award will not exceed two years. Guidelines and application form are available online.
Requirements: The lead agency must be an eligible library, museum, or public broadcasting licensee.
Restrictions: Grant funds may not be used for construction, acquisition of collections, contributions to endowments, social activities, ceremonies, entertainment, or pre-grant costs.
Geographic Focus: All States
Date(s) Application is Due: Mar 1
Amount of Grant: 25,000 - 250,000 USD
Contact: Susan Malbin; (202) 653-4768; fax (202) 606-8591; smalbin@imls.gov
Internet: http://www.imls.gov/applicants/grants/communityCollaboration.shtm
Sponsor: Institute of Museum and Library Services
1800 M Street NW, 9th Floor
Washington, DC 20036-5802

IMLS Save America's Treasures Grants 2521

Administered by the National Park Service in collaboration with the President's Committee on the Arts and the Humanities, Save America's Treasures involves other federal agency partners, including the National Endowment for the Arts, the National Endowment for the Humanities, and the Institute of Museum and Library Services. The National Trust for Historic Preservation has been the program's principal private partner since its inception. Save America's Treasures makes critical investments in the preservation of our nation's most significant and endangered cultural treasures, which illustrate, interpret, and embody the great events, ideas, and individuals that contribute to America's history and culture. This legacy includes the built environment as well as documents, records, artifacts, and artistic works. Collectively, Save America's Treasures projects tell our nation's story and ensure that our legacy is passed on to future generations.
Requirements: The following are eligible: federal agencies funded by the Department of the Interior and Related Agencies Appropriations Act (other federal agencies collaborating with a nonprofit partner to preserve the historic properties or collections owned by the federal agency may submit applications through the nonprofit partner); nonprofit, tax-exempt 501(c), U.S. organizations; units of state or local government; federally recognized Indian tribes; and historic properties and collections associated with active religious organizations.
Restrictions: Grants do not fund acquisition (i.e., purchase in fee simple or interest) of intellectual and cultural artifacts, historic sites, buildings, structures or objects; survey or inventory of historic properties or cataloging of collections; long-term maintenance or curation; interpretive or training programs; reconstruction of historic properties (i.e., recreating all or a significant portion of a structure that no longer exists); moving buildings or work associated with a building that has been moved; historic structure reports and condition assessments, unless they are one component of a larger project to implement the results of these studies; cash reserves, endowments, or revolving funds; costs of fund raising campaigns; or historic properties and collections associated with an active religious organization (i.e., restoration of an historic church that is still actively used as a church).
Geographic Focus: All States
Date(s) Application is Due: May 21
Contact: Christine Henry; (202) 653-4674; fax (202) 606-8591; chenry@imls.gov
Internet: http://www.imls.gov/about/treasures.shtm
Sponsor: Institute of Museum and Library Services
1800 M Street NW, 9th Floor
Washington, DC 20036-5802

Impact 100 Grants 2522

Impact 100 empowers women to dramatically improve lives by collectively funding significant grants that make a lasting impact in the Greater Cincinnati and Northern Kentucky community. During the first few two months of the year, non-profit organizations in the ten-county Greater Cincinnati/Northern Kentucky area region are encouraged to submit grant applications to Impact 100. The Grant Review Committees of Impact 100 review the applications and conduct site visits to narrow their choices. At the end of the review process, a finalist is chosen by each of the five committees (Education, Health & Wellness, Environment/Preservation & Recreation, Culture and Family). These five finalists present their grant requests at the Annual Awards Celebration. After the finalist presentations, each member casts a vote (or has sent an absentee vote in advance). The votes are immediately tabulated, and the Impact 100 grants are awarded at the end of the evening.
Requirements: Applications that are programmatic, endowment, capital, start-up, or research-oriented are excepted. Applications from non-profit organizations headquartered in any of the following counties are available to apply: Ohio - Adams, Brown, Butler, Clermont, Hamilton, Warren; Kentucky - Boone, Campbell, Kenton; Indiana - Dearborn. Every applying agency must have 501(c)3 status with the IRS.
Restrictions: The following types of applications are not available for funding: operating; partisan; individual churches; indigent care subsidy; travel; loans; or for individuals.
Geographic Focus: Indiana, Kentucky, Ohio
Date(s) Application is Due: Mar 1
Amount of Grant: 100,000 USD
Contact: Luann Scherer; (513) 624-9509; Grants@Impact100.org
Internet: http://impact100.org/Grant/Default.aspx
Sponsor: Impact 100
PMB314 2692 Madison Road NI
Cincinnati, OH 45208-1320

Inasmuch Foundation Grants 2523

The foundation was established for charitable, scientific, and educational projects primarily in Oklahoma; however, select projects in Colorado Springs, CO, also are supported. The foundation consistently provides funding and support to educational, health and human service, cultural, artistic, historical, and environmental concerns. This funding is not available to individuals, but is available to formal organizations seeking capital and support for existing programs that meet the emerging needs of the community. In order to initiate a proposal, submit a one-page letter of inquiry by the listed application deadlines. Application information is available online.
Restrictions: The foundation generally does not fund endowments or scholarships.
Geographic Focus: Colorado, Oklahoma
Date(s) Application is Due: Feb 15; Aug 15
Contact: Program Contact; (405) 604-5292
Internet: http://www.inasmuchfoundation.org/application.html
Sponsor: Inasmuch Foundation
210 Park Avenue, Suite 3150
Oklahoma City, OK 73102

Independence Blue Cross Charitable Medical Care Grants 2524

The Independence Blue Cross (IBC) Charitable Medical Care Grant Program awards financial and programmatic grant support to nonprofit, privately funded health clinics that provide free or nominal-fee care to the uninsured and medically underserved communities in Bucks, Chester, Delaware, Montgomery, and Philadelphia counties. See website for grant application.
Requirements: To be eligible for a grant through this program, an applicant must meet the following criteria: the mission of the requesting organization aligns with IBC's Social Mission and its funding priorities; the requesting clinic is a privately funded entity. (Note: A clinic may receive federal funding as part of its revenues.); clinic grantee provides direct medical care for free or for a nominal fee to uninsured and/or underinsured residents of southeastern Pennsylvania; all grantees must be located in Bucks, Chester, Delaware, Montgomery, or Philadelphia counties; organizations must be classified as tax-exempt nonprofit under Section 501(c)3 of the IRS code.
Restrictions: Funding is unavailable to: individuals; private foundations; fund-raising events; conferences or seminars; political causes, candidates, organizations, or campaigns; sports teams; endowments; social organizations; religious groups for religious purposes; organizations that do not meet IBC's Social Mission.
Geographic Focus: Pennsylvania
Amount of Grant: 10,000 - 100,000 USD
Contact: Courtney Smith; (215) 241-4862; fax (215) 241-3543; courtney.smith@ibx.com
Internet: http://www.ibx.com/social_mission/medical_grants/index.html
Sponsor: Independence Blue Cross
1901 Market Street, 28th Floor
Philadelphia, PA 19103-1480

Independence Community Foundation Community Quality of Life Grant 2525

The Foundation makes grants to organizations that engage in community-based efforts that support important institutions or causes. Generally, the grants support: disease awareness and prevention; food pantries; neighborhood greening and graffiti removal; and counseling support for vulnerable populations. Interested applicants should submit an initial letter of inquiry. Application information is available online.
Requirements: Program or project grants are made on a competitive basis to nonprofit organizations located within New York City, Nassau, Suffolk and Westchester counties in New York, and Essex, Bergen, Union, Hudson, Middlesex, Ocean, and Monmouth counties in New Jersey.
Restrictions: The Foundation does not fund: individuals; political contributions; funding for religious purposes; purchase tickets for dinners, golf outings, or similar fundraising events.
Geographic Focus: New Jersey, New York
Date(s) Application is Due: Mar 30; Sep 30
Contact: Program Contact; (718) 722-2300; fax (718) 722-5757; inquiries@icfny.org
Internet: http://www.icfny.org/comm_quality.html
Sponsor: Independence Community Foundation
182 Atlantic Avenue
Brooklyn, NY 11201

Independence Community Foundation Education, Culture & Arts Grant 2526

The Foundation recognizes that cultural and educational institutions create positive change in communities. The Foundation provides program and project support to institutions that seek to bolster economic and social development, and act as stabilizing forces in their communities. Interested applicants should submit a letter of inquiry. Application information is available online.
Requirements: Program or project grants are made on a competitive basis to nonprofit organizations located within New York City, Nassau, Suffolk and Westchester counties in New York, and Essex, Bergen, Union, Hudson, Middlesex, Ocean, and Monmouth counties in New Jersey.
Restrictions: Funding is not available to support individual artists.
Geographic Focus: New Jersey, New York
Date(s) Application is Due: Mar 30; Sep 30
Contact: Program Contact; (718) 722-2300; fax (718) 722-5757; inquiries@icfny.org
Internet: http://www.icfny.org/education_arts.html
Sponsor: Independence Community Foundation
182 Atlantic Avenue
Brooklyn, NY 11201

Independence Community Foundation Neighborhood Renewal Grants 2527

The Foundation makes grants on a competitive basis to nonprofit organizations for programs and projects that fall within the grant programs and are located within the Foundation's geographic giving area. Grant making to neighborhood nonprofit community development and human service organizations forms the core of the Neighborhood Renewal program. Eligible projects and programs include: pre-development and planning grants to convert blighted and vacant properties into affordable housing, commercial uses, open spaces and/or community facilities; workforce development and entrepreneurial training/technical assistance programs; community-based enterprise projects or programs; support for high-quality early childhood development programs and community-based social and human services. Interested organizations should submit an initial letter of inquiry. Application information is available online.
Requirements: Program or project grants are made on a competitive basis to nonprofit organizations located within New York City, Nassau, Suffolk and Westchester counties in New York, and Essex, Bergen, Union, Hudson, Middlesex, Ocean, and Monmouth counties in New Jersey.
Restrictions: Funding is not available for individuals, political contributions, or provide funding for religious purposes. The Foundation does not purchase tickets for dinners, golf outings, or similar fundraising events.

Geographic Focus: New Jersey, New York
Date(s) Application is Due: Mar 30; Sep 30
Contact: Program Contact; (718) 722-2300; fax (718) 722-5757; inquiries@icfny.org
Internet: http://www.icfny.org/grant_eligibility.html
Sponsor: Independence Community Foundation
182 Atlantic Avenue
Brooklyn, NY 11201

Indiana 21st Century Research and Technology Fund Awards 2528

The Indiana 21st Century Research and Technology Fund of the Indiana Economic Development Corporation (IEDC) is open to proposals from all public and private entities for technology-based commercialization activities encompassing science/technology creation, innovation, and transfer intended to have commercial impacts. The fund intends to increase the numbers, and rates of development, of new and expanding technology-based companies by funding promising opportunities that, in some cases, the financial markets might find too risky. The Fund makes awards in two broad categories: Science and Technology Commercialization and Centers of Excellence. In addition, the Fund provides cost-share on behalf of Federal proposals submitted by Indiana-based entities. Generally awards are made in multiples of $50,000 up to $2,000,000. Support for awards in excess of $2,000,000 will be rare.
Requirements: The IEDC defines a technology-based company as one that is involved in transferring advanced technology into products, developing technologies with the near-term intention of creating products, or using new or advanced technologies in its design, development, and/or manufacturing of products. The Fund emphasizes the creation of academic-sector - commercial-sector partnerships. In making awards, the Fund expects significant leverage from the partners involved in the projects. Important: before applying, contact Fund staff (email preferred) to discuss your interest in submitting a proposal and to discuss your technology and commercialization goals. While not a review criterion, the fund encourages the inclusion of interns from any academic institution, or participating commercial sector partner, in order to increase project-related involvement of students at all levels.
Restrictions: Only direct costs will be supported. Institutions will not be provided indirect (overhead) cost support. Entities with previous Fund awards that are not current with regard to financial or technical reporting requirements will be disqualified from making new submissions to the Fund. Resubmissions of previously declined proposals will be considered only if substantive changes have been made to the proposal. Fund staff will determine whether to review resubmissions.
Geographic Focus: Indiana
Amount of Grant: 500,000 - 2,000,000 USD
Contact: Carla Phelps, Financial Manager; (317) 233- 4336; cphelps@21fund.org
Internet: http://www.21fund.org/
Sponsor: Indiana Economic Development Corporation
1 North Capitol Avenue, Suite 900
Indianapolis, IN 46204

Indiana AIDS Fund Grants 2529

Two grant programs are available to Indiana organizations that provide HIV/AIDS advocacy, prevention and direct care services. The Direct Emergency Financial Assistance Fund gives grants to agencies and organizations specifically to help HIV/AIDS patients access emergency financial help for housing, transportation, food, and/or medical care. The Indiana AIDS Fund gives prevention grants in November each year to agencies and organizations that provide persons living with HIV/AIDS direct care services, health education and risk-reduction programs and counseling, testing, and referral programs. Proposal information is available online.
Requirements: Any Indiana-based non-profit 501(c)3 group, organization or agency that provides HIV/AIDS-related programs or services to local constituencies is eligible to apply for grants from the Indiana AIDS Fund. The applicant must function without discrimination or segregation because of race, gender, age, religion, national origin, sexual orientation, disability, military or marital status, in hiring, termination, assignment and promotion of staff, selection of board members or provision of service.
Restrictions: The fund will not make the following types of grants: to individuals; for sectarian religious purposes; to purchase advertising or tickets to events; to support research; for the purpose of deficit reduction; to produce currently available educational materials; to fund endowments; for short- or long-term loans; for multiple-year program funding; for mass media campaigns; for capacity building; or for services not directly related to primary or secondary prevention.
Geographic Focus: Indiana
Contact: Grants Administrator; (317) 630-1805; severett@thfgi.org
Internet: http://www.indianaaidsfund.org/index.cfm?navigationid=1844
Sponsor: Indiana AIDS Fund
429 East Vermont Street, Suite 300
Indianapolis, IN 46202

Indiana Arts Commission American Masterpieces Grants 2530

A major initiative of the National Endowment for the Arts, this program was developed to introduce Americans to the best of their cultural and artistic legacy, through touring, local presentations, and arts education programs across all art forms that will reach all the American people. These activities need to convey the significance of American art and the activity needs to be historically and culturally significant. American Masterpiece applicants must match every dollar provided by the Indiana Arts Commission with one dollar of the organization's own funds. At least 50 percent of the match must be cash. Applicants may request up to 50 percent of the total cost of the project. Letters of Intent must be received by March 3, with final proposals due by 4:30 p.m. on April 1.
Requirements: All applicants for this program must talk with Bobbie Garver on staff to confirm the organization's project meets the criteria for this category. A completed Notice of Intent to Apply form (available at the website) must then be received by the IAC office. All applicant organizations must meet the following eligibility requirements in order to apply: 1) Must be a private tax-exempt nonprofit organization or a public entity; 2) Nonprofit organizations must be incorporated in the state of Indiana at the time of application and have received recognition of tax-exempt status from the Internal Revenue Service; 3) Must be in good standing with the IAC and in compliance with all IAC requirements; 4) Must be Indiana-based and have an Indiana address. Nonprofit corporations that are based in another state must be registered in Indiana as a Foreign Corporation; must have an Indiana address, and must provide all IAC-funded arts activities in Indiana; 5) Must have arts programming and/or service as its primary mission.
Restrictions: IAC-funding cannot be used for any of the following expenses: cash reserves, deficit reduction, or deficit elimination; events in private dwelling places or other locations not open to the general public; consumable supplies and materials not directly related to the project; capital acquisitions (purchase of artwork, etc.); capital expenditures; restoration, or new construction of buildings; costs of receptions, food, or beverages; travel outside the United States; indirect costs or underwriting for ongoing residencies or curricular programs in degree-granting colleges and universities; activities not associated with arts programs and services; projects to be delivered outside the state of Indiana; project expenses outside the state fiscal year and grant period; and activities that are solely for the purpose of fundraising, private functions, religious services, lobbying activities, or any non-public activity.
Geographic Focus: Indiana
Date(s) Application is Due: Mar 3; Apr 1
Contact: Bobbie Garver; (317) 232-1283; fax (317) 232-5595; bgarver@iac.in.gov
Internet: http://www.in.gov/arts/2559.htm
Sponsor: Indiana Arts Commission
150 W Market Street, Suite 618
Indianapolis, IN 46204

Indiana Arts Commission Capacity Building Grants 2531

The program is a stabilization process that provides IAC support, over a 24-month period, for organizational assessment, long range planning, and plan implementation utilizing a standardized assessment tool. It is designed to allow arts providers to comprehensively examine their 'reason for being,' mission, markets, programs, services, and governance and management structures and general operations with the aim of increased organizational effectiveness. The program is not designed to address single issue needs such as developing marketing or fund raising plans, program planning or evaluation, or feasibility studies. Grant amount is 75 percent of project costs or $20,000 over a 24-month period. Grantees must provide at least a 25 percent match. The match may be a combination of cash and in-kind (the value of necessary donated goods and services). However, at least one-half of the matches must be cash. Letters of Intent are due by February 16, with final applications due by April 20.
Requirements: Organizations must meet five basic requirements to apply: 1) Must have arts programming and/or services as its primary mission. 2) Must be a private, nonprofit, tax-exempt organization, incorporated in the state of Indiana. 3) Must have received recognition of tax-exempt status from the Internal Revenue Service. 4) Must be Indiana-based and have an Indiana address. Nonprofit corporations that are based in another state must be registered in Indiana as a Foreign Corporation, have an Indiana address, and provide arts activities in Indiana to be eligible. 5) Must be in good standing with the IAC and in compliance with all IAC requirements. Consider participation if your Indiana-based arts services organization fits into one of the following categories: (a) The organization is healthy and interested in re-evaluating the organization's mission, exploring assumptions about the organization's service and audience, and balancing the need to ensure artistic quality and fostering participation; (b) The organization has recurring problems (i.e. deficit, turnover, poor audience participation) that may relate to overall organizational issues not specific situations, or; (c) The organization has completed some type of overall organizational assessment in the last 5 years. The IAC requires any organization interested in applying to this grant program to submit a Notice of Intent to Apply form. This form can be found at http://www.in.gov/arts/grants/program.html
Restrictions: A complete list of restrictions can be found in the guidelines, instructions, and application packet available at the website.
Geographic Focus: Indiana
Date(s) Application is Due: Feb 16; Apr 20
Amount of Grant: Up to 20,000 USD
Contact: Kristina Davis; (317) 232-1279; fax (317) 232-5595; kdavis-smith@iac.in.gov
Internet: http://www.in.gov/arts/2550.htm
Sponsor: Indiana Arts Commission
150 W Market Street, Suite 618
Indianapolis, IN 46204

Indiana Arts Commission Multi-regional Major Arts Institutions Grants 2532

This program provides annual operating support for the ongoing artistic and administrative functions of eligible arts organizations that provide quality arts and cultural activities on a statewide or multi-regional basis, with special attention to underserved communities. An underserved community is one in which individuals lack access to arts programs due to: geography, economic conditions, ethnic background, disability or age. Operating expenses may include, but are not limited to, salaries, administrative fees, staff development and training, space and equipment rental, promotional costs, and production costs, etc., needed to support the organization's yearly activities. Major Arts Institutions are approved for the two-year grant period; however, grant money will be allocated on a yearly basis. For each year of the biennium, applicants may request up to 10 percent of projected annual cash operating expenses or $100,000, whichever is less. The maximum request amount for the two-year period is $200,000. Major Arts Institutions must match every dollar provided by the Indiana Arts Commission with ten dollars of the organization's own funds. One hundred percent of the match must be cash and cannot include in-kind donations.

Requirements: The IAC requires any organization interested in applying to this grant program to submit a Notice of Intent to Apply form. This form can be found on the web site. Contact sponsor for deadline for the Notice of Intent to Apply. Applications plus any support materials must be submitted electronically prior to the deadline, and the signed original hard copy of the application must be post marked by the deadline. All applicants must also meet with Bobbie Garver on staff to confirm the organization's eligibility to submit an application in this category. All applicant organizations must meet four general eligibility requirements in order to apply: 1) Must be a private tax-exempt nonprofit organization. 2) Nonprofit organizations must be incorporated in the state of Indiana at the time of application and have received recognition of tax-exempt status from the Internal Revenue Service. 3) Must be in good standing with the IAC and in compliance with all IAC requirements. 4) Must be Indiana-based and have an Indiana address. Nonprofit corporations that are based in another state must be registered in Indiana as a Foreign Corporation; must have an Indiana address, and must provide all IAC-funded arts activities in Indiana. Additional requirements apply to Major Arts Institutions.
Restrictions: An organization may not receive Indiana Arts Commission funding from both the IAC and a Regional Arts Partner for operating support in the same fiscal year. Organizations who are funded through the Regional Arts Partner may receive American Masterpiece and/or Capacity Building Program grants from the Indiana Arts Commission.
Geographic Focus: Indiana
Date(s) Application is Due: Mar 1
Amount of Grant: Up to 100,000 USD
Contact: Bobbie Garver; (317) 232-1283; fax (317) 232-5595; bgarver@iac.in.gov
Internet: http://www.in.gov/arts/2553.htm
Sponsor: Indiana Arts Commission
150 W Market Street, Suite 618
Indianapolis, IN 46204

Indiana Arts Commission Statewide Arts Service Organization Grants 2533
This program strengthens the capacity of arts providers and arts providing organizations by providing financial support to organizations that offer quality training and technical assistance services on a statewide or multi-regional basis, with special attention to arts providers in underserved communities. Technical assistance includes workshops, publications and other organizational training. Funding is limited to project support for a distinct aspect of the organization's arts-related technical assistance activities. Organizations may request up to 50 percent of project expenses for two years or $20,000. Applicants must provide a local match. Letters of Intent should be received by March 9, with applications due by April 9.
Requirements: An underserved community is one in which individuals lack access to arts programs due to: geography, economic conditions, ethnic background, disability or age. Organizations must be Indiana-based and have an Indiana address or registered in Indiana as a Foreign Corporation and provide arts activities in Indiana. Indiana public or private, nonprofit, tax-exempt agency or part of an Indiana public agency with a separate organizational structure. In addition to the general eligibility requirements, an organization applying in this category will have: 1) mission to provide arts-related technical assistance; 2) membership or constituency; 3) two-year history of planning and delivering arts-related technical assistance; 4) process for determining the training needs of consumers and an evaluation of the effectiveness; 5) process for planning and evaluation with input from the community; 6) a governing body that is representative of the service area; 7) operated for one year according to a strategic plan adopted by the governing body; 8) statewide presence.
Restrictions: All applicants must provide a local match. In general, applicants must match IAC funds on a dollar-for-dollar basis. In some cases, the match may be a combination of cash and the value of necessary donated goods and services up to 50 percent of the required match amount.
Geographic Focus: Indiana
Date(s) Application is Due: Mar 9; Apr 9
Amount of Grant: 1,000 - 20,000 USD
Contact: Kristina Davis; (317) 232-1279; fax (317) 232-5595; kdavis-smith@iac.in.gov
Internet: http://www.in.gov/arts/2556.htm
Sponsor: Indiana Arts Commission
150 W Market Street, Suite 618
Indianapolis, IN 46204

Indiana Boating Infrastructure Grants (BIG P) 2534
Funds for this program are awarded by the U.S. Fish and Wildlife Service and administered by the Indiana Department of Environmental Management. The program is designed to provide transient dockage for recreational boats 26 feet or more in length for recreational opportunities and safe harbors, as well as to enhance access to recreational, historic, cultural, and scenic resources; strengthen community ties to the water's edge and economic benefits; promote public/private partnerships and entrepreneurial opportunities; provide continuity of public access to the shore; and promote awareness of transient boating opportunities. A 25% matching contribution is required, for which federal funds cannot be used. Typical projects could include construction or renovation as follows: Slips for transient boaters (not more than 10 days); Mooring buoys; Navigational aids limited specifically to direct entry to transient, nontrailerable tie-up facilities; Safe harbors for transients; and initial dredging only to provide transient vessels with safe channel depths. The program offers one application round per year. Prospective applicants may call the Office of Pollution Prevention & Technical Assistance for information on deadlines and how to apply.
Requirements: All public marinas in Indiana which are situated along the shorelines of Lake Michigan and the Ohio River are eligible to apply. All facilities constructed under BIG P must conform to the following *Requirements:* be designed to accommodate boats 26' in length or greater; be used by transient boaters (boaters not at their home port and staying not more than 10 consecutive days); be open to the public; be designed and constructed so as to last at least 20 years; continue to be used for their original stated grant purpose; and be maintained throughout their useful life.
Restrictions: The following activities are ineligible: routine, custodial, and/or janitorial maintenance activities (those that occur regularly on an annual or more frequent basis); construction of slips for long-term rental (more than 10 days); construction or maintenance of facilities designed for trailerable boats; maintenance dredging; dry-land storage or haul-out facilities; activities or construction that does not provide public benefit. Features proposed under BIG P cannot cause damage to the environment, nor to historic features. All facilities must comply with requirements of the Americans with Disabilities Act (ADA).
Geographic Focus: Indiana
Contact: Anthony Sullivan; (317) 232-8172 or (317) 233-6663; asulliva@idem.IN.gov
Internet: http://www.in.gov/idem/5223.htm
Sponsor: Indiana Department of Environmental Management
Indiana Government Center North, 100 N Senate Avenue, Mail Code 50-01
Indianapolis, IN 46204-2251

Indiana Clean Vessel Act Grants 2535
The primary goal of the Clean Vessel Act (CVA) is to reduce overboard sewage discharge from recreational boats. Boat sewage dumped into our waters may affect aquatic plants, fish, and other animals. The nutrients, microorganisms, and chemicals contained in human waste discharged from boats have a negative impact on coastal and inland waters, particularly in sheltered or shallow areas not naturally flushed by tide or current. This program provides funding (on a reimbursement basis) for the construction, renovation, operation and maintenance of pump-out stations for holding tanks and dump stations for portable toilets. A matching contribution is required, 25% of the project cost, and federal funds cannot be used.
Requirements: The Pumpout Program provides funding to private and public marinas for the installation and restoration of boat sewage pumpouts and portable toilet dump stations. Pumpout stations are used to dispose of highly concentrated human waste collected aboard boats. All public marinas in Indiana which support recreational boats which are 26 feet and over in length and have portable or permanent on-board toilets are eligible. Contact the sponsor for guidelines, restrictions and forms.
Geographic Focus: Indiana
Contact: Tony Sullivan, Office of Pollution Prevention & Technical Assistance; (800) 451-6027, ext. 3-6663; tsulliva@idem.in.gov
Internet: http://www.in.gov/idem/resources/grants_loans/cva/index.html
Sponsor: Indiana Department of Environmental Management
Indiana Government Center North, 100 N Senate Avenue, Mail Code 50-01
Indianapolis, IN 46204-2251

Indiana Corn Marketing Council Retailer Grant for Tank Cleaning 2536
More E85 pumps at fuel stations across the state is the goal of a new corn checkoff-funded program offered by the Indiana Corn Marketing Council (ICMC). The new grant program is designed to help fuel retailers with the cost of converting existing fuel storage tanks to hold E85 (85 percent ethanol and 15 percent gasoline). This grant is in addition to the grant offered by the Indiana State Department of Agriculture for the purchase of new E85 refueling equipment or existing pump conversion.
Requirements: Fuel retailers in Indiana are eligible for grants up to $5,000 for the cleaning of fuel storage tanks prior to the introduction of E85 blended fuel. Eligible licensed fuel retailers must be willing to commit to selling and actively promoting E85 for a period of two years. Applicant must be able to demonstrate that cost was incurred for cleaning of fuel tanks by providing a copy of tank cleaning invoice(s). The required application form can be downloaded from the sponsor's website.
Restrictions: Limited to licensed fuel retailers in Indiana.
Geographic Focus: Indiana
Amount of Grant: 5,000 USD
Contact: Mark Walters, (317) 347-3620; mwalters@indianacorn.org
Internet: http://www.incorn.org/index.aspx?ascxid=pagedetail&pid=22664&cid=811
Sponsor: Indiana Corn Marketing Council
5757 W 74th Street
Indianapolis, IN 46278

Indiana Historic Preservation Fund Grants 2537
The program helps to promote historic preservation and archaeology in Indiana by providing assistance to projects that will aid the State in meeting its goals for cultural resource management. Under the HPF matching grants program, grant awards are made in three project categories. When applying for grant funds, applicants must be certain to request and complete the appropriate application packet for their project category. The grant program is limited to the following categories: Architectural and Historical projects, Archaeological projects, and Acquisition and Development projects.
Requirements: Eligible applicants include (a) private, non-profit organizations with 501(c)3 tax exempt status (including local historical societies and preservation organizations), (b) educational institutions (including public and private schools, colleges, and universities), and (c) local governmental units (including city and county agencies and commissions funded by a consortium of local governments). A match is required for this program: 50% federal / 50% local for most projects or 70% federal / 30% local for survey projects. Each category has its own application form; download the forms from the sponsor's website. Properties to be assisted with grant funds (as the focus of an Historic Structure Report, feasibility study, or other planning documents) must be listed in the National Register of Historic Places at the time of application, or they must be in the nomination process and have passed both technical and substantive review at the time of application.
Restrictions: Individuals and private, for-profit entities are not eligible to receive grant funds because federal regulations prohibit grant recipients from making a financial profit as a direct result of the grant-assisted project. Federal regulations do not allow grant funds

to be awarded to active religious organizations, or to be used to assist buildings that are used primarily for religious functions. Note also that state and federal auditing and income tax regulations prevent the DHPA from making a grant award to an organization which is not incorporated, or which does not otherwise exist as a legal entity. Note that properties within the boundaries of historic districts which are designated as non-contributing (NC) are not eligible to receive grant funding. Properties listed in the State Register of Historic Sites and Structures which are not also listed in the National Register of Historic Places are not eligible to receive grant funding.
Geographic Focus: Indiana
Amount of Grant: 50,000 USD
Contact: James A. Glass, Division Director; (317) 232-3492; jglass@dnr.in.gov
Internet: http://www.in.gov/dnr/historic/11816.htm#hpf
Sponsor: Indiana Department of Natural Resources
402 West Washington Street, Room W274
Indianapolis, IN 46204

Indiana Household Hazardous Waste Grants 2538
These grants are designed to help start or expand household hazardous waste (HHW) recycling programs involving the collection, recycling, or disposal of HHW, and conditionally exempt small quantity generator waste (CESQGW). Funds may be used to support educational and outreach programs that inform the public of substitutes for typical household hazardous products, product reuse and exchange programs that help reduce HHW, and the establishment of permanent facilities for the proper handling, collection, storage, recycling or disposal of HHW and CESQGW. HHW projects are eligible for a maximum funding level of $60,000. Regional HHW grants are eligible for up to $100,000. Regional project eligibility requires participation of a minimum of 10 counties or a grant eligible entity or entities serving an area with a population greater than 700,000.
Requirements: A matching contribution of 50% of the total project cost is required (dollar-for-dollar cash or in-kind). Solid waste management districts, counties, municipalities and townships are eligible to apply. Joint applications between two or more units of government are encouraged. Application guides, schedules and forms are available for download at the website.
Restrictions: Funding is not available for projects that stray from the original mission of source reduction and proper disposal of HHW/CESQG waste. Expenses such as personnel expenses, contractor set-up, single-day collection events, permanent structures and site improvements will not be funded through the program. Funding is not available for the recycling or disposal of non-hazardous materials as determined by IDEM, such as alkaline batteries and latex paint.
Geographic Focus: Indiana
Date(s) Application is Due: Jul 27
Contact: Regional Grant Representative; (800) 988-7901; recycling@idem.in.gov
Internet: http://www.in.gov/recycle/funding/hhwg.html
Sponsor: Indiana Department of Environmental Management
100 North Senate Avenue, MC 64-01
Indianapolis, IN 46204-2251

Indiana Humanities Council Initiative Grants 2539
Humanities Initiative Grants may be used for any public humanities program, with participation from a humanities scholar. This grant focuses particularly on strengthening communities through leadership, education, and culture. Eligible projects include workshops, exhibits, film or book discussions, historical presentations, educational materials development, and more. The maximum amount is $1,000.
Requirements: To be eligible for any grant from the Indiana Humanities Council, an applicant must be an Indiana not-for-profit organization with tax-exempt status.
Restrictions: Grants will not be made to individuals, political action or advocacy, social services, construction or renovation, property or major equipment purchases, religious practices or training, scholarships, performance of art unless presenting subject matter in the humanities, operating expenses, microfilming newspapers, or the purchase of alcoholic beverages.
Geographic Focus: Indiana
Date(s) Application is Due: Feb 1; Jun 1; Oct 4
Amount of Grant: 1,000 USD
Contact: Nancy N. Conner, (317) 638-1500; fax (317) 634-9503; nconner@iupui.edu
Internet: http://www.indianahumanities.org/grants.htm
Sponsor: Indiana Humanities Council
1500 North Delaware
Indianapolis, IN 46202

Indianapolis Power & Light Company Community Grants 2540
Indianapolis Power & Light Company (IPL) is committed to the betterment of the communities where it does business. Through various programs and grants, IPL enhances the quality of life for its customers, its employees and its communities. IPL employees generously contribute their time to the community through volunteer efforts. The combination of financial support and human resources affirms IPL's commitment to being a good neighbor. Through the IPL Community Grants Program, IPL makes grants available to organizations that have tax-exempt status of the Internal Revenue code. Contribution dollars are generally limited to the communities where IPL does business, which includes Marion County, the seven surrounding counties and Pike County. IPL targets its support to organizations that fall into one of the following categories: education — Organizations that focus on a variety of educational objectives. A special emphasis is placed on the use of math, science and technology; environmental — organizations that protect, conserve and/or improve the environment; economic development — special requests that encourage economic development within our service territory; community enhancement — organizations that promote diversity and/or an improved quality of life in our community; arts & culture — organizations that offer programs and activities to our community that heighten awareness of the arts and local culture of the community. General inquires or preliminary questions about grant proposals or eligibility should be directed to the Public Affairs department.
Requirements: Grant application procedures — include a proposal summary: briefly summarize the purpose of your organization, including your mission statement; indicate how long your organization has been in existence; explain the community need or problem being addressed; describe the project, program or use for which you are seeking funds. Prepare a sponsorship/donation level page: list IPL donation opportunities in three possible levels and briefly describe how each level would assist your organization; list the benefits to IPL associated with each level. Provide the following attachments: list with names of board members; copy of IRS tax exemption letter; project budget; list of corporations, foundations or individuals providing support. IPL grant guidelines: a grant given in any one year does not ensure future funding; IPL will consider only one grant request per project in a calendar year; grant recipients must use the funds as agreed upon in a timely manner during the grant period specified in the award; a report will be due outlining the use and outcome of the funds used.
Restrictions: Requests for the following will not be considered: health initiatives; organizations without tax exempt status; conferences or seminars; projects benefiting an individual or just a few people; political activities, candidates or organizations; post-event funding; walks and/or runs.
Geographic Focus: Indiana
Contact: Greg Fennig, Vice President; (317) 261-8213; publicaffairs.ipl@aes.com
Internet: http://www.iplpower.com/ipl/index?page=IPLGeneral&Menu=05010000&DocID=0205016c163f01078f72b7310073e8
Sponsor: Indianapolis Power and Light Company
1 Monument Circle, P.O. Box 1595
Indianapolis, IN 46206-1595

Indianapolis Power & Light Company Environmentalist of the Year Award 2541
In memory of Indiana environmentalist Bob Klawitter, IPL created the Environmentalist of the Year Award, which is given to a Hoosier who works or volunteers to improve the environment. Any Indiana resident working in IPL's operating territory is eligible for the IPL Environmentalist of the Year. IPL's operating territory consists of the following counties: Marion, Hamilton, Hendricks, Johnson, Morgan, Boone, Hancock, Shelby and Pike. The recipient will be selected by the Golden Eagle Grant Advisory Panel and the award will include a check for $3,000.
Requirements: Names may be submitted by the potential recipient or by another individual or group. The entry should include: the attached nomination form (see website for form); a photograph (if possible); a description of the individual's activities; examples of how he or she has benefited the environment or worked to preserve or enhance Indiana's natural resources. The entry may include letters of recommendation.
Geographic Focus: Indiana
Date(s) Application is Due: Oct 17
Contact: Cindy Leffler, Administrator of Corporate Contributions; (317) 261-8213
Internet: http://www.iplpower.com/ipl/index?page=IPLGeneral&Menu=06030000&DocID=0205016c163f01078f72b731007433
Sponsor: Indianapolis Power and Light Company
1 Monument Circle, P.O. Box 1595
Indianapolis, IN 46206-1595

Indianapolis Power & Light Company Golden Eagle Environmental Grants 2542
IPL Golden Eagle Grants provide financial grants to not-for-profit organizations and governmental units for projects that will preserve, protect, enhance, or restore environmental and biological resources throughout IPL's operating territory. Grant applications will be reviewed quarterly.
Requirements: Eligible applicants are Indiana nonprofit organizations and units of local or state government, including schools, and parks and recreation departments.
Restrictions: This program is only available to the IPL's operating territory, which consists of the following counties: Marion, Hamilton, Hendricks, Johnson, Morgan, Boone, Hancock, Shelby and Pike.
Geographic Focus: Indiana
Date(s) Application is Due: Nov 6
Contact: Cindy Leffler, Administrator of Corporate Contributions; (317) 261-8213
Internet: http://www.iplpower.com/ipl/index?page=IPLGeneral&Menu=05030000&DocID=0205016c163f01078f72b73100748f
Sponsor: Indianapolis Power and Light Company
1 Monument Circle, P.O. Box 1595
Indianapolis, IN 46206-1595

Indianapolis Preservation Grants 2543
Grants are available for professional architectural and engineering feasibility studies and other preservation consulting services, as well as organizational development and fundraising projects. The foundation makes the preservation grants on a four-to-one matching basis, with four dollars from us matching each local cash dollar. Grants will fund 80% of the total project cost up to $2,000.
Requirements: Nonprofit community preservation organizations and historic neighborhood foundations in Marion County are eligible to apply.
Restrictions: The grants may not be used for physical restoration work.
Geographic Focus: Indiana
Amount of Grant: Up to 2,000 USD
Contact: Chad Lethig, (317) 639-4534; fax (317) 639-6720; flip@historiclandmarks.org
Internet: http://www.historiclandmarks.org/help/grants.html
Sponsor: Historic Landmarks Foundation of Indiana
340 W Michigan Street
Indianapolis, IN 46202

Indiana Preservation Grants 2544
Grants are available for professional architectural and engineering feasibility studies and other preservation consulting services, as well as organizational development and fundraising projects. The foundation makes the preservation Grants on a four-to-one matching basis, with four dollars from us matching each local cash dollar. Grants will fund 80% of the total project cost up to $2,500.
Requirements: Nonprofit organizations in Indiana are eligible to apply. Contact the Historic Landmarks regional office that serves your community (see website for list of regional offices or contact the state headquarters office) for guidelines and forms.
Restrictions: The grants may not be used for physical restoration work.
Geographic Focus: Indiana
Amount of Grant: Up to 2,500 USD
Samples: Clinton, IN (Vermillion County) $3,040 grant for a feasibility study led to a $700,000 restoration of the town's 1905 passenger depot.
Contact: Carla Jones, Receptionist, State Headquarters; (317) 639-4534; fax (317) 639-6734; info@historiclandmarks.org
Internet: http://www.historiclandmarks.org/help/grants.html
Sponsor: Historic Landmarks Foundation of Indiana
340 W Michigan Street
Indianapolis, IN 46202

Indiana Recycling Grants 2545
Indiana Recycling Grants are designed to help start or expand source reduction, recycling, and recycling education programs in Indiana. Funds are available for the costs associated with establishing curbside recycling, drop-off recycling, recycling processing, and yard waste collection and management. These grants are intended to create sustainable projects with no state funding for ongoing program costs.
Requirements: A matching contribution of 50% of the total project cost is required. Solid waste management districts, counties, municipalities, townships, schools, and nonprofit organizations with 501(c) status are eligible. Detailed guidelines, application and forms are available at the website.
Restrictions: Limited to Indiana only.
Geographic Focus: Indiana
Date(s) Application is Due: May 25; Sep 28
Contact: Kristin Brier, Program Officer; (800) 988-7901; kbrier@idem.in.gov
Internet: http://www.in.gov/recycle/funding/irg.html
Sponsor: Indiana Department of Environmental Management
100 North Senate Avenue, MC 64-01
Indianapolis, IN 46204-2251

Indiana Regional Economic Development Partnership Grants 2546
In order to spur further regional economic development initiatives, this program was created to encourage communities to think, plan and act regionally, and to provide additional resource support for regional initiatives. The objective is to build on the work already done to define regional economies, develop regional growth strategies, accelerate effective regional economic development. The purpose of the Regional Economic Development Partnership Program is to increase regional competitiveness in the following areas: Expanding job creation opportunities; Workforce development / Human capital development and retention; Entrepreneurship / Improving access to capital; Targeting and development of industry clusters. Collectively, progress in the areas outlined above will support the broader objective of enhancing regional competitiveness and empowering regional leaders to face the challenges and opportunities of economic growth. Applications will be accepted and reviewed on a rolling basis throughout the year.
Requirements: Regional economic development planning groups shall be eligible to apply for a grant for specific regional economic development initiatives. A regional economic development group ('Group') should comprise area business and community leaders who will work in close coordination with the IEDC, and other appropriate parties, including regional workforce boards and K-12 and higher education representatives. The economic regions that a Group represents are not confined to traditional political or geographical boundaries. Instead, the IEDC encourages a bottom-up approach to defining regional economies that focuses on labor market areas and patterns of commerce. The IEDC strongly promotes the engagement of smaller communities and rural areas in such planning and programmatic efforts. The Group identified in the proposal should represent the collection of those various stakeholders and must include partners from two or more counties cooperatively engaged in projects and/or initiatives intended to support the economic growth of their region. For the purposes of this program, entities eligible to participate in a group may include a not-for-profit organization, an educational institution, a government entity, a local economic development organization, a Chamber of Commerce, or regional workforce board. Proposals must demonstrate a clear strategy for creating or enhancing the opportunities for job creation and economic growth in the State of Indiana and must support the IEDC's goals as articulated in Indiana's strategic plan for economic development, Accelerating Growth. Within those parameters, the IEDC will consider grant proposals addressing one or more of the following: Development of a regional economic development strategy that includes specific implementation actions and metrics for measuring the progress and success of proposal; Development of a regional investment agreement to provide for financial participation of multiple counties in a specific project of regional economic significance; Implementation of specific initiatives identified as part of a regional planning process; Matching of funds provided through a competitive federal or private grant opportunity; Seed capital (not operating expenses) for a Regional Venture Capital Fund that has been or will be approved by the IEDC pursuant to IC 6-3.5-7-13.5. Each grant proposal will be reviewed individually and the match requirement may vary based on the circumstances of the Group and the project being proposed. The following guidelines are generally to be followed, although exceptions may be considered under special circumstances: Grant funds are to be matched on a minimum of a 1:1 basis, with not more than 20% of total matching funds consisting of in-kind contributions; Grant funds can be matched using private, federal or local funds; Grant funds cannot be matched using funds appropriated by the Indiana General Assembly; Proposals demonstrating generous match involvement will be considered more favorably. The maximum award for a single proposal from a Group is $150,000. Not more than 5% of grant funds may be used for payment of grant administration expenses.
Restrictions: A Group may receive more than one grant under this program, but may have no more than one active grant at any time. A county may participate in more than one Group at the same time but cannot be party to more than two grants at any given time. Funding will not be provided for the following uses: Ordinary operating expenses of organizations, such as rent, insurance, utilities and non-program related salaries; Company-specific economic development incentives; Site-specific infrastructure upgrades for development; Purchase or option to purchase property; Reimbursement of proposal preparation costs.
Geographic Focus: Indiana
Amount of Grant: Up to 150,000 USD
Contact: Susan Kleinman, skleinman@iedc.in.gov
Internet: http://www.in.gov/iedc/SpecialPrograms.htm
Sponsor: Indiana Economic Development Corporation
1 North Capitol Avenue, Suite 900
Indianapolis, IN 46204

Indiana Rural Capacity Grants (RCG) 2547
The Rural Capacity Grant program was developed to assist rural Indiana communities in their efforts to expand local capacity by means of grassroots community-development efforts, partnership building, and leveraging regional resources. There are two types of Rural Capacity Grants: Rural Entrepreneurial Support, and Workforce and Educational Development. Projects should seek to build the capacity to support local workforce and educational systems. A competitive project will demonstrate innovative approaches to address workforce development and lifelong learning. Examples of projects include, but are not limited to: training programs designed to meet the job market of the area being served; educational projects intended to increase basic skills, such as literacy and math, of the workforce; projects that seek to increase problem-solving, conflict resolution or other workplace-related soft skills, and other projects which address critical education and workforce-development issues. At the time of this writing, the Office of Community and Rural Affairs (OCRA) is not accepting applications due to funding restraints. Interested organizations are encouraged to contact the Project Manager for information on future funding availability.
Requirements: Not-for-profit organizations properly registered with the Secretary of State, educational or governmental entities, local economic-development organizations, Chambers of Commerce, workforce boards, Small Business Development Centers, community foundations, and other non-profit organizations are eligible to apply.
Restrictions: Grant funds and local match cannot be used for: the purchase of capital equipment over $5,000; administrative expenses in excess of 10% of the grant amount; operational expenses such as rent, utilities, insurance, non-program-related salaries; funding to purchase, improve, or remodel a facility; costs to supplant existing funds (the funding opportunity must be used for expansion of existing services or implementation of new services); or direct financial support to provide start up or operational capital to businesses.
Geographic Focus: Indiana
Date(s) Application is Due: Jun 29
Amount of Grant: Up to 150,000 USD
Contact: Geoff Schomacker, Project Manager; (317) 233-3762 or (800) 824-2476; fax (317) 233-3597; gschomacker@ocra.in.gov
Internet: http://www.in.gov/ocra/2357.htm
Sponsor: Indiana Office of Community and Rural Affairs
1 North Capitol, Suite 600
Indianapolis, IN 46204

Indiana SBIR/STTR Commercialization Enhancement Program (ISCEP) 2548
ISCEP provides funds to enhance commercialization activities of Indiana-based SBIR/STTR (Small Business Innovation Research/Small Business Technology Transfer) awardees. Specific ISCEP goals include: Support of thoughtfully structured commercialization plans of SBIR/STTR Phase II awardees; Accelerate and enhance commercial impacts of SBIR/STTR technologies, and; Establish and enhance successful technology-based businesses in Indiana. Proposals will be accepted from a small business that has received a federal Phase II SBIR or STTR and at least 50% of the federal program dollars must be expended prior to submission of a proposal in response to the RFP. Review considers both the technology development stage and the related business plan. The final stage of review involves a presentation to the IEDC. Between two and four awards of up to $350,000 may be made per funding cycle. The awards will be made with performance periods of up to 2 years and are contingent on the availability of funds.
Requirements: Eligible applicants must have a principal place of business in Indiana and the benefits from commercialization must accrue to an Indiana small business. Applicants must be a small business that has received a federal Phase II SBIR or STTR and at least 50% of the federal program dollars must be expended prior to submission of a proposal in response to the RFP, because an essential metric used in judging suitability for an award will involve assessing current progress toward achievement of Phase II objectives. The technology being commercialized must be directly related to the technology funded under the SBIR or STTR Phase II award. There is no limit as to the number of proposals that a single company can submit. However, only one award per company will be made per RFP cycle. The RFP, proposal tips and application are available at the website.
Restrictions: Awardees must maintain a principal place of business in Indiana for a term of 10 years beginning on the Effective Date of the agreement. Otherwise forfeiture and repayment the award plus interest will be required. Successful applicants must adhere to specific reporting requirements, including: quarterly progress reports, annual reports, annual site visits and a final report.

Geographic Focus: Indiana
Date(s) Application is Due: Jul 20
Amount of Grant: Up to 350,000 USD
Contact: Brooke Pyne; (812) 384-3078; fax (812) 384-3487; bpyne@iedc.in.gov
Internet: http://www.in.gov/iedc/sbir/index.html
Sponsor: Indiana Economic Development Corporation
SBIR/STTR Program Office, 32 E Main Street
Bloomfield, IN 47424

Indiana Space Grant Consortium Grants for Informal Education Partnerships 2549
The National Space Grant Program has a specific charge to provide a means of dissemination of information about NASA and space science opportunities for the development of higher education programs, K-12 education and professional development both for pre- and in-service teachers, and informal education opportunities. The specific purpose of this program is to provide funds to develop new space science related exhibits and improve the evaluation of those exhibits as demonstrations of information education effectiveness. Suggested partnership members include academic, museum, or external entities. Up to $10,000 is available for each applicant.
Requirements: Faculty and students receiving NASA/INSGC funds for direct support (salary or travel) must be U.S. Citizens. A minimum 2 to 1 match is required.
Geographic Focus: Indiana
Date(s) Application is Due: Feb 13
Amount of Grant: Up to 10,000 USD
Contact: Dr. Barrett Caldwell; (765) 494-5873; fax (765) 496-3449; bscaldwell@purdue.edu
Internet: http://www.insgc.org/?q=node/113
Sponsor: Indiana Space Grant Consortium
203 S Martin Jischke Drive, Gerald D. and Edna E Mann Hall, Room 160
West Lafayette, IN 47907-1971

Indiana Space Grant Consortium Workforce Development Grants 2550
The mission of the Indiana Space Grant Consortium is to promote science, technology, engineering and mathematics (STEM) workforce development, formal and informal education, and research by the dissemination of NASA related activities, content, and opportunities to the residents of the State of Indiana. The Workforce Development Program is designed to enhance the workforce capabilities of INSGC affiliate campus students, supporting industries and the State of Indiana by fostering the pursuit of careers in NASA-related aspects of space science and engineering. See the website for details of specific programs and amounts available in this area.
Requirements: Applicants receiving NASA/INSGC funds for direct support (salary or travel) must be U.S. Citizens.
Geographic Focus: Indiana
Date(s) Application is Due: Feb 13
Amount of Grant: 10,000 USD
Contact: Dr. Barrett Caldwell; (765) 494-5873; fax (765) 496-3449; bscaldwell@purdue.edu
Internet: http://www.insgc.org/?q=node/112
Sponsor: Indiana Space Grant Consortium
203 S Martin Jischke Drive, Gerald D. and Edna E Mann Hall, Room 160
West Lafayette, IN 47907-1971

Indiana Waste Tire Fund (WTF) Program Grants 2551
The Indiana Waste Tire Fund (WTF) Program was created to help Indiana businesses undertake research, development, and/or commercial manufacturing projects that develop markets for use of scrap tires. Funds are made available through grants of up to $100,000 with a 50% match requirement are available for innovative research and development projects. Key elements include project partnerships and technology transfer. Provisions will be made for confidentiality of proprietary information.
Requirements: Eligible applicants are limited to Indiana businesses and not-for-profits. Interested applicants must contact OPPTA (Office of Pollution Prevention and Technical Assistance) to receive a grant application. Activities that may be funded through the program include the following: Civil engineering applications using shredded tires; Asphalt-rubber applications using ground rubber; Development of advanced technology and processes for production of products from scrap tires and; Tire-derived-fuel (TDF).
Restrictions: Projects must take place within the state of Indiana.
Geographic Focus: Indiana
Amount of Grant: Up to 100,000 USD
Contact: Regional Grant Representative; (800) 988-7901; recycling@idem.in.gov
Internet: http://www.in.gov/recycle/funding/wtf.html
Sponsor: Indiana Department of Environmental Management
100 North Senate Avenue, MC 64-01
Indianapolis, IN 46204-2251

Indiana Workforce Acceleration Grants 2552
The Workforce Acceleration Grant is designed to help Hoosiers pay for education and training to prepare for 21st Century jobs. The program provides eligible Hoosiers with up to $3,000 per academic year to help cover tuition, fees and book costs for an associate's degree or a vocational certification at more than 50 colleges and universities across the state of Indiana. (See website for a complete list of eligible schools.) Participants in the Workforce Acceleration Grants can pursue areas of study that provide specific career/vocational training leading toward an Associates Degree or certificate program. General Studies and Liberal Arts programs are not covered. The staff at your WorkOne Center can provide more information about approved areas of training.
Requirements: Workers at least 18 years old, who have the legal right to work in the U.S., and are pursuing an Associate Degree or post-secondary certificate that leads to a high wage or high-demand occupation. In addition, workers must fall into one of the two groups: (1) Low-Income participant—Family receives federal, state, or local public assistance (TANF, SNAP, etc); or total family income at or below federal poverty level ($23,239 for family of four); or 70% of lower living-standard income level (based upon previous six months income). (2) Unemployed Worker—Unlikely to return to previous occupation/career field; AND falls into ONE of the following categories: Unemployed through no fault of their own; received notice of impending layoff; spouse of dislocated worker (earning less than 50% of family income); self-employed, but business closed as a result of economic conditions. There is no deadline to enroll in this program, however funding is limited and participants will be accepted on a first-come/first-served basis. To apply visit your local WorkOne Center to pick up an application and bring the following information: Valid Identification – State ID card, Drivers License, etc; Social Security Card or Birth certificate; Proof of Income – Pay stubs, Family or Business Financial Records, Public Assistance Records, Unemployment Insurance Documents, etc. Take application to college financial aid office. Return completed application to WorkOne Center.
Geographic Focus: Indiana
Amount of Grant: Up to 3,000 USD
Contact: Program Supervisor; (800) 891-6499
Internet: http://www.in.gov/dwd/2668.htm
Sponsor: Indiana Department of Workforce Development
Indiana Government Center South, 10 North Senate Avenue
Indianapolis, IN 46204

Infinity Foundation Grants 2553
The foundation awards grants in a broad array of areas including charitable, scientific, religious, educational, and holistic healing activities by organizations and public agencies that work to better the lives of people. Grants also support individuals' research and development of educational materials to improve the authenticity of the portrayal of Indic traditions in the educational system. Proposed projects could result in one or more of the following: books, curriculum development, articles, conferences, CD-Roms, digital slide shows, Internet presentations, and audio/video materials. Topics covered may include philosophy, history, religion, science, art, and sociology, as they pertain to the educational curricula on Indic traditions. Proposals should be submitted by email.
Requirements: Grantee may be a scholar, teacher, visionary, or spiritual leader whose work in the designated topics would be enhanced by a foundation grant.
Geographic Focus: All States
Contact: Rajiv Malhotra; (609) 683-0548; fax (609) 683-0478; rm.infinity@gmail.com
Internet: http://www.infinityfoundation.com/callforgrantproposals.htm
Sponsor: Infinity Foundation
66 Witherspoon Street, Suite 400
Princeton, NJ 08542

Information Society Innovation Fund (ISIF) Grants 2554
The Information Society Innovation Fund (ISIF) is a grants program aimed at stimulating creative solutions to ICT development needs in the Asia Pacific region, placing particular emphasis on the role of the Internet in social and economic development in the region, towards the effective development of the Information Society throughout. Emphasis will be placed on the needs of developing countries of the region which are currently not well serviced in some or all of the respects outlined above. All outcomes of projects funded under this program will be in the public domain. The specific objectives of the fund are to: encourage innovative approaches to the extension of Internet infrastructure and services in the Asia Pacific region; address issues of Internet sustainability and business models in challenging market circumstances; foster innovation and creative solutions to development problems by supporting new and creative uses of ICT applications; help development and public agencies identify new trends and actors in regional ICT development; and generate awareness and foster sharing of innovative approaches to development challenges.
Requirements: ISIF will respond to project proposals from Asia-Pacific-based public or private sector organizations, university or Research and Development (R&D) institutions, and non-government organizations.
Restrictions: Individuals will not be eligible for grants.
Geographic Focus: All States
Date(s) Application is Due: Sep 1
Amount of Grant: Up to 30,000 USD
Contact: Sylvia Cadena; (+617) 38583100; fax (+617) 38583199; info@isif.asia
Internet: http://isif.asia/groups/isif/
Sponsor: Information Society Innovation Fund
APNIC Level 1, 33 Park Road, P.O. Box 2131
Milton, Brisbane Milton 4064 Australia

ING Foundation Grants 2555
The ING Foundation is the charitable giving arm of ING U.S. The Foundation awards grants to non-profit organizations addressing a variety of community needs and resources. The Foundation focuses on four primary areas: financial literacy - ING Foundation is especially interested in programming that empowers individuals to take control of their financial futures through education, financial literacy, and financial planning, with special attention to the needs of young people and minorities; children's education - committed to supporting and improving education for youth in grades K-12, especially children in underserved areas or facing economic disadvantages; diversity - support equity and fairness in societies around the world, funding selected diversity initiatives; and environmental sustainability.
Requirements: Note that the ING Foundation cannot consider funding for organizations that do not have tax-exempt status under Section 501(c)3 of the U.S. Internal Revenue Code.
Restrictions: The Foundation does not grant awards to individuals; private foundations; religious or fraternal organizations and activities; political, legislative, and/or lobbying causes; capital and/or endowment campaigns or building funds; general or administrative operating costs; or organizations that discriminate on the basis of race, color, creed, gender or national origin.

Nor does it support fashion shows, pageants, golf tournaments, sports teams, athletic events, or other funding opportunities that do not align with its strategic areas of giving. Grant requests are reviewed once per quarter by the ING Foundation Advisory Committee.
Geographic Focus: All States
Amount of Grant: 2,500 - 200,000 USD
Contact: Administrator; (770) 980-5417; fax (770) 980-6580; ingfoundation@us.ing.com
Internet: http://ing.us/about-ing/responsibility/ing-foundation-grants
Sponsor: ING Foundation
5780 Powers Ferry Road NW
Atlanta, GA 30327-4349

Initiaive Foundation Inside-Out Connections Grants 2556
Initiaive Foundation Inside-Out Connections Grants are designed to increase the capacity of local communities to address the needs of children of incarcerated parents in central Minnesota. Children with incarcerated parents are among the most vulnerable populations of children, at high risk for neglect, abuse, behavioral health problems, delinquency and substance abuse. These issues, if left unattended, can produce intergenerational patterns of crime and violence. Initial grants of $5,000 are available, and future challenge grants (requiring matching dollars) may be available for projects that are directly related to coalition plans.
Requirements: The Foundation services communities in the following Minnesota counties: Benton, Cass, Chisago, Crow Wing, Isanti, Kanabec, Mille Lacs, Morrison, Pine, Sherburne, Stearns, Todd, Wadena, and Wright. Initial Grant goals are to: create and support multi-sector coalition teams to determine the needs of children with incarcerated parents; increase the capacity of coalition teams to develop and carry out an action plan around issues such as parent education, family support, child mentoring and community engagement; and increase community awareness and support for children who have a parent in jail or prison. Communities interested in participating on an existing team or starting one may contact the Children, Youth and Families Specialist.
Geographic Focus: Minnesota
Contact: Sara Dahlquist; (877) 632-9255; sdahlquist@ifound.org
Internet: http://www.ifound.org/grants_program.php
Sponsor: Initiative Foundation
405 First Street SE
Little Falls, MN 56345

Initiative Foundation Healthy Communities Partnership Grants 2557
Initiative Foundation Healthy Communities Partnership Grants develop the capacity of citizens to create a locally shared vision and plan and to mobilize local and regional assets to implement that plan. The program results in communities that are connected to surrounding communities, able to leverage local, state and national resources, and equipped to drive positive, lasting change. Selected communities receive an initial grant of $10,000 for citizen-based planning, project implementation and related expenses. They also receive training, technical assistance, and referrals to additional resources. After completion communities are encouraged to apply for additional grants and earn priority funding consideration for those projects that help accomplish their plans.
Requirements: The Foundation services communities in the following Minnesota counties: Benton, Cass, Chisago, Crow Wing, Isanti, Kanabec, Mille Lacs, Morrison, Pine, Sherburne, Stearns, Todd, Wadena, and Wright. Selection is a competitive process with the Foundation offering training to four or five communities per year. Interested communities begin the process by contacting the Program Manager for Community Development. A site visit to present information to interested community members will follow. Communities pursuing participation will be invited to complete a formal application. The time from a site visit to actual program participation is often six to twelve months.
Geographic Focus: Minnesota
Contact: Dan Frank; (877) 632-9255; dfrank@ifound.org
Internet: http://www.ifound.org/grants_program.php
Sponsor: Initiative Foundation
405 First Street SE
Little Falls, MN 56345

Initiative Foundation Healthy Lakes and Rivers Partnership Grants 2558
Initiative Foundation Healthy Lakes and Rivers Partnership Grants empower local shoreline associations to improve the quality of their lakes or rivers. Selected associations receive performance-based awards totaling $2,400 after achieving major milestones. Upon completion associations may apply for future challenge-grants (requiring matching dollars) of up to $5,000 for projects that help implement their water management plans.
Requirements: The Foundation services communities in the following Minnesota counties: Benton, Cass, Chisago, Crow Wing, Isanti, Kanabec, Mille Lacs, Morrison, Pine, Sherburne, Stearns, Todd, Wadena, and Wright. Training sessions are offered to eight lake or river groups from the same watershed, county or region. Usually the host (and Grant administrator) is a County's Environmental Services Department or Water Plan Administrator, a nonprofit such as a Coalition of Lake Associations or a watershed district. The Foundation encourages inquiries from individual associations. Contact the Program Manager for Planning and Preservation for more information.
Geographic Focus: Minnesota
Contact: Don Hickman, (320) 632-9255; dhickman@ifound.org
Internet: http://www.ifound.org/grants_program.php
Sponsor: Initiative Foundation
405 First Street SE
Little Falls, MN 56345

Initiative Foundation Innovation Fund Grants 2559
The Initiative Foundation exists to improve the quality of life in central Minnesota. The Foundation's highest priorities are: to strengthen children, youth and families; promote economic stability; preserve space, place and natural resources; build capacity of nonprofit organizations; embrace diversity and reduce prejudice; and increase utilization of technology. Average awards are $5,000 and the maximum is generally $10,000. On occasion higher awards are made for multi-community projects or special initiatives. Requests for funding over $10,000 are accepted on an invitation-only basis.
Requirements: Eligible applicants must be 501(c)3 nonprofits or local units of government that serve the communities of Benton, Cass, Chisago, Crow Wing, Isanti, Kanabec, Mille Lacs, Morrison, Pine, Sherburne, Stearns, Todd, Wadena, and/or Wright Counties in Minnesota. Eligible projects must address at least one of the following areas: help communities address opportunities or barriers to business growth and employment with active participation by private, public and not-for-profit sectors; advance economic self-sufficiency for vulnerable children and families by supporting nonprofits that work in these areas; support training programs for future, displaced or underemployed workers that lead to employment or advancement in growing industries; help small businesses survive and grow through access to consulting services, mentorship and education efforts provided by not-for-profit entities; and help communities improve efficiencies through shared services with other units of government or public-private partnerships resulting in faster, higher quality, or more cost-effective services. Qualified organizations are asked to complete a letter of inquiry, which is found at the website. Inquiries are accepted on an ongoing basis and reviewed quarterly. Organizations with proposed projects which fit priority funding areas and meet funding criteria will be invited to submit a full proposal. The application materials will be provided.
Restrictions: The following are ineligible: grants to individuals; expenses incurred prior to the award; capital expenses; any programs or projects that do not directly benefit residents in the fourteen-county service area; replacement of government funding; religious activities; lobbying or campaigning for a candidate, issue or referendum vote; development or purchase of school curriculum or support for school athletic programs; and arts, health-related and media production applications, unless they are part of a strategic plan developed through a Foundation partnership program.
Geographic Focus: Minnesota
Contact: Grants Director; (877) 632-9255; fax (320) 632-9258; grants@ifound.org
Internet: http://www.ifound.org/grants_index.php
Sponsor: Initiative Foundation
405 First Street SE
Little Falls, MN 56345

Initiative Foundation Minnesota Early Childhood Initiative Grants 2560
Initiative Foundation Minnesota Early Childhood Initiative Grants are a local, regional and statewide partnership with local leaders to ensure that the quality care and education of young children is a top priority. The goal are to: educate citizens about the first five years of rapid brain development that forms lifetime personalities, social skills and learning capacity; promote parents and families as the primary and most important caregivers of young children, and foster the concept that nurturing and educating young children should be also embraced by entire communities; help community coalitions create a shared vision and plan of action around the care and education of young children and their families; provide training, financial and technical assistance and resource/referral services in order to implement quality community-based opportunities for young children; connect with other early childhood-focused communities statewide; promote and advance local, state and national public policy which supports quality care and education for the youngest citizens; and to create and promote "one voice" around the issue of early care and to speak for those who cannot. Selected communities receive an initial grant of $10,000; leadership and planning training; technical assistance; and referrals to resources.
Requirements: The Foundation services communities in the following Minnesota counties: Benton, Cass, Chisago, Crow Wing, Isanti, Kanabec, Mille Lacs, Morrison, Pine, Sherburne, Stearns, Todd, Wadena, and Wright. Selected communities will: build a diverse coalition; survey their community regarding perceptions and awareness around early childhood issues; and create and carry out projects and programs to help children birth to five-years-old. Coalition are community-based teams made up of parents, childcare providers, kindergarten teachers, school administrators, city officials, business owners and other community members. These teams developed a local vision and plan of action to support young children and their families. Selection is a competitive process. The Foundation selects two communities per round. Contact the Children, Youth and Families Specialist for information.
Geographic Focus: Minnesota
Contact: Sara Dahlquist; (877) 632-9255; sdahlquist@ifound.org
Internet: http://www.ifound.org/grants_program.php
Sponsor: Initiative Foundation
405 First Street SE
Little Falls, MN 56345

Institute for Agriculture and Trade Policy Food and Society Fellowships 2561
The IATP Food and Society Fellows Program provides fellowships to professionals in food and agriculture from across North America, enabling them to use mass media channels to inform and shape the public agenda. The goal of the program is to create sustainable food systems that promote good health, vibrant communities, environmental stewardship, worker justice and accessibility for all. Fellows come from many disciplines: chefs, farmers, nutritionists, activists, public health professionals, fishers, policy experts and academics. Together they form an interdisciplinary team that works to: use communication to influence the issues that reach the public agenda, thereby creating policy changes at the personal, organizational and public policy levels that advance sustainable food and farming systems; increase the mass media communications on issues around sustainable food and farming systems that produce healthy, green, fair and affordable foods; raise the profile of the fellows

as food system experts among media and policymakers; and build capacity, leadership, and cohesiveness in a group of experts who collaborate and communicate using mass media channels to bring sustainable food system issues to the public agenda.
Requirements: Applicants should be U.S. residents actively involved in a professional career that involves two or more of the following: agriculture, health promotion, youth development, food production, and/or policy analysis.
Geographic Focus: All States
Contact: Mark Muller, Director; (612) 870-3420; fax (612) 870-4846; mmuller@iatp.org
Internet: http://www.foodandsocietyfellows.org/about/page/about-us
Sponsor: Institute for Agriculture and Trade Policy
2105 First Avenue South
Minneapolis, MN 55404

Intel Community Grants 2562
The corporation is committed to maintaining and enhancing the quality of life in the communities where the company has a major presence. The primary giving focus is education and vigorous support is given to education programs that advance science, math and technology education, particularly for women and underserved populations. The corporation is also committed to the responsible use of natural resources and funding for environmental programs will be considered. Application information is available online.
Requirements: 501(c)3 nonprofit organizations in Arizona, California, Colorado, Massachusetts, New Mexico, Oregon, Texas, Utah, and Washington are eligible to apply.
Restrictions: Funds are not available for: programs outside the site community; endowment or capital-improvement campaigns; unrestricted gifts to national or international organizations; sectarian or denominational religious organizations; foundations that are strictly grant-making bodies; private schools; organizations that practice discrimination; sporting events or teams; health care organizations; arts organizations; special occasion goodwill advertising; scholarship award in the name of another organization; fund raising activities or events, raffles or giveaways; funds for individuals; travel or tours; school extra-curricular activities/clubs; general operating expenses or debt-retirement for organizations.
Geographic Focus: Arizona, California, Colorado, Massachusetts, New Mexico, Oregon, Texas, Utah, Washington
Contact: Morgan Anderson; (503) 264-1868; morgan.anderson@intel.com
Internet: http://www.intel.com/community/grant.htm
Sponsor: Intel Corporation Foundation
AG6-601, 5200 NE Elam Young Parkway
Hillsboro, OR 97124-6497

Intel Finance Internships 2563
Intel offers Operations Finance internship opportunities for undergraduate and MBA candidates, and Accounting internship opportunities for undergraduate candidates. As a member of the Finance Intern team, individuals will have opportunities to analyze business issues, recommend solutions, demonstrate your analytical and problem solving abilities and work with peers and business partners to influence business decisions that maximize shareholder value. The Finance Summer Intern Program is a twelve week assignment within an Intel Finance group where interns undertake a challenging project designed to blend strategic and operational work. Managers will provide a detailed project plan, meet with Interns regularly to provide support as needed, and help to network within the company to ensure a worthwhile internship experience. Interns receive: competitive salaries; vacation and holiday time; access to Intel University classes for professional and personal development; networking with Intel managers and executives; relocation assistance; and earned credit toward sabbaticals. Undergraduate and graduate level internships are available at all our major U.S. sites.
Requirements: Students must be authorized to work in the United States without restriction, and a background investigation and drug screening are required.
Geographic Focus: All States
Contact: Internship Coordinator; (408) 765-8080; fax (408) 765-9904
Internet: http://www.intel.com/jobs/usa/students/internships/finance.htm
Sponsor: Intel Corporation
2200 Mission College Boulevard
Santa Clara, CA 95054-1549

Intel International Community Grants 2564
The corporation is committed to maintaining and enhancing the quality of life in the communities where the company has a major presence. Primary focus is on education with a strong interest in support of K-12/higher education and community programs that deliver the kind of educational opportunities that all students will need to prepare themselves to succeed in the 21st century. Intel will support additional programs that improve the quality of life in its site communities. These requests will be evaluated on the basis of the services offered and the program's impact on the community; its impact on the youth of our community; the cost-effectiveness of the program and its ability to be effectively measured and replicated; and the potential for Intel employee involvement. Current international community giving includes: Costa Rica, China, Ireland, India, Israel, Malaysia, Philippines, and Russia.
Requirements: Grants are made for local programs located in Intel communities in Costa Rica, China, Ireland, India, Israel, Malaysia, Philippines, and Russia.
Restrictions: Requests are denied for: programs outside the site community; endowment or capital-improvement campaigns; unrestricted gifts to national or international organizations; sectarian or denominational religious organizations; foundations that are strictly grant-making bodies; private schools; organizations that practice discrimination; sporting events or teams; health care organizations; arts organizations; special occasion goodwill advertising; scholarship awards in the name of another organization; fund raising activities or events, raffles or giveaways; individuals; travel or tours.
Geographic Focus: All States, China, Israel, Philippines, Russia

Contact: Morgan Anderson; (503) 264-1868; morgan.anderson@intel.com
Internet: http://www.intel.com/community/international.htm
Sponsor: Intel Corporation
2200 Mission College Boulevard
Santa Clara, CA 95054-1549

Intergrys Corporation Grants 2565
Integrys supports the giving initiatives of Wisconsin Public Service Foundation in Michigan, Minnesota and Wisconsin. Other significant giving by Integrys occurs through programs operated by Peoples Gas and North Shore Gas in Illinois, including the city of Chicago and its 54 suburban communities in northeastern Illinois. Areas if interest include: arts and culture; education (all levels); human services and health; community and neighborhood development; and the environment. Employee volunteers allow staff to give back to the neighborhoods they cherish. Matching funds energize charitable involvement. Categories of giving include health and welfare, civic and community, higher education, and cultural. Most corporate contributions are in the form of unrestricted grants. Types of support include capital grants, endowments, general operating grants, matching gifts, and program grants. Before eligibility is determined, consideration will be given to the background of the organization, the organization's legal status, how the program will benefit the community, whether the organization receives broad community support, the quality of the organization's leadership, and the organization's financial status.
Restrictions: Contributions will not be made to individuals; organizations that discriminate by race, color, creed, or national origin; political organizations or campaigns; organizations whose prime purpose is to influence legislation; religious organizations for religious purposes; agencies owned and operated by local, state, or federal governments; or for trips or tours, or special-occasion or special-occasion or goodwill advertising.
Geographic Focus: Illinois, Michigan, Minnesota, Wisconsin
Contact: Contributions Officer; (312) 240-7516 or (800) 699-1269; fax (312) 240-4389
Internet: http://www.integrysgroup.com/corporate/corporate_giving.aspx
Sponsor: Intergrys Corporation
130 E Randolph Drive, 18th Floor
Chicago, IL 60601

International Association of Emergency Managers (IAEM) Scholarships 2566
The scholarship program was established to nurture, promote and develop disaster preparedness and resistance by furthering the education of students studying the field of emergency management. Through donations from individuals, companies and organizations, IAEM's goal is to raise $100,000 to fund scholarship awards to undergraduate or graduate students enrolled in an accredited college program, pursuing a degree that includes courses in emergency management/community planning (most often as part of a program in public or business administration). For each principal amount of approximately $30,000, IAEM should be able to provide a student with a scholarship of $2,000.
Requirements: Scholarships are awarded to students pursuing an associate or diploma baccalaureate, or graduate degree in emergency management or a closely related field.
Geographic Focus: All States
Date(s) Application is Due: Mar 31
Contact: Dawn M. Shiley-Danzeisen; (703) 538-1795; fax (703) 241-5603; shiley@iaem.com
Internet: http://www.iaem.com/resources/scholarships/intro.htm
Sponsor: International Association of Emergency Managers
201 Park Washington Court
Falls Church, VA 22046-4527

International Human Rights Funders Grants 2567
Human rights grantmaking supports a wide range of efforts to ensure that all people have the opportunity to enjoy a genuinely human existence. As affirmed in the Universal Declaration of Human Rights (UDHR) and the international and domestic laws to which it gave rise, the people of the world are endowed with inalienable civil, cultural, economic, political and social rights. What gives human rights work such power is that all governments, including the United States, have a recognized obligation to respect, protect and fulfill these rights, both domestically and internationally. Increasingly, non-state actors corporations and individuals are also being held accountable. Funders contribute to the advancement of human rights around the world through their grantmaking. Grants varying in type and amount support a broad range of approaches, including: public education to inform people about their human rights and how to exercise them; documenting, reporting and fact-finding to expose human rights violations; litigation to uphold human rights and hold abusers accountable; policy advocacy to ensure that states and non-state actors conform to human rights standards; research and scholarship to define the content of rights; networking and coalition building to further the effectiveness of a global human rights movement; and capacity building for organizations engaged in the above work, locally and internationally.
Requirements: The applicant must be an organization that works to defend or promote human rights; and is based in India, Bangladesh, Pakistan, and be working, in whole or in part, on human rights issues in the country in which the organization is based, or is based in Algeria, Tunisia, or Morocco, and be working, in whole or in part, on human rights issues in the country in which the organization is based.
Restrictions: The fund does not support stand-alone conferences, individuals, businesses, scholarships, fundraising events, university-based research, government agencies, or activities directly or indirectly intended to support candidates for political office.
Geographic Focus: All States
Contact: Michael Hirschhorn; (202) 609-2631; fax (202) 609-2633; MichaelH@ihrfg.org
Internet: http://www.hrfunders.org/hrfunding/index.html
Sponsor: International Human Rights Funders Group
1410 Broadway, 23rd Floor
New York, NY 10018

International Paper Company Foundation Grants — 2568

The Foundation supports non-profit organizations in the communities where employees live and work. The primary areas of support are educational initiatives and employee involvement grants. Given the vast nature of education, the Foundation is focusing on environmental education, literacy and minority career development. Limited funding is provided on a short term basis for new critical community needs projects. Application and guidelines are available online. No phone or email inquiries are welcomed.
Requirements: The Foundation makes grants to nonprofit charitable organizations classified under Section 501(c)3 of the United States Internal Revenue Service Code. In addition, certain municipal, county, state and federal entities are eligible, such as school districts and police departments. The Foundation will not review a proposal unless the tax-exempt organization takes full legal, fiscal and administrative responsibility for the request.
Restrictions: The foundation does not provide funds for individuals; academic scholarships; endowments; capital expenses; multi-year commitments; private foundations; veterans or labor groups, religious or political groups, or organizations that have as their primary purpose attempting to influence legislation; organizations that discriminate on the basis of race, color, religion, sex, sexual orientation, or national origin; grants to primarily benefit employees or families of International Paper, or pay for services, subscriptions, tuition, or memberships; sponsorships or advertising; travel expenses for groups or individuals; team sponsorships; national conferences, sporting events, and other one-time events; expansion of educational programs, or summer programs outside of our education focus areas; or more than 20 percent of a charitable organization's total income.
Geographic Focus: All States
Date(s) Application is Due: Feb 1; May 1; Aug 1; Nov 1
Contact: Kim Wirth, Executive Director
Internet: http://www.internationalpaper.com/Our%20Company/IP%20Giving/A_IP%20Foundation/Application_Guidelines.html#
Sponsor: International Paper Company Foundation
6400 Poplar Avenue
Memphis, TN 38197

International Paper Environmental Awards — 2569

This award is presented annually by International Paper, in partnership with The Conservation Fund to an educator who has developed an innovative approach to communicating to students an understanding that the relationship between a healthy environment and a healthy economy is not a mutually exclusive one. This person initiates environmental education that significantly improves student comprehension of environmental issues, fosters an understanding of the link between environmental protection and economic growth, demonstrates leadership and inspires achievement. Nomination forms are available online. Only online submissions are considered.
Requirements: An educator who has developed an innovative approach to environmental education that: results in significantly improved comprehension of environmental issues; fosters understanding of the link between environmental protection and economic growth; demonstrates leadership; and inspires achievement is eligible to apply.
Geographic Focus: All States
Date(s) Application is Due: Apr 15
Contact: Administrator; (703) 525-6300; postmaster@conservationfund.org
Internet: http://www.conservationfund.org/?article=2331
Sponsor: Conservation Fund
1655 N Fort Myer Drive, Suite 1300
Arlington, VA 22209-2156

Internet Society Fellowships — 2570

In its long tradition of helping build technical capacity in less developed countries, ISOC provides a Fellowship program to enable more technologists from developing regions to attend in person at Internet Engineering Task Force (IETF) meetings. The ISOC Fellowship to the IETF covers the cost of attending an IETF meeting for the selected Fellows and pairs each with an IETF veteran who serves as their meeting mentor. As such, the main purposes of the IETF Fellowship program are to: raise global awareness about the IETF and its work; foster greater understanding of and participation in the work of the IETF by technologists from the developing world; provide an opportunity for networking with individuals from around the world with similar technical interests; identify and foster potential future leaders from developing regions, and demonstrate the Internet community's commitment to fostering greater global participation in Internet Forums such as the IETF.
Geographic Focus: All States
Contact: Kevin Craemer; (703) 439-2120; craemer@isoc.org or isoc@isoc.org
Internet: http://www.isoc.org/educpillar/fellowship/
Sponsor: Internet Society
1775 Wiehle Avenue
Reston, VA 20190-5108

Iowa Arts Council Artists in Schools/Communities Residency Grants — 2571

The program helps to bring professional teaching artists into communities to benefit students and teachers. Students learn to be critical and visionary thinkers and grow in confidence and self-esteem. Teachers benefit by enhancing their existing curriculum and discovering new approaches to teaching. Application information is available online.
Requirements: Iowa nonprofits, schools, area education agencies, local, county, state and federal governmental agencies, and tribal councils are eligible to apply.
Restrictions: Funding is not available for: students; applicants who have received Iowa Arts Council grants within the same fiscal year; applicants who have an outstanding late Final Report for a previously funded application.
Geographic Focus: Iowa
Date(s) Application is Due: Apr 1; Oct 1
Amount of Grant: Up to 10,000 USD
Contact: Linda Lee, Grants Assistant; (515) 242-6194; Linda.Lee@iowa.gov
Internet: http://www.iowaartscouncil.org/funding/artist-residency-grant/index.shtml
Sponsor: Iowa Arts Council
600 E Locust, Capitol Complex
Des Moines, IA 50319-0290

IRA Pearson Foundation-IRA-Rotary Literacy Awards — 2572

The Pearson Foundation-IRA-Rotary Literacy Awards will fund literacy projects with IRA and Rotarian members working together to improve the literacy needs of the local community or anywhere in the world. In addition to the cash award, each honoree will identify a literacy organization to receive up to 1,000 books through the digital literacy initiative, We Give Books, created by the Pearson Foundation and Penguin. For each book read at wegivebooks.org, a book will be donated to the predetermined literacy organization. Two awards of $2,500 each are given. Specific guidelines and a current application are available at the website.
Requirements: Applicants must be IRA members or Rotary members in good standing.
Geographic Focus: All States, All Countries
Date(s) Application is Due: Jun 15
Amount of Grant: 2,500 USD
Contact: Awards Contact; (302) 731-1600; fax (302) 731-1057; irawash@reading.org
Internet: http://www.reading.org/Resources/AwardsandGrants/award_pearsonfoundation.aspx
Sponsor: International Reading Association
800 Barksdale Road, P.O. Box 8139
Newark, DE 19714-8139

IRC Community Collaboratives for Refugee Women and Youth Grants — 2573

With support from the Office of Refugee Resettlement through the Community and Family Strengthening Initiative, the International Rescue Committee (IRC) offers funding, technical assistance, and training to refugee service providers nationwide to: provide refugee women and youth with the tools they need to become self-reliant and integrated into their communities; develop model programs that address the unique needs of refugee women and youth; advance awareness of the valuable social and economic contributions refugee women and youth bring to their communities. Applicants should contact the IRC for current applications and deadlines.
Geographic Focus: All States
Contact: Robert Carey; (212) 551-3000; info@theirc.org
Internet: http://www.theirc.org/community
Sponsor: International Rescue Committee
122 East 42nd Street
New York, NY 10168

Ireland Family Foundation Grants — 2574

Established in 2000, the Ireland Family Foundation givings primarily in North Carolina with some funding available in California. The Foundations supports non-profit organizations involved with autism research, human services and education.
Requirements: The initial approach should be in the form of a letter, followed up with a proposal containing : a copy of IRS Determination Letter; a detailed description of project and amount of funding requested.
Restrictions: No grants to individuals.
Geographic Focus: California, North Carolina
Amount of Grant: 10,000 - 60,000 USD
Samples: ARC of Orange County, Chapel Hill, NC., $35,000;
Contact: Lori Ireland, President; (919) 932-3556
Sponsor: Ireland Family Foundation
1434 Arboretum Drive
Chapel Hill, NC 27517-9161

IREX Egypt Media Development Program (MDP) Grants — 2575

In collaboration with Media Development Program (MDP) partners Management Systems International; CARE; and D3 Systems, IREX works with media outlets and training institutes to improve the professionalism and sustainability of Egypt's media sector. MDP offers training, consulting, and equipment assistance to Egyptian print and electronic media as well as to universities and other media support organizations. Key issues are to: build media training capacity in Egypt to promote professional development among mid-career professionals, emerging journalists, and media managers; improve the management and economic viability of Egyptian print and broadcast sectors; strengthen the professionalism and organizational capacity of local and regional media; and strengthen media associations and NGOs in support of media excellence and policy reform.
Geographic Focus: All States
Contact: Program Officer; (202) 628-8188; fax (202) 628-8189; media@irex.org
Internet: http://www.irex.org/programs/mdp/index.asp
Sponsor: International Research and Exchanges Board
2121 K Street NW, Suite 700
Washington, DC 20037

IREX Kosovo Civil Society Project (KCSP) Grants — 2576

The Program is aimed at assisting Kosovo's Nongovernmental Organization (NGO) community in becoming a truly indigenous, viable sector that plays an important role in representing and serving Kosovo's diverse citizenry and shaping public policy. IREX works with individual NGOs and coalitions to strengthen their capacity to advocate for public policy issues while progressing toward forming an inclusive, transparent, and credible Kosovo network of NGOs. In partnership with the Advocacy Training and Resource Center (ATRC), the Program provides grants to support issue-specific campaigns,

coalition-building and training on effective advocacy, coalition-building techniques, and public relations through the media.
Geographic Focus: All States
Contact: Program Officer; (202) 628-8188; fax (202) 628-8189; kcsp@irex.org
Internet: http://www.irex.org/programs/kcsp/index.asp
Sponsor: International Research and Exchanges Board
2121 K Street NW, Suite 700
Washington, DC 20037

IREX MENA Media TV Production Fund Grants   2577
The Program awards small grants twice a year to media outlets, production companies, and individuals based in the Middle East and North Africa or with nationality from the region, for productions that support increasing public dialogue and awareness on current and locally-oriented issues, including those that are under-served by current media production. A list of sample topics includes, but is not exclusive to: employment, elections, education, trade and business, profiles of innovative/emerging leaders, the role of women in society, youth, environment, housing/urban development, minorities and human interest stories. Project applications that include collaboration among television stations, print, radio, or Internet outlets are encouraged.
Geographic Focus: All States
Contact: Program Associate; (202) 628-8188; fax (202) 628-8189; mena@irex.org
Internet: http://www.irex.org/programs/MENAmedia/mena_info.asp
Sponsor: International Research and Exchanges Board
2121 K Street NW, Suite 700
Washington, DC 20037

IREX Moldova Citizen Participation Program (CPP) Grants   2578
This is a five-year program to expand citizen awareness, promote civic engagement and encourage self-reliance while improving living and social conditions throughout Moldova. IREX provides training, mentoring, and funding for citizen-initiated projects. IREX's regional network of local civic trainers assists citizens in mobilizing their communities. The Program funds projects initiated, designed, implemented, and monitored by Moldovan citizens. Initially, IREX funded 52 projects in 50 villages to support infrastructure and civic works, income generation and job creation, and/or social service projects.
Geographic Focus: All States
Contact: Program Officer; (202) 628-8188; fax (202) 628-8189; cpp@irex.org
Internet: http://www.irex.org/programs/cpp/index.asp
Sponsor: International Research and Exchanges Board
2121 K Street NW, Suite 700
Washington, DC 20037

IREX Project Smile Grants   2579
This is a community development program for alumni of select Bureau of Educational and Cultural Affairs (ECA) sponsored programs. Grants are awarded to alumni to implement community service activities that will benefit an underprivileged group in their local community such as children at an orphanage, the disabled or the elderly. Selected projects benefit an under-served population and are community service-oriented. Sample project ideas include cleaning a schoolyard, planning an activity at a children's hospital or orphanage, and coordinating a book drive. The program is completed several times a year. Applicants should contact their local IREX office for the next deadline and a copy of the application.
Requirements: Alumni of the following ECA-sponsored programs are eligible to apply: FSA Undergraduate Program (UGRAD); Edmund S. Muskie Graduate Fellowship Program (Muskie); Freedom Support Act Fellowships in Contemporary Issues (CI); and Russian-U.S. Young Leadership Fellows for Public Service Program (YLF).
Geographic Focus: All States
Contact: Program Officer; (202) 628-8188; fax (202) 628-8189; smiles@irex.org
Internet: http://www.irex.org/programs/smile/index.asp
Sponsor: International Research and Exchanges Board
2121 K Street NW, Suite 700
Washington, DC 20037

IREX Russia Civil Society Support Program (CSSP) Grants   2580
The Program is aimed at strengthening the nongovernmental organization (NGO) sector in Russia, particularly in the Russian Far East. CSSP promotes an environment where the government actively reaches out to involve NGOs in policy development and, in turn, NGOs demonstrate the skills and capacity to advocate their positions in a constructive manner. Small grants support NGO coalitions and alliances for advocacy projects benefiting their constituents. To date, regional and inter-regional coalitions have been initiated to advocate for housing rights, welfare of disabled children, education reform, and environmental protection in twenty regions of the Russian Federation.
Geographic Focus: All States, Russia
Contact: Program Officer; (202) 628-8188; fax (202) 628-8189; csd@irex.org
Internet: http://www.irex.org/programs/cssp/index.asp
Sponsor: International Research and Exchanges Board
2121 K Street NW, Suite 700
Washington, DC 20037

IREX Small Grant Fund for Civil Society Projects in Africa and Asia   2581
IREX will provide a select number of grants of up to US$10,000 to local private, nongovernmental institutions in Africa and Asia. Proposed project must focus on strengthening civic engagement in one of the following ways: institutional development of civil society organizations, to include support for training and technical assistance. Preference given to organizations and/or initiatives focused on advocacy, transparency and accountability, anti-corruption and/or citizen participation; women's empowerment initiatives that promote the full participation of women in all levels of economic, political and /or social life (special use of technology is encouraged); and vocational training or educational programs addressing child labor or trafficking, child soldiers, HIV/AIDS, learning disabilities or special needs. In lieu of a formal application or proposal, IREX requests that interested organizations submit a brief letter of inquiry, of no more than two pages, to help determine whether the proposed project would address IREX's present interests. Inquiry letters will be reviewed on a rolling basis and if they meet current interests, the grant seeker will be asked to submit a formal proposal. Inquiry letters can be sent by mail, fax or email.
Requirements: Applicants must be a private nongovernmental organization based solely in Africa or Asia.
Restrictions: The Program will not fund: grants to individuals; grants for university study, graduate study or research; or grants to attend conferences, trainings or workshops.
Geographic Focus: All States, Algeria, Angola, Benin, Botswana, Burkina Faso, Burundi, Cameroon, Cape Verde, Central African Republic, Chad, Comoros, Congo, Congo, Democratic Republic of, Cote d' Ivoire (Ivory Coast), Djibouti, Egypt, Equatorial Guinea, Eritrea, Ethiopia, Gabon, Gambia, Ghana, Guinea, Guinea-Bissau, Kenya, Lesotho, Liberia, Libya, Madagascar, Malawi, Mali, Mauritania, Mauritius, Morocco, Mozambique, Namibia, Niger, Nigeria, Rwanda, Sao Tome & Principe, Senegal, Seychelles, Sierra Leone, Somalia, South Africa, Sudan, Swaziland
Contact: Program Officers; (202) 628-8188; fax (202) 628-8189; sgfcsd@irex.org
Internet: http://www.irex.org/programs/sgf/index.asp
Sponsor: International Research and Exchanges Board
2121 K Street NW, Suite 700
Washington, DC 20037

IREX Small Grant Fund for Media Projects in Africa and Asia   2582
IREX will provide a select number of grants of up to US$10,000 to local private, nongovernmental institutions in Africa and Asia. Proposed project must focus on promoting professionalism and independence in media in one of the following ways: journalism training, to include basic reporting skills, environmental reporting, business and economics reporting, investigative reporting, and other specialized reporting skills; media advocacy, to include education on the value of professional media, development of media legislation, community outreach, and training in issues related to free media; and institutional development of media and media-related institutions, to include support for equipment and operational costs. In lieu of a formal application or proposal, IREX requests that interested organizations submit a brief letter of inquiry, of no more than two pages, to help determine whether the proposed project would address IREX's present interests. Inquiry letters will be reviewed on a rolling basis and if they meet current interests, the grant seeker will be asked to submit a formal proposal. Inquiry letters can be sent by mail, fax or email.
Requirements: Applicants must be a private nongovernmental organization based solely in Africa or Asia.
Restrictions: The Program will not fund: grants to individuals; grants for university study, graduate study or research; or grants to attend conferences, trainings or workshops.
Geographic Focus: All States, Algeria, Angola, Benin, Botswana, Burkina Faso, Burundi, Cameroon, Cape Verde, Central African Republic, Chad, Comoros, Congo, Congo, Democratic Republic of, Cote d' Ivoire (Ivory Coast), Djibouti, Egypt, Equatorial Guinea, Eritrea, Ethiopia, Gabon, Gambia, Ghana, Guinea, Guinea-Bissau, Kenya, Lesotho, Liberia, Libya, Madagascar, Malawi, Mali, Mauritania, Mauritius, Morocco, Mozambique, Namibia, Niger, Nigeria, Rwanda, Sao Tome & Principe, Senegal, Seychelles, Sierra Leone, Somalia, South Africa, Sudan, Swaziland
Contact: Program Officers; (202) 628-8188; fax (202) 628-8189; sgfmdd@irex.org
Internet: http://www.irex.org/programs/sgf/index.asp
Sponsor: International Research and Exchanges Board
2121 K Street NW, Suite 700
Washington, DC 20037

IREX Yemen Women's Leadership Program (YWLP) Grants   2583
The Yemen Women's Leadership Program (YWLP), launched in 2006, is a three-year program that builds the technical and professional skills of young women, age 22-25, to become leaders in civil society and media. Young Yemen women participate in: intensive English language, computer skills, and organizational management classes; training in life skills, decision making, goal setting, self-confidence building, and negotiation skills; study tours to NGO projects sites, media outlets, and donor offices; and working as volunteer interns at NGOs and media outlets for four to six weeks, honing their skills and gaining exposure to the work environment. All participants have the opportunity to design a grant proposal for civil society and media projects, of which 20 receive program funding. Grant applications should be for expansion of services, creation of pilot projects, and roll-out of proven best practices.
Geographic Focus: All States
Contact: Program Officer; (202) 628-8188; fax (202) 628-8189; ywlp@irex.org
Internet: http://www.irex.org/programs/ywlp/index.asp
Sponsor: International Research and Exchanges Board
2121 K Street NW, Suite 700
Washington, DC 20037

Irving S. Gilmore Foundation Grants   2584
The Irving S. Gilmore Foundation endeavors to develop and to enrich the Greater Kalamazoo community of Michigan and, its residents by supporting the work of nonprofit organizations. The Foundation's funding priorities are: health and well-being; arts; human services; education; community development; culture and humanities. Organizations that are first time Foundation applicants or have not received Foundation funding since 2007 must contact the Foundation at least four weeks prior to an applicable submission deadline.
Requirements: The Foundation supports Kalamazoo County projects, programs, and purposes carried out by charitable institutions, primarily public charities and governmental entities.

Restrictions: Grants are not made to individuals.
Geographic Focus: Michigan
Date(s) Application is Due: Jan 4; Mar 1; May 3; Jul 1; Sep 1; Nov 1
Contact: Janice C. Elliott; (269) 342-6411; fax (269) 342-6465
Internet: http://www.isgilmorefoundation.org/communityinvolvement.htm
Sponsor: Irving S. Gilmore Foundation
136 East Michigan Avenue, Suite 900
Kalamazoo, MI 49007-3912

Irvin Stern Foundation Grants 2585
The Foundation awards grants to nonprofits primarily in the following areas of interest: human services; civic affairs; arts; and Jewish welfare. Other grant requests should be within the Foundation's additional areas of interest which include: aiding the under-served, the poor, and disadvantaged; improving the quality of life in urban communities; and enhancing Jewish community, education and spirituality. Since there are no specified application forms, interested applicants should submit an online letter of inquiry or application letters mailed to the Foundation office.
Requirements: The Foundation makes grants to tax-exempt organizations.
Restrictions: The Foundation does not contribute to endowments, capital campaigns, capital construction projects, and academic or medical research programs of any kind.
Geographic Focus: All States
Samples: Lakeview Pantry, Chicago, Illinois, $10,000 - general operating funds (2011); Celiac Disease Center at Columbia University Medical Center, New York, New York, $10,000 - general operating funds (2011); Generation Rescue, Tarzana, California, $5,000 - general operating funds (2011).
Contact: Christine Flood, (312) 321-9402; christine@irvinstern.org
Internet: http://irvinstern.org/guidelines/
Sponsor: Irvin Stern Foundation
4 East Ohio Street, Studio 6
Chicago, IL 60611

Isabel Allende Foundation Esperanza Grants 2586
The Foundation is guided by a vision of a world in which women have achieved social and economic justice. The vision includes empowerment of women and girls and protection of women and children. The Foundation feels that the way to achieve empowerment is: reproductive self-determination; health care; and education. Application information is available online.
Requirements: 501(c)3 organizations (and equivalent international organizations) are eligible to apply. Priority is given to programs in the San Francisco Bay Area and Chile.
Restrictions: The foundation does not fund capital campaigns, individual trips or tours, conferences, or events; and projects that benefit political, religious, and/or military organizations. Individuals are not eligible to receive grants and should not apply.
Geographic Focus: California
Date(s) Application is Due: Jan 1; Apr 1; Jul 1; Oct 1
Amount of Grant: 1,000 - 5,000 USD
Contact: Lori Barra, (415) 289-0992; lori@isabelallendefoundation.org
Internet: http://www.isabelallendefoundation.org/iaf.php?l=en&p=application
Sponsor: Isabel Allende Foundation
116 Caledonia Street
Sausalito, CA 94965

ISA John Z. Duling Grants 2587
The goal of the program is to provide seed money or partial support for research and technology transfer projects addressing topics that have the potential of benefiting the everyday work of arborists. Proposals in the following priority areas are more likely to be funded: root and soil management; planting and establishment; plant health care; and risk assessment and worker safety. Application information is available online.
Requirements: Proposals must be submitted on the application form or an exact duplicate. No faxed or reduced copies of the original will be accepted. Applications sent electronically will not be accepted.
Restrictions: Funds cannot be used to pay for overhead expenses or student tuition and fees.
Geographic Focus: All States
Amount of Grant: Up to 7,500 USD
Contact: Executive Director; (630) 221-8127; fax (630) 690-0702; treefund@treefund.org
Internet: http://www.treefund.org/grants/Grants.aspx
Sponsor: International Society of Arboriculture
711 East Roosevelt Road
Wheaton, IL 60187

ISI William E. Simon Fellowships for Noble Purpose 2588
The fellowship is an unrestricted cash grant that will be awarded to those graduating college seniors who have demonstrated passion, dedication, a high capacity for self-direction, and originality in pursuit of a goal that will strengthen civil society. Examples of how recipients may use their award include: engage directly in the civic life of their community; help to create opportunity for others, including job creation; advance their expertise; and fund the ultimate realization of their noble purpose. Each year ISI will award three Fellowships for Noble Purpose. One top award and two additional fellowships will be awarded each year. Guidelines and application are available online.
Requirements: Graduating college seniors who embody Mr. Simon's passion to make the most of their talents in such a way that they both realize their own capacities and contribute to larger causes beyond self are eligible.
Geographic Focus: All States
Date(s) Application is Due: Jan 16
Amount of Grant: 40,000 USD
Contact: Coordinator; (800) 526-7022 or (302) 652-4600; simon@isi.org
Internet: http://www.isi.org/programs/fellowships/simon.html
Sponsor: Intercollegiate Studies Institute
3901 Centerville Road, P.O. Box 4431
Wilmington, DE 19807-0431

Ittleson Foundation AIDS Grants 2589
In regards to AIDS, the foundation is particularly interested in new model, pilot, and demonstration efforts: addressing the needs of underserved at-risk populations and especially those programs recognizing the overlap between such programs; responding to the challenges facing community-based AIDS service organizations and those organizations addressing systemic change; providing meaningful school-based sex education; making treatment information accessible, available and easily understandable to those in need of it; or, addressing the psycho-social needs of those infected and affected by AIDS, especially adolescents.
Requirements: Tax-exempt organizations may apply.
Restrictions: The foundation generally does not provide funds for capital building projects, endowments, grants to individuals, scholarships or internships (except as part of a program), direct service programs (especially outside New York City), projects that are local in focus and unlikely to be replicated, continuing or general support, projects and organizations that are international in scope or purpose, or biomedical research.
Geographic Focus: All States
Date(s) Application is Due: Sep 1
Contact: Anthony C. Wood, Executive Director; (212) 794-2008; fax (212) 794-0351
Internet: http://www.ittlesonfoundation.org/aids.html
Sponsor: Ittleson Foundation
15 E 67th Street, 5th Floor
New York, NY 10021

Ittleson Foundation Mental Health Grants 2590
For this program, the foundation is interested in innovative, pilot, model and demonstration projects that are: fighting the stigma associated with mental illness and working to change the public's negative perception of people who have mental illness; utilizing new knowledge and current technological advances to improve programs and services for people who have mental illness; bringing the full benefits of this new knowledge and technology to those who presently do not have access to them; or, advancing preventative mental health efforts, especially those targeted to youth and adolescents, with a special focus on strategies that involve parents, teachers, and others in close contact with these populations.
Requirements: Tax-exempt organizations may apply.
Restrictions: The foundation generally does not provide funds for capital building projects, endowments, grants to individuals, scholarships or internships (except as part of a program), direct service programs (especially outside New York City), projects that are local in focus and unlikely to be replicated, continuing or general support, projects and organizations that are international in scope or purpose, or biomedical research.
Geographic Focus: All States
Date(s) Application is Due: Sep 1
Contact: Anthony C. Wood, Executive Director; (212) 794-2008; fax (212) 794-0351
Internet: http://www.ittlesonfoundation.org/mental.html
Sponsor: Ittleson Foundation
15 E 67th Street, 5th Floor
New York, NY 10021

IYI Responsible Fatherhood Grants 2591
The Institute promotes the healthy development of children and youth by serving the institutions and people of Indiana who work on their behalf. It is IYI's intention to help build the capacity of grassroots coalitions made up of both community and faith-based organizations to provide services that promote responsible fatherhood in their local community or region. The program provides technical assistance and financial awards to five community collaborations that have implemented practical strategies for helping dads become more involved with their children.
Requirements: With federal funding provided by the Promoting Responsible Fatherhood Community Access Grant, IYI seeks to identify and provide grants to five community coalitions of small faith-based and community partnering organizations that will deliver direct services with IYI's coordination. Coalitions must have from six to eight partnering faith-based or community organizations (micro-partners), each having a total annual operating budget of no more than $300,000 OR six or fewer full-time equivalent employees.
Geographic Focus: Indiana
Contact: Nicole Brock; (317) 396-2700 or (800) 343-7060; fax (317) 396-2701; iyi@iyi.org
Internet: http://www.iyi.org/parent-involvement/responsible-fatherhood.aspx
Sponsor: Indiana Youth Institute
603 E Washington Street, Suite 800
Indianapolis, IN 46204-2692

J.B. Reynolds Foundation Grants 2592
The foundation makes grants in the local Kansas City, MO, area, up to a 150-mile radius of the city. Grants are awarded for building and equipment, community development, medical research, social welfare, and the arts and humanities. Some support is given to colleges and universities. Additional types of support include general operating support, continuing support, annual campaigns, endowment funds, publications, and research. The board meets in April and December of each year to consider letters of requests, and only invited proposals are reviewed. All grants are awarded in December.
Requirements: 501(c)3 organizations in the Kansas City area may submit applications.
Geographic Focus: Missouri

Amount of Grant: 5,000 - 50,000 USD
Contact: Richard L. Finn, Secretary-Treasurer; (816) 753-7000; fax (816) 753-1354
Sponsor: J.B. Reynolds Foundation
P.O. Box 219139
Kansas City, MO 64141-6139

J. Bulow Campbell Foundation Grants 2593

The foundation supports nonprofit organizations in Alabama, Florida, Georgia, North or South Carolina, and Tennessee in its areas of interest, including communities, the arts, education, youth, and religious concerns of the Church. Highest priority is given to capital funding rather than providing support for current operating expenses or recurring programs. Application information is available online.
Requirements: Nonprofit organizations in Alabama, Florida, Georgia, North Carolina, South Carolina, and Tennessee may apply. Priority is given to Georgia and almost exclusively in Atlanta.
Restrictions: No grants or loans are made to individuals.
Geographic Focus: Alabama, Florida, Georgia, North Carolina, South Carolina, Tennessee
Date(s) Application is Due: Jan 1; Apr 1; Jul 1; Oct 1
Contact: Betsy Verner, Associate Director; (404) 658-9066
Internet: http://www.jbcf.org
Sponsor: J. Bulow Campbell Foundation
3050 Peachtree Road NW, Suite 270
Atlanta, GA 30303

J.C. Penney Company Grants 2594

The corporate contributions program awards grants to 501(c)3 nonprofit organizations in the company's areas of interest, including improvement of K- through 12th-grade education through curriculum-based after school care, with a priority on JCPenney Afterschool; support/promotion of associate (employee) volunteerism, primarily through the James Cash Penney Awards for Community Service; and United Way (most of JCPenney's support for health and welfare issues is contributed through local United Ways). Funding for other types of programs and projects is limited. Funding is concentrated on projects and organizations that serve a broad sector of the community; national projects that have a multiplier effect by benefiting local organizations across the country; nonprofits offering direct services; and projects with proven track records. Proposals are accepted year-round. There is no formal grant application. Interested applicants should submit a brief letter of inquiry. Submission information is available online.
Requirements: JCPenney only considers grants to organizations with 501(c)3 status or organizations that are a political subdivision of the state as described 170(c)1 of the IRS.
Restrictions: JCPenney refrains from or limits support of: individuals (including family reunions); individual student exchange/travel programs; membership organizations, unless the project benefits the entire community; religious organizations, unless the project benefits the entire community; journal or program advertising; fundraising dinners, luncheons or other types of benefits; merchandise donations; door prizes, gift certificates, or other giveaways; conferences and seminars; capital campaigns and multiyear pledges; international projects except in countries with corporate business locations; pilot projects; film and video projects; research projects; scholarships, except at colleges and universities with which the company has a recruiting relationship; higher education institutions, unless the company has a business or recruiting relationship; individual K-12 schools, unless the company has a business partnership with the school (including proms, graduations, PTOs and PTAs); or donations of returned, damaged or excess merchandise. JCPenney does not offer a matching gifts program at this time.
Geographic Focus: All States
Contact: Jeannette M. Siegel, Community Relations and Contributions Manager; (972) 431-1349; fax (972) 431-1355; jsiegel@jcpenney.com
Internet: http://www.jcpenney.net/about/social_resp/community/default.aspx
Sponsor: J.C. Penney Company
P.O. Box 10001
Dallas, TX 75301-8101

J.E. and L.E. Mabee Foundation Grants 2595

The purpose of the Foundation is to aid Christian religious organizations, charitable organizations, institutions of higher learning, hospitals and other organizations of a general charitable nature. The Foundation favors organizations that combine sound character and stability with progressiveness and purpose. There is no formal application procedure. Proposal submission information is available online.
Requirements: Nonprofit, tax exempt, and not tax- supported organizations in Arkansas, Kansas, Missouri, New Mexico, Oklahoma, and Texas are eligible.
Restrictions: The foundation does not generally favor grants for deficit financing and debt retirement (except a construction contract that was executed prior to the time of application); operating or program funds or annual fundraising campaigns (except Junior Achievement and United Way in Tulsa, OK, and Midland, TX); reserve purposes or for projects likely to be long delayed; endowments; governmental owned or operated institutions and/or facilities (such as state universities and municipal parks and libraries); educational institutions below the college level; furnishing or equipment (except major medical equipment); or churches.
Geographic Focus: Arkansas, Kansas, Missouri, New Mexico, Oklahoma, Texas
Contact: Thomas R. Brett, Director; (918) 584-4286
Internet: http://www.mabeefoundation.com/policies.htm
Sponsor: J.E. and L.E. Mabee Foundation
Mid-Continent Tower, 401 South Boston Avenue, Suite 3001
Tulsa, OK 74103-4017

J. Edwin Treakle Foundation Grants 2596

Incorporated in 1963 in Virginia, the J. Edwin Treakle Foundation awards funding to a number of educational, civic, and community organizations in mostly the Gloucester/Hampton Roads/Norfolk region. Some organizations from other areas in Virginia are also funded. The Foundation's primary fields of interest include: animal welfare, arts, children and youth services, community and economic development, disaster assistance (fire prevention and control), education, health care, human services, public libraries, and Protestant agencies and churches. Types of support include annual campaigns, building and renovation, capital campaigns, continuing support, equipment purchase, general operating support, and scholarship funding. Applicants should begin by contacting the Foundation via telephone or by letter to request an application. Requests should be submitted between January 1 and April 30.
Restrictions: No grant funding is offered to individuals.
Geographic Focus: Virginia
Date(s) Application is Due: Apr 30
Amount of Grant: 500 - 50,000 USD
Contact: John Warren Cooke, President; (804) 693-0881
Sponsor: J. Edwin Treakle Foundation, Inc.
P.O. Box 1157
Gloucester, VA 23061-1157

J. F. Maddox Foundation Grants 2597

The mission of the Foundation is to significantly improve the quality of life in southeastern New Mexico. The Foundation is most interested in supporting initiatives that strive to obtain well-planned project outcomes. The Foundation has redirected its focus toward economic and community development initiatives in an effort to provide opportunities for long-term economic vitality within Lea County. Application information is available online.
Requirements: Nonprofit organizations and governmental agencies seeking grants for the explicit benefit of Lea County, New Mexico are eligible.
Restrictions: Grants are not made to individuals, for the express benefit of an individual, or to other private foundations.
Geographic Focus: New Mexico
Amount of Grant: 5,000 - 700,000 USD
Contact: Jennifer Townsend; (575) 393-6338, ext. 23; jtownsend@jfmaddox.org
Internet: http://www.jfmaddox.org/areas_of_emphasis.asp
Sponsor: J. F. Maddox Foundation
P.O. Box 2588
Hobbs, NM 88241-2588

J. Jill Compassion Fund Grants 2598

The J. Jill Group establishes long-term partnerships with nonprofit organizations whose missions are to aid women and children in need. Organizations serving homeless or at-risk women by providing job training, transitional and/or affordable housing, education, emergency shelter, or other types of aid will be considered upon submission of a grant proposal. Grants are considered for existing programs only. Guidelines are available online.
Requirements: Eligible organizations: community-based organizations serving poor and homeless women in their respective states; federal tax-exempt organizations with 501(c)3 tax-exempt status; organizations located near one or more J. Jill stores in Michigan, Oregon, Washington, Maryland, Pennsylvania and Wisconsin.
Restrictions: Funds are not available for: individuals, including scholarships or travel-related expenses paid to individuals; political, sectarian, fraternal or religious organizations; sponsorship of conferences, sporting events, athletic teams or pageants; advertising in programs, bulletins, yearbooks or brochures; film or television productions; national organizations or their local affiliates; individual clubs, troops or school classrooms; single disease/issue information and research organizations; annual operating expenses; organizations or projects focused outside the United States.
Geographic Focus: All States
Amount of Grant: 5,000 USD
Contact: Program Supervisor; jjill.com
Internet: http://www.jjill.com/jjillonline/compassion/community.aspx?BID=S200812707 325273A414245FA549F090DA25&h=M&sk=M
Sponsor: J. Jill Compassion Fund
4 Batterymarch Park
Quincy, MA 02169

J. Knox Gholston Foundation Grants 2599

The J. Knox Gholston Foundation's mission is to support charitable organizations that provide for the education of children within the City of Comer in Madison County, Georgia. The Foundation is interested in capital and instructional projects that advance academic achievement. The Foundation may also consider at times other charitable organizations serving Comer, Georgia. Grants from the J. Knox Gholston Foundation are primarily one year in duration; on occasion, multi-year support is awarded. Applicants must apply online at the grant website. Applicants are strongly encouraged to do the following before applying: review the downloadable state application procedures for additional helpful information and clarifications; review the downloadable online-application guidelines at the grant website; review the foundation's funding history (link is available from the grant website); review the online application questions in advance; and review the list of required attachments. These will generally include: a list of board members, financial statements (audited, reviewed, or compiled by independent auditor); an organization summary; a list of other funding sources; an IRS Determination letter; and other required documents. All attachments must be uploaded in the online application as PDF, Word, or Excel files. The J. Knox Gholston Foundation application deadlines are January 15 and May 15. Applications must be submitted by 11:59 p.m. on the deadline dates. Applicants will be notified of grant decisions by letter within one to two months after the deadline.

Requirements: Applicants must have 501(c)3 tax-exempt status and serve residents in Madison County, Georgia. A breakdown of number/percentage of people served by county is required on the online application.
Restrictions: The foundation does not support requests from individuals, organizations attempting to influence policy through direct lobbying, or any political campaigns.
Geographic Focus: Georgia
Date(s) Application is Due: Jan 15; May 15
Contact: Quanda Allen, Vice President; (404) 264-1377; quanda.allen@baml.com
Internet: https://www.bankofamerica.com/philanthropic/fn_search.action
Sponsor: J. Knox Gholston Foundation
3414 Peachtree Road, N.E., Suite 1475, GA7-813-14-04
Atlanta, GA 30326-1113

J.L. Bedsole Foundation Grants   2600
The Foundation considers requests that most closely match its overall mission: to improve the quality of life for the citizens of Southwest Alabama and to strengthen the communities in which they live. The Foundation will consider only those grant applications that meet several of the following guidelines. The project addresses needs in at least one of the following areas: education, arts and culture, health and human services and economic development; potential for permanent, enduring benefits that will provide value to the community and the residents of Southwest Alabama; diverse groups are collaborating on the project to achieve common goals; the organization and the project clearly demonstrate sound fiscal management and accountability; the organization attracts multiple sources of support for the project; the project addresses underserved segments of the population, the economically disadvantaged or citizens of rural communities. The Foundation offers a scholarship program as well, see: http://www.jlbedsolefoundation.org/default.asp?ID=7 for details and guidelines.
Requirements: Nonprofit organizations in Mobile, Baldwin, Clarke, Monroe and Washington County, Alabama are eligible to apply.
Restrictions: The Foundation will not support the following: grants that support political activities or attempts to influence action on specific legislation; multiple year pledges nor make grants beyond the current year; grants to endowment funds of other organizations; grants are not made directly to individuals; grants are not made to organizations, programs or projects outside of the State of Alabama.
Geographic Focus: Alabama
Contact: Christopher L. Lee; (251) 432-3369; chrislee@jlbedsolefoundation.org
Internet: http://www.jlbedsolefoundation.org/default.asp?ID=6
Sponsor: J.L. Bedsole Foundation
P.O. Box 1137
Mobile, AL 36633

J.M. Kaplan Fund City Life Grants   2601
Jacob Merrill Kaplan (1891-1987) established The J.M. Kaplan Fund in 1945 and was its president until 1977, his eighty-fifth year. The City Life Program concentrates on public spaces and public services throughout the five boroughs of New York City. It focuses particularly on parks (projects to assure public access to well-maintained parks and greenery in all neighborhoods; enhance public uses of harbor and shoreline; and promote community participation in parks governance and operations) and streets (projects to advocate more and better rail, bus, and water transport; expand pedestrian zones and bikepaths; and regulate truck and automobile traffic).
Requirements: The great majority of projects funded through the four Common Grant programs are solicited by Kaplan Fund staff. Unsolicited written inquiries are welcome, however. Organizations should submit a brief letter – no more than two pages – describing their work and its relevance to the specific program interests of the Fund. Please note that telephone inquiries are discouraged.
Geographic Focus: New York
Contact: Angela D. Carabine, Grants Manager; fax (212) 767-0639; info@jmkfund.org
Internet: http://www.jmkfund.org/grantprograms.html
Sponsor: J.M. Kaplan Fund
261 Madison Avenue, 19th Floor
New York, NY 10016

J.M. Kaplan Fund Migrations Grants   2602
Jacob Merrill Kaplan (1891-1987) established The J.M. Kaplan Fund in 1945 and was its president until 1977, his eighty-fifth year. The Migrations Program aims to support comprehensive immigration policy reform for the United States, pursued through grants for public education and advocacy.
Requirements: The great majority of projects funded through the four Common Grant programs are solicited by Kaplan Fund staff. Unsolicited written inquiries are welcome, however. Organizations should submit a brief letter – no more than two pages – describing their work and its relevance to the specific program interests of the Fund. Please note that telephone inquiries are discouraged.
Geographic Focus: All States
Contact: Angela D. Carabine, Grants Manager; fax (212) 767-0639; info@jmkfund.org
Internet: http://www.jmkfund.org/grantprograms.html
Sponsor: J.M. Kaplan Fund
261 Madison Avenue, 19th Floor
New York, NY 10016

J.M. Long Foundation Grants   2603
The Foundation is focused on providing support to organizations involved with health care, education, and conservation in the communities of Northern California and Hawaii. Preference will be given for new, innovative projects, which can be completed with the Foundation contribution. Applications for new grant requests are given by invitation only. In order to receive an invitation, an organization will need to submit to the Foundation a single page Request for Invitation letter using organization letterhead. This Request for Invitation letter should describe the organization's objective and the specific project for which the grant would be used. The applicant should be sure to include an estimated amount for the grant, as well as contact information including email address if available.
Requirements: Hawaii and Northern California nonprofits are eligible to apply.
Restrictions: Please note that grants will not be made: for the support of solely religious, sacramental or theological functions; in support of political bodies or campaigns; to individuals or foreign organizations; for loans; for purposes of memorializing an individual, although donations may be made to memorial funds as a means of achieving other purposes; for covering operating deficits; to organizations not qualifying as either a federal tax-exempt non-profit private organization or a qualifying public organization; to supporting organizations with a 509(a)(3) designation.
Geographic Focus: California, Hawaii
Amount of Grant: 1,000 - 50,000 USD
Contact: Brenda Kauten, Grants Administrator; (925) 935-4138; fax (925) 935-2092
Internet: http://www.jmlongfoundation.org/Grants.html
Sponsor: J.M. Long Foundation
P.O. Box 3827
Walnut Creek, CA 94598-2827

J. Mack Robinson Foundation Grants   2604
The foundation awards grants to Georgia nonprofits in its areas of interest, including arts, Christian churches and organizations, higher education, and secondary education.
Requirements: Georgia nonprofit organizations are eligible.
Geographic Focus: Georgia
Amount of Grant: 1,000 - 100,000 USD
Contact: J. Mack Robinson, Program Supervisor; (404) 231-2111
Sponsor: J. Mack Robinson Foundation
4370 Peachtree Road NE
Atlanta, GA 30319-3023

J. Marion Sims Foundation Teachers' Pet Grant   2605
The program was designed to assist educators in meeting the evolving needs of students. The programs aim is to inspire and encourage creative concepts that have the potential for enhancing community life through the education of local youth. Awards will be based on merit, innovation, completeness, the enhancement of existing instruction, and the availability of funding. Recipients are limited to one grant per school year. Grant requests must be submitted via email. Application information is available online.
Requirements: Classroom teachers, media specialists, guidance counselors and other certified support staff (exclusive of after-school programs) serving K-12 students in Lancaster County, Fort Lawn and Great Falls, South Carolina, are invited to apply. Requests will not be considered via fax, postal mail, or hand-delivery.
Restrictions: Digital cameras, DVD or VCR equipment, library books, school beautification projects, and transportation will not be funded.
Geographic Focus: South Carolina
Contact: Grants Officer; (803) 286-8772; fax (803) 286-8774; TeachersPet@jmsims.org
Internet: http://www.jmsims.org/grants/teacherspet.html
Sponsor: J. Marion Sims Foundation
800 North White Street, P.O. Box 818
Lancaster, SC 29721

J. Spencer Barnes Memorial Foundation Grants   2606
The J. Spencer Barnes Memorial Foundation was established in Michigan in 1999, with the intent of funding programs in and around Grand Rapids, Michigan. Its primary fields of interest include diabetes, with target populations being children and youth, as well as the general population afflicted with the disease. The major types of support are income development and program development. There are no specific application forms or annual deadlines, and applicants should begin by forwarding a proposal to the office listed. Amounts range from $500 to $2,000.
Requirements: Nonprofits in California are eligible to apply.
Geographic Focus: Michigan
Contact: Robert C. Woodhouse, Jr., President; (616) 949-4854
Sponsor: J. Spencer Barnes Memorial Foundation
3073 East Fulton Street
Grand Rapids, MI 49506-1813

J.W. Kieckhefer Foundation Grants   2607
The Kieckhefer Foundation awards grants to nation-wide 501(c)3 organizations in support of medical research, hospices, and health agencies; family planning services; social services; higher education; youth and child welfare agencies; ecology and conservation; community funds; and cultural programs. Types of support include the following: annual campaigns; building renovation; conferences and seminars; continuing support; emergency funds; endowments; equipment; general operating support; land acquisition; matching and challenge support; program development; publication; and research.
Requirements: Applications are not accepted. Organizations should submit a letter of inquiry to the Foundation, with a description of their project and amount requested.
Restrictions: Grants are not awarded to individuals.
Geographic Focus: All States
Contact: John I. Kieckhefer, Trustee; (928) 445-4010
Sponsor: J.W. Kieckhefer Foundation
116 East Gurley Street
Prescott, AZ 86301-3821

J. Walton Bissell Foundation Grants 2608
The J. Walton Bissell Foundation Grants support 501(c)3 organizations in Connecticut, with emphasis on Hartford. The Foundation gives primarily to the arts and social services, including child welfare and programs for the blind. Funding requests should be submitted four months before funding is needed. Types of support include general operating support, program development, and seed money.
Requirements: Applicants should submit a letter of inquiry, along with a copy of their IRS determination letter, and a copy of their annual report, audited financial statement, or 990.
Restrictions: The Foundation does not grant funding to individuals or endowments.
Geographic Focus: Connecticut
Contact: J. Danford Anthony, Jr., President; (860) 586-8201
Sponsor: J. Walton Bissell Foundation
P.O. Box 370067
West Hartford, CT 06137

J. Willard and Alice S. Marriott Foundation Grants 2609
The J. Willard and Alice S. Marriott Foundation is a private family foundation dedicated to helping youth secure a promising future, especially through education on the secondary and higher education levels, mentoring and youth leadership programs. Equally important are organizations that help provide relief from hunger and disasters; support people with disabilities; and create gainful employment opportunities for vulnerable youth and adults. The Foundation awards grants to nonprofit organizations in its areas of interest: scholarship programs; inner city work and; youth programs, with special interest in employment opportunities for young people with disabilities. Interested applicants should prepare a written request which should include a project narrative and attachments. The Board of Trustees meets two times each year, usually in the Spring and Fall.
Requirements: Nonprofits in Maryland, Virginia and the District of Columbia are eligible.
Restrictions: Individuals are ineligible.
Geographic Focus: District of Columbia, Maryland, Virginia
Contact: Arne Sorenson, President; (301) 380-2246; fax (301) 380-8957; kimberly.howes@marriott.com
Sponsor: J. Willard and Alice S. Marriott Foundation
10400 Fernwood Road
Bethesda, MD 20917

J. Willard Marriott, Jr. Foundation Grants 2610
Established in 1992 in Maryland in the name of the Executive Chairman of Marriott International, the J. Willard Marriott, Jr. Foundation primarily supports residents of New Hampshire, Maryland, and the District of Columbia, although funding is occasionally provided to those outside of this region. Giving is primarily in the areas of health and education, including scholarship awards only to residents of the State of New Hampshire who received their primary and/or secondary education through home schooling and are enrolled in an accredited college or university. Initial approach should be by letter, with all applications being postmarked no later than August 31. Typical awards range from $200 to $5,000.
Geographic Focus: District of Columbia, Maryland, New Hampshire
Date(s) Application is Due: Aug 31
Amount of Grant: 200 - 5,000 USD
Contact: Steven J. McNeil, (301) 380-1765 or (301) 380-3000
Sponsor: J. Willard Marriott, Jr. Foundation
1 Marriott Drive, P.O. Box 925
Washington, DC 20058-0003

Jackson County Community Foundation Unrestricted Grants 2611
The Foundation awards grants to nonprofit organizations covering a full range of charitable activity such as health and human services, education, economic/community development, arts and culture, and environmental quality and protection. All grants are evaluated on a competitive basis and priority is given to those projects that show potential for providing maximum benefit to community members. Application information is available online.
Requirements: The Foundation makes grants to Jackson County, Michigan nonprofit, tax-exempt organizations.
Restrictions: While the Foundation remains flexible in trying to address the needs of the community, it do not make grants to individuals (except scholarships), programs that advocate specific religions, or services which are standard government or school obligations. Applications from organizations not serving Jackson County are not accepted.
Geographic Focus: Michigan
Date(s) Application is Due: Jan 15; May 15; Sep 15
Amount of Grant: 3,000 - 50,000 USD
Contact: Diane McDonald; (517) 787-1321; fax (517) 787-4333; jcf@jacksoncf.org
Internet: http://www.jacksoncf.org/grants.html
Sponsor: Jackson County Community Foundation
1 Jackson Square, 100 E Michigan Avenue, Suite 308
Jackson, MI 49201-1406

Jackson County Community Foundation Youth Advisory Committee Grants 2612
The JCF Youth Advisory Committee (or YAC) is a youth-focused and youth-administered committee within the Jackson Community Foundation (JCF). Its purpose is to address the needs of youth in Jackson County, Michigan by awarding grants to community organizations that benefit youth. At the same time, it provides the students involved in the program an opportunity to volunteer their time and talents to better their community while developing philanthropic leadership skills and valuable experience. This experience will carry over into their adult lives and strengthen philanthropy in the areas communities. The YAC program was established in 1989 through a challenge grant from the Michigan Community Foundation Youth Project (MCFYP) funded by the W.K. Kellogg Foundation. Kellogg's intent was to build community foundation capacity, establish youth as philanthropists and build permanent endowment funds to meet youth-related needs within each community. In addition, the YAC functions as a grant review board, evaluating and making recommendations to the Jackson Community Foundation Board of Trustees for grant requests they receive. See the JCF website for further guidelines and application forms. There are two grant applications, one for up to $5,000 and one for requests over $5,000.
Geographic Focus: Michigan
Contact: Christine Taylor; (517) 787-1321; fax (517) 787-4333; christaylorjcf@yahoo.com
Internet: http://www.jacksoncf.org/grants.html
Sponsor: Jackson County Community Foundation
1 Jackson Square, 100 E Michigan Avenue, Suite 308
Jackson, MI 49201-1406

Jackson Foundation Grants 2613
The Jackson Foundation was established October 1960 pursuant to the last will of Maria C. Jackson. Its purpose is to respond to the requests deemed appropriate to promote the welfare of the public of the City of Portland or the State of Oregon, or both. The Foundation considers projects located outside the Portland metropolitan area only if the project is of statewide appeal, rather than of local concern.
Requirements: Grants are awarded to nonprofit 501(c)3 tax-exempt agencies located within the state of Oregon.
Restrictions: Funding is not available for individuals or private businesses. Grants are generally not made to a K-12 school. Do not contact the Foundation by phone to check the status of an application.
Geographic Focus: Oregon
Date(s) Application is Due: Mar 31; Jun 30; Sep 30; Dec 31
Amount of Grant: 1,000 - 25,000 USD
Contact: Robert H. Depew, c/o U.S. Bank, (503) 275-4414
Internet: http://www.thejacksonfoundation.com
Sponsor: Jackson Foundation
P.O. Box 3168
Portland, OR 97208

Jacksonville Jaguars Foundation Grants 2614
Believing that youth represent the community's future, the Jacksonville Jaguars Foundation is committed to serving the greater Jacksonville area through strategic financial, networking, and volunteer support benefitting economically and socially disadvantaged youth and families.
Requirements: 501(c)3 nonprofits in the greater Jacksonville, FL, area, including Baker, Clay, Duval, Nassau, and Saint Johns counties, are eligible.
Restrictions: In general, the foundation does not support fundraising and sponsorship events; schools; religious organizations for sectarian religious purposes; single-disease organizations; organizations that have applied for support from the foundation within the previous 12 months; and individuals.
Geographic Focus: Florida
Date(s) Application is Due: Feb 19; Jul 16
Amount of Grant: Up to 100,000,000 USD
Contact: Peter M. Racine, (904) 633-5437; foundation@jaguarsnfl.com
Internet: http://www.jaguars.com/foundation/
Sponsor: Jacksonville Jaguars Foundation
1 Stadium Place
Jacksonville, FL 32202-1917

Jacob and Hilda Blaustein Foundation Grants 2615
The Foundation promotes social justice and human rights through its five program areas: Jewish life; strengthening Israeli democracy; health and mental health; educational opportunity; and human rights. Support is provided to organizations in the United States and abroad, with a preference to the Baltimore, Maryland area. The Foundation supports organizations that promote systemic change; involve constituents in planning and decision-making; encourage volunteer and professional development; and engage in ongoing program evaluation. Additional guidelines and application information is available online.
Requirements: Nonprofit organizations are eligible to apply.
Restrictions: Support is unavailable for the following: individuals; scholarships to individuals; unsolicited proposals for academic, scientific, or medical research; direct mail; annual giving; membership campaigns; fundraising; commemorative events.
Geographic Focus: Maryland
Contact: Betsy Ringel; (410) 347-7103; fax (410) 347-7210; info@blaufund.org
Internet: http://www.blaufund.org/foundations/jacobandhilda_f.html
Sponsor: Jacob and Hilda Blaustein Foundation
10 E Baltimore Street, Suite 1111
Baltimore, MD 21202

Jacob G. Schmidlapp Trust Grants 2616
The trust supports tax-exempt organizations in the greater Cincinnati, OH, area. The trust supports charitable or educational purposes; for relief in sickness, suffering, and distress; for the care of young children, the aged, or the helpless; and for the promotion of education to improve living conditions. Support is offered in the form of: endowments; equipment; land acquisition; program development; technical assistance; and seed money grants. An organization interested in submitting a grant proposal should initially contact the Foundation office via a letter of inquiry, an application form is required for proposals. Proposals are reviewed quarterly, March, June, September and, December.
Requirements: Nonprofits in the greater Cincinnati, Ohio area receive the majority of funding, however giving is also available in the surrounding states of Indiana, Kentucky and Michigan.

Restrictions: No support for religious or political purposes. No grants to individuals; no loans.
Geographic Focus: Indiana, Kentucky, Michigan, Ohio
Date(s) Application is Due: Feb 1; May 1; Aug 1; Nov 1
Amount of Grant: 2,000 - 500,000 USD
Contact: Heidi B. Jark, Manager, c/o Fifth Third Bank; (513) 534-4397
Internet: https://www.53.com:443/wps/portal/personal
Sponsor: Jacob G. Schmidlapp Trust
38 Fountain Square Plaza, MD 1090CA
Cincinnati, OH 45263-0001

Jacobs Family Foundation Jabara Learning Opportunities Grants   2617
The Foundation primarily serves the four neighborhoods immediately surrounding The Village at Market Creek: Chollas View, Emerald Hills, Lincoln Park, and Valencia Park; proposals are considered from throughout the Fourth City Council District of southeastern San Diego. The Jabara Learning Opportunities Fund provides grants to send resident to community building trainings.
Requirements: Residents must be working to develop The Village at Market Creek.
Geographic Focus: California
Contact: Program Contact; (619) 527-6161 or (800) 550-6856; fax (619) 527-6162; communications@jacobscenter.org
Internet: http://www.jacobsfamilyfoundation.org/how.htm
Sponsor: Jacobs Family Foundation
Joe & Vi Jacobs Center, 404 Euclid Avenue
San Diego, CA 92114

Jacobs Family Foundation Spirit of the Diamond Grants   2618
The Foundation primarily serves the four neighborhoods immediately surrounding The Village at Market Creek: Chollas View, Emerald Hills, Lincoln Park, and Valencia Park; proposals are considered from throughout the Fourth City Council District of southeastern San Diego. The Spirit of the Diamond Fund provides grants for community projects that enhance the beauty, safety, and spirit of the Diamond Neighborhoods. Funding priority is given to projects that are resident-led, open to the community, and/or strengthen relations among community members. Projects can include art programs, cultural events, historical gatherings, street fairs, health fairs, clean-ups, community gardens, and other neighborhood strengthening programs and activities. Projects that promote cross-cultural understanding are encouraged.
Requirements: Community groups, organizations, or individuals apply do not need to be formal non-profit organizations and may receive up to a total of $5,000 in grants from the Spirit of Diamond Fund during the calender year. Spirit of Diamond Fund applications are accepted six months prior but no later then 60 days before the start of the project
Geographic Focus: California
Amount of Grant: Up to 5,000 USD
Contact: Program Contact; (619) 527-6161 or (800) 550-6856; fax (619) 527-6162; communications@jacobscenter.org
Internet: http://www.jacobsfamilyfoundation.org/how.htm
Sponsor: Jacobs Family Foundation
Joe & Vi Jacobs Center, 404 Euclid Avenue
San Diego, CA 92114

Jacobs Family Foundation Village Neighborhoods Grants   2619
The Foundation primarily serves the four neighborhoods immediately surrounding The Village at Market Creek: Chollas View, Emerald Hills, Lincoln Park, and Valencia Park; proposals are considered from throughout the Fourth City Council District of southeastern San Diego. The Neighborhood Grants Program funds programs or strategies that: strengthen and expand health, environmental, education and family resources; foster opportunities for ownership and building assets through economic and business development; create vibrant places and spaces which express and enhance the cultures and environment of the community; and/or strengthen the ability of the community to get things done and include the voice of residents in decision-making, advocacy, and planning. The Village Neighborhoods Fund makes grants to resident groups and neighborhood organizations that serve or support The Village at Market Creek. Funding is also available for a limited number of grants that support projects outside the neighborhoods that demonstrate innovative community and economic development strategies and a commitment to share what works, what doesn't, and why. Applications are excepted year round, however unsolicited applications are not. Call the Foundation to discuss your project. If the project meets the Foundations criteria, you may be asked to send a brief letter of interest and/or complete a full Village Neighborhoods Fund application.
Requirements: 501(c)3 non-profits may apply that: work with the Jacobs Center to develop The Village at Market Creek in southeastern San Diego; provide programs or services that benefit the neighborhoods surrounding The Village at Market Creek; or provides neighborhood strengthening strategies or models that can inform and advance The Village at Market Creek work.
Geographic Focus: California
Contact: Program Contact; (619) 527-6161; communications@jacobscenter.org
Internet: http://www.jacobsfamilyfoundation.org/how.htm
Sponsor: Jacobs Family Foundation
Joe & Vi Jacobs Center, 404 Euclid Avenue
San Diego, CA 92114

James & Abigail Campbell Family Foundation Grants   2620
The James & Abigail Campbell Family Foundation embraces the values and beliefs of James and Abigail Campbell by investing in Hawwaii's people and the communities that nurture them. The Foundation supports projects in the following areas: Youth—programs that address the challenges of young people; Education—support for public schools, early childhood education and environmental stewardship; Hawaiian—support for programs that promote values and the health and welfare of Hawaiians. Priority is given to programs located in or serving communities in the following areas of West Oahu: Ewa/Ewa Beach, Kapolei, Makakilo and the Wai'anae Coast. The following types of requests are eligible for consideration: support for special projects that are not part of an organization's ongoing operations; program support when unforeseen circumstances have affected the financial base of an organization; financial assistance to purchase items such as office equipment and to fund minor repairs and renovations. Grants range from $5,000 - $50,000. Your grant application must be postmarked by February 1 for the April/May meeting, August 1 for the October/November meeting.
Requirements: The Foundation will only consider requests from organizations which qualify as non-profit, tax-exempt public charities under Section 501(c)3 and 170(b) of the Internal Revenue Code. To apply for a grant, summarize the following information in a two - three page proposal letter: the nature and purpose of your organization; the objectives of your program, include the grant amount requested and the proposed use of funds; a brief outline on how you plan to accomplish your objectives; a statement of a community problem, need or opportunity that this project will address; the duration for which Foundation funds are needed; other sources of funding currently being sought and future funding sources; methods used to measure the program's effectiveness. In addition to the proposal letter, submit a copy of the following: Internal Revenue Service notification of tax-exempt status; most recent annual financial statement; list of the current Board of Directors; the project's proposed budget; one (1) copy of your complete grant proposal package.
Restrictions: The Foundation will not consider funding for: individuals, endowments, sectarian or religious programs, loans, political activities or highly technical research projects. Only one request per organization will ordinarily be considered in a calendar year. Funds are usually not committed for more than one year at a time.
Geographic Focus: Hawaii
Date(s) Application is Due: Feb 1; Aug 1
Amount of Grant: 5,000 - 50,000 USD
Contact: D. Keola; (808) 674-3167; fax (808) 674-3349; keolal@jamescampbell.com
Internet: http://www.campbellfamilyfoundation.org/grant_procedures.cfm
Sponsor: James and Abigail Campbell Family Foundation
1001 Kamokila Boulevard
Kapolei, HI 96707

James A. and Faith Knight Foundation Grants   2621
Primarily serving Jackson and Washtenaw counties, Michigan, the Foundation is dedicated to improving communities by providing grant support to qualified nonprofit organizations including, but not limited to, those that address the needs of women and girls, animals and the natural world, and internal capacity. In general, the foundation supports organizations that believe in good nonprofit practices including sound financial management, developed governance practices, and clarity of mission. Attention to gender, diversity, and outcomes are important. Giving is primarily for human services, including a neighborhood center, women's organizations, and family services; support also for nonprofit management, the United Way, housing, the arts, education, and environmental conservation. Fields of interest include: adult education and literacy; basic skills; GED; arts; environment and natural resources; family services; housing development; human services; nonprofit management; and women's services. There are two annual deadlines, and initial approach should be by letter.
Requirements: Giving is limited to Michigan, with emphasis on Jackson and Washenaw counties.
Restrictions: No support is offered for religious or political organizations. No grants to individuals, or for conferences or special events, or for annual campaigns.
Geographic Focus: Michigan
Date(s) Application is Due: Jan 28; Sep 16
Contact: Margaret A. Talburtt, Executive Director; (734) 769-5653; fax (734) 769-8383; peg@KnightFoundationMi.org or info@knightfoundationmi.org
Internet: http://www.knightfoundationmi.org/guidelines.htm
Sponsor: James A. and Faith Knight Foundation
180 Little Lake Drive, Suite 6B
Ann Arbor, MI 48103-6219

James F. and Marion L. Miller Foundation Grants   2622
The foundation awards single or multiyear grants for projects that advance the arts or education in communities throughout the State of Oregon. The Foundation has also recently adopted several initiatives in the areas of nursing, community college scholarships, new teachers, and sustainability. Requests from the same organization will normally be considered by the trustees only once in a 12-month period and will not be considered until payment of a prior multiyear grant has been completed. Proposals are accepted from eligible applicants throughout the year. The board meets approximately five times annually to review proposals, and applications are reviewed as they are received. Application and guidelines are available online.
Requirements: Oregon 501(c)3 tax-exempt organizations that are not 509(a) private foundations, educational institutions, and governmental entities are eligible.
Restrictions: The foundation generally will not favor proposals seeking funds for direct grants, scholarships, or loans to individuals; endowments; general fund drives or annual appeals; debt retirement or operation deficits; emergency needs; propagandizing or influencing elections or legislation; or projects of religious organizations that principally benefit their own members.
Geographic Focus: Oregon
Contact: Grants Manager; (503) 546-3191; info@millerfnd.org
Internet: http://www.millerfound.org/about/
Sponsor: James F. and Marion L. Miller Foundation
520 SW Yamhill Street, Suite 520
Portland, OR 97205

James Ford Bell Foundation Grants   2623

The Foundation supports organizations primarily in Minnesota. Emphasis is on cultural programs, support is also available for wildlife preservation and conservation, youth agencies, the environment, education, health and human services. A high priority is given to projects with historical connections to the Bell Family. The Trustees meet in the Spring and Fall. Contact the Foundation prior to sending in a proposal. Unsolicited requests for funds are not accepted.
Requirements: Nonprofit organizations in Minnesota are eligible to apply.
Restrictions: No grants are made directly to individuals, nor for scholarships, fellowships, or political campaigns. No funding is available to units of local government. The Foundation does not respond to requests for memberships, annual appeals, or special events and fundraisers.
Geographic Focus: Minnesota
Contact: Ellen George; (612) 377-8400; fax (612) 377-8407; ellen@fpadvisors.com
Internet: http://www.fpadvisors.com/jamesfordbell/jamesfordbell.htm
Sponsor: James Ford Bell Foundation
1818 Oliver Avenue South
Minneapolis, MN 55405-2208

James G.K. McClure Educational and Development Fund Grants   2624

The fund devotes most of its resources to an ongoing scholarship program for the students of western North Carolina. When funds are available, the trustees make grants to organizations in the region, primarily those that enhance the lives of the rural citizens of the area. The trustees look favorably on requests from institutions helping to improve the lives of the people within its geographic area. Hospitals, colleges, libraries, and various schools are common recipients. The trustees meet twice each year, usually in May and October.
Requirements: Applicants must be residents of the following counties: Alleghany, Ashe, Avery, Buncombe, Burke, Caldwell, Cherokee, Clay, Graham, Haywood, Henderson, Jackson, Macon, Madison, McDowell, Mitchell, Polk, Rutherford, Swain, Transylvania, Watauga, and Yancey.
Restrictions: No student may apply for a scholarship unless he or she resides in one of the specified counties, and no grant money will be made to organizations outside this district.
Geographic Focus: North Carolina
Amount of Grant: 1,000 - 5,000 USD
Contact: John Curtis Ager, Executive Director; (704) 628-2114; jager@ioa.com
Sponsor: James G.K. McClure Educational and Development Fund
11 Sugar Hollow Lane
Fairview, NC 28730

James Graham Brown Foundation Quality of Life Grants   2625

The James Graham Brown Foundation fosters the Quality of Life of Louisville by helping to make it a community of choice for families and businesses. The Foundation gives priority to projects that: strengthen the impact of core human services and cultural organizations and agencies in the community; support efforts to improve and sustain quality neighborhoods and a thriving downtown; and support initiatives that strengthen the relationship between business and education to increase growth in human capital and jobs in higher wage, higher knowledge, and high technical areas. It actively supports and funds projects in the fields of education, economic development, health and social services, culture and humanities (excluding performing arts) with an emphasis on community-wide capital campaigns. The Board meets six times annually and determinations are made at the meetings. Funds are dispersed semi-annually.
Requirements: Formal applications must be submitted by the following deadline dates: March 2, Social Services requests; and May 8, Culture and Civic requests. Only organizations that have obtained a tax-exempt designation under Section 501(c)3 of the I.R.S. code may apply. The Foundation grants are limited to the Louisville metropolitan area and the state of Kentucky. Campaigns outside the Jefferson County and Louisville metropolitan area must show evidence of significant local community support before being considered by the foundation for funding.
Restrictions: The Foundation does not support the following: organizations outside of the state of Kentucky; those related either directly or indirectly to the performing arts; requests from religious organizations for religious purposes (including theological seminaries); requests from individuals; requests from political entities; requests from national organizations, even if for local projects.
Geographic Focus: Kentucky
Date(s) Application is Due: Mar 2; May 8
Contact: Dodie L. McKenzie, Grants Director; (502) 896-2440 or (866) 896-5423; fax (502) 896-1774; grants@jgbf.org
Internet: http://www.jgbf.org/Home/Grant-Seeking-Tips/Funding-Areas.aspx
Sponsor: James Graham Brown Foundation
4350 Brownsboro Road, Suite 200
Louisville, KY 40207

James H. Cummings Foundation Grants   2626

The Foundation, gives exclusively for charitable purposes in advancing medical science, research, and education in selected cities in the U.S. and Canada, and for charitable work among underprivileged boys and girls, and aged and infirm persons in designated areas. Priority is given to medical proposals. The funding is limited to: Toronto, Ontario; Canada; Hendersonville, North Carolina and; Buffalo, New York. Grants are available, in the following types of support: building/renovation; capital campaigns; equipment; land acquisition; matching/challenge support; research and seed money.
Requirements: The giving program is limited to the vicinity of the cities of Buffalo, NY; Hendersonville, NC; and Toronto, ON, Canada.
Restrictions: No support for national health organizations. Grants are not awarded to individuals, nor for: loans, annual campaigns, program support, endowment funds, operating budgets, emergency funds, deficit financing, scholarships, fellowships, publications, conferences, or continuing support.
Geographic Focus: New York, North Carolina, Canada
Amount of Grant: 2,000 - 250,000 USD
Contact: William McFarland; (716) 874-0040; cummings.foundation@verizon.net
Sponsor: James H. Cummings Foundation
1807 Elmwood Avenue, Room 112
Buffalo, NY 14207

James Hervey Johnson Charitable Educational Trust Grants   2627

The goal of the trust is to expose religion as against reason, publicize nontheistic views of religion, and publicize James Hervey Johnson's views on health, which are centered primarily in vegetarianism, natural hygiene, and alternative medicine. Interested applicants should contact the Foundation prior to submitting a proposal. The Foundation requires an application form and, will provide guidelines. There are no geographic restrictions, but preference is given to requests from San Diego County, CA.
Requirements: 501(c)3 nonprofits that have been in existence for at least two years are eligible.
Geographic Focus: All States
Date(s) Application is Due: Jun 30
Amount of Grant: 5,000 - 100,000 USD
Contact: Kevin V. Munnelly, Treasurer; (619) 297-9036; promotions@home.com
Sponsor: James Hervey Johnson Charitable Educational Trust
P.O. Box 16160
San Diego, CA 92176-6160

James Irvine Foundation Creative Connections Grants   2628

The Creative Connections Fund supports creativity and the expansion of diverse, relevant cultural offerings in local communities across California and primarily outside San Francisco, San Mateo and Santa Clara counties. The Fund targets small and midsize arts organizations and offers project grants of up to $50,000, over a maximum of 24 months, through an open, competitive review process. The Creative Connections Fund aims to support small and midsize arts organizations with a diversity of projects and ideas. The Foundation's rationale is two-fold. First, small organizations play an important role in the arts ecosystem. They have close ties to the communities they serve, present aesthetics that have particular relevance to their audiences, and involve local artists. In this way, community-based arts organizations support grassroots creativity and add to the cultural offerings of the neighborhoods and cities they serve, which, in turn, adds to the cultural vibrancy of the state. Second, because we frequently partner with organizations that have annual budgets greater than $2 million, the Creative Connections Fund is an important complement to our invitational portfolio and a way to reach arts organizations of all artistic disciplines and aesthetics, located in all geographic locations in California. See Foundations website for additional guidelines.
Requirements: To be considered for a grant organizations and requests must meet all the following *Requirements:* 501(c)3 status or an established relationship with an approved fiscal sponsor; California focus; no more than 50 percent of revenue from government sources; annual revenue of at least $100,000; grant request of no more than $50,000 or 10% of organizations annual budget; no active grant or outstanding reports due to the Foundation.
Restrictions: Irvine does not make direct grants to individual artists.
Geographic Focus: California
Amount of Grant: 50,000 USD
Contact: Fund Coordinator; (800) 374-6851; artsfund@irvine.org
Internet: http://www.irvine.org/grantmaking/our-programs/arts-program/fundingguidelines/creativeconnectionsfund
Sponsor: James Irvine Foundation
575 Market Street, Suite 3400
San Francisco, CA 94105

James Irvine Foundation Leadership Awards   2629

The James Irvine Foundation Leadership Awards highlight and support the work of individuals who are advancing innovative and effective solutions to significant state issues. Award recipients receive $125,000 for their work to benefit the people of California. At least $100,000 is designated for core support of the leader's project or organization, and up to $25,000 may be used for the leader's own professional development. Recipients also receive additional resources for their efforts to share promising approaches to critical state issues with policymakers and practitioners. Additionally, recipients may apply to a special fund for a grant of up to $75,000 annually, over one or two years, to communicate to policymakers and practitioners about their effective model. Additional guidelines are available at the James Irvine Foundation website.
Requirements: Nominees may be working in any field, such as: education; health; housing; economic development; the environment; in the public; private or nonprofit sector. The nominee must be a resident of California, and the nominator must be someone other than the nominee or a family member. The James Irvine Foundation seeks nominees who have not been extensively recognized for their work through other awards.
Geographic Focus: California
Date(s) Application is Due: Oct 19
Amount of Grant: 125,000 USD
Contact: Stephanie Lai, California Democracy Program Associate; (415) 777-2244 or (866) 586-6465; fax (415) 777-0869; leadershipawards@irvine.org
Internet: http://www.irvine.org/leadership/leadership-awards
Sponsor: James Irvine Foundation
575 Market Street, Suite 3400
San Francisco, CA 94105

James J. and Angelia M. Harris Foundation Grants 2630
The foundation's primary areas of interested include: higher and other education, health services and hospitals, social services, youth, Christian organizations and, Presbyterian churches. Types of support include: annual campaigns, building construction/renovation, capital campaigns, challenge/matching grants, program development, seed money and, scholarship funds. There are no application deadlines or forms. The board meets in May and November to consider requests. Letters of inquiry are due in April and October.
Requirements: Nonprofit organizations in Clarke County, GA, and Mecklenburg County, NC, are eligible.
Geographic Focus: Georgia, North Carolina
Amount of Grant: 1,000 - 100,000 USD
Contact: Sherri Harrell, Grants Administrator; fax (704) 364-6046
Sponsor: James J. and Angelia M. Harris Foundation
P.O. Box 220427
Charlotte, NC 28222-0427

James J. McCann Charitable Trust and McCann Foundation, Inc Grants 2631
The foundation's central concern is the vitality of the Dutchess County, NY, area. In supporting the community, the foundation makes grants to support programs and projects of nonprofit educational, health, housing, religious, and recreational organizations. Types of support include annual campaigns, continuing support, building construction/renovation, equipment acquisition, conferences and seminars, publication seed money, fellowships, and scholarship funds. Applications should be in writing and addressed to the trustees.
Requirements: Nonprofit organizations in the Dutchess County, NY, area are eligible.
Restrictions: Grants are not made to individuals or for operating budgets, emergency funds, endowment funds, deficit financing, or matching gifts.
Geographic Focus: New York
Contact: Michael Gartland, President; (845) 452-3085
Sponsor: James J. McCann Charitable Trust and McCann Foundation
35 Market Street
Poughkeepsie, NY 12601

James L. and Mary Jane Bowman Charitable Trust Grants 2632
Established in 1997 in Virginia through a donation by James L. Bowman, the James L. and Mary Jane Bowman Charitable Trust Supports both education and libraries within Virginia. The Trust's primary fields of interest include: Christian agencies and churches, higher education, human services, public libraries, and recreation. There are no specific application forms or deadlines with which to adhere, and applicants should forward a letter of application that includes a needs statement, population to be served, and the project budget.
Requirements: 501(c)3 nonprofit organizations Serving residents of Virginia are eligible.
Restrictions: The foundation does not award grants to individuals in the form of scholarships or other direct support; orpolitical causes or candidates.
Geographic Focus: Virginia
Date(s) Application is Due: Apr 1
Contact: Beverley B. Shoemaker, Trustee; (540) 869-1800; fax (540) 869-4225
Sponsor: James L. and Mary Jane Bowman Charitable Trust
P.O. Box 480
Stephens City, VA 22655-0480

James M. Collins Foundation Grants 2633
The foundation awards grants to Texas nonprofit organizations in its areas of interest, including: arts, economic development, health organizations, association, higher education, human services, museums, Salvation Army, secondary school/education. Types of support include research grants, program support, and social services. There are no application deadlines or forms.
Requirements: Texas nonprofit organizations are eligible.
Restrictions: Individuals are not eligible.
Geographic Focus: Texas
Contact: Dorothy Dann Collins Torbert, President; (214) 691-2032
Sponsor: James M. Collins Foundation
8115 Preston Road, Suite 680
Dallas, TX 75225

James M. Cox Foundation of Georgia Grants 2634
The Foundation awards grants in Cox Enterprises communities in its areas of interest, including journalism, visual and performing arts, child development, education, healthcare, environment, wildlife, and community and family services. Types of support include building construction/renovation, capital campaigns, and program development. There are no application forms or deadlines. Interested applicants should send a request to the Foundation outlining project needs and goals.
Requirements: Nonprofits in Cox Enterprises communities are eligible.
Geographic Focus: All States
Contact: Leigh Ann Launius, Assistant Secretary; (678) 645-0929; fax (678) 645-1708
Internet: http://media.corporate-ir.net/media_files/IROL/76/76341/reports/AR_2003/community.html
Sponsor: James M. Cox Foundation of Georgia
6205 Peachtree Dunwoody Road
Atlanta, GA 30328

James R. Dougherty Jr. Foundation Grants 2635
The James R. Dougherty, Jr. Foundation, established in 1950, gives to organizations primarily in Texas. Areas of interest include: family services, domestic violence, human services and women. Support is offered in the form of: annual campaigns, building/renovation, capital campaigns, continuing support, curriculum development, endowments, equipment, general/operating support, income development, management development/capacity building, matching/challenge support, program development, program evaluation, research, scholarship funds, seed money and, technical assistance grants. The board meets twice a year, in the Spring and Fall. No application form is required, contact the Foundation, before submitting a proposal.
Geographic Focus: Texas
Date(s) Application is Due: Mar 1; Sep 1
Contact: Daren Wilder, Grants Administrator; (512) 358-3560
Sponsor: James R. Dougherty Jr. Foundation
P.O. Box 640
Beeville, TX 78104-0640

James R. Thorpe Foundation Grants 2636
The Foundation is interested in supporting organizations, programs or projects which address the needs of the Elderly and Youth. The Thorpe Foundation is most likely to make general operating or program support grants. In the area of Youth, the Foundation supports organizations and programs that: engage youth in the arts; encourage character development; support academic and social development; provide safety and support to youth. In the area of the Elderly, the Foundation fosters the vital aging of seniors through support of services which help them to live independently. The Foundation will give special consideration to services which address the needs of economically disadvantaged seniors, immigrant seniors and the frail elderly. The Foundation supports organizations and programs that: provide transportation services; assist seniors in remaining in their own homes; educate seniors about housing options; provide social and recreational opportunities for seniors. Additional guidelines are available at: http://www.jamesrthorpefoundation.org/2010procedures.html.
Requirements: The Thorpe Foundation supports 501(c)3 non-profit organizations located in and serving the Minneapolis and the western Minneapolis metro suburbs of the Twin Cities.
Restrictions: The Foundation does not: make multi-year grants or fund individuals; make grants in the east metro area, greater Minnesota, or outside the State of Minnesota; make grants through fiscal agents; support endowment drives, conferences, seminars, tours, or fundraising events; support organizations with operating budgets over $2 million; support organizations with no paid staff.
Geographic Focus: Minnesota
Date(s) Application is Due: Mar 1; Sep 1
Contact: Kerrie Blevins; (612) 822-3412; kerrieblevins@jamesrthorpefoundation.org
Internet: http://www.jamesrthorpefoundation.org/2010guidelines.html
Sponsor: James R. Thorpe Foundation
318 West 48th Street
Minneapolis, MN 55419

James S. Copley Foundation Grants 2637
Incorporated in California in 1953, the Foundation serves as the philanthropic arm of the Copley Press, Inc., publishers of the Copley newspapers. The foundation offers support in the form of: scholarship funds; capital campaigns; equipment; employee matching gifts; endowments; equipment; building and; renovation grants. Funding organizations involved with arts and culture, education, animals and wildlife, health, recreation, and human services should apply. Giving is restricted primarily in areas of company operations in California, Illinois and Ohio.
Requirements: 501(c)3 organizations in the circulation areas of company newspapers/operations are eligible to apply. These areas include: California, Illinois and Ohio.
Restrictions: Ineligible funding opportunities include: religious, fraternal, or athletic organizations, government agencies, local chapters of national organizations, public elementary, secondary schools, public broadcasting systems, individuals, research, publications, conferences, general operating support, large campaigns and loans.
Geographic Focus: California, Illinois, Ohio
Date(s) Application is Due: Jan 2
Contact: Kim Koch, Secretary; (858) 454-0411, ext. 7671
Sponsor: James S. Copley Foundation
P.O. Box 1530
La Jolla, CA 92038-1530

James T. Grady-James H. Stack Award for Interpreting Chemistry for the Public 2638
This Award is given annually to recognize, encourage, and stimulate outstanding reporting directly to the public, which materially increases the knowledge and understanding of chemistry, chemical engineering, and related fields. This information may have been disseminated through the press, radio, television, films, the lecture platform, or books or pamphlets for the lay public. The award consists of $3,000, a medallion with a presentation box, and a certificate.
Requirements: Any individual, except a member of the award committee, may submit one nomination or seconding letter for the award in any given year. The nominating documents consist of a letter of not more than 1000 words containing an evaluation of the nominee's accomplishments and a specific identification of the work to be recognized, a biographical sketch including date of birth, and a list of publications authored by the nominee.
Restrictions: Application or self-nomination is not acceptable.
Geographic Focus: All States
Date(s) Application is Due: Nov 1
Amount of Grant: 3,000 USD
Contact: Felicia Dixon; (800) 227-5558; f_dixon@acs.org or awards@acs.org
Internet: http://portal.acs.org/portal/acs/corg/content?_nfpb=true&_pageLabel=PP_ARTICLEMAIN&node_id=1319&content_id=CTP_004537&use_sec=true&sec_url_var=region1
Sponsor: American Chemical Society
1155 Sixteenth Street, NW
Washington, DC 20036-4801

Jane's Trust Grants 2639

The Jane's Trust has particular interest in organizations and projects which primarily benefit underserved populations and disadvantaged communities. Jane's Trust will support grants for general operating purposes, as well, as it's Fields of Interest, which are: arts and culture, education, the environment, health and welfare. The Trust will make grants in the states of Florida, with a preference for southwest and central Florida; Massachusetts, with a preference for greater Boston and eastern Massachusetts; and in the northern New England states of Maine, New Hampshire and Vermont. Preference will be given to organizations located in those states for projects which will primarily provide benefits within those states. The application process begins by submitting of a concept paper. Guidelines are available at the Trusts website.
Requirements: 501(c)3 tax-exempt organizations in Florida, Maine, Massachusetts, New Hampshire, and Vermont are eligible.
Restrictions: Jane's Trust will not support: loans to charitable organizations; attempts to influence legislation; requests from individuals. Please note: Jane's Trust will normally not support public entities, such as municipalities, municipal departments, or public schools directly, but will entertain applications from tax-exempt fiscal agents or partners for collaborative projects with municipalities or schools. This does not apply to public colleges and universities.
Geographic Focus: Florida, Maine, Massachusetts, New Hampshire, Vermont
Date(s) Application is Due: Jan 25; Jul 15
Amount of Grant: 50,000 - 1,000,000 USD
Contact: Susan Fish; (617) 227-7940, ext. 775; fax (617) 227-0781; sfish@hembar.com
Internet: http://www.hembar.com/selectsrv/janes/index.html
Sponsor: Hemenway and Barnes LLP
60 State Street
Boston, MA 02109-1899

Jane and Jack Fitzpatrick Fund Grants 2640

The Jane and Jack Fitzpatrick Fund was established in Massachusetts in 2005 with the identified purpose of supporting higher education within the State of Massachusetts. The Foundation's primary fields of interest include: arts and art services, economic development, higher education, historic preservation, historical societies, and museums. Types of funding include: building and renovation, equipment purchase, general operating support, management development, and capacity building. A formal application is required, although interested parties should begin by forwarding a letter of interest describing the need in general terms. There are no specified annual deadlines.
Geographic Focus: Massachusetts
Amount of Grant: 50,000 - 100,000 USD
Contact: Jane P. Fitzpatrick, Trustee; (413) 298-1605 or (413) 298-1036
Sponsor: Jane and Jack Fitzpatrick Fund
P.O. Box 1164
Stockbridge, MA 01262-1164

Jane Bradley Pettit Foundation Arts and Culture Grants 2641

The Jane Bradley Pettit Foundation awards grants to initiate and sustain projects in the Greater Milwaukee community, with a focus on programs and projects that serve low-income and disadvantaged individuals, women, children, and the elderly. The Foundation supports the ongoing expenses of arts and cultural organizations through projects which offer guidance as well as individual and social development of young people. An initial application should be in the form of a letter of intent.
Requirements: Milwaukee-area charitable organizations are eligible.
Geographic Focus: Wisconsin
Date(s) Application is Due: Jan 15; May 15; Sep 15
Amount of Grant: 5,000 - 40,000 USD
Contact: Heidi Jones; (414) 982-2880 or (414) 982-2874; hjones@staffordlaw.com
Internet: http://www.jbpf.org/guidelines/index.html
Sponsor: Jane Bradley Pettit Foundation
1200 N. Mayfair Road, Suite 430
Wauwatosa, WI 53226-3282

Jane Bradley Pettit Foundation Community and Social Development Grants 2642

The Jane Bradley Pettit Foundation awards grants to initiate and sustain projects in the Greater Milwaukee community, with a focus on programs and projects that serve low-income and disadvantaged individuals, women, children, and the elderly. The Foundation has designated two areas for special consideration in the area of Community and Social Development Grants: early childhood development and assistance to women and children in poverty. The Foundation also supports programs which enable youth to develop leadership skills, character and self-esteem. An initial application should be in the form of a letter of intent.
Requirements: Milwaukee-area charitable organizations are eligible.
Geographic Focus: Wisconsin
Date(s) Application is Due: Jan 15; May 15; Sep 15
Amount of Grant: 5,000 - 100,000 USD
Contact: Heidi Jones, Director of Administration; (414) 982-2880 or (414) 982-2874; fax (414) 982-2889; hjones@staffordlaw.com
Internet: http://www.jbpf.org/guidelines/index.html
Sponsor: Jane Bradley Pettit Foundation
1200 N. Mayfair Road, Suite 430
Wauwatosa, WI 53226-3282

Jane Bradley Pettit Foundation Health Grants 2643

The Jane Bradley Pettit Foundation awards grants to initiate and sustain projects in the Greater Milwaukee community, with a focus on programs and projects that serve low-income and disadvantaged individuals, women, children, and the elderly. In the area of Health, the Foundation gives priority to community-based health care and prevention programs which address the physical and mental health needs of families, children, persons at-risk and the elderly. Support and advocacy for victims of abuse and neglect are also a priority. An initial application should be in the form of a letter of intent.
Requirements: Milwaukee-area charitable organizations are eligible.
Geographic Focus: Wisconsin
Date(s) Application is Due: Jan 15; May 15; Sep 15
Amount of Grant: 5,000 - 100,000 USD
Contact: Heidi Jones, Director of Administration; (414) 982-2880 or (414) 982-2874; fax (414) 982-2889; hjones@staffordlaw.com
Internet: http://www.jbpf.org/guidelines/index.html
Sponsor: Jane Bradley Pettit Foundation
1200 N. Mayfair Road, Suite 430
Wauwatosa, WI 53226-3282

Janesville Foundation Grants 2644

The Janesville Foundation is dedicated to improving the quality of community living in Janesville, WI, and the surrounding area. The Foundation makes grants to support nonprofit educational, charitable, and health organizations in the area. Capital grants and grants for specific projects or programs will be awarded. Proposals may be submitted at any time. Preliminary inquiries are encouraged. The application and guidelines are available at the Foundation website.
Requirements: Stand-alone ideas are welcome, as are ideas that are part of a larger project. The giving focus is on education, and community and economic development. Ideas that encompass either category have the best change of success. Grants are awarded to 501(c)3 nonprofit groups only. The Foundation will match selected ideas from individuals and businesses to a 501(c)3 nonprofit group suited to implement them.
Geographic Focus: Wisconsin
Contact: Ronald K. Ochs, Grants Coordinator; (608) 752-1032; fax (608) 752-1952
Internet: http://janesvillefoundation.org/
Sponsor: Janesville Foundation
P.O. Box 8123
Janesville, WI 53547-8123

Janirve Foundation Grants 2645

The Janirve Foundation, established in 1954, givings primarily to colleges and universities in western North Carolina. However, the Foundation also supports organizations involved with: children and youth services; community/economic development; environment; environment, natural resources; environment, plant conservation; family services; health organizations, association; higher education; hospitals (general); housing/shelter, development; human services.
Requirements: Applicants should contact Asheville, North Carolina, office for application procedures. Proposals from colleges and universities are considered only in the front quarter. Application form required. Applicants should submit the following: copy of IRS Determination Letter; detailed description of project and amount of funding requested; listing of additional sources and amount of support; how project's results will be evaluated or measured; how project will be sustained once grant support is completed; copy of current year's organizational budget and/or project budget; copy of most recent annual report/audited financial statement/990; listing of board of directors, trustees, officers and other key people and their affiliations; signature and title of chief executive officer; five copies of the proposal.
Restrictions: No support for public and private elementary schools, or churches and religious programs. No grants to individuals (except for scholarships), or generally for operating budgets, endowments or for research programs, publication of books or printed material, theatrical productions, videos, radio or television programs; no loans.
Geographic Focus: North Carolina
Date(s) Application is Due: Mar 1; Jun 1; Sep 1; Dec 1
Amount of Grant: 10,000 - 750,000 USD
Contact: E. Charles Dyson, Chairman; (828) 258-1877; fax (828) 258-1837; janirve@charterinternet.com
Sponsor: Janirve Foundation
1 North Pack Square, Suite 416
Asheville, NC 28801-3409

Janson Foundation Grants 2646

The Janson Foundation was established in 1983 to provide capital grants to deserving charitable organizations located in Skagit County, Washington. Edward W. Janson had a longtime career as a public servant in Skagit County and was committed to the citizens of the county. He established his foundation to assist the ongoing capital needs of deserving charitable organizations for the purchase of equipment, the construction of facilities, or the acquisition of land. In addition, the foundation funds the repair of existing facilities and the replacement of aging equipment. The majority of grants from the Janson Foundation are one year in duration; on occasion, multi-year support is awarded. Application materials are available for download at the grant website. Applicants are strongly encouraged to review the state application guidelines for additional helpful information and clarifications before applying. Applicants are also encouraged to review the foundation's funding history (link is available from the grant website). The application deadline for the Janson Foundation is February 28. Applicants will be notified of grant decisions by April 15.
Requirements: Applicants must have 501(c)3 status. Application must be mailed.
Restrictions: Grant requests for general operating or program support will not be considered. The foundation does not support requests from individuals, organizations attempting to influence policy through direct lobbying, or any political campaigns.
Geographic Focus: Washington
Date(s) Application is Due: Feb 28

Contact: Heidi Gordon, Vice President; (800) 848-7177; heidi.e.gordon@baml.com
Internet: https://www.bankofamerica.com/philanthropic/fn_search.action
Sponsor: Janson Foundation
800 5th Avenue, WA1-501-33-23
Seattle, WA 98104

Janus Foundation Grants 2647
The Foundation strives to help communities reach greater levels of self-sufficiency, and impact the lives of many in each community. The Foundation awards grants to nonprofit organizations in its areas of interest, including: at-risk youth through education; community service and volunteerism; and cultural institutions in the Denver-metro area. Interested applicants should complete the application available online. There is no application deadline. Please note that the Foundation accepts grant applications from nonprofit organizations throughout the U.S. for the first two giving areas. The third giving area only applies to cultural institutions that operate in the Denver, CO metro area.
Requirements: 501(c)3 tax-exempt organizations are eligible.
Geographic Focus: All States
Contact: Traci Papantones; (303) 333-3863; janusfoundation@janus.com
Internet: http://ww4.janus.com/Janus/Retail/StaticPage?jsp=Janushome/JanusFoundation.jsp
Sponsor: Janus Foundation
151 Detroit Street, 4th Floor
Denver, CO 80206-4805

Japan-US Community Education and Exchange (JUCEE) Grants 2648
The program awards grants for joint projects between U.S. and Japanese nonprofit organizations. The program also accomplishes its mission through bilateral nonprofit internships, fellowships, organizational exchanges and professional training. Projects may take place in the United States, Japan, and/or elsewhere, and may address any number of possible issue areas. Preference will be given to community-based projects that can be duplicated or serve as models for international collaboration and that employ online or video technology. The program provides a stipend for each project, as well as linguistic and other support. The matching or leveraging of funds is strongly encouraged. JUCEE will work closely with collaborating organizations throughout the project to provide facilitation and support when necessary and to monitor and document the collaborative processes engaged in the project.
Requirements: Proposals must include at least one Japanese and one U.S. nonprofit organization. All applying U.S. nonprofit organizations must have 501(c)3 status, or be fiscally sponsored by another 501(c)3 organization. Japanese organizations do not need to be incorporated, but must be nonprofit/nonpartisan. Organizations must have been in existence for at least one year as of the application deadline. Organizations need to demonstrate an established relationship between applying organizations.
Geographic Focus: All States
Contact: Conrad Asper, (510) 267-1920; fax (510) 267-1922; info-us@jucee.org
Sponsor: Japan-U.S. Community Education and Exchange
1440 Broadway, Suite 901
Oakland, CA 94612

Japan Foundation Center for Global Partnership (CGP) Grants 2649
Program supports Japan-U.S. collaborative policy-oriented projects in the target areas listed below. In addition, CGP recognizes the value of including a multinational dimension within projects, and therefore gives priority to those that incorporate Asia into its agenda. Prospective grantees must submit letters of inquiry for CGP consideration, 2-3 pages minimum, no later than March 1. Completed applications invited by CGP must be received by May 1.
Requirements: Proposals from U.S. organizations with 501(c)3 status only will be accepted by CGP New York. Appropriate Japan-based institutional collaboration must be demonstrated and secured throughout the course of the project.
Geographic Focus: All States
Date(s) Application is Due: Mar 1; May 1
Contact: Tomoki Akazawa; (212) 489-1255; fax (212) 489-1344; tomoki_akazawa@cgp.org
Internet: http://www.cgp.org/index.php?option=section&id=3
Sponsor: Japan Foundation Center for Global Partnership
152 West 57th Street, 17th Floor
New York, NY 10019-3101

Japan Foundation Center for Global Partnership (CGP) Institutional Grants 2650
With emphasis on academic/intellectual excellence and national and international public consequence, CGP's institutional grant program supports policy-oriented projects conducted by an array of institutions from the United States and Japan, including non-profit organizations, universities, and think tanks as well as policymakers, scholars, and educators, with a view to creating new networks and providing opportunities for advancing research and candid discussion of these issues. Within the mandate of enhancing Japan-U.S. collaboration, CGP recognizes the value of including a multinational dimension within projects, and gives priority to those that incorporate Asia into its agenda. Applicants must submit letters of inquiry for consideration, 2-3 pages minimum, no later than March 3. Full proposals must be received by May 1.
Requirements: Applicants can include: non-profit organizations; universities; think tanks; policymakers; scholars; and educators.
Geographic Focus: All States
Date(s) Application is Due: Mar 3; May 1
Contact: Yukiko Ono; (212) 489-1255; fax (212) 489-1344; yukiko_ono@cgp.org
Internet: http://www.jpf.go.jp/cgp/e/grant/index.html
Sponsor: Japan Foundation Center for Global Partnership
152 West 57th Street, 17th Floor
New York, NY 10019-3101

Japan Foundation Los Angeles Mini-Grants for Japanese Arts & Culture 2651
The Japan Foundation Los Angeles (JFLA) supports projects that will enhance further understanding of Japanese arts and culture, or that produce U.S.-Japan collaborative projects in the following areas: the performing arts, exhibitions, film screenings, lectures, and/or symposia and other cultural events. Successful candidates may be granted up to $1,000. Projects will be evaluated on their artistic quality, their expected impact on the audience and the U.S. arts scene, the strength of the project / organization's educational and community activities, and the organization's ability to carry through with the project and capacity to provide future continuity. Priority will be given to those projects that have secured additional funding from sources other than the Japan Foundation. Downloadable application guidelines and an application form are available at the website. Applications must be received by JFLA at least two months prior to the beginning date of the project. JFNY will contact applicants regarding the result two weeks prior to the project starting date. The Japan Foundation was established in 1972 by the Japanese legislature and became one of Japan's "Independent Administrative Institutions" in October 2003. The foundation maintains its headquarters in Tokyo and operates through a network of 21 overseas offices in 20 countries worldwide including offices in New York and Los Angeles, and a Center for Global Partnership, also in New York. The foundation's mission is to promote international cultural exchange and mutual understanding between Japan and other countries. To do so it offers three major categories of programming: Arts & Culture; Japanese Studies; and Japanese-Language Education.
Requirements: Grants will be made to non-profit U.S.-based organizations for projects that take place in states west of the Rocky Mountains (These include Alaska, Arizona, California, Colorado, Hawaii, Idaho, Montana, Nevada, New Mexico, Oregon, Utah, Washington, and Wyoming.) Grants may be used to cover the following costs: publicity; printing costs of programs, leaflets, or catalogs; honoraria for artists and lecturers; travel expenses for artists and lecturers, including per diem and accommodation expenses; and shipping cost of films, exhibits, and/or other materials related to the proposed event. The applicant should cover theater or space-rental fees, and/or the cost of a reception, if applicable.
Restrictions: Projects must take place in states west of the Rocky Mountains (see list in requirements section). The following entities or activities are not eligible to be funded: individuals and for-profit entities; projects that have already received funding through other Japan Foundation grants; organizations which have received a JFLA grant in the previous fiscal year; language-education programs through Japanese-language workshops and conferences; medical, technical, or scientific projects; and political, religious, social-welfare, fundraising, charitable, and commercial activities. JFLA generally does not fund an organization for more than three consecutive fiscal years.
Geographic Focus: All States
Amount of Grant: Up to 1,000 USD
Contact: Yoshihiro Nihei, Arts & Culture, PR; (213) 621-2267, ext. 109; fax (213) 621-2590; culture@jflalc.org or yoshihiro_nihei@jflalc.org
Internet: http://www.jflalc.org/grants-ac.html
Sponsor: Japan Foundation Los Angeles
333 South Grand Avenue, Suite 2250
Los Angeles, CA 90071

Japan Foundation New York Small Grants for Arts and Culture 2652
The Japan Foundation New York Office (JFNY) Small Grants for Arts and Culture support projects that nurture further understanding of Japanese arts and culture or that produce U.S.-Japan collaborative projects through the performing arts, exhibitions, film screenings, lectures, and/or symposia and other cultural events. Successful candidates may be granted up to $5,000. Projects will be evaluated on their artistic quality, expected impact on the audience and the U.S. arts scene, strength of educational and community activities, and the organization's ability to carry through with the project and capacity to provide future continuity. Priority will be given to those projects that have secured additional funding from sources other than the Japan Foundation. Application guidelines, supporting-documentation requirements, and a downloadable application form are available at the website. Applications must be received by JFNY at least three months prior to the beginning date of the project. JFNY will contact applicants regarding the result two months prior to the project starting date. The Japan Foundation was established in 1972 by the Japanese legislature and became one of Japan's "Independent Administrative Institutions" in October 2003. The foundation maintains its headquarters in Tokyo and operates through a network of 21 overseas offices in 20 countries worldwide including offices in New York and Los Angeles, and a Center for Global Partnership, also in New York. The foundation's mission is to promote international cultural exchange and mutual understanding between Japan and other countries. To do so it offers three major categories of programming: Arts & Culture; Japanese Studies; and Japanese-Language Education.
Requirements: Grants will be made to non-profit U.S.-based organizations for projects that take place in states east of the Rocky Mountains (these include Alabama, Arkansas, Connecticut, District of Columbia, Delaware, Florida, Georgia, Illinois, Indiana, Iowa, Kansas, Kentucky, Louisiana, Massachusetts, Maryland, Maine, Michigan, Minnesota, Missouri, Mississippi, North Carolina, North Dakota, Nebraska, New Hampshire, New Jersey, New York, Ohio, Oklahoma, Pennsylvania, Rhode Island, South Carolina, South Dakota, Tennessee, Texas, Virginia, Vermont, Wisconsin, and West Virginia). Grants may be used to cover the following costs: publicity; printing costs of programs, leaflets, or catalogs; honoraria for artists and lecturers; travel expenses for artists and lecturers, including per diem and accommodation expenses; and shipping cost of films, exhibits, and/or other materials related to the proposed event. The applicant should cover theater or space-rental fees, and/or the cost of a reception, if applicable.
Restrictions: Projects must take place in states east of the Rocky Mountains (see list in requirements section). Individuals and for-profit entities cannot apply. Projects that have already received funding through other Japan Foundation grants cannot apply. Organizations which have received the JFNY Small Grants for Arts and Culture in the previous fiscal year cannot apply. Japanese-language education programs are excluded, along with martial arts- and medical, technical, or scientific projects. (Applicants should contact the Japan

Foundation, Los Angeles for Japanese-language education programs.) The following types of requests are not considered: political; religious; social-welfare; and commercial.
Geographic Focus: All States
Amount of Grant: Up to 5,000 USD
Contact: Yukihiro Ohira; (212) 489-0299; fax (212) 489-0409; info@jfny.org
Internet: http://www.jfny.org/arts_and_culture/smallgrant.html
Sponsor: Japan Foundation in New York
152 W 57th Street, 17th Floor
New York, NY 10019

Jaqua Foundation Grants 2653
The foundation awards grants to nonprofit organizations to fund collegiate education, animal welfare, and the performing arts. There are no application deadlines or forms. Applicants should submit a letter containing the program description, amount of request, and a brief description of the organization.
Requirements: Nonprofit organizations are eligible.
Restrictions: Individuals are ineligible.
Geographic Focus: All States
Contact: Eli Hoffman, Chairperson; (973) 593-7010
Internet: http://fdncenter.org/grantmaker/jaqua
Sponsor: Jaqua Foundation
100 Campus Drive, P.O. Box 944
Florham Park, NJ 07932-0944

Jaquelin Hume Foundation Grants 2654
The Jacquelin Hume Foundation Grants primarily support K-12 education reform efforts that are national in scope. Grants will be made for general operations, project development, and research. Special projects are generally preferred. One request per organization per year will be considered.
Requirements: An application form is not required. Applicants should submit a one-page letter of inquiry along with the following: the qualifications of key personnel; a copy of the IRS determination letter; a copy of the most recent annual report, audited financial statement, or 990; a detailed description of the project and amount of funding requested; a listing of the board of directors, trustees, officers and other key people, with their affiliations; and a list of past and present donors.
Restrictions: The Foundation does not support organizations outside the U.S. or grants to individuals.
Geographic Focus: All States
Date(s) Application is Due: Mar 15; Sep 15
Contact: Gisele Huff, Executive Director; (415) 705-5115
Sponsor: Jaquelin Hume Foundation
600 Montgomery Street, Suite 2800
San Francisco, CA 94111-2803

Jasper Foundation Grants 2655
The purpose of the Foundation is to assist donors in creating assets to meet the ongoing and changing charitable interests of those living in Jasper County, Indiana. Special emphasis is placed on programs that enrich the quality of life of our community in five areas: arts and culture; preservation of historic and cultural resources; education; health; and social concerns. Favored grant requests will generally reflect the following characteristics: projects which propose practical solutions to community needs; projects which promote cooperation among existing agencies without duplicating services; projects that will become self-sustaining without requiring on-going Foundation funds. Applications and guidelines are available at the Foundation office or website. The Foundation has two grant cycles in the spring and fall.
Requirements: Applicants must submit 5 complete copies of the grant application to include the following: the grant application and supporting materials; an outline that addresses the project's goals and objectives, plan of implementation, project budget, staff, method of evaluation, and why the proposal is important to the community; a list of the officers and board of directors; a current financial report; and a copy of the organization's 501(c)3 tax exempt IRS letter.
Restrictions: Grants are not made for budget deficits or sectarian religious activities.
Geographic Focus: Indiana
Date(s) Application is Due: Apr 1; Oct 1
Contact: Linda Reiners; (219) 866-5899; fax (219) 866-0555; jasper@liljasper.com
Internet: http://www.jasperfdn.org/grants.htm
Sponsor: Jasper Foundation
301 N Van Rensselaer Street, P.O. Box 295
Rensselear, IN 47978

Jay and Rose Phillips Family Foundation Grants 2656
The Jay and Rose Phillips Family Foundation has five funding priorities that guide it's grant making: strengthening families; supporting training and education for lifelong success; improving health and wellness; promoting independence and inclusion for people with disabilities and the elderly; and fostering good relations and civic participation. These funding priorities are the combined product of responding to community needs, the legacy of our founders and the current passions and interests of it's Trustees. Across all of these funding priorities, the Foundation place's a high value on supporting efforts that serve the most vulnerable in the community and those with the least access to resources. The Foundation has three program grant rounds each year with deadlines of March 15, July 15 and November 15. All proposals be submitted electronically using an online proposal submission process. The online submission deadline is 11:59 p.m. on the deadline date. The Foundation accepts requests for capital grants once per year through an online Letter of Inquiry (LOI) process. LOI's must be submitted by 11:59 p.m. on January 8.

Requirements: The Foundation awards grants only to organizations which are tax-exempt and publicly supported under Section 501(c)3 of the Internal Revenue Service Code. Grants are awarded primarily in the Twin Cities metropolitan area. Unsolicited proposals are not accepted from organizations located outside of Minnesota.
Restrictions: The foundation does not make grants in support of individuals, for political campaigns, or for lobbying efforts to influence legislation.
Geographic Focus: Minnesota
Date(s) Application is Due: Jan 8; Mar 15; Jul 15; Nov 15
Amount of Grant: 10,000 - 100,000 USD
Contact: Dana Jensen; (612) 623-1652 or (612) 623-1654; djensen@phillipsfnd.org
Internet: http://www.phillipsfnd.org/index.asp?page_seq=15
Sponsor: Jay and Rose Phillips Family Foundation
East Bridge Building, 10 Second Street NE, Suite 200
Minneapolis, MN 55413

Jayne and Leonard Abess Foundation Grants 2657
The Foundation, established in Miami, Florida, in 2004, by the son of City National Bank co-founder, Leonard L. Abess, Sr., supports a variety of causes both locally and nationally. Areas of interest include: design arts education, writer's, human services programs, Jewish agencies and temples, children with special needs, and higher education. The primary type of support is general operating funds. There are no specific applications or deadlines with which to adhere, and applicants should contact the Foundation office directly in writing. This initial contact should include a detailed description of the program, and a budget narrative.
Geographic Focus: All States
Amount of Grant: Up to 50,000 USD
Contact: Leonard L. Abess; (305) 577-7333 or (212) 632-3000; fax (305) 577-7689
Sponsor: Jayne and Leonard Abess Foundation
600 Fifth Avenue
New York, NY 10020-2302

Jean and Louis Dreyfus Foundation Grants 2658
The Jean and Louis Dreyfus Foundation was established in 1979 from the estate of Louis Dreyfus, a music publisher, and that of his wife, Jean. The mission of the Foundation is to enhance the quality of life of New Yorkers, particularly the aging and disadvantaged. The Foundation disburses grants mainly within the five boroughs of New York City, and supports programs in the arts, health and social services (including youth agencies, women, and the elderly), and education (including literacy). Support is given for program development and matching funds. Application forms are not required. The board meets each year in the spring and in the fall. Initial inquiries should consist of a one or two page letter describing the organization and outlining the project in question. The January 15th and July 15th deadlines are for Letters of Intent.
Requirements: New York City nonprofits are eligible.
Restrictions: Grants are never made to individuals.
Geographic Focus: New York
Date(s) Application is Due: Jan 15; Jul 15
Contact: Jessica Keuskamp; (212) 599-1931; jldreyfusfdtn@hotmail.com
Internet: http://foundationcenter.org/grantmaker/dreyfus/guide.html
Sponsor: Jean and Louis Dreyfus Foundation
420 Lexington Avenue, Suite 626
New York, NY 10170

Jean and Price Daniel Foundation Grants 2659
The Jean and Daniel Price Foundation, established in Texas in 1985, has the primary purpose of supporting historical preservation programs. The Foundation's current fields of interest include: historical societies, libraries, archives, protestant agencies and churches, and public health initiatives. Types of support include building and renovation, general operating support, land acquisition, and program development. There are no specific application forms or deadlines with which to adhere, and potential applicants should contact the office initially by letter. Past grants have ranged from $5,000 to $100,000.
Requirements: Applicants should be 501(c)3 organizations located in, or serving the residents of, Texas.
Geographic Focus: Texas
Contact: Jean Daniel Murph, President; (936) 336-7355
Sponsor: Jean and Price Daniel Foundation
P.O. Box 789
Liberty, TX 77575-0789

Jeffris Wood Foundation Grants 2660
The Jeffris Wood Foundation funds grants to community-based organizations working to provide opportunities for urban youth and economically disadvantaged. The Foundation supports programs that: help urban youth improve their futures, explore their creativity and avoid unwanted pregnancies; help Native American youth connect with their cultural traditions; connect low-income urban youth to nature; and provide services for domestic violence survivors. Current deadlines are posted on the website.
Requirements: Organizations must first submit a one-page letter of inquiry that includes a description of the organization and the project. They should also attach a brief budget describing income and expenses, plus complete contact information. If the request is screened for further consideration, the organization will be asked to submit a full proposal. All materials must be sent by U.S. mail.
Restrictions: Grants are not made to: individuals; scholarships; schools; capital expenses or renovation projects; food or shelter programs (except domestic violence); research or publications; video & web productions; religious programs that are not all inclusive; or athletic events and sponsorships.

Geographic Focus: Washington
Amount of Grant: 1,000 - 3,000 USD
Contact: Therese Ogle, Grants Consultant; (206) 781-3472; OgleFounds@aol.com
Internet: http://foundationcenter.org/grantmaker/jeffriswood/guide.html
Sponsor: Jeffris Wood Foundation
6723 Sycamore Avenue NW
Seattle, WA 98117

JELD-WEN Foundation Grants 2661
The Foundation seeks to improve the quality of life in company-operating areas and awards grants in the areas of capital campaigns, education, youth activities, community development, health and medical, and arts and humanities. Types of support include building construction/renovation, equipment, general operating support, land acquisition, matching/challenge support, program development, scholarship funds, and seed money. Prescreening and application information are available online.
Requirements: Nonprofit organizations in the Foundation's area of operations.
Geographic Focus: All States
Amount of Grant: 1,000 - 1,000,000 USD
Contact: JELD-WEN Foundation Headquarters; (503) 478-4478; fax (503) 478-4474
Internet: http://www.jeld-wenfoundation.org/
Sponsor: Jeld-Wen Foundation
200 SW Market Street, Suite 550
Portland, OR 97201

Jenifer Altman Foundation Grants 2662
The foundation is a small foundation working for a socially just and ecologically sustainable future, innovative research and demonstration projects in mind-body health, and improved child care prospects for at-risk children. Small grants are made in two areas: initiatives concerning the impact of endocrine disrupting chemicals on human health and the preservation of the environment and initiatives supporting the global citizens' movement for a just and sustainable future in relation to international governmental decision-making forums. The foundation awards a few grants for innovative research and demonstration programs in mind-body health, especially those focused on cancer. Local initiatives that contribute to the quality of life in Bolinas, CA, are also of interest. Applicants should send a concept letter to determine if their projects align with the foundations areas of interest.
Requirements: Creative and innovative nonprofits are eligible to apply for one-time grants.
Restrictions: Grants are not made to individuals. The foundation rarely funds programs for the conservation of specific species or habitats and rarely funds research at universities on environmental issues. Grants are not made for civic programs, projects in other countries, or projects that are focused entirely on one city or region in the United States.
Geographic Focus: All States
Contact: Marni Rosen; (415) 561-2182 or (415) 561-2187; info@jaf.org or mrosen@jaf.org
Internet: http://www.jaf.org/apply/index.html
Sponsor: Jenifer Altman Foundation
P.O. Box 29209
San Francisco, CA 94129

Jenkins Foundation: Improving the Health of Greater Richmond Grants 2663
The foundation is committed to expanding access to community-based services through programs and organizations that have the potential to make a significant impact on the quality of health, especially for the youth in its local area.
Requirements: The current areas of focus are: Expanding access to health care services for the uninsured and underserved; Substance abuse prevention services that promote healthy lifestyles and increase availability of services; Violence prevention services that promote safe and healthy environments for children and their families and work toward the elimination of violence in the local communities; In addition, the foundation is committed to the long-term viability of the organizations it supports, and will consider capacity building grants that strengthen an agency's ability to better serve its clients. The foundation will also consider a limited number of proposals outside the above stated focus areas.
Restrictions: Proposals will be accepted from charitable organizations, which serve the residents of the City of Richmond and the counties of Chesterfield, Hanover, Henrico, Goochland, and Powhatan.
Geographic Focus: Virginia
Date(s) Application is Due: May 5; Nov 5
Contact: Elaine Summerfield; (804) 330-7400; esummerfield@tcfrichmond.org
Internet: http://www.tcfrichmond.org/Page2954.cfm#Jenkins
Sponsor: Community Foundation Serving Richmond and Central Virginia
7501 Boulders View Drive, Suite 110
Richmond, VA 23225

Jennings County Community Foundation Grants 2664
The Foundation seeks to serve philanthropic and charitable needs in Jennings County, Indiana, by offering endowment services, grant making, scholarships, donor estate and planned gift services to individuals and qualified organizations serving the community of Jennings County, Indiana. The Foundation's fields of interest for all ages include the following: community service; social service; education; health; environment; and the arts. The Foundation reviews proposals in the spring and fall. Applications will be made available at the spring and fall cycle grant explanation meeting as announced in the local media. At this mandatory meeting the grant guidelines and process will be explained. The grant proposal form is available at the website.
Requirements: Nonprofit 501(c)3 organizations, coalitions, community associations, and other civic groups may apply if providing services in Jennings County. Applicants must also attend an explanation meeting of the guidelines for grants.
Restrictions: The Foundation does not fund political activity; sectarian religious activity; endowment purposed except for limited experimental or demonstration periods; operating budgets except for limited experimental or demonstration periods; and salaries.
Geographic Focus: Indiana
Contact: Barb Shaw, Executive Director; (812) 346-5553; jcffdirector@comcast.net
Internet: http://www.jenningsfoundation.net/index.html
Sponsor: Jennings County Community Foundation
111 North State Street
North Vernon, IN 47265-1510

Jennings County Community Foundation Women's Giving Circle Grant 2665
The Women's Giving Circle was established to make a lasting impact in the lives of women and children in Jennings County. Grants are available to nonprofit organizations that have a need for assistance on a community project. Grants are for organizations that meet the needs of women and children in the fields of community service, social service, education, health, environment and the arts. The application is available at the website.
Geographic Focus: Indiana
Contact: Barb Shaw; (812) 523-4483 or (812) 346-5553; jccf@jenningsfoundation.net
Sandy Vance, Grant Contact; (812) 592-1280
Darlene Bradshaw, Grant Contact; (812) 346-1742
Linda Erler, Grant Contact; (812) 873-7421
Internet: http://www.jenningsfoundation.net/php/wgc.php
Sponsor: Jennings County Community Foundation
111 North State Street
North Vernon, IN 47265-1510

Jerome and Mildred Paddock Foundation Grants 2666
The Foundation was established in 1967 to benefit disadvantaged children and elderly populations. Primarily, the foundation is interested in funding programming needs that will improve the quality of life of those less fortunate. Field of interest include: aging; children and youth services; programs for economically disadvantaged; health care support; and human/social services. Though giving is focused in and around Sarasota, the foundation does extend funding beyond Florida. The deadline is January 10th, with final notification by March 15th.
Restrictions: No grants to individuals, or for endowments, debt reduction, operating expenses, conferences or seminars, workshops, travel, surveys, advertising, research, fund raising or for annual campaigns or capital campaigns.
Geographic Focus: All States
Date(s) Application is Due: Jan 10
Amount of Grant: 15,000 USD
Contact: Joan Greenwood, Charitable Associate, Wachovia Bank; (941) 361-5803; joan.greenwood@wachovia.com
Sponsor: Jerome and Mildred Paddock Foundation
Wachovia Bank, NA., P.O. Box 267
Sarasota, FL 34230

Jerome Foundation Grants 2667
The Foundation supports programs in dance, literature, media arts, music, theater, performance art, the visual arts, multidisciplinary work and arts criticism. The Foundation seeks to support artists who exhibit significant potential yet are not recognized as established creators by fellow artists and other arts professionals. Examples of recognition include exhibitions, reviews, commissions, performances, grant awards, residencies, fellowships, publications and productions. Applications are available online.
Requirements: Artists and nonprofit, tax-exempt organizations in Minnesota and New York are eligible.
Geographic Focus: Minnesota, New York
Contact: Program Contact; (800) 995-3766 or (651) 224-9431; fax (651) 224-3439; info@jeromefdn.org
Internet: http://www.jeromefdn.org
Sponsor: Jerome Foundation
400 Sibley Street, Suite 125
Saint Paul, MN 55101-1928

Jerome Foundation Travel and Study Grants 2668
The program awards grants to artists and arts administrators to support periods of travel for the purpose of professional development. The program supports such activities as dialog on aesthetic issues, the experience of seeing artistic work outside of Minnesota, time for reflection and individualized study, the development of collaborations, participation in specific training programs, and research leading to the creation of new work. Awards are made once per year. Grants are available in literature, media arts, and music in odd-numbered years and dance, theater, and visual arts in even-numbered years.
Requirements: Minnesota residents working in literature, media arts, and music are eligible. Applicants must have lived in the state for at least one year.
Geographic Focus: Minnesota
Date(s) Application is Due: Jan 13
Amount of Grant: 1,200 - 5,000 USD
Contact: Vickie Benson, Vice President; (800) 995-3766 or (651) 224-9431; fax (651) 224-3439; vibe@jeromefdn.org
Internet: http://www.jeromefdn.org/IV~Grant_Programs/C~Travel_and_Study
Sponsor: Jerome Foundation
400 Sibley Street, Suite 125
Saint Paul, MN 55101-1928

Jerry L. and Barbara J. Burris Foundation Grants 2669
The Jerry L. and Barbara J. Burris Foundation was established in Indiana in 1994. Its primary fields of interest include: the arts; cancer research; children and youth services; education; hospitals; human services; museums; Protestant agencies and churches; and zoological societies. Funding typically comes in the form of general operating support and scholarship funding. There are no specific applications or annual deadlines, so applicants should begin by contacting the Foundation directly.
Geographic Focus: Florida, Indiana
Amount of Grant: 1,000 - 10,000 USD
Contact: Barbara J. Burris, President; (317) 843-5678
Sponsor: Jerry L. and Barbara J. Burris Foundation
P.O. Box 80238
Indianapolis, IN 46280-0238

Jessie B. Cox Charitable Trust Grants 2670
The Trust is dedicated to improving the environment and the quality of life for people living in the six New England States. To achieve its goals, the Trust pursues initiatives in three key fields of interest: education: early learning, out-of-school time; environment: habitat conservation, concentrating on fresh and marine water protection; health: access to health care. In all of these funding areas, the Trust is mindful of its special status as one of the few funders with an interest in all six of the New England states. Applications for funding are reviewed in light of the important issues of the region. The Grants Committee meets twice per year to award grants, in April and October. The Trust has a two-step system of application, beginning with a concept paper and progressing to a full grant proposal. Concept papers are due on March 15 and September 15. Applicants who have submitted a concept paper and been asked to submit a complete proposal must do so by July 1 (March applicants) or January 5 (September applicants).
Requirements: All grant applicants are asked to demonstrate a plan for measuring their success. This plan should identify benchmarks against which progress towards identified goals can be measured. Grantees must report on their progress within a year of receiving support and on project completion, with reference to the initial benchmarks.
Restrictions: The Cox Trust does not normally support: general operating support and ongoing maintenance; buildings, equipment or land acquisition; endowments, scholarship funds, or fundraising activities; grant requests of under $50,000; projects for which the Trust is the sole or predominant source of support; programs for which the public sector normally assumes funding responsibility; core educational programs of public, private, parochial, or charter schools; requests from individuals; sectarian religious activity.
Geographic Focus: Connecticut, Maine, Massachusetts, New Hampshire, Rhode Island, Vermont
Date(s) Application is Due: Jan 5; Mar 15; Jul 1; Sep 15
Contact: Kirstie David; (617) 391-3081; kdavid@gmafoundations.com
Internet: http://www.jbcoxtrust.org/?page_id=28
Sponsor: Jessie B. Cox Charitable Trust
GMA Foundations, 77 Summer Street, 8th Floor
Boston, MA 02110-1006

Jessie Ball Dupont Fund Grants 2671
The fund is a national foundation having a special, though not exclusive, interest in issues affecting the South. Grants awarded include competitive grants—program grants, institutional development, and capacity building; and feasibility grants—smaller grants that enable institutions to carefully explore and develop new concepts and programs. Areas of interest include six focus areas: strengthening the independent sector; organizing and nurturing philanthropy; building assets of people, families, and communities; building the capacity of eligible organizations; stimulating community problem solving; and helping people hold their communities accountable. The fund supports four initiatives: the religion initiative, the nonprofit initiative, the small liberal arts colleges initiative, and the independent schools initiative. Types of support include general operating support, building construction/renovation, equipment acquisition, program development, seed money grants, publication, consulting services, professorships, curriculum development, matching funds, and technical assistance. Grants are awarded generally for one year. The trustees meet in January, March, May, July, September, and November to consider requests.
Requirements: Applying organizations must have received a contribution from Mrs. DuPont between the five-year period of January 1, 1960, and December 31, 1964.
Amount of Grant: 2,000 - 5,000 USD
Contact: Geana Potter; (904) 353-0890 or (800) 252-3452; contactus@dupontfund.org
Internet: http://www.dupontfund.org
Sponsor: Jessie Ball Dupont Fund
One Independent Drive, Suite 1400
Jacksonville, FL 32202-0511

Jessie Smith Noyes Foundation Grants 2672
The foundation is committed to preventing damage to the natural systems upon which all life depends and to strengthening individuals and institutions committed to protecting natural systems and ensuring a sustainable society. The foundation makes grants primarily in the interrelated areas of environment and reproductive rights. The program components include toxics, sustainable agriculture (both with emphasis on southern and Rocky Mountain states), and U.S. reproductive rights. In addition, a few grants are made in four areas of special concern: sustainable communities, U.S. environmental justice, strengthening the U.S. nonprofit sector, and environmental issues in the metropolitan New York region. Letters of inquiry are received at any time; proposals will be requested from the foundation after review.
Requirements: 501(c)3 tax-exempt organizations are eligible.
Restrictions: Normally, the foundation will not consider requests for direct service, endowments, loans or scholarships to individuals, capital construction funds, conferences, media events, production of media and TV programming, or general fund-raising drives. General research projects are not funded per se.
Geographic Focus: All States
Contact: Millie Buchanan; (212) 684-6577; fax (212) 689-6549; noyes@noyes.org
Internet: http://www.noyes.org
Sponsor: Jessie Smith Noyes Foundation
6 E 39th Street, 12th Floor
New York, NY 10016-0112

Jewish Community Foundation of Los Angeles Cutting Edge Grants 2673
The Jewish Community Foundation's Cutting Edge Grants encourage creative thinkers, social entrepreneurs, and innovative organizations to propose significant and transformative programs of high visibility and impact. The Foundation is interested in funding cutting edge programs for up to $250,000 over a three-year period that address important needs in the Los Angeles Jewish community. The following types of programs that benefit the Los Angeles Jewish community are eligible for consideration: cutting edge programs that have not been tested previously in any location; programs that have been piloted in Los Angeles, proven to be viable, and are proposed for community-wide implementation; programs operating elsewhere in the United States that may be suitable for trial replication or adaptation in the Los Angeles area; and programs developed by a social entrepreneur or group of social activists (where a board of directors and/or nonprofit status have not yet been established), designed to lead to a new charitable organization and partnered in the interim with an appropriate nonprofit fiscal sponsor.
Requirements: Applicants must be an existing nonprofit organization 501(c)3 or a collaboration of nonprofit agencies, or social entrepreneur(s) or group of community activists partnered with an appropriate fiscal sponsor. Organizations are encouraged to review the website for specific requirements for application of funds.
Restrictions: The Foundation does not fund the following: private foundations or endowment programs; previous cutting edge grant awardees whose Foundation grant will still be active in the same year as the request; ongoing general operating support; fundraising campaign; existing financial deficits; programs based on travel; capital projects; or programs implemented outside of Los Angeles.
Geographic Focus: California
Date(s) Application is Due: Mar 1
Contact: Administrator; (323) 761-8700 or 1-877-363-6966; fax (323) 761-8720; info@jewishfoundationla.org
Internet: http://www.jewishfoundationla.org/grants/cutting-edge-grants
Sponsor: Jewish Community Foundation
6505 Wilshire Boulevard, Suite 1200
Los Angeles, CA 90048

Jewish Community Foundation of Los Angeles Israel Grants 2674
The Jewish Community Foundation of Los Angeles is committed to addressing two important issues facing Israelis living in Israel: economic development and self-sufficiency, and Jewish identity.
Requirements: Programs must have a dramatic impact on a large number of people or geographic region, and must include job creation and/or job placement services. They must also work to further participants' ability to engage in non-secular Jewish life, e.g., text study and observance and understanding of Jewish holidays, rituals, and traditions. To apply for the grant, organizations must contact the grant administrator with a brief description of the program, and how its goals relate to either the economic development/economic self-sufficiency or Jewish identity.
Geographic Focus: California
Amount of Grant: 100,000 - 250,000 USD
Contact: Naomi Strongin, Israel Grant Administrator; (323) 761-8700 or (877) 363-6966; fax (323) 761-8720; nstrongin@jewishfoundationla.org
Internet: http://www.jewishfoundationla.org/grants/israel-grants
Sponsor: Jewish Community Foundation
6505 Wilshire Boulevard, Suite 1200
Los Angeles, CA 90048

Jewish Fund Grants 2675
The Fund awards grants to sustain, enrich, and address the overall health care needs of both the Jewish community and general community in the metropolitan Detroit area. The Fund is particularly interested in supporting projects that: address health care and social welfare needs of vulnerable/at-risk populations within the Jewish community; respond to priority capital and equipment needs of the Detroit Medical Center/Sinai Hospital; improve the health and well-being of vulnerable/at risk populations in the general community; support inclusion of people with special needs into the general activities of the community; enhance positive relationships between the Jewish community and the Detroit community. Highest priority is given to requests for programs that: address a critical need; impact the lives of residents of the Wayne, Oakland and Macomb counties; have a defined plan for sustaining the program beyond the grant period; include a financial or in-kind contribution from the organization; involve collaboration with others; have an outcomes-based evaluation plan; and can be funded and replicated by others. Samples of previously funded grants are available on the Fund website.
Requirements: The Jewish Fund will make grants to 501(c)3 organizations and other non-profits qualified as tax exempt under the Internal Revenue Code. Applicant organizations must provide a current audited financial statement. Applicants are encouraged to contact the Fund and discuss their proposed project with the executive director before applying for funding.
Restrictions: The Fund will usually not support: grants made directly to individuals; loans; grants to support religious activities or sectarian education; overseas projects; capital projects or equipment purchases (except equipment at the DMC/Sinai); endowments, annual fund drives, and fundraising events; and past operating deficits.

Geographic Focus: Michigan
Contact: Margo Pernick, Executive Director; (248) 203-1487; fax (248) 645-7879
Internet: http://thejewishfund.org/grant-request-guidelines.html
Sponsor: Jewish Fund
6735 Telegraph Road
Bloomfield Hills, MI 48301-2030

Jewish Funds for Justice Grants 2676
Jewish Funds for Justice recently launched a new grantmaking strategy, The Opportunity Fund which seeks to: Make significant broad-based change within the Jewish community and America; Create strategic partnerships with grantees and other foundations that allow for greater collective impact; Promote new and innovative models of social change whose effects will reverberate on the national level. In addition to financial support, grantees receive technical support from the grantmaking staff. This fund consists of three portfolios: Partnership Portfolio, Transformative Organizing Portfolio and Innovation Portfolio. Partnership grants seek to expand the base of the Jewish social justice movement, within both the progressive and the mainstream communities, strengthen low-income communities and expand the capacity of the Jewish community to act as an anchor and ally in struggles for economic and social justice. Partners range from a variety of organizations, both Jewish and secular. The Transformative Organizing portfolio invests in grassroots organizations engaging in new types of organizing, based on a model of personal, organizational, and field-wide transformation. JFSJ supports organizations that have invested in transformative leadership development and/or are beginning to explore these practices. The Innovation portfolio supports new ideas of organizing groups that have the potential to transform their own work, the field as a whole, or the nation. These grants offer organizing groups the resources to take risks, respond to new opportunities, and invent new approaches. Additionally, Congregation-Based Community Organizing Synagogue challenge grants is a JFSJ grantmaking program contained within the Partnership Portfolio. JFSJ supports synagogues looking to join their local broad-based community organization network by funding half of the membership dues.
Requirements: U.S. nonprofits are eligible. From Jewish organizations, the fund is seeking proposals for Jewish spiritual and cultural renewal, peace, and social change projects. From non-Jewish organizations, the fund is seeking social and economic justice projects that involve organized Jewish activity, such as in outreach efforts, interfaith work, coalition-building, partnerships, governance, daily operations, or other areas.
Geographic Focus: All States
Contact: Rachel Berger , (212) 213-2113; grants@jewishjustice.org
Internet: http://www.jewishjustice.org/jfsj.php?page=2.2
Sponsor: Jewish Funds for Justice
330 7th Avenue, Suite 1902
New York, NY 10001

Jewish Women's Foundation of New York Grants 2677
The foundation provides support for unmet social, economic, and health needs of Jewish females in the New York metropolitan area and beyond. Strategic grants support cutting-edge projects that address Jewish education, training, and culture—projects related to education, training of educators, leadership development, ethics, spirituality, arts, sports, etc; mental and physical health—projects involving genetics, self-esteem, violence prevention, issues concerning the end of life, and other areas that relate to women's health as a quality of life; and economic empowerment—projects that give women more independence, knowledge, competency, and responsibility for their economic situations. Grant requests may address innovative programs, services, and/or research. The projects primary target group must be Jewish females. The foundation expects to award three to four grants. The listed deadline is for concept letters; full proposals are by invitation.
Requirements: 501(c)3 tax-exempt organizations in the New York metropolitan area (the five boroughs of New York City, Long Island and/or Westchester) are eligible.
Restrictions: The foundation will not provide grants for scholarships, equipment, capital campaigns, or ongoing support for existing programs.
Geographic Focus: New York
Date(s) Application is Due: Sep 30
Amount of Grant: Up to 25,000 USD
Contact: Sherri Greenbach, Executive Director; (212) 836-1478; fax (212) 836-1831
Internet: http://www.jewishwomenny.org
Sponsor: Jewish Women's Foundation of New York
130 E 59th Street, Room 563
New York, NY 10022

Jim Blevins Foundation Grants 2678
The purpose of the Jim Blevins Foundation grant program is to support education, Christian, and Presbyterian organizations within the State of Tennessee. Its primary fields of interest include: Christian agencies and churches; health organizations; higher education; human services; Protestant agencies and churches, and youth services. There are no specific deadlines or applications with which to adhere, and applicants should contact the Foundation directly. Giving is limited to Tennessee.
Geographic Focus: Tennessee
Contact: James V. Blevins, Trustee; (615) 298-5000; jwblev@aol.com
Sponsor: Jim Blevins Foundation
P.O. Box 150056
Nashville, TN 37215

Jim Blevins Foundation Scholarships 2679
The purpose of the Jim Blevins Foundation scholarships is to support education within the State of Georgia. The program is open to currently enrolled undergraduate students in the states of Tennessee and Georgia. The annual scholarship amount per individual is $5,000, and is renewable for up to four years total. The award is based on need, and the annual deadline is April 30. Applicants should contact the Foundation directly requesting an application form.
Requirements: Applicants must have a minimum of a 3.0 GPA, and reside in the state of Tennessee or Georgia.
Geographic Focus: Georgia, Tennessee
Date(s) Application is Due: Apr 30
Amount of Grant: Up to 5,000 USD
Contact: James V. Blevins, Trustee; (615) 298-5000; jwblev@aol.com
Sponsor: Jim Blevins Foundation
P.O. Box 150056
Nashville, TN 37215

Jim Moran Foundation Grants 2680
The Jim Moran Foundation Grants award funding to 501(c)3 organizations in Florida. The Foundation seeks to improve the quality of life for youth and families through the support of innovative programs and opportunities that meet the ever-changing needs of the community. The Foundation's funding focuses include: education; elder care programs; family strengthening programs; meaningful after school programs; and youth transitional living programs. Proposals for programs that improve the quality of life for those who are at-risk and economically disadvantaged (without extenuating medical or developmental disabilities) will receive priority consideration. Grants are primarily awarded to the Florida counties of Broward, Palm Beach, and Duval. Applicants submit an online letter of inquiry, and will be notified within 90 days if they qualify to submit the online application.
Requirements: The Foundation will consider only organizations that have received 501(c)3 tax-exempt status under the IRS code. Additionally, the organization must be appropriately recognized by state statutes, laws and regulations that govern tax exempt organizations.
Restrictions: The Foundation will consider requests for operating dollars, but only if they do not exceed 50% of the grant request. The Foundation will not consider requests for capital campaigns, capacity building, healthcare or medical research, or event sponsorships.
Geographic Focus: Florida
Contact: Melanie Burgess, Executive Director; (954) 429-2122; fax (954) 429-2699; information@jimmoranfoundation.org
Internet: http://www.jimmoranfoundation.org/GrantApplication.aspx
Sponsor: Jim Moran Foundation
100 Jim Moran Boulevard
Deerfield Beach, FL 33442

JM Foundation Grants 2681
The foundation awards grants to eligible nonprofit organizations in its areas of interest, including education and research that fosters market-based policy solutions; developing state and national organizations that promote free enterprise, entrepreneurship, and private initiative; and identifying and educating young leaders. Types of support include internships, matching/challenge grants, program grants, publication, research grants, seed grants, and technical assistance. The foundation's board of directors meets bi-annually, usually in May and October. There are no formal proposal deadlines. Inquiries and proposals are processed on an ongoing basis.
Requirements: Public charities, including 501(c)3, 509(a)1, and 170(b)1(a)(vi) nonprofit organizations, that shares the foundation's priority interests is invited to submit a proposal.
Restrictions: Grants do not support individuals, the arts, government agencies, public schools, and international agencies; or requests for operating expenses, annual fundraising campaigns, capital campaigns, equipment, endowment funds, and loans.
Geographic Focus: All States
Amount of Grant: 5,000 - 100,000 USD
Contact: Carl Helstrom, Executive Director; (212) 687-7735; fax (212) 697-5495
Internet: http://foundationcenter.org/grantmaker/jm/guide_jm.html
Sponsor: JM Foundation
654 Madison Avenue, Suite 1605
New York, NY 10065

Joan Bentinck-Smith Charitable Foundation Grants 2682
Established in 1994, the Joan Bentinck-Smith Charitable Foundation offers funding support primarily within its home state of Massachusetts. Its major fields of interest include: children and youth services; education; housing and shelter; human services; and the support of local YMCAs and YWCAs. There are no specified application forms or annual deadlines, so applicants should begin by contacting the Foundation directly. Recent grants have ranged from $500 to $15,000.
Requirements: The Foundation offers funding to 501(c)3 organizations located within, or supporting the residents of, Massachusetts
Geographic Focus: Massachusetts
Amount of Grant: 500 - 15,000 USD
Contact: Joan Bentinck-Smith, Trustee; (508) 420-4250
Sponsor: Joan Bentinck-Smith Charitable Foundation
1340 Main Street
Osterville, MA 02655-0430

Joel L. Fleishman Civil Society Fellowships 2683
The Fellowship provides a select group of leaders from domestic non-profit organizations, international non-governmental organizations, foundations, government, socially responsible businesses, and other civil society groups in the United States and internationally with the opportunity to come in residence at the Sanford Institute for a four-week mini-sabbatical. While at Duke, fellows will perform research and work with institute faculty and other Duke affiliates on issues relating to the development of civil society. Applicants will be selected based upon their proposed research project and how they intend to utilize

Duke's resources to benefit their professional work in civil society. The fellowship provides housing and program expenses; a stipend; and access to the university's library, research centers, and recreational facilities. Download the application online.
Requirements: Employees of nonprofit and nongovernmental groups worldwide are eligible.
Restrictions: Individuals employed at government agencies and academic institutions are not eligible. Full-time academics are not eligible to apply.
Geographic Focus: All States
Date(s) Application is Due: May 1
Amount of Grant: 6,000 USD
Contact: Melynn Glusman, Program Director; (919) 613-7432; melynn.glusman@duke.ed
Internet: http://www.pubpol.duke.edu/centers/civil/
Sponsor: Duke University
P.O. Box 90239
Durham, NC 27708

Joe W. and Dorothy Dorsett Brown Foundation Grants 2684
The foundation awards grants to nonprofit organizations in Louisiana and the Gulf Coast of Mississippi. Areas of interest include medical research; housing for the homeless; support for organizations who care for the sick, hungry or helpless; religious and educational institutions; and organizations and groups concerned with improving the local community. Types of support include operating budgets, research, and student aid. The foundation also supports Service Learning, a learn-by-doing approach to the curriculum. Students receive practical, hands-on experience in the subject matter studied by meeting identified community needs through active participation. The listed deadline date is for Service Learning grants.
Requirements: Louisiana and Mississippi nonprofit organizations, with a focus on South Louisiana, the New Orleans area, and the Mississippi Gulf Coast, are eligible. Service Learning grant applications are available yearly to sixth through 12th grades in the following parishes: Orleans, Jefferson, Plaquemines, Saint Bernard, Saint Charles, Tangipahoa, Saint James, Saint John, Saint Tammany, and Washington.
Geographic Focus: Louisiana, Mississippi
Date(s) Application is Due: Sep 30
Amount of Grant: 5,000 - 25,000 USD
Contact: Beth Buscher, (504) 834-3433; BethBuscher@thebrownfoundation.org
Internet: http://www.thebrownfoundation.org
Sponsor: Joe W. and Dorothy Dorsett Brown Foundation
320 Hammond Highway, Suite 500
Metairie, LA 70005

John and Elizabeth Whiteley Foundation Grants 2685
Incorporated in Michigan in 1955, the Whiteley Foundation sponsors business education scholarships, scholarships for Episcopal seminary students, and grants for community development and religious purposes. Regular grants requests may be submitted at any time. Scholarships are limited to students whose parents reside in Ingham County, Michigan. Previous recipients are allowed to reapply as college students. Application forms are required, though there are no annual deadlines.
Requirements: A letter of intent is required for grants indicating the intended use of funds. Students may request a current application from their high school guidance office or contact the Foundation.
Geographic Focus: Michigan
Contact: Donald B. Lawrence, Jr.; (517) 886-7176, ext. 115; fax (517) 886-1080
Sponsor: John and Elizabeth Whiteley Foundation
5806 W. Michigan Avenue, P.O. Box 80502
Lansing, MI 48908

John and Margaret Post Foundation Grants 2686
The John and Margaret Post Foundation provides support to charitable organizations, which benefit the quality of life for families and society in general and primarily in Northwest New Jersey. The Foundations mission: first consideration for grants is given to organizations based in Northwest New Jersey, or the New Jersey chapters of national organizations; proposals are occasionally considered from groups outside of the state. Priority for funding will be given in the following order: capital needs, specific programs and general operating expenses for smaller organizations who do not have endowments that provide operating support or that can be considered grass roots. Application deadlines are April 1st for a June meeting & October 1st for a December meeting. Grants average $20,000.
Requirements: 501(c)3 organizations based in Northwest New Jersey, or the New Jersey chapters of national organizations are eligible to apply for funding. Contact the Foundation via email for Application Form and Instructions.
Geographic Focus: New Jersey
Date(s) Application is Due: Apr 1; Oct 1
Amount of Grant: 20,000 USD
Contact: Gale Y. Sykes; (908) 598-3576; grantinquiries2@wachovia.com
Internet: https://www.wachovia.com/foundation/v/index.jsp?vgnextoid=af878689fb0aa110VgnVCM1000004b0d1872RCRD&vgnextfmt=default
Sponsor: John and Margaret Post Foundation
190 River Road, NJ3132
Summit, NJ 07901

John Ben Snow Memorial Trust Grants 2687
The mission of the Foundation is to make grants within specific focus areas to enhance the quality of life in Central and Northern New York State. Historically, the Foundation has made grants in the following program areas: arts and culture, community development, education, environment, historic preservation, and journalism. The Foundation responds to the ever-changing needs of various segments of the population, especially to the needs of young people and people who are disadvantaged either physically or economically. It is the Foundation's general policy to give preference to proposals seeking funds for new or enhanced programs, one-time, short-term grants to sustain a program until funding is stabilized, matching grants used to encourage the participation of other donors, and last dollars towards a capital campaign. There are no minimums or maximum grant amounts; however, most grants range from $5,000 to $15,000.
Requirements: Giving is primarily focused in Maryland, Nevada, and central New York.
Restrictions: The Foundation will not accept proposals from individuals or for-profit organizations. Additionally, the Foundation does not encourage proposals from religious organizations or proposals for endowments, contingency funding, or debt reduction.
Geographic Focus: All States
Date(s) Application is Due: Apr 1
Amount of Grant: 5,000 - 25,000 USD
Contact: Jonathan L. Snow, (315) 471-5256; fax (315) 471-5256
Internet: http://www.johnbensnow.com/jbsmt
Sponsor: John Ben Snow Memorial Trust
50 Presidential Plaza, Suite 106
Syracuse, NY 13202

John C. Lasko Foundation Trust Grants 2688
The John C. Lasko Foundation Trust was established to build churches that will last forever and will never deviate or change from God's Mission. Mr. John C. Lasko, founder of the John C. Lasko Foundation Trust, was born November 26, 1920 in Wayne, Michigan. He founded Republic Tool and Die in Belleville, Michigan in 1940. Republic grew to become the largest privately owned tool and die company in North America. Mr. Lasko passed away on February 21, 2011 at the age of ninety. Since its establishment, the John C. Lasko Foundation Trust has supported the construction of churches the world over. The Foundation will continue on in perpetuity as a legacy to Mr. Lasko. Applicants must apply online at the grant website. Applicants are strongly encouraged to do the following before applying: review the downloadable state application procedures for additional helpful information and clarifications; review the downloadable online-application guidelines at the grant website; review the trust's funding history (link is available from the grant website); review the online application questions in advance; and review the list of required attachments. These will generally include: a list of board members, financial statements (audited, reviewed, or compiled by independent auditor); an organization summary; a list of other funding sources; an IRS Determination letter; and other required documents. All attachments must be uploaded in the online application as PDF, Word, or Excel files. The John C. Lasko Foundation Trust has a rolling application deadline. Applicants will be notified of grant decisions four to six months after proposal submission.
Requirements: Applicants to the Lasko Foundation must own the land on which the church will be constructed. A copy of the deed demonstrating ownership of the land, complete financial plans (pre- and post construction), three construction bids from general contractors or construction managers, and complete architectural plans are required. The church will need to fund at least 50% of the project costs.
Restrictions: Grants from the Lasko Foundation are exclusively for the construction of worship space, defined as the sanctuary portion of the church building, and excluding areas such as the fellowship hall, classroom, office area, kitchen, and baptistery. The trust does not provide support for debt repayment.
Geographic Focus: All States, All Countries
Contact: George Thorn; (312) 828-4154; ilgrantmaking@bankofamerica.com
Internet: https://www.bankofamerica.com/philanthropic/fn_search.action
Sponsor: John C. Lasko Foundation Trust
231 South LaSalle Street, IL1-231-13-32
Chicago, IL 60604

John Clarke Trust Grants 2689
Dating from April 20, 1676, this historic trust was created under the will of Dr. John Clarke, a Baptist clergyman and physician and one of the co-founders of the first European settlement on Aquidneck Island in 1638. He was born in 1609 and arrived in Boston in 1637 and was one of some three hundred persons that founded the colony on Aquidneck Island. He was the author of the Royal Charter of 1663 that maintained Rhode Island as a colony. Dr. Clarke had no surviving children. He practiced medicine, was a minister, and held public office, although his chief interest was that of the Christian ministry. He was also very interested in education and is thought to have been involved in establishing a free school for Newport in 1640. Dr. Clarke is buried in a small cemetery on West Broadway in Newport. In his will, written on the date of his death, John Clarke established a perpetual charitable trust. He directed that the income from the trust be used "for the relief of the poor or bringing up of children unto learning from time to time forever." He further instructed the trustees "to have a special regard and care to provide for those that fear the Lord." Applicants must apply online at the grant website. Applicants are strongly encouraged to do the following before applying: review the downloadable state application procedures for additional helpful information and clarifications; review the downloadable online-application guidelines at the grant website; review the trust's funding history (link is available from the grant website); review the online application questions in advance; and review the list of required attachments. These will generally include: a list of board members, financial statements (audited, reviewed, or compiled by independent auditor); an organization summary; a list of other funding sources; an IRS Determination letter; and other required documents. All attachments must be uploaded in the online application as PDF, Word, or Excel files. The semi-annual application deadlines are April 1 and November 1. Applications should be submitted by 11:59 p.m. on the deadline dates. Applicants will be notified of grant decisions by letter within two to three months after the proposal deadline. All applications will be acknowledged. Applicants are encouraged to call the second phone number given if they do not receive an acknowledgment within two to three weeks of proposal submission.

Requirements: The trustees of the John Clarke Trust have established a policy of giving preference to organizations located on Aquidneck Island, Rhode Island, and within the East Bay area. However, applications from any Rhode Island 501(c)3 charitable organizations are acceptable.
Restrictions: Capital grant requests will be considered ONLY for Aquidneck Island. The trust does not support requests from individuals, organizations attempting to influence policy through direct lobbying, or any political campaigns.
Geographic Focus: Rhode Island
Date(s) Application is Due: Apr 1; Nov 1
Contact: Emma Greene; (617) 434-0329 or (888) 703-2345; emma.m.greene@baml.com
Internet: https://www.bankofamerica.com/philanthropic/fn_search.action
Sponsor: John Clarke Trust
225 Franklin Street, 4th Floor, MA1-225-04-02
Boston, MA 02110

John D. and Catherine T. MacArthur Foundation Global Challenges Grants   2690
The global challenges area focuses on emerging opportunities and threats in a period of rapid globalization—the development of complex political, social, and economic interconnections that result from the increased capacity for people, goods, capital, and information to move freely across national borders. Grants are made in the areas of human rights and economic governance. Grants are made throughout the year. Guidelines are available on the Web site.
Requirements: Grants are provided to nonprofit organizations, public agencies, universities, research institutes, and networks of such institutions. Only rarely are grants awarded for individual research projects, preference being given to multifaceted programs.
Restrictions: The foundation will not provide funding for publications and conferences, political activities, attempts to influence legislation, foundation development campaigns, or for programs that are the responsibility of governments.
Geographic Focus: All States
Amount of Grant: 50,000 - 2,000,000 USD
Contact: Grants Management; (312) 726-8000; 4answers@macfound.org
Internet: http://www.macfound.org/programs/gss/GC.htm
Sponsor: John D. and Catherine T. MacArthur Foundation
140 S Dearborn Street, Suite 1100
Chicago, IL 60603-5285

John D. and Katherine A. Johnston Foundation Grants   2691
The John D. and Katherine A. Johnston Foundation was established in 1928 to support charitable organizations that work to improve the lives of physically disabled children and adults. Special consideration is given to organizations that serve low-income individuals. Preference is given to charitable organizations that serve the people of Newport, Rhode Island. Capital requests that fund handicapped assistive devices (wheelchairs, walkers, etc.) or adaptive equipment (lift installation, ramp installation, etc.) are strongly encouraged. Grant requests for general operating or program support will also be considered. The majority of grants from the Johnston Foundation are one year in duration. The Johnston Foundation shares a mission and grantmaking focus with the Vigneron Memorial Fund. Both foundations have the same proposal deadline date of 11:59 p.m. on April 1. Applicants will be notified of grant decisions before May 31. Applicants must apply online at the grant website. Applicants are strongly encouraged to do the following before applying: review the downloadable state application procedures for additional helpful information and clarifications; review the downloadable online-application guidelines at the grant website; review the foundation's funding history (link is available from the grant website); review the online application questions in advance; and review the list of required attachments. These will generally include: a list of board members, financial statements (audited, reviewed, or compiled by independent auditor); an organization summary; a list of other funding sources; an IRS Determination letter; and other required documents. All attachments must be uploaded in the online application as PDF, Word, or Excel files.
Requirements: Applicants must have 501(c)3 tax-exempt status.
Restrictions: The foundation does not support requests from individuals, organizations attempting to influence policy through direct lobbying, or any political campaigns.
Geographic Focus: Rhode Island
Date(s) Application is Due: Apr 1
Contact: Emma Greene, Director; (617) 434-0329; emma.m.greene@baml.com
Internet: https://www.bankofamerica.com/philanthropic/fn_search.action
Sponsor: John D. and Katherine A. Johnston Foundation
225 Franklin Street, 4th Floor, MA1-225-04-02
Boston, MA 02110

John Deere Foundation Grants   2692
The foundation invests in programs in education, health/human services, community improvement, arts and culture. Types of support include annual campaigns, building construction/renovation, continuing support, fellowships, general operating support, scholarship funds, and seed money grants. Foundation interest also includes support for Third World development through US-based nonprofits with international building funds, research grants, general operating purposes, and continuing support. There are no application deadlines.
Requirements: Nonprofit organizations in communities with major John Deere operating units, and employee presence are eligible. Eligible U.S. locations are: Augusta, GA; Quad City Region, IL; Des Moines, IA, Dubuque, IA, Iowa Quad Cities, IA, Ottumwa, IA, Waterloo, IA, Coffeyville, KS, Lenexa, KS, Thibodaux, LA, Springfield, MO, Cary, NC, Fuquay-Varina, NC, Fargo, ND, Greeneville, TN, Madison, WI, Horicon, WI. Exceptions include: accredited colleges and universities; organizations focused on international development initiatives related to John Deere Solutions for World Hunger initiative. Because John Deere dealerships are owned and operated independently, their communities are not included in this geographic scope. Also eligible to apply are organizations and institutions of national or international scope that reflect the foundation's concerns.
Restrictions: Funds are not available for the following organizations or purposes: individual initiatives, including scholarships; sports teams, racing teams, athletic endeavors or scholarships designated for athletes; faith-based organizations for sectarian purposes; political candidates, campaigns or organizations; private clubs, fraternities or sororities; other foundations for purposes of building endowment; tax-supported entities.
Geographic Focus: Georgia, Illinois, Iowa, Kansas, Louisiana, Missouri, North Carolina, Tennessee, Wisconsin, Belarus, Brazil, Canada, Estonia, Latvia, Lithuania, Moldova, Ukraine
Contact: Amy Nimmer, Director; (309) 765-8000
Internet: http://www.deere.com/en_US/globalcitizenship/socialinvestment/index.html
Sponsor: John Deere Foundation
1 John Deere Place
Moline, IL 61265-8098

John Edward Fowler Memorial Foundation Grants   2693
The foundation makes grants to qualified charitable organizations providing grassroots programs for people in need in the Washington, DC, metropolitan area. Preference is given to programs that address the issues of homelessness, hunger, at-risk children and youth (pre-school through high school), adult literacy, free medical care (prenatal to seniors), seniors aging in place, job training and placement. Types of support include general operating support, building construction/renovation, equipment acquisition, program development, and matching funds. The foundation is interested in supporting smaller, well-managed nonprofit organizations that have innovative ideas about how to help people help themselves. Contact the office for application forms. There are no application deadlines.
Requirements: Organizations in Washington, DC, and its close Maryland and Virginia suburbs are eligible.
Restrictions: Grants are not made outside the metropolitan Washington, DC, area, or to/for national health organizations; government agencies; medical research; public school districts; individuals; or arts (except for intensive arts-in-education programs that directly benefit at-risk children and youth).
Geographic Focus: District of Columbia, Maryland, Virginia
Amount of Grant: 5,000 - 20,000 USD
Contact: Suzanne Martin, Grant Consultant; (301) 654-2700
Internet: http://fdncenter.org/grantmaker/fowler/about.html
Sponsor: John Edward Fowler Memorial Foundation
4340 East-West Highway, Suite 206
Bethesda, MD 20814

John F. Kennedy Center for the Performing Arts Rosemary Kennedy Internship   2694
Through the National Rosemary Kennedy Internship Initiative, the VSA and Accessibility Department provides internship opportunities at arts and arts service organizations across the U.S. These programs service youth with disabilities between the ages of 15 and 21 who are seeking careers in the arts, arts administration, and arts education. Existing, new, or innovative programs are encouraged to apply. Proposals are submitted by January 7, with notification on a rolling basis by January 14. Additional submission guidelines are available at the website.
Requirements: Nonprofit contractors must meet the following *Requirements:* at least three years of successful experience operating an internship, apprenticeship, or youth-training program; experience delivering quality internship and/or training opportunities for youth with disabilities between the ages of 15 and 21; identify qualified youth with disabilities to participate in the program; be fiscally sound and have the capacity to manage and execute the proposed program within the designated timeline; comply with any state, local, and, if applicable, school district requirements regarding criminal background checks for program employees, contractors, and volunteers; conduct the program in spaces that are ADA-accessible and be knowledgeable about appropriate accommodations and effective communication for youth with disabilities who choose to participate. Programs must accomplish the following: provide experiential internship, apprenticeship or training opportunities that facilitate the entry and advancement of youth with disabilities into competitive employment in the arts, arts administration or arts education; reflect recognized youth development principles that emphasize the cognitive, social, and behavioral competencies that help youth with disabilities succeed as adults; successfully identify the aptitudes, talents, gifts, competencies, skills necessary to pursue their career or trade pathway of choice in arts-based employment. Programs must have immediate and significant impact with measurable and sustainable outcomes.
Restrictions: The Center will accept only one proposal per contractor. Commercial, for-profit or individual entities, and non-U.S. entities are not eligible.
Geographic Focus: All States
Date(s) Application is Due: Jan 7
Amount of Grant: 5,000 - 25,000 USD
Contact: Sonja Cendak; (202) 416-8823 or (202) 416-8898; scendak@kennedy-center.org
Internet: http://www.kennedy-center.org/accessibility/career.cfm#Rosemary
Sponsor: John F. Kennedy Center for the Performing Arts
2700 F Street NW
Washington, DC 20566

John G. Duncan Trust Grants   2695
The trust awards grants in the following areas of interest: arts; education; health care; human services; religion; and support: building/renovation; capital campaigns; emergency funds; equipment; program development; seed money; and research. Contact the foundation, for the application guidelines and application form.
Requirements: IRS 501(c)3 organizations in Colorado are eligible.
Restrictions: No support for other grantmaking organizations, individuals, endowments, or for general operating expenses.

Geographic Focus: Colorado
Date(s) Application is Due: Jan 31; Apr 30; Jul 31; Oct 31
Amount of Grant: 1,000 - 10,000 USD
Samples: Gospel Shelters for Women, Colorado Springs, CO, $3,250; Boulder Valley Womens Health Center, Boulder, CO, $2,000; Commerce City Community Health Services, Commerce City, CO, $5,000.
Contact: Jason Craig, c/o Wells Fargo Bank, N.A., (720) 947-6820
Sponsor: John G. Duncan Trust
1740 Broadway, MAC C7300-483
Denver, CO 80274-0001

John G. Martin Foundation Grants 2696
The foundation awards grants to eligible Connecticut nonprofit organizations in the areas of education at all levels. Grants may be considered in other areas. Preferential consideration will be given to proposals whose benefits include assistance to the aging and elderly or assistance to youth and adolescents. The foundation is interested in the long-term stabilization and advancement of effective organizations specializing in these areas of interest. Types of support include building construction/renovation, capital campaigns, and matching/challenge grants.
Requirements: Nonprofits serving the Hartford, CT, area may submit applications.
Geographic Focus: Connecticut
Amount of Grant: 10,000 - 65,000 USD
Contact: Frank Loehmann; (860) 677-4574; fax (860) 674-1490; frank@resmgtcorp.com
Sponsor: John G. Martin Foundation
2 Batterson Park Road
Farmington, CT 06032-2553

John Gogian Family Foundation Grants 2697
The Gogian Foundation supports nonprofit organizations in Los Angeles County that provide services and solutions for developmentally disabled adults and children, concentrating on life skills and vocational training, residential group homes, employment, day services, after school programs, and therapeutic services. The Foundation also supports organizations that provides services for abused or neglected youth including: residential group homes; emancipating foster youth; therapeutic, social, and educational services; institutionalized or incarcerated youth; domestic violence; and family preservation. The Foundation makes grants for new, expanding, or sustaining core programming. It also supports improvements, equipment, and vehicle capital expenditures.
Requirements: Applicants must submit the online Letter of Inquiry to request funding, but submit the filled out form by U.S. mail. Organizations will be notified of the outcome of their LOI within 45 of submittal deadline.
Restrictions: The Foundation does not fund the following: national organizations or their affiliates; individuals; care of animals; arts; culture; research; reduction of existing debt; funding of endowments; lending of funds; fundraising events; or political campaigns or projects designed to influence legislation.
Geographic Focus: California
Date(s) Application is Due: Jan 20; Jun 22
Amount of Grant: 5,000 - 20,000 USD
Contact: Lindsey Stammerjohn; (310) 325-0954; jgff@gogianfoundation.org
Internet: http://www.gogianfoundation.org/grant/index.html
Sponsor: John Gogian Family Foundation
3305 Fujita Street
Torrance, CA 90505

John H. and Wilhelmina D. Harland Charitable Foundation Grants 2698
The foundation, offers support for: youth services, community services, cultural programs, education, and health. The focus is local rather than regional or national, and priority is given to institutions with metropolitan Atlanta, Georgia. Grants support: building/renovation; capital campaigns; equipment; general/operating support; matching/challenge support; and scholarship funds. The Foundation prefers a telephone call as opposed to a letter of inquiry for the initial approach.
Requirements: Grant support is available to nonprofit organizations in Georgia, with emphasis on the metropolitan Atlanta area.
Restrictions: Grants are not awarded to individuals.
Geographic Focus: Georgia
Date(s) Application is Due: Mar 1; Sep 1
Amount of Grant: 4,000 - 250,000 USD
Contact: Jane Hardesty, Executive Director; (404) 264-9912
Sponsor: John H. and Wilhelmina D. Harland Charitable Foundation
2 Piedmont Court, Suite 106
Atlanta, GA 30305-1567

John H. Wellons Foundation Grants 2699
Established in 1950, the John H. Wellons Foundation, is a private foundation. The foundation's support is limited to the Dunn, North Carolina, area. The foundation awards student loans to local area residents, provides housing for the elderly and/or handicapped, and contributes to charitable organizations. There are no specific deadlines with which to adhere. Contact the Foundation for further application information and guidelines.
Geographic Focus: North Carolina
Contact: John H. Wellons, President; (910) 892-0436
Sponsor: John H. Wellons Foundation
P.O. Box 1254
Dunn, NC 28335-1254

John I. Smith Charities Grants 2700
The foundation supports nonprofit organizations, primarily in South Carolina. With its areas of interest, including: the visual and performing arts, higher education, medical education, theological education, literacy education and basic skills, Christian agencies and churches, child welfare, and programs for the disabled. Grants support general operations, capital campaigns, endowment funds, scholarship funds, and emergency funds. Application forms are not required. The board meets on a quarterly basis. Mail applications to: P.O. Box 1687, Greer, SC 29652
Requirements: Nonprofit organizations in South Carolina are eligible to apply.
Geographic Focus: South Carolina
Amount of Grant: 2,500 - 200,000 USD
Contact: Jefferson Smith, President; (864) 879-2455
Sponsor: John I. Smith Charities
P.O. Box 40200, FL9-100-10-19
Jacksonville, FL 32203-0200

John J. Leidy Foundation Grants 2701
The John J. Leidy Foundation was established in 1957. The foundation gives primarily in the metropolitan Baltimore, Maryland, area. Funding is available to people with disabilities, education, health, social services, and Jewish organizations in the form of, scholarship funds, building/renovation, equipment, general/operating support, and program development grants.
Requirements: Maryland non-profits are eligible to apply.
Restrictions: No grants to individuals.
Geographic Focus: Maryland
Contact: Robert L. Pierson, President; (410) 821-3006; Leidyfd@attglobal.net
Sponsor: John J. Leidy Foundation
305 W Chesapeake Avenue, Suite 308
Towson, MD 21204-4440

John Jewett and Helen Chandler Garland Foundation Grants 2702
Established in 1959, the John Jewett & Helen Chandler Garland Foundation gives primarily in California, with emphasis on southern California. The foundations area of interest include: the arts, education, health care, children and social services. There are no application deadlines.
Requirements: California nonprofit organizations are eligible.
Restrictions: No telephone inquiries excepted, submit a letter of inquiry.
Geographic Focus: California
Amount of Grant: 2,500 - 610,000 USD
Contact: Lisa M. Hausler, Manager
Sponsor: John Jewett and Helen Chandler Garland Foundation
P.O. Box 550
Pasadena, CA 91102-0550

John Lord Knight Foundation Grants 2703
The Foundation, established in 1957, provides funding for program in the Lucas County, Ohio, region and throughout Florida. Its areas of interest include: cancer research; Christian agencies and churches; education; elementary education; federated giving programs; hospitals; human services; public libraries; and youth services. There are no specific deadlines, and applicants should submit a detailed description of project and amount of funding requested to the listed contact person in care of KeyBank.
Geographic Focus: Florida, Ohio
Contact: Erwin Diener, Key Bank, Trust Officer; (419) 259-8372
Sponsor: John Lord Knight Foundation
Three Seagate, P.O. Box 10099
Toledo, OH 43699-0099

John M. Ross Foundation Grants 2704
The John M. Ross Foundation provides funding to nonprofit organizations operating in the state of Hawaii. Funding priorities include youth services, scholarship funds and federated giving programs, offering support in the form of general/operating grants & scholarships. Grant proposals are due February 1st. Applicants are notified in writing of the Committee's action on their requests. Grants range from $250 - $10,000.
Requirements: Nonprofit organizations operating in the state of Hawaii are eligible. To begin the application process, contact the Foundation's administrative office for a Funding Cover Sheet (FCS) and application form. The (FCS) must accompany each grant proposal. The proposal should be no more then 3 pages in length. Include the following information and documentation with your proposal: 1 copy of IRS determination letter, charter, and bylaw, and annual report and financial statements; how project will be sustained once grantmaker support is completed; qualifications of key personnel; statement of problem project will address; population served; copy of IRS Determination Letter; copy of most recent annual report/audited financial statement/990; how project's results will be evaluated or measured; listing of board of directors, trustees, officers and other key people and their affiliations; detailed description of project and amount of funding requested; organization's charter and by-laws; copy of current year's organizational budget and/or project budget; listing of additional sources and amount of support; 4 copies of proposal. Mail proposal to: John M. Ross Foundation c/o Bank of Hawaii, Corporate Trustee Foundation Administration #758 P. O. Box 3170 Honolulu, Hawaii 96802-3170.
Restrictions: No grants are made for endowments or capital campaigns. The recipient of a grant will be required to submit a narrative report on what has been accomplished as a result of the grant, and a fiscal accounting of the grant expenditures.
Geographic Focus: Hawaii
Date(s) Application is Due: Feb 1
Amount of Grant: 250 - 10,000 USD

Contact: Paula Boyce, Grants Administrator; (808) 694-4945; paula.boyce@boh.com
Sponsor: John M. Ross Foundation
P.O. Box 3170
Honolulu, HI 96802-3170

John M. Weaver Foundation Grants 2705
Established in California in 1997, the John M. Weaver Foundation offers funding support for animals and wildlife, education, and human services throughout the State. There is no specified application form, and no annual deadlines. Interested parties should contact the Foundation directly with a two- or three-page query letter, describing their project, budgetary needs, and overall timeline. Recent grants have been funded in the amount of $100 to $1,200.
Requirements: Any 501(c)3 located in, or serving the residents of, California are eligible.
Geographic Focus: California
Amount of Grant: 100 - 1,200 USD
Contact: John M. Weaver, President; (408) 268-6471
Sponsor: John M. Weaver Foundation
4760 Sherbourne Drive
San Jose, CA 95124-4845

John Merck Fund Grants 2706
The foundation fosters innovative advocacy and problem solving in the fields of Developmental Disabilities, Environment, Reproductive Health, Human Rights and Job Opportunities. Its objective is to act as a catalyst, supporting organizations that can effect constructive and measurable change in each of these areas.
Requirements: The foundation actively seeks out projects and programs that may merit support, then requests grant applications on behalf of those it finds most promising. It does not encourage the submission of unsolicited proposals. However, organizations interested in obtaining support for work they do in one of the foundation's areas of interest are welcome to send a brief letter of inquiry. The foundation favors: outstanding individuals working on promising projects in organizations that may have difficulty attracting funds; pilot projects with potential for widespread application; advocacy, including litigation, capable of setting or protecting important precedents; smaller organizations, start-ups included; one-year grant requests (though multi-year grants of up to three years occasionally are made); matching-grant opportunities, particularly to help broaden support for fledgling initiatives.
Restrictions: The foundation does not provide grants for: endowment or capital-fund projects; large organizations with well-established funding sources (except those that need help launching promising new projects for which funding is not readily available); general support (except in the case of small organizations whose entire mission coincides with one of foundation's areas of interest); individuals (except if his or her project is sponsored by a domestic or foreign educational, scientific or charitable organization).
Geographic Focus: All States
Contact: Ruth G. Hennig; (617) 556-4120; fax (617) 556-4130; info@jmfund.org
Internet: http://www.jmfund.org/program.html
Sponsor: John Merck Fund
2 Oliver Street, 8th Floor
Boston, MA 02108

John P. McGovern Foundation Grants 2707
The John P. McGovern Foundation, established in 1961, supports the charitable interests of the donor to support the activities of established nonprofit organizations, which are of importance to human welfare with special focus on children and family health education and promotion, treatment and disease prevention. The Foundation gives primarily in Texas with an emphasis on the Houston area, but also provides funding in the Southwest region as well. The types of support offered are: building/renovation; conferences/seminars; continuing support; curriculum development; emergency funds; endowments; general/operating support; matching/challenge support; professorships; publication; research; and scholarship funds.
Requirements: Non-profits in Texas are eligible to apply.
Geographic Focus: Texas
Date(s) Application is Due: Aug 31
Amount of Grant: 10,000 - 100,000 USD
Contact: Kathrine G. McGovern, President; (713) 661-4808; fax (713) 661-3031
Sponsor: John P. McGovern Foundation
2211 Norfolk Street, Suite 900
Houston, TX 77098-4044

John P. Murphy Foundation Grants 2708
The Foundation awards grants primarily in Cuyahoga County, Ohio, and its immediately adjacent counties. Areas of interest include education—college level, and primary and secondary education to improve educational programs benefiting low income and minority students, most often in Cleveland public schools; arts and culture; social services; community—community activities, agencies, and events; health—institutions and organizations such as hospitals, clinic, and nursing homes; and religion. Grants to national or regional institutions with broad public support will be made only for start-up programs where time is a factor or where the proposal addresses a specific local community need. Guidelines are available online. Contact the office for an application form.
Requirements: Ohio organizations properly classified by the IRS as being eligible to receive grants may apply. Each applicant must file its most recent IRS letter of classification with each proposal. National or regional institutions with broad public support may submit proposals that address a specific local community need.
Restrictions: No grants will be made to endowment funds or for scholarships.
Geographic Focus: Ohio
Amount of Grant: 5,000 - 75,000 USD
Contact: Allan Zambie, (216) 623-4770 623-4771 or (216) 623-4771; fax (216) 623-4773
Internet: http://fdncenter.org/grantmaker/jpmurphy/interest.html
Sponsor: John P. Murphy Foundation
50 Public Square, Suite 924
Cleveland, OH 44113-2203

John R. Oishei Foundation Grants 2709
The foundation's primary mission is to support medical research and care and education, as well as cultural and social needs existing in the Buffalo Niagara region. The foundation favors creative programs that attempt to advance from the status quo, are strategically sound, and are strongly focused on excellence. Programs that provide opportunities for foundation support to be leveraged into greater support from other sources will be especially favored. The foundation generally does not fund operating expenses, though occasional exceptions may be made for organizations that address basic human needs. Requests for capital funds will not be considered unless they are an integral part of an otherwise eligible proposal. Contact the foundation to discuss eligibility before submitting an application. Grant applications are accepted throughout the year.
Requirements: It is the general policy of the foundation to confine its support to activities located in the Buffalo, NY, metropolitan region.
Restrictions: Grants do not support endowments; capital requests (buildings or equipment); deficit funding or loans; individual scholarships or fellowships (except within specific foundation programs); travel, conferences, seminars, or workshops; fundraising events; or 509(a) private foundations.
Geographic Focus: New York
Amount of Grant: 100,000 - 200,000 USD
Contact: Blythe T. Merrill; (716) 856-9490, ext. 3; btmerrill@oisheifdt.org
Internet: http://www.oisheifdt.org/Home/Fund/WhatWeFundOverview
Sponsor: John R. Oishei Foundation
1 HSBC Center, Suite 3650
Buffalo, NY 14203-2805

John Reynolds and Eleanor B. Allen Charitable Foundation Grants 2710
The Foundation, established in Florida in 2004, is a 501(c)3 dedicated to supporting performing arts programs, particularly instrumental music, as well as other charitable organizations operating in and around Wauchula, Florida. The brainchild of W. Reynolds Allen, founding partner of a Labor and Employment Law firm, the Foundation is interested in offering its support throughout southern Florida. There are no specific application formats or deadlines, and applicants should contact the Foundation for further instructions. Unsolicited or unapproved applications are not accepted.
Requirements: Applicants should be located in Florida.
Geographic Focus: Florida
Amount of Grant: Up to 1,000 USD
Contact: W. Reynolds Allen, (813) 251-1210; fax (813) 253-2006; rallen@anblaw.com
Sponsor: John Reynolds and Eleanor B. Allen Charitable Foundation
324 S Hyde Park Avenue, Suite 225
Tampa, FL 33606-4127

John S. and James L. Knight Foundation Communities Grants 2711
The program aims to improve the quality of life in 26 U.S. communities where the Knight brothers owned newspapers. Grants support six priority areas: education—to gain economic self-sufficiency, remain active learners, be good parents, and effective citizens in a democracy; well-being of children and families; housing and community development—to provide affordable, decent housing in safe, drug-free neighborhoods and to provide services for the homeless as well as affordable opportunities for home ownership; economic development—to help all adults gain access to jobs; civic engagement/positive human relations—to encourage residents to be good citizens, form ties to local institutions, and strengthen relationships with one another; and vitality of cultural life—to provide access to a wide variety of arts and cultural pursuits for all and to nourish creativity in children, youth, and adults. The foundation will work with local advisory committees to craft customized strategies for each Knight community, based on the priority areas, and to identify appropriate nonprofit partners. The foundation encourages interested organizations to send a one- to two-page letter of inquiry before submitting a proposal.
Requirements: Nonprofit organizations and institutions are eligible. The proposed project must serve at least one of the following target areas: Long Beach or San Jose, CA; Boulder, CO; Boca Raton, Bradenton, Miami, or Tallahassee, FL; Columbus, Macon, or Milledgeville, GA; Fort Wayne or Gary, IN; Wichita, KS; Lexington, KY; Detroit, MI; Duluth or Saint Paul, MN; Biloxi, MS; Charlotte, NC; Akron, OH; Philadelphia or State College, PA; Columbia or Myrtle Beach, SC; and Aberdeen, SD. Applicant organizations may be located outside of the project target area.
Geographic Focus: California, Colorado, Florida, Georgia, Indiana, Kansas, Kentucky, Minnesota, Mississippi, North Carolina, Ohio, Pennsylvania, South Carolina, South Dakota
Contact: Anne Corriston; (305) 908-2600 or (305) 908-2673; publications@knightfdn.org
Internet: http://www.knightfoundation.org/programs/communities/
Sponsor: John S. and James L. Knight Foundation
200 S Biscayne Boulevard, Suite 3300
Miami, FL 33131-2349

John S. and James L. Knight Foundation Donor Advised Fund Grants 2712
Competitive grants of about $4,000 or less are available for nonprofits serving Fayette, Bourbon, Clark, Jessamine, Madison, Montgomery, Scott, and Woodford counties of Kentucky in the program areas of education; well-being of children and families; housing and community development; economic development; civic engagement and positive human relations; cultural life. Grants are awarded on an on-going basis to meet community needs in a timely manner.

Geographic Focus: Kentucky
Amount of Grant: 4,000 USD
Contact: Barbara A. Fischer; (859) 225-3343; fax (859) 243-0770; bfischer@bgcf.org
Internet: http://www.bgcf.org/page27526.cfm
Sponsor: Blue Grass Community Foundation
250 W Main Street, Suite 1220
Lexington, KY 40507-1714

John S. and James L. Knight Foundation Grants 2713
The John S. and James L. Knight Foundation offers grants to foster an "informed, engaged" Gary community through Legacy Foundation. The effort is part of Knight Foundation's Community Foundation Initiative, which will help ensure that communities have the information they need to make decisions about their lives. The new approach will modify how Knight Foundation works in the Gary area and other Knight communities. Grant seekers in Gary will apply for funding through Legacy Foundation.
Requirements: To be eligible for funding, an organization must be classified as a 501(c)3 organization and be located in or provide services to residents in Gary, Indiana. Some examples of projects that address the fund's priority include: creating new opportunities to participate; supporting and developing community leadership; creating spaces for engagement; and community influence and solutions. Applicants must fill out the online application, and attach a detailed grant narrative; project budget and budget narrative; a list of board of directors; copy of the organization's current fiscal year operating budget; a copy of the financial audit or review; and the IRS determination letter of federal tax exempt status. The applicant must also be certain that the organization's profile is updated on GuideStar (www.guidestar.org).
Restrictions: The Knight Foundation does not award grants for: on-going requests for general operating support; annual fund-raising campaigns; fund-raising dinners; operating deficits; activities that are normally the responsibility of government; medical research; organizations or projects whose mission is to prevent, eradicate and/or alleviate the effects of specific diseases; requests from hospitals; religious organization or religious activities to propagate a religious faith or restricted to one religion or denomination; support of political candidates; campaigns and memorials; capital campaigns; capital projects; and projects where individuals are merely recipients of services.
Geographic Focus: Indiana
Date(s) Application is Due: Mar 1; Sep 1
Contact: Cara Spicer; (219) 736-1880; cspicer@legacyfoundationlakeco.org
Internet: http://www.legacyfoundationlakeco.org/grantsfundingopps.html
Sponsor: Legacy Foundation
1000 East 80th Place, South Tower 302
Merrillville, IN 46410

John S. and James L. Knight Foundation National and New Initiatives Grants 2714
The National and New Initiatives, (a.k.a. National Venture Fund), support innovative opportunities and initiatives at the national level that relate directly or indirectly to Knight's work in its 26 communities. The fund welcomes proposals from U.S.-based organizations committed to high standards of planning, evaluation and communication. Those interested should submit a letter of inquiry to the foundation.
Requirements: The proposed project must serve at least one of the following target areas: Long Beach or San Jose, CA; Boulder, CO; Boca Raton, Bradenton, Miami, or Tallahassee, FL; Columbus, Macon, or Milledgeville, GA; Fort Wayne or Gary, IN; Wichita, KS; Lexington, KY; Detroit, MI; Duluth or Saint Paul, MN; Biloxi, MS; Charlotte, NC; Grand Forks, ND; Akron, OH; Philadelphia or State College, PA; Columbia or Myrtle Beach, SC; and Aberdeen, SD. Applicant organizations can be outside of the project target area.
Geographic Focus: All States
Contact: Damian Thorman; (305) 908-2667; thorman@knightfoundation.org
Internet: http://www.knightfoundation.org/grants/
Sponsor: John S. and James L. Knight Foundation
200 S Biscayne Boulevard, Suite 3300
Miami, FL 33131-2349

John S. Dunn Research Foundation Grants and Chairs 2715
Established in 1985, the foundation funding area is limited to the Texas, providing support to health and medical-related organizations, especially hospitals; support also for cancer, other medical research, and freestanding clinics.
Requirements: Grants are made to nonprofit organizations within Texas having 501(c)3 tax-exempt status.
Restrictions: No grants to individuals, or for multi-year or seed money grants.
Geographic Focus: Texas
Amount of Grant: 10,000 - 100,000 USD
Contact: Dr. Lloyd Gregory; (713) 626-0368; fax (713) 626-3866
Sponsor: John S. Dunn Research Foundation
3355 West Alabama street, Suite 720
Houston, TX 77098-1718

Johns Manville Fund Grants 2716
The Johns Manville Fund, Inc. gives primarily in areas of company operations in Denver, Colorado, Etowah, Tennessee, and in Canada. The Fund offers support in the areas of: the arts; education; health care; human services; youth services and the American Red Cross. The grants are offered in the form of employee-related scholarships, employee volunteer services, general/operating support, and program development. Contact the Johns Manville Fund, Inc. for a Informational brochure, including application guidelines.
Requirements: Non-profits operating in Denver, Colorado, Etowah, Tennessee, and in Canada are eligible.
Restrictions: No support for religious organizations not of direct benefit to the entire community, hospitals, or non-special needs private educational organizations. No grants for special events.
Geographic Focus: Colorado, Tennessee, Canada
Amount of Grant: 1,000 - 27,000 USD
Contact: Community Relations Manager; (303) 978-3863; fax (303) 978-2108
Internet: http://www.jm.com/corporate/careers/1241.htm
Sponsor: Johns Manville Fund
717 17th Street
Denver, CO 80202-3330

Johnson & Johnson Community Health Care Program Grants 2717
The program provides support for community public health initiatives impacting access and delivery of quality health care services for medically underserved populations, with emphasis on women and children (including infants and adolescents). Additional consideration will be given to programs focusing on the education and prevention of diabetes, obesity, and cardiovascular disease. Grants also will assist organizations in developing a broad-based public and private support network by extending public recognition of their efforts. Second-year continuation grants also are available.
Requirements: Grants are awarded to community/public health care organizations/agencies in Alabama (all areas); Arkansas (all areas); Boston, Massachusetts; Florida (all areas); New Jersey (all areas); Ohio (all areas); San Diego, California; and San Francisco, California.
Restrictions: Proposals from foundations, universities, and political advocacy groups will not be considered.
Geographic Focus: Alabama, Arkansas, California, Florida, Massachusetts, New Jersey, Ohio
Date(s) Application is Due: Oct 17
Amount of Grant: 150,000 USD
Contact: Sierra Veale, (443) 287-5138; fax (410) 510-1974; jandj@jhsph.edu
Internet: http://www.jhsph.edu/johnsonandjohnson/index.html
Sponsor: Johnson and Johnson
615 N Wolfe Street, Room W1100
Baltimore, MD 21205

Johnson & Johnson Corporate Contributions Grants 2718
Johnson & Johnson and its many operating companies support community-based programs that improve health and well-being. The Company works with community-based partners that have the greatest insight into the needs of local populations and the strategies that stand the greatest chances of success. Giving focuses on: saving and improving the lives of women and children; building on the skills of people who serve community health needs, primarily through education; and preventing diseases and reducing stigma and disability in underserved communities where we have a high potential for impact.
Requirements: Grants are awarded to nonprofit and tax-exempt local, national, and international organizations and institutions.
Restrictions: Grants are not awarded to individuals, for deficit funding, capital or endowment funds, demonstration projects, or publications.
Geographic Focus: All States
Contact: Shaun Mickus, (732) 524-2086; smickus@corus.jnj.com
Internet: http://www.jnj.com/connect/caring/corporate-giving/
Sponsor: Johnson and Johnson
1 Johnson & Johnson Plaza
New Brunswick, NJ 08933-0001

Johnson Controls Foundation Arts and Culture Grants 2719
The Johnson Controls Foundation provides financial gifts to select U.S.-based organizations located in the communities in which the company has a presence. In the area of arts and culture, the Foundation supports organizations in the areas of visual, performing and literary arts, public radio and television, libraries, museums, and related cultural activities.
Requirements: In evaluating requests for funds, the Advisory Board has developed policies and guidelines for giving in Culture and the Arts. Contributions will be given to visual, performing, and literary arts, public radio and television, libraries, museums, and other related cultural activities. Priority will be extended to those serving communities in which Johnson Controls employees live and work, and to those in which these employees are involved with their time and/or funds.
Restrictions: In general, no grants will be made to any political campaign or organization; any municipal, state, federal agency, or department, or to any organization established to influence legislation; any private individual for support of personal needs; any sectarian institutions or programs whose services are limited to members of any one religious group or whose funds are used primarily for the propagation of a religion; for testimonial dinners, fund raising events, tickets to benefits, shows, or advertising; to provide monies for travel or tours, seminars and conferences or for publication of books and magazines or media productions; for specific medical or scientific research projects; foreign-based institutions nor to institutions or organizations for use outside of the United States; fraternal orders or veteran groups; private foundations or to endowment funds. The foundation does not donate equipment, products or labor.
Geographic Focus: All States
Amount of Grant: 500 - 40,000 USD
Contact: Charles A. Harvey, President; (414) 524-1200 or (414) 524-2296
Internet: http://www.johnsoncontrols.com/publish/us/en/about/our_community_focus/johnson_controls_foundation.html
Sponsor: Johnson Controls Foundation
5757 North Green Bay Avenue, P.O. Box 591
Milwaukee, WI 53201

Johnson Controls Foundation Civic Activities Grants 2720
The Johnson Controls Foundation provides financial gifts to select U.S.-based organizations located in the communities in which the company has a presence. In the area of civic activities, the Foundation provides assistance to programs in the areas of justice and law, community and neighborhood improvements, the environment, civic activities and equal opportunity, citizenship and safety.
Requirements: In evaluating requests for funds, the Advisory Board has developed policies and guidelines for giving in civic activities. Contributions will be given to programs in the areas of justice and law, community and neighborhood improvements, the environment, civil rights and equal opportunity, citizenship and safety. Requests to finance office equipment and computer systems do not have a high priority.
Restrictions: In general, no grants will be made to any political campaign or organization; any municipal, state, federal agency, or department, or to any organization established to influence legislation; any private individual for support of personal needs; any sectarian institutions or programs whose services are limited to members of any one religious group or whose funds are used primarily for the propagation of a religion; for testimonial dinners, fund raising events, tickets to benefits, shows, or advertising; to provide monies for travel or tours, seminars and conferences or for publication of books and magazines or media productions; for specific medical or scientific research projects; foreign-based institutions nor to institutions or organizations for use outside of the United States; fraternal orders or veteran groups; private foundations or to endowment funds. The foundation does not donate equipment, products or labor.
Geographic Focus: All States
Date(s) Application is Due: Aug 30
Contact: Charles A. Harvey, President; (414) 524-1200 or (414) 524-2296
Internet: http://www.johnsoncontrols.com/publish/us/en/about/our_community_focus/johnson_controls_foundation.html
Sponsor: Johnson Controls Foundation
5757 North Green Bay Avenue, P.O. Box 591
Milwaukee, WI 53201

Johnson Controls Foundation Education and Arts Matching Gift Grants 2721
The Johnson Controls Foundation provides financial gifts to select U.S.-based organizations located in the communities in which the company has a presence. The Education and Arts Matching Gift Program allows current and retired employees to support their desired arts and education organization. Their gift is then supplemented with a matching donation from the Foundation.
Restrictions: In general, no grants will be made to any political campaign or organization; any municipal, state, federal agency, or department, or to any organization established to influence legislation; any private individual for support of personal needs; any sectarian institutions or programs whose services are limited to members of any one religious group or whose funds are used primarily for the propagation of a religion; for testimonial dinners, fund raising events, tickets to benefits, shows, or advertising; to provide monies for travel or tours, seminars and conferences or for publication of books and magazines or media productions; for specific medical or scientific research projects; foreign-based institutions nor to institutions or organizations for use outside of the United States; fraternal orders or veteran groups; private foundations or to endowment funds. The foundation does not donate equipment, products or labor.
Geographic Focus: All States
Contact: Charles A. Harvey, President; (414) 524-1200 or (414) 524-2296
Internet: http://www.johnsoncontrols.com/publish/us/en/about/our_community_focus/johnson_controls_foundation.html
Sponsor: Johnson Controls Foundation
5757 North Green Bay Avenue, P.O. Box 591
Milwaukee, WI 53201

Johnson Controls Foundation Health and Social Services Grants 2722
The Johnson Controls Foundation provides financial gifts to select U.S.-based organizations located in the communities in which the company has a presence. Operating support for organizations in the health and social services category largely occurs in communities where Johnson Controls has a local presence and is often directed through contributions to United Way.
Requirements: In evaluating requests for funds, the Advisory Board has developed policies and guidelines for giving in health and social services. Contributions will be given financial assistance to federated drives, hospitals, youth agencies and other health and human service agencies. Ordinarily, operating support of health and social service agencies is reserved for Johnson Controls communities, and generally directed through contributions to United Way.
Restrictions: In general, no grants will be made to any political campaign or organization; any municipal, state, federal agency, or department, or to any organization established to influence legislation; any private individual for support of personal needs; any sectarian institutions or programs whose services are limited to members of any one religious group or whose funds are used primarily for the propagation of a religion; for testimonial dinners, fund raising events, tickets to benefits, shows, or advertising; to provide monies for travel or tours, seminars and conferences or for publication of books and magazines or media productions; for specific medical or scientific research projects; foreign-based institutions nor to institutions or organizations for use outside of the United States; fraternal orders or veteran groups; private foundations or to endowment funds. The foundation does not donate equipment, products or labor.
Geographic Focus: All States
Date(s) Application is Due: Apr 30
Contact: Charles A. Harvey, President; (414) 524-1200 or (414) 524-2296
Internet: http://www.johnsoncontrols.com/publish/us/en/about/our_community_focus/johnson_controls_foundation.html
Sponsor: Johnson Controls Foundation
5757 North Green Bay Avenue, P.O. Box 591
Milwaukee, WI 53201

Johnson County Community Foundation Grants 2723
The Community Foundation seeks to meet the challenges of the Johnson County, Indiana community as a whole. Special attention is given to requests that increase the capacity of not-for-profit organizations to serve the community and requests that demonstrate community support and in-kind investment. The Foundation generally supports three kinds of requests: projects of service to the general community and pilot projects; seed money to enable projects to demonstrate their potential or enhance services; and emergency funding for community needs. Examples of previously funded projects are available at the website.
Requirements: Applicants must submit a letter of inquiry (2-3 pages), also include a copy of their 501(c)3 Letter of Determination. Letters of inquiry should include: a brief statement of the organization's purpose and goals; a brief description of the project, the need and the target population it addresses; short- and long-term outcomes anticipated and plans for assessing achievements; grant amount needed; a statement about the total agency budget and the project budget; a statement about other funding sources for the agency and/or project, specifying both committed and projected sources of support. Letters of inquiry will be reviewed to determine if the proposed effort fits within the community foundation's grant program. If so, the applicant will be contacted by the Foundation, requesting additional information or a full proposal. The Foundation supports organizations that are tax exempt under Section 501(c)3 of the Internal Revenue Service Code and are not classified as private foundations under Section 509(a) of the Code. In selected cases, it may consider support for projects sponsored by governmental entities.
Restrictions: The Community Foundation does not: take multi-year commitments; support services commonly regarded as the responsibility of government; provide support for political or partisan purposes or for programs in which religious teachings are an integral part; consider more than one proposal from the same organization within a 12-month period; provide discretionary grant support to an organization's ongoing operating budget, building funds, capital campaigns, or endowments; fund raising events and functions; make grants to individuals except for scholarship or special award funds; fund existing obligations or to replenish resources (deficit funding) for such purposes.
Geographic Focus: Indiana
Contact: Kim Minton; (317) 738-2213; fax (317) 738-9113; kimm@jccf.org
Internet: http://www.jccf.org/index.asp?p=37
Sponsor: Johnson County Community Foundation
398 S Main, P.O. Box 217
Franklin, IN 46131-2311

Johnson County Community Foundation Youth Philanthropy Initiative Grants 2724
The Youth Philanthropy Initiative of Johnson County (YPIJC) is the first countywide youth leadership program focused on inspiring excellence in young people. The program equips young people with opportunities, resources, mentors and tools to solve serious community issues while developing a lifelong commitment to philanthropy. The application and samples of previously funded projects are available at the website.
Requirements: Grants are awarded to 501(c)3 nonprofit organizations and other groups including community organizations, schools, classrooms, religious organizations and youth groups for projects that: are youth-led from writing the proposal to implementation of the project; address a serious community need in Johnson County; bring together diverse people and organization; have a learning component on philanthropy; and increase the development assets of young people.
Geographic Focus: Indiana
Amount of Grant: 50 - 500 USD
Contact: Kim Minton; (317) 738-2213; fax (317) 738-9113; kimm@jccf.org
Internet: http://www.jccf.org/Home/GrantsScholarships/YouthGrants/tabid/113/Default.aspx
Sponsor: Johnson County Community Foundation
398 S Main, P.O. Box 217
Franklin, IN 46131-2311

Johnson Foundation Wingspread Conference Support Program 2725
The Johnson Foundation at Wingspread sponsors grants to partially fund conferences focusing on subjects in the public interest, primarily health issues and the environment. Meeting facilities include Wingspread, the home designed by Frank Lloyd Wright, and formerly owned by Herbert Fisk Johnson of the Johnson and Johnson family. Conferences are intensive, one- to four-day meetings of small groups convened in partnership with nonprofit organizations, public agencies, universities, and other foundations. Strategic interests of the Foundation are education, sustainable development and environment, democracy and community, and family. The Foundation's usual contribution to a conference sponsored by one or more other organizations consists of the provision of the full conference facilities of Wingspread, planning and logistical support by the staff, meals and other amenities for the period of the meeting.
Requirements: To be invited to submit a full proposal, applicants first must submit a brief concept letter, consisting of: a clear statement of purpose; a draft agenda; the identification of key participants; and an estimated budget and schedule. The letter should describe how the conference will enhance collaboration and community, include diverse opinions and perspectives, identify solutions, and result in action.
Geographic Focus: All States
Contact: Coordinator; (262) 639-3211; fax (262) 681-3327; info@johnsonfdn.org
Internet: http://www.johnsonfdn.org/guidelines.html
Sponsor: Johnson Foundation
33 East Four Mile Road
Racine, WI 53402

Johnson Scholarship Foundation Grants — 2726

Theodore Johnson and his wife of 52 years, Vivian M. Johnson, placed great faith in education as a means to help people improve their lives. This was based, in part, on personal experience. Mr. Johnson worked his way through college, and after joining United Parcel Service (UPS) in the early 1920s, obtained an MBA at night school. He rose to the position of Vice President of Labor Relations at UPS. He also bought UPS stocks at every opportunity and these appreciated over his lifetime. Mr. Johnson felt that he had been lucky in life and wanted to help deserving people who had been less fortunate. He and his wife created their foundation to fund scholarship and other educational programs which serve people who demonstrate financial need. The foundation's programming is particularly focused on American Indians, people with disabilities, and people who are socially and economically disadvantaged. The foundation's grants committee meets three times/year and considers grant proposals at each of its meetings. Interested applicants should submit a letter of inquiry. Interested applicants may contact the foundation for further information.
Requirements: Educational institutions and organizations whose mission is to serve disadvantaged or disabled people are eligible to apply.
Restrictions: The foundation does not fund the following types of requests: requests from individuals; travel projects or fellowships; capital improvement projects; routine operating expenses; pre-existing debts; political advocacy; and programs outside of the United States or Canada.
Geographic Focus: All States, Canada
Contact: Sharon Wood; (561) 659-2005; fax (561) 659-1054; wood@jsf.bz
Internet: http://www.johnsonscholarships.org/index_new.asp?page=/site/grant_inquiries/index.htm
Sponsor: Johnson Scholarship Foundation
505 South Flagler Drive Suite 1460
West Palm Beach, FL 33401

John W. Alden Trust Grants — 2727

The trust awards grants to Massachusetts nonprofit organizations in its areas of interest, including education and therapy for children who are blind, disabled, retarded, or mentally or physically ill. Grants will normally be made for specific projects rather than general operating purposes. There are no application deadlines. Grant applications should be submitted on-line at www.cybergrants.com/alden. Detailed instructions on the web page will guide you through the process. All questions should be directed to the grants coordinator.
Requirements: Eastern Massachusetts 501(c)3 tax-exempt organizations are eligible.
Restrictions: Grants are not made to individuals.
Geographic Focus: Massachusetts
Date(s) Application is Due: Jan 15; Apr 15; Jul 15; Oct 15
Amount of Grant: Up to 15,000 USD
Contact: Susan Monahan; (617) 951-1108; fax (617) 542-7437; smonahan@rackemann.com
Internet: http://www.cybergrants.com/alden
Sponsor: John W. Alden Trust
160 Federal Street, 13th Floor
Boston, MA 02110-1700

John W. and Anna H. Hanes Foundation Grants — 2728

The trust awards grants, primarily for the arts, to nonprofit organizations in North Carolina. Other interests that are funded are children and youth services; education; environment; health care; historic preservation; and human services. Types of support include annual and capital campaigns; building and renovation; emergency funds; endowments and seed money; equipment and land acquisition; matching and challenge support; and program development. The board meets in January, April, July, and October; application forms are required.
Requirements: 501(c)3 North Carolina nonprofit organizations are eligible.
Restrictions: Giving is limited to North Carolina, with emphasis on Forsyth County. No grants are made to individuals, or for operating expenses.
Geographic Focus: North Carolina
Date(s) Application is Due: Mar 15; Jun 15; Sep 15; Dec 15
Contact: Christopher Spaugh, Vice President, Wachovia Bank NA; (336) 732-5991
Sponsor: John W. and Anna H. Hanes Foundation c/o Wachovia Bank N.A.
1525 West WT Harris Boulevard
Charlotte, NC 28288-5709

John W. Anderson Foundation Grants — 2729

The John W. Anderson Foundation is an independent foundation established in 1967, in Indiana. The trust was established by John W. Anderson, a manufacturing executive and inventor. Mr. Anderson was president of the Anderson Company. The foundation givings primarily to organizations serving youth; higher educational institutions; community funds; scientific or medical research for the purpose of alleviating suffering; care of needy, crippled or orphaned children; care of needy persons who are sick, aged or helpless; improving the health, and quality of life of all persons; human services; and the arts and humanities. The Foundations gives primarily in Lake and Porter counties in northwest Indiana.
Requirements: Applicants should submit the following: signature and title of chief executive officer; copy of IRS Determination Letter; brief history of organization and description of its mission; copy of most recent annual report/audited financial statement/990; listing of board of directors, trustees, officers and other key people and their affiliations; detailed description of project and amount of funding requested; copy of current year's organizational budget and/or project budget.
Restrictions: Applications sent by fax not considered. Application form not required. An organization may submit a request once in a 12-month period. No support for elementary and secondary schools, or for business or any for-profit organization, or for supporting organizations classified 509(a)3. No grants to individuals, or for endowment funds, multi-year grants, fund raising events, advertising, seed money, deficit financing; no loans.
Geographic Focus: Indiana
Date(s) Application is Due: Jan 20; Mar 20; May 20; Jul 20; Sep 20; Nov 20
Amount of Grant: 5,000 - 50,000 USD
Contact: William N. Vinovich, Vice-Chair; (219) 462-4611
Sponsor: John W. Anderson Foundation
402 Wall Street
Valparaiso, IN 46383-2562

John W. Boynton Fund Grants — 2730

The John W. Boynton Fund was established in 1952 by Dora Carter Boynton in memory of her husband. He had a thriving business in tinware in Templeton, MA, and later in his life was a resident of Athol, MA. In her will, Mrs. Boynton asked that "organizations which benefit poor, needy, and deserving persons and particularly those of advanced years and gentility" be considered. She also expressed a desire that special consideration be given to charitable organizations serving the Town of Athol. Grant requests for new or special programs and capital projects are preferred. General operating support also will be considered. In come cases, general operating grants are made to make up for a temporary loss of public or private funding. A typical grant is $5,000. Applicants must apply online at the grant website. Applicants are strongly encouraged to do the following before applying: review the downloadable state application procedures for additional helpful information and clarifications at the grant website; review the downloadable online-application guidelines at the grant website; review the foundation's funding history (link is available from the grant website); review the online application questions in advance; and review the list of required attachments. These will generally include: a list of board members, financial statements (audited, reviewed, or compiled by independent auditor); an organization summary; a list of other funding sources; an IRS Determination letter; and other required documents. All attachments must be uploaded in the online application as PDF, Word, or Excel files. The application deadline is 11:59 p.m. on July 15. Applicants will be notified of decisions by the end of September.
Requirements: Applicants must have 501(c)3 tax-exempt status and serve the residents of Greater Boston.
Restrictions: The fund does not support requests from individuals, organizations attempting to influence policy through direct lobbying, or any political campaigns.
Geographic Focus: Massachusetts
Date(s) Application is Due: Jul 15
Amount of Grant: 2,500 - 25,000 USD
Contact: Michealle Larkins; (866) 778-6859; michealle.larkins@baml.com
Internet: https://www.bankofamerica.com/philanthropic/fn_search.action
Sponsor: John W. Boynton Fund
225 Franklin Street, 4th Floor, MA1-225-04-02
Boston, MA 02110

John W. Gardner Leadership Award — 2731

The award recognizes living Americans, individuals working in or with the voluntary sector, who build, mobilize, and unify people, institutions, or causes. Award recipients are people who have raised the capacity of others to improve society. Their leadership has had national or international impact; if their work has been at the regional or local level, it has attracted wider recognition and imitation. Nominations should be made without the candidate's knowledge and include the candidate's name, organizational affiliation, address, and phone number; the candidate's leadership record, specifically how he or she has been a builder, mobilizer, and unifier of people, institutions, or causes; other past affiliations or achievements; and names and phone numbers of individuals who are in a position to comment on these achievements.
Requirements: Nominations may be submitted by anyone. Recipients may be any age. Guidelines and nomination instructions are available at the website, including an online nomination form.
Geographic Focus: All States
Date(s) Application is Due: Jan 31
Amount of Grant: 10,000 USD
Contact: Claire Wellington; (202) 467-6100; GardnerAward@IndependentSector.org
Internet: http://www.independentsector.org/about/gardneraward.htm
Sponsor: Independent Sector
1200 18th Street NW, Suite 200
Washington, DC 20036

John W. Speas and Effie E. Speas Memorial Trust Grants — 2732

The John W. Speas and Effie E. Speas Memorial Trust was established in 1943 to support and promote quality educational, cultural, human-services, and health-care programming. In the area of arts, culture, and humanities, the trust supports programming that: fosters the enjoyment and appreciation of the visual and performing arts; strengthens humanities and arts-related education programs; provides affordable access; enhances artistic elements in communities; and nurtures a new generation of artists. In the area of education, the trust supports programming that: promotes effective teaching; improves the academic achievement of, or expands educational opportunities for, disadvantaged students; improves governance and management; strengthens nonprofit organizations, school leadership, and teaching; and bolsters strategic initiatives of area colleges and universities. In the area of health, the trust supports programming that improves the delivery of health care to the indigent, uninsured, and other vulnerable populations and addresses health and health-care problems that intersect with social factors. In the area of human services, the trust funds programming that: strengthens agencies that deliver critical human services and maintains the community's safety net and helps agencies respond to federal, state, and local public policy changes. In the area of community improvement, the trust funds capacity-building and infrastructure-development projects including: assessments, planning, and implementation of technology for management and programmatic functions within an

organization; technical assistance on wide-ranging topics, including grant writing, strategic planning, financial management services, business development, board and volunteer management, and marketing; and mergers, affiliations, or other restructuring efforts. Grant requests for general operating support and program support will be considered. Grants from the foundation are one year in duration. Application materials are available for download at the grant website. Applicants are strongly encouraged to review the state application guidelines for additional helpful information and clarifications before applying. Applicants are also encouraged to review the foundation's funding history (link is available from the grant website). There are no application deadlines for the Speas Memorial Trust. Proposals are reviewed on an ongoing basis.
Requirements: Applicants must have 501(c)3 tax-exempt status and serve the residents of the Greater Kansas City Metropolitan area. Applications must be mailed.
Restrictions: Grant requests for capital support will not be considered. The trust does not support requests from individuals, organizations attempting to influence policy through direct lobbying, or any political campaigns.
Geographic Focus: Missouri
Contact: Spence Heddens, (816) 292-4301; Spence.heddens@baml.com
Internet: https://www.bankofamerica.com/philanthropic/fn_search.action
Sponsor: John W. Speas and Effie E. Speas Memorial Trust
1200 Main Street, 14th Floor, P.O. Box 219119
Kansas City, MO 64121-9119

Join Hands Day Excellence Awards 2733
Twenty awardees are selected from thousands of volunteer projects that develop youth and adult partnerships on Join Hands Day (May 7). Each award-winning project receives a check and an engraved glass award. Coordinating groups choose how the funds are used. An additional number of honorable mention projects, up to 30, will receive honorable mention status and an imprinted Certificate of Distinction. Project organizers must post-event register their project. Guidelines are available online.
Requirements: The most important consideration is the quality of the youth and adult partnership in planning and executing the event. Other criteria include the quality of the project to the neighborhood or to persons in need and the effectiveness of the mobilization group.
Geographic Focus: All States
Date(s) Application is Due: Jun 7
Amount of Grant: 1,000 USD
Contact: Director; (877) 687-1329; fax (630) 522-6327; actioncenter@joinhandsday.org
Internet: http://www.joinhandsday.org/scripts/awards_excellence_index.cfm
Sponsor: Join Hands Day
1315 W 22nd Street, Suite 400
Oak Brook, IL 60523

Joseph Alexander Foundation Grants 2734
Established in 1960 in New York, the Foundation supports primarily in the New York region. Fields of interest include the following: higher education; health organizations; medical research, particularly optic nerve research; social services; and Jewish organizations. Types of support also include the following: annual campaigns; building/renovation; capital campaigns; conferences/seminars; curriculum development; endowments; equipment; exchange programs; general/operating support; program development; research; and scholarship funds. Applicants should submit a letter requesting application guidelines before submitting a proposal. There is no deadline, but the board meets in January, April, July, and October.
Requirements: Nonprofit organizations are eligible to apply.
Restrictions: Grants are not made to individuals.
Geographic Focus: New York
Amount of Grant: 5,000 - 50,000 USD
Contact: Robert Weintraub, President; (212) 355-3688
Sponsor: Joseph Alexander Foundation
110 East 59th Street
New York, NY 10022-1304

Joseph Drown Foundation Grants 2735
The foundation makes contributions in the areas of education; community, health and social services; and arts and humanities. It supports programs dealing with such issues as the high school drop-out rate, teen pregnancy, lack of sufficient health care, substance abuse, and violence. Types of support include general operating support, program development, seed money, scholarship funds, and matching funds. Most grant making is limited to programs or organizations in California. Requests are considered each year at March, June, September, and December meetings. The foundation makes grants for both operating support and program support but does not make multiyear commitments. No special application form is required. Proposal should include a letter with information about the organization and the project, a copy of 501(c)3 determination letter, a budget for the organization and the project, the most recent audited financial statements, a copy of the most recent IRS Form 990, and a list of the current board of directors. Any additional materials, such as an annual report, may be attached. Questions should be directed to the program director; proposals should be sent to the foundation president.
Requirements: California 501(c)3 organizations may apply.
Restrictions: The foundation does not provide funds to individuals, endowments, capital campaigns, or annual funds. The foundation does not underwrite annual meetings, conferences, or special events, nor does it fund religious programs or purchase tickets to fund-raising events.
Geographic Focus: California
Date(s) Application is Due: Jan 15; Apr 15; Jul 15; Oct 15
Amount of Grant: 10,000 - 100,000 USD
Contact: Alyssa Eichelberger, Program Administrator; (310) 277-4488, ext. 100; fax (310) 277-4573; alyssa@jdrown.org
Internet: http://www.jdrown.org
Sponsor: Joseph Drown Foundation
1999 Avenue of the Stars, Suite 1930
Los Angeles, CA 90067

Joseph H. and Florence A. Roblee Foundation Grants 2736
The foundation awards grants to enable organizations to promote change by addressing significant social issues in order to improve the quality of life and help fulfill the potential of individuals. The foundation arises out of a Christian framework, and values ecumenical endeavors. The foundation particularly supports programs which work to break down cultural, racial, and ethnic barriers. Organizations and churches are encouraged to collaborate in achieving positive change through advocacy, prevention, and systemic improvements.
Requirements: Giving limited to nonprofit organizations in the greater bi-state St. Louis region, and Miami/Dade, FL. Contact Foundation for additional guidelines.
Restrictions: Support is not given to individuals or for annual campaigns, or research.
Geographic Focus: Florida, Illinois, Missouri
Date(s) Application is Due: Jan 15; Jun 15
Amount of Grant: 1,000 - 30,000 USD
Contact: Peggy Thomas; (314) 466-1304; kathydc@robleefoundation.org.
Sponsor: Joseph H. and Florence A. Roblee Foundation
P.O. Box 14737, MO2-100-07-19
Saint Louis, MO 63178-4737

Josephine G. Russell Trust Grants 2737
The purpose of the trust is for the care, healing, and nursing of the sick and injured, the relief and aid of the poor, the training and education of the young, and any other manner of social service in the city of Lawrence, Massachusetts.
Requirements: Massachusetts nonprofit organizations serving the greater Lawrence metropolitan area are eligible.
Geographic Focus: Massachusetts
Date(s) Application is Due: Jan 31
Amount of Grant: Up to 40,000 USD
Contact: Clifford Elias, Treasurer; (978) 500-3171
Sponsor: Josephine G. Russell Trust
59 Lucerne Drive
Andover, MA 01810-1719

Josephine Goodyear Foundation Grants 2738
The foundation makes grants in the greater Buffalo, NY, area for programs and projects benefiting indigent women and children, particularly with their physical needs. Grants also support hospitals, child welfare organizations, youth agencies, and community funds. Types of support include capital campaigns, building construction/renovation, equipment acquisition, land acquisition, emergency funds, program development, seed grants, research, employee matching gifts, and matching funds. Applicants are requested to submit a two-page proposal including the purpose of the organization, a description of the project/program or need, budget, other sources of funding, and an IRS determination letter.
Requirements: IRS 501(c)3 organizations serving the greater Buffalo area are eligible.
Restrictions: Grants are not awarded in support of individuals, continuing support, annual campaigns, deficit financing, endowment funds, scholarships, fellowships, or loans.
Geographic Focus: New York
Date(s) Application is Due: Apr 15; Aug 15
Amount of Grant: 500 - 30,000 USD
Contact: E.W. Dann Stevens; (716) 566-1465; ewdstevens@hiscockbarclay.com
Internet: http://www.cfgb.org/index.php/affiliates-and-initiatives/josephine-goodyear-foundation/97-josephine-goodyear-grants
Sponsor: Josephine Goodyear Foundation
3 Fountain Plaza, Suite 1100, M & T Center
Buffalo, NY 14203

Josephine S. Gumbiner Foundation Grants 2739
The charitable foundation functions for the benefit of women and children in the Long Beach area. The funder supports a wide array of programs, such as the arts; day care; education health care intervention, prevention, and direct services; housing; and recreation. Organizations are not be eligible for funding more than once in any 12-month period. As a general rule, the foundation will not grant funding to any organization for more than three consecutive years. The two-step application process begins with requesting a letter of intent questionnaire, which should be requested through email. Full applications are by invitation. There are no application deadlines. The board meets three or four times each year.
Requirements: Southern California nonprofit organizations are eligible.
Restrictions: Grants do not support political campaigns, lobbying efforts, programs that supplant tradition schooling, pass-through organizations, or groups with endowments greater than $5 million.
Geographic Focus: California
Amount of Grant: 5,000 - 50,000 USD
Contact: Grants Administrator; (562) 437-2882; fax (562) 437-4212; julie@jsgf.org
Internet: http://www.jsgf.org/
Sponsor: Josephine S. Gumbiner Foundation
333 West Broadway, Suite 302
Long Beach, CA 90802

Joseph P. Kennedy Jr. Foundation Grants 2740
The foundation concentrates its funding in the area of mental retardation. Grants providing seed funding are offered to encourage new methods of service and support for people with mental retardation and their families.
Requirements: Nonprofit organizations may apply.
Restrictions: The foundation will not support capital costs or costs of equipment for projects, nor will it pay for ongoing support or operations of existing programs.
Geographic Focus: All States
Contact: Program Contact; (202) 393-1250; eidelman@jpkf.org or info@jpkf.org
Internet: http://www.jpkf.org/JPKF_Info/GRANT.HTML
Sponsor: Joseph P. Kennedy Jr. Foundation
1133 19th Street NW, 12th Floor
Washington, DC 20036-3604

Joseph S. Stackpole Charitable Trust Grants 2741
The Joseph S. Stackpole Charitable Trust was established in 1957 to support and promote quality educational and human-services programming for underserved populations. Preference is given to charitable organizations that serve the people of Hartford County, Connecticut. The Stackpole Charitable Trust makes approximately 10-15 grants each year. The grant range is $1000-$1500 and grants are one year in duration. Applicants must apply online at the grant website. Applicants are strongly encouraged to do the following before applying: review the downloadable state application procedures for additional helpful information and clarifications; review the downloadable online-application guidelines at the grant website; review the trust's funding history (link is available from the grant website); review the online application questions in advance; and review the list of required attachments. These will generally include: a list of board members, financial statements (audited, reviewed, or compiled by independent auditor); an organization summary; a list of other funding sources; an IRS Determination letter; and other required documents. All attachments must be uploaded in the online application as PDF, Word, or Excel files. The deadline for application to the Joseph S. Stackpole Charitable Trust is 11:59 p.m. on August 15. Applicants will be notified of grant decisions by letter within two to three months after the proposal deadline.
Requirements: First time applicants are asked to contact the Program Officer before applying to the Stackpole Charitable Trust. Applicants must be classified by the Internal Revenue Service (IRS) as a 501(c)3 public charity.
Restrictions: Grant requests for capital projects will not be considered. Applicants will not be awarded a grant for more than 3 consecutive years. The trust does not support requests from individuals, organizations attempting to influence policy through direct lobbying, or any political campaigns.
Geographic Focus: Connecticut
Date(s) Application is Due: Aug 15
Amount of Grant: 1,000 - 1,500 USD
Contact: Kate Kerchaert; (860) 657-7016; kate.kerchaert@baml.com
Internet: https://www.bankofamerica.com/philanthropic/fn_search.action
Sponsor: Joseph S. Stackpole Charitable Trust
200 Glastonbury Boulevard, Suite # 200, CT2-545-02-05
Glastonbury, CT 06033-4056

Josiah W. and Bessie H. Kline Foundation Grants 2742
The foundation was established for charitable, scientific, literary, and educational purposes. The objectives for its grantmaking activities are to aid blind or incapacitated persons or crippled children. Grants are made to Pennsylvania colleges and universities and to hospitals, to institutions for crippled children, or to any other benevolent or charitable institution. Generally, grants are made to such institutions that are located in south-central Pennsylvania. Grants also are made for scientific and medical research. Types of support include continuing support, annual campaigns, capital campaigns, equipment acquisition, building/renovation, curriculum development, scholarship funds, matching funds, research, and emergency funds. The foundation does not have an application form. Instead, a letter of request must be submitted with the following information: a description of the need and purpose of the applicant organization, a project budget, amount requested from the foundation and the dates of the need, and a copy of the 501(c)3 tax-exemption letter. Requests may be submitted at any time. The board generally meets in March and November to consider requests.
Requirements: 501(c)3 organizations serving south-central Pennsylvania are eligible.
Restrictions: The foundation does not make loans and does not make grants to individuals or to normal operational phases of established programs, endowments, campaigns or national organizations, or religious programs.
Geographic Focus: Pennsylvania
Amount of Grant: 500 - 150,000 USD
Contact: John Obrock; (717) 561-0820 or (717) 561-4373; fax (717) 561-0826
Sponsor: Josiah W. and Bessie H. Kline Foundation
515 S 29th Street
Harrisburg, PA 17104

Joukowsky Family Foundation Grants 2743
The Joukowsky Family Foundation supports secondary and higher education, cultural, social, archaeological and historical activities in the northeastern United States. Types of support include capital campaigns; continuing support; endowments; fellowships; general/operating support; and scholarships. The Foundation contributes to pre-selected organizations. Unsolicited proposals are not accepted.
Requirements: Nonprofit 501(c)3 organizations are eligible to apply.
Geographic Focus: Connecticut, Maine, Massachusetts, New Hampshire, New Jersey, New York, Pennsylvania, Rhode Island, Vermont
Amount of Grant: 5,000 - 2,000,000 USD
Contact: Nina Koprulu, President and Director; (212) 355-3151; fax (212) 355-3147
Internet: http://www.joukowsky.org/guidelines.html
Sponsor: Joukowsky Family Foundation
620 Park Avenue, 5th Floor
New York, NY 10022

Journal Gazette Foundation Grants 2744
The foundation awards grants to northeastern Indiana nonprofit organizations in its areas of interest, including community funds, education, higher education, health organizations and hospitals, social services, Christian agencies and churches, and youth. Types of support include general operations and capital campaigns. There are no application deadlines; the board meets quarterly.
Requirements: Indiana nonprofit organizations are eligible. Preference is given to requests from northeastern Indiana.
Restrictions: Grants are not made to individuals.
Geographic Focus: Indiana
Amount of Grant: 25 - 112,000 USD
Contact: Jerry Fox, (260) 424-5257
Sponsor: Journal Gazette Foundation
701 S Clinton
Fort Wayne, IN 46802-1883

Jovid Foundation Grants 2745
The foundation partners with nonprofits in Washington, DC, to help low-income residents of the district learn how to become self-sufficient. Particularly interest is given to funding neighborhood-based efforts that provide programs and services to DC adults. The foundation has a modest budget for the support of the arts. Mini grants are awarded to help increase capacity for small groups through board training, staff development, membership dues, conferences, or Web site development. Potential applicants should initiate contact with the foundation by writing a one- to two-page letter describing the proposed project. Submit a two-page letter of inquiry; full proposals are by request.
Requirements: Washington, DC, nonprofits are eligible.
Geographic Focus: District of Columbia
Date(s) Application is Due: Jan 10; Apr 4; Jul 11; Oct 3
Amount of Grant: Up to 1,000 USD
Contact: Bob Wittig; (202) 686-2616; fax (202) 686-2621; jovidfoundation@yahoo.com
Internet: http://fdncenter.org/grantmaker/jovid
Sponsor: Jovid Foundation
5335 Wisconsin Avenue NW, Suite 440
Washington, DC 20015-2003

Joyce Awards 2746
The awards supports the commissioning of new artwork from artists of color in Chicago, Cleveland, Indianapolis, Detroit, Milwaukee, and Minneapolis/St. Paul. Each artist and nonprofit organization will receive a $50,000 award to support their project and the process of engaging people in its creation. Winners were selected on the merit of their artistic idea, the quality of their body of work, and an artistic process that offers opportunities for innovative community interaction. Joyce Award winners will present works that challenge and engage surrounding communities. Winners' projects will take place in Chicago's Grant Park as well as Milwaukee, Minneapolis and St. Paul, Minnesota.
Requirements: Major cultural organizations whose primary mission is the presentation of art through public programs are eligible for the Awards. Organizations must be located in Chicago, Cleveland, Detroit, Milwaukee, and Saint Paul/Minneapolis. Groups must be well established, demonstrate strong organizational capacity, and have a track record of presenting programs of the highest artistic caliber. Additionally, organizations must demonstrate a commitment to serving diverse audiences through evidence of current programming, community-based education, outreach, and other activities.
Restrictions: Art can take place anywhere and use any media. Additionally, artists may choose to collaborate with any non-profit group, not just art institutions. The artist selection criteria include work that is: rooted in art history, yet fresh and distinct; of high quality, meaning has a high level of creative and innovation, intellectually substantive and challenging as well as relevant and emotionally connective; imaginatively engages diverse communities. Organization selection criteria include an organization that has: the capacity to support the commission and presentation of the work; the ability to appropriately support the artist as the work is being developed; if required, can raise additional funds; can produce the work within a two-year time frame; and, is able to plan and implement that imaginative audience development piece. A letter of interest (LOI) should be submitted describing the concept and plans for the artistic commission; proposed professional artist and creative style; target audiences and engagement plan; projected timeline; estimated budget; organization's ability to carry out the project; plans for evaluating the impact of the project; and, detail of the last two years of programming. The Foundation will notify candidates if a full proposal is requested.
Geographic Focus: All States
Date(s) Application is Due: Jun 17
Amount of Grant: 50,000 USD
Contact: Angelique Power, Senior Program Officer, Culture; (312) 782-2464; fax (312) 595-1350; apower@joycefdn.org
Internet: http://www.joycefdn.org/programs/culture/joyce-awards/
Sponsor: Joyce Foundation
321 North Clark Street, Suite 1500
Chicago, IL 60654

Joyce Foundation Culture Grants 2747
Nurturing a diverse and thriving culture is an important part of the Joyce Foundation's dedication to improving the quality of life in the Midwest. Its Culture grant making has mostly centered on Chicago, and since the mid-1990s has focused on diversity in the arts. That includes supporting community-based arts groups such as Black Ensemble Theater, the Cambodian Heritage Museum, and Luna Negra Dance Theater, and encouraging mainstream arts groups to expand their audiences, boards and staffs to reflect Chicago's diversity. More recently, Joyce grant making has supported expanding opportunities for individual artists through fellowships, residencies and commissions. Since 2003, The Joyce Awards have funded 36 awards to enable Midwest arts groups (and, beginning in 2013, other groups) to commission new works by artists of color. Recognizing that technology creates new possibilities for art-making and community building, in 2012 the Foundation began seeking projects that engage audiences through new media and link the arts to community revitalization efforts.
Requirements: Culture grantmaking is limited primarily to organizations in the Chicago metropolitan area. The nominated artist can be from anywhere in the world. The Culture Program focuses on the following areas: Promoting Access - To encourage mid-sized and major cultural institutions to increase the participation of people of color in their audiences, boards, and staff; Community-based arts - To strengthen the infrastructure and leadership of culturally-specific and community-based arts organizations; Supporting Creativity - To stimulate the commissioning and production of new works that would be relevant to audiences of color, and support the artistic development of artists of color; and, Innovation - To seek and test new ideas emerging in the arts field that heighten digital engagement, use compelling storytelling vehicles to relay the power of art and create partnerships outside of the typical art realm leading to diverse arts audiences. Arts education is not a programmatic priority. However, the program may support some education outreach programs as a part of an organization's overall audience development plan. A letter of interest (LOI) should be submitted first. If acceptable, applicants will be requested to submit a full proposal. Applicants are strongly encouraged to plan their application and proposal submission process for the April or July meetings, since most grant funds will be distributed at those times.
Restrictions: The Joyce Foundation generally does not make grants for capital campaigns, endowment support, or culturally specific groups for organizational management tied to comprehensive strategic plans. Additionally, the Foundation does not award grants to individuals. Grants are made to organizations for projects that support the work of individual artists.
Geographic Focus: Illinois
Date(s) Application is Due: Apr 8; Aug 14; Dec 3
Contact: Veronica Salter, Grants Manager; (312) 782-2464; fax (312) 595-1350; info@joycefdn.org or vsalter@joycefdn.org
Internet: http://www.joycefdn.org/programs/culture/
Sponsor: Joyce Foundation
321 North Clark Street, Suite 1500
Chicago, IL 60654

Joyce Foundation Democracy Grants 2748
The Joyce Foundation has long been interested in ensuring the vibrancy of American democracy, from funding presidential debates to supporting work on such concerns as voter registration and full participation in the U.S Census. Beginning in the mid-1990s, the Foundation focused its efforts on combating the overwhelming influence of big money on most areas of American public life. The Foundation has supported the growth of a strong network of public interest groups in Midwest states, which collaborate through the Midwest Democracy Network; and it has also funded national groups ranging from the Brookings Institution to the Cato Institute. More recently, Joyce's grant making has expanded beyond campaign finance reform to include such issues as fair and open redistricting, protection of voting rights, governmental ethics, and judicial independence – all essential elements of a strong democracy.
Requirements: The overriding goal of the Democracy Program is to preserve and strengthen those values and qualities that are the foundation of a healthy democratic political system: honesty, fairness, transparency, accountability, competition, and maximizing informed citizen participation. Accordingly, the Foundation seeks to create political cultures in Illinois, Michigan, Minnesota, Ohio and Wisconsin which make it possible for more citizens, not just those who are wealthy and well-connected, to run for public office; offer voters real candidate and policy choices at election time; protect voting rights; respect the independence and impartiality of the courts; guarantee the fairness and reliability of elections; and provide citizens with the information needed to make reasoned decisions. To promote these ends, the Foundation supports organizations and coalitions in the Midwest that are willing and have the skills to: (1) Contribute to the development and promotion of broad, multi-issue political reform agendas within the target states, including improvements in the laws and practices governing campaign finance, elections, redistricting, judicial selection, voting rights, and local news coverage of government and politics. (2) Engage in activities necessary for effective advocacy including: policy research and development; public and policy maker education; civic engagement, particularly in underrepresented communities; coalition building; news media outreach; and participation in official proceedings, including litigation. (3) Work collaboratively with other reform and civic groups, academic and legal experts, and policy makers to advance shared goals within their states and across the region. (4) Participate in activities designed to enhance their capacities in the areas of strategic planning, organizing, coalition building, fundraising, advocacy, and communications. A letter of interest (LOI) should be submitted first. If acceptable, applicants will be requested to submit a full proposal. Applicants are strongly encouraged to plan their application and proposal submission process for the April or July meetings, since most grant funds will be distributed at those times. Grants to non-Midwest organizations must be for projects that strengthen the capacity of state-based groups as advocates for comprehensive political reforms, including campaign finance, redistricting, judicial, governmental ethics, lobbying and media reforms.

Geographic Focus: Illinois, Michigan, Minnesota, Ohio, Wisconsin
Date(s) Application is Due: Apr 8; Aug 14; Dec 3
Contact: Veronica Salter, Grants Manager; (312) 782-2464; fax (312) 595-1350; info@joycefdn.org or vsalter@joycefdn.org
Internet: http://www.joycefdn.org/programs/democracy/
Sponsor: Joyce Foundation
321 North Clark Street, Suite 1500
Chicago, IL 60654

Joyce Foundation Employment Grants 2749
The Joyce Foundation believes that equipping workers to succeed in good-paying jobs benefits individuals, their families and communities, and the Midwest economy as a whole. In the last two decades, the Foundation has tested strategies to boost workers' skills and help women on welfare, low-skilled workers, ex-offenders, and others who face significant barriers in joining the workforce. Through it all, Joyce has consistently funded research to evaluate promising strategies and learn from the results; Joyce-supported research on welfare-to-work and transitional jobs were major contributions to the field. Current evaluation research focuses on adult education programs that prepare adults without high school diplomas or the equivalent with skills needed for careers.
Requirements: The Employment Program primarily focuses on federal and state policy grants, but will make some grants to support targeted metro-level progress in Chicago, Indianapolis, and Minneapolis/St. Paul. The current areas of interest are: Basic Foundational Skills - preparing adults with the skills required for jobs in today's market. In particular, the Foundation supports the evaluation and expansion of promising adult education programs that prepare people for post-secondary education and careers; Industry Training Partnerships - The Foundation supports expanding partnerships between industry associations or groups of businesses and educational organizations to create and promote career advancement opportunities. Grants encourage development and promotion of industry-recognized credentials that help low-skilled workers advance in the labor market. The Foundation also supports research into the return on investment relating to employer-sponsored skill development programs; and, Innovation. A letter of interest (LOI) should be submitted first. If acceptable, applicants will be requested to submit a full proposal. Applicants are strongly encouraged to plan their application and proposal submission process for the April or July meetings, since most grant funds will be distributed at those times.
Restrictions: The Foundation does not generally support capital proposals, endowment campaigns, religious activities, commercial ventures, direct-service programs, or scholarships.
Geographic Focus: Illinois, Indiana, Minnesota
Date(s) Application is Due: Apr 8; Aug 14; Dec 3
Contact: Veronica Salter, Grants Manager; (312) 782-2464; fax (312) 595-1350; info@joycefdn.org or vsalter@joycefdn.org
Internet: http://www.joycefdn.org/programs/employment/
Sponsor: Joyce Foundation
321 North Clark Street, Suite 1500
Chicago, IL 60654

Joyce Foundation Environment Grants 2750
The Joyce Foundation is committed to protecting and restoring the Great Lakes and developing cleaner energy for the Midwest region, especially through investments in energy efficiency. Its Great Lakes priorities include reducing polluted runoff into the Lakes through restoration of watersheds in the Milwaukee and Toledo areas and preventing invasive species from devastating the Lakes' ecosystem; a recent Joyce-funded study analyzed the feasibility of breaking the connection between the Lakes and the Mississippi River system, through which many invasives come. Over the decades Joyce has supported a network of advocacy groups that have won major policy advances, including the federally funded Great Lakes Restoration Initiative and the bi-national commitments embodied in Great Lakes Compact. The Foundation has also sought improvements in broader national policies that affect the Lakes, including transportation, agriculture, industrial pollution, and climate change. Its work on energy has included funding on the human health effects of coal and shifts toward high speed rail. Grant making focuses on initiatives that promise to have an impact on the Great Lakes region, specifically the states of Illinois, Indiana, Michigan, Minnesota, Ohio, and Wisconsin. A limited number of environment grants are made to organizations in Canada.
Requirements: Grants will be made for projects that target public policies affecting the Great Lakes region. In the Great Lakes region, The Joyce Foundation will seek and support funding opportunities to protect and restore the Great Lakes by considering proposals at the local, state, regional, and national levels that address the following areas: (1) The introduction and spread of aquatic invasive species in and around the Great Lakes Basin; (2) Polluted, non-point source runoff from agricultural lands and cities. Watershed-based investments related to reducing nonpoint source pollution will continue to focus on the Greater Milwaukee River Watersheds and the Western Lake Erie Basin. The use of green infrastructure as a way to better manage stormwater and reduce combined sewer overflows in urban areas; and (3) Funding of and support for Great Lakes restoration and protection policies. This includes implementation of the Great Lakes-St. Lawrence River Basin Water Resources Compact and Great Lakes Restoration Initiative related work. Support for state and regional work to defend and advance policies to protect and restore the Great Lakes with an emphasis on reducing polluted runoff from cities and farms, promoting the use of green infrastructure and making the case for maintained or increased state and federal investment in Great Lakes restoration. In the other focus area, Energy Efficiency, the Foundation will seek and support funding opportunities to put the Midwest on a path to adopt all energy efficiency measures that are cheaper than generating more power by 2020. Proposals will be considered for work at the local, state, regional and, on a very limited basis, national levels that address the following opportunities: (1) Leveraging state policies—including energy efficiency resource standards, smart grid deployment plans, and decoupling measures—to drive increased and more effectively targeted utility investments in building energy efficiency; and (2)

Identifying, testing, and replicating the most effective building energy efficiency delivery models, whether those are focused at the community level, on a particular type of building, or a group of energy consumers with shared characteristics.
Restrictions: The Environment program generally does not support the following: local-impact projects such as environmental cleanup activities (as part of a comprehensive approach in one watershed, the demonstration projects in the Healthy Rivers Initiative are an exception; environmental education, videos, etc., either through educational institutions or aimed at the general public; efforts to preserve individual species or to purchase land; basic scientific research; and rarely funds conferences. Exceptions would be made only in connection with projects the Foundation is already funding.
Geographic Focus: All States
Date(s) Application is Due: Apr 8; Aug 14; Dec 3
Contact: Veronica Salter; (312) 782-2464; fax (312) 595-1350; info@joycefdn.org
Internet: http://www.joycefdn.org/programs/environment/
Sponsor: Joyce Foundation
321 North Clark Street, Suite 1500
Chicago, IL 60654

Joyce Foundation Gun Violence Prevention Grants 2751

Gun violence claims 30,000 persons in the United States every year, including lives lost in gun homicides, suicides, and accidental shootings. An additional 60,000 Americans are injured by guns annually. This public health and public safety crisis takes an enormous toll on families, and offends the right of all Americans to be safe in their communities. The Joyce Foundation works with law enforcement, policy makers and advocates to develop common sense gun violence reduction and prevention policies that keep our communities safe. The Foundation supports local, state, regional, and national projects that: (1) Advance state-based policy advocacy and organizing to secure effective gun violence prevention policies and practices; (2) Improve public engagement in support of effective gun violence prevention policies and practices; (3) Build effective coalitions to secure support for gun violence prevention policy reform among groups most impacted by gun violence; (4) Support Second Amendment legal strategies to uphold effective gun violence prevention policies and practices; and, (5) Encourage policy-oriented research and data collection to support effective gun violence prevention policies and practices.
Requirements: Grant making focuses on initiatives that promise to have an impact on the Great Lakes region, specifically the states of Illinois, Indiana, Michigan, Minnesota, Ohio, and Wisconsin. The Joyce Foundation is committed to improving public policy through its grant program. Accordingly, the Foundation welcomes grant requests from organizations that engage in public policy advocacy. Federal tax law prohibits private foundations from funding lobbying activities. The Foundation may support organizations engaged in public policy advocacy by either providing general operating support or by funding educational advocacy such as nonpartisan research, technical assistance, or examinations of broad social issues. A letter of interest (LOI) should be submitted first. If acceptable, applicants will be requested to submit a full proposal. Applicants are strongly encouraged to plan their application and proposal submission process for the April or July meetings, since most grant funds will be distributed at those times.
Restrictions: The Foundation does not generally support capital proposals, endowment campaigns, religious activities, commercial ventures, direct-service programs, or scholarships.
Geographic Focus: All States
Date(s) Application is Due: Apr 8; Aug 14; Dec 3
Contact: Veronica Salter; (312) 782-2464; fax (312) 595-1350; info@joycefdn.org
Internet: http://www.joycefdn.org/programs/gun-violence-prevention/
Sponsor: Joyce Foundation
321 North Clark Street, Suite 1500
Chicago, IL 60654

JP Morgan Chase Arts and Culture Grants 2752

The foundation supports programs in the New York tri-state region, across the nation, and around the world that strengthen communities where JP Morgan Chase employees live and work. In its Arts and Culture grantmaking, the Foundation looks for opportunities to integrate the arts into children's educational opportunities and position arts organizations and artists as key drivers of local economic renewal. The Foundation supports: arts programs in schools and after school; building the capacity of community-based arts institutions; initiatives that stimulate the creation and growth of local cultural economies; broadening of access to artistic excellence and diversity by partnering with major arts and culture groups.
Requirements: Only charitable, not-for-profit organizations are eligible to apply. Refer to the website in order to identify the region in which your program will be administered.
Restrictions: The following types of organizations, activities or purposes are not funded: programs outside the geographic markets we serve; individuals; fraternal organizations; athletic teams or social groups; public agencies; private schools; public schools (K-12), unless in partnership with a qualified not-for-profit organization; parent-teacher associations; scholarships or tuition assistance; higher education, unless program is specifically within guidelines; fundraising events (e.g. golf outings, school events); advertising, including ads in event, performance or athletic programs; volunteer-operated organizations; funds to pay down operating deficits; programs designed to promote religious or political doctrines; endowments or capital campaigns (exceptions are made by invitation only); organizations that discriminate on the basis of race, sex, sexual orientation, age or religion; health or medical-related organizations, unless program fits within stated giving guidelines.
Geographic Focus: Arizona, California, Colorado, Connecticut, Delaware, Florida, Illinois, Indiana, Kentucky, Louisiana, Michigan, New Jersey, New York, Ohio, Oklahoma, Texas, Utah, West Virginia, Wisconsin
Contact: Kimberly B. Davis, President; (212) 270-6000
Internet: http://www.jpmorganchase.com/corporate/Corporate-Responsibility/corporate-philanthropy.htm
Sponsor: JP Morgan Chase & Company
270 Park Avenue
New York, NY 10017

JP Morgan Chase Community Development Grants 2753

Working with best-in-class community-based partners, the JP Morgan Chase goal is to help stabilize families living in high-poverty neighborhoods and to make that stability echo through a neighborhood in a manner that improves educational and job opportunities, reduces crime and dramatically raises the community's quality of life. The program supports both resident-focused programs and community-focused programs. Resident-focused programs that address workforce development, asset building, and financial literacy, will support: continuing education courses; adult literacy outreach; job training; money management basics; credit repair; EITC workshops; home ownership and home buyer workshops; and foreclosure prevention programs. Community-focused programming addresses economic development and affordable housing issues.
Requirements: Only charitable, not-for-profit organizations are eligible to apply. Refer to the website in order to identify the region in which your program will be administered.
Restrictions: The following types of organizations, activities or purposes are not funded: programs outside the geographic markets we serve; individuals; fraternal organizations; athletic teams or social groups; public agencies; private schools; public schools (K-12), unless in partnership with a qualified not-for-profit organization; parent-teacher associations; scholarships or tuition assistance; higher education, unless program is specifically within guidelines; fundraising events (e.g. golf outings, school events); advertising, including ads in event, performance or athletic programs; volunteer-operated organizations; funds to pay down operating deficits; programs designed to promote religious or political doctrines; endowments or capital campaigns (exceptions are made by invitation only); organizations that discriminate on the basis of race, sex, sexual orientation, age or religion; health or medical-related organizations, unless program fits within stated giving guidelines.
Geographic Focus: Arizona, California, Colorado, Connecticut, Delaware, Florida, Illinois, Indiana, Kentucky, Louisiana, Michigan, New Jersey, New York, Ohio, Oklahoma, Texas, Utah, West Virginia, Wisconsin
Contact: Kimberly B. Davis, President; (212) 270-6000
Internet: http://servicelearning.org/resources/funding_sources/index.php?popup_id=898
Sponsor: JP Morgan Chase & Company
270 Park Avenue
New York, NY 10017

Judge Isaac Anderson, Jr. Scholarship 2754

This scholarship was established to fund a scholarship to a two- or four-year regionally accredited college or university to a Lee County high school senior who can demonstrate financial need, have a GPA of 3.0 or higher and who can demonstrate strong ties to the community through extracurricular activities, religious endeavors or community service. One scholarship is awarded each year for up to $1,000.
Requirements: In order to be eligible, applicants must: graduate from public or private high school in Lee County; document financial need; maintain a GPA of 3.0 or higher; demonstrate strong ties to the community through extracurricular activities, religious endeavors or community service; and, plan to attend a two- or four-year regionally accredited college or university.
Restrictions: Limited to residents of Lee County.
Geographic Focus: Florida
Date(s) Application is Due: Mar 26
Amount of Grant: Up to 1,000 USD
Contact: Kathyrn Cintron, Donor Services Assistant; (239) 274-5900, ext. 227; fax (239) 274-5930; kcintron@floridacommunity.com
Internet: http://www.floridacommunity.com/scholarships/highschool/
Sponsor: Southwest Florida Community Foundation
8260 College Parkway, Suite 101
Fort Myers, FL 33919

Judith and Jean Pape Adams Charitable Foundation Tulsa Area Grants 2755

The Foundation was established in 2004 as a private foundation and is involved in making distributions to charitable organizations on an annual basis. It encompasses two areas of support: organizations and agencies predominantly in Tulsa County, Oklahoma, and national Amyotrophic Lateral Sclerosis (ALS) research. For the former, primary areas of interest include arts and culture, human services and education. Support is given for operations, programs, capital projects, and maintenance reserve funding. The annual deadline is August 15.
Requirements: Public agencies serving the Tulsa, Oklahoma, region that are classified as a charitable organization described in Section 501(c)3 of the Internal Revenue Code and as a public charity under Section 509(a) of the Internal Revenue Code may apply.
Geographic Focus: Oklahoma
Date(s) Application is Due: Aug 15
Amount of Grant: 500 - 250,000 USD
Contact: Marcia Y. Manhart, Executive Director; (830) 997-7347; fax (830) 997-9888; mmanhart@jjpafoundation.com
Sue Mayhue, (316) 383-1795
Internet: http://www.jjpafoundation.com/guidelines.html
Sponsor: Judith and Jean Pape Adams Charitable Foundation
7030 South Yale Avenue, Suite 600
Tulsa, OK 74136

Judith Clark-Morrill Foundation Grants 2756
Established in Indiana, the Judith Clark-Morrill Foundation has specified its primary fields of interest as: the arts; community and economic development; education; and youth development. An application form is required, and there are two annual deadlines: June 1 and December 1. Amount of awards range from $1,000 to $30,000.
Restrictions: No grants are given to individuals, or for student groups, scholarships, annual campaigns, general operating support, travel, or advertising. There are no loans or multi-year grants.
Geographic Focus: Indiana
Date(s) Application is Due: Jun 1; Dec 1
Amount of Grant: 1,000 - 30,000 USD
Contact: Judith Morrill, President; (260) 357-4141
Sponsor: Judith Clark-Morrill Foundation
P.O. Box 180
Garrett, IN 46738-1350

K. M. Hunter Charitable Foundation Social Welfare Grants 2757
The Foundation provides a number of major grants to social and health services programs in Ontario. In addition, a series of smaller grants are given to organizations, including housing shelters and hospices for the sick. The Foundation requests that applicants make all contacts through its published email address. There are no specific applications or deadlines, and the Board meets two or three times annually to make its funding decisions.
Requirements: Grants are made to registered charitable organizations based in Ontario, with the exception of grants that support AIDS in Africa.
Geographic Focus: Canada
Contact: Judith Hunter; (416) 365-6600; fax (416) 365-0050; turtlart@gmail.com
Internet: http://www.kmhunterfoundation.ca/social.html
Sponsor: K.M. Hunter Charitable Foundation
P.O. Box 38, Station E
Toronto, ON M6H 4E1 Canada

K.S. Adams Foundation Grants 2758
Established in Oklahoma in 1953, the K.S. Adams Foundation offers support primarily in the Bartlesville, Oklahoma region. The Foundation's major fields of interest include: community and economic development, education, philanthropy, and volunteerism. Types of funding come in the form of annual campaign contributions and continuing financial support. A formal application is not required, and interested parties should forward a letter of application. Recently, grants have ranged between $500 and $10,000. There are no specified annual deadlines.
Geographic Focus: Oklahoma
Contact: Trustee; (918) 337-3470 or (918) 337-3279
Sponsor: K.S. Adams Foundation
P.O. Box 1156
Bartlesville, OK 74005

K21 Health Foundation Cancer Care Fund Grants 2759
The Kosciusko County Cancer Care Fund, administered by K21 Health Foundation, provides assistance to financially-eligible residents of Kosciusko County who are suffering from cancer. The purpose of the fund is to relieve some of the financial strain that often accompanies that dreaded diagnosis. The assistance provided includes but is not limited to items such as rent or mortgage payments, utilities, insurance, food, car payments, and prescription medications.
Requirements: Eligibility Requirements for Assistance: documented resident of Kosciusko County; verified cancer diagnosis within the last three months; can demonstrate a financial need; completion of the required application (contact the CCF Director for application).
Geographic Focus: Indiana
Contact: Clare Sessa, CCF Director; (574) 372-3500; csessa@hcfkc.org
Internet: http://www.k21foundation.org/cancer-care-fund/index.cfm
Sponsor: K21 Health Foundation
2170 North Pointe Drive, P.O. Box 1810
Warsaw, IN 46582

K21 Health Foundation Grants 2760
K21 Health Foundation exists for the benefit of Kosciusko County, Indiana citizens to ensure health care services are provided, and to advance prevention and healthy lifestyles. This will be accomplished by identifying health needs in our community, and maintaining an endowment so funding is available, through investments and grants, for those needs. Organizations are strongly encouraged to review K21's mission statement as that is the primary tool used to evaluate each application. When submitting an application, organizations must clearly explain how K21's mission will be advanced by supporting the project, program, or service, and the intended benefit(s) to residents of Kosciusko County.
Requirements: To qualify for a grant from K21, your organization must meet the following *Requirements:* must be a non-profit agency with verified IRS tax-exempt status, or a governmental agency; must be in good standing with the Indiana Secretary of State as indicated in a Business Entity Report; your Bylaws must require term limits for Directors and a rotating board is strongly encouraged.
Restrictions: To qualify for a grant from K21, your request must meet the following *Requirements:* the project, program, or service for which you are seeking funding must benefit residents of Kosciusko County; the project, program, or service for which you are seeking funding should provide direct health services or advance prevention and healthy life solutions.
Geographic Focus: Indiana
Date(s) Application is Due: Feb 1; May 1; Aug 1; Nov 1
Contact: Holly Swoverland; (574) 269-5188, ext. 102; fax (574) 269-5193
Internet: http://www.k21foundation.org/apply-for-grant/index.cfm
Sponsor: K21 Health Foundation
2170 North Pointe Drive, P.O. Box 1810
Warsaw, IN 46582

KaBOOM-CA Playground Challenge Grants 2761
The program awards grants to create and refurbish playgrounds. Grants will support community projects that enlist volunteers and individual donations to build and renovate recreational spaces to encourage children to engage in physical activities. Playgrounds may be built only on federal land or land owned by tax-exempt groups. Guidelines are available online.
Requirements: 501(c)3 nonprofits in the United States, Canada, and Mexico are eligible.
Geographic Focus: All States, Canada, Mexico
Date(s) Application is Due: May 9
Amount of Grant: 2,000 - 47,200 USD
Contact: Program Supervisor; (312) 822-5871; fax (202) 659-0210; info@kaboom.org
Internet: http://www.kaboom.org
Sponsor: KaBOOM!
4455 Connecticut Avenue
Washington, DC 20008

Kahuku Community Fund 2762
The Kahuku Community Fund was established by the Estate of James Campbell in 2005 to be used for charitable and community purposes within the geographic district of Kahuku, bounded by Turtle Bay and Malaekahana. Preference is given to projects that address educational opportunities; recreational opportunities; economic sufficiency; social conditions; health care; strategic action plan around future development of the Kahuku community; housing opportunities; cultural arts, practices and values of the Ko'olauloa moku. Grant range is between $1,000 to $25,000 with an average of $10,000.
Requirements: Nonprofit, 501(c)3 organizations, schools, units of government, neighborhood groups or projects are eligible to apply. Community organizations without 501(c)3 status are eligible to apply for a grant up to $5,000, provided the activities to be supported are charitable. To be eligible for a grant of more than $5,000, a group must be a tax-exempt 501(c)3 organization or have a 501(c)3 fiscal sponsor. Program or project must benefit the Kahuku community.
Restrictions: Projects not likely to be funded: costs relating to establishing a new 501((c)(3) organization; general operating support, although up to 10% for indirect costs will be considered; funds for an endowment; funds for the benefit of specific individuals; except for emergency assistance through a 501(c)3 organization; full personnel costs (staffing costs are less likely to be funded) of a project or program; major capital improvements, although minor capital improvements required to implement a project may be considered; travel out of state.
Geographic Focus: Hawaii
Date(s) Application is Due: Jan 19
Amount of Grant: 1,000 - 25,000 USD
Contact: Amy Luersen, (808) 566-5550; aluersen@hawaiicommunityfoundation.org
Internet: http://www.hawaiicommunityfoundation.org/index.php?id=71&categoryID=22
Sponsor: Hawai'i Community Foundation
1164 Bishop Street, Suite 800
Honolulu, HI 96813

Kaiser Permanente Cares for Communities Grants 2763
Kaiser Permanente partners with nonprofit organizations to improve the health of its members and the communities it serves. The company's four-pronged approach to improve community health includes: increasing access to coverage and care for vulnerable populations, including children and adults who are ineligible for existing state or private programs due to family income or immigration status, and community-based clinics; evidence-based medicine—successful practices in managing chronic diseases such as diabetes, asthma, depression, and heart failure; education of health care professionals and consumers—graduate medical education programs and nursing scholarships, partnerships with national consumer organizations, and educational theater programs; and national public health policy. Application and guidelines are available online.
Requirements: 501(c)3 nonprofit organizations that have national reach are eligible. Organizations must be nonpartisan and nondenominational.
Geographic Focus: All States
Amount of Grant: Up to 100,000,000 USD
Contact: Community Relations Manager; (510) 271-5685; fax (510) 271-6493
Internet: http://www.kaiserpermanentejobs.org/aboutus/community.asp
Sponsor: Kaiser Permanente
1 Kaiser Plaza, 21B
Oakland, CA 94612

Kalamazoo Community Foundation Capacity Building Grants 2764
The Kalamazoo Foundation's Capacity Building Grants provide support that enables nonprofits to identify and address organizational development challenges through resources, training and skill building. These grants are meant to enhance an organization's ability to achieve measurable and sustainable results. Capacity Building Grants generally range in size from $1,500 to $2,500 and have funded activities like strategic planning, merger explorations and training in the areas of fiscal management, diversity, evaluation and leadership. There are no specified annual deadlines for this funding.
Requirements: Kalamazoo, Michigan, organizations recognized (or in the process of applying for recognition) under IRS code 501(c)3 are encouraged to contact foundation staff before submitting a request to determine eligibility.

Restrictions: Generally, the foundation does not provide funding for debt retirement, endowments, individuals, travel for individuals or groups, religious organizations for religious purposes, meetings, conferences, publications, films, or television and radio programming.
Geographic Focus: Michigan
Amount of Grant: 1,500 - 2,500 USD
Contact: Bobbe Luce, (269) 381-4416; fax (269) 381-3146; bluce@kalfound.org *Internet:* http://www.kalfound.org/Grants/OtherGrantOpportunities/tabid/226/Default.aspx
Sponsor: Kalamazoo Community Foundation
151 South Rose Street, Suite 332
Kalamazoo, MI 49007-4775

Kalamazoo Foundation Economic and Community Development Grants 2765

The Kalamazoo Community Foundation envisions a community where physical, social and cultural conditions are continually enhanced for all residents; where people can find meaningful employment and resources for economic growth; where a strong downtown is supported by vibrant neighborhoods; and where quality of life and prosperity are enhanced for all. Therefore, we invest in quality programs that are informed by best practices and: support a vibrant urban core as a platform for economic growth; support redevelopment efforts in the downtown area, surrounding neighborhoods and adjacent communities; provide job training and meaningful job opportunities; and ensure stable housing that contributes to neighborhood health, especially safe and affordable rental and home ownership opportunities. Pre-application conversations about Economic and Community Development grants for the July 1 deadline may be scheduled between May 6 and June 14; for the January 2 deadline, these conversations can be scheduled between November 6 and December 14. Applications for Economic and Community Development grants are accepted in January and July.
Requirements: Kalamazoo, Michigan, organizations recognized (or in the process of applying for recognition) under IRS code 501(c)3 are encouraged to contact foundation staff before submitting a request to determine eligibility.
Restrictions: Generally, the foundation does not provide funding for debt retirement, endowments, individuals, travel for individuals or groups, religious organizations for religious purposes, meetings, conferences, publications, films, or television and radio programming.
Geographic Focus: Michigan
Date(s) Application is Due: Jan 2; Jul 1
Contact: Jessica Aguilera, Community Investment Manager; (269) 381-4416; fax (269) 381-3146; jaguilera@kalfound.org or info@kalfound.org
Internet: http://www.kalfound.org/Grants/OurCommunityInvestmentPriorities/tabid/223/Default.aspx
Sponsor: Kalamazoo Community Foundation
151 South Rose Street, Suite 332
Kalamazoo, MI 49007-4775

Kalamazoo Community Foundation Environment Fund Grants 2766

The Kalamazoo Community Foundation holds three Field-of-Interest Funds that address community needs related to the environment: Spirit of Community Environment Fund, which supports projects that educate and engage citizens about environmental issues; evaluate, protect and improve natural areas and resources; and build healthy, sustainable communities (the application deadline for grants from this fund is the first business day of October); Sustainable Community Endowment Fund, which is dedicated to advancing an environmental ethic that links environmental protection with economic development (applications for grants from this fund can be submitted at any time and are reviewed upon receipt); and Sustainable Community Watershed Endowment Fund, which provides support to projects that address watershed management issues, such as the identification and quantification of pollutant loading from storm water runoff and other nonpoint source discharges (the application deadline for grants from this fund is the first business day of October).
Requirements: Kalamazoo, Michigan, organizations recognized (or in the process of applying for recognition) under IRS code 501(c)3 are encouraged to contact foundation staff before submitting a request to determine eligibility.
Restrictions: Generally, the foundation does not provide funding for debt retirement, endowments, individuals, travel for individuals or groups, religious organizations for religious purposes, meetings, conferences, publications, films, or television and radio programming.
Geographic Focus: Michigan
Date(s) Application is Due: Oct 1
Contact: Jessica Aguilera, Community Investment Manager; (269) 381-4416; fax (269) 381-3146; jaguilera@kalfound.org or info@kalfound.org
Internet: http://www.kalfound.org/Grants/OtherGrantOpportunities/tabid/226/Default.aspx
Sponsor: Kalamazoo Community Foundation
151 South Rose Street, Suite 332
Kalamazoo, MI 49007-4775

Kalamazoo Community Foundation Front Porch Grants 2767

The Kalamazoo Front Porch Grants are based on the custom of neighbors gathering on the front porches of their homes to share conversations about family life, community events, and the latest news, Front Porch Grants provide grants of up to $100 to support activities like block parties, get-togethers and town meetings, which build deeper neighbor-to-neighbor connections. There are no specified deadlines for these grants, and applicants should begin by contacting the Foundation office.
Restrictions: Generally, the foundation does not provide funding for debt retirement, endowments, individuals, travel for individuals or groups, religious organizations for religious purposes, meetings, conferences, publications, films, or television and radio programming.
Geographic Focus: Michigan
Amount of Grant: Up to 100 USD
Contact: Jessica Aguilera, Community Investment Manager; (269) 381-4416; fax (269) 381-3146; jaguilera@kalfound.org or info@kalfound.org
Internet: http://www.kalfound.org/InitiativesImpact/OurInitiatives/BetterTogetherKalamazoo/tabid/245/Default.aspx
Sponsor: Kalamazoo Community Foundation
151 South Rose Street, Suite 332
Kalamazoo, MI 49007-4775

Kalamazoo Community Foundation Good Neighbor Grants 2768

The Good Neighbor Grant program reaches out to individuals and small, grassroots groups to support their efforts in turning their ideas into projects to benefit the Kalamazoo community. These grants place resources for change in the hands of those closest to the issues that need to be addressed, which enables and empowers them to be good neighbors. Grants provide up to $1,000 of support to projects that: enhance bridges between people who are different from each other in some significant way (e.g. race, religion, economic status); engage people—especially those who haven't participated in community activities before—in projects that make a difference in the lives of all those involved; and embrace youths by involving them in project planning and/or providing leadership opportunities.
Requirements: Kalamazoo, Michigan, organizations are encouraged to contact foundation staff before submitting a request to determine eligibility.
Restrictions: Generally, the foundation does not provide funding for debt retirement, endowments, individuals, travel for individuals or groups, religious organizations for religious purposes, meetings, conferences, publications, films, or television and radio programming.
Geographic Focus: Michigan
Amount of Grant: Up to 1,000 USD
Contact: Jessica Aguilera, Community Investment Manager; (269) 381-4416; fax (269) 381-3146; jaguilera@kalfound.org or info@kalfound.org
Internet: http://www.kalfound.org/Grants/GoodNeighborGrants/tabid/291/Default.aspx
Sponsor: Kalamazoo Community Foundation
151 South Rose Street, Suite 332
Kalamazoo, MI 49007-4775

Kalamazoo Community Foundation Individuals and Families Grants 2769

The Kalamazoo Community Foundation envisions a community where individuals and families are fully equipped to meet their basic needs, become self-sufficient, maintain their dignity and thrive. Therefore, we invest in quality programs that are informed by best practices and support basic needs, such as: emergency shelter and transitional housing; safety, food, clothing, transportation and quality child care; access to medical, mental, dental and preventative health care; and skill building to help individuals and families maintain or move toward self-sufficiency. Applications deadlines for Individuals and Families grants are January 2 and July 1.
Requirements: Kalamazoo, Michigan, organizations recognized (or in the process of applying for recognition) under IRS code 501(c)3 are encouraged to contact foundation staff before submitting a request to determine eligibility.
Restrictions: Generally, the foundation does not provide funding for debt retirement, endowments, individuals, travel for individuals or groups, religious organizations for religious purposes, meetings, conferences, publications, films, or television and radio programming.
Geographic Focus: Michigan
Date(s) Application is Due: Jan 2; Jul 1
Contact: Jessica Aguilera, Community Investment Manager; (269) 381-4416; fax (269) 381-3146; jaguilera@kalfound.org or info@kalfound.org
Internet: http://www.kalfound.org/Grants/OurCommunityInvestmentPriorities/tabid/223/Default.aspx
Sponsor: Kalamazoo Community Foundation
151 South Rose Street, Suite 332
Kalamazoo, MI 49007-4775

Kalamazoo Community Foundation John E. Fetzer Institute Fund Grants 2770

The John E. Fetzer Institute Fund is an Advised Fund of the Kalamazoo Community Foundation aimed at enriching the lives of community members. Funding requests of up to $5,000 are considered. A committee of five Fetzer Institute staff members makes recommendations to the Kalamazoo Community Foundation board of trustees for grants based on submitted proposals. Before submitting your grant proposal, you must schedule a pre-application conversation with a member of the Community Investment team. This conversation must be scheduled at least two weeks before the grant application deadline. Grant decisions are made about two months after submission annual deadlines, which are January 2, April 1, July 1, and October 1. To learn more or schedule a pre-application conversation, contact the Foundation directly.
Requirements: Kalamazoo, Michigan, organizations recognized (or in the process of applying for recognition) under IRS code 501(c)3 are encouraged to contact foundation staff before submitting a request to determine eligibility.
Restrictions: Generally, the foundation does not provide funding for debt retirement, endowments, individuals, travel for individuals or groups, religious organizations for religious purposes, meetings, conferences, publications, films, or television and radio programming.
Geographic Focus: Michigan
Date(s) Application is Due: Jan 2; Apr 1; Jul 1; Oct 1
Amount of Grant: Up to 5,000 USD
Contact: Jessica Aguilera; (269) 381-4416; fax (269) 381-3146; jaguilera@kalfound.org

Internet: http://www.kalfound.org/Grants/OtherGrantOpportunities/tabid/226/Default.aspx
Sponsor: Kalamazoo Community Foundation
151 South Rose Street, Suite 332
Kalamazoo, MI 49007-4775

Kalamazoo Community Foundation LBGT Equality Fund Grants 2771
Grants awarded from the LGBT Equality Fund support greater Kalamazoo area nonprofits that promote equality and celebrate appreciation for the lesbian, gay, bisexual, transgender and questioning community members who live, work and raise their families here. The LGBT Equality Fund has four goals: advocate for human rights and equality to positively impact Kalamazoo County's LGBT community; promote social justice and unity; support activities that celebrate the rich social and cultural contributions of the LGBT community; and strengthen organizations that serve the physical, health and social or emotional needs of the gay and transgender community. The Fund's priority areas are people of color, youths, families, transgender, cross-generational, and leadership development. There are no specified deadlines, and applicants should begin by contacting the Foundation.
Requirements: Kalamazoo, Michigan, organizations recognized (or in the process of applying for recognition) under IRS code 501(c)3 are encouraged to contact foundation staff before submitting a request to determine eligibility.
Restrictions: Generally, the foundation does not provide funding for debt retirement, endowments, individuals, travel for individuals or groups, religious organizations for religious purposes, meetings, conferences, publications, films, or television and radio programming.
Geographic Focus: Michigan
Contact: Jessica Aguilera, Community Investment Manager; (269) 381-4416; fax (269) 381-3146; jaguilera@kalfound.org or info@kalfound.org
Internet: http://www.kalfound.org/Grants/OtherGrantOpportunities/tabid/226/Default.aspx
Sponsor: Kalamazoo Community Foundation
151 South Rose Street, Suite 332
Kalamazoo, MI 49007-4775

Kalamazoo Community Foundation Mini-Grants 2772
Kalamazoo Foundation Mini-Grants (usually around $1,500 per grant) are available to nonprofit 501(c)3 organizations for needs that are urgent in nature. These requests must fit within our community investment priorities. Requests generally are reviewed within two weeks of receiving the application.
Requirements: Kalamazoo, Michigan, organizations recognized (or in the process of applying for recognition) under IRS code 501(c)3 are encouraged to contact foundation staff before submitting a request to determine eligibility.
Restrictions: Generally, the foundation does not provide funding for debt retirement, endowments, individuals, travel for individuals or groups, religious organizations for religious purposes, meetings, conferences, publications, films, or television and radio programming.
Geographic Focus: Michigan
Amount of Grant: Up to 2,000 USD
Contact: Bobbe Luce, (269) 381-4416; fax (269) 381-3146; bluce@kalfound.org
Internet: http://www.kalfound.org/Grants/OtherGrantOpportunities/tabid/226/Default.aspx
Sponsor: Kalamazoo Community Foundation
151 South Rose Street, Suite 332
Kalamazoo, MI 49007-4775

Kalamazoo Community Foundation Youth Development Grants 2773
The Kalamazoo Community Foundation envisions a community where young people are nurtured and have their developmental needs met; are productive contributors to the community; and are prepared for life beyond high school, whether they choose to pursue higher education or enter our community's workforce. We invest in quality programs that use effective youth development principles, are informed by best practices and provide youths with: safe access to caring adults through youth/adult partnerships; age-appropriate strategies for growth and development; and opportunities to build social and emotional learning competencies and a positive self identity. Applications deadlines for Youth Development Grants are April 1 and October 1.
Requirements: Kalamazoo, Michigan, organizations recognized (or in the process of applying for recognition) under IRS code 501(c)3 are encouraged to contact foundation staff before submitting a request to determine eligibility.
Restrictions: Generally, the foundation does not provide funding for debt retirement, endowments, individuals, travel for individuals or groups, religious organizations for religious purposes, meetings, conferences, publications, films, or television and radio programming.
Geographic Focus: Michigan
Date(s) Application is Due: Apr 1; Oct 1
Contact: Jessica Aguilera; (269) 381-4416; fax (269) 381-3146; jaguilera@kalfound.org
Internet: http://www.kalfound.org/Grants/OurCommunityInvestmentPriorities/tabid/223/Default.aspx
Sponsor: Kalamazoo Community Foundation
151 South Rose Street, Suite 332
Kalamazoo, MI 49007-4775

Kaneta Foundation Grants 2774
The Foundation's mission is to support children, youth and family ministries that foster the spiritual welfare of its community by sharing hope to those in need. Funding priorities include: education—programs to ensure Christian students access to a quality higher education through scholarships; human services and community development—agencies that foster effective solutions to social and economic challenges; religion and spiritual development—faith based communities and their members that create a more caring community; and youth development—programs that help youth gain confidence, self esteem and become contributing members to our community.
Requirements: Eligible applicants must have 501(c)3 status, or must apply through a fiscal sponsor with 501(c)3 status.
Restrictions: The Foundation does not fund loans or debt service, endowments, funds for re-granting, scholarships, grants to individuals or units of government, or activities that have already occurred.
Geographic Focus: Hawaii
Contact: Christel Wuerfel, (808) 566-5524 or (888) 731-3863; cwuerfel@hcf-hawaii.org
Internet: http://www.kanetafoundation.org/
Sponsor: Kaneta Foundation
1164 Bishop Street, Suite 800
Honolulu, HI 96813

Kansas Arts Commission American Masterpieces Kansas Grants 2775
In order to achieve it's mission, the Kansas Arts Commission, along with the National Endowment for the Arts, sponsors education and access programs in conjunction with the NEA's American Masterpieces: Three Centuries of American Genius. American Masterpieces Kansas will support public arts and cultural events occurring between January 1st, and June 30th, relating to the Kansas 150 commemoration and featuring works by living or deceased recognized Kansas artists. Funding is anticipated to be up to $1,000 per organization and must be matched 1:1.
Requirements: Only Kansas arts and cultural nonprofit organizations and government agencies receiving Operational Support grants (current year) are eligible, and projects must include works by recognized Kansas artists.
Geographic Focus: Kansas
Date(s) Application is Due: Apr 8
Amount of Grant: 1,000 USD
Contact: Raena Sommers, Program Manager; (785) 296-4089; raena@arts.ks.gov
Internet: http://arts.ks.gov/grants/am/index.shtml
Sponsor: Kansas Arts Commission
700 SW Jackson, Jayhawk Tower, Suite 1004
Topeka, KS 66603-3774

Kansas Arts Commission Artist Fellowships 2776
The Commission awards Fellowships that recognize artistic merit, sustained achievement and excellence in the performing and media arts. Fellowships are awarded across all arts disciplines in three categories: Kansas Master Fellowships ($5,000), Kansas Mid-Career Fellowships ($750), and Kansas Emerging Artists Awards ($250).
Requirements: Any working artist who has lived in Kansas since July 1 two years prior July 1 of the current year may apply. The commission expects that recipients will remain in Kansas until July 1 of the current year. This award is for artists who make original work.
Restrictions: Undergraduate or graduate degree-seeking students; and previous recipients of this fellowship are not eligible.
Geographic Focus: Kansas
Date(s) Application is Due: Oct 14
Amount of Grant: 5,000 USD
Contact: Christine Dotterweich Bial; (785) 368-6544; christine@arts.ks.gov
Internet: http://arts.ks.gov/fellowships/index.shtml
Sponsor: Kansas Arts Commission
700 SW Jackson, Jayhawk Tower, Suite 1004
Topeka, KS 66603-3774

Kansas Arts Commission Arts-in-Communities Project Grants 2777
Grants provide financial support for one-time or stand-alone arts projects or series of events that are planned, developed, and presented for the public by arts organizations and non-art organizations. The purpose of the program is to support high-quality arts events, to encourage and expand access to the arts by community audiences, and to support projects that increase work opportunities for artists. This is a competitive grant and funding is determined by an advisory panel.
Requirements: Grants are project-based and are not for general operating expenses. Non-arts organizations, such as, but not limited to, K-12 schools or school districts, libraries, local governmental entities, recreation commissions, community colleges, historical societies or museums, and chambers of commerce, may apply for support of an arts project.
Geographic Focus: Kansas
Date(s) Application is Due: Mar 20
Contact: Christine Dotterweich Bial; (785) 368-6544; christine@arts.ks.gov
Internet: http://arts.state.ks.us/
Sponsor: Kansas Arts Commission
700 SW Jackson, Jayhawk Tower, Suite 1004
Topeka, KS 66603-3774

Kansas Arts Commission Arts-in-Communities Project Mini-Grants 2778
The Commission recognizes the vital roles that community and small, unincorporated organizations play in their respective communities. Many smaller organizations, public agencies, and social service organizations are committed to making the arts accessible to the people who live in their areas. Arts-in-Communities Project Mini-Grants, which are grants of $2,000 or less, support such efforts.
Requirements: Grants are project-based and are not for general operating expenses. Non-arts organizations, such as, but not limited to, K-12 schools or school districts, libraries, local governmental entities, recreation commissions, community colleges, historical societies or museums, and chambers of commerce, may apply for support of an arts project.

Geographic Focus: Kansas
Date(s) Application is Due: Mar 25
Amount of Grant: Up to 2,000 USD
Contact: Christine Dotterweich Bial; (785) 368-6544; christine@arts.ks.gov
Internet: http://arts.ks.gov/grants/aic_mini/index.shtml
Sponsor: Kansas Arts Commission
700 SW Jackson, Jayhawk Tower, Suite 1004
Topeka, KS 66603-3774

Kansas Arts Commission Arts-in-Education Grants — 2779
The Commission is committed to supporting outstanding programs in arts education: programs that enable young people to explore and experience the arts in both broad and focused ways. While it believes that every classroom educator should be able to teach about the arts, the Commission recognize the vital and very powerful role that artists have in education. The Arts-in-Education Grants nurture the integration of the arts in classrooms, community settings, pre-schools and institutions. Through these grants, the Commission supports programs that are innovative, responsive to children, community and classroom needs, and that utilize proven methods of learning and evaluation. The Commission offers three arts-in-education grant programs: Arts-in-Education Grants for Arts Organizations, Arts-Based Early Education and Arts Education for Youth-At-Risk. All three support Kansas communities and arts organizations to bring the arts to our youngest citizens. These grants are competitive, and funding is determined by advisory panels.
Requirements: Organizations must be based in Kansas.
Geographic Focus: Kansas
Date(s) Application is Due: Mar 18
Amount of Grant: 2,000 - 8,000 USD
Contact: Margaret Weisbrod Morris, Program Manager; (785) 368-6545; fax (785) 296-4989; margaret@arts.ks.gov
Internet: http://arts.ks.gov/grants/aie/index.shtml
Sponsor: Kansas Arts Commission
700 SW Jackson, Jayhawk Tower, Suite 1004
Topeka, KS 66603-3774

Kansas Arts Commission Arts on Tour Grants — 2780
Touring program grants are awarded to presenters of concerts, performances for young audiences, workshops, master classes, and other events by performing artists who are listed on the program roster. The purpose of the program is to provide access by Kansas audiences to quality arts events, to provide opportunities for professional Kansas performing artists to perform in communities throughout the state, and to encourage Kansas presenters to share the resources of Kansas' accomplished performing artists. The Commission recommends that organizations submit applications at least six weeks or more prior to the beginning of the project.
Requirements: Qualified Kansas organizations that have scheduled events by commission roster artists during the fiscal year in which the grant application is submitted are eligible. This includes: nonprofit organizations, including arts organizations; schools and school districts; social service agencies; and government agencies.
Geographic Focus: Kansas
Date(s) Application is Due: May 31
Contact: Christine Dotterweich Bial; (785) 368-6544; christine@arts.ks.gov
Internet: http://arts.ks.gov/grants/kat/index.shtml
Sponsor: Kansas Arts Commission
700 SW Jackson, Jayhawk Tower, Suite 1004
Topeka, KS 66603-3774

Kansas Arts Commission Operational Support for Arts & Cultural Organizations — 2781
Through operational support grants, the Commission offers financial assistance to nonprofit arts and cultural organizations with at least a three-year history of incorporation or operation as an independent entity. The award is based upon a percentage of the organization's projected expense budget and the amount of funds available for distribution in this program category. Arts organizations may apply for support of general operating, program, and administrative expenses; and on attached application components, arts organizations may apply for support of arts in education activities, and for support of Kansas touring program events. The purpose of the operational support grants is to strengthen the administrative and programming capability of arts organizations; enable arts organizations to provide high-quality, accessible arts activities, programs, and services to their constituencies; support arts organizations in planning and development of long-term goals; and augment, not supplant, local support for arts organizations.
Requirements: Single or multidisciplinary arts and cultural organizations based in Kansas are eligible to apply. Organizations must have as their primary missions planning, development, support or presentation of arts and cultural programs and services, as evidenced by their mission statement, total fiscal operations, and total activities.
Geographic Focus: Kansas
Date(s) Application is Due: Mar 4
Contact: Raena Sommers; (785) 296-4089; fax (785) 296-4989; raena@arts.state.ks.us
Internet: http://arts.ks.gov/grants/os/index.shtml
Sponsor: Kansas Arts Commission
700 SW Jackson, Jayhawk Tower, Suite 1004
Topeka, KS 66603-3774

Kansas Arts Commission Partnership Agreement Grants — 2782
In order to achieve it's mission, the Kansas Arts Commission and its partners offer services to the arts and arts management field in Kansas. Partnership Agreements support 501(c)3 nonprofit organizations and government agencies in conducting research or offering statewide artistic programs or professional development, training and consulting opportunities for artists, arts and cultural managers, staff and volunteers. The Kansas Arts Commission invites proposals for services to the field. Projects must occur during the current fiscal year of the Kansas Arts Commission (July 1 - June 30). For additional guidelines, refer to: http://arts.ks.gov/grants/pa/index.shtml.
Requirements: Who may apply: a nonprofit, tax-exempt 501(c)3 organization; a local, regional or state government agency; an institution connected to a Kansas university or college that has three-year history of community-oriented programming not connected with the curriculum of the university or college; Kansas college and university foundations or endowments may also apply. Organizations or agencies submitting proposals must have: a functioning, independent board of directors or advisors (does not apply to an agency of the State of Kansas); a demonstrated expertise in an area identified as a priority in the Kansas Arts Commission's current strategic plan.
Geographic Focus: Kansas
Date(s) Application is Due: Apr 8
Amount of Grant: 5,000 - 10,000 USD
Contact: Llewellyn Crain; (785) 368-6548; fax (785) 296-4989; lcrain@arts.ks.gov
Internet: http://arts.ks.gov/grants/pa/index.shtml
Sponsor: Kansas Arts Commission
700 SW Jackson, Jayhawk Tower, Suite 1004
Topeka, KS 66603-3774

Kansas Arts Commission Visual Arts Program Grants — 2783
In order to increase audiences for Kansas visual artists, the Kansas Arts Commission created the Kansas Visual Arts Program. This program supports the exhibition of Kansas artists in arts and cultural organizations throughout the state. Primary objectives are: to promote, develop and support new public exhibitions of Kansas visual artists; to provide opportunities for exhibition by Kansas visual artists; to encourage Kansas arts and cultural organizations to include Kansas artists in exhibitions; and to provide Kansas audiences access to quality visual arts exhibitions.
Requirements: Single or multidisciplinary arts and cultural organizations which have as their primary mission the planning, development, support or presentation of arts and cultural programs and services as demonstrated by their mission statement, total fiscal operations and total activities. Organizations must have at least a three-year history of incorporation and activities and an independent budget. K-12 schools and school districts are also eligible.
Restrictions: An applicant may apply for only one new exhibit per fiscal year. Only exhibits featuring Kansas artists, living or deceased, are eligible for funding.
Geographic Focus: Kansas
Date(s) Application is Due: May 30
Amount of Grant: Up to 1,500 USD
Contact: Christine Dotterweich Bial, Program Manager; (785) 368-6544; fax (785) 296-4989; christine@arts.ks.gov
Internet: http://arts.state.ks.us/
Sponsor: Kansas Arts Commission
700 SW Jackson, Jayhawk Tower, Suite 1004
Topeka, KS 66603-3774

Kansas Health Foundation Recognition Grants — 2784
The Kansas Health Foundation Recognition Grants expand the Foundation's support to a broad range of health-related organizations throughout the state. The Foundation defines health broadly, and looks at all the aspects that affect health, including the social factors that contribute to a healthy population (a state of complete physical, mental, and social well-being and not merely the absence of disease or infirmity). While the majority of the Foundation's funding is through invited proposals, the Recognition Grants program is designed to fund unsolicited requests. It is targeted for organizations and agencies proposing meaningful and charitable projects that fit within the Foundation's mission of improving the health of all Kansans.
Requirements: Kansas 501(c)3 nonprofit health organizations are eligible. The application is at the Foundation website and must be submitted online.
Restrictions: The Foundation does not support: medical research; capital campaigns; operating deficits or retirement of debt; endowment programs not initiated by the Foundation; political advocacy of any kind; vehicles, such as vans or buses; medical equipment; construction projects or real estate acquisitions; direct mental health services; or direct medical services.
Geographic Focus: Kansas
Date(s) Application is Due: Mar 15; Sep 15
Amount of Grant: Up to 25,000 USD
Contact: Nancy Claassen; (800) 373-7681 or (316) 262-7676; info@khf.org
Gina Hess, Grant Assistant; (316) 262-7676 or (800) 373-7681; rinfo@khf.org
Internet: http://www.kansashealth.org/grantmaking/recognitiongrants
Sponsor: Kansas Health Foundation
309 East Douglas
Wichita, KS 67202-3405

Ka Papa O Kakuhihewa Fund — 2785
The purpose of the fund is to promote resource conservation programs for the community that would affect the use of natural resources such as water and land. The goal is to promote and support programs that create and instill a conservation ethic. Preference will be given to projects that: promote natural resource conservation; benefit the geographical community identified by the zip codes of 96707 and 96792; focus on youth (approximately 14-25 years); demonstrate commitment to support the local economy by spending the majority of the funds within the community. Application information is available online.
Requirements: Any nonprofit, tax-exempt 501(c)3 organization, school, unit of government, neighborhood group or project is eligible.

Restrictions: Funding is not available for: costs relating to establishing a new 501(c)3 organization; general operating support, although up to 10% for indirect costs will be considered; funds for an endowment; major capital improvements, although minor capital improvement required to implement the project will be considered; material costs supporting renewable energy without an educational component.
Geographic Focus: Hawaii
Date(s) Application is Due: Mar 30
Amount of Grant: 2,000 - 25,000 USD
Contact: Amy Luersen, (808) 566-5550 or (888) 731-3863; aluersen@hawaiicommunityfoundation.org or aluersen@hcf-hawaii.org
Internet: http://www.hawaiicommunityfoundation.org/index.php?id=71&categoryID=20
Sponsor: Hawai'i Community Foundation
1164 Bishop Street, Suite 800
Honolulu, HI 96813

Kate B. Reynolds Charitable Trust Health Care Grants 2786
The Trust responds to health care and wellness needs and invests in solutions that improve the quality of health for financially needy residents throughout North Carolina. The Health Care Division seeks impact through two program areas: providing treatment and supporting prevention. The trust requires advanced consultation by phone or in writing. Application materials are available online, but applications are not accepted electronically.
Requirements: Nonprofit 501(c)3 organizations in North Carolina are eligible.
Restrictions: Grants are not awarded to individuals.
Geographic Focus: North Carolina
Date(s) Application is Due: Mar 15; Sep 15
Amount of Grant: 20,000 - 200,000 USD
Contact: John H. Frank; (336) 397-5502 or (866) 551-0690; john@kbr.org
Internet: http://www.kbr.org/health-care-division-fund.cfm
Sponsor: Kate B. Reynolds Charitable Trust
128 Reynolda Village
Winston-Salem, NC 27106-5123

Kate B. Reynolds Charitable Trust Poor and Needy Grants 2787
Through the Poor and Needy Division, the trust responds to basic life needs and invests in solutions that improve the quality of life for financially needy residents of Forsyth County. The Poor and Needy division seeks impact through two program areas by providing operating funds: Providing Basic Needs and Increasing Self Reliance. The Grant Application Process is a two-step process involving consultation with a staff Program Officer, followed by formal submission of a grant application. The consultation can be scheduled by calling our Winston-Salem offices.
Requirements: 501(c)3 organizations in Forsyth County, North Carolina, are eligible.
Restrictions: Grants are not awarded to individuals.
Geographic Focus: North Carolina
Date(s) Application is Due: Jan 15; Jul 15
Contact: Joyce T. Adger; (336) 397-5503 or (336) 723-1456; joyce@kbr.org
Internet: http://www.kbr.org/poor-and-needy-division-fund.cfm
Sponsor: Kate B. Reynolds Charitable Trust
128 Reynolda Village
Winston-Salem, NC 27106-5123

Katharine Matthies Foundation Grants 2788
The Katharine Matthies Foundation was established in 1987 to support and promote quality educational, human-services, and health-care programming for underserved populations. Special consideration is given to organizations that work to prevent cruelty to children and animals. The majority of grants from the Matthies Foundation are one year in duration; on occasion, multi-year support is awarded. Applicants must apply online at the grant website. Applicants are strongly encouraged to do the following before applying: review the downloadable state application procedures for additional helpful information and clarifications; review the downloadable online-application guidelines at the grant website; review the foundation's funding history (link is available from the grant website); review the online application questions in advance; and review the list of required attachments. These will generally include: a list of board members, financial statements (audited, reviewed, or compiled by independent auditor); an organization summary; a list of other funding sources; an IRS Determination letter; and other required documents. All attachments must be uploaded in the online application as PDF, Word, or Excel files. The deadline for application to the Katherine Matthies Foundation is 11:59 p.m. on May 1. Applicants will be notified of grant decisions by letter within three to four months after the proposal deadline.
Requirements: Applicant organizations must have 501(c)3 tax-exempt status and serve the people of the following Connecticut towns: Seymour, Ansonia, Derby, Oxford, Shelton, or Beacon Falls. A breakdown of number/percentage of people served by specific towns will be required in the online application. Special consideration will be given to organizations that serve the people of Seymour, Connecticut.
Restrictions: The Matthies Foundation specifically serves people of the Lower Naugatuck Valley. The foundation does not support requests from individuals, organizations attempting to influence policy through direct lobbying, or any political campaigns.
Geographic Focus: Connecticut
Date(s) Application is Due: May 1
Contact: Amy Lynch, Foundation Manager; (860) 657-7015; amy.r.lynch@baml.com
Internet: https://www.bankofamerica.com/philanthropic/fn_search.action
Sponsor: Katharine Matthies Foundation
200 Glastonbury Boulevard, Suite # 200
Glastonbury, CT 06033-4056

Katherine Baxter Memorial Foundation Grants 2789
Established by primary donor Martin B. Ortlieb in California in 1992, the Katherine Baxter Memorial Foundation grants program offers support in the arts, higher education, and YMCAs and YWCAs. Giving is limited to the State of California, with a range of $150 to $20,000. Funding generally supports overall operating costs, and comes in the form of a donation.
Requirements: Applicants must be established 501(c)3 organizations either serving the residents of or located in the State of California.
Geographic Focus: California
Amount of Grant: 150 - 20,000 USD
Contact: Randolph Ortlieb, Trustee; (760) 747-3200
Sponsor: Katherine Baxter Memorial Foundation
970 Canterbury Avenue
Escondido, CA 92025-3836

Katherine John Murphy Foundation Grants 2790
The Katherine John Murphy Foundation was established in 1954 in Atlanta, Georgia by Katherine Murphy Riley. The foundation awards grants to Georgia tax-exempt organizations in its areas of interest, including services for children, education, the environment, and human services. Types of support include annual campaigns, building construction and/or renovation, capital campaigns, continuing support, general operating support, seed grants, and project development. Grants are awarded primarily in Atlanta, Georgia, and select areas of Latin America. Submit a letter of request.
Requirements: Organizations in Atlanta, Georgia, are eligible to apply, as well as select areas of Latin America.
Restrictions: No grants to individuals, or for research, or matching gifts.
Geographic Focus: Georgia, Argentina, Bolivia, Brazil, Chile, Colombia, Costa Rica, Cuba, Dominican Republic, Ecuador, El Salvador, Guatemala, Haiti, Honduras, Mexico, Nicaragua, Panama, Paraguay, Peru, Uruguay, Venezuela
Amount of Grant: 250 - 50,000 USD
Contact: Brenda Rambeau, (404) 589-8090; fdnsvcs.ga@suntrust.com
Internet: http://www.kjmurphyfoundation.org
Sponsor: Katherine John Murphy Foundation
50 Hurt Plaza, Suite 1210
Atlanta, GA 30303

Kathryne Beynon Foundation Grants 2791
Founded in California in 1967, the Kathryne Beynon Foundation provides support primarily for: hospitals (with a special interest in Asthma); youth agencies; child welfare; Roman Catholic church; higher education, Types of support include: general operating support; building construction/renovation; endowment funds; and scholarship funds. The Board meets quarterly to review grant requests. Applicants should contact the office in writing, outlining their proposal. Application is by invitation only, and there is no deadline date when submitting grant proposals. Contact the Foundation directly for additional guidelines before submitting a full proposal.
Requirements: 501(c)3 southern California tax-exempt organizations are eligible. Preference is given to requests from Pasadena. There are no: deadline dates; formal application form required to submit proposal.
Restrictions: No support to individuals.
Geographic Focus: California
Amount of Grant: 500 - 50,000 USD
Contact: Robert D. Bannon, Trustee; (626) 584-8800
Sponsor: Kathryne Beynon Foundation
1111 South Arroyo Parkway, Suite 470
Pasadena, CA 91105-3239

Katie's Krops Grants 2792
This grant opportunity will fund projects for kids ages 9 to 16 to start a vegetable garden to feed people in need in their communities. The winner will be awarded a gift card to a garden center in their area (up to $400), support from Katie's Krops, and a digital camera to document the garden and the harvest. Applications for all types of vegetable gardens, such as a container garden if you live in a city or a vegetable garden located in your neighborhood or at your school, will be considered.
Requirements: Applicants must be between the ages of 9 and 16 as of October 1 and must be residents of the United States. No garden experience is necessary, however a good support system of volunteers and a willingness to give back to the community is. All applications must be filled out completely and signed by a parent or legal guardian. Winners will be notified in January, and the garden must be started in the spring.
Restrictions: Only applications that are mailed will be accepted; emailed or faxed applications will not be accepted.
Geographic Focus: All States
Date(s) Application is Due: Dec 5
Amount of Grant: 400 - 600 USD
Contact: Katie Stagliano, Founder; 843-419-7878; cory@katieskrops.com
Internet: http://www.katieskrops.com/apply-for-a-grant.html
Sponsor: Katie's Krops
P.O. Box 1841
Summerville, SC 29484-1841

Katrine Menzing Deakins Charitable Trust Grants 2793
Katrine Deakins was executive secretary to Amon G. Carter and helped found the Amon G. Carter Foundation. She was the foundation's executive director and throughout her life was very active in numerous professional, social and charitable organizations. Katrine then

established her own trust in 1987, the Katrine Menzing Deakins Charitable Trust to benefit several favored charities in addition to other charitable organization requests selected each year by the trustees. Grants are typically between $1,000 and $25,000.The Katrine Menzing Deakins Charitable Trust has bi-annual application deadlines of March 31 and September 30. Applications must be submitted by 11:29 p.m. on the deadline dates. Applicants must apply online at the grant website. Applicants are strongly encouraged to do the following before applying: review the downloadable state application procedures for additional helpful information and clarifications; review the downloadable online-application guidelines at the grant website; review the trust's funding history (link is available from the grant website); review the online application questions in advance; and review the list of required attachments. These will generally include: a list of board members, financial statements (audited, reviewed, or compiled by independent auditor); an organization summary; a list of other funding sources; an IRS Determination letter; and other required documents. All attachments must be uploaded in the online application as PDF, Word, or Excel files.
Requirements: Applicants must have 501(c)3 tax-exempt status.
Restrictions: The trust does not support requests from individuals, organizations attempting to influence policy through direct lobbying, or any political campaigns.
Geographic Focus: Texas
Date(s) Application is Due: Mar 31; Sep 30
Amount of Grant: 1,000 - 25,000 USD
Contact: Mark J. Smith; (817) 390-6028; tx.philanthropic@baml.com
Internet: https://www.bankofamerica.com/philanthropic/fn_search.action
Sponsor: Katrine Menzing Deakins Charitable Trust
500 West 7th Street, 15th Floor, TX1-497-15-08
Fort Worth, TX 76102-4700

Kawabe Memorial Fund Grants   2794
The Kawabe Memorial Fund was established in 1971 to support and promote quality human-services programming for the economically disadvantaged, children and the elderly. The Fund also provides capital grants to churches as well as scholarships to support teachers and the clergy. The Kawabe Memorial Fund typically supports organizations serving the people of the Puget Sound area. Grant requests for general operating support are strongly encouraged. Program support will also be considered. Small, program-related capital expenses may be included in general operating or program requests. Grants from the Kawabe Memorial Fund are one year in duration. Application materials are available for download at the grant website. Applicants are strongly encouraged to review the state application guidelines for additional helpful information and clarifications before applying. Applicants are also encouraged to review the foundation's funding history (link is available from the grant website). Applications to the Kawabe Memorial Fund are due on the first Friday in February, May or September. Proposals must be post-marked on or before the application deadline and mailed to the address given in the downloadable state guidelines document. In general, applicants will be notified of grant decisions 3 to 4 months after proposal submission.
Geographic Focus: Washington
Contact: Nancy Atkinson, Vice President; (800) 848-7177; nancy.l.atkinson@baml.com
Internet: https://www.bankofamerica.com/philanthropic/fn_search.action
Sponsor: Kawabe Memorial Fund
800 5th Avenue, WA1-501-33-23
Seattle, WA 98104

KEEN Effect Grants   2795
KEEN dedicates time and financial resources to social and environmental organizations actively working towards the greater good. The KEEN Effect is a fan-activated grants program designed to support projects that fuel people's passion for protecting the environment and promoting responsible outdoor participation. Fans and customers nominate organizations in their communities who are doing great work providing ways for people to get outdoors with the goal that the regional Nonprofit organizations receiving funding through the KEEN Effect will multiply this passion for the outdoors though their work inspiring thousands more to get outside and responsibly enjoy our outdoor spaces. Approximately 25 non-profit organizations around the world will be granted a total of $100,000 to bring their projects to life.
Requirements: Grantees nominated by fans must clearly define how their organization or specific program inspires responsible outdoor participation as a way to work towards building a stronger community. KEEN will give special consideration to projects that introduce new audiences to the outdoors through responsible outdoor participation. Non-profit organizations or equivalents outside of the United States, can request up to $2,500 (Tier 1) or up to $10,000 (Tier 2) for submissions that meet stated requirements. Approved proposals will be awarded funding along with technical support and guidance.
Geographic Focus: All States, All Countries
Date(s) Application is Due: Dec 6
Amount of Grant: Up to 10,000 USD
Contact: Chris Enlow; (503) 805-9962; keeneffect@keenfootwear.com
Internet: http://www.keeneffect.com/
Sponsor: KEEN, Inc.
515 NW 13th Avenue
Portland, OR 97209

Kelvin and Eleanor Smith Foundation Grants   2796
The foundation awards grants to northeast Ohio nonprofits in its areas of interest, including nonsectarian education, the performing and visual arts, health care, and environmental conservation and protection. Types of support include general operating support, continuing support, annual campaigns, capital campaigns, building construction/renovation, and equipment acquisition. Since there are no required application forms, each proposal include a cover letter that outlines the reason for the request and the dollar amount. Organizations who have previously received funding from this Foundation may submit a proposal annually. There are no specified annual deadlines.
Requirements: Nonprofit organizations in the greater Cleveland, OH, area are eligible.
Restrictions: Grants are not made in support of individuals or for endowment funds, scholarships, fellowships, matching gifts, or loans.
Geographic Focus: Ohio
Amount of Grant: 3,000 - 150,000 USD
Contact: Carol W. Zett; (216) 591-9111; fax (216) 591-9557; cwzett@kesmithfoundation.org
Internet: http://www.kesmithfoundation.org/grantguidelines.html
Sponsor: Kelvin and Eleanor Smith Foundation
30195 Chagrin Boulevard, Suite 275
Cleveland, OH 44124

Kendrick Foundation Grants   2797
Kendrick Foundation was created to support health-related programs in Morgan County, Indiana. Support includes making grants to health-related organizations and charities, which may include community health care programs, hospice programs, health care education and training, and tax-exempt medical and health programs. Prior to submitting a grant application, a Letter of Intent must be submitted. Letters of Intent are available for download for a limited amount of time during the opening of the grant cycle. Letters of Intent for the spring grant cycle must be physically received in the office of the Community Foundation of Morgan County by March 15, no later than 4 p.m., with invited applications due April 30. Letters of Intent for the fall grant cycle must be physically received in the office of the Community Foundation of Morgan County, Inc. by October 15, no later than 4 p.m., with invited applications due November 30.
Requirements: The Kendrick Foundation will only accept full grant applications from those organizations serving Morgan County, Indiana, which were approved through a Letter of Intent.
Geographic Focus: Indiana
Date(s) Application is Due: Mar 15; Apr 30; Oct 15; Nov 30
Contact: Tom Zoss, (317) 831-1232 or (877) 822-6958; tzoss@cfmconline.org
Internet: http://www.cfmconline.org/kendrick/Grants/tabid/129/Default.aspx
Sponsor: Kendrick Foundation
250 N Monroe Street
Mooresville, IN 46158

Kennedy Center Experiential Education Initiative Internship   2798
The John F. Kennedy Center for the Performing Arts Department of VSA and Accessibility serves youth with disabilities interested in pursuing careers in the arts, arts administration, and arts education. The Department provides this service by investing in effective and innovative internship, apprenticeship, and training programs. The Experiential Education Initiative (EEI) Internship is a program designed to offer meaningful instruction and cultural arts experiences to individuals with intellectual disabilities. The EEI Internship Program provides hands-on internships and opportunities to explore today's complex performing arts environment to six motivated individuals each year. The internships provide exposure to the performing arts, develop social skills, and offer opportunities to improve job-related skills. Candidates may contact the Accessibility office for application information.
Requirements: Applicants must have a documented intellectual disability and be referred to the program through a social service agency. They must also be between the ages of 19 and 30, and demonstrate an interest in the performing arts.
Geographic Focus: All States
Contact: Betty Siegel; (202) 416-8727 or (202) 416-8728; access@kennedy-center.org
Internet: http://www.kennedy-center.org/accessibility/career.cfm#EEI
Sponsor: John F. Kennedy Center for the Performing Arts
2700 F Street NW
Washington, DC 20566

Kennedy Center HSC Foundation Internship   2799
The HSC Foundation Internship has been established to provide opportunities for individuals with disabilities to participate in internships at cultural arts institutions around the Washington, D.C. metropolitan area. Internships are designed to build skills that will enhance the participant's potential for future competitive employment in a career in the arts. Placements will be between 10 and 40 hours per week and of varying length. Deadlines vary by placement and specific internship. All interns will receive a stipend. Current internships are posted at the website. Applications may be emailed or mailed to the post office box in Virginia address listed on the website.
Requirements: Qualified applicants must be between the ages of 18 and 25 with a documented disability or chronic illness, and demonstrate an interest in the cultural arts. Additional requirements vary by placement and specific internship.
Geographic Focus: District of Columbia, Maryland, Virginia
Contact: Betty Siegel; (202) 416-8727 or (202) 416-8728; access@kennedy-center.org
Internet: http://www.kennedy-center.org/accessibility/career.cfm#HSC
Sponsor: John F. Kennedy Center for the Performing Arts
2700 F Street NW
Washington, DC 20566

Kennedy Center Summer HSC Foundation Internship   2800
The HSC Foundation Internship Program has been established to provide opportunities for individuals with disabilities to participate in internships at cultural arts institutions around the Washington, D.C. metropolitan area. Internships are designed to build skills that will enhance the participant's potential for future competitive employment in a career in the arts. Hours vary from 10 to 40 hours a week and of varying length. The Summer HSC Foundation Internship application is due April 30. Internships vary by placement and

deadline. All interns receive a stipend. Applications and currently available internships are posted on the website. Applications may be emailed or mailed to the post office box at the Virginia address listed on the website.
Requirements: Qualified applicants must be between the ages of 18 and 25 with a documented disability or chronic illness, and demonstrate an interest in the cultural arts. Additional requirements and materials submitted will vary by internship.
Geographic Focus: District of Columbia, Maryland, Virginia
Date(s) Application is Due: Apr 30
Contact: Betty Siegel; (202) 416-8727 or (202) 416-8728; access@kennedy-center.org
Internet: http://www.kennedy-center.org/accessibility/career.cfm#hscopps
Sponsor: John F. Kennedy Center for the Performing Arts
2700 F Street NW
Washington, DC 20566

Kenneth A. Scott Charitable Trust Grants 2801
The primary purpose of the Kenneth A. Scott Charitable Trust is to promote the humane treatment of companion animals. Proposals related to other species, including wildlife, may also be considered. The amount of the grant varies.
Requirements: All recipients must be nonprofit organizations with IRS 501(c)3 tax exempt status. Projects outside Ohio should be of national scope or significance. Of particular interest are programs in the following areas: humane education, continuing education for shelter staff and volunteers, prevention of human-animal cruelty or violence, and shelter medicine. For national programs, deadlines are December 1 and June 1. For Ohio programs are March 1 and September 1.
Geographic Focus: All States
Date(s) Application is Due: Mar 1; Jun 1; Sep 1; Dec 1
Contact: H. Richard Obermanns; (216) 752-3301; fax (216) 752-3308; obermanns@aol.com
Sponsor: Kenneth A. Scott Charitable Trust
KeyBank Nonprofit Asset Services, 127 Public Square, 16th Floor
Cleveland, OH 44114-1306

Kenneth T. and Eileen L. Norris Foundation Grants 2802
The foundation supports Los Angeles County nonprofits in the areas of: medicine—to improve access to health care, increase knowledge through research, and provide facilities for those activities to take place; youth—to provide constructive activities, positive role models, and opportunities for disadvantaged, disabled, and misguided children; community—to support law enforcement agencies, good citizenship, and environmental conservation; culture—to support museums, symphony orchestras, and dance and theater companies; and education and science—to focus on private education, especially secondary and college levels. Types of support include general operating support, continuing support, building construction and/or renovation, equipment acquisition, endowment funds, program development, professorships, scholarship funds, research, and matching funds. Education/science and medicine projects are accepted between May 1 and June 30; youth requests are accepted between February 15 and March 31; cultural (the arts) and community requests are accepted between December 1 and January 31; and medicine proposals are due between May 1 and June 30.
Requirements: Grants are awarded to organizations in southern California.
Geographic Focus: California
Date(s) Application is Due: Jan 31; Mar 31; Jun 30
Amount of Grant: 5,000 - 25,000 USD
Contact: Lisa D. Hansen; (562) 435-8444; fax (562) 436-0584; grants@ktn.org
Internet: http://www.norrisfoundation.org/grant.html
Sponsor: Kenneth T. and Eileen L. Norris Foundation
11 Golden Shore, Suite 450
Long Beach, CA 90802

Kenny's Kids Grants 2803
The foundation awards grants to U.S. nonprofits in company-operating locations with a focus on programs that improve life for children and young adults. The primary target of grants is giving support to organizations which seek to give youth greater opportunities outside of the classroom to learn and grow, to teach them skills that will enable them to thrive in a technology-oriented society, and to offer them the guidance and attention necessary to develop such skills. Also consideration for youth-oriented organizations and other organizations that promote the welfare of youth, such as those that offer hope and encouragement to the sick and terminally ill, protect those who have suffered from abuse, and offer after-school programs for the underprivileged. There are no application deadlines. Allow eight to 12 weeks for proposal review.
Requirements: Nonprofits in company operating areas of Illinois are eligible.
Restrictions: No support for private foundations, schools (public or private), or corporations. Grants are not made to individuals, or for political campaigns, film, video, or audio productions.
Geographic Focus: Illinois
Amount of Grant: Up to 573,902 USD
Contact: Nicholas Pontikes, President
Sponsor: Kenny's Kids
1212 W Lill Street
Chicago, IL 60614

Kent D. Steadley and Mary L. Steadley Memorial Trust 2804
The Trust makes contributions to nonprofit organizations in and near Carthage, Missouri, exclusively to support community/economic development; elementary/secondary education; hospitals; human services; and public libraries.
Requirements: Nonprofit organizations operating to promote community well-being of the Carthage, Missouri, area are eligible. Organizations should first send a letter, requesting application materials. There are no application deadlines, and response is usually within six months.
Restrictions: Funding is not available for individuals or national fundraising events.
Geographic Focus: Missouri
Amount of Grant: 5,000 - 200,000 USD
Contact: Lareta Garnier, Program Contact, c/o Bank of America; (417) 227-6237
Sponsor: Kent D. and Mary L. Steadley Memorial Trust
P.O. Box 8300
Springfield, MO 65801-8300

Kentucky Arts Council Access Assistance Grants 2805
The Kentucky Arts Council Access Assistance support arts programs that serve populations whose opportunities to experience the arts may be limited by age, geographic location, ethnicity, economic status, disability, or other factors. A different population is chosen each grant cycle to benefit from these arts programs. Grants are available for up to $10,000, with a 25 percent cash match. The deadline is January 15, with program guidelines and application instructions available at the website. Applicants are encouraged to contact the Arts Council if they are unsure about their organization's eligibility.
Requirements: This grant supports quality arts programming in environments where arts are not the primary emphasis. Public libraries, co-operative extension offices, nursing homes, social service agencies, health departments, state agencies, correctional facilities, college and university programs, and other community-based organizations serving Kentuckians may apply
Restrictions: Organizations receiving general operating support from the Kentucky Arts Council are not eligible.
Geographic Focus: Kentucky
Date(s) Application is Due: Jan 15
Amount of Grant: Up to 10,000 USD
Contact: Sarah Schmitt; (502) 564-8110, ext. 492; sarah.schmitt@ky.gov
Internet: http://artscouncil.ky.gov/Grants/AAA.htm
Sponsor: Kentucky Arts Council
500 Mero Street, 21st Floor, Capital Plaza Tower
Frankfort, KY 40601-1987

Kentucky Arts Council Al Smith Individual Fellowship 2806
The Al Smith Individual Artist Fellowships are given to Kentucky artists who have achieved a high level of excellence and creativity in their work. Application instructions and additional guidelines are available at the website. The application deadline is March 15. The postmark deadline for submission of the hardcopy application and attachments is March 18. Applications are reviewed in April and May. The Arts Council Board reviews recommendations in June, with applicants notified as soon as possible after the board meeting.
Requirements: All applicants must have DUNS numbers (which may take up to 30 days to process). Professional Kentucky artists (writers, composers, choreographers, and visual and media artists) who are responsible for creating their own work, not interpreting the work of others, are eligible to apply. Visual artists, craft artists and media artists (film, video and audio) can apply in odd-numbered years. Writers (fiction, poetry, creative nonfiction, plays/screenwriting), composers, and choreographers can apply in even-numbered years.
Restrictions: The following restrictions apply to the Fellowship: previous Al Smith Fellowship recipients are not eligible; Al Smith recipients may not apply for an Emerging Artist Award; artists may apply only with work samples over which they had complete creative control; work created for commercial or instructional purposes is not eligible; multidisciplinary, interdisciplinary, or multi-category are not eligible; and translations, collaborations, and teams are ineligible. Artists may apply in one category and one medium only per application year. All work samples must be representative of the selected category and medium. With the exception of media arts, all work samples must have been completed within the past three years. Media artists may submit work completed within the past four years.
Geographic Focus: Kentucky
Date(s) Application is Due: Mar 15
Amount of Grant: 7,500 USD
Contact: Tamara Coffey, Individual Artist Director; (502) 564-8110, ext. 479 or (888) 833-2787; fax (502) 564-2839; tamara.coffey@ky.gov
Internet: http://artscouncil.ky.gov/Grants/ASF.htm
Sponsor: Kentucky Arts Council
500 Mero Street, 21st Floor, Capital Plaza Tower
Frankfort, KY 40601-1987

Kentucky Arts Council Emerging Artist Award 2807
The Kentucky Arts Council's Emerging Artist Award is a $1,000 unrestricted award to early career, professional Kentucky artists who demonstrate excellence and creativity in their work. Emerging artists who are responsible for creating their own work, not interpreting the work of others or creating work under the supervision of an instructor, are eligible to apply. Emerging artist is defined as any of the following: a professional artist in the early stages of their career (up to ten years); an artist with some professional experience (exhibitions, sales, contracted/paid performances, publications/reading, etc.), but may not have established a reputation as an artist; or graduating seniors in bachelor's programs, graduate students, or non-matriculating, early stage, professional artists. The Award is based primarily on the quality of the work samples submitted by the artist. Applications are accepted annually on a rotating basis by discipline. Additional guidelines and instructions are available at the website.
Requirements: The Arts Council requests that all applicants have a DUNS number (DUNS applications may take up to 30 days to process). Visual artists, craft artists and media artists (film, video and audio) can apply in odd-numbered years. Writers (fiction, poetry, creative nonfiction and play/screenwriting), composers and choreographers can apply in even-numbered years.

Restrictions: No individual may receive more than two Emerging Artist Awards from the Kentucky Arts Council. Emerging artists who have previously received an Emerging Artist Award ($1,000) in any discipline must wait a total of four years before applying for another Emerging Artist Award. Artists who have received an Emerging Artist Award must wait a total of two years before applying for an Al Smith Fellowship. Artists who have received Al Smith Fellowships may not apply for an Emerging Artist Award. Artists may only apply with work samples over which they had complete creative control and which were not created solely for commercial or instructional purposes. Multi-category, multidisciplinary, or interdisciplinary applications are not eligible. Translations, collaborations, and teams are not eligible to apply. Artists may apply in only one category and one medium per application year. All work samples submitted must be representative of the selected category and medium. With the exception of media arts, all work samples must have been completed within the past three years. Media artists may submit work completed within the past four years.
Geographic Focus: Kentucky
Date(s) Application is Due: Mar 15
Amount of Grant: 1,000 USD
Contact: Tamara Coffey, Individual Artist Director; (502) 564-8110, ext. 479 or (888) 833-2787; fax (502) 564-2839; tamara.coffey@ky.gov
Internet: http://artscouncil.ky.gov/Grants/EAP.htm
Sponsor: Kentucky Arts Council
500 Mero Street, 21st Floor, Capital Plaza Tower
Frankfort, KY 40601-1987

Kentucky Arts Council Folk and Traditional Arts Apprenticeship Grant   2808

The Folk and Traditional Arts Apprenticeship Grant provides up to $3,000, with no match funding requirement, to a Kentucky master traditional artist to teach skills, practices, and culture to a less experienced artist from the same community during the course of a year. The purpose of the grant is to honor traditional artists and encourage the continuation of Kentucky's living traditional arts by funding master artists to teach skills and practices vital to their cultural heritage to less experienced artists within their communities. Performance expectations are reviewed on the excellence of the master artist, excellence of the apprentice, and the apprenticeship work plan. Previously funded projects include storytelling through song, jazz piano, African American traditional gospel, Chinese dance, and basket making. The deadline is February 15, with application review in April. Applicants are notified as soon as possible after the Board Meeting in June. Additional guidelines, application instructions, and a list of previously funded projects are available at the website.
Requirements: Applicant artists must be at least 18 years of age, U.S. citizens, and full time residents of Kentucky for a period of one year immediately prior to the application deadline, and remain a Kentucky resident for one year following the award notification.
Restrictions: Arts Council grant funds may not be used for the following purposes: purchase of equipment, property, library holdings or acquisitions; capital improvements, facility construction, structural renovations and restorations; publications or recordings for commercial purposes; scholarships or other activities related to academic credit or degrees; activities intended primarily for fundraising; food, beverages or other refreshments; requests designed to reduce or eliminate existing deficits; interest on loans, fines, penalties and/or litigation costs; expenses incurred before the starting date of the period covered in the grant request; investments of any kind; performances not available to the general public; programs that have sectarian purposes; or indirect costs.
Geographic Focus: Kentucky
Date(s) Application is Due: Feb 15
Amount of Grant: Up to 3,000 USD
Contact: Mark Brown, Folk and Traditional Arts Program Director; (502) 564-3757, ext. 495 or (888) 833-2787; fax (502) 564-2839; mark.brown@ky.gov
Internet: http://artscouncil.ky.gov/Grants/FAA.htm
Sponsor: Kentucky Arts Council
500 Mero Street, 21st Floor, Capital Plaza Tower
Frankfort, KY 40601-1987

Kentucky Arts Council Partnership Grants   2809

The Kentucky Arts Partnership Grants provide unrestricted operating support to arts organizations to ensure that year-round participation in the arts is available to the people of Kentucky. The amount funded is derived from a formula based on the organization's operating revenues, the panelists' assessment of the application, and the funds available for the program. Additional guidelines, along with the application and a complete list of previously funded projects, are available at the website.
Requirements: Kentucky nonprofit organizations that have had IRS tax-exempt status for at least one year prior to the application deadline, and whose primary purpose is to provide year-round arts services and programs directly for the benefit of the public are eligible to apply.
Restrictions: Internal programs of academic institutions and state or other agencies supported primarily with state or federal funds are not eligible. Partnership Grants cannot be used for the following purposes: purchase of equipment, property, library holdings or acquisitions; capital improvements, facility construction, structural renovations and restorations; publications or recordings for commercial purposes; scholarships or other activities related to academic credit or degrees; activities intended primarily for fundraising; food, beverages or other refreshments; or requests designed to reduce or eliminate existing deficits.
Geographic Focus: Kentucky
Date(s) Application is Due: Jan 15
Contact: Daniel Strauss, Senior Program Analyst; (502) 564-8110, ext. 474 or (888) 833-2787; fax (502) 564-2839; dan.strauss@ky.gov
Internet: http://artscouncil.ky.gov/Grants/KAP.htm
Sponsor: Kentucky Arts Council
500 Mero Street, 21st Floor, Capital Plaza Tower
Frankfort, KY 40601-1987

Kentucky Arts Council Poetry Out Loud Grants   2810

Poetry Out Loud is a national poetry recitation competition created by the National Endowment for the Arts and the Poetry Foundation, and administered in partnership with the state arts agencies. Each participating school receives an artist residency and the opportunity for the school champion to attend the state competition with a chaperone. The application, an informational video, and detailed guidelines are available at the website.
Requirements: All Kentucky high schools, public and private, may apply. Homeschooled students may compete through a participating local high school or a home school regional competition hosted by a local library or community center.
Geographic Focus: Kentucky
Date(s) Application is Due: Oct 15
Contact: Jean St. John, Arts Education Director; (502) 564-8110, ext. 486 or (888) 833-2787; fax (502) 564-2839; jean.stjohn@ky.gov
Internet: http://artscouncil.ky.gov/Grants/P.O.L.htm
Sponsor: Kentucky Arts Council
500 Mero Street, 21st Floor, Capital Plaza Tower
Frankfort, KY 40601-1987

Kentucky Arts Council Teaching Art Together Grants   2811

The Teaching Art Together Grants let teachers collaborate with practicing, professional artists on the design and implementation of innovative one- to four-week residencies. Residencies provide teachers with the tools to continue to incorporate the arts into the curriculum after the residency is completed. The following grants are available: $2,400 for 20-day residencies (applicant match of $1,600); $1,800 for 15 day residencies (applicant match of $1,200); $1,200 for 10 day residencies (applicant match of $800); and $600 for 5 days residencies (applicant match of $400). The artist's fee is $1,000 per five day residency, which includes planning and preparation time. The application and additional guidelines are available at the website.
Requirements: Any teacher or group of teachers presently teaching in a Kentucky public or private school that supports preschool through grade 12 may apply.
Restrictions: All artists must be selected from the arts council's teaching artist directory. No more than two Teaching Art Together applications per school will be accepted for the same application deadline. The following criteria for number of artists must be followed: five-day (20-hour) residencies may only employ one artist; 10-day (40-hour) residencies may employ one or two artists; 15-day (60-hour) residencies may employ one to three artists; and 20-day (80 hour) residencies may use one to four artists. Artist fees may not exceed $1,000 per five days of residency. Classes may not be combined to exceed more than 30 students with the artist during the session. With the exception of professional development, residency hours may not be used for before or after school programming or culminating events. If a school would like to include a culminating assembly or evening program, the school must negotiate the rate of pay with the artist outside of this grant.
Geographic Focus: Kentucky
Date(s) Application is Due: Apr 1; Oct 15
Amount of Grant: 600 - 2,400 USD
Contact: Jean St. John, Arts Education Director; (502) 564-8110, ext. 486 or (888) 833-2787; fax (502) 564-2839; jean.stjohn@ky.gov
Internet: http://artscouncil.ky.gov/Grants/TAT.htm
Sponsor: Kentucky Arts Council
500 Mero Street, 21st Floor, Capital Plaza Tower
Frankfort, KY 40601-1987

Kentucky Arts Council TranspARTation Grant   2812

The TranspARTation Grant enables Kentucky teachers and schools to offer students quality arts experiences by providing transportation funding. Grants are based on the mileage from the school building to the arts organization or performance venue, and the number of buses necessary. There is a minimum grant amount of $100, and specific list of organizations eligible to receive students for the purpose of the travel grant. Funding is approved by the Council Board of Directors who meet two weeks after each quarterly deadline. The application and additional guidelines are available at the website.
Requirements: Any Kentucky school, public or private, that supports grades pre-K through 12 may apply.
Restrictions: There is a minimum grant amount of $100, and one field trip per application.
Geographic Focus: Kentucky
Date(s) Application is Due: Mar 1; Jun 1; Sep 1; Dec 1
Amount of Grant: 100 - 1,400 USD
Contact: Jean St. John, Arts Education Director; (502) 564-8110, ext. 486 or (888) 833-2787; fax (502) 564-2839; jean.stjohn@ky.gov
Internet: http://artscouncil.ky.gov/Grants/TranspARTation.htm
Sponsor: Kentucky Arts Council
500 Mero Street, 21st Floor, Capital Plaza Tower
Frankfort, KY 40601-1987

Ken W. Davis Foundation Grants   2813

The foundation awards grants in company-operating areas to support charities that directly provide for human welfare, basic needs, and quality of life—food, shelter, clothing, healthcare, disabilities, and childcare. Recipients may be asked to submit a post-grant evaluation of the project or program. Requests must be in writing and are reviewed and approved throughout the year. Submit requests as early as possible before October 31, the end of the foundation's fiscal year.
Requirements: Texas nonprofits in Midland-Odessa and Forth Worth are eligible.
Restrictions: The foundation does not support religious organizations for religious purposes; activities in support of social political causes; organizations that receive a substantial amount of federal and/or state funding; or organizations (other than the United Way) that receive wide public support.

Geographic Focus: Texas
Contact: Alan Tucker Davis, (817) 332-4081; fax (817) 332-4095; akd@kwdf.org
Internet: http://fdncenter.org/grantmaker/davis/proposal.html
Sponsor: Ken W. Davis Foundation
P.O. Box 3419
Fort Worth, TX 76113-3419

Kessler Foundation Community Employment Grants　　2814
Kessler Foundation's Community Employment Grant Program seeks to support projects, programs, capacity building, pilot initiatives, and creative solutions that focus on job placement, education, training and retention for New Jersey citizens with disabilities. These solutions improve the employment landscape and lead to full-time or part-time employment, which provides independence and economic self-sufficiency, important factors towards living a purposeful life. Community Employment Grants are awarded for one year. Funding ranges from $25,000 - $50,000. Organizations may apply for indirect cost expenses up to 8% in their project budgets.
Requirements: Nonprofit organizations serving New Jersey residents that are tax-exempt according to the Internal Revenue Code may apply for a Community Employment Grant. This includes nonprofit organizations, public/private schools and public institutions. The Foundation will accept applications from non-NJ based groups as long as the proposed grant projects are based in NJ and serve NJ residents. Some areas of interest are transition to work for youth and adults, vocational training and workplace preparation, employment-related transportation issues, and strategies to support recruitment, hiring, placement and retention. Other related projects or programs may be considered and/or funded at the discretion of our Board of Trustees. It is very important to have a plan for sustaining a funded project beyond the grant period if the proposed project will be ongoing. Additionally, Kessler Foundation is also interested in knowing how the grant will be judged effective at the end of the grant period. Since an affiliation with rehabilitative medicine has been a significant part of Kessler Foundation's history, a priority is placed on serving individuals with mobility disabilities, traumatic brain injury, spinal cord injury, multiple sclerosis, stroke, cerebral palsy, spina bifida, epilepsy or other impairments primarily from neuromuscular disorders. The Foundation requires that 65% of the target grant population meet these criteria.
Restrictions: Any organization awarded a Community Employment Grant for the past three (3) consecutive years is not eligible to apply for this program. Kessler Foundation will not fund projects that discriminate in hiring staff or providing services on basis of race, gender, religion, marital status, sexual orientation, age, or national origin. The foundation does not fund projects for which the primary diagnosis of disability is related to autism, developmental/intellectual disabilities, mental illness, post-traumatic stress, learning disabilities, chemical dependency, or sensory impairments of vision and/or hearing.
Geographic Focus: New Jersey
Date(s) Application is Due: Mar 1
Amount of Grant: 25,000 - 50,000 USD
Contact: Elaine Katz; (973) 324-8367; KFgrantprogram@KesslerFoundation.org
Internet: http://kesslerfoundation.org/grantprograms/communityemploymentgrants.php
Sponsor: Kessler Foundation
300 Executive Drive, Suite 70
West Orange, NJ 07052

Kessler Foundation Hurricane Sandy Emergency Grants　　2815
In the aftermath of Hurricane Sandy, many New Jerseyans with disabilities are experiencing challenges related to recovery. There is an urgent need to address the basic needs of individuals affected by the storm, such as accessibility, transitional housing and home modification, medical equipment and supplies and to offer assistance to disability organizations seeking to restore operations. This emergency grant fund is designed to help non-profit organizations meet the immediate needs of people with disabilities in New Jersey affected by the hurricane. Mini-grants in amounts of $2,500 to $10,000 are available. Applications are accepted and reviewed on a rolling basis. Kessler Foundation expects to process these grants in less than 30 days.
Requirements: Any organization recognized as a tax-exempt entity according to the Internal Revenue Code may apply for funding. This includes non-profit agencies, public or private schools, and public institutions, such as universities and government (state, local, federal) based in the United States or any of its territories and serving New Jersey residents. Each organization is limited to one Rapid Response Grant. Current grantees of Kessler Foundation with open grant projects are also eligible to apply for these emergency funds. Multiple requests from a single organization will not be reviewed. Available grant funding will focus on the immediate needs of disability organizations and individuals served by these organizations within our community. Grants to non-profit organizations may focus on: (1) unrestricted funds to restore operations, including offices, personnel and equipment; (2) funds to address specific, immediate needs for people with disabilities served by a non-profit organization, such as restoring accessibility, providing home modifications, replacement of assistive technology and durable medical products (e.g. mobility, vision and hearing aids, medical supplies), transportation (e.g. medical or para-transport), access to personal assistance providers, and transitional housing. These grants are inclusive of all types of disabilities.
Restrictions: Kessler Foundation will not fund projects that discriminate in hiring staff or providing services on basis of race, gender, religion, marital status, sexual orientation, age, or national origin. Individuals may not apply for these grants. Grant funds are disbursed only to organizations.
Geographic Focus: New Jersey
Contact: Elaine Katz; (973) 324-8367; KFgrantprogram@KesslerFoundation.org
Internet: http://kesslerfoundation.org/grantprograms/hurricanesandyemergencygrants.php
Sponsor: Kessler Foundation
300 Executive Drive, Suite 70
West Orange, NJ 07052

Kessler Foundation Signature Employment Grants　　2816
Kessler Foundation awards Signature Employment Grants yearly to support non-traditional solutions and/or social ventures that increase employment outcomes for individuals with disabilities. Signature Employment Grants are awarded nationally to fund new pilot initiatives, demonstration projects or social ventures that lead to the generation of new ideas to solve the high unemployment and underemployment of individuals with disabilities. Preference is given for interventions that overcome specific employment barriers related to long-term dependence on public assistance, advance competitive employment in a cost-effective manner, or launch a social enterprise or individual entrepreneurship project. Signature grants are not intended to fund project expansions or bring proven projects to new communities, unless there is a significant scale, scope or replicable component. Innovation lies at the core of all signature employment grants. Organizations may apply for up to two years of funding. Yearly funding ranges from $100,000 - $250,000, with maximum project funding at $500,000.
Requirements: The Signature Employment Grant program begins with online concept submission. The concept is scored and reviewed for originality, creativity, feasibility, collaborative stakeholder team. A selected group of candidates will then be invited to submit a full grant proposal. Nonprofit organizations that are tax-exempt according to the Internal Revenue Code may apply for funding. This includes U.S. based non-profit organizations, public/private schools and public institutions, such as universities and government. Application is open to eligible organizations in any state or territories. Priority is placed on serving individuals with mobility disabilities, traumatic brain injury, spinal cord injury, multiple sclerosis, stroke, cerebral palsy, spina bifida, epilepsy or other related impairments. The Foundation requires that 65% of the target grant population meet these criteria. Although matching funds are not required, applicants with additional cash funding provided by the applicant or collaborator(s) will be scored higher. A proven track record managing collaborative grant projects is also desirable.
Restrictions: Kessler Foundation will not fund projects that discriminate in hiring staff or providing services on basis of race, gender, religion, marital status, sexual orientation, age, or national origin. The foundation does not fund projects for which the primary diagnosis of disability is related to autism, developmental/intellectual disabilities, mental illness, post-traumatic stress, learning disabilities, chemical dependency, or sensory impairments of vision and/or hearing.
Geographic Focus: All States
Date(s) Application is Due: May 24
Amount of Grant: 100,000 - 500,000 USD
Contact: Elaine Katz; (973) 324-8367; KFgrantprogram@KesslerFoundation.org
Internet: http://kesslerfoundation.org/grantprograms/signatureemploymentgrants.php
Sponsor: Kessler Foundation
300 Executive Drive, Suite 70
West Orange, NJ 07052

Kettering Family Foundation Grants　　2817
The Kettering Family Foundation (KFF) is a family grant-making organization that supports both Trustee-endorsed and unsolicited proposals that meet specific criteria. Unsolicited requests will be reviewed only one time per KFF fiscal year (ending December 31) from the same requesting organization and/or program. The following categories are of interest to KFF Trustees: cultural and arts; education; environment; medical health; and social/human services. A request summary (letter of interest) is required (by January 31 and July 31) and, if interested, trustees will ask for a full proposal.
Requirements: 501(c)3 tax-exempt organizations are eligible.
Restrictions: Requests for funding for the following areas are not generally approved unless endorsed by a trustee: capital construction; foreign-based or foreign- purpose organizations; religious organizations for religious purposes; individual public elementary or secondary schools or public school districts; local chapters of national organizations; grants, loans, scholarships, fellowships, or memberships; multiyear grants; travel expenses; community drives, event sponsorships; or conduit organizations.
Geographic Focus: All States
Date(s) Application is Due: Jan 31; Mar 1; Jul 31; Sep 1
Contact: Charles F. Kettering; (303) 756-7664; info@ketteringfamilyfoundation.org
Internet: http://www.ketteringfamilyfoundation.org/main.html
Sponsor: Kettering Family Foundation
2833 S Colorado Boulevard
Denver, CO 80222

Kettering Fund Grants　　2818
The mission of the Kettering Fund is to support scientific, medical, social and educational studies and research conducted by nonprofit, charitable organizations that are located and/or provide service in Ohio. The Distribution Committee meets on a semi-annual basis to make funding decisions, generally in May and November. The committee will consider support for the following purposes: capital needs (such as the purchase of land, new construction, renovations and equipment); seed grants for new organizations or programs; project support; endowments; research; and scholarship funds.
Requirements: 501(c)3 nonprofits that provide services in or are located in Ohio may apply.
Restrictions: The fund does not support: religious organizations for religious purposes; activities of specific individuals; public elementary or secondary schools; loans; travel; deficit reduction; benefit events; or efforts to carry on propaganda or otherwise attempt to influence legislation.
Geographic Focus: Ohio
Contact: Judith M. Thompson; (973) 228-1021; info@ketteringfund.org
Internet: http://www.ketteringfund.org/main.html
Sponsor: Kettering Fund
1480 Kettering Tower
Dayton, OH 45423

Kevin P. and Sydney B. Knight Family Foundation Grants 2819

The Foundation, established in 1997 by the founders of Knight Transportation of Phoenix, Arizona, is focused on the greater Phoenix area. Giving programs are aimed at: children and youth; Catholic agencies and churches; athletics/sports activities (particularly baseball); education; health care; and Mormon affiliated groups. Primary types of support include: community development, general research, and youth programs. There are no specific deadlines or application forms, and initial approach should be by letter.
Restrictions: Funding is restricted primarily to 501(c)3 organizations located in Phoenix.
Geographic Focus: Arizona
Amount of Grant: 1,000 - 2,000 USD
Samples: Leukemia and Lymphoma Society, Phoenix, Arizona, $1,000; St. Mary's Food Bank, Phoenix, Arizona, $200; ATA Scholarship Fund, Phoenix, Arizona, $1,500.
Contact: Kevin P. Knight, President; (602) 269-2000; fax (602) 269-8409
Sponsor: Kevin P. and Sydney B. Knight Family Foundation
5601 W Buckeye Road
Phoenix, AZ 85043-4603

KeyBank Foundation Grants 2820

The Foundation's objective is to improve the quality of life and economic vibrancy of the places where KeyCorp customers, employees, and shareholders live and work. The Foundation supports programs with the following funding priorities: financial education - fostering effective financial management and understanding of financial services and tools; workforce development - providing training and placement for people to access job opportunities; diversity - promoting inclusive environments by employing systematic changes to improve the access of individuals of diverse backgrounds. The Foundation typically reviews and decides upon requests quarterly, but there are no deadlines to submit the proposal. Proposal development guidelines and the application are available at the Foundation website. Proposals may be submitted via postal mail or email, but not by fax.
Requirements: Nonprofit 501(c)3 tax-exempt organizations are eligible. Requests for funding from organizations within northeast Ohio are reviewed by the KeyBank Foundation headquarters offices in Cleveland. Other proposals are evaluated by funding committees in district offices throughout the U.S. Requests sent to the KeyBank Foundation headquarters that are more appropriate for district review are forwarded to the appropriate district office.
Restrictions: The Foundation does not contribute to individuals; lobbying or political organizations areas outside its retail operations; selected organizations with IRS 509(a) status; fraternal groups; athletic teams; organizations outside the U.S; or organizations that discriminate in any way with national equal opportunity policies. The Foundation also does not buy journal advertisements or memberships.
Geographic Focus: Alaska, Colorado, Idaho, Indiana, Kentucky, Maine, Michigan, New York, Ohio, Oregon, Utah, Vermont, Washington
Contact: Administrator; (216) 689-5458; key_foundation@keybank.com
Internet: https://www.key.com/about/community/key-foundation-philanthropy-banking.jsp
Sponsor: KeyBank Foundation
127 Public Square, 7th Floor
Cleveland, OH 33113-1306

KeySpan Foundation Grants 2821

The foundation awards grants to eligible nonprofit organizations in its areas of interest, including health and human services; education—K-12 classroom education, scholarships and university partnerships for the underserved, skills training; environment—sustainability of natural resources, educate youth about their connection to the environment, and preserve open spaces for the future; community development; and the arts. Proposals are accepted and reviewed on a first come/first served basis through October. The foundation's board of directors meets on a quarterly basis to review requests and authorize grants.
Requirements: New Hampshire, Massachusetts, and New York nonprofits are eligible.
Restrictions: The foundation does not support religious or political groups, capital or endowment campaigns, advertisements, tables or tickets at dinners, and groups whose combined administrative, management, or fundraising expenses exceed 30 percent of the operating budget.
Geographic Focus: Connecticut, Maine, Massachusetts, New Hampshire, New York, Rhode Island, Vermont
Date(s) Application is Due: Oct 31
Amount of Grant: 5,000 - 25,000 USD
Contact: Robert Keller, Executive Director; (516) 545-5147
Internet: http://www.keyspanenergy.com/corpinfo/community/foundation_all.jsp
Sponsor: KeySpan Foundation
175 E Old Country Road
Hicksville, NY 11801

Kiki Madazine Grow Strong Girls through Leadership Grants 2822

Kiki magazine is making available on a national level matching funds to the leadership grant opportunities offered by the Women's Fund for developing girls' leadership programs. The purpose of this Request for Proposals is therefore two-fold: to support innovative school-based girls' leadership programs that would otherwise not exist and to produce a girls' leadership toolkit, including some of the innovative curricula developed by grant recipients, that will be distributed to schools in kiki region at no cost. This grant program allows educators the opportunity to apply for funding for creative and interesting girls' leadership programs to implement in schools within the United States except within the Greater Cincinnati counties served by The Women's Fund, Hamilton, Butler, Clermont and Warren counties in Ohio; Dearborn County in Indiana; and Campbell, Boone and Kenton counties in Kentucky. The grant pool by The Women's Fund covers those counties. Applications are being accepted through Monday, April 19th for projects with budgets up to $1,500. Schools eligible to submit applications must be full-time, state-chartered schools that enroll girls in grades 6-8. Contact Kiki magazine for additional guidelines at (513) 768-6135 or email: educators@kikimag.com.
Requirements: Schools eligible to submit applications must be full-time, state-chartered schools that enroll girls in grades 6, 7 and/or 8. Applicants must be a subscriber to Kiki magazine. Proof of subscription or paid subscription order must accompany grant application.
Restrictions: Ineligible organizations include: community, G.E.D., or literacy schools; home schools; preschools, day-care centers, and childcare programs; and school auxiliaries, PTAs/PTOs, or clubs.
Geographic Focus: All States
Date(s) Application is Due: Apr 19
Amount of Grant: 1,500 USD
Contact: Tara Block; (513) 833-7416; fax (513) 672-0279; educators@kikimag.com
Internet: http://www.kikimag.com/adults/educators.php
Sponsor: Kiki Magazine
214 East 8th Street
Cincinnati, OH 45202-2191

Kimball International-Habig Foundation Grants 2823

The foundation, which represents Kimball International, Inc., is funded by a percentage of profit earnings of the company. In keeping with the corporate philosophy and Guiding Principles, Kimball International is committed to helping the communities in which they operate to become even better places to live. Supporting that goal, the foundation focuses its funding and resources on grants to organizations and programs that most directly benefit those U.S. communities in which Kimball has operations or facilities, or from which it draws employees.
Requirements: The foundation will consider requests in the following giving categories: Education; Health & Human Services; Civic & Community Programs; Arts & Culture; Religious Institutions (non-denominational, all inclusive); and Other. All requests for funding made to the Kimball Foundation must be made using the online request form. Absolutely no verbal or phone call requests will be processed or acknowledged. All requests must be in writing (via this online form). The foundation board meets quarterly to review and assess those major funding requests submitted during the previous 90 days, in March, June, September, December. Major requests (those over $2,000) are reviewed, assessed and approved quarterly. Standard requests (those under $2,000) are reviewed and approved monthly. Standard requests are reviewed by the foundation board on or about the 25th of each month.
Geographic Focus: California, Florida, Idaho, Indiana, Kentucky, China, Mexico, Poland
Contact: Media Relations Office; (812) 482-8255 or (800) 482-1616; HabigFoundation@Kimball.com
Internet: http://tinyurl.com/cy4ekb
Sponsor: Kimball International-Habig Foundation
1600 Royal Street
Jasper, IN 47549-1001

Kimberly-Clark Community Grants 2824

The corporation contributes significant philanthropic resources to organizations and programs that provide vital information, resources, and services that strengthen today's families; involve parents and others in activities that help children grow physically, mentally, and socially; and develop creative, caring options to cope with the issues facing our older relatives. Kimberly-Clark limits its charitable contributions to organizations serving communities where employees live and work. The corporation also supports YMCA of the USA, UNICEF, United Way, and disaster- relief efforts. Send requests in corporate-operating cities to the site manager's attention. All decisions are made locally, not at the corporate level. Guidelines are available online.
Requirements: Nonprofit organizations in Kimberly-Clark communities are eligible, including Alabama (Mobile), Arkansas (Conway, Maumelle), California (Escondido, Fullerton), Connecticut (New Milford), Georgia (LaGrange, Roswell), Idaho (Pocatello), Kentucky (Owensboro), Michigan (Munising), Mississippi (Corinth, Hattiesburg), North Carolina (Hendersonville, Lexington), Ohio (Piqua), Oklahoma (Jenks), Pennsylvania (Chester), South Carolina (Beech Island), Tennessee (Knoxville, Loudon), Texas (Dallas, Del Rio, Fort Worth, Paris, San Antonio), Utah (Draper, Ogden), Washington (Everett), and Wisconsin (Marinette, Neenah, Whiting).
Restrictions: As a general rule, no unsolicited requests for national or international programs will be considered.
Geographic Focus: Alabama, Arkansas, California, Connecticut, Georgia, Idaho, Kentucky, Michigan, Mississippi, North Carolina, Ohio, Oklahoma, Pennsylvania, South Carolina, Tennessee, Texas, Utah, Washington, Wisconsin
Contact: Contribution Program Manager; (888) 525-8388
Internet: http://www.kimberly-clark.com/aboutus/contrib_program.asp
Sponsor: Kimberly-Clark Corporation
P.O. Box 2020, Department INT
Neenah, WI 54957-2020

King Baudouin International Development Prize 2825

The biennial prize aims to recognize the actions of individuals or organizations that are making a significant contribution to the advancement of developing countries, or mutual support between industrialized and developing countries. The list of prizewinners covers a broad spectrum of fields, from the teaching of adult literacy to the training of the rural poor, and from technology transfer to new forms of credit, or the development of mutual support within the community.
Requirements: The individuals or organizations qualified sumbit nominations are listed in article 11 of the Rules of Procedure for the Prize: members of the Belgian legislative assemblies and the Belgian government; ambassadors of HM the King; senior levels of Belgian or foreign civil service departments responsible for development cooperation;

members of the Belgian Royal Academy of Overseas Sciences and of foreign academies with fields of activity in keeping with the aims of the prize; members of the academic staff of Belgian and foreign university-level institutes, insofar as their teaching or research has a bearing on the precise field of involvement of the candidate proposed by them; the Foreign Affairs or Development Aid Ministers of foreign countries; the heads of diplomatic missions to the royal court; senior levels of the United Nations Organization, the World Bank and Regional Development Banks, together with the regional or specialist institutions affiliated to them; senior levels of world and regional institutions which have activities in keeping with the aims of the prize; European Union bodies with a mandate to handle relations with developing countries; federations of nongovernmental organizations and Belgian nongovernmental organizations with fields of activity coinciding with the theme of the prize; former members of the Selection Committee; holders of the King Baudouin International Development Prize; and individuals, organizations, or companies that the Board invites by name to submit proposals, or recognizes by name as being qualified to do so.
Geographic Focus: All States
Date(s) Application is Due: Feb 1
Amount of Grant: 150,000 EUR
Contact: Prize Administrator; 32-2-549.02.73; fax 32-2-500.54.31; info@kbprize.org
Internet: http://www.kbprize.org/english/prize/prize.htm
Sponsor: King Baudouin Foundation
21 Rue Brederodestraat
Brussels, B-1000 Belgium

Kiplinger Program in Public Affairs Journalism Fellowships 2826
The program in public affairs journalism is dedicated to giving journalists time to produce meaningful work and deepen their knowledge of public affairs issues so they can better inform citizens and contribute to public life. Fellows will have six months to work on an independent public affairs print project of their choice. Fellows who successfully complete the program will receive a Certificate in Public Affairs Journalism from the John Glenn Institute, as well as a transcript reflecting credits for the courses they have taken. Fellows must either be U.S. citizens with five years of relevant professional experience in the United States or abroad, or foreign nationals with five years of professional experience within the United States or working abroad for U.S. organizations. Application and guidelines are available online.
Requirements: Applicants must have at least five years of professional experience in journalism. Those eligible include reporters, editors, and employees from newspapers, wire services, magazines, online publications, and freelancers. Television and radio reporters will also be considered if they seek to produce a print project.
Geographic Focus: All States
Date(s) Application is Due: Jul 20
Amount of Grant: 20,000 USD
Contact: Betsy Hubbard; (614) 247-8845; fax (614) 292-4868; hubbard.160@osu.edu
Internet: http://www.kiplingerprogram.org/kiplinger
Sponsor: Ohio State University
350 Page Hall, 1810 College Road
Columbus, OH 43210

Kirkpatrick Foundation Grants 2827
The Kirkpatrick Foundation lends support to organizations with projects and programs that compliment the vision and mission of the Foundation, within the primary fields of interest of arts and culture, education, natural and built environments, animal research, and conservation. The Foundation encourages preliminary discussion to explore potential project proposals. Grant proposals are considered only from not-for-profit organizations qualified as public charities under Section 501(c)3 of the IRS. Organizations should have at least a three-year track record of programming and have maintained current financial records, a working board of directors and management, governance and accountability structures in place. The Foundation also considers requests from public and private educational institutions and faith-based educational programs. Priority is given to organizations serving Oklahoma with particular emphasis placed on programs and services directly benefiting citizens of the Oklahoma City metropolitan area.
Requirements: Organizations are encouraged to contact the Foundation before beginning the grant application process to determine if the project idea is compatible with Foundation interest areas. First time applicants must complete an on-line eligibility quiz to access the Small Grant Application or Letter of Inquiry. A small proposal of $5,000 or less may be submitted by completing the electronic Small Grant Application. These requests may be submitted throughout the year for future projects not already funded by the Foundation. Small grant requests will typically receive notification of a funding decision within 30 days of submitting the application. The Large Grant application procedure is a two-step electronic process beginning with a Letter of Inquiry. There is no set upper limit on the amount requested, but organizations should seek advice from Foundation staff on an appropriate range, and see the website for further instructions for submission.
Restrictions: Capital campaigns and endowments are not regularly funded. Grants may not be used to fund indirect costs or foundation fees. Grants are also not awarded to: individuals; lobbying organizations; medical and health related causes; social welfare; school trips including for marching bands; and athletic programs.
Geographic Focus: Oklahoma
Date(s) Application is Due: Jan 15; Jul 15
Amount of Grant: 1,000 - 130,000 USD
Contact: Meaghan Hunt Wilson, Program Associate; (405) 608-0934; fax (405) 608-0942; mhuntwilson@kirkpatrickfoundation.com
Internet: http://www.kirkpatrickfoundation.com/Grants/tabid/58/Default.aspx
Sponsor: Kirkpatrick Foundation
1001 West Wilshire Boulevard, Suite 201
Oklahoma City, OK 73116

Knight Foundation Donor Advised Fund Grants 2828
The Fund, administered by the Central Carolina Community Foundation, provides grants that address the following priority areas: education; well-being of children and families; housing and community development; economic development; civic engagement/positive human relations; and vitality of cultural life. Proposals for grants are accepted on a continual basis throughout the year. Grants are due to the Community Foundation office by the fifth of each month. Decisions are typically made by the end of the month. The maximum request amount is $20,000.
Requirements: Grants must serve residents of Richland County, South Carolina.
Geographic Focus: South Carolina
Amount of Grant: Up to 20,000 USD
Contact: Joan Fail Hoffman; (803) 254-5601, ext. 328; joan@yourfoundation.org
Internet: http://www.yourfoundation.org/nonprofits.aspx
Sponsor: Central Carolina Community Foundation
2711 Middleburg Drive, Suite 213
Columbia, SC 29204

Knight Foundation Grants - Georgia 2829
The Foundation, established in 1992, serves a variety of programs and organizations in Savannah, Georgia. Its primary fields of interest include: children and youth services; human services; and Protestant churches and agencies. The primary type of support provided is by way of general operations funding. Applicants should submit: a detailed description of project and amount of funding requested; and the name, address and phone number of organization. The annual deadline is December 1st.
Restrictions: No funding is provided to individuals, and giving is primarily limited to 501(c)3 non-profits operating in Savannah, Georgia.
Geographic Focus: Florida, Georgia
Date(s) Application is Due: Dec 1
Amount of Grant: Up to 10,000 USD
Contact: Stuart G. Knight, President; (912) 925-8092
Sponsor: Knight Foundation
28 Sherborne Road
Savannah, GA 31419-3261

Knight Foundation Grants - Montana 2830
The Foundation, established in 1991, serves programs in and around the Bozeman, Montana, region. Its primary fields of interest include: disaster relief; disaster preparedness; emergency services; and federated giving programs. The type of support generally comes in the form of general operating money. The deadline is April 20th, and the initial approach should be by letter, outlining the need and budgetary details.
Requirements: Applicants should be 501(c)3 organizations operating in Gallatin County, Montana.
Restrictions: No grants are given to individuals.
Geographic Focus: Montana
Date(s) Application is Due: Apr 20
Amount of Grant: 100 - 1,000 USD
Contact: Sarah Nash Zimmer, Secretary; (406) 586-0246
Sponsor: Knight Foundation
P.O. Box 8000
Bozeman, MT 59715-2042

Knox County Community Foundation Grants 2831
The Knox County Community Foundation is a nonprofit, public charity created by and for the people of Knox County, Indiana. The Foundation helps nonprofits fulfill their missions by strengthening their ability to meet community needs through grants that assist charitable programs, address community issues, support community agencies, launch community initiatives, and support leadership development. Grant proposals are accepted once each year according to the grant cycle. Proposal requirements may change from year to year; therefore, grant seekers are advised to contact the foundation or see the foundations website, prior to beginning the grant application process. Grants are normally given as one-time support of a project but may be considered for additional support for expansions or outgrowths of an initial project. At the start of each cycle, a notice is mailed to nonprofit organizations that have applied for grants in the past, have received grants in the past, or have otherwise requested notification of the start of each cycle. Program areas considered for funding are: arts and culture; community development; education; health; human services; other civic endeavors, such as the environment, recreation, and youth development. Proposals will be accepted from January through the March deadline. All organizations that have submitted grant proposals will be notified of the outcome of their application by June 1. Samples of previously funded projects are available at the website.
Requirements: The Foundation welcomes proposals from nonprofit organizations that are deemed tax-exempt under sections 501(c)3 and 509(a) of the Internal Revenue Code and from governmental agencies serving the county. Proposals from nonprofit organizations not classified as a 501(c)3 may be considered provided the project is charitable and supports a community need. Proposals submitted by an entity under the auspices of another agency must include a written statement signed by the agency's board president on behalf of the board of directors agreeing to act as the entity's fiscal sponsor, to receive grant monies if awarded, and to oversee the proposed project.
Restrictions: Project areas not considered for funding are: religious organizations for strictly religious purposes; political parties or campaigns; endowment creation or debt reduction; operating costs; capital campaigns; annual appeals or membership contributions; travel requests for groups or individuals such as bands, sports teams, or classes. A six-month progress report and a final report at project completion are required by organizations whose proposals are approved for funding. Instructions and appropriate forms will be provided at the time the grant is awarded.

Geographic Focus: Indiana
Contact: Jamie Neal; (812) 886-0093; jamie@knoxcountyfoundation.org
Internet: http://www.knoxcountyfoundation.org/disc-grants-program
Sponsor: Knox County Community Foundation
20 N Third Street, Suite 301, P.O. Box 273
Vincennes, IN 47591

Kohl's Cares Scholarships 2832

The program honors young people between the ages of 6 and 18 who have made a difference in their communities. Scholarships are awarded to winners toward their postsecondary education. Awards are made on the store, regional, and national levels. This year, more than 2,200 kids will be recognized with over $440,000 in scholarships and prizes: store winners will receive a $50 Kohl's Gift Card; regional winners will each be awarded a $1,000 scholarship for post-secondary education; and national winners will each be awarded a total of $10,000 in scholarships for post-secondary education. In addition, Kohl's will contribute $1,000 to a nonprofit organization on behalf of each national winner.
Requirements: Nominations may be made online or by visiting a local Kohl's store for a program brochure. To be eligible, the student must meet the following criteria as of March 15: must be between the ages of 6 and 18 and not yet a high school graduate; actions must be described in detail and should document efforts above and beyond what is expected of a child his or her age; and volunteer efforts must have occurred in the last year.
Geographic Focus: All States
Date(s) Application is Due: Mar 15
Contact: Program Coordinator; (319) 341-2932; kohls@act.org
Internet: http://www.kohlscorporation.com/CommunityRelations/scholarship/program-information.asp
Sponsor: Kohl's Department Stores
N56 W 17000 Ridgewood Drive
Menomonee Falls, WI 53051

Kohler Foundation Grants 2833

The Kohler Foundation is a private foundation primarily interested in supporting education, arts and preservation initiatives in Wisconsin. Geographic preference is Sheboygan County, Wisconsin, followed by small towns in Wisconsin. Much of its effort is directed to numerous ongoing programs which were initiated many years ago by Kohler Foundation and which it continues to maintain. Most of the Foundation grants, therefore, do not exceed $5,000. Deadlines for proposals are March 15 and September 15.
Requirements: The Foundation rarely if ever make grants outside the state of Wisconsin. If an organization wishes to submit a proposal, we ask that it furnish the following: copy of IRS designations of organization: 501(c)3 and/or 509(a)1, 2 or 3; description of project (why is it needed? how many people will benefit?); budget and timetable; and credentials and background of project manager.
Geographic Focus: Wisconsin
Date(s) Application is Due: Mar 15; Sep 15
Amount of Grant: Up to 5,000 USD
Contact: Terri Yoho; (920) 458-1972; fax (920) 458-4280; terri.yoho@kohler.com
Internet: http://www.kohlerfoundation.org/grants.html
Sponsor: Kohler Foundation
725 X Woodlake Road
Kohler, WI 53044

Komen Greater NYC Clinical Research Enrollment Grants 2834

Women, especially racial and ethnic minorities, are not adequately represented in cancer research efforts. Multiple barriers — cultural, linguistic, financial, and systematic — hinder their participation in clinical research, and particularly in clinical trials. Through Clinical Research Enrollment Grants, Komen Greater NYC seeks to fund projects that employ effective strategies to overcome these barriers to enrollment and retention in breast cancer clinical research. The funding period is two years, based on the Komen Greater NYC fiscal year — April 1st through March 31st. . Programs applying for the CRE grant may request up to $200,000 over this two-year period. Organizations that have previously received Komen Greater NYC funding are welcome to apply for additional funding.
Requirements: To apply, the organization must be: a not-for-profit organization (a charitable or educational tax-exempt organization), a government agency, or an Indian tribe; conducting National Cancer Institute (NCI) or Department of Defense (DOD) approved breast cancer clinical research (this includes studies through the Clinical Trials Cooperative Group Program including but not limited to ACOSOG, ECOG, SWOG, NSABP, ACRIN, and RTOG; and located in the Komen Greater NYC service area, which includes the five boroughs of New York City, Long Island, Westchester County, and Rockland County.
Geographic Focus: New York
Date(s) Application is Due: Oct 9
Amount of Grant: Up to 200,000 USD
Contact: Michelle Marquez, Director of Development; (212) 461-6186 or (212) 560-9590; fax (212) 560-9598; mmarquez@komennyc.org
Internet: http://www.komennyc.org/site/PageServer?pagename=grants_clinicaltrials
Sponsor: Susan G. Komen for the Cure Foundation
470 Seventh Avenue, 7th Floor
New York, NY 10018

Komen Greater NYC Community Breast Health Grants 2835

The mission of Komen Greater NYC is to eradicate breast cancer as a life-threatening disease by advancing research, education, screening, and treatment. The Greater New York City Affiliate is, therefore, soliciting applications from non-profit organizations that have current or planned breast health programs within the five boroughs of New York City, Long Island, Westchester County, and Rockland County. The purpose of the Community Breast Health Grants Program (formerly known as Screening, Treatment, and Education Program- STEP) is to support community-based programs that provide the medically under-served with access to breast health education, screening coordination, diagnostic, treatment, and support services. The funding period is twelve months, based on the Komen Greater NYC fiscal year — April 1st through March 31st. Programs applying for the CBH grant may request up to $75,000 over this one year period. Organizations that have previously received Komen Greater NYC funding are welcome to apply for additional funding. However, all CBH grant awards are for one year only.
Requirements: Applicant organizations must be: a not-for-profit organization (a charitable or educational tax-exempt organization), a government agency, or an Indian tribe; located in the Komen Greater NYC service area, which includes the five boroughs of New York City, Long Island, Westchester County, and Rockland County; and a current or planned provider of breast health services.
Geographic Focus: New York
Date(s) Application is Due: Oct 9
Amount of Grant: Up to 75,000 USD
Contact: Michelle Marquez, Director of Development; (212) 461-6186 or (212) 560-9590; fax (212) 560-9598; mmarquez@komennyc.org
Internet: http://www.komennyc.org/site/PageServer?pagename=grants_breasthealthgrants
Sponsor: Susan G. Komen for the Cure Foundation
470 Seventh Avenue, 7th Floor
New York, NY 10018

Komen Greater NYC Small Grants 2836

Komen Greater New York City is currently offering small grants up to $5,000 to support small pilot or capacity building projects in breast health. Small Grant Applications are accepted three times a year. Award notifications are generally made within six to eight weeks after the deadline. These grants are for organizations interested in beginning a new program or test new ideas that will increase the innovative capacity and effectiveness of breast health programs that serve low income and uninsured patients. Capacity Building is enhancing an organization's ability to provide services by redesigning processes, implementing new practices, or developing collaborations or partnerships.
Requirements: Applicants and institutions must conform to the eligibility criteria to be considered for funding. Applicants must ensure that all past and current Komen-funded grants or awards are up-to-date and in compliance with Komen requirements. Institutions must be located in or providing services to one or more of the following locations: the five boroughs of New York City; Long Island (Suffolk and Nassau Counties); Westchester County; or Rockland County. Projects must be specific to breast health and/or breast cancer. The applicant must be a non-profit organization with federal tax exemption.
Restrictions: Individuals may not receive grants. Small Grant applicants are restricted to a maximum combined award of $5,000 per Komen Greater NYC grant year (April through March), per program for any type of Small Grant.
Geographic Focus: New York
Date(s) Application is Due: Jan 4; May 1; Sep 1
Amount of Grant: 5,000 USD
Contact: Zenia Dacio-Mesina, Grants Program Coordinator; (212) 560-9590; fax (212) 560-9598; zdmesina@komennyc.org or grants@komennyc.org
Internet: http://www.komennyc.org/site/PageServer?pagename=grants_small_grants_program
Sponsor: Susan G. Komen for the Cure Foundation
470 Seventh Avenue, 7th Floor
New York, NY 10018

Koret Foundation Grants 2837

The Koret Foundation supports projects in the San Francisco Bay Area (Alameda, Contra Costa, Marin, San Francisco, San Mateo, and Santa Clara Counties) related to the following: arts and culture; community development; higher education; Jewish life and culture; primary and secondary education; and youth development. It also supports projects in Israel related to economic development, higher education, and security.
Requirements: Applicants should review grant guidelines, then submit the following: a letter of inquiry; timetable for implementation and evaluation of project; population and geographic area to be served; copy of IRS determination letter; copy of most recent annual report/audited financial statement/990; how project's results will be evaluated or measured; descriptive literature about organization; listing of board of directors, trustees, officers and other key people and their affiliations; detailed description of project and amount of funding requested; and a copy of he current year's organizational budget and/or project budget.
Restrictions: Giving is limited to the Bay Area counties of San Francisco, Alameda, Contra Costa, Marin, Santa Clara, and San Mateo, California. Giving also in Israel and on a national basis for Jewish funding requests. No support for private foundations, or veterans, fraternal, military, religious, or sectarian organizations whose principal activity is for the benefit of their own membership. Funding is not available for individuals, endowment funds, or deficit financing.
Geographic Focus: All States, Israel
Contact: Marina Lum; (415) 882-7740; fax (415) 882-7775; info@KoretFoundation.org
Internet: http://www.koretfoundation.org/apply/application.shtml
Sponsor: Koret Foundation
33 New Montgomery Street, Suite 1090
San Francisco, CA 94105-4526

Kosciusko County Community Foundation Grants 2838

The Kosciusko County Community Foundation serves Kosciusko County, Indiana. Nonprofit organizations serving Kosciusko County are eligible to apply in seven areas of interest: arts and culture, human services, civic projects, recreation, environment, health, and education. Grant applications and guidelines can be obtained at the Foundations office or website. Grant awards are announced nine weeks after each deadline.

Requirements: Grant seekers are strongly encouraged to call the Foundation's program staff to discuss a grant proposal before submitting a formal application. Once the proposal has been discussed, complete and submit a grant application with the required attachments: 6 copies of the original application; 1 copy of the IRS determination letter; 7 copies of the board of directors listing with names and addresses for all; 7 copies of staff listing with names and addresses for all; 7 copies of current internal financial statements; and 7 copies of program/project budget. Do not provide copies of news articles, brochures or other miscellaneous supporting information.

Restrictions: The Foundation will not consider grants for: individuals; political activities or those designated to influence legislation; national organizations (unless the monies are to be used solely to benefit citizens of Kosciusko County); fundraising projects;the direct benefit of the donor or the donor's family; religious organizations for the sole purpose of furthering that religion (this prohibition does not apply to funds created by donors who have specifically designated religious organizations as beneficiaries of the funds); contributions to endowments.

Geographic Focus: Indiana
Date(s) Application is Due: Jan 15; May 15; Sep 15
Contact: Stephanie Overbey, Communication & Program Director; (574) 267-1901; fax (574) 268-9780; stephanie@kcfoundation.org
Internet: http://www.kcfoundation.org/grants.html
Sponsor: Kosciusko County Community Foundation
102 E Market Street
Warsaw, IN 46580

Kosciusko County Community Foundation REMC Operation Round Up Grants 2839

The Kosciusko County Community Foundation serves the residents of Kosciusko County, Indiana. Kosciusko Rural Electric Membership Corporation (REMC) encourages its members to round up their electric bills to the nearest whole dollar. The extra funds are deposited into the Kosciusko REMC Operation Round Up Grants, which supports a variety of charitable causes in communities served by Kosciusko REMC. Applications are due the 15th of the following months: February, April, June, August, October, and December. Grant notifications take place within six weeks after the deadline.

Requirements: Applicants must submit the online application, along with a list of the organization's board of directors, officers, or trustees, and their phone numbers; a one page cover letter that specifies the amount requested and details about how the funds will be used locally; a copy of the organization's 501(c)3 letter; and a copy of the organization's most current financial statements.

Geographic Focus: Indiana
Date(s) Application is Due: Feb 15; Apr 15; Jun 15; Aug 15; Oct 15; Dec 15
Contact: Stephanie Overbey; (574) 946-0906; fax (574) 946-0971; Stephanie@kcfoundation.org
Internet: http://www.kcfoundation.org/seekingfunds/remc.php
Sponsor: Kosciusko County Community Foundation
102 East Market Street
Warsaw, IN 46580

Kovler Family Foundation Grants 2840

The Kovler Family Foundation awards grants in the areas of the arts, children/youth services, medical research (particularly diabetes), education, human services, higher education, human services, and Jewish federated giving programs. General operating or research grants are awarded primarily in the Chicago metropolitan area. There are no application forms. Applicants should submit a one to two page written proposal letter with a copy of their IRS determination letter by mid-November.

Requirements: Illinois nonprofit organizations are eligible to apply.
Restrictions: The Foundation does not award grants to individuals.
Geographic Focus: Illinois
Contact: Jonathan Kovler, President and Treasurer; (312) 664-5050
Sponsor: Kovler Family Foundation
875 North Michigan Avenue
Chicago, IL 60611-1958

Kroger Company Donations 2841

Kroger has a long history of bringing help to the communities they serve. They contribute more than $220 million annually in funds, food, and products to support local communities. They focus on feeding the hungry through more than 80 local Feeding America food bank partners, women's health, American troops and their families, and local schools and grassroots organizations. They are also strong supporters of The Salvation Army, American Red Cross, and organizations that promote the advancement of women and minorities.

Requirements: Organizations may contact their locally owned Kroger store (Kroger, Dillon's, Fred Meyer, Fry's, QFC, Ralph's, Smith's, Baker's, City Market, Food4Less, Foods Co., Gerbes, JayC, King Soopers, Owen's, Pay Less, Kwik Shop, Littman Jewelers, Loaf'n Jug, QuikStop, The Little Clinic, Tom Thumb, Turkey Hill, and Fred Meyer Jewelers) or the Fiscal Administrator at Kroger's corporate office for addition information about requesting a donation.

Geographic Focus: All States
Contact: Fiscal Administraor; (513) 762-4449; fax (513) 762-1295
Internet: http://www.kroger.com/community/Pages/default.aspx
Sponsor: Kroger Foundation
1014 Vine Street
Cincinnati, OH 45202-1100

Kroger Foundation Diversity Grants 2842

The Kroger Foundation provides financial support to local schools, hunger relief agencies, and nonprofit organizations in communities where the company operates stores or manufacturing facilities. Kroger focuses its charitable giving in the following areas: hunger relief; education; diversity; grassroots community support; and women's health. Types of support include grants for general operation, capital gains, and seed money. Diversity grants support organizations that advocate and support the advancement of women and people of color, including local chapters of YWCA, NCCJ, Urban League, and NAACP. At the local level, the Foundation has supported Latino and Native American festivals, the Arab American and Chaldean Council in Detroit, and the Midwest Black Family Reunion in Cincinnati. A list of previously funded projects and organizations across the county is available at the website.

Requirements: Grant applications are not available. Nonprofit organizations may submit grant proposals at any time through the community relations departments at their local Kroger retail store, or contact the fiscal administrator at the corporate office for more information. Proposals must include an IRS tax-exempt letter, a statement of goals and objectives, and a board of trustees list. Support is provided to programs that address a clearly identified need in the community, with specific goals and objectives. Organizations should reflect a strong base of community support.

Restrictions: Only organizations that serve the geographic areas where Kroger owned company operate are eligible to apply. Funding is not available for the following: national or international organizations; for profit organizations; conventions or conference luncheons or dinners; other foundations, except those associated with educational initiatives; endowment campaigns; ongoing operating funding, especially for agencies receiving United Way support (or other federation type support such as a fine arts fund); medical research organizations; sponsorship of golf or other sports events; religious organizationhs or institutions, if the project is for sectarian purposes; individuals; program advertisements; or membership dues.

Geographic Focus: All States
Contact: Fiscal Administrator; (513) 762-4449; fax (513) 762-1295
Internet: http://www.thekrogerco.com/docs/default-document-library/click-here.pdf
Sponsor: Kroger Foundation
1014 Vine Street
Cincinnati, OH 45202-1100

Kroger Foundation Grassroots Community Support Grants 2843

The Kroger Foundation provides financial support to local schools, hunger relief agencies, and nonprofit organizations in communities where the company operates stores or manufacturing facilities. Kroger focuses its charitable giving in the following areas: hunger relief; education; diversity; grassroots community support; and women's health. Types of support includes grants for general operation, capital gains, and seed money. The Grassroots Community Support Grants concentrate on addressing local needs such as assisting with a community environmental issue, building a skateboarding park, or supporting regional youth music or sports programs. The Foundation also offers financial aid when natural disasters such as hurricans strike by supporting the American Red Cross and Salvation Army. Samples of additional project support throughout the U.S. is listed at the Foundation's website.

Requirements: Grant applications are not available. Nonprofit organizations may submit grant proposals at any time through the community relations departments of their local Kroger retail store, or contact the fiscal administrator at the corporate office for more information. Proposals must include an IRS tax-exempt letter, a statement of goals and objecties, and a list of the board of trustees. Support is provided only to programs that address a clearly identified need in the community, with specific goals and objecties. Organizations should reflect a strong base of community support.

Restrictions: Only organizations that serve the geographic areas where Kroger owned companies operate are eligibly to apply. Funding is not available for the following: national or international organizations; for profit organizations; conventions or conferences luncheons or dinner; other foundation, except those associated with educational initiatives; endowment campaigns; ongoing operating funding, especially for agencies receiving United Way support (or other federation type support such as a Fine Arts Fund); medical research organizations; religious organizations or institutions, if the project is for sectarian purposes; individuals; programs advertisements; or membership dues.

Geographic Focus: All States
Contact: Fiscal Administrator; (513) 762-4449; fax (513) 762-1295
Internet: http://www.thekrogerco.com/docs/default-document-library/click-here.pdf
Sponsor: Kroger Foundation
1014 Vine Street
Cincinnati, OH 45202-1100

Kroger Foundation Hunger Relief Grants 2844

The Kroger Foundation provides financial support to local schools, hunger relief agencies, and nonprofit organizations in communities where the company operates stores or manufacturing facilities. Kroger focuses its charitable giving in the following areas: hunger relief; education; diversity; grassroots community support; and women's health. Types of support include grants for general operation, capital gains, and seed money. The Foundation's hunger relief grants support local food banks by purchasing trucks and refrigerators, buying computers to improve their logistics operations, and funding new projects. Kroger is a key partner with Second Harvest, the nation's largest hunger relief organization. Samples of previously funded organizations and projects throughout the U.S. are listed on the Foundation's website.

Requirements: Grant applications are not available. Nonprofit organizations may subject grant proposals at any time through the community relations departments of their local Kroger retail store, or contact the fiscal administrator at the corporate office for more information. Proposals must include an IRS tax-exempt letter, a statement of goals and objectives, and a list of the board of trustees. Support is provided only to programs that

address a clearly identified need in the community, with specific goals and objectives. Organizations should reflect a strong base of community support.
Restrictions: Only organizations that serve the geographic areas where Kroger owned companies operate are eligible to apply. Funding is not available for the following: national or international organzations; for profit organizations; conventions or conference luncheons or dinners; other foundations, except those associated with educational initiatives; endowment campaigns; ongoing operating funding, especially for agencies receiving United Way support (or other federation type support such as a Fine Arts Fund); medical research organizations; sponsorship of sporting events; religious organizations or institutions, if the project is for sectarian purposes; individuals; program advertisements; or membership dues.
Geographic Focus: All States
Contact: Fiscal Administrator; (513) 762-4449; fax (513) 762-1295
Internet: http://www.thekrogerco.com/docs/default-document-library/click-here.pdf
Sponsor: Kroger Foundation
1014 Vine Street
Cincinnati, OH 45202-1100

Kuki'o Community Fund 2845
The Fund is interested in supporting programs that offer out-of-school activities for children, youth and families that contribute to increasing positive social development and reducing risk-taking behaviors by providing: attention from caring adults who can serve as healthy role models; opportunities for exploration of new interests; academic support; a sense of belonging to a group and new friendships; opportunities to take on leadership roles; a sense of self-esteem. Preferences will be given to projects that benefit the residents of West Hawai'i. Application information is available online.
Requirements: Grants will be made to nonprofit, tax exempt 501(c)3 organizations. Community groups without a 501(c)3 will need to apply through a fiscal sponsor.
Geographic Focus: Hawaii
Date(s) Application is Due: Feb 19
Amount of Grant: 5,000 USD
Contact: Marlene Hochuli, (808) 885-2174; dchadwick@hcf-hawaii.org
Internet: http://www.hawaiicommunityfoundation.org/index.php?id=71&categoryID=22
Sponsor: Hawai'i Community Foundation
1164 Bishop Street, Suite 800
Honolulu, HI 96813

L. W. Pierce Family Foundation Grants 2846
Established in 1997, The Foundation supports organizations involved with health, social, and educational services in the areas of alcohol and drug abuse, hospice care and children's welfare. Giving is limited to the Vero Beach, FL and Philadelphia, PA areas.
Requirements: Non-profits in the Vero Beach, FL and Philadelphia, PA areas are eligible.
Restrictions: No grants to individuals.
Geographic Focus: Florida, Pennsylvania
Date(s) Application is Due: Mar 1
Amount of Grant: 1,000 - 50,000 USD
Contact: Constance Buckley, President; (610) 862-2105; fax (610) 862-2120
Sponsor: L. W. Pierce Family Foundation
8 Tower Bridge, Suite 1060, 161 Washington Street
Conshohocken, PA 19428-2060

LA84 Foundation Grants 2847
The Foundation seeks to serve the entire community, but gives special attention to groups and communities under served by traditional sports programs, including girls, ethnic minorities, and the physically challenged and developmentally disabled. Foundation funds are primarily intended for the development of youth sports below the elite level. The Foundation will consider a request from any bona fide Southern California organization devoted to amateur sports.
Requirements: The foundation supports tax-exempt organizations in the area of sports for youth in the eight Southern California counties, including: Imperial, Los Angeles, Orange, Riverside, San Bernardino, San Diego, Santa Barbara, and Ventura.
Restrictions: The current objectives of the board discourage grants for endowments, travel outside Southern California, single public or private school facilities or programs not including sports schools, routine operating expenses, purchase of land, or debt recovery or incurring debt liability. Grants are not made to individuals.
Geographic Focus: California
Date(s) Application is Due: Mar 12; Jun 9; Oct 8
Contact: Jalal Hazzard, Senior Program Officer; (323) 730-4600 or (323) 730-4621; fax (323) 730-9637; jhazzard@la84foundation.org or info@la84foundation.org
Internet: http://www.aafla.org/1gm/grant_frmst.htm
Sponsor: LA84 Foundation
2141 West Adams Boulevard
Los Angeles, CA 90018

Laclede Gas Charitable Trust Grants 2848
The Trust represents Laclede Gas Company's recognition of its civic responsibility to those in its service area. Areas of interest include human needs and services; education and educational institutions; arts and culture; and civic and community projects. The Trust funds operating support, special projects and annual support. Application forms are available on the website. There are no deadlines. The Trustees of the Charitable Trust meet at least semi-annually.
Requirements: Eligible applicants must be 501(c)3 organizations. Only organizations in the Laclede Gas Company's service area are eligible. The service area includes the city of St. Louis and ten other counties in Eastern Missouri. See the website for a map specifying the service area.
Restrictions: The following is not eligible: individuals, family support or family reunions; advertising; political, labor, fraternal or religious organizations or civic clubs; individual K-8 schools or school-affiliated clubs or events (public or private); sports, athletic events or athletic programs; travel related events, including student trips or tours; development or production of books, films, videos or television programs; and endowment or memorial campaigns. No contribution will be made to an organization if the contribution may impair the independence of a member of Laclede's Board of Directors.
Geographic Focus: Missouri
Contact: Grants Administrator; (314) 421-1979
Internet: http://www.lacledegas.com/service/trust.php
Sponsor: Laclede Gas Charitable Trust
720 Olive Street, Room 1517
Saint Louis, MO 63101

Lafayette - West Lafayette Convention and Visitors Bureau Tourist Grants 2849
The Lafayette - West Lafayette Convention and Visitors Bureau (LWLCVB) is the official destination marketing organization of Tippecanoe County that contributes to the economic health of its communities by promoting as a preferred travel destination and by enhancing the visitor experience. This LWLCVB grant program is a matching program that assists local not-for-profit organizations with projects that increase tourism business in Tippecanoe County. Those projects must be used to bring in new business, develop local events, festivals or sporting events. Dollars awarded can only be used for out of town marketing. It is the LWLCVB's philosophy that funding such projects will draw and increase the number of visitors, especially overnight visitors, to Tippecanoe County, thereby providing added economic benefits to the community. Partnerships with Lafayette – West Lafayette tourism industry members are encouraged and will be given high consideration.
Requirements: Qualified organizations must demonstrate how the project for which they are requesting funding ties into the mission of the LWLCVB, and describe the method used to evaluate the success of the project.
Geographic Focus: Indiana
Contact: Lisa Morrow, (765) 447-9999; lmorrow@HomeOfPurdue.com
Internet: http://www.homeofpurdue.com/grants.html
Sponsor: Lafayette - West Lafayette Convention and Visitors Bureau
301 Frontage Road
Lafayette, IN 47905

LaGrange County Community Foundation Grants 2850
The mission of the LaGrange County Community Foundation (LCCF) is to inspire and sustain leadership, generosity and service. Its purpose is to help community service organizations sponsor plans to meet critically important needs. The Foundation funds grants for innovative and creative projects and programs that are responsive to changing community needs in the areas of, but not restricted to: health and human services, environment, arts and culture, and recreation.
Requirements: Non-profit organizations, schools and qualifying government agencies serving the citizens of LaGrange County are invited to apply for a grant through the foundation's application process. In addition to the online application, applicants should submit a complete list of their organization's board of directors and their occupations; a copy of their specific line item budget with projected income and expenses; a copy of the organization's most recent operating budget; documentation to prove the organization's non-profit status.
Restrictions: The foundation does not make grants to individuals, except in the form of academic scholarships. Grants are generally given one-time only for specific purposes and will typically not be awarded to provide annual operating expenses or support. A grant will not be awarded to replenish funds previously expended. Grants are made with the understanding that the foundation has no obligation or commitment to provide additional support to the grantee. Grants may not be used for any political campaign, or to influence legislature of any government body other than through making available the results of nonpartisan analysis, study, and research.
Geographic Focus: Indiana
Date(s) Application is Due: Aug 1
Contact: Laura Lemings; (260) 463-4363; fax (260) 463-4856; llemings@lccf.net
Internet: http://www.lccf.net/grants.html
Sponsor: LaGrange County Community Foundation
109 E Central Avenue, Suite 3
LaGrange, IN 46761

LaGrange Independent Foundation for Endowments 2851
LaGrange Independent Foundation for Endowments, or L.I.F.E., is a philanthropic group of young people in LaGrange County. Representatives from four county schools are selected when they enter grade 8 and serve throughout their high school career as the advisory committee for the donor advised non-permanent fund held by the foundation. Grant applications submitted to the LCCF office are evaluated by the L.I.F.E Youth Pod in order to select recommended recipients.
Requirements: Nonprofit organizations including schools in LaGrange county are eligible to apply. Grants are awarded during the school year. The application is available at the foundation's website.
Geographic Focus: Indiana
Contact: Laura Lemings; (260) 463-4363; fax (260) 463-4856; llemings@lccf.net
Internet: http://www.lccf.net/life.html
Sponsor: LaGrange County Community Foundation
109 E Central Avenue, Suite 3
LaGrange, IN 46761

Laidlaw Foundation Multi-Year Grants 2852
Laidlaw Foundation promotes positive youth development through inclusive youth engagement in the arts, environment and in community. The Foundation offers funding and other support to youth-led groups that have ideas and strategies for tackling issues that affect communities and the broader society. Multi-Year Grants support core operating and capacity strengthening within youth-led groups. Generally, 2-3 Multi-Year Grants are made each year.
Requirements: In order for a group to be eligible for multi-year funding there must be a history of partnering with the Foundation and the group must have received a previous grant. Groups of young people aged 14–25 are eligible to apply. They must be located within the greater Toronto area, specifically in the Greater Golden Horseshoe area. Applicants must have charitable status or partner with an organization with charitable status whose purposes are consistent with the work of the applicant group. Regardless of the type of group applying, young people must write the application, plan the project and make the project happen. Applicants should contact the Foundation about application.
Restrictions: The following is not eligible: projects outside of Canada; local projects outside of Ontario; fundraising campaigns, dinners, benefits, endowments, sponsorships, emergency funding or other special events; one-time or annual conferences, events or workshops; building or capital campaigns, renovations, furnishings, vehicles or other acquisitions; deficit reduction programs; non-secular and faith-based activities; scholarships or bursaries (other than those initiated by the Foundation); personal appeals for financial support; retroactive requests for projects already completed; campus-based or school-based groups and/or in-school programming; youth advisory committees to non-youth-led organizations; and summer camps or youth programs of organizations.
Geographic Focus: Canada
Date(s) Application is Due: Sep 7
Amount of Grant: 50,000 CAD
Contact: Ana Skinner, (416) 964-3614, ext. 307; fax (416) 975-1428; askinner@laidlawfdn.org
Internet: http://www.laidlawfdn.org/youth-organizing-program
Sponsor: Laidlaw Foundation
365 Bloor Street E, Suite 2000
Toronto, ON M4W 3L4 Canada

Laidlaw Foundation Youh Organizing Catalyst Grants 2853
Laidlaw Foundation promotes positive youth development through inclusive youth engagement in the arts, environment and in community. The Foundation offers funding and other support to youth-led groups that have ideas and strategies for tackling issues that affect communities and the broader society. Catalyst Grants are small 'seed' grants for a group of young people to test out an idea; do community research around issues that concern them; to develop partnerships, networks and collaborations; and to respond to a time sensitive situation. Generally 4-6 Catalyst Grants are funded each year. There are no deadlines. Contact the Foundation to discuss the project. The process generally takes 6-8 weeks.
Requirements: Groups of young people aged 14–25 are eligible to apply. They must be located within the greater Toronto area, specifically in the Greater Golden Horseshoe area. Applicants must have charitable status or partner with an organization with charitable status whose purposes are consistent with the work of the applicant group. Regardless of the type of group applying, young people must write the application, plan the project and make the project happen.
Restrictions: The following is not eligible: projects outside of Canada; local projects outside of Ontario; fundraising campaigns, dinners, benefits, endowments, sponsorships, emergency funding or other special events; one-time or annual conferences, events or workshops; building or capital campaigns, renovations, furnishings, vehicles or other acquisitions; deficit reduction programs; non-secular and faith-based activities; scholarships or bursaries (other than those initiated by the Foundation); personal appeals for financial support; retroactive requests for projects already completed; campus-based or school-based groups and/or in-school programming; youth advisory committees to non-youth-led organizations; and summer camps or youth programs of organizations.
Geographic Focus: Canada
Amount of Grant: 5,000 CAD
Contact: Ana Skinner, (416) 964-3614, ext. 307; fax (416) 975-1428; askinner@laidlawfdn.org
Internet: http://www.laidlawfdn.org/youth-organizing-program
Sponsor: Laidlaw Foundation
365 Bloor Street E, Suite 2000
Toronto, ON M4W 3L4 Canada

Laidlaw Foundation Youth Organizaing Initiatives Grants 2854
Laidlaw Foundation promotes positive youth development through inclusive youth engagement in the arts, environment and in community. The Foundation offers funding and other support to youth-led groups that have ideas and strategies for tackling issues that affect communities and the broader society. Initiative Grants support youth-led groups to implement a specific project they have developed; to focus on strengthening their group or organizational capacity; and to develop collaborations, partnerships and networks. Generally 12-20 initiative are funded per year.
Requirements: Groups of young people aged 14–25 are eligible to apply. They must be located within the greater Toronto area, specifically in the Greater Golden Horseshoe area. Applicants must have charitable status or partner with an organization with charitable status whose purposes are consistent with the work of the applicant group. Regardless of the type of group applying, young people must write the application, plan the project and make the project happen. Before developing a full proposal, applicants should contact the Foundation to determine project eligibility. Applications are available on the website.
Restrictions: The following is not eligible: projects outside of Canada; local projects outside of Ontario; fundraising campaigns, dinners, benefits, endowments, sponsorships, emergency funding or other special events; one-time or annual conferences, events or workshops; building or capital campaigns, renovations, furnishings, vehicles or other acquisitions; deficit reduction programs; non-secular and faith-based activities; scholarships or bursaries (other than those initiated by the Foundation); personal appeals for financial support; retroactive requests for projects already completed; campus-based or school-based groups and/or in-school programming; youth advisory committees to non-youth-led organizations; and summer camps or youth programs of organizations.
Geographic Focus: Canada
Date(s) Application is Due: Mar 9; Sep 7
Amount of Grant: 10,000 - 5,000 CAD
Contact: Ana Skinner, (416) 964-3614, ext. 307; fax (416) 975-1428; askinner@laidlawfdn.org
Internet: http://www.laidlawfdn.org/youth-organizing-program
Sponsor: Laidlaw Foundation
365 Bloor Street E, Suite 2000
Toronto, ON M4W 3L4 Canada

Laila Twigg-Smith Art Scholarship 2855
This scholarship is to support Hawaii-based artists in study that furthers their artistic development and offers them exposure to new ideas, influences and opportunities. The program provides scholarships for visual artists to attend summer programs at either the Anderson Ranch Arts Center in Colorado or Pilchuck Glass School in Washington. The award covers tuition and fees, housing and meals, and partial reimbursement for travel. Applications will not be accepted at the Hawaii Community Foundation. Interested applicants will contact the individual schools. The contact for Anderson Ranch is Susan Casebeer, (970) 923-3181, ext. 216 and for Pilchuck Glass School, Tricia Watson (360) 445-3111, ext. 29. The Hawaii Community Foundation will not be involved in the selection process.
Requirements: Eligible applicants must: be legal residents of the State of Hawaii; be a practicing artist, graduate or undergraduate art student; be accepted by the school for admission to its visual arts program; not have received a previous Laila Twigg-Smith Art Fund scholarship to attend the same school. Preference will be given to scholarship applicants with financial need.
Restrictions: Applications will not be accepted at the Hawaii Community Foundation.
Geographic Focus: Hawaii
Contact: Amy Luersen, (808) 566-5550; aluersen@hawaiicommunityfoundation.org
Internet: http://www.hawaiicommunityfoundation.org
Sponsor: Hawai'i Community Foundation
1164 Bishop Street, Suite 800
Honolulu, HI 96813

Lake County Community Fund Grants 2856
The Lake County Community Grant was established to be responsive to community projects throughout Lake County in the areas of arts and culture, civic affairs, community development, education, the environment, health, human services, and youth services. The Foundation will make grants to non-profit organizations implementing projects with the most potential to improve the quality of life of a substantial number of residents of Lake County. Geographic distribution may be considered in awarding grants. Grants typically range from $1,000 to $25,000.
Requirements: Funding priorities include projects that: develop or test new solutions to community problems; address prevention as well as remediation; assist underserved community resources; provide a sustained effect for a substantial number of residents; improve the efficiency of non-profit groups; provide a favorable ratio between the amount of money requested and number of people served; facilitate collaboration among organizations without duplicating services; encourage volunteerism, civic engagement, and development. Applicants must submit the online detailed application, along with the grant narrative, project budget, a list of applicant's board of directors, summary of the organization's current fiscal year operating budget as well as financial audit or review; evidence of Board approval of this application, copy of tax exempt status, and organization's profile on GuideStar (www.guidestar).
Restrictions: The Legacy Foundation does not support: general operating expenses; endowment campaigns, annual campaigns, or fundraising events; travel grants; grants for individual schools or sponsorship of sports teams; previously incurred debt or retroactive funding for current projects; individuals and independent scholarly research projects; and religious or sectarian programs, political parties, or campaigns.
Geographic Focus: Indiana
Date(s) Application is Due: Mar 1; May 1; Sep 1; Nov 1
Amount of Grant: 1,000 - 25,000 USD
Contact: Barry Tyler, Jr., Community Initiatives Officer; (219) 736-1880; fax (219) 736-1940; legacy@legacyfoundationlakeco.org or btyler@legacyfdn.org
Internet: http://www.legacyfoundationlakeco.org/grantsfundingopps.html
Sponsor: Legacy Foundation
1000 East 80th Place, 302 South
Merrillville, IN 46410

Lana'i Community Benefit Fund 2857
The purpose of the Fund is to promote and enrich the lifestyle of the residents of Lanai through the support of educational, cultural and recreational activities for the Lanai community with special emphasis on youth, young adults and senior citizens. Priority will be given to proposals that provide clear objectives and reasonable timelines. Application information is available online.
Requirements: Grants may be made to organizations which are not described as 501(c)3 provided the activities to be supported are charitable and do not involve political lobbying or other non-charitable activities.
Restrictions: Funding for travel and personal expenses or hiring shall be discouraged except to bring speakers, instructors, and other individuals with special talents and abilities from outside of Lanai for activities consistent with the purposes of the Fund.
Geographic Focus: Hawaii

Date(s) Application is Due: May 14
Amount of Grant: 500 - 5,000 USD
Contact: Ginger Gannon, (808) 242-6184; ggannon@hcf-hawaii.org
Internet: http://www.hawaiicommunityfoundation.org/index.php?id=71&categoryID=22
Sponsor: Hawai'i Community Foundation
1164 Bishop Street, Suite 800
Honolulu, HI 96813

Land O'Lakes Foundation California Region Grants   2858
The California Regions Grants were developed specifically for selected Land O'Lakes dairy communities in the Orland, Tulare, Kings, Bakersfield, and Ontario regions. The program works to improve quality of life through donations to valuable projects and charitable endeavors recommended by the Foundation's California dairy member-leaders. Community organizations may be eligible for funding of $500 to $5,000 for local projects and programs. Funds could be used to support such worthwhile projects as: backing local food pantries or emergency feeding efforts; aiding 4-H or FFA programs; building a new park pavilion for the community; or purchasing books for the community library.
Requirements: To be considered, grant proposals must demonstrate how the donation will be used to help improve community quality of life. Grants are restricted to organizations that have been granted tax-exempt status under Section 501(c)3 of the Internal Revenue Code. Foundation awards grants to projects that address the following focus areas: hunger relief; youth and education; civic improvements; and arts and culture. Applicants may refer to the online application for further information about the application process.
Restrictions: Grants will not be awarded for the following purposes: scholarship funds; gifts or fundraisers for individuals; non-public church use; or projects that do not demonstrate a broad application of the principles established in the Foundation's mission statement.
Geographic Focus: California
Contact: Martha Atkins-Sakry; (651) 481-2470; MLAtkins-Sakry@landolakes.com
Internet: http://www.landolakesinc.com/company/corporateresponsibility/foundation/californiagrants/default.aspx
Sponsor: Land O'Lakes Foundation
P.O. Box 64101
St. Paul, MN 55164-0150

Land O'Lakes Foundation Community Grants   2859
Land O'Lakes Foundation Community Grants provide support to nonprofit organizations that are working to improve communities where Land O'Lakes has a large concentration of members or employees. These include organizations that: provide funding to human services; work to alleviate hunger; build knowledge and leadership skills of rural youth; address and solve regional problems; and promote artistic endeavors, especially in underserved rural areas, touring or outreach programs. Special emphasis is directed toward programs that address issues of hunger and are statewide, regional, or national in scope. Requests for more than $5,000 are reviewed in February, June, August, and December. There is no deadline for requests for less than $5,000, but it may take up to three months to fully consider the request. Arts and culture requests are due on May 1. The application is available online.
Requirements: Grants are restricted to organizations that have tax-exempt status under Section 501(c)3 of the Internal Revenue Code. Grants are limited to one per organization per calendar year.
Restrictions: Applications for the following year will only be accepted on or after January 1. Funding generally will not be used for the following categories: lobbying, political and religious organizations; veteran, fraternal and labor organizations; individuals; fundraising events, dinners or benefits; advertising; college/university capital/endowment funds; scholarships; travel expenses for individuals/groups; racing/sports sponsorships; or disease/medical related, including research or treatment.
Geographic Focus: Arkansas, California, Idaho, Illinois, Indiana, Iowa, Kansas, Michigan, Minnesota, Mississippi, Missouri, Nebraska, North Dakota, Ohio, Oregon, Pennsylvania, South Dakota, Texas, Washington, Wisconsin
Amount of Grant: 500 - 10,000 USD
Contact: Martha Atkins-Sakry; (651) 481-2470; MLAtkins-Sakry@landolakes.com
Internet: http://www.landolakesinc.com/company/corporateresponsibility/foundation/communitygrants/description/default.aspx
Sponsor: Land O'Lakes Foundation
P.O. Box 64101
St. Paul, MN 55164-0150

Land O'Lakes Foundation Dollars for Doers   2860
Land O'Lakes Foundation's Dollars for Doers rewards and recognizes local community volunteerism. Through Dollars for Doers, the organization benefits twice: once from the volunteer's contribution of time, and again from the Foundation's financial contribution. Dollars for Doers grants are awarded for a wide variety of volunteer services including, but not limited to: delivering meals to senior citizens; leading a scout troop; teaching reading in a literacy program; volunteer fire fighting; or re-stocking food shelves. Volunteer hours add up to dollars for the organization to which time is donated. The volunteer may apply for grant funds for the nonprofit organization after completing the following number of volunteer hours at one organization: $100 for 16 hours of service; $250 for 50 hours of service; and $500 for 100 hours of service. The application is available at the Foundation website.
Requirements: Full-time, part-time, and retired employees of Land O'Lakes are eligibly to apply. The eligible volunteer organizations must be nonprofit and tax-exempt 501(c)3 under the IRS code.
Restrictions: Ineligible organizations include lobbying, political, religious, fraternal, veteran, and labor organizations.
Geographic Focus: Arkansas, California, Idaho, Illinois, Indiana, Iowa, Kansas, Michigan, Minnesota, Mississippi, Missouri, Nebraska, North Dakota, Ohio, Oregon, Pennsylvania, South Dakota, Texas, Washington, Wisconsin
Date(s) Application is Due: Dec 15
Amount of Grant: Up to 500 USD
Contact: Martha Atkins-Sakry; (651) 481-2470; MLAtkins-Sakry@landolakes.com
Internet: http://www.landolakesinc.com/company/corporateresponsibility/foundation/dollarsdoers/default.aspx
Sponsor: Land O'Lakes Foundation
P.O. Box 64101
St. Paul, MN 55164-0150

Lands' End Corporate Giving Program   2861
The Corporation awards grants to nonprofits for youth and family services programs in their area of company operations in Wisconsin. Areas of interest include education, community development, environment, and health and human services.
Requirements: Wisconsin nonprofits are eligible. Organizations should submit the following: a timetable for implementation and evaluation of the project; statement of the problem that the project will address; population and geographic area to be served; name, address and phone number of organization; copy of IRS determination letter; copy of most recent annual report/audited financial statement/990; how the project's results will be evaluated or measured; list of company employees involved with the organization; detailed description of project and amount of funding requested; contact person; copy of current year's organizational budget and/or project budget; and listing of additional sources and amount of support. Applicants should also include a description of their past involvement with Lands' End, if any.
Restrictions: The Foundation does not consider grants for organizations without nonprofit status; individuals; political organizations, campaigns, or candidates for public office; lobbying groups; advertising in programs, bulletins, yearbooks, or brochures; testimonial/awards dinners; endowments; loans; religious groups for religious purposes; pageants; purchasing of land; salaries; administrative costs; international programs; research programs; or general operating expenses.
Geographic Focus: Wisconsin
Date(s) Application is Due: Mar 31; Jun 30; Sep 30; Dec 31
Contact: Jessica Winzenried, Corporate Giving Manager; (608) 935-6776 or (608) 935-6728; fax (608) 935-6432; donate@landsend.com
Sponsor: Lands' End
2 Lands' End Lane
Dodgeville, WI 53595

Laura Jane Musser Intercultural Harmony Grants   2862
The Laura Jane Musser Grants seek to promote mutual understanding and cooperation between groups and citizens of different cultural backgrounds within defined geographical areas through collaborative, cross-cultural exchange projects. Priority is given to projects that: include members of various cultural communities working together on projects with common goals; build positive relationships across cultural lines; engender intercultural harmony, tolerance, understanding, and respect; enhance intercultural communication, rather than cultural isolation, while at the same time celebrating and honoring the unique qualities of each culture. To be eligible for funding, projects must demonstrate: need in the community for the intercultural exchange project; grassroots endorsement by participants across cultural lines, as well as their active participation in planning and implementation of the project; the ability of the organization to address the challenges of working across the cultural barriers identified by the project; and tangible benefits in the larger community. Projects can be carried out in a number of areas, including, but not limited to the arts, community service, and youth activities. Detailed guidelines for the proposal are available at the Musser website. A list of previously funded grants is also available at the website.
Requirements: Organizations eligible for support include 501(c)3 nonprofits; organizations that are forming if they have a documented fiscal agent relationship; and organizations located within one of the eligible states. Funding will cover new programs or projects within their first three years or the planning and implementation phase of a project.
Restrictions: Capital expenses, general operating expenses, and ongoing program support are not eligible for funding.
Geographic Focus: Colorado, Hawaii, Michigan, Minnesota, Ohio, Wyoming
Date(s) Application is Due: Oct 10
Contact: Mary Karen Lynn-Klimenko; (612) 825-2024; ljmusserfund@earthlink.net
Internet: http://www.musserfund.org/index.asp?page_seq=25
Sponsor: Laura Jane Musser Fund
318 West 48th Street
Minneapolis, MN 55419

Laura Jane Musser Rural Arts Grants   2863
The Musser Rural Arts Grants assist nonprofit arts organizations to develop, implement, or sustain exceptional artistic opportunities for adults and children in the areas of literary, visual, music, and the performing arts. Priority is placed on projects that: increase access to the arts through scholarships, hands-on activities, community venues, workshops, discounts and other innovations; demonstrate capacity to engage their community in the creation of art; demonstrate support from their community (through volunteerism, membership, in-kind, or other types of support). Arts organizations located in rural communities of 20,000 or less in the following states are eligible: Colorado, Hawaii, Wyoming, and specific counties in Michigan, Minnesota, and Ohio (listed on the Musser website). Detailed instructions for applying are posted on the Musser website.
Requirements: Projects eligible for support include: arts organizations with budgets of $200,000 or less; nonprofit 501(c)3 organizations; and organizations that have been in existence for one year at the time of application.

Restrictions: Capital expenses are not eligible for funding. Applications are accepted for one year of funding at a time. It is possible for organizations to apply for and receive funding for up to three consecutive years. But then Grantees may not reapply for funding for one year after the three years of funding.
Geographic Focus: Colorado, Hawaii, Michigan, Minnesota, Ohio, Wyoming
Date(s) Application is Due: Mar 21
Amount of Grant: Up to 10,000 USD
Contact: Mary Karen Lynn-Klimenko; (612) 825-2024; ljmusserfund@earthlink.net
Internet: http://www.musserfund.org/index.asp?page_seq=21
Sponsor: Laura Jane Musser Fund
318 West 48th Street
Minneapolis, MN 55419

Laura Jane Musser Rural Initiative Grants 2864
The Laura Jane Musser Rural Initiative Grants encourage collaborative and participatory efforts among citizens in rural communities in order to strengthen their towns and regions in a number of civic areas including, but not limited to, economic development, business preservation, arts and humanities, public space improvements, and education. Funding is available for planning or implementation (not both). Up to $5,000 is available for planning (consultant or staff time, meeting costs, mailings, secretarial support, refreshments, local travel, etc.). Up to $25,00 is available to implement community based rural projects that originate in, have been planned by, and involve diverse people from the local community. Priority is placed on projects that: bring together a broad range of community members and institutions provide the opportunity for diverse community members to work together; contain measurable short term outcomes within the first 12 to 18 months; include community members actively in all phases of the process; and work toward an outcome of positive change within their community.
Requirements: Projects must demonstrate: support from a diverse cross-section of community members and institutions; matching financial and/or in-kind support from the local community; significant volunteer participation; reasonable plans to complete the project within 18 months. Detailed guidelines to proposal submission are available at the website.
Restrictions: The applicant community must have a population of 10,000 or less and must be able to demonstrate the rural characteristics of their location. Funding is not available for capital campaigns.
Geographic Focus: Colorado, Hawaii, Michigan, Minnesota, Ohio, Wyoming
Date(s) Application is Due: Nov 7
Amount of Grant: 5,000 - 25,000 USD
Contact: Mary Karen Lynn-Klimenko; (612) 825-2024; ljmusserfund@earthlink.net
Internet: http://www.musserfund.org/index.asp?page_seq=6
Sponsor: Laura Jane Musser Fund
318 West 48th Street
Minneapolis, MN 55419

Laura L. Adams Foundation Grants 2865
Established in New York in 2001 with a donation on behalf of Laura L. Adams, offers grants primarily in New Yotk. The Foundation's major field of interest include education, health care, and recreation. Types of support include general operating funds and scholarship funding. Most recent grants have ranged from $875 to $12,500. A formal application is required, and the annual deadline for submission is October 31.
Requirements: 501(c)3 organizations either in, or serving the residents of, New York state are eligible to apply.
Geographic Focus: New York
Date(s) Application is Due: Oct 31
Amount of Grant: 875 - 12,500 USD
Contact: Harold Summar, Director; (716) 854-8000 or (716) 854-2899
Sponsor: Laura L. Adams Foundation
P.O. Box 466
Hamburg, NY 14075-0466

Laura Moore Cunningham Foundation Grants 2866
The Laura Moore Cunningham Foundation is dedicated to advancing the State of Idaho. Priorities include rural healthcare, educational programs for children, programs in underserved communities, and programs for underserved populations. Each year the Foundation accepts applications from throughout the State, allowing organizations of all types to express their need. The Foundation is interested in organizations that run in a cost-effective manner, serving large numbers of people who are truly in need.
Requirements: Eligible applicants must be 501(c)3 Idaho organizations. The Foundation does not limit giving to a certain type of program or need; however administrative costs are not preferred.
Restrictions: Individuals are ineligible.
Geographic Focus: Idaho
Date(s) Application is Due: May 15
Contact: Harry L. Bettis; (208) 472-4066; lmcf_idaho@msn.com
Internet: http://lauramoorecunningham.org/Applying_for_Grants.html
Sponsor: Laura Moore Cunningham Foundation
P.O. Box 1157
Boise, ID 83701

Laurel Foundation Grants 2867
Laurel Foundation Grants focus on programs in Pittsburgh and southwestern Pennsylvania that offer long-term benefits for participants and the community. The Foundation favors programs from nonprofit organizations that foster individual responsibility and self-sufficiency; exhibit a commitment to sound fiscal and program management; implement collaborative efforts; and demonstrate measurable outcomes. Types of funding include those that concentrate in the fields of arts and culture; education; environment; and public/society benefit. Organizations are advised to carefully review the Foundation website to gauge its possible interest prior to submitting a full proposal. If there is uncertainty, a brief, one-page letter of inquiry may be sent to the President, including a summary of the project and related costs.
Requirements: Nonprofit organizations in Pittsburgh and southwestern Pennsylvania may submit applications. The Board meets in June and December. Proposals submitted for consideration at these meetings must be received by April 1 and October 1. Proposals may follow the format of the Common Grant Application, which can be accessed at the Grantmakers of Western Pennsylvania website.
Restrictions: Individuals are not eligible for funding, nor are grants made for scholarships or fellowships. Social and cultural organizations whose services fall outside the Greater Pittsburgh area are not encouraged to submit a request. Laurel Foundation does not ordinarily approve multi-year grants, preferring instead to monitor the status of a program prior to additional funding approval.
Geographic Focus: Pennsylvania
Date(s) Application is Due: Apr 1; Oct 1
Amount of Grant: 5,000 - 55,000 USD
Contact: Elizabeth Tata; (412) 765-2400; laurelcontact@laurelfdn.org
Internet: http://www.laurelfdn.org/grants_program.html
Sponsor: Laurel Foundation
2 Gateway Center, Suite 1800
Pittsburgh, PA 15222

Lawrence J. and Anne Rubenstein Charitable Foundation Grants 2868
The Foundation, established in 1963, supports organizations involved with early childhood services, and higher education, support also for programs for school preparedness. Giving primarily in Boston, MA and Philadelphia, PA. Contact the Foundation for further application information and guidelines.
Requirements: Nonprofits operating in the Boston and Philadelphia area are eligible.
Restrictions: No grants to individuals.
Geographic Focus: Massachusetts, Pennsylvania
Date(s) Application is Due: Apr 1; Oct 1
Contact: Susan W. Hunnewell, Foundation Contact c/o Ridgeway Advisors; (617) 279-8052; fax (617) 279-8059; shunnewelle@ridgewayadvisors.com
Sponsor: Lawrence J. and Anne Rubenstein Charitable Foundation
10 Post Office Square
Boston, MA 02109-4615

Leadership IS Award 2869
The award recognizes a nonprofit organization that develops a culture of investing in the people of the independent sector as they work to build community. The honoree receives an award statuette and monetary gift. Nomination forms are available online; or nominators may submit the name of the organization, the name of its CEO, and contact information.
Requirements: Anyone may nominate any nonprofit organization. Organizations do not need to be members of Independent Sector.
Geographic Focus: All States
Date(s) Application is Due: Feb 15
Amount of Grant: 10,000 USD
Contact: Jennifer Edwards, Executive Assistant; (202) 467-6155; fax (202) 467-6101; leadershipis@independentsector.org
Internet: http://www.independentsector.org/programs/leadership/organizationalaward.htm
Sponsor: Independent Sector
1200 18th Street NW, Suite 200
Washington, DC 20036

Leave No Trace Master Educator Course Scholarships 2870
The Master Course provides participants with a comprehensive overview of Leave No Trace skills and ethics through practical application in a field-based setting. The first day is spent in a classroom, introducing the course and schedule, providing in-depth information on the overall Leave No Trace program and the Center for Outdoor Ethics, reviewing gear, and packing. The remaining days are spent in the field on a short backcountry trip learning and practicing the principles of Leave No Trace.
Requirements: Scholarships are available for private citizens, organization members, and others interested in teaching Leave No Trace. To be eligible, applicants must be enrolled in an approved Leave No Trace Master Educator course prior to subitting the scholarship application. In some cases, scholarships may be retroactive if your course runs prior to one of the two deadlines. If you are awarded a scholarship after you have attended your Master Educator course, you will receive partial reimbursement directly from Leave No Trace Center for Outdoor Ethics If the deadline closest to your course date is missed, your application will be held until the next deadline. Download a copy of the application from the website.
Restrictions: Due to the amount of qualified applications the Center receives, only domestic applicants are eligible.
Geographic Focus: All States
Date(s) Application is Due: Apr 15; Aug 15
Contact: Sarah Folzenlogen; (303) 442-8222, ext. 107; sarah@lnt.org
Internet: http://www.lnt.org/training/mastereducator.php
Sponsor: Leave No Trace Center for Outdoor Ethics
P.O. Box 997
Boulder, CO 80306

Lee and Ramona Bass Foundation Grants — 2871

The Foundation was established in 1993 to support nonprofit organizations that provide important services for people, primarily within the state of Texas. Funding is provided in the following categories: schools, colleges and universities within Texas, with emphasis placed upon faculty development and liberal arts programs; community programs and projects, particularly related to the arts and the environment, such as museums, zoos, and educational/research institutions; and national and regional conservation programs. Preliminary inquiries are requested, in the form of a letter briefly describing the organization and the program or project. Formal proposals are accepted only after the Foundation has responded to the preliminary inquiry.
Requirements: Eligible applicants must have 501(c)3 organizations.
Restrictions: No grants are made to individuals.
Geographic Focus: All States
Contact: Valleau Wilkie Jr.; (817) 336-0494; fax (817) 332-2176; cjohns@sidrichardson.org
Internet: http://www.leeandramonabass.org/grantguidlines.html
Sponsor: Lee and Ramona Bass Foundation
309 Main Street
Fort Worth, TX 76102

Leeway Foundation Art and Change Grants — 2872

The grants provide immediate, short-term grants to women or trans artists in the Philadelphia region who need financial assistance to take advantage of opportunities for art and change that is supported by or in collaboration with a Change Partner. The grant is designed to be inclusive and open to as many types of opportunities as possible. It is acknowledged that the result of every opportunity will not be immediate change, and that change is a process that often involves long-term work. However, it is important that all opportunities have an impact on the work of the artist; have a transformational element; and are important at this particular moment in the artist's life. The program seeks to include artists and work that often fall through the cracks due to a variety of cultural realities, including art by women of color, immigrant women, homosexual women, transgender women, poor and working-class women, women who take risks with art form and content, and other women whose work is often ignored, silenced, and marginalized because of who they are or what they create. One application per deadline will be considered. Application is available online.
Requirements: Applicants must be female (transgender women are eligible); be at least 18 years old; be current residents of Pennsylvania's Bucks, Chester, Delaware, Montgomery, or Philadelphia Counties; and have a commitment from a Change Partner, along with specific dates when the opportunity will happen.
Restrictions: Full-time or matriculated students in art-degree programs and current Art and Change grant or Transformation Award recipients are ineligible.
Geographic Focus: Pennsylvania
Date(s) Application is Due: Mar 24; Jun 16; Sep 8
Amount of Grant: Up to 2,500 USD
Contact: Denise Brown; (215) 545-4078; fax (215) 545-4021; denise@leeway.org
Internet: http://www.leeway.org/grants.php?ID=29
Sponsor: Leeway Foundation
1315 Walnut Street, Suite 832
Philadelphia, PA 19107

Leeway Foundation Transformation Award — 2873

The Transformation Award provides unrestricted annual awards of $15,000 to women and trans artists living in the Delaware Valley region who create art for social change and have done so for the past five years or more, demonstrating a long-term commitment to social change work. The Award is unrestricted (it is not project-based) and open to women and trans people working in any art form, traditional or non-traditional.
Requirements: Eligible applicants are woman- or trans artist who: create art for social change that impacts a larger group, audience, or community; have been creating art for social change for the past five years or more, demonstrating a long-term commitment to this work; have financial need and limited or no access to other financial resources; have lived for the past two or more years in the Delaware Valley region: Bucks, Camden, Chester, Delaware, Montgomery, or Philadelphia County. There is a two-stage application process. Stage 1 is open to all eligible applicants. A panel of community-based artists will review applications and make decisions to invite applicants to submit work samples for Stage 2.
Restrictions: Full-time or matriculated students in art-degree programs are ineligible.
Geographic Focus: Pennsylvania
Date(s) Application is Due: May 5
Amount of Grant: 15,000 USD
Contact: Denise Brown; (215) 545-4078; fax (215) 545-4021; denise@leeway.org
Internet: http://www.leeway.org/grants.php?ID=30
Sponsor: Leeway Foundation
1315 Walnut Street, Suite 832
Philadelphia, PA 19107

Legacy Foundation College Readiness Grant — 2874

The Legacy Foundation established this grant with funding from the Lumina Foundation for Education to improve high school graduation rates and increase the number of students who will attend and succeed in college. The College Readiness Grant supports Lake County organizations that help students gain academic skills to prepare for college, and navigate the college application process. The Grant is particularly interested in serving Lake County students from Hammond, Lake Station, Gary and East Chicago who are low-income or are the first in their family to attend college.
Requirements: The Grant will consider organizations that clearly demonstrate that college readiness or college access is a priority. These programs include, but are not limited to, tutoring, mentoring, academic enrichment programs, college preparation assistance, before and after school care, college tours and visits, and academic or financial aid counseling. Grants can be used to support the following: college readiness or college access staff; professional development and training related to college readiness and college access; program materials and software; test application fees; travel for college visits and related expenses; program participation incentives; and marketing and outreach efforts for college readiness or college access programs. Applicants should submit the online application, along with grant request cover pages; a detailed grant narrative; project budget and budget narrative; a list of the organization's board of directors and officers; summary of the organization's current fiscal year operating budget; copy of current fiscal year financial statements as well as financial audit or review; evidence of the board approval of this application; proof of nonprofit status; and organization's profile on GuideStar (www.guidestar.org).
Restrictions: The Grant concentrates on serving Lake County students from Hammond, Lake Station, Gary, and East Chicago. The proposed college preparatory program must serve youth who are Lake County residents, even though the services provided may take place outside of Lake County. Grant limitations include: endowment campaigns, annual campaigns, fundraising events; sponsorship of sports teams; previously incurred debt or retroactive funding for current projects; individual and independent scholarly research projects; and religious or sectarian programs, political parties or campaigns.
Geographic Focus: Indiana
Date(s) Application is Due: Apr 22
Amount of Grant: 5,000 - 25,000 USD
Contact: Barry Tyler; (219) 736-1880; fax (219) 736-1940; btyler@legacyfoundationlakeco.org
Internet: http://www.legacyfoundationlakeco.org/grantsfundingopps.html
Sponsor: Legacy Foundation
1000 East 80th Place, 302 South
Merrillville, IN 46410

Legacy Partners in Environmental Education Grants — 2875

Legacy provides environmental education grants annually through the Competitive Grants Program. Funds for this program are allocated specifically to assist with helping to create environmentally responsible citizens through education. The application is available at the Legacy website.
Requirements: Any nonprofit tax exempt Alabama organization or school planning a community-based environmental program is encouraged to apply.
Geographic Focus: Alabama
Date(s) Application is Due: Apr 27
Amount of Grant: Up to 10,000 USD
Contact: Paige Moreland; (334) 270-5921 or (800) 240-5115; paige@legacyenved.org
Internet: https://legacyenved.org/index.php/grants-and-scholarships/competitive-grants
Sponsor: Legacy Partners in Environmental Education
P.O. Box 3813
Montgomery, AL 36109

Legacy Partners in Environmental Education Mini-Grants — 2876

The Environmental Education Mini-Grant program provides funding for hands-on environmental education programs to communities in Alabama. Mini-grants assist Alabama citizens with local environmental projects. Although teachers make up the majority of applicants, any non-profit organization wishing to pursue a community-based environmental project in Alabama is encouraged to apply. Applicants may apply for up to $2,500. The application is available at the Legacy website.
Requirements: Both public and private non-profit organizations in Alabama may apply. All applying organizations need proof of tax-exempt status showing specific Internal Revenue Service qualification. Proposals must have a Project Director to implement and guide the proposal. The Director becomes the fiscal agent for the proposal and is responsible for the expenditure of any funds awarded. Two project reports (midterm and final) will be required. These reports will serve as an evaluation mechanism for the project. Failure to comply with reporting requirements and deadlines will result in termination of the current grant, and disqualification from future grant eligibility. The Project Director may be asked to present the project at Legacy's Annual Environmental Partnership Conference.
Geographic Focus: Alabama
Date(s) Application is Due: Apr 27
Amount of Grant: Up to 2,500 USD
Contact: Paige Moreland; (334) 270-5921 or (800) 240-5115; paige@legacyenved.org
Internet: https://legacyenved.org/index.php/grants-and-scholarships/mini-grants
Sponsor: Legacy Partners in Environmental Education
P.O. Box 3813
Montgomery, AL 36109

Legler Benbough Foundation Grants — 2877

The mission of the Foundation is to improve the quality of life of the people in the City of San Diego. To accomplish that mission, the Foundation focuses on three target areas: providing economic opportunity; enhancing cultural opportunity; and providing a focus for health, education and welfare funding. Interested applicants may submit an initial letter requesting funds. When the Foundation wishes to pursue the request, it will provide an application form to the applicant. Initial letters preceding applications are due by February 15 and August 15. Applications (for invited applicants) are due by March 15 and September 15.
Requirements: Funding focuses on activities in support of San Diego city arts and cultural institutions, scientific or research organizations, and health, education and welfare programs.
Restrictions: Awards are made only in the Foundation's focus areas. The following are not funded: capital projects unless there is a special situation where capital expenditure is the best way to achieve a stated objective; awards to individuals; awards for special events, fundraising or recognition events; and projects in the area of the homeless, AIDS, alcohol or drug rehabilitation or treatment and seniors.

Geographic Focus: California
Contact: Peter Ellsworth, President; (619) 235-8099; fax (619) 235-8077; peter@benboughfoundation.org
T*Internet:* http://www.benboughfoundation.org/criteria.php
Sponsor: Legler Benbough Foundation
2550 5th Avenue, Suite 132
San Diego, CA 92103-6622

LEGO Children's Fund Grants 2878
The LEGO Group is committed to helping children develop their creativity and learning skills through constructive play. The LEGO Children's Fund extends this commitment to local and national organizations that support innovative projects and programming to cultivate and celebrate a child's exploration of personal creativity and creative problem-solving in all forms. The Fund will provide quarterly grants for programs, either in part or in total, with a special interest paid to collaborative efforts and in providing matching funds to leverage new dollars into the receiving organization. Priority consideration will be given to programs that both meet the Fund's goals and are supported in volunteer time and effort by LEGO employees.
Requirements: Nonprofit organizations organizations and groups who cater to children ages birth - 14 with 501(c)3 status located anywhere in the United States are eligible to apply. Also eligible are educational organizations as defined in USC 26 § 170 (C) with specific, identifiable needs primarily in these areas of support: (1) Early childhood education and development that is directly related to creativity; (2) Technology and communication projects that advance learning opportunities. Special consideration will be given to applications from the Connecticut and Western Massachusetts area; groups that support disadvantaged children; groups that are supported by LEGO employee volunteers; and, special projects or programs designed to elevate a child's opportunities for exploring creativity. There are no restrictions on grant amounts up to the quarterly allocation. Typical awards, however are between USD $500 and USD $5,000.
Restrictions: The Foundation does not support: Individuals, scholarships, tuition, research, etc; Sectarian or religious oriented activities; Political activities including direct or grass roots lobbying; Offset the costs of tuition for undergraduate, graduate, or post-graduate education; Direct humanitarian and/or disaster relief; Capital campaigns; Debt retirement programs; Debt that has been incurred including mortgages, lines of credit, etc; Ongoing operating costs including completed projects, existing staff costs, existing organizational overhead, etc; Support general or annual fund raising drives; Support institutional benefits; Honorary functions; General endowments, annual appeals or similar appeals; Support overhead costs, operating budgets or staff salaries; Capital projects including, but not limited to, buildings, furniture or renovation projects; Deficit financing; Operating budgets; Efforts routinely supported by government agencies or the general public; Expansion or continuation funding of existing programs.
Geographic Focus: All States
Date(s) Application is Due: Jan 15; Apr 15; Jul 15; Oct 15
Amount of Grant: 500 - 5,000 USD
Contact: Grant Administrator; 860-763-6670; LEGOChildrensFund@lego.com
Internet: http://www.legochildrensfund.org/Guidelines.html
Sponsor: LEGO Children's Fund
P.O. Box 916
Enfield, CT 06083-0916

Leicester Savings Bank Fund 2879
The Fund supports projects that improve the quality of life and build a stronger community in Leicester, Massachusetts. To receive funding, applicants must state how they will use the grant to do the following: make a positive difference for the Leicester community's vulnerable citizens; improve Leicester community life through community development, education, recreation, the arts, or human services; and attract other resources or secure matching funds from public or private sources. Grants are available for capital expenditures (to acquire or renovate property or equipment) or for operating expenses of specific programs or projects undertaken by associations or organizations.
Requirements: Any non-municipal association or nonprofit organization that serves residents of Leicester is invited to apply.
Restrictions: Grants will generally not be awarded to individuals or to municipal agencies.
Geographic Focus: Massachusetts
Date(s) Application is Due: Apr 15
Contact: Pamela B. Kane, (508) 755-0980; pkane@greaterworcester.org
Internet: http://www.greaterworcester.org/grants/LSB.htm
Sponsor: Greater Worcester Community Foundation
370 Main Street, Suite 650
Worcester, MA 01608-1738

Leighton Award for Nonprofit Excellence 2880
The award is intended to celebrate, reward and encourage outstanding achievement in the charitable sector. Each year, this grant will be awarded competitively to a St. Joseph County nonprofit demonstrating superior leadership, management, and programming. The award is a $100,000 endowment challenge grant. Recipients must raise $100,000 in matching funds. The resulting $200,000 will be used to create or add to a fund in the Community Foundation of St. Joseph County for the award recipient's benefit. Foundation staff will also provide technical assistance as needed for raising the required match.
Requirements: Candidates must be nonprofit organizations, organized and operated exclusively for charitable purposes for the benefit of St. Joseph County residents. Recipients of the award may reapply after three years. The winner will be publicly announced each August/September by the foundation. Recipients will have until September 30 of the next year to secure $100,000 in matching gifts and pledges.
Restrictions: If the award recipient fails to raise the full amount within the year, the award will be reduced by the amount of the shortfall.
Geographic Focus: Indiana
Date(s) Application is Due: Jul 1
Amount of Grant: 100,000 USD
Contact: Christopher Nanni; (574) 232-0041; fax (574) 233-1906; chris@cfsjc.org
Internet: http://www.cfsjc.org/initiatives/leighton_award/lane_grants.html
Sponsor: Community Foundation of St. Joseph County
205 W Jefferson Boulevard, P.O. Box 837
South Bend, IN 46624

Lena Benas Memorial Fund Grants 2881
The Lena Benas Memorial Fund was established in 1986 to provide for the health, human services, and housing needs of underserved people living in Litchfield, Connecticut, and its surrounding communities. The deadline for application to the Fund is November 1, and applicants will be notified of grant decisions by letter within 2 months after the proposal deadline. Special consideration is given to organizations that provide housing maintenance and human services programming to needy populations.
Requirements: Preference is given to organizations serving the people of Litchfield, Connecticut. Organizations serving the towns contiguous to Litchfield, including Cornwall, Goshen, Harwinton, Morris, Thomaston, Torrington, Warren, Washington, and Watertown will also be considered.
Restrictions: Grants from the Benas Memorial Fund are 1 year in duration.
Geographic Focus: Connecticut
Date(s) Application is Due: Nov 1
Contact: Kate Kerchaert; (860) 657-7016; kate.kerchaert@baml.com
Internet: https://www.bankofamerica.com/philanthropic/fn_search.action
Sponsor: Lena Benas Memorial Fund
200 Glastonbury Boulevard, Suite #200, CT2-545-02-05
Glastonbury, CT 06033-4056

Leo Goodwin Foundation Grants 2882
The Leo Goodwin Foundation offers grants in the areas of arts, culture, humanities; education; health; human services; and public benefit. Types of support include: capital campaigns for museums and performing arts centers; literacy programs and educational foundations; community college scholarships; cancer research institutes; boys and girls clubs; and child care organizations. There are no deadlines, and organizations may apply at any time. The trustees meet once a month to assess requests for funding.
Requirements: Applicants must be 501(c)3 nonprofit organizations in the state of Florida. All requests must be submitted with the following information: cover letter stating purpose of program and amount requested; objectives, demographics - social and economic status, age, gender, etc; how funds will be used; operating budget, current audited statement and tax return; IRS 501(c)3 status letter; non-recovation statement; funding sources with amounts received; names and information of governing board members; outcome measures and results; and strategic partners or alliances in delivery of services.
Restrictions: Individuals are not eligible.
Geographic Focus: Florida
Amount of Grant: 1,000 - 25,000 USD
Contact: Helen Furia; (954) 772-6863; fax (954) 491-2051; hfurialgj@bellsouth.net
Internet: http://leogoodwinfoundation.org/
Sponsor: Leo Goodwin Foundation
800 Corporate Drive, Suite 500
Fort Lauderdale, FL 33334-3621

Leon and Thea Koerner Foundation Grants 2883
The purpose of the Koerner Foundation is to foster higher education, cultural activities, and public welfare in British Columbia and to stimulate and invigorate cultural and educational life by enabling institutions and individuals to undertake activities that would not normally be possible. Areas of interest include arts and culture, libraries, adult and continuing education, community colleges and universities, social services, special needs groups, community services, family services, and social issues. Applications are available at the Foundation website. Applications require a brief statement of the proposed project, its scope, time required for completion, results sought, total cost, amount requested from the foundation, specific purposes to which the grant will be applied, concise statement of resources available for the project, and a resume of its present state.
Requirements: Grants are made to organizations registered as educational or charitable institutions and organizations.
Restrictions: Individuals may not apply for grant support. Organizations may only receive funding three times within any five year period.
Geographic Focus: Canada
Contact: Grants Contact; (604) 224-2611; fax (604) 224-1059
Internet: http://www.koernerfoundation.ca/eligibility.html
Sponsor: Leon and Thea Koerner Foundation
3695 West 10th Avenue, P.O. Box 39209
Vancouver, BC V6R 4P1 Canada

Leonard L. and Bertha U. Abess Foundation Grants 2884
The Foundation, established in Miami in 1949 by the City National Bank co-founder Leonard L. Abess, Sr., is interested in supporting a number of local programs. Fields of interest include: education at all levels, Jewish agencies and temples, and federated giving programs. The primary type of support offered is for general operations. Applicants should forward a letter describing the program and an overall budget need. There are no particular deadlines with which to adhere, and giving is centered in the Miami, Florida, region.

Geographic Focus: Florida
Amount of Grant: Up to 25,000 USD
Contact: Leonard L. Abess; (305) 577-7333 or (800) 435-8839; fax (305) 577-7689
Sponsor: Leonard L. and Bertha U. Abess Foundation
25 W Flagler Street
Miami, FL 33130-1712

Leo Niessen Jr., Charitable Trust Grants 2885
Leo Niessen lived in Abington Township, Montgomery County, Pennsylvania. In 1993, his Foundation was funded from a testamentary bequest. He was a charitable man, who also made substantial philanthropic gifts to Holy Redeemer Hospital during his lifetime. He had a special affinity for Red Cloud Indian School of Pine Ridge, South Dakota. To this day, the Co-trustees of his Foundation continue to support this school, as well as the Hospital and The Society for the Propagation of the Faith. All grants are made in the memory of Leo Niessen and his family. The Foundation also supports organizations: that provide health services for all ages; which educate the needy and educable at all academic levels, without regard to age; working for and on behalf of youth and the elderly, and which provide assistance to the homeless and economically disadvantaged; which provide spiritual and emotional guidance. Application Deadlines are, January 31 and July 31. Application forms are available online. Applicants will receive notice acknowledging receipt of the grant request, and subsequently be notified of the grant declination or approval.
Requirements: Pennsylvania 501(c)3 nonprofit organizations are eligible to apply. Proposals should be submitted in the following format: completed Common Grant Application Form; an original Proposal Statement; an audited financial report and a current year operating budget; a copy of your official IRS Letter with your tax determination; a listing of your Board of Directors. Proposal Statements (second item in the above Format) should answer these questions: what are the objectives and expected outcomes of this program/project/request; what strategies will be used to accomplish your objective; what is the timeline for completion; if this is part of an on-going program, how long has it been in operation; what criteria will you use to measure success; if the request is not fully funded, what other sources can you engage; an Itemized budget should be included; please describe any collaborative ventures. Prior to the distribution of funds, all approved grantees must sign and return a Grant Agreement Form, stating that the funds will be used for the purpose intended. Progress reports and Completion reports must also be filed as required for your specific grant. All current grantees must be in good standing with required documentation prior to submitting new proposals to any foundation.
Restrictions: Grants are not made for political purposes, nor to organizations which discriminate on the basis of race, ethnic origin, sexual or religious preference, age or gender. The Niessen Foundation normally does not consider grants for endowment.
Geographic Focus: Pennsylvania
Date(s) Application is Due: Jan 31; Jul 31
Amount of Grant: 10,000 - 60,000 USD
Contact: Wachovia Bank, N.A., Trustee; grantinquiries3@wachovia.com
Internet: https://www.wachovia.com/foundation/v/index.jsp?vgnextoid=345852199c0aa110VgnVCM1000004b0d1872RCRD&vgnextfmt=default
Sponsor: Leo Niessen Jr., Charitable Trust
Wachovia Bank, N A. PA 1279, 1234 East Broad Street
Philadelphia, PA 19109-1199

Letha E. House Foundation Grants 2886
Established in Medina, Ohio, in 1967, the Letha E. House Foundation offers support for historical preservation, animal welfare, cemetery and burial services, and the environment. There are no specific deadlines or applications with which to adhere, and applicants should approach the Foundation with a 2-page letter describing the project and budgetary need.
Restrictions: No grants are given to individuals.
Geographic Focus: Ohio
Contact: Charles Clark Griesinger, (330) 723-6404 or (330) 764-7263; fax (330) 723-2007
Sponsor: Letha E. House Foundation
39 Public Square, Suite 100
Medina, OH 44256-2297

Lettie Pate Evans Foundation Grants 2887
Most grants are awarded to tax-exempt organizations in Georgia and occasionally in Virginia, with a strong emphasis on private secondary and higher education; museums, libraries, and the performing arts; and family and child welfare. Traditionally, preference has been given to one-time capital projects. Types of support include capital campaigns, building/renovation, equipment, land acquisition, program development, and seed grants. Awards for basic operating expenses usually are avoided. Grant requests may be submitted at any time. Proposals received by the February deadline will be considered at the April board meeting; those received by the September deadline will be considered at the November meeting. Organizations are encouraged to make an informal inquiry before submitting a proposal.
Requirements: The foundation makes grants to tax-exempt public charities in Georgia and, from time to time, Virginia.
Restrictions: The foundation does not make grants to institutions or agencies for activities attempting to influence legislation. Grants are never made to individuals or organizations for the benefit of a named individual.
Geographic Focus: Georgia, Virginia
Date(s) Application is Due: Feb 1; Sep 1
Contact: Charles McTier; (404) 522-6755; fax (404) 522-7026; fdns@woodruff.org
Internet: http://www.lpevans.org
Sponsor: Lettie Pate Evans Foundation
50 Hurt Plaza, Suite 1200
Atlanta, GA 30303

Lettie Pate Whitehead Foundation Grants 2888
Annual grants are made to accredited educational institutions in the nine specified states in the southeast to fund scholarships for the education of women. The grantee institutions award scholarships on the basis of need to Christian women who reside in one of the named states. Thousands of women receive financial assistance each year in individual amounts determined by the recipient institutions. While most scholarships go toward undergraduate higher education, the foundation maintains a special interest in health education. A significant number of its scholarship grants support education in the medical, nursing, and allied health care fields.
Requirements: Grants are awarded to institutions in Alabama, Florida, Georgia, Louisiana, Mississippi, North Carolina, South Carolina, Tennessee, and Virginia.
Geographic Focus: Alabama, Florida, Georgia, Louisiana, Mississippi, North Carolina, South Carolina, Tennessee, Virginia
Samples: Roanoke College (Salem, VA)—for financial-aid scholarships for women, $138,000; Catawba College (Salisbury, NC)—for scholarships for female students from nine Southern states, $63,000; Wofford College (Spartanburg, SC)—for scholarships, $72,000.
Contact: Program Contact; (404) 522-6755; fax (404) 522-7026; fdns@woodruff.org
Internet: http://www.lpwhitehead.org
Sponsor: Lettie Pate Whitehead Foundation
50 Hurt Plaza, Suite 1200
Atlanta, GA 30303

Lewis H. Humphreys Charitable Trust Grants 2889
The Lewis H. Humphreys Charitable Trust was established in 2004 to support and promote quality educational, cultural, human-services, and health-care programming for underserved and disadvantaged populations. In the area of arts, culture, and humanities, the trust supports programming that: fosters the enjoyment and appreciation of the visual and performing arts; strengthens humanities and arts-related education programs; provides affordable access; enhances artistic elements in communities; and nurtures a new generation of artists. In the area of education, the trust supports programming that: promotes effective teaching; improves the academic achievement of, or expands educational opportunities for, disadvantaged students; improves governance and management; strengthens nonprofit organizations, school leadership, and teaching; and bolsters strategic initiatives of area colleges and universities. In the area of health, the trust supports programming that improves the delivery of health care to the indigent, uninsured, and other vulnerable populations and addresses health and health-care problems that intersect with social factors. In the area of human services, the trust funds programming that: strengthens agencies that deliver critical human services and maintains the community's safety net and helps agencies respond to federal, state, and local public policy changes. In the area of community improvement, the trust funds capacity-building and infrastructure-development projects including: assessments, planning, and implementation of technology for management and programmatic functions within an organization; technical assistance on wide-ranging topics, including grant writing, strategic planning, financial management services, business development, board and volunteer management, and marketing; and mergers, affiliations, or other restructuring efforts. Grant requests for general operating support, program support, and capital support will be considered. Grant requests for capital support, such as for buildings, land, and major equipment should meet a compelling community need and offer a broad social benefit. Grants from the trust are one year in duration. Application materials are available for download at the grant website. Applicants are strongly encouraged to review the state application guidelines for additional helpful information and clarifications before applying. Applicants are also encouraged to review the trust's funding history (link is available from the grant website). Grant applications can be submitted between August 1 and September 30. Applicants will be notified of grant decisions by November 30.
Requirements: Applicants must have 501(c)3 tax-exempt status and serve the residents of Kansas. Grant application materials must be mailed.
Restrictions: The trust does not support requests from individuals, organizations attempting to influence policy through direct lobbying, or any political campaigns.
Geographic Focus: Kansas
Date(s) Application is Due: Sep 30
Contact: James Mueth, Vice President; (816) 292-4342; james.mueth@baml.com
Internet: https://www.bankofamerica.com/philanthropic/fn_search.action
Sponsor: Lewis H. Humphreys Charitable Trust
1200 Main Street, 14th Floor, P.O. Box 219119
Kansas City, MO 64121-9119

Liberty Bank Foundation Grants 2890
The foundation's charitable giving is focused primarily on organizations that provide meaningful programs and activities that benefit people within Liberty Bank's market area. Of particular interest are programs and activities that provide assistance and opportunities to improve the quality of life for people of low income, especially families in crisis or at-risk. Top priorities for funding include community and economic development—affordable housing for low/moderate-income individuals and families, community and neighborhood capacity-building, and community services targeted to low/moderate-income individuals; education—programs that address the needs of low/moderate-income individuals; health care and human services—outreach and educational programs on health issues, quality child care, homeless shelters and services, services for victims of domestic violence, and transitional housing assistance; and arts and culture—programs that increase access to arts and culture for people of low income who might not otherwise be able to participate in them. Grants generally support specific programs rather than capital projects, equipment, or general operating expenses. Organizations that have received funding in two consecutive calendar years should refrain from reapplying for one calendar year. Contact the office to discuss the project prior to applying. Guideline and application are available online.
Requirements: 501(c)3 tax-exempt organizations are eligible.

Restrictions: Individuals, fraternal groups, and organizations that are not open to the general public are ineligible. Grants do not support annual funds of colleges, universities or hospitals; trips, tours, or conferences; scientific or medical research; deficit spending or debt liquidation; lobbying or otherwise influencing the outcome of the legislative or electoral process; religious groups, except for nonsectarian programs; or endowments or other foundations.
Geographic Focus: Connecticut
Date(s) Application is Due: Mar 31; Jun 30; Sep 30; Dec 31
Contact: Grants Administrator; (860) 704-2181; smurphy@liberty-bank.com
Internet: http://www.liberty-bank.com/liberty_foundation.asp
Sponsor: Liberty Bank Foundation
P.O. Box 1212
Middletown, CT 06457

Liberty Hill Foundation Environmental Justice Fund Grants 2891
Liberty Hill's Environmental Justice Fund is dedicated to improving public health in low-income communities that suffer disproportionately from environmental pollution. This fund makes grants to grassroots organizations that are working to decrease exposure to toxic substances in neighborhoods and workplaces, particularly in communities of color and low-income areas. Groups engaged in community organizing, applied research, policy advocacy, litigation, or popular education are eligible. One-year grants, ranging from $7,500 to $35,000 each, and two-year grants, from $50,000 to $70,000 each, are awarded.
Requirements: Los Angeles County, California, grassroots, proactive, community organizations that are committed to diversity, with a record of leadership development through a democratic process, are eligible.
Restrictions: The foundation does not fund social service providers that do not have a strong community organizing component, projects directed at constituencies outside Los Angeles County, individual efforts, film projects, groups that received foundation funding in the previous funding cycle, direct union organizing, nor businesses or profit-making ventures. Liberty Hill generally does not fund travel expenses, equipment purchases, or research.
Geographic Focus: California
Date(s) Application is Due: Nov 1
Amount of Grant: 50,000 - 70,000 USD
Contact: James Williams, (310) 453-3611, ext. 114; jwilliams@libertyhill.org
Internet: http://www.libertyhill.org/donor/environment.html
Sponsor: Liberty Hill Foundation
2121 Cloverfield Boulevard, Suite 113
Santa Monica, CA 90404

Liberty Hill Foundation Fund for a New Los Angeles Grants 2892
The Fund for a New Los Angeles makes grants of $20,000 to $35,000 to organizations with proven track records, mature leadership, and solid constituency that are actively organizing for racial equality, economic justice and community development. The goal is to help these organizations build strong institutions.
Requirements: Los Angeles County, California, grassroots, proactive, community organizations that are committed to diversity, with a record of leadership development through a democratic process, are eligible.
Restrictions: The foundation does not fund social service providers that do not have a strong community organizing component, projects directed at constituencies outside Los Angeles County, individual efforts, film projects, groups that received foundation funding in the previous funding cycle, direct union organizing, nor businesses or profit-making ventures. Liberty Hill generally does not fund travel expenses, equipment purchases, or research.
Geographic Focus: California
Amount of Grant: 20,000 - 35,000 USD
Contact: James Williams, (310) 453-3611, ext. 114; jwilliams@libertyhill.org
Internet: http://www.libertyhill.org/donor/newla.html
Sponsor: Liberty Hill Foundation
2121 Cloverfield Boulevard, Suite 113
Santa Monica, CA 90404

Liberty Hill Foundation Fund for Change Grants 2893
Through this program, the foundation supports high-impact social change that leads to cultivating effective community leaders, seeding emerging organizations, and developing a base of grassroots activists within the areas of economic and racial justice, environmental justice, and lesbian/gay/bisexual/transgender/queer justice. Grants will range from $10,000 to $35,000, paid for one year, and can be applied in one of four areas: capacity building, general support, project-specific support, and seed funding.
Requirements: Eligible applicants must have 501(c)3 status, or be the fiscal sponsor of a nonprofit organization.
Geographic Focus: California
Amount of Grant: 10,000 - 35,000 USD
Contact: James Williams, (310) 453-3611, ext. 114; jwilliams@libertyhill.org
Internet: http://www.libertyhill.org/fundphilosophy/
Sponsor: Liberty Hill Foundation
2121 Cloverfield Boulevard, Suite 113
Santa Monica, CA 90404

Liberty Hill Foundation Lesbian & Gay Community Fund Grants 2894
The fund was created to provide critical support for programs serving the needs of lesbian, gay, bisexual, transgender, and queer (LGBTQ) communities. Grants are targeted to groups actively working for institutional, policy, or public opinion changes that improve LGBTQ life and well-being and build alliances between LGBTQ and straight communities. Grants range from $7,500 to $30,000.
Requirements: Los Angeles County, California, grassroots, proactive, community organizations that are committed to diversity, with a record of leadership development through a democratic process, are eligible.
Restrictions: The foundation does not fund social service providers that do not have a strong community organizing component, projects directed at constituencies outside Los Angeles County, individual efforts, film projects, groups that received foundation funding in the previous funding cycle, direct union organizing, nor businesses or profit-making ventures. Liberty Hill generally does not fund travel expenses, equipment purchases, or research.
Geographic Focus: California
Date(s) Application is Due: Jan 22
Amount of Grant: Up to 30,000 USD
Contact: James Williams, (310) 453-3611, ext. 114; jwilliams@libertyhill.org
Internet: http://www.libertyhill.org/donor/lesbianandgay.html
Sponsor: Liberty Hill Foundation
2121 Cloverfield Boulevard, Suite 113
Santa Monica, CA 90404

Liberty Hill Foundation Queer Youth Fund Grants 2895
The Queer Youth Fund makes multi-year grants to grassroots, local, state or national nonprofit organizations located anywhere in the United States working to improve the quality of life among gay, lesbian, bisexual, transgender, queer and questioning (GLBTQQ) youth. Youth are defined as 24 years old and younger. The Queer Youth Fund awards grants to innovative and effective leadership development programs or organizing projects that empower GLBTQQ youth to improve societal conditions affecting GLBTQQ youth and that make a long-term difference to their movement. Up to four $100,000 grants, payable over three to five years, will be made to grassroots, local, state, national, and international nonprofit organizations that empower queer youth to improve societal conditions for GLBTQQ youth.
Requirements: Eligible organizations must have a total budget for their youth work of $750,000 or less.
Restrictions: Liberty Hill generally does not fund travel expenses, equipment purchases, or research.
Geographic Focus: All States
Date(s) Application is Due: Oct 2
Contact: James Williams, (310) 453-3611, ext. 114; jwilliams@libertyhill.org
Internet: http://www.libertyhill.org/donor/qyf.html
Sponsor: Liberty Hill Foundation
2121 Cloverfield Boulevard, Suite 113
Santa Monica, CA 90404

Liberty Hill Foundation Seed Fund Grants 2896
The hallmark of Liberty Hill's grant making is its Seed Fund, providing one-year grants of $10,000 to $20,000 to organizations tackling social, racial and economic justice issues that are often too new or too controversial to attract funding from more traditional sources. The Seed Fund is often the catalyst that turns someone's vision for a better future into a solid plan of action capable of changing lives as well as communities.
Requirements: Los Angeles County, California, grassroots, proactive, community organizations that are committed to diversity, with a record of leadership development through a democratic process, are eligible.
Restrictions: The foundation does not fund social service providers that do not have a strong community organizing component, projects directed at constituencies outside Los Angeles County, individual efforts, film projects, groups that received foundation funding in the previous funding cycle, direct union organizing, nor businesses or profit-making ventures. Liberty Hill generally does not fund travel expenses, equipment purchases, or research.
Geographic Focus: California
Date(s) Application is Due: Aug 15
Contact: James Williams, (310) 453-3611, ext. 114; jwilliams@libertyhill.org
Internet: http://libertyhill.org/donor/seed.html
Sponsor: Liberty Hill Foundation
2121 Cloverfield Boulevard, Suite 113
Santa Monica, CA 90404

Liberty Hill Foundation Special Opportunity Fund Grants 2897
The Special Opportunity Fund is Liberty Hill's rapid response fund. The fund provides grants of up to $3,000 to help groups respond to special organizational development and training opportunities that are timely and require a modest amount of funding. The fund can fulfill a variety of organizational needs, particularly capacity building, technical assistance, and training. Through this fund, the foundation has supported such projects as strategic planning, organizer training, leadership development, technical assistance, and special and timely education and outreach campaigns.
Requirements: Los Angeles County, California, grassroots, proactive, community organizations that are committed to diversity, with a record of leadership development through a democratic process, are eligible.
Restrictions: No support for direct social service projects, private businesses, profit-making ventures, direct union organizing, or electioneering for candidates for public office. No grants for film or video projects, conferences, one-time events that are not linked to social change organizing strategies, or capital campaigns for land or buildings.
Geographic Focus: California
Contact: James Williams, (310) 453-3611, ext. 114; jwilliams@libertyhill.org
Internet: http://www.libertyhill.org/donor/specialopp.html
Sponsor: Liberty Hill Foundation
2121 Cloverfield Boulevard, Suite 113
Santa Monica, CA 90404

Libra Foundation Future Grants 2898
Libra Future Fund was created to capitalize upon the energy and creativity that Maine's young people embody and to combat youth out-migration by supporting initiatives that increase the number of Maine-based professional opportunities. To that end, Libra Future Fund awards grants to individuals to promote economic development or create job opportunities in Maine. In addition, projects should provide the applicant with substantial professional or educational experience. Projects are typically entrepreneurial in nature, such as fledgling businesses in need of startup capital, but LFF will consider other types of projects that contribute to Maine's economy. In addition, projects should provide the applicant with substantial professional or educational experience. The Libra Future Fund Board of Directors meets in April, July and November to consider grant applications. Once paper applications have been reviewed, the Board schedules meetings with potential grant recipients, and the Directors pose specific questions regarding project ideas. Funding decisions are made based upon both the paper applications and in-person interviews. Once the Board determines which applicants will receive funding, the Directors work with recipients to arrange a funding schedule. This funding schedule reflects the monetary needs of recipient's project at different points during project completion and is based upon the timelines submitted by the grant recipient.
Requirements: Applicants must be between the ages of 18 and 29 and reside in Maine at least 8 months per year. Applicants originally from Maine, but who are attending school out of state, are also eligible to apply.
Geographic Focus: Maine
Date(s) Application is Due: Apr 1; Jul 1; Nov 1
Contact: Erik Hayward; (207) 879-6280; fax (207) 879-6281; erik@librafoundation.org
Internet: http://librafoundation.org/funding-guidelines
Sponsor: Libra Foundation
Three Canal Plaza, Suite 500
Portland, ME 04112-8516

Libra Foundation Grants 2899
The Libra Foundation awards grants to Maine nonprofits in its areas of interest, including art, culture, and humanities; education; health; human services; environment; justice; public/society benefit; and religion. The Foundation makes grants to organizations that it expects to develop innovative and sustainable Maine-based business initiatives and programs that provide for the welfare and betterment of children. The aforementioned activities comprise the majority of the Foundation's charitable giving. The application is available online.
Requirements: Organizations must be in Maine and 501(c)3 nonprofits to apply.
Restrictions: Individuals are ineligible. The Foundation does not provide funding to supplement annual campaigns, regular operating needs, multi-year projects, individuals, scholarships, or travel.
Geographic Focus: Maine
Date(s) Application is Due: Feb 15; May 15; Aug 15; Nov 15
Contact: Elizabeth Flaherty, Executive Assistant; (207) 879-6280
Internet: http://librafoundation.org/application-procedures
Sponsor: Libra Foundation
Three Canal Plaza, Suite 500
Portland, ME 04112-8516

Lied Foundation Trust Grants 2900
The foundation awards grants primarily to Nebraska and Nevada nonprofits in its areas of youth organizations, higher education, and arts and culture. The foundation favors programs that have some educational aspect to them. Types of support include building construction/renovation, equipment acquisition, program development, endowment funds, and scholarship funds.
Requirements: Nonprofit organizations in Nevada, Nebraska, Kansas and Iowa may apply. There is no specific form to complete.
Geographic Focus: Iowa, Kansas, Nebraska, Nevada
Contact: Christina Hixson, Trustee; (702) 878-1559
Sponsor: Lied Foundation Trust
3907 West Charleston Boulevard
Las Vegas, NV 89102

Lillian S. Wells Foundation Grants 2901
The Lillian S. Wells Foundation established in 1976, primarily supports the Fort Lauderdale, Florida, and Chicago, Illinois regions with funding interests that include: medical research, with emphasis on brain cancer research, women's health, substance abuse, and at-risk youth. Additional funding for education and the arts. Contact the Foundation for an application form, the Board meets quarterly in January, April, July, and October.
Requirements: Nonprofit organizations in Chicago, Illinois and Fort Lauderdale, Florida area are eligible to apply.
Geographic Focus: Florida, Illinois
Date(s) Application is Due: Mar 15; Jun 15; Sep 15; Dec 15
Contact: Patricia F. Mulvaney, Executive Director; patricia.mulvaney@thewellsfamily.net
Sponsor: Lillian S. Wells Foundation
600 Sagamore Road
Fort Lauderdale, FL 33301-2215

Lilly Endowment Clergy Renewal Program for Indiana Congregations 2902
The Clergy Renewal Programs awards grants to Indiana congregations that offer a program for the renewal of their pastor, while also giving the congregations themselves an opportunity to better themselves as vital places of worship and mission. The Endowment will provide as many as 40 congregations with up to $50,000. Up to $15,000 of that amount may be used to help the congregation fulfill pastoral duties in the pastor's absence. The program is for ordained pastors who are serious about parish ministry and who can envision this program as a means of renewing a long-term commitment to that congregation and to ordained ministry. Proposal instructions are available at the Foundation website. The website also contains several documents with tips on writing proposals.
Requirements: Indiana congregations may apply for a clergy renewal program grant for any of its ordained pastors. A joint proposal may be submitted for husband-and-wife co-pastors. Spouses serving different congregations may each apply from the congregation they serve and may include each other in the renewal program. Congregations with multiple pastors who are not spouses may submit one application for only one pastor per year. However, three years must have lapsed before an additional grant can be awarded. In addition, all the requirements of the previous grant must have been fulfilled in a satisfactory and timely manner, including final narrative reports from the pastor and the congregation and a financial report from the congregation. A pastor must be a member in good standing of his or her denomination. The congregation must commit to continue the pastor's salary and benefits during the renewal program. The pastor and an authorized congregational leader need to certify the pastor's intent to remain in the congregation at least one year after completing the program.
Restrictions: Four sets of the grant application must be mailed directly to the Endowment. emailed or faxed applications will not be accepted. The Endowment will not accept applications for renewal programs from clergy serving on military bases or for chaplains in colleges, universities, hospitals, or prisons. The clergy renewal program is not intended to be a fellowship program for work toward an academic degree, including the doctor of ministry degree. It is acceptable for some part of the program to involve travel and research. However, if plans are strictly dedicated to work involved in pursuit of a degree, applicants are advised to find support elsewhere. The Endowment does not encourage the use of professional grant writers who are outside the circle of the congregation applying for this grant. Creating and writing the proposal is intended as a collaboration between the pastor and the congregation.
Geographic Focus: Indiana
Date(s) Application is Due: Mar 12
Contact: Jean Smith, Program Director; (317) 916-7350
Internet: http://www.lillyendowment.org/religion_crpic.html
Sponsor: Lilly Endowment
2801 N Meridian Street, P.O. Box 88068
Indianapolis, IN 46208-0068

Lilly Endowment Giving Indiana Funds for Tomorrow Grants 2903
The Giving Indiana Funds for Tomorrow (GIFT) Grants strive to expand the concept of community foundations to Indiana counties and to increase the endowments of existing community foundations in the state. The GIFT Grants also build the capacity of Indiana communities to be self-reliant and better able to shape their own destinies by having local control over their own resources. The Indiana Grantmakers Alliance Foundation (IGAF) provides technical assistance for the GIFT initiative, which includes an annual calendar of programs and on-site visits for community foundations. Technical assistance and training are available to all participants, including board members, staff and volunteers. Organizations are encouraged to
Requirements: Applicants are encouraged to submit a letter of inquiry to see if their project is appropriate for the GIFT grant. Inquiry letters must be submitted through the mail; emailed or faxed letters will not be considered.
Restrictions: Only Indiana organizations are eligible to apply. The Endowment generally does not support loans or cash grants to private individuals; requests to discharge pre-existing debts of individuals or organizations; health-care projects; mass media projects; libraries; or organizations outside of Indianapolis.
Geographic Focus: Indiana
Contact: Ace Yakey, Program Director; (317) 916-7307
Internet: http://www.lillyendowment.org/cd_gift.html
Sponsor: Lilly Endowment
2801 N Meridian Street, P.O. Box 88068
Indianapolis, IN 46208-0068

Lily Auchincloss Foundation Grants 2904
The foundation supports art, education, human services, and preservation/environment programs located within the five boroughs of New York City. The Foundation has three deadlines per year: March 15, August 15, and December 15. The online application is available one month prior to each deadline.
Requirements: The Foundation funds only 501(c)3 organizations located within the five boroughs of New York City.
Restrictions: The foundation is not considering proposals for dance, film, music, or theater programs; does not award grants to individuals; and generally will not support research projects, mental health programs, medical services (including hospitals and nursing homes), substance abuse programs, and private schools.
Geographic Focus: New York
Date(s) Application is Due: Mar 15; Aug 15; Dec 15
Contact: Rossana Martínez; (212) 737-9533; fax (212) 737-9578; info@lilyauch.org
Internet: http://www.lilyauch.org
Sponsor: Lily Auchincloss Foundation
16 East 79th Street, #31
New York, NY 10075

Lily Palmer Fry Memorial Trust Grants 2905
The Lily Palmer Fry Memorial Trust was established in 1954 to support and promote summer camp opportunities for underserved children. Special consideration is given to traditional camp programs that take urban children out of the city to experience the natural environment. The Fry Memorial Trust prefers to fund "camperships" for children and not other expenses of the camp such as supplies, salaries, etc. Grants from the Fry Memorial

Trust are one year in duration. Applicants must apply online at the grant website. Applicants are strongly encouraged to do the following before applying: review the downloadable state application procedures for additional helpful information and clarifications; review the downloadable online-application guidelines at the grant website; review the trust's funding history (link is available from the grant website); review the online application questions in advance; and review the list of required attachments. These will generally include: a list of board members, financial statements (audited, reviewed, or compiled by independent auditor); an organization summary; a list of other funding sources; an IRS Determination letter; and other required documents. All attachments must be uploaded in the online application as PDF, Word, or Excel files. The deadline for application to the Lily Palmer Fry Memorial Trust is 11:59 p.m. on February 1. Applicants will be notified of grant decisions by letter within two to three months after the proposal deadline.
Restrictions: Organizations must serve residents of New York City and Westchester County, New York, and Fairfield and Hartford Counties, Connecticut.
Geographic Focus: Connecticut, New York
Date(s) Application is Due: Feb 1
Contact: Kate Kerchaert; (860) 657-7016; kate.kerchaert@baml.com
Internet: https://www.bankofamerica.com/philanthropic/fn_search.action
Sponsor: Lily Palmer Fry Memorial Trust
200 Glastonbury Boulevard, Suite # 200, CT2-545-02-05
Glastonbury, CT 06033-4056

Lincoln Financial Group Foundation Grants 2906
As one of the country's premier financial services organizations, Lincoln Financial Group is committed to providing its customers with the life insurance, retirement and investment products and services they need to maintain their quality of life. As a concerned corporate citizen, the company's foundation has sustained a strategic philanthropic program to improve the quality of life in the communities where employees live and work. These communities include: Chicago, Illinois; Concord, New Hampshire; Fort Wayne, Indiana; Greensboro, North Carolina; Hartford, Connecticut; Omaha, Nebraska; Philadelphia, Pennsylvania.
Requirements: The Lincoln Financial Foundation welcomes grant applications from organizations that meet our geographic, strategic focus, and eligibility guidelines. Local Charitable Contribution Committees meet and review grant applications. Only nonprofit organizations that have a 501(c)3 designation from the Internal Revenue Service are eligible to apply for funding. To apply for a grant, complete the Lincoln Financial Foundation application by using the online form and submitting it electronically. Grant submission deadlines are: Arts and Culture grants applications must be received by January 15; Education/Workforce Development grant applications must be received by April 21; Human Services grant applications must be received by July 21. Applications are reviewed by the local contribution committees within three to four months after the cycle deadline. Notification will be given soon after decisions are rendered.
Restrictions: Qualified organizations are eligible for one grant per calendar year. In general, the Lincoln Foundation will not award grants to: individuals; religious organizations; public or private elementary or secondary schools or school foundations; hospitals or hospital foundations; fraternal, political, or war veteran organizations; general operating support; capital funding; endowments.
Geographic Focus: Connecticut, Illinois, Indiana, Nebraska, New Hampshire, North Carolina, Pennsylvania, United Kingdom
Date(s) Application is Due: Jan 15; Apr 21; Jul 21
Amount of Grant: 5,000 - 75,000 USD
Contact: Jean Vrabel; (260) 455-3868; fax (260) 455-4004; Jean.Vrabel@LFG.com
Internet: http://www.lfg.com/LincolnPageServer?LFGPage=/lfg/lfgclient/abt/fingrp/hta/index.html
Sponsor: Lincoln Financial Group Foundation
1300 S Clinton Street, P.O. Box 7863
Fort Wayne, IN 46802

Lindbergh Grants 2907
Grants are awarded to individuals whose proposed projects represent a significant contribution toward the achievement of a better balance between technology and our human and natural environment. Nine to 10 grants are awarded each year. The current funding program is interested in increasing representation in the following areas: aviation/aerospace; agriculture; arts and humanities; biomedical research; conservation of natural resources; exploration; health and population sciences; intercultural communication; oceanography; water resources management; waste disposal management; wildlife preservation; and adaptive technology. Grant application can be obtained by writing the fund; enclose a self-addressed, stamped envelope with request. The Web site contains additional information.
Requirements: Grants are international in scope and open to citizens of all countries. Letters of request, proposals, endorser reports, and required progress and final reports must be submitted in English. The fund welcomes candidates who may or may not be affiliated with academic or nonprofit institutions. Grants are made to individuals, not to affiliated institutions for institutional programs. Note: When sending any materials by fax, seven hard copies via mail or delivery are requested. The deadline for grant applications is the second Thursday of June in the year preceding the awarding of funds.
Restrictions: The fund does not provide support for overhead costs of organizations, tuition, scholarships, fellowships, or travel related to such.
Geographic Focus: All States
Date(s) Application is Due: Jun 9
Contact: Coordinator; (763) 576-1596; fax (763) 576-1664; info@lindberghfoundation.org
Internet: http://www.lindberghfoundation.org/grants
Sponsor: Charles A. and Anne Morrow Lindbergh Foundation
2150 Third Avenue N, Suite 310
Anoka, MN 55303-2200

Linden Foundation Grants 2908
The Linden Foundation funds direct program support, general operating support, and occasionally very modest capital needs associated with a particular program. Existing programs, expansion of successful pilot programs, and new programs may all be considered for funding. The Foundation generally makes initial grants for amounts up to $10,000. The Foundation prefers to fund partial support for a project and welcomes the opportunity to join with other philanthropic funders in underwriting an endeavor. Please note that the Linden Foundation is not currently accepting any new inquiries or applications.
Requirements: The Linden Foundation will invite selected organizations to submit proposals. No unsolicited Full Proposals will be considered. Please note that most of the Foundation's grants budget is allocated to renewed funding since much of the Foundation's funding is multi-year. All grant applicants must be non-profit, 501(c)3 organizations, generally serving disadvantaged, low-income communities in the following areas: the northern side of the greater Boston area, with emphasis on communities inside Route 128 and the North Shore to the Gloucester area; and, the counties of the Lakes Region and northern New Hampshire.
Restrictions: No grants will be made to individuals, public schools, charter schools, colleges, or universities. No grants will be made to support community organizing, political lobbying efforts, or stand-alone enrichment activities, such as tickets to artistic and musical performances. Due to limited funding, no grants will be made for computer centers or general operating support for community centers.
Geographic Focus: Massachusetts, New Hampshire
Date(s) Application is Due: Jun 1; Dec 1
Contact: Ruth Victorin; (617) 426-7080 ext. 288; rvictorin@gmafoundations.com
Internet: http://www.lindenfoundation.org/grants.html
Sponsor: Linden Foundation
77 Summer Street, 8th Floor
Boston, MA 02110-1006

Linford and Mildred White Charitable Fund Grants 2909
The Linford and Mildred White Charitable Fund was established in 1956 to support and promote quality educational, human-services, and health-care programming for underserved populations within the city of Waterbury, Connecticut, and its surrounding communities. Grants from the White Charitable Fund are one year in duration. Applicants must apply online at the grant website. Applicants are strongly encouraged to do the following before applying: review the downloadable state application procedures for additional helpful information and clarifications; review the downloadable online-application guidelines at the grant website; review the foundation's funding history (link is available from the grant website); review the online application questions in advance; and review the list of required attachments. These will generally include: a list of board members, financial statements (audited, reviewed, or compiled by independent auditor); an organization summary; a list of other funding sources; an IRS Determination letter; and other required documents. All attachments must be uploaded in the online application as PDF, Word, or Excel files. The deadline for application to the Linford and Mildred White Charitable Fund is 11:59 p.m. on July 1. Applicants will receive notification of grant decisions by letter within two to three months after the proposal deadline.
Requirements: Applicant organizations must have 501(c)3 status and serve the people of Waterbury, Connecticut, and its vicinity.
Restrictions: Grant requests for capital projects will not be considered. Applicants will not be awarded a grant for more than 3 consecutive years. The fund does not support requests from individuals, organizations attempting to influence policy through direct lobbying, or any political campaigns.
Geographic Focus: Connecticut
Date(s) Application is Due: Jul 1
Contact: Carmen Britt; (860) 657-7019; carmen.britt@baml.com
Internet: https://www.bankofamerica.com/philanthropic/fn_search.action
Sponsor: Linford and Mildred White Charitable Fund
200 Glastonbury Boulevard, Suite # 200, CT2-545-02-05
Glastonbury, CT 06033-4056

Lisa and Douglas Goldman Fund Grants 2910
Established in 1992 the Lisa and Douglas Goldman Fund is a private foundation committed to providing support for charitable organizations that enhance society. As natives of San Francisco, the Goldmans place a high priority on projects that have a positive impact on San Francisco and the Bay Area. Interests and priorities include: children and youth; civic affairs; civil and human rights; education; environmental affairs; health; Jewish affairs; literacy; organizational development; population; social and human services; and sports and recreation.
Requirements: After reviewing the Fund's interests and priorities interested applicants may submit an initial letter of inquiry. Applicants who receive a favorable response will be invited to submit a formal proposal with supporting materials. Applicants are encouraged to contact the Fund directly with questions regarding the appropriateness of a project. There are no deadlines.
Restrictions: The following are ineligible: grants to individuals; documentaries and films; events/conferences; books and periodicals; research; and deficit budgets. Applications for annual support are not accepted. Organizations may submit only one request per year.
Geographic Focus: All States
Contact: Nancy D. Kami, Executive Director; (415) 771-1717; fax (415) 771-1797
Internet: http://fdncenter.org/grantmaker/goldman
Sponsor: Lisa and Douglas Goldman Fund
One Daniel Burnham Court, Suite 330C
San Francisco, CA 94109-5460

LISC Financial Opportunity Center Social Innovation Fund Grants   2911
With support from the Social Innovation Fund, this program awards funds to be used to support an integrated service model that focuses on improving the financial situation for low- to moderate-income families by helping people boost earnings, reduce expenses, and make appropriate financial decisions that lead to asset-building. These centers provide individuals and families with services across three critical and interconnected areas: employment placement, job retention, and skill improvement; financial coaching and counseling; and accessing income support and public benefits. Grants of at least $100,000 will be awarded; applicants must demonstrate a 1:1 cash match of non-federal funding.
Requirements: Eligible organizations must have 501(c)3 status and be located in the following cities: Chicago; greater Cincinnati (including northern Kentucky); metropolitan Detroit; Duluth, Minnesota; Houston; Indianapolis; Minneapolis/St. Paul; Providence/Woonsocket, Rhode Island; San Diego; and the San Francisco Bay Area (including Oakland, Richmond, San Francisco, and San Jose).
Geographic Focus: California, Illinois, Indiana, Kentucky, Michigan, Minnesota, Ohio, Rhode Island, Texas
Contact: Stephen Sagner; (212) 455-9800; fax (212) 682-5929; csi@liscnet.org
Internet: http://www.lisc.org/section/ourwork/grants_services
Sponsor: Local Initiatives Support Corporation
501 7th Avenue, 7th Floor
New York, NY 10018-5903

LISC MetLife Foundation Community-Police Partnership Awards   2912
Awarded in conjunction with the MetLife Foundation, these Community-Police Partnership Awards recognize, sustain, and share the work of innovative partnerships between community groups and police to promote neighborhood safety and revitalization. Awards will be given in two categories. Neighborhood Revitalization Awards, ranging from $15,000 to $25,000, will be awarded to exemplary collaborative programs between community groups and police that yield crime reduction as well as economic development outcomes, such as real estate development, business attraction, and job growth. Special Strategy Awards of $15,000 each will be awarded to five partnerships between community and police who have achieved significant accomplishments in one of the following areas: applied technology, aesthetics and greenspace improvement, diversity inclusion and integration, drug market disruption, gang prevention and youth safety, and seniors and safety.
Geographic Focus: All States
Amount of Grant: 15,000 - 25,000 USD
Contact: Stephen Sagner; (212) 455-9800; fax (212) 682-5929; csi@liscnet.org
Internet: http://www.lisc.org/section/ourwork/grants_services
Sponsor: Local Initiatives Support Corporation
501 7th Avenue, 7th Floor
New York, NY 10018-5903

LISC NFL Grassroots Grants   2913
In partnership with the National Football League Youth Football Fund, this program provides nonprofit, neighborhood-based organizations with financial and technical assistance to improve the quality, safety, and accessibility of local football fields. Applicants may request a maximum of $250,000 from the program to be used for capital improvements. Strong preference will be given to those proposals that seek to upgrade existing facilities that are in poor condition or otherwise underutilized; demonstrate active use of the fields; attract matching funding that exceeds the minimum required match of 1:1; involve local partnerships with non-profit community partners (i.e. parks and recreational departments, YMCA branches) to promote youth and community programming on the fields; and provide for continuing maintenance and field safety. There are two levels of funding available. Requests of up to $50,000 will be accepted for general field support (e.g., irrigation, bleachers, lights, etc.); matching grants of up to $200,000 are also available to help finance the resurfacing of football fields. A smaller number of matching grants of up to $100,000 each will be available to help finance the resurfacing of a football field utilizing natural grass/sod surfaces.
Requirements: In order to be eligible, projects must be sponsored by community-based nonprofit 501(c)3 organizations or middle or high schools. In addition, all organizations applying for funds must be located specifically and exclusively within NFL target markets and serve low- to moderate-income areas within those markets.
Geographic Focus: All States
Amount of Grant: Up to 250,000 USD
Contact: Stephen Sagner; (212) 455-9800; fax (212) 682-5929; csi@liscnet.org
Internet: http://www.grantselect.com/editor/view_grant/119281
Sponsor: Local Initiatives Support Corporation
501 7th Avenue, 7th Floor
New York, NY 10018-5903

Liz Claiborne and Art Ortenberg Foundation Grants   2914
The Foundation awards grants in the U.S. Western region and Third World countries for programs addressing the destructive connection between poverty, overpopulation, high infant mortality, cultural traditions that dehumanize women, inequitable land distribution, and the subsequent degradation of the land and the systems the land supports. The Foundation also is actively involved in conservation in the United States, particularly Montana and those Western states historically dependent upon extractive industries and agriculture. It encourages local initiatives addressing the problems of diminishing natural resources, technological change, and job loss. It emphasizes conservation through cooperation, persuasion, and the development of sustainable economic alternatives to resource depletion. Types of support include leveraging funds, multi-year grants, and pilot projects. Projects must satisfy the following criteria: designed with and supported by the local people most directly affected; modest in scale at its inception; clearly stated objectives, with measurable and verifiable levels of success; and designed and justified on sound criteria and firm scientific grounds. There are no application forms or deadlines. The board meets in the spring and fall. Recent world-wide grants are posted on the Foundation website.
Requirements: Nonprofit organizations in the U.S. West, Africa, Asia, Central America, and South America are eligible. The Foundation typically funds modest, carefully designed field activities in which local communities have substantial proprietary interest. Submission to the Foundation must be accompanied by the following information: a clearly stated objective of the project being proposed; the anticipated duration of the project and the scaling of costs as the project develops; the criteria to be used when judging the success of the project; and detailed information as to the local volunteer groups involved in a project as well as information concerning other outside NGOs' activities, either directly concerning the proposed project or working in the area on related projects.
Geographic Focus: Montana, Algeria, Angola, Antigua & Barbuda, Bahamas, Barbados, Belize, Benin, Botswana, Burkina Faso, Burundi, Cameroon, Cape Verde, Central African Republic, Chad, Comoros, Congo, Congo, Democratic Republic of, Costa Rica, Cote d' Ivoire (Ivory Coast), Cuba, Djibouti, Dominica, Dominican Republic, Egypt, El Salvador, Equatorial Guinea, Eritrea, Ethiopia, Gabon, Gambia, Ghana, Grenada, Guatemala, Guinea, Guinea-Bissau, Haiti, Honduras, Jamaica, Kenya, Lesotho, Liberia, Libya, Madagascar, Malawi, Mali, Mauritania, Mauritius, Mexico, Morocco, Mozambique, Namibia, Nicaragua, Niger, Nigeria, Rwanda, Sao Tome & Principe, Senegal, Seychelles, Sierra Leone, Somalia, South Africa, Sudan, Swaziland
Amount of Grant: 5,000 - 600,000 USD
Contact: James Murtaugh; (212) 333-2536; fax (212) 956-3531; lcaof@fcc.net
Internet: http://www.lcaof.org/guidelines.html
Sponsor: Liz Claiborne and Art Ortenberg Foundation
650 Fifth Avenue
New York, NY 10019

Liz Claiborne Foundation Grants   2915
Liz Claiborne Inc.'s founders established the Liz Claiborne Foundation to serve as the company's center for charitable activities. The Liz Claiborne Foundation is a separate nonprofit legal entity, which supports organizations in the U.S. communities where Liz Claiborne Inc.'s primary offices are located. These include the five boroughs of New York City; Hudson County, New Jersey; and Los Angeles County, California. In addition, a small portion of the grants may be directed to national organizations addressing critical issues for women, specifically women's economic independence. The mission of the Liz Claiborne Foundation is as follows: Established in 1981, the Liz Claiborne Foundation supports nonprofit organizations working with women to achieve economic independence by supporting multi-dimensional programs that offer essential job readiness training and increase access to tools that help women, including those affected by domestic violence, transition from poverty into successful independent living.
Requirements: Non-profits in the five boroughs of New York City; Hudson County, New Jersey; and Los Angeles County, California are eligible to apply for funding.
Restrictions: Religious organizations and individuals are ineligible for grants.
Geographic Focus: California, New Jersey, New York
Contact: Melanie Lyons, Vice President; (212) 626-5704; fax (212) 626-5304
Internet: http://www.lizclaiborneinc.com/foundation/default.asp
Sponsor: Liz Claiborne Foundation
1440 Broadway
New York, NY 10018

Lloyd G. Balfour Foundation Attleboro-Specific Charities Grants   2916
The Lloyd G. Balfour Foundation was established in 1973. The Foundation's 3 primary focus areas reflect Mr. Balfour's strong affinity for the employees of the Balfour Company; his commitment to the city of Attleboro, Massachusetts; and his lifelong interest in education. The Foundation supports organizations that specifically serve the people of Attleboro, with special consideration given to organizations that provide educational, human services, and health care programming for underserved populations. The application deadline for Attleboro-specific charities is February 1.
Requirements: 501(c)3 organizations serving the residents of Attleboro, Massachusetts, Maine, New Hampshire, Rhode Island, and Vermont are eligible to apply.
Geographic Focus: Massachusetts
Date(s) Application is Due: Feb 1
Amount of Grant: 75,000 - 200,000 USD
Contact: Miki C. Akimoto, Vice President; (866) 778-6859; miki.akimoto@baml.co
Internet: https://www.bankofamerica.com/philanthropic/fn_search.action
Sponsor: Lloyd G. Balfour Foundation
225 Franklin Street, 4th Floor, MA1-225-04-02
Boston, MA 02110

Local Initiatives Support Corporation Grants   2917
Local Initiatives Support Corporation (LISC) helps local organization become strong and stable neighborhood institutions characterized by effective and responsible fiscal management and capable of carrying out a range of community revitalization activities. Overall, LISC helps community development organizations transform distressed communities and neighborhoods into healthy and sustainable communities that are good places to live, do business, work, and raise families. Through LISC local program offices, it provides grant funding to assist organizations to develop affordable housing, commercial and retail space, and community facilities, as well as other community development activities. Grants are designed and provided consistent with local program office strategies and local community development needs. Grants have typically come in the form of: organizational development grants that assist community organizations to improve its administrative structures, management and financial systems, and real estate development and management capacities; strategic planning grants to cover costs associated with the

creation of new programs that are important to an organization's overall mission and needs of the community's residents; and project grants to help cover costs associated with real estate development that further neighborhood revitalization goals.
Geographic Focus: All States
Amount of Grant: 10,000 - 100,000 USD
Contact: Stephen Sagner; (212) 455-9800; fax (212) 682-5929; csi@liscnet.org
Internet: http://www.lisc.org/section/ourwork/grants_services
Sponsor: Local Initiatives Support Corporation
501 7th Avenue, 7th Floor
New York, NY 10018-5903

Lockheed Martin Philanthropic Grants 2918
Lockheed Martin funds grants that enhance the communities where Lockheed Martin employees work and live. Lockheed Martin will consider grant requests that best support the Corporation's strategic focus areas and reflect effective leadership, fiscal responsibility, and program success. Those focus areas include: education—K-16 science, technology, engineering and math (STEM) education; customer and constituent relations—causes of importance to customers and constituents, including the U.S. military and other government agencies; community relations—building partnerships between employee volunteers and the civic, cultural, environmental, and health and human services initiatives that strengthen the communities where employees work. Applications are accepted year-round. Evaluations are typically performed quarterly.
Requirements: To be considered for grant funding, organizations must meet all of the following criteria: apply through Lockheed Martin's online CyberGrants system; have a non-profit tax exempt classification under Section 501(c)3 of the Internal Revenue Service Code, or equivalent international non-profit classification, or be a public elementary/secondary school, or be a qualifying US-based institute of higher education; align with one or more of Lockheed Martin's three strategic focus areas: delivering standards-based science, technology, engineering and math (STEM) education to students in K-16; investing in programs that support the long term success of the military and their families; and supporting the vitality of the communities where employees live and work; agree to act in accordance with Lockheed Martin's contribution acknowledgement *Requirements:* organization/grantee will comply with all applicable requirements of the Patriot Act and the Voluntary Anti-Terrorist Guidelines and will not use any portion of the grant funds for the support, direct or indirect, of acts of violence or terrorism or for any organization engaged in or supporting such acts; be located or operate in a community in which Lockheed Martin has employees or business interests; demonstrate fiscal and administrative responsibility and have an active, diverse board, effective leadership, continuity and efficiency of administration; be limited to one grant per year, except in unusual circumstances.
Restrictions: Some grant applications may not be able to be considered until the next year's budget cycle, particularly those received in the second half of the year. Grants are generally not made to: organizations that unlawfully discriminate on the basis of race, ethnicity, religion, national origin, age, military veteran's status, ancestry, sexual orientation, gender identity or expression, marital status, family structure, genetic information, or mental or physical disability; private K-12 schools, unless the contribution is in acknowledgement of employee volunteer service provided to the school; home-based child care/educational services; individuals; professional associations, labor organizations, fraternal organizations or social clubs; social events sponsored by social clubs; athletic groups, clubs and teams, unless the contribution is in acknowledgement of employee volunteer service provided to the school; religious organizations for religious purposes; or advertising in souvenir booklets, yearbooks or journals unrelated to Lockheed Martin's business interests.
Geographic Focus: California, Colorado, Florida, Georgia, Louisiana, Maryland, Minnesota, Mississippi, New Jersey, New Mexico, New York, Ohio, Pennsylvania, South Carolina, Texas, Virginia, Canada
Contact: David Phillips, Manager of Corporate Philanthropy; (301) 897-6292; fax (301) 897-6485; david.e.phillips@lmco.com
Internet: http://www.lockheedmartin.com/aboutus/community/philanthropy/funding.html
Sponsor: Lockheed Martin
6801 Rockledge Drive
Bethesda, MD 20817

Lois and Richard England Family Foundation Jewish Community Life Grants 2919
The Lois and Richard England Family Foundation is a private family foundation founded in 1990. The Foundation's Jewish Community Life Grants support organizations working in the following areas: to promote engagement by the Jewish community in Tikkun Olam (repairing the world) through improving the situation of underserved populations and people in crisis; to enhance the democratic nature of Israel by promoting economic empowerment and civil rights for all Israelis; to encourage Jews to become active in Jewish culture, synagogue life, and the Jewish community; to combat anti-Semitism by promoting a positive view of Jews and of Israel through education and dialogue; to build coalitions with non-Jews on areas of common concern and to improve intergroup relations; and to participate in the local Jewish community by supporting local organizations which are valued by trustees of the Foundation. There are no deadlines. The Foundation considers Grants in the fall. Organizations typically will be notified in writing of funding decisions no later than December 30.
Requirements: Applicants must be 501(c)3 organizations. The Foundation supports general operations as well as funding specific programs, capacity building, strategic planning, evaluation, program development, matching grants and endowment/reserve funds. Interested organizations should email the Foundation indicating the organization's mission, budget, website and contact information. A representative from the Foundation will reply via email or phone within 30 days.
Restrictions: Unsolicited proposals are not accepted.
Geographic Focus: All States
Amount of Grant: 5,000 - 50,000 USD
Contact: Sandy Katz, Program Advisor; (301) 657-7737; fax (301) 657-7738; englandfamilyfdn@verizon.net
Internet: http://foundationcenter.org/grantmaker/england/interests.html
Sponsor: Lois and Richard England Family Foundation
P.O. Box 34-1077
Bethesda, MD 20827

Long Island Community Foundation Grants 2920
The Foundation awards grants to eligible New York nonprofit organizations in the following program areas: arts; community development; education; environment; health; mental health; hunger; technical assistance; and youth violence prevention. Projects are preferred that accomplish specific tasks, solve problems, address needs of the disadvantaged, help a large number of people, and use community resources. Specific guidelines for each category and the application are available on the Foundation website. Applicants are encouraged to view recent grants on the website in order to judge if their project is appropriate for the Foundation.
Requirements: New York nonprofit organizations are eligible.
Restrictions: Grants are not made for the following: individuals; building or capital campaigns; medical or scientific research; equipment purchases; budget deficits; endowments; event sponsorships; re-granting purposes; or religious or political purposes.
Geographic Focus: New York
Date(s) Application is Due: Aug 24
Contact: Nancy Arnold; (516) 348-0575; fax (516) 348-0570; narnold@licf.org
Internet: http://www.licf.org/grants
Sponsor: Long Island Community Foundation
1864 Muttontown Road
Syosset, NY 11791

Lotus 88 Foundation for Women and Children Grants 2921
The foundation's mission is to promote the empowerment of women and children through supporting their economic, emotional, and spiritual development. The foundation's focus area is American Indian Country. Grants are awarded in Indian Country for two strategic purposes: revitalizing the council tipis as spiritual, cultural, and service centers; and providing the basic needs through community building. Community building grants are intended to promote and support community building in Indian Country to improve basic living conditions and to encourage a more positive future. Tipi project grants are made to help tribal women living on reservation or off reservation in building community. Grants support cultural and social services, tribal gatherings, educational programs, healing and purification ceremonies, and retreats. Each proposal should identify the specific needs and uses for the tipi and should identify a nonprofit program partner working in the tribal area who will work with the foundation on the project. Contact the Foundation directly for application and additional guideline information.
Requirements: Projects in American Indian communities are eligible.
Geographic Focus: All States
Contact: Patricia Stout; (510) 841-4123; fax (510) 841-4093; benita@lotus88.org
Internet: http://lotus88.net/
Sponsor: Lotus 88 Foundation for Women and Children
127 University Avenue, P.O. Box 10728
Berkeley, CA 94710

Louetta M. Cowden Foundation Grants 2922
The Louetta M. Cowden Foundation was established in 1964 to support and promote quality educational, cultural, human-services, and health-care programming. In the area of culture the foundation supports programming that: fosters the enjoyment and appreciation of the visual and performing arts; strengthens humanities and arts-related education programs; provides affordable access; enhances artistic elements in communities; and nurtures a new generation of artists. In the area of education the foundation supports programming that: promotes effective teaching; improves the academic achievement of, or expands educational opportunities for disadvantaged students; improves governance and management; strengthens nonprofit organizations, school leadership, and teaching; and bolsters strategic initiatives of area colleges and universities. In the area of health the foundation supports programming that: improves the delivery of health care to the indigent, uninsured, and other vulnerable populations; and addresses health and health-care problems that intersect with social factors. In the area of human services, the foundation supports programming that: strengthens agencies that deliver critical human services and maintains the community's safety net; and helps agencies respond to federal, state, and local public policy changes. There are no application deadlines for the Cowden Foundation. Proposals are reviewed on an ongoing basis. Grant requests for general operating support and program support will be considered. Grants from the Foundation are one year in duration. Application materials are available for download at the grant website. Applicants are strongly encouraged to review the downloadable state application guidelines before applying. Applicants are also encouraged to view the foundation's funding history (link is available at the grant website).
Requirements: Applicants must have 501(c)3 tax-exempt status and serve the residents of Kansas City, Missouri.
Restrictions: Grant requests for capital support will not be considered. The foundation does not support requests from individuals, organizations attempting to influence policy through direct lobbying, or any political campaigns.
Geographic Focus: Missouri
Contact: Spence Heddens; (816) 292-4301; Spence.heddens@baml.com
Internet: https://www.bankofamerica.com/philanthropic/fn_search.action
Sponsor: Louetta M. Cowden Foundation
1200 Main Street, 14th Floor, P.O. Box 219119
Kansas City, MO 64121-9119

Louie M. and Betty M. Phillips Foundation Grants 2923
The Foundation supports a variety of organizations in the fields of health, human services, civic affairs, education, and the arts. Types of support include annual operating grants for selected organizations contributing significantly to the Nashville area; one-year project and program grants for specific projects or equipment; and capital support (five-years maximum) for major capital projects of organizations with strong records of community service. The application and a list of previously funded projects are available at the Foundation website.
Requirements: Nonprofit organizations are eligible. With rare exceptions, grants are limited to organizations in the greater Nashville area.
Restrictions: The Foundation does not support individuals or their projects, private foundations, political activities, advertising, or sponsorships. In general, the Foundation does not support projects, programs, or organizations that serve a limited audience; disease-specific organizations; biomedical or clinical research; organizations whose principal impact is outside the Nashville area; or tax-supported institutions.
Geographic Focus: Tennessee
Date(s) Application is Due: Jun 1; Nov 1
Amount of Grant: 500 - 35,000 USD
Contact: Louie Buntin; (615) 385-5949; fax (615) 385-2507; louie@phillipsfoundation.org
Internet: http://www.phillipsfoundation.org
Sponsor: Louie M. and Betty M. Phillips Foundation
3334 Powell Avenue, P.O. Box 40788
Nashville, TN 37204

Louis and Elizabeth Nave Flarsheim Charitable Foundation Grants 2924
The Louis & Elizabeth Nave Flarsheim Charitable Foundation was established to support and promote quality educational, cultural, human-services, and health-care programming. In the area of arts, culture, and humanities, the foundation supports programming that: fosters the enjoyment and appreciation of the visual and performing arts; strengthens humanities and arts-related education programs; provides affordable access; enhances artistic elements in communities; and nurtures a new generation of artists. In the area of education, the foundation supports programming that: promotes effective teaching; improves the academic achievement of, or expands educational opportunities for, disadvantaged students; improves governance and management; strengthens nonprofit organizations, school leadership, and teaching; and bolsters strategic initiatives of area colleges and universities. In the area of health, the foundation supports programming that improves the delivery of health care to the indigent, uninsured, and other vulnerable populations and addresses health and health-care problems that intersect with social factors. In the area of human services, the foundation funds programming that: strengthens agencies that deliver critical human services and maintains the community's safety net and helps agencies respond to federal, state, and local public policy changes. In the area of community improvement, the foundation funds capacity-building and infrastructure-development projects including: assessments, planning, and implementation of technology for management and programmatic functions within an organization; technical assistance on wide-ranging topics, including grant writing, strategic planning, financial management services, business development, board and volunteer management, and marketing; and mergers, affiliations, or other restructuring efforts. Grant requests for general operating support and program support will be considered. Grants from the foundation are one year in duration. Application materials are available for download at the grant website. Applicants are strongly encouraged to review the state application guidelines for additional helpful information and clarifications before applying. Applicants are also encouraged to review the foundation's funding history (link is available from the grant website). There are no application deadlines for the Flarsheim Charitable Foundation. Proposals are reviewed on an ongoing basis.
Requirements: The Flarsheim Foundation supports organizations that serve the residents of Kansas City, Missouri. Applications must be mailed.
Restrictions: Grant requests for capital support will not be considered.
Geographic Focus: Missouri
Contact: Spence Heddens; (816) 292-4301; Spence.heddens@baml.com
Internet: https://www.bankofamerica.com/philanthropic/fn_search.action
Sponsor: Louis & Elizabeth Nave Flarsheim Charitable Foundation
1200 Main Street, 14th Floor, P.O. Box 219119
Kansas City, 64121-9119

Louis Calder Foundation Grants 2925
The Louis Calder Foundation seeks to promote the educational and scholastic development of children and youth by improving academic content at charter and parochial schools and at community based organizations. The Foundation's grant making will focus on opportunities for schools and community based organizations in communities within the Northeast Corridor with populations no greater than 500,000 to undertake such efforts during the regular school hours as well as the out-of-school or extended-day hours. New and existing charter schools, parochial schools and community based organizations are invited to submit a letter of inquiry with a summary of their plans to improve or initiate programs and projects designed to deliver classical education in areas of literacy, history, ethics, mathematics and the sciences. The Foundation has no formal application form and requests that organizations use the Philanthropy New York Common Application Form (available at the Foundation's website).
Requirements: New and existing charter schools, parochial schools and community based organizations are invited to submit a letter of inquiry with a summary of their plans to improve or initiate programs and projects designed to deliver classical education in areas of literacy, history, ethics, mathematics and the sciences. There is no application deadline when applying for funding.
Restrictions: The Foundation does not provide long term continuing program support and requests for renewed support are considered on the basis of reports received, site visits and Foundation priorities.
Geographic Focus: All States
Amount of Grant: 5,000 - 600,000 USD
Contact: Holly Nuechterlein; (203) 966-8925; fax (203) 966-5785; proposals@calderfdn.org
Internet: http://www.louiscalderfdn.org/gguide.html
Sponsor: Louis Calder Foundation
175 Elm Street
New Canaan, CT 06840

Louis R. Cappelli Foundation Grants 2926
The foundation awards grants to eligible New York nonprofit organizations in its areas of interest, including arts—educational programs for at-risk children and youth in the visual and performing arts, art history, and public libraries; education—programs addressing at-risk children and youth; and health—programs that provide innovative, high-quality health education or organized sports programs serving at-risk children and youth. All requests must be in writing; phone and fax requests are not accepted.
Requirements: New York 501(c)3 tax-exempt organizations located in Sullivan or Westchester Counties are eligible.
Geographic Focus: New York
Date(s) Application is Due: Jun 18
Contact: Director; (914) 769-6500; fax (914) 747-9268; jfevola@cappelli-inc.com
Internet: http://www.cappelli-inc.com/lrc.html
Sponsor: Louis R. Cappelli Foundation
115 Suitevens Avenue
Valhalla, NY 10595

Lowe's Charitable and Educational Foundation Grants 2927
The foundation is dedicated to improving the communities it serves through support of public education, community improvement projects, and home safety initiatives. Primary philanthropic focus areas include community improvement projects; K-12 public school initiatives; and vocational trade school scholarships. The foundation requires that all applicants take an eligibility test. Organizations that pass will be considered but not guaranteed a grant. The foundation will only consider an organization's grant application once per calendar year. Guidelines are available online.
Requirements: 501(c)3 nonprofits in Lowe's Inc operating communities are eligible.
Restrictions: The foundation's charitable contributions do not support individuals and families; national health organizations and their local affiliates; academic or medical research; religious organizations, programs, or events; special events, such as conferences, dinners, sport competitions, festivals, or art exhibits; sponsorship of fundraising events (i.e., dinners, walks, golf tournaments and auctions); goodwill advertising or marketing; political, labor, veteran/fraternal organizations, civic clubs, or candidates; sports teams, athletic events, or athletic programs; arts-based programs; animal rescue and support groups; travel-related events, including student trips or tours; development or production of books, films, videos, or television programs; capital campaigns, endowments, or endowed chairs; activities of organizations serving primarily their own membership; private schools; continuing education for teachers and staff; institutional overhead and/or indirect cost; memorial campaigns; multi-year requests; programs outside Lowe???s communities; international programs; or tickets to events.
Geographic Focus: All States
Amount of Grant: 5,000 - 25,000 USD
Contact: Foundation Director; (336) 658-5544; community@lowes.com
Internet: http://www.lowes.com/lowes/lkn?action=frameSet&url=apps.bridgetree.com/funding/default.asp
Sponsor: Lowe's Charitable and Educational Foundation
P.O. Box 1111, MC RPS4
North Wilkesboro, NC 28656

Lowe's Outdoor Classroom Grants 2928
Lowe's Charitable and Educational Foundation, International Paper and National Geographic Explorer classroom magazine have partnered to create an outdoor classroom grant program to provide schools with additional resources to improve their science curriculum by engaging students in hands-on experiences outside the traditional classroom. The program will award grants up to $2,000 to at least 100 schools. In some cases, grants for up to $20,000 may be awarded to schools or school districts with major outdoor classroom projects. The grants can be used to build a new outdoor classroom or to enhance a current outdoor classroom at the school.
Requirements: This program only considers outdoor classroom proposals. All K-12 public schools in the United States are welcome to apply.
Geographic Focus: All States
Amount of Grant: Up to 20,000 USD
Contact: Nikki Lowry, (800) 647-5463; educaiton@nationalgeographic.com
Internet: http://www.lowes.com/lowes/lkn?action=pg&p=AboutLowes/outdoor/apply1.html
Sponsor: Lowe's Charitable and Educational Foundation
P.O. Box 1111, MC RPS4
North Wilkesboro, NC 28656

Lowe Foundation Grants 2929
The foundation awards grants to organizations in Texas, primarily for programs that support the critical needs of women and children. The arts and higher education also receive support. Grants are awarded to support capital campaigns, building construction/renovation, and general operations. The board meets in April of each year. The December 1 deadline listed is for pre-proposals, with full proposals by request due on December 31.
Requirements: 501(c)3 organizations in Texas may apply for grant support.
Geographic Focus: Texas

Date(s) Application is Due: Dec 1; Dec 31
Amount of Grant: 5,000 - 225,000 USD
Contact: Clayton Maebius, Trustee; (512) 322-0041; fax (512) 322-0061; info@thelowefoundation.org
Internet: http://www.thelowefoundation.org/guidelines.htm
Sponsor: Lowe Foundation
1005 Congress Avenue, Suite 895
Austin, TX 78701

Lowell Berry Foundation Grants 2930
Mr. Lowell W. Berry established The Lowell Berry Foundation in 1950 with the primary purpose of assisting in strengthening Christian ministry at the local church level. Mr. Berry's secondary purpose was that of assisting social service programs in the areas in California where he lived and operated his business. Guidelines are available at the Foundation's website.
Requirements: 501(c)3 tax-exempt organizations may apply, The Foundation provides funding primarily in Contra Costa and Alameda counties of California.
Restrictions: No grants to individuals, or for building or capital funds, equipment, seed money, or land acquisition.
Geographic Focus: California
Amount of Grant: 5,000 - 200,000 USD
Contact: Katherine Sanders; (925) 284-4427; info@lowellberryfoundation.org
Internet: http://www.lowellberryfoundation.org/process.html
Sponsor: Lowell Berry Foundation
3685 Mount Diablo Boulevard, Suite 269
Lafayette, CA 94549-3776

Lubbock Area Foundation Grants 2931
The Lubbock Area Foundation is a nonprofit community foundation that manages a pool of charitable endowment funds, the income from which is used to benefit the South Plains community through grants to nonprofit organizations, educational programs and scholarships. Funding priorities are: art and culture; social services; civic and community; education; social services; health and human services. Grants may be made for start-up funding, general operating support, program support and demonstration programs. Typical grant awards range from $500 - $2,500 with $5,000 as the maximum from the unrestricted funds. Grant application and additional guidelines are available on the Foundation's website.
Requirements: The Foundation restricts its support to organizations in Lubbock and the surrounding South Plains area which are 501(c)3 or the government equivalent.
Restrictions: The Foundation does not make grants to individuals, for political purposes, to retire indebtedness or for payment of interest or taxes.
Geographic Focus: Texas
Date(s) Application is Due: Jan 1; Mar 1; May 1; Jul 1; Sep 1; Nov 1
Contact: Kathleen Stocco, Executive Director; (806) 762-8061; fax (806) 762-8551
Internet: http://www.lubbockareafoundation.org/grant.shtml
Sponsor: Lubbock Area Foundation
1655 Main Street, Suite 202
Lubbock, TX 79401

Lubrizol Corporation Community Grants 2932
The Lubrizol Corporation has a long-standing commitment to the local communities in which it operates. The Corporation believes that enhancing the quality of life and building and maintaining positive relationships is the right thing to do. It all began with its founders' corporate philosophy, whose legacy is a culture of active community support. Today, the Corporation continues their model by providing dollars and people to support a wide variety of educational, cultural and charitable organizations. One of the ways that Lubrizol and its employees provide support to its local communities is through various charitable outreach efforts. Employees volunteer their time to offer assistance to local organizations, making use of their individual skills. An annual event in Northeast Ohio that exemplifies this type of charitable outreach is the Building Bonds event. Applicants should contact the Corporate Community Involvement office for further guidelines.
Requirements: IRS 501(c)3 organizations in or serving the following regions may apply: Wickliffe, Ohio; Cleveland, Ohio; Brussels, Belgium; and Hong Kong.
Geographic Focus: Ohio, Belgium, Hong Kong
Contact: Karen Lerchbacher; (440) 347-1797; karen.lerchbacher@lubrizol.com
Internet: http://www.lubrizol.com/CorporateResponsibility/Community.html
Sponsor: Lubrizol Corporation
29400 Lakeland Boulevard
Wickliffe, OH 44092-2298

Lubrizol Foundation Grants 2933
The Lubrizol Foundation makes grants in support of education, health care, human services, civic, cultural, youth and environmental activities of a tax-exempt, charitable nature. Scholarships, fellowships, and awards are generally made in the fields of chemistry and chemical and mechanical engineering at colleges and universities. Types of support include the following: annual campaigns; building/renovation; capital campaigns; continuing support; employee matching gifts; employee volunteer services; equipment; fellowships; general/operating support; scholarship funds. Priority is given to the greater Cleveland, Ohio and Houston, Texas areas. The Lubrizol Foundation typically reviews and decides upon requests quarterly. There are no deadlines by which you need to submit your proposal. Proposals may be submitted via postal mail or email, but not by fax. Applicants will receive written notification of the decision on their proposal.
Requirements: Written applications of established Ohio and Texas nonprofit charitable organizations will be considered on a case by case basis. Grant proposals should include the following: a cover letter that summarizes the purpose of the request, signed by the executive officer of the organization or development office; a narrative of specific information related to the subject of the request; current audited financial statements and a specific project budget, if applicable; documentation of the organization's Federal tax-exempt status, e.g., a copy of the 501(c)3 determination letter. Additional descriptive literature (e.g., an annual report, brochures, etc.) that accurately characterizes the overall activities of the organization is appreciated. Upon review, further information may be requested including an interview and site visit.
Restrictions: Grants are not made for religious or political purposes, to individuals nor, generally, to endowments.
Geographic Focus: Ohio, Texas
Amount of Grant: 2,000 - 250,000 USD
Contact: Karen Lerchbacher; (440) 347-1797; karen.lerchbacher@lubrizol.com
Internet: http://www.lubrizol.com/CorporateResponsibility/Lubrizol-Foundation.html
Sponsor: Lubrizol Foundation
29400 Lakeland Boulevard, 053A
Wickliffe, OH 44092-2298

Lucile Horton Howe and Mitchell B. Howe Foundation Grants 2934
The foundation supports youth organizations, social services, medical research, hospitals, religion, child welfare, drug abuse, education, and family services. Types of support include continuing support, general operating funds, and research. Requests from qualified organizations must be received prior to the second Tuesday of March for the grant year. There is only one consideration meeting a year.
Requirements: Only nonprofit organizations in the Prox-Pasadena area and the San Gabriel Valley of California are eligible. A brief letter and a copy of the organizations 501(c)3 form are the requirements for application.
Restrictions: No restricted grants will be funded by the foundation.
Geographic Focus: California
Date(s) Application is Due: Feb 28
Amount of Grant: 1,000 - 300,000 USD
Contact: Mitchell B. Howe, President; (626) 792-2771; lhmbhowefoun@earthlink.net
Sponsor: Lucile Horton Howe and Mitchell B. Howe Foundation
180 South Lake Avenue
Pasadena, CA 91101-4932

Lucy Downing Nisbet Charitable Fund Grants 2935
The Lucy Downing Nisbet Charitable Fund was established in 2002 to support and promote educational, health-and-human-services, and arts programming for underserved populations. The Foundation specifically serves organizations located in and serving the people of Vermont. Special consideration is given to organizations in the area of healthcare/nursing, domestic violence awareness, heart disease, and endangered species, and organizations located in and serving the people of Morrisville, Vermont. Grants are one year in duration. Applicants must apply online at the grant website. Applicants are strongly encouraged to do the following before applying: review the downloadable state application procedures for additional helpful information and clarifications; review the downloadable online-application guidelines at the grant website; review the foundation's funding history (link is available from the grant website); review the online application questions in advance; and review the list of required attachments. These will generally include: a list of board members, financial statements (audited, reviewed, or compiled by independent auditor); an organization summary; a list of other funding sources; an IRS Determination letter; and other required documents. All attachments must be uploaded in the online application as PDF, Word, or Excel files. The Lucy Downing Nisbet Charitable Fund application deadline is 11:59 p.m. on January 15. Applicants will be notified of grant decisions by letter within two to three months of the deadline.
Requirements: The foundation specifically serves organizations located in and serving the people of Vermont. Applicants must have 501(c)3 tax-exempt status.
Restrictions: The trustees do not make grants for deficit financing, annual giving, endowments or capital projects. The fund does not support requests from individuals, organizations attempting to influence policy through direct lobbying, or any political campaigns.
Geographic Focus: Vermont
Date(s) Application is Due: Jan 15
Amount of Grant: 5,000 - 20,000 USD
Contact: Amy Lynch; (860) 657-7015; amy.r.lynch@baml.com
Internet: https://www.bankofamerica.com/philanthropic/fn_search.action
Sponsor: Lucy Downing Nisbet Charitable Fund
200 Glastonbury Boulevard, Suite # 200, CT2-545-02-05
Glastonbury, CT 06033-4056

Lucy Gooding Charitable Foundation Trust 2936
The trust awards grants to eligible Florida nonprofit organizations in its areas of interest, including child welfare, disabled children, disadvantaged people, homelessness, and hospices. Types of support include building construction/renovation, capital campaigns, equipment and land acquisition, general operating support, seed grants, and United Way. Contact the office for required application form.
Requirements: Florida 501(c)3 nonprofits serving the Jacksonville area are eligible.
Geographic Focus: Florida
Date(s) Application is Due: Sep 30
Amount of Grant: 2,500 - 25,000,000 USD
Contact: Bonnie Smith; (904) 786-4796; fax (904) 786-4796; bhsmith@bellsouth.net
Sponsor: Lucy Gooding Charitable Foundation Trust
P.O. Box 37349
Jacksonville, FL 32236-7349

Lucy Gooding Charitable Foundation Trust Grants 2937
The Foundation, established in 1988, supports organizations involved with children and youth, services, education, human services, residential/custodial care, hospices, economically disadvantaged, people with disabilities, and homelessness. The Foundation gives primarily in the five county area surrounding Jacksonville, Florida.
Requirements: Funding preference is for organizations in the five county area surrounding Jacksonville, FL with projects helping children. Contact the Foundation for application form.
Restrictions: No support for private foundations, religious organizations, or for adults-only services, and individuals.
Geographic Focus: Florida
Date(s) Application is Due: Sep 30
Amount of Grant: 5,000 - 1,000,000 USD
Contact: Bonnie H. Smith; (904) 786-4796; fax (904) 786-4796; bhsmith@bellsouth.net
Sponsor: Lucy Gooding Charitable Foundation Trust
P.O. Box 37349
Jacksonville, FL 32236-7349

Ludwick Family Foundation Grants 2938
The foundation is a California nonprofit public benefit corporation established exclusively for charitable, scientific, literary, and educational purposes. Grants are awarded to United States or U.S. based international organizations in adherence to the mission of Ludwick Family Foundation and its founding documents. The foundation tends to fund tangible types of items that will remain with and can be used repeatedly by the organization.
Requirements: Eligible applicants include U.S. or US-based international organizations, 501(c)3 nonprofit public charities, and government agencies (any level). All grants are to be used exclusively for charitable, public benefit purposes.
Restrictions: The foundation does not grant requests for salaries, general operating expenses, scholarships, endowment funds, fundraising events or capital campaigns, feasibility studies, consulting fees, or advertising. The foundation will no longer accept any unsolicited requests for research or from public/private schools (K-12), universities/colleges, child daycare/development centers, hospitals, or libraries. Grant consideration will be given only to those organizations that have been invited to submit formal proposals and that have completed the application process.
Geographic Focus: All States
Amount of Grant: 5,000 - 50,000 USD
Contact: Trista Campbell; (626) 852-0092; fax (626) 852-0776; ludwickfndn@ludwick.org
Internet: http://www.ludwick.org
Sponsor: Ludwick Family Foundation
203 South Glendora Avenue, Suite B, P.O. Box 1796
Glendora, CA 91740

Luella Kemper Trust Grants 2939
The Luella Kemper Trust was established in 1986 to support and promote quality education and human-services programming for underserved populations. Special consideration is given to charitable organizations that serve the people of Grayson County, Texas. Grants from the Kemper Trust are one year in duration. Applicants must apply online at the grant website. Applicants are strongly encouraged to do the following before applying: review the downloadable state application procedures for additional helpful information and clarifications; review the downloadable online-application guidelines at the grant website; review the trust's funding history (link is available from the grant website); review the online application questions in advance; and review the list of required attachments. These will generally include: a list of board members, financial statements (audited, reviewed, or compiled by independent auditor); an organization summary; a list of other funding sources; an IRS Determination letter; and other required documents. All attachments must be uploaded in the online application as PDF, Word, or Excel files. The Luella Kemper Trust has four deadlines annually: March 1, June 1, September 1, and December 1. Applications must be submitted by 11:59 p.m. on the deadline dates. March deadline applicants will be notified of grant decisions by June 30; June applicants will be notified by September 30; September applicants will be notified by December 31; and December applicants will be notified by March 31 of the following year.
Requirements: Applicants must have 501(c)3 tax-exempt status.
Restrictions: The trust does not support requests from individuals, organizations attempting to influence policy through direct lobbying, or any political campaigns.
Geographic Focus: Texas
Date(s) Application is Due: Mar 1; Jun 1; Sep 1; Dec 1
Contact: David Ross, Senior Vice President; tx.philanthropic@baml.com
Internet: https://www.bankofamerica.com/philanthropic/fn_search.action
Sponsor: Luella Kemper Trust
901 Main Street, 19th Floor, TX1-492-19-11
Dallas, TX 75202-3714

Lumity Technology Leadership Award 2940
The Lumity Technology Leadership Award, presented by Accenture, recognizes Chicago-area nonprofit organizations that demonstrate exemplary use of technology to further their missions. The award winner will receive: a grant of $5,000 from Accenture; and an operations assessment from Lumity, supported by Microsoft software. The runner-up and finalists will also receive a cash grant of $2,500 from Accenture and an operations assessment from Lumity.
Requirements: Chicago-area 501(c)3 charitable organization with the following exceptions: churches, organizations whose primary mission is to promote a religion; public schools, private schools, colleges, or universities; nonprofit hospitals, assisted living health care organizations, or cooperative hospital service organizations; and governmental units are ineligible to apply.
Geographic Focus: All States
Date(s) Application is Due: Nov 9
Amount of Grant: 2,500 - 5,000 USD
Contact: Julie Henderson, Director, Administration & Foundation Relations; (312) 372-4872; fax (312) 372-7962; jhenderson@lumity.org or info@lumity.org
Internet: http://www.lumity.org/images/files/file/TLA/Technology%20Leadership%20Award%202013%20Guidelines%281%29.pdf
Sponsor: Lumity Technology
407 S. Dearborn Street, Suite 800
Chicago, IL 60605

Lumpkin Family Foundation Healthy Environments Grants 2941
Conservation in downstate Illinois has been a central part of the Lumpkin Family Foundation mission since the early 1990s when members of the family first started to plan their philanthropy together. Historically, most of its grants have supported clean water in areas south of Highway 80. In recent more years, however, grants have increasingly gone to encouraging the localization of the food system. As a founder of the Fresh Taste Initiative and an active participant in the Sustainable Agriculture and Food Systems Funders Group, the Foundation's involvement has been deeper in this area than other grant-making areas. The Foundation accepts applications from organizations working to improve environmental health in downstate Illinois. Requests will be evaluated on how well they accomplish one or more of the following: support the creativity of nonprofit organizations by seeding new projects and encouraging experimentation and innovation; support organizations demonstrating outstanding leadership in their field or community; promote the effectiveness of organizations and the nonprofit sector by supporting planning, learning and the professional development of staff and board leaders; facilitate collaboration across traditional organization or sector boundaries for community benefit; and develop public understanding of issues and promote philanthropic support necessary to address issues of community importance.
Requirements: Grants are awarded to nonprofit organizations that serve the community without discrimination on the basis of race, sex, or religion. Special consideration will be given to organizations and programs in East Central Illinois.
Restrictions: Proposals will not be considered from organizations that are not 501(c)3 tax-exempt; organizations whose primary purpose is to influence legislation; political causes, candidates, organizations or campaigns; individuals; or religious organizations, unless the particular program will benefit a large portion of the community and does not duplicate the work of other agencies in the community.
Geographic Focus: Illinois
Amount of Grant: 1,000 - 10,000 USD
Contact: Bruce Karmazin, (217) 234-5915 or (217) 235-3361; Bruce@lumpkinfoundation.org
Internet: http://www.lumpkinfoundation.org/bWHATbwefund/HealthyEnvironments.aspx
Sponsor: Lumpkin Family Foundation
121 South 17th Street
Mattoon, IL 61938

Lumpkin Family Foundation Healthy People Grants 2942
Historically, the Lumpkin Family Foundation has supported entities that provide services that help keep people in its geographic area healthy. Requests will be evaluated on how well they accomplish one or more of the following: support the creativity of nonprofit organizations by seeding new projects and encouraging experimentation and innovation; support organizations demonstrating outstanding leadership in their field or community; promote the effectiveness of organizations and the nonprofit sector by supporting planning, learning and the professional development of staff and board leaders; facilitate collaboration across traditional organization or sector boundaries for community benefit; and develop public understanding of issues and promote philanthropic support necessary to address issues of community importance.
Requirements: Grants are awarded to nonprofit organizations that serve the community without discrimination on the basis of race, sex, or religion. Special consideration will be given to organizations and programs in East Central Illinois.
Restrictions: Proposals will not be considered from organizations that are not 501(c)3 tax-exempt; organizations whose primary purpose is to influence legislation; political causes, candidates, organizations or campaigns; individuals; or religious organizations, unless the particular program will benefit a large portion of the community and does not duplicate the work of other agencies in the community.
Geographic Focus: All States
Amount of Grant: 1,000 - 50,000 USD
Contact: Bruce Karmazin, (217) 234-5915 or (217) 235-3361; fax (217) 258-8444; Bruce@lumpkinfoundation.org
Internet: http://www.lumpkinfoundation.org/bWHATbwefund/HealthyPeople.aspx
Sponsor: Lumpkin Family Foundation
121 South 17th Street
Mattoon, IL 61938

Lumpkin Family Lively Arts and Dynamic Learning Communities Grants 2943
The Lumpkin Family has a proud history of supporting arts and educational institutions in their communities. These organizations contribute significantly to a community's quality of life in themselves and members believe they play a fundamental role in inspiring innovation and creativity in our economy. The Foundation accepts applications through the Regional Grants Program for youth-based arts and/or mentoring programs from organizations in communities where Lumpkin family members live. Members are particularly interested in programs that target disadvantaged young people between grades eight and ten because we understand this to be a critical period in formulating a positive life view and establishing good decision-making patterns. The Lumpkin Family Fund also considers grants to support

community access to the arts throughout east central Illinois radiating out from Coles County. Requests will be evaluated on how well they accomplish one or more of the following: support the creativity of nonprofit organizations by seeding new projects and encouraging experimentation and innovation; support organizations demonstrating outstanding leadership in their field or community; promote the effectiveness of organizations and the nonprofit sector by supporting planning, learning and the professional development of staff and board leaders; facilitate collaboration across traditional organization or sector boundaries for community benefit; and develop public understanding of issues and promote philanthropic support necessary to address issues of community importance.
Requirements: Grants are awarded to nonprofit organizations that serve the community without discrimination on the basis of race, sex, or religion. Special consideration will be given to organizations and programs in East Central Illinois.
Restrictions: Proposals will not be considered from organizations that are not 501(c)3 tax-exempt; organizations whose primary purpose is to influence legislation; political causes, candidates, organizations or campaigns; individuals; or religious organizations, unless the particular program will benefit a large portion of the community and does not duplicate the work of other agencies in the community.
Geographic Focus: Illinois
Amount of Grant: 1,000 - 200,000 USD
Contact: Bruce Karmazin, (217) 234-5915 or (217) 235-3361; fax (217) 258-8444; Bruce@lumpkinfoundation.org
Internet: http://www.lumpkinfoundation.org/bWHATbwefund/LivelyArtsandLearningCommunities.aspx
Sponsor: Lumpkin Family Foundation
121 South 17th Street
Mattoon, IL 61938

Lumpkin Family Foundation Strong Community Leadership Grants 2944
The Lumpkin Family Foundation believes that well managed, mission-driven nonprofit organizations produce more effective and sustainable programs. When organizations work collaboratively on matters of common concern they accomplish more, give greater voice to their concerns, have a deeper impact on their clients and, ultimately, create stronger, more vibrant communities. The Foundation is committed to making grants to support nonprofits in building their leadership and working together on issues impacting the communities it cares about. It accepts applications that address organizational capacity or encourage civic engagement and community leadership. Requests will be evaluated on how well they accomplish one or more of the following: support the creativity of nonprofit organizations by seeding new projects and encouraging experimentation and innovation; support organizations demonstrating outstanding leadership in their field or community; promote the effectiveness of organizations and the nonprofit sector by supporting planning, learning and the professional development of staff and board leaders; facilitate collaboration across traditional organization or sector boundaries for community benefit; and develop public understanding of issues and promote philanthropic support necessary to address issues of community importance.
Requirements: Grants are awarded to nonprofit organizations that serve the community without discrimination on the basis of race, sex, or religion. Special consideration will be given to organizations and programs in East Central Illinois. Other communities receiving consideration for grant funding include: San Francisco, California; Albuquerque, New Mexico; St. Louis, Missouri; Terre Haute, Indiana; Chicago, Illinois; Madison, Wisconsin; Chautauqua County, New York; Silver Creek, New York; Philadelphia, Pennsylvania; and Norwalk, Connecticut.
Restrictions: Proposals will not be considered from organizations that are not 501(c)3 tax-exempt; organizations whose primary purpose is to influence legislation; political causes, candidates, organizations or campaigns; individuals; or religious organizations, unless the particular program will benefit a large portion of the community and does not duplicate the work of other agencies in the community.
Geographic Focus: California, Connecticut, Illinois, Indiana, Missouri, New Mexico, New York, Wisconsin
Amount of Grant: 1,000 - 10,000 USD
Contact: Annie Hernandez, Program Officer; (217) 234-5702 or (217) 235-3361; fax (217) 258-8444; Annie@lumpkinfoundation.org
Internet: http://www.lumpkinfoundation.org/bWHATbwefund/StrongCommunityLeadership.aspx
Sponsor: Lumpkin Family Foundation
121 South 17th Street
Mattoon, IL 61938

Luther I. Replogle Foundation Grants 2945
The foundation focuses its giving on the following areas: programs addressing the needs of youth and children living in, or at risk of, long-term poverty (especially children of inner-city residents and migrant workers); programs to improve educational opportunities for inner- city children, including enrichment programs in the arts and sciences, alternative schools, after-school tutoring and mentoring, and scholarship programs; programs for affordable and supportive housing that reach groups of people frequently left out of traditional shelter programs, including single mothers and families with children, the elderly, ex-offenders, and youth; projects, lectures, and fellowships in classical archaeology; projects and institutions working for the conservation of maps and globes, and dissemination and education in the area of geography; and a modest budget for support of the arts. Types of support include direct service efforts; advocacy at the local, state, and/or federal levels; general operating support, new projects, and capital campaigns (limited). The board meets twice a year to make funding decisions, once in the autumn and once in the spring. Guidelines and application are available online.
Requirements: 501(c)3 nonprofits in Chicago, IL; Minneapolis, MN; Palm Beach County, FL; and Washington, DC, are eligible. Preference is given to organizations with small or modest operating budgets

Geographic Focus: District of Columbia, Florida, Illinois, Minnesota
Date(s) Application is Due: Mar 15; Sep 15
Amount of Grant: 500 - 45,000 USD
Contact: Gwenn Gebhard; (202) 296-3686; fax (202) 296-3948; info@lirf.org
Internet: http://www.lirf.org
Sponsor: Luther I. Replogle Foundation
1111 19th Street NW, Suite 900
Washington, DC 20036

Lydia deForest Charitable Trust Grants 2946
The Lydia Collins deForest Charitable Trust was established in 2002. The deForest Charitable Trust specifically supports: organizations that provide services to those who are visually limited; churches and organizations affiliated with the Protestant Episcopal Church in the United States and other religious organizations in union with or recognized by the Episcopal Church; and organizations that provide services to those who are homeless, unemployed, or substance-dependent. Special consideration is given to the following 3 organizations: The Lighthouse, Inc., in New York, New York; the Calvary Episcopal Church of Summit, New Jersey; and the Salvation Army in Union, New Jersey. Grant requests for general operating support are strongly encouraged. Program support will also be considered. Small, program-related capital expenses may be included in general operating or program requests. To better support the capacity of nonprofit organizations, multi-year funding requests are encouraged. Applicants must apply online at the grant website. Applicants are strongly encouraged to do the following before applying: review the downloadable state application procedures for additional helpful information and clarifications; review the downloadable online-application guidelines at the grant website; review the trust's funding history (link is available from the grant website); review the online application questions in advance; and review the list of required attachments. These will generally include: a list of board members, financial statements (audited, reviewed, or compiled by independent auditor); an organization summary; a list of other funding sources; an IRS Determination letter; and other required documents. All attachments must be uploaded in the online application as PDF, Word, or Excel files. The application deadline for the deForest Charitable Trust is 11:59 p.m., November 30. Applicants will be notified of grant decisions before February 28 of the following year.
Requirements: Applicants must have 501(c)3 status and serve the people of New Jersey. Occasional support is given to organizations within the Metro New York City area.
Restrictions: The trust does not support requests from individuals, organizations attempting to influence policy through direct lobbying, or any political campaigns.
Geographic Focus: New Jersey
Date(s) Application is Due: Nov 30
Contact: Ken Goody, Senior Vice President; (646) 855-0956; kenneth.l.goody@baml.com
Internet: https://www.bankofamerica.com/philanthropic/fn_search.action
Sponsor: Lydia Collins deForest Charitable Trust
One Bryant Park, NY1-100-28-05
New York, NY 10036

Lynde and Harry Bradley Foundation Grants 2947
The foundation aims to encourage projects that focus on cultivating a renewed, healthier, and more vigorous sense of citizenship among the American people and among peoples of other nations. Projects likely to be supported will generally treat free people as self-governing, personally responsible citizens, not as victims or clients; aim to restore the intellectual and cultural legitimacy of common sense, the wisdom of experience, everyday morality, and personal character; seek to reinvigorate and re-empower the traditional, local institutions—families, schools, churches, and neighborhoods—that provide training in and room for the exercise of genuine citizenship, that pass on everyday morality to the next generation, and that cultivate personal character; and encourage decentralization of power and accountability away from centralized, bureaucratic, national institutions back to states, localities, and revitalized mediating structures. Eligible projects may address any arena of public life—economics, politics, culture, or civil society; the problem of citizenship at home or abroad; Milwaukee and Wisconsin community and state projects that aim to improve the life of the community through increasing cultural and educational opportunities, grassroots economic development, and social and health services; the resuscitation of citizenship in the economic, political, cultural, or social realms; policy research and writing about approaches encouraging that resuscitation; academic research and writing that explore the intellectual roots of citizenship; and popular writing and media projects that illustrate for a broader public audience the themes of citizenship. The foundation supports programs that research the needs of gifted children and techniques of providing education for students with superior skills and/or intelligence; research programs investigating how learning occurs in gifted children; and demonstration programs of instruction.
Requirements: As an initial step, tax-exempt and nonprofit organizations should prepare a brief letter of inquiry presenting a concise description of their project, its objectives and significance, and the qualifications of the organizations and individuals involved. If the project appears to fall within the foundation's mandate, the applicant will be invited to submit a formal proposal. If invited to submit a formal proposal, the applicant should submit another letter. It should include a more-thorough, yet still concise description of the project, its objectives and significance, and the qualifications of the groups and individuals involved in it. It should also include a project budget, the specific amount being sought from Bradley, and a list of its other sources of support, philanthropic or otherwise.
Restrictions: The foundation favors projects that are normally not financed by public funds and will consider requests from religious organizations that are not denominational in character. Grants without significant importance to the foundation's areas of interest will only under special conditions be considered for endowment or deficit financing proposals. Grants will not be made to individuals, for overhead costs, or for fund-raising counsel.
Geographic Focus: All States

Date(s) Application is Due: Feb 1; May 1; Aug 1; Nov 1
Amount of Grant: 25,000 - 300,000 USD
Contact: Daniel P. Schmidt; (414) 291-9915; fax (414) 291-9991
Internet: http://www.bradleyfdn.org/program_interests.asp
Sponsor: Lynde and Harry Bradley Foundation
1241 North Franklin Place
Milwaukee, WI 53202-2901

Lynde and Harry Bradley Foundation Prizes: Bradley Prizes 2948
The Bradley Prizes formally recognize individuals of extraordinary talent and dedication who have made contributions of excellence in areas consistent with The Lynde and Harry Bradley Foundation's mission. Up to four Prizes of $250,000 each are awarded annually to innovative thinkers and practitioners whose achievements strengthen the legacy of the Bradley brothers and the ideas to which they were committed. Each year, Bradley Prize nominations are solicited from a national panel of more than 100 prominent individuals involved in academia, public-policy research, journalism, civic affairs, and the arts. All nominees are carefully evaluated by a distinguished selection committee that makes recommendations to the Foundation's Board of Directors, which selects them. The Prize winners are then honored at a celebratory awards ceremony.
Geographic Focus: All States
Amount of Grant: 250,000 USD
Contact: Daniel P. Schmidt; (414) 291-9915; fax (414) 291-9991
Internet: http://www.bradleyfdn.org/bradley_prizes.asp
Sponsor: Lynde and Harry Bradley Foundation
1241 North Franklin Place
Milwaukee, WI 53202-2901

Lyndhurst Foundation Grants 2949
The foundation concentrates its funding on a variety of strategic partnerships that serve to strengthen and enhance the design, animation, ecology, and livability of metropolitan Chattanooga and advance the protection and restoration of the region's forests, watersheds, and natural systems. Contact the Foundation before submitting any requests.
Requirements: Any Chattanooga-based nonprofit organization is eligible to apply.
Geographic Focus: All States
Date(s) Application is Due: Jan 11; Apr 1; Jul 5; Sep 30
Contact: Benic M. Clark III; (423) 756-0767; bclark@lyndhurstfoundation.org
Sponsor: Lyndhurst Foundation
517 E Fifth Street
Chattanooga, TN 37403-1826

M.B. and Edna Zale Foundation Grants 2950
The M.B. & Edna Zale Foundation honors the tradition of its founders through grants that stimulate change. To accomplish this mission, the Foundation acts as a catalyst for collaboration and makes grants in communities where the Directors live or have an interest. Grants are made primarily in the communities of Dallas (Dallas County) and Houston (Harris County), Texas; Boca Raton, Florida; Portland, Oregon; and New York, including Long Island. The Foundation has an interest in four areas of funding: community services; health; education; Jewish heritage.
Requirements: 501(c)3 nonprofits organizations in the communities of Dallas (Dallas County) and Houston (Harris County), Texas; Boca Raton, Florida; Portland, Oregon; and New York, including Long Island are eligible. Contact the Foundation for further application information and guidelines.
Restrictions: The Foundation does not ordinarily provide: major support for the arts; grants to individuals; scholarships and fellowships to individuals (except through colleges and universities).
Geographic Focus: Florida, New York, Oregon, Texas
Amount of Grant: 2,000 - 100,000 USD
Contact: Leonard Krasnow; (214) 855-0627; fax (972) 726-7252; mail@zalefoundation.org
Sponsor: M.B. and Edna Zale Foundation
6360 LBJ Highway, Suite 205
Dallas, TX 75240

M. Bastian Family Foundation Grants 2951
The foundation supports nonprofit organizations in its areas of interest, including music, the arts, higher education, health care and health organizations, religion (Christian and Latter-day Saints), social services, and wildlife conservation. Types of support include general operating support and scholarship funds. Contact the office for application forms. There are no application deadlines.
Requirements: Funding focus is primarily in Utah.
Restrictions: Grants are not made to individuals.
Geographic Focus: All States
Amount of Grant: 2,000 - 200,000 USD
Contact: McKay Matthews, Program Contact; (801) 225-2455
Sponsor: M. Bastian Family Foundation
51 W Center Street, Suite 305
Orem, UT 84057

M.D. Anderson Foundation Grants 2952
The Anderson Foundation funds projects for the improvement of working class conditions among workers, and for the establishment, support and maintenance of hospitals, homes and institutions for the care of the young, sick, the aged, and the helpless. The Foundation also gives for the improvement of general living conditions and for the promotion of health, science, education, and the advancement of knowledge. Funding is given for aging center and services; education; employment; government/public administration; health care; human services; medical specialties public policy and research; and youth services. Types of support include building and/or renovation, equipment, matching/challenge support, research, and seed money.
Requirements: Organizations should submit a letter of inquiry with the following information: a copy of their IRS determination letter; a detailed description of their project and amount of funding requested; a copy of the current year's organizational budget and/or project budget; and a listing of additional sources and amount of support. Applicants should submit five copies of the proposal. There are no deadlines. The Board meets once a month, with organizations contacted within four weeks.
Restrictions: Funding is given primarily in Texas, with emphasis on the Houston area. Grants are not available to individuals, operating funds, or endowments.
Geographic Focus: Texas
Amount of Grant: 25,000 - 200,000 USD
Contact: Karen Jenkins, Grant Contact; (713) 216-1095
Sponsor: M.D. Anderson Foundation
P.O. Box 2558
Houston, TX 77252-8037

M.E. Raker Foundation Grants 2953
The foundation was established in 1984, serving the Allen County, Indiana area. Areas of interest include: children/youth; services; education; environment; natural resources; health care; historic preservation/historical societies; human services people with disabilities. Support is offered in the following areas: building/renovation; general/operating support; matching/challenge support; Program development. No support for the arts or to individuals.
Requirements: Indiana nonprofit organizations are eligible. Emphasis is given to requests from Fort Wayne. Send a letter requesting an application to the foundation office. Application form required for grant proposals.
Geographic Focus: Indiana
Contact: Jennifer Pickard, Grants Coordinator; (260) 436-2182
Sponsor: M.E. Raker Foundation
6207 Constitution Drive
Fort Wayne, IN 46804-1517

M.J. Murdock Charitable Trust General Grants 2954
The M.J. Murdock Charitable Trust General Grants provides support for education, arts and culture, and health and human services. The Trust considers educational projects in formal and informal settings, emphasizing enhancement or expansion, as well as new educational approaches. Of special interest to the Trust are the following: performance and visual arts projects which enrich the cultural environment of the region and educational outreach efforts; and programs that emphasize preventative efforts which address physical, spiritual, social, and psychological needs, with a focus on youth. Grants are awarded for capital projects, program initiation, expansion, or for increased organizational capacity. Organizations are encouraged to view the grants awarded link for examples of previously funded grants.
Requirements: Before proceeding, interested parties should review the General Grant Application Guidelines to see if their organization is eligible or their project is appropriate for application to the Trust. After determining eligibility and appropriateness, organizations must submit a letter of inquiry before proceeding with the application. Upon approval, the organization will use the Trust's General Grant Application form and procedures.
Restrictions: The Trust only funds programs in the Pacific Northwest region: Alaska, Idaho, Montana, Oregon, and Washington. The following requests for funding are not considered: specific individuals and/or their personal benefit; individuals unauthorized to act on behalf of a qualified tax-exempt organization; funds that will ultimately be passed through to other organizations; propagandizing or for influencing legislation and elections; institutions that in policy or practice unfairly discriminate against race, ethnic, origin, sex, creed, or religion; sectarian or religious organizations whose principal activity is for the primary benefit of their own members; or for long-term loans, debt retirement, or operational deficits. The following funding requests are rarely considered: normal ongoing operations or the continuation of existing projects; endowments or revolving funds that act as such; continuation of programs previously financed from other external sources; urgent needs, emergency, or gap funding; organizations organized or operating outside any state or territory of the United States.
Geographic Focus: Alaska, Idaho, Montana, Oregon, Washington
Contact: Marybeth Stewart Goon; (360) 694-8415; fax (360) 694-1819
Internet: http://www.murdock-trust.org/grants/general-grants.php
Sponsor: M.J. Murdock Charitable Trust
703 Broadway, Suite 710
Vancouver, WA 98660

M3C Fellowships 2955
The Midwest Campus Compact Citizen-Scholar (M3C) Fellows Program is a ten-state initiative led by the Wisconsin Campus Compact that is dedicated to implementing institutional change. The M3C Fellows Program is committed to integrating education with civic engagement among campuses across the Midwest. The M3C Fellows Program is an AmeriCorps Education Award Program. Students who are involved in this program will receive an education award to use toward tuition, loan payments, etc. in return for community service.
Requirements: Campuses are selected to participate in the M3C Fellows Program based on a competitive application process. Applications are considered on an ongoing basis in the order that they are received until all slots are filled. Each campus must: (1) be a member of Campus Compact; (2) agree to support a minimum cohort of seven student fellows; (3) identify a new or existing program into which the M3C Fellows Program could naturally be integrated; (4) designate an individual to provide the fellows with regular oversight and guidance (In many cases, the person managing an existing program may also serve as the local M3C fellowship coordinator). Additionally, priority will be given to campuses that

can provide stipends or additional financial support to a cohort of M3C Fellows (through institutional scholarships/stipends, Federal Work Study, or other resources).
Geographic Focus: Illinois, Indiana, Iowa, Kansas, Kentucky, Michigan, Minnesota, Missouri, Ohio, Wisconsin
Contact: Kim White; (262) 595-2514; fax (262) 595-2501; kim.white@uwp.edu
Internet: http://www.wicampuscompact.org/m3c/mabout.php
Sponsor: Midwest Campus Compact Citizen-Scholar (M3C) Fellows Program
P.O. Box 2000
Kenosha, WI 53141-2000

Mabel A. Horne Trust Grants 2956
The Mabel A. Horne Trust was established in 1957 to support and promote quality educational, human-services, and health-care programming for underserved populations. Grant requests for general operating support are strongly encouraged. Program support will also be considered. Small, program-related capital expenses may be included in general operating or program requests. The majority of grants from the Horne Trust are one year in duration; on occasion, multi-year support is awarded. Applicants must apply online at the grant website. Applicants are strongly encouraged to do the following before applying: review the downloadable state application procedures for additional helpful information and clarifications; review the downloadable online-application guidelines at the grant website; review the trust's funding history (link is available from the grant website); review the online application questions in advance; and review the list of required attachments. These will generally include: a list of board members, financial statements (audited, reviewed, or compiled by independent auditor); an organization summary; a list of other funding sources; an IRS Determination letter; and other required documents. All attachments must be uploaded in the online application as PDF, Word, or Excel files. The application deadline for the Mabel A. Horne Trust is 11:59 p.m. on February 1. Applicants will be notified of grant decisions before May 31.
Requirements: Applicants must have 501(c)3 tax-exempt status.
Restrictions: The trust does not support requests from individuals, organizations attempting to influence policy through direct lobbying, or any political campaigns.
Geographic Focus: Massachusetts
Date(s) Application is Due: Feb 1
Contact: Miki C. Akimoto, Vice President; (866) 778-6859; miki.akimoto@baml.com
Internet: https://www.bankofamerica.com/philanthropic/fn_search.action
Sponsor: Mabel A. Horne Trust
225 Franklin Street, 4th Floor, MA1-225-04-02
Boston, MA 02110

Mabel F. Hoffman Charitable Trust Grants 2957
The Mabel F. Hoffman Charitable Trust was established in 1969 to support and promote quality educational, human-services, and health-care programming for underserved populations. Special consideration is given to charitable organizations that serve the people of Hartford, Connecticut. The trust makes approximately twelve, modest size grants per year. Grants from the Hoffman Charitable Trust are one year in duration. Applicants must apply online at the grant website. Applicants are strongly encouraged to do the following before applying: review the downloadable state application procedures for additional helpful information and clarifications; review the downloadable online-application guidelines at the grant website; review the trust's funding history (link is available from the grant website); review the online application questions in advance; and review the list of required attachments. These will generally include: a list of board members, financial statements (audited, reviewed, or compiled by independent auditor); an organization summary; a list of other funding sources; an IRS Determination letter; and other required documents. All attachments must be uploaded in the online application as PDF, Word, or Excel files. The deadline for application to the Mabel F. Hoffman Charitable Trust is 11:59 p.m. on June 15. Applicants will be notified of grant decisions by letter within two to three months after the proposal deadline.
Requirements: First time applicants should contact the Program Officer before applying (see Contact Info below). Applicants must have 501(c)3 tax-exempt status.
Restrictions: Grant requests for capital projects will not be considered. Applicants will not be awarded a grant for more than three consecutive years. The trust does not support requests from individuals, organizations attempting to influence policy through direct lobbying, or any political campaigns.
Geographic Focus: Connecticut
Date(s) Application is Due: Jun 15
Contact: Kate Kerchaert; (860) 657-7016; kate.kerchaert@baml.com
Internet: https://www.bankofamerica.com/philanthropic/fn_search.action
Sponsor: Mabel F. Hoffman Charitable Trust
200 Glastonbury Boulevard, Suite # 200, CT2-545-02-05
Glastonbury, CT 06033-4056

Mabel Louise Riley Foundation Family Strengthening Small Grants 2958
Mabel Louise Riley Foundation Family Strengthening Grants fund activities and projects in the greater Dudley area of Roxbury and Dorchester, Massachusetts that build, strengthen, and support families. The Foundation will give priority to projects and activities which focus on: mending the social fabric of the neighborhood; building, strengthening, and supporting personal and family development; broadening the horizons of individuals and families; removing barriers to employment; increasing parental involvement; beautifying outdoor spaces; and community engagement. Examples include: out-of-school activities for youth or inter-generational activities; parenting seminars; life skills workshops (cooking, sewing, etc.); support groups and services for single parents; community support for reintegrating residents from situations such as recovery, incarceration, etc; or neighborhood cleanups. In addition to resident volunteers, volunteer-run neighborhood groups and associations are eligible. Nonprofit 501(c)3 status is not required, but the organization must be organized for charitable activities for the benefit of the families and neighborhoods.
Requirements: The application is available at the website and must include detailed information about the organization, its proposed project, and budget.
Restrictions: Large social service agencies, community-based organizations, and for-profit entities are not eligible.
Geographic Focus: Massachusetts
Date(s) Application is Due: Apr 25
Amount of Grant: 500 - 5,000 USD
Contact: Nancy Saunders; (617) 399-1850; fax (617) 399-1851; nsaunders@rileyfoundation.com
Internet: http://www.rileyfoundation.com/sginfo.htm
Sponsor: Mabel Louise Riley Foundation
77 Summer Street, 8th Floor
Boston, MA 02110

Mabel Louise Riley Foundation Grants 2959
Mabel Louise Riley Foundation Grants are made to charities incorporated in Massachusetts, with preference for the city of Boston. The Foundation's current priorities include: collaboration with other funders; education and social services for disadvantaged children and adolescents; preschool reading programs; community development that will benefit low-income and minority neighborhoods, including job development and training, and housing; citywide efforts in Boston and vicinity that promote cultural improvements and the arts; grants that, despite some risk, offer high impact or significant benefits for a community; and improvement of race relations and neighborhood safety issues. The Foundation is especially interested in leveraging its grants by funding new programs that can become self-sufficient or which may serve as a model in other geographic areas. Grants from the Foundation normally range from $50,000 to $100,000. Occasionally, when the Foundation decides to pursue a special initiative, the Trustees will consider smaller or larger funding commitments. Multiple year funding may be available, if necessary to fulfill the funding objectives.
Requirements: Applicants are required to submit a proposal of no more than two pages without a cover letter before submitting a formal grant request. This summary should briefly describe the purposes and objectives of the proposal, the history of the applicant, and the amount requested from the Foundation. In addition to the two-page summary, a copy of the IRS 501(c)3 Determination Letter and a program budget should be included. If the filing of a formal grant request is authorized, it must be made using the Common Proposal Form of the Associated Grant Makers (AGM). The narrative portion of the request should not exceed five pages and the attachments required by the Common Proposal Form must be included: AGM Cover Summary;; executive summary (one page snapshot of proposal narrative); current financial statements (balance sheet and P/L); most recent audited financial statement; IRS Form 990, Form 990EZ, or Form 990-N (if applicable); program budget (multi-year, if applicable); organizational budget (multi-year, if applicable); board of trustees/directors (with affiliations); resumes of key project personnel; and sources of funding with amounts (secured and pending). Each formal grant request must contain a clear statement of how the success or failure of the program will be evaluated, including an outcome chart, if applicable. There are no deadlines for these proposal summaries; it is an ongoing process. The Foundation will notify the applicant if the submission of a formal grant request is authorized.
Restrictions: Applicants whose formal grant requests have been denied must wait one full year before reapplying. Grant recipients should expect to wait two full years before submitting a new request. Funding is usually not granted for: grants to defray annual deficits, for regular operating budgets, or as the sole source of support for an agency; grants to governmental agencies or on behalf of individuals for personal needs, travel, research, loans or scholarships, and political purposes.
Geographic Focus: Massachusetts
Amount of Grant: 50,000 - 100,000 USD
Contact: Nancy Saunders; (617) 399-1850; nsaunders@rileyfoundation.com
Internet: http://www.rileyfoundation.com
Sponsor: Mabel Louise Riley Foundation
77 Summer Street, 8th Floor
Boston, MA 02110

Mabel Y. Hughes Charitable Trust Grants 2960
The Trust awards grants to Denver-area nonprofit organizations in its areas of interest, including children and youth services; education; family services; health care; higher education; human services; children's and art museums; performing arts centers; performing arts, opera; and reproductive health and family planning. Types of support include: annual campaigns; continuing support; emergency funds; endowments; equipment; general/operating support; program development; research; and seed money.
Requirements: Organizations should submit a letter of inquiry to the Trust, and if their project is appropriate for funding, they will be asked to submit a proposal.
Restrictions: The Trust does not support funding for individuals, deficit financing, scholarships, fellowships, or loans.
Geographic Focus: Colorado
Amount of Grant: 10,000 - 30,000 USD
Contact: Peggy Toal, c/o Wells Fargo Bank, Private Client Services; (720) 947-6725
Sponsor: Mabel Y. Hughes Charitable Trust
1740 Broadway
Denver, CO 80274

MacArthur Foundation Chicago Arts and Culture General Operations Grants 2961
The MacArthur Foundation's support for arts and culture in the Chicago area is an expression of its civic commitment to Chicago. MacArthur provides multi-year, general operating support to Chicago-area theaters, dance groups, music organizations, art programs, film centers, museums, and libraries. Additional grants support short-term projects that benefit a set of organizations or the field as a whole. In reviewing proposals from arts groups, the Foundation considers: quality of the organization's artistic program; strength of its board

and staff leadership; impact on the organization's neighborhood, the city or the region; sizes and types of audiences served; and community and educational outreach activities.
Requirements: Applicants must be Chicago-based theaters, dance groups, music organizations, art programs, film centers, museums, or libraries.
Geographic Focus: Illinois
Contact: Deepa Gupta, Program Officer; (312) 726-8000; fax (312) 920-6258; dgupta@macfound.org or 4answers@macfound.org
Internet: http://www.macfound.org/info-grantseekers/grantmaking-guidelines/arts-grant-guideline/
Sponsor: John D. and Catherine T. MacArthur Foundation
140 S Dearborn Street, Suite 1100
Chicago, IL 60603-5285

MacArthur Foundation Chicago Arts & Culture International Connections Grants 2962
The MacArthur Foundation's support for over 200 arts and cultural organizations in Chicago and the region is an expression of its civic commitment to the community where the Foundation is headquartered and John and Catherine MacArthur made their home. Grants are designed to help sustain the cultural life of the city and region. To encourage a greater sharing of experiences and international learning, the Foundation has established a $1 million fund to help eligible non-profit arts and culture organizations advance their work by collaborating with peer organizations abroad. Individual grants will range from $5,000 to $50,000. Applications are due to the Foundation between June 1 and July 1.
Requirements: Grant funds must be used in accordance with applicable law. Any travel or expenses associated with the grant including hotels and other accommodations, must be reasonable and necessary to accomplish the grant purposes. Additional expense guidelines will be made available to successful applicants.
Geographic Focus: Illinois, All Countries
Contact: Deepa Gupta, Program Officer; (312) 726-8000; fax (312) 920-6258; dgupta@macfound.org or icf2012@macfound.org
Internet: http://www.macfound.org/info-grantseekers/grantmaking-guidelines/arts-and-culture-international-c/
Sponsor: John D. and Catherine T. MacArthur Foundation
140 S Dearborn Street, Suite 1100
Chicago, IL 60603-5285

MacArthur Foundation Conservation and Sustainable Development Grants 2963
The MacArthur Foundation is concerned about the deteriorating condition of the biosphere that supports life on earth. For the decade 2000-2010, the Foundation pursued a strategy that focused on eight ecological hotspots (places of high biodiversity under threat) in Madagascar, Melanesia, the Andes, Insular Caribbean, Albertine Rift, Eastern Himalayas, and Lower Mekong. In 2011, the Foundation launched a new strategy that is focused on one of the most compelling environmental challenges of the 21st century: the conservation of ecosystems. Ecosystems and their biodiversity underpin human well-being. They provide food and water; regulate floods, drought, and disease; and support soil formation and pollination. They also have intangible value as places of spiritual significance. All these are vital services, essential to economies and nation states. Hence, with the current Conservation and Sustainable Development program, the objective is to slow this degradation of ecosystems and, eventually, to reverse it. The geographical focus will be on three regions: the Great Lakes of East Central Africa, the Greater Mekong and its headwaters, and the watersheds of the Andes. Each is a place of high biodiversity, important freshwater service, and carbon-storage value. MacArthur's conservation and sustainable development program makes grants on a three-year recurring cycle, with one portfolio of grants prepared annually within each region and for the coastal marine initiative.
Geographic Focus: All States
Date(s) Application is Due: Feb 3; Apr 20; Jun 15
Contact: Douglas G. Siegel; (312) 726-8000; fax (312) 920-6258; 4answers@macfound.org
Internet: http://www.macfound.org/programs/conservation/
Sponsor: John D. and Catherine T. MacArthur Foundation
140 S Dearborn Street, Suite 1100
Chicago, IL 60603-5285

MacArthur Foundation Policy Research Grants 2964
Domestic policy-related activities — research, analysis, and the education of policymakers and the general public — are included in both the MacArthur Foundation's Policy Research program area and also in other grantmaking areas such as Juvenile Justice and Community and Economic Development. The purposes of MacArthur's grantmaking in policy research are to: advance the state of knowledge in specific areas, with outcomes that benefit individuals, families and communities, and society as a whole; improve decision making at multiple levels; strengthen the links among research, policy and practice, with each activity informing the others; and apply policy analysis to and foster transparency of complex political processes. The Policy Research area undertakes special initiatives with broad implications for domestic policy. Currently, there are four underway. Three inter-related projects address economic, social, and demographic trends in U.S. society and more data- and evidence-driven policymaking, and a fourth is the capstone to more than a decade of grantmaking in regional policy and practice. Those interested in suggesting a project in this area should submit a letter of inquiry to the Foundation.
Geographic Focus: Illinois
Contact: Valerie Chang; (312) 726-8000; fax (312) 920-6258; vchang@macfound.org
Internet: http://www.macfound.org/info-grantseekers/grantmaking-guidelines/policy_research-grant-guidelines/
Sponsor: John D. and Catherine T. MacArthur Foundation
140 S Dearborn Street, Suite 1100
Chicago, IL 60603-5285

MacDonald-Peterson Foundation Grants 2965
Established in 1995 in Texas, the MacDonald-Peterson Foundation offers funding for health and human services programs in Texas. The Foundation's primary fields of interest include: children's services; Christian agencies and churches; community and economic development; food banks; health organizations; higher education; hospitals; human services; medical research; mental health counseling and support groups; performing arts (orchestras); and youth development and community service clubs. There is no specified application format or annual deadlines, so applicants should begin the process by contacting the Foundation directly. Awards generally range from $5,000 to $20,000, and are given for general operations.
Requirements: Any 501(c)3 organization in or serving residents of Texas are eligible.
Geographic Focus: Texas
Contact: Guy Tabor, (713)579-2355
Sponsor: MacDonald-Peterson Foundation
1 Riverway, Suite 1000
Houston, TX 77056-1944

Macquarie Bank Foundation Grants 2966
The Foundation is one of Australia's oldest and largest corporate foundations contributing more than $150 million to more than 1500 community organizations world-wide since 1985. The Foundation focuses its resources in five core areas - the arts, education, environment, health, and welfare. The Foundation is also committed to projects specifically aimed at supporting indigenous communities. The Foundation's funding criteria is flexible and open. It welcomes applications from a diverse range of community organizations that are working in innovative ways to provide long-term benefits. Funding levels are flexible and are dictated by the needs of the organization and funding availability. Each application is assessed on its individual merit, with priority given to programs which support a broad section of the community at a regional, state or national level; have the involvement or potential for involvement of Macquarie Bank staff through volunteering, fundraising, pro bono work and board and/or management committee involvement; are located in cities/countries where Macquarie Bank staff are located; and deliver long-term benefits and build community sustainability. Prospective applicants are encouraged to check the Foundation website or contact Foundation Staff for more information on how to apply.
Geographic Focus: All States, All Countries
Amount of Grant: 100 - 500,000 USD
Contact: Heather Matwejev, Macquarie Bank Foundation, Asia; +61 2 8232 6951; fax +61 2 8232 0019; heather.matwejev@macquarie.com or foundation@macquarie.com
Internet: http://www.macquarie.com/mgl/com/foundation/about/application-guidelines
Sponsor: Macquarie Bank Foundation
G.P.O. Box 4294
Sydney, NSW 1164 Australia

Maddie's Fund Community Collaborative Projects 2967
Maddie's Fund supports coalitions of animal control agencies, traditional shelters, adoption guarantee organizations, and private practice veterinarians so entire cities, counties, and states can pool their resources to create a community-wide, no-kill safety net for companion animals. Projects are funded in diverse geographic, demographic, and socio-economic regions to demonstrate that models of lifesaving can be created throughout the country. The Foundation is interested in funding communities that are saving all (or a majority) of their healthy shelter dogs and cats and are seeking assistance to save their treatable shelter dogs and cats. Samples of previously funded projects are available at the website. The wide range of funding depends on the particular area and project.
Requirements: Organizations must apply for both programs within the Community Collaborative Project: Maddie's Pet Rescue Project (adoption program) and Maddie's Spay/Neuter Project (spay/neuter program). Organizations should contact Maddie's Fund directly to apply. There are no deadlines and organizations may apply anytime.
Geographic Focus: All States
Amount of Grant: 1,000,000 - 25,000,000 USD
Contact: Joey Bloomfield; (510) 337-8988; fax (510) 337-8989; info@maddies.org
Internet: http://www.maddiesfund.org/Grant_Giving/Community_Collaborative.html
Sponsor: Maddie's Fund
2223 Santa Clara Avenue, Suite B
Alameda, CA 94501-4416

Maddie's Fund Community Shelter Data Grants 2968
The goal of Maddie's Fund is to help build a no-kill nation where all healthy and treatable (underage, sick, injured, and poorly behaved) shelter dogs and cats find loving new homes. Maddie's Fund strives to reach the no-kill nation goal by awarding grants to community collaborations (coalitions of rescue groups, animal control agencies, traditional shelters, and private practice veterinarians), veterinary medical associations, and colleges of veterinary medicine. Coalitions of animal groups operating in any county, region or state in the United States with a human population of 100,000 or greater may be eligible to apply for these grants. This is not a funding opportunity for an individual animal group. The data collection and reporting needs to be community based. Shelter statistics need to be collected from all groups participating in the coalition. At a minimum, the coalition must include all animal control agencies and all traditional shelters located in the target community. The coalition also needs to provide an opportunity for adoption guarantee organizations located in the target community to participate. Each participating group in the coalition must agree to publish their shelter statistics on their website and in at least one major publication (annual report, newsletter, etc.).
Requirements: To apply for a Shelter Data Grant, coalitions must submit a pre-grant inquiry using the Maddie's Fund form. The pre-grant inquiry provides a thumbnail sketch of the target community. It identifies the geographic area comprising the target community, lists the participating groups in the coalition, and reports basic shelter data community-wide for

the most recent calendar year. The form may be submitted by mail or email. Maddie's Fund will then contact the applicant about whether they are eligible to submit an application. Applications may be submitted year round and there are no deadlines.
Restrictions: Animal groups located in Maddie's Fund-supported project areas are not eligible to apply for this grant (see website for current project area locations).
Geographic Focus: All States
Amount of Grant: 10,000 - 40,000 USD
Contact: Joey Bloomfield, Grants Specialist; (510) 337-8988; fax (510) 337-8989; info@maddiesfund.org
Internet: http://www.maddiesfund.org/Grant_Giving/Shelter_Data_Grants.html
Sponsor: Maddie's Fund
2223 Santa Clara Avenue, Suite B
Alameda, CA 94501-4416

Maddie's Fund Lifesaving Awards 2969
Maddie's Community Lifesaving Award acknowledges the outstanding contributions being made by communities that have implemented an adoption guarantee for all healthy shelter pets or have achieved no-kill status (an adoption guarantee for healthy and treatable pets) and are likely to sustain it in the future. These awards are designed to acknowledge the outstanding contributions being made by coalitions consisting of traditional shelters, adoption guarantee organizations, and animal control agencies in which all groups have already implemented: an adoption guarantee for healthy pets in their target community and are likely to sustain it in the future (adoption guarantee community); or an adoption guarantee for all healthy and treatable shelter pets in their target community and are likely to sustain it in the future (no-kill community). Awards range from $200,000 to $3 million, depending on the size of the community. Detailed information about previous awards is located on the website.
Requirements: Awards are community-based and must be applied for on behalf of a coalition. Communities in the United States with a human population of 200,000 or more are eligible to apply. There are no deadlines and organizations may apply any time. Organizations should contact Maddie's Fund directly to apply.
Restrictions: An individual animal welfare organization is not eligible to apply for this award unless it is doing so on behalf of a coalition.
Geographic Focus: All States
Amount of Grant: 200,000 - 3,000,000 USD
Contact: Joey Bloomfield, Grants Specialist; (510) 337-8988; fax (510) 337-8989; info@maddiesfund.org or grants@maddiesfund.org
Internet: http://www.maddiesfund.org/Grant_Giving/Lifesaving_Awards/Lifesaving_Awards.html
Sponsor: Maddie's Fund
2223 Santa Clara Avenue, Suite B
Alameda, CA 94501-4416

Madison Community Foundation Altrusa International of Madison Grants 2970
Altrusa International of Madison, Inc. is a women's service club that has provided direct service and funding for community organizations since 1923. Altrusa established a donor advised fund with the Foundation in 1986 to further its aim of providing service to the community. Grants from the Altrusa Fund are made in the area of literacy and education broadly defined including: projects to help children and youth meet their full educational potential; projects designed to expand opportunities for people returning to school or the workforce or for retraining; projects for people who need assistance to succeed in school so that they are able to be self-supporting; projects that foster parental involvement with their children's schooling; and projects that focus on lifelong learning. Grant applications and guideline are available at the website.
Geographic Focus: Wisconsin
Date(s) Application is Due: Feb 1
Contact: Tom Linfield, Vice President; (608) 232-1768 or (888) 400-7643; fax (608) 232-1772; tlinfield@madisoncommunityfoundation.org
Internet: http://www.madisoncommunityfoundation.org/Page.aspx?pid=274
Sponsor: Madison Community Foundation
2 Science Court, P.O. Box 5010
Madison, WI 53705

Madison Community Foundation Grants 2971
Madison Community Foundation Grants are designed to gather ideas and advance initiatives that impact lives and the community for the long term. Focus areas include arts, children, community development, elderly, environment, learning, and youth. Capital and program grants are offered. Capital grants support the construction, purchase and renovation of facilities, land acquisition, and occasionally the purchase of vehicles or equipment. Program grants support new programs or expansion of existing programs that have a track record of success. Capital grants average $55,000, and program grants average $35,000. Approximately 25 percent of the applications received are funded at some level. The Foundation is rarely the sole financial supporter of projects. Applicants must submit a letter of inquiry. Selected applicants will then be invited to complete a full grant application. Letters of inquiry are due January 18 and July 15. A letter of inquiry form and additional guidelines may be found at the website.
Requirements: Eligible non-profit 501(c)3 organizations or governmental bodies, including schools and municipalities, must serve the people of Dane County and conduct business without discrimination on the basis of race, religion, gender, sexual preference, age, marital status, disability or national origin. Eligible projects will: have a long-term impact on Dane County residents and/or the physical environments in Dane County; include meaningful, reasonable, and measurable outcomes; use innovative approaches to address community issues; strengthen and enhance community assets; build the self-sufficiency of individuals and/or organizations; attract additional funding; and use partnerships and/or collaboration.

Restrictions: The Foundation does not fund: individuals; endowments not held by the Foundation; debt retirement; lobbying; annual campaigns; scholarships; religious organizations for religious purposes; short-term events such as conferences, festivals, fund raising functions and celebrations; substance abuse treatment; health care services, including mental health; and capital grants to support ongoing maintenance.
Geographic Focus: Wisconsin
Contact: Tom Linfield, Vice President; (608) 232-1763 or (888) 400-7643; fax (608) 232-1772; tlinfield@madisoncommunityfoundation.org
Internet: http://www.madisoncommunityfoundation.org/Page.aspx?pid=264
Sponsor: Madison Community Foundation
2 Science Court, P.O. Box 5010
Madison, WI 53705

Madison County Community Foundation City of Anderson Quality of Life Grant 2972
The Madison County Community Foundation - Quality of Life Grant is used as economic development quality of life assistance to non-profits. Generated through the City of Anderson's food and beverage tax, the grant is dispersed to those non-profits who have no voting representation on the committee; are not solely supporting non-secular activities with these funds; carry proof of 501(c)3 status; and are requesting funding for projects with outcomes rather than operational expenses. The grants must be used to increase quality of life for all rather than limited access.
Requirements: Application forms and guidelines are available from the Foundation office or may be downloaded from the Foundation website at www.madisonccf.org. The application will also be available at the City of Anderson website at www.cityofanderson.com.
Restrictions: Funding is limited to the city of Anderson, Indiana. Funding is not available for: annual fund campaigns; individuals; capital debt reduction; sectarian religious purposes; gifts to endowments; political campaigns; medical, scientific, or health research; student loans, scholarship/fellowship programs, or travel grants; programs and/or equipment which were committed prior to the grant application being submitted; organizations without responsible fiscal agents and adequate accounting procedures; schools and government agencies; normal operational expenses of the organization. Funding is limited to grants for one year.
Geographic Focus: Indiana
Date(s) Application is Due: Sep 15
Amount of Grant: 1,000 - 10,000 USD
Contact: Tammy Bowman, (765) 644-0002; fax (765) 662-1438; tbowman@madisoncf.org
Internet: http://www.madisonccf.org/index.php?submenu=grantNO&src=gendocs&ref=GrantProcess&category=Non_Profits
Sponsor: Madison County Community Foundation
33 West 10th Street, Suite 600
Anderson, IN 46015-1056

Madison County Community Foundation General Grants 2973
The Madison County Community Foundation General Grants are made to support projects and programs of non-profit agencies located in or serving residents of Madison County. Grants are typically made in the spring and fall and range from $500 to $10,000 with rare exceptions. Proposals are reviewed by a Grants Committee and those chosen are then approved by the Foundation Board. The priorities of the foundation are arts and culture, education, economic development, civic affairs, and health and human services.
Requirements: Organizations should complete the online application and include the following detailed information: their project and cost; organization information; a project narrative that includes the objective, financial need, justification; constituency; evaluation plan and community impact; additional and/or future funding; professional references and collaborative value. They should also include a list of project expenses and project income. Eight copies of the complete application package should be sent to the Program Director, along with one copy each of the board of directors, IRS tax exempt letter, and financial statement.
Geographic Focus: Indiana
Amount of Grant: 500 - 10,000 USD
Contact: Tammy Bowman, (765) 644-0002; fax (765) 644-3392; tbowman@madisoncf.org
Internet: http://www.madisonccf.org/index.php?submenu=Grants&src=gendocs&ref=Grants&category=Non_Profits
Sponsor: Madison County Community Foundation
33 West 10th Street, Suite 600
Anderson, IN 46015-1056

Maine Community Foundation Baldwin Area Grants 2974
The Foundation's Baldwin Area Grants support nonprofit organizations working in the Baldwin, Maine, area. Funding is provided to assist the residents of Baldwin in finding ways to become more self-reliant and self-sufficient by promoting: public awareness of the importance of forestry and the natural resource economy; education; sustainable management of Baldwin's natural resource-based economy; and volunteerism. Maximum awards are generally $5,000, with larger awards being considered on a case-by-case basis. Applications are available on the Foundation's website, along with examples of previously funded projects.
Requirements: Applicants must be 501(c)3 organizations eligible to accept tax-deductible donations as outlined in Section 170(c) of the Internal Revenue Code. Priority is given if the organization uses the grant to raise additional financial resources, to promote social capital, and if the organization is not likely to received funding from other sources.
Geographic Focus: Maine
Date(s) Application is Due: Jul 1
Contact: Pam Cleghorn; (877) 700-6800; fax (207) 667-0447; pcleghorn@mainecf.org
Internet: http://www.mainecf.org/PFFund.aspx
Sponsor: Maine Community Foundation
245 East Main Street
Ellsworth, ME 04605

Maine Community Foundation Belvedere Animal Welfare Grants — 2975

The Belvedere Animal Welfare Grants support organizations and programs that address population control for cats and dogs. The grants offer project support activities and expenses related to population control or management, including: subsidy or voucher programs for low-income or elderly Maine residents; education and outreach programs for cat and dog owners; and purchase or rental of medical or transport equipment when it is connected to a population control project or program with measurable goals. Capacity building grants support activities that strengthen an animal welfare organization and improve its overall operations, including: training for staff and/or volunteers, with a focus on improving volunteer management; improving fundraising, financial, or general management; expanding services and programs; developing and implementing business plans; and improving board operations. The advisory committee gives priority to proposals that: have clearly defined targets or goals and a practical strategy to measure progress; the greatest potential to positively impact the community or the organization; will be sustained after Foundation funding ends; include other sources of funding to support the proposed work; and specifically address the cat overpopulation problem. The application is available at the Foundation website.
Requirements: All grantees must be eligible to accept tax-deductible donations as outlined in Section 170(c) of the Internal Revenue Code.
Restrictions: Funding is not available for annual appeals, capital campaigns, or endowments; equine programs; training for service animals; animal-assisted therapy programs; purebred rescue efforts; programs that transport adoptable animals from other states; or program expenses that have already accumulated.
Geographic Focus: Maine
Date(s) Application is Due: Jun 15
Amount of Grant: Up to 10,000 USD
Contact: Cathy Melio; (877) 700-6800, ext 1122; fax (207) 667-0447; cmelio@mainecf.org
Internet: http://www.mainecf.org/belvanimal.aspx
Sponsor: Maine Community Foundation
245 East Main Street
Ellsworth, ME 04605

Maine Community Foundation Belvedere Historic Preservation Grants — 2976

The Foundation's Belvedere Historic Preservation Grants support the preservation or restoration of historic buildings, primarily in Washington and Hancock Counties and in under-resourced rural communities in other parts of the state. Grants focus on the preservation and reuse of historic buildings that serve as civic, cultural, or economic hubs for communities. Funding criteria is based on the property's historical significance at the local, state, or national level; the extent to which the property is threatened; the organizational readiness of the applicant to accomplish the proposed work and the likelihood of the project's completion within a year; and geographic location. Strong preference will be given to projects in Hancock and Washington counties, with some consideration for projects in other under-resourced, rural areas of the state. Questions regarding the technical aspects of historic preservation and the eligibility of proposed projects should be directed to the Maine Preservation Commission. Question about the application or review process should be directed to the Maine Community Foundation. The application is available at the Foundation's website, along with the Belvedere Fund for Historic Preservation Grants Manual.
Requirements: Applicants must be 501(c)3 organizations eligible to accept tax-deductible donations as outlined in Section 170(c) of the Internal Revenue Code. All proposed projects must be for historic buildings listed or in the process of being listed on the National Registry. If the project's total budget is larger than $25,000, the application should be for only a portion or phase of the project.
Restrictions: Religious groups are eligible but funding will not be provided for religious purposes. Funding is not provided for the following: political campaigns, or to support attempts to influence legislation of any governmental body other than through making available the results of non-partisan analysis, study and research; ongoing operating support; endowments or capital campaigns; camperships; or capital equipment over $250.
Geographic Focus: Maine
Date(s) Application is Due: Sep 15
Amount of Grant: Up to 22,000 USD
Contact: Kirk Mohney; (207) 287-2132; Kirk.Mohney@maine.gov
Internet: http://www.mainecf.org/belvederehistoric.aspx
Sponsor: Maine Community Foundation
245 East Main Street
Ellsworth, ME 04605

Maine Community Foundation Charity Grants — 2977

The Maine Community Foundation Charity Grants offer funding for the following priorities: start-up money for an organization or project; projects that involve the disabled or economically disadvantaged, as long as the project is not supported by a national campaign or public money; libraries; symphonies; hospice care; projects that are related to the Friendship, Maine area; discrete projects as opposed to general operating support; and small requests from social service organizations for buildings or purchase of necessary equipment. Application is made online from the Foundation's website.
Requirements: Applicants must be 501(c)3 organizations eligible to accept tax-deductible donations as outlined in Section 170(c) of the Internal Revenue Code.
Restrictions: Religious groups are eligible but funding will not be provided for religious purposes. Funding is not provided for the following: political campaigns, or to support attempts to influence legislation of any governmental body other than through making available the results of non-partisan analysis, study and research; ongoing operating support; endowments or capital campaigns; camperships; or capital equipment over $250.
Geographic Focus: Maine
Date(s) Application is Due: Sep 15
Amount of Grant: Up to 5,000 USD
Samples: Big Brothers Big Sisters of Bath/Brunswick, Brunswick, Maine, $1,500, copier and supplies; Community Health and Counseling Services, Bangor, Maine, $4,750, complete a business plan and feasibility study for the development of a hospice house in the greater Bangor area; and Island Community Center, Stonington, Maine $2,500, start-up costs associated with opening The Community Cafe in Stonington.
Contact: Cathy Melio; (877) 700-6800; fax (207) 667-0447; cmelio@mainecf.org
Internet: http://www.mainecf.org/mainecharityfound.aspx
Sponsor: Maine Community Foundation
245 East Main Street
Ellsworth, ME 04605

Maine Community Foundation Community Building Grants — 2978

The Foundation's Community Building Grants support organizations and programs that recognize and build on a community's strengths and assets. Grants are provided for new program development or program expansion and capacity building. Projects must meet at least one of the following priorities: develop community relationships; involve community members; and advance community leadership. Application is made online from the Foundation's website.
Requirements: Applicants must be 501(c)3 organizations eligible to accept tax-deductible donations as outlined in Section 170(c) of the Internal Revenue Code. Projects must meet the following criteria: use of existing community resources (proposed projects must use the skills, services, materials, and/or time that people and organizations in the community can and will provide); ability to strengthen community life (proposed project must make the community stronger by helping it address current or future challenges); and sustainability (proposed projects must continue to affect the community after Foundation funding has been exhausted).
Restrictions: Religious groups are eligible, but funding will not be provided for religious purposes. Funding is not provided for the following: political campaigns, or to support attempts to influence legislation of any governmental body other than through making available the results of non-partisan analysis, study and research; ongoing operating support; endowments or capital campaigns; or capital equipment over $250.
Geographic Focus: Maine
Date(s) Application is Due: Feb 15
Amount of Grant: Up to 10,000 USD
Contact: Amy Pollien, Grants Administrator; (877) 700-6800 or (207) 667-9735, ext. 1109; fax (207) 667-0447; apollien@mainecf.org or info@mainecf.org
Internet: http://www.mainecf.org/CommunityBuilding.aspx
Sponsor: Maine Community Foundation
245 East Main Street
Ellsworth, ME 04605

Maine Community Foundation Edward H. Daveis Benevolent Grants — 2979

The Foundation's Edward H. Daveis Benevolent Grants were established by the will of his daughter, Mabel Stewart Daveis. Grants are awarded for projects that benefit the communities of the greater Portland area. Grants focus on Portland organizations that work with young children, their families, and teachers, in addition to youth leadership program for students through high school. Programs that demonstrate their success may be eligible for funding for up to three years. Collaboration among nonprofits is encouraged. The application is available at the Foundation website. Collaboration among nonprofits is encouraged. A letter from the executive director of each collaborating organization is required, clearly explain the level of involvement and responsibility.
Requirements: Applicants must be 501(c)3 organizations eligible to accept tax-deductible donations as outlined in Section 170(c) of the Internal Revenue Code.
Restrictions: Religious groups are eligible but funding will not be provided for religious purposes. Funding is not provided for the following: political campaigns, or to support attempts to influence legislation of any governmental body other than through making available the results of non-partisan analysis, study and research; ongoing operating support; endowments or capital campaigns; camperships; or capital equipment over $250.
Geographic Focus: Maine
Date(s) Application is Due: Nov 15
Amount of Grant: 7,500 USD
Contact: Pam Cleghorn; (877) 7000-6800, ext. 2205; pcleghorn@mainecf.org
Internet: http://www.mainecf.org/daveisfund.aspx
Sponsor: Maine Community Foundation
245 East Main Street
Ellsworth, ME 04605

Maine Community Foundation Equity Grants — 2980

The mission of the Maine Community Foundation Equity Grants is to strengthen lesbian, gay, bisexual, transgender, and queer (LGBTQ) organizations and community-based initiatives in Maine that address LGBTQ issues and needs. The vision driving the grants is one of inclusive, diverse, prejudice-free communities for the LGBTQ population and for all people in Maine. Two types of proposals encouraged are project grants and capacity building grants. Project grants support a wide variety of projects, particularly those serving people living in rural and underserved communities in Maine. Priority areas are access to health care and reduction of health disparities; support for LGBTQ elders; education to promote respect and understanding of LGBTQ people; equality for LGBTQ families and individuals; reduction of anti-LGBTQ violence; social and cultural community-building activities; and support for LGBTQ youth. Capacity building grants support organizations whose primary mission is to serve Maine's LGBTQ community. Successful applicants will be able to describe how enhancing their organizational capacity will ultimately benefit the communities they serve. A list of previously funded projects are posted on the Foundation website. Applications are available at the Foundation's website.
Requirements: Applicants must be 501(c)3 organizations eligible to accept tax-deductible donations as outlined in Section 170(c) of the Internal Revenue Code.

Restrictions: Religious groups are eligible but funding will not be provided for religious purposes. Funding is not provided for the following: political campaigns, or to support attempts to influence legislation of any governmental body other than through making available the results of non-partisan analysis, study and research; ongoing operating support; endowments or capital campaigns; camperships; or capital equipment over $250.
Geographic Focus: Maine
Date(s) Application is Due: Sep 15
Amount of Grant: 7,500 USD
Contact: Ken Town, Grant Contact; (207) 685-4715; ktown@hotmail.com
Internet: http://www.mainecf.org/equityfund.aspx
Sponsor: Maine Community Foundation
245 East Main Street
Ellsworth, ME 04605

Maine Community Foundation Expansion Arts Grants   **2981**
The Foundation's Expansion Arts Grants support indigenous, ethnic, or rural arts programs or projects, particularly those that serve areas with limited access to arts events. Priority is given to the following: artistic quality of the program; organizations that are developing and promoting the arts of their own communities, using local artists and other resources rather than importing art and artists from outside the region or state; ability of the organization to carry out the project for which funds are requested; evidence of cooperation and coordination with other organizations and programs, within or outside of the arts; evidence of local support for proposed project (financial or in-kind donations); and projects serving underserved areas.
Requirements: Applicants must be 501(c)3 organizations eligible to accept tax-deductible donations as outlined in Section 170(c) of the Internal Revenue Code, with an operating budget of less than $250,000 a year, and a commitment to serving rural audiences and communities. Community-based projects affiliated with school districts are eligible to apply. School-affiliated projects must be open to the public.
Restrictions: The following are ineligible: endowments; capital improvements; scholarships; a regular performance series; production costs of films or annual operating expenses (except for start-up support for new organizations and unusual circumstances where a one-time grant will meet a special need). Projects are rarely funded for a second year. Curriculum-based arts projects from schools or school districts are not eligible to apply. Please contact the Grants Administrator to verify eligibility of school-affiliated projects.
Geographic Focus: Maine
Date(s) Application is Due: Sep 15
Contact: Cathy Melio; (877) 700-6800; fax (207) 667-0447; cmelio@mainecf.org
Internet: http://www.mainecf.org/expansionartsfund.aspx
Sponsor: Maine Community Foundation
245 East Main Street
Ellsworth, ME 04605

Maine Community Foundation Gracie Grants   **2982**
The Foundation's Gracie Grants offer tuition-reimbursement incentives to encourage natives of Washington County, or those who consider Washington County their home, to establish roots in the community following completion of their post-secondary education. Applicants must have graduated from college within five years of the date of application. School loan repayment awards are made to three individuals each year. Grants may be renewed for up to three years. Applications are available at the Foundation's website.
Requirements: Eligible applicants are natives of Washington County, or those who consider Washington County their home, who have recently completed school successfully and are building a professional and personal life in Washington County. Applicants must commit to fulfill their community service obligation by volunteering with a Washington County organization (e.g., social services agency, library, school, church, sports team, etc.). Applicants must commit to active participation in the Gracie program (building an action plan and attending semi-annual meetings of Gracie participants).
Restrictions: Applicants may not be in default on a loan or have deferred loans.
Geographic Focus: Maine
Date(s) Application is Due: Jul 15
Amount of Grant: Up to 5,000 USD
Contact: Cherie Galyean; (877) 700-6800 or (207) 677-9735, ext. 1106; cgalyean@mainecf.org
Internet: http://www.mainecf.org/GracieFund.aspx
Sponsor: Maine Community Foundation
245 East Main Street
Ellsworth, ME 04605

Maine Community Foundation Maine Land Conservation Grants   **2983**
The Foundation's Maine Land Conservation Grants support projects that advance land conservation and strengthen the ability of land conservation organizations and entities to conserve land. Work is supported in the areas of planning, communications, research, outreach and training that advances land conservation. Two types of award are made: grants for new or expanded projects or programs and grants to improve organizational effectiveness. Examples of supported project grant activities include: community outreach and stakeholder involvement; field surveys; volunteer stewardship training; preliminary planning for large-scale conservation projects; and other projects that catalyze and support land conservation. Examples of supported capacity building activities include: exploration of formal partnerships ranging from resource sharing to mergers; strategic conservation planning; strategic planning; membership expansion; board development; and system improvements. Projects that involve collaboration are strongly encouraged. Applications may be made online from the Foundation's website.
Requirements: Applicants must be 501(c)3 organizations eligible to accept tax-deductible donations as outlined in Section 170(c) of the Internal Revenue Code.
Restrictions: The following expenses are ineligible: land acquisition costs; trail construction and associated infrastructure; capital improvements for the general organizational operations or equipment valued at more than $250; capital campaigns or endowments and other activities designed to increase the capital or assets of an organization; ongoing operating costs including overhead, administrative costs, salaries of key staff not directly linked to the proposed project, and activities that are a normal part of the organization's mission and have no clear start or ending dates; and lobbying or religious activities.
Geographic Focus: Maine
Date(s) Application is Due: Nov 15
Amount of Grant: Up to 7,500 USD
Contact: Karen Young, Grants Administrator; (207) 351-0112; kyoung@mainecf.org
Internet: http://www.mainecf.org/landconservation.aspx
Sponsor: Maine Community Foundation
245 East Main Street
Ellsworth, ME 04605

Maine Community Foundation Peaks Island Grants   **2984**
The Foundation's Peaks Island Grants benefit the community of Peaks Island and its residents by supporting the work of local nonprofits and responding to the emerging needs of the island and its residents. A high priority is funding projects that focus on bringing Peaks Island residents together. The intent is that the relationships formed will provide the context for long-term conversations to enhance life on Peaks. Applications are available on the Foundation's website.
Requirements: Applicants must be 501(c)3 organizations eligible to accept tax-deductible donations as outlined in Section 170(c) of the Internal Revenue Code.
Geographic Focus: Maine
Date(s) Application is Due: Jun 21
Amount of Grant: 300 - 10,000 USD
Contact: Pam Cleghorn; (877) 700-6800; fax (207) 667-0447; pcleghorn@mainecf.org
Internet: http://www.mainecf.org/peaksfund.aspx
Sponsor: Maine Community Foundation
245 East Main Street
Ellsworth, ME 04605

Maine Community Foundation People of Color Fund Grants   **2985**
The objective of the People of Color Grants is to help communities of color achieve greater racial equity in Maine. The People of Color Grants support communities seeking to develop their leadership, knowledge, tools, and skills. The targeted beneficiaries of the funding are self-identified people of color. Both project grants (for initiatives that advance racial equity) and organizational development grants (to increase the efficiency and effectiveness of organizations that serve communities of color) are awarded. Priority is given to funding three areas of interest: leadership development, civic engagement, and youth. Applicants can be found at the Foundation's website, along with a list of previously funded projects.
Requirements: Applicants must be 501(c)3 organizations eligible to accept tax-deductible donations as outlined in Section 170(c) of the Internal Revenue Code. Applicants also must provide services or support to an identifiable community of color in Maine and have people of color in leadership positions with significant responsibilities. Only projects in which a majority of the participants or intended recipients are people of color are supported.
Restrictions: General operating support is not funded. Funding is also not available for lobbying or religious activities, program expenses already incurred, annual appeals, or endowment campaigns.
Geographic Focus: Maine
Date(s) Application is Due: Mar 15
Amount of Grant: Up to 7,500 USD
Contact: Leila DeAndrade; (877) 700-6800; fax (207) 667-0447; ldeandrade@mainecf.org
Internet: http://www.mainecf.org/peopleofcolorfund.aspx
Sponsor: Maine Community Foundation
245 East Main Street
Ellsworth, ME 04605

Maine Community Foundation Ram Island Conservation Challenge Grants   **2986**
The Ram Island Conservation Challenge Grants are a one-to-one matching opportunity. Land trusts must raise $25,000 in new funds to secure the $25,000 grant, resulting in $50,000 of new or additional endowment dollars. Technical assistance will be provided to support the organization's efforts to expand development plans to include endowment building, major gift solicitation, and planned giving. Technical assistance is also provided to build staff and board capacity to identify, cultivate, and secure major and planned gifts. Applications are available at the Foundation's website.
Requirements: Applicants must be 501(c)3 organizations eligible to accept tax-deductible donations as outlined in Section 170(c) of the Internal Revenue Code. Applicants must be Maine-based land trusts that either do not currently have a permanent endowment fund or have existing endowment assets of $250,000 or less. Applicant organizations must not be experiencing any overwhelming threats to survival. Organizations should also meet the following criteria: experienced leadership on both the staff and board; organizational experience at the staff or board level in identifying, cultivating, and securing significant gifts from donors; senior staff and board leadership that values a partnership with the Foundation and that can commit the time necessary to complete a successful endowment-building campaign; full participation from the board as donors supporting the mission of the applicant organization; and an established annual fund process or other fundraising program, including goals set and achieved over the past two to three years. Preference is given to land trusts that have been in existence for at least five years and to land trusts that serve larger geographic areas that serve areas and communities with more modest financial resources.
Restrictions: Campaigns should be completed in 18 months.

Geographic Focus: Maine
Date(s) Application is Due: Sep 15
Amount of Grant: 25,000 USD
Contact: Karen Young; (207) 351-0112; fax (207) 667-0447; kyoung@mainecf.org
Internet: http://www.mainecf.org/2525landtrust.aspx
Sponsor: Maine Community Foundation
245 East Main Street
Ellsworth, ME 04605

Maine Community Foundation Rines/Thompson Grants   2987

The Foundation's Rines/Thompson Grants provide support primarily for the benefit of people of the greater Portland community. Established by the children and grandchildren of Henry and Adeline Rines, the grants are designed to give back to the community that has supported the businesses owned by the Rines/Thompson family. Types of support that are considered are new or expanded projects or programs; improved organizational effectiveness; and operating support. Priorities include the areas of Cape Elizabeth, Falmouth, Gorham, Portland, Scarborough, South Portland, Yarmouth, and Westbrook. Arts and culture, environment and conservation, and early childhood and youth programming are also given special attention. For appropriate projects and programs, collaboration between and among organizations is encouraged. The application is available at the website.
Requirements: Applicants must be 501(c)3 organizations eligible to accept tax-deductible donations as outlined in Section 170(c) of the Internal Revenue Code and must serve the greater Portland, Maine, area. A letter from the executive director of each collaborating organization is required and should clearly explain the level of involvement and responsibility. For those organizations partnering with schools, a letter of agreement from the participating teacher(s) is required.
Restrictions: Funding is not available for the following: educational institutions: pre-K through 12 public, independent, parochial, and other private schools, as well as colleges and universities; requests from organizations that are outside the priority areas listed above; expenses that have already been acquired; capital campaigns or endowments and other activities designed to increase the capital or assets of an organization; and scholarships and camperships.
Geographic Focus: Maine
Date(s) Application is Due: Sep 15
Amount of Grant: Up to 7,500 USD
Contact: Pam Cleghorn, (877) 700-6800; fax (207) 667-0447; pcleghorn@mainecf.org
Internet: http://www.mainecf.org/RinesThompsonFund.aspx
Sponsor: Maine Community Foundation
245 East Main Street
Ellsworth, ME 04605

Maine Community Foundation Rose and Samuel Rudman Library Grants   2988

The Foundation's Rose and Samuel Rudman Library Trust was established to help libraries better serve communities in Maine with a population of less than 10,000. Funding is given for lively programming; collections and programs tailored to meet unique local interests; sharing resources through collective purchasing and cooperatives; collaboration with community groups and agencies; and digitizing special collections. Applications can be found at the Foundation's website, along with an additional list of previously funded projects.
Requirements: Applicants must be 501(c)3 organizations eligible to accept tax-deductible donations as outlined in Section 170(c) of the Internal Revenue Code. Applications are invited from libraries serving communities in Maine with a population of less than 10,000 located in the following counties: Aroostook, Hancock, Knox, Penobscot, Piscataquis, Waldo, and Washington.
Restrictions: Grants do not support capital and operational expenses (including staff salaries) or for resources that are otherwise freely available in the state or for refreshments, prize incentives, transportation, or craft supplies for programs. Requests for large-print books or materials and computer hardware or software will not be considered. Kindles, Nooks, and other e-book readers are considered computer hardware and are not eligible for funding. Purchase of e-book titles, however, are considered collection development and will be allowed.
Geographic Focus: Maine
Date(s) Application is Due: Jan 15
Amount of Grant: 300 - 1,000 USD
Contact: Liz Fickett; (877) 700-6800; fax (207) 667-0447; efickett@mainecf.org
Internet: http://www.mainecf.org/rudmantrust.aspx
Sponsor: Maine Community Foundation
245 East Main Street
Ellsworth, ME 04605

Maine Community Foundation Steeples Grants   2989

The Foundation's Steeples Grants support local efforts to assess and restore church steeples of historic, cultural, and community significance to cities and towns in Maine. Funding is a collaboration of Maine Preservation, the Foundation and a donor-advised fund at the Foundation. Maine Preservation provides technical assistance, and the Foundation administers the grants. Grant funding for both assessment and restoration is available. The maximum assessment award is $4,000, and a 10% match of the total cost is required. The maximum restoration award is $40,000, with a 50% match of the total cost. Although assessment applications are accepted at any time, restoration applications are due by November 1. Both applications are available on the Foundation's website.
Requirements: Applicants must be 501(c)3 organizations eligible to accept tax-deductible donations as outlined in Section 170(c) of the Internal Revenue Code. Steeples must be part of a building that is an active or former church with historic, cultural, and community significance in need of restoration and/or repair located in a Maine municipality or township with fewer than 50,000 people. Church buildings must be owned by a religious institution and/or a local nonprofit organization or municipality. The church congregation's or organization's membership must be prepared to match grant dollars received within the specified time period; maintain the steeple after restoration; and follow The Secretary of Interior's Standards for the Preservation of Historic Properties or indicate areas where they may not be able to do so. Interested applicants should first contact the Grants Administrator for general information. Qualifying organizations will then be directed to contact Main Preservation and asked to complete a Steeple Project Information Form (which can be found at the Foundation's website) and to arrange a site visit with its preservation advisors.
Restrictions: Organizations may not apply for a restoration grant without a detailed written assessment of the steeple by a qualified individual.
Geographic Focus: Maine
Contact: Jennifer Southard; (207) 761-2440; jsouthard@mainecf.org
Internet: http://www.mainecf.org/steeplesfund.aspx
Sponsor: Maine Community Foundation
245 East Main Street
Ellsworth, ME 04605

Maine Community Foundation Vincent B. and Barbara G. Welch Grants   2990

The Welch grants are made to institutions primarily in the greater Portland area. Projects and programs in the following areas are given preference: youth, education, health care, alcoholic rehabilitation, and arts and culture. Applications are available at the Community Foundation's website, in addition to an extensive list of previously funded projects and programs.
Requirements: Applicants must be 501(c)3 organizations eligible to accept tax-deductible donations as outlined in Section 170(c) of the Internal Revenue Code.
Restrictions: Funding is not available for program expenses that have already been accumulated.
Geographic Focus: Maine
Date(s) Application is Due: Aug 1
Amount of Grant: Up to 75,000 USD
Contact: Pam Cleghorn, Senior Program Officer; (877) 700-6800, ext 2205; fax (207) 667-0447; pcleghorn@mainecf.org or info@mainecf.org
Internet: http://www.mainecf.org/welch.aspx
Sponsor: Maine Community Foundation
245 East Main Street
Ellsworth, ME 04605

Maine State Troopers Foundation Grants   2991

The major purposes and activities of the Foundation are to provide support for programs designed to prevent or mitigate the effects of domestic violence, child abuse, spousal abuse, substance abuse, and juvenile delinquency. The Foundation further supports programs/projects that promote public safety.
Requirements: No funding to individuals.
Restrictions: The Foundation has a geopgraphic limit to the State of Maine.
Geographic Focus: Maine
Contact: Craig Poulin, President; (207) 622-2277
Sponsor: Maine State Troopers Association
28 Meadow Road
Augusta, ME 04330

Maine Women's Fund Economic Security Grants   2992

Recognizing that women's ability to take care of themselves and their families and to contribute to their communities depend upon their ability to obtain financial security, the Maine Women's Fund provides grants to support projects and organizations that build economic security for Maine women and girls. Specifically, the fund invests in organizations that focus in four strategic areas to create systemic change: education and youth development; entrepreneurship and better jobs and wages; financial literacy and asset building; and policy and leadership. Applicants may request general operating support or program/project support. Downloadable guidelines are available from the grant web page. The fund makes the application available to applicants in early December. Completed applications will be reviewed by a group of women selected from the community for their expertise and commitment to social change. Reviewers will evaluate proposals on several factors including alignment with the Maine Women's Fund values, the likelihood of systemic change occurring, the quality of the project implementation and evaluation plan, and the capacity of the organization or group.
Requirements: Nonprofit organizations or groups that demonstrate tax-exempt status under the Internal Revenue Service Code 501(c)3 or groups that submit an application through a fiscal agent with tax-exempt status that agrees to accept funds on its behalf are eligible to apply. Organizations must serve women and girls who reside in Maine. The fund invests in programs and organizations that are focused on creating tangible social change, and not simply service delivery. The fund prefers to support organizations that have limited access to other donors.
Restrictions: Organizations are limited to receiving one grant per year. The fund will not provide over 10% of an organization's annual budget. The fund will not support the following types of entities or activities: projects that discriminate on the basis of ethnicity, race, color, creed, religion, gender or gender identity, national origin, age, disability, marital status, sexual orientation, or veteran's status; individuals; scholarships; capital or endowment; biomedical research; debt reduction; fundraising events; campaigns for political office; organizations that limit or oppose women's right to self determination; or agencies of state or federal government (unless they are part of an eligible community collaborative). Faith-based organizations are eligible to apply; however, projects and services provided by these must not present or incorporate religion in any manner.
Geographic Focus: Maine
Amount of Grant: Up to 15,000 USD
Contact: Sonya Tomlinson, Office & Grants Manager; (207) 774-5513; fax (207) 774-5533; grants@mainewomensfund.org or thewomen@mainewomensfund.org

Internet: http://www.mainewomensfund.org/grants/economic_security_initiative/
Sponsor: Maine Women's Fund
565 A Congress Street, Suite 306, P.O. Box 5135
Portland, ME 04101

Maine Women's Fund Girls' Grantmaking Initiative 2993
The Girls' Grantmaking Initiative is an opportunity for young women, in grades 8-12, to get hands on with decision-making and philanthropy. In addition to making grants to projects or organizations supporting girls, program participants gain a deeper understanding of philanthropy, practical experience working together to make decisions, and the opportunity to work with other girls who are passionate about social issues. Interested applicants are encouraged to contact the Office and Grants Manager for more information. The Maine Women's Fund is a public grant-making foundation dedicated to creating lasting change by investing in the power of women and the dreams of girls.
Requirements: Nonprofit organizations or groups that demonstrate tax-exempt status under the Internal Revenue Service Code 501(c)3 or groups that submit an application through a fiscal agent with tax-exempt status that agrees to accept funds on its behalf are eligible to apply.
Restrictions: Organizations must serve women and girls who reside in Maine.
Geographic Focus: Maine
Contact: Sonya Tomlinson, Office & Grants Manager; (207) 774-5513; fax (207) 774-5533; grants@mainewomensfund.org or thewomen@mainewomensfund.org
Internet: http://www.mainewomensfund.org/grants/economic_security_initiative/
Sponsor: Maine Women's Fund
565 A Congress Street, Suite 306, P.O. Box 5135
Portland, ME 04101

Manitoba Arts Council Artist in Community Residency Program Grants 2994
The Artist In Community Residency Program will assist incorporated, non-profit organizations in Manitoba with the opportunity to respond to community development needs in, or through, the arts by engaging Manitoba artists to work in Manitoba communities for a specified period of time. In this program artists will engage with the broader community or public in ways that are meaningful and relevant towards the outcome of individual and community development. The artist(s) must be working with a community that would not otherwise be engaged in the arts. This is an opportunity for communities to express themselves through creative collaboration with established and professional artists. There are two possible grant options, developmental and implementation grants. Developing Grants are for up to a maximum of $3,000. For groups having little or no experience planning, coordinating and implementing an Artist in Community Residency, or groups that have experience with coordinating residencies and are developing a new residency project (with a new target group). This grant allows them to undertake a community planning process. Implementation Grants allow up to $10,000 in funding. For groups/communities that have some experience coordinating and implementing an Artist in Community Residency Project, or groups/communities who don't have prior experience but who believe they are ready for an implementation grant. In this case the community group would have to a clear plan, the artist(s) already identified and sources of community support identified.
Requirements: Any incorporated community group or organization can apply, including non-arts organizations. Art organizations that do not receive annual or operating funding from the Manitoba Arts Council can also apply. However, they will need a community based, non-arts group, organization or institution to partner with them in the residency project.
Restrictions: An Artist in Community Residency Project application cannot be submitted by an artist (though it may be initiated or stimulated in the community by the artist at the start, and ideally, jointed planned). Schools, as a major part of many communities, can be a partner in an Artist in Community Residency, but may not apply. This program is not intended to support: ongoing, operational funding; capital, deficit reduction or fund raising projects; proposals having as their sole objective the furthering of formal education; projects which are eligible to support from other programs of the Manitoba Arts Council or the Department of Culture, Heritage or Tourism; art organizations receiving annual or operating funding from the Manitoba Arts Council.
Geographic Focus: Canada
Date(s) Application is Due: Mar 25
Amount of Grant: 3,000 - 10,000 CAD
Contact: Kristen Pauch-Nolin; (204) 945-3384; kpauch-nolin@artscouncil.mb.ca
Internet: http://artscouncil.mb.ca/2010/02/artists-in-community-residency-program/
Sponsor: Manitoba Arts Council
525-93 Lombard Avenue
Winnipeg, MB R3B 3B1 Canada

Manitoba Arts Council Community Connections and Access Grants 2995
The Community Connections and Access Program is designed to address specific needs identified by artists who face barriers to equal opportunities in artistic and professional development and presentation. The program will fund projects to address the needs of the emerging and professional artists in communities that are disadvantaged or under-served. Applications can be submitted by artists, groups, collectives, ensembles and organizations. The maximum award for individual emerging artists is $2,500; for established or professional artists, $5,000; and for ensembles and organizations, $10,000. Some examples of community or group characteristics that may relate to barriers to access are (but not limited to): geographical (rural, northern, inner city/core area); cultural (Aboriginal, Ethnocultural, Francophone); and special populations (people with disabilities, youth, socio-enomically disadvantaged, etc.). Artists are encouraged to identify all the factors or characteristics that create barriers or limits to access. The maximum award for individual emerging professional artists is $2,500; for established or professional artists, $5,000; and for ensembles and organizations, $10,000. Deadline dates for projects beginning after July 1 are March 25, for projects after January 1, the deadline is September 25.
Requirements: Eligible Individuals: are Canadian citizens or permanent residents of Canada; have lived in Manitoba for at least one year immediately prior to applying; are emerging professional artist who face barriers to equal opportunities and who must partner with professional or established artists or with professional arts organizations that have been in operation for one year immediately prior to applying; are professional/established artists who face barriers to equal opportunities in artistic and professional development and presentation. Emerging professional and professional artists who face barriers to equal opportunities in artistic and professional development and presentation as a result of their membership in one or more disadvantaged or under-served communities are eligible for this grants. Organizations who wish to undertake a specific project involving emerging or professional artists who face barriers to equal opportunities in artistic and professional development and presentation as a result of their membership in one or more disadvantaged or under-served communities are also eligible for this grant.
Geographic Focus: Canada
Date(s) Application is Due: Mar 25; Sep 25
Amount of Grant: 2,500 - 10,000 CAD
Contact: Kristen Pauch-Nolin, Program Consultant; (204) 945-3384; fax (204) 945-5925; kpauch-nolin@artscouncil.mb.ca
Internet: http://artscouncil.mb.ca/2010/02/community-connections-and-access-program/
Sponsor: Manitoba Arts Council
525-93 Lombard Avenue
Winnipeg, MB R3B 3B1 Canada

Manitoba Arts Council Literary Arts Publishers Project Grants 2996
The book publishers project grants support the publication of original editions of Manitoba-published books of cultural significance. The periodicals project grants are available to developing and emerging Manitoba periodicals publishers to support a variety of projects related to publishing the periodical. The periodical must focus on aspects of art and culture. Applications for the book publishers project grants are accepted eight weeks prior to project. The deadline for the periodicals publishers project grant is April 15. The deadline for the book publishers project grant December 1.
Requirements: The book publisher must have published at least two books in the past two years and have demonstrated professionalism and editorial quality. The title for which support is requested must be in an eligible genre and of cultural significance. The periodical publisher must have published at least two issues in the past two years, have demonstrated professionalism and editorial quality, have substantial content from contributors who are not principals or employees of the publication, and are not bulletins or newsletters published primarily for membership.
Geographic Focus: All States, Canada
Date(s) Application is Due: Apr 15; Dec 1
Amount of Grant: Up to 3,000 CAD
Contact: Patricia Sanders; (204) 945-0422; psanders@artscouncil.mb.ca
Internet: http://www.artscouncil.mb.ca/english/liter_grantorg.html
Sponsor: Manitoba Arts Council
525-93 Lombard Avenue
Winnipeg, MB R3B 3B1 Canada

Manitoba Arts Council Special Opportunities Grants 2997
The Special Opportunities Grant supports professional Manitoba artists and arts organizations to undertake unique initiatives or take advantage of extraordinary opportunities. It is intended to fund special projects and artistic endeavours that are not served by other programs at the Manitoba Arts Council. Grants levels will be based on the scope of the project and the availability of funds. The maximum grant will normally not exceed $10,000 for organizations and $5,000 for individuals.
Requirements: Eligibility requirements for Individual artists, ensembles, and collectives: be Canadian citizen or landed immigrants; have lived in Manitoba for at least one year immediately prior to making application; be free to devote a concentrated portion of their time to the proposed project; not be full-time students; be recognized by their peers as professionals in their artistic discipline. To be considered a professional, applicants must view the discipline as a vocation, be beyond the level of basic training and have had some work published, produced, or shown in a professionally recognized venue. Eligibility requirements for organizations are: Arts organizations must be not-for-profit corporations that have been in existence for a minimum of one year prior to making application. Publishers eligible for Manitoba Arts Council programs are also eligible to apply. Eligible projects for the Special Opportunities Grant may include (but are not limited to) : unique opportunities for outreach; hosting professional development events; artist-in-residence programs; anniversary or celebration activities; publications not supported by other programs at the Manitoba Arts Council.
Restrictions: The program is not intended to support: projects completed or costs incurred before awards are announced; regular programming of an established group or organization; deficit reduction or fund raising projects; festivals; the hosting of annual business meetings of associations; projects eligible for support from other programs at the Manitoba Arts Council, including activities supported by an organization's operating funding.
Geographic Focus: All States, Canada
Date(s) Application is Due: Jan 15; May 15
Amount of Grant: 5,000 - 10,000 USD
Contact: Kristen Pauch-Nolin, Program Consultant; (204) 945-3384; fax (204) 945-5925; kpauch-nolin@artscouncil.mb.ca
Internet: http://www.artscouncil.mb.ca/english/artsdev_grantind.html
Sponsor: Manitoba Arts Council
525-93 Lombard Avenue
Winnipeg, MB R3B 3B1 Canada

Mann T. Lowry Foundation Grants — 2998

Established in Virginia in 1996, the Mann T. Lowry Foundation has specified in primary fields of interest to include: education; health organizations; human services; and social services. Geographic restrictions for giving are primarily in the State of Virginia, and grants come in the form of general operating support. Amounts have varied most recently from $500 to $21,000. Application forms are not required, and there are no identified annual deadlines. Applicants should provide a two- to three-page letter of request, outlining their program and attaching any pertinent brochures or materials.
Geographic Focus: Virginia
Amount of Grant: 500 - 21,000 USD
Contact: George R. Hinnant, Director; (804) 643-3512
Sponsor: Mann T. Lowry Foundation
1630 Huguenot Road
Midlothian, VA 23113-2427

Marathon Petroleum Corporation Grants — 2999

The Marathon Petroleum Corporation offers grant support within its home-base of Ohio, as well as throughout the states of Illinois, Indiana, Kentucky, Louisiana, Michigan, Texas, and West Virginia. Occasionally, it also gives to national organizations, Its primary purposes are aligned with its core values of health and safety, diversity and inclusion, environmental stewardship and honesty and integrity. With that in mind, special emphasis is also directed toward programs that empower the socially or economically disadvantaged, and provide opportunities for students to reach their full potential. Fields of interest include: the arts, children and youth services, community and economic development, education, the environment, health care, human services, and public affairs. Types of support include: annual campaigns, cause-related marketing, employee matching gifts, general operating support, in-kind donations, and scholarships to individuals.
Geographic Focus: Illinois, Indiana, Kentucky, Louisiana, Michigan, Ohio, Texas, West Virginia
Contact: Bill Conlisk, 419-422-2121; whconlisk@marathonpetroleum.com
Internet: http://www.marathonpetroleum.com/Corporate_Citizenship/
Sponsor: Marathon Petroleum Corporation
539 South Main Street
Findlay, OH 45840-3229

Marcia and Otto Koehler Foundation Grants — 3000

Grants are made to support arts and culture, medical, education, and social organizations in San Antonio, Texas. Proposals must demonstrate leadership in effecting positive change; encourage collaborative effort; serve large and diverse sectors of the population; and demonstrate vision, effectiveness, and good fiscal management. Types of support include general operating support, building construction/renovation, and research. Grants are made for one time only. Applicants must send a letter of request for application by March 1 to receive an application.
Requirements: Grants are awarded only to organizations in Bexar County, Texas.
Restrictions: Grants will not be made to individuals or to support other foundations or endowments; salaries; operating deficits; political organizations; or churches, synagogues, or parishes.
Geographic Focus: Texas
Date(s) Application is Due: Jun 1
Amount of Grant: 2,500 - 50,000 USD
Contact: Thomas K. Killion; (210) 270-5422; thomas.k.killion@ustrust.com
Sponsor: Marcia and Otto Koehler Foundation
P.O. Box 121
San Antonio, TX 78291-0121

Mardag Foundation Grants — 3001

The Mardag Foundation is committed to making grants to qualified nonprofit organizations in Minnesota that help enhance and improve the quality of life, inspire learning, revitalize communities, and promote access to the arts. The Foundation focuses their grantmaking in these priority areas: improving the lives of at-risk families, children, youth, and young adults; supporting seniors to live independently; building the capacity of arts and humanities organizations to benefit their communities; and supporting community development throughout the St. Paul area. Grants normally support; capital projects, program expansion and special projects of a time-limited nature; start-up costs for promising new programs that demonstrate sound management and clear goals relevant to community needs; support for established agencies that have temporary or transitional needs; funds to match contributions received from other sources or to provide a challenge to raise new contributions. Applicants are encouraged to submit a brief summary of their project prior to preparation of a full proposal to see if the project fits the guidelines and interests of the foundation. The Foundation's grantmaking meetings are in April, August, and November. Generally, full proposals must be received three months prior to a meeting date.
Requirements: Nonprofit 501(c)3 organizations are eligible to apply. Organizations must be in the East Metro area of Dakota, Ramsey, or Washington counties.
Restrictions: The Foundation does not fund: programs exclusively serving Minneapolis and the surrounding West Metro area; scholarships and grants to individuals; ongoing annual operating expenses; sectarian religious programs; medical research; federated campaigns; conservation or environmental programs; events and conferences; programs serving the physically, developmentally or mentally disabled; capital campaigns of private secondary schools; and capital and endowment campaigns of private colleges and universities. The Foundation will review, on their own merits, grant applications received from private secondary schools and private colleges and universities for purposes not excluded in the information above.
Geographic Focus: Minnesota
Date(s) Application is Due: May 1; Aug 1; Dec 31
Amount of Grant: 5,000 - 50,000 USD
Contact: Lisa Hansen; (651) 224-5463 or (800) 875-6167; lisa.hansen@mnpartners.org
Internet: http://www.mardag.org/apply_for_a_grant/
Sponsor: Mardag Foundation
55 Fifth Street East, Suite 600
St. Paul, MN 55101

Margaret Abell Powell Fund Grants — 3002

The Margaret Abell Powell Fund of the William S. Abell Foundation makes grants to support traditional classical theater and classical ballet in the Washington, DC, metropolitan area including the counties of Montgomery, Prince George's, Charles, Calvert, St. Mary's and Arlington; and the city of Alexandria. Support will be given to local organizations producing English language, mainstream theater and classical ballet. Emphasis will be given to organizations which support specific performances, the staging or choreography of pieces, and the training of young artists. Applications for this program will be accepted for: the underwriting of specific performances; the training of actors, actresses, performers and dancers; and the staging and choreography of specific pieces. Proposals are reviewed only in June and December. Deadlines are April 15 and October 15. Grants typically do not exceed $25,000.
Requirements: Nonprofit organizations in the District of Columbia and the nearby Maryland counties of Montgomery, Prince George's, Charles, Calvert, and St. Mary's, as well as the city of Arlington, Virginia, are eligible.
Geographic Focus: District of Columbia, Maryland, Virginia
Date(s) Application is Due: Apr 16; Oct 15
Amount of Grant: 5,000 - 65,000 USD
Contact: Carol Doolan, (301) 652-2224; cdoolan@williamsabellfoundation.org
Internet: http://www.williamsabellfoundation.org/margaret_abell_powell_fund
Sponsor: William S. Abell Foundation
8401 Connecticut Avenue, Suite 1204
Chevy Chase, MD 20815-5821

Margaret and James A. Elkins Jr. Foundation Grants — 3003

The Elkins Foundation Grants support nonprofit programs and organizations in the metropolitan Houston, Texas area. Grants are given primarily for charitable, religious, scientific, or educational and literacy programs, including public safety testing, and the prevention of cruelty to children and animals. Fields of interest include: biology/life sciences; child development, education; child development, services; children and youth services; Christian agencies and churches; elementary and secondary education; engineering and technology; health organizations, association; higher education; hospitals (general); medical research, institute; medical education; religion; science; and safety/disasters. The Foundation also supports: building renovation; capital campaigns; emergency funds; endowments; equipment; program development; and research.
Requirements: Applications are not required. Applicants should submit a letter of inquiry, along with a copy of their most recent annual report, audited financial statement, or 990 form. Board meetings vary, and there is no deadline.
Restrictions: Grants are not made to individuals, or to support annual fundraising campaigns or operating deficits.
Geographic Focus: Texas
Amount of Grant: 5,000 - 400,000 USD
Contact: Larry Medford, Secretary-Treasurer; (713) 652-2052
Sponsor: Margaret and James A. Elkins Jr. Foundation
1001 Fannin Street, 1166 First City Tower
Houston, TX 77002

Margaret L. Wendt Foundation Grants — 3004

The foundation awards grants to eligible New York nonprofit organizations in its areas of interest, including education, the arts, social services, churches and religious organizations, health associations, public interest organizations, and youth agencies. There are no application deadlines or forms. The board meets quarterly
Requirements: Western New York nonprofit organizations are eligible. Giving is primarily in Buffalo.
Restrictions: Grants are not awarded to individuals, including scholarships.
Geographic Focus: New York
Contact: Grants Administrator; (716) 855-2146
Sponsor: Margaret L. Wendt Foundation
40 Fountain Plaza, Suite 277
Buffalo, NY 14202

Margaret T. Morris Foundation Grants — 3005

The Margaret T. Morris Foundation awards grants, primarily in Arizona, in its areas of interest, including: animal welfare; arts; children and youth, services; education; environment; higher education; homeless service; human services; marine science; medical research and education; mental health and crisis services; museums; performing arts; reproductive health and family planning; and hospices. The Foundation's types of support include: building renovation; capital campaigns; debt reduction; endowments; general operating support; land acquisition; matching and challenge support; and program development. The Board of Directors meets in August, December, and as needed.
Requirements: Applications are not accepted. Applicants should submit a letter of inquiry with their request for funding and a description of the project.
Geographic Focus: Arizona
Contact: Thomas Polk, Trustee; (928) 445-4010
Sponsor: Margaret T. Morris Foundation
P.O. Box 592
Prescott, AZ 86302-0592

Marie C. and Joseph C. Wilson Foundation Rochester Small Grants   3006
The Marie and Joseph Wilson Foundation strives to improve the quality of life through initiating and supporting projects that measurably demonstrate a means of creating a sense of belonging within the family and community. The Foundation considers 501(c)3 organization requests ranging from $1,000 to $25,000. Grant applications are accepted on an ongoing basis. Foundation board members review applications as they are received. The review committee meets once a month except for July and August. Because the Foundation receives a large number of applications, responses may take up to four months. Prior to the receiving funding, grant recipients are required to sign a grant agreement contract. Written progress reports are required at six months and one year following the date of the grant. Samples of the Foundation's previously funded grants are available online.
Requirements: The Foundation review committee looks for one or more of the following conditions in a proposal: the proposal is a well-planned approach to delivering services; Foundation support would be catalytic to the project's success; the proposal is efficient in its use of funds and expenses are reduced by sharing resources with other agencies or groups; and a collaborative network exists that multiplies the impact of the grant. Applicants may contact the Foundation for a current application form.
Restrictions: Grants are limited to 501(c)3 organizations serving the Rochester, New York area. Grants will not be made to individuals, partisan political organizations, or to support lobbying efforts. Requests for capital projects also will not be considered.
Geographic Focus: New York
Amount of Grant: 1,000 - 25,000 USD
Contact: Megan Bell, Executive Director; (585) 461-4696; fax (585) 473-5206
Internet: http://www.mcjcwilsonfoundation.org/funding.cfm
Sponsor: Marie C. and Joseph C. Wilson Foundation
160 Allens Creek Road
Rochester, NY 14618-3309

Marie H. Bechtel Charitable Remainder Uni-Trust Grants   3007
Established in Scott County, Iowa, in 1987, the Marie H. Bechtel Charitable Remainder Uni-Trust (formerly known as the Marie H. Bechtel Charitable Trust) supports youth services and education. Support is also available for the advancement of health care, maintenance of community cultural activities, and enhancement of the community by restoring its vitality and creating meaningful employment. Contact the Foundation for application forms.
Requirements: 501(c)3 organizations serving residents of Scott County, Iowa, are eligible.
Restrictions: No grants are given for endowment funds, past operating deficit or debt retirement, general or continuing operating support, or basic scholarly research.
Geographic Focus: Iowa
Contact: R. Richard Bittner; (563) 328-3333; fax (563) 328-3352; loseband@blwlaw.com
Sponsor: Marie H. Bechtel Charitable Remainder Uni-Trust
201 West 2nd Street, Suite 1000
Davenport, IA 52801-1817

Marietta McNeill Morgan and Samuel Tate Morgan, Jr. Trust Grants   3008
The Marietta McNeill Morgan & Samuel Tate Morgan, Jr. Trust was established in 1962 to support and promote quality educational and human services programming in the Commonwealth of Virginia. The Morgan Trust only makes grants for specific capital expenditures and not for general capital campaign expenditures. Matching and challenge grants are strongly encouraged. Grants usually are not paid until the grantee has sufficient funds in hand, pledged, or borrowed to complete the proposed project. Grants from the Morgan Trust are one year in duration. Application materials are available for download at the grant website. Applicants are strongly encouraged to review the state application guidelines for additional helpful information and clarifications before applying. Applicants are also encouraged to review the trust's funding history (link is available from the grant website). The Marietta McNeill Morgan & Samuel Tate Morgan, Jr. Trust has biannual deadlines of May 1 and November 1. Applicants for the May deadline will be notified of grant decisions by June 30. Applicants for the November deadline will be notified by February 28 of the following year.
Requirements: Applicants must have 501(c)3 status. Applications must be mailed.
Restrictions: Because requests for support usually exceed available resources, organizations are advised to apply to either the Morgan Trust or the Seay Foundation. While receipt of a grant does not preclude later support, an organization normally will not be considered for another grant from either the Morgan Trust or the Seay Foundation until at least 3 years after the date of the last grant payment. The trust does not support requests from individuals, organizations attempting to influence policy through direct lobbying, or any political campaigns.
Geographic Focus: Virginia
Date(s) Application is Due: May 1; Nov 1
Contact: Sarah Kay, Vice President; (804) 788-2673; sarah.kay@baml.com
Internet: https://www.bankofamerica.com/philanthropic/fn_search.action
Sponsor: Marietta McNeill Morgan and Samuel Tate Morgan, Jr. Trust
1111 E. Main Street, VA2-300-12-92
Richmond, VA 23219

Marie Walsh Sharpe Art Foundation Grants   3009
The Marie Walsh Sharpe Art Foundation was established in June, 1984, by Marie Walsh Sharpe, the culmination of her long-held dream of providing financial assistance to the very gifted in the visual arts. Sharpe charged the Foundation with providing supplemental instruction to art students, through workshops and seminars, beyond that offered in the secondary schools. She also directed the Foundation to offer assistance to gifted individual artists. In the firm belief that successful programs cannot be developed without the ideas and energies of many similarly dedicated people, the Foundation has involved artists, local and national leaders in the arts, art education, and business to participate in meetings to develop ideas on the Foundation's best course.
Geographic Focus: All States
Contact: Kimberly M. Taylor, Program Officer; (719) 635-3220; kim@sharpeartfdn.org or office@sharpeartfdn.org
Internet: http://sharpeartfdn.qwestoffice.net/foundinfo.htm
Sponsor: Marie Walsh Sharpe Art Foundation
830 N Tejon Street, Suite 120
Colorado Springs, CO 80903

Marin Community Foundation Affordable Housing Grants   3010
Marin Community Foundation (MCF) is dedicated to creating housing opportunities in Marin that are affordable and accessible to families and individuals with lower incomes. To support this goal, the Affordable Housing grants fund three strategic areas: increase public support for affordable housing and influence zoning changes that support affordable housing; make investments in affordable housing, both rental properties and owned housing that take advantage of specific market opportunities; and help people at risk of homelessness to remain housed. The grant program manager may be emailed through the grant website.
Requirements: There will not be an open competitive process for these grants. RFPs will be issued to community organizations that are being invited to apply for support under all three strategies. Nonprofit organizations will be invited to submit a Letter of Intent (LOI) in response to a Request for Proposal issued for each of the Strategic Initiatives on the Foundation website. After MCF staff reviews the LOIs, selected applicants will be invited to complete and submit a full proposal. If invited to submit an LOI, nonprofit groups should first register with the Grant Application Center, MCF's online grants application system.
Geographic Focus: California
Contact: Kathleen Harris, Program Director; (415) 44-2549
Internet: http://www.marincf.org/grants-and-loans/grants/strategic-initiatives/increasing-affordable-housing
Sponsor: Marin Community Foundation
5 Hamilton Landing, Suite 200
Novato, CA 94949

Marin Community Foundation Ending the Cycle of Poverty Grants   3011
The goal of the Marin Community Foundation Cycle of Poverty Grant is to end the cycle of poverty experienced by poor and low-income individuals and families. The Foundation believes that low-wage earners can escape the cycle of poverty if they have the tools and resources traditionally available to middle- and high-income earners. This initiative shifts the focus of the Foundation's investment from providing short-term services to people in poverty to creating lasting solutions to poverty and engaging individuals and families, institutions, and the community in efforts to build assets.
Requirements: Nonprofits interested in potential participation for Strategy 1 should contact the program director listed in the contact area for further information.
Geographic Focus: California
Contact: Kathleen Harris, Program Director; (415) 464-2549
Internet: http://www.marincf.org/grants-and-loans/grants/strategic-initiatives/ending-cycle-of-poverty
Sponsor: Marin Community Foundation
5 Hamilton Landing, Suite 200
Novato, CA 94949

Marin Community Foundation Social Justice and Interfaith Understanding Grants   3012
The Marin Community Foundation Social Justice and Interfaith Understanding Grants are committed to supporting efforts that increase awareness, mobilize communities, and catalyze social change to address social inequities in Marin County. The Foundation defines social justice as equal access to social, political, and economic opportunities and resources. It defines interfaith understanding as communication between and among faith communities that crosses religious lines with an aim to explore common ground in beliefs and values. The Foundation funds two strategies depending on the particular program: 1) to increase community engagement to identify and address social justice issues, and 2) to increase collaboration and dialogue among religious institutions, faith-based communities, and community members. The funding varies by strategy (from $10,000 to $70,000 for strategy 1, and from $10,000 to $50,000 for strategy 2), but both strategies have the same deadline and application process. Each strategy funds staff support and operational costs, with strategy one also funding tech assistance. Organizations should refer to the website for specific information about each strategy.
Requirements: Organizations may apply online for either strategy with the same application process. They are also encouraged to contact the program officer by phone or to email directly through the website.
Restrictions: Strategy 1 does not fund the following: direct social or health services; religious programs that are strictly sectarian; and emergency or capital expenditures, such as computer hardware or software. Strategy 2 does not fund the following: individuals; coalitions that do not have a lead organization; endowments or private foundations; religious organizations that are strictly sectarian; federal, state, or municipal agencies; and political campaigns.
Geographic Focus: California
Date(s) Application is Due: Nov 18
Amount of Grant: 10,000 - 70,000 USD
Contact: Shirin Vakharia, Program Director; (415) 464-2523
Internet: http://www.marincf.org/grants-and-loans/grants/community-grants/social-justice-and-interfaith-understanding
Sponsor: Marin Community Foundation
5 Hamilton Landing, Suite 200
Novato, CA 94949

Marin Community Foundation Stinson Bolinas Community Grants 3013
The Stinson/Bolinas Community Grants were created and are supported by a group of local donors. The founders act as advisors, recommending which projects should be supported by this community effort. The maximum grant is $3,000 per grant cycle, and there is no minimum amount. The Foundation assumes that all proposed projects will be completed within twelve months from the beginning of grant support. Although matching funds, donated materials, equipment and services are not required, they are strongly encouraged and will make an application more competitive. If a grant includes a funding request for labor or services, utilizing local resources is encouraged. Priority will be given to applicants who: have received, or expect to receive, funds from other sources that match, or will match, the funds requested in this application (expected receipts need to be based on documented information provided to applicants by other prospective funding sources); and have received significant levels of gifts-in-kind (services, equipment, etc.) for the project to be supported by this application. Application materials are available at the Bolinas and Stinson Beach libraries and from the grant's website. Materials should be mailed to the Stinson Beach contact location.
Requirements: To be eligible, an applicant must be an organization or individual whose project benefits the Stinson Beach and/or Bolinas communities. Organizations are encouraged to contact the grants consultant to discuss their project before submitting an application.
Geographic Focus: California
Date(s) Application is Due: Apr 30; Oct 31
Amount of Grant: Up to 3,000 USD
Contact: Kristen Turek, (415) 464-2531; fax (415) 464-4555
Internet: http://www.marincf.org/grants-and-loans/grants/stinson-bolinas-community-fund
Sponsor: Marin Community Foundation
5 Hamilton Landing, Suite 200
Novato, CA 94949

Marin Community Foundation Successful Aging Grants 3014
The Successful Aging Grants strive to make Marin County a positive and viable place in which to age. Marin Community Foundation defines older adults as individuals who are 60 years of age or older. Given limited resources and the challenging economic climate, Foundation resources will be designated to meet the unique challenges of low-income older adults who are aging in their homes, requiring a coordinated, holistic approach to service delivery. Organizations may view the logic model at the website that the Foundation has developed which further explains the approaches, activities, and desired impact of this goal area. The Foundation's specific goal involves strengthening the delivery of core health and social services through Approach B (Approach A and C are not open, competitive grants). In an effort to strengthen the delivery of services, the Foundation will consider requests that build the capacity of organizations to (1) engage in outcome evaluation and/or (2) strengthen cultural competencies in serving traditionally underserved or marginalized populations (e.g., LGBTQ populations, non-English speaking residents, the frail, elderly populations living in rural communities, people of color, and people who are caregivers for older adults). MCF will continue to support the direct provision of health and social services for low-income older adults living independently in Marin County. Priority consideration will be given to innovative projects that aim to meet the transportation and/or chronic disease management and prevention needs of low-income older adults. Outcome evaluation of the direct services provided is highly encouraged. Organizations are encouraged to review the website for more information and call the program director, who can also be emailed directly through the website.
Requirements: Organizations must be tax-exempt, nonprofit organizations with programs that serve Marin County, California. Organizations must register through the Grant Application Center before submitting a full proposal.
Geographic Focus: California
Date(s) Application is Due: Feb 3
Amount of Grant: 5,000 - 350,000 USD
Contact: Wendy Todd, Program Director; (415) 464-2541; fax (415) 464-4555
Internet: http://www.marincf.org/grants-and-loans/grants/community-grants/successful-aging
Sponsor: Marin Community Foundation
5 Hamilton Landing, Suite 200
Novato, CA 94949

Marion and Miriam Rose Fund Grants 3015
The Marion and Miriam Rose Fund was established to support childcare facilities serving dependent, neglected, indigent, and emotionally disturbed children, and children in foster care. The Marion and Miriam Rose Fund was created under the wills of Mr. George B. Rose and Mrs. Marion Rose. The majority of grants from the Rose Fund are one year in duration. Applicants must apply online at the grant website. Applicants are strongly encouraged to do the following before applying: review the downloadable state application procedures for additional helpful information and clarifications; review the downloadable online-application guidelines at the grant website; review the foundation's funding history (link is available from the grant website); review the online application questions in advance; and review the list of required attachments. These will generally include: a list of board members, financial statements (audited, reviewed, or compiled by independent auditor); an organization summary; a list of other funding sources; an IRS Determination letter; and other required documents. All attachments must be uploaded in the online application as PDF, Word, or Excel files. The application deadline for the Marion and Miriam Rose Fund is 11:59 p.m. on February 1. Applicants will be notified of grant decisions by June 30.
Requirements: Organizations must be located in, or serve the children of Little Rock.
Restrictions: The Fund will consider requests for general operating support only if the organization's operating budget is less than $1 million. In general, grant requests for individuals, endowment campaigns, or capital projects will not be considered.
Geographic Focus: Arkansas
Date(s) Application is Due: Feb 1
Contact: George Thorn; (312) 828-4154; ilgrantmaking@bankofamerica.com
Internet: https://www.bankofamerica.com/philanthropic/fn_search.action
Sponsor: Marion and Miriam Rose Fund
231 South LaSalle Street, IL1-231-13-32
Chicago, IL 60604

Marion County Historic Preservation Fund Grants 3016
The fund makes grants to support nonprofit organizations working to preserve historic buildings and neighborhoods in Marion County. The program is a partnership between The Historic Landmarks Foundation and The Indianapolis Foundation, an affiliate of the Central Indiana Community Foundation. Grants are awarded twice a year.
Requirements: Nonprofit community preservation organizations and historic neighborhood foundations in Marion County are eligible to apply.
Geographic Focus: Indiana
Date(s) Application is Due: Apr 15; Nov 15
Contact: Chad Lethig, Indianapolis Preservation Coordinator, Central Regional Office; (317) 639-4534; fax (317) 639-6720; flip@historiclandmarks.org
Internet: http://www.historiclandmarks.org/help/grants.html
Sponsor: Historic Landmarks Foundation of Indiana
340 W Michigan Street
Indianapolis, IN 46202

Marion Gardner Jackson Charitable Trust Grants 3017
The Marion Gardner Jackson Charitable Trust funds the arts and humanities, education, health, and human service organizations in the Quincy, Illinois area and surrounding communities in Adams County. The trust supports capital, program, and operating grants. The application is available at the trust website through Bank of America.
Restrictions: For program support grants, the yearly request may not be more than 50% of the program's budget. Organizations can submit one application per year and will not receive more than one award from the trust in any given year. Organizations receiving a multi-year award from the trust that continues into the next grant year are not eligible to apply for an additional grant until the end of the grant cycle. The trust does not support requests from individuals, organizations attempting to influence policy through direct lobbying, or any political campaigns.
Geographic Focus: Illinois
Date(s) Application is Due: Jul 31
Contact: Debra Grand; (312) 828-4154; ilgrantmaking@bankofamerica.com
Internet: https://www.bankofamerica.com/philanthropic/fn_search.action
Sponsor: Marion Gardner Jackson Charitable Trust
231 South LaSalle Street, IL1-231-13-32
Chicago, IL 60604

Marion I. and Henry J. Knott Foundation Discretionary Grants 3018
Founded in 1977, the Marion I. and Henry J. Knott Foundation is a Catholic family foundation committed to honoring its founders' legacy of generosity to strengthen the community within the Archdiocese of Baltimore. Henry J. Knott, the eldest of six boys, grew up in a lively household in the Baltimore area. His father was a hard-working carpenter. Marion Isabel Burk, who was orphaned at the age of eleven, grew up cooking and looking after the children in a small boarding house and received little formal education as a result. Henry and Marion met on a blind date arranged by a good friend in 1926, while Henry was taking classes at Loyola College, and were married in 1928. They went on to build a large family (thirteen children, one lost to cancer) and a thriving construction business. Henry was the first developer in Baltimore to employ the practice of prefabricating wall panels in a factory and then sending them out to construction sites. Projects moved at a blistering pace and eventually led Henry to become the President of Arundel Corporation. Henry and Marion who knew firsthand the challenge of raising a large family always practiced philanthropy. The foundation makes awards in five Program categories: Arts and Humanities; Catholic Activities; Education (Catholic schools, nonsectarian private schools specifically catering to special needs, and private colleges and universities); Health Care; and Human Services. Within the five program categories, the foundation funds within five project categories, including capital expenses, development, new and/or ongoing programs, operating expenses, and technology. In addition to its standard granting program, the Knott Foundation provides a limited number of Discretionary Grants (20-30) throughout the year. These grants, ranging between $500 to $2,500, are designed to increase the Foundation's grant-making options as well as its responsiveness to community needs. Grants are awarded based on the proposed project, the availability of funds, and other current requests for funding. To apply for a discretionary grant, applicants should submit a brief (one page) Letter of Inquiry (LOI) on their organization's letterhead. The LOI should describe the applicant's project or program, detail the applicant's needs, and provide a timeframe for use of the award if granted. In addition to the LOI, the applicant should also submit a 501(c)3 status letter, a project budget if applicable, and a list of the board of directors. Discretionary requests are accepted and awarded on a rolling basis throughout the year. Although not guaranteed, approved funds are usually disbursed within one to two weeks of the discretionary grant's approval date. Interested applicants should visit the website for further details and guidelines.
Requirements: Discretionary grant requests must be in alignment with the foundation's areas of geographic and programmatic giving. Funding is limited to 501(c)3 organizations serving Baltimore City and the following counties in Maryland: Allegheny, Anne Arundel, Baltimore, Carroll, Frederick, Garrett, Harford, Howard, and Washington. Applicants may apply through a fiscal sponsor. The fiscal sponsor must be a 501(c)3 nonprofit organization that has a formal relationship and Memorandum of Understanding (MOU) with the applicant. Selected applicants will need to submit a copy of their most recent IRS 990 and/or audited financials.
Restrictions: The following will not be funded: organizations that have not been in operation for at least one year, scholarships, public education/public sector agencies, pro-choice or reproductive health programs, individuals, annual giving, political activities, one-time only

events/seminars/workshops, legal services, environmental activities, medical research, day care centers, endowment funds for arts/humanities, national/local chapters for specific diseases, agencies that redistribute grant funds to other nonprofits, reimbursables or any prior expenses, or government agencies that form 501(c)3 nonprofits to fund public sector projects.
Geographic Focus: Maryland
Amount of Grant: 500 - 2,500 USD
Contact: Kathleen McCarthy, Grants Manager; (410) 235-7068; fax (410) 889-2577; knott@knottfoundation.org or info@knottfoundation.org
Internet: http://www.knottfoundation.org/what_we_do/grant_application_process/discretionary_grant_application_process
Sponsor: Marion I. and Henry J. Knott Foundation
3904 Hickory Avenue
Baltimore, MD 21211-1834

Marion I. and Henry J. Knott Foundation Standard Grants 3019
Founded in 1977, the Marion I. and Henry J. Knott Foundation is a Catholic family foundation committed to honoring its founders' legacy of generosity to strengthen the community within the Archdiocese of Baltimore. Henry J. Knott, the eldest of six boys, grew up in a lively household in the Baltimore area. His father was a hard-working carpenter. Marion Isabel Burk, who was orphaned at the age of eleven, grew up cooking and looking after the children in a small boarding house and received little formal education as a result. Henry and Marion met on a blind date arranged by a good friend in 1926, while Henry was taking classes at Loyola College, and were married in 1928. They went on to build a large family (thirteen children, one lost to cancer) and a thriving construction business. Henry was the first developer in Baltimore to employ the practice of prefabricating wall panels in a factory and then sending them out to construction sites. Projects moved at a blistering pace and eventually led Henry to become the President of Arundel Corporation. Henry and Marion who knew firsthand the challenge of raising a large family always practiced philanthropy. The foundation makes both standard and discretionary awards in five Program categories: Arts and Humanities; Catholic Activities; Education (Catholic Schools, Nonsectarian private schools specifically catering to special needs, and private colleges and universities); Health Care; and Human Services. Within the five program categories, the foundation funds within five project categories, including capital expenses, development, new and/or ongoing programs, operating expenses, and technology. The Knott Foundation uses a two-step online application process for its standard-grants program. Step one requires the submission of an online Letter of Inquiry (LOI) along with a Financial Analysis Form. Applicants whose LOIs are approved will move on to step two which requires online submission of a full proposal. Applicants are given the opportunity to submit a draft of their proposal for comments and feedback prior to their final submission. The review process for the foundation's standard grants program takes approximately four months from the date of the LOI submission until a final funding decision is made. The Knott Foundation accepts standard-grant applications three times per year - February, June and October. LOIs and proposals must be received by 5 p.m. on the applicable deadline date. Complete details, guidelines, and links to the online submission system are available at the grant website.
Requirements: Funding is limited to 501(c)3 organizations serving Baltimore City and the following counties in Maryland: Allegheny, Anne Arundel, Baltimore, Carroll, Frederick, Garrett, Harford, Howard, and Washington. Applicants may apply through a fiscal sponsor. The fiscal sponsor must be a 501(c)3 nonprofit organization that has a formal relationship and Memorandum of Understanding (MOU) with the applicant.
Restrictions: Organizations that are denied funding at the LOI stage of the grant process are eligible to apply again during the next grant cycle; organizations that are denied funding after submitting a full grant proposal must wait one year before reapplying; organizations that receive a grant award must wait two years before reapplying. The following will not be funded: organizations that have not been in operation for at least one year, scholarships, public education/public sector agencies, pro-choice or reproductive health programs, individuals, annual giving, political activities, one-time only events/seminars/workshops, legal services, environmental activities, medical research, day care centers, endowment funds for arts/humanities, national/local chapters for specific diseases, agencies that redistribute grant funds to other nonprofits, reimbursables or any prior expenses, or government agencies that form 501(c)3 nonprofits to fund public sector projects.
Geographic Focus: Maryland
Date(s) Application is Due: Mar 7; Jul 9; Nov 12
Amount of Grant: 35,000 - 45,000 USD
Contact: Kathleen McCarthy, Grants Manager; (410) 235-7068; fax (410) 889-2577; knott@knottfoundation.org or info@knottfoundation.org
Internet: http://www.knottfoundation.org/what_we_do/grant_application_process
Sponsor: Marion I. and Henry J. Knott Foundation
3904 Hickory Avenue
Baltimore, MD 21211-1834

Marion Isabell Coe Fund Grants 3020
The Marion Isabell Coe Fund was established in 1941 to provide quality human services and housing support for underserved adults. Special consideration is given to organizations that encourage individuals to remain in their own homes by aiding them with home repair and maintenance. Preference is given to organizations located in and serving the people of the town of Litchfield, Connecticut. Organizations serving the towns of Morris, Warren, or Goshen will also be considered. Grants from the Coe Fund are one year in duration. Applicants must apply online at the grant website. Applicants are strongly encouraged to do the following before applying: review the downloadable Connecticut state application procedures for additional helpful information, requirements, and restrictions; review the downloadable online-application guidelines at the grant website; review the foundation's funding history (link is available from the grant website); review the online application questions in advance; and review the list of required attachments. These will generally include: a list of board members, financial statements (audited, reviewed, or compiled by independent auditor); an organization summary; a list of other funding sources; an IRS Determination letter; and other required documents. All attachments must be uploaded in the online application as PDF, Word, or Excel files. The deadline for application is 11:59 p.m. on November 1. Applicants will be notified of grant decisions by letter within two months after the proposal deadline.
Requirements: Applicants must have 501(c)3 tax-exempt status and serve the people of the towns of Litchfield, Morris, Warren, and Goshen, in Litchfield County, Connecticut. A breakdown of number/percentage of people served by specific towns will be required in the online application.
Restrictions: Grant requests for capital projects are generally not considered. The fund does not support requests from individuals, organizations attempting to influence policy through direct lobbying, or any political campaigns.
Geographic Focus: Connecticut
Date(s) Application is Due: Nov 1
Contact: Kate Kerchaert, (860) 657-7016; kate.kerchaert@baml.com
Internet: https://www.bankofamerica.com/philanthropic/fn_search.action
Sponsor: Marion Isabell Coe Fund
200 Glastonbury Boulevard, Suite # 200, CT2-545-02-05
Glastonbury, CT 06033-4056

Marjorie Moore Charitable Foundation Grants 3021
The Marjorie Moore Charitable Foundation was established in 1957 to support and promote quality educational, cultural, human-services, environmental, and health-care programming for underserved populations. Grants from the Moore Foundation made in support of operations or programming are one year in duration. Multi-year grants for long-term capital projects will be considered on a case-by-case basis. Applicants must apply online at the grant website. Applicants are strongly encouraged to do the following before applying: review the downloadable state application procedures for additional helpful information and clarifications; review the downloadable online-application guidelines at the grant website; review the foundation's funding history (link is available from the grant website); review the online application questions in advance; and review the list of required attachments. These will generally include: a list of board members, financial statements (audited, reviewed, or compiled by independent auditor); an organization summary; a list of other funding sources; an IRS Determination letter; and other required documents. All attachments must be uploaded in the online application as PDF, Word, or Excel files. The Marjorie Moore Charitable Foundation has biannual deadlines of June 1 and December 1. Applications must be submitted by 11:59 p.m. on the deadline dates. Applicants will be notified of grant decisions by letter within two to three months after each respective proposal deadline.
Requirements: Applicant organizations must have 501(c)3 tax-exempt status and serve the people of Kensington or Berlin, Connecticut. A breakdown of number/percentage of people served by specific towns is required on the online application. Preference is given to organizations that provide human services or health care programming.
Restrictions: The foundation does not support requests from individuals, organizations attempting to influence policy through direct lobbying, or any political campaigns.
Geographic Focus: Connecticut
Date(s) Application is Due: Jun 1; Dec 1
Contact: Kate Kerchaert; (860) 657-7016; kate.kerchaert@baml.com
Internet: https://www.bankofamerica.com/philanthropic/fn_search.action
Sponsor: Marjorie Moore Charitable Foundation
200 Glastonbury Boulevard, Suite # 200, CT2-545-02-05
Glastonbury, CT 06033-4056

Mark Wahlberg Youth Foundation Grants 3022
The foundation was established in May 2001 by Mark Wahlberg, a lifelong member and advocate of the Boys and Girls Clubs of America, for the purpose of raising and distributing funds to youth service and enrichment programs. Its mission is to assist youth in order to ensure that no child is limited or prevented from attaining their lifetime goal or dream due to financial circumstances.
Requirements: Nonprofit organizations serving youth in inner city areas are eligible.
Geographic Focus: All States
Contact: Rose Cortina, Cortina Business Management Contact; (617) 454-1125
Internet: https://www.markwahlbergyouthfoundation.com/about_us.asp
Sponsor: Mark Wahlberg Youth Foundation
P.O. Box 610287
Newton, MA 02461

MARPAT Foundation Grants 3023
The foundation supports nonprofit organizations based in or benefiting the greater Washington metropolitan area. Grants are awarded to support organizations that promote the visual and performing arts; encourage family planning; conserve natural resources or advance knowledge of the natural world; promote international understanding; preserve historic resources or advance knowledge of American history and culture, or; expand opportunities in the District of Columbia's Wards 7 and 8 for low-income youth and adults. Grant support includes general operating support, building funds, equipment, programs/projects, and publications. Stage One summary sheets are due by the listed application deadline; full proposals are by invitation.
Requirements: Organizations determined to be tax-exempt under section 501(c)3 of the U.S. Internal Revenue Code of 1986 and which are not private foundations are eligible. Grants will only be made to organizations based in or benefiting the greater Washington metropolitan area.
Restrictions: The foundation does not make grants for medical research, to endowment funds, to individuals, or to organizations based outside the United States.
Geographic Focus: District of Columbia, Maryland, Virginia

Date(s) Application is Due: May 22
Amount of Grant: 5,000 - 50,000 USD
Contact: Joan Koven, Secretary/Treasurer; jkoven@marpatfoundation.org
Internet: http://fdncenter.org/grantmaker/marpat
Sponsor: MARPAT Foundation
P.O. Box 1769
Silver Spring, MD 20915-1769

Marriott International Corporate Giving Grants 3024

The Marriott International Corporate Giving program is primarily interested in supporting areas of company operations, with emphasis on global and national organizations. The corporations major aim is to make charitable contributions to nonprofit organizations involved with: food and shelter; environmental stewardship; readiness for hotel careers; children, almost exclusively through a partnership with Children's Miracle Network; and organizations that embrace diversity and disabilities. Primary fields of interest mentioned are: agriculture and food; civil and human rights; disabled; minorities; employment and training; the environment; and housing and shelter. Only proposals submitted via email will be accepted. Application forms are not required, so applicants should begin by forwarding a letter. Though there are no specified deadlines, applicants should request funding a minimum of six weeks prior to the need. See the web site for further application details.
Geographic Focus: All States
Contact: Steven J. McNeil, (301) 380-3000; community.engagement@marriott.com
Internet: http://www.marriott.com/corporate-social-responsibility/corporate-responsibility.mi
Sponsor: Marriott International Corporate Giving Grants
10400 Fernwood Road
Bethesda, MD 20817-1102

Mars Foundation Grants 3025

The foundation awards grants to eligible nonprofit organizations primarily within the Washington, DC, metropolitan area, including Virginia, Maryland, and the District of Columbia. Areas of support include arts and culture, animal/wildlife, civic and community, education, environment, health and human services, and historic preservation. Types of support include capital grants, challenge grants, general operating grants, and project grants. Grants are awarded once a year. Requests must be submitted on the foundation's application form.
Requirements: U.S. 501(c)3 nonprofit organizations are eligible.
Geographic Focus: All States
Date(s) Application is Due: Oct 15
Contact: Grants Administrator; (703) 821-4900; fax (703) 448-9678
Internet: http://www.mars.com
Sponsor: Mars Foundation
6885 Elm Street
McLean, VA 22101

Marshall County Community Foundation Grants 3026

The Marshall County Community Foundation (MCCF) was established as a 501(c)3 not-for-profit organization with the defined purpose of serving the citizens of Marshall County, Indiana. The Foundation uses the following criteria when reviewing proposals: is there an established need and will the project achieve the desired result; is it appropriate for Marshall County to fund or is it too large; does it fit the County's areas of interest and geography; is it new or innovative; and does it foster collaboration with multiple impacts. Fund decisions are made within 90 days of each submission deadline. The application is available at the Foundation website.
Requirements: Only charitable organizations with a verifiable 501(c)3 status or equivalent will be considered. If 501(c)3 status is not available, organizations must find another organization to host the project or program.
Restrictions: Funding is not available for individuals; sectarian or religious purposes; long term funding; or for events that have already taken place.
Geographic Focus: Indiana
Date(s) Application is Due: Feb 1; Aug 1
Amount of Grant: Up to 10,000 USD
Contact: Linda Yoder, Executive Director; (574) 935-5159; fax (574) 936-8040
Internet: http://www.marshallcountycf.org/grants.htm
Sponsor: Marshall County Community Foundation
2701 North Michigan Street, P.O. Box 716
Plymouth, IN 46563

Marsh Corporate Grants 3027

The corporate giving program targets nonprofit organizations in corporate communities. Support goes to food banks - financial support and in-kind product donations, and nutrition programs that provide free hot meals for underprivileged children; education and youth programs - operating grants or project support to human service agencies that provide services to people, particularly children, in need in Marsh communities, and projects that directly benefit children, promote the education of children, or encourage the positive development of children; community development - support for operations or projects to community and civic organizations that focus on civic involvement, citizen participation, or positive improvements that benefit the community; arts - cultural and arts organizations that serve broad audiences with programming of the highest quality, and one-time capital grants for arts and cultural facilities; and hometown or neighborhood activities - grass-roots organizations that focus their efforts on improving their immediate community through activities that benefit families in their hometowns or neighborhoods.
Restrictions: Marsh is unable to provide support to for-profit organizations (employee recognition programs, company events, etc.) and third-party organizations.
Geographic Focus: Indiana, Ohio
Contact: Community Relations; (317) 594-2100 or (800) 845-7686; fax (317) 594-2705
Internet: http://www.marsh.net/about/community/marsh-giving/
Sponsor: Marsh Supermarkets
9800 Crosspoint Boulevard
Indianapolis, IN 46256

Martin C. Kauffman 100 Club of Alameda County Survivor Benefits Grants 3028

The mission of the Club is to provide immediate financial assistance to the families of police officers and firefighters killed in the line of duty in Alameda County, California. To that end, the lump sum of $20,000 is available to the family of any Alameda County peace officer or fire fighter who is killed in the line of duty within 48 hours of his/her death to help with burial and other immediate expenses.
Requirements: Recipients must be widows, widowers, and/or dependents of police officers and firefighters who have lost their lives in the line of duty in Alameda County, California.
Geographic Focus: California
Amount of Grant: 20,000 USD
Contact: Bonni L. Hendricks; (510) 818-0337; fax (925) 686-4819; MK100Club@att.net
Internet: http://www.100clubalamedacounty.org/
Sponsor: Martin C. Kauffman 100 Club of Alameda County
781 McKean Place
Concord, CA 94518-2835

Mary's Pence Ministry Grants 3029

Ministry grants are awarded annually with a maximum award of $5,000. A Ministry Project or Organization may receive a maximum of $15,000 awarded over three separate years. The program is available to Catholic women working with projects aimed at self-empowerment among economically poor women and children throughout the Americas. The organization funds small ministries that emerge as women respond urgently to the needs in their own communities. Funding can include general operating expenses, including salaries.
Requirements: A grant applicant must be a Catholic woman who has a clear, personal involvement in creating or expanding a ministry which improves or empowers the lives of economically disadvantaged women and/or women with children. Preference is given to newly developing organizations. In addition, the ministry must operate in North, Central, South America, or the Caribbean; have women of Catholic background prominent in organizational leadership; receive less than 50% of its funding from traditional government, church, parent organization, religious congregation or foundation sources; work on behalf of those who are marginalized in our church and society; have an organizational budget under the amount of $150,000. Organizations in the U.S. must have 501(c)3 status or be in the process of applying for it. The first step is an initial inquiry. Guidelines and the application process are available at the website.
Restrictions: Multi-year awards are not made at this time. Family members of staff, board or major contributors are not eligible. The organization generally does not fund capital campaigns, scholarship funds, and projects that provide charity without addressing systemic change.
Geographic Focus: All States, Antigua & Barbuda, Argentina, Bahamas, Barbados, Belize, Bolivia, Brazil, Canada, Chile, Colombia, Costa Rica, Cuba, Dominica, Dominican Republic, Ecuador, El Salvador, Grenada, Guatemala, Guyana, Haiti, Honduras, Jamaica, Mexico, Nicaragua, Paraguay, Peru
Date(s) Application is Due: Feb 1; Jun 1; Oct 1
Amount of Grant: Up to 4,000 USD
Contact: Katherine Wojtan, Executive Director; (718) 720-8040; fax (718) 720-8041; katherine@maryspence.org or inbox@maryspence.org
Internet: http://www.maryspence.org/ministrygrants.html
Sponsor: Mary's Pence
1000 Richmond Terrace, G-304
Staten Island, NY 10301

Mary's Pence Study Grants 3030

Funding is available to women for theological study at an undergraduate, graduate or certificate level. The study grants are awarded annually with a maximum award of $3,000 per individual and are awarded on a one-time basis. The grant can be used for tuition, books, fees and other expenses, including living expenses.
Requirements: A grant applicant must be a woman of Catholic background who is or will be matriculated in an educational program in order to prepare herself for ministry, expand her skills for current ministry, or re-tool for a new ministry. Applicants must be to women who are studying in North, South or Central America or the Caribbean in preparation for ministry in these regions. An initial inquiry by mail, telephone, or fax must be made prior to completing the application form online. Guidelines and instructions are available at the website.
Restrictions: Family members of staff, board or major contributors are not eligible. Women religious who have the support of a congregation rarely receive funding.
Geographic Focus: All States, Antigua & Barbuda, Argentina, Bahamas, Barbados, Belize, Bolivia, Brazil, Canada, Chile, Colombia, Costa Rica, Cuba, Ecuador, Guyana, Paraguay, Peru
Contact: Katherine Wojtan, (718) 720-8040; fax (718) 720-8041; katherine@maryspence.org
Internet: http://www.maryspence.org/studygrants.html
Sponsor: Mary's Pence
1000 Richmond Terrace, G-304
Staten Island, NY 10301

Mary Black Foundation Active Living Grants 3031

The Mary Black Foundation makes grants to nonprofit organizations in Spartanburg County, South Carolina, region. The Foundation has three applications for active living grants: Programs and Services assist people in becoming more physically active, either for recreation or for transportation; Policies and Places have a direct impact on whether people

have the opportunity to be active; and Planning and Capacity Building for organizations that have as part of their core mission to increase active living. Each area of Active Living has different goals and grant submission procedures. The Foundation accepts applications quarterly: March 1, June 1, September 1, and December 1.
Requirements: Nonprofit organizations in South Carolina's Spartanburg County are eligible. Before submitting an application for a grant in Active Living, potential applicants must meet with the Foundation's program staff.
Restrictions: The Foundation does not accept applications from individuals or general fundraising solicitations.
Geographic Focus: South Carolina
Date(s) Application is Due: Mar 1; Jun 1; Sep 1; Dec 1
Amount of Grant: 2,000 - 200,000 USD
Contact: Amy Page, (864) 573-9500; fax (864) 573-5805; apage@maryblackfoundation.org
Internet: http://www.maryblackfoundation.org/active-living/targeted-results
Sponsor: Mary Black Foundation
349 East Main Street, Suite 100
Spartanburg, SC 29302

Mary Black Foundation Community Health Grants 3032
The Mary Black Foundation makes grants to nonprofit organizations in Spartanburg County, South Carolina, region. The Community Health Fund (CHF) is an annual grantmaking opportunity that supports efforts to promote health and wellness. The CHF is for projects outside of the Foundation's Active Living or Early Childhood Development priority areas and represents 10-20% of the Foundation's total grantmaking. The Foundation accepts applications once each year, with an annual deadline of September 4.
Requirements: Nonprofit organizations in South Carolina's Spartanburg County are eligible. Before submitting an application for a grant in Community Health, potential applicants must meet with the Foundation's program staff.
Restrictions: The Foundation does not accept applications from individuals or general fundraising solicitations.
Geographic Focus: South Carolina
Date(s) Application is Due: Sep 4
Amount of Grant: 1,000 - 5,000 USD
Contact: Amy Page, (864) 573-9500; fax (864) 573-5805; apage@maryblackfoundation.org
Internet: http://www.maryblackfoundation.org/grantmaking/community-health-fund
Sponsor: Mary Black Foundation
349 East Main Street, Suite 100
Spartanburg, SC 29302

Mary Black Foundation Early Childhood Development Grants 3033
The Mary Black Foundation makes grants to nonprofit organizations in Spartanburg County, South Carolina, region. The goals of its investment in early childhood development are: more children in Spartanburg County will enter school ready to learn; and fewer adolescents in Spartanburg County will experience an unintended pregnancy. The Foundation has three applications for early childhood development grants: Programs and Services provide direct assistance, social support, resources, and information to children and teens and their families or to those who work with them; Policies and Places refer to the environmental conditions that affect early childhood development and adolescent pregnancy; and Planning and Capacity Building for organizations that have as part of their core missions the improvement of early childhood development or the reduction of adolescent pregnancy. The Foundation accepts applications quarterly: March 1, June 1, September 1, and December 1.
Requirements: Nonprofit organizations in South Carolina's Spartanburg County are eligible. Before submitting an application for a grant in Early Childhood Development, potential applicants must meet with the Foundation's program staff.
Restrictions: The Foundation does not accept applications from individuals or general fundraising solicitations.
Geographic Focus: South Carolina
Date(s) Application is Due: Mar 1; Jun 1; Sep 1; Dec 1
Amount of Grant: 2,500 - 300,000 USD
Contact: Amy Page, (864) 573-9500; fax (864) 573-5805; apage@maryblackfoundation.org
Internet: http://www.maryblackfoundation.org/early-childhood-development/targeted-results
Sponsor: Mary Black Foundation
349 East Main Street, Suite 100
Spartanburg, SC 29302

Mary C. & Perry F. Spencer Foundation Grants 3034
The Mary C. & Perry F. Spencer Foundation is an independent foundation that was established in 1981. The foundation gives primarily in Fort Wayne, Indiana. Giving primarily for the arts, education, conservation, and human services; some funding available for religious purposes.
Requirements: Applicants should submit a letter for the foundation office, requesting a grant application. Submit the following with your grant application: copy of IRS Determination Letter; detailed description of project and amount of funding requested. Deadline(s): None
Restrictions: The foundation gives primarily in Fort Wayne, Indiana.
Geographic Focus: Indiana
Amount of Grant: 2,000 - 30,000 USD
Samples: Harlan Christian Youth Center, Harlan, IN, $30,000; Youth for Christ, Fort Wayne, IN, $5,000; Taylor University, Fort Wayne, IN, $18,948.
Contact: Denise Andorfer, Director; (260) 462-6218
Sponsor: National City Bank of Indiana
P.O. Box 94651
Cleveland, OH 44101-4651

Mary D. and Walter F. Frear Eleemosynary Trust Grants 3035
Walter Francis Frear was a lawyer and judge in the Kingdom of Hawaii and Republic of Hawaii, and the third Territorial Governor of Hawaii from 1907 to 1913. The Mary D. and Walter F. Frear Eleemosynary Trust was established to sponsor educational projects. Grants are awarded to Hawaii nonprofit organizations in the areas of child welfare and youth, education, social services, music, and the arts. Types of support include building construction and renovation, capital campaigns, conferences and seminars, equipment acquisition, general operating support, matching/challenge grants, program development, and seed grants. There are three annual deadlines specified, and applicants should begin by contacting the Trust administrative office.
Requirements: Grant applications are accepted from qualified tax-exempt charitable organizations in Hawaii.
Restrictions: Grants are not made to individuals, nor for endowments, reserve purposes, deficit financing, or travel.
Geographic Focus: Hawaii
Date(s) Application is Due: Jan 1; Jul 1; Oct 1
Amount of Grant: 5,000 - 25,000 USD
Contact: Paula Boyce, Grants Administrator, c/o Bank of Hawaii; (808) 537-8822; fax (808) 538-4007; pboyce@boh.com
Sponsor: Mary D. and Walter F. Frear Eleemosynary Trust
130 Merchant Street, P.O. Box 3170
Honolulu, HI 96802-3170

Mary Duke Biddle Foundation Grants 3036
The foundation awards grants to eligible New York and North Carolina organizations in its areas of interest, including arts and performing arts (music, dance, and theater), community development, disabled, education (secondary and higher education), and religion. Types of support include conferences and seminars, fellowships, matching/challenge grants, program development, scholarship funds, and seed money grants. There are no application forms. Grant requests are reviewed at quarterly board meetings in March, June, September, and December; contact the office for deadline dates.
Requirements: Only 501(c)3 organizations in New York and North Carolina may apply.
Restrictions: Grants do not support individuals, building construction/renovation, or operating budgets.
Geographic Focus: New York, North Carolina
Contact: Douglas C. Zinn, Executive Director; (919) 493-5591
Internet: http://www.marydukebiddlefoundation.org/
Sponsor: Mary Duke Biddle Foundation
1044 West Forest Hills Boulevard
Durham, NC 27707

Mary E. and Michael Blevins Charitable Trust Grants 3037
Established in 2006 in the State of Missouri, the Mary E. and Michael Blevins Charitable Trust is intended to support Catholic organizations, human service agencies, and service delivery programs within the southeastern United States. There are no specific application or deadlines with which to adhere, and applicants should begin the grant writing process by contacting the Trust directly. Any 501(c)3 organization or church that is located in, or supports the residents of, the southeastern U.S. can apply.
Geographic Focus: Alabama, Arkansas, Georgia, Kentucky, Missouri, North Carolina, South Carolina, Tennessee, Virginia, West Virginia
Amount of Grant: Up to 6,000 USD
Contact: Michael Blevins, Trustee; (636) 368-1413
Sponsor: Mary E. and Michael Blevins Charitable Trust
21 Oak Hill Lane
St. Peters, MO 63376-2158

Mary E. Babcock Foundation 3038
The Mary E. Babcock Foundation was established in Ohio with the specific purposes of supporting community development, economic development, and education within the Johnstown, Ohio, region. An application form is required, and applicants should submit a detailed description of the project and a detailed budget as part of that application. There are no specified annual deadlines, and grant funding ranges up to $8,000.
Requirements: Nonprofit 501(c)3 organizations serving residents of the Johnstown, Ohio, area are eligible to apply.
Geographic Focus: Ohio
Amount of Grant: Up to 8,000 USD
Contact: Stuart Parsons, Treasurer; (740) 366-6561
Sponsor: Mary E. Babcock Foundation
1436 Estates Drive
Newark, OH 43055-1772

Mary E. Ober Foundation Grants 3039
The foundation seeks organizations that have a vision for serving the community at a level that is beyond service numbers. They desire to see long-term impact, and work with those that are a catalyst for change in the areas they identify as core to their mission. Areas of interest include: Marginalized & disenfranchised support; Social justice; Homeless and near-homeless; Youth in crisis situations; Character development; Education; Health/emergency services; Leadership & sustainability; Families educating strong core values.
Requirements: The foundation seeks Christian faith-based or faith-friendly organizations that have a vision for serving the community at a level that is beyond service numbers. It does not have a grant cycle, and does not accept unsolicited grant requests. Instead, it employs a process that may result in a Request For Proposal. Contact the foundation by email, phone or letter, to discuss your organization, program or project. Those organizations

receive invitation to submit a letter of inquiry to the foundation. Be prepared to discuss mission, vision, leadership, sustainability, measured outcomes and community impact for your organization. After the initial discussion, you may be invited to submit a 2-page letter of inquiry including: Brief project description, numbers served, and outcomes; Why you are applying; Why your project fits with our mission; Rationale and the purpose of the project; Project cost estimates. After review of the Letter of inquiry and your organization, you may be invited to submit a full proposal. The foundation will entertain inquiries from organizations located in the U.S. with a core focus on Indiana.
Geographic Focus: All States
Amount of Grant: 1,000 - 20,000 USD
Contact: Charles Wills, Executive Director; (317) 697-7192; info@meofoundation.org
Internet: http://www.meofoundation.org/Grantmaking/tabid/57/Default.aspx
Sponsor: Mary E. Ober Foundation
P.O. Box 186
Nashville, IN 47448-0186

Mary Jane Luick Trust Grants 3040
The Mary Jane Luick Trust was established in Indiana and is administered by Old National Bank of Evansville, Indiana. The funding opportunities from this Trust provide assistance for indigent elderly women who reside in Delaware County, Indiana and are economically disadvantaged.
Requirements: Application form not required for grant proposal and grants are given to individuals only.
Geographic Focus: Indiana
Contact: Trust Coordinator; fax (800) 468-0347
Sponsor: Old National Bank
320 South High Street
Muncie, IN 47305-2325

Mary Jennings Sport Camp Scholarship 3041
The fund is named for New Jersey athlete Mary Jennings who passed away in June of 2006 following a short battle with liver cancer. Although Jennings, 21, was a multi-talented student-athlete who played basketball and ran track, her passion was soccer. The fund is intended to help support young female athletes who would like to attend a sport camp to develop their skills.
Requirements: The fund will provide financial support for female athletes ages 10-14 to attend the sport camp of their choice. Athletes in any sport are eligible to apply. Applications must be received by February 1st of each year (for camps held between mid February and October 1) or October 1st of each year (for camps held between mid October and February 1). A brochure and application form can be downloaded at the website.
Restrictions: Scholarships cannot be applied to transportation, equipment or supplies.
Geographic Focus: All States
Date(s) Application is Due: Feb 1; Oct 1
Contact: Megan McLaughlin; (703) 476-3400, ext. 453; mmclaughling@aahperd.org
Internet: http://www.aahperd.org/nagws/programs/awards/Mary-Jennings-Sport-Camp-Scholarship.cfm
Sponsor: National Association for Girls and Women in Sport
1900 Association Drive
Reston, VA 20191

Mary K. Chapman Foundation Grants 3042
Mary K. Chapman was born in Oklahoma in 1920. She graduated from the University of Tulsa and worked as a nurse before her marriage to Allen Chapman in 1960. After the death of her husband in 1979, Mary Chapman maintained her own personal charitable giving program. Before her death in 2002, she established The Mary K. Chapman Foundation, a charitable trust founded to perpetuate her own charitable giving program. This foundation was fully funded with a bequest from her estate in 2005. Mary K. Chapman was very interested in supporting education, but as a former nurse and a very compassionate person, much of her charity was directed to health, medical research, and educating and caring for the less fortunate and disadvantaged. There are two steps in the process of applying for a grant. The first is a Letter of Inquiry from the applicant. This letter is used to determine if the applicant will be invited to take the second step of submitting a formal Grant Proposal.
Requirements: IRS 501(c)3 non-profits are eligible to apply.
Restrictions: Grant requests for the following purposes are not favored: endowments, except as a limited part of a capital project reserved for maintenance of the facility being constructed; deficit financing and debt retirement; projects or programs for which the Chapman Trusts would be the sole source of financial support; travel, conferences, conventions, group meetings, or seminars; camp programs and other seasonal activities; religious programs of religious organizations; project or program planning; start-up ventures are not excluded, but organizations with a proven strategy and results are preferred; purposes normally funded by taxation or governmental agencies; requests made less than nine months from the declination of a previous request by an applicant, or within nine months of the last payment made on a grant made to an applicant; requests for more than one project.
Geographic Focus: Oklahoma
Amount of Grant: Up to 300,000 USD
Contact: Andie Doyle; (918) 496-7882; fax (918) 496-7887; andie@chapmantrusts.com
Internet: http://www.chapmantrusts.org/grants_programs.php
Sponsor: Mary K. Chapman Foundation
6100 South Yale, Suite 1816
Tulsa, OK 74136

Mary Kay Ash Charitable Foundation Grants 3043
The foundation, whose mission is to enrich women's lives around the world, supports research grants to help find a cure for cancers affecting women (breast, cervical, ovarian, and uterine). It also funds U.S. women's shelters and offers financial support to organizations that raise awareness and address the problem of violence against women. Proposals may be submitted at any time.
Requirements: Cancer research grants are awarded to accredited U.S. medical schools and schools of public health. Shelters must be U.S. tax-exempt entities.
Geographic Focus: All States
Contact: Grants Administrator; (877) 652-2737
Internet: http://www.mkacf.org
Sponsor: Mary Kay Ash Charitable Foundation
P.O. Box 799044
Dallas, TX 75379-9044

Mary Kay Foundation Domestic Violence Shelter Grants 3044
Every October, The Mary Kay Foundation observes National Domestic Violence Awareness Month by awarding grants to deserving women's domestic violence shelters across the United States. During the past year, the Foundation awarded $20,000 grants to more than 150 women's domestic violence shelters across the nation for a total of $3 million. Each year, the Foundation awards a grant to at least one domestic violence shelter in every state. Any remaining funds are distributed based on state population. Grant applications are reviewed by the Domestic Violence Shelter Grant Committee, which makes recommendations to the TMKF Board of Directors. After reviewing these recommendations, the Foundation's Board of Directors selects the final grant recipients. Domestic violence shelter grant applications are available from this Web site or from The Mary Kay Foundation from January to June 30 each year. We announce grant recipients in the fall to coincide with National Domestic Violence Awareness Month in October.
Geographic Focus: All States
Amount of Grant: 20,000 USD
Contact: Lana Rowe, (972) 687-4822 or (877) 652-2737; Lana.Rowe@mkcorp.com Jennifer Cook, (972) 687-5889 or (972) 687-4822; Jennifer.cook@mkcorp.com or MKCares@marykayfoundation.org
Internet: http://www.marykayfoundation.org/Pages/ShelterGrantProgram.aspx
Sponsor: Mary Kay Foundation
P.O. Box 799044
Dallas, TX 75379-9044

Mary M. Aaron Memorial Trust Scholarships 3045
The Trustees of the Mary M. Aaron Memorial Trust Scholarship Fund are committed to primarily helping students that begin their post-secondary education at Yuba College, then move on to other colleges or universities after completing their general education requirements. If funds are available, the Trust grants awards to all qualifying students that are attending Yuba College. When students complete their general education requirements, and are ready to move on to a four-year institution, they may continue to apply for a scholarship.
Requirements: Under the terms of the will of the grantor of the Trust, funds from the Trust are to be awarded to Yuba and Sutter County students who will be attending colleges or universities located within the state of California.
Geographic Focus: California
Date(s) Application is Due: Mar 15
Contact: Tracy Franco, (530) 671-1550; fax (530) 671-3517; tfranco@chipmancpa.com
Sponsor: Mary M. Aaron Memorial Trust
1190 Civic Center Boulevard
Yuba City, CA 95993-3004

Mary Owen Borden Foundation Grants 3046
The Mary Owen Borden Foundation Grants support programs that address the needs of economically disadvantaged youth and their families. This includes needs such as health, family planning, education, counseling, childcare, substance abuse, and delinquency. Other areas of interest for the foundation include affordable housing, conservation, environment, and the arts. Grants average $10,000, and the maximum grant is $15,000. In unique circumstances, the Foundation considers a more significant grant for a program having a major impact in their areas of interests.
Requirements: New Jersey nonprofits in Monmouth and Mercer Counties are eligible. Most of the Foundation's grant go to nonprofit entities in Trenton, Asbury Park, and Long Branch.
Geographic Focus: New Jersey
Date(s) Application is Due: Mar 15; Sep 15
Amount of Grant: Up to 15,000 USD
Contact: Quinn McKean; (732) 741-4645; fax (732) 741-2542; qmckean@aol.com
Internet: http://fdncenter.org/grantmaker/borden/guide.html
Sponsor: Mary Owen Borden Foundation
4 Blackpoint Horseshoe
Rumson, NJ 07760

Mary Reynolds Babcock Foundation Grants 3047
Throughout the southern portion of the U.S., people who live in low-wealth communities and individuals from the public, private and nonprofit sectors are forming creative partnerships to advance economic and social justice. The Mary Reynolds Babcock Foundation invites proposals from local, statewide and regional nonprofits in the Southeastern U.S. that have track records of helping low-wealth people build assets and transform economic conditions in their communities. It supports grassroots groups and networks in low-wealth communities that are poised to expand their scale of impact. The Foundation also supports

statewide or regional organizations and networks that are achieving large-scale impact. It is interested in both new approaches and proven strategies that link together grassroots and larger organizations. Organizations may use grant funds in a variety of ways, including but not limited to: general operating support; project support; glue support for bringing together networks of grassroots and partner organizations; organizational development support; and efforts to bring 18- to 30-year-olds into leadership roles in the organization.
Requirements: The Mary Reynolds Babcock Foundation invites proposals from local, statewide and regional nonprofits in the Southeastern United States that have track records of helping low-wealth people build assets and transform economic conditions in their communities. Applicants must be located in the southeastern U.S., with emphasis on eastern Alabama, Arkansas, Georgia, Louisiana, Mississippi, North Carolina, South Carolina, Tennessee, north and central Florida, and the Appalachian regions of Kentucky and West Virginia.
Restrictions: No grants are given to individuals, or for capital improvements, direct services (such as food or medical assistance), or for satellite operations of organizations outside the southeast.
Geographic Focus: Alabama, Arkansas, Georgia, Kentucky, Louisiana, Mississippi, North Carolina, South Carolina, Tennessee, Virginia, West Virginia
Date(s) Application is Due: Feb 1; Jul 1
Amount of Grant: 1,500 - 6,000,000 USD
Contact: Gayle Williams; (336) 748-9222; fax (336) 777-0095; info@mrbf.org
Internet: http://www.mrbf.org/applyForGrant.aspx
Sponsor: Mary Reynolds Babcock Foundation
2920 Reynolda Road
Winston-Salem, NC 27106-3016

Mary S. and David C. Corbin Foundation Grants 3048
The Corbin Foundation gives primary consideration to charitable organizations and/or local chapters of national charities located in Akron and Summit County, Ohio, although extremely worthy causes outside of this preferred area may be considered. Areas of interest include arts and culture; civic and community; education; health care; housing; social services; medical research; and youth. The Foundation meets in May and November to consider requests. Grant requests must be received no later than March 1 for consideration in May and September 1 for consideration in November. The application and guidelines are available at the Foundation website.
Requirements: The Foundation has a general application cover sheet which applicants must complete. Organizations should also send a brief letter on their letterhead, submitting one original and one copy of all application materials.
Restrictions: Only written applications will be considered. Telephone and personal interviews are discouraged unless requested by the Foundation. The Foundation does not fund individuals; annual fundraising campaigns; ongoing requests for general operating support (although some repeat grants are made); operating deficits; or organizations which in turn make grants to others.
Geographic Focus: Ohio
Date(s) Application is Due: Mar 1; Sep 1
Contact: Erika J. May; (330) 762-6427; fax (330) 762-6428; corbin@nls.net
Internet: http://foundationcenter.org/grantmaker/corbin/guide.html
Sponsor: Mary S. and David C. Corbin Foundation
Akron Central Plaza
Akron, OH 44308-1830

Mary Wilmer Covey Charitable Trust Grants 3049
The Mary Wilmer Covey Charitable Trust was created to support charitable organizations that promote education including instruction and training that help to build human capabilities. It also supports organizations that focus on relieving human suffering due to disease, ill health, physical weakness, disability, or injury; and supports organizations that work to prolong life and improve the quality of life, especially for children. Grants from the Mary Wilmer Covey Charitable Trust are primarily one year in duration; on occasion, multi-year support is awarded. Applicants must apply online at the grant website. The annual application deadline is September 1 at 11:59 p.m. Applicants will be notified of grant decisions by letter within one to two months after the deadline. Applicants are strongly encouraged to do the following before applying: review the downloadable state-specific application procedures at the grant website; review the downloadable online-application guidelines at the grant website; review the trust's funding history (link is available from the grant website); review the online application questions in advance; and review the list of required attachments. These will generally include: a list of board members, financial statements (audited, reviewed, or compiled by independent auditor); an organization summary; a list of other funding sources; an IRS Determination letter; and other required documents. All attachments must be uploaded in the online application as PDF, Word, or Excel files.
Requirements: Applicants must have 501(c)3 tax-exempt status. Preference is given to charitable organizations located in Macon, Georgia; Richmond, Virginia; and Chatham Hall, Virginia.
Restrictions: The trust does not support requests from individuals, organizations attempting to influence policy through direct lobbying, or any political campaigns.
Geographic Focus: Georgia, Virginia
Date(s) Application is Due: Sep 1
Samples: Medical Center of Central Georgia, Macon, Georgia, $50,000; Chatham Hall, Chatham, Virginia, $15,000; Childrens Hospital, Richmond, Virginia, $15,000.
Contact: Quanda Allen, Vice President; (404) 264-1377; quanda.allen@baml.com
Internet: https://www.bankofamerica.com/philanthropic/fn_search.action
Sponsor: Mary Wilmer Covey Charitable Trust
3414 Peachtree Road, N.E., Suite 1475, GA7-813-14-04
Atlanta, GA 30326-1113

Massachusetts Bar Foundation IOLTA Grants 3050
The foundation invites applications from nonprofit organizations in Massachusetts for projects that contribute to the following objectives: provide civil legal services to low-income persons on issues where there is an identifiable and unmet need, or conduct activities contributing directly to the improvement in the administration of justice in Massachusetts; demonstrate an innovative, cost-effective approach that does not duplicate other services; enlist the pro bono support of the private bar; serve particularly underserved areas of the Commonwealth; and include collaborative efforts with both the court system and other organizations. Grants are awarded for innovative initiatives with clear, quantifiable objectives. Consequently, all applicants should include evaluation plans designed to identify program outcomes and impacts. The foundation prefers to support specific projects or programs; it does not provide support for general operating expenses. Organizations are welcome to submit multiple grant applications for distinct programs. Organizations also may submit applications for renewed funding of previously supported programs. Guidelines are available online.
Requirements: The foundation awards grants to organizations. Priority is given to 501(c)3 organizations, although other nonprofit organizations with charitable programs may also receive funding. Typically, grants are awarded to legal service and law-related agencies, as well as to various nongovernment organizations across the state. In rare cases, public agencies, established by governmental entities under statutory authorization, may receive funding for pilot programs that will ultimately receive public funding.
Geographic Focus: Massachusetts
Date(s) Application is Due: Mar 10
Amount of Grant: 24,568 USD
Contact: Administrator; (617) 338-0500; fax (617) 338-0550; foundation@massbar.org
Internet: http://www.massbarfoundation.org/grant_programs/iolta
Sponsor: Massachusetts Bar Foundation
20 West Street
Boston, MA 02111-1204

Massachusetts Bar Foundation Legal Intern Fellowships 3051
The program was established to encourage careers in the law that further the goals of social justice, while contributing valuable legal support to organizations serving the underrepresented in Massachusetts. To assist law students in gaining practical experience in the public sector, the foundation awards four stipends to law students who intern during the summer months at nonprofit organizations providing civil legal services to low-income clients in Massachusetts. Guidelines are available online.
Requirements: Applications are welcome from law students who have secured a volunteer internship with a qualified nonprofit organization in Massachusetts; are currently enrolled in U.S. law schools, with preference given to second- and third-year students; demonstrate a commitment to public interest law, including experience working with low-income clients; and commit to work no less than 10 continuous, full-time weeks between June 1 and October 1.
Geographic Focus: Massachusetts
Date(s) Application is Due: Mar 17
Amount of Grant: 6,000 USD
Contact: Administrator; (617) 338-0534; fax (617) 338-0550; foundation@massbar.org
Internet: http://www.massbarfoundation.org/grant_programs/legal_intern
Sponsor: Massachusetts Bar Foundation
20 West Street
Boston, MA 02111-1204

Massachusetts Cultural Council Adams Arts Program Grants 3052
Business and government leaders agree that Massachusetts' future prosperity is closely tied to the creative economy. Industries such as the arts, architecture, publishing, advertising, and design employ 109,000 workers and generate $4.2 billion in annual economic impact in the Commonwealth. The MCC has been supporting creative economy initiatives throughout Massachusetts for a decade, beginning in the 1990s. In 2004, the Legislature created the Adams Arts Program, which funds projects that create jobs and income, revitalize downtowns, and draw cultural tourists. Adams-funded projects leverage the assets of the creative sector - artists, cultural organizations, and arts-related businesses - inherent in Massachusetts' communities to generate real income. Communities as diverse as Boston, Lowell, New Bedford, and Pittsfield have used these funds to more fully realize these assets for the benefit of residents and visitors alike. There are two grant categories: planning (up to $5,000) and implementation (up to $50,000).
Requirements: Applicants to the grant programs include cultural organizations, individuals, schools, community service organizations, and communities. Organizations must be a 501(c)3 entity based or incorporated in Massachusetts. For implementation grants, a dynamic partnership among stakeholders is a fundamental project component. Partnerships must involve at least three organizations that are prepared to lead the project over time. One of the partners must be a cultural organization incorporated in Massachusetts. Other partners may include: non-cultural organizations, private, for-profit businesses, educational institutions and state and federal agencies. Each organization is expected to make a significant contribution to the project.
Geographic Focus: Massachusetts
Date(s) Application is Due: Apr 19
Amount of Grant: Up to 50,000 USD
Contact: Kylie Sullivan, Program Officer; (617) 727-3668, ext. 269 or (800) 232-0960; fax (617) 727-0044; kylie.sullivan@art.state.ma.us
Internet: http://www.massculturalcouncil.org/programs/adamsarts.asp
Sponsor: Massachusetts Cultural Council
10 St. James Avenue, 3rd Floor
Boston, MA 02116-3803

Massachusetts Cultural Council Cultural Facilities Capital Grants   3053

Governor Deval Patrick has allocated a new appropriation for the Massachusetts Cultural Facilities Fund. These funds will allow the Massachusetts Cultural Council (MCC) and MassDevelopment to support capital projects in the arts, humanities and sciences that create jobs, educate adults and improve the quality of life in cities and towns across the state. The Capital Grant Program provides matching grants to assist with the acquisition, design, construction, repair, renovation, rehabilitation or other capital improvements or deferred maintenance of Cultural Facilities in Massachusetts. The goal of this program is to provide a portion of the resources necessary for our state's cultural facilities to flourish. Through grants and advisory assistance, this program will promote the development of Cultural Facilities that are thoughtfully planned and developed, contribute to the cultural and economic lives of their communities and are supported by significant matching contributions from the private sector. The Capital Grant Program offers grants for: site or facility acquisition; repair, rehabilitation, or renovation of existing facilities (this may include (but is not limited to) efforts to improve physical accessibility, fire safety, and other building safety); expansion of existing facilities; design and construction of new facilities; purchase of major equipment or integrated systems (this may include HVAC systems, sound and light systems, rigging or similar equipment, provided that these are fully integrated elements of a building, structure or site); or any combination of the above. Grants in this program may be used for: acquisition; direct construction costs; costs closely associated with construction such as demolition; architectural, engineering or other design fees; and building permits.
Restrictions: Mobile goods or equipment are generally not eligible for grant reimbursement. Grants in this program may not be used for: non-facilities capital campaigns (e.g., endowment campaigns); regular operating activities of an organization; ongoing staff positions; fundraising or marketing activities; any other costs that are not related to the approved Eligible Project; or mortgage or loan payments.
Geographic Focus: Massachusetts
Date(s) Application is Due: Apr 6
Contact: Jay Paget, Program Director; (617) 727-3668, ext. 263 or (800) 232-0960; fax (617) 727-0044; jay.paget@art.state.ma.us
Internet: http://www.massculturalcouncil.org/facilities/facilities_capital.htm
Sponsor: Massachusetts Cultural Council
10 St. James Avenue, 3rd Floor
Boston, MA 02116-3803

Massachusetts Cultural Council Facilities Feasibility & Tech Assistance Grants   3054

Governor Deval Patrick has allocated a new appropriation for the Massachusetts Cultural Facilities Fund. These funds will allow the Massachusetts Cultural Council (MCC) and MassDevelopment to support capital projects in the arts, humanities and sciences that create jobs, educate adults and improve the quality of life in cities and towns across the state. The purpose of the Feasibility and Technical Assistance Grants is to help managers and board members of cultural organizations get the objective information and analysis they need before they commit their organization's energies and financial resources to a facilities project. Organizations that are contemplating an Eligible Project may apply for funds to support pre-implementation planning - research, fact-finding and analysis that can help them make more informed decisions about their facilities development effort. Types of planning and technical assistance may include (but are not necessarily limited to): market studies; capital campaign feasibility studies; systems replacement plans or other comprehensive facility plans; site selection surveys; preliminary architectural plans and/or schematic drawings; accessibility assessments.
Restrictions: Feasibility and Technical Assistance Grant funds are not available for non-facilities-related planning efforts; site acquisition; regular operating activities; ongoing staff positions; complete architectural drawings; fundraising or marketing activities; or publications.
Geographic Focus: Massachusetts
Date(s) Application is Due: Apr 6
Contact: Jay Paget, Program Director; (617) 727-3668, ext. 263 or (800) 232-0960; fax (617) 727-0044; jay.paget@art.state.ma.us
Internet: http://www.massculturalcouncil.org/facilities/facilities_feasibility.htm
Sponsor: Massachusetts Cultural Council
10 St. James Avenue, 3rd Floor
Boston, MA 02116-3803

Massachusetts Cultural Council Facilities Systems Replacement Plan Grants   3055

Governor Deval Patrick has allocated a new appropriation for the Massachusetts Cultural Facilities Fund. These funds will allow the Massachusetts Cultural Council (MCC) and MassDevelopment to support capital projects in the arts, humanities and sciences that create jobs, educate adults and improve the quality of life in cities and towns across the state. The goal of the Systems Replacement Plan Grants is to provide organizations with the tools they need to prioritize their capital maintenance needs. The Systems Replacement Plan will help managers and board members of cultural organizations get the objective information and analysis they need to address the cycles of maintenance for their facility. With a Systems Replacement Plan Grant, grantees will enter into contract with a pre-approved third party consultant who will survey the building envelope (roof, walls, and entry systems) and the mechanical systems (heating, cooling, ventilation, plumbing, and pool filtration). The survey will provide the estimated usable-life expectancy and the approximate replacement cost of your building systems. At the conclusion of the survey, organizations will receive a 20-year Systems Replacement Plan which forecasts the necessary replacement schedule of specific systems and equipment. The Systems Replacement Plan is priced based on the size of your facility.
Requirements: All projects must provide evidence that they meet these four statutory criteria to be considered for a Systems Replacement Plan Grant: there must be a demonstrated community need for the project; the project must be able to demonstrate that it will benefit tourism in the local area; there must be a demonstrated financial need for a grant; and the project must be able to demonstrate local support.
Geographic Focus: Massachusetts
Date(s) Application is Due: Apr 6
Contact: Jay Paget, Program Director; (617) 727-3668, ext. 263 or (800) 232-0960; fax (617) 727-0044; jay.paget@art.state.ma.us
Internet: http://www.massculturalcouncil.org/facilities/facilities_systems.htm
Sponsor: Massachusetts Cultural Council
10 St. James Avenue, 3rd Floor
Boston, MA 02116-3803

Massachusetts Cultural Council Cultural Investment Portfolio   3056

The primary purpose of MCC's Cultural Investment Portfolio is to strengthen the cultural sector as a whole. State investment in nonprofit arts, humanities, and science organizations yields returns in economic impact and increasing public access, according to the information gathered from the Massachusetts Cultural Data Project. The Cultural Investment Portfolio is not a traditional grant program, but a partnership that will better position the cultural sector as vital components of Massachusetts' economy and the quality of life of our citizens. Providing unrestricted general operating support is a core priority for the Massachusetts Cultural Council (MCC). There are three levels of participation to the Portfolio - Peers, Colleagues, and Partners. Peer grants are designed primarily for organizations new to the MCC operating support funding pool, not fully-cultural organizations, and other groups offering cultural programming who do not meet the requirements for Partners or Colleagues. Colleague grants are available to organizations with a track record of offering public cultural programming in Massachusetts for at least five years, and have received operational support from the MCC for at least four fiscal years. Partner grants are available to given to organizations with a track record of offering public cultural programming in Massachusetts for at least 10 years, and have received operational support from the MCC for at least eight fiscal years since FY1997.
Geographic Focus: Massachusetts
Contact: Cheryl Balukonis, Senior Program Officer; (617) 727-3668, ext. 318 or (800) 232-0960; fax (617) 727-0044; cheryl.balukonis@art.state.ma.us
Internet: http://www.massculturalcouncil.org/programs/cultural_investment_portfolio.asp
Sponsor: Massachusetts Cultural Council
10 St. James Avenue, 3rd Floor
Boston, MA 02116-3803

Massachusetts Cultural Council Local Cultural Council (LCC) Grants   3057

The Local Cultural Council (LCC) Program is the largest grassroots cultural funding network in the nation supporting thousands of community-based projects in the arts, humanities, and sciences annually. The program promotes the availability of rich cultural experiences for every Massachusetts citizen. Each year, local councils award more than $2 million in grants to more than 5,000 cultural programs statewide. These include school field trips, afterschool programs, concerts, festivals, lectures, theater, dance, music, and film. LCC projects take place in schools, community centers, libraries, elder care facilities, town halls, parks, and wherever communities come together. Applicants may apply to the LCC Program for projects, operating support, ticket subsidy programs, artist residencies, fellowships or other activities, based on local priorities and needs. Local councils may also choose to fund cultural field trips for children, grades pre-K through 12, by subsidizing the cost for children to attend programs in the arts, humanities and interpretive sciences (including performances, educational tours and exhibits).
Requirements: Individuals, schools, and cultural organizations are eligible to apply for project support from their local council. Funding for cultural field trips is also available. Applicants should contact their LCC before completing an application.
Geographic Focus: Massachusetts
Date(s) Application is Due: Oct 15
Contact: Jenifer Lawless, Program Manager for Local Cultural Councils; (617) 727-3668, ext. 325 or (800) 232-0960; fax (617) 727-0044; jenifer.lawless@art.state.ma.us
Internet: http://www.massculturalcouncil.org/programs/lccgrants.asp
Sponsor: Massachusetts Cultural Council
10 St. James Avenue, 3rd Floor
Boston, MA 02116-3803

Massachusetts Cultural Council Traditional Arts Apprenticeships   3058

Traditional Arts Apprenticeships is a time-honored method by which an individual learns skills, techniques and artistry under the guidance of a recognized master. Master artists are individuals recognized within their communities as exemplary practitioners of traditional art forms. Apprentices - individuals who learn under the guidance of master artists - typically have prior experience in the traditional art form, significant promise, and a serious long-term commitment to practicing the art. One of the goals of the Apprenticeship Program is to help communities preserve their own cultural heritage. The strongest applications tend to be those that include the pairing of masters and apprentices who are members of the same ethnic, religious, or occupational group. A master artist and an apprentice must apply together. Apprenticeships are awarded every other year to a limited number of master artists. Priority is given to rare or endangered traditions. Funds (up to $6,000 per apprenticeship) are provided to compensate the master artist for teaching time. However, supplies, materials, and travel expenses may also be included in the application.
Geographic Focus: Massachusetts
Date(s) Application is Due: Apr 10
Contact: Maggie Holtzberg, Program Manager; (617) 727-3668, ext. 254 or (800) 232-0960; fax (617) 727-0044; maggie.holtzberg@art.state.ma.us
Internet: http://www.massculturalcouncil.org/programs/apprenticeships.asp
Sponsor: Massachusetts Cultural Council
10 St. James Avenue, 3rd Floor
Boston, MA 02116-3803

Massachusetts Foundation for Humanities Economic Development Grants 3059
The Massachusetts Foundation for the Humanities has created a new category of project grants with $50,000 in funding provided by the Massachusetts Cultural Council's John and Abigail Adams Arts and Humanities Program. According to the enabling legislation, the program is designed to: promote innovations in the arts and humanities that have the capacity to revitalize communities, stimulate income, create or enhance jobs, and attract tourism. roposals may utilize the full range of public humanities program formats, including but not limited to, public conferences, lectures and panel discussions, reading and discussion programs, oral history projects, museum exhibitions, theatrical presentations, documentary films, radio and video productions, professional workshops and seminars, and websites. The maximum grant is $10,000.
Requirements: Proposals are due on or before the first business day of February, May, August, and November. Any non-profit organization, whether or not it has 501(c)3 status, is eligible for MFH funding. Applicants must consult with Hayley Wood before submitting a draft. This consultation must occur at least one month before the deadline of the grant round. See the sponsor's website for specific proposal guidelines and forms to be downloaded.
Geographic Focus: Massachusetts
Amount of Grant: Up to 10,000 USD
Contact: Hayley Wood; (413) 584-8440; fax (413) 584-8454; hwood@mfh.org
Internet: http://www.mfh.org/grants/grantypes/ced.html
Sponsor: Massachusetts Foundation for the Humanities
66 Bridge Street
Northampton, MA 01060

Massachusetts Foundation for the Humanities Project Grants 3060
The Foundation makes project grants to support lecture series, professional development for teachers, public forums, post or pre-performance discussions, film screenings with discussions, reading and discussion programs, oral history projects, and other public humanities activities in Massachusetts. In most cases, the maximum award for a grant for a public program is $5,000, and most proposals the Foundation receives fit under the general category of 'public program'. The current thematic initiative - Liberty and justice for all - gives priority to public humanities programs that explore two fundamental principles in American political life, and their interplay, past and present. Projects that address this theme are eligible for a maximum of $10,000.
Requirements: Proposals are due on or before the first business day of February, May, August, and November. Any non-profit organization, whether or not it has 501(c)3 status, is eligible for MFH funding.
Geographic Focus: Massachusetts
Amount of Grant: Up to 5,000 USD
Contact: Hayley Wood; (413) 584-8440; fax (413) 584-8454; hwood@mfh.org
Internet: http://www.mfh.org/grants/index.htm
Sponsor: Massachusetts Foundation for the Humanities
66 Bridge Street
Northampton, MA 01060

Massage Therapy Foundation Community Service Grants 3061
The Foundation Community Service grants are awarded to organizations that seek to provide massage therapy to communities or groups who currently have little or no access to such services. This program is designed to promote working partnerships between the massage therapy profession and community-based organizations. It benefits the recipient, the massage therapist, and the sponsoring organization by building stronger relationships between these parties. The Community Service deadline is April 1, annually. The normal award for 12 months is $500-$5000 and must be used in the specific time period for which it has been awarded.
Requirements: These grants are available for organizations or affiliates of organizations that have been in existence for at least one year in the respective state or province; are tax-exempt under schedule 501(c)3 in the U.S., non-profit charitable organization in other countries; currently provide some therapeutic or other service programs to the community; and have designated a qualified staff member to oversee the program.
Geographic Focus: All States
Date(s) Application is Due: Apr 1
Amount of Grant: 500 - 5,000 USD
Contact: Alison Pittas, Program Manager of Research and Grants; (847) 869-5019, ext. 167 or (847) 905-1667; fax (847) 864-1178; apittas@massagetherapyfoundation.org
Internet: http://www.massagetherapyfoundation.org/grants_community.html
Sponsor: Massage Therapy Foundation
500 Davis Street, Suite 900
Evanston, IL 60201

Mathile Family Foundation Grants 3062
The Mathile Foundation awards grants to eligible Ohio nonprofit organizations in its areas of interest, including Catholic schools, low income and at-risk children to focus on academic excellence; leadership and professional development; faith formation; finance and governance; and student support. With these initiatives, the Foundation hopes to increase the number of low income post secondary graduates. The Foundation also strives to help nonprofit organizations accomplish meaningful change in the lives of those most vulnerable by investing in opportunities for educational, social-emotional, and physical development for children and their families. The Foundation also considers funding for capital and operating expenses. The Foundation considers proposals for grant amounts of $1,000 and higher. Multi-year funding requests may be considered for up to three years. The size of the request should be 10% of the project's budget. Proposal are accepted four times a year, with funding decisions made within 100 days of submission. Proposal forms with a list of additional information required are available at the Foundation website. For first time applicants, a letter of inquiry is recommended. All letters or applications must be submitted online.
Requirements: Organizations who request funds must be tax-exempt under the IRS Code Section 501(c)3. Ohio nonprofit organizations are eligible. Giving primarily is limited to the Dayton area. Organizations outside this area will only be considered under special circumstances.
Restrictions: Funding is not considered for endowment funds; mass funding appeals; sponsorships; advertising for fundraising events tickets; grants or loans to individuals; or political campaigns or activities.
Geographic Focus: Ohio
Date(s) Application is Due: Feb 1; May 1; Aug 1; Nov 1
Amount of Grant: 1,000 - 250,000 USD
Contact: Mary Walsh; (937) 264-4600; mffinfo@mathilefamilyfoundation.org
Internet: http://mathilefamilyfoundation.org/grantmaking/guidelines
Sponsor: Mathile Family Foundation
P.O Box 13615
Dayton, OH 45413-0615

Maurice Amado Foundation Grants 3063
For several decades the Foundation primarily supported organizations that served members of the Sephardic Jewish community, promoted knowledge of Sephardic Jewish culture and heritage, and expanded knowledge of the contributions of Sephardic Jews to Jewish life. More recently, the Foundation has awarded grants to a wide array of charitable organizations that reflect the philanthropic interests of the Foundation's directors and advisors.
Requirements: Prospective grantees may call the Foundation's Executive Director to determine if the grant seeker's organizational need fit the Foundation's current grantmaking interests. They may email the Executive Director with the name of the organization, its mission, and for what purpose funding is requested. The letter of inquiry should be no more than one page.
Geographic Focus: All States
Contact: Pam Kaizer; (818) 980-9190; pkaizer@mauriceamadofoundation.org
Internet: http://www.mauriceamadofdn.org
Sponsor: Maurice Amado Foundation
12400 Ventura Boulevard, #809
Studio City, CA 91604

Maurice J. Masserini Charitable Trust Grants 3064
The trust awards one-year grants to eligible San Diego County, California nonprofit organizations in its areas of interest, including children and youth, aging, music, higher education, and marine sciences. Types of support include building construction/renovation, equipment acquisition, program development, research grants, matching grants, development grants, internships, and scholarships.
Requirements: San Diego County, California, 501(c)3 tax-exempt organizations are eligible. Interested organizations should contact the trust with a letter of inquiry prior to submitting a formal proposal.
Geographic Focus: California
Amount of Grant: Up to 25,000 USD
Contact: Robert Roszkos, (213) 253-3235
Sponsor: Maurice J. Masserini Charitable Trust
c/o Wells Fargo Bank N.A.
Philadelphia, PA 19106-2112

Max A. Adler Charitable Foundation Grants 3065
The foundation awards grants to eligible New York nonprofit organizations serving the greater Rochester area in its areas of interest, including arts, children and youth services, Jewish services, health care, higher education, and social services. Types of support include building construction/renovation, capital campaigns, general operating support, and program development. There are no application forms or deadlines.
Requirements: New York 501(c)3 nonprofit organizations serving the greater Rochester area are eligible.
Geographic Focus: New York
Amount of Grant: 1,000 - 25,000 USD
Contact: David Gray, President; (585) 232-7290; fax (585) 232-7260
Sponsor: Max A. Adler Charitable Foundation
1010 Times Square Building
Rochester, NY 14614

Max and Anna Levinson Foundation Grants 3066
The Levinson Foundation makes grants to nonprofit organizations committed to developing a more just, caring, ecological, and sustainable world. They seek people and organizations that combine idealism, dedication, and genuine concern with rigorous analysis and strategic plans, and that foster a sense of social connection, mutual recognition, and solidarity. Their funding is distributed among three categories: environment, including ecosystem protection and biological diversity, alternative energy and conversion into the oil economy, alternative agriculture and local green development, climate change, and the development of environmental movements; social, including the promotion of a more democratic, equitable, just and rewarding society, world peace, protection of civil and human rights, alternative media, arts and education, community-based economic development, youth leadership, and violence prevention and response; Jewish/Israel—including Jewish culture, religion, and spirituality, Yiddish, building Jewish community in the Diaspora, Jewish organizations for social change, and peace, social, and environmental issues in Israel. There are no deadlines. Grants are awarded in the $15,000 to $25,000 range. Applicants may refer to the website for types of previous support given to organizations.
Requirements: Applicants within the giving criteria may apply, but grantees must submit the online letter of inquiry to see if they are eligible for funding.

Geographic Focus: All States
Amount of Grant: 15,000 - 25,000 USD
Contact: Charlotte Levinson; (505) 995-8802; info@levinsonfoundation.org
Internet: http://www.levinsonfoundation.org
Sponsor: Max and Anna Levinson Foundation
P.O. Box 6309
Santa Fe, NM 87502-6309

Maximilian E. and Marion O. Hoffman Foundation 3067
The foundation has distributed grants in the areas of medicine, education, the arts, and to various charitable organizations in Connecticut and throughout the country. The principal focus of its philanthropy has been worthy activities in the State of Connecticut.
Geographic Focus: Connecticut
Amount of Grant: 1,000 - 300,000 USD
Contact: Marion Barrak, President; (860) 521-2949
Sponsor: Hoffman Foundation
970 Farmington Avenue, Suite 203
West Hartford, CT 06107-2134

Maxon Charitable Foundation Grants 3068
The Maxon Charitable Foundation is a company-sponsored foundation that was established in 1987 in Indiana. The foundation supports hospitals and organizations involved with higher education, natural resources, recreation, human services, community development, and Christianity and awards college scholarships to individuals in the Muncie, Indiana area.
Requirements: Contact the Foundation's office prior to the initial proposal, the office will provide you with the proper Application form.
Geographic Focus: Indiana
Amount of Grant: 500 - 5,000 USD
Contact: Jeffrey R. Lang, Secretary; (765) 284-3304
Sponsor: Maxon Charitable Foundation
201 E 18th Street
Muncie, IN 47302-4124

May and Stanley Smith Charitable Trust Grants 3069
Created in 1989, the May and Stanley Smith Charitable Trust supports organizations serving people in the United States, Canada, the United Kingdom, Australia, the Bahamas, and Hong Kong – places that May and Stanley Smith lived in or spent time in during their lifetimes. The trust supports organizations that offer opportunities to children and youth, elders, the disabled and critically ill, and disadvantaged adults and families which enrich the quality of life, promote self-sufficiency, and assist individuals in achieving their highest potential. Specific priorities in serving each of these populations are described under the Grant Program Areas section of the trust's website. The trust will fund requests for general-operating, capacity-building, and program support. All grant seekers (including previously-funded organizations) should follow the step-by-step application process laid out at the website to determine eligibility and fit with the trust's funding goals. Eligible organizations whose projects fall within the trust's areas of interest must submit an online Letter of Inquiry (LOI) from the grant website. The trust's staff will review these and invite selected applicants to submit a full proposal. LOIs may be submitted at any time during the year. Processing a grant application from receipt of the LOI to funding notification generally takes between four and six months.
Requirements: Nonprofit organizations in the trust's geographic areas of interest and providing services in its program areas of interest are eligible to apply. U.S. applicants must have tax-exempt status under Section 501(c)3 of the Internal Revenue Service Code and must not be classified as a private foundation under Section 509(a) of the Code; non-U.S. organizations must demonstrate that they would meet the requirements for such status. Organizations can also submit applications through a sponsoring organization that meets the eligibility criteria listed above and that provides written authorization confirming its willingness to act as the fiscal sponsor. The trust prioritizes organizations that exhibit the following characteristics: they meet a demonstrated need; they offer innovative programs and services; they provide direct services to individuals; they offer sustained services that have long-term, lasting impact in the lives of clients; they have a proven track record of success; they have an experienced and engaged staff and an active and committed board of directors; they have a system in place to measure efficacy and success in meeting desired objectives; they operate on a balanced budget and have sufficient cash for operating needs; they maintain reasonable overhead expenses; they receive broad support from a variety of community, institutional, and individual donors; and they partner with other community organizations to meet client needs and to avoid duplication of effort.
Restrictions: The trust rarely supports 100 percent of a project budget, or more than 25 percent of an organization budget, and takes into account award sizes from other foundations. The trust prefers to fund organizations receiving less than 30% of total revenue from government sources. The trust does not fund the following types of organizations or requests: organizations which are not, or would not qualify as, a 501(c)3 public charity; hospitals or hospital foundations; medical clinics or services; scientific or medical research; building funds or capital projects; schools and universities (except those receiving less than 25% of their operating funds from families and those serving a 100% disabled population); endowment funds; individuals; organizations or programs operated by governments; film or media projects; start-up programs or organizations; proselytizing or religious activities that promote specific religious doctrine or that are exclusive and discriminatory; public policy, research, or advocacy; public awareness, education, or information campaigns/programs; debt reduction; conferences or benefit events; projects which carry on propaganda or otherwise attempt to influence legislation; projects which participate or intervene in any political campaign on behalf of or in opposition to any candidate for public office; projects which conduct, directly or indirectly, any voter registration drive; and organizations that pass through funding to an organization or project that would not be eligible for direct funding as described above.
Geographic Focus: All States, Australia, Bahamas, Canada, Hong Kong, United Kingdom
Contact: Janet Ferraiolo, Grants Manager; (415) 332-0166; grantsmanager@adminitrustllc.com or jferraiolo@adminitrustllc.com
Internet: http://www.adminitrustllc.com/may-and-stanley-smith-charitable-trust/
Sponsor: May and Stanley Smith Charitable Trust
c/o Adminitrust LLC
Sausalito, CA 94965

Maytree Foundation Assisting Local Leaders with Immigrant Employment Strategies Grants 3070
ALLIES is a four-year project funded by the J.W. McConnell Family Foundation and the Maytree Foundation. The objectives of the project are to: contribute to the resilience of communities in Canada by enabling citizens and institutions to act on solutions that result in the employment of skilled immigrants, thus contributing to the prosperity and vitality of their communities; create a nation-wide movement and impact through a series of successful community initiatives and national partnerships; create shifts in hiring and other relevant systems and behaviors through these initiatives; and, position leading local employers as agents of change and champions for skilled immigrants. Three types of grants are available to interested communities: Start-Up Grants (phase 1 and phase 2), Partnership Grants, and Innovation Grants. Start-Up Grants in both Phase One and Phase Two are valued at up to $30,000 each. Partnership Grants of up to $90,000 per year over three years will be provided to communities that have successfully completed all elements of developing a multi-stakeholder effort as outlined in Phases One and Two. Applications for all programs will be reviewed on an on-going basis.
Geographic Focus: All States, Canada
Amount of Grant: Up to 30,000 USD
Contact: Stephanie Saunders; (416) 944-2627; fax (416) 944-8915; ssaunders@maytree.com
Internet: http://maytree.com/funding/allies2
Sponsor: Maytree Foundation
170 Bloor Street West, Suite 804
Toronto, ON M5S 1T9 Canada

Maytree Foundation Refugee and Immigrant Grants 3071
The foundation awards grants to community-based programs serving the refugee community in Canada. The purpose of the organization is to support social justice initiatives through the foundation's refugee and immigrant program and special projects program. Direct service grants are awarded at the community level for projects that present new and practical approaches that will lead to improved service delivery or model development and may lead to policy changes. Public education support is available for initiatives that promote awareness of issues facing refugees and immigrants. Capacity building assistance is provided to build on the strengths and capacities of refugee and immigrant organizations and leaders. Amount of support and duration of the grant will depend on the nature of the project and the participation of other funders. Multi-year support is available. Funding decisions are made throughout the year.
Requirements: Applicants should first call the organization to discuss ideas. Applicants should then submit a two- to four-page letter clearly describing the project to be funded, with relevant financial information and a description of the evaluation procedure to judge if the program is meeting stated goals. Canadian community-based organizations are eligible to apply.
Restrictions: The foundation generally does not fund deficit-reduction, equipment purchases, building or renovation costs, capital campaigns or endowments, partisan political activities, religious activities, legal challenges, conferences and workshops, or programs and services which are part of the government's mandate.
Geographic Focus: All States, Canada
Amount of Grant: 2,500 - 25,000 USD
Contact: Katarina Vukobratovic; (416) 944-2627; fax (416) 944-8915; info@maytree.com
Internet: http://maytree.com/funding/refugee-immigrant-grants
Sponsor: Maytree Foundation
170 Bloor Street West, Suite 804
Toronto, ON M5S 1T9 Canada

McCallum Family Foundation Grants 3072
The McCallum Foundation awards grants to Massachusetts nonprofits in its areas of interest, including health and human services, higher education, and to a United Methodist church. Organizations should call the Foundation or submit a letter of inquiry to see if their project is appropriate for the Foundation.
Requirements: Massachusetts nonprofit organizations are eligible.
Geographic Focus: Massachusetts
Amount of Grant: 1,000 - 10,000 USD
Contact: Donna McCallum, Trustee; (978) 649-9132
Sponsor: McCallum Foundation
134 Middle Street
Lowell, MA 01852

McCarthy Family Foundation Grants 3073
The McCarthy Family Foundation is a small private foundation established in 1988. Organized as a California public benefit nonprofit corporation, it operates from San Diego, California. The foundation's current program interest areas have been funded throughout its almost two decades history. These funding areas are: K-12 science education; HIV/AIDS research, education and direct services; assistance to homeless persons; and child abuse prevention and services for victims and families. The board will occasionally fund a special project outside these categorical areas and/or for regional, national or international charitable purposes. A small portion of the grantmaking budget is provided for director matching

grants to encourage and amplify personal philanthropy by the foundation's board of directors. Proposals will be considered in the above general areas or for special project areas established by the Board. Proposals will only be accepted for programs within San Diego County. Multiple year proposals may be considered but it is not the foundation's intention to provide annual support. It is not normally the foundation's desire to be the sole source of funds for a project. Most grants are expected to be small, $5,000-$15,000, reflecting the foundation's limited budget although there are no fixed minimum or maximum amounts. Grant proposals received by March 15 will be considered for decision/funding in June. Grant proposals received by September 15 will be considered for decision/funding in December.
Requirements: Proposals will only be accepted for programs within San Diego County, California. All applicants should first submit a letter of inquiry, which can be submitted directly from the Foundation's web site. The letter (1-2 pages) must contain a brief statement describing the applicant and the need for funds with enough information for the foundation to determine whether or not the application falls within its program areas. Proposals submitted without an initial letter of inquiry will not be reviewed by the foundation. Applicants should briefly and clearly provide a statement of their needs and the specific request to the foundation, taking into account other possible sources of funding. Letters of inquiry will be acknowledged upon their receipt, but because the foundation operates without a professional staff, a more detailed response may be delayed. Applicants who receive a favorable response to their initial inquiry will be invited to submit a grant application. The foundation accepts the Common Grant Application of San Diego Grantmakers, which can be downloaded from the Foundation's web site. Five copies of the application (proposal) should be submitted. Only one copy of required attachments need be submitted. The application should be signed by the organization's board chair or the executive director (or equivalent individuals).
Restrictions: The foundation does not consider grants for individuals, scholarship funds, or sectarian religious activities. Normally the foundation does not consider requests for general fundraising drives. It does not make grants intended directly or indirectly to support political candidates or to influence legislation.
Geographic Focus: California
Date(s) Application is Due: Mar 15; Sep 15
Amount of Grant: 500 - 250,000 USD
Contact: Rachel McCarthy Bender; (858) 485-0129; mail@mccarthyfamilyfdn.org
Internet: http://www.mccarthyfamilyfdn.org/guide.html
Sponsor: McCarthy Family Foundation
P.O. Box 27389
San Diego, CA 92198-1389

McColl Foundation Grants 3074
Established in 1996, the Foundation awards funding in its areas of interest, including: the arts; community and economic development; early childhood education; elementary and secondary education; federated giving programs; health organizations; higher education; and performing arts. Types of support include: annual campaigns, building and renovation, curriculum development, general operations, and scholarship funds. Giving is primarily focused in North Carolina, with an initial approach requesting a Letter of Inquiry. The Board meets twice annually.
Geographic Focus: North Carolina
Contact: Jane McColl Lockwood, President; (704) 376-6978
Sponsor: McColl Foundation
P.O. Box 6144
Charlotte, NC 28207-0001

McCombs Foundation Grants 3075
The McCombs Foundation, established in 1981, makes grants to Texas nonprofit charitable, philanthropic, educational, and benevolent organizations. Areas of interest include arts, athletics, education and higher education, historic preservation, medical research, philanthropy, recreation and sports, youth services, and voluntarism. There are no application deadlines or forms. Applicants should submit a letter of application stating a brief history of the organization, any available printed support materials, and a budget detail. Final notification takes approximately two weeks.
Requirements: Texas nonprofit organizations are eligible. Application form not required.
Restrictions: No grants are given to individuals.
Geographic Focus: Texas
Contact: Gary Woods, Treasurer; (210) 821-6523
Sponsor: McCombs Foundation
755 East Mulberry, Suite 600
San Antonio, TX 78212

McConnell Foundation Grants 3076
The McConnell Foundation awards grants to California nonprofit organizations in its areas of interest, including arts and culture, community development, recreation, social services, children, youth and education, sustainable/livable communities, and the environment. Grants primarily fund the purchase of equipment or building related projects for small and large projects in each county. Requests of up to $50,000 are accepted for projects of benefit to the giving area. Grants are made at three levels, according to the applicant's location. Each county may apply for $1,000 to $10,000. Grants are made to Modoc and Trinity county for $10,000 to $30,000, and grants are made to Shasta, Siskiyou, and Tehama counties for $10,000 to $50,000. Application forms and materials are available at the website for the Shasta Community Foundation who administers the grants.
Requirements: California nonprofit organizations serving Shasta, Siskiyou, Trinity, Tehama, and Modoc counties are eligible.
Restrictions: Grants do not support individuals, religious organizations, research institutions, endowment funds, annual fund drives, budget deficits, or building purchase/construction.
Geographic Focus: California

Date(s) Application is Due: Sep 5
Amount of Grant: Up to 50,000 USD
Contact: Kerry Caranci, Senior Program and Operations Officer; (530) 244-1219 or (530) 926-5486; kerry@shastarcf.org or info@shastarcf.org
Internet: http://www.mcconnellfoundation.org
Sponsor: McConnell Foundation
800 Shasta View Drive
Redding, CA 96003

McCune Charitable Foundation Grants 3077
The Marshall L. and Perrine D. McCune Charitable Foundation is dedicated to enriching the health, education, environment, and cultural and spiritual life of New Mexicans. The Foundation engages in proactive grantmaking that seeks to foster positive social change. Specifically, the Foundation funds projects that benefit New Mexico in the areas of arts, economic development, education, environment, health, and social services. It is working to stimulate economic diversity, nurture sustainability, and bridge the economic gaps that exist in our communities with the aim of creating wealth for all New Mexicans.
Requirements: Grants can be awarded to qualified 501(c)3 nonprofit organizations, federally recognized Indian tribes, public schools, and governmental agencies. Applications are available online via the Foundation's website.
Restrictions: Grants are not awarded to individuals or to support endowments.
Geographic Focus: New Mexico
Date(s) Application is Due: Sep 30
Amount of Grant: Up to 150,000 USD
Contact: Norty Kalishman, M.D., Program Director; (505) 983-8300; fax (505) 983-7887; mccune@nmmccune.org
Internet: http://www.nmmccune.org/
Sponsor: McCune Charitable Foundation
345 East Alameda Street
Santa Fe, NM 87501

McCune Foundation Civic Grants 3078
The McCune Foundation's grants are assigned to one of four program areas, including: education, human services, humanities, and civic. In the area of civic affairs, the Foundation focuses new job growth and generating community wealth, support of core community assets, and quality of life. Community development, public amenities, conservation, and overall regional grants are made in this program area. The civic agenda supports capital projects, research and development, organizational capacity building, and programming with the following strategic priorities: spur investment in Pittsburgh's urban core and metropolitan area; leverage public and private dollars for broad-based support of community assets; revitalize Pittsburgh's neighborhoods by changing blighted market conditions; support broad based community assets improving the livability of the region; and develop a New Economy in Pittsburgh that will return greater prosperity to the region.
Requirements: The foundation supports 501(c)3 organizations in southwestern Pennsylvania and throughout the country, with emphasis on the Pittsburgh area. This area includes the following counties: Allegheny, Beaver, Butler, Armstrong, Westmoreland, and Washington. To apply, an organization should send a brief (2 to 3 page) initial inquiry, preferably using the Foundation's website. The letter should contain: project overview - describe what the proposed efforts are intended to achieve for the region as well as for the organization; what activities/actions are planned to meet the stated goals; project timeline; resources required - total cost of the project; anticipated income, including private and public funders; amount of funding requested; IRS 501(c)3 determination letter - attach a copy (either scanned via email or hard copy via regular mail); and a copy of the organization's latest audit (either scanned via email or hard copy via regular mail).
Restrictions: Grants are not awarded to individuals or for general operating purposes or loans. Unsolicited proposals from outside the funding area are not accepted.
Geographic Focus: All States
Amount of Grant: 1,000 - 1,000,000 USD
Contact: Henry S. Beukema; (412) 644-8779; fax (412) 644-8059; info@mccune.org
Internet: http://www.mccune.org/foundation:Website,mccune,grants
Sponsor: McCune Foundation
750 Sixth PPG Place
Pittsburgh, PA 15222

McCune Foundation Humananities Grants 3079
The McCune Foundation's grants are assigned to one of four program areas, including: education, human services, humanities, and civic. In the area of humanities, the Foundation focuses on culture, preservation, and religion and values. Cultural investments are made from the vantage point of regional economic development and the perspective that a city is more livable with a strong arts and culture sector, and a performance epicenter downtown that attracts patrons and out-of-town visitors. The humanities area supports capital projects, endowment grants, technology, marketing, planning, and programming for the following strategic priorities: promote regional historic and cultural assets; attract new audiences and future generations of residents who appreciate the humanities; contribute to the economic development of the downtown corridor; guard the region's history and religious legacy; and support Christian education through academic institutions.
Requirements: The foundation supports 501(c)3 organizations in southwestern Pennsylvania and throughout the country, with emphasis on the Pittsburgh area. This area includes the following counties: Allegheny, Beaver, Butler, Armstrong, Westmoreland, and Washington. To apply, an organization should send a brief (2 to 3 page) initial inquiry, preferably using the Foundation's website. The letter should contain: project overview - describe what the proposed efforts are intended to achieve for the region as well as for the organization; what activities/actions are planned to meet the stated goals; project timeline; resources required

- total cost of the project; anticipated income, including private and public funders; amount of funding requested; IRS 501(c)3 determination letter - attach a copy (either scanned via email or hard copy via regular mail); and a copy of the organization's latest audit (either scanned via email or hard copy via regular mail).
Restrictions: Grants are not awarded to individuals or for general operating purposes or loans. Unsolicited proposals from outside the funding area are not accepted.
Geographic Focus: All States
Amount of Grant: 1,000 - 1,000,000 USD
Contact: Henry S. Beukema; (412) 644-8779; fax (412) 644-8059; info@mccune.org
Internet: http://www.mccune.org/foundation:Website,mccune,grants
Sponsor: McCune Foundation
750 Sixth PPG Place
Pittsburgh, PA 15222

McCune Foundation Human Services Grants 3080
The McCune Foundation's grants are assigned to one of four program areas, including: education, human services, humanities, and civic. In the area of human services, the Foundation focuses on health, social services, and community improvement. The interdisciplinary approach to grantmaking in this program area works with community-based and regional institutions to address pressing community needs by supporting the critical work of existing programs, as well as new initiatives and programs that seek to find and ameliorate the root causes of community distress and disinvestment. The human services area supports capital projects, research and development, organizational capacity building, and programming with the following strategic priorities: transfer education and research assets into economic opportunities for the region; leverage public and private dollars for broad-based support of community assets; promote self-sufficiency of residents; increase social and economic stability of communities and the region; and test and support effective prevention programs.
Requirements: The foundation supports 501(c)3 organizations in southwestern Pennsylvania and throughout the country, with emphasis on the Pittsburgh area. This area includes the following counties: Allegheny, Beaver, Butler, Armstrong, Westmoreland, and Washington. To apply, an organization should send a brief (2 to 3 page) initial inquiry, preferably using the Foundation's website. The letter should contain: project overview - describe what the proposed efforts are intended to achieve for the region as well as for the organization; what activities/actions are planned to meet the stated goals; project timeline; resources required - total cost of the project; anticipated income, including private and public funders; amount of funding requested; IRS 501(c)3 determination letter - attach a copy (either scanned via email or hard copy via regular mail); and a copy of the organization's latest audit (either scanned via email or hard copy via regular mail).
Restrictions: Grants are not awarded to individuals or for general operating purposes or loans. Unsolicited proposals from outside the funding area are not accepted.
Geographic Focus: All States
Amount of Grant: 1,000 - 1,000,000 USD
Contact: Henry S. Beukema; (412) 644-8779; fax (412) 644-8059; info@mccune.org
Internet: http://www.mccune.org/foundation:Website,mccune,grants
Sponsor: McCune Foundation
750 Sixth PPG Place
Pittsburgh, PA 15222

McGraw-Hill Companies Community Grants 3081
McGraw-Hill focuses its charitable efforts on its goal of financial capability for all. The Corporation partners with nonprofit organizations to help individuals gain the necessary knowledge to make smart savings, credit and spending decisions. McGraw-Hill also extends its support to organizations that share the Corporation's dedication to the arts and culture, education and health and human services. The company gives priority consideration to organizations and projects that: promote and support excellence in education and learning, with a primary emphasis on financial literacy; further financial literacy in the communities and markets where the many diverse businesses of The McGraw-Hill Companies operate; utilize unique applications of innovative and developing technologies; extend their reach globally; can be evaluated and can serve as models elsewhere; are staffed and administered by people with demonstrated competence and experience in their fields; have been determined tax-exempt 501(c)3 organizations and qualify as public charities under IRS rules, or are the local country-specific equivalent of a charitable nonprofit organization.
Requirements: Proposals must include the following: a program narrative (no more than three pages); a detailed organization overview; a concise description of the grant's purpose; and all required attachments. If the request is considered eligible, a meeting may be arranged with the Corporate Responsibility and Sustainability staff. On-site visits may also be made. Proposals are accepted at any time, with funding decisions made quarterly.
Restrictions: McGraw-Hill does not support courtesy advertising, pledges for a walk-a-thon, or similar activities. Funding is also not available for the following: institutions and agencies clearly outside the company's primary geographic concerns and interests; libraries and schools of higher education and K-12; political activities or organizations established to influence legislation; sectarian or religious organizations; member-based organizations, i.e., fraternities, labor, veterans, athletic, social clubs; individuals; endowment funds; or loans. Grants are not renewed automatically. Requests for renewed support must be submitted each year.
Geographic Focus: All States
Contact: Susan Wallman, Manager, Corporate Contributions; (212) 512-6480; fax (212) 512-3611; susan_wallman@mcgraw-hill.com
Internet: http://www.mcgraw-hill.com/site/cr/community/giving#section_2
Sponsor: McGraw-Hill Companies
1221 Avenue of the Americas, 20th Floor
New York, NY 10020-1095

McGregor Fund Grants 3082
The fund makes grants to organizations in the following areas: human services—emphasis on activities in southeastern Michigan addressing emergency needs in housing, food, clothing, and other direct aid; education—early child education and development, colleges and universities in the Detroit metropolitan area, liberal arts colleges and universities in Michigan and Ohio; arts and culture in southeastern Michigan; health care—improving access to primary care for underserved populations in Detroit; and public benefit—civic and community organizations that improve the quality of life in southeastern Michigan. Types of support include project support, operating support, special projects, and capital support. Grant decisions are made by the board of trustees four times annually, in February, May, September, and November. Grant requests may be submitted at any time, but requests may take up to three months for staff review. Application guidelines are available online.
Requirements: Organizations in the metropolitan Detroit, MI area, are eligible. Requests will be considered from organizations located elsewhere for programs or projects that significantly benefit the metropolitan Detroit area (city of Detroit and Wayne, Oakland, and Macomb Counties).
Restrictions: The fund discourages proposals for student scholarships, travel, seminars, conferences, workshops, film or video projects, as well as disease-specific organizations and their local affiliates.
Geographic Focus: Michigan
Amount of Grant: 25,000 - 50,000 USD
Contact: C. David Campbell; (313) 963-3495; fax (313) 963-3512; info@mcgregfund.org
Internet: http://www.mcgregorfund.org/guideline.html
Sponsor: McGregor Fund
333 W Fort Street, Suite 2090
Detroit, MI 48226

McInerny Foundation Grants 3083
The foundation awards grants to Hawaii nonprofit organizations in its areas of interest, including arts and culture, education, environment, health care, youth services, and social services. Types of support include general operating support, continuing support, building construction/renovation, equipment acquisition, program development, seed money, scholarship funds, and matching funds. The July 1 deadline is for capital funds; the November 15 deadline date is for scholarship funds. All other requests are accepted at any time.
Requirements: Hawaii nonprofit organizations are eligible.
Restrictions: Grants are not awarded in support of religious institutions, individuals, endowment funds, deficit financing, or research.
Geographic Focus: Hawaii
Date(s) Application is Due: Jul 1; Nov 15
Amount of Grant: 3,000 - 250,000 USD
Contact: Paula Boyce; (808) 538-4944; fax (808) 538-4006; pboyce@boh.com
Sponsor: McInerny Foundation
P.O. Box 3170, Department 758
Honolulu, HI 96802-3170

McKesson Foundation Grants 3084
The foundation seeks to enhance the health and quality of life in communities where McKesson HBOC operates and its employees live. Emphasis is focused on youth, especially health services for underserved populations, educational enrichment, the environment, recreation, and youth development activities. The foundation also funds emergency services for children and families, and a variety of social, educational and cultural programs. For culture and the arts, support is given primarily to organizations that reach out to youth and other populations that do not have easy access to such programs. Grants are made for specific projects and programs, and general operating support will be considered in some circumstances. Grants are awarded for one to three years. The Foundation does not accept uninvited applications. Initial approach should be to contact the Foundation directly.
Requirements: 501(c)3 tax-exempt organizations are eligible.
Restrictions: Grants are not made to endowment campaigns, individuals or individual scholarships, religious organizations for religious purposes, political causes or campaigns, advertising in charitable publications, research studies or health organizations concentrating on one disease.
Geographic Focus: All States
Amount of Grant: 5,000 - 25,000 USD
Contact: Marcia Argyris, Foundation President; (415) 983-8673 or (415) 983-8300; fax (415) 983-7590; marcia.argyris@mckesson.com or community.relations@mckesson.com
Internet: http://www.mckesson.com/en_us/McKesson.com/About%2BUs/Corporate%2BCitizenship/McKesson%2BFoundation.html
Sponsor: McKesson Foundation
1 Post Street, 32nd Floor
San Francisco, CA 94104-5203

McKnight Foundation Multiservice Grants 3085
The McKnight Foundation assists nonprofit organizations and public agencies to improve the quality of life for all people, particularly those in need. The goal of the Foundation's Multiservice Grants is to support multiservice organizations that provide families with the help they need, while building supportive relationships and providing opportunities for shared learning. The Foundation defines multiservice organizations as those that provide broad services with a focus on families and individuals; increase understanding of how to best support families in the context of their geographic or cultural communities; are embedded in a neighborhood or neighborhoods; and engage and empower families in multiple ways.
Requirements: Applicants must be classified by the Internal Revenue Service as tax-exempt, nonprofit organizations located within the state of Minnesota. Eligible organizations must be grounded in research and best practices about how to support disadvantaged families. They must: approach people holistically, empower them to act on their own behalf, engage

them in decision making, and tailor programs to the varying needs and situations of individuals; have deliberate means for making connections among staff and families and between families; provide a place that people feel welcome and comfortable; look outward and have strong relationships with others in the community, with examples of existing partnerships on behalf of families served; have organizational capacity to effectively support families in a holistic way; and measure success and learn from their work, in both qualitative and quantitative ways, on multiple levels, programmatically, organizationally, and within the community served. Applications are made online.
Restrictions: Grants are not directed for support of organizations with a narrow focus (such as healthcare, domestic violence, chemical dependency, transitional housing, or other specific programmatic areas) although a multiservice organization may have programs that address these issues.
Geographic Focus: Minnesota
Date(s) Application is Due: May 2
Contact: Lee Sheehy, Program Officer; (612) 333-4220; lsheehy@mcknight.org
Internet: http://www.mcknight.org/multiservice/index.aspx
Sponsor: McKnight Foundation
710 S Second Street, Suite 400
Minneapolis, MN 55401

McKnight Foundation Region and Communities Grants 3086
The McKnight Foundation assists nonprofit organizations and public agencies to improve the quality of life for all people, particularly those in need. The goal of the Foundation's Region and Communities Grants is to encourage efficient development within the Twin Cities region that creates livable communities and opportunities for all to thrive. Funding is provided for planning, operating, and projects.
Requirements: Applicants must be classified by the Internal Revenue Service as tax-exempt, nonprofit organizations located within the state of Minnesota. The primary geographic focus is the seven-county Twin Cities metropolitan area. The Grants provide funding to: manage regional growth to minimize sprawl and maximize opportunities; create viable neighborhoods for people, businesses, and communities to thrive; increase family stability through affordable housing; preserve, protect, and restore open spaces; and increase alternative transportation options.
Restrictions: The following are ineligible: health services or policy; scholarships or other types of assistance for individuals; conferences, including attendance or travel (except when related to existing Foundation support); endowments, except in rare cases; activities that have a specific religious purpose; or lobbying prohibited by the Internal Revenue Code. Traditionally activities which are the responsibility of government are not eligible. Capital is funded only in exceptional circumstances and should be discussed with a Program Officer before requested.
Geographic Focus: Minnesota
Date(s) Application is Due: Jan 15; Apr 15; Jul 15; Oct 15
Contact: Lee Sheehy, Program Officer; (612) 333-4220; lsheehy@mcknight.org
Internet: http://www.mcknight.org/region/program.aspx
Sponsor: McKnight Foundation
710 S Second Street, Suite 400
Minneapolis, MN 55401

McKnight Foundation Virginia McKnight Binger Awards in Human Service 3087
The McKnight Foundation assists nonprofit organizations and public agencies to improve the quality of life for all people, particularly those in need. This annual Award recognizes up to six Minnesotans who strive to make life better for other people but receive little or no public recognition. The Foundation seeks individuals who attend, unite, and empower others in communities throughout Minnesota. Individuals who "attend" are defined as those who serve people or organizations directly; who "unite" as those who bring people together around a shared goal; and who "empower" as those who enable people to help themselves and others. Nomination forms are available on the Web site. A committee, composed of human service professionals and volunteers from throughout Minnesota, reviews nominations, checks references, and recommends candidates to the Foundation's Board of Directors. Award recipients are notified in June and honored in August.
Requirements: Nominations are open to the public. Nominees may be volunteers or paid staff involved in providing human services in response to the needs of poor or disadvantaged people in Minnesota. Nominees may be adults or young people and must be current residents of Minnesota. Nominees (and the work for which they are being nominated) do not have to be associated with any specific organization. Tenure of service will be taken into consideration.
Restrictions: Individuals may not nominate themselves and may not be past Human Service Award recipients.
Geographic Focus: Minnesota
Amount of Grant: 10,000 - 10,000 USD
Contact: Tim Hanrahan; (612) 333-4220; thanrahan@mcknight.org
Internet: http://www.mcknight.org/awards
Sponsor: McKnight Foundation
710 S Second Street, Suite 400
Minneapolis, MN 55401

McLean Contributionship Grants 3088
Originally established in 1951 as The Bulletin Contributionship for charitable, educational and scientific purposes, the Contributionship became The McLean Contributionship on May 1, 1980 when the association of the McLean family with the Bulletin ended. Independent Publications, also owned by the McLean family, continues as the main financial supporter of the Contributionship. The Contributionship favors projects that stimulate a better understanding of the natural environment and encourage the preservation of its important features; encourage more compassionate and cost-effective care for the ill and aging in an atmosphere of dignity and self-respect; or promote education, medical, scientific, or on occasion, cultural developments that enhance quality of life. In addition, the Trustees from time to time support projects which motivate promising young people to assess and develop their talents despite social and economic obstacles or encourage those in newspaper and related fields to become more effective and responsible in helping people better understand how events in their communities and around the world affect them. The Trustees meet several times a year. The Contribution accepts and processes applications for grants throughout the year. Applications must be received at least six weeks before a meeting date. Interested organizations may view the annual-meeting schedule on the Application Procedure page at the grant website. The Contributionship accepts the common-grant-application form of Delaware Valley Grantmakers Association (link is provided on the Application Procedure web page). Application may also be made by letter (guidelines are included on the Application Procedure web page).
Requirements: Applicants must show evidence of tax-exempt status.
Restrictions: Geographic area is limited to the following locations: Greater Philadelphia area; Nashua, New Hampshire; Dubois Pennsylvania; and Central Florida. The Contributionship does not fund the costs or expenses of existing staff allocated to a project it is asked to support.
Geographic Focus: Florida, New Hampshire, Pennsylvania
Amount of Grant: 2,000 - 100,000 USD
Contact: Sandra McLean, Executive Director; (610) 527-6330; fax (610) 527-9733
Internet: http://fdncenter.org/grantmaker/mclean
Sponsor: McLean Contributionship
945 Haverford Road, Suite A
Bryn Mawr, PA 19010-3814

McLean Foundation Grants 3089
The sole purpose of the McLean Foundation is to enhance the quality of life for the people of Humboldt county through grantmaking to qualified organizations. The Foundation directs a significant portion of its efforts toward projects that support children and youth, the elderly, social welfare, health and medical needs, as well as supporting the capacity of the local nonprofit sector. Applicants are encouraged to contact the Foundation for further information.
Requirements: Nonprofit organizations in Humboldt county are eligible to apply. Community organizations that meet the needs of the children and youth, the elderly, social welfare, and health and medical needs are also eligible to apply.
Geographic Focus: California
Contact: Leigh Pierre-Oetker; (707) 725-1722; leigh@mcleanfoundation.org
Internet: http://www.northerncalifornianonprofits.org/content/view/102/92/
Sponsor: Mel and Grace McLean Foundation
1336 Main Street
Fortuna, CA 95540

McMillen Foundation Grants 3090
The McMillen Foundation was incorporated in 1947 and serves the Fort Wayne and Allen Counties of Indiana. Fields of interest include: children/youth services; community/economic development; education; health care; health organizations, association; recreation.
Requirements: The foundation requires no application form and proposals may be submitted at anytime. Applicants should submit the following: copy of IRS Determination Letter; brief history of organization and description of its mission; copy of most recent annual report/audited financial statement/990; listing of board of directors, trustees, officers and other key people and their affiliations; detailed description of project and amount of funding requested; copy of current year's organizational budget and/or project budget; listing of additional sources and amount of support; one copy of the proposal.
Restrictions: Giving limited to Fort Wayne and Allen County, Indiana. No support for churches or religious groups. No grants to individuals.
Geographic Focus: Indiana
Amount of Grant: 4,000 - 400,000 USD
Contact: Dorothy J. Robinson, Secretary; (260) 484-8631; fax (260) 484-2141
Sponsor: McMillen Foundation
6610 Mutual Drive
Fort Wayne, IN 46825-4236

MDARD AgD Value Added/Regional Food Systems Grants 3091
The Michigan Department of Agriculture and Rural Development (MDARD) is offering a grant opportunity that will promote and enhance Michigan's agriculture industry. MDARD will accept proposals intended to establish, retain, expand, attract and/or develop value added agricultural processing and/or develop regional food systems by enhancing or facilitating aggregation and distribution of Michigan grown agricultural products. Value-added agriculture refers most generally to manufacturing processes (washing, chopping, packaging, etc.) that increase the value of primary agricultural commodities. Value-added agriculture may also refer to increasing the economic value of a commodity through particular production processes, e.g., organic produce, or through regionally-branded products that increase consumer appeal and willingness to pay a premium over similar but undifferentiated products. Grants will be awarded at a minimum amount of $20,000 and a maximum amount of $200,000. This is a cost reimbursement grant program. Grant dollars can be used to leverage additional funds (ie., Federal funds).
Requirements: Agricultural Cooperatives, Producer Networks, Product Associations, Local Governments, Nonprofit Corporations, Business Entities, Economic Development Organizations, and Regional Farmers Market Authorities are eligible to apply. Only one proposal per applicant will be considered. Regional collaboration is encouraged. Activities appropriate for the Value Added/Regional Food Systems Grants include, but are not limited to, the following: technical assistance; marketing; equipment and innovation; training and outreach. Applicants must provide a minimum of ten (10%) percent in cash matching funds. In-kind contributions will not be counted as part of the required match.

Restrictions: Grant dollars cannot be used to pay for the acquisition of land or the purchase, construction, or structural repair of a building or facility.
Geographic Focus: Michigan
Date(s) Application is Due: Jul 31
Amount of Grant: 20,000 - 200,000 USD
Contact: Nancy Nyquist, (517) 241-4381; fax (517) 335-0628; mda-grants@michigan.gov
Internet: http://www.michigan.gov/mdard/0,4610,7-125-1568_51684—-,00.html
Sponsor: Michigan Department of Agriculture and Rural Development
P.O. Box 30017
Lansing, MI 48909

MDARD County Fairs Capital Improvement Grants 3092
The County Fairs Capital Improvement Program is a competitive grant opportunity for Michigan's county fairs to make building and other capital improvements to their fairground facilities. The grants will range from $1,000 to $20,000 and will require a dollar-for-dollar cash match from the county fair. This grant program provides additional access to funds for county fair officials to help make needed improvements to their fairground facilities; including but not limited to structural improvements or other renovations to buildings. Capital improvements are costs related to making changes to improve capital assets, increase their useful life, or add to the value of these assets. Capital improvements may be structural improvements or other renovations to a building or enhance usefulness or productivity. Building improvements to buildings which are used for fair purposes and are owned by the fair association or political subdivision.
Requirements: Eligible applicants include fairs that are incorporated under Act 80 of 1855 or county owned and operated fairs operating under Act 11 of 1929; and county fairs that have submitted all required year-end reports for the prior two years. Only one grant proposal may be submitted per fair association. The submitted grants will go through a competitive grant process and be reviewed by an evaluation committee.
Geographic Focus: Michigan
Date(s) Application is Due: Nov 15
Amount of Grant: 1,000 - 20,000 USD
Contact: Cinda Karlik, (517) 373-9760; karlikc@michigan.gov
Internet: http://www.michigan.gov/mdard/0,4610,7-125-1568_51684—-,00.html
Sponsor: Michigan Department of Agriculture and Rural Development
P.O. Box 30017
Lansing, MI 48909

MDARD Specialty Crop Block Grant Program-Farm Bill 3093
The Specialty Crop Block Grant Program-Farm Bill (SCBGP-FB) provides grants annually to assist in enhancing the competitiveness of specialty crops (fruits, vegetables, tree nuts, and nursery crops). Specialty crops are defined as fruits, vegetables, tree nuts, dried fruits, horticulture, and nursery crops (including floriculture). Examples of project areas that would qualify for funds include, but are not limited to: food safety; food security; nutrition; trade enhancement; education; research; promotion; marketing; plant health programs; "Buy Local" programs; increased consumption; enhanced innovation; improved efficiency of distribution system; environmental concerns and conservation; product development; and cooperative development. This is a cost reimbursement program.
Requirements: Eligible applicants must be non-profit organizations, local, state, and federal government entities, for-profit organizations, and universities. Organizations must be legal entities recognized by the IRS and must reside, and/or conduct their business or organization in Michigan and must be in good standing. Universities submitting applications for funding (research) must have the application submitted by the commodity group for which the research is being performed. Applications for grant funds should demonstrate how the project potentially impacts and produces measurable outcomes for the specialty crop industry rather than a single organization, institution, or individual. Multi-state organizations proposals are permitted.
Restrictions: Grant funds will not be awarded for projects that directly benefit a particular commercial product or provide a profit to a single organization, institution, or individual, as these projects do not enhance specialty crop industry competitiveness.
Geographic Focus: Michigan
Date(s) Application is Due: Apr 12
Contact: Nancy Nyquist, (517) 241-4381; fax (517) 335-0628; nyquistn@michigan.gov
Internet: http://www.michigan.gov/mdard/0,1607,7-125-1568_51684—-,00.html
Sponsor: Michigan Department of Agriculture and Rural Development
P.O. Box 30017
Lansing, MI 48909

MDEQ Beach Monitoring Grants - Inland Lakes 3094
The Beach Monitoring Grants Program provides funding for more effective monitoring of public bathing beaches. With this funding the goals of the program are to: determine levels of bacteria in select bathing beach waters of the state; notify the public of the results; evaluate the effectiveness of state programs in preventing bacterial contamination of surface waters; and develop methods that can differentiate sources of bacterial contamination. Deadlines may vary from year to year based on funding priorities. Applicants will usually have 60 days to prepare and submit a grant application. Grant awards will be announced following department review. The department reserves 90 days for the review process. In the past, a total of $200,000 was available for grants of up to $25,000.
Requirements: Local county health departments, universities, and non-profit organizations are eligible to apply. The grants require a minimum of 25 percent local match (can include in-kind services). Grant applications are selected for funding by the department based on program priorities and the following criteria: location and frequency of beach use; history of beach monitoring; history of bacterial contamination; access to lab facilities to analyze samples promptly; ability to communicate results to the public in an efficient manner; ability to respond and take appropriate action in an event of beach contamination; proximity of the beach to known contamination source; availability of matching funds; innovativeness and feasibility of the proposed project; and, ability to reduce time delay between sampling and results.
Geographic Focus: Michigan
Amount of Grant: Up to 25,000 USD
Contact: Shannon Briggs, (517) 335-1214; briggss4@michigan.gov
Internet: http://www.michigan.gov/documents/deq/deq-essd-grantsloans-catalog_210643_7.pdf
Sponsor: Michigan Department of Environmental Quality
525 West Allegan Street
Lansing, MI 48909

MDEQ Brownfield Redevelopment and Site Reclamation Grants 3095
The Michigan Department of Environmental Quality offers grants and loans for environmental assessments and cleanups at properties with known or suspected contamination. Funds are targeted to projects that promote economic development and reuse of Brownfield properties. In order to be competitive, proposed projects must document the local financial commitment to the project, and the environmental and economic benefits of the proposed project. A proposed project must result in economic benefit for the community through job creation, private investment, and/or increased tax revenue for the community. Applications are accepted on a continuing basis. A single application is used for all Brownfield Redevelopment Program grants and loans. Maximum grant award is $1 million per project for Brownfield Redevelopment Grants (BRG), and $2 million per project for Site Reclamation Grants (SRG).
Requirements: Any county, city, village, township, Brownfield Redevelopment Authority, or other authority or public body created pursuant to state law may apply for a grant. Evaluation criteria include: the level of economic development; applicant and property owner liability; the anticipated environmental benefit; whether the project demonstrates the principles of site reuse; greenspace preservation; smart growth; storm water runoff management; or other sustainable development concepts. A grant can only be awarded if there is a bona fide development project for the site. The property must meet the definition of a facility under Part 201 of the Natural Resources and Environmental Protection Act, 1994 PA 451, as amended. Prospective applicants are asked to contact the program MDEQ Brownfield Coordinator assigned for the area in which the project is located to discuss eligibility of the proposed project, confirm funding availability and obtain an application. Grant recipients are required to sign a grant agreement prior to commencement of grant eligible work.
Restrictions: Only one grant may be awarded to an applicant during any fiscal year. A liable party may not receive a grant or profit from the expenditure of state funds nor be relieved of responsibility for environmental response activities.
Geographic Focus: Michigan
Amount of Grant: 1,000,000 - 2,000,000 USD
Contact: Sue Erickson, (517) 241-8707; fax (517) 241-9581; ericksons@michigan.gov
Internet: http://www.michigan.gov/deq/0,4561,7-135-3311_4109_29262—-,00.html
Sponsor: Michigan Department of Environmental Quality
525 West Allegan Street
Lansing, MI 48909

MDEQ Clean Diesel Grants 3096
The goal of the Michigan Clean Diesel Program is to reduce diesel engine particulate matter and nitrogen oxide emissions in Michigan, and provide increased health and welfare benefits for populations in areas of the state where the air quality is affected by diesel engine emissions from nearby stationary or mobile emission sources. Grant projects must include the application of a diesel emissions reduction solution that is an emission control technology that has been verified by either the United States Environmental Protection Agency (USEPA) or California Air Resources Board (CARB). All state clean diesel projects are funded as pass through reimbursement grants. This means that grantees must initially assume all costs and then request reimbursement from the DEQ for project activities. All projects will be implemented through grant contracts with the grantees. Administration of the grant contract is the responsibility of the grantee and cannot be contracted out.
Requirements: Eligible applicants in all 83 counties in Michigan may apply. All applicants must be based and doing business in the state of Michigan. All of the following are eligible applicants: cities, townships, and villages; county government agencies; port authorities; public school districts; private schools that are designated as tax exempt under 501(c)3 of the Internal Revenue Code; other non-profit organizations or institutions that have the promotion of transportation or air quality as their focus and are designated as tax exempt under 501(c)3 of the Internal Revenue Code; Metropolitan Planning Organizations (MP.O.s); as well as private business and industry. A single applicant may submit only one application. Each application may contain one or more partners. All applicant and partner entities must have continuous and ongoing business operations that include a permanent physical location in Michigan. Organizations receiving grants are required to match percentages determined by E.P.A program terms and conditions. Grantee contributions may include cash, in-kind goods and services, and/or third party contributions. Deadlines will be determined once a program review is completed and posted on the Clean Diesel Program Web page. All grant proposals should be between $50,000 (the minimum) and $200,000 (the maximum). The maximum amount the DEQ will award is $200,000. The above limitations do not include an applicant's matching funds.
Restrictions: Funds under this award cannot be used for matching funds for other state or federal grants, lobbying, or intervention in state or federal regulatory or adjudicatory proceedings, and cannot be used to sue the state or federal government or any other government entity. Likewise, recipient may not use state or federal funds as matching funds for the Michigan Clean Diesel Grant Program, federal Supplemental Environmental Project Funds or Supplemental Environmental Projects required under a consent order.
Geographic Focus: Michigan

Amount of Grant: 50,000 - 200,000 USD
Contact: Denise Simon; (517) 335-7426 or (800) 662-9278; simond2@michigan.gov
Internet: http://www.michigan.gov/deq/0,4561,7-135-3310-198413—,00.html
Sponsor: Michigan Department of Environmental Quality
525 West Allegan Street
Lansing, MI 48909

MDEQ Coastal Management Planning and Construction Grants 3097
Michigan's Coastal Management Program (MCMP) was developed under the federal Coastal Zone Management Act and approved in 1978. Since then, the Program has assisted organizations in protecting and enhancing their coastal areas, funded studies related to coastal management and helped to increase recreational opportunities in Michigan's Great Lakes coastal area. The goals for the annual grant program are to: create and enhance coastal public access; assist the development of vibrant and resilient coastal communities; protect and restore healthy coastal natural communities, including fish and wildlife habitat; prevent damage from coastal erosion and flood hazards; protect coastal water quality and reduce nonpoint source pollution in coastal watersheds. Planning projects can request a maximum of $60,000. Construction projects can request a minimum of $5,000 and a maximum of $60,000. The Request for Proposal is available in January, with an application deadline of April 1, for funding in the upcoming fiscal year.
Requirements: Coastal units of government including cities, counties, villages and townships; area-wide agencies, including regional planning commissions and conservation districts; universities and school districts; non-profit organizations (non-construction projects only); and tribal governments are eligible to apply. All projects must be within Michigan's coastal boundary that generally lies 1,000 feet inland from the ordinary high water mark of the Great Lakes. Included within the boundary are coastal state parks, coastal lakes, coastal floodplains, Great Lakes connecting waters, coastal river mouths, bays, and designated sand dune areas. Federally-owned lands are excluded from the boundary. Site visits are conducted and projects are selected based on the funds available and how well they further MCMP objectives. The match requirement is 1:1. Local match can be in the form of cash, in-kind services, and other non-federal grant funds sources.
Geographic Focus: Michigan
Date(s) Application is Due: Apr 1
Amount of Grant: 5,000 - 60,000 USD
Contact: Ronda Wuycheck, Chief; (517) 241-7832; wuycheckr@michigan.gov
Internet: http://www.michigan.gov/documents/deq/deq-essd-grantsloans-catalog_210643_7.pdf
Sponsor: Michigan Department of Environmental Quality
525 West Allegan Street
Lansing, MI 48909

MDEQ Community Pollution Prevention Grants: Household Drug Collections 3098
Grant funding is available through the Michigan Community Pollution Prevention (P2) Grant Program for the development of ongoing household drug collection programs. These programs should include strategies and projects that promote environmental stewardship and awareness through the collection and incineration of unused household medications, including controlled and non-controlled substances within Michigan communities. Evidence of pharmaceutical waste has been detected in groundwater and drinking water in the Great Lakes region. The technologies and equipment required to remove these compounds from drinking and waste water are expensive and are currently not widely deployed by communities. Successful drug collection programs will prevent pharmaceutical waste from being released into and accumulating in the environment and reduce the incidence of abuse of prescription drugs. Proposals for projects of various scopes and costs are welcome.
Requirements: Local and tribal governments, non-profit organizations, local health departments, municipalities, and regional planning agencies are eligible to receive funding. This grant request will target the following objectives: (a) develop and implement a household drug collection program that provides a free, convenient, and simple method for the population of a geographically defined area of Michigan to regularly dispose of unused medications, both controlled and non-controlled substances, in an environmentally optimal manner; (b) identify demographic indicators that have an impact on the success or failure of the drug collection program. This will inform citizens regarding the implementation of future drug collection programs in different areas of the state; (c) collect metrics, minimally including collection dates, collection participant numbers, and collection volumes and weights for at least prescription and non-prescription (over the counter) drugs collected; (d) collect questionnaire data from a sample of the population residing in and adjacent to the area served; (e) increase the deployment of equipment needed for the collection of both controlled and non-controlled pharmaceuticals; (f) serve as a resource for other organizations interested in implementing a drug collection program. Organizations receiving grants are required to match state funds by at least 25%. Grantee contributions may include cash, in-kind goods and services, and/or third-party contributions. The maximum dollar amount requested should be based upon what is needed to carry out the identified tasks and products. Total grant fund requests must be no larger than $100,000; however, local match expenditures can bring total project expenditures over the $100,000 limit. Project contracts can run for one or two years and will be on a cost-reimbursement basis.
Geographic Focus: Michigan
Date(s) Application is Due: May 31
Amount of Grant: Up to 100,000 USD
Contact: Karen Edlin, (517) 373-0604; edlink@michigan.gov
Internet: http://www.michigan.gov/deq/0,4561,7-135-3585_62565—,00.html
Sponsor: Michigan Department of Environmental Quality
525 West Allegan Street
Lansing, MI 48909

MDEQ Great Lakes Areas of Concern Land Acquisition Grants 3099
Michigan's Coastal Management Program was developed under the federal Coastal Zone Management Act and approved in 1978. Since then, the Program has assisted organizations in protecting and enhancing their coastal areas, funded studies related to coastal management and helped to increase recreational opportunities in Michigan's Great Lakes coastal area. The goals of the program are to: contribute to the delisting of fish and wildlife habitat-related beneficial use impairments (BUISs) in Great Lakes AOC; yield significant ecological benefits; and provide community benefits such as improved opportunities for recreation, park use, open space, or other tangible community benefits. There is no minimum or maximum amount requirement.
Requirements: Projects must be within a U.S. Great Lakes AOC or its associated watershed and contribute to the removal of either project-based delisting targets or numeric delisting targets for fish and wildlife habitat related BUIs as described in the target AOCs Remedial Action Plan (RAP). The project must be endorsed by the RAP implementation group. Projects should be likely to be completed within 18 months. Local governments may submit proposals provided they have the authority to acquire and manage land for conservation purposes. Local government means a county, municipality, city, town, township local public authority (including any public and Indian housing agency under the United States Housing Act of 1973), school district, special district, intrastate district, council of governments, any other regional or interstate government entity, or any agency or instrumentality of a local government. There is no statutory matching requirement for this program. However, applicants are encouraged to demonstrate a 1:1 non-federal match for land acquisition funds requested to conduct the proposed project. Cost sharing is an element considered in the evaluation criteria. Non-federal match may be derived from state, local, non-governmental or private sources in the form of cash or in-kind contributions.
Geographic Focus: Michigan
Contact: Ronda Wuycheck, Chief; (517) 241-7832; wuycheckr@michigan.gov
Internet: http://www.michigan.gov/deq/0,1607,7-135-3313_3677_3696—,00.html
Sponsor: Michigan Department of Environmental Quality
525 West Allegan Street
Lansing, MI 48909

MDEQ Local Water Quality Monitoring Grants 3100
The water quality monitoring grants are meant to fund water quality monitoring activities to address local issues of concern and to identify new chemicals/issues that may be impacting the quality of Michigan's surface waters. Monitoring activities are limited to surface waters (i.e., rivers, streams, public access lakes, wetlands, the Great Lakes, etc.) and may include ambient chemical, biological, or physical monitoring activities, as well as the development of tools to help with the assessment of such data. Approximately $250,000 is available for water quality monitoring projects (non-beach) under the Clean Michigan Initiative-Clean Water Fund (CMI-CWF). Inland beach grants are available biennially. Disbursement of grant funds is done on a cost-reimbursement basis.
Requirements: Local units of government and nonprofit entities are eligible to receive grant funding. Nonprofit entities are those exempt from taxation under Section 501(c)3 of the Internal Revenue Code. Eligible entities generally include county, city, township, and village agencies, watershed and environmental action councils, universities, regional planning agencies, and other incorporated not-for-profit organizations. Applications must be received no later than 5:00 p.m. of the published deadline date. Eligible groups must have undergone a successful financial audit within the 24-month period immediately preceding the application; and, must not have had a grant revoked or terminated, or demonstrated an inability to manage a grant or meet the obligations in a project contract with the Department of Environmental Quality (DEQ), or its predecessor agencies, within the 24-month period immediately preceding the application. There is no maximum dollar amount for these grants. The dollar amount requested should be based upon what is needed to carry out the tasks identified in the project proposal. This grant requires a minimum 25 percent (%) match of public or private funds. Match may not include other CMI funds or Clean Water Act funds awarded as grants by the state. Project contracts cannot exceed two years.
Geographic Focus: Michigan
Date(s) Application is Due: Mar 22
Contact: Dawn Roush, (517) 335-3307; roushd@michigan.gov
Internet: http://www.michigan.gov/deq/0,1607,7-135-3313_3686_3728—,00.html
Sponsor: Michigan Department of Environmental Quality
525 West Allegan Street
Lansing, MI 48909

MDEQ Wellhead Protection Grants 3101
The primary purpose of the MDEQ Wellhead Protection Grants program is to provide funding to community public water supplies and nonprofit noncommunity public water supplies for the development and implementation of wellhead protection (WHP) programs. A wellhead protection area represents the surface and subsurface area within a ten-year time of travel for groundwater surrounding a water well or well field.
Requirements: Applicant must be a community public water supply or a non-profit non-community water supply. Contract requirements include: development of a local WHP team; meeting minimum eligibility requirements; and completion of grant eligible activities as specified in the administrative rules.
Restrictions: A 50 percent local match is required.
Geographic Focus: Michigan
Contact: Jason Berndt; (517) 241-4796; berndtj1@michigan.gov
Internet: http://www.michigan.gov/documents/deq/deq-essd-grantsloans-catalog_210643_7.pdf
Sponsor: Michigan Department of Environmental Quality
525 West Allegan Street
Lansing, MI 48909

Meacham Foundation Memorial Grants 3102
Each year, AHA awards several grants to shelters for improvements that directly affect the care of the animals in facilities. The grant can help with projects such as kennel or cattery renovation, equipment for veterinary care, capital campaigns, animal environment enrichment, and expansion of facilities. The application and current guidelines are available at the AHA website.
Requirements: Grants can only be made to animal care agencies incorporated and classified at 501(c)3 nonprofit organizations or public (local government) agencies.
Restrictions: Funds may not be used for operating budgets, deficit reduction, vehicle purchases, fund raising efforts (gift shops, etc.), staff areas, or routine maintenance. Agencies receiving grants for construction or capital improvement must either: 1) own the property where improvements are made, or hold a long term lease with a minimum of five years remaining on the property or facility.
Geographic Focus: All States
Amount of Grant: Up to 4,000 USD
Contact: Mark Stubis; (800) 227-4645; info@americanhumane.org
Internet: http://www.americanhumane.org/animals/professional-resources/for-shelter-professionals/grant-programs/meacham-foundation.html
Sponsor: American Humane Association
1400 16th Street NW, Suite 360
Washington, DC 20036

Mead Johnson Nutritionals Evansville-Area Organizations Grants 3103
Evansville area non-profit organizations of all varieties may submit charitable giving applications throughout the year. However, if a request exceeds $1,000 it is highly recommended that the applicant submit an application between June 1 and August 31 in the year prior to when the funds are needed. Requests greater than $1,000 are generally reviewed as a group, one time a year. If approved, funding will be awarded in the following year. Requests greater than $1,000 received after August 31 might not be considered and the applicant might be asked to reapply the following year.
Requirements: Evansville area 501(c)3 designated organizations are eligible to apply.
Geographic Focus: Indiana
Date(s) Application is Due: Aug 31
Contact: Administrator; (812) 429-7831; meadjohnson.grants1@bms.com
Internet: http://www.mjn.com/app/iwp/MJN/Content2.do?dm=mj&id=/MJN_Home2/mjnBtnSocialResponsibility2/mjnBtnCharitableGivingApplication&iwpst=B2C&ls=0&csred=1&cr=3435833953#app
Sponsor: Mead Johnson Nutritionals
2400 West Lloyd Expressway
Evansville, IN 47721-0001

Meadows Foundation Grants 3104
The Meadows Foundation seeks to assist people and institutions of Texas improve the quality and circumstances of life for themselves and future generations. Grants are made in five areas of interest: arts and culture, human services, health, education, and civic and public affairs. Within those three areas, the Foundation seeks to fund programs that: improve educational outcomes of Texas students; preserve and enhance the natural environment; and address the detection and treatment of mental illness. Projects should show the ability to continue and expand after the grant period.
Requirements: Grants are made to qualified organizations in Texas or programs benefiting Texas residents. Applicants must prove one or more of the following conditions in their proposal: Foundation support would be vital or catalytic to a proposed project's success; the project is well planned and the agency has the capacity to execute the plan; and financial support from other sources exists to ensure that the project will be implemented and continue after the grant period. Applications can be found at the website and should be submitted online.
Restrictions: Grants are not made to: individuals; for church or seminary construction; annual fund-raising events or drives; biomedical research; out-of-state performances or competition expenses; single artistic events or performances; or professional conferences and symposia.
Geographic Focus: Texas
Amount of Grant: 10,000 - 600,000 USD
Contact: Cynthia Cass; (214) 826-9431 or (800) 826-9431; grants@mfi.org
Bruce H. Esterline, Vice President for Grants; (214) 826-9431
Internet: http://www.mfi.org
Sponsor: Meadows Foundation of Texas
3003 Swiss Avenue
Dallas, TX 75204-6090

MeadWestvaco Foundation Sustainable Communities Grants 3105
The Foundation began as the Mead Corporation Foundation in 1957 and the Westvaco Foundation in 1953, anchored in shared values for community and environmental enrichment. Since merging in 2003, it has offered more than $36 million in support to targeted programs. Adding to this, company employee volunteers have donated over 572,000 hours to more than 3,000 qualified organizations. Across its diverse efforts, the Foundation focuses on three key areas for strategic grants and volunteer initiatives. In the area of Sustainable Communities, it partners with organizations that help people and families rely on themselves, and offers support to their neighbors. The Foundation's support of central business districts gives communities a strong center around which to grow. And its work with youth programs nurtures tomorrow's community leaders. The Foundation's primary focus is to address important community needs and improve the quality of life in communities where MeadWestvaco operates.
Requirements: Nonprofit 501(c)3 organizations in or serving the following U.S. areas are eligible to apply: Cottonton and Lanett, Alabama; Bentonville, Arkansas; Chino, Corona, and Tecate, California; District of Columbia; Miami and St. Petersburg, Florida; Atlanta, Roswell, Smyrna, and Waynesboro, Georgia; Bartlett, Chicago, Itasca, Lake in the Hills, Schaumburg, and West Chicago, Illinois; Winfield, Kansas; Wickliffe, Kentucky; DeRidder, Louisiana; Minneapolis, Minnesota; Grandview, Missouri; Reno, Nevada; North Brunswick, Rumson, and Tinton Falls, New Jersey; New York, New York; Mebane, North Carolina; Cincinnati and Powell, Ohio; North Charleston and Summerville, South Carolina; Coppell, Evadale, and Silsbee, Texas; Appomattox, Covington, Low Moor, Raphine, and Richmond, Virginia; and Elkins and Rupert, West Virginia. Most areas worldwide are also eligible.
Geographic Focus: Alabama, Arkansas, California, District of Columbia, Florida, Georgia, Illinois, Kansas, Louisiana, Minnesota, Nevada, New Jersey, New York, North Carolina, Ohio, South Carolina, Texas, Virginia, West Virginia, All Countries
Amount of Grant: 250 - 1,500,000 USD
Contact: Christine W. Hale; (804) 444-2531; fax (804) 444-1971; foundation@mwv.com
Internet: http://www.meadwestvaco.com/corporate.nsf/mwvfoundation/applications Guidelines
Sponsor: MeadWestvaco Foundation
501 South 5th Street
Richmond, VA 23219-0501

Mead Witter Foundation Grants 3106
Incorporated in Wisconsin in 1951, the Foundation awards grants to nonprofits in company operating locations, primarily in central and northern Wisconsin. Local community programs are funded, focusing on education, including scholarships in higher education and direct contributions to colleges and universities. Grants also are made to support the arts, health care, human services, youth organizations, environmental programs, and Christian and Roman Catholic organizations for nonreligious purposes. Types of support include general operating support, continuing support, annual campaigns, capital campaigns, building construction and renovation, equipment acquisition, endowment funds, professorships, seed grants, scholarship funds, and employee-matching gifts. The board meets twice annually to consider requests. Full proposal is by invitation only.
Requirements: Wisconsin 501(c)3 organizations may apply.
Restrictions: The foundation does not support religious, athletic, or fraternal groups, except when these groups provide needed special services to the community at large; direct grants or scholarships to individuals; community foundations; or flow-through organizations that redispense funds to other charitable causes.
Geographic Focus: Wisconsin
Amount of Grant: 25,000 - 18,000,000 USD
Contact: Cynthia Henke, President; (715) 424-3004; fax (715) 424-1314
Sponsor: Mead Witter Foundation
P.O. Box 39
Wisconsin Rapids, WI 54495-0039

Medicaid/SCHIP Eligibility Pilots 3107
HCFA is soliciting project proposals from state Medicaid agencies and agencies administering the State Children's Health Insurance Program (SCHIP). The purpose of this project is to identify new and effective ways to simplify the application and enrollment process by piloting and evaluating innovative efforts on a small scale.
Requirements: State Medicaid or SCHIP agencies are eligible to apply. These agencies can collaborate with each other, advocates, schools, community-based organizations, consumers, provider organizations, and other entities.
Geographic Focus: All States
Amount of Grant: Up to 80,000 USD
Contact: Candice Hall, (410) 786-4453; chall2@hcfa.gov
Internet: http://www.cms.hhs.gov/schip/sho-letters/ch62600.asp
Sponsor: Health Care Financing Administration
7500 Security Boulevard
Baltimore, MD 21244-1850

MedImmune Charitable Grants 3108
The program supports educational and charitable activities that ultimately improve patient healthcare and further understanding of disease states and treatment options within the community. While the sponsor will consider initiatives in many areas, priority is given to those in the following areas of interest: (a) health and science education for young people; (b) influenza; (c) immunology; (d) pediatric infectious disease; (e) pediatric respiratory disease.
Requirements: Eligible programs include: (a) Community outreach designed to increase public awareness (e.g, fundraising walk or run, nonprofit community hospital or hospital foundation, etc.); (b) Fellowships; (c) Independent educational/scientific programs, accredited and non-accredited; (d) Medical or Scientific education for Healthcare Professionals; (e) Scholarships; or, (f) Academic Chair Endowments. Applications must be completed online at https://web.medimmune.com/corporategrants/, and must be submitted at least 6 weeks prior to the program date or event.
Restrictions: Applications will not be considered from: (1) individuals, physicians, or physician practices; (2) retroactive support; (3) exhibit or display booths at conventions/conferences; (4) textbooks; (5) operating expenses; (6) fraternal, social, leisure, labor or political organizations; (7) corporate foundations; (8) public or private schools or scholarship funds, except where a grant is specific to a science education initiative.
Geographic Focus: All States
Contact: Grants Office; (866) 396-6235; corporatefunding@medimmune.com
Internet: http://www.medimmune.com/culture_grants.aspx
Sponsor: MedImmune
One MedImmune Way
Gaithersburg, MD 20878

Medtronic Foundation Community Link Arts, Civic, and Culture Grants 3109

At Medtronic, the Foundation makes it a priority to enhance the vitality of the communities where its employees live and work. The CommunityLink program helps the Foundation accomplish this by supporting health, education and community programs throughout the world. The Medtronic Foundation CommunityLink Arts, Civic, and Culture Grants supports programs in the U.S. that celebrate the arts and encourage access to the arts in communities where Medtronic employees live and work. The Foundation looks for opportunities to contribute to programs that increase access to the arts, especially for lower-income families. The Foundation aids cultural organizations making a significant contribution to the life of the community and supports civic organizations addressing the needs of disadvantaged people. The application and current guidelines are available at the website.
Requirements: Only U.S. 501(c)3 nonprofit organizations and equivalent international organizations may apply. Organizations must be located in areas where Medtronic has employees.
Restrictions: The Foundation does not fund the following: Continuing Medical Education (CME) grants; 501(c)3 type 509(a)3 supporting organizations; capital or capital projects; fiscal agents; fundraising events/activities, social events or goodwill advertising; general operating support; general support of educational institutions; greater Twin Cities United Way supported programs; individuals, including scholarships for individuals; lobbying, political or fraternal activities; long-term counseling or personal development; program endowments; purchases of automatic external defibrillators (AEDs); religious groups for religious purposes; private foundations; or research.
Geographic Focus: Arizona, California, Colorado, Florida, Indiana, Massachusetts, Minnesota, Tennessee, Texas, Washington
Date(s) Application is Due: Nov 16
Contact: Deb Anderson; (763) 514-4000 or (800) 633-8766; deb.anderson@medtronic.com
Internet: http://www.medtronic.com/foundation/programs_cl_us.html
Sponsor: Medtronic Foundation
710 Medtronic Parkway
Minneapolis, MN 55432-5604

Medtronic Foundation CommunityLink Education Grants 3110

At Medtronic, the Foundation makes it a priority to enhance the vitality of the communities where its employees live and work. The CommunityLink program helps the Foundation accomplish this by supporting health, education and community programs throughout the world. The CommunityLink Education Grants support educational programs from preschool to higher education in communities where Medtronic has employees. The grants focus on programs and projects that stimulate and sustain the interest of young people in science, engineering, and healthcare. The Foundation considers requests from private and parochial nonprofit schools, school districts and other nonprofit organizations. Priority is given to programs that serve socioeconomically disadvantaged students. Funding varies depending on location. The application and current guidelines are available on the website.
Requirements: Only U.S. 501(c)3 nonprofit organizations and equivalent international organizations may apply. Organizations must be located in areas where Medtronic has employees.
Restrictions: The Foundation does not fund the following: Continuing Medical Education (CME) grants; 501(c)3 type 509(a)3 supporting organizations; capital or capital projects; fiscal agents; fundraising events/activities, social events or goodwill advertising; general operating support; general support of educational institutions; greater Twin Cities United Way supported programs; individuals, including scholarships for individuals; lobbying, political or fraternal activities; long-term counseling or personal development; program endowments; purchases of automatic external defibrillators (AEDs); religious groups for religious purposes; private foundations; or research.
Geographic Focus: Arizona, California, Colorado, Florida, Massachusetts, Minnesota, Puerto Rico, Tennessee, Texas, Washington, Canada, Ireland, Japan, Netherlands
Date(s) Application is Due: Nov 16
Contact: Deb Anderson, (763) 514-4000 or (800) 633-8766; deb.anderson@medtronic.com
Internet: http://www.medtronic.com/foundation/programs_cl_us.html
Sponsor: Medtronic Foundation
710 Medtronic Parkway
Minneapolis, MN 55432-5604

Medtronic Foundation CommunityLink Health Grants 3111

At Medtronic, the Foundation makes it a priority to enhance the vitality of the communities where its employees live and work. The CommunityLink program helps the Foundation accomplish this by supporting health, education and community programs throughout the world. The CommunityLink Health Grants support programs that improve the health and welfare of people, with a focus on Medtronic's areas of expertise. The Foundation gives priority to programs that help people develop and maintain health lifestyles, with particular interest in programs that reduces differences in health care and that support healthy lifestyles, such as nutrition and fitness. The application and guidelines are located on the Foundation website. Guidelines and funding varies depending on location.
Requirements: Only 501(c)3 nonprofits and equivalent international organizations may apply.
Restrictions: The Foundation does not fund the following: Continuing Medical Education (CME) grants; 501(c)3 type 509(a)3 supporting organizations; capital or capital projects; fiscal agents; fundraising events/activities, social events or goodwill advertising; general operating support; general support of educational institutions; greater Twin Cities United Way supported programs; individuals, including scholarships for individuals; lobbying, political or fraternal activities; long-term counseling or personal development; program endowments; purchases of automatic external defibrillators (AEDs); religious groups for religious purposes; private foundations; or research.
Geographic Focus: Arizona, California, Colorado, Florida, Indiana, Massachusetts, Minnesota, Puerto Rico, Tennessee, Texas, Washington, Canada, Ireland, Japan, Netherlands, Switzerland
Date(s) Application is Due: Nov 16
Contact: Deb Anderson; (763) 514-4000 or (800) 633-8766; deb.anderson@medtronic.com
Internet: http://www.medtronic.com/foundation/programs_cl.html
Sponsor: Medtronic Foundation
304 Landmark Center, 75 West Fifth Street
St. Paul, MN 55102

Medtronic Foundation Community Link Human Services Grants 3112

At Medtronic, the Foundation makes it a priority to enhance the vitality of the communities where its employees live and work. The CommunityLink program helps the Foundation accomplish this by supporting health, education and community programs throughout the world. The CommunityLink Human Services Grants support human services in the U.S. that help individuals become more self-sufficient. Programs reach out to a wide range of people, such as: economic literacy programs to help low-income women gain economic stability; peer counseling for teens in crisis situations; homeless shelters; and subsidized childcare programs for low-income parents. The application and current guidelines are available at the website.
Requirements: Only U.S. 501(c)3 nonprofits and equivalent international organizations may apply. Applicants must be located in U.S. areas where Medtronic has employees.
Restrictions: The Foundation does not fund the following: Continuing Medical Education (CME) grants; 501(c)3 type 509(a)3 supporting organizations; capital or capital projects; fiscal agents; fundraising events/activities, social events or goodwill advertising; general operating support; general support of educational institutions; greater Twin Cities United Way supported programs; individuals, including scholarships for individuals; lobbying, political or fraternal activities; long-term counseling or personal development; program endowments; purchases of automatic external defibrillators (AEDs); religious groups for religious purposes; private foundations; or research.
Geographic Focus: Arizona, California, Colorado, Florida, Indiana, Massachusetts, Minnesota, Tennessee, Texas, Washington
Date(s) Application is Due: Nov 16
Contact: Deb Anderson; (763) 514-4000 or (800) 633-8766; deb.anderson@medtronic.com
Internet: http://www.medtronic.com/foundation/programs_cl.html
Sponsor: Medtronic Foundation
710 Medtronic Parkway
Minneapolis, MN 55432-5604

Medtronic Foundation Patient Link Grants 3113

Through Patient Link grants, Medtronic partners with national and international patient organizations that educate, support, and advocate on behalf of patients and their families to improve the lives of people with chronic diseases. Grants are offered in the U.S., Canada, and Europe. In partnership with its Patient Link organizations, the Foundation: empowers patients to become active partners in their health care; engages patients from cultural communities who have not had access to health information and health care; and provides support to patients through what can be difficult emotional times. Each location requires different guidelines and gives a different range of funding.
Requirements: Health grants only fund 501(3)c U.S. or nonprofit international organizations. Public, private, government institutions, and educational institutions are the only exceptions to this rule. U.S. based organizations must gather and complete the application and corresponding documents. Organizations outside the U.S. complete a letter of inquiry to the corresponding contact near their location.
Restrictions: Grants are not available for the following: Continuing Medical Education (CME) grants; 501(c)3 type 509(a)3 supporting organizations; capital or capital projects; fiscal agents; fundraising events/activities, social events or goodwill advertising; general operating support; general support of educational institutions; greater Twin Cities United Way supported programs; individuals, including scholarships for individuals; lobbying, political or fraternal activities; long-term counseling or personal development; program endowments; purchases of automatic external defibrillators; religious groups for religious purposes; private foundations; or research.
Geographic Focus: All States, Belgium, Canada, Denmark, Finland, France, Germany, Great Britain, Iceland, Ireland, Italy, Japan, Lithuania, Luxembourg, Netherlands, Norway, Poland, Portugal, Spain, Sweden, Switzerland, The Netherlands, United Kingdom, Vatican City
Date(s) Application is Due: May 14; Sep 10; Nov 12
Amount of Grant: 10,000 - 175,000 USD
Contact: Deb Anderson; (763) 514-4000 or (800) 633-8766; deb.anderson@medtronic.com
Internet: http://www.medtronic.com/foundation/programs_pl.html
Sponsor: Medtronic Foundation
710 Medtronic Parkway
Minneapolis, MN 55432-5604

Melinda Gray Ardia Environmental Foundation Grants 3114

The foundation's mission is to support educators in developing environmental curricula that integrate field activities and classroom teaching and that incorporate basic ecological principles and problem solving. Grants assist educators in the design and implementation of holistic environmental curricula that fit the foundation's mission statement. Preference is given to grants that benefit public school students. The foundation prefers to support the actual development of a curriculum rather than provide funds to purchase equipment. All funds pass through the school district or nonprofit organization rather than directly to the individual recipients. Guidelines are available online.
Geographic Focus: All States
Contact: Grants Administrator; info@mgaef.org
Internet: http://www.mgaef.org/index.html
Sponsor: Melinda Gray Ardia Environmental Foundation
P.O. Box 621
Skaneateles, NY 13152

Melville Charitable Trust Grants 3115

The Melville Trust was organized in 1990 with the desire to understand the growing problem of homelessness and help eradicate it. The foundation decided to focus its study on Connecticut and to create programs that would alleviate and reduce the impact of homelessness on children, adults and communities. The trust also funds educational, research and advocacy initiatives in the state and on the national level.
Requirements: The Trust does not use a formal application form. Instead, applicants are asked to submit a concept paper of not more than three pages describing the project. If there is interest in pursuing the request after the concept paper has been reviewed, the applicant organization will be contacted to either submit a more formal proposal and/or provide more detailed information to the Board. Applications must be from an organization that has been determined to be tax-exempt under section 501(c)3 of the Internal Revenue Code and not a private foundation under section 509(a) of the Code.
Restrictions: Grants will not be awarded for: direct support to individuals or scholarships; budget deficits; religious organizations for religious purposes; or general fund raising drives or events.
Geographic Focus: All States
Contact: Aimee Hendrigan; (617) 236-2244; fax (617) 482-5624; ahendrigan@melvilletrust.org
Internet: http://www.melvilletrust.org/funding_guidelines.aspx
Sponsor: Melville Charitable Trust
240 Newbury Street, 2nd Floor
Boston, MA 02116-2580

Memorial Foundation for Children Grants 3116

Memorial Foundation for Children Grants are made solely to programs with nonprofit organizations that benefit the care and education of children in the Richmond, Virginia, metropolitan area.
Requirements: Giving is limited to the Richmond, Virginia area, including Chesterfield, Goochland, Hanover, and Henrico counties. Organizations should submit the following: a copy of the IRS determination letter; a brief history of their organization and description of its mission; copy of their most recent annual report, audited financial statement, or 990 form; a detailed description of the project and amount of funding requested; and a copy of the current year's organizational budget and/or project budget.
Geographic Focus: Virginia
Date(s) Application is Due: May 31
Contact: Karl McTaggart, Grants Administrator; (804) 782-7114
Sponsor: Memorial Foundation for Children
P.O. Box 26665
Richmond, VA 23261-6665

Memorial Foundation Grants 3117

The Memorial Foundation awards grants to support nonprofit organizations that provide services only to people who live in the area served by Nashville Memorial Hospital. The Foundation also strives to respond to immediate, critical needs that arise in the community. With assistance from the Foundation, organizations including The Salvation Army, The American Red Cross, Second Harvest Food Bank, Nashville Tree Foundation, and YWCA have received funds. Special emphasis is given to organizations that focus on health; youth and children; senior citizens; education; human and social services; community services; and substance abuse (alcohol, drugs, and tobacco). Types of support include capital projects; general operating support; and start-up projects for new initiatives that address important, unmet community needs and that demonstrate potential for ongoing operational support from other sources.
Requirements: An applicant organization must be exempt from federal taxation under Section 501(c)3 of the Internal Revenue Code and not be a private foundation as described in Section 509(a) in order to be eligible.
Restrictions: The Memorial Foundation does not fund grants for the following: individuals; newsletters, magazines; churches and religious organizations for projects that primarily benefit their own members (exception: church-based programs with broad community support and separate financial statements); disease-specific organizations seeking support for national research projects and programs; sponsor special events, productions, telethons, performances, or similar fundraising and advertising activities (exceptions may be given for approved educational videos); legislative lobbying or other political purposes; retire accumulated debt; bricks and mortar capital projects for colleges, universities, and private or public school education; computer labs and related technologies to schools; or multi-year grants for operating funds.
Geographic Focus: Tennessee
Contact: Joyce Douglas, Grants Contact; (615) 822-9499; fax (615) 822-7797
Internet: http://www.memfoundation.org
Sponsor: Memorial Foundation
100 Bluegrass Commons Boulevard, Suite 320
Hendersonville, TN 37075

Mercedes-Benz USA Corporate Contributions Grants 3118

The company has committed to conducting programs with the concentration of funds geared toward educational causes and organizations, in particular those that help to empower the next generation and underserved groups; diversity programs; and women's initiatives. Specific programs in the categories of health and human services, and civic and community also are supported. There are no application forms or annual deadlines. Applicants should begin by submitting a proposal idea to the nearest company facility.
Requirements: IRS 501(c)3, 4, 6, or 9 organizations whose primary influences and business operations are in the United States and who enhance the quality of life in Mercedes-Benz communities are eligible. These company communities include: Tuscaloosa, Alabama; Carson, California; Irvine, California; Rancho Cucamonga, California; Jacksonville, Florida; Carol Stream, Illinois; Itasca, Illinois; Rosemont, Illinois; Belcamp, Maryland; Baltimore, Maryland; Montvale, New Jersey; Parsippany, New Jersey; Robinsville, New Jersey; and Fort Worth, Texas.
Geographic Focus: Alabama, California, Florida, Illinois, Maryland, New Jersey, Texas
Amount of Grant: 2,500 - 5,000 USD
Contact: Geoff Day, Director of Communications & Events; (201) 573-2270 or (201) 573-0600; fax (201) 573-4787; geoff.day@mbusa.com
Internet: http://www.mbusa.com/mercedes/about_us/mbcommunity
Sponsor: Mercedes-Benz USA
One Mercedes Drive
Montvale, NJ 07645

Merck Family Fund Urban Farming and Youth Leadership Grants 3119

The primary goals of the Merck Family Fund are to restore and protect the natural environment and ensure a healthy planet for generations to come; and to strengthen the social fabric and the physical landscape of the urban community. In the area of Urban Farming and Youth Leadership, the Fund will support programs in low-income urban areas in the Northeast that are harnessing the power of young people to create urban farms and local markets. Specifically, the Fund welcomes proposals that: provide high quality leadership development and employment for youth; support highly productive urban farming projects and increase local access to fresh food; and engage residents in food access and food security issues in the community. Upon submitting a letter of inquiry, applicants will be notified of a decision, by email, typically within one week. If invited, full proposals must be submitted through this online application system no later than August 1, at 5:00pm EST for the November decision, and February 1, at 5:00pm for Spring decision.
Requirements: United States tax-exempt organizations are eligible. Priority will be given to projects that originate in the six New England states, New York, New Jersey and the Delaware Valley region including Philadelphia, Pennsylvania, and Wilmington, Delaware. New and returning requests for support must use the online application system to submit a letter of inquiry prior to a formal application.
Restrictions: The Fund does not support individuals, for-profit organizations, or candidates for political office. The Fund does not generally support: governmental organizations, academic research or books; endowments, debt reduction, annual fund-raising campaigns, capital construction, purchase of equipment, the acquisition of land, or film or video projects.
Geographic Focus: Delaware, Maine, Maryland, Massachusetts, New Hampshire, New Jersey, New York, Pennsylvania, Rhode Island, Vermont
Date(s) Application is Due: Feb 1; Aug 1
Amount of Grant: 3,000 - 50,000 USD
Contact: Jenny Russell; (617) 696-3580; fax (617) 696-7262; merck@merckff.org
Internet: http://www.merckff.org/programs.html
Sponsor: Merck Family Fund
303 Adams Street, P.O. Box 870245
Milton Village, MA 02187

Merck Family Fund Youth Transforming Urban Communities Grants 3120

The primary goals of the Merck Family Fund are to restore and protect the natural environment and ensure a healthy planet for generations to come; and to strengthen the social fabric and the physical landscape of the urban community. In the area of Youth Transforming Urban Communities, the goals have been to support a cadre of young social justice leaders across the country; to link local campaigns with national movements; and to document the impact of their work on communities and themselves. Upon submitting a letter of inquiry, applicants will be notified of a decision, by email, typically within one week. If invited, full proposals must be submitted through this online application system no later than August 1, at 5:00pm EST for the November decision, and February 1, at 5:00pm for Spring decision.
Requirements: United States tax-exempt organizations are eligible. New and returning requests for support must use the online application system to submit a letter of inquiry prior to a formal application.
Restrictions: The Fund does not support individuals, for-profit organizations, or candidates for political office. The Fund does not generally support: governmental organizations, academic research or books; endowments, debt reduction, annual fund-raising campaigns, capital construction, purchase of equipment, the acquisition of land, or film or video projects.
Geographic Focus: All States
Date(s) Application is Due: Feb 1; Aug 1
Amount of Grant: 10,000 - 45,000 USD
Contact: Jenny Russell; (617) 696-3580; fax (617) 696-7262; merck@merckff.org
Internet: http://www.merckff.org/programs.html
Sponsor: Merck Family Fund
303 Adams Street, P.O. Box 870245
Milton Village, MA 02187

Mericos Foundation Grants 3121

The Mericos Foundation primarily awards grants to organizations based in California with emphasis on Santa Barbara. Fields of interest include aging; animals/wildlife; environment; arts and arts education; child development; children and youth; elementary and secondary education; higher education; hospitals; medical care; medical research; libraries; and museums (art and natural history). Types of support include building/renovation, equipment, fellowships, general/operating support, matching/challenge support, and program development. Grants are usually initiated by the foundation. Interested organizations should contact the Vice-President to discuss their project.
Requirements: Nonprofit organizations in California are eligible to apply.
Restrictions: Grants are not made to individuals.
Geographic Focus: California
Amount of Grant: 15,000 - 200,000 USD

Contact: Linda Blinkenberg, Vice President; (626) 441-5188; fax (626) 441-3672
Sponsor: Mericos Foundation
625 South Fair Oaks Avenue, Suite 360
South Pasadena, CA 91030-2630

Meriden Foundation Grants 3122
The foundation awards grants to eligible Connecticut nonprofit organizations in its areas of interest, including arts, children and youth, civic affairs, Christian organizations and churches, health organizations and hospitals, higher education, public libraries, and social services. Types of support include annual campaigns, general operating support, scholarships, and social services delivery. There are no application deadlines. A formal application is required, and the initial approach should be a letter, on organizational letterhead, describing the project and requesting an application.
Requirements: Connecticut nonprofits in the Meriden-Wallingford area are eligible.
Geographic Focus: Connecticut
Contact: Jeffrey F. Otis, Director; (203) 782-4531; fax (203) 782-4530
Sponsor: Meriden Foundation
123 Bank Street
Waterbury, CT 06702-2205

Merkel Family Foundation Grants 3123
The Foundation, established in 1989 in Tulsa, Oklahoma, offers grants primarily in support of the arts, education, and to Christian agencies and churches. Its current fields of interest include Alzheimer's disease, Christian churches and agencies, education, higher education, museums, the Salvation Army, and youth development programs. An application form is required, although there are no specific deadlines. An applicant should begin by contacting the Foundation directly.
Requirements: No grants are given to individuals.
Restrictions: Grants are given only to 501(c)3 organizations in Oklahoma, or those that support the residents of Oklahoma.
Geographic Focus: Oklahoma
Contact: John B. Turner; (918) 744-5222; fax (918) 742-5273; jstuart@tulsacoxmail.com
Sponsor: Merkel Family Foundation
2431 E. 61st Street, Suite 602
Tulsa, OK 74136-1235

Merkel Foundation Grants 3124
The Merkel Foundation, established by Daniel A. and Betty Merkel in Sheboygan, Wisconsin, is interested in supporting a variety of Wisconsin organizations. The Foundation's primary interests are research, religion, education, social services, and relief programs. There are no specific application formats or deadlines with which to adhere. Applicants should begin the process by contacting the Foundation directly. Generally, support is given throughout Wisconsin and, ocassionally, across the country. Amounts range from $100 to $10,000.
Geographic Focus: Wisconsin
Contact: Betty Merkel; (920) 457-5051; fax (920) 457-1485; info@americanortho.com
Sponsor: Merkel Foundation
3712 Bismarck Circle
Sheboygan, WI 53083

Mertz Gilmore Foundation Climate Change Solutions Grants 3125
The Foundation's Climate Change Solutions program builds on past Mertz Gilmore investments to study climate change, promote climate-friendly energy usage, and develop renewable energy sources in the U.S. In 2007, the Board approved a new grants program to help bring about substantial reductions in global warming pollution through targeted investments in sustainable policy and practice. The Foundation is an active member in the U.S. Climate and Energy Funders Group and currently considers grant requests in three strategic categories: (1) Alternatives to coal-fired power plants; (2) New York City; and, (3) New constituencies and approaches for a national climate movement.
Requirements: Submit a letter of inquiry (not a full proposal) of no more than three pages describing the mission of the organization and the purpose of the request. Staff will respond to all communications, and, if appropriate, invite a full proposal. Do not submit videos, DVDs/CDs, press clippings, books, or other materials unless they are requested. Across all funding categories, the Foundation will evaluate the ability of organizations to work in partnership and raise additional funds for proposed work.
Restrictions: The Foundation does not accept proposals for: individuals; endowments, annual fund appeals or fundraising events; conferences, workshops; sectarian religious concerns; scholarships, fellowships, research, loans, or travel; film or media projects; or, publications.
Geographic Focus: All States
Date(s) Application is Due: Jan 13
Contact: Rachael Young, (212) 475-5581; fax (212) 777-5226; ryoung@mertzgilmore.org
Internet: http://www.mertzgilmore.org/index.php/programs/climate-change
Sponsor: Mertz Gilmore Foundation
218 East 18th Street
New York, NY 10003-3694

Mertz Gilmore Foundation NYC Communities Grants 3126
The Mertz Gilmore Foundation supports work in low-income neighborhoods that emerges from, and actively engages, local efforts while looking for opportunities to support collaborative campaigns. The Program'?s grants fall into three categories: (1) Support to community-based organizations working on multiple fronts; (2) Support to technical assistance providers that help community-based organizations address organizational needs; and, (3) Support to collaborative campaigns.
Requirements: Submit a letter of inquiry (not a full proposal) of no more than three pages describing the mission of the organization and the purpose of the request. Staff will respond to all communications, and, if appropriate, invite a full proposal. Do not submit videos, DVDs/CDs, press clippings, books, or other materials unless they are requested. Across all funding categories, the Foundation will evaluate the ability of organizations to work in partnership and raise additional funds for proposed work.
Restrictions: The Foundation does not accept proposals for: individuals; endowments, annual fund appeals or fundraising events; conferences, workshops; sectarian religious concerns; scholarships, fellowships, research, loans, or travel; film or media projects; or, publications.
Geographic Focus: New York
Date(s) Application is Due: Jan 17
Amount of Grant: Up to 150,000 USD
Contact: Rachael Young, (212) 475-5581; fax (212) 777-5226; ryoung@mertzgilmore.org
Internet: http://www.mertzgilmore.org/index.php/programs/nyc-communities
Sponsor: Mertz Gilmore Foundation
218 East 18th Street
New York, NY 10003-3694

Mertz Gilmore Foundation NYC Dance Grants 3127
The Mertz Gilmore Foundation has an extensive history of supporting dance in New York City, reflecting Joyce Mertz Gilmore?'s passion for dance. The Foundation continues to fund contemporary dance presenters located throughout the city?'s five boroughs. Its objective remains to support and invigorate the presenting field to serve New York City?'s artists and audiences. The Program'?s grants fall into two categories: (1) Presenters; and, (2) Advocacy/Support Services.
Requirements: The Foundation will accept proposals from organizations based in New York City. Submit a letter of inquiry (not a full proposal) of no more than three pages describing the mission of the organization and the purpose of the request. Staff will respond to all communications, and, if appropriate, invite a full proposal. Do not submit videos, DVDs/CDs, press clippings, books, or other materials unless they are requested. Across all funding categories, the Foundation will evaluate the ability of organizations to work in partnership and raise additional funds for proposed work.
Restrictions: The Foundation will not make grants for individual artists or companies, or organizations based outside of New York City. Additionally, the Foundation does not accept proposals for: individuals; endowments, annual fund appeals or fundraising events; conferences, workshops; sectarian religious concerns; scholarships, fellowships, research, loans, or travel; film or media projects; or, publications.
Geographic Focus: New York
Date(s) Application is Due: Jan 17
Amount of Grant: Up to 100,000 USD
Contact: Leah Krauss, (646) 723-2225; lkrauss@mertzgilmore.org
Internet: http://www.mertzgilmore.org/index.php/programs/nyc-dance
Sponsor: Mertz Gilmore Foundation
218 East 18th Street
New York, NY 10003-3694

Mervin Bovaird Foundation Grants 3128
The foundation awards grants, with a focus on Tulsa, OK, to nonprofit organizations such as churches, homeless shelters, medical centers, nursing homes, parochial schools, religious welfare organizations, the Salvation Army, and youth organizations. Areas of interest include arts, community development, education, environment, health care and health organizations, and social services. Types of support include general operating support, matching, project, and research grants.
Requirements: Nonprofits in and serving the population of Tulsa, Oklahoma, are eligible. Applicants should submit a brief letter of inquiry, including program and organization descriptions.
Geographic Focus: Oklahoma
Date(s) Application is Due: Nov 15
Amount of Grant: Up to 250,000 USD
Contact: R. Casey Cooper, (918) 592-3300; casey.cooper@cmw-law.com
Sponsor: Mervin Bovaird Foundation
401 South Boston Avenue, Suite 3300
Tulsa, OK 74103

MetLife Foundation Building Livable Communities Grants 3129
MetLife Foundation partners with local, national and global nonprofit organizations to address issues impacting communities worldwide within the following thematic programs. The Foundation that communities are the building blocks of society, a reflection of the attitudes, beliefs and priorities of our families and neighbors. Through its Building Livable Communities program the Foundation provides all people with cultural, social and economic opportunities. The Foundation works to build livable communities through a focus on providing basic needs and promoting access to the arts. In deciding the amount of support, the factors considered include availability of funds, relative priorities and funding patterns. On occasion, the Foundation establishes particular areas of interest for emphasis within a program area. When this is done, the Foundation actively searches out promising opportunities for grants and may issue requests for proposals.
Requirements: To be considered for a MetLife Foundation grant, an organization must be a qualified 501(c)3 organization with a valid IRS Tax ID based in the United States. In the evaluation of the organization, the factors considered include the organization's general structure, objectives, history and management capability; its relationship to the community and the population to be served; its position relative to organizations performing similar functions; and its financial position and sources of income. In the evaluation of a project, the factors considered include the project's goals and implementation plans; length of time for

the project to be complete; the ultimate disposition of the project; benefits of the projects; and the sources of financial and other support.
Restrictions: The Metlife Foundation is not seeking applications for any of the following: private foundations; religious, fraternal, political, athletic or social organizations; hospitals; individuals; local chapters of national organizations; disease-specific organizations; labor groups; organizations primarily engaged in patient care or direct treatment, drug treatment centers and community health clinics; direct contributions to elementary and secondary schools (including charter, parochial and private schools); endowments; courtesy advertising or festival participation; or sponsorships (golf tournaments, dinners, etc.). Grant renewals are not automatic and cannot be guaranteed from year to year.
Geographic Focus: All States
Contact: A. Dennis White; (212) 578-6272; metlifefoundation@metlife.com
Internet: https://www.metlife.com/metlife-foundation/about/index.html?WT.ac=GN_metlife-foundation_about
Sponsor: MetLife Foundation
1095 Avenue of the Americas
New York, NY 10036-6797

MetLife Foundation Empowering Older Adults Grants 3130

The goal of the Metlife Foundation Empowering Older Adults program is to build a secure future for individuals and communities worldwide. MetLife Foundation supports healthy aging programs to ensure older adults remain engaged in their communities. The Foundation also funds Alzheimer's research and public awareness programs in an effort to address the needs of those affected by the disease. In deciding the amount of support, the factors considered include availability of funds, relative priorities and funding patterns. On occasion, the Foundation establishes particular areas of interest for emphasis within a program area. When this is done, the Foundation actively searches out promising opportunities for grants and may issue requests for proposals.
Requirements: To be considered for a MetLife Foundation grant, an organization must be a qualified 501(c)3 organization with a valid IRS Tax ID based in the United States. In the evaluation of the organization, the factors considered include the organization's general structure, objectives, history and management capability; its relationship to the community and the population to be served; its position relative to organizations performing similar functions; and its financial position and sources of income. In the evaluation of a project, the factors considered include the project's goals and implementation plans; length of time for the project to be complete; the ultimate disposition of the project; benefits of the projects; and the sources of financial and other support.
Restrictions: The Metlife Foundation is not seeking applications for any of the following: private foundations; religious, fraternal, political, athletic or social organizations; hospitals; individuals; local chapters of national organizations; disease-specific organizations; labor groups; organizations primarily engaged in patient care or direct treatment, drug treatment centers and community health clinics; direct contributions to elementary and secondary schools (including charter, parochial and private schools); endowments; courtesy advertising or festival participation; or sponsorships (golf tournaments, dinners, etc.). Grant renewals are not automatic and cannot be guaranteed from year to year.
Geographic Focus: All States
Contact: A. Dennis White; (212) 578-6272; metlifefoundation@metlife.com
Internet: https://www.metlife.com/metlife-foundation/about/index.html?WT.ac=GN_metlife-foundation_about
Sponsor: MetLife Foundation
1095 Avenue of the Americas
New York, NY 10036-6797

MetLife Foundation Preparing Young People Grants 3131

MetLife Foundation partners with local, national and global nonprofit organizations to address issues impacting communities worldwide within the following thematic programs. The Foundation's Preparing Young People program helps young people navigate opportunities and obstacles by supporting initiatives focusing on student achievement and youth development. In deciding the amount of support, the factors considered include availability of funds, relative priorities and funding patterns. On occasion, the Foundation establishes particular areas of interest for emphasis within a program area. When this is done, the Foundation actively searches out promising opportunities for grants and may issue requests for proposals.
Requirements: To be considered for a MetLife Foundation grant, an organization must be a qualified 501(c)3 organization with a valid IRS Tax ID based in the United States. In the evaluation of the organization, the factors considered include the organization's general structure, objectives, history and management capability; its relationship to the community and the population to be served; its position relative to organizations performing similar functions; and its financial position and sources of income. In the evaluation of a project, the factors considered include the project's goals and implementation plans; length of time for the project to be complete; the ultimate disposition of the project; benefits of the projects; and the sources of financial and other support.
Restrictions: The Metlife Foundation is not seeking applications for any of the following: private foundations; religious, fraternal, political, athletic or social organizations; hospitals; individuals; local chapters of national organizations; disease-specific organizations; labor groups; organizations primarily engaged in patient care or direct treatment, drug treatment centers and community health clinics; direct contributions to elementary and secondary schools (including charter, parochial and private schools); endowments; courtesy advertising or festival participation; or sponsorships (golf tournaments, dinners, etc.). Grant renewals are not automatic and cannot be guaranteed from year to year.
Geographic Focus: All States
Contact: A. Dennis White; (212) 578-6272; metlifefoundation@metlife.com
Internet: https://www.metlife.com/metlife-foundation/about/index.html?WT.ac=GN_metlife-foundation_about
Sponsor: MetLife Foundation
1095 Avenue of the Americas
New York, NY 10036-6797

MetLife Foundation Promoting Employee Volunteerism 3132

MetLife Foundation partners with local, national and global nonprofit organizations to address issues impacting communities worldwide within the following thematic programs. With this program, MetLife Foundation encourages MetLife employees to contribute their time and talent to improve their communities and help people in need. The Foundation supports the volunteer efforts of MetLife associates through several programs which provide grants to nonprofit organizations where individual MetLife associates or groups of MetLife associates volunteer.
Geographic Focus: All States
Contact: A. Dennis White; (212) 578-6272; metlifefoundation@metlife.com
Internet: https://www.metlife.com/metlife-foundation/about/index.html?WT.ac=GN_metlife-foundation_about
Sponsor: MetLife Foundation
1095 Avenue of the Americas
New York, NY 10036-6797

Metro Health Foundation Grants 3133

The foundation awards grants in southeastern Michigan in its areas of interest, including children and youth, disabled, elderly, health associations, homeless, and women. Types of support include challenge grants, equipment acquisition, general operating support, project development, scholarship funds, seed grants, and federated giving. Obtain application materials from the office; the board meets in April and October.
Requirements: Nonprofit organizations in the metropolitan tri-county Detroit, MI, area are eligible to apply.
Restrictions: Grants do not support advertising, advocacy organizations, athletic groups, individuals, international organizations, political organizations, special events, benefit dinners, or state or local government agencies.
Geographic Focus: Michigan
Date(s) Application is Due: Feb 1; Aug 1
Contact: Theresa Sondys; (313) 965-4220; fax (313) 965-3626; metrohealthfdn@aol.com
Sponsor: Metro Health Foundation
333 W Fort Street, Suite 1370
Detroit, MI 48226-3134

MetroWest Health Foundation Capital Grants for Health-Related Facilities 3134

The MetroWest Health Foundation offers a limited number of capital grants on a highly competitive basis to community-based health organizations within its twenty-five communities. To be competitive for such a grant, the applicant organization must demonstrate a record of outstanding service to the community, strong program and financial management, significant private support, and a demonstrated need for capital funds that will directly impact on the organization's ability to deliver health services. New construction, additions to an existing structure, and extensive renovation of an existing structure will qualify for consideration. In addition, furnishings, equipment and site work associated with any of the above qualified projects are eligible for funding.
Requirements: The Foundation supports programs that directly benefit the health of those who live and work in one of the 25 communities served by the Foundation: Ashland, Bellingham, Dover, Framingham, Franklin, Holliston, Hopedale, Hopkinton, Hudson, Marlborough, Medfield, Medway, Mendon, Milford, Millis, Natick, Needham, Norfolk, Northborough Sherborn, Southborough, Sudbury, Wayland, Wellesley and Westborough. Such support is limited to organizations that qualify as tax-exempt under Section 501(c)3 of the IRS Code, or organizations that are recognized as instrumentalities of state or local government. Applicants are expected to have completed appropriate organizational, financial and facilities planning prior to applying for a capital grant from the Foundation. The Foundation is not positioned to be the sole or major funding of any individual capital project. Therefore, applicants must demonstrate that other funding for the project has been raised or is available through traditional capital financing mechanisms. Organizations seeking capital grants should send a brief 2-3 page letter outlining the proposed project. Requests for full proposals will sent to only those projects the Foundation wishes to consider for funding. Each capital grant is limited to three years in duration.
Restrictions: No single organization shall receive more than one capital grant from the Foundation at a time. Grants will not be made to: projects that supplant or substitute for government funding from local, state, or federal sources; for endowments or debt retirement; program support or fundraising appeals; projects that have been unsuccessfully submitted to the Foundation before.
Geographic Focus: Massachusetts
Contact: Cathy Glover; (508) 879-7625; fax (508) 879-7628; info@mwhealth.org
Internet: http://www.mwhealth.org/GrantsampScholarships/WhatWeFund/tabid/229/Default.aspx
Sponsor: MetroWest Health Foundation
161 Worcester Road, Suite 202
Framingham, MA 01701

MetroWest Health Foundation Grants—Healthy Aging 3135

Since 1999, the MetroWest Health Foundation has provided over funds to non-profit and government organizations to improve health services within its 25-town service area. The Foundation describes its grantmaking efforts as both reactive and proactive. Its reactive grantmaking includes two annual requests for proposals (spring and fall) where

grant applications are solicited from area organizations. These requests for proposals target specific needs or areas of interest, such as access to health care, disease prevention and health promotion. Its proactive grantmaking targets community needs identified by the Foundation. Here the Foundation develops more comprehensive strategies for addressing community health needs. To date, the Foundation's proactive grantmaking has targeted such issues as child obesity, racial and ethnic health disparities, and adolescent substance abuse.
Requirements: The Foundation supports programs that directly benefit the health of those who live and work in one of the 25 communities served by the Foundation: Ashland, Bellingham, Dover, Framingham, Franklin, Holliston, Hopedale, Hopkinton, Hudson, Marlborough, Medfield, Medway, Mendon, Milford, Millis, Natick, Needham, Norfolk, Northborough Sherborn, Southborough, Sudbury, Wayland, Wellesley and Westborough. Such support is limited to organizations that qualify as tax-exempt under Section 501(c)3 of the IRS Code, or organizations that are recognized as instrumentalities of state or local government. The Foundation requires applicants to submit concept papers prior to a full proposal. Concept papers help the Foundation assess whether or not the proposed project is aligned with its funding priorities. Only a limited number of proposals will be funded with a maximum grant amount of $50,000; funding is limited to one year in duration, and funds cannot be used to supplant ongoing government operations or support. Healthy Aging proposals must address one of the following objectives: (1) Decrease the number of MetroWest older adults who are hospitalized each year from injuries due to falls. Funds can be used to expand the use of evidence-based fall prevention programming within the region. (2) Expand older adults participation in local programs and initiatives that actively engage them in their community, including opportunities for socialization; group activities; volunteering; employment and social and civic engagement. Funds can be sued to develop new or expanded programming that reach older adults, especially when they are at greatest risk for becoming isolated (death of a spouse, loss of mobility, etc.). (3) Improve services and supports for caregivers of older adults in the MetroWest region. Funds can be used to support caregiver training, respite services, information sharing or enhanced care management support.
Restrictions: The Foundation does not provide grants to individuals, nor does it provide funds for endowments, fundraising drives and events, retirement of debt, operating deficits, projects that directly influence legislation, political activities or candidates for public office, or programs that are customarily operated by hospitals in Massachusetts. The Foundation does not award grants to organizations that discriminate in the provision of services on the basis of race, color, religion, gender, age, ethnicity, marital status, disability, sexual orientation or veteran status.
Geographic Focus: Massachusetts
Date(s) Application is Due: Apr 12
Amount of Grant: Up to 50,000 USD
Contact: Cathy Glover, Grants Managment Director; (508) 879-7625; fax (508) 879-7628; cglover@mwhealth.org or cglover@mchcf.org
Internet: http://www.mwhealth.org/GrantsampScholarships/Overview/tabid/180/Default.aspx
Sponsor: MetroWest Health Foundation
161 Worcester Road, Suite 202
Framingham, MA 01701

MetroWest Health Foundation Grants to Reduce the Incidence of High Risk Behaviors Among Adolescents 3136
Since 1999, the MetroWest Health Foundation has provided over funds to non-profit and government organizations to improve health services within its 25-town service area. The Foundation describes its grantmaking efforts as both reactive and proactive. Its reactive grantmaking includes two annual requests for proposals (spring and fall) where grant applications are solicited from area organizations. These requests for proposals target specific needs or areas of interest, such as access to health care, disease prevention and health promotion. Its proactive grantmaking targets community needs identified by the Foundation. Here the Foundation develops more comprehensive strategies for addressing community health needs. To date, the Foundation's proactive grantmaking has targeted such issues as child obesity, racial and ethnic health disparities, and adolescent substance abuse.
Requirements: The Foundation supports programs that directly benefit the health of those who live and work in one of the 25 communities served by the Foundation: Ashland, Bellingham, Dover, Framingham, Franklin, Holliston, Hopedale, Hopkinton, Hudson, Marlborough, Medfield, Medway, Mendon, Milford, Millis, Natick, Needham, Norfolk, Northborough Sherborn, Southborough, Sudbury, Wayland, Wellesley and Westborough. Such support is limited to organizations that qualify as tax-exempt under Section 501(c)3 of the IRS Code, or organizations that are recognized as instrumentalities of state or local government. The Foundation requires applicants to submit concept papers prior to a full proposal. Concept papers help the Foundation assess whether or not the proposed project is aligned with its funding priorities. Only a limited number of proposals will be funded with a maximum grant amount of $25,000; applications may be for one, two or three years in duration, and funds cannot be used to supplant ongoing government operations or support. Applications involving schools must submit a letter signed by the Superintendent indicating support for the request. The Foundation will provide grants to municipalities and nonprofit organizations to implement programs that address youth risk behaviors as reported by the MetroWest Adolescent Health Survey. For this grant round, the focus will only be on: (a) efforts to reduce the rate of marijuana use among adolescents; (b) efforts to reduce the incidence of teenage pregnancy. Preference will be given to interventions that are evidence-based or, if no programs meet this criteria, are research-based or recognized as promising practices. In addition, communities with similar risk behavior data and demographics may consider applying for regional approaches in order to maximize impact, although funding will still be subject to the individual grant maximum.
Restrictions: The Foundation does not provide grants to individuals, nor does it provide funds for endowments, fundraising drives and events, retirement of debt, operating deficits, projects that directly influence legislation, political activities or candidates for public office, or programs that are customarily operated by hospitals in Massachusetts. The Foundation does not award grants to organizations that discriminate in the provision of services on the basis of race, color, religion, gender, age, ethnicity, marital status, disability, sexual orientation or veteran status.
Geographic Focus: Massachusetts
Date(s) Application is Due: Apr 12
Amount of Grant: Up to 25,000 USD
Samples: Pelham Apts. Recreation and Computer Network Center, $4,500 to support teen pregnancy prevention programs.
Contact: Cathy Glover, Grants Managment Director; (508) 879-7625; fax (508) 879-7628; cglover@mwhealth.org or cglover@mchcf.org
Internet: http://www.mwhealth.org/GrantsampScholarships/Overview/tabid/180/Default.aspx
Sponsor: MetroWest Health Foundation
161 Worcester Road, Suite 202
Framingham, MA 01701

Metzger-Price Fund Grants 3137
The Metzger-Price Fund, established in New York in 1970, is an independent foundation trust which offers support to the handicapped, health services, child welfare, social service agencies, recreation, and the elderly. Its primary fields of interest include: services and centers for the aged, child and youth services, community and economic development, education, family support services, health care services and health care access, and human services. The Fund's target groups include the elderly, disabled, economically disadvantaged, homeless, women, and other minorities. Funding is directed toward continuing support, general operations, and program development. There are no specific application forms or deadlines, though the board meets to discuss proposals four times each year (January, April, July, and October). An applicant's initial approach should be in the form of an application letter submitted two months prior to each board meeting.
Requirements: 501(c)3 organizations serving the residents of New York, New York, are encouraged to apply.
Restrictions: No grants to individuals, or for capital campaigns or building funds; no multiple grants in single calendar year to same organization.
Geographic Focus: New York
Amount of Grant: 1,000 - 5,000 USD
Contact: Isaac A. Saufer; (212) 867-9501 or (212) 867-9500; fax (212) 599-1759
Sponsor: Metzger-Price Fund, Inc.
230 Park Avenue, Suite 2300
New York, NY 10169-0005

Meyer and Pepa Gold Family Foundation Grants 3138
Established in 1986 and formerly known as the Gold Family Foundation, the revamped Meyer and Pepa Gold Family Foundation offers grant support in New Jersey and New York. Its primary fields of interest include the arts, health organizations, and medical research agencies. The are no specified application forms required or annual deadlines. Interested parties should begin by contacting the Foundation directly, offering an overview of their program and budgetary needs. Recent grants, which predominately support general operations, range up to $35,000.
Requirements: Any 501(c)3 located in, or serving the residents of, New Jersey and/or New York are eligible to apply.
Restrictions: No grants are offered to individuals.
Geographic Focus: New Jersey, New York
Amount of Grant: Up to 35,000 USD
Contact: Pepa Gold, Trustee; (732) 229-0569 or (732) 660-1770
Sponsor: Meyer and Pepa Gold Family Foundation
P.O. Box 777
Oakhurst, NJ 07755

Meyer and Stephanie Eglin Foundation Grants 3139
The Eglin Foundation supports programs in the Philadelphia area. Fields of interest include: cancer research; higher education; hospitals; Jewish agencies, synagogues, and federated giving programs; museums; music and the performing arts; and United Way programs. Applications are not required, and there are no deadlines. Organizations should submit a letter of intent.
Requirements: Along with the letter of intent, organizations should submit an annual report/audited financial statement/990; a 501(c)3 tax-exempt letter; descriptive literature about their organization; and a detailed description of the project, with amount requested.
Geographic Focus: Pennsylvania
Contact: Stephanie Eglin, President; (215) 496-9381
Sponsor: Meyer and Stephanie Eglin Foundation
Eglin Square Garage
Philadelphia, PA 19102

Meyer Foundation Benevon Grants 3140
Eugene Meyer was an investment banker, public servant under seven U.S. presidents, and owner and publisher of the Washington Post. His wife Agnes Ernst Meyer was an accomplished journalist, author, lecturer, and citizen activist. Eugene and Agnes created the Meyer Foundation in 1944. For more than sixty-five years the Meyer Foundation has identified, listened to, and invested in visionary leaders and effective community-based nonprofit organizations that work to create lasting improvements in the lives of low-income people in the Washington, D.C. metropolitan region. The foundation offers program, operating, and capital support to eligible organizations in four priority program areas: education, healthy communities, economic security, and a strong nonprofit sector. Additionally Meyer has developed a partnership with Benevon, a firm that provides training and coaching to help nonprofits implement its proprietary model for raising money from

individual donors. Meyer will make a limited number of grants each year to current Meyer grantees who are planning to implement the Benevon fundraising model. These grants offset the cost of attending either of Benevon's two-day training programs—$15,000 for Benevon 101 and $22,000 for its follow-up Sustainable Funding Program—plus travel and lodging for a seven-member team. Moreover Meyer will consider up to three years of additional grant support to organizations who demonstrate success with the model so that they may continue to participate in Benevon's Sustainable Funding Program, which provides ongoing training and coaching for five years. The deadlines for submitting Benevon applications occur in January and June; exact dates may vary from year to year. Interested organizations should visit the Meyer website to obtain detailed guidelines, downloadable application forms, and current deadline dates. Applications, along with any required attachments, must be submitted electronically via Meyer's online submission system.

Requirements: 501(c)3 organizations who are current Meyer grantees are eligible to apply. Meyer grantees are usually located within and primarily serve the Washington, D.C. region. The foundation defines the Washington, D.C. region to include the following counties and cities: Washington, D.C; Montgomery and Prince George's counties in Maryland; Arlington, Fairfax, and Prince William counties in Virginia; and the cities of Alexandria, Falls Church, and Manassas Park, Virginia.

Restrictions: Only current Meyer grantees are eligible for Benevon grants. Eligibility extends for two years from the date of an organization's last Meyer grant awarded through the foundation's regular grant-making program.

Geographic Focus: District of Columbia, Maryland, Virginia
Date(s) Application is Due: Jan 10; Jun 6
Amount of Grant: 15,000 - 22,000 USD
Contact: Maegan Scott; (202) 534-1860; mscott@meyerfdn.org
Internet: http://www.meyerfoundation.org/our-programs/Benevon
Sponsor: Meyer Foundation
1250 Connecticut Avenue, Northwest, Suite 800
Washington, DC 20036

Meyer Foundation Economic Security Grants   3141

Eugene Meyer was an investment banker, public servant under seven U.S. presidents, and owner and publisher of the Washington Post. His wife Agnes Ernst Meyer was an accomplished journalist, author, lecturer, and citizen activist. Eugene and Agnes created the Meyer Foundation in 1944. For more than sixty-five years the Meyer Foundation has identified, listened to, and invested in visionary leaders and effective community-based nonprofit organizations that work to create lasting improvements in the lives of low-income people in the Washington, D.C. metropolitan region. The foundation offers program, operating, and capital support in four priority program areas: education, healthy communities, economic security, and a strong nonprofit sector. In the area of economic security, the foundation funds organizations that help low-income adults and families to stabilize their lives, build assets, and achieve financial independence. Examples of types of organizations funded are as follows: comprehensive, multi-service, anti-poverty organizations with the capacity to expand their services; legal-service providers that provide both direct legal services and advocacy; and advocacy organizations and coalitions. Specifically the foundation funds the following types of programming; facilitating access to workforce development; facilitating access to legal services and advocacy in matters of legal status, housing, work supports and public benefits, and employment crises; and facilitating access to money-management education and financial literacy. Letters of Intent (LOIs) may be submitted through the foundation's online application system twice a year, in January and June; exact deadline dates may vary from year to year. Applicants will receive an email confirming receipt of their LOI within two to three weeks of submission and will be notified two months after the LOI deadline whether or not they will be invited to submit a full proposal for the board meetings in April and October. Prospective applicants should visit the foundation's website for detailed funding guidelines and current deadline dates before submitting an LOI.

Requirements: Eligible applicants must be 501(c)3 organizations that are located within and primarily serve the Washington, D.C. region defined by the foundation to include the following geographic areas: Washington, D.C; Montgomery and Prince George's counties in Maryland; Arlington, Fairfax, and Prince William counties in Virginia; and the cities of Alexandria, Falls Church, and Manassas Park, Virginia. The foundation looks for organizations that demonstrate visionary and talented leadership, effectiveness, sustainability, and long-term impact.

Restrictions: The foundation does not fund entrepreneurship, microenterprise, small-business-development projects, government agencies, for-profit businesses, individuals (including scholarships or other forms of emergency financial assistance), scientific or medial research, special events or conferences, or endowments.

Geographic Focus: All States
Contact: Julie Rogers; (202) 483-8294; fax (202) 328-6850; jrogers@meyerfdn.org
Internet: http://www.meyerfoundation.org/our-programs/grantmaking/economic-security
Sponsor: Meyer Foundation
1250 Connecticut Avenue, Northwest, Suite 800
Washington, DC 20036

Meyer Foundation Education Grants   3142

Eugene Meyer was an investment banker, public servant under seven U.S. presidents, and owner and publisher of the Washington Post. His wife Agnes Ernst Meyer was an accomplished journalist, author, lecturer, and citizen activist. Eugene and Agnes created the Meyer Foundation in 1944. For more than sixty-five years the Meyer Foundation has identified, listened to, and invested in visionary leaders and effective community-based nonprofit organizations that work to create lasting improvements in the lives of low-income people in the Washington, D.C. metropolitan region. The foundation offers program, operating, and capital support in four priority program areas: education, healthy communities, economic security, and a strong nonprofit sector. In the area of education, the foundation supports a broad range of work, all designed to ensure that young people graduate from high school, go on to earn post-secondary credentials, and enter the skilled work force. This work includes programming that facilitates the following outcomes: successful transitions for children of low-income families throughout their entire education; multiple pathways for children and youth to enter the skilled work force; and education reform in K-12 public education in the D.C. area. Letters of Intent (LOIs) may be submitted through the foundation's online application system twice a year, in January and June; exact deadline dates may vary from year to year. Applicants will receive an email confirming receipt of their LOI within two to three weeks of submission and will be notified two months after the LOI deadline whether or not they will be invited to submit a full proposal for the board meetings in April and October. Prospective applicants should visit the foundation's website for detailed funding guidelines and current deadline dates before submitting an LOI.

Requirements: Eligible applicants must be 501(c)3 organizations that are located within and primarily serve the Washington, D.C. region defined by the foundation to include the following geographic areas: Washington, D.C; Montgomery and Prince George's counties in Maryland; Arlington, Fairfax, and Prince William counties in Virginia; and the cities of Alexandria, Falls Church, and Manassas Park, Virginia. The foundation looks for organizations that demonstrate visionary and talented leadership, effectiveness, sustainability, and long-term impact.

Restrictions: The foundation does not fund short-term or seasonal programs, individual public or private schools, PTAs, organizations that provide out-of-school programs solely for elementary-school children, government agencies, for-profit businesses, individuals (including scholarships or other forms of financial assistance), scientific or medial research, special events or conferences, or endowments.

Geographic Focus: District of Columbia, Maryland, Virginia
Contact: Julie Rogers; (202) 483-8294; fax (202) 328-6850; jrogers@meyerfdn.org
Internet: http://www.meyerfoundation.org/our-programs/grantmaking/education
Sponsor: Meyer Foundation
1250 Connecticut Avenue, Northwest, Suite 800
Washington, DC 20036

Meyer Foundation Healthy Communities Grants   3143

Eugene Meyer was an investment banker, public servant under seven U.S. presidents, and owner and publisher of the Washington Post. His wife Agnes Ernst Meyer was an accomplished journalist, author, lecturer, and citizen activist. Eugene and Agnes created the Meyer Foundation in 1944. For more than sixty-five years the Meyer Foundation has identified, listened to, and invested in visionary leaders and effective community-based nonprofit organizations that work to create lasting improvements in the lives of low-income people in the Washington, D.C. metropolitan region. The foundation offers program, operating, and capital support in four priority program areas: education, healthy communities, economic security, and a strong nonprofit sector. In the area of health, the foundation funds programming that facilitates the following outcomes for low-income people in the Washington, D.C. metropolitan area: access to high-quality primary care that integrates mental and behavioral health care and eliminates health disparities; access to affordable places to live, healthful food to eat, and services that promote health and personal safety; public policies at the state and local level that are aimed at strengthening the safety net, reducing poverty, and improving lives. The foundation funds clinics, social-service organizations, community-organizing groups, and multi-issue research and advocacy groups and gives priority to issues such as homelessness, child abuse, domestic violence, and rape. In the case of service organizations, the foundations gives priority to those who track participant outcomes with quantitative and qualitative measures. Letters of Intent (LOIs) may be submitted through the foundation's online application system twice a year, in January and June; exact deadline dates may vary from year to year. Applicants will receive an email confirming receipt of their LOI within two to three weeks of submission and will be notified two months after the LOI deadline whether or not they will be invited to submit a full proposal for the board meetings in April and October. Prospective applicants should visit the foundation's website for detailed funding guidelines and current deadline dates before submitting an LOI.

Requirements: Eligible applicants must be 501(c)3 organizations that are located within and primarily serve the Washington, D.C. region defined by the foundation to include the following geographic areas: Washington, D.C; Montgomery and Prince George's counties in Maryland; Arlington, Fairfax, and Prince William counties in Virginia; and the cities of Alexandria, Falls Church, and Manassas Park, Virginia. The foundation looks for organizations that demonstrate visionary and talented leadership, effectiveness, sustainability, and long-term impact.

Restrictions: The foundation does not fund medical or scientific research, organizations or programs focused on a single disease or medical condition, capital for construction or development of housing, start-up housing developers, operating support for housing developers, AIDS-related programs (the foundation supports these exclusively through the Washington AIDS Partnership), government agencies, for-profit businesses, individuals (including scholarships or other forms of financial assistance), special events or conferences, or endowments.

Geographic Focus: All States
Contact: Julie Rogers; (202) 483-8294; fax (202) 328-6850; jrogers@meyerfdn.org
Internet: http://www.meyerfoundation.org/our-programs/grantmaking/healthy-communities
Sponsor: Meyer Foundation
1250 Connecticut Avenue, Northwest, Suite 800
Washington, DC 20036

Meyer Foundation Management Assistance Grants   3144

Eugene Meyer was an investment banker, public servant under seven U.S. presidents, and owner and publisher of the Washington Post. His wife Agnes Ernst Meyer was an accomplished journalist, author, lecturer, and citizen activist. Eugene and Agnes created the Meyer Foundation in 1944. For more than sixty-five years the Meyer Foundation has identified, listened to, and invested in visionary leaders and effective community-

based nonprofit organizations that work to create lasting improvements in the lives of low-income people in the Washington, D.C. metropolitan region. The foundation offers program, operating, and capital support to eligible organizations in four priority program areas: education, healthy communities, economic security, and a strong nonprofit sector. Additionally the foundation has a Management Assistance Program (MAP) available to current grantees only. MAP provides grants of up to $25,000 to help Meyer grantees strengthen their management and leadership so they can serve the community more effectively. Organizations generally use MAP grants to hire consultants to help board and staff accomplish work that requires time, energy, expertise, and innovative thinking beyond everyday operations. Examples of such work include strengthening executive and board leadership, conducting organizational planning and assessment, and improving financial management and sustainability. MAP grants have proven especially beneficial to groups experiencing significant organization transitions such as shifts in funding sources, the departure of a founder, or rapid growth. MAP application deadlines coincide with those of the foundation's regular grant-making cycle; however, for time-sensitive or out-of-cycle requests (e.g. executive transition, mergers, and financial planning), organizations should use the MAP email address to get in touch with the foundation. The foundation's regular grant-making cycles start in January and in June when Letters of Intent (LOIs) are accepted through the foundation's online application system; exact deadline dates may vary from year to year. The foundation reviews MAP LOIs within one month of receiving the request. If the proposed project meets the criteria for funding and if sufficient funds remain in the budget, foundation staff will schedule a site visit or meeting to discuss the project with the applicant's executive director and key board members and staff. On the basis of the site visit, applicants will be invited to submit a full proposal. If the foundation approves the grant, the program officer will notify the executive director, usually within three months after the LOI was submitted. Prospective applicants should visit the foundation's website for detailed funding guidelines and current deadline dates before submitting an LOI.
Requirements: 501(c)3 organizations who are current Meyer grantees are eligible to apply. Meyer grantees are usually located within and primarily serve the Washington, D.C. region. The foundation defines the Washington, D.C. region to include the following counties and cities: Washington, D.C; Montgomery and Prince George's counties in Maryland; Arlington, Fairfax, and Prince William counties in Virginia; and the cities of Alexandria, Falls Church, and Manassas Park, Virginia. Grantees are responsible for paying a percentage of the total cost of their MAP project based on their annual budget; matches are as follows: 5% for an annual budget less than $250,000; 10% for an annual budget of $250,000 to $500,000; 15% for an annual budget of $500,000 to $1 million; 20% for an annual budget of $1 million to $2 million; 25% for an annual budget of $2 million to $3 million; 30% for an annual budget of $3 million to $4 million; 40% for an annual budget of $4 million to $5 million; and 50% for an annual budget of over $5 million.
Restrictions: Only current Meyer grantees are eligible for management assistance. Eligibility extends for two years from the date of an organization's last Meyer grant awarded through the foundation's regular grant-making program.
Geographic Focus: District of Columbia, Maryland, Virginia
Amount of Grant: 5,000 - 25,000 USD
Contact: Jane Robinson Ward, Grants Manager; (202) 483-8294; fax (202) 328-6850; map@meyerfdn.org or jward@meyerfdn.org
Internet: http://www.meyerfoundation.org/our-programs/management-assistance/
Sponsor: Meyer Foundation
1250 Connecticut Avenue, Northwest, Suite 800
Washington, DC 20036

Meyer Foundation Strong Nonprofit Sector Grants 3145

Eugene Meyer was an investment banker, public servant under seven U.S. presidents, and owner and publisher of the Washington Post. His wife Agnes Ernst Meyer was an accomplished journalist, author, lecturer, and citizen activist. Eugene and Agnes created the Meyer Foundation in 1944. For more than sixty-five years the Meyer Foundation has identified, listened to, and invested in visionary leaders and effective community-based nonprofit organizations that work to create lasting improvements in the lives of low-income people in the Washington, D.C. metropolitan region. The foundation offers program, operating, and capital support in four program areas: education, healthy communities, economic security, and a strong nonprofit sector—this final area is intended to strengthen nonprofits' leadership, impact, and sustainability. Retention and attraction of capable staff and board members, an increased ability by the nonprofit sector to document and communicate the impact of their work, recognition of nonprofits by government and business leaders as essential partners in improving the lives of low-income people in the D.C. metropolitan region, financial stability of nonprofits, and increased levels of philanthropy from individual and institutional donors are among the desired outcomes of the foundation's Strong Nonprofit Sector Grants. The foundation will fund the following types of programs and/or organizations: professional-development programs (provided these are designed with input from nonprofit executives) for executive directors, emerging leaders, and boards; efforts to increase individual philanthropy in the region and to help nonprofits become more effective at attracting contributions and other types of support; nationally significant research that highlights the unique challenges and needs of nonprofit executive directors and explores how to create stronger support systems for them; programs to build a nonprofit's communications capacity to better demonstrate their impact; region-wide organizations that strengthen the voice and visibility of the nonprofit sector and enable it to serve in broader community leadership roles; and organizations that encourage grant-makers to work together more effectively to be more responsive to needs of grantees and to serve as champions of the region's nonprofit sector. Letters of Intent (LOIs) may be submitted through the foundation's online application system twice a year, in January and June; exact deadline dates may vary from year to year. Applicants will receive an email confirming receipt of their LOI within two to three weeks of submission and will be notified two months after the LOI deadline whether or not they will be invited to submit a full proposal for the board meetings in April and October. Prospective applicants should visit the foundation's website for detailed funding guidelines and current deadline dates before submitting an LOI. The foundation also addresses the desired outcomes for the Strong Nonprofit Sector program area through its Management Assistance Program (MAP), Benevon grants, and the Exponent Award. Participation in these programs is limited to current grantees.
Requirements: Eligible applicants must be 501(c)3 organizations that are located within and primarily serve the Washington, D.C. region defined by the foundation to include the following geographic areas: Washington, D.C; Montgomery and Prince George's counties in Maryland; Arlington, Fairfax, and Prince William counties in Virginia; and the cities of Alexandria, Falls Church, and Manassas Park, Virginia. The foundation looks for organizations that demonstrate visionary and talented leadership, effectiveness, sustainability, and long-term impact.
Restrictions: The foundation does not fund the following types of requests and/or organizations: organizations which provide technology support, hardware, or software for nonprofits; volunteer centers; capacity-building initiatives and organizations that are not region-wide or that serve a small number or a sub-sector of nonprofits (with the exception of initiatives to strengthen the nonprofit sector in Prince George's County, Maryland); government agencies, for-profit businesses, individuals (including scholarships or other forms of financial assistance), scientific or medial research, special events or conferences, or endowments.
Geographic Focus: All States
Amount of Grant: 1,500 - 50,000 USD
Contact: Julie Rogers; (202) 483-8294; fax (202) 328-6850; jrogers@meyerfdn.org
Internet: http://www.meyerfoundation.org/our-programs/grantmaking/strong-nonprofit-sector
Sponsor: Meyer Foundation
1250 Connecticut Avenue, Northwest, Suite 800
Washington, DC 20036

Meyer Memorial Trust Emergency Grants 3146

Emergency Grants are intended for sudden, unanticipated and unavoidable challenges that, if not addressed immediately, could threaten an organization's stability and/or ability to achieve its mission. Examples of emergencies would include: natural disaster; theft or damage to equipment required to operate core programs; or an accident or unexpected occurrence that causes facilities to be inaccessible or programs unable to be operated until the situation is resolved. Emergency proposals can be considered at any program meeting. The application and frequently asked questions are available at the Trust's website.
Requirements: Grants are awarded to 501(c)3 nonprofit organizations in Oregon and Clark County, Washington.
Restrictions: Processing grant requests may take up to 45 days. MMT's Emergency Grants are not intended to address an organization's failure to comply with legal requirements or problems that can be attributed to organizational neglect; failure to plan for likely contingencies, such as the breakdown of aging equipment; or to replace a gradual loss of organizational funding. In addition, the Emergency Grant program cannot be used solely to expedite the standard processing time for a Responsive or Grassroots Grants application.
Geographic Focus: Oregon, Washington
Amount of Grant: 7,500 - 100,000 USD
Contact: Maddelyn High, Grants Administrator; (503) 228-5512; maddelyn@mmt.org
Internet: http://www.mmt.org/program/emergency-grants
Sponsor: Meyer Memorial Trust
425 NW 10th Avenue, Suite 400
Portland, OR 97209

Meyer Memorial Trust Grassroots Grants 3147

The Grassroots Grants program is designed to give smaller organizations (often without development departments) an opportunity to compete for grants from MMT. Focus areas include: health and human services; arts and culture; environmental conservation; education; and public affairs. Applications may be submitted at any time but proposals are collected for consideration on the 15th of March, July and October. Grants of $1,000 to $40,000 are made three to four months later: in June, October and February. Grant periods may be one to two years in length. A list of previous funded projects is available at the Trust's website.
Requirements: Grants are awarded to 501(c)3 nonprofits in Oregon and Clark County, Washington. Organizations must apply through the Trust's online application process.
Geographic Focus: Oregon, Washington
Date(s) Application is Due: Mar 15; Jul 15; Oct 15
Contact: Maddelyn High, Grants Administrator; (503) 228-5512; maddelyn@mmt.org
Internet: http://www.mmt.org/program/grassroots-grants
Sponsor: Meyer Memorial Trust
425 NW 10th Avenue, Suite 400
Portland, OR 97209

Meyer Memorial Trust Responsive Grants 3148

Responsive Grants are awarded in the areas of human services; health; affordable housing; community development; conservation and environment; public affairs; arts and culture; and education. Funding ranges from $40,000 to $300,000, with grants periods from one to three years in length. Responsive grants help support many kinds of projects, including core operating support, building and renovating facilities, and strengthening organizations. There are two stages of consideration before Responsive Grants are awarded. Initial Inquiries are accepted at any time through MMT's online grants application. Applicants that pass initial approval are invited to submit full proposals. The full two-step proposal investigation usually takes five to seven months. Final decisions on Responsive Grants are made by trustees monthly, except in January, April and August. Additional information about the application process, along with the online application, is available at the website.
Requirements: Support is available to 501(c)3 nonprofit organizations in Oregon and Clark County, Washington.

Restrictions: Funding is not available for sectarian or religious organizations for religious purposes, or for animal welfare organizations, or projects that primarily benefit students of a single K-12 school (unless the school is an independent alternative school primarily serving low-income and/or special needs populations). Funding is also not available for individuals or for endowment funds, annual campaigns, general fund drives, special events, sponsorships, direct replacement funding for activities previously supported by federal, state, or local public sources, deficit financing, acquisition of land for conservation purposes (except through Program Related Investments), or hospital capital construction projects (except through Program Related Investments).
Geographic Focus: Oregon, Washington
Amount of Grant: 40,000 - 300,000 USD
Contact: Maddelyn High, Grants Administrator; (503) 228-5512; maddelyn@mmt.org
Internet: http://www.mmt.org/program/responsive-grants
Sponsor: Meyer Memorial Trust
425 NW 10th Avenue, Suite 400
Portland, OR 97209

Meyer Memorial Trust Special Grants 3149

From time to time, Meyer Memorial Trust issues Requests for Proposals (RFPs) in targeted, short-term programs that address immediate pressing needs in the nonprofit community. Nonprofits may subscribe to their email announcements to be notified when RFPs are issued. A list of previously funded projects is posted on the Trust's website.
Requirements: Grants are awarded to 501(c)3 nonprofits in Oregon and Clark County, Washington.
Geographic Focus: Oregon, Washington
Amount of Grant: Up to 50,000 USD
Contact: Maddelyn High, Grants Administrator; (503) 228-5512; maddelyn@mmt.org
Internet: http://www.mmt.org/program/rfp
Sponsor: Meyer Memorial Trust
425 NW 10th Avenue, Suite 400
Portland, OR 97209

MFRI Operation Diploma Grants for Higher Education Institutions 3150

The purpose of this grant program is to enable Indiana higher education institutions to take early steps to improve supports for student service members and veterans. During the first round of funding, grants of up to $15,000 will be awarded; successful applicants in round one will be given special consideration for round two grants of up to $100,000. During the third and final year of funding, grants of up to $50,000 will be available. The goal is to create partnerships and assist institutions in providing quality education to our nation's service members in Indiana.
Requirements: Any institution of higher education located in Indiana that is eligible to receive veterans educational benefits may apply for a grant through Operation Diploma. Only one proposal from any institution will be considered. For the purposes of this program, branch campuses will be considered as individual institutions. Requests for funds will be evaluated according to the following criteria: a. Evidence of need; b. Quality and creativity of plan; c. Likelihood of success.
Geographic Focus: Indiana
Date(s) Application is Due: May 22
Contact: Martina Sternberg, Interim Director; (765) 496-3469; msternbe@purdue.edu
Internet: http://www.mfri.purdue.edu/content.asp?tid=4&id=39
Sponsor: Military Family Research Institute at Purdue University
Purdue West Down Under, 1402 W State Street
West Lafayette, IN 47907-2062

MFRI Operation Diploma Grants for Student Veterans Organizations 3151

One of the primary missions of the Operation Diploma initiative offered by the Military Family Research Institute (MFRI) at Purdue University is to help student veterans organizations (SVOs) in Indiana achieve organizational success, create awareness of SVOs, and increase engagement with academic departments and local communities. The program offers small grants of up to $2,000 to support the creation and sustainability of SVOs through innovative programming and organizational development. These grants will be awarded each semester.
Requirements: Student veterans organizations at higher education institutions in Indiana are eligible to apply. Preference will be given to proposals that demonstrate the development of a student veterans group, increased awareness of student veterans, creation and growth of community partnerships, or to those proposals which are designed to create increased community awareness of the needs of student veterans. Grant applications will need a signature of approval from the student organizations administrator on your campus. The following is a list of several types of projects that the program would consider funding: Organization call-outs designed to attract new members as well as materials and supplies for call-outs; Travel expenses for guest speakers attending SVO meetings; Website maintenance, postage and other communication expenses associated with serving SVO needs; Events on campus that increase awareness of student veterans and their unique needs or issues; Awareness projects focused on the academic community, including workshops, debates, movies, academic speaking series focusing on veterans adjusting to academic life, etc; Orientation and mentoring programs, such as matching upperclassman student veterans and/or prior service faculty with incoming student veteran freshmen to help acclimate to academic life; Organize job fairs to help student veterans translate military experience into civilian career fields, develop a plan of action, and make connections in the professional community; Events to engage student veterans with the community, including charitable fund raising, partnership development with local veteran organizations, and cultivation of community volunteers.
Restrictions: No grant funds can be used for the purchase or consumption of alcoholic beverages, or any other item that is prohibited by your university.
Geographic Focus: Indiana
Amount of Grant: Up to 2,000 USD
Contact: Ryan Carlson, (765) 494-9848; rdcarlso@purdue.edu
Internet: http://www.mfri.purdue.edu/content.asp?tid=4&id=40
Sponsor: Military Family Research Institute at Purdue University
Purdue West Down Under, 1402 W State Street
West Lafayette, IN 47907-2062

MFRI Operation Diploma Small Grants for Indiana Family Readiness Groups 3152

MFRI is offering small monetary grants of up to $2,500 to support Indiana Family Readiness Groups (FRGs). The MFRI Small Grant Program was designed to assist FRGs to do their work more effectively and to strengthen community partnerships that support military families. The goal is to fund projects that will have a lasting impact, and not just fund purely social events, such as homecoming celebrations and holiday parties. Family communication events should include interaction between age groups during activities.
Requirements: This program is open only to Family Readiness Groups in the state of Indiana. Preference will be given to proposals that demonstrate the development and growth of community partnerships, or to proposals which are designed to create increased community awareness of the needs of military families. The grants may be used to award funds to community partners to assist the FRG. For example, if the local library would be willing to create a collection of books aimed at helping military families, the FRG leader and the library could prepare a joint proposal. Examples of potential projects funded by the MFRI Small Grants Program include: Travel expenses for guest speakers attending FRG meetings; Materials and supplies needed for FRG meetings; Childcare and youth engagement activities provided by community partners during FRG meetings (examples include partnering with the YMCA to provide open gym and swimming opportunities, or working with a child care center to provide care during meetings); Postage and other communication expenses associated with serving the needs of family members located in areas outside the immediate vicinity of the FRG; Supplies and materials used for youth projects, such as art projects to mail to deployed parents.
Restrictions: No grant funds can be used for the purchase or consumption of alcoholic beverages. Purdue policy does not allow the use of university funds to purchase gift cards (gas cards, visa or MC gift cards, etc) though gift certificates are an allowable use. Also, no grant funds will be issued to an individual; all checks will be made out to organizations.
Geographic Focus: Indiana
Date(s) Application is Due: Nov 17
Amount of Grant: Up to 2,500 USD
Contact: Joyce (Jo) Vaughan, Outreach Specialist; (765) 496-3403; jivaugha@purdue.edu
Internet: http://www.mfri.purdue.edu/content.asp?tid=3&id=10
Sponsor: Military Family Research Institute at Purdue University
Purdue West Down Under, 1402 W State Street
West Lafayette, IN 47907-2062

MGM Resorts Foundation Community Grants 3153

The MGM Resorts Foundation invites proposals from nonprofit agencies providing direct services to people living in its communities. All of the funds allocated through the Foundation come from employee contributions and their desire to make a difference in the communities where they live and work. Foundation grant allocations are 100% employee-driven. The Foundation empowers MGM Resorts employees to choose to make direct contributions to the agency of their choice, or to contribute to the Community Grant Funds, which provides grants to nonprofits through an annual Request for Proposal (RFP) process. MGM Resorts Foundation grants are for a one-year period and do not automatically renew. Continued or expanded projects and programs (your organization is currently providing these services) can request a per year maximum grant of $65,000 in Southern Nevada; $10,000 in Northern Nevada, Mississippi and the Detroit, Michigan area. New projects and programs (your organization is not currently providing these services) can request a per year maximum grant of $35,000 in Southern Nevada; $5,000 in Northern Nevada, Mississippi and the Detroit, Michigan area.
Requirements: To receive a grant from the Foundation, your agency must meet the following *Requirements:* Operate as an IRS 501(c)3 organization and have been doing so for a minimum of 36 months; provide service within the regions MGM Resorts employees live, work and care for their families (Nevada, Mississippi, and the greater Detroit, Michigan area); your organization's administrative costs must be 25% or under; provide a human service; and, meet the MGM Resorts diversity policy: open to all people, without regard to race, color, creed, sex, sexual orientation, religion, disability, or national origin. Agencies must request funding for projects/programs that provide services in the following focus areas: Strengthening Neighborhoods (self-sufficiency, revitalization of communities); Strengthening Children (early childhood development, success in school, prevention / intervention); and, Strength in Difficult Times (recovery and counseling services). Proposals must be received by the Foundation by 5:00 pm of the deadline date.
Restrictions: The program does not support the following types of organizations or activities: projects/programs that are exclusively for medical research; public schools or privately funded / tuition-based schools; governmental entities; religious organizations that do not have 501(c)3 status; pass-through agencies (organizations whose staff does not provide direct client services but who allocate funding to subsequent organizations to provide projects/programs and services); sponsorship of special events and/or fundraising activities; capital campaigns or endowment funds; political issues, such as, election campaigns, issue endorsements, bill drafts or legislation reform; organizations that require clients to embrace specific beliefs or traditions; projects/programs that are exclusively recreational or athletic sponsorships; membership-based organizations without a sliding fee scale and scholarship system already in place.
Geographic Focus: Michigan, Mississippi, Nevada
Date(s) Application is Due: May 2

Amount of Grant: 5,000 - 65,000 USD
Contact: Shelley Gitomer, Vice President of Philanthropy & Community Engagement; (702) 692-9643; foundation@mgmresorts.com
Internet: http://www.mgmmirage.com/csr/community/foundation.aspx
Sponsor: MGM Resorts Foundation
3260 Industrial Road
Las Vegas, NV 89109

MGN Family Foundation Grants 3154
The MGN Family Foundation makes grants to qualified 501(c)3 organizations specializing in the following areas: education; health care and medical research; children in need; armed service personnel. Areas of particular interest include: colleges, universities and private schools, examples would be: to fund a chair to provide lecturers in literature, philosophy or the arts, and provide scholarships; hospitals and clinics that specialize in excellent patient care and continuing medical research such as Memorial Sloan-Kettering Cancer Center and the Mayo and Cleveland Clinics are other examples, also under consideration would be hospice organizations that provide palliative care to the dying; organizations that support children in need whether due to emotional, physical abuse, neglect or disadvantaged circumstances. Support can be for basic necessities such as food, shelter, education, medical as well as, spiritual and emotional counseling; in light of recent events, this Foundation would like to offer assistance to our servicemen/ servicewomen and their families through those charities which give support to their unique needs. The examples provided above reflect the true mission and goals of the MGN Foundation. There should be no exclusions due to race or creed, provided all applicants have a strong moral base and core values in the areas of education, health care, welfare of children and service personnel and their families. The Foundation Board meets semi-annually in May and November. Applications are due by April 1st and October 1st. Application form is available online.
Requirements: Qualified 501(c)3 organizations specializing in the following areas: education; health care and medical research; children in need; armed service personnel. To apply, submit seven (7) sets of the following items: Grant application form completed, dated, and signed by the Chief Executive Officer or Chairman of the Board of the organization; list of Board of Directors; Financial Statement (audited if available), for the most recent complete fiscal year; copy of IRS 501(c)3 Determination Letter. If you wish, you may submit your proposal in a narrative format of not more than two pages in addition to the completed application form. Optional materials may be submitted but are not required (such as brochures discussing or depicting the activities of the organization).
Restrictions: Do not staple materials or place them in a bound notebook.
Geographic Focus: All States
Date(s) Application is Due: Apr 1; Oct 1
Amount of Grant: 1,000 - 10,000 USD
Contact: Pamela Nothstein; (843) 937-4614; grantinquiries7@wachovia.com
Internet: https://www.wachovia.com/foundation/v/index.jsp?vgnextoid=61078689fb0aa110VgnVCM1000004b0d1872RCRD&vgnextfmt=default
Sponsor: MGN Family Foundation
16 Broad Street (SC1000)
Charleston, SC 29401

Miami County Community Foundation - Boomerang Sisterhood Grant 3155
The Boomerang Sisterhood, a granting project facilitated by Miami County Community Foundation, is a giving circle of Miami County women who pool their resources to support organizations and programs in Miami County, Indiana. The mission of the Boomerang Sisterhood is to inspire Miami County women to reach their full potential to create a better society. The Boomerang Sisters fulfill this mission through an annual contribution of $120 to the Boomerang Sisterhood Fund with the Community Foundation. Half of those funds are distributed each year through grants. The remainder helps build the fund for future grant cycles. All paid members have the opportunity to vote annually on which projects receive funding.
Requirements: Grant projects must be charitable in nature, but organizations are not required to have 501(c)3 status. Applications are available at the Community Resource Center at 13 East Main Street, Peru, Indiana or at the foundations website.
Geographic Focus: Indiana
Date(s) Application is Due: Apr 3
Contact: Mary Alexander; (765) 475-2859 or (877) 432-6423; miami@nicf.org
Internet: http://www.nicf.org/miami/grants.html
Sponsor: Miami County Community Foundation
13 East Main Street
Rochester, IN 46975

Miami County Community Foundation - Operation Round Up Grants 3156
Miami County Community Foundation - Operation Round Up is a national program that allows participating electric cooperatives to partner with their members to provide charitable giving funds in their local community. Each month the total amount of the participating member's bill is rounded up to the nearest dollar and those extra pennies go into the fund designated for distribution to those in need in the area. Areas of consideration include: cultural, education, recreation, human services, health and medical, community development, and environmental awareness. Grant proposals are reviewed by the following criteria: is there an established need; what is the project solving; is it appropriate for the county; are their adequate resources; its benefit and timing to the community; what are the expected results; and will the organization work with other organizations to achieve their goals.
Requirements: Along with the application, organizations must include a one page budget for the amount requested, with justification; proof of 501(s)3 status; their most recent audited financial statement or annual report; and current organizational budget. A total of nine complete sets of applications and documentation must be submitted. Applications are available at the Foundation website and should be mailed to Miami-Cass REMC, Operation Round Up, 3086 West 100 North, P.O. Box 168, Peru, IN 46970.
Restrictions: Operation Round Up funds will not be used for paying utility bills, or funding political or private interests.
Geographic Focus: Indiana
Date(s) Application is Due: Mar 31; Jun 30; Sep 30; Dec 31
Contact: Mary Alexander, Director of Development; (765) 475-2859 or (877) 432-6423; fax (765) 472-7378; miami@nicf.org
Internet: http://www.nicf.org/miami/grantapplications.html
Sponsor: Miami County Community Foundation
13 East Main Street
Peru, IN 46970

Miami County Community Foundation Grants 3157
The Miami County Community Foundation Grants allow the Foundation to assess the greatest needs of Miami County and assist the community's individual programs.
Requirements: Contact the Miami County Community Foundation for additional information and grant applications.
Geographic Focus: Indiana
Samples: Grissom Air Museum, handicap accessible trail, $5,000; Nickel Plate Trail Rest Areas, $2,000; Miami County Helping Hands - Impact Grant $4,000.
Contact: Mary Alexander, Associate Director; (765) 475-2859 or (877) 432-6423; fax (765) 472-7378; miami@nicf.org
Internet: http://www.nicf.org/miami/grants.html
Sponsor: Miami County Community Foundation
13 East Main Street
Peru, IN 46970

Michael and Susan Dell Foundation Grants 3158
The Michael and Susan Dell Foundation's primary goal is to support and initiate programs that directly serve the needs of children living in urban poverty. The Foundation focuses on education, health, and family economic stability to help ensure that underprivileged children escape poverty to become healthy, productive adults. Priority is given to initiatives addressing children's health, education and microfinance, as well as initiatives in India and Central Texas that specifically address the needs of children. Grant amounts vary, but generally the Foundation does not fund more than 25% of a project's budget or more than 10% of an organization's total annual operating expenses.
Requirements: Before beginning a formal grant application, organizations must meet basic eligibility requirements for funding, then submit an online grant proposal via the Foundation website. The proposal will be reviewed, then the organization will receive an emailed response to the proposal within six weeks. Organizations are encouraged to review the Foundation's priorities before beginning the proposal. They are also encouraged to review the master grant list page for more in-depth explanations, including specific instructions for the online grant proposal.
Restrictions: Proposals must be submitted through the Foundation's online form. Proposals by mail are not accepted. In general, the Foundation does not support programs or organizations that fall outside of their key focus areas, nor does it accept proposals to support individuals, medical research projects, event fundraisers or sponsorships, endowments, or lobbying of any kind.
Geographic Focus: Texas, India, South Africa
Contact: Janet Mountain; (512) 732-2765; fax (512) 600-5501; info@msdf.org
Internet: http://www.msdf.org/grants/Grant_Application
Sponsor: Michael and Susan Dell Foundation
P.O. Box 163867
Austin, TX 78716-3867

Michael Reese Health Trust Core Grants 3159
The primary focus of the Michael Reese Health Trust is to improve the health status and well-being of vulnerable populations in the Chicago metropolitan area. The Health Trust is committed to supporting community-based health-related services and education that are effective, accessible, affordable, and culturally competent. It is especially interested in efforts to address the barriers that prevent vulnerable groups from accessing quality health care, and in programs that deliver comprehensive, coordinated services. Each year, the Health Trust awards a small number of Core grants. Core grants are larger, multi-year grants designed to strengthen both program quality and organizational capacity. Organizations approved by Health Trust staff may request up to $100,000 a year for each of three years for a total of up to $300,000.
Requirements: Nonprofit organizations operating in the Chicago metropolitan area are eligible to apply, but preference is given to organizations within the City of Chicago. The applicant must have a 501(c)3 and non-private foundation determination letter from the Internal Revenue Service and be designated as a public charity under section 509(a)1 or 509(a)2, of the Internal Revenue Code. Generally, the Health Trust does not provide grants to 509(a)3 "supporting organizations." Organizations must be non-discriminatory in the hiring of staff and in providing services on the basis of race, religion, gender, sexual orientation, age, national origin or disability. Qualified applicants must have prior approval from Health Trust staff to submit a Core grant request. Contact the Program Officer by phone or by email to discuss how your organization would use a Core grant. Once staff approval has been obtained, the sponsor will send an invitation to submit a Letter of Inquiry for a Core grant through its online application process. The Health Trust awards grants twice a year. The submission deadlines for Letters of Inquiry are June 15 (for grants to run January 1 through December 31) and December 15 (for grants to run July 1 through June 30). If the due date falls on a weekend, they will accept submissions until 5:00pm the following business day. Core grants should focus on the following: quality of services; planning for and

supporting staff, volunteers and activities fundamental to the organization's health-related mission; mission-related infrastructure needs; and/or sustainability of the agency and its health services. Use of evidence-based practices or using the Core grant to systematically learn about and implement evidence-based practices is encouraged. Participation in this program requires a willingness to share findings and lessons learned in order to assist other Health Trust grantees and others in the field.
Restrictions: Grants do not support: lobbying, propaganda, or other attempts to influence legislation; sectarian purposes (programs that promote or require a religious doctrine); capital needs, such as buildings, renovations, vehicles, and major equipment; durable medical equipment; fundraising events, including sponsorship, tickets, and advertising; or, debt reduction; individual and scholarship support. In general, the Health Trust does not provide endowment support.
Geographic Focus: Illinois
Date(s) Application is Due: Jun 15; Dec 15
Contact: Jennifer M. Rosenkranz, (312) 726-1008; jrosenkranz@healthtrust.net
Internet: http://www.healthtrust.net/content/how-apply/new-applicants/application-procedures
Sponsor: Michael Reese Health Trust
150 North Wacker Drive, Suite 2320
Chicago, IL 60606

Michael Reese Health Trust Responsive Grants 3160
The primary focus of the Michael Reese Health Trust is to improve the health status and well-being of vulnerable populations in the Chicago metropolitan area. The Health Trust is committed to supporting community-based health-related services and education that are effective, accessible, affordable, and culturally competent. It is especially interested in efforts to address the barriers that prevent vulnerable groups from accessing quality health care, and in programs that deliver comprehensive, coordinated services. Responsive grants generally range from $25,000-$60,000. The Health Trust will entertain requests for program support and general operating and for both one-year and multi-year projects. However, multi-year grants are generally considered for organizations that have received significant prior Health Trust support. Requests may be for continuation or expansion of a current program, or a new program.
Requirements: Nonprofit organizations operating in the Chicago metropolitan area are eligible to apply, but preference is given to organizations within the City of Chicago. The applicant must have a 501(c)3 and non-private foundation determination letter from the Internal Revenue Service and be designated as a public charity under section 509(a)1 or 509(a)2, of the Internal Revenue Code. Generally, the Health Trust does not provide grants to 509(a)3 "supporting organizations." Organizations must be non-discriminatory in the hiring of staff and in providing services on the basis of race, religion, gender, sexual orientation, age, national origin or disability. The Health Trust awards grants twice a year. The submission deadlines for Letters of Inquiry are June 15 (for grants to run January 1 through December 31) and December 15 (for grants to run July 1 through June 30). If the due date falls on a weekend, they will accept submissions until 5:00pm the following business day.
Restrictions: Grants do not support: lobbying, propaganda, or other attempts to influence legislation; sectarian purposes (programs that promote or require a religious doctrine); capital needs, such as buildings, renovations, vehicles, and major equipment; durable medical equipment; fundraising events, including sponsorship, tickets, and advertising; or, debt reduction; individual and scholarship support. In general, the Health Trust does not provide endowment support.
Geographic Focus: Illinois
Date(s) Application is Due: Jun 15; Dec 15
Contact: Jennifer M. Rosenkranz, Senior Program Officer for Responsive Grants; (312) 726-1008; fax (312) 726-2797; jrosenkranz@healthtrust.net
Internet: http://www.healthtrust.net/content/how-apply/new-applicants/grantmaking-guidelines
Sponsor: Michael Reese Health Trust
150 North Wacker Drive, Suite 2320
Chicago, IL 60606

Micron Technology Foundation Community Grants 3161
The Micron Foundation funds educational and community grants in specific program areas in communities where Micron has manufacturing facilities. These sites are: Boise, Idaho; Manassas, Virginia; Singapore; Avezzano, Italy; and Nishiwaki, Japan. The Foundation's goals are to fund high-impact programs that drive advancements in education, with emphasis on science, math and engineering. Specifically, the Foundation seeks to: provide opportunities for hands-on experiences; improve teacher content knowledge; support extra-curricular science and math opportunities; provide advanced learning opportunities with advanced placement classes; and fund charitable programs that address the priorities and concerns of Micron communities.
Requirements: Applicants must be 501(c)3 organizations or a publicly funded academic group in an area where Micron has a presence. Applications can be downloaded at the website but must be submitted by mail.
Restrictions: Funding is not provided for: general operating costs; individuals; religious, fraternal, veteran or political organizations; luncheons, dinners, auctions, or events; travel and related expenses; courtesy advertisement; endowment campaigns; organizations which promote or practice discrimination; organizations outside of Micron communities; Annual Fund drives; "pass-through" organizations or private foundations; or projects seeking to influence elections or legislation.
Geographic Focus: Idaho, Virginia, Italy, Japan, Singapore
Contact: Kami Faylor, Program Contact; (208) 363-3675; mtf@micron.com
Internet: http://www.micron.com/about/giving/foundation/comgrants.html
Sponsor: Micron Technology Foundation
8000 South Federal Way, P.O. Box 6
Boise, ID 83707-0006

Microsoft Authorized Refurbisher (MAR) Donation Program 3162
The Community Microsoft Authorized Refurbisher (MAR) program provides Microsoft operating system software to PC refurbishers in numerous countries throughout the world. MAR works with U.S. based nonprofit computer refurbishers that recycle donated computers for nonprofits and K-12 schools. Microsoft donates media, certificates of authenticity, and end-user license agreements through the MAR program. The Community MAR program authorizes eligible refurbishers to install the Windows operating system on refurbished computers for eligible recipients: Windows 2000 is available for all computers through the program; and Windows XP is available for computers that were previously installed with Windows XP.
Geographic Focus: All States
Contact: Bruce Brooks, Director of Community Affairs; (425) 936-8185; fax (425) 936-7329; upinfo@microsoft.com or giving@microsoft.com
Internet: http://www.mar.partners.extranet.microsoft.com/
Sponsor: Microsoft Corporation
One Microsoft Way
Redmond, WA 98052-6399

Microsoft Community Affairs Puget Sound Grants 3163
Microsoft provides direct grants and matching support to a broad range of nonprofit organizations that address community needs in the Puget Sound region. Organizations with missions and work that align with funding areas - human services, arts and culture, civic affairs, work-force development, and K-12 math education - can apply. Human services focus is on assisting people in need to move toward self sufficiency. Arts and culture funding supports visual, literary, and performing arts, as well as cultural organizations such as science and history museums. Civic affairs funding supports organizations and projects that promote civic engagement, voter registration, and public policy education. Workforce development funding provides technology that will transform education, foster local innovation, and enable jobs. Education funding helps to improve middle school student academic performance and participation in math. Types of support include employee matching grants to health and human service organizations, general operating support, and capital grants. Applications for donations of software to Washington State nonprofits are considered on an ongoing basis. Grant proposals from community organizations are accepted throughout the year; proposals are requested by the listed application deadline to coincide with meeting schedules.
Requirements: The corporation contributes cash and software to 501(c)3 nonprofits in the Puget Sound, WA, area.
Restrictions: Ineligible organizations and projects include: individuals; private enterprises (for profit); private educational institutions; hospitals or medical clinics (though hospitals or medical clinics designated as Community Health Center Programs by the U.S. Department of Health are eligible to apply); private foundations; political, religious, or fraternal organizations; amateur or professional sports groups, teams, or events; conferences or symposia; or endowments.
Geographic Focus: Washington
Date(s) Application is Due: Oct 31
Contact: Bruce Brooks, Director of Community Affairs; (425) 936-8185; fax (425) 936-7329; upinfo@microsoft.com or giving@microsoft.com
Internet: http://www.microsoft.com/About/CorporateCitizenship/Citizenship/giving/programs/grants.mspx
Sponsor: Microsoft Corporation
One Microsoft Way
Redmond, WA 98052-6399

Microsoft Software Donation Grants 3164
Microsoft awards software product donations to a variety of nonprofit organizations in both the Puget Sound area, where its headquarters are located, and around the country. For this program, grants will be awarded to large nonprofit organizations with multiple locations to help enhance communications, boost organizational efficiency, make use of the Internet, and improve services to clients. Applicants may request a limited number of full-packaged products and up to 1000 licenses per product. Donations are demand-driven, based on the requests of individual nonprofits to meet their organizational needs. The process for requesting a software donations depends on the location of your organization.
Requirements: Eligible are 501(c)3 nonprofit organizations. Applicants must have the hardware capable of running the software requested and must have the IT staff or a technology assistance provider, for both the national and field offices, to implement and maintain the software offered with this award.
Restrictions: Applicants may not be hospitals or medical clinics; political, labor, religious, or fraternal organizations; educational institutions, public or private; or government organizations.
Geographic Focus: All States
Contact: Bruce Brooks, Director of Community Affairs; (425) 936-8185; fax (425) 936-7329; upinfo@microsoft.com or giving@microsoft.com
Internet: http://www.microsoft.com/about/corporatecitizenship/citizenship/giving/apply/default.mspx
Sponsor: Microsoft Corporation
One Microsoft Way
Redmond, WA 98052-6399

Microsoft Unlimited Potential Community Technology Skills Program Grants 3165
These grants provide nonprofit organizations with funding to support technology training programs ranging from learning basic computer skills to using advanced business productivity applications. Donations of cash, software, curriculum, and technical expertise enable individuals to learn about technology and gain the information technology skills needed for employment in the IT field or other industry sectors. UP grants are made through Microsoft's U.S. and international subsidiaries, which work closely with local organizations to identify

community technology centers (CTCs) where IT skills training is a primary focus. Microsoft accepts funding proposals from eligible organizations through Microsoft subsidiary offices located around the world. Funding decisions are made in October of each year.
Requirements: The following types of Community-Based Technology and Learning Center (CTLC) organizations are eligible to apply: nonprofit—in the United States, 501(c)3 designation or a nongovernmental organization that holds charitable status in their country; school-based—a nonprofit or governmental organization that provides services to the community outside of school hours, such as evenings and weekends; and government funded and operated—a nonprofit organization that receives government funding or is a partner with a governmental organization to run its programs.
Restrictions: The following entities are not eligible to receive donations of funding or software: individuals; private foundations; nonprofit organizations without a current 501(c)3 exempt status or nongovernmental organizations without equivalent charitable status in their own country; hospitals; conferences or symposia; sponsors of events, tables, exhibitions, or performances; fund-raising events such as luncheons, dinners, walks, runs, or sports tournaments; K-12 schools; political, labor, and fraternal organizations; or religious organizations without a secular community designation.
Geographic Focus: All States
Contact: Bruce Brooks, Director of Community Affairs; (425) 936-8185; fax (425) 936-7329; upinfo@microsoft.com or giving@microsoft.com
Internet: http://www.microsoft.com/about/corporatecitizenship/citizenship/giving/programs/up/grants.mspx
Sponsor: Microsoft Corporation
One Microsoft Way
Redmond, WA 98052-6399

Mid-America Arts Alliance Community Engagement with Touring Artists Grants   3166
The Mid-America Arts Alliance program for Community Engagement with Touring Artists (CETA) supports and promotes high-quality professional performing artists touring throughout the six-state Mid-America region of Arkansas, Kansas, Missouri, Nebraska, Oklahoma, and Texas.. The program is specifically designed to build new audiences and deepen the impact of performing arts touring. Presenters may apply for a single grant of up to $15,000 covering multiple events, where the applicant organization works with touring artists to promote interaction with local community members and to engage new audiences for professional performance. Applications must be submitted online using the Mid-America Arts Alliance eGrant facility no later than 5 p.m. CST, February 1.
Requirements: Applicant organizations must be based in Arkansas, Kansas, Missouri, Nebraska, Oklahoma, or Texas and be either legally incorporated as a not-for-profit organization with IRS 501(c)3 status or operating as a unit of a state, local, or tribal government.
Restrictions: Organizations receiving a CETA grant are not eligible to receive a Mid-America Regional Touring Program (RTP) grant.
Geographic Focus: Arkansas, Kansas, Missouri, Nebraska, Oklahoma, Texas
Date(s) Application is Due: Feb 1
Amount of Grant: Up to 15,000 USD
Contact: Betty Maltbia; (816) 421-1388, ext. 228; fax (816) 421-3918; ibetty@maaa.org
Internet: http://www.maaa.org/SiteResources/Data/Templates/t7.asp?docid=584&DocName=FY2011%20Grantmaking%20Programs
Sponsor: Mid-America Arts Alliance
2018 Baltimore Avenue
Kansas City, MO 64108

Mid-America Arts Alliance Regional Touring Program Grants   3167
The Mid-America Arts Alliance enriches the cultural life of communities in a 6-state region through support of touring performing arts programs. The Regional Touring Program (RTP), formerly known as Touring Artist Fee Subsidy (TAFS), has been refocused exclusively on the talented registry artists of a six-state region: Arkansas, Kansas, Missouri, Nebraska, Oklahoma, and Texas. RTP funds will be awarded to presenters from the Mid-America region to support performances and residency activities involving Mid-America Artists' Registry members from outside their home state or metropolitan area. Awards will be made on a first-come, first-served basis in response to applications received on two deadlines during the year: April 15, for programs occurring between July 1 and December 31; and October 15, for programs occurring between January 1 and June 30.
Requirements: Nonprofit 501(c)3 organizations or units of federal, state, local, or tribal government in Arkansas, Kansas, Missouri, Nebraska, Oklahoma, and Texas are eligible.
Geographic Focus: Arkansas, Kansas, Missouri, Nebraska, Oklahoma, Texas
Date(s) Application is Due: Apr 15; Oct 15
Contact: Betty Maltbia; (816) 421-1388, ext. 228; fax (816) 421-3918; ibetty@maaa.org
Internet: http://www.maaa.org/SiteResources/Data/Templates/t7.asp?docid=584&DocName=FY2011%20Grantmaking%20Programs
Sponsor: Mid-America Arts Alliance
2018 Baltimore Avenue
Kansas City, MO 64108

Mid-Iowa Health Foundation Community Response Grants   3168
Mid-Iowa Health Foundation awards grants to organizations working towards improving the health of people in greater Des Moines, Iowa. The Foundation is interested in work that affects specific health results and aligns with community-identified priorities. The focus for Community Response grants is the Greater Des Moines Health Safety Net System. The health care safety net provides appropriate, timely and affordable health services to people who experience barriers to accessing services from other providers due to financial, cultural, linguistic, or other issues. These core safety net providers offer care to patients in Greater Des Moines, Iowa regardless of their ability to pay for services, and primarily serve vulnerable, low-income patients who are uninsured, publicly insured or underinsured.

Community Response grants average $10,000 to $30,000. The Foundation may consider partially funding a proposal, if acceptable to the grantee.
Requirements: Applicant organizations must: be tax-exempt, 501(c)3 and/or 509(a) status; serve the greater Des Moines, Iowa area (Polk, Warren, and/or Dallas Counties); and, offer health programs and services aligned with the Foundation's mission. The Foundation will consider proposals from core safety net providers for: preventive and primary safety net health services, including behavioral and oral health; critical elements of the safety net system such as coordinated outreach, system navigation, and culturally competent services; meeting increased demands on a safety net system with capacity, financial and workforce stressors. Mid-Iowa Health Foundation reviews Community Response proposals once annually. Proposals are due by noon on October 1; if the 1st falls on a weekend, proposals are due by noon on the preceding Friday.
Restrictions: The Mid-Iowa Health Foundation does not consider proposals for: individuals; scholarships; conference registration fees; programs that promote religious activities; general operations or special camps of disease- or condition-specific organizations; capital campaigns; endowment campaigns; debt reduction; or, fund raising events.
Geographic Focus: Iowa
Date(s) Application is Due: Oct 1
Contact: Denise Swartz; (515) 277-6411; dswartz@midiowahealth.org
Internet: http://www.midiowahealth.org/grants.html
Sponsor: Mid-Iowa Health Foundation
3900 Ingersoll Avenue, Suite 104
Des Moines, IA 50312

Mid Atlantic Arts Foundation American Masterpieces Grants   3169
American Masterpieces is designed to acquaint audiences in the mid-Atlantic region with the best of their cultural and artistic legacy. Tours supported by Mid Atlantic Arts Foundation highlight the work of artists from within the region that celebrate the excellence and rich evolution of the performing arts in the United States. The Foundation offers fee support grants to presenters booking artists selected for the American Masterpieces roster. This roster of artists changes annually based on the tour theme selected in a given year. The Foundation selects artists for the American Masterpieces Tour Roster based on: artistic excellence, as demonstrated by an artist's record of achievement and national critical recognition; compatibility of the artist's work and genre with the American Masterpieces tour theme identified for a given year; and strong artist representation and/or booking representation capable of identifying appropriate venues and maximizing available resources to fully realize the program's goals of broad regional participation and access to high quality performing arts in underserved communities. Presenters in the mid-Atlantic region are eligible to receive fee support grants toward the contracted artist fees. Artist fees may also include hotel and lodging expenses.
Requirements: All artists selected for the American Masterpieces Tour roster must be based in the mid-Atlantic region (Delaware, District of Columbia, Maryland, New Jersey, New York, Pennsylvania, U.S. Virgin Islands, Virginia, and West Virginia). Supported engagements must include at least one complementary activity that builds appreciation for and a greater understanding of the performance or the art form.
Geographic Focus: Delaware, District of Columbia, Maryland, New Jersey, New York, Pennsylvania, U.S. Virgin Islands, Virginia, West Virginia
Date(s) Application is Due: Jul 15
Contact: Krista Bradley, Program Officer, Performing Arts; (410) 539-6656, ext. 110; fax (410) 837-5517; krista@midatlanticarts.org
Internet: http://www.midatlanticarts.org/funding/pat_presentation/american_masterpieces/american_masterpieces.html
Sponsor: Mid Atlantic Arts Foundation
201 North Charles Street, Suite 401
Baltimore, MD 21201

Mid Atlantic Arts Foundation ArtsConnect Grants   3170
The foundation is a regional nonprofit organization operating in the District of Columbia, U.S. Virgin Islands, Delaware, Maryland, New Jersey, New York, Pennsylvania, Virginia, and West Virginia. Mid Atlantic operates a number of grant programs in the performing and visual arts. ArtsCONNECT provides support for projects in which at least three performing arts presenters in two different states work collaboratively to present a single artist or touring company. Through this program the Foundation supports 12-18 tours of performing arts groups per season that reach 50-75 communities in the mid-Atlantic region. The tours include performances as well as activities, such as artist discussions, lecture demonstrations, master classes, and residencies designed to build appreciation for and an understanding of the work of the touring company. The program is also designed to develop and sustain relationships among the presenters who are working together on a specific tour.
Requirements: Only presenter consortia are eligible to apply to ArtsCONNECT. For the purposes of this program, the Foundation defines a presenter as an organization that selects and engages professional touring artists to perform work before audiences in their communities as an ongoing and significant component of their organization's activity. Presenters manage all the local requirements for the performance and facilitate the interaction between artists and audiences.
Restrictions: Producing organizations, which solely create artistic work or assemble artists to perform as ensembles for performances, are not eligible to apply to ArtsCONNECT.
Geographic Focus: Delaware, District of Columbia, Maryland, New Jersey, New York, Pennsylvania, U.S. Virgin Islands, Virginia, West Virginia
Date(s) Application is Due: Mar 21
Contact: Alan W. Cooper; (410) 539-6656; fax (410) 837-5517; alan@midatlanticarts.org
Internet: http://www.midatlanticarts.org/funding/pat_presentation/arts_connect/index.html
Sponsor: Mid Atlantic Arts Foundation
201 North Charles Street, Suite 401
Baltimore, MD 21201

Mid Atlantic Arts Foundation Folk Arts Outreach Project Grants 3171

The Foundation seeks to strengthen the region's folk and traditional arts infrastructure through the exchange of artistic excellence and best practices through the Folk Arts Outreach Project. The program supports projects in which folklorists and local artists travel from their home communities to host sites in other states or jurisdictions within the mid-Atlantic region to share their work with fellow traditional artists, folklorists, and the public. All projects, which typically take place over a three-to-four day period, are developed collaboratively among participating artists and folklorists.
Requirements: Grants are made to 501(c)3 nonprofit organizations in Delaware, District of Columbia, Maryland, New Jersey, New York, Pennsylvania, U.S. Virgin Islands, Virginia, and West Virginia are eligible for travel–related expenses and professional fees of program participants, and must be matched on a 1:1 basis.
Geographic Focus: Delaware, District of Columbia, Maryland, New Jersey, New York, Pennsylvania, U.S. Virgin Islands, Virginia, West Virginia
Date(s) Application is Due: May 6
Contact: Sally Van de Water, Program Associate, Folk and Traditional Arts/ADA Coordinator; (410) 539-6656, ext 107; fax (410) 837-5517; sally@midatlanticarts.org
Internet: http://www.midatlanticarts.org/funding/pat_presentation/folk_art_outreach_project.html
Sponsor: Mid Atlantic Arts Foundation
201 North Charles Street, Suite 401
Baltimore, MD 21201

Middlesex Savings Charitable Foundation Capacity Building Grants 3172

Since June 2000 the Middlesex Savings Charitable Foundation (MSCF) has provided more than $2 million in grants to over 150 non-profit organizations providing critical community services throughout Eastern and Central Massachusetts. Established as a nonprofit, private charitable foundation to further carry out the philanthropic mission of Middlesex Savings Bank, the Foundation aims to fund eligible organizations in the Bank's CRA market area in any economic environment. Middlesex Savings Bank initially provided $2 million on an endowment basis, and continues to add to the endowment annually. As of this writing, the endowment now totals $6.7 million. MSCF's Capacity Building Grants strengthen and increase the impact of local non-profits by improving their organizational capacity. Desired outcomes for non-profits selected to receive grants through this program include one or more of the following characteristics: improved governance and leadership; improved staff skills; improved management systems and practices; completed strategic plans; improved, expanded, or additional services; and expanded strategic assets, including financial and human resources. Successful applicants will be able to describe how their enhanced capacity will ultimately benefit the communities that they serve. Grant requests of up to $15,000 will be considered. Guidelines are available at the grant website. Applicants must apply online.
Requirements: Eastern Massachusetts 501(c)3 tax-exempt organizations serving one or more communities served by Middlesex Savings Bank, including Acton, Ashland, Ayer, Bedford, Bellingham, Berlin, Bolton, Boxborough, Carlisle, Chelmsford, Concord, Dover, Dunstable, Framingham, Franklin, Groton, Harvard, Holliston, Hopedale, Hopkinton, Hudson, Lexington, Lincoln, Littleton, Marlborough, Maynard, Medfield, Medway, Mendon, Milford, Millis, Natick, Needham, Newton, Norfolk, Northborough, Pepperell, Sherborn, Shirley, Southborough, Stow, Sudbury, Townsend, Tyngsborough, Upton, Walpole, Waltham, Wayland, Wellesley, Westborough, Westford, and Weston, are eligible. Projects for which support is requested should benefit people who live or work in the region. Given the continuing economic challenges faced by MSCF communities, the Board will be focusing upon, and giving preference to, grant submissions from organizations providing basic human services such as food and shelter.
Restrictions: The foundation will not fund political or sectarian activities.
Geographic Focus: Massachusetts
Date(s) Application is Due: Mar 1; Aug 1
Amount of Grant: Up to 15,000 USD
Contact: Dana Neshe, (508) 315-5360
Internet: http://www.middlesexbank.com/community/charitablefoundation/default.asp
Sponsor: Middlesex Savings Charitable Foundation
6 Main Street, P.O. Box 358
Natick, MA 01760

Middlesex Savings Charitable Foundation Community Development Grants 3173

Since June 2000 the Middlesex Savings Charitable Foundation (MSCF) has provided more than $2 million in grants to over 150 non-profit organizations providing critical community services throughout Eastern and Central Massachusetts. Established as a nonprofit, private charitable foundation to further carry out the philanthropic mission of Middlesex Savings Bank, the foundation aims to fund eligible organizations in the Bank's CRA market area in any economic environment. Middlesex Savings Bank initially provided $2 million on an endowment basis, and continues to add to the endowment annually. As of this writing, the endowment now totals $6.7 million. MSCF's Community Development Grants support projects and programs that have a primary goal of improving the lives of low- and moderate-income families and individuals throughout the foundation's communities. Given the continuing economic challenges faced by MSCF communities, the foundation will focus upon, and give preference to, grant submissions from organizations providing basic human services such as food and shelter. Grant requests of up to $15,000 will be considered. Guidelines are available at the grant website. Applicants must apply online.
Requirements: Eastern Massachusetts 501(c)3 tax-exempt organizations serving one or more communities served by Middlesex Savings Bank, including Acton, Ashland, Ayer, Bedford, Bellingham, Berlin, Bolton, Boxborough, Carlisle, Chelmsford, Concord, Dover, Dunstable, Framingham, Franklin, Groton, Harvard, Holliston, Hopedale, Hopkinton, Hudson, Lexington, Lincoln, Littleton, Marlborough, Maynard, Medfield, Medway, Mendon, Milford, Millis, Natick, Needham, Newton, Norfolk, Northborough, Pepperell, Sherborn, Shirley, Southborough, Stow, Sudbury, Townsend, Tyngsborough, Upton, Walpole, Waltham, Wayland, Wellesley, Westborough, Westford, and Weston, are eligible. Projects for which support is requested should benefit people who live or work in the region.
Restrictions: The foundation will not fund political or sectarian activities.
Geographic Focus: Massachusetts
Date(s) Application is Due: Mar 1; Aug 1
Amount of Grant: Up to 15,000 USD
Contact: Dana Neshe, President; (508) 315-5360
Internet: http://www.middlesexbank.com/community/charitablefoundation/default.asp
Sponsor: Middlesex Savings Charitable Foundation
6 Main Street, P.O. Box 358
Natick, MA 01760

Middlesex Savings Charitable Foundation Educational Opportunities Grants 3174

Since June 2000 the Middlesex Savings Charitable Foundation (MSCF) has provided more than $2 million in grants to over 150 non-profit organizations providing critical community services throughout Eastern and Central Massachusetts. Established as a nonprofit, private charitable foundation to further carry out the philanthropic mission of Middlesex Savings Bank, the Foundation aims to fund eligible organizations in the Bank's CRA market area in any economic environment. Middlesex Savings Bank initially provided $2 million on an endowment basis, and continues to add to the endowment annually. As of this writing, the endowment now totals $6.7 million. MSCF's Educational Opportunities Grants provide local youth and adults with unique educational opportunities including (but not limited to) job-training and job-readiness programs, adult-education programs, ESL programs, credit-education and home-buying seminars; and youth-enrichment programs. Grant requests of up to $15,000 will be considered. Guidelines are available at the grant website. Applicants must apply online.
Requirements: Eastern Massachusetts 501(c)3 tax-exempt organizations serving one or more communities served by Middlesex Savings Bank, including Acton, Ashland, Ayer, Bedford, Bellingham, Berlin, Bolton, Boxborough, Carlisle, Chelmsford, Concord, Dover, Dunstable, Framingham, Franklin, Groton, Harvard, Holliston, Hopedale, Hopkinton, Hudson, Lexington, Lincoln, Littleton, Marlborough, Maynard, Medfield, Medway, Mendon, Milford, Millis, Natick, Needham, Newton, Norfolk, Northborough, Pepperell, Sherborn, Shirley, Southborough, Stow, Sudbury, Townsend, Tyngsborough, Upton, Walpole, Waltham, Wayland, Wellesley, Westborough, Westford, and Weston, are eligible. Projects for which support is requested should benefit people who live or work in the region.
Restrictions: The foundation will not fund political or sectarian activities.
Geographic Focus: Massachusetts
Date(s) Application is Due: Mar 1; Aug 1
Amount of Grant: Up to 15,000 USD
Contact: Dana Neshe, President; (508) 315-5360; dneshe@middlesexbank.com
Internet: http://www.middlesexbank.com/community/charitablefoundation/default.asp
Sponsor: Middlesex Savings Charitable Foundation
6 Main Street, P.O. Box 358
Natick, MA 01760

Miguel Aleman Foundation Grants 3175

The foundation operates in Mexico in the fields of conservation and the environment, the arts and humanities, economic development, education, international affairs, medicine and health, science and technology, and social welfare. Types of support include research, grants to organizations, and prizes.
Geographic Focus: All States
Contact: Fernando Castro y Castro; 52-5-250-65-76; 103503.1144@compuserve.com
Internet: http://www.miguelaleman.org.mx
Sponsor: Miguel Aleman Foundation
Ruben Dario 187
Col Chapultepec Morales, 11570 Mexico

Mildred V. Horn Foundation Grants 3176

The Foundation, established in 1988, supports organizations Primarily in Kentucky involved with homeless shelters, education and the preservation of historic homes (built between 1760-1860) open to the public in Illinois, Indiana, Kentucky, Missouri, Ohio, Tennessee, Virginia, and West Virginia.
Requirements: Contact the Foundation for further application information and guidelines.
Geographic Focus: Illinois, Indiana, Kentucky, Missouri, Ohio, Tennessee, Virginia, West Virginia
Date(s) Application is Due: Dec 31
Amount of Grant: 1,000 - 150,000 USD
Contact: H. Scott Davis, Treasurer; (502) 895-2622; fax (502) 895-2622
Sponsor: Mildred V. Horn Foundation
South Highway 53, Suite 3, PMB 2028
La Grange, KY 40031-9119

Military Ex-Prisoners of War Foundation Grants 3177

The Military Ex-Prisoners of War Foundation was founded primarily to assist Military Ex-P.O.W Veterans, and to fund their National Educational Scholarship Program for qualified heirs. The mission of the Military Ex-Prisoners of War Foundation is to support educational programs designed to inform Americans about the P.O.W experience; offer scholarships to children and grandchildren of former P.O.Ws and other such activities as may be approved by the Foundation's board of directors.
Requirements: Children, grandchildren, and great-grandchildren of former prisoners-of-war (P.O.Ws) who served after December 7, 1941 are eligible to apply. Applicants must include the following: completed application (available at the Foundations website); short autobiographical statement (not to exceed one typed page); Transcript *Requirements:* copy of

official transcripts of high school grades including SAT/ACT test scores, official transcripts of college grades; two letters of recommendation, one must be from a present/former teacher; short essay, limited to 1,000 words, on the impact of WWII on society today; statement about your grandparent's experience as a prisoner of war, 1,000 words or less. Completed applications should be mailed to: Dorris Livingstone, Recording Secretary, Military Ex-Prisoners of War Foundation, 1561 Glen Hollow Lane South, Dunedin, FL 34698. If you have any questions, email your inquiry to: Dorris2001@aol.com with Foundation Scholarship Application/Question typed into the Subject line.
Restrictions: No support for individuals not related to former prisoners of war, religious, political causes, or for organizations.
Geographic Focus: All States
Date(s) Application is Due: Apr 1
Contact: F. Paul Dallas; (910) 867-2775; fax (910) 867-0339; threatt273@aol.com
Internet: http://www.militarypowfoundation.org/072409-scholarships.html
Sponsor: Military Ex-Prisoners of War Foundation
916 Bingham Drive
Fayetteville, NC 27803

Milken Family Foundation Grants 3178
The purpose of the Milken Family Foundation is to discover and advance inventive and effective ways of helping people help themselves and those around them lead productive and satisfying lives. The Foundation advances this mission primarily through its work in education and medical research. In education, the Foundation is committed to: strengthening the profession by recognizing and rewarding outstanding educators, and by expanding their professional leadership and policy influence attracting, developing, motivating and retaining the best talent to the teaching profession by means of comprehensive, whole school reform; stimulating creativity and productivity among young people and adults through programs that encourage learning as a lifelong process; and building vibrant communities by involving people of all ages in programs that contribute to the revitalization of their community and to the well-being of its residents. In medical research, the Foundation is committed to: advancing and supporting basic and applied medical research, especially in the areas of prostate cancer and epilepsy, and recognizing and rewarding outstanding scientists in these areas; and supporting basic health care programs to assure the well-being of community members of all ages. Applicants may request funding at any time.
Requirements: Grants are made to 501(c)3 tax-exempt organizations. Grant recipients must have the financial potential to sustain the program for which funding is sought following the period of Foundation support. Preventive programs with long-range goals receive the closest consideration. Applicants should submit a brief written statement that includes: description of project, goals, procedure and personnel; brief background of organization, including number of years in operation, other areas of activity, applicant's qualifications for support, annual operating budget, and previous and current sources of funding; and a letter of exemption from the Internal Revenue Service.
Restrictions: Grants are not made directly to individuals.
Geographic Focus: All States
Contact: Richard Sandler; (310) 570-4800; fax (310) 570-4801; admin@mff.org
Internet: http://www.mff.org/about/about.taf?page=funding
Sponsor: Milken Family Foundation
1250 Fourth Street, 6th Floor
Santa Monica, CA 90401-1353

Miller, Canfield, Paddock and Stone, P.L.C. Corporate Giving Program Grants 3179
The Corporation supports the arts and human/social services programs in the Detroit, Michigan, region. Types of funding includes: annual campaigns; building and renovation; capital campaigns; consulting; equipment donations; endowments; and general operating support. Though unsolicited requests are not encouraged, they are accepted. No formal applications are required, and there are no deadlines.
Restrictions: Giving is primarily in areas of company operations, with emphasis on Detroit, Michigan, and its surrounding suburbs.
Geographic Focus: Michigan
Contact: Amanda Van Dusen, (313) 496-7512 or (313) 963-6420; fax (313) 496-8451; vandusen@millercanfield.com
Internet: http://www.millercanfield.com/
Sponsor: Miller, Canfield, Paddock and Stone, P.L.C.
150 W Jefferson Street, Suite 2500
Detroit, MI 48226

Miller Brewing Corporate Contributions Program Grants 3180
The corporate contributions program funds programs of nonprofit organizations in corporate operating communities. Applicants should call the local Miller community affairs manager to discuss an idea before submitting a proposal. The corporation also supports the Thurgood Marshall Scholarship Fund, which provides four-year merit scholarships to students attending the 44 historically black public colleges and universities, and two-year scholarships to law schools at Texas Southern, North Carolina Central, Southern, and Howard Universities; and ?Adelante! U.S. Education Leadership Fund, which awards scholarships to Hispanic-American students.
Requirements: Nonprofits must be near Miller operating locations, in Irwindale, CA; Albany, GA; Trenton, OH; Eden, NC; Fort Worth, TX; and Milwaukee, WI.
Geographic Focus: California
Contact: Grants Administrator; (414) 931-3110; fax (414) 931-6352
Internet: http://www.millerbrewing.com/inthecommunity/default.asp
Sponsor: Miller Brewing Corporation
3939 W Highland Boulevard
Milwaukee, WI 53201-0482

Miller Foundation Grants 3181
The Miller Foundation focuses on assisting local nonprofit, charitable organizations and governmental agencies with projects that provide the following for the Battle Creek, Michigan, area: economic development; education; health service; human service; neighborhood improvement; arts and culture; recreation and tourism; and leadership. The Miller Foundation Board of Trustees meets every other month to consider grant applications: January, March, May, July, September, and November. Applicants should submit grant applications by the 1st of the month for it to be considered at that month's Board meeting.
Requirements: Nonprofit 501(c)3 organizations located in and working to improve the Battle Creek community are eligible. Organizations should submit a preliminary letter of request, briefly describing their project, its estimated cost, amount requested, and funding from other sources. After reviewing the initial letter, the Foundation staff, if appropriate, will send a formal grant application to the requesting organization.
Restrictions: The Foundation seldom funds an entire project but rather joins with others as they work to improve the quality of life in the Battle Creek community. The Foundation does not make grants to individuals or for continuing operating funds of nonprofit organizations.
Geographic Focus: Michigan
Date(s) Application is Due: Jan 1; Mar 1; May 1; Jul 1; Sep 1; Nov 1
Contact: Sara Wallace, Executive Director; (269) 964-3542; fax (269) 964-8455
Internet: http://themillerfoundation.com/grants.htm
Sponsor: Miller Foundation
310 WahWahTaySee Way
Battle Creek, MI 49015

Millipore Foundation Grants 3182
The foundation supports nonprofit organizations in company operating communities in five main areas: education and research, social services, culture, health care, and public policy. Types of support include general operating support, employee matching gifts, and employee-related scholarships. Applications are accepted throughout the year.
Requirements: 501(c)3 tax-exempt organizations are eligible.
Geographic Focus: All States
Amount of Grant: 2,500 - 5,000 USD
Contact: Charleen Johnson; (978) 715-1268; Charleen_Johnson@millipore.com
Internet: http://www.millipore.com/corporate/milliporefoundation.nsf/foundationhome
Sponsor: Millipore Foundation
290 Concord Road
Billerica, MA 01821-7037

Milton and Sally Avery Arts Foundation Grants 3183
Established in 1983 with a donation from Sally M. Avery, the Foundation supports organizations in New York. Awards are restricted to art education, with emphasis on the visual arts, and to further the development of artists through nonprofit institutions, and to artists' communities and residency programs. Current fields of interest include: arts; arts education; elementary and secondary education; higher education; visual arts (painting and sculpture). There are no particular application forms or deadlines. Initial approach should be by letter. The Board meets once per year on January 9th.
Restrictions: No support is offered for religious or political organizations, and no grants are given to individuals.
Geographic Focus: New York
Contact: March A. Cavanaugh, President; fax (212) 595-2840
Sponsor: Milton and Sally Avery Arts Foundation
360 Lexington Avenue
New York, NY 10017-6502

Milton Hicks Wood and Helen Gibbs Wood Charitable Trust Grants 3184
Milton and Helen Wood were modest people who valued hard work. Milton worked as a chemist for Proctor & Gamble, ultimately funding a charitable trust with money made from company stock. Family was important to Helen, and she spent her time and focus supporting her husband in his work. The Milton Hicks Wood and Helen Gibbs Wood Charitable Trust awards approximately 2-3 grants per year and grants are typically between $5,000 and $10,000. Applicants must apply online at the grant website. Applicants are strongly encouraged to do the following before applying: review the downloadable state application procedures for additional helpful information and clarifications; review the downloadable online-application guidelines at the grant website; review the trust's funding history (link is available from the grant website); review the online application questions in advance; and review the list of required attachments. These will generally include: a list of board members, financial statements (audited, reviewed, or compiled by independent auditor); an organization summary; a list of other funding sources; an IRS Determination letter; and other required documents. All attachments must be uploaded in the online application as PDF, Word, or Excel files. The application deadline is 11:59 p.m. on September 30.
Requirements: Applicants must have 501(c)3 tax-exempt status.
Restrictions: The trust does not support requests from individuals, organizations attempting to influence policy through direct lobbying, or any political campaigns.
Geographic Focus: Texas
Date(s) Application is Due: Sep 30
Amount of Grant: 5,000 - 10,000 USD
Contact: Mark J. Smith; (817) 390-6028; tx.philanthropic@baml.com
Internet: https://www.bankofamerica.com/philanthropic/fn_search.action
Sponsor: Milton Hicks Wood and Helen Gibbs Wood Charitable Trust
500 West 7th Street, 15th Floor, TX1-497-15-08
Fort Worth, TX 76102-4700

Mimi and Peter Haas Fund Grants　　　　　　　　　　　　　　　　3185

The Mimi and Peter Haas Fund supports early childhood development. Their primary focus is for activities that provide San Francisco's young (ages 2-5), low-income children and their families with access to high-quality early childhood programs that are part of a comprehensive, coordinated system. The Fund recognizes the importance of connecting the work of its direct service grants to the ongoing discussions of public policy and seek specific opportunities to collaborate with organizations to improve early childhood settings. The Fund will also continue trustee-initiated grantmaking to arts, education, public affairs, and health and human services organizations. Applicants should contact the trustee office to begin the application process. There are no particular application forms or deadlines with which to adhere.
Geographic Focus: California
Amount of Grant: Up to USD
Contact: Lynn Merz; (415) 296-9249; fax (415) 296-8842; mphf@mphf.org
Sponsor: Mimi and Peter Haas Fund
201 Filbert Street, 5th Floor
San Francisco, CA 94133-3238

Minneapolis Foundation Community Grants　　　　　　　　　　　3186

The foundation awards grants throughout Minnesota. Eligible activities include policy and systems change work in the following areas: affordable housing; economic opportunity; educational achievement; and the health and well-being of children, youth, and families. The foundation also focuses on systems and policy work that addresses the intersection of issues, such as housing and health. Types of support include program/project support, operating support, capital support (limited to the seven-county metro area); and some multiyear grants. Proposals are accepted throughout the year. Guidelines are available online.
Requirements: 501(c)3 nonprofit organizations located in the seven-county metropolitan area of Minneapolis and Saint Paul may apply.
Restrictions: The foundation does not fund individuals, organizations/activities outside of Minnesota, conference registration fees, memberships, direct religious activities, political organizations or candidates, direct fundraising activities, telephone solicitations, courtesy advertising, or financial deficits.
Geographic Focus: Minnesota
Date(s) Application is Due: Mar 15; Sep 15
Contact: Paul Verrette; (612) 672-3836; pverrette@mplsfoundation.org
Internet: http://www.mplsfoundation.org/grants/guidelines.htm
Sponsor: Minneapolis Foundation
800 IDS Center, 80 South Eighth Street
Minneapolis, MN 55402

Minnesota Small Cities Development Grants　　　　　　　　　　　3187

The Small Cities Development Program (SCDP) helps cities and counties with funding for housing, infrastructure and commercial rehabilitation projects that benefit people of low and moderate incomes. Projects must meet one of three objectives: benefit people of low and moderate incomes; eliminate slum and blight conditions; and, eliminate an urgent threat to public health or safety. In addition, need impact and cost effectiveness must be documented and the general public must be involved in the application process. The timeline to complete projects is normally two years, depending on project size and scope. Funds for the Program are provided by the U.S. Department of Housing and Urban Development (HUD), for the benefit of eligible non-entitlement local units of government (cities, counties, townships) through a competitive application process for a variety of community development needs.
Requirements: Cities with fewer than 50,000 residents and counties with fewer than 200,000 residents are eligible. State program rules subdivide grant funds into three general categories: 1) Housing Grants - Funds are granted to local units of government, which, in turn, lend funds for the purpose of rehabilitating local housing stock; 2) Public Facility Grants - Funds are granted for wastewater treatment projects, including collection systems and treatment plants; fresh water projects, including wells, water towers, and distribution systems; storm sewer projects; flood control projects; and, street projects; 3) Comprehensive Grants - Comprehensive projects frequently include housing and public facility activities described above. In addition, comprehensive projects may include an economic development activity, which consists of loans from the grant recipient to businesses for building renovation/construction, purchase of equipment, or working capital. The maximum grant award for a Single Purpose project is $600,000. The maximum grant award for a Comprehensive project is $1.4 million. The amount of other funds required varies and is contingent upon the project type. However, the amount of leveraged resources plays a significant role in determining whether the project is funded. A preliminary proposal is required and must use the form available at the website. Questions or comments should be directed to your Regional SCDP Representative (see the website for the representative responsible for your region of the state).
Geographic Focus: Minnesota
Amount of Grant: 300,000 - 700,000 USD
Contact: Mark Lofthus, Director, Business and Community Development; 651-259-7114
Internet: http://www.positivelyminnesota.com/Government/Financial_Assistance/Community_Development_Funding/Small_Cities_Development_Program.aspx
Sponsor: Minnesota Department of Employment and Economic Development
332 Minnesota Street, Suite E-200
Saint Paul, MN 55101-1351

Minnesota State Arts Board Cultural Community Partnership Grants　3188

The Cultural Community Partnership Grants are designed to enhance the careers of individual artists of color. Any artist can apply for grants to help support collaborative projects. Applicants can collaborate on a project with another Minnesota artist of color or with a Minnesota nonprofit organization. The project must be designed to further the artist's career or enhance the applicant's artistic abilities. Each project must include a community component that will draw visibility to the artist's work. A public performance or exhibition, a published work, or an open workshop or demonstration that the public can attend, are all examples of possible community components. Program funding is eligible for the following: creation and presentation of art work representing the heritage of artists and/or communities of color; creation and exhibition of visual art, either contemporary or traditional; creation and presentation of plays, music, or choreography; public art and design projects for neighborhoods and communities; arts components of neighborhood festivals or celebrations; advanced study or residency for an individual artist with an arts organization; mentorship between a master artist and apprentice; or activities directly related to enhancing an artist's career. The application and application samples are available at the website.
Requirements: Applicants must be professional artists of color, in any stage of their career, working in any discipline. If an artist is collaborating with an organization, the organization can prepare and submit the application. The organization can be either the official applicant or the collaborator. Artists must be Minnesota residents or individuals who have permanent lawful residency status (green card), regardless of whether they are the official applicant or the collaborator. Organizations must be Minnesota nonprofits that are tax-exempt under section 501(c)3 of the Internal Revenue Service code, or have contracted with a fiscal agent that is tax-exempt under the IRS code.
Restrictions: Activities proposed may not begin before May and must be completed by the end of April the following year. Funding is not available for any of the following: costs associated with any degree (i.e., tuition, fees, materials, teaching materials, or teaching programs); collaborations between an artist and an organization by which he or she is employed; costs incurred prior to the official start date of the grant period; literary translation of another artist's work; capital costs (such as construction, property, or equipment costing over $5,000); or work on scholarly manuscripts or standard journalism.
Geographic Focus: Minnesota
Date(s) Application is Due: Oct 26
Amount of Grant: 1,000 - 8,000 USD
Contact: Kathee Foran, Program Officer; (651) 215-1626 or (800) 866-2787; fax (651) 215-1602; kathee.foran@arts.state.mn.us or msab@arts.state.mn.us
Internet: http://www.arts.state.mn.us/grants/cultural-community-partnership.htm
Sponsor: Minnesota State Arts Board
400 Sibley Street
St. Paul, MN 55101-1928

Missouri United Methodist Foundation Ministry Grants　　　　　3189

The foundation awards grants to United Methodist churches, ministries, and agencies across Missouri. The board considers grant applications twice each year. Funding decisions are determined on a case-by-case basis and are dependent on funds available and the merits of each request. Applications must be postmarked by April 1 for Spring consideration or October 1 for Winter consideration. Approximately one year after the grant funds are disbursed, the applicant will be expected to complete an evaluation of the project.
Requirements: Those eligible for ministry grants are Missouri's United Methodist churches and church-related organizations and agencies. Ministry grants are intended to help initiate programs, projects, or activities that are innovative, new, or acutely needed. Grants are made for special one-time funding needs. Proposals seeking funds for capital projects will be considered only after all other grant priorities have been considered and funding allocations determined. Generally, capital funding awards are capped at $10,000. Download the required application form from the sponsor's website.
Restrictions: Applications submitted by fax or email will not be considered.
Geographic Focus: Missouri
Date(s) Application is Due: Apr 1; Oct 1
Contact: David P. Atkins, Executive Director; (800) 332-8238 or (573) 875-4168; fax (573) 875-4595; datkins@mumf.org or foundation@mumf.org
Internet: http://mumf.org/churches-organizations/ministry-grants/
Sponsor: Missouri United Methodist Foundation
P.O. Box 1076
Columbia, MO 65205-1076

Mitsubishi Electric America Foundation Grants　　　　　　　　　3190

The foundation follows a long tradition of philanthropy by the Mitsubishi Electric America companies. It seeks to contribute to the greater good of society by assisting young Americans with disabilities, through education, technology, and other means, to lead fuller and more productive lives. Requests from all areas of the United States will be considered, though priority will be given to communities where MEA companies are located. A major program emphasis is to advance the independence, productivity, and community inclusion of young people with disabilities. Funding is available for projects and general organizational support. The foundation awards matching grants locally. Concept papers are accepted throughout the year. Invited proposals are due by the listed application deadline. Application and guidelines are available online.
Requirements: Grants are made only to 501(c)3 tax-exempt nonprofit organizations.
Restrictions: The foundation does not support individuals; intermediary organizations; ethnic, fraternal, labor, or political organizations; religious organizations for religious purposes; endowments; the purchase of tickets for fundraising; or advertising, mass mailing, or conference expenses.
Geographic Focus: All States
Date(s) Application is Due: Jul 1
Contact: Program Officer; (703) 276-8240; fax (703) 276-8260
Internet: http://www.meaf.org/apply/priorities.html
Sponsor: Mitsubishi Electric America Foundation
1560 Wilson Boulevard, Suite 1150
Arlington, VA 22209

Mix It Up Grants 3191
The program funds youth-directed activist projects that focus on identifying, crossing, and challenging social boundaries in schools and communities. Preference is given to applications that clearly show youth leadership—i.e., projects created and carried out by youth activists; collaborative efforts across social boundaries—i.e., different youth groups or clubs working together, or school-based clubs working with community-based organizations; and continuing efforts to identify, cross, or challenge social boundaries—i.e., the funded project isn't the end of the effort. Download and complete the online application, and return the completed application with the necessary attachments.
Requirements: Individuals proposing youth-directed school or community projects may apply. There is no application deadline.
Restrictions: Grants cannot be renewed and are restricted to one per applicant or school per year.
Geographic Focus: All States
Amount of Grant: 500 USD
Contact: Grants Management Officer; (888) 414-7752; mixitup@tolerance.org
Internet: http://www.tolerance.org/teens/grants.jsp
Sponsor: Southern Poverty Law Center
400 Washington Avenue
Montgomery, AL 36104

Mizuho USA Foundation Grants 3192
The Mizuho USA Foundation is an independent not-for-profit philanthropic organization created by Mizuho Corporate Bank in 2003. The primary mission is to provide Grants to not-for-profit charitable organizations to support community development programs that contribute to the strength and vitality of urban neighborhoods. The Foundation's primary geographic focus is New York City with additional grantmaking in Los Angeles. Program areas include strengthening affordable housing, fostering economic self-sufficiency; and promoting economic development. Applicants should submit a short concept paper for preliminary review. Selected applicants will be invited to submit more detailed proposals. Requests must be received by the first weekday in July to be considered for funding in the same year.
Requirements: Eligible applicants must: be 501(c)3 and classified as a public charity under 509(a)1 or Section 509(a)2 and not a supporting organization under Section 509(a)3; present a proposal that satisfies the Foundation guidelines; not discriminate against a person or group on the basis of age, race, national origin, ethnicity, gender, disability, sexual orientation, political affiliation or religious belief; and be in full compliance with United States anti-terrorism laws and regulations, including the Patriot Act and Executive Order 13224, pertaining to United States based not-for-profit charitable organizations conducting activities outside of the United States.
Restrictions: The Foundation does not fund: general operating support; individuals; religious, sectarian, fraternal, veteran, athletic or labor groups; organizations or programs outside the United States; political organizations, political candidates or political activity; organizations whose primary purpose is to influence legislation; fundraising events; advertising; or endowment or capital campaigns.
Geographic Focus: California, New York
Contact: Lesley Harris Palmer, Executive Director; (212) 282-4192; fax (212) 282-3250; mizuho.usa.foundation@mizuhocbus.com
Internet: http://www.mizuhocbk.com/americas/community/foundation/program.html
Sponsor: Mizuho USA Foundation
1251 Avenue of the Americas, 31st Floor
New York, NY 10020-1104

MLB Tomorrow Fund Grants 3193
The Baseball Tomorrow Grant funds programs, fields, and equipment purchases for youth baseball in the United States and around the world. Grants enable applicants to address needs unique to their communities. The funds may be used to finance a new program, expand or improve an existing program, undertake a new collaborative effort, or obtain facilities or equipment necessary for youth baseball or softball programs. Organizations seeking to implement or improve a youth baseball and/or softball program for youth ages 10 to 16 are encouraged to apply. Grants are awarded on a quarterly basis after a thorough and selective application process which can last from three to six months. The selection process consists of the following steps: letter of inquiry review; application review and evaluation; site visit; and final selection by the Board of Directors. Organizations are encouraged to apply for the grant to fund grant writing for their project, if needed, with information available at the website. The application or letter of inquiry and all supporting materials must be mailed to the MLB New York address.
Requirements: Organizations are encouraged to carefully review the application process before applying. Evaluation criteria are specific to the individual organization's needs, including field lights, travel and and specific instructions and contacts for international applicants. Applicants should also review the frequently asked questions section, application help guide, budget template, and samples of previous grant recipients on the website.
Restrictions: Grants are not a substitute for existing funding or fundraising activities. Grants do not support routine or recurring operating costs or funding for construction or maintenance of buildings.
Geographic Focus: All States, Canada
Date(s) Application is Due: Jan 1; Apr 1; Jul 1; Oct 1
Amount of Grant: 40,000 USD
Contact: Baseball Tomorrow; (212) 931-7800; fax (212) 949-5654; btf@mlb.com
Internet: http://mlb.mlb.com/NASApp/mlb/mlb/official_info/community/btf.jsp
Sponsor: Major League Baseball
245 Park Avenue, 31st floor
New York, NY 10167

MMS and Alliance Charitable Foundation Grants for Community Action and Care for the Medically Uninsured 3194
The Massachusetts Medical Society and Alliance Charitable Foundation, through its Board of Directors, awards grants to nonprofit organizations and works with communities throughout Massachusetts to creatively address issues that affect the health, benefit, and welfare of the community. The Foundation supports physician-led volunteer initiatives to provide free care to uninsured/underinsured patients and increased access to care for the medically underserved. Preference will be given to organizations working with interdisciplinary groups that address health care issues and where strong physician involvement exists.
Requirements: Given the spectrum of issues that influence health, the Foundation, as an organization of physicians and their families, focuses its efforts on programs that directly promote health in the community. Eligible programs may provide direct care services or target public health issues which impact the health care system and the health of communities. Programs applying for grants must address one or more of the following goals: (a) Affect the health and well-being of the community through community-based prevention, screening, early detection, health promotion, and/or increased access to medical care; (b) Promote healthy decision-making around behaviors and lifestyle choices by raising awareness, providing education, improving communication, and/or connecting community members with culturally appropriate programs and services; (c) Support physician-led volunteer initiatives to provide free care to uninsured/underinsured patients and/or increase access to care for the medically underserved; (d) Enable underserved, at-risk populations, to engage in activities that promote health and identify risky behaviors which contribute to diminished health. Applicants should submit a Letter of Inquiry (LOI) (Word Doc, 1 page) and accepted LOIs are invited to submit a full proposal. LOIs are due January 15, and proposals, if invited to submit, are due March 1.
Restrictions: The foundation does not provide funding support for: capital campaigns, endowments, building campaigns; for-profit organizations; fundraising drives and fundraising events; individuals (unless applying for International Health Studies Grant or scholarships through a directed giving program; private or parochial schools, colleges, or universities; government agencies (except in collaboration with community-based, nonprofit organizations which will lead the program and act as fiscal agent); organizations that advocate, support, or practice discrimination based on race, religion, age, national origin, language, sex, sexual preference, or physical handicap; religious organizations for religious purposes; research; or, political or lobbying activities.
Geographic Focus: Massachusetts
Date(s) Application is Due: Mar 1
Contact: Jennifer Day, Manager; (781) 434-7044; foundation@mms.org
Internet: http://www.massmed.org/Charitable_Foundation/Applying_for_Grants/Applying_for_Grants/#.U1gQtccRZlo
Sponsor: Massachusetts Medical Society and Alliance Charitable Foundation
c/o Massachusetts Medical Society
Waltham, MA 02451

MMS and Alliance Charitable Foundation International Health Studies Grants 3195
The primary goal of the International Health Studies Grants is to encourage international education, particularly focusing on underserved populations. This program is supported, in part, by an annual donation from the MMS. Additional monies have been raised through private donations to award a total of five grants annually. The Foundation Board of Directors will consider applications once a year. Applications must be submitted via the online application and be received by 4:00 pm on September 15.
Requirements: Medical students and resident physician members of the Massachusetts Medical Society (MMS) are eligible to apply for grants for up to $2,000 to defray the costs of study abroad. Preference will be given to projects providing health care related work and/or training of staff; and to applicants planning careers serving underprivileged populations in the world.
Restrictions: Research projects that do not involve direct clinical care or teaching will not be considered.
Geographic Focus: Massachusetts
Date(s) Application is Due: Sep 15
Amount of Grant: Up to 2,000 USD
Contact: Jennifer Day, Manager; (781) 434-7044; foundation@mms.org or jday@mms.org
Internet: http://www.massmed.org/Charitable_Foundation/Applying_for_Grants/International_Health_Studies_Program
Sponsor: Massachusetts Medical Society and Alliance Charitable Foundation
c/o Massachusetts Medical Society
Waltham, MA 02451

Mockingbird Foundation Grants 3196
The Mockingbird Foundation (Mockingbird) is a non-profit organization founded by Phish (the rock band) fans in 1996. Since then Mockingbird has distributed over $750,000 to support music-education programs for children. The foundation provides funding through its competitive grants, emergency-related grants, and tour-related grants. Emergency-related grants and tour-related grants are unsolicited grants. Emergency grants come from an Emergency Fund in which 3% of Mockingbird's gross revenues are designated for music-education programs affected by disasters (e.g., hurricanes and tornadoes). Tour-related grants support music-education programs in communities touched by Phish tours and are intended to inspire support for music and arts education and to generate positive press coverage. Competitive grants are awarded to schools and nonprofit organizations through a two-tiered grant-application process. Applicants must first complete an initial inquiry form at Mockingbird's website. If an applicant's project is selected for further consideration, the applicant will then be invited to submit a full and formal proposal. Initial inquiries may be submitted at any time. Mockingbird typically reviews inquiries in August and September, invites full proposals by Halloween, and announces new grants sometime between Christmas

and the end of January. Mockingbird encourages projects with diverse or unusual musical styles, genres, forms, and philosophies; projects with unconventional outlets and forms of instruction as well as instruction in unconventional forms; projects that foster creative expression in any musical form (including composition, instrumentation, vocalization, or improvisation); and projects in which skills, as outcomes, are less assessable or even irrelevant. Projects should be experiential and directly engage students with creating and expressing music. Preference is given to programs that benefit disenfranchised groups, including those with low skill levels, income, education, disabilities, or terminal illness, and/or those in foster-care homes, hospitals, and prisons. Prospective applicants should review the instructions and guidelines given at the website for complete details before making application.
Requirements: Schools and 501(c)3 nonprofit organizations in the United States are eligible. Applicants may apply through a sponsor who meets these qualifications. Mockingbird is particularly interested in organizations with low overhead, innovative approaches, and/or collaborative elements to their work. The foundation encourages geographic diversity and has funded forty-three states to date. Mockingbird is interested in targeting children 18 years or younger, but will consider projects that benefit college students, teachers/instructors, or adult students.
Restrictions: Grants are made on a one-time basis and are non-renewable and non-transferable. Mockingbird does not normally support individuals, fund-raising organizations or events, research, and programs that promote or engage in religious or political doctrine. It is hoped that applicants for Mockingbird grants hire staff and provide services without discriminating on the basis of race, religion, gender, sexual orientation, age, national origin, or disability. Mockingbird supports the provision of instruments, texts, and office materials, and the acquisition of learning space, practice space, performance space, and instructors/instruction. Mockingbird is particularly interested in projects that foster self-esteem and free expression, but does not fund music therapy which is neither education nor music appreciation which does not include participation.
Geographic Focus: All States
Amount of Grant: 100 - 5,000 USD
Contact: Ellis Godard, Executive Director; ellis@mbird.org
Internet: http://mbird.org/funding/guidelines/
Sponsor: Mockingbird Foundation
6948 Luther Circle
Moorpark, CA 93021-2569

Modest Needs Bridge Grants **3197**

Modest Needs offers grants to low-income but generally self-sufficient households, displaced workers struggling to return to the workforce, permanently disadvantaged persons struggling to afford medical care, and small non-profit organizations. To assist persons who've recently returned to work after a period of unemployment, who will probably meet the foundation's self-sufficiency standard once they've received a full month's pay, but who are likely to be evicted from their homes or lose critical services prior to that time, Modest Needs offers the Bridge Grant. The maximum grant available under this program is fixed at $750.00, payable directly to the applicant's creditor (like his or her mortgage lender), but the foundation will work to negotiate with an applicant's creditor of record to resolve his or her issue for the lowest cost possible.
Requirements: The Bridge Grant is available exclusively to persons who are employed in a traditional full-time (32 hours per week) job, started working that job 45 days ago or less, have received at least one paycheck from their new jobs, and have an eviction, repossession or shut-off notice in hand or are at least two month's behind on their mortgage payments at the time of their applications. Applicants should complete the online application. If the responses meet the foundation's self-sufficiency standard, the Application Wizard will direct the applicant to the Bridge Grant application.
Restrictions: Persons who are less than three business days from eviction, foreclosure, repossession or shut-off at the time of their applications (a minimum of ten to fourteen days' lead time is preferable) are not eligible to apply.
Geographic Focus: All States
Amount of Grant: Up to 750 USD
Contact: Keith Taylor, President; (212) 463-7042; kptaylor@modestneeds.org
Internet: https://www.modestneeds.org/about-us/grants-types-bridge.asp
Sponsor: Modest Needs Foundation
115 East 30th Street, FL 1
New York, NY 10016

Modest Needs Hurricane Sandy Relief Grants: Phase 2 **3198**

It is the hope of Modest Needs that by helping low-income homeowners who are now faced with unexpected expenses due to damage from Hurricane Sandy, they can help to speed recovery from the most devastating storm to hit the Northeast in more than a century. Grants will be capped at a maximum of $1,500.00 per household. Under this program, for qualified applicants, Modest Needs will pay either the actual cost the expense with which you request their assistance or up to $1,500.00 towards the cost of that expense, whichever is less.
Requirements: This grant is available only to persons living in New York, New Jersey, and Connecticut. The sponsor will consider requests for assistance only with one of the three, specific types of expenses listed: (1) You may have been forced to relocate to a temporary rental while your home is being repaired; (2) You may have qualified for help from FEMA and other types of aid but still need help to afford the cost of the insurance deductible necessary to begin repairs on your home; or (3) You have have received assistance from FEMA or other state / federal sources, but given the cost of repairs necessary to make your home livable, the assistance you received may not have been sufficient to replace a major appliance or other similar necessity that you lost due to the storm (like a refrigerator, or a bed). If FEMA has identified you as having been affected by Hurricane Sandy and you own your home (you make a monthly mortgage payment, or you own your home 'free and clear'), but you're experiencing financial hardship for one of the specific reasons listed above, Modest Needs' Hurricane Relief Grant may be able to help you. Applicants should complete the online application. If the responses meet the foundation's self-sufficiency standard, the Application Wizard will direct the applicant to the Hurricane Relief Grant application.
Restrictions: Grants are made to qualified applicants on a first-come, first-served basis until funding for this program is exhausted.
Geographic Focus: Connecticut, New Jersey, New York
Amount of Grant: Up to 1,500 USD
Contact: Keith Taylor, President; (212) 463-7042; kptaylor@modestneeds.org
Internet: https://www.modestneeds.org/about-us/grant-types-hurricane-relief.asp
Sponsor: Modest Needs Foundation
115 East 30th Street, FL 1
New York, NY 10016

Modest Needs New Employment Grants **3199**

Modest Needs offers grants to low-income but generally self-sufficient households, displaced workers struggling to return to the workforce, permanently disadvantaged persons struggling to afford medical care, and small non-profit organizations. In offering the New Employment grant, the foundation's goal is to help individuals secure employment that will bring their households to self-sufficiency on an ongoing basis. The maximum grant available under the New Employment grant program is fixed at $750.00, though the foundation will work to negotiate with the vendor named in the applicant's documentation to meet the applicant's needs at the lowest possible cost.
Requirements: Applicants should be aware that they will be asked to document information they provide regarding their identities, housing costs, the position they have been offered (if applicable) and the cost & work-related nature of the expense with which he or she is applying for assistance during the application process. Applicants should complete the online application. If the responses meet the foundation's self-sufficiency standard, the Application Wizard will direct the applicant to the New Employment grant application.
Restrictions: Requests for assistance with regular household expenses, like rent or utility bills, will not be considered. Also, funding cannot be provided to repair cars or to provide transportation for people who are actively seeking but have not yet been offered or recently started new employment.
Geographic Focus: All States
Amount of Grant: Up to 750 USD
Contact: Keith Taylor, President; (212) 463-7042; kptaylor@modestneeds.org
Internet: https://www.modestneeds.org/about-us/grants-types-new-employment.asp
Sponsor: Modest Needs Foundation
115 East 30th Street, FL 1
New York, NY 10016

Modest Needs Non-Profit Grants **3200**

The purpose of the grant is to allow small non-profits to appeal directly to the general public for help to afford expenses that will strengthen the programs and services they provide to the communities that they serve. The maximum grant available under this program is $2,500.00, but the foundation will negotiate with the vendor named in the non-profit's documentation to secure the item the organization has requested at the lowest possible price.
Requirements: This grant type is open only to non-profits with gross incomes of at least $50,000.00 but not more than $500,000.00, that file a Form 990-EZ or Form 990, and that have registered with Modest Needs.
Restrictions: Organizations that file Form 990-N 'postcards' are not eligible to apply for this grant. Under this grant type, non-profits may not apply for help to afford fundraising expenses, like the cost to hire a professional fundraiser or the cost to afford some or all of the expenses involved with an annual fundraising dinner.
Geographic Focus: All States
Contact: Keith Taylor, President; (212) 463-7042; kptaylor@modestneeds.org
Internet: https://www.modestneeds.org/about-us/grants-types-non-profit.asp
Sponsor: Modest Needs Foundation
115 East 30th Street, FL 1
New York, NY 10016

Modest Needs Self-Sufficiency Grants **3201**

The Self-Sufficiency Grant is designed to prevent normally self-sufficient but low-income households from entering the cycle of poverty by helping them to afford short-term emergency expenses that would otherwise pose a tremendous hardship for the grant applicant. Examples of how the grant could be used include: the cost of a medical appointment, an auto repair, an insurance deductible, an unusually large utility bill, or virtually any other type of unexpected emergency expense when remitting payment for the unusual expense would place the grant applicant in a situation where he or she could no longer afford a critical regular bill, like his or her monthly rent; or the cost of a regular monthly bill, like rent, when the applicant can document either that he or she has already received an paid for a short-term emergency expense like those described above, or that he or she has experienced a documentable, short-term loss of income (for example, the loss of income that resulted from an applicant having to take an unpaid week off from work due to illness.)
Requirements: While applicants may request help with virtually any type of short-term emergency expense, serious consideration only to applications for help with expenses that are clearly necessary to the household. The maximum grant available under Modest Needs' Self-Sufficiency grant program is the greater of $750.00 or the 3.75% of the applicant's verifiable annual income. Applicants should complete the online application which will determine if the applicant's household meets the self-sufficiency standard. If so, the Application Wizard will always automatically direct the applicant to the Self-Sufficiency Grant application. Applicants should keep in mind that they will be asked to document information they provide regarding their identities, incomes, housing costs, and the expense with which they would like to apply for help to afford during the application process.

Restrictions: Please note that you cannot apply for a grant or check the status of an application via telephone.
Geographic Focus: All States
Contact: Keith Taylor, President; (212) 463-7042; kptaylor@modestneeds.org
Internet: https://www.modestneeds.org/about-us/grants-types-self-sufficiency.asp
Sponsor: Modest Needs Foundation
115 East 30th Street, FL 1
New York, NY 10016

Moline Foundation Community Grants 3202
The resources and funds of the Moline Foundation are used throughout its community to assist others in times of need, plan for future workforce development, help its neighborhoods grow and prosper, and to better the quality of life with arts and culture. The Moline Foundation provides grants in the following designated charitable categories: Education; Health Care; Social Services; Arts and Humanities; and, Workforce and Economic Development. In general, grants are made for capital and programmatic purposes only, not for operating expenses. Grants are made to non-profit agencies located in the Moline Foundation service area which includes the Quad Cities region. Occasionally, grants may also be allocated to governmental entities such as public libraries and schools.
Requirements: The Moline Foundation grants are intended to support charitable projects that utilize companies, firms or vendors whose principal offices are located within the Moline Foundation area. Since funds that support the Moline Foundation Grantmaking Program are received from local donors, every effort should be made to return these grant dollars to the local community. To apply for a grant, you must be a recognized 501(c)3 not for profit organization as recognized by the Internal Revenue Service. Grants are also awarded on a limited basis to governmental entities such as libraries and schools. The Moline Foundation serves six counties in western Illinois (Henderson, Henry, Mercer, McDonough, Rock Island, and Warren) and Scott County in eastern Iowa including the urban area is known as the Quad Cities.
Restrictions: Grants are not generally available for those agencies and institutions that are funded primarily through tax support.
Geographic Focus: Illinois, Iowa
Date(s) Application is Due: Jan 31; Apr 15; Sep 30
Contact: Linda Martin, Director of Donor and Community Relations; (309) 764-4193
Internet: http://www.molinefoundation.org/Page/Our_Grantmaking.aspx?nt=1152
Sponsor: Moline Foundation
817 11th Avenue
Moline, IL 61265

Monfort Family Foundation Grants 3203
The foundation awards general operating grants to Colorado nonprofit organizations in its areas of interest, including education, health and medical research, arts and culture, agriculture, and general charitable giving. Application forms must be obtained.
Requirements: Colorado nonprofits, primarily in Weld County, are eligible.
Restrictions: Grants are not made to individuals.
Geographic Focus: Colorado
Date(s) Application is Due: May 1; Oct 1
Amount of Grant: 5,000 - 100,000 USD
Samples: U of Northern Colorado, College of Business Administration (Greeley, CO)—to bring nationally prominent business leaders to campus to teach; to create a technology center; and to establish an entrepreneurship institute, a lecture series, and an instruction-improvement fund, $10.5 million.
Contact: Dave Evans, Program Contact; (970) 454-1357
Sponsor: Monfort Family Foundation
Box 337300
Greeley, CO 80633

Monsanto Access to the Arts Grants 3204
The Monsanto Fund works to substantially and meaningfully improve people's lives around the world. In the St. Louis area, the Fund is designed to help arts organizations broaden opportunities for underserved children and adults in the performing, visual or literary arts. Grants help organizations reach underserved groups and communities, identify the barriers, real or perceived, that keep them from participating in the arts, and implement strategies to reduce barriers and engage them in arts education experiences. Most grants range from $25,000 to $50,000.
Requirements: Eligible applicants must be not-for-profit organizations focused on the arts or offering arts education programming located in one of the 16 eligible St. Louis counties. Preference will be given to organizations that have been in operation for 3 or more years. Preference will be given to arts experiences that are ongoing, rather than one-time events, and can demonstrate a change over time in awareness and interest in arts among young people and/or adults. For school-aged students, preference will be given to programming that is tied to and integrated with educational goals.
Restrictions: Schools are not eligible to apply, however programming can take place in a school. Funding is not intended to cover the purchase or creation of new artwork. Up to 20% of the requested grant amount can be utilized for overhead costs. Only one grant per organization per year will be awarded.
Geographic Focus: Missouri
Date(s) Application is Due: Feb 28; Aug 31
Amount of Grant: 150,000 USD
Contact: Deborah J. Patterson; (314) 694-1000; monsantofund@monsanto.com
Internet: http://www.monsantofund.org/grants/st-louis/#access-to-arts
Sponsor: Monsanto Fund
800 North Lindbergh Boulevard
Saint Louis, MO 63167

Monsanto America's Farmers Grow Rural Education Grants 3205
America's Farmers Grow Rural Education Grants is a program to help farmers positively impact their communities and support local school districts. Sponsored by the Monsanto Fund, Grants give farmers the opportunity to nominate their public school district to compete for a grant of up to $25,000.
Requirements: Only farmers who live or farm in an eligible county can nominate a school district. A list of eligible counties can be found at the website (www.GrowRuralEducation.com). Eligible farmers must be 21 years or older and be actively engaged in farming with a minimum of 250 acres of corn, soybeans and/or cotton; or 40 acres of open field vegetables; or at least 10 acres of vegetables grown in protected culture. For these purposes, "vegetables" means one or more of the following: peppers, tomatoes, onions, broccoli, cucumbers, melons, watermelons, spinach, squash, pumpkins, sweet corn, lettuce, peas and garden beans. A nomination form is available (at www.GrowRuralEducation.com) or can be obtained by calling America's Farmers Grow Rural Education.
Restrictions: One nomination may be made per farmer.
Geographic Focus: Illinois, Minnesota
Date(s) Application is Due: Jun 30
Contact: Nomination Coordinator; (877) 267-3332
Internet: http://www.americasfarmers.com/growruraleducation/overview.aspx
Sponsor: Monsanto Fund
800 North Lindbergh Boulevard
Saint Louis, MO 63167

Monsanto Civic Partnership Grants 3206
The Monsanto Fund works to substantially and meaningfully improve people's lives around the world. The Fund has a long history of taking part in major civic initiatives that benefit the greater St. Louis community. Given the scope and complexity of these kinds of transformational initiatives, applications to the Monsanto Fund for civic partnerships are by invitation only.
Geographic Focus: Missouri
Contact: Deborah J. Patterson; (314) 694-1000; monsantofund@monsanto.com
Internet: http://www.monsantofund.org/grants/st-louis/#civic-partnerships
Sponsor: Monsanto Fund
800 North Lindbergh Boulevard
Saint Louis, MO 63167

Monsanto International Grants 3207
The Monsanto Fund works to substantially and meaningfully improve people's lives around the world. Funding for programs outside of the United States is made in two areas. One area is providing basic education support designed to improve education in farming communities around the world, including supporting schools, libraries, science centers, farmer training programs and academic programs that enrich or supplement school programs. A second area is meeting critical needs in communities by supporting nonprofit organizations that help with things such as food security, sanitation, access to clean water, public safety and various other local needs.
Requirements: Eligible organizations include public charities incorporated in the United States and working in a foreign country, indigenous public charities, units of government, private schools primarily serving an economically disadvantaged population, and private hospitals primarily serving an economically disadvantaged population. All applicants must qualify as tax exempt public charities or its equivalent and provide proof of tax-exempt status. Applications for International Grants are by invitation only. Please contact the Fund to learn more.
Restrictions: International Grants are restricted to locations outside of the United States, as the United States is funded by a separate grant program.
Geographic Focus: All Countries
Date(s) Application is Due: Feb 28; Aug 31
Amount of Grant: 25,000 USD
Contact: Deborah J. Patterson; (314) 694-1000; monsantofund@monsanto.com
Internet: http://www.monsantofund.org/grants/international/
Sponsor: Monsanto Fund
800 North Lindbergh Boulevard
Saint Louis, MO 63167

Monsanto Kids Garden Fresh Grants 3208
In partnership with Gateway Greening, the Monsanto Fund is a proud supporter of youth-centered gardens throughout the world. Gardens are invaluable tools in teaching children how to grow food, showing them the important role food plays in health, and an opportunity to integrate hands-on lessons in not only math and science but all subjects. When the fruits and vegetables grown in youth gardens are integrated into home and school meals, they are a source of vitamins and nutrients children need for cognitive development as well as a source of pride for the kids who helped grow them. There is no cash award. Grantees receive the following: assistance with project planning, coordination, and installation; plant materials, seeds, seedlings, plant beds, soil, compost, mulch, garden tools, season extension items such as materials for hoop houses and cold frames, a produce scale, and a garden sign; curricula to use with young people/students; ongoing technical assistance including training for staff, volunteers, and educators, access to Gateway Greening's education library, garden visits, and workshops; and additional volunteers if needed.
Requirements: To be eligible organizations must be located in St. Louis or St. Louis County and be serving children or youth, 60% of whom qualify for free or reduced lunch. K-12 public schools or school districts, K-12 private, charter, or independent schools, licensed child care facilities, or youth-focused nonprofit organizations serving ages 5-21 that meet this criteria are eligible. Preference will be given to organizations that have been in operation for 3 or more years.
Restrictions: Prior grantees may apply every year for an extension or expansion provided all evaluation paperwork has been submitted and all award expectations have been fulfilled.

Geographic Focus: Missouri
Date(s) Application is Due: May 1
Contact: Deborah J. Patterson; (314) 694-1000; monsantofund@monsanto.com
Internet: http://www.monsantofund.org/grants/st-louis/#kids-garden-fresh
Sponsor: Monsanto Fund
800 North Lindbergh Boulevard
Saint Louis, MO 63167

Montana Arts Council Cultural and Aesthetic Project Grants 3209
In 1975, the Montana Legislature set aside a percentage of the Coal Tax to restore murals in the Capitol and support other cultural and aesthetic projects. This unique funding source is a Cultural Trust, with grant money allocated every two years. Grant funds are derived from the interest earned on the Cultural Trust. In 1983, the Legislature established a Cultural and Aesthetic Projects Advisory Committee with 16 members, half appointed by the Montana Arts Council and half by the Montana Historical Society. The committee reviews all grant proposals and makes funding recommendations to the Legislature, which determines who will receive grant funds. Applications must be for cultural and aesthetic projects including, but not limited to, the visual, performing, literary and media arts, history, archaeology, folklore, archives, collections, research, historic preservation and the construction or renovation of cultural facilities. Applications are encouraged for applicants serving rural communities, racial and ethnic groups, people with disabilities, institutionalized populations, youth and the aging.
Requirements: Any person, association, group, or a governmental agency may submit an application for funding. Individuals may apply to special projects using a fiscal agent, which is a 501(c)3 incorporated nonprofit tax-exempt organization that is eligible to apply for Cultural Trust grants. You must contact the Montana Arts Council prior to submitting a grant application if you intend to use a fiscal agent. Proposals must be submitted in one of four categories: (1) Special Projects Requesting $4,500 or Less - organizations that are all-volunteer or employ no more than one half-time person; (2) Special Projects - for the expansion of ongoing programs, adding staff or increasing staff time and for specific cultural and aesthetic activities, services or events of limited duration; (3) Operational Support - for cultural institutions that have been formally organized for at least two years with an ongoing program and with paid professional staff and whose budgets reflect only the cost of continuing their program; (4) Capital Expenditures - for additions to a collection or for acquisition of works of art, artifacts or historical documents, historic preservation, purchase of equipment over $5,000, or the construction or renovation of cultural facilities. For Special Projects $4,500 and Under, Special Projects and Operational Support, each grant dollar is matched with one dollar in cash or in-kind goods and services. For Capital Expenditures, each grant dollar is matched with three dollars in cash or in-kind goods and services. Applications must be received by 5:00 pm of the deadline date.
Restrictions: Hard-copy applications will not be accepted. Applications must be completed online. Funds will not be awarded to support projects created to meet school accreditation standards or other mandated requirements or supplant other funds for current or ongoing programs operated by schools, colleges or universities.
Geographic Focus: Montana
Date(s) Application is Due: Aug 1
Contact: Kristin Han Burgoyne, (406) 444-6449; kburgoyne@mt.gov
Internet: http://art.mt.gov/orgs/orgs_ca.asp
Sponsor: Montana Arts Council
830 North Warren, First Floor
Helena, MT 59620-2201

Montana Community Foundation Big Sky LIFT Grants 3210
The Foundation is committed to improving the lives of Montanans by helping individuals and families achieve their philanthropic goals and by supporting Montana nonprofit organizations. The Foundation administers Big Sky LIFT (Lifting Individuals and Families with Financial Troubles), an emergency relief fund providing grants to families and individuals who are struggling financially due to the economic downturn in Big Sky. Grants will be available in amounts up to $1,000 for individuals and $2,500 for families.
Requirements: Eligible applicants must live or work in the Big Sky area and demonstrate financial hardship. Verify eligibility and application deadlines from the website or by contacting the Foundation.
Geographic Focus: Montana
Date(s) Application is Due: Dec 15
Contact: Cathy Cooney; (406) 443-8313, ext. 108; ccooney@mtcf.org or info@mtcf.org
Internet: http://www.mtcf.org/lift.html
Sponsor: Montana Community Foundation
101 North Last Chance Gulch, Suite 211
Helena, MT 59601

Montana Community Foundation Grants 3211
The Foundation is committed to improving the lives of Montanans by helping individuals and families achieve their philanthropic goals and by supporting Montana nonprofit organizations. The Foundation has discretionary control over a small number of funds for which the organization maintains competitive grantmaking opportunities for community leaders. Grants range from $5,000 to $50,000.
Restrictions: Unsolicited general grant applications are not accepted, but when there is a competitive grant opportunity the application information is posted on the website.
Geographic Focus: Montana
Contact: Cathy Cooney; (406) 443-8313, ext. 108; ccooney@mtcf.org or info@mtcf.org
Internet: http://www.mtcf.org/receive.html
Sponsor: Montana Community Foundation
101 North Last Chance Gulch, Suite 211
Helena, MT 59601

Montana Community Foundation Women's Grants 3212
The Women's Foundation of Montana is an endowed fund of the Montana Community Foundation. The Women's Foundation of Montana is the leading funder of change for women and girls in Montana. The goals of the Women's Foundation Grants are: to fund programs to build economic self-sufficiency for women and help girls to be economically self-sufficient in adulthood; to provide operating support to organizations creating a systemic change that will increase opportunities for economic self-sufficiency for women and girls; and to promote awareness of the issues affecting economic self-sufficiency for women and girls and build support for systemic change to enhance the economic status of women.
Requirements: Grant funds may support current programs, test new ideas and methods, improve organizational efficiency, or support advocacy efforts. Contact the Program Director for funding information.
Geographic Focus: Montana
Amount of Grant: 1,000 - 10,000 USD
Contact: Jen Euell, (406) 443-8313; fax (406) 442-0482; jeuell@mtcf.org or info@mtcf.org
Internet: http://www.mtcf.org/wfmt.html
Sponsor: Montana Community Foundation
101 North Last Chance Gulch, Suite 211
Helena, MT 59601

Montgomery County Community Foundation Grants 3213
The Montgomery County Community Foundation Grants help fund non-profit organizations and agencies in Montgomery County, Indiana. Significant grants have been awarded to organizations such as the Crawfordsville District Public Library, Boys and Girls Club, and the Family Crisis Shelter. Organizations should contact the Foundation for a grant proposal application and other documentation required.
Requirements: A strong proposal will have several or all of the following characteristics: an estimate of who and how many will benefit; show long term potential; address a community problem of some significance for which funding is not covered by the regular budget; present an innovative and practical approach to solve a community problem or project; identify possible future funding, if needed; give evidence of the stability and qualifications of the organization applying; show cooperation within the organization and avoid duplication effort.
Restrictions: The Foundation will usually not fund any of the following: grants to individuals; programs which are religious or sectarian in nature, except when the program is open to the entire community; operating expenses such as salaries and utilities; parades, festivals and sporting events; endowment funds; any propaganda, political or otherwise, attempting to influence legislation or intervene in any political affairs or campaigns; an organization's past debts or existing obligations; or post-event or after-the-fact situations.
Geographic Focus: Indiana
Date(s) Application is Due: May 10
Amount of Grant: Up to 50,000 USD
Contact: Cheryl Keim; (765) 362-1267; fax (765) 361-0562; cheryl@mccf-in.org
Internet: http://www.mccf-in.org/Granthomenewpage.html
Sponsor: Montgomery County Community Foundation
119 East Main Street
Crawfordsville, IN 47933

MONY Foundation Grants 3214
The foundation awards grants in its areas of interest, including after-school community service and volunteer programs for youth, New York, NY; meeting the essential after-school needs of children and teens at risk, Syracuse, NY; and meeting the essential needs of minority children nationwide (with local MONY sales office). Types of support include employee matching gifts, employee-related scholarships, general operating support, in-kind gifts, matching/challenge support, and program development. Contact headquarters or local office by mail to obtain guidelines.
Restrictions: Grants do not support private foundations; fully participating members of the United Way; religious, fraternal, athletic, social, or veterans' organizations; individuals; capital fund drives; endowments; or deficit financing.
Geographic Focus: All States
Amount of Grant: 1,500 - 10,000 USD
Contact: Administrator; (212) 708-2468; fax (212) 708-2001; lynn_stekas@mony.com
Internet: http://www.mony.com
Sponsor: MONY Foundation
1740 Broadway, Mail Drop 10-36
New York, NY 10019

Moody Foundation Grants 3215
The Moody Foundation awards grants in the areas of education; social services; children; and community development. Inquiry letters are accepted at any time. Because the Foundation trustees meet four times a year to consider grant awards, the application process may take up to six months. Up to three projects may be submitted in order of highest priority. The inquiry form is available at the Foundation website.
Requirements: Grants are limited to Texas nonprofit 501(c)3 organizations.
Geographic Focus: Texas
Amount of Grant: 5,000 - 6,000,000 USD
Contact: Colleen Trammell, Assistant to Grants Director; (409) 763-5333; fax (409) 763-5564; colleen@moodyf.org
Internet: http://www.moodyf.org/HTMLversion/grantappset.htm
Sponsor: Moody Foundation
2302 Post Office Street, Suite 704
Galveston, TX 77550

Moran Family Foundation Grants 3216

The Moran Family Foundation supports innovative programs that promote healthy development of at-risk children and at-risk families whose lives are impacted by the challenges of poverty. The foundation is pursuing opportunities to partner with and support organizations focusing on strengthening its surrounding communities by promoting and preserving Catholic values.

Requirements: The Moran Family Foundation supports 501(c)3 tax-exempt organizations in the Greater Washington D.C. area as well as the Greater Cleveland, Ohio region and does not accept unsolicited requests for funding. Eligible organizations should query the foundation prior to submitting a formal proposal. Invited organizations may use the "Common Grant Letter of Intent" and the "Common Grant Application" designed by the Washington Regional Association of Grantmakers. These forms can be found on their web site at www.washingtongrantmakers.org.
Restrictions: The foundation does not make grants to individuals.
Geographic Focus: District of Columbia, Ohio, Virginia
Contact: Grants Administrator; moranfamfdn@aol.com
Internet: http://fdnweb.org/moran/
Sponsor: Moran Family Foundation
1489 Chain Bridge Road, Suite 200
McLean, VA 22101

Morgan Babcock Scholarships 3217

The Helene Morgan Babcock and Alfred L. Babcock Scholarship Trust was established in Massachusetts in 2005 with the purpose of providing scholarship awards to residents of Dunstable, Massachusetts, involved in community service. With that in mind, awards are given volunteers who are involved with community service, economic development programs, or mentoring. These scholarships are given directly to individual students who fulfill the requirements and apply by the annual March 1 deadline. A minimum of 50% of all scholarships awarded will be based on financial need. Amounts range between $2,000 and $4,000.

Requirements: Students must reside in the community of Dunstable, Massachusetts, at the time of graduation.
Geographic Focus: Massachusetts
Amount of Grant: 2,000 - 4,000 USD
Contact: Lee McGovern, Treasurer; (978) 649-7830 or (978) 649-7898
Sponsor: Morgan Babcock Scholarship Trust
588 Main Street
Dunstable, MA 01827-1315

Morris and Gwendolyn Cafritz Foundation Grants 3218

The Morris & Gwendolyn Cafritz Foundation supports IRS-registered, tax-exempt, 501(c)3 organizations with a public charity status of 509(a)(1) or 509(a)(2) only. These organizations must serve residents in the District of Columbia, Prince George's and Montgomery Counties in Maryland, Arlington and Fairfax Counties, and the cities of Alexandria and Falls Church in Virginia. Grants are made in four program areas: Arts and Humanities, Community Services, Education and Health.

Requirements: Nonprofits serving residents in the District of Columbia, Prince George's and Montgomery Counties in Maryland, Arlington and Fairfax Counties, and the cities of Alexandria and Falls Church in Virginia may apply.
Restrictions: The Foundation does not generally fund the following projects: capital campaigns; endowments; multi-year grants; special events or tables for special events. Please also note, the Foundation does not fund: organizations that do not have 501(c)3 tax-exempt status with the IRS; private foundations; public charities with a non-private foundation status of 509(a)(3); individuals; organizations whose missions fall outside the Foundations funding priorities; organizations serving residents outside the Washington, DC metropolitan area.
Geographic Focus: District of Columbia, Maryland, Virginia
Date(s) Application is Due: Mar 1; Jul 1; Nov 1
Contact: Rose Ann Cleveland, (202) 223-3100; fax (202) 296-7567; info@cafritzfoundation.org
Internet: http://www.cafritzfoundation.org/Applicant/app_guidelines.asp
Sponsor: Morris and Gwendolyn Cafritz Foundation
1825 K Sreet NW, Suite 1400
Washington, DC 20006

Morris K. Udall and Stewart L. Udall Foundation Dissertation Fellowships 3219

The foundation awards fellowships to doctoral candidates entering the final year of writing dissertations whose research concerns U.S. environmental public policy and/or environmental conflict resolution. Fellowships are intended to cover both academic and living expenses. Previous fellows' fields of study include political science; economics; government; anthropology; environmental science, policy and management; ecology; environmental justice; regional planning; geography; natural resource policy; and environmental analysis and design.

Requirements: Applicants must have completed all Ph.D. coursework and passed all preliminary exams; have approval for their dissertation research proposal; be entering the final year of writing the dissertation; and be a U.S. citizen, U.S. permanent resident, or U.S. national. Applicants must be enrolled at a U.S. institution of higher education. The primary focus of dissertation research should be U.S. environmental policy or environmental conflict resolution.
Restrictions: U.S. citizens attending universities outside the U.S. are not eligible. It is the foundation's intent that work conducted during the fellowship year be done in the U.S. Ph.D. candidates who hold a fellowship for the purpose of writing the dissertation during the year preceding or coinciding with the fellowship are not eligible.
Geographic Focus: All States
Date(s) Application is Due: Feb 24
Amount of Grant: 24,000 USD
Contact: Jane Curlin, (520) 670-5609; fax (520) 670-5530; curlin@udall.gov
Internet: http://udall.gov/OurPrograms/ECRFellowship/ECRFellowship.aspx
Sponsor: Morris K. Udall and Stewart L. Udall Foundation
130 S Scott Avenue
Tucson, AZ 85701-1922

Morris K. Udall and Stewart L. Udall Foundation Native American Congressional Internships 3220

The foundation provides ten-week summer internships in Washington, D.C., for Native American and Alaska Native students who wish to learn more about the federal government and issues affecting Indian Country. The internship is fully funded providing round-trip airfare, housing, per diem for food and incidentals, and a stipend at the close of the program. Interns work in congressional and agency offices where they have opportunities to research legislative issues important to tribal communities, network with key public officials and tribal advocacy groups, experience an insider's view of the federal government, and enhance their understanding of nation-building and tribal self-governance.

Requirements: Applicants must be a U.S. citizen or U.S. permanent resident. Internships are merit based to Native Americans and Alaska Natives with a college grade-point average of "B" or equivalent who are college juniors or seniors, recent graduates from tribal or four-year colleges, or graduate or law students. A demonstrated interest in fields related to tribal public policy, such as tribal governance, tribal law, Native American education, Native American health, Native American justice, natural resource protection, cultural preservation and revitalization, and Native American economic development is required.
Restrictions: Applicants must be Native Americans or Alaska Natives.
Geographic Focus: All States
Date(s) Application is Due: Jan 31
Amount of Grant: 1,200 USD
Contact: Chia Halpern, Program Coordinator; (520) 901-8500; halpern@udall.gov
Internet: http://udall.gov/OurPrograms/NACInternship/NACInternship.aspx
Sponsor: Morris K. Udall and Stewart L. Udall Foundation
130 S Scott Avenue
Tucson, AZ 85701-1922

Motorola Foundation Grants 3221

Motorola concentrates its giving in the following areas: engineering, technical, science or mathematics programs in K-12 schools or in universities and colleges; programs reaching traditionally under-represented groups in the areas of math, science, engineering and business; programs providing technical assistance, research and statistical information on the state of science and engineering education, or; progams that support the protection and preservation of the environment.

Requirements: All grants are made to 501(c)3 tax-exempt organizations.
Restrictions: Grants may not be made to individuals (scholarships, travel, business loans), religious groups, fraternity or sorority programs, political campaigns, private foundations, benefit events or ads, single disease causes, national health organizations or their local chapters, trade schools, product donations, media projects, capital fund drives, sports sponsorships, or endowment funds.
Geographic Focus: Arizona, California, Florida, Georgia, Illinois, Massachusetts, New Jersey, Pennsylvania, Texas
Contact: Matthew Blakely, (847) 576-7895; fax (847) 576-9440; giving@motorola.com
Internet: http://www.motorola.com/content.jsp?globalObjectId=8152
Sponsor: Motorola Foundation
1303 E Algonquin Road
Schaumburg, IL 60196

Mr. and Mrs. William Foulds Family Foundation Grants 3222

The Mr. and Mrs. William Foulds Family Foundation was established in 1984 to support and promote quality educational, cultural, and recreational programming for underserved populations. Preference is given to charitable organizations that serve the people of Manchester, Connecticut. Grants from the Foulds Family Foundation are one year in duration. The deadline for application is April 30. Applicants will be notified of grant decisions by letter within two to three months after the proposal deadline. Prospective applicants desiring further information regarding the application process should call the second phone number given. Applicants are also encouraged to review the foundation's funding history (link is available from the grant website).

Requirements: Applicants must have 501(c)3 tax-exempt status.
Restrictions: Grant requests for capital projects will not be considered. Applicants will not be awarded a grant for more than 3 consecutive years. The foundation does not support requests from individuals, organizations attempting to influence policy through direct lobbying, or any political campaigns.
Geographic Focus: Connecticut
Date(s) Application is Due: Apr 30
Contact: Carmen Britt; (860) 657-7019 or (860) 952-7392; carmen.britt@baml.com
Internet: https://www.bankofamerica.com/philanthropic/fn_search.action
Sponsor: Mr. and Mrs. William Foulds Family Foundation
200 Glastonbury Boulevard, Suite # 200, CT2-545-02-05
Glastonbury, CT 06033-4056

Ms. Foundation for Women Building Democracy Grants 3223

Through their funding, the Ms. Foundation aims to change systems that prevent people from participating fully in government and civil society. It supports groups that advocate for changes to the criminal justice and immigration systems so that all women, families and communities have the opportunity and resources to lead healthy, safe lives and benefit from the democratic principles of equity and justice. The Foundation promotes the voices

of those who have been excluded from decision making, especially low-income women, women of color, youth, LGBTQ individuals, and immigrants. The Foundation strives to invest in long-term civic engagement and support strategies that bring in new constituencies and expand social movements.
Requirements: Applicants must be nonprofit tax exempt organizations. Organizations can refer to the website for current deadlines, the application process, and previous grant recipients.
Geographic Focus: All States
Contact: Administrator; (212) 742-2300; fax (212) 742-1653; info@ms.foundation.org
Internet: http://ms.foundation.org/our_work/broad-change-areas/building-democracy
Sponsor: Ms. Foundation for Women
12 MetroTech Center, 26th Floor
Brooklyn, NY 11201

Ms. Foundation for Women Ending Violence Grants   3224
The Ms. Foundation works in partnership with grassroots, state, and national organizations to end gender-based violence by transforming policies, beliefs, and behaviors that threaten the well-being of individuals, families and communities nationwide. The Foundation supports a range of community-based strategies to stop violence before it occurs—to prevent violence directed against women, girls, and LGBTQ individuals. The Foundation also supports a movement to advance a community-based, social justice approach to child sexual abuse.
Requirements: Applicants must be tax exempt nonprofits organizations. The application process, current deadlines, and previous grant recipients can be found on the Foundation website.
Geographic Focus: All States
Contact: Administrator; (212) 742-2300; fax (212) 742-1653; info@ms.foundation.org
Internet: http://ms.foundation.org/our_work/broad-change-areas/ending-violence
Sponsor: Ms. Foundation for Women
12 MetroTech Center, 26th Floor
Brooklyn, NY 11201

Ms. Foundation for Women Health Grants   3225
The Ms. Foundation for Women supports organizing at grassroots, state and national levels to promote equitable access to health care and education for women and youth. The Foundation delivers strategic funding, technical assistance, and networking support to organizations that are working in their communities and beyond to address the urgent priorities of those most affected by failed health policies, especially low-income women, women of color, immigrant women, women living with HIV/AIDS, and LGBTQ youth. The Foundation strives to build social movements and advance policy and culture change in key areas: reproductive health, rights and justice; sexuality education; and women and AIDS.
Requirements: Applicants must be tax exempt nonprofit organizations. The application process, current deadlines, and previous grant recipients can be found on the Foundation website.
Geographic Focus: All States
Contact: Grants Contact; (212) 742-2300; fax (212) 742-1653; info@ms.foundation.org
Internet: http://ms.foundation.org/our_work/broad-change-areas/womens-health
Sponsor: Ms. Foundation for Women
12 MetroTech Center, 26th Floor
Brooklyn, NY 11201

Mt. Sinai Health Care Foundation Health of the Jewish Community Grants   3226
The Mt. Sinai Health Care Foundation seeks to assist Greater Cleveland's organizations and leaders to improve the health and well-being of the Jewish and general communities now and for generations to come. The Foundation will support projects that build organizational capacity in those Jewish organizations that address these needs. The Board of Directors of the Foundation meets on a quarterly basis to review proposals.
Requirements: 501(c)3 nonprofits serving greater Cleveland, Ohio may submit proposals for grant support. The foundation welcomes and encourages an informal conversation with program staff prior to the submission of a grant request.
Restrictions: In general, the foundation does not support general operating expenses, direct provision of health services, building or equipment expenses, fund-raising events, projects outside of greater Cleveland, endowment funds, lobbying, program advertising, grants for individuals, or scholarships.
Geographic Focus: Ohio
Date(s) Application is Due: Jan 1; Apr 1; Jul 1; Oct 1
Contact: Ann Freimuth; (216) 421-5500; fax (216) 421-5633; aks17@case.edu
Internet: http://www.mtsinaifoundation.org/whatwefund_jewishcommunity.html
Sponsor: Mount Sinai Health Care Foundation
11000 Euclid Avenue
Cleveland, OH 44106-1714

Mt. Sinai Health Care Foundation Health of the Urban Community Grants   3227
In the tradition of The Mt. Sinai Medical Center, the Foundation is committed to improving the health of Greater Cleveland's most vulnerable individuals and families. To achieve impact in this area, scale is a significant factor. The Foundation seeks to support especially those projects focusing on health promotion and disease prevention that have the potential to access large populations through existing community infrastructure. To optimize impact in large populations, partnering with both public and private funding sources may be appropriate and necessary. Of particular interest are proposals in the areas of health-related early childhood development and health-related aging.
Requirements: 501(c)3 nonprofits serving greater Cleveland, Ohio may submit proposals for grant support. The foundation welcomes and encourages an informal conversation with program staff prior to the submission of a grant request.
Restrictions: In general, the foundation does not support general operating expenses, direct provision of health services, building or equipment expenses, fund-raising events, projects outside of greater Cleveland, endowment funds, lobbying, program advertising, grants for individuals, or scholarships.
Geographic Focus: Ohio
Date(s) Application is Due: Jan 1; Apr 1; Jul 1; Oct 1
Contact: Ann Freimuth; (216) 421-5500; fax (216) 421-5633; aks17@case.edu
Internet: http://www.mtsinaifoundation.org/whatwefund_urbancommunity.html
Sponsor: Mount Sinai Health Care Foundation
11000 Euclid Avenue
Cleveland, OH 44106-1714

Mt. Sinai Health Care Foundation Health Policy Grants   3228
The Mt. Sinai Health Care Foundation seeks to assist Greater Cleveland's organizations and leaders to improve the health and well-being of the Jewish and general communities now and for generations to come. Notwithstanding significant support from the private sector and philanthropy, government at all levels remains the single greatest financial contributor to the health of at-risk populations, including children, the elderly, and the poor. Through strategic initiatives in the area of health policy, the Foundation seeks to support projects that maximize the effectiveness of government in meeting its safety-net obligations and the obligations of the Affordable Care Act.
Requirements: 501(c)3 nonprofits serving greater Cleveland, Ohio may submit proposals for grant support. The foundation welcomes and encourages an informal conversation with program staff prior to the submission of a grant request.
Restrictions: In general, the foundation does not support general operating expenses, direct provision of health services, building or equipment expenses, fund-raising events, projects outside of greater Cleveland, endowment funds, lobbying, program advertising, grants for individuals, or scholarships.
Geographic Focus: Ohio
Date(s) Application is Due: Jan 1; Apr 1; Jul 1; Oct 1
Contact: Jodi Mitchell; (216) 421-5500; fax (216) 421-5633; Jodi.Mitchell@case.edu
Internet: http://www.mtsinaifoundation.org/whatwefund_policy.html
Sponsor: Mount Sinai Health Care Foundation
11000 Euclid Avenue
Cleveland, OH 44106-1714

MTV Think Venturer Community Service Grants   3229
The program awards grants to support young people who are making a difference by creating and leading their own ongoing organizations, clubs, or businesses that address a need in their community. Program activities must focus on discrimination, education, environment, global issues, or sexual health. Each week, one grant will be awarded to a group of young people (two or more) who submit the most compelling and sustainable think venture application. Guidelines, rules and application are available online.
Requirements: To be selected as a Venturer, youth (age 13 and older) must have motivation to make a difference in the community; a youth-lead team that utilizes adults as resources, not as project directors; clear, attainable goals; a credible plan and budget, including a strategy to evaluate progress and community impact (Youth Ventures will help youth develop these); the energy and skills to succeed; an ally (mentor) committed to the organization's independence and success; a plan for how the venture will be sustainable; and ethical standards.
Geographic Focus: All States
Date(s) Application is Due: Dec 31
Amount of Grant: 1,000 USD
Contact: Grants Administrator; (212) 278-8930; thinkventures@youthventure.org
Internet: http://www.youthventure.org/index.php?tg=articles&idx=More&article=1276&topics=368
Sponsor: Youth Venture
690 Eighth Avenue, 6th Floor
New York, NY 10036

Murphy Institute Judith Kelleher Schafer Summer Internship Grants   3230
In the summer between junior and senior years, Political Economy majors may elect to participate in the Murphy Institute Judith Kelleher Schafer Summer Internship Grant Program. The Murphy Institute offers a limited number of internship grants in an open competition for Political Economy majors only. The main criterion for selection is a well-conceived plan of employment in a field related to political economy or public policy. Reading Summer stipends are tailored to need, reflecting current levels of individual financial aid and proximity of the internship to the student's home. In supporting the program, the Murphy Institute emphasizes personal initiative on the part of students in seeking internship opportunities.
Requirements: Political Economy Majors with Tulane University interested in applying to the Schafer Summer Internship Grant Program are asked to first make inquiries with a prospective employer and then apply to the Murphy Institute for internship support. The Schafer Summer Internship Grant Program is administered by Dr. John Howard, Associate Director of the Murphy Institute. Contact Dr. Howard via email
Geographic Focus: Louisiana, Algeria, Angola, Benin, Botswana, Burkina Faso, Burundi, Cameroon, Cape Verde, Central African Republic, Chad, Comoros, Congo, Congo, Democratic Republic of, Cote d' Ivoire (Ivory Coast), Djibouti, Egypt, Equatorial Guinea, Eritrea, Ethiopia, Gabon, Gambia, Ghana, Guinea, Guinea-Bissau, Kenya, Lesotho, Liberia, Libya, Madagascar, Malawi, Mali, Mauritania, Mauritius, Morocco, Mozambique, Namibia, Niger, Nigeria, Rwanda, Sao Tome & Principe, Senegal, Seychelles, Sierra Leone, Somalia, South Africa, Sudan, Swaziland
Contact: John Howard, Associate Director; (504) 862-3234; jhoward2@tulane.edu
Internet: http://murphy.tulane.edu/undergraduate/internships.php
Sponsor: Murphy Institute, Tulane University
108 Tilton Hall
New Orleans, LA 70118

Musgrave Foundation Grants 3231
The foundation awards grants to eligible Missouri tax-exempt organizations in its areas of interest, including civic and public affairs, community development, elementary education, secondary education, higher education, and social services. Types of support include annual campaigns, building construction/renovation, capital campaigns, continuing support, equipment acquisition, general operating support, matching grants, and scholarship funds.
Requirements: 501(c)3 tax-exempt organizations and colleges, universities, and schools in Missouri may apply.
Restrictions: Grants are not made to individuals.
Geographic Focus: Missouri
Date(s) Application is Due: May 31
Amount of Grant: 500 - 61,000 USD
Contact: Jerry Redfern, Program Contact; (417) 841-4698 or (417) 882-9090; fax (417) 882-2529; jredfern@musgravefoundation.org
Internet: http://www.musgravefoundation.org
Sponsor: Musgrave Foundation
P.O. Box 10327
Springfield, MO 65804

NAA Foundation Diversity PowerMind Fellowships 3232
The Newspaper Association of America (NAA) Foundation strives to develop engaged and literate citizens in a diverse society. The Foundation endeavors to help news media companies increase their readership and audience by offering programs that encourage the cultivation of a more diverse work force in the press. Diversity PowerMind Fellowships are a potent professional development tool aimed at cultivating the next generation of newspaper leaders. Fifteen Fellows are chosen for a six-month program which includes monthly teleconferences, webinars, and conversations with individual advisors as well as attendance at the NAA mediaXchange Conference. See the website for an application form and deadlines or contact the Foundation for more information.
Requirements: Applicants must: be managers of color at newspaper companies and have at least five years of total professional experience; commit to four hours of self-development each month during the six-month term of the program; and obtain a recommendation from his/her direct supervisor.
Geographic Focus: All States
Date(s) Application is Due: Nov 4
Contact: Jeanne Fox-Alston, Fellowship Coordinator; (571) 366-1005; fax (571) 366-1158; jeanne.foxalston@naa.org or NAAFoundation@naa.org
Internet: http://www.naafoundation.org/Grants/Diversity/PowerMind.aspx
Sponsor: Newspaper Association of America Foundation
4401 Wilson Boulevard, Suite 900
Arlington, VA 22203

NAA Foundation Minority Fellowships 3233
The Newspaper Association of America (NAA) Foundation strives to develop engaged and literate citizens in a diverse society. The Foundation endeavors to help news media companies increase their readership and audience by offering programs that encourage the cultivation of a more diverse work force in the press. Designed to widen opportunities for people of color to enter or advance in the newspaper industry, Minority Fellowships help participants attend training seminars sponsored by media organizations. Applicants should either be in a management position or demonstrate managerial potential. Fellowships cover event/seminar registration fees and, where applicable, travel, meals and hotel expenses. Minority Fellowships are offered twice a year. See the website for a list of events being offered and the organizations sponsoring them, the application form, and deadlines. Contact the Foundation for more information.
Requirements: Newspaper executives and journalism educators are asked to nominate candidates who demonstrate managerial potential. Supervisor recommendations play a key role in the selection of fellows. For that reason, applicants should work closely with their supervisors when applying.
Geographic Focus: All States
Contact: Jeanne Fox-Alston; (571) 366-1005; jeanne.foxalston@naa.org
Internet: http://www.naafoundation.org/Grants/Diversity/Minority-Fellowship.aspx
Sponsor: Newspaper Association of America Foundation
4401 Wilson Boulevard, Suite 900
Arlington, VA 22203

NAA Foundation Teacher Fellowships 3234
The Foundation strives to develop engaged and literate citizens in a diverse society. The Foundation invests in and supports programs designed to enhance student achievement through newspaper readership and appreciation of the First Amendment. Teacher Fellowships seek teachers, curriculum specialists, media center coordinators, school librarians and other educational professionals who are interested in developing and delivering presentations on their newspaper instructional practices for local, regional and national education gatherings. Teacher Fellowships pay for workshop or conference-related expenses, including travel. See the website for submission deadlines or contact the Foundation with questions.
Requirements: Applicants with a desire to demonstrate and share with other educational professionals should submit a letter of interest that includes: the intended educational audience/event; the event proposal submission deadline; the subject/grade level; a session or workshop title; and a brief session/workshop description, including details about how newspapers are used for instruction.
Geographic Focus: All States
Contact: Sandy Woodcock, Director; (571) 366-1008; fax (571) 366-1195; sandy.woodcock@naa.org or NAAFoundation@naa.org
Internet: http://www.naafoundation.org/Grants/Teacher-Fellowships.aspx
Sponsor: Newspaper Association of America Foundation
4401 Wilson Boulevard, Suite 900
Arlington, VA 22203

NACC David Stevenson Fellowships 3235
The goals of the David Stevenson fellowship are to acknowledge David Stevenson's many contributions to the development of data and information about the nonprofit sector and the important role he played in teaching and working with undergraduate students; and to encourage junior faculty members of color to provide leadership for the field and to assist them in gaining tenure in their respective academic institutions. Two fellowships are awarded annually. Fellowships may be used to support research, travel to present research at conferences, and professional education seminars related to research and teaching. The fellowship must be completed between August 1 and July 31. The award will be made payable to the award recipient's affiliate institution. Guidelines are available online. The Nonprofit Academic Centers Council (NACC) is a membership association comprised of academic centers or programs at accredited colleges and universities that focus on the study of nonprofit organizations, voluntarism and/or philanthropy. Established in 1991, NACC is the first group entirely dedicated to the promotion and networking of centers that provide research and education in philanthropy and the nonprofit sector.
Requirements: Applicants must meet the following eligibility criteria: be junior faculty in a tenure track position; be affiliated with an accredited institution of higher education in the United States or Canada (the institution need not be a member of NACC); be members of the African-American, Latino, Asian/Pacific Islander, or American-Indian/Alaskan-Native communities; be committed to excellence in research and teaching in the field of philanthropic or nonprofit-sector studies or nonprofit management from any one of a variety of academic disciplines; and be willing and able to participate in the annual ARNOVA conference (travel expenses will be paid by NACC). Applications will be evaluated by a selection committee of distinguished scholars in the field and colleagues of David Stevenson using the following criteria: significance and quality of proposed research to the field of philanthropic and nonprofit-sector studies; relationship of the topic to the education of undergraduate students or to the development of relevant data and information systems; merit of the proposed project and use of fellowship funds; ability of the applicant to carry out the proposed activity; and the applicant's ability to present a well-written, thoughtfully-prepared application. Priority consideration will be made for nontenured junior faculty. An emphasis on quality and the potential for a candidate to provide leadership in the field will also be a considering factor.
Restrictions: Travel expenses to attend the ARNOVA conference are not transferable as additional award money. Travel to attend the ARNOVA conference is limited to the year of the award and up to two years after the award to present fellowship-related research results.
Geographic Focus: All States
Date(s) Application is Due: Mar 31
Amount of Grant: 15,000 USD
Contact: Sean W. Shacklett; (216) 368-0969; fax (216) 368-0969; sshacklett-nacc@case.edu
Internet: http://www.nacccouncil.org/stevenson.asp
Sponsor: Case Western Reserve University
10900 Euclid Avenue
Cleveland, OH 44106-7167

NACC William Diaz Fellowships 3236
The goals of the William Diaz Fellowship are to acknowledge William Diaz's contributions to the development of minority leadership for nonprofit organizations, foundations, and the field of philanthropic and nonprofit management studies and to encourage a better understanding of philanthropy from diverse communities. Two fellowships are awarded annually. Fellowships may be used to support research, travel to present research at conferences, professional education seminars related to research and teaching, and course development. All funds must be expended and accounted for within one year after the end of the fellowship. The award will be made payable to the award recipient's affiliate institution. Guidelines are available online. The Nonprofit Academic Centers Council (NACC) is a membership association comprised of academic centers or programs at accredited colleges and universities that focus on the study of nonprofit organizations, voluntarism and/or philanthropy. Established in 1991, NACC is the first group entirely dedicated to the promotion and networking of centers that provide research and education in philanthropy and the nonprofit sector.
Requirements: Applicants must meet the following eligibility criteria: be faculty of any rank (including senior faculty new to philanthropic and nonprofit management studies) whose work focuses on philanthropy, nonprofit organizations, and diversity; be affiliated with an accredited institution of higher education in the United States or Canada (the institution need not be a member of NACC); be members of the African-American, Latino, Asian/Pacific Islander, or American-Indian/Alaskan-Native communities; be committed to excellence in research and teaching in the field of philanthropic or nonprofit-sector studies or nonprofit management from any one of a variety of academic disciplines; be willing and able to participate in the annual ARNOVA Conference (travel expenses will be paid by NACC). Applications will be evaluated by a selection committee of distinguished scholars in the field and colleagues of William Diaz using the following criteria: significance and quality of proposed research; relationship of the proposed research, if any, to the development of minority leadership for nonprofit organizations, foundations, and the field of philanthropic and nonprofit-sector studies; merit of the proposed project and use of fellowship funds; ability of the applicant to carry out the proposed activity; and applicant's ability to present a well-written, thoughtfully-prepared application.
Restrictions: Travel expenses to attend the ARNOVA conference are not transferable as additional award money. Travel to attend the ARNOVA conference is limited to the year of the award and up to two years after the award to present fellowship-related research results.
Geographic Focus: All States
Date(s) Application is Due: Mar 30

Amount of Grant: 15,000 USD
Contact: Sean W. Shacklett; (216) 368-0969; fax (216) 368-0969; sshacklett-nacc@case.edu
Internet: http://www.naccouncil.org/diaz.asp
Sponsor: Case Western Reserve University
10900 Euclid Avenue
Cleveland, OH 44106-7167

NAGC Masters and Specialists Award 3237
The National Association for Gifted Children (NAGC) presents a maximum of three awards to those who have demonstrated at least four of the following: teaching; writing; advocacy; curriculum development; community service in gifted education; juried presentations (local, state, or national); facilitating the social and emotional development of gifted and talented students; mentoring/tutoring of children and adolescents; publication of papers in juried and/or non-juried publications; participation in graduate student research colloquia; teacher in-service/parent workshop.
Requirements: Viable candidates will have a proven record of at least four of the following: teaching; writing; advocacy; curriculum development; community service in gifted education; juried presentations (local, state, or national); facilitating the social and emotional development of gifted and talented students; mentoring/tutoring of children and adolescents; publication of papers in juried and/or non-juried publications; participation in graduate student research colloquia; teacher in-service/parent workshop
Restrictions: An individual may receive this award once. The award must be given within a year of the candidate's graduation. A maximum of one candidate and award can be given to one institution.
Geographic Focus: All States
Date(s) Application is Due: Apr 20
Amount of Grant: 200 USD
Contact: Jeff Danielian; (202) 785-4268; fax (202) 785-4248; danielian@nagc.org
Internet: http://www.nagc.org/index.aspx?id=696
Sponsor: National Association for Gifted Children
1707 L Street NW, Suite 550
Washington, DC 20036

NAR HOPE Awards for Minority Owners 3238
The HOPE (Home Ownership Participation for Everyone) Awards is a national industry awards program that was created in 2001 to recognize individuals and organizations who have made outstanding contributions to increasing minority homeownership, revitalizing communities and expanding affordable housing opportunities. The HOPE Awards are sponsored by a partnership of real estate associations; awards are conferred every other year. The awards honor those who work every day to close the divide in the American dream and help make the face of homeownership in this country look more like America. HOPE Award winners receive a $10,000 honorarium, national media coverage, paid travel expenses to attend and speak at a minority housing symposium, recognition at the HOPE Awards Gala.
Requirements: Nonprofit organizations are eligible.
Geographic Focus: All States
Amount of Grant: 10,000 USD
Contact: Sara Weis, Senior Public Affairs Associate; (202) 383-1013; sweis@realtors.org
Internet: http://www.hopeawards.org/hope/index.htm
Sponsor: National Association of Realtors
500 New Jersey Avenue NW
Washington, DC 20001-2020

NAR Partners in Housing Awards 3239
Grants are available to U.S. nonprofit organizations that partner with local realtor associations on low-income housing projects. This is a joint initiative of the National Association of Realtors and the Fannie Mae Foundation. Projects are evaluated based on the level of realtor involvement, their ability to address a particular affordable housing problem, the need for financial assistance, and the project's potential to serve as a model for other realtor associations. The deadline is in early October.
Requirements: Nominations for the annual award are made by participating realtor association to the National Association of Realtors.
Geographic Focus: All States
Amount of Grant: 2,500 - 10,000 USD
Contact: Sara Weis, Senior Public Affairs Associate; (202) 383-1013; sweis@realtors.org
Internet: http://www.realtor.org/
Sponsor: National Association of Realtors
500 New Jersey Avenue NW
Washington, DC 20001-2020

NAR Realtor Magazine Good Neighbor Awards 3240
The Awards recognize the ongoing efforts of individual realtors who are making exceptional contributions to improve the quality of life in their communities. Among the activities that qualify for consideration are involvement in affordable housing issues, improving the quality of education in an area, supporting initiatives aimed at a community's youth, and work on any other community-based programs. Additional activities may include such things as crime prevention, youth mentoring, and homelessness prevention. Five winners will be announced in Realtor Magazine and will be recognized at the annual convention. The winners will receive travel expenses to the convention, national media exposure for their community cause, and a grant of $10,000. In addition to the winners, five honorable mentions will each receive a grant of $2,500 each. Guidelines and application forms are available online.
Requirements: Nominees must be members of National Aassociation of Realtors in good standing.
Geographic Focus: All States
Date(s) Application is Due: May 22
Amount of Grant: 2,500 - 10,000 USD
Contact: Sara Weis, Senior Public Affairs Associate; (202) 383-1013; sweis@realtors.org
Internet: http://www.realtor.org/rmodaily.nsf/pages/GoodNeighborPrizes?OpenDocument
Sponsor: National Association of Realtors
500 New Jersey Avenue NW
Washington, DC 20001-2020

NASE Foundation Future Entrepreneur Scholarship 3241
The NASE Foundation Future Entrepreneur Scholarship program promotes youth entrepreneurship. The program provides financial aid to selected individuals to assist them in obtaining an undergraduate college or university degree. One NASE Foundation Future Entrepreneur scholarship of up to $24,000 ($12,000 in the first year, with the option for $4,000 renewals in subsequent years if eligible) will be awarded each year, and one NASE Foundation Future Entrepreneur runner-up scholarship of $4,000 will also be awarded annually.
Requirements: Applicants for the NASE Foundation Future Entrepreneur scholarship must own and operate their own business, and must be able to demonstrate through the application how their selected course of study supports their business or career goals.
Geographic Focus: All States
Date(s) Application is Due: Apr 1
Amount of Grant: Up to 24,000 USD
Contact: Kristie Arslan, (800) 649-6273 or (800) 232-6273
Internet: http://www.nase.org/Membership/GrantsandScholarships.aspx
Sponsor: National Association for the Self-Employed
P.O. Box 241
Annapolis Junction, MD 20701-0241

NASE Growth Grants 3242
The National Association for the Self-Employed (NASE) Growth Grants program offers access to capital for micro-business owners who have a specific business need, but lack the finances to carry out that goal. The program was designed after an online NASE Member poll found that a majority of micro-business owners (57 percent) initially fund their businesses using personal savings, and many (40 percent) continue to use personal savings for ongoing financing. Grants (up to $5,000) can be used for marketing, advertising, hiring employees, expanding facilities and other specific business needs.
Requirements: Applicants must: be an NASE Member in good standing; demonstrate a business need that could be fulfilled by the grant; provide a detailed explanation of how you will use the grant proceeds; show how the grant will improve your business growth and success; offer supporting documentation such as a résumé and business plan. There are no specific deadlines.
Geographic Focus: All States
Amount of Grant: Up to 5,000 USD
Contact: Kristie L. Arslan, (800) 649-6273 or (800) 232-6273
Internet: https://www.nase.org/Membership/Benefits/Growth_Grants.aspx
Sponsor: National Association for the Self-Employed
P.O. Box 241
Annapolis Junction, MD 20701-0241

NASE Succeed Scholarships 3243
With the NASE's Succeed Scholarship program, NASE members can apply for a scholarship of up to $4,000 to help pay for continuing education through university or college courses, attend training courses for business licensing and certification, or attend conferences and seminars that will help grow their businesses.
Requirements: To be eligible for an NASE Succeed Scholarship, you must: be an NASE Member in good standing; document the potential of the scholarship to satisfy a business need; demonstrate the potential impact of the course on overall business growth and success; offer supporting documentation such as a résumé and business plan. There are no specific deadlines.
Geographic Focus: All States
Amount of Grant: Up to 4,000 USD
Contact: Kristie L. Arslan, (800) 649-6273 or (800) 232-6273
Internet: http://www.nase.org/Membership/Benefits/Succeed_Scholarships.aspx
Sponsor: National Association for the Self-Employed
P.O. Box 241
Annapolis Junction, MD 20701-0241

Natalie W. Furniss Charitable Trust Grants 3244
The Mission of the Furniss Foundation is to promote the humane treatment of animals by providing funding to societies for the prevention of cruelty to animals.
Requirements: Qualifying tax-exempt 501(c)3 organizations operating in the state of New Jersey are eligible to apply. Applications are accepted Ocotber 1 - December 1. Complete the Common Grant Application form available at the Wachovi website to apply for funding.
Restrictions: Grants are not made for political purposes.
Geographic Focus: New Jersey
Date(s) Application is Due: Dec 1
Contact: Wachovia Bank, N.A., Trustee; grantinquiries6@wachovia.com
Internet: https://www.wachovia.com/foundation/v/index.jsp?vgnextoid=61078689fb0aa110VgnVCM1000004b0d1872RCRD&vgnextfmt=default
Sponsor: Natalie W. Furniss Foundation
100 North Main Street
Winston Salem, NC 27150

Nathan B. and Florence R. Burt Foundation Grants 3245

The Foundation awards funding to organizations primarily in the Denver area that deal with the needs of children and senior citizens. Application and specific guidelines are available online. Deadlines are in the spring and fall each year after Foundation board meetings.
Requirements: Grants are awarded primarily to Colorado 501(c)3 charitable and educational organizations. Applicants should emphasis a specific purpose, program, or need with the online application.
Restrictions: The Foundation does not make grant for general operating or capital construction costs, individuals, or political causes, organizations, or candidates.
Geographic Focus: Colorado
Contact: Gregory Dickson; (303) 393-0615 or (303) 863-8400; fax (303) 832-4703
Internet: http://www.burtfoundation.org/grantapp.htm
Sponsor: Nathan B. and Florence R. Burt Foundation
1660 Lincoln Street
Denver, CO 80264

Nathan Cummings Foundation Grants 3246

The Nathan Cummings Foundation is rooted in the Jewish tradition and committed to democratic values and social justice, including fairness, diversity, and community. It seeks to build a socially and economically just society that values nature and protects the ecological balance for future generations; promotes humane health care; and fosters arts and culture that enriches communities. The Foundation's core programs include arts and culture; the environment; health; interprogram initiatives for social and economic justice; and the Jewish life and values/contemplative practice programs. Basic themes informing the Foundation's approach to grantmaking are: concern for the poor, disadvantaged, and underserved; respect for diversity; promotion of understanding across cultures; and empowerment of communities in need. The Board meets twice a year. Applicants should apply by January 15 to be considered for the spring Board meeting and by August 15 to be considered for the fall Board meeting.
Requirements: Eligible applicants must be 501(c)3 organizations. A two or three page letter of inquiry may be submitted with the following information: basic organizational information; contact person; grant purpose; key personnel; project budget and total organizational budget; amount requested and the length of time for which funds are being requested; and other funding sources. Projects that most closely fit with the Foundation's goals will be invited to submit a complete application.
Restrictions: The following is not funded: individuals; scholarships; sponsorships; capital or endowment campaigns; foreign-based organizations; specific diseases; local synagogues or institutions with local projects; Holocaust related projects; projects with no plans for replication; and general support for Jewish education.
Geographic Focus: All States
Contact: Armanda Famiglietti; (212) 787-7300; info@nathancummings.org
Internet: http://www.nathancummings.org/programs/index.html
Sponsor: Nathan Cummings Foundation
475 10th Avenue, 14th Floor
New York, NY 10018

Nathaniel and Elizabeth P. Stevens Foundation Grants 3247

The Foundation awards funding to eligible Massachusetts nonprofit organizations to improve the quality of life in the greater area comprising Lawrence and Merrimack Valley. Funding includes operating support, program support, special projects, renovations, capital and equipment. The Foundation Trustees generally meet monthly, with the exceptions of July and August. Applicants are encouraged to seek other sources of funding while waiting for funding decisions. Awards range from $250 to $30,000.
Requirements: Eligible applicants must be 501(c)3 Massachusetts charitable organizations. Applications will be considered for experimental and demonstration projects, program expansion, evaluation, renovations, new construction projects and capital funding. Grants may be made to a 501(c)3 organization for the benefit of another organization awaiting its own tax-exempt status. A complete proposal should include: most recent annual financial statement (preferably audited); institutional income and expense budget for current fiscal year; detailed program budget for which support is being requested; and starting and completion dates of proposed program and planned cash flow. If an organization's proposal is complete and fits within the guidelines of the Foundation, the applicant organization may be contacted to provide further information. Contact information should be included with the application.
Restrictions: Awards are not made to the following: individuals; national organizations; annual giving campaigns; and state or federal agencies. The Foundation will not consider a proposal from an organization previously funded until a full report of the expenditures of the previous grant has been submitted. The Trustees will not consider more than one application from an agency in the same calendar year except for summer youth programs.
Geographic Focus: Massachusetts
Contact: Joshua Miner; (978) 688-7211; grantprocess@stevensfoundation.com
Sponsor: Nathaniel and Elizabeth P. Stevens Foundation
P.O. Box 111
North Andover, MA 01845

National 4-H Afterschool Training Grants 3248

The 4-H Afterschool Training Grants, partnering with the MetLife Foundation and National 4-H Council, provide high quality training to at least 5,500 local after-school providers annually. The grants seek to improve the quality of after-school programs; infuse civic engagement into after-school programs; and increase the number of youth engaged in high quality after-school programs. Competitive grants of $15,000 each will be awarded to ten state 4-H programs. Grantees will be expected to provide a minimum of eight hours of training to at least 550 local after-school providers. This enhanced partnership will result in providing underrepresented youth with opportunities to reach their full academic potential through their participation in high quality after-school programs. Through this partnership, National 4-H Council aims to impact more than 200,000 at-risk youth and 11,000 after-school providers nationwide. This grant cycle generally runs from February – November.
Requirements: Organizations should refer to the website for instructions on how to log on and create a password to access the 4-H application system.
Restrictions: Only 4-H state programs may apply.
Geographic Focus: All States
Amount of Grant: 15,000 USD
Contact: Jill Bramble, Vice President for Development; (301) 961-2100
Internet: http://www.4-h.org/resource-library/grants-awards/opportunities/
Sponsor: National 4-H Council
7100 Connecticut Avenue
Chevy Chase, MD 20815

National Book Scholarship Fund 3249

The purpose of the National Book Scholarship Fund (NBSF) is to distribute direct in-kind assistance to local literacy providers throughout the United States. NBSF grants are intended to provide the New Readers Press books and other materials essential to begin a new literacy outreach program or to significantly expand an existing effort. First priority will be given to programs that focus on women and intergenerational or family literacy concerns. Other organizations working in economically disadvantaged urban and rural areas, among homeless populations, in refugee resettlement efforts, in workplace literacy efforts, and English-as-a-second-language initiatives will also receive consideration for support. Types of support include program development grants, research grants, scholarships, technical assistance, and training grants. Applications are accepted from September until December. applicants are encouraged to apply early because NBSF applications are reviewed and awards are made on a first-come, first-served basis.
Requirements: Programs applying for a grant must agree to provide, from local sources, a cash payment equal to 20% of the total amount being requested in the grant application to defray the costs of NBSF administration.
Geographic Focus: All States
Date(s) Application is Due: Apr 14
Amount of Grant: 500 - 8,000 USD
Contact: Michele Diecuch, Program Administrator; (888) 528-2224 or (315) 422-9121, ext. 321; fax (315) 422-6369; mdiecuch@proliteracy.org
Internet: http://www.servicelearning.org/funding-sources#category310
Sponsor: ProLiteracy Worldwide
1320 Jamesville Avenue
Syracuse, NY 13210

National Center for Responsible Gaming Conference Scholarships 3250

The National Center for Responsible Gaming (NCRG) is offering the need-based scholarship program for the NCRG Conference on Gambling and Addiction. Insofar it is able, it is the NCRG's wish to provide fair access to the NCRG Conference to all interested stakeholders, especially those in academia and the clinical and public health sectors. Last year, the NCRG supported almost thirty NCRG Conference attendees. This year, the NCRG will award scholarships to more than fifteen individuals, and a portion of these scholarships may also include travel assistance. Additional scholarship funds may be available at a later time. To apply for a scholarship, interested applicants must submit their application and registration form by June 15.
Geographic Focus: All States
Date(s) Application is Due: Jun 15
Contact: Christine Reilly; (978) 338-6610; fax (978) 522-8452; creilly@ncrg.org
Internet: http://www.ncrg.org/public-education-and-outreach/conference/conference-scholarships
Sponsor: National Center for Responsible Gaming
900 Cummings Center, Suite 418-U
Beverly, MA 01915

National Center for Responsible Gaming Travel Grants 3251

Travel Grants are intended to support the attendance of postdoctoral investigators at scientific meetings at which they will present a paper or a poster on gambling research. Applicants may request up to $1,500 in support of conference registration fees, airfare, ground transportation, meals and lodging. Eligible meetings include academic conferences that employ rigorous peer review in the selection of presentations.
Requirements: Travel Grants are available to scientists who are not more than ten years beyond their doctorate (Ph.D.) or medical residence. The applicant must be the first author of the paper or poster to be presented. Eligible candidates must be based at a U.S. institution.
Restrictions: The Principal Investigator may apply for only one Travel Grant per cycle.
Geographic Focus: All States
Amount of Grant: Up to 1,500 USD
Contact: Christine Reilly; (978) 338-6610; fax (978) 522-8452; creilly@ncrg.org
Internet: http://www.ncrg.org/research-center/apply-ncrg-funding/travel-grants
Sponsor: National Center for Responsible Gaming
900 Cummings Center, Suite 418-U
Beverly, MA 01915

National Endowment for Democracy Reagan-Fascell Democracy Fellowships 3252

The program enables democracy activists, practitioners, scholars, and journalists from around the world to deepen their understanding of democracy and enhance their ability to promote democratic change. Fellows maintain full-time residence at the International Forum for Democratic Studies, the research arm of the Endowment. The Forum hosts 12 to 15 Reagan-Fascell fellows per year for periods ranging from three to ten months. The program offers two

tracks, a practitioner track and a scholarly track. Fellowships on the practitioner track tend to be short-term (three to five months), typically culminating in a strategy memorandum, short article, or op-ed and a presentation of the fellow's analysis and ideas. The scholarly track is principally for professors and researchers from emerging and aspiring democracies. Accomplished scholars from established democracies are also eligible to apply. During their three- to 10-month stay at the Forum, scholars make at least one presentation and complete a substantial piece of writing (a monograph or book) for publication. Each fellow receives a monthly stipend for living expenses, plus health insurance and reimbursement for travel to and from Washington, DC. Fellows also receive a fully equipped office and support services. Application and guidelines are available online.
Requirements: There are no specific degree requirements for applicants selecting the practitioner track; candidates are expected to have substantial practical experience working on behalf of some aspect of democracy building—such as human rights advocacy, political party activism, voter education, election monitoring, journalism and press freedom, ethnic pluralism, civic education, etc. Individuals applying in the scholarly track are expected to possess a PhD or academic equivalent at the time of application, to have published in their field of expertise, and to have developed a detailed research outline for their fellowship project. Examples of eligible candidates for the scholarly track include college and university professors, scholars, analysts at research centers, and independent writers.
Geographic Focus: All States
Date(s) Application is Due: Nov 10
Contact: Coordinator; (202) 378-9700; fax (202) 378-9407; fellowships@ned.org
Internet: http://www.ned.org/forum/reagan-fascell.html
Sponsor: National Endowment for Democracy
1025 F Street NW, Suite 800
Washington, DC 20004

National Endowment for Democracy Visiting Fellows Program 3253
The International Forum for Democratic Studies hosts a small number of Visiting Fellows per year as part of its program. Visiting Fellows are scholars and practitioners who wish to conduct research and writing at the Forum for a limited period of time but do not need any financial assistance. Space permitting, Visiting Fellows may be in residence at the Forum for periods ranging from three to ten months, during which time they are expected to carry out a written or other project related to democracy. While Visiting Fellows do not receive stipend and travel support, the Forum is able to provide use of the Democracy Resource Center and Library and, depending on space availability, a fully equipped office as well. Visiting Fellows have the opportunity to participate in the many events at the Endowment, and to interact with staff and other fellows in residence from around the world. There is no deadline for applying: to receive timely consideration, inquiries and applications must be received at least six months in advance of the proposed starting date of the fellowship.
Geographic Focus: All States
Contact: Coordinator; (202) 378-9700; fax (202) 378-9407; fellowships@ned.org
Internet: http://www.ned.org/forum/visiting_fellows.html
Sponsor: National Endowment for Democracy
1025 F Street NW, Suite 800
Washington, DC 20004

National Endowment for the Arts - Grants to Challenge America Fast-Track 3254
This program supports small and mid-sized organizations for projects that extend the reach of the arts to underserved populations. Underserved population is defined as those whose opportunities to experience the arts are limited by geography, ethnicity, economics, or disability. Grants are available for professional arts programming and for projects that emphasize the potential of the arts in community development. These grants encourages the following two outcomes: engagement - engaging the public with diverse and excellent art, such as a festival, exhibit, recital, reading, performance, screening, broadcast or lecture; or livability - strengthening of communities through the arts, with projects such as streetscapes, wayfinding signage, or landscape architecture, architectural studies, design workshops or competitions, or facility feasibility or predevelopment studies. Activities also may include all design stages for the renovation, restoration, or adaptive reuse of existing structures to be used as cultural facilities. The NEA encourages organizations with operating budgets of less than $50,000 and organizations that have not applied for public funds previously to consider applying to local or state sources to gain practical experience with managing public funds. Application information is available at the NEA website, but organizations must apply through Grants.gov. Organizations are notified within six months of application.
Requirements: School districts, government agencies, and arts and youth-serving organizations may apply.
Restrictions: Grants require a minimum $10,000 match. Funding is not available for activities that occur over an extended period (e.g., projects that span a full season, long-term residencies, and most large-scale projects); competitions other than design competitions; projects that involve curriculum-based instruction in the arts; subgranting or regranting; or the same organization (parent or component) for more than three consecutive years, even if for different projects.
Geographic Focus: All States
Date(s) Application is Due: May 24
Amount of Grant: 10,000 USD
Contact: Stacey Gilchrist, Grants Management Specialist; (202) 682-5403; fax (202) 682-5609; gilchris@arts.gov
Internet: http://www.arts.gov/grants/apply/GAP13/Challenge.html
Sponsor: National Endowment for the Arts
1100 Pennsylvania Avenue NW
Washington, DC 20506-0001

National Endowment for the Arts - National Arts and Humanities Youth Awards 3255
The National Arts and Humanities Youth Program Award is the Nation's highest honor for out-of-school arts and humanities programs that celebrate the creativity of young people, particularly those from underserved communities. This award recognizes and supports excellence in programs that open new pathways to learning, self-discovery, and achievement. Each year, the National Arts and Humanities Youth Program Awards recognize 12 outstanding programs in the U.S., from a wide range of urban and rural settings. Recipients receive a $10,000 grant and the opportunity to visit the White House and accept the award from the First Lady. Awardees also receive a full year of capacity-building and communications support, designed to make their organizations stronger. In addition, 38 exceptional youth-focused arts and humanities programs across the U.S. receive a Finalist Certificate of Excellence. One country each year also receives an International Spotlight Award for a remarkable youth-oriented cultural program. After-school and out-of-school time arts and humanities programs sponsored by museums, libraries, performing arts organizations; educational institutions (e.g., preschools; elementary, middle, and high schools; universities; and colleges), arts centers, community service organizations, businesses, and eligible government entities are encouraged to consider submitting an application. Applications are submitted online at the National Arts and Humanities Youth Program website.
Requirements: Programs are eligible to apply if they meet all of the following *Requirements:* operate as a program for children and youth outside of the school day. Preschool, after-school, weekend, and/or summer programs, however, may have a school-based component or use school space. Multi-site initiatives that meet the criteria also are eligible; use one or more disciplines of the arts or the humanities as the core content of its program(s); concentrate on children and youth who live in family and community circumstances that limit their opportunities—underserved children and youth are the primary participants in the program; involve children and youth as active participants in the arts or humanities experience; cultural programs in which children function only as an audience are not eligible for a National Arts and Humanities Youth Program Award; provide participants with ongoing, regularly scheduled sessions; one-time and occasional programs will not be considered; integrate arts or humanities education programs with youth development goals (e.g., enhanced leadership skills, delf-confidence, and peer relations); have been operational for a minimum of five years; be a nonprofit, tax-exempt 501(c)3 organization, unit of state or local government, or federally recognized tribal community or tribe; and in good standing if a federal grant recipient.
Restrictions: Prior award recipients are not eligible. Programs that concentrate only on preparing youth for an artistic or cultural career are not eligible to apply.
Geographic Focus: All States, All Countries
Date(s) Application is Due: Jan 31
Amount of Grant: 10,000 USD
Contact: Margo Lion; 202) 682-5409; fax (202) 682-5668; pcah@pcah.gov
Internet: http://www.arts.gov/grants/apply/CUT.html
Sponsor: National Endowment for the Arts
1100 Pennsylvania Avenue NW
Washington, DC 20506-0001

National Endowment for the Arts - National Partnership Agreement Grants 3256
Limited funds are available for national services that are provided by membership organizations of state arts agencies and regional arts organizations. Funds are to be used for projects that provide leadership, training, planning, coordination, and information services that increase accountability and transparency. Support for National Services will come out of funds designated by the Congress for the state arts agencies and regional arts organizations. In reviewing requests, the Arts Endowment will use, to the extent applicable, the review criteria for the Regional Arts Organizations. In line with its strategic plan, the Arts Endowment has determined that all National Services projects will address the NEA outcome of Understanding: Public knowledge and understanding about the contributions of the arts are enhanced. The NEA anticipates that national service organizations will be able to address this outcome through activities that include: recognition and promotion of artistic achievement throughout the nation; research and dissemination of reports that demonstrate efforts by SAAs and RAOs to increase public knowledge and understanding about the arts' contributions to social, civic, economic and/or other outcomes; impact analyses of arts and cultural programming; recognition of professional arts workers as a key sector of American industry; efforts by the SAAs and RAOs to nurture and promote innovation; collaborations with other state, regional, or national entities to explore or enhance the role the arts can play in their programming; activities promoting cultural diplomacy with other countries; and the hosting or sponsorship of related convenings, information exchanges, and reports. Organizations must apply through the Grants.gov online application process.
Geographic Focus: All States
Contact: Laura Scanlan, Partnership Team Leader; (202) 682-5583; scanlanl@arts.gov
Internet: http://www.arts.gov/grants/apply/Partnership/national.html
Sponsor: National Endowment for the Arts
1100 Pennsylvania Avenue NW
Washington, DC 20506-0001

National Endowment for the Arts - Our Town Grants 3257
Through the Our Town project, the National Endowment for the Arts provide a limited number of grants, ranging from $25,000 to $150,000, for projects that contribute toward the livability of communities and help transform them into lively, beautiful, and sustainable places with the arts at their core. Our Town invests in creative and innovative projects in which communities, together with their arts and design organizations and artists, seek to improve their quality of life; encourage creative activity; create community identity and a sense of place; and revitalize local economies. All Our Town applications must reflect a partnership that will provide leadership for the project. These partnerships must involve two primary partners: a nonprofit organization and a local government entity. One of the two primary partners must be a cultural (arts or design) organization. Additional partners are encouraged and may include an appropriate

variety of entities such as state level government agencies, foundations, arts organizations and artists, nonprofit organizations, design professionals and design centers, educational institutions, real estate developers, business leaders, and community organizations, as well as public and governmental entities. Projects may include activities such as: planning - creative asset mapping; cultural district planning; the development of master plans or community-wide strategies for public art; support for creative entrepreneurship; creative industry cluster/hub development; design - design of rehearsal, studio, or live/work spaces for artists; design of cultural facilities – new construction or adaptive reuse; design of public spaces, e.g., parks, plazas, streetscapes, landscapes, neighborhoods, districts, infrastructure, bridges; design of wayfinding systems; and community engagement activities including charrettes, competitions, and community design workshops; and arts engagement - innovative programming that fosters interaction among community members, arts organizations, and artists, or activates existing cultural and community assets; festivals and performances in spaces not normally used for such purposes; public art that improves public spaces and strategically reflects or shapes the physical and social character of a community. Applications must be received by the Grants. gov online application process by March 1. Applicants are encouraged to apply at least ten days in advance of the deadline.

Requirements: All applications must have partnerships that involve two primary partners: a nonprofit organization and a local governmental entity. One of the two primary partners must be a cultural (arts or design) organization. Eligible lead applicants are local governments, including counties, parishes, cities, towns, villages, or federally recognized tribal governments; local arts agencies, education agencies (school districts), and government-run community colleges are eligible local governments; and a public entity or a nonprofit tax-exempt 501(c)3 organization with a documented three-year history of programming. To be eligible, the lead applicant organization must have a three-year history of programming prior to the application deadline; meet the Arts Endowment's legal requirements, including nonprofit, tax-exempt status, as detailed in the Grants for Arts Projects guidelines, at the time of application; and have submitted acceptable Final Report packages by the due dates for all Arts Endowment awards previously received. Organizations must request a grant amount at one of the following levels: $25,000, $50,000, $75,000, $100,000, or $150,000.

Restrictions: Funding is not available for projects that do not involve the required partnership to provide leadership for the project; activities that are not tied directly to long-term civic development goals; projects where the arts, design, or cultural activity are not core to the project's plan; capacity building initiatives for artists that are not integral to a broader civic development strategy; construction, purchase, or renovation of facilities (predevelopment, design fees, community planning, and installation of public art are eligible; however, no Arts Endowment or matching funds may be directed to the costs of physical construction or renovation or toward the purchase costs of facilities or land.); subgranting or regranting, except for local arts agencies that are designated to operate on behalf of their local governments or are operating units of city or county government; financial awards to winners of competitions; or fundraising or financing activities. Very few grants are awarded at the $150,000 level. These will be only for projects of significant scale and impact.

Geographic Focus: All States
Date(s) Application is Due: Mar 1
Amount of Grant: 25,000 - 150,000 USD
Contact: Jamie Hand, Our Town Specialist; (202) 682-5566; hand@arts.gov
Internet: http://www.arts.gov/grants/apply/OurTown/index.html
Sponsor: National Endowment for the Arts
1100 Pennsylvania Avenue NW
Washington, DC 20506-0001

National Endowment for the Arts - Regional Partnership Agreement Grants 3258

Regional arts organizations (RAOs) were created by state arts leaders, in partnership with the Arts Endowment and the private sector, in order to transcend state boundaries and give the public access to a greater and richer variety of arts experiences. RAOs encourage the development of the arts and support arts programs at the regional level. They respond to the special needs of each region and assist the Arts Endowment and other funders in distributing programs nationally. One of their roles has been to make excellent dance, theater, musical theater, opera, visual arts, media arts, music, and literature presentations available in underserved communities. The RAOs work cooperatively with the state agencies and the Arts Endowment to achieve common goals and outcomes. With the Arts Endowment's grant making organized around the outcomes below, Partnership Agreement funding enables the RAOs to address priorities identified at the regional level as well as NEA outcomes: creation; engagement; learning; liability; and understanding (detailed information about each of these categories may be found at the NEA website.). Funds will be allotted based on the strength of plans and accomplishments in relation to the review criteria. Funds for activities that strengthen regional support of the folk and traditional arts are awarded competitively and generally range from $20,000 to $45,000. All applications must be submitted through the Grants.gov online process.

Requirements: All awards must be matched at least 1 to 1. In order to enter into a Partnership Agreement with the National Endowment for the Arts, a regional arts organization must: be authorized by three or more state arts agencies to apply for funds on their behalf; meet the Arts Endowment's legal requirements at the time of application; maintain sound fiscal and administrative procedures; base program funding decisions on criteria that rely primarily upon artistic excellence and merit; engage member SAAs in planning and program development; have completed a comprehensive and inclusive planning process and compiled a list of responses to recommendations from that process; establish metrics for accomplishing goals and measuring progress in relation to the region's plan; have submitted acceptable Final Report packages by the due date(s) for all Arts Endowment award(s) previously received, and report on funded activities in accordance with the National Standard for Arts Information Exchange. Regional arts organizations that subgrant must: require their grantees to provide DUNS numbers before a grant can be made; in certain instances, report grants of $25,000 or more in federal funds and information about the compensation of executives related to those grants to the Federal Funding Accountability and Transparency Act Subward Reporting System (FSRS). Nonprofit organizations working in cooperation with their RAO are eligible for support designed to strengthen regional support of the folk & traditional arts. In order to be eligible, such organizations must: meet the Arts Endowment's legal requirements including nonprofit, tax-exempt status at the time of application; have a three-year history of programming prior to the application deadline; have submitted acceptable Final Report packages by the due date(s) for all Arts Endowment grant(s) previously received; and have the support of their RAO for this activity.

Geographic Focus: All States
Date(s) Application is Due: Oct 1
Contact: Laura Scanlan, Partnership Team Leader; (202) 682-5583; scanlanl@arts.gov
Internet: http://www.arts.gov/grants/apply/Partnership/regionals.html
Sponsor: National Endowment for the Arts
1100 Pennsylvania Avenue NW
Washington, DC 20506-0001

National Endowment for the Arts - State Partnership Agreement Grants 3259

By supporting the state arts agencies (SAAs) through Partnership Agreements, the National Endowment for the Arts makes the arts available in more communities than it could through direct grants. The SAAs greatly extend the federal reach and impact, translating national leadership into local benefit. Partnership Agreement funding enables SAAs to address priorities identified at the state level, as well as address the NEA priorities of creation; engagement; learning; livability; and understanding. Funds will be allotted in accordance with the NEA's legislative mandate, and based on the strength of plans and accomplishments in relation to the review criteria. Funds for activities that strengthen state support of the folk and traditional arts are awarded competitively and generally range from $20,000 to $45,000. Organizations must apply through the Grants.gov application process.

Requirements: All awards must be matched at least 1 to 1. State arts agency Partnership Agreements are limited to the fifty state and six jurisdictional arts agencies. In order to enter into a state arts agency Partnership Agreement and receive federal funding from the National Endowment for the Arts, a state arts agency must comply with NEA's authorizing legislation posted on the Endowment website. Additional detailed requirements (legal; organizational entity and capacity; financial support, matching funds, and financial reporting; planning, programming, and evaluation) are posted at the Partnership Agreement website. Organizations must comply with all of these requirements.

Geographic Focus: All States
Date(s) Application is Due: Oct 1
Contact: Laura Scanlan, Partnership Team Leader; (202) 682-5583; scanlanl@arts.gov
Internet: http://www.arts.gov/grants/apply/Partnership/states.html
Sponsor: National Endowment for the Arts
1100 Pennsylvania Avenue NW
Washington, DC 20506-0001

National Endowment for the Arts Artist Communities Grants: Art Works 3260

The National Endowment for the Arts is committed to providing assistance to artist communities for projects that encourage and nurture the development of individual artists and foster and inspire their creative processes. Support is available for artist communities that: provide space, time, and resources to artists for incubation, thought, or creativity in a retreat setting in an urban or rural location; foster and support the creative process of art making by providing studio facilities and assistance with living accommodations to enable artists to live and work concurrently; utilize a competitive application process to recruit and select participants, and rotate a wide range of artists in order to encourage the highest standards of creativity. Art Works encourages and supports the following four outcomes: creation - the creation of art that meets the highest standards of excellence; engagement - public engagement with diverse and excellent art; learning - lifelong learning in the arts; and livability - strengthening communities through the arts. A detailed description of each category and possible projects is available at the NEA website. Innovation is also encouraged within these outcomes, especially through partnerships with organizations in and outside of the arts, if appropriate to their project. All grants require a 1 to 1 nonfederal match. Grants usually range from $10,000 to $100,000. Grants at the highest level are only made for projects that demonstrate exceptional national or regional significance and impact. Applications are submitted through the Grants.gov online process. Additional information about the review process and a list of previously funded projects are available at the NEA website.

Requirements: Eligible applicants include nonprofit, tax-exempt 501(c)3 U.S. organizations; units of state or local government; or federally recognized tribal communities or tribes. Applicants may be arts organizations, local arts agencies, arts service organizations, local education agencies (school districts), and other organizations that can help advance the goals of the Arts Endowment. The applicant organization must have at least a three year history of programming prior to the application deadline. They must also have submitted acceptable final report packages by the due date for all previous Arts Endowment grants.

Restrictions: Funding is not available for: general operating support; seasonal support; costs for the creation of new organizations; direct grants to individuals (although the Arts Endowment encourages applicant organizations to involve individual artists in all possible ways); individual elementary or secondary schools — charter, private, or public — directly; construction, purchase, or renovation of facilities; commercial (for-profit) enterprises or activities; cash reserves and endowments; subgranting or regranting, except for state arts agencies, regional arts organizations, or local arts agencies that are designated to operate on behalf of their local governments or are operating units of city or county government; awards to individuals or organizations to honor or recognize achievement; generally, professional training in degree-granting institutions; work toward academic degrees and the pursuit of academic careers; activities that are designed to supplant existing in-school arts instruction; literary publishing that does not focus on contemporary literature and/or writers; publication of books or exhibition of works by the applicant organization's

staff, board members, faculty, or trustees; exhibitions of, and other projects that primarily involve, single, individually-owned, private collections; projects for which the selection of artists or art works is based upon criteria other than artistic excellence and merit (such as festivals, exhibitions, or publications for which no jury/editorial judgment has been applied); expenditures that are related to compensation to foreign nationals and artists traveling to or from foreign countries when those expenditures are not in compliance with regulations issued by the U.S. Treasury Department Office of Foreign Asset Control; or project costs that are supported by any other federal funds or their match.
Geographic Focus: All States
Date(s) Application is Due: Mar 8
Amount of Grant: 10,000 - 100,000 USD
Contact: Pepper Smith, Artist Communities Specialist; (202) 682-5790; smiths@arts.gov
Internet: http://www.arts.gov/grants/apply/ArtistsCommunities.html
Sponsor: National Endowment for the Arts
1100 Pennsylvania Avenue NW
Washington, DC 20506-0001

National Endowment for the Arts Big Read Grants 3261
The National Endowment for the Arts (NEA) Big Read program is an initiative designed to restore reading to the center of American culture. It provides citizens with the opportunity to read and discuss a single book within their communities. The initiative includes innovative reading programs in selected cities and towns, comprehensive resources for discussing classic literature, an ambitious national publicity campaign, and an extensive website providing comprehensive information on authors and their works. Each community event lasts approximately one month and includes a kick-off event to launch the program locally, ideally attended by the mayor and other local luminaries; major events devoted specifically to the book (panel discussions, author reading, and the like); events using the book as a point of departure (film screenings, theatrical readings, and so forth); and book discussions in diverse locations and aimed at a wide range of audiences. The application and frequently asked questions about The Big Read are available at the NEA website.
Requirements: Applicant organizations for The Big Read must be a 501(c)3 nonprofit; a division of state, local, or tribal government; or a tax-exempt public library. Eligible applicants include such organizations as literary centers, libraries, museums, colleges and universities, art centers, historical societies, arts councils, tribal governments, humanities councils, literary festivals, and arts organizations.
Geographic Focus: All States
Amount of Grant: 2,500 - 20,000 USD
Contact: Angharad Guy, (612) 341-0755, ext. 8054; thebigread@artsmidwest.org
Internet: http://www.neabigread.org/
Sponsor: National Endowment for the Arts
1100 Pennsylvania Avenue NW
Washington, DC 20506-0001

National Endowment for the Arts Dance Grants: Art Works 3262
Dance Grants: Art Works applications are accepted for innovative dance projects twice a year. Spring applications are available for the following NEA outcomes: creation - commissioning and development of dance works; innovative dance projects that create new work through the use of new models, technology, or new media; and residencies and choreography workshops for artists where the primary purpose is to further artistic exploration and/or create new art; and engagement - the restaging of repertory; regional and national tours; home-based performances; the presentation of dance companies; innovative dance presentations that use new models, technology, or new media in the presentation of work or that juxtapose disparate works or genres and engender new connections; dance festivals; and services to dancers, choreographers, and companies, which may include activities such as convening, data collection, information sharing, and technical assistance. Summer application are available for the following NEA outcomes: engagement - touring and performance activity that emphasize outreach to underserved communities; innovative methods of engaging audiences, including collaborations with other organizations, through new models that have the potential to maximize resources and/or the impact on the audience, artists, or the field; the restaging of master works of historical significance; innovative uses of new models, technology, or new media to document and/or perpetuate choreography, technique, or dance process; and documentation, preservation, and conservation of America's dance heritage; learning - education and related activities for children, adults, intergenerational groups, and schools; and professional training including classes, guest artist residenciess; workshops, and mentorship of dance artists; and livability - the development of plans for growth of the dance sector in the local community; the development of artist live/work spaces; the engagement of the dance community in plans and processes to improve community livability; community-based partnerships that integrate dance with livability efforts. Applications are submitted through the Grants.gov online process. Additional instructions, including frequently asked questions, are available at the NEA website.
Requirements: Applicants must choose a first and second choice outcome for their project. Nonprofit, tax-exempt 501(c)3, U.S. organizations; units of state or local government; or federally recognized tribal communities or tribes may apply. Applicants may be arts organizations, local arts agencies, arts service organizations, local education agencies (school districts), and other organizations that can help advance the goals of the Arts Endowment.
Restrictions: Funding is not available for the following: general operating support; seasonal support; costs for the creation of new organizations; direct grants to individuals; individual elementary or secondary schools — charter, private, or public — directly; construction, purchase, or renovation of facilities; commercial enterprises or activities; cash reserves and endowments; subgranting or regranting, except for state arts agencies, regional arts organizations, or local arts agencies that are designated to operate on behalf of their local governments or are operating units of city or county government; awards to individuals or organizations to honor or recognize achievement; professional training in degree-granting institutions; work toward academic degrees and the pursuit of academic careers; activities that are designed to supplant existing in-school arts instruction; literary publishing that does not focus on contemporary literature and/or writers; publication of books or exhibition of works by the applicant organization's staff, board members, faculty, or trustees; exhibitions of, and other projects that primarily involve, single, individually-owned, private collections; projects for which the selection of artists or art works is based upon criteria other than artistic excellence and merit. Examples include festivals, exhibitions, or publications for which no jury/editorial judgment has been applied; expenditures that are related to compensation to foreign nationals and artists traveling to or from foreign countries when those expenditures are not in compliance with regulations issued by the U.S. Treasury Department Office of Foreign Asset Control; and project costs that are supported by any other federal funds or their match.
Geographic Focus: All States
Date(s) Application is Due: Mar 8; Aug 9
Amount of Grant: 10,000 - 100,000 USD
Contact: Janelle Ott Long, Dance Specialist; (202) 682-5739; ottlongj@arts.gov
Juliana Mascelli, Dance Specialist; (202) 682-5656; mascellij@arts.gov
Internet: http://www.arts.gov/grants/apply/GAP13/DanceAW.html
Sponsor: National Endowment for the Arts
1100 Pennsylvania Avenue NW
Washington, DC 20506-0001

National Endowment for the Arts Local Arts Agencies Grants: Art Works 3263
The Art Works Grants encourage and support the following four outcomes: creation - the creation of art that meets the highest standards of excellence; engagement - public engagement with diverse and excellent art; learning - lifelong learning in the arts, and livability - strengthening communities through the arts. Applicants are asked to select the outcome that is most relevant to their project, in addition to selecting a secondary outcome. Creative, innovative projects that extend the arts to underserved populations and areas are encouraged for all outcomes. The Local Arts Agencies Grants are available twice a year. The artistic outcomes for the spring deadline are the following: engagement - coordinated services including marketing campaigns, electronic box office services, and audience development activities; innovative strategies to engage new audiences; conferences, convenings, workshops, technical assistance, leadership training, and other professional development opportunities for artists and arts administrators; and subgranting for service activities on behalf of a local arts agency's constituents; and livability - the development of plans for cultural and/or creative sector growth including cultural assessments, community-wide cultural planning, and specific-issue cultural plans; and the development of artist live/work spaces. The summer deadline outcomes are as follows: creation - artist commissions, including those for public art; artist residencies where the primary purpose is to create new art; and innovative projects using technology, media, new models, or other strategies in the creation of new work; engagement - performing arts events, readings, screenings, broadcasts, and visual arts exhibitions; innovative projects to increase access to the arts or works of art; innovative collaborations that strengthen the field of community arts journalism and arts criticism; and subgranting for programming activities on behalf of a local arts agency's constituents; and documentation and conservation of public and monumental art; learning - artist residencies where the primary purpose is the acquisition of knowledge or skills in the arts; and education and related activities for children, adults, intergenerational groups, and schools; and livability - the enhancement of public spaces through commissioning and/or installation of arts works. Organizations must submit applications through the Grants.gov online system. Additional information, along with a list of frequently asked questions and the review process, is available at the NEA website.
Requirements: A one to one match for funding is required. Nonprofit, tax-exempt 501(c)3, U.S. organizations; units of state or local government; or federally recognized tribal communities or tribes may apply. Applicants may be arts organizations, local arts agencies, arts service organizations, local education agencies (school districts), and other organizations that can help advance the goals of the Arts Endowment. Applicants must have a three year history of programming prior to the application deadline. They must also have submitted acceptable final reports for all Arts grants previously received.
Restrictions: Funding is not available for general operating support; seasonal support; costs for the creation of new organizations; direct grants to individuals; individual elementary or secondary schools directly (schools may participate as partners with other eligible organizations); construction, purchase, or renovation of facilities; commercial enterprises or activities; cash reserves and endowments; subgranting or regranting, except for state arts agencies, regional arts organizations, or local arts agencies that are designated to operate on behalf of their local governments or are operating units of city or county government; awards to individuals or organizations to honor or recognize achievement; professional training in degree-granting institutions; work toward academic degrees and the pursuit of academic careers; activities that are designed to supplant existing in-school arts instruction; literary publishing that does not focus on contemporary literature and/or writers; publication of books or exhibition of works by the applicant organization's staff, board members, faculty, or trustees; exhibitions of, and other projects that primarily involve, single, individually-owned, private collections; projects for which the selection of artists or art works is based upon criteria other than artistic excellence and merit, such as arts festivals, exhibitions, or publications for which no jury/editorial judgment has been applied; expenditures that are related to compensation to foreign nationals and artists traveling to or from foreign countries when those expenditures are not in compliance with regulations issued by the U.S. Treasury Department Office of Foreign Asset Control; and project costs that are supported by any other federal funds or their match.
Geographic Focus: All States
Date(s) Application is Due: Mar 8; Aug 9
Contact: Dinah Walls, Local Arts Agencies Specialist; (202) 682-5586; wallsd@arts.gov
Internet: http://www.arts.gov/grants/apply/Locals.html
Sponsor: National Endowment for the Arts
1100 Pennsylvania Avenue NW
Washington, DC 20506-0001

National Endowment for the Arts Media Arts Grants: Art Works   3264

Art Works Grants encourage and support the following four outcomes for the artistic experience: creation - the creation of art that meets the highest standards of excellence; engagement - public engagement with diverse and excellent art; learning - lifelong learning in the arts, and livability - the strengthening of communities through the arts. Creativity, innovation, and projects that extend the arts to underserved populations and areas are encouraged for all outcomes. Arts Works for Media Arts Grants are available twice a year. Spring deadlines are available for two of the following projected outcomes: engagement - media festivals, showcases, panels, and seminars that include film/video artists, video game and transmedia designers, critics, and/or scholars, and are open to the general public; exhibition of media art including the production of program notes and commentary by visiting artists, scholars, and critics; services to the field including activities that provide media artists and organizations with resources that are essential for artistic growth and development; facilities access that makes production and post-production equipment available to media artists; learning - programs for the media field including workshops/residencies/conferences that are designed for media artists, critics, scholars, and are open to the general public; education and related activities for children, adults, intergenerational groups, and schools; and livability - media arts exhibitions, festivals, and other activities in public spaces that are intended to foster community interaction and/or enhance the unique characteristics of a community. Fall deadlines are available for the following projected outcomes: creation - media art productions: Projects may include high profile multi-part or single television and radio programs (documentaries and dramatic narratives); experimental, animated, transmedia, or interactive work; performance programs; arts-related segments for use within an existing series; multi-part webisodes; installations; and video games. Productions must demonstrate the creative use of media, fulfilling, and when possible, extending their artistic possibilities. All phases of a project are eligible for support including research and development (except narrative scripts), production, completion and distribution costs; engagement - regional, national, or international distribution of media as art or about the arts, including the development of web portals, hubs, mobile apps, or other innovative uses of technology or new models to provide audiences with access to media art works and artists; or distribution projects developed to aggregate artistic content, resources, and knowledge that enable the efficient dissemination of arts-related information; preservation, restoration, or archiving of media art works, and services that support preservation, restoration, or archiving efforts; and publications on issues pertinent to the media arts field, both practical and aesthetic. Applications must be submitted through the Grants.gov online process. Additional information is located at the NEA website.

Requirements: Funding must be met with a 1 to 1 match. Nonprofit, tax-exempt 501(c)3, U.S. organizations; units of state or local government; or federally recognized tribal communities or tribes may apply. Applicants may be arts organizations, local arts agencies, arts service organizations, local education agencies (school districts), and other organizations that can help advance the goals of the Arts Endowment. Applicants must also have a three year history of programming prior to the application deadline, and have submitted acceptable final report packages by the due date for all Endowment grants previously received.

Restrictions: Funding is not available for: productions where the primary purpose is instructional, journalistic (except arts journalism), or promotional; general operating support; seasonal support; costs for the creation of new organizations; direct grants to individuals. (The Arts Endowment encourages applicant organizations to involve individual artists in all possible ways; individual elementary or secondary schools directly; construction, purchase, or renovation of facilities; commercial enterprises or activities; cash reserves and endowments; subgranting or regranting, except for state arts agencies, regional arts organizations, or local arts agencies that are designated to operate on behalf of their local governments or are operating units of city or county government; awards to individuals or organizations to honor or recognize achievement; professional training in degree-granting institutions; work toward academic degrees and the pursuit of academic careers; activities that are designed to supplant existing in-school arts instruction; literary publishing that does not focus on contemporary literature and/or writers; publication of books or exhibition of works by the applicant organization's staff, board members, faculty, or trustees; exhibitions of, and other projects that primarily involve, single, individually-owned, private collections; projects for which the selection of artists or art works is based upon criteria other than artistic excellence and merit, such as festivals, exhibitions, or publications for which no jury/editorial judgment has been applied; expenditures that are related to compensation to foreign nationals and artists traveling to or from foreign countries when those expenditures are not in compliance with regulations issued by the U.S. Treasury Department Office of Foreign Asset Control; and project costs that are supported by any other federal funds or their match.

Geographic Focus: All States
Date(s) Application is Due: Mar 8; Aug 9
Amount of Grant: 10,000 - 100,000 USD
Contact: Mary Smith, Media Arts Specialist; (202) 682-5742; mediaarts@arts.gov
Internet: http://www.arts.gov/grants/apply/Media.html
Sponsor: National Endowment for the Arts
1100 Pennsylvania Avenue NW
Washington, DC 20506-0001

National Endowment for the Arts Museum Grants: Art Works   3265

The National Endowment for the Arts supports museums and other exhibiting institutions and organizations that serve the field and the American public through grants for projects of the highest artistic quality. Grants support projects undertaken by organizations that exhibit, preserve, and interpret visual material through exhibitions, residencies, publications, commissions, public art works, conservation, documentation, services to the field, and public programs. Art Works Grants encourage and support the four outcomes: creation - the creation of art that meets the highest standards of excellence; engagement - public engagement with diverse and excellent art; learning - lifelong learning in the arts; and livability - the strengthening of communities through the arts. Creativity, innovation, and projects that extend the arts to underserved populations and areas are encouraged for all outcomes. Art Works Grants for Museums are offered twice a year. The spring deadline concentrates on creation - commissions or public art; residencies where the primary purpose is to create new art; and innovative uses of technology or new models in the creation of new work; and engagement - exhibitions including planning, implementation, public programs, education, and production of catalogues; and services to the field. The summer deadline concentrates on engagement - conservation; documentation; provenance research; collections management; reinstallation of collections; community outreach activities; permanent collection catalogues; technology projects that provide online or in-museum access to collections, exhibitions, organizational history, and other programming information; innovative uses of technology or new models to exhibit new work or to reach out to audiences; learning - public programs such as lectures and symposia; education and related activities for children, adults, intergenerational groups, and schools; and teaching residencies; and livability - the enhancement of public spaces through commissioning and/or installation of art works; the creation of public spaces such as sculpture parks or gardens to house works of art; and arts exhibitions, festivals, artist residencies, and other activities in public spaces that are intended to foster community interaction and/or enhance the unique characteristics of a community. Applicants must apply through the Grants.gov online process. Additional information, including a list of frequently asked questions and the review process, is located at the NEA website.

Requirements: A funding match of 1 to 1 is required. Nonprofit, tax-exempt 501(c)3, U.S. organizations; units of state or local government; or federally recognized tribal communities or tribes may apply. Applicants may be arts organizations, local arts agencies, arts service organizations, local education agencies (school districts), and other organizations that can help advance the goals of the Arts Endowment. Applicants must also have a three year history of programming prior to the application deadlines, and have submitted acceptable final report packages for any grants previously received.

Restrictions: Funding is not available for the following: general operating support; seasonal support; costs for the creation of new organizations; direct grants to individuals; individual elementary or secondary schools; construction, purchase, or renovation of facilities; commercial enterprises or activities; cash reserves and endowments; subgranting or regranting, except for state arts agencies, regional arts organizations, or local arts agencies that are designated to operate on behalf of their local governments or are operating units of city or county government; awards to individuals or organizations to honor or recognize achievement; professional training in degree-granting institutions; work toward academic degrees and the pursuit of academic careers; activities that are designed to supplant existing in-school arts instruction; literary publishing that does not focus on contemporary literature and/or writers; publication of books or exhibition of works by the applicant organization's staff, board members, faculty, or trustees; exhibitions of, and other projects that primarily involve, single, individually-owned, private collections; projects for which the selection of artists or art works is based upon criteria other than artistic excellence and merit, such as festivals, exhibitions, or publications for which no jury/editorial judgment has been applied; expenditures that are related to compensation to foreign nationals and artists traveling to or from foreign countries when those expenditures are not in compliance with regulations issued by the U.S. Treasury Department Office of Foreign Asset Control; and project costs that are supported by any other federal funds or their match.

Geographic Focus: All States
Date(s) Application is Due: Mar 8; Aug 9
Amount of Grant: 10,000 - 100,000 USD
Contact: Wendy Clark, Museum Specialist; (202) 682-5555; clarkw@arts.gov
Internet: http://www.arts.gov/grants/apply/Museums.html
Sponsor: National Endowment for the Arts
1100 Pennsylvania Avenue NW
Washington, DC 20506-0001

National Endowment for the Arts Music Grants: Art Works   3266

The National Endowment for the Arts (NEA) supports a wide range of music, from classical to contemporary to America's indigenous jazz. It supports both performing ensembles and music presenting institutions including chamber music ensembles, choruses, early music programs, jazz ensembles, music festivals, and symphony orchestras. Organizations of all types and sizes may apply for a variety of music production, presentation, and service projects. The Arts Endowment is particularly interested in innovative presentation methods and the development of skills that can help organizations attract new audiences for music. The Arts Endowment also encourages the commissioning and performance of new American works. The Art Works Grants support the following four outcomes: creation - the creation of art that meets the highest standards of excellence; engagement - public engagement with diverse and excellent art; learning - lifelong learning in the arts, and livability - the strengthening of communities through the arts. Music Art Works Grants are available twice a year. Applicants are asked to apply at the time of the year that most closely matches the outcome of their project. The spring deadline focuses on creation - commissions, residencies, and workshops with artists; development and performances of new works; and innovative creation of music that draws upon a wide range of contemporary resources, emerging practices, and/or technology; engagement - premieres and performances of new musical works; public presentations and performances of artistically excellent works; performance and educational engagements by NEA Jazz Masters that honor their bodies of work, history, or style; provide understanding of their significance to jazz; and broaden audience awareness of the original American art form; innovative musical presentations that juxtapose disparate works or genres and engender new connections; residency activities where the primary purpose is public engagement with art; and services that reach a broad constituency of music organizations, musicians, music educators, and administrators, including workshops, conferences, publications, professional development, technical assistance, networks, or online resources; and learning - professional artistic development and training programs for musicians such as conducting, mentorship, and career development. The summer deadline focuses on engagement - domestic touring;

outreach projects that involve diverse communities or that reach new audiences; innovative methods of engaging audiences, including collaborations with other organizations, through new models that have the potential to maximize resources and/or the impact on the audience, artists, or the field; recordings of works by American composers; technology projects such as online resources and libraries which provide public access to musical works; and documentation, preservation, and archival projects; learning - education and related activities for children, adults, intergenerational groups, and schools; and livability - music festivals, performances, and other activities in public spaces that are intended to foster community interaction and/or enhance the unique characteristics of a community. Creativity, innovative ideas and projects that extend the arts to underserved populations and areas are encouraged for all outcomes. Applications must be submitted through the Grants.gov online system. Additional information, including previously funded projects and a list of frequently asked questions, is located at the NEA website.

Requirements: Applicants are required to do a 1 to 1 funding match. Nonprofit, tax-exempt 501(c)3, U.S. organizations; units of state or local government; or federally recognized tribal communities or tribes may apply. Applicants may be arts organizations, local arts agencies, arts service organizations, local education agencies (school districts), and other organizations that can help advance the goals of the Arts Endowment. Applicants must have a three year history of programming prior to the application deadline. They must also have submitted acceptable final report packages for all Arts grants previously received.

Restrictions: Funding is not available for general operating support; seasonal support; costs for the creation of new organizations; direct grants to individuals; individual elementary or secondary schools; construction, purchase, or renovation of facilities; commercial enterprises or activities; cash reserves and endowment; subgranting or regranting; awards to individuals or organizations to honor or recognize achievement; professional training in degree-granting institutions; work toward academic degrees and the pursuit of academic careers; activities that are designed to supplant existing in-school arts instruction; literary publishing that does not focus on contemporary literature and/or writers; publication of books or exhibition of works by the applicant organization's staff, board members, faculty, or trustees; exhibitions of, and other projects that primarily involve, single, individually-owned, private collections; projects for which the selection of artists or art works is based upon criteria other than artistic excellence and merit, such as festivals, exhibitions, or publications for which no jury/editorial judgment has been applied; expenditures that are related to compensation to foreign nationals and artists traveling to or from foreign countries when those expenditures are not in compliance with regulations issued by the U.S. Treasury Department Office of Foreign Asset Control; or project costs that are supported by any other federal funds or their match.

Geographic Focus: All States
Date(s) Application is Due: Mar 8; Aug 9
Amount of Grant: 10,000 - 100,000 USD
Contact: Court Burns, Music Specialist; (202) 682-5590; burnsc@arts.gov
Anya Nykyforiak, Music Specialist; (202) 682-5487; nykyfora@arts.gov
Katja von Schuttenbach, Music Specialist; (202) 682-5711; vonschuttenbach@arts.gov
Internet: http://www.arts.gov/grants/apply/Music.html
Sponsor: National Endowment for the Arts
1100 Pennsylvania Avenue NW
Washington, DC 20506-0001

National Endowment for the Arts Opera Grants: Art Works 3267

The National Endowment for the Arts supports opera companies and other organizations that professionally produce fully-staged and concert operatic works. Projects of all sizes that involve works from the entire operatic canon are eligible. The Arts Endowment is committed to advancing the highest levels of operatic artistry across the nation's cultural landscape. Support for American opera and the creation of opportunities for American artists also are of interest. The Art Works Grants encourage and support the following four outcomes for artistic projects: creation - the creation of art that meets the highest standards of excellence; engagement - public engagement with diverse and excellent art; learning - lifelong learning in the arts; and livability - the strengthening of communities through the arts. Applicants are asked to select the outcome that is most relevant to their project, in addition to a secondary outcome. Opera Art Works Grants are offered twice a year. Spring deadline outcomes with specific projects include the following: creation - commissions, residencies, and workshops with artists; development and performances of new operatic works. This may include composer and/or librettist fees; and development of innovative new works that cross genres; engagement - world, national, regional, and local premieres; new productions of traditional and contemporary works; remounting of existing productions; and concert opera (performances of the operatic repertoire that are not fully staged). Summer deadline outcomes with specific projects include the following: engagement - festival opera; simulcast performances in public venues; touring and outreach activities that provide access to and experience with the art form for diverse communities and new audiences; artist residency activities where the primary purpose is public engagement with art; recordings of opera works by both American and international composers; technology projects such as online resources and libraries which provide public access to operatic works; documentation, preservation, and conservation of America's opera heritage; and services to opera companies, singers, composers, and librettists. These may include activities such as convening, workshops, data collection, information sharing, networks, online resources, technical assistance, publications, and professional development; learning - educational and related activities for children, adults, intergenerational groups, and schools; and professional development programs that include theatrical training for artists who have finished their conservatory training and are emerging on the professional stage (coaching, conducting, acting, stage movement, diction, language, mentorship, and career development); and livability - operatic performances and other activities in public spaces that are intended to foster community interaction and/or enhance the unique characteristics of a community. Creative, innovative projects that extend the arts to underserved populations and areas are encouraged for all of the outcomes. Applications must be submitted through the Grants.gov online system. Additional information, including a list of frequently asked questions, is available at the NEA website.

Requirements: A one to one funding match is required. Nonprofit, tax-exempt 501(c)3, U.S. organizations; units of state or local government; or federally recognized tribal communities or tribes may apply. Applicants may be arts organizations, local arts agencies, arts service organizations, local education agencies (school districts), and other organizations that can help advance the goals of the Arts Endowment. Applicants must have a three year history of programming prior to the application deadline. They must also have submitted acceptable final reports for all Arts grants previously received.

Restrictions: Funding is not available for general operating support; seasonal support; costs for the creation of new organizations; direct grants to individuals; construction, purchase, or renovation of facilities; commercial enterprises or activities; cash reserves and endowments; subgranting or regranting, except for state arts agencies, regional arts organizations, or local arts agencies that are designated to operate on behalf of their local governments or are operating units of city or county government; awards to individuals or organizations to honor or recognize achievement; professional training in degree-granting institutions; work toward academic degrees and the pursuit of academic careers; activities that are designed to supplant existing in-school arts instruction; literary publishing that does not focus on contemporary literature and/or writers; publication of books or exhibition of works by the applicant organization's staff, board members, faculty, or trustees; exhibitions of, and other projects that primarily involve, single, individually-owned, private collections; projects for which the selection of artists or art works is based upon criteria other than artistic excellence and merit, such as festivals, exhibitions, or publications for which no jury/editorial judgment has been applied; expenditures that are related to compensation to foreign nationals and artists traveling to or from foreign countries when those expenditures are not in compliance with regulations issued by the U.S. Treasury Department Office of Foreign Asset Control; and project costs that are supported by any other federal funds or their match.

Geographic Focus: All States
Date(s) Application is Due: Mar 8; Aug 9
Amount of Grant: 10,000 - 100,000 USD
Contact: Georgianna Paul, Opera Specialist; (202) 682-5600; paulg@arts.gov
Internet: http://www.arts.gov/grants/apply/Opera.html
Sponsor: National Endowment for the Arts
1100 Pennsylvania Avenue NW
Washington, DC 20506-0001

National Endowment for the Arts Presenting Grants: Art Works 3268

The National Endowment for the Arts Presenting Grants support projects and organizations that embrace multiple disciplines from the performing, visual, media, design, and literary arts. These projects and organizations support every stage of the artistic process including arts services, training, residencies, commissioning, presentations, touring and access, documentation, and preservation. The Art Works Grants support the creation of art that meets the highest standards of excellence, public engagement with diverse and excellent art, lifelong learning in the arts, and the strengthening of communities through the arts. Art Works Grants applications are accepted twice a year. The spring deadline features engagement - touring, presenting, and other program activities for underserved communities; and outdoor festivals and programs including site-specific work, outdoor historical dramas, and pageants; and learning - experiential activities in the arts for children and youth and educational activities for adults and intergenerational groups. The fall deadline offers: creation - the creation and commissioning of new works; engagement - the touring and/or presentation of new or existing works (i.e., performances, exhibitions, festivals, residencies, engagements by NEA Jazz Masters, lecture-demonstrations, and workshops); innovative multidisciplinary presenting projects that utilize technology or new models; the documentation, preservation, and conservation of significant material about the field; services to artists and arts organizations (i.e., arts conferences, professional development for artists and arts organizations, and arts technical assistance programs, and arts and business councils or lawyers for arts organizations; learning - training programs for professional artists; and livability - the development of artist live/work spaces; festivals and other activities in public spaces that are intended to foster community interaction and/or enhance the unique characteristics of a community; community-based partnerships that integrate the arts with livability efforts; and the development of plans for growth of the local arts sector. Applicants should choose which outcome most closely matches their project, and apply at that time. Applicants must be submitted through the Grants.gov online system. Additional information, including previously funded grants and a list of frequently asked questions, is available at the NEA website.

Requirements: A one to one match for funding is required. Nonprofit, tax-exempt 501(c)3, U.S. organizations; units of state or local government; or federally recognized tribal communities or tribes may apply. Applicants may be arts organizations, local arts agencies, arts service organizations, local education agencies (school districts), and other organizations that can help advance the goals of the Arts Endowment. Applicants must have a three year history of programming prior to the application deadline. They must also have submitted acceptable final report packages for any Arts grants previously received.

Restrictions: Projects that present or feature a single discipline, such as dance, visual arts, or music, should apply through that discipline at the NEA website. Funding is not available for general operating support; seasonal support; costs for the creation of new organizations; direct grants to individuals; individual elementary or secondary schools directly; construction, purchase, or renovation of facilities; commercial enterprises or activities; cash reserves and endowments; subgranting or regranting, except for state arts agencies, regional arts organizations, or local arts agencies that are designated to operate on behalf of their local governments or are operating units of city or county government; awards to individuals or organizations to honor or recognize achievement; professional training in degree-granting institutions; work toward academic degrees and the pursuit of academic careers; activities that are designed to supplant existing in-school arts instruction; literary publishing that does not focus on contemporary literature and/or writers; publication of books or exhibition

of works by the applicant organization's staff, board members, faculty, or trustees; exhibitions of, and other projects that primarily involve, single, individually-owned, private collections; projects for which the selection of artists or art works is based upon criteria other than artistic excellence and merit, such as festivals, exhibitions, or publications for which no jury/editorial judgment has been applied; expenditures that are related to compensation to foreign nationals and artists traveling to or from foreign countries when those expenditures are not in compliance with regulations issued by the U.S. Treasury Department Office of Foreign Asset Control; or project costs that are supported by any other federal funds or their match.
Geographic Focus: All States
Date(s) Application is Due: Mar 8; Aug 9
Contact: Lara Allee, Presenting Specialist; (202) 682-5698; alleel@arts.gov
Internet: http://www.arts.gov/grants/apply/Presenting.html
Sponsor: National Endowment for the Arts
1100 Pennsylvania Avenue NW
Washington, DC 20506-0001

National Endowment for the Arts Theater and Musical Theater Grants: Art Works 3269
The National Endowment for the Arts (NEA) Art Works Grants encourage and support the following four outcomes: creation - creation of art that meets the highest standards of excellence; engagement - public engagement with diverse and excellent art; learning - lifelong learning in the arts; and livability - strengthening communities through the arts. Applicants choose whichever outcome most closely corresponds to their project. Creative, innovative projects that extend the arts to underserved populations and areas are encouraged for all outcomes. The Theater and Musical Theater Art Works Grants are accepted in the spring and fall, with specific outcomes for each. The spring deadline involves creation - commissioning, development, and production of new work, translations, and adaptations; development programs and labs for new work, which may include the hosting of artist residencies, showcase productions of new work, development workshops, and festivals of new works or works in progress; and development of innovative new works that involve media, technology, or new models; or engagement - production or presentation of existing contemporary or classical work that is planned for the upcoming season. The summer deadline supports engagement - production or presentation of existing contemporary or classical works for the upcoming season; local, regional, and national touring; community based projects; documentation, preservation, conservation, and dissemination of American's theater and musical theater heritage; services to the field that assist organizations or artists in administrative, developmental, technical, and related areas; and innovative methods of engaging audiences, including collaborations with other organizations, through new subscriber or membership models that have the potential to maximize resources and/or the impact on the audience, artists, or the field; or learning - professional training including classes, guest artist residencies, workshops, and mentorship of theater artists; exposure and enrichment projects for children and youth, adults, and intergenerational groups; high-quality, professional productions of Shakespeare's plays performed for middle- and high-school students in underserved schools; or livability - the development of plans for growth of the theater and musical theater sector in the local community; the development of artist live/work spaces; festivals, performances, and other activities in public spaces that are intended to foster community interaction and/or enhance the unique characteristics of a community; the engagement of artists and theater and musical theater organizations in plans and processes to improve community livability; and ommunity-based partnerships that integrate theater and musical theater with livability efforts. Applications must be submitted through the Grants.gov online system. Additional information, including the review process and a list of frequently asked questions, is located at the NEA website.
Requirements: All funding requires a one to one match. Nonprofit, tax-exempt 501(c)3, U.S. organizations; units of state or local government; or federally recognized tribal communities or tribes may apply. Applicants may be arts organizations, local arts agencies, arts service organizations, local education agencies (school districts), and other organizations that can help advance the goals of the Arts Endowment.
Restrictions: Funding is not available for general operating support; seasonal support; costs for the creation of new organizations; direct grants to individuals (although the Endowment encourages applicant organizations to involve individual artists in all possible ways); individual elementary or secondary schools directly; construction, purchase, or renovation of facilities; commercial enterprises or activities; cash reserves and endowments; subgranting or regranting, except for state arts agencies, regional arts organizations, or local arts agencies that are designated to operate on behalf of their local governments or are operating units of city or county government; awards to individuals or organizations to honor or recognize achievement; professional training in degree-granting institutions; work toward academic degrees and the pursuit of academic careers; activities that are designed to supplant existing in-school arts instruction; literary publishing that does not focus on contemporary literature and/or writers; publication of books or exhibition of works by the applicant organization's staff, board members, faculty, or trustees; exhibitions of, and other projects that primarily involve, single, individually-owned, private collections; projects for which the selection of artists or art works is based upon criteria other than artistic excellence and merit such as festivals, exhibitions, or publications for which no jury/editorial judgment has been applied; expenditures that are related to compensation to foreign nationals and artists traveling to or from foreign countries when those expenditures are not in compliance with regulations issued by the U.S. Treasury Department Office of Foreign Asset Control; and project costs that are supported by any other federal funds or their match.
Geographic Focus: All States
Date(s) Application is Due: Mar 8; Aug 9
Contact: Eleanor Denegre; (202) 682-5509; denegree@arts.gov
Internet: http://www.arts.gov/grants/apply/Theater-MusicalTheater.html
Sponsor: National Endowment for the Arts
1100 Pennsylvania Avenue NW
Washington, DC 20506-0001

National Environmental Education Foundation Legacy Award 3270
National Public Lands Day (NPLD) is the nation's largest hands-on volunteer effort to improve and enhance the public lands Americans enjoy. NPLD is a public/private partnership that has garnered approximately 170,000 volunteers who contributed $17 million worth of improvements to over 2,060 public land sites in all 50 states, the District of Columbia and many U.S. territories. NPLD educates individuals about critical environmental, natural and cultural resource issues; promotes the need for shared stewardship of U.S. public lands; builds partnerships between the public sector and the local community; and improves public lands for outdoor recreation, with volunteers assisting land managers in hands-on work. The Department of Defense (DoD) Legacy Resource Management Program and NPLD want to help the many military installations that will be participating in National Public Lands Day on September 29, 2012. The NPLD DoD Legacy Award offers funding of up to $6,500 for base-level volunteer work projects on Department of Defense (DoD) sites that meet all eligibility requirements. The Legacy Award has a special focus on improving habitat for pollinator species such as bees, birds, bats and insects. Projects are not required to involve pollinator habitat improvement, but such projects will be taken into special consideration. Projects can take many forms, including, but not limited to: tree and native vegetation planting; wildflower and native plant seeding; invasive plant removal or weeding; trash and debris cleanup; wildlife habitat improvement and restoration activities; pollinator garden development; wetland, streamside or shoreline restoration and erosion control; trail building and maintenance; restoration or culturally and historically significant areas, buildings, and structures; and nature garden development. Organizations may access the online application process at the Foundation website. Frequently asked questions and previously funded projects are also available at the website.
Requirements: The grant applicant must be a Department of Defense installation site that is open to the public for recreation, including lands managed by the U.S. Army, Air Force, Marine Corps, National Guard or Navy. Projects must be carried out and completed by a specific date.
Restrictions: Lands managed by the U.S. Army Corps of Engineers are not eligible for funding. Funding may not be used for conducting lobbying, carrying on propaganda or otherwise attempting to influence legislation; influencing the outcome of any specific election through any means; budget shortfalls, general support or endowment funds; land acquisitions or real estate purchases; giveaways, such as t-shirts; purchasing food; paying for labor or salary costs; scholarships, fellowships or grants to individuals; or any costs not directly related to the funds requested in the proposal.
Geographic Focus: All States
Date(s) Application is Due: Aug 16
Contact: Jessica Jones; (202) 833-2933; fax (202) 261-6464; jjones@neefusa.org
Internet: http://www.neefusa.org/grants/dod_legacy_awards.htm
Sponsor: National Environmental Education Foundation
4301 Connecticut Avenue NW, Suite 160
Washington, DC 20008

National Environmental Education Foundation Every Day Grants 3271
The public lands of the U.S. need additional support that often comes from nonprofit organizations, whose missions are focused on serving U.S. public land sites. These groups (Friends Groups, Cooperating Associations, or partners) are invaluable in supporting, promoting, and helping maintain public lands. These volunteer organizations are often underfunded and understaffed. The National Environmental Education Foundation (NEEF), with support from Toyota Motor Sales USA, seeks to strengthen these organizations and unleash their potential to serve their public lands. NEEF's Every Day Grants will strengthen the stewardship of public lands by strengthening Friends Groups through funding for organizational capacity building (strategic planning; marketing and communications; leadership capacity; improved fundraising; assessments; and staff training). Twenty-five grants of up to $5,000 each are given in the spring and fall of each year. Applicants who meet all requirements but are not awarded a grant in the first round will be considered for the second round. Organizations may access the online application system at the Foundation website. Detailed guidelines and frequently asked questions are also located at the website.
Requirements: Applicants must be 501(c)3 nonprofit organizations or working through a fiscal agent; in existence for at least two years; be a community-based nonprofit organization whose mission is focused on serving a public land site in the U.S. and the improvement and responsible use of that site. This includes groups that serve more than one site, such as a regional group of parks; have an established collaborative relationship with a local public land site (including federal, state, regional, county, city or other local public land areas) for at least one year. Successful applications will: demonstrate a positive, collaborative partnership with a local public land site that has been in effect for at least one year; describe a needed and well planned project that can be carried out by the applicant and is replicable; demonstrate that the project contributes to the long-term sustainability of the organization; demonstrate that the project strengthens the organization's ability to serve the public land site.
Restrictions: Funds cannot be used for conducting lobbying, carrying on propaganda or otherwise attempting to influence legislation; influencing the outcome of any specific election through any means; purposes other than charitable, scientific or educational; budget shortfalls, general support or endowment funds; landscaping, land acquisition or real estate purchases. Giveaways, such as t-shirts (projects that raise funds by developing items for sale, such as calendars or t-shirts, are allowed); the purchase of food; scholarships, fellowships or grants to individuals; any costs not directly related to the funds requested in the proposal.
Geographic Focus: All States
Date(s) Application is Due: Jun 15
Contact: Teresa Crane; (202) 833-2933; fax (202) 261-6464; tcrane@neefusa.org
Internet: http://www.neefusa.org/grants/every_day_grants.htm
Sponsor: National Environmental Education Foundation
4301 Connecticut Avenue NW, Suite 160
Washington, DC 20008

National Geographic Society All Roads Seed Grants 3272

The All Roads Seed Grant Program funds film projects by and about indigenous and underrepresented minority-culture filmmakers year-round and from all reaches of the globe. The program seeks filmmakers who bring their lives and communities to light through first-person storytelling. Grant funds should be used toward the development and production of a feature film, long documentary, short documentary, shorts, animation or music video. They may be used for equipment, travel for field research, editing time, etc. The program awards up to 16 film projects annually with grants ranging from $1,000 to $10,000. Submission deadlines are quarterly on the 15th of each March, June, September, and December. Award notifications are made approximately six weeks after each of these dates.
Requirements: This grant is open to indigenous and underrepresented minority-culture filmmakers, as well as filmmakers who can demonstrate that they have been designated by indigenous or minority communities to tell their story. Guidelines and application forms also available in Spanish.
Restrictions: This grant may not be used for indirect costs, overhead, and other expenses not directly related to the development and production of a film project. Funds may not be used for travel to film/media-related meetings or conferences, legal actions, land acquisition, endowments, fees or salaries.
Geographic Focus: All States
Date(s) Application is Due: Mar 15; Jun 15; Sep 15; Dec 15
Amount of Grant: Up to 10,000 USD
Contact: Alexandra Nicholson, (202) 857-7660 or (800) 647-5463; allroads@ngs.org
Internet: http://www3.nationalgeographic.com/allroads/seed-grants.html
Sponsor: National Geographic Society
1145 Seventeenth Street NW
Washington, DC 20036-4688

National Geographic Society Conservation Trust Grants 3273

The objective of the trust is to support conservation activities around the world. Grants support projects that contribute significantly to the preservation and sustainable use of the Earth's biological, cultural, and historical resources. Researchers planning work in foreign countries should include at least one local collaborator as part of their research teams. The strength of the program is to identify cutting edge programs that might be overlooked due to inherent risks associated with new investigators and fields. Funds are intended to function as complementary support; the trust strongly encourages applicants to seek additional, concurrent funding from other funding agencies. Before receiving an application form, each principal investigator must submit a pre-application form online. If the pre-application is approved, the principal investigator will be sent an electronic application and instructions.
Requirements: Applicants are not expected to have advanced degrees (PhD or equivalent). However, applicants must provide a record of prior research or conservation action as it pertains to the proposed project.
Restrictions: Society grants may not be used for indirect costs, overhead, and other expenses not directly related to the project. Fringe benefits are also excluded, as are salaries. Funds may be used for travel to scientific/professional meetings or conferences, legal actions, land acquisition, endowments, construction of permanent field stations, or to publish research results.
Geographic Focus: All States
Amount of Grant: 15,000 - 20,000 USD
Contact: Grants Administrator; (800) 647-5463; conservationtrust@ngs.org
Internet: http://www.nationalgeographic.com/conservation
Sponsor: National Geographic Society
1145 Seventeenth Street NW
Washington, DC 20036-4688

National Geographic Society Genographic Legacy Fund Grants 3274

The Genographic Legacy Fund awards grants on a semi-annual basis for community-driven projects directly preserving or revitalizing indigenous or traditional culture. Funded projects have included documenting a traditional language, oral history, or ceremony; creating culturally-specific educational materials and programs; establishing a local museum or archive; inter-generational knowledge sharing; and preserving significant sites and artifacts. Fund does not have a required application form. To apply, send a detailed description of the project and its fulfillment of the GLF criteria, making sure to follow online specifics. Applications are accepted on an ongoing basis and will be reviewed during the subsequent semi-annual review period.
Requirements: To be eligible for funding, projects must be community-driven and deliver a positive, tangible, and timely benefit that is sustainable after GLF funds have been expended. Projects must also show a strong level of local community involvement in their planning, governance, and implementation.
Restrictions: Society grants may not be used for indirect costs, overhead, and other expenses not directly related to the project. Fringe benefits are also excluded, as are salaries. Funds may not be used for travel to scientific/professional meetings or conferences, legal actions, land acquisition, endowments, construction of permanent field stations, or to publish research results.
Geographic Focus: All States
Date(s) Application is Due: Jun 15; Dec 15
Amount of Grant: Up to 25,000 USD
Contact: Terry D. Garcia, Executive Vice President; (800) 647-5463; fax (202) 857-7333; GenographicLegacy@ngs.org
Internet: https://www3.nationalgeographic.com/genographic/legacy_fund.html#information_for_applicants
Sponsor: National Geographic Society
1145 Seventeenth Street NW
Washington, DC 20036-4688

National Geographic Society Young Explorers Grants 3275

Young Explorers Grants (YEG) offer opportunities to individuals between the ages of 18 and 25 to pursue research, conservation, and exploration-related projects consistent with National Geographic's existing grant programs, including: the Committee for Research and Exploration (CRE), the Expeditions Council (EC), and the Conservation Trust (CT). Grants vary in amount depending on significance of the project, though most range between $2,000 and $5,000.
Requirements: Applicants are not expected to have advanced degrees (PhD or equivalent). However, applicants must provide a record of prior research or conservation action as it pertains to the proposed project.
Restrictions: Society grants may not be used for indirect costs, overhead, and other expenses not directly related to the project. Fringe benefits are also excluded, as are salaries. Funds may not be used for travel to scientific/professional meetings or conferences, legal actions, land acquisition, endowments, construction of permanent field stations, or to publish research results.
Geographic Focus: All States
Amount of Grant: 2,000 - 5,000 USD
Contact: Administrator; (800) 647-5463; cre@ngs.org or conservationtrust@ngs.org
Internet: http://www.nationalgeographic.com/field/grants-programs/yeg-application.html
Sponsor: National Geographic Society
1145 Seventeenth Street NW
Washington, DC 20036-4688

National Home Library Foundation Grants 3276

The National Home Library Foundation makes grants to fund books for libraries, schools and literacy programs serving children, teens or adults in need of reading and learning resources. The Trustees meet twice a year to consider applications that address the value of the project to the overall organization requesting support and/or to the community; stability and financial ability of the organization, staff resources and competence to meet the project's objective; and the future ability to maintain the project and its impact, including community support. Samples of previously funded grants are available at the Foundation website.
Requirements: Grants are made only to organizations that are tax exempt under 501(c)3 of the IRS code. Funding requests should include the following information: the legal name and full description of the organization or institution making the application, with list of officers and principal staff; a clear, concise statement of need for which a grant is requested; a proposed budget in detail for use of the requested funds; and evidence of tax-exempt status, along with a financial statement for the preceding year.
Restrictions: Individuals or organizations that seek to influence legislation or intervene in political campaigns are not eligible to apply. Funding is not available for international organizations. Grants are not made for loans, conferences, scholarships, endowments, construction or operating budgets.
Geographic Focus: All States
Amount of Grant: 500 - 5,000 USD
Contact: Joan Sahlgren, Executive Director; (301) 986-4854 or (703) 304-2602; fax (301) 986-4855; natlhomelibrary@yahoo.com
Internet: http://homelibraryfoundation.com/how_to_apply
Sponsor: National Home Library Foundation
3804 Williams Lane, Lower Level
Chevy Chase, MD 20815

National Housing Endowment Challenge/Build/Grow Grant 3277

The National Housing Endowment is the philanthropic arm of the National Association of Home Builders (NAHB). Working with organizations within the NAHB federation, the National Housing Endowment is offering eligible applicants up to $5,000 in matching challenge grant funds (dollar for dollar) for programs and projects addressing NAHB's highest priority areas of Education, Land Use and Labor Shortage/Worker Training.
Requirements: The program/project must address the National Housing Endowment mission of furthering the education, training, and research goals of the home building industry. The program/project can initially be at the local level, but should have the potential to be used as a national model to assist in addressing the education, land use and workforce training/recruitment issue(s). In addition, the program/project should adhere to the IRS regulation definition of ????serving the public interest???? and not exist to serve the sole interests of the home building industry.
Restrictions: Programs and projects are not eligible for support over a multi-year period. HBA projects that have already received funding in 2007 may not apply. Preference will be given to newly created programs/projects especially those that create partnerships in their communities.
Geographic Focus: All States
Date(s) Application is Due: Apr 16
Amount of Grant: Up to 3,000 USD
Contact: Tracy Hensler, (800) 368-5242, ext. 8483; fax (202) 266-8177; nhe@nahb.com
Internet: http://www.nationalhousingendowment.com/CBG.htm
Sponsor: National Housing Endowment
1201 15th Street NW
Washington, DC 20005

National Inclusion Grants 3278

The Program will focus on programs that fulfill the Foundation's mission to bridge the gap that exists between young people with special needs and the world around them, and to support communities as they create environments of full inclusion where opportunities exist, barriers break, and doors open. Eligible programs are ones that focus on the inclusion of children with special needs with their peers. Priorities for funding include but are not limited to: development of inclusion/integration curricula, primarily K-12; educational approaches that engage different learning styles; inclusion strategies for minority

populations including those for whom English is a second language; service learning opportunities and program development, training, and implementation; job training; development, training, and implementation for recreational programs aimed at both paid staff and volunteers; recruitment of special education teachers; assistance to families through eligible programs; continuing education programs/symposia aimed at the development of best practices protocols and strategies; and programs that create awareness, change attitudes and behaviors about the abilities of young people with special needs and foster full life experiences. Applications should be designed to promote the inclusion of children with special needs in school and community settings. The project period may be 1 to 3 years.
Requirements: Applications may originate from public, for profit, or not-for-profit 501(c)3 agencies or organizations.
Geographic Focus: All States
Date(s) Application is Due: Oct 31
Amount of Grant: 1,000 - 20,000 USD
Contact: Aron Hall, (919) 314-5540; fax (919)314-5541; aronhall@inclusionproject.org
Internet: http://www.inclusionproject.org/level_1.php?id=3
Sponsor: National Inclusion Project
104 T.W. Alexander Drive, Building 1, P.O. Box 110104
Durham, NC 27709

National Lottery Community Fund Grants 3279
The organization operates in the United Kingdom and internationally and awards grants to charitable, benevolent, and philanthropic organizations. The organization particularly wants to support projects that help people who face disadvantage that is severe, long-term, difficult to tackle, or who face a combination of needs. Grants support projects that try to prevent or reduce, as far as possible, future disadvantage.
Geographic Focus: All States
Contact: Gerald Oppenheim, Director; 44-020-7-747-5299; fax 44-020-7-747-5214; enquiries.res@biglotteryfund.org.uk
Internet: http://www.community-fund.org.uk/about-us/our-grants-programmes/index.html
Sponsor: National Lottery Community Fund
Saint Vincent House, 16 Suffolk Street
London, SW1Y 4NL England

National Trust for Historic Preservation Diversity Scholarship 3280
This program provides financial assistance to preservationists from diverse, racial, ethnic, and cultural backgrounds to attend the National Preservation Conference. The trust is seeking applicants whose attendance at the conference will benefit their community, whose commitment to historic preservation will be strengthened by their participation, and who will contribute a valuable perspective to conference dialog.
Requirements: Eligible applicants are individual community leaders, preservation and development professionals, and pre-professional college students.
Geographic Focus: Tennessee
Date(s) Application is Due: Jun 15
Contact: Scholarship Administrator; (202) 588-6000 or (800) 944-6847; fax (202) 588-6038; scholarships@nthp.org
Internet: http://www.preservationnation.org/resources/training/npc/npc-scholarships.html
Sponsor: National Trust for Historic Preservation
1785 Massachusetts Avenue NW
Washington, DC 20036-2117

National Urban Fellows Program 3281
The National Urban Fellows leadership development program is a rigorous, 14-month, full-time graduate degree program comprising two semesters of academic course work and a nine-month mentorship assignment. Fellows receive a $25,000 stipend, health insurance, a book allowance, relocation and travel reimbursement, and full payment of tuition, in addition to their ongoing personal and professional development. The program culminates in a Master of Public Administration (MPA) degree from the City of New York's Bernard M. Baruch College, School of Public Affairs. During the mentorship, Fellows complete course work via distance learning. An MPA degree is awarded to Fellows upon completion of all academic and program requirements. Application materials are available at the website.
Requirements: United States citizens who have bachelor's degrees; have three to five years' full-time work experience in an administrative or management capacity; have demonstrated exceptional ability, maturity, leadership potential, and commitment to the solutions of urban and rural problems; and are willing to relocate for the duration of the fellowship year are eligible. An official transcript of all undergraduate and graduate education will be required.
Geographic Focus: All States
Contact: Miguel A. Garcia, Jr., Program Director; (212) 730-1700; fax (212) 730-1823
Internet: http://www.nuf.org/fellows-overview
Sponsor: National Urban Fellows
989 Avenue of the Americas, Suite 400
New York, NY 10018

National Wetlands Awards 3282
Cosponsored by the Environmental Law Institute, U.S. Environmental Protection Agency, U.S. Fish and Wildlife Service, USDA Forest Service, Natural Resources Conservation Service, and National Marine Fisheries Service, the awards recognize individuals who have demonstrated excellence in wetland conservation. Awards will be made in the the following categories: education and outreach; science research; conservation and restoration; landowner stewardship; state, tribal, and local program development; and wetland community leader. Awardees are chosen by a committee of wetland experts representing the conservation and business communities, as well as federal, state, and local governments. Guidelines and nomination form are available online.
Requirements: Nominations must be for individuals—not organizations or groups of individuals—whose programs or projects operate at the regional, state, or local level.
Restrictions: Federal employees are not eligible. Projects not currently in compliance with the Clean Water Act or similar state or local statutes, as well as projects compelled by enforcement actions under these statutes, are not eligible.
Geographic Focus: All States
Date(s) Application is Due: Dec 15
Contact: Roxanne Thomas, Wetlands Program Director; (202) 939-3827; fax (202) 939-3868; thomas@eli.org or wetlandsawards@eli.org
Internet: http://www2.eli.org/nwa/nwaprogram.htm
Sponsor: Environmental Law Institute
2000 L Street NW, Suite 620
Washington, DC 20036

Nation Institute Ridenhour Prizes 3283
Nominations will soon now open for the annual Ridenhour Prizes, which seek to discover and recognize those who persevere in acts of truth-telling that protect the public interest, advance or promote social justice and illuminate a more just vision of society. Winners are granted a $10,000 cash award and receive one of four different awards: the Ridenhour Prize for Truth-Telling; the Ridenhour Book Prize; the Ridenhour Courage Prize; and the Ridenhour Prize for Reportorial Distinction.
Requirements: Nominations are accepted through the web site.
Geographic Focus: All States
Amount of Grant: 10,000 USD
Contact: Taya Kitman, (212) 822-0252; fax (212) 253-5356; taya@nationinstitute.org
Internet: http://www.ridenhour.org/prizes.shtml
Sponsor: Nation Institute
116 E 16th Street, 8th Floor
New York, NY 10003

Nation Institute Robert Masur Fellowship in Civil Liberties 3284
The fellowship competition is open to first-year law students who intend to carry out significant activities during the summer (in between their first and second year) in the areas of civil rights and/or civil liberties. Proposed activities may include a writing or research project, work with a public interest organization in the areas of civil rights or civil liberties, work on a civil rights or civil liberties law case under the supervision of a faculty member or lawyer, or any other work in the areas of civil rights or civil liberties. The fellowship recipient receives a $1,000 honorarium.
Geographic Focus: All States
Date(s) Application is Due: May 15
Amount of Grant: 1,000 USD
Contact: Taya Kitman, (212) 822-0252; fax (212) 253-5356; taya@nationinstitute.org
Internet: http://www.nationinstitute.org/p/masur
Sponsor: Nation Institute
116 E 16th Street, 8th Floor
New York, NY 10003

Nationwide Insurance Foundation Grants 3285
The Nationwide Insurance Foundation's mission is to improve the quality of life in communities in which a large number of Nationwide members, associates, agents and their families live and work. The foundation's grants fall into three categories: General Operating Support, Program and/or Project Support, and Capital Support. Funding priorities are then placed into one of four tiers. Tier 1-Emergency and basic needs: the foundation partners with organizations that provide life's necessities. Tier 2-Crisis stabilization: the foundation partners with organizations that provide resources to prevent crises or help pick up the pieces after one occurs. Tier 3-Personal and family empowerment: Nationwide helps at-risk youth and families in poverty situations who need tools and resources to advance their lives by partnering with organizations that assist individuals in becoming productive members of society. Tier 4-Community enrichment: the foundation partners with organizations that contribute to the overall quality of life in a community.
Requirements: In the following communities, the Nationwide Insurance Foundation will consider funding 501(c)3 organizations from all four tiers of funding priorities: Columbus, Ohio; Des Moines, Iowa; Scottsdale, Arizona. In the following communities, only Tiers 1 and 2 of the foundation's funding priorities will be considered: Sacramento, California; Denver, Colorado; Gainesville, Florida; Atlanta (Metro), Georgia; Baltimore, Maryland; Lincoln, Nebraska; Raleigh/Durham, North Carolina; Syracuse, New York; Canton, Ohio; Cleveland, Ohio; Harrisburg, Pennsylvania; Philadelphia (Metro), Pennsylvania; Nashville, Tennessee; Dallas (Metro), Texas; San Antonio, Texas; Lynchburg, Virginia; Richmond, Virginia; Wausau, Wisconsin.
Restrictions: The Nationwide Insurance Foundation generally does not fund national organizations (unless the applicant is a local branch or chapter providing direct services) or organizations located in areas with less than 100 Nationwide associates. Also, the foundation does not fund the following: Organizations that are not tax-exempt under paragraph 501(c)3 of the U.S. Internal Revenue Code; Fund-raising events such as walk-a-thons, telethons or sponsorships; Individuals for any purpose; Athletic events or teams, bands and choirs (including equipment and uniforms); Debt-reduction or retirement campaigns; Research; Public or private primary or secondary schools; Requests to support travel; Groups or organizations that will re-grant the foundation's gifts to other organizations or individuals (except United Way); Endowment campaigns; Veterans, labor, religious or fraternal groups (except when these groups provide needed services to the community at-large); Lobbying activities.
Geographic Focus: Arizona, California, Colorado, Florida, Georgia, Iowa, Maryland, Nebraska, New York, North Carolina, Ohio, Pennsylvania, Tennessee, Texas, Virginia, Wisconsin

Date(s) Application is Due: Sep 1
Amount of Grant: 5,000 - 50,000 USD
Contact: Chad Jester; (614) 249-4310 or (877) 669-6877; corpcit@nationwide.com
Internet: http://www.nationwide.com/about-us/nationwide-foundation.jsp
Sponsor: Nationwide Insurance Foundation
1 Nationwide Plaza, MD 1-22-05
Columbus, OH 43215-2220

Natonal Endowment for the Arts Research Grants: Art Works 3286

Research into the value and impact of the arts is a core function of the National Endowment for the Arts. Through accurate, relevant, and timely analyses and reports, the NEA elucidates the factors, conditions, and characteristics of the U.S. arts ecosystem and the impact of the arts on other domains of American life. To advance this work further, the NEA welcomes grant applications for projects seeking to use novel research questions and/or techniques to analyze high-quality datasets containing arts variables. The NEA encourages applicants from diverse research fields (e.g., sociology, economics, anthropology) and diverse areas of expertise, including, but not limited to, health, education, and urban and regional planning. Although applicants must be nonprofit organizations, they may partner with for-profit entities, and/or use commercial and/or administrative datasets. The Research Art Works category supports research projects to analyze the value and impact of the arts in the U.S. Through high-quality research, the NEA will expand opportunities for rigorous research that investigates the value of the U.S. arts ecosystem and the impact of the arts on other domains of American life. The NEA will make awards to support research on how "art works." Consistent with its strategic plan, the NEA distinguishes between research projects seeking to define value for the U.S. arts sector, and those seeking to demonstrate the arts' impact on American life. "Value"-oriented research will measure or otherwise clarify one or more components of how Americans participate in the arts. Such research also may probe the underlying conditions and vehicles for arts participation; for instance, it can examine how key inputs such as training, education, and infrastructure, directly affect arts creation, arts audiences, or other aspects of arts engagement. Separately, research on "impact" will investigate the direct benefits of arts participation on individuals and/or communities. A variety of possible types of benefits might be explored, whether cognitive, emotional, social/civic, or economic. The NEA also will consider strong research proposals measuring the effects of arts participation on broader-level outcomes, such as new forms of self-expression, new outlets for creative activity, and the overall creative and expressive capacity of U.S. society. The NEA hopes to spur growth in the number of people experienced in and knowledgeable about arts-related research in the U.S. The NEA recognizes that some of the most compelling research has originated in non-arts specialties: cognitive neuroscience with its discoveries about the role of art in shaping learning-related outcomes; labor economics, with its lessons about art bearing on national and local productivity; urban planning fieldwork that seeks to understand the arts as a marker of community vitality; and psychological studies that posit art's relationship to health and well-being. To this end, the NEA encourages applications from diverse research fields (e.g., sociology, economics, anthropology) and diverse areas of expertise, including health, education, and urban and regional planning. Up to 25 grants will be awarded, ranging from $10,000 to $30,000 each. Applications must be submitted through the Grants.gov online system. It is strongly recommended to submit applications at least two weeks in advance for time to resolve any problems that may occur. Additional information, including an instructional webinar, a list of frequently asked questions, and the review criteria, is located at the NEA website.
Requirements: Nonprofit, tax-exempt 501(c)3, U.S. organizations; units of state or local government; colleges and universities; or federally recognized tribal communities or tribes may apply. For projects that involve multiple organizations, one organization that meets the eligibility requirements must act as the official applicant, and assume full responsibility for the grant. Applications should present novel research questions and/or techniques that will yield valuable information about the utility to arts-related research of various kinds of data. Applicants may propose projects that focus on analyses of qualitative and/or quantitative data, which may be achieved through a broad range of project types such as the following: analyses of existing data; analyses of data for which data collection has not yet occurred; evaluations and assessments of projects, programs, or policies in ways that provide a new and/or deeper understanding of a topic; or meta-analyses of existing bodies of literature in ways that provide a new and/or deeper understanding of a topic. The quality, validity, and reliability of the data used for the proposed analysis will factor greatly in the review of the applications. A list of possible datasets is available at the NEA website.
Restrictions: Indirect costs will be supported, but will be limited to a maximum of 15% of the total award. Although grants do not require matching funds, applicants are strongly encouraged to provide some cash and/or in-kind services in support of their project. The following organizations are not eligible for funding: the designated fifty state and six jurisdictional arts agencies and their regional arts organizations; and any organization whose primary purpose is to channel resources (financial, human, or other) to an affiliated organization if the affiliated organization submits its own application. This prohibition applies even if each organization has its own 501(c)3 status. Additional restrictions are posted at the NEA website.
Geographic Focus: All States
Date(s) Application is Due: Nov 6
Amount of Grant: 10,000 - 30,000 USD
Contact: Jillian Miller; (202) 682-5504; millerj@arts.gov
Internet: http://www.arts.gov/grants/apply/Research.html
Sponsor: National Endowment for the Arts
1100 Pennsylvania Avenue NW
Washington, DC 20506-0001

Nature Hills Nursery Green America Awards 3287

The Green America Awards will be presented annually to groups and organizations that are making a difference in their communities. Nature Hills is looking for community groups who are committed to improving their local environment by planting trees, bushes and shrubs to make their communities a better place to live. Nature Hills Nursery will donate $5,000.00 of plant materials annually to the earth friendly award-winning projects. Awards will be presented to a Grand Prize winner in the amount of $2,500.00 of plant materials. First place winner will receive $1,500 in plant materials and the Second Place winner $1,000.00 in plant materials. The plant materials can contain trees, fruit trees, bushes and shrubs, perennials and vegetable seeds.
Requirements: Eligible submissions will be accepted from charitable or educational organizations that operate as a non profit entity. Awards must be used by the winning organization to complete their project plan and cannot be sold or used in any way other than for the project described in the application submitted by the organization. Applications must be submitted online via the sponsor's website.
Geographic Focus: All States
Date(s) Application is Due: Apr 1
Contact: Jeffrey Dinslage, President; (402) 934-8116, ext. 101; press@naturehills.com
Internet: http://www.naturehills.com/green_america_awards.aspx
Sponsor: Nature Hills Nursery
3334 North 88th Plaza
Omaha, NE 68134

NCFL/Better World Books Libraries and Families Award 3288

Better World Books and the National Center for Family Literacy (NCFL) have teamed up for the annual Libraries and Families Award. Three library literacy programs that serve families will win $10,000 each and scholarships to the National Conference on Family Literacy. As a long-standing partner of Better World Books, NCFL is able to provide the grants by using unrestricted funds they receive from Better World Books. This relationship is a perfect example of Better World Books' dedication to supporting libraries and the important work those libraries do to help the communities they serve. The Libraries and Families Awards will reward innovative library-based literacy programs for families. Existing programs and brand-new programs will be considered.
Requirements: The sponsors are looking for innovative libraries that are passionate about serving families. The preferences are for library literacy programs that: serve parents and children in ways that they can learn together/have a strong intergenerational approach; have a record of success, and a clear plan for a successful project; serve communities and families with high literacy and socioeconomic needs; propose a compelling use of award funding that directly benefits families; and, will likely continue after the grant has been expended. The project must be library-based, implemented by library staff, and grant funds must be awarded directly to a library or library organization (e.g., Friends of the Library groups, library foundations, etc.). Applicant must commit to sharing program and participant stories with NCFL and Better World Books on an ongoing basis. The project must be fully supported by your library director or administrator.
Geographic Focus: All States
Date(s) Application is Due: Feb 6
Amount of Grant: 1,000 USD
Contact: Lisa Avetisian, (502) 584-1133; lavetisian@famlit.org
Internet: http://www.famlit.org/award-grant-opportunities/
Sponsor: National Center for Family Literacy
325 West Main Street, Suite 300
Louisville, KY 40202-4237

Needmor Fund Grants 3289

The fund awards grants to grassroots, community-based organizations for a range of activities in the areas of justice, political liberty, human services (food, shelter, health care, and safety), and education that enables low- and moderate-income individuals to contribute to society and the opportunity to secure productive work with just wages and benefits. Needmor gives to groups that help people take control of their lives and change the conditions that adversely affect them. Preference will be given to groups that have a highly committed membership, develop leadership from within, can determine solutions to major problems facing their communities, and formulate effective strategic plans. Types of support include general operating budgets, seed money, and technical assistance. Grantees are encouraged to develop alternative means of long-term fundraising to promote self-sufficiency. The January 10 deadline is for applicants located in Alabama, Arizona, southern California, Louisiana, Mississippi, New Mexico, and southern Texas (including San Antonio). The June 30 deadline is for applicants in all other states, and required a pre-application process with a deadline of May 31.
Requirements: Nonprofit community-based organizations may apply for support.
Restrictions: Grants do not support individuals, capital funds, scholarships, fellowships, deficit financing, replacement of lost government funding, land acquisition, purchase of buildings or equipment, publications, media, films, TV or radio productions, computer projects, or university research. Nonprofits with access to traditional funding sources generally are denied support.
Geographic Focus: Arizona, California, Colorado, New Mexico, Wyoming
Date(s) Application is Due: Jan 10; Jun 30
Amount of Grant: 15,000 - 40,000 USD
Contact: Mary Sobecki; (419) 255-5560; fax (419) 255-5561; msobecki@needmorfund.org
Internet: http://fdncenter.org/grantmaker/needmor
Sponsor: Needmor Fund
42 South Saint Clair Street
Toledo, OH 43604-8736

Nehemiah Community Foundation Grants 3290

The mission of the Nehemiah Community Foundation is to support faith-based and community-based organizations, and to encourage individual achievement and self-sufficiency. Program areas include affordable housing and neighborhood revitalization; job training and placement for low and moderate-income individuals; education and the arts; culturally diverse leadership training; and financial education. In special cases, requests outside of these areas will considered. Types of support include general operating grants, program-specific grants, and seed grants. Applications are accepted throughout the year, and there are no deadlines. Applicants must submit a one- to two-page letter of intent describing the organization's mission, the purpose of the project for which funds are being requested, and the total amount requested. Funding priority is given to projects that: provide measurable solutions to specific problems; prevent duplication of local services by pursuing collaborative approaches with other non-profit organizations; demonstrate committed, effective leadership and long-term management capacity. Additional application guidelines are available at the Foundation website.
Requirements: Nonprofit 501(c)3 tax-exempt organizations are eligible.
Restrictions: The Foundation does not provide grants for the following: individuals; endowments; start-up nonprofit organizations without a demonstrated, multi-year record of achievement; political, labor, fraternal, or other such activities; marketing activities; promotional merchandise; multiyear grant requests; sports or athletic teams; or organizations without IRS 501(c)3 tax-exempt status.
Geographic Focus: California
Amount of Grant: 1,000 - 15,000 USD
Contact: Melissa Brown, Executive Director; (877) 231-1022; info@nelpleaders.org
Internet: http://www.nehemiahcorp.org/info_ncf.html
Sponsor: Nehemiah Corporation of America
640 Bercut Drive, Suite A
Sacramento, CA 95811-031

NEH Family and Youth Programs in American History Grants 3291

As part of the We the People initiative, NEH invites proposals for public programs that encourage intergenerational learning about and reflection on significant topics in U.S. history and culture. Grants will support programming tailored to youth and/or family audiences at museums, libraries, historical societies and sites, parks, and other places in the community. The projects should: strengthen knowledge and appreciation of American history among young people through activities outside the classroom; or encourage families to explore themes and ideas from American history together. NEH encourages projects that: highlight documents and artifacts significant to American history; make humanities content central to the project; and collaborate with other organizations to extend the reach of the project.
Requirements: Any U.S. nonprofit organization with 501(c)3 tax exempt status is eligible, as are state and local governmental agencies and tribal governments.
Restrictions: Activities that take place at schools during regular school hours or as part of the school curriculum are not eligible. Individuals are not eligible to apply.
Geographic Focus: All States
Date(s) Application is Due: Jan 11
Amount of Grant: 40,000 - 400,000 USD
Contact: Kathy Toavs; (202) 606-8474 or (202) 606-8463; ktoavs@neh.gov
Internet: http://www.neh.gov/grants/guidelines/familyyouthprograms.html
Sponsor: National Endowment for the Humanities
1100 Pennsylvania Avenue NW, Room 511
Washington, DC 20506

NEH Interpreting America's Historic Places Grants 3292

As part of the We the People initiative, NEH seeks proposals for public programs that use one or more historic sites to address themes and issues central to American history. Projects may interpret a single historic site, a series of sites, whole neighborhoods, communities or towns, or larger geographical regions. The place taken as a whole must be significant to American history and the project must convey its importance to visitors. The projects should: increase the public's knowledge and appreciation of American history; encourage historic sites, communities, or regions to develop interpretive programs that address central themes and issues in American history; encourage consultation with humanities scholars and organizations in the development of heritage tourism destinations and itineraries; and focus on the development or implementation of interpretive content that tells a significant national story appropriate to the place. Possible activities include docent tours, publications (e.g., brochures, guidebooks, etc.), driving or walking trails or tours, annotated itineraries, exhibition labeling or trail signage, films, and digital media.
Requirements: Any U.S. nonprofit organization with 501(c)3 tax-exempt status is eligible, as are state and local governmental agencies and federally recognized Indian tribal governments.
Restrictions: Individuals are not eligible to apply.
Geographic Focus: All States
Date(s) Application is Due: Mar 1
Contact: Kathy Toavs; (202) 606-8474 or (202) 606-8463; ktoavs@neh.gov
Internet: http://www.neh.gov/grants/guidelines/historicplaces.html
Sponsor: National Endowment for the Humanities
1100 Pennsylvania Avenue NW, Room 511
Washington, DC 20506

NEH Preservation Assistance Grants for Smaller Institutions 3293

The grants help help small and mid-sized institutions-such as libraries, museums, historical societies, archival repositories, cultural organizations, town and county records offices, and colleges and universities-improve their ability to preserve and care for their humanities collections. These may include special collections of books and journals, archives and manuscripts, prints and photographs, moving images, sound recordings, architectural and cartographic records, decorative and fine art objects, textiles, archaeological and ethnographic artifacts, furniture, historical objects, and digital materials.
Requirements: U.S. nonprofit organizations are eligible, as are state and local governmental agencies and tribal governments. Small and mid-sized institutions that have never received an NEH grant are especially encouraged to apply. Only one application for a Preservation Assistance Grant may be submitted annually by an institution, although distinct collecting entities of a larger organization may apply in the same year, such as the library and museum of a university or two historic sites within a historical society.
Restrictions: Individuals are not eligible to apply. Grants may not be used for projects that focus on collections that fall outside of the humanities; projects that preserve, organize, or describe materials that are not regularly accessible for research, education, or public programming; projects that preserve, organize, or describe materials that are the responsibility of an agency of the federal government; conservation or restoration treatments (including deacidification and encapsulation) or the purchase of conservation or restoration treatment supplies and equipment (e.g., mending tape, erasers, and cleaning supplies), or library binding; graduate-level conservation training or training related to advanced conservation treatment; projects that focus on preserving or restoring buildings or other structures; capital improvements to buildings and building systems, including the purchase of equipment such as air conditioners, dehumidifiers, and security and fire protection systems; projects that seek to catalog, index, or arrange and describe collections; reformatting of collections (e.g., digitizing, photocopying, microfilming, or copying to another medium) or the purchase of equipment for reformatting (e.g., computers, scanners, digital cameras, cassette decks, and CD-ROM drives); development of digitization programs or digital asset management systems; purchase of computers; salaries and fringe benefits for the staff of an institution; attendance at regular meetings of museum, library, archives, or preservation organizations; or the recovery of indirect costs.
Geographic Focus: All States
Date(s) Application is Due: May 18
Amount of Grant: 6,000 USD
Contact: Program Contact; (202) 606-8570; fax (202) 606-8369; preservation@neh.gov
Internet: http://neh.gov/grants/guidelines/pag.html
Sponsor: National Endowment for the Humanities
1100 Pennsylvania Avenue NW, Room 318
Washington, DC 20506

NEH Preservation Microfilming of Brittle Books and Serials Grants 3294

This special initiative's goal is to preserve the knowledge contained in brittle books and other deteriorating paper-based research materials. The endowment's share of the project's total cost will not exceed 67 percent. Applicants must contact the division's staff before developing a proposal.
Requirements: Institutions and individuals are eligible to apply.
Geographic Focus: All States
Contact: Program Contact; (202) 606-8570; fax (202) 606-8639; preservation@neh.gov
Internet: http://www.neh.gov/grants/grants.html
Sponsor: National Endowment for the Humanities
1100 Pennsylvania Avenue NW, Room 318
Washington, DC 20506

NEI Innovative Patient Outreach Programs And Ocular Screening Technologies To Improve Detection Of Diabetic Retinopathy Grants 3295

This Funding Opportunity Announcement (FOA) solicits Small Business Innovation Research (SBIR) grant applications from small business concerns (SBCs) that propose to 1) develop educational outreach programs to create a greater awareness of the blinding consequences of diabetes; and, 2) develop tools and systems to be used for increasing patient access to eye exams for detecting Diabetic Retinopathy (DR). This FOA will utilize the SBIR (R43/R44) grant mechanisms for Phase I, Phase II, and Fast-Track applications. The estimated amount of funds available for support of 2-4 projects awarded as a result of this announcement is $2 million for this fiscal year.
Requirements: Only United States small business concerns (SBCs) are eligible to submit SBIR applications. A small business concern is one that, at the time of award of Phase I and Phase II, meets all of the criteria listed. Any individual(s) with the skills, knowledge, and resources necessary to carry out the proposed research as the PD/PI is invited to work with his/her organization to develop an application for support. Individuals from underrepresented racial and ethnic groups as well as individuals with disabilities are always encouraged to apply for NIH support. See website for details.
Geographic Focus: All States
Date(s) Application is Due: Mar 23; Dec 23
Amount of Grant: 2,000,000 USD
Contact: Jerome R. Wujek, (301) 451-2020; fax (301) 402-0528; wujekjer@nei.nih.gov
Internet: http://grants.nih.gov/grants/guide/rfa-files/RFA-EY-09-001.html
Sponsor: National Eye Institute
5635 Fishers Lane, Suite 1300, MSC 9300
Bethesda, MD 20892-9300

Nelda C. and H.J. Lutcher Stark Foundation Grants 3296

The foundation awards grants in its areas of interest, including education, health and social services, medical and dental, community enrichment, arts and culture. Giving is primarily in Texas, with preference to programs that directly impact Southeast Texas and limited giving in Southwest Louisiana. There are no application forms. Submit a letter of proposal containing the following information: description of the project signed by the president or CEO; brief history, description, programs, and mission of the organization; project time line; specific amount requested; list of other funding sources and amounts; list of board of

directors and occupations; form 990 for most recent year-end; most recent audited financial statements or organization prepared statements; and current copy of IRS determination letter certifying tax-exempt status. Guidelines are available online. All grants from the third quarter of 2008 and for 2009 have been suspended due to recovery efforts in which the Foundation must engage for its own operations as a result of damages from Hurricane Ike, together with the negative impact of the downturn in financial markets on the Foundation's corpus, the Stark Foundation will continue the prior suspension of the grant-making aspect of its operations through the entirety of Year 2009. Therefore, the Stark Foundation will not accept any grant applications for Year 2009, nor will be able to consider any grant applications that may be submitted notwithstanding this suspension.
Requirements: To be eligible for a grant, an organization must: be exempt from taxation under Section 501(c)3 of the Internal Revenue Code; not be a private foundation within the meaning of Section 509(a) of the Code. No grants are made for endowment purposes, to individuals, or to supporting organizations as described in Section 509(a)(3) of the Internal Revenue Code.
Geographic Focus: All States, Canada
Date(s) Application is Due: Mar 1; Jun 1; Oct 1
Contact: Grant Department
Internet: http://www.starkfoundation.org/Grants/Grant-Guidelines.aspx
Sponsor: Nelda C. and H.J. Lutcher Stark Foundation
P.O. Box 909
Orange, TX 77631-0909

Nellie Mae Education Foundation District-Level Change Grants 3297
The Nellie Mae Education Foundation District-Level Systems Change Grants support the shift in high school-level education in New England to prepare students to thrive in a global, complex, fast changing society. Grant programs promote student centered models of schooling that offer a path away from a one size fits all approach to a more customized approach to maximize learning for all students. The initiative focuses on three priority areas: developing school and district designs and practices that enable all learners to achieve high standards; creating sustainable policy change to support these new approaches; and generating public will and increasing demand for changes in practice. Examples of allowable activities for funding include: engaging central office, school administrators, and teachers in identifying current initiatives and how they compete with or support a student centered learning frame; surveying student needs and challenges and what motivates them to achieve academically and personally; creating greater building level autonomy and funding streams based on student needs rather than programs; researching feasibility, designing and planning for the appropriate blended learning model including visits to blended learning schools; using technology as an essential tool in learning environments and professional development; or administrator visits from student centered schools. The Foundation will support self-assessment activities, efforts to build, forge or nurture a common vision and mission for the work, and integration of this work with other school/district initiatives. Funds can support purchasing online and hardcopy literacy materials to support complex Common Core State Standards (CCSS) text demands; engaging a team of district stakeholders to conduct an analysis of culture of the system's various dimensions; or administrative visits from student centered schools. Proposal information, including the request for proposal, a list of supplemental materials and instructions, questions to address in the proposal, a list of frequently asked questions and previously funded projects, and an instructional webinar, is located at the Foundation website.
Requirements: The Foundation's activities include both making grants to the public charities it supports and providing services to those organizations. The Foundation operates exclusively to promote the charitable and educational purposes of nonprofit educational organizations, including universities, colleges, secondary schools, elementary schools and other educational organizations that are described in the IRS Code Section 501(c)3.
Restrictions: Funding for this project is concentrated on urban school districts and learning centers in Connecticut, Massachusetts, and Rhode Island. The Foundation does not fund capital campaigns, endowments, scholarships or fellowships, debt reduction or cash reserves, building construction or renovation, and certain indirect costs.
Geographic Focus: Connecticut, Massachusetts, Rhode Island
Date(s) Application is Due: Oct 18
Amount of Grant: 25,000 - 1,000,000 USD
Contact: Stephanie Cheney, Senior Manager, Grants and Special Programs; (781) 348-4240; fax (781) 348-4299; scheney@nmefdn.org
Internet: http://www.nmefoundation.org/grants/district-level-systems-change
Sponsor: Nellie Mae Education Foundation
1250 Hancock Street, Suite 205N
Quincy, MA 02169

Nellie Mae Education Foundation Public Understanding Grants 3298
The Nellie Mae Education Foundation Public Understanding Grants work to promote awareness of the student-centered approaches that lead to deeper learning for all students, and create the public will to demand greater adoption of these approaches. Grants focus on three areas: educating communities on student-centered approaches to learning, what they are, and why they are critical; transforming public perception of how students learn and why it must change; and building public demand for student-centered learning approaches in communities, districts and states. Funding for projects is posted on the Foundation website when it becomes available. A list of frequently asked questions and previously funded projects are located on the website.
Requirements: The Foundation's activities include both making grants to the public charities it supports and providing services to those organizations. The Foundation operates exclusively to promote the charitable and educational purposes of nonprofit educational organizations, including universities, colleges, secondary schools, elementary schools and other educational organizations as described in the IRS Code Section 501(c)3. Organizations located in the New England area are eligible to apply (Maine, New Hampshire, Vermont, Massachusetts, Rhode Island, and Connecticut). Additionally, the Foundation supports programs, organizations, research and conferences in other states in order to influence policy, and advance knowledge of public opinion toward education.
Restrictions: The Foundation does not fund capital campaigns, endowments, scholarships or fellowships, debt reduction or cash reserves, building construction or renovation, and certain indirect costs. The Foundation also does not support Section 509(a) organizations or individuals.
Geographic Focus: All States
Amount of Grant: 7,500 - 250,000 USD
Contact: Stephanie Cheney, Senior Manager, Grants and Special Programs; (781) 348-4240; fax (781) 348-4299; scheney@nmefdn.org
Internet: http://www.nmefoundation.org/grants/public-understanding
Sponsor: Nellie Mae Education Foundation
1250 Hancock Street, Suite 205N
Quincy, MA 02169

Nellie Mae Education Foundation State Level Systems Change Grants 3299
The Nellie Mae Education Foundation State-Level Systems Change (SLSC) initiative works to remove barriers and shape state and federal policies that promote deeper learning through student-centered approaches. The SLSC focuses on four areas of priority: state accountability systems that include evaluation of new basic skills such as creative thinking and problem solving; high school graduation requirements based more on students demonstrating competency in target areas than on time spent in the classroom; teacher certification requirements that support teachers and help students develop skills and knowledge through relevant, interest-driven experiences; and state funding formulas that enable and support student-centered learning environments. Request for proposals, with supplementary material and instructions, should be posted on the website if funding is currently available and proposals may be submitted. Previously funded projects and a list of frequently asked questions are located at the Foundation website.
Requirements: The Foundation's activities include both making grants to the public charities it supports and providing services to those organizations. The Foundation operates exclusively to promote the charitable and educational purposes of nonprofit educational organizations, including universities, colleges, secondary schools, elementary schools and other educational organizations that are described in IRS Code Section 501(c)3. Funding is concentrated in Connecticut, Maine, New Hampshire, Rhode Island, Vermont, and Massachusetts, but is also available outside the area to support programs, organizations, research, and conference in order to influence policy, and advance knowledge of public opinion toward education.
Restrictions: The Foundation does not fund capital campaigns, endowments, scholarships or fellowships, debt reduction or cash reserves, building construction or renovation, and certain indirect costs.
Geographic Focus: All States
Amount of Grant: 50,000 - 700,000 USD
Contact: Stephanie Cheney, Senior Manager, Grants and Special Programs; (781) 348-4240; fax (781) 348-4299; scheney@nmefdn.org
Internet: http://www.nmefoundation.org/grants/state-level-systems-change
Sponsor: Nellie Mae Education Foundation
1250 Hancock Street, Suite 205N
Quincy, MA 02169

Nell Warren Elkin and William Simpson Elkin Foundation 3300
The foundation awards grants to charitable organizations in its areas of interest, including universities, cancer clinics, specific disease associations, religious groups, and Bible studies. Application form and guidelines are available online.
Requirements: Nonprofit, charitable organizations are eligible.
Geographic Focus: All States
Date(s) Application is Due: Feb 28; Jul 31
Amount of Grant: 2,000 - 10,000 USD
Contact: Dale Welch; (404) 724-3773; rs.foundationinfo@suntrust.com
Internet: http://www.elkinfoundation.org
Sponsor: Nell Warren Elkin and William Simpson Elkin Foundation
P.O. Box 4655, MC 221
Atlanta, GA 30302

Nestle Foundation Training Grant 3301
The Nestlé Foundation supports research in human nutrition with public health relevance in low-income and lower middle-income countries. The results of the research projects should ideally provide a basis for implementation and action which will lead to sustainable effects in the studied populations as generally applicable to the population at large. They should also enable institutional strengthening and capacity building in a sustainable manner in the host country and further cooperation and collaboration between institutions in developed and developing countries. Categories include: training grants, pilot grants, research grants (small and large), and re-entry grants. Training grants support a small research project such as a master's degree in science, Ph.D. thesis project, or a training endeavor. Applications are accepted all year and evaluated twice a year.
Requirements: The Foundation's work is primarily concerned with human nutrition research issues dealing with: maternal and child nutrition, including breastfeeding and complementary feeding; macro- and micronutrient deficiencies and imbalances; interactions between infection and nutrition; and nutrition education and health promotion. Interested scientists should first submit a letter of intent briefly describing the project and the estimated budget. Instructions are available on the Foundation's website. If approved applicants will receive an invitation to submit a full grant proposal. Guidelines and forms are available on our website. The letter of

intent and the grant application should include detailed, evidence-based information about the public health relevance of the project as well as its immediate impact and sustainability. Funding is primarily based on the scientific quality, public health relevance in the short and long term, sustainability, capacity-building component, and budget considerations.
Restrictions: The Foundation expects research proposals to be primarily the initiative of local researchers from developing countries but considers applications jointly made by scientists from developed countries with those from developing countries provided it is clear that the initiative will result in capacity building and human resource development in the latter and the bulk of the budget is spent in the developing country.
Geographic Focus: All Countries
Date(s) Application is Due: Jan 10; May 10
Contact: Catherine Loeb; +41-21-320 33 51; fax +41-21-320 33 92; nf@nestlefoundation.org
Internet: http://www.nestlefoundation.org/e/research.html
Sponsor: Nestle Foundation
4 Place de la Gare
Lausanne, CH-1001 Switzerland

Nestle Purina PetCare Educational Grants 3302
Nestlé Purina PetCare has a rich history of community involvement in greater St. Louis, Missouri, their world headquarters for pet food, and in the cities with manufacturing facilities. The company supports established organizations with diverse boards, effective leadership, clear objectives, sound financial practices and multiple sources of support. Educational Grants are generally given for programs that focus on educational opportunities for disadvantaged youth. Programs might include college readiness, character education, after school programs and field trips.
Requirements: Organizations located in the greater St. Louis area or in a city where the company has manufacturing facilities are eligible. The St. Louis area includes an area within a 100-mile radius of downtown St. Louis. Cities with manufacturing facilities include: Allentown, Pennsylvania; Atlanta, Georgia; Bloomfield, Missouri; Cape Girardeau, Missouri; Clinton, Iowa; Crete, Nebraska; Davenport, Iowa; Denver, Colorado; Dunkirk, New York; Flagstaff, Arizona; Fort Dodge, Iowa; Hager City, Wisconsin; Jefferson, Wisconsin; King William, Virginia; Maricopa, California; Mechanicsburg, Pennsylvania; Oklahoma City, Oklahoma; Springfield, Missouri; St. Joseph, Missouri; Weirton, West Virginia; and Zanesville, Ohio. Application can be made at the website.
Geographic Focus: Arizona, California, Colorado, Georgia, Iowa, Missouri, Nebraska, New York, Ohio, Oklahoma, Pennsylvania, Virginia, West Virginia, Wisconsin
Contact: Public Relations Manager; (314) 982-1000
Internet: http://www.nestlepurina.com/CharitableGiving.aspx
Sponsor: Nestle Purina PetCare Company
Checkerboard Square
Saint Louis, MO 63164

Nestle Purina PetCare Emergency Response and Disaster Relief Grants 3303
Nestle Purina PetCare has a rich history of community involvement and supports established organizations with diverse boards, effective leadership, clear objectives, sound financial practices and multiple sources of support. When floods, fire and ice take their toll on four-legged victims, Purina responds with donations of Purina brand dog and cat foods and Tidy Cats brand litter. In a major disaster, Purina's first response is generally to partner with a nationally recognized rescue agency.
Requirements: Not-for-profit 501(c)3 animal welfare organizations already registered with Purina® Pets For People™ and impacted by a natural disaster or emergency may submit a disaster request. Organizations not registered may first register and then submit a request. Instructions for registration and submitting requests are on the website.
Geographic Focus: All States
Contact: Public Relations Manager; (314) 982-1000; fax (314) 982-2168
Internet: http://www.petsforpeople.com/page?pageid=a0e40000001Sgf1AAC
Sponsor: Nestle Purina PetCare Company
Checkerboard Square
Saint Louis, MO 63164

Nestle Purina PetCare Pet Related Grants 3304
Nestlé Purina PetCare has a rich history of community involvement in greater St. Louis, Missouri, their world headquarters for pet food, and in the cities with manufacturing facilities. The company supports established organizations with diverse boards, effective leadership, clear objectives, sound financial practices and multiple sources of support. Pet Related Grants are generally given to established pet-related organizations for fundraising or responsible pet ownership programs. Small grants may be requested for capital campaigns and education programs.
Requirements: Organizations located in the greater St. Louis area or in a city where the company has manufacturing facilities are eligible. The St. Louis area includes an area within a 100-mile radius of downtown St. Louis. Cities with manufacturing facilities include: Allentown, Pennsylvania; Atlanta, Georgia; Bloomfield, Missouri; Cape Girardeau, Missouri; Clinton, Iowa; Crete, Nebraska; Davenport, Iowa; Denver, Colorado; Dunkirk, New York; Flagstaff, Arizona; Fort Dodge, Iowa; Hager City, Wisconsin; Jefferson, Wisconsin; King William, Virginia; Maricopa, California; Mechanicsburg, Pennsylvania; Oklahoma City, Oklahoma; Springfield, Missouri; St. Joseph, Missouri; Weirton, West Virginia; and Zanesville, Ohio. Application can be made at the website.
Geographic Focus: Arizona, California, Colorado, Georgia, Iowa, Missouri, Nebraska, New York, Ohio, Oklahoma, Pennsylvania, Virginia, West Virginia, Wisconsin
Contact: Public Relations Manager; (314) 982-1000
Internet: http://www.nestlepurina.com/CharitableGiving.aspx
Sponsor: Nestle Purina PetCare Company
Checkerboard Square
Saint Louis, MO 63164

Nestle Purina PetCare Support Dog and Police K-9 Organization Grants 3305
Nestlé Purina PetCare has a rich history of community involvement in greater St. Louis, Missouri, their world headquarters for pet food, and in the cities with manufacturing facilities. The company supports established organizations with diverse boards, effective leadership, clear objectives, sound financial practices and multiple sources of support. Purina acknowledges the benefit that support dog and police K-9 organizations bring to communities and provides limited grant support.
Requirements: Organizations located in the greater St. Louis area or in a city where the company has manufacturing facilities are eligible. The St. Louis area includes an area within a 100-mile radius of downtown St. Louis. Cities with manufacturing facilities include: Allentown, Pennsylvania; Atlanta, Georgia; Bloomfield, Missouri; Cape Girardeau, Missouri; Clinton, Iowa; Crete, Nebraska; Davenport, Iowa; Denver, Colorado; Dunkirk, New York; Flagstaff, Arizona; Fort Dodge, Iowa; Hager City, Wisconsin; Jefferson, Wisconsin; King William, Virginia; Maricopa, California; Mechanicsburg, Pennsylvania; Oklahoma City, Oklahoma; Springfield, Missouri; St. Joseph, Missouri; Weirton, West Virginia; and Zanesville, Ohio.
Geographic Focus: Arizona, California, Colorado, Georgia, Iowa, Missouri, Nebraska, New York, Ohio, Oklahoma, Pennsylvania, Virginia, West Virginia, Wisconsin
Contact: Public Relations Manager; (314) 982-1000
Internet: http://www.nestlepurina.com/CharitableGiving.aspx
Sponsor: Nestle Purina PetCare Company
Checkerboard Square
Saint Louis, MO 63164

Nestle Purina PetCare Youth Grants 3306
Nestlé Purina PetCare has a rich history of community involvement in greater St. Louis, Missouri, their world headquarters for pet food, and in the cities with manufacturing facilities. The company supports established organizations with diverse boards, effective leadership, clear objectives, sound financial practices and multiple sources of support. Youth Grants are generally given for programs that focus on the education and well being of disadvantaged youth. These might include youth camps or youth employment programs.
Requirements: Organizations located in the greater St. Louis area or in a city where the company has manufacturing facilities are eligible. The St. Louis area includes an area within a 100-mile radius of downtown St. Louis. Cities with manufacturing facilities include: Allentown, Pennsylvania; Atlanta, Georgia; Bloomfield, Missouri; Cape Girardeau, Missouri; Clinton, Iowa; Crete, Nebraska; Davenport, Iowa; Denver, Colorado; Dunkirk, New York; Flagstaff, Arizona; Fort Dodge, Iowa; Hager City, Wisconsin; Jefferson, Wisconsin; King William, Virginia; Maricopa, California; Mechanicsburg, Pennsylvania; Oklahoma City, Oklahoma; Springfield, Missouri; St. Joseph, Missouri; Weirton, West Virginia; and Zanesville, Ohio.
Geographic Focus: Arizona, California, Colorado, Georgia, Iowa, Missouri, Nebraska, New York, Ohio, Oklahoma, Pennsylvania, Virginia, West Virginia, Wisconsin
Contact: Public Relations Manager; (314) 982-1000
Internet: http://www.nestlepurina.com/CharitableGiving.aspx
Sponsor: Nestle Purina PetCare Company
Checkerboard Square
Saint Louis, MO 63164

Nestle Very Best in Youth Competition 3307
Nestlé sponsors the biennial Nestlé Very Best In Youth competition which was created to spotlight the best in youth leadership. The competition identifies teens whose efforts are making a profound impact in lives other than their own. Nestlé donates $1,000 in the name of each winner to the charity of his or her choice. Nestlé also awards trips for winners and a parent or guardian to Los Angeles, California for the Nestlé Very Best In Youth awards ceremony. The trip includes round trip coach air travel, hotel accommodations for three nights, and spending money. Each contestant receives a certificate of achievement from Nestlé and samples of Nestlé products.
Requirements: Contestants must be between thirteen and eighteen and have parental or legal guardian permission to submit an entry form. Contestants must demonstrate good citizenship, a strong academic record, and show how they have made a special contribution to their school, church or community. Application include two letters of recommendation, a transcript or current report card, and a consent form signed by a parent or legal guardian. The website provides an-line application and deadline information.
Geographic Focus: All States
Contact: Director; (818) 549-6677; NestleVeryBestInYouth@us.nestle.com
Internet: http://verybestinyouth.nestleusa.com/Public/
Sponsor: Nestle USA
800 North Brand Boulevard
Glendale, CA 91203

Nevada Arts Council Circuit Rider Grants 3308
Nevada Arts Council Circuit Rider grants provide affordable technical assistance to nonprofit arts and cultural organizations. Grant recipients use consultants on the Nevada Circuit Riders Roster to address specific issues and/or challenges such as advocacy, board development, fiscal and management, fundraising, marketing programming, planning or technology. Up to $3,500 may be requested, and a 1:1 match is required. Funding is awarded on a first-come, first-served basis throughout the year while funds are available.
Requirements: Each general psychiatry training program may nominate one PGY-II resident.
Geographic Focus: Nevada
Contact: Ann Libby; (775) 687-7102; fax (775) 687-6688; ann.libby@nevadaculture.org
Internet: http://nac.nevadaculture.org/index.php?option=com_content&view=article&id=1266&Itemid=414
Sponsor: Nevada Arts Council
716 N Carson Street, Suite A
Carson City, NV 89701

Nevada Arts Council Folklife Apprenticeship Grants   3309

Nevada Arts Council Folklife Apprenticeship program encourages the continuation of Nevada's diverse traditional culture by providing grants to skilled master artists to teach committed apprentices through intensive instruction in their art form. A master artist works with one or two apprentices during a one-year period. The master and apprentice are required to present one public program – a demonstration, educational program, or performance – and must arrange in advance for Folklife program staff to attend. A maximum of $2,000, which includes a $1,000 stipend to the master artist for teaching time and up to $750 for supplies and materials, and up to $250 for eligible travel is allowed.
Requirements: A Master Artist must be a Nevada resident, at least 21 years of age and recognized in his or her community as an exemplary practitioner of the particular art form. Apprentices must be Nevada residents, at least 16 years old, with intermediate level experience in the folk art form they wish to continue learning.
Geographic Focus: Nevada
Date(s) Application is Due: May 25
Amount of Grant: Up to 2,000 USD
Contact: Ann Libby; (775) 687-7102; fax (775) 687-6688; ann.libby@nevadaculture.org
Internet: http://nac.nevadaculture.org/index.php?option=com_content&view=article&id=1043&Itemid=412
Sponsor: Nevada Arts Council
716 N Carson Street, Suite A
Carson City, NV 89701

Nevada Arts Council Folklife Opportunities Grants   3310

The Nevada Arts Council Folklife Opportunities program support projects associated with the presentation and preservation of traditional arts, language and other folklife activities. FOG funding may be used to produce festivals, cultural events, concerts, gatherings, master classes, conferences and seminars (including: artist fees, publicity, facility and equipment rentals), and to provide demonstrations at museums, schools, local organizations and community centers, or to support community documentation projects. Applicants can request up to $1,500, and submission deadline is a minimum of 45 days prior to the planned residency.
Requirements: This is an entry-level grant for Nevada's small community 501(c)3 nonprofit organizations only, with budgets of $100,000 or less and that have a record of at least one year of traditional arts programming.
Restrictions: Organizations that have received an NAC Project, Development, or Partners in Excellence Grant within the past five years are not eligible to apply for FOG funds.
Geographic Focus: Nevada
Amount of Grant: Up to 1,500 USD
Contact: Patricia Atkinson; (775) 687-7103; fax (775) 687-6688; patkinson@nevadaculture.org
Internet: http://nac.nevadaculture.org/index.php?option=com_content&view=article&id=1266&Itemid=414
Sponsor: Nevada Arts Council
716 N Carson Street, Suite A
Carson City, NV 89701

Nevada Arts Council Heritage Awards   3311

Nevada Heritage Awards were created to recognize and celebrate our state's living cultural treasures. These individuals embody the highest level of artistic achievement in their work and the highest level of service in the teaching and other work they do in theircommunities to ensure that their traditions stay strong. These awards are given to individuals for their lifelong record of artistic excellence, authenticity, and significance. One or two awards are presented each year, depending on the application pool and availability of funds. Awards are $3,500.
Geographic Focus: Nevada
Amount of Grant: 3,500 USD
Contact: Ann Libby; (775) 687-7102; fax (775) 687-6688; ann.libby@nevadaculture.org
Internet: http://nac.nevadaculture.org/index.php?option=com_content&view=article&id=1043&Itemid=412
Sponsor: Nevada Arts Council
716 N Carson Street, Suite A
Carson City, NV 89701

Nevada Arts Council Jackpot Grants   3312

Jackpots Grants are awarded on a quarterly schedule to eligible individuals and organizations to support new or exemplary arts projects. Jackpots are also designed to support activities that help artists further their careers. Artists must have attained a certain level of proficiency as represented in the quality of work samples submitted with the applications. Examples of eligible Jackpot projects for individuals include arts exhibitions, performances, readings, and concerts; sponsoring of arts-related workshops and conferences; and marketing and promotional activities. Examples of eligible Jackpot projects for organizations include costs associated with attendance at workshops, conferences, seminars, and master classes; preparing portfolios and work samples; and presentation of work (performances, exhibitions, publications, etc.). Grants are evaluated on the artistic merit of the project, the ability of the applicant to complete the project, and if, applicable, evidence of public access to project activities. Individuals are not required to match Jackpot grants. Organizations must have at least a dollar-for-dollar cash match for Jackpot grants, and may not apply for more than 50 percent of a project's allowable costs. Guidelines are available online.
Requirements: Nevada 501(c)3 nonprofit organizations and organizations applying with 501(c)3 fiscal sponsors are eligible. An individual applying in this category must be a Nevada resident, and, in general, may not be a degree candidate student unless he/she can substantiate status as a practicing artist.
Restrictions: Artist fellowship recipients during the entire fellowship year (July 1 through June 30) and recipients of Project, Development, Partners in Excellence, or Arts in Education Professional Development Grants are ineligible for this funding.
Geographic Focus: Nevada
Date(s) Application is Due: Feb 15; May 15; Aug 15; Nov 15
Amount of Grant: Up to 1,000 USD
Contact: Susan Boskoff, Executive Director; (775) 687-6690 or (775) 687-6680; fax (775) 687-6688; sboskoff@nevadaculture.org
Internet: http://nac.nevadaculture.org/index.php?option=com_content&view=article&id=1043&Itemid=412
Sponsor: Nevada Arts Council
716 N Carson Street, Suite A
Carson City, NV 89701

Nevada Arts Council Learning Grants   3313

Arts Learning Grants support imaginative arts education/learning activities and long-term artist residencies that establish, expand and/or enhance lifelong arts learning and increase cultural awareness. A demonstrated planning process and an ongoing evaluation process by teachers, administrators, staff, artists and the community are considered integral parts of a successful arts education/learning project. Whether designed for a school environment or for the general public, these arts education activities must accomplish one or more of the following areas of focus: arts education; arts integration; or arts for social development. Up to $7,500 can be requested, and a 1:1 match is required.
Requirements: Nevada 501(c)3 nonprofit organizations, public institutions, including schools, colleges, community centers, youth organizations, museums, tribal entities, senior centers, park districts, and libraries may apply.
Geographic Focus: Nevada
Date(s) Application is Due: May 25
Amount of Grant: Up to 7,500 USD
Contact: Ann Libby; (775) 687-7102; fax (775) 687-6688; ann.libby@nevadaculture.org
Internet: http://nac.nevadaculture.org/index.php?option=com_content&view=article&id=1266&Itemid=414
Sponsor: Nevada Arts Council
716 N Carson Street, Suite A
Carson City, NV 89701

Nevada Arts Council Professional Development Grants   3314

Nevada Arts Council Professional Development grants are designed to promote the continuing education of Nevada's nonprofit arts industry to advance their work and careers through attendance at regional or national conferences, workshops, or seminars for skills training. For artists, educators, board members, and arts administrators, PDG funds cover costs associated with professional development activities on a reimbursement basis. Must demonstrate travel of at least 100 miles round-trip to qualify. Up to $650 for out-of-state activities, up to $500 for in-state opportunities and up to $350 to attend Nevada Arts Council sponsored activities are allowed.
Requirements: 501(c)3 Nevada arts/cultural organizations applying for the first time to the grants program must apply in this category, no matter the age of the organization or its budget size.
Geographic Focus: Nevada
Contact: Ann Libby; (775) 687-7102; fax (775) 687-6688; ann.libby@nevadaculture.org
Internet: http://nac.nevadaculture.org/index.php?option=com_content&view=article&id=1266&Itemid=414
Sponsor: Nevada Arts Council
716 N Carson Street, Suite A
Carson City, NV 89701

Nevada Arts Council Residency Express Grants   3315

The Nevada Arts Council Residency Express Grant is designed for community and educational sponsors to host a short-term artist residency (three day limit) using an artist on one of the NAC artist rosters. Participatory activities designed collaboratively with professional artists offer rich and engaging experiences and often lead to the implementation of dynamic local cultural programs. The residency design allows the artist to explore his/her discipline with students, teachers and community members through classes, lectures and discussions, rehearsals, performances or community events, and perhaps a final project. Grant amounts of up to $1200 ($400 a day per artist maximum) to support artist fees for a one to three day residency are awarded. In some cases, an artist may charge more than the grant will support. It is up to the sponsor to provide the additional funds to pay the artist(s).
Requirements: Nevada nonprofit 501(c)3 organizations and public institutions such as schools, colleges, community centers, youth organizations, museums, tribal entities, senior centers, park districts and libraries may apply. Organizations in the process of applying for nonprofit 501(c)3 status may apply using a Fiscal Agent.
Restrictions: This is a noncompetitive grant category and is awarded on a first-come, first-served basis to eligible applicants throughout the year as funds are available.
Geographic Focus: Nevada
Contact: Ann Libby; (775) 687-7102; fax (775) 687-6688; ann.libby@nevadaculture.org
Internet: http://nac.nevadaculture.org/index.php?option=com_content&view=article&id=1266&Itemid=414
Sponsor: Nevada Arts Council
716 N Carson Street, Suite A
Carson City, NV 89701

Nevada Community Foundation Grants   3316

The Foundation is committed to improving the lives of southern Nevadans today and for future generations by matching acts of caring to the many needs in the community. The Foundation has committed its discretionary dollars to multi-year funding of programs that are aligned with Ready for Life®, a statewide collaborative movement to ensure that all

Nevada youth are "ready for life" and supported by a community ethic that values education, links youth to workforce opportunities, and creates a safe learning environment for students. There are also corporate granting programs from time to time. Applicants are encouraged to check updates on the website frequently for upcoming grant programs and deadlines.
Geographic Focus: Nevada
Contact: Gian F. Brosco; (702) 892-2326; fax (702) 892-8580; gian.brosco@nevadacf.org
Internet: http://www.nevadacf.org/nonprofits/
Sponsor: Nevada Community Foundation
1635 Village Center Circle, Suite 160
Las Vegas, NV 89134

New Earth Foundation Grants 3317
The New Earth Foundation (NEF) supports nonprofit organizations in the following areas: education, social services, the arts, communication, and the preservation of sacred spaces, among other areas. NEF prefers to fund smaller and newer organizations. Typical grantee organizations are less than 15 years old with annual operating budgets of less than $350,000, including programs and administration. If you are a 501(c)3 organization, or are working under the umbrella of a 501(c)3 organization, you may apply for a grant of between $5,000 and $7,500. If you are working under an umbrella, a clear relationship between that organization and your project must be demonstrated. You must include a letter that shows that the board of directors (not just the staff or chair) agrees that the umbrella organization may act as your funding agent. The letter should address your project's relationship to the organization and be signed by the president/chair.
Requirements: 501(c)3 nonprofit organizations are eligible to apply. To begin the application process submit (electronically) a Letter of Inquiry to the foundation, providing basic information about your organization and about your program/project. After reviewing the Letter of Inquiry, you maybe invited to submit a complete application.
Restrictions: NEF does not fund organizations that: offer mainstream social services or are local organizations that are affiliated with a national organization such as Boys & Girls Clubs, Big Brothers/Big Sisters, Habitat for Humanity, the Cancer Society and other such organizations; are good candidates for governmental funding; are involved in community housing and renovation; have standard forms of after-school programs, outdoor summer camps/expeditions, or gardening programs; are land and building preservation programs; are capital improvement/building projects; are involved in land purchases.
Geographic Focus: All States
Amount of Grant: 5,000 - 7,500 USD
Contact: David Belskis, President; newearthfoundation@foundationsource.com
Internet: http://www.newearthfoundation.org/application.html
Sponsor: New Earth Foundation
Foundation Source, 55 Walls Drive
Fairfield, CT 06824

Newfoundland and Labrador Arts Council Community Arts Grants 3318
The Newfoundland and Labrador Arts Council Community Arts Grants are available to community-based arts organizations and groups. Grants fund projects related to arts workshops, presentations, productions, new creations, adjudicator fees, artist fees, and travel costs.
Requirements: Eligible organizations or groups must: have the development or promotion of the arts as a primary mandate; have been active in Newfoundland and Labrador for a minimum of twelve consecutive months at the time of application; operate in a not-for-profit capacity, or be registered as a not-for-profit organization in the province; have at least half its board members residing in Newfoundland and Labrador; and operate as a community-based organization (i.e. they are run by volunteers and typically do not pay a professional administrator or artistic director). To verify eligibility before applying, applicants are encouraged to contact the Program Manager.
Restrictions: Applicants receiving Grants are not eligible for Professional Project Grants, Professional Festivals Grants, or Sustaining Grants for Professional Arts Organizations. Only one application will be accepted per organization or group per deadline. Applicants are expected to explore other sources of revenue, and they may not be awarded the full amount requested.
Geographic Focus: Canada
Date(s) Application is Due: Sep 30
Amount of Grant: 1,000 - 5,000 CAD
Contact: Ken Murphy; (709 726-2212 or (866) 726-2212; kmurphy@nlac.ca
Internet: http://www.nlac.ca/grants/cap.htm
Sponsor: Newfoundland and Labrador Arts Council
Newman Building, 1 Springdale Street, P.O. Box 98
St Johns, NL A1C 5H5 Canada

Newfoundland and Labrador Arts Council Labrador Cultural Travel Grants 3319
The Newfoundland and Labrador Arts Council Labrador Cultural Travel Grants provide travel assistance to residents of Labrador to participate in arts and heritage activities on the island portion of the province and to Labrador organizations to bring in resource people from the island for seminars, workshops or similar events. Grants will cover up to 90% of the total travel costs to a maximum of $1,500 per individual applicant or $5,000 per group (at least four individuals). Eligible costs include: return airfare; bus tickets; local transportation; hotel accommodations; and per diem. Applications are accepted on an ongoing basis.
Requirements: Eligibility applicants must be: residents of Labrador (minimum of twelve consecutive months immediately prior to the time of application); individuals and groups (including adults and/or children over the age of 12); or Labrador-based arts and heritage organizations. Applicants concerned about eligibility are encouraged to contact the Outreach Officer before applying. Eligible activities include: participating in arts festivals or competitions; attending arts or heritage fairs or workshops; receiving or being nominated for significant cultural awards; participating in major arts performances or heritage presentations; participating in major arts or heritage conferences; or organizations bringing in resource people for seminars, workshops or similar events.
Restrictions: Only one Travel Grant is awarded to an applicant within a 12-month period.
Geographic Focus: Canada
Contact: Donna Roberts; (709) 896-9565 or (888) 896-9565; droberts@nlac.ca
Internet: http://www.nlac.ca/grants/lctf.htm
Sponsor: Newfoundland and Labrador Arts Council
Newman Building, 1 Springdale Street, P.O. Box 98
St Johns, NL A1C 5H5 Canada

Newfoundland and Labrador Arts Council Professional Artists Travel Fund 3320
Newfoundland and Labrador Arts Council Professional Artists Travel Grants are available to professional artists and groups invited to take part in unexpected activities that will enhance their careers. Such activities would include the presentation, development or celebration of the artist's work. Funding up to $750 is available for travel within the province, and up to $1,000 for travel outside the province. Eligible costs include return airfare, bus or train tickets, local transportation, hotel or accommodation and per diems. There are no deadlines but it is recommended that applications be submitted at least two weeks prior to departure.
Requirements: Eligible professional artists are those: who are recognized by their peers as practicing artists; whose work is available to the general public on a regular basis; who earn a portion of their living from their work; and who demonstrate a long-term commitment to their discipline. Applicants must be current residents of Newfoundland and Labrador for a minimum of twelve consecutive months immediately prior to the time of application. Eligible activities include: an invitation to attend a major performance of the artist's work; a significant exhibition of the artist's work; receiving or being nominated for an official regional, national or international honour or award; unexpected opportunities to work under an artist/teacher, or to access specialized equipment not available in Newfoundland and Labrador; an invitation to act as a resource person at a conference, gathering, symposium, seminar, or other event; and an invitation to participate in regional, national, or international auditions or competitions.
Restrictions: Full-time students and arts organizations (or their representatives) are not eligible. Retroactive applications are not considered. Only one travel grant is awarded to an applicant in a 12-month period.
Geographic Focus: Canada
Contact: Donna Roberts, Cultural Outreach Officer; (709) 896-9565 or (888) 896-9565; fax (709) 896-9564; droberts@nlac.ca
Internet: http://www.nlac.ca/grants/patf.htm
Sponsor: Newfoundland and Labrador Arts Council
Newman Building, 1 Springdale Street, P.O. Box 98
St Johns, NL A1C 5H5 Canada

Newfoundland and Labrador Arts Council Professional Festivals Grants 3321
The Newfoundland and Labrador Arts Council Professional Festivals Grants are available to professional not-for-profit arts festivals or series that exclusively run during a concentrated period of time. Applicants can apply for costs related to artist fees, technical costs, venue rental, administration costs, workshop sessions and travel expenses.
Requirements: Eligible professional not-for-profit arts festivals or series: must have the development or promotion of the arts as its primary mandate; must have been active in Newfoundland and Labrador for a minimum of twelve consecutive months at the time of application; must operate in a not-for-profit capacity, or be registered as a not-for-profit organization in the province; must remunerate performers and staff at accepted national rates of pay for services; must have at least half of its board members residing in Newfoundland and Labrador; and would typically employ a paid administrator and/or an artistic director.
Restrictions: Applicants receiving Grants are not eligible to apply for Professional Project Grants, Sustaining Program for Professional Arts Organizations Grants, or Community Arts Program Grants.
Geographic Focus: Canada
Date(s) Application is Due: Feb 15
Contact: Katrina Rice; (709) 726-2212 or (866) 726-2212; krice@nlac.ca
Internet: http://www.nlac.ca/grants/pfp.htm
Sponsor: Newfoundland and Labrador Arts Council
Newman Building, 1 Springdale Street, P.O. Box 98
St Johns, NL A1C 5H5 Canada

Newfoundland and Labrador Arts Council Professional Project Grants 3322
The Newfoundland and Labrador Arts Council Professional Project Grants are available to professional artists, groups and not-for-profit arts organizations. Grants support projects related to creation, production, operating and travel costs, etc. There are three categories with different award maximums. New Professional Artists or Groups (an individual or group in which a majority of members each has less than three years artistic practice post-education) may request up to $3,000. Established Professional Artists or Groups (an individual or group in which a majority of members each has more than three years artistic practice post-education) may request up to $7,500. Professional Not-For-Profit Arts Organization (an organization that has ongoing arts activities throughout the year) may request up to $7,500.
Requirements: Professional individual artists: must be Canadian citizens or have Permanent Resident Status; must be current residents of Newfoundland and Labrador for a minimum of twelve consecutive months immediately prior to the time of application; and must be at least eighteen years of age or hold post-secondary standing. Professional groups and not-for-profit arts organizations: must have the development or promotion of the arts as its primary mandate; must have been active in Newfoundland and Labrador for a minimum of twelve consecutive months at the time of application; must have at least half its members (for groups) or board members (for organizations) residing in Newfoundland and Labrador; and the majority of members must be at least eighteen years of age or hold post-secondary standing.

Restrictions: Only individual artists may apply for living expenses.
Geographic Focus: Canada
Date(s) Application is Due: Mar 15; Sep 15
Contact: Katrina Rice; (709) 726-2212 or (866) 726-2212; krice@nlac.ca
Internet: http://www.nlac.ca/grants/index.htm
Sponsor: Newfoundland and Labrador Arts Council
Newman Building, 1 Springdale Street, P.O. Box 98
St Johns, NL A1C 5H5 Canada

Newfoundland and Labrador Arts Council Sustaining Grants   3323

The Newfoundland and Labrador Arts Council Sustaining Grants are available to professional arts organizations that further the arts of Newfoundland and Labrador. Grants support administration and project costs. Potential applicants should contact the Program Manger to confirm eligibility before applying.
Requirements: Professional arts organizations must: have the development, production, or promotion of the arts as its primary mandate; be based in Newfoundland and Labrador; have at least half its board and/or membership currently residing in Newfoundland and Labrador for a minimum of 12 consecutive months immediately prior to the time of application; be registered as a not-for-profit organization in the province; have completed two consecutive years of significant operations in keeping with the mandate of the organization; have a formal organizational structure including an active board of directors; employ a professional artistic director/executive director or equivalent; have sound administrative and financial management using typical business accounting and organizational management practices; have a good record of providing local employment; pay artist and professional fees in keeping with established national guidelines; have an annual financial statement prepared (minimum acceptable is a review engagement prepared by an independent professional accountant); offer professional development opportunities for staff and/or membership; demonstrate community outreach through workshops, school visits, fundraising, etc; maintain a minimum annual budget of $50,000 ($20,000 for dance and visual art organizations) for the last two years and the current year; maintain a minimum annual budget of $50,000 ($20,000 for dance and visual art organizations) on all proposed budgets included in the application; and maintain a minimum annual budget of $50,000 ($20,000 for dance and visual art organizations) for the overall organizational budget for each fiscal year in which it receives sustaining program funding.
Restrictions: Applicants funded through this program are not eligible to apply for Professional Project Grants, Professional Festivals Grants, or the Community Arts Grants.
Geographic Focus: Canada
Date(s) Application is Due: Feb 15
Amount of Grant: 15,000 USD
Contact: Ken Murphy; (709) 726-2212 or (866) 726-2212; kmurphy@nlac.ca
Internet: http://www.nlac.ca/grants/sppao.htm
Sponsor: Newfoundland and Labrador Arts Council
Newman Building, 1 Springdale Street, P.O. Box 98
St Johns, NL A1C 5H5 Canada

Newfoundland and Labrador Arts Council Visiting Artists Grants   3324

The Newfoundland and Labrador Arts Council Visiting Artists Grants are for schools to bring individual artists, groups of artists, or arts organizations into the school to provide students with direct personal contact with practicing professional artists. Grants cover artist fees, materials, and travel costs. Grants are offered in partnership with the Cultural Connections Strategy of the Newfoundland and Labrador Department of Education, the Newfoundland and Labrador Teachers' Association, and the Newfoundland and Labrador Arts Council. Funding is up to $500 to cover artist fees and up to $200 for art supplies or equipment rental required for a project. Travel subsidies for schools on the island are up to $200 and for schools in Labrador up to $500. There is no deadline, but schools must submit an application at least two weeks before the artist or group is due to come to the school.
Requirements: Eligible applicants include teachers at any school in the provincial K-12 system. Each grade configuration (K-3, 4-6, 7-9, 10-12) in a school is eligible to receive one Grant per school year, or a school can receive one Grant for every 150 students enrolled, to a maximum of four Grants per school year. Each visit must involve at least 10 students.
Restrictions: Teachers or classes with current ArtsSmarts or Learning Through the Arts Grants are not eligible.
Geographic Focus: Canada
Contact: Ken Murphy; (709) 726-2212 or (866) 726-2212; kmurphy@nlac.ca
Internet: http://www.nlac.ca/grants/vap.htm
Sponsor: Newfoundland and Labrador Arts Council
Newman Building, 1 Springdale Street, P.O. Box 98
St Johns, NL A1C 5H5 Canada

New Hampshire Charitable Foundation Grants   3325

The foundation seeks to improve the quality of life for New Hampshire citizens by distributing grants to qualifying organizations and scholarship assistance to the state's residents. Areas of support include arts, humanities, environment and conservation, health, and social and community services. Types of support include seed grants, scholarships and scholarship funds, program development, technical assistance, demonstration grants, development grants, endowments, and training grants. Four regional divisions of the foundation exist to benefit particular areas of the state: Greater Piscataqua Community Foundation, Lakes Region Charitable Foundation, Northern New Hampshire Foundation, and Upper Valley Community Foundation. Although a limited number of multi-year grants are made, awards are not usually repeated or renewed. Grantmaking meetings are held three times each year by the foundation.
Requirements: New Hampshire 501(c)3 tax-exempt organizations are eligible.
Restrictions: Grants are not awarded for capital campaigns, the purchase of major equipment, as operating support for ongoing or annual programs, to replace public funding, for sectarian or religious purposes, for deficit reduction, to support academic research, or for travel out of state by school or youth groups or by individuals for scholarly or professional purposes.
Geographic Focus: New Hampshire
Contact: Jennifer P. Hopkins; (800) 464-6641, ext. 1239; fax (603) 225-1700; jph@nhcf.org
Internet: http://www.nhcf.org/page16898.cfm
Sponsor: New Hampshire Charitable Foundation
37 Pleasant Street
Concord, NH 03301-4005

New Jersey Center for Hispanic Policy, Research and Development Entrepreneur Grants   3326

The Center for Hispanic Policy, Research and Development (CHPRD) was established in 1975 to address the needs of the Hispanic community, recognizing that it was imperative to pay particular attention to this segment of the population, which may have been historically neglected. The CHPRD seeks to empower, provide financial support and technical assistance to primarily Hispanic community-based organizations throughout New Jersey and also ensures the executive and legislative branches are informed of legislative initiatives with potential impact on the Hispanic community. CHPRD seeks to aggressively promote a new model of community development that is focused on making REAL impacts in people's lives while helping community based organizations achieve greater self-sufficiency. In the Hispanic Entrepreneurship area, funding will be made available to organizations to serve as community Hispanic Entrepreneurship Assistance Centers (HEAP), providing entrepreneur development services to Hispanic residents who have recently started a business and in depth assistance to those looking to create a new business. Such assistance is especially important in economically distressed areas where high levels of unemployment and declining infrastructure further limit the ability for these young businesses to develop.
Requirements: Funding for this program is available to public/private non-profit and community-based-organizations whose primary focus is the implementation of programs that address the needs of the Hispanic community of the State of New Jersey. All non-profit, private organizations must be: 501(c)3 Federal non-profit status for at least one year prior to submission of application; a clearly articulated Hispanic mission and focus for the organization and its programs; valid Articles of Incorporation filed prior to July 1, 2008; and, at the time of application, have been in existence and actively providing public programs or services for at least the past three years. Primary consideration for CHPRD funding will be provided to Hispanic community based organizations (HCBOs) that provide direct services and whose staff, board and clientele mirrors the community it will serve.
Restrictions: Ineligible applicants include organizations that are unincorporated, incorporated in another state, or incorporated as profit-making entities. Organizations, agencies, institutions, or projects that do not have organizational goals related to the Hispanic community or a specific Hispanic project to propose will not be considered.
Geographic Focus: New Jersey
Contact: Administrator; (609) 984-3223; fax (609) 633-7141
Internet: http://www.nj.gov/state/programs/dos_program_chprd_grants.html
Sponsor: New Jersey Department of State
225 West State Street, P.O. Box 301
Trenton, NJ 08625-0301

New Jersey Center for Hispanic Policy, Research and Development Governor's Hispanic Fellowships   3327

The Governor's Hispanic Fellows program (formerly the Hispanic Interns in Community Service program) was created in 1988 and implemented in the State of New Jersey with the goals of: exposing Hispanic college students to career opportunities in state government, or other areas of public service, as well as in the nonprofit and private sectors; and allowing students to develop and strengthen professional skills in a conducive working environment. More recently, a new component was added to enhance and complement the experience gained by the program participants. The purpose of this component is to develop and cultivate the leadership skills of the interns through weekly intensive training sessions. It complements the employment component by providing a greater opportunity for leadership development. Past institution curriculum has covered topics such as: dimensions of Hispanic Leadership in the U.S. and N.J. Introduction to public policy and politics; community empowerment; enhancing self-confidence among the young; financial and investment literacy; conflict resolution, negotiation skills and public policy; understanding the legislative process; developing a vision for self and community; identifying personal strengths; handling and understanding diversity; Hispanic issues and demographics; fine-tuning interviewing skills; techniques of public speaking; and the public policy process. In essence, the Governor's Hispanic Fellows program currently provides quality internship experiences to Hispanic college students.
Requirements: Applicants must be residents of New Jersey, of Hispanic descent, and registered at a college or university in New Jersey with grade point averages of 3.0 or higher. Candidates will be selected among applicants on the basis of their overall GPA and class standing. Each qualifying applicant is interviewed by the Review Committee, which normally consists of alumni, staff members of the CHPRD, and Center Board members. Private businesses, government and non-profit organizations interested in participating in the professional development of Hispanic students are invited to submit potential internship opportunities within their organizations.
Geographic Focus: New Jersey
Contact: Administrator; (609) 984-3223; fax (609) 633-7141
Internet: http://www.nj.gov/state/programs/dos_program_chprd_internship.html
Sponsor: New Jersey Department of State
225 West State Street, P.O. Box 301
Trenton, NJ 08625-0301

New Jersey Center for Hispanic Policy, Research and Development Immigration Integration Grants 3328

The Center for Hispanic Policy, Research and Development (CHPRD) was established in 1975 to address the needs of the Hispanic community, recognizing that it was imperative to pay particular attention to this segment of the population, which may have been historically neglected. The CHPRD seeks to empower, provide financial support and technical assistance to primarily Hispanic community-based organizations throughout New Jersey and also ensures the executive and legislative branches are informed of legislative initiatives with potential impact on the Hispanic community. CHPRD seeks to aggressively promote a new model of community development that is focused on making REAL impacts in people's lives while helping community based organizations achieve greater self-sufficiency. In the Immigration Integration area, funding is available to create a new social model of immigrant integration – one that promotes mutual benefits for immigrants and their receiving communities, and that allows newcomers enhanced civic participation and improved economic mobility.

Requirements: Funding for this program is available to public/private non-profit and community-based-organizations whose primary focus is the implementation of programs that address the needs of the Hispanic community of the State of New Jersey. All non-profit, private organizations must have: 501(c)3 Federal non-profit status for at least one year prior to submission of application; a clearly articulated Hispanic mission and focus for the organization and its programs; valid Articles of Incorporation filed prior to July 1, 2008; and, at the time of application, have been in existence and actively providing public programs or services for at least the past three years. Primary consideration for CHPRD funding will be provided to Hispanic community based organizations (HCBOs) that provide direct services and whose staff, board and clientele mirrors the community it will serve.

Restrictions: Ineligible applicants include organizations that are unincorporated, incorporated in another state, or incorporated as profit-making entities. Organizations, agencies, institutions, or projects that do not have organizational goals related to the Hispanic community or a specific Hispanic project to propose will not be considered.

Geographic Focus: New Jersey
Contact: Administrator; (609) 984-3223; fax (609) 633-7141
Internet: http://www.nj.gov/state/programs/dos_program_chprd_grants.html
Sponsor: New Jersey Department of State
225 West State Street, P.O. Box 301
Trenton, NJ 08625-0301

New Jersey Center for Hispanic Policy, Research and Development Innovative Initiatives Grants 3329

The Center for Hispanic Policy, Research and Development (CHPRD) was established in 1975 to address the needs of the Hispanic community, recognizing that it was imperative to pay particular attention to this segment of the population, which may have been historically neglected. The CHPRD seeks to empower, provide financial support and technical assistance to primarily Hispanic community-based organizations throughout New Jersey and also ensures the executive and legislative branches are informed of legislative initiatives with potential impact on the Hispanic community. CHPRD seeks to aggressively promote a new model of community development that is focused on making REAL impacts in people's lives while helping community based organizations achieve greater self-sufficiency. In the area of Innovative Initiatives, funding is available to promote and encourage innovative community service programs that are culturally competent, and whose effective services address specific target areas. The CHPRD will fund nonprofit organizations for start-up monies for innovative initiatives and services that contribute to one of the following target areas: children at risk; prevention of health risks and diseases; Senior Citizen Information and Referral Services; or Mental Health Support Services responsive to cultural needs.

Requirements: Funding for this program is available to public/private non-profit and community-based-organizations whose primary focus is the implementation of programs that address the needs of the Hispanic community of the State of New Jersey. All non-profit, private organizations must have: 501(c)3 Federal non-profit status for at least one year prior to submission of application; a clearly articulated Hispanic mission and focus for the organization and its programs; valid Articles of Incorporation filed prior to July 1, 2008; and, at the time of application, have been in existence and actively providing public programs or services for at least the past three years. Primary consideration for CHPRD funding will be provided to Hispanic community based organizations (HCBOs) that provide direct services and whose staff, board and clientele mirrors the community it will serve.

Restrictions: Ineligible applicants include organizations that are unincorporated, incorporated in another state, or incorporated as profit-making entities. Organizations, agencies, institutions, or projects that do not have organizational goals related to the Hispanic community or a specific Hispanic project to propose will not be considered.

Geographic Focus: New Jersey
Contact: Administrator; (609) 984-3223; fax (609) 633-7141
Internet: http://www.nj.gov/state/programs/dos_program_chprd_grants.html
Sponsor: New Jersey Department of State
225 West State Street, P.O. Box 301
Trenton, NJ 08625-0301

New Jersey Center for Hispanic Policy, Research and Development Workforce Grants 3330

The Center for Hispanic Policy, Research and Development (CHPRD) was established in 1975 to address the needs of the Hispanic community, recognizing that it was imperative to pay particular attention to this segment of the population, which may have been historically neglected. The CHPRD seeks to empower, provide financial support and technical assistance to primarily Hispanic community-based organizations throughout New Jersey and also ensures the executive and legislative branches are informed of legislative initiatives with potential impact on the Hispanic community. CHPRD seeks to aggressively promote a new model of community development that is focused on making REAL impacts in people's lives while helping community based organizations achieve greater self-sufficiency. In the Workforce Development area, funding has been made available to create and develop a comprehensive workforce development system that will engage the entire Hispanic community towards ever increasing levels of self-sufficiency.

Requirements: Funding for this program is available to public/private non-profit and community-based-organizations whose primary focus is the implementation of programs that address the needs of the Hispanic community of the State of New Jersey. All non-profit, private organizations must have: 501(c)3 Federal non-profit status for at least one year prior to submission of application; a clearly articulated Hispanic mission and focus for the organization and its programs; valid Articles of Incorporation filed prior to July 1, 2008; and, at the time of application, have been in existence and actively providing public programs or services for at least the past three years. Primary consideration for CHPRD funding will be provided to Hispanic community based organizations (HCBOs) that provide direct services and whose staff, board and clientele mirrors the community it will serve.

Restrictions: Ineligible applicants include organizations that are unincorporated, incorporated in another state, or incorporated as profit-making entities. Organizations, agencies, institutions, or projects that do not have organizational goals related to the Hispanic community or a specific Hispanic project to propose will not be considered.

Geographic Focus: New Jersey
Contact: Administrator; (609) 984-3223; fax (609) 633-7141
Internet: http://www.nj.gov/state/programs/dos_program_chprd_grants.html
Sponsor: New Jersey Department of State
225 West State Street, P.O. Box 301
Trenton, NJ 08625-0301

New Jersey Office of Faith Based Initiatives Creating Wealth Through Asset Building Grants 3331

The mission of the Office of Faith-based Initiatives is to eliminate all barriers to funding and other resource opportunities, create greater access for partnership and enhance the capacity of faith and community-based organizations to effectively design, implement successful programming and efficiently manage the day-to-day operations of their organizations. The Creating Wealth through Asset building seeks to support demonstration programs to partner with the Asset for Independence project where clients savings will be matched. The savings will be used with the goal of acquiring a first home, post-secondary education, or starting up or expanding a small business. The Creating Wealth through Asset Building project will be an innovative approach to develop and maximize the Assets for Independence (AFI) model and develop financial literacy skills for youth, adults and families. The AFI program provides five-year grants to nonprofit organizations that empower low-income families and individuals to become economically self-sufficient for the long-term. Grantees provide financial education training on money management and they assist participants with saving earned income in special matched savings accounts called Individual Development Accounts. Applications are submitted to the OFBI on the System for Administering Grants Electronically (SAGE) and reviewed by an outside independent panel. Final determinations will be made by the Director. The maximum request is $10,000, and the annual application deadline is July 30.

Requirements: To be eligible to receive a grant under this program, an applicant must submit a joint application as the lead agency in conjunction with a minimum of three collaborating organizations. The lead agency must: be a faith-based non-profit and/or community-based organization; be incorporated in the State of New Jersey as a non-profit corporation or a foreign non-profit corporation; be tax-exempt by determination of the Internal Revenue Service in accordance with Section 501(c)3; be in good standing with the Department of Treasury, Business Service Center; be registered with the New Jersey Division of Consumer Affairs, Charitable Registration and Investigation Section; submit a formal Memorandum of Understanding (MOU) with collaborative partners within 180 days of contract execution; and provide letters of support from all collaborating partners with the application.

Restrictions: Collaborating organizations may not partner with the lead organization's sister organization and/or for profit and non-profit organizations led by the same person or governing entity. Houses of Worship are eligible to partner as a collaborating organization, but cannot receive state funds that are granted to lead organizations.

Geographic Focus: New Jersey
Date(s) Application is Due: Jul 30
Amount of Grant: Up to 10,000 USD
Contact: Administrator; (609) 292-8286 or (609) 984-6952; fax (609) 633-7141
Internet: http://www.nj.gov/state/programs/dos_program_faith_based_funding.html
Sponsor: New Jersey Department of State
225 W. State Street, P.O. Box 456
Trenton, NJ 08625

New Jersey Office of Faith Based Initiatives English as a Second Language Grants 3332

The mission of the Office of Faith-based Initiatives is to eliminate all barriers to funding and other resource opportunities, create greater access for partnership and enhance the capacity of faith and community-based organizations to effectively design, implement successful programming and efficiently manage the day-to-day operations of their organizations. The English as a Second Language program will assist and instruct non-English speaking individuals to learn the Basic English Language with lessons designed around everyday scenarios and circumstances. Applications are submitted to the OFBI on the System for Administering Grants Electronically (SAGE) and reviewed by an outside independent panel. Final determinations will be made by the Director. The maximum request is $20,000, and the annual application deadline is July 30.

Requirements: To be eligible to receive a grant under this program, an applicant must submit a joint application as the lead agency in conjunction with a minimum of three collaborating

organizations. Teachers in the program must be certified and have the necessary ESL credentials. The lead agency must: be a faith-based non-profit and/or community-based organization; be incorporated in the State of New Jersey as a non-profit corporation or a foreign non-profit corporation; be tax-exempt by determination of the Internal Revenue Service in accordance with Section 501(c)3; be in good standing with the Department of Treasury, Business Service Center; be registered with the New Jersey Division of Consumer Affairs, Charitable Registration and Investigation Section; submit a formal Memorandum of Understanding (MOU) with collaborative partners within 180 days of contract execution; and provide letters of support from all collaborating partners with the application.
Restrictions: Collaborating organizations may not partner with the lead organization's sister organization and/or for profit and non-profit organizations led by the same person or governing entity. Houses of Worship are eligible to partner as a collaborating organization, but cannot receive state funds that are granted to lead organizations.
Geographic Focus: New Jersey
Date(s) Application is Due: Jul 30
Amount of Grant: Up to 20,000 USD
Contact: Administrator; (609) 292-8286 or (609) 984-6952; fax (609) 633-7141
Internet: http://www.nj.gov/state/programs/dos_program_faith_based_funding.html
Sponsor: New Jersey Department of State
225 W. State Street, P.O. Box 456
Trenton, NJ 08625

New Jersey Office of Faith Based Initiatives Service to Seniors Grants 3333
The mission of the Office of Faith-based Initiatives is to eliminate all barriers to funding and other resource opportunities, create greater access for partnership and enhance the capacity of faith and community-based organizations to effectively design, implement successful programming and efficiently manage the day-to-day operations of their organizations. The Service to Seniors program is designed to afford seniors and people living with disabilities the opportunity to remain independent in their own homes for as long as possible. Applications are submitted to the OFBI on the System for Administering Grants Electronically (SAGE) and reviewed by an outside independent panel. Final determinations will be made by the Director. The maximum request is $20,000, and the annual application deadline is July 30.
Requirements: To be eligible to receive a grant under this program, an applicant must submit a joint application as the lead agency in conjunction with a minimum of three collaborating organizations. The lead agency must: be a faith-based non-profit and/or community-based organization; be incorporated in the State of New Jersey as a non-profit corporation or a foreign non-profit corporation; be tax-exempt by determination of the Internal Revenue Service in accordance with Section 501(c)3; be in good standing with the Department of Treasury, Business Service Center; be registered with the New Jersey Division of Consumer Affairs, Charitable Registration and Investigation Section; submit a formal Memorandum of Understanding (MOU) with collaborative partners within 180 days of contract execution; and provide letters of support from all collaborating partners with the application.
Restrictions: Collaborating organizations may not partner with the lead organization's sister organization and/or for profit and non-profit organizations led by the same person or governing entity. Houses of Worship are eligible to partner as a collaborating organization, but cannot receive state funds that are granted to lead organizations.
Geographic Focus: New Jersey
Date(s) Application is Due: Jul 30
Contact: Administrator; (609) 292-8286 or (609) 984-6952; fax (609) 633-7141
Internet: http://www.nj.gov/state/programs/dos_program_faith_based_funding.html
Sponsor: New Jersey Department of State
225 W. State Street, P.O. Box 456
Trenton, NJ 08625

Newman W. Benson Foundation Grants 3334
Established in New York in 1990, the Foundation supports both human service programs and religious agencies. Generally, funding comes in the form of operating costs, with giving centered around Bradford and Towanda County, Pennsylvania. A selection of grants are also provided to organizations outside of Pennsylvania. There are no specific application forms or deadlines with which to adhere, and applicants should send a letter of request detailing the program or project, and include both a budget narrative and 501(c)3 letter.
Geographic Focus: All States
Contact: Newman W. Benson, President; (570) 265-3498
Sponsor: Newman W. Benson Foundation
P.O. Box 430, Lake Wesauking
Towanda, PA 18848-0430

New Mexico Women's Foundation Grants 3335
The New Mexico Women's Foundation is dedicated to creating employment opportunities for women that allow them to stay in their communities and produce products that build on local traditions and materials, or by ordering components that can be shipped to them for assembly in or near their homes. The goal is to help establish guilds, or groups of women, in rural areas of the state that can begin to sustain themselves creatively, productively, and financially. Letters of inquiry are due November 15 and September 12 each year; applications are due January 30 and October 25.
Requirements: 501(c)3 groups or organizations, including emerging grassroots groups or organizations (and organizations with 501(c)3 fiscal sponsors), located in New Mexico that help women and/or girls participate in, and/or develop, cottage industries are eligible. Groups must consist of three or more women and have some type of governing body.
Restrictions: Individuals; campaigns to elect public officials; religious organizations for religious purposes; and programs or projects inconsistent with federal, state, and local discrimination or ordinances regarding equal employment opportunity are ineligible.
Geographic Focus: New Mexico
Date(s) Application is Due: Jan 30; Oct 25
Amount of Grant: 200 - 2,000 USD
Contact: Frieda Arth; (505) 983-6155 or (505) 954-4462; nmwomenandgirls@aol.com
Internet: http://www.nmwf.org
Sponsor: New Mexico Women's Foundation
551 Cordova Road, #411
Santa Fe, NM 87505

Newton County Community Foundation Grants 3336
The purpose of the Foundations is to assist donors in creating a source of assets to meet the ongoing needs and interests of the people living in Jasper and Newton County, Indiana communities. The Foundation welcomes grant applications from non-profit organizations whose programs benefit the residents of each county. Grant applications are available in the Foundation office or online at the Foundation's website.
Requirements: Favored grant requests for each county will generally reflect the following characteristics: projects which propose practical solutions to community needs; projects which promote cooperation among existing agencies without duplicating services; and projects that will become self-sustaining without requiring on-going Foundation funds. No restrictions are placed on gifts to these funds, allowing the Board of Directors to address community needs.
Restrictions: Grant are not normally made for budget deficits or sectarian religious activities.
Geographic Focus: Indiana
Date(s) Application is Due: Apr 1; Oct 1
Contact: Linda Harris; (219) 866-5899; fax (219) 866-0555; jasper@liljasper.com
Internet: http://www.jasperfdn.org/newtgrants.htm
Sponsor: Newton County Community Foundation
301 N. Van Rensselaer Street, P.O. Box 295
Rensselaer, IN 47978

New Voices J-Lab Journalism Grants 3337
J-Lab: The Institute for Interactive Journalism offers funding for launching participatory news ventures. Projects can produce news and information for a geographic area such as a small town, city, county, state or region, or they can serve a community of interest. Grantees may receive up to $25,000. They will receive $17,000 the first year and are eligible for $8,000 in matching funds in the second year.
Requirements: Those eligible to receive funding include: 501(c)3 organizations and educational institutions, community groups, public broadcasters, independent media, colleges and universities, and individuals working under the sponsorship of a nonprofit fiscal agent. Projects should serve a defined community and foster an open exchange of journalistically sound information. Projects should showcase their efforts by developing a publicly accessible, regularly updated Web site. They must offer users a way to share or contribute news and opinion, and participate in conversations about their targeted community. New Voices projects need an achievable plan to deliver a steady flow of fresh, original content year-round. Applicants submit a reasonable budget and a strategy for obtaining matching funds and other support from donors, subscribers, foundations, events, advertising, or e-commerce. After New Voices funding has ended, applicants need a strategy for keeping their project alive. Creativity should be shown in the use of new digital technologies. Project leaders post regular brief blogs to the J-NewVoices.org Web site, sharing experiences, challenges and successes along the way. See website for further information.
Restrictions: Only start-up news initiatives can receive funding. Ongoing efforts are not eligible unless they are proposing a new project or product.
Geographic Focus: All States
Date(s) Application is Due: Mar 1
Contact: Jan Schaffer; (202) 885-8100; fax (202) 885-8110; news@j-lab.org
Internet: http://www.j-newvoices.org/site/story/2010rfp/
Sponsor: J-Lab: Institute for Interactive Journalism
3201 New Mexico Avenue, N.W., Suite 330
Washington, DC 20016-8178

New York Foundation Grants 3338
The Foundation supports groups in New York City that are working on problems of urgent concern to residents of disadvantaged communities and neighborhoods. Support is provided to organizations that work in ways that inspire New Yorkers to become more educated and active participants in the overall life of the city. The Foundation places a priority on supporting community organizing and advocacy strategies. While support is given to groups that utilize multiple strategies, including direct service, preference is given to those moving toward incorporating advocacy and organizing. Of particular interest is start-up grants to new, untested programs that have few other sources of support. Interested applicants should send a letter of inquiry outlining the project and the budget.
Requirements: Eligible projects must: involve New York City or a particular neighborhood of the city; address a critical or emerging need, particularly involving youth or the elderly; and articulate how a grant from the Foundation would advance the applicant's work.
Restrictions: The following is not eligible: grants to individuals or to capital campaigns; support of research studies, films, conferences, or publications; requests from outside New York City except from organizations working on statewide issues of concern to youth, the elderly, or the poor; and grants outside of the United States. Letters of inquiry are accepted by mail only, not fax or email.
Geographic Focus: New York
Date(s) Application is Due: Mar 1; Jul 1; Nov 1
Contact: Maria Mottola, Executive Director; (212) 594-8009
Internet: http://www.nyf.org/how/guidelines
Sponsor: New York Foundation
350 Fifth Avenue, Room 2901
New York, NY 10118

New York Landmarks Conservancy City Ventures Grants 3339
The conservancy awards grants to New York nonprofit housing corporations, community development organizations, social service agencies, homesteading organizations, and mutual housing associations for the bricks-and-mortar component of building renovations. Priority is given to essential structural repairs and exterior work that have visual impact on the neighborhood. Grants include technical assistance from conservancy staff, consulting architects, and engineers.
Requirements: New York State 501(c)3 tax-exempt organizations are eligible.
Geographic Focus: New York
Amount of Grant: 5,000 - 50,000 USD
Contact: Karen Ansis; (212) 995-5260; fax (212) 995-5268; karenansis@nylandmarks.org
Internet: http://www.nylandmarks.org/organizations.php3?orgid=79&typeID=643&action=printContentItem&itemID=5042
Sponsor: New York Landmarks Conservancy
One Whitehall Street
New York, NY 10004

New York Landmarks Conservancy Sacred Sites Grants 3340
The Program awards three kinds of grants: Consulting Grants, which allow congregations in New York City only a maximum of $7,500 to retain professional services for the preservation of historic houses of worship; Sacred Sites Fund Grants, which provides congregations up to $10,000 for exterior restoration projects; and Robert W. Wilson Sacred Sites Challenge Grants, which offers matching grants of $25,000 to $50,000 for large-scale church restoration projects (priority will be given to significant restoration of steeples, roofs and related drainage systems, and exterior masonry walls).
Requirements: New York State tax-exempt houses of worship are eligible.
Geographic Focus: New York
Date(s) Application is Due: May 1; Nov 1
Amount of Grant: Up to 50,000 USD
Contact: Colleen Meagher; (212) 995-5260; colleenmeagher@nylandmarks.org
Internet: http://tools.isovera.com/organizations.php3?orgid=79&typeID=643&action=printContentItem&itemID=6520
Sponsor: New York Landmarks Conservancy
One Whitehall Street
New York, NY 10004

New York Life Foundation Grants 3341
The foundation awards grants to nonprofit organizations in its areas of interest. Periodically, the foundation selects an area of special priority. The current focus, Nurturing the Children, directs the majority of the foundation's resources toward organizations, programs, and services aimed at helping young people. This initiative specifically focuses on safe places to learn and grow; educational enhancement; and mentoring. The foundation has initiated a new grant award program for nonprofit organizations based in New York City. Youth In Action recognizes innovative Nurturing the Children programs that engage youth in planning, coordinating and/or helping to provide services.
Requirements: Nonprofit 501(c)3 organizations may submit grant requests. The foundation funds projects in New York City, where New York Life's Home Office is located. The foundation also considers multi-site projects implemented by national organizations. These projects must serve two or more of the following locations: Atlanta; Cleveland; Clinton/Hunterdon County, New Jersey; Dallas; Kansas City; Minneapolis; New York City; Parsippany/Morris County, New Jersey; Tampa; and Westchester County, New York.
Restrictions: The foundation does not support sectarian or religious organizations or activities; fraternal, social, professional, athletic, or veterans groups; seminars or conferences; preschool, primary, or secondary education; endowments; memorials; basic or applied research; capital campaigns; or fund-raising activities.
Geographic Focus: All States
Date(s) Application is Due: Dec 1
Contact: Contact; (212) 576-7341; fax (212) 576-6220; NYLFoundation@newyorklife.com
Internet: http://www.newyorklife.com/foundation/index.html
Sponsor: New York Life Foundation
51 Madison Avenue, Room 1600
New York, NY 10010-1655

NFF Collaboration Support Grants 3342
The intent of the Collaboration Support Program is to promote innovation and advancement in the field of community-based natural resource collaboration, and to support collaborative processes whose work benefits America's National Forests and Grasslands. Grants range up to $5,000 for Capacity grants, and up to $10,000 for Innovation grants. Technical assistance provided includes peer learning, mentoring and coaching opportunities. Examples of grant activities might include: collaborative work on an emerging topic (for example, newly recognized invasive species or private land transfer to public ownership); structured information sharing; new approaches to collaborative stewardship; and multiparty monitoring.
Requirements: Community-based collaborative groups working on stewardship issues on National Forests and Grasslands across the country are eligible to apply.
Geographic Focus: All States
Date(s) Application is Due: Feb 15; Apr 29
Amount of Grant: Up to 10,000 USD
Contact: Adam Liljeblad, Director, Conservation Awards; (406) 542-2805; fax (406) 542-2810; aliljeblad@nationalforests.org
Internet: http://nationalforests.org/conserve/grantprograms
Sponsor: National Forest Foundation
Fort Missoula Road, Building 27, Suite 3
Missoula, MT 59804

NFF Community Assistance Grants 3343
The NFF established the Community Assistance Program (CAP) in 2002 to promote the creation of locally based organizations or groups seeking to resolve natural resource issues through a collaborative, dialogue based process. The program proves support in the form of start-up funds for newly forming (or significantly reorganizing) groups or nonprofit organizations that intend to proactively and inclusively engage local stakeholders in forest management and conservation issues on and around the National Forests and Grasslands. CAP awards provide collaborative groups with start-up grants of $5,000 to $15,000, as well as basic tools and guidance, to enable them to resolve differences and play a more active role in the sustainable management of nearby National Forests, Grasslands and surrounding communities. Organizations applying for funding through CAP will be considered based on need, and will not be required to match the NFF funds. CAP funds can be used for a wide range of tools, including: technical assistance, training, consultants, community outreach, obtaining 501(c)3 status, group facilitation, basic startup and operating costs, materials and equipment, program development, nonprofit management kill building, and communications.
Requirements: In order to qualify for a grant through the CAP, the applicant must be: newly forming or significantly reorganizing collaborative community-based nonprofits or unincorporated groups; engaged in a collaborative process; based in the community in which the collaboration is taking place and be legitimate stakeholders in the collaborative process; working to develop solutions for sustainable management or restoration on and around National Forests and Grasslands that lead to on-the-ground work; specific issues should be related to community-based forest stewardship, recreation, watershed restoration, and/or wildlife habitat; incorporated as a 501(c)3 or utilize a fiscal sponsor organization with that designation; and seeking to build local ecological, social and economic sustainability.
Restrictions: Established organizations, fire safe councils, federal agencies, and state or local governmental entities are not eligible to apply.
Geographic Focus: All States
Date(s) Application is Due: Jan 15; Jul 7
Amount of Grant: 5,000 - 15,000 USD
Contact: Adam Liljeblad; (406) 542-2805; fax (406) 542-2810; aliljeblad@nationalforests.org
Internet: http://nationalforests.org/conserve/grantprograms
Sponsor: National Forest Foundation
Fort Missoula Road, Building 27, Suite 3
Missoula, MT 59804

NFF Matching Grants 3344
The Matching Awards Program (MAP) provides 1:1 matching grants to organizations implementing action-oriented, on-the-ground stewardship and citizen-based science projects that benefit America's National Forests and Grasslands. By matching NFF federal funds to non-federal dollars raised by award recipients, MAP effectively doubles the resources available to nonprofit partners for implementing these projects. A common thread connecting the National Forest Foundation (NFF) program areas is an interest in action-oriented projects that enhance the viability of natural resources while considering benefits to, and the involvement of, surrounding communities.
Requirements: For the Matching Awards Program, the NFF accepts applications from non-governmental, nonprofit 501(c)3 organizations, universities and Native American tribes working on, or adjacent to, national forests and grasslands in an effort to implement on-the-ground conservation, restoration and citizen-based monitoring projects. Proposals for the Matching Awards Program are selected for funding through a two-stage process. Applicants must first submit a pre-proposal (available online) to the National Forest Foundation (NFF) via email by December 8th. After the pre-proposals are evaluated, a subset of the submitting organizations is invited to submit full proposals. The process, from pre-proposal submission to notification of full proposal funding, generally takes four to five months. Pre-Proposal guidelines are provided online. Full proposal guidelines are distributed only to organizations that advance to the full proposal round. Grants typically range from $500 to $125,000, and average award are about $30,000.
Restrictions: All MAP awards require a 1:1 cash match of non-federal funds. Federal funds and in-kind contributions should be documented to show leverage for a project, but cannot be matched by MAP funds.
Geographic Focus: All States
Date(s) Application is Due: Jun 4; Dec 8
Amount of Grant: 500 - 125,000 USD
Contact: Adam Liljeblad; (406) 542-2805; fax (406) 542-2810; aliljeblad@nationalforests.org
Internet: http://nationalforests.org/conserve/grantprograms/ontheground/map
Sponsor: National Forest Foundation
Fort Missoula Road, Building 27, Suite 3
Missoula, MT 59804

NFF Mid-Capacity Assistance Grants 3345
The primary purpose of the Mid-Capacity Assistance Grants is to assist mid-capacity collaborative organizations whose work benefits America's National Forests and Grasslands in building their organizational capacity. Examples of technical assistance and support include: peer learning, mentoring and coaching opportunities; and development of monitoring/outcome plans in coordination with the Western Collaboration Assistance Network (WestCAN). Grant supported activities may include: strategic planning, support for on-going collaborative process needs, training, and board development.
Requirements: Mid-capacity collaborative, community-based groups working on stewardship issues on National Forests and Grasslands are eligible to apply. Applicants may apply for up to $70,000 for a two-year period.
Geographic Focus: All States
Date(s) Application is Due: Feb 15; Apr 29
Amount of Grant: Up to 70,000 USD

Contact: Adam Liljeblad, Director, Conservation Awards; (406) 542-2805; fax (406) 542-2810; aliljeblad@nationalforests.org
Internet: http://nationalforests.org/conserve/grantprograms/capacitybuilding/ccls
Sponsor: National Forest Foundation
Fort Missoula Road, Building 27, Suite 3
Missoula, MT 59804

NFF Wilderness Stewardship Grants — 3346

The National Forest Foundation (NFF), chartered by Congress, engages America in community-based and national programs that promote the health and public enjoyment of the 193-million acre National Forest System, and accepts and administers private gifts of finds and land for the benefit of the National Forests. In 1964, Congress established the national Wilderness Preservation System, under the Wilderness Act. The legislation allows certain federal lands to be set-aside as Wilderness Areas, generally 5,000 acres or larger, that exists largely in their natural state. In celebration of the 40th anniversary of the Wilderness Act, the U.S. Forest Service issued a stewardship challenge, calling for all wilderness areas in the National Forest System designated 2004 and earlier to meet baseline management standards by 2014. To meet this standard, wilderness areas are measured on 10 stewardship elements, and must achieve 60 our of a possible 100 points. The NFF, as an official nonprofit partner of the Forest Service, has increased the resources available to meet this challenge, providing matching grants up to $50,000 to nonprofit partners to implement on-the-ground conservation projects that directly benefit National Forest Wilderness Areas. Refer to the NFF website for an extensive listing of selection criteria for this grant, as well as a complete listing of the ten elements of the Wilderness Stewardship. Additionally, a list of wilderness areas, with information on how well each area is meeting the challenge, is also provided. Applicants are encouraged to address multiple eligible elements of the challenge in their proposal.
Requirements: Applications will be considered from non-federal partners, community-based organizations, Native American tribes and other nonprofit 501(c)3 organizations directly supporting elements of the Wilderness Stewardship Challenge in Congressionally designated Forest Service Wilderness Areas. Proposals should include the following: WSC Cover Sheet (available online); proposal containing: executive summary, project goals and objectives, methods to achieve objectives, environmental compliance, organizational background, budget, budget narrative, youth corps summary (required only for conservation corps and youth employment programs), biographical sketch of professional staff, list of membership of the board of directors, an official, a verifiable better of support from the relevant U.S. Forest Service Forest Supervisors, stating approval and support of the project, basic map (showing location of the proposed project), letter from the IRS demonstrating nonprofit, tax-exempt status, most recent audited financial statement. Send all required documents to the NFF on or before January 26.
Restrictions: Applicants will not be considered from: Federal agencies; regional, state or local governmental entities; for-profit organizations; consultants; educational and research organizations proposing projects that so not show tangible, on-the-ground benefit or collect data relevant to baseline monitoring; organizations seeking general operating support; organizations seeking funding litigation or advocacy; organizations that cannot meet matching funds requirements; organizations proposing work that does not benefit Forest Service Wilderness Areas. Funds awarded through this program: can only be distributed as a 1:1 match to non-federal private-doner funds, up to $50,000; must be used for the purpose of completing work in support of the Challenge, benefitting Forest Service Wilderness Areas; cannot be used for general administrative purposes; cannot be used for litigation or advocacy; cannot be directed back to the U.S. Forest Service or any other federal agency.
Geographic Focus: All States
Date(s) Application is Due: Jan 26
Contact: Adam Liljeblad; (406) 542-2805; fax (406) 542-2810; aliljeblad@nationalforests.org
Internet: http://nationalforests.org/conserve/grantprograms/ontheground/wilderness
Sponsor: National Forest Foundation
Fort Missoula Road, Building 27, Suite 3
Missoula, MT 59804

NFL Charities NFL Player Foundation Grants — 3347

NFL Charities supports the charitable and community service activities of both current and former NFL players by making grants that support the charitable efforts and missions of non-profit organizations of current and former NFL players.
Requirements: This grant is available to current and former NFL Players with non-profit organizations designated as a 501(c)3 or 509 of the IRS code. The organization must be established by the player, or the player must be a full-time, salaried employee of the non-profit organization (former player only). The applying organization must be located within the area of the player's current or former NFL team or in his hometown. Furthermore, the player must demonstrate active involvement with the organization. Former player applicants must be vested in the Bert Bell/Pete Rozelle NFL Retirement Plan in order to apply. Additionally, administrative costs must be less than 35% of the total budget, and the player's foundation must be recognized by the Council on Foundations and practicing under National Standards for U.S. Community Foundations. Grants applications must be completed online through the Grant Application Management System (G.A.M.S.).
Restrictions: Grants cannot be made to memorial foundations that were established on behalf of deceased NFL players. This grant will NOT provide support to organizations that seek funding solely to support a youth football camp.
Geographic Focus: All States
Date(s) Application is Due: Oct 29
Contact: Clare Graff, (212) 450-2435 or (917) 816-2885; clare.graff@nfl.com
Internet: http://www.nflcharities.org/grants/player_foundation
Sponsor: NFL Charities
280 Park Avenue, 17th Floor
New York, NY 10017

NFL Charities Pro Bowl Community Grants in Hawaii — 3348

NFL Charities annually allocates $100,000 in grants to Hawaiian non-profit organizations in support of youth health and education programs. Organizations may provide: Educational and youth literacy services, assistance with study towards college or other post-secondary pursuits, and/or motivation and incentive programs that encourage youth to learn, to stay in school and to complete one's education; mentorship, psychological, therapeutic and/or necessary remedial services to support recovery, individual support or some kind of leadership empowerment; substance and/or physical/emotional abuse prevention and assistance programs; programs that promote good health, nutrition, hygiene, participation in athletics and physical fitness; and medical care, hospice and/or long-term health support services for youth and their families. Applications must be submitted through the online NFL Charities Grant Application Management System (G.A.M.S.) will be accepted.
Requirements: Organizations must be a 501(c)3 located in Hawaii and serve Hawaiian youth.
Restrictions: Only non-profit organization that are defined as tax-exempt under Section 501(c)3 of the IRS Code and are located and dedicated to serving youth in the state of Hawaii are eligible to apply. Grants cannot be made to individuals.
Geographic Focus: Hawaii
Date(s) Application is Due: Dec 23
Amount of Grant: 1,000 - 8,000 USD
Contact: Clare Graff, (212) 450-2435 or (917) 816-2885; clare.graff@nfl.com
Internet: http://www.nflcharities.org/grants/pro_bowl
Sponsor: NFL Charities
280 Park Avenue, 17th Floor
New York, NY 10017

NFL Club Matching Youth Football Field/Stadium Grants — 3349

The NFL Youth Football Fund (YFF) seeks to use football as a catalyst to promote positive youth development, support youth and high school football nationwide, and ensure the health of football in future generations. Through the NFL Club Matching Youth Football Field/Stadium Grant Program, NFL club foundations may apply to the YFF for matching funds of up to $250,000 to either: create youth football fields and stadiums at their team facilities to be dedicated solely toward the support and development of youth and high school football; or refurbish community youth and/or high school football fields located in respective team markets. Both NFL Club Matching Grant opportunities help to create a new level of community excitement for the game.
Requirements: Applicants must serve the residents of respective team markets.
Geographic Focus: All States
Amount of Grant: Up to 250,000 USD
Contact: Joe Browne, Executive Vice President of Communications and Public Affairs; (212) 450-2031 or (212) 450-2000; fax (212) 681-7572; Joe.Browne@nfl.com
Internet: http://www.nflyff.org/grants/fields-equipment/
Sponsor: NFL Youth Football Fund
280 Park Avenue
New York, NY 10017

NFL Grassroots Field Grants — 3350

The NFL Youth Football Fund Grassroots Program (the NFL Grassroots Program) is a partnership of the National Football League Youth Football Fund (NFL YFF), which provides funding for the Program, and the Local Initiatives Support Corporation (LISC), which provides technical assistance and manages the Program. The goal of the NFL Grassroots Program is to provide non-profit, neighborhood-based organizations with financial and technical assistance to improve the quality, safety, and accessibility of local football fields. The NFL Grassroots Program provides grants of up to $200,000 for capital improvement projects.
Requirements: 501(c)3 community-based non-profit organizations and middle or high schools are eligible. Applicant organizations must be located specifically and exclusively within NFL target markets and serve low- to moderate-income areas within those markets.
Geographic Focus: All States
Date(s) Application is Due: Oct 30
Contact: Joe Browne, Executive Vice President of Communications and Public Affairs; (212) 450-2031 or (212) 450-2000; fax (212) 681-7572; Joe.Browne@nfl.com
Internet: http://www.nflyff.org/grants/fields-equipment/
Sponsor: NFL Youth Football Fund
280 Park Avenue
New York, NY 10017

NFL High School Coach of the Week Grant — 3351

The NFL Youth Football Fund (YFF) seeks to use football as a catalyst to promote positive youth development, support youth and high school football nationwide, and ensure the health of football in future generations. The NFL High School Coach of the Week Grant Program aids and promotes high school football by recognizing and honoring high school football coaches and their teams in 32 NFL markets and Los Angeles. The program is designed to recognize high school coaches who, through their hard work and dedication to young people, create successful football teams and players both on and off the field. With the assistance of NFL clubs, it also provides high schools with grants to help maintain and upgrade their football programs.
Geographic Focus: All States
Contact: Joe Browne, Executive Vice President of Communications and Public Affairs; (212) 450-2031 or (212) 450-2000; fax (212) 681-7572; Joe.Browne@nfl.com
Internet: http://www.nflyff.org/grants/coaching/
Sponsor: NFL Youth Football Fund
280 Park Avenue
New York, NY 10017

NFL High School Football Coach of the Year Award 3352
The NFL Youth Football Fund (YFF) seeks to use football as a catalyst to promote positive youth development, support youth and high school football nationwide, and ensure the health of football in future generations. The NFL High School Football Coach of the Year Award Program honors high school football coaches that had a profound impact on the athletic and personal development of current NFL players. NFL Coach of the Year candidates are nominated by current NFL players they have coached, and the winner is selected from among a group of five finalists chosen by a blue-ribbon committee of sports leaders appointed by the NFL. The NFL High School Football Coach of the Year attends the Super bowl as a guest, receives a cash award from the YFF, as well as a $10,000 grant for his high school football program. Four other finalists receive $2,500 cash awards and $5,000 grants for their high school football programs.
Geographic Focus: All States
Amount of Grant: 2,500 - 10,000 USD
Contact: Joe Browne, Executive Vice President of Communications and Public Affairs; (212) 450-2031 or (212) 450-2000; fax (212) 681-7572; Joe.Browne@nfl.com
Internet: http://www.nflyff.org/grants/coaching/
Sponsor: NFL Youth Football Fund
280 Park Avenue
New York, NY 10017

NFL Player Youth Football Camp Grants 3353
The NFL Youth Football Fund (YFF) seeks to use football as a catalyst to promote positive youth development, support youth and high school football nationwide, and ensure the health of football in future generations. Current and former NFL players who organize and host free youth football camps and clinics may apply for YFF support grants up to $4,000 through the NFL Player Football Camp Grant program. This program recognizes NFL players who give back to their communities in their hometowns or team cities while also illustrating how NFL players set positive examples for youngsters by emphasizing the importance of community-wide charitable involvement and sportsmanship.
Requirements: All current and former NFL players who wish to host free, non-contact youth football camps and clinics are eligible to apply for YFF funding. Former NFL players must be vested under the Bert Bell NFL Pension Plan as well as associated with non-profit organizations and/or schools in order to apply for grant support.
Geographic Focus: All States
Date(s) Application is Due: Apr 30
Amount of Grant: Up to 4,000 USD
Contact: Joe Browne, Executive Vice President of Communications and Public Affairs; (212) 450-2031 or (212) 450-2000; fax (212) 681-7572; Joe.Browne@nfl.com
Internet: http://www.nflyff.org/grants/nfl-players/
Sponsor: NFL Youth Football Fund
280 Park Avenue
New York, NY 10017

NFWF/Exxon Save the Tiger Fund Grants 3354
The fund supports a variety of efforts aimed at the conservation of tigers in the wild, including on-the-ground tiger conservation and habitat/prey protection projects in tiger-range countries, as well as education activities both in tiger-range countries and internationally. Applications should demonstrate: anticipated benefits to wild tiger populations; improved management/protection of occupied and/or suitable tiger habitats; enhanced prey protection measures for in situ efforts; cooperation and coordination with other tiger conservation organizations; integration of tiger-range governments and local communities into project; lack of duplication and conflict with other ongoing conservation efforts; and methods for resolving conflicts between tiger conservation and the economic health and day-to-day lives of surrounding communities.
Requirements: U.S. or international nonprofit organizations, academic institutions, and government agencies, excluding U.S. federal agencies, are eligible.
Restrictions: The program will not fund political advocacy or litigation activities; captive tiger projects that are not presently part of approved Species Survival Plan; and general administrative overhead of sponsoring agency.
Geographic Focus: All States
Date(s) Application is Due: Jan 21; Nov 5
Contact: Mahendra Shrestha; (202) 857-0166; Mahendra.Shrestha@nfwf.org
Internet: http://www.savethetigerfund.org/Content/NavigationMenu2/Research/Grantees/Applyforagrant/default.htm
Sponsor: National Fish and Wildlife Foundation #6
1133 15th Street, NW, Suite 1100
Washington, DC 97205

NFWF Acres for America Grants 3355
Acres for America is a partnership between Walmart Stores, Inc. and the National Fish and Wildlife Foundation. The Acres for America program was established to provide funding for projects that conserve important habitat for fish, wildlife, and plants through acquisition of interest in real property. The goal of the Acres for America program is to offset the footprint of Walmart's domestic facilities on at least an acre by acre basis through these acquisitions. Applicants are strongly urged to contact the National Fish and Wildlife Foundation regional director in their area to discuss project ideas prior to submitting pre-proposals. All grant awards require a minimum 1:1 match of cash or contributed goods and services. Federal funds may be considered as match. Higher ratios of matching funds will at times aid in making applications more competitive. All applications to the Acres for America Program will be made through a two-stage process, which includes a pre- and then a full-proposal. Only electronic pre-proposals submitted through the on-line pre-proposal form will be considered. Following a review period of about four weeks, appropriate pre-proposals will be selected and applicants will be invited to submit full proposals.
Requirements: Nonprofit conservation organizations, counties and cities, state government agencies, tribes, federal agencies, and schools are eligible.
Restrictions: The Foundation does not fund political advocacy or litigation of any kind, shortfalls in government agency budgets, general administrative overhead, or indirect costs.
Geographic Focus: All States
Date(s) Application is Due: Aug 1
Amount of Grant: 200,000 USD
Contact: Thomas E. Kelsch, Director; (503) 417-8700, ext. 6008; fax (503) 417-8787; Tom.Kelsch@nfwf.org
Internet: http://www.nfwf.org/AM/Template.cfm?Section=Charter_Programs_List&Template=/TaggedPage/TaggedPageDisplay.cfm&TPLID=60&ContentID=17798
Sponsor: National Fish and Wildlife Foundation #6
1133 15th Street, NW, Suite 1100
Washington, DC 97205

NFWF Alaska Fish and Wildlife Fund Grants 3356
The National Fish and Wildlife Foundation, together with agency and private donor partners, is requesting proposals to further conservation of species and habitats in Alaska and in its near coastal waters. The program is funded with Federal funds provided by the U.S. Fish and Wildlife Service (USFWS), Bureau of Land Management (BLM), U.S.D.A. Forest Service, non-federal funds received as community service payments from court settlements of various federal pollution laws, and non-federal funds contributed by corporate partners, including BP, ConocoPhillips, and Shell. Grants may be awarded using one or more of these sources of funding. Federal funds may be awarded to projects that identify a measureable conservation outcome linked to project activities and achieve at least one of the following: conduct habitat and species studies; benefit species of special concern; evaluate and/or mitigate the impacts of climate change; protect or restore coastal watersheds, estuarine, and nearshore marine habitats; provide benefit for multiple species; or offer opportunities for hands-on volunteer or local citizen-based participation and/or education. Approximately $1,000,000 in grant funds are available.
Requirements: Eligible applicants include: non-profit 501(c) organizations (e.g., watershed organizations, homeowners associations, environmental organizations, private schools, etc.) or local, state, federal, and tribal governments and agencies (e.g., counties, townships, cities, boroughs, conservation districts, planning districts, utility districts, schools and universities). A minimum 1:1 match of non-federal funds or in-kind/contributed goods and services is encouraged for all proposals. All potential sources, including Federal sources, and amounts of match should be listed on the application for consideration during the review process. Matching funds may include cash, in-kind contributions of staff and volunteer time, work performed, materials and services donated, or other tangible contributions to the project objectives and outcomes. The cost of recent land acquisition or easement may also qualify as match for a project involving work at the site.
Restrictions: Individuals and for-profit firms are not eligible for grants under this program. Funds granted under this program may not be used for political advocacy, fund raising, lobbying, litigation or to support projects resulting from legally-mandated mitigation projects.
Geographic Focus: All States
Date(s) Application is Due: May 25
Amount of Grant: 25,000 - 100,000 USD
Contact: Cara Rose, Assistant Director, Western Partnership Office; (503) 417-8700, ext. 6008; fax (503) 417-8787; cara.rose@nfwf.org
Internet: http://www.nfwf.org/AM/Template.cfm?Section=Home&CONTENTID=18629&TEMPLATE=/CM/ContentDisplay.cfm
Sponsor: National Fish and Wildlife Foundation #6
1133 15th Street, NW, Suite 1100
Washington, DC 97205

NFWF Aleutian Islands Risk Assessment Grants 3357
The Aleutian Islands Risk Assessment (AIRA) was created to produce a comprehensive evaluation of the risk of vessel accidents and spills in the Aleutian Islands, with the ultimate goal of identifying risk reduction measures that can be implemented to improve the level of safety related to shipping operations in the region. The Program (AIRA) is soliciting the services of a risk analysis team to perform Phase A of the Risk Assessment. The AIRA Program was created to produce a comprehensive evaluation of the risk of vessel accidents and spills in the Aleutian Islands, with the ultimate goal of identifying risk reduction measures that can be implemented to improve the level of safety related to shipping operations in the region. The AIRA is broken down into two distinct phases. Phase A - Preliminary Risk Assessment and Semi-Quantitative Studies and Phase B - Focused Risk Assessment. This Request for Proposal (RFP) is for Phase A. The purpose of Phase A is to identify the more significant risks related to spills from shipping and provide a basis for the identification and initial ranking of possible risk reduction measures.
Geographic Focus: All States
Date(s) Application is Due: Jul 24
Contact: NFWF Aleutian Islands Risk Assessment Grants, Account Manager, Impact Directed Environmental Accounts (IDEA); (503) 417-8700; fax (503) 417-8787; Jay.Wright@nfwf.org
Internet: http://www.nfwf.org/AM/Template.cfm?Section=Charter_Programs_List&Template=/TaggedPage/TaggedPageDisplay.cfm&TPLID=60&ContentID=16143
Sponsor: National Fish and Wildlife Foundation
806 SW Broadway, Suite 750
Portland, OR 97205

NFWF Bird Conservation Initiative Grants 3358

The National Fish and Wildlife Foundation and its partners have keystone initiatives which are the core portfolio of multi-year initiatives through which they seek to achieve measurable outcomes. The Bird Conservation Initiative focuses on migratory and resident species and habitats that occur in the United States or its territories and that have been identified as high priorities for the nation. The goal is to find the best conservation investments, fund the best solutions, and deliver measurable results for bird conservation. Under this mission statement the Foundation has selected initiatives that focus on making a measurable impact on the status of specific species and their habitats. Individual initiatives are described on the website. Application is made online from the website.

Requirements: Applicants should review the business plans for this initiative and prepare application materials accordingly. Prospective applicants should contact the Director to discuss project ideas prior to submitting proposals to help ensure the relevance of funding requests. The Foundation will consider multi-year funding for important projects, subject to annual performance review of the grantee. A minimum 1:1 match is required for most Foundation grants, and higher ratios of match to Foundation funds are desired and improve the competitiveness of applications.

Geographic Focus: All States

Date(s) Application is Due: Aug 1; Dec 1

Contact: Daniel Petit; (202) 857-0166; fax (202) 857-0162; daniel.petit@nfwf.org

Internet: http://www.nfwf.org/am/template.cfm?section=Bird_

Sponsor: National Fish and Wildlife Foundation #6

1133 15th Street, NW, Suite 1100

Washington, DC 97205

NFWF Bring Back the Natives Grants 3359

The National Fish and Wildlife Foundation is requesting proposals to restore, protect, and enhance native populations of sensitive or listed fish species, especially on lands on or adjacent to federal agency lands. The program is funded with Federal funds provided by the U.S. Fish and Wildlife Service, Bureau of Land Management, and U.S. Forest Service. Grants may be awarded using one or more of these sources of funding. The program will provide funding for projects that identify a measureable conservation outcome for native fish species of special concern. Because the two leading factors in native fish species decline are habitat alteration and invasive species, projects that address either, or both, of these threats are of particular interest. Projects benefitting one or more of the following native fish species will be the priority: upper Colorado native fish (flannelmouth and bluehead suckers, roundtail chub, and Colorado cutthroat trout); Lahontan cutthroat trout; Sierra Nevada native fishes; Apache trout; native brook trout and associated native aquatic species (Chesapeake and Upper Ohio River); Russian River (California) Coho; Klamath suckers, redband trout and Coho; Southeast native bass; river herring; other native fish species identified in state, federal, and tribal fish and wildlife agency planning documents and/or by recognized and candidate National Fish Habitat Board Fish Habitat Partnerships organized under the National Fish Habitat Action Plan; and native fish identified in state Aquatic Invasive Species Management Plans as being at risk from invasive species. Pre-proposals should be submitted electronically through the online application form available on the NFWF website.

Requirements: Eligible applicants are: nonprofit organizations; universities; Native American tribes; and local, state, and federal agencies interested in restoring native populations of sensitive or listed aquatic species. Applicants must provide non-federal match of at least $2 for every $1 of grant funds requested. Eligible non-federal matching sources include cash, in-kind donations, and/or volunteer labor.

Restrictions: No part of a matching grant, either the federal funds from NFWF or the non-federal match, may be used to: support litigation expenses or lobbying activities; cover permanent federal employee salary expenses; supplement shortfalls in government agency budgets; support multi-year grants due to the nature of NFWF's annual appropriations (applicants may apply for funds to continue previous NFWF funded projects if substantial progress has been made on the original grant); support basic research; or support basic planning, outreach, or education projects without an "on-the-ground" component.

Geographic Focus: All States

Date(s) Application is Due: Mar 16

Contact: Cara Rose; (503) 417-8700, ext. 6008; fax (503) 417-8787; Cara.Rosel@nfwf.org

Internet: http://www.nfwf.org/AM/Template.cfm?Section=Browse_All_Programs&Template=/CM/ContentDisplay.cfm&ContentID=3677

Sponsor: National Fish and Wildlife Foundation #6

1133 15th Street, NW, Suite 1100

Washington, DC 97205

NFWF Bronx River Watershed Initiative Grants 3360

The Bronx River Watershed Initiative (BRWI) has funding available for stormwater retrofit projects, including low impact development initiatives, to address the root causes of pollution from stormwater outfalls and improve water quality and river ecology along the Bronx River. The funds come from a $7 million settlement resulting from violations associated with discharges of raw sewage into the Bronx River from storm sewers. See the website to verify availability of funding and application deadlines.

Requirements: Federal, state and local government; non-profit organizations; educational institutions; and interstate entities or regional water pollution control agencies are eligible for funding. Governmental entities are encouraged to partner with local governments or non-profit organizations

Geographic Focus: New York

Contact: Lynn Dwyer; (202) 857-0166; fax (202) 857-0162; Lynn.Dwyer@nfwf.org

Internet: http://www.nfwf.org/AM/Template.cfm?Section=Charter_Programs_List&Template=/TaggedPage/TaggedPageDisplay.cfm&TPLID=60&ContentID=24294

Sponsor: National Fish and Wildlife Foundation #6

1133 15th Street, NW, Suite 1100

Washington, DC 97205

NFWF Budweiser Conservationist of the Year Award 3361

National Fish and Wildlife Foundation and Budweiser are seeking nominations for the Budweiser Conservationist of the Year Award. The award recognizes individuals who have made significant volunteer contributions to the outdoors and conservation. The Budweiser Conservationist of the Year selects a conservation organization to receive a $50,000 grant from Budweiser and the Foundation. The three runners up each direct a $5,000 grant to a conservation organization of their choice. To nominate an individual for the award complete the form on the Foundation's website.

Geographic Focus: All States

Date(s) Application is Due: Oct 19

Amount of Grant: 50,000 USD

Contact: Ellen Gabel; (202) 857-0166; ellen.gabel@nfwf.org or info@nfwf.org

Internet: http://www.nfwf.org/AM/Template.cfm?Section=Who_We_Are&TEMPLATE=/CM/ContentDisplay.cfm&CONTENTID=9637

Sponsor: National Fish and Wildlife Foundation #6

1133 15th Street, NW, Suite 1100

Washington, DC 97205

NFWF California Coastal Restoration Fund Grants 3362

The National Fish and Wildlife Foundation, together with the U.S. Fish and Wildlife Service, is requesting proposals for projects located within the Northern or Central Districts of California that benefit fish and wildlife species and the habitats upon which they depend. Types of project activities may include, but are not limited to, on-the-ground habitat conservation, improvement of public access areas, and projects that encourage collaboration and support local communities. A total of $500,000 is available for which proposals are now being invited. The purposes of the Fund, and for which projects are being solicited, include support of the following activities in the vicinity of the Central and Northern Districts of California: on-the-ground habitat conservation and protection projects to benefit fish and wildlife species and the habitats upon which they depend; improvement of public access areas and other public information/education projects that benefit the U.S. Fish and Wildlife National Wildlife Refuge System; projects that encourage collaboration and support local communities seeking environmentally and economically sustainable solutions for natural resource management; applied research that is directly related to improvement of Northern and Central coastal California's natural resources management; projects that support activities necessary to the collection, research, analysis, study, preservation, storage, display, and protection of historical, cultural, natural, and marine and island resources and wildlife; and purchase of communication and defensive equipment and patrol vessels and vehicles; training; response to and clean up of pollution spills or threats of pollution; preservation and/or construction of facilities enforcement and patrol operations, such as enforcement of Marine Protected Areas (this category applies only to the Northern District, and applicants are limited to appropriate local, state, and tribal agencies; projects in this category will be capped at $40,000).

Requirements: Proposals must meet all of these administrative *Requirements:* projects must be implemented within the Fund's area of impact: the Northern and Central Districts of California (the Northern District of California includes the following three National Marine Sanctuaries: the Monterey Bay, the Gulf of the Farallones, and the Cordell Banks in addition to the California coastal zone between the Port of San Francisco and the Oregon border; the Central District includes coastal areas from Orange to San Luis Obispo Counties); the maximum award amount for any one project will be $175,000; projects should be scheduled to be completed within two years of the award; and while matching funds are not required, applicants are encouraged to include matching funds using cash or in-kind contributions where possible.

Restrictions: The following groups are eligible: non-profit conservation, environmental, or related organizations; counties and cities; state government agencies; tribes; federal agencies; or schools. Funds cannot be used for: political advocacy, litigation, required mitigation, or illegal activities; equipment purchases not primarily related to the intended purpose of the Fund; or website development, or videos not primarily related to the intended purpose of the Fund.

Geographic Focus: All States

Date(s) Application is Due: Apr 24

Contact: Elizabeth Epstein (Broner); (503) 417-8700; fax (503) 417-8787; liz.epstein@nfwf.org or info@nfwf.org

Internet: http://www.nfwf.org/AM/Template.cfm?Section=Charter_Programs_List&TEMPLATE=/CM/ContentDisplay.cfm&CONTENTID=12580

Sponsor: National Fish and Wildlife Foundation #6

1133 15th Street, NW, Suite 1100

Washington, DC 97205

NFWF Chesapeake Bay Conservation Innovation Grants 3363

The National Fish and Wildlife Foundation, in partnership with USDA's Natural Resources Conservation Service, will award grants on a competitive basis of between $75,000 and $1 million each to support the demonstration of innovative natural resource conservation and restoration practices on agricultural lands throughout the Chesapeake Bay watershed. The purpose of the program is to expand the collective knowledge about the most effective ways to engage working farms in protecting and restoring vital natural resources in the Chesapeake Bay region while sustaining agricultural production. This program does not include a pre-proposal round, and full proposals are due February 28.

Requirements: Eligible applicants are either nonprofit 501(c) organizations or local governments (i.e., counties, townships, cities, boroughs, conservation districts, planning districts, utility districts, or other units of local government) from the Virginia, Maryland, Pennsylvania, District of Columbia, New York, West Virginia, and Delaware portions of the Chesapeake Bay watershed.

Restrictions: Individuals, state and federal government agencies, and private for-profit firms are not eligible for grants under this program.

Geographic Focus: Delaware, District of Columbia, Maryland, New York, Pennsylvania, Virginia, West Virginia
Date(s) Application is Due: Feb 28
Amount of Grant: 75,000 - 1,000,000 USD
Contact: Amanda Bassow, (202) 857-0166; fax (202) 857-0162; amanda.bassow@nfwf.org
Internet: http://www.nfwf.org/AM/Template.cfm?Section=Home&Template=/TaggedPage/TaggedPageDisplay.cfm&TPLID=30&ContentID=7982
Sponsor: National Fish and Wildlife Foundation #6
1133 15th Street, NW, Suite 1100
Washington, DC 97205

NFWF Chesapeake Bay Stewardship Fund Small Watershed Grants   3364
The Small Watershed Grants (SWG) Program is administered by the National Fish and Wildlife Foundation (NFWL), in cooperation with the U.S. Environmental Protection Agency, Chesapeake Bay Program. The Chesapeake Bay Program is a partnership among Virginia, Maryland, Pennsylvania, the District of Columbia, the Chesapeake Bay Commission, and the federal government. The partnership has set a number of Bay protection and restoration goals, and it works to mobilize the resources of government and the private sector to achieve the goals. The Chesapeake Bay Program operates as a voluntary, collaborative resource management program. It has set goals related to fisheries, submerged grasses, wetlands, toxins, sustainable development, nutrient reduction, and public participation. Further information can be obtained on the Bay Program's website (www.chesapeakebay.net). The SWG program provides grants to organizations and local governments working on a local level to implement projects that improve small watersheds in the Chesapeake Bay basin, while building citizen-based resource stewardship. The purpose of the Grants is to support protection and restoration actions that contribute to restoring healthy waters, habitat and living resources of the Chesapeake Bay ecosystem. The SWG Program has been designed to encourage the development and sharing of innovative ideas among the many organizations wishing to be involved in watershed protection activities. See the NFWF website for the current request for proposal and current deadlines.
Requirements: Eligible applicants include: non-profit 501(c) organizations or local governments and agencies. Organizations located outside the Chesapeake Bay watershed may apply if their projects will be conducted entirely within the watershed.
Restrictions: Individuals, state and federal government agencies, and private for-profit firms are not eligible
Geographic Focus: All States
Amount of Grant: 20,000 - 200,000 USD
Contact: Amanda Bassow; (202) 857-0166; fax (202) 857-0162; amanda.bassow@nfwf.org
Internet: http://www.nfwf.org/AM/Template.cfm?Section=Chesapeake_Bay_Stewardship_Fund&TEMPLATE=/CM/HTMLDisplay.cfm&CONTENTID=23389
Sponsor: National Fish and Wildlife Foundation #6
1133 15th Street, NW, Suite 1100
Washington, DC 97205

NFWF Chesapeake Bay Targeted Watershed Grants   3365
The overall goal for the Program is to expand the collective knowledge on the most innovative, sustainable and cost-effective strategies - including market-based approaches - for reducing excess nutrient loads within specific tributaries to the Chesapeake Bay. The program seeks to support projects representing the diverse conditions (e.g., urban, rural, suburban) and sources of nutrients (e.g., agricultural, storm water, other non-point sources) that exist throughout the Chesapeake Bay watershed. Priorities for funding include: field-scale demonstrations of innovative technologies, conservation practices and Best Management Practices (BMPs) that have the potential to significantly reduce excess nutrient loads; demonstrations and evaluation, within targeted small watersheds, of the most effective and efficient strategies for implementing nutrient load reductions contained in state Tributary Strategies; water quality trading demonstrations (including point source to non-point source) and other market-based strategies to reduce nutrient loads to the Bay and its tributaries in accordance with EPA policies and guidance and, as appropriate, state policies; and demonstrations of strategies that overcome barriers to adoption of the most effective and efficient BMPs and conservation practices for reducing excess nutrient loads. Pre-proposal applications must be postmarked by November 17, with invitation for Full Proposals announced by December 5 and the Full Proposal deadline January 19.
Requirements: Any project that accelerates the reduction of nutrients from non-point sources within targeted small watersheds may be eligible for funding. Eligible applicants are either non-profit 501(c) organizations, universities, local or state governments (i.e., state conservation agencies, counties, townships, cities, boroughs, conservation districts, planning districts, utility districts, drainage districts, or other units of local government) from the Virginia, Maryland, Pennsylvania, District of Columbia, New York, West Virginia, and Delaware portions of the Chesapeake Bay watershed. Non-profit organizations and universities located outside the Chesapeake Bay watershed may apply only if their projects will be conducted within the watershed. Individuals, federal government agencies, and private for-profit firms are not eligible for grants under this program.
Geographic Focus: Delaware, District of Columbia, Maryland, New York, Pennsylvania, Virginia, West Virginia
Date(s) Application is Due: Jan 19; Nov 17
Amount of Grant: 400,000 - 1,000,000 USD
Contact: Amanda Bassow; (202) 857-0166; fax (202) 857-0162; amanda.bassow@nfwf.org
Internet: http://www.nfwf.org/AM/Template.cfm?Section=Home&Template=/CM/ContentDisplay.cfm&ContentID=3771
Sponsor: National Fish and Wildlife Foundation #6
1133 15th Street, NW, Suite 1100
Washington, DC 97205

NFWF Columbia Basin Water Transactions Program (CBWTP) Grants   3366
The Program intends to address a chronic regional challenge. As a result of legal water withdrawals during the peak growing season, stretches of many streams and rivers run low and sometimes dry with significant consequences for imperiled salmon, steelhead, trout and other creatures. Using permanent acquisitions, leases, investments in efficiency and other incentive-based approaches, the CBWTP supports program partners in Oregon, Washington, Idaho and Montana to assist landowners who wish to restore flows to existing habitat. This program does not include a pre-proposal round. Deadlines for this program vary, please review the program description and RFP for more detail.
Requirements: Programs based in or aimed at addressing the problem in the states of Idaho, Montana, Washington, and Oregon.
Geographic Focus: Idaho, Montana, Oregon, Washington
Contact: Andrew Purkey; (202) 857-0166; fax (202) 857-0162; andrew.purkey@nfwf.org
Internet: http://www.nfwf.org/AM/Template.cfm?Section=Home&TEMPLATE=/CM/ContentDisplay.cfm&CONTENTID=5794
Sponsor: National Fish and Wildlife Foundation #6
1133 15th Street, NW, Suite 1100
Washington, DC 97205

NFWF Columbia River Estuarine Coastal Fund Grants   3367
The Program is aimed at financing: on the ground habitat conservation, restoration and management projects in and along the Columbia River below the Bonneville Dam and the adjacent Coasts of Oregon (up to and including Tillamook Bay) and Washington (up to and including Willapa Bay) that may be affected by estuarine flows to benefit the fish and wildlife resources and the habitats upon which they depend; landowner outreach and incentive programs for restoration and management of natural resources in the same geographic area; public use and natural/cultural projects that benefit the Service's National Wildlife Refuge System; collaborative projects from local communities seeking environmentally and economically sustainable solutions to natural resource problems; and applied research that is directly related to improvement of natural resources management in the same geographic area. Pre-proposals are invited for projects to be funded by: grants for more than $10,000 and up to $200,000; and small grants of $10,000 or less for local conservation or education projects. While matching funds are not required in either category, the National Fish and Wildlife Foundation encourages applicants to include matching funds with cash or in-kind contributions where possible. An approved project should be completed within two years of the award of the grant.
Requirements: Applicants eligible to apply include: 501(c)3 registered non-profit conservation organizations; counties and cities; local, state, and federal government agencies; tribes; schools; soil and water conservation districts; and other special districts.
Restrictions: Funds cannot be used for: political advocacy, litigation expenses, mitigation or terrorist activities; equipment purchases not primarily related to the direct completion of the project; website development or videos; improvement of natural resources for commercial or private profit; required mitigation; required Habitat Conservation Plan activities; or straight percentage of administrative overhead/indirect costs (a portion of the grant may be used for direct project-related administrative expenses, such as salaries, travel, supplies, and telephone, but these must be specifically identified budget line items).
Geographic Focus: Idaho, Montana, Oregon, Washington
Date(s) Application is Due: Sep 29
Amount of Grant: Up to 200,000 USD
Contact: Cara Rose; (503) 417-8700, ext. 21; fax (503) 417-8787; cara.rose@nfwf.org
Internet: http://www.nfwf.org/AM/Template.cfm?Section=Search&Template=/CM/ContentDisplay.cfm&ContentID=3789
Sponsor: National Fish and Wildlife Foundation
806 SW Broadway, Suite 750
Portland, OR 97205

NFWF Community Salmon Fund Partnerships   3368
NFWF has established local partnerships throughout Washington State through the Community Salmon Fund program to engage landowners, community groups, tribes, and businesses in stimulating smaller-scale, community-oriented habitat restoration and protection projects to aid in salmon recovery. Grants made under this program are administered by the Foundation. There are currently three Community Salmon Fund partnership programs. NFWF has partnered with the Washington State Salmon Recovery Funding Board (SRFB) to administer a statewide Community Salmon Fund program that is coordinated with the individual Lead Entity groups. Verify the deadlines from the website.
Requirements: Applicants eligible to apply include: 501(c)3 registered non-profit conservation organizations; counties and cities; local, state, and federal government agencies; tribes; schools; soil and water conservation districts; and other special districts.
Restrictions: Funds cannot be used for: political advocacy, litigation expenses, mitigation or terrorist activities; equipment purchases not primarily related to the direct completion of the project; website development or videos; improvement of natural resources for commercial or private profit; required mitigation; required Habitat Conservation Plan activities; or straight percentage of administrative overhead/indirect costs (a portion of the grant may be used for direct project-related administrative expenses, such as salaries, travel, supplies, and telephone, but these must be specifically identified budget line items).
Geographic Focus: Washington
Contact: Cara Rose; (503) 417-8700, ext. 21; fax (503) 417-8787; cara.rose@nfwf.org
Internet: http://www.nfwf.org/AM/Template.cfm?Section=Browse_All_Programs&Template=/TaggedPage/TaggedPageDisplay.cfm&TPLID=36&ContentID=9865
Sponsor: National Fish and Wildlife Foundation #6
1133 15th Street, NW, Suite 1100
Washington, DC 97205

NFWF ConocoPhillips SPIRIT of Conservation Migratory Bird Grants — 3369

The ConocoPhillips SPIRIT of Conservation Migratory Bird Program provides funding through a competitive application process for projects that benefit migratory birds and their habitats. Priority will be given to projects that: protect or improve management of habitats for migratory birds; result in restoration of habitat through tree or other plantings; benefit declining, threatened or endangered species at the state or federal level; produce measurable benefits to these species that enhance their recovery; and provide opportunities for employee participation and volunteerism. Applicants are strongly encouraged to contact the Program Manager before submitting a pre-proposal.
Requirements: Eligible applicants include non-profit 501(c)3 organizations, educational institutions, and local and state units of governments. Priority will be given to projects in regions where ConocoPhillips has an operating presence, including the following regions in North America: Western Canada; Gulf of Mexico states, including Texas, Louisiana, and Alabama; Prairie states, including Texas, Oklahoma, New Mexico, Colorado, Utah, and Wyoming; and Delaware Bay. International projects will be considered for specific geographic areas. All grant awards require a minimum 1:1 match of cash or contributed goods and services, of which at least 50% should be from non-federal sources.
Geographic Focus: All States
Date(s) Application is Due: Dec 9
Contact: Peter Stangel; (202) 857-0166; fax (202) 857-0162; Peter.Stangel@nfwf.org
Internet: http://www.nfwf.org/AM/Template.cfm?Section=Browse_All_Programs&Template=/CM/ContentDisplay.cfm&ContentID=3791
Sponsor: National Fish and Wildlife Foundation #6
1133 15th Street, NW, Suite 1100
Washington, DC 97205

NFWF Coral Reef Conservation Project Grants — 3370

The Coral Reef Conservation Fund supports the restoration of damaged reef systems and prevents further negative impacts through both on-the-water and up-the-watershed projects. It was created to address the alarming decline in both the quantity and quality of the world's coral reef ecosystems. The U.S. Coral Reef Task Force Partnership Initiative provides grant funding to build local capacity and support for projects that will help restore natural resources. Grant funding is available for the following: enhance watershed management planning, reduce sedimentation, and improve fisheries management. The program requires one-to-one matching funds from project partners. Applicants must submit an on-line pre-proposal application. A limited number of pre-proposal applicants will be invited to submit full proposals.
Requirements: United States and international nonprofits, academic institutions, and government agencies (except United States federal agencies) are eligible.
Geographic Focus: All States
Date(s) Application is Due: Mar 5
Contact: Erin Hoffman; (202) 595-2469; fax (202) 857-0162; erin.hoffman@nfwf.org
Internet: http://www.nfwf.org/AM/Template.cfm?Section=Home&Template=/TaggedPage/TaggedPageDisplay.cfm&TPLID=60&ContentID=24321
Sponsor: National Fish and Wildlife Foundation #6
1133 15th Street, NW, Suite 1100
Washington, DC 97205

NFWF Delaware Estuary Watershed Grants — 3371

This program provides grants to organizations working on a local level to protect and improve watersheds in the Delaware Estuary, while building citizen-based resource stewardship. The purpose of the grants program is to address the living resource and water quality needs of the Delaware Estuary ecosystem. The grants program has been designed to encourage the development and sharing of innovative ideas among the many organizations wishing to be involved in watershed protection activities. The program seeks to support communities in developing and implementing watershed management plans; encourage innovative, locally based programs or projects that restore important habitats and improve water quality within the Delaware Estuary; develop the capacity of local governments, citizens groups, and other organizations to promote community-based stewardship and enhance local watershed management; promote a greater understanding of the Delaware Estuary and the interrelationship between the health of the estuary and the condition of local watersheds; and strengthen the link between communities and the Delaware Estuary Program.
Requirements: 501(c)3 nonprofit organizations or local governments (i.e., counties, townships, cities, boroughs, conservation districts, planning districts, utility districts, or other units of local government) from the Delaware, New Jersey, and Pennsylvania portions of the Delaware Estuary are eligible.
Restrictions: Individuals, state, and federal government agencies; and private for-profit firms are not eligible.
Geographic Focus: Delaware, New Jersey, Pennsylvania
Date(s) Application is Due: Aug 1
Contact: Lynn Dwyer; (202) 857-0166; fax (202) 857-0162; Lynn.Dwyer@nfwf.org
Internet: http://www.nfwf.org/AM/Template.cfm?Section=Who_We_Are&TEMPLATE=/CM/ContentDisplay.cfm&CONTENTID=9977
Sponsor: National Fish and Wildlife Foundation #6
1133 15th Street, NW, Suite 1100
Washington, DC 97205

NFWF Dissolved Oxygen Environmental Benefit Fund Grants — 3372

The mission of the Dissolved Oxygen Environmental Benefit Fund is to restore habitat and improve water quality in the western Long Island Sound and Jamaica Bay. Projects may extend from one to two years. Projects should be ready to begin implementation within three months of the grant award. It is anticipated that $1 million to $1.5 million will be awarded in project grants. The minimum award amount is $25,000 and the maximum award amount is $200,000 per project.
Requirements: Federal, interstate, state and local government, interstate entities, non-profit organizations and educational institutions are eligible to apply. Projects must include: measurable outputs linked to project activities; specific provisions for long-term maintenance, management and protection, as appropriate; activities consistent with the goals of established state and federal protection, conservation, restoration and water quality plans; and education, training, and public outreach components to enhance the benefits of the project.
Restrictions: The geographic scope of the program for the western Long Island Sound is the area of the Sound westward of the line between New Haven, Connecticut and Wading River, New York, and extending to the Whitestone Bridge. The geographic scope of the program for Jamaica Bay includes the tidal creeks and undeveloped upland adjacent to the Bay.
Geographic Focus: All States
Date(s) Application is Due: May 2
Amount of Grant: 25,000 - 200,000 USD
Contact: Lynn Dwyer; (202) 857-0166; fax (202) 857-0162; Lynn.Dwyer@nfwf.org
Internet: http://www.nfwf.org/AM/Template.cfm?Section=Who_We_Are&TEMPLATE=/CM/ContentDisplay.cfm&CONTENTID=9291
Sponsor: National Fish and Wildlife Foundation #6
1133 15th Street, NW, Suite 1100
Washington, DC 97205

NFWF Five-Star Restoration Challenge Grants — 3373

The program awards grants on a competitive basis to support community-based wetland, riparian, and coastal habitat restoration projects that build diverse partnerships and foster local natural resource stewardship through education, outreach, and training activities. Key elements include: ecological restoration (projects must include on-the-ground wetland, riparian, in stream and/or coastal habitat restoration); environmental education (projects must integrate meaningful education into the restoration project either through community outreach, participation and/or integration with K-12 environmental curriculum); and measurable results (projects must result in measurable ecological, educational and community benefits). Grants will vary in size, duration and scale. In general, smaller-scale, one-year projects will be eligible for grants up to $20,000. Two-year larger-scale projects will be eligible for grants up to $40,000.
Requirements: Any public or private entity that can receive grants is eligible. While partnerships are encouraged to include state and federal agencies, those entities may not serve as the grantee unless the community partners demonstrate that the state or federal agency is best suited to coordinate the community-based project.
Geographic Focus: All States
Date(s) Application is Due: Feb 15
Amount of Grant: 10,000 - 40,000 USD
Contact: Claire Thorp; (415) 243-3104; claire.thorp@nfwf.org
Internet: http://www.nfwf.org/AM/Template.cfm?Section=Charter_Programs_List&Template=/TaggedPage/TaggedPageDisplay.cfm&TPLID=60&ContentID=24301
Sponsor: National Fish and Wildlife Foundation #6
1133 15th Street, NW, Suite 1100
Washington, DC 97205

NFWF Freshwater Fish Conservation Initiative Grants — 3374

The National Fish and Wildlife Foundation and its partners have keystone initiatives which are the core portfolio of multi-year initiatives through which they seek to achieve measurable outcomes. The Freshwater Fish Conservation Initiative focuses on species and habitats species that occur in the United States or its territories and that have been identified as high priorities for the nation. Freshwater fish (anadromous and catadromous) and associated aquatic life such as mussels, crayfish, and other invertebrates are included. The goal is to find the best conservation investments, fund the best solutions, and deliver measurable results for fish conservation. Under this mission statement there are selected initiatives that focus on making a measurable impact on the status of specific species and their habitat. Individual initiatives are listed on the website and are focused on conserving freshwater fish, aquatic organisms, and their habitats. Application is made online from the website.
Requirements: Applicants should review the business plans for this initiative and prepare application materials accordingly. Prospective applicants should contact the Director to discuss project ideas prior to submitting proposals to help ensure the relevance of funding requests. The Foundation will consider multi-year funding for important projects, subject to annual performance review of the grantee. A minimum 1:1 match is required for most Foundation grants, and higher ratios of match to Foundation funds are desired and improve the competitiveness of applications.
Geographic Focus: All States
Date(s) Application is Due: Aug 1; Dec 1
Amount of Grant: 50,000 - 375,000 USD
Contact: Jim Sedell, Director, Fish Conservation; (503) 417-8700; fax (503) 417-8787
Internet: http://www.nfwf.org/AM/Template.cfm?Section=Fish_Conservation2
Sponsor: National Fish and Wildlife Foundation #6
1133 15th Street, NW, Suite 1100
Washington, DC 97205

NFWF King County Community Salmon Fund Grants — 3375

The National Fish and Wildlife Foundation (NFWF) and King County have established the Community Salmon Fund to stimulate small-scale, voluntary action by community groups, in cooperation with landowners and businesses, to support salmon recovery on private property in the Cedar River, Lake Washington, Sammamish Watershed (WRIA 8), the Green/Duwamish and Central Puget Sound Watershed (WRIA 9), and southern Snohomish County. The Fund will award grants of up to $75,000. However, only a limited number of awards will be made at that level and requests of $30,000 or less are more the norm. The program's primary focus is smaller, community-based projects that are part of

a larger effort to restore a main stem or a tributary to a level likely to produce, maintain or increase sustainable runs of salmonid, so requests for funds for large-scale restoration projects will not be considered.
Requirements: Projects on public property are also eligible but must include information on how they serve as a pilot for similar projects on private property.
Restrictions: Full fee acquisition, educational projects uncoupled from measurable actions, mitigation or corrective actions, general planning and studies, and legal or lobbying efforts are ineligible. Also, isolated projects (i.e., those with no coordinated link to community-based or government efforts to restore or sustain salmonids in a specified system) will not be considered for funding unless they can serve as a compelling model for widespread adoption.
Geographic Focus: Washington
Date(s) Application is Due: May 23
Amount of Grant: Up to 75,000 USD
Contact: Cara Rose, (503) 417-8700, ext. 21; fax (503) 417-8787; cara.rose@nfwf.org
Internet: http://www.nfwf.org/AM/Template.cfm?Section=Home&Template=/TaggedPage/TaggedPageDisplay.cfm&TPLID=30&ContentID=9511
Sponsor: National Fish and Wildlife Foundation
806 SW Broadway, Suite 750
Portland, OR 97205

NFWF Long Island Sound Futures Fund Grants 3376
The Long Island Sound Futures Fund emphasizes implementation projects focused on protecting and restoring Long Island Sound, particularly projects that restore and protect important fish and wildlife habitats; and implement community-based projects that improve water quality and protect water resources. Grant awards will be made in two categories: large grants between $20,000 and $200,000 and mini-grants between $3,000 and $10,000. Grant awards support projects that span one year to 15 months. An on-line application must be submitted.
Requirements: Eligible applicants include: non-profit 501(c) organizations; state, tribal, and local governments; and academic and educational institutions. To be eligible for consideration habitat restoration or stewardship projects must fall within the coastal area boundary established by the Long Island Sound Study (e.g., the Long Island Sound and its coastal watersheds). Projects must have a minimum match of 50% of the total grant request. Higher match ratios (1:1 or above) are strongly encouraged and will make a proposal significantly more competitive. Projects must fall into one of the following five overall conservation priorities: urban waters, clean water and healthy watersheds, restore and protect habitat and conserve wildlife, engage people and communities around the sound, and improve conservation on private lands.
Geographic Focus: All States
Date(s) Application is Due: Apr 9
Contact: Lynn Dwyer, (202) 857-0166; fax (202) 857-0162; Lynn.Dwyer@nfwf.org
Internet: http://www.nfwf.org/AM/Template.cfm?Section=Charter_Programs_List&Template=/TaggedPage/TaggedPageDisplay.cfm&TPLID=60&ContentID=24304
Sponsor: National Fish and Wildlife Foundation #6
1133 15th Street, NW, Suite 1100
Washington, DC 97205

NFWF Marine & Coastal Conservation Initiative Grants 3377
The National Fish and Wildlife Foundation and its partners have keystone initiatives which are the core portfolio of multi-year initiatives through which they seek to achieve measurable outcomes. The Marine and Coastal Conservation Initiative focuses on building conservation partnerships to overcome the most important challenges to the health of the marine and coastal environment. The goal is to find the best conservation investments, fund the best solutions, and deliver measurable results for a broad cross-section of fish and wildlife representing marine and coastal ecosystem health. Under this mission statement, the Foundation has selected initiatives that are focused on making a measurable impact on specific species and their habitat. Individual initiatives are listed on the website but are focused under three themes that are critical for marine and coastal wildlife in America. The themes are promoting sustainable fishers, protecting marine natural heritage, and climate change and adaptation. Application is made online from the website.
Requirements: Applicants should review the business plans for this initiative and prepare application materials accordingly. Prospective applicants should contact the Director to discuss project ideas prior to submitting proposals to help ensure the relevance of funding requests. The Foundation will consider multi-year funding for important projects, subject to annual performance review of the grantee. A minimum 1:1 match is required for most Foundation grants, and higher ratios of match to Foundation funds are desired and improve the competitiveness of applications.
Geographic Focus: All States
Date(s) Application is Due: Aug 1; Dec 1
Amount of Grant: 50,000 - 375,000 USD
Contact: Anthony C. Chatwin; (202) 857-0166; anthony.chatwin@nfwf.org
Internet: http://www.nfwf.org/am/template.cfm?section=Marine_and_Coastal
Sponsor: National Fish and Wildlife Foundation #6
1133 15th Street, NW, Suite 1100
Washington, DC 97205

NFWF National Whale Conservation Fund Grants 3378
The fund supports research, management, conservation, and education/outreach activities related to the conservation and recovery of whales, particularly projects relating to great whales that are the most endangered (e.g., North Atlantic and North Pacific right whales). Priority will be given to projects that address anthropogenic threats to endangered whales of U.S. waters (i.e., fishing gear entanglement, ship/whale collisions, noise, habitat degradation, contaminants, etc.). Proposals that address tasks or needs identified in endangered whale recovery plans or conservation plans adopted by the National Marine Fisheries Service are encouraged. Applicants are encouraged to show leverage of a one-to-one or greater match to the proposal request. NWCF actively seeks to form new partnerships with corporations, organizations, and individuals to leverage NWCF???s resources sufficiently to meet its aggressive conservation goals. Applications should clearly describe anticipated benefits to whale conservation; project goals, objectives, and methodology, including provisions for monitoring and evaluation; qualifications of key project personnel; detailed budget illustrating use of NWCF grant; cooperation and coordination with other appropriate federal, state, and private organizations; and ability to leverage NWCF grant award.
Restrictions: NWCF will not fund political advocacy, boycotts, litigation, or indirect or unallocated expenses.
Geographic Focus: All States
Contact: Stephanie Pendergrass; (202) 857-0166; Stephanie.Pendergrass@nfwf.org
Internet: http://www.nfwf.org/AM/Template.cfm?Section=Who_We_Are&Template=/TaggedPage/TaggedPageDisplay.cfm&TPLID=30&ContentID=9725
Sponsor: National Fish and Wildlife Foundation #6
1133 15th Street, NW, Suite 1100
Washington, DC 97205

NFWF National Wildlife Refuge Friends Group Program Grants 3379
The National Fish and Wildlife Foundation, along with its partners, recognizes the important role refuge Friends organizations play in building critical community support for the United States Fish and Wildlife Service's National Wildlife Refuge System. As such, proposals are requested for projects that assist organizations to be effective co-stewards of our Nation's important natural resources within the National Wildlife Refuge System. This program provides competitive seed grants to creative and innovative proposals that seek to increase the number and effectiveness of organizations interested in assisting the Refuge System nationwide and their work and projects to support the System. The primary purpose of the Grants is to provide assistance to new and existing Friends organizations. Nuturing and supporting these organizations leads to a stronger National Wildlife Refuge System. Friends organizations are invited to submit proposals that focus on start-up and capacity building projects. Applications are available on the website.
Requirements: Eligible applicants are refuge Friends organizations. Applicants must either be tax exempt under section 501(c), or be in the process of applying for 501(c)3 status.
Restrictions: The Refuge Friends Grant Program will not fund requests for: printing for professional publishing purposes; political advocacy or litigation activities; travel; salaries; non-profit filings; food or beverages; shortfalls in government agency budgets; or multi-year grants (applicant may reapply).
Geographic Focus: All States
Date(s) Application is Due: Apr 30
Amount of Grant: 1,500 - 5,000 USD
Contact: Teal Edelen; (202) 857-0166; teal.edelen@nfwf.org
Internet: http://www.nfwf.org/AM/Template.cfm?Section=Who_We_Are&Template=/CM/ContentDisplay.cfm&ContentID=4639
Sponsor: National Fish and Wildlife Foundation #6
1133 15th Street, NW, Suite 1100
Washington, DC 97205

NFWF Native Plant Conservation Initiative Grants 3380
The Native Plant Conservation Initiative Grants are conducted in cooperation with the Plant Conservation Alliance (PCA), a partnership between the Foundation, ten federal agencies, and more than 270 non-governmental organizations. PCA provides a framework and strategy for linking resources and expertise in developing a coordinated national approach to the conservation of native plants. Grants have funded multi-stakeholder projects that focus on the conservation of native plants and pollinators under any of the following sox focal areas: conservation, education, restoration, research, sustainability, and data linkages. Verify the application deadline from the website.
Requirements: Government agencies and nongovernmental partners are eligible to apply. Preference will be given to projects that involve local communities and volunteers in the conservation efforts.
Geographic Focus: All States
Contact: Teal Edelen; (202) 857-0166; teal.edelen@nfwf.org
Internet: http://www.nfwf.org/AM/Template.cfm?Section=Who_We_Are&CONTENTID=9578&TEMPLATE=/CM/ContentDisplay.cfm
Sponsor: National Fish and Wildlife Foundation #6
1133 15th Street, NW, Suite 1100
Washington, DC 97205

NFWF Nature of Learning Grants 3381
Applications are invited from organizations interested in initiating community-based environmental education. The initiative seeks to: use National Wildlife Refuges and other natural areas as outdoor classrooms to promote a greater understanding of local conservation issues; encourage an interdisciplinary approach to learning that seeks to enhance student academic achievement; utilize field experiences and student-led stewardship projects to connect classroom lessons to real world issues; and involve a partnership among local schools, community groups, natural resource professionals, and local businesses. First year start-up grants are available for up to $10,000, and second year follow-up grants, up to $5,000, are available to support continued implementation of The Nature of Learning program.
Requirements: Collaborative partnerships that include schools or nonprofit organizations and local National Wildlife Refuges are eligible.
Geographic Focus: All States
Date(s) Application is Due: Jun 16
Amount of Grant: Up to 10,000 USD

Contact: Ellen Gabel; (202) 857-0166; fax (202) 857-0162; ellen.gabel@nfwf.org
Internet: http://www.nfwf.org/AM/Template.cfm?Section=Who_We_Are&Template=/CM/ContentDisplay.cfm&ContentID=4784
Sponsor: National Fish and Wildlife Foundation #6
1133 15th Street, NW, Suite 1100
Washington, DC 97205

NFWF One Fly Conservation Partnership Grants   3382
The Jackson Hole One Fly Foundation (One Fly) and the National Fish and Wildlife Foundation (NFWF) have entered into a conservation program partnership to leverage both organizations' funding and interest in cold water fisheries conservation, particularly in the tributaries and mainstem Snake and Yellowstone Basins. The One Fly and NFWF have a long history in fisheries conservation throughout the greater Snake River and Yellowstone region. Both organizations have individually and jointly funded many important projects that are building on this success through this new partnership. A request for proposal is expected to be available on the website in May.
Requirements: Applicants must provide non-federal cash or in-kind match of at least $1 for every $1 funded.
Geographic Focus: Idaho, Montana, Wyoming
Contact: Krystyna Wolniakowski; (503) 417-8700; wolniakowski@nfwf.org
Internet: http://www.nfwf.org/AM/Template.cfm?Section=Charter_Programs_List&TEMPLATE=/CM/ContentDisplay.cfm&CONTENTID=24323
Sponsor: National Fish and Wildlife Foundation #6
1133 15th Street, NW, Suite 1100
Washington, DC 97205

NFWF Oregon Governor's Fund for the Environment Grants   3383
The Oregon Governor's Fund for the Environment is a sustained granting program to benefit Oregon's rivers, streams, and associated fish, wildlife and plants. The goal of the funding is establishing a sustainable revenue source that is dedicated to local environmental clean-up and restoration efforts focused on preserving and protecting Oregon's rivers, watersheds and fish and wildlife. Established in 2005, the Fund is administered by the National Fish and Wildlife Foundation. The grant amounts vary each year based on the interest earned on the principal and new funds deposited through criminal fines and additional private and public donations. The people living in or near such habitats are intended to be the beneficiaries of the fund, on behalf of the habitats and their species. A request for proposals is typically released in late August with pre-proposals due in September and full proposals due in December.
Requirements: Organizations eligible to apply include: 501(c)3 registered non-profit conservation organizations; counties; local, state or federal government agencies; tribes; educational institutions; watershed councils; soil and water conservation districts; and other special districts.
Geographic Focus: Oregon
Contact: Cara Rose; (503) 417-8700, ext. 21; fax (503) 417-8787; cara.rose@nfwf.org
Internet: http://www.nfwf.org/AM/Template.cfm?Section=Who_We_Are&TEMPLATE=/CM/ContentDisplay.cfm&CONTENTID=6492
Sponsor: National Fish and Wildlife Foundation #6
1133 15th Street, NW, Suite 1100
Washington, DC 97205

NFWF Pacific Grassroots Salmonid Initiative Grants   3384
The Pacific Grassroots Salmonid Initiative (PGSI) is a partnership between the National Oceanic and Atmospheric Administration (NOAA) Restoration Center and the National Fish and Wildlife Foundation (the Foundation). PGSI seeks to benefit native anadromous fishes and their habitats along the Pacific Coast of the United States. A broad range of activities are eligible for funding, including: estuary and stream restoration; salmonid habitat conservation planning; applied research; and public education and outreach. The most competitive projects are those that: take place in priority estuaries or watersheds and target key salmon and steelhead populations and essential fish habitat as identified in federal, state, or local conservation management plans; have support from a variety of stakeholders; take a holistic approach; and use science-based, technically defensible methods. Administrative costs directly related to the project may be included. Awards will be focused on Alaska, Oregon, and California. Most grants range from $25,000 to $75,000 in Foundation federal funds, and have a project period between 12 to 18 months.
Requirements: Grantees must raise a minimum of one dollar of matching funds for the project for every dollar of Foundation federal grant funds. However, preference will be given to proposals with two dollars of matching funds to every dollar of Foundation federal grant funds.
Restrictions: Grant funds may not be used for: political advocacy or litigation, general administrative overhead, shortfalls in agency budgets, or basic research. For-profit businesses and federal agencies are not eligible for funding.
Geographic Focus: All States
Date(s) Application is Due: Dec 19
Contact: Claire Thorp; (415)243-3104 or (415) 778-0999; Claire.Thorp@nfwf.org
Internet: http://www.nfwf.org/AM/Template.cfm?Section=Browse_All_Programs&Template=/CM/ContentDisplay.cfm&ContentID=3991
Sponsor: National Fish and Wildlife Foundation
90 New Montgomery Street, Suite 700
San Francisco, CA 94105

NFWF Pierce County Community Salmon Fund Grants   3385
The National Fish and Wildlife Foundation (NFWF) and Pierce County have established the Community Salmon Fund to stimulate smaller-scale, voluntary action by community groups, in cooperation with landowners and businesses, to support salmon recovery on private property in Pierce County. The proposal must target salmon habitat enhancement and demonstrate that such projects will begin within 18 months from the date of the grant award. Grants will be jointly selected by Pierce County and NFWF and administered by the Foundation. This round, funding will also be available for projects aimed at engaging new partners in salmon recovery. The following costs are eligible: restoration of habitat within and along salmon-bearing rivers, streams, and the marine near shore; conservation easements and/or less-than-full-fee acquisitions; and project design and development that is anticipated to lead to an on-the-ground restoration project within 18 months. The Fund will award grants of up to $40,000.
Requirements: Federal, state, tribal, and local governments, educational institutions, and nonprofit conservation organizations are welcome to apply.
Restrictions: Full fee acquisition, freestanding educational projects, mitigation or corrective actions, general planning and studies, and legal or lobbying efforts are ineligible.
Geographic Focus: Washington
Date(s) Application is Due: May 23
Contact: Cara Rose; (503) 417-8700, ext. 21; fax (503) 417-8787; cara.rose@nfwf.org
Internet: http://www.nfwf.org/AM/Template.cfm?Section=Browse_All_Programs&Template=/TaggedPage/TaggedPageDisplay.cfm&TPLID=30&ContentID=6468
Sponsor: National Fish and Wildlife Foundation
806 SW Broadway, Suite 750
Portland, OR 97205

NFWF Pioneers in Conservation Grants   3386
The Pioneers in Conservation grants program is a partnership with the Washington State Conservation Commission. The goal of the program is to fund projects in the Puget Sound area that provide innovative, cost-effective benefits for restoring or protecting salmon habitat and a healthy environment on or directly affecting private agricultural or small private forest lands while complementing and supporting the economic viability of the agriculture or forestry business. The program is designed to help farms and small forest landowners provide on-the-ground benefits for salmon in Puget Sound's watersheds, facilitating the implementation of the Proposal for the Prosperity of Farming and Salmon in the Puget Sound Salmon Recovery Plan (adopted by NOAA Fisheries in January 2007) and strengthening ongoing farm-salmon partnerships. Projects are encouraged to be completed within two years. The following costs are eligible: materials and equipment; salaries, technical assistance; contracting and consulting; printing, copying, postage, etc; travel and transportation; and acquisition of real property interests. The maximum grant award is $75,000, but most grants will range from $25,000 to $50,000.
Requirements: Projects must include matching funds of at least 50% of the total grant request in non-federal funds funds (i.e. for a grant request of $40,000, an applicant would be expected to show at least $20,000 of matching funds, for a total project cost of $60,000).
Geographic Focus: All States
Date(s) Application is Due: Mar 28
Amount of Grant: Up to 75,000 USD
Contact: Cara Rose; (503) 417-8700, ext. 21; fax (503) 417-8787; cara.rose@nfwf.org
Internet: http://www.nfwf.org/AM/Template.cfm?Section=Who_We_Are&Template=/TaggedPage/TaggedPageDisplay.cfm&TPLID=30&ContentID=9121
Sponsor: National Fish and Wildlife Foundation
806 SW Broadway, Suite 750
Portland, OR 97205

NFWF Pulling Together Initiative Grants   3387
The program aims to create partnerships between local agencies, private landowners, and other interested parties in developing long-term weed management projects as part of an integrated pest management strategy. The goals of PTI are: to prevent, manage, or eradicate invasive and noxious plants through a coordinated program of public/private partnerships; and to increase public awareness of the adverse impacts of invasive and noxious plants. Prepoposals should be submitted inline by the October 26 due date, with full proposals due in January.
Requirements: Eligible applicants are partnerships of federal, state, and/or local government agencies, nonprofit organizations, private businesses, and landowners. The foundation makes challenge grants based on a two-to-one nonfederal funding match; awardees are required to supply remaining funds.
Geographic Focus: All States
Date(s) Application is Due: Jan 11; Oct 26
Amount of Grant: 10,000 - 100,000 USD
Contact: Ellen Gabel; (202) 857-0166; fax (202) 857-0162; ellen.gabel@nfwf.org
Internet: http://www.nfwf.org/AM/Template.cfm?Section=Who_We_Are&Template=/CM/ContentDisplay.cfm&ContentID=4790
Sponsor: National Fish and Wildlife Foundation #6
1133 15th Street, NW, Suite 1100
Washington, DC 97205

NFWF Radical Salmon Design Contest   3388
King County and the National Fish and Wildlife Foundation are sponsoring a competition to identify and field-test promising new techniques for salmon habitat restoration. The goal is to fund the design of up to four pilot habitat projects to promote new restoration techniques applicable to central Puget Sound. The design approach should take into consideration constraints and ongoing impacts typically encountered by restorationists. Four winning proposals will each receive up to $5,000 for design work. Designs must focus on habitat restoration on salmon-bearing water bodies in King County, Washington. Projects along Snohomish County streams that flow into King County are also eligible. Designs can range from simple to complex, but should be largely novel, practical, and easily replicable in developed and/or agricultural landscapes. Once designs are complete, the four winners will be evaluated again and the top design will receive a guarantee of funding for the eventual implementation costs of the project, up to $65,000, plus another $5,000 for the design work.

Requirements: Nonprofit organizations, community groups, tribes, and local governments are welcome to apply, as well as students and design consultants. Individuals or for-profit businesses submitting proposals are strongly encouraged to partner with a non-profit organization.
Geographic Focus: Washington
Date(s) Application is Due: Oct 31
Amount of Grant: 5,000 - 65,000 USD
Contact: Cara Rose; (503) 417-8700, ext. 21; fax (503) 417-8787; cara.rose@nfwf.org
Internet: http://www.nfwf.org/AM/Template.cfm?Section=Browse_All_Programs&Template=/TaggedPage/TaggedPageDisplay.cfm&TPLID=30&ContentID=6589
Sponsor: National Fish and Wildlife Foundation
806 SW Broadway, Suite 750
Portland, OR 97205

NFWF Salmon Recovery Funding Board Community Salmon Fund Grants 3389
Established to engage landowners, community groups, tribes, and businesses in salmon recovery within Washington State. NFWF has partnered with the Washington State Salmon Recovery Funding Board (SRFB) to administer a statewide Community Salmon Fund program that is coordinated with the individual Lead Entity groups. The program awards smaller-scale grants for salmon habitat protection and restoration projects that are marked by community involvement and watershed health benefits, and which are consistent with local salmon recovery plans. Salmon Recovery Funding Board Community Salmon Fund grant rounds are coordinated with each of the 27 Lead Entities in Washington State. Each Lead Entity has its own grant round, with its own Request for Proposals and unique timeline. Check the web site for details.
Requirements: Nonprofit organizations, community groups, tribes, and local governments are welcome to apply, as well as students and design consultants. Individuals or for-profit businesses submitting proposals are strongly encouraged to partner with a non-profit organization. *Restrictions:*
Geographic Focus: Washington
Contact: Cara Rose; (503) 417-8700, ext. 21; fax (503) 417-8787; cara.rose@nfwf.org
Internet: http://www.nfwf.org/AM/Template.cfm?Section=Browse_All_Programs&TEMPLATE=/CM/ContentDisplay.cfm&CONTENTID=9895
Sponsor: National Fish and Wildlife Foundation
806 SW Broadway, Suite 750
Portland, OR 97205

NFWF Seafarer's Environmental Education Fund Grants 3390
Together with the U.S. Coast Guard, the Foundation has established the Seafarer's Environmental Education Fund to begin a grant-making program to finance projects in the Commonwealth of Massachusetts and State of New York for the following purposes: to fund non-profit organizations providing environmental education to seafarers visiting or sailing from Massachusetts ports; and to fund non-profit organizations providing environmental education to seafarers visiting or sailing from the Port of New York. The Fund will support projects that have a strong likelihood of reducing the number and severity of violations related to illegal discharges from ships into the marine coastal or marine environment. It is intended that this Fund will support and implement the enforcement of environmental and marine wildlife protection laws in the Commonwealth of Massachusetts and State of New York, to improve fish, plant and wildlife resources. The people of Massachusetts and New York are intended to be the beneficiaries of the Fund, on behalf of the fish, plant and wildlife resources of the Commonwealth of Massachusetts and State of New York. Approximately $450,000 is available for projects addressing the Fund objectives in the Commonwealth of Massachusetts, and approximately $300,000 is available for projects addressing the Fund objectives in the State of New York. The pre-proposal deadline is October 1, with full proposals due on October 31.
Requirements: 501(c)3 registered non-profit organizations (including institutions of higher education) are eligible to apply.
Restrictions: The Fund cannot be used for political advocacy, boycotts, litigation expenses, terrorist activities or activities conducted in violation of the Foreign Corrupt Practices Act.
Geographic Focus: All States
Date(s) Application is Due: Oct 1; Oct 31
Contact: Gillian Harris; (415) 778-0999, ext. 233; gillian.harris@nfwf.org
Internet: http://www.nfwf.org/AM/Template.cfm?Section=Home&Template=/CM/ContentDisplay.cfm&ContentID=4680
Sponsor: National Fish and Wildlife Foundation
90 New Montgomery Street, Suite 700
San Francisco, CA 94105

NFWF Shell Marine Habitat Program Grants 3391
NFWF and Shell Oil Company Foundation fund natural resource conservation projects in the Gulf of Mexico. Projects will be funded that protect, conserve, restore, or enhance the Gulf coasts of Florida, from Tampa north; Mobile Bay, AL; coastal Louisiana, with an emphasis on the La Branche wetlands; and Port Arthur, Galveston Bay, and the Deer Park Ship Channel in Texas. Projects of interest include those that protect or restore estuarine habitat in the above geographic areas. Projects that include opportunities for hands-on participation by volunteers are of special interest. Focal species include brown pelicans, with an emphasis on habitat restoration and conservation of breeding sites. In addition, education programs intended to minimize harm from monofilament entanglement and other human impacts are of particular interest. Priority will be given to projects that build new or enhance existing partnerships and that address conservation needs of species characteristic of southeastern U.S. marine ecosystems. Preproposals must be submitted online by the listed application deadline. Application and guidelines are available online.

Requirements: Nonprofit IRS 501(c)3 tax-exempt organizations are eligible. Entities that are subdivisions of government (federal, state, county/parish, or city) are also eligible. Applicants must be based in the United States.
Restrictions: Individuals are not eligible for grants under this program. The program will not fund international projects, with very limited exceptions. The foundation will not fund political advocacy, lobbying, or litigation of any kind; shortfalls in government agency budgets; general administrative overhead or indirect costs of any kind; multiyear grants (applicant may reapply); or basic research.
Geographic Focus: All States
Date(s) Application is Due: Apr 1; Jun 1
Amount of Grant: 50,000 - 150,000 USD
Contact: Suzanne Sessine; (202) 857-0166; fax (202) 857-0162; Suzanne.Sessine@nfwf.org
Internet: http://www.nfwf.org/AM/Template.cfm?Section=Home&Template=/TaggedPage/TaggedPageDisplay.cfm&TPLID=32&ContentID=9173
Sponsor: National Fish and Wildlife Foundation #6
1133 15th Street, NW, Suite 1100
Washington, DC 97205

NFWF Southern Company Longleaf Legacy Program Grants 3392
The Longleaf Legacy Program is a partnership between the Southern Company and its four operating company affiliates (Alabama Power, Georgia Power, Gulf Power, and Mississippi Power) and the National Fish and Wildlife Foundation. The purpose of this partnership is to provide grants for longleaf pine ecosystem reforestation and conservation within the Southern Company service area of Georgia, Alabama, northwestern Florida, and southeastern Mississippi. Typical grant awards to date have ranged from $75,000 - $250,000. Higher requests will be considered if a multi-year project and/or will result in significant acreage restored. The Project area is Georgia, Alabama, Florida Panhandle (west of the Apalachicola River), southeast Mississippi (23 counties, from Meridian to the coast, with the west boundary running from Pearl River County to Union County). Preproposals are due by April 1, with final proposals due on or before June 1.
Requirements: All grant awards require a minimum 1:1 match of cash or contributed goods and services, of which at least 50% should be from non-federal sources. Nonprofit IRS 501(c)3 tax-exempt organizations are eligible. Entities that are subdivisions of government (federal, state, county/parish, or city) are also eligible. Applicants must be based in the United States.
Restrictions: Individuals are not eligible for grants under this program. The program will not fund international projects, with very limited exceptions. The foundation will not fund political advocacy, lobbying, or litigation of any kind; shortfalls in government agency budgets; general administrative overhead or indirect costs of any kind; multi-year grants (applicant may reapply); or basic research.
Geographic Focus: All States
Date(s) Application is Due: Apr 1; Jun 1
Amount of Grant: 75,000 - 250,000 USD
Contact: Suzanne Sessine; (202) 857-0166; fax (202) 857-0162; Suzanne.Sessine@nfwf.org
Internet: http://www.nfwf.org/AM/Template.cfm?Section=Browse_All_Programs&Template=/CM/ContentDisplay.cfm&ContentID=4027
Sponsor: National Fish and Wildlife Foundation #6
1133 15th Street, NW, Suite 1100
Washington, DC 97205

NFWF Southern Company Power of Flight Bird Conservation Grants 3393
The Power of Flight Bird Conservation Fund is a partnership between the Southern Company and its four operating companies, and the National Fish and Wildlife Foundation. The purpose of this partnership is to provide seed grants for bird conservation projects within the Southern Company service area of Georgia, Alabama, northwestern Florida, and southeastern Mississippi. Projects of interest include: habitat restoration and management; environmental education involving birds, particularly in urban areas; applied research with direct implications for management and conservation, and; nature tourism development. Priority will be given to projects that build new or enhance existing partnerships and that address conservation needs of species characteristic of the southern U.S. The Project area is Georgia, Alabama, Florida Panhandle (west of the Apalachicola River), southeast Mississippi (23 counties, from Meridian to the coast, with the west boundary running from Pearl River County to Union County). Preproposals are due by April 1, with final proposals due on or before June 1.
Requirements: All grant awards require a minimum 1:1 match of cash or contributed goods and services, of which at least 50% should be from non-federal sources. Nonprofit IRS 501(c)3 tax-exempt organizations are eligible. Entities that are subdivisions of government (federal, state, county/parish, or city) are also eligible. Applicants must be based in the United States.
Restrictions: Individuals are not eligible for grants under this program. The program will not fund international projects, with very limited exceptions. The foundation will not fund political advocacy, lobbying, or litigation of any kind; shortfalls in government agency budgets; general administrative overhead or indirect costs of any kind; multi-year grants (applicant may reapply); or basic research.
Geographic Focus: All States
Date(s) Application is Due: Apr 1; Jun 1
Amount of Grant: 30,000 - 100,000 USD
Contact: Suzanne Sessine; (202) 857-0166; fax (202) 857-0162; Suzanne.Sessine@nfwf.org
Internet: http://www.nfwf.org/AM/Template.cfm?Section=Browse_All_Programs&Template=/CM/ContentDisplay.cfm&ContentID=4029
Sponsor: National Fish and Wildlife Foundation #6
1133 15th Street, NW, Suite 1100
Washington, DC 97205

NFWF Southern Company Power of Flight Grants 3394
The Southern Company Power of Flight Program is a partnership between Southern Company, its four operating company affiliates (Alabama Power, Georgia Power, Gulf Power, and Mississippi Power) and the National Fish and Wildlife Foundation (NFWF). The purpose of this partnership is to provide grants that result in measurable benefits to key species and their habitats. The goal of the Grants is to address the conservation needs of high priority bird species characteristic of the southern United States, such as Red-cockaded Woodpecker, Northern Bobwhite, coastal waterbirds, and other imperiled species. Grants are awarded to support this goal and the following objectives: advance implementation of established conservation strategies; support the management of targeted bird species in order to enhance populations and the habitat on which they rely; accomplish on-the-ground habitat restoration projects that directly support targeted bird species; engage the public in education, monitoring and management activities that promote awareness about the importance of protecting and recovering priority bird species; strengthen our scientific understanding of priority species to enhance management decisions by practitioners and policy makers; utilize the East Gulf Coastal Plain Joint Venture Open Pine Decision Support Tool to target projects occurring in open pine systems (see map on website). Approximately a total of $550,000 will be available for annual awards. Applications are available on the website.
Requirements: Southern Company service area of Georgia, Alabama, northwestern Florida, and southeastern Mississippi are eligible.
Geographic Focus: Alabama, Florida, Georgia, Mississippi
Date(s) Application is Due: Apr 9
Contact: Suzanne Sessine; (202) 857-0166; fax (202) 857-0162; Suzanne.Sessine@nfwf.org
Internet: http://www.nfwf.org/AM/Template.cfm?Section=Charter_Programs_List&Template=/TaggedPage/TaggedPageDisplay.cfm&TPLID=60&ContentID=22341
Sponsor: National Fish and Wildlife Foundation #6
1133 15th Street, NW, Suite 1100
Washington, DC 97205

NFWF State Comprehensive Wildlife Conservation Support Grants 3395
The foundation seeks proposals for projects that involve collaboration and strategic coordination for the development and implementation of regional (multistate) and national conservation approaches based on State Comprehensive Wildlife Conservation Strategies (SCWCs). The three-year grant program supports enhancement of the SCWCSs. Projects must involve the coordination of conservation objectives/actions among at least two states and should address priorities identified by at least two SCWCs developed by the respective participating states. Projects may not exceed 18 months in duration, with preference given to projects that do not exceed 12 months. Grant funds may be used for staff salaries or contractual services; workshops; data collection/sharing/synchronization; creation of reports; creation of geo-spatially specific map products; information sharing; plan development assessments of habitat conditions, population demographics; risk analyses; and on-the-ground actions to conserve, manage, and/or enhance habitats or populations. Submit proposals via email. Application and guidelines are available online. Annual deadline dates may vary; contact program staff for exact dates.
Requirements: Eligible recipients include any state fish and wildlife agency (in partnership with at least one other state fish and wildlife agency); International Association of Fish and Wildlife Agencies; Midwest Association of Fish and Wildlife Agencies; Northeast Association of Fish and Wildlife Agencies; Southeastern Association of Fish and Wildlife Agencies; and Western Association of Fish and Wildlife Agencies.
Restrictions: The foundation will not provide grant funding for political advocacy, lobbying, or litigation of any kind. Grant funds may not be used to supplement shortfalls in government agency budgets or to support general administrative overhead or indirect costs. Funds may not be used to supplant or augment the development/implementation of any individual State Comprehensive Wildlife Conservation Strategy.
Geographic Focus: All States
Date(s) Application is Due: May 20
Amount of Grant: Up to 150,000 USD
Contact: Peter Stangel; (202) 857-0166; fax (202) 857-0162; Peter.Stangel@nfwf.org
Internet: http://www.nfwf.org/AM/Template.cfm?Section=Home&Template=/CM/HTMLDisplay.cfm&ContentID=4032
Sponsor: National Fish and Wildlife Foundation #6
1133 15th Street, NW, Suite 1100
Washington, DC 97205

NFWF Sustain Our Great Lakes Grants 3396
Sustain Our Great Lakes is a public-private partnership among ArcelorMittal, U.S. Environmental Protection Agency, U.S. Fish and Wildlife Service, U.S.D.A. Forest Service, National Fish and Wildlife Foundation, National Oceanic and Atmospheric Administration, and Natural Resources Conservation Service. Its mission is to sustain, restore and protect fish, wildlife and habitat in the Great Lakes basin by leveraging funding, building conservation capacity, and focusing partners and resources toward key ecological issues. The purpose of the Grants is to support on-the-ground habitat restoration and enhancement projects that simultaneously improve local habitat conditions and build local conservation capacity. Funding priority is assigned to improving the quality and connectivity of tributary, wetland and coastal habitats through the following action categories: restoration of aquatic connectivity; riparian and in-stream habitat restoration; wetland restoration; and near-shore/shoreline habitat restoration. Projects that receive funding typically: restore or enhance habitats at scales on the order of tens of acres or thousands of stream feet; help build local conservation capacity by incorporating training components into habitat restoration and enhancement work; apply the majority of grant funding to on-the-ground habitat improvement work; have completed planning, design and engineering stages; and include pre- and post-implementation monitoring to document habitat improvements and other project outcomes. Pre-proposal applications must be submitted on-line. Full proposals are by invitation only.
Requirements: Eligible applicants include: non-profit 501(c) organizations; state, tribal, provincial and local governments; and educational institutions. Eligible projects must: occur within the Great Lakes basin and direct the majority of grant funding (more than 50%) toward on-the-ground habitat restoration. The ratio of matching funds offered is one review criterion, and projects that meet or exceed a 1:1 match ratio will tend to be more competitive.
Restrictions: Individuals, federal agencies, and private for-profit firms are not eligible. Grant funding will not be provided for land protection (e.g., acquisition and easement), rain barrels, rain gardens, green roofs, or research. Projects that seek funding for political advocacy, lobbying, litigation, fundraising, or legally mandated mitigation projects are not eligible.
Geographic Focus: All States
Amount of Grant: 25,000 - 150,000 USD
Contact: Todd Hogrefe; (612) 564-7286; todd.hogrefe@nfwf.org
Internet: http://www.nfwf.org/AM/Template.cfm?Section=Home&CONTENTID=22364&TEMPLATE=/CM/ContentDisplay.cfm
Sponsor: National Fish and Wildlife Foundation #6
1133 15th Street, NW, Suite 1100
Washington, DC 97205

NFWF Tampa Bay Environmental Fund Grants 3397
The Tampa Bay Environmental Fund (TBEF) provides funding through a competitive application process for projects that will protect, restore or enhance the natural resources of Tampa Bay. TBEF funds projects that will implement the habitat, species, and nutrient reduction priorities that have been developed by the Tampa Bay Estuary Program and its partners, and outlined in the Comprehensive Conservation and Management Plan. See the website to review the plan. Application requires a pre-proposal with full proposals by invitation only. Check the website for the most recent request for proposal to verify due dates.
Requirements: Local, state, and federal government; non-profit organizations; private firms; and educational institutions are eligible to apply. Projects require a minimum 1:1 match of non-federal funds or contributed goods and services. The geographic focus is the Tampa Bay Watershed (Pinellas, Hillsborough, Manatee, Pasco, and Polk counties within Watershed).
Restrictions: Grants cannot be used for political advocacy, fundraising, lobbying or litigation activities or to support projects resulting from legally mandated mitigation projects.
Geographic Focus: Florida
Amount of Grant: 50,000 - 200,000 USD
Contact: Suzanne Sessine; (202) 857-0166; fax (202) 857-0162; Suzanne.Sessine@nfwf.org
Internet: http://www.nfwf.org/AM/Template.cfm?Section=Who_We_Are&CONTENTID=9966&TEMPLATE=/CM/ContentDisplay.cfm
Sponsor: National Fish and Wildlife Foundation #6
1133 15th Street, NW, Suite 1100
Washington, DC 97205

NFWF Upper Mississippi River Watershed Fund Grants 3398
The Upper Mississippi River Watershed Fund (UMRWF) is a partnership between the USDA Forest Service and the National Fish and Wildlife Foundation. This partnership will provide grants that benefit the stewardship of the forests and the restoration of watersheds in the Upper Mississippi River drainage. See the website to verify availability of funding and application deadlines.
Requirements: Eligible applicants include non-profit 501(c) organizations, and local, and state units of governments. All grant awards require a minimum 1:1 match of cash or contributed goods and services, of which at least 50% should be from non-federal sources.
Restrictions: Grant funds from the UMRWF cannot be used for political advocacy, lobbying, litigation or mitigation projects, general administrative overhead or indirect expenses, clothing, food, and fundraising.
Geographic Focus: All States
Amount of Grant: 15,000 - 75,000 USD
Contact: John Curry; (612) 713-5173; fax (612) 713-5285; john.curry@nfwf.org
Internet: http://www.nfwf.org/AM/Template.cfm?Section=Browse_All_Programs&Template=/CM/ContentDisplay.cfm&ContentID=4037
Sponsor: National Fish and Wildlife Foundation #6
1133 15th Street, NW, Suite 1100
Washington, DC 97205

NFWF Wildlife and Habitat Conservation Initiative Grants 3399
The National Fish and Wildlife Foundation and its partners have keystone initiatives which are the core portfolio of multi-year initiatives through which they seek to achieve measurable outcomes. The Wildlife and Habitat Conservation Initiative addresses conservation needs for mammals, reptiles, amphibians, invertebrates, and plants, as well as landscape-level and issue-based conservation. The goal is to find the best conservation investments, fund the best solutions, and deliver measurable results for wildlife. Under this mission statement, there are selected initiatives focused on making a measureable impact on specific species and their habitats. Individual initiatives are listed on the website and are focused under three themes which are imperiled wildlife species, wildlife movement and migration, and climate change and adaptation. Application is made online from the website.
Requirements: Applicants should review the business plans for this initiative and prepare application materials accordingly. Prospective applicants should contact the Director to discuss project ideas prior to submitting proposals to help ensure the relevance of funding requests. The Foundation will consider multi-year funding for important projects, subject to annual performance review of the grantee. A minimum 1:1 match is required for most Foundation grants, and higher ratios of match to Foundation funds are desired and improve the competitiveness of applications.
Geographic Focus: All States
Date(s) Application is Due: Aug 1; Dec 1

Amount of Grant: 50,000 - 375,000 USD
Contact: Carly Vynne; (202) 857-0166; fax (202) 857-0162
Internet: http://www.nfwf.org/am/template.cfm?section=Wildlife_and_Habitat12
Sponsor: National Fish and Wildlife Foundation #6
1133 15th Street, NW, Suite 1100
Washington, DC 97205

NFWF Wildlife Links Grants　　3400
The purpose of the Wildlife Links program is to fund research, management, and education projects that will enhance wildlife management on golf courses on at least a state-wide, and preferably a region-wide or national basis. Native pollinators, aquatic invertebrates, reptiles and amphibians, birds, and small mammals are all priorities for Wildlife Links. Preference will be given to projects that: build upon previous Wildlife Links grants; support State Comprehensive Wildlife Conservation Strategies; complement other ongoing conservation programs, such as Partners in Flight, Partners for Amphibian and Reptile Conservation, etc; enhance recovery efforts for declining species; help keep common species common; examine course management and design options for increasing biodiversity; determine the roles of habitat characteristics in the designation of golf courses as wildlife corridors or barriers; and study the impact of golf course maintenance activities on wildlife. Preproposals are due April 1, and the deadline for full proposal submission is June 1.
Requirements: Eligible applicants are U.S. 501(c)3 nonprofit organizations and universities. The foundation makes challenge grants based on a two-to-one nonfederal funding match; awardees are required to supply remaining funds.
Restrictions: Funding is not available for habitat improvements on individual courses (butterfly gardens, nest box trails, etc.).
Geographic Focus: All States
Date(s) Application is Due: Apr 1; Jun 1
Amount of Grant: Up to 30,000 USD
Contact: Peter Stangel, (202) 857-0166; fax (202) 857-0162; Peter.Stangel@nfwf.org
Internet: http://www.nfwf.org/AM/Template.cfm?Section=Home&Template=/CM/ContentDisplay.cfm&ContentID=4044
Sponsor: National Fish and Wildlife Foundation #6
1133 15th Street, NW, Suite 1100
Washington, DC 97205

NGA 'Remember Me' Rose School Garden Awards　　3401
Sponsored by All-America Rose Selections, this program is designed to help schools and youth organizations establish gardens to honor the lives of those lost on the attacks of September 11, 2001. These garden programs must also be integrated with education in conflict resolution and mediation skills. The ultimate goal is to give students the skills they need to seek and achieve fair and peaceful solutions. Twenty school gardens will each receive 15 to 20 bare-root rose bushes (valued at about $600) from All-America Rose Selections (AARS), and educational materials from NGA.
Requirements: Schools or community organizations across the United States who plan to garden with at least 15 children between the ages of 3 and 18 are eligible. To apply, download and complete an application form (see website).
Restrictions: Employees of All-America Rose Selections and the National Gardening Association are not eligible for this award.
Geographic Focus: All States
Amount of Grant: 600 USD
Contact: Donna Booska, (800) 538-7476, ext. 115; fax (802) 864-6889; donna@garden.org
Internet: http://www.kidsgardening.com/Dig/DigDetail.taf?ID=2116&Type=Art
Sponsor: National Gardening Association
1100 Dorset Street
South Burlington, VT 05403

NGA Hansen's Natural and Native School Garden Grants　　3402
To promote the benefits of using native plants and foster the installation of naturalized gardens in San Francisco Bay schoolyards, Hansen's is sponsoring the Hansen's Natural and Native School Garden Grants. Through this program, 3 schools in the San Francisco Bay area will receive a Hansen's Natural and Native Planting Kit valued at $1,500, including a variety of native plants and gardening supplies.
Requirements: Preschool, elementary, and middle schools located in the following San Francisco Bay Area counties are eligible: San Francisco, Alameda, Contra Costa, Marin, San Mateo, Santa Clara, Solano, Sonoma, and Napa. Educators must use the garden to teach students about the role of indigenous plants in their local ecosystem, benefits of using native plants in the landscape, and concerns surrounding invasive plant species. Established and start-up garden programs are encouraged to apply. Schools must have 250 square feet available for the new plant materials. The garden must be planted during the fall. Winning schools must be willing to collaborate on press releases and at least 1 school will be selected to host a media event on October 16. No purchase necessary. Purchase of a product does not improve your chances of receiving an award.
Restrictions: Each school will also be required to submit a final report by May, summarizing program accomplishments and impacts.
Geographic Focus: California
Date(s) Application is Due: Sep 25
Contact: Amanda Wiggins; (802) 863-5251; fax (802) 864-6889; amandaw@garden.org
Internet: http://www.kidsgardening.org/grants/naturalandnative.asp
Sponsor: National Gardening Association
1100 Dorset Street
South Burlington, VT 05403

NGA Healthy Sprouts Awards　　3403
The association and Gardener's Supply Company support schools and community organizations that use gardens to teach about nutrition and explore the issue of hunger in the United States. Each of 25 programs receives an award package of seeds, tools, garden products, and educational resources for growing a vegetable garden. Five of these programs also receive a certificate valued at $500; 15 more will each receive a $200 gift certificate. The gift certificates are for the purchase of gardening materials from the sponsoring company, Gardener's Supply.
Requirements: Eligible applicants include schools or nonprofit organizations which must plan to garden with at least 15 children between the ages of 3 and 18. The selection of winners is based on the demonstrated relationship between the garden program and nutrition and hunger issues in the United States. At least 10 percent of the food produced from the program should be donated. Guidelines and application are available online.
Restrictions: Grant awardees will be required to submit a year-end impact report. Programs that do not complete the final report will not be eligible to apply for future awards.
Geographic Focus: All States
Contact: Donna Booska, (800) 538-7476, ext. 115; fax (802) 864-6889; donna@garden.org
Internet: http://www.kidsgardening.com/healthysprouts.asp
Sponsor: National Gardening Association
1100 Dorset Street
South Burlington, VT 05403

NGA Heinz Wholesome Memories Intergenerational Garden Awards　　3404
Recognizing the power of gardens to connect individuals of all ages socially, culturally, and emotionally, the H. J. Heinz Company is proud to sponsor the Heinz Wholesome Memories Intergenerational Garden Award, designed to foster family-focused garden efforts in communities across the country. The award will provide 57 families with the tools needed to embark on a successful gardening adventure that will foster lasting intergenerational memories while growing wholesome food. Winning applicants will receive a $500 award package.
Requirements: The award is open to any adult in the United States who wishes to garden with preschool to high school-aged family member(s) and feels that gardening is a great way to build lasting memories. A focus on nutrition, sustainability, and socialization is a plus. No prior gardening experience necessary. The garden can be established and grown in any suitable outdoor setting such as home, rooftop, deck, school yard, community garden, church garden, etc. No purchase necessary. Purchase of a product does not improve your chances of receiving an award.
Restrictions: Award recipients will be required to submit a one-page summary about their family's gardening experience and at least one photo.
Geographic Focus: All States
Date(s) Application is Due: Jan 10
Contact: Amanda Wiggins; (802) 863-5251; fax (802) 864-6889; amandaw@garden.org
Internet: http://www.kidsgardening.com/grants/heinz.asp
Sponsor: National Gardening Association
1100 Dorset Street
South Burlington, VT 05403

NGA Hooked on Hydroponics Awards　　3405
This program, sponsored by the The Grow Store in conjunction with the Progressive Gardening Trade Association, awards a compact hydroponics package that includes everything required to grow plants successfully indoors. 24 winning schools will each receive: Hydroponic garden systems and indoor light systems (high-intensity discharge or compact fluorescent). Hydroponic garden packages are comprised of various system types, including flood and drain (a.k.a., ebb and flow), nutrient film technique, capillary (a.k.a., wick), and aeroponic systems; curricula and activity books and other supporting materials. Grants are distributed as follows: elementary Schools—6 grants; middle Schools—8 grants; high schools—10 grants.
Requirements: Schools and youth organizations that plan to garden with at least 15 children between the ages of 6 and 18 are eligible to apply. Request an application from the website - applications will be sent only to addresses in Canada, U.S. and U.S. Territories.
Restrictions: Winners must complete and return the Agreement of Use form. Award fulfillment is contingent upon receipt of this form by NGA.
Geographic Focus: All States
Contact: Donna Booska, (800) 538-7476, ext. 115; fax (802) 864-6889; donna@garden.org
Internet: http://www.kidsgardening.com/grants/HOH.asp
Sponsor: National Gardening Association
1100 Dorset Street
South Burlington, VT 05403

NGA Mantis Award　　3406
This program is designed to support and recognize charitable and educational garden programs that enhance the quality of life in their host communities. In the past, winners have included schools, churches, correctional facilities, parks departments, youth camps, community gardens, and many others. The program awards one of 25 Mantis tiller/cultivators (each complete with border edger attachment) for a garden program.
Requirements: The garden program must be charitable or educational in nature.
Restrictions: The award must not use the prize for fundraising (i.e., a raffle or auction). Download the application from the website.
Geographic Focus: All States
Date(s) Application is Due: Mar 1
Contact: Donna Booska, (800) 538-7476, ext. 115; fax (802) 864-6889; donna@garden.org
Internet: http://www.kidsgardening.com/grants/mantis.asp
Sponsor: National Gardening Association
1100 Dorset Street
South Burlington, VT 05403

NGA Midwest School Garden Grants 3407

The Grandchildren of Helene and Mark Eisner will sponsor 10 schools in Midwestern states through the National Gardening Association's Adopt a School Garden program. In addition to receiving technical assistance, and horticultural and garden education consultation from the ASG program, winners will also receive $1,000 in materials and funding to lay the foundation for their garden program.

Requirements: Elementary, middle, and high schools serving low- to middle-income students located in Illinois, Indiana, Iowa, Kansas, Michigan, Minnesota, Missouri, Nebraska, North Dakota, Ohio, South Dakota, and Wisconsin are eligible. Educators should be planning to use the garden to teach students life skills, reinforce academics, develop environmental stewardship, and encourage students to make positive choices for themselves and the planet. Both established and start-up garden programs are encouraged to apply. The required application form can be downloaded from the website. No purchase necessary. Purchase of a product does not improve your chances of receiving an award.

Geographic Focus: Illinois, Indiana, Iowa, Kansas, Michigan, Minnesota, Missouri, Nebraska, North Dakota, Ohio, South Dakota, Wisconsin

Date(s) Application is Due: Feb 12

Amount of Grant: 1,000 USD

Contact: Donna Booska, (800) 538-7476, ext. 115; fax (802) 864-6889; donnab@garden.org

Internet: http://www.kidsgardening.org/grants/MidwestASG.asp

Sponsor: National Gardening Association
1100 Dorset Street
South Burlington, VT 05403

NGA Wuzzleburg Preschool Garden Awards 3408

Wow! Wow! Wubbzy!, an animated television series for preschoolers, is sponsoring this award to give children ages 3-5 valuable gardening opportunities. Such gardening is a hands-on project that allows these children to explore at their own pace and engage in age-appropriate experiential learning. The grants are open to organizations offering structured programs in settings such as preschools, day care centers, and Head Start programs. 75 winners will each receive an assortment of garden tools and garden- and nature-oriented teaching materials valued at $1,000.

Requirements: Applicants must plan to garden with a group of at least 10 children aged 3 to 5 during the implementation stage of the program.

Geographic Focus: All States

Date(s) Application is Due: Mar 15

Amount of Grant: 1,000 USD

Contact: Donna Booska, (800) 538-7476, ext. 115; fax (802) 864-6889; donna@garden.org

Internet: http://www.kidsgardening.com/grants/2008-wubbzy.asp

Sponsor: National Gardening Association
1100 Dorset Street
South Burlington, VT 05403

NGA Youth Garden Grants 3409

Sponsored by Home Depot and Gardening With Kids, the program awards grants to schools and community organizations with child-centered garden programs. In evaluating grant applications, priority will be given to programs that emphasize one or more of these elements: educational focus or curricular/program integration; environmental awareness/education; entrepreneurship; social aspects of gardening such as leadership development, team building, community support, or service-learning. Five (5) programs will receive gift cards valued at $1000 (a $500 gift card to The Home Depot and a $500 gift card to the Gardening with Kids catalog and store) and educational materials; seventy (70) programs will receive a $500 gift card to The Home Depot and educational materials; and fifty (50) programs will receive a $250 gift card to The Home Depot and educational materials.

Requirements: Schools, youth groups, community centers, camps, clubs, treatment facilities, and intergenerational groups throughout the United States are eligible. Applicants must plan to garden in with at least 15 children between the ages of 3 and 18 years. Previous grant winners who wish to reapply must wait one year and have significantly expanded their garden programs. Guidelines and application are available at the website.

Geographic Focus: All States

Date(s) Application is Due: Nov 2

Amount of Grant: 250 - 1,000 USD

Contact: Donna Booska, (800) 538-7476, ext. 115; fax (802) 864-6889; donna@garden.org

Internet: http://www.kidsgardening.com/YGG.asp

Sponsor: National Gardening Association
1100 Dorset Street
South Burlington, VT 05403

NHLBI Ancillary Studies in Clinical Trials 3410

This funding opportunity invites research grant applications to conduct time-sensitive ancillary studies related to heart, lung, and blood diseases and sleep disorders in conjunction with ongoing clinical trials and other large clinical studies supported by NIH or non-NIH entities. The program establishes an accelerated review/award process to support the crucial time frame in which these ancillary studies must be performed. Time-sensitive ancillary studies include those that require active longitudinal data collection and thus need to begin recruiting subjects as close as possible to the start of the parent study. The ancillary study can address any research questions related to the mission of NHLBI for which the parent study can provide participants, infrastructure, and data. The parent studies most often will be a clinical trial, but also can be an observational study or registry that can provide a sufficient cohort of well-characterized patients. Each ancillary study application must demonstrate the time-sensitive nature of the application and must explicitly address why an expedited review is essential to its feasibility. Applications are due May 24, September 24, and January 24 by 5:00 pm local time of applicant.

Requirements: The following may apply: public/state controlled and private institutions of higher education; nonprofits with or without 501(c)3 IRS status (other than institutions of higher education); small businesses; for-profit organizations (other than small businesses); state, county, city or township governments; special district governments; Indian/Native American Tribal governments; eligible agencies of the Federal government; U.S. territory or possession; independent school districts; public housing authorities/Indian housing authorities; faith-based or community-based organizations; regional organizations; non-domestic (non-U.S.) entities (Foreign Institutions). The following types of Higher Education Institutions are always encouraged to apply for NIH support as public or private institutions of higher education: Hispanic-serving institutions; historically Black colleges and universities; Tribally controlled colleges and universities; Alaska Native and Native Hawaiian serving institutions. Non-domestic (non-U.S.) components of U.S. Organizations are eligible to apply. Any individual(s) with the skills, knowledge, and resources necessary to carry out the proposed research as the Program Director/Principal Investigator (PD/PI) is invited to work with his/her organization to develop an application for support. Individuals from underrepresented racial and ethnic groups as well as individuals with disabilities are always encouraged to apply for NIH support. An application may request a budget for direct costs up to $250,000 (10 modules) per year, excluding subcontractor or consortium facilities and administrative (F&A) costs. The scope of the proposed project should determine the project period. The maximum project period is four years.

Geographic Focus: All States, Guam, Marshall Islands, Northern Mariana Islands, Puerto Rico, U.S. Virgin Islands, All Countries, American Samoa

Date(s) Application is Due: Jan 24; May 24; Sep 24

Contact: Suzanne Goldberg, (301) 435-0532; fax (301) 480-3667; goldbergsh@mail.nih.gov

Internet: http://grants.nih.gov/grants/guide/rfa-files/RFA-HL-14-004.html

Sponsor: National Institutes of Health
Building 31, Room 5A48
Bethesda, MD 20892

NHLBI Bioengineering and Obesity Grants 3411

This funding opportunity solicits Research Project Grant (R01) applications from institutions/organizations that propose to solicit applications to develop and validate new and innovative engineering approaches to address clinical problems related to energy balance, intake, and expenditure. Novel sensors, devices, imaging, and other technologies, including technologies to detect biochemical markers of energy balance are expected to be developed and evaluated by collaborating engineers, physical scientists, mathematicians, and scientists from other relevant disciplines with expertise in obesity and nutrition. Because the nature and scope of the proposed research will vary from application to application, it is anticipated that the size and duration of each award will also vary. The total amount awarded and the number of awards will depend upon the mechanism numbers, quality, duration, and costs of the applications received.

Requirements: The following are eligible to apply: public/state controlled and private institutions of higher education; nonprofit with or without 501(c)3 IRS status (other than institution of higher education); small business; for-profit organization (other than small business); state government; U.S. Territory or Possession; Indian/Native American tribal government (federally recognized); Indian/Native American tribal government (other than federally recognized); Indian/Native American tribally designated organization; Non-domestic (non-U.S.) entity (foreign organization); Hispanic-serving institution; historically Black colleges and universities (HBCUs); tribally controlled colleges and universities (TCCUs); Alaska Native and Native Hawaiian serving institutions; regional organizations. Individuals with the skills, knowledge, and resources necessary to carry out the proposed research are invited to work with their institution/organization to develop an application for support. Individuals from underrepresented racial and ethnic groups as well as individuals with disabilities are always encouraged to apply for NIH support. More than one PD/PI, or multiple PDs/PIs, may be designated on the application. Applicants may submit more than one application, provided each application is scientifically distinct.

Geographic Focus: All States, Guam, Marshall Islands, Northern Mariana Islands, Puerto Rico, U.S. Virgin Islands, American Samoa

Date(s) Application is Due: Jan 25

Contact: Abby G. Ershow, (301) 435-0550; fax (301) 480-2858; ErshowA@mail.nih.gov

Internet: http://grants.nih.gov/grants/guide/pa-files/PA-07-354.html

Sponsor: National Institutes of Health
Building 31, Room 5A48
Bethesda, MD 20892

NHLBI Career Transition Awards 3412

The purpose of the NHLBI Career Transition Award (K22) program is to provide highly qualified postdoctoral fellows with an opportunity to receive mentored research experience in the NHLBI Division of Intramural Research and then to provide them with funding to facilitate the transition of their research programs as new investigators to extramural institutions. To achieve these objectives, the NHLBI Career Transition Award will support two phases of research: a mentored intramural phase (two years) and an extramural phase (three years), for a total of five years of combined support. Transition from the intramural phase of support to the extramural phase is not automatic. Approval of the transition will be based on the success of the awardees research program as determined by an NHLBI progress review, which will include an evaluation of a research plan to be carried out at the extramural institution. The total period of support is five years (two years intramural, plus three years extramural). Awards are not renewable. Applications are due by 5:00 pm local time of the applicant organization (see dates below).

Requirements: The following organizations are eligible to apply: public/state controlled and private institutions of higher education; Hispanic-serving institutions; historically black colleges and universities; tribally controlled colleges and universities; Alaska Native and Native Hawaiian serving institutions; nonprofits with or without 501(c)3 IRS status (other

than institutions of higher education); small businesses; for-profit organizations (other than small businesses); state, county, and city/township governments; special district governments; Indian/Native American tribal governments (federally recognized and other than federally recognized); eligible agencies of the Federal government; U.S. territory or possession; independent school districts; public or Indiana housing authorities; Native American tribal organizations (other than federally recognized tribal governments); faith-based or community-based organizations; and regional organizations. Applicant organizations may submit more than one application, provided that each application is scientifically distinct. By the time of award, the individual must be a citizen or a non-citizen national of the United States or have been lawfully admitted for permanent residence. Candidates for this award must have earned a terminal clinical or research doctorate (including PhD, MD, DO, DC, ND, DDS, DVM, ScD, DNS, PharmD., or equivalent doctoral degree), or a combined clinical and research doctoral degree. The candidate must have postdoctoral research experience, during which the potential for highly productive basic or clinical research was demonstrated. Individuals from underrepresented racial and ethnic groups as well as individuals with disabilities are always encouraged to apply for NIH support. During the intramural phase of the award, the candidate will spend full time on research. The required research experience must be completed in an intramural NIH laboratory. To obtain support for the extramural phase, at the time of the award candidates must have a full time formal tenure-track (or equivalent) appointment offer at the academic institution that is the applicant institution. Candidates who have VA appointments may not consider part of the VA effort toward satisfying the full time requirement at the applicant institution. Candidates with VA appointments should contact the NHLBI staff prior to preparing an application to discuss their eligibility. Support for the extramural phase will be provided to the extramural institution. Total direct costs for the extramural phase cannot exceed $249,000, including fringe benefits, per year. The total costs cannot exceed $747,000 for the three-year period.
Restrictions: NIH will not accept any application that is essentially the same as one already reviewed. An individual may not have two or more competing NIH career development applications pending review concurrently. Non-domestic (non-U.S.) entities (foreign institutions) and non-domestic (non-U.S.) components of U.S. organizations are not eligible to apply. Multiple Principal Investigators are not allowed.
Geographic Focus: All States, Guam, Marshall Islands, Northern Mariana Islands, Puerto Rico, U.S. Virgin Islands, American Samoa
Date(s) Application is Due: Feb 12; Jun 11; Oct 12
Amount of Grant: Up to 747,000 USD
Contact: Herbert M. Geller; (301) 451-9440; direducation@nhlbi.nih.gov
Internet: http://grants.nih.gov/grants/guide/pa-files/PAR-12-137.html
Sponsor: National Institutes of Health
Building 31, Room 5A48
Bethesda, MD 20892

NHLBI Investigator Initiated Multi-Site Clinical Trials 3413
The support of multi-site clinical trials is one strategy NHLBI uses to improve the understanding of the clinical mechanisms of disease and to improve prevention, diagnosis, and treatment. The purpose of this opportunity is to provide a vehicle for submitting grant applications for investigator-initiated multi-site randomized controlled clinical trials. The trials may address any research question related to the mission and goals of the NHLBI and may test clinical or behavioral interventions. The funding opportunity is appropriate for applications to conduct phase II and phase III randomized clinical trials where participants are recruited from multiple sites. Large-scale pragmatic trials (such as comparative effectiveness trials) as well as trials designed to test efficacy of an intervention are appropriate. The trials may randomize at the individual (patient) level or at a group level (e.g., randomization of clinics, schools, worksites, etc.). Clinical trials involving NHLBI mission-related rare diseases that require coordination across multiple clinical sites are also suitable for submission to this funding opportunity. In any case, the trial should propose the most efficient study design to complete the specific aims. The maximum project period is 5 years.
Requirements: The following organizations are eligible to apply: public/state controlled and private institutions of higher education; Hispanic-serving institutions; historically black colleges and universities; tribally controlled colleges and universities; Alaska Native and Native Hawaiian serving institutions; Asian American Native American Pacific Islander serving institutions; nonprofits with or without 501(c)3 IRS status (other than institutions of higher education); small businesses; for-profit organizations (other than small businesses); state, county, and city/township governments; special district governments; Indian/Native American tribal governments (federally recognized and other than federally recognized); eligible agencies of the Federal government; U.S. territory or possession; independent school districts; public or Indiana housing authorities; Native American tribal organizations (other than federally recognized tribal governments); faith-based or community-based organizations; regional organizations; and non-domestic (non-U.S.) entities (foreign institutions) and non-domestic (non-U.S.) components of U.S. organizations. Clinical Coordination Center (CCC) and Data Coordination Center (DCC) applications are required to be submitted together when the proposed costs of the clinical trial exceed $500,000 (minus F&A for subcontracts) in any given year. Any individual(s) with the skills, knowledge, and resources necessary to carry out the proposed research as the Program Director(s)/Principal Investigator(s) (PD(s)/PI(s)) is invited to work with his/her organization to develop an application for support. Individuals from underrepresented racial and ethnic groups as well as individuals with disabilities are always encouraged to apply for NIH support.
Geographic Focus: All States, All Countries
Date(s) Application is Due: Feb 12; Jun 12; Oct 12
Contact: David J. Gordon, (301) 435-0564; fax (301) 480-7971; gordond@nhlbi.nih.gov
Internet: http://grants.nih.gov/grants/guide/pa-files/PAR-13-128.html
Sponsor: National Institutes of Health
Building 31, Room 5A48
Bethesda, MD 20892

NHLBI Lymphatics in Health and Disease in the Digestive, Cardiovascular and Pulmonary Systems 3414
This program encourages Exploratory/Developmental Grant (R21) applications for research into aspects of lymphatic vessel physiology and pathophysiology related to health and disease of digestive, cardiovascular and pulmonary system organs and resolution of thromboembolic events, and inflammation and immune responses as they relate to these diseases. However, studies with the major focus on immune mechanisms will not be considered responsive. Studies to understand the factors that control local lymphatic vessel functional anatomy and physiology during health or disease in these organs and systems, and the mechanisms by which alterations of lymphatic vessel function affect organ function, are of interest. Specific areas of interests for the National Heart, Lung, and Blood Institute (NHLBI) include approaches that will identify the genetic, molecular, and cellular defects that contribute to congenital malformation of the lymphatic system; congenital-lymphatic-malformation-induced pulmonary dysfunction; whether and how lymphangiogenesis affects cardiovascular and pulmonary diseases; whether and how lymphatic drainage affects transplant of heart or lungs; whether and how lymphatic vessel hyperplasia in the dermal interstitium is involved in salt-sensitive hypertension; and whether and how the manipulation of platelet-lymphatic endothelial cell interaction may provide clinical benefit during thromboembolic events.
Requirements: The following organizations and institutions are eligible to apply: public/state controlled and private institutions of higher education; Hispanic-serving institutions; historically Black colleges and universities (HBCUs); Tribally controlled colleges and universities (TCCUs); Alaska Native and Native Hawaiian serving institutions; Nonprofits with or without 501(c)3 IRS status; small businesses; for-profit organizations; state, county, or city/township governments; special district governments; Indian/Native American tribal governments; Indian/Native American tribally designated organizations; independent school districts; public housing authorities/Indian housing authorities; U.S. territory or possession; Indian/Native American tribal governments (other than federally recognized); regional organizations; non-domestic (non-U.S.) entities (foreign organizations); other eligible agencies of the federal government; and faith-based or community-based organizations. Non-domestic (non-U.S.) components of U.S. Organizations are also eligible to apply. Applicant organizations may submit more than one application, provided that each application is scientifically distinct. Any individual(s) with the skills, knowledge, and resources necessary to carry out the proposed research as the Program Director(s)/Principal Investigator(s) (PD(s)/PI(s)) is invited to work with his/her organization to develop an application for support. Individuals from underrepresented racial and ethnic groups as well as individuals with disabilities are always encouraged to apply for NIH support.
Geographic Focus: All States, Guam, Marshall Islands, Northern Mariana Islands, Puerto Rico, U.S. Virgin Islands, All Countries
Date(s) Application is Due: Feb 16; Jun 16; Oct 16
Contact: H. Eser Tolunay, Ph.D.; (301) 435-0560; Eser.Tolunay@nih.gov
Internet: http://grants.nih.gov/grants/guide/pa-files/PAR-12-260.html
Sponsor: National Institutes of Health
Building 31, Room 5A48
Bethesda, MD 20892

NHLBI Lymphatics in Health and Disease in the Digestive, Urinary, Cardiovascular and Pulmonary Systems 3415
This program is to encourage Research Project Grant (R01) applications for research into aspects of lymphatic vessel physiology and pathophysiology related to health and disease of digestive system and urinary tract organs, and cardiovascular and pulmonary systems; in resolution of thromboembolic events; and inflammation and immune responses as they relate to these diseases. However, studies with the major focus on immune mechanisms will not be considered responsive. Studies to understand the factors that control local lymphatic vessel functional anatomy and physiology during health or disease in these organs/systems, and the mechanisms by which alterations of lymphatic vessel function affect organ function, are of interest. Applications must be received by 5:00 PM local time of applicant organization.
Requirements: The following organizations and institutions are eligible to apply: public/state controlled and private institutions of higher education; Hispanic-serving institutions; historically Black colleges and universities (HBCUs); Tribally controlled colleges and universities (TCCUs); Alaska Native and Native Hawaiian serving institutions; Nonprofits with or without 501(c)3 IRS status; small businesses; for-profit organizations; state, county, or city/township governments; special district governments; Indian/Native American tribal governments; Indian/Native American tribally designated organizations; independent school districts; public housing authorities/Indian housing authorities; U.S. territory or possession; Indian/Native American tribal governments (other than federally recognized); regional organizations; non-domestic (non-U.S.) entities (foreign organizations); other eligible agencies of the federal government; and faith-based or community-based organizations. Non-domestic (non-U.S.) components of U.S. Organizations are also eligible to apply. Applicant organizations may submit more than one application, provided that each application is scientifically distinct. Any individual(s) with the skills, knowledge, and resources necessary to carry out the proposed research as the Program Director(s)/Principal Investigator(s) (PD(s)/PI(s)) is invited to work with his/her organization to develop an application for support. Individuals from underrepresented racial and ethnic groups as well as individuals with disabilities are always encouraged to apply for NIH support.
Restrictions: NIH will not accept any application that is the same as one already reviewed.
Geographic Focus: All States, Guam, Marshall Islands, Northern Mariana Islands, Puerto Rico, U.S. Virgin Islands, All Countries
Date(s) Application is Due: Feb 5; Jun 5; Oct 5
Contact: H. Eser Tolunay, Ph.D.; (301) 435-0560; Eser.Tolunay@nih.gov
Internet: http://grants.nih.gov/grants/guide/pa-files/PAR-07-420.html
Sponsor: National Institutes of Health
Building 31, Room 5A48
Bethesda, MD 20892

NHLBI Microbiome of the Lung and Respiratory Tract in HIV-Infected Individuals and HIV-Uninfected Controls   3416

The National Heart, Lung, and Blood Institute (NHLBI) solicits grant applications under this Funding Opportunity Announcement (FOA) to characterize the microbiome of the lung (the airways and airspaces below the glottis and the lung parenchyma) alone or in combination with the nasal and/or oropharyngeal cavities in HIV-infected individuals and matched HIV-uninfected controls, including normal healthy controls, using molecular techniques to identify bacteria and if possible other organisms, e.g., viruses, cell-wall deficient organisms, protozoa, and fungi. Investigators should use high-throughput technology platforms to create a data set of sufficient quality and depth to allow analysis of how changes of microbiota relate to HIV lung disease progression/complications. These data will be used to examine the impact of changes in the respiratory microbiome on the pathogenesis and progression of HIV disease, on HIV-related respiratory complications, and the effects of anti-HIV therapies. The NHLBI also invites applications for four Clinical/Sequencing research sites and one supporting Data Coordinating Center (DCC). Each application for a clinical/sequencing research site should propose approaches to characterize the lung microbiome and applicants are encouraged to include at least one hypothesis-driven mechanistic aim. Direct costs up to $525,000 per year for project duration of up to five years may be requested.

Requirements: The following organizations/institutions are eligible to apply: Public/State Controlled Institutions of Higher Education; Private Institutions of Higher Education; Hispanic-serving Institutions; Historically Black Colleges and Universities (HBCUs); Tribally Controlled Colleges and Universities (TCCUs); Alaska Native and Native Hawaiian Serving Institutions; Nonprofits with 501(c)3 IRS Status (Other than Institutions of Higher Education); Nonprofits without 501(c)3 IRS Status (Other than Institutions of Higher Education); Small Businesses; For-Profit Organizations (Other than Small Businesses); State Governments; Indian/Native American Tribal Governments (Federally Recognized); Indian/Native American Tribally Designated Organizations; County Governments; City or Township Governments; Special District Governments; Independent School Districts; Public Housing Authorities/Indian Housing Authorities; U.S. Territory or Possession; Indian/Native American Tribal Governments (Other than Federally Recognized); Regional Organizations; Other Eligible Agencies of the Federal Government; and, Faith-based or Community-based Organizations. Any individual with the skills, knowledge, and resources necessary to carry out the proposed research as the PD/PI is invited to work with his/her institution to develop an application for support. Individuals from underrepresented racial and ethnic groups as well as individuals with disabilities are always encouraged to apply for NIH support. More than one PD/PI, or multiple PDs/PIs, may be designated on the application for projects that require a "team science" approach and therefore clearly do not fit the single-PD/PI model. All PDs/PIs must be registered in the NIH eRA Commons prior to the submission of the application.

Restrictions: Foreign organizations are not eligible, however, domestic institutions may form consortia and enter into subcontracts with Non-domestic (non-U.S.) Entities (Foreign Organizations) if need can be demonstrated – foreign subcontract use the same criteria as are used for justifying foreign grants.
Geographic Focus: All States
Date(s) Application is Due: Feb 5; Jun 5; Oct 5
Amount of Grant: Up to 525,000 USD
Contact: Sandra Colombini Hatch, M.D., (301) 435-0222; Hatchs@nhlbi.nih.gov
Internet: http://grants.nih.gov/grants/guide/rfa-files/RFA-HL-09-006.html
Sponsor: National Institutes of Health
Building 31, Room 5A48
Bethesda, MD 20892

NHLBI Research on the Role of Cardiomyocyte Mitochondria in Heart Disease: An Integrated Approach   3417

The National Heart, Lung, and Blood Institute (NHLBI) invites applications for collaborative research projects to develop an integrated understanding of cardiomyocyte mitochondria and its contributions to myocardial adaptations and heart disease progression by combining functional data with information derived from powerful new technologies. Budgets for direct costs of up to $500,000 per year and a project duration of up to four years may be requested for a maximum of $2,000,000 direct costs over a four-year project period. Because the nature and scope of the proposed research will vary from application to application, it is anticipated that the size and duration of each award will also vary.

Requirements: The following organizations/institutions are eligible to apply: Public/State Controlled Institutions of Higher Education; Private Institutions of Higher Education; Hispanic-serving Institutions; Historically Black Colleges and Universities (HBCUs); Tribally Controlled Colleges and Universities (TCCUs); Alaska Native and Native Hawaiian Serving Institutions; Nonprofits with 501(c)3 IRS Status (Other than Institutions of Higher Education); Nonprofits without 501(c)3 IRS Status (Other than Institutions of Higher Education); Small Businesses; For-Profit Organizations (Other than Small Businesses); State Governments; Indian/Native American Tribal Governments (Federally Recognized); Indian/Native American Tribally Designated Organizations; County Governments; City or Township Governments; Special District Governments; Independent School Districts; Public Housing Authorities/Indian Housing Authorities; U.S. Territory or Possession; Indian/Native American Tribal Governments (Other than Federally Recognized); Regional Organizations; Non-domestic (non-U.S.) Entities (Foreign Organizations); Other Eligible Agencies of the Federal Government; and, Faith-based or Community-based Organizations. Any individual(s) with the skills, knowledge, and resources necessary to carry out the proposed research as the PD/PI is invited to work with his/her organization to develop an application for support. Individuals from underrepresented racial and ethnic groups as well as individuals with disabilities are always encouraged to apply for NIH support. More than one PD/PI (i.e., multiple PDs/PIs) may be designated on the application for projects that require a "team science" approach and therefore clearly do not fit the single-PD/PI model. All PDs/PIs must be registered in the NIH electronic Research Administration (eRA) Commons prior to the submission of the application. Applicants may submit more than one application, provided each application is scientifically distinct. Request for Applications (RFA) Number: RFA-HL-10-002

Restrictions: Applicants are not permitted to submit a resubmission application. Renewals will not be allowed.
Geographic Focus: All States, Guam, Marshall Islands, Northern Mariana Islands, Puerto Rico, U.S. Virgin Islands, All Countries
Date(s) Application is Due: Feb 5; Jun 5; Oct 5
Amount of Grant: Up to 2,000,000 USD
Contact: Isabella Liang, (301) 435-0504; fax (301) 451-5458; Liangi@mail.nih.gov
Internet: http://grants.nih.gov/grants/guide/rfa-files/RFA-HL-10-002.html
Sponsor: National Institutes of Health
Building 31, Room 5A48
Bethesda, MD 20892

NHLBI Ruth L. Kirschstein National Research Service Awards for Individual Postdoctoral Fellows   3418

The National Heart, Lung, and Blood Institute is one of many Institutes in the National Institutes of Health that participate in the Ruth L. Kirschstein National Research Service Awards (NRSA) for Individual Postdoctoral Fellows. This program offers health scientists the opportunity to receive full-time research training for up to 3 years in areas that reflect the national need for biomedical, clinical and behavioral research in cardiovascular, pulmonary, hematologic, and sleep disorders. These grants are not intended for study leading to the M.D., D.O., D.D.S., or equivalent professional degrees, nor do they support residency training. The proposed postdoctoral training must offer an opportunity to enhance the applicant's understanding of the health-related sciences, and must be within the broad scope of biomedical, behavioral, or clinical research or other specific disciplines relevant to the research mission of the participating NIH Institutes and Centers. Applicants with a health professional doctoral degree may use the proposed postdoctoral training to satisfy a portion of the degree requirements for a master's degree, a research doctoral degree or any other advanced research degree program.

Requirements: Any applicant fellow with the skills, knowledge, and resources necessary to carry out the proposed research as the Project Director/Principal Investigator (PD/PI) is invited to work with his/her sponsor and organization to develop an application for support. Individuals from underrepresented racial and ethnic groups as well as individuals with disabilities are always encouraged to apply for NIH support. Applicants must be U.S. citizens, noncitizen nationals, or legal permanent residents of the U.S. Training can be conducted abroad if the site provides opportunities that are not available in this country. Applicants are cautioned that not all NIH Institutes and Centers (ICs) participate in this program, and that consultation with relevant IC staff prior to submission of an application is strongly encouraged. The participating ICs have different emphases and program requirements for this program. Before submitting a fellowship application, the applicant fellow must identify a sponsoring institution. The sponsoring institution must have staff and facilities available on site to provide a suitable environment for performing high-quality research. Eligible sponsoring institutions include: Public/State Controlled and Private Institutions of Higher Education; Nonprofits with or without 501(c)3 IRS Status (Other than Institutions of Higher Education); Small Businesses; For-Profit Organizations (Other than Small Businesses); Eligible Agencies of the Federal Government; and, Non-domestic (non-U.S.) Entities (Foreign Organizations). The following types of Higher Education Institutions are always encouraged to apply for NIH support as Public or Private Institutions of Higher Education: Hispanic-serving Institutions; Historically Black Colleges and Universities (HBCUs); Tribally Controlled Colleges and Universities (TCCUs); and, Alaska Native and Native Hawaiian Serving Institutions. When the fellowship begins, the applicant must have received a doctoral degree and have arranged to work with a sponsor affiliated with an institution that has the staff and facilities needed for the proposed training.

Restrictions: A Kirschstein-NRSA fellowship may not be used to support the clinical years of residency training. However, these awards are appropriate for the research fellowship years of a residency program. Research clinicians must devote full-time to their proposed research training and confine clinical duties to those activities that are part of the research training program.
Geographic Focus: All States, Guam, Marshall Islands, Northern Mariana Islands, Puerto Rico, U.S. Virgin Islands, All Countries
Date(s) Application is Due: Apr 8; Aug 8; Dec 8
Contact: Sandra Colombini Hatch, M.D., (301) 435-0222; hatchs@nhlbi.nih.gov
Internet: http://www.nhlbi.nih.gov/funding/training/redbook/phdf32.htm
Sponsor: National Institutes of Health
Building 31, Room 5A48
Bethesda, MD 20892

NHLBI Ruth L. Kirschstein National Research Service Awards for Individual Predoctoral Fellowships to Promote Diversity in Health-Related Research   3419

NHLBI is one of many Institutes in the NIH that participate in the Ruth L. Kirschstein National Research Service Awards for Individual Predoctoral Fellowships to Promote Diversity in Health-Related Research. This program encourages students from underrepresented racial and ethnic groups, individuals with disabilities, and individuals from disadvantaged backgrounds to seek research doctoral degrees in the biomedical and behavioral sciences to help increase the number of well-trained scientists from underrepresented groups. The fellowship provides up to 5 years of support for research training leading to the Ph.D. or equivalent research degree, the combined M.D./Ph.D. degree, or other combined degrees in the biomedical or behavioral sciences.

Requirements: Individuals with disabilities, or from underrepresented racial and ethnic groups, or individuals from disadvantaged backgrounds pursuing advanced degrees in the biomedical and behavioral sciences are eligible for fellowship awards. The Fellowship applicant must have a baccalaureate degree and be currently enrolled in an eligible doctoral program. At the time

of appointment, students must be U.S. citizens, noncitizen nationals, or lawfully admitted to the U.S. for permanent residence. Individuals on temporary or student visas are not eligible. Before submitting a fellowship application, the applicant fellow must identify a sponsoring institution. The sponsoring institution must have staff and facilities available on site to provide a suitable environment for performing high-quality research. Eligible sponsoring institutions include Public/State Controlled and Private Institutions of Higher Education; Nonprofits with or without 501(c)3 IRS Status (Other than Institutions of Higher Education); Small Businesses; For-Profit Organizations (Other than Small Businesses); Eligible Agencies of the Federal Government; Non-domestic (non-U.S.) Entities (Foreign Organizations). The following types of Higher Education Institutions are always encouraged to apply for NIH support as Public or Private Institutions of Higher Education: Hispanic-serving Institutions; Historically Black Colleges and Universities (HBCUs); Tribally Controlled Colleges and Universities (TCCUs); Alaska Native and Native Hawaiian Serving Institutions.
Restrictions: NIH will not accept any application that is essentially the same as one already reviewed. An individual may not have two or more competing NIH fellowship applications pending review concurrently.
Geographic Focus: All States
Date(s) Application is Due: Apr 8; Aug 8; Dec 8
Contact: Xenia J. Tigno, PhD, Program Director; (301) 435-0202; tignoxt@mail.nih.gov
Internet: http://www.nhlbi.nih.gov/funding/training/redbook/gradf31.htm
Sponsor: National Institutes of Health
Building 31, Room 5A48
Bethesda, MD 20892

NHLBI Ruth L. Kirschstein National Research Service Awards for Individual Predoctoral MD/PhD Fellows and Other Dual Degree Fellows 3420

The NHLBI is interested in supporting individual predoctoral fellowships for combined MD/PhD training in research areas relevant to the NHLBI mission. The purpose of the Ruth L. Kirschstein National Research Service Awards (Kirschstein-NRSA) is to provide support to individuals for combined MD/PhD and other dual doctoral degree training (e.g. DO/PhD, DDS/PhD, AuD/PhD). The participating Institutes award this Kirschstein-NRSA individual fellowship (F30) to qualified applicants with the potential to become productive, independent, highly trained physician-scientists and other clinician-scientists, including patient-oriented researchers in their scientific mission areas. This funding opportunity supports individual predoctoral F30 fellowships with the expectation that these training opportunities will increase the number of future investigators with both clinical knowledge and skills in basic, translational or clinical research. Award budgets are composed of stipends, tuition and fees, and institutional allowance.
Requirements: Domestic for-profit or non-profit institutions/organizations, or public or private institutions, such as universities, colleges, hospitals and laboratories, eligible agencies of the federal government, and NIH intramural laboratories are eligible to apply. The sponsoring institution must have staff and facilities available on site to provide a suitable environment for performing high-quality research training. The PhD phase of the program may be conducted outside the sponsoring institution, e.g. a Federal laboratory including the NIH intramural laboratories. This training, however, must be part of a combined MD/PhD program. Applications to the program will be accepted from students currently enrolled in a formally combined MD/PhD program. By the time of award, all candidates for the Kirschstein-NRSA F30 award must be citizens or non-citizen nationals of the United States, or must have been lawfully admitted to the United States for Permanent Residence.
Restrictions: Foreign institutions are not eligible to apply.
Geographic Focus: All States
Date(s) Application is Due: Apr 8; Aug 8; Dec 8
Contact: Drew E. Carlson; (301) 435-0535; fax (301) 480-7404; carlsonde@nhlbi.nih.gov
Internet: http://www.nhlbi.nih.gov/funding/training/redbook/gradmdphdf30.htm
Sponsor: National Institutes of Health
Building 31, Room 5A48
Bethesda, MD 20892

NHLBI Ruth L. Kirschstein National Research Service Awards for Individual Senior Fellows 3421

The National Heart, Lung, and Blood Institute is one of many Institutes in the National Institutes of Health that participate in the Ruth L. Kirschstein National Research Service Awards (NRSA) for individual Senior Fellows (Parent F33). This program enables experienced scientists to change the direction of their research careers, broaden their scientific background, acquire new research capabilities, or enlarge their command of an allied research field. The purpose of the senior fellowship (F33) award is to provide senior fellowship support to experienced scientists who wish to make major changes in the direction of their research careers or who wish to broaden their scientific background by acquiring new research capabilities as independent research investigators in scientific health-related fields relevant to the missions of the participating NIH Institutes and Centers. These awards will enable individuals with at least seven years of research experience beyond the doctorate (individuals with PhD, MD, OD, associate professors, full professors, etc.), and who have progressed to the stage of independent investigator, to take time from regular professional responsibilities for the purpose of receiving training to increase their scientific capabilities. In most cases, this award is used to support sabbatical experiences for established independent scientists seeking support for retraining or additional career development. This program is not designed for postdoctoral level investigators seeking to enhance their research experience prior to independence. Award budgets are composed of stipends, tuition and fees, and institutional allowance.
Requirements: Applicants must be U.S. citizens, non-citizen nationals, or permanent residents of the U.S. When the fellowship begins, an applicant must have received the Ph.D., M.D., D.O., D.D.S., D.V.M., O.D., D.P.M., Sc.D., D.Eng., DNSc., or equivalent degree. The applicant must arrange to work full-time with a particular sponsor affiliated with an institution that has the staff and facilities needed for the proposed training. Training can be conducted abroad if the site provides opportunities not available in the U.S. The following are eligible sponsoring organizations: public/state controlled and private institutions of higher education; nonprofits with or without 501(c)3 IRS status (other than institutions of higher education); small businesses; for-profit organizations (other than small businesses); eligible agencies of the Federal government; non-domestic (non-U.S.) entities (foreign organizations). The following types of Higher Education Institutions are always encouraged to apply for NIH support as public or private institutions of higher education: Hispanic-serving institutions; historically Black colleges and universities; Tribally controlled colleges and universities; Alaska Native and Native Hawaiian serving institutions.
Restrictions: Multiple Principal Investigators are not allowed.
Geographic Focus: All States, Guam, Marshall Islands, Northern Mariana Islands, Puerto Rico, U.S. Virgin Islands, American Samoa
Date(s) Application is Due: Apr 8; Aug 8; Dec 8
Contact: Charlotte A. Pratt; (301) 435-0382; fax (301) 480-1864; prattc@nhlbi.nih.gov
Internet: http://www.nhlbi.nih.gov/funding/training/redbook/estf33.htm
Sponsor: National Institutes of Health
Building 31, Room 5A48
Bethesda, MD 20892

NHLBI Ruth L. Kirschstein National Research Service Award Short-Term Institutional Research Training Grants 3422

This program provides funds to research institutions to make awards to individuals in health professional schools for research opportunities that would not be available through their regular course of study. Awards are made to training institutions by national competition. Many of the NIH Institutes and Centers (ICs) use this grant mechanism exclusively to support intensive, short-term research training experiences for students in health professional schools during the summer. In addition, the Short-Term Institutional Research Training Grant may be used to support other types of predoctoral and postdoctoral training in focused, often emerging scientific areas relevant to the mission of the funding IC. Grants may be for project periods up to five years in duration and are renewable. Trainees selected for short-term training are required to pursue research training for 2-3 months on a full-time basis.
Requirements: Public and private institutions of higher education; nonprofits with or without 501(c)3 IRS status (other than Institutions of Higher Education); Indian/Native American Tribal Governments; U.S. Territories or Possessions; Native American tribal organizations; and, Faith-based or Community-based Organizations are eligible to apply. The following types of Higher Education Institutions are always encouraged to apply for NIH support as Public or Private Institutions of Higher Education: Hispanic-serving Institutions; Historically Black Colleges and Universities (HBCUs); Tribally Controlled Colleges and Universities (TCCUs); and, Alaska Native and Native Hawaiian Serving Institutions. The proposed training must be in basic, behavioral or clinical research aspects of the health-related sciences. This program is intended to encourage graduate and/or health professional students to pursue research careers by exposure to and short-term involvement in the health-related sciences. The training should be of sufficient depth to enable the trainees, upon completion of the program, to have a thorough exposure to the principles underlying the conduct of research. Trainees are selected by the grantee institution and must be U.S. citizens, noncitizen nationals, or legal permanent residents of the U.S. Trainees should have successfully completed at least one semester at an accredited school of medicine, optometry, osteopathy, dentistry, veterinary medicine, pharmacy, or public health before entering the program. The award can be used to support individuals who already have an M.S. or Ph.D. and have been accepted to health professional schools.
Restrictions: The award cannot be used to support courses that are required for the M.D., D.O., D.D.S., D.V.M., or similar professional degrees. Non-domestic (non-U.S.) Entities (Foreign Organizations) are not eligible to apply. Foreign (non-U.S.) components of U.S. Organizations are not allowed.
Geographic Focus: All States, Guam, Marshall Islands, Northern Mariana Islands, Puerto Rico, U.S. Virgin Islands
Date(s) Application is Due: Jan 25
Contact: Charlotte Pratt, (301) 435-0382; fax (301) 480-1864; PrattC@nhlbi.nih.gov
Internet: http://www.nhlbi.nih.gov/funding/training/redbook/gradt35.htm
Sponsor: National Institutes of Health
Building 31, Room 5A48
Bethesda, MD 20892

NHSCA Artist Residencies in Schools Grants 3423

Artist Residencies in Schools (AIR) provide partial funding to bring juried teaching artists into classrooms and public schools to support creative learning and skills development in the arts. AIR grants support partial costs for artist residencies in a variety of arts disciplines, including all forms of visual arts (ceramics, drawing, painting, printmaking, weaving, etc.), dance, film/video, music, theatre, traditional arts and creative writing. Artist Residencies in Schools projects funded by the State Arts Council are intended to set a model for this work. Therefore, the criteria are extensive and multi-faceted. We encourage schools who have never applied for a State Arts Council funded artist residency to contact the grants coordinator who can help you plan for this exciting opportunity. Participation in the arts increase students' abilities to problem solve, collaborate, use critical thinking skills and make decisions. Research studies show that an education in the arts has broad academic value, enables students to reach high levels of academic achievement, improves overall school performance and supports an environment that is most conducive to overall learning. Teaching artists reach students who may not excel or achieve well in other curriculum areas. Requests may be made for $1,000 to $4,500.
Requirements: At a minimum, grants must be matched on a one-to-one basis. Any public school (pre-Kindergarten to Grade 12), or nonprofit organizations serving as alternative education sites for special needs students (pre-K to age 21) in New Hampshire, that

are publicly funded or have 501(c)3 status from the Internal Revenue Service and are incorporated in the State of New Hampshire may apply.
Restrictions: A school may not receive more than one AIR grant during a school year per school or school level (elementary, middle and high school within a greater school complex). Schools that have been awarded AIR grants of $3,000 or more for three consecutive years must wait one year before applying for an AIR grant again. (This is an effort to encourage new school applicants to apply.) Private or parochial schools are not eligible for AIR grants, due to limited funds.
Geographic Focus: New Hampshire
Date(s) Application is Due: Mar 4
Amount of Grant: 1,000 - 4,500 USD
Contact: Catherine O'Brian, Arts in Education Program Coordinator; (603) 271-0795 or (603) 271-2789; fax (603) 271-3584; Catherine.R.OBrian@dcr.nh.gov
Internet: http://www.nh.gov/nharts/grants/partners/artistresidencies.htm
Sponsor: New Hampshire State Council on the Arts
19 Pillsbury Street, 1st Floor
Concord, NH 03301

NHSCA Arts in Health Care Project Grants 3424
Arts in Health Care grants support arts activities, presentations and artist residencies that occur in health care facilities, rehabilitation centers and in centers serving the needs of the elderly. The overall goal of this grant category is to utilize the arts to enhance the quality of life and promote an environment conducive to healing for patients, residents, and/or clients. This grant category is in response to the Arts Council's commitment to meeting the needs of underserved populations, which can include the elderly, people with disabilities and people with health challenges. Requests may be made for $1,000 - $4,500.
Requirements: At a minimum, grants must be matched on a one-to-one basis. Health care facilities, hospitals, rehabilitation centers and facilities serving the elderly including: assisted living facilities, county and nonprofit nursing homes, veterans' homes, hospice care programs or visiting nurse associations may apply. Applicants must have 501(c)3 tax-exempt status from the IRS and not-for-profit incorporation in the State of New Hampshire and: make their programs accessible to people with disabilities; have submitted all required reports on past State Arts Council grants; and be in good standing with the N.H. Secretary of State's Office and the N.H. Attorney General's Office.
Restrictions: This grant does not fund: projects/activities that are not open to the general public; commercially viable for-profit publications, recordings or films; general operating expenses not directly related to the project; fundraising costs; projects already receiving funds from another State Arts Council grant category; or any cost item listed in the glossary under ineligible expenses.
Geographic Focus: New Hampshire
Date(s) Application is Due: Jun 2
Amount of Grant: 1,000 - 4,500 USD
Contact: Catherine O'Brian, Program Coordinator; (603) 271-0795 or (603) 271-2789; fax (603) 271-3584; Catherine.R.OBrian@dcr.nh.gov
Internet: http://www.nh.gov/nharts/grants/partners/artsinhealthcare.htm
Sponsor: New Hampshire State Council on the Arts
19 Pillsbury Street, 1st Floor
Concord, NH 03301

NHSCA Conservation License Plate Grants 3425
New Hampshire's Conservation License Plates, affectionately called "Moose Plates," help conserve our state's natural, historical and cultural heritage. Since 2001, the Conservation License Plate program has contributed to the ongoing success of more than 150 projects around New Hampshire. All funds raised through the purchase of Conservation License Plates are used for the promotion, protection and investment in New Hampshire's natural, cultural and historic resources. The NH Division of Historical Resources Conservation License Plate Grant Program awards grants through this program for a maximum of $10,000 for the preservation and restoration of publicly owned historic resources. Requests may be made for $2,000 to $20,000. Eligible projects include: projects that conserve publicly owned artwork or arts documents that contribute to New Hampshire's cultural heritage; projects that maintain or preserve artistic elements and function of cultural facilities (e.g. murals, ornamental plaster work, theater curtains, stained glass windows, weather vanes, etc.) while make those facilities and the arts programming that takes place in them, more accessible to the public, including people with disabilities; and projects that improve public access to historic artwork or arts documents while protecting and preserving the originals.
Requirements: New Hampshire municipalities and towns, county agencies, state agencies (other than the Department of Cultural Resources and its Divisions), federal agencies, or *nonprofit organizations that manage publicly owned historic cultural facilities, arts documents or artworks that contribute to the state's cultural heritage that: have submitted all required reports on past State Arts Council grants; and are in good standing with the State Arts Council and the NH Attorney General's Office.
Restrictions: This grant does not support: projects that are receiving other State Arts Council funds; or more than one application per applicant during the grant period (July 1 to June 30).
Geographic Focus: New Hampshire
Date(s) Application is Due: Mar 31
Amount of Grant: 2,000 - 20,000 USD
Contact: Cassandra Erickson Mason, Chief Grants Officer; (603) 271-7926 or (603) 271-2789; fax (603) 271-3584; cassandra.mason@dcr.nh.gov
Internet: http://www.nh.gov/nharts/grants/culturalconservation.htm
Sponsor: New Hampshire State Council on the Arts
19 Pillsbury Street, 1st Floor
Concord, NH 03301

NHSCA Cultural Facilities Grants: Barrier Free Access for All 3426
Cultural Facilities grants will support renovations, maintenance, and purchase of major equipment that supports creating a universal or inclusive environment for the arts where programs, services, and activities are accessible to everyone, including people with and without disabilities. Requests may be made for $1,000 to $8,000. Government agencies, municipalities and towns, county agencies, state agencies, or federal agencies that own a historic cultural facility; or nonprofit organizations that manage publicly owned historic cultural facilities, are encouraged to apply for a Cultural Conservation Grant.
Requirements: At a minimum, grants must be matched on a one-to-one basis. In-kind contributions may comprise one half of the required match and will also be considered by the reviewers as evidence of support and commitment by the community and/or partner organization. Organizations with 501(c)3 tax-exempt status from the IRS and not-for-profit incorporation in the State of New Hampshire may apply, provided that they: own or have a minimum three-year lease on the facility, or demonstrable ability to acquire by deed, or a minimum three-year lease on the proposed facility when it is built or rehabilitated for cultural use; operate or will establish a cultural facility in New Hampshire; have one year of experience in arts programming for the general public prior to the date of application, or have plans for at least one year of arts programming at the facility it plans to operate; must demonstrate that the facility is striving to be in full compliance with the Americans with Disabilities Act (ADA) requirements; have submitted all required reports on past State Arts Council grants; and are in good standing with the N.H. Secretary of State's Office and the N.H. Attorney General's Office.
Restrictions: State Arts Council funds may not be matched by other State Arts Council or National Endowment for the Arts funds.
Geographic Focus: New Hampshire
Date(s) Application is Due: Mar 31
Amount of Grant: 1,000 - 8,000 USD
Contact: Cassandra Erickson Mason, Grants Coordinator; (603) 271-7926 or (603) 271-2789; fax (603) 271-3584; cassandra.mason@dcr.nh.gov
Internet: http://www.nh.gov/nharts/grants/culturalfacilities.htm
Sponsor: New Hampshire State Council on the Arts
19 Pillsbury Street, 1st Floor
Concord, NH 03301

NHSCA General Project Grants 3427
Communities benefit from a lively arts and cultural sector both socially and economically. General Project Grants are designed to help Main Street Programs, municipalities, not-for-profit organizations and schools bring arts presentations and activities into communities to enhance the quality of life for citizens, attract visitors and help stimulate local economies through the arts. This competitive and matching grant category supports a wide range of activities including: performances, concerts, exhibits, workshops, local festivals, collaborative public art projects, etc., that engage the arts and artists for the benefit of New Hampshire residents and communities; short-term arts presentations and activities in schools or after school programs for youth of all ages; and projects that help to preserve, document and showcase heritage & traditional arts. Requests may be made for $750 - $4,500.
Requirements: Any state, federal, county, municipal, or government agency, school, unit of a post secondary educational institution, or cultural organization (e.g. gallery, museum, or television channel), or organization with 501(c)3 tax-exempt status from the IRS and not-for-profit incorporation in the State of New Hampshire may apply that: makes its facilities and programs accessible to people with disabilities; has submitted all required reports on past State Arts Council grants; is in good standing with the N.H. Secretary of State's Office and the N.H. Attorney General's Office; and has at least a one-year history of arts programming prior to application deadline. Organizations that are incorporated within 30 miles of the New Hampshire border, with a significant representation of New Hampshire residents on their board and can demonstrate that over 50% of the individuals who benefit from their work are New Hampshire residents are also eligible. At a minimum, grants must be matched on a one-to-one basis.
Restrictions: Private or parochial schools are eligible to apply for a General Project Grant for fee support to bring artists into the school.
Geographic Focus: New Hampshire
Date(s) Application is Due: Aug 5
Amount of Grant: 750 - 4,500 USD
Contact: Cassandra Erickson Mason, Chief Grants Officer; (603) 271-7926 or (603) 271-2789; fax (603) 271-3584; cassandra.mason@dcr.nh.gov
Internet: http://www.nh.gov/nharts/grants/projectgrantgen.htm
Sponsor: New Hampshire State Council on the Arts
19 Pillsbury Street, 1st Floor
Concord, NH 03301

NHSCA Operating Grants 3428
Operating grants are an investment in the cultural infrastructure and creative economy of New Hampshire. The creative economy is made up of artists, not for profit organizations and creative businesses that positively impact quality of life in communities, generate jobs and produce revenue for municipalities, cities and the state. These competitive and matching grants are awarded in two-year cycles to not-for-profit arts and cultural organizations that demonstrate excellence in planning, administration and programming. Grantees are expected to provide high quality arts experiences, activities and services for New Hampshire citizens and ensure that the arts are accessible to all. They are also expected to maintain close and productive relationships with other community organizations and businesses, ensuring that the arts are integral to community infrastructure.
Requirements: Not-for-profit organizations with incorporation in New Hampshire and a 501(c)3 tax-exempt status from the Internal Revenue Service, whose primary mission is to produce, present or serve the arts. In addition, applicant organizations must: have been in continuous operation as a 501(c)3 non-profit arts organization for at least five years prior to application for an Operating Grant; have an independent board of directors that meets at least

quarterly; have a paid, full-time arts administrator; have a long-range plan in place that covers the two-year grant period; be fully in compliance with the Americans with Disabilities Act requirements; have submitted all required reports on past State Arts Council grants; and be in good standing with the State Arts Council and NH Attorney General's Office.
Restrictions: Requests are for unrestricted operational funds and may be made for up to $15,000 per year. The request for the first year of the grant period may not exceed 10% of income in the organization's last fiscal year prior to application. Applicants also must be able to leverage other support and project a cash match, excluding federal and state funds, of at least $10 for each $1 requested from the State Arts Council. Applicant organizations must be physically located in New Hampshire, not just incorporated in the state. In general, a college, university, library, or school is not eligible for Operating Grants unless its primary mission is the arts and the majority of its arts activities are open to the general public. Grant awards may not be used for previously incurred debts or deficits. Operating Grant awards may not be used for endowments or capital projects, and recipients are ineligible to receive additional General Project Grants, except for the Traditional Arts Project strand, during the Operating Grant period.
Geographic Focus: New Hampshire
Date(s) Application is Due: Mar 11
Amount of Grant: Up to 15,000 USD
Contact: Cassandra Erickson Mason, Chief Grants Officer; (603) 271-7926 or (603) 271-2789; fax (603) 271-3584; cassandra.mason@dcr.nh.gov
Internet: http://www.nh.gov/nharts/grants/organizations/operating.htm
Sponsor: New Hampshire State Council on the Arts
19 Pillsbury Street, 1st Floor
Concord, NH 03301

NHSCA Traditional Arts Apprenticeships 3429
This unique funding opportunity provides assistance for a master traditional artist to teach an experienced apprentice in one-on-one sessions. Individuals interested in applying for this grant should identify a master artist or apprentice they would like to work with and then apply together as a team. In some cases, the Traditional Arts Program can provide contact information on individuals working in a particular traditional art form, but it is up to individuals interested in this grant to contact each other. Grant funds help cover master artist fees for teaching, supplies and some travel funds essential to the apprenticeship. The master artist and apprentice team work together to develop a plan for what they would like to do during the Apprenticeship and then complete the application form together. If funded, the master artist and apprentice team must meet for a minimum of 80 hours and can meet for up to 96 hours over a six to ten month period. Each master and apprentice team is required to give a community presentation within six months of the completion of the Apprenticeship grant. This presentation allows the public to share in the important efforts the artists are making to preserve their heritage and helps people to learn about traditional arts. A master artist and apprentice team may apply for a combined total of up to $3,400 per year. Within that amount, the maximum request for the master artist is $2,400 and the maximum request for the apprentice is $1,000.
Requirements: Individuals representing any cultural or ethnic tradition in New Hampshire may apply for a Traditional Arts Apprenticeship grant. Grant funds may cover: master artist fees for teaching, supplies, and travel costs essential to the Apprenticeship; and apprentice supplies and travel costs essential to the Apprenticeship.
Restrictions: No grant funds are available for apprentice fees. The time invested by the apprentice in learning from the master artist is considered an in-kind match for the project. No other match is required. Each individual applicant, regardless of whether he or she is applying as a master artist or an apprentice, may submit only one application per year. A master artist and apprentice team may apply for and receive funding for two consecutive years. Following this, the team must wait one fiscal year before applying again.
Geographic Focus: New Hampshire
Date(s) Application is Due: Jul 15
Contact: Lynn Martin Graton, Traditional Arts Coordinator; (603) 271-8418 or (603) 271-2789; fax (603) 271-3584; lynn.j.graton@dcr.nh.gov
Internet: http://www.nh.gov/nharts/grants/artists/tradapprenticeships.htm
Sponsor: New Hampshire State Council on the Arts
19 Pillsbury Street, 1st Floor
Concord, NH 03301

NHSCA Youth Arts Project Grants: For Extended Arts Learning 3430
Youth Project Grants fund high-quality arts and cultural education programs that encourage creativity, develop new arts skills and foster academic success for young people (K-12). The overall goal of this grant category is to provide young people opportunities to engage in the arts beyond the normal school day so that they can develop creative problem solving skills and become more engaged in their communities. Activities may take place after regular school hours, in the summer or on weekends, in or outside of the school. Partnerships between schools, arts organizations and community organizations that provide high quality arts learning experiences for youth in under-served communities around the state are encouraged. Requests may be for $1,000 to $4,500.
Requirements: For this purpose, an under-served community is considered one in which individuals lack access to arts programs due to economic conditions, cultural or ethnic background, disability or geographic isolation. At a minimum, grants must be matched on a one-to-one basis. Not-for-profit organizations with incorporation in New Hampshire and a 501(c)3 tax-exempt status from the Internal Revenue Service, schools, school districts or SAUs may apply, who also meet the following conditions: make all their programs and facilities accessible to people with disabilities; have submitted all required reports on past State Arts Council grants; and are in good standing with the NH Secretary of State's Office and the NH Attorney General's Office.
Restrictions: State Arts Council funds may not be matched by other State Arts Council or National Endowment for the Arts funds. This grant does not support: projects already receiving funding from any other State Arts Council grant category; general operating expenses not directly related to the project; or any cost item listed in the glossary under ineligible expenses (see website).
Geographic Focus: New Hampshire
Date(s) Application is Due: Apr 1
Amount of Grant: 1,000 - 4,500 USD
Contact: Catherine O'Brian, Grant Coordinator; (603) 271-0795 or (603) 271-2789; fax (603) 271-3584; Catherine.R.OBrian@dcr.nh.gov
Internet: http://www.nh.gov/nharts/grants/youtharts.htm
Sponsor: New Hampshire State Council on the Arts
19 Pillsbury Street, 1st Floor
Concord, NH 03301

NIAF Anthony Campitelli Endowed Fund Grants 3431
Anthony Campitelli immigrated to the U.S. with his family in 1928. He is a Washington D.C. architect and builder, but has maintained strong ties to his Italian birthplace, providing financial support to many of its local institutions. The Fund will support various humanitarian and community projects in and around Mr. Campitelli's birthplace, Castel Frentano (CH) in Abruzzo, Italy. These will include schools, churches, and eldercare facilities. Applications for scholarships for residents of Castel Frentano and the Chieti province will also be accepted. Grant recipients will be selected based on need and merit.
Geographic Focus: All States, Italy
Date(s) Application is Due: Jun 30
Contact: Alexandra Dall, Scholarships and Grants Manager; (202) 939-3118; fax (202) 387-0800; adall@niaf.org
Internet: http://www.niaf.org/campitellifund/
Sponsor: National Italian American Foundation
1860 19th Street NW
Washington, DC 20009-5501

NIAF Italian Culture and Heritage Grants 3432
The grants are available to individuals or organizations pursuing projects to promote, research, educate, or preserve Italian culture, history, or heritage. As in the past, the NIAF will continue to support grants to organizations and individuals in the fields of the performing arts, the fine arts, history, archeology, other humanities and related heritage and cultural endeavors. Examples of support include documentaries, doctoral research, exhibits, conferences, books, media stereotyping/anti-defamation surveys, campaigns, plays, and course syllabi. The foundation requests that a one-page letter of inquiry describing the project be forwarded prior to final application. The Foundation currently has three monetary categories for its grant program: Category I is $1,000 to $2,500; Category II is $2,501 to $10,000; and Category III is $10,001 and up. Further guidelines are available online.
Geographic Focus: All States
Date(s) Application is Due: Jun 30
Amount of Grant: 1,000 - 15,000 USD
Contact: Alexandra Dall, Scholarships and Grants Manager; (202) 939-3118 or (202) 387-0600; fax (202) 387-0800; adall@niaf.org or grants@niaf.org
Internet: http://www.niaf.org/grants/
Sponsor: National Italian American Foundation
1860 19th Street NW
Washington, DC 20009-5501

NICHD Academic-Community Partnership Conference Series Grants 3433
This announcement solicits NICHD Cooperative Agreement Conference (U13) applications to conduct health disparities-related meetings, workshops, and symposia. The objectives of these meetings will be to establish academic-community partnerships, identify community-research priorities, and develop long-term collaborative agendas. Areas of focus for these partnerships may include one or more of the following community-health issues infant mortality; sudden infant death syndrome (SIDS); violence prevention; techniques for outreach and information dissemination; childhood, adolescent, and/or adult obesity; health literacy; uterine fibroid tumors; and pediatric and maternal HIV/AIDS prevention. An applicant may request a project period of up to three years and a budget for direct costs of up to $30,000 per year.
Requirements: The following organizations and institutions are eligible to apply: individuals; public/state controlled institutions of higher education; private institutions of higher education; Hispanic-serving institutions; historically Black colleges and universities (HBCUs); tribally controlled colleges and universities (TCCUs); Alaska Native and Native Hawaiian serving institutions; nonprofits with 501(c)3 IRS status; nonprofits without 501(c)3 IRS status; for-profit organizations; state governments; Indian/Native American tribal governments (federally recognized); Indian/Native American tribally designated organizations; county governments; city or township governments; special district governments; independent school districts; public housing authorities/Indian housing authorities; U.S. territory or possession; Indian/Native American tribal governments (other than federally recognized); regional organizations; non-domestic (non-U.S.) entities (foreign organizations); other eligible agencies of the federal government; and faith-based or community-based organizations.
Restrictions: Facilities and Administrative (F&A) costs are not allowed.
Geographic Focus: All States
Date(s) Application is Due: Mar 2; Mar 31
Contact: Jean Flagg-Newton; (301) 435-2736; fax (301) 480-0393; flaggnewj@mail.nih.gov
Internet: http://grants.nih.gov/grants/guide/pa-files/PAR-09-092.html
Sponsor: Eunice Kennedy Shriver National Institute of Child Health and Human Development
6100 Executive Boulevard, Room 5E03, MSC 7510
Bethesda, MD 20892-7510

Nicholas H. Noyes Jr. Memorial Foundation Grants 3434

The foundation awards grants to eligible Indiana nonprofit organizations in its areas of interest, including arts and culture, education from early childhood through higher education, disadvantaged, museums, social services, health, hospitals, family services, performing arts, and youth. Types of support include general operating support, endowment funds, and scholarship funds.

Requirements: Proposals are welcomed, and encouraged, to be submitted at any time after January 1st for the first funding cycle or after June 1st for the final funding cycle. Submit the following with your proposal: thirteen copies of the complete grant application (available at the foundations website or office) including attachments (i.e. applicable budget(s) as required). You may recreate the application form for ease in completing, but please limit your response to the space provided and use a minimum font of 12. It is also require that you use both sides of the paper i.e. side one is page 1 with page 2 on the flip-side etc; one copy of your organization's 501(c)3 tax determination letter from the IRS; one copy of your organization's most recent audited financial statement for all organizations requesting $25,000 or more.

Restrictions: Organizations may apply only one time in any calendar year. The Foundation does not make grants to individuals. The principle geographic region served by the Noyes Foundation is the greater Indianapolis area. If you intend to request a grant in excess of $50,000, please contact the Foundation's Program Officer before submitting your grant request.

Geographic Focus: Indiana
Date(s) Application is Due: Feb 1; Aug 29
Contact: Kelly Mills; (317) 844-8009; fax (317) 844-8099; kmills@noyesfoundation.org
Internet: http://www.noyesfoundation.org
Sponsor: Nicholas H. Noyes Jr. Memorial Foundation
1950 E Greyhound Pass, #18
Carmel, IN 46033-7730

Nicor Corporate Contributions 3435

Nicor Gas' philanthropy mission is to apply its charitable funds, company expertise and employee volunteer efforts to help fulfill the educational, health, cultural and community needs of the people who reside in our service territory. Its strategic focus is to help educators and those who support the educational system by providing enrichment opportunities that will assist students in achieving their educational goals.

Requirements: Charitable contributions will be made only to eligible organizations that have a current determination letter exempting them from federal tax under Section 501(c)3 of the Internal Revenue Code. Eligible not-for-profit organizations requesting support from Nicor Gas must prepare and submit the required application form (available for downloading at the website) and all required attachments. Requests may be made for the following types of contributions: (a) General Operating - Only one operating gift will be made to an organization during a year. If an organization receives United Way funding, it will not be eligible for a general operating gift, but may be considered for funding an event if Nicor employees are involved. (b) Events - Requests for support of events in the communities Nicor serves and where Nicor Gas employees are involved will be given consideration. (c) Capital Campaigns - Support may be granted for building and remodeling programs of not-for-profit organizations that best advance Nicor Gas' priorities and add value to the communities where Nicor serves. Capital grants are not multi-year commitments. (d) In-Kind Support - Requests for surplus furniture, equipment or services will be reviewed upon receipt. The response will be based on contribution priorities and availability of the requested gift.

Restrictions: Grants will not be made to: organizations without IRS 501(c)3 designation or equivalent; individuals or foundations; social, athletic, recreational or union groups; endowment or debt reduction drives; churches or religious groups in support of their sacramental or theological functions; organizations with discriminatory practices; political parties, groups or candidates; organizations soliciting advertising space in newspapers or programs; specific schools or foundations supporting specific secondary or primary schools.

Geographic Focus: Illinois
Contact: Julian Brown; (630) 388-2763; jbrown@nicor.com
Internet: http://www.nicor.com/en_us/nicor_inc/nicor_in_the_community/grants_and_donations.htm
Sponsor: Nicor
P.O. Box 3014
Naperville, IL 60566-3014

Nicor Gas Sharing Grants 3436

The Nicor Gas Sharing Program provides one-time annual grants to qualified residential customers. Administered by the Salvation Army, the Sharing Program is funded by direct contributions from Nicor Gas' customers and employees. Eligible customers can receive a Sharing grant of either $400 or $450, depending on age.

Requirements: To qualify for a Sharing grant, you must: (a) Be a residential heating customer of Nicor Gas with a payment due; (b) Be ineligible for state or federal energy assistance programs; (c) Have an annual income above 150 percent but not exceeding 200 percent of the federally established poverty level. Check the Income Guidelines at http://www.nicor.com/en_us/residential/financial_assistance/sharing.htm#guidelines to see if you qualify for a Sharing grant. Applicants must apply in person at their local Salvation Army office and should bring the following documents: (1) Proof of income (check stub, social security letter or unemployment letter); (2) Proof of residence (photo ID, such as a driver's license or state ID); (3) Current Nicor Gas bill.

Restrictions: Only one Sharing grant is awarded per qualifying family per year.
Geographic Focus: Illinois
Contact: Program Coordinator; (888) 642-6748
Internet: http://www.nicor.com/en_us/residential/financial_assistance/sharing.htm
Sponsor: Nicor
P.O. Box 3014
Naperville, IL 60566-3014

NIDRR Field-Initiated Projects 3437

The goals of this project include: developing methods and technologies that maximize the integration of individuals with disabilities into society; employment and family environments; and improving the effectiveness of services authorized under the Rehabilitation Act. Applicants who receive awards under this program may carry out either research or development activities, and applications for each type of project will be reviewed separately. The applicant is responsible for indicating which type of project is being proposed. Projects may last up to three years. Annual deadline dates may vary; contact program staff for exact dates.

Requirements: Proposals will be accepted from any public or private agency or organization.
Geographic Focus: All States
Contact: Donna Nangle, (202) 245-7462; fax (202) 245-7323; Donna.Nangle@ed.gov
Internet: http://www.ed.gov/fund/grant/apply/nidrr/index.html
Sponsor: National Institute on Disability and Rehabilitation Research
550 12th Street SW, 6th Floor, Switzer Building
Washington, DC 20202-6510

NIEHS Hazardous Materials Worker Health and Safety Training Grants 3438

This FOA issued by the National Institute of Environmental Health Sciences (NIEHS) invites applications for cooperative agreements to support the development of model programs for the training and education of workers engaged in activities related to hazardous materials and waste generation, removal, containment, transportation and emergency response. The major objective of this solicitation is to prevent work-related harm by assisting in the training of workers in how best to protect themselves and their communities from exposure to hazardous materials encountered during hazardous waste operations, hazardous materials transportation, environmental restoration of contaminated facilities or chemical emergency response. A variety of sites, such as those involved with chemical waste clean up and remedial action and transportation-related chemical emergency response may pose severe health and safety concerns to workers and the surrounding communities. These sites contain a multiplicity of hazardous substances, sometimes unknown substances, and often the site is uncontrolled. A major goal of the Worker Education and Training Program (WETP) is to provide assistance to organizations in developing their institutional competency to provide appropriate model training and education programs. The total project period for an application submitted in response to this funding opportunity must be 5 years. A new applicant may request a budget for direct costs of up to $700,000 for the first year. Letters of Intent (LOIs) are due by October 23, with full proposals due by November 23.

Requirements: The following organizations and institutions are eligible to apply: public/state controlled institutions of higher education; private institutions of higher education; Hispanic-serving institutions; historically Black colleges and universities (HBCUs); tribally controlled colleges and universities (TCCUs); Alaska Native and Native Hawaiian serving institutions; and nonprofits with 501(c)3 IRS status (other than institutions of higher education).

Geographic Focus: All States
Date(s) Application is Due: Oct 23; Nov 23
Amount of Grant: Up to 700,000 USD
Contact: Joseph Hughes; (919) 541-0217; fax (919) 541-0462; hughes3@niehs.nih.gov
Internet: http://grants.nih.gov/grants/guide/rfa-files/RFA-ES-09-004.html
Sponsor: National Institute of Environmental Health Sciences
Keystone Building, Room 3039, P.O. Box 12233, MD K3-14
Research Triangle Park, NC 27709

Nike and Ashoka GameChangers: Change the Game for Women in Sport 3439

This collaborative competition aims to find innovative solutions and catalyze a community of changemakers around the use of sport to improve community, accelerate development and drive social change for girls and women. Participating in the competition provides the chance to receive feedback on your blueprint from fellow entrants, Changemakers staff, judges and the Changemakers community. The top three entries will win U.S. $5,000 each. After the judges select the 10-15 finalists from the entire competition, the Changemakers online community will vote for 3 winners from among the finalists. Additional prizes will be awarded, including early entry prizes.

Requirements: The competition is open to all types of organizations (charitable organizations, private companies, or public entities) from all countries. All entries that contain the following will be considered: (a) Reflect the theme of the competition - Change the Game for Women in Sport. The scope of the competition is to identify innovative solutions that use sport to improve community, accelerate development and drive social change. Entries are invited from organizations and individuals in all countries. (b) Are beyond the stage of idea, concept, or research, and, at a minimum, are at the demonstration stage and indicate success. While new ideas are supported at every stage, and their entries are encouraged, judges are only able to evaluate programs that are beyond the conceptual stage, and have demonstrated a proof of impact, even at small scale. (c) Complete the entire entry form and submit before the deadline. This contest is open only to those aged thirteen or over, and for whom entry is allowed under the laws of their jurisdiction. Entrants under age 18 affirm that they have their parent's consent to provide personally-identifiable information and to enter the contest.

Restrictions: Ashoka will not make any grant to a company involved in the promotion of tobacco use.
Geographic Focus: All States
Date(s) Application is Due: Feb 11
Amount of Grant: 5,000 USD
Contact: Program Contact; gamechangerswomen@changemakers.net
Internet: http://www.changemakers.com/womeninsport
Sponsor: Nike
One Bowerman Drive
Beaverton, OR 97005

Nike Bowerman Track Renovation Grants   3440

The international program provides matching cash grants to community-based, youth-oriented organizations worldwide that seek to refurbish or construct running tracks. The program provides matching funds of up to $50,000 to youth-oriented nonprofit organizations anywhere in the world. These organizations will demonstrate a need for running track refurbishment or construction and in turn will provide track access to neighboring communities. The program will distribute approximately $200,000 in matching grants each year. Bowerman Track Renovation Program funds must be matched in some amount by other contributors by an agreed upon deadline. Proposals are accepted on an ongoing basis, and are reviewed in January, March, June, and September. Organizations applying for the grant must demonstrate a need for running track refurbishment or construction. Guidelines are available online.
Requirements: 501(c)3 or 509(a) tax-exempt organizations are eligible, including athletic booster clubs, schools, and school districts. Applicants outside the United States should be charitable in purpose and nongovernmental organizations. Applicant organization must be a community-based, nonprofit or nongovernmental organizations serving youth; employ at least one full-time staff person; and maintain a viable track program serving boys and girls ages 14 to 18; consider Nike Grind as the material used for track refurbishment or construction; demonstrate that the track is available in all or most weather conditions and open to and used by members of the community for organized meets and other events; Provide evidence of or an ability to secure matching funds from other organizations by an agreed upon deadline for the completion of track refurbishment or construction; accommodate a site visit by Nike representatives if necessary; mount at the track, at Nike's expense, a plaque commemorating Bill Bowerman; demonstrate a solid commitment to quality construction standards, track maintenance and safety; and indemnify and hold harmless Nike, Inc., its vendors and partners. Special consideration will be given to: existing running tracks in need of repair or refurbishment; and tracks located in low and moderate-income communities.
Restrictions: Projects that have been declined are not eligible for re-submission until the next fiscal year.
Geographic Focus: All States
Date(s) Application is Due: May 31
Amount of Grant: Up to 50,000 USD
Contact: Program Manager; (503) 671-6453; nikeresponsibility@nike.com
Internet: http://www.nikebiz.com/responsibility/community_programs/bowerman_track_program/
Sponsor: Nike
One Bowerman Drive
Beaverton, OR 97005

Nike Foundation Grants   3441

The aim of the foundation is to fund innovation and new ideas in supporting girls in the developing countries, regardless of location. New investments are often directed through Requests for Proposals (RFPs). Proposals are currently under evaluation for the following RFPs: Economic Empowerment Models for Girls - uncovering and refining pioneering models that employ innovation and creativity in the field of economic empowerment of girls; Mentoring Programs for Girls - building girls' social and human capital through quality mentoring programs; Savings Products and Services for Girls - encouraging the development of girl-specific financial products and services; and, Market-based Economic Opportunities for Girls - stimulating both formal and informal market-driven employment opportunities for older girls and young women.
Requirements: The foundation is particularly interested in programs in the current focus countries of Bangladesh, Brazil, China, Ethiopia, India, Kenya, Zambia, Uganda and Liberia. The foundation considers organizations based on the type of project it is pursuing. Some organizations are sought out and some are invited to participate in the RFP process. To be added to the list, send a letter of intent or introductory letter describing your organization and its work to nike.foundation@nike.com. Do not send a formal proposal without being invited to do so.
Geographic Focus: All States, Abkhazia, Afghanistan, Algeria, Angola, Armenia, Azerbaijan, Bahrain, Bangladesh, Benin, Bhutan, Botswana, Brazil, British Indian Ocean Territory, Brunei, Burkina Faso, Burma (Myanmar), Burundi, Cambodia, Cameroon, Cape Verde, Central African Republic, Chad, China, Christmas Island, Cocos, Comoros, Congo, Congo, Democratic Republic of, Cote d' Ivoire (Ivory Coast), Cyprus, Djibouti, Egypt, Equatorial Guinea, Eritrea, Ethiopia, Gabon, Gambia, Georgia, Ghana, Guinea, Guinea-Bissau, Hong Kong, India, Indonesia, Iran, Iraq, Israel, Japan, Jordan, Kazakhstan, Kenya, Kuwait, Kyrgyzstan, Laos, Lebanon, Lesotho, Liberia, Libya, Macau, Madagascar, Malawi, Malaysia, Maldives, Mali, Mauritania, Mauritius, Mongolia, Morocco, Mozambique, Nagorno-Karabakh, Namibia, Nepal, Niger, Nigeria, North Korea, Northern Cyprus, Oman, Pakistan, Palestinian Authority, Philippines, Qatar, Russia, Rwanda, Sao Tome & Principe, Saudi Arabia, Senegal, Seychelles, Sierra Leone, Singapore, Somalia, South Africa, South Korea, South Ossetia, Sri Lanka, Sudan, Swaziland, Syria, Taiwan, Tajikistan, Thailand, Timor-Lester, Turkey, Turkmenistan, United Arab Emirates, Uzbekistan, Vietnam, Yemen
Contact: Ilana Finley, Program Supervisor; (503) 671-6734; nike.foundation@nike.com
Internet: http://www.nikefoundation.org/how_we_fund.html
Sponsor: Nike Foundation
One Bowerman Drive
Beaverton, OR 97005

Nike Giving - Cash and Product Grants   3442

Nike's approach to community investments is pro-active and focused. A significant majority of their investments are targeted toward the Let Me Play program. The remainder goes to support local organizations in Portland, Oregon; Memphis, Tennessee; Hilversum, Holland; Laakdal, Belgium and other corporate offices around the world. In addition, they make local Let Me Play grants through our retail organization.
Requirements: Nike pro-actively seeks out key strategic partners around the world to help drive a three pronged strategy of: (1) Innovation - selectively support grassroots programming that demonstrates innovation in leveraging sport as a vehicle for social change; (2) Skills transfer - seek out social innovators and social entrepreneurs that are thinking of new models to develop sustained grassroots programming and take best practice to scale; (3) Scale - seek partners that will join with us in advocating for shifts in public policy, and open up new channels of funding and other resources for programming and grassroots activities. Because of this strategy of proactive, long term engagement, it is rare that they will accept unsolicited requests. However, organizations are encouraged to share their work via introductory letters. If invited to apply, guidelines are available online for both cash and product grants.
Restrictions: Nike will not support organizations that discriminate against a person or a group on the basis of age, political affiliation, race, national origin, ethnicity, gender, disability, sexual orientation or religious belief. Additionally, the company will not provide charitable support for: Individuals (scholarships, stipends, fellowships, personal assistance); Individual sports teams; For-profit ventures; Religious groups for religious purposes; Capital campaigns, endowment funds or memorials; Lobbying, political or fraternal activities; Team sponsorships; Individual study, research or travel grants; or Awards that require Nike and/or its employees to raise monies on behalf of an organization bestowing the award.
Geographic Focus: All States
Contact: Community Affairs Manager; (503) 671-6453
Internet: http://www.nikebiz.com/responsibility/nike_giving_guidelines.html
Sponsor: Nike
One Bowerman Drive
Beaverton, OR 97005

Nina Mason Pulliam Charitable Trust Grants   3443

The Nina Mason Pulliam Charitable Trust provides grants that focus on the areas of service Nina Pulliam supported during her lifetime: helping people in need; protecting animals and nature; enriching community life. The Trust awards grants for program projects and capital needs, and provides application opportunities three times during the calendar year. The Trust prefers to disperse funds as a one-year grant, but will consider projects of up to three years.
Requirements: Primary consideration is given to 501(c)3 charitable organizations that serve metropolitan Indianapolis and Phoenix. Secondary consideration is given to the states of Indiana and Arizona. National organizations whose programs benefit these priority areas and/or benefit society as a whole are occasionally considered.
Restrictions: Grants are not awarded for international purposes or academic research, Grants are not awarded to individuals, sectarian organizations for religious purposes, or to non-operating private foundations except in extraordinary circumstances.
Geographic Focus: Arizona, Indiana
Date(s) Application is Due: Jan 4; May 4; Sep 4
Contact: David Hillman, (317) 231-6075; fax (317) 231-9208
Internet: http://www.ninapulliamtrust.org
Sponsor: Nina Mason Pulliam Charitable Trust
135 N Pennsylvania Street, Suite 1200
Indianapolis, IN 46204

Nissan Foundation Grants   3444

The Foundation supports educational programs that celebrate and foster appreciation and understanding for our diverse cultural heritage as essential for enhancing human potential and building community. Applicants must submit a letter of intent which includes a brief organizational summary and the proposed project. Applicants may then be invited to submit a proposal. Letters of intent and proposal must be submitted online.
Requirements: Eligible applicants must: be 501(c)3 organizations; support projects compatible with one of their focus areas (education, the environment and humanitarian aid); and serve communities surrounding Nissan's affiliate locations (southern California; middle Tennessee; south central Mississippi; Dallas/Ft. Worth; metro Detroit; New York; and metro Atlanta). All projects must meet the following criteria: reflect the mission and core values of the Foundation; align with the Foundation's funding initiative; demonstrate creative and replicable solutions; and establish clear methodology for measuring results.
Restrictions: The Foundation does not fund: projects serving populations outside of specified geographic areas; disease advocacy, research or religious organizations; fundraising events, sponsorships or political activities; or capital campaigns.
Geographic Focus: California, Georgia, Michigan, Mississippi, New York, Tennessee, Texas
Date(s) Application is Due: Nov 15
Contact: Grants Administrator; (615) 725-1501; nissanfoundation@nissan-usa.com
Internet: http://www.nissanusa.com/about/corporate-info/community-relations.html
Sponsor: Nissan Foundation
P.O. Box 685001, mailstop B5B
Franklin, TN 37076-5001

Nissan Neighbors Grants   3445

Nissan Neighbors is an affiliate-wide, community-focused initiative dedicated to touching lives and improving communities through charitable contributions and in-kind donations to organizations that reflect the diverse interests of employees and also support Nissan's focus areas. which are education, the environment, and humanitarian aid. Through its philanthropic efforts, Nissan seeks to reinforce its commitment to corporate citizenship by making a positive and visible contribution to American neighborhoods. Nissan works closely with select groups to determine the best way to advance their efforts and carefully tailor our assistance to meet each organization's needs. On-line applications are accepted year round.
Requirements: Eligible applicants must: be 501(c)3 organizations; support projects compatible with one of their focus areas (education, the environment, and humanitarian aid); and serve communities surrounding Nissan's affiliate locations (southern California; middle Tennessee; south central Mississippi; Dallas/Ft. Worth; and metro Detroit).

Geographic Focus: California, Michigan, Mississippi, Tennessee, Texas
Contact: Grants Administrator; (615) 725-1501; nissanfoundation@nissan-usa.com
Internet: http://www.nissanusa.com/about/corporate-info/community-relations.html
Sponsor: Nissan Foundation
P.O. Box 685001, mailstop B5B
Franklin, TN 37076-5001

NJSCA Arts Project Support   3446

Arts Project Support (APS) is awarded to New Jersey based, nonprofit, arts-missioned organizations to help underwrite the expense of specific public arts events or series of events such as a concert, festival, a theatre production, an exhibition, dance performance or reading. Applicants must file a Notice of Intent online as well as apply online. Annual deadline dates may vary; contact the program office for exact dates. Deadlines must be met by eFiling by midnight on the deadline date. The deadline for signed originals and support materials is within two business days of the eDeadline and can be met with either a postmark or actual delivery of the materials to NJSCA offices at 225 West State Street, 4th Floor in Trenton by 5:00 p.m on the deadline date. New Jersey State Council on the Arts is a Division in the New Jersey Department of State and Partner Agency with the National Endowment for the Arts.
Requirements: A project is defined as a public activity or event that occurs once during the year either as a single day's or weekend's presentation, or a series of the same presentation occurring within a very limited and specific timeframe generally not to exceed 6 weeks. Applicants must be incorporated in the State of New Jersey as a 501(c)3 organization or be a unit of government; be registered with the New Jersey Charities Registration Bureau; have a clearly articulated mission relating to the arts; have been in existence and actively providing public programs or services for at least the past two years at time of application; have a board of directors empowered to formulate policies and be responsible for the governance and administration of the organization, its programs and finances; demonstrate regional or statewide public impact through the organization's programs or project (regional is defined as serving audiences across a two or more county region of New Jersey). Matching funds are required and must be cash, not in-kind. For each dollar received from the Council, the grantee must show three additional dollars raised and spent, based on operating income. Applicants must apply online and should be advised that the prerequisite pre-registraton process requires up to 72 hours for completion by the system administrator before they can access the system.
Restrictions: Applicants may apply either to the Council or to their County Arts Agency, not both, in a given year. Prospective NJSCA applicants that have been receiving support through their County Arts Agency up to now should attend a scheduled NJSCA grant workshop, work closely with NJSCA staff and their County Arts Agency in filing their Notice of Intent to Apply, and may also want to schedule a meeting early in the process with NJSCA staff. Because the funding periods for the County Arts Agency grants and the NJSCA grants overlap by six months, applicants should discuss their situation in advance of the Notice of Intent to Apply with the NJSCA to determine eligibility. NJSCA General Operating Support and General Program Support applicants/grantees may not apply for APS except in the Folk Arts panel category. K-12 schools and school districts are not eligible to apply, but may be a partner or collaborator on a project with an eligible applicant.
Geographic Focus: New Jersey
Date(s) Application is Due: Feb 23
Contact: Steve Runk; (609) 292-6130; fax (609) 989-1440; steve.runk@sos.state.nj.us
Internet: http://www.njartscouncil.org/grant.cfm
Sponsor: New Jersey State Council on the Arts
225 West State Street, P.O. Box 306
Trenton, NJ 08625-0306

NJSCA Financial and Institutional Stabilization Grants   3447

Financial and Institutional Stabilization grants are offered in collaboration with the New Jersey Cultural Trust created by the Cultural Trust Act of 2000 which established a fund to be used as a permanent source of additional funding for arts, history and humanities organizations. The fund's interest earnings are awarded as grants to support capital projects, endowments, and institutional and financial stabilization and capacity building to help qualified organizations improve their services to the public. The Act directs the New Jersey State Council on the Arts (NJSCA), the New Jersey Historical Commission and the New Jersey Historic Trust to design and administer programs that recommend projects to the Cultural Trust for such grants. NJSCA designs and manages the program that solicits and reviews applications from arts organizations and recommends awards to the Cultural Trust. Priority is given to applicants not previously funded. Collaborative proposals and those on behalf of multiple organizations which seek to address a common or shared challenge are encouraged. Grants will generally range between $10,000 and $40,000, however larger dollar requests will be accepted for collaborative proposals and those on behalf of multiple organizations. Beginning in FY12 the New Jersey Cultural Trust will alternate funding between arts and history annually with arts organizations receiving funding in FY12. NJSCA offers workshops in January to assist organizations in understanding the requirements of the program.
Requirements: To be eligible for these funds, an organization must be a New Jersey-incorporated, nonprofit arts organization (no schools, colleges, units of government or religious organizations) that has been qualified by the Cultural Trust before the proposal is submitted. Applications for qualification are available from the Cultural Trust web site www.njculturaltrust.org or from its office by calling 609-984-6767 and must be submitted by January 31 in order to be qualified by the proposal deadline. In order to become qualified, an organization must demonstrate that it fulfills an arts mission through active programs and services; has been in operation for a minimum of 4 years; is tax-exempt; and has a functioning board that provides financial oversight to the standards set by the Cultural Trust. To be considered for a Financial and Stabilization grant, applicants must demonstrate that they have clearly identified a stabilization challenge or advancement issue, and that they are proposing an appropriate specific strategy to address it and achieve goals that will produce significant and sustainable results. A Notice of Intent to Apply is required for all those interested in applying and will be due in the NJSCA's office by January 31 by 5 p.m. Facsimiles and emailed notices are not accepted. The narrative and forms can be completed on screen, printed, copied and mailed or hand-delivered.
Restrictions: Grants may not replace other funds and must be in addition to funds originally and normally budgeted for or associated with the basic operations of an organization. The following types of projects are ineligible: capital projects (construction, renovations); fundraising events (galas, receptions, etc.); contributions to endowments; international travel; education in a matriculating course of study; public programs, projects and services (performances, and exhibitions, educational programs, readings, etc.). While there is no matching requirement, if an organization's project costs more than the amount requested, the proposal must clearly demonstrate the organization's ability to provide the additional required funds. Cultural Trust funds may not be used to match any other State of New Jersey grant. Indirect and other administrative costs not directly related to the project may not be charged against the grant.
Geographic Focus: New Jersey
Date(s) Application is Due: Mar 21
Contact: Julie Ellen Prusinowski, Director of Programs and Services; (609) 984-7025; fax (609) 989-1440; julie.prusinowski@sos.state.nj.us
Internet: http://www.njartscouncil.org/grant.cfm
Sponsor: New Jersey State Council on the Arts
225 West State Street, P.O. Box 306
Trenton, NJ 08625-0306

NJSCA Folk Arts Apprenticeships   3448

Folk Arts Apprenticeship Grants encourage communities to continue passing on their valued traditions in traditional settings, by providing stipends so that master folk artists and craftsmen can help apprentices develop greater skill. Since 1995, these grants have supported apprenticeships in many different cultural communities, reflecting the rich array of traditional arts in New Jersey. The grant period for the Apprenticeship Program is July 1 to June 30. Application Deadline dates may vary. All potential applicants are encouraged to contact the Folk Arts Program Coordinator to discuss the application and how best to develop it or to register for a technical assistance workshop. New Jersey State Council on the Arts is a Division in the New Jersey Department of State and Partner Agency with the National Endowment for the Arts.
Requirements: Master and apprentice should be members of the same cultural group that shares identity based on religion, occupation, ethnicity, language, or location and have learned the art or craft in traditional community settings rather than formal public institutions. The master folk artist must be someone who has learned a traditional art as part of community life and has attained a high level of excellence in the eyes of other community members. The apprentice must be someone who has demonstrated ability and commitment to learning and practicing the traditional art of the master. Apprentices must be at least eighteen years of age at the time of this grant application deadline and must be residents of New Jersey. Students enrolled in out-of-state educational institutions are eligible as long as they retain their NJ resident status. Verification of residency will be required. At least 80% of the award must be used to compensate the master for his or her time, with the remainder used for travel, materials, or supplies. Public access to folk arts is an important vehicle for increased appreciation and understanding of other cultures. The NJSCA will endeavor to develop public program opportunities and will encourage masters and apprentices to participate.
Restrictions: Apprentices who have received two consecutive years of Council Apprenticeship funds may not reapply to the program for three years. One application per apprentice per year may be submitted. A master artist may be proposed by no more than two apprentice applicants in a single grant cycle. It is the responsibility of the applying apprentice and the master to comply with this requirement. If two apprenticeships that include the same master are funded, the training must still be conducted one-on-one and not in a group or class setting.
Geographic Focus: New Jersey
Date(s) Application is Due: Apr 6
Amount of Grant: Up to 3,000 USD
Contact: Kim Nguyen, Folk Arts Program Coordinator; (609) 292-4495 or (609) 292-6130; fax (609) 989-1440; kim.nguyen@sos.state.nj.us
Internet: http://www.njartscouncil.org/grant.cfm
Sponsor: New Jersey State Council on the Arts
225 West State Street, P.O. Box 306
Trenton, NJ 08625-0306

NJSCA General Program Support Grants   3449

General Program Support (GPS) is awarded to New Jersey based, nonprofit, arts-missioned organizations to help underwrite the expense of presenting major, on-going arts programs. This grant category is open to a variety of organizations which produce or present on-going public arts programs. Receipt of a GPS grant usually carries the commitment of the Council to fund the program over a three-year period, although the funding level will be determined annually. Review and consideration of GPS requests occur only every three years. Applicants must file a Notice of Intent online as well as apply online. Deadline dates may vary; contact the program office for exact dates. Deadlines must be met by eFiling by midnight on the deadline date. The deadline for signed originals and support materials is within two business days of the eDeadline and can be met with either a postmark or actual delivery of the materials to NJSCA offices at 225 West State Street, 4th Floor in Trenton by 5:00 p.m on the deadline date. New Jersey State Council on the Arts is a Division in the New Jersey Department of State and Partner Agency with the National Endowment for the Arts.
Requirements: Applicants must be incorporated in the State of New Jersey as a 501(c)3 organization or be a unit of government; be registered with the New Jersey Charities Registration Bureau; have a clearly articulated mission relating to the arts; have been in existence and actively providing public programs or services for at least the past two years at time of application; have a board of directors empowered to formulate policies and

be responsible for the governance and administration of the organization, its programs and finances; demonstrate regional or statewide public impact through the organization's programs or project (regional is defined as serving audiences across a two or more county region of New Jersey). Matching funds are required and must be cash, not in-kind. For each dollar received from the Council, the grantee must show three additional dollars raised and spent, based on operating income. Applicants must apply online and should be advised that the prerequisite pre-registraton process requires up to 72 hours for completion by the system administrator before they can access the system.
Restrictions: Applicants may apply either to the NJSCA or to their County Arts Agency, not both, in a given year. Prospective NJSCA applicants that have been receiving support through their County Arts Agency up to now should attend a scheduled NJSCA grant workshop, work closely with NJSCA staff and their County Arts Agency in filing their Notice of Intent to Apply, and may also want to schedule a meeting early in the process with NJSCA staff. Because the funding periods for the County Arts Agency grants and the NJSCA grants overlap by six months, applicants should discuss their situation in advance of the Notice of Intent to Apply with the NJSCA to determine eligibility. NJSCA General Operating Support applicants/grantees may not apply for GPS except in the Folk Arts panel category. K-12 schools and school districts are not eligible to apply, but may be a partner or collaborator on a project with an eligible applicant.
Geographic Focus: New Jersey
Date(s) Application is Due: Feb 23
Contact: Steve Runs; (609) 292-6130; fax (609) 989-1440; steve.runk@sos.state.nj.us
Internet: http://www.njartscouncil.org/grant.cfm
Sponsor: New Jersey State Council on the Arts
225 West State Street, P.O. Box 306
Trenton, NJ 08625-0306

NJSCA Projects Serving Artists Grants **3450**

Projects Serving Artists (PSA) grants are awarded to support new or expanded projects whose primary beneficiaries are artists who reside in New Jersey and whose work has or will benefit New Jersey residents. Council funding may be sought annually for the launch and continued expansion of a specific project for up to three years, after which it will be expected that this developed on-going program will be able to be sustained with other resources. Projects can be in the form of programs and services that address artists' needs or the actual commissioning of artists to create new work. The highest priority for funding in the form of programs and services is for projects that provide space for creating, rehearsing, producing and presenting work. Other areas of interest in this category include projects that provide technical assistance or services to artists in the areas of marketing their work, legal issues, and accounting; projects that provide timely, relevant information, particularly about health insurance; projects that provide artists with access to and training on equipment, especially new technologies; and projects that provide networking opportunities, particularly to develop community residencies and secure affordable materials. Projects in the form of commissioning new works may be used to support the planning, production, artistic development, and audience development aspects necessary to a successful launch of a new artistic creation. Applicants must file a Notice of Intent online as well as apply online. Annual deadline dates may vary; contact the program office for exact dates. Deadlines must be met by eFiling by midnight on the deadline date. The deadline for signed originals and support materials is within two business days of the eDeadline and can be met with either a postmark or actual delivery of the materials to NJSCA offices at 225 West State Street, 4th Floor in Trenton by 5:00 p.m on the deadline date. New Jersey State Council on the Arts is a Division in the New Jersey Department of State and Partner Agency with the National Endowment for the Arts.
Requirements: Applicants must be incorporated in the State of New Jersey as a 501(c)3 organization or be a unit of government; be registered with the New Jersey Charities Registration Bureau; have a clearly articulated mission relating to the arts; have been in existence and actively providing public programs or services for at least the past two years at time of application; have a board of directors empowered to formulate policies and be responsible for the governance and administration of the organization, its programs and finances; demonstrate regional or statewide public impact through the organization's programs or project (regional is defined as serving audiences across a two or more county region of New Jersey). Matching funds are required and must be cash, not in-kind. For each dollar received from the Council, the grantee must show three additional dollars raised and spent. Applicants must apply online and should be advised that the prerequisite pre-registraton process requires up to 72 hours for completion by the system administrator before they can access the system.
Restrictions: Applicants may apply either to the NJSCA or to their County Arts Agency, not both, in a given year. Prospective NJSCA applicants that have been receiving support through their County Arts Agency up to now should attend a scheduled NJSCA grant workshop, work closely with NJSCA staff and their County Arts Agency in filing their Notice of Intent to Apply, and may also want to schedule a meeting early in the process with NJSCA staff. Because the funding periods for the County Arts Agency grants and the NJSCA grants overlap by six months, applicants should discuss their situation in advance of the Notice of Intent to Apply with the NJSCA to determine eligibility. K-12 schools and school districts are not eligible to apply, but may be a partner or collaborator on a project with an eligible applicant. Organizations may not apply to commission works from their own artistic leadership. Commissioning projects are intended to fund a single artistic commission, not multiple commissions through one project. Commissioning projects generally involve a single artist or small number of artists creating a single work. NJSCA General Operating Support (GOS)/General Program Support (GPS)/Local Arts Program (LAP) grantees may submit only one application per category each year. Non-GOS/GPS/LAP grantees may submit only one application each year.
Geographic Focus: New Jersey
Date(s) Application is Due: Feb 23
Contact: Steve Runk, Executive Director; (609) 292-6130; fax (609) 989-1440; steve.runk@sos.state.nj.us or njsca@arts.sos.state.nj.us
Internet: http://www.njartscouncil.org/program2.html
Sponsor: New Jersey State Council on the Arts
225 West State Street, P.O. Box 306
Trenton, NJ 08625-0306

NLADA Kutak-Dodds Prizes **3451**

The prestigious award annually honors the accomplishments of civil legal aid attorneys, public defenders, assigned counsel or public interest lawyers who, through the practice of law, are contributing in a significant way to the enhancement of human dignity and quality of life of those persons unable to afford legal representation. The prizes are intended to spotlight legal activity that reinforces the principle and reality of justice for all under the law. Prizes for the current year will honor two legal advocates for equal justice, one from the civil legal aid community and another from the public defense community. Preference is given to the nominee who is involved in legal advocacy and/or active representation of clients on a daily basis in the judicial, legislative, administrative, or public policy arena. No conditions are imposed on the recipient???s expenditure of the cash prize. Nomination guidelines are available online.
Requirements: To qualify for consideration, the nominee must be an attorney employed by or affiliated with an organization serving persons who cannot afford to pay for legal representation in either civil or criminal matters. The nominee also may be an attorney working for a public interest, nonprofit organization. Nominees must have at least 10 years of legal practice in legal services or public interest work and must be currently so engaged.
Geographic Focus: All States
Date(s) Application is Due: Feb 10
Amount of Grant: 10,000 USD
Contact: Tiffany Payne; (202) 452-0620, ext. 232; fax (202) 872-1031; t.payne@nlada.org
Internet: http://www.nlada.org/About/About_Awards_Kutak
Sponsor: National Legal Aid and Defender Association
1140 Connecticut Avenue NW, 9th Floor
Washington, DC 20036

NNEDVF/Altria Doors of Hope Program **3452**

The goal of this initiative is to strengthen the safety net available to survivors of domestic violence through the provision of grant awards that support organizational excellence, innovation, and leadership in the provision of shelter and legal advocacy services. Direct service grants are awarded to domestic violence service providers for shelter services and advocacy/legal services. There is a two stage application process; stage one consists of registration online, which includes key questions that will be used to determine which applicants will be invited to apply for stage two. For the current funding year, grantmaking will be by invitation only. Applicants will be contacted if they are eligible to apply. Additional assistance and information is provided at www.nnedv.org.
Requirements: Eligible organizations must have a primary mission which includes the provision of direct services to survivors of domestic violence; provide shelter and/or legal advocacy services to survivors of domestic violence; be a U.S. based non-profit, non-governmental, tax-exempt organization; have been in operation for a minimum of three years with an organization budget greater than or equal to $250,000; and have nondiscrimination policies that include ethnicity, race, religious creed, national origin, disability, sexual orientation, marital status, age, and gender.
Restrictions: Applications will only be accepted through the online RFP.
Geographic Focus: All States
Amount of Grant: 10,000 - 50,000 USD
Contact: Administrator; (202) 543-5566; fax (202) 543-5626; altriadoorsofhope@nnedv.org
Internet: http://www.altria.com/responsibility/4_9_1_1_2_1_domviolprograms.asp
Sponsor: National Network to End Domestic Violence Fund
660 Pennsylvania Avenue SE, Suite 303
Washington, DC 20003

NOAA Projects to Improve or Amend Coral Reef Fishery Management Plans **3453**

The NOAA Coral Reef Conservation Grant Program/Projects to Improve or Amend Coral Reef Fishery Management Plans (CRFMPGP) provides funding to the Regional Fishery Management Councils for projects to conserve and manage coral reef fisheries, as authorized under the Coral Reef Conservation Act of 2000. Projects funded through the CRFMPGP are for activities that: provide better scientific information on the status of coral reef fisheries resources, critical habitats of importance to coral reef fishes, and the impacts of fishing on these species and habitats; identify new management approaches that protect coral reef biodiversity and ecosystem function through regulation of fishing and other extractive uses; and incorporate conservation and sustainable management measures into existing or new Federal fishery management plans for coral reef species. Proposals selected for funding through this solicitation will be implemented through a Cooperative Agreement. Funding up to $1,050,000 is expected to be available. The NOAA Coral Reef Conservation Program anticipates that awards will range from $175,000 to $525,000.
Requirements: Eligible applicants are limited to the Western Pacific Regional Fishery Management Council, the South Atlantic Fishery Management Council, the Gulf of Mexico Fishery Management Council, and the Caribbean Fishery Management Council.
Geographic Focus: All States
Date(s) Application is Due: Nov 3
Contact: Jennifer Koss, (301) 713-3459, ext. 195; Jennifer.koss@noaa.gov
Internet: http://www07.grants.gov/search/search.do;jsessionid=LQCZGLyvwpgGPznL6jnLRyjK1vpGyTRsfyCJKLZtfJnqhLHphMnJ!280595828?oppId=42308&flag2006=false&mode=VIEW
Sponsor: U.S. Department of Commerce
1401 Constitution Avenue, NW, Room 5128
Washington, DC 20230

NOAA Undersea Research Program Project Grants 3454
NOAA's Undersea Research Program (NURP) is a unique comprehensive research program that provides scientists with the tools and expertise to conduct cutting-edge underwater research using advanced underwater technologies (e.g., human occupied submersibles, remotely operated vehicles, an undersea laboratory, mixed gas and technical diving). Some funds (less than $10,000 per project) are available for developmental projects or small exploratory research grants. These funds are reserved for late-breaking, high priority issues and may be awarded at the discretion of the Center Director. Funding opportunities will be announced through the individual NURP Center or NIUST.
Requirements: Eligible applicants are U.S. Institutions of higher education, not-for-profit institutions, and federal, state, and local governments.
Restrictions: Federal agencies may not charge salary or overhead.
Geographic Focus: All States
Amount of Grant: Up to 10,000 USD
Contact: Karen Kohanowich; (301) 734-1006; karen.kohanowich@noaa.gov
Internet: http://www.nurp.noaa.gov/Funding.htm
Sponsor: U.S. Department of Commerce
1401 Constitution Avenue, NW, Room 5128
Washington, DC 20230

Noble County Community Foundation Celebrate Diversity Project Grants 3455
The Celebrate Diversity Project (CDP) offers competitive grants to support culturally related programs and services throughout Noble County. The project hopes to discourage prejudice and fear regarding diverse populations by encouraging language and communication skills, fostering economic well-being, inspiring education, lifelong learning, and community involvement.
Requirements: The Celebrate Diversity Project will only consider not-for-profit projects that: promote cooperation among organizations without duplicating services; promote volunteer involvement; demonstrate practical approaches to current community issues; enhance or improve an organization's self-sufficiency and effectiveness; emphasize prevention; and promote cultural awareness among people of any age in Noble County, Indiana. Favorable consideration will be given to projects that: affect a broad segment of the population; are clearly replicable pilot programs; have a sustainability plan; serve people whose needs are not being met by existing services and that encourage independence; and move the community to a higher cultural awareness. When submitting the proposal, attach a cover sheet, not to exceed three pages, which includes: name of organization; contact person's name, address, and phone number; and signature of Board President/Director/Principal. Note: Teachers must have a signature from their school corporation's central office. Proposals should include the following: the need for and importance of this project and the number of people affected by it; brief description of the project and how it pertains to cultural diversity awareness; description of past projects that Celebrate Diversity Project has funded for the organization and the year received; timeline for project; a detailed budget for the amount requested, with justification. Budgets must include at least a 25% dollar match. Match may include: Other committed or applied for funding for project, organizational cash contribution, in-kind services and materials; and a copy of IRS Non-Profit Status letter. Applicants awarded a grant are required to send a representative(s) to the Taste of Noble County Ethnic Festival to showcase their project. Representative may be teachers, students, parents, or other volunteers who have been involved with the project.
Restrictions: Grants will not support: multi-year funding; research; uniforms and performance apparel; travel/transportation; salaries; meals/food. Grants will not be used under any circumstances to support: segregation programs; projects that don't serve residents of Noble County, Indiana; political/lobbying purposes; underwriting for fundraising events; projects not related to the promotion of cultural awareness.
Geographic Focus: Indiana
Date(s) Application is Due: Jun 15
Amount of Grant: Up to 15,000 USD
Contact: Margarita White, Diversity Director; (260) 894-9078; fax (260) 894-9906; margarita@noblecountycf.org or info@noblecountycf.org
Internet: http://www.noblecountycf.org/body.cfm?lvl1=servic&lvl2=progra&lvl3=pgmcdp
Sponsor: Noble County Community Foundation
1599 Lincolnway South
Ligonier, IN 46767

Noble County Community Foundation Grants 3456
The Noble County Community Foundation makes grants for innovative, creative projects and programs responsive to changing community needs in the areas of health and human services, education, arts and culture, and civic affairs. The funding is not limited to these areas and grant seekers are encouraged to respond to emerging community needs. The Foundation considers only not-for-profit projects that: promote cooperation among organizations without duplicating services; promote volunteer involvement; demonstrate practical approaches to current community issues; enhance or improve an organization's self-sufficiency and effectiveness; emphasize prevention. In addition, the Foundation considers projects that: affect a broad segment of the population; are pilot programs clearly replicable in their design and have reasonable prospects for future support; serve people whose needs are not being met by existing services and which encourage independence; move the community to a higher cultural awareness. The Foundation offers grants in April, June, August, and December, with decisions made 60 days after each deadline. Applicants are encouraged to contact the Foundation before submitting a proposal to find out if the project is appropriate for funding. Applicants should refer to the website for further information.
Requirements: In applying for grants, the following points must be addressed (with explanation if information is not available): the specific purpose and the need for the funds requested; the need for the program/project in the community; the amount requested; a detailed description of how the money would be spent; a statement of how the project will improve life in Noble County and how the outcomes will be measured; recent grants received and applications pending for this program/project; a listing of the current board and/or project organizers and their contact information; a copy of the organization's IRS tax-exempt letter stating 501(c)3 status; and for schools applying, a letter of support from the organization's superintendent/principal. After the organization's request has been received, it may be contacted by a Foundation representative requesting a site visit or additional information.
Restrictions: Discretionary funds will not be used under any circumstances to support: deficit spending; political purposes; annual fund campaigns; lobbying; organizations whose primary function is to allocate funds to other charitable organizations or projects; projects that do not serve residents of Noble County; travel; augmenting endowments; underwriting for fundraising events; loans.
Geographic Focus: Indiana
Date(s) Application is Due: Mar 2; May 2; Jul 2; Nov 2
Amount of Grant: 500 - 5,000 USD
Contact: Linda Yerick, Executive Director; (260) 894-3335; fax (260) 894-9020; linda@noblecountycf.org or info@noblecountycf.org
Internet: http://www.noblecountycf.org/body.cfm?lvl1=servic&lvl2=grants&lvl3=how2ap
Sponsor: Noble County Community Foundation
1599 Lincolnway South
Ligonier, IN 46767

Nokomis Foundation Grants 3457
From time to time, Nokomis Foundation will send out Requests for Proposals specifically related to their focus areas of women's economic self-sufficiency as well as civic engagement. Nokomis Foundation does not accept unsolicited proposals. Questions about the grantmaking process may be directed to the Program Director.
Geographic Focus: All States
Contact: Anne Hagen, Program Director; (616) 451-0267; fax (616) 451-9914; ahagen@nokomisfoundation.org
Internet: http://www.nokomisfoundation.org/grantmaking
Sponsor: Nokomis Foundation
161 Ottawa NW, Suite 305-C
Grand Rapids, MI 49503

Nonprofit Management Fund Grants 3458
The mission of the Nonprofit Management Fund is to improve the management effectiveness and efficiency of nonprofit organizations and to increase the resources for nonprofit management in the greater Milwaukee area. The expectations are that grantees will become more effective and efficient in serving clients, program participants, their audience, or the community-at-large. The specific costs associated with technical assistance that are eligible for funding include: consulting services, training, technology upgrades or graphic design assistance that builds the capacity of nonprofit organizations. Three general categories of technical assistance have been established: management assistance, organizational alternatives, and diagnostic clinics. The Fund considers applications during the first 10 days of the even months of the year. Proposals are due in the first 10 days of the odd months of the year for consideration. Grants will be project-specific, non-renewable, and range from $1,000 to $10,000. The application is available as an online process through the Fund website. Additional information, including previously funded projects and an extended list of eligible funding projects, is also located at the website.
Requirements: Small and medium-sized private, nonprofit, 501(c)3 tax-exempt organizations, which have been incorporated for at least two years, and serve Milwaukee, Ozaukee, Washington or Waukesha counties are eligible to apply. The priority target groups of the Funds are smaller organizations that lack the capacity to underwrite technical assistance within their operating budgets. Applicants are expected to have Milwaukee, Ozaukee, Washington, or Waukesha county as their primary target area, with at least 70% of the organization's work conducted in the greater Milwaukee area.
Restrictions: Organizations with annual operating budgets of over $3 million will not be considered. Grants will not be made for the following activities: general operating support, office equipment and furnishings (except for computer hardware and software), construction or rehabilitation of facilities, emergency repairs, payroll needs, debt liquidation, or routine financial audits. The Nonprofit Management Fund does not support program planning, program evaluation, or community needs assessments. The Fund will not underwrite expenses associated with capital campaigns, including feasibility studies. Projects that request support for independent contractors to perform staff functions will not be considered. The Fund also will not fund activities that have taken place prior to the date of the committee's funding decision.
Geographic Focus: Wisconsin
Contact: Patricia Wyzbinski, Fund Advisor; (414) 271-4869; fax (414) 271-5023; fundadvisors@nonprofitmanagementfund.org
Internet: http://www.nonprofitmanagementfund.org/GrantApplication.aspx
Sponsor: Nonprofit Management Fund
2212 South Kinnickinnic Avenue
Milwaukee, WI 53207

Norcliffe Foundation Grants 3459
The Norcliffe Foundation is a private nonprofit family foundation established in 1952 by Paul Pigott for the purpose of improving the quality of life for all people in the Puget Sound region. The foundation provides grants in the areas of health, education, social services, civic improvement, religion, culture and the arts, the environment, historic preservation and youth programs. Foundation funding types include capital campaigns for building and equipment, certain operating budgets, endowments, challenge/matching grants, land acquisition, new projects, start-up funds, renovation, and research. Requests for publication, videos/films, and website production may be considered as may scholarships, fellowships / chairs, conferences / seminars, social enterprise development, and technical assistance.

Multi-year and renewable funding may be considered. Applications are accepted year-round. One copy of a letter proposal and/or common grant application form should be directed to the President in care of the Foundation Manager at the contact information given. An initial phone call is optional. Guidelines, instructions, and a copy of the common grant proposal form are provided at the website. Funding decisions and notification generally occur three to six months after receipt of request.
Requirements: 501(c)3 organizations in the Puget Sound region in and around Seattle, Washington are eligible to apply.
Restrictions: The Norcliffe Foundation does not provide the following types of assistance: deficit financing, emergency funds, grants to individuals, matches to employee-giving, Program-Related Investments / Loans (PRIs), in-kind services, volunteer / loaned executive, and internships. Applicants may only submit one request per year from date of funding or denial. Applicants who have previously received grants of $50,000 or more from the Foundation must wait two years from final payment before submitting a new application.
Geographic Focus: Washington
Amount of Grant: 1,000 - 25,000 USD
Contact: Arline Hefferline; (206) 682-4820; arline@thenorcliffefoundation.com
Internet: http://www.thenorcliffefoundation.com/
Sponsor: Norcliffe Foundation
999 Third Avenue, Suite 1006
Seattle, WA 98104-4001

Norcross Wildlife Foundation Grants　　　　　　　　　　　　　　　　3460
Norcross makes only restricted grants: for land protection, program-related office and field equipment/technology, public education materials. They support a very limited amount of community-service work, confined to the New York City metropolitan area and the towns near the Norcross Wildlife Sanctuary. Requests for no more than $10,000 will be considered; grants average less then $5,000 though.
Requirements: Nonprofit organizations are eligible. Norcross will generally consider only one grant request per organization per year. Small, grassroots organizations with limited staff and ability to raise funds are given preference.
Restrictions: The foundation does not support research, conferences, general operating expenses, salaried positions, animal welfare, or wildlife rehabilitation; nor does it renew earlier grants, make grants to individuals, match other funders' support, or make multi-year commitments of funds. Grant requests will not be considered from large national organizations, endowed colleges and universities, or regional NGO's with professional development staff and/or considerable invested assets or a large gap between income and program expenses. Requests for land-purchase funds are discouraged.
Geographic Focus: All States
Amount of Grant: Up to 10,000 USD
Contact: John G. McMurray; (212) 362-4831 or (718) 791-2094; john@norcrossws.org
Internet: http://norcrossws.org/Foundation%20Infor/Foundmain.html
Sponsor: Norcross Wildlife Foundation
250 W 88th Street, #806
New York, NY 10024

Nord Family Foundation Grants　　　　　　　　　　　　　　　　3461
The Nord Family Foundation, in the tradition of its founders, Walter and Virginia Nord, endeavors to build community through support of projects that bring opportunity to the disadvantaged, strengthen the bond of families, and improve the quality of people's lives. Grants are awarded in the fields of arts and culture, civic affairs, education and health and social services. Most grants are made for program related activities, with some grants to support capital improvements and capital campaigns when special criteria are met. Projects that are directed at the root causes of social problems are of special interest. Grants range from $2,000 to $50,000.
Requirements: Applicants must be 501(c)3 non-profit organizations or selected public sector activities. Awards are made primarily in the environs of Lorain County, Ohio, with additional support in Cuyahoga County, Ohio. Particular attention is given to Cuyahoga County non-profits that provide services to Lorain County residents. Occasionally awards are made outside of this area, to organizations located in areas where voting members of the Foundation reside or to organizations with a national or international focus. Application is made online from the Foundation's website.
Restrictions: The Foundation does not support debt reduction, research projects, and tickets or advertising for fundraising activities.
Geographic Focus: Ohio
Date(s) Application is Due: Apr 1; Aug 1; Dec 1
Contact: John Mullaney, Executive Director; (800) 745-8946 or (440) 984-3939; fax (440) 984-3934; execdir@nordff.org or info@nordff.org
Internet: http://www.nordff.org
Sponsor: Nord Family Foundation
747 Milan Avenue
Amherst, OH 44001

Nordson Corporation Foundation Grants　　　　　　　　　　　　　　　　3462
The corporate foundation awards grants to nonprofit organizations in geographic areas where Nordson facilities and employees are located: Cuyahoga and Lorain counties in Ohio; the Greater Atlanta, Georgia area; California, Rhode Island and Southeastern Massachusetts. The foundation provides a source of stable funding for community programs and projects in the areas of education, human welfare, civic, and arts and culture. Educational support is generally limited to improving elementary and secondary schools and certain programs for public and private higher education. Human welfare grants focus on children and youth. The foundation considers other funding areas, including urban affairs, volunteerism, public policy, health and health organizations, and literacy. Grants are awarded for general operating support, continuing support, annual campaigns, capital campaigns, building construction/renovation, equipment acquisition, emergency funds, seed money, scholarship funds, employee matching gifts, and technical assistance. The board meets four times each year. Deadlines vary by state; contact program staff for appropriate deadlines. Application forms are available on the website and may only be submitted online.
Requirements: Private, nonprofit organizations in California, Georgia, Ohio, Rhode Island, and southeastern Massachusetts may apply.
Restrictions: Funding is not provided for organizations whose services are not provided within the foundation's geographic areas of interest; direct grants or scholarships to individuals; organizations not eligible for tax-deductible support; organizations not exempt under Section 501(c)3 of the Internal Revenue Code; political causes, candidates, organizations or campaigns; organizations that discriminate on the basis of race, sex, or religion; or special occasion, goodwill advertising, i.e., journals or dinner programs.
Geographic Focus: California, Georgia, Massachusetts, Ohio, Rhode Island
Date(s) Application is Due: Feb 15; May 15; Aug 15; Nov 15
Amount of Grant: Up to 15,000,000 USD
Contact: Cecilia H. Render, Director; (440) 892-1580, ext. 5172; crender@nordson.com
Internet: http://www.nordson.com/Corporate/Community/Foundation
Sponsor: Nordson Corporation Foundation
28601 Clemens Road
Westlake, OH 44145-1119

Norfolk Southern Foundation Grants　　　　　　　　　　　　　　　　3463
The Norfolk Southern Foundation awards grants to nonprofits in the territory served by Norfolk Southern Railway Company. The foundation offers grants in four principal areas: educational programs, primarily at the post-secondary level; community enrichment focusing on cultural and artistic organizations; environmental programs; and health and human services (primarily food banks, homeless programs, and free clinics). Decision are made by December 31 for the following year's discretionary funding program, and applicants are notified early in the following calendar year.
Requirements: Applicants should include the following in their information packet: a valid 501(c)3 or 170(c)1 letter from the IRS; a short request outlining objectives of the organization, project, and intended use of funds; a listing of the applicant's board of directors; current and potential sources of funding; audited financial statements from the last three years; and the applicant's contact name, phone number, and email address.
Restrictions: Grant requests are only accepted between July 15 and September 30 for funding in the following calendar year. Applications will not be accepted from: organizations not in the NS territory (must be served by Norfolk Southern to be considered); organizations that do not have a 501(c)3 or 170(c)(1) IRS letter; individuals or organizations established to help individuals; religious, fraternal, social or veterans organizations; political or lobbying organizations; public or private elementary and secondary schools; fundraising events, telethons, races or benefits; sports or athletic organizations or activities; community or private foundations, or other organizations that merely redistribute to other eligible organizations aggregated contributions; disease-related organizations and hospitals; mentoring programs; Boys and Girls Scout programs or similar organizations; animal organizations; non-U.S. based charities; and organizations whose programs have national scope
Geographic Focus: Alabama, Connecticut, Delaware, District of Columbia, Florida, Georgia, Illinois, Indiana, Iowa, Kentucky, Louisiana, Maine, Maryland, Massachusetts, Michigan, Mississippi, Missouri, New Hampshire, New Jersey, New York, North Carolina, Ohio, Pennsylvania, Rhode Island, South Carolina, Tennessee, Texas, Vermont, Virginia, West Virginia, Wisconsin
Date(s) Application is Due: Sep 30
Amount of Grant: Up to USD
Contact: Katie Fletcher; (757) 629-2881; fax (757) 629-2361; katie.fletcher@nscorp.com
Internet: http://www.nscorp.com/nscportal/nscorp/Community/NS%20Foundation/
Sponsor: Norfolk Southern Foundation
P.O. Box 3040
Norfolk, VA 23514-3040

Norman Foundation Grants　　　　　　　　　　　　　　　　3464
The Norman Foundation supports efforts that strengthen the ability of communities to determine their own economic, environmental and social well-being, and that help people control those forces that affect their lives. These efforts may: promote economic justice and development through community organizing, coalition building and policy reform efforts; work to prevent the disposal of toxics in communities, and to link environmental issues with economic and social justice; link community-based economic and environmental justice organizing to national and international reform efforts. The following is considered when evaluating grant proposals: does the project arise from the hopes and efforts of those whose survival, well-being and liberation are directly at stake; does it further ethnic, gender and other forms of equity; is it rooted in organized, practical undertakings; and is it likely to achieve systemic change. In pursuing systemic change, the Foundation would hope that: the proposed action may serve as a model; the spread of the model may create institutions that can survive on their own; their establishment and success may generate beneficial adaptations by other political, social and economic institutions and structures. The Foundation provides grants for general support, projects, and collaborative efforts. We also welcome innovative proposals designed to build the capacity of social change organizations working in our areas of interest. Priority is given to organizations with annual budgets of under $1 million.
Requirements: Programs must be 501(c)3 tax-exempt organizations that focused on domestic United States issues. Prospective grantees should initiate the application process by sending a short two or three page letter of inquiry to the Program Director (fax, email or regular mail). There are no set deadlines, and letters of inquiry are reviewed throughout the year. The Foundation only accepts full proposals upon positive response to the letter of inquiry. The letter of inquiry should briefly explain: the scope and significance of the problem to be addressed; the organization's proposed response and (if appropriate) how this strategy

builds upon the organization's past work; the specific demonstrable effects the project would have if successful, especially its potential to effect systemic (fundamental, institutional and significant) change; how the project promotes change on a national level and is otherwise related to the foundation's guidelines; the size of the organization's budget. All inquiries will be acknowledged and, if deemed promising, the Foundation will request a full proposal.
Restrictions: The Foundation does not make grants to individuals or universities; or to support conferences, scholarships, research, films, media and arts projects; or to capital funding projects, fundraising drives or direct social service programs, such as shelters or community health programs. The Foundation's grant making is restricted to U.S.-based organizations.
Geographic Focus: All States
Amount of Grant: 5,000 - 30,000 USD
Contact: June Makela, Program Director; (212) 230-9830; fax (212) 230-9849; norman@normanfdn.org
Internet: http://www.normanfdn.org/
Sponsor: Norman Foundation
147 East 48th Street
New York, NY 10017

North American Wetlands Conservation Grants 3465
The North American Wetlands Conservation Council provides matching grants to private and public organizations and to individuals to carry out wetlands conservation projects in the United States, Canada, and Mexico. The council is accepting applications to support partnerships to conserve wetlands and wetland-dependent fish and wildlife. The council also administers a small grants program to encourage participation by new grantees. Federal dollars must be matched on a one-to-one ratio for both types of grants. Applications for small grants must meet an April deadline. Traditional grants applications may be submitted at any time but no later than the first Friday in April or August. Annual deadline dates may vary; contact the program office to confirm exact dates.
Requirements: Eligible applicants include federal agencies, state and local governments, nongovernmental nonprofits, Native American tribal groups, private profit-making agencies, and individuals who have established partnerships to contribute funds, services, and resources to develop wetlands conservation projects.
Restrictions: The small grants program only funds projects in the United States.
Geographic Focus: All States
Amount of Grant: 40,000 - 1,000,000 USD
Contact: Chief, Division of Bird Habitat Conservation; (703) 358-1784
Internet: http://www.fws.gov/grants/state.html
Sponsor: U.S. Fish and Wildlife Service
1849 C Street NW
Washington, DC 20240

North Carolina Arts Council Arts and Audiences Grants 3466
This category provides funds to organizations to increase and enhance participation in the arts by linking the content of art programs they wish to produce with the interests and experiences of the audiences they wish to engage. Grant funds will be awarded to support strong artistic programs with clear audience goals. Audience goals can be designed to: broaden participation by attracting more people; diversify participation by attracting audiences different from those the organization is already attracting; and deepen participation by increasing current participants' levels of involvement. Grant funds may be used for artist fees, marketing, interpretive materials, contractual fees (including contractual personnel), and other related costs. Up to 25-percent of the grant amount requested may be used for operating expenses including salaries that are directly related to the project. Grant amounts range from $5,000-$15,000 and rarely exceed $10,000. General support organizations and organizations applying for two-year projects must file letters of intent with the Arts Council by January 15. All regular applications are due by the March 2 deadline.
Requirements: Grants must be matched dollar for dollar by the organization.
Restrictions: Projects that take place primarily in schools or focus primarily on children are not eligible in this category.
Geographic Focus: North Carolina
Date(s) Application is Due: Jan 15; Mar 2
Contact: Jeff Pettus, (919) 807-6513; jeff.pettus@ncdcr.gov
Internet: http://www.ncarts.org/freeform_scrn_template.cfm?ffscrn_id=265
Sponsor: North Carolina Arts Council
Department of Cultural Resources, 109 East Jones Street, MSC #4632
Raleigh, NC 27601-2807

North Carolina Arts Council Arts Folklife Internship 3467
This three-month internship provides intensive, directed training with the Arts Council's Folklife staff. The intern receives a $4,000 stipend for the three-month period. The internship takes place for twelve weeks between April and August. Applicants must have completed at least one year of graduate study in folklife or related fields (ethnomusicology, anthropology, history, etc.) or have experience with traditional arts and culture. The next application deadline is March 2.
Requirements: Applicants must have completed at least one year of graduate study in folklife or related fields (ethnomusicology, anthropology, history, etc.) or have otherwise gained significant experience with traditional arts and culture. Applicants must be North Carolina residents.
Geographic Focus: North Carolina
Date(s) Application is Due: Mar 2
Contact: Wayne Martin; (919) 807-6506; wayne.martin@ncmail.net
Internet: http://www.ncarts.org/freeform_scrn_template.cfm?ffscrn_id=119
Sponsor: North Carolina Arts Council
Department of Cultural Resources, 109 East Jones Street, MSC #4632
Raleigh, NC 27601-2807

North Carolina Arts Council Arts in Education Artist Residencies Grants 3468
This category provides support for artist residencies of at least five days and up to a full year. Residency days and weeks do not have to be consecutive. Applicants may request funding for up to two artist residencies in their application. Grant funds may be used for artist fees, marketing, contractual fees, artist/contractor travel, and other project-related costs. Priority is given to requests for artist fees. (Fees for student artists and ensembles are not eligible for funding.) Up to 25 percent of the funds requested may be used to support administrative expenses including personnel. The minimum grant amount is $5,000. Generally, grant amounts range from $5,000 to $10,000 and will not exceed $15,000. Organizations and schools may hire performing, visual, literary, or traditional artists or companies from within the state or from outside the state.
Requirements: North Carolina pre K-12 schools, school systems, nonprofit arts, community organizations, or partnership teams consisting of at least one school and one arts group may apply. All grants must be matched dollar for dollar except those serving rural, low wealth counties which are eligible for 75 percent to 100 percent funding.
Restrictions: This category is not intended to provide support for guest artists to direct, choreograph, or conduct school based productions or performances.
Geographic Focus: North Carolina
Date(s) Application is Due: Mar 2
Amount of Grant: Up to 15,000 USD
Contact: Linda Bamford; (919) 807-6502; linda.bamford@ncmail.net
Internet: http://www.ncarts.org/freeform_scrn_template.cfm?ffscrn_id=17
Sponsor: North Carolina Arts Council
Department of Cultural Resources, 109 East Jones Street, MSC #4632
Raleigh, NC 27601-2807

North Carolina Arts Council Arts in Education Initiatives Grants 3469
This grant provides support to a variety of educational programs. The following programs and projects are fundable in this category: afterschool and summer arts in education programs designed specifically for underserved students; and professional development workshops and institutes for pre K-12 educators and teaching artists that focus on increasing skills in arts and education or integrating the arts into the curriculum. Funding can support a series of workshops or a multiple day institute. The training must include these follow-up components: opportunity to demonstrate acquired knowledge and skills through follow-up activities observed by a trainer or designated mentor; print and Web site based resources (multiple year projects only); and documentation and assessment by a professional evaluator (multiple year projects only). Project costs may include fees for planning and evaluation meetings, artists, consultants, workshop leaders, instructors, contract personnel, space rental, artist or contractor travel costs, marketing, and supplies. (Fees for student artists and ensembles are not eligible for funding.) The minimum grant amount is $5,000. Generally, grant amounts range from $5,000 to $10,000 and will not exceed $20,000. Up to 25 percent of the funds requested may be used to support administrative expenses including personnel, but funds cannot be requested solely for project administration or salary assistance. Priority is given for fees that support the work of professional artists in educational settings and programs. Priority will be given to replicable projects designed as multiple year initiatives; however, an applicant must reapply each year.
Requirements: North Carolina pre K-12 schools, school systems, nonprofit arts, community organizations, or partnership teams consisting of at least one school and one arts group may apply. All grants must be matched dollar for dollar except those serving rural, low wealth counties which are eligible for 75 percent to 100 percent funding.
Restrictions: This category is not designed to provide annual support for on-going projects.
Geographic Focus: North Carolina
Date(s) Application is Due: Mar 2
Amount of Grant: Up to 20,000 USD
Contact: Linda Bamford; (919) 807-6502; linda.bamford@ncmail.net
Internet: http://www.ncarts.org/freeform_scrn_template.cfm?ffscrn_id=17
Sponsor: North Carolina Arts Council
Department of Cultural Resources, 109 East Jones Street, MSC #4632
Raleigh, NC 27601-2807

North Carolina Arts Council Arts in Education Rural Development Grants 3470
This category provides entry-level support to establish or improve arts in education programs in rural communities. Funding is available to rural schools and organizations to support a three-year approach to program development as follows: Planning Year (first year)—grant amounts of $3,000 are awarded for this planning year and matching funds are not required; Pilot Year (second year)—participants may receive up to $5,000 to pilot the approved new arts program, and a match is required; and Implementation Year (third year)—participants who successfully complete the second year may submit a third year request for up to $7,500.
Requirements: Pre K-12 schools, school systems, and nonprofit arts or community organizations located in rural areas listed below. Applicants in this category may not apply in other AIE categories.
Geographic Focus: North Carolina
Date(s) Application is Due: Mar 2
Amount of Grant: 3,000 - 7,500 USD
Contact: Linda Bamford; (919) 807-6502; linda.bamford@ncmail.net
Internet: http://www.ncarts.org/grants_category.cfm?ID=29&CFID=4457728&CFTOKEN=11501724&jsessionid=28302898591231777988333
Sponsor: North Carolina Arts Council
Department of Cultural Resources, 109 East Jones Street, MSC #4632
Raleigh, NC 27601-2807

GRANT PROGRAMS | 529

North Carolina Arts Council Community Arts Administration Internship   3471
This program provides two individuals with a three-month intensive, supervised internship with one of the state's local arts councils or arts centers. At each location, the intern is under the supervision of the executive director or other designated staff member who, in collaboration with the intern, designs a training program taken from the spectrum of community arts administration — e.g., programming, fund raising, marketing, grantmaking, planning, facility management, financial management, etc. Interns also spend time with Council staff for information and evaluation sessions. Interns receive a $5,000 stipend to cover living expenses. The host organizations are responsible for assisting interns in locating housing; however, interns may make their own living arrangements if they prefer.
Requirements: An individual must be a U.S. citizen or holder of permanent resident alien status to be eligible to apply. Applicants must have at least a four-year college degree and demonstrate a strong interest in a career in community arts administration. North Carolina applicants are given priority consideration, but qualified individuals living outside the state are also encouraged to apply.
Geographic Focus: North Carolina
Date(s) Application is Due: May 1
Contact: Katherine Reynolds, fax (919) 807-6505; katherine.reynolds@ncmail.net
Internet: http://www.ncarts.org/freeform_scrn_template.cfm?ffscrn_id=119
Sponsor: North Carolina Arts Council
Department of Cultural Resources, 109 East Jones Street, MSC #4632
Raleigh, NC 27601-2807

North Carolina Arts Council Community Public Art and Design Dev Grants   3472
A grant through this category supports consultants' fees, artists' fees, travel, and other expenses associated with: development of a master plan to incorporate art or design features into public space. Consultants recommended by N.C. Arts Council staff will lead the master planning process; or development of a specific public art or design project through planning, artist selection, and preliminary design phases up to, but not including, commission, final plans, and implementation. The minimum grant amount is $5,000, and the maximum grant amount is $10,000.
Requirements: Nonprofit arts or community organizations, as well as municipal or county government agencies, may apply. Non-arts organizations and agencies must apply with an arts partner. Applicants must match grants dollar, with the exception of programs serving rural, low wealth areas. Applicants from these designated areas may request 75 percent to 100 percent of the project costs.
Geographic Focus: North Carolina
Date(s) Application is Due: Mar 2
Contact: Brendan Greaves; (919) 807-6509; brendan.greaves@ncdcr.gov
Internet: http://www.ncarts.org/freeform_scrn_template.cfm?ffscrn_id=125
Sponsor: North Carolina Arts Council
Department of Cultural Resources, 109 East Jones Street, MSC #4632
Raleigh, NC 27601-2807

North Carolina Arts Council Community Public Art and Design Implem Grants   3473
A grant through this category supports; fees for artists, project managers, and consultants; fabrication and installation costs; travel; and other expenses associated with final design and implementation of a public art or design project. Fundable phases may include: artist or designer commissions; advanced design proposals, including renderings, blueprints, and models; the creation of the final work, including materials, fabrication, and installation; and workshops and educational programming to ensure the community relevance of the project. The minimum grant amount is $5,000 and the maximum grant award is $15,000.
Requirements: Nonprofit arts or community organizations, as well as municipal or county government agencies, may apply. Non-arts organizations and agencies must apply with an arts partner. Applicants must match grants dollar for dollar, with the exception of programs serving rural, low wealth areas. Applicants from these designated areas may request 75 percent to 100 percent of the project costs.
Geographic Focus: North Carolina
Date(s) Application is Due: Mar 2
Contact: Brendan Greaves; (919) 807-6509; brendan.greaves@ncdcr.gov
Internet: http://www.ncarts.org/freeform_scrn_template.cfm?ffscrn_id=125
Sponsor: North Carolina Arts Council
Department of Cultural Resources, 109 East Jones Street, MSC #4632
Raleigh, NC 27601-2807

North Carolina Arts Council Facility Design Grants   3474
This category is divided into two levels that support all phases of facility design. Level I is Project Feasibility, which provides consultants to lead a preliminary planning process to determine the feasibility of an arts facility renovation or building project. Level II is Architectural Design, which provides support for the design phases of renovating or building an arts facility. Level I grant awards will be $5,000, and the applicant must match with $3,000 (applicants in designated rural, low wealth areas may apply for the full $8,000). In Level II, the minimum grant amount is $5,000, and the maximum grant amount is $10,000.
Requirements: Nonprofit arts or community organizations, as well as municipal or county government agencies, may apply. Non-arts organizations and agencies must apply with an arts partner. In Level II, grants must be matched dollar for dollar by the applicant, with the exception of programs serving rural, low wealth areas.
Geographic Focus: North Carolina
Date(s) Application is Due: Mar 2
Contact: Brendan Greaves; (919) 807-6509; brendan.greaves@ncdcr.gov
Internet: http://www.ncarts.org/grants_category.cfm?ID=25
Sponsor: North Carolina Arts Council
Department of Cultural Resources, 109 East Jones Street, MSC #4632
Raleigh, NC 27601-2807

North Carolina Arts Council Folklife Documentary Project Grants   3475
Documentary projects support: folklife fieldwork that creates primary source materials that documents North Carolina's traditional arts; or artists' projects that produce, publicize, and distribute materials that promote an individual traditional artist, ensemble, or group. Materials created may include sound recordings, videography, photography, transcribed interviews, disc recordings, Web site development, brochures and pamphlets, podcasts, and video projects, among others. Grant funds support project-related costs including stipends for project personnel, honoraria for folk artists, travel, supplies, and materials. Primary source materials created through the grant should be deposited in a publicly accessible archive.
Requirements: North Carolina organizations and individuals who have demonstrated a substantial knowledge of North Carolina's folk art traditions and expertise in professional documentation techniques are eligible. Applicants must contact the staff before applying to this category.
Geographic Focus: North Carolina
Date(s) Application is Due: Mar 2
Amount of Grant: Up to 10,000 USD
Contact: Sally Peterson, Folklife Specialist; (919) 807-6507; sally.peterson@ncdcr.gov
Internet: http://www.ncarts.org/grants_programs.cfm?ID=6
Sponsor: North Carolina Arts Council
Department of Cultural Resources, 109 East Jones Street, MSC #4632
Raleigh, NC 27601-2807

North Carolina Arts Council Folklife Public Program Grants   3476
Public programs support: exhibitions, performances and workshops, publications, and radio and television programs that promote public knowledge and appreciation of the state's traditional arts; or salary assistance to organizations that create a staff position for a professional folklorist. Grant funds also support expenses directly related to the project including production costs, stipends, honoraria, marketing, travel, supplies, telephone, and postage.
Requirements: North Carolina nonprofit organizations are eligible.
Geographic Focus: North Carolina
Date(s) Application is Due: Mar 2
Amount of Grant: Up to 10,000 USD
Contact: Sally Peterson, Folklife Specialist; (919) 807-6507; sally.peterson@ncdcr.gov
Internet: http://www.ncarts.org/grants_programs.cfm?ID=6
Sponsor: North Carolina Arts Council
Department of Cultural Resources, 109 East Jones Street, MSC #4632
Raleigh, NC 27601-2807

North Carolina Arts Council General Support Grants   3477
This category provides funds to arts organizations to support their ongoing artistic and administrative functions. Fundable expenses may include, but are not limited to, salaries, artists fees, production, travel, promotion, postage, telephone, and facility operation. This category is designed to support groups that, over time, have consistently produced strong artistic programs and demonstrated responsible administrative practices. All grant-funded activities must take place between July 1 of the current year and June 30 of the next. Application materials are available on the Web site.
Requirements: North Carolina dance, literary, music, theater, and visual arts organizations may apply. Grants must be matched dollar for dollar from the organization's budget. Organizations not previously funded in this category must contact the council staff to discuss eligibility before submitting applications.
Restrictions: University museums or galleries are not eligible to apply in this category.
Geographic Focus: North Carolina
Date(s) Application is Due: Mar 2
Amount of Grant: 5,000 - 70,000 USD
Contact: Linda Bamford; (919) 807-6502; linda.bamford@ncmail.net
Internet: http://www.ncarts.org/grants_programs.cfm?ID=7
Sponsor: North Carolina Arts Council
Department of Cultural Resources, 109 East Jones Street, MSC #4632
Raleigh, NC 27601-2807

North Carolina Arts Council New Realities Program Grants   3478
With the New Realities Program, arts leaders are asked to consider the changing conditions and environment, to describe their reality and to develop a plan addressing or altering that reality. This plan addresses how each organization will make its art or produce arts programs, how it will connect with its community, and how it will develop the human and financial resources it needs. The program requires the organization's staff leadership to participate and be prepared to explore new and different approaches to organizational structure and operation. The organization's board leadership is also expected to participate in various aspects of the program. Applicants will submit the form electronically through North Carolina ARTS Grants Online (AGO), and must also submit a print version of the form by 5 p.m. on the deadline day.
Requirements: North Carolina nonprofit organizations are eligible.
Geographic Focus: North Carolina
Date(s) Application is Due: Mar 2
Contact: Nancy Trovillion, Deputy Director; (919) 807-6526; nancy.trovillion@ncdcr.gov
Internet: http://www.ncarts.org/grants_category.cfm?ID=14&menu_sel=4&sub_sel=15&CFID=4457522&CFTOKEN=92501306&jsessionid=28302898591231777988333
Sponsor: North Carolina Arts Council
Department of Cultural Resources, 109 East Jones Street, MSC #4632
Raleigh, NC 27601-2807

North Carolina Arts Council Outreach Program Grants — 3479
The Program has two distinct categories: technical assistance to organizations that have an operating budget of at least $10,000 and that have been producing arts programs for two or more years; and funds to support the ongoing artistic and administrative functions of organizations that have operating budgets of $50,000 or higher and have been producing arts programs for three or more years.
Requirements: North Carolina nonprofit, tax-exempt arts organizations, primarily based in and focused on the African American, Asian American, Hispanic, or Native American communities, may apply. Single-discipline organizations that are not the primary constituents of other council sections are eligible for support, as well as multidisciplinary organizations that serve a wide range of art forms including the performing, visual, and literary arts in their cultures.
Geographic Focus: North Carolina
Date(s) Application is Due: Mar 2
Amount of Grant: 2,500 - 20,000 USD
Contact: Janie Wilson, Outreach Coordinator; (919) 807-6508; janie.wilson@ncmail.net
Internet: http://www.ncarts.org/freeform_scrn_template.cfm?ffscrn_id=153
Sponsor: North Carolina Arts Council
Department of Cultural Resources, 109 East Jones Street, MSC #4632
Raleigh, NC 27601-2807

North Carolina Arts Council Regional Artist Project Grants — 3480
This program funds regional consortia of local arts councils to award project grants to artists in their regions. These grants support professional artists in any discipline and at any stage in their careers to pursue projects that further their artistic development. Types of fundable projects include: creation of a new work; purchase of equipment; professional development workshops; travel support for expenses associated with a professional opportunity such as participating in an exhibition or a conference; and development or upgrading of promotional materials such as brochures, DVDs, CDs, and Web sites. Grant awards to artists generally range from $500 to $3,000, while grant amounts to consortia generally range from $5,000 to $12,500.
Requirements: Any community-based North Carolina nonprofit, tax-exempt local arts council or commission may apply. Artists may apply to participating local arts councils for small grants to assist them in furthering their careers. Grants must be matched dollar-for-dollar by the applicant consortia.
Geographic Focus: North Carolina
Date(s) Application is Due: Mar 2
Amount of Grant: 500 - 12,500 USD
Contact: Jeff Pettus, Visual Arts Director; (919) 807-6513; jeff.pettus@ncmail.net
Internet: http://www.ncarts.org/grants_category.cfm?ID=2
Sponsor: North Carolina Arts Council
Department of Cultural Resources, 109 East Jones Street, MSC #4632
Raleigh, NC 27601-2807

North Carolina Arts Council Residency Center Grants — 3481
The N.C. Arts Council sponsors one- and two-month residencies for artists in a variety of disciplines at residency centers in California and Vermont. The purpose of the N.C. Arts Council's residency program is to provide both emerging and established North Carolina artists with time for their work. Two artists will be selected for residencies at Headlands Center for the Arts and for residencies at Vermont Studio Center as part of this program. The deadline for Headlands is June 6, and the deadline for Vermont is June 16.
Requirements: North Carolina poets, fiction writers, playwrights, storytellers, and visual artists may apply.
Geographic Focus: North Carolina
Date(s) Application is Due: Jun 6; Jun 16
Amount of Grant: 1,000 - 7,500 USD
Contact: Jeff Pettus, Visual Arts Director; (919) 807-6513; jeff.pettus@ncmail.net
Internet: http://www.ncarts.org/grants_category.cfm?ID=36&CFID=4457402&CFTOKEN=25653586&jsessionid=28302898591231777988333
Sponsor: North Carolina Arts Council
Department of Cultural Resources, 109 East Jones Street, MSC #4632
Raleigh, NC 27601-2807

North Carolina Arts Council Technical Assistance Grants — 3482
Funds are provided to organizations to: hire knowledgeable consultants to strengthen an organization's management and programs or conduct planning meetings for a specific project; sponsor workshops or conferences; develop a resource publication; develop a community-wide cultural plan; provide scholarships to send staff members to conferences, workshops or short-term programs (available on a limited basis). Examples of issues consultants may address include, but are not limited to, staff development, community relations, fund-raising, audience development, and financial management. Organizations should contact the council staff before applying in this category.
Requirements: Any North Carolina nonprofit arts organization or organization that provides arts programs, such as schools or community organizations, may apply. Grants must be matched dollar-for-dollar by the applicant, except in cases of demonstrated need.
Geographic Focus: North Carolina
Date(s) Application is Due: Mar 2
Amount of Grant: 2,500 USD
Contact: Janie Wilson, Outreach Coordinator; (919) 807-6508; janie.wilson@ncmail.net
Internet: http://www.ncarts.org/freeform_scrn_template.cfm?ffscrn_id=121
Sponsor: North Carolina Arts Council
Department of Cultural Resources, 109 East Jones Street, MSC #4632
Raleigh, NC 27601-2807

North Carolina Arts Council Touring/Presenting Grants — 3483
This category provides support to organizations to hire artists or companies to engage audiences in their community for a Performance Series or a Community-based Residency. Performance Series Performance Series includes support for a discreet and clearly defined series of performances and related outreach and educational activities. Community-based Residencies must be at least 2 days in length and must include activities that are hands-on participatory experiences for a targeted audience group.
Requirements: Nonprofit organizations in North Carolina that present artists for performances, presentations, and residencies as a primary function of their overall operations are eligible.
Restrictions: Artists and companies may not apply for Series Support to self-present a tour or series.
Geographic Focus: North Carolina
Date(s) Application is Due: Mar 2
Amount of Grant: 2,500 - 10,000 USD
Contact: Vicki Vitiello; (919) 807-6504; vicki.vitiello@ncmail.net
Internet: http://www.ncarts.org/grants_programs.cfm?ID=19&CFID=4457677&CFTOKEN=20384898&jsessionid=28302898591231777988333
Sponsor: North Carolina Arts Council
Department of Cultural Resources, 109 East Jones Street, MSC #4632
Raleigh, NC 27601-2807

North Carolina Arts Council Visual Arts Program Support Grants — 3484
The program provides funds to North Carolina nonprofit organizations that: support innovative performing (dance, music, and theater) or visual arts programming and services; provide programs or services to the state's arts community or promote awareness about the arts in the state; advance public discussion and understanding of an artist or art form; and support innovative arts programming for public public television. All grant-funded activities must take place between July 1 of the current year and June 30 of the next. Grant funds support artistic and administrative expenses directly related to the project. Both first-time and experienced applicants are encouraged to contact council staff early in the planning of their grant proposals to receive information on preparing competitive applications and to discuss proposed projects.
Requirements: North Carolina nonprofit organizations that produce literary, performing, or visual arts programs may apply. Statewide service organizations also may apply. Grants must be matched dollar-for-dollar by the organization. Organizations may apply for projects spanning more than one year; applicants must reapply each year for funding of a multiyear project.
Geographic Focus: North Carolina
Date(s) Application is Due: Mar 2
Contact: Jeff Pettus, Visual Arts Director; (919) 807-6513; jeff.pettus@ncmail.net
Internet: http://www.ncarts.org/grants_category.cfm?ID=11&CFID=4457835&CFTOKEN=61825421&jsessionid=28302898591231777988333
Sponsor: North Carolina Arts Council
Department of Cultural Resources, 109 East Jones Street, MSC #4632
Raleigh, NC 27601-2807

North Carolina Biotechnology Center Event Sponsorship Grants — 3485
This popular Biotechnology Center grant promotes and supports events advancing the understanding or application of biotechnology to benefit North Carolina. Events must promote information sharing and personal interaction focused on biotechnology research, education, or business. The highest amount awarded is $3,000. Awards typically cover costs such as speaker fees, travel expenses, event-site rental and publicity.
Requirements: All award money is disbursed directly to the applicant's organization. The money must be used solely to support the event outlined in this application.
Restrictions: This sponsorship does not provide money either to promote a specific product to benefit a few companies or individuals. This sponsorship does not cover food or refreshments for event attendees.
Geographic Focus: North Carolina
Contact: Ginny DeLuca, (919) 549-8842; fax (919) 549-9710; virginia_deluca@ncbiotech.org
Internet: http://www.ncbiotech.org/services_and_programs/grants_and_loans/biotechnology_event_sponsorship/index.html
Sponsor: North Carolina Biotechnology Center
15 T.W. Alexander Drive, P.O. Box 13547
Research Triangle Park, NC 27709-3547

North Carolina Biotechnology Center Meeting Grants — 3486
This grant promotes and supports national and international meetings which advance the understanding or application of biotechnology and focus national and international attention on the North Carolina scientific community. Meetings must promote information sharing and personal interaction focused on biotechnology research, education, or business. The highest amount awarded is $10,000. Awards typically cover costs such as speaker fees, travel expenses, event-site rental and publicity.
Requirements: All award money is given to the applicant's organization. The money must be used solely to support the event outlined in this application.
Restrictions: This sponsorship does not provide money either to promote a specific product to benefit a few companies or individuals. This sponsorship does not cover food or refreshments for event attendees.
Geographic Focus: North Carolina
Contact: Ginny DeLuca, (919) 549-8842; fax (919) 549-9710; virginia_deluca@ncbiotech.org
Internet: http://www.ncbiotech.org/services_and_programs/grants_and_loans/BiotechnologyMeetingGrant.html
Sponsor: North Carolina Biotechnology Center
15 T.W. Alexander Drive, P.O. Box 13547
Research Triangle Park, NC 27709-3547

North Carolina Biotechnology Center Multidisciplinary Research Grants 3487
The Multidisciplinary Research Grant is designed to encourage collaboration between North Carolina scientists from at least three distinct fields of study working together for advancement of the state of the art in biotechnology. This grant is intended to support development of preliminary data for federal grant applications. Each scientist must directly contribute approximately equal percent effort to the project.
Requirements: Proposed programs and activities must clearly relate to biotechnology research, development, commercialization, education, or training. Priority will be giving to proposals requesting support for innovative programs or activities in biotechnology. Only North Carolina academic institutions, non profit research organizations, or businesses may apply.
Restrictions: Awards are not made to individuals.
Geographic Focus: North Carolina
Date(s) Application is Due: Jul 16
Amount of Grant: Up to 300,000 USD
Contact: Ginny DeLuca, (919) 549-8842; fax (919) 549-9710; virginia_deluca@ncbiotech.org
Internet: http://www.ncbiotech.org/services_and_programs/grants_and_loans/multi disciplinary_research/index.html
Sponsor: North Carolina Biotechnology Center
15 T.W. Alexander Drive, P.O. Box 13547
Research Triangle Park, NC 27709-3547

North Carolina Biotechnology Center Regional Development Grants 3488
The goal of the Regional Development Grant Program (PDF) is to build capacity through collaborative projects, providing a foundational resource for biotechnology development in the community that was not there previously and that the community could not have achieved without Biotechnology Center funding. Prepoposals are required: cycle 1 prepoposals are due no later than January 28, while cycle 2 prepoposals should be received by August 20. The deadlines for final proposals are April 1 (cycle 1) and October 15 (cycle 2).
Requirements: Proposed programs and activities must clearly relate to biotechnology research, development, commercialization, education, or training. Priority will be giving to proposals requesting support for innovative programs or activities in biotechnology. Only North Carolina academic institutions, non profit research organizations, or businesses may apply.
Restrictions: Awards are not made to individuals.
Geographic Focus: North Carolina
Date(s) Application is Due: Jan 28; Apr 1; Aug 20; Oct 15
Amount of Grant: Up to 75,000 USD
Contact: Deborah De; (919) 549-9845; fax (919) 549-9710; deborah_de@ncbiotech.org
Internet: http://www.ncbiotech.org/services_and_programs/grants_and_loans/regional_ development/index.html
Sponsor: North Carolina Biotechnology Center
15 T.W. Alexander Drive, P.O. Box 13547
Research Triangle Park, NC 27709-3547

North Carolina Community Foundation Grants 3489
The community foundation exists to meet the needs of nonprofit organizations and improve the lives of citizens of North Carolina counties, including Allegheny, Caldwell, Cherokee, Clay, Craven, Eastern Bank of Cherokee Indians, Franklin Community, Franklin, Graham, Harnett, Haywood, Jackson, Johnston, Madison, Montgomery, Moore, Pender, Pitt, Randolph, Rockingham, Swain, Wake, Watauga, and Wilkes. Support is available for programs that enrich the quality of life in the areas of civic affairs, education, health, religion, social services, arts, and the conservation and preservation of environmental, historical preservation, and cultural resources. Grants will be awarded to support programs and projects, endowments, conferences and seminars, and consulting services. Grants are awarded in local communities; use the Affiliate Webpage link to contact the office serving your area.
Requirements: Nonprofit organizations throughout North Carolina are eligible to apply.
Geographic Focus: North Carolina
Contact: Jennifer Tolle Whiteside, President; (800) 201-9533 or (919) 828-4387; fax (919) 828-5495; jtwhiteside@nccommunityfoundation.org
Internet: http://nccommunityfoundation.org/05_grants_available.php
Sponsor: North Carolina Community Foundation
4601 Six Forks Road, Suite 524
Raleigh, NC 27609

North Carolina GlaxoSmithKline Foundation Grants 3490
The foundation supports activities primarily in North Carolina that help meet the needs of today's society and future generations by funding programs that emphasize the understanding and application of health, science, and mathematics at all educational and professional levels. Although providing seed funds for new and worthwhile educational programs is the foundation's primary focus, requests for funding of ongoing projects will also receive consideration. Types of support include operating budgets, professorships, and conferences and seminars. Proposals may be submitted for either one-year or multi-year funding with a maximum of five years' duration. The foundation's board of directors meets four times a year to consider and award grants. Completed applications must be received by the listed deadline dates. If the stated deadline falls on a weekend or holiday, the next business day serves as the official deadline. All applicants will be notified of the board's decisions within 15 days of the board meeting.
Requirements: The foundation makes grants only to North Carolina 501(c)3 tax-exempt organizations and institutions or to governmental agencies.
Restrictions: Grants are not made to individuals for construction or restoration projects, or for international programs unless specifically exempted by the board. Funds are not ordinarily provided to programs that benefit a limited geographic region.
Geographic Focus: North Carolina
Date(s) Application is Due: Jan 1; Apr 1; Jul 1; Oct 1
Amount of Grant: 25,000 - 1,000,000 USD
Contact: Marilyn Foote-Hudson, Executive Director; (919) 483-2140; fax (919) 315-3015; community.partnership@gsk.com
Internet: http://us.gsk.com/html/community/community-grants-foundation.html
Sponsor: North Carolina GlaxoSmithKline Foundation
5 Moore Drive, P.O. Box 13398
Research Triangle Park, NC 27709

North Central Health Services Grants 3491
North Central Health Services is committed to addressing a wide range of health issues, and to enhancing the quality of life for individuals, families, and communities in our eight county Service Area. NCHS will support not-for-profit organizations and agencies that share our commitment to Health and Healthy Communities, primarily through grants for capital projects. NCHS prefers to fund projects that have a significant potential for positive impact on the community. NCHS encourages collaboration among agencies and organizations that efficiently utilize resources, and provide programs and services that are not duplicative. The first step for an organization to apply for a grant is to submit a written letter of inquiry. This letter should include a concise description of the organization, a statement of the problem or need being addressed, and an explanation of the project, estimated total costs, and the amount being requested from NCHS. Grants have ranged from $600 to $5,000,000.
Requirements: Applicants should be 501(c)3 not-for-profit organizations who serve Benton, Carroll, Clinton, Fountain, Montgomery, Tippecanoe, Warren, and White Counties.
Geographic Focus: Indiana
Amount of Grant: Up to 5,000,000 USD
Contact: Rita Smith, Program Director; (765) 423-1604
Internet: http://www.nchsi.com/grantmaking.cfm
Sponsor: North Central Health Services
P.O. Box 528
Lafayette, IN 47902

North Central Health Services Grants 3492
North Central Health Services (NCHS) was created in 1984 to serve as the parent company of a family of corporations which included Lafayette Home Hospital, Home Hospital Foundation, and Service Frontiers Incorporated. Today, NCHS is a medical services company whose primary purpose is to operate an ambulatory surgery center, where sterilization services are made available to the Greater Lafayette community. NCHS also is a grant making organization providing primarily capital grants to 501(c)3 organizations serving the citizens of Benton, Carroll, Clinton, Fountain, Montgomery, Tippecanoe, Warren, and White counties in Indiana. Grants are awarded to organizations for projects that relate to Health, and Healthy Communities. NCHS prefers to fund projects that have a significant potential for positive impact on the community. NCHS encourages collaboration among agencies and organizations that efficiently utilize resources, and provide services that are not duplicative of existing programs. NCHS provides grants that will: advance technology and scientific development in health care; develop and promote community health education; provide direct, individual social welfare and human service; promote a Healthy Community; improve the quality of life for all the communities people.
Requirements: The first step for an organization to apply for a grant is to submit a written letter of inquiry. This letter should include a concise description of the organization, a statement of the problem or need being addressed, and an explanation of the project, estimated total costs, and the amount being requested from NCHS. The letter should be addressed to: North Central Health Services, Inc., Attn: Rita Smith, Program Director, P.O. Box 528, Lafayette, In. 47902. Upon receipt of the letter of inquiry, initial review will determine whether or not the request meets the funding focus and priorities of NCHS. You will be promptly notified in writing of the initial determination, and informed of application opportunities.
Restrictions: Beginning in 2008, NCHS implemented the following grant categories and cycles. Grant requests and cycles: letter of inquiry requesting funds in excess of $250,000, accepted May 1 to August 15 of each calendar year. If approved, funding would be available for distribution after January 1 of the following year; letter of inquiry requesting funds of $100,000 to $250,000 will be accepted throughout the calendar year. If approved, funding would generally be available for distribution within 90 days of board approval; letter of inquiry requesting funds of $25,000 to $100,000 will be accepted throughout the calendar year. If approved, funding would generally be available within 60 days of board approval; letter of inquiry requesting funds of less than $25,000 will be accepted throughout the calendar year. If approved, funding would generally be available within 60 days of approval.
Geographic Focus: Indiana
Contact: Rita Smith, Program Director; (765) 423-1604
Internet: http://www.nchsi.com/grantmaking.cfm
Sponsor: North Central Health Services
201 Main Street, Suite 606, P.O. Box 528
Lafayette, IN 47902

North Dakota Community Foundation Grants 3493
The Foundation serves North Dakota communities statewide with the goal of improving the quality of life for the state's citizens. The Foundation does not have a narrow area of focus. Each project is reviewed on its own merits with an emphasis on helping applicants who have limited access to other sources of funding. Applicants may submit a concise letter of request not to exceed two pages describing the organization, the project, the approximate project cost, and the amount requested from the Foundation. If the Board is interested in additional information, formal application materials will be sent.
Requirements: Eligible applicants must be 501(c)3 organizations in North Dakota.
Restrictions: The Foundation accepts applications by mail but not by fax or email. Only one request per agency per year may be submitted. The following is not funded: grants to organizations and projects that exist to influence legislation, carry on propaganda,

participate in political campaigns, or which threaten to cause significant controversy or divisiveness; grants to individuals; and multi-year grant commitments. Low priority is given to the following: projects already substantially supported by government, or which in the opinion of the Board, can and should be provided for by taxes; grants for sectarian projects; grants to national organizations; and organizations which field substantial fund-raising each year with paid and volunteer staff.
Geographic Focus: North Dakota
Date(s) Application is Due: Aug 15
Contact: Kevin Dvorak; (701) 222-8349; fax (701) 222-8349; kdvorak@ndcf.net
Internet: http://www.ndcf.net/Information/GrantGuidelines.asp
Sponsor: North Dakota Community Foundation
309 North Mandan Street, Suite 2, P.O. Box 387
Bismarck, ND 58502-0387

North Dakota Council on the Arts Community Access Grants 3494
As a community-based grant program, Community Arts Access is designed to benefit nonprofit organizations that present arts programming in small and rural communities in North Dakota. It also supports nonprofit organizations in communities of all sizes whose arts programming makes a deliberate and focused effort to serve a special constituency or an under-served audience in that community. Funds for the program are appropriated by the state of North Dakota. Some of the program goals are to strengthen existing arts organizations and art forms, provide start-up funds for new or emerging arts organizations, and expand new audiences. Examples of supported activities include general operating costs, production costs, honoraria for artistic or technical directors, musical scores/performance rights, printing costs for programs and catalogs, and artist services. Grant requests may not exceed $2,000, and $650 is the minimum request. Applicants are encouraged to submit a notice of intent to apply. While this is not a requirement, it will assist the Council on the Arts in the planning of review panels and other matters.
Requirements: Applicant must be registered as a non-profit organization with the state of North Dakota, or be a community or county government entity. Organizations may form partnerships with state agencies, for-profit businesses, and other entities, but the non-profit organization must be the applicant. A 1:1 match is required. Of this, up to half may be documented in-kind.
Restrictions: Organizations supported through the Institutional Support and Mini-Grant programs, requests for Artists in Residence or LEAP activities, reduction of a deficit, and projects completed at the time of the application are ineligible.
Geographic Focus: North Dakota
Date(s) Application is Due: Apr 1; Nov 1
Amount of Grant: 650 - 2,000 USD
Contact: Amy Schmidt; (701) 328-7594; fax (701) 328-7595; amschmid@nd.gov
Internet: http://www.nd.gov/arts/grants/CAAguidelines.html
Sponsor: North Dakota Council on the Arts
1600 E Century Avenue, Suite 6
Bismarck, ND 58503-0649

North Dakota Council on the Arts Individual Artist Fellowships 3495
The Individual Fellowship Program was established to recognize practicing artists residing in North Dakota with a monetary fellowship award. This program is designed to support professional artists with outstanding talent and ability to improve their artistic skills and enhance their career opportunities. Two fellowships of $2,500 are annually awarded. An applicant will be considered professional if they are pursuing their original artwork on an ongoing basis within an artistic discipline, and if they are pursuing it as a means of livelihood, either on a partial or total basis. Works in progress are acceptable with an explanation of the work's goal in the Artist's Statement.
Requirements: To be eligible for a fellowship the applicant must: be at least 18 years of age and a resident of the state of North Dakota as of January of the grant year and agree to maintain that residency during the fellowship period; submit a completed application and samples of work on or before the deadline; not be enrolled as an undergraduate or graduate degree-seeking student during the fellowship period; submit samples of work completed within the last three years prior to the application deadline.
Restrictions: Collaborative works will not be accepted. Artists may submit collaborative work as evidence of artistic skill only if the applicant's role in the creation of the work is clearly defined.
Geographic Focus: North Dakota
Date(s) Application is Due: Feb 15
Amount of Grant: 2,500 USD
Contact: Rebecca Engelman; (701) 328-7593; fax (701) 328-7595; rengelman@nd.gov
Internet: http://www.nd.gov/arts/grants/IAFguidelines.html
Sponsor: North Dakota Council on the Arts
1600 E Century Avenue, Suite 6
Bismarck, ND 58503-0649

North Dakota Council on the Arts Institutional Support Grants 3496
The Institutional Support program is designed to benefit artists, arts organizations, and the general public. The program provides general support for local arts councils and other arts organizations, as well as support for performances, exhibitions, publications, classes, workshops, and special events in all arts disciplines. The program's goals are to assist arts institutions and cultural organizations in improving artistic or administrative standards; encourage arts organizations to attain financial stability by developing a diversified funding base; expand cultural opportunities to new audiences and under-served areas; and increase opportunities for local artists and others to participate in a wide range of arts activities. Examples of funded activities include general operating expenses; honoraria for artistic and technical staff/services; and production costs for performances, exhibitions, and publications. Letter of intent is due by January 15; application must be received by March 15. Application materials are available on the website.
Requirements: Applicant North Dakota-based organizations must comply with all NDCA general policy guidelines; comply with applicable state and federal laws; submit complete and accurate applications and provide at least 50 percent of the total cash cost of the project; and submit current long-range plans that include goals and measurable objectives for the organization. Applicants whose operating budgets exceed $200,000 must be tax-exempt and submit independent audits for the most recently completed fiscal year. Presentation, production, or service of the arts must be the primary activity of the applicant organization.
Restrictions: The following are ineligible: organizations supported through Access; capital architectural improvements or purchase or long-term rental of equipment or property; benefits or hospitality costs; fellowships, scholarships, or tuition fees; activities restricted to an organization's membership; and proposals which match federal funds with federal funds.
Geographic Focus: North Dakota
Date(s) Application is Due: Mar 15
Amount of Grant: 2,000 - 10,000 USD
Contact: Jan Webb; (701) 328-7592; fax (701) 328-7595; comserv@state.nd.us
Internet: http://www.nd.gov/arts/grants/ISguidelines.html
Sponsor: North Dakota Council on the Arts
1600 E Century Avenue, Suite 6
Bismarck, ND 58503-0649

North Dakota Council on the Arts Presenter Support Grants 3497
Presenter Support is designed to benefit nonprofit organizations that are not eligible for other major grant programs through the North Dakota Council on the Arts, offers financial support for arts events and programming, and supports organizations in communities with a population of 6,000 or more. Goals of the program include: to encourage existing arts organizations to build upon themselves, enhance the artistic quality of their programming, and expand their audience; to promote knowledge and appreciation of the arts in North Dakota's communities; to provide start-up funds or general operating support for new or emerging arts programs; and to provide opportunities for North Dakota artists. Grant requests may not exceed $2,000. Annual deadlines are April 1 and November 1.
Requirements: Applicants are encouraged to submit a notice of intent to apply. While this is not a requirement, it will assist the Council on the Arts in the planning of review panels and other matters.
Restrictions: Applicant must be registered as a 501(c)3 non-profit organization with the state of North Dakota, or be a community or county government entity. Organizations may form partnerships with state agencies, for-profit businesses, and other entities, but the non-profit organization must be the applicant. An applicant must be from a community with a population of 6,000 or more, according to the most recent census available. A 1:1 cash match is required. Requested funds can cover no more than half of the total expenses for the programming.
Geographic Focus: North Dakota
Date(s) Application is Due: Apr 1; Nov 1
Amount of Grant: Up to 2,000 USD
Contact: Amy Schmidt; (701) 328-7594; fax (701) 328-7595; amschmid@nd.gov
Internet: http://www.nd.gov/arts/grants/PRSguidelines.html
Sponsor: North Dakota Council on the Arts
1600 E Century Avenue, Suite 6
Bismarck, ND 58503-0649

Northeast Utilities Foundation Grants 3498
The Northeast Utilities Foundation Grants strive to improve the quality of life in the communities where their customers and employees are located. Their grant funding supports the following issues: economic and community development (new job creation, small business development, and smart growth); workforce development (training and education); and environmental leadership and stewardship (protecting, preserving, or improving the environment, including natural habitats and biological diversity, renewable energy, and energy efficiency). All proposals are evaluated on the following criteria: objectives that fit within the Foundation's priority areas; the potential impact on the community, and benefits to the region served; the potential for employee participation; and demonstrated leadership and effectiveness. All inquires and proposal for the Foundation should be submitted to the appropriate state representative.
Requirements: Applicants must be tax exempt organizations, and be located within the three state area that the Foundation serves (Connecticut, Massachusetts, and New Hampshire).
Restrictions: Grants do not support individuals; corporations that do not qualify as charitable organizations according to IRS codes; private foundations or endowments; projects benefiting limited groups (religious, fraternal, political); athletic outings; reducing or eliminating a preexisting debt; or athletic outings.
Geographic Focus: Connecticut, Massachusetts, New Hampshire
Amount of Grant: Up to 175,000 USD
Contact: Amanda Scheyd; (888) 682-4639 or (860) 728-4501; amanda.scheyd@nu.com
Internet: http://www.northeastutilitiesfoundation.org/what/index.html
Sponsor: Northeast Utilities Foundation
P.O. Box 270
Hartford, CT 06141-0270

Northern Chautauqua Community Foundation Community Grants 3499
The foundation awards grants to nonprofit, tax-exempt organizations located in Northern Chautauqua County, New York. Priority will be given to programs representing innovative and efficient approaches to serving community needs and opportunities, projects that assist citizens whose needs are not met by existing services, projects that expect to test or demonstrate new approaches and techniques in the solutions of community problems, and projects that promote volunteer participation and citizen involvement in the community.

Consideration will be given to the potential impact of the request and the number of people who will benefit. Seed grants will be awarded to initiate promising new programs in the foundation's field of interest as well as challenge grants to encourage matching gifts. Except in unusual circumstances, grants are approved for one year at a time. Contact the foundation office for an application.
Requirements: 501(c)3 organizations in Northern Chautauqua County, New York, are eligible.
Restrictions: Areas generally not funded are capital campaigns to establish or add to endowment funds, general operating budgets for existing organizations, publication of books, conferences, or annual fund-raising campaigns.
Geographic Focus: New York
Date(s) Application is Due: Mar 23; Sep 21
Amount of Grant: 12,500 USD
Contact: Diane E. Hannum, Executive Director; (716) 366-4892; fax (716) 366-3905; dhannum@nncfoundation.org or info@nccfoundation.org
Internet: http://www.nccfoundation.org/Grantseekers/ApplyforaGrant/tabid/256/Default.aspx
Sponsor: Northern Chautauqua Community Foundation
212 Lake Shore Drive West
Dunkirk, NY 14048

Northern Chautauqua Community Foundation DFT Communications Community Betterment Grants 3500
The Northern Chautauqua Community Foundation awards grants to nonprofit, tax-exempt organizations located in Northern Chautauqua County, New York. DFT Communications has earned a reputation as a strong supporter of the community they serve. In 2001, the Foundation began administering their DFT Communications Community Betterment Fund. Priority will be given to programs representing innovative and efficient approaches to serving community needs and opportunities, projects that assist citizens whose needs are not met by existing services, projects that expect to test or demonstrate new approaches and techniques in the solutions of community problems, and projects that promote volunteer participation and citizen involvement in the community. Grants are awarded from this fund on a monthly basis.
Geographic Focus: New York
Date(s) Application is Due: Jan 20; Feb 20; Mar 20; Apr 20; May 20; Jun 20; Jul 20; Aug 20; Sep 20; Oct 20; Nov 20; Dec 20
Contact: Diane E. Hannum, Executive Director; (716) 366-4892; fax (716) 366-3905; dhannum@nncfoundation.org or info@nccfoundation.org
Internet: http://www.nccfoundation.org/Grantseekers/ApplyforaGrant/tabid/256/Default.aspx
Sponsor: Northern Chautauqua Community Foundation
212 Lake Shore Drive West
Dunkirk, NY 14048

Northern Chautauqua Community Foundation Environmental Grants 3501
The purpose of the Northern Chautauqua Community Foundation Environmental fund is to increase public knowledge of environmental issues in Chautauqua County, particularly those relating to Lake Erie and its watershed. A broad range of educational activities will be funded, including educational events, hands-on educational experiences, stipends for internships and lectures. Research projects are permitted, providing that the research is shared in a useful manner. Priority will be given to applications involving Lake Erie or its watershed. In most instances, grants will be no greater than $500.
Requirements: Environmental organizations that are recognized as non-profit tax exempt under section 501(c)3 of the Internal Revenue Code are eligible to apply. Educational institutions and other public agencies (agencies of the state, county or local government) are also eligible to apply. Individuals interested in applying for a grant must be affiliated with an eligible organization.
Restrictions: Grants will not be made for lobbying or political purposes.
Geographic Focus: New York
Date(s) Application is Due: Jan 9
Contact: Diane E. Hannum, Executive Director; (716) 366-4892; fax (716) 366-3905; dhannum@nncfoundation.org or info@nccfoundation.org
Internet: http://www.nccfoundation.org/Grantseekers/ApplyforaGrant/tabid/256/Default.aspx
Sponsor: Northern Chautauqua Community Foundation
212 Lake Shore Drive West
Dunkirk, NY 14048

Northern Chautauqua Community Foundation Lake Shore Savings and Loan Community Reinvestment Grants 3502
The foundation awards grants to nonprofit, tax-exempt organizations located in Northern Chautauqua County, New York. Priority will be given to programs representing innovative and efficient approaches to serving community needs and opportunities, projects that assist citizens whose needs are not met by existing services, projects that expect to test or demonstrate new approaches and techniques in the solutions of community problems, and projects that promote volunteer participation and citizen involvement in the community. Lake Shore Savings is known throughout the region for its commitment to the community. Lake Shore Savings' Community Reinvestment Fund makes money available for area organizations to help fund programs to benefit the community. Lake Shore Savings is also a strong supporter of SUNY Fredonia through gifts to the Fredonia College Foundation. Such gifts made possible the purchase of the campus's first clock tower and carillon among other projects.
Geographic Focus: New York
Contact: Diane E. Hannum; (716) 366-4892; dhannum@nncfoundation.org
Internet: http://www.nccfoundation.org/Grantseekers/ApplyforaGrant/tabid/256/Default.aspx
Sponsor: Northern Chautauqua Community Foundation
212 Lake Shore Drive West
Dunkirk, NY 14048

Northern New York Community Foundation Grants 3503
The foundation is looking for innovative programs that address problems to be solved, or opportunities to be seized, in the northern New York area. Grants are made only for capital items and for seed money for new agencies, or new projects by established agencies.
Requirements: Grants are made to nonprofit, tax-exempt organizations in or serving Jefferson and/or Lewis counties in New York State. Governmental units are also eligible provided that the purpose of the grant goes beyond the expected limits of government service. The foundation does not make grants to churches and religious organizations except in cases where projects clearly benefit the entire community. Applicants should contact the office to provide a brief summary of the project and needs. The applicant will be notified of grant award or denial by letter after the board of directors meets, which is generally one month following application deadline dates. Grant requests under $5,000 may be approved at the committee level. Larger grant requests are referred to the board of directors with a committee recommendation.
Restrictions: Individuals are ineligible. The foundation does not fund operations or pay off deficits.
Geographic Focus: New York
Date(s) Application is Due: Jan 30; Apr 24; Aug 28; Oct 23
Contact: Alex Velto, (315) 782-7110; fax (315) 782-0047; info@nnycf.org
Internet: http://www.nnycf.org/grantguidelines.asp?mm=5
Sponsor: Northern New York Community Foundation
120 Washington Street, Suite 400
Watertown, NY 13601

Northern Trust Company Charitable Trust and Corporate Giving Program 3504
Contributions from the Charitable Trust support program, general operating, capital, or endowment priorities. Grants usually are confined to programs and agencies that focus on advancing the well-being of disadvantaged women and children, and people with disabilities. Priority is given to programs or agencies that serve the following Chicago neighborhoods: Chatham, Englewood, Humboldt Park, Logan Square, Loop, Washington Park, and West Town. Applications, including all material specified in the checklist must be received in the Community Affairs office before 5:00 pm on the deadline date. Deadlines for requests for funding are determined by area of service, as follows: social welfare—January 13 and August 12, education—May 13; and arts and culture—May 13.
Requirements: Nonprofit organizations in Illinois are eligible. A proposal should include a short cover letter, an operating budget for the current year, a copy of the agency's most recent audited financial statement, a list of members of the agency's governing board, a list of Chicago-based corporate and foundation contributors and amounts each has contributed in the last calendar year, and a letter from the IRS indicating tax-exempt status.
Geographic Focus: Illinois
Date(s) Application is Due: Jan 13; May 13; Aug 12
Amount of Grant: 2,500 - 5,000 USD
Contact: Dawn McGovern, Program Contact; (312) 444-4059
Internet: http://www.northerntrust.com/aboutus/community/charitable/index.html
Sponsor: Northern Trust Company
50 S LaSalle Street, Suite L-7
Chicago, IL 60675

North Georgia Community Foundation Grants 3505
The foundation serves Banks, Dawson, Fannin, Forsyth, Franklin, Habersham, Hall, Hart, Jackson, Lumpkin, Rabun, Stephens, Towns, Union, and White counties. The foundation looks favorably at efforts which promise to affect a broad constituency in its service area. The foundation is interested in those organizations which can demonstrate that they have planned their projects in light of overall community need, and that similar projects by other organizations do not duplicate the proposed services. A request which asks the foundation to provide a portion of the support for a project generally will receive greater priority than one which looks to it as the single funding source. The foundation is especially interested in leveraging additional income from other sources.
Requirements: Grants are made only to Georgia nonprofit tax-exempt organizations in the counties listed for charitable purposes, unless donor-advised funds are designated to qualifying entities outside the foundation's area of emphasis.
Restrictions: Funding is not generally provided for annual fund campaigns, lobbying, operating support other than start-up, or to individuals.
Geographic Focus: Georgia
Amount of Grant: Up to 3,000 USD
Contact: Program Officer; (770) 535-7880; fax (770) 503-0439; info@ngcf.org
Internet: http://www.ngcf.org/main.asp
Sponsor: North Georgia Community Foundation
615F Oak Street, Suite 1300
Gainesville, GA 30501

Northland Foundation Grants 3506
The Northland Foundation provides resources to programs that value children and families and help the next generation develop into responsible, caring adults; provide individuals and families with the tools to become self-reliant through economic and social justice; and encourage older adults to share their vitality and wisdom. Eligible projects must address one of the following three priority areas: Connecting Kids and Communities/Strengthening Families; Opportunities for Self-Reliance; Aging with Independence.
Requirements: Non-profit 501(c)3 organizations in the seven-county area of Aitkin, Carlton, Cook, Itasca, Koochiching, Lake, and Saint Louis Counties of Minnesota are eligible. Interested applicants should contact Grants Program staff to determine if the project is a promising candidate. A pre-application form (available online) may be submitted for review. The Foundation's Board reviews pre-applications monthly. Pre-applications received by the 15th of the month are reviewed the following month. After review applicants are notified

by letter if a full proposal is requested and when it is due. On average, consideration of a full proposal takes sixty to ninety days.
Restrictions: Grants do not support individuals, religious programs, endowments, fundraising campaigns, buildings or major equipment, festivals, traditional government services, or programs for which public support has been cut.
Geographic Focus: Minnesota
Contact: Erik Torch; (800) 433-4045 or (218) 723-4040; erik@northlandfdn.org
Internet: http://www.northlandfdn.org/Grants/
Sponsor: Northland Foundation
202 West Superior Street, Suite 610
Duluth, MN 55802

Northrop Grumman Corporation Grants 3507
Northrop Grumman is committed to supporting communities throughout the U.S., especially those where its employees live and work. The Contributions Program seeks to address critical issues and needs by providing financial assistance to accredited schools and 501(c)3 nonprofit organizations. The majority of these contributions address education, services for veterans and the military, health and human services, and the environment.
Requirements: The following information must be included in the grant request: Tax Exempt Number; non-profit contact name, title, address, phone number, fax number; brief history of the organization, mission statement, goals and objectives; type and scope of services offered, and the geographical area served; specific details as to how requested funds would be used; project budget and amount requested; demographic impact; current operating budget including latest financial statement; list of other corporate funders; list of directors and/or officers, and their affiliations; Northrop Grumman employee sponsor, if applicable (name and phone number); and contact information.
Restrictions: Grants are not awarded to: religious organizations; political groups; fraternal organizations; individuals; athletic groups or activities, including charity-benefit sporting events; charter schools, unless they have open enrollment and hold the same standards as public schools; bands or choirs; capital campaigns; organizations providing services primarily to animals; communities outside of the United States; or organizations whose programs discriminate based on race, color, age, sex, religion, national origin, sexual orientation, disability, veteran status or any other characteristic protected by law.
Geographic Focus: All States
Date(s) Application is Due: Apr 30; Sep 30
Contact: Cheryl Horn, cheryl.horn@ngc.com
Internet: http://www.northropgrumman.com/corporate-responsibility/corporate-citizenship/contribution-guidelines.html
Sponsor: Northrop Grumman Corporation
1840 Century Park East
Los Angeles, CA 90067

Northwest Airlines KidCares Medical Travel Assistance 3508
The program provides air travel to children age 18 and younger who are unable to receive treatment in their home area. The KidCares program is fueled by generous mileage donations of Northwest's WorldPerks members. Availability of the program is based on that donated WorldPerks mileage, and consideration of each request is based on the guidelines below. Each application received must be evaluated on a case-by-case basis.
Requirements: Guidelines are as follows: (1) Only one round-trip per family is permitted. (2) A letter from the child's physician must accompany the application, stating: (a) patient's diagnosis; (b) confirmation of the need for travel; (c) the patient has medical clearance for air travel; (d) dates of appointments/surgery; and (e) length of stay. (3) The patient must be 18 years old or younger at the time the travel request is made. (4) The medical treatment for which the child is traveling must be unavailable in the child's home location. (5) KidCares travel can only be provided by Northwest Airlines or one of its airline partners. (6) Families demonstrating financial need are given priority consideration for KidCares travel. (7) One adult companion may accompany the child on KidCares travel at no additional cost. Applications may be found on Northwest's Web site, nwa.com at the following location http://www.nwa.com/corpinfo/aircares/about/KidCares_Application.pdf. You may also call (612) 726-4206 and leave detailed information regarding where the application should be sent and to whom.
Restrictions: KidCares travel is not available to families with insurance coverage that covers the cost of travel for medical treatment. KidCares travel is not eligible for Northwest Airlines WorldPerks bonus mileage credit. KidCares travel is not provided to St. Jude Children's Research Hospital, which is covered by a separate Northwest Airlines travel program.
Geographic Focus: All States
Contact: Community Manager; (612) 726-4206; fax (612) 726-3942; aircares@nwa.com
Internet: http://www.nwa.com/corpinfo/aircares/feature/
Sponsor: Northwest Airlines
2700 Lone Oak Parkway, Department A1300
St. Paul, MN 55121

Northwestern Mutual Foundation Grants 3509
The people of Northwestern Mutual have a long history of community involvement. To carry out its corporate contributions program, Northwestern Mutual created a private foundation, The Northwestern Mutual Foundation. The Northwestern Mutual Foundation focuses its funding in Milwaukee, where the company is headquartered. Therefore, applying for a grant from the Northwestern Mutual Foundation is limited to Milwaukee-area nonprofit organizations with programs centered on Education, Health & Human Services or Arts & Culture.
Requirements: Northwestern Mutual Foundation does not accept unsolicited grant requests. Groups new to the Foundation are asked to submit a written letter of intent, describing the organization, funding request, and provide information about the program for which you are seeking support. The Foundations team will review your letter of intent and, if they are interested in learning more about your project, you will receive an application form. Groups that have an active relationship with the Foundation and currently receive funding are allowed to apply annually for support. Once an organization submits an application, the review process takes about 90 days. The Foundation review's Milwaukee-area grants on a monthly basis.
Restrictions: Milwaukee-area nonprofits are eligible to apply. The Foundation defines the Milwaukee-area as Milwaukee County, with limited programmatic grants in Waukesha, Racine and Ozaukee Counties.
Geographic Focus: Wisconsin
Amount of Grant: 10,000 - 800,000 USD
Contact: Edward J. Zore , President; (414) 271-1444
Internet: http://www.nmfn.com/tn/aboutus—fd_intro
Sponsor: Northwestern Mutual Foundation
720 East Wisconsin Avenue
Milwaukee, WI 53202-4797

Northwest Fund for the Environment Grants 3510
The Northwest Fund for the Environment is designated to be spent promoting change in the uses of natural resources to increase their protection and preservation in the state of Washington. Emphasis is placed on the protection of wild fish, native wildlife, natural forests, wetlands and shorelines, and the preservation of pure and free-flowing waters. Special program areas of interest include aquatic ecosystem protection of freshwater and saltwater; growth management to promote smart growth land use policies and to prevent damage to environmentally sensitive areas; and community response in support of grassroots work that feeds into the fund's goals or supports emergent issues and opportunities not covered by previous funding. The Foundation requires grantees to propose a scope of work lasting up to 16 months, complete the entire 16 month grant period, and submit a final report prior to applying for a new standard grant. Standard grants range from $3,000 to $20,000. The Community Response Fund Grants range from $500 to $3,000. Application deadlines vary according to particular funding requested. Samples of previous funding are available at the website.
Requirements: Applicants must follow the online application process, which includes calling the Foundation to discuss whether it may be eligible for funding. Unsolicited applications or letters of inquiry will not be accepted. Only nonprofit organizations classified as 501(c)3 public charities serving Washington state are eligible. First time applicants may only apply for project support.
Restrictions: The following are not eligible for funding: individuals or for profit organizations; endowments or capital campaigns; debt reduction or loans to organizations; capital projects, such as building acquisition or construction, large equipment purchases or vehicle acquisition; land acquisition; structural restoration, such as tree planting or culvert removal; purely educational activities (except when an integral part but only one component of your application); organization of, scholarships for, or support of public conferences, as distinct from invited meetings or convening of groups engaged in related efforts; youth group support; production of publications and videos for the general public; web page development; museum displays; art projects, including performances; visual art projects and arts education; partisan political activities; academic scholarships or fellowships; academic research; university overhead costs; or field research (except when an integral part but only one component of your application).
Geographic Focus: Washington
Date(s) Application is Due: Feb 1
Contact: Pam Fujita-Yuhas, (206) 386-7220; fax (206) 386-7223; staff@nwfund.org
Internet: http://www.nwfund.org
Sponsor: Northwest Fund for the Environment
1904 Third Avenue, Suite 615
Seattle, WA 98101

Northwest Minnesota Foundation Asset Building Grants 3511
The purpose of the Northwest Minnesota Foundation Asset Building Grants is to help organizations develop new networks, foster coalition building and promote collaborations between human service providers, other organizations, and/or public agencies. The Foundation will consider projects that address joint ventures leading to increased effectiveness and efficiency among organizations and/or public agencies; and/or cooperative planning and implementation, including shared resources, staffing, programs or possible mergers between organizations and/or public agencies. There are three types of grants. Community Planning Grants will be considered for the design and implementation of plans that address one or more of the following priorities: comprehensive community development, including plans for recreational parks and trails; effective management of community growth; and economic development. Caring Communities Grants will be considered for new, innovative efforts, including faith-based initiatives, that address the needs of children, families and the elderly, and that focus on one or more of the following priorities: reducing the incidence of physical and emotional violence among children; alleviating childhood dysfunction in the areas of learning, social development and health; preventing at risk behaviors (such as eating disorders, promiscuity, depression, suicidal tendencies and the use of alcohol, tobacco and other drugs) among children and adolescents; and enabling the elderly to remain healthy, integrated members of their communities. Natural Resource Grants will be considered for projects that address one or more of the following priorities: research to promote sustainable development strategies and new processing methods that add value to local resources; and promoting the sustainable use and preservation of the natural resource base. All grants are awarded for a two-year period or less and usually do not exceed $25,000. The Foundation typically funds no more than half of the total project.
Requirements: Applicants must be qualified nonprofit organizations or public agencies located and/or conducting activities within the Foundation's twelve-county service area. The twelve counties are: Beltrami; Clearwater; Hubbard; Kittson; Lake of the Woods; Mahnomen; Marshall; Norman; Pennington; Polk; Red Lake; and Roseau. Applicants must be public agencies, local governments, or private nonprofits with a 501(c)3 federal tax-exempt status. A pre-proposal with a brief project description may be submitted at any time. Before submission applicants are encouraged to contact Grants Program staff to

discuss potential projects. Pre-proposals will be accepted at any time and are reviewed on a regular basis. If the applicant's project is determined to be eligible, a full application is invited. Eligible expenses include typical project-related expenses such as salary and fringe benefits, consultant contracts, local travel, technology, supplies, and equipment essential to complete a project. Applicants must provide matching funds in the form of cash and in-kind support. Applicants must show grassroots support, the need for Foundation funding and plans for future sustainability.
Restrictions: Ineligible expenses include: capital campaigns; annual fund drives; endowments; building construction; religious activities; past operating deficits; general operating expenses; lobbying; and publicity or advertising.
Geographic Focus: Minnesota
Amount of Grant: 25,000 USD
Contact: Jim Steenerson; (800) 659-7859 or (218) 759-2057
Internet: http://www.nwmf.org/grants.html
Sponsor: Northwest Minnesota Foundation
4225 Technology Drive NW
Bemidji, MN 56601

Northwest Minnesota Foundation Women's Fund Grants 3512
Formed in 1997 as a tax exempt charitable component of the Northwest Minnesota Foundation (NMF), the Women's Fund serves as a catalyst for improving the quality of life for women and girls by promoting ideas and supporting programs for the continued strengthening and empowerment of all women. The Women's Fund will consider grant requests of up to $2,500 addressing one or more of the following areas meeting the needs of females: cultural interactions; economic development; education; healthcare; and housing.
Requirements: Minnesota counties served by NMF are Beltrami, Clearwater, Hubbard, Kittson, Lake of the Woods, Mahnomen, Marshall, Norman, Pennington, Polk, Red Lake, and Roseau. Priority is given to applications supporting the following goals: developing entrepreneurial and economic opportunities for women; supporting programs that lead to a safer environment for women and girls; building networks of women in leadership positions throughout the region; and encouraging and equipping women and girls to achieve their full potential.
Geographic Focus: Minnesota
Date(s) Application is Due: May 1
Amount of Grant: 2,500 USD
Contact: Lisa Peterson, Communications Director; (800) 659-7859; lisap@nwmf.org
Internet: http://www.nwmf.org/component-funds/community-fund-websites/nw-mn-womens-fund/womens_fund_grants_and_programs.html
Sponsor: Northwest Minnesota Foundation
4225 Technology Drive NW
Bemidji, MN 56601

Northwest Minnesota Foundation Women's Fund Scholarships 3513
Northwest Minnesota Foundation Women's Fund Scholarships are offered to women from the twelve counties in their service area who are pursuing post-secondary education at a public higher education institution in the area (Bemidji State University, Northwest Technical College in Bemidji, Northland Community and Technical College at Thief River Falls and East Grand Forks, the University of Minnesota Crookston, and the White Earth Tribal College). Preference will be given to women who intend to remain in the region upon graduation. Scholarship funds are to be used for tuition and books or direct educational material expenses. One scholarship is designated for a woman attending the University of Minnesota, Crookston, with preference given to an older than average woman student.
Requirements: Eligible students must reside in the twelve-county service region of the Women's Fund (Beltrami, Clearwater, Hubbard, Kittson, Lake of the Woods, Mahnomen, Marshall, Norman, Pennington, Polk, Red Lake, and Roseau) and must intend to pursue post secondary education at a public higher education institution in the region within six months of the award. Financial need may be considered in awarding the scholarship, but is not an eligibility requirement. Students must have a minimum "C", or its equivalent, high school grade point average, and demonstrate a willingness to advance in education. Successful candidates will have some participation, involvement, or demonstrated positive leadership qualities in the following types of activities: community service; school organized extra-curricular or volunteer activities; and non-school work positions. Previous recipients may reapply for a second year scholarship but renewal is not guaranteed.
Geographic Focus: Minnesota
Date(s) Application is Due: May 1
Amount of Grant: 500 - 500 USD
Contact: Lisa Peterson; (800) 659-7859 or (218) 759-2057; lisap@nwmf.org
Internet: http://www.nwmf.org/component-funds/community-fund-websites/nw-mn-womens-fund/womens_fund_grants_and_programs.html
Sponsor: Northwest Minnesota Foundation
4225 Technology Drive NW
Bemidji, MN 56601

Norton Foundation Grants 3514
The Mission of the Norton Foundation, is to make grants designed to meet the needs of children and adolescents in Louisville, Kentucky. The Foundation supports experiential and holistic education that encourages their social, emotional, intellectual, physical and ethical development. The Foundation gives priority to programs that use the arts to achieve this goal. The Foundation also supports social services benefiting children and adolescents which are protective and preventative in nature. Civic projects in Louisville and Jefferson County which enhance the lives of children and adolescents are also considered for funding. The Board of Trustees meets three times per year. Applications must precede the meeting by approximately one month. Deadlines and meeting days fluctuate. Current deadline may be learned by calling or emailing the office. Grant application is available at the Foundation's website.

Requirements: Grants are made to IRS qualified 501(C)3 public charities (but not private foundations) that carry out activities primarily in the greater metropolitan Louisville area.
Restrictions: The Foundation does not make grants to individuals, nor may it designate funds for legislation or support activities that seek to influence the legislative process, except as allowed by the Internal Revenue Code of 1986, as amended.
Geographic Focus: Kentucky
Amount of Grant: 5,000 - 60,000 USD
Contact: Lucy Crawford; (502) 893-9549; lcrawford@nortonfoundation.com
Internet: http://www.nortonfoundation.com/application.html
Sponsor: Norton Foundation
4350 Brownsboro Road, Suite 133
Louisville, KY 40207-1679

Norwin S. and Elizabeth N. Bean Foundation Grants 3515
The Norwin S. and Elizabeth N. Bean Foundation was established in 1967 as a general purpose foundation to serve the communities of Manchester and Amherst and, consistent with the wishes of the founders, grants are made in the fields of arts and humanities, education, environment, health, human services, and public/society benefit.
Requirements: Applications are accepted from nonprofit 501(c)3 organizations and municipal and public agencies serving the communities of Manchester and Amherst, New Hampshire. Priority consideration is given to organizations operating primarily in those two communities. However, the Foundation will consider applications from statewide or regional organizations which provide a substantial and documented level of service to Manchester and Amherst.
Restrictions: The foundation does not make grants to individuals or provide scholarship aid.
Geographic Focus: New Hampshire
Date(s) Application is Due: Apr 1; Sep 1; Dec 1
Contact: Kathleen Cook, Grant Manager; (603) 493-7257; KCook@BeanFoundation.org
Internet: http://www.beanfoundation.org/grants/bean-foundation-grant/application-criteria.aspx
Sponsor: Norwin S. and Elizabeth N. Bean Foundation
40 Stark Street
Manchester, NH 03301

Notsew Orm Sands Foundation Grants 3516
The Notsew Orm Sands Foundation was established in 1995 via an initial donation from Charles Burnett, III, a British-born race car driver who set the steam-powered land speed record in 2009. Giving is on a national and international basis, with some emphasis on Houston, Texas, and the United Kingdom. Primary fields of interest are: higher education, hospitals, human services, medical research, and Protestant agencies and churches. There are no specific deadlines, and applicants should submit a detailed description of project and amount of funding requested, along with a copy of current year's organizational budget and/or project budget.
Restrictions: No grants are given to individuals.
Geographic Focus: All States
Amount of Grant: 250 - 75,000 USD
Samples: Baylor College of Medicine, Houston, Texas, $75,000; University of Saint Thomas, Houston, Texas, $61,000; Yale University, New Haven, Connecticut, $55,636; Centurion Ministries, Princeton, New Jersey, $20,000.
Contact: Charles Burnett, III, President and Secretary; (281) 497-0744
Sponsor: Notsew Orm Sands Foundation
2470 S. Dairy Ashford Street, Suite 802
Houston, TX 77077-5716

NRA Foundation Grants 3517
Grant requests must conform to, and foster the purposes set forth in The NRA Foundation's Articles of Incorporation. These purposes are as follows: to promote, advance and encourage firearms and hunting safety; to educate individuals, including the youth of the United States, with respect to firearms and firearms history and hunting safety and marksmanship, as well as with respect to other subjects that are of importance to the well-being of the general public; to conduct research in furtherance of improved firearms safety and marksmanship facilities and techniques; to support activities of the National Rifle Association of America, but only to the extent that such activities are in furtherance of charitable, educational or scientific purposes within the meaning of section 501(c)3 of the Internal Revenue Code; to engage in any other activity that is incidental to, connected with, or in advancement of the foregoing purposes and that is within the scope of allowable purposes under 26 U.S.C. 501(c)3.
Requirements: Any organization, association or other entity, whether formally incorporated or not, that has, as a minimum, a unique federal employer identification number (EIN) issued by the Internal Revenue Service. Eligible organizations may apply for an NRA Foundation grant for a qualifying project. Additionally, allowable projects must qualify under IRS 501(c)3 regulations in one of the following categories: charitable; scientific; testing for public safety; literary; educational; fostering national/international amateur sports competition (cannot include the provision of athletic facilities or equipment.)
Restrictions: The following organizations are not eligible for grants: political candidates or organizations; labor organizations; state fund committees; friends of NRA committees; private business/private enterprise; other organizations or groups that have not been assigned a federal employer identification number by the Internal Revenue Service. The following activities are not eligible for funding: projects which confer private benefit upon the applying organization/group; deficit financing; projects for commercial ventures; projects which require membership in the NRA or in the applying organization/group; applications from organizations or groups that have not submitted a final report for a previously awarded grant. In addition, the following limitations/restrictions apply to grants which are otherwise eligible for funding: no funding will be awarded to an applicant for payment of administrative

fees, office overhead, or other similar charges; the Foundation does not approve multi-year funding of projects; requests must be submitted for consideration each year. Funding cannot be given for competitions requiring NRA or other club or association membership. In addition, although grants may be sought for the purpose of fostering national or international amateur sports competition, grant awards cannot be made for the purpose of providing facilities or equipment to be used in such competitions.
Geographic Focus: All States
Amount of Grant: 5,000 - 9,000,000 USD
Contact: Wayne Sheets; (800) 423-6894; fax (703) 267-3985; nraf@nrahq.org
Internet: http://www.friendsofnra.org/National.aspx?cid=9
Sponsor: National Rifle association Foundation
11250 Waples Mill Road
Fairfax, VA 22030

NSERC Brockhouse Canada Prize for Interdisciplinary Research in Science and Engineering Grant   3518

The Brockhouse Canada Prize for Interdisciplinary Research in Science and Engineering recognizes outstanding Canadian teams of researchers from different disciplines who have combined their expertise to produce achievements of outstanding international significance in the natural sciences and engineering. The prize, accompanied by a team research grant of $250,000, reflects NSERC's commitment to supporting Canadian research through strategic investments in people, discovery and innovation. The grant supports the direct costs of university-based research and/or the enhancement of research facilities. The grant may be distributed in one lump sum or up to five instalments, depending on the needs of the recipients.
Requirements: Research teams nominated for the Brockhouse Canada Prize must have at least two members who are independent researchers, one of whom must hold an NSERC grant. The team can be part of an international effort, but the majority of the nominated team members must be employed at a Canadian university or public or private organization. NSERC recognizes that teams may change between the time of the specific research achievements and the time of nomination. Nominations will be accepted when changes have occurred but only as long as the core of the team remains intact. Contributions must be primarily in the natural sciences and engineering, and of an interdisciplinary and collaborative nature.
Restrictions: Any Canadian citizen may nominate a research team for the Brockhouse Canada Prize. Self nominations will not be accepted. Current NSERC Council members cannot be nominated. Since the prize is for interdisciplinary research, nominators should consult NSERC's Guidelines for the Preparation and Review of Applications in Interdisciplinary Research. Nominators should also consult NSERC's Guidelines for the Preparation and Review of Applications in Engineering and the Applied Sciences. See website for deadline & hyper links to above mentioned guidelines.
Geographic Focus: All States, Canada
Date(s) Application is Due: Jun 1
Amount of Grant: 250,000 USD
Contact: Administrator; (613) 995-5829; brockhouse@nserc-crsng.gc.ca
Internet: http://www.nserc-crsng.gc.ca/Prizes-Prix/Brockhouse-Brockhouse/Index-Index_eng.asp
Sponsor: Natural Sciences and Engineering Research Council of Canada
350 Albert Street
Ottawa, ON K1A 1H5 Canada

NSERC Michael Smith Awards   3519

The Michael Smith Awards for Science Promotion focus on people and groups who are inspirational in the way they promote science to the general public. The Awards are an opportunity for Canada's science community to recognize, support and encourage outstanding science promoters.
Requirements: Any individual, organization or company within Canada may be nominated for the award. Nominees will have made a successful and sustained effort to encourage public interest in and an understanding of the natural sciences and engineering (including math and technology) outside the formal education system. Science promotion activities with award potential could include activities such as: organizing science camps, fairs, clubs or programs with youth organizations; creating new learning materials; developing science and engineering related co-op programs or job shadowing initiatives; arranging demonstrations, visits and lectures; creating new learning materials;writing books and articles;creating radio or television programs and generating public involvement through multi-media programs.
Geographic Focus: All States, Canada
Date(s) Application is Due: Sep 1
Contact: Administrator; (613) 996-1417; michaelsmithawards@nserc-crsng.gc.ca
Internet: http://www.nserc-crsng.gc.ca/Prizes-Prix/Smith-Smith/Index-Index_eng.asp
Sponsor: Natural Sciences and Engineering Research Council of Canada
350 Albert Street
Ottawa, ON K1A 1H5 Canada

NSF Accelerating Innovation Research   3520

To accelerate the process of innovation, NSF is undertaking two related, new activities. The first will encourage the translation of the numerous, technologically-promising, fundamental discoveries made by NSF researchers, while drawing upon and building the entrepreneurial spirit of the researchers and students. The second activity will foster connections between an existing NSF innovation research alliance (including consortia such as Engineering Research Centers (ERC), Industry University Cooperative Research Centers (I/UCRC), Partnerships for Innovation (PFI), Science and Technology Centers (STC), Nanoscale Science and Engineering Centers (NSEC), Materials Research Science and Engineering Centers (MRSEC) grantees) and other institutions, whose complementary focus will spur the development of discoveries into innovative technologies through collaboration. Both of these activities are designed to strengthen the U.S. innovation ecosystem.
Requirements: For the Technology Translation Competition, the Principal Investigator or a co-PI must be a current or prior NSF awardee and a faculty member at a U.S. college or university at the time of award in the current competition. Subject technology must be derived from a discovery research project already conducted or initiated by the National Science Foundation. For the Research Alliance Competition, one of the partners must be an NSF funded innovation research alliance (including Centers for Analysis and Synthesis, Centers for Chemical Innovation, Engineering Research Centers, Industry/University Collaborative Research Centers, Materials Research Science and Engineering Centers, Nanoscale Science and Engineering Centers, Science and Technology Centers, and Science of Learning Centers). The research alliance must be active at the time of award in the current competition. The other partner(s) may be another research entity (either NSF-funded, other government agency funded, or privately funded), a small business consortium, or a local or regional innovation entity.
Geographic Focus: All States
Date(s) Application is Due: Feb 1
Amount of Grant: 350,000 - 1,000,000 USD
Contact: Rathindra DasGupta; (703) 292-8353; fax (703) 292-9057; rdasgupt@nsf.gov
Internet: http://www.nsf.gov/funding/pgm_summ.jsp?pims_id=503553
Sponsor: National Science Foundation
4201 Wilson Boulevard
Arlington, VA 22230

NSF Atmospheric Sciences Mid-Size Infrastructure Opportunity Grants   3521

The Division of Atmospheric Sciences (ATM) at the National Science Foundation recognizes the need for new experimental infrastructure that directly enables areas of research traditionally supported by the Division. For the purpose of this program, mid-size infrastructure is defined as research equipment costing between $4M and $25M. The development of mid-size infrastructure is intended to be a long-term effort in ATM to phase in high priority science-enabling tools consistent with community needs, ATM goals, and the NSF strategic vision. The potential for broad community usage and support is essential. Projects to be funded as mid-size infrastructure must be multi-user facilities that have demonstrable broad community support and directly enable research activities traditionally supported by ATM. Broad community advocacy for proposed projects is essential, as evidenced by the results of decadal surveys, focused workshops, and relevant steering or advisory committee recommendations. Selected projects will be funded for one to five years. NSF 07-602
Requirements: Proposals may be submitted by: (a) Academic Institutions located in the U.S. - U.S. universities and colleges located in the U.S; for-profit organizations - U.S. commercial organizations, especially small businesses with strong capabilities in scientific or engineering research or education; non-profit, non-academic organizations - Independent museums, observatories, research labs, professional societies and similar organizations in the U.S. associated with educational or research activities. Selected projects will be funded for one or more years, not to exceed five years. The development of mid-size infrastructure is intended to be a long-term effort in ATM to phase in high priority science-enabling tools consistent with community needs, ATM goals, and the NSF strategic vision. Design, engineering, and prototyping of mid-size infrastructure will be considered for funding only if there is valid justification for why this activity cannot be funded at the program level.
Restrictions: FFRDC's (Federally Funded Research and Development Centers) affiliated with agencies other than the National Science Foundation are NOT eligible to submit a proposal to this competition.
Geographic Focus: All States
Date(s) Application is Due: Jan 11; Jun 2
Amount of Grant: 4,000,000 - 25,000,000 USD
Contact: Robert M. Robinson, (703) 292-8529; rmrobins@nsf.gov
Internet: http://www.nsf.gov/publications/pub_summ.jsp?ods_key=nsf07602
Sponsor: National Science Foundation
4201 Wilson Boulevard
Arlington, VA 22230

NSF CISE Communicating Research to Public Audiences Grants   3522

The purpose of Communicating Research to Public Audiences grants is to promote the discovery, integration, dissemination, and employment of new knowledge in service to society and to achieve excellence in U.S. science, technology, engineering, and mathematics (STEM) education at all levels. These grants will provide an opportunity for Principal Investigators (PIs) to explain in non-technical terms the methods and/or results of their research to a broad and diverse audience. Projects with funding levels up to $75,000 will be supported to communicate the processes and results of current research awards from any NSF directorate or the Office of Polar Programs to public audiences in order to assist in the broader dissemination of research results and to promote science and technological literacy for the general public in an out-of-school setting. The grant can be used for any activity that falls within the definition of an informal science education activity such as media presentations, exhibits, or youth-based activities, in order to disseminate research results, research in progress, or research methods.
Requirements: Individuals and organizations in the following categories may submit proposals: U.S. universities and two-and four-year colleges (including community colleges) acting on behalf of their faculty members; independent museums, observatories, research laboratories, professional societies and similar organizations in the U.S. that are directly associated with educational or research activities; U.S. commercial organizations (especially small businesses with strong capabilities in scientific or engineering research or education); state and local governments; scientists, engineers or educators in the U.S. and U.S. citizens; foreign organizations; and a limited number of other types of Federal agencies.
Restrictions: NSF rarely provides support to foreign organizations. However, NSF will consider proposals for cooperative projects involving U.S. and foreign organizations, provided support is requested only for the U.S. portion of the collaborative effort.
Geographic Focus: All States

Amount of Grant: Up to 75,000 USD
Contact: Sylvia M. James; (703) 292-5333; fax (703) 292-9044; sjames@nsf.gov
Internet: http://www.nsf.gov/pubs/2003/nsf03509/nsf03509.html
Sponsor: National Science Foundation
4201 Wilson Boulevard
Arlington, VA 22230

NSF CISE Community-Based Data Interoperability Networks Grants   3523

This NSF crosscutting program supports community efforts to provide for broad interoperability with the goal of enhancing interaction and information sharing across all of the areas of science and engineering research and education represented at the National Science Foundation. The program supports the formation of community-based Data Interoperability Networks groups that enable communities to work together in the development of effective data interoperability strategies. Each Network holds dual responsibilities for: enabling broad community engagement in the development of consensus and agreement on strategies, priorities, and best approaches for achieving broad interoperability; and providing the technical expertise necessary to turn consensus and agreement into robust interoperability frameworks along with the appropriate tools and resources for their broad use and implementation.
Requirements: Individuals and organizations in the following categories may submit proposals: U.S. universities and two-and four-year colleges (including community colleges) acting on behalf of their faculty members; independent museums, observatories, research laboratories, professional societies and similar organizations in the U.S. that are directly associated with educational or research activities; U.S. commercial organizations (especially small businesses with strong capabilities in scientific or engineering research or education); state and local governments; scientists, engineers or educators in the U.S. and U.S. citizens; foreign organizations; and a limited number of other types of Federal agencies.
Restrictions: NSF rarely provides support to foreign organizations. However, NSF will consider proposals for cooperative projects involving U.S. and foreign organizations, provided support is requested only for the U.S. portion of the collaborative effort.
Geographic Focus: All States
Date(s) Application is Due: Jul 23
Amount of Grant: 750,000 - 1,250,000 USD
Contact: Maria Burka, (703) 292-7030; mburka@nsf.gov
Internet: http://www.nsf.gov/pubs/2007/nsf07565/nsf07565.htm
Sponsor: National Science Foundation
4201 Wilson Boulevard
Arlington, VA 22230

NSF CISE Computer and Network Systems (CNS): Core Programs Grants   3524

CISE's Division of Computer and Network Systems (CNS) supports research and education projects that develop new knowledge in two core programs: the Computer Systems Research (CSR) program; and the Networking Technology and Systems (NeTS) program. Proposers are invited to submit proposals in three project classes, which are defined as follows: Small Projects—up to $500,000 total budget with durations up to three years; Medium Projects—$500,001 to $1,200,000 total budget with durations up to four years; and Large Projects—$1,200,001 to $3,000,000 total budget with durations up to five years. Small Project proposals are due by December 17, Medium Project proposals are due by August 31, and Large Project proposals are due by November 28.
Requirements: Proposals may only be submitted by the following: non-profit, non-academic organizations—independent museums, observatories, research labs, professional societies and similar organizations in the U.S. associated with educational or research activities; and universities and two- and four-year colleges (including community colleges) located and accredited in the US, acting on behalf of their faculty members.
Geographic Focus: All States
Date(s) Application is Due: Aug 31; Nov 28; Dec 17
Amount of Grant: 500,000 USD
Contact: Krishna Kant, (703) 292-4776; kkant@nsf.gov
Internet: http://www.nsf.gov/pubs/2008/nsf08576/nsf08576.htm
Sponsor: National Science Foundation
4201 Wilson Boulevard
Arlington, VA 22230

NSF CISE Computing and Communication Foundations Core Programs Grants   3525

CISE's Division of Computing and Communication Foundations (CCF) supports research and education projects that develop new knowledge in three core programs: the Algorithmic Foundations program; the Communications and Information Foundations program; and the Software and Hardware Foundations program. Proposers are invited to submit proposals in three project classes, which are defined as follows: Small Projects—up to $500,000 total budget with durations up to three years; Medium Projects—$500,001 to $1,200,000 total budget with durations up to four years; and Large Projects—$1,200,001 to $3,000,000 total budget with durations up to five years. Small Project proposals are due by December 17, Medium Project proposals are due by August 31 (except for October 31 in 2008), and Large Project proposals are due by November 28.
Requirements: Proposals may only be submitted by the following: non-profit, non-academic organizations—independent museums, observatories, research labs, professional societies and similar organizations in the U.S. associated with educational or research activities; and universities and two- and four-year colleges (including community colleges) located and accredited in the US, acting on behalf of their faculty members.
Geographic Focus: All States
Date(s) Application is Due: Aug 30; Nov 28; Dec 17
Amount of Grant: 500,000 USD
Contact: Richard Beigel, (703) 292-8910; rbeigel@nsf.gov

Internet: http://www.nsf.gov/pubs/2008/nsf08577/nsf08577.htm
Sponsor: National Science Foundation
4201 Wilson Boulevard
Arlington, VA 22230

NSF CISE Computing Research Infrastructure (CRI) Grants   3526

The CISE Computing Research Infrastructure (CRI) program drives discovery and learning in the computing disciplines by supporting the creation, enhancement and operation of world-class computing research infrastructure. Further, through the CRI program CISE seeks to ensure that individuals from a diverse range of academic institutions, including minority-serving and predominantly undergraduate institutions, have access to such infrastructure. The CRI program supports two classes of awards: (1) Institutional Infrastructure awards support either the creation of new computing research infrastructure or the enhancement of existing computing research infrastructure to enable world-class research and education opportunities at the awardee and collaborating institutions. (2) Community Infrastructure awards support the planning for computing research infrastructure, or the creation of new computing infrastructure, or the enhancement of existing computing research infrastructure to enable world-class research and education opportunities for broadly-based communities of researchers and educators that extend well beyond the awardee institutions. Furthermore, CI awards support the operation of such infrastructure, ensuring that awardee institutions are well-positioned to provide a high quality of service to community researchers and educators expected to use the infrastructure to realize their research and education goals. NSF 08-570
Requirements: Individuals and organizations in the following categories may submit proposals: U.S. universities and two-and four-year colleges (including community colleges) acting on behalf of their faculty members; independent museums, observatories, research laboratories, professional societies and similar organizations in the U.S. that are directly associated with educational or research activities; U.S. commercial organizations (especially small businesses with strong capabilities in scientific or engineering research or education); state and local governments; scientists, engineers or educators in the U.S. and U.S. citizens; foreign organizations; and a limited number of other types of Federal agencies.
Restrictions: NSF rarely provides support to foreign organizations. NSF will consider proposals for cooperative projects involving U.S. and foreign organizations, provided support is requested only for the U.S. portion of the collaborative effort. NSF does not normally support research or education activities by scientists, engineers or educators employed by Federal agencies or Federally Funded Research and Development Centers (FFRDCs).
Geographic Focus: All States
Date(s) Application is Due: Aug 5; Sep 22
Amount of Grant: 200,000 - 750,000 USD
Contact: Tanya Korelsky, Program Director; (703) 292-8930; tkorelsk@nsf.gov
Internet: http://www.nsf.gov/funding/pgm_summ.jsp?pims_id=12810&govDel=USNSF_39
Sponsor: National Science Foundation
4201 Wilson Boulevard
Arlington, VA 22230

NSF Communicating Research to Public Audiences   3527

Communicating Research to Public Audiences is a component of the Informal Science Education program (ISE) in the Division of Elementary, Secondary, and Informal Education. ISE projects provide rich and stimulating contexts and experiences for individuals of all ages, interests, and backgrounds to increase their appreciation for, and understanding of, science, technology, engineering, and mathematics (STEM) in out-of-school settings. Requests for up to $75,000 will be considered to support projects that communicate to public audiences the process and results of current research that is being supported by any NSF directorate through informal science education activities, such as media presentations, exhibits, or youth-based activities. The purpose of these efforts is to disseminate research results, research in progress, or research methods. NSF 03-509
Requirements: The Principal Investigator (PI) must have an active NSF research award; a letter of support from the cognizant Program Officer for the research award is required. (NSF research awards do not include Small Grants for Exploratory Research Awards; Conference, Symposia, and Workshops grants; Dissertation Improvement Awards; or Post-doc Fellowships.) There is no fixed deadline. Proposals may be submitted at anytime, but at least six months prior to anticipated start date. The maximum award amount is $75,000. The maximum award period is 24 months. It is expected that the product (e.g. exhibit, film, program) will have a life beyond the expiration of the award. Estimated program budget, number of awards, and average award size/duration are subject to the availability of funds.
Restrictions: One proposal per active research award.
Geographic Focus: All States
Amount of Grant: Up to 75,000 USD
Contact: Sylvia M. James; (703) 292-5333; fax (703) 292-9044; sjames@nsf.gov
Internet: http://www.nsf.gov/funding/pgm_summ.jsp?pims_id=5362&org=DGE&sel_org=DGE&from=fund
Sponsor: National Science Foundation
4201 Wilson Boulevard
Arlington, VA 22230

NSF Decision, Risk, and Management Science Research Grants   3528

This program supports scientific research directed at increasing the understanding and effectiveness of decision making by individuals, groups, organizations, and society. Disciplinary and interdisciplinary research, doctoral dissertation research, and workshops are funded in the areas of judgment and decision making; decision analysis and decision aids; risk analysis; perception, and communication; societal and public policy decision making; management science and organizational design. The program also supports small grants for exploratory research of a time-critical or high-risk, potentially transformative

nature. Funded research must be relevant to an operational or applied context, grounded in theory, based on empirical observation, or subject to empirical validation, and generalizable. Proposals are accepted at any time from investigators in all fields of science. The target dates indicate the proximity of panel review meetings. Refer to NSF brochure PD 98-1321 for program announcement. Full Proposal Target dates are January 18 and August 18.
Geographic Focus: All States
Date(s) Application is Due: Jan 11; Aug 11
Amount of Grant: 1,000 - 1,000,000 USD
Contact: Robert O'Connor; (703) 292-7263; fax (703) 292-9068; roconnor@nsf.gov
Internet: http://www.nsf.gov/funding/pgm_summ.jsp?pims_id=5423
Sponsor: National Science Foundation
4201 Wilson Boulevard
Arlington, VA 22230

NSF Partnership for Advancing Technologies in Housing Grants   3529
The objective of this program is to support the objectives of the PATH program, which are to: improve the quality, affordability, durability, environmental performance, and energy efficiency of today's new and existing homes; strengthen the technology infrastructure of the United States; and help create the next generation of American housing. In addition to proposals in the above areas of technology and technology management, NSF and PATH are also interested in proposals involving partnerships between research institutions, industrial enterprises, local government, and/or other broadly-defined research and development participants relevant to the home building industry. NSF 01-45
Requirements: Proposals may be submitted by U.S. academic institutions in support of individual investigators or small groups.
Geographic Focus: All States
Date(s) Application is Due: Apr 17
Contact: Robert Wellek, Deputy Division Director; (703) 292-8370; rwellek@nsf.gov
Internet: http://www.nsf.gov/pubs/2001/nsf0145/nsf0145.htm
Sponsor: National Science Foundation
4201 Wilson Boulevard
Arlington, VA 22230

NSS Foundation Hunting Heritage Partnership Grants   3530
The program designed to build a strong partnership between the foundation, the Congressional Sportsmen's Foundation, and state wildlife agencies by providing funding to state wildlife agencies to create greater hunting opportunities and put more hunters in the field. Grants support a range of hunter-related programs—increasing hunter access, hunter retention, hunter recruitment, programs that create more opportunities to hunt, and communications programs geared toward retaining or recruiting hunters. The deadline for submitting proposals normally falls in early spring, and NSSF will notify grant recipients within two months following the deadline. Priority consideration is given to projects that will be completed by March 1st of the year following signing of the official grant documentation. Application materials and instructions are available online.
Requirements: State wildlife agencies are eligible. Eligible projects must address one or more of the following: recruitment of new hunters in the state; retention of current hunters in the state; increased hunter access; and/or communications or outreach geared toward retaining or recruiting hunters.
Restrictions: The following are ineligible: projects including activities other than hunting with a firearm; projects that include the purchase of land; projects that focus specifically on the management of wildlife habitats or ecosystems; projects that focus on the planning of meetings, symposia, conferences, etc; projects that involve building or improving existing structures; or all other projects that are not directly related to the above-stated project eligibility requirements as determined by the foundation.
Geographic Focus: All States
Contact: Steve Wagner, (203) 426-1320; swagner@nssf.org or info@nssf.org
Internet: http://www.nssf.org/grants/index.cfm?AoI=generic
Sponsor: National Shooting Sports Foundation
Flintlock Ridge Office Center, 11 Mile Hill Road
Newtown, CT 06470-2359

NSTA Distinguished Informal Science Education Award   3531
This award honors one NSTA member who has made extraordinary contributions to the advancement of science education in an informal or nontraditional school setting, such as a science-technology center, museum, or community science center. The award consists of three nights' hotel accommodation and $500 toward expenses to attend the NSTA National Conference on Science Education. Awardees will be honored at the Awards Banquet held during the NSTA conference. The application is available for download at the website.
Requirements: This award is open to NSTA members who are not classroom teachers and who have demonstrated their dedication to informal science education.
Restrictions: Applicants may apply for more than one award but are eligible to win only one NSTA award per year. Each application must be based on a unique program and process. Submission of the same idea and materials to different NSTA award programs will result in the disqualification of all applications. If an applicant's idea or project has received an NSTA award in the past, that idea or project is not eligible to receive an additional award.
Geographic Focus: All States
Date(s) Application is Due: Nov 30
Contact: Amanda Upton, Manager, NSTA Nominations and Teacher Awards Programs; (703) 312-9217; fax (703) 243-7177; nominations@nsta.org or awards@nsta.org
Internet: http://www.nsta.org/about/awards.aspx#distinformal
Sponsor: National Science Teachers Association
1840 Wilson Boulevard
Arlington, VA 22201

Nuffield Foundation Africa Program Grants   3532
The Commission for Africa highlighted the importance of strengthening Africa's science capacity, recommending that donors develop incentives for research and development in health that meet Africa's needs, and increase funding to African-led research. With that in mind, the Foundation has recently replaced its Commonwealth Program with Africa Program grants, which aims to improve services in health, education and civil justice in Southern and Eastern Africa through the development of the expertise and experience of practitioners and policy makers.
Geographic Focus: All States, Algeria, Angola, Benin, Botswana, Burkina Faso, Burundi, Cameroon, Cape Verde, Central African Republic, Chad, Comoros, Congo, Congo, Democratic Republic of, Cote d'Ivoire (Ivory Coast), Djibouti, Egypt, Equatorial Guinea, Eritrea, Ethiopia, Gabon, Gambia, Ghana, Guinea, Guinea-Bissau, Kenya, Lesotho, Liberia, Libya, Madagascar, Malawi, Mali, Mauritania, Mauritius, Morocco, Mozambique, Namibia, Niger, Nigeria, Rwanda, Sao Tome & Principe, Senegal, Seychelles, Sierra Leone, Somalia, South Africa, Sudan, Swaziland, United Kingdom
Contact: Sarah Lock, 44-171-631-0566; africaprogram@nuffieldfoundation.org
Internet: http://www.nuffieldfoundation.org/go/grants/commonwealth/page_100.html
Sponsor: Nuffield Foundation
28 Bedford Square
London, WC1B 3JS England

Nuffield Foundation Children and Families Grants   3533
The foundation was founded for the advancement of health through medical research and teaching and for the care of the elderly through scientific research and education. The Children and Families program supports work to help ensure that the legal and institutional framework is best adapted to meet the needs of children and families. At present, particular interests include (but are not limited to): work that links education and child development, either in the case of adolescent mental health or younger children; work that considers policies relevant to child welfare in a broader institutional context: parents' paid working patterns; childcare and early years provision; work that considers especially the well-being of children growing up in adverse conditions, and what institutional responses may be appropriate; work in family law, including cohabitation, child contact, child support; and work in child protection and placement (adoption and fostering) but only when it raises significant issues. Where a proposal is for a research study, Trustees are interested in the dispassionate examination of evidence. It notes that evidence is likely to be different in different cases, for different types of children and families, and are more likely to support work that takes this approach.
Requirements: Usually grants are made only to United Kingdom organizations, and support work that will be mainly based in the UK, although the Trustees welcome proposals for collaborative projects involving partners in European or Commonwealth countries.
Restrictions: The Foundation does not make grants for the running costs of voluntary bodies but will consider making a contribution to voluntary sector overheads on funded projects.
Geographic Focus: All States, United Kingdom
Date(s) Application is Due: Jan 8; May 7; Sep 3
Amount of Grant: 5,000 - 150,000 GBP
Contact: Sharon Witherspoon, 44-171-631-0566; sfwpa@nuffieldfoundation.org
Internet: http://www.nuffieldfoundation.org/go/grants/cplfj/page_30.html
Sponsor: Nuffield Foundation
28 Bedford Square
London, WC1B 3JS England

Nuffield Foundation Open Door Grants   3534
The Foundation keeps an open door to proposals of exceptional merit for research projects or practical innovations that lie outside our main program areas, but that meet Trustees' wider interests. These must have some bearing on the Foundation's widest charitable object. Particular interest is given to projects which identify change or interventions which will have a practical implications for policy or practice, or that will improve the quality of research evidence in areas of public debate. Through the Open Door, the Foundation may also identify emerging areas that justify more sustained attention.
Requirements: Usually grants are made only to United Kingdom organizations, and support work that will be mainly based in the UK, although the Trustees welcome proposals for collaborative projects involving partners in European or Commonwealth countries.
Geographic Focus: All States, United Kingdom
Date(s) Application is Due: Jan 8; May 7; Sep 3
Amount of Grant: 5,000 - 150,000 GBP
Contact: Sharon Witherspoon, 44-171-631-0566; sfwpa@nuffieldfoundation.org
Internet: http://www.nuffieldfoundation.org/go/grants/opendoor/page_115.html
Sponsor: Nuffield Foundation
28 Bedford Square
London, WC1B 3JS England

Nuffield Foundation Small Grants   3535
Most recently, the Foundation has decided that it will no longer try to fund across the full range of all social sciences, but will focus on work that more closely matches the wider interests of the Foundation. As a consequence, the budgetary ceiling for individual grants will be raised from the current maximum of 12,000GBP.
Geographic Focus: All States, United Kingdom
Date(s) Application is Due: Jul 17
Amount of Grant: 12,000 GBP
Contact: Sarah Lock, 44-171-631-0566; smallgrants@nuffieldfoundation.org
Internet: http://www.nuffieldfoundation.org/go/grants/smallgrants/page_123.html
Sponsor: Nuffield Foundation
28 Bedford Square
London, WC1B 3JS England

Nu Skin Force for Good Foundation Grants　　　　　　　　　　　3536
The foundation's mission is to create a better world for children by improving human life, continuing indigenous cultures, and protecting fragile environments. Funding decisions are made by a committee comprising a cross-section of Nu Skin Enterprises officers and employees. Each project is thoroughly researched, and the needs of the children and community that the project will affect are taken into consideration. Funding requests should be submitted with a letter of inquiry highlighting the project and should include a description of the organization and the nature of its work, as well as a brief summary of achievements, particularly as they relate to the program or issue to be addressed; a statement of the problem or need to be addressed and a brief explanation of how it will be addressed; a description of the time frame of the proposed activities; estimated costs for the activity and the amount requested; and proof of nonprofit status.
Requirements: Nonprofit organizations are eligible.
Restrictions: The foundation does not support capital campaigns, seed funding, ad space in benefit programs, individuals, fraternal organizations, religious purposes, political lobbyists, or travel.
Geographic Focus: All States
Contact: Sydney Fox, Public Relations; shfox@nuskin.com
Internet: http://www.forceforgood.org/giving/index.shtml
Sponsor: Nu Skin Enterprises
75 W Center Street
Provo, UT 84601

NWHF Health Advocacy Small Grants　　　　　　　　　　　3537
Awards of up to $10,000 will be available for 15-20 projects dedicated to one of the following areas: grassroots organizing; coalition building; communications; and policy analysis. For example, organizations may request funds to develop communications materials or enhance their Web site, dedicate staff time to keep abreast of health-reform related activity in Salem during the legislative session, or build their organizational capacity to develop a coalition focused on health reform. In addition to grant dollars, organizations can apply for approximately two days of technical assistance from the Consumer Voices for Coverage team in one or more of the areas listed above.
Requirements: 501(c)3 educational institutions and governmental entities are eligible. Generally speaking, foundation programs serve the entire state of Oregon, and the following Washington counties: Clark, Cowlitz, Pacific, Skamania, and Wahkiakum. Specific programs and funds may have additional geographic restrictions. Applying organizations must sign a statement of nondiscrimination in leadership, staffing, and services.
Restrictions: Support will not be considered for basic operations, or for salaries or other expenses associated with ongoing programs.
Geographic Focus: Idaho, Oregon, Washington
Date(s) Application is Due: Feb 4
Amount of Grant: Up to 10,000 USD
Contact: Chris DeMars; (971) 230-1292 or (503) 220-1955; cdemars@nwhf.org
Internet: http://www.nwhf.org/index.php?/apply/access
Sponsor: Northwest Health Foundation
221 NW Second Avenue, Suite 300
Portland, OR 97209

NWHF Kaiser Permanente Community Fund Grants　　　　　　　　　　　3538
The Kaiser Permanente Community Fund (KPCF) at Northwest Health Foundation was established in late 2004 to advance the health of the communities served by Kaiser Permanente Northwest. The Fund intends to achieve this goal by addressing those factors in the social, policy, and physical environment that impact community health. Often referred to as the social determinants of health, these factors have been shown to play a major role in the development of health disparities based on race, ethnicity, and socio-economic status.
Requirements: To be eligible to apply for a grant from the Kaiser Permanente Community Fund, the service area of your project must fall within the geographic region roughly spanning from Longview, Washington to Salem, Oregon and portions of the Willamette Valley.
Geographic Focus: Oregon, Washington
Date(s) Application is Due: Jul 2
Contact: Judith Woodruff; (503) 220-1955; fax (503) 220-1355; judith@nwhf.org
Internet: http://www.nwhf.org/index.php?/apply/kaiser
Sponsor: Northwest Health Foundation
221 NW Second Avenue, Suite 300
Portland, OR 97209

NWHF Partners Investing in Nursing's Future Grants　　　　　　　　　　　3539
Partners Investing in Nursing's Future is a collaborative initiative of the RWJ Foundation and Northwest Health Foundation that will address nursing issues at the local level through funding partnerships with community and regional foundations. The goal of this initiative is to enable local foundations to act as catalysts in developing the comprehensive strategies that are vital to establishing a stable, adequate nursing workforce. Grants support the capacity, involvement, and leadership of local foundations to advance nursing workforce solutions in their communities. Local foundations must match funds with at least $1 for every $1 provided by the program. Proposals must be submitted online. Guidelines are available online. Letters of Intent are due by October 2, and invited proposals are due on December 19.
Requirements: U.S. local or regional private, family, or community foundations are eligible. Eligible foundations are those classified under IRS codes as 501(c)3 tax exempt, a nonexempt charitable trust treated as a private foundation under 4947(a)1, or organizations claiming status as a private operating foundation under 4942(j)3 or 5. Government entities, corporations, or corporate grantmakers may participate in funding collaboratives but may not serve as the applicant organization.
Geographic Focus: All States
Date(s) Application is Due: Oct 2; Dec 19
Amount of Grant: Up to 250,000 USD
Contact: Judith Woodruff; (503) 220-1955; fax (503) 220-1355; judith@nwhf.org
Internet: http://www.partnersinnursing.org/grants.html
Sponsor: Northwest Health Foundation
221 NW Second Avenue, Suite 300
Portland, OR 97209

NWHF Physical Activity and Nutrition Grants　　　　　　　　　　　3540
The Foundation is soliciting applications from organizations engaged in creating community environments and policies that support healthy lifestyles, specifically with regards to healthy food choices and opportunities for regular physical activity. It is looking to fund initiatives that: identify the social, policy or environmental factors to be addressed, and how they will support healthy physical activity and nutrition behaviors; articulate goals, strategies and priorities that have been developed in full partnership with the community to be served; build and mobilize constituencies to advocate for improved physical activity and nutrition policies, practices and environments; reduce health disparities related to unequal access to healthy food and opportunities for daily physical activity; involve collaboration among different organizations or agencies, especially across different sectors, to achieve common goals; and implement recommendations proposed in peer-reviewed national and state reports on physical activity and nutrition. The Foundation's intent is to award a portfolio of five to eight grants of various sizes in the $25,000 to $100,000 range (total award amount - not per year). Projects will be funded for up to three years.
Requirements: The Northwest Health Foundation invites proposals from non-profit organizations, local government agencies and/or tribal organizations
Restrictions: For this RFP, the Foundation is not interested in funding curriculum development, research studies, clinical interventions, exercise or cooking classes, educational programs, capital construction costs or general operating support.
Geographic Focus: Oregon, Washington
Date(s) Application is Due: Mar 16
Amount of Grant: 25,000 - 100,000 USD
Contact: Judith Woodruff; (503) 220-1955; fax (503) 220-1355; judith@nwhf.org
Internet: http://www.nwhf.org/index.php?apply/obesity
Sponsor: Northwest Health Foundation
221 NW Second Avenue, Suite 300
Portland, OR 97209

NYCH Together Grants　　　　　　　　　　　3541
The New York Council for the Humanities Together Book Talk for Kids and Parents program offers a forum for parents and their 9-to-11 year old children to come together to talk about books and ideas at their local library. Each of the six 90-minute Together sessions is co-facilitated by a librarian and a humanities scholar from the local community. The sessions alternate between picture books and novels, all of which explore key themes in American life such as courage, freedom, and being American. To host a Together series at your library, find a humanities scholar who is willing to serve as co-facilitator and submit your application to the Council. If your application is successful, the Council will supply all the books, contract directly with your scholar co-facilitator, and provide your library with a $1000 stipend to cover necessary expenses such as childcare and materials.
Requirements: Steps required to apply for a Together series at your library: 1- Find a humanities scholar from your community to serve as the series co-facilitator. Libraries are responsible for identifying a humanities scholar (or graduate student) to co-facilitate the six 90-minute discussions with a librarian; 2- Choose a librarian to serve as co-facilitator. Libraries are also responsible for identifying a librarian who is willing to co-facilitate the six 90-minute discussions with the scholar co-facilitator; 3- Designate spaces in your library. Find a space in your library where group discussions can be held uninterrupted. Also, make sure that there is a designated space for your childcare provider to watch younger siblings; 4- Apply to the Council. Complete and submit the Together application (see NYCH website). Include the resume of the scholar you have identified with your application; 5- Participate in a training session. If your application is accepted, the scholar co-facilitator and the librarian co-facilitator will both be required to attend the Together training session. The Council will cover all transportation costs; 6- Schedule, promote and host a Together series.
Geographic Focus: New York
Date(s) Application is Due: Jun 15; Nov 1
Contact: Jane McNamara, Director; (646) 302-4937 or (212) 233-1131, ext. 24; fax (212) 233-4607; education@nyhumanities.org
Internet: http://www.nyhumanities.org/discussion_groups/kids_and_parents/together/
Sponsor: New York Council for the Humanities
150 Broadway, Suite 1700
New York, NY 10038

NYCT AIDS/HIV Grants　　　　　　　　　　　3542
The Trust supports projects that strengthen preventive health care, improve access to services, promote the efficient use of health resources, and develop the skills and independence of people with special needs. The goal of this program is to address the complex social, medical, and legal problems of people with HIV. Since this issue cuts across a number of program areas, projects may fall within a number of funding categories. A limited amount of support is available specifically for policy research and advocacy efforts that: increase public understanding of AIDS and HIV infection; improve the funding and delivery of services; and improve coordination among service organizations. The grant review process takes from two to six months. Grants range from $5,000 to $100,000; an average grant is around $60,000.
Requirements: Grants are made primarily to nonprofit organizations located in the five boroughs of New York City. Grants for programs outside the area are generally from funds designated for specific charities or have been made at the suggestion of donors.

Restrictions: The trust does not make grants to individuals, offer general or capital funding, endowments, building construction/renovation, deficit financing, films, or religion.
Geographic Focus: New York
Date(s) Application is Due: Sep 14
Amount of Grant: 5,000 - 100,000 USD
Contact: Joyce M. Bove; (212) 686-0010, ext. 552; info@nycommunitytrust.org
Internet: http://www.nycommunitytrust.org/HowtoApply/RequestsforProposals/NewYorkCityAIDSFund/tabid/408/Default.aspx
Sponsor: New York Community Trust
909 Third Avenue, 22nd Floor
New York, NY 10022

NYCT Blindness and Visual Disabilities Grants 3543

The Trust supports projects that strengthen preventive health care, improve access to services, promote the efficient use of health resources, and develop the skills and independence of people with special needs. The goals of this program are to support program innovation and reform and eliminate service gaps. Specifically, grants are made to projects that: improve services to those people with visual disabilities who are presently underserved, such as the elderly, minorities, people with multiple disabilities, people in institutions, and youth in transition from school to work (projects need not be limited to direct service, and may include advocacy and organizational improvement); involve people with visual disabilities more fully in community activities; expand programs that identify people with vision problems at an early stage and link them with appropriate resources; empower persons with visual disabilities by enabling them to participate in planning programs that affect them; and support research in the prevention and treatment of blindness (this may include clinical, epidemiological, and applied studies). The grant review process takes from two to six months. Grants range from $5,000 to $100,000; an average grant is around $60,000.
Requirements: Grants are made primarily to nonprofit organizations located in the five boroughs of New York City. Grants for programs outside the area are generally from funds designated for specific charities or have been made at the suggestion of donors.
Restrictions: The trust does not make grants to individuals, offer general or capital funding, endowments, building construction/renovation, deficit financing, films, or religion.
Geographic Focus: New York
Amount of Grant: 5,000 - 100,000 USD
Contact: Joyce M. Bove; (212) 686-0010, ext. 552; info@nycommunitytrust.org
Internet: http://www.nycommunitytrust.org/ForGrantSeekers/GrantmakingGuidelines/HealthandPeoplewithSpecialNeeds/tabid/207/Default.aspx
Sponsor: New York Community Trust
909 Third Avenue, 22nd Floor
New York, NY 10022

NYCT Children and Youth with Disabilities Grants 3544

The Trust supports projects that strengthen preventive health care, improve access to services, promote the efficient use of health resources, and develop the skills and independence of people with special needs. The goals of this program are to stimulate policymakers and service providers to improve existing services for children with disabilities and to encourage a service approach that emphasizes independence and the development of full potential. Specifically, grants are made to projects that: foster integration into community life, independent living, and improved self-image; improve early identification of disability, encourage early intervention, and increase access to early childhood education; provide comprehensive treatment, planning, and referral programs for children and their families; and assess needs, develop policy, and advocate to improve the delivery and coordination of services. The grant review process takes from two to six months. Grants range from $5,000 to $100,000; an average grant is around $60,000.
Requirements: Grants are made primarily to nonprofit organizations located in the five boroughs of New York City. Grants for programs outside the area are generally from funds designated for specific charities or have been made at the suggestion of donors.
Restrictions: The trust does not make grants to individuals, offer general or capital funding, endowments, building construction/renovation, deficit financing, films, or religion.
Geographic Focus: New York
Amount of Grant: 5,000 - 100,000 USD
Contact: Joyce M. Bove; (212) 686-0010, ext. 552; info@nycommunitytrust.org
Internet: http://www.nycommunitytrust.org/ForGrantSeekers/GrantmakingGuidelines/HealthandPeoplewithSpecialNeeds/tabid/207/Default.aspx
Sponsor: New York Community Trust
909 Third Avenue, 22nd Floor
New York, NY 10022

NYCT Civic Affairs Grants 3545

The Trust works in partnership with government and private agencies to develop the strengths of families and young people; to improve their living and working conditions; to improve family and child welfare services; and to advance social work practice. The goals of this program are to ensure a representative political process and improve the functioning of government. The first goal of the Program is to encourage voting through projects that: support reform of election administration and voting infrastructure; remove obstacles to voting, especially for groups that have historically not voted; and disseminate nonpartisan information about candidates and elected officials. The second goal of the Program is to make local and state government more accountable through projects that: support efforts to make Albany work better for the citizens of the City and the State; strengthen nonprofit civic groups; and provide citizens and advocates with information and skills needed to promote effective governance. The final goal of the Program is to promote civic literacy in children and civic learning for our newest citizens through projects that: encourage good citizenship among immigrants and their children; enrich civic learning opportunities for children and youth; and target neighborhoods and constituencies with low levels of civic participation. The grant review process takes from two to six months. Grants range from $5,000 to $100,000; an average grant is around $60,000.
Requirements: Grants are made primarily to nonprofit organizations located in the five boroughs of New York City. Grants for programs outside the area are generally from funds designated for specific charities or have been made at the suggestion of donors.
Restrictions: The trust does not make grants to individuals, offer general or capital funding, endowments, building construction/renovation, deficit financing, films, or religion.
Geographic Focus: New York
Amount of Grant: 5,000 - 100,000 USD
Contact: Joyce M. Bove; (212) 686-0010, ext. 552; info@nycommunitytrust.org
Internet: http://www.nycommunitytrust.org/ForGrantSeekers/GrantmakingGuidelines/CommunityDevelopmentandtheEnvironment/tabid/204/Default.aspx
Sponsor: New York Community Trust
909 Third Avenue, 22nd Floor
New York, NY 10022

NYCT Community Development Grants 3546

The Trust focuses on relieving New York's chronic shortage of affordable housing, strengthening the local economy, and protecting the environment. It supports community-based agencies working on these issues at the neighborhood level, and government and nonprofit institutions developing strategies for the City as a whole. The goals of this program are to build and sustain strong communities and create economic opportunities for residents of low-income neighborhoods. The Program supports a mix of citywide and local community development activities as well as citywide technical assistance, policy research, and advocacy. It give priority to projects that promote community participation. Specifically, grants are made to projects that: preserve affordable housing in low- income neighborhoods; promote strategies for job creation and linking low-income residents to jobs; develop new sources of capital and innovative community development tools; enhance the capacity of community development organizations to function effectively; and monitor and document the effects of community and economic development policies on poor communities. The grant review process takes from two to six months. Grants range from $5,000 to $100,000; an average grant is around $60,000.
Requirements: Grants are made primarily to nonprofit organizations located in the five boroughs of New York City. Grants for programs outside the area are generally from funds designated for specific charities or have been made at the suggestion of donors.
Restrictions: The trust does not make grants to individuals, offer general or capital funding, endowments, building construction/renovation, deficit financing, films, or religion.
Geographic Focus: New York
Amount of Grant: 5,000 - 100,000 USD
Contact: Joyce M. Bove; (212) 686-0010, ext. 552; info@nycommunitytrust.org
Internet: http://www.nycommunitytrust.org/ForGrantSeekers/GrantmakingGuidelines/CommunityDevelopmentandtheEnvironment/tabid/204/Default.aspx
Sponsor: New York Community Trust
909 Third Avenue, 22nd Floor
New York, NY 10022

NYCT Fund for New Citizens Grants 3547

The Trust concentrates on projects that: improve New York City's public education system; promote diversity, equity, and access in the arts; and advocate for the rights of all people. The Fund is a consortium of foundations that assists immigrant and refugee groups on issues related to the Immigration Act of 1990. The grant review process takes from two to six months. Grants range from $5,000 to $100,000; an average grant is around $60,000.
Requirements: Grants are made primarily to nonprofit organizations located in the five boroughs of New York City. Grants for programs outside the area are generally from funds designated for specific charities or have been made at the suggestion of donors.
Restrictions: The trust does not make grants to individuals, offer general or capital funding, endowments, building construction/renovation, deficit financing, or films.
Geographic Focus: New York
Contact: Joyce M. Bove; (212) 686-0010, ext. 552; info@nycommunitytrust.org
Internet: http://www.nycommunitytrust.org/AboutTheTrust/Donorcollaboratives/TheFundforNewCitizens/tabid/397/Default.aspx
Sponsor: New York Community Trust
909 Third Avenue, 22nd Floor
New York, NY 10022

NYCT Girls and Young Women Grants 3548

The Trust works in partnership with government and private agencies to develop the strengths of families and young people; to improve their living and working conditions; to improve family and child welfare services; and to advance social work practice. The goal of this Program is to improve conditions and opportunities for those who are poor and disadvantaged, particularly minorities and young, single mothers. Specifically, the program funds projects that: prepare girls and young women for economic self-sufficiency by providing the economic and personal support necessary to gain access to jobs and promoting innovative ways to include indigent and vulnerable young women in the workplace; and reduce the effects of health and social problems that threaten the lives and well-being of girls and young women through direct services and policy and advocacy efforts. Particular emphasis is placed on projects addressing the issues of teen pregnancy, homelessness, and AIDS. The grant review process takes from two to six months. Grants range from $5,000 to $100,000; an average grant is around $60,000.
Requirements: Grants are made primarily to nonprofit organizations located in the five boroughs of New York City. Grants for programs outside the area are generally from funds designated for specific charities or have been made at the suggestion of donors.

Restrictions: The trust does not make grants to individuals, offer general or capital funding, endowments, building construction/renovation, deficit financing, films, or religion.
Geographic Focus: New York
Amount of Grant: 5,000 - 100,000 USD
Contact: Joyce M. Bove; (212) 686-0010, ext. 552; info@nycommunitytrust.org
Internet: http://www.nycommunitytrust.org/ForGrantSeekers/GrantmakingGuidelines/ChildrenYouthandFamilies/tabid/205/Default.aspx
Sponsor: New York Community Trust
909 Third Avenue, 22nd Floor
New York, NY 10022

NYCT Grants for the Elderly 3549
The Trust supports projects that strengthen preventive health care, improve access to services, promote the efficient use of health resources, and develop the skills and independence of people with special needs. The goals of this program are to enable elderly people to remain active in their communities and to meet the basic needs of those who are vulnerable and dependent. Resources are primarily targeted toward the most underserved elderly and those whose needs are most acute, including members of racial and ethnic minorities, the poor, and those with chronic illnesses or mental or functional disabilities. Specifically, grants are made to projects that: increase the number of elderly who are able to participate in community activities, particularly those involving contact with young people; enable the elderly to assume a leadership role in planning, influencing, or changing the programs that serve them; improve the management, capacity, and resources of government and voluntary agencies serving the elderly, and encourage collaboration among agencies; and assess need, develop policy, and advocate to improve the delivery and coordination of services. The grant review process takes from two to six months. Grants range from $5,000 to $100,000; an average grant is around $60,000.
Requirements: Grants are made primarily to nonprofit organizations located in the five boroughs of New York City. Grants for programs outside the area are generally from funds designated for specific charities or have been made at the suggestion of donors.
Restrictions: The trust does not make grants to individuals, offer general or capital funding, endowments, building construction/renovation, deficit financing, films, or religion.
Geographic Focus: New York
Amount of Grant: 5,000 - 100,000 USD
Contact: Joyce M. Bove; (212) 686-0010, ext. 552; info@nycommunitytrust.org
Internet: http://www.nycommunitytrust.org/ForGrantSeekers/GrantmakingGuidelines/HealthandPeoplewithSpecialNeeds/tabid/207/Default.aspx
Sponsor: New York Community Trust
909 Third Avenue, 22nd Floor
New York, NY 10022

NYCT Health Services, Systems, and Policies Grants 3550
The Trust supports projects that strengthen preventive health care, improve access to services, promote the efficient use of health resources, and develop the skills and independence of people with special needs. The primary goal of this program is to improve the effectiveness, responsiveness, and equity of health care in New York City. Specifically, the program makes grants: for services, policy research, advocacy, and technical assistance that promote the accessibility of basic health services, especially in minority and immigrant communities; to strengthen health service providers, especially those serving the city's poorest residents; and to promote healthy lifestyles. The grant review process takes from two to six months. Grants range from $5,000 to $100,000; an average grant is around $60,000.
Requirements: Grants are made primarily to nonprofit organizations located in the five boroughs of New York City. Grants for programs outside the area are generally from funds designated for specific charities or have been made at the suggestion of donors.
Restrictions: The trust does not make grants to individuals, offer general or capital funding, endowments, building construction/renovation, deficit financing, films, or religion.
Geographic Focus: New York
Amount of Grant: 5,000 - 100,000 USD
Contact: Joyce M. Bove; (212) 686-0010, ext. 552; info@nycommunitytrust.org
Internet: http://www.nycommunitytrust.org/ForGrantSeekers/GrantmakingGuidelines/HealthandPeoplewithSpecialNeeds/tabid/207/Default.aspx
Sponsor: New York Community Trust
909 Third Avenue, 22nd Floor
New York, NY 10022

NYCT Historic Preservation Grants 3551
The Trust concentrates on projects that: improve New York City's public education system; promote diversity, equity, and access in the arts; and advocate for the rights of all people. The goals of this program are to support preservation in low-income and minority communities and the boroughs outside of Manhattan, and restore historic places that represent significant and overlooked aspects of New York City's history. Specifically, it supports programs that: foster collaborations between preservation organizations and minority, ethnic, and other community groups; incorporate preservation efforts into neighborhood revitalization initiatives and increase the preservation expertise of community organizations; promote the adaptive use of historic buildings for social, cultural, and civic purposes; and help groups develop alternative sources of financial support for capital, maintenance, and repairs. The grant review process takes from two to six months. Grants range from $5,000 to $100,000; an average grant is around $60,000.
Requirements: Grants are made primarily to nonprofit organizations located in the five boroughs (in this case, excluding Manhattan) of New York City. Grants for programs outside the area are generally from funds designated for specific charities or have been made at the suggestion of donors.
Restrictions: To ensure maximum impact from the limited funds, the Trust will not make grants directly for maintenance or capital projects. The trust does not make grants to individuals, offer general or capital funding, endowments, deficit financing, films, or religion.
Geographic Focus: New York
Amount of Grant: 5,000 - 100,000 USD
Contact: Joyce M. Bove; (212) 686-0010, ext. 552; info@nycommunitytrust.org
Internet: http://www.nycommunitytrust.org/GrantSeekers/Grantmakingguidelines/ArtsEducationandHumanJustice/tabid/206/Default.aspx
Sponsor: New York Community Trust
909 Third Avenue, 22nd Floor
New York, NY 10022

NYCT Human Justice Grants 3552
The Trust concentrates on projects that: improve New York City's public education system; promote diversity, equity, and access in the arts; and advocate for the rights of all people. The goals of this program are to improve the operations of the justice system; to increase access to the system for vulnerable populations; to protect civil rights; and to promote harmony among different racial and ethnic groups. Specifically, grants are made to projects that: overcome interracial and intergroup conflict, particularly among young people; protect the civil rights of minorities and disenfranchised groups; and support court reform projects and expand civil legal services for the poor. The grant review process takes from two to six months. Grants range from $5,000 to $100,000; an average grant is around $60,000.
Requirements: Grants are made primarily to nonprofit organizations located in the five boroughs of New York City. Grants for programs outside the area are generally from funds designated for specific charities or have been made at the suggestion of donors.
Restrictions: The trust does not make grants to individuals, offer general or capital funding, endowments, building construction/renovation, deficit financing, films, or religion.
Geographic Focus: New York
Amount of Grant: 5,000 - 100,000 USD
Contact: Joyce M. Bove; (212) 686-0010, ext. 552; info@nycommunitytrust.org
Internet: http://www.nycommunitytrust.org/GrantSeekers/Grantmakingguidelines/ArtsEducationandHumanJustice/tabid/206/Default.aspx
Sponsor: New York Community Trust
909 Third Avenue, 22nd Floor
New York, NY 10022

NYCT Hunger and Homelessnes Grants 3553
The Trust works in partnership with government and private agencies to develop the strengths of families and young people; to improve their living and working conditions; to improve family and child welfare services; and to advance social work practice. The goals of this program are to improve the institutions serving people who are homeless and hungry, and to promote the independence and reintegration into society of homeless families and adults. Specifically, grants are made to projects that: conduct policy analyses, needs assessments, and advocacy to increase public understanding of hunger and homelessness, and to improve funding and services; prepare homeless heads of household and other adults for economic self-sufficiency through education, employment and training programs, and related support services; and increase the capacity of community organizations to integrate relocated formerly homeless families into their neighborhoods. The grant review process takes from two to six months. Grants range from $5,000 to $100,000; an average grant is around $60,000.
Requirements: Grants are made primarily to nonprofit organizations located in the five boroughs of New York City. Grants for programs outside the area are generally from funds designated for specific charities or have been made at the suggestion of donors.
Restrictions: The trust does not make grants to individuals, offer general or capital funding, endowments, building construction/renovation, deficit financing, films, or religion.
Geographic Focus: New York
Amount of Grant: 5,000 - 100,000 USD
Contact: Joyce M. Bove; (212) 686-0010, ext. 552; info@nycommunitytrust.org
Internet: http://www.nycommunitytrust.org/ForGrantSeekers/GrantmakingGuidelines/ChildrenYouthandFamilies/tabid/205/Default.aspx
Sponsor: New York Community Trust
909 Third Avenue, 22nd Floor
New York, NY 10022

NYCT Mental Health and Mental Retardation Grants 3554
The Trust supports projects that strengthen preventive health care, improve access to services, promote the efficient use of health resources, and develop the skills and independence of people with special needs. The goals of this program are to foster the independence of people with mental illness and mental retardation, and to encourage a community-based system of care. Specifically, grants are made to projects that: improve the quality and availability of community housing and services for people with chronic mental illnesses; improve and expand the delivery of mental health services to children and adolescents, especially those that stress the early identification and remediation of problems; strengthen advocacy groups that promote reimbursement practices and allocation of mental health resources that correspond to community needs; and direct the attention of service providers, policy makers, and the general public to the mental health concerns of racial and ethnic minorities. The grant review process takes from two to six months. Grants range from $5,000 to $100,000; an average grant is around $60,000.
Requirements: Grants are made primarily to nonprofit organizations located in the five boroughs of New York City. Grants for programs outside the area are generally from funds designated for specific charities or have been made at the suggestion of donors.
Restrictions: The trust does not make grants to individuals, offer general or capital funding, endowments, building construction/renovation, deficit financing, films, or religion.
Geographic Focus: New York
Amount of Grant: 5,000 - 100,000 USD
Contact: Joyce M. Bove; (212) 686-0010, ext. 552; info@nycommunitytrust.org

Internet: http://www.nycommunitytrust.org/ForGrantSeekers/GrantmakingGuidelines/HealthandPeoplewithSpecialNeeds/tabid/207/Default.aspx
Sponsor: New York Community Trust
909 Third Avenue, 22nd Floor
New York, NY 10022

NYCT Neighborhood Revitalization Grants 3555
The Trust focuses on relieving New York's chronic shortage of affordable housing, strengthening the local economy, and protecting the environment. It supports community-based agencies working on these issues at the neighborhood level, and government and nonprofit institutions developing strategies for the City as a whole. Each fall, the Trust operates a special competitive grants initiative to strengthen the capacity of local community development organizations. Designed for organizations with strong board and community involvement, these grants support local efforts to protect and expand neighborhood investments and link residents to a full range of services. Proposals are reviewed each year through a Request for Proposals, the focus of which may change from year to year. The grant review process takes from two to six months. Grants range from $5,000 to $100,000; an average grant is around $60,000.
Requirements: Grants are made primarily to nonprofit organizations located in the five boroughs of New York City. Grants for programs outside the area are generally from funds designated for specific charities or have been made at the suggestion of donors.
Restrictions: The trust does not make grants to individuals, offer general or capital funding, endowments, building construction/renovation, deficit financing, films, or religion. No faxed or emailed proposals will be accepted.
Geographic Focus: New York
Date(s) Application is Due: Aug 13
Amount of Grant: 5,000 - 100,000 USD
Contact: Joyce M. Bove; (212) 686-0010, ext. 552; info@nycommunitytrust.org
Internet: http://www.nycommunitytrust.org/GrantSeekers/RequestsforProposals/NeighborhoodRevitalizationProgram/tabid/409/Default.aspx
Sponsor: New York Community Trust
909 Third Avenue, 22nd Floor
New York, NY 10022

NYCT New York City Environment Grants 3556
The New York City program focuses on four urban environmental issues: promoting a more effective and sustainable solid waste management program through consumer education, research, and advocacy, with an emphasis on waste reduction and equitable distribution of solid waste facilities; expanding open space and parks through advocacy, constituency building, and support of local planning and greening activities; reclaiming the waterfront and brownfields through technical assistance, advocacy, and partnerships between community development and environmental groups; reducing air pollutants and other environmental toxins through cleaner fuels and engines, mass transit improvements, and elimination of indoor pollutants and the concentration of polluting facilities in poor communities. In the New York metropolitan region, the NYCT aims are, to preserve and restore habitat, promote a more sustainable transportation system, protect open space and drinking water, and redevelop brownfields.
Requirements: Grants are made primarily to nonprofit organizations located in the five boroughs of New York City. Grants for programs outside the area are generally from funds designated for specific charities or have been made at the suggestion of donors.
Restrictions: The trust does not make grants to individuals, offer general or capital funding, endowments, building construction/renovation, deficit financing, films, or religion.
Geographic Focus: New York
Contact: Joyce M. Bove; (212) 686-0010, ext. 552; info@nycommunitytrust.org
Internet: http://www.nycommunitytrust.org/ForGrantSeekers/GrantmakingGuidelines/CommunityDevelopmentandtheEnvironment/tabid/204/Default.aspx
Sponsor: New York Community Trust
909 Third Avenue, 22nd Floor
New York, NY 10022

NYCT Social Services and Welfare Grants 3557
The Trust works in partnership with government and private agencies to develop the strengths of families and young people; to improve their living and working conditions; to improve family and child welfare services; and to advance social work practice. The goals of this program are to help poor families become more self-sufficient and to preserve the safety of the most vulnerable children. Specifically, the program supports efforts that: link social service agencies with employment programs and provide the support to help poor people get access to and keep jobs (e.g., training, child care, placement assistance); safeguard the welfare of children through services and advocacy; monitor and document the effects of policy and program changes on poor children, families, and communities, and their implications for social work practice; and enhance the capacity of social service agencies to deliver quality services. Priority is given to projects that: have specific plans for achieving and documenting results in a specified time period; serve the neediest neighborhoods; and employ multidisciplinary, collaborative approaches that build on efforts where comprehensive neighborhood planning structures are in place. The grant review process takes from two to six months. Grants range from $5,000 to $100,000; an average grant is around $60,000.
Requirements: Grants are made primarily to nonprofit organizations located in the five boroughs of New York City. Grants for programs outside the area are generally from funds designated for specific charities or have been made at the suggestion of donors.
Restrictions: The trust does not make grants to individuals, offer general or capital funding, endowments, building construction/renovation, deficit financing, films, or religion.
Geographic Focus: New York
Contact: Joyce M. Bove; (212) 686-0010, ext. 552; info@nycommunitytrust.org

Internet: http://www.nycommunitytrust.org/ForGrantSeekers/GrantmakingGuidelines/ChildrenYouthandFamilies/tabid/205/Default.aspx
Sponsor: New York Community Trust
909 Third Avenue, 22nd Floor
New York, NY 10022

NYCT Substance Abuse Grants 3558
The Trust works in partnership with government and private agencies to develop the strengths of families and young people; to improve their living and working conditions; to improve family and child welfare services; and to advance social work practice. The goal of this program is to address the treatment needs of the most under-served, with a focus on women, ex-offenders, and adolescents. Specifically, grants are made to projects that: promote coordinated drug treatment, particularly between treatment providers and other systems such as mental health and child welfare; expand treatment by building the capacity of mid-sized drug treatment programs. We will help groups strengthen and increase existing services and develop new capacity to accommodate people not being treated; and promote strategies that reduce or prevent substance abuse among elders. The grant review process takes from two to six months. Grants range from $5,000 to $100,000; an average grant is around $60,000.
Requirements: Grants are made primarily to nonprofit organizations located in the five boroughs of New York City. Grants for programs outside the area are generally from funds designated for specific charities or have been made at the suggestion of donors.
Restrictions: The trust does not make grants to individuals, offer general or capital funding, endowments, building construction/renovation, deficit financing, films, or religion.
Geographic Focus: New York
Contact: Joyce M. Bove; (212) 686-0010, ext. 552; info@nycommunitytrust.org
Internet: http://www.nycommunitytrust.org/ForGrantSeekers/GrantmakingGuidelines/ChildrenYouthandFamilies/tabid/205/Default.aspx
Sponsor: New York Community Trust
909 Third Avenue, 22nd Floor
New York, NY 10022

NYCT Technical Assistance Grants 3559
The Trust focuses on relieving New York's chronic shortage of affordable housing, strengthening the local economy, and protecting the environment. It supports community-based agencies working on these issues at the neighborhood level, and government and nonprofit institutions developing strategies for the City as a whole. The goal of this program is to improve the management capacity of nonprofits and strengthen the nonprofit sector. Specifically, The Trust provides grants: up to $10,000 to current and prospective grantees to hire consultants to help with specific management needs; to advance public and nonprofit service by developing skills and expertise of professionals in the field; and to support service and umbrella organizations providing technical assistance to groups of nonprofits. The grant review process takes from two to six months. Grants range from $5,000 to $100,000; an average grant is around $60,000.
Requirements: Grants are made primarily to nonprofit organizations located in the five boroughs of New York City. Grants for programs outside the area are generally from funds designated for specific charities or have been made at the suggestion of donors.
Restrictions: The trust does not make grants to individuals, offer general or capital funding, endowments, building construction/renovation, deficit financing, films, or religion.
Geographic Focus: New York
Contact: Joyce M. Bove; (212) 686-0010, ext. 552; info@nycommunitytrust.org
Internet: http://www.nycommunitytrust.org/ForGrantSeekers/GrantmakingGuidelines/CommunityDevelopmentandtheEnvironment/tabid/204/Default.aspx
Sponsor: New York Community Trust
909 Third Avenue, 22nd Floor
New York, NY 10022

NYCT Workforce Development Grants 3560
The NYCT Workforce Development Program's primary goal is to improve the workforce development system in New York City for disadvantaged job seekers. Grants are made to projects that: advocate for policies and programs that expand access to skills training, career guidance services, and job placement assistance for disadvantaged job seekers; build the capacity of workforce development agencies to serve the needs of employers while helping employees get requisite skills in economic sectors where job growth is anticipated, such as energy efficiency, renewable energy, and health care; address the particular needs of groups with serious barriers to employment, for example, those with limited English, few basic skills, and ex-offenders.
Requirements: Grants are made primarily to nonprofit organizations located in the five boroughs of New York City. Grants for programs outside the area are generally from funds designated for specific charities or have been made at the suggestion of donors.
Restrictions: The trust does not make grants to individuals, offer general or capital funding, endowments, building construction/renovation, deficit financing, films, or religion.
Geographic Focus: New York
Contact: Joyce M. Bove; (212) 686-0010, ext. 552; info@nycommunitytrust.org
Internet: http://www.nycommunitytrust.org/ForGrantSeekers/GrantmakingGuidelines/CommunityDevelopmentandtheEnvironment/tabid/204/Default.aspx
Sponsor: New York Community Trust
909 Third Avenue, 22nd Floor
New York, NY 10022

NYCT Youth Development Grants 3561
The Trust focuses on relieving New York's chronic shortage of affordable housing, strengthening the local economy, and protecting the environment. It supports community-based agencies working on these issues at the neighborhood level, and government and nonprofit institutions developing strategies for the City as a whole. The goal of this program

is to help young people (up to age 24) become better prepared for adulthood. Resources are targeted to low-income neighborhoods where disadvantaged, minority, and poor youth face the most serious obstacles. Specifically, grants are made to projects that: help the hardest-to-reach youth, ages 13 to 18, assume leadership roles and prepare for careers and long-term self-sufficiency, particularly youth involved in the juvenile justice system, immigrant youth, and youth in foster care; and provide technical assistance to help youth organizations build program capacity and monitor outcomes. The grant review process takes from two to six months. Grants range from $5,000 to $100,000; an average grant is around $60,000.
Requirements: Grants are made primarily to nonprofit organizations located in the five boroughs of New York City. Grants for programs outside the area are generally from funds designated for specific charities or have been made at the suggestion of donors.
Restrictions: The trust does not make grants to individuals, offer general or capital funding, endowments, building construction/renovation, deficit financing, films, or religion.
Geographic Focus: New York
Contact: Joyce M. Bove; (212) 686-0010, ext. 552; info@nycommunitytrust.org
Internet: http://www.nycommunitytrust.org/ForGrantSeekers/GrantmakingGuidelines/ChildrenYouthandFamilies/tabid/205/Default.aspx
Sponsor: New York Community Trust
909 Third Avenue, 22nd Floor
New York, NY 10022

NYFA Artists in the School Community Planning Grants 3562
Planning grants emphasize collaborations between schools, teaching artists, and/or cultural organizations to prepare for first-time Implementation projects or to further develop existing Implementation projects. Planning Grants offer schools the opportunity to assess needs, identify resources, and explore pilot program ideas. Applicants may apply for one year of planning support with the intent to apply for an Implementation grant in the same fiscal year. Funding of Planning grants does not guarantee funding of Implementation grants. The award is not designed to support artist-student contact, though pilot activities are acceptable. Awards are matching grants and range from $500 to $2,000. NYFA contributes up to 50% of total project costs.
Requirements: Schools, school districts, BOCES, Teacher Centers, colleges and universities or on Indian reservation land in New York State are eligible to apply. Applicants must provide, through in-kind resources and cash, matching support for artist fees, materials and supplies, teacher release time, teacher compensation and all other project costs. In-kind contributions cannot exceed 1/3 of the applicant's match.
Restrictions: Nonprofit cultural organizations are not eligible to apply. New York State non-profit organizations may work collaboratively with schools and artists; however the school must be the lead organization. Planning Grants can only be used for artist fees and/or artist materials and supplies.
Geographic Focus: New York
Date(s) Application is Due: Nov 5
Contact: Susan Ball, Interim Director of Programs; (212) 366-6900, ext. 321; fax (212) 366-1778; sball@nyfa.org or ASC_Plannning@nyfa.org
Internet: http://www.nyfa.org/level3.asp?id=35&fid=2&sid=22
Sponsor: New York Foundation for the Arts
20 Jay Street, 7th Floor
Brooklyn, NY 11201

NYFA Building Up Infrastructure Levels for Dance (BUILD) Grants 3563
The BUILD program sustains New York City dance companies with small- and mid-sized budgets by offering choreographers and their dancers an opportunity to access the financial support necessary to build and maintain infrastructure and longevity. BUILD identifies and awards artistic merit, fosters long-term strategies to develop and sustain organizational health, and strengthens the organizational environment so that time and resources are available to create, conceive, and advance dance companies' artistic missions. BUILD supports, but is not limited to, requests for administrative costs; consultant fees; press and/or booking agent fees; company promotional materials; studio or space rental; and computers/equipment.
Requirements: New York City 501(c)3 tax-exempt organizations (or organizations with a 501(c)3 fiscal sponsor) are eligible to apply under category 1 (have a three-year-average budget between $16,000 and $80,000 per annum; and have performed work at least twice during the past three years) and category 2 (have a three-year-average budget between $81,000 and $160,000 per annum; and have produced at least three seasons of choreography with one season produced by a presenter other than the company itself). Additionally, BUILD provides stability grants of $1,000 to $2,500.
Restrictions: BUILD will not support requests for production costs associated with the performance of work including costumes, lighting, set design, or music fees; touring or traveling costs; or compensation for dancers, musicians, choreographers, teachers, or accompanists.
Geographic Focus: New York
Date(s) Application is Due: Apr 29
Contact: Pter Cobb, (212) 366-6900, ext. 212; fax (212) 366-1778; pcobb@nyfa.org
Internet: http://www.nyfa.org/level2.asp?id=78&fid=2
Sponsor: New York Foundation for the Arts
20 Jay Street, 7th Floor
Brooklyn, NY 11201

NYFA Deutsche Bank Americas Fellowship 3564
The New York Foundation for the Arts (NYFA) was founded in 1971 to empower artists at critical stages in their creative lives. Deutsche Bank Americas Foundation supports one Fellowship in the visual arts. Considering cultural commitment as part of its business and social responsibility, Deutsche Bank seeks to contribute vital support to contemporary artists in a variety of ways.
Requirements: Applicants must have resided in New York State for two years prior to application. Each recipient will be required to provide public service within the state of New York.
Geographic Focus: New York
Date(s) Application is Due: Nov 5
Contact: Susan Ball; (212) 366-6900, ext. 321; fax (212) 366-1778; sball@nyfa.org
Internet: http://www.nyfa.org/level3.asp?id=46&fid=1&sid=1
Sponsor: New York Foundation for the Arts
20 Jay Street, 7th Floor
Brooklyn, NY 11201

NYFA Gregory Millard Fellowships 3565
The New York Foundation for the Arts (NYFA) was founded in 1971 to empower artists at critical stages in their creative lives. The Gregory Millard Fellowships were established by the New York City Department of Cultural Affairs in 1984 in memory of poet and playwright Gregory Millard. As Assistant Commissioner of Cultural Affairs from 1978 until his death in 1984, Mr. Millard championed the cause of individual artists. Recipients are New York City residents chosen in several categories from those recommended by the various panels.
Requirements: Applicants must have resided in New York State for two years prior to application. Each recipient will be required to provide public service within the state of New York.
Geographic Focus: New York
Date(s) Application is Due: Nov 5
Contact: Susan Ball; (212) 366-6900, ext. 321; fax (212) 366-1778; sball@nyfa.org
Internet: http://www.nyfa.org/level3.asp?id=46&fid=1&sid=1
Sponsor: New York Foundation for the Arts
20 Jay Street, 7th Floor
Brooklyn, NY 11201

NYFA Strategic Opportunity Stipends 3566
Strategic Opportunity Stipends (SOS), a project of the New York Foundation for the Arts, working in collaboration with arts councils and cultural organizations across New York State, are designed to help individual artists of all disciplines take advantage of unique opportunities that will significantly benefit their career development. Literary, media, visual, music and performing artists may request support ranging from $200 to $1,500 for specific, forthcoming opportunities that are distinct from work in progress. Artists can devise an opportunity and approach a third-party to assist with its execution and apply for funds to realize it; recipients may also use funds for a significant professional development opportunity such as taking a class if, the application describes the substantial/significant impact the opportunity will have on the applicant's career.
Restrictions: There is a geographic restriction for SOS. It is only available to New York State artists excluding residents of the five boroughs of New York City.
Geographic Focus: New York
Date(s) Application is Due: Apr 5; Sep 12
Amount of Grant: 200 - 1,500 USD
Contact: Susan Ball; (212) 366-6900, ext. 321; fax (212) 366-1778; sball@nyfa.org
Internet: http://www.nyfa.org/level2.asp?id=21&fid=1
Sponsor: New York Foundation for the Arts
20 Jay Street, 7th Floor
Brooklyn, NY 11201

NYHC Major and Mini Grants 3567
Founded in 1975, the New York Council for the Humanities helps all New Yorkers lead vibrant lives by strengthening traditions of cultural literacy, critical inquiry, and civic participation. The Council is a private, not-for-profit organization and an independent affiliate of the National Endowment for the Humanities, from which it receives major support. The Council awards Major Grants (up to $20,000) and Mini Grants (up to $2,500). The two post-mark deadlines for Major Grants are March 16 and September 15; Mini Grants are accepted on a rolling basis. Council grants are meant to provide financial support for public programs presented by not-for-profit organizations across New York State that bring humanities scholars and scholarship to a general public audience. Special consideration is given to projects that reach underserved populations; to projects that, without our funding, might not happen; and to organizations that need financial seed money so that they may secure long-term support from other sources.
Requirements: Any not-for-profit organization or institution with tax-exempt status in New York State is eligible to apply for a grant. All projects must be rooted in one or more of the humanities disciplines, integrally feature humanities scholars, and be intended for the general public.
Geographic Focus: New York
Date(s) Application is Due: Mar 15; Sep 15
Amount of Grant: 250 - 20,000 USD
Contact: Jane McNamara, Director; (646) 302-4937 or (212) 233-1131, ext. 24; fax (212) 233-4607; education@nyhumanities.org
Internet: http://www.nyhumanities.org/grants/
Sponsor: New York Council for the Humanities
150 Broadway, Suite 1700
New York, NY 10038

NYHC Reading and Discussion Grants 3568
Founded in 1975, the New York Council for the Humanities helps all New Yorkers lead vibrant lives by strengthening traditions of cultural literacy, critical inquiry, and civic participation. The Council is a private, not-for-profit organization and an independent affiliate of the National Endowment for the Humanities, from which it receives major support. The Council awards Reading and Discussion (R&D) Grants of up to $1,000 to support text-based facilitated discussion programs hosted by New York state tax-exempt

organizations. A collaboration between the host site and a local scholar-facilitator, R&D Grants are intended to help organizations both large and small conduct reading and discussion programs that engage community members in meaningful conversation around humanities-based texts. Applicant organizations must have previously hosted the Council's Reading Between the Lines program.
Requirements: R&D Grants are available by application (see NYHC website) to any New York state tax-exempt organization that has previously hosted and successfully completed at least one of the Council's Reading Between the Lines series. A resume including a proposed scholar-facilitator and a budget for the proposed program must be submitted with the application.
Geographic Focus: New York
Date(s) Application is Due: Jun 19
Amount of Grant: 1,000 USD
Contact: Anna Links, (646) 302-4937 or (212) 233-1131, ext. 28; education@nyhumanities.org
Internet: http://www.nyhumanities.org/discussion_groups/grants/index.php
Sponsor: New York Council for the Humanities
150 Broadway, Suite 1700
New York, NY 10038

NYHC Speakers in the Humanities Grants 3569
Founded in 1975, the New York Council for the Humanities helps all New Yorkers lead vibrant lives by strengthening traditions of cultural literacy, critical inquiry, and civic participation. The Council is a private, not-for-profit organization and an independent affiliate of the National Endowment for the Humanities, from which it receives major support. Launched in 1983, the Speakers in the Humanities program brings the best in humanities scholarship to thousands of people at hundreds of cultural organizations in virtually every corner of New York. To host a lecture in your town, just select a topic, contact the Speaker, and apply for funding through the Council. If your application is successful, the Council covers the cost of the Speaker's honorarium and travel expenses.
Requirements: Any not-for-profit organization in New York State is eligible to use the program. See NYHC website for application. Applications must be received at least eight (8) weeks prior to proposed lecture date along with the correct processing fee: $35 for the first event of the calendar year, $50 for the second event
Restrictions: Speakers events must be open to the public and free of charge.
Geographic Focus: New York
Contact: Jane McNamara, Director; (646) 302-4937 or (212) 233-1131, ext. 24; fax (212) 233-4607; education@nyhumanities.org
Internet: http://www.nyhumanities.org/speakers/adult_audiences/
Sponsor: New York Council for the Humanities
150 Broadway, Suite 1700
New York, NY 10038

NYSCA Architecture, Planning, and Design: Capital Fixtures and Equipment Purchase Grants 3570
Capital Fixtures and Equipment Purchase grants support the purchase of facility-related items that are essential to the production of a particular art form, such as theatrical lighting or sound sound systems, theatre seats, gallery lighting, etc. Equipment is generally defined as any physical item that is not fixed in place and is depreciable, widely available, and generally not "made-to-order."
Requirements: Applicants must be registered with NYSCA by February 22 to receive funding the following fiscal year. In order to receive funding for Capital Fixtures and Equipment purchases, organizations must have received NYSCA funding for ongoing programs and activities for the previous three consecutive years. In addition, applicants must prove ownership of the facility or leasehold with an unexpired period of at least six years at the time of application. Organizations must own their facility to apply for any exterior rehabilitation projects, such as roof replacement and facade restoration. Applicants must be nonprofit organizations registered in New York State. First time applicants must contact program staff before the registration deadline. Applications are available at the website and should be submitted online.
Restrictions: Ineligible requests include: non-depreciable audiovisual equipment; office furniture; office shelving; stackable chairs; computers and software; and telephones. NYSCA will only award up to 50% of the costs of construction material and labor. Organizations may not include other New York State funds in their project budgets, but may include in-kind goods and services. Also, religious institutions or arts organizations requesting funds for a facility they share with or lease from a religious institution, and public school districts, public universities or state agencies are not eligible for funding.
Geographic Focus: New York
Date(s) Application is Due: Apr 1
Amount of Grant: 7,500 - 50,000 USD
Contact: Kristin Herron; (212) 741-7848; kherron@nysca.org or fchiu@nysca.org
Internet: http://www.nysca.org/public/guidelines/facilities/capital_fixtures.htm
Sponsor: New York State Council on the Arts
175 Varick Street
New York, NY 10014-4604

NYSCA Architecture, Planning, and Design: Capital Project Grants 3571
Support is available for renovation, expansion, or restoration projects. NYSCA funding priorities include projects that (in order of importance): improve, expand, or rehabilitate existing buildings to provide access for all; address known health and safety deficiencies; address issues of building stabilization; further cultural development in rural or minority communities; reduce an organization's operating costs; and demonstrate environmental stewardship and/or sustainable building practices.
Requirements: Applicants must have received NYSCA funding for ongoing programs and activities for the previous three consecutive years. In addition, applicants must prove ownership of the facility or leasehold with an unexpired period of at least six years at the time of application. Organizations must own their facility to apply for any exterior rehabilitation projects, such as roof replacement and facade restoration. Applicants must be nonprofit organizations registered in New York State. First time applicants must contact program staff before the registration deadline.
Restrictions: Applicants must be registered with NYSCA by February 22 to be eligible for funding the following fiscal year. NYSCA will only award up to 50% of the costs of construction material and labor. Organizations may not include other New York State funds in their project budgets, but may include in-kind goods and services. Also, religious institutions or arts organizations requesting funds for a facility they share with or lease from a religious institution, and public school districts, public universities or state agencies are not eligible for funding.
Geographic Focus: New York
Date(s) Application is Due: Apr 1
Amount of Grant: 7,500 - 50,000 USD
Contact: Kristin Herron; (212) 741-7848; kherron@nysca.org or fchiu@nysca.org
Internet: http://www.nysca.org/public/guidelines/facilities/capital_projects.htm
Sponsor: New York State Council on the Arts
175 Varick Street
New York, NY 10014-4604

NYSCA Architecture, Planning, and Design: Design and Planning Studies Grants 3572
Funding is available for any nonprofit arts or cultural organization or local government agency which manages a cultural facility in New York State to engage the services of an architect, designer, or historic preservation professional for a wide variety of planning and design studies. NYSCA funding priorities include projects that (in order of importance): improve, expand, or rehabilitate existing buildings to provide access for all; address known health and safety deficiencies; address issues of building stabilization; further cultural development in rural or minority communities; reduce an organization's operating costs; and demonstrate environmental stewardship and/or sustainable building practices. Funds awarded may cover consultants' fees for the design phases of a project, expenses related to site analysis, program evaluation, schematic design, design development, working drawings, and/or cost-estimating phases of a project.
Requirements: Applicants are required to register with NYSCA by February 22 to be eligible for funding the following fiscal year. NYSCA awards grants to nonprofit organizations incorporated in New York State, Indian tribes, and units of local government. First time applicants are required to call program staff before the registration deadline. Also, applicants must own the facility or have a long-term lease on the proposed project. Applications can be found at the website and should be submitted online.
Restrictions: The Design and Planning Studies Grant does not support bid negotiation, public colleges or universities, construction administration, purchase of real estate or capital construction costs, out-of-state travel, salaries or overhead of public agencies, religious institutions or arts organizations requesting funds for a facility they share with or lease from a religious institution, public school districts, state agencies, or student projects. In addition to these restrictions, the request amount should not exceed 50% of the total project budget. NYSCA is unlikely to fund maintenance projects and capital projects that have resulted from deferred maintenance.
Geographic Focus: New York
Date(s) Application is Due: Apr 1
Contact: Kristin Herron; (212) 741-7848; kherron@nysca.org or fchiu@nysca.org
Internet: http://www.nysca.org/public/guidelines/facilities/design.htm
Sponsor: New York State Council on the Arts
175 Varick Street
New York, NY 10014-4604

NYSCA Architecture, Planning, and Design: General Operating Support Grants 3573
General Operating Support grants represent an investment by NYSCA in an organization's ongoing work, rather than a specific project program in order to help organizations become more effective in fulfilling their mission. The Council examines the nature, scope, and quality of an organization's programs and activities when considering the provision and level of support. Support for this grant is awarded on a multi-year basis.
Requirements: Applicants must register with NYSCA before February 22 to be eligible for funding the following fiscal year. An applicant for general operating support must also meet the following conditions: have a primary focus in the discipline in which the organization is seeking support; have an organizational mission that is primarily devoted to arts and culture with a prior record of accomplishment in producing or presenting cultural activities; demonstrate fiscal stability as indicated by such factors as a positive fund balance, an absence of substantial, recurring organizational deficits, a realistic and balanced organizational budget, diverse revenue sources, and strong controls; one or more qualified, salaried administrative staff; a viable board of directors and officers that exercises oversight and accountability for governance, operations, programming and finances; and must have ongoing programs, exhibitions, productions or other art and cultural activities that are open to the general public. First time applicants are required to call program staff before the registration deadline. Applications are available at the website and should be submitted online.
Restrictions: General Operating Support grants will be no less than $5,000 and shall not exceed 25% of an organization's budget, based on the income and expense statement for the organization's most recently completed fiscal year. Applicants cannot apply for both General Operating Support and General Program Support. In addition, NYSCA does not fund: major expenditures for the establishment of new organizations; accumulate deficits; debt reductions; programs of public universities or New York state agencies or departments; programs of public school districts or their affiliates; activities restricted to an organization's membership; operating expenses or fellowships at professional training schools that are not open to the general public; programs that are essentially recreational, rehabilitation, or therapeutic; operating expenses of privately owned facilities, such as homes or studios;

components of an organization's budget that are not directed toward programs in New York State; competitions or contests; out-of-state travel expenses; or hospitality or entertainment costs of receptions, performance or museum openings, or fundraising benefits.
Geographic Focus: New York
Date(s) Application is Due: Apr 1
Contact: Kristin Herron, Senior Program Officer; (212) 741-7848; kherron@nysca.org
Internet: http://www.nysca.org/public/guidelines/architecture/general_operating.htm
Sponsor: New York State Council on the Arts
175 Varick Street
New York, NY 10014-4604

NYSCA Architecture, Planning, and Design: General Program Support Grants   3574
General Program Support grants fund activities of arts and cultural programs that are operated as independent entities within their own organization, or for significant arts programming within a nonprofit whose mission is not art-based. The Council examines the nature, scope, and quality of an organization's programs and activities, its managerial and fiscal competence, and its public service when considering the provision and level of support.
Requirements: Applicants must register with NYSCA before February 22 to be eligible for funding the following fiscal year. An applicant for General Program Support must also meet the following conditions: have significant ongoing activities that address a focus in architecture, planning and design; substantial commitment to arts and culture, with a prior record of accomplishment in producing or presenting cultural activities; demonstrate fiscal stability as indicated by such factors as a positive fund balance, an absence of substantial, recurring organizational deficits, a realistic and balanced organizational budget, diverse revenue sources, and strong controls; one or more qualified, salaried administrative staff; a viable board of directors and officers that exercises oversight and accountability for governance, operations, programming and finances; and must have ongoing programs, exhibitions, productions or other art and cultural activities that are open to the general public. First time applicants are required to call program staff before the registration deadline. Applications are available at the website and should be submitted online.
Restrictions: General Program Support grants will be no less than $5,000 and shall not exceed 25% of an organization's budget, based on the income and expense statement for the organization's most recently completed fiscal year. In addition, applicants cannot apply for both General Operating Support and General Program Support. In addition, NYSCA does not fund: major expenditures for the establishment of new organizations; accumulate deficits; debt reductions; programs of public universities or New York state agencies or departments; programs of public school districts or their affiliates; activities restricted to an organization's membership; operating expenses or fellowships at professional training schools that are not ope to the general public; programs that are essentially recreational, rehabilitation, or therapeutic; operating expenses of privately owned facilities, such as homes or studios; components of an organization's budget that are not directed toward programs in New York State; competitions or contests; out-of-state travel expenses; or hospitality or entertainment costs of receptions, performance or museum openings, or fundraising benefits.
Geographic Focus: New York
Date(s) Application is Due: Apr 1
Samples: Friends of the High Line, New York, New York, $24,923 - program development and exhibitions (2011).
Contact: Kristin Herron, Senior Program Officer; (212) 741-7848; kherron@nysca.org
Internet: http://www.nysca.org/public/guidelines/architecture/general_program.htm
Sponsor: New York State Council on the Arts
175 Varick Street
New York, NY 10014-4604

NYSCA Architecture, Planning, and Design: Independent Project Grants   3575
Independent Projects allow for individuals (or a team) to creatively explore or research an issue or problem in the design, planning and/or historic preservation fields which advances that field and contributes to the public's understanding of the built environment. The category seeks projects that are innovative in nature and emphasize the artistry of design excellence.
Requirements: Applicants must register with NYSCA online before February 22 to be eligible for funding the following fiscal year. Independent Project grants must originate with the individual (or team), but applications can only be submitted through a sponsoring organization. In addition: only design planning and historic preservation professionals who are New York State residents are eligible; and individuals may be associated with only one project request per year. Applications can be found at the website.
Restrictions: Student projects are not eligible. Funds cannot be used for out-of-state travel
Geographic Focus: New York
Date(s) Application is Due: Apr 1
Amount of Grant: Up to 10,000 USD
Contact: Kristin Herron; (212) 741-7848; kherron@nysca.org or fchiu@nysca.org
Internet: http://www.nysca.org/public/guidelines/architecture/independent_projects.htm
Sponsor: New York State Council on the Arts
175 Varick Street
New York, NY 10014-4604

NYSCA Architecture, Planning, and Design: Project Support Grants   3576
Project Support grants awards projects of programs which promote an understanding of the design and planning fields, and may be directed at a general or professional audience. Such arts and cultural programming might include: exhibitions, publications, workshops, conferences, public programs, or services to the field. Emerging Architecture, Planning and Design organizations may seek salary support for a senior design, planning or historic preservation professional with whom the organization's growth and development would be advanced.
Requirements: Applicants must register with the Council before February 22 to be considered for funding in that fiscal year. New York State organizations that present documented proof of nonprofit status are eligible to apply. Applications are available at the website and must be submitted online. First time applicants should contact NYSCA before registering with the Council.
Restrictions: Requests for personnel for site-specific restoration projects are not eligible. Organizations applying for or receiving General Operating or General Program Support are not eligible for funding under this program.
Geographic Focus: New York
Date(s) Application is Due: Apr 1
Contact: Kristin Herron; (212) 741-7848; kherron@nysca.org or fchiu@nysca.org
Internet: http://www.nysca.org/public/guidelines/architecture/projects.htm
Sponsor: New York State Council on the Arts
175 Varick Street
New York, NY 10014-4604

NYSCA Arts Education: Community-based Learning Grants   3577
Community-based Learning grants support a range of projects that provide in-depth and sustained experiences to learners of all ages for the creation and understanding of art through ongoing arts learning activities in community settings. Participants may include children, adults, families, and life- long learners in community and/or inter-generational settings. Grants are particularly focused on rural and under-served communities who have limited access to arts programming. Activities may include workshops, classes, and training in the arts. Eligible projects may be offered by arts organizations or community-based organizations with established arts activities, in partnership with artists and arts groups. Funds may be used for art materials, documentation of the project, transportation of art materials or instruments necessary for the project, and a percentage of the applicant organization's administrative staff time.
Requirements: All participating artists must be guaranteed a fee, which applicants are expected to indicate in the project budget. Projects must be in-depth, sequential learning projects. First-time applicants are required to call the program staff before the registration deadline.
Restrictions: Workshops and training programs for professional artists, as well as programs that are primarily therapeutic in nature are ineligible for support. This grant does not support one-time workshops, single performances, or one-time visits to cultural institutions. Professional training of artists is not supported with this grant. The grant may not exceed 50% of the total project cost.
Geographic Focus: New York
Date(s) Application is Due: Apr 1
Contact: Kathleen Masterson; (212) 741-2622; kmasterson@nysca.org
Internet: http://www.nysca.org/public/guidelines/arts_education/community.htm
Sponsor: New York State Council on the Arts
175 Varick Street
New York, NY 10014-4604

NYSCA Arts Education: General Operating Support Grants   3578
General Operating Support grants fund an organization's ongoing work, rather than a specific project or program in order to help organizations become more effective in fulfilling their mission, especially in arts education. The Council examines the nature, scope, and quality of an organization's programs and activities, its managerial and fiscal competence, and its public service when considering the provision and level of support.
Requirements: Applicants must register before February 22 to be considered for funding that fiscal year. In addition, applicant's must meet the following conditions: have a primary focus in arts education; have an organizational mission primarily devoted to arts and culture with a prior record of accomplishment in producing or presenting cultural activities; demonstrate fiscal stability as indicated by such factors as a positive Fund Balance, have an absence of substantial and recurring organizational deficits, a realistic and balanced organizational budget, have diverse revenue sources, and strong internal controls; one or more qualified staff; a viable board of directors and officers that exercises oversight and accountability for governance, operations, programming and finances; and must have ongoing programs, exhibitions, productions, or other art and cultural activities that are open to the general public. Applications can be found at the website and must be completed online. First time applicants must contact program staff before registration deadline.
Restrictions: Applicants cannot apply for both General Operating Support and General Program Support. Grants will be no less than $5,000 and shall not exceed 25% of an organization's budget.
Geographic Focus: New York
Date(s) Application is Due: Apr 1
Contact: Kathleen Masterson; (212) 741-2622; kmasterson@nysca.org
Internet: http://www.nysca.org/public/guidelines/arts_education/general_operating.htm
Sponsor: New York State Council on the Arts
175 Varick Street
New York, NY 10014-4604

NYSCA Arts Education: General Program Support Grants   3579
The purpose of General Program Support (GPS) is to offer unrestricted support for ongoing activities of arts and cultural programs that are operated as independent entities within their own organization or for significant arts programming within a non-profit whose mission is not art-based (for example, a performing arts center that is operated as a separate entity within a college). The Council examines the nature, scope, and quality of an organization's programs and activities, its managerial and fiscal competence, and its public service when considering the provision and level of GPS support.
Requirements: To be eligible to apply, an organization must meet each of the following conditions: significant ongoing activities that address the focus in the discipline in which the organization is seeking General Program Support; organization makes evident a substantial commitment to arts and culture, with a prior record of accomplishment in producing or presenting cultural activities; demonstrate fiscal stability as indicated by such

factors as a positive fund balance, an absence of substantial and/or recurring organizational deficits, a realistic and balanced organizational budget, diverse revenue sources, a significant ongoing financial commitment by the applicant to its arts and cultural program, and strong internal controls; at least one qualified, salaried administrative staff responsible for the program; a viable board of directors, advisory board, or other governance structure specifically responsible for oversight and accountability for operations, programming and finances of this program; and must have ongoing programs, exhibitions, productions or other arts and cultural activities that are open to the general public. In addition, applicants must register with the Council before February 22 to be considered for funding that fiscal year. Applications are available at the website and must be submitted online. First time applicants must contact the Council before the registration deadline.
Restrictions: Organizations receiving General Program Support from the Arts in Education Program are not eligible for General Operating Support. Grants will be no less than $5,000 and shall not exceed 25% of the arts or cultural program's budget.
Geographic Focus: New York
Date(s) Application is Due: Apr 1
Contact: Kathleen Masterson; (212) 741-2622; kmasterson@nysca.org
Internet: http://www.nysca.org/public/guidelines/arts_education/general_program.htm
Sponsor: New York State Council on the Arts
175 Varick Street
New York, NY 10014-4604

NYSCA Arts Education: K-12 In-School Programs Grants   3580
The K-12 In-School Programs grant supports projects that directly serve students. Projects should provide in-depth experiences for students in the process of creating and/or understanding art. Projects may be formulated in order to enhance learning in the arts or non-arts disciplines, but the arts must be central to the learning experience. The project may be directed toward development of affective, cognitive or aesthetic objectives.
Requirements: Applicants must register with the Council by February 22 to be considered for funding that fiscal year. Projects must involve a minimum of 10 artist contact sessions and must occur during the regular or extended school day, but not as part of a recreational after-school program. Cultural organizations are required to apply with an educational partner such as an individual school, a group of schools, a district, or a BOCES. In addition, applications must include written documentation of the planning process that addresses the clearly articulated goals and learning objectives of each project partner, and participating artists must be guaranteed a fee which is to be indicated in project budget.
Restrictions: This grant will not fund partnerships that replace, or appear to replace the role of certified arts teachers in schools. Arts Education funds a maximum of 50% of the project's total cash expenses. In addition, this grant does not support extracurricular projects that take place after school, in the summer, or during non-school hours.
Geographic Focus: New York
Date(s) Application is Due: Apr 1
Contact: Kathleen Masterson; (212) 741-2622; kmasterson@nysca.org
Internet: http://www.nysca.org/public/guidelines/arts_education/school_programs.htm
Sponsor: New York State Council on the Arts
175 Varick Street
New York, NY 10014-4604

NYSCA Arts Education: Local Capacity Building Grants (Regrants)   3581
Local Capacity Building grants offer support to organizations to administer regrant programs that support arts partnerships between schools and cultural organizations or individual artists. Local Capacity Building programs generally support projects that are small and represent first-time or new forays into arts in education on the part of the school applicants. Each Local Capacity Building program site serves a specific region of the state and is expected to promote the regrant program, coordinate application and panel review processes, and provide ongoing technical assistance and professional development.
Requirements: Applicants must have: a full-time, paid executive director; a designated, qualified staff member (preferably not the executive director) to serve as coordinator of the program; and resources to provide appropriate technical assistance, outreach, and professional development opportunities for constituent schools, artists, and cultural organizations in the service area. First time applicants are required to call program staff before the registration deadline. Applications are at the website and must be submitted online.
Restrictions: NYSCA does not fund: operating expenses of privately owned facilities, such as homes or studios; components of an organization's budget that are not directed toward programs in New York State; and competitions or contests.
Geographic Focus: New York
Date(s) Application is Due: Apr 1
Contact: Kathleen Masterson; (212) 741-2622; kmasterson@nysca.org
Internet: http://www.nysca.org/public/guidelines/arts_education/local_capacity.htm
Sponsor: New York State Council on the Arts
175 Varick Street
New York, NY 10014-4604

NYSCA Arts Education: Services to the Field Grants   3582
The Services to the Field grant is designed to support innovative projects of statewide or regional scope, and statewide significance, which support the development of the arts education field. Projects supported through this category must provide tangible services to multiple organizations statewide, or within a specific region(s). Funding may be requested to support professional development for field-specific capacity-building within multiple organizations. Research projects are ineligible for support.
Requirements: New and returning applicants are required to consult with NYSCA staff in advance of the registration deadline to discuss eligibility. Eligible projects must focus on: 1) building the capacity of cultural organizations and the field in general to engage in arts education and lifelong learning partnerships; or 2) improving the practice and knowledge base of the field at large. Applications can be found at the website and must be submitted online.
Restrictions: The requested amount should not exceed 50% of the total project budget. NYSCA does not fund: operating expenses of privately owned facilities, such as homes or studios; components of an organization's budget that are not directed toward programs in New York State; and competitions or contests. Research projects are also ineligible for support.
Geographic Focus: New York
Date(s) Application is Due: May 1
Contact: Kathleen Masterson; (212) 741-2622; kmasterson@nysca.org
Internet: http://www.nysca.org/public/guidelines/arts_education/services.htm
Sponsor: New York State Council on the Arts
175 Varick Street
New York, NY 10014-4604

NYSCA Dance: Commissions Grants   3583
NYSCA Commissions grants support choreographers and companies to collaborate in order to broaden their repertories. Commissioned works may be revivals, reconstructions of existing works or new works by guest choreographers.
Requirements: Organizations must register with the Council by February 22 to be considered for funding. The company must schedule the premiere of the commissioned work in New York State, preferably during a home season, within the company's grant period. Professional dance companies and alternative spaces that present dance and have a prior funding history with Dance are eligible to apply. Performances must also be open to the public and consist of at least one hour of programming by the company. In addition, dance company applicants must have an established record of paying artists' salaries. Applications are at the website and should be submitted online.
Restrictions: Support is generally awarded for choreographers' fees only. Requests may include 100% of the choreographer's fee. An organization may request a maximum of two commissioned artists under this category in any given year.
Geographic Focus: New York
Date(s) Application is Due: Apr 1
Contact: Beverly D'Anne, Senior Program Officer; (212) 741-3232 or (212) 741-3331; bdanne@nysca.org or dlim@nysca.org
Internet: http://www.nysca.org/public/guidelines/dance/commissions.htm
Sponsor: New York State Council on the Arts
175 Varick Street
New York, NY 10014-4604

NYSCA Dance: General Operating Support Grants   3584
General Operating Support grants sponsor an organization's ongoing work, rather than a specific project, in order to help organizations become more effective in fulfilling their mission. The Council examines the nature, scope, and quality of an organization's programs and activities, its managerial and fiscal competence, and its public service when considering the provision and level of support. Support is awarded on a multi-year basis.
Requirements: Applicants must register with the Council before February 22 to be considered for funding. In addition, all applicants must: have a primary focus in dance; have an organizational mission that is primarily devoted to arts and culture with a prior record of accomplishment in producing or presenting cultural activities; demonstrate fiscal stability as indicated by such factors as a positive Fund balance, an absence of substantial and/or recurring organizational deficits, a realistic and balanced organizational budget, diverse revenue sources, and strong internal controls; one or more qualified, salaried administrative staff; a viable board of directors and officers that exercises oversight and accountability for governance, operations, programming and finances; have ongoing programs, exhibitions, productions or other art and cultural activities that are open to the general public; demonstrate significant services or activity in New York State, which is defined as a home season of at least 7 performances within the last three years. Applications can be found at the website and should be submitted online. First-time applicants are required to call staff before the registration deadline.
Restrictions: General Operating Support will be no less than $5,000 and shall not exceed 25% of an organization's budget. Applicants cannot apply for both General Operating Support and General Program Support.
Geographic Focus: New York
Date(s) Application is Due: Apr 1
Contact: Beverly D'Anne, Senior Program Officer; (212) 741-3232 or (212) 741-3331; bdanne@nysca.org or dlim@nysca.org
Internet: http://www.nysca.org/public/guidelines/dance/general_operating.htm
Sponsor: New York State Council on the Arts
175 Varick Street
New York, NY 10014-4604

NYSCA Dance: General Program Support Grants   3585
General Program Support grants offer awards to sponsor ongoing activities of arts and cultural programs that are operated as independent entities within their own organization or for significant arts programming within a non-profit whose mission is NOT art-based. The Council examines the nature, scope, and quality of an organization's programs and activities, its managerial and fiscal competence, and its public service when considering the provision and level of support. General Program support is awarded on a multi-year basis.
Requirements: Applicants must register with the Council before February 22 to be considered for funding. Organizations must: have significant ongoing activities that address the focus in the discipline in which the organization is seeking General Program Support; make evident a substantial commitment to arts and culture, with a prior record of accomplishment in producing or presenting cultural activities; demonstrate fiscal stability as indicated by such factors as a positive fund balance, an absence of substantial and/or recurring organizational deficits, a realistic and balanced organizational budget, diverse revenue sources, a significant

ongoing financial commitment by the applicant organization to its arts and cultural program, and strong internal controls; one or more qualified, salaried administrative staff responsible for this program; a viable board of directors, advisory board or other governance structure specifically responsible for this program that exercises oversight and accountability for governance, operations, programming and finances; and have ongoing programs, exhibitions, productions or other arts and cultural activities that are open to the general public. Applications are available at the website and should be submitted online. Also, first-time applicants are required to call staff before the registration deadline.
Restrictions: Grants will be no less than $5,000 and shall not exceed 25% of the arts or cultural program's budget. Applicants cannot apply for both General Operating Support and General Program Support.
Geographic Focus: New York
Date(s) Application is Due: Apr 1
Contact: Beverly D'Anne, Senior Program Officer; (212) 741-3232 or (212) 741-3331; bdanne@nysca.org or dlim@nysca.org
Internet: http://www.nysca.org/public/guidelines/dance/general_program.htm
Sponsor: New York State Council on the Arts
175 Varick Street
New York, NY 10014-4604

NYSCA Dance: Long-Term Residency in New York State Grants 3586
Long-Term Residency in New York State grants supports artists' fees and some administrative costs for a 3 to 6-week residency by a New York-based dance company in a targeted area outside New York City. The residency must be of consecutive weeks and take place in a location in New York State that is not within a company's home county. The goals of this grant are: to develop audiences outside New York City; to encourage and develop the cultural resources of a community through interaction and collaboration between the resident company and interdisciplinary professional groups and/or individuals in the area; and to support a New York-based dance company with a substantial period of work during which it may be involved not only in conducting classes, workshops, open rehearsals, and community programs, but also in the creation of a new piece of choreography and in the presentation of public performances at the culmination of the residency.
Requirements: Applicants must register by February 22 to be considered for funding. In addition to being a dance company, organizations must confirm residency host and location in the application, have previously received support from Dance, have had previous touring experience, and have the administrative resources to conduct a residency for a minimum of three weeks. First time applicants for this grant are required to call program staff before the registration deadline. Applications can be found at the website and should be submitted online.
Restrictions: Only dance companies, not host organizations are eligible to apply. In addition, this grant does not fund: requests that are greater than an organization's total operating expenses minus total operating income; out-of-state travel expenses; competitions or contests; and/or hospitality or entertainment costs for receptions, performance or museum openings, or fundraising benefits.
Geographic Focus: New York
Date(s) Application is Due: Apr 1
Contact: Beverly D'Anne, Senior Program Officer; (212) 741-3232 or (212) 741-3331; bdanne@nysca.org or dlim@nysca.org
Internet: http://www.nysca.org/public/guidelines/dance/longterm_residency.htm
Sponsor: New York State Council on the Arts
175 Varick Street
New York, NY 10014-4604

NYSCA Dance: Services to the Field Grants 3587
Services to the Field grants provides support to service organizations that offer professional services for the advancement of dance groups and individuals. Services may include technical assistance in administrative and/or new technological areas, cooperative management, booking and promotional services, research facilities, archival documentation, projects that utilize technology, and performance spaces.
Requirements: Applicants must register with the Council before February 22 to be considered for funding. In addition, applicants should demonstrate how Council support would meet the needs of the professional dance field. A paid administrator on staff is required. Applications can be obtained at the website and should be submitted online. First-time applicants are required to call staff before the registration deadline.
Restrictions: The request amount should not exceed 50% of the total project budget.
Geographic Focus: New York
Date(s) Application is Due: Apr 1
Contact: Beverly D'Anne, Senior Program Officer; (212) 741-3232 or (212) 741-3331; bdanne@nysca.org or dlim@nysca.org
Internet: http://www.nysca.org/public/guidelines/dance/services.htm
Sponsor: New York State Council on the Arts
175 Varick Street
New York, NY 10014-4604

NYSCA Electronic Media and Film: Film Festivals Grants 3588
Film Festivals grants are available for the public presentation of film, video and new media offered in cinemas, community centers, galleries, libraries and museums. The presentation of work by New York State artists is strongly encouraged. Programming including youth media is also welcome. Touring exhibitions that circulate to three or more sites throughout New York State are also encouraged.
Requirements: Applicants must register with the Council by February 22 to be considered for funding. In addition, applicants must have completed three years of festival programming to a public audience. First-time applicants are required to call program staff before the registration deadline. All grants are also two year, multiyear awards.
Restrictions: Projects will not be considered for support when screenings and the use of technology is in the service of another discipline or objective other than film and electronic media as an art form. Also, requests should not exceed 50% of the total project budget.
Geographic Focus: New York
Date(s) Application is Due: Apr 1
Contact: Karen Helmerson; (212) 741-3003; khelmerson@nysca.org
Internet: http://www.nysca.org/public/guidelines/electronic_media/festivals.htm
Sponsor: New York State Council on the Arts
175 Varick Street
New York, NY 10014-4604

NYSCA Electronic Media and Film: General Exhibition Grants 3589
General Exhibition grants are for the public presentation of film, video, installation work, sound art and new media offered in cinemas, community centers, galleries, libraries and museums, or through a variety of communications technologies, including radio and the Internet. The presentation of work by New York State artists is strongly encouraged. Programming including youth media is also welcome. Touring exhibitions that circulate to three or more sites throughout New York State are also encouraged.
Requirements: Applicants must register with the Council before February 22 to be considered for funding. Also, this grant supports sound work, moving image media, video and/or film installations in a gallery, museum, or outdoor venue, including radio and internet. If the project is interdisciplinary in nature, strong evidence of technology as an art form and as a distinct component must be presented. Applications can be found at the website and should be submitted online. First-time applicants are required to call staff before the registration deadline.
Restrictions: Organizations may not apply to the Electronic Media and Film if applying to another NYSCA discipline area for the same project. Also, projects will not be considered for support when the use of technology is in the service of another discipline or objective other than film and electronic media. Also, the request for funding should not exceed 50% of the total project budget.
Geographic Focus: New York
Date(s) Application is Due: Apr 1
Contact: Karen Helmerson; (212) 741-3003; khelmerson@nysca.org
Internet: http://www.nysca.org/public/guidelines/electronic_media/exhibition.htm
Sponsor: New York State Council on the Arts
175 Varick Street
New York, NY 10014-4604

NYSCA Electronic Media and Film: General Operating Support 3590
General Operating Support sponsors an organization's ongoing work, rather than a specific project or program. The Council examines the nature, scope, and quality of an organization's programs and activities, its managerial and fiscal competence, and its public service when considering the provision and level of support. Support is awarded on multi-year basis.
Requirements: Applicants must register with the Council before February 22 to be considered for funding. In addition, applicants must have: a primary focus in Electronic Media and Film; an organizational mission that is primarily devoted to arts and culture with a prior record of accomplishment in producing or presenting cultural activities; demonstrated fiscal stability as indicated by such factors as a positive Fund Balance, an absence of substantial and/or recurring organizational deficits, a realistic and balanced organizational budget, diverse revenue sources, and strong internal controls; one or more qualified, salaried administrative staff; a viable board of directors and officers that exercises oversight and accountability for governance, operations, programming and finances; and ongoing programs, exhibitions, productions or other art and cultural activities that are open to the general public. First-time applicants are required to call staff before the registration deadline.
Restrictions: General Operating Support grants will be no less than $5,000 and shall NOT exceed 25% of the applicant organization's budget. Also, applicants CANNOT apply for both General Operating Support and General Program Support.
Geographic Focus: New York
Date(s) Application is Due: Apr 1
Contact: Karen Helmerson; (212) 741-3003; khelmerson@nysca.org
Internet: http://www.nysca.org/public/guidelines/electronic_media/general_operating.htm
Sponsor: New York State Council on the Arts
175 Varick Street
New York, NY 10014-4604

NYSCA Electronic Media and Film: General Program Support 3591
General Program Support grants fund activities of arts and cultural programs that are operated as independent entities within their own organization, or for significant arts programming within a nonprofit whose mission is not art-based. The Council examines the nature, scope, and quality of an organization's programs and activities, its managerial and fiscal competence, and its public service when considering the provision and level of support.
Requirements: Applicants must register with NYSCA before February 22 to be eligible for funding the following fiscal year. An applicant for General Program Support must also meet the following conditions: have significant ongoing activities that address a focus in Electronic Media and Film; substantial commitment to arts and culture, with a prior record of accomplishment in producing or presenting cultural activities; demonstrate fiscal stability as indicated by such factors as a positive fund balance, an absence of substantial, recurring organizational deficits, a realistic and balanced organizational budget, diverse revenue sources, and strong controls; one or more qualified, salaried administrative staff; a viable board of directors and officers that exercises oversight and accountability for governance, operations, programming and finances; and must have ongoing programs, exhibitions, productions or other art and cultural activities that are open to the general public. First time applicants are required to call program staff before the registration deadline. Applications are available at the website and should be submitted online.

Restrictions: General Program Support grants will be no less than $5,000 and shall not exceed 25% of the program's budget, based on the income and expense statement for the organization's most recently completed fiscal year. In addition, applicants cannot apply for both General Operating Support and General Program Support. NYSCA does not fund: major expenditures for the establishment of new organizations; accumulate deficits; debt reductions; programs of public universities or New York state agencies or departments; programs of public school districts or their affiliates; activities restricted to an organization's membership; operating expenses or fellowships at professional training schools that are not ope to the general public; programs that are essentially recreational, rehabilitation, or therapeutic; operating expenses of privately owned facilities, such as homes or studios; components of an organization's budget that are not directed toward programs in New York State; competitions or contests; out-of-state travel expenses; or hospitality or entertainment costs of receptions, performance or museum openings, or fundraising benefits.
Geographic Focus: New York
Date(s) Application is Due: Apr 1
Contact: Karen Helmerson; (212) 741-3003; khelmerson@nysca.org
Internet: http://www.nysca.org/public/guidelines/electronic_media/general_program.htm
Sponsor: New York State Council on the Arts
175 Varick Street
New York, NY 10014-4604

NYSCA Electronic Media and Film: Screenings Grants 3592
Screenings grants are available for the public presentation of film, video and new media offered in cinemas, community centers, galleries, libraries and museums. Funding is available to a variety of screenings, including series and year-round programming. The presentation of work by New York State artists is strongly encouraged. Programming including youth media is also welcome. Touring exhibitions that circulate to three or more sites throughout New York State are also encouraged.
Requirements: Applicants must register with the Council by February 22 to be considered for funding. Film Screenings grants only support moving image media, film, or video programs and series in a cinematic setting for public audiences, including outdoor venues. All applicants are encouraged to contact the Council before submitting a proposal, but first-time applicants MUST contact the program staff. Applications are at the website and should be submitted online.
Restrictions: Film screenings on DVD or through the Internet are rarely supported. Projects will not be considered for support when screenings and the use of technology are in the service of another discipline or objective other than film and electronic media as an art form. Also, the request amount should NOT exceed 50% of the total project budget.
Geographic Focus: New York
Date(s) Application is Due: Apr 1
Contact: Karen Helmerson; (212) 741-3003; khelmerson@nysca.org
Internet: http://www.nysca.org/public/guidelines/electronic_media/screenings.htm
Sponsor: New York State Council on the Arts
175 Varick Street
New York, NY 10014-4604

NYSCA Electronic Media and Film: Workspace Grants 3593
The Workspace grants fund public workshops, production facilities, artists' residencies and workspace (virtual as well as physical), and technical assistance at low cost. This category also supports equipment purchase. Workspace proposals with an emphasis on reaching underserved populations are encouraged. The Workspace grant also encourages the participation of media artists as educators and mentors in the development of programs and in facilities design. Electronic Media and Film welcomes proposals that help professional and mature media artists advance their knowledge and use of new technologies. Support for facilities, residencies and workshops may be incorporated into a single request.
Requirements: Applicants must register with the Council by February 22 to be eligible for funding. Requests should demonstrate an integrated view of technology planning, management and program design, and demonstrate capacity for salaried administrative staff, technical support and the ability to maintain regular business hours. Proposals must also show strong evidence of film and electronic media as an art form in production standards and training curriculum. Training and workshops at the Workspace must address the art as well as the craft of teaching film, new media, sound art, and video. In addition, if this grant serves youth, participants must be at least 15 years old in after-school, pre-professional training programs for young artists and/or independent youth media summer workshops. If applying for a Residency Request, applicants should facilitate networking and professional development opportunities through interaction with other artists, arts professionals and the local community, as well as allow maximum flexibility for artists to do their work. First-time applicants are required to call program staff before the registration deadline.
Restrictions: This grant does not support youth media projects in K-12 schools. Also, request amounts should not exceed 50% of the total project budget.
Geographic Focus: New York
Date(s) Application is Due: Apr 1
Contact: Karen Helmerson; (212) 741-3003; khelmerson@nysca.org
Internet: http://www.nysca.org/public/guidelines/electronic_media/workspace.htm
Sponsor: New York State Council on the Arts
175 Varick Street
New York, NY 10014-4604

NYSCA Folk Arts: Exhibitions Grants 3594
Exhibition grants are offered for an exhibition of the work of living folk artists, to explore issues in the folk arts, or to interpret the traditional culture of a specific community through its folk arts. The proposed exhibition should enhance understanding and appreciation of the folk arts for general audiences as well as communities represented in the exhibition. The exhibition may include objects of folk art, photographic representations of folk culture, and/or multimedia kiosks or other installations in the exhibition utilizing new technologies. Requests may include field research expenses for the development of an exhibition and expenses for an exhibition catalog.
Requirements: Applicants must register with the Council before February 22 to be considered for funding. The proposed exhibition should focus on traditions currently practiced or within living memory, and may incorporate relevant historical works of folk art. First-time applicants must call program staff before the registration deadline.
Restrictions: Funding awarded for exhibitions cannot exceed 50% of project expenses. Support is not available for programming involving artists who appropriate, interpret, or revive the traditions of other communities. Folk Arts emphasizes support for presentations grounded in the traditional modes of practicing folk art, and not programming involving choreography, theatricality, or stylization that significantly alters traditions.
Geographic Focus: New York
Date(s) Application is Due: Apr 1
Contact: Robert Baron; (212) 741-7755 or (212) 741-7143; rbaron@nysca.org
Internet: http://www.nysca.org/public/guidelines/folk_arts/exhibitions.htm
Sponsor: New York State Council on the Arts
175 Varick Street
New York, NY 10014-4604

NYSCA Folk Arts: General Program Support Grants 3595
General Program Support grants fund activities of arts and cultural programs that are operated as independent entities within their own organization, or for significant arts programming within a nonprofit whose mission is not art-based. The Council examines the nature, scope, and quality of an organization's programs and activities, its managerial and fiscal competence, and its public service when considering the provision and level of support.
Requirements: Applicants must register with NYSCA before February 22 to be eligible for funding the following fiscal year. An applicant for General Program Support must also meet the following conditions: have significant ongoing activities that address a focus in Folk Arts; substantial commitment to arts and culture, with a prior record of accomplishment in producing or presenting cultural activities; demonstrate fiscal stability as indicated by such factors as a positive fund balance, an absence of substantial, recurring organizational deficits, a realistic and balanced organizational budget, diverse revenue sources, and strong controls; one or more qualified, salaried administrative staff; a viable board of directors and officers that exercises oversight and accountability for governance, operations, programming and finances; and must have ongoing programs, exhibitions, productions or other art and cultural activities that are open to the general public. First time applicants are required to call program staff before the registration deadline. Applications are available at the website and should be submitted online.
Restrictions: Applicants cannot apply for both General Operating Support and General Program Support. Grants will be no less than $5,000 and shall not exceed 25% of an organization's budget. Folk Arts emphasizes support for presentations grounded in the traditional modes of practicing folk art, and not programming involving choreography, theatricality, or stylization that significantly alters traditions. Support is also not available for programming involving artists who appropriate, interpret, or revive the traditions of other communities.
Geographic Focus: New York
Date(s) Application is Due: Apr 1
Contact: Robert Baron; (212) 741-7755 or (212) 741-7143; rbaron@nysca.org
Internet: http://www.nysca.org/public/guidelines/folk_arts/general_program.htm
Sponsor: New York State Council on the Arts
175 Varick Street
New York, NY 10014-4604

NYSCA Folk Arts: Presentation Grants 3596
The Presentation grants support activities that present folk arts and artists to the public, including concerts, festivals, lecture/demonstrations, residencies, and programs presenting oral narratives. Applications may involve one type of activity or a series of thematically related activities that may involve different modes of presentation. Folk arts events and series are also supported.
Requirements: Applicants must register with the Council by February 22 to be considered for funding. Applications should demonstrate a clearly articulated thematic focus for the event or series requested. Also, artists must receive appropriate fees for their presentations, and when travel is involved, adequate per diem. Presentations should also involve personnel and consultants with appropriate cultural expertise and technical skills. These may include, but are not limited to: folklorists, ethnomusicologists, graphic designers, publicists and specialists in lighting, sound reinforcement, stage management, promotion and marketing. In addition, the folk art activity being presented must have its own interpretive materials, and promotion for the program should substantially publicize the folk arts event and the artists involved in the activity. First-applicants must contact program staff before the registration deadline. Applications can be found at the website and should be submitted online.
Restrictions: This grant will not fund more than 50% of the project expenses. Applicants may submit no more than one application in this funding category. Folk Arts emphasizes support for presentations grounded in the traditional modes of practicing folk art, and not programming involving choreography, theatricality, or stylization that significantly alters traditions. Support is also not available for programming involving artists who appropriate, interpret, or revive the traditions of other communities.
Geographic Focus: New York
Date(s) Application is Due: Apr 1
Contact: Robert Baron; (212) 741-7755 or (212) 741-7143; rbaron@nysca.org
Internet: http://www.nysca.org/public/guidelines/folk_arts/presenting.htm
Sponsor: New York State Council on the Arts
175 Varick Street
New York, NY 10014-4604

NYSCA Folk Arts: Regional and County Folk Arts Programs Grants 3597

Folk Arts, in partnership with regional and local cultural organizations, supports folk arts programs which are regional and county-wide in scope. Support for these programs is intended to generate field research and programming for diverse audiences on an ongoing basis, directed by qualified individuals with experience and expertise in the public folklore field. Grants may be used towards the salaries of staff folklorists employed year-round and expenses associated with their production of public programs, field research on local traditions, and assistance to individual folk artists and other organizations interested in developing folk arts activities.

Requirements: Applicants must register with the Council by February 22 to be considered for funding. In addition, an applicant must have: received support from Folk Arts for the past three years; a minimum of four significant public programs that are organized each year; programs to be based to a significant extent upon field research, and work plans that include sufficient time for field research. Also, field research materials collected must be maintained in a locally accessible archive. Staff folklorists supported through this category must have experience organizing folk arts public programs and academic training in folklore or ethnomusicology. The staff folklorist must be employed for a minimum of three days each week. Applicant organizations are also expected to have a long-term commitment to folk arts services and programming. Program income should come from a variety of sources. First-time applicants are required to call staff before the registration deadline.

Restrictions: The request amount should not exceed 50% of the total project budget. Folk Arts emphasizes support for presentations grounded in the traditional modes of practicing folk art, and not programming involving choreography, theatricality, or stylization that significantly alters traditions. Support is also not available for programming involving artists who appropriate, interpret, or revive the traditions of other communities.

Geographic Focus: New York
Date(s) Application is Due: Apr 1
Contact: Robert Baron; (212) 741-7755 or (212) 741-7143; rbaron@nysca.org
Internet: http://www.nysca.org/public/guidelines/folk_arts/regional.htm
Sponsor: New York State Council on the Arts
175 Varick Street
New York, NY 10014-4604

NYSCA Literature: General Operating Support Grants 3598

General Operating Support grants sponsor an organization's ongoing work, rather than a specific project, in order to help organizations become more effective in fulfilling their mission. The Council examines the nature, scope, and quality of an organization's programs and activities, its managerial and fiscal competence, and its public service when considering the provision and level of support. Support is awarded on a multi-year basis.

Requirements: Applicants must register with the Council before February 22 to be considered for funding. In addition, all applicants must: have a primary focus in Literature; have an organizational mission that is primarily devoted to arts and culture with a prior record of accomplishment in producing or presenting cultural activities; demonstrate fiscal stability as indicated by such factors as a positive Fund balance, an absence of substantial and/or recurring organizational deficits, a realistic and balanced organizational budget, diverse revenue sources, and strong internal controls; one or more qualified, salaried administrative staff; a viable board of directors and officers that exercises oversight and accountability for governance, operations, programming and finances; and have ongoing programs, exhibitions, productions or other art and cultural activities that are open to the general public. Applications can be found at the website and should be submitted online. First-time applicants are required to call staff before the registration deadline.

Restrictions: General Operating Support will be no less than $5,000 and shall not exceed 25% of an organization's budget. Applicants cannot apply for both General Operating Support and General Program Support.

Geographic Focus: New York
Date(s) Application is Due: Apr 1
Contact: Robert Zukerman; (212) 741-7077; rzukerman@nysca.org
Internet: http://www.nysca.org/public/guidelines/literature/general_operating.htm
Sponsor: New York State Council on the Arts
175 Varick Street
New York, NY 10014-4604

NYSCA Literature: General Program Support Grants 3599

General Program Support grants fund activities of arts and cultural programs that are operated as independent entities within their own organization, or for significant arts programming within a nonprofit whose mission is not art-based. The Council examines the nature, scope, and quality of an organization's programs and activities, its managerial and fiscal competence, and its public service when considering the provision and level of support.

Requirements: Applicants must register with NYSCA before February 22 to be eligible for funding the following fiscal year. An applicant for General Program Support must also meet the following conditions: have significant ongoing activities that address a focus in Literature; substantial commitment to arts and culture, with a prior record of accomplishment in producing or presenting cultural activities; demonstrate fiscal stability as indicated by such factors as a positive fund balance, an absence of substantial, recurring organizational deficits, a realistic and balanced organizational budget, diverse revenue sources, and strong controls; one or more qualified, salaried administrative staff; a viable board of directors and officers that exercises oversight and accountability for governance, operations, programming and finances; and must have ongoing programs, exhibitions, productions or other art and cultural activities that are open to the general public. First time applicants are required to call program staff before the registration deadline. Applications are available at the website and should be submitted online.

Restrictions: Applicants cannot apply for both General Operating Support and General Program Support. Grants will be no less than $5,000 and shall not exceed 25% of an organization's budget.

Geographic Focus: New York
Date(s) Application is Due: Apr 1
Contact: Robert Zukerman; (212) 741-7077; rzukerman@nysca.org
Internet: http://www.nysca.org/public/guidelines/literature/general_program.htm
Sponsor: New York State Council on the Arts
175 Varick Street
New York, NY 10014-4604

NYSCA Literature: Public Programs 3600

The Public Programs grant offers project support to organizations that present professional writers to the public as part of a reading series. It also offers support for other public literary programs including workshops, book discussion groups led by published writers, lectures by writers, writers' tours, and literary programs involving electronic media. This category serves new applicants and organizations whose primary focus is not literary. Funding in this category is directed toward writers'/curators' fees and promotional activities.

Requirements: Applicants must register with the Council by February 22 to be considered for funding. In addition, applicants offering literary programs to the public must have completed at least one year of programming and should present a minimum of four literary readings per year. Applicants holding writing workshops should offer a minimum of eight consecutive sessions per year taught by professional writers and be open to the public. Reading series at colleges and universities are eligible to apply if they are promoted to and attended by the general public, and provided they are not offered for college credit to students. Applications can be found at the website and should be submitted online. First-time applicants are required to call staff before the registration deadline.

Restrictions: The requested amount should not exceed 50% of the total project budget.
Geographic Focus: New York
Date(s) Application is Due: Apr 1
Contact: Robert Zukerman; (212) 741-7077; rzukerman@nysca.org
Internet: http://www.nysca.org/public/guidelines/literature/public_programs.htm
Sponsor: New York State Council on the Arts
175 Varick Street
New York, NY 10014-4604

NYSCA Literature: Services to the Field Grants 3601

Services to the Field grants offer support to organizations for projects that provide managerial, artistic, or information services to individual writers and/or literary organizations. These services may include professional development, administrative support, shared informational resources such as database compilations, projects that utilize technology, and field-wide initiatives beyond the scope of an organization's core activities.

Requirements: Applicants must register with the Council by February 22 to be considered for funding. Also, applicants must have paid project staff in order to be eligible for this grant. First-time applicants are required to call the Literature staff before the registration deadline. Applications are available at the website and should be submitted online.

Restrictions: Request amounts should not exceed 50% of the total project budget.
Geographic Focus: New York
Date(s) Application is Due: Apr 1
Contact: Robert Zukerman; (212) 741-7077; rzukerman@nysca.org
Internet: http://www.nysca.org/public/guidelines/literature/services.htm
Sponsor: New York State Council on the Arts
175 Varick Street
New York, NY 10014-4604

NYSCA Museum: General Operating Support Grants 3602

General Operating Support grants sponsor an organization's ongoing work, rather than a specific project, in order to help organizations become more effective in fulfilling their mission. The Council examines the nature, scope, and quality of an organization's programs and activities, its managerial and fiscal competence, and its public service when considering the provision and level of support. Support is awarded on a multi-year basis.

Requirements: Applicants must register with the Council before February 22 to be considered for funding. Museums must have been open to the public for a minimum of one year prior to the registration deadline and provide a minimum of 120 days per year. In addition, all applicants must: have a primary focus in Museums; have an organizational mission that is primarily devoted to arts and culture with a prior record of accomplishment in producing or presenting cultural activities; demonstrate fiscal stability as indicated by such factors as a positive Fund balance, an absence of substantial and/or recurring organizational deficits, a realistic and balanced organizational budget, diverse revenue sources, and strong internal controls; one or more qualified, salaried administrative staff; a viable board of directors and officers that exercises oversight and accountability for governance, operations, programming and finances; and have ongoing programs, exhibitions, productions or other art and cultural activities that are open to the general public. Applications can be found at the website and should be submitted online. First-time applicants are required to call staff before the registration deadline.

Restrictions: General Operating Support will be no less than $5,000 and shall not exceed 25% of an organization's budget. Applicants cannot apply for both General Operating Support and General Program Support. Organizations open to the public by appointment only do not meet this requirement.

Geographic Focus: New York
Date(s) Application is Due: Apr 1
Contact: Kristin Herron, Senior Program Officer; (212) 741-7848; kherron@nysca.org
Internet: http://www.nysca.org/public/guidelines/museums/general_operating.htm
Sponsor: New York State Council on the Arts
175 Varick Street
New York, NY 10014-4604

NYSCA Museum: General Program Support Grants **3603**

General Program Support grants fund activities of arts and cultural programs that are operated as independent entities within their own organization, or for significant arts programming within a nonprofit whose mission is not art-based. The Council examines the nature, scope, and quality of an organization's programs and activities, its managerial and fiscal competence, and its public service when considering the provision and level of support.

Requirements: Applicants must register with NYSCA before February 22 to be eligible for funding the following fiscal year. Museums must have have been open to the public for a minimum of one year prior to the registration and provide services to the public for a minimum of 120 days per year. An applicant for General Program Support must also meet the following conditions: have significant ongoing activities that address a focus in Museums; substantial commitment to arts and culture, with a prior record of accomplishment in producing or presenting cultural activities; demonstrate fiscal stability as indicated by such factors as a positive fund balance, an absence of substantial, recurring organizational deficits, a realistic and balanced organizational budget, diverse revenue sources, and strong controls; one or more qualified, salaried administrative staff; a viable board of directors and officers that exercises oversight and accountability for governance, operations, programming and finances; and must have ongoing programs, exhibitions, productions or other art and cultural activities that are open to the general public. First time applicants are required to call program staff before the registration deadline. Applications are available at the website and should be submitted online.

Restrictions: Applicants cannot apply for both General Operating Support and General Program Support. Grants will be no less than $5,000 and shall not exceed 25% of an organization's budget.

Geographic Focus: New York

Date(s) Application is Due: Apr 1

Contact: Kristin Herron, Senior Program Officer; (212) 741-7848; kherron@nysca.org

Internet: http://www.nysca.org/public/guidelines/museums/general_program.htm

Sponsor: New York State Council on the Arts

175 Varick Street

New York, NY 10014-4604

NYSCA Museum: Project Support Grants **3604**

Project Support grants offer an opportunity for museums or related service organizations to seek support for projects or programs which are essential to maintain and/or increase service to their audience/communities. Such arts and cultural projects may include, but are not limited to: exhibitions, education programs, public programs, salary support for a curator or educator, interpretation, collections research, catalogs, audience development, and services to the field. Salary Support prioritizes museums which are poised to move forward in their development by adding an additional staff member for a professional collections-based or education position.

Requirements: Applicants must register with the Council by February 22 to be considered for funding. Museums must have been open to the public for a minimum of one year prior to the registration deadline and must provide services at least 120 days per year. Applications can be found at the website and should be submitted online. First-time applicants must contact the Museum staff before the registration deadline.

Restrictions: The requested amount shall not exceed 50% of the total project budget. In addition, awards cannot be made for more than three years, and salary support can only partially cover salary and benefits. Organizations applying for or receiving Museum General Operating Support or General Program Support are not eligible for funding in this category. Also, applicants may only submit one Museum request.

Geographic Focus: New York

Date(s) Application is Due: Apr 1

Contact: Kristin Herron, Senior Program Officer; (212) 741-7848; kherron@nysca.org

Internet: http://www.nysca.org/public/guidelines/museums/projects.htm

Sponsor: New York State Council on the Arts

175 Varick Street

New York, NY 10014-4604

NYSCA Music: Community Music Schools Grants **3605**

Community Music Schools grants support the multiple core activities of community music schools. Although the school may have a single or multidisciplinary focus, for the purpose of this category, the school's principal focus should be music instruction. In addition, residencies, performances, and presentations by professional artists should serve the instructional components of the school and provide additional opportunities for the broader community to engage in arts activities.

Requirements: Applicants must register with the Council by February 22 to be considered for funding. To be eligible, a community music school must be a permanent, non-degree granting nonprofit institution that has been in operation for a minimum of two years. Also, the institution must own or operate an accessible cultural facility, have a cumulative enrollment of at least 100 students, offer year-round instruction and programming, have professional artists on staff, have sequential curriculum to serve a multifaceted enrollment, and articulate standards of mastery to allow beginning and advanced students. First-time applicants must contact Music staff before registration deadline. Applications are available at the website and should be submitted online.

Restrictions: Requested support will not exceed 25% of the project budget. PreK-12 classes during school hours are not eligible for support.

Geographic Focus: New York

Date(s) Application is Due: Apr 1

Contact: Beverly D'Anne, Senior Program Officer; (212) 741-3232; bdanne@nysca.org

Internet: http://www.nysca.org/public/guidelines/music/community_schools.htm

Sponsor: New York State Council on the Arts

175 Varick Street

New York, NY 10014-4604

NYSCA Music: General Operating Support Grants **3606**

General Operating Support grants represent an investment by NYSCA in an organization's ongoing work, rather than a specific project or program, in order to help organizations become more effective in fulfilling their mission. The Council examines the nature, scope, and quality of an organization's programs and activities when considering the provision and level of support. Support for this grant is awarded on a multi-year basis.

Requirements: Applicants must register with NYSCA before February 22 to be eligible for funding. An applicant for general operating support must also meet the following conditions: have a primary focus in Music; have an organizational mission that is primarily devoted to arts and culture with a prior record of accomplishment in producing or presenting cultural activities; demonstrate fiscal stability as indicated by such factors as a positive fund balance, an absence of substantial, recurring organizational deficits, a realistic and balanced organizational budget, diverse revenue sources, and strong controls; one or more qualified, salaried administrative staff; a viable board of directors and officers that exercises oversight and accountability for governance, operations, programming and finances; and must have ongoing programs, exhibitions, productions or other art and cultural activities that are open to the general public. First time applicants are required to call program staff before the registration deadline. Applications are available at the website and should be submitted online.

Restrictions: Applicants cannot apply for both General Operating Support and General Program Support. Grants will be no less than $5,000 and shall not exceed 25% of an organization's budget.

Geographic Focus: New York

Date(s) Application is Due: Apr 1

Contact: Beverly D'Anne, Senior Program Officer; (212) 741-3232; bdanne@nysca.org

Internet: http://www.nysca.org/public/guidelines/music/general_operating.htm

Sponsor: New York State Council on the Arts

175 Varick Street

New York, NY 10014-4604

NYSCA Music: General Program Support Grants **3607**

The purpose of General Program Support (GPS) is to offer unrestricted support for ongoing activities of arts and cultural programs that are operated as independent entities within their own organization or for significant arts programming within a non-profit whose mission is not art-based (for example, a performing arts center that is operated as a separate entity within a college). The Council examines the nature, scope, and quality of an organization's programs and activities, its managerial and fiscal competence, and its public service when considering the provision and level of GPS support.

Requirements: Applicants must register with NYSCA before February 22 to be eligible for funding the following fiscal year. An applicant for General Program Support must also meet the following conditions: have significant ongoing activities that address a focus in Music; substantial commitment to arts and culture, with a prior record of accomplishment in producing or presenting cultural activities; demonstrate fiscal stability as indicated by such factors as a positive fund balance, an absence of substantial, recurring organizational deficits, a realistic and balanced organizational budget, diverse revenue sources, and strong controls; one or more qualified, salaried administrative staff; a viable board of directors and officers that exercises oversight and accountability for governance, operations, programming and finances; and must have ongoing programs, exhibitions, productions or other art and cultural activities that are open to the general public. First-time applicants are required to call program staff before the registration deadline. Applications are available at the website and should be submitted online.

Restrictions: General Program Support grants will be no less than $5,000 and shall not exceed 25% of the program's budget, based on the income and expense statement for the organization's most recently completed fiscal year. In addition, applicants cannot apply for both General Operating Support and General Program Support.

Geographic Focus: New York

Date(s) Application is Due: Apr 1

Contact: Beverly D'Anne, Senior Program Officer; (212) 741-3232; bdanne@nysca.org

Internet: http://www.nysca.org/public/guidelines/music/general_program.htm

Sponsor: New York State Council on the Arts

175 Varick Street

New York, NY 10014-4604

NYSCA Music: New Music Facilities **3608**

New Music Facilities grants are available to institutions that provide musicians with residencies, studio time, technical instruction, and access to equipment. Support is also available for the completion of a specific musical project, including collaborative works. A studio or host organization may apply for support to fully or partially subsidize up to eighty hours of studio time on behalf of one or more specific artists or for a specific number of artists selected through a fair selection process.

Requirements: Applicants must register with the Council by February 22 to be considered for funding. First-time applicants are required to call the Music staff before the registration deadline. Applications are available at the website and should be submitted online.

Restrictions: The funding request shall not exceed 50% of the project budget. In addition, NYSCA does not fund: major expenditures for the establishment of new organizations; accumulate deficits; debt reductions; programs of public universities or New York state agencies or departments; programs of public school districts or their affiliates; activities restricted to an organization's membership; operating expenses or fellowships at professional training schools that are not open to the general public; programs that are essentially recreational, rehabilitation, or therapeutic; operating expenses of privately owned facilities, such as homes or studios; components of an organization's budget that are not directed toward programs in New York State; competitions or contests; out-of-state travel expenses; or hospitality or entertainment costs of receptions, performance or museum openings, or fundraising benefits.

Geographic Focus: New York

Date(s) Application is Due: Apr 1

Contact: Beverly D'Anne, Senior Program Officer; (212) 741-3232; bdanne@nysca.org
Internet: http://www.nysca.org/public/guidelines/music/facilities.htm
Sponsor: New York State Council on the Arts
175 Varick Street
New York, NY 10014-4604

NYSCA Presenting: General Operating Support Grants 3609
General Operating Support grants sponsor an organization's ongoing work, rather than a specific project or program. The Council examines the nature, scope, and quality of an organization's programs and activities, its managerial and fiscal competence, and its public service when considering the provision and level of support.
Requirements: Applicants must register with the Council by February 22 to be considered for funding. Also, an organization must meet the following conditions: a primary focus in presenting; an organizational mission primarily devoted to arts and culture with a prior record of accomplishment in producing or presenting cultural activities; a minimum of ten discrete presentations by ten different professional performing artists; demonstrate fiscal stability as indicated by such factors as a positive Fund balance, an absence of substantial and/or recurring organizational deficits, a realistic and balanced organizational budget, diverse revenue sources and strong internal controls; one or more qualified, salaried administrative staff; a viable board of directors and officers that exercises oversight and accountability for governance, operations, programming and finances; and must have on going programs, exhibitions, productions, or other art and cultural activities that are open to the general public. Applications can be found at the website and must be submitted online. First-time applicants are required to call the Presenting staff before the registration deadline.
Restrictions: Total requested amounts may not exceed 25% of the total project budget and must be more than $5,000. Applicants may not apply for both General Operating Support and General Program Support grants. In addition, the following activities are not eligible: single- and two-day festivals (unless incorporated within a larger presenting season); competitions, contests, talent showcases or parades; poetry readings (unless incorporated within a performance context) or staged readings; magic shows or ventriloquists; lectures, in-school classroom activity, master classes, or workshops; presentations or events that include the presentation of the organization's own work or work of their staff or board members, even when the project includes guest artists; and student work.
Geographic Focus: New York
Date(s) Application is Due: Apr 1
Contact: Leanne Tintori Wells; (212) 741-2227; lwells@nysca.org
Internet: http://www.nysca.org/public/guidelines/presenting/general_operating.htm
Sponsor: New York State Council on the Arts
175 Varick Street
New York, NY 10014-4604

NYSCA Presenting: General Program Support Grants 3610
General Program Support grants sponsor an organization's ongoing activities of arts and cultural programs that are operated as independent entities within their own organization or for significant arts programming within a non-profit whose mission is not art based. The Council examines the nature, scope, and quality of an organization's programs and activities, its managerial and fiscal competence, and its public service when considering the provision and level of support.
Requirements: Applicants must register with the Council by February 22 to be considered for funding. Also, organizations must: have significant ongoing activities that address a focus in presenting; make evident a substantial commitment to arts and culture, with a prior record of accomplishment in producing or presenting cultural activities; have a minimum of ten discrete presentations by ten different professional performing artists; demonstrate fiscal stability as indicated by such factors as a positive fund balance, an absence of substantial, recurring organizational deficits, a realistic and balanced organizational budget, diverse revenue sources, and strong controls; one or more qualified, salaried administrative staff; a viable board of directors and officers that exercises oversight and accountability for governance, operations, programming and finances; and must have ongoing programs, exhibitions, productions or other art and cultural activities that are open to the general public. First-time applicants are required to call program staff before the registration deadline. Applications are available at the website and should be submitted online.
Restrictions: Total requested amounts may not exceed 25% of the total project budget and must be more than $5,000. Applicants may not apply for both General Operating Support and General Program Support grants. In addition, the following activities are not eligible: single- and two-day festivals (unless incorporated within a larger presenting season); competitions, contests, talent showcases or parades; poetry readings (unless incorporated within a performance context) or staged readings; magic shows or ventriloquists; lectures, in-school classroom activity, master classes, or workshops; presentations or events that include the presentation of the organization's own work or work of their staff or board members, even when the project includes guest artists; and student work.
Geographic Focus: New York
Date(s) Application is Due: Apr 1
Contact: Leanne Tintori Wells; (212) 741-2227; lwells@nysca.org
Internet: http://www.nysca.org/public/guidelines/presenting/general_program.htm
Sponsor: New York State Council on the Arts
175 Varick Street
New York, NY 10014-4604

NYSCA Presenting: Presenting Grants 3611
NYSCA Presenting grants offer support to experienced presenters of live professional performing arts. Funding is directed toward costs of specific professional performing arts presentations.
Requirements: Applicants must register with the Council by February 22 to be eligible for funding. Also, applicants are required to present a minimum of five performances by five different professional artists over five separate dates. NYSCA considers a festival day to be a single performance even when several artists are presented throughout the day. Festival-only presenters must present a minimum of three multiple performance days. Applications can be found at the website and should be submitted online. First-time applicants must contact Presenting staff before the registration deadline.
Restrictions: The requested amount should not exceed 50% of the total project budget. In addition, the following activities are not eligible: single- and two-day festivals (unless incorporated within a larger presenting season); competitions, contests, talent showcases or parades; poetry readings (unless incorporated within a performance context) or staged readings; magic shows or ventriloquists; lectures, in-school classroom activity, master classes, or workshops; presentations or events that include the presentation of the organization's own work or work of their staff or board members, even when the project includes guest artists; and student work.
Geographic Focus: New York
Date(s) Application is Due: Apr 1
Contact: Leanne Tintori Wells; (212) 741-2227; lwells@nysca.org
Internet: http://www.nysca.org/public/guidelines/presenting/index.htm
Sponsor: New York State Council on the Arts
175 Varick Street
New York, NY 10014-4604

NYSCA Presenting: Services to the Field Grants 3612
The Services to the Field grants provide funding to advance the presenting field in all areas of management and presentation. Requests are welcome from organizations interested in conducting and/or administering projects and activities that provide professional services to New York State performing arts presenters. Such services may focus on programmatic, informational, or managerial areas and may include professional development workshops, roundtable discussions, symposia, artist showcases, or projects that utilize new technologies. Priority is given to services carried out on a regional or statewide basis.
Requirements: Applicants must register with the Council by February 22 to be eligible for funding. Priorities of the grant are focused on programs or activities that present contemporary and new commissioned works; programming that represents a broad range of culturally diverse work, particularly work by international artists, lesser known artists, women artists, or artists of color; projects that explore new directions involving performing artists, multimedia, and hybrid art forms; co-presentation efforts in which two or more partners share in the expenses and income; and presenters that operate in economically depressed communities, as well as presenters that own and/or operate theatrical facilities. First-time applicants must contact the Presenting staff before the registration deadline.
Restrictions: Requested amounts may not exceed 50% of the total proposed budget. In addition, the following activities are not eligible: single- and two-day festivals (unless incorporated within a larger presenting season); competitions, contests, talent showcases or parades; poetry readings (unless incorporated within a performance context) or staged readings; magic shows or ventriloquists; lectures, in-school classroom activity, master classes, or workshops; presentations or events that include the presentation of the organization's own work or work of their staff or board members, even when the project includes guest artists; and student work.
Geographic Focus: New York
Date(s) Application is Due: Apr 1
Contact: Leanne Tintori Wells; (212) 741-2227; lwells@nysca.org
Internet: http://www.nysca.org/public/guidelines/presenting/services.htm
Sponsor: New York State Council on the Arts
175 Varick Street
New York, NY 10014-4604

NYSCA Special Art Services: Project Support Grants 3613
Project Support grants offer support for ongoing programming and related activities involving performing, visual, literary arts, film, and/or electronic media. These activities must be professionally directed and take place in, or tour, communities of color or communities of a specific ethnic character.
Requirements: Applicants must register with the Council before February 22 to be considered for funding. Priority is given to organizations that pay fees to artists and curators and those that provide ongoing programming that is not available elsewhere in that community. Applications are available at the website and should be submitted online. First-time applicants are required to call the Special Art Services staff before the registration deadline.
Restrictions: Requested funds may not exceed 50% of the total proposed budget. This grant does not support single, one-time activities such as a single exhibition or festival. Organizations may not require or request artists to pay a fee of any kind to participate in exhibitions.
Geographic Focus: New York
Date(s) Application is Due: Apr 1
Contact: Robert Baron, Senior Program Officer; (212) 741-7755; rbaron@nysca.org
Internet: http://www.nysca.org/public/guidelines/special_arts_services/project.htm
Sponsor: New York State Council on the Arts
175 Varick Street
New York, NY 10014-4604

NYSCA Special Arts Services: General Operating Support Grants 3614
General Operating Support grants sponsor an organization's ongoing work, rather than a specific project or program. The Council examines the nature, scope, and quality of an organization's programs and activities, its managerial and fiscal competence, and its public service when considering the provision and level of support. This grant specifically helps to ensure the quality, viability, and productivity of artists and institutions within communities of color and other specific cultures. Special Arts Services also welcomes requests from

organizations serving the disabled community by offering professionally-directed training in an arts discipline with the goal of more advanced study or career entry.
Requirements: Applicants must register with the Council by February 22 to be considered for funding. Also, an organization must meet the following conditions: a primary focus of providing cultural programs within and for communities of color or other ethnic communities; an organizational mission primarily devoted to arts and culture with a prior record of accomplishment in producing or presenting cultural activities; demonstrate fiscal stability as indicated by such factors as a positive Fund balance, an absence of substantial and/or recurring organizational deficits, a realistic and balanced organizational budget, diverse revenue sources and strong internal controls; one or more qualified, salaried administrative staff; a viable board of directors and officers that exercises oversight and accountability for governance, operations, programming and finances; and must have on going programs, exhibitions, productions, or other art and cultural activities that are open to the general public. Applications can be found at the website and must be submitted online. First-time applicants are required to call the Presenting staff before the registration deadline.
Restrictions: Total requested amounts cannot exceed 25% of the total project budget and will be no less than $5,000. Applicants cannot apply for both General Operating Support and General Program Support. In addition, organizations whose projects are directed toward general audiences or organizations in which artists do not represent those communities previously mentioned are not eligible for support and should consult the guidelines of other areas of support.
Geographic Focus: New York
Date(s) Application is Due: Apr 1
Contact: Robert Baron, Senior Program Officer; (212) 741-7755; rbaron@nysca.org
Internet: http://www.nysca.org/public/guidelines/special_arts_services/general_operating.htm
Sponsor: New York State Council on the Arts
175 Varick Street
New York, NY 10014-4604

NYSCA Special Arts Services: General Program Support Grants 3615
General Program Support grants sponsor an organization's ongoing activities of arts and cultural programs that are operated as independent entities within their own organization or for significant arts programming within a non-profit whose mission is not art based. The Council examines the nature, scope, and quality of an organization's programs and activities, its managerial and fiscal competence, and its public service when considering the provision and level of support.
Requirements: Applicants must register with the Council by February 22 to be considered for funding. Also, organizations must: have significant ongoing activities that address a focus in Special Arts Services; make evident a substantial commitment to arts and culture, with a prior record of accomplishment in producing or presenting cultural activities; demonstrate fiscal stability as indicated by such factors as a positive fund balance, an absence of substantial, recurring organizational deficits, a realistic and balanced organizational budget, diverse revenue sources, and strong controls; one or more qualified, salaried administrative staff; a viable board of directors and officers that exercises oversight and accountability for governance, operations, programming and finances; and must have ongoing programs, exhibitions, productions or other art and cultural activities that are open to the general public. Organizations applying to Special Arts Services should have appropriate representation at the staff and board level reflecting the communities served. First-time applicants are required to call program staff before the registration deadline. Applications are available at the website and should be submitted online.
Restrictions: Total requested amounts may not exceed 25% of the total project budget and must be more than $5,000. Applicants may not apply for both General Operating Support and General Program Support grants. Also, organizations whose projects are directed toward general audiences or organizations in which artists do not represent those communities previously mentioned are not eligible for support and should consult the guidelines of other areas of support.
Geographic Focus: New York
Date(s) Application is Due: Apr 1
Contact: Robert Baron, Senior Program Officer; (212) 741-7755; rbaron@nysca.org
Internet: http://www.nysca.org/public/guidelines/special_arts_services/general_program.htm
Sponsor: New York State Council on the Arts
175 Varick Street
New York, NY 10014-4604

NYSCA Special Arts Services: Instruction and Training Grants 3616
Instruction and Training grants offer an opportunity for study aimed toward professional careers in the arts and/or instruction in the traditional art of an ethnic community for members of that community. The goal of this category is to foster professional development in a variety of arts disciplines and techniques, including those with a particular interest in preserving the traditions of specific cultures. Support is offered in three distinct courses of study of professionally-directed instruction and training in any art discipline. These are, in order of priority: Professional Development, Traditional Arts Study, and Pre-Professional Development.
Requirements: Applicants must register with the Council by February 22 to be eligible for funding. Also, organizational priorities must serve African/Caribbean, Asian/Pacific Islander, Latino/Hispanic, and Native American/Indian populations, as well as organizations serving the disabled community whose members seek career development opportunities. Applicant organizations must state which course of study they are providing. Classes must be ongoing and taught by accomplished artists in community-based venues. Application organizations must also provide guidance through all levels of artistic development. In all cases, organizations are required to provide documentation of the results of their programs. First-time applicants are required to call Special Arts Services staff before the registration deadline.
Restrictions: Total requested amounts should not exceed 50% of the total project budget. In addition, the following programs are not eligible for support: single-instructor programs; programs offered in cooperation with schools, school districts, or BOCES, and offered during school hours, or which take place immediately after school hours in school facilities; programs that are essentially recreational, rehabilitative or therapeutic; one-time workshops or programs of very short duration; summer camp activities that are not an integral part of year-round instruction and training programs.
Geographic Focus: New York
Date(s) Application is Due: Apr 1
Contact: Robert Baron, Senior Program Officer; (212) 741-7755; rbaron@nysca.org
Internet: http://www.nysca.org/public/guidelines/special_arts_services/instruction_training.htm
Sponsor: New York State Council on the Arts
175 Varick Street
New York, NY 10014-4604

NYSCA Special Arts Services: Professional Performances Grants 3617
Professional Performances grants are offered for performances of professionally-directed, community-based dance, theatre, and music organizations. Support is also available for performing companies of color or other ethnic companies to tour communities of color and/or other ethnic communities throughout the state. Such activities must serve audiences of color or other ethnic audiences and be performed in community-based venues serving the relevant ethnic groups.
Requirements: Applicants must register with the Council by February 22 to be considered for funding. First-time applicants are required to call Special Arts Services staff before the registration deadline. Applications are available at the website and should be submitted online.
Restrictions: Requested amounts cannot exceed 50% of the total proposed project budget. Activities that do not serve audiences of color or other ethnic audiences and are not performed in community-based venues are not eligible to apply.
Geographic Focus: New York
Date(s) Application is Due: Apr 1
Contact: Robert Baron, Senior Program Officer; (212) 741-7755; rbaron@nysca.org
Internet: http://www.nysca.org/public/guidelines/special_arts_services/performances.htm
Sponsor: New York State Council on the Arts
175 Varick Street
New York, NY 10014-4604

NYSCA State and Local Partnerships: Administrative Salary Support Grants 3618
Administrative Salary Support grants are designed for new applicants to begin the process of professionalizing the organization. Funds awarded in this entry-level category are directed toward the salary of a professional staff position that helps ensure organizational capacity to carry out essential programmatic and developmental activities. Funding is awarded on a single-year basis for up to three years with the expectation that the organization will develop the capability to sustain the position.
Requirements: Applicants must register with the Council before February 22 to be considered for funding. State and Local Partnership grants primarily support multi-arts centers, local arts councils, and multi-arts service organizations. First-time applicants must contact State and Local Partnerships staff before the registration deadline. Applications are available at the website and should be submitted online.
Restrictions: Requested funds may not exceed 50% of the professional's salary.
Geographic Focus: New York
Date(s) Application is Due: Apr 1
Contact: Leanne Tintori Wells; (212) 741-2227; lwells@nysca.org
Internet: http://www.nysca.org/public/guidelines/state_partnerships/admin_support.htm
Sponsor: New York State Council on the Arts
175 Varick Street
New York, NY 10014-4604

NYSCA State and Local Partnerships: General Operating Support Grants 3619
General Operating Support grants sponsor an organization's ongoing work, rather than a specific project or program. The Council examines the nature, scope, and quality of an organization's programs and activities, its managerial and fiscal competence, and its public service when considering the provision and level of support. Specifically, State and Local Partnerships grants seek to: strengthen the leadership role of local/regional arts organizations in encouraging local cultural development and increasing resources available for the arts; encourage greater participation in the arts through support of a wide range of local, regional, and statewide programs and services responding to assessed cultural needs and reaching the full diversity of each community served; and enhance the professional capability of multi-arts organizations operating on the local levels and arts service organizations promoting the development of the arts and providing arts services statewide.
Requirements: Applicants must register with the Council by February 22 to be considered for funding. Also, an organization must meet the following conditions: a primary focus of providing local arts and cultural initiatives; an organizational mission primarily devoted to arts and culture with a prior record of accomplishment in producing or presenting cultural activities; demonstrate fiscal stability as indicated by such factors as a positive Fund balance, an absence of substantial and/or recurring organizational deficits, a realistic and balanced organizational budget, diverse revenue sources and strong internal controls; one or more qualified, salaried administrative staff; a viable board of directors and officers that exercises oversight and accountability for governance, operations, programming and finances; and must have on going programs, exhibitions, productions, or other art and cultural activities that are open to the general public. Applications can be found at the website and must be submitted online. First-time applicants are required to call the State and Local Partnerships staff before the registration deadline.
Restrictions: Total requested amounts cannot exceed 25% of the total project budget and will be no less than $5,000. Applicants cannot apply for both General Operating Support and General Program Support.

Geographic Focus: New York
Date(s) Application is Due: Apr 1
Contact: Leanne Tintori Wells, (212) 741-2227; lwells@nysca.org
Internet: http://www.nysca.org/public/guidelines/state_partnerships/general_operating.htm
Sponsor: New York State Council on the Arts
175 Varick Street
New York, NY 10014-4604

NYSCA State and Local Partnerships: General Program Support Grants   3620
General Program Support grants sponsor an organization's ongoing activities of arts and cultural programs that are operated as independent entities within their own organization or for significant arts programming within a non-profit whose mission is not art based. The Council examines the nature, scope, and quality of an organization's programs and activities, its managerial and fiscal competence, and its public service when considering the provision and level of support.
Requirements: Applicants must register with the Council by February 22 to be considered for funding. Also, organizations must: have significant ongoing activities that address a focus in local and regional cultural and arts services; make evident a substantial commitment to arts and culture, with a prior record of accomplishment in producing or presenting cultural activities; demonstrate fiscal stability as indicated by such factors as a positive fund balance, an absence of substantial, recurring organizational deficits, a realistic and balanced organizational budget, diverse revenue sources, and strong controls; one or more qualified, salaried administrative staff; a viable board of directors and officers that exercises oversight and accountability for governance, operations, programming and finances; and must have ongoing programs, exhibitions, productions or other art and cultural activities that are open to the general public. First-time applicants are required to call program staff before the registration deadline. Applications are available at the website and should be submitted online.
Restrictions: Total requested amounts may not exceed 25% of the total project budget and must be more than $5,000. Applicants may not apply for both General Operating Support and General Program Support grants.
Geographic Focus: New York
Date(s) Application is Due: Apr 1
Contact: Leanne Tintori Wells; (212) 741-2227; lwells@nysca.org
Internet: http://www.nysca.org/public/guidelines/state_partnerships/general_program.htm
Sponsor: New York State Council on the Arts
175 Varick Street
New York, NY 10014-4604

NYSCA State and Local Partnerships: Services to the Field Grants   3621
Services to the Field grants advance the professional/organizational development of a defined arts constituency or service area. This grant supports the delivery of specific service initiatives focusing on long-term developmental objectives of the targeted constituency(ies). Services may include legal and accounting issues, fiscal and organization management, projects that utilize technology to serve the field, professional development for individual artists, and cultural data gathering and analysis that report on the impact of the arts in communities or statewide. State and Local Partnerships encourages collaboration between two or more organizations within this category.
Requirements: Applicants are required to register with the Council by February 22 to be considered for funding. First-time applicants must contact the State and Local Partnerships staff before the registration deadline. Applications are available at the website and should be submitted online.
Restrictions: Total requests should not be more than 50% of the total project budget.
Geographic Focus: New York
Date(s) Application is Due: Apr 1
Contact: Lisa Johnson, Senior Program Officer; (212) 741-6562; ljohnson@nysca.org
Internet: http://www.nysca.org/public/guidelines/state_partnerships/services.htm
Sponsor: New York State Council on the Arts
175 Varick Street
New York, NY 10014-4604

NYSCA State and Local Partnerships: Workshops Grants   3622
Workshops grants are designated for expenses of providing a structured program of workshops, classes, or seminars in a range of arts disciplines. Participatory workshops must offer ongoing, professional instruction, and be widely publicized and economically accessible to all segments of the community. Workshops should be designed either for the general public or for the professional development of individual artists from a range of disciplines. Funds may also be requested for outreach and scholarship support to reach the diversity of the community, assuring access to quality programs.
Requirements: Applicants must register with the Council by February 22 to be eligible for funding. In order to be eligible for funding, proposed workshops must offer ongoing, professional instruction, and be widely publicized and economically accessible to all segments of the community. First-time applicants are required to call the State and Local Partnerships staff before the registration deadline. Applications can be found at the website and should be submitted online.
Restrictions: Requested funds may not exceed 50% of the total project budget. The Council also does not fund: debt reductions; programs of public Universities or of New York State agencies or departments; programs of public schools or their components or affiliates; programs that are essentially rehabilitative and/or therapeutic; or activities restricted to an organization's membership.
Geographic Focus: New York
Date(s) Application is Due: Apr 1
Contact: Lisa Johnson, Senior Program Officer; (212) 741-6562; ljohnson@nysca.org
Internet: http://www.nysca.org/public/guidelines/state_partnerships/workshops.htm

Sponsor: New York State Council on the Arts
175 Varick Street
New York, NY 10014-4604

NYSCA Theatre: General Operating Support Grants   3623
General Operating Support grants sponsor an organization's ongoing work, rather than a specific project or program. The Council examines the nature, scope, and quality of an organization's programs and activities, its managerial and fiscal competence, and its public service when considering the provision and level of support. Producing organizations must offer seasonal production activity that is open to the general public and may include main-stage performances, readings and developmental workshops. Priority will be given to main-stage production activity.
Requirements: Applicants must register with the Council by February 22 to be considered for funding. Also, an organization must meet the following conditions: a primary focus in theatre and/or dramatic arts; an organizational mission primarily devoted to arts and culture with a prior record of accomplishment in producing or presenting cultural activities; demonstrate fiscal stability as indicated by such factors as a positive Fund balance, an absence of substantial and/or recurring organizational deficits, a realistic and balanced organizational budget, diverse revenue sources and strong internal controls; one or more qualified, salaried administrative staff; a viable board of directors and officers that exercises oversight and accountability for governance, operations, programming and finances; and must have on going programs, exhibitions, productions, or other art and cultural activities that are open to the general public. Applications can be found at the website and must be submitted online. First-time applicants are required to call the Theatre staff before the registration deadline.
Restrictions: Total requested amounts cannot exceed 25% of the total project budget and will be no less than $5,000. Applicants cannot apply for both General Operating Support and General Program Support. Applicants may make only ONE request in the Theatre Program. In addition, Theatre support will not be available for community theatre, commercial or student productions, carnivals, sideshows, parades, variety shows, or drama therapy programs.
Geographic Focus: New York
Date(s) Application is Due: Apr 1
Contact: Robert Zukerman; (212) 741-7077; rzukerman@nysca.org
Internet: http://www.nysca.org/public/guidelines/theatre/general_operating.htm
Sponsor: New York State Council on the Arts
175 Varick Street
New York, NY 10014-4604

NYSCA Theatre: General Program Support Grants   3624
General Program Support represents an investment by NYSCA for ongoing activities of arts and cultural programs that are operated as independent entities within their own organization or for significant arts programming within a non-profit whose mission is not art-based. Specifically, NYSCA offers support to professional theatre companies with ongoing production and development programs, and to service organizations that build and reinforce administrative and institutional skills, provide resources and information, assist in the professional development of artists, and enhance education about and access to theatre for all audiences.
Requirements: Applicants must register with the Council by February 22 to be considered for funding. Also, organizations must: have significant ongoing activities that address a focus in theatre; make evident a substantial commitment to arts and culture, with a prior record of accomplishment in producing or presenting cultural activities; demonstrate fiscal stability as indicated by such factors as a positive fund balance, an absence of substantial, recurring organizational deficits, a realistic and balanced organizational budget, diverse revenue sources, and strong controls; one or more qualified, salaried administrative staff; a viable board of directors and officers that exercises oversight and accountability for governance, operations, programming and finances; and must have ongoing programs, exhibitions, productions or other art and cultural activities that are open to the general public. First-time applicants are required to call program staff before the registration deadline. Applications are available at the website and should be submitted online.
Restrictions: Total requested amounts cannot exceed 25% of the total project budget and will be no less than $5,000. Applicants cannot apply for both General Operating Support and General Program Support. Applicants may make only ONE request in the Theatre Program. In addition, Theatre support will not be available for community theatre, commercial or student productions, carnivals, sideshows, parades, variety shows, or drama therapy programs.
Geographic Focus: New York
Date(s) Application is Due: Apr 1
Contact: Robert Zukerman; (212) 741-7077; rzukerman@nysca.org
Internet: http://www.nysca.org/public/guidelines/theatre/general_program.htm
Sponsor: New York State Council on the Arts
175 Varick Street
New York, NY 10014-4604

NYSCA Theatre: Professional Performances Grants   3625
Professional Performances grants offers support to professional theatre companies with ongoing production and development programs, and to service organizations that build and reinforce administrative and institutional skills, provide resources and information, assist in the professional development of artists, and enhance education about and access to theatre for all audiences. NYSCA also encourages and supports the development of emerging theatre companies that demonstrate artistic potential and/or accomplishment. Funding can be directed toward artists' fees, salaries and production expenses.
Requirements: Applicants must register with the Council by February 22 to be considered for funding. In addition, theatre companies: must have produced for two seasons before applying for support; must stage at least one public production per year; must have an artistic director; and must be able to document payment to artistic personnel in their budgets.

First-time applicants are required to call Theatre staff before the registration deadline. Applications are available at the website and should be submitted online.
Restrictions: Request funds should not exceed 50% of the total proposed project budget. Also, Theatre support will not be available for community theatre, commercial or student productions, carnivals, sideshows, parades, variety shows, or drama therapy programs.
Geographic Focus: New York
Date(s) Application is Due: Apr 1
Contact: Robert Zukerman; (212) 741-7077; rzukerman@nysca.org
Internet: http://www.nysca.org/public/guidelines/theatre/performances.htm
Sponsor: New York State Council on the Arts
175 Varick Street
New York, NY 10014-4604

NYSCA Theatre: Services to the Field Grants 3626
Services to the Field offers support for service organizations and for activities that provide managerial, artistic or information services to individual theatre artists and/or organizations. These services may include publications, professional development through workshops, symposia and roundtables, managerial support, information resources, projects that utilize technology, subsidized space for rehearsals and performances, festivals, and initiatives extending beyond the scope of an organization's general programming.
Requirements: Applicants must register with the Council before February 22 to be eligible for funding. In addition, applicants must be able to document a history of providing services to the Theatre field of New York State. Producing organizations must also offer seasonal production activity that is open to the general public and may include main-stage performances, readings and developmental workshops. Priority will be given to main-stage production activity. First-time applicants are required to call the Theatre staff before the registration deadline. Applications can be found at the website and should be submitted online.
Restrictions: Requested funds should not exceed 50% of the total proposed project budget. Applicants may make only ONE request under the Theatre category at NYSCA. Also, Theatre support will not be available for community theatre, commercial or student productions, carnivals, sideshows, parades, variety shows, or drama therapy programs.
Geographic Focus: New York
Date(s) Application is Due: Apr 1
Contact: Robert Zukerman; (212) 741-7077; rzukerman@nysca.org
Internet: http://www.nysca.org/public/guidelines/theatre/services.htm
Sponsor: New York State Council on the Arts
175 Varick Street
New York, NY 10014-4604

NYSCA Visual Arts: Exhibitions and Installations Grants 3627
Exhibitions and Installations grants provide support to organizations that offer exhibitions and installations of original work by living artists. Visual Arts encourages professional curatorial practice - staff or guest curators should not include their own work in the proposed exhibitions. Funds are available for fees to participating artists, materials, curator fees, catalogue expenses, and essayists' fees. The applicant organization, not the artists, is responsible for all shipping, preparatory expenses of artwork, press and publicity costs.
Requirements: Applicants must register with the Council by February 22 to be eligible for funding. Organizations must have a minimum of four exhibitions scheduled during the applicant's request year. In addition, exhibitions must demonstrate a sound intellectual premise and advance the public's understanding of contemporary art practices. Material that provides a curatorial explanation of each exhibition is required of all applicants. Also, direct payment of fees to artists is required for all activities that include artists, and New York State based artists must be included in the ongoing programming. First-time applicants must contact the Visual Arts staff before the registration deadline. Applications are available at the website and should be submitted online.
Restrictions: The requested amount may not exceed 50% of the total proposed budget. Also, organizations cannot require or request artists to pay a fee for participation in the project. Commissions on sales of art in projects funded by the NYSCA cannot exceed 25% of the sale price, and projects and exhibitions featuring membership, board members, staff, faculty, or enrolled students are not eligible. Events such as festivals and open studios are not supported.
Geographic Focus: New York
Date(s) Application is Due: Apr 1
Contact: Karen Helmerson; (212) 741-3003; khelmerson@nysca.org
Internet: http://www.nysca.org/public/guidelines/visual_arts/exhibitions.htm
Sponsor: New York State Council on the Arts
175 Varick Street
New York, NY 10014-4604

NYSCA Visual Arts: General Operating Support Grants 3628
General Operating Support grants sponsor an organization's ongoing work, rather than a specific project or program. The Council examines the nature, scope, and quality of an organization's programs and activities, its managerial and fiscal competence, and its public service when considering the provision and level of support. Visual Arts supports a wide range of contemporary art activity for the benefit of the public and the advancement of the field with a goal of assisting New York State artists in their efforts to create and exhibit new work, interpret the work of contemporary visual artists to the public, and encourage dialogue and critical commentary about the visual arts.
Requirements: Applicants must register with the Council by February 22 to be considered for funding. Also, an organization must meet the following conditions: a primary focus in visual arts; an organizational mission primarily devoted to arts and culture with a prior record of accomplishment in producing or presenting cultural activities; demonstrate fiscal stability as indicated by such factors as a positive Fund balance, an absence of substantial and/or recurring organizational deficits, a realistic and balanced organizational budget, diverse revenue sources and strong internal controls; one or more qualified, salaried administrative staff; a viable board of directors and officers that exercises oversight and accountability for governance, operations, programming and finances; and must have on going programs, exhibitions, productions, or other art and cultural activities that are open to the general public. Applications can be found at the website and must be submitted online. First-time applicants are required to call the Visual Arts staff before the registration deadline.
Restrictions: Total requested amounts cannot exceed 25% of the total project budget and will be no less than $5,000. Applicants cannot apply for both General Operating Support and General Program Support. In addition, organizations cannot require or request artists to pay a fee for participation in projects funded by Visual Arts, and commissions on sales of art in projects funded by NYSCA cannot exceed 25% of the sale price. Events such as festivals and open studios are not supported.
Geographic Focus: New York
Date(s) Application is Due: Apr 1
Contact: Karen Helmerson; (212) 741-3003; khelmerson@nysca.org
Internet: http://www.nysca.org/public/guidelines/visual_arts/general_operating.htm
Sponsor: New York State Council on the Arts
175 Varick Street
New York, NY 10014-4604

NYSCA Visual Arts: General Program Support Grants 3629
General Program Support represents an investment by NYSCA for ongoing activities of arts and cultural programs that are operated as independent entities within their own organization or for significant arts programming within a non-profit whose mission is not art-based. Visual Arts supports a wide range of contemporary art activity for the benefit of the public and the advancement of the field with a goal of assisting New York State artists in their efforts to create and exhibit new work, interpret the work of contemporary visual artists to the public, and encourage dialogue and critical commentary about the visual arts.
Requirements: Applicants must register with the Council by February 22 to be considered for funding. Also, organizations must: have significant ongoing activities that address a focus in visual arts; make evident a substantial commitment to arts and culture, with a prior record of accomplishment in producing or presenting cultural activities; demonstrate fiscal stability as indicated by such factors as a positive fund balance, an absence of substantial, recurring organizational deficits, a realistic and balanced organizational budget, diverse revenue sources, and strong controls; one or more qualified, salaried administrative staff; a viable board of directors and officers that exercises oversight and accountability for governance, operations, programming and finances; and must have ongoing programs, exhibitions, productions or other art and cultural activities that are open to the general public. First-time applicants are required to call program staff before the registration deadline. Applications are available at the website and should be submitted online.
Restrictions: Total requested amounts cannot exceed 25% of the total project budget and will be no less than $5,000. Applicants cannot apply for both General Operating Support and General Program Support. In addition, organizations cannot require or request artists to pay a fee for participation in projects funded by Visual Arts, and commissions on sales of art in projects funded by NYSCA cannot exceed 25% of the sale price. Events such as festivals and open studios are not supported.
Geographic Focus: New York
Date(s) Application is Due: Apr 1
Contact: Karen Helmerson; (212) 741-3003; khelmerson@nysca.org
Internet: http://www.nysca.org/public/guidelines/visual_arts/general_program.htm
Sponsor: New York State Council on the Arts
175 Varick Street
New York, NY 10014-4604

NYSCA Visual Arts: Services to the Field Grants 3630
Services to the Field provides support for managerial, artistic, or information services that strengthen the nonprofit infrastructure for the visual arts in New York State. Eligible projects include convening opportunities, publications and support for ongoing collaborative relationships. Funds from this category may cover consultants' fees, administrative fees, and/or travel expenses within New York State as applicable. Applicants should confer with NYSCA staff before the registration deadline.
Requirements: Applicants must register with the Council by February 22 to be considered for funding. Also, direct payment of fees to artists is required for all activities that include artists, and New York State artists must be included in the ongoing programming of organizations. First-time applicants must contact the Visual Arts staff before the registration deadline. Applications can be found at the website and should be submitted online.
Restrictions: Requested amounts may not exceed 50% of the total project budget. This grant cannot be used to commission public art projects or support an individual artist's project.
Geographic Focus: New York
Date(s) Application is Due: Apr 1
Contact: Karen Helmerson; (212) 741-3003; khelmerson@nysca.org
Internet: http://www.nysca.org/public/guidelines/visual_arts/services.htm
Sponsor: New York State Council on the Arts
175 Varick Street
New York, NY 10014-4604

NYSCA Visual Arts: Workspace Facilities Grants 3631
Workspace Facilities grants provide support for ongoing professional workspace facilities that provide New York based visual artists with a positive working environment and enable artists to advance their work. Support in this category includes access to technical staff, use of equipment, access to other discipline-specific resources, residencies and a stipend. The goals of this grant are to assure that artists have the time to focus on the creative process and/or to experiment with new materials and techniques as well as to interact with the local community,

and have interchange with mentors and peers. Special consideration is given to organizations offering opportunities to artists at any stage of their career who have not received exposure or recognition for their work. Funds are available for direct payment of fees to participating artists, for ensuring the ongoing availability of technical expertise, and for providing materials used by artists during the residency. The applicant organization is expected to cover transportation needs and housing costs if selected artists are not within commuting distance.
Requirements: Applicants must register with the Council by February 22 to be eligible for funding. In addition, direct payment of fees to artists is required for all activities that include artists, and New York State artists must be included in the ongoing programming of an organization. First-time applicants must contact the Visual Arts staff by the registration deadline. Applications are available at the website and should be submitted online.
Restrictions: Request amounts should not exceed 50% of the total project budget. Also, Organizations cannot require or request artists to pay a fee for participation in projects funded by Visual Arts or take more than 25% of the sale price on commissions of art sales in projects funded by NYSCA. Events such as festivals and open studios are also not eligible for funding.
Geographic Focus: New York
Date(s) Application is Due: Apr 1
Contact: Karen Helmerson; (212) 741-3003; khelmerson@nysca.org
Internet: http://www.nysca.org/public/guidelines/visual_arts/workspace.htm
Sponsor: New York State Council on the Arts
175 Varick Street
New York, NY 10014-4604

Oak Foundation Child Abuse Grants 3632
The foundation awards grants worldwide to address international social and environmental issues, particularly those that have a major impact on the lives of the disadvantaged. In the Child Abuse Program, the Foundation envisions a world in which all children are protected from sexual abuse and sexual exploitation. Recognising that for many children these forms of abuse do not exist in isolation from other forms of abuse and violence, Oak supports initiatives that: directly address sexual abuse and sexual exploitation; and/or diminish other forms of abuse and violence that are related to or impact upon sexual abuse and sexual exploitation. Oak has a particular interest in promoting and supporting learning from the work of partners. This is done through the identification of learning opportunities within its existing partnerships, as well as through new partnerships specifically designed to drive learning forward across the sector.
Requirements: Within this program, Oak funds organizations in the United States, Canada, Brazil, Bulgaria, Ethiopia, Latvia, Mexico, Moldova, Netherlands, South Africa, Switzerland, Tanzania, and Uganda.
Restrictions: Oak does not provide support to individuals, and does not provide funding for scholarships or tuition assistance for undergraduate or postgraduate studies. The Foundation also does not fund religious organizations for religious purposes, election campaigns, or general fund-raising drives.
Geographic Focus: All States, Brazil, Bulgaria, Canada, Ethiopia, Latvia, Mexico, Moldova, Netherlands, South Africa, Switzerland, Tanzania, Uganda, United Kingdom
Amount of Grant: 25,000 - 2,000,000 USD
Contact: Florence Bruce, Director, Child Abuse Programs; cap@oakfnd.ch
Internet: http://www.oakfnd.org/node/1296
Sponsor: Oak Foundation
Case Postale 115 58, Avenue Louis Casai
Geneva, Cointrin 1216 Switzerland

Oak Foundation Housing and Homelessness Grants 3633
The foundation awards grants worldwide to address international social and environmental issues, particularly those that have a major impact on the lives of the disadvantaged. In the Housing and Homelessness Program, the Foundation aims to promote economic self-sufficiency, increase the availabilty and supply of affordable housing, and prevent homelessness.
Requirements: Within this program, Oak's geographic focus is currently on: Boston, New York and Philadelphia in the United States; London, Belfast, South Wales and Glasgow in the United Kingdom; and Ranchi and Kolkata in India. Projects which have national impact in the U.S. and the United Kingdom are also funded.
Restrictions: Oak does not provide support to individuals, and does not provide funding for scholarships or tuition assistance for undergraduate or postgraduate studies. The Foundation also does not fund religious organizations for religious purposes, election campaigns, or general fund-raising drives.
Geographic Focus: All States, India, United Kingdom
Amount of Grant: 25,000 - 2,000,000 USD
Contact: Amanda Beswick; hhp@oakfnd.org
Internet: http://www.oakfnd.org/node/1298
Sponsor: Oak Foundation
Case Postale 115 58, Avenue Louis Casai
Geneva, Cointrin 1216 Switzerland

Oakland Fund for Children and Youth Grants 3634
Grants support Oakland, CA, nonprofit organizations in two categories. The general grants program awards grants to organizations serving children and youth ages 0-20 in four priority areas: support for children's success in school, child health and wellness, healthy transitions to adulthood, and youth empowerment. The Community Promotions Program for Service Organizations and the Youth Violence/Drug Prevention Program award grants to organizations providing parent/caregiver support services, youth drug prevention services, or work to prevent youth violence. Annual deadline dates may vary; contact program staff for exact date.
Requirements: Oakland, CA, nonprofits serving children and youth are eligible.
Geographic Focus: California
Date(s) Application is Due: Jan 6
Amount of Grant: 20,000 - 250,000 USD
Contact: Ayako Miyashita; (510) 238-4913; amiyashita@oaklandnet.com
Internet: http://www.ofcy.org
Sponsor: East Bay Community Foundation, Oakland Fund for Children and Youth
De Domenico Building, 150 Frank H. Ogawa Plaza, Suite 4216
Oakland, CA 94612

Ober Kaler Community Grants 3635
The Ober Kaler Community Grants aid nonprofit organizations dedicated to addressing the education and welfare needs of at-risk children and youth in Washington, D.C. and Baltimore. The Grants are administered by a group of employees within the firm who then review and award the three annual grants. Applications and a list of previous recipients are available online.
Requirements: Tax-exempt 501(c)3 nonprofit organizations are eligible. Churches, synagogues, parochial, and public schools also may apply if their umbrella organizations have tax-exempt status.
Restrictions: Individuals, government agencies and religious organizations requesting funds for sectarian activities are not eligible for funding. The following are also not eligible for grant consideration: start-up funding; capital campaigns; fund raising; galas; advertising; political campaigns and supporting events/tournaments; and scholarships.
Geographic Focus: District of Columbia, Maryland
Date(s) Application is Due: Aug 1
Contact: Grants Coordinator; (410) 230-7185; fax (410) 547-0699; oberkalergrants@ober.com or info@ober.com
Internet: http://www.ober.com/our_firm/community-grants
Sponsor: Ober Kaler Grimes and Shriver
100 Light Street
Baltimore, MD 21202

OceanFirst Foundation Grants 3636
The foundation awards two types of grants (small and major) to nonprofit organizations in OceanFirst Bank's service area and its neighboring communities for programs that expand home ownership opportunities and provide access to affordable rental housing; support youth development programs to improve life options through education and work skills; support community organizations that contribute to the quality of life; and support nonprofit medical facilities. There are no application deadlines; requests are considered in the first, second, and fourth quarters of the year.
Requirements: New Jersey nonprofit organizations serving Middlesex, Monmouth, and Ocean Counties are eligible.
Geographic Focus: New Jersey
Contact: Katherine Durante; (732) 341-4676; fax (732) 473-9641; kdurante@oceanfirstfdn.org
Internet: http://www.oceanfirstfdn.org
Sponsor: OceanFirst Foundation
1415 Hooper Avenue, Suite 304
Toms River, NJ 08753

Oceanside Charitable Foundation Grants 3637
The Oceanside Charitable Foundation will focus on supporting projects that inspire and strengthen Civil Society in its communities; in particular, projects that foster community participation, consensus-building and collective problem solving in the field of children and youth programs. The Oceanside Charitable Foundation will fund Civil Society projects for school-aged (K-12) children and youth that are managed by non-profit organizations or government agencies.
Requirements: Projects for which funding is requested must serve children and/or youth in the geographical limits of the City of Oceanside.
Restrictions: The Oceanside Charitable Foundation does not make grants for: annual campaigns and fund raising events for non-specific purposes; capital campaigns for buildings or facilities; stipends for attendance at conferences; endowments or chairs; for-profit organizations or enterprises; individuals unaffiliated with a qualified fiscal sponsor; projects that promote religious or political doctrine; research projects (medical or otherwise); scholarships; or existing obligations or debt.
Geographic Focus: California
Date(s) Application is Due: Dec 18
Contact: Trudy Amstrong, Regional Manager; (619) 814-1384; trudy@sdfoundation.org
Internet: http://www.endowoceanside.org/grants.html
Sponsor: Oceanside Charitable Foundation / San Diego Foundation
2508 Historic Decatur Road, Suite 200
San Diego, CA 92106

ODKF Athletic Grants 3638
The purpose of the program is to sponsor, promote and encourage participation in state, national and international competitions in the sports of canoeing, surfing, kayaking, swimming, water polo and volleyball. Applicants (individuals, teams or events) should: provide personal history in the event; describe the applicant's training program; describe up to three years of previous competition; provide documented results of competition with records and times; provide a grant budget; and describe other forms of fundraising being pursued. Note that the Foundation awards only one grant per person, event or group per fiscal year (October through September).
Requirements: To qualify an applicant must: be a resident of Hawai'i and an American citizen; demonstrate financial need; have participated in competitive sports and can produce a record of accomplishments; and be applying for a specific upcoming event.

Geographic Focus: Hawaii
Date(s) Application is Due: Jan 15; May 15; Aug 15; Oct 15
Contact: Roberta Cullen; (808) 545-4880; fax (808) 532-0560; info@dukefoundation.org
Internet: http://www.dukefoundation.org/index.php?option=com_content&task=view&id=15&Itemid=31
Sponsor: Outrigger Duke Kahanamoku Foundation
P.O. Box 2498
Honolulu, HI 96804

Office Depot Foundation Caring is Sharing Grants 3639

One of the key ways in which the Office Depot Foundation makes a difference in the communities it serves is through in-kind donations of office products, school supplies and other items. During the past decade, the Foundation has donated millions of dollars worth of new products to charities across the United States and beyond. Through its Caring is Sharing Product Donation Program, the Foundation partners with two national non-profit organizations - Feed The Children and the National Association for the Exchange of Industrial Resources (NAEIR) - to ensure that products Office Depot no longer can use are donated to charities that serve children in need. The Caring is Sharing Program enables the non-profit recipients of product donations to stretch their budgets, thus allowing them to focus on their core programs. These donations also benefit communities by conserving resources and keeping items out of landfills that might have been thrown away in the past. An online eligibility survey and grant application can be found on the Grant Making Guidelines page. Applications are retrieved on a monthly basis and are reviewed by a committee. Applicants should allow at least twelve weeks for a response. Grant amounts will be a minimum of $50 and a maximum of $3,000 (very limited). The majority of grants issued are in the vicinity of $1,000 and are supported by in-kind donations when inventory allows.
Requirements: 501(c)3 nonprofit organizations are eligible to apply.
Restrictions: Office Depot does not contribute to individuals and does not make donations in return for advertising. In addition, grants do not support athletic teams or events; fashion shows; project graduation; capital campaigns; individual or group travel; political causes; film/video projects; or nonprofit organizations that spend more than 25 percent of their revenue on management overhead and fundraising expenses.
Geographic Focus: All States
Amount of Grant: 50 - 3,000 USD
Contact: Mary Wong; (561) 438-2895 or (561) 438-4276; mwong@jkggroup.com
Sabrina Conte, (561) 438-8752; Sabrina.conte@officedepot.com
Internet: http://devel.jkggroup.com/od/foundation/caring.asp
Sponsor: Office Depot Foundation
6600 North Military Trail
Boca Raton, FL 33496

Office Depot Foundation Disaster Relief Grants 3640

With its origins rooted in the devastation of Hurricane Andrew, today's Office Depot Foundation seizes the opportunity to help when natural disasters strike. The Foundation supports relief, recovery and rebuilding efforts in the wake of hurricanes, floods, tornadoes, earthquakes, forest fires and similar catastrophic events and works to assist community-based organizations and initiatives through grants and in-kind donations. A special grant program exists for Office Depot associates who are in need of shelter, food and clothing following natural disasters.
Restrictions: Office Depot does not contribute to individuals and does not make donations in return for advertising. In addition, grants do not support athletic teams or events; fashion shows; project graduation; capital campaigns; individual or group travel; political causes; film/video projects; or nonprofit organizations that spend more than 25 percent of their revenue on management overhead and fundraising expenses.
Geographic Focus: All States, All Countries
Contact: Mary Wong; (561) 438-2895 or (561) 438-4276; mwong@jkggroup.com
Sabrina Conte, (561) 438-8752; Sabrina.conte@officedepot.com
Internet: http://devel.jkggroup.com/od/foundation/disaster_relief.asp
Sponsor: Office Depot Foundation
6600 North Military Trail
Boca Raton, FL 33496

Ogden Codman Trust Grants 3641

The trust awards grants to eligible Massachusetts nonprofit organizations in its areas of interest, including environmental conservation, historic preservation, cultural activities, health care, and social services. Grants support special programs intended to improve the quality of life. Matching funds are sometimes requested
Requirements: Lincoln, MA, nonprofit organizations are eligible to apply.
Restrictions: General operating grants are rarely awarded.
Geographic Focus: All States
Contact: Susan Monahan; (617) 951-1108; fax (617) 542-7437; smonahan@rackemann.com
Sponsor: Ogden Codman Trust
160 Federal Street, 13th Floor
Boston, MA 02110-1700

Ohio Artists on Tour Fee Support Requests 3642

The fee support program enables Ohio's arts organizations to tap into the creative potential of Ohio artists to enrich their programming and the vitality of their communities. To learn more about the touring artists listed in the Ohio Artists on Tour Directory visit http://www.oac.state.oh.us/search/ArtistsOnTour/.
Requirements: Organizations applying for funds to present an artist listed in the directory must be incorporated in Ohio and be located in Ohio. Applicants must intend their program or project to be nonprofit. Refer to the Legal Requirements listed in the Guidelines.

Presenters may request one third of an artist/ensemble's fee including travel, lodging and outreach activities. A fully executed contract for each request must be submitted to the Ohio Arts Council. Each contract should include dates of engagement, contracted fee, number of performances and outreach activities if applicable. Each contract must be signed and dated by the presenter and artist or artist management.
Geographic Focus: Ohio
Date(s) Application is Due: May 1
Amount of Grant: 10,000 - 15,000 USD
Contact: Regional Program Coordinator; (614) 466-2613
Internet: http://www.oac.state.oh.us/grantsprogs/guidelines/guide_other.asp#OAOTfs
Sponsor: Ohio Arts Council
30 E. Broad Street, 33rd Floor
Columbus, OH 43215-3414

Ohio Arts Council Artist Express Grants 3643

The Artist Express program was created to provide an opportunity for schools or community organizations to collaborate with an artist for one, two or three days in order to explore an arts discipline or to see what it might be like to host an artist for the first time. Applicants should exhibit an interest in the work of a particular artist from the Arts Learning Artist Directory that supports collaborative learning and also have a basic level of readiness for the artist's visit. The program supports one-, two- or three-day artist visits for schools, arts organizations and other community organizations. The program is for applicants who have never hosted an OAC artist in residence or for experienced residency sponsors who want to expand learning opportunities through an art discipline that is new for the site. The current fee for an artist in the Artist Express program is $300 per day. Grants will be awarded for either $250 (one day), $500 (two days) or $750 (three days). The sponsor is responsible for the remaining $50, $100 or $150 per day as well as the artist's lunch and supplies.
Requirements: Eligible organizations include—but are not limited to—public, private, charter or parochial schools (pre-kindergarten through secondary schools) and other community organizations or social service organizations that provide arts programming. All organizations that apply to this program must have nonprofit status or nonprofit intent.
Restrictions: Applicants may receive only one Artist Express grant per year.
Geographic Focus: Ohio
Amount of Grant: 250 - 750 USD
Contact: Dia Foley, Grants Office Director; (614) 728-4429 or (614) 466-2613; fax (614) 466-4494; dia.foley@oac.state.oh.us
Internet: http://www.oac.state.oh.us/grantsprogs/guidelines/ArtistExpress.asp
Sponsor: Ohio Arts Council
30 E. Broad Street, 33rd Floor
Columbus, OH 43215-3414

Ohio Arts Council Artist in Residence Grants for Artists 3644

Professional artists in all arts disciplines who are interested in working with individuals, from young children through senior citizens, may apply to the program. A limited number of out-of-state artists are accepted into program each year. Out-of-state artists must contact the Arts Learning staff before submitting an application. Grants awarded to the residency sponsor cover two-thirds of the artist's fee. The sponsor is responsible for the remaining one-third. The total professional fee for an artist is $1,200 per week for up to eight weeks.
Requirements: The Arts Learning/Artist in Residence program application for artists is not part of OLGA. Artists applying for the Artist in Residence Roster must submit a paper application. Download the proper forms from the website.
Restrictions: The program will consider professional artists, persons who devote a major portion of their time to practicing, performing or teaching any of the arts, with strong preference to those living and working in the state of Ohio. Refer to the 'Arts Learning Residency Handbook' before applying. The handbook describes the roles each person plays in the residency and the selection process for artists.
Geographic Focus: Ohio
Date(s) Application is Due: Jul 1
Contact: Dia Foley, Grants Office Director; (614) 728-4429 or (614) 466-2613; fax (614) 466-4494; dia.foley@oac.state.oh.us
Internet: http://www.oac.state.oh.us/grantsprogs/guidelines/ArtistinResidenceArtists.asp
Sponsor: Ohio Arts Council
30 E. Broad Street, 33rd Floor
Columbus, OH 43215-3414

Ohio Arts Council Artist in Residence Grants for Sponsors 3645

The Artist in Residence program brings schools and community organizations together with artists to share in-depth, engaging, personal and sustained arts learning experiences. Using experienced artists listed in the Arts Learning Artist Directory, the Artist in Residence program offers opportunities for learners of all ages to participate in the creative process, bridge cultural differences and cultivate fresh ways of seeing, responding to and learning through the arts. Applicants should demonstrate that they value collaborative learning and show that they are prepared to host an artist in residence by providing evidence of broad-based planning efforts, flexibility, appropriate evaluation strategies and strong organizational support. The OAC also recognizes the hard work of established residency sponsors by allowing them to apply for two-year grants, reducing their administrative burden. By bringing together artists and members of the public to cultivate creativity, the Artist in Residence program transforms lives and contributes to the growth of individuals, communities and society as a whole. The Artist in Residence program (AIR) provides one- or two-year grants to place accomplished professional artists in a variety of educational and community settings to facilitate learning in, through and about the arts.
Requirements: Applicant organizations must have nonprofit status. They include, but are not limited to, public, charter or parochial schools (prekindergarten through university

level) and other community organizations such as neighborhood centers, senior centers, arts organizations, faith-based organizations, libraries and social service agencies. Sponsors must provide one-third of the artist's fee, daily lunch and supplies. Budgets for supplies typically range from $25 to $300 per week, depending on the discipline and the length of the residency. Sponsors should find free or reduced-rate housing for the artist(s). All applications to the OAC must be submitted via the online application system, OLGA. Notify the OAC about your organization's intention to apply. You are also strongly encouraged to submit a draft application to the Arts Learning Office at least 30 days before the final deadline date. To submit a draft, simply follow the instructions at the beginning of the application form through OLGA.
Restrictions: Residency-related activities designed in preparation for or in conjunction with competitions or residencies that typically are part of the ongoing program responsibilities of an organization or institution (usually higher education) are ineligible. Residencies may be planned for a minimum of two weeks to a maximum of eight weeks in length. A maximum of four classes or contact sessions per day may be scheduled with the artist in residence.
Geographic Focus: Ohio
Date(s) Application is Due: Mar 1
Amount of Grant: Up to 6,400 USD
Contact: Dia Foley, Grants Office Director; (614) 728-4429 or (614) 466-2613; fax (614) 466-4494; dia.foley@oac.state.oh.us
Internet: http://www.oac.state.oh.us/grantsprogs/guidelines/ArtistinResidence.asp
Sponsor: Ohio Arts Council
30 E. Broad Street, 33rd Floor
Columbus, OH 43215-3414

Ohio Arts Council Artists with Disabilities Access Program Grants   3646
The program is designed to help artists with disabilities move to a higher level of artistic development. Developing an artistic career is a long-term process that requires different types of assistance at different times. Therefore, funds may be used for a variety of services and materials. Applicants may request up to $500; however, most grants average $300. Applicants do not need to show a cash match.
Requirements: Artists with disabilities must: (1) be residents of Ohio, (2) have lived in the state continuously for one year, and; (3) have exhibited, performed or published work within the past three years. All applicants should read 'Legal Requirements and Ohio Arts Council Rules' before applying to this program. Because funds are limited, artists are strongly encouraged to call the OAC Accessibility Coordinator before submitting an application.
Restrictions: Equipment or supplies not related to the production or presentation of creative works will not be covered by the grant.
Geographic Focus: Ohio
Amount of Grant: Up to 500 USD
Contact: Ohio Relay Service; (800) 750-0750
Internet: http://www.oac.state.oh.us/grantsprogs/guidelines/IndividualCreativity.asp#DWhatProgramSupports
Sponsor: Ohio Arts Council
30 E. Broad Street, 33rd Floor
Columbus, OH 43215-3414

Ohio Arts Council Arts Access Program Grants   3647
The program provides funds for organizations that have never before applied for OAC funding, startup organizations, community-driven one-time projects, and organizations with budgets under $25,000. Because the OAC seeks to improve access to arts experiences for all Ohioans, this grant category was developed to provide for the unique needs typically exhibited by these applicants, including operational expenses and special project costs. Grants generally range between $500 and $3,000. The grant amount does not exceed one-third of the total cost of the arts programming or project budget. There is a 1:1 match required for all organizational grants. Cash and some documented in-kind donations are allowable as part of that match.
Requirements: All applications to the OAC must be submitted via its online application system, OLGA. No paper applications are accepted. Organizations applying are encouraged to notify an OAC staff member of their intent to apply. All applicants are strongly encouraged to submit a draft application at least 30 days before the final deadline date. Arts Access grants are available to both arts organizations and non-arts organizations with an arts component. To be eligible, an organization must fulfill one of the following criteria: Organization's most recently completed fiscal year income is under $25,000. For non-arts organizations doing arts programming, this criterion is based on the organization's arts programming budget, not the overall organizational budget; -OR- Organization is a first-time applicant to the OAC. The OAC defines a first-time applicant as an organization that has not received funding at least twice through an OAC panel process in the past five fiscal years. Note: In the event that an organization with no prior funding history receives a second year of Arts Access support during an even-numbered fiscal year, that organization will be considered a new applicant and thus eligible to apply to the Arts Access program for one additional year. All applicants should read 'Legal Requirements and Ohio Arts Council Rules' before applying to this program.
Restrictions: Organizations that receive Sustainability support are ineligible for Arts Access grants. Applicants may receive only one Arts Access grant per OAC fiscal year. See Funding Restrictions. Contact the OAC with any questions regarding eligibility.
Geographic Focus: Ohio
Date(s) Application is Due: Mar 1
Amount of Grant: 500 - 3,000 USD
Contact: Dan Katona, Director of Organizational Services; (614) 995-1662 or (614) 466-2613; fax (614) 466-4494; dan.katona@oac.state.oh.us
Internet: http://www.oac.state.oh.us/grantsprogs/guidelines/ArtsAccess.asp
Sponsor: Ohio Arts Council
30 E. Broad Street, 33rd Floor
Columbus, OH 43215-3414

Ohio Arts Council Arts Individual Excellence Awards   3648
The awards are peer recognition of creative artists for the exceptional merit of a body of work that advances or exemplifies the discipline and the larger artistic community. These awards support artists' growth and development and recognize their work in Ohio and beyond. Awards are offered in the following areas: choreography, crafts, fiction/nonfiction, poetry, playwriting/screenplays, criticism, design arts/illustration, interdisciplinary/performance art, media arts, music composition, photography and visual arts. The anonymous review process is not project-based; awards are based solely on the quality of past work. The awards are either $5,000 or $10,000. Grant amounts are determined by the review panel. Recipients are required to sign a Grant Agreement with the OAC. The awards may be used for any purpose designated by the receiving artists except to pursue a degree-granting program.
Requirements: To be eligible to apply for an award, an artist must be a resident of Ohio, have lived in the state continuously for one year before the deadline and remain an Ohio resident during the term of the award. The Ohio Arts Council defines an Ohio resident as someone who spends at least eight months of the year living and working in Ohio. The Board retains the right to determine if Ohio is an applicant's primary state of residence. All applicants should read 'Legal Requirements and Ohio Arts Council Rules' before applying to this program.
Restrictions: An applicant may not be a student enrolled in any degree-or certificate-granting program. An applicant must be a creative artist; performing artists are ineligible to apply.
Geographic Focus: Ohio
Date(s) Application is Due: Sep 1
Amount of Grant: 5,000 - 10,000 USD
Contact: Kathy Signorino, Program Officer; (614) 728-6140 or (614) 466-2613; fax (614) 466-4494; kathy.signorino@oac.state.oh.us
Internet: http://www.oac.state.oh.us/grantsprogs/guidelines/IndividualCreativity.asp#IWhatProgramSupports
Sponsor: Ohio Arts Council
30 E. Broad Street, 33rd Floor
Columbus, OH 43215-3414

Ohio Arts Council Arts Innovation Program Grants   3649
The OAC believes that encouraging Ohio's arts and cultural institutions to innovate, be original and take calculated risks in their programming and service delivery sustains Ohio's communities and citizens. These grants are designed to support proposals including special, one-time projects, development of new projects for new constituencies, experimental program designs and pioneering initiatives being offered for the first time. Eligible activities can include, and are not limited to: One-time program from a local arts center that features a new or contemporary art form, such as digital media design or electronic music composition; Collaborative project, featuring artists with disabilities, that involves art-making and includes the community in showcases, design and instruction; Series designed to reach new audiences that features performances in nontraditional spaces such as faith-based institutions and shopping plazas; Residency project by a local arts council to bring an internationally recognized artist to the community to work with students and adult learners. Grants are awarded for up to one year, and are made in amounts of $5,000, $10,000, $15,000 and $20,000 and require a 1:1 cash match.
Requirements: All applicants are strongly encouraged to submit a draft application at least 30 days before the final deadline date. Arts Innovation grants are designed to support projects that are truly progressive and that represent a departure from the programming norm for their institutions. All nonprofit arts, cultural and community-based organizations that demonstrate a strong commitment to using the arts effectively and authentically in their programming may apply to this program. However, due to limited funding, small, emerging, and midsized arts and cultural organizations generally are given priority to receive these funds. Applicants should call the OAC before submitting an application. Only new projects, or direct continuations of previously funded Arts Innovation projects, are eligible for funding in this program. All applicants should read 'Legal Requirements and Ohio Arts Council Rules' before applying to this program. Applications must be submitted via its online application system, OLGA. No paper applications are accepted.
Restrictions: All applicants should read Legal Requirements and Ohio Arts Council Rules and Grants Process for Organizations before applying to this program.
Geographic Focus: Ohio
Amount of Grant: 5,000 - 20,000 USD
Contact: Dan Katona, Director of Community Development; (614) 995-1662 or (614) 466-2613; fax (614) 466-4494; dan.katona@oac.state.oh.us
Internet: http://www.oac.state.oh.us/grantsprogs/guidelines/ArtsInnovation.asp
Sponsor: Ohio Arts Council
30 E. Broad Street, 33rd Floor
Columbus, OH 43215-3414

Ohio Arts Council Arts Partnership Grants   3650
The Arts Partnership program provides one or two year grants to support activities that enhance the quality of and access to learning in the arts for learners of all ages, backgrounds, experience levels and abilities. Effective and sustainable arts learning projects and programs are achieved through strong collaborations or partnerships. In this category, priority is given to collaborative efforts that emphasize skill acquisition and direct participation in and access to quality arts experiences. Additional priorities include fostering commitment to arts learning in school and community settings and supporting research, evaluation, and scholarship about teaching and learning in the arts. Grant amounts in this program generally do not exceed 50% of the project budget. The Arts Partnership program requires a 1:1 cash match. Applicants may request a minimum of $4,000 and as much as $25,000 per year.
Requirements: Collaborating organizations and individual organizations are encouraged to apply. These nonprofit organizations include, but are not limited to, public, private, charter or parochial schools (prekindergarten through university level), and other community

organizations with arts programming, such as arts organizations, neighborhood centers, senior centers, libraries, faith-based organizations, adult or juvenile detention centers and social service agencies. All applicants must read the Legal Requirements and Ohio Arts Council Rules (available at website) before applying. Organizations should inform the OAC of their intent to apply no later than six weeks before the application deadline. This can be done through an email, phone call or letter to the appropriate coordinator or during a visit to the OAC offices; please call for an appointment. Notification should identify the program and give a contact person's name, phone numbers and a title or brief description of the project or program. All Arts Partnership grants require at least a 1:1 cash match.
Restrictions: Organizations applying must be incorporated in Ohio and/or be located in Ohio. Applicants must intend their program or project to be nonprofit.
Geographic Focus: Ohio
Date(s) Application is Due: Mar 1
Amount of Grant: Up to 20,000 USD
Contact: Dia Foley, Grants Office Director; (614) 728-4429 or (614) 466-2613; fax (614) 466-4494; dia.foley@oac.state.oh.us
Internet: http://www.oac.state.oh.us/grantsprogs/guidelines/ArtsPartnership.asp
Sponsor: Ohio Arts Council
30 E. Broad Street, 33rd Floor
Columbus, OH 43215-3414

Ohio Arts Council Building Cultural Diversity Initiative Grants 3651
The Building Cultural Diversity Initiative supports the development and viability of culturally diverse arts organizations whose mission, programs, and staff are representative of the Black/African American, Appalachian, Asian/Pacific Islander, Hispanic/Latino, American Indian, or other culturally specific perspectives. The program also supports arts organizations in the training of emerging minority arts administrators. Because the OAC seeks to ensure that Ohio has a strong culturally diverse arts sector, this program was developed to address the wide range of needs faced by diverse arts groups, such as operational expenses, leadership development, organizational planning, program development, and special project costs. Funded activities may include, but are not limited to: long-range or strategic planning sessions; attendance or presentation at a conference, workshop, or seminar; development of fiscal management systems; development of fundraising or marketing plans; creation/expansion of a Web site; equipment purchase (not to exceed $500); facility rental; assistance in becoming a 501(c)3 organization; artists' fees or assistance in the creation or presentation of artistic work; professionally significant internships (10-16 weeks) for emerging minority arts leaders in all areas of arts administration; and seed funding for a new staff position. Applications must be received no later than 5 p.m. on the second Friday of any given month.
Requirements: Building Cultural Diversity grants are available to both established and emerging culturally diverse arts organizations and non-arts organizations with an arts component. Organizations must have a non-profit status or be non-profit in intent. Due to limited funding, priority generally will be given to small, emerging, and mid-sized arts and cultural organizations and organizations that have shown a commitment over time to arts and cultural programming.
Restrictions: All applicants should read Legal Requirements and Ohio Arts Council Rules and Grants Process for Organizations before applying to this program.
Geographic Focus: Ohio
Amount of Grant: 5,000 - 20,000 USD
Contact: Katherine Eckstrand, Director of Community Development; (614) 728-4467 or (614) 466-2613; fax (614) 466-4494; katherine.eckstrand@oac.state.oh.us
Internet: http://www.oac.state.oh.us/grantsprogs/guidelines/ArtsInnovation.asp
Sponsor: Ohio Arts Council
30 E. Broad Street, 33rd Floor
Columbus, OH 43215-3414

Ohio Arts Council Capacity Building Grants for Organizations and Communities 3652
Capacity building funds are designed to strengthen Ohio's nonprofit arts and cultural sector by helping applicants improve internal governance and leadership, cultivate strategic community linkages, and develop financial and human resources for long-term stability. Building organizational capacity is a long-term, evolutionary process that organizations must engage in purposefully. The program provides funding for work in three areas of capacity: (1) Organizational Governance and Leadership; (2) Strategic Community Linkages; and, (3) Assets and Resources Development. For other topics appropriate to your organization, contact and discuss with the Program Coordinator. Grants for capacity building generally range from $500 to $5,000. Organizations must show a 1:1 match, half of which may be from allowable, appropriate in-kind donations.
Requirements: All nonprofit arts, cultural and community-based organizations in Ohio that demonstrate a strong commitment to using the arts effectively and authentically in their programming may apply to this program. However, due to limited funding, small, emerging, and mid-sized arts and cultural organizations generally are given priority. Call the OAC before submitting an application. Applications must be received in OLGA (online grant application system) no later than 5 p.m. on the second Friday of any given month. Because effective capacity building activities require careful planning, applications will be accepted only through the second Friday of April (for activities occurring May 15-June 30), except in rare circumstances. Beginning June 1 of each year, applications will be accepted for the next fiscal year.
Geographic Focus: Ohio
Amount of Grant: 500 - 5,000 USD
Contact: Katherine Eckstrand, Director of Community Development; (614) 728-4467 or (614) 466-2613; fax (614) 466-4494; katherine.eckstrand@oac.state.oh.us
Internet: http://www.oac.state.oh.us/grantsprogs/guidelines/CapacityBuilding.asp#top
Sponsor: Ohio Arts Council
30 E. Broad Street, 33rd Floor
Columbus, OH 43215-3414

Ohio Arts Council International Partnership Grants 3653
The program provides a limited number of small grants to assist Ohio nonprofit arts and cultural organizations and universities and colleges to develop exemplary international arts projects and innovative partnerships in countries where the OAC has signed agreements or established collaborative partnership projects. OAC's international funding priorities are focused on Argentina, Chile, India, Israel, Japan, Mexico, Austria, the Czech Republic, Germany, Hungary, Korea and Estonia. The list of partnerships may change from year to year. Contact the Ohio Arts Council for the most current list of partnership agreements. An organization may request up to $10,000; a 1:1 match is required.
Requirements: Ohio nonprofit arts and cultural organizations and universities and colleges. All applicants should read 'Legal Requirements and Ohio Arts Council Rules' and 'Grants Process for Organizations' before applying to this category. Both documents are available at the website.
Restrictions: Grants are paid after the grant activities are complete.
Geographic Focus: Ohio
Contact: Julie S. Henahan, Executive Director; (614) 728-4445 or (614) 466-2613; fax (614) 466-4494; julie.henahan@oac.state.oh.us
Internet: http://www.oac.state.oh.us/grantsprogs/guidelines/International.asp
Sponsor: Ohio Arts Council
30 E. Broad Street, 33rd Floor
Columbus, OH 43215-3414

Ohio Arts Council Sustainability Program Grants 3654
Funding from this program supports organizations that provide essential arts programming to their community and are integral to its cultural legacy. Through direct financial support of ongoing programming by arts, non-arts and cultural organizations, the OAC sustains the vitality of Ohio economically, educationally and culturally. The program allows organizations to plan and conduct ongoing arts programs - either a full year of activities or recurring projects - in both traditional spaces (galleries, concert halls, theaters, museums) and nontraditional venues (hospitals, shopping malls, retirement centers, places of worship). Grants are based on the arts program's budget (see website for formula), not the organization's total budget. Indirect costs may be shown as in-kind but not as part of the cash match. The application deadline is for odd-numbered years only.
Requirements: This funding program provides two-year grants to organizations for annual arts programming or a recurring single project or activity. Repeated events, such as a yearly festival, are eligible. The program supports organizations that offer broad-based arts programming in any discipline (multiarts, performing arts, literature, traditional arts, visual arts) that is produced and presented by nonprofit arts and cultural organizations, other nonprofit or government entities, and colleges or universities that offer arts programming. Applicants to the Sustainability program must have received OAC funds at least twice in the past five years. This previous support must have come from an OAC funding program that evaluated and scored the application through a panel process. First-time applicants to the OAC and organizations with budgets of $25,000 or less should refer to the Arts Access Program. Applicants may be: nonprofit arts and cultural organizations; social service agencies; other nonprofit organizations that provide arts programming; educational organizations that demonstrate a commitment to arts programming in a larger community setting; non-arts organizations such as colleges and universities, government entities and social service organizations may apply to the Sustainability program only for their ongoing arts component or programming.
Restrictions: Please read Legal Requirements and Ohio Arts Council Rules and Grants Process for Organizations before applying to this program. Both documents are available for download at the website.
Geographic Focus: Ohio
Date(s) Application is Due: Feb 1
Contact: Dan Katona, Director of Organizational Services; (614) 995-1662 or (614) 466-2613; fax (614) 466-4494; dan.katona@oac.state.oh.us
Internet: http://www.oac.state.oh.us/grantsprogs/guidelines/Sustainability.asp
Sponsor: Ohio Arts Council
30 E. Broad Street, 33rd Floor
Columbus, OH 43215-3414

Ohio Arts Council Traditional Arts Apprenticeship Grants 3655
This program strives to keep alive Ohio's traditional and folk arts by supporting collaborations between master artists and dedicated apprentices who are preserving their ethnic, occupational, regional group, community, or family traditions that have been passed down for generations. The program provides support for a master artist and one or more apprentices to work together in an intensive individual study program that preserves traditional art forms of Ohio residents. Examples of traditional arts include, but are not limited to, Polish paper cutting, blues music, stone carving, Appalachian fiddling, embroidery, Laotian khene playing, icon painting, Irish step dancing, woodcarving, Chicano corridor singing, quilting, tamburitza music and polka. Grants are up to $2,500 for a master and apprentice(s) to work together, regardless of the number of apprentices. The master artist's fee should make up at least $1,250 of the budget, with some funds for supplies and necessary.
Requirements: Applicants are requested to submit an Intent to Apply notice and are strongly encouraged to submit a draft application at least 30 days before the actual deadline date. The master artist is the eligible applicant and practices an art form that represents and has been preserved by their ethnic, occupational or regional group, or within their community or family for generations. Apprentices should demonstrate a desire to learn by practical experience from a master artist. The Ohio Arts Council gives preference to apprentices who wish to study their own traditions. Apprentices must live in Ohio. Master artists may be from another state if there is no suitable master living near the apprentice. Masters and apprentices must be U.S. citizens or permanent resident aliens and must have lived in the United States for at least eight months before the application deadline date. All applicants should read 'Legal Requirements and Ohio Arts Council Rules' before applying to this program.

Restrictions: Funds are not available for apprentices who wish to travel and study with master artists who live outside the United States.
Geographic Focus: Ohio
Date(s) Application is Due: Jan 15
Amount of Grant: Up to 4,000 USD
Contact: Kathy Signorino, Program Officer; (614) 728-6140 or (614) 466-2613; fax (614) 466-4494; kathy.signorino@oac.state.oh.us
Internet: http://www.oac.state.oh.us/grantsprogs/guidelines/IndividualCreativity.asp#TWhatProgramSupports
Sponsor: Ohio Arts Council
30 E. Broad Street, 33rd Floor
Columbus, OH 43215-3414

Ohio County Community Foundation Board of Directors Grants 3656
The Ohio County Community Foundation may, on occasion, find it necessary to issue discretionary small grants from the unrestricted funds outside the Grants Committee recommendations and full Board approval. These grants are on a first come, first serve basis until allotted funding for the current calendar year has been exhausted. Each grant application will be reviewed after submission to ensure the application is complete and the organization is eligible to make application. Specifically, Board of Directors Grants are given in an amount not to exceed $300 per application with a maximum of $600 per year per organization and a maximum of four Board Grants per year.
Requirements: Grants will only be awarded for projects and programs that benefit the residents of Ohio County. Applicants must qualify as an exempt organization under the IRS Code 501(c), or be sponsored by such organizations, or qualify as a governmental or educational entity or possess similar attributes per IRS Code Section 509(a). Grants applied for brick and mortar projects must be only for charitable purposes, to further the mission of a public charity.
Restrictions: No grants will be made solely to individuals but can be made for the benefit of certain individuals for such purposes as scholarships and special programs through educational institutions and other sponsoring recipient organizations. In addition, no grants will be made specifically for sectarian religious purposes but can be made to religious organizations for general community programs.
Geographic Focus: Indiana
Amount of Grant: Up to 300 USD
Contact: Stephanie Scott; (812) 438-9401; fax (812) 438-9488; sscott@occfrisingsun.com
Internet: http://www.occfrisingsun.com/CombineApplicationSmallGrants.htm
Sponsor: Ohio County Community Foundation
591 Smart Drive, P.O. Box 170
Rising Sun, IN 47040

Ohio County Community Foundation Conference/Training Grants 3657
The Ohio County Community Foundation may, on occasion, find it necessary to issue discretionary small grants from the unrestricted funds outside the Grants Committee recommendations and full Board approval. These grants are on a first come, first serve basis until allotted funding for the current calendar year has been exhausted. Conference/Training Grants will be in an amount not to exceed $150 per application with a maximum of $300 per year per organization and a maximum of two Conference/Training Grants per year. This grant may be used for the purpose of training and/or attending conferences which support and enhance the goals of non-profit organizations serving Ohio County.
Requirements: Grants will only be awarded for projects and programs that benefit the residents of Ohio County. Applicants must qualify as an exempt organization under the IRS Code 501(c), or be sponsored by such organizations, or qualify as a governmental or educational entity or possess similar attributes per IRS Code Section 509(a). Grants applied for brick and mortar projects must be only for charitable purposes, to further the mission of a public charity.
Restrictions: No grants will be made solely to individuals but can be made for the benefit of certain individuals for such purposes as scholarships and special programs through educational institutions and other sponsoring recipient organizations. In addition, no grants will be made specifically for sectarian religious purposes but can be made to religious organizations for general community programs.
Geographic Focus: Indiana
Amount of Grant: Up to 150 USD
Contact: Stephanie Scott; (812) 438-9401; fax (812) 438-9488; sscott@occfrisingsun.com
Internet: http://www.occfrisingsun.com/CombineApplicationSmallGrants.htm
Sponsor: Ohio County Community Foundation
591 Smart Drive, P.O. Box 170
Rising Sun, IN 47040

Ohio County Community Foundation Grants 3658
The Ohio County Community Foundation is charged with assisting donors in building, managing, and distributing a lasting source of charitable funds for the good of Ohio County. The Foundation funds projects and programs for economic development, education, human services, cultural affairs, and health. The Foundation will: offer grant awards that strive to anticipate the changing needs of the community and be flexible in responding to them; focus on those types of grants which will have the greatest benefit per dollar granted; encourage the participation of other contributions by using matching, challenge and other grant techniques; offer funding that closely relates and coordinates with the programs of other sources for funding, such as the government, other foundations, and associations; induces grant recipients to achieve certain objectives such as becoming more efficient, increasing fundraising capabilities, and delivering better products; and consider grants in the form of technical assistance and staff assisted special projects which are intended to respond to a variety of needs in the county.
Requirements: Grants will be made only to organizations whose programs benefit the residents of Ohio County. The Foundation uses the following criteria when evaluating proposals: is there an established need for the program or project; are there other more compatible sources for potential funding; does the Foundation have adequate sources to respond: and does the grant support a charitable purpose.
Restrictions: Funding is not available to individuals. Grants are not made to enable individuals or groups to take trips except where there are special circumstances which will benefit the larger community.
Geographic Focus: Indiana
Date(s) Application is Due: Apr 15; Oct 15
Amount of Grant: Up to 3,000 USD
Contact: Stephanie Scott; (812) 438-9401; fax (812) 438-9488; sscott@occfrisingsun.com
Internet: http://www.occfrisingsun.com/GrantApplicationNew.htm
Sponsor: Ohio County Community Foundation
591 Smart Drive, P.O. Box 170
Rising Sun, IN 47040

Ohio County Community Foundation Junior Grants 3659
The Ohio County Community Foundation may find it necessary to issue junior grants from the unrestricted funds outside the Grants Committee recommendations on occasion. This may occur if an occasion arises that would not require full committee and board approval. Each Junior Grant Application will be reviewed, after submission, by the Program Coordinator to ensure the application is complete and the organization is eligible to make application. Amounts should not to exceed $500, with a maximum of $500 per year per organization or a maximum of two Junior Grants per year totaling $500.
Requirements: The Foundation will seek and accept Junior Grant Applications from area non-profit organizations whose programs benefit the residents of Ohio County. Applications must be approved by a majority of the Foundation's Future Grant Committee. Applicants must qualify as an exempt organization under the IRS Code 501(c), or be sponsored by such organizations, or qualify as a governmental or educational entity or possess similar attributes per IRS Code Section 509(a). Grants applied for brick and mortar projects must be only for charitable purposes, to further the mission of a public charity.
Restrictions: No grants will be made solely to individuals but can be made for the benefit of certain individuals for such purposes as scholarships and special programs through educational institutions and other sponsoring recipient organizations. In addition, no grants will be made specifically for sectarian religious purposes but can be made to religious organizations for general community programs.
Geographic Focus: Indiana
Contact: Stephanie Scott; (812) 438-9401; fax (812) 438-9488; sscott@occfrisingsun.com
Internet: http://www.occfrisingsun.com/juniorgrantapplication.html
Sponsor: Ohio County Community Foundation
591 Smart Drive, P.O. Box 170
Rising Sun, IN 47040

Ohio County Community Foundation Mini-Grants 3660
The Ohio County Community Foundation assists donors in building, managing and distributing a lasting source of charitable funds for the good of Ohio County. The Foundation Mini-Grants fund projects and programs for economic development, education, human services, cultural affairs, and health. Amounts do not exceed $100 per application with a maximum of $200 per year per organization and a maximum of four mini-grants per year. These grants are on a first come, first serve basis until allotted funding for the current calendar year has been exhausted.
Requirements: Grants will be made only to organizations whose programs benefit the residents of Ohio County. The Foundation uses the following criteria when evaluating proposals: is there an established need for the program or project; are there other more compatible sources for potential funding; does the Foundation have adequate sources to respond; and does the grant support a charitable purpose.
Restrictions: Funding is not available to individuals. Grants are not made to enable individuals or groups to take trips except where there are special circumstances which will benefit the larger community.
Geographic Focus: Indiana
Amount of Grant: Up to 100 USD
Contact: Stephanie Scott; (812) 438-9401; fax (812) 438-9488; sscott@occfrisingsun.com
Internet: http://www.occfrisingsun.com/CombineApplicationSmallGrants.htm
Sponsor: Ohio County Community Foundation
591 Smart Drive, P.O. Box 170
Rising Sun, IN 47040

Ohio River Border Initiative Grants 3661
The Ohio River Border Initiative (ORBI) is a joint project of the West Virginia Commission on the Arts and the Ohio Arts Council to support the arts community in the Ohio River valley. ORBI's programs are open to artists, arts groups and community arts programs in all Ohio and West Virginia counties that touch the Ohio River. These counties are Wayne, Cabell, Mason, Jackson, Wood, Pleasants, Tyler, Wetzel, Marshall, Ohio, Brooke and Hancock in West Virginia, and Lawrence, Gallia, Meigs, Athens, Washington, Monroe, Belmont, Jefferson and Columbiana in Ohio. The program offers grants to fund projects that encourage active collaborations among artists, communities and/or organizations on both sides of the Ohio River. The maximum grant award is $3,000 to any one group or artist.
Geographic Focus: Ohio
Date(s) Application is Due: Feb 1
Amount of Grant: Up to 3,000 USD
Contact: Bill Howley, ORBI Project Director; (304) 655-8255; billhowley@hughes.net
Internet: http://www.oac.state.oh.us/grantsprogs/guidelines/guide_other.asp#ohioriver
Sponsor: Ohio Arts Council
30 E. Broad Street, 33rd Floor
Columbus, OH 43215-3414

Ohio Valley Foundation Grants 3662

The foundation awards grants to Ohio nonprofit organizations in its areas of interest, including arts and culture, community service organizations, education, and youth development. Types of support include building construction/renovation and capital campaigns. The board meets quarterly to review grant applications.
Requirements: Ohio 501(c)3 nonprofit organizations are eligible. Preference is given to requests in the greater Cincinnati, OH, area. To begin the application process submit a letter of inquiry to the Foundation. After review, full proposals will be accepted by invitation only. Organizations will be given an Ohio Common Grant Application Form to complete. There is no deadline date for submitting these applications.
Restrictions: Grants do not support religious organizations for religious activities, individuals, endowments, or operating budgets.
Geographic Focus: Ohio
Amount of Grant: 10,000 - 30,000 USD
Contact: Heidi B. Jark, Vice President, c/o Fifth Third Bank; (513) 534-7001
Sponsor: Ohio Valley Foundation
38 Fountain Square Plaza, MD 1090CA
Cincinnati, OH 45263-0001

OJJDP Gang Prevention Coordination Assistance Program Grants 3663

The OJJDP FY Gang Prevention Coordination Assistance Program provides funding for localities to enhance coordination of Federal, state, and local resources in support of community partnerships implementing the following antigang strategies: primary prevention, secondary prevention, gang intervention, and targeted gang enforcement. This application must be submitted through Grants.gov. All applications are due by 8:00 p.m., Eastern Time, on March 4.
Requirements: Applicants are limited to public agencies (including state agencies, units of local government, public universities and colleges, and tribal governments) and private organizations (including faith-based and community organizations).
Geographic Focus: All States
Date(s) Application is Due: Mar 4
Contact: Stephanie Rapp, Program Manager; (202) 514-9123; stephanie.rapp@usdoj.gov
Internet: http://ojjdp.ncjrs.org/funding/FundingDetail.asp?fi=116
Sponsor: Office of Juvenile Justice and Delinquency Prevention
810 7th Street NW
Washington, DC 20531

OJJDP National Mentoring Program Grants 3664

This solicitation invites eligible applicants to propose the enhancement or expansion of initiatives that will assist in the development and maturity of community programs to provide mentoring services to high-risk populations that are underserved due to location, shortage of mentors, special physical or mental challenges of the targeted population, or other analogous situations identified by the community in need of mentoring services. The due date for applying for funding under this announcement is 8:00 p.m., Eastern Time, February 25. Applicants are urged to submit their application at least 72 hours prior to the due date of the application to allow time to receive the validation message and to correct any problems that may have caused rejection.
Requirements: Applicants are limited to national organizations, including faith-based and community nonprofit organizations.
Geographic Focus: All States
Date(s) Application is Due: Feb 25
Contact: Eric Stansbury, Program Manager; (202) 305-1826; Eric.Stansbury@usdoj.gov
Internet: http://ojjdp.ncjrs.org/funding/FundingDetail.asp?fi=111
Sponsor: Office of Juvenile Justice and Delinquency Prevention
810 7th Street NW
Washington, DC 20531

OJJDP Tribal Juvenile Accountability Discretionary Grants 3665

OJJDP will award funds under its Tribal Juvenile Accountability Discretionary Grants (Tribal JADG) Program to federally recognized tribal communities to develop and implement programs that hold AI/AN youth accountable for delinquent behavior and strengthen tribal juvenile justice systems. The due date for applying for funding under this announcement is 8:00 p.m. E.T., March 12. Applicants are urged to submit their application at least 72 hours prior to the due date of the application to allow time to receive the validation message and to correct any problems that may have caused rejection.
Requirements: Applicants are limited to federally recognized tribal governments.
Geographic Focus: All States
Date(s) Application is Due: Mar 12
Contact: Brecht Donoghue; (202) 305-1270; Brecht.Donoghue@usdoj.gov
Internet: http://ojjdp.ncjrs.org/funding/FundingDetail.asp?fi=117
Sponsor: Office of Juvenile Justice and Delinquency Prevention
810 7th Street NW
Washington, DC 20531

Oklahoma City Community Programs and Grants 3666

The community foundation functions to enhance the quality of life in Oklahoma by awarding grants to nonprofits in its areas of interest, including arts and cultural programs, education, health care, health associations, and human services. Types of support include general operating support, continuing support, annual campaigns, building/renovation, equipment, emergency funds, program development, seed grants, fellowships, scholarship funds, research, and matching funds. The grants assist organizations with activities that provide new or expanded services to the community in response to new opportunities and changing circumstances. The community foundation views its role as a partner with other organizations and regards contributions and participation by other individuals and groups as an essential element in grant activities. Especially encouraged are programs and services that are oriented toward the entire population and are not restricted only to those people who live in a particular geographic location or who are members of a particular organization. The foundation encourages nonprofit organizations to cooperate and pool their resources to meet community needs. The use of volunteers as a significant program component is considered favorably as is active participation of the agency's board of directors and a broad base of financial support in the community. Grants are generally made for a specified time period and are nonrenewable. Applications and guidelines for each program are available on the Web site.
Requirements: 501(c)3 nonprofit organizations serving the greater Oklahoma City area, and programs that benefit persons living in the greater Oklahoma City metropolitan area, are eligible.
Restrictions: Grants are not awarded to individuals or to benefit specific individuals. No faxed or emailed proposals are accepted.
Geographic Focus: Oklahoma
Contact: Grants Manager; (405) 235-5603; fax (405) 235-5612; info@occf.org
Internet: http://www.occf.org/occf/community_programs/index.php
Sponsor: Oklahoma City Community Foundation
P.O. Box 1146
Oklahoma City, OK 73103-1146

Oleonda Jameson Trust Grants 3667

The trust awards grants to New Hampshire nonprofit organizations in its areas of interest, including arts/culture, community foundations, children and youth, health care, housing, social sciences, human services, federated giving programs and, social services. Types of support include capital campaigns, building construction/renovation, equipment acquisition, emergency funds, and scholarship funds. There are no application forms or deadlines. The board meets in March, June, September, and December.
Requirements: New Hampshire nonprofit organizations are eligible. Requests from Concord nonprofits receive preference.
Restrictions: Grants do not support endowments or general operating expenses.
Geographic Focus: New Hampshire
Amount of Grant: 1,000 - 60,000 USD
Contact: Grants Management Officer; (603) 226-0400
Sponsor: Oleonda Jameson Trust
11 South Main Street, Suite 500
Concord, NH 03301-4945

Olga Sipolin Children's Fund Grants 3668

The Olga Sipolin Children's Fund was established in 1998 to provide for the basic needs of underserved children. Preference is given to charitable organizations that have a direct impact on the social welfare of children through the provision of housing, clothing, food, medical care, or education. Grants from the Sipolin Children's Fund are one year in duration. Applicants must apply online at the grant website. Applicants are strongly encouraged to do the following before applying: review the downloadable state application procedures for additional helpful information and clarifications; review the downloadable online-application guidelines at the grant website; review the fund's funding history (link is available from the grant website); review the online application questions in advance; and review the list of required attachments. These will generally include: a list of board members, financial statements (audited, reviewed, or compiled by independent auditor); an organization summary; a list of other funding sources; an IRS Determination letter; and other required documents. All attachments must be uploaded in the online application as PDF, Word, or Excel files. The deadline for application to the Olga Sipolin Children's Fund is 11:59 p.m. on November 1. Applicants will be notified of grant decisions by letter within two to three months after the proposal deadline.
Requirements: Applicants must have 501(c)3 tax-exempt status.
Restrictions: Grant requests for capital projects are generally not considered. Applicants will not be awarded a grant for more than 3 consecutive years. The fund does not support requests from individuals, organizations attempting to influence policy through direct lobbying, or any political campaigns.
Geographic Focus: Connecticut
Date(s) Application is Due: Nov 1
Contact: Kate Kerchaert; (860) 657-7016; kate.kerchaert@baml.com
Internet: https://www.bankofamerica.com/philanthropic/fn_search.action
Sponsor: Olga Sipolin Children's Fund
200 Glastonbury Boulevard, Suite # 200, CT2-545-02-05
Glastonbury, CT 06033-4056

Olin Corporation Charitable Trust Grants 3669

The charitable trust supports nonprofits in company-operating areas. Grants focus on three priority categories: education, with a science and technology emphasis; programs that include Olin employees as volunteers and that impact communities in which Olin employees work and live; and conservation, environmental education, and environmental research. Types of support include general operating budgets, continuing support, annual campaigns, seed money, emergency funds, building funds, equipment, land acquisition, special projects, research, publications, conferences and seminars, internships, scholarship funds, employee-related scholarships, fellowships, and employee matching gifts. US-based nonprofits with an international focus are supported primarily through matching gifts. There are no application deadlines. Applicants should submit a letter of request. The board meets in January to consider requests.
Requirements: Support is directed primarily to communities where Olin has a major employee presence.
Restrictions: Grants are not awarded to individuals or for endowments.

Geographic Focus: All States
Amount of Grant: 50 - 50,000 USD
Contact: Program Contact; (314) 480-1400
Internet: http://www.olin.com/about/charitable.asp
Sponsor: Olin Corporation Charitable Trust
190 Carondelet Plaza, Suite 1530
Clayton, MO 63105-3443

Olive B. Cole Foundation Grants 3670
The Foundation provides funding to organizations located within or serving residents of DeKalb, LaGrange, Noble and Steuben counties in Indiana. Job creation, entrepreneurism, and education are areas of interest. Applicants may submit a one-page preliminary letter which includes a description of the organization, the proposed project, and the funding needed. Some applicants may be asked to submit a full proposal. All applicants will receive a written response to their funding request.
Requirements: Indiana nonprofit organizations or government entities are eligible.
Restrictions: Faxed requests will not be considered. Loans or cash grants are not made to individuals. Normally the Foundation does not make grants to religious organizations, to endowments, or to national fund drives. The Foundation does not encourage grants where the Foundation is asked to fund the entire project.
Geographic Focus: Indiana
Amount of Grant: 100 - 120,000 USD
Contact: Maclyn T. Parker, President; (260) 436-2182
Internet: http://colefoundationonline.org/Guidlines.html
Sponsor: Olive B. Cole Foundation
6207 Constitution Drive
Fort Wayne, IN 46804

Olive Smith Browning Charitable Trust Grants 3671
Established in 1991, the Olive Smith Browning Charitable Trust offers funding to organizations located in the Twin Falls, Idaho, region. Its primary fields of interest have been: the arts; education; and health care. There are no specified application formats or annual deadlines, so applicants should begin by sending their proposal overview directly to the trustee in charge of managing the trust. Most recent grants have ranged from $1,000 to $8,000.
Requirements: Applicants should be 501(c)3 organizations either located in, or serving the residents of, Twin Falls, Idaho.
Restrictions: No grants are given to individuals.
Geographic Focus: Idaho
Amount of Grant: 1,000 - 8,000 USD
Contact: Carla Colfack, Trust Officer; (208) 736-1217 or (888) 730-4933
Sponsor: Olive Smith Browning Charitable Trust
P.O. Box 53456, MAC S4101-22G
Phoenix, AZ 85072-3456

Onan Family Foundation Grants 3672
The Onan Family Foundation is a private philanthropy located in Minneapolis, Minnesota making grants to tax-exempt organizations in the areas of education, social welfare, cultural and civic affairs, and religion. Special interest is given to programs that are centered in Minneapolis and Saint Paul, Minnesota. Grant requests should be sent to the foundation well in advance of the semi-annual board of trustees meetings in May and October. Grant requests should be made using the Minnesota Common Grant.
Requirements: The Onan Family Foundation makes grants only to pre-selected organizations located in Minneapolis and Saint Paul, Minnesota, and does not accept unsolicited grant requests. The purpose of this statement is twofold: 1) Information to those from whom we have requested a grant proposal; 2) A reminder to our ongoing recipients that we want a request from them each year.
Restrictions: Grants are not made to individuals or to organizations that attempt to influence legislation, carry on propaganda, or participate or intervene in a New York political campaign. Grants for endowment purposes, to capital funds, or for trips or tours are generally not supported.
Geographic Focus: Minnesota
Contact: Patricia Onan, Executive Director; (612) 544-4702; office@onanfamily.org
Internet: http://www.onanfamily.org/~onanfami/index.php?id=9
Sponsor: Onan Family Foundation
P.O. Box 50667
Minneapolis, MN 55405

OneFamily Foundation Grants 3673
The foundation awards grants to eligible Washington nonprofit organizations working to improve the lives of women living in poverty and at-risk youth, for support services for abused women, and for efforts to end sexual abuse against women and children. Consideration is given to programs that provide training and skills development to low-income women and services providing basic needs such as shelter, counseling, food, and childcare; educational and mentoring projects to help prevent teen pregnancy; job-training programs for youth and school/community-based programs to help low-income youth complete their education; parenting, training, and education programs to help break the cycle of family violence; shelters and services to support abused and neglected children and women; and hands-on programs to encourage philanthropy among children and youth. Grants will support operating expenses, special projects, and minor capital costs necessary to assure the success of a funded project. For general grants, two-page preapplication letters are due on the third Friday in March, July, and November and final proposals are due the second Friday in January, May, and September. Annual deadlines may vary; contact program staff for exact dates.
Requirements: Nonprofit 501(c)3 organizations based in King County, Snohomish County, or the Olympic Peninsula of Washington State are eligible to apply for funding.
Restrictions: Grants are not made to: individuals, scholarships, schools, research, summer camps, athletic events, video or film projects, website development, book publications. No multi-year requests are considered. Groups who have been declined three times are ineligible to reapply.
Geographic Focus: Washington
Amount of Grant: 5,000 - 12,000 USD
Contact: Therese Ogle; (206) 781-3472; fax (206) 784-5987; Oglefounds@aol.com
Internet: http://fdncenter.org/grantmaker/onefamily
Sponsor: OneFamily Foundation
6723 Sycamore Avenue NW
Seattle, WA 98117

OneStar Foundation AmeriCorps Grants 3674
OneStar NSC seeks to fund programs that engage members to address health, public safety, homeland security, education, or human service needs in Texas communities. Funds support the state priority grant, professional corps grant, and education award grant. AmeriCorps education awards for members who successfully complete their full term of service will also be supported. Guidelines are available online.
Requirements: Local or statewide nonprofit organizations, state and local units of government, and institutions of higher education are eligible.
Geographic Focus: All States
Contact: Administrator; (512) 287-2000; onestar@onestarfoundation.org
Internet: http://www.onestarfoundation.org/page/americorpstexas
Sponsor: OneStar Foundation
816 Congress, Stuite 900
Austin, TX 78701

Ontario Arts Council Aboriginal Arts Project Grants 3675
The primary purpose of the Program is to develop opportunities for Aboriginal artists to engage with Aboriginal communities and to strengthen the relationship of Aboriginal organizations and communities with the arts and Aboriginal artists.
Requirements: The program is open to professional, Ontario-based Aboriginal artists, including artists' collectives and not-for-profit Aboriginal organizations, centers and councils.
Restrictions: The OAC does not fund activities, events or projects that have taken place before the program deadline date or that have been completed before the results of the competition have been announced.
Geographic Focus: All States, Canada
Date(s) Application is Due: Feb 15; Sep 17
Contact: Wanda Nanibush, English Services Officer; (416) 969-7454 or (800) 387-0058, ext. 7454; wnanibush@arts.on.ca
Internet: http://www.arts.on.ca/Page92.aspx
Sponsor: Ontario Arts Council
151 Bloor Street West, 5th Floor
Toronto, ON M5S 1T6 Canada

Ontario Arts Council Artists in the Community/Workplace Grants 3676
This program encourages individual artists and arts organizations from all art forms to work with communities and trade unions through a collaborative creative process. Grants are designed to integrate the arts into community life through artistic projects.
Requirements: This program is open to Ontario-based, individual professional artists, groups of artists, community organizations, arts organizations, and trade unions. Projects may take place in various communities or workplaces.
Geographic Focus: All States, Canada
Date(s) Application is Due: Mar 17; Aug 15
Amount of Grant: Up to 10,000 USD
Contact: Bushra Junaid; (416) 969-7425 or (800) 387-0058, ext. 7425; bjunaid@arts.on.ca
Internet: http://www.arts.on.ca/Page95.aspx
Sponsor: Ontario Arts Council
151 Bloor Street West, 5th Floor
Toronto, ON M5S 1T6 Canada

Ontario Arts Council Compass Grants 3677
The objective of the program is to assist arts organizations to increase their self-reliance, capacity-building and sustainability by covering some or all of the costs of engaging appropriate specialists and mentors to help them increase their effectiveness. The program funds activities that contribute to arts education, public participation and community involvement in the arts in Ontario. The program aims to reflect the range of artistic practices in the arts community and to support excellence, regional activity, linguistic and cultural diversity and Aboriginal and Franco-Ontarian identity. The program helps organizations pay outside experts who have management knowledge and experience. Areas may include but are not limited to: artistic planning; artists' development; arts education; audience development; board development/governance; change management; crisis management/intervention; developing partnerships; marketing; organizational transformation; outreach; public relations/communications; resource development (financial, artistic, human); strategic and business planning; sustainability; and technology development strategies.
Requirements: To be eligible for OAC project funding: incorporated not-for-profit organizations and book and magazine publishers must be located in Ontario; and ad hoc groups, collectives or unincorporated organizations must operate on a not-for-profit basis and be mainly composed of professional artists or arts professionals with at least 50% of the members located in Ontario. Colleges, universities and municipalities are eligible to apply to this program.

Restrictions: The following are not eligible for project funding: events/activities that take place before the deadline date; events/activities that have been completed before the results of the competition have been announced, which will be approximately 3 months after the deadline date; fundraising activities; or capital expenses. In addition, you must: be an arts organization specifically engaged in not-for-profit professional arts activity in Ontario and be eligible to apply to OAC granting programs; be a book or magazine publisher eligible to apply to OAC's literature programs; or be a group or consortium working together on a joint initiative that would be eligible to OAC programs.
Geographic Focus: All States, Canada
Date(s) Application is Due: Mar 17; Jun 16; Sep 17; Dec 17
Contact: Larissa Momryk; (416) 969-7412 or (800) 387-0058; lmomryk@arts.on.ca
Internet: http://www.arts.on.ca/Page127.aspx
Sponsor: Ontario Arts Council
151 Bloor Street West, 5th Floor
Toronto, ON M5S 1T6 Canada

Ontario Arts Council Integrated Arts Grants 3678
The Program supports a wide range of integrated arts practice and interdisciplinary work through the research, development, creation, production and presentation of original work. This includes new practices, hybrid forms and performance. Integrated arts are creative art forms, artistic processes or practices that use two or more artistic disciplines including visual arts, music, theater, literature, film and dance. Applicants may also choose to combine these above-mentioned disciplines with design, architecture or disciplines outside the arts. Each of these disciplines has expanded over the years to include aspects of the others. The program seeks to fund innovative integration of disciplines where there is a contribution to the development of each discipline and the artist(s). This program funds: artistic research; exploration and experimentation (including workshops/residencies where the artist(s) are integrating disciplines); collaborations fusing film making, visual/installation art, literature, dance, theater, music, architecture, design or any other disciplines; creation/presentation/production of new artistic work integrating two or more art forms; interdisciplinary performance pieces; and projects that combine artificial and natural processes. Aboriginal, culturally diverse, francophone and regional organizations receiving operating grant support are eligible to apply for additional project funding in any program outside their granting offices. Grants in research and development are generally awarded in the $3,000 to $8,000 range depending on the stage of development. Production or Presentation grants are generally awarded in the $5,000 to $15,000 range.
Requirements: This program is open to professional Ontario-based artists, collectives, teams of artists and not-for-profit organizations engaged in integrated arts development, production and presentation. Music theater and opera projects are no longer eligible in this program.
Restrictions: The following are not eligible for project funding: events/activities that take place before the deadline date; events/activities that have been completed before the results of the competition have been announced, which will be approximately 4 months after the deadline date; capital expenses;
Geographic Focus: All States, Canada
Date(s) Application is Due: Mar 17; Nov 1
Amount of Grant: Up to 20,000 USD
Contact: Georgina Braoudakis; (416) 969-7417; gbraoudakis@arts.on.ca
Internet: http://www.arts.on.ca/Page120.aspx
Sponsor: Ontario Arts Council
151 Bloor Street West, 5th Floor
Toronto, ON M5S 1T6 Canada

Ontario Arts Council Orchestras Grants 3679
The Project supports a range of orchestral activity in Ontario, including factors such as: repertoire and programming across the entire classical tradition, geographic location, and performance and development opportunities provided for orchestral players. The program funds activities that contribute to arts education, public participation and community involvement in the arts in Ontario. Grants support the costs of engaging professional Canadian artists (conductors, extra-musicians, guest soloists, etc.). $2,000 to $10,000 is the general range of grants that have been awarded to orchestras located outside Northern Ontario (south of North Bay), while $15,000 to $25,000 is the general range of grants that have been awarded to orchestras located in Northern Ontario (North Bay and above).
Requirements: This program is open to Canadian orchestras that have completed at least three full seasons, with a minimum of two self-presented concerts in each season. Programming must include professional Canadian musicians. Orchestras must also provide their communities with activities such as concert series, educational programs, and satellite and touring series.
Restrictions: The following are not eligible for project funding: events/activities that take place before the deadline date; events/activities that have been completed before the results of the competition have been announced, which will be approximately 4 months after the deadline date; fundraising activities; capital expenses; organizations funded by OAC operating or programming grants; colleges, universities and municipalities, including orchestras that are attached to, or affiliated with, educational institutions (e.g. university music departments, conservatories or schools of music); youth orchestras; orchestras that operate under the umbrella of a parent organization that is currently funded through another OAC program, (e.g. as part of an opera company); orchestras contracted for special events without continuity of membership, ongoing artistic activity or organizational and community development; tours and exchange programs; or recording projects.
Geographic Focus: All States, Canada
Date(s) Application is Due: Mar 17
Amount of Grant: Up to 25,000 USD
Contact: Georgina Braoudakis, Music Officer - French Services; (416) 969-7417 or (800) 387-0058, ext. 7417; gbraoudakis@arts.on.ca

Internet: http://www.arts.on.ca/Page113.aspx
Sponsor: Ontario Arts Council
151 Bloor Street West, 5th Floor
Toronto, ON M5S 1T6 Canada

Ontario Arts Council Presenter/Producer Grants 3680
The program supports a range of music performance/concert presentation and production around Ontario, encompassing a wide diversity of genres, styles and artistic objectives. OAS offers grants to music presenters for single public performances/concerts or series of performances/concerts. The program also offers grants to music organizations for the production of music festivals. As well, the program offers grants to professional music collectives for public performance/concert presentation and/or rehearsal activity. The average grant range $2,000 to $12,000.
Requirements: This program is open to Ontario-based music organizations that present and/or produce work for the benefit of their communities. Organizations applying for funding through this program may include series, festivals, or ensembles. Programming must include professional Canadian artists.
Restrictions: The following are not eligible for project funding: events/activities that take place before the deadline date; events/activities that have been completed before the results of the competition have been announced, which will be approximately 4 months after the deadline date; fund raising or benefit activities; capital expenses; applications from individual artists; activity already funded by other OAC grants; performances that are part of another event; faculty and/or student series/festivals at colleges, universities and conservatories; regular programming by radio/TV stations; organizations or programming attached to, or which operate directly as part of, religious institutions; organizations where the presentation of music programming is not the primary purpose/mandate; entertainment/variety presenters; trade shows and conferences; record labels; recording studios; music competitions or award shows; nightclub programmers and activity proposed by independent promoters, agents and managers; multidisciplinary projects where music is not the primary focus; touring projects; recording projects/expenses; or music video or film production.
Geographic Focus: All States, Canada
Date(s) Application is Due: Apr 2; Nov 1
Amount of Grant: Up to 20,000 USD
Contact: Georgina Braoudakis, Music Officer - French Services; (416) 969-7417 or (800) 387-0058, ext. 7417; gbraoudakis@arts.on.ca
Internet: http://www.arts.on.ca/Page109.aspx
Sponsor: Ontario Arts Council
151 Bloor Street West, 5th Floor
Toronto, ON M5S 1T6 Canada

Ontario Arts Council Theatre Creators' Reserve Grants 3681
The program assists Ontario-based professional theater creators, and informal collectives of creators, by funding them to create work. This is a third-party recommender program. Applications are made to and funding decisions are made by the theater companies. The program aims to reflect the range of artistic practices in the theater community and to support excellence, regional activity, cultural diversity and Aboriginal identity.
Requirements: To be eligible for project funding, individuals must: be Canadian citizens or permanent residents of Canada; have been resident in Ontario for at least a year before the application is made and live in Ontario for at least eight months a year; and be professional artists. To be eligible for project funding, collectives must operate on a not-for-profit basis and be composed mainly of professional artists or arts professionals with at least 50% of the members located in Ontario.
Restrictions: The following are not eligible for funding: applications from individuals or collectives whose reports for previously awarded OAC grants are overdue or incomplete; work that has been completed before you have received notification by the recommender; the cost of buying equipment such as computers or printers; professional expenses such as the costs of translation, dramaturgy, etc; creation of non-theater work (e.g. fiction, poetry, film, radio or TV, etc.); or production or workshop costs.
Geographic Focus: All States, Canada
Amount of Grant: 1,000 - 5,000 USD
Contact: Pat Bradley; (416) 969-7433 or (800) 387-0058, ext. 7433; pbradley@arts.on.ca
Internet: http://www.arts.on.ca/Page86.aspx
Sponsor: Ontario Arts Council
151 Bloor Street West, 5th Floor
Toronto, ON M5S 1T6 Canada

Ontario Arts Council Travel Assistance Grants 3682
The program provides support to facilitate exchange among representatives from Ontario-based arts groups and organizations to increase touring, distribution, circulation and presentation of the work of Ontario-based artists and arts organizations. The program is open to arts organizations in all disciplines including literary, media, performing and visual arts. Support is available for travel to Ontario destinations where there is the potential for future co-productions, exhibitions, readings, remounts, residencies, runouts, screenings or tours. The program funds activities that have the potential to contribute to arts education, public participation and community involvement in the arts in Ontario. $1,000 is the maximum per person up to a maximum of $5,000 if more than one person is involved; $2,000 is the maximum per person for travel to and from northern Ontario fly-in locations up to a maximum of $10,000 if more than one person is involved.
Requirements: To be eligible for project funding, applicants must be: incorporated not-for-profit organizations and book and magazine publishers located in Ontario; or ad hoc groups, collectives or unincorporated organizations operating on a not-for-profit basis and mainly composed of professional artists or arts professionals with at least 50% of the members located in Ontario. In addition, in order to apply to the program, an applicant

must be a not-for-profit arts organization or collective working in any of the disciplines supported at the OAC including dance, literature, media arts, multi-disciplinary arts, music, theater or visual arts.
Restrictions: Individual artists are not eligible to apply. The following are not eligible for project funding: travel that takes place before the notification; costs of accommodation, per diem, general operating costs, etc; fund raising activities; capital expenses; out-of-province travel; support to appear at or attend trade shows such as book fairs and Contact events; travel for the purpose of attending meetings such as annual general meetings, board retreats, etc; or attendance at professional development activities.
Geographic Focus: All States, Canada
Amount of Grant: Up to 10,000 USD
Contact: Larissa Momryk; (416) 969-7412 or (800) 387-0058; lmomryk@arts.on.ca
Internet: http://www.arts.on.ca/Page87.aspx
Sponsor: Ontario Arts Council
151 Bloor Street West, 5th Floor
Toronto, ON M5S 1T6 Canada

Open Meadows Foundation Grants 3683
Open Meadows Foundation is a grant-making organization for projects that are led by and benefit women and girls, particularly those from vulnerable communities. It funds projects that do not discriminate on the basis of race, religion, national origin, gender identity and expression, sexual identity and expression, age or ability.
Requirements: Grants up to $2,000 are offered to projects that: are designed and implemented by women and girls; reflect the diversity of the community served by the project in both its leadership and organization; promote building community power; promote racial, social, economic and/or environmental justice; and, have limited financial access or have encountered obstacles in their search for funding. Small and start-up organizations are strongly encouraged to apply. Proposals from organizations not previously funded have priority. Download the required cover sheet from the website.
Restrictions: email proposals are not accepted. Organizational budget should not exceed $150,000. Please note that applications postmarked on the deadline date or received after the deadline date will not be considered.
Geographic Focus: All States
Date(s) Application is Due: Feb 15; Aug 15
Amount of Grant: Up to 2,000 USD
Contact: Melanie Hope, Community Board Member; openmeadows@igc.org
Internet: http://www.openmeadows.org
Sponsor: Open Meadows Foundation
P.O. Box 150-607, Van Brunt Station
Brooklyn, NY 11215-0607

Open Spaces Sacred Places National Awards 3684
The initiative offers planning grant support for cross-disciplinary teams to develop proposals for integrated design and research studies to understand the impact of contemplative greenspace on urban dwellers. The awards will directly support the design and implementation of significant new Open Spaces Sacred Places sites designed to address critical human factors related to the physical, mental, and spiritual well-being of individuals living in challenging urban environments. The awards will simultaneously sponsor research on the human impact of encountering and experiencing these open, sacred places in nature in the urban setting.
Requirements: Eligible grantees include any 501(c)3 tax-exempt charitable organizations that are classified as public charities and not as private foundations. Such public charities include: a. Institutions that serve a large number of constituents, such as universities, schools, hospitals, medical research organizations, religious institutions, and governmental units and agencies as more specifically described in Section 170 (b)(1)(A)(i-vi) of the Internal Revenue Code (IRC); b. Publicly supported organizations that receive more than one-third of their revenues from modest donors and/or fees and sales of services and goods performed in conducting their charitable activities for a large number of persons as more specifically described in Section 509 (a)(2) of the IRC; c. Organizations created to support and benefit one or more other public charities as more specifically described in Section 509 (a)3 of the IRC. Eligible teams must be cross-disciplinary in makeup and must include an identified Firesoul or Firesouls. Eligible projects must have both an institutional and a community-based partner.
Geographic Focus: All States
Date(s) Application is Due: Jun 30; Sep 1
Amount of Grant: Up to 50,000 USD
Contact: Christine Tanabe, Director of Communications & Program Development; (410) 268-1376; fax (410) 268-1379; info@tkffdn.org
Internet: http://www.opensacred.org/grants/request-for-proposal
Sponsor: TKF Foundation
410 Severn Avenue, Suite 216
Annapolis, MD 21403

Oppenstein Brothers Foundation Grants 3685
Grants are awarded in the metropolitan area of Kansas, City, Missouri, primarily for social services and early childhood, elementary, secondary, adult-basic, vocational, and higher education; family planning and services; social services and welfare agencies; Jewish welfare organizations; and programs for youth, the handicapped, disadvantaged, mentally ill, homeless, minorities, and elderly. Additional areas of interest include arts/cultural programs, the performing arts, museums, health care and health organizations, and AIDS research. The foundation considers requests for building and renovation, capital campaigns, curriculum development, emergency funds, equipment, general operating support, program development, seed money, technical support, conferences and seminars, consulting services, and matching funds. Application guidelines are available on request. The board meets every other month. Deadlines are generally three weeks prior to board meetings. Notification of award will take place within two to four months.
Requirements: Nonprofit organizations serving the metropolitan area of Kansas City, Missouri are eligible to apply.
Restrictions: The foundation primarily supports 501(c)3 nonprofit organizations serving the metropolitan area of Kansas City, Missouri. Grants are not awarded to support individuals or for annual campaigns.
Geographic Focus: Missouri
Amount of Grant: 5,000 - 15,000 USD
Contact: Beth Radtke, Program Officer; (816) 234-2577
Sponsor: Oppenstein Brothers Foundation
922 Walnut Street, Suite 200
Kansas City, MO 64106-1809

Oracle Corporate Contributions Grants 3686
The corporation awards grants for medical research in the areas of cancer, AIDS, and neuroscience; endangered animal protection; environmental protection, specifically for education and preservation of important open space; and K-12 education, with emphasis on mathematics, science, and technology programs. Grants are awarded in February and August.
Requirements: Nonprofits nationwide and in operating communities are eligible.
Restrictions: Grants generally do not support fundraising benefits, charitable dinners, sporting events, and marketing brochures. The corporation does not award multiyear grants and rarely approves funds for more than three consecutive years.
Geographic Focus: All States
Contact: Corporate Giving Coordinator; (650) 506-7000
Internet: http://www.oracle.com/corporate/giving/community/index.html?giveform.html
Sponsor: Oracle Corporation
500 Oracle Parkway, MS 50P11
Redwood City, CA 94065

Orange County Community Foundation Grants 3687
The Orange County Community Foundation makes grants for a variety of purposes, including education, the arts, youth and recreation, health and human services, and the environment. Grants that receive the highest priority include programs or projects that reach the highest percentage of Orange County as a whole; are preventative rather than remedial; increase individual access to community resources and promote independence; examine and address the underlying causes of local problems and issues; attract volunteer resources and support; strengthen the non-profit sector; encourage collaboration among organizations; build the capacity of the organization; and offer services not already available in the community. Applications and specific guidelines for individual grants are available at the website.
Requirements: Grants must meet legal and tax requirements as to purpose and may be made only to non-profit organizations and government agencies. However, for-profit entities which apply will be considered if their project or program serves a charitable purpose.
Restrictions: Funding is not available for the following: political parties or political campaigns; sectarian religious purposes (but can be made to religious organizations for general community programs); endowment creation or debt reduction; programs or equipment that were committed to prior to the grant application being submitted; new or routine maintenance construction projects (except renovations of existing facilities that enable the organization to provide a better quality of service to Orange County); annual giving or capital campaigns; or normal operating expenses (except start-up expenses).
Geographic Focus: Indiana
Date(s) Application is Due: Jul 7
Contact: Imojean Dedrick, Executive Director; (812) 723-4150; fax (812) 723-7304; imodedrick@orangecountyfoundation.org
Internet: http://184.172.138.191/~orange/services/grants/
Sponsor: Orange County Community Foundation - Indiana
112 West Water Street
Paoli, IN 47454

Orange County Community Foundation Grants 3688
The Foundation's mission is to encourage, support and facilitate philanthropy in Orange County, California. One of our most important strategic priorities is strengthening the capacity of Orange County's nonprofit sector. Foundation Grants are made possible by the income earned from unrestricted, field-of-interest endowment funds and legacy funds. Grants funding is determined through research of community needs and approved by the Board. In addition, Grants are periodically administered in partnership with statewide and national foundations as well as Foundation donors to advance special projects and initiatives in Orange County. Fields of interest include arts and culture, environment, education, health, an human services.
Requirements: Nonprofits agencies in Orange County, California, are eligible. Unsolicited grant proposals are not accepted. Nonprofit agencies wishing to apply should pay special attention to the website for requests for proposal and deadlines. Every grant has a formal application and its own annual cycle.
Geographic Focus: California
Contact: Patricia Benevenia; (949) 553-4202, ext. 37; penevenia@oc-cf.org
Internet: http://www.oc-cf.org/Page.aspx?pid=496
Sponsor: Orange County Community Foundation
4041 MacArthur Boulevard, Suite 510
Newport Beach, CA 92660

ORBI Artist Fast Track Grants 3689
The Artist Fast Track grant program is jointly administered by the Ohio River Border Initiative (ORBI), a joint program of the Ohio Arts Council and the West Virginia Commission on the Arts of the West Virginia Division of Culture and History, and the Appalachian Arts Program (AAP) of the Ohio Arts Council. Grants are intended to support immediate, short-term projects that have a positive impact upon the career development of

artists by helping them: (1) increase access to audiences and venues, (2) develop new skills and insights, (3) investigate new artistic ideas and approaches. Projects must have a specific beginning point and a specific end point. Artists and craftspeople may apply for grants of up to $500. Funds may be used for professional and artistic development for attendance at workshops, conferences, seminars, master classes, exhibits, exchange programs; presentation opportunities - preparation of portfolios and slides, printing of brochures or marketing materials and demonstration tapes; rental expenses for rehearsal or studio space for time periods of less than one month; shipping and crating of art works for a show or exhibit; lodging and transportation costs for a training session, workshop, conference, or exhibit; rental of equipment or purchase of supplies required for showing and displaying art works.
Requirements: The program is open to artists and craftspeople, part-time or full time with professional experience who live and work in the Ohio counties of Adams, Athens, Belmont, Brown, Carroll, Clermont, Coshocton, Columbiana, Gallia, Guernsey, Harrison, Highland, Hocking, Holmes, Jackson, Jefferson, Lawrence, Meigs, Monroe, Morgan, Muskingum, Noble, Perry, Pike, Ross, Scioto, Tuscarawas, Vinton, Washington or the West Virginia counties of Wayne, Cabell, Mason, Jackson, Wood, Pleasants, Tyler, Wetzel, Marshall, Ohio, Brooke, Hancock. Organizations are also eligible and must be located in any of the counties named above. Applications must be received by ORBI or AAP no later than 60 days before the proposed project's start date. Grants are available on first come first served basis. Once the total budgeted for the current fiscal year runs out, no grants will be awarded until the next fiscal year.
Restrictions: Grants are not intended for long term or open ended projects such as the purchase tools or equipment or for long term training or education. You may not apply for more than one grant in the state fiscal year period, July 1 to June 30. Additionally, funds cannot be used for tools such as musical instruments, brushes or art supplies used directly by the artist; tickets or admission to performances or exhibits by other artists; tools or equipment used to produce artworks; long term training or apprenticeships; or, expenses associated with research.
Geographic Focus: Ohio, West Virginia
Amount of Grant: Up to 500 USD
Contact: Bill Howley, Project Director; (304) 655-8255
Internet: http://www.orbi.org/news.html#fast%20track
Sponsor: Ohio River Border Initiative
P.O. Box 3
Chloe, WV 25235

Orchard Foundation Grants 3690
The foundation makes grants to eligible New York and New England nonprofit organizations in its areas of interest, including environment (air quality, biodiversity, fresh and coastal waters, forests, toxic substances, and pollution prevention); children, youth, and families (child welfare systems, literacy, and pregnancy prevention); and campaign finance reform. The foundation will occasionally provide seed money, operating support, and start-up capital to smaller home-grown organizations provided that strong local support has been obtained for a project in the form of membership and contributions, and that the entire mission of the organization coincides with a field of interest to the foundation. The listed deadlines are for concept letters.
Requirements: The foundation focuses on Massachusetts, Maine, New Hampshire, New York, Vermont, Connecticut, and Rhode Island. The foundation accepts letters of inquiry from groups in those seven states as well as from national groups with regional offices or projects in the area.
Restrictions: Grants are not made to individuals or for endowments, annual or capital campaigns, religious programs, any religion-affiliated organization, conference participation/travel unrelated to current foundation grant, research efforts unrelated to advocacy interests of the foundation, scholarships, fellowships, building projects, equipment needs, film and video projects, land acquisition, animal hospitals/rehabilitation centers, or groups that focus on specific diseases or conditions. Loans are not made.
Geographic Focus: Connecticut, Maine, Massachusetts, New Hampshire, New York, Rhode Island, Vermont
Date(s) Application is Due: Mar 1; Sep 1
Amount of Grant: 3,000 - 15,000 USD
Contact: Executive Director; (207) 799-0686; orchard@maine.rr.com
Internet: http://home.maine.rr.com/orchard
Sponsor: Orchard Foundation
P.O. Box 2587
Portland, ME 04116

Ordean Foundation Grants 3691
The Foundation, established in 1933, supports organizations involved with alcoholism, children/youth, services, crime/violence prevention, youth, education, family services, food services, health care, homeless, human services, housing/shelter, human services, medical care, rehabilitation, mental health/crisis services, substance abuse, services, YM/YWCAs & YM/YWHAs, aging, disabilities, economically disadvantaged. Grants will be awarded for up to three years. Applications are reviewed on an ongoing basis; the deadline is the 15th of each month.
Requirements: Non-profits in the Duluth and contiguous cities and townships in St. Louis County, Minnesota are eligible. The Foundation accepts the Minnesota Common Grant Application Form.
Restrictions: No support for direct religious purposes, or for political campaigns or lobbying activities. No grants to individuals (directly), or for endowment funds, travel, conferences, seminars or workshops, telephone solicitations, benefits, dinners, research, including biomedical research, deficit financing, national fund raising campaigns, or to supplant government funding.
Geographic Focus: Minnesota
Amount of Grant: 1,000 - 290,000 USD
Contact: Stephen A. Mangan, Executive Director; (218) 726-4785; fax (218) 726-4848; ordean@computerpro.com
Sponsor: Ordean Foundation
501 Ordean Building
Duluth, MN 55802-4725

Oregon Youth Soccer Foundation Grants 3692
The foundation awards grants to support soccer-related projects for youth in Oregon. Participation in the Oregon Youth Soccer program enables children to grow physically, mentally and socially, developing the invaluable tools of character, discipline, teamwork, leadership, and self-esteem. It is the goal of the Oregon Youth Soccer Foundation to foster these values for the years to come, providing children with healthy, exciting and rewarding adult-supervised activity. Areas of interest include increasing the number of participants, increasing the availability of fields and facilities, improving the quality of play, enhancing gender equity, promoting participation by minority and disadvantaged youth, and encouraging recreational soccer programs and activities for youth in economically disadvantaged families. Requests for field development projects are favored if they are collaborative and foundation funds are critical to the project's success. Proposals for hard assets receive priority over requests for operating or ongoing maintenance costs.
Geographic Focus: Oregon
Date(s) Application is Due: Dec 15
Contact: Chuck Keers; (800) 275-7353 or (503) 626-4625; info@oysf.org
Internet: http://www.oregonyouthsoccer.org/service/oysfoundation.aspx
Sponsor: Oregon Youth Soccer Foundation
4840 SW Western Avenue, Suite 800
Beaverton, OR 97005

Organic Farming Research Foundation Grants 3693
The mission of the foundation is to sponsor research related to organic farming practices. Grants support research into organic farming methods, dissemination of research results to organic farmers and to growers interested in making the transition to organic production systems, and education of the general public about organic farming issues.
Requirements: Farmers, researchers, organic advocacy organizations, and other individuals or entities may apply. Projects should involve farmers in both design and execution and take place on working organic farms whenever possible and appropriate.
Geographic Focus: All States
Date(s) Application is Due: Jul 15; Dec 15
Amount of Grant: Up to 15,000 USD
Contact: Jane Sooby, (831) 426-6606; fax (831) 426-6670; jane@ofrf.org
Internet: http://www.ofrf.org/research/index.html
Sponsor: Organic Farming Research Foundation
303 Potrero Street, Suite 29-203, P.O. Box 440
Santa Cruz, CA 95061

Oscar Rennebohm Foundation Grants 3694
The foundation awards grants to nonprofit organizations in the Madison, WI area. Areas of interest, include: higher education, the arts, environmental conservation, health and social service agencies. Types of support include building construction/renovation, equipment acquisition, and research. There are no application forms or deadlines.
Geographic Focus: Wisconsin
Contact: Grants Administrator; (608) 274-5991
Sponsor: Oscar Rennebohm Foundation
P.O. Box 5187
Madison, WI 53705

OSF-Baltimore Community Fellowships 3695
The Baltimore Community Fellowships program works to meet the challenges facing Baltimore's most needy communities by identifying and supporting social innovators of unusual promise and providing them with the ingredients to ensure their ideas have a stable foundation and long-term viability. The Fellowships program seeks dynamic activists and social entrepreneurs interested in implementing projects that address problems in underserved communities in Baltimore City. Funding of $60,000 is available over 18 months. The application is available at the OSF-Baltimore website, and candidates may be placed on an application mailing list.
Requirements: Fellowships are for initiatives that take place in Baltimore City. Applicants may come from any field, including—but not limited to—business, management, the arts, law, medicine, education, architecture, and engineering. Individuals from underserved communities and people of color are strongly encouraged to apply. Applicants need not be from Baltimore City, but should be knowledgeable about social and economic justice issues affecting Baltimore's communities. Fellows must be willing to participate fully in meetings scheduled for the Community Fellows.
Restrictions: Individuals already receiving wages or a salary for the proposed project from a host organization are not eligible. Fellows may not use stipends to supplant funding for activities or projects that the host organization is already implementing. The program does not award fellowships to conduct research or to implement lobbying initiatives.
Geographic Focus: All States
Contact: Pamela King, Director, Baltimore Fellowships and Initiatives; (410) 234-1091, ext. 210; fax (410) 234-2816; pamela.king@opensocietyfoundations.org
Internet: http://www.opensocietyfoundations.org/grants/baltimore-community-fellowships
Sponsor: Open Society Foundations
201 North Charles Street, Suite 1300
Baltimore, MD 21201

GRANT PROGRAMS | 565

OSF-Baltimore Criminal and Juvenile Justice Grants   **3696**
The Open Society Foundations–Baltimore Criminal and Juvenile Justice Program seeks to reduce the overuse of incarceration and its social and economic costs without compromising public safety and promote justice systems that are fair, are used as a last resort, and offer second chances. It supports advocacy, public education, research, grassroots organizing, litigation and demonstration projects that focus on reforming racial and social inequities at critical stages of the criminal and juvenile justice systems: arrest, detention and pre-trial/pre-adjudication; sentencing, incarceration, and pre-release; and reentry and reintegration into the community. Funding supports initiatives and organizations that seek to: increase the number of Baltimore residents who are diverted from the criminal and juvenile justice systems, particularly those accused of non-violent offenses; promote systemic reform of unfair criminal and juvenile justice policies and practices relating to arrests, pre-trial procedures, sentencing, conditions of confinement, and parole and probation; and ensure that individuals with criminal and juvenile records successfully reenter and reintegrate into Baltimore City. Applications are accepted at any time.
Requirements: Applicants should submit a copy of the IRS letter stating tax-exempt status and a two to three page letter of inquiry. If OSF-Baltimore determines that the proposal is of interest, it will invite the applicant to submit a full proposal. Additional guidelines, including a detailed list of the proposal requirements, are posted on the website.
Geographic Focus: Maryland
Contact: Kiera Edwards, Program Associate, Criminal and Juvenile Justice Program; (410) 234-1091; fax (410) 234-2816; kiera.edwards@opensocietyfoundations.org
Internet: http://www.opensocietyfoundations.org/grants/criminal-and-juvenile-justice-baltimore
Sponsor: Open Society Foundations
201 North Charles Street, Suite 1300
Baltimore, MD 21201

OSF-Baltimore Education and Youth Development Grants   **3697**
The Baltimore Education and Youth Development Grants aim to increase the knowledge and skills of Baltimore's children and youth through improved public education and enhanced after-school and summer programs, so that they can become successful citizens, workers, and parents. Grants have the following funding priorities: keep children connected to school, pre-k through graduation; support school reform efforts to create new schools; and expand opportunities for learning when school is not in session. Applications are accepted at any time.
Requirements: Applicants should submit a copy of the IRS letter stating tax-exempt status, along with a two to three page letter of inquiry. If it is determined that the proposal is of interest, applicants will be invited to submit a full proposal. Additional guidelines, including format and attachments required, are posted on the website.
Restrictions: OSF-Baltimore generally does not fund individual after-school programs, but concentrates its out-of-school time funding on city wide efforts to improve the quality and quantity of programs.
Geographic Focus: Maryland
Contact: Kiera Edwards, Program Associate, Educaton and Youth Development; (410) 234-1091; fax (410) 234-2816; kiera.edwards@opensocietyfoundations.org
Internet: http://www.opensocietyfoundations.org/grants/education-and-youth-development-baltimore
Sponsor: Open Society Foundations
201 North Charles Street, Suite 1300
Baltimore, MD 21201

OSF-Baltimore Tackling Drug Addiction Grants   **3698**
The Tackling Drug Addiction Treatment Initiative of the Open Society Foundations–Baltimore seeks to ensure universal access to treatment services for all in need regardless of income or insurance status. The Tackling Drug Addiction Treatment Initiative funds grantees who focus on the following three priorities: using the opportunity of health care reform to help Baltimore City and Maryland as a whole reach nearly universal access to a comprehensive, high-quality public treatment system; ensuring access to high quality public substance use disorder services for those that remain uninsured after the implementation of health care reform; and facilitating the creation or help to sustain a strong, diverse addition treatment advocacy community, inclusive of those most affected by substances use disorder services policies. Applications are accepted at any time.
Requirements: Applicants should submit a copy of the IRS letter stating tax-exempt status and a letter of inquiry not exceeding three pages. If OSF-Baltimore determines that the proposal is of interest, the applicant is invited to submit a full proposal. Additional guidelines are available at the website.
Geographic Focus: Maryland
Contact: Ruzana Hedges, Program Associate, Tackling Drug Addiction Iniative; (410) 234-1091; fax (410) 234-2816; ruzana.hedges@opensocietyfoundations.org
Internet: http://www.opensocietyfoundations.org/grants/tackling-drug-addiction
Sponsor: Open Society Foundations
201 North Charles Street, Suite 1300
Baltimore, MD 21201

OSF Advancing the Rights and Integration of Roma Grants   **3699**
The purpose of this call is to support responses to the challenges and to increase the foundations of hope. OSF aims to focus on organized activities that seek to change the policies, regulations and practices that perpetuate the exclusion of Roma. To realize such change, projects should generate strategic capacity among Roma NGOs, organizations from the broader civil society and grassroots constituencies. This may mean changing or advancing a new policy, or ensuring enforcement of an existing one. Potential applicants should focus on one or more of the following priority policy areas: elections, with a focus on voter protection; ending anti-Gypsyism and discrimination; transparency and accountability of public spending on Roma integration; rights of Roma women; the right of Roma to adequate housing; employment and income generation for Roma; and rights of migrants including internally displaced persons (IDPs), refugees, returnees, asylum seekers and migrants of Roma origin. Applicants will be encouraged to consider using a wide range of advocacy methods and tools, such as: voter empowerment, coalition building, community organizing, litigation and legal advocacy, traditional and social media, research and policy analysis, the use of existing demonstration or pilot projects, and the use of arts, culture and sports as platforms for constituency building. The deadline for receiving concept papers is March 19.
Requirements: Nongovernmental organizations registered in the following countries are eligible to apply: Albania, Bosnia and Herzegovina, Bulgaria, Croatia, the Czech Republic, France, Hungary, Italy, Kosovo, Macedonia, Montenegro, Romania, Serbia, Slovakia and Spain.
Geographic Focus: Albania, Bosnia & Herzegovina, Bulgaria, Croatia, Czech Republic, France, Hungary, Italy, Kosovo, Macedonia, Moldova, Montenegro, Romania, Serbia, Slovakia, Spain
Date(s) Application is Due: Mar 19
Contact: Adem Ademi; +36-1-882-3100; fax +36-1-882 3101; gholman@osi.hu
Internet: http://www.opensocietyfoundations.org/grants/advancing-rights-and-integration-roma
Sponsor: Open Society Foundations
400 West 57th Street, 3rd Floor
New York, NY 10019

OSF Affordable Access to Digital Communications Initiative   **3700**
Affordable access to communications networks is a basic requirement for the effective functioning of governance, civil society, and education as well as for economic development. Public policy is a fundamental factor in hindering or enabling the investment and business models needed to provide affordable access. Although the media and many development agencies trumpet a "mobile miracle" across Africa, monopolies and poorly managed liberalization as well as inappropriate regulatory regimes are still posing a barrier to affordable access. The aim of this component of the Information Program is to broaden affordable access to communications networks in Africa and other strategically important countries in the South by supporting policy analysis, policy interventions and the staging of new models. The program intends to advance this aim with a particular focus on the following priorities: affordable access to mobile phones; and spectrum reform.
Geographic Focus: All States, All Countries
Contact: Elizabeth Eagen, Program Manager; (212) 548-0600; fax (212) 548-4600; informationprogram.grants@opensocietyfoundations.o
Orsolya Cseh, Administrative and Financial Coordinator; +36-1-882-3100; fax +36-1-882-3101; informationprogram.grants@opensocietyfoundations.o
Internet: http://www.opensocietyfoundations.org/grants/affordable-access-digital-communications-initiative
Sponsor: Open Society Foundations
400 West 57th Street, 3rd Floor
New York, NY 10019

OSF Arab Regional Office Grants   **3701**
The Open Society Foundations Arab Regional Office welcomes unsolicited grant proposal outlines, or concept notes, on a rolling basis throughout the year. Concept notes should fall within the following focus areas: rights and governance; media and information; women's rights; and knowledge and education. The criteria for successful proposals are their relevance to the Arab Regional Office's priority focal areas and their attempt to raise standards and promote new ideas in their respective fields. Additional guidelines are posted on the website.
Requirements: Professional organizations, universities, NGOs, and other institutions may apply for support. Once a grant is approved, the office places no conditionality or "strings attached" on grantee recipients. Grantee reports are required twice annually or once a year to insure a grantees compliance with the terms of the approved proposal.
Restrictions: Individuals are not eligible for funding.
Geographic Focus: Algeria, Bahrain, Comoros, Djibouti, Egypt, Iraq, Jordan, Kuwait, Lebanon, Libya, Mauritania, Morocco, Oman, Palestinian Territory, Qatar, Saudi Arabia, Somalia, Sudan, Syria, Tunisia, United Arab Emirates, Yemen
Contact: Abier Al Khateeb, Grants Manager; +962-6-582-7395; abier.khateeb@opensocietyfoundations.org or proposals@osimena.org
Internet: http://www.opensocietyfoundations.org/grants/arab-regional-office
Sponsor: Open Society Foundations
400 West 57th Street, 3rd Floor
New York, NY 10019

OSF Burma Project/Southeast Asia Initiative Grants   **3702**
The Burma Project, established by the Open Society Foundations in 1994, is dedicated to increasing international awareness of conditions in Burma and helping the country make a successful transition from a closed to an open society. To this end, the Burma Project prioritizes projects supporting marginalized communities including ethnic minorities, women, and youth. It supports efforts to: address and prevent human rights abuses; promote independent media and access to information; encourage peace and reconciliation; empower women, youth, and ethnic minorities; and encourage an end to discrimination. The Southeast Asia Initiative provides grants to civil society organizations, nongovernmental organizations, academic institutions and think tanks to promote constructive engagement with national and regional institutions in Southeast Asia and to develop new talent among young leaders in the fields of access to justice, freedom of expression and participation, freedom of information, migrant and citizenship rights, public interest media, and protection of human rights defenders.
Requirements: The Burma Project does not invite proposals from international groups, but will solicit them when a need is identified. The Southeast Asia Initiative's priority

countries are Cambodia, Malaysia, and Thailand, but we will accept concept papers from organizations working on other countries in the Southeast Asia region.
Restrictions: Ineligible projects include support for the following: governments or political parties, agriculture or rural development projects, social welfare projects (including schools, orphanages, and basic service provision) construction costs, micro-finance loans, film production, individual education or research costs. The Burma Project/Southeast Asia Initiative also does not support cultural or environmental projects, unless directly connected to the protection and promotion of civil and political rights.
Geographic Focus: Burma (Myanmar), Cambodia, East Timor, Laos, Malaysia, Philippines, Singapore, Thailand, Timor-Lester, Vietnam
Contact: Jeffrey Stein; (212) 548-0600 or (212) 548-0632; fax (212) 548-4600; jeffrey.stein@opensocietyfoundations.org or burma@opensocietyfoundations.org
Internet: http://www.opensocietyfoundations.org/grants/southeast-asia-initiative
Sponsor: Open Society Foundations
400 West 57th Street, 3rd Floor
New York, NY 10019

OSF Campaign for Black Male Achievement Grants **3703**
The Open Society Campaign for Black Male Achievement aims to create hope and opportunities for black men and boys who are significantly marginalized from U.S. economic, social, and political life. Campaign grantmaking seeks to: promote education equity, and dismantle of the school-to-prison pipeline; strengthen low-income black families through responsible fatherhood initiatives, policy advocacy, and supporting efforts that lift barriers facing single mothers raising black boys; expand and ensure family supportive wage work opportunities for black males; integrate strategic communications into the campaign's work to promote positive messages about black men and boys; promote leadership development and advocacy/organizing training for young black males; serve as a catalyst in the field of philanthropy; and develop strategies that build local coalitions. The Campaign provides funding for a wide range of policy advocacy strategies including the following: grassroots organizing and mobilization; coalition building; public awareness and strategic communications; impact litigation; policy-driven research and analysis; leadership development; and model programs. The letter of interest template is available at the website. Letters of interest are accepted at any time.
Requirements: The Campaign will consider letters of inquiry from advocacy groups, community groups, scholarly or research institutions, government agencies, associations of elected officials, and nonprofit business associations or initiatives. Funding is available for national, state, and local organizations focused on outcomes in the U.S. regions of Baltimore, Maryland; Philadelphia, Pennsylvania; Jackson, Mississippi; New Orleans, Louisiana; Chicago, Illinois; and Milwaukee, Wisconsin. Letters of inquiry are considered from organizations or projects outside of these regions only if the proposed activities have clear and demonstrable potential for national impact and/or replication in other localities or regions.
Restrictions: Funding is not available for: direct services that do not also advance one of the advocacy strategies listed in the program description; lobbying activities; annual fundraising drives; projects undertaken by individuals; capital costs, including equipment or real estate purchases/renovations; or film production or post-production.
Geographic Focus: All States
Contact: Shawn Dove; (212) 548-0356; shawn.dove@opensocietyfoundations.org
Internet: http://www.opensocietyfoundations.org/grants/campaign-black-male-achievement
Sponsor: Open Society Foundations
400 West 57th Street, 3rd Floor
New York, NY 10019

OSF Central Eurasia Project Grants **3704**
The Open Society Central Eurasia Project uses grantmaking to international and regional NGOs, academic institutions, think tanks, and other structures to support their work, help build local capacity, bring international expertise to bear on the region and promote cooperation between local activists and international civic movements. The ultimate goal of such activity is to strengthen civic leaders in the region and to construct support networks for them within international structures and movements. The Central Eurasia Project's grantmaking generally joins with its research and advocacy agenda. Project funding is available for human rights; labor migration; transparency and consumer protection; transparency of Western military and security cooperation; Turkmenistan; and Uzbekistan. The Central Eurasia Project does not limit the amount that can be requested in a grant application and both single and multi-year proposals are accepted. Projects are encouraged to demonstrate funding from multiple sources. With the exception of Turkmenistan and Uzbekistan, the Central Eurasia Project only funds proposals with activity in two or more countries in the region.
Requirements: Applicants may submit a one-page letter of inquiry in English, summarizing the organization's mission and proposed project's statement of purpose, main activities, and requested budget. Letters of inquiry are accepted on a rolling basis throughout the year. Letters of inquiry may be submitted in Russian if they are accompanied by an English translation. Upon reception of the letter of inquiry, the Central Eurasia Project will consider the proposed project. Should the proposal meet the Central Eurasia Project's criteria, organizations will be invited to submit a full grant application within six weeks of receiving the letter of inquiry. Full applications will be accepted in either English or Russian. When submitting the application, anticipate a project start date of four to six months from date of submission, if approved.
Restrictions: The Open Society Foundations are prohibited from funding any electioneering, including the support for or, opposition to, political candidates or parties, and from the earmarking of grant funds for lobbying activities in any country. Lobbying is defined as an attempt to influence federal, state, local legislative bodies, or the outcome of referenda and ballot initiatives. This proscription includes attempts to influence treaty ratification by legislative bodies. The prohibition against lobbying includes, but may not necessarily be limited to, communications with legislators or legislative staff that express a view on pending legislation or specific legislative proposals, and communications with the general public reflecting a view on specific legislation or a specific legislative proposal where such communication includes a "call to take action" by the public.
Geographic Focus: Kazakhstan, Kyrgyzstan, Tajikistan, Turkmenistan, Uzbekistan
Contact: Kristin Whitehead, Program Coordinator; (212) 548-0600; fax (212) 548-4679; kristin.whitehead@opensocietyfoundations.org or cepgrants@sorosny.org
Internet: http://www.opensocietyfoundations.org/grants/central-eurasia-project
Sponsor: Open Society Foundations
400 West 57th Street, 3rd Floor
New York, NY 10019

OSF Civil Service Awards **3705**
The Civil Service Awards provide fellowships for master's degree study, offering professional training and development to public sector employees engaged in policy analysis and implementation. The program is offered in Georgia and Moldova. The program is designed to meet the professional development needs of mid- to top-level staff of governmental ministries and agencies. The fellowship targets career civil servants who demonstrate both academic and professional excellence and the potential to become leaders, decision-makers, and agents of change in their home countries. Upon completing the degrees, grantees return to employment at a position determined by the home government for a commitment of three years. Applications and additional guidelines for each country are available at the website.
Requirements: For Georgia, the awards are open to employees of the two cooperating federal ministries and their associated agencies: The Ministry of Labor, Health and Social Affairs of Georgia; and The Ministry of Environmental Protection and Natural Resources of Georgia. For Moldova, the awards are open to public sector employees and are intended to benefit the following federal entities and their associated agencies: Ministry of Education; Ministry of Labor, Social Protection, and Family; Ministry of the Economy; Ministry of Transportation; Ministry of Agriculture; Ministry of Foreign Affairs and European Integration; and The State Chancellery.
Geographic Focus: Georgia, Moldova
Contact: Nino Chinchaladze, Program Coordinator; +995 32 252615; cie@osgf.ge
Internet: http://www.opensocietyfoundations.org/grants/civil-service-awards
Sponsor: Open Society Foundations
400 West 57th Street, 3rd Floor
New York, NY 10019

OSF Documentary Photography Project Audience Engagement Grant **3706**
The Audience Engagement Grant supports photographers to take an existing body of work on a social justice or human rights issue and devise an innovative and effective way of using that work as a tool for social change. We are looking for projects that serve as interventions on pressing problems and provide concrete ways for photographers, organizations, and their target audiences to create a positive impact. The Project is interested in well-designed projects that: inspire audiences visually and create meaningful interactions with photographic content; utilize photography as the basis for programming or tools that directly connect people to processes that lead to social change; provide deeper, more nuanced understanding of human rights and social justice issues; and pairs photographers with organizations that are connected to the target audience and currently working on related issues. Between five and eight grants from $10,000 to $30,000 will be provided. The application, which included detailed guidelines, is available at the website.
Requirements: The grant supports photographers who are partnering with organizations on collaborative projects. Each project partner should have the skills and track record to realize the project and must commit time and resources to implement it. The partnership should include: photographer or curator/project organizer, whose expertise is in the production or presentation of documentary photography; or audience engagement partner(s), with expertise in a specific issue and already connected to the target audience. A distribution partner with expertise in the dissemination or presentation method are optional. Grant funding is also seeking projects that include the following: an existing body of compelling photographs that documents a human rights or social justice issue (preference will be given to projects that address issues and geographical areas of concern to the Open Society Foundations); effective and innovative ideas for using photography to spark deeper engagement with a particular community on a social justice or human rights issue; well-designed dissemination strategies that are uniquely tailored to meet the needs and interests of a target audience; and a detailed plan for engaging targeted audiences in concrete ways.
Restrictions: The following projects are not eligible for funding: requests to shoot new work; dated material, unless the purpose is to collect and preserve untold, alternative, or historically; significant narratives about a particular community or historical event; projects whose only goal is to fundraise and/or raise awareness in a general way; projects geared toward "the general public," and do not identify a primary target audience; exhibitions that serve only the interests of the photographer or the gallery; book production; documentary film or video; or lobbying activities.
Geographic Focus: All States, All Countries
Date(s) Application is Due: Jun 28
Contact: Anna Overstrom-Coleman, Program Assistant; (212) 548-0600; anna.overstrom-coleman@opensocietyfoundations.org
Internet: http://www.opensocietyfoundations.org/grants/audience-engagement-grant
Sponsor: Open Society Foundations
400 West 57th Street, 3rd Floor
New York, NY 10019

OSF European Commission Internships for Young Roma Graduates **3707**
The Open Society Roma Initiatives offer five-month internships at the European Commission for five Roma University graduates from the following EU member states: Albania, Bosnia and Herzegovina, Croatia, Kosovo, Macedonia, Montenegro, and Serbia. The internship has the following main goals: give Roma interns a general idea of the

objectives and problems of European integration; provide them with practical knowledge of the working of the Commissions' Directorates-General; enable them to acquire personal experience by means of the contacts made in the course of their everyday work; allow them to enrich and put into practice the knowledge they have acquired during their studies or professional careers; and promote the active citizenship of young Roma in Central and Eastern Europe by exposing them to advocacy and community service work. Additional information is available in the call for proposals and application at the website.
Requirements: Candidates should demonstrate willingness to return to their home country after the internship and complete a community-based service project. Applicants must have a working knowledge of English or French, and ability to draft reports in one of these languages. The maximum age for interns is 25. However, the Selection Committee may, if there is a good reason, make exceptions to this age limit at the candidate's request (in which case, a cover letter should be submitted with the application form). The internship at the Commission is open to candidates who have not yet benefited from in-service training in another European institution or body.
Geographic Focus: Albania, Bosnia & Herzegovina, Croatia, Kosovo, Macedonia, Montenegro, Serbia
Date(s) Application is Due: Jun 29
Contact: Bernard Rorke, Research and Advocacy Director; +36 1 327 3100 or +36 1 882 3100; fax +36 1 327 3101; bernard.rorke@opensocietyfoundations.org
Internet: http://www.opensocietyfoundations.org/grants/european-commission-internship-young-roma-university-graduates
Sponsor: Open Society Institute
Oktober 6 u 12
Budapest, H-1051 Hungary

OSF Human Rights and Governance Grants 3708
The Human Rights and Governance Grants fund national and international organizations to advance governmental accountability in Central and Eastern Europe, the former Soviet Union, and Mongolia. The program supports efforts to promote public participation in and oversight of governmental activity, at both the national and local levels, including in the delivery of services. The program provides funding to national and international NGOs to monitor public administration and to curb corrupt behavior by state authorities. Additional guidelines are available at the OSF website.
Requirements: National and international advocacy organizations that promote political and civil rights locally and internationally are eligible. Prior to sending a full proposal, potential applicants should submit a brief concept paper of no more than 2-3 pages to determine whether projects meet the Human Rights and Governance Grants Program's current funding priorities and guidelines.
Geographic Focus: All States, Austria, Belarus, Czech Republic, Estonia, Germany, Hungary, Latvia, Liechtenstein, Lithuania, Moldova, Mongolia, Poland, Russia, Slovakia, Slovenia, Switzerland, Ukraine
Contact: Magda Adamowicz, Program Coordinator; (+011) (361) 327-3027 or (+011) (361) 327-3100; fax (+01) (361) 235-6167; madamowicz@opensocietyfoundations.org
Internet: http://www.opensocietyfoundations.org/grants/human-rights-fund
Sponsor: Open Society Foundations
400 West 57th Street, 3rd Floor
New York, NY 10019

OSF Mental Health Initiative Grants 3709
The Mental Health Initiative provides grants to projects that stimulate the reform of national health, social welfare, education, and employment policies. The initiative also provides technical assistance and training in substantive areas to its grantees. Many grantees provide high-quality, community-based services which demonstrate that people with intellectual disabilities can live in their communities when they receive appropriate support. The Initiative supports projects that include community-based housing, early intervention, inclusive education, and supported employment for people with intellectual disabilities. The Initiative also provides support for organizations working on policy-based advocacy at local or national levels with the aim of promoting community living for people with intellectual disabilities.
Requirements: The Mental Health Initiative provides funding to non-governmental organizations in Central and Eastern Europe and the former Soviet Union, or to organizations based in other countries that focus their activities in this region. The Initiative has an open pre-application process. To be considered for an invitation to submit a full proposal, organizations may write a one page letter containing the following information: its purpose and goals; full description of the project and amount requested; organization's total income for the past fiscal year; and biographical information about the organization's leadership.
Restrictions: The Mental Health Initiative does not fund projects which are connected to increasing the capacity of or to improving residential institutions for people with disabilities. This includes renovations or any other upgrades, equipment, charitable contributions or humanitarian aid, events organized within an institution, and any other form of core support to residential institutions.
Geographic Focus: Albania, Bosnia & Herzegovina, Bulgaria, Croatia, Czech Republic, Estonia, Germany, Hungary, Kosovo, Latvia, Lithuania, Macedonia, Montenegro, Poland, Romania, Russia, Serbia, Slovakia, Slovenia
Contact: Jens Trummer, Program Officer; (212) 547-6919; fax (212) 548-4676; jens.trummer@opensocietyfoundations.org or mhi@osi.hu
Internet: http://www.soros.org/initiatives/health/focus/mhi/focus_areas
Sponsor: Open Society Foundations
400 West 57th Street, 3rd Floor
New York, NY 10019

OSI After Prison Initiative Grants 3710
The Initiative works to decrease U.S. over-reliance on mass incarceration and harsh punishment by advancing policies and practices that support the successful reentry of people after prison. The Initiative funds projects that: reorient the mission and resources of criminal justice and prison systems to maximize successful reentry and minimize incarceration; strengthen civil society institutions and infrastructure in high-impact communities; promote civic and political inclusion and re-enfranchisement; and rethink crime and punishment for the 21st century. The program provides funding for projects that address one or more of the above focus areas and strategies through at least one of the following tactics: policy advocacy; coalition-building; community organizing; public education; impact litigation; and policy-driven research and analysis. Letters of inquiry for new projects will be accepted May 1-August 1 only. Applicants will be notified via email within 1-2 weeks of receipt that their request has been received. Decisions will be made by September 1, after which time candidates will receive a letter of declination or an invitation to submit a full proposal.
Requirements: The Initiative will consider proposals from advocacy groups, community groups, scholarly or research institutions, government agencies, associations of elected officials, and nonprofit business associations or initiatives.
Restrictions: The Initiative does not provide funding for: programs or direct services; lobbying activities; start-up costs or seed monies; annual fund raising drives; projects undertaken by individuals; general support (for first-time grantees); capital costs (including equipment or real estate purchases/renovations); or film production or post-production.
Geographic Focus: All States
Date(s) Application is Due: Aug 1
Contact: Leonard Noisette; (212) 548-0600; fax (212) 548-4679; lnoisette@sorosny.org
Internet: http://www.soros.org/initiatives/usprograms/focus/justice/programs/after_prison/
Sponsor: Open Society Foundations
400 West 57th Street, 3rd Floor
New York, NY 10019

OSI Sentencing and Incarceration Alternatives Project Grants 3711
The mission of the Project is to reduce the scale of incarceration in the United States. To that end, the Project offers grants to organizations that advance campaigns, research initiatives, and policies that seek to eliminate race and class disparities in sentencing and incarceration; reduce the length of criminal sentences and promote judicial discretion in sentencing; promote alternatives to incarceration that emphasize rehabilitation and treatment; limit prison growth and prison privatization; and empower communities most affected by mass incarceration to develop and advocate for alternative policies that address underlying social, racial, and economic inequality. The Project provides funding for policy reform, including the following strategies: grassroots/community-led advocacy, constituency-building, and mobilization; coalition-building; public education; impact litigation; policy-driven research and analysis; and leadership development. Letters of Inquiry must include a preliminary project budget and amount requested (there is no minimum or maximum request).
Requirements: The Project will consider Letters of Inquiry from advocacy groups, community groups, scholarly or research institutions, government agencies, associations of elected officials, and nonprofit business associations or initiatives.
Restrictions: The Project does not provide funding for: lobbying activities; programs or direct services; start-up costs or seed monies; annual fund raising drives; projects undertaken by individuals; capital costs, including equipment or real estate purchases/renovations; or film production or post-production.
Geographic Focus: All States
Contact: Christina Voight; (212) 548-0600; fax (212) 548-4666; cvoight@sorosny.org
Internet: http://www.soros.org/initiatives/usprograms/focus/justice/programs/sentencing/guidelines
Sponsor: Open Society Foundations
400 West 57th Street, 3rd Floor
New York, NY 10019

Ottinger Foundation Grants 3712
The Ottinger Foundation is a private family foundation that funds non-profit organizations that promote innovative policies and citizen activism to build a movement for change. It supports organizations that address structural or root causes of social problems and focus on systemic social change rather than direct services. Organizations and projects funded by the Ottinger Foundation include a sound strategic vision, a concrete action plan, and strong components of advocacy and grassroots organizing. Projects must have national significance. The Foundation also favor organizations that are involved in coalition building as well as building leadership and organizational infrastructure. The Foundation continues its program area focusing on economic security issues and is only accepting proposals in the form of a brief letter of intent in this area. Grants generally range from $10,000 to $50,000.
Requirements: IRS 501(c)3 tax-exempt organizations may apply. Due to the large number of proposals received, initial letters of inquiry are discouraged and will not receive a response. email proposals will also not be accepted.
Restrictions: The foundation does not make grants to organizations that traditionally enjoy popular support, such as universities, museums, hospitals, or schools. The foundation does not support individuals, academic research, film or video projects, the construction or restoration of buildings, conferences, books, or local programs that do not have national significance.
Geographic Focus: All States
Amount of Grant: 10,000 - 50,000 USD
Contact: Michele Lord, Executive Director; (212) 764-1508; fax (917) 438-4639; info@ottingerfoundation.org
Internet: http://www.ottingerfoundation.org/guidelines.html
Sponsor: Ottinger Foundation
80 Broad Street, 17th Floor
New York, NY 10004

Otto Bremer Foundation Grants 3713
The foundation concentrates its grantmaking activity in communities served by Bremer-affiliated banks and provides financial assistance to nonprofit organizations whose work contributes to the well-being of these towns. The foundation looks to support programs that promote civil and political rights, including freedom of assembly, speech, and religion; economic and social rights, including the right to education, food, health care, and shelter; and cultural and environmental rights, including the right to live in a clean environment and participate in the cultural and political events of one's community. Types of support include program development, operating support, capital (including building and equipment), matching or challenge grants, and internships. Applications are accepted throughout the year. Most grants are given for a one-year period, although some multiyear grants are awarded. The foundation encourages initial telephone or written inquiries concerning its interest in a particular project. Applicants are also encouraged to contact foundation staff for assistance in the development of a proposal.
Requirements: Private nonprofit or public 501(c)3 tax-exempt organizations whose beneficiaries are residents of Minnesota, North Dakota, or Wisconsin with priority given to those communities or regions served by Bremer affiliates.
Restrictions: Requests for the following types of projects are discouraged: annual fund drives; benefit events; camps; commercial and business development; K-12 education; medical research; sporting activities; building endowments other than for the development of community foundations; capital requests for hospitals and nursing homes; theatrical productions, including motion pictures, books, and other artistic or media projects; municipal and government services; or historical preservation, museums, and interpretive centers.
Geographic Focus: Minnesota, North Dakota, Wisconsin
Amount of Grant: 552 - 259,235 USD
Contact: Danielle Cheslog, Grants Manager; (651) 312-3717 or (651) 227-8036; fax (651) 312-3665; danielle@ottobremer.org or obf@ottobremer.org
Sponsor: Otto Bremer Foundation
445 Minnesota Stret, Suite 2250
Saint Paul, MN 55101-2107

OUT Fund for Lesbian and Gay Liberation Grants 3714
The organization is dedicated to a range of social justice, race, class, gender, and sexuality issues and supports radical organization projects to build community among lesbians, gay men, bisexuals, and transgender people. Proposals are sought that originate in marginalized communities like the poor, young, old, or disabled; serve rural areas; develop long-term coalitions in and out of diverse communities; organize antiracism efforts; foster organization through cultural projects; and focus on HIV health policy, prevention, and education efforts. Proposals that identify and target multi-issues, such as race, class, gender, and poverty, are preferred.
Requirements: 501(c)3 tax-exempt organizations and organizations with a 501(c)3 fiscal sponsor are eligible. 501(c)4 lobbying organizations may be eligible under very specific circumstances.
Geographic Focus: All States
Contact: Grants Administrator; (212) 529-5300; fax (212) 982-9272; info@fex.org
Internet: http://www.fex.org/grantmaking.shtml
Sponsor: Funding Exchange
666 Broadway, Suite 500
New York, NY 10012

Overbrook Foundation Grants 3715
The foundation strives to improve the lives of people by supporting projects that protect human and civil rights, advance the self-sufficiency and well being of individuals and their communities, and conserve the natural environment. The foundation's environment program supports organizations working to develop better consumption and production habits in the United States and in Latin America (currently Brazil, Mexico and Ecuador only). In Latin America the primary objective is to conserve the planet's dwindling biodiversity. The foundation's human and civil rights program is multifaceted and provides support to the following: reproductive health rights; domestic criminal system reform efforts; lesbian, gay, bisexual, and transgender rights; gun violence prevention and international human rights. An emphasis is placed on work that protects the rights of children and women. The foundation supports projects both domestically and internationally (with a particular focus in Latin America and South Africa). Generally speaking, the foundation's domestic programs support policy development, advocacy, coalition building, research, legal and other strategies likely to impact large classes of people or shape issues important to the foundation's mission. In its international funding, the foundation also supports organizations providing direct services. The first step in the application process is to Submit a letter of inquiry; full application is by invitation. Guidelines are available online.
Requirements: 501(c)3 tax-exempt organizations are eligible.
Restrictions: The foundation does not make grants to individuals and rarely for endowments, building campaigns, deficit financing, or religious purposes. Grant funds may not be used to participate in or intervene in any political campaign on behalf of or in opposition to any candidate for public office or to conduct, directly or indirectly, any voter registration drive (within 4945(d)2 of the IRS code). Grants are not made for debt reduction. Funding for conferences, publications, and media is limited to projects directly related to priorities in the foundation's program areas.
Geographic Focus: All States
Contact: Administrator; (212) 661-8710; fax (212) 661-8664; apply@overbrookfoundation.org
Internet: http://www.overbrook.org
Sponsor: Overbrook Foundation
122 E 42nd Street, Suite 2500
New York, NY 10168

Owen County Community Foundation Grants 3716
The Owen County Community Foundation was established in 1996 and serves the Owen County, Indiana area. The Foundation connects donors with the causes they care about. The Foundation provides support for organizations involved with arts and culture, education, animal welfare, health care, human services, and community development.
Requirements: A letter of intent is required prior to submitting a grant request, in addition to a tax-exempt verification. Applicants will be contacted within 30 days as to whether they should submit a full proposal. A full proposal should include the following: grant application and agreement page; the organization's background, including history, mission statement, number of staff, and number of persons served by agency or program; proposed program. Submitted information should also include desired outcomes; program methods; evaluation; funding the program; timetable; project budget; agency budget; governing organization; and financial statement and balance sheet.
Restrictions: Giving is limited to Owen County, Indiana. No grants for endowments, deficit funding, conferences, publications, films, television, or radio programs, travel, annual appeals, religious purposes or membership contributions.
Geographic Focus: Indiana
Date(s) Application is Due: Sep 15
Amount of Grant: Up to 30,000 USD
Contact: Marilyn Hart; (812) 829-1725; fax (812) 829-9958; marilyn@owencountycf.org
Internet: http://www.owencountycf.org/Grants.asp
Sponsor: Owen County Community Foundation
201 W. Morgan Street, Suite 202, P.O. Box 503
Spencer, IN 47460

Owens Corning Foundation Grants 3717
The Owens Corning Foundation's giving programs are made directly to non-profit organizations that most effectively provide direct service on behalf of disadvantaged children and families in the following areas: affordable housing; K-16 education; federated giving programs; arts and culture; and civic betterment. Funding emphasis is given to projects and organizations that promote diversity and social welfare, serve a broad sector of the community, and have a proven record of success.
Requirements: Applications are not accepted and there are no specific deadlines. Request for contributions (both financial and in-kind) must be made in writing on agency letterhead and include the following: description of the mission and work of the organization, including the audience and community the organization it serves; an outline of the specific request and a statement explaining how it accomplishes and measures the organization's goals; a description of the organization's anticipated outcome and benefits resulting from this grant; the amount requested; an outline of services or promotional opportunities available to the Owens Corning Foundation for contribution; proof of tax exempt status or tax exempt number; and other funding commitments to project.
Restrictions: In general, funding is not considered for the following organizations or types of activities: religious, political or discriminatory organizations; travel funds of any kind; capital campaigns and ongoing operations support; grants to individuals; special events such as conferences and sports competitions; organizations or projects in countries where the U.S. government restricts business dealings; or agencies that receive United Way support to the degree which we are already contributing. Giving is on a national basis in areas of company operations, with emphasis on Ohio.
Geographic Focus: All States
Contact: Simone Hayes; (419) 248-8000; OCFoundation@owenscorning.com
Internet: http://sustainability.owenscorning.com/contents/community-alliances/oc-foundation/
Sponsor: Owens Corning Foundation
1 Owens Corning Parkway
Toledo, OH 43659

Owens Foundation Grants 3718
The Owens Foundation, established in 1985, supports organizations involved with housing/shelter; development; human services; secondary school/education; economically disadvantaged; homelessness. Giving is primarily in Chicago, IL. area. There are no specific deadlines with which to adhere. Contact the Foundation for further application information and guidelines.
Requirements: Must be a non-profit in Chicago, IL.
Restrictions: No grants to individuals, or for capital campaigns, building funds, or raffles.
Geographic Focus: Illinois
Amount of Grant: 10,000 - 300,000 USD
Contact: Mary M. Owens, President; (708) 361-8845
Sponsor: Owens Foundation
7804 College Drive, Suite 3SW
Palos Heights, IL 60463-1473

PACCAR Foundation Grants 3719
The PACCAR Foundation is a private foundation which usually directs its grants to organizations in those communities within the service area of a significant PACCAR presence, such as a factory or a major office. Grant recipients in locations where there is a significant PACCAR presence usually include United Way, universities, hospitals and programs for the arts and economic education. The balance of the Foundation's grants is normally reserved for capital campaigns involving acquisition or improvement of facilities used for social and health services, education and cultural affairs.
Requirements: Organizations submitting a proposal should include the following information: complete name, mailing address and website of the organization; contact name, title, phone number and email address; information on the organization's history and goals; background data on the organization, personnel and Board of Directors or Board of Trustees; most recent annual report and audited financial statements; a list of sources

for ongoing operational support; evidence of 501(c)3 tax-exempt status specific amount requested; description of the specific project; an overall budget for the project to be funded and a total annual budget; a time schedule for project commencement and completion; and other project funding sources.
Restrictions: Proposals for program funds, support of operation budgets, and fundraising events are seldom funded. Although applications are taken anytime, the Foundation does not accept more than one request per organization per year; provide financial support by purchasing sponsorships, dinner or event tickets; purchase advertising space for charitable causes in yearbooks, programs or other publications; accept telephone solicitations; support specific churches for the purpose of religious advocacy; automatically renew a contribution from year to year; award scholarships or other grants for individuals; or grant personal interviews with trustees.
Geographic Focus: Oklahoma, Texas, Washington, Australia, Canada, Mexico, Netherlands, United Kingdom
Contact: Ken Hastings, (425) 468-7400; fax (425) 468-8216; ken.hastings@paccar.com
Internet: http://www.paccar.com/company/foundation.asp
Sponsor: PACCAR Foundation
777 106th Avenue N.E.
Bellevue, WA 98009

Pacers Foundation Be Drug-Free Grants 3720
The foremost priority of the Pacers Foundation is to help Indiana's youth through the nonprofit organizations that serve them. The foundation's areas of interest are youth programs that address childhood obesity, keep kids in school, prevent and treat adolescent and teenage alcohol/drug abuse, encourage tolerance and prevent bullying, and that help girls build self-esteem during the crucial preteen and teenage years. The foundation's Be Drug-Free grants support the efforts of Indiana groups that help young substance abusers to achieve and maintain their sobriety, help youth who are at serious risk of substance abuse to stay drug and alcohol free, and that educate high-risk youth about the potential consequences of drug and/or alcohol abuse (chronic dependence and links to criminal behavior, high-risk sexual activity, etc.). Substance abuse treatment programs, substance abuse education programs, counseling programs, after-school programs that focus on creating positive alternatives to "the streets," and other similarly focused groups should consider applying. Other types of organizations focused on youth substance abuse may also apply. Grants are one year in length and range from $5,000 - $20,000. Organizations that achieve the results set forth in their applications may apply for continued support in subsequent years. A link to application guidelines and forms is provided at the grant website.
Requirements: 501(c)3 tax-exempt organizations are eligible.
Restrictions: Pacers Foundation does not provide support for: individuals, emergency funds, political candidates or parties, fundraisers, or corporate memberships. Requests to support fundraisers are reviewed by Pacers Sports & Entertainment, not Pacers Foundation. These requests should be directed to Marilynn Wernke, Pacers Sports & Entertainment, at the sponsor address given. Although the foundation will occasionally support efforts of national significance or efforts outside of the state, it remains primarily committed to its hometown of Indianapolis and its home state of Indiana.
Geographic Focus: All States
Date(s) Application is Due: Dec 30
Amount of Grant: 5,000 - 20,000 USD
Contact: Rick Fuson; (317) 917-2864; fax (317) 917-2599; foundation@pacers.com
Internet: http://www.pacersfoundation.org/grants.php
Sponsor: Pacers Foundation
125 S Pennsylvania Street
Indianapolis, IN 46204

Pacers Foundation Be Educated Grants 3721
The foremost priority of the Pacers Foundation is to help Indiana's youth through the nonprofit organizations that serve them. The foundation's areas of interest are youth programs that address childhood obesity, keep kids in school, prevent and treat adolescent and teenage alcohol/drug abuse, encourage tolerance and prevent bullying, and that help girls build self-esteem during the crucial preteen and teenage years. The foundation's Be Educated grants support the efforts of Indiana groups that help struggling students to stay in school and out-of-school youth to re-engage in learning. Mentoring and/or tutoring programs, alternative schools, and after-school programs with an emphasis on learning should consider applying. Other types of organizations with a focus on youth education may also apply. Grants are one year in length and range from $5,000 - $20,000. Organizations that achieve the results set forth in their applications may apply for continued support in subsequent years. A link to application guidelines and forms is provided at the grant website.
Requirements: 501(c)3 tax-exempt organizations are eligible.
Restrictions: Pacers Foundation does not provide support for: individuals, emergency funds, political candidates or parties, fundraisers, or corporate memberships. Requests to support fundraisers are reviewed by Pacers Sports & Entertainment, not Pacers Foundation. These requests should be directed to Marilynn Wernke, Pacers Sports & Entertainment, at the sponsor address given. Although the foundation will occasionally support efforts of national significance or efforts outside of the state, it remains primarily committed to its hometown of Indianapolis and its home state of Indiana.
Geographic Focus: All States
Date(s) Application is Due: Sep 30
Amount of Grant: 5,000 - 20,000 USD
Contact: Rick Fuson; (317) 917-2864; fax (317) 917-2599; foundation@pacers.com
Internet: http://www.pacersfoundation.org/grants.php
Sponsor: Pacers Foundation
125 S Pennsylvania Street
Indianapolis, IN 46204

Pacers Foundation Be Healthy and Fit Grants 3722
The foremost priority of the Pacers Foundation is to help Indiana's youth through the nonprofit organizations that serve them. The foundation's areas of interest are youth programs that address childhood obesity, keep kids in school, prevent and treat adolescent and teenage alcohol/drug abuse, encourage tolerance and prevent bullying, and that help girls build self-esteem during the crucial preteen and teenage years. The foundation's Be Healthy and Fit grants support the efforts of Indiana groups that help overweight and obese youth and/or those who are at serious risk of becoming overweight to make healthier choices with respect to diet and exercise and to cope with the psychosocial effects of, and the stigma associated with, being overweight or obese; and that help educate schools and families about the root causes of obesity and the importance of nutrition and exercise in preventing and fighting obesity. School-based programs, health centers (including mental health programs focused on the psychosocial effects of childhood obesity), organizations focused on fighting and/or treating obesity, and groups focused on educating others about obesity should consider applying. Grants are one year in length and range from $5,000 - $20,000. Organizations that achieve the results set forth in their applications may apply for continued support in subsequent years. A link to application guidelines and forms is provided at the grant website.
Requirements: 501(c)3 tax-exempt organizations are eligible.
Restrictions: Pacers Foundation does not provide support for: individuals, emergency funds, political candidates or parties, fundraisers, or corporate memberships. Requests to support fundraisers are reviewed by Pacers Sports & Entertainment, not Pacers Foundation. These requests should be directed to Marilynn Wernke, Pacers Sports & Entertainment, at the sponsor address given. Although the foundation will occasionally support efforts of national significance or efforts outside of the state, it remains primarily committed to its hometown of Indianapolis and its home state of Indiana.
Geographic Focus: All States
Date(s) Application is Due: Jun 30
Amount of Grant: 5,000 - 20,000 USD
Contact: Rick Fuson; (317) 917-2864; fax (317) 917-2599; foundation@pacers.com
Internet: http://www.pacersfoundation.org/grants.php
Sponsor: Pacers Foundation
125 S Pennsylvania Street
Indianapolis, IN 46204

Pacers Foundation Be Tolerant Grants 3723
The foremost priority of the Pacers Foundation is to help Indiana's youth through the nonprofit organizations that serve them. The foundation's areas of interest are youth programs that address childhood obesity, keep kids in school, prevent and treat adolescent and teenage alcohol/drug abuse, encourage tolerance and prevent bullying, and that help girls build self-esteem during the crucial preteen and teenage years. The foundation's Be Tolerant grants support the efforts of Indiana groups that teach tolerance and respect for diversity; that focus on breaking down racial, ethnic, religious and other barriers by bringing youth from "all walks of life" together and exposing youth to cultures and "ways of life" other than their own; and that carry out anti-bullying and anti-stigma programs. School-based programs, faith-based programs, and other non-profit organizations focused on teaching tolerance should consider applying. Grants are one year in length and range from $5,000 - $20,000. Organizations that achieve the results set forth in their applications may apply for continued support in subsequent years. A link to application guidelines and forms is provided at the grant website.
Requirements: 501(c)3 tax-exempt organizations are eligible.
Restrictions: Pacers Foundation does not provide support for: individuals, emergency funds, political candidates or parties, fundraisers, or corporate memberships. Requests to support fundraisers are reviewed by Pacers Sports & Entertainment, not Pacers Foundation. These requests should be directed to Marilynn Wernke, Pacers Sports & Entertainment, at the sponsor address given. Although the foundation will occasionally support efforts of national significance or efforts outside of the state, it remains primarily committed to its hometown of Indianapolis and its home state of Indiana.
Geographic Focus: All States
Date(s) Application is Due: Mar 30
Amount of Grant: 5,000 - 20,000 USD
Contact: Rick Fuson; (317) 917-2864; fax (317) 917-2599; foundation@pacers.com
Internet: http://www.pacersfoundation.org/grants.php
Sponsor: Pacers Foundation
125 S Pennsylvania Street
Indianapolis, IN 46204

Pacers Foundation Indiana Fever's Be Younique Fund Grants 3724
The foremost priority of the Pacers Foundation is to help Indiana's youth through the nonprofit organizations that serve them. The foundation's areas of interest are youth programs that address childhood obesity, keep kids in school, prevent and treat adolescent and teenage alcohol/drug abuse, encourage tolerance and prevent bullying, and that help girls build self-esteem during the crucial preteen and teenage years. The Indiana Fever's Be Younique Fund grants support the efforts of Indiana groups that help girls build self-esteem; that promote positive body imagery; and that educate girls about dating violence and/or provide services to those who have experienced such violence. School-based programs and other non-profit organizations focused on empowering girls should consider applying. Grants are one year in length and range from $5,000 - $20,000. Organizations that achieve the results set forth in their applications may apply for continued support in subsequent years. A link to application guidelines and forms is provided at the grant website.
Requirements: 501(c)3 tax-exempt organizations are eligible.
Restrictions: Pacers Foundation does not provide support for: individuals, emergency funds, political candidates or parties, fundraisers, or corporate memberships. Requests to support fundraisers are reviewed by Pacers Sports & Entertainment, not Pacers Foundation. These

requests should be directed to Marilynn Wernke, Pacers Sports & Entertainment, at the sponsor address given. Although the foundation will occasionally support efforts of national significance or efforts outside of the state, it remains primarily committed to its hometown of Indianapolis and its home state of Indiana.
Geographic Focus: All States
Date(s) Application is Due: Mar 30
Amount of Grant: 5,000 - 20,000 USD
Contact: Rick Fuson; (317) 917-2864; fax (317) 917-2599; foundation@pacers.com
Internet: http://www.pacersfoundation.org/grants.php
Sponsor: Pacers Foundation
125 S Pennsylvania Street
Indianapolis, IN 46204

PacifiCare Foundation Grants 3725
The foundation's mission is to improve the quality of life for residents of areas where PacifiCare Health Systems does business. The foundation's focus areas are: child/youth, including child care, youth activity programs, at-risk youth, and counseling programs; education, including school programs that promote self-esteem, encourage academic achievement and the development of specific skills, literacy programs, training programs, and programs that improve the effectiveness of the educational system; health, including prevention, health education, access to health care, and improved quality of health care of targeted populations; human/social services, including housing, shelters, education, protection, community development, crime prevention, food, transportation, and other social services for targeted populations; and senior, including social services, nutrition, education, volunteer, and and adult day care. Preference will be given to proposals for specific projects. Requests for operating costs will be considered if the request is very specific and clearly defined. Seed grant requests also receive consideration. Organizations funded by the foundation are welcome to reapply annually. Application forms are available on the foundation's website.
Requirements: IRS 501(c)3 nonprofit organizations serving residents of PacifiCare regions in Arizona, California, Colorado, Nevada, Oklahoma, Oregon, Texas, and Washington are eligible. The proposal must include two copies of the following: application form; checklist form; cover letter accompanying the proposal, signed by either the CEO or appointee of the organization, summarizing the proposed project, the problem addressed, the amount requested, and the name and phone number of the contact person; the written proposal, which should not exceed 2-5 pages in length and should include background information, description of the problem, need or issue being addressed, and a complete description of the proposed project; most recent audited financial statement and 990; current operating budget and line item budget for the specific project; list of major funders and amounts; list of board of directors; and one paragraph summary of previous support from the PacifiCare Foundation.
Restrictions: The foundation will not consider grants for arts/cultural programs, associations, annual campaigns, associations (professional/technical), capital campaigns, challenge/matching grants, hosting/supporting conferences, individual support, private foundations, programs that promote religious doctrine, research, scholarships, or sponsorship of special events.
Geographic Focus: Arizona, California, Colorado, Nevada, Oklahoma, Oregon, Texas, Washington
Date(s) Application is Due: Jan 1; Jul 1
Amount of Grant: 2,000 - 10,000 USD
Contact: Riva Gebel, Director, (714) 825-5233
Internet: http://www.pacificare.com/vgn/images/portal/cit_60701/127503Guidelines_for_Charitable_Giving.pdf
Sponsor: PacifiCare Foundation
P.O. Box 25186, MS LC03-159
Santa Ana, CA 92799

Pacific Life Foundation Grants 3726
Pacific Life has long recognized the importance of helping communities where their employees reside and work and has a record of community involvement that spans the history of the company. The Foundation accepts proposals from agencies seeking funds for programs and projects in the areas of health and human services; education; arts and culture; and civic, community, and environment. Grant proposals are generally accepted from July 15 through August 15. See the Foundation's website to verify deadlines.
Requirements: Funding is made primarily in areas with large concentrations of Pacific Life employees: generally, the greater Orange County, California, area and other areas, such as Omaha, Nebraska. Ideally, agencies should serve a large area, usually including more than one city or community. Some California statewide and national organizations also receive support. General grants range from $5,000 to $10,000 for a one-year period of funding and are given to support programs, operating expenses, or collaborative programs with other agencies. Capital grants range from $10,000 to $100,000 and are paid over multiple years. Capital grants are generally given to an agency with an organized campaign already under way to raise substantial funds. More than fifty percent of the campaign goal (excluding in-kind donations, anonymous gifts and loans) must be pledged prior to consideration by the Foundation.
Restrictions: The following is not funded: individuals; political parties, candidates, or partisan political organizations; labor organizations, fraternal organizations, athletic clubs, or social clubs; K-12 schools, school districts, or school foundations; sectarian or denominational religious organizations, except for programs that are broadly promoted, available to anyone, and free from religious orientation; fundraising events; sports leagues or teams; and advertising sponsorship or conference underwriting/sponsorship.
Geographic Focus: All States
Contact: Brenda Hardwig; (949) 219-3787; PLFoundation@PacificLife.com
Internet: http://www.pacificlife.com/About+Pacific+Life/Foundation+or+Community
Sponsor: Pacific Life Foundation
700 Newport Center Drive
Newport Beach, CA 92660

PacifiCorp Foundation for Learning Grants 3727
The foundation awards grants to eligible nonprofit organizations in four broad areas, including educational and research institutions, both public and private, from early childhood through university level; youth organizations; cultural enrichment organizations dedicated to the performing arts, the visual arts, historic preservation, cross-cultural education, and other such activities; and health and human services organizations, including chemical dependency treatment and prevention programs, senior citizen centers, runaway youth services, and domestic violence treatment and prevention programs. Deadline for education organizations is March 15; for civic, community, and organizations not covered in other categories, June 15; for culture and arts organizations, September 15; for health, welfare, and social service organizations, December 15. Guidelines and application are available online.
Requirements: 501(c)3 community organizations in Idaho, Oregon, Utah, California, Washington, and Wyoming are eligible.
Restrictions: Organizations and activities not eligible for foundation support include religious groups for religious purposes; political organizations, ballot measure campaigns, or candidates for public office; organizations that discriminate against individuals on the basis of creed, color, sex, age, national origin, or veteran status; individuals; contributions to or memberships in chambers of commerce, service clubs, taxpayer associations, and other similar bodies; or any non-charitable purpose. As a general rule, the foundation also will not support establishment or support of endowments; coverage of operating deficits; capital campaigns; conferences, conventions, and events; projects that do not have a bearing on communities within the six-state region served by PacifiCorp subsidiaries or communities served by PacifiCorp Power Marketing.
Geographic Focus: California, Idaho, Oregon, Utah, Washington, Wyoming
Date(s) Application is Due: Mar 15; Jun 15; Sep 15; Dec 15
Amount of Grant: 1,000 - 10,000 USD
Contact: Grants Manager; (503) 813-7257; pacificorpfoundation@pacificorp.com
Internet: http://www.pacificorpfoundation.org/Article/Article25110.html
Sponsor: PacifiCorp Foundation for Learning
825 NE Multnomah, Suite 2000
Portland, OR 97232-4116

Pacific Rainbow Foundation Grants 3728
Established in Hawaii in 2005 by primary donor Patrick Joseph Sullivan, the Foundation primarily supports educational and health care programs in Hawaii. There are no specific applications or deadlines with which to adhere, and potential applicants should begin by forwarding a letter in narrative form detailing the project and funding requested.
Requirements: Any 501(c)3 organization serving residents of Hawaii is eligible to apply.
Geographic Focus: Hawaii
Amount of Grant: Up to 10,000 USD
Contact: Elliot H. Loden, (808) 524-8099; fax (808) 526-0968
Sponsor: Pacific Rainbow Foundation
737 Bishop Street, Suite 2990
Honolulu, HI 96813-3219

Packard Foundation Local Grants 3729
The Foundation supports an array of nonprofit organizations in geographic areas that are significant to the Packard family. These include the five California counties that surround the Foundation's headquarters in Los Altos, California (San Mateo, Santa Clara, Santa Cruz, Monterey, and San Benito) as well as Pueblo, Colorado, the birthplace of David Packard. The goal in supporting these communities is to help make them stronger and more vibrant places where all families can thrive and reach their potential. To achieve this goal, Local Grants focus resources on addressing five fundamental issue areas: arts; children and youth; conservation and science; food and shelter; and population and reproductive health. There are no deadlines. Samples of previously funded projects are discussed at the Foundation website.
Requirements: The Foundation accepts grant proposals only for charitable, educational, or scientific purposes, primarily from tax-exempt, charitable organizations. An online letter of inquiry form is available at the Foundation's website. Applicants typically receive a response within three to six weeks. If accepted, further details about completing a full proposal will be provided.
Restrictions: The following is not funded: public policy work, capital campaigns, specific performances or productions, one-time events, event sponsorships, religious or business organizations, and individuals. Requests should generally not exceed 25% of the organization's operating budget.
Geographic Focus: California, Colorado
Amount of Grant: 15,000 - 150,000 USD
Contact: Linda Schuurmann Baker, Program Officer, Santa Cruz and Monterey Counties; (650) 917-7238; fax (650) 948-1361; local@packard.org
Internet: http://www.packard.org/what-we-fund/local-grantmaking/
Sponsor: David and Lucile Packard Foundation
343 Second Street
Los Altos, CA 94022

Packard Foundation Organizational Effectiveness and Philanthropy Grants 3730
The Organizational Effectiveness and Philanthropy Grants support the Packard Foundation's current grantees to allow them to undertake projects that transform their organizations in a sustained and meaningful way. These grants address the many organizational and capacity challenges that affect nonprofits, from strategic planning and board development needs to mergers and executive transitions. To this end, the Foundation advances the organizational effectiveness of current grantees by supporting projects that improve their management, governance, and leadership by developing strategies, systems, structures, and skills. The Foundation also makes grants to help advance and support the field of private philanthropy. Funding is primarily used to cover the cost of outside consultants in the following efforts:

organization or network assessment, which may include social network analysis or mapping; strategic planning, business, or operational planning; financial and executive coaching; mergers or other restructuring efforts; fund development planning and feasibility studies; executive search services during senior leadership transitions; cultural competence or diversity initiatives; board development and governance; training for network coordinators (e.g., facilitation skills); strategic communications planning, including planning for use of social media; and building the organization or network's capacity to evaluate its work. Samples of previously funded projects are discussed at the Foundation website.
Restrictions: Only current Packard Foundation grantees are eligible to apply. The following are not eligible for funding: organizations or networks that are not current Packard Foundation grantees; project already underway or for expenses already incurred; and projects to build the field of organization or network effectiveness. The Foundation does not support core operating costs to sustain organizations or networks and related expenses such as staff salaries; administrative overhead; computers or software; rent or other occupancy expenses; website design, financial audits; tuition for degree programs; conference costs; recurring staff training expenses; printing of strategic plans or other reports; and legal fees.
Geographic Focus: All States
Contact: Cheryl Chang; (650) 948-7658; fax (650) 948-1361
Internet: http://www.packard.org/what-we-fund/organizational-effectiveness-and-philanthropy/
Sponsor: David and Lucile Packard Foundation
343 Second Street
Los Altos, CA 94022

Pajaro Valley Community Health Health Trust Insurance/Coverage & Education on Using the System Grants 3731
The Trust provides grants for projects that advance our mission to improve the health and quality of life for all people of the greater Pajaro Valley. The primary goals of the Health Insurance/Coverage & Education on Using the System Initiative are to increase the number of Pajaro Valley residents with health insurance, increase residents understanding and appropriate use of a medical home (family practitioner), and decrease inappropriate use of the emergency department. The Trust will support programs that increase the number of Pajaro Valley residents that have health insurance, as well as programs that improve access to health care for our community's more vulnerable populations. Additionally, the Trust will look at community-wide solutions to these issues.
Requirements: Applicant organizations must provide or plan to provide programs/services benefiting the health of residents in the Trust's primary geographic service area. Communities within this service area include Watsonville, Pajaro, Freedom, and Aromas. The home office of the applicant organization need not be located in the Pajaro Valley, but the applicant organization must demonstrate that it provides or plans to provide services that directly benefit residents of the Pajaro Valley. The applicant organization must be a nonprofit, 501(c)3 tax-exempt organization; a school-based health program; or have a 501(c)3, tax-exempt organization as a fiscal sponsor.
Restrictions: In general, the Trust's Board of Directors prefers not to fund programs or projects administered by a city, county, state, or federal government with the exception of school-based health programs. In general, the Trust does not give grants to: projects that do not substantially benefit residents of the Pajaro Valley; projects and proposals unrelated to the Trust's mission, eligibility requirements, and current strategic plan funding priorities and objectives; individuals, with the exception of the Trust's scholarship programs; religious organizations for secular purposes; endowments, building campaigns, annual fund appeals, fundraising events, or celebrations; or commercial ventures.
Geographic Focus: California
Contact: Raquel Ramirez Ruiz, Director of Programs; (831) 763-6456 or (831) 761-5639; fax (831) 763-6084; info@pvhealthtrust.org or raquel_dhc@pvhealthtrust.org
Internet: http://www.pvhealthtrust.org/grants_core.html
Sponsor: Pajaro Valley Community Health Trust
85 Nielson Street
Watsonville, CA 95076

Pajaro Valley Community Health Trust Diabetes and Contributing Factors Grants 3732
The Trust provides grants for projects that advance our mission to improve the health and quality of life for all people of the greater Pajaro Valley. The primary goals of the Diabetes and Contributing Factors Initiative are to reduce the risk factors associated with diabetes, reduce complications related to diabetes, and decrease the prevalence of childhood and adult obesity in the Pajaro Valley. The Trust will mobilize communities in the tri-county area to prevent the increase of type-2 diabetes in youth and young adult populations; teach diabetes self-management, and provide medical nutrition therapy to people living with diabetes thereby preventing the life-threatening complications associated with diabetes. Further, the Trust will promote "best practices" in clinical management of diabetes throughout the region. The Trust will seek to minimize factors that contribute to diabetes, including obesity, poor nutrition, and lack of physical activity.
Requirements: Applicant organizations must provide or plan to provide programs/services benefiting the health of residents in the Trust's primary geographic service area. Communities within this service area include Watsonville, Pajaro, Freedom, and Aromas. The home office of the applicant organization need not be located in the Pajaro Valley, but the applicant organization must demonstrate that it provides or plans to provide services that directly benefit residents of the Pajaro Valley. The applicant organization must be a nonprofit, 501(c)3 tax-exempt organization; a school-based health program; or have a 501(c)3, tax-exempt organization as a fiscal sponsor.
Restrictions: In general, the Trust's Board of Directors prefers not to fund programs or projects administered by a city, county, state, or federal government with the exception of school-based health programs. In general, the Trust does not give grants to: projects that do not substantially benefit residents of the Pajaro Valley; projects and proposals unrelated to the Trust's mission, eligibility requirements, and current strategic plan funding priorities and objectives; individuals, with the exception of the Trust's scholarship programs; religious organizations for secular purposes; endowments, building campaigns, annual fund appeals, fundraising events, or celebrations; or commercial ventures.
Geographic Focus: California
Amount of Grant: 5,000 - 30,000 USD
Contact: Raquel Ramirez Ruiz, Director of Programs; (831) 763-6456 or (831) 761-5639; fax (831) 763-6084; info@pvhealthtrust.org or raquel_dhc@pvhealthtrust.org
Internet: http://www.pvhealthtrust.org/grants_core.html
Sponsor: Pajaro Valley Community Health Trust
85 Nielson Street
Watsonville, CA 95076

Palm Beach and Martin Counties Grants 3733
The community foundation supports nonprofit organizations serving Florida's Palm Beach and Martin Counties in eight program areas: arts and culture, education, environment, health, human services, community development, the conservation and preservation of historical and cultural resources, and human and race relations. Guidelines and forms are available online.
Requirements: Florida organizations based in and serving Palm Beach and Martin Counties are eligible to apply.
Restrictions: Proposals will not be funded for routine operating expenses, endowments, building campaigns, computers, fund-raising events, celebration functions, feasibility studies, religious organizations for religious purposes, or recurring requests for the same purpose.
Geographic Focus: Florida
Amount of Grant: Up to 25,000 USD
Contact: Linda Raybin; (561) 659-6800; fax (561) 832-6542; lraybin@cfpdmc.org
Internet: http://www.cfpbmc.org/grant/Guidelines.asp
Sponsor: Community Foundation for Palm Beach and Martin Counties
700 S Dixie Highway, Suite 200
West Palm Beach, FL 33401

PAMA Awards Program 3734
PAMA's awards program honors those individuals or companies who have promoted the tenets of professionalism and integrity on behalf of the aviation maintenance technician while exemplifying honor and diligence for outstanding achievements. Currently, the awards include: Award of Excellence; Award of Merit; Award of Special Merit; Chapter of the Year Award; Company Appreciation Award; Member Service Award; The Joe Chase Award; and the PAMA/ATP Award. Guidelines and nomination forms are available online.
Geographic Focus: All States
Date(s) Application is Due: Nov 30
Amount of Grant: Up to 1,000 USD
Contact: Administrator; (866) 865-7262 or (724) 772-4091; pamaawards@sae.org
Internet: http://www.pama.org/content.asp?contentid=71
Sponsor: Professional Aviation Maintenance Association Foundation
400 Commonwealth Drive
Warrendale, PA 15096

Parke County Community Foundation Grants 3735
The Parke County Community Foundation Grants fund fields of interest which are community-enhancing such as agricultural interests, family support, fine arts/culture, handicapped persons, historic preservation, individual township interests, religion, scholarship/education, and youth/recreation. The Foundation accepts grant applications year-round.
Requirements: Applications for grants are accepted from any new or existing charitable organization or community agency with a charitable purpose in Parke County. Organizations should fill out the online application with the following information: a detailed description of their organization, project, and budget required; other organizations who might partner with them with a similar project. For requests of $1,000 or less, a one-page letter or email is acceptable. This letter should describe the project, sharing the organization's perception of need. It should also describe who and how many are likely to benefit and the factors the organization will use to evaluate its success. Applicants are encouraged to contact the Foundation to discuss if their project is appropriate for funding before submitting the application.
Restrictions: The Foundation usually funds only to nonprofit organizations, but may fund other organizations if the project is designed to assist the needy and promote well-being in Parke County.
Geographic Focus: Indiana
Contact: Brad Bumgardner, Executive Director; (765) 569-7223; fax (765) 569-5383; bradbum@yahoo.com or parkeccf@yahoo.com
Internet: http://www.parkeccf.org/Grants.html
Sponsor: Parke County Community Foundation
115 North Market Street
Rockville, IN 47872

Parker Foundation (California) Grants 3736
The Parker Foundation was founded for charitable purposes leading to the betterment of life for all people of San Diego County, California. Areas of grant support include culture (visual arts, performing arts, museums/zoos), adult and youth services, medical, education, community activities, and environmental. Initial grant proposals must be submitted in writing. The format can be found on the website. Generally proposals are considered at the next Board meeting, which is generally monthly. Meeting dates can be found on the website under Board Schedule.
Requirements: Applicants must be 501(c)3 organizations.
Restrictions: While occasional grant support is given to religious organizations, those grants are only made for direct support to nonsectarian educational or service projects.
Geographic Focus: California

Contact: Program Contact; (760) 720-0630; fax (760) 420-1239
Internet: http://www.TheParkerFoundation.org
Sponsor: Parker Foundation: California
2604-B El Camino Real, Suite 244
Carlsbad, CA 92008

Parker Foundation (Virginia) Grants to Support Christian Evangelism   3737

The foundation awards grants nationwide to Christian agencies and churches that are working for redemptive purposes in accordance with Biblical truth, morality, and mission. Grants support specific projects that aim to make successful organizations more effective or for the start up of a new project. Areas of interest include world evangelism, evangelical leadership development, and Christian social relief and public persuasion. Contact the Foundation for application materials. There are no deadlines.
Requirements: 501(c)3 organizations are eligible.
Geographic Focus: All States
Contact: Brian Broadway, Program Contact; (804) 285-5416
Sponsor: Parker Foundation: Virginia
701 East Byrd Street, 17th Floor
Richmond, VA 23219

Parkersburg Area Community Foundation Action Grants   3738

Community Action Grants help organizations by supporting vital projects in the fields of arts and culture, education, health and human services, community and economic development, youth and family services, and recreation. The Foundation accepts applications for the spring deadline on March 1 and for the fall deadlines on September 1. Applicants are encouraged to contact the Foundation with any questions about the grants or the application process.
Requirements: Grants are awarded to 501(c)3 tax-exempt nonprofit organizations in specific counties of West Virginia (Calhoun; Doddridge; Gilmer; Jackson; Pleasants; Mason; Ritchie; Roane; Wirt; and Wood) and Washington County, Ohio.
Restrictions: Grants do not support religious purposes, travel, meetings, seminars, student exchange programs, annual campaigns, endowment funds, operating budgets, or debt reduction.
Geographic Focus: Ohio, West Virginia
Date(s) Application is Due: Mar 1; Sep 1
Amount of Grant: 1,000 - 10,000 USD
Contact: Marian Clowes; (866) 428-4438 or (304) 428-4438; info@pacfwv.com
Internet: http://www.pacfwv.com
Sponsor: Parkersburg Area Community Foundation
501 Avenuery Street, P.O. Box 1762
Parkersburg, WV 26102-1762

Park Foundation Grants   3739

The foundation awards grants to nonprofit organizations in central New York and areas in the U.S. Southeast. Areas of interest include education and higher education, animal welfare, environment, television, and general charitable giving. Types of support include general operating support, program development, professorships, seed money, fellowships, scholarship funds, research grants, and matching funds. There are no application deadlines. The board meets in March, June, August, October, and December. Obtain application forms.
Requirements: 501(c)3 nonprofits in he eastern US, primarily in central NY, Washington, DC, and North Carolina are eligible.
Restrictions: For-profit organizations and individuals are not eligible.
Geographic Focus: All States
Amount of Grant: 5,000 - 100,000 USD
Contact: Linda Madeo, Executive Director; (607) 272-9124; fax (607) 272-6057
Sponsor: Park Foundation
P.O. Box 550
Ithaca, NY 14851

Partnership Enhancement Program (PEP) Grants   3740

The mission of the National Tree Trust continues through the Arbor Day Foundation, a nonprofit, environmental education organization with a mission of inspiring people to plant, nurture, and celebrate trees. The Partnership Enhancement Program (PEP) makes dollar-for-dollar matching monetary grants to qualifying nonprofits involved in a wide range of tree-related projects. Grants are made in four categories: tree planting and maintenance; education and training; overhead and administration; and national and regional programs. Applications for projects usually become available in June.
Requirements: To be eligible, the applying organization must: be a currently certified 501(c)3 nonprofit organization located within the United States; have been in existence for a minimum of two years; demonstrate that tree planting, maintenance, and education are components of the organization; and be volunteer based.
Geographic Focus: All States
Amount of Grant: Up to 25,000 USD
Contact: Mark Derowitsch; (888) 448-7337; mderowitsch@arborday.org
Internet: http://www.arborday.org/generalinfo/
Sponsor: Arbor Day Foundation
100 Arbor Avenue
Nebraska City, NE 68410

Pasadena Foundation Average Grants   3741

The community foundation serves the greater Pasadena, CA, area and awards grants for capital improvements to agencies serving children, the elderly, and the disabled. Fields of interest include child development, the elderly, disabled, youth, drug abuse, family planning, education, arts and the humanities, mental health, community development, and the environment. Challenge/matching grants also are awarded. The deadline is the first business day in March.
Restrictions: Schools, religious institutions, and political organizations are ineligible.
Geographic Focus: California
Amount of Grant: Up to 8,000 USD
Contact: Program Contact; (626) 796-2097; fax (626) 583-4738; pcfstaff@pasadenacf.org
Internet: http://www.pasadenacf.org/grant_reg.htm
Sponsor: Pasadena Foundation
260 S Los Robles Avenue, #119
Pasadena, CA 91101

PAS Internship   3742

The Percussive Arts Society (PAS) is a music service organization promoting percussion education, research, performance and appreciation throughout the world. PAS offers six-month internships during the spring and fall semesters for percussion students who wish to gain music industry experience. PAS interns acquire broad industry experience by assisting with a variety of staff projects, including those relating to music products, teaching, concert production, publishing, artist management, and marketing. Spring internship(s) begin in January. Interns receive a $1,200 stipend each month. Application guidelines are available at the grant website. Applicants and faculty advisors are encouraged to contact PAS for additional information.
Requirements: All percussion students who wish to gain music industry experience and promote career goals are eligible to apply.
Geographic Focus: All States
Date(s) Application is Due: Nov 4
Amount of Grant: 7,200 USD
Contact: Otice Sircy; (317) 974-4488; fax (317) 974-4499; osircy@pas.org
Internet: http://www.pas.org/experience/internship.aspx
Sponsor: Percussive Arts Society
110 W. Washington Street, Suite A
Indianapolis, IN 46204

Paso del Norte Health Foundation Grants   3743

The Paso del Norte Health Foundation (PdNHF) is one of the largest private foundations on the U.S. - Mexico border. It was established in 1995 from the sale of Providence Memorial Hospital to Tenet Healthcare Corporation for $130 million. The purpose of the Foundation is to improve the health and promote the wellness of the people living in West Texas, Southern New Mexico, and Ciudad Juárez, Mexico through education and prevention. The foundation currently issues RFPs for the following initiatives: physical activity and balanced nutrition; tobacco, alcohol, and illicit drug use; health care and mental health services; healthy families and social environments; and leadership. Interested organizations can sign up for the foundation's RFP mailing list at the grant website. The foundation does not accept unsolicited proposals but offers workshops when new RFPs are issued and also encourages organizations to contact the Program Officer with suggestions and ideas for new programs, especially as they relate to the foundation's initiatives. At the time of this writing, the foundation has an active RFP entitled "A Smoke-free Paso del Norte" which may be downloaded from the grant website. The application must be received by 2 p.m. on the due date. It may be hand-delivered or emailed in PDF format directly to the Program Director, but not faxed.
Requirements: Proposals must be solicited, and must be linked to an established initiative. Applicants must be 501(c)3 or equivalent organizations operated for charitable, educational, or religious purposes. Funding is principally for in-field intervention projects. Research, studies, or planning activities may be considered only if they directly assist in the implementation of a project. Ineligible expenses include general operating and overhead expenses, capital acquisition or construction (such as property or buildings), purchase of motorized vehicles, and the direct provision of medical services and medicines for acute care.
Restrictions: Funding is not provided to individuals. Proposals are only considered from the Paso del Norte region which encompasses El Paso and Hudspeth Counties in West Texas; Doña Ana, Luna, and Otero Counties in Southern New Mexico; and Ciudad Juárez and Chihuahua in Northern Mexico.
Geographic Focus: Texas, Mexico
Date(s) Application is Due: Jan 10
Contact: Jon Law; (915) 544-7636; fax (915) 544-7713; jlaw@pdnhf.org
Internet: http://www.pdnhf.org/grantcenter.asp
Sponsor: Paso del Norte Health Foundation
221 N. Kansas, Suite 1900
El Paso, TX 79901

PAS PASIC Scholarships   3744

The Percussive Arts Society (PAS) is a music service organization promoting percussion education, research, performance and appreciation throughout the world. PAS provides several scholarships assisting students to attend the annual Percussive Arts Society International Convention (PASIC), which features over 120 concerts, clinics, master classes, labs, workshops, panels and presentations. Each scholarship recipient will receive a PASIC registration, a PASIC souvenir t-shirt, and $500 toward the cost of transportation/lodging. A downloadable application is available at the grant website.
Requirements: Applicants must be active PAS members at time of application and during the convention.
Geographic Focus: All States
Date(s) Application is Due: Jun 15
Contact: Heath Towson; (317) 974-4488; fax (317) 974-4499; percarts@pas.org
Internet: http://www.pas.org/experience/grantsscholarships.aspx
Sponsor: Percussive Arts Society
110 W. Washington Street, Suite A
Indianapolis, IN 46204

Pathways to Nature Conservation Fund Grants 3745
The fund makes grants to enhance environmental education activities and bird and wildlife viewing opportunities at significant nature tourism destinations in the United States and Canada. Projects of interest include, but are not limited to, boardwalks, viewing platforms and blinds, educational displays, and interactive exhibits. Grants will be managed by the foundation and will include a mix of federal and private funds. Grantees must match awards with a minimum one-to-one ratio of third-party cash or contributed goods and services. The Pathways To Nature grant funds are currently committed to funding only projects within the National Wildlife Refuge System.
Requirements: Eligible project sites include public and private nature tourism destinations that attract at least 100,000 visitors annually from multi-states, provinces, and countries.
Restrictions: Applicants must be located within the National Wildlife Refuge System.
Geographic Focus: All States
Date(s) Application is Due: Jul 15
Amount of Grant: Up to 50,000 USD
Contact: Heather C. Alexander, Director, Grants and Contract Management; (202) 857-0166 or (404) 679-7099; fax (202) 857-0162; pathways@nfwf.org
Internet: http://www.wbu.com/pathways/about.html
Sponsor: National Fish and Wildlife Foundation
1875 Century Boulevard, Suite 200
Atlanta, GA 30345

Patricia Price Peterson Foundation Grants 3746
Established in 1964, the foundation awards grants to eligible California 501(c)3 nonprofit organizations and Central American countries in its areas of interest, including environmental protection and conservation (including agricultural university scholarships, orphanages, environmental education, community development, and nature reserve-conservation), science education, and federated giving. Types of support include program grants and general operating grants. Funding can be used for emergency programs, equipment, general operations, land acquisition, management development, capacity building, professorships, program development, scholarship funds, or seed money. The application deadline is in early May; call for the specific date. the applicant's initial approach should be via email, followed by the submission of a written application. Final proposals should be submitted in Spanish.
Requirements: California nonprofit organizations serving the San Francisco Bay area or Central American organizations are eligible to apply.
Geographic Focus: California, Belize, Costa Rica, Cuba, El Salvador, Guatemala, Honduras, Jamaica, Mexico, Nicaragua, Panama
Contact: Stephen W. Bennett, President; (831) 684-0958; fax (415) 622-5388; epeterson@aureos.co.cr or neyastv@aol.com
Sponsor: Patricia Price Peterson Foundation
17 Aqua View Drive
Selva Beach, CA 95076-1625

Patrick and Aimee Butler Foundation Community Arts and Humanities Grants 3747
The Butler Family Foundation makes grants through Community Grants, the Foundation Initiative Fund, and Special Projects programs. Community Grants are competitive and primarily support the Twin Cities metropolitan area of St. Paul and Minneapolis. The Foundation has an interest in making the arts and cultural programs accessible to all communities in the Twin Cities region. Funding will be granted to organizations that emphasize artistic quality, reflect the diversity of the community, and demonstrate stable programming, within the following areas: Historical Societies, primarily in Ramsey County, Minnesota; Humanities programs or organizations; Museums, and Music Education. The Foundation is most likely to make general operating or program support grants.
Requirements: Minnesota 501(c)3 nonprofits are eligible to apply.
Restrictions: The Butler Family Foundation does not make grants to organizations through fiscal agents. The Foundation does not make loans or grants to individuals. No grants are made outside of the United States. The Foundation does not fund criminal justice, economic development or education, work or vocational programs, films or videos, health care, hospitals, medical research, elementary or secondary education, and music or dance.
Geographic Focus: Minnesota
Date(s) Application is Due: Feb 7; Jun 6
Amount of Grant: 5,000 - 30,000 USD
Contact: Kerrie Blevins; (651) 222-2566; kerrieb@butlerfamilyfoundation.org
Internet: http://www.butlerfamilyfoundation.org/guidelines2011.html
Sponsor: Patrick and Aimee Butler Family Foundation
332 Minnesota Street, Suite E-1420
Saint Paul, MN 55101-1369

Patrick and Aimee Butler Family Foundation Community Environment Grants 3748
The Butler Family Foundation makes grants through Community Grants, the Foundation Initiative Fund, and Special Projects programs. Community Grants are competitive and primarily support the entire State of Minnesota. The Foundation seeks to preserve and promote stewardship of the natural environment for present and future generations. Funding will be granted to programs that positively impact environmental quality and encourage citizen participation in environmental issues. Granting will be limited to organizations and programs operating in Minnesota, whose primary mission is to address one of these issues: Water Quality of the Upper Mississippi Watershed; Environmental Education (with a preference for programs providing in-depth learning experiences); Land Preservation and Use. The Foundation is most likely to make general operating or program support grants.
Requirements: Minnesota 501(c)3 nonprofits are eligible to apply.
Restrictions: The Butler Family Foundation does not make grants to organizations through fiscal agents. The Foundation does not make loans or grants to individuals. No grants are made outside of the United States. The Foundation does not fund criminal justice, economic development or education, work or vocational programs, films or videos, health care, hospitals, medical research, elementary or secondary education, and music or dance.
Geographic Focus: Minnesota
Date(s) Application is Due: Feb 7; Jun 6
Amount of Grant: 5,000 - 30,000 USD
Contact: Kerrie Blevins; (651) 222-2566; kerrieb@butlerfamilyfoundation.org
Internet: http://www.butlerfamilyfoundation.org/guidelines2011.html
Sponsor: Patrick and Aimee Butler Family Foundation
332 Minnesota Street, Suite E-1420
Saint Paul, MN 55101-1369

Patrick and Aimee Butler Family Foundation Community Human Services Grants 3749
The Butler Family Foundation makes grants through Community Grants, the Foundation Initiative Fund, and Special Projects programs. Community Grants are competitive and primarily support the Twin Cities metropolitan area of St. Paul and Minneapolis. The Foundation has a special concern for the condition of women and children in society, particularly those living in poverty. The Foundation seeks to foster a supportive environment for all families to ensure children's healthy development. Priority will be given to enhance the ability of individuals and families to break dependencies and achieve self-reliance in the following areas: Abuse - including domestic and family violence, pornography, and prostitution; Chemical dependency; Affordable housing - including housing and services for homeless youth; Children and Families - with an emphasis on early childhood development and parenting education. Strategies that offer both practical help to those in need and advocate for systems change will be favored. The Foundation is most likely to make general operating or program support grants.
Requirements: Minnesota 501(c)3 nonprofits are eligible to apply.
Restrictions: The Butler Family Foundation does not make grants to organizations through fiscal agents. The Foundation does not make loans or grants to individuals. No grants are made outside of the United States. The Foundation does not fund criminal justice, economic development or education, work or vocational programs, films or videos, health care, hospitals, medical research, elementary or secondary education, and music or dance.
Geographic Focus: Minnesota
Date(s) Application is Due: Feb 7; Jun 6
Amount of Grant: 5,000 - 30,000 USD
Contact: Kerrie Blevins; (651) 222-2566; kerrieb@butlerfamilyfoundation.org
Internet: http://www.butlerfamilyfoundation.org/guidelines2011.html
Sponsor: Patrick and Aimee Butler Family Foundation
332 Minnesota Street, Suite E-1420
Saint Paul, MN 55101-1369

Patrick and Aimee Butler Family Foundation Community Philanthropy & the Non-Profit Management Grants 3750
The Butler Family Foundation makes grants through Community Grants, the Foundation Initiative Fund, and Special Projects programs. Community Grants are competitive and primarily support the Twin Cities metropolitan area of St. Paul and Minneapolis. Through its Philanthropy and Non-Profit Management program, the Foundation seeks to foster a vital non-profit sector by supporting regranting through community funds committed to social change; and by supporting intermediary organizations that enhance the management capacity of non-profit organizations. The Foundation is most likely to make general operating or program support grants.
Requirements: Minnesota 501(c)3 nonprofits are eligible to apply.
Restrictions: The Butler Family Foundation does not make grants to organizations through fiscal agents. The Foundation does not make loans or grants to individuals. No grants are made outside of the United States. The Foundation does not fund criminal justice, economic development or education, work or vocational programs, films or videos, health care, hospitals, medical research, elementary or secondary education, and music or dance.
Geographic Focus: Minnesota
Date(s) Application is Due: Feb 7; Jun 6
Amount of Grant: 5,000 - 30,000 USD
Contact: Kerrie Blevins; (651) 222-2566; kerrieb@butlerfamilyfoundation.org
Internet: http://www.butlerfamilyfoundation.org/guidelines2011.html
Sponsor: Patrick and Aimee Butler Family Foundation
332 Minnesota Street, Suite E-1420
Saint Paul, MN 55101-1369

Patrick and Anna M. Cudahy Fund Grants 3751
The Patrick and Anna Cudahy Fund is a general purpose foundation which primarily supports organizations in Wisconsin and the metropolitan Chicago area. The principal areas of interest are social service, youth, and education with some giving for the arts, and other areas. Some support is also given for local and national programs concerned with public interest and environmental issues. A few grants are given for international programs but only to those which are represented by a United States based organization.
Requirements: Nonprofits organizations in Wisconsin and the metropolitan Chicago area are eligible. See Foundations website for additional guidelines and application form: http://www.cudahyfund.org/Guideliines.htm
Restrictions: Organizations may submit only one proposal during any calendar year. Requests are not considered for: organizations and projects primarily serving a local constituency outside of Wisconsin and the Chicago metropolitan area; organizations outside the United States who are not represented by a United States based 501 [c]3 organization; grants to individuals; loans or endowments.
Geographic Focus: Illinois, Wisconsin
Date(s) Application is Due: Jan 5; Apr 5; Jul 5; Oct 5
Amount of Grant: 5,000 - 25,000 USD

Contact: Janet S. Cudahy, President; (847) 866-0760; fax (847) 475-0679
Internet: http://www.cudahyfund.org/Guideliines.htm
Sponsor: 1609 Sherman Avenue, #207
Evanston, IL 60201

Patrick John Bennett, Jr. Memorial Foundation Grants 3752

The Patrick John Bennett, Jr. Memorial Foundation, which was established in Maryland in 2004, offers support primarily to assist the disabled with specific educational needs throughout Maryland and Pennsylvania. Therefore, its major fields of interest are education and human services. A specific application form is required, and can be secured from the Foundation officer. This application should include a detailed description of the project, along with the amount of funding needed. There are no annual deadlines. Most recently, grants have ranged from $250 to $2,000.
Geographic Focus: Maryland, Pennsylvania
Amount of Grant: 250 - 2,000 USD
Contact: Deborah Bennett, Trustee; (410) 971-3302 or (410) 527-0207
Sponsor: Patrick John Bennett, Jr. Memorial Foundation
11508 Hunters Run Drive
Cockeysville, MD 21030

Patron Saints Foundation Grants 3753

The Patron Saints Foundation is a private foundation that provides grants to public charities that improve the health of individuals residing in the West San Gabriel Valley through health care programs which are consistent with the moral and religious teachings of the Roman Catholic Church. Grants will be made to qualified public charities to sponsor charitable, scientific or educational health care programs which are not inconsistent with the moral and religious teachings of the Roman Catholic Church, in the following health care categories: community health services (direct health care services); community health care education; capital expenditures; equipment and supplies; medical research. Grants typically range from $5,000 to $15,000. Larger or smaller grants are at the discretion of The Patron Saints Foundation Board of Directors based on the merits of the project.
Requirements: California 501(c)3 tax-exempt organizations serving the West San Gabriel Valley are eligible, including: the cities of Alhambra, Arcadia, Duarte, El Monte, La Canada Flintridge, Monrovia, Monterey Park, Pasadena, Rosemead, San Gabriel, San Marino, Sierra Madre, South El Monte, South Pasadena, Temple City and the unincorporated areas of Los Angeles County known as Altadena and South San Gabriel along with the unincorporated portions of Los Angeles County within the West San Gabriel Valley.
Restrictions: Grants are not awarded for endowment funds, political activities, travel, surveys or fund raising activities.
Geographic Focus: California
Date(s) Application is Due: Mar 1; May 1
Contact: Kathleen T. Shannon; (626) 564-0444; patronsaintsfdn@sbcglobal.net
Internet: http://www.patronsaintsfoundation.org/index.php?nav=Grant%20Guidelines
Sponsor: Patron Saints Foundation
260 S Los Robles Avenue, Suite 201
Pasadena, CA 91101-3614

Paul and Daisy Soros Fellowships for New Americans 3754

The program offers support for graduate study by New Americans, individuals who hold Green Cards or who have been naturalized as U.S. citizens or are children of two parents who are both naturalized citizens. The program offers maintenance and tuition grants for up to two years of graduate study in the United States. Fellows must have shown potential in the fields for which they seek further education; the capacity for creativity, initiative, originality, and work; and the commitment to the values of the U.S. Constitution and Bill of Rights. Applications are available from college academic advisors, the program's Web site, or by contacting the program directly.
Requirements: Applicants must have either the bachelor's degree or be in the final year of undergraduate study and must not be older than 30 years of age as of the listed application deadline.
Geographic Focus: All States
Date(s) Application is Due: Nov 1
Contact: Administrator; (212) 547-6926; fax (212) 548-4623; pdsoros_fellows@sorosny.org
Internet: http://www.pdsoros.org
Sponsor: Paul and Daisy Soros Fellowships for New Americans
400 W 59th Street
New York, NY 10019

Paul and Edith Babson Foundation Grants 3755

The focus of the Foundation is to provide opportunities for the people of Greater Boston. Grants are awarded for specific types of activities in the following areas: entrepreneurship and economic development (programs focused on providing and encouraging youth and community entrepreneurship education, community economic development, job training for youth, and urban youth business and enterprise initiatives); culture, education and leadership development (programs focused on education and leadership development opportunities for young people through team sports, art, dance, music and theater); and environment and community building (programs focused on community building through urban community gardens and urban greenspace initiatives).
Requirements: IRS 501(c)3 tax-exempt organizations in the Greater Boston, Massachusetts, area are eligible. Applicants must telephone or email prior to applying, and then a preliminary letter may be sent. After review the Board may request a full proposal.
Restrictions: Only one preliminary letter may be submitted in a 12-month period. The following is ineligible: support for specific individuals, scholarships, films, videos, conferences, fundraising or donor cultivation events.
Geographic Focus: Massachusetts
Date(s) Application is Due: Feb 6; Sep 9
Amount of Grant: 5,000 - 40,000 USD
Contact: Elizabeth Nichols, Program Officer; (617) 523-8368; fax (617) 523-8949; pebabsonfdn@babsonfoundations.org
Internet: http://www.babsonfoundations.org/peguidelines.htm
Sponsor: Paul and Edith Babson Foundation
50 Congress Street
Boston, MA 02109-4017

Paul and Mary Haas Foundation Contributions and Student Scholarships 3756

Grants are given to tax-exempt organizations in six areas: civic and charitable, education (including adult basic education, adult/family literacy training, curriculum development, and vocational programs), health, religion, the arts, and college scholarships. Funding is generally seed money for innovative services in the Corpus Christi, TX, area. Creative, innovative, and exploratory projects are encouraged, with less interest in building projects and areas covered by normal budgets. Additional types of support include general operating support, equipment acquisition, program development, conferences and seminars, and scholarship funds and scholarships to individuals. Requests for support are normally reviewed on a year-round basis in the order in which they are received. All grants are made for one year and are not automatically renewed. Applications for scholarships are due in August at the beginning of senior high school year; application for other grants are accepted at any time.
Requirements: Grants are made to Texas organizations with 501(c)3 status. Initial inquiries should be made in the form of a one- to two-page written proposal.
Geographic Focus: Texas
Amount of Grant: 35 - 250,000 USD
Contact: Karen Wesson; (361) 887-6955; fax (361) 883-5992; haasfdn@aol.com
Sponsor: Paul and Mary Haas Foundation
P.O. Box 2928
Corpus Christi, TX 78403

Paul Balint Charitable Trust Grants 3757

The trust operates in the United Kingdom and internationally and awards grants to nonprofit charities in the fields of Jewish charities, medicine, disability, with a specific interest in aging and elderly and improving the daily lives of those with disabilities.
Geographic Focus: All States
Contact: Andrew Balint, 020 7624 2098
Sponsor: Paul Balint Charitable Trust
26 Church Crescent
London, N20 0JP England

Paul E. and Klare N. Reinhold Foundation Grants 3758

The foundation makes grants in Clay County, Florida, for projects in health, religion, children and youth, music appreciation and education, art appreciation and education, and public improvement. Types of support include building construction/renovation, capital campaigns, emergency funds, equipment, land acquisition, matching/challenge grants, operating grants, and seed money grants. Details are available on the Web site.
Requirements: 501(c)3 tax-exempt organizations in Florida's Clay County are eligible.
Restrictions: Grants do not support advertising for fund-raising campaigns, tickets, debt reduction, endowments, attempts to influence legislation, or basic operating costs.
Geographic Focus: Florida
Amount of Grant: Up to 10,000 USD
Contact: Program Contact; (904) 269-5857; fax (904) 269-8382; lhoke@reinhold.net
Internet: http://www.reinhold.org/html/guidelines.htm
Sponsor: Paul E. and Klare N. Reinhold Foundation
1845 Town Center Boulevard, Suite 105
Orange Park, FL 32003

Paul G. Allen Family Foundation Grants 3759

The single foundation, created through the consolidation of Allen's six previous foundations (The Allen Foundation for the Arts, The Paul G. Allen Charitable Foundation, The Paul G. Allen Foundation for Medical Research, The Paul G. Allen Forest Protection Foundation, The Allen Foundation for Music, and The Paul G. Allen Virtual Education Foundation), will continue to focus on the Allen family's philanthropic interests in the areas of arts and culture, youth engagement, community development and social change, and scientific and technological innovation. The Arts and Culture Program fosters creativity and promotes critical thinking by helping strong arts organizations become sustainable and supporting projects that feature innovative and diverse artistic forms. The Youth Engagement Program improves the way young people learn by supporting organizations that use innovative teaching strategies and provide opportunities for children to address issues relevant to their lives. The Community Development and Social Change Program promotes individual and community development by supporting initiatives and organizations that provide access to resources and opportunities. The Scientific and Technological Innovation Program advances promising scientific and technology research that has the potential to enhance understanding and stewardship of the world in which we live. Organizations may only receive one grant per year. Organizations must not have any delinquent final reports due to any of the Paul G. Allen Foundations for previous grants. Grantseekers are encouraged to apply through the online application process, where basic organizational and project information will be requested. Guidelines are available online.
Requirements: 501(c)3 tax-exempt organizations, status from the Internal Revenue government entities, and IRS-recognized tribes are eligible. Eligible organizations must be located in, or serving populations of, the Pacific Northwest, which includes Alaska, Idaho, Montana, Oregon, and Washington.

Restrictions: In general, the foundation will not consider requests for general fund drives, annual appeals, or federated campaigns; special events or sponsorships; direct grants, scholarships, or loans for the benefit of specific individuals; projects of organizations whose policies or practices discriminate on the basis of race, ethnic origin, sex, creed, or sexual orientation; contributions to sectarian or religious organizations whose principle activity is for the benefit of their own members or adherents; loans or debt retirement; projects that will benefit the students of a single school; general operating support for ongoing activities; or projects not aligned with the foundation's specified program areas. 509(a) private foundations are ineligible.
Geographic Focus: Alaska, Idaho, Montana, Oregon, Washington
Date(s) Application is Due: Mar 31; Sep 30
Contact: Grants Administrator; (206) 342-2030; fax (206) 342-3030; info@pgafamilyfoundation.org
Internet: http://www.pgafamilyfoundation.org
Sponsor: Paul G. Allen Family Foundation
505 Fifth Avenue S, Suite 900
Seattle, WA 98104

Paul Green Foundation Efforts to Abolish the Death Penalty in North Carolina Grants 3760
The Paul Green Foundation was established in 1982 to perpetuate the vision of playwright and activist Paul Green, whose commitment to the arts and human rights continues today through the mission of the Foundation. In 2007 the Paul Green Foundation established two funds at the Triangle Community Foundation and now gives the majority of its grants through these funds. The Efforts to Abolish the Death Penalty in North Carolina grants are awarded, in conjunction with the ACLU of North Carolina, to individuals or nonprofits whose efforts accomplish the stated goal.
Requirements: 501(c)3 organizations and/or individuals with a goal of abolishing the death penalty in North Carolina are eligible to apply.
Geographic Focus: North Carolina
Contact: Marsha Warren, (919) 929-6244; paulgreenfdn@earthlink.net
Internet: http://www.paulgreen.org/foundation.html
Sponsor: Paul Green Foundation
P.O. Box 2624
Chapel Hill, NC 27515

Paul Green Foundation Human Rights Project Grants 3761
The Paul Green Foundation was established in 1982 to perpetuate the vision of playwright and activist Paul Green, whose commitment to the arts and human rights continues today through the mission of the Foundation. In 2007 the Paul Green Foundation established two funds at the Triangle Community Foundation and now gives the majority of its grants through these funds. Human Rights Project grants are intended to promote racial harmony, free expression, humane treatment of prisoners and international peace and cooperation.
Requirements: Human Rights Project grants are awarded only to North Carolina-based 501(c)3 organizations.
Geographic Focus: North Carolina
Contact: Marsha Warren, (919) 929-6244; paulgreenfdn@earthlink.net
Internet: http://www.paulgreen.org/foundation.html
Sponsor: Paul Green Foundation
P.O. Box 2624
Chapel Hill, NC 27515

Paul Green Foundation Playwrights Fellowship 3762
The Paul Green Foundation was established in 1982 to perpetuate the vision of playwright and activist Paul Green, whose commitment to the arts and human rights continues today through the mission of the Foundation. In 2007 the Paul Green Foundation established two funds at the Triangle Community Foundation and now gives the majority of its grants through these funds. Specifically, the Paul Green Playwrights Fellowship nurtures playwrights through professional theaters in the 10 southeastern states.
Requirements: 501(c)3 theaters in Alabama, Florida, Georgia, Kentucky, Mississippi, North Carolina, South Carolina, Tennessee, Virginia, and West Virginia are eligible.
Geographic Focus: Alabama, Florida, Georgia, Kentucky, Mississippi, North Carolina, South Carolina, Tennessee, Virginia, West Virginia
Date(s) Application is Due: Oct 1
Amount of Grant: 4,000 USD
Contact: Marsha Warren, (919) 929-6244; paulgreenfdn@earthlink.net
Internet: http://www.paulgreen.org/foundation.html
Sponsor: Paul Green Foundation
P.O. Box 2624
Chapel Hill, NC 27515

Pauline E. Fitzpatrick Charitable Trust 3763
The Pauline E. Fitzpatrick Charitable Trust was established in Connecticut in 1991 with a primary purpose of supporting aged citizens of Norwalk, Connecticut. The Trust's major fields of interest include: Catholic agencies and churches, as well as other religious groups supporting human services for the aged. Funding comes in the form of general operating support. There are no specified application forms or annual deadlines, and interested partied should contact the Trust office directly. Typical grants range from $1,000 to $2,500.
Requirements: 505(c)3 organizations supporting the aged in Norwalk, Connecticut, are eligible to apply.
Geographic Focus: Connecticut
Amount of Grant: 1,000 - 2,500 USD
Contact: John B. Devine, (203) 838-0665 or (203) 327-3112
Sponsor: Pauline E. Fitzpatrick Charitable Trust
P.O. Box 411
Norwalk, CT 06852-0411

Paul Ogle Foundation Grants 3764
The Paul Ogle Foundation, Inc., was incorporated as an Indiana non-profit corporation in 1979 and is qualified under the IRS 501(c)3 as a private foundation. The Foundation's founder and original benefactor was Paul W. Ogle, who lived in Clark County, Indiana. The Foundation is headquartered in Jeffersonville, Indiana, and provides grants to deserving IRS 501(c)3 organizations in Clark, Floyd, Harrison, Switzerland, Scott, and Washington Counties in Indiana and Jefferson County, Kentucky. The Board of Directors has established guidelines for programs which they will consider for grant funding of capital projects and endowments. The guidelines are published on the Foundations website and make up the current basis for recognized charities to apply for grant funding.
Requirements: First read guidelines prior to contacting the foundations office, then send a letter of intent to the office. The letter should be typed on your institutions letterhead and should not exceed for typewritten pages in length. It should contain the following information about the proposed project: a brief description of the need that will be addressed by the proposal; a statement of the project's principal objectives; how the need will be met; the total estimated project budget and other sources of support that may be forthcoming, including a list of donors and amounts; the staff that will carry out the project and their qualifications; a timetable for the project; brief background on the organization; list of board members; the name of the primary contact person for follow-up; copy of IRS 501(c)3 exemption letter. Based on review of your letter of intent, the foundation may request a full proposal. If a proposal is requested, you will be provided with a grant form along with specific instructions. All projects are funded only on the authorization of the Foundation's Board of Director, this may take up to six months. Formal written communications from the foundation is the ONLY way you will be advised of a favorable funding decision.
Restrictions: Grants are not made to: private foundations; religious organizations for religious purposes; individuals; primary or secondary schools; political entities; national organizations, even if for local projects; annual operating support or debt reduction.
Geographic Focus: Indiana, Kentucky
Contact: Robert W. Lanum, Chair; (812) 284-5519; klanum@ogle-fdn.org
Internet: http://www.ogle-fdn.org/Guidelines.htm
Sponsor: Paul Ogle Foundation
321 East Court Avenue, P.O. Box 845
Jeffersonville, IN 47131

Paul Rapoport Foundation Grants 3765
The Paul Rapoport Foundation was established in 1987 with funds from the estate of Paul Rapoport, a founder of both New York City's LGBT Community Services Center and GMHC. For its final years of grantmaking the Foundation's focus will be on three populations of low or no income: transgender communities of color; LGTBQ youth of color, ages 24 and under; and LGTB seniors of color aged 60 and over. The Foundation will also consider funding programs of organizations not focused exclusively on the LGTB community if the number of LGTBQ clients of color served by the program is at least 50%. The foundation awards grants to nonprofits in the metropolitan area of New York, New York. Types of support include general operating support, continuing support, building construction and renovation, program development, conferences and seminars, publications, seed money, technical assistance, and matching funds. There are no application forms. The board meets in February, June, and October to consider requests. Grants of $50,000 and higher, per year are awarded.
Requirements: The Foundation funds only non-profit, charitable organizations as defined by the Internal Revenue Service Code Section 509(a). The Foundation funds primarily within the five boroughs of New York City, as well as on Long Island, in Westchester and nearby New Jersey. It will only fund national organizations when they request funding for programs specific to the New York metropolitan area.
Restrictions: The Foundation will no longer support start-up organizations. The Foundation does not support medical research, cultural and artistic activities, major building campaigns, endowments, grants or scholar-ships to individuals or to other foundations. The Foundation does not make grants for purposes of influencing elections or legislation, or for any other activity that may jeopardize the Foundation's tax-exempt status.
Geographic Focus: New York
Date(s) Application is Due: Feb 1; Jun 1; Oct 1
Contact: Jane D. Schwartz, Executive Director; (212) 888-6578; fax (212) 980-0867
Ona M. Winet, Program Director; (212) 888-6578; fax (212) 980-0867
Internet: http://www.paulrapoportfoundation.org/guide.html
Sponsor: Paul Rapoport Foundation
220 E 60th Street, Suite 3H
New York, NY 10022

Paul Stock Foundation Grants 3766
The foundation awards grants in Park County, WY, for higher education, university support, recreation, and human services. Types of support include annual campaigns, building construction/renovation, research grants, and scholarships to individuals. The board meets in July and December. There are no application forms.
Requirements: Giving primarily in Park County, WY; student aid is limited to those who have resided in WY for one year or more.
Geographic Focus: Wyoming
Contact: Charles Kepler, President; (307) 587-5275
Sponsor: Paul Stock Foundation
P.O. Box 2020
Cody, WY 82414-2020

Paul V. Sherlock Center on Disabilities Access for All Abilities Mini Grants 3767

The mission of the Paul V. Sherlock Center on Disabilities is to promote membership of individuals with disabilities in school, work and community. The purpose of this grant program is to: Increase access (physical, financial, programmatic) for people with various disabilities to existing social, leisure, recreational and cultural activities in the community; Increase participation of people with disabilities alongside people without disabilities in scheduled activities; Support Rhode Island leisure organizations and businesses in expanding their customer base to include more people with disabilities. The Sherlock Center has $10,000 to award up to four grants. Organizations may apply for up to $2,500.

Requirements: Applicants must be businesses and organizations offering social, leisure, recreational, and/or cultural activities to the general public in Rhode island. non-profit organizations and business, city, or town government agencies are welcome to apply. Examples of supportable projects include: purchase or development of specialized equipment or product to enhance accessibility; sensitivity or specific skill training for employees; modifications to an existing program to accommodate people with disabilities; seed money for a larger project or strategic planning.

Restrictions: AAA grants will not fund: Development of a disability-only program (e.g., 'karate for kids with autism,' 'dance classes for adults with disabilities,' 'hiking for the visually impaired,' etc.); Proposals from entities whose primary client base is already people with disabilities; A service or product which will only benefit a single individual (e.g., equipment needing to be custom fit for a particular person, funding a one-on-one assistant, etc.).

Geographic Focus: Rhode Island

Date(s) Application is Due: Mar 5

Amount of Grant: Up to 2,500 USD

Contact: Mary Anne Pallack, (401) 456-8072; mpallack@ric.edu

Internet: http://www.ric.edu/sherlockcenter/aaa.html

Sponsor: Paul V. Sherlock Center on Disabilities at Rhode Island College
600 Mount Pleasant Avenue
Providence, RI 02908

Pay It Forward Foundation Mini Grants 3768

The Pay It Forward Foundation was established by author Catherine Ryan Hyde and others to educate and inspire students to realize that they can change the world, and provide them with opportunities to do so. By bringing the author's vision and related materials into classrooms internationally, students and their teachers are encouraged to formulate their own ideas of how they can pay it forward. Pay It Forward Mini-Grants are designed to fund one-time-only service-oriented projects identified by youth as activities they would like to perform to benefit their school, neighborhood, or greater community.

Requirements: Projects must contain a "pay it forward" focus - that is, they must be based on the concept of one person doing a favor for others, who in turn do favors for others, with the results growing exponentially - to be considered in the grant making process. Proposals should be no more than 3 pages in length and need to include the educational benefit to students/teachers, the integration of the proposed project with school curriculum, and the number of people impacted.

Restrictions: The Pay It Forward Foundation does not fund general educational grants for the improvement of schools, the purchase of educational materials, or other standard classroom needs.

Geographic Focus: All States

Date(s) Application is Due: Feb 15; Sep 15

Amount of Grant: 500 USD

Contact: Grants Administrator; (805) 924-1180; info@payitforwardfoundation.com or PayItForwardFoundation@hotmail.com

Internet: http://www.payitforwardfoundation.org/educators/grant.html

Sponsor: Pay It Forward Foundation
P.O. Box 4543
San Luis Obispo, CA 93403-4543

PCA-PCD Organizational Short-Term Professional Development and Consulting Grants 3769

The Pennsylvania Council on the Arts (PCA) is a state agency whose mission is to foster the arts in Pennsylvania and broaden the availability and appreciation of those arts throughout the state. Through its Preserving Cultural Diversity (PCD) Division, PCA supports development of organizations from the African-American, Asian-American, Hispanic/Latino, and Native-American communities. Eligible organizations may submit requests up to $2,000 to engage consultants to address specific artistic, programmatic, administrative, or technical needs. PCD's Organizational Short-Term Professional Development and Consulting program does not have its own section on the PCD webpage at the time of this writing but is discussed in the downloadable guide for PCD's Strategies for Success grants and may share the application used for PCA's general professional development grants. Both documents are available from the download section of the website. Applicants are encouraged to contact the Program Director or Program Associate for more information on eligibility and how to apply.

Requirements: PCD's Organizational Short-Term grants are intended to extend organizational development opportunities to African-American, Asian-American, Latino/Hispanic, and Native-American organizations that may be ineligible to participate in PCD's Strategies for Success Program. Requests must be postmarked at least 8 weeks before the assistance is needed.

Geographic Focus: Pennsylvania

Contact: Charon Battles, Preserving Diverse Cultures Program Director; (717) 787-6883 or (717) 787-1521; fax (717) 783-2538; cbattles@pa.gov

Internet: http://pacouncilonthearts.org/pca.cfm?id=47&level=Third&sid=48

Sponsor: Pennsylvania Council on the Arts
216 Finance Building
Harrisburg, PA 17120

PCA-PCD Professional Development for Individual Artists Grants 3770

The Pennsylvania Council on the Arts (PCA) is a state agency whose mission is to foster the arts in Pennsylvania and broaden the availability and appreciation of those arts throughout the state. Through its Preserving Cultural Diversity (PCD) Division, PCA supports development of individual artists from the African-American, Asian-American, Hispanic/Latino, and Native-American communities. Individual artists may request up to $200 for conferences and other professional development opportunities. In the past funds have have been used to cover conference fees, non-credit career advancement, and promotional materials. Priority is given to artists who were not funded by PCD's program in the prior year. PCD's Professional Development for Individual Artists program does not have its own section on the PCD webpage at the time of this writing but is discussed in the downloadable guide for PCD's Strategies for Success grants and may share the application used for PCA's general professional development grants. Both documents are available from the download section of the website. Applicants are encouraged to contact the Program Director or Program Associate for more information.

Requirements: Individual artists working within the communities targeted by PCD's Strategies for Success program and African Americans, Asian Americans, Hispanic/Latinos, and Native Americans in Pennsylvania are eligible to apply.

Geographic Focus: Pennsylvania

Amount of Grant: Up to 200 USD

Contact: Charon Battles, Preserving Diverse Cultures Program Director; (717) 787-6883 or (717) 787-1521; fax (717) 783-2538; cbattles@pa.gov

Internet: http://pacouncilonthearts.org/pca.cfm?id=47&level=Third&sid=48

Sponsor: Pennsylvania Council on the Arts
216 Finance Building
Harrisburg, PA 17120

PCA Art Organizations and Art Programs Grants for Presenting Organizations 3771

The Pennsylvania Council on the Arts (PCA) is a state agency in the Office of the Governor. The mission of PCA is to foster the excellence, diversity, and vitality of the arts in Pennsylvania and to broaden the availability and appreciation of those arts throughout the state. Funding for the Council on the Arts comes through the General Assembly and from the National Endowment for the Arts. PCA offers various funding tracks for organizations that offer arts programming. The Arts Organizations and Arts Programs (AOAP) funding track has been created to provide continuous support for established organizations who have offered arts programming for a year or longer. Organizations must be invited by the PCA to apply for AOAP grants. The invitation usually is extended to organizations in PCA's Entry Track or Strategies for Success programs who have consistently received positive reviews by PCA advisory panels. Organizations on the AOAP track receive annual funding in renewable three-year blocks (subject to past performance); applicants submit full applications every three years and interim applications in intervening years. Organizations may also be removed from the AOAP track for various reasons. The AOAP track is divided into thirteen categories: art museums; arts in education organizations; arts service organizations; crafts; dance; folk and traditional arts; literature; theatre; film and electronic media; local arts; music; presenting organizations; and visual arts. In the presenting organizations category, the PCA supports organizations that present professional performing artists. These presentations may occur in a variety of settings. A performing arts presenter has the following responsibilities: engaging professional touring artists; paying their fees; handling the local presentation, promotion, and ticket sales; and arranging for the facilities and technical support for the event(s). Presenters work with artists, managers, educators, and community groups to bring artists into a community in concerts and less formal arrangements. The presenting field includes the following types of organizations: cultural centers; theatres; galleries and museums; arts centers; libraries; college and university artist series; festivals; concert, music, dance and theatre associations; and civic or cultural groups and programs that promote cooperative programming and activity between Pennsylvania presenting organizations. Both interim and full applications for AOAP grants for Presenting Organizations must be completed using various online systems (available from the grant website), then printed, assembled, and mailed by the postmark date. The PCA encourages applicants to upload any required work samples and attachments through their online system. DVDs must be mailed. The application process is explained in the complete guide (PDF document) which may be accessed from the download section of the website. Application deadlines may vary from year to year. Applicants should visit the calendar section of the website to verify current deadline dates.

Requirements: The AOAP Grants for Presenting Organizations support organizations that present professional performing artists. Organizations and programs that exclusively present local artists should apply for AOAP Grants in the Local Arts category. Pennsylvania artists or ensembles who self-produce their home seasons or local performances should apply for AOAP Grants in one of the arts genre categories (Dance, Music, Theatre, etc.). In general, the PCA supports the following types of organizations: 501(c)3 corporations; units of government; or school districts providing arts programming and/or arts services in Pennsylvania. Organizations are required to provide proof of incorporation and activity in Pennsylvania before applications are reviewed or funds awarded. Unincorporated groups (and in some instances, individuals) may apply to the PCA through a nonprofit organization that acts as a fiscal sponsor. Applicants applying through a fiscal sponsor organization must meet the same requirements as other applicants except for nonprofit status. Unless otherwise specified in the guidelines, PCA awards must be matched on a dollar-for-dollar basis in cash. In-kind goods and services may not be used to match PCA funds. The PCA generally will support no more than 25% of an organizational budget, and usually considerably less.

Restrictions: The AOAP Grants for Presenting Organizations do not fund presenters who present nonprofessional, avocational, student, or school-related artists or ensembles (faculty) seasons. In general, the PCA does not fund nor can the match for PCA funds be used for the following expenses or activities: capital expenditures, including equipment costing $500 per item or more; activities for which academic credit is given; activities that have already

been completed; activities that have a religious purpose; performances and exhibitions not available to the general public; performances and exhibitions outside Pennsylvania; cash prizes and awards; benefit activities; hospitality expenses (e.g. receptions, parties, gallery openings); lobbyists' payments; and competitions.
Geographic Focus: Pennsylvania
Date(s) Application is Due: Jan 13
Contact: Philip Horn, Executive Director and Presenting Organizations Program Director; (717) 787-6883 or (717) 787-1530; fax (717) 783-2538; phorn@pa.gov
Internet: http://www.pacouncilonthearts.org/pca.cfm?id=1&level=Third&sid=48
Sponsor: Pennsylvania Council on the Arts
216 Finance Building
Harrisburg, PA 17120

PCA Arts in Education Residencies 3772

The Pennsylvania Council on the Arts (PCA) is a state agency whose mission is to foster the arts in Pennsylvania and broaden the availability and appreciation of those arts throughout the state. PCA develops and supports quality arts-education programs in schools and community settings for all Pennsylvanians by providing artist-in-residency grants. Schools and community organizations interested in hiring a resident artist may submit applications for either a single-residency or a multi-residency. Multi-residencies are more complex than single-residencies in that they are conducted at multiple sites with multiple artists under the management of a single organization. Multi-residencies may include residencies within individual schools, in-service workshops, other professional development for artists and/or educators, and other arts-education programming and are intended to leverage arts-in-education programs in rural and other areas where access to the arts has been limited. PCA's artists-in-residency program is administered regionally by eleven Arts in Education (AIE) partners throughout the state. Organizations interested in obtaining the services of an artist in residence are encouraged to apply through their AIE partner organization (contact information is available at the grant website in the form of a regional map). Organizations may apply directly to PCA as well (organizations in regions of Pennsylvania that still remain to be covered by an AIE Partner must apply to the PCA directly). The direct application process is explained in the complete guide (PDF document) which may be accessed from the download section of the website. Applicants applying through an AIE partner should also download the guide but should contact the partner or visit the partner's website as well. (Applicants should note that details of the application process may vary not only among partners but from the central PCA as well). Annual deadlines for artists-in-education residencies may vary; applicants should contact their AIE partner or visit the calendar section of the PCA website to verify current deadline dates. PCA maintains an annual Directory of Artists in Education from which applicants may select artists. Applicants may access the Directory online or contact PCA or their AIE Partner for a printed copy. Artists who would like to be included in the Directory should contact the AIE Partner in their region for guidelines and application materials. AIE Partners recruit, select, train, place and evaluate the artists in their regions. Interested artists are also encouraged to visit PCA's Arts-in-Education website for more information on the Directory and PCA's residency grants.
Requirements: Pennsylvania schools, institutions, arts organizations, government agencies, local arts agencies, institutions of higher education and other 501(c)3 nonprofit organizations are eligible for Arts In Education funding. Organizations receiving support through other funding areas of the PCA are eligible to apply for AIE funding. Resident and visiting artists must be paid at a minimum rate of $175 per day for the residency. Grant awards from the PCA under the Arts In Education Division are matching grants. A twenty-day minimum residency is required for a 1:1 PCA match. Residencies under 20 days in length require the applicant to fund up to 70% of the total project. The focus of residency activities should be on developing students' creative capabilities and technical skills (as opposed to producing a finished product, performance, or exhibition, although these activities may be included in the residency). Residency projects must be developed collaboratively by both the host organization and the artist(s) who take part. The application must be signed by both the host organization and the artist(s) who will take part in the residency. Organizations coordinating their residency through their AIE Partner should also coordinate their artist selection with their AIE Partner. Artists not listed in the annual Directory of Artists in Education must submit five samples of their work and a resume with the application. Applicants must list a host coordinator on the application. Host-coordinators serve as a liaison between artist(s), site(s), and the groups involved and are responsible for the management of all elements of the residency including consulting with the artist to schedule the overall residency, residency activities, and appropriate groups for workshops and performances. In the instance of a multi-residency application, a host-coordinator must be designated to serve as a central contact for participating schools and the AIE Division. It is helpful if this person is the one responsible for coordinating with local schools/sites in developing and writing the multi-residency application. In a multi-residency application, each school/site must identify an on-site coordinator to assist the host coordinator and artist(s) with scheduling, identification of core groups, requisition of supplies, equipment or custodial services, and publicity for staff, students and the community.
Restrictions: Artists outside of Pennsylvania may participate. The work of the teaching artist in a residency or project is seen as an enhancement of the work of the professional educator in the educational setting; therefore residency artists may NOT be used to replace staff or faculty or to substitute teach. The PCA will not fund residencies less than ten days. Expenses for residencies are limited to: artists' fees, including those of visiting artists; artist travel expenses; and multi-residency host-coordinator administrative expenses of up to twenty five percent (25%) of the residency funding. Funds may be used only for eligible expenses.
Geographic Focus: Pennsylvania
Date(s) Application is Due: Apr 2
Amount of Grant: 600 - 4,400 USD
Contact: Jamie Dunlap; (717) 787-6883 or (717) 525-5542; jadunlap@pa.gov
Internet: http://www.pacouncilonthearts.org/aie/educators.cfm

Sponsor: Pennsylvania Council on the Arts
216 Finance Building
Harrisburg, PA 17120

PCA Arts Management Internship 3773

The Pennsylvania Council on the Arts (PCA) is a state agency whose mission is to foster the arts in Pennsylvania and broaden the availability and appreciation of those arts throughout the state. Through its Arts Management Internships, PCA's Preserving Cultural Diversity Division enables novice and intermediate arts administrators in culturally specific organizations to sharpen their management skills. Participation includes a four-phase instructional program that provides classroom, laboratory, and field experience. The program begins in the month of June with a three-day certification workshop (six hours per day) in the fundamentals of management. University faculty will supervise each participant's progress. In phase two (four to six weeks in duration), participants will view firsthand the operations of the PCA. During this phase, participants will assist PCA program directors in the review and processing of grant applications. Participants will gain further knowledge during this phase through supervised site visits to the field. PCA will award a $5,000 stipend and up to $500 housing stipend for the PCA residency. Phase three will place participants in a four-month internship with a regional host organization that has an annual budget of $100,000 or more and two independent PCA-approved readings in arts management. During this phase interns will focus on multi-cultural funding, programming, marketing, and audience outreach as a part of the host organization's management team. The skills and confidence learned in the prior phases will enable the intern to make valuable contributions to the host-site program. The final phase is participation in an online course in Arts Management administered by the Arts Extension Service, a national, nonprofit arts service organization. Prospective applicants should visit the grant website and also contact the Program Director or the Program Associate for information on how to apply. Organizations interested in hosting an intern should visit the grant website and contact the Program Director or Program Associate for an AMI Site Manual. Host organizations receive a four-month intern and a $750 stipend.
Requirements: Prospective interns should contact the Program Director or Program Associate for eligibility criteria. Prospective host organizations should be deeply rooted in and reflective of the African-American, Asian-American, Hispanic/Latino, and Native-American perspectives and have programs and staff that are representative of those communities. Generally, these organizations should have current or proposed multi-cultural programming, annual operating budgets of $100,000 or more, 501(c)3 status, and a minimum of two administrative staff with a minimum of twenty (20) hours per week per staff position.
Geographic Focus: Pennsylvania
Amount of Grant: 750 - 5,500 USD
Contact: Charon Battles, Preserving Diverse Cultures Program Director; (717) 787-6883 or (717) 787-1521; fax (717) 783-2538; cbattles@pa.gov
Internet: http://pacouncilonthearts.org/pca.cfm?id=47&level=Third&sid=48
Sponsor: Pennsylvania Council on the Arts
216 Finance Building
Harrisburg, PA 17120

PCA Arts Organizations and Arts Program Grants for Music 3774

The Pennsylvania Council on the Arts (PCA) is a state agency in the Office of the Governor. The mission of PCA is to foster the excellence, diversity, and vitality of the arts in Pennsylvania and to broaden the availability and appreciation of those arts throughout the state. Funding for the Council on the Arts comes through the General Assembly and from the National Endowment for the Arts. PCA offers various funding tracks for organizations that offer arts programming. The Arts Organizations and Arts Programs (AOAP) funding track has been created to provide continuous support for established organizations who have offered arts programming for a year or longer. Organizations must be invited by the PCA to apply for AOAP grants. The invitation usually is extended to organizations in PCA's Entry Track or Strategies for Success programs who have consistently received positive reviews by PCA advisory panels. Organizations on the AOAP track receive annual funding in renewable three-year blocks (subject to past performance); applicants submit full applications every three years and interim applications in intervening years. Organizations may also be removed from the AOAP track for various reasons. The AOAP track is divided into thirteen categories: art museums; arts in education organizations; arts service organizations; crafts; dance; folk and traditional arts; literature; theatre; film and electronic media; local arts; music; presenting organizations; and visual arts. In the music category, the PCA supports music organizations and programs the primary purpose of which includes public performances. Both interim and full applications for AOAP grants for music must be completed using various online systems (available from the grant website), then printed, assembled, and mailed by the postmark date. The PCA encourages applicants to upload any required work samples and attachments through their online system. DVDs must be mailed. The application process is explained in the complete guide (PDF document) which may be accessed from the download section of the website. Application deadlines may vary from year to year. Applicants should visit the calendar section of the website to verify current deadline dates.
Requirements: In general, the PCA supports the following types of organizations: 501(c)3 corporations; units of government; or school districts providing arts programming and/or arts services in Pennsylvania. Organizations are required to provide proof of incorporation and activity in Pennsylvania before applications are reviewed or funds awarded. Unincorporated groups (and in some instances, individuals) may apply to the PCA through a nonprofit organization that acts as a fiscal sponsor. Applicants applying through a fiscal sponsor organization must meet the same requirements as other applicants except for nonprofit status. Unless otherwise specified in the guidelines, PCA awards must be matched on a dollar-for-dollar basis in cash. In-kind goods and services may not be used to match PCA funds. The PCA generally will support no more than 25% of an organizational budget, and usually considerably less.

Restrictions: In general, the PCA does not fund nor can the match for PCA funds be used for the following expenses or activities: capital expenditures, including equipment costing $500 per item or more; activities for which academic credit is given; activities that have already been completed; activities that have a religious purpose; performances and exhibitions not available to the general public; performances and exhibitions outside Pennsylvania; cash prizes and awards; benefit activities; hospitality expenses (e.g., receptions, parties, gallery openings); lobbyists' payments; and competitions.
Geographic Focus: Pennsylvania
Date(s) Application is Due: Jan 13
Contact: Lori Frush Schmelz, Music Program Director; (717) 787-6883 or (717) 787-1523; fax (717) 783-2538; lschmelz@pa.gov
Internet: http://www.pacouncilonthearts.org/pca.cfm?id=1&level=Third&sid=48
Sponsor: Pennsylvania Council on the Arts
216 Finance Building
Harrisburg, PA 17120

PCA Arts Organizations and Arts Programs Grants for Art Museums   3775
The Pennsylvania Council on the Arts (PCA) is a state agency in the Office of the Governor. The mission of PCA is to foster the excellence, diversity, and vitality of the arts in Pennsylvania and to broaden the availability and appreciation of those arts throughout the state. Funding for the Council on the Arts comes through the General Assembly and from the National Endowment for the Arts. PCA offers various funding tracks for organizations that offer arts programming. The Arts Organizations and Arts Programs (AOAP) funding track has been created to provide continuous support for established organizations who have offered arts programming for a year or longer. Organizations must be invited by the PCA to apply for AOAP grants. The invitation usually is extended to organizations in PCA's Entry Track or Strategies for Success programs who have consistently received positive reviews by PCA advisory panels. Organizations on the AOAP track receive annual funding in renewable three-year blocks (subject to past performance); applicants submit full applications every three years and interim applications in intervening years. Organizations may also be removed from the AOAP track for various reasons. The AOAP track is divided into thirteen categories: art museums; arts in education organizations; arts service organizations; crafts; dance; folk and traditional arts; literature; theatre; film and electronic media; local arts; music; presenting organizations; and visual arts. In the art museums category, PCA supports organizations whose primary mission is to present, interpret, and preserve fine art objects of outstanding aesthetic quality. The PCA seeks to ensure the enlightened interpretation and care of the state's artistic heritage and to foster the relationships between museums and their communities through support for exhibitions, educational programs, collections care programs, and institutional operations. Both interim and full applications for AOAP grants for Art Museums must be completed using various online systems (available from the grant website), then printed, assembled, and mailed by the postmark date. The PCA encourages applicants to upload any required work samples and attachments through their online system. DVDs must be mailed. The application process is explained in the complete guide (PDF document) which may be accessed from the download section of the website. Application deadlines may vary from year to year. Applicants should visit the calendar section of the website to verify current deadline dates.
Requirements: In general, the PCA supports the following types of organizations: 501(c)3 corporations; units of government; or school districts providing arts programming and/or arts services in Pennsylvania. Organizations are required to provide proof of incorporation and activity in Pennsylvania before applications are reviewed or funds awarded. Unincorporated groups (and in some instances, individuals) may apply to the PCA through a nonprofit organization that acts as a fiscal sponsor. Applicants applying through a fiscal sponsor organization must meet the same requirements as other applicants except for nonprofit status. Unless otherwise specified in the guidelines, PCA awards must be matched on a dollar-for-dollar basis in cash. In-kind goods and services may not be used to match PCA funds. The PCA generally will support no more than 25% of an organizational budget, and usually considerably less.
Restrictions: The AOAP Grants for Art Museums do not fund organizations that provide only ongoing exhibition programs. Those organizations may be able to apply for AOAP Craft or Visual Arts Grants, depending on the focus of the exhibition series. In general, the PCA does not fund nor can the match for PCA funds be used for the following expenses or activities: capital expenditures, including equipment costing $500 per item or more; activities for which academic credit is given; activities that have already been completed; activities that have a religious purpose; performances and exhibitions not available to the general public; performances and exhibitions outside Pennsylvania; cash prizes and awards; benefit activities; hospitality expenses (e.g., receptions, parties, gallery openings); lobbyists' payments; and competitions.
Geographic Focus: Pennsylvania
Date(s) Application is Due: Jan 13
Contact: Bryan Holtzapple, Art Museums Program Director; (717) 787-6883 or (717) 787-1520; fax (717) 783-2538; bholtzappl@pa.gov
Internet: http://www.pacouncilonthearts.org/pca.cfm?id=1&level=Third&sid=48
Sponsor: Pennsylvania Council on the Arts
216 Finance Building
Harrisburg, PA 17120

PCA Arts Organizations and Arts Grants for Arts Education Organizations   3776
The Pennsylvania Council on the Arts (PCA) is a state agency in the Office of the Governor. The mission of PCA is to foster the excellence, diversity, and vitality of the arts in Pennsylvania and to broaden the availability and appreciation of those arts throughout the state. Funding for the Council on the Arts comes from the citizens of Pennsylvania and from the National Endowment for the Arts. PCA offers various funding tracks for organizations that offer arts programming. The Arts Organizations and Arts Programs (AOAP) funding track has been created to provide continuous support for established organizations that have offered arts programming for a year or longer. Organizations must be invited by the PCA to apply for AOAP grants. The invitation usually is extended to organizations in PCA's Entry Track or Strategies for Success programs who have consistently received positive reviews by PCA advisory panels. Organizations on the AOAP track receive annual funding in renewable three-year blocks (subject to past performance); applicants submit full applications every three years and interim applications in intervening years. Organizations may also be removed from the AOAP track for various reasons. The AOAP track is divided into thirteen categories: art museums; arts in education organizations; arts service organizations; crafts; dance; folk and traditional arts; literature; theatre; film and electronic media; local arts; music; presenting organizations; and visual arts. In the arts education organizations category, the PCA supports organizations or departments whose primary mission and activities include arts education or arts-in-education programs with a significant public participation component. Arts-education programming can consist of arts workshops, classes, and/or programs. Both interim and full applications for AOAP grants for arts education organizations must be completed using various online systems (accessible from the grant website), then printed, assembled, and mailed by the postmark date. The PCA encourages applicants to upload any required work samples and attachments through the online system. DVDs must be mailed. The application process is explained in the complete guide (PDF document) which may be accessed from the download section of the website. Application deadlines may vary from year to year. Applicants should visit the calendar section of the website to verify current deadline dates.
Requirements: Single-discipline arts organizations or organizations providing art-education programming and activities are eligible to apply for these grants. In general, the PCA supports the following types of organizations: 501(c)3 corporations; units of government; or school districts providing arts programming and/or arts services in Pennsylvania. Organizations are required to provide proof of incorporation and activity in Pennsylvania before applications are reviewed or funds awarded. Unincorporated groups (and in some instances, individuals) may apply to the PCA through a nonprofit organization that acts as a fiscal sponsor. Applicants applying through a fiscal sponsor organization must meet the same requirements as other applicants except for nonprofit status. Unless otherwise specified in the guidelines, PCA awards must be matched on a dollar-for-dollar basis in cash. In-kind goods and services may not be used for match. The PCA generally will support no more than 25% of an organizational budget, and usually considerably less.
Restrictions: AOAP Grants for Arts Education Organizations do not fund public schools, school districts, intermediate units, other local educational agencies, or private and parochial schools (however, these organizations may apply to PCA's Arts-In-Education Division for artist residencies). In general, the PCA does not fund nor can the match for PCA funds be used for the following expenses or activities: capital expenditures, including equipment costing $500 per item or more; activities for which academic credit is given; activities that have already been completed; activities that have a religious purpose; performances and exhibitions not available to the general public; performances and exhibitions outside Pennsylvania; cash prizes and awards; benefit activities; hospitality expenses (e.g., receptions, parties, gallery openings); lobbyists' payments; and competitions.
Geographic Focus: Pennsylvania
Date(s) Application is Due: Jan 13
Contact: Jamie Dunlap; (717) 787-6883 or (717-525-5542; jadunlap@pa.gov
Internet: http://www.pacouncilonthearts.org/pca.cfm?id=1&level=Third&sid=48
Sponsor: Pennsylvania Council on the Arts
216 Finance Building
Harrisburg, PA 17120

PCA Arts Organizations and Arts Grants for Arts Service Organizations   3777
The Pennsylvania Council on the Arts (PCA) is a state agency in the Office of the Governor. The mission of PCA is to foster the excellence, diversity, and vitality of the arts in Pennsylvania and to broaden the availability and appreciation of those arts throughout the state. Funding for the Council on the Arts comes through the General Assembly and from the National Endowment for the Arts. PCA offers various funding tracks for organizations that offer arts programming. The Arts Organizations and Arts Programs (AOAP) funding track has been created to provide continuous support for established organizations who have offered arts programming for a year or longer. Organizations must be invited by the PCA to apply for AOAP grants. The invitation usually is extended to organizations in PCA's Entry Track or Strategies for Success programs who have consistently received positive reviews by PCA advisory panels. Organizations on the AOAP track receive annual funding in renewable three-year blocks (subject to past performance); applicants submit full applications every three years and interim applications in intervening years. Organizations may also be removed from the AOAP track for various reasons. The AOAP track is divided into thirteen categories: art museums; arts in education organizations; arts service organizations; crafts; dance; folk and traditional arts; literature; theatre; film and electronic media; local arts; music; presenting organizations; and visual arts. In the arts service organizations category, the PCA supports organizations whose primary mission is to provide services to Pennsylvania arts organizations and artists (national service organizations can only be funded for arts services provided in Pennsylvania). Both interim and full applications for AOAP Arts Service Organization grants must be completed using various online systems (available from the grant website), then printed, assembled, and mailed by the postmark date. The PCA encourages applicants to upload any required work samples and attachments through their online system. DVDs must be mailed. The application process is explained in the complete guide (PDF document) which may be accessed from the download section of the website. Application deadlines may vary from year to year. Applicants should visit the calendar section of the website to verify current deadline dates.
Requirements: In general, the PCA supports the following types of organizations: 501(c)3 corporations; units of government; or school districts providing arts programming and/or arts services in Pennsylvania. Organizations are required to provide proof of incorporation and activity in Pennsylvania before applications are reviewed or funds

awarded. Unincorporated groups (and in some instances, individuals) may apply to the PCA through a nonprofit organization that acts as a fiscal sponsor. Applicants applying through a fiscal sponsor organization must meet the same requirements as other applicants except for nonprofit status. National service organizations may occasionally be supported if they provide services in Pennsylvania. Unless otherwise specified in the guidelines, PCA awards must be matched on a dollar-for-dollar basis in cash. In-kind goods and services may not be used to match PCA funds. The PCA generally will support no more than 25% of an organizational budget, and usually considerably less.
Restrictions: In general, the PCA does not fund nor can the match for PCA funds be used for the following expenses or activities: capital expenditures, including equipment costing $500 per item or more; activities for which academic credit is given; activities that have already been completed; activities that have a religious purpose; performances and exhibitions not available to the general public; performances and exhibitions outside Pennsylvania; cash prizes and awards; benefit activities; hospitality expenses (e.g. receptions, parties, gallery openings); lobbyists' payments; and competitions.
Geographic Focus: Pennsylvania
Date(s) Application is Due: Jan 13
Contact: Jamie Dunlap; (717) 787-6883 or (717) 525-5542; jadunlap@pa.gov
Internet: http://www.pacouncilonthearts.org/pca.cfm?id=1&level=Third&sid=48
Sponsor: Pennsylvania Council on the Arts
216 Finance Building
Harrisburg, PA 17120

PCA Arts Organizations and Arts Programs Grants for Crafts   3778
The Pennsylvania Council on the Arts (PCA) is a state agency in the Office of the Governor. The mission of PCA is to foster the excellence, diversity, and vitality of the arts in Pennsylvania and to broaden the availability and appreciation of those arts throughout the state. Funding for the Council on the Arts comes through the General Assembly and from the National Endowment for the Arts. PCA offers various funding tracks for organizations that offer arts programming. The Arts Organizations and Arts Programs (AOAP) funding track has been created to provide continuous support for established organizations who have offered arts programming for a year or longer. Organizations must be invited by the PCA to apply for AOAP grants. The invitation usually is extended to organizations in PCA's Entry Track or Strategies for Success programs who have consistently received positive reviews by PCA advisory panels. Organizations on the AOAP track receive annual funding in renewable three-year blocks (subject to past performance); applicants submit full applications every three years and interim applications in intervening years. Organizations may also be removed from the AOAP track for various reasons. The AOAP track is divided into thirteen categories: art museums; arts in education organizations; arts service organizations; crafts; dance; folk and traditional arts; literature; theatre; film and electronic media; local arts; music; presenting organizations; and visual arts. In the crafts category, the PCA supports a wide range of organizations who have a mission to present exhibitions and provide instruction, criticism, long-term residencies, and other professional development to craft artists. Both interim and full applications for AOAP grants for crafts must be completed using various online systems (accessible from the grant website), then printed, assembled, and mailed by the postmark date. The PCA encourages applicants to upload any required work samples and attachments through the online system. DVDs must be mailed. The application process is explained in the complete guide (PDF document) which may be accessed from the download section of the website. Application deadlines may vary from year to year. Applicants should visit the calendar section of the website to verify current deadline dates.
Requirements: In general, the PCA supports the following types of organizations: 501(c)3 corporations; units of government; or school districts providing arts programming and/or arts services in Pennsylvania. Organizations are required to provide proof of incorporation and activity in Pennsylvania before applications are reviewed or funds awarded. Unincorporated groups (and in some instances, individuals) may apply to the PCA through a nonprofit organization that acts as a fiscal sponsor. Applicants applying through a fiscal sponsor organization must meet the same requirements as other applicants except for nonprofit status. Unless otherwise specified in the guidelines, PCA awards must be matched on a dollar-for-dollar basis in cash. In-kind goods and services may not be used for match. The PCA generally will support no more than 25% of an organizational budget, and usually considerably less.
Restrictions: In general, the PCA does not fund nor can the match for PCA funds be used for the following expenses and activities: capital expenditures, including equipment costing $500 per item or more; activities for which academic credit is given; activities that have already been completed; activities that have a religious purpose; performances and exhibitions not available to the general public; performances and exhibitions outside Pennsylvania; cash prizes and awards; benefit activities; hospitality expenses, i.e. receptions, parties, gallery openings; lobbyists' payments; and competitions.
Geographic Focus: Pennsylvania
Date(s) Application is Due: Jan 13
Contact: Bryan Holtzapple, Crafts Program Director; (717) 787-6883 or (717) 787-1520; fax (717) 783-2538; bholtzappl@pa.gov
Internet: http://www.pacouncilonthearts.org/pca.cfm?id=1&level=Third&sid=48
Sponsor: Pennsylvania Council on the Arts
216 Finance Building
Harrisburg, PA 17120

PCA Arts Organizations and Arts Programs Grants for Dance   3779
The Pennsylvania Council on the Arts (PCA) is a state agency in the Office of the Governor. The mission of PCA is to foster the excellence, diversity, and vitality of the arts in Pennsylvania and to broaden the availability and appreciation of those arts throughout the state. Funding for the Council on the Arts comes through an annual state appropriation by the General Assembly and from the National Endowment for the Arts. PCA offers various funding tracks for organizations that offer arts programming. The Arts Organizations and Arts Programs (AOAP) funding track has been created to provide continuous support for established organizations who have offered arts programming for a year or longer. Organizations must be invited by the PCA to apply for AOAP grants. The invitation usually is extended to organizations in PCA's Entry Track or Strategies for Success programs who have consistently received positive reviews by PCA advisory panels. Organizations on the AOAP track receive annual funding in renewable three-year blocks (subject to past performance); applicants submit full applications every three years and interim applications in intervening years. Organizations may also be removed from the AOAP track for various reasons. The AOAP track is divided into thirteen categories: art museums; arts in education organizations; arts service organizations; crafts; dance; folk and traditional arts; literature; theatre; film and electronic media; local arts; music; presenting organizations; and visual arts. In the dance category, the PCA supports nonprofit dance organizations whose primary purpose includes public performances. The PCA supports ethnic, modern, classical, jazz, tap, and vernacular dance projects. Both interim and full applications for AOAP grants for Dance must be completed using various online systems (available from the grant website), then printed, assembled, and mailed by the postmark date. The PCA encourages applicants to upload any required work samples and attachments through their online system. DVDs must be mailed. The application process is explained in the complete guide (PDF document) which may be accessed from the download section of the website. Application deadlines may vary from year to year. Applicants should visit the calendar section of the website to verify current deadline dates.
Requirements: In general, the PCA supports the following types of organizations: 501(c)3 corporations; units of government; or school districts providing arts programming and/or arts services in Pennsylvania. Organizations are required to provide proof of incorporation and activity in Pennsylvania before applications are reviewed or funds awarded. Unincorporated groups (and in some instances, individuals) must apply to the PCA through a nonprofit organization that acts as a fiscal sponsor. Applicants applying through a fiscal sponsor organization must meet the same requirements as other applicants except for nonprofit status. Unless otherwise specified in the guidelines, PCA awards must be matched on a dollar-for-dollar basis in cash. In-kind goods and services may not be used to match PCA funds. The PCA generally will support no more than 25% of an organizational budget, and usually considerably less.
Restrictions: The AOAP dance program does not fund dance schools, civic ballets, training institutions, or nonprofessional dance companies, except for those activities which engage professional guest teachers and choreographers; nor does it fund programs in which a professional performing organization is contracted by another organization to perform. (In the latter case, the presenting organization should apply under the Presenting Organizations category.) In general, the PCA does not fund nor can the match for PCA funds be used for the following expenses or activities: capital expenditures, including equipment costing $500 per item or more; activities for which academic credit is given; activities that have already been completed; activities that have a religious purpose; performances and exhibitions not available to the general public; performances and exhibitions outside Pennsylvania; cash prizes and awards; benefit activities; hospitality expenses (e.g. receptions, parties, gallery openings); lobbyists' payments; and competitions.
Geographic Focus: Pennsylvania
Date(s) Application is Due: Jan 13
Contact: Charon Battles; (717) 787-1521 or (717) 787-6883; cbattles@pa.gov
Internet: http://www.pacouncilonthearts.org/pca.cfm?id=1&level=Third&sid=13
Sponsor: Pennsylvania Council on the Arts
216 Finance Building
Harrisburg, PA 17120

PCA Arts Organizations and Arts Grants for Film and Electronic Media   3780
The Pennsylvania Council on the Arts (PCA) is a state agency in the Office of the Governor. The mission of PCA is to foster the excellence, diversity, and vitality of the arts in Pennsylvania and to broaden the availability and appreciation of those arts throughout the state. Funding for the Council on the Arts comes from the citizens of Pennsylvania (through an annual state appropriation by the General Assembly) and from the National Endowment for the Arts. PCA offers various funding tracks for organizations that offer arts programming. The Arts Organizations and Arts Programs (AOAP) funding track has been created to provide continuous support for established organizations who have offered arts programming for a year or longer. Organizations must be invited by the PCA to apply for AOAP grants. (Applicants to PCA's Entry Track or Strategies for Success programs may be invited to apply to the AOAP Track; transition to the AOAP Track begins with constant positive reviews by PCA advisory panels.) Organizations on the AOAP track receive annual funding in three-year blocks, subject to past performance; organizations may also be removed from the AOAP Track for various reasons. Applicants must submit full applications every three years and interim applications in intervening years. The AOAP track grants are divided into thirteen categories: art museums; arts in education organizations; arts service organizations; crafts; dance; folk and traditional arts; literature; theatre; film and electronic media; local arts; music; presenting organizations; and visual arts. In the Film and Electronic Media category, the PCA supports organizations or programs that create, produce, exhibit or distribute media arts and have a commitment to advancing the field through an emphasis on the creative use of the medium. (NOTE: past applicants to the Broadcast of the Arts Project category must contact the Film and Electronic Media Program Director for guidance.) Both interim and full applications for AOAP grants for Film and Electronic Media must be completed using various online systems (available from the grant website), then printed, assembled, and mailed by the postmark date. The PCA encourages applicants to upload any required work samples and attachments through their online system. DVDs must be mailed. The application process is explained in the complete guide (PDF document) which may be accessed from the download section of the website. Application deadlines may vary from year to year. Applicants should visit the calendar section of the website to verify current deadline dates.
Requirements: In general, the PCA supports the following types of organizations: 501(c)3 corporations; units of government; or school districts providing arts programming and/or arts services in Pennsylvania. Organizations are required to provide proof of incorporation and activity

in Pennsylvania before applications are reviewed or funds awarded. Unincorporated groups (and in some instances, individuals) may apply to the PCA through a nonprofit organization that acts as a fiscal sponsor. Applicants applying through a fiscal sponsor organization must meet the same requirements as other applicants except for nonprofit status. Unless otherwise specified in the guidelines, PCA awards must be matched on a dollar-for-dollar basis in cash. In-kind goods and services may not be used to match PCA funds. The PCA generally will support no more than 25% of an organizational budget, and usually considerably less.
Restrictions: AOAP Grants for Film and Electronic Media do not support commercial, strictly instructional, promotional, or archival projects; profit-making theatres/exhibitors; student organizations; or public TV or radio. In general, the PCA does not fund nor can the match for PCA funds be used for the following expenses and activities: capital expenditures, including equipment costing $500 per item or more; activities for which academic credit is given; activities that have already been completed; activities that have a religious purpose; performances and exhibitions not available to the general public; performances and exhibitions outside Pennsylvania; cash prizes and awards; benefit activities; hospitality expenses, i.e. receptions, parties, gallery openings; lobbyists' payments; and competitions.
Geographic Focus: Pennsylvania
Date(s) Application is Due: Jan 13
Contact: Lori Frush Schmelz, Film and Electronic Media Program Director; (717) 787-6883 or (717) 787-1523; fax (717) 783-2538; lschmelz@pa.gov
Internet: http://www.pacouncilonthearts.org/pca.cfm?id=1&level=Third&sid=48
Sponsor: Pennsylvania Council on the Arts
216 Finance Building
Harrisburg, PA 17120

PCA Arts Organizations and Arts Programs Grants for Literature 3781
The Pennsylvania Council on the Arts (PCA) is a state agency in the Office of the Governor. The mission of PCA is to foster the excellence, diversity, and vitality of the arts in Pennsylvania and to broaden the availability and appreciation of those arts throughout the state. Funding for the Council on the Arts comes through an annual state appropriation by the General Assembly and from the National Endowment for the Arts. PCA offers various funding tracks for organizations that offer arts programming. The Arts Organizations and Arts Programs (AOAP) funding track has been created to provide continuous support for established organizations who have offered arts programming for a year or longer. Organizations must be invited by the PCA to apply for AOAP grants. The invitation usually is extended to organizations in PCA's Entry Track or Strategies for Success programs who have consistently received positive reviews by PCA advisory panels. Organizations on the AOAP track receive annual funding in renewable three-year blocks (subject to past performance); applicants submit full applications every three years and interim applications in intervening years. Organizations may also be removed from the AOAP track for various reasons. The AOAP track is divided into thirteen categories: art museums; arts in education organizations; arts service organizations; crafts; dance; folk and traditional arts; literature; theatre; film and electronic media; local arts; music; presenting organizations; and visual arts. In the literature category, the PCA supports publications, readings, and other activities that deliver programs and services. Funds are awarded to publishers of fiction and poetry, creative nonfiction, children's literature, and for public readings that make the work of contemporary writers more available in the state. College-based literature programs and publications will be considered if the activity is not for academic credit and if the applicant can demonstrate broad community participation. Applicants should provide a clear editorial vision and the literary impact of the publication(s), the diversity of authors, and clear evidence that writers are paid fees generally accepted as fair and in cash. Circulation and marketing strategies, production quality and quality-cost ratio, and design are considered. PCA Panelists consider the diversity and excellence of the writers that have been presented, the applicant's demonstrated ability to expand or develop new and diverse audiences, the quality of previous programming, and the effectiveness of promotional strategies. Both interim and full applications for AOAP grants for Literature must be completed using various online systems (available from the grant website), then printed, assembled, and mailed by the postmark date. The PCA encourages applicants to upload any required work samples and attachments through their online system. DVDs must be mailed. The application process is explained in the complete guide (PDF document) which may be accessed from the download section of the website. Application deadlines may vary from year to year. Applicants should visit the calendar section of the website to verify current deadline dates.
Requirements: In general, the PCA supports the following types of organizations: 501(c)3 corporations; units of government; or school districts providing arts programming and/or arts services in Pennsylvania. Organizations are required to provide proof of incorporation and activity in Pennsylvania before applications are reviewed or funds awarded. Unincorporated groups (and in some instances, individuals) may apply to the PCA through a nonprofit organization that acts as a fiscal sponsor. Applicants applying through a fiscal sponsor organization must meet the same requirements as other applicants except for nonprofit status. Unless otherwise specified in the guidelines, PCA awards must be matched on a dollar-for-dollar basis in cash. In-kind goods and services may not be used to match PCA funds. The PCA generally will support no more than 25% of an organizational budget, and usually considerably less.
Restrictions: AOAP Grants for Literature do not fund nor may the match for PCA funds be used for the following expenses or activities: scholarly writing; publications printing primarily student work; student-run publications; vanity press or self publications; literary projects for which academic credit is given; writing competitions, prizes or awards; capital expenditures, including equipment costing $500 per item or more; activities that have already been completed; activities that have a religious purpose; performances and exhibitions not available to the general public; performances and exhibitions outside Pennsylvania; benefit activities; hospitality expenses (e.g. receptions, parties, gallery openings); and lobbyists' payments.
Geographic Focus: Pennsylvania
Date(s) Application is Due: Jan 13
Contact: Philip Horn, Executive Director and Literature Program Director; (717) 787-6883 or (717) 787-1530; fax (717) 783-2538; phorn@pa.gov
Internet: http://www.pacouncilonthearts.org/pca.cfm?id=1&level=Third&sid=48
Sponsor: Pennsylvania Council on the Arts
216 Finance Building
Harrisburg, PA 17120

PCA Arts Organizations and Arts Programs Grants for Local Arts 3782
The Pennsylvania Council on the Arts (PCA) is a state agency in the Office of the Governor. The mission of PCA is to foster the excellence, diversity, and vitality of the arts in Pennsylvania and to broaden the availability and appreciation of those arts throughout the state. Funding for the Council on the Arts comes through the General Assembly and from the National Endowment for the Arts. PCA offers various funding tracks for organizations that offer arts programming. The Arts Organizations and Arts Programs (AOAP) funding track has been created to provide continuous support for established organizations who have offered arts programming for a year or longer. Organizations must be invited by the PCA to apply for AOAP grants. The invitation usually is extended to organizations in PCA's Entry Track or Strategies for Success programs who have consistently received positive reviews by PCA advisory panels. Organizations on the AOAP track receive annual funding in renewable three-year blocks (subject to past performance); applicants submit full applications every three years and interim applications in intervening years. Organizations may also be removed from the AOAP track for various reasons. The AOAP track is divided into thirteen categories: art museums; arts in education organizations; arts service organizations; crafts; dance; folk and traditional arts; literature; theatre; film and electronic media; local arts; music; presenting organizations; and visual arts. In the local arts category, the PCA supports organizations and programs that provide a wide range of arts activities and significant public participation in the arts in a specified community or region. These agencies support, coordinate, and provide a broad range of arts programs and administrative services based on the needs and resources of the designated community. Both interim and full applications for AOAP grants for local arts must be completed using various online systems (accessible from the grant website), then printed, assembled, and mailed by the postmark date. The PCA encourages applicants to upload any required work samples and attachments through the online system. DVDs must be mailed. The application process is explained in the complete guide (PDF document) which may be accessed from the download section of the website. Application deadlines may vary from year to year. Applicants should visit the calendar section of the website to verify current deadline dates.
Requirements: Applicants to the local arts program must be a multi-discipline arts center, multi-discipline arts council, multi-discipline arts festival, and/or a multi-discipline arts program in a social service center or other nonprofit organization or a government agency. In general, the PCA supports the following types of organizations: 501(c)3 corporations; units of government; or school districts providing arts programming and/or arts services in Pennsylvania. Organizations are required to provide proof of incorporation and activity in Pennsylvania before applications are reviewed or funds awarded. Unincorporated groups (and in some instances, individuals) may apply to the PCA through a nonprofit organization that acts as a fiscal sponsor. Applicants applying through a fiscal sponsor organization must meet the same requirements as other applicants except for nonprofit status. Unless otherwise specified in the guidelines, PCA awards must be matched on a dollar-for-dollar basis in cash. In-kind goods and services may not be used to match PCA funds. The PCA generally will support no more than 25% of an organizational budget, and usually considerably less.
Restrictions: The AOAP Grants for Local Arts do not fund single-discipline arts organizations or programs. In general, the PCA does not fund nor can the match for PCA funds be used for the following expenses or activities: capital expenditures, including equipment costing $500 per item or more; activities for which academic credit is given; activities that have already been completed; activities that have a religious purpose; performances and exhibitions not available to the general public; performances and exhibitions outside Pennsylvania; cash prizes and awards; benefit activities; hospitality expenses (e.g., receptions, parties, gallery openings); lobbyists' payments; and competitions.
Geographic Focus: Pennsylvania
Date(s) Application is Due: Jan 13
Contact: Lori Frush Schmelz, Local Arts Program Director; (717) 787-6883 or (717) 787-1523; fax (717) 783-2538; lschmelz@pa.gov
Internet: http://www.pacouncilonthearts.org/pca.cfm?id=1&level=Third&sid=48
Sponsor: Pennsylvania Council on the Arts
216 Finance Building
Harrisburg, PA 17120

PCA Arts Organizations and Arts Programs Grants for Theatre 3783
The Pennsylvania Council on the Arts (PCA) is a state agency in the Office of the Governor. The mission of PCA is to foster the excellence, diversity, and vitality of the arts in Pennsylvania and to broaden the availability and appreciation of those arts throughout the state. Funding for the Council on the Arts through the General Assembly and from the National Endowment for the Arts. PCA offers various funding tracks for organizations that offer arts programming. The Arts Organizations and Arts Programs (AOAP) funding track has been created to provide continuous support for established organizations that have offered arts programming for a year or longer. Organizations must be invited by the PCA to apply for AOAP grants. The invitation usually is extended to organizations in PCA's Entry Track or Strategies for Success programs who have consistently received positive reviews by PCA advisory panels. Organizations on the AOAP track receive annual funding in renewable three-year blocks (subject to past performance); applicants submit full applications every three years and interim applications in intervening years. Organizations may also be removed from the AOAP track for various reasons. The AOAP track is divided into thirteen categories: art museums; arts in education organizations; arts service organizations; crafts; dance; folk and traditional arts; literature; theatre; film and electronic

media; local arts; music; presenting organizations; and visual arts. In the theatre category, the PCA supports production and presentation of plays, the writing and production of new plays, the exploration of new theatre forms, touring, ticket subsidy, and other programs that make theatre more available to Pennsylvania citizens of all ages. Both interim and full applications for AOAP grants for Theatre must be completed using various online systems (available from the grant website), then printed, assembled, and mailed by the postmark date. The PCA encourages applicants to upload any required work samples and attachments through their online system. DVDs must be mailed. The application process is explained in the complete guide (PDF document) which may be accessed from the download section of the website. Application deadlines may vary from year to year. Applicants should visit the calendar section of the website to verify current deadline dates.

Requirements: In general, the PCA supports the following types of organizations: 501(c)3 corporations; units of government; or school districts providing arts programming and/or arts services in Pennsylvania. Organizations are required to provide proof of incorporation and activity in Pennsylvania before applications are reviewed or funds awarded. Unincorporated groups (and in some instances, individuals) may apply to the PCA through a nonprofit organization that acts as a fiscal sponsor. Applicants applying through a fiscal sponsor organization must meet the same requirements as other applicants except for nonprofit status. Unless otherwise specified in the guidelines, PCA awards must be matched on a dollar-for-dollar basis in cash. In-kind goods and services may not be used to match PCA funds. The PCA generally will support no more than 25% of an organizational budget, and usually considerably less.

Restrictions: In general, the PCA does not fund nor can the match for PCA funds be used for the following expenses or activities: capital expenditures, including equipment costing $500 per item or more; activities for which academic credit is given; activities that have already been completed; activities that have a religious purpose; performances and exhibitions not available to the general public; performances and exhibitions outside Pennsylvania; cash prizes and awards; benefit activities; hospitality expenses (e.g. receptions, parties, gallery openings); lobbyists' payments; and competitions.

Geographic Focus: Pennsylvania
Date(s) Application is Due: Jan 13
Contact: Philip Horn, Executive Director and Theatre Program Director; (717) 787-6883 or (717) 787-1530; fax (717) 783-2538; phorn@pa.gov
Internet: http://www.pacouncilonthearts.org/pca.cfm?id=1&level=Third&sid=48
Sponsor: Pennsylvania Council on the Arts
216 Finance Building
Harrisburg, PA 17120

PCA Arts Organizations and Arts Programs Grants for Traditional and Folk Arts 3784
The Pennsylvania Council on the Arts (PCA) is a state agency in the Office of the Governor. The mission of PCA is to foster the excellence, diversity, and vitality of the arts in Pennsylvania and to broaden the availability and appreciation of those arts throughout the state. Funding for the Council on the Arts comes through an annual state appropriation by the General Assembly and from the National Endowment for the Arts. PCA offers various funding tracks for organizations that offer arts programming. The Arts Organizations and Arts Programs (AOAP) funding track has been created to provide continuous support for established organizations who have offered arts programming for a year or longer. Organizations must be invited by the PCA to apply for AOAP grants. The invitation usually is extended to organizations in PCA's Entry Track or Strategies for Success programs who have consistently received positive reviews by PCA advisory panels. Organizations on the AOAP track receive annual funding in renewable three-year blocks (subject to past performance); applicants submit full applications every three years and interim applications in intervening years. Organizations may also be removed from the AOAP track for various reasons. The AOAP track is divided into thirteen categories: art museums; arts in education organizations; arts service organizations; crafts; dance; folk and traditional arts; literature; theatre; film and electronic media; local arts; music; presenting organizations; and visual arts. In the folk and traditional arts category, the PCA supports traditional arts programming, services to artists and communities practicing traditional arts and customs, and the conservation of the traditional arts and customs found in the Commonwealth. Both interim and full applications for AOAP grants for Traditional and Folk Arts must be completed using various online systems (available from the grant website), then printed, assembled, and mailed by the postmark date. The PCA encourages applicants to upload any required work samples and attachments through their online system. DVDs must be mailed. The application process is explained in the complete guide (PDF document) which may be accessed from the download section of the website. Applicants are strongly encouraged to contact the PCA or the Institute for Cultural Partnerships for technical support, if needed. Application deadlines may vary from year to year. Applicants should visit the calendar section of the website to verify current deadline dates.

Requirements: In general, the PCA supports the following types of organizations: 501(c)3 corporations; units of government; and school districts providing arts programming and/or arts services in Pennsylvania. Organizations are required to provide proof of incorporation and activity in Pennsylvania before applications are reviewed or funds awarded. Unincorporated groups (and in some instances, individuals) may apply to the PCA through a nonprofit organization that acts as a fiscal sponsor. Applicants applying through a fiscal sponsor organization must meet the same requirements as other applicants except for nonprofit status. Unless otherwise specified in the guidelines, PCA awards must be matched on a dollar-for-dollar basis in cash. In-kind goods and services may not be used to match PCA funds. The PCA generally will support no more than 25% of an organizational budget, and usually considerably less.

Restrictions: This program does not fund oral history programs that do not include contemporary traditions, nor does it fund the production or marketing of historical crafts, or other traditions that are not part of the living heritage of particular communities. In general, the PCA does not fund nor can the match for PCA funds be used for the following expenses or activities: capital expenditures, including equipment costing $500 per item or more; activities for which academic credit is given; activities that have already been completed; activities that have a religious purpose; performances and exhibitions not available to the general public; performances and exhibitions outside Pennsylvania; cash prizes and awards; benefit activities; hospitality expenses (e.g. receptions, parties, gallery openings); lobbyists' payments; and competitions.

Geographic Focus: Pennsylvania
Date(s) Application is Due: Jan 13
Contact: Philip Horn; (717) 787-6883 or (717) 787-1530; phorn@pa.gov
Internet: http://www.pacouncilonthearts.org/pca.cfm?id=1&level=Third&sid=48
Sponsor: Pennsylvania Council on the Arts
216 Finance Building
Harrisburg, PA 17120

PCA Arts Organizations and Arts Programs Grants for Visual Arts 3785
The Pennsylvania Council on the Arts (PCA) is a state agency in the Office of the Governor. The mission of PCA is to foster the excellence, diversity, and vitality of the arts in Pennsylvania and to broaden the availability and appreciation of those arts throughout the state. Funding for the Council on the Arts comes through the General Assembly and from the National Endowment for the Arts. PCA offers various funding tracks for organizations that offer arts programming. The Arts Organizations and Arts Programs (AOAP) funding track has been created to provide continuous support for established organizations who have offered arts programming for a year or longer. Organizations must be invited by the PCA to apply for AOAP grants. The invitation usually is extended to organizations in PCA's Entry Track or Strategies for Success programs who have consistently received positive reviews by PCA advisory panels. Organizations on the AOAP track receive annual funding in renewable three-year blocks (subject to past performance); applicants submit full applications every three years and interim applications in intervening years. Organizations may also be removed from the AOAP track for various reasons. The AOAP track is divided into thirteen categories: art museums; arts in education organizations; arts service organizations; crafts; dance; folk and traditional arts; literature; theatre; film and electronic media; local arts; music; presenting organizations; and visual arts. In the visual arts category, the PCA supports contemporary visual arts organizations and programs that have a primary mission to provide high-quality exhibitions, programs, and activities such as publications and education/instruction. The PCA defines visual arts as including (but not limited to) painting, sculpture, graphic art, photography, architecture, interdisciplinary arts, and electronic and digital art. Both interim and full applications for AOAP grants for visual arts must be completed using various online systems (accessible from the grant website), then printed, assembled, and mailed by the postmark date. The PCA encourages applicants to upload any required work samples and attachments through the online system. DVDs must be mailed. The application process is explained in the complete guide (PDF document) which may be accessed from the download section of the website. Application deadlines may vary from year to year. Applicants should visit the calendar section of the website to verify current deadline dates.

Requirements: In general, the PCA supports the following types of organizations: 501(c)3 corporations; units of government; or school districts providing arts programming and/or arts services in Pennsylvania. Organizations are required to provide proof of incorporation and activity in Pennsylvania before applications are reviewed or funds awarded. Unincorporated groups (and in some instances, individuals) may apply to the PCA through a nonprofit organization that acts as a fiscal sponsor. Applicants applying through a fiscal sponsor organization must meet the same requirements as other applicants except for nonprofit status. Unless otherwise specified in the guidelines, PCA awards must be matched on a dollar-for-dollar basis in cash. In-kind goods and services may not be used for match. The PCA generally will support no more than 25% of an organizational budget, and usually considerably less.

Restrictions: In general, the PCA does not fund nor can the match for PCA funds be used for the following expenses and activities: capital expenditures, including equipment costing $500 per item or more; activities for which academic credit is given; activities that have already been completed; activities that have a religious purpose; performances and exhibitions not available to the general public; performances and exhibitions outside Pennsylvania; cash prizes and awards; benefit activities; hospitality expenses (e.g., receptions, parties, and gallery openings); lobbyists' payments; and competitions.

Geographic Focus: Pennsylvania
Date(s) Application is Due: Jan 13
Contact: Bryan Holtzapple, Visual Arts Program Director; (717) 787-6883 or (717) 787-1520; fax (717) 783-2538; bholtzappl@pa.gov
Internet: http://www.pacouncilonthearts.org/pca.cfm?id=1&level=Third&sid=48
Sponsor: Pennsylvania Council on the Arts
216 Finance Building
Harrisburg, PA 17120

PCA Busing Grants 3786
The Pennsylvania Council on the Arts (PCA) is a state agency in the Office of the Governor. The mission of PCA is to foster the excellence, diversity, and vitality of the arts in Pennsylvania and to broaden the availability and appreciation of those arts throughout the state. Funding for the Council on the Arts comes from the citizens of Pennsylvania (through an annual state appropriation by the General Assembly) and from the National Endowment for the Arts. The PCA's Busing Program provides grants of up to $250 to assist groups attending arts events of artistic merit that might otherwise be inaccessible because of transportation problems. The program primarily serves groups living a distance from major cities, inner-city audiences for whom public transportation is inadequate, and special groups (i.e. people with disabilities or the elderly) for whom transportation is a problem. Requests may be submitted at any time, but must be postmarked at least 30 days prior to the beginning of the event for which funding is requested. Applications are available from the downloads section of the website.

Requirements: The group must make its own provisions for the purchase of tickets to the events. In most cases, the group attending the arts event and not the arts organization attended should apply. If the group attending is not incorporated, the organization

producing the event may apply on their behalf, if a letter of intent from the attending group is enclosed. This is a non-matching award.
Restrictions: Trips to events outside of Pennsylvania will not be supported.
Geographic Focus: Pennsylvania
Amount of Grant: Up to 250 USD
Contact: Charon Battles, Preserving Diverse Cultures Program Director; (717) 787-6883 or (717) 787-1521; cbattles@pa.gov
Internet: http://pacouncilonthearts.org/pca.cfm?id=48&level=Third&sid=48
Sponsor: Pennsylvania Council on the Arts
216 Finance Building
Harrisburg, PA 17120

PCA Entry Track Arts Organizations and Arts Programs Grants for Art Museums   3787
The Pennsylvania Council on the Arts (PCA) is a state agency in the Office of the Governor. The mission of PCA is to foster the excellence, diversity, and vitality of the arts in Pennsylvania and to broaden the availability and appreciation of those arts throughout the state. Funding for the Council on the Arts comes from the citizens of Pennsylvania (through an annual state appropriation by the General Assembly) and from the National Endowment for the Arts. PCA offers various funding tracks for organizations that offer arts programming. The Entry Track for Arts Organizations and Arts Programs is the point of entry for organizations wishing to eventually receive on-going support from PCA's multi-year/renewable Arts Organizations and Arts Programs Grants. Entry-Track grants support eligible organizations that generally have a history of at least one-year consistent arts/cultural programming. Entry-Track grants fall into three categories: Community Arts, Performance and Presenting, and Visual Arts and Electronic Media. The Community Arts category includes arts-education, arts-service, folk and traditional arts, local multi-discipline arts center, arts-council, and arts-festival programs. The Performance and Presenting category includes dance, literature, music, presenting-organization, and theatre programs. The Visual Arts and Electronic Media category includes art-museum, crafts, film and electronic media, interdisciplinary-arts, and visual-arts programs. Within the Visual Arts and Electronic Media/art-museums category, PCA supports organizations whose primary mission is to present, interpret, and preserve fine art objects of outstanding aesthetic quality. The PCA seeks to ensure the enlightened interpretation and care of the state's artistic heritage and to foster the relationships between museums and their communities through support for exhibitions, educational programs, collections care programs, and institutional operations. The application for an Entry-Track grant for art museums must be completed using various online systems (available from the grant website), then printed, assembled, and mailed by the postmark date. The PCA encourages applicants to upload any required work samples and attachments through their online system. DVDs must be mailed. The application process is explained in the complete guide (PDF document) which may be accessed from the download section of the website. Application deadlines may vary from year to year. Applicants should visit the calendar section of the website to verify current deadline dates.
Requirements: All applicants must contact PCA's Entry Track Coordinator prior to applying for the first time to discuss eligibility. Generally, organizations are eligible to apply to the Entry Track if they meet the folowing criteria: their average operating budget is over $200,000; they have at least one year of ongoing stable arts programming; and they are a nonprofit, tax-exempt corporation, unit of government, or school district providing arts programming and/or arts services in Pennsylvania. Organizations are required to provide proof of incorporation and activity in Pennsylvania before applications are reviewed or funds awarded. Non-arts organizations must clearly define an ongoing arts program that has been in existence for at least one year and submit with their application a board resolution demonstrating clear commitment to the applicant's art program. Unincorporated groups (and in some instances, individuals) may apply to the PCA through a nonprofit organization that acts as a fiscal sponsor. Applicants applying through a fiscal sponsor organization must meet the same requirements as other applicants except for nonprofit status. Unless otherwise specified in the guidelines, PCA awards must be matched on a dollar-for-dollar basis in cash. In-kind goods and services may not be used to match PCA funds. The PCA generally will support no more than 25% of an organizational budget, and usually considerably less. Interested organizations who may not meet the eligibility requirements of the Entry Track may be eligible to apply for grants from PCA's Pennsylvania Partners in the Arts (PPA), a decentralized funding program which offers both ongoing support and arts projects funding opportunities.
Restrictions: PCA's Entry-Track grants for Art Museums do not fund organizations that provide only ongoing exhibition programs. Those organizations may be able to apply for AOAP Craft or Visual Arts Grants, depending on the focus of the exhibition series. Ensembles and/or organizations from the African-American, Asian- American, Hispanic/Latino, and Native-American communities may apply for either a PCA Strategies-for-Success grant or an Entry-Track grant, but not for both. Organizations planning a one-time-only arts project should apply for PCA's Pennsylvania Partners in the Arts grants. In general, the PCA does not fund nor can the match for PCA funds be used for the following expenses and activities: capital expenditures, including equipment costing $500 per item or more; activities for which academic credit is given; activities that have already been completed; activities that have a religious purpose; performances and exhibitions not available to the general public; performances and exhibitions outside Pennsylvania; cash prizes and awards; benefit activities; hospitality expenses, i.e. receptions, parties, gallery openings; lobbyists' payments; and competitions.
Geographic Focus: Pennsylvania
Date(s) Application is Due: Jan 13
Contact: Jamie Dunlap, Entry Track Program Director; (717) 787-6883 or (717) 525-5542; fax (717) 783-2538; jadunlap@pa.gov
Internet: http://www.pacouncilonthearts.org/pca.cfm?id=2&level=Third&sid=48
Sponsor: Pennsylvania Council on the Arts
216 Finance Building
Harrisburg, PA 17120

PCA Entry Track Arts Organizations and Arts Programs Grants for Arts Education Organizations   3788
The Pennsylvania Council on the Arts (PCA) is a state agency in the Office of the Governor. The mission of PCA is to foster the excellence, diversity, and vitality of the arts in Pennsylvania and to broaden the availability and appreciation of those arts throughout the state. Funding for the Council on the Arts comes from the citizens of Pennsylvania (through an annual state appropriation by the General Assembly) and from the National Endowment for the Arts. PCA offers various funding tracks for organizations that offer arts programming. The Entry Track for Arts Organizations and Arts Programs is the point of entry for organizations wishing to eventually receive on-going support from PCA's multi-year/renewable Arts Organizations and Arts Programs Grants. Entry-Track grants support eligible organizations that generally have a history of at least one-year consistent arts/cultural programming. Entry-Track grants fall into three categories: Community Arts, Performance and Presenting, and Visual Arts and Electronic Media. The Community Arts category includes arts-education, arts-service, folk and traditional arts, local multi-discipline arts center, arts-council, and arts-festival programs. The Performance and Presenting category includes dance, literature, music, presenting-organization, and theatre programs. The Visual Arts and Electronic Media category includes art-museum, crafts, film and electronic media, interdisciplinary-arts, and visual-arts programs. Within the Community Arts/arts-education organizations category, the PCA supports organizations or departments whose primary mission and activities are arts education or arts-in-education that include a significant public participation component. Arts-education programming can be arts workshops, classes, and/or programs. The application for an Entry-Track grant for arts-education organizations must be completed using various online systems (available from the grant website), then printed, assembled, and mailed by the postmark date. The PCA encourages applicants to upload any required work samples and attachments through their online system. DVDs must be mailed. The application process is explained in the complete guide (PDF document) which may be accessed from the download section of the website. Application deadlines may vary from year to year. Applicants should visit the calendar section of the website to verify current deadline dates.
Requirements: Single-discipline arts organizations or organizations providing programs whose primary mission is to provide art-education programming and activities can apply for these grants. All applicants must contact PCA's Entry Track Coordinator prior to applying for the first time to discuss eligibility. Generally, organizations are eligible to apply to the Entry Track if they meet the folowing criteria: their average operating budget is over $200,000; they have at least one year of ongoing stable arts programming; and they are a nonprofit, tax-exempt corporation, unit of government, or school district providing arts programming and/or arts services in Pennsylvania. Organizations are required to provide proof of incorporation and activity in Pennsylvania before applications are reviewed or funds awarded. Non-arts organizations must clearly define an ongoing arts program that has been in existence for at least one year and submit with their application a board resolution demonstrating clear commitment to the applicant's art program. Unincorporated groups (and in some instances, individuals) may apply to the PCA through a nonprofit organization that acts as a fiscal sponsor. Applicants applying through a fiscal sponsor organization must meet the same requirements as other applicants except for nonprofit status. Unless otherwise specified in the guidelines, PCA awards must be matched on a dollar-for-dollar basis in cash. In-kind goods and services may not be used to match PCA funds. The PCA generally will support no more than 25% of an organizational budget, and usually considerably less. Interested organizations who may not meet the eligibility requirements of the Entry Track may be eligible to apply for grants from PCA's Pennsylvania Partners in the Arts (PPA), a decentralized funding program which offers both ongoing support and arts projects funding opportunities.
Restrictions: Ensembles and/or organizations from the African-American, Asian-American, Hispanic/Latino, and Native-American communities may apply for either a PCA Strategies-for-Success grant or an Entry-Track grant, but not for both. Organizations planning a one-time-only arts project should apply for PCA's Pennsylvania-Partners-in-the-Arts grants. Entry-Track grants for arts-education organizations do not fund public schools, school districts, intermediate units, other local educational agencies, or private and parochial schools (however, these organizations may apply to PCA's Arts-In-Education Division for artist residencies). In general, the PCA does not fund nor can the match for PCA funds be used for the following expenses and activities: capital expenditures, including equipment costing $500 per item or more; activities for which academic credit is given; activities that have already been completed; activities that have a religious purpose; performances and exhibitions not available to the general public; performances and exhibitions outside Pennsylvania; cash prizes and awards; benefit activities; hospitality expenses, i.e. receptions, parties, gallery openings; lobbyists' payments; and competitions.
Geographic Focus: Pennsylvania
Date(s) Application is Due: Jan 13
Contact: Jamie Dunlap, Entry Track Program Director; (717) 787-6883 or (717) 525-5542; fax (717) 783-2538; jadunlap@pa.gov
Internet: http://www.pacouncilonthearts.org/pca.cfm?id=2&level=Third
Sponsor: Pennsylvania Council on the Arts
216 Finance Building
Harrisburg, PA 17120

PCA Entry Track Arts Organizations and Arts Programs Grants for Arts Service Organizations   3789
The Pennsylvania Council on the Arts (PCA) is a state agency in the Office of the Governor. The mission of PCA is to foster the excellence, diversity, and vitality of the arts in Pennsylvania and to broaden the availability and appreciation of those arts throughout the state. Funding for the Council on the Arts comes from the citizens of Pennsylvania (through an annual state appropriation by the General Assembly) and from the National Endowment for the Arts. PCA offers various funding tracks for organizations that offer arts programming. The Entry Track for Arts Organizations and Arts Programs is the point of entry for organizations wishing to

eventually receive on-going support from PCA's multi-year/renewable Arts Organizations and Arts Programs Grants. Entry-Track grants support eligible organizations that generally have a history of at least one-year consistent arts/cultural programming. Entry-Track grants fall into three categories: Community Arts, Performance and Presenting, and Visual Arts and Electronic Media. The Community Arts category includes arts-education, arts-service, folk and traditional arts, local multi-discipline arts center, arts-council, and arts-festival programs. The Performance and Presenting category includes dance, literature, music, presenting-organization, and theatre programs. The Visual Arts and Electronic Media category includes art-museum, crafts, film and electronic media, interdisciplinary-arts, and visual-arts programs. Within the Community Arts/arts-service category, the PCA supports organizations whose primary mission is to provide services to Pennsylvania arts organizations and artists (national service organizations can only be funded for arts services provided in Pennsylvania). The application for an Entry-Track grant for arts service organizations must be completed using various online systems (available from the grant website), then printed, assembled, and mailed by the postmark date. The PCA encourages applicants to upload any required work samples and attachments through their online system. DVDs must be mailed. The application process is explained in the complete guide (PDF document) which may be accessed from the download section of the website. Application deadlines may vary from year to year. Applicants should visit the calendar section of the website to verify current deadline dates.
Requirements: All applicants must contact PCA's Entry Track Coordinator prior to applying for the first time to discuss eligibility. Generally, organizations are eligible to apply to the Entry Track if they meet the folowing criteria: their average operating budget is over $200,000; they have at least one year of ongoing stable arts programming; and they are a nonprofit, tax-exempt corporation, unit of government, or school district providing arts programming and/or arts services in Pennsylvania. Organizations are required to provide proof of incorporation and activity in Pennsylvania before applications are reviewed or funds awarded. Non-arts organizations must clearly define an ongoing arts program that has been in existence for at least one year and submit with their application a board resolution demonstrating clear commitment to the applicant's art program. Unincorporated groups (and in some instances, individuals) may apply to the PCA through a nonprofit organization that acts as a fiscal sponsor. Applicants applying through a fiscal sponsor organization must meet the same requirements as other applicants except for nonprofit status. Unless otherwise specified in the guidelines, PCA awards must be matched on a dollar-for-dollar basis in cash. In-kind goods and services may not be used to match PCA funds. The PCA generally will support no more than 25% of an organizational budget, and usually considerably less. Interested organizations who may not meet the eligibility requirements of the Entry Track may be eligible to apply for grants from PCA's Pennsylvania Partners in the Arts (PPA), a decentralized funding program which offers both ongoing support and arts projects funding opportunities.
Restrictions: Ensembles and/or organizations from the African-American, Asian-American, Hispanic/Latino, and Native-American communities may apply for either a PCA Strategies-for-Success grant or an Entry-Track grant, but not for both. Organizations planning a one-time-only arts project should apply for PCA's Pennsylvania Partners in the Arts grants. In general, the PCA does not fund nor can the match for PCA funds be used for the following expenses and activities: capital expenditures, including equipment costing $500 per item or more; activities for which academic credit is given; activities that have already been completed; activities that have a religious purpose; performances and exhibitions not available to the general public; performances and exhibitions outside Pennsylvania; cash prizes and awards; benefit activities; hospitality expenses, i.e. receptions, parties, gallery openings; lobbyists' payments; and competitions.
Geographic Focus: Pennsylvania
Date(s) Application is Due: Jan 13
Contact: Bryan Holtzapple; (717) 787-6883 or (717) 787-1520; bholtzappl@pa.gov
Internet: http://www.pacouncilonthearts.org/pca.cfm?id=2&level=Third
Sponsor: Pennsylvania Council on the Arts
216 Finance Building
Harrisburg, PA 17120

PCA Entry Track Arts Organizations and Arts Programs Grants for Dance   3791
The Pennsylvania Council on the Arts (PCA) is a state agency in the Office of the Governor. The mission of PCA is to foster the excellence, diversity, and vitality of the arts in Pennsylvania and to broaden the availability and appreciation of those arts throughout the state. Funding for the Council on the Arts comes from the citizens of Pennsylvania (through an annual state appropriation by the General Assembly) and from the National Endowment for the Arts. PCA offers various funding tracks for organizations that offer arts programming. The Entry Track for Arts Organizations and Arts Programs is the point of entry for organizations wishing to eventually receive on-going support from PCA's multi-year/renewable Arts Organizations and Arts Programs Grants. Entry-Track grants support eligible organizations that generally have a history of at least one-year consistent arts/cultural programming. Entry-Track grants fall into three categories: the Community Arts category includes arts-education organizations, arts-service organizations, folk and traditional arts, local arts (multi-discipline arts centers), arts councils, and arts festivals; the Performance and Presenting category includes dance, literature, music, presenting organizations, and theatre; and the Visual Arts and Electronic Media category includes art museums, crafts, film and electronic media, interdisciplinary arts, and visual arts. In the dance sub-category, the PCA supports nonprofit dance organizations whose primary purpose includes public performances. The PCA supports ethnic, modern, classical, jazz, tap, and vernacular dance projects. The application for an Entry-Track grant for dance must be completed using various online systems (available from the grant website), then printed, assembled, and mailed by the postmark date. The PCA encourages applicants to upload any required work samples and attachments through their online system. DVDs must be mailed. Applicants are strongly encouraged to visit the grant website for complete information, guidelines, and deadlines and to contact the PCA for technical support, if needed.
Requirements: All applicants must contact PCA's Entry Track Coordinator prior to applying for the first time to discuss eligibility. Generally, organizations are eligible to apply to the Entry Track if: their average operating budget is over $200,000; they have at least one year of ongoing stable arts programming; and if they are a nonprofit, tax-exempt corporation, unit of government, or school district providing arts programming and/or arts services in Pennsylvania. Organizations are required to provide proof of incorporation and activity in Pennsylvania before applications are reviewed or funds awarded. Non-arts organizations must clearly define an ongoing arts program that has been in existence for at least one year and submit with their application a board resolution demonstrating clear commitment to the applicant's art program. Unincorporated groups (and in some instances, individuals) may apply to the PCA through a nonprofit organization that acts as a fiscal sponsor. Applicants applying through a fiscal sponsor organization must meet the same requirements as other applicants except for nonprofit status. Unless otherwise specified in the guidelines, PCA awards must be matched on a dollar-for-dollar basis in cash. In-kind goods and services may not be used to match PCA funds. The PCA generally will support no more than 25% of an organizational budget, and usually considerably less. Interested organizations who may not meet the eligibility requirements of the Entry Track may be eligible to apply for grants from PCA's Pennsylvania Partners in the Arts (PPA), a decentralized funding program which offers both ongoing support and arts projects funding opportunities.

Contact: Jamie Dunlap, Entry Track Program Director, Accessibility Programs Director; (717) 787-6883 or (717) 525-5542; fax (717) 783-2538; jadunlap@pa.gov
Internet: http://www.pacouncilonthearts.org/pca.cfm?id=2&level=Third
Sponsor: Pennsylvania Council on the Arts
216 Finance Building
Harrisburg, PA 17120

PCA Entry Track Arts Organizations and Arts Programs Grants for Crafts   3790
The Pennsylvania Council on the Arts (PCA) is a state agency in the Office of the Governor. The mission of PCA is to foster the excellence, diversity, and vitality of the arts in Pennsylvania and to broaden the availability and appreciation of those arts throughout the state. Funding for the Council on the Arts comes from the citizens of Pennsylvania (through an annual state appropriation by the General Assembly) and from the National Endowment for the Arts. PCA offers various funding tracks for organizations that offer arts programming. The Entry Track for Arts Organizations and Arts Programs is the point of entry for organizations wishing to eventually receive on-going support from PCA's multi-year/renewable Arts Organizations and Arts Programs Grants. Entry-Track grants support eligible organizations that generally have a history of at least one-year consistent arts/cultural programming. Entry-Track grants fall into three categories: Community Arts, Performance and Presenting, and Visual Arts and Electronic Media. The Community Arts category includes arts-education, arts-service, folk and traditional arts, local multi-discipline arts center, arts-council, and arts-festival programs. The Performance and Presenting category includes dance, literature, music, presenting-organization, and theatre programs. The Visual Arts and Electronic Media category includes art-museum, crafts, film and electronic media, interdisciplinary-arts, and visual-arts programs. Within the Visual Arts and Electronic Media/crafts category, the PCA supports a wide range of organizations who have a mission to present exhibitions and provide instruction, criticism, long-term residencies, and other professional development to craft artists. The application for an Entry-Track grant for crafts must be completed using various online systems (available from the grant website), then printed, assembled, and mailed by the postmark date. The PCA encourages applicants to upload any required work samples and attachments through their online system. DVDs must be mailed. The application process is explained in the complete guide (PDF document) which may be accessed from the download

Restrictions: The Entry-Track dance sub-category does not fund dance schools, civic ballets, training institutions, or nonprofessional dance companies, except for those activities which engage professional guest teachers and choreographers; or programs in which a professional performing organization is contracted by another organization to perform. In the last instance, the presenting organization should apply under the Entry-Track presenting organizations sub-category. Ensembles and/or organizations from the African-American, Asian- American, Hispanic/Latino, and Native-American communities may apply for either a PCA Strategies-for-Success grant or an Entry-Track grant, but not for both. Organizations planning a one-time-only arts project should apply for PCA's Pennsylvania Partners in the Arts grants. In general, the PCA does not fund the following nor can the match for PCA funds be used for these expenses: capital expenditures, including equipment costing $500 per item or more; activities for which academic credit is given; activities that have already been completed; activities that have a religious purpose; performances and exhibitions not available to the general public; performances and exhibitions outside Pennsylvania; cash prizes and awards; benefit activities; hospitality expenses, i.e. receptions, parties, gallery openings; lobbyists' payments; and competitions.
Geographic Focus: Pennsylvania
Date(s) Application is Due: Jan 13
Contact: Jamie Dunlap, Entry Track Program Director, Accessibility Programs Director; (717) 787-6883 or (717) 525-5542; fax (717) 783-2538; jadunlap@pa.gov
Internet: http://www.pacouncilonthearts.org/pca.cfm?id=2&level=Third
Sponsor: Pennsylvania Council on the Arts
216 Finance Building
Harrisburg, PA 17120

PCA Entry Track Arts Organizations and Arts Programs Grants for Film and Electronic Media 3792

The Pennsylvania Council on the Arts (PCA) is a state agency in the Office of the Governor. The mission of PCA is to foster the excellence, diversity, and vitality of the arts in Pennsylvania and to broaden the availability and appreciation of those arts throughout the state. Funding for the Council on the Arts comes from the citizens of Pennsylvania (through an annual state appropriation by the General Assembly) and from the National Endowment for the Arts. PCA offers various funding tracks for organizations that offer arts programming. The Entry Track for Arts Organizations and Arts Programs is the point of entry for organizations wishing to eventually receive on-going support from PCA's multi-year/renewable Arts Organizations and Arts Programs Grants. Entry-Track grants support eligible organizations that generally have a history of at least one-year consistent arts/cultural programming. Entry-Track grants fall into three categories: Community Arts, Performance and Presenting, and Visual Arts and Electronic Media. The Community Arts category includes arts-education, arts-service, folk and traditional arts, local multi-discipline arts center, arts-council, and arts-festival programs. The Performance and Presenting category includes dance, literature, music, presenting-organization, and theatre programs. The Visual Arts and Electronic Media category includes art-museum, crafts, film and electronic media, interdisciplinary-arts, and visual-arts programs. Within the Visual Arts and Electronic Media/film and electronic media category, the PCA supports organizations or programs that create, produce, exhibit or distribute media arts and have a commitment to advancing the field through an emphasis on the creative use of the medium. The application for an Entry-Track grant for film and electronic media must be completed using various online systems (available from the grant website), then printed, assembled, and mailed by the postmark date. The PCA encourages applicants to upload any required work samples and attachments through their online system. DVDs must be mailed. The application process is explained in the complete guide (PDF document) which may be accessed from the download section of the website. Application deadlines may vary from year to year. Applicants should visit the calendar section of the website to verify current deadline dates.
Requirements: All applicants must contact PCA's Entry Track Coordinator prior to applying for the first time to discuss eligibility. Generally, organizations are eligible to apply to the Entry Track if they meet the folowing criteria: their average operating budget is over $200,000; they have at least one year of ongoing stable arts programming; and they are a nonprofit, tax-exempt corporation, unit of government, or school district providing arts programming and/or arts services in Pennsylvania. Organizations are required to provide proof of incorporation and activity in Pennsylvania before applications are reviewed or funds awarded. Non-arts organizations must clearly define an ongoing arts program that has been in existence for at least one year and submit with their application a board resolution demonstrating clear commitment to the applicant's art program. Unincorporated groups (and in some instances, individuals) may apply to the PCA through a nonprofit organization that acts as a fiscal sponsor. Applicants applying through a fiscal sponsor organization must meet the same requirements as other applicants except for nonprofit status. Unless otherwise specified in the guidelines, PCA awards must be matched on a dollar-for-dollar basis in cash. In-kind goods and services may not be used to match PCA funds. The PCA generally will support no more than 25% of an organizational budget, and usually considerably less. Interested organizations who may not meet the eligibility requirements of the Entry Track may be eligible to apply for grants from PCA's Pennsylvania Partners in the Arts (PPA), a decentralized funding program which offers both ongoing support and arts projects funding opportunities.
Restrictions: Ensembles and/or organizations from the African-American, Asian- American, Hispanic/Latino, and Native-American communities may apply for either a PCA Strategies-for-Success grant or an Entry-Track grant, but not for both. Organizations planning a one-time-only arts project should apply for PCA's Pennsylvania Partners in the Arts grants. In general, the PCA does not fund nor can the match for PCA funds be used for the following expenses and activities: capital expenditures, including equipment costing $500 per item or more; activities for which academic credit is given; activities that have already been completed; activities that have a religious purpose; performances and exhibitions not available to the general public; performances and exhibitions outside Pennsylvania; cash prizes and awards; benefit activities; hospitality expenses, i.e. receptions, parties, gallery openings; lobbyists' payments; and competitions.
Geographic Focus: Pennsylvania
Date(s) Application is Due: Jan 13
Contact: Jamie Dunlap, Entry Track Program Director, Accessibility Programs Director; (717) 787-6883 or (717) 525-5542; fax (717) 783-2538; jadunlap@pa.gov
Internet: http://www.pacouncilonthearts.org/pca.cfm?id=2&level=Third
Sponsor: Pennsylvania Council on the Arts
216 Finance Building
Harrisburg, PA 17120

PCA Entry Track Arts Organizations and Arts Programs Grants for Literature 3793

The Pennsylvania Council on the Arts (PCA) is a state agency in the Office of the Governor. The mission of PCA is to foster the excellence, diversity, and vitality of the arts in Pennsylvania and to broaden the availability and appreciation of those arts throughout the state. Funding for the Council on the Arts comes from the citizens of Pennsylvania (through an annual state appropriation by the General Assembly) and from the National Endowment for the Arts. PCA offers various funding tracks for organizations that offer arts programming. The Entry Track for Arts Organizations and Arts Programs is the point of entry for organizations wishing to eventually receive on-going support from PCA's multi-year/renewable Arts Organizations and Arts Programs Grants. Entry-Track grants support eligible organizations that generally have a history of at least one-year consistent arts/cultural programming. Entry-Track grants fall into three categories: Community Arts, Performance and Presenting, and Visual Arts and Electronic Media. The Community Arts category includes arts-education, arts-service, folk and traditional arts, local multi-discipline arts center, arts-council, and arts-festival programs. The Performance and Presenting category includes dance, literature, music, presenting-organization, and theatre programs. The Visual Arts and Electronic Media category includes art-museum, crafts, film and electronic media, interdisciplinary-arts, and visual-arts programs. Within the Performance and Presenting/literature category, the PCA supports publications, readings and other activities that deliver programs and services. Funds are awarded to publishers of fiction, poetry, creative nonfiction, and children's literature as well as for public readings that make the work of contemporary writers more available in the state. College-based literature programs and publications will be considered if the activity is not for academic credit and if the applicant can demonstrate broad community participation. Applicants should provide a clear editorial vision, make a case for the literary impact of the publication(s, show the diversity of authors, and demonstrate clear evidence that writers are paid fees generally accepted as fair and in cash. Circulation and marketing strategies, production quality and quality-cost ratio, and design are considered. PCA Panelists consider the diversity and excellence of the writers that have been presented, the organization's demonstrated ability to expand or develop new and diverse audiences, the quality of previous programming, and the effectiveness of promotional strategies. The application for an Entry-Track grant for literature must be completed using various online systems (available from the grant website), then printed, assembled, and mailed by the postmark date. The PCA encourages applicants to upload any required work samples and attachments through their online system. DVDs must be mailed. The application process is explained in the complete guide (PDF document) which may be accessed from the download section of the website. Application deadlines may vary from year to year. Applicants should visit the calendar section of the website to verify current deadline dates.
Requirements: All applicants must contact PCA's Entry Track Coordinator prior to applying for the first time to discuss eligibility. Generally, organizations are eligible to apply to the Entry Track if they meet the folowing criteria: their average operating budget is over $200,000; they have at least one year of ongoing stable arts programming; and they are a nonprofit, tax-exempt corporation, unit of government, or school district providing arts programming and/or arts services in Pennsylvania. Organizations are required to provide proof of incorporation and activity in Pennsylvania before applications are reviewed or funds awarded. Non-arts organizations must clearly define an ongoing arts program that has been in existence for at least one year and submit with their application a board resolution demonstrating clear commitment to the applicant's art program. Unincorporated groups (and in some instances, individuals) may apply to the PCA through a nonprofit organization that acts as a fiscal sponsor. Applicants applying through a fiscal sponsor organization must meet the same requirements as other applicants except for nonprofit status. Unless otherwise specified in the guidelines, PCA awards must be matched on a dollar-for-dollar basis in cash. In-kind goods and services may not be used to match PCA funds. The PCA generally will support no more than 25% of an organizational budget, and usually considerably less. Interested organizations who may not meet the eligibility requirements of the Entry Track may be eligible to apply for grants from PCA's Pennsylvania Partners in the Arts (PPA), a decentralized funding program which offers both ongoing support and arts projects funding opportunities.
Restrictions: Entry-Track grants for literature do not fund nor may the match for PCA funds be used for the following expenses or activities: scholarly writing; publications printing primarily student work; student-run publications; vanity press or self publications; literary projects for which academic credit is given; writing competitions, prizes or awards; activities that have already been completed; activities that have a religious purpose; performances and exhibitions not available to the general public; performances and exhibitions outside Pennsylvania; benefit activities; capital expenditures, including equipment costing $500 per item or more; hospitality expenses (eg., receptions, parties, and gallery openings); and lobbyists' payments. Ensembles and/or organizations from the African-American, Asian- American, Hispanic/Latino, and Native-American communities may apply for either a PCA Strategies-for-Success grant or an Entry-Track grant, but not for both. Organizations planning a one-time-only arts project should apply for PCA's Pennsylvania Partners in the Arts grants.
Geographic Focus: Pennsylvania
Date(s) Application is Due: Jan 13
Contact: Jamie Dunlap; (717) 787-6883 or (717) 525-5542; jadunlap@pa.gov
Sponsor: Pennsylvania Council on the Arts
216 Finance Building
Harrisburg, PA 17120

PCA Entry Track Arts Organizations and Arts Programs Grants for Local Arts 3794

The Pennsylvania Council on the Arts (PCA) is a state agency in the Office of the Governor. The mission of PCA is to foster the excellence, diversity, and vitality of the arts in Pennsylvania and to broaden the availability and appreciation of those arts throughout the state. Funding for the Council on the Arts comes from the citizens of Pennsylvania (through an annual state appropriation by the General Assembly) and from the National Endowment for the Arts. PCA offers various funding tracks for organizations that offer arts programming. The Entry Track for Arts Organizations and Arts Programs is the point of entry for organizations wishing to eventually receive on-going support from PCA's multi-year/renewable Arts Organizations and Arts Programs Grants. Entry-Track grants support eligible organizations that generally have a history of at least one-year consistent arts/cultural programming. Entry-Track grants fall into three categories: Community Arts, Performance and Presenting, and Visual Arts and Electronic Media. The Community Arts category includes arts-education, arts-service, folk and traditional arts, local multi-discipline arts center, arts-council, and arts-festival programs. The Performance and Presenting category includes dance, literature, music, presenting-organization, and theatre programs. The Visual Arts and Electronic Media category includes art-museum, crafts, film and electronic media, interdisciplinary-arts, and visual-arts programs. In the Community Arts/local, multi-discipline arts-center category, the PCA supports organizations and programs that provide a wide range of arts activities and significant public participation in the arts in a specified community or region. These agencies support, coordinate, and provide a broad range of arts programs and administrative services based on the needs and resources of the designated community. The application for an Entry-Track grant for local arts must be completed using various online systems (available from the grant website), then printed, assembled, and mailed by the postmark date. The PCA encourages applicants to upload any required work samples and attachments through their online system. DVDs must be mailed. The application process is explained in the complete guide (PDF document) which may be accessed from the download section of the website. Application deadlines may vary from year to year. Applicants should visit the calendar section of the website to verify current deadline dates.

Requirements: Applicants for this category must be a multi-discipline arts center, multi-discipline arts council, multi-discipline arts festival, and/or a multi-discipline arts program in a social service center or other nonprofit organization or a government agency. All applicants must contact PCA's Entry Track Coordinator prior to applying for the first time to discuss eligibility. Generally, organizations are eligible to apply to the Entry Track if they meet the folowing criteria: their average operating budget is over $200,000; they have at least one year of ongoing stable arts programming; and they are a nonprofit, tax-exempt corporation, unit of government, or school district providing arts programming and/or arts services in Pennsylvania. Organizations are required to provide proof of incorporation and activity in Pennsylvania before applications are reviewed or funds awarded. Non-arts organizations must clearly define an ongoing arts program that has been in existence for at least one year and submit with their application a board resolution demonstrating clear commitment to the applicant's art program. Unincorporated groups (and in some instances, individuals) may apply to the PCA through a nonprofit organization that acts as a fiscal sponsor. Applicants applying through a fiscal sponsor organization must meet the same requirements as other applicants except for nonprofit status. Unless otherwise specified in the guidelines, PCA awards must be matched on a dollar-for-dollar basis in cash. In-kind goods and services may not be used to match PCA funds. The PCA generally will support no more than 25% of an organizational budget, and usually considerably less. Interested organizations who may not meet the eligibility requirements of the Entry Track may be eligible to apply for grants from PCA's Pennsylvania Partners in the Arts (PPA), a decentralized funding program which offers both ongoing support and arts projects funding opportunities.

Restrictions: Entry-Track grants for local arts do not fund single-discipline arts organizations or programs. Ensembles and/or organizations from the African-American, Asian- American, Hispanic/Latino, and Native-American communities may apply for either a PCA Strategies-for-Success grant or an Entry-Track grant, but not for both. Organizations planning a one-time-only arts project should apply for PCA's Pennsylvania Partners in the Arts Projects grants. In general, the PCA does not fund the following nor can the match for PCA funds be used for the following expenses or activities: capital expenditures, including equipment costing $500 per item or more; activities for which academic credit is given; activities that have already been completed; activities that have a religious purpose; performances and exhibitions not available to the general public; performances and exhibitions outside Pennsylvania; cash prizes and awards; benefit activities; hospitality expenses, i.e. receptions, parties, gallery openings; lobbyists' payments; and competitions.

Geographic Focus: Pennsylvania

Date(s) Application is Due: Jan 13

Contact: Jamie Dunlap, Entry Track Program Director, Accessibility Programs Director; (717) 787-6883 or (717) 525-5542; fax (717) 783-2538; jadunlap@pa.gov

Internet: http://www.pacouncilonthearts.org/pca.cfm?id=2&level=Third

Sponsor: Pennsylvania Council on the Arts
216 Finance Building
Harrisburg, PA 17120

PCA Entry Track Arts Organizations and Arts Programs Grants for Music 3795

The Pennsylvania Council on the Arts (PCA) is a state agency in the Office of the Governor. The mission of PCA is to foster the excellence, diversity, and vitality of the arts in Pennsylvania and to broaden the availability and appreciation of those arts throughout the state. Funding for the Council on the Arts comes from the citizens of Pennsylvania (through an annual state appropriation by the General Assembly) and from the National Endowment for the Arts. PCA offers various funding tracks for organizations that offer arts programming. The Entry Track for Arts Organizations and Arts Programs is the point of entry for organizations wishing to eventually receive on-going support from PCA's multi-year/renewable Arts Organizations and Arts Programs Grants. Entry-Track grants support eligible organizations that generally have a history of at least one-year consistent arts/cultural programming. Entry-Track grants fall into three categories: Community Arts, Performance and Presenting, and Visual Arts and Electronic Media. The Community Arts category includes arts-education, arts-service, folk and traditional arts, local multi-discipline arts center, arts-council, and arts-festival programs. The Performance and Presenting category includes dance, literature, music, presenting-organization, and theatre programs. The Visual Arts and Electronic Media category includes art-museum, crafts, film and electronic media, interdisciplinary-arts, and visual-arts programs. Within the Performance and Presenting/music category, the PCA supports music organizations and programs whose primary purpose includes public performances. The application for an Entry-Track grant for music must be completed using various online systems (available from the grant website), then printed, assembled, and mailed by the postmark date. The PCA encourages applicants to upload any required work samples and attachments through their online system. DVDs must be mailed. The application process is explained in the complete guide (PDF document) which may be accessed from the download section of the website. Application deadlines may vary from year to year. Applicants should visit the calendar section of the website to verify current deadline dates.

Requirements: All applicants must contact PCA's Entry Track Coordinator prior to applying for the first time to discuss eligibility. Generally, organizations are eligible to apply to the Entry Track if they meet the folowing criteria: their average operating budget is over $200,000; they have at least one year of ongoing stable arts programming; and they are a nonprofit, tax-exempt corporation, unit of government, or school district providing arts programming and/or arts services in Pennsylvania. Organizations are required to provide proof of incorporation and activity in Pennsylvania before applications are reviewed or funds awarded. Non-arts organizations must clearly define an ongoing arts program that has been in existence for at least one year and submit with their application a board resolution demonstrating clear commitment to the applicant's art program. Unincorporated groups (and in some instances, individuals) may apply to the PCA through a nonprofit organization that acts as a fiscal sponsor. Applicants applying through a fiscal sponsor organization must meet the same requirements as other applicants except for nonprofit status. Unless otherwise specified in the guidelines, PCA awards must be matched on a dollar-for-dollar basis in cash. In-kind goods and services may not be used to match PCA funds. The PCA generally will support no more than 25% of an organizational budget, and usually considerably less. Interested organizations who may not meet the eligibility requirements of the Entry Track may be eligible to apply for grants from PCA's Pennsylvania Partners in the Arts (PPA), a decentralized funding program which offers both ongoing support and arts projects funding opportunities.

Restrictions: Ensembles and/or organizations from the African-American, Asian-American, Hispanic/Latino, and Native-American communities may apply for either a PCA Strategies-for-Success grant or an Entry-Track grant, but not for both. Organizations planning a one-time-only arts project should apply for PCA's Pennsylvania Partners in the Arts grants. In general, the PCA does not fund nor can the match for PCA funds be used for the following expenses and activities: capital expenditures, including equipment costing $500 per item or more; activities for which academic credit is given; activities that have already been completed; activities that have a religious purpose; performances and exhibitions not available to the general public; performances and exhibitions outside Pennsylvania; cash prizes and awards; benefit activities; hospitality expenses, i.e. receptions, parties, gallery openings; lobbyists' payments; and competitions.

Geographic Focus: Pennsylvania

Date(s) Application is Due: Jan 13

Contact: Jamie Dunlap, Entry-Track Program Director, Accessibility Programs Director; (717) 787-6883 or (717) 525-5542; fax (717) 783-2538; jadunlap@pa.gov

Internet: http://www.pacouncilonthearts.org/pca.cfm?id=2&level=Third

Sponsor: Pennsylvania Council on the Arts
216 Finance Building
Harrisburg, PA 17120

PCA Entry Track Arts Organizations and Arts Programs Grants for Presenting Organizations 3796

The Pennsylvania Council on the Arts (PCA) is a state agency in the Office of the Governor. The mission of PCA is to foster the excellence, diversity, and vitality of the arts in Pennsylvania and to broaden the availability and appreciation of those arts throughout the state. Funding for the Council on the Arts comes from the citizens of Pennsylvania (through an annual state appropriation by the General Assembly) and from the National Endowment for the Arts. PCA offers various funding tracks for organizations that offer arts programming. The Entry Track for Arts Organizations and Arts Programs is the point of entry for organizations wishing to eventually receive on-going support from PCA's multi-year/renewable Arts Organizations and Arts Programs Grants. Entry-Track grants support eligible organizations that generally have a history of at least one-year consistent arts/cultural programming. Entry-Track grants fall into three categories: Community Arts, Performance and Presenting, and Visual Arts and Electronic Media. The Community Arts category includes arts-education, arts-service, folk and traditional arts, local multi-discipline arts center, arts-council, and arts-festival programs. The Performance and Presenting category includes dance, literature, music, presenting-organization, and theatre programs. The Visual Arts and Electronic Media category includes art-museum, crafts, film and electronic media, interdisciplinary-arts, and visual-arts programs. Within the Performance and Presenting/presenting-organizations category, the PCA supports organizations that present professional performing artists. These presentations may occur in a variety of settings. A performing arts presenter organization engages professional touring artists, pays their fees, handles the local presentation, promotion and ticket sales, and arranges for the facilities and technical support for the event(s). Presenters work with artists, managers, educators, and community groups to bring artists into a community in concerts and less formal arrangements. The presenting field includes cultural centers, theatres, galleries and museums, arts centers, libraries, college and university artist series, festivals, concert, music, dance or theatre associations, and civic or cultural organizations and programs that promote cooperative programming and activity between Pennsylvania presenting organizations. The application for an Entry-Track grant for presenting organizations must be completed using various online systems (available from the grant website), then printed, assembled, and mailed by the postmark date. The PCA encourages applicants to upload any required work samples and attachments through their online system. DVDs must be mailed. Applicants are strongly encouraged to visit the grant website for complete information, guidelines, and deadlines and to contact the PCA for technical support, if needed.

Requirements: Entry-Track grants in the presenting organizations sub-category support organizations that present professional performing artists. Organizations and programs that exclusively present local artists should apply for Entry-Track grants in the local arts sub-category. Pennsylvania artists or ensembles who self-produce their home seasons or local performances should apply in one of the Entry-Track arts genre sub-categories (Dance, Music, Theatre, etc.). All applicants must contact PCA's Entry Track Coordinator prior to applying for the first time to discuss eligibility. Generally, organizations are eligible to apply to the Entry Track if they meet the folowing criteria: their average operating budget is over $200,000; they have at least one year of ongoing stable arts programming; and they are a nonprofit, tax-exempt corporation, unit of government, or school district providing arts programming and/or arts services in Pennsylvania. Organizations are required to provide proof of incorporation and activity in Pennsylvania before applications are reviewed or funds awarded. Non-arts organizations must clearly define an ongoing arts program that has been in existence for at least one year and submit with their application a board resolution demonstrating clear commitment to the applicant's art program. Unincorporated groups (and in some instances, individuals) may apply to the PCA through a nonprofit organization that acts as a fiscal sponsor. Applicants applying through a fiscal sponsor organization must meet the same requirements as other applicants except for nonprofit status. Unless otherwise specified in the guidelines, PCA awards must be matched on a dollar-for-dollar basis in cash. In-kind goods and services may not be used to match PCA funds. The PCA generally will support no more than 25% of an organizational budget, and usually considerably less. Interested organizations who may not meet the eligibility requirements of the Entry Track may be eligible to apply for grants from PCA's Pennsylvania Partners in the Arts (PPA), a decentralized funding program which offers both ongoing support and arts projects funding opportunities.

Restrictions: Entry-Track grants in the presenting organizations sub-category do not fund presenters who present nonprofessional, avocational, student, or school-related artists or ensembles (faculty) seasons. Ensembles and/or organizations from the African-American, Asian-American, Hispanic/Latino, and Native-American communities may apply for either a PCA Strategies-for-Success grant or an Entry-Track grant, but not for both. Organizations planning a one-time-only arts project should apply for PCA's Pennsylvania Partners in the Arts grants. In general, the PCA does not fund nor can the match for PCA funds be used for the following expenses and activities: capital expenditures, including equipment costing $500 per item or more; activities for which academic credit is given; activities that have already been completed; activities that have a religious purpose; performances and exhibitions not available to the general public; performances and exhibitions outside Pennsylvania; cash prizes and awards; benefit activities; hospitality expenses, i.e. receptions, parties, gallery openings; lobbyists' payments; and competitions.

Geographic Focus: Pennsylvania
Date(s) Application is Due: Jan 13
Contact: Jamie Dunlap, Entry Track Program Director, Accessibility Programs Director; (717) 787-6883 or (717) 525-5542; fax (717) 783-2538; jadunlap@pa.gov
Internet: PCA Entry Track Arts Organizations and Arts Programs Grants for Presenting Organizations
Sponsor: Pennsylvania Council on the Arts
216 Finance Building
Harrisburg, PA 17120

PCA Entry Track Arts Organizations and Arts Programs Grants for Theatre   3797
The Pennsylvania Council on the Arts (PCA) is a state agency in the Office of the Governor. The mission of PCA is to foster the excellence, diversity, and vitality of the arts in Pennsylvania and to broaden the availability and appreciation of those arts throughout the state. Funding for the Council on the Arts comes from the citizens of Pennsylvania (through an annual state appropriation by the General Assembly) and from the National Endowment for the Arts. PCA offers various funding tracks for organizations that offer arts programming. The Entry Track for Arts Organizations and Arts Programs is the point of entry for organizations wishing to eventually receive on-going support from PCA's multi-year/renewable Arts Organizations and Arts Programs Grants. Entry-Track grants support eligible organizations that generally have a history of at least one-year consistent arts/cultural programming. Entry-Track grants fall into three categories: Community Arts, Performance and Presenting, and Visual Arts and Electronic Media. The Community Arts category includes arts-education, arts-service, folk and traditional arts, local multi-discipline arts center, arts-council, and arts-festival programs. The Performance and Presenting category includes dance, literature, music, presenting-organization, and theatre programs. The Visual Arts and Electronic Media category includes art-museum, crafts, film and electronic media, interdisciplinary-arts, and visual-arts programs. Within the Performance and Presenting/theater category, the PCA supports production and presentation of plays, the writing and production of new plays, the exploration of new theatre forms, touring, ticket subsidy, and other programs that make theatre more available to Pennsylvania citizens of all ages. The application for an Entry-Track grant for theatre must be completed using various online systems (available from the grant website), then printed, assembled, and mailed by the postmark date. The PCA encourages applicants to upload any required work samples and attachments through their online system. DVDs must be mailed. The application process is explained in the complete guide (PDF document) which may be accessed from the download section of the website. Application deadlines may vary from year to year. Applicants should visit the calendar section of the website to verify current deadline dates.

Requirements: All applicants must contact PCA's Entry Track Coordinator prior to applying for the first time to discuss eligibility. Generally, organizations are eligible to apply to the Entry Track if they meet the folowing criteria: their average operating budget is over $200,000; they have at least one year of ongoing stable arts programming; and they are a nonprofit, tax-exempt corporation, unit of government, or school district providing arts programming and/or arts services in Pennsylvania. Organizations are required to provide proof of incorporation and activity in Pennsylvania before applications are reviewed or funds awarded. Non-arts organizations must clearly define an ongoing arts program that has been in existence for at least one year and submit with their application a board resolution demonstrating clear commitment to the applicant's art program. Unincorporated groups (and in some instances, individuals) may apply to the PCA through a nonprofit organization that acts as a fiscal sponsor. Applicants applying through a fiscal sponsor organization must meet the same requirements as other applicants except for nonprofit status. Unless otherwise specified in the guidelines, PCA awards must be matched on a dollar-for-dollar basis in cash. In-kind goods and services may not be used to match PCA funds. The PCA generally will support no more than 25% of an organizational budget, and usually considerably less. Interested organizations who may not meet the eligibility requirements of the Entry Track may be eligible to apply for grants from PCA's Pennsylvania Partners in the Arts (PPA), a decentralized funding program which offers both ongoing support and arts projects funding opportunities.

Restrictions: Ensembles and/or organizations from the African-American, Asian-American, Hispanic/Latino, and Native-American communities may apply for either a PCA Strategies-for-Success grant or an Entry-Track grant, but not for both. Organizations planning a one-time-only arts project should apply for PCA's Pennsylvania Partners in the Arts grants. In general, the PCA does not fund nor can the match for PCA funds be used for the following expenses and activities: capital expenditures, including equipment costing $500 per item or more; activities for which academic credit is given; activities that have already been completed; activities that have a religious purpose; performances and exhibitions not available to the general public; performances and exhibitions outside Pennsylvania; cash prizes and awards; benefit activities; hospitality expenses, i.e. receptions, parties, gallery openings; lobbyists' payments; and competitions.

Geographic Focus: Pennsylvania
Date(s) Application is Due: Jan 13
Contact: Jamie Dunlap, (717) 787-6883 or (717) 525-5542; jadunlap@pa.gov
Internet: http://www.pacouncilonthearts.org/pca.cfm?id=2&level=Third
Sponsor: Pennsylvania Council on the Arts
216 Finance Building
Harrisburg, PA 17120

PCA Entry Track Arts Organizations and Arts Grants for Traditional & Folk Arts   3798
The Pennsylvania Council on the Arts (PCA) is a state agency in the Office of the Governor. The mission of PCA is to foster the excellence, diversity, and vitality of the arts in Pennsylvania and to broaden the availability and appreciation of those arts throughout the state. Funding for the Council on the Arts comes from the citizens of Pennsylvania (through an annual state appropriation by the General Assembly) and from the National Endowment for the Arts. PCA offers various funding tracks for organizations that offer arts programming. The Entry Track for Arts Organizations and Arts Programs is the point of entry for organizations wishing to eventually receive on-going support from PCA's multi-year/renewable Arts Organizations and Arts Programs Grants. Entry-Track grants support eligible organizations that generally have a history of at least one-year consistent arts/cultural programming. Entry-Track grants fall into three categories: Community Arts, Performance and Presenting, and Visual Arts and Electronic Media. The Community Arts category includes arts-education, arts-service, folk and traditional arts, local multi-discipline arts center, arts-council, and arts-festival programs. The Performance and Presenting category includes dance, literature, music, presenting-organization, and theatre programs. The Visual Arts and Electronic Media category includes art-museum, crafts, film and electronic media, interdisciplinary-arts, and visual-arts programs. Within the Community-Arts/folk and traditional arts category, the PCA supports traditional arts programming, services to artists and communities practicing traditional arts and customs, and the conservation of the traditional arts and customs found in the Commonwealth. The application for an Entry-Track grant for traditional and folk arts must be completed using various online systems (available from the grant website), then printed, assembled, and mailed by the postmark date. The PCA encourages applicants to upload any required work samples and attachments through their online system. DVDs must be mailed. The application process is explained in the complete guide (PDF document) which may be accessed from the download section of the website. Application deadlines may vary from year to year. Applicants should visit the calendar section of the website to verify current deadline dates.

Requirements: All applicants must contact PCA's Entry Track Coordinator prior to applying for the first time to discuss eligibility. Generally, organizations are eligible to apply to the Entry Track if they meet the folowing criteria: their average operating budget is over $200,000; they have at least one year of ongoing stable arts programming; and they are a nonprofit, tax-exempt corporation, unit of government, or school district providing arts programming and/or arts services in Pennsylvania. Organizations are required to provide proof of incorporation and activity in Pennsylvania before applications are reviewed or funds awarded. Non-arts organizations must clearly define an ongoing arts program that has been in existence for at least one year and submit with their application a board resolution demonstrating clear commitment to the applicant's art program. Unincorporated groups (and in some instances, individuals) may apply to the PCA through a nonprofit organization that acts as a fiscal sponsor. Applicants applying through a fiscal sponsor organization must meet the same requirements as other applicants except for nonprofit status. Unless otherwise specified in the guidelines, PCA awards must be matched on a dollar-for-dollar basis in cash. In-kind goods and services may not be used to match PCA funds. The PCA generally will support no more than 25% of an organizational budget, and usually considerably less. Interested organizations who may not meet the eligibility requirements of the Entry Track may be eligible to apply for grants from PCA's Pennsylvania Partners in the Arts (PPA), a decentralized funding program which offers both ongoing support and arts projects funding opportunities.

Restrictions: Entry-Track grants do not support oral history programs that do not include contemporary traditions, or the production or marketing of historical crafts, or other

traditions that are not part of the living heritage of particular communities. Ensembles and/or organizations from the African-American, Asian- American, Hispanic/Latino, and Native-American communities may apply for either a PCA Strategies-for-Success grant or an Entry-Track grant, but not for both. Organizations planning a one-time-only arts project should apply for PCA's Pennsylvania Partners in the Arts grants. In general, the PCA does not fund nor can the match for PCA funds be used for the following expenses and activities: capital expenditures, including equipment costing $500 per item or more; activities for which academic credit is given; activities that have already been completed; activities that have a religious purpose; performances and exhibitions not available to the general public; performances and exhibitions outside Pennsylvania; cash prizes and awards; benefit activities; hospitality expenses, i.e. receptions, parties, gallery openings; lobbyists' payments; and competitions.
Geographic Focus: Pennsylvania
Date(s) Application is Due: Jan 13
Contact: Jamie Dunlap, Entry Track Program Director, Accessibility Programs Director; (717) 787-6883 or (717) 525-5542; fax (717) 783-2538; jadunlap@pa.gov
Internet: http://www.pacouncilonthearts.org/pca.cfm?id=2&level=Third
Sponsor: Pennsylvania Council on the Arts
216 Finance Building
Harrisburg, PA 17120

PCA Entry Track Arts Organizations and Arts Programs Grants for Visual Arts   3799
The Pennsylvania Council on the Arts (PCA) is a state agency in the Office of the Governor. The mission of PCA is to foster the excellence, diversity, and vitality of the arts in Pennsylvania and to broaden the availability and appreciation of those arts throughout the state. Funding for the Council on the Arts comes from the citizens of Pennsylvania (through an annual state appropriation by the General Assembly) and from the National Endowment for the Arts. PCA offers various funding tracks for organizations that offer arts programming. The Entry Track for Arts Organizations and Arts Programs is the point of entry for organizations wishing to eventually receive on-going support from PCA's multi-year/renewable Arts Organizations and Arts Programs Grants. Entry-Track grants support eligible organizations that generally have a history of at least one-year consistent arts/cultural programming. Entry-Track grants fall into three categories: Community Arts, Performance and Presenting, and Visual Arts and Electronic Media. The Community Arts category includes arts-education, arts-service, folk and traditional arts, local multi-discipline arts center, arts-council, and arts-festival programs. The Performance and Presenting category includes dance, literature, music, presenting-organization, and theatre programs. The Visual Arts and Electronic Media category includes art-museum, crafts, film and electronic media, interdisciplinary-arts, and visual-arts programs. Within the Visual Arts and Electronic Media/visual-arts category, the PCA supports contemporary visual arts organizations and ongoing programs whose primary mission is to provide high-quality exhibitions and other programs and activities such as publications and education/instruction. The PCA defines visual arts as including, but not limited to, painting, sculpture, graphic art, photography, architecture, interdisciplinary arts, electronic and digital art. The application for an Entry-Track grant for visual arts must be completed using various online systems (available from the grant website), then printed, assembled, and mailed by the postmark date. The PCA encourages applicants to upload any required work samples and attachments through their online system. DVDs must be mailed. The application process is explained in the complete guide (PDF document) which may be accessed from the download section of the website. Application deadlines may vary from year to year. Applicants should visit the calendar section of the website to verify current deadline dates.
Requirements: All applicants must contact PCA's Entry Track Coordinator prior to applying for the first time to discuss eligibility. Generally, organizations are eligible to apply to the Entry Track if they meet the folowing criteria: their average operating budget is over $200,000; they have at least one year of ongoing stable arts programming; and they are a nonprofit, tax-exempt corporation, unit of government, or school district providing arts programming and/or arts services in Pennsylvania. Organizations are required to provide proof of incorporation and activity in Pennsylvania before applications are reviewed or funds awarded. Non-arts organizations must clearly define an ongoing arts program that has been in existence for at least one year and submit with their application a board resolution demonstrating clear commitment to the applicant's art program. Unincorporated groups (and in some instances, individuals) may apply to the PCA through a nonprofit organization that acts as a fiscal sponsor. Applicants applying through a fiscal sponsor organization must meet the same requirements as other applicants except for nonprofit status. Unless otherwise specified in the guidelines, PCA awards must be matched on a dollar-for-dollar basis in cash. In-kind goods and services may not be used to match PCA funds. The PCA generally will support no more than 25% of an organizational budget, and usually considerably less. Interested organizations who may not meet the eligibility requirements of the Entry Track may be eligible to apply for grants from PCA's Pennsylvania Partners in the Arts (PPA), a decentralized funding program which offers both ongoing support and arts projects funding opportunities.
Restrictions: Ensembles and/or organizations from the African-American, Asian-American, Hispanic/Latino, and Native-American communities may apply for either a PCA Strategies-for-Success grant or an Entry-Track grant, but not for both. Organizations planning a one-time-only arts project should apply for PCA's Pennsylvania Partners in the Arts grants. In general, the PCA does not fund nor can the match for PCA funds be used for the following expenses and activities: capital expenditures, including equipment costing $500 per item or more; activities for which academic credit is given; activities that have already been completed; activities that have a religious purpose; performances and exhibitions not available to the general public; performances and exhibitions outside Pennsylvania; cash prizes and awards; benefit activities; hospitality expenses, i.e. receptions, parties, gallery openings; lobbyists' payments; and competitions.
Geographic Focus: Pennsylvania
Date(s) Application is Due: Jan 13
Contact: Bryan Holtzapple, Visual Arts Program Director; (717) 787-6883 or (717) 787-1520; fax (717) 783-2538; bholtzappl@pa.gov
Internet: http://www.pacouncilonthearts.org/pca.cfm?id=2&level=Third
Sponsor: Pennsylvania Council on the Arts
216 Finance Building
Harrisburg, PA 17120

PCA Management/Technical Assistance Grants   3800
The Pennsylvania Council on the Arts (PCA) is a state agency in the Office of the Governor. The mission of PCA is to foster the excellence, diversity, and vitality of the arts in Pennsylvania and to broaden the availability and appreciation of those arts throughout the state. Funding for the Council on the Arts comes from the citizens of Pennsylvania (through an annual state appropriation by the General Assembly) and from the National Endowment for the Arts. The PCA's Management/Technical Assistance Grants are available to organizations to address specific artistic, programmatic, administrative, or technical needs throughout the year. Up to $2,000 in funding may be requested to engage consultants to address specific issues and recommend action in the following areas: cultural, financial, or strategic planning; creating and improving the artistic quality of the documentation for an organization (i.e. slides, tapes, etc.); mission, board, staff, or program development; audience development or marketing; fundraising; and evaluating and planning to make facilities, programs, and staff accessible to individuals with disabilities. Requests of $2,000 or less may be submitted at any time, but must be postmarked at least 30 days prior to the beginning of the project for which funding is requested. Applications are available from the downloads section of the website.
Requirements: Most awards are non-matching. Organizations are encouraged to contact the Program Director or Program Assistant to clarify any eligibility questions.
Restrictions: Generally, the PCA will only fund to a maximum of $4,000 per year.
Geographic Focus: Pennsylvania
Amount of Grant: Up to 2,000 USD
Contact: Charon Battles, Preserving Diverse Cultures Program Director; (717) 787-6883 or (717) 787-1521; fax (717) 783-2538; cbattles@pa.gov
Internet: http://pacouncilonthearts.org/pca.cfm?id=48&level=Third&sid=48
Sponsor: Pennsylvania Council on the Arts
216 Finance Building
Harrisburg, PA 17120

PCA Pennsylvania Partners in the Arts Program Stream Grants   3801
Pennsylvania Partners in the Arts (PPA) is a partnership between local organizations and the Pennsylvania Council on the Arts (PCA) that has the aim of making arts programs available to communities that may have been underserved by state arts funding. Administered by thirteen regional partners across the state, the PPA re-grants funds to support a wide variety of local and community arts activities in every county in Pennsylvania. The PPA offers two streams of funding opportunities, the Project Stream and the Program Stream. The Project Stream provides grants of up to $3,000 to eligible organizations or individuals to conduct arts projects. The Program Stream provides ongoing support to eligible organizations with an established history of PCA support. Applications for PPA Program Stream grants must be completed using various online systems (available from the grant website), then printed, assembled, and mailed along with any required attachments/work samples by the postmark date to the applicant's regional PPA Partner (contact information is available at the grant website in the form of a regional map). The application process is explained in the complete guide (PDF document) which may be accessed from the download section of the website. Application deadlines may vary from year to year. Applicants should visit the calendar section of the website to verify current deadline dates.
Requirements: Organizations must have been notified by the PCA or a PPA Partner that they have met the eligibility requirements and have been invited to apply to the PPA Program Stream. In general, the PCA supports the following types of organizations: nonprofit, 501(c)3, tax-exempt corporations; units of government; or school districts providing arts programming and/or arts services in Pennsylvania. Organizations are required to provide proof of incorporation and activity in Pennsylvania before applications are reviewed or funds awarded. Unincorporated groups (and in some instances, individuals) may apply to the PCA through a nonprofit organization that acts as a fiscal sponsor, but they must satisfy all requirements except for nonprofit status. The PCA may also accept applications from national service organizations based outside of Pennsylvania that have a strong presence in Pennsylvania. Unless otherwise specified in the guidelines, PCA awards must be matched on a dollar-for-dollar basis in cash. The PCA generally will support no more than 25% of an organizational budget, and usually considerably less. Organizations or individuals who do not meet the eligibility criteria for Entry Track or PPA Program Stream, may be eligible for PPA Project Stream funding.
Restrictions: Applicants are permitted to submit one application per year to Program Stream. Applicants for PPA Program Stream funding may not also apply for PPA Project funding or the PCA's Arts Organizations and Arts Programs (AOAP) Track, or Entry Track for the same time period. In general, the PCA does not fund the following nor can the match for PCA funds be used for these expenses: capital expenditures, including equipment costing $500 per item or more; activities for which academic credit is given; activities that have already been completed; activities that have a religious purpose; performances and exhibitions not available to the general public; performances and exhibitions outside Pennsylvania; cash prizes and awards; benefit activities; hospitality expenses, i.e. receptions, parties, gallery openings; lobbyists' payments; and competitions. In-kind goods and services may not be used to match PCA funds. PPA Program Stream funds cannot be used to match other PCA grants.
Geographic Focus: Pennsylvania
Date(s) Application is Due: Mar 5
Contact: Lori Frush Schmelz, Pennsylvania Partners in the Arts Program Director; (717) 787-6883 or (717) 787-1523; fax (717) 783-2538; lschmelz@pa.gov
Internet: http://pacouncilonthearts.org/pca.cfm?id=36&level=Third&sid=48
Sponsor: Pennsylvania Council on the Arts
216 Finance Building
Harrisburg, PA 17120

PCA Pennsylvania Partners in the Arts Project Stream Grants 3802

Pennsylvania Partners in the Arts (PPA) is a partnership between local organizations and the Pennsylvania Council on the Arts (PCA) that has the aim of making arts programs available to communities that may have been underserved by state arts funding. Administered by thirteen regional partners across the state, the PPA re-grants funds to support a wide variety of local and community arts activities in every county in Pennsylvania. The PPA offers two streams of funding opportunities, the Program Stream and the Project Stream. The Program Stream offers ongoing support to arts organizations and arts programs with an established history of PPA support while the Project Stream provides grants of up to $3,000 to eligible organizations or individuals to conduct one-time arts projects. Preference is weighted (75% of available funding vs. 25% of available funding) to art projects not conducted with or in venues already supported by the PCA. A list of arts organizations and programs the PCA already supports is available at the grant website or from the PPA Partner Organizations. Applications for PPA Project Stream grants must be completed using various online systems (available from the grant website), then printed, assembled, and mailed along with any required attachments/work samples by the postmark date to the applicant's regional PPA Partner (contact information is available at the grant website in the form of a regional map). The application process is explained in the complete guide (PDF document) which may be accessed from the download section of the website. Application deadlines may vary from year to year. Applicants should visit the calendar section of the website to verify current deadline dates.

Requirements: In general, the PCA supports the following types of organizations: 501(c)3 corporations; units of government; or school districts providing arts programming and/or arts services in Pennsylvania. Organizations are required to provide proof of incorporation and activity in Pennsylvania before applications are reviewed or funds awarded. Unincorporated groups and individuals may apply to the PCA through a nonprofit organization that acts as a fiscal sponsor, but they must satisfy all requirements except for nonprofit status. Organizations or individuals who do not meet the eligibility criteria for PCA Entry Track or PPA Program Stream may be eligible for PPA Project Stream funding. (Alternatively, organizations who have received Project Stream funding for multiple years may qualify to transition to the PPA Program Stream if they have consistent arts programming and good assessments from the Project Stream review panels.) Proposed projects for Project Stream must be arts activities conducted for the benefit of the public (for-profit organizations are ineligible) and take place in the applicant's PPA service region. First- and second-time PPA Project Stream recipients are not required to match the requested amount; however third-time recipients must show a 1:1 cash match of funds requested for their third and any subsequent projects.

Restrictions: Applicants may submit one Project Stream application per PPA service region per grant period. PPA Project Stream applicants may not apply to the following grant programs for the same period: PPA Program Stream, PCA Arts Organizations Arts Programs (AOAP) track; or PCA Entry Track. PPA Project Stream applicants may apply to the following PCA grant programs during the same period: Arts in Education Residencies; Preserving Diverse Cultures; and Professional Development and Consulting. Applicants, if individuals, must be at least eighteen years old. In general, the PCA does not fund nor can the match for PCA funds be used for the following expenses: capital expenditures, including equipment costing $500 per item or more; activities for which academic credit is given; activities that have already been completed; activities that have a religious purpose; performances and exhibitions not available to the general public; performances and exhibitions outside Pennsylvania; cash prizes and awards; benefit activities; hospitality expenses, i.e. receptions, parties, gallery openings; lobbyists' payments; and competitions. In-kind goods and services may not be used to match PCA funds. PCA funds may not be used as match for other PCA funds.

Geographic Focus: Pennsylvania
Date(s) Application is Due: Jun 15
Amount of Grant: Up to 3,000 USD
Contact: Lori Frush Schmelz, Pennsylvania Partners in the Arts Program Director; (717) 787-6883 or (717) 787-1523; fax (717) 783-2538; lschmelz@pa.gov
Internet: http://pacouncilonthearts.org/pca.cfm?id=42&level=Third&sid=48
Sponsor: Pennsylvania Council on the Arts
216 Finance Building
Harrisburg, PA 17120

PCA Professional Development Grants 3803

The Pennsylvania Council on the Arts (PCA) is a state agency in the Office of the Governor. The mission of PCA is to foster the excellence, diversity, and vitality of the arts in Pennsylvania and to broaden the availability and appreciation of those arts throughout the state. Funding for the Council on the Arts comes from the citizens of Pennsylvania (through an annual state appropriation by the General Assembly) and from the National Endowment for the Arts. The PCA's Professional Growth Opportunities Grants are available to individual artists for peer to peer consultations and for registration and travel fees for arts conferences, seminars and workshops. More than one person may be included on the application. Requests may be submitted at any time, but must be postmarked at least 30 days prior to the beginning of the project for which funding is requested. Applications are available from the downloads section of the website.

Requirements: Individuals are encouraged to contact the PCA with any questions.
Geographic Focus: Pennsylvania
Amount of Grant: Up to 500 USD
Contact: Charon Battles, Preserving Diverse Cultures Program Director; (717) 787-6883 or (717) 787-1521; fax (717) 783-2538; cbattles@pa.gov
Internet: http://pacouncilonthearts.org/pca.cfm?id=48&level=Third&sid=48
Sponsor: Pennsylvania Council on the Arts
216 Finance Building
Harrisburg, PA 17120

PCA Strategies for Success Grants - Advanced Level 3804

The Pennsylvania Council on the Arts (PCA) is a state agency whose mission is to foster the arts in Pennsylvania and broaden the availability and appreciation of those arts throughout the state. Through its Strategies for Success grants, PCA's Preserving Cultural Diversity Division supports development of organizations from the African-American, Asian-American, Hispanic/Latino, and Native-American communities. PCA offers its Strategies for Success grants at three different levels: Basic, Intermediate, and Advanced. Funding at each level depends on an annual evaluation. The Advanced Level focuses on arts organizations that have consistent arts and cultural programming and are viewed as institutions within their communities. This level recognizes an organization's preparedness for institutional status. Such organizations must document a track record of quality presentations and commitment to and from their community. The PCA awards up to $20,000 to support the following types of projects: fundraising, long-range planning, program development, facility development, board development, and expansion. Recipients must present a budget that shows $40,000 ($20,000 PCA and $20,000 match) of activity for a combination of staffing and/or program activity. Prospective applicants may download a detailed guide (PDF document) and grant application (Microsoft Excel) from the downloads section of the grant website. Application deadlines may vary from year to year. Applicants are encouraged to view the calendar at the grant website to verify current deadline dates.

Requirements: To be eligible to apply at the advanced level, organizations must have been in operation for a minimum of ten consecutive years and have all the following: an average fiscal budget of approximately $125,000; a Federal I.D. Number and 501(c)3 status; a formal, structured board of directors; a salaried staff with at least two full-time staff members; a demonstrated use of volunteers; a formal bookkeeping system; a yearly audit; regular office hours and an accessible place of business; an established long-range plan (for at least three years); a demonstrated marketing program; evidence of structured annual fund-raising activities; and an established community support and awareness program.

Restrictions: Eligibility for Strategies for Success Grants is restricted to organizations and artists from the African-American, Asian-American, Latino/Hispanic and Native-American communities. Generally, the combined length of an organization's participation in the Strategies for Success program at the Basic and Intermediate Levels may not exceed 6 years with no more than three years spent at the same level. Generally, the maximum length of an organizations' participation in the Advanced level is 2 years. However, graduates of the Program or organizations experiencing difficulty in advancing to the next level may request an extension.

Geographic Focus: Pennsylvania
Date(s) Application is Due: Mar 3
Contact: Charon Battles, Preserving Diverse Cultures Program Director; (717) 787-6883 or (717) 787-1521; fax (717) 783-2538; cbattles@pa.gov
Internet: http://pacouncilonthearts.org/pca.cfm?id=47&level=Third&sid=48
Sponsor: Pennsylvania Council on the Arts
216 Finance Building
Harrisburg, PA 17120

PCA Strategies for Success Grants - Basic Level 3805

The Pennsylvania Council on the Arts (PCA) is a state agency whose mission is to foster the arts in Pennsylvania and broaden the availability and appreciation of those arts throughout the state. Through its Strategies for Success grants, PCA's Preserving Cultural Diversity Division supports development of organizations from the African-American, Asian-American, Hispanic/Latino, and Native-American communities. PCA offers its Strategies for Success grants at three different levels: Basic, Intermediate, and Advanced. Funding at each level depends on an annual evaluation. Basic-Level grants support organizations seeking assistance in the development of a formal board structure, more consistent arts programming, and establishment of 501(c)3 status. The PCA awards up to $2,500 in non-matching funds for consultants (as assigned by agreement/consent of the PCA), and up to $2,500 in non-matching funds for programs for a maximum total of $5,000. Eligible expenses include: staff development materials (fiscal management systems, publications, and workshops); conference costs (fees, lodging, and transportation not to exceed $500); artists' fees; equipment/facility rental (not to exceed $500); printing; and other needs as determined by the assigned consultants. Prospective applicants may download a detailed guide (PDF document) and grant application (Microsoft Excel) from the downloads section of the grant website. Application deadlines may vary from year to year. Applicants are encouraged to view the calendar at the grant website to verify current deadline dates.

Requirements: Applicants must have at least a two-year history of arts/cultural programming; be an unincorporated ensemble or arts program or organization interested in organization/program development; and have a 2-3 year average arts/cultural fiscal budget of less than $24,000. Basic-Level applicants may also submit an application for a Pennsylvania Partners in the Arts grant or to the Arts Organizations Arts Programs track (provided the applicant meets eligibility requirements for those programs). First-time applicants are encouraged to contact the Preserving Diverse Cultures Division Director prior to completing an application.

Restrictions: Eligibility for Strategies for Success Grants is restricted to organizations and artists from the African American, Asian American, Latino/Hispanic and Native American communities. Generally, the combined length of an organization's participation in the Strategies for Success program at the Basic and Intermediate Levels may not exceed 6 years with no more than three years spent at the same level. Generally, the maximum length of an organizations' participation in the Advanced level is 2 years. However, graduates of the Program or organizations experiencing difficulty in advancing to the next level may request an extension.

Geographic Focus: Pennsylvania
Date(s) Application is Due: Mar 5
Contact: Charon Battles; (717) 787-6883 or (717) 787-1521; cbattles@pa.gov
Internet: http://pacouncilonthearts.org/pca.cfm?id=47&level=Third&sid=48
Sponsor: Pennsylvania Council on the Arts
216 Finance Building
Harrisburg, PA 17120

PCA Strategies for Success Grants - Intermediate Level 3806
The Pennsylvania Council on the Arts (PCA) is a state agency whose mission is to foster the arts in Pennsylvania and broaden the availability and appreciation of those arts throughout the state. Through its Strategies for Success grants, PCA's Preserving Cultural Diversity Division supports development of organizations from the African-American, Asian-American, Hispanic/Latino, and Native-American communities. PCA offers its Strategies for Success grants at three different levels: Basic, Intermediate, and Advanced. Funding at each level depends on an annual evaluation. The Intermediate level is designed for arts organizations or programs within social service, community, and non-arts organizations interested in developing professionally-staffed arts programs (with active boards of directors and professional staff). The primary focus of the Intermediate level is capacity building and assisting in administrative and programmatic stabilization. To that end PCA awards up to $2,500 in non-matching funds for consultants (as assigned by agreement/consent of the PCA), up to $2,500 in non-matching funds for program assistance; and up to $5,000 in matching funds for the implementation or augmentation of one administrative staff position or long-term contracted service. The intent of the funded staff position is to assist the organization in developing professional staff who are committed to the growth of the organization. Allowable programmatic expenses include printing, staff training, conference expenses (fees, lodging, and transportation not to exceed $500), and artists' fees. Prospective applicants may download a detailed guide (PDF document) and grant application (Microsoft Excel) from the downloads section of the grant website. Application deadlines may vary from year to year. Applicants are encouraged to view the calendar at the grant website to verify current deadline dates.
Requirements: To be eligible for Intermediate Level Strategies for Success grants, organizations must meet the following criteria: have an average fiscal budget of $24,000 to $100,000; have a Federal I.D. Number and pending 501(c)3 status; have a formal board of directors with committee structure and regular meetings; use a formal bookkeeping system; keep regular office hours and an accessible place of business; show evidence of fund-raising; demonstrate consistent community and audience support; provide annual programming that is artistically significant and that effectively presents cultural activities; have been in operation for three consecutive years; and have at least one staff position (20 hours per week or more).
Restrictions: Eligibility for Strategies for Success Grants is restricted to organizations and artists from the African American, Asian American, Latino/Hispanic and Native American communities. Generally, the combined length of an organization's participation in the Strategies for Success program at the Basic and Intermediate Levels may not exceed 6 years with no more than three years spent at the same level. Generally, the maximum length of an organizations' participation in the Advanced level is 2 years. However, graduates of the Program or organizations experiencing difficulty in advancing to the next level may request an extension.
Geographic Focus: Pennsylvania
Date(s) Application is Due: Mar 5
Amount of Grant: Up to 10,000 USD
Contact: Charon Battles, Preserving Diverse Cultures Program Director; (717) 787-6883 or (717) 787-1521; fax (717) 783-2538; cbattles@pa.gov
Internet: http://pacouncilonthearts.org/pca.cfm?id=47&level=Third&sid=48
Sponsor: Pennsylvania Council on the Arts
216 Finance Building
Harrisburg, PA 17120

PDF Community Organizing Grants 3807
Peace Development Fund awards Community Organizing Grants to any organization in the United States, Haiti and/or Mexico that fit into PDF's guidelines. Specifically, this award sponsors organizations that focus on social justice, organizing to shift powers, working to build a movement, dismantling oppression, and creating new structures in these geographical areas.
Requirements: Applications are available at PDF's website and must be emailed to grants@peacefund.org by 5:00 pm Pacific Standard Time on the due date. This grant is highly competitive and the Fund will only award grants to organizations that align with PDF's guidelines.
Restrictions: PDF will not fund programs outside the U.S., Mexico or Haiti unless specified for a special initiative or Donor Advised fund. Also, PDF will not fund: individuals and/or organizations with strong leadership from only one person; conferences and other one-time events; audio-visual productions and distribution, including TV, radio, publications, films, etc; research that is NOT directly linked to an organizing strategy; academic institutions or scholarships; other grant-making organizations; or organizations with large budgets ($300,000 or more) or who have access to other sources of funding.
Geographic Focus: All States, Puerto Rico, Haiti, Mexico, Virgin Islands (U.S.)
Date(s) Application is Due: May 20
Amount of Grant: 2,000 - 5,000 USD
Contact: Kazu Haga, Program Coordinator; (415) 642-0900 or (415) 205-6776; fax (415) 642-8200; kazu@peacefund.org or grants@peacefund.org
Internet: http://www.peacedevelopmentfund.org/page/commorg
Sponsor: Peace Development Fund
44 N Prospect Street, P.O. Box 1280
Amherst, MA 01004

PDF Fiscal Sponsorship Grant 3808
The Peace Development Fund's Fiscal Sponsorship grant seeks to support programs that are dedicated to equality and social justice. Specifically, this award supports organizations that focus on social justice, organizing to shift powers, working to build a movement, dismantling oppression, and creating new structures in these geographical areas.
Requirements: Applications must be downloaded at PDF's website. Applications will only be accepted in English, and must be submitted at fiscal@peacefund.org to be considered for funding. In addition, projects must involve public education and/or other charitable 501(c)3 organizations.
Restrictions: PDF does not fund: programs whose primary geographic focus is outside of the United States, U.S. Territories, Latin America and the Caribbean Basin; individuals and/or organizations with strong leadership from only one person; conferences and other one-time events; audio-visual productions and distribution, including TV, radio, publications, films, etc; research that is NOT directly linked to an organizing strategy; academic institutions or scholarships; other grant-making organizations; and projects with a primary focus on "conflict resolution."
Geographic Focus: All States, Puerto Rico, U.S. Virgin Islands, Caribbean, Haiti, Mexico
Contact: Jaime Arsenault; (413) 256-8306 ext. 112; fiscal@peacefund.org
Internet: http://www.peacedevelopmentfund.org/page/fiscalsponsorship
Sponsor: Peace Development FUnd
44 N Prospect Street, P.O. Box 1280
Amhert, MA 01004

Peacock Foundation Grants 3809
Established by Henry B. Peacock, Jr. in 1947, the mission of Peacock Foundation, Inc. is to enhance and promote the good health and well being of children, families, and underprivileged persons in Southeast Florida, through contributions, gifts, and grants to eligible nonprofit organizations. The priorities of Peacock Foundation, Inc. include: making grants to human services providers that promote youth development, assist abused or neglected children, women, and the elderly, and seek to reduce abuse, prevent homelessness, and end hunger in our community; supporting educational programs in the arts and the environment, as well as special education for disabled persons; contributing to medical research, health care organizations, and hospitals.
Requirements: All applicants must be IRS recognized 501(c)3 public charities classified as not a private foundation, registered with the Department of Agriculture to solicit funds in Florida, when applicable, and located in and/or of significant benefit to residents to the Southeast Florida counties of Miami-Dade, Broward, or Monroe. In order for a proposal to be considered for funding, the applicant first must send a brief letter of inquiry. See Foundations website for letter of inquiry guidelines: http://www.peacockfoundationinc.org/review_progress.html.
Restrictions: Peacock Foundation, Inc. does not fund: capital campaigns, construction, or renovation projects; deficit financing or debt reduction; conferences or festivals; fundraising events or advertising; special events or athletic events; individuals; lobbying to influence legislation; religious organizations, unless engaged in a significant project benefiting the entire community.
Geographic Focus: Florida
Contact: Joelle Allen, Executive Director; (305) 373-1386
Internet: http://www.peacockfoundationinc.org/eligibility.html
Sponsor: Peacock Foundation
100 SE Second Street, Suite 2370
Miami, FL 33131

Pegasus Foundation Grants 3810
The Pegasus Foundation improves animal welfare through effective grantmaking and education in the United States, the Caribbean, Native American lands and Kenya. The program awards challenge grants for companion animal spay-neuter surgeries and related services. Proposals are sought that identify collaborations with dollar-for-dollar matches in cash or in-kind contributions. Pegasus would prefer to issue one or two larger grants to a single grantee, who would then coordinate and support initiatives for multiple islands. The recipient of a larger grant would work collaboratively with other organizations that could receive sub-grants from the primary grantee. However, the foundation is open to reviewing proposals for smaller grants from individual grantees providing services, as long as these proposals include collaborations with dollar-for-dollar matches in cash or in-kind contributions.
Geographic Focus: All States
Amount of Grant: Up to 50,000 USD
Contact: Anne Ostberg, Senior Program Officer; (603) 225-3918; fax (603) 225-4624; aostberg@pegasusfoundation.org or info@pegasusfoundation.org
Internet: http://www.pegasusfoundation.org/index.html
Sponsor: Pegasus Foundation
27 Merrimack Street
Concord, NH 03301

PennPAT Artist Technical Assistance Grants 3811
Created as a unique public/private partnership and administered by the Mid Atlantic Arts Foundation, Pennsylvania Performing Arts on Tour (PennPAT) increases opportunities for professional Pennsylvania-based performing artists to obtain successful touring engagements in Pennsylvania and other states. Artists may apply directly for two types of grants: Artist Technical Assistance Grants and Strategic Opportunity Grants. Artist Technical Assistance Grants support projects that advance tour readiness and improve marketing and other tour-management capabilities. Projects may include the following types of expense: hiring a consultant on a short-term basis to assist or advise on various artistic, management, and marketing-related aspects of touring; costs to attend or participate in workshops or conferences that address issues and practices of touring; development of newly designed marketing materials (video, audio, web, press pack, brochure, etc.) that raise the level of quality, communication, and professionalism in the artist's presentation to presenters; registration, travel, and showcase fees for artists adjudicated into a major showcase; travel and registration costs for an artist to exhibit at a regional booking conference for the first time; and expanding the artist's ability to tour by making the artist more affordable or more attractive to presenters. Prospective applicants must first contact the PennPAT Director to discuss the project. If the project is deemed eligible, PennPAT will email or mail the guidelines and application to the applicant. Artists may submit applications on an ongoing basis, at least six weeks prior to the start of the proposed project. Grants will generally

be awarded for up to 50% of project costs, up to a maximum of $5,000 per calendar year. Applicants may include documented in-kind contributions as part of their match.
Requirements: Applicants must be included in the PennPAT artist roster for the time in which the project will take place. Information on how to be included in the artist roster is available at the PennPAT website. In addition, the applicant must have submitted all final reports on previous projects by the report due date.
Restrictions: Technical Assistance Grants will not support the following expenses: purchase of equipment, supplies or other costs related to normal business activities; compensation for staff; travel, lodging, or fees related to a touring engagement; and projects related to artistic development. Artists may apply for and receive multiple grants in each category (Artist Technical Assistance and Strategic Opportunity), but may not receive more than $5,000 in each category during a calendar year (maximum $10,000 per year, per artist).
Geographic Focus: Pennsylvania
Amount of Grant: Up to 5,000 USD
Contact: Katie West; (215) 496-9424 ext. 4; katie@pennpat.org or info@pennpat.org
Internet: http://www.pennpat.org/Grants.aspx?id=124&ekmensel=216_submenu_284_btnlink
Sponsor: Pennsylvania Performing Arts on Tour
230 South Broad Street, Suite 1003
Philadelphia, PA 19102

PennPAT Fee-Support Grants for Presenters **3812**
Created as a unique public/private partnership and administered by the Mid Atlantic Arts Foundation, Pennsylvania Performing Arts on Tour (PennPAT) increases opportunities for professional Pennsylvania-based performing artists to obtain successful touring engagements in Pennsylvania and other states. To this end, PennPAT provides grants and marketing support to both presenters and artists, as well as training for artists. PennPat offers three types of grants to presenting organizations: Fee-Support Grants, New Directions Grants, and Presenter Travel Grants. Fee-Support Grants provide funding to presenters in support of touring engagements with artists listed on the PennPAT Artist Roster. Fee-Support Grants have two application deadlines: February 15 for projects that fall within a two year period beginning the following June; and October 15 for projects that fall within a two-year and three-month period beginning the following February. Applications must be submitted through the Mid Atlantic Arts Foundation eGrant system (link is available from the PennPAT website) by the deadline date. Applications must also be mailed to PennPAT and postmarked by the deadline date. Fee-Support Grants will fund up to 50% of the contracted artist fees, travel, and lodging. This amount is often capped at $20,000 per grant. Complete application guidelines (PDF) can be downloaded from the grant website. Applicants are also encouraged to read the FAQ section of the website.
Requirements: To be eligible for Fee-Support grants, applicants must meet PennPat's definition of a presenting organization; be a 501(c)3 organization or a unit of government; and be located in Delaware, the District of Columbia, Maryland, New Jersey, New York, Ohio, Pennsylvania, the U.S. Virgin Islands, Virginia, or West Virginia. Eligible projects must include a tentative contract for an engagement with a PennPAT roster artist (who lives or is based outside the community where the presentation will take place); and include at least one public performance at a venue within the eligible states/jurisdictions listed above. Complementary activities (e.g. master classes, workshops, lecture/demonstrations, school performances) are also strongly encouraged and should be included in the artist's contract. A presenting organization is defined as an organization that selects, engages and pays touring performing artists to perform works created elsewhere by those or other artists, which will be performed in many locations. Presenters manage all local arrangements for the performance (e.g. providing space, local technical support, advertising/promotion) and facilitate the interaction between artists and audiences.
Restrictions: Presenters may apply at more than one deadline for Fee-Support and New Directions grants. Presenters may request funds for more than one artist, however, they must submit a separate application for each separately contracted engagement. Applicants must not have any overdue outstanding reports from previous PennPAT or Mid Atlantic Foundation grants. PennPAT will not fund the following activities: programs or events that primarily serve a confined audience (e.g. K-12 schools, university classes, summer camps, nursing homes); arts-in-education projects; programs or events in which the roster artist is not the primary focus of the performance; fundraising events; programs or events that are commercial in nature or in which the arts are not the primary focus (e.g. sidewalk sales, food festivals, fireworks displays); or home-season engagements. Applications for engagements that are less than 50 miles from the artist's home community must explain why the project should be considered a touring engagement. K-12, college, and university projects must include substantive participation and attendance from outside the school population.
Geographic Focus: Delaware, District of Columbia, Maryland, New Jersey, New York, Ohio, Pennsylvania, U.S. Virgin Islands, Virginia, West Virginia
Date(s) Application is Due: Feb 15; Oct 15
Amount of Grant: Up to 20,000 USD
Contact: Katie West; (215) 496-9424 ext. 4; katie@pennpat.org or info@pennpat.org
Internet: http://www.pennpat.org/Grants.aspx?id=114&ekmensel=216_submenu_228_btnlink
Sponsor: Pennsylvania Performing Arts on Tour
230 South Broad Street, Suite 1003
Philadelphia, PA 19102

PennPAT New Directions Grants for Presenters **3813**
Created as a unique public/private partnership and administered by the Mid Atlantic Arts Foundation, Pennsylvania Performing Arts on Tour (PennPAT) increases opportunities for professional Pennsylvania-based performing artists to obtain successful touring engagements in Pennsylvania and other states. To this end, PennPAT provides grants and marketing support to both presenters and artists, as well as training for artists. PennPat offers three types of grants to presenting organizations: Fee-Support Grants, New Directions Grants, and Presenter Travel Grants. New Directions Grants provide funding to presenters in support of touring engagements with artists listed on the PennPAT Artist Roster. Unlike the Fee-Support Grants, New Directions Grants provide support for more complex projects that fall outside the scope of traditional presenting models. These longer-term projects should offer an opportunity for both creative and audience development for the roster artist involved and should build relationships among artists, presenters and community members through collaborative activities while presenting at least one public performance. New Directions have two application deadlines: February 15 for projects that fall within a two year period beginning the following June; and October 15 for projects that fall within a two-year and three-month period beginning the following February. Applications must be submitted through the Mid Atlantic Arts Foundation eGrant system (link is available from the PennPAT website) by the deadline date. Applications must also be mailed to PennPAT and postmarked by the deadline date. New Directions Grants will fund up to to 50% of the total project costs. Eligible project costs may include the following expenses for planning and implementing the project: artist fees and travel expenses, marketing and publicity, printing, space rental, technical costs, and reasonable administrative costs. Project costs are often capped at $30,000 per grant. Complete application guidelines (PDF) can be downloaded from the grant website. Applicants are also encouraged to read the FAQ section of the website.
Requirements: Presenters applying for New Directions grants must contact the PennPAT Director in advance. To be eligible for New Directions grants, applicants must meet PennPat's definition of a presenting organization; be a 501(c)3 organization or a unit of government; and be located in Delaware, the District of Columbia, Maryland, New Jersey, New York, Ohio, Pennsylvania, the U.S. Virgin Islands, Virginia, or West Virginia. Eligible projects must be jointly submitted and include a tentative contract for an engagement with a PennPAT roster artist (who lives or is based outside the community where the presentation will take place); include at least one public performance at a venue within the eligible states/jurisdictions listed above; provide the PennPAT roster artist with an extended residency (at least seven days) that will allow time and conditions conducive to the artist's personal creative development; and include activities that will promote greater understanding of the roster artist's work and/or increase or broaden audiences for the roster artist's public performance. A presenting organization is defined as an organization that selects, engages and pays touring performing artists to perform works created elsewhere by those or other artists, which will be performed in many locations. Presenters manage all local arrangements for the performance (e.g. providing space, local technical support, advertising/promotion) and facilitate the interaction between artists and audiences.
Restrictions: Generally, a roster artist will not be funded for more than one New Directions project per year. Presenters may apply at more than one deadline for Fee-Support and New Directions grants. Presenters may request funds for more than one artist, however, they must submit a separate application for each separately contracted engagement. Applicants must not have any overdue outstanding reports from previous PennPAT or Mid Atlantic Foundation grants. PennPAT will not fund the following activities: programs or events that primarily serve a confined audience (e.g. K-12 schools, university classes, summer camps, nursing homes); arts-in-education projects; programs or events in which the roster artist is not the primary focus of the performance; fundraising events; programs or events that are commercial in nature or in which the arts are not the primary focus (e.g. sidewalk sales, food festivals, fireworks displays); or home-season engagements. Applications for engagements that are less than 50 miles from the artist's home community must explain why the project should be considered a touring engagement. K-12, college, and university projects must include substantive participation and attendance from outside the school population.
Geographic Focus: Delaware, District of Columbia, Maryland, New Jersey, New York, Ohio, Pennsylvania, U.S. Virgin Islands, Virginia, West Virginia
Date(s) Application is Due: Feb 15; Oct 15
Amount of Grant: Up to 30,000 USD
Contact: Katie West; (215) 496-9424 ext. 4; katie@pennpat.org or info@pennpat.org
Internet: http://www.pennpat.org/Grants.aspx?id=114&ekmensel=216_submenu_228_btnlink
Sponsor: Pennsylvania Performing Arts on Tour
230 South Broad Street, Suite 1003
Philadelphia, PA 19102

PennPAT Presenter Travel Grants **3814**
Created as a unique public/private partnership and administered by the Mid Atlantic Arts Foundation, Pennsylvania Performing Arts on Tour (PennPAT) increases opportunities for professional Pennsylvania-based performing artists to obtain successful touring engagements in Pennsylvania and other states. To this end, PennPAT provides grants and marketing support to both presenters and artists, as well as training for artists. PennPat offers three types of grants to presenting organizations: Presenter Travel Grants, Fee-Support Grants, and New Directions Grants. Presenter Travel Grants are provided to U.S. presenters who are interested in booking a PennPAT roster artist and would like to first see a live performance by that artist. Funds may be used to attend a full public performance by a PennPAT roster artist, either at home or on tour (presenter may be based anywhere in the U.S.). Grants are available for up to $500 and may cover, on a reimbursement basis, up to 100% of reasonable travel/lodging cash expenses related to this project. Applications must be received at the PennPAT office at least six weeks prior to the performance date. Applicants will be notified on the status of their proposal within four weeks of the application receipt date. The grant application may be downloaded from the grant website.
Requirements: Applicants must be 501(c)3 organizations or units of governments based within the United States that present touring performing artists and groups.
Restrictions: Conference registration fees are NOT eligible. Organizations may receive up to two Presenter Travel Grants per year. Applicants must not have any overdue outstanding reports from previous PennPAT or Mid Atlantic Foundation grants.
Geographic Focus: All States
Amount of Grant: Up to 500 USD
Contact: Katie West; (215) 496-9424 ext. 4; katie@pennpat.org or info@pennpat.org
Internet: http://www.pennpat.org/Grants.aspx?id=114&ekmensel=216_submenu_228_btnlink

Sponsor: Pennsylvania Performing Arts on Tour
230 South Broad Street, Suite 1003
Philadelphia, PA 19102

PennPAT Strategic Opportunity Grants 3815
Created as a unique public/private partnership and administered by the Mid Atlantic Arts Foundation, Pennsylvania Performing Arts on Tour (PennPAT) increases opportunities for professional Pennsylvania-based performing artists to obtain successful touring engagements in Pennsylvania and other states. Artists may apply directly for two types of grants: Artist Technical Assistance Grants and Strategic Opportunity Grants. Strategic Opportunity Grants support artists' overseas travel costs for international touring engagements that represent a strategic opportunity for the artist to expand his/her future touring ability. Prospective applicants must first contact the PennPAT Director to discuss the project. If the project is deemed eligible, PennPAT will email or mail the guidelines and application to the applicant. Artists may submit applications on an ongoing basis, at least six weeks prior to the start of the proposed project. Grants will generally be awarded for up to 50% of reasonable cash expenses for travel and lodging, up to a maximum of $5,000 per calendar year.
Requirements: Projects MUST include at least one performance that is open to and marketed to the general public. Applicants must be included in the PennPAT artist roster for the time in which the project will take place. Information on how to be included in the artist roster is available at the PennPAT website. In addition, the applicant must have submitted all final reports on previous PennPAT and Mid Atlantic Foundation projects by the report due date.
Restrictions: Mid Atlantic Arts Foundation also provides grants for international touring engagements through the USArtists International (USAI) program. PennPAT roster artists must explore PennPAT Strategic Opportunity Grants as a first option for support of international touring engagements. If a PennPAT roster artist also chooses to apply to USAI, the maximum amount of support for a single project through both programs combined will not exceed $15,000. Grants will NOT support the following activities and expenses: engagements that consist primarily of workshops, training or conference sessions; engagements in which the artist must produce their own performances (e.g. artists who are self-selected, have no established venue, or receive no artistic fee other than percentage of box office receipts); events that are academic in nature, are competitions, or for which ensembles must pay a participation, registration, or tuition fee; and purchase of equipment, supplies, or other costs related to normal business activities.
Geographic Focus: Pennsylvania
Contact: Katie West; (215) 496-9424 ext. 4; katie@pennpat.org or info@pennpat.org
Internet: http://www.pennpat.org/Grants.aspx?id=126&ekmensel=216_submenu_286_btnlink
Sponsor: Pennsylvania Performing Arts on Tour
230 South Broad Street, Suite 1003
Philadelphia, PA 19102

Pentair Foundation Education and Community Grants 3816
The Pentair Foundation focuses awards in two focus areas: education and community projects. Educational projects should focus on: supporting science and math education; providing "school-to-work" initiatives that prepare a student for the professional world; projects that offer alternative education; and programs that support art education. Community programs should focus on: water quality education, conservation and action; assistance to individuals in achieving self-sufficiency; entrepreneurial opportunities; opportunities for youth to gain life skills; services for youth in crisis; access to health care services; and assistance, education and rehabilitation services for those suffering from mental and/or physical disabilities and life-threatening illness.
Requirements: Nonprofit organizations, including schools and school districts, in communities where Pentair has a presence may apply. Application must be completed online and is located at the Foundation's website.
Restrictions: The foundation does not support individuals; political, lobbying, or fraternal activities; religious groups for religious purposes; medical research by individuals; scholarships to individuals; fundraising events, sponsorships, or advertising support; travel or tour expenses; conferences, seminars, workshops, or symposiums; athletic or sports-related organizations; non 501(c)3 organizations or those operating under a fiscal agent.
Geographic Focus: Wisconsin
Date(s) Application is Due: Mar 1; Jun 1; Oct 1
Contact: Susan Carter, Grants Administrator; (763) 656-5237; susan.carter@pentair.com
Internet: http://www.pentair.com/About_pentair_foundation.aspx
Sponsor: Pentair Foundation
5500 Wayzata Boulevard, Suite 800
Minneapolis, MN 55416

Peoples Bancorp Foundation Grants 3817
The corporate foundation makes charitable donations to community organizations that assist low- to moderate-income families in Peoples Bank's service areas. Grants focus on community investment and community development; youth and education; social services programs that improve the social needs of low- and moderate-income communities and individuals; and arts and culture. Grant applications are reviewed on a quarterly basis. Grants should be in writing with the required completed application and supporting documentation requested. Guidelines and application are available online.
Requirements: Kentucky, Ohio, and West Virginia nonprofit organizations are eligible.
Geographic Focus: Kentucky, Ohio, West Virginia
Date(s) Application is Due: Feb 10; May 10; Aug 10; Nov 10
Contact: Kristi Close; (740) 376-7128; kclose@peoplesbancorp.com
Internet: http://www.pebo.com/investors/PeoplesBankFoundationForm.htm
Sponsor: Peoples Bancorp
P.O. Box 738
Marietta, OH 45750

PeopleSoft Community Relations Grants 3818
The company awards grants and provides volunteer support to nonprofits that benefit the community, particularly innovative programs that empower people to help themselves. PeopleSoft prefers to support organizations that devote a high percentage of their budget to direct services rather than to administrative overhead. Preference is given to requests that offer employees opportunities to volunteer or a request that is presented by an employee. Generally, large educational organizations and foundations are receive preference over requests from individual schools.
Requirements: 501(c)3 tax-exempt organizations are eligible.
Geographic Focus: All States
Date(s) Application is Due: Jun 1; Dec 1
Contact: Wanda Brackins, Community Relations; (925) 694-2705; fax (925) 694-2633; community_relations@peoplesoft.com
Internet: http://www.peoplesoft.com/corp/en/public_index.jsp
Sponsor: PeopleSoft Corporation
4460 Hacienda Drive, P.O. Box 8015
Pleasanton, CA 94588-8615

PepsiCo Foundation Grants 3819
The foundation's three focus areas include health (food security, improved and optimum nutrition, and energy balance), environment (water security, sustainable agriculture, and adaptive approaches to climate change), and education (access to education, dropout prevention, women's empowerment, and skills training for the under-served). Additionally the foundation provides financial assistance, in-kind product donations, and human-resource contributions to help respond to people and communities affected by major disasters. The foundation divides its grants into two categories: major requests (over $100,000) and other requests ($100,000 and under). Foundation staff must solicit proposals for all major grants. All other requests must be submitted as a Letter of Interest (LOI) to the email address given. Specific guidelines for LOI contents are available at the website. LOIs are reviewed on a rolling basis. Consideration regularly takes several months, especially during peak periods. PepsiCo Foundation was established in 1962 for charitable and educational purposes. In the 1970s, the Foundation began to support fitness research, and by the 1980s had established a focus on preventive medicine. Later, the Foundation's focus was expanded to funding fitness education for youth. Today the foundation has evolved its goals to reflect the needs of under-served populations and has extended its grant-making to the global community.
Requirements: Eligible organizations must have official tax-exempt status under Section 501(c)3 of the Internal Revenue Code (or the equivalent of such status) and have a primary focus in the areas of health, environment, or education. In evaluating requests, the foundation will consider the following criteria: the extent to which the request addresses specific goals, methodologies, and approaches; the degree to which the request advances or fulfills PepsiCo Foundation's stated goals and priorities; evidence of proven success in the field or scope of work specific to the request; and a method by which to measure and track impact and progress.
Restrictions: PepsiCo Foundation does not fund the following entities (or causes): individuals; private charities or foundations; organizations not exempt under Section 501(c)3 of the Internal Revenue Code and not eligible for tax-deductible support; religious organizations; political causes, candidates, organizations, or campaigns; organizations that discriminate on the basis of age, race, citizenship or national origin, disability or disabled-veteran status, gender, religion, marital status, sexual orientation, military service or status, or Vietnam-era veteran status; organizations whose primary purpose is to influence legislation; endowments or capital campaigns; playgrounds, sports fields, or equipment; film, music, TV, video, and media production companies; sports sponsorships; performing arts tours; and association memberships.
Geographic Focus: All States, All Countries
Contact: Maura Smith, President; (914) 253-3153 or (914) 253-2000; fax (914) 253-2788; pepsico.foundation@pepsico.com
Internet: http://www.pepsico.com/Purpose/PepsiCo-Foundation/Grants.html
Sponsor: PepsiCo Foundation
700 Anderson Hill Road
Purchase, NY 10577

Percy B. Ferebee Endowment Grants 3820
Grants from the Percy B. Ferebee Endowment are awarded to support charitable, scientific and literary projects, and in particular, governmental and civic projects designed to further the cultural, social, economic and physical well-being of residents of Cherokee, Clay, Graham, Jackson, Macon and Swain Counties of North Carolina and the Cherokee Indian Reservation. Grants are also awarded in the form of scholarships to assist worthy and talented young men and women who reside in said counties in pursuing their college/university degree education within the state of North Carolina. The deadline for the submission of a grant application is September 30. The deadline for scholarship applications is January 31. Application forms are available online. Applicants will receive notice acknowledging receipt of the grant request, and subsequently be notified of the grant declination or approval.
Requirements: 501(c)3 non-profits in the Cherokee, Clay, Graham, Jackson, Macon and Swain Counties of North Carolina are eligible to apply for grants. Proposals should be submitted in the following format: completed Common Grant Application Form; an original Proposal Statement; an audited financial report and a current year operating budget; a copy of your official IRS Letter with your tax determination; a listing of your Board of Directors. Proposal Statements (second item in the above Format) should answer these questions: what are the objectives and expected outcomes of this program/project/request; what strategies will be used to accomplish your objective; what is the timeline for completion; if this is part of an on-going program, how long has it been in operation; what criteria will you use to measure success; if the request is not fully funded, what other sources can you engage; an Itemized budget should be included; please describe any collaborative ventures. Prior to the distribution of funds, all approved grantees must sign and return a Grant Agreement Form, stating that the funds will

be used for the purpose intended. Progress reports and Completion reports must also be filed as required for your specific grant. All current grantees must be in good standing with required documentation prior to submitting new proposals to any foundation. Scholarship recipients must be a resident of these areas and must attend a college or university in the state of North Carolina. Contact the Foundation for additional application requirements.
Restrictions: Grants are not made for political purposes, nor to organizations which discriminate on the basis of race, ethnic origin, sexual or religious preference, age or gender.
Geographic Focus: North Carolina
Date(s) Application is Due: Jan 31; Sep 30
Contact: Wachovia Bank, N.A., Trustee; grantinquiries6@wachovia.com
Internet: https://www.wachovia.com/foundation/v/index.jsp?vgnextoid=5d6852199c0aa110VgnVCM1000004b0d1872RCRD&vgnextfmt=default
Sponsor: Percy B. Ferebee Endowment
Wachovia Bank, NC6732, 100 North Main Street
Winston Salem, NC 27150

Perkin Fund Grants 3821
The Perkin Fund supports projects and programs in the fields of astronomy, medicine, and scientific research, as well as limited giving to leading organizations in the arts, education, and social services. Most grants are awarded to well-established institutions. However, small and medium-sized institutions doing significant work in the fields of interest also are encouraged to apply. Deadlines are March 15 and September 15, with board meetings in May and November. Final notification of funding is usually two to four weeks.
Requirements: U.S. nonprofit institutions and organizations are eligible. Applicants should submit a letter with a detailed description of their project, the amount of funding requested, and a copy of their IRS determination letter.
Restrictions: The Fund does not grant to individuals or institutions outside the United States. Funding is limited to Connecticut, Massachusetts, and New York.
Geographic Focus: Connecticut, Massachusetts, New York
Date(s) Application is Due: Mar 15; Sep 15
Contact: Winifred Gray, Treasurer; (978) 468-2266; theperkinfund@verizon.net
Sponsor: Perkin Fund
176 Bay Road, P.O. Box 2220
South Hamilton, MA 01982-2232

Perkins-Ponder Foundation Grants 3822
The mission of the Perkins-Ponder Foundation is to assist charitable organizations that provide for the aid and assistance of dependent and economically disadvantaged, aged females and under-privileged children of Bibb County. Grants from the Perkins-Ponder Foundation are primarily one year in duration; on occasion, multi-year support is awarded. Applicants must apply online at the grant website. Applicants are strongly encouraged to do the following before applying: review the downloadable state application procedures for additional helpful information and clarifications; review the downloadable online-application guidelines at the grant website; review the foundation's funding history (link is available from the grant website); review the online application questions in advance; and review the list of required attachments. These will generally include: a list of board members, financial statements (audited, reviewed, or compiled by independent auditor); an organization summary; a list of other funding sources; an IRS Determination letter; and other required documents. All attachments must be uploaded in the online application as PDF, Word, or Excel files. The Perkins-Ponder Foundation application deadline is 11:59 p.m. on February 1. Applicants will be notified of grant decisions by letter within one to two months after the deadline.
Requirements: Applicants must have 501(c)3 tax-exempt status.
Restrictions: Applicants must serve the residents of Bibb County, Georgia. The foundation does not support requests from individuals, organizations attempting to influence policy through direct lobbying, or any political campaigns.
Geographic Focus: Georgia
Date(s) Application is Due: Feb 1
Contact: Quanda Allen, Vice President; (404) 264 1377; quanda.allen@baml.com
Internet: https://www.bankofamerica.com/philanthropic/fn_search.action
Sponsor: Perkins-Ponder Foundation
3414 Peachtree Road, N.E., Suite 1475, GA7-813-14-04
Atlanta, GA 30326-1113

Perkins Charitable Foundation Grants 3823
The Perkins Charitable Foundation Trust was established in 1950, by members of the Perkins family. The Foundation gives primarily for education, the arts, environmental conservation, animals, wildlife, health and medical care, and children, youth and social services. They offer funding on a national basis, with some emphasis on Ohio and Vermont.
Requirements: Contact the Foundation's office by letter or phone prior to your proposal. No Application form is required.
Restrictions: No grants to individuals.
Geographic Focus: All States
Contact: Marilyn Best, Secretary; (216) 621-0465
Sponsor: Perkins Charitable Foundation
1030 Hanna Building, 1422 Euclid Avenue
Cleveland, OH 44115-2001

Perl 6 Microgrants 3824
The program was established by a donation from Best Practical Solutions to help support Perl 6 development. Grants of $500 will be awarded to a range of Perl 6-related projects over the life of the grant program. Proposals will be accepted on a rolling schedule.
Requirements: Accepted grants might be for coding, documentation, testing or even writing articles about Perl 6. The program isn't tied to any one implementation of Perl 6 — they are interested in seeing proposals related to Pugs, Perl 6 on Parrot, Perl 6 on Perl 5 or any other Perl 6 implementation, and in general, projects that can be completed in 4-6 calendar weeks. To submit a grant proposal, send an email to perl6- microgrants@perl.org with the following information: a) A two to three paragraph summary of the work you intend to do; b) A quick bio; c) A brief description of what 'success' will mean for your project (How will we know you're done?); d) Where (if anywhere) you've discussed your project in the past; e) Where you'll be blogging about your progress. (Twice-weekly blog posts are a requirement for getting your grant money.)
Geographic Focus: All States
Amount of Grant: 500 USD
Contact: Jesse Vincent, Grant Manager; jesse@bestpractical.com
Internet: http://www.perlfoundation.org/patrick_michaud_awarded_perl_6_development_grant_as_a_joint_initiative_by_the_perl_foundation_and_mozilla_foundation
Sponsor: Perl Foundation
6832 Mulderstraat
Grand Ledge, MI 48837

Perl Foundation Grants 3825
The Perl Foundation (TPF) is dedicated to the advancement of the Perl programming language through open discussion, collaboration, design, and code.
Requirements: Projects do not have to be large, complex, or lengthy. If you have a good idea and the means and ability to accomplish it, the project will be considered. As a general rule, a properly formatted grant proposal is more likely to be approved if it meets the following criteria: it has widespread benefit to the Perl community or a large segment of it; you can convince TPF that you can accomplish your goals; and, the project can be accomplished in the published funding range ($500 - $3,000). To submit a proposal see the guidelines at http://www.perlfoundation.org/how_to_write_a_proposal and TPF rules of operation at http://www.perlfoundation.org/rules_of_operation. Then send your proposal to tpf-proposals@perl-foundation.org. Note that proposals should be properly formatted accordingly with the required P.O.D template.
Geographic Focus: All States
Date(s) Application is Due: May 31
Amount of Grant: 500 - 3,000 USD
Contact: Richard Dice, President; rdice@perlfoundation.org
Internet: http://news.perlfoundation.org/2009/04/2009q2_call_for_grant_proposal.html
Sponsor: Perl Foundation
6832 Mulderstraat
Grand Ledge, MI 48837

Perpetual Trust for Charitable Giving Grants 3826
The Perpetual Trust for Charitable Giving was established in 1957 to support and promote quality educational, human-services, and health-care programming for underserved populations. Special consideration is given to medical aid and medical research organizations, as well as to institutions of higher learning. Grant requests for general operating support are strongly encouraged. Program support will also be considered. Small, program-related capital expenses may be included in general operating or program requests. To better support the capacity of nonprofit organizations, multi-year funding requests are strongly encouraged. Applicants must apply online at the grant website. Applicants are strongly encouraged to do the following before applying: review the downloadable state application procedures for additional helpful information and clarifications; review the downloadable online-application guidelines at the grant website; review the trust's funding history (link is available from the grant website); review the online application questions in advance; and review the list of required attachments. These will generally include: a list of board members, financial statements (audited, reviewed, or compiled by independent auditor); an organization summary; a list of other funding sources; an IRS Determination letter; and other required documents. All attachments must be uploaded in the online application as PDF, Word, or Excel files. The application deadline for the Perpetual Trust is 11:59 p.m. on September 1. Applicants will be notified of grant decisions before November 30.
Restrictions: The trust does not support requests from individuals, organizations attempting to influence policy through direct lobbying, or any political campaigns.
Geographic Focus: Massachusetts
Date(s) Application is Due: Sep 1
Contact: Miki C. Akimoto, Vice President; (866) 778-6859; miki.akimoto@baml.com
Internet: https://www.bankofamerica.com/philanthropic/fn_search.action
Sponsor: Perpetual Trust for Charitable Giving
225 Franklin Street, 4th Floor, MA1-225-04-02
Boston, MA 02110

Perry County Community Foundation Grants 3827
The Perry County Community Foundation is a nonprofit, public charity created for the people of Perry County, Indiana. We connect donors with the causes they care about. The Foundation will accept grant proposals from all charitable organizations seeking funding; however, special attention will be given to projects that promote healthy living and that offer training and/or support to potential small business entrepreneurship. Funding priority areas include arts and culture; community development; education; health; human services; environment; recreation; and youth development. The Foundation considers proposals for grants on a yearly cycle which begins each July. At the start of each cycle, a notice is mailed to nonprofit organizations that have applied for or received grants in the past, or have otherwise requested notification of the start of each cycle. The Foundation's grant cycle runs from July through November each year. Proposals are accepted from July through September. The grant committee makes its recommendations on funding to the Foundation's Board of Trustees, which will make final funding recommendations to the board of directors of the Community Foundation Alliance. All organizations who submit

proposals are notified committee's decision no later than December 1. The application is available at the Foundation's website.
Requirements: The Foundation welcomes proposals from nonprofit organizations that are 501(c)3 and 509(a) tax-exempt under the IRS code and from governmental agencies serving the county. Proposals from nonprofit organizations not classified as a 501(c)3 public charity may be considered if the project is charitable and supports a community need. Proposals submitted by an entity under the auspices of another agency must include a written statement signed by the agency's board president on behalf of the board of directors agreeing to act as the entity's fiscal sponsor, to receive grant monies if awarded, and to oversee the proposed project.
Restrictions: Project areas not considered for funding: religious organizations for religious purposes; political parties or campaigns; endowment creation or debt reduction; operating costs; capital campaigns; annual appeals or membership contributions; travel requests for groups or individuals such as bands, sports teams, or classes.
Geographic Focus: Indiana
Contact: Renate Warner; (812) 547-3176; renate@perrycommunityfoundation.org
Internet: http://www.perrycommunityfoundation.org/disc-grants-program
Sponsor: Perry County Community Foundation
817 12th Street, P.O. Box 13
Tell City, IN 47586

Pet Care Trust Fish in the Classroom Grant 3828
Incorporated in Washington, D.C. in 1990, The Pet Care Trust is a non-profit, charitable, public foundation. The purpose of The Pet Care Trust is to help promote public understanding regarding the value of and right to enjoy companion animals, to enhance knowledge about companion animals through research and education, and to promote professionalism among members of the companion animal community. The Pet Care Trust's Fish in the Classroom (FIC) was created to educate and enhance the experiences of grade school students. The FIC supports their learning about fish and how to care for them. Use contact information to obtain deadline dates.
Geographic Focus: All States
Amount of Grant: 250 USD
Contact: Steve Hellem, Executive Director; (202) 530-5910; shellem@navista.net
Internet: http://www.petcaretrust.org/i4a/pages/index.cfm?pageid=3327
Sponsor: Pet Care Trust
1155 Fifteenth Street NW, Suite 500
Washington, DC 20005

Pet Care Trust Sue Busch Memorial Award 3829
Incorporated in Washington, D.C. in 1990, The Pet Care Trust is a non-profit, charitable, public foundation. The purpose of The Pet Care Trust is to help promote public understanding regarding the value of and right to enjoy companion animals, to enhance knowledge about companion animals through research and education, and to promote professionalism among members of the companion animal community. The Pet Care Trust invites you submit a letter of recommendation for a graduating veterinary technician student who has been selected by your faculty as having a keen interest in companion animals (dogs, cats, small pet mammals, birds, reptiles, amphibians or pond and aquarium fish) as well as dedicating time to community service related to animals while maintaining a high academic standard. Please include instances relating to the above mentioned criteria. If selected, the student you have recommended will receive one of three $500 Sue Busch Memorial Awards for the year. Our goal is not only to bring recognition to a fine student but recognition as well to the institution instrumental in educating that student. Please submit your recommendations on or before Feb 1 You will be notified on or before April 30 in order for the Check and Certificate to be presented at your graduation ceremony.
Geographic Focus: All States
Date(s) Application is Due: Feb 1
Contact: Steve Hellem, Executive Director; (202) 530-5910; shellem@navista.net
Internet: http://www.petcaretrust.org/i4a/pages/index.cfm?pageid=3297
Sponsor: Pet Care Trust
1155 Fifteenth Street NW, Suite 500
Washington, DC 20005

Petco Foundation 4 Rs Project Support Grants 3830
The Petco Foundation's mission is to raise the quality of life for pets and people who love and need them. The foundation accomplishes this by providing monetary grants directly to more than 7,500 local animal-welfare organizations in communities nationwide, in most cases to help support day-to-day operations and special projects. These are mostly small humane non-profits, who collectively provide the majority of animal rescue work today. The 4 Rs Project Support Grant program is specifically for projects that support the Petco Foundation 4Rs: Reduce (spay and/or neuter); Rescue (adoptions); Rehabilitate (training); Rejoice (promote and assist with the human/animal bond). Items covered by this type of grant include: general veterinary services; spay and neuter services; trap/neuter/return programs (for feral animals); sponsorship of an event; animal adoptions; training; animal assisted therapy; dog parks; emergency rescue; humane education; and equipment purchase (can also be applied for under Capital Grants program).
Geographic Focus: All States
Contact: Susan Rosenberg, National Grants Manager; (858) 453-7845, ext. 3348; fax (858) 909-2618; susanrn@petco.com or petcofoundation@petco.com
Internet: http://www.petco.com/Petco_Page_PC_foundationabout.aspx?CoreCat=LN_Petcofoundation_about
Sponsor: Petco Foundation
7262 North Rosemead Boulevard
San Gabriel, CA 91775

Petco Foundation Capital Grants 3831
The Petco Foundation's mission is to raise the quality of life for pets and people who love and need them. The foundation accomplishes this by providing monetary grants directly to more than 7,500 local animal-welfare organizations in communities nationwide, in most cases to help support day-to-day operations and special projects. These are mostly small humane non-profits, who collectively provide the majority of animal rescue work today. Capital Grants are larger funding opportunities utilized for buildings, construction or equipment, rather than program or operating expenses.
Requirements: 501(c)3 nonprofits that fulfill one of the four areas of interest are eligible.
Geographic Focus: All States
Contact: Susan Rosenberg, National Grants Manager; (858) 453-7845, ext. 3348; fax (858) 909-2618; susanrn@petco.com or petcofoundation@petco.com
Internet: http://www.petco.com/Petco_Page_PC_foundationabout.aspx?CoreCat=LN_Petcofoundation_about
Sponsor: Petco Foundation
7262 North Rosemead Boulevard
San Gabriel, CA 91775

Petco Foundation Product Support Grants 3832
The Petco Foundation's mission is to raise the quality of life for pets and people who love and need them. The foundation accomplishes this by providing monetary grants directly to more than 7,500 local animal-welfare organizations in communities nationwide, in most cases to help support day-to-day operations and special projects. These are mostly small humane non-profits, who collectively provide the majority of animal rescue work today. Petco Foundation Product Support Grants come in the form of products to be donated. These donations can be used for general operations, special events, goodie bags, feeding programs, food banks, disaster relief, silent auction, animal transport, animal holding, animal adoptions, and more.
Requirements: 501(c)3 nonprofits that fulfill one of the four areas of interest are eligible.
Geographic Focus: All States
Contact: Susan Rosenberg, National Grants Manager; (858) 453-7845, ext. 3348; fax (858) 909-2618; susanrn@petco.com or petcofoundation@petco.com
Internet: http://www.petco.com/Petco_Page_PC_foundationabout.aspx?CoreCat=LN_Petcofoundation_about
Sponsor: Petco Foundation
7262 North Rosemead Boulevard
San Gabriel, CA 91775

Petco Foundation We Are Family Too Grants 3833
The Petco Foundation's mission is to raise the quality of life for pets and people who love and need them. The foundation accomplishes this by providing monetary grants directly to more than 7,500 local animal-welfare organizations in communities nationwide, in most cases to help support day-to-day operations and special projects. These are mostly small humane non-profits, who collectively provide the majority of animal rescue work today. We Are Family Too Grants are short-term and seed funding for animal welfare groups to help pet owners who have lost their homes or are experiencing temporary financial hurdles. We Are Family Too funds such programs as pet food banks, product donations, referral lists of pet-friendly housing, short-term foster pet care, and veterinary services.
Requirements: 501(c)3 nonprofits that fulfill one of the four areas of interest are eligible.
Geographic Focus: All States
Contact: Susan Rosenberg, National Grants Manager; (858) 453-7845, ext. 3348; fax (858) 909-2618; susanrn@petco.com or petcofoundation@petco.com
Internet: http://www.petco.com/Petco_Page_PC_foundationabout.aspx?CoreCat=LN_Petcofoundation_about
Sponsor: Petco Foundation
7262 North Rosemead Boulevard
San Gabriel, CA 91775

Peter and Elizabeth C. Tower Foundation Annual Intellectual Disabilities Grants 3834
Elizabeth Nelson Clarke was born in Mt. Vernon, New York, in 1920, and Peter Tower in Niagara Falls, New York, in 1921. They met while attending Cornell University and married in the summer of 1942. Two daughters, Mollie and Cynthia, were born in 1944 and 1947. Peter entered the Army Air Force in January 1943. After service in Texas and Europe, he hoped to find work in the fledgling air transport business which he expected to thrive. Taking a "temporary" clerk job for the family's customhouse broker business C. J. Tower and Sons, he stayed on to see the partnership evolve into a corporation. In 1986 it processed a total of $45 billion worth of merchandise and Peter then sold the business to McGraw-Hill Inc. who later sold it to the Federal Express Company, which utilizes Tower skills and systems worldwide. Meanwhile, Liz, who had studied art at Cornell, had become a notable artist, working mostly in oils. True to other personal philosophies, Peter and Liz knew that with prosperity came responsibility. Their desire was to assure that the resources they had acquired over the years were put to good use and to see the benefits spread among many. Formed December 31, 1990, the Peter and Elizabeth C. Tower Foundation seeks to support community programming that will help children, adolescents, and young adults affected by substance abuse, learning disabilities, mental illness, and intellectual disabilities achieve their full potential. The foundation's funding objective in the intellectual disabilities category is to improve service delivery for children, adolescents, and young adults to age 26 with intellectual disabilities. The foundation defines an intellectual disability as a disability characterized by significant limitations both in intellectual functioning and adaptive behavior, which covers many everyday social and practical skills. This disability originates before the age of 18. The Foundation will give preference to projects addressing one or more of the following priority areas: reducing obstacles to seeking services/treatment; stigma reduction; transitional services; early identification and linkage to services; effective treatment/programming; co-occurring disorders; and provider workforce shortage and readiness (capacity building).

The foundation will also consider other project ideas that have the potential to advance its objective in the category. Typical funding range is $25,000 - $75,000 per year. Multi-year grants are encouraged; projects should be sustainable after grant funding ends. Preference is given to projects where the majority of costs are both new to the organization and directly related to the proposed initiative. Interested organizations must submit a letter of inquiry by 5:00 p.m. June 8 to the Chief Program Officer. Guidelines for the letter of inquiry are provided at the grant website. Applicants will be notified by July 27 of the result of their letters of inquiry. Selected applicants must submit a full grant application by June 22. Final grantees will be informed by September 14. Deadline dates may vary from year to year. Interested organizations should visit the grant website to verify current deadline dates.
Requirements: Letters of inquiry must be mailed or hand-delivered. emailed and faxed copies will not be accepted. Signature of organization's Executive Director, Superintendent or Headmaster is required; designee signatures are not acceptable.
Restrictions: The Foundation accepts only one letter of inquiry per applicant. The Foundation makes grants only to: tax-exempt organizations with 501(c)3 tax-exempt status from the Internal Revenue Service that are neither private foundations nor described as 509(a)3 organizations; diocesan and public school districts; charter schools; and to nonprofit public benefit corporations. Organizations must be located in and primarily serve residents of one of the following geographic areas: Barnstable County, Massachusetts; Dukes County, Massachusetts; Essex County, Massachusetts; Nantucket County, Massachusetts; Erie County, New York; or Niagara County, New York. The Foundation does not provide funds that: may be used for the private benefit of any grant recipient or affiliated person; attempt to influence legislation; attempt to influence or intervene in any political campaign; support capital campaigns or improvements; support individual scholarships; provide general operating support; or that subsidize individuals for the cost of care.
Geographic Focus: Massachusetts, New York
Date(s) Application is Due: Sep 14
Contact: Tracy A. Sawicki, Executive Director; (716) 689-0370; fax (716) 689-3716; info@thetowerfoundation.org or tas@thetowerfoundation.org
Internet: http://www.thetowerfoundation.com/WhatWeFund/ID/IDGrantGuidelines
Sponsor: Peter and Elizabeth C. Tower Foundation
2351 North Forest Road
Getzville, NY 14068-1225

Peter and Elizabeth C. Tower Foundation Annual Mental Health Grants 3835
Elizabeth Nelson Clarke was born in Mt. Vernon, New York, in 1920, and Peter Tower in Niagara Falls, New York, in 1921. They met while attending Cornell University and married in the summer of 1942. Two daughters, Mollie and Cynthia, were born in 1944 and 1947. Peter entered the Army Air Force in January 1943. After service in Texas and Europe, he hoped to find work in the fledgling air transport business which he expected to thrive. Taking a "temporary" clerk job for the family's customhouse broker business C. J. Tower and Sons, he stayed on to see the partnership evolve into a corporation. In 1986 it processed a total of $45 billion worth of merchandise and Peter then sold the business to McGraw-Hill Inc. who later sold it to the Federal Express Company, which utilizes Tower skills and systems worldwide. Meanwhile, Liz, who had studied art at Cornell, had become a notable artist, working mostly in oils. True to other personal philosophies, Peter and Liz knew that with prosperity came responsibility. Their desire was to assure that the resources they had acquired over the years were put to good use and to see the benefits spread among many. Formed December 31, 1990, the Peter and Elizabeth C. Tower Foundation seeks to support community programming that will help children, adolescents, and young adults affected by substance abuse, learning disabilities, mental illness, and intellectual disabilities achieve their full potential. The foundation has a particular interest in serious mental illnesses, including major depression, schizophrenia, bipolar disorder, obsessive-compulsive disorder (OCD), panic disorder, post-traumatic stress disorder (PTSD) and borderline personality disorder. The foundation's annual mental health grants seek to prevent or alleviate psychological disorders in children, adolescents, and young adults to age 26. The foundation will give preference to projects involving one or more of the following priorities: providing direct benefit to individuals with serious mental illness; reducing barriers to seeking treatment or services; reducing stigma and prejudice often associated with mental illness; fostering social and emotional development; providing early identification and linkage to services; treating co-occurring disorders; offering life-skills programming for persons with serious mental illness; building provider workforce readiness (capacity building); providing indicated or selected prevention programming; and providing effective treatment/programming. The foundation will also consider other project ideas that have the potential to advance its objective in the category. Typical funding range is $25,000 - $75,000 per year. Multi-year grants are encouraged; projects should be sustainable after grant funding ends. Preference is given to projects where the majority of costs are both new to the organization and directly related to the proposed initiative. Interested organizations must submit a letter of inquiry by 5:00 p.m. March 30 to the Chief Program Officer. Guidelines for the letter of inquiry are provided at the grant website. Applicants will be notified by May 11 of the result of their letters of inquiry. Selected applicants must submit a full grant application by June 22. Final grantees will be informed by September 7. Deadline dates may vary from year to year. Interested organizations should visit the grant website to verify current deadline dates.
Requirements: To be eligible to apply, organizations must operate programs that provide services for children, adolescents, or young adults to age 26 with psychological disorders; and/or offer programming to prevent the onset of psychological disorders in children, adolescents, and young adults to age 26 who, based on a range of socio-economic factors, have a higher-than-average likelihood of developing these conditions. Letters of inquiry must be mailed or hand-delivered. emailed and faxed copies will not be accepted. Signature of organization's Executive Director, Superintendent or Headmaster is required; designee signatures are not acceptable.
Restrictions: The Foundation accepts only one letter of inquiry per applicant. Universal programs (programs applied to general population groups without reference to or identification of those at particular risk) will not be considered for funding. Certain general restrictions apply to all grant-seeking organizations. The Foundation makes grants only to: tax-exempt organizations with 501(c)3 tax-exempt status from the Internal Revenue Service that are neither private foundations nor described as 509(a)3 organizations; diocesan and public school districts; charter schools; and to nonprofit public benefit corporations. Organizations must be located in and primarily serve residents of one of the following geographic areas: Barnstable County, Massachusetts; Dukes County, Massachusetts; Essex County, Massachusetts; Nantucket County, Massachusetts; Erie County, New York; or Niagara County, New York. The Foundation does not provide funds that: may be used for the private benefit of any grant recipient or affiliated person; attempt to influence legislation; attempt to influence or intervene in any political campaign; support capital campaigns or improvements; support individual scholarships; provide general operating support; or that subsidize individuals for the cost of care.
Geographic Focus: Massachusetts, New York
Amount of Grant: 25,000 - 75,000 USD
Contact: Tracy A. Sawicki, Executive Director; (716) 689-0370; fax (716) 689-3716; info@thetowerfoundation.com or tas@thetowerfoundation.org
Internet: http://www.thetowerfoundation.com/WhatWeFund/MentalHealth/AnnualMentalHealthGrantGuidelines
Sponsor: Peter and Elizabeth C. Tower Foundation
2351 North Forest Road
Getzville, NY 14068-1225

Peter and Elizabeth C. Tower Foundation Learning Disability Grants 3836
Elizabeth Nelson Clarke was born in Mt. Vernon, New York, in 1920, and Peter Tower in Niagara Falls, New York, in 1921. They met while attending Cornell University and married in the summer of 1942. Peter entered the Army Air Force in January 1943. After serving in Texas and Europe, he took a "temporary" clerk job for the family's customhouse broker business C. J. Tower and Sons. Two daughters, Mollie and Cynthia, were born in 1944 and 1947. Although he had hoped to find work in the fledgling air transport business which he expected to thrive, he stayed with Tower and Sons to see the partnership evolve into a corporation. In 1986 it processed a total of $45 billion worth of merchandise and Peter then sold the business to McGraw-Hill Inc. who later sold it to the Federal Express Company, which utilizes Tower skills and systems worldwide. Meanwhile, Liz, who had studied art at Cornell, had become a notable artist, working mostly in oils. True to other personal philosophies, Peter and Liz knew that with prosperity came responsibility. Their desire was to assure that the resources they had acquired over the years were put to good use and that the benefits were spread among many. Formed December 31, 1990, the Peter and Elizabeth C. Tower Foundation supports community programming that helps children, adolescents, and young adults affected by substance abuse, learning disabilities, mental illness, and intellectual disabilities achieve their full potential. Learning disabilities are defined as neurological disorders affecting the brain's ability to receive, process, store, and respond to information. These constitute disorders in one or more of the basic psychological processes involved in understanding or using language, spoken or written, and may manifest themselves in the imperfect ability to listen, think, speak, read, write, spell or do mathematical calculations. These disorders do not include learning problems that are primarily the result of visual, hearing, or motor abilities, of mental retardation, of emotional disturbance, of traumatic brain injury, or of environmental, cultural, or economic disadvantage. The Tower Foundation is conducting research on the current state of the field. The foundation plans to offer grant opportunities to organizations that offer programming to help the learning disabled after it completes the study. These organizations are encouraged to check the grant website in 2012.
Requirements: Eligible organizations must focus on providing services and programming that will help children, adolescents, and young adults affected by substance abuse, learning disabilities, mental illness, and intellectual disabilities achieve their full potential.
Restrictions: Certain general restrictions apply to all grant-seeking organizations. The Foundation makes grants only to the following: tax-exempt organizations with 501(c)3 tax-exempt status that are neither private foundations nor described as 509(a)3 organizations; diocesan and public school districts; charter schools; and nonprofit public benefit corporations. Organizations must be located in and primarily serve residents of one of the following geographic areas: Barnstable County, Massachusetts; Dukes County, Massachusetts; Essex County, Massachusetts; Nantucket County, Massachusetts; Erie County, New York; or Niagara County, New York. The Foundation does not provide funds for the following purposes: the private benefit of any grant recipient or affiliated person; attempts to influence legislation; attempts to influence or intervene in any political campaign; capital campaigns or improvements; individual scholarships; general operating support; or subsidy of individuals for the cost of care.
Geographic Focus: Massachusetts, New York
Contact: Tracy A. Sawicki, Executive Director; (716) 689-0370; fax (716) 689-3716; info@thetowerfoundation.org or tas@thetowerfoundation.org
Internet: http://www.thetowerfoundation.com/WhatWeFund/LearningDisabilities
Sponsor: Peter and Elizabeth C. Tower Foundation
2351 North Forest Road
Getzville, NY 14068-1225

Peter and Elizabeth C. Tower Foundation Mental Health Reference and Resource Materials Mini-Grants 3837
Elizabeth Nelson Clarke was born in Mt. Vernon, New York, in 1920, and Peter Tower in Niagara Falls, New York, in 1921. They met while attending Cornell University and married in the summer of 1942. Two daughters, Mollie and Cynthia, were born in 1944 and 1947. Peter entered the Army Air Force in January 1943. After service in Texas and Europe, he hoped to find work in the fledgling air transport business which he expected to thrive. Taking a "temporary" clerk job for the family's customhouse broker business C. J. Tower and Sons, he stayed on to see the partnership evolve into a corporation. In 1986 it processed a total of $45 billion worth of merchandise and Peter then sold the business to

McGraw-Hill Inc. who later sold it to the Federal Express Company, which utilizes Tower skills and systems worldwide. Meanwhile, Liz, who had studied art at Cornell, had become a notable artist, working mostly in oils. True to other personal philosophies, Peter and Liz knew that with prosperity came responsibility. Their desire was to assure that the resources they had acquired over the years were put to good use and to see the benefits spread among many. Formed December 31, 1990, the Peter and Elizabeth C. Tower Foundation seeks to support community programming that will help children, adolescents, and young adults affected by substance abuse, learning disabilities, mental illness, and intellectual disabilities achieve their full potential. The Mental Health Mini-Grant initiative seeks to prevent or alleviate psychological disorders in children, adolescents, and young adults up to age 26, as well as to build mental health providers' capacity. The mini-grants will provide funds for the purchase of clinical reference and resource materials for these purposes. Grant requests of up to $7,500 will be considered for mental health providers requesting reference materials for multiple sites within an agency. Grant requests of up to $3,000 will be considered for mental health providers requesting reference materials for one site. The Foundation anticipates making 30-45 awards. Applicants must mail or hand-deliver a letter of application (along with required supporting materials) by October 31. Guidelines are available at the grant website. Questions may be directed to the Program Officer. A FAQ is also available at the grant website. Award checks are distributed November 30.
Requirements: Letters of application from community-based organizations must have the Executive Director/CEO's original signature. Requests from school districts, private schools, or charter schools must have the Superintendent/School Headmaster's original signature.
Restrictions: Only one request per community-based organization, charter school, private school or school district will be accepted. Mini-grant monies may not be used for: the purchase of office equipment, furniture or supplies; computers or smart boards; non-mental health reference materials or consumable items; screening or assessment tools; subscriptions to journals/newsletters; professional development or staff training; staff salaries or other general operating expense; or for capital improvements. Certain general restrictions apply to all grant-seeking organizations. The Foundation makes grants only to: tax-exempt organizations with 501(c)3 tax-exempt status from the Internal Revenue Service that are neither private foundations nor described as 509(a)3 organizations; diocesan and public school districts; charter schools; and to nonprofit public benefit corporations. Organizations must be located in and primarily serve residents of one of the following geographic areas: Barnstable County, Massachusetts; Dukes County, Massachusetts; Essex County, Massachusetts; Nantucket County, Massachusetts; Erie County, New York; or Niagara County, New York. The Foundation does not provide funds that: may be used for the private benefit of any grant recipient or affiliated person; attempt to influence legislation; attempt to influence or intervene in any political campaign; support capital campaigns or improvements; support individual scholarships; provide general operating support; or that subsidize individuals for the cost of care.
Geographic Focus: Massachusetts, New York
Date(s) Application is Due: Oct 31
Contact: Tracy A. Sawicki, Executive Director; (716) 689-0370; fax (716) 689-3716; info@thetowerfoundation.org or tas@thetowerfoundation.org
Internet: http://www.thetowerfoundation.com/WhatWeFund/MentalHealth/MH-RRMaterialsMiniGrant
Sponsor: Peter and Elizabeth C. Tower Foundation
2351 North Forest Road
Getzville, NY 14068-1225

Peter and Elizabeth C. Tower Foundation Organizational Scholarships 3838
Elizabeth Nelson Clarke was born in Mt. Vernon, New York, in 1920, and Peter Tower in Niagara Falls, New York, in 1921. They met while attending Cornell University and married in the summer of 1942. Peter entered the Army Air Force in January 1943. After serving in Texas and Europe, he took a "temporary" clerk job for the family's customhouse broker business C. J. Tower and Sons. Two daughters, Mollie and Cynthia, were born in 1944 and 1947. Although he had hoped to find work in the fledgling air transport business which he expected to thrive, he stayed with Tower and Sons to see the partnership evolve into a corporation. In 1986 it processed a total of $45 billion worth of merchandise and Peter then sold the business to McGraw-Hill Inc. who later sold it to the Federal Express Company, which utilizes Tower skills and systems worldwide. Meanwhile, Liz, who had studied art at Cornell, had become a notable artist, working mostly in oils. True to other personal philosophies, Peter and Liz knew that with prosperity came responsibility. Their desire was to assure that the resources they had acquired over the years were put to good use and that the benefits were spread among many. Formed December 31, 1990, the Peter and Elizabeth C. Tower Foundation seeks to support community programming that will help children, adolescents, and young adults affected by substance abuse, learning disabilities, mental illness, and intellectual disabilities achieve their full potential. Recognizing the benefits of using existing community programming aimed at building organizational infrastructure, the Tower Foundation partners with local providers to offer organizational scholarships for selected programs at the Canisius College Center for Professional Development, the University at Buffalo Institute for Nonprofit Agencies, the Boston University Institute for Nonprofit Management and Leadership, the Merrimack College's Non-Profit Certificate Program, and the Martha's Vineyard Donors Collaborative. More information is available at the grant website.
Restrictions: Funding is limited to organizations whose service recipients are children, adolescents, and young adults to age 26 affected by mental illness, intellectual disabilities, learning disabilities, and/or substance abuse. The Foundation makes grants only to 501(c)3 organizations that are neither private foundations nor described as 509(a)3 organizations, diocesan and public school districts, charter schools, and nonprofit public benefit corporations. Organizations must be located in and primarily serve residents of one of the following geographic areas: Barnstable County, Massachusetts; Dukes County, Massachusetts; Essex County, Massachusetts; Nantucket County, Massachusetts; Erie County, New York; or Niagara County, New York.

Geographic Focus: Massachusetts, New York
Contact: Tracy A. Sawicki, Executive Director; (716) 689-0370; fax (716) 689-3716; info@thetowerfoundation.org or tas@thetowerfoundation.org
Internet: http://www.thetowerfoundation.com/WhatWeFund/OrganizationalCapacity-Building/OrganizationalScholarships
Sponsor: Peter and Elizabeth C. Tower Foundation
2351 North Forest Road
Getzville, NY 14068-1225

Peter and Elizabeth C. Tower Foundation Phase II Technology Initiative Grants 3839
The Peter and Elizabeth C. Tower Technology Initiative program connects not-for-profit organizations to technological expertise in order to develop and execute a strategic technology plan. A strategic technology plan aligns an organization's administrative and business needs (as outlined in the organization's strategic plan) with its technology needs thus allowing it to function more efficiently and effectively. The application process for the technology initiative grants occurs in two phases: in Phase I, the foundation provides funds to hire a technology consultant to conduct a technology inventory and needs assessment and to assist an organization in developing a three-to-five-year technology plan; in Phase II, the foundation provides a dollar-for-dollar match (up to $125,000) to organizations wishing to implement their technology plans. The Tower Foundation anticipates making multiple Phase II awards in each of the geographic areas it serves. Each matching grant will be for a time period of up to three years; funds will be disbursed each year, not as a single lump sum. Grant awards will vary. The foundation does not accept unsolicited proposals. Applicants must first call the foundation to clarify the intent, scope, and details of the technology initiative; establish the organization's eligibility for the initiative; and to discuss their capacity and readiness to implement their strategic technology plan. Based on this telephone call, the foundation will determine whether or not it wishes to request a full application from the organization. Arrangements for this pre-screening telephone call must be made prior to January 6 for the summer cycle, or July 6 for the winter cycle. The deadline for full proposals is March 14 for the summer cycle and September 12 for the winter cycle. Successful applicants will be notified by June 15 or December 15. More thorough information on the application process is available at the grant website. Details on Phase I of the application process are also available at the website.
Requirements: Organizations must be located in and primarily serve residents of one of the following geographic areas: Barnstable County, Massachusetts; Dukes County, Massachusetts; Essex County, Massachusetts; Nantucket County, Massachusetts; Erie County, New York; or Niagara County, New York. Organizations must focus on the following: providing services for children, adolescents and young adults to age 26 with intellectual disabilities; treating mental illness among children, adolescents and young adults to age 26; or preventing or treating substance abuse among children, adolescents and young adults to age 26. To be eligible for Phase II technology initiative grants, organizations must have already developed a strategic technology plan (based on an up-to-date strategic plan) that recommends specific technologies/policies/practices, identifies their relationship to administrative needs, and provides an estimated implementation budget for each recommendation. Preference will be given to technology plans that also do the following: identify the current state of the organization's technology (including network infrastructure, desktop/server hardware and software, staff skills and training needs, end-user support, periodic systems maintenance, and current practices, policies, procedures, and documentation); place a priority on each recommendation, as well as identify benefits associated with each recommendation and consequences of failing to implement recommendations; and propose an implementation timeline and replacement schedule. Organizations funded through this initiative are expected to provide dollar for dollar matching funds for the Tower Foundation's award. These funds may be obtained through any source of unrestricted funds or awards designated for the technology implementation project specifically.
Restrictions: The foundation makes technology initiative grants only to private and charter schools, nonprofit public benefit corporations, and organizations with 501(c)3 tax-exempt status that are neither private foundations nor described as 509(a)3 organizations. Diocesan and public school districts are not eligible to apply for technology initiative grants. Phase II grant money may not used for the following: the private benefit of any grant recipient or affiliated person; endowments; non-technology capital projects or campaigns; the development of an organization's strategic plan; the development of a strategic technology plan; the development of custom software applications or websites; advanced information technology training or certifications; general operating support; or individual scholarships. Please note that the RFP does not provide funds for hiring new staff nor does it provide funds for existing staff to conduct Phase II technology-initiative-grant activities.
Geographic Focus: Massachusetts, New York
Date(s) Application is Due: Mar 14; Sep 12
Amount of Grant: Up to 125,000 USD
Contact: Tracy A. Sawicki, Executive Director; (716) 689-0370; fax (716) 689-3716; info@thetowerfoundation.org or tas@thetowerfoundation.org
Internet: http://www.thetowerfoundation.com/WhatWeFund/OrganizationalCapacity-Building/TechnologyInitiative/PhaseII2012
Sponsor: Peter and Elizabeth C. Tower Foundation
2351 North Forest Road
Getzville, NY 14068-1225

Peter and Elizabeth C. Tower Foundation Phase I Technology Initiative Grants 3840
The Peter and Elizabeth C. Tower Technology Initiative program connects not-for-profit organizations to technological expertise in order to develop and execute a strategic technology plan. A strategic technology plan aligns an organization's administrative and business needs (as outlined in the organization's strategic plan) with its technology needs thus allowing it to function more efficiently and effectively. The application process for the technology initiative grants occurs in two phases: in Phase I, the foundation provides funds to hire a technology consultant to conduct a technology inventory and needs assessment

and to assist an organization in developing a three-to-five-year technology plan; in Phase II, the foundation provides a dollar-for-dollar match (up to $125,000) to organizations wishing to implement their technology plans. The Tower Foundation anticipates making multiple Phase I awards in each of the geographic areas it serves. Each grant will be for a one-year time period. Grant awards will range from $10,000 to $50,000 depending on the size of the organization and the complexity of its business needs. The foundation does not accept unsolicited proposals. Applicants must first call the foundation to clarify the intent, scope, and details of the technology initiative; establish the organization's eligibility for the initiative; and to discuss their capacity and readiness to undertake the technology planning process. Based on this telephone call, the foundation will determine whether or not it wishes to request a full application from the organization. Arrangements for this pre-screening telephone call must be made prior to January 6 for the summer funding cycle, or July 6 for the winter funding cycle. The deadline for full proposals is March 14 for the summer cycle and September 12 for the winter cycle. Successful applicants will be notified by June 15 or December 15. More information on the application process is available at the grant website. Details on Phase II of the application process are also available at the website.
Requirements: Organizations must be located in and primarily serve residents of one of the following geographic areas: Barnstable County, Massachusetts; Dukes County, Massachusetts; Essex County, Massachusetts; Nantucket County, Massachusetts; Erie County, New York; or Niagara County, New York. Organizations must focus on the following: providing services for children, adolescents and young adults to age 26 with intellectual disabilities; preventing or treating mental illness among children, adolescents and young adults to age 26; or preventing or treating substance abuse among children, adolescents and young adults to age 26. Additionally, organizations must have completed a strategic planning document within the past 36 months explicitly identifying technology as a focal area.
Restrictions: The foundation makes technology initiative grants only to private and charter schools, nonprofit public benefit corporations, and organizations with 501(c)3 tax-exempt status that are neither private foundations nor described as 509(a)3 organizations. Diocesan and public school districts are not eligible to apply for technology initiative grants. Phase I grant money may not used for the following: the private benefit of any grant recipient or affiliated person; endowments; capital projects or campaigns; staffing costs associated with technology planning or implementation; the development of an agency's strategic plan; general operating support; individual scholarships; or the purchase of computer hardware or software.
Geographic Focus: Massachusetts, New York
Date(s) Application is Due: Mar 14; Sep 12
Amount of Grant: 10,000 - 50,000 USD
Contact: Tracy A. Sawicki, Executive Director; (716) 689-0370 x206; fax (716) 689-3716; info@thetowerfoundation.org or tas@thetowerfoundation.org
Internet: http://www.thetowerfoundation.com/WhatWeFund/OrganizationalCapacity-Building/TechnologyInitiative/PhaseI-2012
Sponsor: Peter and Elizabeth C. Tower Foundation
2351 North Forest Road
Getzville, NY 14068-1225

Peter and Elizabeth C. Tower Foundation Social and Emotional Preschool Curriculum Grants 3841

Elizabeth Nelson Clarke was born in Mt. Vernon, New York, in 1920, and Peter Tower in Niagara Falls, New York, in 1921. They met while attending Cornell University and married in the summer of 1942. Two daughters, Mollie and Cynthia, were born in 1944 and 1947. Peter entered the Army Air Force in January 1943. After service in Texas and Europe, he hoped to find work in the fledgling air transport business which he expected to thrive. Taking a "temporary" clerk job for the family's customhouse broker business C. J. Tower and Sons, he stayed on to see the partnership evolve into a corporation. In 1986 it processed a total of $45 billion worth of merchandise and Peter then sold the business to McGraw-Hill Inc. who later sold it to the Federal Express Company, which utilizes Tower skills and systems worldwide. Meanwhile, Liz, who had studied art at Cornell, had become a notable artist, working mostly in oils. True to other personal philosophies, Peter and Liz knew that with prosperity came responsibility. Their desire was to assure that the resources they had acquired over the years were put to good use and to see the benefits spread among many. Formed December 31, 1990, the Peter and Elizabeth C. Tower Foundation seeks to support community programming that will help children, adolescents, and young adults affected by substance abuse, learning disabilities, mental illness, and intellectual disabilities achieve their full potential. The foundation's Social and Emotional Preschool Curriculum Grants provide funds to implement selected preschool curricula to enhance the social-emotional development of preschool children. Eligible social-emotional curricula include: "Al's Pals: Kids Making Healthy Choices"; "The Incredible Years: Dina Dinosaur Classroom Curriculum Preschool"; "PATHS Preschool (Promoting Alternative-Thinking Strategies)"; "Second Step"; and "Tools of the Mind." Grants awards will be for two or three years with grant payments made annually. Funding levels will depend on the specific curriculum selected. In general funds may be used for the cost of training and technical assistance from program developers or publishers, including travel expense; direct program expense including materials and equipment supporting curriculum implementation; and substitute teacher or stipends for out-of-school time training expenses, if applicable. The Social and Emotional Preschool Curriculum Grants have a two-step application process. Applicants must submit a pre-application by 5:00 p.m. on December 1; selected applicants must submit a full proposal by February 9; grantees will be notified by May 6. Further information on the grant application process, including downloadable forms, are available at the grant website. Deadline dates may vary from cycle to cycle. Interested organizations are encouraged to visit the website to verify current deadline dates.
Requirements: The pre-application must be mailed or hand-delivered to the Chief Program Officer. The foundation requires organizations to commit to the highest level of staff training available. However, only those costs associated with the specific training and technical assistance recommended and provided by program developers or publishers will be permitted.
Restrictions: emailed or faxed proposals are not accepted. Social and Emotional Preschool Curriculum Grants do not provide funds for existing personnel expense or to hire new staff. The foundation will accept only one request for a single curriculum from each eligible organization. Certain general restrictions apply to all grant-seeking organizations. The Foundation makes grants only to: tax-exempt organizations with 501(c)3 tax-exempt status from the Internal Revenue Service that are neither private foundations nor described as 509(a)3 organizations; diocesan and public school districts; charter schools; and to nonprofit public benefit corporations. Organizations must be located in and primarily serve residents of one of the following geographic areas: Barnstable County, Massachusetts; Dukes County, Massachusetts; Essex County, Massachusetts; Nantucket County, Massachusetts; Erie County, New York; or Niagara County, New York. The Foundation does not provide funds that: may be used for the private benefit of any grant recipient or affiliated person; attempt to influence legislation; attempt to influence or intervene in any political campaign; support capital campaigns or improvements; support individual scholarships; provide general operating support; or that subsidize individuals for the cost of care.
Geographic Focus: Massachusetts, New York
Date(s) Application is Due: Feb 9
Contact: Tracy A. Sawicki, Executive Director; (716) 689-0370; fax (716) 689-3716; info@thetowerfoundation.org or tas@thetowerfoundation.org
Internet: http://www.thetowerfoundation.com/WhatWeFund/MentalHealth/2011SocialandEmotionalPreschoolRFPs
Sponsor: Peter and Elizabeth C. Tower Foundation
2351 North Forest Road
Getzville, NY 14068-1225

Peter and Elizabeth C. Tower Foundation Substance Abuse Grants 3842

Elizabeth Nelson Clarke was born in Mt. Vernon, New York, in 1920, and Peter Tower in Niagara Falls, New York, in 1921. They met while attending Cornell University and married in the summer of 1942. Peter entered the Army Air Force in January 1943. After serving in Texas and Europe, he took a "temporary" clerk job for the family's customhouse broker business C. J. Tower and Sons. Two daughters, Mollie and Cynthia, were born in 1944 and 1947. Although he had hoped to find work in the fledgling air transport business which he expected to thrive, he stayed with Tower and Sons to see the partnership evolve into a corporation. In 1986 it processed a total of $45 billion worth of merchandise and Peter then sold the business to McGraw-Hill Inc. who later sold it to the Federal Express Company, which utilizes Tower skills and systems worldwide. Meanwhile, Liz, who had studied art at Cornell, had become a notable artist, working mostly in oils. True to other personal philosophies, Peter and Liz knew that with prosperity came responsibility. Their desire was to assure that the resources they had acquired over the years were put to good use and that the benefits were spread among many. Formed December 31, 1990, the Peter and Elizabeth C. Tower Foundation supports community programming that helps children, adolescents, and young adults affected by substance abuse, learning disabilities, mental illness, and intellectual disabilities achieve their full potential. Substance Abuse is defined as the use of illegal drugs or the use of prescription or over-the-counter drugs or alcohol for purposes other than those prescribed, or in excessive amounts. Substance abuse may lead to social, physical, emotional, and job-related problems. The Tower Foundation is conducting research on the current state of the field. The foundation plans to offer grant opportunities to organizations that offer treatment/programming for substance abusers after it completes the study. These organizations are encouraged to check the grant website in 2012.
Requirements: Eligible organizations must focus on providing services and programming that help children, adolescents, and young adults affected by substance abuse, learning disabilities, mental illness, and intellectual disabilities to achieve their full potential.
Restrictions: Certain general restrictions apply to all grant-seeking organizations. The Foundation makes grants only to: tax-exempt organizations with 501(c)3 tax-exempt status that are neither private foundations nor described as 509(a)3 organizations; diocesan and public school districts; charter schools; and to nonprofit public benefit corporations. Organizations must be located in and primarily serve residents of one of the following geographic areas: Barnstable County, Massachusetts; Dukes County, Massachusetts; Essex County, Massachusetts; Nantucket County, Massachusetts; Erie County, New York; or Niagara County, New York. The Foundation does not provide funds for the following purposes: the private benefit of any grant recipient or affiliated person; attempts to influence legislation; attempts to influence or intervene in any political campaign; capital campaigns or improvements; individual scholarships; general operating support; or subsidy of individuals for the cost of care.
Geographic Focus: Massachusetts, New York
Contact: Tracy A. Sawicki, Executive Director; (716) 689-0370; fax (716) 689-3716; info@thetowerfoundation.org or tas@thetowerfoundation.org
Internet: http://www.thetowerfoundation.com/WhatWeFund/SubstanceAbuse
Sponsor: Peter and Elizabeth C. Tower Foundation
2351 North Forest Road
Getzville, NY 14068-1225

Peter and Georgia Angelos Foundation Grants 3843

The foundation awards grants, primarily in Baltimore, MD, in its areas of interest, including higher education, scholarships, philanthropy, and Roman Catholic churches and organizations.
Geographic Focus: Maryland
Amount of Grant: 10,000 - 40,000 USD
Contact: Grants Administrator
Sponsor: Peter and Georgia Angelos Foundation
100 N Charles Street, 22nd Floor
Baltimore, MD 21201

Peter F. Drucker Award for Canadian Nonprofit Innovation 3844
The award honors the development of leadership and projects aimed at improving the performance of nonprofit organizations, particularly those aimed at dismantling the walls separating the nonprofit, business, and government arenas. The winning program receives a monetary prize, recognition at a special ceremony, and documentation of the program's story.
Requirements: Registered Canadian nonprofit organizations are eligible. The program or project submitted must have been started no earlier than January 1, 1998, and only one entry may be submitted by an organization.
Geographic Focus: All States, Canada
Amount of Grant: 2,000 - 20,000 CAD
Contact: Jacline Nyman, Chairperson; (416) 979-3939; canada@innovation-award.ca
Internet: http://www.innovation-award.ca/aboutdruckeraward.html
Sponsor: Peter F. Drucker Canadian Foundation
215 Spadina Avenue, Suite 120
Toronto, ON M5T 2C7 Canada

Peter Kiewit Foundation General Grants 3845
The foundation supports nonprofits and individuals in designated geographic areas for arts and cultural programs, higher and other education, health care, human services, youth services, rural development, community development, and government/public administration. In the general purpose grants program, there are no limitations on the size or duration of the grants that may be requested. Any applicant may submit a total of up to two applications, for two separate projects, in any 12 month period. All Peter Kiewit Foundation grants are awarded on a matching funds basis.
Requirements: Grant application guidelines and application forms are required to submit a funding request and these materials are available through the Foundation office only. Potential applicants should contact the Foundation to establish an organization's eligibility to apply and to discuss the proposed project. Nonprofit 501(c)3 organizations in Rancho Mirage, California; western Iowa; Nebraska; and Sheridan, Wyoming are eligible for a maximum of 50% of the total project cost. Units of government (tax supported) in Rancho Mirage, California; western Iowa; Nebraska; and Sheridan, Wyoming may apply for a maximum of 25% of the total project cost.
Restrictions: Grants are not awarded to support elementary or secondary schools, churches, or religious groups. Grants are not awarded to individuals (except for scholarships), or for endowment funds or annual campaigns.
Geographic Focus: California, Iowa, Nebraska, Wyoming
Date(s) Application is Due: Jan 15; Apr 15; Jul 15; Oct 15
Amount of Grant: 10,000 - 500,000 USD
Contact: Lynn Wallin Ziegenbein, (402) 344-7890; fax (402) 344-8099
Internet: http://www.peterkiewitfoundation.org/page.aspx?id=13&pid=3
Sponsor: Peter Kiewit Foundation
8805 Indian Hills Drive, Suite 225
Omaha, NE 68114-4096

Peter Kiewit Foundation Neighborhood Grants 3846
Peter Kiewit Neighborhood Grants are awarded annually to help organized Omaha neighborhood associations develop or complete projects that enhance or improve neighborhood safety, appearance, beautification, and organization. Projects should also encourage neighborhood participation. Grants are awarded on a matching funds basis or issued as a challenge. No more than 50% of the total project cost will be considered. The maximum award is $10,000. Application materials are available from the Peter Kiewit Foundation office. The current application deadline for this program is February 1.
Requirements: Grant application guidelines and application forms are required to submit a funding request and these materials are available through the Foundation office only. Potential applicants should contact the Foundation to establish an organization's eligibility to apply and to discuss the proposed project. Organized neighborhood associations in Omaha, Nebraska are eligible to apply.
Restrictions: Grants are not awarded to support elementary or secondary schools, churches, or religious groups. Grants are not awarded to individuals (except for scholarships), or for endowment funds or annual campaigns.
Geographic Focus: Nebraska
Date(s) Application is Due: Feb 1
Contact: Lynn Wallin Ziegenbein, (402) 344-7890; fax (402) 344-8099
Internet: http://www.peterkiewitfoundation.org/page.aspx?id=15&pid=3
Sponsor: Peter Kiewit Foundation
8805 Indian Hills Drive, Suite 225
Omaha, NE 68114-4096

Peter Kiewit Foundation Small Grants 3847
The foundation supports nonprofits and individuals in designated geographic areas for arts and cultural programs, higher and other education, health care, human services, youth services, rural development, community development, and government/public administration. The small grants program allows the Trustees to assist a large number of worthy organizations with a broad array of small projects which are limited in scope but significant for the organization. Small grants are rarely awarded to large organizations. Small grants range in size from $500 to $10,000. The Trustees created this category of grants to support small, defined projects; not to contribute small amounts to much larger budgets.
Requirements: Grant application guidelines and application forms are required to submit a funding request and these materials are available through the Foundation office only. Potential applicants should contact the Foundation to establish an organization's eligibility to apply and to discuss the proposed project. Nonprofit 501(c)3 organizations in Rancho Mirage, California; western Iowa; Nebraska; and Sheridan, Wyoming are eligible for a maximum of 50% of the total project cost. Units of government (tax supported) in Rancho Mirage, California; western Iowa; Nebraska; and Sheridan, Wyoming may apply for a maximum of 25% of the total project cost.
Restrictions: Grants are not awarded to support elementary or secondary schools, churches, or religious groups. Grants are not awarded to individuals (except for scholarships), or for endowment funds or annual campaigns.
Geographic Focus: California, Iowa, Nebraska, Wyoming
Date(s) Application is Due: Jan 15; Apr 15; Jul 15; Oct 15
Contact: Lynn Wallin Ziegenbein, (402) 344-7890; fax (402) 344-8099
Internet: http://www.peterkiewitfoundation.org/page.aspx?id=14&pid=3
Sponsor: Peter Kiewit Foundation
8805 Indian Hills Drive, Suite 225
Omaha, NE 68114-4096

Peter M. Putnam Foundation Grants 3848
The Peter M. Putnam Foundation is a 501(c)3 organization which supports programs for children and youth of northwest communities that are affected by the crisis of poverty and lack of opportunity. It works to help young boys and girls to discover organized sports, a safe and healthy alternative to risky behaviors during the after-school hours, which are the peak times for youth violence and victimization. Sports activities are often the catalyst for these kids to develop leadership and teamwork skills that will be necessary throughout the rest of their lives. There are no specific deadlines, and an online application is available at the website.
Geographic Focus: Idaho, Oregon, Washington
Contact: Chris Turnley; (206) 790-1315; fax (206) 770-7253; cturnley@putnamfoundation.org
Internet: http://www.putnamfoundation.com/index.asp
Sponsor: Peter M. Putnam Foundation
4580 Klahanie Drive SE, #195
Issaquah, WA 98029

Peter Norton Family Foundation Grants 3849
Created by the founder of Norton Utilities, the Foundation's grantmaking focuses primarily on the support of contemporary visual art. The Foundation also targets a small amount of funds to programs dealing with women and children, education, and parenting projects. There are no deadlines although the Foundation has a monthly funding cycle. The average grant ranges from $1,000 to $50,000. Typically, the board meets at the end of each month to consider pending requests. If the board decides to award a grant, additional documentation will be requested, including 501(c)3 documentation, a board list, and financial statement. An informal report of grant expenditures is required at the end of the grantee's fiscal year. The foundation also offers technical assistance and equipment grants to local nonprofits.
Geographic Focus: California
Contact: Anne Etheridge, Executive Director; (310) 576-7700; fax (310) 576-7701
Sponsor: Peter Norton Family Foundation
225 Arizona Avenue, Suite 350
Santa Monica, CA 90401

Petra Foundation Fellows Awards 3850
The foundation's mission is to recognize, encourage, and support unsung individuals who are making distinctive contributions to human freedom. Fellows are selected on the basis of their work in support of racial justice; the autonomy of individuals, groups, families, or communities; and the defense of freedom of speech and expression. While most nominations and fellows come from within the United States, a few individuals from outside the country have received awards. Award decisions are reached in mid-April. A formal announcement and awards ceremony is held in Washington, DC, each June. Nomination guidelines and form are available online.
Geographic Focus: All States
Date(s) Application is Due: Feb 12
Contact: Meg Fidler; (212) 665-6673; fax (212) 864-4924; info@petrafoundation.org
Internet: http://www.petrafoundation.org/nominations.html
Sponsor: Petra Foundation
315 Duke Ellington Boulevard, 16C
New York, NY 10025

PetSmart Charities Conference Sponsorship Grants 3851
PetSmart Charities is an independent, nonprofit 501(c)3 organization that creates and supports programs to save the lives of homeless pets, raise awareness of companion animal welfare issues, and promote healthy relationships between people and pets. PetSmart Charities is the largest funder of animal-welfare efforts in North America. Grants are available to organizers of national, regional, or statewide training conferences. Conference sponsorships are available to non-profit, municipal or tribal organizations in the United States and Canada that organize or host training events for the animal welfare community. Priority is given to training opportunities which focus on the issues of caring for homeless pets, spay/neuter, pet adoptions, animal non-profit management, and other topics that assist animal welfare agencies with their primary work. There are no deadlines.
Restrictions: Funding is limited each year. Apply at least three months before the conference date. Grants do not support individual conference attendance fees, building projects, general operating budgets, endowments, or programs that protect wildlife or endangered species. Grants cannot provide assistance with fundraising events or donation of items.
Geographic Focus: All States
Contact: Meredith Jones, Program Contact; (800) 423-7387 or (623) 580-6100; fax (623) 580-6561; mjones@charities.org or info@petsmartcharities.org
Internet: http://www.petsmartcharities.org/grants/types/conference-sponsorship-grants.html
Sponsor: PetSmart Charities
19601 N 27th Avenue
Phoenix, AZ 85027

PetSmart Charities Free-Roaming Cat Spay-Neuter Grants 3852

The free-roaming cat grant offered by PetSmart Charities provides funding, strategic planning, and mentoring for a comprehensive trap-neuter-return (TNR) program for free-roaming cats. The goal is to build a program that is community-wide in scope, effective in reducing the local feral and stray cat population, efficient in its use of resources, measurable in impact and sustainable over a period of years to come. Grant recipients are expected to complete a detailed assessment of the conditions and resources in their community related to free-roaming cats. Upon completion of the assessment, the applicant will work with PetSmart Charities staff to formulate a strategic plan for building an effective TNR program in the applicant's community. Grant recipients will also receive ongoing mentoring during the grant period. Applicants should check the grant website for current summer/fall and winter/spring deadlines. The grant application is available online.
Requirements: Applicants are strongly encouraged to view the webinars posted on the website, as well as the Grants FAQs for helpful hints in the application process. The quality and detail of the application and strategic plan, as well as the applicant's capacity and willingness to collect and report data before and after the grant, is important. Follow up reports require data to track the progress of the project, particularly if the problem improved as a result of the grant and mentoring provided by PetSmart. Applicants should update their organization's profile on GuideStar.org as information pertinent to the application is obtained from this site.
Restrictions: Organizations are eligible to apply for only one of the two spay/neuter grants (targeted spay/neuter and free-roaming cat) at a time. Because of the length of time to review and process grant applications, applicants are encouraged to apply early within the application period.
Geographic Focus: All States
Amount of Grant: 10,000 - 100,000 USD
Contact: Meredith Jones, Program Contact; (800) 523-7586 or (623) 580-6100; fax (623) 580-6561; mjones@charities.org or info@petsmartcharities.org
Internet: http://www.petsmartcharities.org/grants/types/free-roaming-cat-neuter-program.html
Sponsor: PetSmart Charities
19601 N 27th Avenue
Phoenix, AZ 85027

PetSmart Charities Grants for Canadian Agencies 3853

Grants are available to organizers of national, regional, or statewide training conferences. Conference sponsorships are available to non-profit, municipal or tribal organizations in the United States and Canada that organize or host training events for the animal welfare community. Priority is given to training opportunities which focus on the issues of caring for homeless pets, spay/neuter, pet adoptions, animal non-profit management, and other topics that assist animal welfare agencies with their primary work. There are no deadlines. PetSmart Charities offers Canadian grants separately from U.S. grants. The website posts updated information and webinars for the current application process, including what "high impact" projects PetSmart is seeking. See website for details on the application process and examples of awarded grants.
Restrictions: The grant is limited to Canada only. Limited funding is available for each province, and competition is high. Grants are not guaranteed and are only open to registered charities.
Geographic Focus: Canada
Contact: Meredith Jones, Program Contact; (800) 523-7586; canadiangrants@petsmartcharities.org or info@petsmartcharities.org
Internet: http://www.petsmartcharities.org/grants/types/canada-grants.html
Sponsor: PetSmart Charities
19601 N 27th Avenue
Phoenix, AZ 85027

PetSmart Charities Model Volunteering Grants 3854

The PetSmart Charities Model Volunteering Grants reward agencies for innovative volunteer programs that best utilize the time, skills, and passion of their volunteers for outstanding results. PetSmart is looking for creative solutions to maximize volunteer contributions in animal welfare agencies so they can share these programs with other agencies across the United States. Each quarter, PetSmart selects one winning agency from submitted volunteer programs. The winning agency receives $1,000, will be featured on PetSmart's website and in Quarterly, the newsletter for and about PetSmart's animal welfare partners.
Requirements: Applicants should discuss their agency's stellar volunteer programs, showcasing the ways it utilizes volunteers by answering the following questions: how they challenge volunteers to work smarter, not just harder; and how their agency demonstrates the leadership to guide their volunteers into strong programs that impact adoptions, fundraising, and day-to-day operations. See website for examples of programs recently funded.
Geographic Focus: All States
Contact: Meredith Jones, Program Contact; (800) 523-7586 or (623) 580-6100; fax (623) 580-6561; mjones@charities.org or info@petsmartcharities.org
Internet: http://www.petsmartcharities.org/grants/types/model-volunteering-program.html
Sponsor: PetSmart Charities
19601 N 27th Avenue
Phoenix, AZ 85027

PetSmart Charities Spay/Neuter Clinic Equipment Grant 3855

PetSmart Charities offers funding toward the purchase of equipment and consumables for start-up or expansion of high-volume spay/neuter clinics in which at least 75% of surgeries are done on public animals (owned cats and dogs and feral and free-roaming cats). The applicant must be able to perform a minimum of 5,000 surgeries per year. PetSmart generally recommends that the applicant's community has a population of 250,000 or more within a 60 mile radium to accomplish this. Eligible funding includes medical/office equipment and consumables (suture material, gloves, etc.) necessary to open or expand a high-volume clinic. There are no deadlines for applying. Applications are accepted year round.
Requirements: Applicants should refer to the website for the appropriate pre-application questionnaire, then view the Starting a High-Volume Spay/Neuter Clinic webinar. Applicants should apply when they are six months or less from opening their clinic. They must have secured their building by lease or purchase and submit a signed copy of the lease or deed with the application. Applicants must have approximately $35,000 or three months of operating funds in reserve. Applicants should agree to provide data for a minimum of 36 months after the funding date to allow PetSmart to measure the results of the program. This includes sharing surgical data by category (species, zip code, age/weight, etc.).
Restrictions: The following equipment is not funded: equipment that has already been purchased on credit or equipment for which the applicant is seeking reimbursement; equipment to replace or update existing items to maintain the current level of surgeries; outfitting of surgery suites solely for in-house shelter or foster animals; salaries and operating costs; start up costs such as the cost to send the team to train at Humane Alliance, renovations, pre-opening salaries, or purchase/rent of a building; and equipment and consumables for clinics primarily serving shelter or foster animals.
Geographic Focus: All States
Contact: Meredith Jones, Program Contact; (800) 523-7586 or (623) 580-6100; fax (623) 580-6561; mjones@charities.org or info@petsmartcharities.org
Internet: http://www.petsmartcharities.org/grants/types/spayneuter-clinic-equipment.html
Sponsor: PetSmart Charities
19601 N 27th Avenue
Phoenix, AZ 85027

PetSmart Charities Targeted Spay/Neuter Grants 3856

PetSmart offers funding for a comprehensive targeted spay/neuter program identifying a segment of the community (geographic, demographic or animal specific) that has a critical need for low-cost spay/neuter services. This critical need must be documented by a combination of indicators that include shelter intake and/or euthanasia data, other assessments, and anecdotal evidence. The final program proposal must include the information about how the applicant's need was determined; a detailed plan to reach the targeted community; the resources in place to provide the surgeries; and the plan to make the community outreach sustainable beyond the grant's time frame. The grantee organization will be required to supply data at the beginning and the end of the project and for a specified time following the grant to help determine the ongoing effects of the targeted program. Success and potential two-year funding will be measured by the organization's ability to meet its stated goals and to accurately document progress made. The grant application is available online. Contact PetSmart for specific quarterly deadlines.
Requirements: Applicants are strongly encouraged to view the webinars posted on the website, as well as the Grants FAQs for helpful hints in the application process. The quality and detail of the application and strategic plan, as well as the applicant's capacity and willingness to collect and report data before and after the grant, is important. Follow up reports require data to track the progress of the project, particularly if the problem improved as a result of the grant and mentoring provided by PetSmart. Applicants should update their organization's profile on GuideStar.org as information pertinent to the application is obtained from this site.
Restrictions: Organizations are eligible to apply for only one of the two spay/neuter grants (targeted spay/neuter and free-roaming cat) at a time.
Geographic Focus: All States
Amount of Grant: 10,000 - 100,000 USD
Contact: Meredith Jones, Program Contact; (800) 523-7586 or (623) 580-6100; fax (623) 580-6561; mjones@charities.org or info@petsmartcharities.org
Internet: http://www.petsmartcharities.org/grants/types/targeted-spay-neuter-program.html
Sponsor: PetSmart Charities
19601 N 27th Avenue
Phoenix, AZ 85027

Pew Charitable Trusts Arts and Culture Grants 3857

The Pew Charitable Trusts supports a broad spectrum of institutions, artists, projects, and cultural marketing initiatives. The Trusts also helps cultural organizations take advantage of technical assistance and professional development opportunities, which has proven to be an effective means of extending the impact of its investments. Pew's objectives in supporting arts and culture are twofold: to nurture artistic excellence and to expand public participation. its efforts have been successful in Philadelphia, where a thriving arts environment has helped raise the city's profile on the world stage and infused new life and energy into the region.
Requirements: Grants are made only to 501(c)3 tax-exempt organizations that are not private foundations.
Restrictions: Grants are not made to individuals or for endowments, capital campaigns, unsolicited construction requests, debt reduction, or scholarships or fellowships that are not part of a program initiated by the Trusts.
Geographic Focus: All States
Contact: Susan A. Magill, Managing Director; (202) 552-2129 or (202) 552-2000; fax (202) 552-2299; smagill@pewtrusts.org or info@pewtrusts.com
Internet: http://www.pewtrusts.org/our_work_category.aspx?id=18
Sponsor: Pew Charitable Trusts
2005 Market Street, Suite 1700
Philadelphia, PA 19103-7077

Pew Charitable Trusts Children and Youth Grants 3858

The Pew Charitable Trusts seeks to study and promote nonpartisan policy solutions for pressing and emerging problems that affect the next generation. Pew supports initiatives, grounded in research and evidence, that aim to help children and youth become active, contributing members of society both in Philadelphia and around the country. At the national level, Pew supports efforts to prevent children from languishing in foster care

without safe, permanent families. Pew works to provide access to high-quality preschool for all three- and four-year-olds, and supports a public health initiative that seeks to reduce young people's exposure to alcohol advertising. Locally, the Pew Fund for Health and Human Services in Philadelphia offers operating and project-specific support to a number of nonprofits that aid youth in the city and four nearby counties.
Requirements: Grants are made only to 501(c)3 tax-exempt organizations that are not private foundations.
Restrictions: Grants are not made to individuals or for endowments, capital campaigns, unsolicited construction requests, debt reduction, or scholarships or fellowships that are not part of a program initiated by the Trusts.
Geographic Focus: All States
Contact: Susan A. Magill, Managing Director; (202) 552-2129 or (202) 552-2000; fax (202) 552-2299; smagill@pewtrusts.org or info@pewtrusts.com
Internet: http://www.pewtrusts.org/our_work_category.aspx?id=4
Sponsor: Pew Charitable Trusts
2005 Market Street, Suite 1700
Philadelphia, PA 19103-7077

Pew Charitable Trusts Special Civic Project Grants 3859
The Pew Charitable Trusts supports initiatives that illuminate our nation's rich history and contribute to an increased understanding of American democracy. Examples of Pew's national civic work include support for a new museum and visitor center at Gettysburg National Military Park and for a new project by noted documentary filmmaker Ken Burns, titled America's Best Idea: Our National Parks. Pew also works to make a difference in the lives of the nation's citizens. It has been a major supporter of the substantial relief efforts undertaken in the aftermath of Hurricane Katrina and other natural disasters, both locally and worldwide.
Requirements: Grants are made only to 501(c)3 tax-exempt organizations that are not private foundations.
Restrictions: Grants are not made to individuals or for endowments, capital campaigns, unsolicited construction requests, debt reduction, or scholarships or fellowships that are not part of a program initiated by the Trusts.
Geographic Focus: All States
Contact: Susan A. Magill, Managing Director; (202) 552-2129 or (202) 552-2000; fax (202) 552-2299; smagill@pewtrusts.org or info@pewtrusts.com
Internet: http://www.pewtrusts.org/our_work_category.aspx?id=42
Sponsor: Pew Charitable Trusts
2005 Market Street, Suite 1700
Philadelphia, PA 19103-7077

Pew Fellowships in the Arts 3860
Fellowships support artists working in a wide variety of performing, visual, and literary disciplines. Awards are made to artists working in 12 different discipline categories, which rotate on a four-year cycle. Applications are accepted annually for the three discipline categories under consideration in that year. Fields of application for the current year are performance art; poetry; and sculpture and installation. The grants provide financial support directly to the artists so that they may have the opportunity to dedicate themselves to creative pursuits exclusively. The program aims to provide such support at moments in artists' careers when a concentration on artistic growth and exploration is most likely to have the greatest impact on an artist's long-term professional development. Guidelines and application are available online. Annual deadline dates may vary; contact program staff for exact dates.
Requirements: All applicants must be practicing artists of demonstrated commitment and professional accomplishment, and be able to provide evidence of such. Refer to specific eligibility requirements under appropriate field of application. Applicants must be verifiable Pennsylvania residents of Bucks, Chester, Delaware, Montgomery, or Philadelphia County for two years or longer immediately prior to the application deadline; and maintain permanent residence in the five-county Philadelphia area through the selection process. Artists who are granted fellowships must maintain permanent residence in the five-county Philadelphia area during their fellowship period.
Restrictions: Artists are not eligible if they are: not able to provide evidence of their professional achievements within their field of application; a matriculated student (full-time or part-time) in a degree-granting program or equivalent at the time of application or during the selection process; a current employee of PFA or The Pew Charitable Trusts, or immediate family member of such an individual; or a previous recipient of a Pew Fellowship in the Arts.
Geographic Focus: Pennsylvania
Date(s) Application is Due: Dec 2
Amount of Grant: 50,000 USD
Contact: Administrator; (215) 875-2285; fax (215) 875-2276; pewarts@mindspring.com
Internet: http://www.pewarts.org/apply.html
Sponsor: Pew Charitable Trusts
2005 Market Street, Suite 1700
Philadelphia, PA 19103-7077

PeyBack Foundation Grants 3861
The PeyBack Foundation was established by NFL quarterback Peyton Manning with the purpose of promoting the future success of disadvantaged youth by assisting programs that provide leadership and growth opportunities for children at risk (ages 6-18). The nature of the programs and their immediate long-term benefit shall be guiding considerations in funding grants. Although the foundation does not have a dollar limit on grant requests, most grant amounts range between $1,500 and $10,000. The deadline to submit a PeyBack Foundation Grant Application is February 1 each year. In order to be considered, all applications must be submitted in entirety to the PeyBack Foundation by this date.
Requirements: Due to the close association of Peyton Manning with the Indiana, Tennessee, Denver, and the New Orleans Metropolitan area, programs and projects related to the youth in these areas are of primary concern to the foundation. Proposals will be only considered from organizations that have tax-exempt status under Section 501(c)3 of the Internal Revenue Code. A proposal asking to consider providing a portion of the support for a project will generally receive greater preference than one seeking exclusive funding. Download the required application form at the website.
Restrictions: The following are not areas that the PeyBack Foundation supports: organizations without 501(c)3 tax-exempt status will immediately be eliminated; Fundraising and sponsorship events (e.g., golf tournaments, telethons, banquets); Groups outside of Indiana, Tennessee and New Orleans, LA; Projects/groups benefiting an individual or just a few persons; Building/renovating expenses of any kind; To defray meeting, conferences, workshops or seminars expenses; Payment of travel of individuals or groups; Re-granting organizations; Post-event fundraising; Multi-year gifts.
Geographic Focus: Colorado, Indiana, Louisiana, Tennessee
Date(s) Application is Due: Feb 1
Amount of Grant: 1,500 - 10,000 USD
Contact: Elizabeth Ellis; (877) 873-9225; PeyBack@PeytonManning.com
Internet: http://www.peytonmanning.com/peyback-foundation/requests/funding-requests
Sponsor: PeyBack Foundation
6325 North Guilford, Suite 201
Indianapolis, IN 46220

Peyton Anderson Foundation Grants 3862
The Peyton Anderson Foundation initiates projects to meet needs in the community and reacts to requests from charitable organizations in Macon, Bibb County, and Middle Georgia.
Requirements: Applicants must serve Macon and/or Bibb County Georgia in order to be considered for funding. Preference is given to organizations that have a substantial presence in Bibb County. Applications can be downloaded from the Foundation's website and must contain the original application plus five (5) copies, including copies of all required application items. In addition, organizations must submit one (1) copy of the organization's current annual operating budget, IRS determination letter, and most recent annual financial statement.
Restrictions: Grants may not be made to private foundations, individuals, private schools, endowments, churches, or for festivals and trips. Grants are also only awarded to organizations with current 501(c)3 status that benefit Macon and Bibb County, Georgia. DO NOT include any forms or information other than what is required above.
Geographic Focus: Georgia
Date(s) Application is Due: Apr 1; Aug 1
Amount of Grant: 1,000 - 500,000 USD
Contact: Juanita T. Jordan; (478) 743-5359; fax (478) 742-5201; jtjordan@pafdn.org
Internet: http://www.peytonanderson.org
Sponsor: Peyton Anderson Foundation
577 Mulberry Street, Suite 830
Macon, GA 31201

Pfizer Healthcare Charitable Contributions 3863
Pfizer's healthcare charitables contributions support the following types of requests/projects: patient education (including health screening); patient advocacy for disease awareness; and improving patient access to care. Funding is currently available in the following clinical areas to support healthcare charitable contributions: arthritis & pain management; Gaucher disease; growth disorders; hemophilia; infectious disease (bacterial, pneumococcal disease prevention); neurology; amyloidosis; dementia; diabetic peripheral neuropathy; fibromyalgia; multiple sclerosis; oncology; breast cancer; gastrointestinal stromal tumors; leukemia (CML and ALL); lung cancer; non-Hodgkin's lymphoma; pancreatic neuroendocrine tumors; renal cell carcinoma; pulmonary arterial hypertension; respiratory (COPD, smoking cessation); rheumatoid arthritis; transplantation (kidney transplant); urology (overactive bladder); and women's health (menopause, cardiovascular risk, depression, bladder health, and sexual health). Applicants have four opportunities during the year to apply for Pfizer's Healthcare Charitable Contributions: from December 1 through January 15 for activities starting in April; March 1 through April 15 for activities starting in July; June 1 through July 15 for activities starting in October; and September 1 through October 15 for activities starting in January. Interested applicants must apply through the Pfizer Grants Application System. Applicants can register and log into the system from the grant webpage. Pfizer, Inc. is an American multinational research-based pharmaceutical company that was founded in 1849 by two cousins Charles Pfizer and Charles Erhart. It topped the 2009 list of America's most generous companies, giving $2.3 billion in products and cash. Most of Pfizer's philanthropic activities are managed by its Corporate Responsibility Department through two foundations, the Pfizer Foundation and the Pfizer Patient Assistance Foundation. Pfizer's philanthropic activities are generally divided among its global health programs, its various grants and contributions programs, and its work with health care professionals. Pfizer's grants and contributions include the following types of support: support for medical, scientific, and patient organizations; lobbying and political contributions; medical education grants; medical and academic partnerships; healthcare charitables; sponsorships; and special events.
Requirements: 501(c)3 organizations are eligible to apply.
Restrictions: Pfizer must not receive any significant value in terms of good or services in return for their donation.
Geographic Focus: All States, All Countries
Date(s) Application is Due: Jan 15; Apr 15; Jul 15; Oct 15
Contact: Caroline Roan; (866) 634-4647 or (212) 209-8997; healthcharitables@pfizer.com
Internet: https://www.pfizerhealthcharitables.com/
Sponsor: Pfizer
235 East 42nd Street
New York, NY 10017-5755

Pfizer Medical Education Track One Grants 3864
The mission of the Pfizer medical-education-grants program is to cooperate with healthcare delivery organizations and professional associations to narrow professional-practice gaps through support of continuing education, learning, and continuous-improvement strategies that result in measurable improvement in competence, performance, or patient outcomes. Applicants may apply for two types of medical-education grants: healthcare quality improvement (track one) grants; and annual meetings for purposes of emerging science/knowledge exchange (track two) grants. For track one the Pfizer Medical Education Group (MEG) will identify, on an annual basis, public health concerns (for which education is likely to improve patient care) and issue Requests for Proposals (RFPs) for training, continuing education, and/or certification in these areas. (As of this update, identified priorities are vaccines, oncology, smoking cessation, pain and inflammation, infectious disease, and women's health.) MEG will post the RFPs at the website and also disseminate them through email to all registered organizations. Application must be made through MEG's online Grant Management System (GMS) which is available at the website. To be considered, applicants must first register with the GMS. Only applicants whose registration has been approved by MEG will be able to submit a letter of intent (LOI) in response to an RFP. From the submitted LOIs, MEG will select semi-finalists who will be invited to submit full proposals. Each published RFP will include submission timelines and a Letter of Intent template. Interested applicants are encouraged to visit the Pfizer website and register with the GMS to receive notice of new RFPs. Pfizer, Inc. is an American multinational research-based pharmaceutical company that was founded in 1849 by two cousins Charles Pfizer and Charles Erhart. It topped the 2009 list of America's most generous companies, giving $2.3 billion in products and cash. Most of Pfizer's philanthropic activities are managed by its Corporate Responsibility Department through two foundations, the Pfizer Foundation and the Pfizer Patient Assistance Foundation. Pfizer's philanthropic activities are generally divided among its global health programs, its various grants and contributions programs, and its work with health care professionals. Pfizer's grants and contributions include the following types of support: support for medical, scientific, and patient organizations; lobbying and political contributions; medical education grants; medical and academic partnerships; healthcare charitables; sponsorships; and special events.
Geographic Focus: All States, All Countries
Contact: Caroline Roan; (866) 634-4647 or (212) 209-8997; healthcharitables@pfizer.com
Internet: www.pfizermededgrants.com
Sponsor: Pfizer
235 East 42nd Street
New York, NY 10017-5755

Pfizer Special Events Grants 3865
Pfizer, Inc. provides limited support to external, independent, not-for-profit organizations for special events, e.g. fundraising dinners, walks, biking and golf events, galas, awards ceremonies, and other similar events that do not provide Pfizer with a tangible benefit. Requests must be submitted at least sixty days prior to the event. Applicants must submit their requests via email to the contact information given. Interested applicants can download a special event brochure from the grant webpage to obtain detailed information about application requirements, processes, and materials. Pfizer, Inc. is an American multinational research-based pharmaceutical company that was founded in 1849 by two cousins Charles Pfizer and Charles Erhart. It topped the 2009 list of America's most generous companies, giving $2.3 billion in products and cash. Most of Pfizer's philanthropic activities are managed by its Corporate Responsibility Department through two foundations, the Pfizer Foundation and the Pfizer Patient Assistance Foundation. Pfizer's philanthropic activities are generally divided among its global health programs, its various grants and contributions programs, and its work with health care professionals. Pfizer's grants and contributions include the following types of support: support for medical, scientific, and patient organizations; lobbying and political contributions; medical education grants; medical and academic partnerships; healthcare charitables; sponsorships; and special events.
Requirements: External, independent, not-for-profit organizations - e.g. patient advocacy groups, professional medical associations, trade associations and other charitable organizations with a 501(c)3 or similar status, are eligible to apply. Events must provide broad public benefit and primarily benefit patient care, advance medical science, or otherwise align with Pfizer's policy or business goals.
Restrictions: Pfizer will not provide funding for the following types of activities: special events that have already occurred; activities aimed at improperly influencing any entity, including but not limited to healthcare professionals and government officials; activities to improperly influence prescribing, formulary positioning, or recommendation of Pfizer products; activities that may result in off-label promotion of Pfizer products; activities that would undermine in any way an organization's independence; activities offered as quid pro quo for service or support; capital support for an organization, including building costs or other similar requests related to "start up" costs; proposals from individual persons; and non-research proposals from individual healthcare professionals or group practices.
Geographic Focus: All States, All Countries
Contact: Sally Susman; (212) 733-2323; publicaffairssupport@pfizer.com
Internet: http://www.pfizer.com/responsibility/grants_contributions/special_events.jsp
Sponsor: Pfizer
235 East 42nd Street
New York, NY 10017-5755

PG&E Bright Ideas Grants 3866
Bright Ideas grants are designed to tap into the expertise and commitment of our teachers and to foster environmental stewardship in our future leaders. This year, PG&E will be awarding more than $400,000 in grants to green school campuses, providing unique environmental learning opportunities for students.
Requirements: Credentialed teachers, professors, instructors, principals, deans, department heads, distinct administrators and facilities managers of K-12 public schools served by PG&E may all apply to receive a $1,000, $2,500, $5,000, or $10,000 grant to promote environmental stewardship in any of the five following categories: educational solar projects; youth energy and environmental programs; renewable energy or science related field trips; green your school projects; and professional development, service learning projects and workforce development programs.
Geographic Focus: California
Date(s) Application is Due: Mar 20; Sep 20
Amount of Grant: 1,000 - 10,000 USD
Contact: Linda Romero; (415) 973-4951 or (800) 743-5000; LMRH@pge.com
Internet: http://www.pge.com/about/community/education/brightideasgrants/
Sponsor: Pacific Gas and Electric Corporation Foundation
P.O. Box 770000, MC B32
San Francisco, CA 94177-0001

PG&E Community Investment Grants 3867
The Community Investment Program focuses on three areas: education, local environment, and community vitality. The education area supports innovative programs that give students and teachers opportunities to learn and prepare for their future, the future of California, and the future of the energy industry. The local environment area supports energy sustainability, environmental conservation, and stewardship of our lands and resources. The grant supports partnerships focused on renewables and energy efficiency as well as local Earth Day projects that help ensure our neighborhoods, parks, and recreation areas remain clean, safe and viable for future generations. Community vitality concentrates on providing assistance to income-qualified families through programs that reduce their utility bills. It partners with local organizations to support emergency preparedness efforts and investments in local economic and energy-related workforce development initiatives. In addition, it supports civic initiatives that bring value to the communities.
Requirements: Applicants must be a 501(c)3 nonprofit organization. They should also provide an opportunity for employee volunteerism, address a demonstrated community need, and live in PG&E's service area. Applicants must complete an online application. Coordination with a PG&E representative is encouraged (see website for area specific program contacts).
Restrictions: PG&E will not fund organizations who discriminate on the basis of race, color, religion, age, sex, national origin, ancestry, physical or mental disability, medical condition, veteran status, marital status, pregnancy, sexual orientation, gender identity, or any basis prohibited by applicable law. Grants may be used for charitable purposes only. Applicants must be, and remain, in compliance with all federal, state, and local laws, rules, and regulations, including if applicable the California Nonprofit Integrity Act of 2004. Applicants and each of their grantees, if any, must be in full compliance with all statutes. See website for further information.
Geographic Focus: California
Date(s) Application is Due: Sep 30
Amount of Grant: Up to 5,000 USD
Contact: Linda Romero, Program Contact; (415) 973-4951; LMRH@pge.com
Internet: http://www.pge.com/about/community/contributions/
Sponsor: Pacific Gas and Electric Corporation Foundation
P.O. Box 770000, MC B32
San Francisco, CA 94177-0001

PG&E Community Vitality Grants 3868
With the goal to strengthen the economic development and social vitality of its communities, the company awards grants to eligible nonprofit organizations located in its service area of northern and central California. Grant making is focused in four primary areas: environmental stewardship—including projects to improve or restore habitat, air and water quality projects, solar and other alternative energy development, and energy efficiency projects; aid to schools—including public schools serving pre-school and K-12 students, universities, teacher training, after-school programs, and kids safety training; emergency preparedness—including efforts to improve community and family disaster preparedness, nonprofit emergency planning, and recovery projects; and, economic vitality—including efforts to retain and expand jobs in local communities, workforce development programs, and policy planning activities. The contributions program is funded throughout the calendar year, however, applications are requested in the fall. Multi-year grants are not awarded. Current grantees must submit a new request for annual funding. An application may be downloaded online. Corporate employee associations also sponsor scholarship programs for college-bound high school students and employees of the company, including the Asian Employees Association, Black Employees Association, Filipino Employees Association, and PrideNetwork.
Requirements: Northern and central California 501(c)3 nonprofit organizations and government programs/agencies in the corporation's service area are eligible.
Restrictions: Grants do not support individuals; tickets for contests, raffles, or other activities with prizes; religious organizations (unless the request specifically supports a program offered to the public on a nondiscriminatory basis and without regard to the recipient's religious affiliation); film, television, or video productions; capital campaigns, endowment funds, academic chairs, or fellowships; debt-reduction campaigns; political and partisan organizations or events; sports tournaments; trips or tours for individuals or groups; talent or beauty contests; or conferences.
Geographic Focus: California
Amount of Grant: 1,000 - 200,000 USD
Contact: Contributions Administrator; (415) 973-4951; charitablecontributions@pge.com
Internet: http://www.pge.com/about_us/community/charitable/index.html
Sponsor: Pacific Gas and Electric Corporation Foundation
P.O. Box 770000, MC B32
San Francisco, CA 94177-0001

PGE Foundation Grants 3869
The foundation awards grants to Oregon nonprofit organizations in its areas of interest, including preschool through college education, healthy families, arts and cultural events, and the environment. The foundation also supports Community 101, a signature program of the foundation that helps high school youth experience the value of community service learning and philanthropy. The program includes student volunteerism and student grant making and is student-led. A PGE Foundation Grant request consists of two steps, both of which are submitted online: Letter of Inquiry (open to all who qualify); and Full Application (at the invitation of the PGE Foundation). Letters of Inquiry are due on: January 12, April 6, July 13, and November 16. The Foundation considers just one request per year from an organization.
Requirements: Applicant organizations must be a 501(c)3 charitable, nonprofit, tax-exempt organizations; and domiciled in Oregon to serve Oregonians.
Restrictions: The following types of requests are not eligible: bridge grants, debt retirement, or operational deficits; endowment funds; general fund drives or annual appeals; requests to support political entities, ballot-measure campaigns, or candidates for political office; requests from organizations that discriminate against individuals on the basis of creed, color, gender, sexual orientation, age, religion, or national origin; requests from fraternal, sectarian, and religious organizations if the grant is intended for the principal benefit of the organization's own members or adherents; any activities or organizations for which support would violate IRS regulations for private foundations; direct grants to individuals; travel expenses; conferences, symposiums, festivals, events, team sponsorships, or user fees; or salaries of employees, with the exception of costs relating directly to the funded project. The foundation generally does not fund capital requests that include building improvements, equipment purchases, or anything considered an asset of the organization.
Geographic Focus: Oregon
Amount of Grant: 1,000 - 25,000 USD
Contact: Carole Morse; (503) 464-8818; fax (503) 464-2929; pgefoundation@pgn.com
Internet: http://www.pgefoundation.org/eligibility.html
Sponsor: PGE Foundation
One World Trade Center, 3rd Floor, 121 SW Salmon Street
Portland, OR 97204

Phelps County Community Foundation Grants 3870
The Phelps County Community Foundation's grants program provides a means by which not-for-profit charitable organizations may secure financial assistance for projects and programs which will enhance the quality of life for residents of Phelps County, Nebraska. The foundation awards grants in the areas of education, culture, human services, health and recreation, and community. Priority is given to seed grants to initiate promising new projects or programs, programs representing innovative and efficient approaches to serving community needs and opportunities, challenge grants, organizations that work cooperatively with other community agencies, projects or programs where a moderate amount of grant money can effect a significant result, and projects or programs that enlist volunteer participation and citizen involvement. Types of support include general operating grants, continuing support grants, building construction/renovation, equipment acquisition, program development, publication, seed money, scholarship funds, and matching grants. Applicants must have a plan for future funding and support from other sources.
Requirements: Grants are made to 501(c)3 nonprofit organizations in Phelps County, Nebraska, and sometimes to governmental agencies for capital expenditures and/or capital improvements within Phelps County.
Restrictions: Grants are not made to individuals, to support political activities, to support operating expenses of well-established organizations or public service agencies, to establish new endowment funds, for travel or related expenses for individuals or groups, for operating support of governmental agencies, to religious groups for religious purposes, to profit-making enterprises, or to agencies serving a populace outside of Phelps County. In addition, grants are not made to support annual fund drives or to eliminate previously incurred deficits.
Geographic Focus: Nebraska
Date(s) Application is Due: Apr 1; Oct 1
Amount of Grant: Up to 25,000 USD
Contact: Vickie Klein; (308) 995-6847; fax (308) 995-2146; vlpccf@phelpsfoundation.org
Internet: http://www.phelpsfoundation.org/grants.html
Sponsor: Phelps County Community Foundation
504 4th Avenue
Holdrege, NE 68949

Phi Kappa Phi Scholar Award 3871
The Phi Kappa Phi Scholar Award honors those who demonstrate the ideals of the Society through their activities, achievements, and scholarship. The Award recognizes excellence in teaching, research, and public service. The Award is given every three years. Chapters and active members are encouraged to nominate an individual for this award; self-nominations are encouraged. Although nominees are often faculty members at colleges and universities, a chapter or any active member may nominate an active Society member who is not institution-affiliated provided all criteria are met. The Award recipient will be presented with a check for $1,000, a one year active membership in Phi Kappa Phi, a recognition certificate, and an invitation to the annual Convention. Travel, lodging and meal expenses incurred by the recipient are reimbursed. Specific criteria and a nomination form are located at the website.
Requirements: Applicants must be Society members in good standing; hold a distinguished record of past scholarly achievements; possess documented evidence of national or international prominence and visibility; demonstrated consistency of excellence in teaching and/or service; and a distinguished record of honors, publications, patents, inventions or other types of recognition for excellence and scholarly achievement.
Geographic Focus: All States, All Countries
Date(s) Application is Due: Feb 15
Amount of Grant: 1,000 USD
Contact: Scholar Award Contact; (800) 804-9880; Scholar@PhiKappaPhi.org
Internet: http://www.phikappaphi.org/Web/Awards/PKP_Scholar_and_Artist.html
Sponsor: Phi Kappa Phi Foundation
7576 Goodwood Boulevard
Baton Rouge, LA 70806

Philadelphia Foundation Organizational Effectiveness Grants 3872
Organizational Effectiveness Grants are designed to strengthen and improve the business and operational practices of nonprofit organizations in Bucks, Chester, Delaware, Montgomery and Philadelphia counties. As in business, these practices are critical to the success of nonprofits' ability to lead, adapt, manage and effectively operate their organizations. These core competencies are critical to nonprofits at all stages of development and size for the effective delivery of services, implementation of best practices, utilization of data to drive decision-making and the ability to adapt to new demands, risks and opportunities. new applications for General Operating Support or Organizational Effectiveness cannot be accepted until January 1st.
Requirements: IRS 501(c)3 tax-exempt organizations located in Bucks, Chester, Delaware, Montgomery, and Philadelphia Counties of Pennsylvania are eligible.
Restrictions: Grants are rarely made to affiliates of national or international organizations, government agencies, organizations not located in Southeastern Pennsylvania, organizations with budgets of more than $1.5 million, private schools, or umbrella-funding organizations. Requests usually are denied for capital campaigns, conferences, deficit financing, endowments, publications, research projects, tours, and trips. Individuals are ineligible.
Geographic Focus: Pennsylvania
Amount of Grant: 3,000 - 30,000 USD
Contact: Libby Walsh, Program Associate; (215) 563-6417; fax (215) 563-6882; lwalsh@philafound.org or oeapplications@philafound.org
Internet: https://www.philafound.org/ForNonprofits/DiscretionaryGrantmaking/OrganizationalEffectiveness/tabid/238/Default.aspx
Sponsor: Philadelphia Foundation
1234 Market Street, Suite 1800
Philadelphia, PA 19107

Philadelphia Foundation YOUTHadelphia Grants 3873
YOUTHadelphia is the youth advisory committee of the Fund for Children. Comprised of a dozen high school students and adult coaches from a diverse set of Philadelphia neighborhoods, schools, and youth organizations, YOUTHadelphia engages youth in grantmaking activities, where they distribute $100,000 annually and develop leadership skills. The Program provides grants of up to $15,000 for youth led and youth engaged projects.
Requirements: IRS 501(c)3 tax-exempt organizations located in Bucks, Chester, Delaware, Montgomery, and Philadelphia Counties of Pennsylvania are eligible.
Geographic Focus: Pennsylvania
Contact: Shawn Mooring, (215) 563-6417; fundforchildren@philafound.org
Internet: https://www.philafound.org/ForNonprofits/DiscretionaryGrantmaking/FundforChildren/tabid/249/Default.aspx
Sponsor: Philadelphia Foundation
1234 Market Street, Suite 1800
Philadelphia, PA 19107

Philanthrofund Foundation Grants 3874
Founded in 1987 the Philanthrofund Foundation (PFund) is one of only a handful of foundations in the nation created specifically by and for LGBT communities. It provides grants to emerging non-profit organizations and projects that would otherwise not get funded, awards scholarships, develops leaders, and inspires giving. PFund manages more than $1.3 million in assets, enjoying the support of committed donors and dedicated volunteers from LGBT and allied communities. PFund awards over $140,000 annually to LGBT-related individuals and organizations throughout the Upper Midwest — in Minnesota, Iowa, North Dakota, South Dakota and Wisconsin. PFund funds nonprofits that focus their programming or projects within one of the following three pillars of social justice: achieving equal rights through advocacy and civic engagement; ensuring access, safety and security in such areas as housing, schools and healthcare; and creating power through community as a result of organizing, events and the arts. Interested organizations must submit a letter of inquiry through PFund's online inquiry system. Guidelines for content are available to download from the grant web page. Letters of inquiry are accepted from June 1 to August 1. From these applicants are selected to submit a full proposal which is due October 1.
Requirements: Eligible organizations must support PFund's mission and vision and satisfy the following criteria: have a program or service area in Minnesota, Iowa, North Dakota, South Dakota and/or Wisconsin; complete and submit a final report for any past grants from PFund; complete PFund's Certificate of Non-discrimination; and have proof of 501(c)3 or 501(c)4 status or a fiscal agent with 501(c)3 or 501(c)4 status. In the selection process, PFund considers the following criteria: whether an applicant's programs benefit LGBT and allied communities; whether a proposal addresses the depth and complexity of critical issues in LGBT communities; whether a proposed program has a clear vision of social change that address intersections of multiple forms of oppression; whether an applicant offers a wide variety of programs, including those that serve targeted populations, e.g., by gender, race and age; whether organizations and programs represent a broad range of fields, e.g., the arts, social change, advocacy, health and wellness, and education; whether organizations and programs have limited appeal to traditional funding sources; and whether genuine collaboration exists among organizations with similar goals that will, whenever possible, result in uniqueness of efforts.
Restrictions: PFund's grant program does not fund the following activities/entities: religious organizations for religious purposes; political campaigns; individual persons; fundraising

events; for-profit organizations; public agencies for mandated services; and projects for the fulfillment of requirements toward a degree-granting program. PFund recognizes the importance of grassroots and direct lobbying efforts for many LGBT organizations and will consider proposals for lobbying efforts on behalf of LGBT issues as a limited part of its annual grant-making cycle, within the limits set by the 501(h) section of the tax code-legislation which allows a certain amount of expenditures by nonprofits to be used for lobbying and advocacy activities. Organizations with an annual budget of less than $500,000 and a mission focus on LGBT people and issues may apply for general operating funds and/or project support. Larger organizations may apply only for project-specific support and are limited to receiving annual support for the same project for no more than three (3) consecutive years. (This is not multi-year project funding; new grant applications must be made annually). In assessing such applications, the foundation is positively influenced by an organization's demonstrated commitment to including LGBT communities and individuals at all levels of the organization and in its activities and programming.
Geographic Focus: Iowa, Minnesota, North Dakota, South Dakota, Wisconsin
Date(s) Application is Due: Oct 1
Amount of Grant: Up to 10,000 USD
Contact: Kayva Yang, Program Officer; (800) 435-1402 or (612) 870-1806; fax (612) 871-6587; kyang@PFundOnline.org or info@PFundOnline.org
Internet: http://www.pfundonline.org/grants.html
Sponsor: Philanthrofund Foundation
1409 Willow Street, Suite 109
Minneapolis, MN 55403

Phil Hardin Foundation Grants 3875
The foundation targets its funding to education. Specific priorities are to strengthen the capacity of communities to nurture and educate young children; the capacity of higher education institutions to renew communities and their economies; the capacity of communities for locally initiated educational improvement and economic development; and state- and local-level policy and leadership initiatives that fit with foundation goals. Types of support include general operating support, continuing support, building construction/renovation, equipment acquisition, endowment funds, program development, conferences and seminars, professorships, publication, seed grants, fellowships, scholarship funds, research, and matching funds. The foundation also operates four K-12 fellowship programs. Deadlines vary between programs; contact program staff for specific fellowship deadlines.
Requirements: Applicants must either be based in Mississippi or the project must benefit Mississippi, depending on the program. Contact program staff for eligibility.
Geographic Focus: All States
Amount of Grant: Up to 6,000,000 USD
Contact: C. Thompson Wacaster, (601) 483-4282; info@philhardin.org
Internet: http://www.philhardin.org
Sponsor: Phil Hardin Foundation
1921 24th Avenue
Meridian, MS 39301

Philip L. Graham Fund Grants 3876
The Philip L. Graham Fund awards grants to organizations in the Washington, D.C. metropolitan area, including Maryland and Virginia to groups providing educational, social, community enrichment, and arts programs and services to communities in and around Washington, D.C. The Fund also supports improvements in journalism on a national scale. Specifically, the Philip L. Graham fund concentrates funding on the areas of arts and humanities, community endeavors, education, health and human services, and journalism and communication.
Requirements: Applicants are required to submit a letter of inquiry through the Fund's online application system before one of three deadline dates (see Key Dates). Organizations must be a tax-exempt 501(c)3 organization to apply and located within the greater Washington D.C. metropolitan area.
Restrictions: Proposals for the following purposes are not considered: advocacy or litigation; research; endowments; special events, conferences workshops or seminars; travel expenses; annual giving campaigns, benefits or sponsorships; courtesy advertising; and production of films or publications. Also, independent schools, institutions of post-secondary education, national or international organizations, and hospitals are not eligible to apply. Grants are also not made to: individuals; religious, political or lobbying activities; to membership organizations; or to any organization that has received a grant from the Fund within the previous thirty-six months.
Geographic Focus: District of Columbia, Maryland, Virginia
Amount of Grant: 5,000 - 150,000 USD
Contact: Eileen F. Daly; (202) 334-6640; fax (202) 334-4498; plgfund@washpost.com
Internet: http://www.plgrahamfund.org/
Sponsor: Philip L. Graham Fund
1150 15th Street NW
Washington, DC 20071

Phi Upsilon Omicron Florence Fallgatter Distinguished Service Award 3877
Phi Upsilon Omicron National Honor Society was founded in 1910 at the University of Minnesota in the area of Family and Consumer Sciences. The society's Florence Fallgatter Distinguished Service Award is granted biennially to a qualified alumni member of the society for outstanding achievement in family and consumer sciences. The recipient's expenses to attend the society's biennial meeting will be paid, and the member will be recognized with a plaque at the meeting. The nomination deadline is November 1. Interested applicants should contact the society for information on nomination procedures.
Requirements: A nominee must exhibit the following characteristics: be an alumni member of the society; have finished his or her bachelor's degree no less than ten years ago; have demonstrated excellence in business, dietetics/nutrition, education, cooperative extension; journalism; research; social services, or volunteer services; and have had a significant positive impact on the family and consumer sciences profession.
Geographic Focus: All States
Date(s) Application is Due: Nov 1
Contact: Susan Rickards; (304) 368-0612; rickards@phiu.org or info@phiu.org
Internet: http://phiu.org/awards.htm
Sponsor: Phi Upsilon Omicron, Inc.
P.O. Box 329
Fairmont, WV 26555

Phi Upsilon Omicron Frances Morton Holbrook Alumni Award 3878
Phi Upsilon Omicron National Honor Society was founded in 1910 at the University of Minnesota in the area of Family and Consumer Sciences. The society grants its Frances Morton Holbrook Alumni Award biennially to a qualified alumni member of the society for fulfilling personal and professional goals which promote the purposes of family and consumer sciences. Criteria includes demonstrated excellence in one of the areas of family and consumer sciences. The recipient's expenses to attend the society's biennial meeting will be paid, and the member will be recognized with a plaque at the meeting. The nomination deadline is November 1. Interested applicants should contact the society for information on nomination procedures.
Requirements: Nominees must be alumni members of the society to be eligible for the award.
Geographic Focus: All States
Date(s) Application is Due: Nov 1
Contact: Susan Rickards; (304) 368-0612; rickards@phiu.org or info@phiu.org
Internet: http://phiu.org/awards.htm
Sponsor: Phi Upsilon Omicron, Inc.
P.O. Box 329
Fairmont, WV 26555

Phoenix Coyotes Charities Grants 3879
Coyotes Charities seeks to enhance the quality of life throughout Arizona communities by supporting non-profit organizations that promote healthcare, educational, cultural, arts, and sports-related programs for children. The Charities will fund activities that accomplish the following goals: to focus on the health and well-being of youth through community awareness, information dissemination, and treatment or prevention; to promote the value of quality education through provision of in-school or after-school enrichment programs that equip children for the future; to develop the artistic potential of youth, allow youth to share in the vital cultural currents of the Arizona community, and help youth learn to create with their hands; to encourage physical activities, exercise, teamwork, self-esteem, goal setting, and a healthy lifestyle through community outreach, organized sports, or mentorship programs. Interested organizations may download an application from the grant website. Mailed applications must be postmarked by the deadline date. Hand-delivered applications must be received by a Coyotes Charities representative in the Phoenix Coyotes offices by 5:00 p.m. on the deadline date. Deadlines may vary from year to year. Applicants are encouraged to verify the current deadline date at the grant website.
Requirements: Organizations must be classified as a public charity and exempt from federal taxes under 501(c)3 of the Internal Revenue Code. Organizations must align with the Coyotes Charities mission statement by being focused on improving the lives of children in Arizona.
Restrictions: Giving is limited to the state of Arizona. The foundation will not support the following entities: individuals; sports teams or leagues; religious, fraternal, or political institutions; schools or their affiliated organizations (booster clubs, PTAs, etc.); governmental municipalities; or environmental groups.
Geographic Focus: Arizona
Date(s) Application is Due: Jun 24
Amount of Grant: Up to 5,000 USD
Contact: Doug Moss, President; (623) 772-3200; fax (623) 872-2000; coyotes.charities@phoenixcoyotes.com
Internet: http://coyotes.nhl.com/club/page.htm?id=32747
Sponsor: Phoenix Coyotes Charities
6751 N. Sunset Boulevard #200
Glendale, AZ 85305

Phoenix Neighborhood Block Watch Grants 3880
Neighborhood Block Watch Grants are available to community organizations and Block Watch groups for projects that fight crime and improve the safety and quality of life within neighborhoods. Funding is directed for community groups to undertake new and innovative programs and activities aimed at preventing and reducing crime in the community by detecting, detering, and/or delaying crime.
Requirements: Only neighborhood/homeowners/Block Watch organizations listed with the City of Phoenix Neighborhood Services Department or Block Watch groups registered with the Phoenix Police Department by deadline date may apply as the primary applicant. Co-applicants can be any educational or religious organizations, non-profit agencies within a specific geographic area, and City of Phoenix departments by section or division. Primary applicants must submit copies of neighborhood meeting agendas from four neighborhood meetings held in separate months during the previous year where crime prevention topics were discussed, as well as the number of people in attendance. Primary applicants that are formal Homeowners' Associations (HOAs), incorporated neighborhoods, or neighborhood associations with a 501(c)3 need to complete the HOA Checklist (found in the Additional Grant Forms section of this website). If one of these organizations applies as a co-applicant, they must still submit the required documents listed on the HOA Checklist. The application is available at the program's website.

Restrictions: Primary applicants may submit two applications only if one is for applicant's neighborhood and the second is with a co-applicant. Co-applicants cannot apply by themselves as a single applicant. The service area of the proposed project must be within the corporate limits of the city of Phoenix or the impacted population must be Phoenix citizens. The following is a list of ineligible items for the grant: administration of the grant; alcoholic beverages; awards and raffle prizes; bulletproof vests; entertainment, parties, and recognition dinners; entrance or admission fees for any in-state or out-of-state non-educational field trips, including water and amusement parks; food or beverages of any kind, including consumable prizes or incentives in the form of food or beverages; motor vehicles; out-of-state field trips or travel; surveillance equipment, including night vision and listening devices; vehicle overhead emergency light bars; or weapons of any type, including firearms, pepper spray, mace, knives, stun guns, etc.
Geographic Focus: Arizona
Date(s) Application is Due: Feb 4
Amount of Grant: Up to 10,000 USD
Contact: Daisy Lowry; (602) 262-6543; nbwgrant@phoenix.gov
Internet: http://phoenix.gov/police/nbwgrant.html
Sponsor: City of Phoenix
200 W. Washington Street
Phoenix, AZ 85003

Phoenix Suns Charities Grants 3881
Ranging in size from $1,000 to $10,000, Phoenix Suns Charities Program Grants are intended for Arizona non-profit organization whose programs and activities focus on helping children and families maximize their potential. The foundation's largest annual gift, the Playmaker Award, is a one-time $100,000 grant which can be used for capital or programs, or a combination of both. For this grant, Suns Charities looks favorably on collaborative ideas and naming or branding opportunities.
Requirements: Applications and supporting documents must be submitted electronically through ZoomGrants at the Suns website. Organizations must consider the prerequisites, answer all questions and carefully follow directions. Applications are available in November, evaluated by Suns board members in April and May, with funding in June.
Geographic Focus: Arizona
Date(s) Application is Due: Apr 1
Amount of Grant: 1,000 - 10,000 USD
Contact: Kathryn Pidgeon; (602) 379-7948; fax (602) 379-7990; kpidgeon@suns.com
Internet: http://www.nba.com/suns/charities.html
Sponsor: Phoenix Suns
201 East Jefferson Street
Phoenix, AZ 85004

Piedmont Health Foundation Grants 3882
The Piedmont Health Care Foundation was established in 1985 through the sale of the first HMO in Greenville County, South Carolina. During the past 25 years, the foundation has invested more than $3.4 million in dozens of nonprofit organizations in the Greenville, South Carolina area. The Piedmont Health Care Foundation has played an important role in catalyzing and providing seed funding to critical projects, and it has provided operating and programmatic funds needed by local health-service organizations. In looking ahead, the foundation recognizes that much of what makes a healthy community takes place outside of the health-care system. So for its 25th anniversary, the foundation decided to change its name to the Piedmont Health Foundation. The foundation currently focuses on the area of policy, system, and environmental change to reduce childhood obesity rates. Applications are accepted on a quarterly basis. Downloadable guidelines and editable forms are provided at the foundation website. Applicants should email their completed forms to the address given by midnight of the deadline date.
Requirements: Nonprofit organizations that serve Greenville County are eligible to apply.
Geographic Focus: South Carolina
Date(s) Application is Due: Jan 31; Apr 10; Jul 10; Oct 10
Contact: Katy Smith, Executive Director; (864) 370-0212; fax (864) 370-0212; katypughsmith@bellsouth.net or katysmith@piedmonthealthfoundation.org
Internet: http://www.phcfdn.org/grantmaking.php
Sponsor: Piedmont Health Foundation
P.O. Box 9303
Greenville, SC 29604

Piedmont Natural Gas Corporate and Charitable Contributions 3883
Piedmont Natural Gas supports local non-profit organizations sponsored by its employees through matching gifts, financial assistance and volunteer support.
Requirements: Piedmont supports 501(c)3 organizations that are sponsored or assisted by its employees. Eligible organizations with employee sponsors are also able to apply for Employee Matching Gifts. Applications are available at Piedmont's website.
Restrictions: As a general rule, grants do not support: individuals or non-501(c)3 organizations; pre-college level private schools except through employee matching gifts; travel and conferences; third-party professional fund-raising organizations; controversial social causes; fraternal and veterans organizations or private clubs; religious organizations with programs limited to or expressly for their membership only; agencies already receiving corporate support through United Way or a united arts drive, with the exception of approved capital campaigns; or athletic events and programs.
Geographic Focus: North Carolina, South Carolina, Tennessee
Contact: George Baldwin; (704) 731-4063; george.baldwin@piedmontng.com
Internet: http://www.piedmontng.com/ourcommunity/communityoutreach.aspx
Sponsor: Piedmont Natural Gas Corporation
4720 Piedmont Row Drive
Charlotte, NC 28210

Piedmont Natural Gas Foundation Environmental Stewardship and Energy Sustainability Grant 3884
Piedmont Natural Gas Foundation awards one grant to organizations in North Carolina, South Carolina and Tennessee that provide one or more of the following objectives: increase access to interaction with nature and the environment; promote local accountability or actions to create cleaner cities, reduce emissions and incorporate conscious environmental decision-making; incorporate energy and/or environmental education in K-12 schools and curriculum; promote a general awareness about environmental and energy-related issues for the public; and/or preserve or restore a community's existing natural resources, including green/open space.
Requirements: Organizations are invited to apply for Environmental Stewardship and Energy Sustainability grants through a Request for Proposal process. Also, organizations must be a 501(c)3 non-profit organization or a qualified government entity. All grant requests must be submitted through Piedmont's online grant application form located at Piedmont's website.
Restrictions: Piedmont Natural Gas Foundation will not fund: religious, fraternal, political or athletic groups; four-year colleges and universities; private foundations; or social or veterans' organizations. In addition to these restrictions, contributions will generally not be made to or for: individuals; pre-college level private schools, except through the Employee Matching Gifts program; travel and conferences; third-party professional fundraising organizations; controversial social causes; religious organizations with programs limited to or expressly for their membership only; athletic events and programs; agencies already receiving Piedmont support through United Way or a united arts drive, with the exception of an approved capital campaign; or any proposal outside of the geographic area where Piedmont Natural Gas does business.
Geographic Focus: North Carolina, South Carolina, Tennessee
Amount of Grant: 500 - 30,000 USD
Contact: George Baldwin; (704) 731-4063; george.baldwin@piedmontng.com
Internet: http://www.piedmontng.com/ourcommunity/ourfoundation.aspx#guidelines
Sponsor: Piedmont Natural Gas Foundation
4720 Piedmont Row Drive
Charlotte, NC 28210

Piedmont Natural Gas Foundation Health and Human Services Grants 3885
Piedmont Natural Gas Foundation's Health and Human Services grant focuses funding toward: organizations providing outreach services to community members with basic needs, including shelter, food and clothing; substance abuse or mental illness; organizations providing services or programs for a range of human service needs including youth engagement and mentoring, special needs and disability assistance, substance abuse or mental illnesses, transitional housing and situational homelessness support, and gang violence prevention; organizations providing emergency/disaster relief; increased access to critical healthcare services and comprehensive medical treatment including preventative care, prescription medication, medical exams, screenings, immunizations and dental care; and increased access to mental health services.
Requirements: Organizations must be a 501(c)3 non-profit organization or a qualified government entity. All grant requests must be submitted through Piedmont's online grant application form located at Piedmont's website.
Restrictions: Piedmont Natural Gas Foundation will not fund: religious, fraternal, political or athletic groups; four-year colleges and universities; private foundations; or social or veterans' organizations. In addition to these restrictions, contributions will generally not be made to or for: individuals; pre-college level private schools, except through the Employee Matching Gifts program; travel and conferences; third-party professional fundraising organizations; controversial social causes; religious organizations with programs limited to or expressly for their membership only; athletic events and programs; agencies already receiving Piedmont support through United Way or a united arts drive, with the exception of an approved capital campaign; or any proposal outside of the geographic area where Piedmont Natural Gas does business.
Geographic Focus: North Carolina, South Carolina, Tennessee
Amount of Grant: 500 - 30,000 USD
Contact: George Baldwin; (704) 731-4063; george.baldwin@piedmontng.com
Internet: http://www.piedmontng.com/ourcommunity/ourfoundation.aspx#guidelines
Sponsor: Piedmont Natural Gas Foundation
4720 Piedmont Row Drive
Charlotte, NC 28210

Piedmont Natural Gas Foundation Workforce Development Grant 3886
Piedmont Natural Gas Foundation's Workforce Development Grant is directed toward programs and projects that: coordinate with economic development efforts and activities to promote the region's availability of qualified workers; provide high quality, affordable and easily accessible training to those entering the workforce with the skills necessary to obtain employment; provide training programs that serve to upgrade employee skills and wages; create and develop strategies to encourage life-long learning and opportunities to engage in professional development. in addition to these goals, the grant supports programs that incorporate vocational and technical training through community colleges.
Requirements: Organizations must be a 501(c)3 non-profit organization or a qualified government entity. All grant requests must be submitted through Piedmont's online grant application form located at Piedmont's website.
Restrictions: Piedmont Natural Gas Foundation will not fund: religious, fraternal, political or athletic groups; four-year colleges and universities; private foundations; or social or veterans' organizations. In addition to these restrictions, contributions will generally not be made to or for: individuals; pre-college level private schools, except through the Employee Matching Gifts program; travel and conferences; third-party professional fundraising organizations; controversial social causes; religious organizations with programs limited to or expressly for their membership only; athletic events and programs; agencies already

receiving Piedmont support through United Way or a united arts drive, with the exception of an approved capital campaign; or any proposal outside of the geographic area where Piedmont Natural Gas does business.
Geographic Focus: North Carolina, South Carolina, Tennessee
Amount of Grant: 500 - 30 USD
Contact: George Baldwin; (704) 731-4063; george.baldwin@piedmontng.com
Internet: http://www.piedmontng.com/ourcommunity/ourfoundation.aspx#guidelines
Sponsor: Piedmont Natural Gas Foundation
4720 Piedmont Row Drive
Charlotte, NC 28210

Pier 1 Imports Grants 3887
Pier 1 Imports has established long-standing relations with select organizations, which receive the majority of charitable funds. With few exceptions, funds not already committed to the above causes are given to Fort Worth, Tarrant County, Texas programs making a difference in community services, children's education, and the arts. There are no application deadlines. Applicants are contacted with a funding decision within six weeks. Applications are located at the Pier 1 website.
Requirements: Applicants requesting less than $1000 or a Pier 1 gift card may submit a brief letter describing the organization's mission, the request, proposed use of funds, total project cost, number of people served by the project, contact information, and proof of tax-exempt status. For requests of above $1,000, applicants should complete the online giving request form.
Restrictions: Funding is not available for individuals; religious, political, or fraternal organizations; individual school activities, such as carnivals, graduation, prom, or PTA/PTOs; private schools; journal or program advertising; amateur or professional sporting groups; beauty or talent contests; endowments; conferences or seminars; travel; scholarships; or requests for returned, damaged or excess merchandise.
Geographic Focus: Texas
Contact: Charitable Giving Contact; (800) 252-8808
Internet: http://www.pier1.com/Philanthropy/pr_philanthropy,default,pg.html
Sponsor: Pier 1 Imports
301 Commerce Street, Suite 600
Fort Worth, TX 76102

Pike County Community Foundation Grants 3888
The Pike County Community Foundation is a charitable organization formed to strengthen the Pike County, Indiana community by awarding grants to local nonprofits, by bringing individuals together to address community needs, and by offering personalized charitable gift planning services to donors. At the start of each cycle, a notice is mailed to nonprofit organizations that have previously applied for and received grants, or have otherwise requested notification of each cycle. Proposals are accepted from July through the September deadline. The grants committee will make its recommendations on funding to the Foundation's Board of Trustees, which will make final funding recommendations to the board of directors of the Community Foundation Alliance. All organizations that have submitted grant proposals are notified of the final outcome no later than December 1. Application instructions and samples of previously funded projects are available at the website.
Requirements: The Foundation welcomes proposals from nonprofit organizations that are deemed tax-exempt under sections 501(c)3 and 509(a) of the Internal Revenue Code and from governmental agencies serving Pike County. Proposals from nonprofit organizations not classified as a 501(c)3 public charity may be considered provided the project is charitable and supports a community need. Proposals submitted by an entity under the auspices of another agency must include a written statement signed by the agency's board president on behalf of the board of directors agreeing to act as the entity's fiscal sponsor, to receive grant monies if awarded, and to oversee the proposed project.
Restrictions: Project areas NOT considered for funding: religious organizations for religious purposes; political parties or campaigns; endowment creation or debt reduction; operating costs; capital campaigns; annual appeals or membership contributions; travel requests for groups or individuals such as bands, sports teams, or classes.
Geographic Focus: Indiana
Date(s) Application is Due: Nov 1
Contact: Foundation Director; (812) 354-6797; director@pikecommunityfoundation.org
Internet: http://www.pikecommunityfoundation.org/disc-grants
Sponsor: Pike County Community Foundation
714 Main Street, P.O. Box 587
Petersburg, IN 47567

Pi Lambda Theta Anna Tracey Memorial Award 3889
The Anna Tracey Memorial Award is presented in recognition of producers of a communications medium that enhances the image of the elderly. The award consists of a cash payment of four hundred dollars ($400) and a framed certificate. The award was established in 1975. It is sustained by a restricted fund established in the Pi Lambda Theta Educational Endowment pursuant to a contribution by Lillian Tracey Barry, of Rho Chapter, to honor the memory of her mother.
Requirements: A nomination must be made by a member in good standing or by a non-member with the endorsement of a member in good standing. A complete nomination includes: a Pi Lambda Theta universal application/nomination cover sheet; an abstract of the individual's or chapter's qualifying book, study, journal article, documentary film, filmstrip, slide-tape presentation, etc; a letter citing tangible evidence of improvements in the lives of the targeted individuals or groups and attesting to the impact the medium has had on the public to bring about an improved image of the elderly and a list of the source(s) of financial support for the project, if any.
Geographic Focus: Indiana
Date(s) Application is Due: Feb 10

Contact: Pam Todd, Manager; (812) 339-3411; fax (812) 339-3462; pam@pilambda.org
Internet: http://www.pilambda.org/benefits/awards/ScholarshipsAwards.html
Sponsor: Pi Lambda Theta
4101 E Third Street, P.O. Box 6626
Bloomington, IN 47407-6626

Pi Lambda Theta Lillian and Henry Barry Award in Human Relations 3890
The Lillian and Henry Barry Award in Human Relations is presented in recognition of outstanding service to people with disabilities. The award consists of a cash payment of four hundred dollars ($400) and a framed certificate. The award was established in 1977. It is sustained by a restricted fund established in the Pi Lambda Theta Educational Endowment pursuant to a contribution by Lillian Tracey Barry, of Rho Chapter.
Requirements: A nominee must be a member or chapter of Pi Lambda Theta. A nomination must include evidence that the nominee has demonstrated outstanding service to people with disabilities, resulting in the development of the ability to lead useful, fulfilling lives and/or a better understanding of the needs of people with disabilities by the public.
Restrictions: A nomination must be made by a member in good standing or by a non-member with the endorsement of a member in good standing. Self-nomination/endorsement is not permitted.
Geographic Focus: Indiana
Date(s) Application is Due: Feb 10
Amount of Grant: 400 USD
Contact: Pam Todd, Manager; (812) 339-3411; fax (812) 339-3462; pam@pilambda.org
Internet: http://www.pilambda.org/benefits/awards/ScholarshipsAwards.html
Sponsor: Pi Lambda Theta
4101 E Third Street, P.O. Box 6626
Bloomington, IN 47407-6626

Pinellas County Grants 3891
The Pinellas Community Foundation was established in 1969, it distributes grants twice annually to a wide variety of non-profit agencies, organizations and programs that enhance and support the quality of life in Pinellas County, Florida. Areas of interest are: art, culture, health care, environment, community development, employment opportunities, the underserved, and social services.
Requirements: Eligibility: a non-profit, 501(c)3; be headquartered in Pinellas County; provide social services to people in Pinellas County; not have a large endowment or fund raising staff; provide recent audited financial statements. For Grant Applications call Pinellas Community Foundation: (727)531-0058.
Geographic Focus: Florida
Date(s) Application is Due: Jun 15; Oct 1
Contact: Julie Scales; (727) 531-0058; fax (727) 531-0053; info@pinellasccf.org
Internet: http://www.pinellasccf.org/pinellas-community-foundation-pcf-clearwater-fl-our-grants-programs.htm
Sponsor: Pinellas County Community Foundation
5200 East Bay Drive, Suite 202
Clearwater, FL 33764

Pinkerton Foundation Grants 3892
The Pinkerton Foundation is an independent grantmaking foundation established in 1966 by Robert Allan Pinkerton with the broad directive to reduce the incidence of crime and to prevent juvenile delinquency. The Foundation's principal program interests are focused on economically disadvantaged children, youth and families, and severely learning disabled children and adults of borderline intelligence. The Foundation supports efforts to strengthen and expand community-based programs for children, youth and families in New York City. The Foundation also occasionally funds research, demonstration and evaluation projects in its principal program areas. While grants for direct service projects are usually limited to New York City, those with potential for national impact or replication may go beyond this geographic limitation. The Foundation's Board of Directors have two grantmaking meetings per year, in May and in December. Letters of inquiry are welcome throughout the year. Additional guidelines are available at the Foundation's website.
Requirements: Grants are awarded primarily to New York City 501(c)3 nonprofit public charitable organizations.
Restrictions: The foundation does not grant requests for emergencies, medical research, direct provision of health care, religious education, conferences, publications, or capital projects.
Geographic Focus: All States
Date(s) Application is Due: Feb 1; Sep 1
Contact: Joan Colello; (212) 332-3385; fax (212) 332-3399; pinkfdn@pinkertonfdn.org
Internet: http://fdncenter.org/grantmaker/pinkerton
Sponsor: Pinkerton Foundation
610 Fifth Avenue, Suite 316
New York, NY 10020

Pinnacle Entertainment Foundation Grants 3893
The Pinnacle Entertainment Foundation awards grants in its primary fields of interest, including: the arts; children and youth services; food banks; community foundations; health care; patient services; higher education; hospitals; the humanities; performing arts; and recreation programs. Types of support include: general operating funds; program development; scholarship funds; and sponsorships. Applications are limited to two per calendar year, per organization. An online application form is required, and should include: plans for acknowledgement; a detailed description of project and amount of funding requested; a brief history of organization and description of its mission; contact information; and a copy of the IRS Determination Letter.
Requirements: 501(c)3 organizations serving the residents of Louisiana or Nevada are eligible to apply.

Restrictions: The Foundation does not support: organizations that are not 501(c)3 entities; political causes, candidates, organizations or campaigns; organizations whose primary purpose is to influence legislation; organizations that discriminate on the basis of age, color, disability, disabled veteran status, gender, race, religion, national origin, marital status, sexual orientation or military service; administrative expenses or programs with administrative expenses in excess of 15%; capital project funding; purchase of uniforms or trips for school-related organizations and booster clubs, youth athletics or amateur sports teams; activities whose sole purpose is promotion or support of a specific religion, denomination or religious institution; fraternal, alumni, trade, professional or social organizations; individuals; medical fundraisers; political or partisan organizations or candidates; or study or travel grants (scholarships, stipends, writing allowances).
Geographic Focus: Louisiana, Nevada
Contact: Shelly Peterson, (702) 541-7777 or (818) 710-2719
Internet: https://www.pnkinc.com/pinnacle-entertainment-foundation/
Sponsor: Pinnacle Entertainment Foundation
8918 Spanish Ridge Avenue
Las Vegas, NV 89148-1302

Pinnacle Foundation Grants 3894
The Pinnacle Foundation was established in the State of Washington with a primary interest in family, military family support, critical housing, and homeless programs. Although there are no specified annual deadlines, a formal application is required. The standard application should include contact information, a description of the charitable function, and an overview of the project.
Geographic Focus: All States
Contact: Stanley J. Harrelson, President; (206) 215-9700 or (206) 215-9747
Sponsor: Pinnacle Foundation
2801 Alaskan Way, Suite 310
Seattle, WA 98121-1136

Pioneer Hi-Bred Community Grants 3895
The international corporation supports community-based projects in the areas of agriculture, education, farm safety, and the environment. Priority consideration is given to projects located in Pioneer facility communities or rural agricultural regions and to organizations with active Pioneer management/employee participation and company-related expertise and interest. Types of support include capital grants, general operating grants, program development grants, and seed money grants. The company accepts proposals from nonprofit organizations nationwide but favors programs in its operating communities. Pioneer prefers to make direct contributions to organizations, rather than sponsorships, ticket or table purchases. This allows more funding to go directly toward the non-profit organization; however, we are willing to consider sponsorships when Pioneer employees are actively involved with the organization. The employee must present the request to Community Investment at least one month in advance. Due to the number of non-profit events held annually, there is a $1,000 maximum contribution level per event per year. The company favors proposals that demonstrate cooperation with other community-based programs, broad-based funding, community need, and positive results. Grant proposals are reviewed on a quarterly basis.
Requirements: Nonprofit organizations are eligible. All requests should be directed to the Pioneer Hi-Bred office within the local area. Otherwise, send to the contact listed. Pioneer does not respond favorably to verbal requests.
Restrictions: Grants are not made to individuals, religious or political organizations that promote a particular doctrine, elected officials, company marketing or advertising, or organizations where there is a conflict of interest with Pioneer Hi-Bred.
Geographic Focus: All States
Contact: Administrator; (800) 247-6803, ext. 3915; community.investment@pioneer.com
Internet: http://www.pioneer.com/web/site/portal/menuitem.bb020a6d93d9d318bc0c0a03d10093a0/
Sponsor: Pioneer Hi-Bred International
6900 NW 62nd Avenue, P.O. Box 246
Johnston, IA 50131

Pioneer Hi-Bred Conferences and Meetings Grants 3896
The primary purpose of the grant is to support research conferences and meetings addressing topics of relevance to Pioneer Hi-Bred. Areas of interest include: plant science research, global agronomy, germplasm preservation, and plant biotechnology. Funding decisions are made by the Research Awards Committee Chair and Research Management, based on input from PHI scientists. For further information, applicants should forward an email to the listed contact person.
Geographic Focus: All States
Contact: David Bubeck, (515) 270-3200 or (800) 247-6803, ext. 3915; fax (515) 334-4415; David.Bubeck@pioneer.com
Internet: http://www.pioneer.com/web/site/portal/menuitem.07196fe7964ae318bc0c0a03d10093a0/
Sponsor: Pioneer Hi-Bred International
6900 NW 62nd Avenue, P.O. Box 246
Johnston, IA 50131

PIP American Dream Fund Grants 3897
The ADF is an immigrant-integration initiative of the John S. and James L. Knight Foundation (Knight), a charter donor to the Public Interest Projects' (PIP) Four Freedoms Fund. The ADF is the locally focused component of Knight's New Americans Initiative, which supports grassroots organizations that help immigrants become engaged, naturalized citizens in its 26 grantmaking communities (see below). The ADF provides multiyear general and project support, in grants of $20,000 to $25,000 per year, to organizations working to foster naturalization and civic participation among foreign-born residents. Funded activities include: conducting community outreach and referrals to citizenship services to encourage naturalization; coordination with local, regional and national citizenship efforts; providing citizenship-preparedness and English-language classes, tutoring, and workshops; assisting with naturalization applications and screenings; providing legal support for naturalization filings; and anticipating in efforts to reduce the barriers to naturalization.
Requirements: 501(c)3 tax-exempt organizations and organizations applying through 501(c)3 fiscal sponsors are eligible.
Geographic Focus: All States
Amount of Grant: 20,000 - 25,000 USD
Contact: Cynthia Brothers; (212) 764-1508; cbrothers@publicinterestprojects.org
Internet: http://www.publicinterestprojects.org/projects/partner-and-collaborative-funds/american-dream-fund
Sponsor: Public Interest Projects
80 Broad Street, 17th Floor
New York, NY 10004

PIP Communities for Public Education Reform Grants 3898
Communities for Public Education Reform (CPER) is a partnership of local and national foundations working to improve educational opportunities and outcomes for students in low-income communities. CPER supports the growing field of education organizing through grants and technical assistance to community organizations working to ensure that parents and students have a strong voice in shaping the policies that affect their public schools. By bringing new resources to at least four sites for a minimum of three years, CPER promotes innovation and supports systemic reforms that address educational inequities. CPER links a wide range of funders to: increase the visibility of and support for effective education-organizing strategies at the local, state and national levels; leverage local dollars with national funds; engage in mutual learning and strategizing; facilitate collaboration among the grantees to form a more strategically connected group with a related set of messages and stories; and facilitate the emergence of new voices in public discourse around public-education reform.
Requirements: 501(c)3 tax-exempt organizations and organizations applying through 501(c)3 fiscal sponsors are eligible.
Geographic Focus: All States
Contact: Julie K. Kohler, Program Manager; (212) 764-1508, ext. 231; fax (917) 438-4639; jkohler@publicinterestprojects.org
Internet: http://www.publicinterestprojects.org/projects/partner-and-collaborative-funds/cper
Sponsor: Public Interest Projects
80 Broad Street, 17th Floor
New York, NY 10004

Piper Jaffray Foundation Communities Giving Grants 3899
The foundation supports organizations and programs that enhance the lives of people living and working in communities in which the company has offices. Of primary interest is support for organizations that increase opportunities for individuals to improve their lives and help themselves. Highest priority is given to family stability programs (including housing, family violence, responsible parenting), early childhood development, job training/career development, youth development, and adult education services. The foundation will also consider requests from organizations that work to increase citizen understanding or involvement in civic affairs or that enhance the artistic and cultural life of the community. Requests for general operating support from proven nonprofit organizations will be considered. Requests for project and capital support will be considered on a very selective basis. Support for higher education and K-12 public and private schools is provided primarily through the company gift-matching program. Contact the foundation for deadline dates.
Requirements: IRS 501(c)3 organizations located in the Minneapolis/Saint Paul metropolitan area should submit requests directly to the foundation. Organizations located outside the Minneapolis/Saint Paul metropolitan area should submit requests to the nearest Piper Jaffray office for forwarding to the foundation. Offices are located in communities in Arizona, California, Colorado, Idaho, Illinois, Iowa, Kansas, Kentucky, Minnesota, Missouri, Montana, Nebraska, Nevada, North Dakota, Ohio, Oregon, South Dakota, Tennessee, Utah, Washington, Wisconsin, and Wyoming.
Restrictions: Requests will not be considered from newly formed nonprofit organizations; individuals; teams; religious, political, veterans, or fraternal organizations; or organizations working to treat or eliminate specific diseases. Support is not available for basic or applied research, travel, event sponsorship, benefits or tickets, or to eliminate an organization's operating deficit.
Geographic Focus: Arizona, Arkansas, California, Colorado, Idaho, Illinois, Iowa, Kansas, Kentucky, Minnesota, Missouri, Montana, Nebraska, Nevada, North Dakota, Ohio, Oregon, South Dakota, Tennessee, Utah, Washington, Wisconsin, Wyoming
Date(s) Application is Due: Mar 18
Amount of Grant: 1,000 - 5,000 USD
Contact: Connie McCuskey; (612) 303-1309; communityrelations@pjc.com
Internet: http://www.piperjaffray.com/2col_largeright.aspx?id=127
Sponsor: Piper Jaffray Foundation
800 Nicollet Mall, Suite 800
Minneapolis, MN 55402

Piper Trust Arts and Culture Grants 3900
The Piper Trust's grantmaking focuses on Virginia Galvin Piper's commitment to improving the quality of life for residents of Maricopa County. Piper Trust's particular interest lies with projects that benefit young children, adolescents and older adults in Maricopa County. The Trust makes grants to faith-based organizations that serve these target populations in a manner consistent with program guidelines. For Arts and Culture grants, the trust is focused on improved business and financial operations; collaborations for greater effectiveness and efficiencies; and, revenue generation, cost reduction, and mergers.

Requirements: Piper Trust makes grants to actively operating Section 501(c)3 organizations in Maricopa County. These organizations must have been in operation for at least three years from the effective date of their IRS ruling. Special rules apply to private foundations and 509(a)3 (Type III) organizations. There are no deadlines on initial proposals, and letters of inquiry throughout the year are reviewed throughout the year. If the Trust asks for a full proposal, its disposition depends on its completeness and the meeting schedule of the Piper trustees. Virginia G. Piper Charitable Trust requires all arts and culture grantees to participate in the Arizona Cultural Data Project (Arizona CDP). The Arizona CDP is a powerful online management tool designed to strengthen arts and cultural organizations by providing an amazing array of reports designed to increase management capacity, inform decision-making, and document the economic value of the arts.
Restrictions: Individuals are not eligible.
Geographic Focus: Arizona
Amount of Grant: Up to 350,000 USD
Contact: Ellen Solowey, Program Officer; (480) 556-7133; esolowey@pipertrust.org
Internet: http://pipertrust.org/our-grants/arts-culture/
Sponsor: Virginia G. Piper Charitable Trust
1202 East Missouri Avenue
Phoenix, AZ 85014

Piper Trust Children Grants — 3901
The Piper Trust's grantmaking focuses on Virginia Galvin Piper's commitment to improving the quality of life for residents of Maricopa County. Piper Trust's particular interest lies with projects that benefit young children, adolescents and older adults in Maricopa County. The Trust makes grants to faith-based organizations that serve these target populations in a manner consistent with program guidelines. For Children grants, the trust is focused on improved parent and caregiver child-rearing know-how; assistance for children without resources or with special needs; enhanced child care practices and after school care; and, integrated early childhood policies and practices.
Requirements: Piper Trust makes grants to actively operating Section 501(c)3 organizations in Maricopa County. These organizations must have been in operation for at least three years from the effective date of their IRS ruling. Special rules apply to private foundations and 509(a)3 (Type III) organizations. There are no deadlines on initial proposals, and letters of inquiry throughout the year are reviewed throughout the year. If the Trust asks for a full proposal, its disposition depends on its completeness and the meeting schedule of the Piper trustees.
Geographic Focus: Arizona
Contact: Terri Leon, Program Officer; (480) 556-7121; tleon@pipertrust.org
Internet: http://pipertrust.org/our-grants/children/
Sponsor: Virginia G. Piper Charitable Trust
1202 East Missouri Avenue
Phoenix, AZ 85014

Piper Trust Education Grants — 3902
The Piper Trust's grantmaking focuses on Virginia Galvin Piper's commitment to improving the quality of life for residents of Maricopa County. Piper Trust's particular interest lies with projects that benefit young children, adolescents and older adults in Maricopa County. The Trust makes grants to faith-based organizations that serve these target populations in a manner consistent with program guidelines. For Education grants, the trust is most interested in proposals that address improved early learning environments, academic enhancements for youth, and engagement of older adults in learning.
Requirements: Piper Trust makes grants to actively operating Section 501(c)3 organizations in Maricopa County. These organizations must have been in operation for at least three years from the effective date of their IRS ruling. Special rules apply to private foundations and 509(a)3 (Type III) organizations. There are no deadlines on initial proposals, and letters of inquiry throughout the year are reviewed throughout the year. If the Trust asks for a full proposal, its disposition depends on its completeness and the meeting schedule of the Piper trustees.
Geographic Focus: Arizona
Contact: Terri Leon, Program Officer; (480) 556-7121; tleon@pipertrust.org
Sponsor: Virginia G. Piper Charitable Trust
1202 East Missouri Avenue
Phoenix, AZ 85014

Piper Trust Healthcare and Medical Research Grants — 3903
The Piper Trust's grantmaking focuses on Virginia Galvin Piper's commitment to improving the quality of life for residents of Maricopa County. Piper Trust's particular interest lies with projects that benefit young children, adolescents and older adults in Maricopa County. The Trust makes grants to faith-based organizations that serve these target populations in a manner consistent with program guidelines. For Healthcare and Medical Research grants, the trust is most interested in proposals that address improved facilities for children, adolescents and older adults; better trained healthcare workforce; increased access to basic healthcare; and, centers for advancement in personalized medicine.
Requirements: Piper Trust makes grants to actively operating Section 501(c)3 organizations in Maricopa County. These organizations must have been in operation for at least three years from the effective date of their IRS ruling. Special rules apply to private foundations and 509(a)3 (Type III) organizations. There are no deadlines on initial proposals, and letters of inquiry throughout the year are reviewed throughout the year. If the Trust asks for a full proposal, its disposition depends on its completeness and the meeting schedule of the Piper trustees.
Geographic Focus: Arizona
Contact: Terri Leon, Program Officer; (480) 556-7121; tleon@pipertrust.org
Internet: http://pipertrust.org/our-grants/healthcare-medical-research/
Sponsor: Virginia G. Piper Charitable Trust
1202 East Missouri Avenue
Phoenix, AZ 85014

Piper Trust Older Adults Grants — 3904
The Piper Trust's grantmaking focuses on Virginia Galvin Piper's commitment to improving the quality of life for residents of Maricopa County. Piper Trust's particular interest lies with projects that benefit young children, adolescents and older adults in Maricopa County. The Trust makes grants to faith-based organizations that serve these target populations in a manner consistent with program guidelines. For Older Adults grants, the trust is most interested in proposals that address disease and disability prevention; assistance for older adults to remain independent; and, volunteerism, "recareering" and community engagement.
Requirements: Piper Trust makes grants to actively operating Section 501(c)3 organizations in Maricopa County. These organizations must have been in operation for at least three years from the effective date of their IRS ruling. Special rules apply to private foundations and 509(a)3 (Type III) organizations. There are no deadlines on initial proposals, and letters of inquiry throughout the year are reviewed throughout the year. If the Trust asks for a full proposal, its disposition depends on its completeness and the meeting schedule of the Piper trustees.
Geographic Focus: Arizona
Contact: Terri Leon, Program Officer; (480) 556-7121; tleon@pipertrust.org
Internet: http://pipertrust.org/our-grants/older-adults/
Sponsor: Virginia G. Piper Charitable Trust
1202 East Missouri Avenue
Phoenix, AZ 85014

Piper Trust Reglious Organizations Grants — 3905
The Piper Trust's grantmaking focuses on Virginia Galvin Piper's commitment to improving the quality of life for residents of Maricopa County. Piper Trust's particular interest lies with projects that benefit young children, adolescents and older adults in Maricopa County. Grantmaking for religious organizations reflects Piper's objectives and strategies in the Children, Older Adults, Education, and Healthcare program areas. For Religious Organizations grants, the trust is most interested in proposals that address assessments of learning environments in faith-based preschools and quality improvement projects and housing alternatives for older adults.
Requirements: Piper Trust makes grants to actively operating Section 501(c)3 organizations in Maricopa County. These organizations must have been in operation for at least three years from the effective date of their IRS ruling. Special rules apply to private foundations and 509(a)3 (Type III) organizations. There are no deadlines on initial proposals, and letters of inquiry throughout the year are reviewed throughout the year. If the Trust asks for a full proposal, its disposition depends on its completeness and the meeting schedule of the Piper trustees.
Geographic Focus: Arizona
Contact: Terri Leon, Program Officer; (480) 556-7121; tleon@pipertrust.org
Internet: http://pipertrust.org/our-grants/religious-organizations/
Sponsor: Virginia G. Piper Charitable Trust
1202 East Missouri Avenue
Phoenix, AZ 85014

PIP Four Freedoms Fund Grants — 3906
The Four Freedoms Fund (FFF) is a national funding collaborative founded in July 2003 to energize American democracy by supporting and engaging immigrants and refugees. The FFF connects local, often ethnic-specific groups to coordinated state and national campaigns for immigration reform, civic engagement and integration, and protection of civil liberties and human rights. The FFF makes grants to foster a strong, national immigrant-rights field by: supporting a coherent infrastructure of effective local, state and regional organizations; providing multi-year, capacity-building funding and peer-learning opportunities to anchor coalitions through its Capacity Building Initiative and other efforts; regularly commissioning strategic research to identify funding opportunities; sponsoring in-person and telephonic briefings for funders; building the communications capacities of key grantees through its Strategic Communications Initiative; and operating as a link tank, coordinating with other grant makers and grantee networks.
Requirements: 501(c)3 tax-exempt organizations and organizations applying through 501(c)3 fiscal sponsors are eligible.
Geographic Focus: All States
Contact: Naomi Abraham, Program Officer; (212) 764-1508, ext. 215; fax (917) 438-4639; nabraham@publicinterestprojects.org
Internet: http://www.publicinterestprojects.org/projects/partner-and-collaborative-funds/fff
Sponsor: Public Interest Projects
80 Broad Street, 17th Floor
New York, NY 10004

PIP Fulfilling the Dream Fund — 3907
The Fulfilling the Dream Fund (Dream Fund) is a funders' collaborative to support affirmative action and other efforts to promote full inclusion of people of color and women in our society, consistent with our core democratic values. The Dream Fund focuses on eliminating systemic barriers to opportunity in three areas: education, employment and contracting. The Dream Fund was established in 2004 with a $10 million pledge by the Ford Foundation. Funds raised by other donors are matched on a one-to-one basis. The Dream Fund supports efforts that: improve public understanding of systemic barriers to opportunity and the benefits to society of increased racial and gender diversity; expand philanthropic support for affirmative action; demonstrate the links between racial/gender exclusion and systemic flaws in education and employment that affect the broader public, and create more platforms to explore the nation's commitment to opportunity.
Requirements: 501(c)3 tax-exempt organizations and organizations applying through 501(c)3 fiscal sponsors are eligible.
Geographic Focus: All States
Contact: Ingrid Benedict, Program Officer; (212) 764-1508; fax (917) 438-4639; ibenedict@publicinterestprojects.org

Internet: http://www.publicinterestprojects.org/projects/partner-and-collaborative-funds/fulfilling-dream-fund
Sponsor: Public Interest Projects
80 Broad Street, 17th Floor
New York, NY 10004

PIP Racial Justice Collaborative Grants 3908
The Racial Justice Collaborative (RJC) funds partnerships of lawyers and community organizations that use legal and other tools to achieve equity and fairer policies for communities marginalized by race, ethnicity, and immigrant or citizenship status. The RJC is a partnership of foundations and individual donors consisting of a national fund and three state and regional grant making funds (in California, North Carolina and Massachusetts-Rhode Island). In addition to its grant making, the RJC incorporates intensive peer learning for both grantees and donors
Requirements: 501(c)3 tax-exempt organizations and organizations applying through 501(c)3 fiscal sponsors are eligible.
Geographic Focus: All States
Amount of Grant: 50,000 - 100,000 USD
Contact: Elizabeth Lee; (212) 764-1508, ext. 243; fax (917) 438-4639; info@lordross.com
Internet: http://www.rjcollab.org/about.html
Sponsor: Public Interest Projects / Racial Justice Collaborative
80 Broad Street, 17th Floor
New York, NY 10004

PIP U.S. Human Rights Fund Grants 3909
The U.S. Human Rights Fund (USHRF) arose from a sense shared by a group of foundations and individual donors that greater U.S. adherence to the principles of human rights and humanitarian law benefits not only the United States but the wider world as well. The USHRF is a national funding collaborative, launched on July 4, 2005, to provide strategic, field-building support to U.S. human rights work. The USHRF seeks to promote human-rights organizing and advocacy in the United States and to increase awareness of and support for this work among its own members and other donor partners. The Fund focuses in particular on domestic social justice groups actively engaged in U.S. human rights work and, more generally, to their links to the U.S. rights, legal and policy communities. The USHRF provides support to domestic human rights organizations in four strategic areas that the field has identified as relating most directly to its core capacity needs: human rights education and training; regional and national networks; communications; and strategic thinking and advocacy. The USHRF also supports donor education on effective U.S. human rights grantmaking.
Requirements: 501(c)3 tax-exempt organizations and organizations applying through 501(c)3 fiscal sponsors are eligible.
Geographic Focus: All States
Contact: Tanya E. Coke; (212) 764-1508, ext. 236; fax (917) 438-4639
Internet: http://www.publicinterestprojects.org/projects/partner-and-collaborative-funds/ushrf
Sponsor: Public Interest Projects
80 Broad Street, 17th Floor
New York, NY 10004

Pittsburgh Foundation Community Fund Grants 3910
The Pittsburgh Foundation, established in 1945, is the 14th largest community foundation in the county. The foundation awards grants to organizations operating primarily in the Pittsburgh area and Allegheny County, PA. The Foundation supports five targeted areas of impact: education; economic development; families, children and youth; health care; arts.
Requirements: Grants in the five targeted areas for impact are awarded to nonprofit organizations that are defined as tax-exempt under Section 501(c)3 of the Internal Revenue Code and are located within Allegheny County, or can demonstrate that a significant majority of their population served is from Allegheny County.
Geographic Focus: Pennsylvania
Amount of Grant: 30,000 - 150,000 USD
Contact: Jane Downing; (412) 391-5122; fax (412) 391-7259; downingj@pghfdn.org
Internet: http://www.pittsburghfoundation.org/page8894.cfm
Sponsor: Pittsburgh Foundation
5 PPG Place, Suite 250
Pittsburgh, PA 15222-5414

Planet Dog Foundation Grants 3911
The Planet Dog Foundation strives to support worthy organizations through a grant-making program designed to financially support 501(c)3 not-for-profit partners across the U.S. The goal of the grant program is to fund programs that train, place and support dogs helping people in need. Funding is allocated nationwide to promote and financially support service-oriented canine programs such as assistance dogs, therapy dogs, search and rescue programs or police, fire and military dogs. The application with specific instructions is available at the Foundation website.
Requirements: Applicants must be classified as 501(c)3 tax-exempt organizations. They must also be involved with assistance dog, therapy dog, or other canine service programs. Programs applying for a therapy dog grant must require membership of their volunteer teams by the Delta Society, Therapy Dogs International, Therapy Dogs, Inc. or other nationally recognized certification program.
Restrictions: The Foundation is not able to fund any of the following: spay/neuter programs; adoption, shelter or rescue program operating expenses; individuals; political groups; religious groups or groups with any religious affiliation; for-profit organizations; scholarship programs; government agencies; non-profit agencies that are not 501(c)3; programs spending more than 35% of expenses on administrative costs; or any program engaged in animal testing or animal cruelty.
Geographic Focus: All States
Date(s) Application is Due: Mar 31
Amount of Grant: Up to 7,500 USD
Contact: Executive Director; (207) 761-1515, ext 101; pdf@planetdog.com
Internet: http://www.planetdogfoundation.org/grantmaking.aspx
Sponsor: Planet Dog Philanthropy
85 Bradley Drive
Westbrook, ME 04092

Playboy Foundation Freedom of Expression Award 3912
The $25,000 cash award will be made to a nominee who has a project or program dedicated to defending, advocating, or supporting the First Amendment through their personal or professional pursuits. In addition, a successful nominee should demonstrate a promising future as a First Amendment advocate based on their history of accomplishment and the potential for the award to facilitate additional work. Emphasis will be placed on nominees who would benefit from having financing to relieve inhibitions or burdens of pursing the First Amendment ideals of their project or program. Nominations are accepted via email by filling out the form at the website.
Geographic Focus: All States
Amount of Grant: 25,000 USD
Contact: Director; (312) 373-2437 or (312) 751-8000; giving@playboy.com
Internet: http://www.playboyenterprises.com/home/content.cfm?content=t_title_as_division&ArtTypeID=0008B752-BBD0-1C76-8FEA8304E50A010D&packet=0001F2B3-75D2-1C7A-9B578304E50A011A&MmenuFlag=foundation&viewMe=1
Sponsor: Playboy Foundation
680 North Lake Shore Drive
Chicago, IL 60611

Playboy Foundation Grants 3913
The Playboy Foundation seeks to foster social change by confining its grants and other support to projects of national impact and scope involved in fostering open communication about, and research into, human sexuality, reproductive health and rights; protecting and fostering civil rights and civil liberties in the United States for all people, including women, people affected and impacted by HIV/AIDS, gays and lesbians, racial minorities, the poor and the disadvantaged; and eliminating censorship and protecting freedom of expression and First Amendment rights. The Foundation does not accept unsolicited proposals, but welcomes letters of inquiry via post for the areas of interest noted above. Grants awarded by the Foundation are typically up to $10,000.
Restrictions: The foundation will not consider religious programs, individual needs, capital campaigns, endowments, scholarships, or fellowships; social services, including residential care, clinics, treatment, or recreation programs; national health, welfare, educational, or cultural organizations, or their state affiliates; or government agencies or projects.
Geographic Focus: All States
Amount of Grant: 5,000 - 10,000 USD
Contact: Director; (312) 373-2437 or (312) 751-8000; giving@playboy.com
Internet: http://www.playboyenterprises.com/foundation
Sponsor: Playboy Foundation
680 North Lake Shore Drive
Chicago, IL 60611

Playboy Foundation Social Change Documentary Film Grants 3914
The Playboy Foundation seeks to foster social change by confining its grants and other support to projects of national impact and scope involved in fostering open communication about, and research into, human sexuality, reproductive health and rights; protecting and fostering civil rights and civil liberties in the United States for all people, including women, people affected and impacted by HIV/AIDS, gays and lesbians, racial minorities, the poor and the disadvantaged; and eliminating censorship and protecting freedom of expression and First Amendment rights. The Foundation is interested in social change documentary film projects that have nationwide impact and scope. Its grants are modest and range from $1000-$5000. For that reason, its film grants are limited to projects in post production and distribution. The Foundation will evaluate social change documentary film grant proposals once per calendar year. Submissions can be made from May 1 to June 30 for evaluation in July and August.
Requirements: Applicants should include the Internal Revenue Service verification from the sponsoring organization that states the organization is not a private foundation and is exempt from taxation under Internal Revenue Service sections 509(a) and 501(c)3.
Restrictions: Grants are not made to individual filmmakers.
Geographic Focus: All States
Date(s) Application is Due: Jun 30
Amount of Grant: 1,000 - 5,000 USD
Contact: Director; (312) 373-2437 or (312) 751-8000; giving@playboy.com
Internet: http://www.playboyenterprises.com/home/content.cfm?content=t_template&packet=000DA063-D005-1CA9-9B578304E50A011A&artTypeID=0001D5D6-CFD3-1CA9-9B578304E50A011A
Sponsor: Playboy Foundation
680 North Lake Shore Drive
Chicago, IL 60611

Plough Foundation Grants 3915
The foundation awards grants to nonprofit organizations in Shelby County, Tennessee, (emphasis on Memphis) for charitable purposes that will benefit the greatest number of people in the state. Areas of interest include early childhood and elementary education, crime, health care, economic development, social service agencies, housing and homelessness, and the arts. Types of support include building/renovation, capital

campaigns, endowments, equipment, land acquisition, management development/capacity building, matching/challenge support, professorships, program-related investments/loans, program development, program evaluation, and seed money. Applicants should submit a brief letter of three pages or less explaining the specific project for which funds are needed and the results anticipated if the project is funded. Organizations whose projects are within the focus area will be invited to submit full proposals. The board meets in February, May, August, and November to review requests.
Requirements: Nonprofit organizations in Shelby County, TN, with particular emphasis on Memphis, may submit letters of request.
Restrictions: Funding requests are denied for annual operating expenses, individuals, and projects outside the Memphis, TN, area.
Geographic Focus: Tennessee
Date(s) Application is Due: Jan 10; Apr 10; Jul 10; Oct 10
Amount of Grant: 1,000 - 1,250,000 USD
Contact: Scott McCormick, Executive Director; (901) 529-4063; mail@plough.org
Sponsor: Plough Foundation
62 North Main Street, Suite 201
Memphis, TN 38103

Ploughshares Fund Grants 3916
Ploughshares Fund supports organizations and individuals working to build a safe, secure, nuclear weapons-free world. The organization places very few restrictions on our grantmaking—there are no geographical limitations on their grants; Ploughshares funds direct lobbying programs and makes grants to individuals.
Requirements: U.S. and international nonprofit organizations and individuals may apply. Ploughshares gives grants that: (1) promote the elimination of nuclear weapons (Building a consensus among the world's leaders creates a global norm against nuclear weapons and increases the momentum toward zero. Along the way, concrete steps to limit and reduce current arsenals must be realized as well.); (2) prevent the emergence of new nuclear states (The Fund focuses on the two most significant threats to the global nonproliferation regime – Iran and North Korea. Ploughshares believes that, though difficult, solutions are possible through effective diplomacy and engagement grounded in well-informed and strategic analysis. The Fund is investing significant resources over the next year on a special Iran Campaign that will promote non-military solutions to the Iran case.); and (3) build regional peace and security (South Asia represents perhaps the most dangerous region on earth given the long-standing conflict between India and Pakistan and the fact that both nations possess substantial nuclear arsenals. Ploughshares' investments support fact-finding missions, on-the-ground analysis, high-level dialogue, confidence-building measures, policy advocacy and media outreach to advance the transformation of conflicts in South and Southwest Asia.).
Restrictions: Ploughshares does not fund the production of films, videos, books, art projects or the research and writing of academic dissertations.
Geographic Focus: All States, All Countries
Date(s) Application is Due: Mar 15; Jul 15; Sep 15
Amount of Grant: 5,000 - 80,000 USD
Contact: Lorely Bunoan, Grants and Technology Manager; (415) 668-2244; fax (415) 668-2214; proposals@ploughshares.org or lorely@ploughshares.org
Internet: http://www.ploughshares.org/grants.php?a=2&b=0&c=0
Sponsor: Ploughshares Fund
The Presidio of San Francisco
San Francisco, CA 94129

Plum Creek Foundation Grants 3917
The corporate foundation awards grants to improve the quality of life in company operating areas. The foundation supports human services for children, at-risk youth, seniors, low-income, and abused individuals; education, particularly public and private colleges; youth organizations; hospitals, equipment, and medical programs; arts and cultural organizations; environmental education and conservation efforts; and civic affairs such as crime prevention, parks, and community development. Applications are reviewed quarterly. Application materials are available on the Web site.
Geographic Focus: Alabama, Arkansas, Florida, Georgia, Idaho, Louisiana, Maine, Mississippi, Montana, North Carolina, Oklahoma, Oregon, Pennsylvania, South Carolina, Texas, Virginia, Washington, West Virginia, Wisconsin
Amount of Grant: 1,000 - 10,000 USD
Contact: Administrator; (206) 467-3600; fax (206) 467-3799; foundation@plumcreek.com
Internet: http://www.plumcreek.com/community/default.php
Sponsor: Plum Creek Foundation
999 Third Avenue, Suite 4300
Seattle, WA 98104-4096

PMI Foundation Grants 3918
The PMI Foundation awards grants nationally, with emphasis on California, to a wide range of organizations with the goal of expanding homeownership. The foundation also contributes generously to deserving causes and charities in the areas of arts and culture, health and human services, education, civic organizations, and community development. Application guidelines are available for download from the PMI website. There are no application deadlines. Check with foundation staff to verify whether they are currently accepting applications.
Requirements: 501(c)3 organizations are eligible. Requests must target the disadvantaged, the poor, and distressed populations. Requests must either focus on increasing affordable housing opportunities or directly contribute to the quality of life in under-served communities.
Restrictions: The PMI Foundation does not accept requests for the following purposes: individuals; fraternal, veteran, labor, athletic or religious organizations serving a limited constituency; political or lobbying organizations, or those supporting the candidacy of a particular individual; travel funds; and films, videotapes or audio productions.
Geographic Focus: All States
Amount of Grant: 200 - 200,000 USD
Contact: Laura Kinney, Foundation Grant Administrator; (925) 658-6562
Internet: http://www.pmifoundation.org/index.html
Sponsor: PMI Foundation
3003 Oak Road
Walnut Creek, CA 94597-2098

PMP Professional Development Grants 3919
Annual grants of up to $5,000 are available to current recipients of adjudicated grants from the Philadelphia Music Project. Accordingly, applicant organizations have been vetted by PMP regrant panels. Professional development grants are intended to develop professional opportunities for the artistic leadership of Philadelphia music organizations. Early submissions for PMP professional development grants are encouraged, as available funding will be distributed to qualified applicants on a strictly first-come, first-served basis. Applications should be submitted at least four weeks prior to the project start date. Examples of projects eligible for funding include, but are not limited to, costs to attend workshops, lectures, performances, and conferences; or fees for visiting consultants that supports the professional artistic skills development of the leadership of the organization. Travel fees may be included in this request.
Requirements: Prior to submitting a full application, please submit a brief (not to exceed one page) letter of inquiry summarizing your proposed project to PMP's Director. Pending approval, proceed as follows: A. a narrative of no more than three typewritten pages on the applicant organization's letterhead, signed and dated by an authorizing official of the applicant organization. Address and number your responses according to the following points: request amount and objectives; activities; outcomes; impact; evaluation; B. a project budget; C. a single-page resume for each person named in the application.
Restrictions: Although professional development grants are intended to support artistic and curatorial capacity building, they may not be used to subsidize fees or pay for expenses related to artistic engagements (e.g., performances, showcases, residencies, recording projects, commissions).
Geographic Focus: Pennsylvania
Contact: Matthew Levy; (267) 350-4960; fax (267) 350-4998; mlevy@pcah.us
Internet: http://www.philadelphiamusicproject.org/professionaldevgrants.php
Sponsor: Philadelphia Music Project, the Pew Center for Arts and Heritage
1608 Walnut Street, 18th Floor
Philadelphia, PA 19103

PMP Project Grants 3920
The PMP primary goal is to enhance the cultural life of the community and further establish Greater Philadelphia as a cultural destination, by addressing the following priorities: fund music projects of increasing significance, creativity, and diversity; foster and promote musical excellence in our region; to augment and enrich organizations ideas and activities.
Requirements: Professional nonprofit 501(c)3status, music performing and presenting organizations are eligible to apply. Prior to submitting a full application, please submit a letter of inquiry and a Project Status Report (current PMP grantees only),deadline date, November 1. Complete application and PMP Summary Report of PACDP Cultural Data Profile, deadline date January 15. See website for application forms and guidelines.
Restrictions: An applicant organization must have been in operation for at least two years prior to the application deadline.
Geographic Focus: Pennsylvania
Date(s) Application is Due: Jan 15; Nov 1
Contact: Matthew Levy; (267) 350-4960; fax (267) 350-4998; mlevy@pcah.us
Internet: http://www.philadelphiamusicproject.org/projectgrants.php
Sponsor: Philadelphia Music Project, the Pew Center for Arts and Heritage
1608 Walnut Street, 18th Floor
Philadelphia, PA 19103

PNC Charitable Trust and Foundation Grants 3921
The PNC Charitable Trust Grant Review Committee serves over thirty perpetual charitable trusts and private foundations for which PNC is trustee. PNC's mission is to implement the legacies set forth by the individual donors who established these trust relationships with PNC. The Committee distributes grants from these charitable trusts to worthy 501(c)3 non-profit organizations. In accordance with the provisions of the trust agreements, the Committee funds grant requests that demonstrate a capacity and commitment to charitable service and enhance the quality of life for the people and their communities. Inquiries and proposals should be directly addressed to the local PNC representative. Names and contact information are listed on an interactive map on the website.
Requirements: Priority is given to the following: organizations that are direct providers of services, with projects and programs that meet donors' intent; organizations that demonstrate a capacity to meet the stated objectives, with objectives that are clearly articulated and measurable; the critical nature of the need being addressed; and organizations with strong leadership, diversified income streams, and long-term sustainability that have demonstrated efficiencies in delivering services. PNC seeks to support projects and programs that: reflect the core social mission of the applicant organization; address a community need; have broad impact, or benefit under-served populations; have measurable outcomes and a plan for documenting results; have detailed project budgets and demonstrate effective financial accountability; involve collaboration with other organizations; are of longer duration than events, conferences, or seminars; and complements rather than duplicate the work of other non-profit organizations.
Restrictions: Funding is provided in communities where donors lived and/or engaged. See the website to verify specific locations. The following are ineligible: general operating costs;

event, conference or seminar sponsorships or entry fees; pilot or new programming; multi-year commitments; for-profit organizations; individuals or private foundations; fraternal, political, advocacy or labor organizations; and organizations that discriminate based on race, color, creed, gender, or national origin.
Geographic Focus: District of Columbia, Indiana, Kentucky, Maryland, New Jersey, Ohio, Pennsylvania
Date(s) Application is Due: Feb 1; May 1; Aug 1; Oct 1
Contact: Eva T. Blum, Chairman; (412) 705-3584; eva.blum@pnc.com
Internet: http://www.pncsites.com/pncfoundation/charitable_trusts.html
Sponsor: PNC Foundation
630 Liberty Avenue, Tenth Floor
Pittsburg, PA 15222-2705

PNC Ecnomic Development Grants 3922
The PNC Foundation's priority is to form partnerships with community-based nonprofit organizations within the markets PNC serves. One priority is to promote the growth of targeted communities through economic development initiatives. Economic development organizations, including those which enhance the quality of life through neighborhood revitalization, cultural enrichment and human services are given support. Priority is given to community development initiatives that strategically promote the growth of targeted low-and moderate-income communities and/or provide services to these communities. Supported areas include affordable housing, community development, community services, revitalization and stabilization of low- and moderate-income areas, and arts and culture. All philanthropic giving is directed regionally. Inquiries and proposals should be directly addressed to the local PNC representative. Names and contact information are listed on an interactive map on the website. See the website for further proposal instructions.
Requirements: Organizations receiving support from the PNC Foundation must have a current Internal Revenue Service tax-exempt designation and be eligible to receive charitable contributions. In addition, the proposed activity must occur in a community where PNC has a significant presence. See the interactive map on the website to verify PNC locations.
Restrictions: The following is not supported: organizations that discriminate by race, color, creed, gender or national origin; religious organizations, except for non-sectarian activities; advocacy groups; operating funds for agencies that receive funds through PNC United Way allocation; individuals or private foundations; annual funds of hospitals or colleges and universities; conferences and seminars; and tickets and goodwill advertising.
Geographic Focus: Delaware, District of Columbia, Florida, Illinois, Indiana, Maryland, Michigan, Missouri, New Jersey, Ohio, Pennsylvania, Wisconsin
Contact: Eva T. Blum, Chairman; (412) 705-3584; eva.blum@pnc.com
Internet: http://www.pncsites.com/pncfoundation/foundation_grantProcess.html
Sponsor: PNC Foundation
630 Liberty Avenue, Tenth Floor
Pittsburg, PA 15222-2705

PNC Foundation Green Building Grants 3923
The PNC Foundation's priority is to form partnerships with community-based nonprofit organizations within the markets PNC serves. One priority is green building. The Foundation provides support to environmental projects and green building in the community. All philanthropic giving is directed regionally. Inquiries and proposals should be directly addressed to the local PNC representative. Names and contact information are listed on an interactive map on the website. See the website for further proposal instructions.
Requirements: Organizations receiving support from the PNC Foundation must have a current Internal Revenue Service tax-exempt designation and be eligible to receive charitable contributions. In addition, the proposed activity must occur in a community where PNC has a significant presence. See the interactive map on the website to verify PNC locations.
Restrictions: The following is not supported: organizations that discriminate by race, color, creed, gender or national origin; religious organizations, except for non-sectarian activities; advocacy groups; operating funds for agencies that receive funds through PNC United Way allocation; individuals or private foundations; annual funds of hospitals or colleges and universities; conferences and seminars; and tickets and goodwill advertising.
Geographic Focus: Delaware, District of Columbia, Florida, Illinois, Indiana, Maryland, Michigan, Missouri, New Jersey, Ohio, Pennsylvania, Wisconsin
Contact: Eva T. Blum, Chairman; (412) 705-3584; eva.blum@pnc.com
Sponsor: PNC Foundation
630 Liberty Avenue, Tenth Floor
Pittsburg, PA 15222-2705

PNC Foundation Grow Up Great Grants 3924
PNC and the PNC Foundation have long histories of strengthening and enriching the lives of their neighbors in communities in which they live and work. To build on this commitment, PNC developed PNC Grow Up Great, a 10-year, $100 million investment to help improve the school readiness of millions of children from birth to age five. As part of this initiative, the PNC Foundation has earmarked funds for grants to nonprofit organizations which work to directly improve children's school readiness by providing support in one of the following key areas: social and emotional development, teacher training and arts and culture. By focusing support in these critical areas, PNC's hope is to achieve greater results in school readiness, which will yield stronger, smarter and healthier children, families and communities.
Requirements: Organizations applying for support from the PNC Foundation must have a current Internal Revenue Service tax-exempt designation and be eligible to receive charitable contributions. In addition, the proposed activity must occur in a community where PNC has a meaningful presence. Available states are: Delaware; Kentucky; Indiana; New Jersey; Ohio; Pennsylvania; Washington. See PNC website for proposal guidelines and a complete listing of state contacts.
Geographic Focus: Delaware, Indiana, Kentucky, Maryland, New Jersey, Ohio, Pennsylvania, Washington

Contact: Eva T. Blum; (412) 762-2748; fax (412) 705-3584; eva.blum@pnc.com
Internet: https://www.pnc.com/webapp/unsec/ProductsAndService.do?siteArea=/PNC/Home/About+PNC/Our+Organization/Community+Involvement/PNC+Foundation/PNC+Foundation
Sponsor: PNC Foundation
One PNC Plaza, 249 5th Avenue, P1-P.O.PP-20-1
Pittsburgh, PA 15222

PNM Power Up Grants 3925
The PNM Fund of the PNM Resources Foundation created a the grant program, PNM Power Up Grants, to vitalize communities. The program seeks innovative and creative proposals, which will improve the quality of life in New Mexican communities. Grants will be awarded to nonprofits that propose the best projects for community and neighborhood revitalization, corridor, street or median improvements, green space creation, or creation of meaningful public spaces. Projects from parks to streetscapes will be considered.
Requirements: 501(c)3 nonprofit organizations are eligible to apply. Applications will be awarded throughout the state in communities PNM serves or where PNM has a significant presence. As the state's largest electricity provider, PNM serves more than 500,000 New Mexico residential and business customers in Greater Albuquerque, Rio Rancho, Los Lunas and Belen, Santa Fe, Las Vegas, Alamogordo, Ruidoso, Silver City, Deming, Bayard, Lordsburg and Clayton. It also serves the New Mexico tribal communities of the Tesuque, Cochiti, Santo Domingo, San Felipe, Santa Ana, Sandia, Isleta and Laguna Pueblos. Four principal grants will be awarded in the amount of $50,000 and twenty grants will be awarded in the amount of $15,000. Grant applications must be submitted online. All applications must be submitted by 5:00 pm MST of the deadline date.
Restrictions: PNM Power Up Grants will not be awarded to any of the following groups, programs or activities: sectarian or religious programs for religious purposes; veterans, labor and political organizations or campaigns; organizations outside of PNM Resources and its subsidiaries' service territories or communities where the company has business interests; organizations that are not registered with the appropriate state registration agency (New Mexico Attorney General, IRS) or are not in good standing with the registration body; organizations that limit membership and services based on race, religion, color, creed, sex, sexual orientation, age or national origin; or, organizations without current or active IRS 501(c)3 status.
Geographic Focus: New Mexico
Date(s) Application is Due: May 31
Amount of Grant: 15,000 - 50,000 USD
Contact: Jennifer Scacco; (505) 241-2864; Jennifer.Scacco@pnmresources.com
Internet: https://www.pnm.com/powerup
Sponsor: PNM Resources Foundation
414 Silver Avenue SW
Albuquerque, NM 87102

PNM Reduce Your Use Grants 3926
Reduce Your Use Grants help nonprofit organizations put their energy-saving ideas into action with grants up to $5,000. Since its inception in 2008, this program has awarded more than $1.5 million to nonprofits around the state of New Mexico to help them decrease their energy use in order to free up funds for their mission-based programs.
Requirements: All Reduce Your Use Grant submissions should include activities designed to educate your employees, clients and community about the importance of energy conservation. Priority will be given to organizations that have PNM employees and retirees actively volunteering with them. 501(c)3 nonprofit organizations are eligible to apply. Applications will be awarded throughout the state in communities PNM serves or where PNM has a significant presence. As the state's largest electricity provider, PNM serves more than 500,000 New Mexico residential and business customers in Greater Albuquerque, Rio Rancho, Los Lunas and Belen, Santa Fe, Las Vegas, Alamogordo, Ruidoso, Silver City, Deming, Bayard, Lordsburg and Clayton. It also serves the New Mexico tribal communities of the Tesuque, Cochiti, Santo Domingo, San Felipe, Santa Ana, Sandia, Isleta and Laguna Pueblos.
Restrictions: Reduce Your Use Grants will not be awarded to any of the following groups, programs or activities: individual teachers, schools or school districts; individuals; organizations without current or active IRS 501(c)3 status; payments of loans, interest, taxes or debt retirement; sectarian or religious programs for religious purposes; special events, annual events, camps or one-time only events; veterans, labor and political organizations or campaigns; municipalities (however, if a municipality uses a 501(c)3 nonprofit organization as a fiscal agent, they may qualify); organizations outside of PNM Resources service territory; organizations that are not registered with the appropriate state registration agency or are not in good standing with the registration body; organizations that limit membership and services based on race, religion, color, creed, sex, sexual orientation, age or national origin.
Geographic Focus: New Mexico
Amount of Grant: Up to 5,000 USD
Contact: Jennifer Scacco; (505) 241-2864; Jennifer.Scacco@pnmresources.com
Internet: https://www.pnm.com/reduceyouruse
Sponsor: PNM Resources Foundation
414 Silver Avenue SW
Albuquerque, NM 87102

Poets & Writers Readings/Workshops Grants 3927
Since its inception in 1970, Poets & Writers has provided fees to writers who give readings or conduct writing workshops. Organizations that sponsor readings and workshops in New York State or California, or Atlanta, Chicago, Detroit, Houston, New Orleans, Seattle, Tucson, or Washington, D.C. may apply for grants to be used for writers' fees. Grants for readings or spoken word performances range from $50-$350. Grants for workshops range from $100-$200 (In California, generally no more than $500 total for a workshop series)

per session. Organizations are encouraged to match the sponsor's payments to writers, but this requirement may be waived if there are extenuating circumstances.
Requirements: Organizations that may apply for grants include: colleges, cultural centers, museums, libraries, correctional facilities, hospitals, small presses, community centers, senior centers, places of worship, bookstores, cafes, galleries, and theaters. Nonprofit status is not required. Priority will be given to organizations that: (a) serve a culturally diverse audience; (b) feature culturally diverse writers; (c) feature writers who have not previously presented at that venue; (d) present programs in rural or other underserved areas; (e) have not previously received P&W support (If an organization has received P&W funding in the past, they will consider whether it has followed the grant guidelines and returned reports in a timely manner.); (f) are able to match P&W's payment to the writer (not including in-kind contributions such as meals, lodging, or travel); (g) have a publicity plan and/or strong publicity samples from past events. Published poets, fiction writers, creative nonfiction writers, and performance poets are eligible to receive fee payments from P&W. If the writer is not listed in P&W's Directory of American Poets and Writers (see http://www.pw.org/directory), the organization must submit a bio for the writer that includes verifiable publication or performance credits for the writer's original works. See the application guidelines and download the application form at the sponsor's website. Grants are approved on a rolling basis, however applications must be submitted at least eight weeks before the proposed event.
Restrictions: The project director and employees of the organization sponsoring the event are not eligible for funding.
Geographic Focus: Arizona, California, District of Columbia, Georgia, Illinois, Louisiana, Michigan, New York, Texas, Washington
Amount of Grant: 50 - 1,500 USD
Contact: Nicole Sealey, East Program Coordinator; (212) 226-3586; rwny@pw.org
Internet: http://www.pw.org/content/funding_readingsworkshops
Sponsor: Poets and Writers
90 Broad Street, Suite 2100
New York, NY 10004

Pohlad Family Foundation 3928
The Pohlad Foundation concentrates their funding on the arts, health and human services, capital grants, and youth programs. The Foundation strives to support programs that: support all types and sizes of art programs of interest to diverse audiences; provide essential and effective human services to disadvantaged children and families, fund a range of services from emergency needs to workforce development, and have a positive multi-year impact;
Requirements: Applications are considered only in response to a request for proposal or an invitation to apply. Organizations must be 501(c)3 non-profit organizations. Priority is given to organizations that demonstrate a commitment to their communities by ensuring that their governing bodies include representatives from within the community and projects that directly benefit communities in need. Organizations may view sample grant recipients and specific instructions on how to apply on the website.
Restrictions: Grants are focused in Minnesota, primarily St. Paul and Minneapolis. Funding is not available for: direct funding to individuals; health or housing-related emergency assistance to individuals; benefits, fundraisers, walk-a-thons, telethons, galas, or other revenue generating events; advertising; organizations that discriminate on the basis of race, gender, religion, culture, age, physical ability or disability, sexual orientation, gender identity, status as a military veteran or genetic information; veterans' and fraternal organizations; political or lobbying organizations; replacement of government funding.
Geographic Focus: Minnesota
Contact: Rose Peterson; (612) 661-3903; fax (612) 661-3715; rpeterson@pohladfamilygiving.org
Internet: http://pohladfoundation.org/giving/grant-guidelines.html
Sponsor: Pohlad Family Foundation
60 South Sixth Street, Suite 3900
Minneapolis, MN 55402

Polk Bros. Foundation Grants 3929
The primary focus of the Foundation is programs that work with populations of need, particularly children, youth, and families in underserved Chicago communities. Very few awards are made to organizations located outside the city of Chicago. Grants are made for both new and ongoing initiatives in four program areas: social service, education, culture and health care. In all areas, proposals should address increased access to services and improvement of the quality of life for area residents. Grants are seldom made for capital support.
Requirements: Illinois 501(c)3 nonprofit organizations are eligible. Preference is given to requests from Chicago. An organization that has not previously received a grant from the Foundation should first call the Foundation office or complete the pre-application form available on the Foundation website. The Foundation will then mail an application form or contact the organization with further questions.
Restrictions: The Polk Bros. Foundation will not support: organizations that devote a substantial portion of their activities to attempting to influence legislation or to participating in campaigns on behalf of candidates for public office; religious institutions seeking support for programs whose participants are restricted by religious affiliation or whose services promote a particular creed; purchase of dinner or raffle tickets or advertising in dinner programs; medical, scientific, or academic research; grants to individuals; tax-generating entities (municipalities, school districts, etc.) for services within their normal responsibilities. The Foundation will not consider more than one request from an organization or its affiliates in a 12-month period, nor will it generally fund more than eight percent of an organization's operating budget.
Geographic Focus: Illinois
Contact: Suzanne Doombos Kerbow; (312) 527-4684; questions@polkbrosfdn.org
Internet: http://www.polkbrosfdn.org/guidelines.htm
Sponsor: Polk Brothers Foundation
20 West Kinzie Street, Suite 1110
Chicago, IL 60611

Pollock Foundation Grants 3930
The foundation awards grants to Texas nonprofit organizations in its areas of interest, including cultural programs, dental education and schools, health care and health organizations, Jewish organizations and temples, libraries and library science, nursing, public health education and schools, social services, and youth development. Grants support program develoment and general operating expenses. There are no application deadlines. Contact the office for application materials.
Requirements: Texas nonprofits are eligible. Preference is given to requests from Dallas.
Geographic Focus: Texas
Amount of Grant: 1,000 - 300,000 USD
Contact: Robert Pollock, Trustee; (214) 871-7155; fax (214) 871-8158
Sponsor: Pollock Foundation
2626 Howell Street, Suite 895
Dallas, TX 75204

Porter County Community Foundation Grants 3931
The Porter County Community Foundation seeks to enhance the quality of life in Porter County by providing funds through an open grant making process for humanitarian, cultural, education and environmental purposes. The Foundation will consider grants in three categories: Program Enhancement with a maximum grant of $10,000; Program Operations with a maximum grant of $5,000; Capital Campaign Support with a maximum grant of $20,000. Refer to the Foundations website for a detailed description of each category. The Foundation offers two grant cycles per year. Organizations receive notice of whatever action is taken on their application within 45 days of application deadline.
Requirements: All applications must contain the following information: a grant request cover page; a grant narrative; a project budget; a copy of the organization's current year operating budget; a copy of the most recent financial statement; names and principal occupations of the Board of Directors; copy of the organization's 501(c)3 tax exempt ruling; and a letter of support or memo of understanding if the grant request is for a program that will be conducted at a facility not controlled by requesting organization.
Restrictions: The Foundation generally does not fund: annual appeals or membership contributions; event sponsorships; programs that are sectarian or religious in nature; political organizations or candidates; contributions to endowment campaigns; campaigns to reduce previously incurred debt; individuals (except scholarships from scholarship funds); programs already completed and/or equipment already contracted for; travel for bands, sports teams and similar groups; and camp scholarships or fees related to camp programs.
Geographic Focus: Indiana
Date(s) Application is Due: Feb 16; Aug 15
Amount of Grant: 5,000 - 20,000 USD
Contact: Brenda A. Sheetz; (219) 465-0294; bsheetz@portercountyfoundation.org
Internet: http://www.portercountyfoundation.org/index2.php#
Sponsor: Porter County Community Foundation
57 South Franklin Street, Suite 207, P.O. Box 302
Valparaiso, IN 46384

Porter County Emergency Grants 3932
The Foundation will consider emergency grants at any time during the year. An emergency grant may be awarded when an organization encounters uninsured damage to their physical facilities such as flooding, wind or fire damages. An emergency grant may be awarded to an organization that provides emergency assistance to individuals and families if there is a significant increase in the demand for assistance due to a natural disaster or other unanticipated occurrence. Under extremely rare circumstances, an organization may apply for assistance if they have experienced an unanticipated expenditure or revenue shortfall that has placed an extreme burden on the organization.
Requirements: To apply for an emergency grant, applicants should submit a letter describing the cause of the emergency, detailing the expenses anticipated or revenue lost, and any other relevant information. Upon receipt of the letter, the Foundation will review the request and, if necessary, schedule a meeting or site visit with the organization.
Restrictions: The amount of grant dollars will vary from time to time, and there is no guarantee that funds will be available.
Geographic Focus: Indiana
Contact: Brenda Sheetz; (219) 465-0294; bsheetz@portercountyfoundation.org
Internet: http://www.portercountyfoundation.org/grantprograms.html
Sponsor: Porter County Community Foundation
57 South Franklin Street, Suite 207, P.O. Box 302
Valparaiso, IN 46384

Porter County Health and Wellness Grant 3933
The Porter County Health and Wellness Fund awards grants to nonprofit organizations that promote, support, and/or advance health care in Porter County. Funding priorities include: increasing health care access for the underserved; improving and promoting healthy lifestyles for youth; and improving the nonprofit's operational capabilities to provide health care services. The maximum grant amount is $25,000.
Requirements: In addition to the application, all grant application packets must include the following information: a grant request cover page; a grant narrative; a project budget; a current operating budget and financial statement; the names and principal occupations of the organization's Board of Directors; the organization's grant application approval by their Board of Directors; and a copy of the organization's 501(c)3 tax exemption ruling.
Restrictions: Grants will not be made to: individuals; membership contributions; event sponsorships; programs that are sectarian or religious in nature; political organizations or candidates; contributions to endowment campaigns; campaigns to reduce previously incurred debt; and programs already completed.
Geographic Focus: Indiana

Date(s) Application is Due: Jun 15
Amount of Grant: 25,000 USD
Contact: Brenda Sheetz, Health/Wellness Fund Contact; (219) 465-0294; fax (219) 464-2733; bsheetz@portercountyfoundation.org
Internet: http://www.portercountyfoundation.org/grantprograms.html
Sponsor: Porter County Community Foundation
57 South Franklin Street, Suite 207, P.O. Box 302
Valparaiso, IN 46384

Porter County Women's Grant 3934
The Women's Grant of Porter County seeks to improve the quality of life for women and children in Porter County by collectively funding high impact grants for charitable initiatives with the same purpose. The group will award a $45,000 grant to a nonprofit organization in support of a project or program that addresses the issues of women and children and is sustainable. Priority will be given to innovative programs that demonstrate positive outcomes in one of the following areas: education and training to promote economic security and self-sufficiency; leadership development and programs designed to build self-esteem; access to women's health services and healthy lifestyles; safe environments and freedom from violence; and access to affordable daycare services that will expand hours of service, increase the number served on a sustainable basis and/or improve quality.
Requirements: In addition to the online application form, all application packets must include the following information: a grant request cover page; a grant narrative (see application for narrative details); a project budget; a copy of the organization's current year operating budget; the organization's most recent financial statement; names and principal occupations of the Board of Directors; evidence of Board approval for this application; a copy of the organization's 501(c)3 tax exemption.
Restrictions: The grant will not fund the following: projects or programs that do not address issues facing women and/or children; scholarship programs including daycare and program participation fees; annual appeals or membership contributions; event sponsorships; programs that are sectarian or religious in nature; political organizations or candidates; contributions to endowment campaigns; campaigns to reduce previously incurred debt; individuals; programs already completed and/or equipment already contracted for; and travel for bands, sports teams and similar groups.
Geographic Focus: Indiana
Date(s) Application is Due: Apr 15
Amount of Grant: 45,000 USD
Contact: Brenda Sheetz; (219) 465-0294; bsheetz@portercountyfoundation.org
Internet: http://www.portercountyfoundation.org/grantprograms.html
Sponsor: Porter County Community Foundation
57 South Franklin Street, Suite 207, P.O. Box 302
Valparaiso, IN 46384

Portland Foundation - Women's Giving Circle Grant 3935
The mission of The Portland Foundation Women's Giving Circle is to build a community of women philanthropists through the pooling of knowledge and resources for the purpose of providing grants to Jay County organizations and initiatives that address mutually-agreeable issues. The Circle awards grants which focus on enhancing the capacity of Jay County's not-for-profit organizations to support programming that addresses needs for youth and families. The Circle strives to fund innovative endeavors to benefit Jay County residents from toddlers to senior citizens.
Requirements: Organizations are encouraged to contact the Foundation to discuss whether their project is appropriate for funding. The application is available at the Foundation site. In addition to the application, proposals should include 10 copies of the following information: a copy of the IRS determination letter confirming tax-exempt status; organization's most recent financial statement, including budget and year-to-date income and expenses; and a detailed list of the Board of Directors.
Restrictions: The following are excluded from funding: organizations for religious or sectarian purposes; make-up of operating deficits, post-event or after-the-fact situations; endowment or capital projects and campaigns; for any propaganda, political or otherwise, attempting to influence legislation or intervene in any political affairs or campaigns; and dinner galas, advertising or other special fundraising events.
Geographic Focus: Indiana
Amount of Grant: 200 - 1,000 USD
Contact: Douglas Inman; (260) 726-4260; fax (260) 726-4273; tpf@portlandfoundation.org
Internet: http://www.portlandfoundation.org/womens-giving-circle-grant
Sponsor: Portland Foundation
112 East Main Street
Portland, IN 47371

Portland Foundation Grants 3936
The Portland Foundation Community Grants are particularly interested in proposals for start-up costs for new programs; one-time projects or needs; and capital needs beyond an applicant's capabilities and means. In addition, limited funding is available in the following areas: emergency service agencies; programs that benefit the elderly of Jay County; needy families; libraries; historical facilities; care and prevention of cruelty to animals; handicapped children; and education of sensory impaired children. The Foundation funds twice yearly in the summer and winter. Both applications are available on the website.
Requirements: The grant application is available on the Foundation website, and must be sent electronically. Ten complete proposal packages are then mailed to the Foundation and must include: a completed, computer-generated application (typed or handwritten applications cannot be accepted); copy of the 501(c)3 IRS determination letter; the organization's most recent financial statements; current budget reflecting year-to-date income and expenses; purchase estimates and/or project bids, if applicable; phone number where contact person can be reached; requested signatures; completed Counterterrorism Compliance form; and an explanation of why any of the above is not included.
Restrictions: The Foundation will not normally consider grants for the following purposes: individuals other than scholarships; organizations for religious or sectarian purposes; make-up of operating deficits, post-event or after-the-fact situations; endowment campaigns; or for any propaganda, political or otherwise, attempting to influence legislation or intervene in any political affairs or campaigns. The Foundation is reluctant to approve grants for the purpose of maintaining an on-going operating budget or for multi-year grants requests. However, exceptions to this may be made at the discretion of the Foundation.
Geographic Focus: Indiana
Date(s) Application is Due: Jan 6; Jul 6
Amount of Grant: 1,000 - 25,000 USD
Contact: Douglas Inman; (260) 726-4260; fax (260) 726-4273; tpf@portlandfoundation.org
Internet: http://www.portlandfoundation.org/winter-grants-scholarships
Sponsor: Portland Foundation
112 East Main Street
Portland, IN 47371

Portland General Electric Foundation Grants 3937
Portland General Electric is committed to improving the quality of life for all Oregonians. The Foundation focuses giving in three areas: education, arts and culture, and healthy families. Education funding dedicates awards to scholarships, innovation in classroom instruction, transitional bridges between grade levels, career readiness and at-risk youth programs. Arts and Culture awards support youth programs and adult cultural programs that enhances understanding in communities. Healthy Families funding promotes access and services in areas of health, domestic violence, parenting, foster care, and other services that benefit families.
Requirements: 501(c)3 nonprofits in Oregon that address issues in the three focus areas of the Foundation are eligible for funding. Applicants must first submit a Letter of Inquiry to the Foundation; applicants may then be invited to submit a full application. Both of these steps must be completed online.
Restrictions: The foundation does not fund: bridge grants, debt retirement or operational deficits; endowment funds; general fund drives or annual appeals; political entities, ballot measure campaigns or candidates for political office; organizations that discriminate against individuals on the basis of creed, color, gender, sexual orientation, age, religion or national origin; fraternal, sectarian and religious organizations; individuals; travel expenses; or conferences, symposiums, festivals, events, team sponsorships or user fees. The Foundation also does not directly fund public K-12 education.
Geographic Focus: Oregon
Date(s) Application is Due: Jan 11; Apr 5; Jul 5; Nov 1
Contact: Paige Haxton; (503) 464-8818; fax (503) 464-2929; pgefoundation@pgn.com
Internet: http://www.pgefoundation.org/how_we_fund.html
Sponsor: Portland General Electric Foundation
121 SW Salmon Street, One World Trade Center, 3rd Floor
Portland, OR 97204

Posey Community Foundation Women's Fund Grants 3938
The Posey County Community Foundation is a nonprofit, public charity created by and for the people of Posey County, Indiana. The Posey County's Women's Fund makes yearly grants to support a variety of projects or programs serving women and girls in Posey County, Indiana. These programs include those that prevent domestic violence, secure family-supporting jobs, promote health and education, and develop confidence. Grant proposals are accepted once each year. Grants are normally given as one time support of a project but may be considered for additional support for expansions or outgrowths of an initial project. The application form and examples of previously funded projects available at the website.
Requirements: Projects must address the needs which support the Fund's mission by providing opportunities, encouragement, knowledge, information, and hope for the community's women and girls. The Women's Fund welcomes proposals from non-profit organizations that are tax-exempt under sections 501(c)3 and 509(a) of the Internal Revenue Code and from governmental agencies serving Posey County women and girls. Proposals from other non-profit organizations that address issues facing women and girls in the county may be accepted. Proposals submitted by an entity under the auspices of another agency must include a written statement signed by the agency's board president on behalf of the board of directors agreeing to act as the entity's fiscal sponsor, to receive grant monies if awarded, and to oversee the proposed project.
Geographic Focus: Indiana
Date(s) Application is Due: Jul 5
Contact: Johnna Denning; (812) 838-0288; johnna@poseycommunityfoundation.org
Internet: http://www.poseycommunityfoundation.org/wf-grantmaking
Sponsor: Posey County Community Foundation
402 Main Street, P.O. Box 746
Mt. Vernon, IN 47620

Posey County Community Foundation Grants 3939
The Posey County Community Foundation is a nonprofit, public charity created by and for the people of Posey County, Indiana. Grant proposals are accepted once each year as a one-time project support. At the beginning of each cycle in January, notices are sent to nonprofit organizations that have previously applied for grants, have received grants in the past, or have otherwise requested notification. Applicants are encouraged to schedule a meeting with the Foundation's director to receive an overview of the grant process. Proposals are accepted from January through March. The grant application is available at the website.
Requirements: The Foundation welcomes funding requests from nonprofit organizations that are 501(c)3 tax exempt. For those organizations not tax exempt, requests may be considered if the project is charitable and supports a community need.

Restrictions: Funding is not available for religious organizations for religious purposes; political parties or campaigns; endowment creation or debt reduction; operating costs; capital campaigns; annual appeals or membership contributions; or travel requests for groups or individuals such as bands, sports teams, or classes.
Geographic Focus: Indiana
Date(s) Application is Due: Mar 6
Amount of Grant: Up to 5,000 USD
Contact: Johnna Denning; (812) 838-0288; johnna@poseycommunityfoundation.org
Internet: http://www.poseycommunityfoundation.org/disc-grants
Sponsor: Posey County Community Foundation
402 Main Street, P.O. Box 746
Mt. Vernon, IN 47620

Pott Foundation Grants 3940
Established in 1963 by Herman T. Pott, The Pott Foundation is a non-profit organization supporting children, education and health and human services. Most of the grant recipients are located in Herman Pott's adopted city of St. Louis, Missouri. The Foundation distributes approximately $1.5 million annually to over 100 charities.
Requirements: Non-profit 501(c)3 organization are eligible to apply in Missouri. Mail grant applications to: The Pott Foundation, C/O U.S. Bank, N.A., The Private Client Reserve, Attn: Carol Eaves, Mail Loc: SL-MO-CTCS, 10 North Hanley, Clayton, MO 63105.
Geographic Focus: Missouri
Date(s) Application is Due: Apr 1
Contact: Carol Eaves, (314) 418-8317
Sponsor: Pott Foundation
10 North Hanley
Clayton, MO 63105

Powell Family Foundation Grants 3941
The foundation awards grants to nonprofits in the Kansas City area for support of programs in the areas of environment, civic affairs, and youth. Types of support include general operating support, continuing support, annual campaigns, capital campaigns, equipment acquisition, and program/project development. There are no application forms. Letters of intent must be received 30 days preceding board meetings. The foundation prefers written inquiries and will send guidelines if the project meets foundation criteria.
Requirements: Nonprofits in, or serving the residents of, Missouri are eligible.
Restrictions: The foundation does not support welfare or social services programs.
Geographic Focus: Missouri
Amount of Grant: 2,500 - 25,000 USD
Contact: George Powell, Jr., President; (913) 236-0003; fax (913) 262-0058
Sponsor: Powell Family Foundation
4350 Shawnee Mission Parkway, Suite 280
Fairway, KS 66205-2528

Powell Foundation Grants 3942
The purpose of the Powell Foundation is to distribute funds for public charitable purposes, principally for the support, encouragement and assistance to education, health, conservation, and the arts with a direct impact within the Foundation's geographic zone of interest The Foundation places priority on organizations and programs that serve residents in Harris, Travis and Walker counties, Texas, principally in the fields of education, the arts, health and conservation. The Foundation's current emphasis is in the field of public education in the broadest sense. Other areas of interest continue to be community service projects focused on the needs of children, the disadvantaged, the urban environment, and the visual and performing arts, especially in the Greater Houston, Texas area. The Foundation operates on a calendar year and its Board meets twice a year in the spring and in the fall. Submission of proposals is required at least two months prior to a meeting for consideration at that meeting. To allow for optimum consideration and due diligence, those seeking grants are encouraged to apply to the foundation on an ongoing basis. Grants that do not make the deadline for one meeting will be carried forward to the next meeting. Each request must be in writing and should be accompanied by the proposal summary and the required list of attachments. See the foundation's website for additional guidelines.
Requirements: Texas IRS 501(c)3 tax-exempt organizations serving Harris, Walker, and Travis counties are eligible to apply.
Restrictions: Normally, the Foundation will not support: requests for building funds or grant commitments extending into successive calendar years; grants to religious organizations for religious purposes; fund raising events or advertising; grants to other private foundations; grants to cover past operating deficits or debt retirement; grants for support to individuals; grants that impose the exercise of responsibility upon the Foundation. For example: private operating foundations or certain supporting organizations.
Geographic Focus: Texas
Amount of Grant: 1,000 - 20,000 USD
Contact: Caroline J. Sabin; (713) 523-7557; fax (713) 523-7553; info@powellfoundation.org
Internet: http://www.powellfoundation.org/powellguide.htm
Sponsor: Powell Foundation of Houston
2121 San Felipe, Suite 110
Houston, TX 77019-5600

PPG Industries Foundation Grants 3943
Funding requests for a variety of project proposals that advance the foundation's interests are eligible for consideration. These may include capital projects, operating grants and special projects. In general, the foundation gives priority to applications from organizations dedicated to enhancing the welfare of communities in which PPG is a resident. Each grant application is reviewed with regard to the: compatibility of the applicant's goals with the foundation's priorities and available resources; financial needs of the organization; past practices of the foundation with respect to that organization; capability and reputation of the applicant; funds available to the applicant from other sources; extent to which the work of the applicant duplicates that of other organizations; public scope and impact of the applicant's proposal; and the interest of other corporate foundations with respect to the applicant. Historically the foundation has supported nonprofits in the areas of human services, health and safety, civic and community affairs, education, and cultural and arts. Requests for funding are accepted year-round. Determinations are made by the foundation's screening committee and board of directors.
Requirements: Applicants must use PPG's online grant making system to apply. The link is on the website. PPG Industries Foundation will review applications on a regular basis and will contact all grantseekers with proposals of interest. Organizations located in the Pittsburgh area and organizations of national scope should direct any questions to the executive director of the foundation. Organizations serving communities where PPG facilities are located should direct any questions to the local PPG Industries Foundation agent in their area. A list of these may be found at the PPG Foundation website under the Foundation Governance link.
Restrictions: The foundation will not award grants for: advertising or sponsorships; endowments; political or religious purposes; projects which would directly benefit PPG Industries, Inc; or special events and telephone solicitations. Operating grants are not made to United Way agencies.
Geographic Focus: All States, Pennsylvania
Contact: Sue Sloan; (412) 434-2453; fax (412) 434-4666; foundation@ppg.com
Internet: http://www.ppg.com/en/ppgfoundation/Pages/Grant_Policies.aspx
Sponsor: PPG Industries Foundation
One PPG Place
Pittsburgh, PA 15272

Praxair Foundation Grants 3944
The foundation supports nonprofit organizations primarily in the communities where Praxair operates. Preference is given to projects in the following areas: higher education—science, engineering, and environmental studies and programs that encourage minority students to pursue studies in these areas; community service—United Way (matching employee donations), public Libraries (technology upgrading, acquiring new materials, or initiating innovative programs), employee volunteer grants (grants to nonprofit organizations where employees volunteer); public policy and the environment; and international organizations operating in countries where Praxair is expanding its presence, primarily in Asia. All proposals should describe projects that serve the needs of the community at large. Special attention will be given to innovative programs that can be started and completed within one year of the award. Goals should be clearly defined and measurable. The level of support varies depending upon the nature of the project and how closely it fits with foundation guidelines. To apply for a grant, complete the Praxair Foundation Funding Request form.
Requirements: 501(c)3 tax-exempt organizations are eligible.
Geographic Focus: All States
Amount of Grant: 1,000 - 50,000 USD
Contact: Grants Administrator; (800) 772-9247; fax (716) 879-2040
Internet: http://www.praxair.com/praxair.nsf/AllContent/1E607B9456292F1185256BF800779733?OpenDocument
Sponsor: Praxair Foundation
39 Old Ridgebury Road
Danbury, CT 06810

Premera Blue Cross CARES Grants 3945
Premera CARES, a corporate giving program of Premera Blue Cross, focuses on health promotion and disease prevention in the communities it serves in Washington and Alaska. The program supports action-oriented events and programs which promote wellness and prevent major health conditions (e.g., diabetes, heart disease and cancer) as well as supporting initiatives which address the emotional and social well-being of community members and organizations which provide services to people with low and no income. Eligible organizations can submit funding requests through Premera's online grants-application tool on an ongoing basis. Guidelines and a link to the online-application tool are available at the grant website. Organizations should allow 90 days for processing of each request.
Requirements: Applicants must assist residents in areas served by Premera in Alaska and Washington, and must be a 501(c)3 organization, a government agency (or program), or a public school or school district. Funds must be used exclusively for public purposes. In addition, preference will be given to proposals that do the following: focus on health or wellness, including exercise and stress management, as a means of addressing common risk factors and preventing such health conditions as diabetes, heart disease, and cancer; address issues of access to healthcare for uninsured, low-income and underserved; and/or meet a special regional community-health need. Premera is a corporate contributor to United Way. In general, proposals from individual agencies already funded by the United Way will be given lower priority than proposals from other eligible organizations that are not receiving United Way support.
Restrictions: Grant awards are limited to areas of company operations in Alaska and Washington. Premera funds do not support the following entities: individuals; organizations that are for profit; arts organizations; religious organizations (unless the award is designated to an ongoing secular community-service program such as a food bank, shelter, homelessness project, or low-income health clinic and is not used to propagate a belief in a specific faith); or organizations that discriminate against individuals on any impermissible basis. Premera funds are not used for capital campaigns.
Geographic Focus: Alaska, Washington
Contact: Johanna Raisch, Grants Coordinator; (917) 677-2426
Internet: https://www.premera.com/stellent/groups/public/documents/xcpproject/social_responsibility.asp

Sponsor: Premera Blue Cross
7001 220th Street, S.W., Building 1
Mountlake Terrace, WA 98043-2160

Presbyterian Church USA Sam and Helen R. Walton Award 3946
In late December 1991, Sam and Helen R. Walton made a generous gift through the Presbyterian Church (U.S.A.) Foundation of $6 million. This gift included an endowment in the amount of $3 million, the earned interest to be used by new church developments that have placed an emphasis on site acquisition. The program offers an opportunity annually to sessions, presbyteries and synods to nominate new church developments that are working in creative ways to bring the gospel to their local communities. Those chosen will receive a one-time financial award of $50,000.
Geographic Focus: All States
Date(s) Application is Due: Jan 31
Amount of Grant: 50,000 USD
Contact: Tim McCallister, Associate for Program Grants; (888) 728-7228, ext. 5251
Internet: http://www.pcusa.org/missionprogramgrants/walton.htm
Sponsor: Presbyterian Church USA
100 Witherspoon Street, Room M042
Louisville, KY 40202-1396

Presbyterian Health Foundation Bridge, Seed and Equipment Grants 3947
The primary objective of bridge grants is to provide funding of limited duration to enhance faculty competitiveness for national extramural funding. The seed grant program provides start-up funding for young investigators or for investigators launching into a new research direction. The equipment grants program provides the funding for laboratory equipment needed to advance research.
Requirements: Oklahoma nonprofit organizations are eligible. Submit a letter of application. Applications are due the last week in March, June, September, and December.
Restrictions: Grants are not made to individuals, private foundations, for-profit organizations or for operating funds of organizations.
Geographic Focus: Oklahoma
Amount of Grant: 25,000 - 250,000 USD
Contact: Michael D. Anderson; (405) 319-8150; manderson@phfokc.com
Internet: http://www.phfokc.com/bridge.htm
Sponsor: Presbyterian Health Foundation
655 Research Park Way, Suite 500
Oklahoma City, OK 73104-3603

Preservation Maryland Heritage Fund Grants 3948
The Preservation Maryland Heritage Fund provides direct assistance for the protection of endangered cultural resources and promotes innovative demonstration projects that can be successfully replicated to meet Maryland's historic preservation needs. The Fund is intended to serve the needs of tangible cultural resources in Maryland that are not likely to be met through existing Preservation Maryland and Maryland Historical Trust programs. Along with historic sites, buildings, districts, and objects, projects benefiting archaeological resources are eligible for funding. Each year one or more special needs will be identified as additional priority funding areas. Projects eligible for funding include: stabilization or acquisition of endangered historic properties; feasibility studies, architectural plans, structural assessments and historic structure reports; projects benefiting archaeological resources including curatorial services; bricks and mortar repairs and restoration; and educational, research, and planning efforts related to resource preservation.
Requirements: Maryland organizations and local jurisdictions are eligible to apply.
Geographic Focus: Maryland
Date(s) Application is Due: Feb 1; Jun 1; Oct 1
Amount of Grant: Up to 5,000 USD
Contact: Marilyn Benaderet, Director of Preservation Services; (410) 685-2886; fax (410) 539-2182; mbenaderet@preservationmaryland.org
Internet: http://www.preservemd.org/html/fundingopps.html
Sponsor: Preservation Maryland
24 W Saratoga Street
Baltimore, MD 21201

President's Student Service Scholarships 3949
The program offers a service scholarship to one high school junior or senior from every high school in the country. The scholarship is made up of $500 from the Corporation for National Service and a $500 match from the local community. In addition to the scholarship, students receive an award certificate, a letter from the president, and the President's Student Service Award gold pin. Principals, counselors, and teachers should work with representatives of community organizations to determine how applications will be solicited and how scholarship recipients will be selected. The school must complete the scholarship certification form; this form may also be used as a student application form. Nominations will be accepted on an ongoing basis; however, no student may receive more than one award in a year. Nomination forms must be submitted by June 28. All entries submitted before April 1 will be reviewed in time for end-of-the-year award ceremonies. Nomination forms are available online.
Requirements: High school juniors and seniors who contribute at least 100 hours of service to their community within a 12-month period are eligible. Students must attend a public, private, charter, or parochial school within the 50 states, the District of Columbia, an Indian tribe, a U.S. territory, or a Department of Defense school. No minimum grade point average is required.
Geographic Focus: All States
Amount of Grant: 1,000 USD
Contact: Scholarship Administrator; (866) 291-7700 or (202) 742-5390; info@studentservicescholarship.org
Internet: http://www.nationalservice.org
Sponsor: President's Student Service Challenge
1150 Connecticut Avenue NW, Suite 1100
Washington, DC 20036

Price Chopper's Golub Foundation Grants 3950
Price Chopper's Golub Foundation provides financial support to eligible charitable organizations with a current 501(c)3 tax exempt status. Contributions are made through planned, continued giving programs in the areas of health and human services, arts, culture, education, and youth activities, within Price Chopper marketing areas. To be considered for funding, mail a written request, on letterhead for the organization seeking the donation, six to eight weeks prior to needed support or response deadlines. The Foundation reviews capital campaign requests quarterly, so please allow three to four months for a response.
Requirements: The Foundation's six state marketing area includes a specific mile radius around its stores in New York (Albany, Broome, Cayuga, Chenango, Clinton, Columbia, Cortland, Delaware, Dutchess, Essex, Franklin, Fulton, Greene, Hamilton, Herkimer, Jefferson, Lewis, Madison, Montgomery, Oneida, Onondaga, Orange, Oswego, Otsego, Rensselaer, St. Lawrence, Saratoga, Schenectady, Schoharie, Sullivan, Tioga, Tompkins, Ulster, Warren, and Washington counties), Massachusetts (Berkshire, Hampden, Hampshire, Middlesex, and Worcester counties), Vermont (Addison, Bennington, Caledonia, Chittenden, Essex, Franklin, Grand Isle, Lamoille, Orange, Orleans, Rutland, Washington, Windham, and Windsor counties), Pennsylvania (Lackawanna, Luzerne, Pike, Susquehanna, Wayne, and Wyoming counties), Connecticut (Hartford, Litchfield, New Haven, Tolland, and Windham counties) and New Hampshire (Cheshire, Grafton, and Sullivan counties).
Restrictions: The Foundation does not support: individuals; annual meetings; endowments; film and video projects; program advertising; funding for travel; organizations or events outside of its marketing area; events to raise funds for groups outside of its local community; conferences, conventions, or symposiums; publishing; operating expenses; scholarship programs outside of its own; or capital campaigns of national, religious or political organizations.
Geographic Focus: Connecticut, Massachusetts, New Hampshire, New York, Pennsylvania, Vermont
Contact: Deborah Tanski; (518) 356-9450 or (518) 379-1270; fax (518) 374-4259
Internet: http://www.pricechopper.com/GolubFoundation/GolubFoundation_S.las
Sponsor: Price Chopper's Golub Foundation
P.O. Box 1074
Schenectady, NY 12301

Price Chopper's Golub Foundation Two-Year Health Care Scholarship 3951
The Foundation annually awards the two-year $2,000 total college scholarship to a graduating high school senior planning to attend a degree-granting community or junior college to study within the health care field. The applicant must have demonstrated either outstanding leadership, entrepreneurial ability, or a commitment to humanity, as well as scholastic ability. As part of the application process, a Personal Essay Topic should describe the educational course of study chosen and specifically how the chosen future occupation or profession will aid the community in which the applicant lives. The applicant should also include why he/she believes Price Chopper's Golub Foundation should award this scholarship to them. To be eligible to apply for the scholarship, the applicant must plan to attend an accredited two year community or junior college in Connecticut, Massachusetts, New Hampshire, New York, Pennsylvania, or Vermont.
Requirements: An application form is required for scholarships, and a personal interview may be required. The Foundation's six state marketing area includes a specific mile radius around its stores in New York (Albany, Broome, Cayuga, Chenango, Clinton, Columbia, Cortland, Delaware, Dutchess, Essex, Franklin, Fulton, Greene, Hamilton, Herkimer, Jefferson, Lewis, Madison, Montgomery, Oneida, Onondaga, Orange, Oswego, Otsego, Rensselaer, St. Lawrence, Saratoga, Schenectady, Schoharie, Sullivan, Tioga, Tompkins, Ulster, Warren, and Washington counties), Massachusetts (Berkshire, Hampden, Hampshire, Middlesex, and Worcester counties), Vermont (Addison, Bennington, Caledonia, Chittenden, Essex, Franklin, Grand Isle, Lamoille, Orange, Orleans, Rutland, Washington, Windham, and Windsor counties), Pennsylvania (Lackawanna, Luzerne, Pike, Susquehanna, Wayne, and Wyoming counties), Connecticut (Hartford, Litchfield, New Haven, Tolland, and Windham counties) and New Hampshire (Cheshire, Grafton, and Sullivan counties).
Geographic Focus: Connecticut, Massachusetts, New Hampshire, New York, Pennsylvania, Vermont
Date(s) Application is Due: Mar 15
Amount of Grant: 2,000 USD
Contact: Deborah Tanski; (518) 356-9450 or (518) 379-1270; fax (518) 374-4259
Internet: http://www2.pricechopper.com/scholarships/
Sponsor: Price Chopper's Golub Foundation
P.O. Box 1074
Schenectady, NY 12301

Price Family Charitable Fund Grants 3952
Established in 1983, the Price Family Charitable Fund serves the San Diego, Carlsbad and, San Marcos, California region. The foundation is interested in supporting the economically disadvantaged, giving primarily for education and philanthropy purposes. The types of support include: annual campaigns; fellowships; program evaluation; scholarship funds; scholarships to individuals and; general operating support. There's no formal application to submit. Potential grantees much first submit a letter of Inquiry including: project goals, objectives and expected results (maximum of one page); project narrative (maximum of five pages); project budget (maximum of one page); a list of grants, if any, received by

organization in the last 12 months for this program/project (sources and amounts); a list of the organization's current board of directors, including each member's name, profession, and office help on the board, if any.
Requirements: Non-profit organizations with 501(c)3 status or governmental units such as public schools or city departments in are available for funding. The Foundation gives primarily in the following region of: San Diego; Carlsbad; San Marcos, California.
Restrictions: Grants are not made: to organizations whose primary purpose is religious, or for propagandizing, influencing legislation and/or elections, promoting voting registration, for political candidates, political campaigns or organizations engaged in political activities; or to federal appeals or to organizations the collect funds for redistribution to other non-profit groups. Unsolicited requests for funds are not accepted.
Geographic Focus: California
Contact: Terry Malavenda, (858) 551-2330
Sponsor: Price Family Charitable Fund
7979 Ivanhoe Avenue, Suite 520
La Jolla, CA 92037-4513

Price Gilbert, Jr. Charitable Fund Grants   3953
The Price Gilbert, Jr. Charitable Fund was established under the will of Price Gilbert, Jr. in 1973. During his life, Gilbert made bequests to the Georgia Tech Foundation with preference for the Price Gilbert Memorial Library, the Atlanta Speech School, the University of Georgia Foundation for the Gilbert Infirmary, and Northside Methodist Church. The remainder of his estate funded the Price Gilbert, Jr. Charitable Fund. Wells Fargo Bank serves as Trustee to a portion of this successor fund. The purpose of the Price Gilbert, Jr. Charitable Fund is to distribute to such charitable and/or educational institutions in the Atlanta area as selected by said Trustee as are recognized by the Internal Revenue Service.
Requirements: All grants are made to qualified 501(c)3 organizations in the Atlanta area, taking into consideration the charitable intent of Mr. Gilbert. Consideration will be given to the Georgia Tech Foundation and the Atlanta Speech School in grantmaking decisions. Proposals should be submitted in the following format: completed Common Grant Application Form; an original Proposal Statement; an audited financial report and a current year operating budget; a copy of your official IRS Letter with your tax determination; a listing of your Board of Directors. Proposal Statements (second item in the above Format) should answer these questions: what are the objectives and expected outcomes of this program/project/request; what strategies will be used to accomplish your objective; what is the timeline for completion; if this is part of an on-going program, how long has it been in operation; what criteria will you use to measure success; if the request is not fully funded, what other sources can you engage; an Itemized budget should be included; please describe any collaborative ventures. Prior to the distribution of funds, all approved grantees must sign and return a Grant Agreement Form, stating that the funds will be used for the purpose intended. Progress reports and Completion reports must also be filed as required for your specific grant. All current grantees must be in good standing with required documentation prior to submitting new proposals to any foundation.
Restrictions: Grants are not made for political purposes, nor to organizations which discriminate on the basis of race, ethnic origin, sexual or religious preference, age or gender.
Geographic Focus: Georgia
Date(s) Application is Due: Aug 1
Amount of Grant: 2,000 - 100,000 USD
Contact: Joyce Yamaato; (888) 234-1999; grantadministration@ wellsfargo.com
Internet: https://www.wachovia.com/foundation/v/index.jsp?vgnextoid=13d852199c0aa110VgnVCM1000004b0d1872RCRD&vgnextfmt=default
Sponsor: Price Gilbert, Jr. Charitable Fund
3280 Peachtree Road NE, Suite 400
Atlanta, GA 30305

Priddy Foundation Capital Grants   3954
The Priddy Foundation is a general purpose foundation, interested primarily in programs that have the potential for lasting and favorable impact on individuals and organizations. Considerations for funding include the geographic area served by the project, the individuals and groups served, the problem being addressed, the availability of existing resources and the degree of need. The Foundation board will consider capital projects for buildings and major items of equipment. Approval is more likely if the project has broad support from organizations and individuals to the extent that Foundation's requested share of the project does not exceed 20% of the total project budget. Before a capital grant is funded, the organization must attain the project fund-raising goal and document that funds raised are sufficient to complete the project as presented in the grant application. Deadlines for preliminary applications are February 1 and August 1, while final applications are due March 1 and September 1.
Requirements: 501(c)3 Texas and Oklahoma nonprofit organizations are eligible. The foundation considers grant applications from organizations in the Wichita Falls, Texas area. In Texas, this includes the following counties: Archer, Baylor, Childress, Clay, Cottle, Foard, Hardeman, Haskell, Jack, King, Knox, Montague, Stonewall, Throckmorton, Wichita, Wilbarger, Wise, and Young. In Oklahoma, it includes the following counties: Comanche, Cotton, Jackson, Jefferson, Stephens, and Tillman.
Restrictions: The Priddy Foundation does not normally make grants for the following purposes: operating deficits; endowments; debt retirement; organizations that make grants to others; charities operated by service clubs; a request for capital funds for a project previously supported; any grant that would tend to obligate the foundation to future funding; fund raising programs and events; grants that impose expenditure responsibility on the foundation; grants to individuals, including individual scholarship awards; start-up funding for new organizations; individual public elementary or secondary schools (K-12); religious institutions except for non-sectarian, human service programs offered on a non-discriminatory basis; basic or applied research; media productions or publications; school trips; conferences or other educational events except through an organizational development grant; or direct grants to volunteer fire departments.
Geographic Focus: Oklahoma, Texas
Date(s) Application is Due: Mar 1; Sep 1
Amount of Grant: 30,000 - 1,500,000 USD
Contact: Debbie C. White, Grants Director; (940) 723-8720; fax (940) 723-8656; debbiecw@priddyfdn.org
Internet: https://priddyfdn.org/policy/
Sponsor: Priddy Foundation
807 Eighth Street, Suite 1010
Wichita Falls, TX 76301-3310

Priddy Foundation Operating Grants   3955
The Priddy Foundation is a general purpose foundation, interested primarily in programs that have the potential for lasting and favorable impact on individuals and organizations. Considerations for funding include the geographic area served by the project, the individuals and groups served, the problem being addressed, the availability of existing resources and the degree of need. Although the Foundation is wary of fostering annual budget dependency on the part of a grantee agency, its board recognizes that there are circumstances in which a grant for general operating purposes might be critical to an organization's success or viability. Such grants would be for a limited period of time. Among other conditions which might be imposed, based on a specific organization's application, a grantee organization will be required to present a practicable plan to achieve self-sufficiency without additional foundation funding. During the term of the grant the grantee organization might also be required to enter into a formal consulting arrangement with a Center for Non-profit Management, or a similar organization, also with the objective of becoming self-sufficient. Deadlines for preliminary applications are February 1 and August 1, while final applications are due March 1 and September 1.
Requirements: 501(c)3 Texas and Oklahoma nonprofit organizations are eligible. The foundation considers grant applications from organizations in the Wichita Falls, Texas area. In Texas, this includes the following counties: Archer, Baylor, Childress, Clay, Cottle, Foard, Hardeman, Haskell, Jack, King, Knox, Montague, Stonewall, Throckmorton, Wichita, Wilbarger, Wise, and Young. In Oklahoma, it includes the following counties: Comanche, Cotton, Jackson, Jefferson, Stephens, and Tillman.
Restrictions: The Priddy Foundation does not normally make grants for the following purposes: operating deficits; endowments; debt retirement; organizations that make grants to others; charities operated by service clubs; a request for capital funds for a project previously supported; any grant that would tend to obligate the foundation to future funding; fund raising programs and events; grants that impose expenditure responsibility on the foundation; grants to individuals, including individual scholarship awards; start-up funding for new organizations; individual public elementary or secondary schools (K-12); religious institutions except for non-sectarian, human service programs offered on a non-discriminatory basis; basic or applied research; media productions or publications; school trips; conferences or other educational events except through an organizational development grant; or direct grants to volunteer fire departments.
Geographic Focus: Oklahoma, Texas
Date(s) Application is Due: Mar 1; Sep 1
Amount of Grant: 20,000 - 120,000 USD
Contact: Debbie C. White; (940) 723-8720; fax (940) 723-8656; debbiecw@priddyfdn.org
Internet: https://priddyfdn.org/policy/
Sponsor: Priddy Foundation
807 Eighth Street, Suite 1010
Wichita Falls, TX 76301-3310

Priddy Foundation Organizational Development Grants   3956
The Priddy Foundation is a general purpose foundation, interested primarily in programs that have the potential for lasting and favorable impact on individuals and organizations. Considerations for funding include the geographic area served by the project, the individuals and groups served, the problem being addressed, the availability of existing resources and the degree of need. In the area of Organizational Development, the Foundation will consider grants to organizations for such things as board and staff development, planning initiatives, technical assistance, technology enhancements, and capital projects. Organizational development grants will be dependent on a comprehensive plan supported by the organization's board, outside professional assistance (e.g., Center for Non-profit Management), if appropriate, and absolute linkage between the development plan and the ability of the organization to achieve its mission more effectively. Deadlines for preliminary applications are February 1 and August 1, while final applications are due March 1 and September 1.
Requirements: 501(c)3 Texas and Oklahoma nonprofit organizations are eligible. The foundation considers grant applications from organizations in the Wichita Falls, Texas area. In Texas, this includes the following counties: Archer, Baylor, Childress, Clay, Cottle, Foard, Hardeman, Haskell, Jack, King, Knox, Montague, Stonewall, Throckmorton, Wichita, Wilbarger, Wise, and Young. In Oklahoma, it includes the following counties: Comanche, Cotton, Jackson, Jefferson, Stephens, and Tillman.
Restrictions: The Priddy Foundation does not normally make grants for the following purposes: operating deficits; endowments; debt retirement; organizations that make grants to others; charities operated by service clubs; a request for capital funds for a project previously supported; any grant that would tend to obligate the foundation to future funding; fund raising programs and events; grants that impose expenditure responsibility on the foundation; grants to individuals, including individual scholarship awards; start-up funding for new organizations; individual public elementary or secondary schools (K-12); religious institutions except for non-sectarian, human service programs offered on a non-discriminatory basis; basic or applied research; media productions or publications; school trips; conferences or other educational events except through an organizational development grant; or direct grants to volunteer fire departments.
Geographic Focus: Oklahoma, Texas
Date(s) Application is Due: Mar 1; Sep 1

Amount of Grant: 1,500 - 120,000 USD
Contact: Debbie C. White; (940) 723-8720; fax (940) 723-8656; debbiecw@priddyfdn.org
Internet: https://priddyfdn.org/policy/
Sponsor: Priddy Foundation
807 Eighth Street, Suite 1010
Wichita Falls, TX 76301-3310

Priddy Foundation Program Grants 3957
The Priddy Foundation is a general purpose foundation, interested primarily in programs that have the potential for lasting and favorable impact on individuals and organizations. Considerations for funding include the geographic area served by the project, the individuals and groups served, the problem being addressed, the availability of existing resources and the degree of need. In the area of Program Grants, the Foundation gives highest priority to organizations seeking funds for service extension or implementation of new services. Projects should make a difference in the lives of people served by dealing effectively with known problems or opportunities. Results should be capable of evaluation against defined standards of measurement. Proposals should be realistic concerning the ability of the organization to conduct the program and to sustain the program beyond the period a grant from the Foundation may cover. Deadlines for preliminary applications are February 1 and August 1, while final applications are due March 1 and September 1.
Requirements: 501(c)3 Texas and Oklahoma nonprofit organizations are eligible. The foundation considers grant applications from organizations in the Wichita Falls, Texas area. In Texas, this includes the following counties: Archer, Baylor, Childress, Clay, Cottle, Foard, Hardeman, Haskell, Jack, King, Knox, Montague, Stonewall, Throckmorton, Wichita, Wilbarger, Wise, and Young. In Oklahoma, it includes the following counties: Comanche, Cotton, Jackson, Jefferson, Stephens, and Tillman.
Restrictions: The Priddy Foundation does not normally make grants for the following purposes: operating deficits; endowments; debt retirement; organizations that make grants to others; charities operated by service clubs; a request for capital funds for a project previously supported; any grant that would tend to obligate the foundation to future funding; fund raising programs and events; grants that impose expenditure responsibility on the foundation; grants to individuals, including individual scholarship awards; start-up funding for new organizations; individual public elementary or secondary schools (K-12); religious institutions except for non-sectarian, human service programs offered on a non-discriminatory basis; basic or applied research; media productions or publications; school trips; conferences or other educational events except through an organizational development grant; or direct grants to volunteer fire departments.
Geographic Focus: Oklahoma, Texas
Date(s) Application is Due: Mar 1; Sep 1
Amount of Grant: 1,500 - 1,500,000 USD
Contact: Debbie C. White; (940) 723-8720; fax (940) 723-8656; debbiecw@priddyfdn.org
Internet: https://priddyfdn.org/policy/
Sponsor: Priddy Foundation
807 Eighth Street, Suite 1010
Wichita Falls, TX 76301-3310

Pride Foundation Grants 3958
The Pride Foundation works to strengthen the lesbian, gay, transgender, and bisexual community primarily in Washington state and extending to the four neighboring states of Alaska, Idaho, Montana, and Oregon. The Foundation awards grants to projects in arts and recreation; education, advocacy, and outreach; health and community service; HIV/AIDS service delivery and prevention; lesbian health; and youth and family services. Applicants will first submit the letter of inquiry online applications by August 19. If organizations are invited to submit the full application, they will be notified by September 23. Funds will be available in December.
Requirements: IRS 501(c)3 tax-exempt organizations or organizations affiliated with tax-exempt organizations are eligible. Projects or programs must directly benefit the lesbian, gay, bisexual, and transgender community; people affected by HIV/AIDS; and/or their friends and families.
Restrictions: Grants to individuals cannot be considered.
Geographic Focus: Alaska, Idaho, Montana, Oregon, Washington
Date(s) Application is Due: Sep 20
Amount of Grant: Up to 5,000 USD
Contact: Jeff Hedgepeth; (800) 735-7287 or (206) 323-3318; jeff@pridefoundation.org
Internet: http://www.pridefoundation.org/grants/overview/
Sponsor: Pride Foundation
1122 East Pike, PMB 1001
Seattle, WA 98122

Prince Charitable Trusts Chicago Grants 3959
The trusts awards grants to eligible Chicago nonprofit organizations in its areas of interest: arts and culture, education, environment, health, and social services.
Requirements: The Trusts Chicago program only funds organizations within the city limits of Chicago (with the exception of grants made through the MacArthur Fund for Arts and Culture at Prince). The Trusts make grants only to charitable organizations that are exempt from federal income tax under Section 501(c)3 of the Internal Revenue Code and are classified as public charities under Sections 509(a)(1) or 509(a)(2). All grant applications must include a Prince Charitable Trusts cover sheet, see the Trusts website, http://foundationcenter.org/grantmaker/prince/chi_app.html for proper form and additional guidelines.
Restrictions: The Trusts do not fund projects that promote or proselytize any religion. While the Trusts do fund the projects of faith-based organizations, those projects must be secular in nature. The Trusts do not fund organizations that discriminate on the basis of ethnicity, race, color, creed, religion, gender, national origin, age, disability, marital status, sexual orientation, gender identity, or any veteran's status.
Geographic Focus: Illinois
Date(s) Application is Due: Jan 13; May 1; Jun 1
Contact: Sharon Robison; (312) 419-8700; fax (312) 419-8558; srobison@prince-trusts.org
Internet: http://www.fdncenter.org/grantmaker/prince/chicago.html
Sponsor: Prince Charitable Trusts
303 West Madison Street, Suite 1900
Chicago, IL 60606

Prince Charitable Trusts District of Columbia Grants 3960
The trusts awards grants to eligible Washington D.C. nonprofit organizations in its areas of interest: arts and culture, community, environment, health, emergency services, youth and provide a limited number of capital grants each year.
Requirements: The Trusts make grants only to charitable organizations that are exempt from federal income tax under Section 501(c)3 of the Internal Revenue Code and are classified as public charities under Sections 509(a)(1) or 509(a)(2). Electronic proposals are preferred. Attachments may be mailed separately. Proposals should include the Prince Charitable Trust Grant Application Cover Sheet and the Common Grant Application Format of Washington Grantmakers. These forms and additional guidelines may be obtained at the Trusts website, http://foundationcenter.org/grantmaker/prince/dc_app.html.
Restrictions: The Trusts do not make grants to individuals, nor does it fund projects that promote or proselytize any religion. While the Trusts do fund the projects of faith-based organizations, those projects must be secular in nature.
Geographic Focus: District of Columbia
Date(s) Application is Due: Feb 1; Aug 10; Sep 1
Amount of Grant: 10,000 - 30,000 USD
Contact: Kristin Pauly; (202) 728-0646; fax (202) 466-4726; kpauly@princetrusts.org
Internet: http://www.fdncenter.org/grantmaker/prince/dc_interest.html
Sponsor: Prince Charitable Trusts
816 Connecticut Avenue NW
Washington, DC 20006

Prince Charitable Trusts Rhode Island Grants 3961
The trusts awards grants to eligible Rhode Island nonprofit organizations in its areas of interest: arts and culture, environment and social services. In Rhode Island, the Trusts support programs that improve the quality of life for residents of the city of Newport and Aquidneck Island. Generally, the Trusts only support programs that are regional or statewide when these programs have a direct or indirect impact on Newport or Aquidneck Island.
Requirements: The Trusts make grants only to charitable organizations that are exempt from federal income tax under Section 501(c)3 of the Internal Revenue Code and are classified as public charities under Sections 509(a)(1) or 509(a)(2). All grant applications must include a Prince Charitable Trusts cover sheet, see the Trusts website, http://foundationcenter.org/grantmaker/prince/ri_app.html for proper form and additional guidelines.
Restrictions: The Trusts do not fund organizations that discriminate on the basis of ethnicity, race, color, creed, religion, gender, national origin, age, disability, marital status, sexual orientation, gender identity, or any veteran's status. The Trusts do not fund projects that promote or proselytize any religion. While the Trusts do fund the projects of faith-based organizations, those projects must be secular in nature. The Trusts also do not make grants to individuals.
Geographic Focus: Rhode Island
Date(s) Application is Due: Jun 1
Contact: Sharon Robison; (312) 419-8700; fax (312) 419-8558; srobison@prince-trusts.org
Internet: http://fdncenter.org/grantmaker/prince/ri.html
Sponsor: Prince Charitable Trusts
303 West Madison Street, Suite 1900
Chicago, IL 60606

Princeton Area Community Foundation Fund for Women and Girls Grants 3962
The Princeton Area Community Foundation created the Fund for Women and Girls to promote philanthropy by and for girls and the women who raise them. A $100,000 challenge from the Bristol-Myers Squibb Company in 2001 accelerated the Fund's growth. The Fund supports projects that help girls ages 5 to 18 years who reside in Greater Mercer attain success in their personal, academic, family and community lives. The Fund also encourages women to think of themselves as philanthropists, and provides them with an effective vehicle to collectively make a real difference in their communities.
Requirements: Funding must support programs that benefit girls and the women who raise them in Mercer County, New Jersey, and the immediately adjoining areas of surrounding counties.
Geographic Focus: New Jersey
Contact: Deborah Thomas, (609) 219-1800; fax (609) 219-1850; daubert-thomas@pacf.org
Internet: http://www.pacf.org/grants/polCalendarEvent.cfm?Program_Code=4
Sponsor: Princeton Area Community Foundation
15 Princess Road
Lawrenceville, NJ 08648

Princeton Area Community Foundation Greater Mercer Grants 3963
The Greater Mercer Grants Program is a competitive program for projects benefiting residents of Mercer County, New Jersey, and the immediately adjoining areas of surrounding counties. There are three distinct categories. In addressing the needs of low-income individuals and families (Category 1), grants up to $15,000 are made to nonprofit organizations only. In support of community organizing in low-income neighborhoods (Category 2), grants of $500 to $20,000 are made to 501(c)3 nonprofit organizations, neighborhood associations, and groups of residents forming a neighborhood association to work on a project. And in support of building community within and among municipalities (Category 3), grants generally range from $10,000 to $35,000, but may be as much as $50,000, made to nonprofit organizations only.

Requirements: Nonprofit organizations that have tax-exempt status under Section 501(c)3 of the Internal Revenue Code are eligible. They must be registered with the State of New Jersey as a charity, unless they are religious organizations, or schools that file their curricula with the Department of Education and are exempt from the provisions of the New Jersey Charitable Registration and Investigation Act.
Restrictions: Nonprofits may submit one application per calendar year in each category, for a maximum of three. Neighborhood associations or groups of residents who will form a neighborhood association may apply only once annually for a Community Organizing in Low-Income Neighborhoods grant.
Geographic Focus: New Jersey
Amount of Grant: 500 - 35,000 USD
Contact: Deborah Thomas; (609) 219-1800; fax (609) 219-1850; daubert-thomas@pacf.org
Internet: http://www.pacf.org/grants/polCalendarEvent.cfm?Program_Code=12
Sponsor: Princeton Area Community Foundation
15 Princess Road
Lawrenceville, NJ 08648

Princeton Area Community Foundation Rebecca Annitto Service Opportunities for Students (SOS) Award   3964

The award rewards and encourages youth volunteerism and is presented annually to a Mercer County middle or upper school student. A grant will be made to the nonprofit organization suggested by the award recipient. The winner will have: made a difference at home, in school, and/or in the community; lived out the ambition to serve, not to be served; inspired others to make volunteering a central part of their lives; and demonstrated motivation, leadership, creativity, and commitment in pursuing service. Students must be nominated for the award. No formal application is required.
Restrictions: Self-nominations and nominations from family members are disqualified.
Geographic Focus: California
Date(s) Application is Due: Sep 11
Contact: Deborah Thomas; (609) 219-1800; fax (609) 219-1850; daubert-thomas@pacf.org
Internet: http://www.pacf.org/grants/awards.cfm
Sponsor: Princeton Area Community Foundation
15 Princess Road
Lawrenceville, NJ 08648

Princeton Area Community Foundation Thomas George Artists Fund Grants   3965

Through this grants program, the Thomas George Artists Fund will assist artists at the outset of their careers. One $5,000 grant will be awarded to support an artist engaged in drawing and painting for up to six months directly following his or her graduation from art school or college; or for a student studying art but not seeking a degree, directly following his or her completion of the school or college's art program coursework. The purpose of the grant is to cover living and/or other expenses for an artist engaged in drawing and painting so that he or she will have the financial freedom to dedicate their attention full-time to drawing and painting for a limited period after graduation or completion of art program coursework. This respite from the demands of school and workplace is intended to provide a time for career reflection and planning, and an opportunity to do art. Grant monies may be used for routine living expenses, including rent, utilities, transportation, insurances, food and the like. They may also be used for art supplies; travel and accommodations at locations that will facilitate the artist's drawing and painting; and for non-traditional art study.
Requirements: To qualify for the grant, the applicant must: be a year-round resident of New Jersey, and a citizen or permanent resident of the United States; be studying art at The College of New Jersey, Mercer County Community College or Rider University; be enrolled in an arts program that has provided traditional training in drawing and painting; be on track to graduate with an Associate or Bachelor of Fine Arts degree during the spring or summer, or (for students studying art but not seeking a degree) to have completed all of the required art program classes of one of the above schools during the spring or summer; agree to participate in an interview with the Grant Selection Committee if chosen as a finalist; and agree to show a minimum of two drawings and two paintings completed during the grant period to the Grant Selection Committee if chosen to receive the award.
Geographic Focus: New Jersey
Date(s) Application is Due: Dec 11
Amount of Grant: 5,000 USD
Contact: Deborah Thomas; (609) 219-1800; fax (609) 219-1850; daubert-thomas@pacf.org
Internet: http://www.pacf.org/grants/awards.cfm
Sponsor: Princeton Area Community Foundation
15 Princess Road
Lawrenceville, NJ 08648

Principal Financial Group Foundation Grants   3966

The foundation addresses concerns in the areas of health and human services, education, arts and culture, environment, and recreation and tourism. The primary objective is to support, through charitable contributions, selected nonprofit organizations primarily located in the greater Des Moines, IA, area. The foundation also will consider requests from organizations located in areas where the corporation has offices, including Des Moines, Mason City and Cedar Falls, IA; Grand Island, NE; Spokane, WA; Wilmington, DE; Appleton, WI; and Phoenix, AZ. The objectives, priorities, and programs seek to reflect the needs and concerns of communities in which the corporation operates. Support is given for annual campaigns, building funds, capital campaigns, continuing support, employee matching gifts, in-kind gifts, performances and exhibitions, conferences and workshops, adult basic education, vocational programs, operating budgets, internships, demonstration grants, matching grants, and seed grants. Contribution requests are considered on a quarterly basis, in accordance with the following schedule: health and human services, March 1; education, June 1; arts and culture, September 1; and environment, recreation, and tourism, December 1.

Requirements: 501(c)3 organizations in company operating locations may apply.
Restrictions: Proposals for athletic groups, conferences, endowments, fellowships, festivals, fraternal organizations, health care facility fund drives, libraries, or religious groups are denied.
Geographic Focus: Delaware, Iowa, Nebraska, Washington
Date(s) Application is Due: Mar 1; Jun 1; Sep 1; Dec 1
Amount of Grant: 1,000 - 50,000 USD
Contact: Laura Sauser; (515) 247-7227; fax (515) 246-5475
Internet: http://www.principal.com/about/giving/grant.htm
Sponsor: Principal Financial Group Foundation
711 High Street
Des Moines, IA 50392-0150

Procter and Gamble Fund Grants   3967

The fund supports nonprofit organizations in company-operating locations in the areas of education, health and social services, civic projects, cultural organizations, disaster relief, and environmental efforts. Grants are awarded to education initiatives in local communities, such as teacher training efforts, with a focus on economic teaching; and other efforts by public policy, research, and economic education organizations. Employee voluntarism is prevalent in many K-12 initiatives. Most health and human services funding supports the United Way. The Salvation Army, Red Cross, hospitals, food banks, and other social service organizations receive support. Community support is awarded through grants that bolster economic growth and enrichment, including support for a youth jobs program, libraries, zoos, and local chambers of commerce. Support is awarded to a variety of arts organizations, including theater, dance, music, and visual arts. Major environmental groups also receive support. Grant Application Cycles are July 1 through September 30 and December 1 through February 28, grant requests are only accepted during those times.
Requirements: 501(c)3 organizations in communities where Procter and Gamble Company manufacturing plants are located are eligible.
Geographic Focus: All States
Amount of Grant: Up to 25,000,000 USD
Contact: Brenda Ratliff; (513) 945-8454; fax (513) 945-5211; pgfund.im@pg.com
Internet: http://www.pg.com/company/our_commitment/grant_application_guidelines.shtml
Sponsor: Procter and Gamble Fund
P.O. Box 599
Cincinnati, OH 45201

Progress Energy Corporate Contributions Grants   3968

Corporate grants support a variety of nonprofit organizations and programs that improve the quality of life in the company's communities. Typically, these programs serve a single community up to a few counties, although they may sometimes have a statewide impact. The grants range in size from several hundred dollars up to $10,000. There are no submission deadlines for corporate grants, which are reviewed on an ongoing basis.
Requirements: Florida, North Carolina, and South Carolina nonprofits are eligible.
Restrictions: Grants are limited to organizations that serve Progress Energy customers in Florida, North Carolina or South Carolina. No support for religious organizations not of direct benefit to the entire community, political candidates or organizations, lobbying organizations, athletic, labor, or fraternal groups, or individual K-12 schools. No grants to individuals, or for political causes or campaigns, endowments, or capital campaigns.
Geographic Focus: Florida, North Carolina, South Carolina
Amount of Grant: Up to 10,000 USD
Contact: Contributions Specialist; (919) 508-5400; grants@pgnmail.com
Internet: https://www.progress-energy.com/commitment/community/grant-programs/index.page?
Sponsor: Progress Energy Corporation
P.O. Box 1551
Raleigh, NC 27602-2591

Progress Energy Foundation Economic Vitality Grants   3969

The foundation partners with nonprofits in North Carolina, South Carolina and Florida to help Progress Energy customer communities understand and adapt to the new realities posed by the shifting energy landscape. Grants focus on energy education, workforce development and the environment, with priority given to energy-related grants. Economic vitality grants support major arts organizations that make a significant contribution to the economic vitality of our headquarter cities in Raleigh, North Carolina and St. Petersburg, Florida. Nonprofit organizations providing services to Progress Energy customers in the focus areas may apply online.
Requirements: 501(c)3 nonprofit organizations in Raleigh, North Carolina, and St. Petersburg, Florida are eligible.
Restrictions: Grants are limited to nonprofit organizations that serve Progress Energy customer areas. No support for religious organizations not of direct benefit to the entire community, political candidates or organizations, lobbying organizations, athletic, labor, or fraternal groups, or individual K-12 schools. No grants to individuals, or for political causes or campaigns, endowments, or capital campaigns.
Geographic Focus: Florida, North Carolina
Date(s) Application is Due: May 1
Amount of Grant: 10,000 - 100,000 USD
Contact: Grants Manager; (919) 546-6189; fax (919) 546-4338; grants@pgnmail.com
Internet: https://www.progress-energy.com/commitment/community/grant-programs/index.page?
Sponsor: Progress Energy Foundation
P.O. Box 2591
Raleigh, NC 27602-2591

Progress Energy Foundation Environmental Stewardship Grants 3970
The foundation partners with nonprofits in Florida, North Carolina, and South Carolina to help customer communities understand and adapt to the new realities posed by the shifting energy landscape. Grants focus on energy education, workforce development and the environment, with priority given to energy-related grants. Environmental stewardship grants advance technologies relating to greenhouse gas reduction/avoidance, alternative/renewable energy and energy efficiency/conservation. Nonprofit organizations providing services to Progress Energy customers in the focus areas may apply online.
Requirements: Florida, North Carolina, and South Carolina nonprofit organizations serving the residents of the corporation's service area are eligible. Nonprofits applying for a foundation grant must be exempt under Section 501(c)3 of the IRS code.
Restrictions: Grants are limited to nonprofit organizations that serve Progress Energy customer areas. No support for religious organizations not of direct benefit to the entire community, political candidates or organizations, lobbying organizations, athletic, labor, or fraternal groups, or individual K-12 schools. No grants to individuals, or for political causes or campaigns, endowments, or capital campaigns.
Geographic Focus: Florida, North Carolina, South Carolina
Date(s) Application is Due: Oct 1
Contact: Grants Manager; (919) 546-6189; fax (919) 546-4338; grants@pgnmail.com
Internet: https://www.progress-energy.com/commitment/community/grant-programs/index.page?
Sponsor: Progress Energy Foundation
P.O. Box 2591
Raleigh, NC 27602-2591

Project AWARE Foundation Grants 3971
The foundation's grant program supports worthwhile aquatic conservation projects. Grants are awarded to projects that have a direct benefit to the aquatic environment such as: public education (formal and informal); grassroots conservation and enhancement projects; environmentally focused research that leads to conservation measures; public awareness initiatives; environmental assessment and monitoring projects; and volunteer-supported community activism. Micro grants provide funding for localized grassroots efforts, including but not limited to, beach and underwater cleanups, mooring buoy programs, research projects, local education, and public awareness programs. Macro grants support large-scale regional, national, or international efforts, including but not limited to, broad-based education and public awareness programs and high profile conservation projects. Quarterly board meetings are typically scheduled during the third week of the month. The program operates in the United States, Australia, and the United Kingdom.
Restrictions: Grants do not support legislative advocacy to influence policy; political campaigns; projects whose methods are not environmentally accepted; overhead expenses including salaries, stipends, benefits or tuition; capital expenses including computer hardware/software or office furnishings; travel and living expenses; dive equipment or instruction; or products designed for resale.
Geographic Focus: All States
Date(s) Application is Due: Feb 15; May 15; Aug 15; Nov 15
Contact: Grants Administrator; information@projectaware.org
Internet: http://www.projectaware.org/americas/english/grants.asp
Sponsor: Project AWARE Foundation
30151 Tomas Street
Rancho Santa Margarita, CA 92688

Project Orange Thumb Grants 3972
Within U.S. and Canada twenty (20) grant recipients will be selected. Each will receive up to $1,500 in Fiskars garden tools and up to $800.00 in gardening-related materials (i.e. green goods). Four grant recipients will also be awarded within Australia. Each of these recipients will receive up to $1,000 in Fiskars Tools and up to $1,000 in gardening related materials (i.e. green goods).
Requirements: Gardens and/or gardening projects geared toward community involvement, neighborhood beautification, sustainable agriculture and/or horticultural education in the 50 United States, DC, Canada, Australia and New Zealand are eligible. Community garden groups, as well as schools, youth groups, community centers, camps, clubs, treatment facilities are all encouraged to apply. Only group applications will be considered; single individuals are not eligible for a Project Orange Thumb grant. This is not a contest or sweepstakes. Applications must be submitted electronically on or before the deadline.
Restrictions: Prizes are not transferable, or substitutable, except by Sponsor at its sole discretion. Failure to collect or properly claim grant in accordance with these rules or to comply with these rules will result in forfeiture of the grant. If forfeited for any reason, recipients will not receive any other substitution or compensation. All federal, state/provincial and local taxes related to any prize are the sole responsibility of grant recipients.
Geographic Focus: All States, Australia, Canada, New Zealand
Date(s) Application is Due: Feb 19
Contact: Program Contact; orangethumb@fiskars.com
Internet: http://projectorangethumb.com/pot/
Sponsor: Fiskars Brands
780 Carolina Street
Sauk City, WI 53583

Proteus Fund Grants 3973
Proteus Fund is a foundation committed to advancing justice through democracy, human rights and peace. Proteus Fund collaborative grant making initiatives work on some of the most cutting edge issues of our time. Each initiative is uniquely structured and focused to achieve the goals of its funding partners and led by experienced program staff. Proteus Fund works to connect this work to other social movements and resources while providing a full compliment of services to support the work, including partnership development, marketing, grants and financial management and administrative support.
Geographic Focus: All States
Contact: Beery Adams Jimenez, Grants Manager; (413) 256-0349; info@proteusfund.org
Internet: http://www.proteusfund.org/initiatives
Sponsor: Proteus Fund
101 University Drive, Suite A2
Amherst, MA 01002

Prudential CARES Volunteer Grants 3974
Prudential CARES Volunteer Grants recognize Prudential active and retired associates and Prudential Real Estate Affiliates (PREA) broker/owners, employees, or sales staff who volunteer in their communities. Award grants are provided to organizations for which the winners serve as volunteers. Winners receive an award certificate. Annually, employees and retirees around the globe who have volunteered their time fill out applications that result in awards to the nonprofit organizations they have served. This year's grants of $250 to $5,000 added up to a total of $407,500 and well over $10 million since the program began in 1991. Individual applications will be considered for all grant levels.
Requirements: To apply, the minimum time requirement is 40 hours of volunteer service per individual during the previous calendar year.
Geographic Focus: All States
Amount of Grant: 1,000 - 5,000 USD
Contact: Virginia Esteves; (973) 802-7353; fax (973) 802-3345; spirit@prudential.com
Patricia Dieterly, Community Resources; (215) 784-8147; fax (215) 784-2813
Tricia Gravatt, Community Resources; (904) 313-3078; fax (904) 313-6561
Internet: http://www.prudential.com/view/page/public/12315
Sponsor: Prudential Insurance Company
751 Broad Street, 15th Floor
Newark, NJ 07102

Prudential Foundation Arts and Culture Grants 3975
The Prudential Foundation's areas of interest are ready-to-learn programs, ready-to-work programs, and ready-to-live programs. In order to promote sustainable communities and improve social outcomes for community residents, the Foundation focuses its strategy in the following Arts and Culture areas: arts as an economic engine and as a quality-of-life issue to ensure that residents have access to quality arts programs; and capacity building activities for nonprofit organizations to ensure their sustainability and growth. Types of support include operating support, continuing support, annual campaigns, seed money, matching funds and employee matching gifts, consulting services, technical assistance, employee-related scholarships, research, capital campaigns, conferences and seminars, and projects/programs. Results the Foundation seeks from their investments include: successful contributions by arts and culture organizations to the economic development and vitality of the community they serve; increased quality and diversity of artistic creations that reflect emerging ethnic and historically underserved populations; and underserved community members that increase their participation or experiences of the arts. Funds are targeted to areas where Prudential has a strong presence. Applicant should make initial contact with a brief letter to determine whether a more detailed proposal would be acceptable.
Requirements: The Prudential Foundation supports nonprofit, charitable organizations, and programs whose mission and operations are broad and non-discriminatory. The Foundation focuses its resources to support organizations whose activities address social needs or benefit underserved groups and communities. The Foundation funds programs in Newark, New Jersey; Hartford, Connecticut; Los Angeles, California; Chicago, Illinois; Phoenix, Arizona; Jacksonville, Florida; Dubuque, Iowa; Minneapolis, Minnesota; Philadelphia and Scranton, Pennsylvania; and Houston and Dallas, Texas.
Restrictions: The Foundation does not fund organizations that are not tax-exempt under paragraph 501(c)3 of the U.S. Internal Revenue Code; labor, religious, political, lobbying, or fraternal groups—except when these groups provide needed services to the community at large; direct grants or scholarships to individuals; support for single-disease health groups; or good will advertising.
Geographic Focus: Arizona, California, Connecticut, Florida, Georgia, Illinois, Iowa, Minnesota, New Jersey, New York, Pennsylvania, Texas
Amount of Grant: Up to 1,000,000 USD
Contact: Lata Reddy, Director of Programs and Operations; (973) 802-4791; community.resources@prudential.com
Internet: http://www.prudential.com/view/page/public/12373
Sponsor: Prudential Foundation
751 Broad Street, 15th Floor
Newark, NJ 07102-3777

Prudential Foundation Economic Development Grants 3976
The Prudential Foundation's areas of interest are ready-to-learn programs, ready-to-work programs, and ready-to-live programs. In order to promote sustainable communities and improve social outcomes for community residents, the Foundation focuses its strategy in the following economic development areas: workforce development programs to train and place individuals in high-demand occupations; business development opportunities to create and grow businesses; and community revitalization initiatives to strengthen community development corporations (CDCs). Types of support include operating support, continuing support, annual campaigns, seed money, matching funds and employee matching gifts, consulting services, technical assistance, employee-related scholarships, research, capital campaigns, conferences and seminars, and projects/programs. The Foundation is especially interested in proposals that anticipate and address potential major problems. Funds are targeted to areas where Prudential has a strong presence. Applicant should make initial contact with a brief letter to determine whether a more detailed proposal would be acceptable.

Requirements: The Prudential Foundation supports nonprofit, charitable organizations, and programs whose mission and operations are broad and non-discriminatory. The Foundation focuses its resources to support organizations whose activities address social needs or benefit underserved groups and communities. Funding locations include Newark, New Jersey, and surrounding communities; Los Angeles, California; Jacksonville, Florida; Chicago, Illinois; Dubuque, Iowa; Phoenix, Arizona; New York, New York; Minneapolis, Minnesota; Philadelphia and Scranton, Pennsylvania; New Orleans, Louisiana; Houston and Dallas, Texas. Third priority are national programs that can be implemented or replicated in the above cities.
Restrictions: The Foundation does not fund: organizations that are not tax-exempt under paragraph 501(c)3 of the U.S. Internal Revenue Code; labor, religious, political, lobbying, or fraternal groups—except when these groups provide needed services to the community at large; direct grants or scholarships to individuals; support for single-disease health groups; or good will advertising.
Geographic Focus: Arizona, California, Connecticut, Florida, Georgia, Iowa, Louisiana, Minnesota, New Jersey, New York, Pennsylvania, Texas
Contact: Lata Reddy; (973) 802-4791; community.resources@prudential.com
Internet: http://www.prudential.com/view/page/public/12373
Sponsor: Prudential Foundation
751 Broad Street, 15th Floor
Newark, NJ 07102-3777

Prudential Foundation Education Grants 3977
The Prudential Foundation's areas of interest are ready-to-learn programs, ready-to-work programs, and ready-to-live programs. In order to promote sustainable communities and improve social outcomes for community residents, the Foundation focuses its strategy in the following educational areas: education leadership to support reform in public education by increasing the capacity of educators, parents, and community residents to implement public school reform; and youth development to build skills and competencies needed for young people to be productive citizens (this includes expanding arts education opportunities and supporting effective out-of-school-time programs for young people). Finally, the Foundation also funds organizations whose efforts influence policy that adapts promising practices and evidence-based approaches to instruction and learning in schools. Types of support include operating support, continuing support, annual campaigns, seed money, matching funds and employee matching gifts, consulting services, technical assistance, employee-related scholarships, research, capital campaigns, conferences and seminars, and projects/programs. The Foundation is especially interested in proposals that anticipate and address potential major problems. Funds are targeted to areas where Prudential has a strong presence. Applicant should make initial contact with a brief letter to determine whether a more detailed proposal would be acceptable.
Requirements: The Prudential Foundation supports nonprofit, charitable organizations, and programs whose mission and operations are broad and non-discriminatory. The Foundation focuses its resources to support organizations whose activities address social needs or benefit underserved groups and communities. Priority in order of preference goes to programs in Newark, New Jersey, and surrounding communities; Los Angeles, California; Hartford, Connecticut; New York, New York; Chicago, Illinois; Jacksonville, Florida; Atlanta, Georgia; Minneapolis, Minnesota; Philadelphia and Scranton, Pennsylvania; Houston and Dallas, Texas; Dubuque, Iowa; Phoenix, Arizona; and New Orleans, Louisiana.
Restrictions: The Foundation does not fund: organizations that are not tax-exempt under paragraph 501(c)3 of the U.S. Internal Revenue Code; labor, religious, political, lobbying, or fraternal groups—except when these groups provide needed services to the community at large; direct grants or scholarships to individuals; support for single-disease health groups; or good will advertising.
Geographic Focus: Arizona, California, Connecticut, Florida, Georgia, Illinois, Iowa, Louisiana, Minnesota, New Jersey, New York, Pennsylvania, Texas
Contact: Lata Reddy; (973) 802-4791; community.resources@prudential.com
Internet: http://www.prudential.com/view/page/public/12373
Sponsor: Prudential Foundation
751 Broad Street, 15th Floor
Newark, NJ 07102-3777

Prudential Spirit of Community Awards 3978
The Prudential Spirit of Community Awards program is the United States' largest youth recognition program based exclusively on volunteer community service. The program was created in 1995 by Prudential in partnership with the National Association of Secondary School Principals (NASSP) to honor middle level and high school students for outstanding service to others at the local, state, and national level. The program's goals are to applaud young people who already are making a positive difference in their towns and neighborhoods, and to inspire others to think about how they might contribute to their communities. The award recognizes middle- and high-school students for volunteer community service. Honorees will receive a monetary award and a trip to Washington, DC. Ten national honorees will each receive an additional monetary prize, and a monetary prize will be given to a charitable organization of his or her choice. Applications are available at more than 40,000 public and private middle and high schools throughout the United States. The Prudential Spirit of Community Awards program is also conducted in Japan, South Korea, Taiwan, Ireland, and India, where Prudential has significant business operations.
Requirements: Any student in grades five through 12 as of November 1 who resides in one of the 50 states, the District of Columbia, or Puerto Rico, and has engaged in volunteer activities since September 1 of last year is eligible.
Geographic Focus: All States, India, Ireland, Japan, South Korea, Taiwan
Date(s) Application is Due: Oct 31
Contact: Awards Coordinator; (888) 450-9961; spirit@prudential.com
Internet: http://spirit.prudential.com/view/page/soc
Sponsor: Prudential Insurance Company
751 Broad Street, 15th Floor
Newark, NJ 07102

PSEG Corporate Contributions Grants 3979
PSEG's contributions program supports nonprofit organization proposals that address its three funding priorities: children and families; community and economic development; and the environment. Examples include pre-collegiate education, environmental education, job readiness, and urban revitalization. Within funding priorities, additional criteria apply: consideration is given to the organization's scope, i.e., geographic area served and the number of people to benefit; and effectiveness/results of the program are also considered, as well as availability of funding sources and program budgets. Priority consideration is given to organizations/programs in PSEG's service area. Limited funding is available for arts, sports, community fairs, and other community functions. Funding requests are accepted from January through October.
Requirements: 501(c)3 nonprofit organizations in PSEG's service territory are eligible.
Restrictions: Grants do not support individuals; organizations not exempt under Section 501(c)3 of the IRS code; organizations outside PSEG service area; sectarian purpose programs that promote religious doctrines or exclude participants based on religion; political causes, candidates, organizations, or campaigns; organizations that discriminate on the basis of race, sex, or religion; organizations with a primary purpose of influencing legislation; athletic, labor, or fraternal groups; organizations that address single-health issues; endowments; or programs/organizations for which PSEG is asked to serve as the sole funder.
Geographic Focus: New Jersey
Date(s) Application is Due: Oct 31
Contact: Shauwea Hamilton, Community Affairs Manager; (800) 436-7734
Internet: http://www.pseg.com/community/request_faqs.jsp
Sponsor: Public Service Enterprise Group
80 Park Plaza, 10C
Newark, NJ 07102

PSEG Environmental Education Grants 3980
The program helps to inspire teachers to implement an interdisciplinary approach to teaching about the environment, and fosters new ideas. Funds may be applied to equipment, materials and field trips that would not normally be provided by the school or school district. Specific budget criteria are provided on the grant application.
Requirements: The program is open to educators of grades K-9 who teach in: PSE&G's electric or gas service areas (see http://tinyurl.com/ch22pa for a complete list); New Jersey schools within PSEG's Estuary Enhancement Program Areas; or, schools in New Jersey and Delaware located within PSEG's Emergency Planning Zone. Grants are available to teachers who can successfully link their students' understanding of science, mathematics, computer science and/or technology concepts with an enthusiasm and appreciation for the environment. The following types of proposals will be considered: ideas for the development of one or more classroom units; expansion or refinement of an existing course or curriculum; extension of classroom work to community or after-school activities. The school or school district is required to conduct the grant project for at least two years. Grant funding may also be spread over a two-year period if the school/school district deems it necessary. The school/school district is also encouraged to continue the project after this source of external funding expires.
Restrictions: Grant recipients will be expected to assist other educators by sharing the results of their successful projects, in a format that can be posted at the sponsor's web site.
Geographic Focus: Delaware, New Jersey
Date(s) Application is Due: Jun 6
Contact: JoAnn Dow-Breslin, (973) 430-7000; JoAnn.Dow-Breslin@pseg.com
Internet: http://www.pseg.com/community/grants.jsp
Sponsor: Public Service Enterprise Group
80 Park Plaza, P.O. Box 570
Newark, NJ 07102

Public Education Power Grants 3981
Mary and Robert Pew of North Palm Beach, Florida and Grand Rapids, Michigan created the Mary and Robert Pew Public Education Fund in 1998 as a supporting organization to the Community Foundation for Palm Beach and Martin Counties. The Pews' primary philanthropic objective is to positively impact children's lives by providing access to high-quality instruction and educational enhancements. The fund supports initiatives that improve public education for economically-disadvantaged children through professional development for teachers, leadership development, and improving best practices in early childhood development. Most proposals are invited by the Pew Fund staff; however, interested parties wishing to share ideas may submit a brief description of their innovation through an online form at the grant website.
Restrictions: Giving is limited to Martin and Palm Beach counties, Florida.
Geographic Focus: Florida
Contact: Louise Grant; (561) 659-6800 or (561) 691-6044; louigrant1@aol.com
Internet: http://pewfund.org/?q=node/4
Sponsor: Mary and Robert Pew Public Education Fund
601 Heritage Drive Suite 206
Jupiter, FL 33458

Public Interest Law Foundation Community Grants 3982
The Public Interest Law foundation (PILF) is a not-for-profit organization of law students, faculty, and alumni that raises funds to promote the practice of public interest law at Columbia Law School and across the country. Each year, through the Community Grants program, PILF awards grants to organizations committed to providing legal services to communities in need. Since its inception, PILF has awarded over $1 million to public interest legal organizations. In selecting projects for funding, we are guided by PILF's commitment to supporting public interest activities, including but not limited to: reforming the criminal and civil justice systems, eradicating discrimination, expanding educational and economic opportunities, improving living standards, and increasing citizen access to legal

forums. PILF prefers to fund discrete projects that can be completed on a measurable time frame. Proposals should be innovative, well conceived, and practical to implement. Special consideration will be given to projects: addressing issues or aiding groups that currently receive inadequate attention or representation by individuals, organizations, or government bodies; that are discrete and will be completed on a measurable time-frame; or proposed by graduates of Columbia Law School. In recent years, PILF has awarded four to five grants per year ranging from $1,500 to $15,000, with the typical grant being approximately $10,000.
Requirements: All organizations performing work that benefits the public interest through the mechanism of law are eligible.
Restrictions: PILF does not fund: organizations seeking general funding for standard operating expenses; private practice on behalf of particular clients or any other profit-seeking activity; or activities that replicate recognized governmental functions or which duplicate projects that are principally supported by governmental and other public funds.
Geographic Focus: All States
Date(s) Application is Due: Feb 28
Amount of Grant: 1,500 - 15,000 USD
Contact: Michael Pfautz, Community Grants Coordinator; pilf.grants@gmail.com
Internet: http://www.columbia.edu/cu/pilf/communitygrants.html
Sponsor: Public Interest Law Foundation
435 W 116th Street
New York, NY 10027

Public Safety Foundation of America Grants 3983
The Public Safety Foundation of America (PSFA) makes grants to organizations supporting public safety communications function and issues. Eligible applicants include: Association of Public Safety Communications Officials (APCO) international committees and approved project groups and task forces; APCO partner organizations (nonprofit only); and APCO subsidiary organizations and parent. The PSFA funds new or ongoing projects for the betterment of the public safety communications community. Eligible projects include: planning and coordination – expenses related to determining how best to plan for or coordinate a major organizational public safety communications project; strategic initiatives – expenses related to high level programs addressing organizational challenges and issues related to improving the overall quality of a public safety communications agency or organization; PSAP equipment and technology – expenses associated with the physical equipment required for an acquisition or upgrade within a public safety communications agency or organization; education – expenses associated with developing and implementing programs to educate public safety agencies and other stakeholders about the importance of public safety communications or public safety communications issues. The Foundation works with recognized organizations to structure programs specific to the funding parameters set forth by the Board of Directors. Applications are subsequently reviewed by the Grant Review Working Group and approved or denied by the Board of Directors on an ongoing basis. A detailed list of proposal requirements and a scoring criteria for the proposal are available at the PSFA website.
Geographic Focus: All States
Contact: Mark Cannon, Grants Administrator; (571) 312-4400; cannonm@apcointl.org
Internet: http://psfa.us/Grantseekers.html
Sponsor: Public Safety Foundation of America
1426 Prince Street
Alexandria, VA 22314

Public Welfare Foundation Grants 3984
Grants are awarded primarily to grassroots organizations in the United States and abroad, with emphasis on the environment, disadvantaged elderly and youth, population and reproductive health, economic development, welfare reform, health, human rights and global security, criminal justice, and community development. Programs must serve low-income populations, with preference to short-term needs. Types of support include matching funds, operating budgets, seed money, continuing support, and special projects. Grant guidelines are available upon request. Proposal with cover letter should be addressed to the Steering Committee at the address listed.
Requirements: Nonprofit organizations and, in certain cases, organizations without 501(c)3 status, may apply for grant support. Eligible exceptions are listed in the guidelines (available upon request).
Restrictions: Grants will not be made to individuals or for religious purposes, building funds, capital improvements, endowments, scholarships, graduate work, foreign study, conferences, seminars, publications, research, workshops, consulting services, annual campaigns, or deficit financing.
Geographic Focus: All States
Amount of Grant: 25,000 - 50,000 USD
Contact: Administrator; (202) 965-1800; reviewcommittee@publicwelfare.org
Internet: http://www.publicwelfare.org/about/about.asp
Sponsor: Public Welfare Foundation
1200 U Street NW
Washington, DC 20009

Publix Super Markets Charities Local Grants 3985
Publix Super Markets Charities has long focused on youth and education. The Foundation supports efforts on the areas of youth, education (specifically literacy), and the plight of the homeless and hungry.
Requirements: The Foundation's charitable focus is toward nonprofit agencies and it supports many other efforts in Florida, Georgia, South Carolina, Alabama and Tennessee. Grant requests may be made writing and should include the following: organizational information including a brief history and mission; a copy of the Internal Revenue Service 501(c)3 determination letter; a brief budget; and a list of the Board of Directors. If requesting support for a particular project, include the total cost, the amount committed by the applicant, the amount requested, and the support received from other community organizations. Any applicable deadlines should be specified. The Foundation Board meets monthly and generally it takes six to eight weeks to process a request.
Restrictions: No grants funding is made to individuals.
Geographic Focus: Alabama, Florida, Georgia, South Carolina, Tennessee
Contact: Sharon Miller, Executive Director; (863) 680-5339
Internet: http://www.publix.com/about/CommunityInvolvement.do
Sponsor: Publix Super Markets Charities
P.O. Box 407
Lakeland, FL 33802-0407

Puerto Rico Community Foundation Grants 3986
The Foundation wishes to develop the capacities of communities in Puerto Rico so that they may achieve social transformation and economic self-sufficiency, by stimulating investment in communities and maximizing the impact and yield of each contribution. Grants are awarded in the areas of: education; community development; financial development; development of social interest housing; and philanthropy. Types of support include: general operating support; emergency funds; conferences and seminars; professorships; publications; research; technical assistance; consulting services; and matching funds. There are no application deadlines; the board meets in March, June, September, and December to consider requests.
Requirements: Organizations applying for grants must comply with the conditions below in order to demonstrate eligibility: be duly incorporated and registered as a nonprofit organization, according to the laws of the Commonwealth of Puerto Rico; be located and offer services in Puerto Rico. Present a copy of the following documents: certificate of good standing from the State Department; certificate from the Treasury Department; statement of organization's total budget for the year for which funds are solicited; financial statements; list of current members of Board of Directors. Should include each member's address and phone number; resume or curriculum vitae of the Project Director.
Restrictions: The foundation does not make grants to support individuals, annual campaigns, seed money, endowments, deficit financing, scholarships, or building funds.
Geographic Focus: Puerto Rico
Amount of Grant: 1,000 - 40,000 USD
Contact: Grants Administrator; (787) 721-1037; fax (787) 721-1673; fcpr@fcpr.org
Internet: http://www.fcpr.org/
Sponsor: Puerto Rico Community Foundation
P.O. Box 70362
San Juan, PR 00936-8362
Puerto Rico

Puffin/Nation Prize for Creative Citizenship 3987
This unique award is given to an individual who has challenged the status quo through distinctive, courageous, imaginative and socially responsible work of significance. Candidates are found in a broad range of occupations and pursuits, including academia, journalism, organizing, public health, environmental sciences, literature, art and the humanities. The prize is intended to encourage the recipients to continue their work and to inspire others to challenge the prevailing orthodoxies they face in their own careers. The Prize is an annual $100,000 award administered by the Nation Institute and endowed by the Puffin Foundation.
Requirements: The recipient must be a U.S. citizen.
Restrictions: The recipient cannot currently be holding or seeking public office.
Geographic Focus: All States
Amount of Grant: 100,000 USD
Contact: Taya Kitman, (212) 822-0252; fax (212) 253-5356; taya@nationinstitute.org
Internet: http://www.nationinstitute.org/puffinnation/prize.html
Sponsor: Puffin Foundation / Nation Institute
116 E 16th Street, 8th Floor
New York, NY 10003

Pulaski County Community Foundation Grants 3988
The Pulaski County Community Foundation was established to serve the citizens of Pulaski County, Indiana. The Foundation welcomes grant requests from any nonprofit organization in Pulaski County. The Foundation also invites applications to help fund new organizations who meet demonstrated needs or benefit the community through creative and innovative projects and programs. Grant seekers may access the online application but are also encouraged to discuss their project with the Foundation office before submitting a grant proposal.
Requirements: The Foundation favors grant requests which: impact a substantial number of people in the Pulaski community; propose practical solutions to current problems or address a current community interest; examine and address underlying causes of local needs; encourage cooperation and elimination of duplicate services; build the capacity of the applying organization; are from established non-profit organizations.
Restrictions: Grants are made only to organizations that serve the Pulaski county area. As a general rule, the Foundation does not make grants from its discretionary funds for the following: ongoing operating expenses or annual fund raising drives; existing obligations, debt reduction or building campaigns; individuals or travel expenses; loans or endowments; political purposes. Grantees are required to complete a Final Report (program and financial) detailing how the grant funds were spent.
Geographic Focus: Indiana
Contact: Wendy Rose, (574) 946-0906; fax (574) 946-0971; wrose@pulaskionline.org
Internet: http://www.pulaskionline.org/content/view/97/432/
Sponsor: Pulaski County Community Foundation
127 E. Pearl Street, P.O.Box 407
Winamac, IN 46996

Pulte Homes Corporate Contributions 3989

The charitable giving program is committed to addressing the life challenges facing individuals and families by partnering with organizations that have a significant positive impact on the future of society. Pulte's focus is in four primary categories: housing—funds are allocated for this category through 2006; education—major capital improvements or professorship endowments to improve programs targeted toward the residential homebuilding industry at U.S. universities; environmental—sustainable conservation projects or major initiatives to improve the environment; and health and human services. In the health and human services category, requests for funds benefiting the metropolitan Detroit area will be considered at the listed office location. Requests for funds for other geographic areas should be forwarded to the local Pulte market office. Guidelines and application are available online.
Requirements: 501(c)3 tax-exempt organizations are eligible.
Restrictions: Grants do not support individuals (except for residential homebuilding-industry scholarships); organizations that discriminate on the basis of race, religion, ethnicity, sexual preference, or other unlawful classification; or religious, fraternal, or veterans' organizations unless they benefit the community at large. Appeals for unrestricted funds or for organizations that distribute funds to other charities will not be considered.
Geographic Focus: All States
Contact: Charitable Giving Administrator; (248) 433-4534
Internet: http://www.pulte.com/about_us/contributions_missionstatement.asp?ss={4F1CC3DE-CDDA-4CA2-BBE7-800009464021}
Sponsor: Pulte Homes Corporation
100 Bloomfield Hills Parkway, Suite 300
Bloomfield Hills, MI 48304

Putnam County Community Foundation Grants 3990

The Putnam County Community Foundation is a nonprofit public charity established to administer funds, award grants and provide leadership, enriching the quality of life and strengthening community in Putnam County. The Foundation makes grants to qualified nonprofit organizations seeking to make a different in Putnam County and its residents. Grants are made in the following areas: animal welfare; arts and culture; civic and community; economic development; education; environment; health and human services; recreation; and youth. The application and samples of previously funded grants are available at the website.
Requirements: To be considered for funding, organizations must first submit a preliminary grant application form. The Grants Committee will review all preliminary applications to determine who will be invited to submit a full grant application.
Restrictions: Funding is not allowed for the following: individuals; ongoing operational expenses, i.e. salaries, rent, and utilities; projects that do not serve Putnam County citizens; projects normally fully funded by units of government; programs to build or fund an endowment; religious activities or programs that appear to serve one denomination and not the community at large; political organizations or campaigns; national and state-wide fund raising projects; for-profit companies; or projects requesting retroactive funding.
Geographic Focus: Indiana
Date(s) Application is Due: Feb 1; Mar 9; Aug 1; Sep 9
Contact: M. Elaine Peck; (765) 653-4978; epeck@pcfoundation.org or info@pcfountation.org
Internet: http://www.pcfoundation.org/grant_what_we_fund.html
Sponsor: Putnam County Community Foundation
2 South Jackson Street, P.O. Box 514
Greencastle, IN 46135

Putnam Foundation Grants 3991

The foundation, established in 1952, awards grants to eligible New Hampshire nonprofit organizations in its areas of interest, including civic and public affairs, cultural programs, ecology and environmental protection, education, historic preservation, public affairs and government, and youth programs. Types of support include capital campaigns (including endowments), general operating grants, and project grants. There are no application deadlines or forms.
Requirements: New Hampshire nonprofits serving the Monadnock region are eligible.
Geographic Focus: New Hampshire
Contact: Rosamond P. Delori, Secretary; (603) 352-2448; fax (603) 355-9954
Sponsor: Putnam Foundation
20 Central Square, 2nd Floor, P.O. Box 323
Keene, NH 03431-0323

Quaker Oats Company Kids Care Clubs Grants 3992

The Kids Care Clubs supports the organization's mission to raise compassionate, community-minded kids. The program aims to promote youth volunteerism, increase the number of Kids Care Clubs and build a network of moms, teachers, youth leaders and others interested in sharing experiences and insights. In the first year, Quaker awarded more than $25,000 in grants to deserving Kids Care Clubs to bring good moments to more than 10,000 people in need. In addition, more than 575 new facilitators signed up and started new Kids Care Clubs to help young volunteers get involved. Quaker is looking forward to continuing to inspire youth volunteerism through its partnership with Kids Care Clubs. Projects are eligible for mini-grants and in-kind donations from the sponsors.
Geographic Focus: All States
Date(s) Application is Due: Feb 1
Contact: Maureen Byrne; (203) 656-8052 or (866) 269-0510; fax (203) 656-8062; MByrne@generationOn.org or kidscare@generationOn.org
Internet: http://www.quakeroats.com/about-quaker-oats/content/community-programs/kids-care.aspx
Sponsor: Quaker Oats Company
P.O. Box 049003
Chicago, IL 60604-9003

Qualcomm Grants 3993

The philanthropic endeavors of Qualcomm develop and strengthen communities worldwide. Qualcomm invests human and financial resources in inspirational, innovative programs that serve diverse populations. Specifically their goal is to create educated, healthy, sustainable, culturally vibrant communities and to support employees' commitment to global communities through various programs. The company focuses primarily in geographic regions where they have a business presence. There are three focus areas. First is educated communities. The company is committed to improving science, technology, engineering and math education for students during their primary, secondary, and higher education years, and to expanding educational opportunities for under-represented students. Second is healthy, sustainable communities. The company strives to better the lives of underserved populations by providing basic human needs, with a focus on enhancing the welfare of children. They are also committed to protecting and enhancing our global environment. Third is culturally vibrant communities. Through their support of arts education and outreach programs, they help young people develop innovative minds and expand cultural enrichment opportunities to in-need populations. Applicants may submit a letter of inquiry form online and some organizations will be invited to submit a proposal for funding consideration. The submission deadlines are based on the grantmaking focus areas. The schedule can be found on the website.
Requirements: Eligible applicants must be 501(c)3 organizations.
Restrictions: The following are not eligible: individuals; sporting events without a charitable beneficiary; sectarian or denominational religious groups; faith-based schools unless the school accepts students from all religious and non-religious backgrounds and the students are not required to adhere to or convert to any religious doctrine; faith-based organizations unless the programs are broadly promoted and the program's beneficiaries are not encouraged or required to learn about, adhere, or convert to any religious doctrine; organizations that advocate, support, or practice activities inconsistent with Qualcomm's non-discrimination policies, whether based on race, religion, color, national origin, ancestry, mental or physical disability, age, gender, gender identity and/or expression, sexual orientation, veteran status, pregnancy, medical condition, marital status, or other basis protected by law; primary and secondary schools (note, however, these entities may be eligible for employee matching grants as long as they are not deemed ineligible by other exclusions and restrictions); and political contributions.
Geographic Focus: California, Colorado, Georgia, New Jersey, North Carolina, Texas
Contact: Administrator; (858) 651-3200; fax (858) 651-3255; giving@qualcomm.com
Internet: http://www.qualcomm.com/citizenship/global-social-responsibility/philanthropy/guidelines
Sponsor: Qualcomm
5775 Morehouse Drive
San Diego, CA 92121

Quality Health Foundation Grants 3994

The Quality Health Foundation (QHF) awards grants to eligible organizations that work to improve healthcare for individuals and communities through measurable outcome improvement projects. The Foundation is the mission arm of Quality Health Strategies, a group of companies with 40 years of experience in conducting and evaluating health care quality improvement initiatives. QHF will fund various projects, including service, demonstration, education and clinical programs producing high impact results on health outcomes. Funding will be prioritized based on a project's potential impact on healthcare improvements and access for individuals and communities, particularly the uninsured and under-served population, and/or projects that can be replicated. Customarily, grant awards are for one year with the potential for additional funding in subsequent years. These awards may be up to $50,000.
Requirements: Applicants must be from Maryland or the District of Columbia. All organizations focused on improving the health of individuals at the community level are encouraged to apply. Priority areas include: improved treatment through the use of "best practices"; improved access to health care services; improved understanding of health issues.
Restrictions: QHF will not fund: reimbursable direct patient care services; facility construction/remodeling of facilities; lobbying; or fundraising activities.
Geographic Focus: District of Columbia, Maryland
Date(s) Application is Due: Jan 16
Amount of Grant: Up to 50,000 USD
Contact: Glennda Moragne El; (410) 872-9632; moragneelg@dfmc.org
Internet: http://www.qualityhealthfoundation.org/funding
Sponsor: Quality Health Foundation
9240 Centreville Road
Easton, MD 21601

Quantum Corporation Snap Server Grants 3995

The Snap Server Donation program focuses its charitable efforts on increasing access to storage technology by supporting organizations in the areas of human services and civic development. Quantum makes grants of storage appliances to nonprofit organizations worldwide. Its goal is to help bring the benefits of storage technology to people and their communities, to provide support to the communities in which its employees live, and to support its employees by taking an active role in their community. Snap Server donations are focused on youth organizations, local community programs, science and technology organizations, and humanitarian causes.
Geographic Focus: California
Contact: Sean Lamb, Public Relations Manager; (408) 879-8776; fax (408) 371-1783; sean.lamb@quantum.com
Internet: http://www.quantum.com
Sponsor: Quantum Corporation
2001 Logic Drive
San Jose, CA 95035

Quantum Foundation Grants 3996

The foundation makes grants to approved charitable organizations, as well as state and local governmental entities, serving Palm Beach County, Florida, in the areas of health—improving access to insurance, health care, and prevention programs and reforming the health care delivery system; education—early childhood development, along with academic and career achievement for K-12 students; and community betterment (by invitation only)—promoting diversity, helping special needs populations, reducing family violence, and reducing child abuse and neglect. Types of support include capital grants, challenge/matching grants, program development grants, and seed money grants. Submit concept papers before full proposals.
Requirements: Nonprofits serving West Palm Beach, Florida, are eligible.
Geographic Focus: Florida
Contact: Christine Koehn; (561) 832-7497; fax (561) 832-5794; chrisk@quantumfnd.org
Internet: http://www.quantumfnd.org
Sponsor: Quantum Foundation
2701 North Australian Avenue, Suite 200
West Palm Bach, FL 33407

Questar Corporate Contributions Grants 3997

The corporation funds health and social services in the West, including some parts of Colorado, Oklahoma, Utah, and Wyoming. Grants have been awarded to hospitals, especially to build emergency rooms; substance abuse prevention programs, especially in the schools; child abuse prevention programs; and HIV/AIDS prevention and care. Questar determines the size of the grants based on the number of its employees in its facilities in the area, as well as how many other organizations of the same type it has funded nearby. Requests should be submitted in writing and describe the problem, outline the project, and state the amount sought. Applications are accepted at any time.
Requirements: Nonprofits in the West are eligible.
Geographic Focus: Colorado, Oklahoma, Utah, Wyoming
Amount of Grant: 5,000 - 20,000 USD
Contact: Jan Bates; (801) 324-5132 or (801) 324-5202; Jan.Bates@Questar.com
Internet: http://www.questar.com/about_us/community/contributions.html
Sponsor: Questar Corporation
180 East 100 South, P.O. Box 45433, Mailstop QB 811
Salt Lake City, UT 84145-0433

QuikTrip Corporate Contributions Grants 3998

QuikTrip allocates 5 percent of its profits to support nonprofit organizations in its service area. The corporation's charitable giving priority is to contribute where the need is critical and effect is long-term, with the resulting rewards to society measuring several times that of the original investment. Community-building efforts also are favored. There are no application deadlines. Proposals are accepted throughout the year, but staff encourage submissions between January and May.
Requirements: Corporate-operating communities are in: Tulsa, Oklahoma; Kansas City, Missouri; Kansas City, Kansas; Wichita, Kansas; Des Moines, Iowa; Omaha, Nebraska; Dallas-Fort Worth, Texas; St. Louis, Missouri; Atlanta, Georgia; and Phoenix, Arizona.
Geographic Focus: Arizona, Georgia, Iowa, Kansas, Missouri, Nebraska, Oklahoma, Texas
Contact: Community Relations Manager; (918) 615-7872; fax (918) 615-7408; Contributions@QuikTrip.com
Internet: http://www.quiktrip.com/community/contributions.asp
Sponsor: QuikTrip Corporation
P.O. Box 3475
Tulsa, OK 74101

R.C. Baker Foundation Grants 3999

The foundation makes grants to U.S. nonprofit organizations for projects and programs that support social services for youth and the elderly, crime prevention, education, religion (Christian, Episcopal, Friends, Jewish, Methodist, and Presbyterian), scientific research, culture, and health. Support will be provided for fellowships and scholarships, general operating grants, challenge/matching grants, emergency funds, building funds, equipment, continuing support, annual campaigns, capital campaigns, renovation projects, and special projects. Submit cover letter with proposal. The board meets in June and November to consider requests.
Requirements: Nonprofit organizations are eligible. $25,000 to
Restrictions: Anaheim Memorial Medical Center, Anaheim, CA - $40,000; Harvey Mudd College, Claremont, CA - $25,000;
Date(s) Application is Due: May 1; Oct 1
Amount of Grant: 1,000 - 280,000 USD
Contact: Frank Scott, Chairman; (714) 750-8987
Sponsor: R.C. Baker Foundation
P.O. Box 6150
Orange, CA 92863-6150

R.E.B. Awards for Distinguished Educational Leadership 4000

The award recognizes those principals who go beyond the day-to-day demands of their position to create an exceptional educational environment. Four principals will be publicly recognized, one in each school district of the Richmond metropolitan area (i.e. the counties of Chesterfield, Hanover, Henrico and the City of Richmond). Each award will consist of a $7,500 cash grant to the principal and an additional $7,500 for the principal's school for projects chosen by the principal.
Requirements: Nominations may be submitted from the school community and from the public at-large. However, principals may not nominate themselves. Nominees must be principals who: [1] Manage effectively to promote excellence in education. [2] Demonstrate leadership and exemplify commitment. [3] Inspire their students and are advocates for their school and faculty. [4] Encourage team spirit. [5] Foster cooperation between the school and the community. [6] Maintain dialogue with students, parents, faculty and staff. [7] Have been a principal of their school for at least 3 years.
Geographic Focus: Virginia
Date(s) Application is Due: Oct 27
Amount of Grant: 15,000 USD
Contact: Susan Hallett; (804) 330-7400; fax (804) 330-5992; shallett@tcfrichmond.org
Internet: http://www.tcfrichmond.org/Page8759.cfm#REBD
Sponsor: Community Foundation Serving Richmond and Central Virginia
7501 Boulders View Drive, Suite 110
Richmond, VA 23225

R.J. McElroy Trust Grants 4001

The R.J. McElroy Trust was founded in 1965. Its benefactor was a pioneer Iowa broadcaster. Grant funding is provided to organizations which provide educational benefits to deserving youth. The Trust gives higher priority to funding programs than it does to funding capital projects. It prefers to provide seed money for new projects with organizations building a firm financial basis including other funding sources after one to three years.
Requirements: Eligible applicants must be 501(c)3 non-profit organizations. Governmental entities are eligible. Organizations must be in the following areas of Iowa: Allamakee, Benton, Black Hawk, Bremer, Buchanan, Butler, Chickasaw, Clayton, Delaware, Dubuque, Fayette, Floyd, Franklin, Grundy, Howard, Hardin, Tama, Winneshiek, and rural Linn county. Before applying applicants are asked contact the Executive Director by phone or email to ensure eligibility. Applications are available on the website.
Restrictions: The Trust does not make grants to individuals or to religious organizations for religious programming.
Geographic Focus: Iowa
Date(s) Application is Due: Mar 1; Jun 1; Sep 1; Dec 1
Contact: Stacy Van Gorp; (319) 287-9102; fax (319) 287-9105; vangorp@mcelroytrust.org
Internet: http://mcelroytrust.org/grantProposalGuidlines.html
Sponsor: R.J. McElroy Trust
425 Cedar Street, Suite 312
Waterloo, IA 50701

R.S. Gernon Trust Grants 4002

The R.S. Gernon Trust was established in 1975 to support and promote quality educational, human-services, and health-care programming for underserved populations. Grants from the R.S. Gernon Trust are primarily one year in duration. On occasion, multi-year support is awarded. Applicants must apply online at the grant website. Applicants are strongly encouraged to do the following before applying: review the downloadable state application procedures for additional helpful information and clarifications; review the downloadable online-application guidelines at the grant website; review the trust's funding history (link is available from the grant website); review the online application questions in advance; and review the list of required attachments. These will generally include: a list of board members, financial statements (audited, reviewed, or compiled by independent auditor); an organization summary; a list of other funding sources; an IRS Determination letter; and other required documents. All attachments must be uploaded in the online application as PDF, Word, or Excel files. The R. S. Gernon Trust has biannual deadlines of February 15 and August 15. Applications must be submitted by 11:59 p.m. on the deadline dates. Applicants will be notified of grant decisions by letter within two to three months after each respective proposal deadline.
Requirements: Applicants must have 501(c)3 tax-exempt status and serve the people of Norwich, Connecticut.
Restrictions: Grant requests for capital projects are generally not considered. Applicants will not be awarded a grant for more than 3 consecutive years. The trust does not support requests from individuals, organizations attempting to influence policy through direct lobbying, or any political campaigns.
Geographic Focus: Connecticut
Date(s) Application is Due: Feb 15; Aug 15
Contact: Kate Kerchaert; (860) 657-7016; kate.kerchaert@baml.com
Internet: https://www.bankofamerica.com/philanthropic/fn_search.action
Sponsor: R.S. Gernon Trust
200 Glastonbury Boulevard, Suite # 200, CT2-545-02-05
Glastonbury, CT 06033-4056

Rachel Alexandra Girls Grants 4003

The Girls Grant Project Team is dedicated to funding programs that fulfill the needs and interests of girls and young women. It strives to fund programs that have visible evidence of girl-involvement. The Foundation is looking for programs that allow girls and young women participants to have an active voice in decision-making and program planning. Some components of girl-involvement might be, but are not limited to: girls and young women being utilized in leadership positions with adult support; girls and young women serving in an advisory committee capacity to decision-makers in a given agency/organization; and girls and young women having some responsibilities for program planning, grant writing, budgeting and/or evaluating.
Requirements: Agencies and organizations in Cass, Clay, Jackson, Platte and Ray counties in Missouri; Johnson, Leavenworth and Wyandotte Counties in Kansas may apply.
Restrictions: The Program does not fund individuals or scholarships.
Geographic Focus: Kansas, Missouri
Date(s) Application is Due: Sep 12
Contact: Jackie Loya-Torres; (913) 831-0711, ext. 26; fax (913) 831-0881; women@wfgkc.org
Internet: http://www.wfgkc.org/grants_girls.html
Sponsor: Women's Foundation of Greater Kansas City
6950 Squibb Road, Suite 220
Mission, KS 66202

Radcliffe Institute Individual Residential Fellowships   4004
The Radcliffe Institute Fellowship Program is a scholarly community where individuals pursue advanced work across a wide range of academic disciplines, professions, and creative arts. Radcliffe Institute fellowships are designed to support scholars, scientists, artists, and writers of exceptional promise and demonstrated accomplishment who wish to pursue work in academic and professional fields and in the creative arts. In recognition of Radcliffe's historic contributions to the education of women and to the study of issues related to women, the Radcliffe Institute sustains a continuing commitment to the study of women, gender, and society. Applicants need not focus on gender, however. Women and men from across the United States and throughout the world are encouraged to apply. email fellowships@radcliffe.edu for questions regarding humanities, social sciences, or creative arts fellowships. email sciencefellowships@radcliffe.edu for questions regarding natural science and mathematics fellowships.
Requirements: Scholars in any field with a doctorate or appropriate terminal degree at least two years prior to appointment (by December of the prior year) in the area of the proposed project are eligible to apply. Only scholars who have published at least two articles or monographs are eligible to apply. Artists and writers need not have a PHD or an MFA to apply; however, they must meet other specific eligibility requirements. Fellows are expected to be free of their regular commitments so they may devote themselves full time to the work. Applicants must reside in the Boston area, with their primary office at the Institute. Applications are available online, but applicants should refer to website for current deadlines and application requirements for each academic discipline.
Restrictions: Former fellows of the Radcliffe Institute Fellowship Program (1999 to present) are not eligible to apply.
Geographic Focus: All States, All Countries
Amount of Grant: 35,000 - 70,000 USD
Contact: (617) 496-1324
Internet: http://www.radcliffe.edu/fellowships/apply.asp
Sponsor: Radcliffe Institute for Advanced Study
10 Garden Street
Cambridge, MA 02138

RadioShack StreetSentz Community Grants   4005
The grant program is designed to offer answers—answers that bring community impact through programs or projects conducted by local nonprofit organizations. The program currently focuses on two areas: prevention of family violence/abuse, and/or child abduction. Guidelines are available online.
Requirements: 501(c)3 tax-exempt organizations and municipalities, including local police departments, are eligible. Applicant organization must offer solutions to help prevent family violence/abuse and/or child abduction; and directly impact or benefit, through programs and/or services, a RadioShack community.
Restrictions: Grants cannot be considered for individuals; endowments or private foundations that are themselves grant-making organizations; construction or major renovation projects; to fund advertising or marketing programs; fundraising events and sponsorships (i.e., golf tournaments, dinners, auctions); multiyear grants; religious, political, and fraternal organizations; or trips, sporting events, tours, and transportation.
Geographic Focus: All States
Date(s) Application is Due: Mar 15; Jun 15; Sep 15; Dec 15
Amount of Grant: Up to 500 USD
Contact: Community Relations Manager; (817) 415-3699; fax (817) 415-0939; corporate.citizenship@radioshack.com
Internet: http://www.radioshackcorporation.com/cc/contributions.html
Sponsor: RadioShack Corporation
200 RadioShack Circle, MS CF3-323
Fort Worth, TX 76102-1964

Rainbow Academy Foundation Grants   4006
In 2001, the Rainbow Academy Child Care Centers formed a 501c non-profit organization called the Rainbow Foundation with one primary goal: Contribute to the health, education and overall well being of children. The Rainbow Academy corporate offices donates all of the administrative costs so that all of the money raised is available for distribution to local and national children's charities. The new mission is to help connect parents with their children. Some of the areas available for grants include: family education (book programs for needy families and sign language classes for a family member of a deaf child); family health and well being (medical costs, autism therapy, hearing aids costs and family therapy); family planning (adoption, in-vitro and fertility expenses); and rainbow Dreams (vacations for a child with terminal illnesses, travel expenses for adoption and making dreams come true).
Requirements: Families or programs located in the New Jersey regions where there are Rainbow Academy centers can apply, which include the communities of: Brick, Cranford, Flemington, Iselin, North Brunswick, Piscataway, Rutherford, Summit, Whippany, and Woodbridge. An applicant must be sponsored by a Rainbow Academy parent, staff or investor.
Geographic Focus: New Jersey
Contact: Guy Falzarano, President; (732) 388-9866 or (866) 470-0262; fax (732) 388-9876; guy@rainbowacademy.com or foundation@rainbowacademy.com
Internet: http://www.rainbowacademy.com/foundation1.shtml
Sponsor: Rainbow Academy Foundation
80 Kingsbridge Road
Piscataway, NJ 08854

Rainbow Endowment Grants   4007
Once a year, the Rainbow Endowment invites non-profit organizations having a national impact on the LGBT community to submit a request for funding. The proposals are reviewed by the Endowment's Grant Committee, which makes funding recommendations to the Board of Directors. The endowment supports national efforts to encourage positive physical and mental health; promote increased visibility; and advance full participation and access to social, cultural, and civic life for the gay and lesbian community. The Endowment seeks to support LGBT organizations whose efforts are national in scope in the areas of health and community. Priority is given to efforts that have practical implications or applications. In the area of health, grants are made to promote awareness of gay and lesbian mental and physical health issues among consumers and health care providers; to advocate for and develop public policy for equal health care treatment or equal access to health care treatment; and to advocate for and develop public policy to prevent further HIV/AIDS infection and to improve the lives of people with HIV/AIDS. In the area of community, grants are made to protect lesbian and gay rights; promote coalitions that work to strengthen advocacy efforts to improve conditions for lesbians and gays; and to develop policies that benefit lesbian and gay youth and the children of lesbian and gay families. Proposals can be submitted at anytime; however, they are reviewed only once per year. The deadline is the third Friday in May.
Requirements: U.S. nonprofit 501(c)3 organizations are eligible to apply.
Restrictions: The endowment does not support direct services, state or local projects, government agencies, individuals, regularly held meetings, fund-raising events, K-12 schools, religious purposes, endowments, or capital projects. Organizations may not apply more than once each calendar year.
Geographic Focus: All States
Amount of Grant: 5,000 - 20,000 USD
Contact: Jean E. Bochnowski, Executive Director; (215) 241-7280; fax (215) 241-7278; jeb35@aol.com or endowment@rainbowcard.com
Internet: http://www.rainbowendowment.org/what.html
Sponsor: Rainbow Endowment
1501 Cherry Street
Philadelphia, PA 19102-1403

Rainbow Families Foundation Grants   4008
The Rainbow Families Foundation, established by Pat and Bob Grisar, is a non profit-humanitarian relief organization founded to organize efforts to provide humanitarian relief to families, primarily in the Dominican Republic. In addition to clothing and shoes, the Foundation stresses the need for school supplies, coloring books, pencils, pens, candles, toothpaste, toothbrushes, surgical gloves, blankets, and soap. Applications can be made on behalf of the needy.
Geographic Focus: All States
Contact: Patricia M. Grisar, (440) 256-4825; pgrisar@rainbowfamilies.org
Internet: http://www.rainbow-families.org/index.html
Sponsor: Rainbow Families Foundation
8543 Hemlock Ridge Drive
Kirtland, OH 44094

Rainbow Fund Grants   4009
The Trust was established in 1954 in Georgia. Giving is primarily focused on theological education and other Christian endeavors. Support is also offered for substance abuse treatment and music education through mentoring high school students and conservatory musicians. There are no specific guidelines or application forms, and potential applicants are advised to contact the office directly.
Requirements: Eligible applicants from Florida, Georgia, Kentucky, Mississippi, and Texas can apply.
Geographic Focus: Florida, Georgia, Kentucky, Mississippi, Texas
Amount of Grant: 25,000 - 2,000,000 USD
Contact: Burton S. Luce; (954) 764-7724; fax (954) 764-3603; lluce@drmail.com
Sponsor: Rainbow Fund
2408 Sunrise Key Boulevard
Fort Lauderdale, FL 33304

Rainbow Media Holdings LLC Corporate Giving Program Grants   4010
Rainbow Media is a leading producer of targeted, multi-platform content for global distribution, creating and managing some of the world's most compelling and dynamic entertainment brands. Its corporate giving program makes charitable contributions to nonprofit organizations involved with the arts, culture and education. Types of support include: annual campaigns, conferences/seminars, general operating support, in-kind gifts, scholarship funds, and sponsorships. There is no application form to be submitted. Applicants should, instead, send a detailed description of the project and amount of funding requested. Support is given primarily in the states of New York, New Jersey, and Connecticut, and typically notification occurs within one month of submission.
Requirements: 501(c)3 organizations serving the folks of New York, New Jersey, and Connecticut are eligible to apply.
Geographic Focus: Connecticut, New Jersey, New York
Contact: Matthew Frankel, Director; (917) 542-6390 or (516) 803-5154; fax (516) 803-5143; mdfrankel@rainbow-media.com
Internet: http://www.rainbow-media.com/default
Sponsor: Rainbow Media Holdings LLC
200 Jericho Quadrangle
Jericho, NY 11753-2701

Rajiv Gandhi Foundation Grants   4011
The foundation conducts activities in India in the areas of the arts and humanities, conservation and the environment, economic affairs, education, international affairs, law and human rights, medicine and health, science and technology, and social welfare. Main projects are concerned with literacy and primary education, empowering women and children, aid for the disabled, health care services in rural and poor urban areas, and decentralized government. Types of support include research grants to institutions and scholarships, fellowships, and prizes to individuals.

Geographic Focus: All States
Contact: Jawahar Bhawan, Director; (091-11) 23755117 or (091-11) 23312456; fax (091-11) 23755119; info@rgfindia.org
Internet: http://www.rgfindia.com
Sponsor: Rajiv Gandhi Foundation
Dr. Rajendra Prasad Road
New Delhi, 110 001 India

Ralph and Virginia Mullin Foundation Grants 4012
The foundation provides small grants to animal welfare and shelter organizations. The foundation also gives a few gifts annually to organizations that are working to become incorporated and obtain 501(c)3 status. Those grant recipients must use funds for costs directly related to achieving these goals.
Requirements: The foundation currently does not have a website. Contact the sponsor by mail or email for any additional guidelines or questions.
Geographic Focus: All States
Date(s) Application is Due: Sep 30
Amount of Grant: Up to 2,000 USD
Contact: Rob Rauh, (520) 881-6607; fax (520) 881-6775; rob@hrtucson.com
Sponsor: Ralph and Virginia Mullin Foundation
2401 E Speedway Boulevard
Tucson, AZ 85719

Ralph M. Parsons Foundation Grants 4013
The Ralph M. Parsons Foundation strives to support and facilitate the work of the region's best nonprofit organizations, recognizing that many of those in need today will go on to shape the future of Southern California, to define it, redefine it, and help it set and achieve new goals. The Foundation focuses on four areas: social impact, civic and cultural programs, health, and higher education. Applicants may submit a letter of inquiry, and there are no deadlines. If the Foundation decides to explore specifics of the request in more detail, applicants will be asked to submit a full proposal. Guidance will be provided in writing. Approximately 200 awards are made per year ranging from $25,000 to $50,000.
Requirements: Eligible applicants are 501(c)3 organizations located in Los Angeles County. Some occasional exceptions are made in the area of higher education. Excellence, access for disadvantaged populations, and the active participation of volunteers, board and staff are key characteristics the Foundation seeks in its applicants. Funding of direct services is a priority.
Restrictions: The following is ineligible: fundraising events, dinners and mass mailings; direct aid to individuals; conferences, seminars, workshops, etc; sectarian, religious or fraternal purposes; federated fundraising appeals; support of candidates for political office or to influence legislation; for-profit organizations or businesses; organizations outside of Los Angeles County (with occasional exceptions in the area of higher education); animal welfare; environment; documentary filmmaking; and scientific and/or medical research. Scholarship support is provided only to nonprofit institutions; individuals are not eligible to apply.
Geographic Focus: California
Contact: Wendy Garen, President and Chief Executive Officer; (213) 362-7600
Internet: http://www.rmpf.org
Sponsor: Ralph M. Parsons Foundation
1888 West Sixth Street, Suite 700
Los Angeles, CA 90017

Ralphs Food 4 Less Foundation Grants 4014
The foundation supports nonprofits primarily in areas of company operations in southern California, from Santa Barbara to San Diego, for programs and activities to improve the well-being of youth through education, recreation, and health-related programs; expand cultural awareness and appreciation of the arts; strengthen neighborhoods; and assist communities in the aftermath of local disasters. Types of support include special projects and general operating expenses. There are no application deadlines. Applicants should submit a letter of application.
Requirements: To be eligible, your organization must be: a 501(3) tax exempt nonprofit; located in Southern California; working in one of the focus areas. Requests for funding must arrive eight (8) weeks prior to the event date or date of need.
Restrictions: Funding is not available to: individuals; capital campaigns; travel expenses; projects of sectarian or religious organizations whose principal benefit is for their own members or adherents; organizations that discriminate on the basis of sex, race, religion, sexual orientation or national origin; third party giving.
Geographic Focus: California
Contact: Michelle Williams, Executive Director; (310) 884-6205 or (310) 900-3522
Internet: http://www.ralphs.com/corpnewsinfo_charitablegiving_art5.htm
Sponsor: Ralph's-Food 4 Less Foundation
P.O. Box 54143
Los Angeles, CA 90054

Rancho Bernardo Community Foundation Grants 4015
The Foundation focus will be providing financial support for organizations serving the Rancho Bernardo community. Currently, funding sources available through the Foundation include: arts and culture—Symphony on the Green Fund for organizations wanting funds for music related activities and programs (grants must be $1,000 or less); human services—discretionary grants for projects benefiting the community (grants can be up to $1,000); and the Kathryn Staab Fund—for organizations providing services to disabled seniors (grants can be up to $1,500). The deadline for all three categories is September 22.
Requirements: Any 501(c)3 organization serving the residents of Rancho Bernardo, California, are eligible to apply.
Restrictions: The Rancho Bernardo Charitable Foundation does not make grants for: annual campaigns and fund raising events for non-specific purposes; capital campaigns for buildings or facilities; stipends for attendance at conferences; endowments or chairs; for-profit organizations or enterprises; individuals unaffiliated with a qualified fiscal sponsor; projects that promote religious or political doctrine; research projects (medical or otherwise); scholarships; or existing obligations or debt.
Geographic Focus: California
Date(s) Application is Due: Sep 22
Amount of Grant: 1,500 USD
Contact: Kerry Helmer, (619) 814-1384; kerry@sdfoundation.org
Internet: http://www.endowrb.org/grants.html
Sponsor: Rancho Bernardo Community Foundation / San Diego Foundation
2508 Historic Decatur Road, Suite 200
San Diego, CA 92106

Rancho Santa Fe Foundation Grants 4016
Each year, we identify organizations or issues in the community or in our region, that deserve special funding from our unrestricted endowments. Generally, the Foundation will provide stimulus funds to begin the process and we then seek additional funding from our donor advisors, private foundations in the community, or individuals who we know support these causes.
Requirements: California 501(c)3 nonprofits benefiting Rancho Santa Fe residents are eligible.
Geographic Focus: California
Amount of Grant: 1,000 - 20,000 USD
Contact: Christy Wilson; (858) 756-6557; fax (858) 756-6561; info@rsffoundation.org
Internet: http://www.rsffoundation.org/grants/index.html
Sponsor: Rancho Santa Fe Foundation
P.O. Box 811
Rancho Santa Fe, CA 92067

Randall L. Tobias Foundation Grants 4017
The Randall L. Tobias Foundation was established in 1994 in Indiana, and gives support to learning for children and youth through opportunity and experience.
Requirements: Funding is offered in geographic areas where the Tobias family has particular interests, primarily the Indianapolis, IN, area.
Geographic Focus: Indiana
Samples: Indiana University Foundation, Bloomington, IN - $200,000.
Contact: Paige N. Tobias-Button; info@rltfound.org or snh@rltfound.org
Internet: http://www.rltfound.org/main.html
Sponsor: Randall L. Tobias Foundation
500 E 96th Street, Suite 110
Indianapolis, IN 46240

RAND Corporation Graduate Student Summer Associateships 4018
The program introduces outstanding graduate students to RAND, an institution that conducts research on a wide range of national security problems and domestic and international social policy issues. Students receive a stipend and are given the opportunity to conduct research that can be completed during the three months they are at RAND. The program receives about 500 applications each year for the 20+ positions. The associates who end up finding matches with a research project do so because their skill sets match the needs of the project. The program runs in the summer months only. Summer associates work at RAND full time for a 12-week period. Positions are available in RAND's three major U.S. offices - Santa Monica, Arlington, and Pittsburgh. All summer associates are collocated with project mentors. The location of the project mentor determines the location of the summer associate. The summer stipend in 2008 was about $12,000 (before taxes) for the 12 weeks of full time research.
Requirements: The program is designed for full time students who have completed at least two years of graduate work leading to a doctorate or professional degree (e.g., law or medical degree, professional engineer certificate). Students must be enrolled full time in a graduate degree program during the spring and fall of the current school year to be considered for the program. U.S. citizenship is not necessary except for positions that require security clearances. Most of RAND's professional hiring is at the PhD level, so the summer program is oriented toward individuals who are generally within a year or two of completing their doctorates. However, sometimes there are projects that match with the skills of graduate students in other stages of their education who also have significant work experience. To apply, go to the website at http://www.rand.org/jobs/. Click Find a Job, click Advanced Search, select Research-Summer Associate Prog under Job Families, and click the Search button. Click on the position and click the Apply Now button. Follow the prompts for application submission.
Restrictions: The program does not hire undergraduates for the summer. Also, those students graduating prior to the summer of employment are not eligible to apply. The program typically does not consider Master's degree students without significant work or research experience. Postdoctoral fellows are not eligible for the summer program.
Geographic Focus: All States
Date(s) Application is Due: Jan 31
Contact: Summer Director; (310) 393-0411; Summer_Director@rand.org
Internet: http://www.rand.org/about/edu_op/fellowships/gsap/
Sponsor: RAND Corporation
1776 Main Street, P.O. Box 2138
Santa Monica, CA 90407-2138

Raskob Foundation for Catholic Activities Grants 4019
The Raskob Foundation is an independent private Catholic family foundation that makes grants worldwide for projects and programs associated with the Catholic Church. Grants support elementary and secondary education, community action and development, missionary activities, ministries (including youth and parish), health care, social concerns, AIDS victims, finance and development, and relief services. Types of support include

operating budgets, seed money, emergency funds, equipment, land acquisition, conferences and seminars, program-related investments, renovation projects, special projects, and matching funds. Deadlines are June 8 and August 8 for the fall meeting; and December 8 and February 8 for the spring meeting.
Requirements: Roman Catholic organizations listed in the Kenedy Directory of Official Catholic Organizations may apply. Organizations should refer to the application guidelines for specific instruction on how to apply and information to submit.
Restrictions: The Foundation does not accept applications for the following purposes: tuition, scholarships or fellowships; reduction of debt; endowment funds; grants made by other grantmaking organizations; individual scholarly research; lobbying or legislation; or projects completed prior to our board meetings (mid-May and late November).
Geographic Focus: All States, All Countries
Amount of Grant: 5,000 - 15,000 USD
Contact: Maureen Horner; (302) 655-4440; fax (302) 655-3223; info@rfca.org
Internet: http://www.rfca.org/en/Grantmaking/tabid/63/Default.aspx
Sponsor: Raskob Foundation for Catholic Activities
P.O. Box 4019
Wilmington, DE 19807

Rasmuson Foundation Capital Grants   4020
The Rasmuson Foundation supports non-profit organizations which strive to improve the quality of life for people throughout the state of Alaska. Capital Grants provide funding for assets such as furnishings, buildings, audio and video equipment, books, medical equipment, technology, art supplies, sports equipment, musical instruments, and vehicles. The Foundation encourages applicants to discuss proposals prior to submission. Applications are available on the website and are accepted at any time.
Requirements: Alaskan organizations that have received 501c(3) status and are classified as not a private foundation under section 509(a) of the Internal Revenue Service Code, units of government, and federally-recognized tribes are eligible.
Restrictions: For religious organizations, only projects with a broad community impact are considered. For units of government and tribes, only projects with a broad community impact beyond traditional government functions are considered. The following is not eligible: general operations, administrative, indirect, or overhead costs; deficits or debt reduction; endowments; scholarships; fundraising events or sponsorships; in general, K-12 education; reimbursement for items already purchased; and electronic health records and other emerging technologies.
Geographic Focus: Alaska
Amount of Grant: 25,000 USD
Contact: Barbara Bach, Director of Grant Management; (877) 366-2700 or (907) 297-2700; fax (907) 297-2770; bbach@rasmuson.org or rasmusonfdn@rasmuson.org
Internet: http://www.rasmuson.org/index.php?switch=viewpage&pageid=32
Sponsor: Rasmuson Foundation
301 W Northern Lights Boulevard, Suite 400
Anchorage, AK 99503

Rasmuson Foundation Creative Ventures Grants   4021
The Rasmuson Foundation supports non-profit organizations which strive to improve the quality of life for people throughout the state of Alaska. Creative Venture Grants seek to expand the creative reach of cultural organizations by encouraging innovation and exploration. Grants provide matching funds to pursue new ideas and activities or to expand current programs. Grants are designed to be awarded early in the project planning process in order to provide a financial platform for programmatic risk-taking. All projects must involve a public performance, exhibit, or other presentation. Applicants are encouraged to contact the Foundation to discuss their project before applying. Applications are available on the website and may be submitted at any time.
Requirements: Alaskan-based arts and/or cultural organizations that have received 501c(3) status and are classified as not a private foundation under section 509(a) of the Internal Revenue Service Code are eligible. Organizations must have been in existence at least three years and have a performance/exhibition record of at least two years. Organization must have an active board of directors and at least one paid part-time staff person. Eligible project categories are: the creation of new work; the expansion of existing programs; and collaborations that present a financial or artistic risk.
Restrictions: Applicants may request up to 50% of the costs of the expansion, collaboration or creation project. Awards must be matched on a one-to-one basis. Matching requirements may be met through a combination of cash and in-kind sources. However, no more than 50% of matching funds may come from in-kind sources.
Geographic Focus: Alaska
Contact: Jayson Smart, (877) 366-2700 or (907) 297-2882; jsmart@rasmuson.org
Internet: http://www.rasmuson.org/index.php?switch=viewpage&pageid=115
Sponsor: Rasmuson Foundation
301 W Northern Lights Boulevard, Suite 400
Anchorage, AK 99503

Rasmuson Foundation Individual Artists Awards   4022
The Foundation honors the merit and significance of a life dedicated to serious artistic exploration and growth. The Foundation funds individual Alaskan artists whose work is defined by excellence and reflects any of the diverse cultural and aesthetic communities in the state. Awards provide artists the resources to concentrate and reflect on their work; to immerse themselves in a creative endeavor; and to experiment, explore, and develop their artistry more fully. There are three Individual Artists Awards for artists living and working in Alaska: project awards (up to $5,000 for emerging, midcareer, and mature artists for specific, short-term projects that have a clear benefit to the artist and the development of his/her work; artist fellowships ($12,000 for midcareer or mature artists to focus their energy and attention for a one-year period on developing their creative work; and distinguished artist award ($25,000 for a mature artist of recognized stature with a history of creative excellence and accomplishment in the arts). Deadlines for project awards are March 1 and September 1; fellowship award applications, and distinguished artist award applications are due September 1. Guidelines and application cover sheets are available on the website.
Requirements: Eligible applicants must be: a full-time Alaskan resident at the time of application and for the duration of the grant period; 18 years of age or older; and an artist who is currently producing work.
Restrictions: Artists may apply for only one of the three awards per deadline. Artists receiving an Rasmuson Individual Artist Award must wait three years before re-applying. Artist Fellowships are in ten artistic disciplines that rotate on a two-year cycle. Cycle one includes: media arts; multidiscipline/new genre; music composition; presentation/interpretation; and visual arts . Cycle two includes: choreography, crafts, folk and traditional arts; literary arts/scriptworks; and performing art.
Geographic Focus: Alaska
Contact: Barbara Bach, Director of Grant Management; (877) 366-2700 or (907) 297-2700; fax (907) 297-2770; bbach@rasmuson.org or rasmusonfdn@rasmuson.or
Internet: http://www.rasmuson.org/index.php?switch=viewpage&pageid=92
Sponsor: Rasmuson Foundation
301 W Northern Lights Boulevard, Suite 400
Anchorage, AK 99503

Rasmuson Foundation Organizational Advancement Grants   4023
The Rasmuson Foundation supports non-profit organizations which strive to improve the quality of life for people throughout the state of Alaska. The Foundation recognizes that healthy, stable organizations are critical to the development of a diverse and vibrant cultural community in Alaska. The ability of organizations to deliver quality arts and cultural programs is greatly affected by their leadership, fiscal health, and management capacity. Organizational Advancement Grants were created to strengthen the effectiveness and impact of organizations that provide arts and cultural experiences to the citizens of Alaska by encouraging sustainable operations and strong leadership. Three competitive funding programs are offered to strengthen management and governance, increase resources, build effective systems, and align the mission and programs of applicant organizations. Programs are not tied to the size of an organization's budget, but rather to the unique needs of organizations at various stages of development and maturity. The programs available are: Management Assistance (awards up to $5,000 for activities that address pressing organizational needs or opportunities to build the internal capacity of organizations that provide arts and cultural services to their communities); Cultural Leadership (awards up to $3,000 for professional development opportunities which are designed to help professional staff, board, and/or volunteers); and Effective Organizations (a structured technical assistance and grant program to help arts and cultural organizations address critical internal issues and make them better equipped to fulfill their missions and improve service to their communities). Management Assistance and Cultural Leadership must be submitted no later than 90 days prior to the scheduled activity. A letter of inquiry is required for Effective Organizations by November 1.
Requirements: Alaskan-based organizations that have received 501(c)3 status from the Internal Revenue Service and are classified as "not a private foundation" under section 509(a) or the Code, or organizations with equivalent status. Organizations must have been in existence at least two years and have a record of public arts or cultural programming.
Restrictions: Management Assistance and Cultural Leadership Grants are limited to one per organization per year. Effective Organizations Assistance and Grants are limited to one per organization every five years.
Geographic Focus: Alaska
Contact: Barbara Bach, Director of Grant Management; (877) 366-2700 or (907) 297-2700; fax (907) 297-2770; bbach@rasmuson.org or rasmusonfdn@rasmuson.org
Internet: http://www.rasmuson.org/index.php?switch=viewpage&pageid=133
Sponsor: Rasmuson Foundation
301 W Northern Lights Boulevard, Suite 400
Anchorage, AK 99503

Rasmuson Foundation Sabbatical Grants   4024
For 50 years, the Foundation has been honored to help improve the quality of Alaskan's lives. Through its competitive grantmaking programs, the Foundation awards grants both to organizations serving Alaskans through a base of operations in Alaska, and to individuals for projects, fellowships and sabbaticals. The Sabbatical Program is designed to provide time away from the job for nonprofit and tribal leaders to engage in activities for personal renewal or professional growth. The Foundation believes that nonprofit CEOs/executive directors and tribal administrators better serve their organization when they have extended opportunities to reflect on their work, gain insight into what they want to accomplish in their careers, learn better ways to run their organizations, and renew their personal energy. To achieve these objectives and help prevent job related stress and burnout, the Foundation endorses the concept of sabbaticals and has committed funds to support time off for outstanding nonprofit and tribal professionals in Alaska. This program recognizes the value the Foundation places on high-performing and accomplished organization leaders. The sabbatical not only is a reward for achievement, it is a motivating factor to keep the best people in their field. This award is for the personal growth or renewal of the applicant, with no bias toward either reason. Activities dedicated to personal renewal as defined by the recipient may include travel, study, time for reflection, or simply rest. Awards will support sabbaticals of a minimum of 60 continuous and a maximum of 180 continuous days. Although Grants are awarded to the organization, funds are to be used specifically for the individual taking the sabbatical to cover salary and expenses during the sabbatical. No distinction is made between large and small organizations. Applications are available on the website.
Requirements: The organization must be an Alaska 501(c)3 health and human service nonprofit or equivalent. The participant must be an Alaska resident with at least five years

in the nonprofit sector and at least three years in his/her current position. The applicant must be the CEO or executive director of his/her organization.
Geographic Focus: Alaska
Amount of Grant: 30,000 USD
Contact: Sammye Pokryfki, Grants Administrator; (877) 366-2700 or (907) 297-2700; fax (907) 297-2770; spokryfki@rasmuson.org or rasmusonfdn@rasmuson.or
Internet: http://rasmuson.org/index.php?switch=viewpage&pageid=112
Sponsor: Rasmuson Foundation
301 W Northern Lights Boulevard, Suite 400
Anchorage, AK 99503

Rasmuson Foundation Special Project Grants 4025
The Rasmuson Foundation supports non-profit organizations which strive to improve the quality of life for people throughout the state of Alaska. Special Project Grants support the expansion or start-up of innovative programs that address issues of broad community or statewide significance, such as capital projects (assets such as furnishings, buildings, audio and video equipment, books, medical equipment, technology, art supplies, sports equipment, musical instruments, vehicles) and special projects (including the expansion or start-up of innovative programs that address issues of broad community or statewide significance). Projects must demonstrate long-term benefits or impacts and be initiated by an established organization with a history of accomplishment. Applications are available on the website and are accepted on an ongoing basis.
Requirements: Alaskan organizations that have received 501c(3) status and are classified as not a private foundation under section 509(a) of the Internal Revenue Service Code, units of government, and federally-recognized tribes are eligible. The Foundation is rarely the first, the largest or the only contributor to any project. The Foundation expects that the community in which the project is located will provide significant financial support.
Restrictions: For religious organizations, only projects with a broad community impact are considered. For units of government and tribes, only projects with a broad community impact beyond traditional government functions are considered. The following is not eligible: general operations, administrative, indirect, or overhead costs; deficits or debt reduction; endowments; scholarships; fundraising events or sponsorships; in general, K-12 education; reimbursement for items already purchased; and electronic health records and other emerging technologies.
Geographic Focus: Alaska
Contact: Barbara Bach, Director of Grant Management; (877) 366-2700 or (907) 297-2700; fax (907) 297-2770; bbach@rasmuson.org or rasmusonfdn@rasmuson.org
Internet: http://www.rasmuson.org/index.php?switch=viewpage&pageid=33
Sponsor: Rasmuson Foundation
301 W Northern Lights Boulevard, Suite 400
Anchorage, AK 99503

Rathmann Family Foundation Grants 4026
The foundation's main funding areas are education, with priority given to science and math; the arts; children and youth health organizations; and preservation of the environment. Types of support include general operating support, continuing support, capital campaigns, equipment acquisition, endowment funds, program development, conferences and seminars, seed grants, curriculum development, fellowships, internships, scholarship funds, research, and matching funds. There are no specific deadlines or application forms, and interested parties should begin by contacting the Foundation directly.
Requirements: Grants are awarded to organizations in the San Francisco Bay, California area; the Annapolis, Maryland area; the Seattle, Washington area; the Philadelphia, Pennsylvania area: and metropolitan Minneapolis/Saint Paul, Minnesota.
Restrictions: Grants are not awarded to/for private foundations; religious organizations for religious activities; civil rights; social action; advocacy organizations; fraternal groups; political purposes; mental health counseling; individuals; or fundraisers, media events, public relations, annual appeals, or propaganda.
Geographic Focus: California, Maryland, Minnesota, Pennsylvania, Washington
Contact: Rick Rathmann, (410) 349-2376; fax (410) 349-2377
Sponsor: Rathmann Family Foundation
1290 Bay Dale Drive, P.O. Box 352
Arnold, MD 21012

Ray Foundation Grants 4027
The Foundation wishes to encourage creativity, responsibility, and self-reliance on the part of the grant recipients. The Foundation has a particular interest in aviation and the development of strategies and programs which address the involvement and education of children and young adults in aviation and flight. There are no submission deadlines.
Requirements: Eligible applicants must be 501(c)3 organizations. Interested applicants should send a letter, not to exceed two pages, summarizing their request and including the following: applicant's name as recognized by the Internal Revenue Service; applicant's address and telephone number; the date of the application; the nature, history and purpose of the organization; the organization's tax exempt status, including a copy of the Internal Revenue Service determination letter; a brief general description of the organization's need or problem to be addressed; a brief preliminary budget for the project, including the amount requested from the Foundation and proposed sources and amounts of other funding; plans for cooperation with other institutions and organizations, if any; the signature and title of the organization's project director and chief administrative officers indicating approval of the request.
Geographic Focus: All States
Contact: James C. Ray, President; (239) 649-5733
Sponsor: Ray Foundation, Inc.
100 Aviation Drive South
Naples, FL 34104

Raymond John Wean Foundation Grants 4028
The foundation awards grants to children's nonprofits in northeast Ohio and southwest Pennsylvania in the areas of education and human services. In education, the foundation supports programs helping teachers and schools prepare students for life and work, especially projects improving educational opportunities, standards, performance, and achievement. In the human services category, the foundation prefers programs strengthening families, providing opportunities for at-risk youth, and helping disadvantaged people. The foundation also is interested in improving healthcare access.
Requirements: Nonprofits serving northeast Ohio and southwest Pennsylvania are eligible.
Geographic Focus: Ohio, Pennsylvania
Date(s) Application is Due: Mar 1; Jun 1; Sep 1; Dec 1
Amount of Grant: 1,000 - 5,000 USD
Contact: Administrator; (330) 394-5600; fax (330) 394-5601; info@rjweanfoundation.org
Internet: http://www.rjweanfoundation.org
Sponsor: Raymond John Wean Foundation
108 Main Avenue SW, Suite 1005
Warren, OH 44481-1058

Ray Solem Foundation Grants to Help Immigrants Learn English in Innovative Ways 4029
The foundation is offering one-time grants of up to $10,000 to non-profit organizations that have found creative ways to help immigrants in the United States further their verbal English language skills - listening comprehension and oral communications. A grant is to be used to continue ongoing work performed by the organization; there are no restrictions on its use.
Requirements: Grants will be awarded based on the following criteria: (1) The degree of creativity, imaginativeness, innovation and success shown in the approach to learning verbal English. The approach must be one that has been in place for at least a year. (2) The percentage of the organization's expenses that are overhead, as shown on Internal Revenue Service form 990 and associated audited financial statement, as submitted to the Combined Federal Campaign. Applications can be emailed but must be received by the posted deadline. Guidelines and application instructions are available at the website.
Restrictions: All organizations with any personal connection to Ray Solem's family or the Ray Solem Foundation are ineligible for consideration.
Geographic Focus: All States
Date(s) Application is Due: Jul 31
Contact: Marianne Emerson; (202) 625-6448; fax (202) 625-0343; rraysol@aol.com
Internet: http://www.raysolemfund.org/grants.html
Sponsor: Ray Solem Foundation
P.O. Box 3589
Washington, DC 20027

Raytheon Grants 4030
Raytheon is committed to its employees and the communities where they are located. It supports community organizations through volunteering and providing grants. Raytheon's philanthropic interests are focused on math and science education, and they give preference to regional projects that serve the broader community in locations where their major facilities are located.
Requirements: Eligible applicants must be: a non-profit 501(c)3 organization based in the United States or a valid non-profit organization located outside of the United States. Funding requests focusing on math and science education are eligible. To submit an application for a community organization, see Raytheon's website.
Restrictions: The following are ineligible: private foundations; religious, fraternal, political or athletic organizations; health and disease-specific organizations; private elementary or secondary schools; basic research projects; sponsorships of athletic teams, golf tournaments, band competitions; and grants to individuals, clubs, social groups or social events. Only requests made through Raytheon's website are accepted.
Geographic Focus: All States
Contact: Community Relations; (781) 522-3000; corporatecontributions@raytheon.com
Internet: http://www.raytheon.com/responsibility/community/local/grants/index.html
Sponsor: Raytheon Company
870 Winter Street
Waltham, MA 02451

RBC Dain Rauscher Foundation Grants 4031
The foundation awards grants to youth education efforts, social services programs, and the arts. In youth education, K-12 programs that serve students of color or disadvantaged children, and programs that help children understand the country's economic system are funded. The emphasis in social services giving is programs that foster economic independence and self-sufficiency and that help families. Types of support include general operating support, continuing support, annual campaigns, building construction/renovation, seed grants, and matching gifts.
Requirements: Organizations in Arizona, California, Illinois, Iowa, Kansas, Louisiana, Minnesota, Montana, Nebraska, North Dakota, Oklahoma, Oregon, South Dakota, Texas, Utah, Washington, and Wyoming are eligible.
Geographic Focus: Arizona, California, Illinois, Iowa, Kansas, Louisiana, Minnesota, Montana, Nebraska, North Dakota, Oklahoma, Oregon, South Dakota, Texas, Utah, Washington, Wyoming
Contact: Sherry Koster, Program Manager; (612) 371-2765 or (612) 371-2936; fax (612) 371-7933; sherry.koster@rbcdain.com
Internet: http://www.rbcwm-usa.com/DRP_1.0/Public_Site/Common_Pages/DRP_1.0VSectionIndex/1,73394,4-3-2-0,00.html
Sponsor: RBC Dain Rauscher Foundation
60 South 6th Street, P2
Minneapolis, MN 55402-4422

RCF General Community Grants 4032

Six times a year, the Richland County Foundation awards General Community Grants to nonprofit organizations through a competitive process. In doing so, the Foundation looks to partner with nonprofit organizations to respond to current community needs in the following areas: education; health services; arts and culture; community services; children, youth and families; human services; environment; and employment and economic development. Application deadlines are 5:00 p.m. on the first Friday of January, March, May, July, September, and November. Applications must be at the Foundation Office by 5:00 p.m. on the due date to meet the deadline. Final decisions on all grant applications are made by the Board of Trustees approximately 6 – 8 weeks following the grant deadline.

Requirements: 501(c)3 public charities, government entities, schools, and nonprofit medical facilities serving residents of Richland County are eligible to apply. The application procedure should begin with a telephone call to the Program Officer to schedule an initial meeting to discuss the project. The Foundation typically looks for several of the following key elements in submitted applications: a one-time grant, especially for a pilot project which can serve as a model or be replicated; a project in which the Foundation is a funding partner, rather than the sole funder; a project or program which promotes volunteer involvement; an organization which can demonstrate the ability to sustain the project in the future when Foundation grant dollars end; projects or programs which are a collaborative effort(s) among nonprofit organizations in the community which eliminate duplication of services; a project which is likely to make a clear difference in the quality of life of a substantial number of people; an organization which is proposing a practical approach to a solution of a current community problem; a project or program which is focusing on prevention; and a worthy community project for which a grant from the Foundation will most likely leverage additional financial support. Applicants who have a program or project that meets these criteria are encouraged to contact the Foundation to discuss submitting an application.

Restrictions: Community grants are awarded from endowed, unrestricted and field of interest funds. Richland County Foundation typically does not provide funding from unrestricted funds for the following: sectarian activities of religious organizations; operating expenses for annual drives or to eliminate debt; medical, scientific or academic research; individuals other than for college scholarships; travel to or in support of conferences, or travel for groups such as bands, sports teams and classes (unless through special grant programs such as Summertime Kids or the Teacher Assistance Program); capital improvements to building and property not owned by the organization or covered by a long term lease; computer systems; projects that taxpayers support or expected to support; and political issues.

Geographic Focus: Ohio
Contact: Bradford Groves; (419) 525-3020; fax (419) 525-1590; bgroves@rcfoundation.org
Internet: http://www.richlandcountyfoundation.org/grant-information/types-of-grants/community
Sponsor: Richland County Foundation
24 West Third Street, Suite 100
Mansfield, OH 44902-1209

RCF Individual Assistance Grants 4033

Twice a year, the Richland County Foundation awards Individual Assistance Grants to nonprofit organizations which operate programs that assist the needy. Grant dollars may be used for emergency assistance, basic human needs and sustaining basic health. Application deadlines are 5:00 p.m. on the first Friday of March and September. Applications must be at the Foundation Office by 5:00 p.m. on the due date to meet the deadline. Final decisions on all grant applications are made by the Board of Trustees approximately 6 – 8 weeks following the grant deadline. Community grants are awarded from endowed, unrestricted and field of interest funds.

Requirements: 501(c)3 public charities, government entities, schools, and nonprofit medical facilities providing emergency assistance, basic human needs, and basic health programs for residents of Richland County are eligible to apply. The application procedure should begin with a telephone call to the Program Officer to schedule an initial meeting to discuss the project.
Geographic Focus: Ohio
Contact: Bradford Groves; (419) 525-3020; fax (419) 525-1590; bgroves@rcfoundation.org
Internet: http://www.richlandcountyfoundation.org/grant-information/types-of-grants/community
Sponsor: Richland County Foundation
24 West Third Street, Suite 100
Mansfield, OH 44902-1209

RCF Summertime Kids Grants 4034

Richland County Foundation's Summertime Kids Grants provide funding to nonprofit organizations that develop creative, educational and fun-filled activities for Richland County children throughout the summer months. Proposals are due the second Friday in February and must be at the Foundation Office by 5:00 p.m. on the due date to meet the deadline. The application with original signatures plus 18 copies must be submitted (the Foundation requests that applicants refrain from attachments). Awards will be announced in early April.

Requirements: 501(c)3 organizations, schools, churches, government entities and health service organizations serving residents of Richland County are eligible to apply. Collaborating applicants should submit only one application and note on it the lead agency.
Restrictions: Grant dollars should be used for direct programming expenses rather than operational expenses.
Geographic Focus: Ohio
Contact: Becky Smith; (419) 525-3020; fax (419) 525-1590; bsmith@rcfoundation.org
Internet: http://richlandcountyfoundation.spirecms.com/grant-information/types-of-grants/summertime-kids
Sponsor: Richland County Foundation
24 West Third Street, Suite 100
Mansfield, OH 44902-1209

RCF The Women's Fund Grants 4035

Richland County Foundation makes grants annually from "The Women's Fund" a permanent endowment established in 1996 to promote the physical, intellectual, emotional, social, economic, and cultural growth of women of all ages. While the current grant cycle is open to any nonprofit organization for programs which benefit women and girls in Richland County, a preference will be given to programs addressing childhood obesity, which exclusively target girls up to the age of (18) eighteen. The Foundation offers a workshop in August for interested applicants. Details are available at the grant website. Grant applications will be available at the workshop and will be made available for download from the website afterwards. Awards will be announced at the annual Women's Fund Luncheon in November.

Requirements: 501(c)3 public charities, government entities, schools, and nonprofit medical facilities serving residents of Richland County are eligible to apply. Deadline dates may vary from year to year. Interested applicants are encouraged to check the website, call the Program Officer with any questions and attend the Foundation's annual workshop for this grant.
Geographic Focus: Ohio
Date(s) Application is Due: Sep 16
Amount of Grant: 250 - 10,000 USD
Contact: Bradford Groves; (419) 525-3020; fax (419) 525-1590; bgroves@rcfoundation.org
Internet: http://richlandcountyfoundation.spirecms.com/womens-fund/womens-fund-application-process
Sponsor: Richland County Foundation
24 West Third Street, Suite 100
Mansfield, OH 44902-1209

Reader's Digest Partners for Sight Foundation Grants 4036

The Reader's Digest Partners for Sight (PFS) Foundation welcomes proposals for initiatives that further its charge to devote resources to assist the visually impaired and blind. The foundation is seeking to fund projects or programs with broad, practical applications and measurable outcomes as opposed to outcomes that are pure research, narrow in geographical scope, or otherwise very limited i potential reach and scale. The preference is for funding new initiatives, but in select cases, the foundation my support projects in the development phase that require additional funding in order to bring them to completion. The initial grant will be up to $300,000 in year one, and up to $200,000 for two to three subsequent years based on proven results.

Requirements: 501(c)3 nonprofits are eligible, however other options may be considered.
Restrictions: PFS will not fund individuals, lobbying organizations, medical research, endowments, charities operating outside the United States, and/or organizations or entities whose primary function is fundraising activities.
Geographic Focus: All States
Date(s) Application is Due: Sep 30
Amount of Grant: Up to 700,000 USD
Contact: Dianna Kelly, Grant Program Manager; (914) 244-5830 or (800) 877-5293; fax (914) 244-7481; dianna@partnersforsight.org or susan@partnersforsight.org
Internet: http://www.partnersforsight.org/grants.shtml
Sponsor: Reader's Digest Partners for Sight Foundation
100 South Bedford Road, Suite 340
Mount Kisco, NY 10549

RealNetworks Foundation Grants 4037

The foundation considers requests for funding to help underserved communities get better access to technology and to requests that enhance the quality of life in communities where Real Networks employees live and work. Priority is given to projects using the Internet in innovative ways to achieve project goals.

Requirements: Nonprofits in areas where Real Networks employees live and work (California, Illinois, Maryland, New Jersey, New York, and Washington) are eligible to apply.
Geographic Focus: California
Date(s) Application is Due: Feb 1; Aug 1
Contact: Ellen Stearns; (206) 892-6644; fax (206) 956-8249; info@realfoundation.org
Internet: http://www.realfoundation.org/grants/index.html
Sponsor: RealNetworks Foundation
P.O. Box 91123
Seattle, WA 98111-9223

Red Robin Foundation U-ACT Grants 4038

U-ACT, which stands for Unbridled Acts, or random acts of kindness, is a character-building initiative specifically for grades K-8, which aims to inspire and encourage students to be kind to others. The goal of the Red Robin Foundation U-ACT Program is to create a sense of neighborliness inside and outside of school settings and eliminate bullying through Unbridled Acts. Through monthly monetary grants, the U-ACT Program honors schools that exemplify kindness to others and show support in their community through Unbridled Acts. Categories are as follows: Class Awards—if one class participates in the project, that class is eligible to earn a $150 grant; Grade Awards—if one grade level participates in the project, that grade level is eligible to earn a $500 grant; and, School Awards—if the entire school participates in the project, the school is eligible to earn a $2,500 grant. In May, all schools that completed their program and received a school award grant (of $2,500) will have the opportunity to be named the U-ACT Champion School for the year and earn an additional award of $5,000.

Requirements: The U-ACT Program is open to all elementary, middle and junior high schools (grades K-8) located in the fifty (50) United States and the District of Columbia. Entrants must fully disclose any family relationship between an entrant's supervisory personnel and a director, officer or key employee of the Red Robin Foundation, of Red Robin Gourmet Burgers, Inc. or of the company's affiliates. Project proposals may be submitted to the Red Robin Foundation anytime between August and March. From September through April the Red Robin Foundation U-ACT Committee will hold a monthly grant meeting around the 15th of every month to review project proposals and to pick the grant recipients.

Restrictions: The U-ACT Program is void where prohibited or restricted by law. No school will be awarded more than one grant per category during the school year.
Geographic Focus: All States
Date(s) Application is Due: Mar 31
Contact: Program Coordinator; 303-846-5492; fax 720-493-2724
Internet: http://www.redrobin.com/rrfoundation/uactprogram.aspx
Sponsor: Red Robin Foundation
6312 S. Fiddler's Green Circle
Greenwood Village, CO 80111

Regence Foundation Access to Health Care Grants 4039
Grants in this category support the health care safety-net and insurance access programs, including efforts to: increase access to health and medical care for low-income, uninsured or underinsured individuals; provide a medical home to those who would otherwise go without; improve medical outcomes; and help eligible individuals and families navigate the process of accessing available health insurance coverage.
Requirements: The Foundation funds: organizations that are nonprofit and tax-exempt under 501(c)3 of the Internal Revenue Service Code (IRC) and defined as a public charity under 509(a) 1, 2, or 3 (types I, II, or a functionally integrated type III); organizations that serve residents of Idaho, Oregon, Washington and/or Utah; accredited schools or universities; units of government and public agencies; and programs and services that align with our mission and program areas.
Restrictions: The Foundation does not fund: capital construction; award dinners, athletic events, competitions, special events or tournaments; conferences or seminars; religious organizations for religious purposes; political causes, candidates, organizations or campaigns; grants to individuals; grants to 509(a)3, type III supporting organizations that are not functionally integrated; or grants to organizations that are not doing significant work in Idaho, Oregon, Washington and/or Utah.
Geographic Focus: Idaho, Oregon, Utah, Washington
Contact: Monique Barton; (503) 276-1965; mxbarto@regence.com
Internet: http://www.regencefoundation.org/programs/transformation.html
Sponsor: Regence Foundation
100 SW Market Street, MS E-8T
Portland, OR 97201

Regence Foundation Health Care Community Awareness and Engagement Grants 4040
At the core of this program area is a laser-focus on increasing the accessibility and usability of information for consumers to make informed health care decisions. Grants in this category support efforts that encourage consumers to seek information about the value and quality of their health care, and develop tools to access that information, such as: community collaborative pilot projects; campaigns promoting consumer education and engagement; and research on consumer use of health care information.
Requirements: The Foundation funds: organizations that are nonprofit and tax-exempt under 501(c)3 of the Internal Revenue Service Code (IRC) and defined as a public charity under 509(a) 1, 2, or 3 (types I, II, or a functionally integrated type III); organizations that serve residents of Idaho, Oregon, Washington and/or Utah; accredited schools or universities; units of government and public agencies; and programs and services that align with our mission and program areas.
Restrictions: The Foundation does not fund: capital construction; award dinners, athletic events, competitions, special events or tournaments; conferences or seminars; religious organizations for religious purposes; political causes, candidates, organizations or campaigns; grants to individuals; grants to 509(a)3, type III supporting organizations that are not functionally integrated; or grants to organizations that are not doing significant work in Idaho, Oregon, Washington and/or Utah.
Geographic Focus: Idaho, Oregon, Utah, Washington
Contact: Monique Barton; (503) 276-1965; mxbarto@regence.com
Internet: http://www.regencefoundation.org/programs/transparency.html
Sponsor: Regence Foundation
100 SW Market Street, MS E-8T
Portland, OR 97201

Regence Foundation Health Care Connections Grants 4041
Grants in this category support general health programs that are innovative and solve community-identified problems, including efforts to: manage chronic conditions; make healthy lifestyle choices; and serve a target population whose health care needs may be unmet and/or who may be experiencing health disparities.
Requirements: The Foundation funds: organizations that are nonprofit and tax-exempt under 501(c)3 of the Internal Revenue Service Code (IRC) and defined as a public charity under 509(a) 1, 2, or 3 (types I, II, or a functionally integrated type III); organizations that serve residents of Idaho, Oregon, Washington and/or Utah; accredited schools or universities; units of government and public agencies; and programs and services that align with our mission and program areas.
Restrictions: The Foundation does not fund: capital construction; award dinners, athletic events, competitions, special events or tournaments; conferences or seminars; religious organizations for religious purposes; political causes, candidates, organizations or campaigns; grants to individuals; grants to 509(a)3, type III supporting organizations that are not functionally integrated; or grants to organizations that are not doing significant work in Idaho, Oregon, Washington and/or Utah.
Geographic Focus: Idaho, Oregon, Utah, Washington
Amount of Grant: 15,000 - 50,000 USD
Contact: Monique Barton; (503) 276-1965; mxbarto@regence.com
Internet: http://www.regencefoundation.org/programs/transformation.html
Sponsor: Regence Foundation
100 SW Market Street, MS E-8T
Portland, OR 97201

Regence Foundation Improving End-of-Life Grants 4042
The Regence Foundation works to transform health care and address core problems in our health care system with innovative solutions. The Foundation supports a transformational health care system where consumers partner with their physicians and other providers to make health care decisions based on what's valuable to them - such as end-of-life decisions - just as they do when making other economic decisions.
Requirements: The Foundation funds: organizations that are nonprofit and tax-exempt under 501(c)3 of the Internal Revenue Service Code (IRC) and defined as a public charity under 509(a) 1, 2, or 3 (types I, II, or a functionally integrated type III); organizations that serve residents of Idaho, Oregon, Washington and/or Utah; accredited schools or universities; units of government and public agencies; and programs and services that align with our mission and program areas.
Restrictions: The Foundation does not fund: capital construction; award dinners, athletic events, competitions, special events or tournaments; conferences or seminars; religious organizations for religious purposes; political causes, candidates, organizations or campaigns; grants to individuals; grants to 509(a)3, type III supporting organizations that are not functionally integrated; or grants to organizations that are not doing significant work in Idaho, Oregon, Washington and/or Utah.
Geographic Focus: Idaho, Oregon, Utah, Washington
Contact: Monique Barton; (503) 276-1965; mxbarto@regence.com
Internet: http://www.regencefoundation.org/programs/endOfLife.html
Sponsor: Regence Foundation
100 SW Market Street, MS E-8T
Portland, OR 97201

Regence Foundation Tools and Technology Grants 4043
At the core of this program area is a laser-focus on increasing the accessibility and usability of information for consumers to make informed health care decisions. Grants in this category support innovative technology solutions that work to overcome practical barriers and improve the quality and safety of health care. Projects might include: multi-stakeholder technology collaborations; not-for-profit technology initiatives that include providers in development and testing; research on the usage and effects of technology collaborations in health care; and approaches that address patients who receive services from multiple providers across the spectrum.
Requirements: The Foundation funds: organizations that are nonprofit and tax-exempt under 501(c)3 of the Internal Revenue Service Code (IRC) and defined as a public charity under 509(a) 1, 2, or 3 (types I, II, or a functionally integrated type III); organizations that serve residents of Idaho, Oregon, Washington and/or Utah; accredited schools or universities; units of government and public agencies; and programs and services that align with our mission and program areas.
Restrictions: The Foundation does not fund: capital construction; award dinners, athletic events, competitions, special events or tournaments; conferences or seminars; religious organizations for religious purposes; political causes, candidates, organizations or campaigns; grants to individuals; grants to 509(a)3, type III supporting organizations that are not functionally integrated; or grants to organizations that are not doing significant work in Idaho, Oregon, Washington and/or Utah.
Geographic Focus: Idaho, Oregon, Utah, Washington
Contact: Monique Barton; (503) 276-1965; mxbarto@regence.com
Internet: http://www.regencefoundation.org/programs/transparency.html
Sponsor: Regence Foundation
100 SW Market Street, MS E-8T
Portland, OR 97201

Regents Professional Opportunity Scholarships 4044
Students pursuing a career in one of several professions may be eligible to apply for the scholarships. Degree programs include: associate degree, available at two-year community colleges and some four-year colleges—dental hygiene, dietetics/nutrition, massage therapy assistant, ophthalmic dispensing, physical therapy assistant, registered physician assistant, and veterinary technician; baccalaureate degree, available at four-year colleges only—certified public accountancy, architecture, athletic trainer, dietetics/nutrition, professional engineering, interior design, landscape architecture, registered nurse, occupational therapy, pharmacy, physical therapy, registered physician assistant, and veterinary technician; master's degree, graduate programs—acupuncture, architecture, audiology, landscape architecture, midwifery, occupational therapy, physical therapy, registered physician assistant, social work, speech language, and pathology; doctoral degree (Drive, PhD, PharmD)—chiropractic, optometry, pharmacy, podiatry, psychology, and veterinary medicine; and doctor of law (JD). Priority is given to individuals who are economically disadvantaged and/or who are members of a minority group that is historically underrepresented in the chosen profession; and enrolled in or graduate from SEEK, College Discovery, EOP, or HEOP opportunity programs.
Requirements: Students must study full time and be matriculated in an approved program of study in New York State, be New York State residents, and be U.S. citizens or qualifying noncitizens. Upon completion of study, the student must work as a licensed professional one year for each annual payment received. Employment must be in the studied profession and must be in New York State.
Geographic Focus: New York
Amount of Grant: 1,000 - 5,000 USD
Contact: Program Coordinator; (518) 486-1319 or (518) 473-1574
Internet: http://www.hesc.com/Content.nsf/SFC/2/NYS_Regents_Professional_Opportunity_Scholarships
Sponsor: New York State Higher Education Services Corporation
Education Building Addition, Room 1071
Albany, NY 12255

Regional Arts and Cultural Council General Support Grants 4045
RACC supports the region's vital arts and culture community through a variety of grant programs. The General Support Grants Program aims to provide general financial support to arts organizations in Multnomah, Washington, and Clackamas Counties, based on their artistic excellence, proven service to the community, administrative and fiscal competence and RACC grant compliance. The General Support Grants Program seeks to fund arts organizations and provide a wide range of high quality arts programming made available to the public. The General Support application process is bi-annual. General Support grants are for arts organizations with eligible expenses between $80,000 and $500,000.
Requirements: Some of the basic eligibility requirements for General Support are: be an arts organization; have IRS 501(c)3 tax status; have been in existence for a minimum of three years or be the result of merging organizations with at least a three-year history each; have minimum eligible income of $80,000; have at least one paid professional administrative staff; and have continuous administration throughout the year. The General Support Grant program provides financial support to Multnomah, Washington and Clackamas County not-for-profit organizations and individual artists.
Geographic Focus: Oregon
Contact: Tonisha Toler; (503) 823-5866 or (503) 823-5111; ttoler@racc.org
Internet: http://www.racc.org/grants/general-support-grants
Sponsor: Regional Arts and Cultural Council
108 NW 9th Avenue, Suite 300
Portland, OR 97209-3318

Regional Arts and Cultural Council Opportunity Grants 4046
The Opportunity Grant Program is funded by the City of Portland and is designed to provide grants to Portland-based nonprofit arts and cultural organizations to help meet special opportunities or assist organizations with emergencies that arise during the year and that are not part of the applicant's annual budget or regular programming. There will be multiple cycles of this grant throughout the fiscal year. It is meant to supplement but not be a substitute for any other existing RACC grant.
Requirements: Portland-based nonprofit arts and culture organizations are eligible to apply for the Opportunity Grant provided that they meet all the following *Requirements:* is a nonprofit arts and culture organization that regularly presents arts and/or cultural events or arts projects; has current tax-exempt status under Section 501(c)3 of the Internal Revenue Service and regularly produces financial statements; is headquartered and has a physical address in the City of Portland; provides arts and culture programs and events that are advertised and open to the public; and is current on all RACC grant agreements and has submitted final reports for all completed RACC grants.
Restrictions: Applicants receiving funds from this program will not be eligible to apply again for a period of 24 months from the date of the final report submission to RACC.
Geographic Focus: Oregon
Date(s) Application is Due: Sep 7
Contact: Tonisha Toler; (503) 823-5866 or (503) 823-5111; ttoler@racc.org
Internet: http://www.racc.org/grants/opportunity-grants
Sponsor: Regional Arts and Cultural Council
108 NW 9th Avenue, Suite 300
Portland, OR 97209-3318

Regional Arts and Cultural Council Professional Development Grants 4047
RACC supports the region's vital arts and culture community through a variety of grant programs. The Professional Development Grant program assists artists or arts administrators with opportunities that specifically improve their business management development skills and/or brings the artist or the arts organization to another level artistically. Professional Development Grants are strictly intended to assist artists and arts administrators with unique experiences directly related to career or organizational development. These grants are available to residents in Clackamas, Multnomah and Washington Counties, in Oregon and are offered in two Cylces - Spring and Fall. The Council requests a letter of intent be submitted by September 21st. The electronic application deadline is September 28th, and the physical submission deadline is October 5th.
Requirements: The Professional Development Grant program provides financial support to Multnomah, Washington and Clackamas County not-for-profit organizations and individual artists. Proposals in the Professional Development Grant Program cannot be geared toward the creation of a specific art project, but must clearly demonstrate how the proposal will benefit the organization or individual long-term.
Geographic Focus: Oregon
Date(s) Application is Due: Sep 28; Oct 5
Contact: Tonisha Toler; (503) 823-5866 or (503) 823-5111; ttoler@racc.org
Internet: http://racc.org/grants/professional-development-grants
Sponsor: Regional Arts and Cultural Council
108 NW 9th Avenue, Suite 300
Portland, OR 97209-3318

Regional Arts and Cultural Council Project Grants 4048
RACC supports the region's vital arts and culture community through a variety of grant programs. The Project Grant program provides financial support to Multnomah, Washington and Clackamas County not-for-profit organizations and individual artists for Project Based Arts programming. Grants are awarded up to $6,000 and are available in three categories: Artistic Focus, Community Participation and Arts-In-Schools. A project is a specific art presentation, exhibit or creation of work that is fully executed within a specified timeline and contains a public component. A project possesses artistic quality, imaginative scope and vision, and is fully executed within a specified timeline. The Council requests a letter of intent be submitted by August 3rd. The electronic application deadline is August 17th, and the physical submission deadline is August 24th.
Requirements: The Project Grant program provides financial support to Multnomah, Washington and Clackamas County not-for-profit organizations and individual artists.
Geographic Focus: Oregon
Date(s) Application is Due: Aug 17; Aug 24
Amount of Grant: Up to 6,000 USD
Contact: Tonisha Toler; (503) 823-5866 or (503) 823-5111; ttoler@racc.org
Internet: http://www.racc.org/grants/project-grants
Sponsor: Regional Arts and Cultural Council
108 NW 9th Avenue, Suite 300
Portland, OR 97209-3318

Regional Fund for Digital Innovation in Latin America and the Caribbean Grants 4049
The FRIDA Program provides financial support for projects in the form of small grants. This means that each project is allocated a small sum, which allows their funding to be complemented by other sources; that these grants are not repayable (no money or interest must be paid back); that their allocation is decided through a competitive process in which a public invitation is made for the presentation of proposals, and these proposals are later evaluated and the best are awarded the grants; and that they allow flexible management, as they do not involve important bureaucratic mechanisms. The projects that will be selected must address at least one of the following issues: formation and development of local capacities; innovations for improving productivity and employment; electronic government, social fairness; network security; wireless communication and networks; and public policies and regulation.
Requirements: The proposals must: originate from legally constituted non-profit organizations, either from the public or the private sectors; be presented by organizations having their head office and main activities in Latin American or Caribbean countries; and further one or more of the Fund's goals. These goals include: developing or adapting new technologies and standards; modernization of public policies and regulation; and social innovation in the use of new technologies for development.
Geographic Focus: All States, Antigua & Barbuda, Argentina, Bahamas, Barbados, Belize, Bolivia, Brazil, Caribbean, Chile, Colombia, Costa Rica, Cuba, Ecuador, Guyana, Paraguay, Peru
Date(s) Application is Due: Aug 15
Amount of Grant: 12,500 - 25,000 USD
Contact: Program Coordinator; +598 2 6042222; fax +598 2 6042222, int. 112; convocatoria2008@programafrida.net
Internet: http://programafrida.net/en/index.html
Sponsor: Regional Fund for Digital Innovation in Latin America and the Caribbean
Rambla Republica de Mexico 6125
Montevideo, 11400 Uruguay

Rehab Therapy Foundation Grants 4050
The foundation awards grants to North Carolina nonprofit organizations. Areas of priority include organizations that serve children with developmental disabilities and their families; and impact inadequately insured or underserved children with developmental disabilities and their families. Grant applications are available year round at the Foundations website however, applications will only be accepted once a year beginning in January and must be received by February 28th. Award recipients will be notified by mail on or about May 15th.
Requirements: Applicant must be a nonprofit 501(c)3 organization or public school in North Carolina.
Restrictions: Proposals benefiting religious organizations, university level education, research, events, individuals, trusts, or political causes will not be funded.
Geographic Focus: North Carolina
Date(s) Application is Due: Feb 28
Amount of Grant: Up to 50,000 USD
Contact: Kimberly D. Reilly; info@rehabtherapyfoundation.org
Internet: http://www.rehabtherapyfoundation.org/grant.htm
Sponsor: Rehab Therapy Foundation
150 Fayetteville Street, Seventh Floor
Raleigh, NC 27602

REI Conservation and Outdoor Recreation Grants 4051
The program seeks to engage communities in active stewardship of the environment. REI wants to ensure that we take care of the outdoor places where we love to play. Therefore, its grant funding encourages volunteer stewardship of public lands and waterways where people enjoy outdoor recreation.
Requirements: REI will only fund organizations in the communities in which they do business. Organizations are invited to submit proposals only after receiving nominations from its employees. As a result, they do not accept unsolicited grant requests and proposals. If an REI employee is directly involved in your non-profit organization, please ask him or her to submit a nomination for a grant. REI accepts nominations from its employees for projects or programs that focus on protecting outdoor places for recreation or helping increase participation in outdoor activities—especially among youth.
Geographic Focus: Alaska, Arizona, California, Colorado, Connecticut, District of Columbia, Georgia, Idaho, Illinois, Maryland, Massachusetts, Michigan, Minnesota, Missouri, Montana, Nevada, New Jersey, New Mexico, North Carolina, Oregon, Pennsylvania, Rhode Island, Tennessee, Texas, Utah, Virginia, Washington, Wisconsin
Samples: Alaska Geographic, Anchorage, AK, $5,000—grant will support Explorer's Ridge Trail, a project designed to engage younger generations with the Chugach National Forest and create responsible stewards of wild places by incorporating youth into the process of updating and designing recreation and trail features in the area; Friends of the Chicago River, Chicago, IL, $10,000—The Friends of the Chicago River's, River Volunteer Stewardship Program (RVSP) seeks to increase the number of high-functioning volunteer stewards enabling the Friends to better restore and improve natural lands along the Chicago River.

Contact: David Jayo, Secretary; (253) 395-5928
Internet: http://www.rei.com/aboutrei/grants02.html
Sponsor: Recreational Equipment
1700 45th Street, East
Sumner, WA 98352

Reinberger Foundation Grants 4052

Clarence T. Reinberger was born in 1894 on Cleveland's west side, and began his business career in the 1920's as a pioneer in the automobile replacement parts field. Starting as a clerk in the Cleveland retail store of the National Automotive Parts Association's (NAPA) Automotive Parts Company, he became president of that company in 1948. In the 1960's the Automotive Parts Company merged with the Genuine Parts Company of Atlanta. Mr. Reinberger held the position of Chairman of the Board of Genuine Parts Company until his death in 1968. Louise Fischer Reinberger was born in Germany. After graduation from high school in the United States, she was employed by the Halle Brothers Company, a large Cleveland department store. The Reinberger Foundation was established by Mr. and Mrs. Reinberger in 1966. Mr. Reinberger left a substantial bequest to the Foundation at his death in 1984. Upon Mrs. Reinberger's death in 1968, the major portion of her estate was also bequeathed to the Foundation. Although the Reinbergers had no children, the foundation continues to be managed by several generations of Mr. Reinberger's family. Since its inception, the foundation has distributed over $91,000,000 to the non-profit community. The foundation divides its support among the following program areas: Arts, Culture, and Humanities; Education; Human Service - Health; and Human Service - Other. Categories supported under Arts, Culture and Humanities include museums, visual arts, performing arts, media and communication, arts education, zoos, and public recreation. Categories supported under Education include K-12 schools, early childhood education, adult education/literacy, libraries, and workforce development. Categories supported under Human Service - Health include hospitals and clinics, substance abuse prevention/treatment, medical and disease research, disease prevention, and speech and hearing. Categories supported under Human Service - Other include children and youth services, residential and home care, emergency food programs, youth development, domestic violence, and temporary housing/homeless shelters. Letters of Inquiry for grants of any type may be submitted according to the following program-area schedule: Education - March 1; Human Service (Health) - June 1; Human Service (Other) - September 1; and Arts, Culture, and Humanities - December 1. Letters of Inquiry may either be sent by U.S. Mail or emailed and are due in the foundation office by the deadline date. Full proposals are accepted only at the request of the foundation.
Requirements: Applicants must be 501(c)3 organizations. Preferential consideration is given to organizations serving Northeast Ohio, or the greater-Columbus area.
Restrictions: No loans are made, nor are grants given to individuals. The Reinberger Foundation does not make more than one grant to a particular organization during a given calendar year, nor will new proposals be considered until existing multi-year commitments have been paid.
Geographic Focus: Ohio
Date(s) Application is Due: Mar 1; Jun 1; Sep 1; Dec 1
Contact: Karen R. Hooser, President; (216) 292-2790; fax (216) 292-4466; info@reinbergerfoundation.org
Internet: http://reinbergerfoundation.org/apply.html
Sponsor: Reinberger Foundation
30000 Chagrin Boulevard #300
Cleveland, OH 44122

Research Program at Earthwatch Grants 4053

The program considers proposals for field research in any discipline that can gainfully employ nonspecialists in the implementation of a carefully constructed pure or applied research project. The volunteers, who are recruited and screened to meet scientists' needs, are highly educated citizens dedicated to improving environmental understanding. The center encourages proposals that are interdisciplinary and/or transnational. Specific requests for proposals include the life sciences, earth sciences, social sciences, and interdisciplinary. A typical project would employ five to 10 volunteers each on three to six sequential teams. Teams normally spend one to three weeks in the field. Shorter and longer teams are encouraged where appropriate, as are larger or smaller teams. Preliminary proposals should be submitted 12 to 14 months in advance of anticipated field dates. Full proposals are invited upon review of preliminary materials and will be peer reviewed. Proposals are accepted and reviewed year-round.
Requirements: Earthwatch primarily supports postdoctoral or equivalent scholarship, including principal investigators with commensurate life experience. Proposals are welcomed from advanced scholars of any nationality, covering any geographic region. Applicants intending to conduct research in foreign countries must include host-country nationals in their research staffs.
Geographic Focus: All States
Contact: Center for Field Research; (800) 776-0188 or (978) 461-0081; fax (978) 461-2332; research@earthwatch.org
Internet: http://www.earthwatch.org/research/grantslists.html
Sponsor: Earthwatch Institute
3 Clock Tower Place, Suite 100, Box 75
Maynard, MA 01754-0075

RESIST Accessibility Grants 4054

RESIST, founded in 1967, was originally formed to oppose the war in Vietnam and to support draft resistance. By the 1970s, RESIST expanded its scope dramatically by making the connection between the unequal distribution of power and money at home, and a system of U.S. domination abroad. Accessibility grants provide up to $4,000 to support projects that enable all people to participate in the movement for social justice. RESIST will fund the additional costs of projects or events which will make them accessible to people with disabilities. Application procedures are the same as for general support grants and decisions are based on the potential success of the underlying project. Organizations which receive an accessibility grant may also apply for a general support grant.
Restrictions: RESIST does not fund: organizations with annual budgets over $150,000; individuals; groups that primarily provide direct services (to individuals, families or communities) that are not part of progressive organizing activities; research, litigation or legal organizations unless they are directly connected to progressive organizing campaigns; organizations located outside the United States; the development or production of films, videos or radio projects; media or cultural organizations not directly connected to progressive organizing campaigns; organizations with access to traditional sources of funding; or other foundations or grant giving organizations.
Geographic Focus: All States
Date(s) Application is Due: Feb 4; Apr 1; Jun 3; Aug 5; Sep 30; Dec 3
Contact: Robin Carton, Director of Grants; (617) 623-5110; robin@resistinc.org
Internet: http://www.resistinc.org/grants/programs
Sponsor: RESIST
259 Elm Street
Somerville, MA 02144

RESIST Arthur Raymond Cohen Memorial Fund Grants 4055

RESIST, founded in 1967, was originally formed to oppose the war in Vietnam and to support draft resistance. By the 1970s, RESIST expanded its scope dramatically by making the connection between the unequal distribution of power and money at home, and a system of U.S. domination abroad. The Arthur Raymond Cohen Memorial Fund Grant is designed to support the causes to which Arthur Cohen (1918-1986) was committed: opposition to the arms race, the cold war, and American intervention abroad; and support for civil liberties, the fight against racism; and the struggle of workers and unions at home.
Restrictions: RESIST does not fund: organizations with annual budgets over $150,000; individuals; groups that primarily provide direct services (to individuals, families or communities) that are not part of progressive organizing activities; research, litigation or legal organizations unless they are directly connected to progressive organizing campaigns; organizations located outside the United States; the development or production of films, videos or radio projects; media or cultural organizations not directly connected to progressive organizing campaigns; organizations with access to traditional sources of funding; or other foundations or grant giving organizations.
Geographic Focus: All States
Date(s) Application is Due: Feb 4; Apr 1; Jun 3; Aug 5; Sep 30; Dec 3
Contact: Robin Carton, Director of Grants; (617) 623-5110; robin@resistinc.org
Internet: http://www.resistinc.org/node/1528
Sponsor: RESIST
259 Elm Street
Somerville, MA 02144

RESIST Emergency Grants 4056

RESIST, founded in 1967, was originally formed to oppose the war in Vietnam and to support draft resistance. By the 1970s, RESIST expanded its scope dramatically by making the connection between the unequal distribution of power and money at home, and a system of U.S. domination abroad. Emergency grants provide up to $500 to help groups respond quickly to unexpected organizing needs. While it is impossible to precisely define an emergency, these grants are generally given to provide support for demonstrations or other events arising from a political crisis. These grants are not intended to provide a safety net for groups who have failed to adequately plan for their financial needs, or who have missed the regular funding deadline.
Geographic Focus: All States
Date(s) Application is Due: Feb 4; Apr 1; Jun 3; Aug 5; Sep 30; Dec 3
Contact: Robin Carton, Director of Grants; (617) 623-5110; robin@resistinc.org
Internet: http://www.resistinc.org/grants/programs
Sponsor: RESIST
259 Elm Street
Somerville, MA 02144

RESIST Freda Friedman Salzman Memorial Fund Grants 4057

RESIST, founded in 1967, was originally formed to oppose the war in Vietnam and to support draft resistance. By the 1970s, RESIST expanded its scope dramatically by making the connection between the unequal distribution of power and money at home, and a system of U.S. domination abroad. The Freda Friedman Salzman Memorial Fund is dedicated to the purpose of supporting organized resistance to the institutions and practices that rob people of their dignity as full human beings, giving a high priority to the efforts of Native American peoples to resist cultural as well as actual genocide.
Restrictions: RESIST does not fund: organizations with annual budgets over $150,000; individuals; groups that primarily provide direct services (to individuals, families or communities) that are not part of progressive organizing activities; research, litigation or legal organizations unless they are directly connected to progressive organizing campaigns; organizations located outside the United States; the development or production of films, videos or radio projects; media or cultural organizations not directly connected to progressive organizing campaigns; organizations with access to traditional sources of funding; or other foundations or grant giving organizations.
Geographic Focus: All States
Date(s) Application is Due: Feb 4; Apr 1; Jun 3; Aug 5; Sep 30; Dec 3
Contact: Robin Carton, Director of Grants; (617) 623-5110; robin@resistinc.org
Internet: http://www.resistinc.org/node/1528
Sponsor: RESIST
259 Elm Street
Somerville, MA 02144

RESIST General Support Grants 4058

RESIST, founded in 1967, was originally formed to oppose the war in Vietnam and to support draft resistance. By the 1970s, RESIST expanded its scope dramatically by making the connection between the unequal distribution of power and money at home, and a system of U.S. domination abroad. Organizations with an annual budget of $150,000 or less may apply for a one-year grant with the maximum amount requested not to exceed $3,000. RESIST provides funds for general support as a means of enabling grantees to build infrastructure and capacity while engaged in on-going social justice activism. Up to $4,000 is given for general support as a means of building infrastructure and capacity while engaged in on-going social justice activism.

Requirements: Organizations with a budget of approximately $125,000 or less may apply for a one-year grant.

Restrictions: RESIST does not fund: organizations with annual budgets over $150,000; individuals; groups that primarily provide direct services (to individuals, families or communities) that are not part of progressive organizing activities; research, litigation or legal organizations unless they are directly connected to progressive organizing campaigns; organizations located outside the United States; the development or production of films, videos or radio projects; media or cultural organizations not directly connected to progressive organizing campaigns; organizations with access to traditional sources of funding; or other foundations or grant giving organizations.

Geographic Focus: All States
Date(s) Application is Due: Feb 4; Apr 1; Jun 3; Aug 5; Sep 30; Dec 3
Amount of Grant: 500 - 4,000 USD
Contact: Robin Carton, Director of Grants; (617) 623-5110; robin@resistinc.org
Internet: http://www.resistinc.org
Sponsor: RESIST
259 Elm Street
Somerville, MA 02144

RESIST Hell Yes! Award 4059

RESIST, founded in 1967, was originally formed to oppose the war in Vietnam and to support draft resistance. By the 1970s, RESIST expanded its scope dramatically by making the connection between the unequal distribution of power and money at home, and a system of U.S. domination abroad. To honor the moral clarity, courage and political commitment of its founders, RESIST created a new tribute grant in 2008: the Hell Yes! Award. This grant recognizes inspiring, radical activism that cuts to the heart of RESIST's mission to challenge illegitimate authority.

Restrictions: RESIST does not fund: organizations with annual budgets over $150,000; individuals; groups that primarily provide direct services (to individuals, families or communities) that are not part of progressive organizing activities; research, litigation or legal organizations unless they are directly connected to progressive organizing campaigns; organizations located outside the United States; the development or production of films, videos or radio projects; media or cultural organizations not directly connected to progressive organizing campaigns; organizations with access to traditional sources of funding; or other foundations or grant giving organizations.

Geographic Focus: All States
Date(s) Application is Due: Feb 4; Apr 1; Jun 3; Aug 5; Sep 30; Dec 3
Contact: Robin Carton, Director of Grants; (617) 623-5110; robin@resistinc.org
Internet: http://www.resistinc.org/node/1528
Sponsor: RESIST
259 Elm Street
Somerville, MA 02144

RESIST Ken Hale Tribute Grants 4060

RESIST, founded in 1967, was originally formed to oppose the war in Vietnam and to support draft resistance. By the 1970s, RESIST expanded its scope dramatically by making the connection between the unequal distribution of power and money at home, and a system of U.S. domination abroad. The Ken Hale Tribute Grant is given in memory of the life and work of Ken Hale (1934-2001), one of the world's foremost linguists, a RESIST founder and a passionate activist for justice. This grant is given to support organizations which ensure that the voices of those most affected are given primacy in the struggle to protect and expand civil, cultural and political rights.

Restrictions: RESIST does not fund: organizations with annual budgets over $150,000; individuals; groups that primarily provide direct services (to individuals, families or communities) that are not part of progressive organizing activities; research, litigation or legal organizations unless they are directly connected to progressive organizing campaigns; organizations located outside the United States; the development or production of films, videos or radio projects; media or cultural organizations not directly connected to progressive organizing campaigns; organizations with access to traditional sources of funding; or other foundations or grant giving organizations.

Geographic Focus: All States
Date(s) Application is Due: Feb 4; Apr 1; Jun 3; Aug 5; Sep 30; Dec 3
Contact: Robin Carton, Director of Grants; (617) 623-5110; robin@resistinc.org
Internet: http://www.resistinc.org/node/1528
Sponsor: RESIST
259 Elm Street
Somerville, MA 02144

RESIST Leslie D'Cora Holmes Memorial Fund Grants 4061

RESIST, founded in 1967, was originally formed to oppose the war in Vietnam and to support draft resistance. By the 1970s, RESIST expanded its scope dramatically by making the connection between the unequal distribution of power and money at home, and a system of U.S. domination abroad. The Leslie D'Cora Holmes Memorial Fund Grant was established in 1999 to honor the life's work and legacy of Leslie D'Cora Holmes. This fund supports activities and organizations that embody the characteristics, values, and principles that reflect her spirit-filled mission, including: empowerment for communities and individuals; self-determination through education and community organizing; harmonization of diverse communities of interest; actualization and recognition of individual potential; courage of conviction; and pride in culture, community and self.

Restrictions: RESIST does not fund: organizations with annual budgets over $150,000; individuals; groups that primarily provide direct services (to individuals, families or communities) that are not part of progressive organizing activities; research, litigation or legal organizations unless they are directly connected to progressive organizing campaigns; organizations located outside the United States; the development or production of films, videos or radio projects; media or cultural organizations not directly connected to progressive organizing campaigns; organizations with access to traditional sources of funding; or other foundations or grant giving organizations.

Geographic Focus: All States
Date(s) Application is Due: Feb 4; Apr 1; Jun 3; Aug 5; Sep 30; Dec 3
Contact: Robin Carton, Director of Grants; (617) 623-5110; robin@resistinc.org
Internet: http://www.resistinc.org/node/1528
Sponsor: RESIST
259 Elm Street
Somerville, MA 02144

RESIST Mike Riegle Tribute Grants 4062

RESIST, founded in 1967, was originally formed to oppose the war in Vietnam and to support draft resistance. By the 1970s, RESIST expanded its scope dramatically by making the connection between the unequal distribution of power and money at home, and a system of U.S. domination abroad. The Mike Riegle Tribute Grant is given in memory of the life and work of Boston activist Mike Riegle, a supporter of prisoners' rights, gay and lesbian liberation, and the radical movement for justice.

Restrictions: RESIST does not fund: organizations with annual budgets over $150,000; individuals; groups that primarily provide direct services (to individuals, families or communities) that are not part of progressive organizing activities; research, litigation or legal organizations unless they are directly connected to progressive organizing campaigns; organizations located outside the United States; the development or production of films, videos or radio projects; media or cultural organizations not directly connected to progressive organizing campaigns; organizations with access to traditional sources of funding; or other foundations or grant giving organizations.

Geographic Focus: All States
Date(s) Application is Due: Feb 4; Apr 1; Jun 3; Aug 5; Sep 30; Dec 3
Contact: Robin Carton, Director of Grants; (617) 623-5110; robin@resistinc.org
Internet: http://www.resistinc.org/node/1528
Sponsor: RESIST
259 Elm Street
Somerville, MA 02144

RESIST Multi-Year Grants 4063

RESIST, founded in 1967, was originally formed to oppose the war in Vietnam and to support draft resistance. By the 1970s, RESIST expanded its scope dramatically by making the connection between the unequal distribution of power and money at home, and a system of U.S. domination abroad. Grantees who have been funded by RESIST at least two times during the preceding five years may apply for a multi-year grant. Of the two prior grant awards, the most recent must have been for the full amount given out during that cycle. Multi-year grants will cover a three-year period and are designed to provide general support to eligible grantee organizations.

Requirements: All multi-year applicants must: submit answers to the Multi-Year Grant Questionnaire; and be currently eligible to receive grant awards under RESIST's Funding Guidelines. All applicants must provide specific, measurable objectives as part of their proposal. These objectives should demonstrate the capacity to plan at least one to three years ahead. In addition, groups must submit evidence of their past performance, examples of which might include prior Progress or Annual Reports, with their proposal.

Restrictions: RESIST does not fund: organizations with annual budgets over $150,000; individuals; groups that primarily provide direct services (to individuals, families or communities) that are not part of progressive organizing activities; research, litigation or legal organizations unless they are directly connected to progressive organizing campaigns; organizations located outside the United States; the development or production of films, videos or radio projects; media or cultural organizations not directly connected to progressive organizing campaigns; organizations with access to traditional sources of funding; or other foundations or grant giving organizations.

Geographic Focus: All States
Date(s) Application is Due: Feb 4; Apr 1; Jun 3; Aug 5; Sep 30; Dec 3
Contact: Robin Carton, Director of Grants; (617) 623-5110; robin@resistinc.org
Internet: http://www.resistinc.org/node/1527
Sponsor: RESIST
259 Elm Street
Somerville, MA 02144

RESIST Sharon Kurtz Memorial Fund Grants 4064

RESIST, founded in 1967, was originally formed to oppose the war in Vietnam and to support draft resistance. By the 1970s, RESIST expanded its scope dramatically by making the connection between the unequal distribution of power and money at home, and a system of U.S. domination abroad. In 2008, the friends and family of Sharon Kurtz chose RESIST as the home of a new fund in her name. The Sharon Kurtz Memorial Fund commemorates the life of Sharon Kurtz, a community organizer who dedicated her life to making the world a more just and humane place.

Restrictions: RESIST does not fund: organizations with annual budgets over $150,000; individuals; groups that primarily provide direct services (to individuals, families or communities) that are not part of progressive organizing activities; research, litigation or legal organizations unless they are directly connected to progressive organizing campaigns; organizations located outside the United States; the development or production of films, videos or radio projects; media or cultural organizations not directly connected to progressive organizing campaigns; organizations with access to traditional sources of funding; or other foundations or grant giving organizations.
Geographic Focus: All States
Date(s) Application is Due: Feb 4; Apr 1; Jun 3; Aug 5; Sep 30; Dec 3
Contact: Robin Carton, Director of Grants; (617) 623-5110; robin@resistinc.org
Internet: http://www.resistinc.org/node/1528
Sponsor: RESIST
259 Elm Street
Somerville, MA 02144

RESIST Technical Assistance Grants 4065
RESIST, founded in 1967, was originally formed to oppose the war in Vietnam and to support draft resistance. By the 1970s, RESIST expanded its scope dramatically by making the connection between the unequal distribution of power and money at home, and a system of U.S. domination abroad. Technical Assistance grants provide up to $500 to enable current grantees to increase their internal organizational skills and capacity.
Requirements: All multi-year applicants must: submit answers to the Multi-Year Grant Questionnaire; and be currently eligible to receive grant awards under RESIST's Funding Guidelines.
Restrictions: Only grantees who have been funded at least two times during the preceding five years may apply for a Technical Assistance grant. RESIST does not fund: organizations with annual budgets over $150,000; individuals; groups that primarily provide direct services (to individuals, families or communities) that are not part of progressive organizing activities; research, litigation or legal organizations unless they are directly connected to progressive organizing campaigns; organizations located outside the United States; the development or production of films, videos or radio projects; media or cultural organizations not directly connected to progressive organizing campaigns; organizations with access to traditional sources of funding; or other foundations or grant giving organizations.
Geographic Focus: All States
Date(s) Application is Due: Feb 4; Apr 1; Jun 3; Aug 5; Sep 30; Dec 3
Amount of Grant: Up to 500 USD
Contact: Robin Carton, Director of Grants; (617) 623-5110; robin@resistinc.org
Internet: http://www.resistinc.org/grants/programs
Sponsor: RESIST
259 Elm Street
Somerville, MA 02144

Retirement Research Foundation Accessible Faith Grants 4066
Through the Accessible Faith Grant Program, the Foundation makes funds available to Chicago area houses of worship for accessibility improvements to their facilities. Such improvements should allow increased participation of older adults in the programs, services, and activities that occur in the facilities. Grants will be awarded for up to 50 percent of a project's total cost. Accessible Faith Grants may be used for the following purposes: construction projects; purchase and installation of accessibility-related equipment.
Requirements: To be eligible for an Accessible Faith Grant, the facility and congregation must meet the following criteria: be registered as a certified 501(c)3 religious organization; be located within Cook, Lake, or DuPage County in Illinois; provide programs and activities beyond worship services that benefit older adults; demonstrate a need for financial assistance to carry out the accessibility project; demonstrate the ability to raise sufficient funds to complete the project if awarded a grant; own the facility where improvements would be made.
Restrictions: Grants will not be made for: chairlifts because they do not provide accessibility for all people who have difficulty climbing stairs; used equipment; purchase of accessible vehicles or individual mobility aids, such as wheelchairs or walkers; projects that are already completed; constructing entirely new buildings, entirely new multi-room additions to existing buildings, or for overall large-scale facility renovations that include many elements unrelated to accessibility.
Geographic Focus: Illinois
Date(s) Application is Due: Apr 17; Jun 26
Amount of Grant: 1,000 - 30,000 USD
Contact: Irene Frye; (773) 714-8080; fax (773) 714-8089; info@rrf.org
Internet: http://www.rrf.org/accessibleFaithGrantProgram.htm
Sponsor: Retirement Research Foundation
8765 W Higgins Road, Suite 430
Chicago, IL 60631-4170

Retirement Research Foundation General Program Grants 4067
The Retirement Research Foundation, based in Chicago, was established in the 1950s and endowed in 1978 by the late John D. MacArthur. The Foundation is devoted solely to serving the needs of older persons in the U.S. and enhancing their quality of life. The Foundation supports a range of programs and special initiatives designed to: improve access to and quality of community-based and residential health and long-term care; promote economic security for all older adults by strengthening social insurance, pension, and personal savings programs; and support adequate training of, and compensation for, those already working directly with older persons and their families to bring higher quality of care to larger numbers of older adults. The Foundation's historic interest in innovative projects continues. RRF also has a strong interest in projects that implement or adapt proven models that address clearly identified needs and gaps. Requests for support of projects focusing on advocacy, research, or education and training will be considered from anywhere in the United States. Direct service requests will be considered only from organizations in these seven states: Illinois, Indiana, Iowa, Kentucky, Missouri, Wisconsin, and Florida.
Requirements: The Retirement Research Foundation does not use a standard application form, proposals for funds should include the following elements: cover page; Summary; project significance; statement of objectives; description of methodology; dissemination; budget and timetable; plans for continued support; list of personnel; applicant organization; tax exempt status. Application submission must include: the signature of the chief executive officer of the applicant organization; the proposal and attachments must be submitted in triplicate; only one copy of the annual report and financial/audit are needed.
Restrictions: Funding for vans is limited to applicants from Illinois and Florida. Funding is not generally available for: biomedical research; computer equipment; conferences, publications or travel unless they are components of other larger Foundation-funded projects; construction of facilities; dissertation research; endowment or developmental campaigns; general operating expenses of established organizations; grants or scholarships to individuals; production of films and videos; projects of governmental organizations except for state universities, area agencies on aging, and programs of the Veterans Administration; projects outside the United States
Geographic Focus: All States
Date(s) Application is Due: Feb 1; May 1; Aug 1
Contact: Irene Frye; (773) 714-8080; fax (773) 714-8089; info@rrf.org
Internet: http://www.rrf.org/generalProgram.htm
Sponsor: Retirement Research Foundation
8765 W Higgins Road, Suite 430
Chicago, IL 60631-4170

Reynolds American Foundation Grants 4068
The Reynolds American Foundation focuses its grant resources in several areas. The Foundation funds birth-12 public education programs that focus on improving academic performance for at-risk and economically disadvantaged students. It contributes funding to local community campaigns, such as support for United Way and Arts Council campaigns in target communities. The Foundation also supports the following programs for children of employees and retirees: the Matching Grants Program, the Community Involvement Plan, the Leadership in Education Program, and the Scholarship Program. The Foundation awards grants on a quarterly basis. Notification will be received within 60 days of the proposal deadline.
Requirements: To be eligible for grant consideration, an applicant must be: a nonprofit agency with tax-exempt status under section 501(c)3 of the Internal Revenue Code or an appropriate government agency; serving residents in communities where significant numbers of Reynolds American employees live and/or work; and, operated and organized so that it does not discriminate on the basis of race, religion, gender, national origin, sexual orientation, age, or disability, in terms of hiring practices, service provisions or board-member selection.
Restrictions: The Foundation generally will not consider funding requests for the following: endowments; support for individuals; general operating expenses; requests from churches; programs that promote religious doctrine; requests for political candidates and organizations; requests for travel expenses for individuals or organizations; sponsorship of most special events; and request for programs that have already received support from the Foundation for three consecutive years. Individual day-care centers are not eligible for grants.
Geographic Focus: All States
Date(s) Application is Due: Feb 1; May 1; Aug 1; Nov 1
Contact: Stephen R. Strawsburg, President; (336) 741-5315
Internet: http://www.rjrt.com/fndnguide.aspx
Sponsor: Reynolds American Foundation
P.O. Box 2959, Reynolds Building, 14th Floor
Winston-Salem, NC 27102

Reynolds and Reynolds Associate Foundation Grants 4069
Reynolds has a long-standing reputation as a leading corporate citizen within the communities where it has a large presence. The company encourages its associates to roll up their sleeves and get involved in organizations they believe in, and in which they often are involved personally. The mission of The Foundation is to provide a vehicle for Dayton associates to improve health and human services in the local communities. Since 1956, the Foundation has provided financial support to area health and human service agencies throughout an eight-county area. Focus areas include: health and human services with emphasis on domestic violence and child abuse; youth-at-risk; hunger; issues of the elderly; homelessness; literacy; and life-threatening illnesses.
Requirements: Giving is limited to the eight-county region in and around Dayton, Ohio.
Restrictions: There is no support available for non 501(c)3 organizations, sectarian organizations with a predominately religious purpose, fraternal or veterans' organizations, individual primary or secondary schools (except for occasional special projects), or tax-supported universities and colleges (except for occasional special projects) No grants are offered to individuals, or for endowments, courtesy advertising, fund raising events, deficit or debt retirement, or capital campaigns.
Geographic Focus: Ohio
Date(s) Application is Due: Jan 7; Mar 11; Jun 10; Sep 9
Amount of Grant: Up to 40,000 USD
Contact: Alice Davisson; (937) 485-4409 or (937) 485-8138; alice_davisson@reyrey.com
Internet: http://www.reyrey.com/company/community/associate_foundation.asp
Sponsor: Reynolds and Reynolds Associate Foundation
P.O. Box 2608
Dayton, OH 45401-2608

Reynolds and Reynolds Company Foundation Grants 4070

The Foundation has a strong tradition of giving. The Company Foundation traditionally has funded support in three specific areas; arts and culture—programs designed to promote the enrichment of quality of life for regional residents; community betterment—programs designed to promote strategic economic development, downtown revitalization, and regional growth; and education—programs designed to promote education, with special emphasis directed toward higher education.
Requirements: Giving is limited to the eight-county region in and around southwest Ohio, specifically the communities of Dayton and Celina.
Restrictions: There is no support available for non 501(c)3 organizations, sectarian organizations with a predominately religious purpose, fraternal or veterans' organizations, individual primary or secondary schools (except for occasional special projects), or tax-supported universities and colleges (except for occasional special projects) No grants are offered to individuals, or for endowments, courtesy advertising, fund raising events, deficit or debt retirement, or capital campaigns.
Geographic Focus: Ohio
Date(s) Application is Due: Feb 15; May 16; Aug 15; Nov 14
Amount of Grant: Up to 200,000 USD
Contact: Alice Davisson; (937) 485-4409 or (937) 485-8138; alice_davisson@reyrey.com
Internet: http://www.reyrey.com/company/community/company_foundation.asp
Sponsor: Reynolds and Reynolds Company Foundation
P.O. Box 2608
Dayton, OH 45401-2608

Reynolds Family Foundation Grants 4071

The Foundation, established in California in support of its residents, is primarily aimed at supporting educational programs, human services, and international affairs. Funding most often comes in the form of general operating support. Although there are no specific grant applications required, applicants should contact the Foundation initially by either letter or telephone, followed by a detailed letter of application outlining the project and amount of funding requested.
Geographic Focus: California
Amount of Grant: 500 - 3,000 USD
Samples: Angel Kiss Foundation, Reno, Nevada, $300,; Saint Johns Health Center Foundation, Santa. Monica, California, $3,000.
Contact: Paula M. Golden, President; (310) 600-0598 or (310) 829-8433; fax (310) 556-7986; paula@paulagolden.net
Internet: http://paulagolden.net/about_us
Sponsor: Reynolds Family Foundation
2132 Century Park Lane, #209
Los Angeles, CA 90067-3312

RGK Foundation Grants 4072

RGK Foundation awards grants in the broad areas of Education, Community, and Medicine/Health. The foundation's primary interests within Education include programs that focus on formal K-12 education (particularly mathematics, science and reading), teacher development, literacy, and higher education. Within Community, the foundation supports a broad range of human services, community improvement, abuse prevention, and youth development programs. Human service programs of particular interest to the foundation include children and family services, early childhood development, and parenting education. The foundation supports a variety of Community Improvement programs including those that enhance non-profit management and promote philanthropy and voluntarism. Youth development programs supported by the foundation typically include after-school educational enrichment programs that supplement and enhance formal education systems to increase the chances for successful outcomes in school and life. The foundation is also interested in programs that attract female and minority students into the fields of mathematics, science, and technology. The foundation's current interests in the area of Medicine/Health include programs that promote the health and well-being of children, programs that promote access to health services, and Foundation-initiated programs focusing on ALS.
Requirements: Although there are no geographic restrictions to the foundation's grantmaking program, the foundation no longer accepts unsolicited requests for international agencies or programs. All applicants must complete an electronic Letter of Inquiry from the Web site as the first step. RGK Foundation will entertain one electronic Letter of Inquiry (LOI) per organization in a twelve-month period. While the foundation occasionally awards grants for operating expenses, capital campaigns, endowments, and international projects, such grants are infrequent and usually initiated by the foundation. Grants are made only to nonprofit organizations certified as tax exempt under Sections 501(c)3 or 170(c) of the IRS code. Hospitals, educational institutions, and governmental institutions meeting these requirements are eligible to apply.
Restrictions: The foundation refrains from funding annual funds, galas or other special-event fundraising activities; debt reduction; emergency or disaster relief efforts; dissertations or student research projects; indirect/administrative costs; sectarian religious activities, political lobbying, or legislative activities; institutions that discriminate on the basis of race, creed, gender, or sexual orientation in policy or in practice; or loans, scholarships, fellowships, or grants to individuals; unsolicited requests for international organizations or programs or for ALS research projects.
Geographic Focus: All States
Amount of Grant: 1,000 - 25,000 USD
Contact: Suzanne Haffey; (512) 474-9298; fax (512) 474-7281; shaffey@rgkfoundation.org
Internet: http://www.rgkfoundation.org/public/guidelines
Sponsor: RGK Foundation
1301 West 25th Street, Suite 300
Austin, TX 78705-4236

Rhode Island Foundation Grants 4073

The foundation seeks to promote philanthropic activities that will improve the living conditions and well-being of the inhabitants of Rhode Island. Grants for capital and operating purposes principally to agencies working in the fields of education, health care, the arts and cultural affairs, youth, the aged, social services, urban affairs, historic preservation, and the environment.
Requirements: Rhode Island nonprofits organizations may apply. See Foundations website for additional guidelines.
Restrictions: The foundation does not make grants for endowments, research, religious groups for religious purposes, hospital equipment, capital needs of health organizations, or to educational institutions for general operating expenses.
Geographic Focus: Rhode Island
Contact: Owen Heleen, Vice President for Grant Programs; (401) 427-4009 or (401) 274-4564; fax (401) 331-8085; oheleen@rifoundation.org
Internet: http://www.rifoundation.org/Nonprofits/GrantOpportunities/tabid/175/Default.aspx
Sponsor: Rhode Island Foundation
1 Union Station
Providence, RI 02903

Rice Foundation Grants 4074

The foundation awards grants to Illinois nonprofit organizations in its areas of interest, including civic affairs, higher education, hospitals, libraries, medical education, and youth programs. Project and operating support are available. There are no application forms or deadlines.
Requirements: Applicants should submit a proposal with directly to the Foundation including the following: statement of problem project will address; copy of IRS Determination Letter; brief history of organization and description of its mission; detailed description of project and amount of funding requested.
Geographic Focus: Illinois
Amount of Grant: 25,000 - 1,000,000 USD
Contact: Peter Nolan, President; (847) 581-9999
Sponsor: Daniel F. and Ada L. Rice Foundation
8600 Gross Point Road
Skokie, IL 60077-2151

Richard and Caroline T. Gwathmey Memorial Trust Grants 4075

The Richard and Caroline T. Gwathmey Memorial Trust was established by Mrs. Elizabeth Gwathmey Jeffress in 1981 in memory of her parents. Mrs. Jeffress was particularly interested in the history, literature, art, and architecture of Virginia. Preference will be given to specific, well-defined project requests for which the results can be evaluated. In general, requests for general operating support, capital support, and endowments are rarely awarded. Grants from the Gwathmey Memorial Trust are one year in duration. Application materials are available for download at the grant website. Applicants are strongly encouraged to review the state application guidelines for additional helpful information and clarifications before applying. Applicants are also encouraged to review the trust's funding history (link is available from the grant website). The Gwathmey Memorial Trust has biannual deadlines of March 1 and September 1. Applicants for the March deadline will be notified of grant decisions by June 15. Applicants for the September deadline will be notified by December 31. Grants from the Gwathmey Trust are awarded on the advice of an allocations committee comprised of five Virginia residents appointed for a limited term by one of the following organizations: the Virginia Academy of Science, the Medical Society of Virginia, the Executive Committee of the Bar Association of the City of Richmond, the Virginia State Chamber of Commerce, and Bank of America (as Trustee).
Requirements: Applicants must have 501(c)3 tax-exempt status.
Restrictions: Contributions are not made to periodic campaigns for funds by national or community organizations. Requests for support from an organization that has received a grant will be considered no sooner than three years from the date of the first payment of the previous grant. The trust does not support requests from individuals, organizations attempting to influence policy through direct lobbying, or any political campaigns.
Geographic Focus: Virginia
Date(s) Application is Due: Mar 1; Sep 1
Contact: Sarah Kay, Vice President; (804) 788-3698; fax (804) 788-2700
Internet: https://www.bankofamerica.com/philanthropic/fn_search.action
Sponsor: Richard and Caroline T. Gwathmey Memorial Trust
1111 E. Main Street, VA2-300-12-92
Richmond, VA 23219

Richard and Helen DeVos Foundation Grants 4076

The foundation supports nonprofit organizations primarily in western Michigan and central Florida in its areas of interest, including religious agencies and churches and education and outreach, social services, the arts, public policy, and health care. Types of support include general operating support, continuing support, annual campaigns, capital campaigns, building construction/renovation, program development, seed grants, and matching funds.
Requirements: Application forms are not required. Applicants should submit the following: copy of IRS Determination Letter; copy of current year's organizational budget and/or project budget. The Board meets every 3 months, submit your proposal two weeks prior to the review (contact Foundation for deadline dates). Mail applications to: 126 Ottawa Avenue, N.W., Suite 500, Grand Rapids, MI 49503
Restrictions: No grants to individuals.
Geographic Focus: Florida, Michigan
Contact: Ginny Vander Hart; (616) 643-4700; fax (616) 774-0116; virginiav@rdvcorp.com
Sponsor: Richard and Helen DeVos Foundation Grants
P.O. Box 230257
Grand Rapids, MI 49523-0257

Richard and Rhoda Goldman Fund Grants 4077
The fund is interested in supporting programs that will have a significant positive impact in an array of fields, including culture, the environment, population, Jewish affairs, violence prevention, children and youth, the elderly, and social and human services. Types of support include general operating support, continuing support, capital campaigns, program development, and seed money. Funds will be allocated primarily in the San Francisco Bay area of California and to organizations benefiting this area. There are no application deadlines.
Requirements: Nonprofit organizations serving primarily the San Francisco Bay area of California are eligible.
Restrictions: The fund does not accept applications for research or award grants or scholarships for individuals, conferences, documentary films, or fund-raisers. Unsolicited proposals for support of arts organizations or institutions of primary, secondary, or higher education will not be accepted.
Geographic Focus: California
Amount of Grant: 1,000 - 500,000 USD
Contact: Sam Salkin; (415) 345-6300; fax (415) 345-9686; info@goldmanfund.org
Internet: http://www.goldmanfund.org
Sponsor: Richard and Rhoda Goldman Fund
211 Lincoln Boulevard, P.O. Box 29924
San Francisco, CA 94129

Richard and Susan Smith Family Foundation Grants 4078
The foundation awards grants to Massachusetts nonprofit organizations in its areas of interest, including arts and culture, children and youth, disadvantaged (economically), education (early childhood, elementary, and higher), minorities, biomedical research, health care and social services delivery. Types of support include annual campaigns, building construction/renovation, capital campaigns, curriculum development, general operating grants, program/project support, seed grants, and service delivery programs. There are no application forms.
Requirements: Massachusetts nonprofits serving the greater Boston area are eligible.
Restrictions: Grants do not support political activities; religious activities; individuals; or requests for deficit financing or endowment funds.
Geographic Focus: Massachusetts
Date(s) Application is Due: Mar 15; Aug 15
Amount of Grant: 5,000 - 238,000 USD
Contact: David Ford; (617) 278-5200; fax (617) 278-5250; dford@smithfamilyfoundation.net
Internet: http://www.smithfamilyfoundation.net
Sponsor: Richard and Susan Smith Family Foundation
1280 Boylston Street, Suite 100
Chestnut Hill, MA 02467

Richard D. Bass Foundation Grants 4079
The Richard D. Bass Foundation's area of interest include: arts/cultural-programs, including music and dance companies; Catholic/Protestant agencies & churches; community/economic development; education; health organizations, association. The type of support available include: annual campaigns; building/renovation; capital campaigns; general/operating support. Giving primarily in the metropolitan Dallas, Texas area. Grants range from $500 - $15,000. Application deadlines are March 31 and September 30 annually.
Requirements: IRS 501(c)3 nonprofit organizations are available to apply. The Foundations gives primarily to the Dallas, Texas region of the United States but funding is not limited to Texas. Grant proposals are available through out the U.S., contact the Foundation directly before submitting a proposal to access the likely hood of funding for your project. There is no application form required when applying for funding. Submit the proposal with one copy of the organizations IRS Determination Letter.
Restrictions: Funding is not available for: private foundations; individuals.
Geographic Focus: All States
Date(s) Application is Due: Mar 31; Sep 30
Amount of Grant: 500 - 10,000 USD
Contact: Barbara B. Moroney, Treasurer; (214) 351-6994
Sponsor: Richard D. Bass Foundation
4516 Wildwood Road
Dallas, TX 75209-1926

Richard Davoud Donchian Foundation Grants 4080
The Richard Davoud Donchian Foundation was founded after Mr. Donchian's death in April of 1993. Extending Mr. Donchian's lifetime passion, its mission is to help others meet their potential and achieve high degrees of personal and professional success. The Foundation's Board of Directors is continuous in its efforts to preserve the Donchian legacy of leadership and integrity, as well as its commitment to learning and personal growth. Consequently, the Foundation concentrates its primary giving activities in the areas of ethical leadership in business and community affairs; education, personal development and literacy; and moral, ethical and spiritual advancement in all areas of life. Applications are accepted throughout the year and are reviewed in the order they are received. The Foundation encourages pilot initiatives that test new program models.
Requirements: The majority of the Foundation's grantmaking is focused in the northeastern United States, although, occasionally, grants may be made in other regions of the country and/or abroad. All applicants must have tax-exempt 501(c)3 status as a non-profit organization as defined by the Internal Revenue Service. The applicant must have an active board of directors with policy-making authority. Grants may range from a few thousand dollars up to $50,000. In unique circumstances, the Foundation does consider a more significant grant for a program having a major impact in one or more of our areas of interest. Of particular interest to the Foundation are organizations that promote partnerships and collaborative efforts among multiple groups and organizations. Priority will be given to requests that show specific plans for funding beyond the present and program innovation and tangible outcomes, with an emphasis on opportunities for significant and lasting social improvement.
Restrictions: The Foundation generally will not provide grants for the following: organizations not determined to be tax-exempt under section 501(c)3 of the Internal Revenue Code; individuals; general fundraising drives; endowments; government agencies; or organizations that subsist mainly on third party funding and have demonstrated no ability or expended little effort to attract private funding.
Geographic Focus: Connecticut, Delaware, District of Columbia, Florida, Maine, Maryland, New Jersey, New York, North Carolina, South Carolina, Vermont, Virginia
Amount of Grant: Up to 50,000 USD
Contact: Donchian Administrator, (203) 629-8552; fax (203) 547-6112; rdd@fsllc.net
Internet: http://www.foundationservices.cc/RDD2/grantrequests.htm#Guidelines
Sponsor: Richard Davoud Donchian Foundation
640 W. Putnam Avenue, 3rd Floor
Greenwich, CT 06830

Richard E. Griffin Family Foundation Grants 4081
The Foundation, established in 1997, is dedicated to supporting higher education, human and social services, and federated giving programs. Funding most often comes in the form of general operating support. Though there are no specific application forms or deadlines with which to adhere, applicants should make an initial approach by letter outlining the project and budgetary need.
Geographic Focus: All States
Amount of Grant: 1,000 - 100,000 USD
Contact: Richard E. Griffin, (603) 472-4652
Sponsor: Richard E. Griffin Family Foundation
75 Federal Street, Suite 413
Boston, MA 02110-1904

Richard F. and Janice F. Weaver Educational Trust Grants 4082
The Richard F. and Janice F. Weaver Educational Trust was established in Kentucky with the primary purpose of supporting higher education institutions in Kentucky. Support typically comes in the form of funding for general operating costs. Since no formal application is required, interested parties should send a letter of request to the Trust officer. There are no annual deadlines, and typical grant amounts are up to $1,000.
Requirements: Colleges and Universities in Kentucky are eligible to apply.
Geographic Focus: Kentucky
Amount of Grant: Up to 1,000 USD
Contact: Richard F. Weaver, Chief Executive Officer; (270) 753-2899
Sponsor: Richard F. and Janice F. Weaver Educational Trust
1608 Sycamore Street
Murray, KY 42071

Richard Florsheim Art Fund Grants 4083
During his lifetime, Richard Florsheim's career was distinguished by a sustained commitment to producing art, and an equally continuous dedication to improving conditions under which artists work. In his will, he established a small trust fund to assist meritorious older American artists in the pursuit of their careers in art. Since the inception of the Richard Florsheim Art Fund twenty years ago, the Fund has made over 500 grants in support of deserving older artists.
Geographic Focus: All States
Contact: Kimberly M. Taylor; (719) 635-3220; kim@sharpeartfdn.org
Internet: http://sharpeartfdn.qwestoffice.net/FlorsheimMerger.htm
Sponsor: Marie Walsh Sharpe Art Foundation
830 N Tejon Street, Suite 120
Colorado Springs, CO 80903

Richard H. Driehaus Foundation Grants 4084
The Richard H. Driehaus Foundation, founded in 1983 and as a family foundation in 1992, benefits individuals and communities primarily by supporting the preservation and enhancement of the built and natural environments through historic preservation, encouragement of quality architectural and landscape design, and conserving open space. The Foundation also supports the performing and visual arts and makes grants to organizations that provide opportunities for working families who remain poor. The foundation currently provides funding in the areas of the Built Environment, Economic Opportunity for the Working Poor, Government Accountability/Investigative Reporting, Small Museums and Cultural Centers. The Foundation accepts no unsolicited proposals, but welcomes letters of inquiry and phone calls. Proposals are encouraged from companies that emphasize presentation instead of education or community outreach. Guidelines and application information are available online.
Requirements: Dance and theater companies in the Chicago metropolitan area that have produced at least one show in the Chicago area and that have annual operating budgets of less than $100,000 are eligible.
Restrictions: The Foundation tends not to fund large organizations with multi-million dollar budgets; arts education or arts outreach; community theater and community dance; public, private or parochial education; or health care.
Geographic Focus: Illinois
Date(s) Application is Due: Mar 1; Jul 1; Nov 1
Contact: Sonia Fischer; (312) 641-5772; sunnyfischer@driehausfoundation.org
Internet: http://www.driehausfoundation.org
Sponsor: Richard H. Driehaus Foundation
333 North Michigan Avenue, Suite 510
Chicago, IL 60601

Richard H. Driehaus Foundation MacArthur Fund for Arts and Culture 4085
The fund will make multiyear, general operating support grants to organizations that have budgets of $500,000 or less and that reside in, and serve, the Chicago metropolitan area (the counties of Cook, DuPage, Lake, McHenry, Kane, and Will). Most grants will be in the range of $5,000 to $15,000. Most of the grants will be for general operating support. The deadline for receipt of proposals from performing arts organizations (music, theater and dance groups) is 5 p.m. on March 1. The deadline for receipt of proposals from all other groups: literary arts, visual and media arts, interdisciplinary arts, special projects, museums as well as service, policy or advocacy groups is 5 p.m. on June 1. Letters of inquiry must be: received by the listed deadline date; limited to five pages; the first four pages should include a brief description of your organization and your request; the final page should be a summary of your organization's budgets for this year. Full proposals are by invitation only.
Requirements: The following arts and culture organizations may apply: performing arts; visual and media arts; literary arts; interdisciplinary arts; special projects; museums, and service, policy or advocacy groups.
Restrictions: This program is not intended for arts education programs. Nor is it intended, for professional theater and dance companies with operating budgets of less than $150,000; those companies should visit the MacArthur Foundation website to review the guidelines for the Small Theater and Dance Group Funding Program.
Geographic Focus: Illinois
Date(s) Application is Due: Mar 1; Jun 1
Amount of Grant: 5,000 - 15,000 USD
Contact: Richard Cahan, Program Oficer; (312) 641-5772 or (847) 722-9244; fax (312) 641-5736; RichardCahan@aol.com
Internet: http://www.driehausfoundation.org/support
Sponsor: Richard H. Driehaus Foundation
333 North Michigan Avenue, Suite 510
Chicago, IL 60601

Richard H. Driehaus Foundation Small Theater and Dance Grants 4086
The Richard H. Driehaus Foundation, founded in 1983 and as a family foundation in 1992, benefits individuals and communities primarily by supporting the preservation and enhancement of the built and natural environments through historic preservation, encouragement of quality architectural and landscape design, and conserving open space. This program addresses the needs of small theater and dance companies in the Chicago area. Companies that emphasize professional presentation instead of education or community outreach are encouraged to apply. Use of grants may be unrestricted.
Requirements: Dance and theater companies that reside in the Chicago metropolitan area, have produced at least one show in the Chicago area, and have annual operating budgets of less than $150,000 are eligible.
Geographic Focus: Illinois
Date(s) Application is Due: Apr 25; Sep 12
Amount of Grant: 2,500 - 10,000 USD
Contact: Peter Handler; (312) 641-5772; peterhandler@driehausfoundation.org
Internet: http://www.driehausfoundation.org/support
Sponsor: Richard H. Driehaus Foundation
333 North Michigan Avenue, Suite 510
Chicago, IL 60601

Richard King Mellon Foundation Grants 4087
On a national basis, the foundation makes grants to acquire and preserve key tracts of land in danger of being lost to urban growth and environmentally insensitive development. Mellon gives to nonprofits in Pittsburgh and throughout southwestern Pennsylvania to improve human services, education, medical care, civic affairs, and cultural activities. Types of support include capital grants, challenge/matching grants, general operating grants, project grants, and seed money grants. Application and guidelines are available online.
Requirements: Projects originating in Pittsburgh and southwestern Pennsylvania are given special priority.
Restrictions: The Foundation gives priority to projects and programs that have clearly defined outcomes and an evaluation component. It does not consider requests on behalf of individuals, or from outside the Untied States. The Foundation does not encourage requests from outside Pennsylvania.
Geographic Focus: Pennsylvania
Contact: Michael Watson, Senior Vice President; (412) 392-2800; fax (412) 392-2837
Internet: http://foundationcenter.org/grantmaker/rkmellon/
Sponsor: Richard King Mellon Foundation
500 Grant Street, Suite 4106
Pittsburgh, PA 15219-2502

Richard M. Fairbanks Foundation Grants 4088
The Richard M. Fairbanks Foundation, Inc. was established in 1986 by Richard M. Fairbanks, founder and owner of Fairbanks Communications. An independent private foundation granting funds to qualifying nonprofit organizations, programs, and projects in the greater Indianapolis, Indiana area. Exceptions to this geographic limitation are normally made only for organizations historically supported by the Fairbanks family or for national disasters. If you are interested in learning if your organization and project/program matches the Richard M. Fairbanks Foundation's areas of interest and funding guidelines, you may contact the foundation by telephone, email or brief written letter of inquiry. Please note that the Fairbanks Foundation does not accept unsolicited proposals.
Requirements: The Foundation: makes grants only to tax exempt public charities as defined in Sections 501(c)3 & 509(a)(1)(2)(3) of the Internal Revenue Code, except as prohibited for 509(a)(3) Type III organizations; will not consider requests for loans and grants to individuals; does not make grants or give support to conferences, seminars, media events, or workshops unless they are an integral part of a broader program; ordinarily considers grant requests only from organizations located in Greater Indianapolis, Indiana.
Geographic Focus: Indiana
Contact: Claire Fiddian-Green, Grants Officer; (317) 663-4189 or (317) 846-7111; fax (317) 844-0167; Fiddiangreen@rmfairbanksfoundation.org
Internet: http://www.rmfairbanksfoundation.org/default.asp?p=3
Sponsor: Richard M. Fairbanks Foundation
9292 North Meridian Street, Suite 304
Indianapolis, IN 46260

Richards Foundation Grants 4089
Founded by Roy Richards, Jr. in 1990, the Richards Foundation supports organizations in Carrollton, Georgia, and other communities that are working to break the cycles that create economic disadvantage and social needs. The children of Roy Richards, Sr., continue the tradition of community involvement and caring begun long ago by Mr. and Mrs. Richards.
Requirements: Awards are made to groups and individuals who give service to others. Application should be made in writing with information regarding how funds will be used.
Geographic Focus: All States
Contact: Judy Windom, (770) 832-4097; Judy_Windom@southwire.com
Sponsor: Richards Foundation
P.O. Box 800
Carrollton, GA 30112

Rich Foundation Grants 4090
The foundation awards grants to nonprofit organizations in Atlanta, GA, to support community funds, performing arts, cultural programs, higher education, social services, homeless, youth, hospitals, heart disease, theater, and AIDS. Types of support include annual campaigns, building funds, continuing support, equipment acquisition, operating budgets, technical assistance, and research. Contact the office for application forms. The board meets quarterly to review requests.
Requirements: Nonprofits in the Atlanta, GA, area are eligible for grant support.
Geographic Focus: Georgia
Date(s) Application is Due: Mar 15; Jun 15; Sep 15; Dec 15
Amount of Grant: 5,000 - 100,000 USD
Contact: Anne Poland Berg, Grant Consultant; (404) 262-2266
Sponsor: Rich Foundation
11 Piedmont Center, Suite 204
Atlanta, GA 30305

Richland County Bank Grants 4091
The Richland County Bank has had a long tradition of community involvement, dedication and volunteerism. The Bank is committed to supporting the community in which it serves. In addition to monetary contributions, the bank encourages its employees to take an active role in our community. As a corporate sponsor, we support various organizations in Richland and surrounding counties, including: Vernon, Crawford, Grant, Iowa, and Sauk counties. Areas of interest include: health care; higher education; agricultural agencies; community development; children and youth programs; and scholarship funds.
Requirements: Applicants must be 501(c)3 organizations serving the Wisconsin counties of Richland, Vernon, Crawford, Grant, Iowa, or Sauk.
Geographic Focus: Wisconsin
Contact: Gail Surrem, Vice President; (608) 647-6306
Internet: http://www.richlandcountybank.com/aboutInvolvement.cfm
Sponsor: Richland County Bank
195 West Court Street
Richland Center, WI 53581

Richmond Eye and Ear Fund Grants 4092
The fund is committed to serving the city of Richmond, Colonial Heights, Hopewell and Petersburg, and the counties of Chesterfield, Hanover, Henrico, Goochland, New Kent, Charles City, Lancaster, Northumberland, Richmond, Westmoreland and Powhatan in the fields of ophthalmology, otolaryngology, and oral maxillofacial surgery for qualified organizations. Grantmaking focuses on underserved, uninsured, or medically indigent children and adults in need of ophthalmological (eye), otolaryngological (ear, nose, and throat), and/or oral maxillofacial services (conditions, defects, injuries, and aesthetic aspects of the mouth, teeth, and jaws); improving access and outreach as it relates to the stated services mentioned; and healthcare education/preventive care consistent with purposes of this fund. Guidelines are available online. The Fund???s grantmaking focuses on: Underserved, uninsured or medically indigent children and adults in need of ophthalmological (eye), otolaryngological (ear, nose and throat), and/or oral maxillofacial services (conditions, defects, injuries, and aesthetic aspects of the mouth, teeth, and jaws). Improving Access and Outreach as it relates to the services mentioned above. Healthcare Education/preventive care consistent with purposes of this fund.
Requirements: Proposals will be accepted from charitable organizations, which serve the residents of the focus area.
Geographic Focus: Virginia
Date(s) Application is Due: May 5; Nov 5
Amount of Grant: Up to 50,000 USD
Contact: Elaine Summerfield, Program Officer; (804) 330-7400; fax (804) 330-5992; esummerfield@tcfrichmond.org
Internet: http://www.tcfrichmond.org/Page2954.cfm#ear
Sponsor: Community Foundation
7501 Boulders View Drive, Suite 110
Richmond, VA 23225

Righteous Persons Foundation Grants 4093

The foundation, established by Steven Spielberg, makes grants nationally for projects to revitalize Jewish life, help young people learn about Judaism, and promote tolerance among people of all faiths and ethnicities. Many of the awards are for projects that explore new ideas and opportunities with a special emphasis on young people and that include many projects that may have otherwise had a difficult time obtaining funding. Projects that are national in scope or can serve as models for other communities will receive preference.
Requirements: U.S. 501(c)3 nonprofits are eligible.
Restrictions: Grants are not awarded to support endowments, capital campaigns, building funds, university faculty chairs, individual synagogues or day schools, research, or the publication of books or magazines.
Geographic Focus: All States
Amount of Grant: 5,000 - 400,000 USD
Contact: Rachel Levin, Program Officer; (310) 314-8393; fax (310) 314-8396
Sponsor: Righteous Persons Foundation
2800 28th Street, Suite 105
Santa Monica, CA 90405

Riley Foundation Grants 4094

The foundation's purpose is to make grants, distributions, and/or loans to charitable and governmental organizations for charitable purposes and to provide financial resources and assistance for community wide projects and programs in health care; education; and the betterment of cultural, environmental, and economic conditions for the people of Meridian and Lauderdale County, Mississippi. Applications are reviewed at quarterly meetings in January, April, July, and October and must be in by noon on the listed deadline days.
Requirements: Mississippi governmental agencies and 501(c)3 organizations that are not private foundations as defined under Section 509(a) are eligible.
Restrictions: Best of Both Worlds Addiction Center, Inc. $75,000 - Operating Support; Meridian Community College $5,000 - Lucile Reisman Rosenbaum Memorial Scholarship Endowmen;
Geographic Focus: Mississippi
Date(s) Application is Due: Feb 15; May 15; Aug 15; Nov 15
Amount of Grant: 2,000 - 300,000 USD
Contact: Becky Lewis, (601) 481-1430; fax (601) 481-1434; info@rileyfoundation.org
Internet: http://www.rileyfoundation.org/guide.htm?46,10
Sponsor: Riley Foundation
4518 Poplar Springs Drive
Meridian, MS 39305

Ripley County Community Foundation Grants 4095

The Ripley County Community Foundation (RCCF) was established to improve the quality of life for Ripley County, Indiana residents. The mission of the Ripley County Community Foundation is to assist donors in building an enduring source of charitable assets to benefit the citizens and qualified organizations of Ripley County. The RCCF strives to provide responsible stewardship of the gifts donated; to promote leadership in addressing Ripley County's issues; and to make grants in the fields of community service, social service, education, health, environment, and the arts. The application and samples of previously funded projects are available at the website.
Requirements: Grant applicants must qualify as 501(c)3 or 509(a) tax exempt organizations or hold sponsorship with such organizations. Because the grant guidelines and policies are brief and do not address every aspect of the RCCF granting program, the most effective means of making initial contact with the RCCF is through a letter or phone call of inquiry to the RCCF.
Restrictions: Funding is not available for the following: individuals; travel or lodging expenses to enable individuals or groups to attend seminars or take trips; endowment purposes of recipient organizations; programs funded prior to the RCCF date for grant decisions; to repay acquisition costs for equipment already purchased or paid for; for acquisition of weapons, firearms or destructive devices; sectarian religious purposes; to attempt to influence legislation or to intervene in any political campaign. RCCF reserves the right to refuse any and all grant applications.
Geographic Focus: Indiana
Date(s) Application is Due: Sep 14
Amount of Grant: Up to 2,500 USD
Contact: Jane Deiwert; (877) 234-5220 or (812) 933-1098; jdeiwert@rccfonline.org
Internet: http://www.rccfonline.org/grants.asp
Sponsor: Ripley County Community Foundation
4 South Park, Suite 210
Batesville, IN 47006

Ripley County Community Foundation Small Project Grants 4096

Small Project Grants are available throughout the year (not just during the traditional Fall Granting Cycle) for amounts up to $500. The projects must meet the Foundation's charitable guidelines for traditional grants. Organizations may only apply for one small project grant each year; they may also apply for a grant during the traditional fall granting cycle if they receive a small project grant. Organizations may only apply for one larger grant in the fall. Applications will be accepted anytime during the year but decisions will only be made by the 30th of April, June, August, and October.
Requirements: To be considered, application must be made by the second Friday of each of these months. Applications not received by the second Friday will be held for the next Small Project Grant period.
Geographic Focus: Indiana
Date(s) Application is Due: Apr 30; Jun 30; Aug 30; Oct 30
Amount of Grant: Up to 500 USD
Contact: Jane Deiwert; (877) 234-5220 or (812) 933-1098; jdeiwert@rccfonline.org
Internet: http://www.rccfonline.org/grants.asp
Sponsor: Ripley County Community Foundation
4 South Park, Suite 210
Batesville, IN 47006

RISCA Design Innovation Grant 4097

Rhode Island State Council on the Arts (RISCA) recognizes that Rhode Island is home to a wealth of talented design professionals who are skilled innovators, entrepreneurs and problem solvers. RISCA will offer one $6000 competitive Design Innovation Grant (DIG) annually to Rhode Island designers for design ideas that are highly creative and show potential for innovation and/or implementation. Grant proposals should address one of the following goals: innovation of a specific kind of design, process or application; or creation of a product or service that has a potential public benefit. Awards are based upon samples of past work and proposals for future work. Grant recipients are not required to pursue implementation of winning design proposals or completion of design projects. However, award recipients will be asked to pursue the next phase of their project such as meeting with potential partners, creating more detailed schematics, or creating a project development plan, for example. Artists may submit the same support materials for a DIG grant and a Project Grant for Individuals if they are applying for both. Applicants are strongly encouraged to attend a DIG grants information session or contact the Director of Individual Artist Programs to discuss their application in detail.
Requirements: Applicants must be at least eighteen years of age and residents of the State of Rhode Island for at least twelve consecutive months prior to the date of application. Applicants must submit work that has been created within the three years prior to the date of application (with the exception of film and video, which must be completed within the past five years). Applicants must register and apply through RISCA's online grant application system which may be accessed at the grant website. Proposals must be submitted online by 4:30 pm on the application deadline date. All required supporting materials are likewise due by 4:30 pm on the application deadline date whether mailed, hand-carried, or submitted through the online system.
Restrictions: DIG grant recipients will be ineligible to apply for two deadlines following receipt of an award (for example, if an awardee was funded for a 2009 application, that individual may not apply again until October 1, 2012). Students pursuing graduate or undergraduate degrees in an arts discipline or an arts-related subject area at the time of application may not apply. Applicants must be the primary creative force behind the work; consequently, no other artist may submit the same piece as support material at the same deadline or in any future RISCA application.
Geographic Focus: Rhode Island
Date(s) Application is Due: Oct 1
Amount of Grant: 6,000 USD
Contact: Christina Di Chiera; (401) 222-3881; cristina@arts.ri.gov
Internet: http://www.arts.ri.gov/grants/guidelines/
Sponsor: Rhode Island State Council on the Arts
One Capitol Hill, Third Floor
Providence, RI 02908

RISCA Folk Arts Apprenticeships 4098

Folk Arts Apprenticeships are designed to foster the sharing of traditional (folk) artistic skills between a master and an apprentice who is already familiar with the genre. The program creates this opportunity specifically for individuals who share a common cultural heritage. The folk arts are defined as those artistic practices that are community or family-based and express that community's aesthetic heritage and tradition. The learning process is informal and is passed on from generation to generation by word of mouth, apprenticeship, and imitation. The Folk Arts Apprenticeship Program is not designed as a classroom but rather as a one-on-one teaching/learning experience. Most of the award will go towards the master's fee. Requests for materials, travel, and for the apprentice(s) stipend, however, will be considered. At the end of the apprenticeship, the Program requires a public component (display or performance). Applicants who need assistance completing an application and/or who require an interpreter should contact RISCA well in advance of the deadline.
Requirements: Applicants must be current, legal residents of the state of Rhode Island for a minimum of twelve consecutive months prior to the date of application. There is no age requirement to participate, however applicants under the age of 16 must submit a parent's or legal guardian's release or permission form as part of the application process. Apprentices should seek a master artist in the genre of their choice and are encouraged to verify master artist residency requirements with RISCA. Applicants needing assistance locating master artists should call or email the RISCA Community Arts Program Director. Applications must be submitted online using the RISCA online grant application system (http://www.arts.ri.gov/grants/guidelines/) or by completing RISCA's Folk Arts Application Form and submitting it with the appropriate supplemental information/budget sheet(s) and any required supporting documents. Applications must be typed. All materials are due by 4:30p of the deadline date, whether submitted online, mailed or hand-delivered. Facsimiles will not be accepted. The National Endowment for the Arts and RISCA support should be acknowledged in all marketing and publicity materials.
Restrictions: Only one Folk Arts Apprenticeship application is allowed per person per deadline, whether to the Rhode Island Folk Arts Apprenticeship Program or to the Southern New England Folk and Traditional Arts Apprenticeship Program. Apprentices who have been funded for three consecutive years by this program are ineligible to reapply for one fiscal year. RISCA Council members, full- or part-time employees, or their families are ineligible to apply during or for two years after their employment. Students pursuing graduate or undergraduate degrees at the time of application or during the award period are ineligible. Former grantees who have outstanding Final Reports are ineligible.
Geographic Focus: Rhode Island
Date(s) Application is Due: Oct 1
Amount of Grant: 1,000 - 3,000 USD

Contact: Elena Calderon Patino, Community Arts Program Director; (401) 222-6996; fax (401) 521-1351; epatino@Arts.RI.gov or info@risca.state.ri.us
Internet: http://www.arts.ri.gov/folkarts/FolkandTraditionalArtsGrantInfo.php
Sponsor: Rhode Island State Council on the Arts
One Capitol Hill, Third Floor
Providence, RI 02908

RISCA Professional Arts Development Grants 4099

Rhode Island State Council on the Arts (RISCA) Professional Arts Development (PAD) grants provide funds to entrepreneurial artists to help address their business and professional development needs. Preference will be given to individuals who have not received a RISCA grant or RISCA Fellowship Award in the past. The goal of the PAD grants is to enable artists to engage in specific professional and business development activities that will build their capacity and strengthen their ability to meet the goals of their arts business. Professional development activities should enhance the applicant's knowledge and skills; extend the reach of their products and services; and/or support strategic partnership projects that serve to expand audience or capacity for artists and their collaborators. Ways in which PAD funds may be used, for example, are: for documentation of artwork or performance; for the creation of a professional or business plan; for print and online marketing materials; for professional conferences and workshops; for registration and exhibition fees; and for certain travel expenses. Applications will be accepted quarterly. Applicants should allow 30 days for notification of grant award. Applicants are strongly encouraged to attend a PAD grant information session or contact the Director of Individual Artists Programs to discuss their applications in detail.
Requirements: Individual artists who are pursuing a livelihood through their artwork are eligible to apply. Applicants must use the online application system at the grant website to register and apply. Online applications must be submitted by 5:00 PM on the deadline date. Support materials must be postmarked or hand delivered by 4:30 pm EST on the deadline date. Applicants must be at least 18 years of age and be residents of the State of Rhode Island for at least twelve consecutive months prior to the date of application. Applicants must submit a business or professional development plan with their grant application, with the exception of those artists who are applying for funds to create such a plan. All grant proposals should address specific goals in an applicant's professional or business plan, unless the individual is seeking funds for the creation of such a plan. All requests must be matched 1 to 1 with applicant cash being an acceptable match. All grant-funded activities must take place AFTER the approval of the grant application.
Restrictions: Funding for the PAD grant program is limited. Until further notice, successful applicants may not reapply for a PAD grant, however applicants who do not receive funding may reapply at subsequent deadlines. Students pursuing graduate or undergraduate degrees in an arts discipline or an arts-related subject area at the time of application may not apply. PAD grants do not support: the creation of new work, performances or exhibitions; costs associated with international travel; equipment costs including computers, cameras, paintbrushes, frames, etc; bricks and mortar activities and capital improvements including permanent equipment purchase and installation; the elimination or reduction of existing debt; contributions to an endowment fund; fundraising efforts, such as social events or benefits; prizes and awards; hospitality expenses, such as food and beverages for openings or receptions; the purchase of alcoholic beverages; applications where the purpose is to "regrant" or award funds using some or all of the RISCA grant funds; activities which are part of a graduate or undergraduate degree program, or for which academic credit is received; applications for projects that proselytize or promote religious activities, or which take place as part of a religious service; and activities that are inaccessible to people with disabilities.
Geographic Focus: Rhode Island
Amount of Grant: 250 - 750 USD
Contact: Cristina Di Chiera; (401) 222-3881; cristina@arts.ri.gov
Internet: http://www.arts.ri.gov/grants/guidelines/
Sponsor: Rhode Island State Council on the Arts
One Capitol Hill, Third Floor
Providence, RI 02908

RISCA Project Grants for Organizations, Individuals and Education 4100

Rhode Island State Council of the Arts (RISCA) Project Grants are competitive funds available to artists, non-profit organizations, schools and educators. These grants support programs and projects that engage Rhode Islanders in arts learning, arts participation, arts experiences and appreciation of the arts. Project Grants in Education (PGE and PGA) provide support to artists and cultural organizations collaborating with schools and other educational entities in order to: increase access to high quality curriculum-based arts learning for all RI children and youth; foster the professional development of artists and educators; engage the participation of families and other community members in arts learning for children and youth; and help to ensure that all RI youth are able to demonstrate proficiency in one or more art forms at or before graduation from high school. Project Grants for Individuals (PGI) provide support to highly creative and talented artists who seek to produce, perform, teach or share their work with the public. This might include the coordination of community arts events, public performances, arts workshops, creative collaborations, and exhibitions and installations with a strong public component. Project Grants for Organizations (PGO) provide support for arts and non-profit organizations involved in programming that ensures that the arts are an integral part of life in Rhode Island. Applications in the Project Grants category are accepted twice a year on April 1 (for activities taking place from July 1 to June 30) and October 1 (for activities taking place from January 1 to June 30). RISCA strongly recommends that first time applicants meet with RISCA staff at least six weeks prior to the deadline to orient new applicants and review draft applications.
Requirements: Individual artists must be at least 18 years of age and a current, legal resident of the State of Rhode Island to apply for RISCA Project Grants for Individual Artists. Additionally an individual artist must have established legal residence in Rhode Island for a minimum of twelve consecutive months prior to the date of application. All Rhode Island nonprofit arts, cultural and community-based organizations that demonstrate a strong commitment to using the arts effectively and as an integral part of their programming may apply for RISCA Project Grants to Organizations. Non-profit organizations must be incorporated in and conduct business in the State of Rhode Island, with 501(c)3 tax exempt status from the Internal Revenue Service, governed by a revolving board of directors, trustees or advisory board drawn from the community at large and shown to be actively involved in the governance of the organization. Units of local government (cities and towns) may apply for support. Organizations which have not yet received the appropriate IRS non-profit determination letter may be sponsored by an eligible nonprofit organization, however, the sponsoring organization is financially, administratively and programmatically responsible for all conditions of the grant and for signing all pertinent documents and report forms. All organizations applying to RISCA Project Grants for Education must comply with the requirements already listed for organizations. In addition, public schools, colleges or universities with tax-exempt status, state-run schools (such as Rhode Island School for the Deaf or Davies Career Technical High School), and tax-exempt private and parochial schools may apply. Individuals applying for RISCA Project Grants for Education must comply with requirements already listed for individuals and must be experienced teaching artists, either on the RISCA Education/Folk Arts roster or with a resume and supporting materials demonstrating significant teaching experience with the population targeted in the application. All grants to organizations and education require a dollar-for-dollar cash match, meaning that grant requests in this category may not exceed 50% of the project budget. Applicants may request up to a maximum of $10,000, or up to half the cost of the project, whichever is less. 25% of match for education projects can be in-kind. Individuals applying for individual project grants or education grants do not need a match, but cash and in-kind contributions are encouraged to demonstrate support for the project. Only one application per applicant will be accepted at each deadline. All applicants must register first at http://www.arts.ri.gov/register, after which applications must be submitted online at http://www.arts.ri.gov/apply. All applications must be submitted online and support materials received at the RISCA offices by no later than 4:30PM on the deadline date. If applicants plan to send support materials by mail, they should include one print copy of their complete application with those materials.
Restrictions: Students attending high school or students pursuing undergraduate or graduate degrees in an arts discipline or an arts-related subject area at the time of application may not apply. Individuals who are paid staff of a non-profit organization that receives General Operating Support or Project Grant Support from RISCA cannot apply for funding for projects that are part of that organization's programming. Individuals who are paid staff or proprietors of a for-profit organization cannot apply for funding for projects that are a product or service of that organization. Individuals and organizations cannot apply for funding for the same project at the same deadline. Members of the RISCA staff, Council and their spouses and immediate relatives are also ineligible to apply. State and quasi-public state government agencies are ineligible to apply. RISCA support may not be used for: bricks and mortar activities and capital improvements; the purchase of permanent equipment; eliminating or reducing existing debt; contributions to an endowment fund; fundraising efforts; prizes and awards; hospitality expenses, such as food and beverages for openings or receptions; purchase of alcoholic beverages; expenses incurred prior to or after the grant cycle in which the grant has been awarded; applications where the purpose is to "regrant" or award funds using some or all of the RISCA grant funds; activities which are part of a graduate or undergraduate degree program, or for which academic credit is received; projects that proselytize or promote religious activities, or which take place as part of a religious service; and performances and exhibitions not available to the general public or which are inaccessible to people with disabilities.
Geographic Focus: Rhode Island
Date(s) Application is Due: Apr 1; Oct 1
Amount of Grant: Up to 10,000 USD
Contact: Daniel L. Kahn; (401) 222-1146; fax (401) 521-1351; dan@arts.ri.gov
Internet: http://www.arts.ri.gov/grants/guidelines/
Sponsor: Rhode Island State Council on the Arts
One Capitol Hill, Third Floor
Providence, RI 02908

Rite Aid Corp Grants 4101

The Rite Aid Foundation, founded in July 2001, is a not-for-profit foundation dedicated to helping people in the communities Rite Aid serves lead happier, healthier lives. We support specific programs of non-profit organizations that are classified and exempt from federal tax under section 501(c)3 of the Internal Revenue Service Code. We limit our funding to programs that focus on health and wellness in the communities in which Rite Aid operates. Grants are awarded for one year at a time, and no organization can receive a grant from the Foundation more than two years in a row. Organizations that receive two consecutive grants must wait 24 months to apply to the Foundation again. While The Rite Aid Foundation accepts proposals throughout the year, our committee reviews them as soon as possible after July 1, October 1, January 1 and April 1.
Requirements: See website for funding proposal requirements and restrictions. Funding requests are mailed directly to the Rite Aid Foundation.
Geographic Focus: All States
Contact: Customer Service; (800) 748-3243
Internet: http://www.riteaid.com/company/community/foundation.jsf
Sponsor: Rite Aid Foundation
P.O. Box 3165
Harrisburg, PA 17105

Roberta Leventhal Sudakoff Foundation Grants 4102

The Foundation, established in 1996, offers funding primarily in the forms of ongoing support and capital campaigns. Focus areas include: the arts; community development; education of children and youth; environmental issues; human/social service programs that support families and seniors; and science. Of particular interest are the performing

arts, including dance, music, and theater. The geographic focus is Sarasota, Florida, with an initial approach by Letter of Interest (LOI). The annual deadline for applications is July 1, with final notification by September 30th.
Requirements: Grantees must be 501(c)3 organizations with a sound track record.
Restrictions: Generally the Foundation will not provide grants for: endowments, deficit financing, debt reduction, or ordinary operating expenses; conferences, seminars, workshops, travel, surveys, advertising, fund-raising costs or research; annual giving campaigns; individuals; or projects that have already been completed.
Geographic Focus: Florida
Amount of Grant: 107,636 USD
Contact: Debra M. Jacobs, (941) 957-0442; fax (941) 957-3135; djacobs@selbyfdn.org
Internet: http://www.selbyfdn.org/
Sponsor: Roberta Leventhal Sudakoff Foundation
1800 Second Street, Suite 750
Sarasota, FL 34236-5900

Robert and Helen Haddad Foundation Grants 4103
The Robert and Helen Haddad Foundation, established in Indiana in 2002, supports the arts, Christian agencies and churches, education, and health care. There is a specific application form, though no deadlines with which to adhere. Applicants should submit a letter of application, which includes a copy of the IRS determination letter, a brief history of the organization and its mission, and a detailed description of the project and amount of funding requested.
Requirements: 501(c)3 organizations that serve residents of Indiana are welcome to apply.
Geographic Focus: Indiana
Amount of Grant: 1,000 - 20,000 USD
Contact: Kevin Alerding, (317) 236-2435; kevin.alerding@icemiller.com
Sponsor: Robert and Helen Haddad Foundation
3460 Commerce Drive
Columbus, IN 47201-2204

Robert and Joan Dircks Foundation Grants 4104
The foundation supports non-profit organizations that enrich and improve the quality of life for individuals primarily located in the New Jersey area. The focus is to encourage innovative programs and projects that benefit and improve the lives of children and individuals who are physically mentally or economically disadvantaged.
Requirements: Submit your inquiry online, using the Grant Request Information form provided on the Robert and Joan Dircks Foundation website: http://www.dircksfoundation.org/application2.asp
Restrictions: The Robert and Joan Dircks Foundation does not award grants for political or lobbying activities, environmental or cultural projects, capital or annual campaigns, endowments, operating budgets, deficit or debt reduction, loans or housing projects. Also, grants are not made to programs of national or international scope.
Geographic Focus: Connecticut, Maine, Massachusetts, New Hampshire, Rhode Island, Vermont
Amount of Grant: 1,000 - 15,000 USD
Contact: Grants Administrator; grants@dircksfoundation.org
Internet: http://www.dircksfoundation.org/guidelines.html
Sponsor: Robert and Joan Dircks Foundation
P.O. Box 6
Mountain Lakes, NJ 07046

Robert and Polly Dunn Foundation Grants 4105
The foundation awards grants in the U.S. Southeast, with emphasis on the Atlanta, GA, area, for projects in the area of youth, child development, and higher education. Types of support include capital campaigns, general operating support, and scholarship funds. There are no application forms. The board meets in June and December to consider requests.
Restrictions: Grants do not support individuals and not awarded to support endowment funds, loans, or program-related investments
Geographic Focus: Georgia
Date(s) Application is Due: Apr 30; Sep 30
Amount of Grant: Up to 587,925 USD
Contact: Karen Wilbanks, Executive Director; (404) 816-2883; fax (404) 816-2883
Sponsor: Robert and Polly Dunn Foundation
P.O. Box 723194
Atlanta, GA 31139

Robert B McMillen Foundation Grants 4106
The Robert B McMillen Foundation is a non-profit charitable foundation. The Foundation offers funding in the states of Washington and Alaska. The two areas of intent are: medical and social enhancement. Fifty percent of the annual funding is earmarked for medical research. The Foundation will consider making grants to non-profit organizations involved in researching cardiology, lipid and organ transplants. Twenty-five percent of annual giving is earmarked for social areas including, but not limited to, Goodwill, Salvation Army & United Way. Preference is given to organizations and/or programs that use art as the vehicle to impact communities and change individual lives.
Requirements: The Foundation does not accept uninvited medical or social proposals. Contact the Foundations office for information on, how to be invited to make a medical or social proposal to the McMillen Foundation.
Restrictions: The Foundation do not make grants to: religious, fraternal or other organizations primarily benefiting their own members; other private foundations nor political organizations; for-profit entities; other than scholarships, the foundation will not make multi-year grants.
Geographic Focus: Alaska, Washington

Contact: Cassandra Town, President; (425) 313-5711; fax (425) 313-8955; cassandra@mcmillenfoundation.org
Internet: http://www.mcmillenfoundation.org/mission.htm
Sponsor: Robert B McMillen Foundation
55 1st Place NW, Suite 2, P.O. Box 1523
Issaquah, WA 98027

Robert Bowne Foundation Fellowships 4107
Fellowships are dedicated to building capacity in youth program staff to design and conduct research in the areas of youth development and education during the out-of-school hours. The goals of the fellowships include generating and disseminating research in the area of education in community-based organizations serving youth, building a network of scholars, contributing to basic knowledge, improving practice, and informing policy.
Requirements: Robert Bowne Foundation Research Fellows are selected by application and work in youth programs in New York City. They meet twice monthly for six months and monthly for the remainder of the year. Fellows become members of a community of researchers, learn methods of qualitative research, read and discuss research articles, and conduct site-specific research projects. Fellows participate in a writing institute where they write a research article or article for publication and present at a research roundtable. Contact foundation for application.
Geographic Focus: New York
Contact: Anne Lawrence; (212) 792-6250; anne.lawrence@bownefoundation.org
Internet: http://bownefoundation.org/index.php?option=com_content&view=category&layout=blog&id=74&Itemid=96
Sponsor: Robert Bowne Foundation
6 East 39th Street, 10th Floor
New York, NY 10016

Robert Bowne Foundation Literacy Grants 4108
The foundation awards grants to out-of-school-time programs that support literacy. The foundation defines literacy as engagement in reading, writing, listening, and speaking in order to better understand ourselves, others, and the world around us. The foundation seeks to have a long-term and substantial effect on the field of out-of-school-time education. The priority is supporting individual programs that make literacy education an integral part of their work, provide quality experiences for young people, and seek to evolve as learning opportunities by supporting ongoing development of participants, staff, families and community leaders. The foundation seeks to build program capacity to support literacy development.
Requirements: Grants awarded to 501(c)3 agencies located within one of the five boroughs of New York City or in rare instances to an agency located outside the City if it serves New York City children. Agencies must serve youth (preschool to age 21).
Restrictions: Grants are not awarded to religious organizations, primary or secondary schools, colleges or universities, individuals, to support in-school projects or projects following a traditional remedial model of instruction or to support capital campaigns or endowments.
Geographic Focus: New York
Amount of Grant: 20,000 - 30,000 USD
Contact: Anne Lawrence; (212) 792-6250; anne.lawrence@bownefoundation.org
Internet: http://bownefoundation.org/index.php?option=com_content&view=article&id=54&Itemid=69
Sponsor: Robert Bowne Foundation
6 East 39th Street, 10th Floor
New York, NY 10016

Robert Bowne Foundation Youth-Centered Grants 4109
The foundation awards grants to youth-centered programs with a clear mission that encourage participants to express their emerging identities. The foundation recognizes that learning and development require ongoing feedback and that assessment and program evaluation are integrated throughout programs. Supported programs will include activities, techniques and material tailored to the interests, strengths and needs of the youth being served. Successful programs will have high quality content and instruction and celebrate young people's achievements.
Requirements: Grants awarded to 501(c)3 agencies located within one of the five boroughs of New York City or in rare instances to an agency located outside the City if it serves New York City children. Agencies must serve youth (preschool to age 21).
Restrictions: Grants are not awarded to religious organizations, primary or secondary schools, colleges or universities, individuals, to support in-school projects or projects following a traditional remedial model of instruction or to support capital campaigns or endowments.
Geographic Focus: New York
Contact: Anne Lawrence; (212) 792-6250; anne.lawrence@bownefoundation.org
Internet: http://bownefoundation.org/index.php?option=com_content&view=article&id=54&Itemid=69
Sponsor: Robert Bowne Foundation
6 East 39th Street, 10th Floor
New York, NY 10016

Robert E. and Evelyn McKee Foundation Grants 4110
The foundation awards grants in the following categories: civic, cultural, and religion; education and scholarships; hospitals; medical and medical research; welfare, rehabilitation, and mental health; United Way; and youth activities. Grants awarded for scholarships are made to a few selected high schools and universities, who select scholarship recipients. Religious contributions are basically limited to the local Episcopal churches. The majority of funding is made to local charitable organizations or through local affiliates of national or statewide organizations.

Requirements: 501(c)3 tax-exempt organizations are eligible.
Restrictions: Funding is not available to organizations outside the United States or those limited by race or ethnic origin. The foundation refrains from awarding grants for endowments or deficit financing. Grants are not made to other foundations, except for a local community foundation.
Geographic Focus: Texas
Date(s) Application is Due: Dec 15
Amount of Grant: 1,000 - 10,000 USD
Contact: Administrator; (915) 581-4025; mckeefoundation@directway.com
Internet: http://www.mckeefoundation.org
Sponsor: Robert E. and Evelyn McKee Foundation
5835 Cromo Drive, Suite 1
El Paso, TX 79912

Robert F. Kennedy Human Rights Award 4111
The award was established to honor creative individuals who are engaged, often at great personal risk, in strategic and nonviolent efforts to overcome serious human rights violations. Those working within their own country's social change process and who have worked strategically and effectively to address serious human rights problems are given the highest priority. If given to more than one individual in any given year, the award will be divided equally among the recipients. The award ceremony is held in Washington, DC, on a date in November as close as possible to November 20, the birthday of Robert F. Kennedy.
Requirements: Persons working to promote and protect human rights of any race, creed, religion, nationality, gender, or sexual orientation are eligible to receive the award. The laureate does not need to be widely known; should have an established reputation for integrity, creativity, and commitment to principles of human rights; and be associated with or lead a nongovernmental organization contributing to a social movement working to achieve a specific social change.
Geographic Focus: All States
Date(s) Application is Due: Apr 15
Amount of Grant: 30,000 USD
Contact: Fernanda Katz Ellenberg, (202) 463-7575; nominations@rfkmemorial.org
Internet: http://www.rfkmemorial.org/legacyinaction/humanrightsawardadvocacy/
Sponsor: Robert F. Kennedy Memorial
1367 Connecticut Avenue NW, Suite 200
Washington, DC 20036

Robert F. Stoico / FIRSTFED Charitable Foundation Grants 4112
The foundation was established to support the local communities of southeastern Massahusetts and Rhode Island. The foundation's main areas of interest are affordable housing, economic/job development, educational programs, arts and cultural programs that benefit the public or the traditionally underserved, and accessible health care for all. Small grants (under $2501) are reviewed throughout the year on a rolling basis. Large grant requests are reviewed four times a year (in April, July, October and January). Application and guidelines are available online.
Requirements: Massachusetts and Rhode Island 501(c)3 nonprofit organizations in the counties where FIRSTFED America Bancorp had business involvement are eligible.
Restrictions: The foundation does not support sports programs, political organizations, individual schools, individuals, or organizations that are not classified 501(c)3.
Geographic Focus: Massachusetts, Rhode Island
Contact: Stacie Charbonneau; (508) 235-1368; info@stoicofirstfed.org
Internet: http://www.stoicofirstfed.org/apply.htm
Sponsor: Robert F. Stoico / FIRSTFED Charitable Foundation
P.O. Box 438
Swansea, MA 02777

Robert G. Cabell III and Maude Morgan Cabell Foundation Grants 4113
The foundation supports capital projects of Virginia nonprofit organizations in the areas of arts and culture, community development, higher education, historic preservation, the arts and culture, religion (Christian, Episcopal, Protestant, and Roman Catholic), social services, and community welfare. Preference will be given to the Richmond, Virginia, area. There are no application forms. Applicants may submit a written proposal that includes a brief description of the overall mission of the organization, a brief description of how the specific project supports the overall mission, a project budget, the level and type of support for the project from the local area, applicant's current operating budget and most recent budget, list of governing board and its officers, evidence of 501(c)3 status, and cover letter. Proposals are considered at grant review meetings each spring and fall.
Requirements: Virginia 501(c)3 tax-exempt organizations that are not classified as private foundations or private operating foundations are eligible.
Restrictions: The foundation does not make grants to individuals, primary or secondary schools, or state-supported organizations; nor will grants be made for debt reduction, endowments (except for faculty development), general operating expenses, research, or scholarships.
Geographic Focus: District of Columbia, Maryland, Virginia
Date(s) Application is Due: Apr 1; Oct 1
Amount of Grant: 25,000 - 500,000 USD
Contact: Jill A. McCormick; (804) 780-2050; Cabell.foundation@gmail.com
Sponsor: Robert G. Cabell III and Maude Morgan Cabell Foundation
901 E Cary Street, Suite 1402
Richmond, VA 23219-4037

Robert Lee Adams Foundation Grants 4114
Established in 1993, the Robert Lee Adams Foundation offers general operating support funding throughout the State of California, though its region of concentration is the Los Angeles metropolitan area. The Foundation's primary fields of interest have been youth camps and human services. Applications are required and accepted at any time, though interested parties should first contact the office with a one- to two-page letter of interest delineating the need and budgetary desires.
Geographic Focus: California
Contact: Julian Eli Capata, Trustee; (213) 739-2022
Sponsor: Robert Lee Adams Foundation
3580 Wilshire Boulevard, 10th Floor
Los Angeles, CA 90010-2543

Robert Lee Blaffer Foundation Grants 4115
Established in Indiana in 2001, the Robert Lee Blaffer Foundation offers support primarily in the State of Indiana. The Foundations primary fields of interest include: education; operating support for community charities; and human services. There is no specific application form, and organizations interested in applying should contact the office directly. Final submissions should be in the form of a letter which includes: name and description of the requesting organization; and purpose of the grant; budget detail. The annual deadline is March 31
Geographic Focus: Indiana
Date(s) Application is Due: Mar 31
Contact: Gary Gerard, Secretary; (812) 682-3631
Sponsor: Robert Lee Blaffer Foundation
P.O. Box 399
New Harmony, IN 47631-0399

Robert M. Hearin Foundation Grants 4116
The foundation awards grants to four-year colleges and universities in Mississippi. Areas of interest include program development and improvement, research, scholarships, and faculty development. There are no application deadlines or forms.
Geographic Focus: Mississippi
Amount of Grant: 200,000 - 650,000 USD
Contact: Daisy Blackwell, (601) 366-8363; fax (601) 961-6876
Sponsor: Robert M. Hearin Foundation
P.O. Box 16505
Jackson, MS 39207

Robert P. & Clara I. Milton Fund for Senior Housing 4117
The purpose of this fund is to support innovative programs focusing on issues related to senior housing. Projects will be considered that make a meaningful impact while promoting dignity, independence and quality of life. This fund strives to make St. Joseph County a regional model for senior housing by acting as a catalyst through the funding of innovative approaches. Senior housing may range from institutional care to in-home care, as well as the various services related to this issue. Special consideration will be given to projects that serve the most vulnerable of the aging population. Priorities for funding include education/training; home and community based services; programs and project serving vulnerable seniors; and public policy issues. Grants are judged by community impact, concept/idea, improved solutions to current and projected needs, the ability to implement the project, the quality of need, and its sustainability.
Requirements: In addition to the online application, the following attachments are required: up to a two page proposal narrative; a detailed project budget; current board roster with officers identified; and proof of nonprofit status. Detailed guidelines and application are available at the website.
Restrictions: Annual appeals or membership contributions, grants to individuals directly or special event underwriting will not be funded.
Geographic Focus: Indiana
Date(s) Application is Due: May 1; Nov 1
Contact: Christopher Nanni; (574) 232-0041; fax (574) 233-1906; chris@cfsjc.org
Internet: http://www.cfsjc.org/initiatives/senior/milton_grants.html
Sponsor: Community Foundation of St. Joseph County
205 W Jefferson Boulevard, P.O. Box 837
South Bend, IN 46624

Robert R. McCormick Tribune Foundation Civics Grants 4118
The McCormick Foundation Civics area supports initiatives that help build the foundation of knowledge, skills, attitudes, and experiences that lead to lifelong civic participation. Funding concentrates on Chicago area youth ages 12-22. Civics grantmaking focuses on four areas: civic education to improve civic knowledge, skills, and attitudes through classroom based programs and curriculum; civic engagement - to help youth development lifelong civic habits and provide meaningful opportunities for them to becomes positive change agents in their communities; professional development and training for educators - to support programs that provide educators with the knowledge, capacity, and efficacy necessary to develop or implement high quality, relevant, and engaging civic coursework and activities; and policy change - to change civic education policy and strengthen the civic education system in local school districts. The Foundation accepts requests up to $50,000 at any time. These proposals are reviewed monthly by foundation staff. For requests over $50,000, letters of inquiry should be submitted no later than December 1 for consideration at the February board of directors meeting.
Requirements: Nonprofit 501(c)3 organizations may apply. Before submitting a full proposal, organizations should send a letter of inquiry that describes their organization's mission, the amount of funding requested, and the nature and purpose of the proposed program or project.
Restrictions: Funding is focused on the Chicago area, but the Foundation also supports some national advocacy efforts with the potential for local impact.

Geographic Focus: Illinois
Contact: Andrea Jett Fletcher, Senior Program Officer; (312) 445-5000; fax (312) 445-5001; ajett@mccormickfoundation.org or info@mccormickfoundation.org
Internet: http://www.mccormickfoundation.org/page.aspx?pid=575
Sponsor: Robert R. McCormick Tribune Foundation
205 North Michigan Avenue, Suite 4300
Chicago, IL 60601

Robert R. McCormick Tribune Foundation Community Grants   4119
The Communities Program helps to transform communities by giving under-served people access to programs which improve their lives. The McCormick Foundation partners with media outlets, sports teams and philanthropic organizations to raise money for local needs and provides matching funds to increase the impact of charitable giving. Through the partnership, grants are made to qualified nonprofit organization with programs that help transition low-income children, adults and families to self-sufficiency. To achieve greater impact, the Foundation focuses on programs for children and youth in education, literacy, health & wellness and abuse prevention; hunger & housing; and adult workforce development and literacy. The McCormick Foundation is committed to measurable change with these projects and monitors the impact of all grants made. Community grants are made on the basis of requests received from 501(c)3 organizations in each local community where the Foundation has fundraising partners (Chicago, Denver, Fort Lauderdale, Los Angeles, Orlando, Washington, D.C., and Long Island, New York). Each fund partner has a unique set of guidelines that emphasize the needs of the particular community. Areas of focus include: child abuse prevention and treatment; child and youth education; health and wellness; housing; hunger; literacy; workforce development; and youth sports.
Requirements: Organizations must apply through the individual funding partners listed on the Foundation website.
Restrictions: Funding is not available for individuals or for-profit organizations.
Geographic Focus: California, Colorado, District of Columbia, Florida, Illinois, New York
Contact: Lesley Kennedy, Communities Program Officer; (312) 445-5000; info@mccormickfoundation.org
Internet: http://www.mccormickfoundation.org/page.aspx?pid=594
Sponsor: Robert R. McCormick Tribune Foundation
205 North Michigan Avenue, Suite 4300
Chicago, IL 60601

Robert R. McCormick Tribune Veterans Initiative Grants   4120
The mission of the McCormick Foundation Veterans Initiative is to create welcoming and inclusive communities for returning military and their families where each is able to reach their maximum potential. Current initiatives include workforce development programs to create pathways to careers for new veterans; a peer to peer model to assist veterans in finding pathways to information, services, and connection with other veterans; and strategic partnerships with medical centers across the country, local VA medical centers, and research institutions to explore innovative strategies to engage veterans and their families in mental health services that are user friendly, free of stigma, and readily accessible. A detailed list of previously funded project is available at the Foundation website. The application process and deadlines vary according to individual program.
Requirements: Grantees are solicited through a request for proposal (RFP) process at the Foundation website.
Restrictions: Support is concentrated in the Chicago area, but other locations are considered for funding.
Geographic Focus: Illinois
Contact: Anna LauBach, Director of Veterans Initiatives; (312) 445-5000; fax (312) 445-5001; ALauBach@mccormickfoundation.org
Internet: http://donate.mccormickfoundation.org/page.aspx?pid=627
Sponsor: Robert R. McCormick Tribune Foundation
205 North Michigan Avenue, Suite 4300
Chicago, IL 60601

Robert R. Meyer Foundation Grants   4121
The Robert R. Meyer Foundation is a private foundation established in 1949 by Mr. Robert R. Meyer and further funded by bequests from the wills of Robert R. Meyer and John Meyer. Mr. Meyer desired that assets from his foundation be used to address needs in Birmingham and its vicinity. The foundation has made awards in the areas of arts and culture, education, environment, health, human services, and public/society benefit. The foundation meets twice a year in the spring and fall to review proposals. Applicants should contact the Trustee for application forms and guidelines.
Requirements: Giving is limited to 501(c)3 organizations in the metropolitan Birmingham, Alabama area. All applicant organizations are encouraged (but not required) to join the Alabama Association of Nonprofits.
Geographic Focus: Alabama
Date(s) Application is Due: Mar 1; Sep 1
Amount of Grant: 5,000 - 100,000 USD
Contact: Carla B. Gale, Vice President and Trust Officer; (205) 326-5382
Sponsor: Robert R. Meyer Foundation
P.O. Box 11647
Birmingham, AL 35202-1647

Robert Sterling Clark Foundation Arts and Culture Grants   4122
For more than two decades, the Foundation has provided support for the arts in deference to Robert Sterling Clark's lifelong love of art and the world of collecting. The Foundation has determined that that the most constructive way to provide support is to help arts organizations manage what resources they have in the most effective way possible to achieve their artistic goals. These management issues are supported within the context of capacity building. Capacity building activities fall into several broad categories including defining one's mission, planning strategically, promoting good governance, developing resources, and managing the day to day activities that help transform inspiration into art. Activities supported include: program assessment and long-range strategic planning; board recruitment and development; development of individual contributions; generation of related and non-related earned income; marketing of artistic programs and services; implementation of effective accounting and financial reporting systems; high technology applications; and joint marketing aimed at reducing expenses of participating organizations. Capacity building grants are limited to organizations based in New York City having an annual operating budget of $500,000 or more.
Requirements: Capacity building grants are limited to organizations based in New York City having an annual operating budget of $500,000 or more.
Restrictions: Grants are not awarded to support individuals or arts in education programs.
Geographic Focus: New York
Amount of Grant: 1,000 - 200,000 USD
Contact: Margaret C. Ayers; (212) 288-8900; fax (212) 288-1033; rcsf@rsclark.org
Internet: http://www.rsclark.org/index.php?page=art-and-culture
Sponsor: Robert Suiterling Clark Foundation
135 East 64th Street
New York, NY 10065-7045

Robert Sterling Clark Foundation Government Accountability Grants   4123
The underlying premise of the Foundation's interest in government performance is that government agencies and employees will deliver better services to the public in a more cost-effective manner if their activities are examined, evaluated and held up to public view. In supporting advocacy organizations, the first of the Foundation's objectives is to safeguard the well-being of those who are most dependent on government programs. Thus, many of its grantees seek to improve policies that affect low-income New Yorkers and other vulnerable individuals served by publicly funded agencies (e.g. children in foster care, the elderly, and families attempting to move from welfare to work). With regard to the last of these, the Foundation is particularly interested in promoting the implementation of programs to help the adults in such families obtain education, training, and job placement as well as access to child care. A second objective of this grant-making program is to help ensure that all children in the State receive an adequate education. Finally, the Foundation's grant-making also supports some efforts to improve city and state policies in areas such as solid waste management, land use planning, and protection of parks and open space.
Geographic Focus: New York
Amount of Grant: 1,000 - 200,000 USD
Contact: Margaret C. Ayers; (212) 288-8900; fax (212) 288-1033; rcsf@rsclark.org
Internet: http://www.rsclark.org/index.php?page=government-accountability
Sponsor: Robert Suiterling Clark Foundation
135 East 64th Street
New York, NY 10065-7045

Robert W. Woodruff Foundation Grants   4124
The foundation is interested in supporting programs and projects in the areas of elementary, secondary, and higher education; health care and education; Human services, particularly for children and youth; economic development and civic affairs; art and cultural activities; and conservation of natural resources and environmental education. Preference is given to one-time capital projects, matching/challenge grants, specific projects, construction, land acquisition, and equipment purchases.
Requirements: Most grants are awarded to tax-exempt organizations in Georgia. Grants to qualified public charities headquartered outside Georgia are considered when it is demonstrated that the proposed project or program will have particular impact in Georgia. Application forms are not required. Proposals should be made in letter form and describe the organization, including its purposes, staffing, and governing board; latest financial statement and most recent audit report; description of the proposed project and justification for funding; itemized project budget, including other sources of support; and evidence of tax-exempt status. The board meets in April and November to consider requests.
Restrictions: Grants are not awarded to support individuals, annual operating support, festivals and performances, conferences, films and documentaries, start-up funding or seed money, churches or their denominational programs, or youth services outside Atlanta.
Geographic Focus: Georgia
Date(s) Application is Due: Feb 1; Sep 1
Amount of Grant: 50,000 - 750,000 USD
Contact: P. Russell Hardin; (404) 522-6755; fax (404) 522-7026; fdns@woodruff.org
Internet: http://www.woodruff.org/appGuidelines_rww.aspx
Sponsor: Robert W. Woodruff Foundation
50 Hurt Plaza, Suite 1200
Atlanta, GA 30303

Robin Hood Foundation Grants   4125
The foundation's mission is to end poverty in New York City. Robin Hood makes grants to poverty-fighting organizations that are direct service providers operating in the five boroughs of New York City and has a continuing commitment to community-based programs and strong leaders in the city's poorest neighborhoods. First time grant requests are generally in the area of $100,000 to $200,000. Robin Hood will consider requests for a variety of purposes, including specific programs, salaries or start-up costs. Capital, renovation and general operating funds are given only to those groups already receiving Robin Hood support.
Requirements: Robin Hood seeks to fund 501(c)3 tax-exempt nonprofits in New York City with the following characteristics: proven track record; bold idea that is feasible; clear sense of mission and the steps needed to accomplish that mission; strong, committed leadership;

existing evaluation procedures or willingness to evaluate programs and measure outcomes; commitment to, and knowledge of, the population served; high quality, dedicated staff; financial stability; and, respect or standing in its community and relationships with other organizations in the community. Applications are accepted year-round, and grant decisions will be made on a quarterly basis although decisions may take up to one year. Contact the Grants Manager before completing an application.
Restrictions: Programs that do not wish to evaluate the outcomes of their efforts should not apply to Robin Hood for funds. In general, Robin Hood does not make grants to technical assistance providers, other funders, or individuals. Robin Hood does not give grants to distribute propaganda, to attempt to influence legislation or the outcome of any public election or to engage in any activity that is not exclusively charitable, scientific or educational. Robin Hood will not support organizations that discriminate against people seeking either services or employment based on race, sex, religion, age, sexual orientation or physical disability.
Geographic Focus: New York
Amount of Grant: Up to 200,000 USD
Contact: Karen Moody, (212) 227-6601; fax (212) 227-6698; grants@robinhood.org
Internet: https://www.robinhood.org/programs/get-funding
Sponsor: Robin Hood Foundation
826 Broadway, 9th Floor
New York, NY 10003

Robins Foundation Grants 4126
The foundation awards grants to nonprofit organizations in the Richmond, VA, area. Areas of interest include general grants—including cultural, charitable, scientific, environmental, and educational programs, and at-risk youth; and early childhood/quality improvement grants— for organizations that devote a major portion of their resources to young children and their families. The goal is to help improve the quality of services by providing funding for accreditation, staff training, facilities improvements, and similar initiatives. The foundation seeks projects that meet well-defined community needs, use effective approaches that build on proven programs, develop models with potential for wider application, foster self-reliance and/or end dependency, and focus on prevention as well as treatment. Types of support include capital grants and endowments.
Requirements: 501(c)3 organizations based in Virginia are eligible. Organizations based in Virginia that have or support programs outside Virginia or the United States also are eligible.
Restrictions: In general, the foundation does not make grants to support annual operating funds or budgets, special events or fundraising benefits, or religious purposes unless they are otherwise compatible with the objectives of the foundation.
Geographic Focus: Virginia
Contact: William Roberts Jr., Executive Director; (804) 697-6917; fax (804) 697-6797; wlrjr@robins-foundation.org
Internet: http://www.robins-foundation.org
Sponsor: Robins Foundation
Capitol Station, P.O. Box 1124
Richmond, VA 23218-1124

Rochester Area Community Foundation Grants 4127
The foundation seeks to improve the quality of life in the community and awards grants in the areas of child development, education, the environment, arts and cultural programs, health services, community development, and social services and general charitable giving. Types of support include general operating support, building construction/renovation, equipment acquisition, program development, conferences and seminars, publication, seed grants, scholarship funds, technical assistance, consulting services, and scholarships to individuals. There are no application deadlines. The board meets in January, February, March, May, June, July, October, and November.
Requirements: Nonprofits in Monroe, Livingston, Ontario, Orleans, Genessee, and Wayne Counties, NY, are eligible.
Restrictions: Grants do not support partisan political organizations or religious projects, individuals, annual campaigns, deficit financing, land acquisition, endowments, or emergency funds.
Geographic Focus: New York
Contact: Marlene Cole; (585) 341-4333; fax (585) 271-4292; mcole@racf.org
Internet: http://www.racf.org/page10000903.cfm
Sponsor: Rochester Area Community Foundation
500 East Avenue
Rochester, NY 14607-1912

Rochester Area Foundation Grants 4128
The foundation makes grants in the fields of arts and culture, community development, education, human services and recreation in the greater Rochester, Minnesota area.
Requirements: Organizations must be one of the following to be eligible to receive grant funding: a tax-exempt 501(c)3 organization, a government unit (city, township, county), or a government-created organization such as a public agency. Download the required pre-application form from the website. If your pre-application is approved, you will be notified and asked to submit a full application to the foundation. (The required full application form is also available at the website.)
Geographic Focus: Minnesota
Date(s) Application is Due: Jan 2; May 1; Sep 1
Contact: Steve Thornton, Executive Director; (507) 424-2400 or (507) 424-3755, ext. 102; fax (507) 282-4938; Steve@RochesterArea.org
Internet: http://www.rochesterarea.org/grant-resources/index.html
Sponsor: Rochester Area Foundation
400 South Broadway, Suite 300
Rochester, MN 55904

Rockefeller Brothers Fund Charles E. Culpeper Arts and Culture Grants in New York City 4129
The Fund seeks to foster an environment in which artists and the creative process can flourish by supporting organizations that assist individual artists and the creative process, provide infrastructure to sustain the artistic life, and offer additional opportunities to artists for developing skills complementary to their creative talents. In addition, the Fund seeks to sustain and advance small and mid-size cultural organizations, particularly those that are community based and/or culturally specific through the following strategies: supporting core operations by providing non-renewable, two-year capacity-building grants of up to $50,000 per year; strengthening long-term financial viability by providing endowment grants and cash reserve grants of up to $250,000 to cultural and arts organizations that demonstrate the potential for long-term leadership and excellence in the presentation of creative work to the broadest possible audiences; enhancing institutional leadership through competitive awards to arts and cultural organizations for innovative, team-based leadership conferences designed to strengthen long-range organizational management and governance; and offering grants of up to $15,000 to cover the costs of the leadership conference, including the participation of professional consultants, advisors, or facilitators (following completion of a leadership conference, the Fund may make an additional award of up to $25,000 to support the participating organization's efforts to implement some aspects of what was learned through the conference.
Requirements: A prospective grantee must be located in New York City, and must be either a tax-exempt organization or an organization seeking support for a project that would qualify as educational or charitable.
Restrictions: The fund does not make grants to individuals, nor does it as a general rule support research, graduate study, or the writing of books or dissertations by individuals.
Geographic Focus: New York
Amount of Grant: Up to 250,000 USD
Contact: Ben Rodriguez-Cubenas; (212) 812-4200; fax (212) 812-4299; info@rbf.org
Internet: http://www.rbf.org/programs/
Sponsor: Rockefeller Brothers Fund
437 Madison Avenue, 37th Floor
New York, NY 10022-7001

Rockefeller Brothers Fund Cross-Programmatic Initiative: Energy Grants 4130
In 2006, the Fund decided to examine the issue of sustainable energy as a cross-cutting programmatic theme that would connect RBF's core interests in sustainable development, peace and security, and democratic practice. By overlaying the RBF program structure lens on the energy challenges of the 21st century, the Fund can focus on energy as a pivotal issue and explore the strategic opportunities to accelerate a transition to an alternative energy future. On October 12, 2006, RBF trustees approved grantmaking in the area called Cross-Programmatic Initiative: Energy. Work within this pivotal issue offers the opportunity to reshape the energy system by advancing conservation and efficiency and by accelerating the development and implementation of alternatives in order to enhance security, promote development and economic growth, and protect against the devastating impacts of global warming.
Requirements: A prospective grantee in the United States or foreign counterpart must be either a tax-exempt organization or an organization seeking support for a project that would qualify as educational or charitable.
Restrictions: The fund does not make grants to individuals, nor does it as a general rule support research, graduate study, or the writing of books or dissertations by individuals.
Geographic Focus: All States
Contact: Elizabeth C. Campbell, (212) 812-4200; fax (212) 812-4299; info@rbf.org
Internet: http://www.rbf.org/programs/programs_show.htm?doc_id=512777
Sponsor: Rockefeller Brothers Fund
437 Madison Avenue, 37th Floor
New York, NY 10022-7001

Rockefeller Brothers Fund Democratic Practice Grants 4131
The Fund's Democratic Practice program has two parts: the health of democracy in the United States and the strength of democracy in global governance. Each focus has two distinct goals. Based on a careful assessment of local needs and priorities, the Fund may also pursue one or more of these goals in a limited number of its pivotal places. Recognizing that there is no single model of effective democratic practice, the Fund emphasizes flexibility and adaptability to different contexts in these pivotal places.
Requirements: A prospective grantee in the United States or foreign counterpart must be either a tax-exempt organization or an organization seeking support for a project that would qualify as educational or charitable.
Restrictions: The fund does not make grants to individuals, nor does it as a general rule support research, graduate study, or the writing of books or dissertations by individuals.
Geographic Focus: All States
Contact: Benjamin R. Shute; (212) 812-4200; fax (212) 812-4299; info@rbf.org
Internet: http://www.rbf.org/programs/
Sponsor: Rockefeller Brothers Fund
437 Madison Avenue, 37th Floor
New York, NY 10022-7001

Rockefeller Brothers Fund Fellowship in Nonprofit Law 4132
The fellowship permits one fellow each year to spend one year in residence at the Vera Institute of Justice in New York City, working closely with Vera's general counsel and special counsel on legal issues. The fellowship will provide a law school graduate with exposure to a wide variety of legal and organizational issues encountered by nonprofit organizations. It also will provide the opportunity to identify an emerging or changing area of law with particular significance for nonprofits. Fellows will be selected without regard to race, color, religion, gender, political beliefs, national origin, disability, age, or sexual orientation.

Requirements: Graduates of accredited U.S. law schools are eligible.
Geographic Focus: All States
Date(s) Application is Due: Dec 5
Amount of Grant: 47,000 USD
Contact: Erin Bainbridge Ortiz; (212) 998-6168; fax (212) 995-3149; ncpl.info@nyu.edu
Internet: http://www.rbf.org/grantsdatabase/grantsdatabase_show.htm?doc_id=616213
Sponsor: National Center on Philanthropy and the Law
110 W Third Street, Room 205
New York, NY 10012

Rockefeller Brothers Fund Peace and Security Grants 4133
The Fund's Peace and Security Program focuses on two factors that may be key to advancing or undermining global problem solving: the content and style of U.S. global engagement in the face of new perils and opportunities; and the strength and quality of relationships between Muslim and Western societies. In addition, peace and security is a theme that may be identified for attention in one or more of the Fund's pivotal places. Two specific goals have emerged: to advance U.S. policies and behaviors that reflect a broadly shared vision of constructive, cooperative, principled, farsighted, and effective global engagement; and to reduce the divisive and destabilizing tensions that exist between much of the Islamic world and the West, particularly the United States, and to increase the potential for collaboration among Muslim and Western societies on behalf of a better, safer world.
Requirements: A prospective grantee in the United States or foreign counterpart must be either a tax-exempt organization or an organization seeking support for a project that would qualify as educational or charitable.
Restrictions: The fund does not make grants to individuals, nor does it as a general rule support research, graduate study, or the writing of books or dissertations by individuals.
Geographic Focus: All States
Amount of Grant: 25,000 - 300,000 USD
Contact: Benjamin R. Shute; (212) 812-4200; fax (212) 812-4299; info@rbf.org
Internet: http://www.rbf.org/programs/
Sponsor: Rockefeller Brothers Fund
437 Madison Avenue, 37th Floor
New York, NY 10022-7001

Rockefeller Brothers Fund Pivotal Places Grants: New York City 4134
Three of the Fund's four program interests are reflected in the RBF's engagement with New York City as a pivotal place. Aside from its programs supporting human advancement, the Fund also supports building sustainable communities and encouraging civic engagement. Specifically, the Fund seeks to improve the safety, aesthetic quality, and the spiritual and community life of New York City neighborhoods by: assisting community-based initiatives that encourage respect and care for the natural and built environment and that enhance or reclaim public space; supporting opportunities for community engagement in local development and planning processes; and advancing innovative ideas and projects that promote the concept of New York as a sustainable city. Further, the Fund seeks to improve the quality of life in disadvantaged neighborhoods by: supporting civic initiatives and community processes that address locally identified priorities; strengthening community leadership capacity, particularly among immigrant populations; encouraging collaboration among local institutions and across sectors.
Requirements: A prospective grantee must be located in New York City, and must be either a tax-exempt organization or an organization seeking support for a project that would qualify as educational or charitable.
Restrictions: The fund does not make grants to individuals, nor does it as a general rule support research, graduate study, or the writing of books or dissertations by individuals.
Geographic Focus: New York
Contact: Ben Rodriguez-Cubenas; (212) 812-4200; fax (212) 812-4299; info@rbf.org
Internet: http://www.rbf.org/programs/
Sponsor: Rockefeller Brothers Fund
437 Madison Avenue, 37th Floor
New York, NY 10022-7001

Rockefeller Brothers Fund Pivotal Places Grants: Serbia, Montenegro, and Kosova 4135
The Fund has been engaged in grantmaking in Serbia, Montenegro, and Kosovo, and will continue to focus primarily on those three places, while reserving flexibility to support exceptional regional and cross-frontier efforts. The Fund now concentrates its grantmaking on two of its four programmatic themes: Democratic Practice and Sustainable Development. This reflects the Fund's assessment that helping to build tolerant and pluralistic democracy and to promote sustainable development in the region represent top priorities and opportunities for significant impact. Major goals of this Fund include: improving the performance, accountability, and transparency of government; strengthening constituencies of citizens actively engaged in building democracy; and supporting efforts to nurture economically, ecologically, and socially sustainable urban and rural communities through processes that actively engage diverse stakeholders.
Requirements: A prospective grantee in the United States or foreign counterpart must be either a tax-exempt organization or an organization seeking support for a project that would qualify as educational or charitable.
Restrictions: The fund does not make grants to individuals, nor does it as a general rule support research, graduate study, or the writing of books or dissertations by individuals.
Geographic Focus: All States
Contact: William S. Moody; (212) 812-4200; fax (212) 812-4299; info@rbf.org
Internet: http://www.rbf.org/programs/
Sponsor: Rockefeller Brothers Fund
437 Madison Avenue, 37th Floor
New York, NY 10022-7001

Rockefeller Brothers Fund Sustainable Development Grants 4136
The Fund's sustainable development grant making endeavors to address global challenges by supporting environmental stewardship that is ecologically based, economically sound, socially just, culturally appropriate, and consistent with intergenerational equity. The Fund encourages government, business, and civil society to work collaboratively on environmental conservation and to make it an integral part of all development planning and activity. Recognizing the global nature of many environmental problems, the Fund also promotes international cooperation in addressing these challenges. Some of the Fund's sustainable development strategies are pursued at the global level, while others are pursued primarily in North America. The Russian Far East is the focus of a modest program of grant making. Major goals include: combating global warming; protecting ecosystems; and conserving biodiversity. In all regions where the RBF is engaged in sustainable development grant making, it monitors the social and environmental effects of development programs and fiscal policies that are associated with global economic integration and seeks to integrate activities across geographic areas to promote maximum impact.
Requirements: A prospective grantee in the United States or foreign counterpart must be either a tax-exempt organization or an organization seeking support for a project that would qualify as educational or charitable.
Restrictions: The fund does not make grants to individuals, nor does it as a general rule support research, graduate study, or the writing of books or dissertations by individuals.
Geographic Focus: All States
Amount of Grant: 25,000 - 300,000 USD
Contact: Michael Northrop; (212) 812-4200; fax (212) 812-4299; info@rbf.org
Internet: http://www.rbf.org/programs/
Sponsor: Rockefeller Brothers Fund
437 Madison Avenue, 37th Floor
New York, NY 10022-7001

Rockefeller Family Fund Grants 4137
The fund makes grants in four program areas: citizen participation and government accountability, economic justice for women, the environment, institutional responsiveness, and self-sufficiency. Grants support advocacy efforts within these program areas that are action-oriented and likely to yield tangible public policy results. Funding is also given to organizations that seek to maintain or expand their financing in innovative ways or from non-foundation sources. Applicants should submit a letter of inquiry of no more than two pages summarizing the goals of the project; the strategy or plan for achieving the goals; and the amount of funding requested. There are no application deadlines. Guidelines are available online.
Requirements: Tax-exempt organizations engaged in activities of national significance are eligible. The fund does not ordinarily consider projects that pertain to a single community, except in the rare instance where a project is unique, strategically placed to advance a national issue, or is likely to serve as a national model.
Restrictions: Grants do not support academic or scholarly research, or social or human service programs. Nor are grants made to support individuals, scholarships, international programs, domestic programs dealing with international issues, profit-making businesses, construction or restoration projetcs, or to reduce an organization's debt. In addition, grants are normally made to the same organization for no more than two years at a time, and except in extraordinary cases, are not given to the same organization for more than three or four consecutive years.
Geographic Focus: All States
Amount of Grant: 25,000 - 30,000 USD
Contact: Administrator; (212) 812-4252; fax (212) 812-4299; mmccarthy@rffund.org
Internet: http://www.rffund.org
Sponsor: Rockefeller Family Fund
437 Madison Avenue, 37th Floor
New York, NY 10022

Rockefeller Foundation Grants 4138
The foundation provides grants to institutions and individuals seeking to improve the lives of poor people with a focus on the issues and region where the foundation works. The foundation works globally but provides the majority of its grants to organizations whose work is focused in Southern and Eastern Africa, Southeast Asia, and North America through programs that address agriculture, health, employment, housing, education, arts and culture, and global policy. The foundation also operates special programs, including a conference and study program at its Bellagio Center, the Program Venture Experiment, and the Philanthropy Workshop.
Requirements: Nonprofit organizations are eligible.
Restrictions: The foundation does not give or lend money for personal aid to individuals, support attempts to influence legislation, or, except in rare cases, provide general institutional support, fund endowments, or contribute to building and operating funds.
Geographic Focus: All States
Contact: Grants Administrator; (212) 869-8500; fax (212) 764-3468
Internet: http://www.rockfound.org/grants/grants.shtml
Sponsor: Rockefeller Foundation
420 Fifth Avenue
New York, NY 10018-2702

Rockefeller Foundation Partnerships Affirming Commun Transformation Grants 4139
This program supports projects in any medium in which local arts and community organizations use their artistic and organization skills to advance the development of an identified community. Projects must draw on the cultural backgrounds and experiences of participants, encouraging social and cultural creativity in shaping the project itself and contributing to community cultural development. Preference will be given to projects that most directly and comprehensively give voice to poor and excluded peole; allow cultural

democracy and exchange on an equal basis; provide a critical examination of cultural values; endeavor to frame public discourse; strive to effect change at the core of society; and explore or expand the social role of the artist. Applications should outline proposed partnerships and the projected roles of partners.
Requirements: The grant application must be made by a tax-exempt organization that is a partner in the process and acts in a fiduciary capacity as the formal grant recipient.
Geographic Focus: All States
Amount of Grant: 10,000 - 50,000 USD
Contact: Program Contact; (212) 852-8286; pact@rockfound.org
Internet: http://www.rockfound.org/grants/grants.shtml
Sponsor: Rockefeller Foundation
420 Fifth Avenue
New York, NY 10018-2702

Rockwell Fund, Inc. Grants 4140
Rockwell Fund, Inc. was founded in 1931 from the estate of James M. Rockwell. Rockwell's grant making is concentrated on the following issue areas: community health, concentrating on health issues that affect the broader community, including mental and behavioral health; education, concentrating on dropout prevention strategies that target the intermediate and middle school years; employment, concentrating on training/placement and jobs creation/enterprise development opportunities; and supportive housing, concentrating on affordable housing coupled with onsite, sustained services to support individuals and families in achieving self-sufficiency.
Requirements: Eligible applicants must be nonprofit tax exempt organizations. To be eligible, an organization must: have a determination letter from the Internal Revenue Service indicating that it is an organization described in Section 501(c)3 of the Internal Revenue Code or be a church or political subdivision that is not required to obtain a Section 501(c)3 designation in order to be a permitted donee of a private foundation. Funding is provided for the Houston area or in some cases for a purpose that will benefit a Houston cause. Interested applicants must first complete an on-line inquiry form. Applicants will then either be invited to submit a full grant application for further consideration or declined. Inquiries are accepted throughout the year.
Restrictions: The following projects or programs are ineligible: feasibility studies; annual fund drives; direct mail or other mass solicitations; grants that impose the exercise of "expenditure responsibility" upon Rockwell Fund, for example, private operating foundations or certain support organizations; houses of worship; individuals; medical or scientific research projects or organizations that target a specific disease; parochial or private primary and secondary schools; and underwriting for benefits, dinners, galas, golf tournaments or other fundraising or special events.
Geographic Focus: Texas
Contact: Judy Ahlgrim; (713) 341-5338; fax (713) 629-7702; jahlgrim@rockfund.org
Internet: http://www.rockfund.org/giving/howToApply.shtml
Sponsor: Rockwell Fund, Inc.
770 S. Post Oak Lane, Suite 525
Houston, TX 77056

Rockwell International Corporate Trust Grants 4141
Grants are awarded in the areas of education and youth development, with emphasis in math, science, and engineering; and culture and the arts, with emphasis on youth educational programs. Rockwell also contributes to health, human services, and civic organizations and also gives special consideration to qualifying organizations in which employees are involved as volunteers. Types of support include capital grants, challenge/matching grants, conferences and seminars, development grants, endowments, research grants, scholarship funds, and general operating grants. Awards include single-year, multiple-year, and provisional continuing support of specific programs. Applicants should submit full, detailed proposals. Proposals are accepted at any time. At the Web site, click on About Us, then Corporate Citizenship, and then Rockwell Automation Corporation Trust.
Restrictions: Organizations are not eligible if they have not received a permanent, tax-exempt ruling determination from the federal government; if they cannot provide current full, certified, audited financial statements; or if they are private foundations. Funding will not be considered for the following purposes: general endowments, deficit reduction, grants to individuals, federated campaigns, organizations or projects outside the United States, religious organizations for religious purposes, or fraternal or social organizations.
Geographic Focus: All States
Amount of Grant: 1,000 - 50,000 USD
Contact: Rockwell International Corporation General Information; (562) 797-3311
Internet: http://www.rockwell.com
Sponsor: Rockwell International Corporate Trust
1201 S Second Street
Milwaukee, WI 53204

Roeher Institute Research Grants 4142
The institute, through the support of the Scottish Rite Charitable Foundation of Canada, offers research grants to associates, associations, and agencies in a broad range of fields relating to human services and intellectual disability. The renewable grants are offered for one year. Research projects must be under the direction of the Roeher Institute academic associates or other university faculty or under researchers approved by the Roeher Institute. Areas constituting research priorities for the Roeher Institute are issues affecting people with intellectual disabilities; integration of people who have an intellectual disability into society; prevention, early identification, and minimization of disabling conditions; and strategies for social change that improve the quality of life of persons with intellectual disabilities. Applicants are asked to submit a summary of their research project, budget, and financial requirements.
Requirements: Applications are invited from university faculty, department heads, supervisors, Roeher Institute associates, and/or consultants.
Geographic Focus: All States
Amount of Grant: Up to 10,000 CAD
Contact: Cameron Crawford, President; (416) 661-9611; fax (416) 661-5701; cameronc@roeher.ca or cameronc@worldchat.com
Internet: http://www.roeher.ca/english/about/about.htm
Sponsor: Roeher Institute
4700 Keele Street, York University, Kinsmen Building.
North York, ON M3J 1P3 Canada

Roger L. and Agnes C. Dell Charitable Trust II Grants 4143
The trust's major purpose is to assist education, the arts, and human service programs. The trust awards grants to eligible Minnesota nonprofit organizations in its areas of interest, including arts and culture, education, human services, Jewish agencies and temples, YMCAs, YWCAs, youth, and service programs. Types of support include funding for general operations and for specific project proposals.
Requirements: Minnesota 501(c)3 tax-exempt organizations in Fergus Falls and the surrounding area are eligible.
Restrictions: Individuals are not eligible for grants.
Geographic Focus: Minnesota
Date(s) Application is Due: Jun 15; Oct 15
Amount of Grant: 100 - 50,000 USD
Contact: Richard C. Hefte; (218) 998-3355; fax (218) 736-3950; dell@prtel.com
Sponsor: Roger L. and Agnes C. Dell Charitable Trust II
110 North Mill Street
Fergus Falls, MN 56537

Rogers Family Foundation Grants 4144
The Rogers Family Foundation funds nonprofit organizations that provide educational, medical, artistic, and religious services within Massachusetts' Merrimack Valley and North Shore and southeastern New Hampshire. See website for specific areas served.
Requirements: Applicants must be tax exempt under section 501(c)3 of the Internal Revenue Code and classified as "not a private foundation" under Section 509(a) of the Code. All applications are submitted on-line. The online application follows the Common Proposal designed and published by Associated Grant Makers, Inc. See website for detailed online application and instructions.
Restrictions: Traditionally the Foundation awards grants to organizations located in Massachusetts' Merrimack Valley and North Shore and southeastern New Hampshire. From time to time grants may be made outside of this normal geographic area.
Geographic Focus: Massachusetts, New Hampshire
Date(s) Application is Due: Mar 1; Sep 1
Amount of Grant: 25,000 USD
Contact: Susan Haff, (617) 426-7080; fax (617) 426-7087
Internet: http://www.rogersfamilyfoundation.com/app/
Sponsor: Rogers Family Foundation
c/o GMA Foundations
Boston, MA 02110

Rohm and Haas Company Grants 4145
The company awards grants in five key philanthropic categories: education, environment, civic and community, health and human services, and arts and culture. Education grants support programs linking education in science, technology, and math to workplace and career opportunities; and educational enrichment for students, particularly in the areas of math, science, technology, and the environment either during or after school hours (including weekends, summer, and other times when school is not in session). Environment grants support after-school programs that build environmental awareness and understanding; sustainability programs that educate and promote development that meets the needs of the present society without compromising the ability of future generations to meet their own needs; pollution prevention and waste management, environmental conservation and biodiversity, and energy and water conservation; and community beautification. Civic and community grants support regional efforts that build local competitiveness and strengthen the economic and social base in Rohm and Haas host communities; programs that cut across multiple giving categories and/or that impact key stakeholders in Rohm and Haas communities; and programs that focus on volunteerism. Health and human services grants support public safety awareness; disaster preparedness; structured youth development such as leadership training; and structured youth activities and recreation. Arts and culture grants support organizational capacity building in the form of plan implementation—technology implementation and/or enhancement, communications and marketing, outreach and audience development, financial management and fundraising, board development, strategic development, professional development, and educational program development. Application and guidelines are available online.
Requirements: Eligible national and international organizations include performing and visual arts, humanities and historical societies, and museums. Preference is given to requests from Chicago, IL, and the greater Philadelphia area.
Restrictions: Grants are not awarded to individuals or for fundraising, advertising, or testimonials.
Geographic Focus: All States
Amount of Grant: 250 - 50,000 USD
Contact: Alexandra Samuels, (215) 592-3644; alexandra_samuels@rohmhaas.com
Internet: http://www.rohmhaas.com/community/giving/guidelines/guidelines.html
Sponsor: Rohm and Haas Company
100 Independence Mall W
Philadelphia, PA 19106-2399

Rollin M. Gerstacker Foundation Grants 4146
The primary purpose of the foundation is to furnish financial aid to charities of all types supported by Mr. and Mrs. R.M. Gerstacker during their lifetimes. These charities are concentrated in Michigan and Ohio. The foundation's areas of interest include churches, community development, education, environment, health care, music and arts, research, social services, and youth, and grants are also awarded for services to the elderly and the emotionally disturbed. Some funds are designated for cultural programs and for colleges. Applications are accepted at any time.
Restrictions: Grants are not awarded to individuals, or for scholarships or fellowships
Geographic Focus: Michigan, Ohio
Date(s) Application is Due: Apr 15; Aug 15; Nov 15
Contact: E.N. Brandt, Vice President; (989) 631-6097; fax (989) 832-8842
Sponsor: Rollin M. Gerstacker Foundation
P.O. Box 1945
Midland, MI 48641-1945

Rollins-Luetkemeyer Foundation Grants 4147
The Foundation awards grants to eligible Maryland nonprofit organizations in its areas of interest, including education (early childhood, elementary school, and higher education), health care and health organizations, historic preservation/societies, and social services. Types of support include annual campaigns, building construction/renovation, general operating support, and project support.
Requirements: Applications are not required. Letters of intent are accepted at any time.
Restrictions: Maryland nonprofit organizations, with preference given to the Baltimore area, are eligible. No grants to individuals.
Geographic Focus: Maryland
Amount of Grant: 2,000 - 2,000,000 USD
Contact: John A. Luetkemeyer, Jr., President; (443) 921-4358
Sponsor: Rollins-Luetkemeyer Foundation
1427 Clarkview Road, Suite 500
Baltimore, MD 21209

Romic Environmental's Charitable Contributions Grants 4148
Romic's corporate giving program is designed to support effective local programs that enable the local community to develop its own long-term solutions for meeting residents' needs. This program gives the highest priority to effective local programs designed to keep children in school and build self-esteem; programs that introduce local youth to the world of computers, provide after-school tutoring, match mentors with at-risk youth, keep teenage mothers in school, and more; develop marketable job skills or job opportunities; and programs that abate drug abuse and crime.
Requirements: Programs must serve primarily East Palo Alto residents and be sponsored by IRS tax-exempt organizations.
Restrictions: Romic will not make contributions to individuals; religious, political, or fraternal organizations; fund-raising events; program advertisements; trips or tours.
Geographic Focus: California
Date(s) Application is Due: May 1; Nov 1
Contact: Chris Stampolis; (650) 462-2315; fax (650) 462-2311; chriss@romic.com
Sponsor: Romic Environmental
2081 Bay Road
East Palo Alto, CA 94303

Ronald McDonald House Charities Grants 4149
Ronald McDonald House Charities provides grants to nonprofit, tax-exempt organizations whose national or global programs help improve the health and well being of children under 21. Types of support include capital grants, challenge/matching grants, formula grants, professorships, program grants, research grants, scholarships, seed money grants, and visiting scholars. The board meets quarterly to review, select, and award grants to organizations that have demonstrated an ability to respond to the needs of specific groups of children in a definitive, hands-on manner that yields measurable results.
Requirements: To be considered for funding, an applicant must be designated a not-for-profit, tax-exempt charitable organization. U.S. charities must have a current 501(c)3 tax-exempt status letter on file with the Internal Revenue Service. Organizations seeking funding should have: a broad base of funding support; management and staff capacity to effectively execute the project; a longer-term organizational strategic plan (evidence to ensure program and organization sustainability); and a clear, concise plan for project evaluation with outcome measurement that shows potential for meaningful change. Organizations seeking funding should have a specific program that: directly improves the health and well being of children; addresses a significant funding gap or critical opportunity; has long-term impact in terms of replication or reach; produces measurable results; and is sustainable without relying on RMHC funding. Prior to submitting a full proposal, organizations must submit a letter of inquiry which will be reviewed by the Board. If interested, the Board will invite organizations to submit a formal grant proposal.
Restrictions: The charity does not fund projects/programs that are local in scope and that do not benefit children under 21; to reduce debt; for annual fund appeals; for medical research; for for-profit organizations; for fundraising sponsorships; for programs/projects administered by activist groups; for projects that have already been completed; for sectarian or religious purposes; for scholarships and fellowships to individuals; to propagandize or influence elections or legislation; for advertising or fundraising drives; to intermediary funding agencies; for endowment campaigns; for individuals.
Geographic Focus: All States
Date(s) Application is Due: Mar 5; Sep 7
Contact: Michael Singer; (630) 623-7048; fax (630) 623-7488; grants@rmhc.org
Internet: http://rmhc.org/what-we-do/grants/how-to-apply/
Sponsor: Ronald McDonald House Charities
1 Kroc Drive
Oak Brook, IL 60523

Roney-Fitzpatrick Foundation Grants 4150
The Roney-Fitzpatrick Foundation was established to offer support in the central region of New Jersey (although grants are sometimes given throughout the United States). Its primary fields of interest include both education and human service programs. Types of funding are limited to general operating costs. There are no specified application formats or annual deadlines, and interested parties should begin by contacting the grant office with a letter describing the program and financial need. Recent funding amounts have ranged from $300 to $6,000.
Requirements: Nonprofit organizations throughout the United States are eligible to apply, although emphasis is on central New Jersey.
Restrictions: Foundation grants are not given to individuals.
Geographic Focus: All States
Amount of Grant: 4,600 - 200,000 USD
Contact: Edwin J. Fitzpatrick, Trustee; (212) 922-8189
Sponsor: Roney-Fitzpatrick Foundation
P.O. Box 185
Pittsburgh, PA 15230-0185

Rosalynn Carter Institute Georgia Caregiver of the Year Awards 4151
To honor their work and to focus public attention on the contributions of caregivers throughout the State of Georgia, the Rosalynn Carter Institute on Caregiving in cooperation with the Georgia CARE-NETS initiated the Georgia Caregiver of the Year Awards in 2007. Awardess are presented with a gilded rose and a check for $1,000.
Requirements: Nominees must be caregivers from the State of Georgia.
Geographic Focus: Georgia
Amount of Grant: 1,000 USD
Contact: Laura Bauer Granberry; (229) 931-2034; fax (229) 931-2663; lbgran@gsw.edu
Internet: http://www.rosalynncarter.org/caregiver2/
Sponsor: Rosalynn Carter Institute for Caregiving
800 GSW Drive
Americus, GA 31709-4379

Rose Community Foundation Aging Grants 4152
In its Aging program area, Rose Community Foundation promotes change in how communities organize care and support for both seniors and caregivers, with particular attention to the needs of low- and moderate-income seniors. In addition to funding community-based programs, the Foundation plays a leadership role in strengthening the existing network of aging resources, including initiatives that bring together community and government partners to address key issues in aging. The Foundation is especially interested in projects that address the following priorities: direct in-home and community-based services; transportation; and end-of-life care.
Requirements: Colorado 501(c)3 tax-exempt organizations serving the residents of Adams, Arapahoe, Boulder, Denver, Douglas, and Jefferson Counties are eligible.
Geographic Focus: Colorado
Contact: Therese Ellery; (303) 398-7413 or (303) 398-7400; tellery@rcfdenver.org
Internet: http://www.rcfdenver.org/programs_aging.htm
Sponsor: Rose Community Foundation
600 South Cherry Street, Suite 1200
Denver, CO 80246-1712

Rose Community Foundation Child and Family Development Grants 4153
Through its Child and Family Development program, the Rose Community Foundation invests resources in developing and improving early childhood care outside the home, including advocacy initiatives aimed at increasing public awareness of and access to high-quality child care. It also supports parent education programs that help parents raise children who are physically and emotionally healthy, and mentally prepared to learn. Recognizing that economic self-sufficiency is the key to strong families, the Foundation supports employment and training programs that help people find stable jobs, and support services that help them advance up the career ladder. In addition, the Foundation funds organizations that offer family support services, such as child care, health care, affordable housing and other efforts essential to parents who need to work full-time.
Requirements: Colorado 501(c)3 tax-exempt organizations serving the residents of Adams, Arapahoe, Boulder, Denver, Douglas, and Jefferson Counties are eligible.
Geographic Focus: Colorado
Contact: Elsa Holguin; (303) 398-7414 or (303) 398-7400; eholguin@rcfdenver.org
Internet: http://www.rcfdenver.org/programs_child_development.htm
Sponsor: Rose Community Foundation
600 South Cherry Street, Suite 1200
Denver, CO 80246-1712

Rose Community Foundation Health Grants 4154
The Rose Community Foundation recognizes that improving access to quality care requires well-informed, visionary leaders. For this reason, the Foundation promotes initiatives that develop health-policy and public-health leadership. While the Foundation invests in health leadership that can improve access to quality care over the long term, it also works to effect more immediate change. Committed to improving access to care for low-income children, youth and families, the Foundation continues to support efforts to enroll them in programs such as Child Health Plan Plus (CHP+), a publicly supported health insurance program. Because at least half of all premature deaths are the result of lifestyle choices

that individuals may be able to change, the Foundation also supports health promotion and disease prevention programs that encourage healthy choices and discourage behaviors that lead to illness and injury. In addition, the Foundation funds community organizations that provide information about the steps individuals can take to prevent such conditions as diabetes, teen pregnancy, HIV, heart disease and cancer.
Requirements: Colorado 501(c)3 tax-exempt organizations serving the residents of Adams, Arapahoe, Boulder, Denver, Douglas, and Jefferson Counties are eligible.
Geographic Focus: Colorado
Contact: Whitney G. Connor; (303) 398-7410 or (303) 398-7400; wconnor@rcfdenver.org
Internet: http://www.rcfdenver.org/programs_health.htm
Sponsor: Rose Community Foundation
600 South Cherry Street, Suite 1200
Denver, CO 80246-1712

Rose Community Foundation Jewish Life Grants — 4155
The Jewish Life program area supports efforts to create and sustain a vibrant Jewish community. The Foundation funds new ideas that connect Jews to Jewish life and to each other, promoting partnerships and addressing emerging needs, while also strengthening institutions so that they can respond to change. The four highest priorities in Jewish Life are outreach to unconnected Jews, experiences that promote Jewish growth, leadership development and organizational development. The Foundation is also dedicated to building bridges within the Jewish community.
Requirements: Colorado 501(c)3 tax-exempt organizations serving the Jewish organizations of Adams, Arapahoe, Boulder, Denver, Douglas, and Jefferson Counties are eligible.
Geographic Focus: Colorado
Contact: Lisa Farber Miller, Senior Program Officer; (303) 398-7420 or (303) 398-7400; fax (303) 398-7430; lfmiller@rcfdenver.org
Internet: http://www.rcfdenver.org/programs_jewishlife.htm
Sponsor: Rose Community Foundation
600 South Cherry Street, Suite 1200
Denver, CO 80246-1712

Rose Foundation For Communities and the Environment Consumer Privacy Rights Grants — 4156
The Rose Foundation supports grassroots initiatives to inspire community action to protect the environment, consumers and public health. The purpose of the Consumer Privacy Rights Fund is to support projects that relate to the preservation or promotion of privacy rights of California consumers or residents, among others. This includes, but is not limited to, grants to strengthen the organizational capacity of groups whose core mission is privacy rights.
Requirements: The applicant must demonstrate that it has the experience and expertise to promote the goals of the fund, and the capability to carry out the proposed project. The applicant must have 501(c)3 non-profit status, or a fiscal sponsor. Funds may not be used for litigation or lobbying purposes. All applicants must submit a letter of inquiry (2-pages maximum) before submitting a full proposal. Letters of inquiry are due August 31. This allows the Foundation to determine if the project will fit within the guidelines of any currently-available restitution fund. Letters of inquiry may be sent by either regular mail or email. Letters should be addressed to Karla James, Managing Director. Rose Foundation staff will contact you either by phone or email within one week of receiving your letter. At that time, the Foundation will either invite a proposal, or decline a proposal. If invited to, submit a full proposal which explains your project in detail. Full proposals are due on October 1.
Geographic Focus: California
Date(s) Application is Due: Aug 31; Oct 1
Contact: Tim Little; (510) 658-0702; fax (510) 658-0732; tlittle@rosefdn.org
Internet: http://rosefdn.org/article.php?list=type&type=76
Sponsor: Rose Foundation For Communities and the Environment
6008 College Avenue, Suite 10
Oakland, CA 94618

Rose Foundation For Communities and the Environment Kern County Air Pollution Mitigation Grants — 4157
The Rose Foundation supports grassroots initiatives to inspire community action to protect the environment, consumers and public health. The Kern County Air Pollution Mitigation Fund supports direct, pro-active projects in Kern County designed to reduce particulate or ozone air pollution, such as clean fueled school buses or other alternatives to large diesel engines. Preferred Projects: more cost-effective projects will receive preference; projects whose air quality benefits can be reasonably projected to last longer than the 5 year minimum will receive preference. In addition to the required five year calculation, these longer-lasting projects are encouraged to supply a separate estimate of their total life span and their cost-effectiveness over their total life span; projects designed to reduce the greatest amount of total air pollution over a 5 year period going forward from the initiation of the project will receive preference. Projects with the potential to reduce air pollution beyond five years will also receive preference. These longer-lasting projects are encouraged to supply an estimate of the total air pollution reduced over the entire project lifespan; projects located in areas of Kern County that are the most impacted by air pollution, such as Arvin, Lamont and southeast Bakersfield, will receive preference; projects that reduce both particulates and ozone will receive preference; projects that have secondary air quality benefits, such as reducing greenhouse gases or toxic air contaminants, will receive preference; projects that reduce impacts to disadvantaged or impacted communities will receive preference; projects that maximize public health benefit, especially benefits to sensitive populations such as children or seniors, will receive preference.
Requirements: Requirements: projects must relate to reductions of state or federal non-attainment pollutants (ie - particulates, particulate precursors or ozone precursors (NOX or ROG); projects must be located in the valley portion of Kern County; projects must be technologically feasible (CARB certified or equivalent); projects must supply their estimated cost-effectiveness per ton of pollution reduced over a 5 year period going forward from the initiation of the project. The calculation must conform to SJVAPCD standards, using the link to the SJVAPCD calculation spreadsheet provided with the application; eligible projects must go beyond any existing legal requirements. The Fund will not support projects that are already mandated by law; any air quality credits generated by the project must be permanently retired.
Restrictions: No funding available for: advocacy, organizing or research.
Geographic Focus: California
Contact: Tim Little; (510) 658-0702; fax (510) 658-0732; tlittle@rosefdn.org
Internet: http://rosefdn.org/article.php?list=type&type=86
Sponsor: Rose Foundation For Communities and the Environment
6008 College Avenue, Suite 10
Oakland, CA 94618

Rose Foundation For Communities and the Environment Northern California Environmental Grassroots Grants — 4158
The Rose Foundation supports grassroots initiatives to inspire community action to protect the environment, consumers and public health. The Grassroots Fund supports small groups throughout greater northern California that are tackling tough environmental problems including toxic pollution, urban sprawl, environmental degradation of rivers, wild places, as well as the communities health. Most grant are for a one year period. Grassroots Fund grantees are also eligible to receive up to $200 of training scholarships per year. The scholarships cover 80% of the registration cost of training. Grantees traveling more than 75 miles round trip will also receive a travel stipend. See Foundations website for further guidelines.
Requirements: To be eligible for a grassroots grant, the applicant must meet the following criteria: geographic scope - project impact must be in Northern California (includes the entire Sierra Nevada Mountains, Bay Area, Central Valley, Central Coast, and North Coast); organization size - annual income or expenses of $100,000 or less; issues supported - include, but are not limited to; environmental health and justice, land management and urban sprawl, habitat and wilderness protection, sustainable forestry, water resources, agriculture, sustainability, and pollution; strategies supported - general support for organizations with an environmental mission, or project support for strategies such as community-based advocacy, technical assistance, litigation, restoration projects, organizing expenses, grassroots campaigns, and environmental education; tax status - applicants may be a nonprofit, be fiscally sponsored by another nonprofit, or ask for fiscal sponsorship from the fund. An application form is available for download on the Foundations website. Mail application in by deadline, emailed or faxed applications will not be accepted.
Restrictions: Not eligible for support: capital campaigns, annual fundraising appeals, government agencies, colleges or universities and individuals.
Geographic Focus: California
Date(s) Application is Due: Feb 1; May 1; Aug 1; Nov 1
Amount of Grant: Up to 5,000 USD
Contact: Tim Little; (510) 658-0702; fax (510) 658-0732; tlittle@rosefdn.org
Internet: http://rosefdn.org/article.php?list=type&type=36
Sponsor: Rose Foundation For Communities and the Environment
6008 College Avenue, Suite 10
Oakland, CA 94618

Rose Foundation For Communities and the Environment Southeast Madera County Responsible Growth Grants — 4159
The Rose Foundation supports grassroots initiatives to inspire community action to protect the environment, consumers and public health. The Southeast Madera County Responsible Growth Fund was created to advocate for responsible growth in Madera County through adherence to California land use laws and Madera County General Plan policies, to promote comprehensive and integrated planning, and to ensure full compliance with the requirements of the California Environmental Quality Act, within, or pertaining to, the southeastern portion of Madera County. This Target Area is bounded on the West by State Route 99, on the North by SR 145 and on the East and South by the Millerton Reservoir and the San Joaquin River.
Requirements: Eligible applicants include governmental, public agency, quasi-governmental, or non-profit entities qualified pursuant to the requirements of the California Franchise Tax Board and the Internal Revenue Code whose purposes include advocating for or engaging in comprehensive planning within, or for the benefit of, Madera County. Initial contact should be through a Letter of Inquiry, no more than three pages concisely describing each of the following: proposed project; project goals; explain your strategy and why this project is important; time frame; funding need; other anticipated sources of support; and a brief description of the organization requesting funds. If invited to submit a full proposal include the following: 1 page cover sheet consisting of: applicant's name, address, telephone number and website; primary contact person's name, address, telephone number, and email; amount of funds requested; EIN number; 1 - 2 paragraph short description of the proposed project; proposed start date for the project; specific statement of authorization of the application by the applicant's executive officer, including executive officer's signature. Narrative project description, not more than 5 pages long. The narrative description should describe the applicant, proposed project, overall strategic considerations, specific project workplan, key deliverables, and any other factors for consideration, such as urgency of need for support. Required Attachments: project budget; identification of other potential sources of project funding; organizational budget for the current year; balance sheet and profit/loss statement for the most recently completed year; description of lead project staff; Board of directors roster; timetable of activities; description of how the applicant will evaluate progress and any key metrics that will be used to measure performance towards grant objectives; IRS 501(c)3 determination letter or other acceptable documentation of nonprofit purpose or fiscal sponsorship. Optional Attachments: press clippings or other material describing the organization and key past accomplishments (limit 3); Letters of Reference (limit 3); submit the original application, plus 5 copies, by U.S. mail or delivery service to the Foundation.

Geographic Focus: California
Amount of Grant: 12,000 - 100,000 USD
Contact: Tim Little; (510) 658-0702; fax (510) 658-0732; tlittle@rosefdn.org
Internet: http://rosefdn.org/article.php?list=type&type=114
Sponsor: Rose Foundation For Communities and the Environment
6008 College Avenue, Suite 10
Oakland, CA 94618

Rose Foundation For Communities and the Environment Watershed Protection Grants   4160

The Rose Foundation supports grassroots initiatives to inspire community action to protect the environment, consumers and public health. The Watershed Protection Fund accepts applications for projects designed to benefit the water quality and ecosystem of San Francisco Bay, the San Francisco-San Joaquin Bay/Delta, and tributaries to the Bay/Delta Water system. From time to time, the Foundation is also able to accept proposals to benefit Southern California watersheds, and other coastal areas. If you have a project that benefits other watersheds, contact the executive director to make sure there is a fit before submitting a Letter of Inquiry. The Watershed Protection Fund has grant cycles twice per year. Summer docket deadlines: Letter of Inquiry due February 15; full proposals due April 1; decisions in May. Winter docket deadlines: Letter of Inquiry due August 15; full proposals due October 1; decisions in November. You may submit Letters of Inquiry via email to the executive director. Proposals must be mailed; emailed or faxed proposals will not be accepted.
Requirements: Submit a Letter of Inquiry of no more than three pages concisely describing each of the following: proposed project; project goals; explain your strategy and why this project is important; time frame; funding need; other anticipated sources of support; and a brief description of the organization requesting funds. To be eligible for a grant from the Watersheds Protection Fund you must be able to demonstrate that your project will benefit the water quality of the San Francisco Bay/Delta watershed. This is a large watershed, and includes the San Joaquin River, Sacramento River and their tributaries. Many factors affect water quality, therefore, projects do not necessarily need to have an explicit water quality focus to be eligible. However, a successful applicant will be able to clearly demonstrate the linkages between their project and water quality. Eligible projects must demonstrate 501(c)3 status. Non 501(c)3 projects may apply through fiscal sponsors. Governmental agencies and resource conservation districts are also eligible. If you are invited to submit a full proposal, see the Foundation's website: http://rosefdn.org/article.php?id=243 for complete proposal guidelines.
Geographic Focus: California
Date(s) Application is Due: Feb 15; Aug 15
Amount of Grant: 5,000 - 20,000 USD
Contact: Tim Little; (510) 658-0702; fax (510) 658-0732; tlittle@rosefdn.org
Internet: http://rosefdn.org/article.php?list=type&type=84
Sponsor: Rose Foundation For Communities and the Environment
6008 College Avenue, Suite 10
Oakland, CA 94618

ROSE Fund Grants   4161

The fund is committed to recognizing, assisting, and empowering women who have broken the cycle of domestic violence. The bulk of grants are made to small organizations with annual budgets under $500,000. Priority is given to organizations in the Northeast. Grants are made for one year. Guidelines are available online.
Requirements: 501(c)3 tax-exempt organizations are eligible.
Geographic Focus: All States
Date(s) Application is Due: Oct 1
Amount of Grant: Up to 10,000 USD
Contact: John Brisbin; (617) 482-5400; fax (617) 482-3443; jbrisbin@rosefund.org
Internet: http://www.grantselect.com/gs/editorial/
Sponsor: Rose Fund
200 Harvard Mill Square, Suite 310
Wakefield, MA 01880

Rose Hills Foundation Grants   4162

The Rose Hills Foundation accepts and processes applications for grants throughout the year with the expectation of grant distributions every six months. Depending on timing, requests are reviewed at six annual Board Meetings. At times, there may be an approximate wait of up to six months prior to a request being reviewed. Grants range from $5,000 to million dollar commitments. Foundation directors may opt to grant less than the amount requested, depending upon resources available, or spread payments over more than one year.
Requirements: Preferential attention is given to organizations that exhibit the following criteria: a history of achievement, good management, and a stable financial condition; self-sustaining programs that are unlikely to depend on future Foundation funding; significant programs that make a measurable impact; funding that is matched or multiplied by other sources; projects or programs that benefit people of southern California; and programs that reach the greatest number of people at the most reasonable cost. Organizations should send a two page letter of introduction (LOI) addressed to the Foundation's President. Initial correspondence should include the following information: brief purpose and history of organization; brief outline of program/project for which funds are being sought; program/project budget; specific amount being requested from Foundation; geographic area, demographics of population, and the number of individuals served annually; list of Board of Directors; current operating budget and most recent audited financials (if not available, please provide most recent financial statement); copy of IRS determination letter; and a detailed funding history.
Restrictions: Funding is not available for propagandizing, influencing legislation and/or elections or promoting voter registration; political candidates, political campaigns or organizations engaging in political activities; programs which promote religious doctrine; individuals (except as permitted by the IRS); governmental agencies; or endowments.
Geographic Focus: California
Amount of Grant: 5,000 - 1,000,000 USD
Contact: Victoria Rogers, President; (626) 696-2220; fax (626) 696-2210; vbrogers@rosehillsfoundation.org
Internet: http://www.rosehillsfoundation.org/AppProcedures.htm
Sponsor: Rose Hills Foundation
225 South Lake Avenue, Suite 1250
Pasadena, CA 91101

Rosie's For All Kids Foundation Grants   4163

The foundation awards grants to nonprofit organizations dedicated to helping children and their families through child care, early childhood education, literacy, and other essential programs. In order of preference, grants support infant, toddler, and preschool programs; education, after school and literacy programs; and emergency assistance, crisis intervention, cultural development programs, and services for children with special needs. Letters of intent are accepted on a rolling basis. The foundation has two funding cycles per year with disbursements typically occurring in February/March and in September/October. Organizations that are invited to submit full applications will be informed at the time they apply as to which funding cycle they will fall into.
Requirements: 501(c)3 nonprofit organizations are eligible.
Restrictions: The foundation does not give support in the following areas: general operating support, salaries, or administrative needs, grants to individuals, school districts, municipalities or programs outside the United States. Requests for annual fundraising appeals, event sponsorships and items for auction are not considered.
Geographic Focus: All States
Amount of Grant: 5,000 - 10,000 USD
Contact: Grant Review Committee; grants@forallkids.org
Internet: http://www.forallkids.org/html/grants.cfm
Sponsor: Rosie's For All Kids Foundation
P.O. Box 225
Allendale, NJ 07401

Ross Foundation Grants   4164

The Ross Foundation, established in 1966, supports organizations involved with education, arts and cultural enrichment, community beautification and improvement, historical preservation, mental health and people who are developmentally disabled, and forestry research and conservation management. Giving is limited to the Arkadelphia and Clark County, Arkansas region. Contact the Foundation for an application form to begin your proposal.
Requirements: Non-profits operating in the Arkadelphia and Clark County, Arkansas region are eligible to apply for funding. Applicants submit the following: copy of IRS Determination Letter; brief history of organization and description of its mission; copy of most recent annual report/audited financial statement/990; listing of board of directors, trustees, officers and other key people and their affiliations; detailed description of project; amount of funding requested, and 6 copies of the proposal.
Geographic Focus: Arkansas
Date(s) Application is Due: Jan 1; Mar 31; May 1; Jul 31; Sep 1; Nov 30
Amount of Grant: 3,000 - 20,000 USD
Contact: Mary Elizabeth Eldridge, Director of Programs; (870) 246-9881; fax (870) 246-9674; meeldridge@rossfoundation.us
Sponsor: Ross Foundation
P.O. Box 335
Arkadelphia, AR 71923

Royal Caribbean Cruises Ocean Fund   4165

The Royal Caribbean Cruises Ocean Fund supports efforts to restore and maintain a healthy marine environment, minimize the impact of human activity on the environment, and promote awareness of ocean and coastal issues and respect for marine life. Ocean Fund grants are made to a variety of nonprofit groups and institutions whose activities are directly related to marine conservation, including initiatives in research, education and innovative technologies. Previous funding for organizations around the world include include projects that relate to ocean science, climate change, key marine species, education and innovative technologies. Previously funded projects are available at the Ocean Fund website.
Requirements: Organizations seeking grant funding from the Ocean Fund are welcome to email throughout the year to introduce their organization, mission, programs and potential projects relevant to the mission of the Ocean Fund within the body of the email. Due to the volume of email inquiries, only those organizations who are requested to submit a letter of interest will receive a personalized response to their email. The Ocean Fund grant selection process is by invitation only.
Restrictions: Any attachments to emails will not be reviewed.
Geographic Focus: All States
Amount of Grant: 20,000 - 40,000 USD
Contact: Ocean Fund Administrator; (305) 539-6573; oceanfund@rccl.com
Internet: http://www.theoceanfund.com/about
Sponsor: Royal Caribbean Cruises
1050 Caribbean Way
Miami, FL 33132-2096

Roy and Christine Sturgis Charitable Trust Grants   4166

The Roy and Christine Sturgis Charitable Trust was established in 1981 to support and promote quality educational, cultural, human-services, and health-care programming for all people. Roy Sturgis was one of ten children of an Arkansas farmer and homemaker. He dropped out of school after the tenth grade to join the Navy during World War I. Mr. Sturgis returned to his family home in southern Arkansas after the war and went to work in the local

sawmills. In 1933, he married Texas native Christine Johns. They became very successful in the timber, lumber, and sawmill industries in Arkansas, owned other prosperous business enterprises, and had notable success managing their investments. Mr. and Mrs. Sturgis spent most of their lives in Arkansas and Dallas, Texas. They did not have children, but were particularly interested in educational opportunities for young people. In addition, Mr. and Mrs. Sturgis supported organizations working in the areas of health, social services, and the arts. The Sturgis Charitable Trust encourages requests for the following types of grants: capital, project-related, medical research, and endowment campaign. Funding for start-up programs and limited general-operating requests will also be considered. Approximately 65% of the trust's annual distributions are made within the state of Arkansas. The remaining 35% of grants are distributed within the state of Texas with strong preference given to organizations located in the Dallas area. The majority of grants from the Sturgis Charitable Trust are one year in duration; on occasion, multi-year support is awarded. Applicants must apply online at the grant website. Applicants are strongly encouraged to do the following before applying: review the downloadable state application procedures for additional helpful information and clarifications; review the downloadable online-application guidelines at the grant website; review the trust's funding history (link is available from the grant website); review the online application questions in advance; and review the list of required attachments. These will generally include: a list of board members, financial statements (audited, reviewed, or compiled by independent auditor); an organization summary; a list of other funding sources; an IRS Determination letter; and other required documents. All attachments must be uploaded in the online application as PDF, Word, or Excel files. The application deadline for the Roy and Christine Sturgis Charitable Trust is 11:59 p.m. on December 31. Applicants will be notified of grant decisions before July 31.
Requirements: 501(c)3 nonprofit organizations in Texas and Arkansas are eligible.
Restrictions: Former grantees must skip a year before submitting a subsequent application. The trust does not support requests from individuals, organizations attempting to influence policy through direct lobbying, or any political campaigns.
Geographic Focus: Arkansas, Texas
Date(s) Application is Due: Dec 31
Contact: David Ross, Senior Vice President; (214) 209-1965; tx.philanthropic@baml.com
Internet: https://www.bankofamerica.com/philanthropic/fn_search.action
Sponsor: Roy and Christine Sturgis Charitable Trust
901 Main Street, 19th Floor, TX1-492-19-11
Dallas, TX 75202-3714

Roy J. Carver Charitable Trust Youth Program Grants 4167
Projects receiving Trust funding under the youth program designation are typically designed to complement curriculum-based education and encourage individual development and physical well-being. Of the grants awarded within this category, a significant portion has been directed toward the efforts of organizations advocating for disadvantaged and disabled youth and their families. As an example, improving the conditions at adolescent residential facilities in Iowa has represented an important area of Trust charitable giving. In addition, grants to help communities establish safe and affordable recreation opportunities are also part of the youth-directed programming. The Trust offers strategic funding for the development of public recreation facilities and related activities for children.
Requirements: Priority is given to projects in the Iowa counties of Muscatine, Louisa and Scott, as well as Rock Island and Mercer Counties in Illinois. Overall, grants are made to 501(c)3 tax-exempt organizations in Iowa and western Illinois.
Restrictions: The trust does not support annual campaigns or ongoing operations, direct grants to individuals, religious activities, organizations without 501(c)3 status, fund-raising benefits or program advertising, or political parties or candidates.
Geographic Focus: Illinois, Iowa
Amount of Grant: 10,000 - 200,000 USD
Contact: Dr. Troy Ross; (563) 263-4010; fax (563) 263-1547; info@carvertrust.org
Internet: https://www.carvertrust.org/index.php?page=37
Sponsor: Roy J. Carver Charitable Trust
202 Iowa Avenue
Muscatine, IA 52761-3733

RR Donnelley Community Grants 4168
The foundation makes monetary grants to organizations in the communities where RR Donnelley has a presence. The foundation evaluates all grant proposals against two priorities. Special consideration is given to any grant which gives a high priority to activities that support the written word and ensures the future strength of communities by promoting reading and literacy. Occasionally grants are made beyond the top priorities. Proposals are accepted between January 1 and November 1 each year.
Requirements: Nonprofits working in areas of company operations are eligible.
Restrictions: Scholarships are awarded only to children of employees and retirees. Health care is not a priority, therefore grants are not made for specific diseases, clinical care, medical research or equipment. Grants are not made to individuals or to religious organizations. Special event support is only made under circumstances where there is high correlation with program priorities and active employee involvement. The foundation does not contribute printing.
Geographic Focus: Illinois, Nevada, New York
Date(s) Application is Due: Nov 1
Contact: Calvin Butler; (312) 326-8712; fax (312) 326-7156; communityrelations@rrd.com
Internet: http://www.banta.com/wwwRRD/AboutUs/ExternalAffairs/TheRRD Foundation/CommunityGrants.asp
Sponsor: RR Donnelley
111 South Wacker Drive
Chicago, IL 60606-4301

RRF Accessible Faith Grants 4169
The foundation will make funds available to Chicago-area houses of worship for accessibility improvements to their facilities. Such improvements should allow increased participation of elderly persons and people with disabilities in the programs, services, and activities of the facilities. Grants may be used used for the following purposes: planning/scoping/design projects involving design consultation with a licensed architect or engineer; construction projects; and purchase and installation of program-related equipment. Guidelines and application are available online.
Requirements: Certified 501(c)3 religious organizations in Illinois's Cook, DuPage, and Lake Counties are eligible; must provide or host programs and activities — beyond worship services — that benefit elderly persons.
Restrictions: Grants will not be made for chairlifts because they do not provide accessibility for all people who have difficulty climbing stairs; used equipment; or the purchase of accessible vehicles or individual mobility aids, such as wheelchairs or walkers. Grants are not provided for constructing entirely new buildings or entirely new multi-room additions to existing buildings or or projects that are already completed.
Geographic Focus: Illinois
Date(s) Application is Due: Apr 17; Jun 26
Amount of Grant: Up to 30,000 USD
Contact: Grants Administrator; (773) 714-8080; fax (733) 714-8089; info@rrf.org
Internet: http://www.rrf.org/accessibleFaithGrantProgram.htm
Sponsor: Retirement Research Foundation
8765 W Higgins Road, Suite 430
Chicago, IL 60631-4170

RRF General Program Grants 4170
The program funds service, education, research, and advocacy projects. The foundation is particularly interested in innovative projects that have the potential to change practice, policy, or delivery systems. The foundation's programs seek to improve the availability and quality of community-based and institutional long-term care programs; expand opportunities for older persons to play meaningful roles in society; support selected basic, applied, and policy research into the causes and solutions of significant problems of the aged; and increase the number of professionals and paraprofessionals adequately prepared to serve the elderly. Proposals fall into three general categories: research, model projects and service, and education and training. Guidelines are available online.
Requirements: Direct service projects that seek to improve the availability and quality of community-based and institutional long-term care programs; expand opportunities for older persons to play meaningful roles in society; support selected applied and policy research into the causes and solutions of significant problems of the aged; increase the number of professionals and paraprofessionals adequately prepared to serve the elderly.
Restrictions: The foundation will only consider proposals from applicants in Illinois, Indiana, Iowa, Kentucky, Missouri, Wisconsin, and Florida. Priority is given to nonprofit organizations serving the Chicago metropolitan area.
Geographic Focus: Florida, Illinois, Indiana, Iowa, Kentucky, Missouri, Wisconsin
Date(s) Application is Due: Feb 1; May 1; Aug 1
Amount of Grant: Up to 15,000,000 USD
Contact: Marilyn Hennessy, President; (773) 714-8080; fax (773) 714-8089; info@rrf.org
Internet: http://www.rrf.org/generalProgram.htm
Sponsor: Retirement Research Foundation
8765 W Higgins Road, Suite 430
Chicago, IL 60631-4170

Rucker & Margaret Agee Fund Grants 4171
The Fund, in the care of the Regions Bank in Birmingham, Alabama, supports 501(c)3 organizations situated in the metropolitan area and throughout the state. Its primary fields of interest include: the arts; education; the environment; and human resources. The Fund offers general operating support. There are no specific deadlines or application formats. Applicants should include a copy of their IRS determination letter, along with an outline/description of their program need.
Restrictions: No grants are given to individuals.
Geographic Focus: Alabama
Contact: Laura Wainwright, Trust Officer, Regions Bank; (205) 801-0380; fax (205) 581-7433; laura.wainwright@regions.com
Sponsor: Rucker and Margaret Agee Fund
P.O. Box 11426
Birmingham, AL 35202

Rucker-Donnell Foundation Grants 4172
The Foundation, established in 2001, is involved with the support of community expansion and development throughout the Murfreesboro, Tennessee, region. It would appear that, in the past, the Foundation's primary fields of interest include: community development/expansion, the arts, and the environment. Specific support is given for general operations. There are no particular deadlines or guidelines, and potential applicants should contact the office before proceeding.
Geographic Focus: Tennessee
Contact: Rick G. Mansfield, Trustee; (615) 890-5700
Internet: http://ruckerdonnellfoundation.org/templates/System/default.asp?id=37512
Sponsor: Rucker-Donnell Foundation
110 S Maple Street
Murfreesboro, TN 37130-3530

Rudy Bruner Award for Urban Excellence 4173

American cities embody our nation's greatest triumphs and most daunting challenges. At their best they showcase the rich diversity, cultural achievement, and democratic values that characterize the American spirit. At their worst they reflect our country's most persistent social ills: economic disparity, hopelessness, neglect and abandonment. Yet there are those places that are developed with such vision and imagination that they transform urban problems into creative solutions. The Rudy Bruner Award for Urban Excellence (RBA) seeks to discover those special places, to celebrate and publicize their achievement. Excellence exists in every city. It can be found in downtowns, neighborhoods, and parks. The Rudy Bruner Award is a search for examples of this often overlooked excellence, and a celebration of their contribution to the richness and diversity of the urban experience. Often these places transcend the boundaries between architecture, urban design, and planning. They are born through processes of transformation, the renewal of something old, or the creation of something new that resonates in the history of community life. The Rudy Bruner Award considers form only one aspect of urban excellence. An excellent urban place involves the interplay of process, place and values. Processes may be inclusive, innovative, or participatory. Places may be grandiose or modest, new or historic, but must be well designed. Values guide the inevitable trade offs involved in bringing a project to life. The Award recognizes that these relationships are not simple. It seeks to illuminate the complex process of urban placemaking, so that it may be strengthened to better reflect the balance between form and use; opportunity and cost; preservation and change. The Gold Medal is a $50,000 award, and the Silver medals are $10,000 each.
Requirements: The criteria are: the project must be a real place, not just a plan or program; since site visits are integral to the award process, the project must have been in operation for a sufficient amount of time to demonstrate success; the project must be located in the continental United States. It is not feasible to conduct site visits at other locations; there are no distinct categories. Projects may include any type of place that makes a positive contribution to the urban built environment; urban environment is broadly defined to include cities, towns, villages, neighborhoods, counties and/or regions; previous applicants and Honorable Mention winners may apply up to three times.
Restrictions: Previous winners are not eligible.
Geographic Focus: All States
Date(s) Application is Due: Dec 15
Amount of Grant: 10,000 - 50,000 USD
Contact: Program Contact; (617) 492-8404; application@brunerfoundation.org
Internet: http://www.brunerfoundation.org/rba/index.php?page=aboutRBA&sidebar=1
Sponsor: Bruner Foundation
130 Prospect Street
Cambridge, MA 02139

Rush County Community Foundation Grants 4174

The Rush County Community Foundation, is a nonprofit public charity established in 1991 to serve donors, award grants and scholarships, and provide leadership to enrich and enhance the quality of life in Rush County, Indiana. The Rush County Community Foundation now holds over 130 funds, and have permanent endowment assets of over $6.5 million. As a public foundation, it helps donors provide grant making dollars for not-for-profit organizations that serve Rush County citizens. For additional information contact the Foundations office.
Requirements: Funding projects must serve the Rush County citizens.
Geographic Focus: Indiana
Contact: Garry Cooley; (765) 938-1177; garryc@rushcountyfoundation.org
Internet: http://www.rushcountyfoundation.org/funds.php
Sponsor: Rush County Community Foundation
117 North Main Street
Rushville, IN 46173

Russell Berrie Foundation Grants 4175

The foundation supports nonprofit organizations primarily in Israel and the New York and New Jersey metropolitan areas. Grants are awarded for education (colleges and universities, Jewish education, divinity schools, parochial elementary and secondary schools, and religious higher education), health care (hospitals and respite homes), international programs (development programs, ministries, and missions), religious organizations (religious welfare, synagogues, and temples), social issues, and youth welfare. Types of support include capital support and general operating support. Applicants should submit a brief letter of inquiry and include a description of the program and the organization, including a financial statement. There are no application deadlines.
Requirements: Christian, Jewish, and Roman Catholic organizations in New York, New Jersey, and Israel are eligible.
Geographic Focus: New Jersey, New York, Israel
Amount of Grant: 5,000 - 20,000 USD
Contact: Susan Strunk, Administrative Director; (201) 928-1880
Internet: http://www.russberrie.com/foundation.html
Sponsor: Russell Berrie Foundation
300 Frank Burr Boulevard, Building E, 7th Floor
Teaneck, NJ 07666-6704

Ruth Anderson Foundation Grants 4176

The Ruth Anderson Foundation awards grants to Florida nonprofit organizations in Dade County. The Foundation's funding interests include AIDS research; children and youth services; homeless/housing shelters; human services; and substance abuse services. There are no application forms or deadlines. The initial approach should consist of a brief exploratory letter; full proposals will be by invitation only. The board meets throughout the year to consider requests for funding.
Requirements: Miami Dade County 501(c)3 tax-exempt organizations are eligible.
Restrictions: Grants are not awarded to individuals. Funding is limited to the Miami area.
Geographic Focus: Florida
Amount of Grant: 1,000 - 10,000 USD
Contact: Funding Contact; (305) 789-4929
Sponsor: Ruth Anderson Foundation
1525 W. W.T. Harris Boulevard, D1114-044
Charlotte, NC 28288-1161

Ruth and Vernon Taylor Foundation Grants 4177

The foundation awards grants to nonprofit organizations in the areas of arts and humanities, civic and public affairs, secondary schools, higher education, environment, hospitals, human services, health, youth services, and social services. Types of support include general operating support, building construction and renovation, endowment funds, and research. The foundation suggests that initial contact be made in writing, since unsolicited requests for funds are not accepted. The Board meets in May and September.
Requirements: Organizations located in Colorado, Illinois, Montana, New Jersey, New York, Pennsylvania, Texas, or Wyoming are eligible.
Restrictions: Grants are not awarded to individuals.
Geographic Focus: Colorado, Illinois, Montana, New Jersey, New York, Pennsylvania, Texas, Wyoming
Amount of Grant: 1,000 - 20,000 USD
Contact: Douglas Taylor, Trustee; (303) 893-5284; fax (303)893-8263
Sponsor: Ruth and Vernon Taylor Foundation
518 17th Street, Suite 1670
Denver, CO 80202

Ruth Eleanor Bamberger and John Ernest Bamberger Foundation Grants 4178

The Foundation is dedicated to fulfilling the Founders' desires to help people reach their individual potential. The Foundation assists people of all ages, but especially children and young people through educational opportunities and scholarships, supporting crisis care and protective services, dental aid, after school programs, etc.
Requirements: Only residents of Utah may apply.
Restrictions: Grants and scholarships are given only to organizations, not to individuals.
Geographic Focus: Utah
Date(s) Application is Due: Mar 16; Sep 28
Amount of Grant: 1,000 - 20,000 USD
Contact: Eleanor Roser, Treasurer; (801) 364-2045; bambergermemfdn@qwestoffice.net
Internet: http://www.ruthandjohnbambergermemorialfdn.org/
Sponsor: Ruth Eleanor Bamberger and John Ernest Bamberger Memorial Foundation
136 S Main, Suite 418
Salt Lake City, UT 84101-1690

Ruth H. and Warren A. Ellsworth Foundation Grants 4179

The foundation awards grants to nonprofits in Massachusetts in support of the arts, children and youth, community development, education and higher education, and health care and hospitals. Types of support include general operating support, continuing support, annual campaigns, building construction/renovation, equipment acquisition, emergency funds, and seed grants. There are no application forms.
Requirements: Nonprofits in the Worcester, MA, area are eligible.
Restrictions: Grants are not awarded to individuals or for endowment funds, scholarships, fellowships, research, publications, conferences, matching gifts, or loans.
Geographic Focus: Massachusetts
Amount of Grant: 500 - 100,000 USD
Contact: Sumner Tilton Jr., Trustee; (508) 798-8621
Sponsor: Ruth H. and Warren A. Ellsworth Foundation
370 Main Street, 12th Floor, Suite 1250
Worcester, MA 01608-1723

Ruth Mott Foundation Grants 4180

The community is invited to submit grant requests for the program areas of arts—culture, music, theater, dance, media, graphics, photography, storytelling, and crafts; beautification—enhance neighborhoods and quality of life in the greater Flint area; and health promotion—healthy and active lifestyles and environments such as physical activity, proper nutrition, responsible sexual behavior, and overall well-being. Types of support include special projects, capacity building (planning, technical assistance, and resource development), evaluation, and general purposes. Priority is given to requests that bring diverse segments of the community together to share ideas and common interests and to respectfully address and resolve differences; enable the engagement of citizens in civic life, community service and leadership; ensure that all stakeholders are informed and involved in decisions affecting them; promote life-long learning and involvement; share and celebrate community members' unique talents, histories, cultures, and contributions; and benefit low-income segments of the community and reduce social, economic, and racial disparities. Concept papers may be submitted at any time throughout the year; full proposals are by invitation.
Requirements: Michigan nonprofits are eligible. Preference is given to requests from Flint,.
Geographic Focus: All States
Amount of Grant: Up to 65,000,000 USD
Contact: Grants Administrator; (810) 233-0170
Internet: http://www.ruthmottfoundation.org
Sponsor: Ruth Mott Foundation
111 E Court Street, Suite 3C
Flint, MI 48502-1649

Rutter's Children's Charities Grants　　　4181

The mission of Rutter's Children's Charities is to improve the lives of children in the Rutter's market area. Each year, Rutter's will make financial awards to a select number of children's organizations in York, Adams and Franklin counties of Pennsylvania. Non-profit organizations should send an application letter describing its mission and purpose, the amount the organization is seeking, and how the funds will be used. There are no annual deadlines.

Requirements: Rutter's has established the following criteria for non-profit organizations interested in applying for funds through its Rutter's Children's Charities: must benefit children; must be located within Rutter's marketing area; must spend monies within Rutter's marketing area; must use monies for tangible items, not for general operating and overhead expenses; and must provide accounting information and any other proof of how funds are used as requested by Rutter's.

Geographic Focus: Pennsylvania
Amount of Grant: Up to 50,000 USD
Contact: Scott Hartman, President; (717) 771-5933; fax (717) 815-2833
Internet: http://www.rutters.com/aboutus/childrenscharities.html
Sponsor: Rutter's Farm Stores Corporation
2100 N George Street
York, PA 17404

RWJF Changes in Health Care Financing and Organization Grants　　　4182

The Robert Wood Johnson Foundation, through its Changes in Health Care Financing and Organization (HCFO) initiative, supports research, policy analysis and evaluation projects that provide policy leaders timely information on health care policy, financing and organization issues. Supported projects include: examining significant issues and interventions related to health care financing and organization and their effects on health care costs, quality and access; and exploring or testing major new ways to finance and organize health care that have the potential to improve access to more affordable and higher quality health services. Grants will be awarded in two categories: small grants for projects requiring $100,000 or less and projected to take up to twelve months or less; and large grants for projects requiring more than $100,000 and/or projected to take longer than twelve months.

Requirements: Researchers, as well as practitioners and public and private policy-makers working with researchers, are eligible to submit proposals through their organizations. Projects may be initiated from within many disciplines, including health services research, economics, sociology, political science, public policy, public health, public administration, law and business administration. RWJF encourages proposals from organizations on behalf of researchers who are just beginning their careers, who can serve either individually as principal investigators or as part of a project team comprising researchers or other collaborators with more experience. Only organizations and government entities are eligible to receive funding under this program. Preference will be given to applicants that are either public entities or nonprofit organizations that are tax-exempt under Section 501(c)3 of the Internal Revenue Code and are not private foundations as defined under Section 509(a). Proposals for this solicitation must be submitted via the RWJF online system. Applicants should direct inquiries to the national program office.

Restrictions: Grants are not available for ongoing general operating expenses or existing deficits; endowment or capital costs, including construction, renovation, or equipment purchases; basic biomedical research; conferences, symposia, publications, or media projects, unless they are clearly related to the foundation's goals; research on unapproved drug therapies or devices; international programs and institutions; or direct support to individuals.

Geographic Focus: All States
Amount of Grant: Up to 500,000 USD
Contact: Bonnie J. Austin; (202) 292-6700 or (202) 292-6756; fax (202) 292-6800; bonnie.austin@academyhealth.org or hcfoproposals@academyhealth.org
Internet: http://www.hcfo.org/funding
Sponsor: Robert Wood Johnson Foundation
Route 1 and College Road East, P.O. Box 2316
Princeton, NJ 08543-2316

RWJF Community Health Leaders Awards　　　4183

Each year, the RWJF Community Health Leaders Award program honors outstanding individuals who overcome daunting odds to expand access to health care and social services to under-served and isolated populations in communities across the United States. Awards include a personal stipend and a grant for program enhancement. Potential nominators must submit a letter of intent; if a letter of intent is approved, a packet is sent to the nominator. For more information, contact the program office directly.

Requirements: Candidates must be residents of the United States, be affiliated with a 501(c)3 tax-exempt organization, have a five- to 15-year record of work in the community-health field, have experience as a direct provider of health-care services or be involved in the improvement of health-care access and delivery, demonstrate a full-time commitment to working with needy people, and have received no significant national recognition.

Restrictions: Nominations are not accepted from development and public relations departments or professional grant writers. Self-nominations are not accepted.

Geographic Focus: All States
Date(s) Application is Due: Oct 15
Amount of Grant: 125,000 USD
Contact: Janice Ford Griffin, National Program Director; (832) 319-7380; fax (832) 319-7385; info@communityhealthleaders.org
Internet: http://www.communityhealthleaders.org/
Sponsor: Robert Wood Johnson Foundation
Route 1 and College Road East, P.O. Box 2316
Princeton, NJ 08543-2316

RWJF Health Policy Fellowships　　　4184

The purpose of RWJF Health Policy Fellowships is to give outstanding mid-career health professionals in academic and community-based settings an opportunity to learn more about the legislative process through direct participation. Fellows actively contribute to the formulation of national health policies and accelerate their careers as leaders in health policy. Up to six grants of up to $165,000 each will be made. Each fellow will receive up to $94,000 for the Washington stay in salary plus fringe benefits or fellowship stipend. Fellows will receive an additional allowance for relocation subject to limitations provided in detail on the program's Web site. November 13 is the deadline for receipt of applications submitted online.

Requirements: Applicants may have backgrounds in the following disciplines: allied health professions; biomedical sciences; dentistry; economics or other social sciences; health services organization and administration; medicine; nursing; public health; or social and behavioral health. Applicants must be U.S. citizens or have permanent residency status at the time of application. Potential applicants must obtain documented sponsorship from an eligible institution to support their application. Nonprofit health care organizations and academic centers are eligible sponsors. Eligible institutions may sponsor more than one candidate, but no more than one individual will be selected from any one sponsoring organization.

Restrictions: No additional direct costs (such as laptops or PDAs) or indirect costs are paid for during the first year of this program.

Geographic Focus: All States
Date(s) Application is Due: Nov 13
Amount of Grant: Up to 165,000 USD
Contact: Marie Michnich, Director; (202) 334-1506; fax (202) 334-3862; mmichnich@nas.edu or info@healthpolicyfellows.org
Internet: http://www.rwjf.org/content/rwjf/en/grants/calls-for-proposals/2013/health-policy-fellows-.html
Sponsor: Robert Wood Johnson Foundation
Route 1 and College Road East, P.O. Box 2316
Princeton, NJ 08543-2316

RWJF Jobs to Careers: Promoting Work-Based Learning for Quality Care　　　4185

The Jobs to Careers program supports partnerships to advance and reward the skill and career development of incumbent (currently employed) workers providing care and services on the front lines of our health and health care systems. The program seeks to develop and redesign systems that support and institutionalize learning and career advancement and test new models of work-based learning. The implementation grants fund partnerships of health and health care employers and educational institutions to promote learning, career advancement and testing of new models of work-based learning. Recent grants range from $400,000 to $1,000,000

Requirements: Jobs to Careers will support projects that involve emerging or existing partnerships of at least one health or health care employer and at least one educational institution (e.g., a community college) that provides academic credit or an industry-recognized credential. Eligible applicant organizations include employers, educational institutions or other organizations within the partnership that are public entities or nonprofit organizations that are tax-exempt under Section 501(c)3 of the Internal Revenue Code. Only one organization representing the partnership may submit a proposal. All proposals must be submitted only through the RWJF Grantmaking Online system.

Restrictions: Grant funds may not be used to subsidize individuals for the costs of their health care, to support clinical trials of unapproved drugs or devices, to construct or renovate facilities, for lobbying, or as a substitute for funds currently being used to support similar activities.

Geographic Focus: All States
Amount of Grant: Up to 1,000,000 USD
Contact: Maria Kniesler Flynn, Program Director; (617) 728-4446; mflynn@jff.org
Internet: http://www.rwjf.org/en/grants/programs-and-initiatives/J/jobs-to-careers—promoting-work-based-learning-for-quality-care.html
Sponsor: Robert Wood Johnson Foundation
Route 1 and College Road East, P.O. Box 2316
Princeton, NJ 08543-2316

RWJF Local Funding Partnerships Grants　　　4186

The foundation awards matching grants to establish funding partnerships with local grantmakers in support of innovative, community-based projects that focus on the health and health care of underserved and at-risk populations. Priority will be given to projects that involve cooperation among public- and private-sector service providers; have other financial sponsors; include continuation of the proposed innovation after support expires; and have local government support. Grants are awarded for 36 to 48 months and must be matched one-to-one. Grant funds may be used for project staff salaries, consultant fees, data collection and analysis, meetings, supplies, project-related travel, and other direct project expenses, including a limited amount of equipment deemed essential to the project. The full RFP is available online.

Requirements: Applicants may be either 501(c)3 public entities or nonprofit organizations and not classified as a private foundation under Section 509(a).

Restrictions: In-kind services and money to pay for capital costs or renovation may not be used to match funds.

Geographic Focus: All States
Amount of Grant: 50,000 - 200,000 USD
Contact: Pauline M. Seitz; (609) 275-4128; pseitz@localfundingpartnerships.org
Internet: http://www.lifp.org/index.html
Sponsor: Robert Wood Johnson Foundation
Route 1 and College Road East, P.O. Box 2316
Princeton, NJ 08543-2316

RWJF New Jersey Health Initiatives Grants 4187

The RWJF New Jersey Health Initiatives program funds grants that promote the development of innovative, community-based health services in New Jersey. Special emphasis is placed on projects that improve access to primary health care, address the complex service needs of people with chronic health conditions, and reduce substance abuse. Grant funds may be used for staff salaries, project-related travel, data processing, supplies, a limited amount of equipment, and other expenses essential to the project. The primary emphasis of the program is the demonstration of new service delivery approaches, although a limited amount of funding will be available for planning, feasibility, and program development. The program will also support a small number of health services research or evaluation projects in the goal areas. Projects funded through NJHI are generally three years in duration with proposals submitted annually through calls for proposals issued by the Robert Wood Johnson Foundation.
Requirements: Public entities or IRS 501(c)3 organizations located in New Jersey are eligible for funding. Applicants are asked to propose projects that respond to one of the following RWJF interest areas: addiction prevention and treatment; childhood obesity; or vulnerable populations. Projects must address all of the following: reach people who are not served by traditional health and social services; focus on meeting the needs of individuals and families, touching their lives directly; and address the lack of policy, financing and service integration among state and local agencies that creates barriers to helping people.
Restrictions: Private 509(a) foundations are not eligible. Grant funds may not be used for capital costs (including construction, renovation, and most equipment purchases), to support ongoing general operating expenses or existing deficits, or to substitute for funds currently supporting similar services. No hard-copy brief or full proposals will be accepted.
Geographic Focus: New Jersey
Date(s) Application is Due: Jan 15
Contact: Bob Atkins; (856) 225-6734 or (856) 225-6733; info@njhi.org
Internet: http://njhi.org/about-njhi
Sponsor: Robert Wood Johnson Foundation
Route 1 and College Road East, P.O. Box 2316
Princeton, NJ 08543-2316

RWJF Partners Investing in Nursing's Future Grants 4188

The Partners Investing in Nursing's Future Grants program is a collaborative initiative of the Robert Wood Johnson Foundation (RWJF) and the Northwest Health Foundation (NWHF), with the intention of addressing nursing issues at the community level through funding partnerships with local and regional foundations. Up to ten awards of up to $250,000 each will be made for projects lasting up to 24 months. Local foundations, with other partners (such as state workforce investment boards, hospital and long-term-care associations, foundations and other funding sources) will match these awards with at least $1 for every $2 provided by the program. Funding will be commensurate with the size and scope of the proposed activity and the foundation's experience with nursing issues. Funding is not intended to support the continuation of ongoing projects, but it may support new programs led by foundations that are already working in the field of nursing.
Requirements: Eligible institutions include local or regional private, family or community foundations and public charities. Eligible foundations are those classified as tax-exempt under Section 501(c)3 as a public charity or private foundation, a nonexempt charitable trust treated as a private foundation under Section 4947(a)(1), or organizations that claim status as private operating foundations under Section 4942(j)3 or 4942(j)5 of the Internal Revenue Code. Government entities, corporate grant-makers and others may participate as part of funding collaboratives; however, they may not serve as the applicant institution. All proposals to this program must address one or more of these topics: Diversity; Educational Infrastructure and Faculty Development; Public Health; Long-Term Care; and/or Mid-Level Management. Proposals for planning as well as implementation projects will be considered.
Geographic Focus: All States
Contact: Renee' Jensen Reinhardt, Program Officer; (971) 230-0093; fax (503) 220-1335; renee@nwhf.org or info@PartnersInNursing.org
Internet: http://www.partnersinnursing.org/
Sponsor: Robert Wood Johnson Foundation
Route 1 and College Road East, P.O. Box 2316
Princeton, NJ 08543-2316

RWJF Pioneer Portfolio Grants 4189

The Pioneer Portfolio Grant program aims to support novel, high-return ideas that may have far-reaching impact on people's health, the quality of care they receive and the systems through which that care is provided. It seeks ideas not only from the mainstream of health and health care but also looks to sources outside of these fields for innovations that might have transformative impact. Several projects apply approaches from diverse sectors such as finance, design and entertainment to forge new solutions in health and health care arenas.
Requirements: Preference is given to public agencies, public charities or are tax-exempt under section 501(c)3 of the Internal Revenue Code. Organizations must be located in the United States or one of its territories.
Restrictions: The organization does not fund any of the following: Ongoing general operating expenses or existing deficits; Endowment or capital costs; Basic biomedical research; Research on drug therapies or devices; International programs; Direct support of individuals; Lobbying of any kind. Additionally, RWJF no longer funds projects in the following areas: End-of-life care; Long-term care; Specific chronic conditions (that are not part of the strategies of other Program Areas); Physical activity for adults age 50 or older.
Geographic Focus: All States
Contact: Deborah H. Bae; (609) 627-5812 or (877) 843-7953; dbae@rwjf.org
Internet: http://www.rwjf.org/en/grants/what-we-fund.html
Sponsor: Robert Wood Johnson Foundation
Route 1 and College Road East, P.O. Box 2316
Princeton, NJ 08543-2316

RWJF Vulnerable Populations Portfolio Grants 4190

Programs within the Vulnerable Populations Portfolio have four elements in common: they offer an opportunity to improve health by taking a fresh approach to a long standing problem; they address poor health status in the context of other factors like housing, education and poverty; they make fundamental changes in how services are organized and delivered; and they address the lack of policy, financing, or service integration among local service providers and state and federal agencies. While RWJF awards most of its grants in response to calls for proposals, it also award grants in response to unsolicited proposals in the Vulnerable Populations Portfolio.
Requirements: Preference is given to public agencies, public charities or are tax-exempt under section 501(c)3 of the Internal Revenue Code. Organizations must be located in the United States or one of its territories.
Restrictions: This program will not provide funding for efforts that do not incorporate the social factors that drive health status as part of their proposed model. Additionally, the program does not fund documentaries, research, programs that address a single medical condition, or provide core support for free or safety net clinics, disease management models, or well-tested models whose effectiveness have already been established and that have been widely disseminated.
Geographic Focus: All States
Contact: Kristin B. Schubert; (888) 631-9989; kschubert@rwjf.org
Internet: http://www.rwjf.org/en/about-rwjf/program-areas/vulnerable-populations/Programs-and-Grants.html
Sponsor: Robert Wood Johnson Foundation
Route 1 and College Road East, P.O. Box 2316
Princeton, NJ 08543-2316

Ryder System Charitable Foundation Grants 4191

The Ryder System Charitable Foundation was established in 1984 in Florida. The Foundation supports zoological societies and organizations involved with arts and culture, education, animal welfare, health, cystic fibrosis, and human services. Giving is limited to Los Angeles, CA, southern FL, Atlanta, GA, St. Louis, MO, Cincinnati, OH, and Dallas, TX.
Requirements: Organizations in California, Florida, Georgia, Missouri, Ohio, and Texas are eligible to apply. There is no application form, Applicants should submit the following: brief history of organization and description of its mission; copy of most recent annual report/audited financial statement/990; explanation of why grantmaker is considered an appropriate donor for project; listing of board of directors, trustees, officers and other key people and their affiliations; detailed description of project and amount of funding requested; copy of IRS Determination Letter.
Geographic Focus: California, Florida, Georgia, Missouri, Ohio, Texas
Amount of Grant: 100 - 100,000 USD
Contact: Administrator; (305) 500-3031; fax (305) 500-4579; foundation@ryder.com
Sponsor: Ryder System Charitable Foundation
11690 NW 105th Street
Miami, FL 33178-1103

S. D. Bechtel, Jr. Foundation Stephen Bechtel Environmental Education Grants 4192

The Foundations believe that environmental education is vital to the development of a knowledgeable, skilled, and responsible California population that takes individual and collective actions to protect and improve the environment, human health, and economic prosperity. The Directors have a particular interest in supporting environmental education in order to further the goals of the STEM education, environment, character and citizenship development, and preventive healthcare program areas by improving access to high-quality programs and engaging all Californians in environmental learning and behavior. The Foundation supports organizations working to achieve the following objectives: building the research base to advance environmental education teaching and learning; expanding support for environmental education and promote environmental behavior; inspiring personal connections to the natural world and interest in STEM learning by strengthening systems that serve students in the San Francisco Bay Area; and encouraging local stewardship and develop new environmental leaders from urban communities in the San Francisco Bay Area.
Requirements: The primary geographic focus of the Foundation/Fund is the San Francisco Bay area. The Foundation/Fund: support non-profit organizations providing quality programs in science, technology, engineering and math (STEM) education, environment, environmental education, character and citizenship development and preventive healthcare and selected research; provide capital support; provide operational support; and provide project support.
Restrictions: The Foundation/Fund do not provide endowment funding, international grants, or grants for individuals.
Geographic Focus: California
Date(s) Application is Due: Oct 1
Amount of Grant: 5,000 - 25,000 USD
Contact: Coordinator; (415) 284-8675; fax (415) 284-8571; sdbjr@sdbjrfoundation.org
Internet: http://www.sdbjrfoundation.org/program_areas.htm#enviro_ed
Sponsor: S. D. Bechtel, Jr. Foundation / Stephen Bechtel Fund
P.O. Box 193809
San Francisco, CA 94119-3809

S.E.VEN Fund $50k VINE Project Prizes 4193

The VINE (Virtual Integrated Networking Experience) Project will award $50,000 in prizes to individuals or teams of contributors for developing investment indicators for emerging market SMEs (Small and Medium-sized Enterprises) through an online competition that invites anyone with ideas to submit, collaborate, and refine them. The end result will be an index of factors that the SEVEN Fund will release to the public to assist in broader analysis of investment opportunities for emerging market investment. The $50,000 will be awarded to participants at critical nodes along the 'vine' of the evolution of the winning idea; for

example, the originator of the winning proposal might receive $20,000, with $10,000 each for two key editors/future contributors, and $2,500 each for the other four finalists.
Requirements: This competition is open to anyone who wishes to participate. Participants must register at http://www.sevenfund.org/vine-form.php. The SEVEN Fund is putting out a challenge, a question to be answered by anyone and everyone:'What indicators can outside investors measure to help them predict the potential success of emerging market SMEs?' Phase I - Initial Submission: The first step to participating in the competition is to submit an idea. Participants may submit their ideas using the form at http://www.sevenfund.org/vine-form.php. Submitted ideas can take any form individual indicators, a complete framework for evaluation, an equation that can be used to input indicative information, anything you can come up with. Registrants may submit more than one idea. Initial submissions are limited to a maximum of 750 words, and should include a 100 word abstract. Phase II - Collaboration: All submitted ideas will be posted to a wiki and everyone who has submitted an idea will receive a username and password. During this period of collaboration, new and existing contributors can: post new ideas; comment on an existing idea; combine ideas; and/or, refine and change ideas. Phase III - Voting and Awards: The wiki will be closed to further edits registrations. $50,000 in prizes will be awarded. The online community will be asked to select the top five finalists. From there, an expert panel of judges will make the final selection of awards.
Geographic Focus: All States
Date(s) Application is Due: Nov 15
Amount of Grant: Up to 50,000 USD
Contact: Elizabeth Hooper, Executive Director; info@sevenfund.org
Internet: http://www.sevenfund.org/vine/
Sponsor: Social Equity Venture Fund (S.E.VEN)
1770 Massachusetts Avenue, 247
Cambridge, MA 02140

S.E.VEN Fund 'In The River They Swim' Essay Competition 4194
The SEVEN Fund is sponsoring a global competition seeking the best essays written in the spirit of 'In the River They Swim: Essays from Around the World on Enterprise Solutions to Poverty'. The top essay will be awarded a $10,000 prize; the best submissions will be published on www.inthirivertheyswim.com to be read by a global audience, and, perhaps, in a future book. There are no restrictions on the prize money.
Requirements: Anyone may participate in this essay competition. The winning author will be required to enter into a contract with SEVEN prior to final award. Applicants from every field of study, discipline, level and area of professional experience, and geographic region are welcome. Submissions should be 2000 words or less; should be well written and a pleasure to read; deeply introspective and probe the author's emotions and journey within development, globalization, and enterprise solutions to poverty. Take a theme from the book, or from life, and make it your own by infusing it with your insights and your story.
Restrictions: Each author may submit only one essay.
Geographic Focus: All States
Date(s) Application is Due: Sep 1
Amount of Grant: 10,000 USD
Contact: Elizabeth Hooper, Executive Director; info@sevenfund.org
Internet: http://www.sevenfund.org/book-river/
Sponsor: Social Equity Venture Fund (S.E.VEN)
1770 Massachusetts Avenue, 247
Cambridge, MA 02140

S.E.VEN Fund Annual Grants 4195
The sponsor is a virtual non-profit entity run by entrepreneurs whose strategy is to markedly increase the rate of diffusion of enterprise-based solutions to poverty. This is accomplished by targeted investment that fosters thought leadership through books, films and websites; supporting role models - whether they are entrepreneurs or innovative firms - in developing nations; and shaping a new discourse in government, the press and the academy around private-sector innovation, prosperity and progressive human values. This program is intended to catalyze, support and disseminate research on questions of economic development, prosperity and entrepreneurship. Funding is particularly targeted toward new frontiers in enterprise-based solutions to poverty and innovative ideas that are unlikely to be supported by conventional funding sources.
Requirements: S.E.VEN welcomes the participation of entrepreneurs, business people, investors, academics, laypeople, and philanthropists. To begin the process, add your name to the database online. Further information will be emailed to you.
Geographic Focus: All States
Amount of Grant: Up to 100,000 USD
Contact: Elizabeth Hooper, Executive Director; info@sevenfund.org
Internet: http://www.sevenfund.org/research-funding-areas.html
Sponsor: Social Equity Venture Fund (S.E.VEN)
1770 Massachusetts Avenue, 247
Cambridge, MA 02140

S.E.VEN Fund Mini-Grants 4196
The sponsor is a virtual non-profit entity run by entrepreneurs whose strategy is to markedly increase the rate of diffusion of enterprise-based solutions to poverty. This is accomplished by targeted investment that fosters thought leadership through books, films and websites; supporting role models - whether they are entrepreneurs or innovative firms - in developing nations; and shaping a new discourse in government, the press and the academy around private-sector innovation, prosperity and progressive human values. Mini-grant requests should align with the S.E.VEN Fund's funding priorities and do not exceed $10,000. The sponsor considers funding requests for mini-grants on an ongoing basis; the competition runs three times annually.
Requirements: This program's funding is intended to catalyze, support and disseminate research on questions of economic development, prosperity and entrepreneurship. Funding is particularly targeted toward new frontiers in enterprise-based solutions to poverty and innovative ideas that are unlikely to be supported by conventional funding sources. Funded projects are typically research-based or involve the creative use of the media - books, film, the Web, organizing conferences, etc. You can apply for funding by filling out the online mini-grant request form.
Restrictions: The sponsor is unable to provide funding for direct services.
Geographic Focus: All States
Amount of Grant: Up to 10,000 USD
Contact: Elizabeth Hooper, Executive Director; info@sevenfund.org
Internet: http://www.sevenfund.org/submit-mini-grants.php
Sponsor: Social Equity Venture Fund (S.E.VEN)
1770 Massachusetts Avenue, 247
Cambridge, MA 02140

S.E.VEN Fund Open Enterprise Solutions to Poverty RFP Grants 4197
The RFP competition focuses on academic and scientific research in the field of Enterprise-based Solutions to Poverty. The competition will award up to two (2) research grants of no more than $100,000 each for a duration of no more than twelve months. There is no geographic or other limitation on who may compete for these funds - anyone may compete for these funds.
Requirements: Anyone may submit an Initial Proposal in order to compete for a SEVEN RFP grant as long as the proposal reflects the scope and guidelines stated in the call for RFPs. The winning parties will be required to enter into a contract with SEVEN prior to final award. Since this is a program run by both practitioners and academics, SEVEN may be a bit more flexible than traditional funding agencies in the definition of a Principal Investigator. Thus, they may accept applications from non-academics as the PI or a co-investigator if his/her experience and background warrant it. Acceptable use of grant funds include: student or postdoctoral salary and benefits for part of the academic year; summer salary and teaching buyout for academics; support for specific projects during sabbaticals; assistance in writing or publishing books; modest allowance for justifiable equipment, computers, publication charges, and other supplies; modest travel allowance; development of workshops, conferences, or lecture series for professionals; or, justified overhead of at most 20%.
Geographic Focus: All States
Date(s) Application is Due: Oct 15
Amount of Grant: 100,000 USD
Contact: Elizabeth Hooper, Executive Director; info@sevenfund.org
Internet: http://www.sevenfund.org/enterprise-solutions-poverty/index.php
Sponsor: Social Equity Venture Fund (S.E.VEN)
1770 Massachusetts Avenue, 247
Cambridge, MA 02140

S.E.VEN Fund WHY Prize 4198
The sponsor's objective with The WHY Prize is to stimulate innovation in the specific domain of Enterprise Solutions to Poverty by encouraging collaboration; specifically, they will support collaboration between macroeconomists and anthropologists. The WHY Prize intends to catalyze cross-fertilization across disciplines and spur progress in finding sustainable solutions to poverty. The prize is a one-time award of $50,000.
Requirements: Anyone may submit a nomination in order to compete for The WHY Prize as long as the proposal reflects the scope and guidelines stated in the call for nominations. Individuals may nominate themselves or others for consideration. Nominated teams must include one individual who holds a masters or doctoral degree in economics and anthropology respectively. Other disciplines may join the collaboration to broaden the perspective beyond these two disciplines. The WHY prize will reward a team that has published in either a major venue like the Atlantic Monthly, New York Times Magazine, Financial Times, Businessweek, Forbes, Foreign Policy, Foreign Affairs etc. or in a peer reviewed journal, with a view toward producing further work such as a book or additional articles in a peer reviewed format. The published piece must add to the dialogue around enterprise solutions to poverty by proposing solutions that represent the best integration of actionable insights and thought leadership. Nominees may submit an article, paper, or book for consideration by applying on the sponsor's website.
Restrictions: Only applications submitted through the form on the website are accepted.
Geographic Focus: All States
Date(s) Application is Due: Oct 7
Contact: Elizabeth Hooper, Executive Director; info@sevenfund.org
Internet: http://www.sevenfund.org/press-release-mar-2008-WHY-prize.html#qanda
Sponsor: Social Equity Venture Fund (S.E.VEN)
1770 Massachusetts Avenue, 247
Cambridge, MA 02140

S.H. Cowell Foundation Grants 4199
The foundation awards grants for a wide variety of causes to nonprofit organizations in northern California. Projects of interest include those that support children, youth, and families; education; housing; alcohol abuse prevention; religious organizations, education, and welfare; school-to-work employment training; population and environment; family planning; and conventional arms control. Applicants are encouraged to obtain most of their operating and project funding from other sources. Matching and challenge grants will be awarded under appropriate circumstances. The foundation prefers to award grants for one-time capital needs or for specific projects that are time-definite in nature and likely to become self-sufficient within several years. The application process should begin with a phone call. If interested, the foundation will request a short letter and then a formal proposal.
Requirements: Grants are made only to 501(c)3 tax-exempt organizations primarily in northern California.
Restrictions: The foundation does not normally make grants to individuals, for start-up of new organizations, for academic or other research, for general support, for annual fund-

raising, to governmental agencies, to churches for religious support, to hospitals for medical research or treatment, for conferences, for media projects, or for political lobbying.
Geographic Focus: California
Amount of Grant: Up to 500,000 USD
Contact: Susan Vandiver; (415) 397-0285; fax (415) 986-6786; info@shcowell.org
Internet: http://www.shcowell.org/grant/grant.php
Sponsor: S.H. Cowell Foundation
120 Montgomery Street, Suite 2570
San Francisco, CA 94104

S. Livingston Mather Charitable Trust Grants 4200
The S. Livingston Mather Charitable Trust was established in 1953 in Ohio by Cleveland-Cliffs vice-president Samuel Livingston Mather. The Trust's primary areas of interest include cultural programs, education, child welfare, and social services. Support is also available for youth programs, the environment, and natural resources. Giving is primarily restricted to the northeastern Ohio area. Applicants should contact the Trust prior to submitting an application.
Requirements: Unsolicited requests for funds not accepted, contact the Trust before sending a proposal.
Restrictions: No support is available for: endowments; science; medical research programs; in areas appropriately supported by the government and/or the United Way; individuals; or deficit financing.
Geographic Focus: Ohio
Amount of Grant: 100 - 100,000 USD
Contact: Janet W. Havener, Director, c/o Glenmede Trust Company; (215) 419-6000
Sponsor: S. Livingston Mather Charitable Trust
1 Corporate Exchange, 25825 Science Park Drive, Suite 110
Beachwood, OH 44122

S. Mark Taper Foundation Grants 4201
The S. Mark Taper Foundation, founded in 1989, is a private family foundation dedicated to enhancing the quality of people's lives by supporting nonprofit organizations and their work in the Los Angeles, Long Beach, Santa Ana, California communities. Areas of interest are broad and include but are not limited to education, the environment, independent living for the disabled, abused women, immigrant health care, children, hunger, housing, AIDS, teenage pregnancy prevention, job creation and economic revitalization, individuals with visual impairments, and the arts. Types of support include capital grants, challenge/matching grants, general operating grants, research grants, program/project grants, seed money grants, and scholarships. Grants are made generally for one year.
Requirements: 501(c)3 nonprofit organizations in California are eligible for grant support. Application forms are required therefore your initial approach should be a Letter of Inquiry containing one copy of the proposal and the following: brief history of organization and description of its mission; copy of most recent annual report/audited financial statement/990; detailed description of project and amount of funding requested; list of source(s) of last three years of funding for the specific project (if any) and, the organization.
Geographic Focus: California
Date(s) Application is Due: Dec 1
Amount of Grant: 5,000 - 500,000 USD
Contact: Raymond Reister, Executive Director; (310) 476-5413; fax (310) 471-4993; rreisler@smtfoundation.org or info@smtfoundation.org
Internet: http://www.smtfoundation.org/
Sponsor: S. Mark Taper Foundation
12011 San Vicente Boulavard, Suite 400
Los Angeles, CA 90049

S. Spencer Scott Fund Grants 4202
Established in New York in 1949, the S. Spencer Scott Fund serves the residents of Connecticut, Rhode Island, New York, Vermont, Maine, Maryland, New Hampshire, Pennsylvania, and Massachusetts. Its primary fields of interest include the arts, museums, education, and religion. There are no particular application forms or annual deadlines, and applicants are advised to contact the Fund directly. Funding general is given for general operations, and amounts range from $250 to $5,000.
Requirements: Any 501(c)3 organization serving the residents of Connecticut, Rhode Island, New York, Vermont, Maryland, Maine, New Hampshire, Pennsylvania, and Massachusetts are eligible to apply.
Geographic Focus: Connecticut, Maine, Maryland, Massachusetts, New Hampshire, New York, Pennsylvania, Rhode Island, Vermont
Amount of Grant: 250 - 5,000 USD
Contact: Suzette Hearn, Treasurer; (212) 286-2600
Sponsor: S. Spencer Scott Fund
60 E. 42nd Street, Suite 3600
New York, NY 10165-0006

Safeco Insurance Community Grants 4203
The program supports the enhancement of neighborhoods. Grants are awarded to programs and organizations that play a role in building an economic foundation for strong neighborhoods—programs that encourage small business development and growth, and homebuyer education programs for low- and moderate-income populations that include homeowners insurance education; protecting the foundation of strong neighborhoods—loss-prevention programs for homeowners, and safety and disaster preparedness programs; helping neighborhoods flourish and thrive—neighborhood festivals that attract diverse audiences, community clean-ups and neighborhood beautification projects, and the creation or enhancement of pocket parks and gathering spaces. Priority is given to programs serving disadvantaged and diverse populations. Grant seekers are encouraged to email a general overview of the funding request prior to developing a full proposal.
Requirements: 501(c)3 organizations located in Puget Sound, WA; Golden, CO; Richmond, VA; Aliso Viejo, CA; Hartford, CT; Rochester, NY; Atlanta, GA; Indianapolis, IN; Spokane, WA; Chicago, IL; Nashville, TN; Saint Louis, MO; Cincinnati, OH; Orlando, FL; Dallas, TX; and Portland, OR, are eligible.
Restrictions: Proposals are not accepted for amateur arts; amateur sports teams or athletic scholarships; capital campaigns; conferences; colleges or universities; endowment funds; film or video production; fraternal or political projects; general fundraising and advertising; health education, research or prevention; hospitals or hospital foundations; individuals; individual K-12 public and private schools; loans and investments; operating deficits, debt retirement, or emergency funding; projects of a national nature; research; or theological functions or church-sponsored nonsecular programs.
Geographic Focus: California, Colorado, Connecticut, Florida, Georgia, Illinois, Indiana, Missouri, New York, Ohio, Oregon, Tennessee, Texas, Virginia, Washington
Date(s) Application is Due: Feb 25; May 27; Aug 12; Oct 31
Contact: Grants Coordinator; (206) 545-5015; fax (206) 545-5730; comrel@safeco.com
Internet: http://www.safeco.com/safeco/in_the_community/corporate_giving/community_grants.asp
Sponsor: Safeco Insurance Corporation
4333 Brooklyn Avenue, Safeco Plaza, T-8
Seattle, WA 98185

Sage Foundation Grants 4204
The foundation awards grants nationwide, with emphasis on the Midwest, to nonprofit organizations in support of higher education, legal education, and secondary education; seniors; hospitals; disabled; Catholic giving and welfare; youth; child welfare; social services; and cultural programs. Types of support include annual campaigns, building construction/renovation, capital campaigns, challenge grants, endowments, equipment acquisition, general operating grants, multi-year support, project development, research, and scholarship funds. There are no application deadlines or forms; submit a letter of inquiry. The board meets quarterly.
Geographic Focus: All States
Amount of Grant: 1,000 - 250,000 USD
Contact: Melissa Sage Fadim, Grants Administrator; (810) 227-7660 or (212) 737-7311
Sponsor: Sage Foundation
P.O. Box 1919
Brighton, MI 48116

Saginaw Community Foundation Discretionary Grants 4205
Saginaw Community Foundation's Discretionary Grants are designed to meet the needs of a wide variety of nonprofit organizations. The Foundation's grants are intended to help residents build a strong community by addressing pressing needs in the County.
Requirements: Applicants must first call the Foundation to discuss the project with the staff. To be eligible for funding, organizations must have a nonprofit status and directly benefit Saginaw County. Grants are ordinarily only made for one year. Applications must be received by mail, or dropped off at the agency.
Restrictions: The Saginaw Community Foundation does not support: operating budgets; basic municipal services; basic educational functions; endowment campaigns; previously incurred debt; or sectarian religious programs.
Geographic Focus: Michigan
Date(s) Application is Due: Feb 1; May 1; Aug 1; Nov 1
Amount of Grant: Up to 10,000 USD
Contact: Kendra Kempf, Program Associate/FORCE Coordinator; (989) 755-0545; fax (989) 755-6524; kendra@saginawfoundation.org
Internet: http://www.saginawfoundation.org/grants_and_scholarships/grants/
Sponsor: Saginaw Community Foundation
100 South Jefferson, Suite 201
Saginaw, MI 48602

Saginaw Community Foundation Senior Citizen Enrichment Fund 4206
The Senior Citizens Enrichment Fund assists programs supporting charitable purposes that benefit the elderly in Saginaw County. The priority of this grant is to assist programs and projects that enhance the quality of life for seniors maintaining an independent residence.
Requirements: Applicants must first call the Foundation to discuss the project with the staff. To be eligible for funding, organizations must have a nonprofit status and directly benefit Saginaw County. Grants are ordinarily only made for one year. Applications can be downloaded at the website but must be received by mail or dropped off at the agency.
Restrictions: The Saginaw Community Foundation does not support: operating budgets; basic municipal services; basic educational functions; endowment campaigns; previously incurred debt; or sectarian religious programs.
Geographic Focus: Michigan
Date(s) Application is Due: Feb 1; May 1; Aug 1; Nov 1
Amount of Grant: Up to 10,000 USD
Contact: Kendra Kempf, Program Associate/FORCE Coordinator; (989) 755-0545; fax (989) 755-6524; kendra@saginawfoundation.org
Internet: http://www.saginawfoundation.org/grants_and_scholarships/grants/
Sponsor: Saginaw Community Foundation
100 South Jefferson, Suite 201
Saginaw, MI 48602

Saginaw Community Foundation YWCA Fund for Women and Girls Grants   4207
YWCA Fund for Women and Girls Grants support projects and programs that benefit women and girls of Saginaw County. Specifically, its goals are: to support the physical, intellectual, emotional, social and spiritual needs of women, children and families; and to foster the elimination of racism and sexism.
Requirements: Applicants must first call the Foundation to discuss the project with the staff. To be eligible for funding, organizations must have a nonprofit status and directly benefit Saginaw County. Grants are ordinarily only made for one year. Applications can be downloaded at the website but must be received by mail or dropped off at the agency.
Restrictions: The Saginaw Community Foundation does not support: operating budgets; basic municipal services; basic educational functions; endowment campaigns; previously incurred debt; or sectarian religious programs.
Geographic Focus: Michigan
Date(s) Application is Due: Feb 1; May 1; Aug 1; Nov 1
Amount of Grant: Up to 5,000 USD
Contact: Kendra Kempf, Program Associate/FORCE Coordinator; (989) 755-0545; fax (989) 755-6524; kendra@saginawfoundation.org
Internet: http://www.saginawfoundation.org/grants_and_scholarships/grants/
Sponsor: Saginaw Community Foundation
100 South Jefferson, Suite 201
Saginaw, MI 48602

Saginaw County Community Foundation Youth FORCE Grants   4208
Saginaw County Youth FORCE Grants directly benefit young people. Priority of this grant is placed on projects that: include youth in the planning and implementation; empower youth and increase their awareness of community issues; and are first-time funding requests.
Requirements: Applicants must contact the Community Foundation before submitting a grant application to discuss the proposed project. Student organizations applying for FORCE funds must have an adult supervisor. Also, organizations must be 501(c)3 and the proposed program must directly benefit Saginaw County. Applications can be downloaded at the website but must be sent by mail or hand-delivered at the office.
Restrictions: Applicants to FORCE grants must be 20 years of age or younger. In addition, Saginaw Community Foundation does not fund: operating budgets; basic municipal services; basic educational functions; endowment campaigns; previously incurred debt; or sectarian religious programs.
Geographic Focus: Michigan
Date(s) Application is Due: Feb 1; Nov 1
Amount of Grant: Up to 10,000 USD
Contact: Kendra Kempf; (989) 755-0545; fax (989) 755-6524; kendra@saginawfoundation.org
Internet: http://www.saginawfoundation.org/grants_and_scholarships/grants/
Sponsor: Saginaw Community Foundation
100 South Jefferson, Suite 201
Saginaw, MI 48602

SAG Motion Picture Players Welfare Fund Grants   4209
The Motion Picture Players Welfare Fund (MPPWF) is an emergency financial assistance fund of the Screen Actors Guild New York region designed to assist eligible members who are struggling with a financial, personal or medical crisis. The Screen Actors Guild contracts with The Actors Fund to administer the MPPWF as well as provide an array of services to meet each members needs. Services include counseling and referrals for personal, family or work-related problems. Linkage to community resources for legal services, elder care, entitlement benefits or childcare. Workshops are offered on locating affordable housing, financial education as well as health insurance options. Financial assistance is available for rent, utilities, mental health and medical care as well as other basic living expenses. Grants are approved on a case-by-case basis based on need.
Requirements: All SAG members should feel free to call The Actors Fund for information, referrals and access to our social services. To be eligible for financial assistance from MPPWF you must be: living in the New York Tri-State area; a SAG member for at least six dues periods; a member in good standing at the time of application or be vested for pension purposes; and, able to document a need for emergency financial assistance.
Geographic Focus: New York
Contact: Program Director; (212) 221-7300, ext. 119
Internet: http://new.actorsfund.org/services/Partner_Programs/Motion_Picture_Players/index_html
Sponsor: Screen Actors Guild
360 Madison Avenue, 12th Floor
New York, NY 10017

Saigh Foundation Grants   4210
Fred M. Saigh was born in Springfield, Illinois on June 27, 1905, the son of Lebanese immigrants who owned a chain of grocery stores. He passed away in 1999. Although he is best known as the owner of the St. Louis Cardinals (1948 - 1953), many of his friends and acquaintances will always remember him as a perceptive and caring benefactor - "a one-man charity fund," in the words of sportswriter Mike Eisenbath. The Saigh Foundation continues the important work begun by Mr. Saigh by assisting St. Louis-area organizations that benefit children and youth, particularly in the areas of education and healthcare. The foundation is particularly interested in stimulating the development of new ventures, as well as in supporting organizations that feature innovative approaches or programs. Like Mr. Saigh, the foundation is especially dedicated to aiding those who might not otherwise receive assistance. Proposals are requested at least three months before any quarterly meeting. These are normally held in January, April, July, and October. The foundation uses a customized version of the Missouri Common Grant Application (CGA). It is available at the grant website along with guidelines and budget templates and should be submitted via mail or fax to the address given.
Requirements: Saint Louis-area nonprofit organizations are eligible.
Restrictions: The foundation does not participate in annual appeals, dinner functions, and fundraising events; capital campaigns; loans and deficits; grants for films and travel; or nonprofit organizations outside of the metropolitan Saint Louis area.
Geographic Focus: Missouri
Contact: JoAnn Hejna; (314) 862-3055; fax (314) 862-9288; saigh@thesaighfoundation.org
Internet: http://www.thesaighfoundation.org/grant_guide.html
Sponsor: Saigh Foundation
7777 Bonhomme Avenue, Suite 2007
Saint Louis, MO 63105

Sailors' Snug Harbor of Boston Elder Programs Grants   4211
Sailors' Snug Harbor of Boston began its formal grantmaking program with a focus on assisting seamen and their families. In 1970, the Trustees voted to extend eligibility for grants to agencies that serve low-income elderly men and women in the Greater Boston area. The SSH trustees typically set aside approximately one-half of the Foundation's annual allocations budget for Elder Programs. Examples of qualified programs include, but are not limited to, the following: advocacy for and provision of suitable housing for the elderly; health and social services to help the elderly live independently in their homes for as long as possible; services, including transportation, which increase elders' access to community health and social services; improved coordination of services for the elderly; and technical assistance and training, for both volunteer/family caregivers and human service providers, which will improve the quality of life for the elderly.
Geographic Focus: Massachusetts
Date(s) Application is Due: Dec 15
Contact: Gracelaw Simmons, Administrator; (617) 426-7080, ext. 312 or (617) 426-7080; fax (617) 426-5441; gsimmons@gmafoundations.com
Internet: http://home.comcast.net/~sailorssnug/
Sponsor: Sailors' Snug Harbor of Boston
77 Summer Street, 8th Floor
Boston, MA 02110-2449

Sailors' Snug Harbor of Boston Fishing Communities Initiative Grants   4212
The focus of this initiative is to help current and former fishing families in Massachusetts achieve sustainable self-sufficiency during this period of transition in their industry. It is the trustees' hope that funded programs will work with fishermen and their families through the immediate crisis and beyond. The trustees are interested in making grants to 501(c)3 organizations that are presently providing services to fishermen and their families. They are also interested in supporting agencies that would like to expand or develop new programs to serve the onshore needs of fishermen and their families. Organizations that received funding from this initiative in prior years are eligible to reapply this year. The deadline is the last Monday in August annually.
Requirements: Massachusetts 501(c)3 tax-exempt organizations are eligible.
Geographic Focus: Massachusetts
Date(s) Application is Due: Aug 31
Amount of Grant: 5,000 - 25,000 USD
Contact: Gracelaw Simmons, Administrator; (617) 426-7080, ext. 312 or (617) 426-7080; fax (617) 426-5441; gsimmons@gmafoundations.com
Internet: http://home.comcast.net/~sailorssnug/
Sponsor: Sailors' Snug Harbor of Boston
77 Summer Street, 8th Floor
Boston, MA 02110-2449

Saint George's Society of New York Scholarships   4213
The Society's funds will be directed to matriculate undergraduate upperclassmen/women (with a minimum of 60-plus earned credits) at four senior colleges of the City University of New York. The colleges which are the initial targets for the SGS Program are: Brooklyn, City, Lehman, and Queens. These institutions have the largest local concentration of British Commonwealth immigrants or first generation British Commonwealth descendants. The SGS Grant is renewable for an additional (Senior) year if the recipient is in his or her Junior Year of study as long as the 3.75 GPA is maintained.
Requirements: Recipients must have a combined Grade Point Average of 3.75 (on a 4.0 system) in order to qualify for SGS assistance.
Geographic Focus: New York
Contact: John Shannon; (212) 682-6110; john.shannon@stgeorgessociety.org
Internet: http://www.stgeorgessociety.org/scholarships.php
Sponsor: Saint George's Society of New York
216 East 45th Street, Suite 901
New York, NY 10017-3304

Saint Louis Rams Foundation Community Donations   4214
The foundation supports nonprofits that help inspire positive change for youth in the Saint Louis area. Programs that impact youth in the general fields of education, literacy, health, and recreation will be considered. Annually, the Rams provide to charitable groups more than 3,500 items, helping recipient organizations raise thousands of dollars through raffles, auctions and other fundraising endeavors. Other types of financial support include program development grants and general operating grants. The foundation does not accept unsolicited requests, but initial information may be sent for the office to keep on file for future opportunities.
Requirements: Nonprofits in the metropolitan Saint Louis, Missouri, area, including southern Illinois and eastern Missouri, are eligible. Preference is given to organizations that partner with other local nonprofits and offer creative approaches for more than grants (i.e., personnel involvement or in-kind support) and ways the Rams can participate.

Restrictions: The Rams do not provide monetary contributions or merchandise donations for the following: businesses, retail and otherwise; capital campaigns/start-up funding for new businesses; on-line auctions; chamber of commerce/city/neighborhood festivals such as homecoming celebrations and carnivals that do not directly benefit a charitable organization; class reunions; family reunions; pageant contestants (beauty and otherwise); student ambassador/exchange programs; or non-charity events and organizations such as company picnics, employee golf tournaments, employee recognition/incentive programs, card clubs, car shows, "poker runs", and organized adult leisure sports teams.
Geographic Focus: Missouri
Date(s) Application is Due: Jan 1; Jul 1
Contact: Donations Coordinator; (314) 516-8788 or (314) 982-7267; fax (314) 770-0392
Internet: http://www.stlouisrams.com/community/donations.html
Sponsor: Saint Louis Rams Foundation
1 Rams Way
Saint Louis, MO 63045

Saint Luke's Foundation Grants 4215
The foundation exists to improve the health and well being of individuals and families living in Greater Cleveland. Proposals are invited for activities intended to enhance community involvement and ownership; promote healthy behaviors and life styles by education and outreach programs aimed at increasing the capacity of individuals and families to protect and improve their own health; increase and improve health care by improving access to affordable, high-quality, comprehensive, culturally competent and appropriate health care; educate health care professionals to increase their capacity in serving the health and health care needs of inner-city residents; and increase knowledge by furthering research on: the determinants of health; innovative systems, strategies, and collaborations designed to improve health and well being in the community; and the underlying causes of diseases and disabilities particularly prevalent in the communities.
Requirements: 501(c)3 tax-exempt organizations and governmental units/agencies are eligible. The grant application is a 3 step process: step 1: Letter of Inquiry; step 2: site visit; step 3: proposal submission. See website for detailed description of each step. The deadlines posted are for the Letter of Inquiry.
Restrictions: The Foundation does not fund: individuals; religious organizations for religious or evangelical purposes; projects outside Greater Cleveland that do not directly benefit Cleveland residents; fundraising events; endowment funds; biomedical research; debt retirement; lobbying.
Geographic Focus: Ohio
Date(s) Application is Due: Jan 5; Apr 1; Jul 1; Aug 1; Oct 1
Contact: Peg Butler; (216) 431-8010; fax (216) 431-8015; pbutler@saintlukesfoundation.org
Internet: http://www.saintlukesfoundation.org/grants/community-grants.html
Sponsor: Saint Luke's Foundation of Cleveland, Ohio
4208 Prospect Avenue
Cleveland, OH 44103

Saint Luke's Health Initiatives Grants 4216
The trust was established for the purpose of addressing critical health needs in Maricopa County, AZ. Community grants support innovative approaches that address community health from a broad perspective, including funding for such projects as professional education and training, public education/advocacy demonstration projects, program planning and expansion, and equipment to address the health needs of populations that are considered underserved and vulnerable. Community grants are awarded for up to two years. Bridge grants support small, emerging organizations or new programs of larger organizations that have infrastructure or developmental needs. Grants support strategic planning, technical training, purchasing equipment, or convening discussion groups on community health issues. Bridge grants are awarded for one year. Inquiries are encouraged prior to proposal submission.
Requirements: To be eligible for a community partnership grant, a prospective organization must: demonstrate tax-exempt status under Section 501(c)3 of the Internal Revenue Service Code or be recognized as an instrumentality of state/local government; be located in Arizona. Preference is given to organizations within Maricopa County, although a statewide program with impact on Maricopa County will be considered.
Restrictions: The trust does not fund individuals, participate in large capital campaigns or endowment drives, provide grants for ongoing annual operating support, or fund projects of sectarian or religious organizations.
Geographic Focus: Arizona
Date(s) Application is Due: Feb 12; Aug 14
Amount of Grant: 10,000 - 100,000 USD
Contact: Jane Pearson, Associate Director; (602) 385-6500; fax (602) 385-6510; Jane.Pearson@slhi.org or info@slhi.org
Internet: http://www.slhi.org/community_grants/how_to_apply.shtml
Sponsor: Saint Luke's Health Initiatives
2929 North Central Avenue, Suite 1550
Phoenix, AZ 85012

Saint Paul Companies Foundation Grants 4217
Saint Paul Companies is dedicated to strengthening the communities in which its employees live and work. Grants are considered for programs that fall under one or more of the following focus areas: enrich lives and celebrate diversity through arts and culture; revitalize communities; and educate underserved populations to create social and economic opportunities. Grants are made for operating,support, program/project support, capital support, start-up funding, and transitional support. Grantmaking is restricted to the Twin Cities (primarily Saint Paul), the Baltimore area, the United Kingdom, and selected locations where the corporation has a significant business presence. An organization seeking funds for new programs should begin the application process by submitting a one-page letter describing the request. The foundation no longer accepts paper applications; all applications must be made online. Application guidelines at the Travelers website.
Geographic Focus: Minnesota, United Kingdom
Date(s) Application is Due: Sep 1
Amount of Grant: 15,000 - 250,000 USD
Contact: Ronald McKinley, Community Affairs; (651) 310-2623 or (800) 328-2189
Internet: http://www.travelers.com/corporate-info/about/community/foundation.aspx
Sponsor: Saint Paul Companies
385 Washington Street
Saint Paul, MN 55102-1396

Saint Paul Foundation Community Sharing Fund Grants 4218
The purpose of the Community Sharing Fund is to provide funding to individuals, families and organizations with verifiable emergency needs when other services or funds are unavailable. Grants are approved for rent, damage deposit, utility costs, medical expenses, child care, transportation, and other critical needs. Grant amounts range from $20 to $500. The average grant is $320; the maximum grant may vary depending on the availability of funds.
Requirements: The applicant must be a resident of Dakota, Ramsey or Washington County, Minnesota.
Restrictions: Grants are not provided to applicants that have received a grant from the Community Sharing Fund within the last 18 months.
Geographic Focus: Minnesota
Amount of Grant: 20 - 500 USD
Contact: Michael J. Conaboy, Program Associate; (651) 224-5463; fax (651) 379-5326; mjc@saintpaulfoundation.org
Internet: http://www.saintpaulfoundation.org/grants/community_sharing_fund/
Sponsor: Saint Paul Foundation
55 Fifth Street E, Suite 600
Saint Paul, MN 55101-1797

Saint Paul Foundation Grants 4219
The community foundation serves the greater Saint Paul, Minnesota, area and makes grants to support educational (including adult basic education and literacy programs), charitable, or cultural programs/projects that benefit residents of Ramsey, Washington, and Dakota Counties. The foundation's grantmaking vehicles include project/program, start-up costs, general operating support, capital projects, and matching funds. Support will ordinarily not exceed three years. There are no application deadlines; however, full proposals must be received approximately three and one-half months prior to the meeting date. The board meets in April, August, and December.
Requirements: Minnesota 501(c)3 tax-exempt organizations are eligible.
Restrictions: The foundation will not consider requests for ongoing annual operating expenses; sectarian religious programs; grants to individuals; capital projects located outside Ramsey, Dakota, and Washington Counties; or programs not serving residents of Ramsey, Dakota, and Washington Counties.
Geographic Focus: Minnesota
Amount of Grant: 250 - 500,000 USD
Contact: John G. Couchman, Vice-President; (651) 224-5463; fax (651) 224-8123; jgc@saintpaulfoundation.org or inbox@saintpaulfoundation.org
Internet: http://www.saintpaulfoundation.org/grants/apply_for_a_foundation_grant/
Sponsor: Saint Paul Foundation
55 Fifth Street E, Suite 600
Saint Paul, MN 55101-1797

Saint Paul Foundation Lowertown Future Fund Grants 4220
Grants will be made to nonprofit organizations or neighborhood groups with a nonprofit fiscal agent working on projects to improve or enrich the Lowertown neighborhood, including grants for programs, studies for neighborhoods, or possibly even assisting construction of small buildings or other amenities. The Fund can and may make multiple year commitments but is not likely to accept endowment requests. There are virtually no limits to the range of opportunity or imagination offered to grant requests as long as there is a reasonable and not contrived relationship to Lowertown. Grant proposals should define expected outcomes and the means to measure or evaluate the success of a program. Grants will be considered in a range of $1,000 to $100,000 - although thoughtful exceptions will be reviewed. The grantmaking schedule will follow a calendar cycle with two review meetings scheduled each year during the second week of April and October.
Requirements: Minnesota 501(c)3 tax-exempt organizations are eligible.
Geographic Focus: Minnesota
Amount of Grant: 1,000 - 100,000 USD
Contact: Sally Seiberlich, (651) 325-4237; sjs@saintpaulfoundation.org
Internet: http://www.saintpaulfoundation.org/grants/lowertown_future_fund/
Sponsor: Saint Paul Foundation
55 Fifth Street E, Suite 600
Saint Paul, MN 55101-1797

Saint Paul Foundation Management Improvement Fund Grants 4221
The Management Improvement Fund, a special project of The Saint Paul Foundation, provides grants to nonprofit organizations operating in, or serving a substantial portion of their clients in Ramsey, Dakota and Washington counties. This Fund makes grants to nonprofit organizations to finance the cost of consultation or technical assistance to improve organizational capacity and management capabilities to better serve the community. The staff of the Saint Paul Foundation provides assistance to potential grant applicants to help them define needs appropriate for funding and works closely with grant recipients to monitor their progress on their projects. A percentage of matching funds is recommended

based on an organization's budget. Generally, larger organizations are asked to secure more matching funds than those with smaller budgets. Annual operating budget matching guidelines: $0-$1 million—no match required; $1 million to $2.5 million—25% of project budget; and $2.5 million or higher—50% of the project budget.
Requirements: Minnesota 501(c)3 tax-exempt organizations are eligible.
Geographic Focus: Minnesota
Contact: Jerry Timian; (651) 325-4286; fax (651) 379-5386; gct@saintpaulfoundation.org
Internet: http://www.saintpaulfoundation.org/grants/management_improvement_fund/
Sponsor: Saint Paul Foundation
55 Fifth Street E, Suite 600
Saint Paul, MN 55101-1797

Saint Paul Foundation SpectrumTrust Grants 4222
The SpectrumTrust Endowments are Minnesota statewide funds that include a Multicultural Endowment as well as four community-specific endowments (Asian Pacific Community, El Fondo de Nuestra Comunidad, Pan African Community, and Two Feathers Community). Each endowment is operated by a committee made up of volunteers from the respective cultural community. These committees develop their own grantmaking guidelines specific to the unique characteristics of their communities. Proposals that meet guidelines are solicited widely from within each of the communities. Applicants should note that the application process and accompanying materials are specific to each endowment. Deadlines and amounts vary from guidelines to guidelines.
Requirements: Minnesota 501(c)3 tax-exempt organizations are eligible.
Geographic Focus: Minnesota
Contact: Anne Pierre, (651) 325-4229 or (651) 224-5463; ajp@saintpaulfoundation.org
Internet: http://www.saintpaulfoundation.org/grants/spectrumtrust/
Sponsor: Saint Paul Foundation
55 Fifth Street E, Suite 600
Saint Paul, MN 55101-1797

Salem Foundation Charitable Trust Grants 4223
The Foundation provides funding for a large variety of community based programs that serve the greater Salem area. In partnership with donors, the Foundation supports nonprofit and other community organizations with funds for health and human services, affordable housing, early childhood development, community arts, culture and other important areas of need. Grant making decisions are made by the Distribution Committee, comprised of five Salem area residents.
Requirements: Must be a community-based organization that serves the greater Salem region. Grants may be made only to organizations which have received appropriate determination letters from the Internal Revenue Service that they are exempt under the Internal Revenue Code.
Geographic Focus: Oregon
Date(s) Application is Due: May 1; Dec 1
Contact: Trustee; (503) 363-3136; salemfoundation@pioneertrustbank.com
Internet: http://www.pioneertrustbank.com/salemfoundation/index.html
Sponsor: Salem Foundation Charitable Trust
109 Commercial Street NE, P.O. Box 2305
Salem, OR 97308

Salisbury Community Foundation Grants 4224
The foundation was created to address the needs of the Salisbury, NC, community and its residents. Nonprofit organizations may apply for project support in the categories of arts, education, environment, historic preservation, human services, health and medical research, public and civic affairs, religion, the elderly, and youth services. Applications are accepted throughout the year.
Requirements: Tax-exempt, charitable organizations in Salisbury, NC, and Rowan county are eligible.
Geographic Focus: North Carolina
Date(s) Application is Due: Jan 31; Apr 30; Jul 31; Oct 31
Amount of Grant: 10,000 USD
Contact: McCray Benson; (704) 973-4559; fax (704) 973-4946; mvbenson@fftc.org
Internet: http://www.fftc.org/affiliates/community/nc/salisbury
Sponsor: Salisbury Community Foundation
217 S Tryon Street
Charlotte, NC 28202

Salmon Foundation Grants 4225
Established in New York in 1991, the Salmon Foundation provides funding to nonprofit organizations for programs providing for children and youth programs, family services, and education. Grants are awarded for projects, scholarship support, operating support, and capital funding. Funding ranges from $2,000 to $40,000.
Requirements: Funding provided to nonprofit organizations. Organizations tend to be on the east coast and include Connecticut, New Hampshire, Vermont, Ohio, Pennsylvania, Alabama, Tennessee, Virginia, California, Maryland, Colorado and District of Columbia.
Restrictions: No individual scholarships are made.
Geographic Focus: Alabama, California, Colorado, Connecticut, District of Columbia, Maryland, New Hampshire, Pennsylvania, Tennessee, Virginia
Amount of Grant: 2,000 - 40,000 USD
Contact: Emily Grand, Administrator; (212) 708-9316 or (212) 812-4362
Sponsor: Salmon Foundation, Inc.
6 West 48th Street, 10th Floor
New York, NY 10036-1802

Salt River Project Civic Leadership Grants 4226
Salt River Project (SRP) is an energy/utilities company serving electric customers and water shareholders in the Phoenix metropolitan area. SRP provides funding to nonprofit organizations that address critical needs within its service communities. Civic Leadership Grants increase the local community's ability to identify and train local residents to serve in leadership positions; sponsor select special community events; and support community forums which enhance the quality of life through discussion of emerging issues and strategic planning.
Requirements: Eligible applicants must be 501(c)3 nonprofit, organizations within SRP's service area. SRP's service area is central Arizona and includes the following cities and towns: Phoenix, Mesa, Tempe, Paradise Valley, Fountain Hills, Scottsdale, Apache Junction, Peoria, Queen Creek, Avondale, Chandler, Gilbert, Glendale, Guadalupe, and Tolleson. There are no specific grant deadlines. Requests are reviewed in an on-going process which typically takes eight weeks.
Restrictions: The following are ineligible: individuals, including support for specific students, researchers, travel expenses, conference fees; organizations that discriminate on the basis of race, creed, color, sex, or national origin; endowment programs; medical research projects or medical procedures for individuals; professional schools of art, academic art programs, individual high school or college performing groups; political or lobbying groups or campaigns; fraternal organizations, veterans' organizations, professional associations, and similar membership groups; public or commercial broadcasting programs; religious activities or church-sponsored programs limited to church membership; and debt-reduction campaigns. SRP does not donate services, including water or electricity, or equipment for which a fee is normally charged.
Geographic Focus: Arizona
Contact: Corporate Contributions Administrator; (602) 236-5900; webmstr@srpnet.com
Internet: http://www.srpnet.com/community/contributions/guidelines.aspx
Sponsor: Salt River Project
1521 North Project Drive
Tempe, AZ 85281-1298

Salt River Project Environmental Quality Grants 4227
Salt River Project (SRP) is an energy/utilities company serving electric customers and water shareholders in the Phoenix metropolitan area. SRP provides funding to nonprofit organizations that address critical needs within its service communities. SRP believes in stewardship of Arizona's natural resources and protecting the water and air quality of Arizona. Environmental Quality Grants focus on improving the environmental quality of neighborhoods and supporting programs that promote the awareness and understanding of technical environmental issues.
Requirements: Eligible applicants must be 501(c)3 nonprofit, organizations within SRP's service area. SRP's service area is central Arizona and includes the following cities and towns: Phoenix, Mesa, Tempe, Paradise Valley, Fountain Hills, Scottsdale, Apache Junction, Peoria, Queen Creek, Avondale, Chandler, Gilbert, Glendale, Guadalupe, and Tolleson. There are no specific grant deadlines. Requests are reviewed in an on-going process which typically takes eight weeks.
Restrictions: The following are ineligible: individuals, including support for specific students, researchers, travel expenses, conference fees; organizations that discriminate on the basis of race, creed, color, sex, or national origin; endowment programs; medical research projects or medical procedures for individuals; professional schools of art, academic art programs, individual high school or college performing groups; political or lobbying groups or campaigns; fraternal organizations, veterans' organizations, professional associations, and similar membership groups; public or commercial broadcasting programs; religious activities or church-sponsored programs limited to church membership; and debt-reduction campaigns. SRP does not donate services, including water or electricity, or equipment for which a fee is normally charged.
Geographic Focus: Arizona
Contact: Corporate Contributions Administrator; (602) 236-5900
Internet: http://www.srpnet.com/community/contributions/guidelines.aspx
Sponsor: Salt River Project
1521 North Project Drive
Tempe, AZ 85281-1298

Salt River Project Health and Human Services Grants 4228
Salt River Project (SRP) is an energy/utilities company serving electric customers and water shareholders in the Phoenix metropolitan area. SRP provides funding to nonprofit organizations that address critical needs within its service communities. SRP is committed to safe and healthy communities. Health and Human Services Grants support programs that reach out to underserved communities to promote the individual's ability to overcome barriers and be self-sufficient; increase the community's ability to care for individuals who are in need of food, shelter, and safety from violent or crisis situations; increase the ability of children to participate in youth programs which promote personal development and positive life choices; support increasing underserved communities' access to hospitals and medical care as an integral part of a thriving community; and sponsor programs that seek to highlight the never ceasing need for water and electric safety.
Requirements: Eligible applicants must be 501(c)3 nonprofit, organizations within SRP's service area. SRP's service area is central Arizona and includes the following cities and towns: Phoenix, Mesa, Tempe, Paradise Valley, Fountain Hills, Scottsdale, Apache Junction, Peoria, Queen Creek, Avondale, Chandler, Gilbert, Glendale, Guadalupe, and Tolleson. There are no specific grant deadlines. Requests are reviewed in an on-going process which typically takes eight weeks.
Restrictions: The following are ineligible: individuals, including support for specific students, researchers, travel expenses, conference fees; organizations that discriminate on the basis of race, creed, color, sex, or national origin; endowment programs; medical research projects or medical procedures for individuals; professional schools of art, academic art programs, individual high school or college performing groups; political or lobbying groups or campaigns; fraternal organizations, veterans' organizations, professional associations, and similar membership

groups; public or commercial broadcasting programs; religious activities or church-sponsored programs limited to church membership; and debt-reduction campaigns. SRP does not donate services, including water or electricity, or equipment for which a fee is normally charged.
Geographic Focus: Arizona
Contact: Corporate Contributions Administrator; (602) 236-5900; webmstr@srpnet.com
Internet: http://www.srpnet.com/community/contributions/guidelines.aspx
Sponsor: Salt River Project
1521 North Project Drive
Tempe, AZ 85281-1298

SAMHSA Campus Suicide Prevention Grants 4229
The purpose of this program is to facilitate a comprehensive approach to preventing suicide in institutions of higher education. This program is designed to assist colleges and universities in their efforts to prevent suicide attempts and completions and to enhance services for students with mental and behavioral health problems, such as depression and substance abuse, which put them at risk for suicide and suicide attempts. Applications are due by November 25.
Requirements: Eligibility for SAMHSA's Campus Suicide Prevention Grant program is limited to institutions of higher education. Applicants from both public and private institutions may apply, including State universities, private four-year colleges and universities (including those with religious affiliations), Minority Serving Institutions of higher learning, and community colleges.
Geographic Focus: All States
Date(s) Application is Due: Nov 25
Amount of Grant: 100,000 USD
Contact: Scott J. Salvatore, (240) 276-1866; Scott.Salvatore@samhsa.hhs.gov
Internet: http://www.samhsa.gov/Grants/2009/sm_09_001.aspx
Sponsor: Substance Abuse and Mental Health Services Administration
1 Choke Cherry Road, Room 7-1085
Rockville, MD 20857

SAMHSA Drug Free Communities Support Program Grants 4230
This Program is a collaborative initiative sponsored by ONDCP in partnership with SAMHSA in order to achieve two major goals: establish and strengthen collaboration among communities, private nonprofit agencies, and Federal, State, local, and tribal governments to support the efforts of community coalitions to prevent and reduce substance abuse among youth; and reduce substance abuse among youth and, over time, among adults by addressing the factors in a community that increase the risk of substance abuse and promoting the factors that minimize the risk of substance abuse. Substances include, but are not limited to, narcotics, depressants, stimulants, hallucinogens, cannabis, inhalants, alcohol, and tobacco, where their use is prohibited by Federal, State, or local law. Approximately $17 million for 130 FY 2009 DFC grants will be awarded through this RFA. DFC grants will be available to eligible coalitions in amounts of up to $125,000 per year over a five-year period. Applications are due by March 20.
Requirements: DFC grant funds are intended to support eligible community-based coalitions.
Geographic Focus: All States
Date(s) Application is Due: Mar 30
Amount of Grant: Up to 125,000 USD
Contact: Dan Fletcher, (240) 276-1270; dfcnew2009@samhsa.hhs.gov
Internet: http://www.samhsa.gov/grants/2009/sp_09_002.aspx
Sponsor: Substance Abuse and Mental Health Services Administration
1 Choke Cherry Road, Room 7-1085
Rockville, MD 20857

SAMHSA Strategic Prevention Framework State Incentive Grants 4231
The purpose of the SPF SIG program is to provide funding to States, Federally recognized Tribes and U.S. Territories in order to: prevent the onset and reduce the progression of substance abuse, including childhood and underage drinking; reduce substance abuse-related problems; and build prevention capacity and infrastructure at the State, tribal, territorial and community-levels. Applications are due by November 7.
Requirements: Eligible applicants are the immediate Office of the Chief Executive (e.g., Governor) in the States, U.S. Territories or District of Columbia; and Federally recognized Tribes. The Chief Executive of the State, Territory, or District of Columbia; or of the Federally recognized Tribe must sign the application.
Geographic Focus: All States
Date(s) Application is Due: Nov 7
Amount of Grant: Up to 23,000,000 USD
Contact: Mike Lowther; (240) 276-2581; mike.lowther@samhsa.hhs.gov
Internet: http://www.samhsa.gov/Grants/2009/sp_09_001.aspx
Sponsor: Substance Abuse and Mental Health Services Administration
1 Choke Cherry Road, Room 7-1085
Rockville, MD 20857

Samuel Huntington Public Service Award 4232
The award provides an annual stipend for a graduating college senior to pursue public service anywhere in the world. This allows recipients to engage in a meaningful public service activity for one year before proceeding on to graduate school or a career. Students are encouraged to develop proposals for public service here or abroad. The proposal may encompass any activity that furthers the public good. It can be undertaken by the student alone or by working through established charitable, religious, educational, governmental, or other public service organizations. Applications must be accompanied by a proposal, budget, transcript, and three letters of recommendation. Application and guidelines are available online.
Requirements: Graduating college seniors are eligible.
Geographic Focus: All States
Date(s) Application is Due: Feb 15
Amount of Grant: 10,000 USD
Contact: Award Administrator; (508) 389-2000; fax (508) 389-3198
Internet: http://www.nationalgridus.com/commitment/d4-1_award.asp
Sponsor: National Grid
25 Research Drive
Westborough, MA 01582

Samueli Foundation Human Security Grants 4233
The Foundation considers grants to agencies, primarily in Orange County, California, that serve the community, and whose programs meet the guidelines listed. Grants are usually approved for a defined period of time, but may be paid over a multi-year period. In the area of Human Security, its goals are to: support initiatives that address threats to the personal security of the most vulnerable individuals in developing countries; and work internationally to provide opportunity for people in chronic poverty to transform their lives through job creation, asset building and strengthening communities. The Foundation has a two-phase application process, the first of which is a Letter of Inquiry. If there is interest upon review of the Letter, the Foundation will contact applicants for further information and may request submission of a formal application for funding consideration.
Requirements: 501(c)3 tax-exempt organizations are eligible.
Restrictions: The foundation does not fund umbrella fund raising organizations, political campaigns, or grants to individuals.
Geographic Focus: All States
Amount of Grant: 1,000 - 50,000 USD
Contact: Maggie Sherer; (949) 760-4400; fax (949) 759-5707; Info@samueli.org
Internet: http://www.samueli.org/humansecurity.aspx
Sponsor: Samueli Foundation
2101 East Coast Highway, 3rd Floor
Corona del Mar, CA 92625

Samueli Foundation Youth Services Grants 4234
The Foundation considers grants to agencies, primarily in Orange County, California, that serve the community, and whose programs meet the guidelines listed. Grants are usually approved for a defined period of time, but may be paid over a multi-year period. In the area of Youth Services, its goals are to provide: mentoring, educational and enrichment opportunities to at risk youth; and comprehensive services and support for foster care youth. The Foundation has a two-phase application process, the first of which is a Letter of Inquiry. If there is interest upon review of the Letter, the Foundation will contact applicants for further information and may request submission of a formal application for funding consideration.
Requirements: 501(c)3 tax-exempt organizations are eligible.
Restrictions: The foundation does not fund umbrella fund raising organizations, political campaigns, or grants to individuals.
Geographic Focus: All States
Amount of Grant: 1,000 - 50,000 USD
Contact: Maggie Sherer; (949) 760-4400; fax (949) 759-5707; Info@samueli.org
Internet: http://www.samueli.org/socialservices.aspx
Sponsor: Samueli Foundation
2101 East Coast Highway, 3rd Floor
Corona del Mar, CA 92625

Samuel L. Phillips Family Foundation Grants 4235
The Samuel L. Phillips Family Foundation was funded to benefit the Mitchell County region of the western North Carolina Appalachian Mountains. The mission of this Foundation is to improve the quality of life for the people, by supporting the charitable organizations that are active in this area. This may extend to surrounding areas of Western North Carolina upon special consideration, but the emphasis should be squarely upon the well-being, growth, and enhancement of Mitchell County. Applications must be submitted by June 30th for annual summer meeting.
Requirements: The applicant must be a 501(c)3 tax-exempt non-profit entity. The programs and services of the applicant must be consistent with the Foundation's mission and values. The benefits of the grant must have a measurable impact within Mitchell County, North Carolina, and, upon special consideration, the surrounding areas of Western North Carolina. Each applicant must complete a prescribed application form (available online) and attach required documentation. All forms and information must be submitted in a hard copy format. Each successful grant applicant will be required to sign a statement agreeing to the following conditions: grant funds must be used entirely for the purposes approved by the Board of the Samuel L. Phillips Family Foundation; any funds not expended or committed for the purposes of the grant must be returned to the Foundation; each grantee must submit a progress report upon the earlier of completion of the project for which the grant was awarded or within one year of the date of the grant. To submit the application form and attachments, collate five (5) complete sets of your grant materials in the following order: optional cover letter; signed grant application form; optional detail regarding project (up to two pages); project budget spreadsheet; optional detail regarding organization (up to two pages); list of Board of Directors; copy of IRS 501(c)3 determination letter; financial statement (audited if available) for the most recent complete fiscal year; optional brochures or other printed material regarding the organization or the grant project. Completed applications should be mailed, as follows: Samuel L. Phillips Family Foundation, c/o Wachovia Bank, N.A., Nonprofit & Philanthropic Services D3310-022, P.O. Box 969, Greenville, SC 29602.
Restrictions: The Foundation normally does not fund requests for the following purposes: annual appeals or membership drives; unrestricted endowment funds; operating expenses of established organizations; debt retirement of established organizations supported by the United Way; grants to individuals; recurring type grants. All applicants must have the financial ability to sustain the funded program or project on a continuing basis.

Geographic Focus: North Carolina
Date(s) Application is Due: Jun 30
Contact: Wachovia Trust Nonprofit & Philanthropic Services; (864) 255-8231; fax (864) 467-2865; grantinquiries7@wachovia.com
Internet: https://www.wachovia.com/foundation/v/index.jsp?vgnextoid=3d3478a32dd93210VgnVCM200000627d6fa2RCRD&vgnextfmt=default
Sponsor: Samuel L. Phillips Family Foundation
P.O. Box 969
Greenville, SC 29602

Samuel N. and Mary Castle Foundation Grants 4236
The Foundation is committed to providing resources to improve the life of Hawaii's children and families by improving the quality and quantity of early education. Efforts are concentrated on creating greater social equality and opportunity through improving access to high quality pre-K education. Secondarily, the Foundation provides limited support for independent K-12 education, the arts, health, and historical and cultural projects. Grants generally range from $5,000 to $25,000. Grants for major capital improvements typically range from $10,000 to $100,000.
Requirements: Eligible organizations must be tax exempt, publicly supported and charitable as determined by the Internal Revenue Service. Grants are primarily awarded to organizations located within the state of Hawaii, for programs and projects benefiting the people of Hawaii. Proposed programs or projects must be in response to a documented community need, and not solely an organizational need. Grants may be awarded for innovative programs, demonstration projects and "start-up" funding. Program and project support does not generally exceed three years, and funding must be applied for on a yearly basis. Applicants must contact the Foundation's Executive Director by letter, email, phone or a personal visit before making fund application. A site visit may be required if the organization has not applied before or in many years.
Restrictions: The following are ineligible: charter schools; endowments; regular operating costs such as salaries, rents, or maintenance; more than forty to fifty percent of total project costs; programs not open to all racial and ethnic groups; projects in which parents and the community have not been appropriately involved in planning and funding; publication projects; general student scholarships for tuition, travel, or conferences; video projects; and annual fund drives or sponsorships.
Geographic Focus: Hawaii
Date(s) Application is Due: Feb 1; Jun 1; Oct 1
Contact: Alfred L. Castle, (808) 522-1101; fax (808) 522-1103; acastle@aloha.net
Internet: http://foundationcenter.org/grantmaker/castle/prior.html
Sponsor: Samuel N. and Mary Castle Foundation
733 Bishop Street, Suite 1275
Honolulu, HI 96813

Samuel Rubin Foundation Grants 4237
The Rubin Foundation is dedicated to the pursuit of peace and justice and the search for an equitable reallocation of the world's resources and believes these objectives can be achieved only through the fullest implementation of social, economic, political, civil, and cultural rights for all the world's people. Grants are awarded to support projects that reach toward the solutions to bring about this state. Types of support include general operating support and seed money. Applications should be in the form of a letter and include a budget and tax determination letter. The Board of Directors normally meets three times a year. Application deadlines are the first Friday in January, September, and May. Applicants are notified of the Foundation's decision within a week of its meeting. Faxed or emailed applications will not be accepted, nor will phone solicitations.
Restrictions: Funds are not granted to individuals or for buildings, endowments, or scholarships.
Geographic Focus: All States
Amount of Grant: 5,000 - 10,000 USD
Contact: Lauranne Jones, Grants Administrator; (212) 697-8945; fax (212) 682-0886; joneslauranne@gmail.com
Internet: http://www.samuelrubinfoundation.org/guidelines.html
Sponsor: Samuel Rubin Foundation
777 United Nations Plaza
New York, NY 10017-3521

Samuel S. Fels Fund Grants 4238
Since the Fels Fund has a small budget - approximately $2.5 million in the next few years - it could not possibly provide ongoing operating support to hundreds of organizations. Instead, the Fund tries to make grants at critical junctures. Critical junctures are points in an organization's life when there is a need to change methodologies. This could mean growing, shrinking, trying a new type of programming, experimenting with staffing, piloting a project that might support itself eventually, opening a satellite, seeking new accreditation, retraining staff or board or rethinking the physical plant. The fund supports activities or projects in the fields of education, the arts, and community services, which are intended to improve the quality of life in Philadelphia, Pennsylvania. Applicant organizations also must be located in Philadelphia. Types of support include general operating support, continuing support, program development, seed funding, curriculum development, internships, matching funds, and technical assistance. Grants at Fels range in size from $3,000 to $30,000. Occasionally, the Fund will make a larger grant in an exceptional situation. Applications are accepted at any time (with the exception of Arts and Humanities projects which are due by 5 p.m. on January 15th or May 15th).
Requirements: Philadelphia nonprofits may apply.
Restrictions: Grants are not awarded to support multi-year projects, umbrella-funding groups, scholarships, travel, research, capital funds, major equipment, endowments, deficit financing, ticket purchases, ads, fund-raising events, or emergency aid.
Geographic Focus: Pennsylvania
Amount of Grant: 3,000 - 30,000 USD
Contact: Helen Cunningham; (215) 731-9455; fax (215) 731-9457; helenc@samfels.org
Internet: http://www.samfels.org/apps.html
Sponsor: Samuel S. Fels Fund
1616 Walnut Street, Suite 800
Philadelphia, PA 19103-5313

Samuel S. Johnson Foundation Grants 4239
The Samuel S. Johnson Foundation was incorporated in 1948 and supports organizations primarily in Oregon and Clark County, Washington region. The Foundation gives to: formal education programs leading to an R.N. status or baccalaureate or higher college/university degree in nursing; vocational education programs targeting high school dropouts and high school grads who are not able to pursue junior college or higher formal education and which offer them job-specific technical training, mentoring or coaching; emergency food assistance programs; rural mobile health screening/care projects benefiting the uninsured medically needy; environmental programs, coastal & marine ecosystems, sustainable agriculture and communities.
Requirements: Grants are awarded to non-profit organizations in Oregon and Clark County, Washington. Contact the Foundation for current focus and guidelines with a phone call before submitting a proposal. No Application form is required, however you must include the following in your proposal: copy of IRS Determination Letter; brief history of organization and description of its mission; copy of most recent annual report/audited financial statement/990; listing of board of directors, trustees, officers and other key people and their affiliations; detailed description of project and amount of funding requested; contact person; copy of current year's organizational budget and/or project budget; listing of additional sources and amount of support. Include one copy of the proposal. The board meets twice a year, in May and October, with no deadline date for the submitting of proposals. If your proposal is accepted, you will receive notification within 2 - 3 weeks after the board meets.
Restrictions: No support for foreign organizations. No grants or scholarships to individuals, or for leadership training or staff development, campaigns to retire debt, annual campaigns, deficit financing, construction, sole underwriting of major proposals or projects, demolition or endowments.
Geographic Focus: Oregon, Washington
Amount of Grant: 400 - 100,000 USD
Contact: Mary A. Krenowicz; (541) 548-8104; fax (541) 548-2014; mary@tssjf.org
Sponsor: Samuel S. Johnson Foundation
P.O. Box 356
Redmond, OR 97756-0079

San Antonio Area Foundation Grants 4240
Grants are usually awarded in the areas of health care and biomedical research, community and social services, arts and culture, education (early childhood education, higher education, medical schools, nursing schools, adult basic education and literacy), and animal services. Types of support include operating budgets, continuing support, annual campaigns, seed grants, emergency funds, equipment acquisition, matching funds, scholarship funds, research, lectureships, professorships, and building renovations. Applicants must submit a letter of intent to apply; if the letter is approved, the foundation will send a request for a proposal to the applicant. The foundation only reviews full proposals from applicants whose letters of intent have been approved. If asked to submit a proposal, the applicant will be sent an application package with a letter of notification in early February.
Requirements: Grants are made to organizations in the San Antonio, Texas, area.
Geographic Focus: Texas
Date(s) Application is Due: Nov 15
Contact: Lydia R. Saldana, Program Officer; (210) 228-3753 or (210) 225-2243; fax (210) 225-1980; lsaldana@saafdn.org or info@saafdn.org
Internet: http://www.saafdn.org/NetCommunity/Page.aspx?pid=254
Sponsor: San Antonio Area Foundation
110 Broadway Street, Suite 230
San Antonio, TX 78205-1948

San Diego County Bar Foundation Grants 4241
The foundation was established to improve the administration of justice and the delivery of legal services. Applications will be accepted to achieve the following: promote public understanding of the law; improve the administration of justice and the San Diego court system; promote and preserve the highest of ethical standards and quality legal services in the profession; facilitate and expand the availability of legal services; and provide for the acquisition, preservation, and exhibition of historical objects related to law. Consideration will be given to requests for seed money (start-up) for projects, projects supported by volunteer efforts of members of various Bar Associations in San Diego County, and special projects/needs for established organizations. Decisions generally are made in June and December. Potential applicants are encouraged to call foundation staff to discuss their proposal prior to submission; application is by invitation only. Guidelines and application are available online.
Restrictions: Grants will not be made to support organizations that are not tax exempt as described in section 509(a)1 and 170B(1)a of the Internal Revenue Code; religious, political, or lobbying purposes; organizations whose primary function is to allocate funds to other charitable organizations or projects; projects outside of San Diego County; or loans.
Geographic Focus: California
Contact: Briana. Wagner, (619) 231-7015; bwagner@sdcbf.org
Internet: http://www.sdcbf.org/
Sponsor: San Diego County Bar Foundation
1333 Seventh Avenue, Suite 101
San Diego, CA 92101-4309

San Diego Foundation After-the-Fires Fund Grants 4242
Following best practices in disaster philanthropy, the San Diego Regional Disaster Fund Board will seek out agencies/organizations which have the capacity to meet one or more of the needs identified in the Community Needs Assessment Report. Foundation staff will work closely with potential grantees to support the development of responsive proposals that will be submitted to the Regional Disaster Board for review and approval. No specific deadlines or guidelines have been identified.
Requirements: To be eligible, organizations must be providing services in San Diego County. The organizations must have a 501(c)3 IRS tax exempt status. An organization may serve as a fiscal sponsor for a charitable organization that does not have a 501(c)3 status if a cooperative relationship between the two can clearly be demonstrated. The fiscal sponsor must be willing to administer the grant if awarded.
Restrictions: Generally, the Foundation does not make grants for: organizations that have previously received funding from the Foundation but have not submitted required final reports; major building/capital campaigns; scholarships; endowments; for-profit organizations; projects that promote religious doctrine; individuals; organizations outside San Diego County; marketing and/or promotional materials (annual reports, brochures, video productions); re-granting dollars to other nonprofit organizations or individuals; short-term, annual or one time events, including festivals, performances and conferences; travel outside of the San Diego region, or; existing obligations or debt.
Geographic Focus: California
Contact: Kerri Favela, (619) 235-2300, ext. 1329; kerri@sdfoundation.org
Internet: http://www.sdfoundation.org/fire2007/grantguidelines.shtml
Sponsor: San Diego Foundation
2508 Historic Decatur Road, Suite 200
San Diego, CA 92106

San Diego Foundation Arts & Culture Grants 4243
The Foundation's grant-making process in the area of arts and culture will distribute funds to organizations working collaboratively to create innovative new works and/or processes. It anticipates making six to eight high-impact grants in the community in this grant cycle, with grants between $10,000 and $50,000. This Art Works for San Diego program supports projects that can achieve the following results: provide San Diego residents and visitors with high quality arts and culture experiences; incorporate arts and culture into community problem solving; enable people to come together and connect with each other; build bridges between the arts and culture community and the community at large; and increase cultural patronage including hands-on involvement, audience participation and philanthropy.
Requirements: To be eligible, organizations must be providing services in San Diego County. The organizations must have a 501(c)3 IRS tax exempt status. An organization may serve as a fiscal sponsor for a charitable organization that does not have a 501(c)3 status if a cooperative relationship between the two can clearly be demonstrated. The fiscal sponsor must be willing to administer the grant if awarded.
Restrictions: Generally, the Foundation does not make grants for: organizations that have previously received funding from the Foundation but have not submitted required final reports; major building/capital campaigns; scholarships; endowments; for-profit organizations; projects that promote religious doctrine; individuals; organizations outside San Diego County; marketing and/or promotional materials (annual reports, brochures, video productions); re-granting dollars to other nonprofit organizations or individuals; short-term, annual or one time events, including festivals, performances and conferences; travel outside of the San Diego region, or; existing obligations or debt.
Geographic Focus: California
Date(s) Application is Due: Jan 16
Contact: Kerri Favela, (619) 235-2300, ext. 1329; kerri@sdfoundation.org
Internet: http://www.sdfoundation.org/communityimpact/cycle2006.html#ac
Sponsor: San Diego Foundation
2508 Historic Decatur Road, Suite 200
San Diego, CA 92106

San Diego Foundation Civil Society Grants 4244
The San Diego Foundation's Civil Society Working Group was established with the mission to foster civic engagement in community problem solving leading to an improved quality of life for all residents. The San Diego region requires a shared vision to enable effective and inclusive dialogue for the purpose of planning for balanced and equitable future growth. The goal of this initiative is to establish a framework to address the need for housing across the San Diego region resulting in livable communities with choices for all. Preference will be given to applicants with strategic partnerships that demonstrate the experience, skills, and capacity to achieve stated results and commit to sharing best practices and lessons learned to advance initiative goals. Applicants are encouraged to apply for grants generally between $25,000 and $50,000.
Requirements: To be eligible, organizations must be providing services in San Diego County. The organizations must have a 501(c)3 IRS tax exempt status. An organization may serve as a fiscal sponsor for a charitable organization that does not have a 501(c)3 status if a cooperative relationship between the two can clearly be demonstrated. The fiscal sponsor must be willing to administer the grant if awarded.
Restrictions: Generally, the Foundation does not make grants for: organizations that have previously received funding from the Foundation but have not submitted required final reports; major building/capital campaigns; scholarships; endowments; for-profit organizations; projects that promote religious doctrine; individuals; organizations outside San Diego County; marketing and/or promotional materials (annual reports, brochures, video productions); re-granting dollars to other nonprofit organizations or individuals; short-term, annual or one time events, including festivals, performances and conferences; travel outside of the San Diego region, or; existing obligations or debt.
Geographic Focus: California
Date(s) Application is Due: Jan 16
Amount of Grant: 25,000 - 50,000 USD
Contact: Shelley Lyford; (619) 235-2300; Shelley@sdfoundation.org
Internet: http://www.sdfoundation.org/communityimpact/cycle2006.html#ac
Sponsor: San Diego Foundation
2508 Historic Decatur Road, Suite 200
San Diego, CA 92106

San Diego Foundation Environment Blasker Grants 4245
The Blasker-Rose-Miah Fund was established at the San Diego Foundation to nurture and develop unique and innovative discoveries and experiences which may be of benefit to all mankind, and to support and encourage individuals with high potential in the scientific, engineering, and medical fields to reach their full potential in their chosen areas of study, work, and analysis. Emphasis is placed on supporting students and young scientists. Blasker Grants are awarded in two areas: environment and science; and technology. Grants support programs and projects that have the potential to improve the quality of life in the San Diego region and to support and encourage San Diegans to reach their full potential. Preference will be given to programs or projects that facilitate collaboration between university researchers and local nonprofits whose work helps to advance either of the above listed program areas. Projects may include but are not limited to: internships, fellowships, and promotion of mentorship, but not scholarships. Preference will be given to individuals who have attended and graduated from a high school in San Diego County and are continuing their studies at an institution in San Diego. Additional preference will be given to projects or programs that enhance collaboration between university researchers, local nonprofits and/or community residents engaged in environmental work. Applicants are encouraged to apply for grants up to $75,000.
Requirements: To be eligible, organizations must be providing services in San Diego County. The organizations must have a 501(c)3 IRS tax exempt status. An organization may serve as a fiscal sponsor for a charitable organization that does not have a 501(c)3 status if a cooperative relationship between the two can clearly be demonstrated. The fiscal sponsor must be willing to administer the grant if awarded.
Restrictions: Generally, the Foundation does not make grants for: organizations that have previously received funding from the Foundation but have not submitted required final reports; major building/capital campaigns; scholarships; endowments; for-profit organizations; projects that promote religious doctrine; individuals; organizations outside San Diego County; marketing and/or promotional materials (annual reports, brochures, video productions); re-granting dollars to other nonprofit organizations or individuals; short-term, annual or one time events, including festivals, performances and conferences; travel outside of the San Diego region, or; existing obligations or debt.
Geographic Focus: California
Date(s) Application is Due: Jan 16
Amount of Grant: Up to 75,000 USD
Contact: Kerri Favela, (619) 235-2300, ext. 1329; kerri@sdfoundation.org
Internet: http://www.sdfoundation.org/communityimpact/cycle2006.html#ac
Sponsor: San Diego Foundation
2508 Historic Decatur Road, Suite 200
San Diego, CA 92106

San Diego Foundation Environment Community Grants 4246
The vision of the San Diego Foundation's Environment Working Group is to ensure that all generations enjoy clean air, safe water, wildlife, natural and culturally-sensitive areas. Within the next three years, the Environment Working Group will help strengthen the capacity and financial viability of environmental and environmental health and justice organizations to ensure the protection of the public trust - our air, land, water and other resources - so people can live, work, play and learn in a clean and healthy environment. To this end, the Working Group will accept proposals requesting up to $50,000, focusing on the following two initiatives: land and watershed conservation initiatives; and clean environments, healthy communities initiatives.
Requirements: To be eligible, organizations must be providing services in San Diego County. The organizations must have a 501(c)3 IRS tax exempt status. An organization may serve as a fiscal sponsor for a charitable organization that does not have a 501(c)3 status if a cooperative relationship between the two can clearly be demonstrated. The fiscal sponsor must be willing to administer the grant if awarded.
Restrictions: Generally, the Foundation does not make grants for: organizations that have previously received funding from the Foundation but have not submitted required final reports; major building/capital campaigns; scholarships; endowments; for-profit organizations; projects that promote religious doctrine; individuals; organizations outside San Diego County; marketing and/or promotional materials (annual reports, brochures, video productions); re-granting dollars to other nonprofit organizations or individuals; short-term, annual or one time events, including festivals, performances and conferences; travel outside of the San Diego region, or; existing obligations or debt.
Geographic Focus: California
Date(s) Application is Due: Jan 16
Amount of Grant: Up to 50,000 USD
Contact: Kerri Favela, (619) 235-2300, ext. 1329; kerri@sdfoundation.org
Internet: http://www.sdfoundation.org/communityimpact/cycle2006.html#ac
Sponsor: San Diego Foundation
2508 Historic Decatur Road, Suite 200
San Diego, CA 92106

San Diego Foundation for Change Grants 4247
The foundation seeks funding proposals from grassroots community organizations who work to achieve social, economic, and environmental justice in San Diego County. Foundation concerns cover the range of progressive social issues, including: ending discrimination in any form; halting environmental pollution; promoting peace; expanding immigrant rights;

improving San Diego's neighborhoods and workplaces; working toward racial equality; fighting for women's rights; developing youth projects; addressing domestic violence; and preventing violence in the community. Priority goes to projects with limited access to other sources of funding. In addition to the general funds, the foundation has the following special grants: the Danzig Award; and the James Mitsuo Cua Award. Organizations submitting a general application will be considered for these special grants with no additional application necessary. Letters of Intent are due on February 5, while full proposals are due by April 2.
Requirements: California nonprofit organizations in San Diego are eligible.
Restrictions: Grants do not support social or human service organizations that do not have a strong community organizing component; individual efforts; national or statewide projects unless there is a strong local focus; direct union organizing; private businesses or profit-making organizations; or electoral campaigns or candidates.
Geographic Focus: All States
Date(s) Application is Due: Feb 5; Apr 2
Contact: John Fanestil, Executive Director; (619) 692-0527; fax (619) 255-3640; john@foundation4change.org or info@foundation4change.org
Internet: http://www.foundation4change.org/forapplicants.php
Sponsor: San Diego Foundation for Change
3758 30th Street
San Diego, CA 92104

San Diego Foundation Health & Human Services Grants 4248
The San Diego Foundation's Health and Human Services Working Group was established with the vision to improve the health, well-being and self-sufficiency of individuals, families and communities in the San Diego region. The Health and Human Services Working Group's research, investigation and grant awards to date indicate that families who are vulnerable to episodic homelessness benefit from financial education that leads to budget management, traditional banking relationships, reduction of debt improved credit, and increased savings. This initiative will support financial education and asset building programs of community-based organizations that serve the residents of the San Diego region.
Requirements: To be eligible, organizations must be providing services in San Diego County. The organizations must have a 501(c)3 IRS tax exempt status. An organization may serve as a fiscal sponsor for a charitable organization that does not have a 501(c)3 status if a cooperative relationship between the two can clearly be demonstrated. The fiscal sponsor must be willing to administer the grant if awarded.
Restrictions: Generally, the Foundation does not make grants for: organizations that have previously received funding from the Foundation but have not submitted required final reports; major building/capital campaigns; scholarships; endowments; for-profit organizations; projects that promote religious doctrine; individuals; organizations outside San Diego County; marketing and/or promotional materials (annual reports, brochures, video productions); re-granting dollars to other nonprofit organizations or individuals; short-term, annual or one time events, including festivals, performances and conferences; travel outside of the San Diego region, or; existing obligations or debt.
Geographic Focus: California
Date(s) Application is Due: Jan 16
Amount of Grant: 30,000 USD
Contact: Shelley Lyford; (619) 235-2300; Shelley@sdfoundation.org
Internet: http://www.sdfoundation.org/communityimpact/cycle2006.html#ac
Sponsor: San Diego Foundation
2508 Historic Decatur Road, Suite 200
San Diego, CA 92106

San Diego Foundation Paradise Valley Hospital Community Fund Grants 4249
The Foundation has created a joint process managed by the San Diego Foundation and Alliance Healthcare Foundation for the distribution of funds to tax-exempt community-based health and social service organizations. Grant making decisions and oversight of funded projects will be provided by an advisory committee comprised of diverse individuals representing stakeholders in the PVH service area, as well as members of The San Diego Foundation's Health & Human Services Working Group.
Requirements: To be eligible, organizations must be providing services in San Diego County. The organizations must have a 501(c)3 IRS tax exempt status. An organization may serve as a fiscal sponsor for a charitable organization that does not have a 501(c)3 status if a cooperative relationship between the two can clearly be demonstrated. The fiscal sponsor must be willing to administer the grant if awarded.
Geographic Focus: California
Contact: Anahid Brakke; fax (619) 235-2300; anahid@sdfoundation.org
Internet: http://sdfoundation.org/communityimpact/healthservices/pvhfund.html
Sponsor: San Diego Foundation
2508 Historic Decatur Road, Suite 200
San Diego, CA 92106

San Diego Foundation Science & Technology Blasker Grants 4250
The Blasker-Rose-Miah Fund was established at the San Diego Foundation to nurture and develop unique and innovative discoveries and experiences which may be of benefit to all mankind, and to support and encourage individuals with high potential in the scientific, engineering, and medical fields to reach their full potential in their chosen areas of study, work, and analysis. Blasker Grants are awarded in two areas: environment; and science and technology. Along with supporting innovative research, projects may include but are not limited to: internships, fellowships, and promotion of mentorship, but not scholarships. Preference will be given to individuals who have attended and graduated from a high school in San Diego County and are continuing their studies or research at an institution in San Diego. Grant applicants are encouraged to apply for grants up to $75,000.

Requirements: To be eligible, organizations must be providing services in San Diego County. The organizations must have a 501(c)3 IRS tax exempt status. An organization may serve as a fiscal sponsor for a charitable organization that does not have a 501(c)3 status if a cooperative relationship between the two can clearly be demonstrated. The fiscal sponsor must be willing to administer the grant if awarded.
Restrictions: Generally, the Foundation does not make grants for: organizations that have previously received funding from the Foundation but have not submitted required final reports; major building/capital campaigns; scholarships; endowments; for-profit organizations; projects that promote religious doctrine; individuals; organizations outside San Diego County; marketing and/or promotional materials (annual reports, brochures, video productions); re-granting dollars to other nonprofit organizations or individuals; short-term, annual or one time events, including festivals, performances and conferences; travel outside of the San Diego region, or; existing obligations or debt.
Geographic Focus: California
Date(s) Application is Due: Jan 16
Contact: Sedra Shapiro, Director; (619) 235-2300; sedra@sdfoundation.org
Internet: http://www.sdfoundation.org/communityimpact/cycle2006.html#ac
Sponsor: San Diego Foundation
2508 Historic Decatur Road, Suite 200
San Diego, CA 92106

San Diego HIV Funding Collaborative (SDHFC) Grants 4251
The mission of the Collaborative is to raise, leverage and collaboratively allocate private funds to reduce the impact of HIV in the San Diego region. Donations are pooled and re-granted to local service organizations to help people affected by HIV/AIDS. Funds from the local community are used to make grants to local organizations and assist grantees with technical support. All grant applicants must start by submitting a Letter of Intent.
Requirements: The Foundation does not fund projects and programs outside San Diego and Imperial Counties.
Restrictions: The Foundation does not fund: research; lobbying; underwriting of medical expenses; general operating expenses we deem to be excessive; construction or renovation; the purchase of costly equipment; development activities, such as fund raising events, capital campaigns or annual fund drives; projects or proposals from individuals; or organizations that do not have 501(c)3 status.
Geographic Focus: California
Contact: Hamse Warfa, Program Officer; (858) 614-4892 or (858) 874-3788; fax (858) 874-3656; hwarfa@alliancehf.org
Internet: http://www.alliancehf.org/sdhiv/who_we_are.html
Sponsor: Alliance Healthcare Foundation
9325 Sky Park Court, Suite 350
San Diego, CA 92123

San Diego Women's Foundation Grants 4252
The San Diego Women's Foundation (SDWF) strengthens and improves women's capacities to engage in significant philanthropy in the San Diego region. The foundation chooses one focus area of grant making each year. Its primary focus areas include: education, arts and culture, environment, employment and economic development, civil society, and health and human services. Check the web site each September for that year's focus guidelines.
Requirements: Only 501(c)3 organization within San Diego County should apply.
Geographic Focus: California
Date(s) Application is Due: Dec 6
Contact: Tracy Johnson; (619) 814-1374 or (619) 235-2300; tracy@sdfoundation.org
Internet: http://www.sdwomensfoundation.org/
Sponsor: San Diego Women's Foundation
2508 Historic Decatur Road, Suite 200
San Diego, CA 92106

SanDisk Corporation Community Sharing Program 4253
Since being established in May 2003, the SanDisk Corporate Fund has linked SanDisk's corporate giving program with the Silicon Valley Community Foundation (SVCF), a non-profit organization that specializes in philanthropic and charitable giving programs. This is just one way that SanDisk shares its financial success, and growing resources, with the communities served by their employees. SanDisk is committed to being an asset in the communities where their employees live and work. The Community Sharing Committee acts as a facilitator to carry out this vision by making donations to non-profit organizations, foundations, and community groups. To maximize the results of their efforts, SanDisk focus on programs that support individuals and families, education, youth development, and community enrichment through the arts. The above areas are the Community Sharing Committee's primary focus, however, the committee will also consider applications that fall under the following focus areas: environmental; animal rescue needs; disaster recovery efforts. The application form is available at the SanDisk Corporation website.
Requirements: Grant applications should be sent to: SanDisk Corporation c/o Silicon Valley Community Foundation, 2440 West El Camino Real, Suite 300, Mountain View, CA 94040. If you have any questions regarding your application, contact Patti Pace, Corporate Philanthropy Manager with the Silicon Valley Community Foundation at (650)450-5488 or email her at papace@siliconvalleycf.org.
Geographic Focus: All States
Date(s) Application is Due: Jan 1; Apr 1; Jul 1; Oct 1
Contact: Corporate Office; (408) 801-1000; fax (408) 801-8657
Internet: http://www.sandisk.com/Corporate/Default.aspx?CatID=1015
Sponsor: SanDisk Corporation
601 McCarthy Boulevard
Milpitas, CA 95035

Sands Foundation Crisis Fund Grants 4254
The Venetian Foundation (now the Sands Foundation) was formed December 7, 2000, by the Venetian Casino Resort. Today, the Las Vegas Sands Corporation's primary philanthropic initiative is pursued through Sands Foundation, a non-profit 501(c)3 organization. Through the Crisis Fund, any member of the Las Vegas community facing a crisis is eligible to receive assistance from the fund. This crisis may consist of immediate family disasters such as fire, accident, sudden illness, personal tragedy, or other life-altering events in which the individual suffers severe financial hardship. Requests for assistance are considered on a case-by-case basis. Applicants must have first exhausted all other sources of financial assistance. Mortgage/rent, utilities, and needs for living expenses are funded only in the case of an emergency. All assistance through the foundation will be paid directly to the source providing the service needed.
Geographic Focus: Nevada, Pennsylvania, Macau, Singapore
Contact: Community Development; (702) 607-1677; foundation@venetian.com
Internet: http://www.lasvegassands.com/LasVegasSands/Sands_Foundation/Donation_Request.aspx
Sponsor: Sands Foundation
3355 Las Vegas Boulevard South
Las Vegas, NV 89109-8941

Sands Foundation Grants 4255
The Venetian Foundation (now the Sands Foundation) was formed December 7, 2000, by the Venetian Casino Resort. Today, the Las Vegas Sands Corporation's primary philanthropic initiative is pursued through Sands Foundation, a non-profit 501(c)3 organization. Sands Foundation pursues a mission of supporting charitable organizations and endeavors that concentrate on assisting youth, promoting health, and expanding educational opportunities within the local communities. The Foundation also supports causes that empower minority communities and improve underprivileged areas, as well as other valuable charitable and philanthropic activities permitted under relevant tax-exempt laws. Sands Foundation pursues a mission of supporting charitable organizations and endeavors that concentrate on assisting youth, promoting health, and expanding educational opportunities within our local communities. The Foundation also supports causes that empower minority communities and improve underprivileged areas, as well as other valuable charitable and philanthropic activities permitted under relevant tax-exempt laws. Charitable requests along with supporting documents may either be faxed or mailed.
Requirements: All charitable requests must be submitted in writing. Written requests should include the following: agency/organization information (brochures, information packet, list of the board of directors, history, background, or other helpful information); 501(c)3 tax identification number; contact person; mailing address and telephone number; overview of project or event at hand; date, time, location for event requests; purpose of request; very specific information about the amount/item(s) requested; and target population which will benefit from support.
Geographic Focus: Nevada, Pennsylvania, Macau, Singapore
Amount of Grant: 5,000 - 100,000 USD
Contact: Community Development; (702) 607-1677; foundation@venetian.com
Internet: http://www.lasvegassands.com/LasVegasSands/Sands_Foundation/Donation_Request.aspx
Sponsor: Sands Foundation
3355 Las Vegas Boulevard South
Las Vegas, NV 89109-8941

Sands Memorial Foundation Grants 4256
The foundation awards grants to Montana nonprofits in the area of companion animal protection and care, including spay/neuter programs and cruelty-prevention programs. Types of support include general operating support, continuing support, building construction/renovation, equipment acquisition, emergency funds, and seed grants. Application forms are required.
Requirements: Montana nonprofit organizations may apply.
Restrictions: Individuals are ineligible.
Geographic Focus: Montana
Date(s) Application is Due: Oct 30
Contact: Cynthia Bryson; (406) 265-4271; fax (406) 265-4271; smf@hi-line.net
Sponsor: Sands Memorial Foundation
P.O. Box 1450
Havre, MT 59501-1450

Sandy Hill Foundation Grants 4257
The Sandy Hill Foundation offers awards to eligible nonprofit organizations in the areas of education, health care, and social services. The foundation gives primarily to the arts and culture, higher education, hospitals, health associations, social services, and federated giving programs. Their areas of interest include the arts; child and youth services; community and economic development; health organizations and associations; higher education; hospitals; human services; Protestant agencies and churches; recreation camps; and United Way and Federated Giving Programs. It also offers college scholarships for designated local area schools.
Requirements: There is no application or specific deadline for nonprofit giving. See contact information for current scholarship application due April 1.
Restrictions: The foundation gives primarily to the greater Hudson Falls, NY area. No grants are given to individuals.
Geographic Focus: New York
Date(s) Application is Due: Apr 1
Amount of Grant: Up to USD
Contact: Nancy Juckett Brown, Trustee; (518) 791-3490
Sponsor: Sandy Hill Foundation
P.O. Box 30
Hudson Falls, NY 12839-0030

San Francisco Foundation Art Awards James Duval Phelan Literary Award 4258
The distinguished James Duval Phelan Literary Award, sponsored by The San Francisco Foundation and administered by Intersection for the Arts since 1991, is offered annually in the amount of $2,000 each to encourage young writers (20 to 35 years old), who are either California-born or currently residing in Northern California or Nevada, for an unpublished manuscript-in-progress. In addition to the cash award, winners will be invited to participate in a public reading at Intersection for the Arts, and the winning manuscripts will be permanently housed at UC Berkeley's Bancroft Library. Applicants must have been born in the state of California, but need not be current residents. The unpublished work-in-progress submitted may be fiction, nonfiction prose, poetry, or drama.
Requirements: The Foundation makes grants to organizations that are exempt under Section 501(c)3 of the Internal Revenue Code and are classified as not a private foundation under Section 509(a). The Foundation also provides grants to government and public agencies, as well as to independent projects that have a qualified tax-exempt fiscal sponsor.
Geographic Focus: California
Date(s) Application is Due: Mar 31
Amount of Grant: 2,000 USD
Contact: John Killacky, Program Officer; (415) 733-8523; jrk@sff.org
Internet: http://www.sff.org/programs/awards-programs/art-awards
Sponsor: San Francisco Foundation
225 Bush Street, Suite 500
San Francisco, CA 94104-4224

San Francisco Foundation Art Awards Joseph Henry Jackson Literary Award 4259
Joseph Henry Jackson Literary Award Applicants must be residents of northern California or the state of Nevada for three consecutive years immediately prior to the contest deadline. The unpublished work in progress may be fiction (novel or short stories), nonfiction prose, or poetry. Sponsored by The San Francisco Foundation and administered by Intersection for the Arts since 1991, are offered annually in the amount of $2,000 each to encourage young writers (20 to 35 years old), who are either California-born or currently residing in Northern California or Nevada, for an unpublished manuscript-in-progress. In addition to the cash award, winners will be invited to participate in a public reading at Intersection for the Arts, and the winning manuscripts will be permanently housed at UC Berkeley's Bancroft Library.
Requirements: The Foundation makes grants to organizations that are exempt under Section 501(c)3 of the Internal Revenue Code and are classified as not a private foundation under Section 509(a). The Foundation also provides grants to government and public agencies, as well as to independent projects that have a qualified tax-exempt fiscal sponsor.
Geographic Focus: California
Date(s) Application is Due: Mar 31; Mar 31
Amount of Grant: 2,000 USD
Contact: John Killacky, Program Officer; (415) 733-8523; jrk@sff.org
Internet: http://www.sff.org/programs/awards-programs/art-awards
Sponsor: San Francisco Foundation
225 Bush Street, Suite 500
San Francisco, CA 94104-4224

San Francisco Foundation Art Awards Mary Tanenbaum Literary Award 4260
The Mary Tanenbaum Literary Award, sponsored by The San Francisco Foundation and administered by Intersection for the Arts since 1991, are offered annually in the amount of $2,000 each to encourage young writers (20 to 35 years old), who are either California-born or currently residing in Northern California or Nevada. In addition to the cash award, the winner will be invited to participate in a public reading at Intersection for the Arts, and the winning manuscripts will be permanently housed at UC Berkeley's Bancroft Library. Tanenbaum Award in Nonfiction Applicants must be residents of northern California or the state of Nevada for three consecutive years immediately prior to the contest deadline.
Requirements: The Foundation makes grants to organizations that are exempt under Section 501(c)3 of the Internal Revenue Code and are classified as not a private foundation under Section 509(a). The Foundation also provides grants to government and public agencies, as well as to independent projects that have a qualified tax-exempt fiscal sponsor.
Geographic Focus: California
Date(s) Application is Due: Mar 31
Amount of Grant: 2,000 USD
Contact: John Killacky, Program Officer; (415) 733-8523; jrk@sff.org
Internet: http://www.sff.org/programs/awards-programs/art-awards
Sponsor: San Francisco Foundation
225 Bush Street, Suite 500
San Francisco, CA 94104-4224

San Francisco Foundation Bay Area Documentary Fund Grants 4261
Many award-winning documentaries have emerged from the San Francisco Bay Area. In recognition of this fine tradition, we have created The San Francisco Foundation Bay Area Documentary Fund. Four or five awards ranging from $20,000 to $25,000 will be distributed annually to support documentary projects in early production phases by experienced filmmakers with an esteemed body of previously created work. TSFF is interested in documentaries exploring issues that have been historically underexposed, misinterpreted, or ignored and that are pertinent to the five Bay Area counties. The counties included are: Martin, Contra Costa, San Francisco, Alameda and San Mateo.
Requirements: The Foundation makes grants to organizations that are exempt under Section 501(c)3 of the Internal Revenue Code and are classified as not a private foundation under Section 509(a). The Foundation also provides grants to government and public agencies, as well as to independent projects that have a qualified tax-exempt fiscal sponsor. Applications will be available in Fall, check website for application deadline.
Geographic Focus: California

Amount of Grant: 20,000 - 25,000 USD
Contact: John Killacky, Program Officer; (415) 733-8523; jrk@sff.org
Internet: http://www.sff.org/programs/arts-culture/fund-for-artists
Sponsor: San Francisco Foundation
225 Bush Street, Suite 500
San Francisco, CA 94104-4224

San Francisco Foundation Community Development Grants 4262

The San Francisco Foundation welcomes unsolicited applications twice a year. The Community Development Program focuses on solutions to poverty in the five counties we serve. The goal is to stabilize families and individuals by investing in an expanded supply of affordable housing to address homelessness, and to prevent displacement due to high housing costs. The foundation also strives to increase the economic security of households struggling to make ends meet through our investment in workforce development and micro-enterprise entrepreneurial training. Additionally, by supporting safety-net services, the foundations aim is to assist those who are homeless or in crises by providing access to services to meet basic needs. To leverage the greatest change, the foundation makes targeted investments in policy and advocacy that addresses the root causes of poverty. By supporting the foundations of stable lives and families homes, quality jobs, and safety-net services, we build community and help make the Bay Area an even better place for us all. The Bay Area counties included are: Martin, Contra Costa, San Francisco, Alameda and San Mateo.
Requirements: The Foundation makes grants to organizations that are exempt under Section 501(c)3 of the Internal Revenue Code and are classified as not a private foundation under Section 509(a). The Foundation also provides grants to government and public agencies, as well as to independent projects that have a qualified tax-exempt fiscal sponsor.
Geographic Focus: California
Date(s) Application is Due: Jan 16; Jul 1
Amount of Grant: 5,000 - 30,000 USD
Contact: Jessica Pitt, Program Coordinator; (415) 733-8560; jmp@sff.org
Internet: http://www.sff.org/programs/community-development
Sponsor: San Francisco Foundation
225 Bush Street, Suite 500
San Francisco, CA 94104-4224

San Francisco Foundation Community Health Grants 4263

The San Francisco Foundation welcomes unsolicited applications twice a year. The Community Health Program works to expand access to health services and promote health prevention in the five counties we serve. Community Health's efforts focus on improving health on a community level and providing the social supports for communities to improve health. The Bay Area counties included are: Martin, Contra Costa, San Francisco, Alameda and San Mateo.
Requirements: Grants are made to nonprofit organizations in Alameda, Contra Costa, Marin, San Francisco, and San Mateo Counties of California.
Restrictions: The foundation generally does not fund projects outside the Bay Area community; long-term operating support; medical, academic, or scientific research; religious activities (religious institutions may apply for nonsectarian programs); direct assistance to individuals; or conferences or one-time events.
Geographic Focus: California
Date(s) Application is Due: Jan 16; Jul 1
Amount of Grant: 15,000 - 80,000 USD
Contact: Denise Martin; (415) 733-8500 or (415) 733-8569; dkm@sff.org
Internet: http://www.sff.org/programs/community-health
Sponsor: San Francisco Foundation
225 Bush Street, Suite 500
San Francisco, CA 94104-4224

San Francisco Foundation Community Leadership Awards 4264

Individuals and nonprofit organizations in Alameda, Contra Costa, Marin, San Francisco, and San Mateo Counties may be nominated. Individuals from all sectors, from government agencies, nonprofits, corporations, or the private sector are eligible for these awards. Up to four awards are made each year. One of the four awards is designated for an under-recognized, mature artist who has made a significant and ongoing contribution in the Bay Area. Artists from the performing, literary, media, and visual arts including craft, folk, and traditional forms will be considered. This award is made in the honor of Helen Crocker Russell. The three additional awards are: The San Francisco Foundation Award, John R. May Award & the Robert C. Kirkwood Award.
Requirements: Individuals and nonprofit organizations in California's Alameda, Contra Costa, Marin, San Francisco, and San Mateo counties are eligible.
Geographic Focus: California
Amount of Grant: 1,500 - 5,000 USD
Contact: Awards Coordinator; (415) 733-8500; fax (415) 477-2783; srh@sff.org
Internet: http://www.sff.org/programs/awards-programs/community-leadership-awards
Sponsor: San Francisco Foundation
225 Bush Street, Suite 500
San Francisco, CA 94104-4224

San Francisco Foundation Disability Rights Advocate Fund Emergency Grants 4265

The program awards emergency grants to positively impact large populations of people with disabilities in the Bay Area and northern California. Grants are available to organizations to assist mobilizing people with disabilities to act upon time-sensitive and urgent matters affecting the disability community. For example, funds may be used to cover the transportation and/or personal assistant costs associated with a community mobilization effort. Requests are accepted throughout the year; decisions are made, based on availability of funds, within four to six weeks of submission. Requests should be submitted via electronic mail. Guidelines are available online.
Requirements: Organizations located in the Bay Area and northern California are eligible.
Geographic Focus: California
Amount of Grant: 10,000 USD
Contact: Denise Martin; (415) 733-8500 or (415) 733-8569; dkm@sff.org
Internet: http://www.sff.org
Sponsor: San Francisco Foundation
225 Bush Street, Suite 500
San Francisco, CA 94104-4224

San Francisco Foundation Environment Grants 4266

The San Francisco Foundation welcomes unsolicited applications twice a year. The Foundation's strategic goals and objectives, and projects must benefit residents in the five Bay Area counties. The counties included are: Martin, Contra Costa, San Francisco, Alameda and San Mateo. The Environment Program relates directly to the mission of the Foundation, which is echoed in the Environment Program's overarching goal to promote environmentally sustainable practices and equitable development that guarantee livable communities and healthy environments. This Program has many natural intersections with other elements of the Foundation's work due to the multidisciplinary nature of environmental issues.
Requirements: The Foundation makes grants to organizations that are exempt under Section 501(c)3 of the Internal Revenue Code and are classified as not a private foundation under Section 509(a). The Foundation also provides grants to government and public agencies, as well as to independent projects that have a qualified tax-exempt fiscal sponsor.
Geographic Focus: California
Date(s) Application is Due: Jan 16; Jul 1
Contact: Arlene Rodriguez, Program Officer; (415)733-8517; amr@sff.org
Internet: http://www.sff.org/programs/environment
Sponsor: San Francisco Foundation
225 Bush Street, Suite 500
San Francisco, CA 94104-4224

San Francisco Foundation Faith Program and Arts and Culture Program 4267

The San Francisco Foundation benefit residents in five Bay Area counties. The counties included are: Martin, Contra Costa, San Francisco, Alameda and San Mateo. The San Francisco Foundation's FAITHS Program and Arts and Culture Program have given the FAITHS Arts and Culture Mini-Grants for the past three years. These mini-grants will support faith-based organizations and groups in providing free, community-based artistic and cultural activities, with a priority focus on immigrant, refugee, and grassroots communities.
Requirements: The Foundation makes grants to organizations that are exempt under Section 501(c)3 of the Internal Revenue Code and are classified as not a private foundation under Section 509(a). The Foundation also provides grants to government and public agencies, as well as to independent projects that have a qualified tax-exempt fiscal sponsor.
Geographic Focus: California
Date(s) Application is Due: Feb 24
Contact: Michelle Myles Chambers, Program Assistant; (415) 733-8539; mmc@sff.org
Internet: http://www.sff.org/programs/arts-culture/grants-awards/?searchterm=Koshland/20Program/20arts/20and/20culture/20mini-grants
Sponsor: San Francisco Foundation
225 Bush Street, Suite 500
San Francisco, CA 94104-4224

San Francisco Foundation FAITHS Arts and Culture Mini Grants 4268

The program awards mini grants to faith-based organizations and congregations in the five Bay Area counties served by the foundation (Alameda, Contra Costa, Marin, San Francisco, and San Mateo Counties). These grants will support free, community-based artistic and cultural activities, with a priority focus on immigrant, refugee, and grassroots communities. Outreach and cultural exchange efforts with communities outside the congregation also are eligible. Application and guidelines are available online.
Geographic Focus: California
Amount of Grant: 5,000 USD
Contact: Tessa Rouverol Callejo, Program Coordinator; (415) 733-8541; trc@sff.org
Internet: http://www.sff.org/initiatives/faith.html
Sponsor: San Francisco Foundation
225 Bush Street, Suite 500
San Francisco, CA 94104-4224

San Francisco Foundation Fund for Artists Arts Teacher Fellowships 4269

The Fund for Artists Arts Teacher Fellowship Program is a regional initiative to support the artistic revitalization of outstanding arts teachers in Bay Area middle and high schools. Arts teachers often lack time and resources to reconnect with other arts professionals and with the artistic processes they teach. Through the FFAATF, fellows will design individualized courses of study that foster their own creative work and the opportunity to interact with other professional artists in their fields. See website for application deadline.
Requirements: The Foundation makes grants to organizations that are exempt under Section 501(c)3 of the Internal Revenue Code and are classified as not a private foundation under Section 509(a). The Foundation also provides grants to government and public agencies, as well as to independent projects that have a qualified tax-exempt fiscal sponsor.
Geographic Focus: California
Contact: John R. Killacky; (415) 733-8523; artsinfo@sff.org or jrk@sff.org
Internet: http://www.sff.org/programs/arts-culture/fund-for-artists
Sponsor: San Francisco Foundation
225 Bush Street, Suite 500
San Francisco, CA 94104-4224

GRANT PROGRAMS | 661

San Francisco Foundation Fund For Artists Award For Choreographers   4270
The San Francisco Foundation benefits residents in the five Bay Area counties. The Fund For Artists gives awards to outstanding individuals, ranging in size from $1,500 to $15,000. The awards provide the artists with money, exposure to other artists and arts institutions, and public recognition of their excellence. This $5,000 awards given to outstanding choreographers through World Arts West. See website for application deadline.
Requirements: The Foundation makes grants to organizations that are exempt under Section 501(c)3 of the Internal Revenue Code and are classified as not a private foundation under Section 509(a). The Foundation also provides grants to government and public agencies, as well as to independent projects that have a qualified tax-exempt fiscal sponsor.
Geographic Focus: California
Amount of Grant: 5,000 USD
Contact: John R. Killacky; (415) 733-8523; artsinfo@sff.org or jrk@sff.org
Internet: http://www.sff.org/programs/arts-culture/fund-for-artists
Sponsor: San Francisco Foundation
225 Bush Street, Suite 500
San Francisco, CA 94104-4224

San Francisco Foundation Fund for Artists Award for Composers and Music Ensembles   4271
The San Francisco Foundation benefits residents in the five Bay Area counties. The Fund For Artists gives awards to outstanding individuals, ranging in size from $1,500 to $15,000. The awards provide the artists with money, exposure to other artists and arts institutions, and public recognition of their excellence. The Fund For Artists Award for Composers and Music Ensembles $5,000 awards are given to outstanding composers working with music ensembles through American Composers Forum.
Requirements: The Foundation makes grants to organizations that are exempt under Section 501(c)3 of the Internal Revenue Code and are classified as not a private foundation under Section 509(a). The Foundation also provides grants to government and public agencies, as well as to independent projects that have a qualified tax-exempt fiscal sponsor. See website for application deadline.
Geographic Focus: California
Amount of Grant: 5,000 USD
Contact: John R. Killacky; (415) 733-8523; artsinfo@sff.org or jrk@sff.org
Internet: http://www.sff.org/programs/arts-culture/fund-for-artists
Sponsor: San Francisco Foundation
225 Bush Street, Suite 500
San Francisco, CA 94104-4224

San Francisco Foundation Fund For Artists Award For Playwrights and Theatre Ensembles   4272
The San Francisco Foundation benefits residents in the five Bay Area counties. The Fund For Artists gives awards to outstanding individuals, ranging in size from $1,500 to $15,000. The awards provide the artists with money, exposure to other artists and arts institutions, and public recognition of their excellence. This $10,000 awards given to outstanding playwrights working with theatre companies through Theatre Bay Area. See website for application deadline.
Requirements: The Foundation makes grants to organizations that are exempt under Section 501(c)3 of the Internal Revenue Code and are classified as not a private foundation under Section 509(a). The Foundation also provides grants to government and public agencies, as well as to independent projects that have a qualified tax-exempt fiscal sponsor.
Geographic Focus: California
Amount of Grant: 10,000 USD
Contact: John R. Killacky; (415) 733-8523; artsinfo@sff.org or jrk@sff.org
Internet: http://www.sff.org/programs/arts-culture/fund-for-artists
Sponsor: San Francisco Foundation
225 Bush Street, Suite 500
San Francisco, CA 94104-4224

San Francisco Foundation Fund for Artists Award for Visual and Media Artists   4273
The San Francisco Foundation benefits residents in the five Bay Area counties. In partnership with local and national arts organizations, The Fund For Artists gives awards to outstanding individual visual and media artists and arts organizations through Artadia. See website for application deadlines.
Requirements: The Foundation makes grants to organizations that are exempt under Section 501(c)3 of the Internal Revenue Code and are classified as not a private foundation under Section 509(a). The Foundation also provides grants to government and public agencies, as well as to independent projects that have a qualified tax-exempt fiscal sponsor.
Geographic Focus: California
Amount of Grant: 1,500 - 15,000 USD
Contact: John R. Killacky; (415) 733-8523; artsinfo@sff.org or jrk@sff.org
Internet: http://www.sff.org/programs/arts-culture/fund-for-artists
Sponsor: San Francisco Foundation
225 Bush Street, Suite 500
San Francisco, CA 94104-4224

San Francisco Foundation Fund For Artists Matching Commissions Grants   4274
The San Francisco Foundation benefits residents in the five Bay Area counties. The Fund For Artists gives awards to outstanding individuals, ranging in size from $1,500 to $15,000. Seeking to support the development of new work by Bay Area artist and at the same time help small to mid-sized arts groups diversify funding by attracting individual donors, in 2007, The San Francisco Foundation sent out an RFP to more than 200 arts organizations with budgets under $2 million in San Francisco and San Mateo Counties (augmenting similar programs sponsored by Marin Arts Council and East Bay Community Foundation in their respective counties). Grants of up to $5,000 were offered to support the commissioning of new works by Bay Area artists, but had to be matched on a one-to-one basis with contributions from individuals.
Requirements: The Foundation makes grants to organizations that are exempt under Section 501(c)3 of the Internal Revenue Code and are classified as not a private foundation under Section 509(a). The Foundation also provides grants to government and public agencies, as well as to independent projects that have a qualified tax-exempt fiscal sponsor. See website for application deadline.
Geographic Focus: California
Amount of Grant: 1,000 - 5,000 USD
Contact: John R. Killacky; (415) 733-8523; artsinfo@sff.org or jrk@sff.org
Internet: http://www.sff.org/programs/arts-culture/fund-for-artists
Sponsor: San Francisco Foundation
225 Bush Street, Suite 500
San Francisco, CA 94104-4224

San Francisco Foundation Fund Shenson Performing Arts Fellowships   4275
The San Francisco Foundation benefits residents in the five Bay Area counties. The Fund For Artists gives awards to outstanding individuals, ranging in size from $1,500 to $15,000. With Shenson Performing Arts Fellowships is awarded through a pre-selected group of arts organizations that provide excellent professional-track performing arts training and performance opportunities were invited to nominate an exemplary pre-professional performing artist (above 18 yrs of age) for a $5,000 award to assist with their professional advancement. Fellowships were based on the nominee's artistic merit and their potential for future excellence and impact in his or her performing arts discipline.
Requirements: The Foundation makes grants to organizations that are exempt under Section 501(c)3 of the Internal Revenue Code and are classified as not a private foundation under Section 509(a). The Foundation also provides grants to government and public agencies, as well as to independent projects that have a qualified tax-exempt fiscal sponsor. NEXT APPLICATION DEADLINE: The Shenson Fellowships are awarded through nominations by select arts teaching organizations, and no general public applications are available. Please check the SFF website after January 1, 2009, for information on the March 2009 deadline.
Geographic Focus: California
Amount of Grant: 5,000 USD
Contact: John Killacky, Program Officer; (415) 733-8523; jrk@sff.org
Internet: http://www.sff.org/programs/arts-culture/fund-for-artists
Sponsor: San Francisco Foundation
225 Bush Street, Suite 500
San Francisco, CA 94104-4224

San Francisco Foundation James D. Phelan Art Award in Photography   4276
The James D. Phelan Art Awards were established by the trust of James D. Phelan (1861-1930), former San Francisco Mayor, United States Senator, and arts supporter, to recognize the achievements of California-born artists in a variety of disciplines. The San Francisco Foundation sponsors the annual competitions to recognize the achievements of California-born artists in four different disciplines: film, photography, printmaking, and video. Winning applicants will be asked to provide copies of their birth certificates. There are no age restrictions for these awards. Up to six awards are made each year. The competitions are administered in partnership with four community-based arts organizations and are only open to California-born artists. The Phelan Award in Photography is awarded in odd-numbered years. Applications for the award are due to SF Camerawork by February 28. Please visit http://www.sfcamerawork.org/phelan_award/phelan_award2009.html for eligibility requirements, award guidelines, and to submit your application. All application questions should be directed to SF Camerawork.
Requirements: The Foundation makes grants to organizations that are exempt under Section 501(c)3 of the Internal Revenue Code and are classified as not a private foundation under Section 509(a). The Foundation also provides grants to government and public agencies, as well as to independent projects that have a qualified tax-exempt fiscal sponsor.
Geographic Focus: California
Date(s) Application is Due: Feb 28
Amount of Grant: 3,750 USD
Contact: John Killacky, Program Officer; (415) 733-8523; jrk@sff.org
Internet: http://www.sff.org/programs/awards-programs/art-awards
Sponsor: San Francisco Foundation
225 Bush Street, Suite 500
San Francisco, CA 94104-4224

San Francisco Foundation James D. Phelan Art Award in Printmaking   4277
The James D. Phelan Art Awards were established by the trust of James D. Phelan (1861-1930), former San Francisco Mayor, United States Senator, and arts supporter, to recognize the achievements of California-born artists in a variety of disciplines. The San Francisco Foundation sponsors the annual competitions to recognize the achievements of California-born artists in four different disciplines: film, photography, printmaking, and video. Winning applicants will be asked to provide copies of their birth certificates. There are no age restrictions for these awards. Up to six awards are made each year. The competitions are administered in partnership with four community-based arts organizations and are only open to California-born artists. The Phelan Award in Printmaking is administered by The Kala Art Institute. Two artists will receive $5,000 each and be invited to participate in a group exhibition in the Kala Art Institute's gallery. The Phelan Award in Printmaking is awarded in odd-numbered years. Applications for the award are due by May 8 to Kala Art Institute. Please visit http://www.kala.org/call/phelan/phelan.html for eligibility

requirements, award guidelines, and to submit your application. All application questions should be directed to Kala Art Institute.
Requirements: The Foundation makes grants to organizations that are exempt under Section 501(c)3 of the Internal Revenue Code and are classified as not a private foundation under Section 509(a). The Foundation also provides grants to government and public agencies, as well as to independent projects that have a qualified tax-exempt fiscal sponsor.
Geographic Focus: California
Date(s) Application is Due: May 8
Amount of Grant: 5,000 USD
Contact: John Killacky, Program Officer; (415) 733-8523; jrk@sff.org
Internet: http://www.sff.org/programs/awards-programs/art-awards
Sponsor: San Francisco Foundation
225 Bush Street, Suite 500
San Francisco, CA 94104-4224

San Francisco Foundation James D. Phelan Award in Film, Video, and Digital Media 4278
The James D. Phelan Art Awards were established by the trust of James D. Phelan (1861-1930), former San Francisco Mayor, United States Senator, and arts supporter, to recognize the achievements of California-born artists in a variety of disciplines. The San Francisco Foundation sponsors the annual competitions to recognize the achievements of California-born artists in four different disciplines: film, photography, printmaking, and video. Winning applicants will be asked to provide copies of their birth certificates. There are no age restrictions for these awards. The San Francisco Foundation is honored to announce the 13th biennial James D. Phelan Art Award in Video, Film, and Digital Media. In partnership with the Bay Area Video Coalition and the Film Arts Foundation, we will award one $10,000 prize and two $5,000 prizes. The Phelan Awards are given to California-born media artists whose body of work merits recognition for its creativity, innovation, and contribution to the fields of film, video, and digital media. Eligible platforms include film, analog and digital time-based video, installation work, web, interactive and mobile media, and hybrid projects. Applications and work samples will be due in March.
Requirements: The Foundation makes grants to organizations that are exempt under Section 501(c)3 of the Internal Revenue Code and are classified as not a private foundation under Section 509(a). The Foundation also provides grants to government and public agencies, as well as to independent projects that have a qualified tax-exempt fiscal sponsor.
Geographic Focus: California
Amount of Grant: 5,000 - 10,000 USD
Contact: John Killacky, Program Officer; (415) 733-8523; jrk@sff.org
Internet: http://www.sff.org/programs/awards-programs/art-awards
Sponsor: San Francisco Foundation
225 Bush Street, Suite 500
San Francisco, CA 94104-4224

San Francisco Foundation John Gutmann Photography Fellowship Award 4279
The San Francisco Foundation is proud to sponsor a variety of artistic awards that help foster individual growth within our community through its Art Awards Program. Established by the internationally recognized photographer, John Gutmann (1905-1998), the John Gutmann Photography Fellowship awards $5,000 to $10,000 annually to an emerging artist who exhibits professional accomplishment, serious artistic commitment, and need in the field of creative photography. The Gutmann award is determined by nomination only, and nominees are selected by jurors who were appointed by John Gutmann. For more information on John Gutmann, the award, and the jurors, visit: www.johngutmann.org/jurors. There are no applications for this award. Only applicant names submitted by a nominating jury will be considered.
Requirements: The Foundation makes grants to organizations that are exempt under Section 501(c)3 of the Internal Revenue Code and are classified as not a private foundation under Section 509(a). The Foundation also provides grants to government and public agencies, as well as to independent projects that have a qualified tax-exempt fiscal sponsor.
Geographic Focus: California
Amount of Grant: 5,000 - 10,000 USD
Contact: John R. Killacky, Program Officer; (415) 733-8500; artsinfo@sff.org
Internet: http://www.sff.org/programs/awards-programs/art-awards
Sponsor: San Francisco Foundation
225 Bush Street, Suite 500
San Francisco, CA 94104-4224

San Francisco Foundation Koshland Program Arts and Culture Mini-Grants 4280
The Arts and Culture program collaborates with The San Francisco Foundation's Koshland Civic Unity Program to award arts mini-grants of up to $3,000 for grassroots arts projects based in key Bay Area neighborhoods. The Koshland Program recognizes Bay Area grassroots risk-takers, those social innovators of bold spirit who accept the most stubborn neighborhood problems as a personal challenge and who work collaboratively to overcome them. In recognizing these individuals, the Koshland Committee of The San Francisco Foundation seeks to promote civic unity by building mutual respect among diverse people in the community and encouraging small, voluntary efforts to address neighborhood problems.
Requirements: The Foundation makes grants to organizations that are exempt under Section 501(c)3 of the Internal Revenue Code and are classified as not a private foundation under Section 509(a). The Foundation also provides grants to government and public agencies, as well as to independent projects that have a qualified tax-exempt fiscal sponsor. See website for application deadlines.
Geographic Focus: California
Amount of Grant: 3,000 USD
Contact: Jason Torres Hancock, Program Assistant; (415) 733-8564; jth@sff.org

Internet: http://www.sff.org/programs/arts-culture/grants-awards/?searchterm=Koshland/20Program/20arts/20and/20culture/20mini-grants
Sponsor: San Francisco Foundation
225 Bush Street, Suite 500
San Francisco, CA 94104-4224

San Francisco Foundation Multicultural Fellowship 4281
The San Francisco Foundation's Multicultural Fellowship Program aims to increase diversity in the philanthropic and nonprofit sectors. The Program provides young professionals of color with challenging work experiences and leadership opportunities in the areas of grant making and community building. The Fellowship includes an intensive curriculum and dynamic hands-on professional experience.
Requirements: The Foundation makes grants to organizations that are exempt under Section 501(c)3 of the Internal Revenue Code and are classified as not a private foundation under Section 509(a). The Foundation also provides grants to government and public agencies, as well as to independent projects that have a qualified tax-exempt fiscal sponsor.
Geographic Focus: California
Date(s) Application is Due: Jan 16; Jul 1
Contact: John Killacky, Program Officer; (415) 733-8523; jrk@sff.org
Internet: http://www.sff.org/programs/multicultural-fellowship-program
Sponsor: San Francisco Foundation
225 Bush Street, Suite 500
San Francisco, CA 94104-4224

San Francisco Foundation Murphy and Cadogan Fellowships in the Fine Arts 4282
In support of emerging student artists, the Murphy and Cadogan Fellowships in the Fine Arts offer multiple awards of $3,500 to Bay Area fine arts graduate students for continued academic study. These fellowships assist local artists in developing and exploring their artistic potential. In addition to the monetary award, the San Francisco Arts Commission Gallery sponsors an annual exhibit featuring the work of the Murphy and Cadogan Fellowship winners. The number of awards vary per year. Applicants must be a graduate fine arts student at one of the following eight Bay Area colleges and universities: Academy of Art College, California College of the Arts, John F. Kennedy University, Mills College, San Francisco Art Institute, San Francisco State University, Stanford University, University of California at Berkeley.
Requirements: The Foundation makes grants to organizations that are exempt under Section 501(c)3 of the Internal Revenue Code and are classified as not a private foundation under Section 509(a). The Foundation also provides grants to government and public agencies, as well as to independent projects that have a qualified tax-exempt fiscal sponsor.
Geographic Focus: California
Date(s) Application is Due: May 2
Amount of Grant: 3,500 USD
Contact: John Killacky, Program Officer; (415) 733-8523; jrk@sff.org
Internet: http://www.sff.org/programs/awards-programs/art-awards
Sponsor: San Francisco Foundation
225 Bush Street, Suite 500
San Francisco, CA 94104-4224

San Juan Island Community Foundation Grants 4283
The foundation's mission is to enhance the quality of life on San Juan Island and make a positive difference in the community. The foundation awards grants to tax-exempt organizations in its areas of interest, including arts and culture, health and wellness, local economy, community infrastructure, environment, education, and basic social needs.
Requirements: The Foundation only gives grants to tax-exempt organizations which include 501(c)3's, local non-profit branches of 501(c)1's, government agencies, non-profit schools and religious organizations (but only for non-religious purposes). Faith-based organizations are eligible but only for non-religious and unrestricted public service projects. Foundation grants, by policy, are targeted to the local community and would usually only be given to an outside nonprofit for work that affected the local community. A meeting with Foundation representatives is required before a grant application is submitted. Call the office to request a "pre-grant application 1-on-1 meeting". Partner funding will be a critical component of each required, pre-submission meeting including careful identification of the resources that will be allocated by the applying organization itself. The required grant application can be downloaded from the website or requested by phone. Applications may be submitted at anytime following the required online registration and the pre-submission 1:1 meeting with Foundation representatives.
Restrictions: Grants do not support religious organizations where the funds would be used to further the organization's religious purposes; individuals; other endowments; political purposes; or any purpose that discriminates as to race, creed, ethnic group, or gender.
Geographic Focus: Washington
Date(s) Application is Due: Apr 28; Jul 22; Oct 27; Dec 30
Amount of Grant: 500 USD
Contact: Jeanne Peihl; (360) 378-1001; info@sjicf.org
Internet: http://sjicf.org/for-nonprofits/
Sponsor: San Juan Island Community Foundation
P.O. Box 1352
Friday Harbor, WA 98250

Santa Barbara Foundation Monthly Express Grants 4284
Since its inception in 1928, the Santa Barbara Foundation has partnered with local nonprofits to provide a vast array of services throughout Santa Barbara County. The foundation seeks to fund a diverse group of nonprofits to help bring about the vision of making Santa Barbara County a more vibrant community. Express Grants support nonprofit organizations with up to $10,000 for organizational development, defined projects, to leverage community resources/matching funds, and emergencies. Applications may be submitted at any time in the calendar year through November 3.

Requirements: Organizations must be a 501(c)3 serving Santa Barbara County or use a fiscal sponsor with the 501(c)3 tax status. Applications that do not contain a valid EIN (tax ID) number will automatically be declined. The Santa Barbara Foundation uses Guidestar.org to verify nonprofit EIN numbers. Be sure your organization's contact information is accurate on this website, as the Santa Barbara Foundation is obligated to mail award checks to the address associated with the EIN number that is listed. Organizations may submit one application for an Express Grant during a calendar year. This includes applicants funded through the foundation's partnership with The Valley Foundation. An organization may submit more than one application in a calendar year if the proposed project is a Collaborative Grant. Organizations requesting funds to be used in the Santa Ynez Valley region must submit an application through the Santa Ynez Valley Foundation. The region includes Santa Ynez, Los Olivos, Solvang, Buellton, and Los Alamos. A different application is required to be filled out and submitted to the Santa Ynez Valley Foundation for consideration.
Restrictions: Express Grant requests for the following will not be considered: one-time events, religious based programs, fundraisers, direct contributions to capital campaigns, deferred infrastructure and equipment maintenance, general support operating funds, workshops, conferences and training, strategic planning for individual organizations, and public sector projects, unless aligned with foundation initiatives or developing areas of interest.
Geographic Focus: California
Amount of Grant: Up to 10,000 USD
Contact: Jack Azar; (805) 963-1873; fax (805) 966-2345; jazar@sbfoundation.org
Internet: http://www.sbfoundation.org/page.aspx?pid=574
Sponsor: Santa Barbara Foundation
1111 Chapala Street, Suite 200
Santa Barbara, CA 93101

Santa Barbara Foundation Strategy Grants - Capital Support 4285

As the community foundation for all of Santa Barbara county, the foundation funds a wide range of initiatives and projects that address community needs, strengthen the nonprofit sector, develop community leadership, and encourage collaboration. Strategy Grants are distributed annually and aim to help nonprofit organizations fulfill their important missions so that community needs and affect positive change can be addressed. Capital Grants support fundraising plans to raise a significant amount of funds – by a nonprofit, over a specified period of time, or to meet the infrastructure needs of an organization. Specific projects may include construction of new buildings, renovation or expansion of existing buildings, purchase of a building, or to make land improvements (improvements that have indefinite life, such as drainage systems, roads, dredging, grading, site excavating, and paving to ready land for its intended use). The maximum award for a Capital Grant is $50,000. Grants are one year in length.
Requirements: The foundation provides grants to nonprofit organizations serving Santa Barbara County. Organizations must have 501(c)3 tax-exempt status or operate under a fiscal agent. Organizations may submit one Strategy Grant application (Core Support, Capital, or Innovation), as well as be part of one or more Collaborative Strategy Grant applications. Organizations must have thoroughly vetted all aspects of the campaign and must demonstrate the feasibility of the project (assessment of the overall community to support the project and the mission of the organization), and that the community understands the value of the proposed project. Organizations must have the financial infrastructure to handle the rigors of fundraising for the project. Organizations must provide critical information regarding the sustainability of the organization to support the on-going operation after the project has been completed. Consideration will be given to all aspects of a capital campaign's timeline and phases, including the planning and implementation phases. Consideration will be given to organizations who have a long-term lease of 20-30 years. Applications must be received by the foundation by 5:00 pm of the deadline date.
Restrictions: The foundation does not make grants for the following purposes or activities: debt; endowment; fundraising events; individuals; religious organizations for religious purposes; government entities (including schools) for basic services or capital needs; projects that discriminate on the basis of ethnicity, race, color, creed, religion, gender, national origin, age, disability, marital status, sexual orientation, gender identity, gender expression, or any veteran status; or, activities that occurred prior to the beginning date of the grant.
Geographic Focus: California
Amount of Grant: Up to 50,000 USD
Contact: Jack Azar; (805) 963-1873; fax (805) 966-2345; jazar@sbfoundation.org
Internet: http://www.sbfoundation.org/page.aspx?pid=779
Sponsor: Santa Barbara Foundation
1111 Chapala Street, Suite 200
Santa Barbara, CA 93101

Santa Barbara Foundation Strategy Grants - Core Support 4286

As the community foundation for all of Santa Barbara county, the foundation funds a wide range of initiatives and projects that address community needs, strengthen the nonprofit sector, develop community leadership, and encourage collaboration. Strategy Grants are distributed annually and aim to help nonprofit organizations fulfill their important missions so that community needs and affect positive change can be addressed. Core Support Grants are available to nonprofit organizations looking to sustain their organizational infrastructure. Core support is defined as unrestricted funding that enables an organization to carry out its mission. A Core Support Grant can be used to underwrite administrative infrastructure and/or to maintain core programs and essential staff. The foundation's philanthropic purpose for offering core support at this time is to maintain organizations that provide safety net services for the poor and underserved members of our community, and to support increased demand for services whether due to sustained need and/or significant reductions in funding that impact the delivery of core programs and services.
Requirements: The foundation provides grants to nonprofit organizations serving Santa Barbara County. Organizations must have 501(c)3 tax-exempt status or operate under a fiscal agent. Organizations may submit one Strategy Grant application (Core Support, Capital, or Innovation), as well as be part of one or more Collaborative Strategy Grant applications. The organization must be addressing issues of hunger or shelter, or providing primary or behavioral health care for vulnerable populations. The organization must demonstrate increasing demand for services and/or significant reductions in funding over the past three years. Priority for Core Support Grants will be given to organizations that are providing direct services to address hunger, shelter, and primary and/or behavioral health care; are established, well-managed, financially viable, and operate effective programs that primarily serve the needs of poor and underserved communities; and, have developed short- and long-term strategies for addressing identified organizational needs. Applications must be received by the foundation by 5:00 pm of the deadline date.
Restrictions: The foundation does not make grants for the following purposes or activities: debt; endowment; fundraising events; individuals; religious organizations for religious purposes; government entities (including schools) for basic services or capital needs; projects that discriminate on the basis of ethnicity, race, color, creed, religion, gender, national origin, age, disability, marital status, sexual orientation, gender identity, gender expression, or any veteran status; or, activities that occurred prior to the beginning date of the grant.
Geographic Focus: California
Amount of Grant: Up to 50,000 USD
Contact: Jack Azar; (805) 963-1873; fax (805) 966-2345; jazar@sbfoundation.org
Internet: http://www.sbfoundation.org/page.aspx?pid=778
Sponsor: Santa Barbara Foundation
1111 Chapala Street, Suite 200
Santa Barbara, CA 93101

Santa Barbara Foundation Strategy Grants - Innovation 4287

As the community foundation for all of Santa Barbara county, the foundation funds a wide range of initiatives and projects that address community needs, strengthen the nonprofit sector, develop community leadership, and encourage collaboration. Strategy Grants are distributed annually and aim to help nonprofit organizations fulfill their important missions so that community needs and affect positive change can be addressed. Innovation Grants support compelling projects, approaches, or organizational structures that provide effective pathways to problem solving in order to improve community outcomes. The foundation is interested in innovative ideas and new approaches that transform how the community addresses the critical problems of our time. Innovation Grants are available for new programs or projects that address timely or relevant issues or opportunities, or for existing programs or projects taking a fresh approach or new twist to solving problems. Competitive projects will be collaborative in nature and should be beyond the exploratory and planning phases. Projects should be ready to pilot or for full implementation. Grants may exceed one year in length. Smaller grant awards with a one year time frame are also available.
Requirements: The foundation provides grants to nonprofit organizations serving Santa Barbara County. Organizations must have 501(c)3 tax-exempt status or operate under a fiscal agent. Organizations may submit one Strategy Grant application (Core Support, Capital, or Innovation), as well as be part of one or more Collaborative Strategy Grant applications. The maximum award for Innovation Grants is $250,000. Priority is given to projects that transform how an organization or program operates, approaches problems, or delivers services; create new structures, partnerships, or collaborations for greater efficiencies, better delivery of services, or fresh approaches to solve problems or address needs, gaps, or opportunities; serve as a model for future scaling up to reach more people, other sectors, or additional organizations; incorporate a strong financial model for long-term sustainability.
Restrictions: The foundation does not make grants for the following purposes or activities: debt; endowment; fundraising events; individuals; religious organizations for religious purposes; government entities (including schools) for basic services or capital needs; projects that discriminate on the basis of ethnicity, race, color, creed, religion, gender, national origin, age, disability, marital status, sexual orientation, gender identity, gender expression, or any veteran status; or, activities that occurred prior to the beginning date of the grant. Applications must be received by the foundation by 5:00 pm of the deadline date.
Geographic Focus: California
Amount of Grant: Up to 250,000 USD
Contact: Jack Azar; (805) 963-1873; fax (805) 966-2345; jazar@sbfoundation.org
Internet: http://www.sbfoundation.org/page.aspx?pid=781
Sponsor: Santa Barbara Foundation
1111 Chapala Street, Suite 200
Santa Barbara, CA 93101

Santa Barbara Foundation Towbes Fund for the Performing Arts Grants 4288

The Towbes Fund for the Performing Arts, a field of interest fund of the Santa Barbara Foundation, has been created to support performing arts organizations and programs primarily serving Santa Barbara County. Grants will be made two to three times per calendar year from a pool of qualified performing arts organizations and are awarded based on a process of research, due diligence, and evaluation by an internal grant committee consisting of senior level foundation staff. Funds may be used for general operating support or for a specific program, project, or initiative. Award amounts generally range from $2,000 to $50,000 and are commensurate to organizational size and scale of work.
Requirements: The foundation provides grants to nonprofit organizations serving Santa Barbara County. Organizations must have 501(c)3 tax-exempt status or operate under a fiscal agent. Grant selection will be based on alignment with the donor's interest and history of giving in the performing arts as well as foundation initiatives. To be included in the pool of qualified organizations for funding consideration, organizations must provide the following to the foundation: Qualification letter (two page maximum) that includes organizational mission statement or purpose, description of organization and program offerings (performances, outreach and education, numbers served, demographics, etc.), and highlight of a specific program, initiative, or campaign you would like considered for

funding; Annual operating budget and balance sheet; and, Board roster. Qualification materials can be submitted at any time in the calendar year.
Restrictions: The foundation does not make grants for the following purposes or activities: debt; endowment; fundraising events; individuals; religious organizations for religious purposes; government entities (including schools) for basic services or capital needs; projects that discriminate on the basis of ethnicity, race, color, creed, religion, gender, national origin, age, disability, marital status, sexual orientation, gender identity, gender expression, or any veteran status; or, activities that occurred prior to the beginning date of the grant.
Geographic Focus: California
Amount of Grant: 2,000 - 50,000 USD
Contact: Jack Azar; (805) 963-1873; fax (805) 966-2345; jazar@sbfoundation.org
Internet: http://www.sbfoundation.org/page.aspx?pid=906
Sponsor: Santa Barbara Foundation
1111 Chapala Street, Suite 200
Santa Barbara, CA 93101

Santa Fe Community Foundation root2fruit Santa Fe 4289
SFCF root2fruit provides resources for local, small organizations to build their capacity to thrive and succeed. The program provides funding, mentoring and peer partnerships to grantees. Three organizations will be selected per year to receive up to $10,000 per year for three years. Project-specific proposals will not be funded within this program.
Requirements: Organizations must be located in the County of Santa Fe and/or provide a significant amount of their services to Santa Fe residents. This is an initiative for smaller organizations with annual operating budgets of approximately $150,000 or smaller. Contact the Foundation and discuss your ideas prior to submitting a proposal.
Restrictions: The foundation does not award grants for religious purposes, capital campaigns or endowments, scholarships, or individuals.
Geographic Focus: New Mexico
Date(s) Application is Due: Aug 20
Amount of Grant: Up to 30,000 USD
Contact: Katie Dry, Fund Coordinator; (505) 988-9715 x 7016; kdry@santafecf.org
Internet: http://www.santafecf.org/nonprofits/grantseekers/root2fruit
Sponsor: Santa Fe Community Foundation
501 Halona Street
Santa Fe, NM 87505

Santa Fe Community Foundation Seasonal Grants-Fall Cycle 4290
Through its outreach to nonprofits, donors and community leaders, the Foundation organizes its annual grants cycle into a two-season grants program. Each season (Spring and Fall) focuses on its own specific goals and strategies. The Foundation is devoted to building healthy and vital communities in the region where: racial, cultural or economic differences do not limit access to health, education or employment; diverse audiences enjoy the many arts and cultural heritages of our region; and, all sectors of its community take responsibility for ensuring a healthy environment. The areas of interest for the Fall Cycle are Arts, Animal Welfare, and Health and Human Services. For Arts proposals, projects should: increase public engagement in the arts; and, support public policy, community organizing or public information to strengthen the arts segment of the creative economy locally. For Health and Human Services proposals, projects should: improve the health of underserved residents of the Santa Fe region; improve access to affordable healthy food; strengthen the delivery of homelessness services; improve safety for children, women, families, sexual minorities and the elderly; and/or, support public policy, civic engagement, community organizing or public information to improve the health and well-being of local residents. For Animal Welfare proposals, the Foundation has approximately $25,000 available for animal welfare-related grants, and will include summaries of all animal welfare proposals (that meet basic due diligence) in the 'Giving Together' catalogue that accompanies the Fall Community Grant Cycle. The Giving Together catalogue is then shared with the Foundation's fundholders who are invited to make grants toward any proposal in the catalogue.
Requirements: Applications will be accepted from organizations that: are located in or serve the people of Santa Fe, Rio Arriba, Taos, Los Alamos, San Miguel or Mora Counties; are tax-exempt under Section 501(c)3 of the Internal Revenue Code or are a public or governmental agency or a federally recognized tribe in the state of New Mexico, or that have a fiscal sponsor; employ staff and provide services without discrimination on the basis of race, religion, sex, age, national origin, disability, or sexual orientation; and, are at least three years old. Each nonprofit entity may only apply for funding once per year. All grants will be $5,000, $10,000 or $15,000, depending on your annual budget. For organizations whose annual budget is under $150,000, you may apply for a $5,000 grant; for organizations whose annual budget is between $150,000 and $500,000, you may apply for a $10,000 grant; for organizations with an annual budget over $500,000, you may apply for a $15,000 grant. Grant applications will be accepted online only. Applications must be received by 5:00 pm of the deadline date.
Restrictions: The foundation does not award grants for religious purposes, capital campaigns or endowments, scholarships, or individuals. Organizations that received a community grant from SFCF in the last calendar year are not eligible to apply for a community grant in the current calendar year.
Geographic Focus: New Mexico
Date(s) Application is Due: Aug 26
Amount of Grant: 5,000 - 15,000 USD
Contact: Christa Coggins, Vice President for Community Philanthropy; (505) 988-9715 x 7002; ccoggins@santafecf.org
Internet: http://www.santafecf.org/nonprofits/grantseekers/general-grant-information
Sponsor: Santa Fe Community Foundation
501 Halona Street
Santa Fe, NM 87505

Santa Fe Community Foundation Seasonal Grants-Spring Cycle 4291
Through its outreach to nonprofits, donors and community leaders, the Foundation organizes its annual grants cycle into a two-season grants program. Each season (Spring and Fall) focuses on its own specific goals and strategies. The Foundation is devoted to building healthy and vital communities in the region where: racial, cultural or economic differences do not limit access to health, education or employment; diverse audiences enjoy the many arts and cultural heritages of our region; and, all sectors of its community take responsibility for ensuring a healthy environment. The areas of interest for the Spring Cycle are Economic Opportunity, Education and Environment. For Economic Opportunity proposals, the projects should: increase the number of low-income individuals who have achieved stable housing; measurably improve the outcomes of and access to job training programs and the income of low- wage earners; assist low-income families and individuals to save for and invest in future economic success through education, achieving affordable and sustainable housing, and building entrepreneurial skills and activities; and/or support public policy, civic engagement, community organizing or public information to improve economic opportunity. For Education (Closing the Educational Achievement Gap) proposals, projects should: increase the number of low-income children who are prepared for academic success in school through an investment in all learning experiences, parent involvement, and extended time spent learning; increase the number of low-income students who access post-secondary education ready to succeed through an investment in student preparation, college access, and coordination of providers; and/or support public policy, civic engagement, community organizing or public information to improve education. For Environment proposals, projects should: strengthen infrastructure for local food production and availability; support programs supporting sustainable agriculture; increase number of youth and adults engaged in agricultural and ecological restoration; expand support for groups engaged in advocacy and policy development for regional resource management, including land, air and water; and/or support promotion of and advocacy for local, renewable energy.
Requirements: Applications will be accepted from organizations that: are located in or serve the people of Santa Fe, Rio Arriba, Taos, Los Alamos, San Miguel or Mora Counties; are tax-exempt under Section 501(c)3 of the Internal Revenue Code or are a public or governmental agency or a federally recognized tribe in the state of New Mexico, or that have a fiscal sponsor; employ staff and provide services without discrimination on the basis of race, religion, sex, age, national origin, disability, or sexual orientation; and, are at least three years old. Each nonprofit entity may only apply for funding once per year. All grants will be $5,000, $10,000 or $15,000, depending on your annual budget. For organizations whose annual budget is under $150,000, you may apply for a $5,000 grant; for organizations whose annual budget is between $150,000 and $500,000, you may apply for a $10,000 grant; for organizations with an annual budget over $500,000, you may apply for a $15,000 grant. Grant applications will be accepted online only. Applications must be received by 5:00 pm of the deadline date.
Restrictions: The foundation does not award grants for religious purposes, capital campaigns or endowments, scholarships, or individuals. Organizations that received a community grant from SFCF in the last calendar year are not eligible to apply for a community grant in the current calendar year.
Geographic Focus: New Mexico
Date(s) Application is Due: Mar 3
Amount of Grant: 5,000 - 15,000 USD
Contact: Christa Coggins; (505) 988-9715 x 7002; ccoggins@santafecf.org
Internet: http://www.santafecf.org/nonprofits/grantseekers/general-grant-information
Sponsor: Santa Fe Community Foundation
501 Halona Street
Santa Fe, NM 87505

Santa Fe Community Foundation Special and Urgent Needs Grants 4292
The Foundation created the Special and Urgent Needs (SUN) grants to address the short-term needs of nonprofits. With a relatively small amount of funding, SUN grants help an organization take advantage of an unbudgeted, unforeseen, and time-sensitive opportunity or emergency that will enhance or preserve the ability of the organization to meet its mission. There is no deadline - you may apply anytime. Only electronic applications are accepted. Decisions are made within 14 days of receiving application. Grants funds awarded will be up to $2,500.
Requirements: Applications will be accepted from organizations that are located in and serve the people of Santa Fe, Rio Arriba, Taos, Los Alamos, San Miguel or Mora Counties. Organizations must be tax-exempt under Section 501(c)3 of the Internal Revenue Code or be a public agency in the state of New Mexico. Nonprofit organizations or community groups who do not have 501(c)3 status may apply for grant awards if another tax-exempt organization acts as a fiscal sponsor. Applicants must employ staff and provide services without discrimination on the basis of race, religion, sex, age, national origin, disability, or sexual orientation.
Restrictions: The Foundation will not generally make SUN grants for: organizations with an operating budget larger than $1.5 million; independent/private schools; endowments; capital campaigns (except for initial planning expenses); religious purposes; individuals; debts; equipment (unless it is an integral part of an otherwise eligible project); and SFCF does not fund work that has already been completed. SFCF also cannot consider applications for budget deficits or shortfalls.
Geographic Focus: New Mexico
Amount of Grant: Up to 2,500 USD
Contact: Christa Coggins; (505) 988-9715 x 7002; ccoggins@santafecf.org
Internet: http://www.santafecf.org/nonprofits/grantseekers/SUN-grants
Sponsor: Santa Fe Community Foundation
501 Halona Street
Santa Fe, NM 87505

Sapelo Foundation Environmental Protection Grants 4293
The Sapelo Foundation is a private family foundation focusing its funding within the State of Georgia. The Foundation is particularly interested in projects that involve multiple groups that work cooperatively toward common goals, accomplish systemic reform, and have a statewide impact. In addition, the Foundation gives special attention to low-resource regions in the state and innovative, community-based projects within the Foundation's focus areas. The Foundation believes that the preservation of Georgia's finite natural resources benefits all species of life and is essential to their health and long-term survival. Currently, the Foundation's primary focus is a strategic campaign addressing water resource management and policy in Georgia. The Foundation was instrumental in the creation of the Georgia Water Coalition and its active members currently receive priority for funding. Grants range from $1,000 to $60,000, and the average award is between $5,000 and $25,000.
Requirements: Georgia 501(c)3 nonprofit organizations are eligible.
Restrictions: The Foundation does not give priority to: academic research; land acquisition; environmental education centers and nature centers; wildlife parks or animal rehabilitation center; or museums. The Foundation does not support projects operating solely within the Metro Atlanta Area. The Foundation does not fund the following: brick-and-mortar, building projects or renovations, including construction materials and labor costs; endowment funds; fraternal groups or civic clubs; health care initiatives or medical research; individuals; national or regional organizations, unless their programs specifically benefit Georgia and all funds are spent within the state; organizations that are not tax-exempt; or payment of debts.
Geographic Focus: Georgia
Date(s) Application is Due: Mar 1; Sep 1
Amount of Grant: 1,000 - 60,000 USD
Contact: Phyllis Bowen, Executive Director; (912) 265-0520; fax (912) 254-1888; info@sapelofoundation.org or sapelofoundation@mindspring.com
Internet: http://www.sapelofoundation.org/index.html
Sponsor: Sapelo Foundation
1712 Ellis Street, 2nd Floor
Brunswick, GA 31520

Sapelo Foundation Social Justice Grants 4294
The Sapelo Foundation is a private family foundation focusing its funding within the State of Georgia. The Foundation is particularly interested in projects that involve multiple groups that work cooperatively toward common goals, accomplish systemic reform, and have a statewide impact. In addition, the Foundation gives special attention to low-resource regions in the state and innovative, community-based projects within the Foundation's focus areas. The Foundation believes that the development of sound public policy is crucial to effective government and the empowerment of the citizenry. Therefore, it is the aim of the Foundation to strengthen representative democracy in Georgia through efforts that educate the public about government institutions and policies, promote civic engagement and responsibility, and monitor government performance. Currently, the Foundation's primary focus is a strategic campaign advocating for fairness for children in the state's justice system. Grants range from $1,000 to $60,000, and the average award is between $5,000 and $25,000.
Requirements: Georgia 501(c)3 nonprofit organizations are eligible.
Restrictions: The Foundation does not give priority to: academic research; local government entities; human services programs; criminal justice programs designed to rehabilitate and/or punish individuals; senior citizen's programs; after-school mentoring/tutoring programs; single-site day care facilities; homeless shelters or programs; affordable housing; or programs serving the physically or developmentally disabled. The Foundation does not support projects operating solely within the Metro Atlanta Area. The Foundation does not fund the following: brick-and-mortar, building projects or renovations, including construction materials and labor costs; endowment funds; fraternal groups or civic clubs; health care initiatives or medical research; individuals; national or regional organizations, unless their programs specifically benefit Georgia and all funds are spent within the state; organizations that are not tax-exempt; or payment of debts.
Geographic Focus: Georgia
Date(s) Application is Due: Mar 1; Sep 1
Amount of Grant: 1,000 - 60,000 USD
Contact: Phyllis Bowen, Executive Director; (912) 265-0520; fax (912) 254-1888; info@sapelofoundation.org or sapelofoundation@mindspring.com
Internet: http://www.sapelofoundation.org/index.html
Sponsor: Sapelo Foundation
1712 Ellis Street, 2nd Floor
Brunswick, GA 31520

Sarah Scaife Foundation Grants 4295
Approximately 80 percent of the annual grants are made to public policy programs that address major domestic and international issues. There are no geographic restrictions. Other grants are made in the fields of education and culture, health and medicine, scientific research, public affairs, and recreation and equipment in all geographic areas, but primarily in western Pennsylvania. Types of support include general operating support, continuing support, program development, conferences and seminars, publication, seed grants, fellowships, research, and matching funds. Applications are accepted at any time. Foundation staff considers requests in February, May, September, and November.
Restrictions: Grants are not made to individuals or to national organizations for general fund-raising purposes.
Geographic Focus: All States
Amount of Grant: 25,000 - 200,000 USD
Contact: Michael Gleba, Vice President of Programs; (412) 392-2900
Internet: http://www.scaife.com/sarah.html
Sponsor: Sarah Scaife Foundation
1 Oxford Center, 301 Grant Street, Suite 3900
Pittsburgh, PA 15219

Sara Lee Foundation Grants 4296
The foundation's cash grants program concentrates on the Chicago metropolitan area. Special interests include organizations that serve the disadvantaged with emphasis on programs concerning hunger and homelessness, job placement, housing, and women's issues; education, including child development education, adult basic education, and literacy skills; and arts and cultural institutions including libraries. The foundation also funds a scholarship program and youth ambassador program for employees of the Sara Lee Corporation and its subsidiaries. Additional types of support include employee matching gifts, special projects, operating budgets, annual campaigns, and continuing support. The annual leadership awards recognize and support nonprofit organizations that demonstrate innovative leadership in improving life for the disadvantaged in communities where Sara Lee Corporation divisions have facilities; two to four awards are presented each year. Leadership awards are not restricted to Illinois nonprofits. Annual deadline may vary; contact program officer for exact date.
Requirements: IRS 501(c)3 nonprofit organizations in Illinois that have been in existence for at least two years at the time of application and that are located in a community where a Sara Lee Corporation division has facilities are eligible.
Restrictions: Grants do not support individuals; organizations with a limited constituency, such as fraternities or veterans groups; organizations that limit their services to members of one religious group, or those whose services propagate religious faith or creed, including churches, seminaries, bible colleges, and theological institutions; political organizations or those having the primary purpose of influencing legislation or promoting a particular ideological point of view; elementary and secondary schools, either private or public; units of government or quasi-governmental agencies; or hospitals and health organizations concentrating their research and/or treatment in one area of human disease.
Geographic Focus: Illinois
Date(s) Application is Due: Jan 10; Jul 10
Amount of Grant: Up to 15,000 USD
Samples: Steppenwolf Theatre Co (Chicago, IL)—for its campaign to build endowment and to support key programs, $1 million.
Contact: Robin Tryloff, Executive Director; (312) 558-8448; fax (312) 419-3192
Internet: http://www.saraleefoundation.org/funding/focus.cfm
Sponsor: Sara Lee Foundation
3 First National Plaza
Chicago, IL 60602-4260

Sarkeys Foundation Grants 4297
Governed by a dedicated Board of Trustees, the foundation that bears SJ Sarkeys' name is deeply committed to furthering his vision to improve the quality of life in Oklahoma. The Foundation provides grants to a diverse group of nonprofit organizations and institutions, almost all of which are located in Oklahoma. Major areas of foundation support include education, arts and cultural endeavors, scientific research, animal welfare, social service and human service needs, and cultural and humanitarian programs of regional significance. Grant proposals are considered at the April and October meetings of the board of trustees.
Requirements: Most organizations classified by the IRS as being a 501(c)3 that is not a private foundation and is headquartered and offering services in Oklahoma may apply. Preference is given to organizations that have been in operation at least 3 years. Organizations are required to submit a Letter of Inquiry to determine whether they meet the criteria and priorities for funding. Representatives are encouraged to speak with a program officer for more information and to ask any questions about the process. An organization may submit one request in a twelve month period.
Restrictions: The Sarkeys Foundation will not fund: local programs appropriately financed within the community; direct mail solicitations and annual campaigns; out of state institutions; hospitals; operating expenses; purchase of vehicles; grants to individuals; responsibility for permanent financing of a program; programs whose ultimate intent is to be profit making; start-up funding for new organizations; feasibility studies; grants which trigger expenditure responsibility by Sarkeys Foundation; direct support to government agencies; individual public or private elementary or secondary schools, unless they are serving the needs of a special population which are not being met elsewhere; and religious institutions and their subsidiaries.
Geographic Focus: Oklahoma
Date(s) Application is Due: Feb 3; Aug 1
Amount of Grant: Up to 50,000 USD
Contact: Susan Frantz; (405) 364-3703; susan@sarkeys.org or sarkeys@sarkeys.org
Internet: http://www.sarkeys.org/grant_guidelines.html
Sponsor: Sarkeys Foundation
530 East Main Street
Norman, OK 73071

Sartain Lanier Family Foundation Grants 4298
The Sartain Lanier Family Foundation awards grants to Georgia nonprofits in support of education, health and human services, arts, environment, and community development, with the majority of new grantmaking in the area of education. Types of support include building and renovation; capital campaigns; endowments; general operating support; program development; and program-related investments and loans. The foundation's board meets in May and November of each year to consider grant requests, which will be by invitation only. Interested applicants should provide an organizational overview for consideration purposes. Prior to submitting a full proposal, interested parties should submit a letter limited to two pages summarizing the request. The letter should include a brief description of the organization and its purpose, the project for which funding is requested, the total cost of the project, and the amount being requested.
Requirements: Nonprofit organizations in the southeastern United States are eligible to apply if invited to do so; however, the majority of recipients are located in Georgia and specifically the Atlanta metro area.

Restrictions: The foundation does not make grants for individuals; churches or religious organizations for projects that primarily benefit their own members; partisan political purposes; tickets to charitable events or dinners, or to sponsor special events or fundraisers.
Geographic Focus: Georgia
Contact: Patricia E. Lummus, Associate Director; (404) 564-1259; fax (404) 564-1251; plummus@lanierfamilyfoundation.org
Internet: http://lanierfamilyfoundation.org/funding-priorities/
Sponsor: Sartain Lanier Family Foundation
25 Puritan Mill, 950 Lowery Boulevard NW
Atlanta, GA 30318

Sasakawa Peace Foundation Grants 4299
The nonprofit foundation sponsors a wide range of programs designed to address international issues and to promote global peace via nonprofit sector initiatives worldwide. The foundation aims to contribute to the welfare of humankind and development of a sound international community. A statement of the proposed activity must be submitted on three to four pages of A-4 size paper. A full proposal will then be requested if the project is deemed appropriate. There is no prescribed application form or format. Applications are accepted at any time; no submission deadline and no grant ceiling have been set. Proposals are accepted in English or Japanese only. Further information about grant programs is available on the Web site in both English and Japanese.
Restrictions: Ineligible are acquisition of real estate or other capital assets, construction of buildings, subsidization of operating expenses for an organized body, non-applied research, and disaster relief.
Geographic Focus: All States
Contact: Mika Sekiguchi; 81-3-6229-5457; fax 81-3-6229-5473; pr@spf.or.jp
Internet: https://www.spf.org/e/grants/index.html
Sponsor: Sasakawa Peace Foundation
1-2-2-4F Akasaka, Minato-ku
Tokyo, 107-8523 Japan

SAS Institute Community Relations Donations 4300
SAS (pronounced "sass") once stood for "statistical analysis system," and began at North Carolina State University as a project to analyze agricultural research. As demand for such software grew, SAS was founded in 1976 to help all sorts of customers - from pharmaceutical companies and banks to academic and governmental entities. Coming from such beginnings, SAS is committed to corporate citizenship and supports the community through a generous financial program, in-kind giving, and employee volunteerism. SAS's donations program focuses primarily on strategic educational initiatives in the geographic area surrounding SAS world headquarters in Cary, South Carolina, that increase interest and achievement in the science, technology, engineering, and math (STEM) disciplines. In particular, SAS supports programs that focus on the integration of technology with teaching and learning in ways that will strengthen the education system and increase the number of students entering STEM careers. Programs must also show that their efforts have a long-term impact and affect significant numbers of people, without discrimination. Acting on the philosophy of reduce-reuse-recycle, SAS donates surplus computer hardware, office equipment, and other tangible items to organizations that can benefit from the donation. Priority goes to schools, other educational organizations, and organizations with which SAS employees are personally involved. SAS also offers several products and services at no cost to K-12 schools as well as to colleges and universities. Application guidelines and an interactive application form for SAS's donation program are available at the company website. To apply, applicants must complete and print the form and mail it (along with any required supporting documentation) to the address given.
Requirements: Eligible organizations must meet the following criteria: have 501(3)c status with the IRS; have a responsible board of directors serving without compensation; show financial stability as evidenced by annual financial statements; employ ethical methods of publicity, promotion, and solicitation of funds; raise funds without payment of commissions, street solicitations or mailing of unordered tickets; operate from a detailed annual budget; request funds for programs or operations with a minimal portion applied to overhead; and use SAS in-kind donations to benefit organizational members or constituents.
Restrictions: The following programs and activities are not funded: sponsorship of professional athletic or amateur sports teams or individuals; single events such as walk-a-thons, fundraisers, workshops, seminars, etc; religious causes; political parties, candidates or issues; organizations that are in any way exclusive; trips and tours; independent film/video productions; and requests from individuals.
Geographic Focus: North Carolina
Contact: George Farthing, (919) 677-8000; CommunityRelations@sas.com
Internet: http://www.sas.com/company/csr/education.html#s1=4
Sponsor: SAS Institute
100 SAS Campus Drive
Cary, NC 27513-2414

Saucony Run for Good Foundation Grants 4301
The mission of the foundation is to encourage active and healthy lifestyles for children to combat obesity, and applications that involve running programs will be given priority consideration. The grants are open to non-profit organizations that initiate and support running and fitness programs for kids which in turn will help them live longer, healthier lives. There are two grant cycles per year, with up to seven awards granted each cycle.
Requirements: Programs whose participants are 18 years of age or less, have 501(c)3 status and can demonstrate their program positively impacts the lives of participants through their increased participation in running. Salaries and/or stipends can be included in the budget. Selection of grant recipients will be based on the following: Utilization of running participation for health and/or well-being in children; Serves youth populations not traditionally exposed to running programs; Demonstrates support and inspiration in creating a program that exemplifies the Saucony Run For Good Program's mission of inspiring the community of runners.
Restrictions: Grant monies may not be used to cover expenses incurred prior to the award date of the grant. Employees or relatives of Saucony, Inc., the Stride Rite Corporation, and/or any of its affiliates are not eligible to apply and/or receive grants.
Geographic Focus: All States
Date(s) Application is Due: Jun 13; Dec 12
Amount of Grant: Up to 10,000 USD
Contact: Pat Oakley, Saucony Consumer Specialist; (800) 365-4933
Internet: http://www.sauconyrunforgood.com/
Sponsor: Saucony Run for Good Foundation
191 Spring Street
Lexington, MA 02420

SCBWI Don Freeman Memorial Grant 4302
An important function of the SCBWI is providing assistance and support to those working in the children's book field; to encourage continuing excellence in the creation of children's literature, the Society of Children's Book Writers and Illustrators has instituted grant programs. The Don Freeman Memorial Grant-In-Aid has been established by the SCBWI to enable picture-book artists to further their understanding, training, and work in the picture-book genre. One grant of $1,500 will be awarded annually. One Runner-Up grant of $500 will also be awarded.
Requirements: The grant is available to both full and associate members of the SCBWI who, as artists, seriously intended to make picture books their chief contribution to the field of children's literature. Membership is open to anyone with an active interest in children's literature or media. Applicants will be required to submit artwork: either a rough book-dummy accompanied by two finished illustrations or ten finished illustrations suitable for picture-book portfolio presentation. Art work specifications are included with the application instructions.
Restrictions: Members can apply for only one SCBWI grant in a given year.
Geographic Focus: All States
Date(s) Application is Due: Feb 2
Amount of Grant: 500 - 1,500 USD
Contact: Kim Turrisi; (323) 782-1010; fax (323) 782-1892; kimturrisi@scbwi.org
Internet: http://www.scbwi.org/Pages.aspx/Don-Freeman-Grant
Sponsor: Society of Children's Book Writers and Illustrators
8271 Beverly Boulevard
Beverly Hills, CA 90048

Schering-Plough Foundation Community Initiatives Grants 4303
The Schering-Plough Foundation, a non-profit membership corporation established in 1955, is dedicated to working with the citizens of our communities to help them realize their full potential and enhance their quality of life. Support for community development takes many forms and allows the Foundation to reach out to numerous, highly diverse groups within its communities. The Foundation continues to support organizations that promote culture and the arts, environmental issues, legal services, etc. and are always seeking out new and innovative ways to serve the citizens of its communities.
Requirements: The Foundation considers requests from tax-exempt, 501(c)3 non-profit organizations located in the United States, or its possessions, whose goals and activities fall within its stated objectives and areas of interest. All requests for funding must be made online. National organizations are eligible to apply.
Restrictions: Grants are not made to individuals.
Geographic Focus: All States
Amount of Grant: 5,000 - 200,000 USD
Contact: Christine Fahey, Assistant Secretary; (908) 298-7232; fax (908) 298-7349
Internet: http://www.schering-plough.com/company/foundation.aspx
Sponsor: Schering-Plough Foundation
2000 Galloping Hill Road
Kennilworth, NJ 07033-0530

Schering-Plough Foundation Health Grants 4304
The Schering-Plough Foundation, a non-profit membership corporation established in 1955, is dedicated to working with the citizens of our communities to help them realize their full potential and enhance their quality of life. The Foundation's interest in improving the health and well-being of its communities remains a top priority and is reflected in the numerous initiatives that have been developed to benefit these communities. The Foundation invests in the future of those communities by building meaningful partnerships that enhance the quality of life. Currently, the Foundation is involved in several partnerships that seek to expand the quality and availability of health care in its underserved communities.
Requirements: The Foundation considers requests from tax-exempt, 501(c)3 non-profit organizations located in the United States, or its possessions, whose goals and activities fall within its stated objectives and areas of interest. All requests for funding must be made online. National organizations are eligible to apply.
Restrictions: Grants are not made to individuals.
Geographic Focus: All States
Amount of Grant: 5,000 - 200,000 USD
Contact: Christine Fahey, Assistant Secretary; (908) 298-7232; fax (908) 298-7349
Internet: http://www.schering-plough.com/company/foundation.aspx
Sponsor: Schering-Plough Foundation
2000 Galloping Hill Road
Kennilworth, NJ 07033-0530

Scherman Foundation Grants 4305
The main areas of interest for the foundation are the environment, peace and security, reproductive rights and services, human rights and liberties, the arts, and social welfare. Priority is given to organizations in New York City in the areas of the arts and social welfare. Requests for support should be made in a brief letter addressed to the President (Mike Pratt) outlining the purpose for the funds being sought; program description; budget; list of directors and staff; audited financial statement; sources of support; and evidence of tax status. The board meets four times a year to consider applications.
Restrictions: The foundation does not accept applications through fax. Funding is not given to: individuals; colleges, universities, or professional schools; medical, science, or engineering research; capital campaigns; conferences; or specific media or arts productions. Do not submit video or audio cassettes or CD's, unless requested to do so.
Geographic Focus: All States, New York
Amount of Grant: 1,000 - 60,000 USD
Contact: Mike Pratt; (212) 832-3086; fax (212) 838-0154; mpratt@scherman.org
Internet: http://www.scherman.org/html2/approc.html
Sponsor: Scherman Foundation
16 East 52nd Street, Suite 601
New York, NY 10022-5306

Scheumann Foundation Grants 4306
Established in Indiana in 2002, the Scheumann Foundation offers grants in support of youth services, recreation, camps, and housing development within the State of Indiana. There are no specific application forms or annual deadlines. With that in mind, applicants should forward a two- to three-page letter of application outlining their program and budgetary needs. Most recent awards have ranged from $500 to $400,000.
Requirements: Giving is restricted to non-profit programs serving youth and families within Indiana.
Geographic Focus: Indiana
Amount of Grant: 500 - 400,000 USD
Contact: John B. Scheumann, President; (765) 742-0300
Sponsor: Scheumann Foundation
P.O. Box 811
Lafayette, IN 47902-0811

Schlessman Family Foundation Grants 4307
The foundation awards grants to Colorado nonprofits in its areas of interest: education, disadvantaged youth programs and services, elderly/senior programs, special needs groups, and established cultural institutions (such as museums, libraries and zoos). Performing arts grants are available but are very limited.
Requirements: Grants are limited to Colorado charities, primarily greater metro-Denver organizations. The Foundation accepts, but does not require, the Colorado Common Grant Application. All requests must be in writing and discourages lengthy proposals with multiple attachments. If additional information is required, you will be contacted. Proposals are accepted throughout the year, however they must be postmarked on or before the deadline date if they are to be considered in time for the once-a-year distributions on March 31.
Restrictions: The following are ineligible: individuals, start-ups, support for benefits or conferences, public/private/charter schools.
Geographic Focus: Colorado
Date(s) Application is Due: Dec 31
Contact: Patricia Middendorf, (303) 831-5683; contact@schlessmanfoundation.org
Internet: http://www.schlessmanfoundation.org
Sponsor: Schlessman Family Foundation
1555 Blake Street, Suite 400
Denver, CO 80202

Scholastic Book Grants 4308
Scholastic will select three to five national nonprofit organizations each year to receive large donations of books. Smaller grants will be disbursed. Each grantee is expected to distribute the books it receives to the children it serves in a creative and unique way. Projects must be directed at children from preschool to high school. Book grants are granted on a quarterly basis during the following months: January, April, July, and October. See Scholastic website for application form.
Requirements: Grants are given to literacy organizations that have tax-exempt classification under sections 170 (c) or 501(c)3 of the IRS code. Requests from organizations that serve the needs of at-risk children or families, particularly those living in inner city or rural areas, are more likely to be granted.
Restrictions: The company does not grant requests for the following: individuals, individual schools, scholarships, scholarship funds, political, labor, religious, fraternal or sports groups, special events, fundraisers or capital campaigns.
Geographic Focus: All States
Contact: Kyle Good, Vice President; (212) 343-4563
Internet: http://www.scholastic.com/aboutscholastic/communitybookgrants.htm
Sponsor: Scholastic
557 Broadway, 5th Floor
New York, NY 10012

Scholastic Welch's Harvest Grants 4309
As a family-farmer owned company that is proud grow and nuture grapes, Welch's is here to help teach healthy eating habits. In partnership with Scholastic, Welch's is supporting school garden programs through Welch's Harvest Grants. Winning schools will receive a customized indoor or outdoor garden package filled with a variety of tools, seeds, educational materials, and more. Entries will be judged by experts from the National Gardening Association and Scholastic, and two schools in every state will be selected to receive a grant. The Sponsor will award a total of one hundred (100) school gardens. Five (5) $1,000 garden packages; twenty-five (25) $500 garden packages; and seventy (70) $250 garden packages will be awarded. Winning applicants will have the option of receiving an indoor or outdoor garden package.
Requirements: Eligible schools/organizations are public and private schools and accredited home school associations (K-8), public libraries, religious educational centers and Head Start centers having any of the grades K through 8 and a minimum of 15 students in the classroom located in the 50 United States and District of Columbia ('Eligible Institutions'). Entries must be received from 'School Officials' in order to be valid. 'School Officials' may be any of the following: U.S. residents who are at least 18 years of age and employees or volunteers on behalf of any Eligible Institution, including teachers, administrators, assistants and teacher's aides, as well as any parent or guardian of any student who is designated by the school to be a 'School Official' for purposes of this of Contest.
Restrictions: Each Eligible Institution may win only one prize. Employees, officers, directors, agents, representatives and independent contractors of the Sponsor, (including Scholastic Inc., Welch's, and the National Gardening Association) and each of their respective parent, subsidiary and affiliated companies, together with the immediate family members and members of the same households (whether related or not) of each of the foregoing are not eligible to participate. This Contest is subject to all federal, state and local laws and regulations. Void where prohibited or restricted by law, including but not limited to those jurisdictions with laws that would require registration and/or trust account or posting of a bond, or any other requirements.
Geographic Focus: All States
Date(s) Application is Due: Feb 6
Contact: Contest Administrator; (212) 343-6100 or (800) SCHOLASTIC; P&Cconnects@scholastic.com
Internet: http://www2.scholastic.com/browse/article.jsp?id=3752778
Sponsor: Scholastic
557 Broadway, 5th Floor
New York, NY 10012

Schramm Foundation Grants 4310
The foundation awards grants to Colorado nonprofit organizations in its areas of interest, including arts and culture, civic affairs, community development, education (elementary, secondary, and higher), health care, housing, humanities, medical research, science, social services delivery, technology, women's issues, and youth. Types of support include building construction/renovation, continuing support, equipment acquisition, general operating support, matching/challenge grants, program development, and scholarship funds. Applications are accepted from July 1 through August 31 (postmarked).
Requirements: Colorado 501(c)3 nonprofit organizations are eligible. Preference is given to requests from the Denver area. Applications must clearly express the reason(s) for the request, attach financial statements and copy of exemption letter.
Restrictions: Grants do not support advertising, advocacy organizations, individuals, international organizations, political organizations, religious organizations, school districts, special events, or veterans organizations.
Geographic Focus: Colorado
Date(s) Application is Due: Aug 31
Amount of Grant: 500 USD
Contact: Gary Kring, President; (303) 861-8291
Sponsor: Schramm Foundation
800 Grant Street, Suite 330
Denver, CO 80203-2944

Schumann Fund for New Jersey Grants 4311
The Schumann Fund for New Jersey is a tax exempt, private foundation, incorporated as a corporation not for pecuniary profit under the laws of the State of New Jersey. Schumann Fund program priorities fall into four categories: Early Childhood Development; Environmental Protection; Essex County; and Public Policy.
Requirements: There is no standard application form to be used in presenting a request to the Schumann Fund for New Jersey, but organizations may use the New York/New Jersey Common Application Form if they choose. The Foundation asks that a written proposal be submitted which includes a clear description of the purpose of the grant, the need or problem that will be addressed, the work to be undertaken, the staffing plan for project implementation, any collaborative efforts underway or contemplated, and the means of evaluating progress. The proposal must include the following items: a copy of the organization's latest audited financial statement; current organizational and project budgets identifying all sources of revenue and categories and amounts of expenditures; brief resumes of key organization and project staff; the project time frame and projected sources of future funding; a list of the organization's board of directors; Internal Revenue Service documents confirming the organization's status as a 501(C)3 organization. The Schumann Fund Board of Trustees meets quarterly.
Restrictions: In general, the Schumann Fund for New Jersey does not accept applications for capital campaigns, annual giving, endowment, direct support of individuals, or local programs in counties other than Essex. Projects in the arts, health care, and housing development normally fall outside the fund's priority areas.
Geographic Focus: New Jersey
Date(s) Application is Due: Jan 15; Apr 15; Jul 15; Oct 15
Amount of Grant: 15,000 - 100,000 USD
Contact: Barbara Reisman, Executive Director; (973) 509-9883; fax (973) 509-1149
Internet: http://foundationcenter.org/grantmaker/schumann/program_guidelines.html
Sponsor: Schumann Fund for New Jersey
21 Van Vleck Street
Montclair, NJ 07042

Schurz Communications Foundation Grants 4312
The Schurz Communications Foundation, Inc. is a company sponsored foundation which was incorporated in 1940. The Foundations donors are: Schurz Communications, Incorporated; South Bend Tribune Corporation; WSBT, Incorporated. The Foundation supports community service clubs and organizations involved with arts and culture, higher education, youth development and disabled people.
Requirements: Giving is limited to the South Bend Indiana area.
Geographic Focus: Indiana
Amount of Grant: 1,000 - 40,000 USD
Contact: David C. Ray, President; (574) 235-6241
Sponsor: Schurz Communications Foundation
225 West Colfax Avenue
South Bend, IN 46624

Scott B. and Annie P. Appleby Charitable Trust Grants 4313
The trust supports programs and projects of nonprofit organizations in the categories of higher education, cultural programs, and child welfare. Types of support include general operating support, continuing support, capital campaigns, building construction/renovation, and scholarship funds.
Requirements: The foundation awards grants to nonprofit organizations in the United States. There are no deadlines. Interested applicants are encouraged to submit a letter describing the intent and purpose of the organization with a specific proposal for allocation of funds.
Geographic Focus: All States
Amount of Grant: 2,000 - 50,000 USD
Contact: Benjamin N. Colby, Co-Trustee; (941) 329-2628; bncolby@uci.edu
Sponsor: Scott B. and Annie P. Appleby Charitable Trust
c/o The Northern Trust Company
Sarasota, FL 34236

Scott County Community Foundation Grants 4314
The purpose of the Scott County Community Foundation is to improve the quality of life of the residents of Scott County, Indiana. Grant funding will focus on the encouragement of programs that enhance cooperating and collaboration among institutions within the Scott County community. Funding focuses on effectiveness of special non-recurring projects which enrich health, education, cultural or recreational situations in Scott County. Specific areas of interest include community service; social service; education; the arts; environment; and entrepreneurship. Special consideration is given to agencies who partner with other organizations to complete a unified project. Funding will seek to offer leverage funds through the use of seed money, match and challenge grants. Applications are typically accepted in the spring and recipients announced during the summer. The application and additional guidelines are available at the Foundation website.
Restrictions: The Foundation does not typically fund: on going operational expenses; existing obligations; services primarily supported by tax dollars or responsibility of a public agency; individuals or travel expenses; multi-year grants or repeat funding; advocacy or political purposes; religious or sectarian purposes; and loans or endowments.
Geographic Focus: Indiana
Contact: Jaime Toppe; (812) 752-2057; fax (812) 752-9257; info@scottcountyfoundation.org
Internet: http://www.scottcountyfoundation.org/grants.htm
Sponsor: Scott County Community Foundation
60 North Main Street, P.O. Box 25
Scottsburg, IN 47170

Scotts Company Give Back to Grow Awards 4315
The awards honor individuals who take pride in giving back to their communities through gardening. One winner and two finalists will be selected in each of the following categories: classroom gardener of the year, good neighbor gardener of the year, urban greenup gardener of the year, and community beautification gardener of the year. Each winner and two finalists in each category receive cash prizes and public recognition for their work. Nomination forms are available online, or applicants may sign up to have nomination forms sent to them by mail.
Requirements: Individuals may nominate as many individuals in any or all categories as they wish.
Geographic Focus: All States
Date(s) Application is Due: Dec 1
Amount of Grant: 2,500 - 5,000 USD
Contact: Award Coordinator; (866) 565-3554 or (937) 644-0011
Internet: http://www.scotts.com/index.cfm/event/Article.Detail/documentId/B2B7085F5E339CA8055EA996030ED7B1
Sponsor: Scotts Company
515 Olive Street, Suite 1900
Saint Louis, MO 63101

Seabury Foundation Grants 4316
In general, The Seabury Foundation makes one-time, special project grants, rather than general operating support. Areas of interest of the Foundation include: Arts, Culture and Humanities; Human Capacity-building; Health; Education; Conservation and Environment; Children, Youth and Families. On occasion, the Foundation may invite grant renewal requests for up to two consecutive succeeding years. After that period, the Foundation will not consider a request for funding from that organization until a minimum of two full years have passed since the final grant was awarded. Please note that all grants awarded are within the City of Chicago with the exception of projects personally sponsored by family members.
Requirements: Chicago, IL, nonprofit organizations are eligible. Initial contact should be through a Letter of Inquiry, letters need only be 1-2 pages in length. Deadline dates for Letter of Inquiry are: September 15; January 15; June 15. If after reviewing the Letter of Inquiry, if your organization is invited to submit a full proposal, the deadline dates are: November 1; March 1; August 1.
Restrictions: The Seabury Foundation do not entertain grants in support of gala events, annual fundraising events, or annual fundraising drives.
Geographic Focus: Illinois
Date(s) Application is Due: Jan 15; Mar 1; Jun 15; Aug 1; Sep 15; Nov 1
Contact: Boyd McDowell III, Director; (312) 587-7146; fax (312) 587-7332; bmcdowell@seaburyfoundation.org
Internet: http://www.seaburyfoundation.org/apply.htm
Sponsor: Seabury Foundation
1111 North Wells Street, Suite 503
Chicago, IL 60610-7633

Seagate Technology Corporation Capacity to Care Grants 4317
Seagate's community engagement program addresses the varied interests of employees and the growing needs of its local communities. Known as Capacity to Care, the program aligns Seagate's giving with employees' localized interests, leveraging the impact of combined financial, product and volunteer contributions. Seagate focuses its giving on K-12 science and technology education. Innovative programs that enhance creativity, encourage hands-on learning, and reach all populations (specifically low-income and minority communities where fewer opportunities exist) are sought. Programs that support and assist people in extreme need of shelter, food, healthcare, and support services are given preference. Arts and culture, civic, environmental, and diversity-focused programs are valuable to building a well-balanced, healthy community. Volunteerism is an important component of Seagate's philanthropic program, and consideration will be given to proposals that offer employee involvement opportunities. The company offers support through donations of cash; excess furniture, computer and office equipment; in-kind donations of disc drives, tape drives and software; and by encouraging employee volunteerism. There are no application deadlines. Submit requests on organization letterhead.
Requirements: Nonprofit organizations must: maintain program expenses at or below 20 percent; demonstrate a clear objective and have tools in place to measure, track, and report the impact of a contribution; and operate within 50 miles of those communities where Seagate maintains a significant business presence. This includes: Silicon Valley, California; Longmont, Colorado; Bloomington and Normandale, Minnesota; Oklahoma City, Oklahoma; Shrewbury, Massachusetts; Londondary, Northern Ireland; Singapore; China; Indonesia; Malaysia; Mexico; and Thailand.
Restrictions: Grants do not support organizations that raise funds for redistribution to other organizations; organizations, or events sponsored by organizations, that discriminate by race, creed, gender, disability, sexual orientation, age, religion or nationality; political parties, religious, or labor organizations (exceptions occasionally made for programs sponsored for the direct benefit of the community); luncheons, banquets or other forms of indirect support; private foundations; endowment funds or capital fund drives; fundraising organizations; special interest groups; athletic teams or events; individuals; travel funds; or courtesy advertising-related projects.
Geographic Focus: California, Colorado, Massachusetts, Minnesota, Oklahoma, China, Ireland, Malaysia, Mexico, Singapore, Thailand
Contact: Community Involvement Director; (405) 324-4700 or (800) 732-4283; community.involvement@seagate.com
Internet: http://www.seagate.com/about/global-citizenship/?navtab=community-involvement
Sponsor: Seagate Tecdhnologies Corporation
10200 South De Anza Boulevard
Cupertino, CA 95014

Search Dog Foundation Rescue Dog Assistance 4318
The Search Dog Foundation is a non-profit, non-governmental organization based in Ojai, California. Its primary mission is to strengthen disaster preparedness in America by partnering rescued dogs with firefighters to find people buried alive in the wreckage of disasters. The teams are provided at no cost to fire departments and other emergency service agencies throughout the country. There are no specified application forms or deadlines, and interested qualified organizations should begin by contacting the Foundation directly.
Requirements: Fire departments (public and volunteer), as well as other emergency service agencies, are eligible to apply.
Geographic Focus: All States
Contact: Debra Tosch, Executive Director; (888) 459-4376, ext. 104 or (805) 646-1015; fax (805) 640-1848; ExecDirector@SearchDogFoundation.org
Internet: http://www.searchdogfoundation.org/about/
Sponsor: Search Dog Foundation
501 E. Ojai Avenue
Ojai, CA 93023

Seattle Foundation Annual Neighborhoods and Communities Grants 4319
The Foundation's Neighborhoods & Communities Annual Grants Program will prioritize organizations or programs that are aligned with one or both of the following funding strategies: support organizations or programs that increase civic engagement, develop local leadership, or encourage community organizing and advocacy; or support organizations or programs that build relationships and trust within and across communities (geographic and non-geographic). Some project examples include: local community spaces or events that provide programming and opportunities for people to meet and build relationships; programs or organizations that work to increase interfaith, intergenerational or cross-cultural understanding; and neighborhood or cultural groups that bring people together to share resources and build social networks. The Foundation's Annual Grants Program typically provides general operating support grants, but may also award program/project funding when

the overall organization's work does not align with the specific strategies. Capital campaign funding is also awarded in some cases, but is not a priority for the Foundation.
Requirements: To qualify for a grant from the Foundation's Grantmaking program, an organization must: be a 501(c)3 tax-exempt nonprofit organization; serve residents of King County, Washington; and provide programming in neighborhood and community funding needs that align with one or both of the Foundation's two strategies.
Restrictions: Capital campaign funding requests are typically considered a low priority. Organizations that have an annual operating budget less than $100,000 as reflected in the most recently filed IRS Form 990 are considered a lower priority for the Annual Grants Program, but may be eligible for Neighbor to Neighbor funding, which focuses on the White Center, South Seattle and Kent neighborhoods. Multi-year grants are not currently considered. Grants are not made to individuals or to religious organizations for religious purposes. Grants will not be awarded for: endowment; funding of conferences or seminars; operating expenses for public or private elementary and secondary schools, colleges and universities; fundraising events such as walk-a-thons, tournaments, auctions and general fundraising solicitations; or the production of books, films, or videos.
Geographic Focus: Washington
Date(s) Application is Due: Jan 15
Amount of Grant: 15,000 - 50,000 USD
Contact: Ceil Erickson, Grantmaking Director; (206) 515-2131 or (206) 515-2109; fax (206) 622-7673; grantmaking@seattlefoundation.org or c.erickson@seattlefoundation.org
Internet: http://www.seattlefoundation.org/nonprofits/grantmaking/communities/Pages/NeighborhoodsCommunities.aspx
Sponsor: Seattle Foundation
1200 Fifth Avenue, Suite 1300
Seattle, WA 98101-3151

Seattle Foundation Arts and Culture Grants 4320
The Seattle Foundation believes that the arts play a crucial role in the health of the community. The Foundation awards grants to nonprofits in all fields that improve the quality of life for King County residents, and is currently looking to fund organizations working to make significant progress towards the following three arts and culture strategies: broaden community engagement in the arts; support a continuum of arts education for students; and preserve and fully utilize arts space. The Foundation awards grants to provide general support to organizations. The next deadline for Arts and Culture is February 1.
Requirements: To qualify for a grant from the Foundation's Grantmaking program, an organization must: be a 501(c)3 tax-exempt nonprofit organization; serve residents of King County, Washington; and provide programming in arts and culture that aligns with one of the Foundation's three strategies.
Restrictions: Grants are not made to individuals or to religious organizations for religious purposes. Grants will not be awarded for: endowment; funding of conferences or seminars; operating expenses for public or private elementary and secondary schools, colleges and universities; fundraising events such as walk-a-thons, tournaments, auctions and general fundraising solicitations; or the production of books, films, or videos.
Geographic Focus: Washington
Date(s) Application is Due: Feb 1
Amount of Grant: 10,000 - 25,000 USD
Contact: Ceil Erickson, Grantmaking Director; (206) 515-2131 or (206) 515-2109; fax (206) 622-7673; grantmaking@seattlefoundation.org or c.erickson@seattlefoundation.org
Internet: http://www.seattlefoundation.org/nonprofits/grantmaking/artsandculture/Pages/GrantmakingforArtsCulture.aspx
Sponsor: Seattle Foundation
1200 Fifth Avenue, Suite 1300
Seattle, WA 98101-3151

Seattle Foundation Basic Needs Grants 4321
The Seattle Foundation is committed to providing the most vulnerable people in the region with tools to strengthen their economic resilience. Foundation work focuses on ensuring that no one falls between the cracks by supporting organizations that prevent homelessness, ensure the availability of affordable housing, and make sure that everyone has access to nutritious food. Its goals are to: support efforts to provide nutritious food and increase healthier options for vulnerable populations year-round; provide support services to get people back into housing; and support people who are struggling to stay housed. The next deadline for Basic Needs is September 1.
Requirements: To qualify for a grant from the Foundation's Grantmaking program, an organization must: be a 501(c)3 tax-exempt nonprofit organization; serve residents of King County, Washington; and provide programming in basic needs that aligns with one of the Foundation's three strategies.
Restrictions: Capital campaign funding requests are considered a low priority. Organizations that have less than a three-year operating history after receiving its 501(c)3 classification are considered a low priority. Multi-year grants are not considered.
Geographic Focus: Washington
Date(s) Application is Due: Sep 1
Amount of Grant: 15,000 - 50,000 USD
Contact: Ceil Erickson, Grantmaking Director; (206) 515-2131 or (206) 515-2109; fax (206) 622-7673; grantmaking@seattlefoundation.org or c.erickson@seattlefoundation.org
Internet: http://www.seattlefoundation.org/nonprofits/grantmaking/basicneeds/Pages/GrantsforBasicNeeds.aspx
Sponsor: Seattle Foundation
1200 Fifth Avenue, Suite 1300
Seattle, WA 98101-3151

Seattle Foundation Benjamin N. Phillips Memorial Fund Grants 4322
The Benjamin N. Phillips Memorial Fund was established by the estate of Joy Phillips to honor her late husband in 2006 as an area of interest fund of The Seattle Foundation. The goal of the Fund is to make grants to organizations improving the lives of Clallam County, Washington, residents. The Benjamin N. Phillips Memorial Fund is interested in supporting organizations that have: a mission statement that clearly defines the organization's purpose and reflects its understanding of the communities they serve; a clear articulation of why it believed what it is doing is important and that it will be effective and produce desired results; clearly defined priorities, goals and measurable outcomes; experienced and highly qualified staff and volunteer leadership; a skilled governing board whose knowledge includes management, fundraising and the community served; a funding plan appropriate to agency size and developmental state-guiding development efforts; sound financial management practices; support in the community and constituent involvement; and proven ability to mobilize financial and in-kind support, including volunteers. Grants are predominately made for one year, with no implied renewal funding. However, a two-year grant will be considered if a case is made for why funding is required for a longer period. An example of this exception is a planning or capacity-building process occurring over a two-year period of time. Approximately $250,000 will be distributed annually, with grants ranging in size from $1,000 to $25,000; the average grant size is $11,000.
Requirements: To qualify for a grant from the Foundation, an organization must: be a 501(c)3 tax-exempt nonprofit organization serving residents of Clallam County, Washington.
Geographic Focus: Washington
Date(s) Application is Due: Jul 1
Amount of Grant: 1,000 - 25,000 USD
Contact: Ceil Erickson, Grantmaking Director; (206) 515-2131 or (206) 515-2109; fax (206) 622-7673; c.erickson@seattlefoundation.org or phillips@seattlefoundation.org
Internet: http://www.seattlefoundation.org/nonprofits/phillips/Pages/benjaminphillipsmemorialfund.aspx
Sponsor: Seattle Foundation
1200 Fifth Avenue, Suite 1300
Seattle, WA 98101-3151

Seattle Foundation C. Keith Birkenfeld Memorial Trust Grants 4323
Keith Birkenfeld was an educator, world traveler and philanthropist who died September 7, 2005. He retired from the Bellevue School District, where he spent 20 years as a high school teacher of international relations and U.S. history, and later as an administrator. He spent his last 25 years living on Bainbridge Island and traveling the world, meeting interesting and famous people. He was raised in Bremerton and was well-known around Kitsap County for his generous spirit. The C. Keith Birkenfeld Memorial Trust was established in 2006 as an Area of Interest Fund of The Seattle Foundation. The goal of the Trust is to make one-time grants to organizations improving the quality of life for Puget Sound residents. Grants are awarded annually, with Kitsap County charitable organizations receiving first consideration. Previous grants made by the Trust range from $3,000 to $400,000, with an average grant size of $96,000.
Requirements: Eligible applicants are organizations: that have current status as a tax-exempt 501(c)3 public charity, as determined by the IRS, or have a fiscal sponsor with this status; and working in the arts, horticulture, wildlife, maritime and human service sectors, particularly agencies serving Kitsap County residents;
Restrictions: Organizations with religious affiliations will be considered for grants only if their activities address the needs of the wider community without regard to religious belief; proposed projects may not contain any content or activity intended to proselytize, even when participation in such activities is voluntary. In general, the entirety of a project's costs will not be awarded and only one grant will be made by the Trust over the course of the project.
Geographic Focus: Washington
Amount of Grant: 3,000 - 400,000 USD
Contact: Ceil Erickson, Grantmaking Director; (206) 515-2131 or (206) 515-2109; fax (206) 622-7673; grantmaking@seattlefoundation.org or c.erickson@seattlefoundation.org
Internet: http://www.seattlefoundation.org/nonprofits/birkenfeld/Pages/CKeithBirkenfeldMemTrust.aspx
Sponsor: Seattle Foundation
1200 Fifth Avenue, Suite 1300
Seattle, WA 98101-3151

Seattle Foundation Doyne M. Green Scholarships 4324
Doyne M. Green Scholarships are intended to support and honor female graduate students of medicine, law or social and public services. This scholarship is available to students who have completed at least one year of graduate work. The scholarship amount is $4,000, and two awards are given each year. The annual application deadline is March 1.
Geographic Focus: Washington
Date(s) Application is Due: Mar 1
Amount of Grant: 4,000 USD
Contact: Ceil Erickson, Grantmaking Director; (206) 515-2131 or (206) 515-2109; fax (206) 622-7673; c.erickson@seattlefoundation.org
Internet: https://fortress.wa.gov/hecb/thewashfound/ScholarshipDetails/The+Seattle+Foundation/2012-2013/Doyne+M+Green+Scholarship
Sponsor: Seattle Foundation
1200 Fifth Avenue, Suite 1300
Seattle, WA 98101-3151

Seattle Foundation Economy Grants 4325
The security of the King County, Washington, region depends on its economy. The Foundation believes that a strong economy is the essential engine that fuels all other elements of a healthy community. The Foundation awards grants to nonprofits in all fields that improve the quality of life for King County residents. The Foundation is currently

looking to provide funding to scale up innovative programs or project with proven success in the following three strategies: supporting education and training for low-income adults, particularly organizations that demonstrate a link to career pathways and living wage employment for participants; improving financial stability for individuals; and increasing access to resources for underserved businesses. Funding will be unrestricted and is intended to help build the capacity to expand proven innovative programs or projects. Proposals must demonstrate cultural competency and stakeholder engagement. Grant awards will likely range from $20,000 to $50,000. All proposals and back-up materials must be received at the Foundation by 5:00 p.m. on May 1.
Requirements: To qualify for a grant: the applicant must be a 501(c)3 tax-exempt nonprofit organization or be sponsored by a tax-exempt nonprofit organization; the applicant must serve residents of King County; the applicant's' mission and core services must align with one or more of our three strategies in the economy element; and the applicant's projects/programs must demonstrate a track record of success (new program or pilots are not eligible).
Geographic Focus: Washington
Date(s) Application is Due: May 1
Amount of Grant: 20,000 - 50,000 USD
Contact: Ceil Erickson, Grantmaking Director; (206) 515-2131 or (206) 515-2109; fax (206) 622-7673; grantmaking@seattlefoundation.org or c.erickson@seattlefoundation.org
Internet: http://www.seattlefoundation.org/nonprofits/grantmaking/economy/Pages/Economy.aspx
Sponsor: Seattle Foundation
1200 Fifth Avenue, Suite 1300
Seattle, WA 98101-3151

Seattle Foundation Education Grants 4326

The Seattle Foundation is committed to providing every child with a high-quality education. Because educational attainment is among the most powerful factors in determining whether children will reach their potential as healthy, productive adults, the Foundation feels that it is critical to provide the region's most vulnerable youth with a robust continuum of support at all stages of their education, from cradle to career. To realize this vision, grantmaking supports strong public schools at the systems level and student success at the individual level. Within the education element, the Foundation's goals are to: prepare young people for college and career success; promote parent and community involvement in helping students succeed in school; and advocate for high-quality public schools through authentic community engagement and effective professional development for teachers and school leaders.
Requirements: To qualify for a grant from The Seattle Foundation's Grantmaking Program, an organization must: be a 501(c)3 tax-exempt nonprofit organization or public agency (including educational institutions); serve residents of King County; and provide programming that aligns with one of the Foundation's three education strategies.
Restrictions: Operating expenses for public or private elementary and secondary schools, colleges and universities are not considered. The following are typically considered a low priority: capital campaign funding requests; organizations that have less than a three-year operating history after receiving their 501(c)3 classification; organizations that have an annual operating budget less than $100,000 as reflected in the most recently filed IRS Form 990; and youth-serving organizations that don't target and track outcomes related to education success. Grants are not made to individuals or to religious organizations for religious purposes. Grants will not be awarded for: endowment; funding of conferences or seminars; operating expenses for public or private elementary and secondary schools, colleges and universities; fundraising events such as walk-a-thons, tournaments, auctions and general fundraising solicitations; or the production of books, films, or videos.
Geographic Focus: Washington
Date(s) Application is Due: Nov 1
Amount of Grant: 15,000 - 50,000 USD
Contact: Ceil Erickson, Grantmaking Director; (206) 515-2131 or (206) 515-2109; fax (206) 622-7673; grantmaking@seattlefoundation.org or c.erickson@seattlefoundation.org
Internet: http://www.seattlefoundation.org/nonprofits/grantmaking/education/Pages/Education.aspx
Sponsor: Seattle Foundation
1200 Fifth Avenue, Suite 1300
Seattle, WA 98101-3151

Seattle Foundation Environment Grants 4327

The Seattle Foundation believes that the environment is central to our region's quality of life and our economy. To protect the environment and create a healthy region for the future, the Foundation supports organizations that work to improve the health of Puget Sound, promote sustainable growth, and that engage everyone in the community in environmental issues – including people from diverse backgrounds and cultures. The Foundation's primary goals are to: foster efforts to restore and preserve Puget Sound, as well as educate the public about protecting the health of the Sound; support efforts that address environmental disparities, train workers for a clean economy, and foster efforts to engage youth through environmental education; educate the public on residents' impact on the environment; and support sustainable growth by bringing together many parties and varied interests across elements and sectors to create a livable region for decades to come.
Requirements: To qualify for a grant from the Foundation's Grantmaking program, an organization must: be a 501(c)3 tax-exempt nonprofit organization; serve residents of King County, Washington; and provide programming in environmental needs that aligns with one of the Foundation's three strategies.
Restrictions: Capital campaign funding requests are considered a low priority. Organizations that have less than a three-year operating history after receiving its 501(c)3 classification are considered a low priority. Organizations that have an annual operating budget less than $100,000 as reflected in the most recently filed IRS Form 990 are considered a low priority.
Geographic Focus: Washington
Date(s) Application is Due: Aug 1
Amount of Grant: 15,000 - 50,000 USD
Contact: Ceil Erickson, Grantmaking Director; (206) 515-2131 or (206) 515-2109; fax (206); grantmaking@seattlefoundation.org or c.erickson@seattlefoundation.org
Internet: http://www.seattlefoundation.org/nonprofits/grantmaking/environment/Pages/Environment.aspx
Sponsor: Seattle Foundation
1200 Fifth Avenue, Suite 1300
Seattle, WA 98101-3151

Seattle Foundation Health and Wellness Grants 4328

The Seattle Foundation is committed to fostering health and wellness for people throughout the King County, Washington, region. The Foundation awards grants to nonprofits in all fields that improve the quality of life for county residents, and is focused on making sure that everyone in the county has access to quality care, including physical and dental health, cognitive, emotional, and mental health. Goals within the Health and Wellness element are to: improve access to: basic healthcare, especially services and treatment for those who are low-income, uninsured and/or underinsured; support efforts designed to reduce and/or eliminate disparities in health status due to poverty and/or race; foster efforts to strengthen the ability and capacity of providers to deliver quality services; and support efforts that protect the safety net for the vulnerable in our community through case management, treatment, and counseling services. The fields of interest and populations captured in this element include: healthcare, dental care, mental health, domestic violence, developmentally disabled, physically disabled, seniors, and birth to three programs, substance abuse programs and child welfare programs. The deadline for Health and Wellness is May 1.
Requirements: To qualify for a grant from the Seattle Foundation's Grantmaking Program, an organization must: be a 501(c)3 tax-exempt nonprofit organization; serve residents of King County; and provide programming in Health and Wellness that aligns with one of our three strategies.
Restrictions: The Foundation does not support disease-specific organizations and does not support health research projects. Multi-year grants are not considered.
Geographic Focus: Washington
Date(s) Application is Due: May 1
Amount of Grant: 15,000 - 50,000 USD
Contact: Ceil Erickson, Grantmaking Director; (206) 515-2131 or (206) 515-2109; fax (206) 622-7673; grantmaking@seattlefoundation.org or c.erickson@seattlefoundation.org
Internet: http://www.seattlefoundation.org/nonprofits/grantmaking/healthwellness/Pages/HealthWellness.aspx
Sponsor: Seattle Foundation
1200 Fifth Avenue, Suite 1300
Seattle, WA 98101-3151

Seattle Foundation Medical Funds Grants 4329

The Seattle Foundation administers the Medical Funds program to support medical research of potential benefit to the community and to address specific healthcare needs. In the area of medical research, grants are available in the fields of cancer, cardio-pulmonary disease, multiple sclerosis and diabetes. Special consideration will be given to research projects related to immunology, oncology, neurology, molecular biology and genetics. Grants will also be given to requests for specific equipment. Grants are also available to organizations that are administering projects addressing the healthcare needs of low-income children. In this area, grants will be given to requests for specific equipment and support for capital campaigns or facility renovation projects. A total amount of $200,000 is available for grants annually in this entire program. Typically no more than $50,000 is disbursed to any one organization.
Requirements: Preference will be given to organizations/institutions with the capacity to disseminate research findings and who receive regular support from other recognized funding sources (including the federal government).
Restrictions: These funds are not to be used for patient care. Research activities can include patient care, but the primary purpose of these grants is to support the purchase of equipment used in medical research.
Geographic Focus: Washington
Contact: Ceil Erickson, Grantmaking Director; (206) 515-2131 or (206) 515-2109; fax (206) 622-7673; grantmaking@seattlefoundation.org or c.erickson@seattlefoundation.org
Internet: http://www.seattlefoundation.org/nonprofits/medicalfunds/Pages/MedicalFunds.aspx
Sponsor: Seattle Foundation
1200 Fifth Avenue, Suite 1300
Seattle, WA 98101-3151

Seattle Foundation Neighbor to Neighbor Small Grants 4330

Neighbor to Neighbor, the Seattle Foundation's Small Grants program will prioritize organizations or programs that are aligned with one or both of the following funding strategies: organizations or programs that increase civic engagement, develop local leadership, or encourage community organizing and advocacy; or organizations or programs that build relationships and trust within and across communities (geographic and non-geographic). The quarterly deadlines for submitting applications are January 15, April 15, July 15 and October 15.
Requirements: To qualify for the Neighbor to Neighbor Small Grants program, an applicant must: be a 501(c)3 tax-exempt nonprofit organization, or be fiscally sponsored by one; have a small budget (generally under $100,000); and have a presence in South Seattle, White Center or Kent, and engage diverse, low-income community members to address disparities in these neighborhoods (South Seattle is defined as areas south of Interstate 90, west of Lake Washington, and north of Seattle's southern border; White Center is defined as the unincorporated area between the cities of Burien and Seattle).

Geographic Focus: Washington
Date(s) Application is Due: Jan 15; Apr 15; Jul 15; Oct 15
Amount of Grant: Up to 15,000 USD
Contact: Ceil Erickson, Grantmaking Director; (206) 515-2131 or (206) 515-2109; fax (206) 622-7673; grantmaking@seattlefoundation.org or c.erickson@seattlefoundation.org
Internet: http://www.seattlefoundation.org/nonprofits/neighbortoneighbor/Pages/Neighbor2NeighborFund.aspx
Sponsor: Seattle Foundation
1200 Fifth Avenue, Suite 1300
Seattle, WA 98101-3151

Seaver Institute Grants 4331
The Institute's focuses its giving in four primary areas: scientific and medical research, education, public affairs, and the cultural arts. Seed grants are awarded to nonprofit organizations for projects that offer the potential for a significant advancement in their fields. The institute seeks proposals that incorporate state-of-the-art scientific research, exceptional educational development, unique approaches to the creative arts, and the ramifications of shifting societal realities. There are no application deadlines.
Requirements: U.S. 501(c)3 nonprofits are eligible. Interested applicants should submit an inquiry letter of two or three pages and include the goals of the project, a preliminary budget, and the qualifications of the organization and principal investigator. If interested, the institute will invite a full proposal.
Restrictions: Grants are not made for construction, endowments, ongoing projects, operating budgets, deficits, or individual scholarships.
Geographic Focus: All States
Amount of Grant: 1,000 USD
Contact: Victoria Seaver Dean, President; (310) 979-0298; vsd@theseaverinstitute.org
Sponsor: Seaver Institute
12400 Wilshire Boulevard
Los Angeles, CA 90025

SeaWorld and Busch Gardens Conservation Fund Grants 4332
The fund's grants support wildlife conservation projects conducted by recognized charitable organizations and noted scientists throughout the world. Grants support projects in the areas of species research, terrestrial; species research, aquatic; habitat protection; animal rescue and rehabilitation; and conservation education. Grants are awarded on a semiannual basis. Both guidelines and application are available online.
Requirements: Charitable organizations and scientists worldwide are eligible.
Geographic Focus: All States
Date(s) Application is Due: Jun 1; Dec 1
Amount of Grant: 5,000 - 25,000 USD
Contact: Fred Jacobs, Senior Director; (314) 613-6077 or (877) 792-4332; fax (314) 613-6079; fred.jacobs@anheuser-busch.com or mailbox@swbgfund.org
Internet: http://www.seaworld.com/conservation-matters/conservation-fund/index.htm
Sponsor: SeaWorld and Busch Gardens Conservation Fund
423 Lynch Street, Building 260-2
Saint Louis, MO 63118

SEJ Annual Awards for Reporting on the Environment 4333
SEJ's awards honor the best environmental journalism in seven categories, bringing recognition to the most important stories on the planet. Journalism broadcast, published in print, or online submissions are eligible. Multimedia links may be included in the cover letter. SEJ's annual contest offers $500 in each of seven categories. Cover letters should include a description of the reporting's impact and must not exceed 1,000 words. The annual deadline is April 1. SEJ awards are presented at the Annual Conference, typically held in October of each year.
Requirements: You must already be a member of SEJ to enter at the member rate.
Restrictions: Members of SEJ's board of directors and awards committee and SEJ staff may not enter. Exception will be made for group entries including an SEJ board member, if that member did not play a significant role.
Geographic Focus: All States
Date(s) Application is Due: Apr 1
Amount of Grant: 500 USD
Contact: Christine Bruggers, Director of Awards; (502) 641-1844 or (215) 884-8174; fax (215) 884-8175; chrisbruggers@icloud.com or sej@sej.org
Internet: http://www.sej.org/initiatives/awards-fellowships/sej-annual-awards-reporting-environment
Sponsor: Society of Environmental Journalists
P.O. Box 2492
Jenkintown, PA 19046

Selby and Richard McRae Foundation Grants 4334
The Foundation offers grants primarily for social services, religion, and education. Its fields of interest include: Christian agencies and churches; educational programs; and human/social service programs. Applicants should begin by sending a Letter of Interest. There are no deadlines or official application forms, and giving is limited to organizations located in Mississippi.
Geographic Focus: Mississippi
Contact: Richard D. McRae Sr., President; (601) 968-4200; fax (601) 968-4354
Sponsor: Selby and Richard McRae Foundation
P.O. Box 20080
Jackson, MS 39289-0080

Self Foundation Grants 4335
The Self Family Foundation primarily serves the Greenwood, South Carolina and surrounding counties. The Self Family Foundation will consider requests from other regions of South Carolina, if they have statewide impact. The Foundation supports non-profit organizations in the following areas of interest: Education - enhancing children's school readiness and ability to achieve educational goals with success; working together with schools, families, youth-serving organizations and other community organizations to support the intellectual and social development of young people; Arts, Culture & History - increasing awareness of and access to activities that broaden the horizons and knowledge of all residents, within Greenwood, South Carolina; Civic & Community - improving neighborhood resources and community attitudes and services, emphasizing the utilization of existing facilities, skills and talents to create a stronger, more unified community through collaboration with organizations, businesses, public institutions and residents; Health and Human Services - promoting individual and community wellness, prevention and literacy.
Requirements: IRS 501(c)3 tax-exempt or 509(a) nonprofit organizations in South Carolina are eligible. Letters of Inquiry or requests for information may be emailed to: application@selffoundation.org or mailed to Foundation. Contact Foundation Program Officer by email or phone prior to submitting proposal. All applicants must have the financial potential to sustain the project on a continuing basis after any funding is approved.
Restrictions: No grants to individuals and no loans available.
Geographic Focus: South Carolina
Date(s) Application is Due: Feb 15; May 15; Aug 15; Nov 15
Contact: Grants Administrator; (864) 953-2441 or (864) 941-4036; fax (864) 941- 4091; info@selffoundation.org
Internet: http://www.selffoundation.org/grantmaking4.htm
Sponsor: Self Family Foundation
P.O. Box 1017
Greenwood, SC 29648-1017

Seneca Foods Foundation Grants 4336
The Seneca Foods Foundation was established in 1988 in New York and is sponsored by the Seneca Foods Corporation. The foundation supports fire departments and organizations involved with education, health, Down Syndrome, agriculture and food, recreation, and youth. Funding is primarily in areas of company processing facilities, with emphasis on New York.
Requirements: Nonprofit organizations in Seneca Foods operating locations are eligible. Contact foundation for application form.
Restrictions: Grants are not made to individuals.
Geographic Focus: All States
Contact: Kraig H. Kayser, President; (315) 926-8100; foundation@senecafoods.com
Sponsor: Seneca Foods Corporation
3736 South Main Street
Marion, NY 14505-9751

Sensient Technologies Foundation Grants 4337
The foundation supports organizations involved with arts and culture; children/youth, services; community/economic development; education; education, fund raising/fund distribution; education, research; family services; food services; general charitable giving; health care; higher education; homeless, human services; hospitals (general); human services; medical research, institute; mental health/crisis services; nutrition; performing arts; residential/custodial care, hospices; United Ways and Federated Giving Programs; Urban/community development; and voluntarism promotion. The foundation's types of support include: annual campaigns; capital campaigns; emergency funds; endowments; general operating support; matching/challenge support; program development; research; and scholarship funds.
Requirements: An application form is not required. Submit a letter of inquiry as an initial approach. The advisory board meets in January and June/July or as needed, with deadline for proposal review one month prior to board meetings.
Restrictions: The foundation gives primarily to its areas of interest in Indianapolis, Indiana; St. Louis, Missouri; and Milwaukee, Wisconsin. It does not support sectarian religious, fraternal, or partisan political organizations. It does not give grants to individuals.
Geographic Focus: Indiana, Missouri, Wisconsin
Contact: Douglas L. Arnold, (414) 271-6755; fax (414) 347-4783
Sponsor: Sensient Technologies Foundation
777 E Wisconsin Avenue
Milwaukee, WI 53202-5304

Seybert Institution for Poor Boys and Girls Grants 4338
The charitable foundation supports nonprofit organizations providing services for disadvantaged youth in Philadelphia. The foundation is interested in projects for abused, deprived children and youth counseling services. The institute also supports special projects that encourage disadvantaged children in Philadelphia public elementary schools to develop leadership and academic skills. Generally grants range up to $7,500 and are made on a one-year basis. Recipients must provide a detailed narrative and financial report on how the funds were spent. The deadline for requests for after school and summer programs is March 17. The deadlines for other grant requests are January 2 and October 1.
Requirements: IRS 501(c)3 tax-exempt nonprofit organizations operating to benefit poor boys and girls in Philadelphia, PA, are eligible.
Geographic Focus: Pennsylvania
Date(s) Application is Due: Jan 2; Mar 17; Oct 1
Contact: Judith L. Bardes, Manager; (610) 828-8145; fax (610) 834-8175; judy1@aol.com
Internet: http://www.grants-info.org/seybert/guidelines.htm
Sponsor: Adam and Maria Sarah Seybert Institution for Poor Boys and Girls
P.O. Box 540
Plymouth Meeting, PA 19462-0540

Shared Earth Foundation Grants 4339
The foundation is committed to the tenet that all creatures have an enduring claim to sustainable space on this planet. The foundation will fund organizations that promote protection and restoration of habitat for the broadest possible biodiversity, that foster respect for other species and individual creatures, that work to limit detrimental human impact on the planet, and that further the inherent right of all creatures to share the Earth. The foundation looks to fund primarily, though not exclusively, small organizations. It will provide administrative as well as project funds, with possibility for renewal or continuation, in the United States and abroad, to groups working in the natural and political worlds. The Foundation will fund a few applications for projects only, in the $5,000 to $10,000 range. The Foundation will acknowledge the request within one month, and respond within two months with a request for a full proposal, or declination. The Foundation will make grant decisions by December 15 of each year.
Restrictions: The Foundation will not fund individuals, scholarships, fellowships, or financial aid to students.
Geographic Focus: All States
Date(s) Application is Due: Dec 1
Amount of Grant: 5,000 - 10,000 USD
Contact: Caroline D. Gabel; (410) 778-6868; fax (410) 778-9050; sharedearth@aol.com
Internet: http://www.sharedearth.org
Sponsor: Shared Earth Foundation
113 Hoffman Lane
Chestertown, MD 21620

Share Our Strength Grants 4340
Share Our Strength awards grants to nonprofit organizations, schools, and other eligible organizations who are involved in the following activities: increasing access to after school snack and meal programs, or child care programs, supported through the Child and Adult Care Food Program (CACFP); increasing access to summer meal programs supported through the Summer Food Service Program or the National School Lunch "Seamless Summer" Program; educating and enrolling more eligible families in SNAP/WIC; increasing the availability of Universal School Breakfast through alternative models such as in-classroom breakfast and grab-n-go; and advocacy around any of the above anti-hunger issues. Proposals are typically accepted in the spring and early summer. There are no specific limitations on what type of expenses are allowed.
Requirements: Organizations that have received grants within the past two years will be automatically notified of available grant opportunities. All others should submit a letter of inquiry (no more than 2 pages; one page preferred), describing how the proposed project will help increase access to the programs outlined in the Share Our Strength grants' programs initiatives. Letters of inquiry should be emailed to grants@strength.org, with the subject line "NKH proposal - name of organization - program" (i.e. summer, afterschool, SNAP, etc.). Share Our Strength will notify the organization within two weeks if they will be inviting a full proposal. Applicants should refer to the website for guidelines and frequently asked questions before submitting a proposal.
Geographic Focus: All States
Amount of Grant: 5,000 - 10,000 USD
Contact: Chuck Scofield, Chief Development Officer; (800) 761-4227 or (202) 393-2925; fax (202) 347-5868; info@strength.org
Internet: http://www.strength.org/grants/
Sponsor: Share Our Strength
1730 M Street NW, Suite 700
Washington, DC 20036

Shastri Indo-Canadian Institute Action Research Project Grants 4341
The Shastri Indo-Canadian Institute (Shastri) is a unique bi-national non-profit organization that builds academic and cultural relationships between India and Canada by providing programs and services that will enable, facilitate and sustain bi-national dialogue, understanding and interaction. More specifically, Shastri: enables and facilitates linkages as a bi-national network of leading academic institutions and knowledge partners; invests in students and researchers for knowledge and skills enhancement; and collects and disseminates practical information, data, and research findings with a renewed emphasis on international development and information on higher education in India and Canada. Based upon this mandate Shastri, with funding assistance from Canadian International Development Agency (CIDA), announces the Call for Applications for the Action Research Project Grants (ARPG) with a specific objective of supporting applied and participatory research to find local solutions that will have lasting impacts on communities in India by improving the human condition. The overall goal of the ARP is to generate knowledge about developmental needs in India that are to lead to specific interventions. With the above objectives, Shastri wishes to develop an approach to research on poverty alleviation, which views poverty in its totality. Shastri believes that there is a need for society to recognize that the needs of economically disadvantaged people go beyond adequate income and other basic requirements of life such as food, health, education and shelter, and encompass other areas such as justice, equality, women empowerment, good governance, human rights, healthy environment, security, culture, opportunity for creative and aesthetic pursuits, etc. Applied research should help to bring focus on this reality. Acceptable expenses include; travel and accommodation for participants; meals; communications costs (audio, video conferencing, promotional materials); organizational support; translation; copying and printing; dissemination of research; research assistant allowance; and reasonable out of pocket expenses. Travel expenses may either be for Canadians going to India or for Indians going to Canada or domestic travel for research purposes.
Requirements: The lead applicant must be an individual researcher and/or faculty member or research team affiliated with a Canadian or Indian member institution of the Shastri Indo-Canadian Institute. The applicant must have a development partner (NGO) in India that has a long and good reputation of working in the development field directly.
Restrictions: The Shastri Institute is not allowed by the funding agency to pay institutional overhead.
Geographic Focus: Canada, India
Date(s) Application is Due: Apr 10
Amount of Grant: Up to 10,000 CAD
Contact: Mahmuda Aldeen; (403) 220-7467; fax (403) 289-0100; sici@ucalgary.ca
Internet: http://www.sici.org/programmes/details/action-research-project-grants-arpg-2011-12/
Sponsor: Shastri Indo-Canadian Institute
1402 Education Tower, 2500 University Drive NW
Calgary, AB T2N 1N4 Canada

Shaw's Supermarkets Donations 4342
Shaw's focuses its support on not-for-profit 501(c)3 organizations that help create healthy, thriving communities. Shaw's provides financial support, volunteer support and in-kind product donations to organizations that benefit communities in areas where they operate, and meet the following focus areas: (1) Hunger Relief - Ending hunger in the stores' local communities via both product and financial support to hunger-relief organizations. (2) Nutrition Education - support for organizations that educate and promote healthy lifestyles and nutrition by emphasizing disease management and prevention through diet. (3) Environmental Stewardship - environmental stewardship and sustainable operations and that will continually work to use energy more efficiently and reduce waste. Shaw's supports local efforts towards sustainability. (4) Community Connections - select local events that build strong communities by broadly engaging community pride and spirit.
Requirements: 501(c)3 tax-exempt organizations in Connecticut, Maine, Massachusetts, New Hampshire, Rhode Island, and Vermont are eligible. If the grant request involves an event, the request should be sent at least 8 weeks prior to event date. Download the application form from the website.
Restrictions: Shaw's will generally not support: individuals; travel or research expenses; fees for participation in competitive programs; veteran, fraternal or labor organizations; lobbying, political or religious programs; or, organizations that are not tax-exempt.
Geographic Focus: Connecticut, Maine, Massachusetts, New Hampshire, Rhode Island, Vermont
Contact: Donation Committee; shaws.donations@shaws.com
Internet: http://www.shaws.com/pages/community/donationRequests.php
Sponsor: Shaw's Supermarkets
P.O. Box 600
East Bridgewater, MA 02333

Shell Oil Company Foundation Grants 4343
Shell makes monetary grants to nonprofit organizations within the U.S. Priority consideration will be given to organizations in or near communities where Shell Oil Company or its affiliates in the United States have a major presence. Shell Oil Company and the Shell Oil Company Foundation will consider charitable contributions to eligible nonprofit organizations for select programs that fall within our focused areas of contributions: health and welfare; community outreach; workforce development / education and; environment. There are no deadline dates for submitting a proposal, proposals are reviewed on a regular basis.
Requirements: Nonprofit organizations in company operating locations are eligible.
Restrictions: Shell Oil Company and the Shell Oil Company Foundation will not consider contributions for the following purposes: individuals; private Foundations; non-profit organizations without a current 501(c)3 exempt status; conferences or symposia; endowment funds; fraternal and labor organizations; capital campaigns; conferences, workshops, or seminars not directly related to Shell business interests; religious organizations that do not serve the general public on a non-denominational basis; organizations located in or benefiting nations other than U.S. and its territories; organizational operating expenses.
Geographic Focus: All States
Contact: A.H. Myres; (713) 241-3616; fax (713) 241-3329; socfoundation@shellus.com
Internet: http://www.shell.us/home/content/usa/responsible_energy/shell_in_the_society/giving_back/grant/grant_request_060208.html
Sponsor: Shell Oil Company Foundation
One Shell Plaza, 910 Louisiana, Suite 4478A
Houston, TX 77002

Sheltering Arms Fund Grants 4344
The purpose of the fund is to complement and extend Sheltering Arms Hospital's mission by funding health related initiatives that serve uninsured and underinsured adults who are experiencing physical or cognitive disabilities or who are at risk for developing functional limitations. Emphasis will be placed on responding to the needs of individuals with a Rehab Impairment Category diagnosis as defined by the Centers for Medicaid and Medicare (CMS)
Requirements: Proposals will be accepted from charitable organizations, which serve the residents of the metropolitan Richmond and Central Virginia. Proposed programs should align with the goals of the fund: Improve access to health and related support services such as Primary Care, Specialty clinics (Diabetes, Podiatry, Dental, Women's Health, etc.), and Nutritional Support; Increase functional independence (Home care, Day care, Transportation, Use of assistive devices and technology, Facility renovations to improve handicapped access); Promote disability prevention for at risk populations through education and/or public health initiatives.
Geographic Focus: Virginia
Date(s) Application is Due: May 5
Amount of Grant: Up to 100,000 USD
Contact: Susan Hallett; (804) 330-7400; fax (804) 330-5992; shallett@tcfrichmond.org
Internet: http://www.tcfrichmond.org/page2954.cfm#SAF

Sponsor: Community Foundation Serving Richmond and Central Virginia
7501 Boulders View Drive, Suite 110
Richmond, VA 23225

Shirley W. & William L. Griffin Charitable Foundation Grants 4345
The Foundation, established in 2004, is intended to assist Catholic agencies and churches, as well as human services programs. Grants are given on a national basis, and typically range from $500 up to $2,500. Although there are no formal guidelines or application forms, applicants should forward a letter of request specifying the amount needed and purpose of the organization.
Geographic Focus: New York
Amount of Grant: 500 - 2,500 USD
Contact: Charles J. Schoff, Treasurer; (315) 336-4400; fax (315) 336-0005
Sponsor: Shirley W. and William L. Griffin Charitable Foundation
512 W Court Street
Rome, NY 13440-4010

Shopko Foundation Community Charitable Grants 4346
The Shopko Foundation is proud of Shopko's roots as a retail health and optical care provider. To maximize its impact, the Foundation has a narrow focus on areas of giving that support the health of Shopko customers, teammates and communities. The Foundation also recognizes that education is fundamental to an individual's health and functionality in society. To achieve its vision, the Shopko Foundation believes in supporting community projects that may be accessed by, and its contribution made well known to, customers and teammates of Shopko. Funds will support established non-profit organizations with a proven record of success in maintaining solid, critical programs or innovative new organizations and programs supported by established non-profits or successful leadership. Grant funding will be $1,000 or less.
Requirements: Nonprofit 501(c)3 organizations located within 25 miles of a Shopko store are eligible to apply. Grants to accredited publicly/privately funded schools, colleges, and universities will be considered. Grant requests must contain all required information and be submitted at least 45 days prior to the date of the scheduled event to ensure sufficient time for review. Requests should be related to a specific program or project, rather than related to general fundraising.
Restrictions: In general, the Shopko Foundation does not support the following: Programs or events that do not support the Foundation's mission; Programs or events outside of Shopko communities; Sponsorship of cultural exhibits; Events which provide assistance to a specific individual; Advertising in event programs or yearbooks; Religious organizations (however gifts designated for, and restricted to, human services or humanitarian purposes may be eligible); Political or fraternal organizations; Events with multiple or competing business sponsors; Organizations that discriminate on the basis of sex, creed, national origin or religion; Charitable requests in support of raffle, auctions, benefits or similar fundraising events. Applications via postal mail will not be accepted.
Geographic Focus: California, Idaho, Illinois, Indiana, Iowa, Kansas, Kentucky, Michigan, Minnesota, Missouri, Montana, Nebraska, North Dakota, Ohio, Oregon, South Dakota, Utah, Washington, Wisconsin, Wyoming
Amount of Grant: Up to 1,000 USD
Contact: Michelle Hansen, Program Director; (920) 429-4054; fax (920) 496-4225; shopkofoundation@shopko.com or michelle.hansen@shopko.com
Internet: http://www.shopko.com/thumbnail/Company/Community-Giving/Shopko-Foundation/pc/2176/c/2181/2185.uts?&pageSize=
Sponsor: Shopko Foundation
700 Pilgrim Way
Green Bay, WI 54304

Shopko Foundation Green Bay Area Community Grants 4347
The Shopko Foundation is proud of Shopko's roots as a retail health and optical care provider. To maximize its impact, the Foundation has a narrow focus on areas of giving that support the health of Shopko customers, teammates and communities. The Foundation also recognizes that education is fundamental to an individual's health and functionality in society. The Foundation strives to enhance the quality of life in the Green Bay area through charitable causes, events and activities that support healthy lifestyles for residents. Its goal is to make Shopko communities a better place to live by supporting programs and services that improve the health and education of its residents. Grants awarded through this program support larger or long-term community wide projects.
Requirements: Nonprofit 501(c)3 organizations located in the Green Bay area are eligible to apply. Grants to accredited publicly/privately funded schools, colleges, and universities will be considered. Requests should be related to a specific program or project, rather than related to general fundraising.
Restrictions: In general, the Shopko Foundation does not support the following: Programs or events that do not support the Foundation's mission; Programs or events outside of Shopko communities; Sponsorship of cultural exhibits; Events which provide assistance to a specific individual; Advertising in event programs or yearbooks; Religious organizations (however gifts designated for, and restricted to, human services or humanitarian purposes may be eligible); Political or fraternal organizations; Events with multiple or competing business sponsors; Organizations that discriminate on the basis of sex, creed, national origin or religion; Charitable requests in support of raffle, auctions, benefits or similar fundraising events. Applications via postal mail will not be accepted.
Geographic Focus: Wisconsin
Contact: Michelle Hansen, Program Director; (920) 429-4054; fax (920) 496-4225; shopkofoundation@shopko.com or michelle.hansen@shopko.com
Internet: http://www.shopko.com/thumbnail/Company/Community-Giving/Shopko-Foundation/pc/2176/c/2181/2185.uts?&pageSize=
Sponsor: Shopko Foundation
700 Pilgrim Way
Green Bay, WI 54304

Sidgmore Family Foundation Grants 4348
The Sidgmore Family Foundation honors the legacy of John W. Sidgmore by taking a proactive approach to helping others succeed. The Foundation desires to use its resources to find creative and innovative solutions so that people may achieve their full potential and become responsible, healthy and productive members of society. In recognition that an impoverished environment limits the possibilities for people to develop and thrive, the Sidgmore Family Foundation is particularly interested in funding organizations that: improve the quality of education and teacher training; further the advancement of knowledge in the field of medicine with a special emphasis on hearing and cardiology; utilize entrepreneurial skills to explore and develop creative, scalable, and sustainable solutions to critical social problems; and, provide support and services to those in need in the Washington DC area. Grants are awarded to organizations that have a clear, replicable plan for success, measured sustainable results, and high approval ratings from charity evaluator organizations, such as Charity Navigator. The Foundation also awards multi-year grants that can sustain a program or project.
Requirements: Nonprofit 501(c)3 organizations are eligible. Preference is given to organizations that serve residents in the Washington, D.C. metropolitan area, Maryland, and Virginia. Applicants must begin the process with an initial Letter of Inquiry (LOI). LOIs will receive a response if the Foundation wishes to receive a proposal from your organization.
Restrictions: The Sidgmore Family Foundation does not make grants to individuals, national health organizations, government agencies, or political and public policy advocacy groups.
Geographic Focus: All States
Contact: M. Gelbwaks, Director; (516) 541-2713; SidgmoreFound@aol.com
Internet: http://www.sidgmorefoundation.com/#application_process
Sponsor: Sidgmore Family Foundation
71 Leewater Avenue
Massapequa, NY 11758

Sidney Stern Memorial Trust Grants 4349
The Sidney Stern Memorial Trust provides grants and funding to various non-profit organizations. The board of the trust meets regularly to review grant applications and make funding decisions. Areas of interest for grants include civil rights, children, community development, disabled causes, education, health, science, social services and Native Americans. Recipients of grants include local public media outlets, educational programs, archaeological centers, international aid organizations and performing arts programs for children.
Requirements: The trust prefers all correspondence to be sent by mail. No personal or email requests will be entertained. All organizations applying for funding must be recognized by the IRS as 501(c)3 certified, verifiable via GuideStar Charity Check. Folders containing lengthy brochures, pictorial pamphlets or CDs should not be included. Although the foundation supports projects and organizations across the country, most grants are offered to proposals from California.
Restrictions: The trust does not award grants to individuals, political candidates or campaigns, lobbying projects or programs to directly influence legislation, or for conferences or redistribution.
Geographic Focus: California
Amount of Grant: 750 USD
Contact: Betty Hoffenberg, Chairperson; (800) 352-3705
Internet: http://sidneysternmemorialtrust.org/uploads/Application_and_Guidelines_for_Grant_FINAL.pdf
Sponsor: Sidney Stern Memorial Trust
P.O. Box 457
Pacific Palisades, CA 90272

Sid W. Richardson Foundation Grants 4350
Grants are provided to tax-exempt organizations in Texas in the areas of education (museums, learning centers, day schools, K-12 schools, higher education institutions, and business and economic education), health (medical schools, organ donor registries, hospitals, disease prevention, health science centers, and nursing associations), arts (arts councils, visual and performing arts festivals, museums, ballet, symphony orchestra, and arts education programs), and human services (boys' and girls' clubs, united funds, the elderly, crime prevention, the disabled, housing opportunities, food programs, and drug and alcohol abuse prevention); specific goals within these larger areas change periodically. Types of support include operating budgets, seed grants, building construction funds, equipment acquisition, endowment funds, research, publications, conferences and seminars, matching funds, continuing support, and projects/programs. Award amounts vary depending on proposed projects.
Requirements: Proposals must cover programs and projects within Texas.
Restrictions: Grants are not made to individuals.
Geographic Focus: Texas
Date(s) Application is Due: Jan 15
Amount of Grant: 10,000 - 100,000 USD
Contact: Valleau Wilkie Jr., Executive Director; (817) 336-0494; fax (817) 332-2176
Internet: http://www.sidrichardson.org/GrantInfo.html
Sponsor: Sid W. Richardson Foundation
309 Main Street
Fort Worth, TX 76102

Siebert Lutheran Foundation Grants 4351

Specific areas of interest vary from time to time. At present, the Foundation is supportive of the following: Clergy and lay education and training, community development and outreach, health ministry, evangelism and youth. Grants are occasionally made to provide seed money or start-up costs for a program or project. In such instances, the participation of other donors is desired. Grants are made only to Lutheran organizations exempt under Section 501(c)3 of the Internal Revenue Code and are generally awarded for a one-year period.
Requirements: The Foundation utilizes an on-line grant application. Potential grant applicants, who represent Wisconsin congregations or Wisconsin recognized service organizations in the Lutheran church, may complete the Foundation's formal, online, letter of inquiry. A telephone call is not necessary prior to completing the letter of inquiry for Lutheran organizations in Wisconsin. If your organization does not meet the above criteria and you would like to discuss possible funding, contact the Foundation office (262-754-9160).
Restrictions: The Foundation does not approve grants for the following: endowment funds, fellowships and scholarships, trusts, and other grant-making foundations. Grants are generally not made to churches for capital or operating expenses. No grants are made outside the United States.
Geographic Focus: Wisconsin
Date(s) Application is Due: Mar 1; Jun 1; Sep 1; Dec 1
Contact: Deborah Engel, Administrative Assistant; (262) 754-9160; fax (262) 754-9162; contactus@Siebertfoundation.org
Internet: http://www.siebertfoundation.org/grants.htm
Sponsor: Siebert Lutheran Foundation
300 North Corporate Drive, Suite 200
Brookfield, WI 53045

Sierra Fund Grants 4352

The Sierra Fund is a non-profit community foundation providing philanthropic stewardship and charitable support services to support environmental conservation in the Sierra Nevada region. We partner with private donors and public agencies to increase and organize investment in the land, air, water and human resources of the Sierra Nevada.
Requirements: Non-profitss from the Sierra Nevada region are eligible to apply.
Geographic Focus: Nevada
Amount of Grant: 1,000 - 100,000 USD
Contact: Elizabeth Martin, Chief Executive Officer; (530) 265-8454, ext. 11; izzy.martin@sierrafund.org
Internet: http://www.sierrafund.org/philanthropy/grantmaking
Sponsor: Sierra Fund
432 Broad Street
Nevada City, CA 95959

Sierra Health Foundation Responsive Grants 4353

The Sierra Health Foundation Responsive Grants are designed to promote health and well-being in Northern California communities. Fields of interest include: AIDS; alcoholism; biomedicine; child development, education; child development, services; children/youth, services; community/economic development; crime/violence/ prevention, youth; family services; health care; health organizations, association; human services; leadership development; medical care, rehabilitation; mental health/crisis services; nutrition; substance abuse, services; and youth development. The Foundation funds employee matching gifts, in-kind gifts, program development, program evaluation; and technical assistance. Examples of Foundation funding include food banks, homeless shelters, senior citizen agencies, youth and family centers, job readiness programs, and faith based organizations.
Requirements: Organizations may contact the Foundation for current application procedures and deadlines.
Restrictions: The Foundation funds the following northern California counties: Alpine, Amador, Butte, Calaveras, Colusa, El Dorado, Glenn, Lassen, Modoc, Mono, Nevada, Placer, Plumas, Sacramento, San Joaquin, Shasta, Sierra, Siskiyou, Solano (eastern), Stanislaus, Sutter, Tehama, Trinity, Tuolumne, Yolo and Yuba. The Foundation does not fund individuals or endowments.
Geographic Focus: California
Amount of Grant: Up to 25,000 USD
Contact: Kathy Mathews, Grants Administrator; (916) 922-4755; fax (916) 922-4024; kmathews@sierrahealth.org or grants@sierrahealth.org
Internet: http://www.sierrahealth.org/doc.aspx?129
Sponsor: Sierra Health Foundation
1321 Garden Highway
Sacramento, CA 95833-9754

Silicon Valley Community Foundation Donor Circle for the Arts Grants 4354

Silicon Valley Community Foundation's Donor Circle for the Arts Fund is inviting grant requests from emerging artists and arts groups in San Mateo and Santa Clara counties. The goal is to encourage the creation and appreciation of professional quality artistic works that reflect the diverse cultural communities of the Silicon Valley region. Grants are available for a wide range of artistic disciplines and will range from $2,500 to $5,000.
Requirements: San Mateo and/or Santa Clara County-serving organizations are eligible.
Geographic Focus: California
Date(s) Application is Due: Nov 13
Amount of Grant: 2,500 - 5,000 USD
Contact: Lisa Snider, (650) 450-5534; donorcircleforthearts@siliconvalleycf.org
Internet: http://www.siliconvalleycf.org/donor-circle-for-the-arts.html
Sponsor: Silicon Valley Community Foundation
2440 West El Camino Real, Suite 300
Mountain View, CA 94040

Silicon Valley Community Foundation Economic Security Grants 4355

Silicon Valley Community Foundation announces an RFP targeting programs that include: financial education and asset-building components; foreclosure prevention counseling. Asset building requires financial education, the availability of affordable financial products and services, protective public policies and public awareness of the availability and value of these products and services. All of these elements are key, particularly for low-income families who are cash-strapped and have little cushion for emergencies such as a health crisis or job loss. Together, assetbuilding assistance, financial education, and foreclosure prevention counseling enable families to have more options in life and to pass on opportunities to future generations. Up to 15 grants will be awarded under this RFP. Each successful applicant will receive grants in the range of $50,000-$250,000 for a minimum of one year; multi-year grants may be awarded in certain cases at the discretion of the community foundation.
Requirements: San Mateo and/or Santa Clara County-serving organizations are eligible. Organizations headquartered outside the two-county region must demonstrate significant service to the area. Organizations with a 501(c)3 designation or those that have a fiscal sponsor with a 501(c)3 designation, public institutions or other entities that have a designated charitable purpose are also eligible.
Geographic Focus: California
Date(s) Application is Due: Jun 30
Amount of Grant: 50,000 - 250,000 USD
Contact: Ellen Clear; (650) 450-5400; fax (650) 450-5401; ehclear@siliconvalleycf.org
Internet: http://www.siliconvalleycf.org/grantmaking-strategies/index.html#COF
Sponsor: Silicon Valley Community Foundation
2440 West El Camino Real, Suite 300
Mountain View, CA 94040

Silicon Valley Community Foundation Education Grants 4356

Silicon Valley Community Foundation is pleased to announce an RFP that targets closing the middle school achievement gap in mathematics through in-school and out-of-school strategies. By using an RFP approach, the community foundation aims to solicit the best thinking of public school districts and other public sector agencies, nonprofit service providers, professional and research institutions and other entities serving San Mateo and Santa Clara counties. Most of the proposals funded will focus on program implementation, while the Foundation also welcomes requests for planning grants as stand-alone endeavors where a compelling case can be made for them. The Foundation expects to award approximately 15 grants in the range of $50,000-$250,000 for a minimum of one year; multi-year grants may be awarded in certain cases at the discretion of the community foundation. Out-of-school proposals are due on January 23 and in-school proposals are due on February 20.
Requirements: San Mateo and/or Santa Clara County-serving organizations are eligible. Organizations headquartered outside the two-county region must demonstrate significant service to the area. Organizations with a 501(c)3 designation (such as teacher education/curriculum support organizations) or those that have a fiscal sponsor with a 501(c)3 designation, public institutions (such as schools or school districts) or other entities that have a designated charitable purpose are also eligible.
Geographic Focus: California
Date(s) Application is Due: Jan 23; Feb 20
Amount of Grant: 50,000 - 250,000 USD
Contact: Ellen Clear; (650) 450-5400; fax (650) 450-5401; ehclear@siliconvalleycf.org
Internet: http://www.siliconvalleycf.org/grantmaking-strategies/index.html#E-CMSAG
Sponsor: Silicon Valley Community Foundation
2440 West El Camino Real, Suite 300
Mountain View, CA 94040

Silicon Valley Community Foundation Elizabeth Anabo BRICC Awards 4357

Silicon Valley Community Foundation recognizes creative, resourceful and inspirational neighborhood groups in Santa Clara County with the Elizabeth Anabo BRICC Awards. Since 2001, The Elizabeth Anabo BRICC Awards commemorates the late Elizabeth Anabo, former senior program officer at Community Foundation Silicon Valley, one of our parent foundations. Elizabeth was extremely dedicated to and passionate about neighborhood groups and made tremendous contributions to them over the four years she worked at the community foundation. BRICC awards of $1,000 are given to one or two neighborhood groups in Santa Clara County that have made outstanding contributions to their community. The two categories for the award are seasoned groups and new emerging groups. Previous BRICC Award recipients may apply two years after receiving the award. Neighborhood groups may nominate themselves. A review panel composed of community representatives, including past award recipients, selects the BRICC award recipients.
Requirements: San Mateo and/or Santa Clara County-serving organizations are eligible.
Geographic Focus: California
Amount of Grant: 1,000 USD
Contact: Ellen Clear; (650) 450-5400; fax (650) 450-5401; ehclear@siliconvalleycf.org
Internet: http://www.siliconvalleycf.org/grants_bricc_awards.html
Sponsor: Silicon Valley Community Foundation
2440 West El Camino Real, Suite 300
Mountain View, CA 94040

Silicon Valley Community Foundation Immigrant Integration Grants 4358

In Silicon Valley, one-third of the residents are immigrants, nearly half of the workforce is foreign born, and close to two-thirds of those under the age of 18 are the children of immigrants. Given this demographic reality, a new social model of immigrant integration - one that promotes mutual benefits for immigrants and their receiving community and that allows newcomers enhanced civic participation and improved economic mobility is critical. Current thinking on immigrant integration supports not only the immigrant taking responsibility for the adaptation process, but also that the immigrant's new home

community, known as the receiving community, should also take responsibility for the adaptation process. This two-way model does not place the entire burden on the individual, but rather emphasizes that both mainstream institutions and community members have important roles to play. The goals behind immigrant integration are for the individual immigrant to take responsibility and to be supported in order to be productive and contribute fully, and for the community to acknowledge the differences among community members and work towards becoming a cohesive whole. The community foundation will award a limited number of planning grants. Each successful applicant will receive a grant up to $50,000 for a minimum of one year. Up to 15 successful applicants will receive grants in the range of $50,000-$250,000 for a minimum of one year; multi-year grants may be awarded in certain cases at the discretion of the community foundation.
Requirements: San Mateo and/or Santa Clara County-serving organizations are eligible. Organizations headquartered outside the two-county region must demonstrate significant service to the area. Organizations with a 501(c)3 designation or those that have a fiscal sponsor with a 501(c)3 designation, public institutions or other entities that have a designated charitable purpose are also eligible.
Geographic Focus: California
Date(s) Application is Due: Nov 20
Amount of Grant: 50,000 - 250,000 USD
Contact: Ellen Clear; (650) 450-5400; fax (650) 450-5401; ehclear@siliconvalleycf.org
Internet: http://www.siliconvalleycf.org/grantmaking-strategies/index.html#II-SLSI
Sponsor: Silicon Valley Community Foundation
2440 West El Camino Real, Suite 300
Mountain View, CA 94040

Silicon Valley Community Foundation Regional Planning Grants 4359
Silicon Valley Community Foundation is focused on innovative solutions that solve problems and improve the quality of life throughout San Mateo and Santa Clara counties. As a new community foundation, we have examined the diverse needs across our region, evaluated the best practices of our parent foundations and incorporated community input before launching a new set of grantmaking strategies. By using an RFP approach for Regional Planning grants, the community foundation aims to solicit the best thinking of nonprofit service providers, public sector agencies, research institutions and other entities serving San Mateo and Santa Clara counties.
Requirements: San Mateo and/or Santa Clara County-serving organizations are eligible. Organizations headquartered outside the two-county region must demonstrate significant service to the area. Organizations with a 501(c)3 designation or those that have a fiscal sponsor with a 501(c)3 designation, public institutions or other entities that have a designated charitable purpose are also eligible.
Geographic Focus: California
Date(s) Application is Due: Apr 7
Contact: Ellen Clear; (650) 450-5400; fax (650) 450-5401; ehclear@siliconvalleycf.org
Internet: http://www.siliconvalleycf.org/grantmaking-strategies/index.html#II-BCG
Sponsor: Silicon Valley Community Foundation
2440 West El Camino Real, Suite 300
Mountain View, CA 94040

Simmons Foundation Grants 4360
The foundation awards grants to Maine nonprofits in its areas of interest, including arts, higher education, family services, health care, food services, health organizations, human services, children and youth, services and women. Types of support include general operating support, building construction/renovation, equipment acquisition, and scholarship funds.
Requirements: There are no application forms or deadlines however your initial approach should be in the form of a letter. Applicants should submit the following: detailed description of project and amount of funding requested; brief history of organization and description of its mission; descriptive literature about organization; copy of IRS Determination Letter.
Geographic Focus: Maine
Contact: Suzanne McGuffey, Treasurer; (207) 774-2635
Sponsor: Simmons Foundation
1 Canal Plaza
Portland, ME 04101-4098

Simple Advise Education Center Grants 4361
The Simple Advise Education Center supports organizations, centers & services, primarily in North Carolina. Giving to improve the quality of life of citizens with developmental disabilities.
Requirements: There are no specific deadlines with which to adhere. Contact the Foundation for further application information and guidelines.
Geographic Focus: North Carolina
Contact: Barbara J. Spigner, Director; (800) 677-7306
Sponsor: Simple Advise Education Center c/o BJ Hills and Assoc.
P.O. Box 758
Fayetteville, NC 28302-0758

Simpson Lumber Charitable Contributions 4362
Simpson has been in the forest products business since 1890 and currently has two operating subsidiaries: Simpson Door Company and Simpson Tacoma Kraft Company, LLC. The mission of Simpson's contributions program is to improve the quality of life in communities where the company has a significant number of employees living and working; and to serve as a catalyst for employees to become involved and to provide leadership in their communities. The company's broad areas of interest include education, health and human services, and efforts to enhance its operating communities. Contributions are generally made in locations where the company has operations. To the extent possible, contributions will support organizations of interest to, or recommended by, Simpson employees. Simpson prefers to make capital contributions that will benefit the operating communities for the long term as opposed to contributing operating funds. Generally, support is committed for one year at a time and in amounts less than $5,000. Interested applicants should write to Simpson's Public Affairs department to request application materials. Simpson's review committees meet once per year to consider funding applications. The application deadline is May 15. For requests less than $1,000, applicants should contact Simpson's Public Affairs department.
Requirements: 501(c)3 organizations that serve Pierce, Thurston, Lewis, Mason, Grays Harbor, and Cowlitz counties in Washington are eligible to apply. Criteria taken into account in determining the amount of any contributions are as follows: degree of support from company employees; relative size and importance of company operations in the community (balance among Simpson communities); needs of organization or program for which funding is requested; amount of previous company contributions to the organization; amount committed by other companies, foundations, and/or governments (projects should demonstrate broad-based community support); and proximity of the requesting organization to Simpson operations or administrative offices.
Geographic Focus: Washington
Date(s) Application is Due: May 15
Amount of Grant: Up to 5,000 USD
Contact: Raymond P. Tennison, President; (253) 779-6400
Internet: http://www.simpson.com/communitycontribute.cfm
Sponsor: Simpson Lumber Company, LLC
917 East 11th Street
Tacoma, WA 98421

Singing for Change Foundation Grants 4363
The Singing for Change Foundation offers annual competitive grants to progressive U.S. nonprofit organizations that address the root causes of social or environmental problems. SFC is interested in funding projects that improve the quality of life for people and that empower individuals to effect positive change in their communities. Most likely to be considered are organizations that keep their overhead low and collaborate with other groups in their community to find innovative ways of solving common problems. Areas of interest include children and youth—health, education, and protection of children and their families; disenfranchised groups—projects that help people overcome social or economic barriers to education or employment, promote the empowerment of individuals toward self-sufficiency and provide opportunities for personal growth, and demonstrate human equality and encourage people to cross boundary lines to help others and the environment; and the environment—programs that promote environmental awareness and teach people methods of conservation, protection and the responsible use of natural resources. Submit a one-page letter of interest describing the organization and project; full proposals are by invitation.
Requirements: U.S. nonprofit organizations are eligible.
Restrictions: The Singing for Change Foundation does not consider grants to: individuals; government agencies; public or private schools; art, music, or recreational programs, even if offered to disenfranchised groups; political organizations; religious organizations; medical research or disease treatment organizations; basic-needs programs (that exist to supply food or clothing); single service programs such as individual counseling.
Geographic Focus: All States
Amount of Grant: 1,000 - 10,000 USD
Contact: Judith Ranger Smith, Executive Director; (843) 388-7730; judithrangersmith@gmail.com or info@singingforchange.com
Internet: http://www.singingforchange.org/grant_information.html
Sponsor: Singing for Change Foundation
P.O. Box 729
Sullivan's Island, SC 29482

Sioux Falls Area Community Foundation Community Fund Grants (Unrestricted) 4364
The purpose of the Sioux Falls Area Foundation (SFACF)'s unrestricted grantmaking program is to provide support across a wide spectrum of charitable needs and interests. Grantmaking categories include Arts and Humanities (e.g., theatre, music, arts, dance, cultural development, historic preservation, library programs, and museums); Community Affairs and Development (e.g., citizen participation, public use of parks and recreation, administration of justice, economic development, employment, and training); Education (e.g., lifelong-learning activities in formal educational settings, support of educational facilities and systems, and scholarships); Environment (e.g., protection of natural areas, conservation of energy, prevention and elimination of pollution or hazardous waste, wildlife protection, and water quality); Health (e.g., improvement of healthcare, prevention of substance abuse; support of mental-health needs, and medical research); Human Services (e.g., assistance to families, youth, the elderly, disabled, special groups, social service providers, and those who stand in need); and Religion (e.g., support for churches, religious institutions, and religion programs). SFACF offers two grant programs from its unrestricted funds: Spot Grants for projects up to $3,000 and Community Fund Grants for projects over $3,000. The majority of Community Fund Grants are made in the range of $5,000 - $10,000. Proposals for Community Fund Grants must be submitted using a standard application form (available from the SFACF office or downloadable from the website). Applications are accepted anytime and will be reviewed by the Grants Committee at their next scheduled meeting. Meetings take place six times a year: January, March, May, July, September, and November (a schedule is posted at the SFACF website).
Requirements: Nonprofit organizations serving residents in the Sioux Falls, South Dakota area (Minnehaha, Lincoln, McCook, and Turner counties) are eligible to apply. SFACF considers grant requests for programs that require start-up funds to address important community needs or opportunities, expansion of programs that meet important community needs or opportunities, assistance to organizations weathering unforeseen or unusual financial crises; programs that increase an organization's capacity to advance its mission

more efficiently or effectively; and programs or studies that inform the community's understanding of needs or opportunities. Requests are evaluated by the following criteria: comparative benefit to the community; the organization's capacity to achieve the stated objectives; the amount of support requested versus the number of people benefited; a well-planned approach to achieving stated objectives; a reasonable expectation that the program can be sustained over time (where applicable); the organization's history of working collaboratively to address community needs and opportunities; and when applicable, the organization's past SFACF grant performance.
Restrictions: SFACF does not consider grant requests for individuals, national fundraising efforts, political advocacy, and sectarian religious programs. The following types of requests are discouraged: large capital improvements or construction drives; ongoing operational support; reduction or elimination of organizational deficits; reimbursement of expenses undertaken prior to submission of a grant application; computer hardware and software, unless these are the focus of a new or enhanced program; public art for which approval and placement has not yet been secured; and multi-year requests.
Geographic Focus: South Dakota
Date(s) Application is Due: Jan 1; Mar 1; May 1; Jul 1; Sep 1; Nov 1
Contact: Candy Hanson; (605) 336-7055 ext. 12; fax (605) 336-0038; chanson@sfacf.org
Internet: http://www.sfacf.org/AboutGrants.aspx
Sponsor: Sioux Falls Area Community Foundation
300 N Philips Avenue, Suite 102
Sioux Falls, SD 57104-6035

Sioux Falls Area Community Foundation Field-of-Interest and Donor-Advised Grants   4365

The Sioux Falls Area Community Foundation (SFACF) manages over 800 grant-making funds from donors who have specified a particular field of interest (e.g., youth enrichment, the arts, animal welfare, or outdoor recreation) or a specific neighborhood organization or nonprofit. Application guidelines and due dates may vary from donor to donor. Interested applicants are encouraged to call the SFACF's program officer for specific application forms or further information.
Requirements: Requirements may vary from donor to donor. Interested applicants are encouraged to call the SFACF's program officer for further information.
Restrictions: Restrictions may vary from donor to donor. Interested applicants are encouraged to call the SFACF's program officer for further information.
Geographic Focus: South Dakota
Date(s) Application is Due: Aug 15
Contact: Patrick Gale; (605) 336-7055 ext. 20; fax (605) 336-0038; pgale@sfacf.org
Internet: http://www.sfacf.org/News.aspx
Sponsor: Sioux Falls Area Community Foundation
300 N Philips Avenue, Suite 102
Sioux Falls, SD 57104-6035

Sioux Falls Area Community Foundation Spot Grants (Unrestricted)   4366

The purpose of the Sioux Falls Area Foundation (SFACF)'s unrestricted grantmaking program is to provide support across a wide spectrum of charitable needs and interests. Grantmaking categories include Arts and Humanities (e.g., theatre, music, arts, dance, cultural development, historic preservation, library programs, and museums); Community Affairs and Development (e.g., citizen participation, public use of parks and recreation, administration of justice, economic development, employment, and training); Education (e.g., lifelong-learning activities in formal educational settings, support of educational facilities and systems, and scholarships); Environment (e.g., protection of natural areas, conservation of energy, prevention and elimination of pollution or hazardous waste, wildlife protection, and water quality); Health (e.g., improvement of healthcare, prevention of substance abuse; support of mental-health needs, and medical research); Human Services (e.g., assistance to families, youth, the elderly, disabled, special groups, social service providers, and those who stand in need); and Religion (e.g., support for churches, religious institutions, and religion programs). SFACF offers two grant programs from its unrestricted funds: Community Fund Grants for projects over $3,000 and Spot Grants for projects up to $3,000. Spot Grant proposals may be submitted at any time and do not require SFACF's standard application form. Applicants should include the following components in their requests: a typed summary of their program in two pages or fewer; signatures of the organization's executive director and board chair; a board of directors roster; a copy of the organization's IRS tax determination letter; and a project budget. In most cases, SFACF will review and respond to Spot Grant requests within two weeks of receipt. SFACF has provided complete guidelines and an informative FAQ at their website.
Requirements: Nonprofit organizations serving residents in the Sioux Falls, South Dakota area (Minnehaha, Lincoln, McCook, and Turner counties) are eligible to apply. SFACF considers grant requests for programs that require start-up funds to address important community needs or opportunities, expansion of programs that meet important community needs or opportunities, assistance to organizations weathering unforeseen or unusual financial crises; programs that increase an organization's capacity to advance its mission more efficiently or effectively; and programs or studies that inform the community's understanding of needs or opportunities. Requests are evaluated by the following criteria: comparative benefit to the community; the organization's capacity to achieve the stated objectives; the amount of support requested versus the number of people benefited; a well-planned approach to achieving stated objectives; a reasonable expectation that the program can be sustained over time (where applicable); the organization's history of working collaboratively to address community needs and opportunities; and when applicable, the organization's past SFACF grant performance.
Restrictions: SFACF does not consider grant requests for individuals, national fundraising efforts, political advocacy, and sectarian religious programs. The following types of requests are discouraged: large capital improvements or construction drives; ongoing operational support; reduction or elimination of organizational deficits; reimbursement of expenses undertaken prior to submission of a grant application; computer hardware and software, unless these are the focus of a new or enhanced program; public art for which approval and placement has not yet been secured; and multi-year requests.
Geographic Focus: South Dakota
Contact: Candy Hanson; (605) 336-7055 ext. 12; fax (605) 336-0038; chanson@sfacf.org
Internet: http://www.sfacf.org/sfacf/aboutgrants.aspx
Sponsor: Sioux Falls Area Community Foundation
300 N Philips Avenue, Suite 102
Sioux Falls, SD 57104-6035

Siragusa Foundation Arts & Culture Grants   4367

The Siragusa Foundation, established in 1950 by Ross D. Siragusa, is a private family foundation that is committed to honoring its founder by sustaining and developing Chicago's extraordinary nonprofit resources. The Foundation's Arts and Culture Program is committed to broadening audience involvement and access to Chicago's cultural institutions in an effort to foster a life-long engagement with the arts. More specifically, the Foundation supports community outreach initiatives and curriculum enrichment programs. The Foundation also supports projects designed to sustain and develop Chicago's artistic and cultural resources.
Requirements: Nonprofit 501(c)3 organization in Chicago are eligible to apply. Before submitting a formal proposal to the Foundation, prospective applicants should submit a two-page letter of inquiry outlining the background of the organization and the proposed project. The letter of inquiry should describe succinctly the project for which funding is requested, including how it relates to the Foundation's interests, the target audience, the estimated budget and request amount. After reviewing the letter of inquiry, the Foundation may or may not request a formal proposal.
Restrictions: The Foundation limits potential grantees from applying for funds to once per calendar year. The Foundation does not accept unsolicited proposals from outside the Chicago area and does not support individuals or political advocacy. The foundation typically does not support capital expenditures or endowments.
Geographic Focus: Illinois
Contact: Kristen M. Buerster, Grants Administrator; (312) 755-0064; fax (312) 755-0069
Internet: http://www.siragusa.org/pages/program_areas/13.php
Sponsor: Siragusa Foundation
1 East Wacker Drive, Suite 2910
Chicago, IL 60601

Siragusa Foundation Health Services & Medical Research Grants   4368

The Siragusa Foundation, established in 1950 by Ross D. Siragusa, is a private family foundation that is committed to honoring its founder by sustaining and developing Chicago's extraordinary nonprofit resources. The Foundation's Health Services and Medical Research Program is balanced between medical research organizations, which are concerned with scientific inquiry and the exploration of treatment methods, and health service organizations, which provide direct social and clinical care. The Foundation primarily funds fellowships, single-disease research programs and clinical treatment services. The Foundation believes it is critical to fund research efforts, health support services, patient care services and treatment, and advocacy programs for both adults and youth, all of which are highly complementary to each other.
Requirements: Nonprofit 501(c)3 organization in Chicago are eligible to apply. Before submitting a formal proposal to the Foundation, prospective applicants should submit a two-page letter of inquiry outlining the background of the organization and the proposed project. The letter of inquiry should describe succinctly the project for which funding is requested, including how it relates to the Foundation's interests, the target audience, the estimated budget and request amount. After reviewing the letter of inquiry, the Foundation may or may not request a formal proposal.
Restrictions: The Foundation limits potential grantees from applying for funds to once per calendar year. The Foundation does not accept unsolicited proposals from outside the Chicago area and does not support individuals or political advocacy. The foundation typically does not support capital expenditures or endowments.
Geographic Focus: Illinois
Contact: Kristen M. Buerster, Grants Administrator; (312) 755-0064; fax (312) 755-0069
Internet: http://www.siragusa.org/pages/program_areas/13.php
Sponsor: Siragusa Foundation
1 East Wacker Drive, Suite 2910
Chicago, IL 60601

Siragusa Foundation Human Services Grants   4369

The Siragusa Foundation, established in 1950 by Ross D. Siragusa, is a private family foundation that is committed to honoring its founder by sustaining and developing Chicago's extraordinary nonprofit resources. The Foundation's Human Services Program funds a large number of organizations that address a wide range of current and pressing social needs. We are primarily interested in sustaining programs that, in the words of our founder, help people help themselves. The Human Services Program targets underserved populations in the following areas: poverty, hunger, and homelessness; programs for children and youth; programs for women and girls; services for the disabled; services for the elderly; employment assistance and life skills programs.
Requirements: Nonprofit 501(c)3 organization in Chicago are eligible to apply. Before submitting a formal proposal to the Foundation, prospective applicants should submit a two-page letter of inquiry outlining the background of the organization and the proposed project. The letter of inquiry should describe succinctly the project for which funding is requested, including how it relates to the Foundation's interests, the target audience, the estimated budget and request amount. After reviewing the letter of inquiry, the Foundation may or may not request a formal proposal.
Restrictions: The Foundation limits potential grantees from applying for funds to once per calendar year. The Foundation does not accept unsolicited proposals from outside

the Chicago area and does not support individuals or political advocacy. The foundation typically does not support capital expenditures or endowments.
Geographic Focus: Illinois
Contact: Kristen M. Buerster, Grants Administrator; (312) 755-0064; fax (312) 755-0069
Internet: http://www.siragusa.org/pages/program_areas/13.php
Sponsor: Siragusa Foundation
1 East Wacker Drive, Suite 2910
Chicago, IL 60601

Sir Dorabji Tata Trust Grants for NGOs or Voluntary Organizations   4370
Thoughtful and committed programs initiated by organizations in priority areas are considered for financial support. The Trust draws on the expertise of its staff and specialist consultants who travel widely, study project proposals and keep abreast of developments in each of the sectors (see below).
Requirements: The trust limits its funding to projects within India. This program focuses on specific sectors for its funding: Management of Natural Resources; Livelihood; Education; Health; and Social Development Initiatives. While no specific format is prescribed, applications should preferably include: (a) description of the proposed project with clearly articulated objectives, plans/programs or activities, and mechanisms for impact assessment; (b) profile of the project holder (qualifications, achievements, experience) and a brief background of the core team; (c) Registration Certificates of the organization and Income-tax Exemption Certificates; (d) The financial audited statements of the last three years and Annual Reports.
Geographic Focus: All States, Albania, Andorra, Armenia, Austria, Azerbaijan, Belarus, Belgium, Bosnia & Herzegovina, Bulgaria, Croatia, Cyprus, Czech Republic, Denmark, Estonia, Finland, France, Georgia, Germany, Greece, Hungary, Iceland, Ireland, Italy, Kosovo, Latvia, Liechtenstein, Lithuania, Luxembourg, Macedonia, Malta, Moldova, Monaco, Montenegro, Norway, Poland, Portugal, Romania, Russia, San Marino, Serbia, Slovakia, Slovenia, Spain, Sweden, Switzerland, The Netherlands, Turkey, Ukraine, United Kingdom, Vatican City
Contact: R.M. Lala; 91 22 6665 8282; fax 91 22 2204 5427; sdtt@sdtatatrust.com
Internet: http://www.dorabjitatatrust.org/ngo/ngo_grants.asp
Sponsor: Sir Dorabji Tata Trust
Bombay House, 24 Homi Mody Street
Mumbai, 400 001 India

Sister Fund Grants for Women's Organizations   4371
The Sister Fund is a private foundation that supports and gives voice from a faith based perspective to the marginalized, especially women working for healing in the world. The Sister Fund believes that women can transform faith, and faith can transform feminism. It funds this kind of transformation in a variety of contexts. They are committed to woman-centered philanthropy and the empowerment of faith-based women, because the Fund believes the energy of love heals. The Sister Fund provides grants, technical support, communication tools and networking opportunities in a variety of forms. Some of the activities they support are: naming and validating both historical and contemporary examples of faith-fueled feminism; building bridges between faith-based and secular women; bolstering women's leadership in all sectors of society, especially faith-based institutions; fostering the emergence of young women's voices in leadership spheres; decreasing domestic violence; supporting the rights of incarcerated women; and empowering women economically. The Fund does not accept or respond to unsolicited requests for funding. Contact the Fund for further information.
Requirements: Nonprofit organizations are eligible to apply.
Geographic Focus: All States
Contact: Sunita Mehta; (212) 260-4446; fax (212) 260-4633; info@sisterfund.org
Internet: http://www.sisterfund.org/
Sponsor: Sister Fund
79 Fifth Avenue, 4th Floor
New York, NY 10003

Sisters of Charity Foundation of Canton Grants   4372
The Sisters of Charity Foundation of Canton's initiatives focus on health, education, and social services. The Foundation strives to fund innovative, effective programs within these areas that exemplify its mission and guiding principles. In its attempts to address the root causes of poverty and to reach out to youth and families, the Foundation focuses its resources on programs designed to make a measurable impact in one or more of the following areas: the needs of the poor and underserved; enhancing organizational capacity; innovative ways of supporting children and families; and health care access.
Requirements: The Foundations primary service area is Stark County. However, proposals will be considered from the surrounding counties including Carroll, Holmes, Tuscarawas, and Wayne. The programs and services of the organization requesting funding must be consistent with the Foundation's Mission and Guiding Principles. The applicant must be a 501(c)3 nonprofit organization and the request must be in compliance with local, state, and federal laws. Organizations must first complete the two-page concept form at the Foundation website that explains the purpose of the organization's request. Foundation representatives will review and respond to concept forms within two weeks, when organizations may be invited to submit a proposal.
Restrictions: The Foundation generally does not fund requests for the following, unless it can be demonstrated that program services will have a significant effect on the root causes of poverty: debt reduction; annual appeals or membership drives; general endowments; or grants to individuals.
Geographic Focus: Ohio
Contact: Anne Savastano; (330) 454-5800; fax (330) 454-5909; asavastano@sfcanton.org
Internet: http://www.scfcanton.org/grantguidlines.html
Sponsor: Sisters of Charity Foundation of Canton
400 Market Avenue North, Suite 300
Canton, OH 44702-1556

Sisters of Charity Foundation of Cleveland Good Samaritan Grants   4373
The Sisters of Charity Foundation of Cleveland provides support each year to organizations meeting the basic needs such as food, clothing, shelter, and transportation of those living in poverty in Cuyahoga County. The Good Samaritan Grants are intended for programs that provide direct goods and services for individuals living in poverty. To celebrate the foundation's 15th anniversary, the foundation has increased the Good Samaritan funding to establish a unique transportation project this year called Ride Your Way. Grant funds may be used for program support, operating support, program-related capital support, planning, or capacity building. Grant periods will vary depending upon the particular grant. Most grants are for one year. Grant periods for planning may be shorter, and multi-year grants are possible.
Requirements: Organizations must be tax-exempt, nonprofit organizations that primarily serve the Cuyahoga County region.
Restrictions: The Foundation does not make grants to support endowments, fundraising campaigns (including annual appeals), membership drives, debt retirement, and individual scholarships. Further, the Foundation does not make grants to individuals.
Geographic Focus: Ohio
Date(s) Application is Due: Jun 2
Amount of Grant: Up to 10,000 USD
Contact: Ursula Craig; (216) 241-9300; fax (216) 241-9345; ucraig@socfdncleveland.org
Internet: http://www.socfdncleveland.org/RespondingToOurCommunity/GoodSamaritanGrantProgram/tabid/148/Default.aspx
Sponsor: Sisters of Charity Foundation of Cleveland
The Halle Building, 1228 Euclid Avenue, Suite 330
Cleveland, OH 44115-1834

Sisters of Charity Foundation of Cleveland Reducing Health and Educational   4374
Disparities in the Central Neighborhood Grants
The Sisters of Charity Foundation of Cleveland is committed to helping families and individuals overcome the challenges of poverty. In this grant opportunity the Foundation focuses on health, housing and education as key components to building stronger families and stable neighborhoods. The Foundation seeks to reduce both health and educational disparities in Cuyahoga County. Grant funds may be used for program support, operating support, program-related capital support, planning, or capacity building. Grant periods will vary depending upon the particular grant. Most grants are for one year. Grant periods for planning may be shorter, and multi-year grants are possible.
Requirements: Applicants must be 501(c)3 organizations or governmental units or agencies (such as schools) that primarily serve the Cuyahoga County region.
Restrictions: The Foundation does not make grants to support endowments, fundraising campaigns (including annual appeals), membership drives, debt retirement, and individual scholarships. Further, the Foundation does not make grants to individuals.
Geographic Focus: Ohio
Date(s) Application is Due: Apr 7
Amount of Grant: 40,000 - 150,000 USD
Contact: Ursula Craig; (216) 241-9300; fax (216) 241-9345; ucraig@socfdncleveland.org
Internet: http://www.socfdncleveland.org/sistersofcharity/OurFocusAreas/HealthDisparities/HealthintheCentralNeighborhood/tabid/344/Default.aspx
Sponsor: Sisters of Charity Foundation of Cleveland
The Halle Building, 1228 Euclid Avenue, Suite 330
Cleveland, OH 44115-1834

Sisters of Mercy of North Carolina Foundation Grants   4375
The foundation provides grants to tax-exempt health care, educational, and social service organizations that assist women, children, the elderly, and the poor to improve the quality of their lives. Types of support include start-up grants for new organizations or programs, ongoing operating expenses for individual organizations, program or project expenses, building renovation, and equipment acquisition. Preference will be given to organizations whose efforts are collaborative, ecumenical, and multicultural. Particular attention will be given to organizations that serve the unserved or underserved. Annual deadline dates may vary; contact program staff for exact dates.
Requirements: Tax-exempt health care, education, and social service organizations in North and South Carolina are eligible to apply.
Restrictions: The Foundation does not ordinarily support projects, programs, or organizations that serve a limited audience; biomedical or clinical research; units of the federal government; political activities; publication of newsletters, magazines, books and the production of videos; conferences and travel; endowment funds; capital fundraising campaigns; annual giving campaigns; or social events or similar fundraising activities.
Geographic Focus: North Carolina, South Carolina
Date(s) Application is Due: Apr 1; Aug 1; Dec 1
Amount of Grant: 25,000 - 150,000 USD
Contact: Administrator; (704) 366-0087; fax (704) 366-8850; contact@somncfdn.org
Internet: http://www.somncfdn.org/grantseekers.html
Sponsor: Sisters of Mercy of North Carolina Foundation
2115 Rexford Road, Suite 401
Charlotte, NC 28211

Sisters of Saint Joseph Charitable Fund Grants   4376
The charitable fund awards community support grants to nonprofits in West Virginia and Ohio counties in three areas: Healthy Communities grants support efforts to mobilize resources and citizen energy for communitywide health promotion, environmental protection, and local development; Healthy Families funding goes to efforts to provide children and youth with sustained, caring adult relationships that will encourage responsible behavior and positive self-identity; Healthy Senior Citizens grants support efforts to engage the elderly in the community by promoting wellness and preventive health care,

independent living, voluntary service, and growth through learning. Community Initiative grants support grassroots community-based groups that are addressing health and human service needs directly affecting their local areas. The listed application deadline dates are for one-page letters of inquiry. If interested, the fund will send an application packet. Annual deadline dates may vary; contact program staff for exact dates.
Requirements: 501(c)3 tax-exempt organizations in Calhoun, Jackson, Pleasants, Ritchie, Roane, Tyler, Wirt, and Wood counties of West Virginia; and Athens, Meigs, and Washington counties of Ohio may apply for grant support. Eligible volunteer groups, such as neighborhood associations or church outreach communities, must be sponsored by a 501(c)3 organization.
Restrictions: The fund is unable to make grants to organizations without a 501(c)3 designation, whose projects do not benefit residents of the SSJCF service area, or whose projects do not promote health and wellness in the community it serves. Individuals are not eligible. Organizations that promote proselytizing or religious conversion as a goal of their programming or proposal; or Endowment funds.
Geographic Focus: Ohio, West Virginia
Date(s) Application is Due: Jan 9; Jul 12
Amount of Grant: 18,000 USD
Contact: Manager; (304) 424-6080; fax (304) 424-6081; info@ssjcharitablefund.org
Internet: http://www.ssjcharitablefund.org/grant_program.htm
Sponsor: Sisters of Saint Joseph Charitable Fund
P.O. Box 4440
Parkersburg, WV 26104-4440

Sisters of St. Joseph Healthcare Foundation Grants 4377
The Sisters of St. Joseph Healthcare Foundation is a non-profit, public benefit corporation, which addresses the needs of the working and indigent poor in: Southern California; San Francisco Bay Area; Humboldt County; Fresno County. The Sisters of St. Joseph Healthcare Foundation funds programs which directly serve the needs of the underserved, especially families and children at risk. The Foundation sponsors or supports long-term efforts which are closely identified with the Sisters of St. Joseph of Orange and their mission of bringing unity and healing where divisiveness and oppression exist. The foundation supports the concept of Healthy Communities and desire to fund programs and organizations that: provide direct health-related services; support and transform the individual, social, economic, institutional, and cultural aspects of communities; provide change within larger societal systems to benefit low-income and at-risk populations; and develop the leadership and capacity for self-determination of those served by our funding. The Sisters of St. Joseph Healthcare Foundation is particularly interested in proposals which fall into these funding categories: mental health services; health services; homeless services; violence prevention.
Requirements: Southern California, Humbolt County, Fresno County and San Francisco bay area nonprofits are eligible.
Restrictions: The Foundation does not fund direct support to individuals, annual fund drives, or capital campaigns.
Geographic Focus: California
Amount of Grant: 1,000 - 50,000 USD
Contact: Sister Regina Fox; (714) 633-8121, ext. 7109; rfox@csjorange.org
Sponsor: Sisters of St. Joseph Healthcare Foundation
440 South Batavia Street
Orange, CA 92868-3998

Skaggs Foundation Grants 4378
The Skaggs Foundation was established in 1962 in California, and currently provides funding in Alaska. The foundations area of interest include: animals/wildlife; preservation/protection; children services; special education; environmental education; environment; natural resources; marine science. Types of support available with these funds include: continuing support; endowments; equipment; general/operating support; internship funds; land acquisition; matching/challenge support; program evaluation; research; technical assistance.
Requirements: Nonprofit organizations are eligible, preference is given to requests from Alaska. The initial approach should be a one or two page letter of inquiry. There is no formal application form. Applicants should submit the following: copy of IRS Determination Letter; copy of current year's organizational budget and/or project budget; one copy of the proposal.
Restrictions: No grants to individuals.
Geographic Focus: Alaska
Date(s) Application is Due: May 1; Oct 1
Contact: Samuel D. Skaggs Jr., President; (907) 463-4843
Sponsor: Skaggs Foundation
P.O. Box 20510
Juneau, AK 99802-0510

Skillman Foundation Community Connections Small Grants 4379
The Skillman Foundation typically awards grants to nonprofit organizations with federal tax-exempt status and revenues greater than $100,000. However, through the Community Connections Small Grants program, the Foundation has the flexibility to provide opportunities beyond these limitations. Volunteer community groups and residents, working in the Detroit neighborhoods of Brightmoor, Cody/Rouge, the Northend, Osborn, and Chadsey/Condon and Vernor in Southwest Detroit, can receive grants toward achieving community goals. Small grants provide support for innovative grassroots efforts to impact community change in neighborhoods. The Foundation is able to respond quickly to community needs, build resident leadership and empower residents and small nonprofits to help implement programs that will support their community goal. Small grants range between $500 to $5,000.
Requirements: The applicant schools or organizations must be tax exempt and may not be a 509(a) private foundation. The foundation's primary geographic area of focus is the Detroit metropolitan area, comprising Wayne, Macomb, and Oakland Counties.
Restrictions: The foundation does not award grants directly to individuals or provide loans of any kind; nor does it support sectarian religious activities, political lobbying, political advocacy, legislative activities, endowments, annual fund drives, basic research, or support of past operating deficits.
Geographic Focus: Michigan
Amount of Grant: 500 - 5,000 USD
Contact: Tonya Allen; (313) 393-1185; fax (313) 393-1187; info@skillman.org
Internet: http://www.skillman.org/grants/small-grants/
Sponsor: Skillman Foundation
100 Talon Centre Drive, Suite 100
Detroit, MI 48207

Skillman Foundation Good Neighborhoods Grants 4380
The Good Neighborhoods program encourages the creation of safe, healthy, and vibrant neighborhoods where children with the support of caring adults, programs, and experiences can develop fully. Launched in January 2006, the program provides full-scale support to six Detroit neighborhoods where more than 65,000 children live, roughly 30% of the city's child population. Half of the children in these neighborhoods live in poverty. This program encourages the creation of safe, healthy and vibrant neighborhoods where children, with support of caring adults, programs and experiences, can develop fully. The six neighborhoods are: Brightmoor; Cody/Rouge; Northend (also known as Central); Osborn; Chadsey/Condon, in Southwest Detroit; and Vernor, in Southwest Detroit. The goal of the Good Neighborhoods program is to ensure that children experience safe, healthy and high-quality environments where they can thrive: neighborhoods with resources, opportunities and assets for children to develop fully and pursue prosperity.
Requirements: The applicant organizations must be tax exempt and may not be a 509(a) private foundation. The foundation's primary geographic area of focus is the Detroit metropolitan area.
Restrictions: The foundation does not award grants directly to individuals or provide loans of any kind; nor does it support sectarian religious activities, political lobbying, political advocacy, legislative activities, endowments, annual fund drives, basic research, or support of past operating deficits.
Geographic Focus: Michigan
Amount of Grant: 10,000 - 2,000,000 USD
Contact: Tonya Allen; (313) 393-1185; fax (313) 393-1187; info@skillman.org
Internet: http://www.skillman.org/good-neighborhoods/
Sponsor: Skillman Foundation
100 Talon Centre Drive, Suite 100
Detroit, MI 48207

Skillman Foundation Good Opportunities Grants 4381
The goal of the Good Opportunities program is to respond to special needs and opportunities that have great return for children, further the Foundation's Good Neighborhoods and Good Schools work, or support the longtime interests of founder, Rose Skillman. Grantmaking in this area will: leverage investments in schools and neighborhoods; create citywide infrastructure and champions for the Foundation's work; and support organizations that serve Detroit's neediest children and families.
Requirements: The applicant schools or organizations must be tax exempt and may not be a 509(a) private foundation. The foundation's primary geographic area of focus is the Detroit metropolitan area, comprising Wayne, Macomb, and Oakland Counties.
Restrictions: The foundation does not award grants directly to individuals or provide loans of any kind; nor does it support sectarian religious activities, political lobbying, political advocacy, legislative activities, endowments, annual fund drives, basic research, or support of past operating deficits.
Geographic Focus: Michigan
Amount of Grant: 10,000 - 2,000,000 USD
Contact: Tonya Allen; (313) 393-1185; fax (313) 393-1187; info@skillman.org
Internet: http://www.skillman.org/good-opportunities/
Sponsor: Skillman Foundation
100 Talon Centre Drive, Suite 100
Detroit, MI 48207

Skillman Foundation Good Schools Grants 4382
The Good Schools: Making the Grade initiative has, in the past four years, developed and implemented an application process to identify and recognize Good Schools in Detroit. Schools are invited, on an annual basis, to participate in the application process that uses nine indicators of student and school success to help identify Good Schools. Michigan State University provides technical assistance to the program through the Good Schools Resource Center. The Resource Center provides technical assistance to schools throughout the application process and coordinates application submission and site visits.
Requirements: The applicant schools or organizations must be tax exempt and may not be a 509(a) private foundation. The foundation's primary geographic area of focus is the Detroit metropolitan area, comprising Wayne, Macomb, and Oakland Counties.
Restrictions: The foundation does not award grants directly to individuals or provide loans of any kind; nor does it support sectarian religious activities, political lobbying, political advocacy, legislative activities, endowments, annual fund drives, basic research, or support of past operating deficits.
Geographic Focus: Michigan
Contact: Tonya Allen; (313) 393-1185; fax (313) 393-1187; info@skillman.org
Internet: http://www.skillman.org/good-schools/
Sponsor: Skillman Foundation
100 Talon Centre Drive, Suite 100
Detroit, MI 48207

Skoll Foundation Awards for Social Entrepreneurship   4383
The Skoll Foundation presents the Skoll Awards for Social Entrepreneurship each year to a select few social entrepreneurs who are solving the world's most pressing problems. The Skoll Award includes a core support grant to the organization to be paid over three years, and a non-cash award to the social entrepreneur presented at the Skoll World Forum on Social Entrepreneurship every spring. The Foundation's focus on the following areas stems from a belief that many of the world's most pressing problems are worsened by inequality between the rich and the poor. Social entrepreneurs provide solutions that address this inequality at a systematic level. This list serves as a guide and is not meant to be comprehensive: economic and social equity; environmental sustainability; health; institutional responsibility; peace and security; and tolerance, justice, and human rights. Qualifying organizations are evaluated against the following criteria for their proposed project: its impact potential, proven approach, innovation, specific issue; leverage; its social entrepreneur; and the project's sustainability. Applications are accepted from January 4 through March 1 of each year.
Requirements: The application process includes several stages. The eligibility quiz helps applicants assess whether they should apply for the award. Organizations that pass the eligibility quiz will be given a URL to the application. Selected applicants (usually ten or fewer each year) will be invited by the program officer to submit a full proposal. This processes includes interviews, a site visit, reference checks, follow-up questions, in-depth financial review, and a discussion of grant objectives. Approximately ten award winners will then be selected.
Restrictions: The Foundation Awards will not support: individuals; programs promoting religious or ideological doctrine, such as those principally sectarian in nature; lobbying (beyond that allowed by law for charitable organizations); film financing; endowments, cash reserves or deficit reductions; government agencies; university-based projects; public schools and school districts; land, site acquisition or facilities construction; institutions that discriminate on the basis of race, creed, age, gender or sexual orientation in policy or practice; grantmaking to other organizations or individuals; event sponsorship; political campaigns; new or early-stage business plans or ideas; organizations whose missions and work focus on a single municipality, province or state; or local offices of parent organizations or specific programs within organizations.
Geographic Focus: All States
Date(s) Application is Due: Mar 1
Contact: Administrator; (650) 331-1031; fax (650) 331-1033; info@skollfoundation.org
Internet: http://www.skollfoundation.org/about/skoll-awards/
Sponsor: Skoll Foundation
250 University Avenue, Suite 200
Palo Alto, CA 94301

Slow Food in Schools Micro-Grants   4384
Slow Food in Schools projects are based on the three building blocks of pleasure, tradition, and sustainability. SFIS projects are diverse, yet all involve the fundamental principles of Slow Food itself; namely to provide healthy, nutritious, and delicious foods to children while simultaneously educating them about the ecological and cultural traditions of the foods they are eating and enjoying the pleasures of taste.
Requirements: At website is a link to download the steps to starting a Slow Foods in Schools project. For requests under $500, contact the SFUSA office. SFUSA gives annual micro-grants to SFIS projects across the country, and allocates funds to each project from national fundraising efforts for Slow Food in Schools. In addition to these funds, SFUSA often sends materials such as seeds and tools to SFIS projects, and works with national companies to secure sponsorship.
Geographic Focus: All States
Contact: Deena Goldman; (718) 260-8000; fax (718) 260-8068; info@slowfoodusa.org
Internet: http://www.slowfoodusa.org/index.php/programs/details/in_schools/
Sponsor: Slow Foods USA
20 Jay Street, Suite M04
Brooklyn, NY 11201

Smith Richardson Foundation Direct Service Grants   4385
The Smith Richardson Foundation makes a small number of direct service grants to organizations in North Carolina and Connecticut that provide innovative services for disadvantaged children and families. Applicants seeking direct service grants should prepare a short letter describing the mission of the organization, the population it serves, and the nature of the services it delivers. Applicants should also indicate the size of their organization's budget and the costs of the program for which they are seeking support from the Foundation.
Requirements: Direct service organizations located outside of North Carolina or Connecticut, as well as national direct service charities, will not be considered.
Restrictions: The Foundation does not provide support for the following: deficit funding or previously established projects; building or construction projects; arts and humanities projects; historic restoration projects; research projects in the physical sciences; evaluations of direct service organizations conducted internally; or educational or other support to individuals.
Geographic Focus: Connecticut, North Carolina
Contact: Mark Steinmeyer; (203) 222-6222; fax (203) 222-6282; msteinmeyer@srf.org
Internet: http://www.srf.org/grants/domesticservicegrants.php
Sponsor: Smith Richardson Foundation
60 Jesup Road
Westport, CT 06880

Smith Richardson Foundation Domestic Public Research Fellowship   4386
The Domestic Public Policy program supports projects that will help the public and policy makers understand and address critical challenges facing the United States. An overarching goal of the Foundation's grant making is to support projects that help stimulate and inform important public policy debates. To that end, the Foundation supports research on and evaluation of existing public policies and programs, as well as projects that inject new ideas into public debates. The Foundation is interested in a wide range of topics. Education and school reform have been central to the Foundation's grant making in recent years, including efforts to assess the effectiveness of various school reform initiatives, such as charter schools. The Foundation has expanded on its interest in public finance issues by beginning to explore the future of the Medicare program and the larger challenge of coping with expected increases in the costs of federal entitlement programs. The Foundation also provides support for projects that assess the impact of immigration on American society, examine the effectiveness of our regulatory policies, and explore the interaction between the policy making process and the political process through support for projects on congressional redistricting and the conduct and financing of political campaigns. The Foundation continues to support projects that inform the debate over policies designed to assist disadvantaged families.
Requirements: Fellowships will only be awarded to individual researchers and not to research teams. He or she must hold a position as a full-time faculty member at a college or university or as a full-time fellow at a public policy think tank or research organization in the United States. An applicant should explain how he or she meets these requirements in the cover letter to his or her research proposal.
Geographic Focus: All States
Amount of Grant: 60,000 USD
Contact: Mark Steinmeyer; (203) 222-6222; fax (203) 222-6282; msteinmeyer@srf.org
Internet: http://www.srf.org/grants/domestic.php
Sponsor: Smith Richardson Foundation
60 Jesup Road
Westport, CT 06880

Snee Reinhardt Charitable Foundation Grants   4387
The foundation awards a large variety of grants that have an impact on the social issues that Americans face every day. Recent grantees have included children's museums, universities, health agencies, theaters, schools, hospitals, youth issues, and environmental causes. Precedence is given to organizations situated within or whose activities are concentrated in, first, southwestern Pennsylvania, then northern West Virginia, northern Maryland, the Commonwealth of Pennsylvania and, lastly, the United States. Application and guidelines are available online.
Requirements: 501(c)3 nonprofit organizations are eligible.
Restrictions: Organizations, activities, and/or programs excluded from support include general capital improvement; general operating expenses, including salaries and fringe benefits; chairs or professorships; endowment funding; grants to individuals; political contributions; highly specialized health or medical programs that do not have specific impact on the community; organizations and programs designed to influence legislation or elect candidates to public office; organizations that discriminate by race, color, creed, gender, or national origin; or programs that promote, research, or support the prevention of life, abortion, the practice of euthanasia, or cruelty to animals.
Geographic Focus: All States
Date(s) Application is Due: Apr 15; Aug 15
Amount of Grant: Up to 50,000 USD
Contact: Grants Administrator; (412) 390-2690; fax (412) 390-2686
Internet: http://www.snee-reinhardt.org/index.html
Sponsor: Snee Reinhardt Charitable Foundation
River Park Commons Two, 2425 Sidney Street
Pittsburgh, PA 15203

SOBP A.E. Bennett Research Award   4388
The Society of Biological Psychiatry offers an annual award of $2,000 each in basic science and in clinical science for the purpose of stimulating international research in biological psychiatry by young investigators. Candidates must be actively engaged in the research for which the award is sought. Applicants need only write a brief description of their research, submit 2-3 published or submitted papers and arrange for two letters of support (at least one of the letters needs to be from a member of the Society). Although the research is not to be judged in comparison with the work of the more senior investigators, special consideration will be given to the originality of the approach and independence of thought evident in the submission. Nominations should be submitted on-line on or before November 29.
Requirements: Submissions are welcomed from laboratory researchers in any country who have not passed their 45th birthday or have not been engaged in research for greater than 10 years following award of their terminal degree or the end of formal clinical/fellowship training, whichever is later by deadline date; candidates need not be current members of the society.
Geographic Focus: Wisconsin
Date(s) Application is Due: Feb 1; Mar 15; Aug 1; Sep 13; Sep 15; Nov 29
Amount of Grant: 2,000 USD
Contact: Director; (904) 953-2842; fax (904) 953-7117; maggie@mayo.edu
Internet: http://www.sobp.org/i4a/pages/index.cfm?pageID=3379
Sponsor: Society of Biological Psychiatry
4500 San Pablo Road, Birdsall 310
Jacksonville, FL 32224

Sobrato Family Foundation Grants   4389
Foundation Grants are targeted toward strong community-based organizations that promote self-reliance and economic independence, and positively contribute to the quality of life for economically, physically and/or emotionally challenged individuals in Santa Clara, Southern San Mateo and Southern Alameda Counties. The Foundation's interests include, but are not limited to, the areas of: education; health; human services including crime and legal related services, employment training, housing and shelter, human services and food programs, and youth development; and public/societal benefit organizations, specifically nonprofit capacity building agencies. The Foundation generally awards operating support in the range of one to eight percent of an agency's three-year average renewable private cash contributed income (excluding unique one-time gifts, bequests, capital campaign

and endowment contributions). Grants range from $20,000 to over $400,000. To apply applicants take an eligibility questionnaire on line at the Foundation's website. Eligible applicants will then be instructed on how and when to apply.
Requirements: Eligible applicants must: be a 501(c)3 organization; have locally raised renewable private cash contributed income of at least $300,000 per year over a three-year average; serve at least fifty percent of their primary clients in the California counties of Santa Clara, Southern San Mateo and Southern Alameda; serve clients who are economically, emotionally and/or physically challenged; and have a primary mission that is aligned with the Foundation's priorities of education, health, human services and public/ societal benefit organizations.
Restrictions: The following are ineligible: agencies whose largest program expense supports mental health, the environment or the arts; fiscally-sponsored programs or organizations; fundraising events or endowment campaigns; school-managed clubs or individual schools, unless an invitation is extended; medical research or specific diseases; projects created or operated by public government agencies or departments; and public libraries or their foundations.
Geographic Focus: California
Contact: Mara Williams Low, Manager; (408) 996-9500; fax (408) 996-9516; MLow@Sobrato.org or grants@Sobrato.org
Internet: http://www.sobrato.com/foundation
Sponsor: Sobrato Family Foundation
10600 N De Anza Boulevard, Suite 225
Cupertino, CA 95014

Sobrato Family Foundation Meeting Space Grants 4390
The Sobrato Family Foundation is dedicated to helping create and sustain a vibrant and healthy community, where all Silicon Valley residents have equal opportunity to live, work and be enriched. To accomplish this purpose, the Foundation invests in strong community-based nonprofits that promote self-reliance and economic independence, and positively contribute to the quality of life for economically, physically and/or emotionally challenged individuals in Santa Clara, Southern San Mateo and Southern Alameda Counties. There are three Conference Center locations. The Redwood Shores Center is located at 330-350 Twin Dolphin Drive in Redwood City; the San Jose Center is located at 1400 Parkmoor Avenue in San Jose; and the Milpitas Center is located at 600 Valley Way in Milpitas.
Requirements: All Bay Area 501(c)3 organizations and local public agencies are eligible to use the Foundation's nonprofit conference facilities at no charge, on a first-come, first-served reservation basis. All activities must be related to and support the charitable mission of their agency. A $1 million General Liability Certificate of Insurance naming the Sobrato Foundation, Silicon Valley Community Foundation, The Sobrato Family Foundation and The Sobrato Organization and their related entities as additionally insured is required for every meeting use. Reservation can be made by sending an email request which includes: contact name, phone and email address; the nonprofit's legal name and employer identification number; the date and start and end time of the meeting (including set up & take down); the number of expected meeting attendees; and the preferred Conference Center.
Restrictions: Commercial, religious, and partisan political activities are prohibited. The rooms are not available for use by individuals, groups without 501(c)3 status, or those that cannot produce the required certificate of insurance.
Geographic Focus: California
Contact: Community Conference Coordinator; (408) 466-0700; fax (408) 996-9516; Meetings@Sobrato.org
Internet: http://www.sobrato.org/what-we-do/meeting-space-grants-eligibility
Sponsor: Sobrato Family Foundation
10600 N De Anza Boulevard, Suite 225
Cupertino, CA 95014

Sobrato Family Foundation Office Space Grants 4391
The Sobrato Family Foundation is dedicated to helping create and sustain a vibrant and healthy community, where all Silicon Valley residents have equal opportunity to live, work and be enriched. To accomplish this purpose, the Foundation invests in strong community-based nonprofits that promote self-reliance and economic independence, and positively contribute to the quality of life for economically, physically and/or emotionally challenged individuals in Santa Clara, Southern San Mateo and Southern Alameda Counties. The Foundation has two office business parks available for multi-tenant nonprofit centers: Sobrato Center for Nonprofits Milpitas, and Sobrato Center for Nonprofits San Jose. A third center in Redwood Shores is scheduled for future opening.
Requirements: There is a competitive review process for Office Space Grants. Awards are based on the following: alignment with the Foundation's mission and client service priorities; the organization's capacity to support its mission, including program quality and effectiveness, staff and board leadership, and the organization's reputation and experience; the organization's capital structure to support its mission; and the organization's effective use of space relative to the available unit(s) open. Application can be made on-line from the Foundation's website.
Geographic Focus: California
Contact: Mara Williams Low, Manager; (408) 466-0700; fax (408) 996-9516; MLow@Sobrato.org or grants@Sobrato.org
Internet: http://www.sobrato.org/what-we-do/office-space-grants
Sponsor: Sobrato Family Foundation
10600 N De Anza Boulevard, Suite 225
Cupertino, CA 95014

SOCFOC Catholic Ministries Grants 4392
The Sisters of Charity Foundation of Cleveland belongs to a community of Catholic health and social service organizations inspired to service by the healing ministry of Jesus Christ. As a supporting foundation to the congregation of the Sisters of Charity of St. Augustine, the Foundation gives priority to the ministries of the Sisters of Charity Health System. A limited amount of remaining funds may be available to other Catholic ministries in health and human services in Cuyahoga County. Funding is limited to Invited Proposals.
Requirements: Each proposal to the Foundation must include a completed application form, proposal narrative, budget, and Budget Narrative. The application form and guidelines for the proposal narrative may be found on this website under the specific program area. Eligible organizations are 501(c)3 organizations or governmental agencies or units.
Restrictions: The Foundation does not make grants to individuals.
Geographic Focus: Ohio
Amount of Grant: 10,000 - 150,000 USD
Contact: Lynn Berner; (216) 241-9300; fax (216) 241-9345; lberner@socfdncleveland.org
Internet: http://www.socfdncleveland.org/RespondingToOurCommunity/CatholicMinistries/tabid/313/Default.aspx
Sponsor: Sisters of Charity Foundation of Cleveland
The Halle Building, 1228 Euclid Avenue, Suite 330
Cleveland, OH 44115-1834

SOCFOC Community Collaborations Grants 4393
Frequently, the philanthropic community initiates collaboration, sometimes with government partners, to address a particular challenge facing our community. These collaborations create opportunities for greater efficiency, stronger advocacy, and more robust funding than a single foundation. The Sisters of Charity Foundation of Cleveland is open to participation in those collaborations which align with our mission of improving the lives of people in need.
Requirements: Eligible are 501(c)3 organizations or governmental agencies or units.
Geographic Focus: Ohio
Amount of Grant: 5,000 - 100,000 USD
Contact: Lynn Berner; (216) 241-9300; fax (216) 241-9345; lberner@socfdncleveland.org
Internet: http://www.socfdncleveland.org/RespondingToOurCommunity/CommunityCollaborations/tabid/321/Default.aspx
Sponsor: Sisters of Charity Foundation of Cleveland
The Halle Building, 1228 Euclid Avenue, Suite 330
Cleveland, OH 44115-1834

Social Justice Fund Northwest Criminal Justice Giving Project Grants 4394
Social Justice Fund Northwest is a public membership foundation that supports organizations working for structural change, to improve the lives of people most affected by political, economic and social inequities. The Criminal Justice Giving Project is a diverse group of people who have committed to building community together, learning about intersections of race and class in the systems that criminalize poor people of people of color and about the movement for social justice, and working together to fund strategic, inspiring, and under-resourced community organizing. Criminal Justice Giving Project grants are one-year awards of up to $15,000 each to support social change in Idaho, Montana, Oregon, Washington and Wyoming, specifically focused on criminal justice issues. Such issues are defined broadly to include all of the systems which criminalize the lives of people of color and poor people. Examples include, but are not limited to, immigration, school discipline, child protective services and foster care, in addition to issues which directly involve the criminal justice system.
Requirements: To be eligible for any Social Justice Fund grant program, an organization must: be a nonprofit organization with 501(c)3 or 501(c)4 status as determined by the IRS, or be a federally recognized American Indian tribal government or agency; be led by people who are most directly affected by the problems that the organization or project is addressing; carry out most of its work in Idaho, Montana, Oregon, Washington, and/or Wyoming; and satisfy evaluation requirements for all previous Social Justice Fund grants. The committee welcomes applications from people with all levels of English fluency and formal education; therefore, grammatical and spelling errors will not negatively impact scores. In addition, small and/or new organizations are encouraged to apply. If your organization does not have tax-exempt status or sponsorship, but might otherwise be a good fit for this grant, contact Social Justice Fund staff so that they can assist you with your eligibility.
Geographic Focus: Idaho, Montana, Oregon, Washington, Wyoming
Date(s) Application is Due: May 11
Amount of Grant: Up to 15,000 USD
Contact: Mijo Lee; (206) 624-4081; fax (206) 382-2640; mijo@socialjusticefund.org
Karen Toering, (206) 624-4081; fax (206) 382-2640; karen@socialjusticefund.org
Internet: http://www.socialjusticefund.org/apply-grant
Sponsor: Social Justice Fund Northwest
1904 Third Avenue, Suite 806
Seattle, WA 98101

Social Justice Fund Northwest Economic Justice Giving Project Grants 4395
Social Justice Fund Northwest is a public membership foundation that supports organizations working for structural change, to improve the lives of people most affected by political, economic and social inequities. Economic Justice Giving Project grants are one-year awards of up to $10,000 each to support social change in Idaho, Montana, Oregon, Washington and Wyoming, specifically focused on economic justice issues. Such issues are defined broadly to include work that addresses the root causes of economic inequity using community led solutions to build power among its members (ie. workers, families, faith communities etc.) to advocate for and create thriving communities. Examples of this activity include, but are not limited to: worker and consumer protections, transportation access, healthcare solutions, affordable housing, tax policy, and impacts of the wealth divide on low income, people of color, immigrants, disability and LGBTQ populations.
Requirements: To be eligible for any Social Justice Fund grant program, an organization must: be a nonprofit organization with 501(c)3 or 501(c)4 status as determined by the IRS, or be a federally recognized American Indian tribal government or agency; be led by people who are most directly affected by the problems that the organization or project is addressing;

carry out most of its work in Idaho, Montana, Oregon, Washington, and/or Wyoming; and satisfy evaluation requirements for all previous Social Justice Fund grants.
Geographic Focus: Idaho, Montana, Oregon, Washington, Wyoming
Date(s) Application is Due: Jun 8
Amount of Grant: 10,000 USD
Contact: Kylie Gursky; (206) 624-4081; fax (206) 382-2640; kylie@socialjusticefund.org
Internet: http://www.socialjusticefund.org/apply-grant
Sponsor: Social Justice Fund Northwest
1904 Third Avenue, Suite 806
Seattle, WA 98101

Social Justice Fund Northwest Environmental Justice Giving Project Grants   4396
Social Justice Fund Northwest is a public membership foundation that supports organizations working for structural change, to improve the lives of people most affected by political, economic and social inequities. Environmental Justice Giving Project grants are one-year grants of up to $10,000 each to support social change in Idaho, Montana, Oregon, Washington and Wyoming specifically working for environmental justice. Grants are defined in the environmental justice movement as the spaces where we live, work, learn, play, pray, and heal. For the purpose of this grant, environmental justice organizations: strive for equitable access to a clean and healthy environment; work for sustainability, including racial and economic justice; and are community-based and led by the people who are most disproportionally affected by environmental justice issues. Some examples are: safe and healthy housing, workplaces, and schools; transportation; access to healthy food; air, water, soil, light, and noise pollution; health care; waste disposal; distribution of natural resources and the benefits of a green economy; preservation and restoration of wildlife and wildlands; and climate change. This granting committee is open to considering other environmental justice issues not identified here, particularly as they relate to the fundamental rights to air, water, land, and food.
Requirements: To be eligible for any Social Justice Fund grant program, an organization must: be a nonprofit organization with 501(c)3 or 501(c)4 status as determined by the IRS, or be a federally recognized American Indian tribal government or agency; be led by people who are most directly affected by the problems that the organization or project is addressing; carry out most of its work in Idaho, Montana, Oregon, Washington, and/or Wyoming; and satisfy evaluation requirements for all previous Social Justice Fund grants. The committee welcomes applications from people with all levels of English fluency and formal education; therefore, grammatical and spelling errors will not negatively impact scores. In addition, small and/or new organizations are encouraged to apply. If your organization does not have tax-exempt status or sponsorship, but might otherwise be a good fit for this grant, contact Social Justice Fund staff so that they can assist you with your eligibility.
Geographic Focus: Idaho, Montana, Oregon, Washington, Wyoming
Date(s) Application is Due: Jun 8
Amount of Grant: Up to 10,000 USD
Contact: Mijo Lee, Project Manager; (206) 624-4081; fax (206) 382-2640; mijo@socialjusticefund.org or generalgrant@socialjusticefund.org
Internet: http://www.socialjusticefund.org/apply-grant
Sponsor: Social Justice Fund Northwest
1904 Third Avenue, Suite 806
Seattle, WA 98101

Social Justice Fund Northwest General Grants   4397
Social Justice Fund Northwest is a public membership foundation that supports organizations working for structural change, to improve the lives of people most affected by political, economic and social inequities. General Grants are one-year grants of up to $10,000 each to support social change in Idaho, Montana, Oregon, Washington and Wyoming. These grants may be for general support or for specific projects.
Requirements: To be eligible for any Social Justice Fund grant program, an organization must: be a nonprofit organization with 501(c)3 or 501(c)4 status as determined by the IRS, or be a federally recognized American Indian tribal government or agency; be led by people who are most directly affected by the problems that the organization or project is addressing; carry out most of its work in Idaho, Montana, Oregon, Washington, and/or Wyoming; and satisfy evaluation requirements for all previous Social Justice Fund grants. The committee welcomes applications from people with all levels of English fluency and formal education; therefore, grammatical and spelling errors will not negatively impact scores. In addition, small and/or new organizations are encouraged to apply. If your organization does not have tax-exempt status or sponsorship, but might otherwise be a good fit for this grant, contact Social Justice Fund staff so that they can assist you with your eligibility.
Geographic Focus: Idaho, Montana, Oregon, Washington, Wyoming
Date(s) Application is Due: Jul 13
Amount of Grant: Up to 10,000 USD
Contact: Kylie Gursky, Project Manager; (206) 624-4081; fax (206) 382-2640; kylie@socialjusticefund.org or generalgrant@socialjusticefund.org
Internet: http://www.socialjusticefund.org/apply-grant
Sponsor: Social Justice Fund Northwest
1904 Third Avenue, Suite 806
Seattle, WA 98101

Social Justice Fund Northwest LGBTQ Giving Project Grants   4398
Social Justice Fund Northwest is a public membership foundation that supports organizations working for structural change, to improve the lives of people most affected by political, economic and social inequities. The LGBTQ (lesbian, gay, bisexual, transgender, and queer) Giving Project is a diverse group of LGBTQ-identified people who have committed to building community across race and class and generations, learning about a multi-issue movement for justice, and working together to fund strategic, inspiring, and underfunded LGBTQ organizing in the Northwest. The members of the Giving Project each make a donation of an amount that is meaningful to them, develop skills as donor organizers, raise the money for this grant, screen grant proposals, participate in site visits, and make the final granting decisions. LGBTQ Giving Project Grants are one-year grants of $10,000 each to support community organizing by and for LGBTQ people in Idaho, Montana, Oregon, Washington and Wyoming. This grant will prioritize LGBTQ organizing that is commonly overlooked by mainstream funders, especially work that is led by and focused on communities of color.
Requirements: To be eligible for any Social Justice Fund grant program, an organization must: be a nonprofit organization with 501(c)3 or 501(c)4 status as determined by the IRS, or be a federally recognized American Indian tribal government or agency; be led by people who are most directly affected by the problems that the organization or project is addressing; carry out most of its work in Idaho, Montana, Oregon, Washington, and/or Wyoming; and satisfy evaluation requirements for all previous Social Justice Fund grants. This particular grant is open to LGBTQ organizations, as well as organizations who do not necessarily consider themselves to be LGBTQ organizations, but whose membership and leadership includes LGBTQ-identified people, and whose work supports struggles for LGBTQ justice in meaningful ways and helps to build a strong, multi-issue, progressive movement. The committee welcomes applications from people with all levels of English fluency and formal education; therefore, grammatical and spelling errors will not negatively impact scores. In addition, small and/or new organizations are encouraged to apply. If your organization does not have tax-exempt status or sponsorship, but might otherwise be a good fit for this grant, contact Social Justice Fund staff so that they can assist you with your eligibility.
Geographic Focus: Idaho, Montana, Oregon, Washington, Wyoming
Date(s) Application is Due: May 11
Amount of Grant: 10,000 USD
Contact: Kylie Gursky; (206) 624-4081; fax (206) 382-2640; kylie@socialjusticefund.org
Mijo Lee, (206) 624-4081; fax (206) 382-2640; mijo@socialjusticefund.org
Internet: http://www.socialjusticefund.org/apply-grant
Sponsor: Social Justice Fund Northwest
1904 Third Avenue, Suite 806
Seattle, WA 98101

Social Justice Fund Northwest Montana Giving Project Grants   4399
Social Justice Fund Northwest is a public membership foundation that supports organizations working for structural change, to improve the lives of people most affected by political, economic and social inequities. The Montana Giving Project is a diverse group of people who have committed to building community together, learning about a multi-issue movement for justice, and working together to fund strategic, inspiring, and under-resourced community organizing in Montana. Montana Giving Project grants are one-year grants of up to $10,000 each to support community organizing for social change in Montana only. These grants may be for general support or for specific projects.
Requirements: To be eligible for this Social Justice Fund grant program, an organization must: be a nonprofit organization with 501(c)3 or 501(c)4 status as determined by the IRS, or be a federally recognized American Indian tribal government or agency; be led by people who are most directly affected by the problems that the organization or project is addressing; carry out most of its work in Montana; and satisfy evaluation requirements for all previous Social Justice Fund grants.
Geographic Focus: Montana
Date(s) Application is Due: Jun 29
Amount of Grant: Up to 10,000 USD
Contact: Kylie Gursky, Project Manager; (206) 624-4081; fax (206) 382-2640; kylie@socialjusticefund.org or mtgp@socialjusticefund.org
Internet: http://www.socialjusticefund.org/apply-grant
Sponsor: Social Justice Fund Northwest
1904 Third Avenue, Suite 806
Seattle, WA 98101

Sodexo Foundation STOP Hunger Scholarships   4400
The scholarship program was created to recognize and reward the great steps young people are taking to fight hunger in our communities across the country. Up to five students will each receive a $5,000 scholarship award and a matching $5,000 grant in their name, for the hunger-related charity of their choice. The scholarships will be presented at the Sodexo Foundation Dinner in Washington, D.C. In addition, up to 20 regional honorees will receive a $1,000 grant in their name, for the hunger-related charity of their choice.
Requirements: The scholarships are open to students (kindergarten through college graduate school) enrolled in accredited educational institutions in the United States. Applicants must have demonstrated on-going commitment to their community by performing volunteer services impacting hunger in the United States at least within the last 12 months. Volunteer services must help non-family members. Applicants must obtain a Community Service Recommendation as part of the application process. The Community Service Recommendation must be completed by a third party; this person must be at least 21 years old and may not be a parent, guardian or family member. All applicants must be citizens or permanent residents of the United States. Eligible students can apply online at http://www.applyists.net/ (Access Key: SDXF).
Restrictions: Employees of Sodexo are not eligible to receive a scholarship, but their family members who are not employees of Sodexo may apply. Previous STOP Hunger Scholarship recipients are not eligible. Previous regional STOP Hunger Honorees are eligible to apply.
Geographic Focus: All States
Date(s) Application is Due: Feb 26
Contact: Stephen J. Brady; (800) 763-3946; STOPHunger@sodexofoundation.org
Internet: http://www.sodexofoundation.org/hunger_us/scholarships/scholarships.asp
Sponsor: Sodexo Foundation
9801 Washingtonian Boulevard
Gaithersburg, MD 20878

Solo Cup Foundation Grants 4401
The foundation awards grants to Illinois nonprofit organizations in its areas of interest, including higher education, health, social services, and Christian organizations and churches. Types of support include capital campaigns, general operating support, and scholarship funds. There are no application deadlines or forms.
Requirements: Illinois nonprofit organizations are eligible.
Geographic Focus: Illinois
Amount of Grant: 5,000 - 85,000 USD
Contact: Robert M. Korzenski; (847) 831-4800; fax (847) 579-3245; info@solocup.com
Sponsor: Solo Cup Foundation
1700 Old Deerfield Road
Highland Park, IL 60035

Solutia Fund Grants 4402
The fund was established to aid and support qualified organizations in communities in which Solutia Inc. operates within the United States. The fund represents the corporation's commitment to help improve its operating communities, especially by furthering the growth of science education and environmental stewardship, and providing new avenues for community health and development. There are no application forms or deadlines. Applicants should provide a short description of the program and the reason for the request; the amount requested; and the timeframe in which the contribution is needed.
Requirements: Solutia Fund grants money to U.S. 501(c)3 organizations located in Solutia communities (Alabama, California, District of Columbia, Florida, Georgia, Illinois, Massachusetts, Michigan, Missouri, New York, Ohio, South Carolina, Tennessee, Texas, Virginia, and Washington).
Restrictions: The fund does not consider applications for advocacy groups; individuals; fraternal, social, veterans, or military organizations; lobbying efforts to influence legislation; travel for individuals or groups; for-profit organizations; or endowment funds. Generally, the fund does not award grants for organizations not located in Solutia communities; fundraising, testimonial, or athletic events; emergency operating support; funding more than 10 percent of an organization's annual budget or campaign goal; funding a program or project for multiple years; or capital campaigns.
Geographic Focus: Alabama, California, District of Columbia, Florida, Georgia, Illinois, Massachusetts, Michigan, Missouri, New York, Ohio, South Carolina, Tennessee, Texas, Virginia, Washington
Contact: Grants Administrator; (314) 674-3083; fax (314) 674-1585
Internet: http://www.solutia.com/pages/corporate/about/mission.asp
Sponsor: Solutia Fund
575 Maryville Center Drive, P.O. Box 66760
Saint Louis, MO 63166-6760

Sonoco Foundation Grants 4403
The Sonoco Products Company is the company sponsor of the Sonoco Foundation. The foundation was established in 1983, in the state of South Carolina. The foundation supports organizations involved with education, crime and violence prevention, human services, youth, and community development. Giving primarily in areas of company operations, with emphasis on Hartsville, South Carolina.
Requirements: South Carolina nonprofit organizations are eligible to apply for these grants. There is no application form required. Applicants should submit a detailed description of project and amount of funding requested.
Restrictions: The foundation does not support religious, political, or lobbying organizations. Grants aren't available to individuals, or for educational capital funds programs, endowments, trips, or tours.
Geographic Focus: South Carolina
Amount of Grant: 1,000 - 600,000 USD
Samples: University of South Carolina, Columbia, SC, $600,000; Boy Scouts of America, Florence, SC, $60,000; United Way of Florence County, Florence, SC, $14,000;
Contact: Joyce Beasley, (800) 377-2692 or (843) 383-7501
Internet: http://www.sonoco.com
Sponsor: Sonoco Foundation
1 North Second Street, MS A09
Hartsville, SC 29550-3300

Sonora Area Foundation Competitive Grants 4404
The Foundation's governing board has a pool of discretionary funds, and regularly awards grants to qualified non-profit and public agencies. These grants are competitive and are awarded for worthy projects that help improve the quality of life in Tuolumne County, whether for education, human services, recreation, arts or the environment. The Foundation seeks opportunities to stretch its funding impact by making grants which will work in combination with other funds. This might involve requiring an applicant to provide matching funds from other sources. In addition, the Foundation may choose to make a challenge grant, where additional funds must be secured before Foundation monies are released. The Foundation considers several types of competitive grant requests: Pilot or Demonstration Project (intended to promote creativity, such a project is based on the concept of setting up, testing and evaluating a model approach to dealing with challenges found in the community), New or Expanded Program (based on challenges or needs within Tuolumne County), and Capacity Building (strengthening an applicant organization's ability to achieve its mission or purposes).
Requirements: Nonprofit organizations serving Tuolumne County, CA, may submit applications. Public sector entities or units of government primarily serving Tuolumne County residents are also eligible to apply. Informal associations, community groups or collaboratives may apply through an eligible lead organization acting as the fiscal sponsor. The Sonora Area Foundation Board of Directors reviews grant applications at their scheduled Board meetings (usually the fourth Tuesday) in February, April, June, August, October, December. Applications are due at the Foundation office by the end of the month preceding these Board Meetings.
Restrictions: Grants are not awarded to/for sectarian purposes, private foundations, political purposes, annual or capital campaigns, endowment funds, existing financial obligations or debt retirement, or programs or services for other than Tuolumne County residents.
Geographic Focus: California
Date(s) Application is Due: Jan 31; Mar 31; May 31; Jul 31; Sep 31; Nov 30
Amount of Grant: Up to 200,000 USD
Contact: Lin Freer, Program Manager; (209) 533-2596; fax (209) 533-2412
Internet: http://www.sonora-area.org/grantapplication.html
Sponsor: Sonora Area Foundation
362 South Stewart Street
Sonora, CA 95370

Sony Corporation of America Corporate Philanthropy Grants 4405
Sony Corporation of America consists of three operating companies as well as the corporate headquarters, which is based in New York City: Sony Electronics, Inc. (headquarters in San Diego, California); Sony Pictures Entertainment, Inc. (headquarters in Culver City, California); and Sony Music Entertainment, Inc. (headquarters in New York City). Each company, as well as the overall corporation, has its own philanthropic priorities and resources (e.g. grants, product donations, and recordings and screenings) that benefit a multitude of causes. Taken together the corporation's areas of interest cover arts and culture; health and human services; civic and community outreach, education; the environment; disaster response; and volunteerism. The core of Sony's various corporate philanthropy programs are their contributions to the communities in which Sony employees work and live; however, the corporation and subsidiaries contribute to national nonprofits as well. In the past, types of support have included general operating budgets, continuing support, annual campaigns, seed grants, building construction, equipment acquisition, endowment funds, employee matching gifts, internships, and employee-related scholarships. Sony Corporation of America and its subsidiaries welcome requests for support throughout the year. There is no grant application form. Requests must be submitted in writing to the corporation or its operating companies. Contact information is given on this page and at the website. Guidelines for what to include in the application as well as more information on types of programs the corporation and/or its subsidiaries have supported are available at the grant website. Notification of grant-request approval or rejection will be made in writing within one month of receipt of all proposed materials.
Requirements: U.S. nonprofits, including schools and school districts, are eligible.
Restrictions: The corporation does not consider multi-year requests for support. The following types of organizations will not be funded: organizations that discriminate on the basis of race, color, creed, gender, religion, age, national origin, or sexual orientation; partisan political organizations, committees, or candidates and public office holders; religious organizations in support of their sacramental or theological functions; labor unions; endowment or capital campaigns of national origin; organizations whose prime purpose is to influence legislation; testimonial dinners in general; for-profit publications or organizations seeking advertisements or promotional support; individuals seeking self-advancement; foreign or non-U.S.-based organizations; and organizations whose mission is outside of the U.S.
Geographic Focus: All States
Amount of Grant: 1,000 - 100,000 USD
Contact: Janice Pober, (310) 244-7737
Internet: http://www.sony.com/SCA/philanthropy/guidelines.shtml
Sponsor: Sony Corporation of America
550 Madison Avenue, 33rd Floor
New York, NY 10022-3211

Sophia Romero Trust Grants 4406
The Sophia Romero Trust was established in 1948 to support and promote quality human-services and health-care programming for underserved elders living in Bristol County, Massachusetts. Special consideration will be given to organizations that serve older women living in Bristol County, Massachusetts. Grant requests for general operating support or program support are strongly encouraged. The majority of grants from the Romero Trust are one year in duration. Applicants must apply online at the grant website. Applicants are strongly encouraged to do the following before applying: review the downloadable state application procedures for additional helpful information and clarifications; review the downloadable online-application guidelines at the grant website; review the trust's funding history (link is available from the grant website); review the online application questions in advance; and review the list of required attachments. These will generally include: a list of board members, financial statements (audited, reviewed, or compiled by independent auditor); an organization summary; a list of other funding sources; an IRS Determination letter; and other required documents. All attachments must be uploaded in the online application as PDF, Word, or Excel files. The application deadline for the Sophia Romero Trust is 11:59 p.m. on February 1. Applicants will be notified of grant decisions before April 30.
Requirements: Applicants must have 501(c)3 tax-exempt status and serve the residents of Bristol County, Massachusetts.
Restrictions: The fund does not support requests from individuals, organizations attempting to influence policy through direct lobbying, or any political campaigns.
Geographic Focus: Massachusetts
Date(s) Application is Due: Feb 1
Contact: Emma Greene, Director; (617) 434-0329; emma.m.greene@baml.com
Internet: https://www.bankofamerica.com/philanthropic/fn_search.action
Sponsor: Sophia Romero Trust
225 Franklin Street, 4th Floor, MA1-225-04-02
Boston, MA 02110

Sorenson Legacy Foundation Grants 4407

The foundation has a broad spectrum of philanthropic interests and supports endeavors that: encourage and support the long-term preservation and enhancement of the quality of life of all humankind, especially of families and children; assist the disenfranchised of society, such as but not limited to, abused spouses and children, in order that they receive the full benefits of membership in society and fulfill their potential as human beings; promote medical research and the development of innovative medical technologies for saving lives and alleviating pain and suffering; promote the development of the arts, including art education in schools, assistance of promising young artists, and support of performing arts organizations; promote community development and security, adequate and affordable housing, and education and job training; promote law and order generally and provide youth with alternatives to gangs, crime and socially nonproductive behavior; protect and enhance the environment, preserve wild and open spaces, and promote development of parks and green spaces; promote the development of science, culture and recreation; promote world peace and unity through a greater understanding, tolerance and harmony among religious, national and ethnic groups; advance the programs at private and state universities and colleges that are consistent with the foundation's charter; and, advance the mission of the Church of Jesus Christ of Latter-day Saints in all its places.
Geographic Focus: All States
Contact: Executive Director, (801) 461-9700; (801) 461-9722
Internet: http://www.sorensoncompanies.com/giving_back.html
Sponsor: Sorenson Foundation
2511 South West Temple Street
Salt Lake City, UT 84115

Sosland Foundation Grants 4408

The foundation awards grants to nonprofit organizations in the metropolitan bistate Kansas City area. Areas of interest include arts and culture, higher education, health care, Jewish services, and social services. Types of support include program development, building construction/renovation, equipment acquisition, development grants, endowments, general operating grants, and matching gifts. There are no application forms or deadlines. Applicants should send a letter including a description of the program and the organization, a list of board and staff, and proof of tax-exempt status.
Requirements: Metro bistate Kansas City 501(c)3 nonprofit organizations are eligible.
Restrictions: Individuals and publications or conferences are ineligible.
Geographic Focus: Kansas, Missouri
Amount of Grant: 1,000 - 5,000 USD
Contact: Program Contact; (816) 756-1000; fax (816) 756-0494
Internet: http://www.soslandfoundation.org
Sponsor: Sosland Foundation
4800 Main Street, Suite 100
Kansas City, MO 64112

Southbury Community Trust Fund 4409

The Fund awards grants in the areas of arts, community and economic development, education, the environment, and health and human services. High priority is given to program development, program implementation, organizational capacity building, and policy change addressing root causes of problems. Interested applicants should complete a letter of inquiry. Information for submission is available online.
Requirements: Organizations with IRS 501(c)3 status serving Southbury are eligible to submit letters of inquiry.
Restrictions: Funding is not available for: religious purposes; political campaigns; annual appeals; building fund/capital, endowment or memorial campaigns; loans or deficit financing; federal, state, or municipal agencies or departments supported by taxation; individuals.
Geographic Focus: Connecticut
Date(s) Application is Due: Jan 15
Contact: Anne Watkins; (203) 334-7511; fax (203) 333-4652; awatkins@gbafoundation.org
Internet: http://www.gbafoundation.org/grants/apply.asp
Sponsor: Greater Bridgeport Area Foundation
211 State Street, 3rd Floor
Bridgeport, CT 06604

South Carolina Arts Commission Accessibility Grants 4410

The program was created to help South Carolina arts organizations make programs and existing facilities accessible to persons with disabilities. Funds may be used for a variety of programs as well as facilities improvements that address accessibility. There is a required 1:1 match, and 50% of the applicant's match must be cash.
Requirements: Applicant must be one of the following: (1) a SC organization with primary mission focused on the arts (or an organization that serves as the primary arts provider in its community); (2) designated South Carolina Department of Disabilities and Special Needs board; or, (3) an organization that will commit to a project that connects the arts to persons who have disabilities. Applicant must ALSO be one of the following: (1) a charitable organization currently registered with the Office of the Secretary of State that has its own federal tax exempt status with the Internal Revenue Service; (2) a charitable organization currently registered with the Office of the Secretary of State applying through a tax exempt fiscal agent organization; or, (3) a unit of government. Applications must be received at least 6 weeks before the project begins. Projects must be completed by the close of current SC Arts Commission fiscal year (June 30).
Restrictions: Applicants are limited to one grant award per fiscal year. Funds for capital improvements (bricks and mortar) are limited to renovations to existing facilities. If the existing facility is on The National Register of Historic Places or deemed eligible, all work must conform with the Secretary of the Interior's Standards for Rehabilitation. All construction documents must be stamped by the architect and/or engineer and must meet all local and state building codes. If applying for capital improvements, applicant must include a copy of deed or letter from property owner acknowledging approval of project.
Geographic Focus: South Carolina
Amount of Grant: Up to 5,000 USD
Contact: Rusty Sox, Coordinator; (803) 734-8696; rsox@arts.sc.gov
Internet: http://www.southcarolinaarts.com/grants/organizations/accessibility.shtml
Sponsor: South Carolina Arts Commission
1800 Gervais Street
Columbia, SC 29201

South Carolina Arts Commission AIE Residency Plus Individual Site Grants 4411

program provides support for schools collaborating with artists concerning residencies, performances and workshops. Awards in this category may be used to cover residency/performance/workshop fees, but may not be used to cover travel expenses or supplies. Residency Plus Individual Site is designed to serve individual schools that are not served through a Residency Plus Multi-site or ABC Advancement grant award. Please note that Residency Plus Individual Site grants are awarded for work scheduled to take place during the following school year.
Requirements: Applicants must be one of the following: pre-K-12 SC public or private school; nonprofit after school program in partnership with a pre-K-12 SC public or private school; or, a unit of government or charitable organization currently registered with the SC Office of the Secretary of State that either has its own federal tax-exempt status with the IRS or is applying through a fiscal agent - in partnership with a pre-K-12 SC public or private school that has not previously received funding through the SC Arts Commission's Arts in Education or Arts Education Initiatives grant programs during the current fiscal year. Parent/Teacher Organizations (PTOs) may submit/administer grants on behalf of their schools, but the individual school must be listed as the grant applicant and the school district as the fiscal receiver. Applicants may request one half of the artist(s) fees, not to exceed $750. A 1:1 match is required - the applicant's match must be cash. Applications must be received by November 15 for residencies planned for the upcoming fiscal year (July 1 - June 30).
Restrictions: The SCAC will not fund programs for which the sum of all artist(s) fees is less than $750. Funds may not be used to cover travel expenses or supplies. Residency sites may not apply as individual sites if they are included in multi-site applications. ABC sites are not eligible to apply for Residency Plus funding. The SCAC will not consider requests from applicants who have failed to submit the required final report documents on previous grants.
Geographic Focus: South Carolina
Date(s) Application is Due: Nov 15
Amount of Grant: Up to 750 USD
Contact: Katie Fox; (803) 734-8767; kfox@arts.sc.gov
Internet: http://www.southcarolinaarts.com/grants/aie/residencyplusindividual.shtml
Sponsor: South Carolina Arts Commission
1800 Gervais Street
Columbia, SC 29201

South Carolina Arts Commission AIE Residency Plus Multi-Site Grants 4412

The program provides support for school districts and local arts partnerships that wish to provide residencies, performances, and workshops at multiple schools in collaboration with teachers and teaching artists. Awards in this category may be used to cover residency/performance/workshop fees, but may not be used to cover travel expenses or supplies. Residency Plus Multi-Site is designed to serve schools that are not served through a Residency Plus Individual-site or ABC Advancement grant award. grant covers a two-year cycle. However, when applying, the applicant should only account for the first year of the grant. The applicant's award will be based on that account; upon completion of a final report for the first year of the grant, similar funding is assured for the second year of the cycle, as long as the SC Arts Commission's funding remains stable.
Requirements: Individual schools may be included in a multi-site grouping of schools. Schools that are part of Gifted and Talented Consortia (RES) may apply as individual sites or as part of multi-sites in addition to their participation in consortia applications. Applicants must be: a SC school district; a Gifted and Talented Consortium (group); a Private school (pre-K-12); a nonprofit after school program- in partnership with pre-K-12 schools or a school district; or, a unit of government or charitable organization currently registered with the Office of the Secretary of State that either has its own federal tax-exempt status with the IRS or is applying through a fiscal agent - in partnership with pre-K-12 schools or a school district. Awards are based on the projected total artist fees paid and the total number of schools served. Applicants may request up to 1/3 of the total artists fees for all grant activities, but requests cannot exceed $750 per site served. Applicants should use the Grant Request Worksheet to calculate the amount that they can request. Gifted & Talented Consortia (RES) awards may not exceed a total of $7,500. Multi-site applicants may request an additional ten percent for program administration. Requests for administrative fees must be included in the initial application. Grantees who do not request the ten percent administrative fees in their application may not include administrative fees in their request for payment. A 2:1 match is required - the applicant's match must be cash.
Restrictions: The SCAC will not consider requests from applicants who have failed to submit the required final report documents on previous grants.
Geographic Focus: South Carolina
Date(s) Application is Due: Nov 15
Amount of Grant: Up to 750 USD
Contact: Katie Fox; (803) 734-8767; kfox@arts.sc.gov
Internet: http://www.southcarolinaarts.com/grants/aie/residencyplusmulti.shtml
Sponsor: South Carolina Arts Commission
1800 Gervais Street
Columbia, SC 29201

South Carolina Arts Commission American Masterpieces in South Carolina Grants 4413

This program will provide grant funds to help qualified performing groups and presenters acquire, prepare, and present to the public significant American works of choral music, musical theatre, and dance. The project will capitalize on the 'American Masterpieces' branding that has been developed by the National Endowment for the Arts through an integrated, statewide marketing effort and will engage local schools and school districts to develop K-12 educational links with funded projects. Funds support a project's development and restaging expenses. See the website for more detailed guidelines.

Requirements: Applicant must be: a nonprofit, charitable organization that is currently registered with the Office of the Secretary of State of South Carolina that has its own federal tax exempt status with the Internal Revenue Service; OR a nonprofit, charitable organization that is currently registered with the Office of the Secretary of State of South Carolina that applies through a tax exempt fiscal agent organization; OR a unit of government. College and university departments are eligible, but only one application per department will be accepted. All grants must be matched at least 1:1. Before applying you are strongly advised to discuss the project with your county coordinator to determine whether your project meets the guidelines. Applications must be postmarked or hand-delivered to the SC Arts Commission offices before 5:00 PM, no later than the stated date, or, when the deadline occurs on a weekend or holiday, no later than the next business day.
Geographic Focus: South Carolina
Date(s) Application is Due: Jun 15
Amount of Grant: Up to 10,000 USD
Contact: Rusty Sox, Coordinator; (803) 734-8696; rsox@arts.sc.gov
Internet: http://www.southcarolinaarts.com/grants/organizations/americanmasterpieces.shtml
Sponsor: South Carolina Arts Commission
1800 Gervais Street
Columbia, SC 29201

South Carolina Arts Commission Operating Support for Organizations Grants 4414

This program provides twelve-month operational support to SC arts organizations with primary missions involving these artistic functions: Producing, Service, Presenting, Education. Support is broad in scope and can be used for a variety of arts programs, salaries, artist fees, supplies, and other operating expenses at the discretion of the organization within the eligibility and legal requirements defined in these guidelines. There is no pre-set funding range. Awards will be based on organizational budgets, application reviews, and the availability of funds.

Requirements: Organizations requesting Annual Operating Support must have completed one fiscal year of programming in order to be eligible to apply. Applicant must be a SC organization with primary mission focused on the arts (or an organization that serves as the primary arts provider in its community). Applicant must also be (1) a charitable organization currently registered with the Office of the Secretary of State that has its own federal tax exempt status with the Internal Revenue Service; or, (2) a charitable organization currently registered with the Office of the Secretary of State applying through a tax exempt fiscal agent organization; or, (3) a unit of local government. Applicant must have a valid DUNS number. A minimum of 2:1 cash match is required. No in-kind expenses are allowed as part of applicant's match in this category. Applications must be submitted via the Online SC Arts Resources (OSCAR) application process by 5:00 PM on the posted deadline date. NOTE: This grant requires a filing fee of $15.00, payable by check made out to South Carolina Arts Commission OR online credit card payment.
Restrictions: No in-kind expenses are allowed as part of applicant's match in this category. Payment will be on a reimbursement basis only. Organizations requesting Annual Operating Support may not apply for Long Term or Quarterly Support (except for requests for staff professional development under Quarterly Support grants).
Geographic Focus: South Carolina
Date(s) Application is Due: Feb 15
Contact: Rusty Sox, Coordinator; (803) 734-8696; rsox@arts.sc.gov
Internet: http://www.southcarolinaarts.com/grants/organizations/annual.shtml
Sponsor: South Carolina Arts Commission
1800 Gervais Street
Columbia, SC 29201

South Carolina Arts Commission Artists Fellowships 4415

Fellowships recognize and award the artistic achievements of South Carolina's exceptional artists by rewarding their career achievements. Six fellowships are awarded each year according to the fellowship rotation cycle (see website). Fellowship awards are made through a highly competitive process and are based on artistic excellence. See the website for application materials and guidelines.

Requirements: Applicant must: be a legal resident of the U.S. and SC with a permanent residence in the state for two years prior to the application date and throughout the fellowship period; be a practicing individual artist (duos, collaborative works, and other ensembles are not eligible); not be a degree-seeking, full-time student during the award period; be 18 years of age or older at the time of application. Support material submitted must include work that has been completed within the last five years.
Restrictions: Full-time degree-seeking students, members and staff of the commission, and artists under contract to the commission are ineligible. There is a limit of three fellowships in an artist's career and a period of ineligibility of ten years after the first fellowship is awarded. An artist may apply in more than one category, but is only eligible to receive one fellowship. Fellows may not receive any other SCAC grant awards during their fellowship year. A minimum of five applications must be received in a fellowship category in order for the discipline category to undergo panel review.
Geographic Focus: South Carolina
Date(s) Application is Due: Oct 1
Amount of Grant: 2,000 USD
Contact: Jeanette Guinn, Dance Supervisor; (803) 734-8677; jguinn@arts.sc.gov
Internet: http://www.southcarolinaarts.com/grants/artists/fellowships.shtml
Sponsor: South Carolina Arts Commission
1800 Gervais Street
Columbia, SC 29201

South Carolina Arts Commission Arts and Economic Impact Study Assistance 4416

Funding is available to Arts Councils who wish to undertake economic impact studies for their counties. Studies may be provided by Americans for the Arts or by any other qualified group or individual. Only contractual fees to providers and other direct costs of the studies are eligible for reimbursement.

Requirements: Applicant must be: (1) an Arts Council that is currently registered with the Office of the Secretary of State of South Carolina, and that either has its own federal tax-exempt status with the IRS or applies through a fiscal agent. If a fiscal agent is used, SCAC requires that the fiscal agent and the applicant organization enter into a formal agreement that outlines the working relationship and responsibilities of both parties. This letter must be submitted with the application; or, (2) the primary provider of general, multidisciplinary arts programs and/or services within a particular community or region. Applicant must also: have completed at least three full fiscal years in operation prior to application; be a current Annual Operating Support or Long Term Operating Support grantee; make available copies of study results to SCAC and to local representation or delegation. All grants must be matched at least 1:1.
Restrictions: Payment will be on an expense reimbursement basis only.
Geographic Focus: South Carolina
Date(s) Application is Due: Aug 15
Amount of Grant: Up to 2,500 USD
Contact: Rusty Sox, Coordinator; (803) 734-8696; rsox@arts.sc.gov
Internet: http://www.southcarolinaarts.com/grants/organizations/economicimpactstudy.shtml
Sponsor: South Carolina Arts Commission
1800 Gervais Street
Columbia, SC 29201

South Carolina Arts Commission Arts Facility Projects Grants 4417

The program is intended to assist SC arts organizations with construction and renovation of arts facilities. Funds may be used for purchase and/or construction of arts facilities, including: improvements to existing administrative, performance, exhibition, gallery, studio space, workshops, or classrooms; new administrative, performance, exhibition, gallery, studio space, workshops, or classrooms; making existing facilities accessible to persons with disabilities; or, outstanding payments for such projects undertaken within the past three years.

Requirements: Applicants must be a SC organization with primary mission focused on the arts (or an organization that serves as the primary arts provider in its community). Applicant must also be: (1) charitable organization currently registered with the Office of the Secretary of State that has its own federal tax exempt status with the Internal Revenue Service (Applicant may not use a fiscal agent); or, (2) a unit of government. A match of 2:1 is required - 100% of the applicant's match must be cash; no in-kind expenses are allowed.
Restrictions: Applicant may not be a college, university, or K-12 public or private school. No in-kind expenses are allowed. Funds may not be used for: feasibility or fundraising studies; cosmetic work such as interior painting and furnishings; or, landscape projects or monuments. Payment will be on an expense reimbursement basis only.
Geographic Focus: South Carolina
Amount of Grant: Up to 200,000 USD
Contact: Rusty Sox, Coordinator; (803) 734-8696; rsox@arts.sc.gov
Internet: http://www.southcarolinaarts.com/grants/organizations/facilities.shtml
Sponsor: South Carolina Arts Commission
1800 Gervais Street
Columbia, SC 29201

South Carolina Arts Commission Arts in Education After School Arts Grants 4418

The initiative supports arts-based after school programs in non-profit, tax-exempt facilities with programs for middle school and/or high school students who self-select participation. Participating programs will be required to track indicators of students' social, artistic, creative and intellectual growth. An arts-based after school program is one wherein the majority of time is spent in study and practice of the visual, literary, or performing arts. There may be a portion of time designated for homework help or snacks, but the programming focus must be on the arts. In addition, funded programs may be housed in the same facility as non-arts programs and/or share transportation and resources, but must function as independent, arts-focused courses of activity. An after school program, for the purposes of this grant, may be housed at a school or an outside facility. It may take place 1-5 days per week. The program's start time does not have to coincide with the end of the school day, but at least a portion of the program must take place during the hours of 3:00-6:00 pm. Grants will be awarded up to $10,000 per site per year for up to 3 years. This funding is contingent upon continued availability of funds allocated to the Commission.

Requirements: An applicant must be a non-profit, tax exempt school-year or year-round after school program that offers arts-based programs for middle school or high school students. This includes both school and non-school entities. Programs must be those for which students self-select participation. Participation fees and transportation may not serve as obstacles to participation in programs. A match is required for each year: Years 1 and 2 - 1:1; Year 3 - 2:1.
Restrictions: For-profit organizations and after school programs that do not serve middle school or high school students are not eligible to apply. Non-arts based programs are not eligible to apply. Programs to which students are involuntarily assigned are not eligible to apply. Payment will be on an expense reimbursement basis only.
Geographic Focus: South Carolina

Date(s) Application is Due: Feb 1
Amount of Grant: 10,000 - 30,000 USD
Contact: Katie Fox; (803) 734-8767; kfox@arts.sc.gov
Internet: http://www.southcarolinaarts.com/grants/aie/afterschool.shtml
Sponsor: South Carolina Arts Commission
1800 Gervais Street
Columbia, SC 29201

South Carolina Arts Commission Cultural Tourism Initiative Grants 4419
The SC Arts Commission established a cultural tourism initiative in 2005 which helps to link arts and tourism in communities across the state, understanding that the promotion of arts and cultural projects serves to attract new cultural tourists, stimulate local economies, and create renewed pride and recognition of the value of the arts and cultural resources of South Carolina communities. Grants are intended to fund: market research or marketing activities; new cultural tourism products that stimulate community economic impact by attracting cultural tourists, generating direct visitor expenditures; existing cultural tourism products that stimulate community economic impact by attracting new cultural tourists, increasing expenditures, lengthening stays, or extending seasons; collaborative/partnership projects involving multiple organizations across different sectors (arts, tourism, travel, hospitality, retail, etc.) that attract new cultural tourists, increase expenditures, lengthen stays, or extend tourism seasons; and, projects that increase cultural tourists' awareness of and participation in the arts and result in increased expenditures, lengthened stays, or extended tourism seasons. Awarded grants can be used for either Planning (up to $5,000) or Implementation (up to $10,000). Guidelines for each type of grant are available at the website.
Requirements: Applicant must have production or presentation of arts events or service to the arts as its primary organizational mission; or be the primary provider of general, multidisciplinary arts programs and/or services within a particular community or region. Also, applicant must be: (1) a nonprofit, charitable arts organization that is currently registered with the Office of the Secretary of State of South Carolina that has its own federal tax exempt status with the Internal Revenue Service; or, (2) a nonprofit, charitable arts organization that is currently registered with the Office of the Secretary of State of South Carolina that applies through a tax exempt fiscal agent organization; or, (3) a unit of local government that has production or presentation of arts events or service to the arts as its primary organizational mission. Applicant must have completed at least one full fiscal year in operation prior to application. A 1:1 match is required - 50% of the applicant's match must be cash.
Restrictions: Applicant must not be a college, university or state agency. Funding for this grant category is limited to a total of three grant awards to a single organization with an ineligibility period of two years after the last award.
Geographic Focus: South Carolina
Amount of Grant: Up to 10,000 USD
Contact: Rusty Sox, Coordinator; (803) 734-8696; rsox@arts.sc.gov
Internet: http://www.southcarolinaarts.com/grants/organizations/culturaltourism.shtml
Sponsor: South Carolina Arts Commission
1800 Gervais Street
Columbia, SC 29201

South Carolina Arts Commission Cultural Visions Grants 4420
The mission of Cultural Visions is to work with local organizations to strengthen leadership, advocacy, and grassroots activism to achieve the vision. Planning Grants are available for initial planning to help determine project potential, and advanced planning to aid in developing a plan that leads to a project. Initial planning grants are made up to $2,500 and advanced planning grants up to $10,000. Implementation Grants are for use to help create a cultural and arts project that has an economic impact of some kind. Because there is an economic component, the application asks you to think of the project as a business. Consequently the narrative solicits information not dissimilar to what a business would prepare in a business plan. Implementation grants are made up to $20,000.
Requirements: A preliminary Intent to Apply questionnaire and proposed project description (see website) must be submitted before you are eligible to apply for a Planning or Implementation grant. Applicant must be: located in an underserved area* as defined by the Cultural Visions Council; a unit of government; or, a charitable organization currently registered with the Office of the Secretary of State of South Carolina that either has its own federal tax-exempt status with the IRS or applies through a fiscal agent. *For the purposes of this program, an underserved area is defined as one that does not have an extensive history of or involvement with cultural programs, services, resources or economic development initiatives. Deadlines: May 15 for projects beginning July through September; August 15 for projects beginning October through December; November 15 for projects beginning January through March; February 15 for projects beginning in April through June. Intents to Apply must be submitted 30 days before the next quarterly application deadline. A 1:1 match is required - 50% of the applicant's match must be cash.
Restrictions: Payment will be on an expense reimbursement basis only.
Geographic Focus: South Carolina
Amount of Grant: Up to 20,000 USD
Contact: Rusty Sox, Coordinator; (803) 734-8696; rsox@arts.sc.gov
Internet: http://www.southcarolinaarts.com/grants/organizations/culturalvisions.shtml
Sponsor: South Carolina Arts Commission
1800 Gervais Street
Columbia, SC 29201

South Carolina Arts Commission Folklife & Traditional Arts Grants 4421
The program supports non-profit organizations that seek to promote and preserve the traditional arts practiced across the state. Priority for funding is given to projects that provide recognition and support for South Carolina's traditional art forms and their practitioners. SCAC will fund the projects that may include the following: (1) Presentation of Traditional Artists through workshops, concerts, festivals, exhibitions, radio programs, recordings, etc; (2) Documentation of Traditional Arts and/or Folklife of South Carolina - such a project must result in some form of public presentation (3) Cultural Survey - fieldwork done to identify traditions and traditional artists; (4) Production, Documentation and/or Distribution of a traditional artist's work; for example, the production of publicity materials; (5) Acquisition of difficult-to-obtain materials or equipment needed to create traditional art; or, (6) Conservation - projects, such as apprenticeships, that serve to keep a traditional art form vibrant and visible.
Requirements: Before applying, you are strongly advised to discuss your project with the Folklife & Traditional Arts director in order to determine if your project meets the guidelines. Applicants must be: a nonprofit, charitable organization that is currently registered with the Office of the Secretary of State of South Carolina that has its own federal tax exempt status with the Internal Revenue Service; a nonprofit, charitable organization that is currently registered with the Office of the Secretary of State of South Carolina that applies through a tax exempt fiscal agent organization; or, a unit of government. A 1:1 match is required - 50% of the applicant's match must be cash.
Restrictions: Modern interpretations of traditional art and revivals of traditions that have ceased to exist within the originating culture are not funded. Individual artists are not eligible to apply to this program. General oral history projects, projects that are limited to an historical focus and projects that present historical recreations of past lifestyles are not eligible. Projects that have a multi-year existence and have been supported by previous SCAC Folklife and Traditional Arts grants will not be a funding priority. Payment will be on an expense reimbursement basis only.
Geographic Focus: South Carolina
Date(s) Application is Due: Mar 15
Amount of Grant: Up to 7,500 USD
Contact: Julianne Carroll; (803) 734-8764; fax (803) 734-8526; jcarroll@arts.sc.gov
Internet: http://www.southcarolinaarts.com/grants/organizations/folklife.shtml
Sponsor: South Carolina Arts Commission
1800 Gervais Street
Columbia, SC 29201

South Carolina Arts Commission Incentive Grants for Employer Benefits 4422
Many arts organizations are facing difficulties recruiting and retaining qualified staff because they lack the capacity to compete with larger organizations when it comes to benefits packages. Competitive salaries or bonuses are no longer enough to recruit and retain staff. Today's market requires an attractive package which includes employer sponsored benefits which are a direct cost to the organization. The bottom line for many organizations looking to build organizational capacity through staff recruitment and retention is whether or not the organization is able to afford basic health insurance coverage as an employee benefit. And, for organizations that do offer benefits, there is need to control the costs. In an effort to assist organizations, SCAC is offering a grant program to encourage employer sponsored benefits.
Requirements: Applicant must be a SC organization with primary mission focused on the arts (or an organization that serves as the primary arts provider in its community). Applicant must also be: (1) a charitable organization currently registered with the Office of the Secretary of State that has its own federal tax exempt status with the Internal Revenue Service; (2) a charitable organization currently registered with the Office of the Secretary of State applying through a tax exempt fiscal agent organization; or, (3) a unit of local government with primary mission focused on the arts. This program requires a match: 1:1 - up to 50% of benefits for year 1; 2:1 - up to 33% of benefits for year 2.
Restrictions: Applicant may not be a unit of state or federal government, college, university, or K-12 public or private school. Funds may not be used for employee bonuses or salary increases. Payment will be on an expense reimbursement basis only.
Geographic Focus: South Carolina
Amount of Grant: Up to 2,000 USD
Contact: Rusty Sox, Coordinator; (803) 734-8696; rsox@arts.sc.gov
Internet: http://www.southcarolinaarts.com/grants/organizations/benefits.shtml
Sponsor: South Carolina Arts Commission
1800 Gervais Street
Columbia, SC 29201

South Carolina Arts Commission Leadership and Organizational Devel Grants 4423
The program was established to support arts leaders' (professional administrators and board members) acquisition of skills and practical tools which hone their ability to lead, develop, and sustain the overall health and vitality of South Carolina's arts organizations. Funding is targeted to professional arts administrators and board members of arts organizations. Grantees will identify a set of critical individual or operational capacity-building issues toward which the funds will be used. For the purpose of this initiative, capacity-building is defined as activities that either strengthen individual ability to lead or improve organizational functioning and sustainability. Leadership Development funding includes: costs for individuals to receive professional development; costs involved in coordinating and/or conducting professionally facilitated learning for individuals or groups across position or discipline. Organizational Development funding includes: costs for professional consultant/consulting firms providing services in areas such as fundraising, financial management, marketing, executive transition, public relations, board development, strategic planning, program development, technology, etc; costs involved with coordinating and/or conducting professionally facilitated learning for individuals or groups across position or discipline.
Requirements: Before applying, you are strongly advised to discuss the project with your county coordinator to determine whether your project meets the guidelines. Applicants must: (1) be a nonprofit, charitable arts organization that is currently registered with the Office of the Secretary of State of South Carolina, and that either has its own federal tax-exempt status with the IRS or applies through a fiscal agent; (2) have the production or presentation of arts events or service to the arts as its primary organizational mission; OR be the primary provider of general, multidisciplinary arts programs and/or services within a particular community or region; and, (3) have completed at least one full fiscal year in

operation prior to application. Applications must be received at least six weeks before the start of the project or activity. Projects must be completed by June 30. Applications received after May 15 must be for projects beginning after July 1. A 1:1 match is required - 50% of the applicant's match must be cash.
Restrictions: Applicants may not be a unit of SC State government. Individual artists are not eligible to apply to this program. Applicants may submit only one application per project per year. This category is not intended to fund annual or recurring projects. However, organizations/individuals previously funded under this category and intending to apply for funds to support the same or a similar project must demonstrate how receiving additional funds will substantially improve organizational functioning and sustainability or strengthen an individual's ability to lead the organization. Payment will be on an expense reimbursement basis only.
Geographic Focus: South Carolina
Amount of Grant: Up to 2,000 USD
Contact: Joy Young, Program Director; (803) 734-8203; jyoung@arts.sc.gov
Internet: http://www.southcarolinaarts.com/grants/organizations/leadershiporgdev.shtml
Sponsor: South Carolina Arts Commission
1800 Gervais Street
Columbia, SC 29201

South Carolina Arts Commission Long Term Operating Support for Organizations Grants 4424

The purpose of Long Term Operating Support is to strengthen arts organizations that bring ongoing arts experiences and services to individuals and other organizations throughout the state, by providing consistent, unrestricted support for basic operations. There is no pre-set funding range. Awards will be based on organizational budgets, application reviews, and the availability of funds. Grant awards may change from year to year due to availability of funds.
Requirements: Applicants must be a SC organization with primary mission focused on the arts (or an organization that serves as the primary arts provider in its community). Applicants must also be: (1) a unit of local government; (2) a charitable organization currently registered with the Office of the Secretary of State that has its own federal tax exempt status with the Internal Revenue Service; or, (3) a charitable organization currently registered with the Office of the Secretary of State applying through a tax exempt fiscal agent organization. Organizations must have been in operation for at least one fiscal year in order to be eligible to apply. Applications must be submitted via the Online SC Arts Resources (OSCAR) application process by 5:00 PM of the posted deadline date. A minimum of 3:1 cash match is required. No in-kind expenses are allowed as part of applicant's match in this category. NOTE: A filing fee of $30.00 is required, payable by check made out to South Carolina Arts Commission or online credit card payment.
Restrictions: Organizations requesting Long Term Operating Support may not apply for Annual or Quarterly Support during the three-year grant cycle (except for requests for staff professional development under Quarterly Support grants).
Geographic Focus: South Carolina
Contact: Rusty Sox, Coordinator; (803) 734-8696; rsox@arts.sc.gov
Internet: http://www.southcarolinaarts.com/grants/organizations/longterm.shtml
Sponsor: South Carolina Arts Commission
1800 Gervais Street
Columbia, SC 29201

South Carolina Arts Commission Statewide Arts Participation Initiative Grants 4425

The participation project grant is intended to fund arts projects that meet one or more of these goals: broaden participation of audience, creators, or stewards; deepen participation of audience, creators or stewards; diversify participation of audience, creators or stewards. South Carolina arts organizations, individual artists and independent arts programmers may apply for funding for participation grants (up to $15,000). An independent arts programmer is any person within the state of South Carolina, who is not employed by any organization, but whose work includes the creation and/or implementation of arts events, art exhibits, and/or arts programs that are open to the general public. Applicants that receive funding will demonstrate best cases for broadening, deepening and/or diversifying participation in the arts.
Requirements: The program is open to arts providers in South Carolina interested in building participation in the arts. Applicant must be: (1) a charitable organization currently registered with the Office of the Secretary of State of South Carolina and have its own federal tax-exempt status with the IRS or is applying through a qualified fiscal agent; (2) a unit of government; or, (3) an individual artist or independent arts programmer who resides in South Carolina, working in partnership with a qualified organization (see #1 above). Individual artists and arts programmers will be required to partner with a 501(c)3 non-profit organization for their projects. A 1:1 match is required - 50% of the applicant's match must be cash.
Restrictions: K-12 schools are not eligible for funding in this program. Payment will be on an expense reimbursement basis only.
Geographic Focus: South Carolina
Date(s) Application is Due: Jun 1
Contact: Rusty Sox, Coordinator; (803) 734-8696; rsox@arts.sc.gov
Internet: http://www.southcarolinaarts.com/grants/participation.shtml
Sponsor: South Carolina Arts Commission
1800 Gervais Street
Columbia, SC 29201

South Carolina Arts Commission Subgranting Grants 4426

Subgranting provides funds to local arts councils for subgranting quarterly grants to organizations and artists in their region. The Arts Commission does not review or fund quarterly grant applications from a county that has a subgranting arts council, except when the Commission has pre-determined that a project has a statewide impact. Funding is for the twelve-month period of July 1 - June 30.
Requirements: Subgranting is only available to arts councils. Applicants must be a SC organization with primary mission focused on the arts (or an organization that serves as the primary arts provider in its community). Applicants must also be; (a) a charitable organization currently registered with the Office of the Secretary of State that has its own federal tax exempt status with the Internal Revenue Service; (b) a charitable organization currently registered with the Office of the Secretary of State applying through a tax exempt fiscal agent organization; or, (c) a unit of government. Applicants must have at least a part-time staff (paid or volunteer) responsible for artistic, administrative and programmatic functions of the organization. Applicants must utilize a subgranting process approved by the Arts Commission that includes: (a) Review of local applications by a panel that is representative of the community (i.e. business, education, minorities, government, artists) of no less than three members, including some individuals not directly associated with the subgranting organization (no more than 1/3 of the review panel can be members of your board); (b) at least four application review periods per year; (c) appropriate publicity for grant availability and deadlines; (d) a single grant award that is at least $1,000; (e) limit of two awards per organization or artist per year; (e) match of at least 1:1 required of all individuals and groups receiving funding from the subgranting arts council; (f) notification to SCAC Regional Arts Coordinator of all subgrant review meetings.
Restrictions: Funding is not intended to support school-based artist residencies.
Geographic Focus: South Carolina
Date(s) Application is Due: Mar 15
Amount of Grant: Up to 10,000 USD
Contact: Rusty Sox, Coordinator; (803) 734-8696; rsox@arts.sc.gov
Internet: http://www.southcarolinaarts.com/grants/organizations/subgranting.shtml
Sponsor: South Carolina Arts Commission
1800 Gervais Street
Columbia, SC 29201

South Carolina Arts Commission Traditional Arts Apprenticeship Grants 4427

The purpose of the Traditional Arts Apprenticeship Initiative is three-fold: it is meant to support Master Artists who seek to pass their artistic and cultural knowledge to qualified Apprentices; to provide Apprentices with an opportunity to advance their cultural and artistic knowledge to a higher level so that they may continue to pursue the art form beyond the life of the apprenticeship; and to document the work and instruction of the Master Artist. Apprenticeship projects are required to have a Project Coordinator to handle the details of the project so that the Master and Apprentice may concentrate on the lessons. Award funds of $2,750 will be distributed - $2,000 for the Master Artist to compensate for his/her time; $250 for the Apprentice to assist with travel and supplies; and $500 for the Project Coordinator to assist with the cost of travel and necessary materials and to compensate for his/her time. Apprenticeships last 10 months and all activities must occur between July 1 and May 1, leaving time for completion and submission of the final report.
Requirements: Applicants must be residents of South Carolina and reside in the state during the apprenticeship period. Before applying, you are strongly advised to discuss your project with the program director. Priority for funding is given to projects focusing on traditional arts considered to be endangered. The Project Coordinator must be a graduate of the Institute for Community Scholars (ICS) or have cultural documentation experience. If the project coordinator is not an ICS graduate, contact the program director to discuss his/her qualifications.
Restrictions: Modern interpretations of traditional art and revivals of traditions that have ceased to exist within the originating culture will not be funded. This program does not support beginning-level students.
Geographic Focus: South Carolina
Date(s) Application is Due: Mar 15
Amount of Grant: 2,750 USD
Contact: Julianne Carroll; (803) 734-8764; fax (803) 734-8526; jcarroll@arts.sc.gov
Internet: http://www.southcarolinaarts.com/grants/artists/folklifeapprentice.shtml
Sponsor: South Carolina Arts Commission
1800 Gervais Street
Columbia, SC 29201

Southern California Edison Civic Affairs Grants 4428

Southern California Edison (SCE) is committed to helping customers when they need it the most. Since 1982, SCE has provided financial assistance to income-qualified customers through the Energy Assistance Fund (EAF), SCE's non-profit and only direct payment assistance program. EAF helps customers who meet income guidelines, many of whom are seniors, disabled, or are facing financial hardships. This fund is an important part of customer outreach efforts - especially in today's challenging economic environment - providing critical support to customers who are having difficulty paying their electric bills. A maximum of $100 is available to qualified customers once in a 12-month period.
Restrictions: Edison's grant programs do not support: individuals; private charities or foundations not aligned with our principle areas of charitable giving; religious organizations, unless the particular program will benefit a large portion of a community without regard to religious affiliation; political causes, candidates, organizations or campaigns; organizations whose primary purpose is to influence legislation; fraternities or sororities; endowments or capital campaigns; research studies or video projects, including student films and documentaries, unless related to initiatives Edison International is already supporting; local, regional or national sports teams or activities; medical research and disease-specific initiatives; medical procedures for individuals; tickets for contests, raffles or other activities with prizes; promotional merchandise; any group whose activities are not in the best interest of Edison International, its affiliates, employees, shareholders, customers or the communities it serves; or donations to charities in lieu of compensation to an individual for services rendered to the company (or any of its affiliates).
Geographic Focus: California

Amount of Grant: Up to 100 USD
Contact: Tammy Tumbling; (800) 990-7788 or (866) 840-6438; edison.gifts@sce.com
Internet: http://www.sce.com/CommunityandRecreation/CommunityGrantsandVolunteerSupport/CoreGivingAreas/civic.htm
Sponsor: Southern California Edison
P.O. Box 800
Rosemead, CA 91770

Southern California Edison Environmental Grants 4429
Edison invests significant resources in developing and nurturing partnerships with community-based organizations in SCE's service territory through targeted philanthropic giving in three areas of priority: education, the environment and the underserved. In the area of environment, Edison believes that protecting the environment makes good business sense for its customers, its shareholders and its long-term corporate interests. The corporation seeks to minimize its own environmental footprint, encourage energy efficiency, and support the work of organizations that educate and engage their communities in preserving a healthy and sustainable environment. Edison provides grants and sponsorships, typically up to $25,000. Applications for grants are accepted during the following funding cycles: March 1 to March 31; May 1 to May 31; August 1 to August 31; and October 1 to October 31 The majority of funding requests generally take between six and eight weeks for review. Organizations are eligible to receive one grant per calendar year.
Requirements: Eligibility for grants is open to non-profit and non-governmental organizations whose efforts align with the three focus areas of the company's philanthropic giving.
Restrictions: Edison's grant programs do not support: individuals; private charities or foundations not aligned with our principle areas of charitable giving; religious organizations, unless the particular program will benefit a large portion of a community without regard to religious affiliation; political causes, candidates, organizations or campaigns; organizations whose primary purpose is to influence legislation; fraternities or sororities; endowments or capital campaigns; research studies or video projects, including student films and documentaries, unless related to initiatives Edison International is already supporting; local, regional or national sports teams or activities; medical research and disease-specific initiatives; medical procedures for individuals; tickets for contests, raffles or other activities with prizes; promotional merchandise; any group whose activities are not in the best interest of Edison International, its affiliates, employees, shareholders, customers or the communities it serves; or donations to charities in lieu of compensation to an individual for services rendered to the company (or any of its affiliates).
Geographic Focus: California
Date(s) Application is Due: Mar 31; May 31; Aug 31; Oct 31
Amount of Grant: Up to 5,000 USD
Contact: Tammy Tumbling; (800) 990-7788 or (866) 840-6438; edison.gifts@sce.com
Internet: http://www.sce.com/CommunityandRecreation/CommunityGrantsandVolunteerSupport/CoreGivingAreas/environment.htm
Sponsor: Southern California Edison
P.O. Box 800
Rosemead, CA 91770

Southern California Edison Public Safety and Preparedness Grants 4430
Safety is the highest priority for Southern California Edison and is a constant in everything the company does. SCE is committed to the safety of the public and its employees. Preparedness is key to being able to best cope with emergencies, especially in the event of a major disaster or catastrophe. Whether its communities face downed power lines, an earthquake, fire or flood, preparedness will help to reduce the risks and enable a swift rescue, recovery or rebuilding effort to take place. SCE is committed to assisting communities to best prepare for the inevitable. Applications for grants are accepted during the following funding cycles: March 1 to March 31; May 1 to May 31; August 1 to August 31; and October 1 to October 31 The majority of funding requests generally take between six and eight weeks for review. Organizations are eligible to receive one grant per calendar year.
Restrictions: Edison's grant programs do not support: individuals; private charities or foundations not aligned with our principle areas of charitable giving; religious organizations, unless the particular program will benefit a large portion of a community without regard to religious affiliation; political causes, candidates, organizations or campaigns; organizations whose primary purpose is to influence legislation; fraternities or sororities; endowments or capital campaigns; research studies or video projects, including student films and documentaries, unless related to initiatives Edison International is already supporting; local, regional or national sports teams or activities; medical research and disease-specific initiatives; medical procedures for individuals; tickets for contests, raffles or other activities with prizes; promotional merchandise; any group whose activities are not in the best interest of Edison International, its affiliates, employees, shareholders, customers or the communities it serves; or donations to charities in lieu of compensation to an individual for services rendered to the company (or any of its affiliates).
Geographic Focus: California
Date(s) Application is Due: Mar 31; May 31; Aug 31; Oct 31
Contact: Tammy Tumbling; (800) 990-7788 or (866) 840-6438; edison.gifts@sce.com
Internet: http://www.sce.com/CommunityandRecreation/CommunityGrantsandVolunteerSupport/CoreGivingAreas/public-safety-preparedness.htm
Sponsor: Southern California Edison
P.O. Box 800
Rosemead, CA 91770

Southern Minnesota Initiative Foundation AmeriCorps Leap Grants 4431
Southern Minnesota Initiative Foundation has been a catalyst for economic growth in twenty Minnesota counties since 1986. The Foundation works to build a prosperous region with vibrant communities and innovative businesses. To accomplish this, the Foundation invests in strategic efforts in early childhood education and economic development. There are Grant opportunities for individuals and organizations/groups that focus on the social and emotional development of young children. Programs may engage an AmeriCorps member in service for eleven months. Members are recruited, connected, and matched to site service partner positions. Placements are made as members are engaged in the program. Members begin the LEAP service term the the last week in August and serve through the following July.
Requirements: Southern Minnesota 501(c)3 nonprofit organizations in existence for at least one year, local units of government, or public school districts serving the residents of the following counties are eligible: Blue Earth, Brown, Dodge, Faribault, Fillmore, Freeborn, Goodhue, Houston, Le Sueur, Martin, Mower, Nicollet, Olmsted, Rice, Sibley, Steele, Wabasha, Waseca, Watonwan, and Winona. For more information contact the Early Childhood Coordinator.
Geographic Focus: Minnesota
Contact: Teri Steckelberg; (507) 455-3215, ext. 132; teris@smifoundation.org
Internet: http://smifoundation.org/childed.php?sec=3#leap
Sponsor: Southern Minnesota Initiative Foundation
525 Florence Avenue, P.O. Box 695
Owatonna, MN 55060-0695

Southern Minnesota Initiative Foundation BookStart Grants 4432
Southern Minnesota Initiative Foundation has been a catalyst for economic growth in twenty Minnesota counties since 1986. The Foundation works to build a prosperous region with vibrant communities and innovative businesses. To accomplish this, the Foundation invests in strategic efforts in early childhood education and economic development. The Foundation's BookStart Grants provide books to organizations committed to distributing books and literacy programming directly to young people.
Requirements: Southern Minnesota 501(c)3 nonprofit organizations in existence for at least one year, local units of government, or public school districts serving the residents of the following counties are eligible: Blue Earth, Brown, Dodge, Faribault, Fillmore, Freeborn, Goodhue, Houston, Le Sueur, Martin, Mower, Nicollet, Olmsted, Rice, Sibley, Steele, Wabasha, Waseca, Watonwan, and Winona. Applications are available in March of each year. For more information about the Grants and the application process, contact the Early Childhood Coordinator.
Geographic Focus: Minnesota
Contact: Teri Steckelberg; (507) 455-3215, ext. 132; teris@smifoundation.org
Internet: http://smifoundation.org/childed.php?sec=3#bookstart
Sponsor: Southern Minnesota Initiative Foundation
525 Florence Avenue, P.O. Box 695
Owatonna, MN 55060-0695

Southern Minnesota Initiative Foundation Community Growth Initiative Grants 4433
Southern Minnesota Initiative Foundation has been a catalyst for economic growth in twenty Minnesota counties since 1986. The Foundation works to build a prosperous region with vibrant communities and innovative businesses. To accomplish this, the Foundation invests in strategic efforts in early childhood education and economic development. The Foundation's Community Growth Initiative Grants bring community members together to evaluate the assets of the community, set goals, and accomplish a project of choice. The Foundation provides facilitation, technical assistance, and up to $15,000 to assist asset based community development efforts that lead to economic growth and prosperity.
Requirements: Southern Minnesota 501(c)3 nonprofit organizations in existence for at least one year, local units of government, or public school districts serving the residents of the following counties are eligible: Blue Earth, Brown, Dodge, Faribault, Fillmore, Freeborn, Goodhue, Houston, Le Sueur, Martin, Mower, Nicollet, Olmsted, Rice, Sibley, Steele, Wabasha, Waseca, Watonwan, and Winona. Communities are selected through a request for proposal process. For information about applying including deadlines, contact the Grants Associate.
Geographic Focus: Minnesota
Contact: Jennifer Heien; (507) 455-3215; jenniferh@smifoundation.org
Internet: http://smifoundation.org/applications.php
Sponsor: Southern Minnesota Initiative Foundation
525 Florence Avenue, P.O. Box 695
Owatonna, MN 55060-0695

Southern Minnesota Initiative Foundation Home Visiting Grants 4434
Southern Minnesota Initiative Foundation has been a catalyst for economic growth in twenty Minnesota counties since 1986. The Foundation works to build a prosperous region with vibrant communities and innovative businesses. To accomplish this, the Foundation invests in strategic efforts in early childhood education and economic development. The Foundation's Home Visiting Grants enhance and increase visitation services. The Foundation is committed to ensuring that all young children thrive and have a healthy life of learning, achieving, and succeeding. Through home visiting programs, families expecting a child or having an infant voluntarily meet with a trained professional who provides information about the child's development, parenting support, and community resources. Measurable results of effective home visitation programs include increased immunization rates, increased enrollment in early learning classes and fewer incidences of abuse and neglect.
Requirements: Tax-exempt nonprofit organizations or units or agencies of local, state, or federal government located in or serving residents of the Foundation's twenty-county service area (Blue Earth, Brown, Dodge, Faribault, Fillmore, Freeborn, Goodhue, Houston, Le Sueur, Martin, Mower, Nicollet, Olmsted, Rice, Sibley, Steele, Wabasha, Waseca, Watonwan, and Winona counties) are eligible. For information about applying including deadlines, contact the Grants Associate.
Geographic Focus: Minnesota
Contact: Teri Steckelberg; (507) 455-3215, ext. 132; teris@smifoundation.org
Internet: http://smifoundation.org/childed.php?sec=3#homevisitation
Sponsor: Southern Minnesota Initiative Foundation
525 Florence Avenue, P.O. Box 695
Owatonna, MN 55060-0695

Southern Minnesota Initiative Foundation Incentive Grants 4435

Southern Minnesota Initiative Foundation has been a catalyst for economic growth in twenty Minnesota counties since 1986. The Foundation works to build a prosperous region with vibrant communities and innovative businesses. To accomplish this, the Foundation invests in strategic efforts in early childhood education and economic development. The Foundation's Incentive Grants support new asset-based approaches to current opportunities. Support for early childhood development projects prepare young children for a life of learning, achieving and succeeding. This may include early literacy projects, health promotion, kindergarten transition programs, programs that support social and emotional development, programs that support skilled and knowledgeable child care providers, or similar projects. Support for economic development projects help communities grow local business while building on the assets of the region. In particular, support is provided for partnerships which help increase the capacity of community/organizational efforts to support entrepreneurs and advance the development of bio science initiatives. Projects may include training, collaboration development and technical assistance programs, or similar projects.

Requirements: Tax-exempt nonprofit organizations or units or agencies of local, state, or federal government located in or serving residents of the Foundation's twenty-county service area (Blue Earth, Brown, Dodge, Faribault, Fillmore, Freeborn, Goodhue, Houston, Le Sueur, Martin, Mower, Nicollet, Olmsted, Rice, Sibley, Steele, Wabasha, Waseca, Watonwan, and Winona counties) are eligible. Priority consideration is given to applications which best demonstrate: asset-based approaches (projects that maximize the strengths, talents, and resources of the local community); collaboration and partnership (projects that work with other organizations in unique and effective ways); measurable results (projects that can show quantitative results in the Foundation's focus areas); sustainability of local or other funding streams (projects that have solid plans for continuation outside of Foundation funding); and leveraged funding (projects that access all available resources and maximize the Foundation's investment). All Grants require dollar-for-dollar match. At least twenty-five percent of the match must be cash in hand at the time of the award. No more than seventy-five percent of the match can be in-kind support. In-kind support is defined as goods or services (rather than cash) that are used to directly benefit the project. Grant applications are reviewed twice annually, with submission deadlines in February and August. For information about applying including deadlines, contact the Grants Associate.

Restrictions: The following are excluded: individuals, businesses, or other for-profit organizations; general operating expenses; capital campaigns or endowments; existing deficits or projects already in progress or completed; organizations that have not satisfied a past grant obligation; replacement of discontinued government funding; and funds for re-granting or to establish loan pools.
Geographic Focus: Minnesota
Amount of Grant: 20,000 USD
Contact: Jennifer Heien; (507) 455-3215, ext. 133; jenniferh@smifoundation.org
Internet: http://smifoundation.org/entre.php?sec=2#incgrants
Sponsor: Southern Minnesota Initiative Foundation
525 Florence Avenue, P.O. Box 695
Owatonna, MN 55060-0695

Southern Minnesota Initiative Foundation Youth Explorer Grants 4436

Southern Minnesota Initiative Foundation has been a catalyst for economic growth in twenty Minnesota counties since 1986. The Foundation works to build a prosperous region with vibrant communities and innovative businesses. To accomplish this, the Foundation invests in strategic efforts in early childhood education and economic development. Early childhood partners may apply to receive a "kid friendly" early learning computer station with science, math, reading and literacy focused software.

Requirements: Tax-exempt nonprofit organizations or units or agencies of local, state, or federal government located in or serving residents of the Foundation's twenty-county service area (Blue Earth, Brown, Dodge, Faribault, Fillmore, Freeborn, Goodhue, Houston, Le Sueur, Martin, Mower, Nicollet, Olmsted, Rice, Sibley, Steele, Wabasha, Waseca, Watonwan, and Winona counties) are eligible. Applications are available in the fall. For more information contact the Early Childhood Coordinator.
Geographic Focus: Minnesota
Date(s) Application is Due: Oct 1
Contact: Teri Steckelberg, (507) 455-3215, ext. 132; teris@smifoundation.org
Internet: http://smifoundation.org/childed.php?sec=3#youngexplorers
Sponsor: Southern Minnesota Initiative Foundation
525 Florence Avenue, P.O. Box 695
Owatonna, MN 55060-0695

Southern Minnesota Initiative Fund Grants 4437

Since 1986, Southern Minnesota Initiative Foundation (SMIF) has been a catalyst for economic growth in 20 Minnesota counties. It works to build a prosperous region with vibrant communities, innovative businesses and a skilled and valued workforce. To accomplish this, the Foundation invests in strategic efforts in emerging business and emerging workforce. It helps businesses, local governments and nonprofit organizations collaborate to find common ground, pool resources and achieve more. There are two funding periods, with pre-applications due March 2 and September 1, respectively.

Requirements: Eligible applicants include 501(c)3 nonprofits, government units serving the southern Minnesota area. The counties are: Blue Earth, Fillmore, Le Sueur, Olmsted, Wabasha, Brown, Freeborn, Martin, Rice, Waseca, Dodge, Goodhue, Mower, Sibley, Watonwan, Faribault, Houston, Nicollet, Steele, and Winona.
Geographic Focus: Minnesota
Date(s) Application is Due: Mar 2; Apr 17; Sep 1; Oct 16
Amount of Grant: Up to 20,000 USD
Contact: Suzy Meneguzzo; (507) 455-3215, ext. 118; suzym@smifoundation.org
Internet: http://smifoundation.org/new.php
Sponsor: Southeastern and Southcentral Minnesota Initiative Fund
525 Florence Avenue, P.O. Box 695
Owatonna, MN 55060-0695

Southern New England Folk and Traditional Arts Apprenticeship Grants 4438

Folk or traditional arts are those artistic practices that have an occupational, geographic, ethnic, community or family base, and are shared and understood by all as part of that community's aesthetic heritage. The apprenticeship grants are designed to foster the sharing of traditional artistic skills through the apprenticeship learning model of regular, intensive, one-on-one teaching by a master artist to a student/apprentice, both of whom share a common base, as defined above. Sponsored by the Institute for Community Research (Connecticut Cultural Heritage Arts Program), Rhode Island State Council on the Arts (Folk Arts Program) and Massachusetts Cultural Council (Folk and Traditional Arts Program), the apprenticeship grants enable masters and apprentices to travel and teach across state lines. Master artists may also apply to share their skills or repertoires with an equally accomplished master artist from the same community in another of the three states. Only one application is allowed per person. This year six to nine master/apprentice pairs will be selected to receive teaching contracts. The amount each pair will receive will depend on the number of contracts awarded. Previous amounts have been around $2000. Applicants are encouraged to contact the sponsor to verify current proposal deadline and submission requirements.

Requirements: Massachusetts, Rhode Island, and Connecticut residents may apply as master artists or apprentices. Master and apprentice artists must share an occupational, geographic, ethnic, community or family base. Most of the funding should go towards the master artist's fee. Modest materials and/or travel costs may be allowable. The Institute for Community Research generates and carefully monitors all contract work.
Geographic Focus: Connecticut, Massachusetts, Rhode Island
Date(s) Application is Due: Oct 13
Amount of Grant: 2,000 USD
Contact: Lynne Williamson, M.Litt., Director, Connecticut Cultural Heritage Arts Program; (860) 278-2044 ext. 251; fax (860) 278-2141; lynne.williamson@icrweb.org
Internet: http://www.arts.ri.gov/folkarts/FolkandTraditionalArtsGrantInfo.php
Sponsor: Rhode Island State Council on the Arts
One Capitol Hill, Third Floor
Providence, RI 02908

Southern Poverty Law Center Strategic Litigation Grants 4439

The program provides monetary grants to cover out-of-pocket litigation costs (such as expert fees, depositions, etc.) to help attorneys bring civil rights and other important cases that otherwise might not move forward. Project grants typically range from $2,500 to $10,000. The sponsor generally makes grants to cases that fall within the Legal Agenda (see http://www.splcenter.org/legal/agenda.jsp) or are commensurate with its legal history (see http://www.splcenter.org/legal/landmark/challenge.jsp).

Requirements: This program is available to attorneys only. Funds are available only for out-of-pocket case costs - not for attorney's fees or overhead expenses. To apply for a grant, attorneys must submit the following items: (1) Cover letter that states - nature of the case; importance of the case; why it would be difficult to bring the case without the Center's financial help; amount requested; and total estimated out-of-pocket case costs. (2) Draft Complaint - The project will consider requests for assistance in cases that have already been filed; however, the preference is to fund new cases.
Restrictions: The project will not consider financial assistance requests for cases on appeal that were lost at trial or on summary judgment.
Geographic Focus: All States
Amount of Grant: 2,500 - 10,000 USD
Contact: Rhonda Brownstein, Litigation and Legal Affairs Director; fax (334) 956-8200
Internet: http://www.splcenter.org/legal/assist/grant.jsp
Sponsor: Southern Poverty Law Center
400 Washington Avenue
Montgomery, AL 36104

South Madison Community Foundation Grants 4440

The South Madison Community Foundation (SMCF) Grants serves the residents in Adams, Fall Creek, Green, and Stony Creek Townships of Madison County. The Foundation has developed a procedure for submission and evaluation of grant proposals. The Grants Committee makes its recommendation to the Board of Directors who give final approval for funding. Applicants are notified within one month of the submission deadline of approval or denial of their request for funding. Online applications are available at the Foundation website. Organizations are encouraged to read the Tips for Submitting Effective Proposals on the Foundation website.

Requirements: With limited funds, the Foundation must distribute grant funding that gives the greatest positive impact on the needs and growth of South Madison county. Applicants should focus on projects that: focus on the prevention of problems rather than the symptoms, and make a significant improvement to the community; maintain a proactive focus and an ability to respond to creative ideas; respond to the changing needs of the community; encourage programs that enhance cooperation and collaboration among institutions within the community; and leverage funds through the use of match and challenge grants.
Restrictions: Note that Cycle One of the funding deadlines is funded with a smaller budget than the other funding cycle dates, so that applicants should apply for no more than $1,000. Because of time constraints, all proposals to the Foundation must be submitted in writing, so that no personal presentations are accepted. The following items will not be funded: operational expenses of existing programs; endowments or deficit funding; funds for redistribution by the grantee; conferences, publication, films, television and radio programs unless integral to the project for which the grant is sought; religious or political purposes; travel for individuals or groups such as bands, sports teams, and classes; annual appeals and membership contributions; and major capital improvements.

Geographic Focus: Indiana
Date(s) Application is Due: Feb 1; Jun 1; Oct 1
Amount of Grant: 150 - 10,000 USD
Contact: Barbara Switzer; (765) 778-8444; barbara@southmadisonfoundation.org
Internet: http://www.southmadisonfoundation.org/grants.html
Sponsor: South Madison Community Foundation
233 South Main Street
Pendleton, IN 46064

Southwest Florida Community Foundation Arts & Attractions Grants   4441
The program was established to use existing resources in Lee County to assist arts and attractions agencies, especially to encourage repeat visits, strengthen a need in the arts, provide the financial foundation that will encourage additional and create greater resources for growth, and partner with motivated professionals to maximize the expenditure and ensure a quality return on investments. Two types of grants will be offered: Marketing & Visitor Enhancement Grants and Basic Operating Grants.
Requirements: Marketing and Visitor Enhancement Grants: All Tourist Development Council funds will be granted to this grant category. Only Lee County 501(c)3 agencies will be eligible. Basic Operating Grants: These grants provide unrestricted funds for the general administration, operations and programs of arts and attractions organizations located in Lee County. These grants can be allocated for capital improvement purchases. Guidelines and the required application can be found at the sponsor's website.
Geographic Focus: Florida
Date(s) Application is Due: Jun 12
Contact: Carol McLaughlin, Chief Program Officer; (239) 274-5900, ext. 225; fax (239) 274-5930; cmclaughlin@floridacommunity.com
Internet: http://www.floridacommunity.com/grantseekers/applications/
Sponsor: Southwest Florida Community Foundation
8260 College Parkway, Suite 101
Fort Myers, FL 33919

Southwest Florida Community Foundation Competitive Grants   4442
Program/project grants are primarily for new or expanded programs and pilot or demonstration projects, which meet a documented need. Capital grants primarily support the construction, acquisition and renovation of facilities. The foundation offers competitive grants for programs and projects in eight focus areas: animal welfare, arts and culture, community development, conservation and preservation, education, the environment, health, and human services.
Requirements: IRS 501(c)3 tax-exempt organizations undertaking programs to improve the quality of life in Florida's Lee County and contiguous counties, including Charlotte, Collier, Gledes, and Hendry, are eligible. (NOTE: Agencies located in Collier County must also serve one of the other four counties in order to be eligible.) Applicants must employ staff, elect a governing board, and conduct business without discrimination on the basis of race, religion, gender, sexual orientation, age, national origin or disability.
Restrictions: The foundation generally will not fund: Normal operating expenses or existing obligations; Annual campaigns; Endowments; Sectarian purposes (i.e. programs that promote or require a religious doctrine except where designated by a donor); Debt retirement Monetary awards; Professional conferences, sports team travel, class trips, etc; Individuals; Fraternal organizations, societies, etc; Political organizations or campaigns; Fund-raising or feasibility studies; Research; or, Re-granting.
Geographic Focus: Florida
Date(s) Application is Due: Jun 19
Contact: Carol McLaughlin, Chief Program Officer; (239) 274-5900, ext. 225; fax (239) 274-5930; cmclaughlin@floridacommunity.com
Internet: http://www.floridacommunity.com/grantseekers/
Sponsor: Southwest Florida Community Foundation
8260 College Parkway, Suite 101
Fort Myers, FL 33919

Southwest Florida Community Foundation Good Samaritan Grants   4443
A limited amount of funding is available each year for one-time emergencies not covered by other sources. The foundation receives recommendations from charitable agencies, which have verified the need in advance. After consideration, the foundation determines its ability to make the grant. Grants are ordinarily in the range of $50 - $250 and must be made to the charitable 501(c)3 agency, which will be responsible for dispersing the funds to the individuals.
Requirements: Applications must be made by a charitable agency. Individual requests cannot be honored. Telephone requests from agencies are acceptable.
Restrictions: Limited to organizations in Lee, Charlotte, Hendry, Glades and Collier Counties.
Geographic Focus: Florida
Contact: Kathyrn Cintron, Donor Services Assistant; (239) 274-5900, ext. 227; fax (239) 274-5930; kcintron@floridacommunity.com
Internet: http://www.floridacommunity.com/grantseekers/
Sponsor: Southwest Florida Community Foundation
8260 College Parkway, Suite 101
Fort Myers, FL 33919

Southwest Florida Community Foundation Undergraduate and Grad Scholarships 4444
The foundation offers scholarships to undergraduate and graduate student in need of financial assistance to complete their college-level education. More than 17 scholarships are available in a directory listing at the foundation's website. Each scholarship is listed with the specific parameters as well as an application for that specific scholarship. Students may be eligible to apply for more than one scholarship.
Requirements: Scholarship eligibility requirements vary according to the specific wishes of each scholarship fund's donor. (Download the directory at http://www.floridacommunity.com/scholarships/college/.) Please look at each scholarship for information regarding specific eligibility requirements, scholarship dollar amount and whether the scholarship is for one year or four years of higher education. When applying for more than one scholarship, students must submit a separate set of back up documentation for each scholarship including transcripts.
Geographic Focus: Florida
Contact: Kathryn Cintron; (239) 274-5900, ext. 227; kcintron@floridacommunity.com
Internet: http://www.floridacommunity.com/scholarships/college/
Sponsor: Southwest Florida Community Foundation
8260 College Parkway, Suite 101
Fort Myers, FL 33919

Southwest Gas Corporation Foundation Grants   4445
The corporate foundation supports nonprofit organizations in its service communities. General support grants and employee matching gifts are made in the areas of education (universities, colleges, and literacy programs) and social services (United Way organizations, youth groups, community service, and volunteer organizations). Additional areas of interest are arts/culture and health. Types of support include general operating grants, projects grants, conferences and seminars, building construction/renovation, capital campaigns, emergency funds, employee matching gifts, research grants, donated equipment, and in-kind services. In southern Arizona, contact Marty Looney, P.O. Box 26500, Tucson, AZ 85726-6500; (520) 794-6416.
Requirements: Nonprofit organizations in Arizona; San Bernardino County, CA; and Nevada may apply.
Geographic Focus: Arizona, California, Nevada
Amount of Grant: Up to 620,567 USD
Contact: Suzanne Farinas; (702) 876-7247; fax (702) 876-7037
Internet: http://www.swgas.com
Sponsor: Southwest Gas Corporation
P.O. Box 98510
Las Vegas, NV 89193-8510

Southwest Initiative Foundation Grants   4446
The Southwest Initiative Foundation is a regional community foundation dedicated to advancing southwest Minnesota through leadership, relationship building, program development, and philanthropy. The Foundation works to ensure that southwest Minnesota is a highly productive and engaged region where growing numbers of people choose to live. Most Grants awarded have a strong connection to their current initiatives including: renewable energy; entrepreneurship; connected communities; early childhood; the Paul & Alma Schwan Aging Trust Fund; and the Student Enrichment Fund. Grants generally range from $1,000 to $20,000 and require a fifty percent match through in-kind and other cash contributions.
Requirements: Proposals must demonstrate a benefit within the following eighteen counties in southwest Minnesota: Big Stone, Chippewa, Cottonwood, Jackson, Kandiyohi, Lac qui Parle, Lincoln, Lyon, McLeod, Meeker, Murray, Nobles, Pipestone, Redwood, Renville, Rock, Swift, and Yellow Medicine. The Foundation prefers applicants located within the eighteen-county area it serves and that ideas and visions are generated locally. Applicants must be a 501(c)3 organization, a unit of government, or a public agency. Successful proposals should: include involvement early in the proposed project and throughout implementation by targeted and diverse populations; incorporate an innovative approach and avoid duplication of efforts; have clearly stated goals and measurable outcomes; and exhibit evidence of appropriate partnerships. Applicants complete an online pre-application questionnaire and after submission are either invited to make a full application or declined. Contact the Senior Administration and Grants Officer with questions.
Restrictions: Funding for the following is generally ineligible: capital expenditures; religious purposes or activities; lobbying or political activities; for-profit businesses; debt retirement; ongoing, open ended grant funding; administrative budgets for existing organizations; arts; programs or services mandated by law or to replace government funding; and national fundraising campaigns, ticket sales, fundraising dinners, endowment drives, or other similar activities. Churches and religious organizations may apply for support for activities that benefit the larger community but not for activities that have a sectarian religious purpose.
Geographic Focus: Minnesota
Contact: Nancy Fasching, Senior Administration and Grants Officer; (320) 587-5858 or (800) 594-9480; fax (320) 587-3838; nancyf@swifoundation.org
Internet: http://www.swifoundation.org/grants.html
Sponsor: Southwest Initiative Foundation
15 3rd Avenue NW
Hutchinson, MN 55350

Southwire Company Grants   4447
The company awards grants to nonprofits located in company-operating communities in Cleburne and Randolph Counties, AL; Mississippi County, AR; Mohave County, AZ; Carroll, Clarke and Oconee, GA; Daviess and Hancock Counties, KY; Oktibeeha County, MS; and Clay County, IL. Corporate community relations supports local community health and development, families in need, at-risk youth, disadvantaged youth, youth education, and religious development. The one-year grants vary in size. Requests are reviewed monthly. Interested applicants should apply at least 45 days prior to the date funding is needed.
Requirements: Requests must be in writing. In Georgia and Alabama: Southwire Company, 1 Southwire Drive, Carrollton, GA 30119; in Arkansas: Southwire Company, Arkansas Plant, P.O. Box 685, Osceola, AR 72370; in Kentucky: Southwire Company, Kentucky Plant, P.O. Box 500, Hawesville, KY 42348; in Illinois: Southwire Company, Flora Plant, Eash Road, Flora, IL 62839; in Mississippi: Southwire Company, Starkville Plant, 103 Airport Road, P.O. Box 967, Starkville, MS 39759; in Texas: Integral Corporation, P.O.

Box 151369, Dallas, TX 75223; and in Utah: Southwire Company, Utah Plant, 3295 West 8600 S, West Jordon, UT 84088.
Restrictions: The company does not make contributions to individuals; political, labor, athletic, or social groups; advertising campaigns; or fundraising benefits.
Geographic Focus: Alabama, Arkansas, Georgia, Illinois, Kentucky, Mississippi, Texas, Utah
Contact: Community Relations Manager; (800) 444-1700 or (770) 832-4242; fax (770) 832-4929; gift@southwire.com
Internet: http://www.southwire.com
Sponsor: Southwire Company
1 Southwire Drive
Carrollton, GA 30119

Spartan Foundation Grants 4448
Established in 2006 in West Virginia, the Spartan Foundation gives primarily throughout the State of West Virginia. Its foremost area of interest is the support of public libraries. Types of support include: equipment purchase, ongoing operations, and materials securement. A specific application form is required, and applicants should begin by contacting the Foundation by mail. There are no specific deadlines.
Requirements: 501(c)3 organizations serving the residents of West Virginia should apply.
Restrictions: Grants are not given to individuals.
Geographic Focus: West Virginia
Date(s) Application is Due: Feb 8
Contact: Harry H. Esbenshade, Junior President; (304) 295-3311
Sponsor: Spartan Foundation
166 60th Street
Parkersburg, VA 26105-8002

Special Olympics Project UNIFY Grants 4449
Following the groundswell of enthusiasm and interest from the 2009 Global Youth Activation Summit, Special Olympics Project UNIFY has announced funding opportunities for youth advocates across North America. Special Olympics' Project UNIFY is a U.S. national program, funded by the U.S. Department of Education. The goal of Project UNIFY is to activate youth around the country in an effort to develop school communities where all young people are agents of change - fostering respect, dignity and advocacy for people with intellectual disabilities by utilizing the programs and initiatives of Special Olympics. The Program's intent is to provide Sub Award (Grant) opportunities of up to $5,000 for youth to implement projects that demonstrate the principles of Project UNIFY and the eight motions of the Global Youth Activation Summit Assembly.
Requirements: To be eligible for consideration for this sub award (grant), you must be at least 12 years of age up to 20 years, or a current undergraduate student in college. A Special Olympics North America Program is required to be your main partner organization.
Geographic Focus: All States
Date(s) Application is Due: Dec 31
Contact: Oscar J. Harrell; (202) 824-0269; oharrell@specialolympics.org
Internet: http://www.specialolympics.org/project_unify_grants.aspx
Sponsor: Special Olympics
1133 19th Street, NW
Washington, DC 20036-3604

Speer Trust Grants 4450
The purpose of the Trust is to assist organizations in Delaware or the Eastern Shore of Maryland addressing poverty by encouraging the poor to gain responsibility and control over their lives. Projects or programs should provide an opportunity to partner with members of the Presbyterian Church. An online application is available at the website.
Requirements: Eligible applicants must be a 501(c)3 organization with a Board of Directors; provide services in Delaware or the Eastern Shore of Maryland; and work in partnership with a Presbyterian church on the proposed project.
Restrictions: Organizations are funded only once a year. A second year of funding is provided only if there is an expansion or new component of the previous project. Organizations that are not 501(c)3 tax-exempt or that do not have a Board of Directors are not necessarily denied but may not qualify for the amount requested.
Geographic Focus: Delaware, Maryland
Date(s) Application is Due: Apr 1; Oct 15
Contact: Jacqueline Taylor; (302) 366-0595; SpeerOffice@ncpresbytery.org
Internet: http://www.speertrust.org/Apply.asp
Sponsor: Speer Trust
256 Chapman Road, Suite 205
Newark, DE 19702

Spencer County Community Foundation Grants 4451
The Spencer County Community Foundation is a nonprofit, public charity created for the people of Spencer County, Indiana. The Foundation helps nonprofits fulfill their missions by strengthening their ability to meet community needs through grants that assist charitable programs, address community issues, support community agencies, launch community initiatives, and support leadership development. Priority funding areas include arts and culture; community development; education; health; human services; environment; recreation; and youth development. Grant proposals are accepted once each year according to the grant cycle. Grants are normally given as one time support of a project but may be considered for additional support for expansions or outgrowths of an initial project. Proposals will be accepted from mid-January through mid-March. Grant awards will be presented in June. The application, supporting materials, and examples of previously funded project are available at the Foundation website.
Requirements: The Foundation welcomes proposals from nonprofit organizations that are tax exempt under sections 501(c)3 and 509(a) and from governmental agencies serving the county. Proposals from nonprofit organizations not classified as a 501(c)3 public charity may be considered if the project is charitable and supports a community need. Proposals submitted by an entity under the auspices of another agency must include a written statement signed by the agency's board president on behalf of the board of directors agreeing to act as the entity's fiscal sponsor, to receive grant monies if awarded, and to oversee the proposed project.
Restrictions: Project areas not considered for funding: religious organizations for religious purposes; political parties or campaigns; endowment creation or debt reduction; operating costs; capital campaigns; annual appeals or membership contributions; travel requests for groups or individuals such as bands, sports teams, or classes.
Geographic Focus: Indiana
Contact: Laura Harmon; (812) 649-5724; laura@spencercommunityfoundation.org
Internet: http://www.spencercommunityfoundation.org/disc-grants
Sponsor: Spencer County Community Foundation
Lincoln Commerce Center
Rockport, IN 47635

Sport Manitoba Athlete/Team Travel Assistance Grants 4452
Individual sport athletes trying out for a Provincial Team or participating in a sanctioned Provincial or Manitoba High Schools Athletic Association Championship are eligible to receive assistance of up to $100. Teams participating in a sanctioned Provincial or Manitoba High Schools Athletic Association Championship are eligible to receive assistance of up to $300. Individual sport athletes and teams from remote communities traveling to events in the Norman Region are eligible to receive up to $150 for individuals and $500 for teams. Individual athletes and teams are eligible to receive one grant per sport annually.
Requirements: It is expected that the championship or camp will be targeted at youth, generally from ages 7 to 21. Athletes/Teams are required to travel a minimum of 300 kms total at their own expense. Any travel over and above the minimum 300 kms is eligible for assistance up to the maximums stated in the funding levels. If a championship is 150 kms from residence and the event is three days long, the total distance traveled would be 900 kms. Travel assistance would be available for 900kms - 300kms = 600 kms. Individual sport athletes traveling from a community/club to a provincial championship (i.e. Swim Club) may be grouped under team sport funding levels to a maximum of $300. Guidelines and application are available at the website.
Restrictions: All travel will be confirmed with the appropriate Provincial Sport Organization.
Geographic Focus: All States, Canada
Amount of Grant: 100 - 500 CAD
Contact: Regional Manager; (204) 925-5907; fax (204) 925-5916; info@sport.mb.ca
Internet: http://sportmanitoba.ca/communitysports/grants.php
Sponsor: Sport Manitoba
200 Main Street
Winnipeg, MB R3C 4M2 Canada

Sport Manitoba Athlete Skill Development Clinics Grants 4453
Funding of up to $300 CAN is available to a community sport partner working with a Provincial Sport Organization (PSO) for hosting a skill development clinic targeted at youth. Remote communities are eligible for a grant of up to $500 CAN. Funding is cost-shared between the community (50%) and Sport Manitoba (50%). Elgible expenses can inlcude: Clinicians honoraria; travel, accommodations and meals if required; Facility rental; Expendable equipment (i.e. tennis balls, pucks etc.); Advertising and promotion costs; and/or Administration costs.
Requirements: It is expected that the program/clinic/camp will be targeted at youth, generally from ages 7 to 21. Only community based, not for profit, sport-recreation groups that are recognized by Sport Manitoba may apply. This includes the following Community Sport Partners: a) Local sport teams/clubs and regional sport associations who are affiliated with their respective Provincial Sport Organization; b) Regional Sport Specific Associations who are associated to their respective PSO; c) General Council of Winnipeg Community Centres' member clubs d) Elementary, Junior-Middle and Senior High Schools; e) Municipal Recreation departments and recreation districts which are recognized and supported by the Province of Manitoba's Culture, Heritage and Tourism's Recreation Department & Regional Services Branch and Aboriginal and Northern Affairs; f) City of Winnipeg's Community Services Department or City of Winnipeg's Community Services Department and co-Sponsored Organizations; g) First Nations and Aboriginal & Northern Affairs Communities; h) Community Sport Alliances.
Restrictions: Funds cannot be used for: Participant meals, awards, t-shirts/gifts, participant travel; or non-expendable equipment (i.e. permanent club or organization owned equipment like volleyball standards, tennis nets, softball/baseball bases, bats etc.). There is a maximum of one clinic/camp sport per community sport partner/per year. All Instructors must be recognized by the PSO.
Geographic Focus: All States, Canada
Contact: Regional Manager; (866) 774-2220; fax (204) 925-5916; info@sport.mb.ca
Internet: http://www.sportmanitoba.ca/communitysports/grants.php
Sponsor: Sport Manitoba
200 Main Street
Winnipeg, MB R3C 4M2 Canada

Sport Manitoba Bingo Allocations Grants 4454
Funding of up to $3,000 is available to a community sport partner working with a Provincial Sport Organization through a Sport Manitoba allocated bingo event. Funding must be used to support the hosting of a major event or championship or for sport development opportunities that leave a sport or equipment legacy in the community.
Requirements: Regional Sport Council bingos will be allocated to support any/all of the following: special grants to support the hosting of major events/championships that will

leave a legacy for sport; special grants to support sport development opportunities that will leave a legacy for sport; new or existing programs that your Regional Sport Council would deliver with a sport partner. Before applying, contact your regional manager.
Geographic Focus: All States, Canada
Amount of Grant: Up to 3,000 USD
Contact: Regional Manager; (866) 774-2220; fax (204) 925-5916; info@sport.mb.ca
Internet: http://www.sportmanitoba.ca/communitysports/grants.php
Sponsor: Sport Manitoba
200 Main Street
Winnipeg, MB R3C 4M2 Canada

Sport Manitoba Coaches/Officials Travel Assistance Grants 4455
Assistance of up $200 is available to coaches attending recognized National Coaches Certification Clinics (Theory or Technical), to coaches participating in Coaching Manitoba or PSO (Provincial Sport Organization) sponsored seminars/conferences and volunteer officials attending recognized Officials Certification Clinics.
Requirements: Courses offered outside Manitoba may be eligible based upon circumstances within sport and or level of course. Coaches/Officials are eligible for 10 cents per km up to a maximum of $200.00 per sport per year.
Restrictions: All travel will be confirmed with each respective Provincial Sport Organization.
Geographic Focus: All States, Canada
Amount of Grant: Up to 200 CAD
Contact: Regional Manager; (866) 774-2220; fax (204) 925-5916; info@sport.mb.ca
Internet: http://sportmanitoba.ca/communitysports/grants.php
Sponsor: Sport Manitoba
200 Main Street
Winnipeg, MB R3C 4M2 Canada

Sport Manitoba Hosting Regional Championships Grants 4456
Funding of up to $300 is available to community sport partners for the hosting of a regional championship for youth athletes that leads to a sanctioned Provincial Championship, supports Manitoba Games competition in a non-Games year or supports regional team selection for the Manitoba Indigenous Summer Games. Funding is cost-shared between the community and Sport Manitoba. Funds can be used for facility rental, expendable field of play equipment (i.e. tennis balls, pucks etc.), officials honoraria, or travel, meals and accommodations if required.
Requirements: It is expected that the championship will be targeted at youth, generally from ages 7 to 21. Regional championships must be a separate competition from league play. The event must either lead to a Provincial Sport Organization sanctioned provincial championship; or will support Manitoba Games Competitions in a non-games year. The age category and competition format must allow for participants to be eligible for the next Manitoba Games Competition. (i.e. if the age category for the Manitoba Games in baseball is 13-14 years old, the competition that takes place the year before the Manitoba Games should be 12-13 years old.). Sport Manitoba may provide funding for hosting events for the purpose of selecting regional teams/athletes to participate in the Manitoba Indigenous Games (M.I.G.).
Restrictions: League competitions are not eligible for assistance. Funds cannot be used for awards, t-shirts/gifts, banquets/meals, or for non-expendable equipment (i.e. permanent club or organization owned equipment like volleyball standards, tennis nets, softball/baseball bases, bats etc.)
Geographic Focus: All States, Canada
Amount of Grant: Up to 300 CAD
Contact: Regional Manager; (866) 774-2220; fax (204) 925-5916; info@sport.mb.ca
Internet: http://www.sportmanitoba.ca/communitysports/grants.php
Sponsor: Sport Manitoba
200 Main Street
Winnipeg, MB R3C 4M2 Canada

Sport Manitoba Introduction of a New Sport Grants 4457
Funding of up to $300 is available to a community sport partner working with a Provincial Sport Organization for the introduction of a new sport through establishment of a team, club or league in the community. Remote communities are eligible for a grant of up to $500. Funding is cost-shared between the community and Sport Manitoba.
Requirements: The introduction of a sport means that the sport must not have been offered at any level in the community for the past two years. In relation to a school based 'introduction of a new sport,' the sport must be extracurricular based (not curriculum based) and the new sport must demonstrate training, competitions and led by a qualified coach. It is expected that the program will be targeted at youth, generally ages 7 - 21. Applicants are responsible for at least 50% of eligible expenses. Funds may be used for purchase of new non-expendable equipment that meets the sport's minimum technical/field of play standards and/or organizational costs (promotion, advertising, facility rental). A Community Sport Partner may apply for 2 consecutive years. Guidelines and application are available at the website.
Restrictions: Communities are eligible to receive one grant per sport annually. Any equipment purchased with the grant may not be personally owned, and must be organization or club owned, equipment. The funds are not for the purchase of expendable equipment such as balls, player uniforms or warm up clothes, etc. If the Club/Organization ceases operation the equipment must be returned to the appropriate regional sport office.
Geographic Focus: All States, Canada
Amount of Grant: 300 - 500 CAD
Contact: Regional Manager; (866) 774-2220; fax (204) 925-5916; info@sport.mb.ca
Internet: http://www.sportmanitoba.ca/communitysports/grants.php
Sponsor: Sport Manitoba
200 Main Street
Winnipeg, MB R3C 4M2 Canada

GRANT PROGRAMS | 691

Sport Manitoba KidSport Athlete Grants 4458
KidSport is national charity administered by Sport Manitoba that helps to remove barriers and assist less fortunate children participate in sport - so all kids can play. Based on demonstrated need, assistance of up to $300 per individual is available to children between the ages of 5 and 18 to help offset the cost of registration fees. Provincial Sport Organizations must recognize planned activities. Application deadlines for all regions are April 30th and October 15th of each year. Winnipeg Region also has an additional application deadline of July 15th. Applicants who have been identified by their provincial sport organization as a high performance provincial level athlete are eligible for assistance of up to $500 per individual based on demonstrated need.
Requirements: Financial assistance to individual athletes is designed to help children ages 5-18 who would not play a sport without KidSport. Preference is given to children being introduced to a sport. Sport activities must be affiliated with organizations recognized by Sport Manitoba. Funds are given for structured sport activities led by a qualified coach. Financial assistance is disbursed up to a maximum of $300 in a calendar year per athlete. Sport activities must be affiliated with organizations recognized by Sport Manitoba. Costs relating to camps, travel, championships, etc. do not qualify. For high performance athletes, other requirements apply - the maximum amount is $500 and costs relating to camps, travel, championships etc. do qualify. Applications are available for download at the website.
Restrictions: Funds are sent directly to the sport organization.
Geographic Focus: All States, Canada
Contact: Regional Manager; (866) 774-2220; fax (204) 925-5916; info@sport.mb.ca
Internet: http://sportmanitoba.ca/programs/kidsport.php
Sponsor: Sport Manitoba
200 Main Street
Winnipeg, MB R3C 4M2 Canada

Sport Manitoba Sport Special Initiatives Grants 4459
Funding of up to $500 is available to a community sport partner working with a Provincial Sport Organization for a project, activity or event that would assist in the development of community based sport and is not eligible under any other Sport Manitoba grant. Projects should contain an educational component. Funding is cost-shared between the community and Sport Manitoba. Communities are eligible to receive one grant annually.
Requirements: Only community based, not for profit, sport-recreation groups that are recognized by Sport Manitoba may apply. This includes the following Community Sport Partners: a) Local sport teams/clubs and regional sport associations who are affiliated with their respective Provincial Sport Organization; b) Regional Sport Specific Associations who are associated to their respective PSO; c) General Council of Winnipeg Community Centres' member clubs d) Elementary, Junior-Middle and Senior High Schools; e) Municipal Recreation departments and recreation districts which are recognized and supported by the Province of Manitoba's Culture, Heritage and Tourism's Recreation Department & Regional Services Branch and Aboriginal and Northern Affairs; f) City of Winnipeg's Community Services Department or City of Winnipeg's Community Services Department and co-Sponsored Organizations; g) First Nations and Aboriginal & Northern Affairs Communities; h) Community Sport Alliances. The funding request must clearly outline how that initiative will assist in meeting the needs of the athletes, coaches, officials or volunteers. The project, event or activity should contain an educational component. Regional Sport Specific Associations are eligible to apply for developmental funding. Before applying please contact your respective regional manager.
Geographic Focus: All States, Canada
Contact: Regional Manager; (866) 774-2220; fax (204) 925-5916; info@sport.mb.ca
Internet: http://www.sportmanitoba.ca/communitysports/grants.php
Sponsor: Sport Manitoba
200 Main Street
Winnipeg, MB R3C 4M2 Canada

Sport Manitoba Women to Watch Grants 4460
A major initiative is the Women to Watch Grant Program. Working in partnership with Provincial Sport Organizations and Coaching Manitoba, Sport Manitoba provides a monthly grant of $500 to a female athlete, team, official or volunteer to assist them in enhancing their women in sport career. A $500 monthly grant is also awarded to a female coach to assist them in further developing the skills necessary to attain a higher level of coaching or increased level of coaching experience. Grants may be used to offset costs such as training, travel, certification, sport equipment, competitions/tournaments, camps, leadership development, professional development and child care costs related to future development in their sport.
Requirements: Applicants must be female and a member of their provincial sport organization in good standing as an athlete, coach, official or in a leadership position either as a volunteer or paid staff. The application must be endorsed by the PSO with a commitment to matching the $250 grant from Sport Manitoba/Coaching Manitoba.
Geographic Focus: All States, Canada
Date(s) Application is Due: Mar 15; Jul 15; Nov 30
Contact: Shawnee Scatliff; (204) 885-7400; fax (204) 925-5916; sscatliff@mts.net
Internet: http://sportmanitoba.ca/programs/womensport.php
Sponsor: Sport Manitoba
200 Main Street
Winnipeg, MB R3C 4M2 Canada

Sprague Foundation Grants 4461
Grants are made to hospitals, arts and cultural organizations, civic and community affairs, educational institutions, and health and human service organizations and charities located in New York and Massachusetts. Types of support include general operating support, matching and challenge funds, and program development. The initial approach should be a letter requesting the foundation's guidelines. Grants are awarded at the June and December board meetings.

Requirements: Only residents of New York and Massachusetts may apply.
Restrictions: No grants are provided to individuals, for building funds, or for loans.
Geographic Focus: Massachusetts, New York
Date(s) Application is Due: Apr 15; Oct 1
Amount of Grant: 1,000 - 55,000 USD
Contact: Linda Franciscovich, c/o U.S. Trust Company of New York, (212) 852-3377
Sponsor: Seth Sprague Educational and Charitable Foundation
114 W 47th Street
New York, NY 10036-1532

Springs Close Foundation Grants 4462

Since it was chartered in 1942, the Springs Close Foundation has contributed over $85 million to a wide variety of charitable and educational causes designed to improve the quality of life and well-being of the people in Chester, Lancaster and York Counties. Support includes, but is not limited to, food, shelter and medical assistance. This temporary change in focus is in response to high levels of unemployment and economic distress in the Foundation's service areas. The Foundation also makes occasional statewide grants in South Carolina. There are three major areas of program interest: Recreation and Environment, Public Education and Early Childhood Development, Community Service and Health
Requirements: Grants are made only to organizations that are tax-exempt under Section 501(c)3 of the Internal Revenue Code. No grants are made to individuals.
Restrictions: The Foundation will only consider grant requests from eligible nonprofit organizations that can effectively deliver emergency and basic support to citizens in Chester and Lancaster counties and a portion of York County.
Geographic Focus: South Carolina
Date(s) Application is Due: Mar 1; Oct 1
Amount of Grant: 5,000 - 50,000 USD
Contact: Angela McCrae, President; (803) 548-2002; fax (803) 548-1797
Internet: http://www.thespringsclosefoundation.org/grants.htm
Sponsor: Springs Close Foundation
1826 Second Baxter Crossing
Fort Mill, SC 29708

Sprint Foundation Grants 4463

The foundation's charitable giving program emphasizes support of nonprofit local and regional organizations in those communities in which the corporation has a major presence. The foundation focuses its contributions in four major areas of interest. Education—programs that increase and improve student achievement, family engagement and professional development for educators; K-12 education; and higher education through its Matching Gift program, as well as through partnerships with the United Negro College Fund, the Hispanic College Fund, and targeted MBA programs and undergraduate institutions to provide financial assistance and employment opportunities for students pursuing degrees in business and technology-related fields. Unsolicited scholarship requests will not be considered for funding. Arts and Culture—visual and performing arts organizations, theater, symphonies, museums, and other cultural organizations and activities that contribute to a thriving and diverse community. Youth Development—mentoring programs, minority youth endeavors, broad-scale community youth activities focused on building leadership and social skills, and programs that support business and economic education for youth. Community Development—regional initiatives that contribute to a strong civic infrastructure and a vibrant, healthy community; and, on a national level, the foundation matches funds raised for its national food drive and United Way pledges made by Sprint employees who participate in the corporation's national campaign. Types of support include general operating support, continuing support, annual campaigns, capital campaigns, program development, and employee matching gifts. The foundation accepts proposals throughout the year.
Requirements: 501(c)3 organizations in Atlanta, Boston, Chicago, Dallas, Kansas City, Las Vegas, Los Angeles, New York City, Orlando, San Francisco and the District of Columbia are eligible; however, these areas are subject to change. Support of national organizations with a broad sphere of interests will be considered on a case-by-case basis. The foundation's geographic focus is primarily domestic.
Restrictions: Organizations generally excluded from the foundation's grantmaking activities include political, religious, fraternal, labor, and veterans organizations; hospitals; and neighborhood associations. No grants are made to individuals.
Geographic Focus: All States
Contact: David Thomas, Executive Director; (913) 624-3343; fax (913) 624-3490
Internet: http://www.sprint.com/community/sprint_foundation/index.html
Sponsor: Sprint Foundation
2330 Shawnee Mission Parkway
Westwood, KS 66205

Square D Foundation Grants 4464

The foundation makes donations for operating support, capital development needs, and special projects to nonprofit organizations in the areas of education, social welfare, arts and cultural and civic affairs, and health. Each year the foundation supports United Way in communities where the company and its domestic subsidiaries have significant operations. Donations are not normally made to organizations already receiving support through United Way. Support of higher education is achieved through scholarships, endowments for faculty and acquisition or expansion of equipment or facilities, unrestricted operating support, and the matching gift program. Submit letters of application between June and August.
Requirements: Giving primarily to 501(c)3 tax-exempt organizations in areas of company operations, with emphasis on: Illinois; Indiana; Iowa; Kentucky; Missouri; Nebraska; North Carolina; Ohio; South Carolina; Tennessee; and Wisconsin.
Restrictions: Grants are not made to religious organizations for religious purposes, political groups and organizations, labor unions and organizations, organizations making requests by telephone, organizations listed by the U.S. attorney general as subversive, or to individuals.
Geographic Focus: Illinois, Indiana, Iowa, Kentucky, Nebraska, North Carolina, Tennessee, Texas, Wisconsin
Date(s) Application is Due: Aug 31
Amount of Grant: Up to 27,000,000 USD
Contact: Harry Wilson, Secretary; (847) 397-2600
Internet: http://www.squared.com
Sponsor: Square D Foundation
1415 South Roselle Road
Palatine, IL 60067

SSA Work Incentives Planning and Assistance (WIPA) Projects 4465

The overall goal of the Work Incentives Planning and Assistance (WIPA) Program is to better enable SSA's beneficiaries with disabilities to make informed choices about work. The major purpose of these projects is to disseminate accurate information to beneficiaries with disabilities (including transition-to-work aged youth) about work incentives programs and issues related to such programs, to enable them to make informed choices about working and whether or when to assign their Ticket to Work, as well as how available work incentives can facilitate their transition into the workforce. Subject to the availability of funds, SSA anticipates minimum awards of $100,000 for individual state WIPA projects (minimum awards for territories will remain at $50,000) and a maximum of $300,000 will be available to fund specific WIPA projects annually. Awardees are required to contribute a non-Federal match of project costs of at least 5% of the total project cost. The non-Federal share may be cash or in-kind (property or services). Awards made under this announcement may be renewed annually through FY 2009. A cooperative agreement may be awarded to any State or local government (excluding any State administering the State Medicaid program), public or private organization, or nonprofit or for-profit organization (for profit organizations may apply with the understanding that no cooperative agreement funds may be paid as profit to any awardee), as well as Native American tribal organizations that the Commissioner determines is qualified to provide work incentives planning, assistance and outreach services to all SSDI and SSI beneficiaries with disabilities, within the targeted geographic area. The deadline is July 1, with Letters of Intent due by May 30.
Requirements: States, local governments, the District of Columbia, Puerto Rico, U.S. territories, and nonprofit and for-profit organizations are eligible to apply.
Geographic Focus: All States
Date(s) Application is Due: Jul 1
Amount of Grant: 50,000 - 300,000 USD
Contact: Regina Bowden, Project Officer, Office of Employment Support Programs; (410) 965-7145 or (800) 772-1213; regina.bowden@ssa.gov
Internet: http://www.socialsecurity.gov/work/ServiceProviders/wipafactsheet.html
Sponsor: Social Security Administration
6401 Security Boulevard, 107 Altmeyer Building
Baltimore, MD 21235-6401

SSHRC Therese F. Casgrain Fellowship 4466

The Therese F. Casgrain Fellowship supports research on women and social change in Canada. This Fellowship supports research in the field of social justice, particularly in defense of individual rights and the promotion of the economic and social interests of Canadian women. The Foundation is particularly interested in research that includes a discussion of public policy options and makes concrete recommendations for change. The non-renewable Fellowship, tenable for 12 months and only in Canada, is available every fourth year. The award consists of a $40,000 stipend, paid in three installments, of which up to $10,000 may be used for travel and research expenses. The successful applicant must take up the award between April 1 and October 1 following the announcement of awards.
Requirements: Applicants must be Canadian citizens or permanent residents of Canada, hold a doctorate degree or equivalent advanced professional degree, have at least five years of proven research experience, and not be under SSHRC sanction for financial or research misconduct. Affiliation with a university or an appropriate research institute or similar organization is desirable, but is not a condition of the award.
Geographic Focus: Canada
Contact: Grants Contact; (613) 943-7777; fax (613) 943-1329; fellowships@sshrc-crsh.gc.ca
Internet: http://www.sshrc-crsh.gc.ca/funding-financement/programs-programmes/fellowships/casgrain-eng.aspx
Sponsor: Social Sciences and Humanities Research Council of Canada
350 Albert Street, P.O. Box 1610
Ottawa, ON K1P 6G4 Canada

SSRC-Van Alen Fellowships 4467

The SSRC-Van Alen New York Prize Fellowships support work on the intersection between social dynamics and the built environment. Since its inception, two rounds of Fellowships have been offered in collaboration with the Van Alen Institute, an independent nonprofit architectural organization, on issues of urban sustainability and the 'spatialization' of information policy. Grants are awarded to partnerships between social scientists and architectural/design specialists. Investigations may take a range of formats, including installations, demonstrations, performances, and workshops, but are by their involvement of the general public. Additional information is available at the SSRC website.
Geographic Focus: All States
Contact: Joe Karaganis; (718) 517-3673 or (212) 377-2700; karaganis@ssrc.org
Internet: http://www.ssrc.org/fellowships/ssrc-van-alen-fellows-program/
Sponsor: Social Science Research Council
One Pierrepont Plaza, 15th Floor
Brooklyn, NY 11201

St. Joseph Community Health Foundation Catherine Kasper Award   4468
The Blessed Mary Catherine Kasper Award for Outstanding Service to the Poor. This is a $1,500 award established in honor of the Foundress of the Poor Handmaids of Jesus Christ. These awards are given to agencies who typically do not qualify for the Foundation's regular health care access grants, but who provide exceptional service and /or basic needs for the poor in Allen County, Indiana. The Foundation will consider requests for program, program-related equipment, staff continuing education, and technical assistance. The Foundation will commit support on an annual basis only.
Requirements: Applicants should have a demonstrated history of serving poor and powerless populations residing in Allen County, Indiana. Applicants should be not-for-profit entities classified as 501(c)3 by the Internal Revenue Service.
Restrictions: Grant applications will not be accepted for building projects, elimination of deficits, support of political activities, individuals, or projects all ready completed.
Geographic Focus: Indiana
Date(s) Application is Due: Mar 1; Jun 1; Sep 1; Dec 1
Amount of Grant: 1,500 USD
Contact: Meg Distler; (260) 969-2001, ext. 201; fax (260) 969-2004; mdistler@sjchf.org
Internet: http://www.stjosephhealthfdn.org/index.php?option=com_content&view=article&id=84&Itemid=69
Sponsor: St. Joseph Community Health Foundation
2826 South Calhoun Street
Fort Wayne, IN 46807

St. Joseph Community Health Foundation Improving Healthcare Access Grants   4469
The St. Joseph Community Health Foundation was established in 1998 when the Poor Handmaids of Jesus Christ sold the St. Joseph Medical Center and reorganized the St. Joseph Community Health Foundation with a significant share of the proceeds. Proceeds from the Foundation's endowment are redistributed as grants typically ranging from $5,000 to $35,000 to advance programs, projects and partnerships that improve the access to quality health care and the health of the poor and powerless of Allen County, Indiana. Typically, only programs that can demonstrate that greater than 51 percent of their clients are very low income with health issues are considered for these grants. The Foundation also considers these values of the Poor Handmaids as a part of its grant review process: respecting and valuing each person; standing with the poor and powerless; using our talents and resources to respond to the emerging needs of society; nurturing leadership in our efforts to bring peace to the world. The Foundation will consider requests for program support, operations, seed monies, program-related equipment, staff continuing education, technical assistance, and matching funds. The Foundation will commit support on an annual basis only. Additional funding will be contingent upon program performance.
Requirements: Applicants should have a demonstrated history of serving poor and powerless populations with medical, dental, mental, and/or spiritual health care and wellness services. Applicants should be not-for-profit entities classified as 501(c)3 by the Internal Revenue Service. Partnerships between not-for-profits are encouraged. The proposed grant must be operated for the benefit of residents of Allen County, Indiana.
Restrictions: Grant applications will not be accepted for building projects, elimination of deficits, support of political activities, individuals, or projects already completed.
Geographic Focus: Indiana
Date(s) Application is Due: Mar 1; Sep 1
Amount of Grant: 5,000 - 35,000 USD
Contact: Meg Distler; (260) 969-2001, ext. 201; fax (260) 969-2004; mdistler@sjchf.org
Internet: http://www.stjosephhealthfdn.org/index.php?option=com_content&view=article&id=79&Itemid=70
Sponsor: St. Joseph Community Health Foundation
2826 South Calhoun Street
Fort Wayne, IN 46807

St. Louis-Jefferson Solid Waste Management Waste Reduction and Recycling Grants   4470
The St. Louis-Jefferson Solid Waste Management District is a regional agency created to assist the public, private, and not-for-profit sectors in establishing and expanding waste reduction and recycling. The District includes the City of St. Louis, St. Louis County, Jefferson County and St. Charles County. A major tool of the District to expand waste reduction and recycling is the Waste Reduction and Recycling Grant Program. The annual District Grant Program provides valuable assistance to local governments, private businesses and not-for-profit organizations in the implementation and expansion of a wide variety of waste reduction and recycling projects. Funds may be used for a variety of costs associated with a project, from equipment to operating expenses. The District Grant Program provides an excellent opportunity to expand local recycling efforts throughout the region. The grant program deadlines will be announced in the fall of this year, for the following year, see website.
Requirements: Any municipality, county, public institution, not-for-profit organization, private business or individual currently operating in the City of St. Louis, St. Louis County, Jefferson County or St. Charles County, or who will be operating in these areas, is eligible to apply. The District encourages the submission of cooperative projects or proposals which address regional or multi-jurisdictional waste reduction and recycling needs.
Geographic Focus: Missouri
Contact: David Berger; (314) 645-6753; fax (314) 645-6504; david@swmd.net
Internet: http://www.swmd.net/grants.html
Sponsor: St. Louis-Jefferson Solid Waste Management District
7525 Sussex Avenue
St. Louis, MO 63143

Stackner Family Foundation Grants   4471
The foundation awards grants concentrated in the Milwaukee metropolitan area for building programs and equipment acquisition, medical research, programs at all levels of education, social welfare, child welfare, and programs that assist the physically disabled. Additional categories of support include general operating support, continuing support, annual campaigns, capital campaigns, and program development. The board meets each year in January, April, July, and October. Application forms are not required.
Requirements: Nonprofits in the greater Milwaukee, WI, area may request grant support.
Geographic Focus: Wisconsin
Date(s) Application is Due: Mar 15; Jun 15; Sep 15; Dec 15
Amount of Grant: 25 - 25,000 USD
Contact: Paul Tillman, (414) 646-5409; Stackner@MSH.com
Sponsor: Stackner Family Foundation
411 E Wisconsin Avenue
Milwaukee, WI 53202-4497

Stackpole-Hall Foundation Grants   4472
The Stackpole-Hall Foundation awards grants to nonprofit organizations and institutions designed to enhance the social welfare of the Pennsylvania area. The Foundation concentrates on the areas of education, health care, cultural, youth development, social welfare, environmental, and community development. Priority is given to Elk County. Grants are awarded in support of matching, seed, partnership, and under certain circumstances, operational grants. The Foundation trustees meet four times a year to award grants. Proposals are due a month prior to the meeting for which they will be considered. Application forms are not required. Detailed instructions about information to include with the letter of inquiry are located at the Foundation website.
Requirements: The Foundation considers requests from organizations which qualify as churches; governmental organizations; or 501(c)3 organizations; or are classified as not being a private foundation under section 509(a) of the federal tax code.
Restrictions: Unless usual circumstances exist, requests for operating or endowment grants are given low priority. Funding is not available for individuals.
Geographic Focus: Pennsylvania
Amount of Grant: Up to 50,000 USD
Contact: William Conrad; (814) 834-1845; fax (814) 834-1869; stackpolehall@windstream.net
Internet: http://www.stackpolehall.org/application.html
Sponsor: Stackpole-Hall Foundation
44 South St. Marys Street
St. Marys, PA 15857

Stan and Sandy Checketts Foundation   4473
Established by Stan and Sandy Checketts in 1998, the Foundation's primary focus is on human services and helping individuals defray medical expenses. Primary fields of interest include: children and youth programs, health care, housing and shelter programs, human services, and recreation. Types of support are general operating funds and grants to individuals. Applicants should submit a detailed description of the project, along with the amount of funding requested. There are no deadlines, and the primary geographic focus is Utah.
Geographic Focus: Utah
Contact: Stan Checketts, President; (435) 752-1987; fax (435) 752-1948
Sponsor: Stan and Sandy Checketts Foundation
350 West 2500 North
Logan, UT 84341-1734

Stanley Smith Horticultural Trust Grants   4474
The Stanley Smith Horticultural Trust was created in 1970 by May Smith, in honor of her late husband. The trust typically makes grants to botanical gardens, arboreta, and universities primarily in North and South America to support education and research in ornamental horticulture. Specifically, the trust is interested in funding organizations pursuing the following activities: the advancement of research in ornamental horticulture and the publication of the results of such research; assisting in the creation, development, preservation, and maintenance of gardens accessible to the public for educational purposes; promotion of the environmentally responsible introduction, cultivation, and distribution of plants which have ornamental horticultural value; assisting in the publication of books or other works relating to the science of horticulture; and informal and/or formal educational activities which further ornamental horticulture. The trust typical awards grants in the amount of $20,000. Organizations seeking funding should first confirm that their projects meet the trust's funding interests and eligibility requirements by taking the eligibility quiz which is accessible from the grantseeker's webpage at the trust's website. Grant seekers meeting the qualifications should send an email to the Grants Director with a brief description of their project. Organizations with projects that appear to be qualified and that are of interest to the trust will be sent current application guidelines along with an invitation to submit a full proposal. Proposals are accepted until August 15 and are reviewed by the trustees once a year in November. Funding of approved grants occurs in December for use in the following calendar year.
Requirements: Organizations that are recognized as 501(c)3 public charities by the United States Internal Revenue Service and non-U.S. organizations that can demonstrate that they would meet the requirements for such status are eligible to apply. The trust provides support for projects in North and South America in the following areas: development of programs and projects; salaries; physical improvements; signage; access; equipment; publications; and, under some circumstances, general operations.
Restrictions: The trust does not fund endowments, indirect costs, or projects concerned primarily with agriculture, environmental issues, science education, or horticultural therapy.
Geographic Focus: All States, All Countries
Date(s) Application is Due: Aug 15
Amount of Grant: Up to 20,000 USD

Contact: Dr. Thomas F. Daniel, Grants Director, Stanley Smith Horticultural Trust; (415) 379-5350; tdaniel@calacademy,org
Janet Ferriaolo, Grants Manager; (415) 332-0166; jferraiolo@adminitrustllc.com
Internet: http://www.adminitrustllc.com/stanley-smith-horticultural-trust/
Sponsor: Stanley Smith Horticultural Trust
c/o Adminitrust LLC
Sausalito, CA 94965

Staples Foundation for Learning Grants 4475

The mission of foundation is to provide funding to programs that support or provide job skills and/or education for all people, with a special emphasis on disadvantaged youth. Grants will support efforts to teach, train, and inspire. Grant decisions are made on a quarterly basis, and all requests must be submitted at least four weeks prior to the foundation's meeting. Application submissions guidelines are available online.
Requirements: 501(c)3 nonprofit organizations are eligible. Projects must align with the foundations mission and give focus on job skills and education.
Restrictions: Contributions do not support the following: individuals; educational loans; organizations that discriminate on the basis of race, religion, creed, gender, or national origin; international organizations; travel expenses or fees to conferences or conventions; political organizations; books, research papers, or articles in professional journals; medical research projects or medical procedures for individuals; religious organizations, unless they are engaged in a significant project that benefits a broad base of the community; fraternal organizations, veterans' organizations, professional associations, and similar membership groups; or public or commercial broadcasting programs.
Geographic Focus: All States
Contact: Grants Administrator; (508) 253-9600; foundationinfo@staples.com
Internet: http://www.staplesfoundation.org
Sponsor: Staples Foundation for Learning
500 Staples Drive, 4W
Framingham, MA 01702-4478

Starbucks Foundation Shared Planet Youth Action Grants 4476

In 2008, The Starbucks Foundation began supporting young people as they strived to create change in their local communities through the Starbucks Shared Planet Youth Action Grants. This program helps young people improve communities around the world through new ideas, volunteerism and civic action and is the primary vehicle through which the Starbucks Foundation invests in communities globally. Grants will range from $10,000 to $25,000 each for one year. Funding will be considered based on numbers of clients served, geographic reach, organizational capacity, and size of operating budget.
Requirements: The foundation will solicit applications from organizations that provide young people (ages 6 to 24) with a continuum of service opportunities in social entrepreneurship. To be eligible, U.S. applicants must be tax-exempt, 501(c)3 nonprofit organizations. Applicants outside the United States must be charitable in purpose and identified as nongovernmental organizations or the equivalent of a tax-exempt nonprofit organization. The foundation does not accept unsolicited proposals. Interested organizations may submit an online profile. The foundation reviews these profiles periodically and will contact those organizations about which it is interested in learning more. Submissions are reviewed on a quarterly basis; there are no deadlines for the submission of organization profiles. The Starbucks Foundation will give priority funding to organizations that can demonstrate sustainability.
Restrictions: Starbucks will not support organizations that discriminate against a person or a group on the basis of age, political affiliation, race, national origin, ethnicity, gender, disability, sexual orientation or religious belief. Additionally, the following types of activities are not eligible for funding: Events, tables, exhibitions, performances or sports tournaments and one time volunteer events not connected to a program curriculum; Capital campaigns (including use of grant funds for exclusive purchase of technology and materials); Trips and travel; Contests, festivals or parades; Sponsorship of fundraising or other events; Advertising; Tickets to events; Supply drives.
Geographic Focus: All States
Amount of Grant: 10,000 - 25,000 USD
Contact: Vivek Varma, Senior Vice President, Public Affairs; (206) 318-1575
Internet: http://www.starbucksfoundation.com/index.cfm?objectid=BE688C92-1D09-317F-BBA1CDA8E271C9CB
Sponsor: Starbucks Foundation
2401 Utah Avenue S, Suite 800, Mail Stop S-SR1
Seattle, WA 98134

Stark Community Foundation Grants 4477

Generally the Foundation awards charitable grants to help launch new programs, initiatives, or capital needs not addressed by existing organizations. The Foundation requires year-end evaluative reports for all charitable grants, and collects specific data to track outcomes of our Board directed Impact Areas: After school, Affordable Housing and Economic Development, and Neighborhood Capacity Building. Guidelines and application information are available at the Foundation's website.
Requirements: Grants are made to: tax-exempt private agencies, 501(c)3 organizations which are public charities, and government entities located within Stark County, Ohio only or directly benefiting Stark County.
Restrictions: Stark Community Foundation normally does not approve grants to support: operating expenses of well-established organizations; deficit financing for programs or capital expenditures; endowment funds; religious organizations for religious purposes; annual appeals and membership contributions; conferences and recognition events; grants to individuals except through scholarship funds.
Geographic Focus: Ohio
Date(s) Application is Due: Jan 4; Aug 2
Contact: Cindy Lazor; (330) 454-3426; fax (330) 454-5855; cmlazor@starkcf.org
Internet: http://www.starkcf.org/competitive_grants_for_nonprofits.asp
Sponsor: Stark Community Foundation
400 Market Avenue N, Suite 200
Canton, OH 44702

Stark Community Foundation Neighborhood Community and Economic Development Technical Assistance Grants 4478

Available to (CDC's) Canton City Community Development Corporations, and NBO's Neighborhood Based Organizations that have received their 501(c)3. The purpose of this grant is to increase the capacity and expertise of local Community Development Corporations and Neighborhood Based Organizations through attending educational seminars or conferences to learn more about securing, managing, and reporting on State and Federal funds to revitalize city neighborhoods.
Requirements: Criteria for funding: CDC and NBO 501(c)3 organizations must be working directly with Canton City neighborhoods to qualify for these Technical Assistance grants; request letter should be sent to the Foundation at least three weeks prior to the beginning of the conference; funding will be limited to two individuals (daily) from each CDC or NBO applying; A Stark Community Foundation NCED technical assistance application should be completed by the Director or Chairman of the CDC or NBO and must include a completed copy of the application(s) required for the conference; an already established CDC may apply to the Foundation for a grant to equal one-half of the amount required for registration and hotel. Food and travel/gasoline expenses will be the responsibility of the applicant; a neighborhood-based organization (NBO) may apply to the Foundation for a grant to cover all of the registration and hotel plus $25 per day/per person for food. Travel/gasoline expenses will be the responsibility of the applicant.
Geographic Focus: Ohio
Contact: Marilyn Thomas Jones; (330) 454-3426; fax (330) 454-5855; mtjones@starkcf.org
Internet: http://www.starkcf.org/neighborhood_tech_assistance.asp
Sponsor: Stark Community Foundation
400 Market Avenue N, Suite 200
Canton, OH 44702

Stark Community Foundation Neighborhood Partnership Grants 4479

The purpose of this grant is to: encourage groups of people within a neighborhood to identify and work on important issues relative to their neighborhood concerns; provide resources for community projects to build the capacity of neighbor—hood organizations; leverage grass roots volunteer involvement and additional community resources; provide lasting community improvements for neighborhood residents by making Canton neighborhoods better places to live, work, play and raise families; provide an opportunity for neighbors to celebrate, and share their neighborhood revitalization success. Refer to the Foundation or it's website for additional guidelines regarding this program: http://www.starkcf.org/neighborhood_partnership.asp
Geographic Focus: Ohio
Date(s) Application is Due: Jan 23
Amount of Grant: 500 - 7,000 USD
Contact: Marilyn Thomas Jones; (330) 454-3426; fax (330) 454-5855; mtjones@starkcf.org
Internet: http://www.starkcf.org/neighborhood_partnership.asp
Sponsor: Stark Community Foundation
400 Market Avenue N, Suite 200
Canton, OH 44702

Stark Community Foundation SummerTime Kid Grants 4480

SummerTime Kids is a grant initiative of Stark Community Foundation. Guided by a volunteer oversight committee and Foundation staff, it provides charitable grants of $500 to $2,000 to imaginative and unique summer programs with an emphasis on character and community service. These types of programs not only enrich the lives of the youth that participate but also benefit the community as a whole.
Requirements: Grants are made to: tax-exempt private agencies, 501(c)3 organizations which are public charities, and government entities located within Stark County, Ohio only or directly benefiting Stark County.
Restrictions: Stark Community Foundation normally does not approve grants to support: operating expenses of well-established organizations; deficit financing for programs or capital expenditures; endowment funds; religious organizations for religious purposes; annual appeals and membership contributions; conferences and recognition events; grants to individuals except through scholarship funds.
Geographic Focus: Ohio
Date(s) Application is Due: Mar 12
Contact: Cindy Lazor; (330) 454-3426; fax (330) 454-5855; cmlazor@starkcf.org
Internet: http://www.starkcf.org/summertime_kids.asp
Sponsor: Stark Community Foundation
400 Market Avenue N, Suite 200
Canton, OH 44702

Stark Community Foundation Women's Fund Grants 4481

The Women's Fund is a permanent endowment to benefit future generations and increase vital funding for programs which advance the economic, educational, physical, emotional, social, artistic, and personal growth of women and to educate and inspire women to become leaders in philanthropy. The interest area of this fund includes nonprofit agencies and their programs or projects that meet the needs of women and children in the Stark County area.
Requirements: The Women's Fund would like to fund grassroots nonprofit organizations, churches, and educational components that have unique projects serving women and/or women and children, and their basic needs for daily living.

Geographic Focus: Ohio
Date(s) Application is Due: Mar 5
Amount of Grant: 500 - 3,000 USD
Contact: Cindy Lazor; (330) 454-3426; fax (330) 454-5855; cmlazor@starkcf.org
Internet: http://www.starkcf.org/the_womens_fund.asp
Sponsor: Stark Community Foundation
400 Market Avenue N, Suite 200
Canton, OH 44702

Starke County Community Foundation Grants 4482
The Starke Community Foundation offers grants to schools and teachers with the maximum amount of $500 per school. The following school systems are eligible to apply: Knox, North Judson-San Pierre and Oregon-Davis. Areas of interest include: community development; education; health and human services; youth; environment and recreation; and arts and culture. Applicants may fill out the online application, but are advised to contact the program coordinator to discuss their project before applying.
Requirements: The Foundation favors activities that: reach a broad segment of the community, especially those citizens whose needs are not being met by existing services that are normally expected to be provided by private rather than government sources; request seed money to realize innovative opportunities to meet needs in the community; stimulate and encourage additional funding; promote cooperation and avoid duplication of effort; help make a charitable organization more effective and efficient and better able to be self-sustaining; and one time projects or needs.
Restrictions: The Foundation will not consider grants for: religious organizations for the sole purpose of furthering that religion (this prohibition does not apply to funds created by donors who have specifically designated religious organizations as beneficiaries of the funds); political activities or those designated to influence legislation; national organizations (unless the monies are to be used solely to benefit citizens of Starke County); grants that directly benefit the donor or the donor's family; fundraising projects; and contributions to endowments.
Geographic Focus: Indiana
Date(s) Application is Due: Sep 30
Amount of Grant: 500 USD
Contact: Grants Coordinator; (574) 223-2227 or (877) 432-6423
Internet: http://www.nicf.org/starke/grants.html
Sponsor: Starke County Community Foundation
1512 South Heaton Street
Knox, IN 46534

Starr Foundation Grants 4483
The foundation awards grants to nonprofit organizations in the areas of education, medicine and health care, human needs, public policy, and culture. Education grants support scholarships for deserving students, groups that offer need-based financial aid, and international-exchange programs. Human needs grants support food programs for the poor, job training, literacy, adequate housing, and programs for the disabled. Medicine and health care grants include capital grants to hospitals, significant research grants, and grants to assist in the provision of health care to underserved communities. Public policy grants support international relations and democratic institutions around the world. Culture grants go to exchange programs and provide services to the elderly and/or disabled. The foundation rarely funds local charities outside of New York City but may fund national organizations that serve communities outside of New York. Types of support include multiyear grants, general operating grants, and capacity-building grants. There are no application deadlines. The board meets throughout the year.
Geographic Focus: All States
Amount of Grant: Up to 70,000,000 USD
Contact: Florence Davis; (212) 770-6882; florence.davis@starrfdn.org
Internet: http://fdncenter.org/grantmaker/starr
Sponsor: Starr Foundation
70 Pine Street, 14th Floor
New York, NY 10270

State Farm Companies Safe Neighbors Grants 4484
State Farm values the importance of keeping our neighbors safe, with funding directed toward: improving driver, vehicle, and roadway safety; shielding homes from fires, criminals, and natural disasters; supporting disaster preparedness programs and recovery services, and; enhancing personal financial security. In general, grants are awarded for specific programs in the giving categories described, rather than for one-time events or capital campaigns. Grant requests must be submitted in writing on the requesting organization's letterhead. One proposal per organization per year will be considered if it meets the guidelines. Guidelines are available online.
Requirements: U.S. and Canadian 501(c)3 educational organizations are eligible.
Restrictions: The foundation does not fund individuals seeking personal; politically partisan programs; religious programs; or organizations outside the United States and Canada.
Geographic Focus: All States
Contact: Safe Neighbors Grants Coordinator; (309) 766-2161; fax (309) 766-2314; home.sf-foundation.494b00@statefarm.co
Internet: http://www.statefarm.com/about/part_spos/grants/cogrants.asp
Sponsor: State Farm Insurance Company
1 State Farm Plaza, B-4
Bloomington, IL 61710-0001

State Farm Companies Strong Neighborhoods Grants 4485
State Farm is committed to helping maintain the vibrancy and culture of neighborhoods in various communities throughout the U.S. and Canada. They demonstrate this commitment by supporting nonprofit organization programs that: make housing affordable; promote first-time homeownership; eliminate barriers to homeownership; educate homebuyers about insurance, loss mitigation, and homeownership; foster sustainable communities, and; rehabilitate neighborhoods or communities.
Restrictions: The company does not fund: organizations that are not a governmental entity, a stable nonprofit 501(c)3 organization with a diverse funding base, an educational institution, or a Canadian charitable organization; individuals seeking personal help or scholarships; religious programs; politically partisan programs, or; organizations outside the U.S. and Canada.
Geographic Focus: All States
Contact: Strong Neighborhoods Grants Coordinator; (309) 766-2161; fax (309) 766-2314; home.sf-foundation.494b00@statefarm.co
Internet: http://www.statefarm.com/about/part_spos/grants/cogrants.asp
Sponsor: State Farm Insurance Company
1 State Farm Plaza, B-4
Bloomington, IL 61710-0001

State Farm Foundation Grants 4486
The foundation is primarily committed to education, helping to raise the level of student achievement in elementary and secondary schools, as well as supporting key higher education initiatives. The foundation provides funding for its Education Excellence (education) initiatives that are national in scope. Its primary focus includes: K-12 public schools; service learning program initiatives; systemic improvement, and; teacher excellence. Guidelines and application are available online.
Requirements: K-12 school districts are eligible.
Geographic Focus: All States
Contact: Grants; (309) 766-2161; home.sf-foundation.494b00@statefarm.co
Internet: http://www.statefarm.com/about/part_spos/grants/foundati.asp
Sponsor: State Farm Foundation
1 State Farm Plaza, B-4
Bloomington, IL 61710-0001

State Farm Project Ignition Grants 4487
Sponsored by State Farm and coordinated by the National Youth Leadership Council(NYLC), Project Ignition is a grant program that uses service-learning to help address teen driver safety issues. These grants support students in grades 9 through 12 and their teachers or advisors to work together to develop a campaign to address the issue of teen driver safety in your community. Grants will be awarded to a maximum of twenty-five (25) selected programs. The grantee's school will receive a $2,000 grant, funded by State Farm, to implement their program in the fall. Each year, schools whose campaigns are judged to be among the top 10 in the nation receive $5,000 to help cover expenses to come to The National Service-Learning Conference. There, they showcase their great work, one campaign is named the Best of the Best and that team presented with a $10,000 grant to continue its teen driver safety efforts.
Requirements: Public schools (including public charter and public alternative schools) in the United States that educate students in grades 9 through 12, ages 13 and older, are eligible to participate and receive project awards. All applications require a teacher and principal signature. Participation is not limited to service-learning schools, but schools already implementing service-learning in their curricula are encouraged to participate.
Restrictions: Project Ignition is offered only in the U.S. Void where prohibited by law.
Geographic Focus: All States
Date(s) Application is Due: Jun 30
Amount of Grant: 2,000 USD
Contact: Michael VanKeulen, NYLC Contact; (888) 856-7026; mvankeulen@nylc.org
Internet: http://www.sfprojectignition.com
Sponsor: State Farm Insurance
1 State Farm Plaza, B-4
Bloomington, IL 61710-0001

State Justice Institute Curriculum Adaptation and Training Grants 4488
Curriculum Adaptation and Training (CAT) Grants are intended to: enable courts and regional or national court associations to modify and adapt model curricula, course modules, or conference programs to meet States' or local jurisdictions' educational needs; train instructors to present portions or all of the curricula; pilot-test them to determine their appropriateness, quality, quality and effectiveness; or conduct judicial branch education and training programs, led by either expert or in-house personnel, designed to prepare judges and court personnel for innovations, reforms, and/or new technologies recently adopted by grantee courts.
Requirements: State and local courts and their agencies, national nonprofit organizations operating with and serving the state courts, and national nonprofit education and training organizations are eligible. Applicants for CAT Grants will be required to contribute a match of not less than 50% of the grant amount requested, of which 20% must be cash. Applicants considering cash match well in excess of $2,000 should consider applying for Project Grants and are strongly urged to consult with SJI prior to applying.
Restrictions: CAT grants may not exceed $30,000. Grant periods for CAT Grants ordinarily may not exceed 12 months.
Geographic Focus: All States
Date(s) Application is Due: Feb 1; May 1; Aug 1; Nov 1
Amount of Grant: Up to 30,000 USD
Contact: Janice Munsterman; (703) 684-6100, ext. 202; janice.munsterman@sji.gov
Internet: http://www.sji.gov/grant-curriculum.php
Sponsor: State Justice Institute
1650 King Street, Suite 600
Alexandria, VA 22314

State Justice Institute Partner Grants 4489
Partner Grants allow SJI and Federal, State, or local agencies or foundations, trusts, or other private entities to combine financial resources in pursuit of common interests. Partner Grants are intended to support innovative research, demonstration, education, or technical assistance projects with a high probability of national impact. SJI is interested in funding both innovative programs and programs of proven merit that can be replicated in other jurisdictions. SJI is especially interested in funding projects that: formulate new procedures and techniques, or creatively enhance existing procedures and techniques; address aspects of the State judicial systems that are in special need of serious attention; have national significance by developing products, services, and techniques that may be used in other States; and create and disseminate products that effectively transfer the information and ideas developed to relevant audiences in State and local judicial systems, or provide technical assistance to facilitate the adaptation of effective programs and procedures in other State and local jurisdictions. There is no limit to the size of a Partner Grant, and may be submitted at any time.
Requirements: State and local courts and their agencies, national nonprofit organizations operating with and serving the state courts, and national nonprofit education and training organizations are eligible. Partner Grants assume that grantees are unable to contribute a cash match of not less than 50%.
Geographic Focus: All States
Date(s) Application is Due: Feb 1; May 1; Aug 1; Nov 1
Contact: Janice Munsterman, Executive Director; (703) 684-6100, ext. 202; fax (703) 684-7618; janice.munsterman@sji.gov
Internet: http://www.sji.gov/grant-partner.php
Sponsor: State Justice Institute
1650 King Street, Suite 600
Alexandria, VA 22314

State Justice Institute Project Grants 4490
SJI was established by federal law in 1984 to improve the quality of justice in State courts, facilitate better coordination between State and Federal courts, and foster innovative, efficient solutions to common issues faced by all courts. Project Grants are the centerpiece of the SJI Board's efforts to improve the administration of justice in State courts nationwide. Ordinarily, Project Grants may not exceed $300,000; however, grants in excess of $200,000 may be awarded only to support highly promising projects likely to have a significant national impact. Project Grants are intended to support innovative research, demonstration, education, or technical assistance projects. Grant periods for Project Grants ordinarily may not exceed 36 months. SJI is interested in funding both innovative programs and programs of proven merit that can be replicated in other jurisdictions.
Requirements: State and local courts and their agencies, national nonprofit organizations operating with and serving the state courts, and national nonprofit education and training organizations are eligible. Applicants for Project Grants will be required to contribute a cash match of not less than 50% of the total cost of the proposed project. Applicants may contribute the required cash match directly or in cooperation with third parties. SJI may waive the cash match requirements only in the most extraordinary circumstances.
Restrictions: Absent extraordinary circumstances, no grant will continue for more than five years.
Geographic Focus: All States
Date(s) Application is Due: Feb 1; May 1; Aug 1; Nov 1
Amount of Grant: Up to 300,000 USD
Contact: Janice Munsterman, Executive Director; (703) 684-6100, ext. 202; fax (703) 684-7618; janice.munsterman@sji.gov
Internet: http://www.sji.gov/grant-project.php
Sponsor: State Justice Institute
1650 King Street, Suite 600
Alexandria, VA 22314

State Justice Institute Scholarships 4491
SJI supports the Scholarship program for State court judges and court managers. Scholarships will be awarded to individuals to attend out-of-State, court-related educational programs within the United States or online court-related educational programs. The purpose of the scholarship program is to enhance the skills, knowledge, and abilities of judges and court managers by supporting attendance at programs sponsored by national and State providers that they could not otherwise attend because of limited State, local, and personal budgets; and provide States, judicial educators, and court staff with evaluative information on a range of judicial and court-related education programs. An SJI scholarship may cover the costs of tuition, transportation to and from the educational program, and reasonable lodging (up to $150 per night, including taxes), up to a maximum total of $1,500 per scholarship.
Requirements: Scholarships can be awarded only to: full-time judges of State or local trial and appellate courts; full-time professional State or local court personnel with management responsibilities; and supervisory and management probation officials in judicial branch probation offices. Senior judges, part-time judges, quasi-judicial hearing officers including referees and commissioners, administrative law judges, staff attorneys, law clerks, line staff, law enforcement officers, and other executive branch personnel are not eligible to receive scholarships.
Geographic Focus: All States
Amount of Grant: Up to 1,500 USD
Contact: Janice Munsterman, Executive Director; (703) 684-6100, ext. 202; fax (703) 684-7618; janice.munsterman@sji.gov
Internet: http://www.sji.gov/grant-scholarship.php
Sponsor: State Justice Institute
1650 King Street, Suite 600
Alexandria, VA 22314

State Justice Institute Strategic Initiative Grants 4492
The Strategic Initiatives Grants (SIG) program provides SJI the flexibility to address national court issues as they occur, and develop solutions to those problems. This is an innovate approach to doing business where SJI is no longer simply making grants and hoping that a grant application covers a major issue facing the courts; rather, SJI is actively addressing these issues. In this way, SJI uses its expertise and the expertise and knowledge of its grantees to address key issues facing State courts across the United States. The program is handled at the discretion of the SJI Board of Directors and Staff outside the normal grant application process (i.e. SJI will initiate the project), and there is no cash match requirement.
Requirements: State and local courts and their agencies, national nonprofit organizations operating with and serving the state courts, and national nonprofit education and training organizations are eligible.
Geographic Focus: All States
Date(s) Application is Due: Feb 1; May 1; Aug 1; Nov 1
Contact: Janice Munsterman, Executive Director; (703) 684-6100, ext. 202; fax (703) 684-7618; janice.munsterman@sji.gov
Internet: http://www.sji.gov/grants.php
Sponsor: State Justice Institute
1650 King Street, Suite 600
Alexandria, VA 22314

State Justice Institute Technical Assistance Grants 4493
Technical Assistance Grants are designed to provide State and local courts with funding to obtain expert assistance to diagnose a problem, develop a response to that problem, and initiate implementation of any needed changes. Technical Assistance Grants are limited to no more than $50,000 each, and may cover the cost of obtaining the services of expert consultants; travel by a team of officials from one court to examine a practice, program, or facility in another jurisdiction that the applicant court is interested in replicating; or both.
Requirements: Only State or local courts may apply for Technical Assistance grants. Normally, the technical assistance must be completed within 12 months after the start date of the grant. A cash and in-kind match must be provided equal to at least 50% of the grant amount, of which 20% of the match must be in cash.
Restrictions: Technical Assistance Grant funds ordinarily may not be used to support production of a videotape.
Geographic Focus: All States
Date(s) Application is Due: Feb 1; May 1; Aug 1; Nov 1
Amount of Grant: Up to 50,000 USD
Contact: Janice Munsterman; (703) 684-6100, ext. 202; janice.munsterman@sji.gov
Internet: http://www.sji.gov/grant-tech.php
Sponsor: State Justice Institute
1650 King Street, Suite 600
Alexandria, VA 22314

State Strategies Fund Grants 4494
The program supports state-based strategies to increase civic participation in political life, empower disadvantaged constituencies, and promote political reform. Areas of interest include campaign finance reform, fair tax policy, affordable health care, and the environment. Permanent state-based coalitions that have a long-term strategy for uniting diverse constituencies with a grassroots base and that have a common vision and policy agenda for economic and social justice receive grants. The grant program supports organizations with the following goals: to build strong and effective relationships and collaboration among diverse groups; to integrate a broad array of issues into a common progressive agenda; to develop the collective power of constituents to implement this common agenda; to increase the capacity of underrepresented constituencies to have greater impact on public policy and governance at the state level; to enhance the capacity of grassroots organizations to mobilize their members; and to develop new public leaders representing and accountable to disadvantaged constituencies. Applications should be submitted by email. Attachments and/or mailed applications must be postmarked by the listed application deadline.
Geographic Focus: All States
Date(s) Application is Due: Aug 25
Contact: Amy Clough; (413) 256-0349, ext. 12; aclough@proteusfund.org
Internet: http://www.proteusfund.org/grantmaking/ssf
Sponsor: State Strategies Fund
264 N Pleasant Street
Amherst, MA 01002

State Street Foundation Grants 4495
The foundation focuses grantmaking worldwide on three areas: neighborhood revitalization, education and job training and development, and youth programs. Of special interest are projects that strengthen organizations' capacity to address community needs. In addition, the foundation provides funding for health and human needs and civic improvement projects that support its areas of focus. Types of support include annual campaigns, employee matching gifts, general operating budgets, matching funds, special projects, affordable housing rehabilitation projects, and technical assistance to achieve nonprofit performance improvement. Creative partnerships are encouraged between the public and private sectors. Contact the office for proposal guidelines.
Requirements: 501(c)3 organizations that are not private foundations and are located in Alameda, Los Angeles, and San Francisco, CA; Connecticut; Florida; Atlanta, GA; Illinois; Boston and the Cape Cod, MA, area; Saint Louis and Kansas City, MO; New Hampshire; New Jersey; and New York are eligible.
Restrictions: The foundation does not make grants for scholarships or fellowships; research projects; emergency cash flow, deficit spending, or debt liquidation situations; seed money/start-up programs; trips, tours, and transportation expenses; or films or videos.

Geographic Focus: California, Connecticut, Florida, Georgia, Illinois, Massachusetts, Missouri, New Hampshire, New Jersey, New York
Amount of Grant: 3,000 - 25,000 USD
Contact: Grants Administrator; (617) 664-1937; gabowman@statestreet.com
Internet: http://www.statestreet.com/company/community_affairs/global_philanthropy/overview.html
Sponsor: State Street Foundation
225 Franklin Street, 12th Floor
Boston, MA 02110

Staunton Farm Foundation Grants 4496
The Staunton Farm Foundation is a family foundation established in 1937 in accordance with the wishes of Matilda Staunton Craig, who wanted her estate to be used to benefit people with mental illness. The Foundation awards grants in the field of mental health in southwestern Pennsylvania. Projects that represent new and different approaches for organizations and ultimately affect patient care are encouraged. Support may be for more than one year, but the project must become self-sustaining following the grant period. Applicants should submit a letter of intent; full proposals are by invitation.
Requirements: Nonprofit organizations in the 10-county area in southwestern Pennsylvania including Washington, Greene, Fayette, Westmoreland, Armstrong, Butler, Lawrence, Beaver, Indiana, and Allegheny are eligible.
Geographic Focus: Pennsylvania
Date(s) Application is Due: Jun 1; Dec 1
Contact: Joni S. Schwager; (412) 281-8020; jschwager@stauntonfarm.org
Internet: http://www.stauntonfarm.org
Sponsor: Staunton Farm Foundation
650 Smithfield Street, Suite 210
Pittsburgh, PA 15222

Steelcase Foundation Grants 4497
The foundation make grants to nonprofit organizations, projects, and programs in corporate communities. Grants are awarded in the areas of human service, health, education, community development, the arts, and the environment. Preference is given to programs designed to improve the quality life for disadvantaged, disabled, young, and elderly people. Matching gifts are made to educational, arts, and environment programs supported by Steelcase employees, retirees, and directors. To obtain a grant application, send a letter on letterhead, signed by the organization's chief executive officer. Include the following items in the letter: description of the organization or project; expected results of the project; amount of grant funds requested; and a copy of 501(c)3 nonprofit certification. Guidelines are available online.
Requirements: The foundation makes grants to IRS-certified nonprofit organizations in areas where Steelcase manufacturing plants are located (Grand Rapids, MI; Fletcher, NC; City of Industry, CA; Athens, AL; Toronto, Canada; and Tijuana, Mexico.)
Restrictions: The foundation does not provide grants to individuals or to organizations that discriminate on the basis of race, religion, sex, disability, or national origin; have received a Steelcase foundation grant within the past 12 months; request support for a conference or seminar; or request support for religious programs (nonsectarian programs for humanitarian purposes are eligible for consideration.)
Geographic Focus: Alabama, California, Michigan, Canada, Mexico
Amount of Grant: 2,000 - 673,000 USD
Contact: Director; (616) 475-2009; fax (616) 475-2200; sbroman@steelcase.com
Internet: http://www.steelcase.com/na/ourcompany.aspx?f=10042&c=10022
Sponsor: Steelcase Foundation
P.O. Box 1967, CH4E
Grand Rapids, MI 49501

Steele-Reese Foundation Grants 4498
The foundation's available income is divided equally for grants to operating charities in southern Appalachia (particularly Kentucky) and in the Northwest (particularly Idaho). In both areas the funds are devoted to education, health, welfare, and the humanities. Types of support include general operating support, equipment, endowment funds, matching funds, professorships, scholarship funds, and capital campaigns. The foundation gives preference to projects that have, among others, the following characteristics: rural, modest in ambition, narrow in function, unglamorous, based on experience, enjoying community financial support, and essential rather than merely desirable. While the foundation considers southern Kentucky and Idaho to be its territories of primary concern, it makes grants to organizations operating throughout southern Appalachia and in Oregon, Montana, and Wyoming.
Requirements: Applicant should submit a letter requesting guidelines. Only residents of Georgia, Idaho, Kentucky, Montana, North Carolina, Texas, and Wyoming are eligible to apply. Personal and telephone inquiries are not encouraged.
Restrictions: The foundation does not make grants to individuals, to community chest or similar drives, for conferences or workshops, for efforts to influence elections or legislation, for planning purposes or experimental projects, for emergencies, or for permanent support except for occasional endowment grants to organizations where stability is critically important.
Geographic Focus: Georgia, Idaho, Kentucky, Montana, North Carolina, Texas, Wyoming
Date(s) Application is Due: Mar 1
Amount of Grant: 10,000 - 50,000 USD
Contact: Charles U. Buice, (212) 505-2696; charlesbuice@hotmail.com
Internet: http://www.steele-reese.org/what.html
Sponsor: Steele-Reese Foundation
32 Washington Square West
New York, NY 10011

Sterling-Turner Charitable Foundation Grants 4499
The charitable foundation awards grants to Texas organizations, primarily for higher and secondary education, adult basic education and literacy, social services, youth, the elderly, fine and performing arts groups and other cultural programs, church support and religious programs (Catholic, Jewish, and Protestant), hospitals and health services, hospices, research, conservation, and civic and urban affairs. Grants are awarded for general operating support, annual campaigns, capital campaigns, continuing support, building construction/renovation, equipment acquisition, endowment funds, program and project development, conferences and seminars, curriculum development, fellowships, scholarship funds, research, and matching funds. The board meets in April.
Requirements: Nonprofit Texas organizations in the following counties are eligible to apply: Fort Bend, Harris, Kerr, Tom Green, and Travis. Only those 501(c)3 organizations with offices located within the counties being considered within the State of Texas may submit and all funds must be managed, used and services provided within those counties in the State of Texas. All funds must be used within the requesting county. If the organization is a 509(a)3, there is a template for a required letter of explanation as to why your organization falls under the category that must be submitted for consideration. All documents must be received by 5:00 pm of the deadline date.
Restrictions: Individuals are ineligible.
Geographic Focus: Texas
Date(s) Application is Due: Mar 1
Amount of Grant: 5,000 - 25,000 USD
Contact: Patricia Stilley; (713) 237-1117; fax (713) 223-4638; pstilley@stfdn.org
Internet: http://sterlingturnerfoundation.org/information_and_instructions.htm
Sponsor: Sterling-Turner Charitable Foundation
5850 San Felipe Street, Suite 125
Houston, TX 77057-3292

Stettinius Fund for Nonprofit Leadership Awards 4500
The fund will award cash grants to outstanding professional leaders employed by a recognized 501(c)3 nonprofit organizations that serve the greater Richmond or Tri-Cities communities. It is expected that up to 5 awards will be made each year. The award may be used to pursue professional development opportunities of the candidate's own design, including executive seminars, advanced degree course work, best practice or applied research, on-site practica, professional exchange programs and travel.
Requirements: The selection committee seeks to identify emerging leaders from the nonprofit sector including: executive directors, directors, program managers or project managers from area nonprofits and consortia. Nominees should demonstrate: (1) commitment to the nonprofit sector; (2) leadership capabilities; (3) success in contributing to their own organizations; and (4) aptitude for continuous learning, innovation, and management of change.
Restrictions: Nominee shall be a current employee of a locally recognized 501(c)3 nonprofit organization in the metropolitan Richmond area (as defined by The Community Foundation service area); Nominee may be employed by a national or regional nonprofit with responsibilities and operations in foundation's service area; Nominees from faith-based organizations, which are separately incorporated as a 501(c)3 publicly supported charity are eligible, provided the organization is primarily engaged in providing human services, educational programs, arts or other secular services to clients and communities on a nondiscriminatory basis; Nominees whose primary responsibilities are related to religious or public sector (government) matters are ineligible.
Geographic Focus: Virginia
Date(s) Application is Due: Mar 16
Contact: Susan Brown Davis; (804) 330-7400
Internet: http://www.tcfrichmond.org/Page8759.cfm#stet
Sponsor: Community Foundation Serving Richmond and Central Virginia
7501 Boulders View Drive, Suite 110
Richmond, VA 23225

Steuben County Community Foundation Grants 4501
The Steuben County Community Foundation works to preserve and enhance the lifestyle and assets of Steuben County, Indiana, for current and future generations by providing ongoing assessment and financial support of identified needs through philanthropic giving and endowment building. The Foundation grants funding for arts and culture, education, health, environment, human services, recreation, and community development. Grants are not limited to these areas, and grant seekers are encouraged to respond to emerging community needs.
Requirements: Prospective applicants are strongly encouraged to discuss their grant requests with Community Foundation staff before beginning the application process. Applications can be obtained on the Foundation's website. The Steuben County Community Foundation encourages projects that: address priority community concerns; encourage more effective use of community resources; test or demonstrate new approaches and techniques in the solution of community problems; are intended to strengthens the management capabilities of agencies, and; promote volunteer participation and citizen involvement in community affairs.
Restrictions: If approved, each grant recipient must sign an agreement that includes the following obligations: public acknowledgment of the Foundation's support; expenditure of the monies as specified in the proposal; return of any unused portion of the grant; completion of an evaluation report; any special conditions as mutually agreed (failure to do so can adversely affect any subsequent requests).
Geographic Focus: Indiana
Date(s) Application is Due: Feb 28; Apr 29; Jun 30; Aug 31; Oct 31; Dec 30
Contact: Bill Stockberger, Program Officer; (260) 665-6656; fax (260) 665-8420
Internet: http://www.steubenfoundation.org/grants/index.html
Sponsor: Steuben County Community Foundation
1701 N Wayne Street
Angola, IN 46703

Steven B. Achelis Foundation Grants 4502
The Steve B. Achelis Foundation is a small private foundation with limited resources. Typical grants range between $500 and $5,000 with an average grant of $2,000. Total annual grants are approximately $50,000. Applicants should include: a description of the services provided; a copy of their 501(c)3 IRS ruling letter; and a breakdown of revenue sources and expenditures. There are no specified annual deadlines.
Geographic Focus: All States
Amount of Grant: 500 - 5,000 USD
Contact: Steven B. Achelis, Treasurer; (801) 560-5733; fax (801) 272-1148; info@eMedic.com or steve@rescuerigger.com
Internet: http://stevesfoundation.org/guidelines.htm
Sponsor: Steven B. Achelis Foundation
6154 Oak Canyon Drive, P.O. Box 71342
Salt Lake City, UT 84121-6344

Steve Young Family Foundation Grants 4503
The major fields of interest of the foundation include philanthropy, voluntarism, and recreation programs. Areas of most recent giving has concentrated its efforts on assisting children in need, focusing on family togetherness and welfare, as well as major health issues. The foundation's geographic focus is of a national scope.
Restrictions: 501(c)3 organizations that have a national appeal.
Geographic Focus: All States
Samples: $10,000, Twin Towers Orphan Fund, Bakersfield, CA; National Brain Tumor Foundation, San Francisco, CA;
Contact: Jon Steven Young, (800) 994-3837
Sponsor: Steve Young Family Foundation
559 W 500th Street South
Bountiful, UT 84010

Steward of the Land Award 4504
An annual award was created to recognize the many farmers and farm families throughout America who have demonstrated outstanding stewardship of their farms and ranches. Preference is given to nominees who have played an active role in promoting or developing farmland conservation practices and local, state, or federal farmland protection policies. Nomination forms are available on the website. Those interested in making a nomination should check the website to verify the availability of the award.
Requirements: Nominees must be actively engaged in farming in the United States and employ management practices or other farming methods consistent with good land stewardship on their farms and ranches. Nominees need not be Farmland Trust (AFT) members, but they must support AFT's mission and program objectives.
Restrictions: Individuals or families may not nominate themselves. Current or former AFT staff and board members may not participate.
Geographic Focus: All States
Contact: Jennifer Morrill; (202) 378-1255; fax (202) 659-8339; jmorrill@farmland.org
Internet: http://www.farmland.org/steward/index.htm
Sponsor: American Farmland Trust
1200 18th Street NW, Suite 800
Washington, DC 20036

Stewart Huston Charitable Trust Grants 4505
The purpose of the Trust is to provide funds, technical assistance and collaboration on behalf of non-profit organizations engaged exclusively in religious, charitable or educational work; to extend opportunities to deserving needy persons. Giving primarily in the Savannah, GA, area and Coatesville, PA.
Requirements: 501(c)3 nonprofit organizations are eligible.
Restrictions: Grants are not awarded for scholarship support to individuals, endowment purposes, purchases of tickets or advertising for benefit purposes, coverage of continuing operating deficits, or document publication costs. Support is not provided to intermediate or pass-through organizations (other than United Way) that in turn allocate funds to beneficiaries or to fraternal organizations, political parties or candidates, veterans, labor or local civic groups, volunteer fire companies, or groups engaged in influencing legislation.
Geographic Focus: Georgia, Pennsylvania
Date(s) Application is Due: Jan 15; Mar 1; Sep 1
Amount of Grant: 1,000 - 15,000 USD
Contact: Scott Huston; (610) 384-2666; fax (610) 384-3396; admin@stewarthuston.org
Internet: http://www.stewarthuston.org
Sponsor: Stewart Huston Charitable Trust
50 South First Avenue
Coatesville, PA 19320

Stinson Foundation Grants 4506
Sue Stinson's life was guided by a philosophy of optimism and cheerfulness. Before moving from her native Virginia to Midland in the mid-1930s, she taught in a one-room school in a Virginia Mennonite farming community and lived in a tent in the Arizona desert. She found humor and beauty in adverse situations, and the good in her life always took precedence and kept her going. The Stinson Foundation focuses on charitable organizations dedicated to children and families, and arts and education. This foundation makes approximately ten awards each year. Applicants must apply online at the grant website. Applicants are strongly encouraged to do the following before applying: review the downloadable state application procedures for additional helpful information and clarifications; review the downloadable online-application guidelines at the grant website; review the foundation's funding history (link is available from the grant website); review the online application questions in advance; and review the list of required attachments. These will generally include: a list of board members, financial statements (audited, reviewed, or compiled by independent auditor); an organization summary; a list of other funding sources; an IRS Determination letter; and other required documents. All attachments must be uploaded in the online application as PDF, Word, or Excel files. The application deadline is 11:59 p.m. on May 15.
Requirements: Applicants must have 501(c)3 tax-exempt status and serve residents of the Permian Basin Area.
Restrictions: The foundation does not support requests from individuals, organizations attempting to influence policy through direct lobbying, or any political campaigns.
Geographic Focus: Texas
Date(s) Application is Due: May 15
Amount of Grant: 2,000 - 10,000 USD
Contact: Mark J. Smith, (817) 390-6028; tx.philanthropic@baml.com
Internet: https://www.bankofamerica.com/philanthropic/fn_search.action
Sponsor: Stinson Foundation
500 West 7th Street, 15th Floor, TX1-497-15-08
Fort Worth, TX 76102-4700

Stocker Foundation Grants 4507
The Stocker Foundation aims to lessen the achievement-gap for under-resourced prekindergarten through third grade public school students by investing in programs that strengthen reading literacy. The foundation remains an all-family board, headquartered in Lorain, Ohio. Annual grant distributions focus first on Lorain County, Ohio, the place where assets were generated. Then, in communities where other trustees reside (see below).
Requirements: The Stocker Foundation provides grants to nonprofit organizations qualified under Section 501(c)3 of the Internal Revenue Code, and to selected public sector activities. Grants are considered and decided upon one time annually in the area of improved reading literacy outcomes for under-resourced prekindergarten through fifth grade public school students. Funds are made to organizations in Lorain and Cuyahoga counties, Ohio; Pima County, Arizona; Alameda and San Francisco counties, California; Bernalillo and Dona Ana counties, New Mexico; King County, Washington; and Hartford County, Connecticut. Areas of interest include: supplemental programs that move students toward grade-level reading mastery; comprehensive intervention strategies that increase overall literacy achievement by fourth grade; book distribution programs that increase students' access to print materials, encourage students' reading outside of the classroom, and develops students' life-long love of reading; and, programs that support emerging literacy and reading skills among prekindergarten (children enter kindergarten ready to read). Some limited funding is available for services that can help remove barriers toward reading success. All organizations seeking funding must first submit a Letter of Inquiry (LOI). The specific guidelines for the LOI can be downloaded from the sponsor's website. LOIs are due no later than July 1. For those LOIs moving forward, a full proposal is due by October 1 for a spring decision.
Restrictions: In general, the foundation does not award grants toward: debt reduction, research projects, tickets or advertising for fundraising events, individuals, religious exclusivism, or capital campaigns.
Geographic Focus: Arizona, California, Connecticut, New Mexico, Ohio, Washington
Date(s) Application is Due: Oct 1
Amount of Grant: Up to 100,000 USD
Contact: Patricia O'Brien; (440) 366-4884; fax (440) 366-4656; pobrien@stockerfoundation.org
Internet: http://www.stockerfoundation.org/grants.aspx
Sponsor: Stocker Foundation
201 Burns Road
Elyria, OH 44035

Stockton Rush Bartol Foundation Grants 4508
The foundation promotes cultural activities in Philadelphia. Its highest priority is serving children (arts education efforts that promote social development), communities (broaden access to high-quality experiences at the neighborhood level), and the arts community (arts groups at critical junctures in their artistic or organizational development). Grants also go to diversify audiences, help artists produce or exhibit work, create new works, or provide services to a broad cultural community. The foundation encourages art that involves experimentation and risk.
Requirements: Nonprofit organizations in the Philadelphia area are eligible to apply.
Restrictions: Grants do not support capital projects (except as part of historic preservation efforts), religious organizations, or political activities.
Geographic Focus: Pennsylvania
Date(s) Application is Due: May 3
Samples: To be divided among 32 groups in Philadelphia (PA)—to support local arts and cultural organizations, with an emphasis on arts-education and community-based arts programs, $176,000.
Contact: Beth Feldman Brandt; (215) 557-7225; fax (215) 557-7316; info@bartol.org
Internet: http://www.bartol.org
Sponsor: Stockton Rush Bartol Foundation
1811 Chestnut Street, The Belgravia, Suite 301
Philadelphia, PA 19103

Stonyfield Farm Profits for the Planet Program Grants 4509
The program annually awards 10 percent of the company's profits to environmental protection and resource conservation efforts. Priority is given to proposed projects that aim to protect and restore the planet; generate measurable results; and promote Stonyfield Farm via sampling opportunities, collateral, media relations, etc. The program also donates products. Written product requests should include an estimated number of recipients, date of the event, and a brief description of the organization. Product requests should be submitted at least one month prior to the event to Kim Brugger at the listed address.
Requirements: Section 501(c)3 of the Internal Revenue Code

Geographic Focus: All States
Contact: Mary Townsend, Director; (603) 437-7594; mtownsend@stonyfield.com
Internet: http://www.stonyfield.com/EarthActions/GivingProfitstothePlanet.cfm
Sponsor: Stonyfield Farm
10 Burton Drive
Londonderry, NH 03053

Stowe Family Foundation Grants 4510
The Foundation focuses on giving primarily for community development, higher education, the arts, natural resource conservation, children, youth, social services and Christian churches. The geographic focus is on Brunswick, Maine, New York City, and Pennsylvania. There are no specific deadlines and no formal application processes.
Restrictions: Giving primarily to 501(c)3 organizations located in the State of Pennsylvania, New York City, and Brunswick, Maine.
Geographic Focus: Maine, New York, Pennsylvania
Samples: The Episopal School, New York, NY, $22,000; Bowdoin College, Brunswick, ME, $50,000.
Contact: Richard H. Stowe, Treasurer; (212) 879-6727
Sponsor: Stowe Family Foundation
912 5th Avenue, Suite 6B
New York, NY 10021-4159

Strake Foundation Grants 4511
The Foundation supports hospitals, schools, colleges, and Catholic charities, as well as projects focusing in adult basic education and literacy, museums, and arts and culture. Support is considered for operating budgets, capital campaigns, special projects, research, matching funds and general purposes.
Requirements: Awards are made to 501(c)3 organizations located only in the United States, primarily in Texas. Organizations may submit only one request per calendar year. There are no set amounts for requests, however awards generally range between $2,000 and $20,000 with a few exceptions as high as $50,000.
Restrictions: Awards are not made to support individuals, nor for deficit financing, consulting services, technical assistance, publications, or loans.
Geographic Focus: All States
Contact: George Strake, Jr., President; (713) 216-2400; foundation@strake.org
Sponsor: Strake Foundation
712 Main Street, Suite 3300
Houston, TX 77002

Stranahan Foundation Grants 4512
The Stranahan Foundation was created in 1944 by brothers Frank D. and Robert A. Stranahan, founders of the Champion Spark Plug Company in Toledo, Ohio. The purpose of the foundation is to assist individuals and groups in their efforts to become more self-sufficient and contribute to the improvement of society and the environment. The foundation supports a multitude of important programs that fit within five priority areas of interest: Human Services, Ecological Well-Being, Arts & Culture, Education, and Mental & Physical Health. Grant funds may be used for start up support for a new program, operating support, expansion or capacity building, or capital support.
Requirements: Nonprofit organizations with 501(c)3 tax-exempt status are eligible to apply. While the foundation awards funds nationwide, its focus is on the Toledo, Ohio area. All applicants must, as a first step, submit a letter of inquiry to the Stranahan Foundation. Full proposals are by invitation only and may only be submitted by organizations that are invited to apply after their letter of inquiry has been accepted and reviewed. The Foundation will contact those organizations invited to submit a full proposal and notify those that are not eligible to apply. Instructions and forms for letters of inquiry and full grant proposals can be found on the website.
Restrictions: The Stranahan Foundation does not normally consider proposals for funding in the following areas: personal businesses; reduction or elimination of deficits; projects that are located outside of the United States; endowment fund campaigns; government sponsored or controlled projects; or individuals. Additionally, the foundation will not support organizations that discriminate in the leadership, staffing or service provision on the basis of age, gender, race, ethnicity, sexual orientation, disability, national origin, political affiliation or religious beliefs.
Geographic Focus: All States
Date(s) Application is Due: Jul 1
Amount of Grant: 1,000 USD
Contact: Pam Roberts; (419) 882-5575; fax (419) 882-2072; proberts@stranahanfoundation.org
Internet: http://www.stranahanfoundation.org/index.php?src=gendocs&ref=GrantmakingPriorities&category=Main
Sponsor: Stranahan Foundation
4169 Holland-Sylvania Road, #201
Toledo, OH 43623

Strengthening Families - Strengthening Communities Grants 4513
The foundation is committed to improving the quality of life for residents of metropolitan Richmond. Competitive grantmaking focuses on building or enhancing the resources of the charitable sector to address: basic human needs for children and families who are impoverished; child and youth development, with an emphasis on young people who are at moderate or high risk of experiencing problems in school, in their social interactions, or with lifestyle choices; community development that promotes affordable housing and safe neighborhoods; opportunities to broadly enrich family and community life; and collaborative models of service, volunteerism, and community leadership development. Generally, projects undertaken in collaboration with other nonprofits receive a higher priority. These may include requests that address unmet or emerging community needs or allow for program expansion or enhancement. Collaboratives that include current recipient organizations or that minimize duplication of services will be considered. The foundation will give preference to those organizations that seek to develop or enhance their work through a cohesive regional strategy. Guidelines are available online.
Requirements: Proposals will be accepted from charitable organizations that serve the residents of metropolitan Richmond and Central Virginia. Generally, projects undertaken in collaboration with other nonprofits receive a higher priority. These may include requests that address unmet or emerging community needs or allow for program expansion or enhancement. Collaboratives that include current recipient organizations or that minimize duplication of services will be considered. The foundation will give preference to those organizations that seek to develop or enhance their work through a cohesive regional strategy.
Geographic Focus: Virginia
Date(s) Application is Due: May 5; Nov 5
Amount of Grant: 5,000 - 100,000 USD
Contact: Susan Hallett; (804) 330-7400; fax (804) 330-5992; shallett@tcfrichmond.org
Internet: http://www.tcfrichmond.org/page2954.cfm#CF
Sponsor: Community Foundation Serving Richmond and Central Virginia
7501 Boulders View Drive, Suite 110
Richmond, VA 23225

Strolling of the Heifers Scholarships for Farmers 4514
The purpose of the scholarship program is to encourage farmers' ongoing education in the agricultural field, and will award funding to farmers and agricultural students who want to take a course, attend workshops or conferences, or pursue other educational opportunities related to farming. Applicants may apply for funding to cover registration or other fees. Scholarship money also can be used to cover the cost of the time on the farm lost by farmers pursuing further education.
Requirements: Farmers, farm employees, and agriculture students are eligible to receive scholarships. More than one applicant from a farm may apply for funding. All applicants must complete a separate application form. To be eligible, applicants must apply no later than 2 months after the date of the educational opportunity. Applications must be accompanied by a copy of the paperwork related to the educational opportunity. Application forms are available at the foundation's web site.
Geographic Focus: Vermont
Amount of Grant: Up to 250 USD
Contact: Laurie Garland, (802) 257-1646
Internet: http://www.strollingoftheheifers.org
Sponsor: Strolling of the Heifers Foundation
105 Partridge Road
East Dummerston, VT 05346

Strowd Roses Grants 4515
Strowd Roses, Inc. is a private charitable foundation which was established in 2001 under the will of Mrs. Irene Harrison Strowd of Chapel Hill, North Carolina. The Board of Directors of Strowd Roses, Inc. makes grants to qualified tax-exempt charitable, educational, religious and public organizations that are based in Chapel Hill or Carrboro, or are devoted primarily to benefiting the citizens of those communities. Grants may also be made to individuals engaged in projects designed to enhance the Chapel Hill/Carrboro community. Grants may, at the Board's discretion, include support for operating as well as capital expenditures, seed money and matching grants. Grants to individuals may be used for scholarships or fellowships; to produce a report or similar product; or to improve or enhance a literary, artistic, musical, scientific, teaching or similar capacity, skill or talent which will be used to benefit the life of the community. Particular consideration is given to those projects and purposes which further the interests of Mr. and Mrs. Strowd, including the welfare of children and youth, the enhancement of the environment, and the promotion of a sense of civic duty.
Requirements: Applicants should submit the appropriate application form (see foundations website), along with a proposed budget and evidence of their tax-exempt status (IRS determination letter or comparable documentation) to: Board of Directors, Strowd Roses, Inc., P.O. Box 3558, Chapel Hill, NC, 27515-3558.
Geographic Focus: North Carolina
Date(s) Application is Due: Jan 31; Apr 30; Jul 31; Oct 31
Contact: Jennifer Boger; (919) 929-1984; fax (919) 929-1990; jboger@strowdroses.org
Internet: http://www.strowdroses.org/grantApp.htm
Sponsor: Strowd Roses
P.O. Box 3558
Chapel Hill, NC 27515-3558

Stuart Foundation Grants 4516
The foundation's mission is to help children and youth in California and the state of Washington become capable, responsible citizens. Areas of interest include strengthening communities that serve families (community building, service integration, institutional and community partnerships, professional development, and technical assistance), strengthening the child welfare system (permanency, supportive services for youth, comprehensive assessment and services, prevention, or volunteering), strengthening public schools (teacher development, public policy, early learning, systemic school reform, and other opportunities), and policy analysis and advocacy. The foundation is interested in funding programs that promote collaboration and integrated services to improve children's outcomes. Grants also include assistance with community engagement, conflict resolution, research, technology, and training. Types of support include seed money, operating support, and special projects. Programs receive funding each year; renewal is subject to board and staff decisions. Obtain a guidelines brochure from the office.
Requirements: The foundation supports programs serving California and Washington.
Restrictions: The foundation does not make grants to support political activities, endowments, building campaigns, fundraising events, material acquisition, or operating funds.

Geographic Focus: California, Washington
Date(s) Application is Due: Mar 1; Jun 1; Sep 1; Dec 1
Amount of Grant: 5,000 - 100,000 USD
Contact: Stephanie Titus, Grants Manager; (415) 393-1551; fax (415) 393-1552
Internet: http://www.stuartfoundation.org/how.html
Sponsor: Stuart Foundation
50 California Street, Suite 3350
San Francisco, CA 94111-4735

Subaru Adopt a School Garden Grants 4517
Through a grant to the National Gardening Association, Subaru of America Foundation is sponsoring the National Gardening Association's Adopt a School Garden (ASG) program in 9 southern New Jersey schools. In addition to receiving technical assistance, horticultural and garden education consultation from the ASG program, winners will also receive $1,000 in materials and funding to lay the foundation for their garden program. In addition to receiving technical assistance and horticultural and garden education consultation from the ASG program, winners will also receive $1,000 in materials and funding to lay the foundation for their garden program.
Requirements: Elementary, middle, and high schools serving low to middle income students located in the following southern New Jersey counties are eligible: Burlington, Camden, Cumberland, Gloucester, and Salem Counties, with preference given to Burlington and Camden Counties. Educators should be planning to use the garden to teach students life skills, reinforce academics, develop environmental stewardship, and encourage students to make positive choices for themselves and the planet. Established and start-up garden programs are encouraged to apply. The garden program must be implemented by June 30. No purchase necessary. Purchase of a product does not improve your chances of receiving an award. Download the required application at the website.
Geographic Focus: New Jersey
Date(s) Application is Due: Feb 9
Amount of Grant: 1,000 USD
Contact: Donna Booska, (800) 538-7476, ext. 115; fax (802) 864-6889; donna@garden.org
Internet: http://www.kidsgardening.org/grants/SubaruASG.asp
Sponsor: National Gardening Association
1100 Dorset Street
South Burlington, VT 05403

Subaru of America Foundation Grants 4518
The Subaru of America Foundation was established in 1984 to support the communities where facilities are located. The Foundation seeks partnerships and awards grants in the area of education to nonprofit organizations that: engage youth and encourage their active participation in the learning experience, including (but not limited to) professional development for educators, programs that enhance math and science education, and literacy improvement and education; promote environmental stewardship and education for youth, including (but not limited to) school gardens and science exploration as it pertains to the environment; and benefit youth through grade 12. Listed application deadline dates are for letters of inquiry; full proposals are by invitation. Application and guidelines are available online.
Requirements: 501(c)3 nonprofits in the following regions are eligible to apply: southern New Jersey (mainly Camden and Burlington counties); Philadelphia, Pennsylvania; Westhampton, New Jersey; Orlando, Florida; Atlanta, Georgia; Washington, DC; Itasca and Chicago, Illinois; Minneapolis, Minnesota; Columbus, Ohio; Dallas, Texas; Denver, Colorado; Phoenix, Arizona; San Diego, California; Los Angeles, California; San Francisco, California; Portland, Oregon and Seattle, Washington.
Restrictions: Consideration will not be given to organizations whose fund balances exceed $5 million. The trustees prefer not to fund individuals; veterans, fraternal, and labor organizations; government agencies; direct support of churches, religious, or sectarian groups; social, membership, or other groups that serve the special interests of their constituency; advertising; sponsorships of special events, purchase of tables, and athletic campaigns; capital campaigns; political organizations, campaigns, or candidates running for public office; organizations that benefit individuals outside the United States; or organizations that, in policy or practice, discriminate against a person or group on the basis of age, political affiliation, race, national origin, ethnicity, gender, religious belief, disability, or sexual orientation. Vehicle donations will not be considered. As a general rule, national organizations are not eligible.
Geographic Focus: Colorado, Georgia, Illinois, New Jersey
Date(s) Application is Due: Jan 30; Aug 31
Amount of Grant: 1,000 - 10,000 USD
Contact: Manager; (856) 488-8500; fax (956) 488-3274; foundation@subaru.com
Internet: http://www.subaru.com/company/soa-foundation/index.html
Sponsor: Subaru of America Foundation
P.O. Box 6000, Subaru Plaza
Cherry Hill, NJ 08034-6000

Subaru of Indiana Automotive Foundation Grants 4519
The Subaru of Indiana Automotive Foundation is committed to making gifts to qualifying organizations, institutions, or entities within Indiana that will improve the quality of life and help meet the needs of the residents of the state. The foundation awards cash grants that are used to support the funding of specific capital projects in the areas of: arts and culture, education, and health and welfare. Grants must be used for investments in facilities, equipment, or real estate made by qualifying organizations. Grant requests must be for $1,000 or more, with a maximum requested amount of $10,000. Funding can be used for investments in facilities, equipment, or real estate (non-operation funding). Applications for grants will be accepted from January 1 through March 31 to be considered for a grant to be dispersed by June 15. Applications will be accepted from July 1 through September 30 to be considered for a grant to be dispersed by December 15.
Requirements: Applying organizations must be 501(c)3 tax-exempt, with a chapter or office in Indiana; an education institution located in Indiana; or an Indiana governmental or quasi-governmental entity.
Restrictions: Support will not be provided for operating costs, routine expenses, or deficit reduction; endowments or memorials; fundraising events, conferences, meals, or travel; or annual fund drives. Support will not be provided to individuals; organizations located outside of Indiana or organizations that are not tax-exempt; for-profit businesses; organizations whose primary purpose is to influence legislation or support political candidates; religious institutions for religious purposes or fraternal organizations; or organizations that discriminate in the provision of services on the basis of race, sex, color, national origin, disability, age, religious affiliation, or any other unlawful basis.
Geographic Focus: Indiana
Date(s) Application is Due: Mar 31; Sep 30
Amount of Grant: 1,000 - 10,000 USD
Contact: Shannon Walker; (765) 449-6565; shannon.walker@subaru-sia.com
Internet: http://www.siafoundation.org
Sponsor: Subaru of Indiana Automotive Foundation
P.O. Box 6479
Lafayette, IN 47903

Subaru Rainbow Leadership Award 4520
The award honors an individual or organization whose work has benefited gay, lesbian, bisexual, and transgender people. The winner will receive a monetary contribution to further his/her work and goals. Nomination forms and additional information are available online.
Requirements: Individuals or organizations working to advance causes of importance to gay, lesbian, bisexual, and transgender people are eligible.
Geographic Focus: All States
Date(s) Application is Due: May 22
Amount of Grant: 10,000 USD
Contact: Jean E. Bochnowski, Executive Director; (215)241-7280
Internet: http://www.rainbowendowment.org/apply.html
Sponsor: Rainbow Endowment
1501 Cherry Street
Philadelphia, PA 19102-1403

Suffolk County Office of Film and Cultural Affairs Cultural Arts Grants 4521
The Suffolk County Office of Film and Cultural Affairs announces a streamlined grant program for small community arts organizations, to be administered by the Suffolk County Alliance of Arts Councils, which includes: Babylon Citizens Council on the Arts, Brookhaven Arts and Humanities Council, East End Arts Council, Greater Port Jefferson-Northern Brookhaven Arts Council, Huntington Arts Council, and Smithtown Township Arts Council. The County will appropriate $12,000 to each of the seven County arts councils to distribute in amounts of $500 to $5000 to community arts groups performing or exhibiting in each of the seven service areas.
Restrictions: Applicants must be 501(c)3 organizations supporting programs in Suffolk County, New York.
Geographic Focus: New York
Date(s) Application is Due: Nov 27
Amount of Grant: 500 - 5,000 USD
Contact: Michelle Isabelle-Stark, Director; (631) 853-4800; fax (634) 853-4888; michelle.stark@suffolkcountyny.gov
Internet: http://www.suffolkartsandfilm.com/ca_grants.html
Sponsor: Suffolk County Office of Film and Cultural Affairs
H. Lee Dennison Building, 100 Veterans Memorial Highway, 2nd Floor
Hauppauge, NY 11788

Sulzberger Foundation Grants 4522
The foundation awards grants to eligible nonprofit organizations in its areas of interest, including arts and culture, education, environmental protection and natural resource conservation, hospitals, and social services delivery. Types of support include annual campaigns, building construction/renovation, endowments, general operating support, multiyear grants, programs and projects, and scholarship funds. There are no application forms or deadlines. Preference is given to requests from New York City and Chatanooga.
Restrictions: Individuals are not eligible. Loans and matching grants are not awarded.
Geographic Focus: All States
Contact: Marian Heiskell, President; (212) 556-1400
Sponsor: Sulzberger Foundation
229 W 43rd Street, Suite 1031
New York, NY 10036

Summerlee Foundation Grants 4523
Created in 1988 by Dallas philanthropist Annie Lee Roberts, the purpose of Summerlee Foundation is restricted to programs in animal protection and Texas history. Animal protection funding is geographically restricted to communities which are most underserved and the most challenged, with an emphasis on the west and mid-west regions of the United States. Programmatically, the Foundation focuses on cats with special emphasis on the feral and free-roaming. They continue to support work with Mexico and the Associacion Internacional Protectora de Animales. Their wildlife program continues its emphasis on mountain lions, bobcats, coyotes and bears, funding only those programs which protect with advocacy and ethical research. They continue to support Earth Island Institute and the Sunny Initiative, an anti-captivity program protecting dolphins and whales. Texas history programs have funded a wide variety of Texas history programs in a multitude of disciplines, ranging from academic research to field archaeology, throughout every region

of the state. The Foundation is a strong advocate of collaborative projects between historical organizations. The Foundation requires contact with the appropriate program director prior to submitting a proposal. Proposals are reviewed three times a year. After receipt of a proposal, applicants will be notified of the review date.
Requirements: 501(c)3 tax-exempt organizations are eligible.
Restrictions: The following is not eligible: awards for religious purposes; individuals; courthouse restoration; planning and construction of monuments or memorials; and indirect costs to educational institutions.
Geographic Focus: All States
Contact: John W. Crain; (214) 363-9000 or (888) 363-9003; info@summerlee.org
Internet: http://www.summerlee.org/grant.apps.html
Sponsor: Summerlee Foundation
5556 Caruth Haven Lane
Dallas, TX 75225

Summit Foundation Grants 4524
The Summit Foundation supports charitable organizations that enhance the quality of life in Summit County, Colorado, and neighboring communities. Grants are awarded twice each year, in June and in December, to agencies providing programs or services in the areas of health and human service, art and culture, education, environment and sports. The Foundation funds specific projects and programs which have measurable results.
Requirements: Applicants for funding must be tax exempt under the provisions of section 501(c)3 and 170(b)1(a)(i.V.I.) of the Internal Revenue Code.
Restrictions: The Foundation will not fund any political campaign on behalf of any issue or candidate. Additionally, The Foundation does not fund religious programs. Organizations requesting funding support will only be considered for funding once in a calendar year. Requests for programs or projects already completed are not eligible for funding.
Geographic Focus: Colorado
Contact: Lee Zimmerman; (970) 453-5970; fax (970) 453-1423; sumfound@colorado.net
Internet: http://www.summitfoundation.org/gRequest.php
Sponsor: Summit Foundation
111 Lincoln Avenue, P.O. Box 4000
Breckenridge, CO 80424

Sun Academic Excellence Grants 4525
The Sun Academic Excellence Grant program has helped numerous schools kick-start their projects by providing equipment grants and access to free training and certifications. Funding for grants focus on areas such as: curriculum integration—the integration of Sun Technology in undergraduate and graduate level courses through the development and use of model curricula; community development—the sponsorship of a Sun or Open Source community development projects that align with the academic and research interests of your students, faculty and researchers and result in put-backs to the code; localization—the localization of the code or development tools and resources to languages other than English; community outreach—to promote broad awareness of Sun technologies on campus and participation of faculty, students and other members of the academic community in Sun communities through events, workshops and end-user communications; Java software development—NetBeans IDE plug-ins that result in put backs to the Net Beans community; application development—development of an application, technology or solution using the Sun platform which can be deployed in the Education, Life Science, Healthcare or Government industry; and thin client—deployment of Sun Ray thin clients; ideally 100 or more seats. Grants are made on a published quarterly calendar and are for hardware donations only.
Requirements: In the United States, higher education eligible institutions must have: 3304(f) or a 501(c)3 or Section 115 tax exempt status; and be a degree granting institution or be involved in basic research. Outside of the United States, higher education institutions must either be degree-granting or involved in basic research and be recognized as a non-commercial enterprise by their national government. To be eligible as a primary or secondary educational institution, the following guidelines must be met: public or private formal full-time educational institution offering classes in the range or equivalence of grades Primary and Secondary (K12); or licensed, certified or accredited to operate as a school or school administrative unit in the state or country of operation.
Restrictions: Grants do not include maintenance, service or technical support. Non-profit institutions with 501(c)3 status which are neither degree-granting nor directly involved with basic research may be eligible if they directly support the academic and research communities in their mission to create and disseminate knowledge, and if they can demonstrate financial need.
Geographic Focus: All States
Date(s) Application is Due: Feb 26; May 31; Aug 31; Nov 30
Contact: Linda Rogers, Senior Director of Strategy; (650) 336-0487 or (650) 960-1300; fax (650) 856-2114; corpaffrs@corp.sun.com
Internet: http://www.sun.com/solutions/landing/industry/education/aeg.xml
Sponsor: Sun Microsystems Corporation
4150 Network Circle
Santa Clara, CA 95054

Sunbeam Products Grants 4526
The corporation awards grants and donates products, with priority given to requests from its operating areas, to support(Youth & Education; Health & Health Services; Community & Civic; Arts & Culture; Environment & Conservation) Programs in which employees volunteer are encouraged. There are no application deadlines. Guidelines are available online.
Requirements: 501(c)3 nonprofit organizations are eligible.
Restrictions: The company does not generally make contributions to individuals or individuals' research projects; organizations without 501(c)3 status; political activities; trips, travel, or cultural exchange programs; or endowment campaigns.
Geographic Focus: All States
Contact: Corporate Philanthropy Coordinator; (561) 912-4585; fax (561) 912-4668; corpaffairs@sunbeam.com
Internet: http://www.sunbeam.com
Sponsor: Sunbeam Products
2381 NW Executive Center Drive
Boca Raton, FL 33431

Sunderland Foundation Grants 4527
The foundation makes grants annually to publicly supported charitable organizations in its areas of interest, including higher education; churches; youth serving agencies; health facilities; community buildings; museums; civic projects; and and low maintenance, energy efficient housing projects sponsored by qualified tax-exempt organizations. The Foundation generally awards grants to larger, well-established nonprofit organizations. The Sunderland Foundation primarily makes grants in the geographic areas that have connections to the Ash Grove Cement Company. Grants are awarded in Western Missouri, Kansas, Nebraska, Arkansas, and Western Iowa, and to a lesser extent, in Idaho, Oregon, Washington, Utah and Montana.
Requirements: All grant requests should be submitted in writing, and proposals should include the following: a clear description of the project for which funds are being requested, including program goals and objectives, documentation of need and expected outcomes; a brief background on the proposing organization or agency; a detailed expense budget for the project indicating how the funds would be spent and over what time period; an income statement showing other sources of project support, public and/or private, which have been or will be solicited, including a statement of funds that have been received or pledged to date; a financial plan showing how the project will be supported beyond the grant period; the organization's current board of directors and their terms of office; a copy of the organization's most recent 501(c)3 tax-exempt ruling from the IRS; the organization's most recent certified audit or audited financial statement, where applicable. Proposals should be submitted by mail to the address listed in the "Sponsoring Organization" catagory. Proposals will also be accepted by email. Send a PDF file to the following address: sunderlandfoundation@ashgrove.com.
Restrictions: The Foundation does not award grants: for annual operating expenses; for programs or endowments; provide sponsorship for special events; to primary and secondary schools are generally not considered; to individuals. No scholarships are available from the Foundation.
Geographic Focus: Arkansas, Idaho, Iowa, Kansas, Missouri, Montana, Nebraska, Oregon, Utah, Washington
Contact: Kent Sunderland; (913) 451-8900; sunderlandfoundation@ashgrove.com
Internet: http://www.sunderlandfoundation.org
Sponsor: Sunderland Foundation
P.O. Box 25900
Overland Park, KS 66225

Sunflower Foundation Bridge Grants 4528
Bridge Grant funding is intended to provide core transitional financial support for new or expanded medical, mental, dental and/or public health services that provide primary care or primary prevention services to the uninsured and the underinsured. Funds are available for: salaries, benefits, allowable indirect expenses appropriate to the health care practitioners needed for the program; administrative services (e.g. financial & medical record clerks, clerical staff) resulting from the new or expanded services for which funding is being requested from the Foundation. Applicants must demonstrate a cost share in the project through a cash match of $1 to $1 of the total amount requested. Grants will not exceed $200,000 each and may be for projects up to three years in length.
Requirements: Proposals are invited from private nonprofit or public organizations that have a mission to improve health status or access to quality, affordable health care for Kansans.
Restrictions: The foundation will not fund ongoing general operating expenses or existing deficits; capital, endowment or specific fund-raising campaigns; fund raising events; routine continuing education; travel to conferences not directly related to the project; programs that are not Kansas-based; programs that require additional staff but demonstrate no clear means of sustainability after foundation funding; individual medical care or support; medical equipment; capital equipment (except for allowable technology); political purposes; or support of organizations that practice discrimination. Additional exclusions include: requests for new construction; and facility renovations. Any Safety Net clinic that qualifies for the Dental Hub initiative should contact the Sunflower Foundation program staff prior to application (there may be some restrictions for Dental Bridge Grant funding for organizations eligible for Dental Hub funding).
Geographic Focus: Kansas
Date(s) Application is Due: Oct 23
Amount of Grant: Up to 200,000 USD
Contact: Cheryl Bean; (785) 232-3000, ext. 104; cbean@sunflowerfoundation.org
Internet: http://www.sunflowerfoundation.org/areas_of_interest-health_care_access.php
Sponsor: Sunflower Foundation: Health Care for Kansans
1200 SW Executive Drive, Suite 100
Topeka, KS 66615-3850

Sunny and Abe Rosenberg Foundation Grants 4529
The Rosenberg Foundation awards grants to New York City area nonprofit organizations. Funding priorities include programs that promote excellence in public education; artistic and cultural education for public school students; and activities that promote learning for disadvantaged children and youth. The Foundation also awards support to supplementary services for children currently in foster care and young adults moving out of the foster system. Typically, an awarded grant ranges from $10,000 to $50,000. The Foundation does not accept unsolicited proposals.

Requirements: New York City-area nonprofit organizations are eligible. Applicants should contact the Foundation to see if their project may be eligible for funding.
Restrictions: The Foundation does not support advocacy, litigation, or political causes. Funding is also not available for individuals or other private foundations.
Geographic Focus: New York
Contact: Maryanne Passafiume; (212) 993-6230; mpassafiume@rosenbergfoundation.org
Internet: http://www.rosenbergfoundation.org/
Sponsor: Sunny and Abe Rosenberg Foundation
Ansonia Station
New York, NY 10023

Sunoco Foundation Grants 4530
The Sunoco Foundation invests in projects that promote local education and workforce development or that make communities great places to live and work. Grants are primarily awarded to nonprofits located where Sunoco has a major presence. The foundation considers all types of efforts, including homelessness, housing, community development, seniors and education. The Sunoco Foundation aligns giving and business strategy with focus on three key areas—Fueling Minds: Educate and Develop Skills for the Workforce; Fueling the Planet: Promote Environmental Stewardship and Responsibility; and, Fueling Communities: Make them great places to live and work.
Requirements: Applicants must successfully complete an eligibility quiz before submitting an online letter of inquiry. If the letter of inquiry matches the foundation's priorities, the applicant will be invited to submit a full proposal. The Foundation prefers to fund specific projects rather than operating budgets.
Restrictions: Requests for deficit funding, individuals, benefit fundraisers, endowments, surveys, studies, religious groups, fraternal organizations, athletic groups, schools, single diseases, and non-tax exempt organizations are generally not considered.
Geographic Focus: Alabama, Connecticut, Delaware, District of Columbia, Florida, Georgia, Indiana, Kentucky, Maine, Maryland, Massachusetts, Michigan, New Hampshire, New Jersey, New York, North Carolina, Ohio, Pennsylvania, Rhode Island, South Carolina, Tennessee, Vermont, Virginia, West Virginia
Contact: Ruth Clauser; (215) 977-3000; fax (215) 977-3409; raclauser@sunocoinc.com
Internet: https://online.foundationsource.com/public/home/sunoco
Sponsor: Sunoco Foundation
1735 Market Street, Suite Ll
Philadelphia, PA 19103

Suntrust Bank Atlanta Foundation Grants 4531
Grants are made to nonprofit metropolitan Atlanta organizations that have legitimate needs and a worthwhile purpose. The foundation will consider requests for grants for capital improvements such as buildings, furniture and equipment, and alterations to existing structures. Applications will be considered for special projects of a community nature, special studies, surveys, research and pilot programs which do not commit the funds to recurring expenditures. Applications are available on the Web site.
Requirements: The foundation makes grants to nonprofits in the metropolitan Atlanta area only. Usually grants will only be made to organizations with records of successful operation without a deficit for at least a year.
Restrictions: The fund will not consider requests for general operating support such as salaries, maintenance, and debt service, and requests by political organizations, churches, or individuals.
Geographic Focus: Georgia
Contact: Renee Barnett, (404) 588-8250
Internet: http://www.suntrustatlantafoundation.org
Sponsor: Suntrust Bank Atlanta Foundation
P.O. Box 4418, MC 041
Atlanta, GA 30302

Supreme Court Fellows Commission Fellowships 4532
The Supreme Court Fellows Commission seeks outstanding individuals who are interested in working in Washington, DC, within the federal judiciary. Fellows spend one calendar year (late August through early September) at the Supreme Court of the United States, the Federal Judicial Center, the Administrative Office of the United States Courts, or the U.S. Sentencing Commission working on various projects concerning the federal court system and the administration of justice. Up to four fellowships are awarded each year. Candidates must submit a resume, 700-word essay explaining their interest in the program, copies of two publications or other writing samples, and three reference letters. Additional information, an online application, and complete instructions are available online.
Requirements: Candidates must be familiar with the judicial system and have at least one postgraduate degree and two or more years of professional experience with high achievement. Multidisciplinary training and experience is desirable.
Geographic Focus: All States
Date(s) Application is Due: Nov 10
Contact: Administrative Director, Judicial Fellows Program; (202) 479-3415
Internet: http://www.fellows.supremecourtus.gov/index.html
Sponsor: Supreme Court of the United States
1 First Street NE
Washington, DC 20543

Surdna Foundation Sustainable Environments Grants 4533
The Surdna Foundation seeks to create just and sustainable communities where consumption and conservation are balanced and innovative solutions to environmental problems improve people's lives. It works from a sustainable development perspective to demonstrate that a healthy environment is the backbone of a healthy economy and a democratic society. The Foundation funds three key related priority areas - Climate Change, Green Economy, and Transportation and Smart Growth - that aim to transform how Americans work, consume, and move. Together these will help make the theory of a carbon free society into a practical and achievable reality for communities across the United States. The Surdna Foundation accepts applications on an ongoing basis. However, grants are approved three times per year: in February, May and September. Applicants should use the online letter of inquiry to apply for funding.
Requirements: 501(c)3 organizations may apply. The foundation urges applicants to send two- to three-page letters of intent before sending proposals. IRS nonprofit status certification, recent audited financial statements, and project budget should also be included.
Restrictions: Generally, the Surdna Foundation does not support: programs addressing toxics, hazardous waste, land and habitat conservation; animal welfare, biodiversity and ocean management; individuals; or academic fellowships.
Geographic Focus: All States
Amount of Grant: 15,000 - 1,000,000 USD
Contact: Edward Skloot, Executive Director; (212) 557-0010; fax (212) 557-0003; grants@surdna.org or executivedirector@surdna.org
Internet: http://www.surdna.org/what-we-fund/sustainable-environments.html
Sponsor: Surdna Foundation
330 Madison Avenue, 30th Floor
New York, NY 10017-5001

Susan A. and Donald P. Babson Charitable Foundation Grants 4534
The Foundation's focus is the enrichment and empowerment of people of all ages around the world, so as to prevent exploitation, poverty, and injustice. Applicants may submit a two-page concept letter by the deadline. Selected applicants will be asked to provide additional information. Grants range was $1,000 to $10,000, and the average size is $3,121. Verify guidelines and deadlines on the website.
Requirements: Applicants must be 501(c)3 organizations.
Restrictions: The Foundation does not make capital grants. A limited number of multi-year grants might be considered in each grant cycle.
Geographic Focus: All States
Date(s) Application is Due: Feb 28
Amount of Grant: 1,000 - 10,000 USD
Contact: Michelle Jenney; (617) 391-3087; mjenney@gmafoundations.com
Internet: http://www.babsonfoundation.org/?page_id=5
Sponsor: Susan A. and Donald P. Babson Charitable Foundation
77 Summer Street, 8th Floor
Boston, MA 02110

Susan G. Komen Breast Cancer Foundation Challege Grants: Breast Cancer and the Environment 4535
Major advances have been made in understanding the biology and diversity of breast cancer, but much more remains to be discovered about the many causes of breast cancer – particularly what contributions a diverse array of environmental factors may be making – and how to prevent it. The challenges are many: The scientific community has been presented with conflicting and inconclusive results from past studies. With increased knowledge of the complexity of breast cancer biology, it has become apparent that future research into environmental influences will need to focus on early-life exposures, associations with specific tumor types, and gene-environment interactions. Adding to the complexity of this task is the fact that for a wide array of exposures the assessment methodologies, tools and resources are limited. Through its Challenge Grants: Breast Cancer and the Environment program, the Foundation seeks to address key research needs in the field of environmental contributions to breast cancer risk. Susan G. Komen for the Cure and its Scientific Advisory Board have requested that the Institute of Medicine (IOM) review the current evidence on environmental risk factors for breast cancer, consider gene-environment interactions in breast cancer, explore evidence-based actions that might reduce the risk of breast cancer, and recommend research needed in these areas. At the conclusion of their report, the IOM issued 13 recommendations for further research, of which three have been chosen by the Komen Scientific Advisory Board as the subject of Challenge Grants: Studies of Occupational Cohorts and Other Highly Exposed Populations; New Exposure Assessment Tools; and Minimizing Exposure to Ionizing Radiation.
Requirements: U.S. nonprofits and international institutions will be eligible to apply.
Geographic Focus: All States
Amount of Grant: Up to 250,000 USD
Contact: Director; (972) 855-1600; fax (972) 855-1605; grants@komen.org
Internet: http://ww5.komen.org/ResearchGrants/FundingOpportunities.html
Sponsor: Susan G. Komen Breast Cancer Foundation
5005 LBJ Freeway, Suite 250
Dallas, TX 75244

Susan Mott Webb Charitable Trust Grants 4536
The trust awards grants to eligible Alabama nonprofit organizations in its areas of interest, including the arts, civic and public affairs, animals/wildlife, community development, education, health care, religion, social services, youth programs and homelessness. Types of support include annual campaigns, building construction/renovation, capital campaigns, continuing support, curriculum development, emergency funds, endowments, equipment, general/operating support, internship funds, program development, publication, and technical assistance. Contact the Foundation for further application information and guidelines.
Requirements: Giving limited to the greater Birmingham, AL, area.
Restrictions: Grants do not support advertising, individuals, international organizations, or political organizations.
Geographic Focus: Alabama
Date(s) Application is Due: Apr 1; Oct 1
Amount of Grant: 2,000 - 100,000 USD

Samples: Alabama Symphonic Association, Birmingham, AL, $40,000; Crisis Resource Center of Southeast Kansas, Pittsburg, KS, $25,000;
Contact: Laura Wainwright, Vice President, c/o Regions Bank; (205) 801-0380; fax (205) 581-7433; laura.wainwright@regions.com
Sponsor: Susan Mott Webb Charitable Trust
P.O. Box 11426
Birmingham, AL 35202-1426

Susan Vaughan Foundation Grants 4537
The Susan Vaughan Foundation established in 1952, supports non-profits involved with: education, particularly to a library; arts; environment, natural resources; higher education; human services. The Foundation gives primarily in Houston and Austin Texas area with support in the form of: annual campaigns; building/renovation; capital campaigns; general/operating support; matching/challenge support.
Requirements: There is no formal application form required, applicant must be a non-profit in the Houston and Austin, Texas region. Initial contact should be made through a Letter of Inquiry.
Geographic Focus: Texas
Amount of Grant: 2,500 - 630,000 USD
Contact: Jennifer Grosvenor; (713) 651-8980; jgrosvenor@legacytrust.com
Sponsor: Susan Vaughan Foundation
600 Jefferson Street, Suite 300
Houston, TX 77002-7377

SVP Early Childhood Development and Parenting Grants 4538
The foundation has established education and children's issues as grantmaking priorities and awards grants to Puget Sound nonprofits to support positive outcomes for children (prenatal through 18 years old). There are two grant cycles: a fall children's grant cycle and a spring education grant cycle. Types of support include curriculum development/teacher training, institutional development, education programs, general operating support, materials/equipment acquisition, seed grants, service delivery programs, and technical assistance. Letters of inquiry are invited. The letter of inquiry should not exceed two pages in length and have no attachments, with the following information: one paragraph summarizing the organization's mission, history, and goals; a summary of goals and specific activities to be supported by the grant (include population served); a description of how success will be measured; a description of how SVP volunteer or professional services will be used; and budget figures, including the amount requested, the total budget for the project, and the organization's operating budget for the current year. Letters of inquiry may be sent by fax, email as a Word attachment, and mail. Full proposals will be invited.
Requirements: Programs must serve King County in Washington. Applicants must be classified as nonprofit 501(c)3 public charities or public schools or school districts qualifying under section 170(c) of the IRS code.
Restrictions: The foundation does not consider requests from individuals, organizations that discriminate, religious organizations for sectarian purposes, sports teams, and political or lobbying organizations. The foundation does not consider requests for auctions or fund-raising events, debt reduction, endowment funds or capital campaigns, litigation or legal expenses, land acquisition, productions, or performances.
Geographic Focus: Washington
Date(s) Application is Due: Dec 2
Amount of Grant: 40,000 USD
Contact: Paul Shoemaker, Executive Director; (206) 374-8757; fax (206) 728-0552; paulshoe@svpseattle.org or info@svpseattle.org
Internet: http://www.svpseattle.org/grant_guidelines/early_childhood.htm
Sponsor: Social Venture Partners
1601 Second Avenue, Suite 605
Seattle, WA 98101-1541

SVP Environment Grants 4539
The program seeks to promote a healthy future for all life in the Pacific Northwest by fostering environmental stewardship that is ecologically based and economically sound. Environmental grantmaking priorities include: fostering a population of environmentally informed, responsible, proactive citizens; encouraging people from a wide range of interests and disciplines to work together in addressing environmental issues; supporting programs that eliminate problems at the source and promote systemic change; and supporting programs that have a broad societal impact. In addition to cash grants, SVP provides strategic consulting assistance (both volunteer and paid) to help build the organizational, management, and technology infrastructure of its nonprofit partners.
Requirements: Applicants must be classified as 501(c)3 public charities or public schools or school districts qualifying under Section 170(c) of the Internal Revenue Code.
Restrictions: SVP will not consider grant requests from individuals; religious organizations for sectarian purposes; sports teams; or organizations that discriminate on the basis of race, sexual orientation, gender, age, marital status, national origin, or physical ability. SVP also will not make grants intended to influence legislation or to support candidates for political office, auctions or fundraising events, debt reduction, endowment funds or capital campaigns, litigation or legal expenses, land acquisition, or productions or performances.
Geographic Focus: Idaho, Oregon, Washington
Date(s) Application is Due: Feb 10
Amount of Grant: 40,000 USD
Contact: Program Contact; (206) 728-0552; info@svpseattle.org
Internet: http://www.svpseattle.org/grant_guidelines/environment.htm
Sponsor: Social Venture Partners
1601 Second Avenue, Suite 605
Seattle, WA 98101-1541

Swaim-Gause-Rucker Foundation Grants 4540
The Foundation, established in May of 1979, offers general charitable giving throughout the Mart, Texas, region. Funding comes in the form of gifts, grants, and general loans that support 501(c)3 organizations' general operations and new projects. There are no specific application forms or deadlines with which to adhere. Applicants seeking support should submit: a copy of their IRS determination letter; a detailed description of the project; and a budgeted amount of funding requested.
Geographic Focus: Texas
Contact: Wells Fargo Private Client Services; (254) 714-6160
Sponsor: Swaim-Gause-Rucker Foundation
P.O. Box 2626
Waco, TX 76702-2626

Sweet Water Trust Grants 4541
Since its establishment in 1992, Sweet Water Trust has been actively involved in conservation work in New England and Upstate New York, focusing in recent years on the forests of the Northern Appalachians, including neighboring lands in Canada. This funding program gives grants to conservation groups who love and protect wild places. The Trust works with conservation non-profits, government agencies, foundations, businesses, and individual landowners to help find the means and instruments to convert some of the private land at risk in the region into conservation land protected forever as wild.
Requirements: Eligible applicants must be publicly supported, tax-exempt non-profit organization and a qualified organization under Sections 501(c)3 and 170(h) of the Internal Revenue Code, within New York, New England and parts of Canada. The Trust does not accept unsolicited proposals, contact Eve Endicott, Executive Director for an interview prior to submitting any material.
Geographic Focus: Connecticut, Maine, Massachusetts, New Hampshire, New York, Rhode Island, Vermont, Canada
Contact: Eve Endicott; (617) 263-7776; fax (617) 263-7774; eendicott@sweetwatertrust.org
Internet: http://www.sweetwatertrust.org/article/articleview/2556/1/297/
Sponsor: Sweet Water Trust
Faneuil Hall Marketplace, 4 South Market Building, 4th Floor
Boston, MA 02109-1610

Swindells Charitable Foundation 4542
The Swindells Charitable Foundation was established in 1933 to support and promote quality health and human-services programming for underserved children and adults. The Swindells Charitable Foundation also makes grants to public charitable hospitals. Preference is given to organizations that serve sick or economically disadvantaged children or older adults. Special consideration is given to organizations that provide for the "basic human needs" of individuals. Grants from the Swindells Charitable Foundation are one year in duration. Applicants must apply online at the grant website. Applicants are strongly encouraged to do the following before applying: review the downloadable state application procedures for additional helpful information and clarifications; review the downloadable online-application guidelines at the grant website; review the foundation's funding history (link is available from the grant website); review the online application questions in advance; and review the list of required attachments. These will generally include: a list of board members, financial statements (audited, reviewed, or compiled by independent auditor); an organization summary; a list of other funding sources; an IRS Determination letter; and other required documents. All attachments must be uploaded in the online application as PDF, Word, or Excel files. The Swindells Charitable Foundation has biannual deadlines of February 1 and August 1. Applications are by 11:59 p.m. on the deadline dates. Applicants will be notified of grant decisions by letter within two to three months after each respective proposal deadline.
Requirements: Applicants must have 501(c)3 tax-exempt status.
Restrictions: Applicants will not be awarded a grant for more than three consecutive years. The trust does not support requests from individuals, organizations attempting to influence policy through direct lobbying, or any political campaigns. Capital requests will not be considered.
Geographic Focus: Connecticut
Date(s) Application is Due: Feb 1; Aug 1
Contact: Kate Kerchaert; (860) 657-7016; kate.kerchaert@baml.com
Internet: https://www.bankofamerica.com/philanthropic/fn_search.action
Sponsor: Swindells Charitable Foundation
200 Glastonbury Boulevard, Suite # 200, CT2-545-02-05
Glastonbury, CT 06033-4056

Sylvia Adams Charitable Trust Grants 4543
The Sylvia Adams Charitable Trust supports organizations that work with: children and young people; those with a disability; and those living in poverty or who are disadvantaged. In the area of children and young people, the Trust is particularly interested in: work which addresses the needs of children at risk of neglect and who are affected by lack of appropriate parenting; and work with young people that will give them the chance to acquire essential life skills such as communication, self discipline, motivation and empathy (this includes projects that focus on challenging activities, sport, the arts and access to the natural environment). For those with disability, the Trust has a particular emphasis on: innovations that have the potential to bring about significant improvements (excluding medical research); sporting and cultural activities, and access to the natural environment; and conditions that are less publicized or generally known and therefore attract less public support. For those experiencing poverty or social exclusion, the Trust includes: work which addresses homelessness; and particular problems facing some rural communities. Primary fields of interest include: education; water and sanitation; high impact health initiatives; and projects to help small scale farmers. Grants will normally be in the range of 5,000 pounds to 30,000 pounds. Occasionally the Trustees may make a grant up to 50,000 pounds. Most grants will be for one or two years, though in certain circumstances a grant may be made over three years.

Requirements: The Trust supports residents of Hertfordshire (local projects), the United Kingdom (rural poverty), and overseas (far reaching poverty). For work in Hertfordshire and the United Kingdom, most of the organizations that the Trust will make grants to will be registered charities. However it will also consider applications from organizations that are delivering work which is legally charitable. For overseas work, the Trust will only make grants to United Kingdom registered charities, but seek those whose activities are strengthening the capacity of local NGO's.
Restrictions: The Trust will not consider localized United Kingdom projects outside Hertfordshire. It will only consider United Kingdom work which has a wider impact. The Trust does not fund: individuals; overseas countries other than those specified in Current Specific Areas of Concern; work that solely benefits elderly people; or support to organizations helping animals, medical research or environmental causes.
Geographic Focus: United Kingdom
Amount of Grant: 5,000 - 50,000 EUR
Contact: Jane Young; 01707 259259; fax 01707 259268; info@sylvia-adams.org.uk
Internet: http://www.sylvia-adams.org.uk/what_we_will_fund/index.php
Sponsor: Sylvia Adams Charitable Trust
24 The Common, Sylvia Adams House
Hatfield, HERTS AL10 0NB United Kingdom

Symantec Community Relations and Corporate Philanthropy Grants 4544
Symantec's Community Relations and Corporate Philanthropy Program strives to have a positive impact on our local communities around the globe. Symantec supports four main philanthropic areas, all with the objective of creating a sustainable and diverse future for the technology industry; science, technology, engineering, and math education; equal access to education; diversity in engineering; environmental responsibility; and online safety.
Requirements: 501(c)3 entities and/or educational institutions that have philosophy programs that benefit the lives of children are encouraged to apply. Nonprofit organizations in Minneapolis, Minnesota; San Francisco Bay Area, California; Orlando, Florida; and Vienna, Virginia, are eligible.
Restrictions: Grants will not be made for political or religious purposes. Grants will not be made to organizations that discriminate on the basis of age, disability, religion, ethnic origin, sex or sexual orientation.
Geographic Focus: California, Florida, Minnesota, Virginia
Contact: Grants Director; (800) 327-2232 or (650) 527-8000; fax (650) 527-2908; community_relations@Symantec.com
Internet: http://www.symantec.com/about/profile/responsibility/community/index.jsp
Sponsor: Symantec Corporation
350 Ellis Street
Mountain View, CA 94043

T. James Kavanagh Foundation Grants 4545
A large percentage of funding supports the Catholic church and religious associations, along with support for U.S. Roman Catholic schools, with emphasis on Pennsylvania and southern New Jersey. The foundation also makes music awards. Types of support include annual campaigns, continuing support, equipment, general operating support, program development, research, and scholarship funds. Proposals should be submitted preferably by the end of February, July, or October. The board meets in March, August, and November to consider requests.
Requirements: Giving is strictly limited to the US, with emphasis on southern NJ and PA. Any Roman Catholic affiliate, church, school, college, or hospital will be considered.
Restrictions: Grants will not be awarded outside of the United States, not even to U.S. missions or to help their agencies abroad. No funding will be given for individuals; endowment funds; seed money; deficit financing; land acquisition; publications; conferences; scholarships or fellowships; matching gifts; or loans.
Geographic Focus: All States
Amount of Grant: 2,000 - 10,000 USD
Contact: Thomas Kavanagh, Trustee; (610) 356-4606
Sponsor: T. James Kavanagh Foundation
234 E State Street
Sharon, PA 16146

T.L.L. Temple Foundation Grants 4546
The T.L.L. Temple Foundation was established in 1962 by Georgie Temple Munz in honor of her father, Thomas Lewis Latané Temple, an East Texas lumberman and founder of Southern Pine Lumber Company, which later became Temple Industries. It was her wish to create a charitable foundation that would operate primarily to improve the quality of life for the inhabitants of Deep East Texas. The foundation supports organizations devoted to programs in the areas in education, public health, public affairs, human services, arts and culture, and the environment. Since its inception, the T.L.L. Temple Foundation has been committed to supporting environmental initiatives devoted to the conservation of forest lands and river systems, and the preservation of native plant and wildlife species—to protect and ensure the perpetuity of these significant natural resources.
Requirements: The foundation primarily makes grants to projects located and/or to be operated in the area constituting the East Texas pine timber belt and Miller County, Arkansas in which T.L.L. Temple founded and operated his timber production and manufacturing enterprises. Governmental units exempt under the IRS code and 501(c)3 nonprofit organizations (not classified as a private foundation) are eligible to apply. There are no specific deadlines.
Restrictions: Grants do not support private foundations. Grants are not made to individuals for scholarships, research or other purposes.
Geographic Focus: Arkansas, Texas
Contact: Millard F. Zeagler, Executive Director; (936) 634-3900; fax (936) 639-5199

Sponsor: T.L.L. Temple Foundation
204 Champions Drive
Lufkin, TX 75901-7321

T. Raymond Gregory Family Foundation Grants 4547
The Foundation, established in 1991, is supported by Gregory Galvanizing & Metal Processing and Gregory Industries. Offering general operating support primarily in the Canton, Ohio, Region, the Foundation supports service clubs and organizations involved with nursing education and human services. Fields of interest include: child and youth services; community development; service clubs; family and human services; nursing school programs; and service delivery programs. A formal application is not required, and an applicant should contact the Foundation initially with a letter of inquiry. There are no specific deadlines.
Geographic Focus: Ohio
Amount of Grant: 1,800 - 12,000 USD
Contact: T. Raymond Gregory, (330) 477-4800; fax (330) 453-9691
Sponsor: T. Raymond Gregory Family Foundation
1723 Cleveland Avenue SE
Canton, OH 44707

T. Rowe Price Associates Foundation Grants 4548
T. Rowe Price has a long tradition of philanthropy and investment in the communities where our associates live and work. Central to this tradition is the T. Rowe Price Foundation. Launched in 1981, the Foundation provides direct grants to U.S.-based nonprofit organizations that enhance community life through education, arts and culture, human services, and civic and community initiatives. Globally, nonprofit organizations receive support from the Foundation's associates through a Matching Gift Program. The Foundation's history of giving in its communities is strong—and consistent with the firm's goals and values.
Requirements: Although not limited to, giving is primarily made in the metropolitan Baltimore, Maryland, area.
Restrictions: No support provided for religious or political organizations; hospitals or health care providers; recreational sports leagues and sports related fundraisers; private foundations; or grants to individuals.
Geographic Focus: Maryland
Amount of Grant: 25 - 275,000 USD
Contact: Christine Stein, Program Director; (410) 345-3603; fax (410) 345-2848
Internet: http://corporate.troweprice.com/ccw/home/ourCompany/aboutUs/communityInvolvement.do
Sponsor: T. Rowe Price Associates Foundation
100 E Pratt Street, 8th Floor
Baltimore, MD 21202

TAC Arts Access Grant 4549
The Arts Access (AA) grants are made possible through the National Endowment for the Arts. AA grants offer direct support for projects to arts organizations of color and to non-arts organizations whose programs and services primarily benefit persons of color. Award amounts range from $500 to $9,000 for arts organizations of color and from $500 to $7,000 for non-arts organizations whose programs and services primarily benefit persons of color. Arts Access grants must be matched one-to-one (1:1). Applications must contain a clear, single-project focus and must be limited to only one expense category on the budget. A project may start no earlier than July 1 and must end no later than June 15 of the applicable fiscal year. The following are examples of single-project focused activities and expenditures that are consistent with the funding philosophy for Arts Access: projects that involve and promote professional Tennessee artists; visiting artists conducting master classes; specific aspects of workshops, festivals, and conferences; public performances, productions, and exhibitions produced by the applicant; exhibitions of art by Tennessee artists and artists from outside Tennessee; promotion, publicity, and newsletters; administrative and artistic staff support; research and documentation as part of a project or program development; consultancies and residencies for administrative and artistic activities; the development of long-range planning documents; touring projects that bring professional performers to communities across the state; improved program accessibility for underserved constituencies, e.g., children, people living in rural communities or isolated settings, people with disabilities, people of color, and senior citizens; art in public places (additional information available from the Director of Visual Arts); extensions of literary projects, journals with continuing publication, or juried anthologies; apprenticeship programs; computer software/training; technical/production support; and technical assistance projects. The following are examples of activities and expenditures not fundable for Arts Access projects: insurance premiums; endowments; space rental; janitorial service and general physical plant maintenance; food and hospitality; permanent equipment purchases; scholarships; payment of accumulated deficits; capital improvements; vanity publications; out-of-state travel; scholarly arts-related research and writing; cash awards; purchase of local public art; legal fees; planned fundraising activities; events to which the general public is not invited; payments to members of the organization's board; and payments to an employee or official of the State of Tennessee (exceptions exist - contact TAC for details). Most applicants will be asked to participate in an on-site review conducted by a member of the TAC's staff and/or an independent consultant. NOTE: New applicants may not submit an application without prior consultation with TAC's Director of Arts Access. The consultation deadline is January 14 at 4:30pm (CST). Deadline dates may vary from year to year; applicants are encouraged to call the Director of Arts Access or check the TAC website for current deadlines.
Requirements: Any applicant is eligible for support of its arts activities if it is a nonprofit arts organization of color or if it is a nonprofit organization whose programs and services primarily benefit persons of color. In either case, the applicant must be legally chartered in Tennessee and in possession of a determination letter from the Internal Revenue Service declaring the organization exempt from federal income tax under section 501(c)3 of the Internal Revenue Code. At least 51% of the organization's Board must reflect the culture

of the target population. Before or at the time of application, all first-time 501(c)3 grant applicants must provide the TAC with copies of their non-profit status documentation including a copy of the organization's: Tennessee State Charter; IRS 501(c)3 Determination Letter; and a recent copy of the organization's by-laws. All applicants must provide a valid IRS Employer Identification Number that is issued in the name of the applicant organization. Three deadlines exist for the Arts Access Grants: first, new applicants must consult with TAC staff members (in person) before 4:30 p.m. (CST), January 14; second, the application must be completed and submitted via TAC's eGRANT system by January 18, 4:30 p.m. (CST); third, the required number of hard copies mentioned in the application guidelines (available at the grant website) including all supplemental materials must be postmarked or hand-delivered to the TAC by January 18th, 4:30 p.m. (CST). NOTE: Proposed art projects must involve one or more TAC recognized classical art forms including: visual art, craft, media, music, theater, dance, folk and ethnic, or literary arts.
Restrictions: K-12 schools are not eligible to apply for Arts Access grants. Applicants eligible to apply in more than one TAC grant category in a single fiscal year must apply for unrelated projects each time. It is the responsibility of all applicants to read the legal requirements section at the TAC website (under the Grants tab) for further restrictions and requirements before making application.
Geographic Focus: Tennessee
Date(s) Application is Due: Jan 18
Amount of Grant: 500 - 9,000 USD
Contact: Rod Reiner, Deputy Director and Director of Arts Access; (615) 741-2093; fax (615) 741-8559; rod.reiner@tn.gov
Internet: http://www.tn.gov/arts/grant_categories.htm
Sponsor: Tennessee Arts Commission
401 Charlotte Avenue, Citizens Plaza Building
Nashville, TN 37243-0780

TAC Arts Access Technical Assistance Grants 4550

Arts Access Technical Assistance (AA-TA) grants are primarily used to bring in an outside consultant for intensive work needed to strengthen Tennessee arts organizations of color or arts organizations chartered in the state of Tennessee to serve people with disabilities. Example projects include: contracting with a consultant to address the organization's short- and long-term planning, marketing and promotion, board/staff development, financial management, technical skills, personnel needs, or similar administrative and managerial topics; facilities or activities assessment; assistance in grants making, fundraising, and other fiscal development; computer software purchase in conjunction with computer training; and web site development or redesign (support of expenses related to ongoing Web site updates and maintenance is not allowed). An organization may use in-state or out-of-state consultants for the project, but these must be approved by the Tennessee Arts Commission (TAC). TAC's Capacity Building Services program offers a list of trained peer advisors, professional consultants and other resources that may be utilized with AA-TA funding. For more information, click on "Capacity Building" under the Resources tab at the TAC website. A cash match from the grantee is not required but demonstrates commitment from the applicant organization toward the project and may affect the award amount. Applications should be submitted at least 30 days prior to the beginning of the actual technical assistance activity. After the TAC's approval of the grant request, AA-TA grantees may request 40% of the grant amount. The final payment shall be made only after the grantee has completed the project and has submitted a final financial report of the expenditures and other required documents. AA-TA grants are available until June 15 OR until all TAC funds in this category are expended ("first come, first served"). Prior to submitting an application, qualifying organizations must check on the status of funding availability and discuss their project proposal with the Arts Access Director.
Requirements: Tennessee arts organizations of color or arts organizations chartered in the state of Tennessee to serve people with disabilities are eligible to apply. Arts organizations of color must have a Board of Directors whose membership is composed of at least 51% people of color. Arts organizations in neighboring states which are located within five (5) miles of the Tennessee state border, meet the criteria described above and significantly serve Tennesseans may also be eligible. Applicants must electronically submit a AA-TA eGRANT application at least thirty (30) days prior to the beginning of the technical assistance activity. The link to the eGrant form is available at the grant website. In addition, applicants MUST submit the required number of sets of the printed eGrant application and any required accompanying documents. These sets must be postmarked or hand-delivered to the TAC at least thirty (30) days prior to the beginning of the activity. The earliest starting date for a project is July 1. The latest end date for a project is June 15. Applicants should contact the Arts Access Director for any questions or clarifications on eligibility.
Restrictions: Non-arts organizations may not apply in this category. TAC offers two categories of technical assistance grants. These are the AA-TA grants and the general Technical Assistance (TA) grants. Except in unusual circumstances, only one technical assistance grant will be awarded to any one applicant in a single fiscal year. Applicants should contact the Director of Arts Access and/or review the guidelines at the grant website for more information on TAC's technical assistance grants.
Geographic Focus: Alabama, Arkansas, Georgia, Kentucky, Mississippi, Missouri, North Carolina, Tennessee, Virginia
Amount of Grant: 500 - 3,500 USD
Contact: Beverly Scott; (615) 532-9797; fax (615) 741-8559; beverly.scott@tn.gov
Internet: http://www.tn.gov/arts/grant_categories.htm
Sponsor: Tennessee Arts Commission
401 Charlotte Avenue, Citizens Plaza Building
Nashville, TN 37243-0780

TAC Arts Build Communities Grants 4551

Arts Build Communities (ABC) Grants are funded by the Tennessee General Assembly and administered in cooperation with the Tennessee Arts Commission (TAC) and designated agencies in different regions of the state. The short-term objective of this grant is to create a decentralized decision-making and distribution process for certain State dollars. A long-term objective is to build communities by nurturing artists, arts organizations (including local arts agencies) and arts supporters in each of Tennessee's ninety-five counties. The ABC grants require at least a one-to-one (1:1) dollar match meaning the applicant must cover at least half the cost of a project or program through other income sources. Proposed projects must take place and grants funds used between October 15 and June 15. Applications must contain a clear, single-project focus and must be limited to only one expense category in the grant request. The following are examples of single-project focus activities and expenditures that are consistent with the funding philosophy for ABC grants: projects that involve and promote Tennessee artists; visiting artists conducting master classes; workshops, festivals and conferences; public performances, productions and exhibitions produced by the applicant; exhibitions of art by Tennessee artists and artists from outside Tennessee; promotion, publicity and newsletters; administrative and artistic staff support; research and documentation as part of a project or program development; consultancies and residencies for administrative and artistic activities; the development of long-range planning documents; touring projects that bring professional performers to communities across the state; improved program accessibility for special constituencies such as children, people living in rural communities or isolated settings, people with disabilities, people of color and senior citizens; art in public places (in accordance with specific regulations available from the TAC's Director of Visual Arts); extensions of literary projects, journals with continuing publication and juried anthologies; apprenticeship programs; computer software/training; technical/production support; and technical assistance projects.
Requirements: Individuals are not eligible to apply directly for ABC grants. Organizations are eligible to apply for funding of arts activities if they are legally chartered in Tennessee and have 501(c)3 not-for-profit tax-exemption status, or if they are entities of government (such as city/county government departments, public libraries, public schools, etc. Nonprofit private schools which meet the same tax exemption criteria are also eligible. School projects must include a component that is open to the general public (such as a public performance, exhibit or workshop). Colleges and universities are eligible only for activities that clearly serve the needs of surrounding communities or the State and are designed to involve a broad audience (activities that are credit-producing or oriented primarily to students and the academic community are not eligible). Applications from institutions of higher education must emphasize non-academic community involvement in the planning and implementation of the project. Before or at the time of application, all first-time 501(c)3 grant applicants must provide the TAC with copies of their non-profit status documentation including a copy of the organization's: Tennessee State Charter; IRS 501(c)3 Determination Letter; and a recent copy of the organization's by-laws. All applicants must provide a valid IRS Employer Identification Number that is issued in the name of the applicant organization. Applicants must apply directly to the designated agency in their area. A list of designated agencies along with the counties they serve can be found in the ABC grant guidelines (available at the grant website). Prior to submitting an application, qualifying organizations should discuss their program or project proposal with their designated agency or with the TAC. ABC grant application forms are available electronically from any designated agency or for download from the grant website. These should be filled out at the computer and then printed for submission (alteration of official grant application forms is not allowed; handwritten or partially handwritten applications will not be accepted; applicants should contact their designated agency for technical assistance filling out the electronic forms). All applicants must have an elected or appointed governing board that is representative of the community served. All events sponsored in part or entirely with ABC funds must be open to the general public.
Restrictions: Only one grant application may be submitted per applicant per year in this program. Any organization currently receiving Major Cultural Institution, Cultural Education Partnership, or Partnership Support funding is not eligible to apply for an ABC grant. Please contact the TAC if you have questions about this restriction. ABC funds may not be used: to support a project already funded by the Tennessee Arts Commission; for capital improvements (buildings or construction); for equipment purchases; or for the elimination of an accumulated deficit. Such expenditures that relate to the proposed project may be used as matching expenses up to $2,500. Additionally, ABC funds may not be used: as "seed money" for starting new organizations; to begin, match, add to or complete any type of endowment campaign or program; for in-school, curriculum-based projects; and for out-of-state travel expenses, insurance premiums, office space rental, janitorial service and general physical plant maintenance, food and hospitality, scholarships, vanity publications, scholarly arts-related research and writing, cash awards, purchase of local public art, legal fees, planned fundraising events, events to which the general public is not invited, and payments to members of the organization's board. In-kind contributions cannot be used for the one-to-one (1:1) dollar match requirement, but the ABC program wants to know about such contributions. The GRANT REQUEST & MATCH page of the ABC application form provides a space for estimating the value of in-kind contributions. Such contributions should include those services and supplies for which the applicant under normal circumstances would have to pay, but are being donated without charge for the project. It is the responsibility of all applicants to read the legal requirements section at the TAC website (under the Grants tab) for further restrictions and requirements before making application.
Geographic Focus: Tennessee
Date(s) Application is Due: Aug 31
Contact: Shannon Ford, Director of Community Arts Development; (615) 532-9796; fax (615) 741-8559; shannon.ford@tn.gov
Internet: http://www.tn.gov/arts/grant_categories.htm
Sponsor: Tennessee Arts Commission
401 Charlotte Avenue, Citizens Plaza Building
Nashville, TN 37243-0780

TAC Arts Education Community-Learning Grants 4552

Arts Education Community Learning (AE-CL) grants from the Tennessee Arts Commission (TAC) provide funding for projects that demonstrate creative and innovative arts education programming in community settings or non-traditional school environments for populations of all ages. Examples of projects may include, but are not limited to, after-school programs for at-risk youth, projects involving adults as the primary learners, community-wide events with strong arts learning components and short-term teacher training activities. Professional visual, performing, folk and ethnic, or literary artists must be used. The Commission gives priority to funding the fees of professional artists. Applications MUST have a single project focus. Organizations with expansive education programs should narrow their focus to one component of their overall educational programming. Funds may be requested for only ONE of the following: professional artist fees, in-state travel and/or lodging for artists, space rental (for locations in which the applicant must pay to use), marketing and consumable supplies related to the project. The applications that are most competitive are often those that request funding for professional artist fees. Arts Education grants do not require a dollar for dollar match; however, applicants are strongly encouraged to match the grant as much as possible to strengthen the competitiveness of the application. In-kind contributions cannot be used for matching purposes, but will strengthen the application. The eGRANT application provides a space for estimating the value of all in-kind contributions. Such contributions should include those services and supplies for which the applicant under normal circumstances would have to pay, but are being donated to the program.

Requirements: Three deadlines exist for AE-LC grant applications: first, applicants must notify the Director of Arts Education at least one week prior to submitting an application; second, the application must be submitted via TAC's eGRANT system by January 10th at 4:30pm CST (the eGRANT link is available at the grant website); third, the required number of printed copies of the eGRANT application and any required attachments must be postmarked or hand-delivered to the TAC by January 10th at 4:30pm CST. Because deadlines vary from year to year, applicants should check with the Director of Arts Education or the TAC website for current deadlines. Projects may not begin until July 1 and must conclude by June 15. In order to be eligible for AE-LC funds, applicants must be non-profit arts organizations, arts councils, libraries, non-profit non-arts organizations, government agencies and human service organizations whose primary mission is education. Private preK-12 schools may also apply. All non-profit applicants must possess 501(c)3 status and be chartered in the state of Tennessee. Private educational institutions must be non-profit and meet the same tax-exemption requirements. Arts organizations located within five miles of the Tennessee border in neighboring states may also apply if there is clear demonstration that the projects and activities for which funds are being requested significantly serve Tennesseans. These out-of-state organizations must meet all eligibility requirements of Tennessee-based organizations including being chartered in the state. Additionally, residents of Tennessee must be appropriately represented on the organization's governing board. All applicants should read the legal section at the TAC website (under the Grants tab) for further requirements. In order to be eligible for AE-LC funds, projects must: serve a population defined by the organization's mission; directly involve participants in a hands-on learning experience focused on performing, visual and/or literary arts (projects in which learners are primarily spectators will not be considered); demonstrate a clear and beneficial educational focus that reflects thorough planning and implementation; clearly define the instructional goals, objectives, hands-on activities, problem-solving or critical-thinking components, and evaluation methods; explain how any state or national standards, if listed, relate to outcomes being evaluated; provide learners with historical and/or social context; and demonstrate and/or reinforce the skill sets needed for the artistic medium being used. Applicants are encouraged (but not required) to link content to state and/or national curriculum standards (state standards may be accessed from the Tennessee Department of Education's website). Applicants should include an appropriate evaluation component that measures the planning, implementation, and successes of the program and addresses improvements or expansion of future projects.

Restrictions: Public preK-12 schools and school systems may NOT apply in this category. The AE-LC grant category is not intended to provide support for guest artists to direct, choreograph, or conduct productions or performances. Funds may NOT be used for: projects in which the artist is to serve as the arts teacher in the absence of any on-going arts education programs; permanent staff of an organization; incentives for participation including cash awards; projects designed primarily as performances, demonstrations, or exhibits with only minimal impact and limited hands-on participation; field trips; competitions and/or tours in which students are presenting, performing, and/or exhibiting; out-of-state travel; individual private lesson instruction; payment for apprentices or interns; capital outlay for permanent or non-consumable materials or equipment purchases (such as musical instruments, books, cameras, easels, etc.); planned fundraising activities; after-school clubs; scholarships or competitions; food; grant writing fees; non-classical art forms including, but not limited to culinary arts, martial arts, healing arts, exercise programs, acrobatics or gymnastics; and payments to an employee or official of the State of Tennessee (exceptions exist - contact TAC for details). AE funds cannot be used for salary support for full-time employees but a portion of the employee's salary related to the amount of time spent on the AE project/program may be used as part of the applicant's cash match. This type of match is called a "soft match." Expenditures for capital improvements (buildings or construction), for equipment purchases including but not limited to musical instruments, cameras, computers, etc., food or refreshments, or for elimination of an accumulated deficit may be used as matching funds up to $2,500 if these are related to the project. Expenditures for field trips may be used as a match. TAC does not allow the use of federally assigned indirect cost ratios in calculating grant requests or matching TAC funds. TAC will not make grants to an organization with a standing deficit unless a plan to reduce that deficit is submitted with the application.

Geographic Focus: Alabama, Arkansas, Georgia, Kentucky, Mississippi, Missouri, North Carolina, Tennessee, Virginia
Date(s) Application is Due: Jan 10
Amount of Grant: 500 - 5,000 USD
Contact: Kim Leavitt, (615) 532-5934; fax (615) 741-8559; kim.leavitt@tn.gov
Internet: http://www.tn.gov/arts/grant_categories.htm
Sponsor: Tennessee Arts Commission
401 Charlotte Avenue, Citizens Plaza Building
Nashville, TN 37243-0780

TAC Arts Education Mini Grants 4553

Tennessee Arts Commission (TAC) Mini Grants are smaller grants designed to introduce new applicants to the grant making process or to provide support to arts education providers who have unanticipated short-term (maximum one week) or one-day arts education projects. Projects may consist of, but are not limited to, community activities for adult learners, after-school programs for at-risk youth, in-school curriculum-based opportunities, arts-based service learning, or teacher training. Funds may only be used for professional teaching artist fees. Applicants may apply for mini grants throughout TAC's fiscal year OR until all funds are expended. Funding is on a first-come, first-serve basis. Arts Education Mini Grant applications are reviewed "in-house" by TAC members and staff. Funding notification will take approximately 30 days from the time the application is submitted. Applicants have 30 days from the end of the project to submit receipts and all required close-out paperwork. The earliest start date for a project is July 1. The latest end date for a project is May 15.

Requirements: Applicants must contact the Director of Arts Education before making application. Projects must utilize a Commission-approved Artist-in-Residence. A roster of approved Artists-in-Residence may be found on TAC's website: click "Arts Education" on the Programs tab pop-up menu and then click "Roster" on the Artist Roster button's pop-up menu. Information for artists interested in participating in education residencies may be found here as well. Click "Arts Education" on the Programs tab pop-up menu and then click "Overview" on the Artist Roster button's pop-up menu to get the "Teaching Artist Program" page. Three deadlines exist for the Mini Grants: first, applicants must notify the Director of Arts Education prior to submitting an eGrant; second, the application must be completed and submitted via TAC's eGRANT system at least (30) days prior to the beginning of the project; third, the required number of hard copies including all supplemental materials must be postmarked or hand-delivered to the TAC at least thirty (30) days prior to the beginning of the project. An organization is eligible to apply for funding of its arts activities if it is legally chartered in Tennessee and has 501(c)3 not-for-profit tax-exemption status, or if it is a public or private educational institution (such as an elementary or secondary school), a school board, a governmental agency or a college or university. Private educational institutions must be not-for-profit and meet the same tax-exemption criteria. Colleges and universities are eligible only for activities that clearly serve the needs of surrounding communities or the State and are designed to involve a broad audience. Activities that are credit-producing or are oriented primarily to students and the academic community are not eligible. Arts organizations located within five miles of the Tennessee border in neighboring states may apply if there is clear demonstration that the projects and activities for which funds are being requested significantly serve Tennesseans. These out-of-state organizations must meet all eligibility requirements of Tennessee-based organizations including being chartered in the state. Additionally, residents of Tennessee must be appropriately represented on the organization's governing board. It is the responsibility of all applicants to read the legal requirements section at the TAC website (under the Grants tab) for further requirements before making application. Before or at the time of application, all first-time 501(c)3 grant applicants must provide the TAC with copies of their non-profit status documentation including a copy of the organization's: Tennessee State Charter; IRS 501(c)3 Determination Letter; and a recent copy of the organization's by-laws. All applicants must provide a valid IRS Employer Identification Number that is issued in the name of the applicant organization. AE Mini Grant, projects must: directly involve participants in a hands-on learning experience (applications that are performance or demonstration based where learners are primarily spectators will not be considered); have a clear and beneficial educational focus; include an instructional component that defines the goals and objectives of the project; explains how any referenced state or national standards are included in the instruction and related to outcomes being evaluated; provides learners with historical and/or social context; and demonstrates and/or reinforces the skill set needed for the artistic medium being used.

Restrictions: Requests may NOT be made for artists to direct and/or conduct performances or to mount exhibitions. Projects in which the artist is primarily performing, demonstrating or exhibiting work with minimal hands-on instruction and/or impact will not be considered. Funds may only be used for teaching artist fees. Projects must be a minimum of one day (6 hours of instruction) in length up to a maximum of one week. Organizations applying for any other TAC Arts Education grant may not apply for a Mini Grant in the same fiscal year. Organizations may not apply for more than one Mini Grant in any fiscal year. Funds may not be used for permanent staff of an organization.

Geographic Focus: Alabama, Arkansas, Georgia, Kentucky, Mississippi, Missouri, North Carolina, Tennessee, Virginia
Amount of Grant: 500 - 1,000 USD
Contact: Kim Leavitt, (615) 532-5934; fax (615) 741-8559; kim.leavitt@tn.gov
Internet: http://www.tn.gov/arts/grant_categories.htm
Sponsor: Tennessee Arts Commission
401 Charlotte Avenue, Citizens Plaza Building
Nashville, TN 37243-0780

TAC Arts Projects Grants 4554

The Tennessee Arts Commission (TAC) Arts Project Support (APS) grants supply funding to organizations which are located in urban areas of Tennessee and which provide a wide variety of public-value arts projects and programs such as: projects that involve and promote professional Tennessee artists; visiting artists conducting master classes; specific aspects of workshops, festivals, and conferences; public performances, productions, and exhibitions produced by the applicant; exhibitions of art by Tennessee artists and artists from outside Tennessee; promotion, publicity, and newsletters; administrative and artistic staff support; research and documentation as part of an arts project or program development; consultancies and residencies for administrative and artistic activities; the development of long-range planning documents; touring projects that bring professional performers to communities across the state; improved program accessibility for underserved constituencies, e.g., children, people living in rural communities or isolated settings, people with disabilities, people of color and senior citizens; art in public places (additional information available from the Director of Visual Arts); extensions of literary projects, journals with continuing publication or juried anthologies; apprenticeship programs; computer software/training; technical/production support; and technical assistance projects. APS grant amounts range from $500 to $7,000 for non-arts organizations and $500 to $9,000 for arts-focused groups. Arts organizations serving a statewide audience may apply for up to $10,000. Applicants should contact the Tennessee Arts Commission to verify current submission dates and requirements.

Requirements: The following entities are eligible to apply for APS grants: 501(c)3 not-for-profit organizations in urban areas of and chartered in Tennessee; and Tennessee colleges and universities who meet the tax-exempt requirements just described for not-for-profit organizations. Entities bordering Tennessee (and serving urban areas in Tennessee) are also eligible to apply if they meet the criteria described for instate applicants. First time applicants must contact the TAC prior to submitting an application to verify eligibility. All first time 501(c)3 applicants must provide the TAC with copies of all of the basic nonprofit status documentation, which includes a copy of the organization's Tennessee State Charter, the IRS 501(c)3 Determination Letter and a recent copy of the by-laws of the organization. Proposed projects must involve one or more TAC recognized classical art forms, including visual art, crafts, media, music, theater, dance, folk and ethnic art, or literary arts. Applicants who apply in more than one TAC grant category in a single fiscal year must submit entirely unrelated projects for each proposal. All APS applicants must submit an online eGRANT application by January 18 at 4:30 pm. The link to the eGRANT form is available at the grant website. Additionally, hard copies and required supporting documents described in the guidelines at the grant website must be mailed or hand-delivered to the TAC by Jan 18 at 4:30 pm to complete the application process. Applications must contain a clear, single- project focus. Requested funds should be listed under one expense category on the budget page (and should correspond with the Activity Code indicated on the application). Grant funds must be matched one-to-one (1:1). A project may start no earlier than July 1 and must end no later than June 15. For more requirements, applicants should read the guidelines at the grant website. Additionally applicants should read the legal requirements page at http://www.tn.gov/arts/legal.htm.

Restrictions: An APS application may be submitted only by an organization chartered in Tennessee and located in an urban county (for a list of TAC's urban and rural designations, see the downloadable guidelines at the grant website). K-12 schools are not eligible to apply. Colleges and universities are eligible only for activities that clearly serve the needs of surrounding communities or the state and are designed to involve a broad audience. Activities that are credit-producing or are oriented primarily to students and the academic community are not eligible. An eligible organization may submit only one APS application for the current fiscal year. APS applicants may not apply for a Partnership Support, Cultural Education Partnership or Major Cultural Institution grant. Additional restrictions on funding are listed on the legal requirements page at http://www.tn.gov/arts/legal.htm.

Geographic Focus: Alabama, Arkansas, Georgia, Kentucky, Mississippi, Missouri, North Carolina, Tennessee, Virginia
Date(s) Application is Due: Jan 18
Amount of Grant: 500 - 10,000 USD
Contact: Kim Leavitt, (615) 532-5934; fax (615) 741-8559; kim.leavitt@tn.gov
Internet: http://www.tn.gov/arts/grant_categories.htm
Sponsor: Tennessee Arts Commission
401 Charlotte Avenue, Citizens Plaza Building
Nashville, TN 37243-0780

TAC Rural Arts Project Support Grants 4555
The Tennessee Arts Commission (TAC) Rural Arts Project Support (RAPS) grants supply funding to organizations which are located in rural areas of Tennessee and which provide a wide variety of public-value arts projects and programs such as: projects that involve and promote professional Tennessee artists; visiting artists conducting master classes; specific aspects of workshops, festivals, and conferences; public performances, productions, and exhibitions produced by the applicant; exhibitions of art by Tennessee artists and artists from outside Tennessee; promotion, publicity, and newsletters; administrative and artistic staff support; research and documentation as part of an arts project or program development; consultancies and residencies for administrative and artistic activities; the development of long-range planning documents; touring projects that bring professional performers to communities across the state; improved program accessibility for underserved constituencies, e.g., children, people living in rural communities or isolated settings, people with disabilities, people of color and senior citizens; art in public places (additional information available from the Director of Visual Arts); extensions of literary projects, journals with continuing publication or juried anthologies; apprenticeship programs; computer software/training; technical/production support; and technical assistance projects. RAPS grant amounts range from $500 to $7,000 for non-arts organizations and $500 to $9,000 for arts-focused groups. Applicants should contact the Tennessee Arts Commission to verify current submission dates and requirements.

Requirements: The following entities are eligible to apply for RAPS grants: 501(c)3 not-for-profit organizations in rural areas of and chartered in Tennessee; and Tennessee colleges and universities who meet the tax-exempt requirements just described for not-for-profit organizations. Entities bordering Tennessee (and serving rural areas in Tennessee) are also eligible to apply if they meet the criteria described for instate applicants. First time applicants must contact the TAC prior to submitting an application to verify eligibility. All first time 501(c)3 applicants must provide the TAC with copies of all of the basic nonprofit status documentation, which includes a copy of the organization's Tennessee State Charter, the IRS 501(c)3 Determination Letter and a recent copy of the by-laws of the organization. Proposed projects must involve one or more TAC recognized classical art forms, including visual art, crafts, media, music, theater, dance, folk and ethnic art, or literary arts. Applicants who apply in more than one TAC grant category in a single fiscal year must submit entirely unrelated projects for each proposal. All RAPS applicants must submit an online eGRANT application by January 18 at 4:30 pm. The link to the eGRANT form is available at the grant website. Additionally, hard copies and required supporting documents described in the guidelines at the grant website must be mailed or hand-delivered to the TAC by Jan 18 at 4:30 pm to complete the application process. Applications must contain a clear, single- project focus. Requested funds should be listed under one expense category on the budget page (and should correspond with the Activity Code indicated on the application). Grant funds must be matched one-to-one (1:1). A project may start no earlier than July 1 and must end no later than June 15. For more requirements, applicants should read the guidelines at the grant website. Additionally applicants should read the legal requirements page at http://www.tn.gov/arts/legal.htm.

Restrictions: A RAPS application may be submitted only by an organization chartered in Tennessee and located in a rural county (for a list of TAC's urban and rural designations, see the downloadable guidelines at the grant website). K-12 schools are not eligible to apply. Colleges and universities are eligible only for activities that clearly serve the needs of surrounding communities or the state and are designed to involve a broad audience. Activities that are credit-producing or are oriented primarily to students and the academic community are not eligible. An eligible organization may submit only one RAPS application for the current fiscal year. RAPS applicants may not apply for a Partnership Support, Cultural Education Partnership or Major Cultural Institution grant. Additional restrictions on funding are listed on the legal requirements page at http://www.tn.gov/arts/legal.htm.

Geographic Focus: Alabama, Arkansas, Georgia, Kentucky, Mississippi, Missouri, North Carolina, Tennessee, Virginia
Date(s) Application is Due: Jan 18
Amount of Grant: 500 - 9,000 USD
Contact: Kim Leavitt, (615) 532-5934; fax (615) 741-8559; kim.leavitt@tn.gov
Internet: http://www.tn.gov/arts/grant_categories.htm
Sponsor: Tennessee Arts Commission
401 Charlotte Avenue, Citizens Plaza Building
Nashville, TN 37243-0780

TAC Technical Assistance Grants 4556
The Technical Assistance (TA) grants provide funds for technical assistance during the Tennessee Arts Commission (TAC)'s fiscal year (July 1 – June 30). TA funds are primarily used to bring in an outside consultant for intensive work needed to strengthen the applicant arts organization. Example projects include: contracting with a consultant to address the organization's short- and long-term planning, marketing and promotion, board/staff development, financial management, technical skills, personnel needs, or similar administrative and managerial topics; facilities or activities assessment; assistance in grants making, fundraising, and other fiscal development; computer software purchase in conjunction with computer training; and web site development or redesign (support of expenses related to ongoing Web site updates and maintenance is not allowed). An organization may use in-state or out-of-state consultants for the project, but these must be approved by the TAC. TAC's Capacity Building Services program offers a list of trained peer advisors, professional consultants and other resources that may be utilized with TA funding. For more information, click on "Capacity Building" under the Resources tab at the TAC website. A cash match from the grantee is not required but demonstrates commitment from the applicant organization toward the project and may affect the award amount. Applications should be submitted at least 30 days prior to the beginning of the actual technical assistance activity. After the TAC's approval of the grant request, TA grantees may request 40% of the grant amount. The final payment shall be made only after the grantee has completed the project and has submitted a final financial report of the expenditures and other required documents. TA grants are available until June 15 OR until all TAC funds in this category are expended ("first come, first served"). Prior to submitting an application, qualifying organizations must check on the status of funding availability and discuss their project proposal with the Deputy Director.

Requirements: Any 501(c)3 non-profit arts organization or non-profit private art school chartered in Tennessee or entities of government with an arts focus (such as an arts council or commission) are eligible to apply. Arts organizations located within five miles of the Tennessee border in neighboring states may apply if there is clear demonstration that the activiies for which funds are being requested significantly benefit Tennesseans. These out-of-state organizations must meet all eligibility requirements of Tennessee-based organizations including being chartered in the State of Tennessee. Additionally, residents of Tennessee must be appropriately represented on an out-of-state organization's governing board. Before or at the time of application, all first-time 501(c)3 grant applicants must provide the TAC with copies of their non-profit status documentation including a copy of the organization's: Tennessee State Charter; IRS 501(c)3 Determination Letter; and a recent copy of the organization's by-laws. Applicants must electronically submit a TA eGRANT application at least thirty (30) days prior to the beginning of the technical assistance activity. The link to the eGrant form is available at the grant website. In addition, the required number of sets of the printed eGrant application with required accompanying documents must be postmarked or hand-delivered to the TAC at least thirty (30) days prior to the beginning of the activity. The earliest starting date for a project is July 1. The latest end date for a project is June 15.

Restrictions: Non-arts organizations may not apply in this category. TAC offers two categories of technical assistance grants. These are the TA grants and the Arts Access Technical Assistance (AA-TA) grants. Except in unusual circumstances, only one technical assistance grant will be awarded to any one applicant in a single fiscal year. Applicants should contact the Deputy Director and/or review the guidelines at the grant website for more information on TAC's technical assistance grants. It is the responsibility of all applicants to read the legal requirements section at the TAC website (under the Grants tab) for further requirements before making application.

Geographic Focus: Alabama, Arkansas, Georgia, Kentucky, Mississippi, Missouri, North Carolina, Tennessee, Virginia
Amount of Grant: 500 - 3,500 USD
Contact: Rod Reiner; (615) 741-2093; fax (615) 741-8559; rod.reiner@tn.gov
Internet: http://www.tn.gov/arts/grant_categories.htm
Sponsor: Tennessee Arts Commission
401 Charlotte Avenue, Citizens Plaza Building
Nashville, TN 37243-0780

TAC Touring Arts and Arts Access Touring Arts Grants   4557
The Tennessee Art Commission (TAC)'s Touring Arts Program bring professional artists (primarily from Tennessee) to communities across the state by providing financial assistance to qualified presenters/sponsors. The Touring Arts Program offers two categories of funding: the Touring Arts (TOUR) grants and the Arts Access Touring Arts (AA-TR) grants. The AA-TR grants are funded in part by the National Endowment for the Arts and are designed to stimulate and encourage the presentation of performing, visual and literary arts by professional Tennessee artists of color or artists with disabilities. One-to-one (1:1) dollar matching may be required from the applicant. TOUR grants support professional Tennessee performing artists and groups; however, TOUR applicants may apply to engage one out-of-state artist or group per fiscal year. Both AA-TR and TOUR funds are used to pay a portion of the artist's fee, which is established by the artist. Prior to submitting an application, the applicant must contact the artist or his/her manager and book the artist with a binding contract containing a clause stating the performance will occur contingent upon Tennessee Arts Commission funding, or a letter of intent to hire (see guidelines at the grant website for further details). AA-TR and TOUR grant requests will be paid by reimbursement after the event. Due to reporting requirements, artist fees funded under these grants must be paid directly to the artist by the grantee (and not to an artist representative or management company). Tennessee presenters who receive National Endowment for the Arts/South Arts Regional Touring funding through South Arts may apply for matching support for one out-of-state artist through the TOUR category. AA-TR grant applicants must contact the Deputy Director before submitting an application. New TOUR grant applicants must contact the Director of Performing Arts before submitting an application. AA-TR and TOUR applications must be submitted electronically through the eGRANT system at the grant website a minimum of thirty (30) days prior to the beginning of the presentation. Also, the printed eGrant application and all required documents and materials must be postmarked or hand-delivered to the TAC office a minimum of thirty (30) days prior to the beginning of the presentation. The earliest starting date for a presentation project is July 1. The latest end date for a presentation project is June 15. This program is open until June 15 or until all funds are expended ("first come, first served").
Requirements: A Tennessee organization is eligible for funding support of its presenting activities if it meets the following criteria: it is legally chartered in Tennessee and has 501(c)3 not-for-profit tax-exemption status; it is an entity of government (such as a park, recreational organization or library); it is a public or private school; it is a college or university. Private educational institutions must be not-for-profit and meet the tax-exemption criteria described above. Arts organizations located within five miles of the Tennessee border in neighboring states may apply if there is clear demonstration that the presentations for which funds are being requested significantly serve Tennesseans. These out-of-state organizations must meet all eligibility requirements of Tennessee-based organizations including being chartered in the State of Tennessee. Additionally, residents of Tennessee must be appropriately represented on an out-of-state organization's governing board. It is the responsibility of all applicants to read the legal requirements section at the TAC website (under the Grants tab) for further requirements before making application. Before or at the time of application, all first-time 501(c)3 grant applicants must provide the TAC with copies of their non-profit status documentation including a copy of the organization's: Tennessee State Charter; IRS 501(c)3 Determination Letter; and a recent copy of the organization's by-laws. Sponsored artists and performing groups must have a history of being financially compensated for their artistic work. This compensation must be a major source of support for their livelihood. They must also have a history of touring and have high quality promotional materials, e.g. printed information, CD's, DVD's and Web sites. An educational/outreach activity must be included in the proposal. This activity needs to be separate from the live public performance, and include interaction between the artist(s) and an audience (not necessarily the same audience that attended the public performance). Examples of educational/outreach activities are pre- or post-performance talkbacks, lecture/demonstrations, hands-on workshops, or master classes. Criteria (in addition to the availability of funds and eligibility of the applicant) include evidence that the presenter is introducing new or untried performing arts events that will broaden audience appreciation for a variety of art forms; evidence of cooperation with other sponsors/presenters through "block" (group) booking; evidence that the presenter is serving audiences in rural communities or isolated settings and/or other underserved constituencies; evidence of one or more education/outreach activities; evidence of promotion efforts toward filling the house; and evidence of generating substantial percentage of expenses.
Restrictions: A sponsored artist or group (two or more persons) may receive up to $8000 in combined awards from both AA-TR and TOUR grants in the applicable fiscal year. Presenters may not apply for both AA-TR and TOUR grants for the same project. Colleges and universities are eligible only for activities that clearly serve the needs of surrounding communities or the State and that are designed to involve a broad audience. Activities that are credit-producing or are oriented primarily to students and the academic community are not eligible. Schools, colleges, and universities must schedule public performances outside of school hours, and demonstrate that they are open and marketed to the public. The following activities are not eligible for funding under the Touring Arts Program: any activity used as a planned fundraising event; projects that do not include a public performance component and an additional education/outreach component; and guest artist appearances that are part of a producing arts organization (e.g. orchestra, theater company, dance company or opera company)'s own performance, concert or production. Only one public performance and outreach activity by an artist or group residing within the presenter's county will be allowed per organization in both the AA-TR and TOUR categories.
Geographic Focus: Alabama, Arkansas, Georgia, Kentucky, Mississippi, Missouri, North Carolina, Tennessee, Virginia
Contact: Hal Partlow; (615) 741-2093; fax (615) 741-8559; hal.partlow@tn.gov
Rod Reiner, Deputy Director; (615) 741-2093; fax (615) 741-8559; rod.reiner@tn.gov
Internet: http://www.tn.gov/arts/grant_categories.htm
Sponsor: Tennessee Arts Commission
401 Charlotte Avenue, Citizens Plaza Building
Nashville, TN 37243-0780

Talbert and Leota Abrams Foundation   4558
The Talbert and Leota Abrams Foundation awards grants to organizations in Michigan in its fields of interest, including higher education, adult basic education and literacy programs, libraries and reading, and community funds. Grants support research and program development. The board meets in May to consider requests.
Requirements: Nonprofit organizations in Michigan, primarily central Michigan, are eligible. Applicants submit a two page letter of inquiry, along with a copy of their 501(c)3 exemption. Churches may apply for nonsectarian, nonreligious grants.
Restrictions: Grants do not support athletic activities, churches for sectarian use, individuals, operating expense, loans, or traveling expenses. The Foundation does not fund the maintenance of existing programs or services.
Geographic Focus: Michigan
Date(s) Application is Due: May 31
Contact: Joe Foster Jr., Secretary; (517) 706-5791
Sponsor: Talbert and Leota Abrams Foundation
400 Lake Lansing Road, Suite F
Lansing, MI 48912-3674

Tanner Humanities Center Research Fellowships   4559
The Tanner Humanities Center awards fellowships to encourage, support, and disseminate important humanistic research. Each fellow will spend one year or one semester conducting research full-time, in residence at the center. In addition, fellows will present work-in-progress talks throughout the year. The deadline for faculty applicants is October 1 to their department chair and October 15 to the center. Visiting faculty must apply by December 1. The deadline for graduate students to apply for doctoral fellowships is March 1. Guidelines and application forms for each fellowship are available online.
Requirements: Applicants must have received the PhD by August two years prior to the year of application. Eligible fields include anthropology, communication, history (including art history and criticism, film history, musicology, and theater history), comparative religion, ethnic studies, jurisprudence, languages and linguistics, literature, philosophy, women's studies, and historical or philosophical applications of the social and natural sciences.
Restrictions: The center does not consider applications for projects leading to completion of advanced degrees.
Geographic Focus: All States
Date(s) Application is Due: Mar 1; Oct 1; Oct 15; Dec 1
Contact: Office Manager; (801) 581-7989; Tanner.Humanities@hum.utah.edu
Internet: http://vegeta.hum.utah.edu/humcntr/applications.html
Sponsor: University of Utah
380 S 1400 E, Room 201
Salt Lake City, UT 84112-0312

Taproot Foundation Capacity-Building Service Grants   4560
The program seeks to strengthen the capacity of strong charitable organizations that provide effective, high-quality programs. Applicant organizations must have a mission that fits in one of four categories: education—organizations that strengthen the public education (pre-K and K-12) system or enhance the educational success of students; environment—organizations that preserve or restore the environment; health—organizations that improve people's physical or emotional health; and social services—organizations that provide social services to those who suffer hardship or who have been unable to participate fully in the social and economic life of the community. The foundation makes grants of high-quality professional services that target capacity-building needs nonprofit organizations, including fundraising, marketing, information technology, and talent management. Each grant is staffed by professionals from the business community who donate their time and expertise to help the community. The grant also includes a project plan with estimated timing based on volunteers donating five hours per week. Guidelines and application are available online.
Requirements: 501(c)3 nonprofit organizations that provide direct benefits primarily or entirely to residents of the five boroughs of New York City (Manhattan, Bronx, Queens, Staten Island, and Brooklyn) and the six counties of the California Bay Area (Alameda, San Francisco, San Mateo, Santa Clara, Marin, and Contra Costa counties) are eligible. The organization must also have its headquarters in one of these areas.
Restrictions: The foundation does not support nonprofits with other than 501(c)3 status, for-profit corporations, or individuals. Service Grants are not expressly intended to support candidates for political office, or to influence legislation. Grants are not awarded to support religious purposes. (Agencies operated by religious organizations that serve secular needs are eligible.)
Geographic Focus: California, New York
Date(s) Application is Due: Mar 1; Jun 1; Sep 15; Dec 1
Contact: Grants Administrator; (415) 359-0226; national@taprootfoundation.org
Internet: http://taprootfoundation.org/npo/index.shtml
Sponsor: Taproot Foundation
466 Geary Street, Suite 300
San Francisco, CA 94102

Target Corporation Local Store Grants 4561
Grants focus on arts, reading, and family violence prevention. In the area of arts, the company's goal is to make the arts more accessible and affordable for the entire family. Grants support programs that provide art exhibits, classes, or performances. Programs that bring arts to schools or kids to the arts are encouraged. In the area of reading, the company funds programs that promote a love of reading or encourage children to read together with their families. Preference is given to programs that focus on programs that inspire young readers (birth through third grade). The corporation also awards All-Around Scholarships—including four national scholarships and two smaller scholarships for each Target store—to high school seniors and college students age 24 or younger. The scholarships recognize volunteer work as well as academic achievement. In the area of family violence prevention, the company funds programs that help prevent family violence, such as parent education, family counseling, support groups, and shelters. Organizations making efforts to reduce domestic violence or prevent child abuse and neglect receive preference.
Requirements: IRS 501(c)3 organizations in company-operating areas are eligible.
Restrictions: Grants do not support capital drives, religious organizations, medical or health-related causes, housing or rehabilitation programs, treatment programs (i.e., substance abuse), athletic teams or events, or fundraisers/benefits. Organizations in Alaska, Hawaii, and Vermont are not eligible.
Geographic Focus: All States
Date(s) Application is Due: Apr 30
Amount of Grant: 1,000 - 3,000 USD
Contact: Bridget McGinnis; (612) 696-6098; fax (612) 696-5088; guidelines@target.com
Internet: http://sites.target.com/site/en/corporate/page.jsp?contentId=PRD03-001818
Sponsor: Target Corporation
1000 Nicollet Mall, TPS-3080
Minneapolis, MN 55403

Target Foundation Grants 4562
The foundation welcomes applications from nonprofit organizations in the Minneapolis/Saint Paul metropolitan area. Types of support include operating, project, and capital grants. The foundation is specifically interested in partnering with arts and cultural institutions to make special exhibitions, performances, and events visible and accessible to the community; and supporting direct service organizations that sustain the basic shelter, food, and clothing needs of individuals or families at risk. Proposals are accepted throughout the year; the preferred submission time is February through November. Organizations that fit foundation guidelines may apply for funding by submitting a grant request via U.S. postal mail.
Requirements: 501(c)3 nonprofits in the Minneapolis/Saint Paul metropolitan area are eligible.
Restrictions: The foundation does not make grants to individuals or to religious groups for religious purposes; usually support national ceremonies, memorials, conferences, fundraising dinners, testimonials, or other similar events; usually support health, recreation, therapeutic programs; living subsidies; or care of disabled persons.
Geographic Focus: Minnesota
Date(s) Application is Due: Oct 1
Amount of Grant: 10,000 - 50,000 USD
Contact: Bridget McGinnis; (612) 696-6098; fax (612) 696-5088; guidelines@target.com
Internet: http://sites.target.com/site/en/corporate/page.jsp?contentId=PRD03-001819
Sponsor: Target Foundation
1000 Nicollet Mall, TPS-3080
Minneapolis, MN 55403

Tauck Family Foundation Grants 4563
The Tauck Family Foundation Grants focus on organizations and programs that are committed to Bridgeport's elementary school children, and to strengthening their capacity to help these children build the social and emotional skills they need to succeed throughout their educations. The desire is to help create better outcomes for children from low?income families and to focus the foundation's efforts in a way that would strengthen its nonprofit investees over time.
Requirements: The Tauck Family Foundation has selected its first portfolio of investees and has made a multi-year commitment to those organizations. As a result the foundation is not accepting proposals at this time. However, the Tauck Family Founation continues to be interested in learning about organizations developing the essential life skills of Bridgeport children. Nonprofit 501(c)3 organizations that meet the eligibility guidelines are free to submit an inquiry (via the foundation's website). Eligibility guidelines are as follows: be a non-profit, 501(c)3 organization; work (or have a specific strategy to work) with elementary (kindergarten through fifth grade) students in Bridgeport, Connecticut (organizations may be based in other cities/towns as long as they work with a significant number - more than 100 - of Bridgeport children in grades K-5); have an operating budget of $300,000 or more; consider the development of life skills of youth from low-income families to be core to the organization's mission; be interested in developing organizationally and receiving capacity building support, as needed and including: (a) going through an intensive Theory of Change process with the Tauck Family Foundation's consultants, and (b) implementing performance management systems to measure and monitor the development of children's self-control, persistence, mastery orientation, and academic self-efficacy.
Geographic Focus: Connecticut
Contact: Mirellise Vazquez, Program Officer; (203) 899-6824; fax (203) 286-1340; mirellise@tauckfoundation.org
Internet: http://www.tauckfamilyfoundation.org/how-to-apply
Sponsor: Tauck Family Foundation
P.O. Box 5020
Norwalk, CT 06856

Taylor S. Abernathy and Patti Harding Abernathy Charitable Trust Grants 4564
The Taylor S. Abernathy and Patti Harding Abernathy Charitable Trust was established in 1988 to support religious, charitable, scientific, and educational purposes. To that end, the trust provides grants that support and promote quality educational, cultural, human services, and health care programming. Grant requests for general operating support and program support will be considered. The Trust generally supports organizations that serve residents of the Greater Kansas City Metropolitan area. There are no application deadlines for the Abernathy Charitable Trust. Proposals are reviewed on an ongoing basis. Grants are one year in duration. Grant requests for general operating support and program support will be considered.
Requirements: 501(c)3 organizations serving the residents of the Greater Kansas City Metropolitan area are welcome to apply.
Restrictions: Grant requests for capital support will not be considered.
Geographic Focus: Kansas, Missouri
Amount of Grant: Up to 25,000 USD
Contact: Spence Heddens; (816) 292-4300; Spence.heddens@baml.com
Internet: https://www.bankofamerica.com/philanthropic/grantmaking.action
Sponsor: Taylor S. Abernathy and Patti Harding Abernathy Charitable Trust
1200 Main Street, 14th Floor, P.O. Box 219119
Kansas City, MO 64121-9119

TCF Bank Foundation Grants 4565
The foundation awards grants to community-based, nonprofit organizations operating in the areas served by TCF Bank. Areas of interest include education, human services, economic and community development, youth development, financial literacy, and the arts. Guidelines, which vary by state, are available online.
Requirements: Minnesota, Illinois, Michigan, Wisconsin, Colorado, and Indiana 501(c)3 tax-exempt organizations are eligible.
Geographic Focus: Colorado, Illinois, Indiana, Michigan, Minnesota, Wisconsin
Amount of Grant: 2,500 - 7,500 USD
Contact: Grants Administrator; (952) 745-2757
Internet: http://www.tcfexpress.com/About/about_community_relations.jsp
Sponsor: TCF Bank Foundation
200 Lake Street E
Wayzata, MN 55391

TD4HIM Foundation Grants 4566
The San Francisco 49ers Foundation is the non-profit community funding extension of the San Francisco 49ers. Now in its 16th year, the 49ers Foundation supports development programs for underserved youth that keep them safe, on track and in school. A significant portion of its funding goes toward family violence prevention programs and activities that teach youth leadership and respect.
Requirements: 501(c)3 organizations and programs in the greater Bay Area that are in alignment with the mission of the 49ers Foundation: keeping kids safe, on track and in school, are eligible to apply.
Restrictions: Please be advised that the 49ers Foundation does not fund the following areas: land, building or vehicle purchase; endowments; political campaigns; religious organizations (projects to promote religion); loans of any type; personal scholarships; travel; drives; specific individuals; organizations based outside the greater San Francisco Bay Area.
Geographic Focus: All States
Contact: TD4HIM Program Coordinator; (408) 829-3381
Internet: http://www.49ers.com/community/foundation.html
Sponsor: TD4HIM Foundation
60 Shoreline Circle
Incline Village, NV 89451-9529

Teaching Tolerance Grants 4567
The program offers grants of up to $10,000 for programs that engage collaboration between educators, researchers, parents/guardians and student groups that aim to equalize students' experience in schools. Programs should promote racial, ethnic, and religious harmony. The grants will target small-scale, resourceful, student-focused projects that promote acceptance of diversity, peace making, community service, or any other aspect of tolerance education. Applicants should submit a cover letter with name, grade and subject taught, school and home addresses, and phone numbers; and a typed 500-word description of project idea and a detailed proposed budget. There are no application deadlines.
Requirements: These grants require a two-stage application procedure, beginning with a Letter of Inquiry and, on invitation, followed by the submission of a full proposal. Guidelines are available at the sponsor's website. Letters of Inquiry are accepted at any time. Grants are restricted to one per applicant or school per school year. Grants are not renewable, and application materials are non-returnable.
Restrictions: Salaries, stipends, overhead costs, travel expenses, food items and computer hardware are not normally within the realm of funding. Field trips or speaker fees will be considered for funding, but they should not comprise more than 25% of the budget and should support a broader scope of experiences. When a grant is a fraction of a much larger proposal, or is sought to underwrite the cost of other tolerance-related programs, funding is unlikely.
Geographic Focus: All States
Amount of Grant: Up to 10,000 USD
Contact: Annie Bolling; (334) 264-0286, ext. 374; fax (334) 264-3121
Internet: http://www.tolerance.org/teach/grants/schoolgrants.jsp
Sponsor: Southern Poverty Law Center
400 Washington Avenue
Montgomery, AL 36104

Teaching Tolerance Mix-it-Up Grants 4568
The program funds youth-directed activist projects that focus on identifying, crossing, and challenging social boundaries in schools and communities. Preference is given to applications that clearly show: youth leadership—i.e., projects created and carried out by youth activists; collaborative efforts across social boundaries—i.e., different youth groups or clubs working together, or school-based clubs working with community-based organizations; and continuing efforts to identify, cross, or challenge social boundaries—i.e., the funded project isn't the end of the effort. Application and guidelines are available online.
Requirements: Individuals proposing youth-directed school or community projects are eligible.
Geographic Focus: All States
Amount of Grant: 500 USD
Contact: Annie Bolling; (334) 264-0286, ext. 374; fax (334) 264-3121
Internet: http://www.tolerance.org/teens/grants.jsp
Sponsor: Teaching Tolerance
400 Washington Avenue
Montgomery, AL 36104

Teagle Foundation Grants 4569
The Teagle Foundation's commitment to promoting and strengthening liberal education grounds their grant funding. Awards generally encourage collaboration among institutions, seeking to generate new knowledge on issues of importance to higher education. The Foundation is committed to widely disseminating this knowledge. The Foundation's signature Outcomes and Assessment initiative grows from their conviction that nothing has as much potential to affect students' educational experience as a sustained and systematic assessment of what and how they learn. The College-Community Connections program provides grants to community-based organizations in New York City that help disadvantaged young people prepare for and succeed in college, and works to build closer ties between these organizations and area colleges and universities.
Requirements: Requests for proposals are published on the Foundation's website .
Restrictions: The Foundation does not accept unsolicited proposals.
Geographic Focus: All States
Contact: Richard L. Morrill, President; (212) 373-1972; info@teaglefoundation.org
Internet: http://www.teaglefoundation.org/grantmaking/overview.aspx
Sponsor: Teagle Foundation
570 Lexington Avenue
New York, NY 10020-1903

TechFoundation TechGrants 4570
TechGrants is a grant program and newsletter that provides nonprofits with access to capital to help fulfill their technology needs. TechGrants focuses on directly funding critical technology needs while using its electronic newsletter to publicize innovative ways to find capital. As one of the only technology-focused granting programs in the US, TechFoundation aspires to implement an increasing number of highly successful projects that will bring quality technology resources to select nonprofits in the US; show that effectively deployed technology can have a great impact on the ability of a nonprofit to achieve their mission; and increase awareness of and support for the nonprofit technology assistance providers (NTAPs) community, which provides technology services to thousands of nonprofits in the US.
Geographic Focus: All States
Contact: Administrator; (617) 354-7500; fax (617) 354-7510; techgrants@techfoundation.org
Internet: http://www.techfoundation.org/techgrants
Sponsor: TechFoundation
20 University Road, 6th Floor
Cambridge, MA 02138

Technology Enhancement Certification for Hoosiers (TECH) 4571
To help Indiana companies meet the ever-growing demands of the new information economy, the state has designed a program to help workers gain new technology skills. The Technologies Enhancement Certification for Hoosiers, or TECH, Fund is a reimbursement grant program which provides financial assistance to existing companies that are committed to training their workers in the latest information technology skills. The maximum grant award for any one company or nonprofit organization is $50,000, $2,500 per employee, or 50 percent of training costs, whichever is less.
Requirements: Indiana companies or nonprofit organizations that employ Indiana residents in advanced information technology occupations are eligible to participate in this program. Training activities eligible for reimbursement under the guidelines are those offered by industry-certified training providers, which result in a full-time employee receiving a portable certification in systems administration, systems engineering, software development, professional certifications or other certifications in advanced e-business-enabling applications.
Restrictions: Limited to Indiana companies or nonprofit organizations.
Geographic Focus: Indiana
Amount of Grant: Up to 50,000 USD
Contact: Charlie Sparks; (317) 233-5122; fax (317) 232-4146; csparks@iedc.in.gov
Internet: http://www.in.gov/iedc/workforce/tech.html
Sponsor: Indiana Economic Development Corporation
1 North Capitol Avenue, Suite 700
Indianapolis, IN 46204

TE Foundation Grants 4572
The foundation provides grants to nonprofit organizations in geographic areas where Tyco Electronics has a significant employee population and for specific projects or programs in broad categories, including education (with an emphasis on math and science), community impact, and arts and culture. In addition to a matching gifts program for employee contributions to accredited high schools, colleges, and universities, the foundation makes direct grants for programs that address a business or community concern of Tyco Electronics. Organizations that support pre-college math and science education receive special attention. Agencies that promote personal growth, career opportunities, and economic self-sufficiency are encouraged to apply, as are local chapters of health- and civic-related organizations. Special attention is given to community-wide arts organizations that solicit and allocate funds for a number of arts groups and institutions. Local public television and radio stations are encouraged to apply for funding of specific education initiatives. Capital campaigns of significant arts and cultural organizations serving communities in which the corporation has a major presence also will receive consideration. Grants also are awarded to support general operations, program development, and employee matching gifts. Applications are accepted throughout the year but are considered on the listed application deadlines.
Requirements: The TE Foundation limits grants to U.S. organizations that qualify as nonprofit under Section 501(c)3 of the Internal Revenue Code. Requests receive preferential review if the organization is supported by TE employees as volunteers.
Restrictions: The foundation generally will not support organizations in geographic areas where Tyco Electronics has few or no employees; individuals, private foundations, national organizations, or service clubs; fraternal, social, labor or trade organizations; organizations that discriminate on the basis of race, religion, color, national origin, physical or mental conditions, veteran or marital status, age, or sex; churches or religious organizations, with the exception of nondenominational programs sponsored by a church or religious group such as a food bank, youth center or non-sectarian education programs; political campaigns; loans or investments; or programs that pose a potential conflict of interest.
Geographic Focus: California, Massachusetts, Michigan, North Carolina, Pennsylvania, South Carolina, Texas, Virginia
Date(s) Application is Due: Mar 15; Jun 15; Sep 15; Dec 15
Amount of Grant: 250 - 25,000 USD
Contact: Mary Rakoczy, (717) 592-4869; fax (717) 592-4022; TEfoundation@te.com
Internet: http://www.te.com/en/about-te/responsibility/community.html
Sponsor: Tyco Electronics Foundation
c/o TE Corporation
Harrisburg, PA 17105-3608

Telluride Foundation Community Grants 4573
The foundation offers an annual granting cycle for nonprofit organizations that serve people living and/or working in Colorado's San Miguel County. The foundation awards grants to local nonprofit organizations involved in the arts, education, athletics, childcare, land conservation, environmental, minority programs, and other community-based efforts. Additionally, the foundation provides local nonprofits with technical assistance, such as training seminars, grant writing and consulting and capacity building services. Foundation grants are awarded once a year, at the end of December, with grant awards being distributed the following year. Grants will fall generally in the range of $500 and above, depending on the amount available for distribution.
Requirements: The Telluride Foundation will consider grant applications from 501(c)3 organizations meeting the following eligibility *Requirements:* conduct activities and programs consistent with the Foundation's mission; serve people living or working in San Miguel County (primary emphasis of grant making is to organizations based in San Miguel, Ouray and west Montrose counties—all other organizations must document a strong case to meet "serving people that live and/or work in San Miguel County."). Applicants without 501(c)3 status, but which have applied to the IRS for such status, may apply. Applicants without 501(c)3 status, but which are operating under an organization qualified as a 501(c)3 organization, may apply separately if they have their own advisory board and have the written consent of the qualified organization.
Restrictions: Grants will not be awarded for building/renovation; equipment that could be capitalized on a financial statement; capital campaigns; debt reduction or retiring past operating deficits; fellowships or other grants to individuals; loans; non-educational publications; litigation; political campaigns; operating support for organizations that conduct lobbying or political action campaigns, economic development, endowment funds, religious organizations for religious purposes, graduate and post-graduate research, or candidates for political office.
Geographic Focus: Colorado
Date(s) Application is Due: Oct 28
Amount of Grant: 500 USD
Contact: April Montgomery; (970) 728-8717; fax (970) 728-9007; april@telluridefoundation.org
Internet: http://www.telluridefoundation.org/index.php?page=community-grants
Sponsor: Telluride Foundation
220 E. Colorado Avenue, Suite 106
Telluride, CO 81435

Telluride Foundation Emergency/Out of Cycle Grants 4574
The Telluride Foundation Board of Directors recognizes that there will be times when its annual grant cycle does not work for all organizations and their needs. Out-of-cycle grants are requests that fall out of the Foundation's annual cycle of granting. Because of timing issues or emergencies that arise, not all organizations can fit their request into the regular October to December cycle. Out-of-cycle grants are not intended to be a catch-all for organizations that fail to anticipate the October-December cycle or to meet a budget crises, which occur from poor financial planning. The grants are intended to address needs that arise through external or uncontrollable emergencies and that present a compelling story of an unmet and necessary need.
Requirements: The Telluride Foundation will consider grant applications from 501(c)3 organizations meeting the following eligibility *Requirements:* conduct activities and programs consistent with the Foundation's mission; serve people living or working in San Miguel County (primary emphasis of grant making is to organizations based in San Miguel, Ouray and west Montrose counties—all other organizations must document a strong case to meet "serving people that live and/or work in San Miguel County."). Only two types of

needs will be considered: Timing-needs which arise because of timing issues on the part of the organization; and, Human Emergencies. Needs which do not fall into one of these two narrow categories will be considered and the request must be for a project or program described under "Types of Support" in the regular grant guidelines.
Restrictions: Grants will not be awarded for building/renovation; equipment that could be capitalized on a financial statement; capital campaigns; debt reduction or retiring past operating deficits; fellowships or other grants to individuals; loans; non-educational publications; litigation; political campaigns; operating support for organizations that conduct lobbying or political action campaigns, economic development, endowment funds, religious organizations for religious purposes, graduate and post-graduate research, or candidates for political office.
Geographic Focus: Colorado
Contact: April Montgomery; (970) 728-8717; fax (970) 728-9007; april@telluridefoundation.org
Internet: http://www.telluridefoundation.org/index.php?page=emergency-out-of-cycle-grants
Sponsor: Telluride Foundation
220 E. Colorado Avenue, Suite 106
Telluride, CO 81435

Telluride Foundation Technical Assistance Grants 4575
The Telluride Foundation offers local nonprofits with the option of applying for a Technical Assistance Grant. The grants provide an easy, effective way for nonprofit organizations to improve their operational efficiency through a proven, turnkey program for assessing and addressing individual organization's needs. The objective is to provide the nonprofit a professional third part assessment of their current needs then a professional nonprofit consultant to assist through the solution process. The assessment may identify the need for an updated business plan, strategic plan, marketing plan, Board of Directors development, etc. The consultant will assist the organizations staff and Board through the development of the plan. The Assessment will be conducted by the Community Resource Center or a consultant choosen by the nonprofit, if approved by the Telluride Foundation, and will be shared with the Telluride Foundation. The Telluride Foundation will pay for the assessment and will fund part or the entire consultant fees. If selected for a TA, the non-profit will not be eligible for future funding from the Telluride Foundation until they have completed the TA process.
Requirements: The Telluride Foundation will consider grant applications from 501(c)3 organizations meeting the following eligibility *Requirements:* conduct activities and programs consistent with the Foundation's mission; serve people living or working in San Miguel County (primary emphasis of grant making is to organizations based in San Miguel, Ouray and west Montrose counties—all other organizations must document a strong case to meet "serving people that live and/or work in San Miguel County."). Applicants without 501(c)3 status, but which have applied to the IRS for such status, may apply. Applicants without 501(c)3 status, but which are operating under an organization qualified as a 501(c)3 organization, may apply separately if they have their own advisory board and have the written consent of the qualified organization. A request for a Technical Assistance Grant may be included in a Community Grant application requesting project or general operating funds or a nonprofit may only request Technical Assitance Funds using the Community Grant application.
Restrictions: Grants will not be awarded for building/renovation; equipment that could be capitalized on a financial statement; capital campaigns; debt reduction or retiring past operating deficits; fellowships or other grants to individuals; loans; non-educational publications; litigation; political campaigns; operating support for organizations that conduct lobbying or political action campaigns, economic development, endowment funds, religious organizations for religious purposes, graduate and post-graduate research, or candidates for political office.
Geographic Focus: Colorado
Date(s) Application is Due: Oct 28
Contact: April Montgomery; (970) 728-8717; fax (970) 728-9007; april@telluridefoundation.org
Internet: http://www.telluridefoundation.org/index.php?page=technical-assistance-grants
Sponsor: Telluride Foundation
220 E. Colorado Avenue, Suite 106
Telluride, CO 81435

Temple-Inland Foundation Grants 4576
The foundation makes grants to IRS 501(c)3 tax-exempt organizations located in geographic operating areas of Temple-Inland Inc's subsidiary companies. Areas of interest include services for children and youth, Christian churches and organizations, education at all levels, health care and organizations, human services, and arts and culture. Types of support include general operating support, research, employee matching gifts, and employee-related scholarships. Requests should be received two weeks prior to quarterly board meetings. Submit a written request for guidelines and specific application deadlines. The listed deadline date is for scholarships.
Restrictions: Ineligible applicants include fraternal, veterans, political, local social, and service organizations.
Geographic Focus: All States
Date(s) Application is Due: Mar 15
Contact: Richard Warner, (936) 829-1721; fax (936) 829-7727
Internet: http://www.templeinland.com
Sponsor: Temple-Inland Foundation
1300 S Mopac
Austin, TX 78749

Temple University George D. McDowell Fellowship 4577
The fellowship provides a stipend and access to photographs and newspaper clippings in the archives of the Philadelphia Evening Bulletin newspaper, a resource for research on the Philadelphia metropolitan area. The program provides support for a six-week fellowship to do research and study that results in a scholarly work. Application and guidelines are available online.
Requirements: Undergraduate and graduate students, independent scholars, educators, writers, filmmakers, and anyone interested in the history of Philadelphia are invited to apply.
Restrictions: Current employees of Temple University are ineligible.
Geographic Focus: All States
Date(s) Application is Due: Feb 15
Amount of Grant: 3,000 USD
Contact: Margaret Jerrido; (215) 204-5750; fax (212) 204-3681; urban@library.temple.edu
Internet: http://library.temple.edu/collections/urbana
Sponsor: Temple University
1210 W Berks Street
Philadelphia, PA 19122

Tension Envelope Foundation Grants 4578
Incorporated in 1954, the Tension Envelope Foundation supports nonprofits in company-operating areas, with an emphasis on Jewish welfare funds, community funds, higher education, health, civic affairs, culture and the arts, and youth. Funding typically is provided for general operating costs. There are no annual deadlines or guidelines, and the foundation does not distribute an annual report. To apply for a grant, send proposal with an overview of the project, budget, and proof of 501(c)3 status, requesting an application form in the process. The board meets several times a year.
Requirements: 501(c)3 nonprofits in California, Iowa, Kansas, Minnesota, Missouri, North Carolina, Tennessee, and Texas are eligible.
Geographic Focus: California, Iowa, Kansas, Minnesota, Missouri, North Carolina, Tennessee, Texas
Contact: William Berkley, Director; (816) 471-3800
Sponsor: Tension Envelope Foundation
819 E 19th Street, 5th Floor
Kansas City, MO 64108-1781

Texas Commission on the Arts Arts Education Project 1 Grants 4579
This program provides funding support for projects demonstrating artistic merit and best practices in arts education. This program is directed toward the advancement of arts education curriculum, student achievement through hands on activity, teacher training, and assessment. See website for deadline date.
Requirements: To be eligible for TCA grants, an organization must be: a tax-exempt nonprofit organization as designated by the Internal Revenue Service and/or must be an entity of government; be incorporated in Texas; have fulfilled all its outstanding contractual obligations to the State of Texas (i.e. student loans, child support, taxes, etc.); and comply with regulations pertaining to federal grant recipients including Title VI of the Civil Rights Act of 1964, Section 504 of the Rehabilitation Act of 1973, the Age Discrimination Act of 1975, the Education Amendments of 1972, the Americans with Disabilities Act of 1990, and the Drug Free Workplace Act of 1988. All Arts Education Projects must be curriculum based and aligned with the Texas Essential Knowledge and Skills to be considered eligible. Performances for youth and/or adults without these components will not be accepted as an Arts Education Project. The Arts Education - Resource Catalogue includes eligible projects for this category.
Geographic Focus: Texas
Contact: Director of Programs; (512) 463-5535 or (800) 252-9415; fax (512) 475-2699; front.desk@arts.state.tx.us
Internet: http://www2.arts.state.tx.us/tcagrant/TXArtsPlan/AEP1.htm
Sponsor: Texas Commission on the Arts
P.O. Box 13406
Austin, TX 78711-3406

Texas Commission on the Arts Arts in Education Team Building/Texas Music Project Grants 4580
This program provides funding for strategic development in arts education. Texas Music Project (TMP) grants are directed to K-12 schools to provide music education in the classroom. Priority is given to Title I public schools.
Requirements: To be eligible for TCA grants, an organization must be: a tax-exempt nonprofit organization as designated by the Internal Revenue Service and/or must be an entity of government; be incorporated in Texas; have fulfilled all its outstanding contractual obligations to the State of Texas (i.e. student loans, child support, taxes, etc.); and comply with regulations pertaining to federal grant recipients including Title VI of the Civil Rights Act of 1964, Section 504 of the Rehabilitation Act of 1973, the Age Discrimination Act of 1975, the Education Amendments of 1972, the Americans with Disabilities Act of 1990, and the Drug Free Workplace Act of 1988.
Geographic Focus: Texas
Date(s) Application is Due: May 1
Contact: Director of Programs; (512) 463-5535 or (800) 252-9415; fax (512) 475-2699; front.desk@arts.state.tx.us
Internet: http://www2.arts.state.tx.us/tcagrant/TXArtsPlan/AEP1.htm
Sponsor: Texas Commission on the Arts
P.O. Box 13406
Austin, TX 78711-3406

Texas Commission on the Arts Arts Respond Project Grants 4581
This program provides project assistance grants on a short-term basis and may include administrative costs directly related to the project. Projects must address one of the following priority areas: education, health and human services, economic development, public safety, criminal justice, natural resources, or agriculture. Organizations that are eligible are: Arts Organizations, Established Arts Organizations, Minority Arts Organizations, Rural Arts Providers.
Requirements: To be eligible for TCA grants, an organization must be: a tax-exempt nonprofit organization as designated by the Internal Revenue Service and/or must be an

entity of government; be incorporated in Texas; have fulfilled all its outstanding contractual obligations to the State of Texas (i.e. student loans, child support, taxes, etc.); and comply with regulations pertaining to federal grant recipients including Title VI of the Civil Rights Act of 1964, Section 504 of the Rehabilitation Act of 1973, the Age Discrimination Act of 1975, the Education Amendments of 1972, the Americans with Disabilities Act of 1990, and the Drug Free Workplace Act of 1988.
Geographic Focus: Texas
Amount of Grant: Up to 45,000 USD
Contact: Director of Programs; (512) 463-5535 or (800) 252-9415; fax (512) 475-2699; front.desk@arts.state.tx.us
Internet: http://www.arts.state.tx.us/index.php?option=com_wrapper&view=wrapper&Itemid=86
Sponsor: Texas Commission on the Arts
P.O. Box 13406
Austin, TX 78711-3406

Texas Commission on the Arts County Arts Expansion Program 4582
This program provides project support for arts activities and may include administrative costs directly related to the project. The intent is to advance the creative economy of Texas by investing in arts activities in counties with populations under 50,000. Nonprofits, schools, universities, and units of government in designated counties are eligible. See website, http://www.arts.state.tx.us/index.php?option=com_content&view=article&id=67:county-arts-expansion-program&catid=55:account-holders&Itemid=84 for a complete listing of eligible counties.
Requirements: To be eligible for TCA grants, an organization must: be a tax-exempt nonprofit organization as designated by the Internal Revenue Service and/or must be an entity of government; be incorporated in Texas; have fulfilled all its outstanding contractual obligations to the State of Texas (i.e. student loans, child support, taxes, etc.); and comply with regulations pertaining to federal grant recipients including Title VI of the Civil Rights Act of 1964, Section 504 of the Rehabilitation Act of 1973, the Age Discrimination Act of 1975, the Education Amendments of 1972, the Americans with Disabilities Act of 1990, and the Drug Free Workplace Act of 1988.
Geographic Focus: Texas
Date(s) Application is Due: May 1
Amount of Grant: 3,000 USD
Contact: Director of Programs; (512) 463-5535 or (800) 252-9415; fax (512) 475-2699; front.desk@arts.state.tx.us
Internet: http://www2.arts.state.tx.us/tcagrant/TXArtsPlan/AEP1.htm
Sponsor: Texas Commission on the Arts
P.O. Box 13406
Austin, TX 78711-3406

Texas Commission on the Arts Create-1 Program Grants 4583
To advance the creative economy of Texas by investing in arts organizations. This program provides multi-year operational support. Applicants write their grant for a one year period, and if funded, will provide an update for the second year. Established Arts Organizations with a budget between $50,000 and $1 million may apply. Depending on the availability of funds, the organization's award amount will be the same for two fiscal years. New organizations may only apply in odd numbered years.
Requirements: To be eligible for TCA grants, an organization must: be a tax-exempt nonprofit organization as designated by the Internal Revenue Service and/or must be an entity of government; be incorporated in Texas; have fulfilled all its outstanding contractual obligations to the State of Texas (i.e. student loans, child support, taxes, etc.); and comply with regulations pertaining to federal grant recipients including Title VI of the Civil Rights Act of 1964, Section 504 of the Rehabilitation Act of 1973, the Age Discrimination Act of 1975, the Education Amendments of 1972, the Americans with Disabilities Act of 1990, and the Drug Free Workplace Act of 1988.
Geographic Focus: Texas
Date(s) Application is Due: Mar 1
Amount of Grant: 3,000 - 40,000 USD
Contact: Director of Programs; (512) 463-5535 or (800) 252-9415; fax (512) 475-2699; front.desk@arts.state.tx.us
Internet: http://www.arts.state.tx.us/index.php?option=com_wrapper&view=wrapper&Itemid=86
Sponsor: Texas Commission on the Arts
P.O. Box 13406
Austin, TX 78711-3406

Texas Commission on the Arts Create-2 Program Grants 4584
Established Minority Arts Organizations with a budget over $50,000. To advance the creative economy of Texas by investing in arts organizations. This program provides multi-year operational support. Applicants write their grant for a one year period, and if funded, will provide an update for the second year. Depending on the availability of funds, the organization's award amount will be the same for two fiscal years. One application per organization for this program. New organizations may only apply in odd numbered years.
Requirements: To be eligible for TCA grants, an organization must: be a tax-exempt nonprofit organization as designated by the Internal Revenue Service and/or must be an entity of government; be incorporated in Texas; have fulfilled all its outstanding contractual obligations to the State of Texas (i.e. student loans, child support, taxes, etc.); and comply with regulations pertaining to federal grant recipients including Title VI of the Civil Rights Act of 1964, Section 504 of the Rehabilitation Act of 1973, the Age Discrimination Act of 1975, the Education Amendments of 1972, the Americans with Disabilities Act of 1990, and the Drug Free Workplace Act of 1988.
Geographic Focus: Texas
Date(s) Application is Due: Mar 15
Amount of Grant: 3,000 - 35,000 USD
Contact: Director of Programs; (512) 463-5535 or (800) 252-9415; fax (512) 475-2699; front.desk@arts.state.tx.us
Internet: http://www.arts.state.tx.us/index.php?option=com_wrapper&view=wrapper&Itemid=86
Sponsor: Texas Commission on the Arts
P.O. Box 13406
Austin, TX 78711-3406

Texas Commission on the Arts Create-3 Program Grants 4585
This program provides multi-year operational support for Established Arts Organizations with a budget between $1 million and $5 million dollars. Applicants write their grant for a one year period, and if funded, will provide an update for the second year. Depending on the availability of funds, the organization's award amount will be the same for two fiscal years. New organizations may only apply in odd numbered years.
Requirements: To be eligible for TCA grants, an organization must: be a tax-exempt nonprofit organization as designated by the Internal Revenue Service and/or must be an entity of government; be incorporated in Texas; have fulfilled all its outstanding contractual obligations to the State of Texas (i.e. student loans, child support, taxes, etc.); comply with regulations pertaining to federal grant recipients including Title VI of the Civil Rights Act of 1964, Section 504 of the Rehabilitation Act of 1973, the Age Discrimination Act of 1975, the Education Amendments of 1972, the Americans with Disabilities Act of 1990, and the Drug Free Workplace Act of 1988.
Geographic Focus: Texas
Date(s) Application is Due: Mar 15
Amount of Grant: 3,000 - 40,000 USD
Contact: Director of Programs; (512) 463-5535 or (800) 252-9415; fax (512) 475-2699; front.desk@arts.state.tx.us
Internet: http://www.arts.state.tx.us/index.php?option=com_wrapper&view=wrapper&Itemid=86
Sponsor: Texas Commission on the Arts
P.O. Box 13406
Austin, TX 78711-3406

Texas Commission on the Arts Create-4 Program Grants 4586
Established Arts Organizations with a budget over $5 million may apply for this grant. The intent is to advance the creative economy of Texas by investing in arts organizations. This program provides multi-year operational support. Applicants write their grant for a one year period, and if funded, will provide an update for the second year. Depending on the availability of funds, the organization's award amount will be the same for two fiscal years. New organizations may only apply in odd numbered years.
Requirements: To be eligible for TCA grants, an organization must: be a tax-exempt nonprofit organization as designated by the Internal Revenue Service and/or must be an entity of government; be incorporated in Texas; have fulfilled all its outstanding contractual obligations to the State of Texas (i.e. student loans, child support, taxes, etc.); comply with regulations pertaining to federal grant recipients including Title VI of the Civil Rights Act of 1964, Section 504 of the Rehabilitation Act of 1973, the Age Discrimination Act of 1975, the Education Amendments of 1972, the Americans with Disabilities Act of 1990, and the Drug Free Workplace Act of 1988.
Geographic Focus: Texas
Date(s) Application is Due: Mar 15
Amount of Grant: 3,000 - 40,000 USD
Contact: Director of Programs; (512) 463-5535 or (800) 252-9415; fax (512) 475-2699; front.desk@arts.state.tx.us
Internet: http://www.arts.state.tx.us/index.php?option=com_wrapper&view=wrapper&Itemid=86
Sponsor: Texas Commission on the Arts
P.O. Box 13406
Austin, TX 78711-3406

Texas Commission on the Arts Create-5 Program Grants 4587
The intent of this grant is to advance the creative economy of Texas by investing in arts organizations. This program provides multi-year operational support. Applicants write their grant for a one year period, and if funded, will provide an update for the second year. Depending on the availability of funds, the organization's award amount will be the same for two fiscal years. New organizations may only apply in odd numbered years.
Requirements: To be eligible for TCA grants, an organization must: Be a tax-exempt nonprofit organization as designated by the Internal Revenue Service and/or must be an entity of government Be incorporated in Texas Have fulfilled all its outstanding contractual obligations to the State of Texas (i.e. student loans, child support, taxes, etc.) Comply with regulations pertaining to federal grant recipients including Title VI of the Civil Rights Act of 1964, Section 504 of the Rehabilitation Act of 1973, the Age Discrimination Act of 1975, the Education Amendments of 1972, the Americans with Disabilities Act of 1990, and the Drug Free Workplace Act of 1988.
Geographic Focus: Texas
Date(s) Application is Due: Mar 15
Amount of Grant: 3,000 - 50,000 USD
Contact: Director of Programs; (512) 463-5535 or (800) 252-9415; fax (512) 475-2699; front.desk@arts.state.tx.us
Internet: http://www.arts.state.tx.us/index.php?option=com_wrapper&view=wrapper&Itemid=86
Sponsor: Texas Commission on the Arts
P.O. Box 13406
Austin, TX 78711-3406

Texas Commission on the Arts Cultural Connections-Performance Support Grants 4588

All Texas nonprofits, schools, colleges, and units of government are eligible for this grant. This program provides professional artist fees to schools, libraries, and nonprofit organizations for hiring an artist from the TCA Touring Roster to do a performance. See website for a hyper link to the TCA Touring Roster. The application deadline is also listed on website.
Requirements: To be eligible for TCA grants, an organization must: Be a tax-exempt nonprofit organization as designated by the Internal Revenue Service and/or must be an entity of government Be incorporated in Texas Have fulfilled all its outstanding contractual obligations to the State of Texas (i.e. student loans, child support, taxes, etc.) Comply with regulations pertaining to federal grant recipients including Title VI of the Civil Rights Act of 1964, Section 504 of the Rehabilitation Act of 1973, the Age Discrimination Act of 1975, the Education Amendments of 1972, the Americans with Disabilities Act of 1990, and the Drug Free Workplace Act of 1988.
Restrictions: Multiple applications can be submitted, but only $12,000 cumulatively will be awarded to an organization per fiscal year (Sept.-Aug.)
Geographic Focus: Texas
Amount of Grant: 8,000 USD
Contact: Director of Programs; (512) 463-5535 or (800) 252-9415; fax (512) 475-2699; front.desk@arts.state.tx.us
Internet: http://www2.arts.state.tx.us/tcagrant/TXArtsPlan/AEP1.htm
Sponsor: Texas Commission on the Arts
P.O. Box 13406
Austin, TX 78711-3406

Texas Commission on the Arts Cultural Connections-Visual & Media Arts Touring Exhibits Grants 4589

All Texas nonprofits, schools, colleges, and units of government are eligible for this grant. This program provides funding for organizations to present art exhibitions, film series, documentary films, or other media series curated by an outside organization. This program is limited to traveling exhibitions funded through TCA's Exhibition Preparation Program or Exhibits USA. Priority will be given to first time TCA applicants, rural and underserved areas. See website for hyper links to the Exhibition Preparation Program and Exhibits USA. Application deadlines can also be found on the website.
Requirements: To be eligible for TCA grants, an organization must: Be a tax-exempt nonprofit organization as designated by the Internal Revenue Service and/or must be an entity of government Be incorporated in Texas Have fulfilled all its outstanding contractual obligations to the State of Texas (i.e. student loans, child support, taxes, etc.) Comply with regulations pertaining to federal grant recipients including Title VI of the Civil Rights Act of 1964, Section 504 of the Rehabilitation Act of 1973, the Age Discrimination Act of 1975, the Education Amendments of 1972, the Americans with Disabilities Act of 1990, and the Drug Free Workplace Act of 1988.
Geographic Focus: Texas
Amount of Grant: 2,000 USD
Contact: Director of Programs; (512) 463-5535 or (800) 252-9415; fax (512) 475-2699; front.desk@arts.state.tx.us
Internet: http://www2.arts.state.tx.us/tcagrant/TXArtsPlan/AEP1.htm
Sponsor: Texas Commission on the Arts
P.O. Box 13406
Austin, TX 78711-3406

Texas Commission On The Arts Cultural Connections Consultant/Simply Solutions Grants 4590

This program provides support for professional training, organizational assessment, and development. Support is provided for a solution to a problem through a consultant. Priority will be given to first-time TCA applicants, unforeseen opportunities, rural and under served areas. Arts Organizations, Established Arts Organizations, Minority Arts Organizations are eligible to apply.
Requirements: To be eligible for TCA grants, an organization must: Be a tax-exempt nonprofit organization as designated by the Internal Revenue Service and/or must be an entity of government Be incorporated in Texas Have fulfilled all its outstanding contractual obligations to the State of Texas (i.e. student loans, child support, taxes, etc.) Comply with regulations pertaining to federal grant recipients including Title VI of the Civil Rights Act of 1964, Section 504 of the Rehabilitation Act of 1973, the Age Discrimination Act of 1975, the Education Amendments of 1972, the Americans with Disabilities Act of 1990, and the Drug Free Workplace Act of 1988.
Geographic Focus: Texas
Date(s) Application is Due: May 1
Amount of Grant: 2,000 USD
Contact: Director of Programs; (512) 463-5535 or (800) 252-9415; fax (512) 475-2699; front.desk@arts.state.tx.us
Internet: http://www2.arts.state.tx.us/tcagrant/TXArtsPlan/AEP1.htm
Sponsor: Texas Commission on the Arts
P.O. Box 13406
Austin, TX 78711-3406

Texas Commission on the Arts Cultural Connections Grants 4591

This program provides opportunities for professional training and development. Support is provided through the use of travel/registration subsidies to attend a conference on the TCA list of approved conferences. Arts Organizations, Established Arts Organizations, Minority Arts Organizations are eligible to apply. See website for complete listing of these approved conferences.
Requirements: To be eligible for TCA grants, an organization must: Be a tax-exempt nonprofit organization as designated by the Internal Revenue Service and/or must be an entity of government Be incorporated in Texas Have fulfilled all its outstanding contractual obligations to the State of Texas (i.e. student loans, child support, taxes, etc.) Comply with regulations pertaining to federal grant recipients including Title VI of the Civil Rights Act of 1964, Section 504 of the Rehabilitation Act of 1973, the Age Discrimination Act of 1975, the Education Amendments of 1972, the Americans with Disabilities Act of 1990, and the Drug Free Workplace Act of 1988.
Geographic Focus: Texas
Date(s) Application is Due: May 1
Contact: Director of Programs; (512) 463-5535 or (800) 252-9415; fax (512) 475-2699; front.desk@arts.state.tx.us
Internet: http://www2.arts.state.tx.us/tcagrant/TXArtsPlan/CC1.htm
Sponsor: Texas Commission on the Arts
P.O. Box 13406
Austin, TX 78711-3406

Texas Commission On The Arts GPA1 4592

The intent of this grant is to advance the creative economy of Texas by investing in arts organizations. This program provides multi-year operational support. Applicants write their grant for a one year period, and if funded, will provide an update for the second year. Depending on the availability of funds, the organization's award amount will be the same for two fiscal years. New organizations may only apply in odd numbered years. Established Arts Organizations with a budget between $50,000 and $1 million are eligible for this grant.
Requirements: To be eligible for TCA grants, an organization must: Be a tax-exempt nonprofit organization as designated by the Internal Revenue Service and/or must be an entity of government Be incorporated in Texas Have fulfilled all its outstanding contractual obligations to the State of Texas (i.e. student loans, child support, taxes, etc.) Comply with regulations pertaining to federal grant recipients including Title VI of the Civil Rights Act of 1964, Section 504 of the Rehabilitation Act of 1973, the Age Discrimination Act of 1975, the Education Amendments of 1972, the Americans with Disabilities Act of 1990, and the Drug Free Workplace Act of 1988.
Geographic Focus: Texas
Date(s) Application is Due: Mar 1
Contact: Director of Programs; (512) 463-5535 or (800) 252-9415; fax (512) 475-2699; front.desk@arts.state.tx.us
Internet: http://www2.arts.state.tx.us/tcagrant/TXArtsPlan/AEP1.htm
Sponsor: Texas Commission on the Arts
P.O. Box 13406
Austin, TX 78711-3406

Texas Commission on the Arts Special Opportunities Grants 4593

All Texas nonprofits, schools, colleges, and units of government are eligible for this grant. The intent of this grant is to advance the creative economy of Texas by investing in arts activities. Based on available funding, TCA will fund unique opportunities that advance the arts in Texas. Emphasis will be placed on projects that advance cultural tourism and designated dollars received from an external funder for programs and initiatives the Commission occasionally undertakes. Interested applicants may email a one-page description of the project to: opportunities@arts.state.tx.us. Letters must include: indication of organization's nonprofit status in Texas; a description of the project including a project timeline; expected outcomes and benefits to the state of Texas and an indicator of how those outcomes will be tracked and measured and a budget indicating revenue secured and expenditures. Approved proposals will be invited to formally apply after the quarterly board meeting. See website for application deadlines. This grant program will end on August 31, 2009.
Requirements: To be eligible for TCA grants, an organization must: Be a tax-exempt nonprofit organization as designated by the Internal Revenue Service and/or must be an entity of government Be incorporated in Texas Have fulfilled all its outstanding contractual obligations to the State of Texas (i.e. student loans, child support, taxes, etc.) Comply with regulations pertaining to federal grant recipients including Title VI of the Civil Rights Act of 1964, Section 504 of the Rehabilitation Act of 1973, the Age Discrimination Act of 1975, the Education Amendments of 1972, the Americans with Disabilities Act of 1990, and the Drug Free Workplace Act of 1988.
Geographic Focus: Texas
Contact: Director of Programs; (512) 463-5535 or (800) 252-9415; fax (512) 475-2699; front.desk@arts.state.tx.us
Internet: http://www2.arts.state.tx.us/tcagrant/TXArtsPlan/AEP1.htm
Sponsor: Texas Commission on the Arts
P.O. Box 13406
Austin, TX 78711-3406

Texas Commission on the Arts Young Masters Program Grants 4594

This grant is available every other year to Texas 8th to 12th grade students (or home schooled students who have achieved a comparable status towards high school graduation) who are legal U.S. and Texas residents are eligible for this grant. The intent of this grant is to advance the creative economy of Texas by investing in the future of the arts. This program awards grants to talented young artists to further their studies in their chosen field. This grant is not a college scholarship. The most talented young artists will receive the title of Young Master and will be awarded grants of up to $2,500 per year to further their studies in their chosen arts disciplines.
Requirements: Students are eligible to receive the grant for up to three years, but not beyond their senior year, and they must reapply annually. Students must be participating in a school-based arts program, summer institute, a specialized course of study, or receiving private lessons from a qualified instructor. Students must maintain passing grades in all academic areas. Applications will be from the student, his or her parent/guardian, and his or her arts instructor.

Geographic Focus: Texas
Date(s) Application is Due: Nov 15
Amount of Grant: 2,500 USD
Contact: Director of Programs; (512) 463-5535 or (800) 252-9415; fax (512) 475-2699; front.desk@arts.state.tx.us
Internet: http://www2.arts.state.tx.us/tcagrant/TXArtsPlan/AEP1.htm
Sponsor: Texas Commission on the Arts
P.O. Box 13406
Austin, TX 78711-3406

Texas Filmmakers Production Grants 4595
The Texas Filmmakers Production Grants are awarded to emerging film and video artists in the state of Texas. Awards are provided to artists whose work shows promise, skill, and creativity. Grant recipients have shown their films at renowned festivals like Sundance, Cannes, Toronto, Tribeca, Venice and SXSW and have been nominated for Gotham Awards, won Independent Spirit Awards and Student Academy Awards. Several have been released theatrically or in the cable and home video markets. In August, an independent panel of highly esteemed professionals from the national film community convene in Austin to review applications and administer awards. Award announcements are posted on the society's website at the conclusion of the panel session, and grant disbursements are made in early September. The application, other required attachments, and grant guidelines are available online.
Requirements: Emerging film and video artists in Texas are eligible. The applicant must have lived in Texas for at least one year prior to the deadline; and must be the person with primary creative control over the proposed project. This is usually defined as the director.
Restrictions: The program does not fund multimedia projects or television series. Funding is not available for pre-production or development of the film.
Geographic Focus: Texas
Date(s) Application is Due: Jun 1
Contact: Rebecca Campbell, Executive Director; (512) 322-0145; fax (512) 322-5192; rebecca@austinfilm.org or afs@austinfilm.org
Internet: http://www.austinfilm.org/page.aspx?pid=300
Sponsor: Austin Film Society
1901 East 51st Street
Austin, TX 78723

Texas Instruments Corporation Arts and Culture Grants 4596
The Corporation offers grant support for artistic and cultural programs at Texas Instrument plant-site locations. Programs must enhance the quality of life in the community by helping draw and retain employees to the plant-site locations. The Corporation board meets quarterly, and funding decisions are made within three weeks of each meeting. Corporate grant funding is prioritized based on opportunities for TI employee/retiree involvement.
Requirements: Applicants must be 501(c)3 tax-exempt nonprofit organizations. Grant applications are only accepted online. Applicants access the eligibility quiz at the website and if they are eligible, they gain access to the application.
Restrictions: The Corporation does not support the following: organizations that are not 501(c)3 charities; grants to individuals, including sponsorships; private foundations or endowment funds; sectarian or denominational religious organizations; political activities, parties or candidates; veteran organizations; hospitals; fraternal or labor organizations; courtesy advertising, including program books and yearbooks; entertainment events, scholarships or conferences; sporting events or teams; golf tournaments; unrestricted gift to national or international organizations; travel or tours; or table sponsorships.
Geographic Focus: Arizona, California, Illinois, Maryland, Massachusetts, New Hampshire, Texas, Australia, Austria, Belgium, Brazil, Canada, China, Czech Republic, Denmark, Finland, France, Germany, Hungary, India, Ireland, Israel, Italy, Japan, Korea, Malaysia, Mexico, Netherlands, Norway, Philippines, Poland, Portugal, Romania, Russian Federation, Singapore, Spain, Sweden, Switzerland, Taiwan, Thailand, Turkey, Vietnam
Contact: Andy Smith; (214) 480-3462; fax (214) 480-2920; wasmith@ti.com
Internet: http://www.ti.com/corp/docs/csr/giving.shtml
Sponsor: Texas Instruments Corporation
12500 TI Boulevard
Dallas, TX 75266-0199

Texas Instruments Corporation Civic and Business Grants 4597
The Corporation strives to improve the quality of the TI plant-site communities by enriching civic and business climates. Such programs are funded based on community and economic impact, and opportunities for TI employee/retiree involvement. The Corporation board meets quarterly to discuss funding, then awards are given within three weeks of each meeting. Corporate grant funding is prioritized based on opportunities for TI employee/retiree involvement.
Requirements: Applicants must be 501(c)3 nonprofit organizations. Grant applications are only accepted online. Applicants access the eligibility quiz at the website and if they are eligible, they gain access to the application.
Restrictions: The Corporation does not support the following: organizations that are not 501(c)3 charities; grants to individuals, including sponsorships; private foundations or endowment funds; sectarian or denominational religious organizations; political activities, parties or candidates; veteran organizations; hospitals; fraternal or labor organizations; courtesy advertising, including program books and yearbooks; entertainment events, scholarships or conferences; sporting events or teams; golf tournaments; unrestricted gifts to national or international organizations; travel or tours; or table sponsorships.
Geographic Focus: Arizona, California, Illinois, Maryland, Massachusetts, New Hampshire, Texas, Australia, Austria, Belgium, Brazil, Canada, China, Czech Republic, Denmark, Finland, France, Germany, Hungary, India, Ireland, Israel, Italy, Japan, Korea, Malaysia, Mexico, Netherlands, Norway, Philippines, Poland, Portugal, Romania, Russian Federation, Singapore, Spain, Sweden, Switzerland, Taiwan, Thailand, Turkey, Vietnam
Contact: Andy Smith; (214) 480-3462; fax (214) 480-2920; wasmith@ti.com
Internet: http://www.ti.com/corp/docs/csr/giving.shtml
Sponsor: Texas Instruments Corporation
12500 TI Boulevard
Dallas, TX 75266-0199

Texas Instruments Corporation Health and Human Services Grants 4598
The Corporation builds healthy communities by funding health and human service programs that address the needs of the community. The Health and Human Services grants are primarily program specific, with limited support to United Way agencies. The Corporation board meets quarterly, and funding decisions are made within three weeks of each meeting.
Requirements: Applicants must be 501(c)3 tax-exempt nonprofit organizations. Grant applications are only accepted online. Applicants access the eligibility quiz at the website and if they are eligible, they gain access to the application.
Restrictions: Corporate grant funding is prioritized based on opportunities for TI employee/retiree involvement. Due to the TI Foundation's and TI employees' long-time support of United Way, only limited support of United Way agencies will be considered. The Corporation does not support the following: organizations that are not 501(c)3 charities; grants to individuals, including sponsorships; private foundations or endowment funds; sectarian or denominational religious organizations; political activities, parties or candidates; veteran organizations; hospitals; fraternal or labor organizations; courtesy advertising, including program books and yearbooks; entertainment events, scholarships or conferences; sporting events or teams; golf tournaments; unrestricted gifts to national or international organizations; travel or tours; or table sponsorships.
Geographic Focus: Texas
Contact: Andy Smith; (214) 480-3462; fax (214) 480-2920; wasmith@ti.com
Internet: http://www.ti.com/corp/docs/csr/giving.shtml
Sponsor: Texas Instruments Corporation
12500 TI Boulevard
Dallas, TX 75266-0199

Texas Instruments Foundation Arts and Culture Grants 4599
The Foundation supports arts and cultural institutions that will boost the economic growth to attract and retain employees at the Texas Instrument plant site locations. Some examples include the Dallas Museum of Art, the AT&T Performing Arts Center, and the Museum of Nature and Science. The Foundation board meets on a quarterly basis, then funding is finalized within three weeks of each meeting.
Requirements: All applicants must be 501(c)3 nonprofit organizations. Grant applications are only accepted online. Applicants access the eligibility quiz at the website and if they are eligible, they gain access to the application.
Restrictions: The Foundation does not support the following: organizations that are not 501(c)3 charities; grants to individuals, including scholarships; private foundations or endowment funds; sectarian or denominational religious organizations; political activities, parties or candidates; veteran organizations; hospitals; fraternal or labor organizations; courtesy advertising, including program books and yearbooks; entertainment events, scholarships or conferences; sporting events or teams; golf tournaments; unrestricted gifts to national or international organizations; travel or tours; or table sponsorships.
Geographic Focus: Arizona, California, Illinois, Maryland, Massachusetts, New Hampshire, Texas, Australia, Austria, Belgium, Brazil, Canada, China, Czech Republic, Denmark, Finland, France, Germany, Hungary, India, Ireland, Israel, Italy, Japan, Korea, Malaysia, Mexico, Netherlands, Norway, Philippines, Poland, Portugal, Romania, Russian Federation, Singapore, Spain, Sweden, Switzerland, Taiwan, Thailand, Turkey, Vietnam
Contact: Ann Pomykal, Director; (214) 480-6873; fax (214) 480-6820; giving@ti.com
Internet: http://www.ti.com/corp/docs/csr/giving.shtml
Sponsor: Texas Instruments Foundation
12500 TI Boulevard
Dallas, TX 75266-0199

Texas Instruments Foundation Community Services Grants 4600
The Foundation offers funding to enrich health and human services programs that meet the greatest community needs. This includes capital or civic campaigns. The Foundation considers supporting such campaigns based on community needs and economic impact. The Foundation primarily supports services through its annual United Way donations. Beyond United Way, it also provides limited support to organizations meeting the greatest community needs. The Foundation board meets quarterly (March, June, September, and November) and makes funding decisions within three weeks of each meeting.
Requirements: Applicants must be 501(c)3 nonprofit organizations. Grant applications are only accepted online. Applicants access the eligibility quiz at the website and if they are eligible, they gain access to the application. The Foundation primarily supports programs in the Dallas area.
Restrictions: The Foundation does not support the following: organizations that are not 501(c)3 charities; grants to individuals, including sponsorships; private foundations or endowment funds; sectarian or denominational religious organizations; political activities, parties or candidates; veteran organizations; hospitals; fraternal or labor organizations; courtesy advertising, including program books and yearbooks; entertainment events, scholarships or conferences; sporting events or teams; golf tournaments; unrestricted gifts to national or international organizations; travel or tours; or table sponsorships.
Geographic Focus: Texas
Contact: Ann Pomykal, Director; (214) 480-6873; fax (214) 480-6820; giving@ti.com
Internet: http://www.ti.com/corp/docs/csr/giving.shtml
Sponsor: Texas Instruments Foundation
12500 TI Boulevard
Dallas, TX 75266-0199

Textron Corporate Contributions Grants 4601

Textron Inc. was founded in 1923 as a small textile company and has since become one of the world's best known multi-industry companies. Textron focuses philanthropic giving in the following areas: workforce development and education; healthy families/vibrant communities; and sponsorships. In the area of workforce development and education, the company focuses on job-training and employment development (eg., school-to-work, welfare-to-work, job-training for underserved-audiences, literacy, and English-as a-Second-Language programs). In the area of healthy families/vibrant communities, the company focuses on arts and culture (with emphasis on outreach programs that enhance learning and target low- and moderate-income individuals), community revitalization (eg., affordable housing and economic development in low-income areas), and health and human-service organizations (eg., food pantries, homeless shelters, and services for low-income residents). In the area of sponsorships, the company encourages volunteerism and sponsors worthwhile events that benefit the communities where employees live and work. Textron's grant history has included funding of general-operating costs, capital campaigns, building construction/renovation, equipment acquisition, program development, conferences and seminars, publication, seed money, fellowships, scholarship funds, research, technical assistance, consulting services, and matching funds. Downloadable guidelines (PDF) and application (Word document) are available online. The completed application and required accompanying documentation must be received via mail by the deadline date.
Requirements: Textron targets its giving to nonprofit agencies located in its headquarters state of Rhode Island and those locations where the company has divisional operations. Organizations outside of Rhode Island should contact the Textron company in their area; a listing of Textron businesses along with their contact information can be accessed by clicking the "Contact Us" link at the Textron website.
Restrictions: Textron will review only one request per organization during a 12-month period. Contributions will not be made to the following types of organizations: organizations without 501(c)3 status as defined by the Internal Revenue Service; individuals; political, fraternal or veterans organizations; religious institutions when the grant would support sectarian activities; and organizations that discriminate by race, creed, gender, ethnicity, sexual orientation, disability, age or any other basis prohibited by law.
Geographic Focus: Georgia, Illinois, Kansas, Louisiana, Maryland, Massachusetts, New York, North Carolina, Pennsylvania, Rhode Island, Texas, Germany, Great Britain
Date(s) Application is Due: Mar 1; Sep 1
Contact: Karen Warfield; (401) 421-2800; fax (401) 457-2225
Internet: http://www.textron.com/about/commitment/corp-giving/
Sponsor: Textron Charitable Trust
40 Westminster Street
Providence, RI 02903

Thanks Be to Grandmother Winifred Foundation Grants 4602

The foundation offers financial support to encourage the creativity of women, 54 years of age and older, in projects that empower and enrich the lives and well-being of adult women. Funding enables women to create, develop, and implement ideas and concepts that will improve the lives of women in one or more aspects, including: activities that allow women to achieve a specific objective; produce a report; and improve a literary, artistic, or scientific skill or talent. The foundation prefers to receive requests in writing.
Geographic Focus: All States
Amount of Grant: 500 - 5,000 USD
Contact: Rev. Deborah Ann Light, (631) 725-0323 or (631) 725-0323
Sponsor: Thanks Be to Grandmother Winifred Foundation
210 Division Street, P.O. Box 2669
Sag Harbor, NY 11963-0119

Thelma Braun and Bocklett Family Foundation Grants 4603

The Thelma Braun and Bocklett Family Foundation was established in 1980 to support and promote quality education, cultural, human-services, and health-care programming for underserved populations. Miss Braun was a gifted musician who spent many years playing the organ and piano for area organizations and churches. She never married and had no children of her own, but she truly loved the young people in the area. Special consideration is given to charitable organizations that serve the people of Grayson County, Texas, especially in the areas of arts and education. Applicants must apply online at the grant website. The Thelma Braun and Bocklett Family Foundation has rolling deadlines and decision dates. Applicants are strongly encouraged to do the following before applying: review the downloadable state application procedures at the grant website; review the downloadable online-application guidelines at the grant website; review the foundation's funding history (link is available from the grant website); review the online application questions in advance; and review the list of required attachments. These will generally include: a list of board members, financial statements (audited, reviewed, or compiled by independent auditor); an organization summary; a list of other funding sources; an IRS Determination letter; and other required documents. All attachments must be uploaded in the online application as PDF, Word, or Excel files.
Requirements: Applicants must have 501(c)3 tax-exempt status.
Restrictions: The foundation does not support requests from individuals, organizations attempting to influence policy through direct lobbying, or any political campaigns.
Geographic Focus: Texas
Samples: Denison Independent School District, Denison, Texas, $30,000; Grayson County Shelter, Denison, Texas, $25,000; Downtown Improvement Company of Denison, Denison, Texas, $15,000.
Contact: David Ross, Senior Vice President; tx.philanthropic@baml.com
Internet: https://www.bankofamerica.com/philanthropic/fn_search.action
Sponsor: Thelma Braun and Bocklett Family Foundation
901 Main Street, 19th Floor, TX1-492-19-11
Dallas, TX 75202-3714

Thelma Doelger Charitable Trust Grants 4604

The trust awards grants in the San Francisco Bay area to zoos, hospitals, and organizations supporting animal welfare and senior citizens. Grants are awarded for general purposes and to support operating budgets. There are no application deadlines. Application forms are required.
Requirements: Nonprofit organizations in the San Francisco Bay area of northern California may submit grant requests.
Restrictions: Individuals are not eligible.
Geographic Focus: California
Amount of Grant: 2,000 - 75,000 USD
Contact: D. Eugene Richard, Trustee; (650) 755-2333
Sponsor: Thelma Doelger Charitable Trust
950 Daly Boulevard, Suite 300
Daly City, CA 94015-3004

Theodore Edson Parker Foundation Grants 4605

The Theodore Edson Parker Foundation's primary goal is to make effective grants that benefit the city of Lowell, Massachusetts, and its residents. Grants are made for a variety of purposes including social services, cultural programs, community development activities, education, community health needs, and urban environmental projects. The Foundation funds specific needs including special programs and projects, capital improvements and equipment purchases, and technical assistance. In his will, Mr. Parker suggested that his trustees give special consideration to the welfare of children, disadvantaged young women, and the elderly. The Foundation is especially committed to assisting these and other underserved individuals including refugees, immigrants, and people of color. Preference is given to applicants who have formulated creative approaches to societal problems and can provide leverage for Foundation funds. The Foundation favors projects that can demonstrate good prospects for continuation after the conclusion of Foundation funding. Interested applicants are welcome to contact staff prior to applying. All applications are accepted online.
Requirements: Eligible applicants are 501(c)3 organizations in Lowell, Massachusetts.
Restrictions: The Foundation does not usually fund the operating expenses of charitable organizations, endowments, or fund deficits. Applicants are limited to one per year. Grant recipients should expect to wait two years before submitting a new request.
Geographic Focus: Massachusetts
Date(s) Application is Due: Jan 15; May 15; Sep 15
Amount of Grant: 10,000 - 50,000 USD
Contact: Philip Hall; (617) 391-3097 or (617) 426-7087; phall@grantsmanagement.com
Internet: http://parkerfoundation.gmafoundations.com/
Sponsor: Theodore Edson Parker Foundation
77 Summer Street, 8th Floor
Boston, MA 02110-1006

The World Food Prize 4606

The international prize recognizes — without regard to race, religion, nationality, or political beliefs — the achievements of individuals who have advanced human development by improving the quality, quantity, or availability of food in the world. The award recognizes contributions in any field involved in the world food supply—food and agriculture science and technology, manufacturing, marketing, nutrition, economics, poverty alleviation, political leadership, and the social sciences. The prize emphasizes the importance of a nutritious and sustainable food supply for all people. Nomination form and complete details are available online. Annual deadline dates may vary; contact program staff for exact dates.
Geographic Focus: All States
Date(s) Application is Due: Mar 1
Amount of Grant: 250,000 USD
Contact: Judith Pim, Director of Secretariat Operations; (515) 245-3796; fax (515) 245-3785; jpim@worldfoodprize.org
Internet: http://worldfoodprize.org/Home/tonominate.htm
Sponsor: World Food Prize Foundation
666 Grand Avenue, Suite 1700
Des Moines, IA 50309

Third Millennium Foundation Grants 4607

The Third Millennium Foundation's principal goal is to support programs and initiatives designed to promote tolerance, particularly among the young. Its work is focused on developing young children's understanding of and respect for the differences that exist among themselves, especially those related to culture, ethnicity, gender, race, and socioeconomic status. The Foundation emphasizes art in its grant making and continues to explore creative new avenues for unlearning intolerance. Foundation programs build on research findings demonstrating that gaining self-control and the ability to relate positively to others is developed in early childhood and that family, educators, and child caregivers play significant roles in shaping lifelong attitudes. The Foundation makes grants in the United States and internationally, and supports arts and human rights programs. Its programmatic emphasis is on education, children's rights and capacity building for grassroots organizations.
Geographic Focus: All States
Contact: Grants Manager; (212) 421-5244; fax (212) 421-5243; tmf.usa@verizon.net
Internet: http://www.seedsoftolerance.org/initiative-grantmaking.html
Sponsor: Third Millennium Foundation
340 West 12th Street
New York, NY 10014

Third Sector New England Inclusion Initiative Grants 4608

The Third Sector New England Inclusion Initiative was established in 1990, and it provides technical assistance and funding to Greater Boston nonprofits committed to increasing their capacity to meet their mission more effectively through: greater racial, ethnic and cultural diversity within their staff and boards; inclusion of diverse perspectives reflected in the development of programs and delivery of services; and affecting shifts in their institutional cultures through strategic planning and application of inclusive practices. Since the first diversity grants were given, the program has held collaborative learning as a core value. Fundamental to the work of the diversity and inclusion is an acknowledgement that as in society, institutional racism exists within non-profit organizations.
Requirements: Greater Boston area nonprofit organizations are eligible. Preference is given to applicants that do not have organizational budgets in excess of $2 million.
Geographic Focus: Massachusetts
Contact: Vickie Burns, Program Department Administrator; (617) 523-6565 or (800) 281-7770; fax (617) 523-2070; info@inclusioninitiative.org or info@tsne.org
Internet: http://www.tsne.org/site/c.ghLUK3PCLoF/b.1354305/k.C62D/Diversity__Inclusion_Initiative__Grantmaking_to_Build_Your_Nonprofits_Capacity_and_Valuing_Differences.htm
Sponsor: Third Sector New England
89 South Street, Suite 700
Boston, MA 02111-2670

Third Wave Foundation Lela Breitbart Memorial Fund Grants 4609

Third Wave Foundation will use this endowed fund to offer an annual grant of $3,000 in memory of Lela Breitbart to innovative organizations working on issues of reproductive justice around the country. This grant will be given to programs that are developed and led by women and transgender people between the ages of 15 and 30, with an emphasis on supporting and strengthening young women, transgender youth and their allies working for gender, racial, social, and economic justice.
Requirements: Applicant organizations and/or programs must be based in the United States.
Geographic Focus: All States
Amount of Grant: 3,000 USD
Contact: Director; (212) 228-8311; fax (212) 780-9181; info@thirdwavefoundation.org
Internet: http://www.thirdwavefoundation.org/grant-making/breitbart
Sponsor: Third Wave Foundation
25 East 21st Street
New York, NY 10010

Third Wave Foundation Organizing and Advocacy Grants 4610

Third Wave is a feminist, activist foundation that works nationally to support young women and transgender youth ages 15 to 30. Through strategic grantmaking, leadership development, and philanthropic advocacy, it supports groups and individuals working towards gender, racial, economic, and social justice. The Organizing and Advocacy (O&A) Fund supports work that challenges sexism, racism, homophobia, transphobia, economic injustice, and other forms of oppression in interesting ways. Grants are provided for both specific projects and general operating support.
Requirements: Applicant organizations and/or programs must be based in the United States.
Geographic Focus: All States
Date(s) Application is Due: Apr 1; Oct 1
Contact: Monique Mehta, Executive Director; (212) 228-8311; fax (212) 780-9181; info@thirdwavefoundation.org
Internet: http://www.thirdwavefoundation.org/grant-making/organizing-and-advocacy
Sponsor: Third Wave Foundation
25 East 21st Street
New York, NY 10010

Third Wave Foundation Reproductive Health and Justice Grants 4611

The foundation supports work, organizing, and activism that exists to challenge sexism, racism, homophobia, economic injustice, and other forms of oppression. The Reproductive Health and Justice Initiative is grounded in the view that reproductive rights are a fundamental human right, and that these rights cannot be fully expressed or enjoyed unless people have access to the means to fulfill them. The initiative works to help build solidarity and movement between young people, particularly young women of color and transgender youth, who have been overlooked, unheard, or tokenized within the larger movement. Proposed projects should benefit, focus on, and be developed and led by women between the ages of 15 and 30, with an emphasis on low-income women, differently abled women, women of color, and lesbian and bisexual women. Grants are made for project support and for general operating support. One grant proposal per organization will be accepted each year.
Requirements: Applicant organizations and/or programs must be based in the United States.
Geographic Focus: All States
Date(s) Application is Due: Apr 1; Oct 1
Amount of Grant: 1,000 - 10,000 USD
Contact: Monique Mehta; (212) 228-8311; fax (212) 780-9181; info@thirdwavefoundation.org
Internet: http://www.thirdwavefoundation.org/grant-making/reproductive-health-and-justice
Sponsor: Third Wave Foundation
25 East 21st Street
New York, NY 10010

Thomas and Dorothy Leavey Foundation Grants 4612

Thomas Leavey and partner John C. Tyler began the Farmer's Insurance Company in 1928. The foundation was begun in 1952 by Leavey and his wife, Dorothy. Thomas Leavey died in 1980 and Dorothy actively led the foundation until her death in 1998. Giving primarily in southern California, the Foundation offers support for: hospitals, medical research, higher and secondary education, Catholic church groups; and provides scholarships to children of employees of Farmers Group.
Requirements: The foundation gives primarily in southern California.
Geographic Focus: California
Amount of Grant: 10,000 - 2,000,000 USD
Contact: Kathleen Leavey McCarthy, Chair; (310) 551-9936
Sponsor: Thomas and Dorothy Leavey Foundation
10100 Santa Monica Boulevard, Suite 610
Los Angeles, CA 90067-4110

Thomas Austin Finch, Sr. Foundation Grants 4613

The purpose of the Finch Foundation is the improvement of the mental, moral and physical well-being of the inhabitants of Thomasville, North Carolina, with emphasis on improving education, improving health related facilities and attracting new business to the community. However, grants are made for a wide variety of charitable causes throughout the greater Thomasville area. In general, grants are awarded for seed money, matching funds and general purposes. Primary consideration is given to projects of a non-recurring nature or to start up funding of limited duration. The foundation meets twice a year to review grant requests. Requests must be submitted by February 15th for the Spring Meeting and October 15th for the Fall Meeting. Application forms are available online. Applicants will receive notice acknowledging receipt of the grant request, and subsequently be notified of the grant declination or approval.
Requirements: Eligible applicants are IRS 501(c)3 non-profit organizations located within the corporate limits of the City of Thomasville, North Carolina or, organizations where the benefits of the grant will inure primarily to the residents of Thomasville. Proposals should be submitted in the following format: completed Common Grant Application Form; an original Proposal Statement; an audited financial report and a current year operating budget; a copy of your official IRS Letter with your tax determination; a listing of your Board of Directors. Proposal Statements (second item in the above Format) should answer these questions: what are the objectives and expected outcomes of this program/project/request; what strategies will be used to accomplish your objective; what is the timeline for completion; if this is part of an on-going program, how long has it been in operation; what criteria will you use to measure success; if the request is not fully funded, what other sources can you engage; an Itemized budget should be included; please describe any collaborative ventures. Prior to the distribution of funds, all approved grantees must sign and return a Grant Agreement Form, stating that the funds will be used for the purpose intended. Progress reports and Completion reports must also be filed as required for your specific grant. All current grantees must be in good standing with required documentation prior to submitting new proposals to any foundation.
Restrictions: Grants are generally not made for typical operational or maintenance-oriented purposes, political purposes, nor to organizations which discriminate on the basis of race, ethnic origin, sexual or religious preference, age or gender.
Geographic Focus: North Carolina
Date(s) Application is Due: Feb 15; Oct 15
Amount of Grant: 1,500 - 100,000 USD
Contact: Wachovia Bank, N.A., Trustee; grantinquiries6@wachovia.com
Sponsor: Thomas Austin Finch, Sr. Foundation
Wachovia Bank, NC6732, 100 North Main Street
Winston Salem, NC 27150

Thomas B. and Elizabeth M. Sheridan Foundation Grants 4614

The foundation awards grants to 501(c)3 organizations in the Greater Baltimore area with an emphasis on private secondary schools and cultural arts.
Requirements: Nonprofit organizations in the Greater Baltimore area are eligible. Applications should send a letter of inquiry prior to submitting a proposal. There are no deadlines—applications are reviewed as received.
Restrictions: Grants are not awarded to individuals, for employee matching, or for loans.
Geographic Focus: District of Columbia, Maryland, Virginia
Amount of Grant: 500 USD
Contact: John Sinclair, President; (410) 771-0475; jbs@sheridanfoundation.org
Sponsor: Thomas B. and Elizabeth M. Sheridan Foundation
11350 McCormick Road, Executive Plaza II, Suite 704
Hunt Valley, MD 21031

Thomas C. Ackerman Foundation Grants 4615

The Thomas C. Ackerman Foundation was founded on August 6, 1991. By Spring, 1992, substantial assets had been received from the Thomas C. Ackerman Trust, funded as a result of Mr. Ackerman's death on February 13, 1991; the Board of Directors was fully constituted; and the guidelines and objectives for grant making were adopted. The Foundation's areas of interest include: arts and culture; education; and health and human services. To be considered for a grant from the Thomas C. Ackerman Foundation, an organization must initially submit a Letter of Intent online. Directions for completing the grant application will be provided to an organization, if it is invited to submit one. Awards generally range from $1,000 to $40,000.
Requirements: California nonprofits, primarily in San Diego County, are eligible.
Restrictions: It is a policy of the Foundation not to provide continuous support for any project to the extent that the project becomes dependent upon the Foundation for its continued existence. The Foundation may make multi-year commitments on occasion. Grants are not made to individuals. Generally, the Foundation does not support conferences or symposia. While occasional grant support is given to religious organizations, those grants are made for direct support of nonsectarian educational or service projects and not for projects which are of primary benefit to members of a particular religion or belief or which primarily promote a particular religion or belief. The Foundation will not consider grants relating to human medical or biomedical research.

Geographic Focus: California
Amount of Grant: 1,000 - 40,000 USD
Contact: Lynne Newman; (619) 741-0113; info@AckermanFoundation.org
Internet: http://www.ackermanfoundation.org/
Sponsor: Thomas C. Ackerman Foundation
600 W Broadway, Suite 2600
San Diego, CA 92101-3391

Thomas D. McGrain Cedar Glade Foundation Grants 4616
The Thomas D. McGrain Cedar Glade Foundation for the Needy of Harrison County is an Independent foundation. The Foundation was established in 1996 and serves the residents of Harrison County, Indiana by awarding grants to the needy.
Requirements: The Foundation awards grants only to individuals economically disadvantaged and residing in Harrison County, Indiana. Contact the Foundation by letter for your initial approach.
Geographic Focus: Indiana
Amount of Grant: Up to 15,700 USD
Contact: William H. Davis, Director; (812) 738-3201
Sponsor: Thomas D. McGrain Cedar Glade Foundation
102 Capitol Avenue
Corydon, IN 47112-1164

Thomas J. Atkins Memorial Trust Fund Grants 4617
The Thomas J. Atkins Memorial Trust Fund was established in 1946 to support and promote quality educational, human services, and health care programming for underserved populations. The Trust Fund specifically serves the people of Middlesex County, Connecticut. Preference is given to organizations and programs that provide for the relief of human distress and suffering. The deadline for application is October 1. Applicants will be notified of grant decisions by letter within 2 to 3 months after the proposal deadline. Grants from the Atkins Memorial Trust Fund are 1 year in duration.
Requirements: 501(c)3 organizations serving the residents of Middlesex, Connecticut, are eligible to apply.
Geographic Focus: Connecticut
Date(s) Application is Due: Oct 1
Contact: Kate Kerchaert; (860) 657-7016; kate.kerchaert@baml.com
Internet: https://www.bankofamerica.com/philanthropic/grantmaking.action
Sponsor: Thomas J. Atkins Memorial Trust Fund
200 Glastonbury Boulevard, Suite #200, CT2-545-02-05
Glastonbury, CT O6033-4056

Thomas J. Long Foundation Community Grants 4618
Through its Community Grants Program, the Foundation practices responsive grant making and awards grants to charitable organizations in the San Francisco East Bay, and in five selected fields of interest — Arts & Culture, Conservation, Education, Health, and Human Services. The Foundation gives preference to proposals received from organizations that provide direct benefit to low income children and youth, the elderly and disabled persons. Safety net services, and programs focused on economic self-sufficiency are also favored.
Requirements: The Foundation awards grants to selected tax-exempt charitable organizations that have been recognized by the IRS as being described in Section 501(c)3 and 509(a)1 or 509(a)2 of the Internal Revenue Code. The Foundation primarily funds charitable programs and services which are of particular benefit to residents of the East Bay counties of Alameda and Contra Costa. Organizations that are considering a proposal for grant support should have an established presence in these communities including an office and/or dedicated staff permanently assigned to the East Bay. Proposals which do not focus on the East Bay are unlikely to be funded and it is rarely worthwhile to submit a proposal.
Restrictions: The Foundation does not ordinarily award grants for the following: 509(a)3 supporting organizations; government entities; individuals; advocacy or influencing public policy; endowments; international grants; loan repayments; research or studies; capital campaigns (invitation only); projects or programs that have already taken place; or, national organizations headquartered outside of the San Francisco Bay Area. The Thomas J. Long Foundation uses a formal grant process to administer its grant making program. All forms used in the grant process are available only through the Foundation's on-line grants management system. Requests for funding or reports submitted in any other manner will not be accepted. Grant proposals are accepted on a continuous basis throughout the year.
Geographic Focus: California
Contact: Nancy Shillis, Program Officer; (925) 944-3800; fax (925) 944-3573
Internet: http://www.thomasjlongfdn.org/?q=grants
Sponsor: Thomas J. Long Foundation
2950 Buskirk Avenue, Suite 160
Walnut Creek, CA 94597

Thomas Sill Foundation Grants 4619
Mr. Sill lived his entire life in Winnipeg and practiced as a chartered accountant for many years. He was an astute investor who built a fortune which became the basis for the Thomas Sill Foundation. The foundation provides encouragement and financial support to qualifying Manitoba organizations that strive to improve the quality of life in the province. The foundation awards grants in the following areas of interest: Responses to Community (agencies addressing poverty, women's shelters, qualifying daycares, mentally and physically challenged people, and community well-being); Health (eye care, palliative care, mental illness); Education (students at risk, including adults); Arts and Culture; Heritage (museums, architecture, projects); and, Environment (water issues). Grants awarded may be capital, operating or project in nature.
Requirements: Registered charities may obtain an application form by phoning the foundation office, at which time a preliminary discussion will determine eligibility. There are no deadlines by which applications must be submitted. Applicants should allow four months, from the submission of a request, to receive a response.
Restrictions: Successful applicants must wait two years before submitting another request.
Geographic Focus: Canada
Amount of Grant: 1,000 - 50,000 CAD
Contact: Hugh Arklie; (204) 947-3782; fax (204) 956-4702; hugha@tomsill.ca
Internet: http://thomassillfoundation.com/guidelines/
Sponsor: Thomas Sill Foundation
206-1661 Portage Avenue
Winnipeg, MB R3J 3T7 Canada

Thomas Thompson Trust Grants 4620
The Thompson Trust limits its distribution of funds to organizations located in Windham County, Vermont, (primarily the Town of Brattleboro) or in Dutchess County, New York (primarily the Town of Rhinebeck) which predominately serve residents located in those areas. The Will of Thomas Thompson was executed in 1867 and defined his charitable purposes rather narrowly as was the practice with 19th Century philanthropy. By successive court decrees in the 20th Century, the Trustees are now authorized to make grants to charitable organizations whose work and purposes promote health, education or the general social or civic betterment in the stated geographical areas; but the Trustees will continue to place particular emphasis on healthcare and other social services. The Trustees generally meet on the fourth Thursday in January, April, July and October. Applications are due by the first day of the month of the meeting.
Requirements: Organizations must have operated for three consecutive years before applying and be located in Windham County, VT, with preference given to Brattleboro; or Duchess County, New York, with preference given to Rhinebeck.
Restrictions: Grants are not made for general operating support, seed money, endowment purposes, or loans.
Geographic Focus: New York, Vermont
Date(s) Application is Due: Jan 1; Apr 1; Jul 1; Oct 1
Amount of Grant: 1,000 - 20,000 USD
Contact: Susan T. Monahan; (617) 951-1108; fax (617) 542-7437; smonahan@rackemann.com
Internet: http://www.cybergrants.com/thompson/grant.html
Sponsor: Thomas Thompson Trust
160 Federal Street, 13th Floor
Boston, MA 02110-1700

Thomas W. Briggs Foundation Grants 4621
The Foundation provides gifts that help serve the needs of thousands in the Memphis area. The focus of the funding includes youth projects and programs, education, social services, arts and cultural organizations and civic organizations that promote quality of life. Although some grants are multi-year pledges, many fall in the one-year $5,000 to $25,000 range.
Requirements: Applicants are asked to submit a proposal letter of not more than two pages, giving a brief history of the organization, stating goals and services provided and a list of present sources of funding. Tennessee nonprofit organizations are eligible to apply.
Restrictions: The Foundation does not support public and private schools, churches and synagogues, nationally affiliated organizations and seminars as well as special events. New applicants are required to set up an appointment before applying for a grant.
Geographic Focus: Tennessee
Date(s) Application is Due: Feb 1; Aug 1
Amount of Grant: 5,000 - 25,000 USD
Contact: Joanne Tilley, Executive Director; (901) 680-0276; fax (901) 767-1135
Internet: http://www.thomaswbriggsfoundation.com/funding.html
Sponsor: Thomas W. Briggs Foundation
6075 Poplar Avenue, Suite 330
Memphis, TN 38119

Thompson Charitable Foundation Grants 4622
Established in 1987, the Foundation supports organizations involved with education, Christian organizations, Autism research, health, human services, youth, including funding for capital and building improvements for human service organizations and educational institutions. Giving is limited to Bell, Clay, Laurel, and Leslie counties, Kentucky; Anderson, Blount, Knox, and Scott counties, Tennessee; and Buchanan and Tazewell counties, Virginia.
Requirements: Nonprofits operating in Bell, Clay, Laurel, and Leslie counties, Kentucky; Anderson, Blount, Knox, and Scott counties, Tennessee; and Buchanan and Tazewell counties, Virginia are eligible to apply. Initial contact should be a letter, no more then 2 pages long. The letter should include: a statement of the problem, the project will address; a detailed description of project, and amount of funding requested.
Restrictions: No support for religious or political organizations, budget deficits or endowments.
Geographic Focus: Kentucky, Tennessee, Virginia
Date(s) Application is Due: Mar 31; Sep 1
Amount of Grant: 2,000 - 500,000 USD
Contact: Debbie Black; (865) 588-0491; fax (865) 588-4496; debbie@cf.org
Sponsor: Thompson Charitable Foundation
800 South Gay Street, Suite 2021
Knoxville, TN 37929-9710

Thompson Foundation Grants 4623
With $3,500 in savings, Bob and Ellen Thompson - along with Thompson's uncle, Wilford McCully - started the Thompson-McCully Company, a contract road paving company, in 1959. The Thompson Foundation's mission is to help low-income people rise out of poverty and become self-sufficient. The foundation awards grants to eligible Michigan nonprofit organizations that support economically disadvantaged residents and help them rise out of poverty. Types of support include emergency funds, general operating grants, program development, scholarship funds, and seed grants. There are no application forms. The board meets in February, April, June, August, October, and December.
Requirements: Although the Foundation serves a seven-county region (Wayne, Oakland, Macomb, St. Clair, Livingston, Washtenaw, and Monroe), the vast majority of its funds are used to serve those who live in Detroit, Highland Park and Hamtramck.
Geographic Focus: Michigan
Contact: John Ziraldo; (734) 453-6412; fax (734) 453-6475; cebejer@thompsonfdn.org
Internet: http://www.thompsonfdn.org/
Sponsor: Thompson Foundation
P.O. Box 6349
Plymouth, MI 48170

Thornton Foundation Grants 4624
The foundation awards grants to California nonprofit organizations in its areas of interest, including arts/ and culture and higher/secondary education. Types of support include annual campaigns, building construction/renovation, continuing support, endowment funds, and research. There are no application deadlines.
Requirements: California nonprofit organizations are eligible.
Geographic Focus: California
Amount of Grant: 1,000 - 200,000 USD
Contact: Charles Thornton Jr., President; (213) 629-3867
Sponsor: Thornton Foundation
523 W Sixth Street, Suite 636
Los Angeles, CA 90014

Threshold Foundation Election Integrity Grants 4625
The Threshold Foundation serves the social-change movement through collaborating with and funding innovative American and international nonprofit organizations and individuals working toward social justice, environmental sustainability, humane economic systems, and peaceful coexistence. The Election Integrity Funding Circle seeks to ensure that every American can vote, that votes will be counted as cast, and works to eliminate voter suppression and barriers to voting. Funding targets specific efforts to protect the democratic process from threats of election manipulation and fraud. Projects funded will address the following issues: whistle blower protection; citizen exit polls to engage civic participation; and meaningful prosecution of election fraud crimes.
Requirements: Proposals are accepted by invitation, with invitations issues in mid-December.
Restrictions: The Election Integrity Funding Circle does not support work outside the U.S., and does not support projects whose primary purpose is election year voter registration.
Geographic Focus: All States
Contact: Craig Harwood; (415) 561-6400; fax (415) 561-6401; tholdgrants@tides.org
Internet: http://www.thresholdfoundation.org/?id=320
Sponsor: Threshold Foundation
P.O. Box 29903
San Francisco, CA 94129-0903

Threshold Foundation Justice and Democracy Grants 4626
The Threshold Foundation Justice and Democracy grants support organizations working for human rights for youth impacted by the criminal justice and drug policy systems. Grants fund organizations or programs aimed at reforming criminal justice systems and drug policy, with a focus on youth, either directly through civic action and legislative initiatives or through the development and implementation of specific rehabilitation programs or alternatives to incarceration. This focus includes but is not limited to policies that negatively impact youth (the "school-to-prison" pipeline), sentencing reform, substituting treatment for incarceration, and decriminalization of specific currently illegal drugs. Grants also support organizations working on civic participation, aimed at expanding political rights for those who live in historically disenfranchised communities. Focus will be on organizations incorporating a sustainable, bottom-up model of electoral power-building led by and for historically under-represented constituencies. Core strategies could include leadership development, community organizing, civic engagement and coalition building. Up to four $100,000 grants are made, payable over three to four years. Organizations should contact the Foundation for current dates and guidelines for letter of inquiry submission.
Requirements: Funding is made to 501(c)3 organizations and programs, as well as programs and organizations with a 501(c)3 fiscal sponsor. The applicant's actual budget for the last completed fiscal year, as well as projected budgets for the three fiscal years in which the first, second, and third annual grant payments would be used, must be below $800,000. If the organization has both a 501(c)3 and a 501(c)4, their combined organizational budgets must be below $800,000. Requested amount for year one should be between $25,000 and $40,000. Funding in the second and succeeding years is conditional on the grantee's compliance with reporting requirements, continued progress toward the stated goals and outcomes, and demonstrated impact of activities.
Geographic Focus: All States
Contact: Craig Harwood; (415) 561-6400; fax (415) 561-6401; tholdgrants@tides.org
Internet: http://www.thresholdfoundation.org/?id=268
Sponsor: Threshold Foundation
P.O. Box 29903
San Francisco, CA 94129-0903

Threshold Foundation Sustainable Planet Grants 4627
The Threshold Foundation serves the social-change movement through collaborating with and funding innovative American and international nonprofit organizations and individuals working toward social justice, environmental sustainability, humane economic systems, and peaceful coexistence. The Sustainable Planet grants strive to meet the needs of people now without compromising the needs of future generations. Projects should bring all human activities into harmony with nature for the benefit of everyone. This implies transforming both human culture and technology to live within the physical limits of the local and global ecosystems. Most urgently, this implies protecting threatened ecosystems to preserve biodiversity and prevent extinction. This in turn will require addressing global ecological issues such as climate change, empowering local and indigenous communities and deploying new clean technologies. Letters of inquiry are requested periodically, with requests for proposals sent directly to invited organizations. Organizations should contact the Foundation for current dates and guidelines.
Geographic Focus: All States
Contact: Craig Harwood; (415) 561-6400; fax (415) 561-6401; tholdgrants@tides.org
Internet: http://www.thresholdfoundation.org/?id=263
Sponsor: Threshold Foundation
P.O. Box 29903
San Francisco, CA 94129-0903

Threshold Foundation Thriving Resilient Communities Funding Circle 4628
The Thriving Resilient Communities Funding Circle's intention is to build collective wisdom, map the field, and fund best practices and leading-edge work in community resilience. Priority will be given to replicable whole-systems approaches that promote inclusive economic models, social interconnectedness, and vibrant health and well-being. An integral approach fosters compassion, inner resilience (healthy, caring relationships) and outer resilience (fair, sustainable sharing systems) within an eco-social region. The resilient community movement includes community initiatives with similar visions using a variety of names such as Healthy, Livable, Local, Peace, Resilient, Sustainable, Thrive, and Transition. An open letter of inquiry submission process is periodically reassessed for future grantmaking cycles.
Requirements: Proposals are accepted by invitation, with invitations issued in early December.
Geographic Focus: All States
Contact: Craig Harwood; (415) 561-6400; fax (415) 561-6401; tholdgrants@tides.org
Internet: http://www.thresholdfoundation.org/index.php?id=326
Sponsor: Threshold Foundation
P.O. Box 29903
San Francisco, CA 94129-0903

Thrivent Financial for Lutherans Foundation Grants 4629
The Thrivent Financial for Lutherans Foundation was founded in 1982 and operates exclusively for charitable, educational and religious purposes to help improve the health and vitality of the Lutheran community and the communities of the Fox Cities of Wisconsin and the Twin Cities of Minnesota. The primary charitable interest of the Foundation is the economic security and sustainability of nonprofit organizations and those they serve. Lutheran community grants support Lutheran nonprofits across the country in efforts that focus on strengthening the health and vitality of the Lutheran community. Areas of focus include helping Lutheran nonprofit organizations become more secure and sustainable in delivering their mission by helping them to understand, expand and strengthen their capacity and resources. Corporate community grants provide financial support to nonprofit organizations that address the changing needs of communities, with a particular focus on economic self-sufficiency. For information about future grant programs and opportunities contact the Foundation.
Requirements: Community grants support Lutheran nonprofits across the country and corporate community grants support nonprofit organizations in the Fox Cities of Wisconsin and the Twin Cities of Minnesota.
Restrictions: The foundation does not provide grants to individuals.
Geographic Focus: All States
Contact: Grants Administrator; (800) 847-4836; fax (920) 380-5900; mail@thrivent.com
Internet: https://www.thrivent.com/foundations/tflfoundation/index.html
Sponsor: Thrivent Financial for Lutherans Foundation
4321 N Ballard Road
Appleton, WI 54919-0001

Tides Foundation California Wildlands Grassroots Fund 4630
The program supports conservationists advocating for the permanent protection of intact wildlands on both public and private lands in order to help preserve California's wilderness and native biological diversity. Priority is given to small, nonprofit organizations with budgets of $100,000 or less, and individual activists with a sponsoring organization; and geographic areas and advocacy efforts that have not received significant foundation support. The fund targets project-specific requests and does not typically provide general support (such as overhead costs including rent, staff salaries). Grant-supported activities include, but are not limited to, mailings; paid advertising; advocacy-related travel; research; hiring technical, legal, or scientific experts; consultants; equipment purchase or rental; training; retreats; monitoring; mapping; and advocacy-related personal expenses (i.e., childcare). Guidelines and application are available online.
Requirements: California 501(c)3 and 501(c)4 tax-exempt organizations with budgets of $100,000 or less are eligible.
Geographic Focus: California
Contact: Malisa Tsang, (415) 561-6400; fax (415) 561-6401; mtsang@tides.org
Internet: http://www.calwildlandsfund.org/index.cfm
Sponsor: Tides Foundation
P.O. Box 29903
San Francisco, CA 94129-0903

Tides Foundation Death Penalty Mobilization Fund Grants   4631

The fund supports efforts to abolish the death penalty in individual states and as a federal policy. Projects supported may focus on intermediate steps aimed at mitigating aspects of the death penalty, including working toward a moratorium on executions. The fund supports short-term, concrete projects rather than providing general operating or organizational development support. Priority is given to projects that entail collaboration between groups and aim to achieve maximum impact in a short time. Examples include media campaigns, research such as polling leading to a larger community education and organizing strategy, and short-term projects within larger organizational goals. Preference is given to projects that commence within six months of funding rather than those that have already begun. The proposal deadline is the first day of each month at 5 pm Pacific Time. Grant decisions will be made by the first day of the following month.
Requirements: Strategic collaborations of local, regional, and national nonprofit 501(c)3 and 501(c)4 organizations working on the death penalty are eligible.
Geographic Focus: All States
Contact: Michelle Coffey, (212) 509-1049; fax (212) 509-1059; mcoffey@tides.org
Internet: http://www.tidesfoundation.org/dpmf_rapidresp_rfp.cfm
Sponsor: Tides Foundation
55 Exchange Place, Suite 402
New York, NY 10005-1965

Tides Foundation Grants   4632

The foundation actively promotes change toward a healthy society and channels its grantmaking to the following issue areas: arts, culture and alternative media; civic participation; death penalty abolishment; drug policy reform; economic development; economic and racial justice; environmental justice; gay, lesbian, bisexual, and transgender issues; HIV/AIDS; Native communities; peace strategies; women's empowerment and reproductive health; youth development and organizing; and violence prevention. The foundation prefers to fund creative, effective solutions to problems.
Requirements: Nonprofit organizations are eligible. Preference is given to nonprofits engaged in grassroots organizing.
Restrictions: Tides does not accept requests from universities, schools, individuals, or corporations; nor for capital campaigns, endowments, or film production.
Geographic Focus: All States
Contact: Idelise Malave; (415) 561-6366; fax (415) 561-6401; imalave@tides.org
Internet: http://www.tidesfoundation.org/index_tf.cfm
Sponsor: Tides Foundation
P.O. Box 29903
San Francisco, CA 94129-0903

Tifa Foundation Grants   4633

The Tifa Foundation has two grant making mechanism. The first, known as Pro-Active Grants, is through a proactive approach in which Tifa assumes an active role in working together with other organizations that correspond with Tifa's mission. The second, known as Open Grants, is through the endorsement of program proposals that conform to Tifa's strategic direction and priority/supporting programs.
Requirements: Grants are awarded to: organizations with proposed program activities that are in accordance with Tifa's vision and mission; organizations that possess unblemished an track record during their involvement with Tifa as well as with other donor institutions; organizations with legal entities; organizations that cooperate with government agencies; and institutions under the control of a particular university.
Restrictions: Grants are not eligible for: individuals, including proposals for scholarships, trips, conferences and others; all government agencies, legislative and judiciary bodies, political parties, military or those with affiliation/direct relationship with the aforementioned bodies; all organizations with profit-seeking interests; program proposals where the end product or outcome is sold to the public (except upon Tifa's approval); organizations that are still engaged in cooperation with Tifa for the ongoing period except upon prior approval.
Geographic Focus: All States
Date(s) Application is Due: Jan 15; Jul 15
Contact: Yayasan Tifa, (62) 021 829 2776; fax (62) 021 837 83648; public@tifafoundation.org
Internet: http://www.tifafoundation.org/
Sponsor: Tifa Foundation
Jl. Jaya Mandala II No. 14 E
Menteng Dalam, South Jakarta, 12870 Indonesia

Tiger Woods Foundation Grants   4634

Tiger Woods Foundation grants focus on providing opportunities to under served youth, ages 8-18, with the average grant range between $2,500 and $25,000. The following are approved programmatic areas of funding: education, programs that enhance the learning process for youth; youth development, year-round mentoring and/or tutoring programs. (please note, Junior Golf Programs are not eligible)
Requirements: 501(c)3 nonprofit organizations, including schools and school districts, may submit grant proposals.
Geographic Focus: California, District of Columbia, Florida, Maryland, Nevada, Pennsylvania, Texas, Virginia
Date(s) Application is Due: Feb 1; May 1; Aug 1; Nov 1
Amount of Grant: 2,500 - 25,000 USD
Contact: Michelle Kim; (949) 725-3003; grant@tigerwoodsfoundation.org
Internet: http://www.tigerwoodsfoundation.org/grants.php
Sponsor: Tiger Woods Foundation
121 Innovation, Suite 150
Irvine, CA 92617

Time Warner Diverse Voices in the Arts Initiative Grants   4635

In early 2004, Time Warner launched its Diverse Voices in the Arts Initiative to help nurture emerging storytellers that represent diverse perspectives. Included in this initiative are Time Warner supported programs at three renowned New York City theaters known for their work in cultivating emerging playwrights: Playwrights Horizons, the Public Theater, and Second Stage Theatre. In 2007, in conjunction with the Sundance Institute, the program launched the Time Warner Storytelling Advancement Fund, a new program which seeks to cultivate the works of diverse writers so their stories may be brought to the stage or film. This program was conceived and developed with the input of executives from HBO and Warner Brothers. To help meet the needs of smaller arts organizations, the program created the Diverse Voices Small Theater Fund which provides support to community based theater and arts groups in New York City that present or develop work by artists from diverse backgrounds.
Restrictions: Organizations and projects that fall in the following categories are not eligible for consideration: organizations that do not have 501(c)3 tax-exempt status; individuals; political, labor, religious or fraternal organizations; amateur or professional sports groups; or publications of books or the production of films and music.
Geographic Focus: All States
Amount of Grant: 1,000 - 50,000 USD
Contact: Lisa Quiroz, Senior Vice President; (212) 484-6903 or (212) 484-8000; corporate.responsibility@timewarner.com
Internet: http://www.timewarner.com/corp/citizenship/community/education_arts/index.html
Sponsor: Time Warner Corporation
1 Time Warner Center
New York, NY 10019-8016

Time Warner Youth Media and Creative Arts Grants   4636

Through the Youth Media and Arts Fund, launched in 2005, the company supports high-quality New York City-based after-school programs that engage underserved youth in a variety of arts disciplines - from visual arts to performing arts to film-making. These programs work with teens to give them the opportunity to develop and express their voices while using the arts to help them acquire learning skills that prepare them for success in school, work and life. A 2006 independent survey of Time Warner's youth-focused grantees conducted by Policy Studies Associates indicated that, as a result of Time Warner funding, 71% of youth arts grantees reported increased self-confidence and self-esteem in their students and 64% of grantees reported improved learning skills of participants. In 2007, annual reports from two Time Warner grantees, Reel Works and Urban Word NYC, stated that 86% of Reel Works alums are still in high school or higher education and 90% of Urban Word's core students finished high school and went on to college.
Restrictions: Organizations and projects that fall in the following categories are not eligible for consideration: organizations that do not have 501(c)3 tax-exempt status; individuals; political, labor, religious or fraternal organizations; amateur or professional sports groups; or publications of books or the production of films and music.
Geographic Focus: New York
Amount of Grant: 1,000 - 50,000 USD
Contact: Lisa Quiroz, Senior Vice President; (212) 484-6903 or (212) 484-8000; corporate.responsibility@timewarner.com
Internet: http://www.timewarner.com/corp/citizenship/community/education_arts/index.html
Sponsor: Time Warner Corporation
1 Time Warner Center
New York, NY 10019-8016

TJX Foundation Grants   4637

The primary mission of the contribution program is to contribute to programs that provide basic-need services to disadvantaged children, women, and families in communities in which TJX does business. Support is focused on programming consistent with the foundatio's mission and designed to strengthen the development of children, women and families in need. Emergency assistance programs, such as disaster relief intervention projects, are also supported. The TJX Foundation does not have a typical grant award range, but one of its goals is to support as many nonprofit organizations as possible within a fiscal year. The foundation holds three allocation meetings per fiscal year. Completed proposal must be received by The TJX Foundation 12 weeks prior to a meeting.
Requirements: IRS 501(c)3 tax-exempt organizations are eligible. Support is focused on organizations in communities where one or more of TJX's divisions operates a home office, a store or distribution facility, and whose programs help to: promote strong families, provide emergency shelter, enhance education/job readiness, and build community ties.
Restrictions: The foundation will not fund international organizations, other giving organizations, prison populations/offenders and ex-offenders, capital campaign requests, cash reserves, computer purchases, conferences/seminars, consultant fees/salaries, conventions, education loans, endowments, fellowships, films/photography, individual requests, new construction, political organizations, programs in operation for less than 12 months, publications, public policy research/advocacy, renovations, building expansions, salary-only requests, seed money/start-up costs, training money/stipend, travel grants/transportation, and unrestricted grants.
Geographic Focus: All States
Date(s) Application is Due: Mar 3; Jul 7
Contact: Christine Strickland, TJX Foundation Manager; (774) 308-3199 or (774) 308-5722; tjx_foundation@tjx.com
Internet: http://www.tjx.com/corprespons/commsupp.html
Sponsor: TJX Foundation
770 Cochituate Road, Route 300-1BN
Framingham, MA 01701

Toby Wells Foundation Grants 4638
The Toby Wells Foundation welcomes funding requests from recognized 501(c)3 non-profit organizations operating programs within San Diego County for initiatives that support the Foundation's work in enhancing the lives of youth, people with disabilities, and animals. Specific areas of interest include programs that: assist youth in developing a positive self-image; bring youth and animals together for mutual benefit; enhance the lives of individuals with spinal cord injuries; and support the "No Kill" philosophy of animals by providing animals with a second chance.
Requirements: Proposals must be submitted in hard-copy format by mail only. If an organization is uncertain whether the program for which they are requesting funding qualifies, they may submit an online letter of inquiry. The Foundation will respond to the submission and help the organization determine whether to submit a full proposal.
Restrictions: Letters of inquiry and proposals are accepted throughout the year, but funding decisions are not determined until December. The Foundation does not provide funding to individual or endowments. All of its funding is limited to programs or organizations in San Diego County.
Geographic Focus: California
Date(s) Application is Due: Sep 5
Contact: Adrienne Wells Castaneda; (858) 391-2973; adrienne@tobywells.org
Internet: http://www.tobywells.org/funding-guidelines
Sponsor: Toby Wells Foundation
P.O. Box 519
Poway, CA 92074

Todd Brock Family Foundation Grants 4639
Established in Texas in 2007, the Todd Brock Family Foundation offers support for educational programs, children, athletics, research, and community projects, as well Protestant agencies and churches. A formal application is required, and applicants should forward the entire proposal to the office. The Foundation rarely offers funding outside of Texas. There are no deadlines for submitting a completed proposal, and grants have most recently ranged from $300 to $250,000.
Geographic Focus: Texas
Contact: Todd O. Brock, President; (409) 833-6226; fax (409) 832-3019
Sponsor: Todd Brock Family Foundation
1670 E Cardinal Drive, P.O. Box 306
Beaumont, TX 77704-0306

Tom's of Maine Grants 4640
The company awards grants in Maine and nationally in the areas of education, the environment, the arts, and human services. In the area of education, the company seeks to fund innovative programs for children and adults, especially projects that encourage community involvement and foster environmental awareness. Art grants support the performing and visual arts, programs and resources for the arts, and artistic cultural programs with interactive and educational components. Company grants also address social issues, especially those affecting youths, people with disabilities, and indigenous peoples. Environmental projects, with a focus on animal welfare, conservation, wildlife, and biodiversity, also are considered. The company gives priority to projects that integrate two or more of its giving categories. Applications are accepted between November 1st and February 1st.
Geographic Focus: All States
Amount of Grant: 1,000 - 10,000 USD
Contact: Project Manager; (207) 985-2944 or (800) 367-8667; fax (207) 985-5656; info@tomsofmaine.com
Internet: http://www.toms-of-maine.com
Sponsor: Tom's of Maine
302 Lafayette Center
Kennebunk, ME 04043

Tony Hawk Foundation Grants 4641
The foundation awards grants to promote and establish high-quality public skateboard parks throughout the United States. The foundation seeks to fund the construction of skateparks that are designed and built by qualified and experienced skatepark contractors; include local skaters in the design process; are in low-income areas, or areas with a high population of at-risk youth; can demonstrate grassroots commitment to the project; have a creative mix of street obstacles and transition/vert terrain; do not require skaters or their parents to sign waivers; encourage skaters to look after their own safety and the safety of others; are open during daylight hours throughout the year; are free of charge; and are in areas that currently have no skateboarding facilities. Priority is given to grassroots organizations.
Requirements: 501(c)3 or 170(b)(1)(a) tax-exempt organizations; and state or local agencies, including public school systems or public projects, are eligible.
Geographic Focus: All States
Date(s) Application is Due: Mar 1; Sep 1
Amount of Grant: 1,000 - 25,000 USD
Contact: Steve Hawk, (760) 477-2479; questions@tonyhawkfoundation.org
Internet: http://www.tonyhawkfoundation.org/grant_application.asp
Sponsor: Tony Hawk Foundation
1611-A S Melrose Drive, Suite 360
Vista, CA 92081

Topeka Community Foundation Boss Hawg's Charitable Giving Grants 4642
he Boss Hawg's Charitable Giving Fund with the Topeka Community Foundation is a donor advised fund that was established by the Boss Hawg's Restaurant and Catering Co. to provide financial assistance to organizations that support the Fund's area of interest which is children's programs.
Geographic Focus: Kansas
Contact: Marsha Pope; (785) 272-4804; pope@topekacommunityfoundation.org
Internet: http://www.topekacommunityfoundation.org/newsarticle.cfm?articleid=130350&ptsidebaroptid=0&returnto=page31525.cfm&returntoname=Grant Information&siteid=1897&pageid=31520&sidepageid=31525
Sponsor: Topeka Community Foundation
5431 SW 29th Street, Suite 300
Topeka, KS 66614

Topeka Community Foundation Building Families Grants 4643
The Building Families Fund offers grant support to Kansas Christian families adopting internationally and domestically. The fund has two deadlines each year. Applicants are encouraged to have a completed homestudy before applying. Successful grant applications will receive a maximum of one-half of verified adoption costs, including but not limited to the agency fee, orphanage donation, a homestudy and reasonable travel. Personal items including but not limited to physical exams necessary for adoption, postage, photocopying, and gifts to the birth mother will be excluded from the total of adoption costs. Income tables in accordance with the IRS regulations allowing for an adoption deduction will be followed to determine if less grant money will be awarded.
Requirements: Kansas residents or those with Kansas ties will be given first preference. Then grants will be given to others as funds allow. Those applying must have a professed Christian faith and a letter of reference from their pastor. Those applying must have a completed homestudy. Single parents will be considered. Both domestic and international adoptions will be considered. Private adoptions will be considered, but not given priority. Payments would go directly to the attorney. Adoption agencies may be contacted to get recommendations about specific applicants. A release form (included in application) must be signed to allow for this communication. Families must have a referral before completing the application and being considered for a grant.
Restrictions: Completed adoptions will not be considered.
Geographic Focus: Kansas
Date(s) Application is Due: Apr 30
Contact: Marsha Pope; (785) 272-4804; pope@topekacommunityfoundation.org
Internet: http://www.topekacommunityfoundation.org/newsarticle.cfm?articleid=10031703&ptsidebaroptid=0&returnto=page31525.cfm&returntoname=Grant Information&siteid=1897&pageid=31520&sidepageid=31525
Sponsor: Topeka Community Foundation
5431 SW 29th Street, Suite 300
Topeka, KS 66614

Topeka Community Foundation Grants 4644
The foundation awards grants to Kansas nonprofits in its areas of interest, including arts and culture, early childhood education, education, environment, substance abuse services, children and youth services, family services, community development, and public affairs. Types of support include general operating support, continuing support, annual campaigns, capital campaigns, building construction/renovation, emergency funds, program development, seed money, scholarship funds and scholarships to individuals, and matching funds. The board meets bimonthly to consider requests.
Requirements: Grants are awarded to Topeka and Shawnee County, KS, nonprofits.
Restrictions: Grants are not awarded to religious organizations for religious purposes or for scientific, medical, or academic research.
Geographic Focus: Kansas
Contact: Roger K. Viola, President; (785) 272-4804; fax (785) 272-4644; viola@topekacommunityfoundation.org
Internet: http://www.topekacommunityfoundation.org/page31525.cfm
Sponsor: Topeka Community Foundation
5431 SW 29th Street, Suite 300
Topeka, KS 66614

Topeka West Rotary Youth Enrichment Grants 4645
The Topeka West Rotary Club established a Charitable Fund in the early 1990's administered by the Topeka Community Foundation to endow assets for charitable purposes. In 2005, the Club chose to designate the Fund to be available for Youth Enrichment activities. The Club wishes to support youth in their endeavors to improve themselves spiritually, culturally, physically or athletically. Grants are funded by May 31 each year.
Requirements: Grant applications may be obtained at the Topeka Community Foundation website.
Geographic Focus: Kansas
Date(s) Application is Due: Mar 15; May 15
Contact: Marsha Pope; (785) 272-4804; pope@topekacommunityfoundation.org
Internet: http://www.topekacommunityfoundation.org/newsarticle.cfm?articleid=129824&ptsidebaroptid=0&returnto=page31525.cfm&returntoname=Grant Information&siteid=1897&pageid=31520&sidepageid=31525
Sponsor: Topeka Community Foundation
5431 SW 29th Street, Suite 300
Topeka, KS 66614

Topfer Family Foundation Grants 4646
The mission of the foundation (TFF) is to fund programs and organizations that connect people to the tools and resources they need to build self-sufficient and fulfilling lives. Programs areas of interest include child abuse prevention and treatment; youth enrichment; job training and support services; children's health; and aging in place. The Topfer family is keenly interested in understanding the unique needs of the communities in which they invest foundation resources. Therefore, contributions are limited to the communities in

which the family resides: the greater Austin, TX, and the greater Chicago, IL, metropolitan areas. In Illinois, preference is given to organizations serving Du Page and Cook Counties. Note to Chicago area applicants: The foundation is not accepting unsolicited applications in the Job Training or Children's Health program areas from the Chicago area at this time. Guidelines and application are available online.
Requirements: 501(c)3 nonprofit organizations in Illinois and Texas are eligible.
Restrictions: The foundation does not generally support: grants or loans to individuals; loans to charitable organizations; more than 20 percent of an organization's operating budget; administrative costs; organizations that exclude participants based on race or religion; the purchase of dinner, gala, or raffle tickets; school fundraisers or events (including sports and other extracurricular activities); tax-generating entities (municipalities, school districts, etc.) for services within their normal responsibilities; public or private educational institutions for recurrent operating, administrative, or capital expenses (i.e., acquisition, construction, improvement, and maintenance of buildings and equipment), or scholarships that subsidize existing funding base; academic or scientific research; advertising or marketing efforts; political campaigns or purposes; or any one program more than once a calendar year.
Geographic Focus: Illinois, Texas
Contact: Grants Administrator; (866) 897-0298 or (512) 329-0009
Internet: http://www.topferfamilyfoundation.org
Sponsor: Topfer Family Foundation
5000 Plaza on the Lake, Suite 170
Austin, TX 78746

Toro Foundation Grants 4647
The foundation supports nonprofit organizations in corporate operating areas to improve the quality of life for employees and customers. The foundation's primary giving focus is to support organizations that preserve the outdoor environment. The foundation also contributes to programs that enhance education, health and welfare, culture, the arts, and civic projects. Preference is given to requests for program funds over endowment or capital fund requests and to organizations where Toro employees volunteer. Grants are evaluated based on criteria such as mission, employee involvement, geographical area, environmental component, industry relevance, and the presence of United Way funds. Proposals are accepted throughout the years. Guidelines are available online.
Requirements: 501(c)3 tax-exempt organizations in corporate communities are eligible, including Minneapolis/Saint Paul, and Windom, MN; El Cajon, Madera, and Riverside, CA; Oxford, MS; Beatrice, NE; Baraboo, Tomah, and Plymouth, WI; and Abilene, and El Paso, TX.
Restrictions: Grants do not support religious or political activities; general, capital, or endowment support for educational institutions; health treatment, scientific research, or substance abuse treatment programs; travel for individuals or groups; fundraising events or activities, social events, or goodwill advertising, except where Toro employees are participating; individuals or for-profit organizations; or organizations funded by the United Way.
Geographic Focus: California, Minnesota, Mississippi, Nebraska, Texas, Wisconsin
Contact: Grants Administrator; (800) 348-2424 or (952) 887-8870; fax (952) 887-8258
Internet: http://www.thetorocompany.com/community/foundation.html
Sponsor: Toro Foundation
8111 Lyndale Avenue S
Bloomington, MN 55420-1196

Tourism Cares Professional Development Scholarships 4648
Tourism Cares manages the scholarship funds endowed by both individual donors and the following travel, tourism, and hospitality industry organizations, which include the American Society of Travel Agents (ASTA) and the International Airlines Travel Agent Network (IATAN) funds. The Professional Development Scholarships work on a reimbursement basis. The award may be used to reimburse the cost of the completed certificate program or the conference or symposium attended.
Requirements: Each applicant must have either: completed and fully paid for the travel-and-tourism or hospitality certificate program at the accredited or state-licensed educational institution in the United States, Guam, Puerto Rico, or Canada; or attended the conference or symposium held by the U. S. accredited or state-licensed educational institution, no more than 12 months prior to the scholarship application deadline to be eligible to receive the scholarship award. Applicants will need to provide: proof of citizenship or permanent residency; evaluation form and letter of recommendation from a faculty member, or evaluation form and letter of recommendation from an industry professional, with the exception of the ASTA Chapter Scholarships; resume; proof of certificate program completion or conference attendance, and proof of full payment for certificate program or conference. Additionally, a one-page essay is required.
Geographic Focus: All States
Contact: Amanda D'Aiuto, Student Programs Manager; (781) 821-5990 ext. 215; fax (781) 821-8949; Amandad@Tourismcares.org
Internet: http://tourismcares.org/student-programs/scholarship-programs/2012-professional-development-scholarships
Sponsor: Tourism Cares
275 Turnpike Street, Suite 307
Canton, MA 02021

Tourism Cares Worldwide Grants 4649
The Tourism Cares Worldwide Grant Program provides grants to nonprofit, tax-exempt organizations for conservation, preservation, restoration, or education at cultural, historic and natural tourism-related sites of exceptional significance around the world. Funding is designed to ensure that exceptional sites are preseved for future travelers. Tourism Cares grants have supported both capital improvements or educational programs.
Requirements: Grant recipients must be classified as non-profit, tax-exempt organizations under section 501(c)3 of the United States Internal Revenue Code (or the equivalent in the case of non-U.S. organizations).
Geographic Focus: All States, All Countries
Date(s) Application is Due: Sep 1
Amount of Grant: 5,000 - 20,000 USD
Contact: Bruce Beckham, (781) 821-5990; fax (781) 821-8949; bruceb@tourismcares.org
Internet: http://tourismcares.org/grants/worldwide-grant-program
Sponsor: Tourism Cares
275 Turnpike Street, Suite 307
Canton, MA 02021

Town Creek Foundation Grants 4650
The foundation awards grants in four general areas: preservation and enhancement of the nation's environment and the monitoring of federal, state, and local officials and bodies responsible for the enforcement of legislation enacted to protect the environment; the dissemination, via public radio and television, of news and commentary; the search for ways to secure a peaceful and democratic society, supporting projects that challenge and redirect the military economy, reduce the risk of war, and promote a government responsive and accountable to its citizens; and the improvement of the quality of life and the opportunity for advancement for the people of Talbot County, MD, where such opportunities have been adversely affected by economic and social conditions. Types of support include continuing support, operating support, program development, seed money, and matching funds. The foundation will consider proposals at any time during the year. The foundation can be reached, customarily, on Mondays and Wednesdays.
Requirements: IRS 501(c)3 tax-exempt organizations are eligible. Social service grants are limited to nonprofits in Talbot County, Maryland.
Restrictions: The Foundation does not provide grants for the following: programs or organizations outside of the United States; individuals; primary and secondary schools; colleges or universities, except when some aspect of their work is an integral part of a program supported by the Foundation; hospitals or health care institutions; ministry or religious programs; endowment, capital or building fund campaigns, or the purchase of land and/or buildings; research or scholarship programs; conferences not part of a program supported by the Foundation; publication of books and periodicals; or visual or performing arts projects.
Geographic Focus: All States
Amount of Grant: 10,000 - 250,000 USD
Contact: Stuart Alan Clarke, Executive Director; (410) 763-8171; fax (410) 763-8172; info@towncreekfdn.org or sclarke@towncreekfdn.org
Internet: http://www.towncreekfdn.org/tcfsite/tguides.html
Sponsor: Town Creek Foundation
121 N. West Street
Easton, MD 21601

Toyota Motor Engineering & Manufacturing North America Grants 4651
Toyota Motor Engineering & Manufacturing North America oversees the various North American manufacturing operations of Toyota Motor Corporation. Funding from this facility is centered in the tri-state region of Greater Cincinnati, Northern Kentucky and southeastern Indiana, primarily supporting education, environment and safety, but also funding civic groups, health and human services, arts and culture. TEMA prefers to support programs, rather than events. Grants are provided to support the development and implementation of programs that generally range from $50,000 to $200,000. Submission deadlines for applications are January 1, April 1, July 1, October 1. The review process can take up to six months.
Requirements: Communities served must be in Greater Cincinnati, Northern Kentucky or Southeast Indiana.
Restrictions: EMA does not make grants for publications, lobbying activities, advertising, capital campaigns or endowments. Individuals are ineligible to apply. Toyota will not make grants to the following types of organizations: those not recognized as 501(c)3 by the Internal Revenue Service; those that practice discrimination by race, creed, color, sex, age or national origin; those that serve only their own memberships, such as fraternal organizations, labor organizations or religious groups; or political parties or candidates.
Geographic Focus: Indiana, Kentucky, Ohio
Date(s) Application is Due: Jan 1; Apr 1; Jul 1; Oct 1
Amount of Grant: 50,000 - 200,000 USD
Contact: Grants Administrator; (859) 746-4000; fax (859) 746-4190
Internet: http://www.toyota.com/about/philanthropy/guidelines/index.html#tmmk
Sponsor: Toyota Motor Engineering & Manufacturing North America
25 Atlantic Avenue
Erlanger, KY 41018

Toyota Motor Manufacturing of Alabama Grants 4652
Established in 2001, Toyota Motor Manufacturing of Alabama manufactures V6 and V8 engines for light trucks, with operations include machining and assembly. TMMAL believes in becoming an integral part of the community by improving the quality of life where its team members live and work. TMMAL provides funding to education, health and human services, civic affairs, arts and culture, and environmental organizations. TMMAL prefers to support programs that are sustainable, diverse, and have an educational focus. Grants are provided to support the development and implementation of programs that generally range from $50,000 to $200,000. Applications are reviewed quarterly, in May, August, November, and February. Submission deadlines for applications are April 15, July 15, October 15, and January 15. The review process can take up to six months.
Requirements: Applicant organizations must have 501(c)3 tax-exempt status, be located within or serve population(s) of Madison County, Alabama, and present a proposal that satisfies the mission, guidelines and limitations of the corporation.

Restrictions: The Toyota Motor Manufacturing of Alabama does not make grants for publications, lobbying activities, advertising, capital campaigns or endowments. Individuals are ineligible to apply. Toyota will not make grants to the following types of organizations: those not recognized as 501(c)3 by the Internal Revenue Service; those that practice discrimination by race, creed, color, sex, age or national origin; those that serve only their own memberships, such as fraternal organizations, labor organizations or religious groups; or political parties or candidates.
Geographic Focus: Alabama
Date(s) Application is Due: Jan 15; Apr 15; Jul 15; Oct 15
Amount of Grant: 50,000 - 200,000 USD
Contact: Grants Administrator; (256) 746-5000; fax (256) 746-5906
Internet: http://www.toyota.com/about/our_business/engineering_and_manufacturing/tmmal/
Sponsor: Toyota Motor Manufacturing of Alabama
1 Cottonvalley Drive
Huntsville, AL 35810

Toyota Motor Manufacturing of Indiana Grants   4653
Toyota Motor Manufacturing of Indiana offers funding in support of residents from the Indiana counties of Daviess, Dubois, Gibson, Knox, Pike, Posey, Spencer, Warrick, and Vanderburgh. Counties in Illinois include Wabash and White, as well as the Kentucky counties of Daviess and Henderson. TMMI supports a variety of programs, including youth and education, health and human services, civic and community, the environment, and arts and culture. Grants are provided to support the development and implementation of programs that generally range from $50,000 to $200,000. Submission deadlines for applications are February 15, May 15, August 15, and November 15, with notification of results by the end of the month following the deadline.
Requirements: Applicant organizations must have 501(c)3 tax-exempt status, and be located within or serve population(s) of: Indiana, specifically Daviess, Dubois, Gibson, Knox, Pike, Posey, Spencer, Warrick, and Vanderburgh counties; Illinois, specifically Wabash and White counties; or Kentucky, specifically Daviess and Henderson ountiesdoes not make grants for publications, lobbying activities, advertising, capital campaigns or endowments. Individuals are ineligible to apply. Toyota will not make grants to the following types of organizations: those not recognized as 501(c)3 by the Internal Revenue Service; those that practice discrimination by race, creed, color, sex, age or national origin; those that serve only their own memberships, such as fraternal organizations, labor organizations or religious groups; or political parties or candidates. . Applicants must present a proposal that satisfies the mission, guidelines and limitations of the corporation.
Restrictions: Toyota Motor Manufacturing of Indiana does not make grants for publications, lobbying activities, advertising, capital campaigns or endowments. Individuals are ineligible to apply. Toyota will not make grants to the following types of organizations: those not recognized as 501(c)3 by the Internal Revenue Service; those that practice discrimination by race, creed, color, sex, age or national origin; those that serve only their own memberships, such as fraternal organizations, labor organizations or religious groups; or political parties or candidates.
Geographic Focus: Illinois, Indiana, Kentucky
Date(s) Application is Due: Feb 15; May 15; Aug 15; Nov 15
Amount of Grant: 50,000 - 200,000 USD
Contact: Grants Administrator; (812) 387-2000 or (812) 387-2266; fax (812) 387-2002
Internet: http://www.toyota.com/about/philanthropy/guidelines/index.html#limitations
Sponsor: Toyota Motor Manufacturing of Indiana
4000 Tulip Tree Drive
Princeton, IN 47670

Toyota Motor Manufacturing of Kentucky Grants   4654
Toyota Motor Manufacturing of Kentucky proves its commitment to the community, as well as to the state, through both monetary contributions and personal involvement of TMMK team members. Besides being a major contributor to United Way of the Bluegrass, which serves eight central Kentucky counties, many employees are members of and serve on community organization boards. Its funding priorities include: the committed to the education of people of all ages - in particular, TMMK participates in educational programs that will help ensure the success of Kentucky's reform related programs; health and human services, by supporting the advancement of physical and mental health for people of all ages; arts and culture, by preservation and advancement of the arts and culture, particularly for our children; the environment, by supporting a variety of efforts to provide for the education, sustainability and preservation of our environment; civic and community progress, by helping make a difference by supporting groups that address local and state issues as well as provide leadership programs for developing human capital; and minorities and diversity, by supporting the advancement and growth of opportunity, inclusion, respect, equality and justice for all people. Grants are provided to support the development and implementation of programs that generally range from $50,000 to $200,000. Submission deadlines for applications are February 1, May 1, August 1, and November 1.
Requirements: Applicant organizations must have 501(c)3 tax-exempt status, and be located within or serve population(s) of any county in Kentucky, with the exception of Boone, Kenton and Campbell. Applicants must also present a proposal that satisfies the mission, guidelines and limitations of the corporation.
Restrictions: Toyota Motor Manufacturing of Kentucky does not make grants for publications, lobbying activities, advertising, capital campaigns or endowments. Individuals are ineligible to apply. Toyota will not make grants to the following types of organizations: those not recognized as 501(c)3 by the Internal Revenue Service; those that practice discrimination by race, creed, color, sex, age or national origin; those that serve only their own memberships, such as fraternal organizations, labor organizations or religious groups; or political parties or candidates.
Geographic Focus: Kentucky
Date(s) Application is Due: Feb 1; May 1; Aug 1; Nov 1
Amount of Grant: 50,000 - 200,000 USD
Contact: Grants Administrator; (502) 868-2000; fax (502) 868-3060
Internet: http://www.toyotageorgetown.com/comm2.asp
Sponsor: Toyota Motor Manufacturing of Kentucky
1001 Cherry Blossom Way
Georgetown, KY 40324

Toyota Motor Manufacturing of Mississippi Grants   4655
Toyota Motor Manufacturing of Mississippi supports sustainable and diverse programs and organizations focusing on youth and education, health and human services, civic and community, the environment, and arts and culture. TMMMS prefers to support program specific grants rather than event sponsorships. Grants are provided to support the development and implementation of programs that generally range from $50,000 to $200,000. Submission deadlines for applications are February 1, May 15, August 15, and November 15. Grant request status notification will be provided to applicants within 45 days of the application deadline.
Requirements: The geographic scope of funding is centered around Pontotoc County, Union County, and Lee County, all in West Virginia.
Restrictions: Toyota Motor Manufacturing of Mississippi does not make grants for publications, lobbying activities, advertising, capital campaigns or endowments. Individuals are ineligible to apply. Toyota will not make grants to the following types of organizations: those not recognized as 501(c)3 by the Internal Revenue Service; those that practice discrimination by race, creed, color, sex, age or national origin; those that serve only their own memberships, such as fraternal organizations, labor organizations or religious groups; or political parties or candidates.
Geographic Focus: All States
Date(s) Application is Due: Feb 1; May 15; Aug 15; Nov 15
Amount of Grant: 50,000 - 200,000 USD
Contact: Grants Administrator; (662) 317-3281 or (662) 538-5902
Internet: http://www.toyota.com/about/philanthropy/guidelines/index.html#limitations
Sponsor: Toyota Motor Manufacturing of Mississippi
1200 Magnolia Drive
Blue Springs, MS 38828

Toyota Motor Manufacturing of Texas Grants   4656
As a good corporate citizen, Toyota Motor Manufacturing of Texas contributes to economic and social development in local communities. Giving back to the communities where its team members live and work is a priority. The corporation believes in helping people improve the quality of life in their communities through educational and family literacy programs. It also partners with leading organizations that educate children and their families about creating a cleaner, greener and healthier world. TMMTX makes grants to support programs and events benefiting the following categories: youth and education, health and human services, arts and culture, civic and community, and the environment. Requests are reviewed quarterly. Grants are provided to support the development and implementation of programs that generally range from $50,000 to $200,000. Submission deadlines for applications are January 31, April 30, September 30, and October 31 of every calendar year.
Requirements: Applicant organizations must have 501(c)3 tax-exempt status, and be located within or serve population(s) of Bear County, Texas, and its adjacent counties. Applicants must also present a proposal that satisfies the mission, guidelines and limitations of the corporation.
Restrictions: TMMTX does not donate vehicles. Nor does it make grants for publications, lobbying activities, advertising, capital campaigns or endowments. Individuals are ineligible to apply. Toyota will not make grants to the following types of organizations: those not recognized as 501(c)3 by the Internal Revenue Service; those that practice discrimination by race, creed, color, sex, age or national origin; those that serve only their own memberships, such as fraternal organizations, labor organizations or religious groups; or political parties or candidates.
Geographic Focus: Texas
Date(s) Application is Due: Jan 31; Apr 30; Sep 30; Oct 31
Amount of Grant: 50,000 - 200,000 USD
Contact: Grants Administrator; (210) 263-4000
Internet: http://www.toyotatexas.com/index.php?option=com_content&view=article&id=5&Itemid=4
Sponsor: Toyota Motor Manufacturing of Texas
1 Lone Star Pass
San Antonio, TX 78264

Toyota Motor Manufacturing of West Virginia Grants   4657
Toyota Motor Manufacturing of West Virginia is committed to continuing the worldwide Toyota tradition of community involvement and support. In response to the needs and interests of its team members and the community, Toyota has designed a corporate donations program focusing on specific issues and geographic areas with its first priority of improving the quality of life in the community in which it operates. TMMWV provides funding to education, health and human services, civic and community, arts and culture, and environmental organizations. TMMWV's education donations focus primarily on projects that serve K-12 students in the public setting. Community development activities must improve the economy or the quality of life for the people in the region. Health and human services projects must be aimed at significantly improving health or health care, or providing assistance to families in need. Environmental activities must be designed to preserve, restore, or improve the quality of air, natural or wildlife resources. Grants are provided to support the development and implementation of programs that generally range from $50,000 to $200,000. Grants are reviewed quarterly, in March, June, September, and December. Submission deadlines for applications are March 1, June 1, October 1, and January 1.

Requirements: Top priority is given to Putnam County; second priority is given to Cabell, Jackson, Kanawha, Lincoln and Mason counties; and there is a limited participation in important statewide projects.
Restrictions: Toyota Motor Manufacturing of West Virginia does not make grants for publications, lobbying activities, advertising, capital campaigns or endowments. Individuals are ineligible to apply. Toyota will not make grants to the following types of organizations: those not recognized as 501(c)3 by the Internal Revenue Service; those that practice discrimination by race, creed, color, sex, age or national origin; those that serve only their own memberships, such as fraternal organizations, labor organizations or religious groups; or political parties or candidates.
Geographic Focus: West Virginia
Date(s) Application is Due: Jan 1; Mar 1; Jun 1; Oct 1
Amount of Grant: 50,000 - 200,000 USD
Contact: Grants Administrator; (304) 937-7000
Internet: http://www.toyota.com/about/philanthropy/guidelines/index.html#limitations
Sponsor: Toyota Motor Manufacturing of West Virginia
1 Sugar Maple Lane
Buffalo, WV 25033

Toyota Motor North America of New York Grants — 4658
Toyota Motor North America offers grant funding nationally, focusing on three primary areas: the environment, safety, and education. National programs in these areas must have a broad reach by impacting several major U.S. cities, communities or groups. In the local New York City area, Toyota also focuses on those three major areas, and provides other local assistance as well, including arts and culture, civic and community, health and human services and leadership development. Toyota prefers to support programs, rather than sponsor events. Organizations must apply for each new grant requested, and subsequent funding is contingent upon evaluation of previous activities. The geographic scope is the continental U.S. for programs national in scope and the New York City area for community-based programs. Only online applications are accepted.
Requirements: Applicant organizations must have 501(c)3 tax-exempt status, be located within or serve population(s) either on a national scope or specifically in the New York City area, and present a proposal that satisfies the mission, guidelines and limitations of the corporation.
Restrictions: Toyota Motor North America of New York does not make grants for publications, lobbying activities, advertising, capital campaigns or endowments. Individuals are ineligible to apply. Toyota will not make grants to the following types of organizations: those not recognized as 501(c)3 by the Internal Revenue Service; those that practice discrimination by race, creed, color, sex, age or national origin; those that serve only their own memberships, such as fraternal organizations, labor organizations or religious groups; or political parties or candidates.
Geographic Focus: All States
Amount of Grant: 50,000 - 200,000 USD
Contact: Grants Administrator; (212) 223-0303; fax (212) 759-7670
Internet: http://www.toyota.com/about/philanthropy/guidelines/index.html
Sponsor: Toyota Motor North America
601 Lexington Avenue, 49th Floor
New York, NY 10022

Toyota Motor Sales, USA Grants — 4659
Toyota Motor Sales, USA, offers grant funding within the Torrance, California for community?based programs. The program's funding scope primarily supports education, environment and safety, but also funds civic groups, arts and culture, health and human services. Toyota Motor Sales prefers to support programs, rather than sponsor events. Organizations must apply for each new grant requested, and subsequent funding is contingent upon evaluation of previous activities. Only online applications are accepted.
Requirements: Applicant organizations must have 501(c)3 tax-exempt status, be located within or serve population(s) in the Torrance, California, region, and present a proposal that satisfies the mission, guidelines and limitations of the corporation.
Restrictions: Toyota Motor Sales, USA does not make grants for publications, lobbying activities, advertising, capital campaigns or endowments. Individuals are ineligible to apply. Toyota will not make grants to the following types of organizations: those not recognized as 501(c)3 by the Internal Revenue Service; those that practice discrimination by race, creed, color, sex, age or national origin; those that serve only their own memberships, such as fraternal organizations, labor organizations or religious groups; or political parties or candidates.
Geographic Focus: California
Amount of Grant: 50,000 - 200,000 JPY
Contact: Grants Administrator; (310) 468-5249 or (310) 468-4216; fax (310) 468-7840
Internet: http://www.toyota.com/about/philanthropy/guidelines/index.html
Sponsor: Toyota Motor Sales, USA
19001 S. Western Avenue
Torrance, 90501

Toyota Technical Center Grants — 4660
For more than 35 years, Toyota Technical Center, a division of Toyota Motor Engineering and Manufacturing, has been the driving force behind Toyota's North American engineering and research and development activities. Established in 1977 and headquartered in Michigan, TTC has Research and Development facilities in Ann Arbor, Saline, Plymouth and Livonia. TTC focuses on education (specifically math and science), environment, and safety, as well as programs that enrich the lives of children, families and the communities within the specified locations listed. Grants are provided to support the development and implementation of programs that generally range from $50,000 to $200,000. Submission deadlines for applications are March 1, June 1, September 1, and December 1. The review process can take up to six months.
Requirements: Applicant organizations must have 501(c)3 tax-exempt status, and be located within or serve population(s) of: Michigan, specifically Washtenaw County; Arizona, specifically Maricopa County; or California, specifically Los Angeles County. Applicants must present a proposal that satisfies the mission, guidelines and limitations of the corporation.
Restrictions: The Toyota Technical Center does not make grants for publications, lobbying activities, advertising, capital campaigns or endowments. Individuals are ineligible to apply. Toyota will not make grants to the following types of organizations: those not recognized as 501(c)3 by the Internal Revenue Service; those that practice discrimination by race, creed, color, sex, age or national origin; those that serve only their own memberships, such as fraternal organizations, labor organizations or religious groups; or political parties or candidates.
Geographic Focus: Arizona, California, Michigan
Date(s) Application is Due: Mar 1; Jun 1; Sep 1; Dec 1
Amount of Grant: 50,000 - 200,000 USD
Contact: Grants Administrator; (734) 695-2600
Internet: http://www.toyota.com/about/philanthropy/guidelines/index.html#tmmk
Sponsor: Toyota Technical Center
8777 Platt Road
Saline, MI 48176

Toyota USA Foundation Environmental Grants — 4661
The Toyota USA Foundation is committed to environmental causes. It supports nonprofit organizations that promote environmental stewardship, education and research. Its Environmental programs also reflect our commitment to representing and engaging diverse populations and communities. In 2008, the Foundation launched TogetherGreen, a $20 million, five-year alliance with Audubon to fund conservation projects, train environmental leaders, and offer volunteer opportunities to significantly benefit the environment. Grants are provided to support the development and implementation of programs that generally range from $50,000 to $200,000. Foundation reviews applications continually and does not have deadlines. The review process can take up to six months.
Requirements: Applicant organizations must have 501(c)3 tax-exempt status, be located within and serve population(s) in the United States, and present a proposal that satisfies the guidelines and limitations of the foundation.
Restrictions: The foundation does not support routine institutional expenses, general operating costs, annual fund drives, or deficit reductions; endowments, capital campaigns, or any building and/or construction costs; fund-raising events, dinners or lunches, advertising, mass mailings; travel; lobbying organizations, fraternal groups, veteran organizations, religious groups, or labor organizations; equipment (unless a small component of an otherwise eligible program); conferences; or publication subsidies. The Foundation will only fund a program one time; however, a grant recipient may present a new program for consideration after three years.
Geographic Focus: All States
Contact: Patricia Salas Pineda, Foundation Administrator; (212) 715-7486
Internet: http://www.toyota.com/about/philanthropy/environment/index.html
Sponsor: Toyota USA Foundation
9 West 57th Street, Suite 4900
New York, NY 10019

Toyota USA Foundation Safety Grants — 4662
At the Toyota USA Foundation, safety is a priority from the vehicles the Corporation puts on the road to the people who drive them. Since 2004, the Foundation has sponsored and created programs that educate drivers and passengers of all ages across the U.S. on critical safety behaviors. Its signature program is Toyota Driving Expectations (TDE), a free program for teen drivers and their parents. The goal of TDE is to proactively take America's driving youth through a safe driving experience. Grants are provided to support the development and implementation of programs that generally range from $50,000 to $200,000. Foundation reviews applications continually and does not have deadlines. The review process can take up to six months.
Requirements: Applicant organizations must have 501(c)3 tax-exempt status, be located within and serve population(s) in the United States, and present a proposal that satisfies the guidelines and limitations of the foundation.
Restrictions: The foundation does not support routine institutional expenses, general operating costs, annual fund drives, or deficit reductions; endowments, capital campaigns, or any building and/or construction costs; fund-raising events, dinners or lunches, advertising, mass mailings; travel; lobbying organizations, fraternal groups, veteran organizations, religious groups, or labor organizations; equipment (unless a small component of an otherwise eligible program); conferences; or publication subsidies. The Foundation will only fund a program one time; however, a grant recipient may present a new program for consideration after three years.
Geographic Focus: All States
Contact: Patricia Salas Pineda, Foundation Administrator; (212) 715-7486
Internet: http://www.toyota.com/about/philanthropy/safety/index.html
Sponsor: Toyota USA Foundation
9 West 57th Street, Suite 4900
New York, NY 10019

TRDRP Participatory Research Awards: CARA/SARA — 4663
The purpose of the Community Academic Research Awards (CARA) and the School Academic Research Awards (SARA) is to stimulate and support collaborations between community-based organizations/ schools with academic investigators. These awards are for a collaborative partnership to perform scientifically rigorous research into tobacco control issues that are identified as important and meaningful to specific communities/schools in the state.
Requirements: The applicant partners must demonstrate the use of methods that are relevant, culturally sensitive, and appropriate in terms defined and accepted by the participating

communities/schools. Applicants are encouraged to consider TRDRP's Primary research areas and the TEROC recommended research strategies that lend themselves to a participatory research approach.
Restrictions: All submitted applications will be screened for their direct relevance to tobacco use or tobacco-related disease. Proposed research that is not relevant will not undergo peer review for scientific merit. It is incumbent on the applicant to make a compelling case that the proposed work is directly relevant to the mission of TRDRP.
Geographic Focus: California
Date(s) Application is Due: Jan 15
Amount of Grant: 100,000 - 300,000 USD
Contact: M.F. Bowen, (510) 987-9811; mf.bowen@ucop.edu
Internet: http://www.trdrp.org/fundingopps/callawardmechs.asp
Sponsor: Tobacco-Related Disease Research Program
Office of the President, 300 Lakeside Drive, 6th Floor
Oakland, CA 94612-3550

TRDRP Research Grants 4664
TRDRP will consider unsolicited requests to support research-related activities that build research infrastructure, disseminate research findings, or stimulate new research directions. Support can be requested for scientific conferences to assess tobacco's impact on California's population; or to allow tobacco investigators to evaluate, in a timely manner, new and breaking trends in tobacco control or tobacco-related disease research. The TRDRP Scientific Advisory Committee will make recommendations regarding funding. These opportunities will be limited in number, scope, cost, and duration. Contact a TRDRP research administrator regarding the appropriateness of your proposal prior to submission.
Requirements: In order to qualify for funding, the planned activities must be directly related to one or more of TRDRP's Priority research areas. The activity must primarily take place in California, involve California investigators, and include, where applicable, discussants and speakers funded by TRDRP. Unsolicited requests may be submitted at any time. Requests will be evaluated expeditiously by ad-hoc peer review when appropriate.
Restrictions: All submitted applications will be screened for their direct relevance to tobacco use or tobacco-related disease. Proposed research that is not relevant will not undergo peer review for scientific merit. It is incumbent on the applicant to make a compelling case that the proposed work is directly relevant to the mission of TRDRP.
Geographic Focus: California
Contact: M.F. Bowen, (510) 987-9811; mf.bowen@ucop.edu
Internet: http://www.trdrp.org/fundingopps/callawardmechs.asp
Sponsor: Tobacco-Related Disease Research Program
Office of the President, 300 Lakeside Drive, 6th Floor
Oakland, CA 94612-3550

Tri-County Electric People Fund Grants 4665
The fund awards grants for charitable purposes to benefit people and organizations in the Tri-County Electric service area. Grants are awarded for food, shelter, clothing, health, and other humane needs for programs or services that benefit a significant segment of a community. An organization's financial statements, bylaws, and nonprofit status must be submitted with its application. Individuals or families must submit copies of previous federal income tax forms. The fund has the right to fully audit the use of donations at any time. Guidelines and application are available online.
Requirements: Individuals and organizations in mid-Michigan, including Ionia, Eaton, Ingham, Clinton, Gratiot, Montcalm, Isabella, and Mcosta Counties, are eligible.
Restrictions: No funds shall in any fashion be used to support any candidate for political office or any political purpose. An applicant may not reapply within six months from a previous application.
Geographic Focus: Michigan
Amount of Grant: 2,500 - 10,000 USD
Contact: People Fund Supervisor; (877) 466-3957, ext. 1; tricoenergy@homeworks.org
Internet: http://www.tricoenergy.com/people_fund1/guidelines.htm
Sponsor: Tri-County Electric People Fund
P.O. Box 503
Portland, MI 48875

Tri-State Community Twenty-first Century Endowment Fund Grants 4666
The Foundation for the Tri-State Community makes grants in support of educational, cultural, scientific and other charitable purposes in Kentucky, Ohio, and West Virginia. Specifically, the Foundation encourages project proposals with the following goals: improve the quality of life in the Tri-State area; test or demonstrate new approaches and techniques to find solutions to important community problems; promote community volunteerism; strengthen non-profit agencies and institutions by reducing operating costs, increasing public financial support, and/or improving internal management; and use community resources to promote coordination, cooperation, and sharing among organizations to eliminate duplicate services.
Requirements: 501(c)3 tax-exempt organizations that serve Boyd and Greenup Counties, Kentucky; Lawrence County, Ohio; and Cabell and Wayne Counties, West Virginia are eligible. Applicants should contact the Foundation to obtain a copy of the grant application and to discuss the proposed project.
Restrictions: The foundation does not fund general operating support grants, endowment funds, individuals, operational deficits, or sectarian activities of religious organizations. Also, organizations may submit only one application per funding cycle, and past awardees should wait at least 12 months from the approval of their award to submit another request. The 21st Century Endowment grants also do not provide funding for components of projects begun before grant award decisions are made.
Geographic Focus: Kentucky, Ohio, West Virginia
Date(s) Application is Due: Jan 15; Apr 15; Jul 15; Oct 15
Amount of Grant: 250 - 5,000 USD
Contact: Mary Witten Wiseman, President; (304) 942-0046; fax (304) 942-0048; FTSC_MWWiseman@yahoo.com
Internet: http://www.tristatefoundation.org/html/grants.html
Sponsor: Foundation for the Tri-State Community
P.O. Box 2096
Ashland, KY 41105-2096

Triangle Community Foundation Community Grants 4667
Established in 1983, the Triangle Community Foundation is a nonprofit organization that serves Chatham, Durham, Orange and Wake counties of North Carolina. The Community Grantmaking Program provides funding through an open, competitive, discretionary process, Triangle Community Foundation provides funding to Triangle-based nonprofits with annual budgets of less than $750,000. Grants, ranging from $10,000 to $15,000, are awarded in both the spring and fall of each year to initiatives promoting Civic Engagement and Youth Leadership & Development.
Requirements: 501(c)3 nonprofit organizations, government entities and faith-based groups based in Chatham, Durham, Orange and Wake counties with total annual organizational budgets of $750,000 or less are eligible to apply. Organizations wishing to submit a proposal must use the Foundation's Community Grantmaking Program application. The application is available at: http://www.trianglecf.org/page33709.cfm. Applications should be emailed as an attachment to cgp@trianglecf.org.
Restrictions: The Foundation does not accept additional supporting materials, such as letters of support.
Geographic Focus: North Carolina
Date(s) Application is Due: Feb 15; Dec 15
Amount of Grant: 10,000 - 15,000 USD
Contact: Robyn Fehrman; (919) 474-8370, ext. 128; robyn@trianglecf.org
Internet: http://www.trianglecf.org/page33699.cfm
Sponsor: Triangle Community Foundation
324 Blackwell Street, Suite 1220
Durham, NC 27701

Triangle Community Foundation Donor-Advised Grants 4668
Established in 1983, the Triangle Community Foundation is a nonprofit organization that serves Chatham, Durham, Orange and Wake counties of North Carolina. There's no application process for the donor-advised grants, rather, fundholders advise Foundation staff as to where they would like their grants made. Often, fundholders seek guidance from staff about which nonprofits are doing work matching their charitable interests. For this reason, it is important nonprofits keep members of the Philanthropic Services Team informed about their organizations, including special projects and funding needs. For more information, nonprofit organizations should contact the following staff: Arts, Culture, & Humanites - Lori O'Keefe, lori@trianglecf.org; Community Building - Agnes Vishnevkin, agnes@trianglecf.org; Education & Youth Development - Robyn Fehrman, robyn@trianglecf.org; Health & Human Services - Sandra Rodriguez, sandra@trianglecf.org; Law, Justice, & Public Action - Robyn Fehrman, robyn@trianglecf.org; Natural Resources - Tracy Joseph, tracy@trianglecf.org; Volunteerism & Community Support - Libby Long, libby@trianglecf.org; Religious & Spiritual Development - Tracy Joseph, tracy@trianglecf.org.
Requirements: North Carolina 501(c)3 tax-exempt organizations, government units, and religious congregations planning projects that benefit residents of Chatham, Durham, Orange and Wake counties of North Carolina are eligible.
Geographic Focus: North Carolina
Contact: Lori O'Keefe, Director of Philanthropic Services; (919) 474-8370, ext. 144; fax (919) 941-9208; lori@trianglecf.org
Internet: http://www.trianglecf.org/page33699.cfm
Sponsor: Triangle Community Foundation
324 Blackwell Street, Suite 1220
Durham, NC 27701

Trinity Foundation Grants (Arkansas) 4669
The Foundation, established in 1952, supports organizations involved with arts and culture, education, boys & girls clubs, environment, children/youth, services, higher education, and scholarships/ financial aid. Giving is limited to the state of Arkansas. Contact the Foundation for further application information and guidelines.
Geographic Focus: Arkansas
Date(s) Application is Due: Mar 1
Contact: Drew Atkinson, Secretary; (870) 534-7120
Sponsor: Trinity Foundation
P.O. Box 7008
Pine Bluff, AR 71611-7008

Trinity Foundation Grants (Iowa) 4670
The Foundation, established in 1990, supports organizations involved with the American Red Cross, human services, and religion. Giving is primarily centered in the Des Moines, Iowa area. There are no specific deadlines with which to adhere. Contact the Foundation for further application information and guidelines.
Geographic Focus: Iowa
Contact: Carmelita M. Blackman, President; (515) 226-1706
Sponsor: Trinity Foundation
4900 West Park Drive
West Des Moines, IA 50266-4946

Trinity Trust Community Response Grants 4671

The Trinity Trust makes grants exclusively for the benefit of citizens in Trinity County, California. The Trust is an affiliate of the Humboldt Area Foundation, who manages the Trinity Trust Endowment and administers Trinity Trust grants. Grant decision are made by a committee of Trinity Country residents who have shown long-term interest in improving their community. The Trinity Trust's Community Response Grant Program is designed to respond to urgent, unexpected or one-time needs where a small investment can make a lasting difference in the community. Grants are made for projects that do one or more of the following: build collaborative relationships and partnerships; integrate youth in ways that build their commitment to community and civic responsibility; engage community members who will benefit in the planning; develop community leadership; leverage matching funding or resources for the organization; and increase the long-term capacity of an organization to improve or expand their services. The application and additional information are available at the website.
Requirements: Applicants must be nonprofit charitable or tax exempt organizations, public schools, government agencies, Indian tribal governments, or have a qualified fiscal sponsor. Projects must benefit the communities within Trinity County, California. Any organizations from outside this service area must demonstrate that they are working with a locally based group to develop and implement the project.
Restrictions: This grant program should not be viewed as an ongoing or yearly source of support. Funding is not available for any of the following: expenses outside the service area such as travel expenses of school or groups for trips out of the area; cultural groups going on tour; good will ambassadors; scholarships or fellowships to other countries; deferred maintenance or annual operating costs of public institutions, churches, services or special tax districts, government, or cemeteries; religious activities or projects that exclusively benefit the members of sectarian or religious organizations; or expenses that have already been incurred.
Geographic Focus: California
Contact: Duane Heryford, Trinity Trust Administrator; (530) 623-0320
Internet: http://www.trinity-trust.org/content/view/92/83/
Sponsor: Trinity Trust
P.O. Box 3216
Weaverville, CA 96093

Trinity Trust Summer Youth Mini Grants 4672

The Trinity Trust is committed to supporting children and youth, and values programs that offer opportunities for them to learn, play and develop in a safe, productive setting while school is not in session. The Trust recognizes that organizations offering summer programs for children and youth are integral to providing those opportunities. Small grants are awarded so that agencies may expand and enrich summer recreation programs serving Trinity County children operating between June and September. Funding is based on the following criteria: a high number of low-income, disabled or other disadvantaged youth are served; youth in outlying areas would have few summer alternatives for productive activities; operating hours are extensive throughout the summer; and high numbers of at-risk youth are served. Additional funding may be considered for the following organization: a large number of scholarships to the organization's summer program are provided; the program requires no fee; good use is made of available resources and/or collaborations; programs provide developmental as well as well recreational opportunities; and organizations request items to help ensure the safety of program participants. Grants are normally provided to support expenses such as sports and recreational equipment, arts and craft supplies, special events, and field trips and camperships for low-income participants. The average grant is $400, but may increase with some circumstances. The application and additional information is available at the website.
Requirements: Nonprofit organizations serving Trinity County youth programs offered between June 1 and September 1 are eligible to apply.
Geographic Focus: California
Date(s) Application is Due: Mar 15
Amount of Grant: 400 USD
Contact: Duane Heryford, Trinity Trust Administrator; (530) 623-0320
Internet: http://www.trinity-trust.org/content/view/92/83/
Sponsor: Trinity Trust
P.O. Box 3216
Weaverville, CA 96093

Trull Foundation Grants 4673

The Trull Foundation was established to share God's bounty in Texas and beyond. The Foundation supports organizations involved with: health care, the coastal Texas environment, seniors, child abuse, neglect, farming, ranching, agriculture, birds, hunger, substance abuse, religion, charity, education, improving the quality of life, especially for those living in poor or oppressed conditions, with a special concern for the needs of Palacios and Matagorda County where the Foundation has its roots.
Requirements: 501(c)3 tax-exempt organizations and departments, agencies, and other services operated within federal, state, or local government agencies and institutions and agencies affiliated with organized religions and religious bodies are eligible. Proposals should be mailed directly to the foundation, faxed or emailed proposals will not be excepted. See foundation's website for additional proposal guidelines and application forms.
Restrictions: The foundation usually will not make long term commitments; make grants for buildings, endowments, or research; repeat grants to the same project longer than three years; or fund operational expenses except during initial years. Any scholarship funds granted are made to institutions and are administered by those institutions. No scholarships or other funds are granted to individuals.
Geographic Focus: All States
Amount of Grant: 250 - 20,000 USD
Contact: E. Gail Purvis; (361) 972-5241; gpurvis@trullfoundation.org
Internet: http://www.trullfoundation.org
Sponsor: Trull Foundation
404 Fourth Street
Palacios, TX 77465

TSA Advanced Surveillance Grants 4674

On February 17, 2009, the American Recovery and Reinvestment Act of 2009 was enacted to assist those most impacted by the recession by creating and preserving jobs and promoting economic recovery. The funding was specified for multiple areas of national interest. The Transportation Security Administration received $1 billion specifically for the procurement and installation of checked baggage explosives detection systems and checkpoint explosives detection equipment to accelerate the installations at locations with completed design plans. It is estimated that five (5) awards will be given, with estimated total program funding around $7.8 million.
Requirements: Eligibility is limited to state, local, or other public institution/organizations responsible for commercial airport operations as the certificate holder at airports within their jurisdiction.
Geographic Focus: All States
Date(s) Application is Due: Jun 30
Contact: Patricia Masterson; (571) 227-1587; Patricia.Masterson@dhs.gov
Internet: http://www.tsa.gov/what_we_do/grants/index.shtm
Sponsor: U.S. Department of Homeland Security
2650 Park Tower Drive, 2nd Floor - Metroplace 1
Vienna, VA 22180-7300

TSYSF Individual Scholarships 4675

Teemu Selänne, nicknamed "The Finnish Flash," is a Finnish professional ice hockey winger. An offensive player known for his skill and speed, Selänne has led the NHL in goal-scoring three times and has been named to the league's First All-Star Team on two occasions. He has won the Stanley Cup once with the Ducks in 2007. The Teemu Selänne Youth Sports Foundation (TSYSF) provides financial, educational and inspirational opportunities for children and their families through structured sports programs. Individual scholarships are available for youth (and their families) who want to play in organized sports but lack the financial means to do so.
Requirements: The required scholarship application must be filled out (available at website) and submitted with copies of: current Federal tax return; proof of current income status (copies of last 3 months' paycheck stubs, etc.); and a return envelope for the foundation's decision. Families submitting for more than one child need to submit only one copy of the requested supporting documents. There are no specific deadlines. Scholarship applications take a minimum of eight weeks before the Board makes a decision.
Geographic Focus: All States
Contact: Scholarship Coordinator, (949) 544-3110; fax (949) 309-3845; info@tsysf.org
Internet: http://tsysf.org/tsysf-grant-scholarship-application/
Sponsor: Teemu Selänne Youth Sports Foundation
22431 Antonio Parkway, Suite B160-800
Rancho Santa Margarita, CA 92688

TSYSF Team Grants 4676

Teemu Selänne, nicknamed "The Finnish Flash," is a Finnish professional ice hockey winger. An offensive player known for his skill and speed, Selänne has led the NHL in goal-scoring three times and has been named to the league's First All-Star Team on two occasions. He has won the Stanley Cup once with the Ducks in 2007. The Teemu Selänne Youth Sports Foundation (TSYSF) provides financial, educational and inspirational opportunities for children and their families through structured sports programs. Team grants are available for youth athletic teams.
Requirements: The required grant application form must be filled out (available at website) and submitted with copies of: documentation of any scholarships, grants or fundraising revenues received by team and/or players and/or projected revenue if not yet received; confirmed team travel schedule; and a return envelope for the foundation's decision. Organizations with multiple teams may submit just one application instead of one for each team within the organization. There are no specific deadlines. Scholarship applications take a minimum of eight weeks before the Board makes a decision.
Geographic Focus: All States
Contact: Grants Administrator, (949) 544-3110; fax (949) 309-3845; info@tsysf.org
Internet: http://tsysf.org/tsysf-grant-scholarship-application/
Sponsor: Teemu Selänne Youth Sports Foundation
22431 Antonio Parkway, Suite B160-800
Rancho Santa Margarita, CA 92688

Tulane University Community Service Scholars Program 4677

The Tulane University Community Service Scholars program is a four year program that includes community service and leadership to incoming freshmen who performed exceptional community service in high school and commit to continued service during their college experience. Supported by the Center for Public Service, Student Affairs, and the Admissions office, the Community Service Scholarship is renewable for four years and provides $5,000 to $42,000 (full tuition) support to approximately 20 students per class year who demonstrate a commitment to community service and fulfill the program requirements. Community Service Scholars Program is a structured program that includes ongoing training and enrichment activities, community service reflection, peer mentorship, and leadership development. See website for application form.
Requirements: Scholars must: maintain 2.7 cumulative GPA every semester for a partial scholarship and a 3.0 cumulative GPA for a full scholarship; complete a total of 50 hours of community service and 2 service events throughout the academic year; attend Group

Meetings once a month and Pair Meetings three times a year within the mentoring program; submit a reflection essay at the end of each semester.
Geographic Focus: Louisiana
Date(s) Application is Due: Jan 15
Amount of Grant: 5,000 - 42,000 USD
Contact: Avery Brewton; (504) 862-8060; abrewton@tulane.edu
Internet: http://tulane.edu/cps/students/scholars-program-overview.cfm
Sponsor: Tulane University
210 Gibson Avenue
New Orleans, LA 70118

Tulane University Public Service Fellows 4678
The Public Service Fellows (PSF) program honors the Center for Public Service's mission to merge academic inquiry with civic engagement by promoting public service leadership. The program aims to recruit, train, and supervise student leaders who will assist faculty members with the coordination of service-learning projects.
Requirements: The program is open to all Tulane juniors and seniors students. The applicant must: be in good standing; submit a completed application; and have completed the first tier of the public service graduation requirement or demonstrate experience in service learning or community service. Public Service Fellows are matched with faculty members either by direct nomination or in consultation with Center staff.
Geographic Focus: Louisiana
Contact: Craig Willie, Program Coordinator; (504) 862-3357; cwillie@tulane.edu
Internet: http://tulane.edu/cps/programs/fellows-index.cfm
Sponsor: Tulane University
327 Gibson Hall, 6823 St. Charles Avenue
New Orleans, LA 70118

Tull Charitable Foundation Grants 4679
Priority interest areas for awarding grants, in Georgia, are education, health and human services, youth development, and the arts. Requests for major capital projects are eligible for consideration. Requests for endowments and for the start-up of new initiatives are sometimes considered.
Requirements: The Foundation's Trustees limit grant awards to 501(c)3 organizations based in the State of Georgia. Requests from organizations located outside of Georgia are not considered. It is preferred that an applicant organization be able to demonstrate a broad base of financial support for a proposed project from its own community and constituency prior to asking for support of that project from the Foundation. Prior to submitting a full proposal, it is recommended (but not required) that an applicant organization contact the Foundation via a concise letter-of-intent in order to determine the potential eligibility of the request.
Restrictions: Grants are not available for operating support, research, conferences and seminars, legislative lobbying or other political purposes, special events, or individuals; nor to churches, sports booster clubs, to sponsor events or to retire accumulated debt. The Foundation does not utilize fiscal agents to handle funds for organizations that do not have an IRS certification letter.
Geographic Focus: Georgia
Date(s) Application is Due: Mar 3; Jun 2; Sep 2; Dec 2
Contact: Carol D. Aiken, (404) 659-7079; carol@tullfoundation.org
Internet: http://www.tullfoundation.org/app_procedures.asp
Sponsor: Tull Charitable Foundation
50 Hurt Plaza, Suite 1245
Atlanta, GA 30303

Turner B. Bunn, Jr. and Catherine E. Bunn Foundation Grants 4680
The Foundation, established in North Carolina in 2000, gives primarily to children and youth services, Christian agencies and churches, educational programs, and human services supporting residents of North Carolina. An application form is not required, and applicants should submit the following: brief history of organization and description of its mission; copy of IRS Determination Letter; and a detailed description of project and amount of funding requested. There are no annual deadlines, and applicants should submit the entire proposal via mail.
Geographic Focus: North Carolina
Samples: Barton College Scholarship Fund, Wilson, North Carolina, $8,600; Boys and Girls Club of Coastal Carolina, Morehead City, North Carolina, $3,800; Hope Station Renovation, Wilson, North Carolina
Contact: Turner B. Bunn III; (252) 243-3136; fax (252) 243-8293; tbb3@nc.rr.com
Sponsor: Turner B. Bunn, Jr. and Catherine E. Bunn Foundation
P.O. Box 3299
Wilson, NC 27895-3299

Turner Foundation Grants 4681
The Turner Foundation believes each organization to be important and that the best person to convey the passion for your organization is you. The Foundation supports initiatives that enhance the quality of life in the greater Springfield/Clark County community through artistic, educational, environmental, recreational, family, healthcare, historic preservation, community beautification and revitalization programs. In most cases, discretionary grants fall in the range of $5,000 to $15,000.
Requirements: To be considered for a discretionary grant, each organization must serve the people of Clark County Ohio, be a tax-exempt non-profit with a 501(c)3 classification from the IRS, and have a governing board.
Restrictions: The Turner Foundation does not fund individuals, churches, legislative action groups, annual fundraising campaigns, scholarships, fraternal groups or political groups and issues.
Geographic Focus: Ohio
Date(s) Application is Due: Sep 14
Amount of Grant: 5,000 - 30,000 USD
Contact: Director; (937) 325-1300; fax (937) 325-0100; email@hmturnerfoundation.org
Internet: http://www.hmturnerfoundation.org/grants.html
Sponsor: Turner Foundation
4 West Main Street, Suite 800
Springfield, OH 45502

Turner Voices Corporate Contributions 4682
Turner Voices, its signature corporate philanthropy program, brings together the company's commitment to the communities in which its employees live and work and its belief in the power of story to effect positive change in the world. Through the financial support of organizations focused on high school-aged youth and the arts, and by leveraging our greatest assets — its people, products, technology and services — Turner Voices identifies and develops the next generation of storytellers.
Requirements: Programs supporting high schooled-aged youth or the arts are welcome to submit a corporate funding proposal. Although Turner Voices accepts unsolicited proposals, funding is typically awarded to 501(c)3 tax-exempt organizations that its Corporate Contributions department has proactively sought for partnerships in which Turner executives and employees have direct leadership and involvement. Corporate funding proposals are accepted throughout the year, but annual plans are formulated in the fall for major projects.
Restrictions: Turner Broadcasting System, Inc. does not make charitable contributions to: Individuals; Religious organizations; Fraternal organizations; Athletic organizations; Social or veterans groups; Charities sponsored solely by a single civic organization; Courtesy or journal advertising campaigns; Multi-year commitments; Seminars, conferences or trips.
Geographic Focus: California, District of Columbia, Florida, Georgia, Illinois, Louisiana, Massachusetts, Michigan, New York, Texas, Argentina, Australia, Brazil, Chile, China, Colombia, Cuba, Denmark, Egypt, France, Germany, Hong Kong, Hungary, Iceland, India, Indonesia, Israel, Italy, Japan, Korea, Lebanon, Mexico, Norway, Pakistan, Panama, Poland, Romania, Russia, Singapore, South Africa, Spain, Sweden, Taiwan, Thailand, Turkey, United Arab Emirates, United Kingdom
Contact: Betsy Holland, Director, Corporate Responsibility & Civic Affairs; (404) 827-1170; betsy.holland@turner.com
Internet: http://www.turner.com/community/contributions-and-grants
Sponsor: Turner Broadcasting System, Inc.
1 CNN Center
Atlanta, GA 30303

TWS Foundation Grants 4683
The foundation awards grants to eligible nonprofit organizations in its areas of interest, including community development, arts, health care, public policy, research, and human services. Types of support include general operating support and scholarship funds. There are no application forms or deadlines.
Requirements: Nonprofit organizations, primarily in Connecticut, New York, Rhode Island, and Texas, are eligible.
Geographic Focus: Connecticut, New York, Rhode Island, Texas
Amount of Grant: 100 - 230,000 USD
Contact: Thomas Smith, Trustee
Sponsor: TWS Foundation
323 Railroad Avenue
Greenwich, CT 06830-6306

Tyler Aaron Bookman Memorial Foundation Trust Grants 4684
The Tyler Aaron Bookman Memorial Foundation was established by Neil and Jill Bookman in memory of their eleven-year-old son, Tyler, who died of a brain tumor. His parents, based on Tyler's love of learning, started the Foundation with the money they had saved for his college education. To them, education is key to breaking the cycle of poverty. With funding centered in Camden, New Jersey, and adjoining states, the Foundation's primary fields of interest is support of health care and research, Catholic churches and agencies, and children and youth education. There are no specific deadlines with which to adhere, and applicants should initially approach the Foundation by way of letter requesting an application form.
Restrictions: No grants are given to individuals.
Geographic Focus: New Jersey, North Carolina, Pennsylvania
Amount of Grant: Up to 30,000 USD
Contact: Neil S. Bookman; (215) 646-2192 or (267) 216-7718; fax (215) 654-6060
Sponsor: Tyler Aaron Bookman Memorial Foundation
426 Newbold Road
Jenkintown, PA 19046-2851

U.S. Army ROTC Scholarships 4685
Army ROTC offers two-, three- and four-year scholarships, which pay full tuition and fees, include a separate allowance for books, and a monthly stipend of up to $5,000 a year. Army ROTC is one of the only college programs that teaches leadership. This training is invaluable for any career that involves leading, managing and motivating people or fostering teamwork. Young Army Officers are typically responsible for hundreds of Soldiers and millions of dollars in equipment; this kind of management experience can be very attractive for post-Army employers.
Requirements: If you are applying for a scholarship, you first will need to create a MY GOARMY account. The college four-year Scholarship is for high school students planning on attending a four-year college program. The three-year scholarship is available for students already enrolled in a college or university with three academic years remaining. The two-

year scholarship is available for those who have two academic years of college remaining. To be eligible, you must: be a U.S. citizen; be between the ages of 17 and 26; have a high school GPA of at least 2.50; have a high school diploma or equivalent; ccore a minimum of 920 on the SAT (math/verbal) or 19 on the ACT (excluding the required writing test scores); meet physical standards; agree to accept a commission and serve in the Army on Active Duty or in a Reserve Component (Army Reserve or Army National Guard).
Restrictions: If you are awarded a scholarship, you will be expected to serve full time in the Army for four years. Selected Cadets may choose to serve part time in the Army Reserve or Army National Guard while pursuing a civilian career. Army ROTC scholarships are not retroactive.
Geographic Focus: All States
Contact: Scholarship Coordinator; (888) 944-2769
Internet: http://www.goarmy.com/rotc/scholarships.jsp
Sponsor: U.S. Army Cadet Command
55 Patch Road
Fort Monroe, VA 23651

U.S. Bank Foundation Grants   4686
The Foundation contributes to the strength and vitality of communities through charitable contributions. They seek to build strong partnerships and lasting value in communities by supporting organizations that improve the educational and economic opportunities of low- and moderate-income individuals and families and enhance the cultural and artistic life of communities. Funding priorities include: economic opportunity (including affordable housing, self-sufficiency and economic development); education; culture and artistic enrichment; and human services. Support is provided for unrestricted general operating support, program support, capital support, contributions of equipment and property. Application deadlines vary by state. See website for states deadlines and state contacts.
Requirements: Applicants must be 501(c)3 not for profit organizations and located in a community with a U.S. Bank office.
Restrictions: The Foundation will not provide funding for: organizations that are 501(c)3 not for profits; fraternal organizations, merchant associations, chamber memberships or programs, or 501(c)4 or 6 organizations; section 509(a)3 supporting organizations; fundraising events or sponsorships; "pass through" organizations or private foundations; organizations outside U.S. Bancorp communities; programs operated by religious organizations for religious purposes; political organizations or organizations designed primarily to lobby; individuals; travel and related expenses; endowment campaigns; deficit reduction; organizations receiving primary funding from United Way; and organizations whose practices are not in keeping with the company's equal opportunity policy.
Geographic Focus: Arizona, Arkansas, California, Colorado, Idaho, Illinois, Iowa, Kansas, Kentucky, Minnesota, Missouri, Montana, Nebraska, Nevada, New Mexico, North Dakota, Ohio, Oregon, South Dakota, Tennessee, Utah, Washington, Wisconsin, Wyoming
Contact: Grants Administrator; 612-659-2000
Internet: http://www.usbank.com/cgi_w/cfm/about/community_relations/grant_guidelines.cfm
Sponsor: U.S. Bank Foundation
800 Nicollet Mall, 23rd Floor
Minneapolis, MN 55402

U.S. Department of Education 21st Century Community Learning Centers   4687
This program supports the creation of community learning centers that provide academic enrichment opportunities for children, particularly students who attend high-poverty and low-performing schools. The program helps students meet state and local student standards in core academic subjects, such as reading and math; offers students a broad array of enrichment activities that can complement their regular academic programs; and offers literacy and other educational services to the families of participating children.
Requirements: Awards are made to State Education Agencies (SEAs). Local education agencies (LEAs) and nonprofit organization may apply to states for subgrants. Formula grants are awarded to State educational agencies, which in turn manage statewide competitions and award grants to eligible entities. For this program, eligible entity means a local educational agency, community-based organization, another public or private entity, or a consortium of two or more of such agencies, organizations, or entities. States must give priority to applications that are jointly submitted by a local educational agency and a community-based organization or other public or private entity. Consistent with this definition of eligible entities, faith-based organizations are eligible to participate in the program. Each eligible entity that receives an award from the state may use the funds to carry out a broad array of before- and after-school activities (including those held during summer recess periods) to advance student achievement. Many states around the country are conducting competitions to award 21st Century Community Learning Center grants. The State Contact List (http://www.ed.gov/programs/21stcclc/contacts.html#state) now includes links to State websites and application due dates.
Geographic Focus: All States
Contact: Peter Eldridge, Acting Program Contact; (202) 260-2514; fax (202) 260-8969; 21stCCLC@ed.gov or Peter.Eldridge@ed.gov
Internet: http://www.ed.gov/programs/21stcclc/index.html
Sponsor: U.S. Department of Education
400 Maryland Avenue SW, Room 3E246
Washington, DC 20202-6200

U.S. Department of Education Centers for Independent Living   4688
This program supports centers for independent living that are designed and operated within a local community by individuals with disabilities and provide an array of independent living services, including the core services of information and referral, independent living skills training, peer counseling, and individual and systems advocacy. The purpose of the program is to maximize the leadership, empowerment, independence, and productivity of individuals with disabilities and to integrate these individuals into the mainstream of American society.
Requirements: Consumer-controlled, community-based, cross-disability, nonresidential private nonprofit agencies are eligible to apply. Only eligible organizations from states and outlying areas holding competitions may apply.
Geographic Focus: All States
Date(s) Application is Due: Jun 8
Contact: Veronica Hogan, (202) 245-7378; fax (202) 245-7593; Veronica.Hogan@ed.gov
Internet: http://www.ed.gov/programs/cil/index.html
Sponsor: U.S. Department of Education
400 Maryland Avenue SW, Room 5051, PCP
Washington, DC 20202-2700

U.S. Department of Education Child Care Access Means Parents in School Grants   4689
This program supports the participation of low-income parents in postsecondary education through the provision of campus-based child care services. Funds are used to support or establish campus-based child care programs primarily serving the needs of low-income students enrolled in IHEs. Grants may be used for before- and after-school services. In addition, grants may be used to serve the child care needs of the community served by the institution.
Requirements: Any institution of higher education that during FY 2008 awarded a total of $350,000 or more of Federal Pell Grant funds to students enrolled at the institution is eligible to apply. Priority is given to institutions of higher education that submit applications describing child care programs that: (1) Leverage significant local or institutional resources, including in-kind contributions, to support the activities assisted under section 419N of the HEA; and (2) Utilize a sliding fee scale for child care services provided under this program in order to support a high number of low-income parents pursuing postsecondary education at the institution.
Geographic Focus: All States
Date(s) Application is Due: May 8
Amount of Grant: 10,000 - 300,000 USD
Contact: Josephine Hamilton, (202) 502-7583; josephine.hamilton@ed.gov
Internet: http://www.ed.gov/programs/campisp/index.html
Sponsor: U.S. Department of Education
1990 K Street NW, Room 7041
Washington, DC 20006-8510

U.S. Department of Education Disability and Rehabilitation Research Projects   4690
The purpose of the program is to plan and conduct research, demonstration projects, training, and related activities to improve the lives of individuals with disabilities. The projects are quite varied, though all are aimed at fulfilling NIDRR's (National Institute on Disability and Rehabilitation Research) overarching goals of inclusion, integration, employment, and self-sufficiency for people with disabilities.
Requirements: Institutions of Higher Education, States, Nonprofit Organizations are eligible to apply. Public or private agencies—including for-profit agencies, Indian tribes, and tribal organizations may also apply.
Geographic Focus: All States
Contact: Donna Nangle, (202) 245-7462; fax (202) 245-7323; donna.nangle@ed.gov
Internet: http://www.ed.gov/programs/drrp/index.html
Sponsor: U.S. Department of Education
400 Maryland Avenue SW, Room 6030, PCP
Washington, DC 20202-2700

U.S. Department of Education Early Reading First Grants   4691
Early Reading First, part of the President's 'Good Start, Grow Smart' initiative, is designed to transform existing early education programs into centers of excellence that provide high-quality, early education to young children, especially those from low-income families. The overall purpose of the Early Reading First Program is to prepare young children to enter kindergarten with the necessary language, cognitive, and early reading skills to prevent reading difficulties and ensure school success. Grants are designed to help early childhood centers improve their programs, by creating centers of excellence that provide preschool-age children with language and cognitive skills, and an early reading foundation. Funds must be used to: Enhance children's language, cognitive, and early reading skills through professional development for teachers; Provide early language and reading development and instructional materials as developed from scientifically based reading research; Provide preschool-age children with cognitive learning opportunities in high quality language and literature-rich environments; Use screening assessments to effectively identify preschool children who may be at risk for reading failure; and improve existing early childhood programs by integrating scientifically based reading research into all aspects of the program (including instructional materials, teaching strategies, curricula, parent engagement, and professional development).
Requirements: All applicants must submit a pre-application that briefly addresses certain key concepts. Applicants invited to submit full applications will be expected to respond to more specific selection criteria. Institutions of Higher Education (IHEs), Local Education Agencies (LEAs), Nonprofit Organizations, Other Organizations and/or Agencies, State Education Agencies (SEAs), LEAs eligible for a Reading First subgrant and public or private organizations or agencies located in a community served by an eligible LEA may apply. In order to be eligible to apply for an Early Reading First Grant, an applicant must be: 1. One or more eligible LEAs; 2. One or more public or private organizations or agencies, including faith based organizations, located in a community served by an eligible LEA. Unless the public or private organization is a preschool program applying on its own behalf, it must apply on behalf of one or more programs that serve preschool-age children, 3. One or more of the eligible LEAs applying in collaboration with one or more of the eligible organizations or agencies.
Geographic Focus: All States
Date(s) Application is Due: Jun 16
Amount of Grant: 1,500,000 - 4,500,000 USD

Contact: Deborah Spitz; (202) 260-3793; fax (202) 260-8969; Deborah.Spitz@ed.gov
Internet: http://www.ed.gov/programs/earlyreading/index.html
Sponsor: U.S. Department of Education
400 Maryland Avenue SW
Washington, DC 20202-5960

U.S. Department of Education Innovative Strategies in Community Colleges for Working Adults and Displaced Workers Grants 4692

The Fund for the Improvement of Postsecondary Education (FIPSE) supports innovative grants and cooperative agreements to improve postsecondary education. It supports reforms, innovations, and significant improvements of postsecondary education that respond to problems of national significance and serve as national models. Under this area of special focus they are particularly interested in projects that propose innovative strategies to benefit working adults and displaced workers who are pursuing degrees or credentials in community colleges. Projects may include, but are not limited to, activities that improve: academic remediation; tutoring; academic and personal counseling; registration processes; students' course selection and scheduling; instructional delivery; student support services related to childcare, transportation, or educational costs, such as textbook rental; and career counseling. Applicants should focus on meeting the unique needs of community college students and adult learners and preparing them for high-growth occupations and to meet employer needs. The estimated range for awards is $300,000-$750,000 for a three-year project period. $132,000-$330,000 for the first year.
Requirements: Institutions of Higher Education, other Public and Private Nonprofit Institutions and Agencies, and combinations of these Institutions and Agencies.
Geographic Focus: All States
Date(s) Application is Due: Aug 4
Amount of Grant: 300,000 - 750,000 USD
Contact: Levenia Ishmell, (202) 502-7500; Levenia.Ishmell@ed.gov
Internet: http://www.ed.gov/programs/fipsecc/index.html
Sponsor: U.S. Department of Education
1990 K Street NW, Room 6147
Washington, DC 20006-8544

U.S. Department of Education Migrant and Seasonal Farmworkers Grants 4693

The program is administered in coordination with other programs serving migrant agricultural workers and seasonal farm workers. The program provides grants for vocational rehabilitation (VR) services, which include vocational evaluation, counseling, mental and physical restoration, vocational training, work adjustment, job placement, and postemployment services. Projects also develop innovative methods for reaching and serving this population. Emphasis is given in these projects to outreach, specialized bilingual rehabilitation counseling and coordination of VR services with services from other sources. The goal of this program is to increase employment opportunities for migrant or seasonal farmworkers who have disabilities. Projects provide VR services to migrant and seasonal farmworkers and to members of their families when such services will contribute to the rehabilitation of the worker with a disability. Discretionary grants are limited to 90 percent of the costs of the projects providing these services.
Requirements: Local Education Agencies (LEAs), Nonprofit Organizations, Other Organizations and/or Agencies, State Education Agencies (SEAs). Applicants may include a state-designated agency interpreted to mean designated state agencies as defined in Sec. 7(8) of the Rehabilitation Act of 1973, as amended, a nonprofit agency working in collaboration with a state agency, or a local agency working in collaboration with a state agency.
Geographic Focus: All States
Date(s) Application is Due: May 20
Contact: Sonja Turner, (202) 245-7557; fax (202) 245-7593; Sonja.Turner@ed.gov
Internet: http://www.ed.gov/programs/rsamigrant/index.html
Sponsor: U.S. Department of Education
400 Maryland Avenue SW, Room 5051, PCP
Washington, DC 20202-2700

U.S. Department of Education Native Hawaiian Education Grants 4694

The purpose of this program is to develop innovative education programs to assist native Hawaiians and to supplement and expand programs and authorities in the area of education. Authorized activities include, among others: early education and care programs; family-based education centers; beginning reading and literacy programs; activities to address the needs of gifted and talented native Hawaiian students; special education programs; professional development for educators; and activities to enable native Hawaiian students to enter and complete postsecondary education programs.
Requirements: Nonprofit Organizations, Native Hawaiian education organizations; Native Hawaiian community-based organizations; public and private nonprofit organizations, agencies, and institutions (including State Education Agencies [SEAs], Local Education Agencies [LEA]s, and Institutions of Higher Education [IHEs]) with experience in developing or operating Native Hawaiian programs or programs of instruction in the Native Hawaiian language; and consortia thereof may apply.
Geographic Focus: All States
Date(s) Application is Due: Mar 24
Contact: Stephen Balkcom, (202) 260-2737; Stephen.Balkcom@ed.gov
Internet: http://www.ed.gov/programs/nathawaiian/index.html
Sponsor: U.S. Department of Education
400 Maryland Avenue SW, Room 3E214
Washington, DC 20202-6200

U.S. Department of Education Parent Information and Training 4695

The program provides training and information to enable individuals with disabilities, and their parents, family members, guardians, advocates, or other authorized representatives, to participate more effectively in meeting their vocational, independent living, and rehabilitation needs.
Requirements: Private nonprofit organizations may apply that either are governed by a board of directors that meets the requirements in Sec. 303(c)(4)(B) of the Rehabilitation Act of 1973 or that have a membership that represents the interests of individuals with disabilities and a special governing committee that meets the requirement in Sec. 303(c)(4)(B). To the extent practicable, technical assistance grants will be awarded to parent training and information centers established pursuant to Sec. 682(a) of the Individuals with Disabilities Education Act. Eligible projects are designed to meet the unique information and training needs of individuals with disabilities who live in the area to be served, particularly those who are members of populations who have been unserved or underserved.
Geographic Focus: All States
Date(s) Application is Due: Mar 14
Amount of Grant: 100,000 - 160,000 USD
Contact: Ellen Chesley; (202) 205-9481; ellen.chesley@ed.gov
Internet: http://www.ed.gov/programs/rsaptp/index.html
Sponsor: U.S. Department of Education
400 Maryland Avenue SW, Room 5018, PCP
Washington, DC 20202-2800

U.S. Department of Education Programs for Native Hawaiians 4696

The purpose of this program is to make financial assistance available to organizations primarily serving and representing Native Hawaiians to plan, conduct, and administer programs designed for the benefit of Native Hawaiians. Organizations must be organized to: prevent violence in and around schools; prevent the illegal use of alcohol, tobacco, and drugs; involve parents and communities; coordinate with related Federal, State, school, and community efforts and resources to foster a safe and drug-free learning environment that supports student academic achievement; and, establish performance measures for their projects. These performance measures must assess the effectiveness of the Safe and Drug-Free Schools Programs for Native Hawaiians, and include measures related to changes in student behaviors or risk or protective factors related to youth drug use or youth violence.
Requirements: Organizations primarily serving and representing Native Hawaiians for the benefit of Native Hawaiian youth are eligible to apply. Applicants must include information in their application as to how they primarily serve and represent Native Hawaiians for the benefit of Native Hawaiian youth. This could include: Independent school districts, State controlled institutions of higher education, Nonprofits other than institutions of higher education [includes community action agencies and other organizations having a 501(c)3 status with the IRS], for profit organizations other than small businesses. Projects must be implemented by eligible organization primarily serving and representing Native Hawaiians, for the benefit of Native Hawaiians, to plan, conduct, and administer programs that prevent or reduce violence, the use, possession and distribution or illegal drugs, or delinquency.
Geographic Focus: All States
Date(s) Application is Due: Jul 30
Amount of Grant: 250,000 - 300,000 USD
Contact: Pat Rattler, (202) 245-7893; fax (202) 245-7166; Pat.Rattler@ed.gov
Internet: http://www.ed.gov/programs/dvpnathawaii/index.html
Sponsor: U.S. Department of Education
400 Maryland Avenue SW, Room 10073, PCP
Washington, DC 20202-6450

U.S. Department of Education Promoting Postbaccalaureate Opportunities for Hispanic Americans (PP.O.HA) Grants 4697

The Promoting Postbaccalaureate Opportunities for Hispanic Americans (PP.O.HA) Program provides grants to: (1) expand postbaccalaureate educational opportunities for, and improve the academic attainment of, Hispanic students; and (2) expand the postbaccalaureate academic offerings as well as enhance the program quality in the institutions of higher education that are educating the majority of Hispanic college students and helping large numbers of Hispanic and low-income students complete postsecondary degrees.
Requirements: There are two application processes for this program — one for eligibility and one for grant funding. You must be designated an eligible institution before applying for funding under this program. Institutions of higher education that offer a postbaccalaureate certificate or degree program and qualify as eligible Hispanic-serving institutions are welcome to apply. PP.O.HA grants shall be used for one or more of the following activities: (1) Purchase, rental, or lease of scientific or laboratory equipment for educational purposes, including instructional and research purposes. (2) Construction, maintenance, renovation, and improvement of classrooms, libraries, laboratories, and other instructional facilities, including purchase or rental of telecommunications technology equipment or services. (3) Purchase of library books, periodicals, technical and other scientific journals, microfilm, microfiche, and other educational materials, including telecommunications program materials. (4) Support for low-income postbaccalaureate students including outreach, academic support services, mentoring, scholarships, fellowships, and other financial assistance to permit the enrollment of such students in postbaccalaureate certificate and postbaccalaureate degree granting programs. (5) Support of faculty exchanges, faculty development, faculty research, curriculum development, and academic instruction. (6) Creating or improving facilities for Internet or other distance education technologies, including purchase or rental of telecommunications technology equipment or services. (7) Collaboration with other institutions of higher education to expand postbaccalaureate certificate and postbaccalaureate degree offerings. (8) Other activities that contribute to carrying out the purposes of the program and are approved by the Secretary as part of the review and acceptance of the grant application.

Geographic Focus: All States
Date(s) Application is Due: Jul 20
Amount of Grant: 518,000 USD
Contact: Dr. Maria E. Carrington, (202) 502-7548; Maria.Carrington@ed.gov
Internet: http://www.ed.gov/programs/ppoha/index.html
Sponsor: U.S. Department of Education
1990 K Street NW, Room 6033
Washington, DC 20006-8500

U.S. Department of Educ Rehabilitation Engineering Research Centers Grants 4698
RERCs support activities that: (1) lead to the development of methods, procedures, and devices that will benefit individuals with disabilities, especially those with the most severe disabilities; or (2) involve technology for the purposes of enhancing opportunities for meeting the needs of and addressing the barriers confronted by individuals with disabilities in all aspects of their lives. Types of activities supported include: the development of technological systems for persons with disabilities; stimulation of the production and distribution of equipment in the private sector; and clinical evaluations of equipment. Awards are for five years, except that grants to new recipients or to support new or innovative research may be made for fewer than five years.
Requirements: States, Institutions of Higher Education (IHEs), Nonprofit Organizations, public or private agencies, including for-profit agencies, Indian tribes, and tribal organizations may apply. RERCs must be operated by or in collaboration with one or more institutions of higher education or nonprofit organizations.
Geographic Focus: All States
Date(s) Application is Due: Apr 1; Aug 1
Amount of Grant: 850,000 - 1,000,000 USD
Contact: Donna Nangle, (202) 245-7462; fax (202) 245-7323; donna.nangle@ed.gov
Internet: http://www.ed.gov/programs/rerc/index.html
Sponsor: U.S. Department of Education
400 Maryland Avenue SW, Room 5051, PCP
Washington, DC 20202-2700

U.S. Department of Education Rehabilitation Research Training Centers 4699
The RRTCs conduct coordinated and advanced programs of research, training, and information dissemination. Each RRTC has a major program of research in a particular area, such as mental illness, vocational rehabilitation (VR), or independent living, which is specified by the National Institute on Disability and Rehabilitation Research (NIDRR). The RRTCs must serve as centers of national excellence and national or regional resources for providers and individuals with disabilities and their representatives. RRTC awards are for five years, except that grants to new recipients or to support new or innovative research may be made for fewer than five years.
Requirements: Note: Each year, competitions are held in specific areas that determine the types of projects. Eligible applicants include Institutions of Higher Education and Nonprofit Organizations, States, public or private agencies - including for-profit agencies, Indian tribes, and tribal organizations may also apply. Rehabilitation research and training centers must be operated by or in collaboration with: (1) one or more institutions of higher education or (2) one or more providers of rehabilitation or other appropriate services.
Geographic Focus: All States
Date(s) Application is Due: Aug 21; Aug 22
Amount of Grant: Up to 675,000 USD
Contact: Donna Nangle, (202) 245-7462; fax (202) 245-7323; donna.nangle@ed.gov
Internet: http://www.ed.gov/programs/rrtc/index.html
Sponsor: U.S. Department of Education
400 Maryland Avenue SW, Room 5051, PCP
Washington, DC 20202-2700

U.S. Department of Educ Rehabilitation Training—Rehabilitation Continuing Education Programs (RCEP)—Institute on Rehabilitation Issues 4700
The purpose of the Technical Assistance and Dissemination To Improve Services and Results For Children With Disabilities program is to promote academic achievement and to improve results for children with disabilities by providing technical assistance (TA), supporting model demonstration projects, disseminating useful information, and implementing activities that are supported by scientifically based research. The purpose of this priority is to support the establishment and operation of State Technical Assistance Projects To Improve Services and Results for Children Who Are Deaf-Blind (projects). Grants are available to support projects in the District of Columbia; Puerto Rico; and the Virgin Islands.
Requirements: Eligible applicants include: SEAs; LEAs, including public charter schools that are considered LEAs under State law; IHEs; other public agencies; private nonprofit organizations; outlying areas; FAS; Indian tribes or tribal organizations; and for-profit organizations. The projects funded under this competition must make positive efforts to employ and advance in employment qualified individuals with disabilities (see section 606 of IDEA). Applicants and grant recipients funded under this competition must involve individuals with disabilities or parents of individuals with disabilities ages birth through 26 in planning, implementing, and evaluating the projects (see section 682(a)(1)(A) of IDEA).
Restrictions: Funds awarded under this priority may not be used to provide direct early intervention services under Part C of IDEA, or direct special education and related services under Part B of IDEA. The Department will reject an application for a State project that proposes a budget exceeding the funding level for any single budget period of 12 months.
Geographic Focus: District of Columbia, Puerto Rico, U.S. Virgin Islands
Date(s) Application is Due: Jul 17
Amount of Grant: 30,000 - 65,000 USD
Contact: Donna Nangle, (202) 245-7462; fax (202) 245-7323; donna.nangle@ed.gov
Internet: http://www.ed.gov/programs/rsatrain/applicant.html#84264c

Sponsor: U.S. Department of Education
400 Maryland Avenue SW, Room 5038, PCP
Washington, DC 20202-2800

U.S. Department of Education Special Education—National Activities—Parent Information Centers 4701
The purpose of this program is to ensure that parents of children with disabilities receive training and information to help improve results for their children. Awards are made for parent information centers, community parent centers, and for technical assistance to such centers. This program includes the following grants competitions: Community Parent Resource Centers (CFDA 84.328C); Parent Training and Information Centers (CFDA 84.328M); and, Technical Assistance for the Parent Centers (CFDA 84.328R).
Requirements: Nonprofit organizations are eligible to apply. For Parent Training and Information (PTI) Centers (# 84.328M), parent organizations may apply. A parent organization is a private nonprofit organization (other than an institution of higher education [IHE]) that: (a) has a board of directors (1) the majority of whom are parents of children with disabilities ages birth through 26; (2) that includes (i) individuals working in the fields of special education, related services, and early intervention, (ii) individuals with disabilities, and (iii) the parent and professional members of which are broadly representative of the population to be served, including low-income parents of limited English proficient (LEP) children; and (b) has as its mission serving families of children with disabilities who are ages birth through 26, and have the full range of disabilities described in Sec. 602(3) of the Individuals with Disabilities Education Act(IDEA). For Community Parent Resource Centers (CPRC; # 84.328C), local parent organizations may apply (same requirements as listed above for PTI Centers). Additionally, "Community to be served" refers to a community whose members experience significant isolation from available sources of information and support as a result of cultural, economic, linguistic, or other circumstances deemed appropriate by the secretary of education. For Technical Assistance for Parent Training and Information Centers (# 84.328R), state education agencies (SEAs); local education agencies (LEAs); public charter schools that are LEAs under state law; IHEs; other public agencies; private nonprofit organizations; outlying areas (American Samoa, Guam, the Northern Mariana Islands, and the U.S. Virgin Islands); freely associated states; Indian tribes or tribal organizations; and for-profit organizations may apply.
Geographic Focus: All States
Date(s) Application is Due: Feb 26; Apr 18
Amount of Grant: 100,000 - 500,000 USD
Contact: Lisa Gorove, (202) 245-7357; fax (202) 245-7617; Lisa.Gorove@ed.gov
Internet: http://www.ed.gov/programs/oseppic/index.html
Sponsor: U.S. Department of Education
400 Maryland Avenue SW, Room 5051, PCP
Washington, DC 20202-2700

U.S. Department of Education Vocational Rehabilitation Services Projects for American Indians with Disabilities Grants 4702
The program provides financial assistance for the establishment and operations of vocational rehabilitation (VR) services programs for American Indians with disabilities living on or near a federal or state reservation. The purpose of this program is to assist tribal governments to develop or to increase their capacity to provide a program of vocational rehabilitation services, in a culturally relevant manner, to American Indians with disabilities residing on or near federal or state reservations. The program's goal is to enable these individuals, consistent with their individual strengths, resources, priorities, concerns, abilities, capabilities, and informed choice, to prepare for and engage in gainful employment. Program services are provided under an individualized plan for employment and may include native healing services.
Requirements: The governing body of an Indian tribe or consortia of such governing bodies located on federal and state reservations may apply.
Geographic Focus: All States
Date(s) Application is Due: May 5; Jun 12
Amount of Grant: 350,000 - 450,000 USD
Contact: Alfreda Reeves, (202) 245-7485; alfreda.reeves@ed.gov
Internet: http://www.ed.gov/programs/vramerind/index.html
Sponsor: U.S. Department of Education
400 Maryland Avenue SW, Room 5051, PCP
Washington, DC 20202-2700

U.S. Lacrosse Emerging Groups Grants 4703
In 2008, the U.S. Lacrosse Board of Directors approved the launch of the program, Emerging Groups, in order to allow U.S. Lacrosse to better serve groups in inner-city or underserved communities. This program provides those groups with financial and resource assistance to build and sustain a lacrosse program. The benefits of applying for an Emerging Group grant include: discounted U.S. Lacrosse membership for players (includes insurance coverage and Lacrosse Magazine); equipment (four package choices; discounted access to Coaches Education Program Level 1 and 2 online courses and clinics; additional discounts on CEP educational DVD's and resource materials; NCSI Background checks for coaches/administrators; and PCA online training.
Geographic Focus: All States
Date(s) Application is Due: Oct 2
Contact: Sarah Newman, Programs Manager; (410) 235-6882; fax (410) 366-6735; snewman@uslacrosse.org
Internet: http://www.uslacrosse.org/programs/emerginggroups.phtml
Sponsor: U.S. Lacrosse
113 W University Parkway
Baltimore, MD 21210

U.S. Lacrosse Equipment Grants 4704

The U.S. Lacrosse Equipment Grant can include a full team's worth of equipment (sticks and protective gear) and are awarded to programs within their first year of operation. Applicant programs must demonstrate a financial need and priority is given to those residing in a state or region where lacrosse opportunities are currently limited or absent. June 16 is the postmark deadline for submitting completed application.

Geographic Focus: All States

Date(s) Application is Due: Jun 16

Contact: Sarah Newman, (410) 235-6882; fax (410) 366-6735; snewman@uslacrosse.org

Internet: http://www.uslacrosse.org/programs/equipmentgrants.phtml

Sponsor: U.S. Lacrosse
113 W University Parkway
Baltimore, MD 21210

UNCFSP TIEAD Internship 4705

The Training in Education, Affairs and Development (TIEAD) Program strengthens the career opportunities of students and professionals seeking experiences and advancement in international affairs and development. TIEAD offers citizens of diverse nations the opportunity to work together on development issues that significantly affect human life, critical language training and cultural immersion, and the competitive edge to diversify the current and next generation of international public service professionals. The length of internship is nine-weeks during the summer at a Department of Energy laboratory or research facility.

Requirements: The applicant's GPA must be a minimum 3.0 on a 4.00 grading scale. Applicants must be: a member of an underrepresented group, including ethnic minorities and persons with disabilities; a U.S. citizen, including residents of Puerto Rico, the Virgin Islands, and other U.S. territories; pursuing a STEM degree (i.e., biology, chemistry, physics, engineering, environmental science, etc.)

Restrictions: Permanent residents and students with dual citizenship will not be eligible.

Geographic Focus: All States

Date(s) Application is Due: Feb 1

Contact: Jacqueline Howard-Matthews, Director; (703) 205-8145 or (703) 677-3400; fax (703) 205-7645; jhowardmatthews@uncfsp.org

Internet: http://www.uncfsp.org/spknowledge/default.aspx?page=program.view&areaid=2&contentid=176&typeid=tiad

Sponsor: United Negro College Fund Special Programs Corporation
2750 Prosperity Avenue, Suite 600
Fairfax, VA 22031

UNESCO World Heritage Fund Grants 4706

The World Heritage Fund provides about $4 million annually to support activities requested by States Parties in need of international assistance. The Fund includes compulsory and voluntary contributions from the States Parties, as well as from private donations. The World Heritage Committee allocates funds according to the urgency of requests, with priority given to the most threatened sites. International Assistance from the World Heritage Fund can support requests falling under one of the following three categories: emergency assistance; conservation and management (technical cooperation, training and research assistance, and promotional and educational assistance, up to $10,000); and preparatory assistance (up to $30,000). Requests may be submitted through the online application process, but the application and attachments must be sent by regular mail. Additional guidelines and specific instructions are posted at the website.

Requirements: All States Parties to the Convention are eligible in principle. However, the Operational Guidelines state that when funds available are limited and a selection has to be made, preference should be given to the following: a least developed country or low income economy (as defined by the United Nations Economic and Social Council's Committee for Development Policy; or a lower middle income country (as defined by the World Bank); or a small island developing state (SIDS); or a state party in a post-conflict situation. International Assistance requests must be transmitted by a State Party National Commission for UNESCO or Permanent Delegation to UNESCO, or an appropriate governmental Department or Ministry.

Restrictions: States Parties in arrears of payment of their compulsory or voluntary contributions to the World Heritage Fund are not eligible for international assistance. Individuals, foundations, IGOs and NGOs are not eligible.

Geographic Focus: All Countries

Amount of Grant: Up to 30,000 USD

Contact: Irina Bokova, Director-General; +33 (0) 1 45 68 24 96; fax +33 (0) 1 45 68 55 70; wh-info@unesco.org

Internet: http://whc.unesco.org/en/funding/

Sponsor: United Nations Educational, Scientific, and Cultural Organization
7 place de Fontenoy
Paris 07 SP, 75352

UniBank 911 Emergency Personnel Education Fund 4707

The UniBank September 11th Emergency Personnel Education Fund was created to honor the everyday heroes who responded to the September 11th tragedy and to help local emergency personnel become better prepared. The education program must be made available to counterpart organizations in all other towns of the Blackstone Valley. The total amount available for distribution from this Fund is $1,400.

Requirements: Organizations that deploy emergency service teams in the towns of the Blackstone Valley, Millbury, Grafton, Northbridge, Upton, Hopedale, Mendon, Blackstone, Millville, Uxbridge, Douglas and Sutton are eligible to apply.

Geographic Focus: Massachusetts

Date(s) Application is Due: Feb 15

Contact: Pamela B. Kane, (508) 755-0980; pkane@greaterworcester.org

Internet: http://www.greaterworcester.org/grants/Unibank.htm

Sponsor: Greater Worcester Community Foundation
370 Main Street, Suite 650
Worcester, MA 01608-1738

Union Bank, N.A. Corporate Sponsorships and Donations 4708

As part of its ten-year community committment, Union Bank has pledged to annually distribute at least two percent of its annual after-tax net profit to help meet the needs of the communities it serves, a commitment that has resulted in donations exceeding $72 million dollars during the first six years. This two-percent charitable commitment is achieved through contributions and sponsorships made directly by the bank (through the corporate contribution program) and through grants and investments made by the bank's foundation (Union Bank Foundation). The bank's corporate contributions program is intended to enhance the bank's reputation and visibility by supporting the charitable work of its employees and clients. The bank funds donations and sponsorships supporting a broad range of charitable categories, including community economic development, affordable housing, education, health and human services, culture and arts, emergency services, and the environment. The bank is particularly interested in donations and sponsorships that support low-income populations and promote and enhance diversity in all its forms. The bank's local-area contribution committees consider applications at their monthly meetings. Applications are accepted via an online application system accessible from the bank website. Please note that event-sponsorship applications should be submitted at least ninety days in advance of the event date. Prospective applicants should review the bank's application guidelines and instructions, which are available at the website. Questions may be directed to the foundation officers listed on this page.

Requirements: 501(c)3 nonprofits in company-operating areas in California and the Pacific Northwest are eligible (e.g., San Diego, San Francisco, Los Angeles, Anaheim, Berkeley, Del Mar, Fresno, Irvine, Mission Grove, Pasadena, Sacramento, Salinas, San Jose, Santa Ana, and Torrance, California). A branch locator is available at the bank's website.

Restrictions: The bank does not support the following requests from the following entities or for the following items: individuals; veterans, military, fraternal, or professional organizations; political organizations or programs; service club activities; other intermediary foundations (i.e., foundations which, in turn, make grants to other charities); churches or religious groups (except separately incorporated community development corporations); educational institution operating funds; and individual elementary or secondary schools.

Geographic Focus: California, Oregon, Washington

Contact: J.R. Raines; (619) 230-3105; CSRGroup@unionbank.com

Internet: https://www.unionbank.com/global/about/corporate-social-responsibility/foundation/foundation-grants.jsp#products-tab-item-2

Sponsor: Union Bank, N.A.
350 California Street
San Francisco, CA 94104

Union Bank, N.A. Foundation Grants 4709

As part of its ten-year community committment, Union Bank has pledged to annually distribute at least two percent of its annual after-tax net profit to help meet the needs of the communities it serves, a commitment that has resulted in donations exceeding $72 million dollars during the first six years. The two-percent charitable commitment is achieved through contributions and sponsorships made directly by the bank and through grants and investments made by the Union Bank Foundation, a nonprofit public-benefit corporation which serves as an agent for the bank. Because of its belief that the long-term success of the Union Bank business-model is dependent upon the existence of healthy communities, Union Bank Foundation focuses its philanthropy on building innovative initiatives and partnerships to cultivate healthy communities, which it identifies as possessing the following characteristics: stable families with high rates of home ownership; availability of affordable housing; livable-wage job opportunities; accessible public transportation; convenient access to professional services (e.g., doctors, lawyers, and accountants); adequate public services (e.g., police, fire, and sanitation); safe public places to relax and recreate (e.g., parks, libraries, theaters); clean air and water supplies; a high level of civic engagement; a community constituency possessing diverse income levels; well-funded public schools; successful small business owners who live in the community; a variety of retail shops and restaurants; and traditional financial institutions providing access to capital in or adjacent to the community. With an eye toward being an agent of positive change in Union Bank communities, the foundation focuses on the following strategic program areas (targeting resources especially to benefit low- to moderate-income populations): Affordable Housing; Community Economic Development; Education; and Environment. In the area of Affordable Housing, the foundation focuses on for-sale housing, rental housing, special-needs housing, senior housing, transitional-living facilities, emergency/homeless shelters, youth housing, self-help housing, farm-worker housing, pre-development funding to nonprofit developers, and capacity building for nonprofit housing organizations. In the area of Community Economic Development area, the foundation focuses on small business development, individual development, and neighborhood development. Small business development includes micro-enterprise development and support, technical assistance/entrepreneurial training, organizations that promote access to capital for business or farms meeting Small Business Administration criteria, and job creation. Individual development includes job training/apprenticeship, welfare-to-work programs, wealth-accumulation/asset-building programs, life-skills training, financial-literacy/credit-counseling programs, mortgage credit counseling, business education, and intervention/prevention programs for at-risk youth. Neighborhood Development includes gang prevention/gang intervention programs, crime prevention, dispute resolution/mediation/violence prevention, reduction of liquor outlets, improved quality of food in local markets, childcare and daycare programs, drug- and alcohol-rehabilitation programs, independent living programs, organizational capacity building and funding for operating/administrative expenses, and community organizing to engage, inform and empower citizenry. In the

area of Education, the foundation focuses on scholarship programs, tutoring programs, general education degree (GED) preparation, English as a second language (ESL) programs, computer education, support for the teaching profession, teacher training, literacy programs, parent education, visual- and performing-arts-organizations outreach programs, enrichment programs, and capacity-building. In the area of Environment the foundation focuses on brown-field remediation, science and education relevant to green building, energy upgrade and conservation, rehabilitation and cleanup, coastal/creek- and reserve-cleanup and preservation, urban green-space projects, environmental education, aquariums and museums, ecology and recycling centers, and state parks, nature centers, conservancy centers, botanical gardens, and wildlife centers. The Union Bank Foundation prefers program grants, but will consider requests for core operating support and/or capacity-building grants to support exceptional work within its strategic funding categories. The foundation considers applications at its bimonthly board meetings. Applications are accepted via an online application system accessible from the foundation website. Applicants must choose from three categories when they apply. These are requests for $1,000 or less, requests for $1001 to $25,000, and requests for over $25,000. Prospective applicants should review the foundation's application guidelines and instructions, which are available at the foundation website. Questions may be directed to the foundation officers listed on this page.
Requirements: 501(c)3 nonprofits in company-operating areas in California and the Pacific Northwest are eligible (e.g., San Diego, San Francisco, Los Angeles, Anaheim, Berkeley, Del Mar, Fresno, Irvine, Mission Grove, Pasadena, Sacramento, Salinas, San Jose, Santa Ana, and Torrance, California). A branch locator is available at the sponsor website.
Restrictions: The foundation does not support the following requests from the following entities or for the following items: individuals; veterans, military, fraternal, or professional organizations; political organizations or programs; service club activities; other intermediary foundations (i.e., foundations which, in turn, make grants to other charities); churches or religious groups (except separately incorporated community development corporations); educational institution operating funds; and individual elementary or secondary schools.
Geographic Focus: California, Oregon, Washington
Amount of Grant: 5,000 - 25,000 USD
Contact: J.R. Raines; (619) 230-3105; charitablegiving@unionbank.com
Internet: https://www.unionbank.com/global/about/corporate-social-responsibility/foundation/foundation-grants.jsp
Sponsor: Union Bank Foundation
P.O. Box 45174
San Francisco, CA 94145-0174

Union Benevolent Association Grants 4710
The Union Benevolent Association attempts to distribute its limited resources as widely as is consistent with the needs of its recipients. It tends to select projects that aid large groups of individuals among the disadvantaged. Grants have frequently been given to help support summer camping and educational experiences for inner city youths, to aid programs for the elderly and handicapped, to assist those involved in legal, medical, and social difficulties, to improve the quality of life in deteriorating neighborhoods, and to provide deprived young people with employable skills and artistic and cultural experiences. The Board prefers to make grants for specific projects and, as a rule, does not contribute toward general operating revenues or major building programs. It limits its grants to projects serving the needs of residents of Philadelphia. Preference is given to organizations with budgets of 2 million and below, and which leverage the use of volunteers.
Requirements: The Association makes grants only to 501(c)3 non-profit organizations,that work with people in need, within the city of Philadelphia, PA. Submitted proposals must be on the Delaware Valley Grantmakers Common Application Form (available on the Union Benevolent Association website) and be received (not posted) by email AND regular mail on or before 5:00PM on the deadline date.
Restrictions: The Association does not make grants for capital renovations or to individuals.
Geographic Focus: Pennsylvania
Date(s) Application is Due: Apr 30; Sep 30
Contact: Fernando Chang-Muy; (215) 763-7670; fax (215) 731-9457; info@uba1831.org
Internet: http://www.uba1831.org/grant_guide.html
Sponsor: Union Benevolent Association
1616 Walnut Street, Suite 800
Philadelphia, PA 19103

Union County Community Foundation Grants 4711
Established in 1989, the Union County Community Foundation is a regional affiliate of Foundation for the Carolinas. The Foundation assists donors in making charitable gifts to the community, provides services for nonprofit organizations to create new or manage existing endowments and makes grants for new projects. Preference will be given to programs that meet the following criteria: serve those who are mentally or physically challenged as a result of visual and/or hearing impairments; provide professional development for Union County public school teachers; or address community needs through innovative approaches (funding available only to programs that cannot be covered by normal budgets of existing charitable agencies). Giving limited for the benefit of Union County, NC.
Requirements: Non-profits in or benefiting the community of Union County, North Carolina are eligible to apply. Contact the Foundation, an application form is required to submit a proposal. Applicants should submit the following: signature and title of chief executive officer; copy of most recent annual report/audited financial statement/990; copy of current year's organizational budget and/or project budget; listing of board of directors, trustees, officers and other key people and their affiliations; copy of IRS Determination Letter.
Restrictions: No grants to individuals, or for capital campaigns, ongoing operating budgets beyond the seed level, publication of books, conferences, or endowment funds.
Geographic Focus: North Carolina
Contact: Karen Coppadge, Grants Specialist; (704) 973-4559; kcoppadge@fftc.org

Sponsor: Union County Community Foundation
217 South Tryon Street
Charlotte, NC 28202-3201

Union County Foundation Grants 4712
The Union County Foundation's main purpose is to distribute the donated funds for philanthropic purposes and thus improve and enrich the quality of life in Union County. Grants are awarded on a quarterly basis, with applications due March 31, June 30, September 30, and December 31. The application and additional guidelines is available at the website.
Requirements: Applicants must submit proof of the 501(c)3 status along with the application. In keeping with the mission of the Foundation, grants should: strive to anticipate the changing needs of the community and be flexible in responding to them; be change-oriented and problem-solving in nature with emphasis on seed money or pilot project support rather than for ongoing general operating support; focus on grants which will have the greatest benefit per dollar granted and benefit the greatest number of people; encourage the participation of other contributions by using matching, challenge, and other grant techniques; coordinate with the programs of other sources for funding such as government, other foundations, and associations.
Restrictions: Funding is not available for individuals or religious purposes that do not include the general community. No grants are made for partisan political programs or activities, or previously incurred debt.
Geographic Focus: Indiana
Date(s) Application is Due: Mar 31; Jun 30; Sep 30; Dec 31
Contact: Danka Klein, Executive Director; (765) 458-7664; fax (765) 458-0522; dklein@ucfoundationinc.org or gmurray@ucfoundationinc.org
Internet: http://www.ucfoundationinc.org/8.html
Sponsor: Union County Foundation
404 Eaton Street
Liberty, IN 47353

Union Labor Health Foundation Community Grants 4713
The Union Labor Health Foundation Community Grants support health programs that make a difference in the lives of Humboldt County residents. The Foundation provides funding to projects or institutions that nurture, foster, encourage, support and educate in order to enhance the wellbeing of each individual within the Humboldt County region. The Foundation is interested in projects that concentrate on the following: nurture, foster, encourage, support and educate, in order to enhance the wellbeing of residents of the County of Humboldt; increase access and/or service delivery for underserved populations; and have a lasting impact or a plan for sustainability after the Foundation grant funding is expended. Detailed instructions about application submission are available at the website.
Requirements: Applicants must be nonprofit charitable or federal tax exempt organizations, public schools, government agencies, Indian tribal governments or have a qualified fiscal sponsor. Projects must benefit the communities within Humboldt County. All organizations from outside this service area must demonstrate that they are working with a county based group to develop and implement the proposed project.
Restrictions: Grants cannot be made for the following: expenses outside the service area such as travel expenses of schools or groups for trips, good will ambassadors, or scholarships and fellowships to other countries; infrastructure, deferred maintenance or annual operating costs of public institutions, churches, services of special tax districts, or government agencies; religious activities or projects that exclusively benefit the members of sectarian or religious organizations; or expenses that have already been incurred.
Geographic Focus: California
Date(s) Application is Due: Sep 4
Amount of Grant: 4,500 - 10,000 USD
Contact: Amy Jester, Program Manager, Health and Nonprofit Resources; (707) 442-2993, ext. 374; fax (707) 442-9072; amyj@hafoundation.org
Internet: http://www.ulhf.org/content/view/92/83/
Sponsor: Union Labor Health Foundation
363 Indianola Road
Bayside, CA 95524

Union Pacific Foundation Community and Civic Grants 4714
The Foundation has a strong interest in promoting organizational effectiveness among nonprofits. To that end, this Foundation dedicates the majority of their grants to help nonprofit organizations build their capacity, increase their impact, and operate more efficiently and effectively. Grants are made primarily to proposals in the areas of community and civic, and health and human services. The community and civic grants category focuses on assisting community-based organizations and related activities that improve and enrich the general quality of life in the community. This category includes organizations such as aquariums, botanical gardens, children's museums, history/science museums, public libraries, public television and radio, and zoos.
Requirements: The Foundation will accept only online applications; printed copies of the application are not available and will not be accepted. Grants are made to institutions located in communities served by Union Pacific Corporation and its operating company Union Pacific Railroad Company.
Restrictions: The Foundation will not consider a request from or for: individuals; organizations/projects/programs that do not fit within the Foundation's funding priorities; organizations without a Section 501(c)3 public charity determination letter from the Internal Revenue Service; organizations that channel grant funds to third parties; organizations whose dominant purpose is to influence legislation or participate/intervene in political campaigns on behalf of or against any candidate for public office; organization/projects/programs for which the Foundation is asked to serve as the sole funder; organizations that already have an active multi-year Union Pacific Foundation grant; religious organizations

for non-secular programs (i.e. programs which promote religious doctrine); organizational deficits; local affiliates of national health/disease-specific organizations; non-U.S.-based charities; organizations whose program activities are mainly international; elementary or secondary schools; athletic programs or events; donations of railroad equipment; conventions, conferences or seminars; fellowships or research; loans; labor organizations; or organizations whose programs have a national scope.
Geographic Focus: Arizona, Arkansas, California, Colorado, Idaho, Illinois, Iowa, Kansas, Louisiana, Minnesota, Missouri, Montana, Nebraska, Nevada, New Mexico, Oklahoma, Oregon, Tennessee, Texas, Utah, Washington, Wisconsin, Wyoming
Date(s) Application is Due: Aug 15
Contact: Darlynn Myers, Director; (402) 271-5600; fax (402) 501-2291; upf@up.com
Internet: http://www.up.com/found/grants.shtml
Sponsor: Union Pacific Foundation
1400 Douglas Street, Stop 1560
Omaha, NE 68179

Union Pacific Foundation Health and Human Services Grants 4715
The Foundation has a strong interest in promoting organizational effectiveness among nonprofits. To that end, this foundation dedicates the majority of their grants to help nonprofit organizations build their capacity, increase their impact, and operate more efficiently and effectively. Grants are made primarily to proposals in the areas of community and civic, and health and human services. The health and human services category assists organizations dedicated to improving the level of health care or providing human services in the community. Types of support include general operating support, continuing support, capital campaigns, building construction and renovation, curriculum development, equipment acquisition, program development, and matching funds.
Requirements: The Foundation will accept only online applications; printed copies of the application are not available and will not be accepted. Grants are made to institutions located in communities served by Union Pacific Corporation and its operating company Union Pacific Railroad Company.
Restrictions: The Foundation generally will not consider a request from or for: individuals; organizations/projects/programs that do not fit within the Foundation's funding priorities; organizations without a Section 501(c)3 public charity determination letter from the Internal Revenue Service; organizations that channel grant funds to third parties; organizations whose dominant purpose is to influence legislation or participate/intervene in political campaigns on behalf of or against any candidate for public office; organization/projects/programs for which the Foundation is asked to serve as the sole funder; organizations that already have an active multi-year Union Pacific Foundation grant; religious organizations for non-secular programs; organizational deficits; local affiliates of national health/disease-specific organizations; non U.S.-based charities; organizations whose program activities are mainly international; elementary or secondary schools; athletic programs or events; donations of railroad equipment; conventions, conferences or seminars; fellowships or research; loans; labor organizations; or organizations whose programs have a national scope.
Geographic Focus: Arizona, Arkansas, California, Colorado, Idaho, Iowa, Kansas, Louisiana, Minnesota, Missouri, Montana, Nebraska, Nevada, New Mexico, Oklahoma, Oregon, Tennessee, Texas, Utah, Washington, Wisconsin, Wyoming
Date(s) Application is Due: Aug 15
Contact: Darlynn Myers, Director; (402) 271-5600; fax (402) 501-2291; upf@up.com
Internet: http://www.up.com/found/grants.shtml
Sponsor: Union Pacific Foundation
1400 Douglas Street, Stop 1560
Omaha, NE 68179

Union Square Arts Award 4716
The Union Square Arts Award recognizes the central leadership role played by arts and culture in providing educational opportunities for young people, building collaborations and promoting social change. The Arts Award supports organizations working with youth and families in low-income communities across New York City in all artistic disciplines: creative writing, dance, music, theater, visual and media arts. Each Arts Award consists of a grant of up to $35,000, comprehensive technical assistance, and the opportunity to apply for re-grants to help build long-term organizational sustainability and community engagement.
Requirements: Candidates for Union Square Arts Award are identified through a nomination process. Nominations are reviewed throughout the year and may be submitted by anyone familiar with the organization's contributions and accomplishments. Submissions must describe the nominee's work and outline why the organization should be considered for an Award. Nominations may be made online, by mail, or fax.
Restrictions: Recipient organizations are less than ten-years-old with annual operating budgets under $1 million.
Geographic Focus: New York
Amount of Grant: Up to 35,000 USD
Contact: Denise Beek, Program Associate; (212) 213-6140; fax (212) 213-6372
Internet: http://www.unionsquareawards.org/arts-program
Sponsor: Union Square Awards
9 East 38th Street, 2nd floor
New York, NY 10016

Union Square Award for Social Justice 4717
Recipients of the the Union Square Award have changed public policies, litigated landmark cases, created innovative models of service, and built important community institutions. Award recipients address concerns and build organizations that bring diverse communities into public discourse. Specifically, the Union Square Award supports work in the following areas: homelessness and hunger; HIV/AIDS prevention, education, and treatment; family and community development; youth leadership and organizing; economic self-sufficiency; and conflict resolution. The Award identifies organizations that have not yet received substantial funding and public recognition. It consists of a general operating support grant of $50,000, comprehensive technical assistance, and the opportunity to apply for re-grants to help build long-term organizational sustainability and community engagement.
Requirements: Candidates for the Award are identified through a nominations process. Nominations are reviewed throughout the year and may be submitted by anyone familiar with the organization's contributions and accomplishments. Submissions must describe the nominee's work and outline why the organization should be considered for an Award. Nominations may be made through the online form and are accepted online, by mail, or fax.
Restrictions: Only organizations in the New York City area are eligible for nomination.
Geographic Focus: New York
Amount of Grant: 50,000 USD
Contact: Denise Beek, Program Associate; (212) 213 6140; fax (212) 213-6372
Internet: http://www.unionsquareawards.org/awards-program
Sponsor: Union Square Awards
9 East 38th Street, 2nd floor
New York, NY 10016

Union Square Awards Grants 4718
Union Square Awards Grants support community outreach, ongoing campaigns, services and advocacy work in New York City. The goal is to assist organizations in building long-term sustainability by making general operating support available to previous award recipients.
Requirements: The Union Square Awards staff sends information and guidelines to all eligible organizations about available grant opportunities.
Restrictions: Union Square Awards grants are open to Union Square Award recipients only.
Geographic Focus: New York
Contact: Denise Beek, Program Associate; (212) 213-6140; fax (212) 213-6372
Internet: http://www.unionsquareawards.org/grants-program/overview
Sponsor: Union Square Awards
9 East 38th Street, 2nd floor
New York, NY 10016

United Methodist Committee on Relief Global AIDS Fund Grants 4719
The United Methodist Global AIDS Fund supports education, prevention and care programs for people living with HIV and AIDS around the world. The fund currently supports over 200 HIV/AIDS church oriented and Christ centered ministries in 37 countries, including the United States. The Fund develops appropriate promotional materials and funding guidelines, advocates for social justice, and encourages partnerships between congregations and organizations globally that are engaged in the struggle against HIV/AIDS. The Fund is guided by an inter-agency committee comprised of representatives from the Council of Bishops, General Board of Church and Society, General Board of Global Ministries, General Commission on Communications, the Division on Ministries with Young People and the Office of Christian Unity and Interreligious Concerns.
Requirements: Overseas programs fitting the mission of the Global AIDS Fund may apply to receive a grant. The application should propose work in one or more of the following types of activities: promoting HIV/AIDS awareness and prevention by education and information; behavior modification; voluntary testing and counseling; treatment of persons with AIDS; home based care; and care of orphans and vulnerable children.
Restrictions: This program is only for grants covering primarily United Methodist or Methodist-related projects for up to a one-year period.
Geographic Focus: All States
Contact: Shannon Trilli; (212) 870-3870 or (212) 870-3951; strilli@umcor.org
Internet: http://www.umcor.org/UMCOR/Programs/Global-Health/HIV-AIDS
Sponsor: United Methodist Committee on Relief
475 Riverside Drive, Room 1520
New York, NY 10115

United Methodist Committee on Relief Hunger and Poverty Grants 4720
The United Methodist Committee on Relief provides grants to organizations that work to eradicate the root causes of hunger and poverty. The Committee supports these initiatives both in the United States and around the world, and has provided grants to partners such as Agricultural Missions, Grassroots International, the United Methodist Church of Sierra Leone, and Abraham's Table. At this time, grant applications are by invitation only, so interested parties should begin by contacted the Committee to discuss their proposal.
Geographic Focus: All States, All Countries
Contact: Shannon Trilli; (212) 870-3870 or (212) 870-3951; strilli@umcor.org
Internet: http://www.umcor.org/UMCOR/Programs/Global-Development/Hunger-and-Poverty-Grants/Hunger-and-Poverty-Grants
Sponsor: United Methodist Committee on Relief
475 Riverside Drive, Room 1520
New York, NY 10115

United Methodist Health Child Mental Health Grants 4721
Brain imaging research reveals the astonishing impact early childhood experiences have on the physical architecture of the brain. Other research shows the indivisible interrelationship of early growth in cognitive, physical and mental health. The foundational importance of social and emotional development in early childhood to success in learning, regulating behavior, and building positive relationships throughout life is increasingly recognized. The neuroscience of the first five years of a child's life is clear. Public policies and programs intended to support the healthy development of children have not kept pace with the science. Establishing systems for identifying potential social and emotional development issues as early as possible and assuring access to timely and appropriate early intervention is not only more economical and effective than treating a problem later - such as school failure

or incarceration - but early support also minimizes the damage to a child's potential and a family's well-being. The Child Mental Health Grants funding opportunity is intended to support the design and implementation of a coordinated system of early screening and intervention for the healthy social and emotional development of young children in three to four Kansas communities. The specific goals of the funding are: to stimulate coordinated community-wide screening of pregnant women, new mothers, and young children; and to improve coordination among relevant child-serving organizations to assure timely and appropriate promotion, prevention, and treatment for young children's social and emotional development. The maximum individual grant award will be $200,000.
Requirements: Grants can be awarded only to 501(c)3 organizations or governmental entities with projects to benefit the health of Kansas residents. Grants have one or more of the following purposes: to develop new or expanded, sustainable program resources to provide quality services; to change the delivery system to meet demands, improve access/quality, or reduce cost; to test innovative ideas for improved service delivery; to offer public education for improvement of individual and community health care; to provide group opportunities for health care providers to improve critical skills; or to develop technical expertise, collaborations, and similar supports for improvement and change in health care service delivery and education. Contact the sponsor before beginning a grant application - the Health Fund will not accept unsolicited and unauthorized applications, and will be automatically rejected them without consideration.
Restrictions: Grants are not awarded to individuals or for individual medical, dental, or other personal care treatment. Generally, capital projects and endowments are not funded. The fund does not provide regular operating expenses of on-going projects. The Health Fund does not fund projects in other U.S. states (outside of Kansas) or foreign nations.
Geographic Focus: Kansas
Contact: Virginia Elliott; (620) 662-8586; fax (620) 662-8597; velliot@healthfund.org
Kim Moore, President; (620) 662-8586; fax (620) 662-8597; kmoore@healthfund.org
Internet: http://www.healthfund.org/ycsed2012.php
Sponsor: United Methodist Health Ministry Fund
100 East First Avenue, P.O. Box 1384
Hutchinson, KS 67504-1384

United Methodist Health Ministry Fund Grants 4722
Grantmaking is the Health Fund's primary means of achieving its mission, and we see each grant as an opportunity to move toward the goal of healthy Kansans. To maximize impact with available resources, the Health Fund is targeting the following three areas for funding: access; fit kids; ready for life. In addition to these general focus areas, the Health Fund seeks to support Kansas United Methodist churches in health ministry work through the Healthy Congregations Covenant program. Grants are awarded to health care projects proposed by eligible organizations to respond to needs and build on assets of local, regional, and state situations. These grants generally have one or more of the following purposes: develop new or expanded, sustainable program resources to provide quality services; change the delivery system to meet demands, improve access/quality, or reduce cost; test innovative ideas for improved service delivery; offer public education for improvement of individual and community health care; provide group opportunities for health care providers to improve critical skills; and develop technical expertise, collaborations, and similar supports for improvement and change in health care service delivery and education.
Geographic Focus: Kansas
Contact: Virginia Elliott; (620) 662-8586; fax (620) 662-8597; velliott@healthfund.org
Kim Moore, President; (620) 662-8586; fax (620) 662-8597; kmoore@healthfund.org
Internet: http://www.healthfund.org/funding.php
Sponsor: United Methodist Health Ministry Fund
100 East First Avenue, P.O. Box 1384
Hutchinson, KS 67504-1384

United Methodist Women Brighter Future for Children and Youth Grants 4723
United Methodist Women offers grants of up to $4,000 for projects that address the needs of young people five to eighteen years of age in the areas of violence and/or abuse prevention and/or treatment. Preference will be given to organizations that have significant involvement of women and youth at the grassroots level; demonstrate the ability to raise additional funds from other sources; provide direct, comprehensive services to young people; promote respect for and appreciation of racial/ethnic diversity; and cultivate spiritual life and values. Funding proposals in Spanish are accepted. Interested parties should contact the Foundation to first discuss their proposal, and full grant applications are by invitation only.
Requirements: The Women's Division funds small-scale, community and church-based programs and projects. New or existing projects are eligible to apply. Projects should demonstrate the ability to raise additional funds from other sources.
Restrictions: Groups affiliated with national organizations, hospitals, organizations with budgets totaling more than $3,000,000 are not normally within the realm of funding. Building improvements, computer hardware, one-time only events, or summer events and activities are not eligible for funding.
Geographic Focus: All States
Amount of Grant: Up to 4,000 USD
Contact: Marva Usher-Kerr, Executive Secretary; (212) 870-3738; fax (212) 870-3736; MUsherke@unitedmethodistwomen.org
Internet: http://new.gbgm-umc.org/umw/give/brighterfuture/
Sponsor: United Methodist Women
475 Riverside Drive, Room 1503
New York, NY 10115

United States Institute of Peace - National Peace Essay Contest for High School Students 4724
The United States Institute of Peace (USIP) National Peace Essay Contest is intended to promote serious discussion among high school students, teachers, and national leaders about international peace and conflict resolution today and in the future; complement existing curricula and other scholastic activities; and strengthen students' research, writing, and reasoning skills. Students may take part in the contest with the sponsorship of any school, school club, youth group, community group, or religious organization. There must be a contest coordinator, someone in the school or community who can review essays and act as the key contact between participants and the institute. First-place state winners will receive college scholarships. First-place state winners will also compete for national awards of $10,000, $5,000, and $2,500 for first, second, and third place respectively. All first-place state winners are invited to attend an all-expense-paid awards program in Washington, D.C. in June.
Requirements: Students are eligible to participate if they are in grades nine through 12 in any of the 50 states, the District of Columbia, or the U.S. territories, or if they are U.S. citizens attending high school overseas. Students may be attending a public, private, or parochial school or participating in a high school correspondence program. Entries from home-schooled students are also accepted.
Restrictions: Students who graduate from high school before the application deadline are not eligible.
Geographic Focus: All States
Date(s) Application is Due: Feb 1
Contact: National Peace Essay Contest Coordinator; (202) 429-3854 or (202) 457-1700; fax (202) 429-6063; essay_contest@usip.org
Internet: http://www.usip.org/education-training/domestic/national-peace-essay-contest-high-school-students/awards-and-eligibility
Sponsor: United States Institute of Peace
2301 Constitution Avenue, NW
Washington, DC 20037

United Technologies Corporation Grants 4725
United Technologies Corporation (UTC) grant-making is centered on the geographic regions where its employees live and work. Additionally the corporation focuses its grants on the following four areas of interest: supporting vibrant communities, building sustainable cities, advancing STEM education, and investing in emerging markets. A more detailed description of each area follows. UTC supports vibrant communities by supporting community revitalization initiatives, health and human service programs, and arts and culture. UTC defines sustainable cities as those that are safe and energy efficient to protect people, assets, and natural resources. In support of sustainable cities, UTC focuses on sustainable building practices, urban green space, and preservation of natural habitats to offset green-house gas emissions. To advance science, technology, engineering, and mathematics (STEM) education and to develop the next generation of engineers and scientists, UTC targets programs that include employee volunteerism to spark students' interest and inspire innovation, especially in minorities and women. As it invests in emerging markets, UTC seeks to lay a foundation for responsible citizenship from the inception of business expansion by supporting communities through employee engagement in China and India. Grant seekers have the option of applying either to UTC corporate headquarters or to a UTC business unit (Pratt & Whitney, Otis, Carrier, Sikorsky, UTC Fire & Security, and Hamilton Sundstrand). Either way, application is made online at the grant website given. Grant applications are accepted between January 1 and June 30 each year. Awardees will receive notification within one quarter of their application submission (or in the case of a UTC-business-unit application, in the first quarter of the calendar year in which funding will occur).
Requirements: 501(c)3 organizations in the U.S. and equivalent nonprofit organizations in the corporation's emerging markets are eligible.
Restrictions: Non-profit organizations may apply only once a year and to only one UTC business - either Corporate Headquarters or one of the UTC business units (see description section). UTC will not fund individuals, religious activities or organizations, municipalities, alumni groups (unless the award is distributed to the eligible higher education institution), booster clubs, sororities or fraternities, political groups, organizations engaged in or advocating illegal action, or any organization determined by UTC to have a conflict of interest. Additionally the corporation will not support fees for publication or merchandise.
Geographic Focus: All States, All Countries
Date(s) Application is Due: Jun 30
Contact: Andrew Olivastro; (860) 728-7000; contribu@corphq.utc.com
Internet: http://www.utc.com/Corporate+Responsibility/Community/Apply+for+a+grant
Sponsor: United Technologies Corporation
United Technologies Building
Hartford, CT 06101

Unity Foundation Of LaPorte County Grants 4726
The Unity Foundation of LaPorte County makes discretionary and field of interest grants to charitable organizations in the area of the arts, education, health and human services, the environment, and the community for the benefit of the citizens of LaPorte County, Indiana. The Foundation is particularly interested in funding: projects that are not adequately being serviced by existing community resources; start-up costs for new programs; one-time projects or needs; projects that provide leverage for generating other funds and community resources; projects that facilitate cooperation and collaboration between organizations and the communities within LaPorte County.
Requirements: Only charitable organizations with a verifiable 501(c)3 IRS status operating or offering programs in LaPorte County will be considered for funding.
Restrictions: No grants will be made: to churches for sectarian religious programs; for operating budgets or for basic municipal or educational functions and services; for

endowment campaigns or for previously incurred debts; to provide long-term funding. No grants will be made for post-event or after-the-fact situations.
Geographic Focus: Indiana
Date(s) Application is Due: Jul 18
Contact: Margaret Spartz; (219) 879-0327 or (888) 898-6489; mspartz@uflc.net
Internet: http://uflc.net/grants-scholarships/
Sponsor: Unity Foundation of LaPorte County
619 Franklin Street, P.O. Box 527
Michigan City, IN 46361

UPS Corporate Giving Grants 4727
As a complement to its foundation, UPS also makes charitable contributions to nonprofit organizations directly. UPS is focused on creating opportunities for its customers and supporting communities around the world. As part of this commitment, the Corporation sponsors numerous sports teams, as well as community and cultural events in the neighborhoods where it does business. Current sponsorships include: motorsports; the Chinese women's volleyball team; golf; and a wide variety of community programs around the globe.
Requirements: Due to the high volume of requests that the Corporation receives, all opportunities must be submitted via the website for consideration. UPS does not accept hard copy sponsorship proposals.
Geographic Focus: All States
Contact: Ken Sternad, President; (404) 828-6374; fax (404) 828-7435
Internet: http://www.upssponsorships.com/#
Sponsor: United Parcel Service (UPS) Foundation
55 Glenlake Parkway NE
Atlanta, GA 30328

UPS Foundation Community Safety Grants 4728
The work of the UPS Foundation brings together UPS expertise and philanthropic dollars to address areas of critical importance to improving the safety of communities and the effectiveness of organizations committed to assisting them in times of need. UPS has a long-standing reputation as a leading provider of transportation and logistics services in times of disaster. The Foundation is supporting organizations that are injecting new thinking and innovative solutions to further leverage UPS's skills in this area.
Requirements: IRS 501(c)3 tax-exempt organizations are eligible to apply.
Restrictions: The foundation does not award grants to individuals, religious organizations or theological functions, or church-sponsored programs limited to church members. Grants supporting capital campaigns, endowments, or operating expenses are seldom approved.
Geographic Focus: All States
Amount of Grant: 1,000 - 200,000 USD
Contact: Ken Sternad, President; (404) 828-6374; fax (404) 828-7435
Internet: http://responsibility.ups.com/UPS+Foundation/Focus+On+Giving/Community+Safety
Sponsor: United Parcel Service (UPS) Foundation
55 Glenlake Parkway NE
Atlanta, GA 30328

UPS Foundation Diversity Grants 4729
As a company, UPS brings together people, cultures, and commerce. A commitment to diversity and inclusion are deeply entrenched in all facets of its organization. Through day-to-day activities, it demonstrates that diversity is a business imperative. The UPS Foundation reflects this commitment to the diverse communities UPS serves. From empowering women and girls to obtain an education and become productive members of their society to providing equal opportunity for the under served and underprivileged, the UPS Foundation has supported nonprofit organizations dedicated to inclusion and diversity since the 1960s. The Foundation's support for these organizations helps them in their efforts to demonstrate the true value of diversity communities around the world. Countries, communities and companies become stronger when they embrace the diversity of ideas, beliefs, ethnic groups, and abilities of their people. UPS Foundation grants have long supported organizations dedicated to equality, inclusion, accessibility, and civil liberties.
Requirements: IRS 501(c)3 tax-exempt organizations are eligible to apply.
Restrictions: The foundation does not award grants to individuals, religious organizations or theological functions, or church-sponsored programs limited to church members. Grants supporting capital campaigns, endowments, or operating expenses are seldom approved.
Geographic Focus: All States
Amount of Grant: 1,000 - 200,000 USD
Contact: Ken Sternad, President; (404) 828-6374; fax (404) 828-7435
Internet: http://responsibility.ups.com/UPS+Foundation/Focus+On+Giving/Diversity
Sponsor: United Parcel Service (UPS) Foundation
55 Glenlake Parkway NE
Atlanta, GA 30328

UPS Foundation Economic and Global Literacy Grants 4730
Since 1989, the UPS Foundation has committed more than $26.4 million addressing the variety of challenges presented by illiteracy. Initially focused on adult literacy and later on workforce and family literacy, today the foundation builds on UPS's knowledge to enable global commerce by teaching people how to effectively compete by enhancing their economic and global literacy. The goal of the Foundation's current grant making is enhancing the economic literacy in communities through programming that teaches the fundamentals of free enterprise and the foundations of economic education. In addition to helping people around the world learn the basics of entrepreneurship and self-sufficiency, the UPS Foundation will also support emerging entrepreneurs through grants to innovative micro enterprise organizations who teach the business skills necessary for success in today's global economy.
Requirements: IRS 501(c)3 tax-exempt organizations are eligible to apply.
Restrictions: The foundation does not award grants to individuals, religious organizations or theological functions, or church-sponsored programs limited to church members. Grants supporting capital campaigns, endowments, or operating expenses are seldom approved.
Geographic Focus: All States
Amount of Grant: 1,000 - 200,000 USD
Contact: Ken Sternad, President; (404) 828-6374; fax (404) 828-7435
Internet: http://responsibility.ups.com/UPS+Foundation/Focus+On+Giving/Economic+and+Global+Literacy
Sponsor: United Parcel Service (UPS) Foundation
55 Glenlake Parkway NE
Atlanta, GA 30328

UPS Foundation Environmental Sustainability Grants 4731
While UPS has long been considered a pioneer in developing ways of reducing its environmental impact, protecting and conserving the natural world is a new area of focus for the UPS Foundation. Operating on a global scale, the foundation will pursue opportunities that help build understanding about the challenges confronting the environment, support programming that helps conserve nature and its bounty, and strengthen the ability of people to enjoy the bounty of our planet. Over the years, the UPS Foundation has periodically supported environmental programming. From clean water initiatives in Africa to support for enhancing Keep America Beautiful's volunteer capacity, foundation grants have been effective in this focus area. The Foundation launched its philanthropic focus on environmental sustainability in 2008 with more than $1.7 million in grants to support a variety of environmental programs and organizations worldwide. These grants support tree planting, conservation efforts, youth education and volunteerism.
Requirements: IRS 501(c)3 tax-exempt organizations are eligible to apply.
Restrictions: The foundation does not award grants to individuals, religious organizations or theological functions, or church-sponsored programs limited to church members. Grants supporting capital campaigns, endowments, or operating expenses are seldom approved.
Geographic Focus: All States
Amount of Grant: 1,000 - 200,000 USD
Contact: Ken Sternad, President; (404) 828-6374; fax (404) 828-7435
Internet: http://responsibility.ups.com/UPS+Foundation/Focus+On+Giving/Environmental+Sustainability
Sponsor: United Parcel Service (UPS) Foundation
55 Glenlake Parkway NE
Atlanta, GA 30328

UPS Foundation Nonprofit Effectiveness Grants 4732
Since the launch of its Volunteer Impact Initiative in 1999, the UPS Foundation has focused on helping nonprofit organizations operate more effectively and efficiently. Widely regarded as a well-run company, UPS provides non-profits a variety of management and operational expertise in areas such as human resources management, technology, and other knowledge resources. This provides a robust hands on component that supports the foundation's philanthropy. It's the perfect example of taking the core assets of the corporation and applying them in a way that helps the independent sector address society's many challenges. Most nonprofit agencies face daunting tasks in raising funds, analyzing needs, managing volunteers and measuring results. With its employees and families volunteering more than 1.2 million hours of their time each year, UPS understands these challenges first hand. Helping nonprofit agencies more effectively manage them can further the impact of the services they provide to local communities. The UPS Foundation is currently focusing its resources on such areas as volunteer management, leadership development, social enterprise, and capacity building through new technology.
Requirements: IRS 501(c)3 tax-exempt organizations are eligible to apply.
Restrictions: The foundation does not award grants to individuals, religious organizations or theological functions, or church-sponsored programs limited to church members. Grants supporting capital campaigns, endowments, or operating expenses are seldom approved.
Geographic Focus: All States
Amount of Grant: 1,000 - 200,000 USD
Contact: Ken Sternad, President; (404) 828-6374; fax (404) 828-7435
Internet: http://responsibility.ups.com/UPS+Foundation/Focus+On+Giving/Nonprofit+Effectiveness
Sponsor: United Parcel Service (UPS) Foundation
55 Glenlake Parkway NE
Atlanta, GA 30328

Ursula Thrush Peace Seed Grants 4733
Ursula Thrush founded the Maria Montessori School of the Golden Gate and Teacher Training Center in San Francisco and helped to establish several other Montessori programs, including The Science of Peace Task Force and the Montessori Peace Academy. Her dedication to fulfilling Maria Montessori's vision for peace through children opened doors to many Montessori educators, inspiring them to include peace education in their classrooms and communities. Since 2004, the AMS Peace Committee has awarded annual Peace Seed Grants to encourage educators to promote peace through their teaching. Lesley Nan Haberman, headmistress of The Family Schools in New York City, initiated the grant in memory of her dear friend Ursula Thrush.
Requirements: Montessorians who have formulated a project fostering education for peace are invited to apply. Applicants must have a Montessori background. The project must further education for peace and must reach a significant number of children and/or educators. The recipient of the grant must share the results of his/her project with the AMS community. The project goal must be accomplished in the year following receipt of the grant. The recipient must show how he/she will be accountable for the use of the funds.
Geographic Focus: All States

Date(s) Application is Due: Feb 1
Amount of Grant: 1,100 USD
Contact: Judi Bauerlein, (212) 358-1250; fax (212) 358-1256; Judi4trees@sbcglobal.net
Internet: http://www.amshq.org/peaceseedconnection.htm#thrushGrant
Sponsor: American Montessori Society
281 Park Avenue South
New York, NY 10010-6102

USAA – Ann Hoyt / Jim Easton JOAD Grants 4734
The Ann Hoyt/Jim Easton Junior Olympic Archery Development (JOAD) Program is made possible by archery legend, Ann Hoyt and current supporter of youth archery, Jim Easton. Through contributions from the Ann Hoyt Legacy Fund and the Easton Sports Development Foundation, JOAD Clubs can request funds for items such as, target butts, stands, archery equipment, general supplies and coaching certification.
Requirements: Applicants do not need to be a qualified 501(c)3 organization in order to receive funding; however, they do need to be an active JOAD club in good standing. Requests may be submitted at any time. USAA will review grants once a quarter. Applications will be reviewed March 1st, June 1st, September 1st, December 1st. Applications must be submitted at least 15 days prior to these deadlines in order to be considered during the upcoming review. Grantees (USAA JOAD Clubs) are required to plan programs, submit grant proposals, respond to inquiries, keep scrupulous records of finances and program participants, and produce written reports to the grantor (USAA) on finances, program goals, and accomplishments.
Geographic Focus: All States
Amount of Grant: Up to 5,000 USD
Contact: Diane Watson, USA Archery JOAD Coordinator; dwatson@usarchery.org
Internet: http://www.esdf.org/apply-for-grant/usaa-ann-hoytjim-easton-joad-grant-application/
Sponsor: Easton Foundations
7855 Haskell Avenue, Suite 260
Van Nuys, CA 91406

USA Football Equipment Grants 4735
As the sport's National Governing Body, and Official Youth Football Development Partner of the NFL and NFL Players Association, USA Football is committed to enhancing the football experience for all at the youth and amateur levels through its Equipment Grants Program. Each year, USA Football awards $1 million in equipment to youth and high school football programs throughout the country. USA Football enables eligible youth football organizations and school-sponsored programs to apply for the following grants: Youth Football Equipment Grant (retail value about $1,000); or High School Equipment Grant (retail value about $1,500).
Geographic Focus: All States
Amount of Grant: 1,000 - 1,500 USD
Contact: Nick Inzerello, Director of Football Development; (877) 536-6822 or (703) 918-0007, ext. 102; ninzerello@usafootball.com
Internet: http://www.nflyff.org/grants/fields-equipment/
Sponsor: USA Football
8300 Boone Boulevard, Suite 625
Vienna, VA 22182

USAID/Cambodia Maternal and Child Health, Tuberculosis, HIV/AIDS. and Malaria Grants 4736
USAID/Cambodia encourages creativity and innovative approaches in the design of the project(s) proposed under this request. Applicants are free to submit more than one concept paper; however, each concept should address one of the four specific areas: maternal and child health; tuberculosis; HIV/AIDS; or malaria. Concept papers must include an illustrative basic budget for the entire proposed program period (not to exceed one year). A detailed budget will be negotiated with accepted concepts during the second step of the application process. The budget for the applicant's program should be within the range stated for each discrete program area. The maximum funding available for this program for a single project is $100,000, and USAID expects to issue one or more awards under this APS.
Requirements: Application eligibility is unrestricted.
Geographic Focus: All States, All Countries
Amount of Grant: 25,000 - 100,000 USD
Contact: Honey Sokry; (855-23) 728 345; hsokry@usaid.gov
Internet: http://www07.grants.gov/search/search.do;jsessionid=Y8hyRkShSpQkpL0lpV1zQMMRWm1GJwQmLsyDjZQJYpyNVJYSk1dy!-1168907641?oppId=211073&mode=VIEW
Sponsor: U.S. Agency for International Development
Ronald Reagan Building
Washington, DC 20523-1000

USAID Accelerating Progress Against Tuberculosis in Kenya Grants 4737
The United States Agency for International Development (USAID) is seeking applications for a Cooperative Agreement to provide funding in support of a program entitled Accelerating Progress Against TB (APA-K) in Kenya. The main objective of this program is to extend access to quality-assured TB services in all districts and for all forms of TB, through the identification and implementation of evidence-based activities that support and/or complement the activities of the Government of Kenya's Division of Leprosy, TB and Lung Diseases. It is expected that a single grant with be funded in the amount of $40,000,000. The deadline for application is April 15.
Requirements: In response to this RFA, only local Kenyan organizations are eligible.
Geographic Focus: Kenya
Date(s) Application is Due: Apr 15
Amount of Grant: 40,000,000 USD
Contact: Jennifer Kiiru, Acquisitions and Assistance Specialist; +254-20-862-2848 or +254-20-862-2000; fax +254-20-862-2680; jkiiru@usaid.gov or usaidke@usaid.gov
Internet: http://www.grants.gov/search/search.do;jsessionid=Ty6nRyTfyLlh9Bp501FpjptxyhJL02HR2D01sPWcc1s9JVyBsr3x!1962156644?oppId=223813&mode=VIEW
Sponsor: U.S. Agency for International Development
Ronald Reagan Building
Washington, DC 20523-1000

USAID African Institutions Innovation Mechanism Grants 4738
A key objective of Feed the Future and the new USAID Forward initiative is to support the CAADP agenda by building the capacity of African regional organizations, private firms, regional trade associations and civil society. USAID is committed to new ways of doing business – shifting away from large contracts with American consulting firms to contracts and grants with more and varied local partners, including NGO's, private sector associations, and small businesses. At the same time, the Mission will continue to support and strengthen host regional systems in the public sector. Over the past years, USAID/East Africa has focused on building the capacity of African institutions, both through direct grants and through short term technical assistance and sub-grants managed by contractors. As part of the Feed the Future strategy, the regional mission will establish a new African Institutions Innovation Mechanism (AIIM). It will have two components: an Annual Program Statement (APS) that will provide an opportunity for African organizations and firms to write proposals to participate in the regional Feed the Future agenda; and a group of professionals available to provide technical services to missions and their partners. AIIM will complement and add value to ongoing support to the Regional Economic Communities and other African regional organizations. Funding ranges from $100,000 to $2,500,000, and the annual deadline is January 1
Requirements: This opportunity is restricted to applicants that are operational in at least two of the following countries and legally registered in one: Burundi, Democratic Republic of the Congo, Djibouti, Ethiopia, Kenya, Rwanda, South Sudan, Sudan, Tanzania, and/or Uganda.
Geographic Focus: All States, Burundi, Congo, Democratic Republic of, Djibouti, Ethiopia, Kenya, Rwanda, Sudan, Tanzania, Uganda
Date(s) Application is Due: Jan 1
Amount of Grant: 100,000 - 2,500,000 USD
Contact: Michael Makosala, Acquisitions and Assistance Specialist; +254-20-862-2848 or +254-20-862-2000; fax +254-20-862-2680; mmakosala@usaid.gov
Internet: http://www.grants.gov/search/search.do;jsessionid=Ty6nRyTfyLlh9Bp501FpjptxyhJL02HR2D01sPWcc1s9JVyBsr3x!1962156644?oppId=147073&mode=VIEW
Sponsor: U.S. Agency for International Development
Ronald Reagan Building
Washington, DC 20523-1000

USAID African Institutions Innovation Mechanism Grants 4739
The objective of the USAID African Institutions Innovation Mechanism Grants program is to seek applications from regional organizations in East Africa for programs that support the U.S. Government's Feed the Future (FTF) strategy for East Africa. The expected number of awards is six (6), and each will range between $100,000 and $1,000,000. The current closing date for applications to be submitted is January 1.
Requirements: Successful applicants must be operational in at least two of the following countries and legally registered in one: Burundi, Democratic Republic of the Congo, Djibouti, Ethiopia, Kenya, Rwanda, Somalia, South Sudan, Sudan, Tanzania, and/or Uganda. Given that this APS is designed to support the regional FTF strategy, applicants and/or their partners must have the experience, presence and organizational mandate to operate in a regional context and contribute to the strategy's regional goals and objectives.
Geographic Focus: Burundi, Congo, Democratic Republic of, Djibouti, Ethiopia, Kenya, Rwanda, Somalia, Sudan, Tanzania, Uganda
Date(s) Application is Due: Jan 1
Amount of Grant: 100,000 - 1,000,000 USD
Contact: Michael Makosala; 254-20-8622000; MMakosala@usaid.gov
Internet: http://www07.grants.gov/search/search.do;jsessionid=1v8kR3HpjBFsc7Z47pRgjfSFjbcHqr2Jf6p2BXMYZTRdnTrpWtT4!1321711693?oppId=230933&mode=VIEW
Sponsor: U.S. Agency for International Development
Ronald Reagan Building
Washington, DC 20523-1000

USAID Albania Critical Economic Growth Areas Grants 4740
The objective of this APS is to support targeted small and medium-scale development activities that serve as catalysts for job creation, increased trade, and economic growth. By strengthening critical elements of Albania agriculture, this program will contribute to economic stabilization and reintegration efforts of returnees in the context of the Eurozone crisis. The range of awards is $500,000 to $1,500,000, and the application deadline is December 28.
Requirements: Local Albanian organizations are eligible to apply.
Geographic Focus: All States, Albania
Date(s) Application is Due: Dec 28
Amount of Grant: 500,000 - 1,500,000 USD
Contact: Brian Aaron; (36-1) 475-4400; fax (36-1) 475-4764; baaron@usaid.gov
Internet: http://www.grants.gov/search/search.do;jsessionid=6wkXRm4XlPrL2gnTXwynW1rnnBXH1gDJQDZdGVySjBTTpwmYrsQT!1762381823?oppId=213133&mode=VIEW
Sponsor: U.S. Agency for International Development
Ronald Reagan Building
Washington, DC 20523-1000

USAID Bengal Tiger Conservation Activity Grants 4741

The United States Agency for International Development in Bangladesh (USAID/Bangladesh) is seeking applications for a four year Cooperative Agreement from qualified Bangladeshi entities to implement a project entitled Bengal Tiger Conservation Activity (Bagh) in Bangladesh. Bagh's approach will protect and improve key tiger habitats, focusing primarily on the Sundarbans but potentially including the habitats of other charismatic species. Healthy, improved ecosystems will provide diversified sustainable livelihoods to communities and better shelter Bangladesh's vulnerable population from tropical cyclones and other negative impacts of climate change. Intact forests and wetlands will also sequester CO_2 and other greenhouse gases to mitigate the effects of climate change. Bagh will be similarly aligned with Government of Bangladesh (GOB) strategies and action plans. Specifically, Bagh is very closely aligned with the Bangladesh Tiger Action Plan. The development hypothesis is that improved wildlife conservation is an effective means to conserve the bio-diverse habitats that millions – especially women and the poor rural population – depend on for their livelihoods. One award/contract will be given, ranging from $10,800,000 to $12,000,000. The application deadline is May 15.
Requirements: To be eligible to receive this Cooperative Agreement, prime applicants must: be organized under the laws of the recipient country; have its principal place of business in the recipient country; be majority owned by individuals who are citizens or lawful permanent residents of the recipient country or be managed by a governing body, the majority of whom are citizens or lawful permanent residents of a recipient country; and not be controlled by a foreign entity or by an individual or individuals who are not citizens or permanent residents of the recipient country.
Geographic Focus: Bangladesh
Date(s) Application is Due: May 15
Amount of Grant: 10,800,000 - 12,000,000 USD
Contact: M. Sirajam Munir, Senior Acquisitions and Assistance Specialist; (880-2) 885-5500; fax (880-2) 882-3648; akarapetyan@usaid.gov
Internet: http://www07.grants.gov/search/search.do;jsessionid=Y8hyRkShSpQkpL0lpV1zQMMRWm1GJwQmLsyDjZQJYpyNVJYSk1dy!-1168907641?oppId=228673&mode=VIEW
Sponsor: U.S. Agency for International Development
Ronald Reagan Building
Washington, DC 20523-1000

USAID Call for Public-Private Alliance Proposals in Serbia 4742

As a development agency established to address poverty, economic growth and governance concerns, USAID strives to maximize the development impact of all its programs. In order to address emerging concerns regarding economic growth in Serbia, USAID/Serbia seeks to engage private sector partners in joint activities intended to accelerate the transition of the Serbian economy and support the EU integration process, in addition to related activities already being implemented in Serbia. In particular, USAID would like to identify ways in which collaboration with the private sector can improve workforce development in Serbia and provide the country with the mix of human capital needed to promote broad-based economic growth, accelerate the transition of the Serbian economy and support the EU integration process. Through this solicitation, USAID/Serbia is looking for proposals that describe and develop approaches that encourage innovative, substantial, and sustainable improvements in the quality and relevance of skills in the workforce.
Requirements: For-profit private companies, qualified locally-registered Serbian Civil Society Organizations (CSOs), non-profit or voluntary organizations, academic institutions, and consulting firms are eligible to apply.
Geographic Focus: All States, Serbia
Contact: Branislav Bulatovic, Acquisitions and Assistance Assistant; +(381) 11 306-4736 or +(381) 11 306-4675; bbulatovic@usaid.gov
Internet: http://serbia.usaid.gov/opportunities/grant-opportunities.1074.html
Sponsor: U.S. Agency for International Development
Ronald Reagan Building
Washington, DC 20523-1000

USAID Civic Participation Program Grants 4743

USAID/West Bank and Gaza intends to provide approximately $18 Million in total USAID funding for this activity to be allocated over a three- year period. USAID reserves the right to fund any or none of the applications submitted. Although it is planned to make an award of one Cooperative Agreement under this RFA, USAID/West Bank and Gaza in its discretion may make awards to more than one organization or no award. The purpose of the Civic Participation Program is to reinvigorate civic participation in the Palestinian Authority (PA) decision-making process, in the monitoring and oversight of government institutions, and in the broader public sector discourse in order to ensure a more vibrant and robust democratic dialogue between the government and the citizens of the future Palestinian state. The three major program objectives are: increased institutional capacity of targeted civil society organizations; increased public awareness of how to participate in public sector decision making with targeted PA institutions and local governmental entities; and new strategic partnerships among government institutions, citizens, civil society actors, and other stakeholders. This activity will support the USAID/West Bank and Gaza Mission's Assistance Objective 11: to reinforce Palestinian efforts to strengthen the performance and democratic practices of selected public sector institutions and non-state actors as outlined in the Mission's Democracy and Governance Strategy. It will be managed by the USAID/WBG's Democracy and Governance Office (DGO). The four program components are as follows: civic participation and CSO capacity buildingp; coalition building; windows of opportunity; and a robust monitoring and evaluation.
Requirements: Qualified U.S. Non-Governmental Organizations (NGOs), U.S. Private Voluntary Organizations (PVOs) registered with USAID, Public International Organizations, or U.S. for profit firms (provided they forgo profit) are eligible to apply.
Geographic Focus: Israel
Date(s) Application is Due: Apr 30
Amount of Grant: 6,000,000 - 18,000,000 USD
Contact: Nevine Zakariya, Acquisitions and Assistance Specialist; +972-3-511-4861 or +972-3-511-4848; fax +972-3-511-4888; spervaiz@usaid.gov
Internet: http://www07.grants.gov/search/search.do;jsessionid=rkvMR4JXpflyGGVJhyMcvClxFntKpQd5YlMn1HLnhMtNGjCG1t2Q!1321711693?oppId=54170&mode=VIEW
Sponsor: U.S. Agency for International Development
Ronald Reagan Building
Washington, DC 20523-1000

USAID Civil Society Sustainability Project (CSSP) Grants in Bosnia and Herzegovina 4744

The United States Agency for International Development (USAID), through the Regional Contracting Office in Kosovo is seeking applications from local Bosnian Non-Governmental Organizations (NGOs) for a Cooperative Agreement to fund a program entitled Civil Society Sustainability Project (CSSP) in Bosnia and Herzegovina (BiH). The authority for this Request for Applications (RFA) is found in the Foreign Assistance Act of 1961, as amended.In support of USAID's efforts to develop local capacity and promote sustainability, eligibility to submit applications under this solicitation is limited to local entities. Subject to the availability of funds, USAID anticipates awarding one cooperative agreement, not to exceed the approximate amount of $8,850,000 in total funding, to a local Bosnian Non-Governmental Organization to be allocated over a five (5) year period. USAID reserves the right to fund any or none of the applications submitted, and will determine the resulting level of funding for the award. Eligible local Bosnian Non-Governmental Organizations interested in submitting an application are encouraged to read the RFA thoroughly to understand the type of program sought and the application submission and evaluation process. The chosen recipient(s) will be responsible for ensuring achievement of the program objectives. The deadline for application is May 12.
Requirements: Local Bosnian non-governmental organizations are eligible to apply.
Geographic Focus: Bosnia & Herzegovina
Date(s) Application is Due: May 12
Amount of Grant: 8,850,000 USD
Contact: Viktoria Hollosy, Acquisitions and Assisstance Specialist; (36-1) 475-4626 or (36-1) 475-4400; fax (36-1) 475-4764; vhollosy@usaid.gov
Internet: http://www.grants.gov/search/search.do;jsessionid=6wkXRm4XlPrL2gnTXwynW1rnnBXH1gDJQDZdGVySjBTTpwmYrsQT!1762381823?oppId=227573&mode=VIEW
Sponsor: U.S. Agency for International Development
Ronald Reagan Building
Washington, DC 20523-1000

USAID Community Infrastructure Development Program Grants 4745

The Community Infrastructure Development Program would respond to small to medium scale infrastructure needs identified by the PA and the USAID/West Bank and Gaza Mission to support improved physical infrastructure. Activities considered under this program will include, but not be limited to, the construction and renovation of schools and kindergartens; upgrade of vocational education schools facilities; rehabilitation and development of youth/women and recreational centers; rehabilitation and development of roads, sidewalks and public parks; and upgrading and renovation of NGO/private health facilities. The objectives are to: provide basic multi-sector infrastructure packages to remote communities in order to raise their standard of living; support requests to increase the impact of USAID-funded programs in health, democracy and governance, education and the private sector by addressing underlying infrastructure needs which may be limiting the impact of those programs; and to the full extent practicable, provide employment opportunities to Palestinian communities, enhance local government capacity to respond to urgent infrastructure needs, and encourage community participation and empowerment in the planning, design, construction, and maintenance of public infrastructure.
Requirements: U.S. Non-Governmental Organizations (U.S. NGOs), U.S. Private Voluntary Organization (PVO), Public International Organizations (PIO), or a U.S. for profit firm (provided they forgo profit) actively engaged in activities consistent with the program objectives may submit applications.
Geographic Focus: All States
Date(s) Application is Due: Apr 16
Amount of Grant: 15,000,000 - 100,000,000 USD
Contact: Sandy Sakran, Grantor; +972-3-511-4870 or +972-3-511-4848; fax +972-3-511-4888; ssakran@usaid.gov or wbg@usaid.gov
Internet: http://www07.grants.gov/search/search.do;jsessionid=rkvMR4JXpflyGGVJhyMcvClxFntKpQd5YlMn1HLnhMtNGjCG1t2Q!1321711693?oppId=53806&mode=VIEW
Sponsor: U.S. Agency for International Development
Ronald Reagan Building
Washington, DC 20523-1000

USAID Community Livelihoods Project in Yemen Grant 4746

The Community Livelihoods Project in Yemen will be expected to build on and complement ongoing activities during the transition phase between the existing portfolio of USAID/Yemen projects and this flagship initiative. Very close coordination and collaboration with the Mission's future National Governance Project (NGP) will be extremely important during the implementation of the CLP. The implementer also will partner with and make extensive use of local, Yemeni organizations during the implementation of the project. The implementer also will coordinate with USAID's future Monitoring and Evaluation Project to help ensure that program results are tracked against stability measures. The strategy will be released when this solicitation is released for bid. USAID anticipates an award for a base period of three years with the potential for follow-on activities dependent on performance

and availability of funding. Subject to the availability of funds, the estimated budget for the three year base period is approximately $65 million. A single award is expected in the amount of $65,000,000 and, at the present, there is no designated application deadline.
Geographic Focus: All States, All Countries
Amount of Grant: 65,000,000 USD
Contact: Botros Wilson, Acquisitions Specialist; +20-2-516-6921 or +20-2-522-7000; fax +20-2-522-7197; YemenNGPRFA1@usaid.gov
Internet: http://www.grants.gov/search/search.do;jsessionid=6wkXRm4XlPrL2gnTXwynW 1rnnBXH1gDJQDZdGVySjBTTpwmYrsQT!1762381823?oppId=50471&mode=VIEW
Sponsor: U.S. Agency for International Development
Ronald Reagan Building
Washington, DC 20523-1000

USAID Comprehensive District-Based Support for Better HIV/TB Patient Outcomes Grants   **4747**
The United States Government, as represented by the United States Agency for International Development (USAID) Mission to Southern Africa, is seeking applications from organizations interested in implementing a five-year comprehensive district-based HIV-related services support program for better patient outcomes, as fully described in this Request for Applications (RFA). The purpose of this program is to strengthen SAG systems in order to improve patient outcomes and prevent HIV by supporting comprehensive clinic-based HIV-related services in select districts. All support will be in line with SAG national, provincial and district policies, standards, guidelines, and implementation plans as well as the Partnership Framework between the USG and SAG. The program will build and capitalize on the accomplishments and lessons learned since the national ARV rollout began in 2004. It will focus on institutionalization of routine and consistent use of systems designed to improve efficiencies in district and sub-district management that ultimately improve patient and public health outcomes.
Requirements: Any local South African non-governmental organizations (NGOs), private voluntary organizations (PVOs), Faith-based and community organizations, and for-profit companies willing to forego profit will be eligible for award under this RFA. In support of the Agency's interest in fostering a larger assistance base and expanding the number and sustainability of development partners, USAID encourages applications from potential new partners.
Geographic Focus: South Africa
Amount of Grant: Up to 20,000,000 USD
Contact: Beatrice Lumanade, Acquisitions and Assistance Specialist; +27 12 452 2377 or +27 12 452 2000; blumande@usaid.gov or applications4@usaid.gov
Internet: http://www07.grants.gov/search/search.do;jsessionid=1v8kR3HpjBFsc7Z47pRgj fSFjbcHqr2Jf6p2BXMYZTRdnTrpWtT4!1321711693?oppId=169154&mode=VIEW
Sponsor: U.S. Agency for International Development
Ronald Reagan Building
Washington, DC 20523-1000

USAID Development Assistance Fund Grants   **4748**
The United States Agency for International Development (USAID) Mission in Peru is seeking applications from for-profit, not-for-profit, and public Peruvian organizations to implement activities that support USAID/Peru's development objectives under the Development Assistance Fund (DAF). The objective of this APS is to support small-scale development activities that benefit underserved Peruvian communities and/or populations suffering social inequities. DAF crosscuts all USAID/Peru program areas and seeks funding applications from organizations and local communities with project applications that: advance local economic growth; promote health and education; foster stronger democratic practices and community level organizations; pursue licit livelihoods in former coca-growing regions; and increase awareness of and resiliency to the impact of climate change. Up to fourteen (14) grants will be awarded, ranging from $5,000 to $50,000. The deadline for application is June 6.
Requirements: Applicants must be legally registered to operate in Peru and may include private entities, Non-Governmental Organizations (NGOs), as well as other non-profit organizations including: universities, research organizations, professional associations, community-based organizations, municipalities, regional and local government bodies, and/or relevant special interest associations. For-profit companies may also apply for DAF grants.
Geographic Focus: Peru
Date(s) Application is Due: Jun 6
Amount of Grant: 5,000 - 50,000 USD
Contact: Jose Antonio Zarzar, Acquisitions and Assistance Specialist; (511) 618-1253; limasolicitations@usaid.gov
Internet: http://www.grants.gov/search/search.do;jsessionid=n9BzRwGpSrYLypK2VY2L L16RLylhQ7lSqgvlxnVBdbzT7pwv85QQ!-1898900577?oppId=175214&mode=VIEW
Sponsor: U.S. Agency for International Development
Ronald Reagan Building
Washington, DC 20523-1000

USAID Development Innovation Ventures Grants   **4749**
As part of its commitment to increase investments and engagement in cost-efficient innovations, USAID launched Development Innovation Ventures (DIV) as a way of producing development outcomes more effectively and cost-efficiently while managing risk and obtaining leverage. Through DIV, USAID seeks to identify and rigorously test promising projects with the potential to significantly (rather than incrementally) improve development outcomes, and help replicate and scale projects that are proven successful. USAID/DIV expects its most successful of investments will have an accelerated growth path to reach tens of millions of beneficiaries worldwide within 10 years. DIV Grants will support projects at three stages: Stage 1, the development needed to support proof of concept and feasibility; Stage 2, implementing the project at large scale with rigorous impact testing; and Stage 3, transitioning innovations to widespread adoption throughout one country and/or additional adoption in other countries. For Stage 1 applicants, a Concept Paper and its attachments are the only application documents required. Stage 2 and 3 applicants may submit a Concept Paper and wait to be invited (or not) to submit a Full Application. Alternatively Stage 2 and 3 applicants may elect to forego the Concept Paper and submit a Full Application. Interested applicants must first submit an Letters of Interest using the LOI form posted. Only invited applicants will receive the Full Application form.
Requirements: USAID/DIV welcomes applications from many types of organizations, including: U.S. non-governmental organizations (NGOs); non-U.S. NGOs; faith-based organizations; U.S. private businesses; non-U.S private businesses; business and trade associations; international organizations; U.S. colleges and universities (public and private); non-U.S. colleges and universities (public and private); civic groups; regional organizations; and foundations.
Restrictions: All applicants must be legally recognized organizational entities under applicable law. Individuals and governments are not eligible to apply directly at this time. The participation of foreign government organizations under this APS is possible only through an approved subaward agreement with a prime recipient.
Geographic Focus: All States, All Countries
Date(s) Application is Due: Apr 12
Amount of Grant: 100,000 - 15,000,000 USD
Contact: Tameka Laws, Grantor; (202) 567-5066; DIVApplications@usaid.gov
Internet: http://idea.usaid.gov/organization/div
Sponsor: U.S. Agency for International Development
Ronald Reagan Building
Washington, DC 20523-1000

USAID Economic Prospectsfor Armenia-Turkey Normalization Grants   **4750**
The primary objective of activities under this Annual Program Statement (APS) is to increase mutually beneficial economic partnerships and linkages between Armenian and Turkish organizations to promote longer-term economic development and Armenia-Turkey reconciliation. The APS allows for a range of ideas, focusing on various mutually-beneficial partnership opportunities and economic prospects to foster Armenia-Turkey reconciliation. This is an Annual Program Statement and applications are due to USAID/Armenia on October 15. Applications received from the initial posting date through March 18, will be reviewed and considered for award in the current fiscal year; applications received from March 19, through October 15, will be reviewed and considered for award in the next fiscal year. Grants will range from $100,000 to $500,000.
Requirements: Potential partners include Armenian registered organizations owned and operated by Armenians, such as private businesses, business and trade organizations, think-tanks, business-oriented NGOs and private for-profit companies willing to forego profit. Potential local private for-profit applicants should note that the payment of fee/profit to the prime recipient under grants and cooperative agreements is not allowed. Only those applications that identify agreed upon partnerships with Turkish counterpart organizations will be eligible for award.
Geographic Focus: All States, All Countries
Date(s) Application is Due: Oct 15
Amount of Grant: 100,000 - 500,000 USD
Contact: Narine Sarkisian, Acquisition Specialist; (374 10) 494 364 or (374 10) 464 700; fax (374 10) 464 728; nsarkisian@usaid.gov or armeniacontact@usaid.gov
Internet: http://armenia.usaid.gov/en/node/48
Sponsor: U.S. Agency for International Development
Ronald Reagan Building
Washington, DC 20523-1000

USAID Family Health Plus Project Grants   **4751**
The purpose of this activity is to expand contraceptive choices in family planning and reproductive health by increasing the availability of long acting methods of family planning in Nigeria. This activity will support USAID/Nigeria's goal of increasing the use of high impact interventions, within the Investing in People Foreign Assistance objective. The project will identify suitable training venues to provide experience in implants and IUDs and adopt a practical curriculum to cover these topics. The project will visit the proposed training venues to ensure that there is adequate patient flow and that good quality procedures are being used and taught. Project staff themselves do not need to provide this training but must be able to assess the capacity of other trainers to provide good quality training. If possible, sites within the trainees' own state would be preferred; especially those also used as training sites for nursing or midwife schools. A single funding award is anticipated in the amount of $9,000,000. The annual posted deadline for applications is May 23.
Requirements: Nigerian non-governmental organizations are eligible to submit applications. Applicants must have established financial management, monitoring and evaluation, internal control systems, and policies and procedures that comply with established U.S. Government standards, laws, and regulations. All potential awardees will be subject to a responsibility determination (this may include a pre-award survey) issued by a warranted Agreements Officer in USAID.
Geographic Focus: Nigeria
Amount of Grant: 9,000,000 USD
Contact: Ugo Oguejiofor; +234 803 900 9300; abujafhplus@usaid.gov
Internet: http://www07.grants.gov/search/search.do;jsessionid=3YLtRvGZL1CMpzgyybZ8 WNC1DsyRSGC97kmvZ9BS6c5VQ1SvFSbL!1866286003?oppId=229613&mode=VIEW
Sponsor: U.S. Agency for International Development
Ronald Reagan Building
Washington, DC 20523-1000

USAID Food Security, Nutrition, Biodiversity and Conservation Grants 4752

USAID continues its commitment to foster more strategic alliances with the private sector's "solution holders" who are often well positioned to address specific development challenges. USAID-Uganda Food Security, Nutrition, Biodiversity and Conservation Grants will fund a limited number of Public Private Alliances to enhance food security and address issues of biodiversity and conservation. There are two key priority areas: food security and nutrition; and biodiversity and conservation. In regards to food security and nutrition, USAID-Uganda is seeking priority partnerships that include promising methods for substantially advancing coffee, maize, beans, agro-inputs, nutritional food products, financial services, and information and communication technologies solutions. Biodiversity priorities include innovative methods for promoting ecotourism as well as averting ecological and transboundary threats. Grants will be offered for two years. The number of awards is variable and subject to change. Competition is a two-step process where applicants first submit a Concept Paper. After review USAID will invite successful applicants to submit a Full Application. The Full Application will offer the applicant the opportunity to explain its technical approach in more detail.
Requirements: Applicants are expected to leverage USAID resources on at least a one-to-one basis, with a strong preference for realizing a three-to-one leverage ratio. Place of performance for these Grants is Uganda. Application eligibility is unrestricted.
Geographic Focus: All States, All Countries
Date(s) Application is Due: Jun 14
Amount of Grant: Up to 17,000,000 USD
Contact: Sarah Acio, Acquisitions and Assistance Specialist; +256 414-306-001; sacio@uganda.gov or KampalaUSAIDAPS@usaid.gov
Internet: http://www07.grants.gov/search/search.do;jsessionid=rkvMR4JXpflyGGVJhyMcvClxFntKpQd5YlMn1HLnhMtNGjCG1t2Q!1321711693?oppId=90013&mode=VIEW
Sponsor: U.S. Agency for International Development
Ronald Reagan Building
Washington, DC 20523-1000

USAID Global Development Alliance Grants 4753

The U.S. Agency for International Development (USAID) is committed to increasing the sustainable impact of its development assistance programs through strategic alliances with the private sector. Such alliances enable the Agency to leverage private sector markets, expertise, interests, and assets in a manner that solves critical development problems and promotes effective market led development. They also enable the private sector to leverage USAID's expertise, assets and working relationships in a manner that advances business success and fosters the broader economic growth and poverty reduction that is vital to sustaining such success. Through strategic and ongoing collaboration, the private sector and USAID are better able to increase the impact, reach, efficiency, and effectiveness of our respective investments in developing countries worldwide. This Global Development Alliance (GDA) Annual Program Statement (APS) is designed to catalyze, facilitate and support such collaboration.
Requirements: USAID seeks to develop new and innovative alliances with the private sector, including local and multinational corporations, foundations, non-governmental organizations, and academia.
Restrictions: Proposals that do not leverage resources by at least matching the amount requested will not be considered.
Geographic Focus: All States, All Countries
Date(s) Application is Due: Jan 31
Contact: Suhaib Khan, Contracting Officer; (202) 567-5059; sukhan@usaid.gov
Internet: http://www07.grants.gov/search/search.do;jsessionid=kGnXRdGLdv3SbzZvRgnNLtS1jvTlZ8qs4Tcf1kvwg8y5TtT8hcN1!1884755759?oppId=223974&mode=VIEW
Sponsor: U.S. Agency for International Development
Ronald Reagan Building
Washington, DC 20523-1000

USAID Grant for Operationalizing a Neighborhood Approach to Reduce Urban Disaster Risk in Latin America and the Caribbean 4754

The objective of this APS is to support innovative and/or proven ways to reduce the risk of disasters to populations living in in hazard-prone, marginalized and vulnerable urban settlements, through applying the Neighborhood Approach. Applicants demonstrating expertise and strong contextual understanding of proposed locations based on prior comprehensive participatory urban risk assessments will receive preference. Furthermore, OFDA will give preference to proposals that take a multi-hazard approach. OFDA is interested in supporting activities that would minimize the interruption of key services and livelihoods during a major disaster. While the primary goal of proposed interventions will be the reduction of communal disaster risk, activities funded under this APS may also provide secondary benefits in the form of improved safety of individual households' housing stock, reduction of households' risk of contracting waterborne diseases, and improvements to livelihoods.
Requirements: OFDA will not accept applications from individuals. All applicants must be legally recognized organizational entities under applicable law. Applicants must complete all required steps (if any) with the host government to legally operate their program before implementing their program.
Geographic Focus: All States
Date(s) Application is Due: May 8
Amount of Grant: Up to 2,000,000 USD
Contact: Acquisitions Specialist; support@grants.gov
Internet: http://www.grants.gov/search/search.do;jsessionid=Ty6nRyTfyLlh9Bp501FpjptxyhJL02HR2D01sPWcc1s9JVyBsr3x!1962156644?oppId=224273&mode=VIEW
Sponsor: U.S. Agency for International Development
Ronald Reagan Building
Washington, DC 20523-1000

USAID Grants for Building Disaster-Resilient Communities in Southern Africa 4755

OFDA's mandate is to save lives, alleviate human suffering, and reduce the social and economic impact of disasters worldwide. In order to achieve this goal, OFDA is seeking applications that address our strategic priorities and aim to reduce disaster risks and strengthen preparedness of vulnerable individuals and families and their communities throughout vulnerable areas of the Southern Africa region. All proposed interventions must be targeted at populations that are demonstrated to be particularly vulnerable to drought or flooding. Under this APS, OFDA is looking for innovative and proven ways of: building on the substantial investments in agriculture and nutrition interventions, by supporting complementary water, sanitation and hygiene (WASH) programming and community-based disaster risk management programming for the same at-risk populations to help fill gaps and address unmet needs; or further increasing resilience of the target population by integrating interventions that aim to enhance agriculture and food security, foster improved nutrition uptake through WASH waterborne disease mitigation; and improve community preparedness to natural disasters through community-based disaster risk management programs. The program duration is for up to 24 months from the date of award. OFDA anticipates that up to approximately USD 6.5 million will be available to support the program(s) or activity(ies) described herein. While no ceiling has been established on the magnitude of individual applications, applicants are encouraged to keep costs reasonable in relation to the scope of their proposed activities, recognizing that the total funding under this APS will cover a range of efforts.
Requirements: All applicants must be legally recognized organizational entities under applicable law. Eligible applicants include: public and state controlled institutions of higher education; Native American tribal governments (Federally recognized); nonprofits having a 501(c)3 status with the IRS, other than institutions of higher education; private institutions of higher education; for profit organizations other than small businesses; or small businesses.
Restrictions: OFDA will not accept applications from individuals.
Geographic Focus: All States
Date(s) Application is Due: Jul 11
Amount of Grant: Up to 6,500,000 USD
Contact: Agreement Specialist; OFDA_APS@ofda.gov
Internet: http://www07.grants.gov/search/search.do;jsessionid=kGnXRdGLdv3SbzZvRgnNLtS1jvTlZ8qs4Tcf1kvwg8y5TtT8hcN1!1884755759?oppId=215273&mode=VIEW
Sponsor: U.S. Agency for International Development
Ronald Reagan Building
Washington, DC 20523-1000

USAID Haiti Disaster Risk Reduction Capacity Building Grants 4756

Pursuant to the Foreign Assistance Act of 1961, as amended (FAA), the United States Government (USG), as represented by the U.S. Agency for International Development (USAID), Bureau for Democracy, Conflict, and Humanitarian Assistance (DCHA), Office of U.S. Foreign Disaster Assistance (OFDA) is seeking to support or stimulate the activities described in this Annual Program Statement (APS). The scope of the APS is to build capacity of the Directorate of Civil Protection (DPC) with: institutional support while complementing the current efforts of the Government of Haiti and international community, notably OFDA, USAID/Haiti, and SOUTHCOM; and a rapid response mechanism for helping meet urgent needs following a disaster in the department. The project will fall under OFDA's Risk Management Policy and Practice sector and both the Capacity Building/Training and Building Community Awareness/Mobilization subsectors. For more information, please review the full announcement of this APS. The maximum amount of funding support being offered is $250,000.
Requirements: Eligibility to apply is unrestricted.
Geographic Focus: All States, All Countries
Date(s) Application is Due: Sep 16
Amount of Grant: Up to 250,000 USD
Contact: Agreement Specialist; (800) 518-4726; OFDA_APS_FY13_009@ofda.gov or support@grants.gov
Internet: http://www07.grants.gov/search/search.do;jsessionid=kGnXRdGLdv3SbzZvRgnNLtS1jvTlZ8qs4Tcf1kvwg8y5TtT8hcN1!1884755759?oppId=227161&mode=VIEW
Sponsor: U.S. Agency for International Development
Ronald Reagan Building
Washington, DC 20523-1000

USAID HIV Prevention with Key Populations - Mali Grants 4757

The USAID/Mali HIV Prevention Program aims to provide HIV prevention services to one or more of the following key populations (KPs): men who have sex with men (MSM); commercial sex workers (CSWs); and/or HIV positive individuals through Positive Health Dignity and Prevention (PHDP). The primary goal is to reduce HIV prevalence among KPs in Mali and among the general population through behavior change communication (BCC), HIV counseling and testing, sexually transmitted infections (STI) management, and distribution and promotion of condoms and lubricants. Activities to be funded through this RFA should be in line with the U.S. Government (USG) Mali HIV/AIDS Strategic Plan 2010-2015 and will support the United States' President's Emergency Plan for AIDS Relief (PEPFAR) initiative. It is anticipated that three (3) awards will be funded, ranging from $600,000 to $2,000,000. The next upcoming deadline is May 8.
Requirements: All local Mali organizations are eligible to apply.
Geographic Focus: Mali
Date(s) Application is Due: May 8
Amount of Grant: 600,000 - 2,000,000 USD
Contact: Zachary Clarke, Contracting and Agreement Officer; +223 20 70 27 78 or +223 20 70 23 00; fax +223 20 22 39 33; zclarke@usaid.gov
Internet: http://www.grants.gov/search/search.do;jsessionid=k9ywRnXcGzJNZf5yyFK5MkJyHQhBHGTQlcyJyyVN9yBxlqx5pC5V!1866286003?oppId=225213&mode=VIEW

Sponsor: U.S. Agency for International Development
Ronald Reagan Building
Washington, DC 20523-1000

USAID Implementation Science for Strengthening Use of Evidence in Family Planning/Reproductive Health Programming Grants 4758

The United States Agency for International Development (USAID), the Office of Population and Reproductive Health (PRH), in the Bureau of Global Health (GH), seeks applications for a Cooperative Agreement from eligible for-profit, not-for-profit, or private voluntary organizations (PVO) (and any combination of those organizations) for a program titled Implementation Science for Strengthening Use of Evidence in FP/RH Programming (ISSUE FP/RH). The authority for the RFA can be found in the Foreign Assistance Act of 1961, as amended. USAID's objective with this solicitation is strategic generation, translation, and use of new and existing evidence to improve FP/RH programming worldwide. Specifically, USAID seeks assistance to: generate evidence through high quality research to increase the effectiveness of FP/RH programming; synthesize and share existing and new evidence to accelerate scale-up of evidence-based FP/RH programming; and provide technical assistance for use of evidence to improve FP/RH programming worldwide. The Agency expects to award a single grant in the amount of $150,000,000.
Requirements: For-profit organizations, non-profit organizations, and private voluntary organizations are eligible to apply.
Geographic Focus: All States
Date(s) Application is Due: May 16
Amount of Grant: 100,000,000 USD
Contact: Franklin Goode, Agreement Specialist; (202) 567-5316; fgoode@usaid.gov
Internet: http://www07.grants.gov/search/search.do;jsessionid=kGnXRdGLdv3SbzZvRgn NLtS1jvTlZ8qs4Tcf1kvwg8y5TtT8hcN1!1884755759?oppId=228953&mode=VIEW
Sponsor: U.S. Agency for International Development
Ronald Reagan Building
Washington, DC 20523-1000

USAID In-Support for Teacher Education Program (In-STEP) Grants 4759

USAID/India seeks a U.S. School of Education (SOE) to implement a three to five month customized teacher training program for approximately 100-110 teacher educators from India. The first group of 50 plus teacher educators would arrive in the U.S. on or around September 15, and the second group on or around September 15 the following year. The purpose of the proposed project, the India – Support for Teacher Education Program (In-STEP), is to build the capacity of Indian teacher educators (and administrators) by exposing them to the talent, methodologies, and expertise offered by U.S. Schools of Education (SOEs). It is expected that these teacher educators will take the practices and methodologies learned in the U.S. and apply them to the Indian context. One award will be approved for $4,300,000. The application deadline is May 10.
Requirements: Applicants must be legally established U.S. Public or Private Colleges (Schools of Education) that specialize in formal educator training.
Geographic Focus: All States
Date(s) Application is Due: May 10
Amount of Grant: 4,300,000 USD
Contact: Sumit Dutta, Acquisitions and Assisstance Specialist; 91-11-24198547 or 91-11-24198000; fax 91-11-24198612; sdutta@usaid.gov
Internet: http://www.grants.gov/search/search.do;jsessionid=6wkXRm4XlPrL2gnTXwynW 1rnnBXH1gDJQDZdGVySjBTTpwmYrsQT!1762381823?oppId=228393&mode=VIEW
Sponsor: U.S. Agency for International Development
Ronald Reagan Building
Washington, DC 20523-1000

USAID India-Africa Agriculture Innovation Bridge Grants 4760

The purpose of this Annual Program Statement (APS) is to invite applicants to propose the sharing of proven Indian agriculture innovations in Kenya, Liberia, and Malawi, which are the USAID Feed the Future focus countries in Africa. The APS is open for submission of concept papers until December 30, with four rounds of concept paper submissions on a quarterly basis. Concept papers received until the deadlines provided on the cover page of the APS will be evaluated by USAID to decide which of these warrant an invitation to submit a full application. At the discretion of USAID, concept papers received after the first round of evaluations may be considered on a rolling basis or as a part of another round of evaluations. The process will be repeated for all concept papers received up to Dec 30, 2013. Submission instructions for the concept papers and full application are provided in Section III of the APS. USAID does not guarantee that any award shall be made against this APS. The expected number of awards is four, with funding ranging from $500,000 to $2,000,000.
Requirements: Prime recipients should be local Indian organizations that are private, non-profit organizations (or for-profit companies willing to forego profits), including private voluntary organizations, universities, research organizations, professional associations, and relevant special interest associations.
Geographic Focus: All States, India
Date(s) Application is Due: Dec 30
Contact: Sumit Dutta, Acquisitions and Assistance Specialist; 91-11-24198568 or 91-11-24198000; fax 91-11-24198612; vvats@usaid.gov or indiarco@usaid.gov
Internet: http://www.grants.gov/search/search.do;jsessionid=Ty6nRyTfyLlh9Bp501Fpjptx yhJL02HR2D01sPWcc1s9JVyBsr3x!1962156644?oppId=212173&mode=VIEW
Sponsor: U.S. Agency for International Development
Ronald Reagan Building
Washington, DC 20523-1000

USAID India Partnership Grants 4761

USAID/India's invitation goes out to prospective implementing partners (e.g. NGOs, private sector concerns, and others) who can engage and work with resource partners (e.g. corporations, local businesses, foundations, and others). USAID/India is specifically seeking Indian implementing organizations (for-profit and not-for-profit) and non-traditional Indian development partners, to reach out to Indian resource partners and explore ways in which collaboration with USAID/India might help each partner – private sector, NGO, and public sector contributors – to more effectively address key issues, advance shared development goals, and achieve exceptional development results and impacts in India and beyond. For greater sustainability and country ownership, USAID/India seeks Partnerships in which Indian organizations would lead implementation in collaboration with others. The expected number of awards is five, and funding will be approximately $1,000,000 for each. The posted deadline February 28.
Requirements: This funding opportunity is unrestricted.
Geographic Focus: All States, All Countries
Date(s) Application is Due: Feb 28
Contact: Vandana Vats, Acquisitions and Assistance Specialist; 91-11-24198568 or 91-11-24198000; fax 91-11-24198612; vvats@usaid.gov or indiarco@usaid.gov
Internet: http://www.grants.gov/search/search.do;jsessionid=Ty6nRyTfyLlh9Bp501Fpjptx yhJL02HR2D01sPWcc1s9JVyBsr3x!1962156644?oppId=222653&mode=VIEW
Sponsor: U.S. Agency for International Development
Ronald Reagan Building
Washington, DC 20523-1000

USAID Integration of Care and Support within the Health System to Support Better Patient Outcomes Grants 4762

The purpose of the USAID Integration of Care and Support within the Health System to Support Better Patient Outcomes Grants program is to support and strengthen integration of care and support services within the broader health system, and to strengthen community systems and organizations to ensure the provision of a continuum of comprehensive care and support services (palliative care). Two awards are anticipated, with each ranging up to $25,000,000. The posted annual application deadline is May 16.
Requirements: Any local South African non-governmental organization (NGO) and for-profit organization meeting the criteria in section III is eligible to apply.
Geographic Focus: South Africa
Date(s) Application is Due: May 16
Contact: Martha Zhou, Grantor; +012-452-2179; mzhou@usaid.gov
Internet: http://www07.grants.gov/search/search.do;jsessionid=1v8kR3HpjBFsc7Z47pRgj fSFjbcHqr2Jf6p2BXMYZTRdnTrpWtT4!1321711693?oppId=230173&mode=VIEW
Sponsor: U.S. Agency for International Development
Ronald Reagan Building
Washington, DC 20523-1000

USAID International Emergency Food Assistance Grants 4763

USAID's Office of Food for Peace (FFP) is the United States Government leader in international food assistance. FFP manages the Emergency Food Security Program which provides cash that can be used for local and regional purchase of food and other interventions such as food vouchers and cash transfers. The program provide emergency food assistance to address needs arising from natural disasters, such as floods or droughts, and complex emergencies often characterized by insecurity and population displacement. FFP emergency resources are prioritized for use in relief activities that address acute needs as well as early recovery activities. Applicants may submit concept papers, and approved applicants will be invited to submit a full proposal.
Requirements: The following are eligible: nonprofits having a 501(c)3 status with the IRS, other than institutions of higher education; nonprofits that do not have a 501(c)3 status with the IRS, other than institutions of higher education; private institutions of higher education; for profit organizations other than small businesses; and small businesses.
Geographic Focus: All States
Date(s) Application is Due: Sep 30
Contact: Agreement Officer; FFPEmergency@macf.com
Internet: http://www07.grants.gov/search/search.do;jsessionid=pT8wPqGTTngC6tQHhh 2yQmGGf1mtN8xJ52fjQnL76xz7C18M1Ysn!748281696?oppId=88013&mode=VIEW
Sponsor: U.S. Agency for International Development
Ronald Reagan Building
Washington, DC 20523-1000

USAID International Food Relief Partnership Grants 4764

The International Food Relief Partnership (IFRP) is a U.S. Agency For International Development (USAID) program to support the production, stockpiling, transportation, delivery, and distribution of shelf-stable, prepackaged foods by U.S. non-profit and Public International Organizations (PIO). This request for applications (RFA) applies to applications for grants for the transportation, delivery and distribution of IFRP products. Grants range up to $150,000, and the application deadline is May 8.
Requirements: Nonprofits having a 501(c)3 status with the IRS, other than institutions of higher education, are eligible to apply.
Geographic Focus: All States
Date(s) Application is Due: May 8
Contact: Ben Vogler, Program Manager; ifrp@amexdc2.com
Internet: http://www07.grants.gov/search/search.do;jsessionid=1v8kR3HpjBFsc7Z47pRgj fSFjbcHqr2Jf6p2BXMYZTRdnTrpWtT4!1321711693?oppId=230574&mode=VIEW
Sponsor: U.S. Agency for International Development
Ronald Reagan Building
Washington, DC 20523-1000

USAID Knowledge for Health II Grants 4765
Through its Knowledge for Health II program, USAID proposes a global cooperative agreement focused on strengthening knowledge and information use and exchange among health program managers and service providers, particularly in the areas of family planning and reproductive health (FP/RH). The proposed project, Knowledge for Health Phase II (K4Health-II), is expected to build on USAID's efforts to facilitate knowledge and information use and exchange among key audiences—health program managers and service providers—by developing, improving, and promoting the use of robust knowledge management (KM) practices and services. One award in the amount of $40,000,000 is expected.
Requirements: U.S. based-non-profit, for profit, private voluntary organization, Institution of Higher Education and Non-U.S. nongovernmental international organizations are eligible to apply.
Geographic Focus: All States, All Countries
Date(s) Application is Due: Apr 23
Amount of Grant: 40,000,000 USD
Contact: Samuel Bishop, Agreements Specialist; (202) 567-5298; sbishop@usaid.gov
Internet: http://www07.grants.gov/search/search.do;jsessionid=kGnXRdGLdv3SbzZvRgn NLtS1jvTlZ8qs4Tcf1kvwg8y5TtT8hcN1!1884755759?oppId=228373&mode=VIEW
Sponsor: U.S. Agency for International Development
Ronald Reagan Building
Washington, DC 20523-1000

USAID Leadership Initiative for Good Governance in Africa Grants 4766
The purpose of the Leadership Initiative for Good Governance in Africa (LIGGA) is to promote a culture of good governance and leaders of integrity who eschew corruption in Africa. Strengthening good governance, developing leadership capacity, modeling integrity, and promoting accountability is the focus of LIGGA, with emphasis on transparency, oversight mechanisms, representativeness and responsiveness, respect for human rights, and principles of inclusion, participation, and public service. Applications should be designed to enhance benefiting individuals and organizations ability to contribute positively and demonstrably to such aspects of democratic governance. Successful applications under this funding opportunity will describe an approach that leads to concrete, measurable, and sustainable improvements in democratic good governance in Africa. Interventions could include but are not limited to exchange programs; extended trainings, educational programs, or fellowships; small grant incentive funds; study tours; short courses or workshops; or other creative means to be proposed. All applicants should promote a participatory approach appropriate for professional adult learners and describe a cohesive methodology targeted at a specific impact. Applications should offer programs that include participation from multiple African countries. Awards will range from $200,000 to $1,500,000.
Requirements: Eligible applicants include: U.S. and non-U.S. non-profit organizations; U.S. and non-U.S. for-profit organizations; U.S. and non-U.S. colleges and universities.
Geographic Focus: All States, All Countries
Date(s) Application is Due: Apr 24
Amount of Grant: 200,000 - 1,500,000 USD
Contact: LIGGA Team; LIGGAAPS@usaid.gov
Internet: http://www.grants.gov/search/search.do;jsessionid=JLnfQ2dXjGsLJMk6qcndyn ccd2Y8QYb2vGLdchNvr5WhGqZ80RGb!99807221?oppId=167133&mode=VIEW
Sponsor: U.S. Agency for International Development
Ronald Reagan Building
Washington, DC 20523-1000

USAID Malawi Local Capacity Development Initiative Grants 4767
The purpose of this Annual Purpose Statement (APS) is to disseminate information to prospective applicants so that they may develop and submit applications for USAID funding. This APS may provide funding opportunities in the following four (4) program areas: Sustainable Economic Growth – Malawi Agriculture Policy Strengthening (MAPS) Program; Education - Strengthening Early Grade Reading for Malawi Children Program; Health, Nutrition and Population – Further details will be provided via an amendment to this APS; and Mainstreaming Activities involving the Disabled. The funding range is $150,000 to $1,500,000, and the annual deadline is listed as April 26.
Requirements: Registered local (Malawian) and regional (East or Southern African) non-governmental organizations, non-profit organizations and for-profit organizations may apply.
Geographic Focus: Angola, Botswana, Kenya, Malawi, Namibia, South Africa, Tanzania
Date(s) Application is Due: Apr 26
Amount of Grant: 150,000 - 1,500,000 USD
Contact: Joseph Chisoni Tembo, +2-6517-72-45; jtembo@usaid.gov
Craig Lamberton, (202) 712-4314; clamberton@usaid.gov
Internet: http://www.grants.gov/search/search.do;jsessionid=k9ywRnXcGzJNZf5yyFK5M kJyHQhBHGTQlcyJyyVN9yBxlqx5pC5V!1866286003?oppId=168937&mode=VIEW
Sponsor: U.S. Agency for International Development
Ronald Reagan Building
Washington, DC 20523-1000

USAID Media and Elections Program in Rwanda Grants 4768
The United States Government, as represented by the United States Agency for International Development in Rwanda (USAID/Rwanda) is seeking applications from qualified organizations for an eighteen-month Media and Elections Program. The goal of the Media and Elections Program in Rwanda is to build the confidence and capacity of media professionals and to provide higher quality, transparent and balanced reporting in the period around the September Parliamentary Elections and leading up to the much anticipated 2017 Presidential Elections. It is anticipated that one award of up to $500,000 will be offered. The application deadline is April 25.
Requirements: Application eligibility is unrestricted.
Geographic Focus: All States, All Countries
Amount of Grant: Up to 500,000 USD
Contact: Geraldine Kyazze, Acquisitions and Assistance Specialist; +250 252 596400; fax +250 252 596591; gkyazze@usaid.gov or kigali@usaid.gov
Internet: http://www.grants.gov/search/search.do;jsessionid=1hyNR1ZCCTTR82b1LCtk GHdD32b2Jb4LRf6fPLTx1BpbKydjvGpB!657861682?oppId=225353&mode=VIEW
Sponsor: U.S. Agency for International Development
Ronald Reagan Building, 1300 Pennsylvania Avenue, NW
Washington, DC 20523-1000

USAID Mekong Partnership for the Environment Project Grants 4769
The United States Agency for International Development (USAID), is seeking applications (proposals for funding) from U.S. institutions of higher education and U.S. non-governmental organizations (NGOs) and/or a consortia to provide technical support to a new Mekong Partnership for the Environment Project (MPE) to foster integrated sub-regional cooperation and capacity building among Cambodia, Laos, Thailand, and Vietnam, in the areas of education, health, environment and water, and connectivity. One award is anticipated, ranging up to a maximum of $13,000,000. The posted deadline for applications is June 10.
Requirements: U.S. institutions of higher education and U.S. non-governmental organizations (NGOs) and/or a consortia are eligible.
Geographic Focus: All States
Date(s) Application is Due: Jun 10
Amount of Grant: Up to 13,000,000 USD
Contact: Praveena ViraSingh; (66-2) 263-3000; pvirasingh@usaid.gov
Internet: http://www07.grants.gov/search/search.do;jsessionid=1v8kR3HpjBFsc7Z47pRgj fSFjbcHqr2Jf6p2BXMYZTRdnTrpWtT4!1321711693?oppId=230153&mode=VIEW
Sponsor: U.S. Agency for International Development
Ronald Reagan Building
Washington, DC 20523-1000

USAID National Governance Project Grant 4770
This is a pre-solicitation notice that in the near future USAID-Yemen intends to announce a full and open competition to implement a National Governance Project (NGP) Grant. The announcement is subject to the availability of funds. The NGP is intended to facilitate more equitable socio-economic development by strengthening public policies and institutions that will contribute to mitigating the drivers of instability in Yemen. A more equitable, representative, transparent, responsive, and reliable Yemeni government that meets the needs of its most vulnerable citizens is one way to help achieve USAID's objectives. As the needs in Yemen are great, the implementer will focus on initiatives that directly satisfy the needs identified in USAID's strategy, that are supported by the Republic of Yemen Government's or that would require relatively little effort to garner support, and that will have the biggest strategic impact for the resources expended. Activities will quickly and effectively mitigate critical threats to stability in Yemen by reestablishing trust, respect, and, in some communities, legitimacy for the Government of Yemen. Youth will be a particularly important demographic group throughout implementation. The implementer will partner with and make extensive use of local, Yemeni organizations during the implementation of the project. The estimated budget for the three year base period is approximately $20 million. Staff are unable to entertain meetings or respond to queries with prospective implementers at this stage. Please check the website for updated information including the application date. One award of $20,000,000 will be funded.
Geographic Focus: All States, All Countries
Amount of Grant: 20,000,000 USD
Contact: Botros Wilson, Acquisitions Specialist; +20-2-516-6921 or +20-2-522-7000; fax +20-2-522-7197; YemenNGPRFA1@usaid.gov
Internet: http://www.grants.gov/search/search.do;jsessionid=6wkXRm4XlPrL2gnTXwynW 1rnnBXH1gDJQDZdGVySjBTTpwmYrsQT!1762381823?oppId=50473&mode=VIEW
Sponsor: U.S. Agency for International Development
Ronald Reagan Building
Washington, DC 20523-1000

USAID NGO Health Service Delivery Program Grants 4771
The United States Agency for International Development (USAID), is seeking applications (proposals for funding) from local organizations as primary recipients to improve the health status of vulnerable populations in target provinces within Cambodia to increase utilization of high-quality reproductive health/family planning (RH/FP), maternal and child health, and HIV/AIDS services. The eight target provinces include Phnom Penh, Kampong Speu, Kampong Cham, Battambang, Kandal, Bantey Mean Chey, Siem Reap, and Prey Veng. Target populations include: youth, garment industry workers, men who have sex with men, entertainment workers, and urban and peri-urban poor, including low-income formal and informal workers, such as migrant laborers, who have limited access to quality, affordable health services. One cooperative agreement worth a total estimated amount of $6,600,000 will be funded, for a program not to exceed five years.
Requirements: This award is limited to local organizations as the primary recipient.
Geographic Focus: All States, Cambodia
Amount of Grant: Up to 6,600,000 USD
Contact: Honey Sokry; (855-23) 728 345; hsokry@usaid.gov
Internet: http://www07.grants.gov/search/search.do;jsessionid=Y8hyRkShSpQkpL0lpV1zQM MRWm1GJwQmLsyDjZQ JYpyNVJYSk1dy!-1168907641?oppId=225133&mode=VIEW
Sponsor: U.S. Agency for International Development
Ronald Reagan Building
Washington, DC 20523-1000

USAID Pakistan Private Investment Initiative Grants 4772
USAID Pakistan seeks interest in its project which provides for investment fund management companies to co-fund, with USAID, equity or quasi-equity investment in potential high growth small and medium sized businesses (SME's) in Pakistan. USAID Pakistan intends to enter into multiple agreements with an investment by USAID of 15 to 20 million dollars per investment fund. USAID will require a match of at least dollar for dollar with greater matches viewed favorably. Evidence of investment commitments from prospective partner/investors will be required to satisfy this requirement. The window for investments will be 5 years with investments liquidated after an anticipated 5 year holding period. The compensation of the fund management company for its service would be market based and subject to negotiation. This procurement will be conducted as a multi-tiered assistance procurement with concept papers initially being accepted and full applications sought from the highest evaluated initial applications. It is expected that four (4) grants will be awarded, with a maximum award of $24,000,000. The Application deadline is September 12.
Requirements: Eligibility to apply is unrestricted.
Geographic Focus: All States, All Countries
Amount of Grant: Up to 24,000,000 USD
Contact: Sufyan Javaid, Contract Assistant; +92-51-208-1273; sjaved@usaid.gov
Internet: http://www.grants.gov/search/search.do;jsessionid=sc1DRwpLDV4C4tmQM2Q6mJBf3SHMkwKghf75HcJlrrhtqHvTfTzN!-1898900577?oppId=199453&mode=VIEW
Sponsor: U.S. Agency for International Development
Ronald Reagan Building
Washington, DC 20523-1000

USAID Palestinian Community Assistance Grants 4773
The USAID/West Bank and Gaza Palestinian Community Assistance Program has been one of the leading donors of humanitarian assistance to the people of Gaza since the onset of military operations in December 2008. USAID assistance has focused on the delivery of food and non-food items (including clothing, household items, and hygiene kits), school and classroom supplies for private schools, and emergency supplies (blankets, plastic sheeting, and medical supplies). This assistance was a critical lifeline for the people of Gaza in the immediate aftermath of Operation Cast Lead and throughout the ensuing months. Humanitarian assistance and disaster response remain key pillars of USG support for Gaza. Additionally, USAID planning for future assistance has increasingly focused on recovery programs that both meet basic human needs and address the recovery of livelihoods for Gazan families. USAID/West Bank and Gaza will be releasing an RFA that intends to award one Cooperative Agreement to an organization that would manage and oversee humanitarian and recovery sub-grants over a multi-year period. The RFA will fund complex programming in Gaza which promotes long-term food security, safe and secure housing options, improved infrastructure, household-level economic recovery, and other economic recovery opportunities. These efforts are in line with the priorities established in the Palestinian Authority's Early Recovery and Reconstruction Plan for Gaza. Projects funded under this RFA may include activities in the health, education, agriculture, infrastructure, or economic sectors. Examples of potential activities may include constructing agricultural infrastructure, rehabilitating irrigation systems, providing emergency food and non-food items, constructing or rehabilitating private schools/health clinics, building women's centers, weatherizing private homes, or providing educational programming for school age children.
Requirements: U.S. Non-Governmental Organizations (U.S. NGOs), U.S. Private Voluntary Organization (PVO), Public International Organizations (PIO), or a U.S. for profit firm (provided they forgo profit) are eligible to apply.
Geographic Focus: Israel
Contact: Sandy Sakran, Grantor; +972-3-511-4870 or +972-3-511-4848; fax +972-3-511-4888; ssakran@usaid.gov or wbg@usaid.gov
Internet: http://www07.grants.gov/search/search.do;jsessionid=rkvMR4JXpflyGGVJhyMcvClxFntKpQd5YlMn1HLnhMtNGjCG1t2Q!1321711693?oppId=55065&mode=VIEW
Sponsor: U.S. Agency for International Development
Ronald Reagan Building
Washington, DC 20523-1000

USAID Palestinian Community Infrastructure Development Grants 4774
The Palestinian Community Infrastructure Development (PCID) Program aims to increase Palestinian access to water, sanitation and other small and medium scale community infrastructure in the West Bank. This focus will be complemented by a minimum stand-by capability to respond rapidly to needs in Gaza should political and security conditions require. Any interventions in Gaza will be identified and discussed by USAID and the implementing partner on a case by case basis after award. No interventions in Gaza are contemplated at this time. Accordingly, PCID will meet the following objectives: increase access to water and sanitation systems, reduce water losses and enhance water and sanitation system sustainability; increase the impact of USAID-funded programs in health, democracy and governance, education and the private sector by addressing underlying infrastructure needs which may be limiting the impact of those programs; and respond rapidly to urgent water, sanitation and other public infrastructure needs. The estimated ceiling for this RFA is $100 million.
Requirements: U.S.-based non-governmental organizations are eligible to submit applications. Applicants must have established financial management, monitoring and evaluation, internal control systems, and policies and procedures that comply with established U.S. Government standards, laws, and regulations.
Restrictions: Applications from non-U.S. organizations as well as Public International Organizations will not be considered.
Geographic Focus: All States
Date(s) Application is Due: Mar 9
Amount of Grant: Up to 100,000,000 USD
Contact: Claudia Koziol, Agreements Officer; 972-3-519-8507 or 972-3-511-4868; fax ckoziol@usaid.gov; WBG-OCM-packages@usaid.gov
Internet: http://www07.grants.gov/search/search.do;jsessionid=kGnXRdGLdv3SbzZvRgnNLtS1jvTlZ8qs4Tcf1kvwg8y5TtT8hcN1!1884755759?oppId=148373&mode=VIEW
Sponsor: U.S. Agency for International Development
Ronald Reagan Building
Washington, DC 20523-1000

USAID Public-Private Alliance Proposals in Burma, Thailand, and Vietnam 4775
USAID/OFDA seeks partnerships that bring together the private and public sectors in ways that contribute to the reduction of natural disaster risks in the EAP region. Through this announcement and in support of USAID/OFDA's overall programming, USAID/OFDA invites humanitarian agencies, the private sector, and the public sector to develop new and innovative alliances that focus on the first element of its three-pronged approach: investing in early warning, preparedness, mitigation, and prevention efforts. Specifically, alliances proposed under this Addendum should address one or more of the following objectives: increasing the effectiveness of early warning systems to communities at risk of natural disasters in Burma, Thailand, and/or Vietnam; improving the preparedness of vulnerable communities to natural disasters in Burma, Thailand, and/or Vietnam; improving the risk/hazard assessments throughout the country(ies) or in specific highly vulnerable areas of each country in coordination with the lead national government agency and other relevant agencies in Burma, Thailand, and/or Vietnam; and improving settlement planning and construction practices that contribute to reducing the risks of vulnerable communities, based on their specific hazard exposure, in Burma, Thailand, and/or Vietnam.
Requirements: Eligibility to apply is unrestricted
Geographic Focus: All States, All Countries
Date(s) Application is Due: May 8
Contact: Elizabeth Stickman, estickman@usaid.gov
Ken Lee, kenlee@usaid.gov
Internet: http://www07.grants.gov/search/search.do;jsessionid=kGnXRdGLdv3SbzZvRgnNLtS1jvTlZ8qs4Tcf1kvwg8y5TtT8hcN1!1884755759?oppId=226114&mode=VIEW
Sponsor: U.S. Agency for International Development
Ronald Reagan Building
Washington, DC 20523-1000

USAID Rapid Response for Sudan Grants 4776
OFDA's mandate is to save lives, alleviate human suffering, and reduce the social and economic impact of disasters worldwide. As part of USAID/OFDA's strategy for Sudan, USAID/OFDA seeks to establish a rapid response funding mechanism with stand-by capacity, whereby international and local organizations will be supported to respond to acute humanitarian needs stemming from disasters and localized emergencies through timely, short-term, quick-impact and effective interventions as emergencies occur over the duration of this award. The rapid response funding mechanism is not intended to address chronic poverty or long-term needs. Potential shocks resulting in new humanitarian needs in Sudan for the duration of the award period which might require an emergency response under the rapid response mechanism include: inter- and intra-state conflict and inter or intra-state violence; natural disasters such as flood and drought; sudden shortages of water or food; disease outbreaks; significant new population displacements or returns; and other localized emergencies and/or shocks that result in acute needs. The anticipated program duration is 24 months from the date of award. OFDA plans to make a single award.
Requirements: Eligibility to apply is unrestricted.
Geographic Focus: All States, All Countries
Date(s) Application is Due: Apr 19
Contact: Contract Specialist; (800) 518-4726; OFDA_APS_FY13_007@ofda.gov
Internet: http://www07.grants.gov/search/search.do;jsessionid=kGnXRdGLdv3SbzZvRgnNLtS1jvTlZ8qs4Tcf1kvwg8y5TtT8hcN1!1884755759?oppId=226034&mode=VIEW
Sponsor: U.S. Agency for International Development
Ronald Reagan Building
Washington, DC 20523-1000

USAID Rapid Response to Pakistanis Affected by Disasters - Phase Two Grants 4777
The United States Government(USG), as represented by the U.S. Agency for International Development (USAID), Bureau for Democracy, Conflict, and Humanitarian Assistance (DCHA), Office of U.S. Foreign Disaster Assistance (OFDA) is seeking to support or stimulate the activities described in this Annual Program Statement (APS). The scope and objective of the Rapid Response to Pakistanis Affected by Disasters - Phase Two(RAPID II) program to be funded under the award(s) resulting from this APS are to establish a funding mechanism for the award of sub-grants to local and international non-government organizations (NGOs) so they will be able to address urgent humanitarian and early recovery needs of persons affected throughout Pakistan whether due to natural disasters or conflict. The framework created will thus support quick impact, innovative responses to emergency situations appropriate to needs identified immediately after the occurrence of a natural disaster or as the result of new or ongoing displacement due to conflict. It will be flexible and responsive to constantly changing needs. It will reflect an understanding and sensitivity to the real or perceived impact that gender and other personal attributes such as disability or age may have on personal security and access to relief assistance. One award is expected in an amount up to $8,000,000.
Requirements: Eligibility requirements are unrestricted.
Geographic Focus: All States, All Countries
Date(s) Application is Due: Aug 12
Contact: Agreement Specialist; (800) 518-4726; ofda_aps@ofda.gov
Internet: http://www07.grants.gov/search/search.do;jsessionid=kGnXRdGLdv3SbzZvRgnNLtS1jvTlZ8qs4Tcf1kvwg8y5TtT8hcN1!1884755759?oppId=220173&mode=VIEW
Sponsor: U.S. Agency for International Development
Ronald Reagan Building
Washington, DC 20523-1000

USAID Reading Enhancement for Advancing Development Grants   4778
The United States Agency for International Development (USAID), Bangladesh is issuing this Request for Applications (RFA) for a four year Cooperative Agreement entitled USAID's Reading Enhancement for Advancing Development (READ) activity in Bangladesh. This activity will support improved early grade reading skills in selected low performing districts in Bangladesh. The primary objective of the activity is: improved reading skills in early grade students, as measured by an increase in oral reading fluency. The activity is comprised of four related intermediate results: IR 1 - increased use of evidence-based, interactive reading instruction; IR 2 - improved use of early grade reading assessment; IR 3 - expanded provision and use of supplementary reading materials; and IR 4 - increased community support of early grade literacy. The award will range from $14,000,000 to $15,400,000, and the deadline for applications is May 14.
Requirements: Funding eligibility is unrestricted.
Geographic Focus: All States
Date(s) Application is Due: May 14
Amount of Grant: 14,000,000 - 15,400,000 USD
Contact: Kaiser Parvez Ali, Acquisitions and Assistance Specialist; (880-2) 885-5500, ext. 2722; fax (880-2) 882-3648; kali@usaid.gov
Internet: http://www07.grants.gov/search/search.do;jsessionid=Y8hyRkShSpQkpL0lpV1zQM MRWm1GJwQmLsyDjZQ JYpyNVJYSk1dy!-1168907641?oppId=228833&mode=VIEW
Sponsor: U.S. Agency for International Development
Ronald Reagan Building
Washington, DC 20523-1000

USAID Resilience and Economic Growth in the Sahel Enhanced Resilience Grants   4779
The United States Agency for International Development (USAID) Senegal Regional Mission is seeking applications to fund one organization through a Cooperative Agreement for a five year period. The REGIS-ER program is designed around three interwoven objectives: increased and sustainable economic well-being; strengthened institutions and governance; and improved health and nutrition status. It is anticipated that the successful applicant will be funded in a range between $67,000,000 and $72,000,000. USAID encourages application from potential new partners. The application deadline is May 9.
Requirements: This is a full and open competition, under which any type of organization, large or small, commercial (for- and nonprofit), faith-based and partnerships may apply. All international nongovernmental organizations (NGOs), private voluntary organizations (PVOs) and consortium of local and international firms are also eligible to submit their application(s) against the RFA. Applicants must be a legal entity accredited or able to obtain accreditation to operate in Niger and Burkina Faso. Applicants must submit with their applications, the status of their application for registration with the host governments of Niger and Burkina Faso.
Geographic Focus: All States, All Countries
Date(s) Application is Due: May 9
Amount of Grant: 67,000,000 - 72,000,000 USD
Contact: Victor Bushamuka, Regional Advisor; (221) 33-869-61-00 or (221) 33-879-40-00; fax (221) 33-869-61-01; rfajpcregiser@usaid.gov or usaid-senegal@usaid.gov
Internet: http://www07.grants.gov/search/search.do;jsessionid=qGTQR1Cfh7mp196zMJy LGPqzYv1nC7JMb67WwJpTvY2z0qSz2J8M!-982222471?oppId=228496&mode=VIEW
Sponsor: U.S. Agency for International Development
Ronald Reagan Building
Washington, DC 20523-1000

USAID Scholarships for Youth and Teachers   4780
USAID is providing scholarships for youth and teachers from rural and/or indigenous communities to study for one to two years at U.S. community colleges in programs designed to improve their technical skills so that they can better contribute to Mexico's development. The fields of study supported through the provision of scholarships for youth and teachers in Mexico include, but are not limited to: Quality Control; Integrated Natural Resource Technology; Agribusiness for Export; Electronics Technology for Manufacturing; Strengthening Rural Primary Education; and Small and Medium Enterprise Management and Marketing. Upon their return, youth are assisted in obtaining employment and teachers apply newly-gained skills in rural classrooms. All scholarship recipients lead and implement community development projects.
Requirements: Scholarship recipients have been selected from rural and/or indigenous areas of Chiapas, Chihuahua, Distrito Federal, Guanajuato, Guerrero, Jalisco, Michoacán, Nayarit, Oaxaca, Querétaro, and San Luis Potosí.
Geographic Focus: Mexico
Contact: Tom Delaney; +52 (55) 5080-2257 or +52 (55) 5080-2000; fax +52 (55) 5080-2574
Internet: http://transition.usaid.gov/mx/scholarshipseng.html
Sponsor: U.S. Agency for International Development
Ronald Reagan Building
Washington, DC 20523-1000

USAID Service Delivery and Support for Families Caring For Orphans and   4781
Vulnerable Children Grants
The purpose of the USAID-South Africa Service Delivery and Support for Families Caring For Orphans and Vulnerable Children Grants is to improve the well-being of families and their vulnerable children through comprehensive and coordinated evidence-based interventions that strengthen the capacity of families and communities to care for vulnerable children in sub-districts and districts with high HIV prevalence, high maternal mortality, and a high number of orphans and vulnerable children. Five grant awards are anticipated, ranging up to a maximum of $20,000,000.
Requirements: Any local South African non-governmental organization (NGO) and for-profit organization meeting the criteria in section III is eligible to apply.
Geographic Focus: South Africa
Amount of Grant: Up to 75,000,000 USD
Contact: Martha Zhou, Grantor; +012-452-2179; mzhou@usaid.gov
Internet: http://www07.grants.gov/search/search.do;jsessionid=1v8kR3HpjBFsc7Z47pRgj fSFjbcHqr2Jf6p2BXMYZTRdnTrpWtT4!1321711693?oppId=169333&mode=VIEW
Sponsor: U.S. Agency for International Development
Ronald Reagan Building
Washington, DC 20523-1000

USAID Strengthening Democratic Local Governance in South Sudan Grants   4782
The USAID Strengthening Democratic Local Governance Program in South Sudan is intended to strengthen democratic local governance through improving local government's ability to perform its core functions and supporting the development of strong and credible state and local systems. Specifically, the program will engender a bottom-up and inclusive public participatory approach in the decision-making, implementation and accountability of government service delivery and further strengthen linkages within national, state, and local (payam) governments and International/NGOs for better coordination, delivery of services and accountability to the people. This competitively awarded five-year cooperative agreement will focus on implementing projects primarily in high conflict, disaster prone and low resource areas. USAID will advise applicants of project objectives and desired outcome; however, applicants must provide the methodology or approach for implementation of the project. Applicants will have the opportunity to propose a sound, cost effective approach for the program. Applicants are strongly encouraged to consider implementation through a consortium with other organizations including PIOs and local organizations; however, principal responsibility for implementation of the program should rest with the applicant who should act as prime and have final responsibility for implementation and performance monitoring of the program.
Requirements: Qualified foreign and domestic for-profit companies that forego profit, foreign and domestic non-profit organizations, faith-based organizations, foundations, academic institutions, civic groups and regional organizations are eligible to apply.
Geographic Focus: All States, All Countries
Amount of Grant: 25,000,000 - 75,000,000 USD
Contact: Claudia Koziol , Agreement Officer; ckoziol@usaid.gov
Internet: http://www07.grants.gov/search/search.do;jsessionid=1v8kR3HpjBFsc7Z47pRgj fSFjbcHqr2Jf6p2BXMYZTRdnTrpWtT4!1321711693?oppId=231353&mode=VIEW
Sponsor: U.S. Agency for International Development
Ronald Reagan Building
Washington, DC 20523-1000

USAID Strengthening Free and Independent Media in South Sudan Grants   4783
This competitively awarded five-year cooperative agreement will focus on strengthening the independence, professionalism, production capacities, self-sustainability and regulatory framework of the media sector in South Sudan. Media assistance will build on the transition to self-sustainability of five currently USAID-supported local partner radio stations. Due to its unique potentials for communicating with virtually the entire population, media can enable a much needed national conversation to vitally contribute to the building of this new nation. The media, be it print, broadcast, internet, or other form, represent an integral part of accountability systems that, in turn, are critical to the effective functioning of democratic governance. USAID will advise applicants of project objectives and desired outcome; however, applicants must provide the methodology or approach for implementation of the project. Applicants will have the opportunity to propose a sound, cost effective approach for the Program.
Requirements: Qualified foreign and domestic for-profit companies that forego profit, foreign and domestic non-profit organizations, faith-based organizations, foundations, academic institutions, civic groups and regional organizations are eligible to apply. Applicants are strongly encouraged to consider implementation through a consortium with other organizations including but not limited to PIOs and local organizations; however, principal responsibility for implementation of the program should rest with the applicant who should act as prime and have final responsibility for implementation and performance monitoring of the program.
Geographic Focus: All States, All Countries
Amount of Grant: 25,000,000 - 60,000,000 USD
Contact: John Gemenze, Acquisitions and Assistance Specialist; +211 (0)912 105 188; jgemenze@usaid.gov or jubainfo@usaid.gov
Internet: http://www07.grants.gov/search/search.do;jsessionid=1v8kR3HpjBFsc7Z47pRgj fSFjbcHqr2Jf6p2BXMYZTRdnTrpWtT4!1321711693?oppId=231354&mode=VIEW
Sponsor: U.S. Agency for International Development
Ronald Reagan Building
Washington, DC 20523-1000

USAID Strengthening RMNCH Through Indian Health Professional Associations   4784
and Scaling Up Uptake Grants
USAID Strengthening RMNCH Through Indian Health Professional Associations and Scaling Up Uptake Grants generally targets India's vulnerable, marginalized, and underserved populations spread across rural areas, urban slums, and tribal pockets – including those currently outside the realm of effective service provision for reasons related to economics, gender, and social inclusion (notably females across the life cycle). The expected number of awards is six, and each will range from $3,650,000 to $8,000,000. The annual deadline date is April 9.
Requirements: USAID seeks applications from local India organizations.
Geographic Focus: All States, India
Date(s) Application is Due: Apr 9
Amount of Grant: 3,650,000 - 8,000,000 USD
Contact: Vandana Vats, Acquisitions and Assisstance Specialist; 91-11-24198568 or 91-11-24198000; fax 91-11-24198612; vvats@usaid.gov or indiarco@usaid.gov

GRANT PROGRAMS | 743

Internet: http://www.grants.gov/search/search.do;jsessionid=6wkXRm4XlPrL2gnTXwynW
1rnnBXH1gDJQDZdGVySjBTTpwmYrsQT!1762381823?oppId=229933&mode=VIEW
Sponsor: U.S. Agency for International Development
Ronald Reagan Building
Washington, DC 20523-1000

USAID Systems Strengthening for Better HIV/TB Patient Outcomes Grants   **4785**
USAID-South Africa Systems Strengthening for Better HIV/TB Patient Outcomes Grants are intended to strengthen South African Government systems in order to improve patient outcomes and prevent HIV by supporting comprehensive clinic-based (hospitals, community health centers, and primary health care clinics) HIV-related services. Applicants may submit a concept paper, and approved applicants will be invited to submit a full application. Eight awards are anticipated, ranging from $10,000,000 to $150,000,000 each.
Requirements: Any local South African non-governmental organizations, private voluntary organizations, faith-based and community organizations, and for-profit companies willing to forego profit is eligible. Applications from potential new partners are encouraged.
Geographic Focus: South Africa
Date(s) Application is Due: Jan 6
Contact: Beatrice Lumanade, Acquisitions and Assisstance Specialist; +27 12 452 2377; fax Applications4@usaid.gov
Internet: http://www07.grants.gov/search/search.do;jsessionid=1v8kR3HpjBFsc7Z47pRgj
fSFjbcHqr2Jf6p2BXMYZTRdnTrpWtT4!1321711693?oppId=133033&mode=VIEW
Sponsor: U.S. Agency for International Development
Ronald Reagan Building
Washington, DC 20523-1000

USAID Unsolicited Proposal Grants   **4786**
USAID is engaged in a comprehensive development program in Armenia, supporting democratic principles and a free market economy. The main objectives of the Mission are to increase Armenia's competitiveness, strengthen democratic institutions, ensure energy security, increase access to primary healthcare, and protect socially vulnerable population. USAID/Armenia generally undertakes direct assistance programs design in consultations with Armenian counterparts and through competitive grants and cooperative agreements. Therefore, only exceptional unsolicited applications can be considered for funding on a noncompetitive basis—ones which present a unique approach, are fully supportive of USAID/Armenia development objectives, and demonstrate a unique capacity by the applicant to carry out proposed activities and where there is clear support for such activities. The application is to be submitted in two stages: unsolicited concept paper and, in case of positive notification from USAID, unsolicited detailed application.
Requirements: Unsolicited concept papers should be submitted directly to USAID/Armenia Program Office. Two copies of the application must be submitted in English.
Geographic Focus: All States, All Countries
Contact: Armen Karapetyan, Acquisitions Specialist; (374 10) 494 493 or (374 10) 464 700; fax (374 10) 464 728; akarapetyan@usaid.gov
Internet: http://armenia.usaid.gov/en/node/34
Sponsor: U.S. Agency for International Development
Ronald Reagan Building
Washington, DC 20523-1000

USAID Workforce Development Program in Mexico Grants   **4787**
The United States Agency for International Development in Mexico (USAID) intends to award a Cooperative Agreement for a 36-month activity focusing on Mexico's northern border region entitled Workforce Development (WFD) for Youth in Mexico: Strengthening Education-to-Employment Systems. The overall goal of this activity is to support Mexican initiatives at a systemic level to increase labor market skills acquisition among youth, adapt upper- and post-secondary education and training programs to labor market needs, and increase portability of skills across the education, training and labor market systems. The award range is $3,000,000 to $4,000,000, and the annual deadline for application is April 30.
Requirements: This is a full and open competition, under which all potential applicants may apply, large or small commercial (for profit) firms and non-profit organizations (including public or private universities) in partnerships or consortia.
Geographic Focus: All States
Date(s) Application is Due: Apr 30
Contact: Beatriz Chinchilla; +52 (55) 5080-2000 or +52 (55) 5080-2000; fax +52 (55) 5080-2574; bchinchilla@usaid.gov or usaidmexico@usaid.gov
Internet: http://www.grants.gov/search/search.do;jsessionid=k9ywRnXcGzJNZf5yyFK5M
kJyHQhBHGTQlcyJyyVN9yBxlqx5pC5V!1866286003?oppId=227637&mode=VIEW
Sponsor: U.S. Agency for International Development
Ronald Reagan Building
Washington, DC 20523-1000

US Airways Community Contributions   **4788**
U.S. Airways invests in community organizations and initiatives to enhance quality of life in markets served by the airline. The airline's funding priorities include arts and culture, health and human services, and education and environment in the following hub markets and focus cities: Boston, Charlotte, Las Vegas, New York, Philadelphia, Phoenix, Pittsburgh and Washington, DC.
Requirements: Tax exempt organizations in the airline's market areas are eligible to apply. All requests must be submitted in writing on the organization's letterhead 6-8 weeks prior to the event and any print deadlines. All completed proposals will receive a written response within 6-8 weeks from receipt. The Contributions Committee meets bi-weekly to review requests.
Restrictions: Funding will not be considered for: Pass through and start-up organizations; Individuals, including support for specific students, researchers or conference fees; Endowment programs; Foundations which are themselves grant-making entities; Professional associations; Debt-reduction campaigns; Fundraising activities related to individual sponsorship (i.e. walk-a-thons); Service clubs (i.e. Lions, Rotary, Kiwanis); Sports teams, political, labor or fraternal organizations, scouting groups and religious organizations; Organizations or programs funded 50% or more by government sources; Individual schools; district and system-wide education programs will be considered; Capital and building campaigns.
Geographic Focus: Arizona, District of Columbia, Massachusetts, Nevada, New York, North Carolina, Pennsylvania
Contact: Community Relations Manager; community.relations@usairways.com
Internet: http://www.usairways.com/awa/content/aboutus/corporategiving/default.aspx
Sponsor: U.S. Airways Community Foundation
4000 E Sky Harbor Boulevard
Phoenix, AZ 85034

US Airways Community Foundation Grants   **4789**
The community foundation supports multi-year capital and building campaigns by 501(c)3 non-profit organizations operating in U.S. Airways' hub markets of Charlotte, Philadelphia and Phoenix. Grant application deadlines are April 1 and October 1 of each year. Grants will be made in late May and November.
Requirements: Grantees must be 501(c)3 nonprofit organizations that operate in one of U.S. Airways' hub cities (Charlotte, Philadelphia and Phoenix) and improve the quality and availability of charitable health care; artistic and cultural organizations; education; and/or community services. Support includes multi-year capital and building campaigns only
Restrictions: The foundation will not consider funding for endowment programs; professional associations; debt-reduction campaigns; service clubs (i.e. Lions, Rotary and Kiwanis); political, labor/fraternal or sports organizations; individual schools; general operating support; staff/consultant fees; hardware, software; infrastructure; religious activities.
Geographic Focus: Arizona, North Carolina, Pennsylvania
Date(s) Application is Due: Apr 1; Oct 1
Contact: Julie Coleman; (480) 693-3652; community.relations@usairways.com
Internet: http://www.usairways.com/awa/content/aboutus/corporategiving/default.aspx
Sponsor: U.S. Airways Community Foundation
4000 E Sky Harbor Boulevard
Phoenix, AZ 85034

US Airways Education Foundation Grants   **4790**
The foundation was established to support educational initiatives in communities the airline serves by promoting employee engagement and funding college scholarships to dependents of airline employees and community education grants to nonprofit organizations. Hub markets and focus cities include Boston, Charlotte, Las Vegas, New York, Philadelphia, Phoenix, Pittsburgh and Washington, DC. The foundation places a high value on educational programs that respond to social issues, especially those that directly or indirectly strive to improve education or increase skills for its participants.
Requirements: Nonprofit organizations (exempt under section 501(c)3 of the IRS Code) in which their nearest major airport is served by U.S. Airways or its wholly owned subsidiaries (Piedmont and PSA) are eligible to apply. Proposed programs educational programs that include any of the following criteria: a) Educational programs that respond to the special needs of disadvantaged or disabled individuals; b) Educational programs that teach or enhance social responsibility; c) Educational programs that facilitate parental and/or community involvement; d) Educational programs that enhance academic achievement.
Restrictions: Funding shall not be provided for: Organizations that discriminate on the basis of race, color, gender, national origin, marital status, age, disability, or veteran status; Programs that are purely denominational in purpose; Political campaigns or activities; Endowment funds or foundations which are themselves grant-making entities; Grants for travel expenses or transportation costs; Grants for debt retirement or operational costs; Grants for general operational budgets; Purchase of program advertisements; Air transportation donations; Purchase of tickets or tables for dinners and/or benefits; Stipends for personal expenses; Start-up organizations; Individuals, including support for specific students, researchers or conference fees; Capital or Building Projects.
Geographic Focus: Arizona, District of Columbia, Massachusetts, Nevada, New York, North Carolina, Pennsylvania
Date(s) Application is Due: Jul 1
Contact: Community Relations Manager; (480) 693-0800
Internet: http://www.usairways.com/awa/content/aboutus/corporategiving/default.aspx
Sponsor: U.S. Airways Education Foundation
4000 E Sky Harbor Boulevard
Phoenix, AZ 85034

USA Volleyball Foundation Educational Grants   **4791**
The USA Volleyball Foundation will accept grant applications from organizations and individuals for volleyball educational projects benefiting groups not individuals. At the present time grants are limited to a maximum of $5000 annually.
Requirements: Preference will be extended but not limited to non-profit organizations. Download the required application form and include the organization's current operating budget and year-to-date financial statements; the last certified audit; and a copy of the latest verification of tax-exempt status from the IRS. There are no deadlines.
Geographic Focus: All States
Contact: Fred Wendelboe, Chairman; (719) 228-6800; fred.wendelboe@usav.org
Internet: http://volleyball.teamusa.org/content/index/1692
Sponsor: USA Volleyball Foundation
4240 Briar Creek Road
Clemmons, NC 27012

USBC Annual Zeb Scholarship 4792

The Annual Zeb Scholarship commemorates the dedication and enthusiasm for youth bowling exemplified by Jim Zebehazy. Zeb was the executive director of the Young American Bowling Alliance for eight years prior to the organization's merger with the United States Bowling Congress. Under his leadership, YABA expanded the opportunities for its members to earn scholarships, develop their leadership abilities and compete in national championship tournaments in both scratch and handicap play. The Annual Zeb Scholarship is awarded to a USBC Youth member who achieves academic success and gives back to his or her community through service. One person will be selected to receive a $2,500 scholarship which will be formally presented at the USBC Junior Gold Championships award ceremony. USBC will pay travel and hotel expenses for the winner and one guest to attend the award ceremony. The selection is based on the candidate's grades, academic and community involvement, letters of reference and essay.

Requirements: Applicants must be in their 11th or 12th grade year in high school, must be USBC Youth members in good standing, and may be male or female. This scholarship is based mainly on community service and very strong academic success. Bowling successes do not factor into the selection process.
Geographic Focus: All States
Date(s) Application is Due: Apr 1
Amount of Grant: 2,500 USD
Contact: Breanne Eoff, (800) 514-2695, ext. 8422; breanne.eoff@bowl.com
Internet: http://bowl.com/scholarships/index.jsp
Sponsor: United States Bowling Congress
621 Six Flags Drive
Arlington, TX 76011

USBC Earl Anthony Memorial Scholarships 4793

USBC awards five annual scholarships of $5,000 each to recognize male and female bowlers for their community involvement and academic achievements, both in high school and college. The American Bowling Congress, in cooperation with the Young American Bowling Alliance (YABA), presents this prestigious scholarship in honor of Earl Anthony. This legendary professional bowler was inducted into the bowling Hall of Fame, the winner of numerous ABC and PBA Championships, and one of the greatest ambassadors for the sport of bowling.

Requirements: Eligible candidates must be current members of YABA, in good standing, as of June 1 and never have competed in a professional bowling tournament (Pro-AMs excluded). In addition, candidates must have a minimum cumulative GPA of 2.5 based on a 4.0 scale, or equivalent. Financial need will also be considered.
Restrictions: Individuals may win this award only once.
Geographic Focus: All States
Date(s) Application is Due: May 1
Amount of Grant: 5,000 USD
Contact: Contact Coordinator; (800) 514-2695, ext. 3168; smart@bowl.com
Internet: http://bowl.com/scholarships/index.jsp
Sponsor: United States Bowling Congress
621 Six Flags Drive
Arlington, TX 76011

USCM HIV/AIDS Prevention Grants 4794

The USCM HIV Prevention Grants Program, in cooperation with the Centers for Disease Control and Prevention, provides financial and technical assistance to local health departments and community-based organizations to implement HIV prevention programs. The goal of this effort is to strengthen the capacity of local service providers to carry out effective HIV/AIDS prevention activities.

Requirements: Grants are awarded on the recommendation of an independent external review panel composed of HIV/AIDS experts drawn from local and state health departments, national organizations, and local community-based organizations.
Geographic Focus: All States
Contact: Crystal D. Swann, Assistant Executive Director; (202) 861-6707; fax (202) 293-2352; cswann@usmayors.org
Internet: http://www.usmayors.org/hivprevention/hiv_prevention_grant.asp
Sponsor: United States Conference of Mayors
1620 I Street NW
Washington, DC 20006

US CRDF Science and Technology Entrepreneurship Program (STEP) Business Partnership Grant Competition Armenia 4795

The U.S. Civilian Research and Development Foundation (CRDF) is a nonprofit organization authorized by the U.S. Congress and established in 1995 by the National Science Foundation. This unique organization promotes international scientific and technical collaboration through grants, technical resources, and training. The STEP Business Partnership Grants Competition, conducted by CRDF, the Ministry of Economy of RA and Enterprise Incubator Foundation (EIF), promotes research and development (R&D) partnerships between companies (Company) and teams of researchers/scientists (Technology Team) to develop new commercial opportunities of economic benefit to both parties.

Requirements: Projects must have R&D as their core task and must include preliminary market assessment, customer needs analysis and business development components. Projects that demonstrate their ability to enable revenue creation and/or attract non-STEP Partner organization sources of funding will be given priority consideration in the selection process. All goals and outcomes of the projects must be defined and measurable. STEP BPG projects are limited to a maximum of 12 months. Funds for projects are provided by the CRDF and the Ministry of Economy of RA. Funds are limited to $15,000. At least 10% of company cash contribution is mandatory. New Science Team/Company Partnership is preferable. All funds must be used for Science Team expenses. At first, written proposals should be submitted to EIF for review on eligibility and completeness of information provided. Complete proposals must be submitted to CRDF via electronic proposal submission (EPS) and emailed to the EIF by (18:00) local time on the following submission deadlines to be eligible. Proposals for EIF should be both in English and Armenian. Each proposal submitted to the STEP BPG is required to have a single Principal Investigator (PI) from a Company and a single Principal Investigator (PI) from the Science Team who will be responsible for coordinating all participating personnel, organizations, and work. Scientists and engineers may participate concurrently on more than one EIF/CRDF grant, but cannot be the PI on more than one active EIF/CRDF project or exceed full-time work status on the combined EIF/CRDF projects. Projects are required to be in research and development fields that are oriented toward commercial, non-military objectives and must be carried out in a civilian research environment. The participants of the Science Team are required to be scientists or engineers at institutes, universities, companies, or other organizations involved in research and development. The PIs and all participants of the Science Team are required to be citizens of and must currently reside and work in Armenia. The primary partner of the Company Team is required to be a for-profit company based in Armenia. In order to be considered Armenia-based, a company must have registered offices in Armenia and its facilities and personnel associated with the project must be located in this country. Joint U.S. - Armenia for-profit ventures are eligible to participate. The PI of the Company Team is required to be a citizen of Armenia and must currently reside and work in Armenia.
Restrictions: The Company and the organization employing the team of scientists may not be subsidiaries of or owned, either wholly or partially, by one another. Organizations and individuals of the Science Team working for organizations that are barred by the U.S. Government from receiving U.S. financial support, materials, or services are not eligible to participate in BPG program.
Geographic Focus: All States, Ukraine
Date(s) Application is Due: Oct 5
Amount of Grant: 15,000 USD
Contact: Natalia Pipia; (703) 526-9720; fax (703) 526-9721; step@crdf.org
Internet: http://www.crdf.org/funding/funding_show.htm?doc_id=990740
Sponsor: U.S. Civilian Research and Development Foundation
1530 Wilson Boulevard, 3rd Floor
Arlington, VA 22209

US CRDF STEP Business Partnership Grant Competition Ukraine 4796

The U.S. Civilian Research and Development Foundation (CRDF) is a nonprofit organization authorized by the U.S. Congress and established in 1995 by the National Science Foundation. This unique organization promotes international scientific and technical collaboration through grants, technical resources, and training. The Science and Technology Entrepreneurship Program Business Partnership Grants competition (STEP BPG), conducted by CRDF and the Ministry of Education and Science (MES) promotes research and development (R&D) partnerships between companies (Company) and teams of scientists (Science Team) to develop new commercial opportunities of economic benefit to both parties. At the first stage of the STEP Program, two workshops will be carried out in Lviv and Sevastopol, Ukraine which will provide basic training on technology commercialization, and intellectual property protection. Workshops will also further clarify STEP program goals and objectives and will introduce the BPG competition terms and conditions.

Requirements: STEP BPG projects must have research and development (R&D) as their core task and must include a preliminary market assessment; a customer needs analysis, and business development components. Projects that demonstrate their ability to enable revenue creation and/or attract non-STEP Partner organization sources of funding will be given priority consideration in the selection process. All goals and outcomes of the projects must be well defined and measurable. STEP BPG projects are limited to a maximum of 12 months. Funds for projects are provided by the CRDF and MES. Funds are limited to $24,000. All funds must be used for Science Team expenses. In support of the goals of the Business Partnership Grant competition to increase the number of linkages between the science and business sectors, preference will be given to newly-formed science- business partnerships. Preference will also be given to projects with at least 10% company cash contribution. Each proposal submitted to the STEP BPG competition is required to have a single Principal Investigator (PI) from a Company and a single Principal Investigator (PI) from the Science Team who will be responsible for coordinating all participating personnel, organizations, and work. Scientists and engineers may participate concurrently on more than one CRDF grant, but cannot be the PI on more than one active CRDF project or exceed full-time work status on the combined CRDF projects. The STEP BPG projects are required to be in research and development fields that are oriented toward commercial, non-military objectives and must be carried out in a civilian research environment. All proposals are required to be submitted to CRDF in English. Two copies of all proposals should be submitted in printed form to the MES in Ukrainian. The participants of the Science Team are required to be scientists or engineers at institutes, universities, companies, or other organizations involved in research and development. The PIs and all participants are required to be citizens of and must currently reside and work in Ukraine. The primary partner is required to be a for-profit company based in Ukraine or in the U.S; thus, a company must have registered offices in Ukraine or in the U.S. and its facilities and personnel associated with the project must be located in these countries. Joint U.S.-Ukrainian for-profit ventures are eligible to participate. The PI of the Company Team is required to be a citizen of and must currently reside and work in Ukraine. Note: The MES and CRDF discourage the inclusion of an 'administrative' superior in a proposal in any role for which individual financial support is requested. An 'Administrative Superior' is defined as an individual who has direct administrative authority over the Principal Investigator, and who works within the same division, laboratory, or unit as the Principal Investigator. Institutional leadership including university rectors and vice rectors and institute directors and deputy directors are also defined as 'administrative superiors.' This definition does not apply to other individuals of higher 'rank' within the institution but who work outside the division, laboratory or unit of the Principal Investigator.

Restrictions: The Company and the organization employing the team of scientists may not be subsidiaries of or owned, either wholly or partially, by one another. Organizations and individuals working for organizations that are barred by the U.S. Government from receiving U.S. financial support, materials, or services are not eligible to participate in CRDF programs. No grant funds can be used for company expenses.
Geographic Focus: All States, Ukraine
Date(s) Application is Due: Dec 20
Amount of Grant: 24,000 USD
Contact: Natalia Pipia; (703) 526-9720; fax (703) 526-9721; step@crdf.org
Internet: http://www.crdf.org/funding/funding_show.htm?doc_id=1034127
Sponsor: U.S. Civilian Research and Development Foundation
1530 Wilson Boulevard, 3rd Floor
Arlington, VA 22209

USDA 1890 Land Grant Colleges and Universities Initiative Grants 4797
USDA Rural Development and the 1890 Land-Grant Universities are working together on a new approach to support the development of businesses that create quality jobs. The 1890 Institutions have some of the best agricultural science and business education programs in the nation. USDA is building on the strength of these programs to ensure that quality education related to small business development is also available in these communities. The primary program goals are to: develop income-producing projects for under-developed rural communities; create self-sustaining, long-term economic development in targeted areas of high unemployment through partnerships with the Universities and community-based organizations; and assist and guide these communities in becoming self-sustainable. Rural Development 1890 institutions can use grant money to: sponsor business conferences and workshops; finance rural businesses; provide technical assistance to new and existing businesses, including cooperatives; assist communities in leveraging other resources via state, local, private, and/or public funding; assist businesses through the application process; offer courses in business development; provide computer labs where community members can have access to other rural economic development sources on the Internet; and establish business incubator services.
Requirements: Identified 1890 Institutions are eligible to apply.
Geographic Focus: All States
Contact: Claudette Fernandez; (202) 690-4730; claudette.fernandez@wdc.usda.gov
Internet: http://www.rurdev.usda.gov/BCP_1890LandGrant.html
Sponsor: U.S. Department of Agriculture
1400 Independence Avenue, SW
Washington, DC 20250

USDA Agricultural and Rural Economic Research Grants 4798
USDA Agricultural and Rural Economic Research project grant program is to provide economic and other social science information and analysis for public and private decisions on agriculture, food, natural resources, and rural America. ERS produces such information for use by the general public and to help the executive and legislative branches develop, administer, and evaluate agricultural and rural policies and programs. ERS performs economic research and analyses related to U.S. and world agriculture that addresses a multitude of economic concerns and decision making needs of Federal, State, and local governments, farmers, farm organizations, farm suppliers, marketers, processors, and consumers.
Requirements: Any individual or organization in the U.S. and its Territories is eligible to receive the popular or technical research publications that convey the research results, although there may be a fee.
Restrictions: There are no restrictions on the use of ERS produced information.
Geographic Focus: All States
Contact: Nancy A. Thomas; (202) 694-5008; fax (202) 245-5318; nthomas@ers.usda.gov
Internet: http://www.ers.usda.gov/
Sponsor: U.S. Department of Agriculture
355 E Street SW, Room 7-174
Washington, DC 20024-3231

USDA Bioenergy Program for Advanced Biofuel Payments to Advanced Biofuel Producers 4799
The Advanced Biofuel Payment Program provides payments to producers to support and expand production of advanced biofuels refined from sources other than corn kernel starch. The Program supports and helps to ensure the expanding production of advanced biofuels by providing payments to eligible advanced biofuel producers. Additional incentive payments may be made to certain producers who have increased their biofuel output over the previous year's production. Advanced biofuels are produced from renewable biomass crops such as cellulose, sugar and starch (other than ethanol derived from corn kernel starch), hemicelluloses, lignin, waste materials, biogas, butanol, diesel-equivalent fuel, sugarcane, and nonfood crops such as poplar trees or switchgrass.
Requirements: To be eligible for the Advanced Biofuel Producer Program, an applicant must produce and sell an advanced biofuel. Conditions need to be met for the producer and for the biofuel.
Restrictions: Funding is only available to advanced biofuel producers in rural areas.
Geographic Focus: All States
Contact: Cindy Mason; (202) 690-4730; fax (202) 690-4737; cindy.mason@wdc.usda.gov
Internet: http://www.rurdev.usda.gov/BCP_Biofuels.html
Sponsor: U.S. Department of Agriculture
1400 Independence Avenue, SW
Washington, DC 20250

USDA Child and Adult Care Food Program 4800
The Child and Adult Care Food Program approves the quality of day care by making it more affordable for many low income families. Each day millions of children receive nutritious meals and snacks through the program. The program also provides meals and snacks to over 100,000 adults who receive care in nonresidential adult day care centers. The program alo provides meals to children residing in emergency shelters, and snacks and suppers to youths participating in eligible after school care programs. Disbursement is made on the basis of the number of lunches, suppers, breakfasts, and snacks served, using annually adjusted reimbursement rates specified by law. Program institutions may receive reimbursement for not more than three meals per day per participant. Specific guidelines and current applications are available at the website.
Requirements: City, local or county governments; other public entities; or private nonprofit organizations are eligible to apply. Each site operated must meet applicable state and local health, safety, and sanitation standards. Meals must meet minimum requirements of the United States Department of Agriculture (USDA). Organizations desiring to participate must agree to operate a nonprofit food service that is available to all eligible children.
Geographic Focus: All States
Contact: Tim O'Connor, Associate Administrator; (703) 305-2054
Internet: http://www.fns.usda.gov/cnd/care/CACFP/aboutcacfp.htm
Sponsor: U.S. Department of Agriculture
1400 Independence Avenue SW
Washington, DC 20250

USDA Community Facility Grants 4801
Community Programs provides grants to assist in the development of essential community facilities in rural areas and towns of up to 20,000 in population. Grants are authorized on a graduated scale. Applicants located in small communities with low populations and low incomes will receive a higher percentage of grants. Grants are available to public entities such as municipalities, counties, and special-purpose districts, as well as non-profit corporations and tribal governments. In addition, applicants must have the legal authority necessary for construction, operation, and maintenance of the proposed facility and also be unable to obtain needed funds from commercial sources at reasonable rates and terms. Grant funds may be used to assist in the development of essential community facilities. Grant funds can be used to construct, enlarge, or improve community facilities for health care, public safety, and community and public services. This can include the purchase of equipment required for a facility's operation. A grant may be made in combination with other CF financialassistance such as a direct or guaranteed loan, applicant contributions, or loans and grants from other sources. The Community Facilities Grant program is typically used to fund projects under special initiatives, such as Native American community development efforts; child care centers linked with the Federal government's Welfare-to-Work initiative; Federally-designated Enterprise and Champion Communities, and the Northwest Economic Adjustment Initiative area. Grant assistance may be available for up to 75% of project costs. Grant funding limitations are based on population and income, economic feasibility, and availability of funds.
Restrictions: Grant funds cannot be used to: pay any annual recurring costs, including purchases or rentals that are generally considered to be operating and maintenance expenses; construct or repair electric generating plants, electric transmission lines, or gas distribution lines to provide services for commercial sale; pay costs to construct facilities to be used for commercial rental where the applicant has no control over tenants and services offered; construct facilities primarily for the purpose of housing State, Federal or quasi-Federal agencies; or finance recreational facilities or community antenna television services or facilities.
Geographic Focus: All States
Contact: Rob Nelson, Acting Director; (202) 720-9647 or (202) 720-0654; fax (202) 690-0500; rob.nelson@wdc.usda.gov
Internet: http://www.rurdev.usda.gov/HAD-CF_Grants.html
Sponsor: U.S. Department of Agriculture
1400 Independence Avenue, SW
Washington, DC 20250

USDA Community Food Projects Competitive Grants 4802
The Community Food Projects Competitive Grant Program (CFPCGP) has existed since 1996 as a program to fight food insecurity through developing community food projects that help promote the self-sufficiency of low-income communities. Community Food Projects are designed to increase food security in communities by bringing the whole food system together to assess strengths, establish linkages, and create systems that improve the self-reliance of community members over their food needs. The program is designed to: meet the needs of low-income people by increasing their access to fresher, more nutritious food supplies; increase the self-reliance of communities in providing for their own food needs; and promote comprehensive responses to local food, farm, and nutrition issues. Additionally, projects should: meet specific state, local, or neighborhood food and agricultural needs for infrastructure improvement and development; plan for long-term solutions; and create innovative marketing activities that mutually benefit agricultural producers and low-income consumers. These grants are intended to help eligible private nonprofit entities that need a one-time infusion of federal assistance to establish and carry out multipurpose community food projects. Projects are funded from $10,000-$300,000 and from 1 to 3 years. They are one-time grants that require a dollar-for-dollar match in resources.
Geographic Focus: All States
Amount of Grant: 10,000 - 300,000 USD
Contact: Ila Blue; (202) 401-0628 or (202) 720-4423; iblue@nifa.usda.gov
Internet: http://www.nifa.usda.gov/nea/food/in_focus/hunger_if_competitive.html
Sponsor: U.S. Department of Agriculture
1400 Independence Avenue, SW, Stop 2201
Washington, DC 20250-2201

746 | GRANT PROGRAMS

USDA Cooperative Extension System Education Grants   4803
The program seeks to help people improve their lives and communities through an educational process that uses scientific knowledge focused on issues critical to the economic, agricultural, societal, health/safety, and environmental progress of all Americans. In addition, the program seeks to identify and solve farm, home, and community problems through the practical application of research findings of the USDA and land-grant colleges and universities. The cooperative extension system is a future-oriented, self-renewing, national educational network providing excellence in programs that focus on contemporary issues and needs of people.
Requirements: Grants are available to designated 1862, 1890, and 1994 land-grant institutions in the 50 states and Puerto Rico, Guam, the Virgin Islands, American Samoa, Micronesia, Northern Marianas, and the District of Columbia.
Geographic Focus: All States
Amount of Grant: 890,000 - 20,000,000 USD
Contact: Andrea L. Brandon; (202) 720-9181 or (202) 720-4423; abrandon@nifa.usda.gov
Internet: http://www.csrees.usda.gov/nea/education/education.cfm
Sponsor: U.S. Department of Agriculture
1400 Independence Avenue, SW, Stop 2201
Washington, DC 20250-2201

USDA Delta Health Care Services Grants   4804
The Delta Health Care Services Grant Program is designed to provide financial assistance to address the continued unmet health need in the Delta Region through cooperation among health care professionals, institutions of higher education, research institutions, and other entities in the Delta Region. Each fiscal year, applications are solicited through a Notice of Funds Availability (NOFA) published in the Federal Register. Grant funds must be used for projects in rural areas within the Delta Region to develop: a health care cooperative; health care services; health education programs; health care training programs; and expand public health-related facilities in the Delta Region to address longstanding and unmet health needs of the region.
Requirements: Consortiums of regional institutions of higher education, academic health and research institutes, and economic development entities located in the Delta Region that have experience in addressing the health care issues in the region are eligible. The Delta region includes specified counties in: Alabama, Arkansas, Illinois, Kentucky, Louisiana, Mississippi, Missouri, and Tennessee.
Restrictions: Individuals are not eligible for this program.
Geographic Focus: Alabama, Arkansas, Illinois, Kentucky, Louisiana, Mississippi, Missouri, Tennessee
Contact: Claudette Fernandez; (202) 690-4730; claudette.fernandez@wdc.usda.gov
Internet: http://www.rurdev.usda.gov/BCP_DeltaHealthCare.html
Sponsor: U.S. Department of Agriculture
1400 Independence Avenue, SW
Washington, DC 20250

USDA Denali Commission High Energy Cost Grants   4805
The High Energy Cost Grant Program provides financial assistance for the improvement of energy generation, transmission, and distribution facilities servicing eligible rural communities with home energy costs that are over 275 percent of the national average. Denali Commission High Energy Cost Grants (CFDA 10.857) are made to the Denali Commission for energy generation, transmission, and distribution facilities serving rural Alaskan communities with average home costs exceeding 275% of the national average.
Requirements: To be eligible an applicant must be: a legally-organized for-profit or nonprofit organization such as, but not limited to, a corporation, association, partnership (including a limited liability partnership), cooperative, or trust; a sole proprietorship; a State or local government, or any agency or instrumentality of a State or local government, including a municipal utility or public power authority; an Indian tribe, a tribally-owned entity, and Alaska Native Corporation; an individual or group of individuals; or any of the above entities located in a U.S. Territory or other area authorized by law to participate in programs of the Rural Utilities Service or under the Rural Electrification Act.
Geographic Focus: Alaska
Contact: Kristi Kubista-Hovis, Rural Development Electric Programs; (202) 720-9545 or (202) 884-7700; fax (202) 690-0717; Kristi.Kubista-Hovis@wdc.usda.gov
Internet: http://www.rurdev.usda.gov/UEP_Our_grant_programs.html
Sponsor: U.S. Department of Agriculture
1400 Independence Avenue, SW
Washington, DC 20250

USDA Distance Learning and Telemedicine Grants   4806
The Distance Learning and Telemedicine (DLT) Grants are designed to meet the rural educational and health care needs of residents in rural areas. The purpose of the program is to encourage and improve the use of telemedicine, telecommunications, computer networks, and related advanced technologies. Funds may be used for telecommunications, computer networks, and related advanced technologies that provide educational and/or medical benefits to students, teachers, medical professionals, and rural residents. Eligible uses for funding include: acquisition of capital assets, such as interactive video equipment; audio and video equipment; computer terminals; data terminal equipment; inside wiring; computer hardware and software; network components; and other facilities that further DLT services. Acquisition of instructional programming, technical assistance, and instruction for using the equipment is also eligible. Specific guidelines, application materials, and current deadlines (usually after the first of the year) are available on the web site.
Requirements: The following are eligible for funding: entities providing education and medical care via telecommunications including corporations or partnerships; federally recognized tribes; state or local units of government; consortia; and private for-profit or not-for profit corporations. There is a match requirement minimum of 15%.
Restrictions: Individuals are not eligible for funding.
Geographic Focus: All States
Amount of Grant: 50,000 - 500,000 USD
Contact: Sam Morgan, Program Contact; (202) 720-0665; sam.morgan@wdc.usda.gov
Internet: http://www.rurdev.usda.gov/UTP_DLT.html
Sponsor: U.S. Department of Agriculture
1400 Independence Avenue, SW
Washington, DC 20250

USDA Emergency Community Water Assistance Grants   4807
The USDA Emergency Community Water Assistance Grants help rural residents who have experienced a significant decline in quantity or quality of water to obtain adequate quantities of water that meet the standards of the Safe Drinking Water Act. Examples of emergencies include a drought, earthquake, flood, tornado, hurricane, disease outbreak or chemical spill, leakage or seepage. There are two levels of funding limits. In order for a project to be considered under the $500,000 limit, the project must be used to alleviate a significant decline in quantity and quality of water available. Funds will be used for the construction of a water source up to and including the treatment plant, such as new wells, reservoirs, transmission lines, treatment plants, and/or other sources of water. Grants to be considered under the $150,000 limit will be made for distribution waterline extensions, breaks or repairs on distribution waterlines, and operation and maintenance type items that remedy an acute shortage or significant decline in the quantity or quality of potable water. Examples are a washed out river crossing in a distribution system, and/or construction of distribution lines to individuals not currently on the system whose wells have gone dry. Applications are accepted any time through state and area offices. Specific guidelines, applications, and lists of state contacts are available at the website.
Requirements: Grants may be made to public bodies, non-profit corporations, and federally recognized tribes serving rural areas. The material submitted with the application should include the Preliminary Engineering Report, Environmental Review, population and median household income of the area to be served, description of project, and the nature of the emergency that caused the problem(s) being addressed by the project.
Restrictions: Grants provided under this program shall not be used to assist a rural area or community with a population in excess of 10,000; to assist a rural area that has a median household income in excess of the statewide non-metropolitan median household income; to finance facilities that are not modest in size, design, and cost; to pay loan or grant finder's fees; to pay any annual recurring costs considered to be operational expenses; to pay rental for the use of equipment or machinery owned by the rural community; to purchase existing systems; to refinance existing indebtedness; and to make reimbursement for projects developed with other grant funds.
Geographic Focus: All States
Amount of Grant: 150,000 - 500,000 USD
Contact: Scott Barringer, Director, Water and Environmental Program; (202) 720-9583; fax (202) 690-0649; scott.barringer@wdc.usda.gov
Internet: http://www.rurdev.usda.gov/UWP-ecwag.htm
Sponsor: U.S. Department of Agriculture
1400 Independence Avenue, SW
Washington, DC 20250

USDA Farmers Market Promotion Grants   4808
The Farmers Market Promotion Program (FMPP) offers grants to help improve and expand domestic farmers' markets, roadside stands, community-supported agriculture programs, agri-tourism activities, and other direct producer-to-consumer market opportunities. The maximum amount awarded for any one proposal cannot exceed $100,000.
Requirements: Agricultural cooperatives, producer networks, producer associations, local governments, nonprofit corporations, public benefit corporations, economic development corporations, regional farmers' market authorities and Tribal governments are among those eligible to apply.
Geographic Focus: All States, Guam, Marshall Islands, Northern Mariana Islands, Puerto Rico, U.S. Virgin Islands, American Samoa, Micronesia
Amount of Grant: Up to 100,000 USD
Contact: Trista Etzig, Program Contact; (202) 690-4942; trista.etzig@ams.usda.gov
Internet: http://www.ams.usda.gov/AMSv1.0/ams.fetchTemplateData.do?template=TemplateN&navID=WholesaleandFarmersMarkets&leftNav=WholesaleandFarmersMarkets&page=FMPP&description=Farmers%20Market%20Promotion%20Program&acct=fmpp
Sponsor: U.S. Department of Agriculture
1400 Independence Avenue, SW
Washington, DC 20250

USDA Farm Labor Housing Grants   4809
The Rural Development (RD) Farm Labor Housing Grants are available to buy, build, improve, or repair housing for farm laborers, including persons whose income is earned in aquaculture (fish and oyster farms) and those engaged in on-farm processing. Funds can be used to purchase a site or a leasehold interest in a site; to construct housing, day care facilities, or community rooms; to pay fees to purchase durable household furnishings; and to pay construction loan interest. Grants may cover up to 90% of development costs. State RD directors can award grants with the prior approval of the National Office. The Program Director has the authority to approve loans to individuals of up to $100,000, and the State Director can approve loans of up to $400,000. Larger loans must receive prior approval from the National Office.
Requirements: Grants are made to farmworker associations, nonprofit organizations, federally recognized tribes, and public agencies. Funds may be used in urban areas for nearby farm labor.
Geographic Focus: All States, Guam, Puerto Rico, U.S. Virgin Islands, American Samoa
Date(s) Application is Due: Aug 22

Amount of Grant: Up to 400,000 USD
Contact: Rob Nelson, Deputy Director; (202) 720-9619 or (202) 720-0654; fax (202) 690-0500; rob.nelson@wdc.usda.gov
Internet: http://www.rurdev.usda.gov/HAD-Farm_Labor_Grants.html
Sponsor: U.S. Department of Agriculture
1400 Independence Avenue, SW
Washington, DC 20250

USDA Federal-State Marketing Improvement Grants 4810
The Federal-State Marketing Improvement Program (FSMIP) provides matching funds to state departments of agriculture, state agricultural experiment stations, and other appropriate state agencies to assist in exploring new market opportunities for U.S. food and agricultural products, and to encourage research and innovation aimed at improving the efficiency and performance of the marketing system. FSMIP funds a wide range of applied research projects that address barriers, challenges, and opportunities in marketing, transporting, and distributing U.S. food and agricultural products domestically and internationally. Proposals may address issues throughout the marketing chain including direct, wholesale, and retail. Proposals may involve small, medium or large-scale agricultural entities, but should potentially benefit multiple producers or agribusinesses. Proposals that address issues of importance at the state, multi-state, or national level are appropriate for FSMIP. FSMIP also seeks unique and innovative proposals on a smaller scale that may serve as pilot projects or case studies useful as models for other states. Of particular interest are proposals that reflect a collaborative approach between the states, academia, the farm sector, and other appropriate entities and stakeholders. Eligible agricultural categories include livestock, livestock products, food and feed crops, fish and shellfish, horticulture, viticulture, apiary, and forest products and processed or manufactured products derived from such commodities. FSMIP also funds projects dealing with nutraceuticals, bioenergy, compost and products made from agricultural residue. FSMIP funds may be awarded for projects for up to two years.
Requirements: Eligible applicants include state governments, and public or private institutions of higher education.
Restrictions: Proprietary proposals that benefit one business or individual will not be considered for funding.
Geographic Focus: All States
Date(s) Application is Due: May 28
Amount of Grant: 25,000 - 100,000 USD
Contact: Janise Zygmont; (202) 720-5024; janise.zygmont@ams.usda.gov
Internet: http://www.grants.gov/search/search.do;jsessionid=3pHcRCtLmgJnBFrgyL0Xx
FXKWp5FfdkQZgy1kZJ5VYgHrh3kj48K!-943438780?oppId=231855&mode=VIEW
Sponsor: U.S. Department of Agriculture
1400 Independence Avenue, SW
Washington, DC 20250

USDA Foreign Market Development Grants 4811
The Foreign Market Development Program (FMD), also known as the cooperator program, is administered by the Foreign Agricultural Service (FAS) of the U.S. Department of Agriculture (USDA). The goal of the program is to develop, maintain, and expand long-term export markets for U.S. agricultural products. The Cooperator program is designed to create, expand, and maintain foreign markets for U.S. agricultural commodities and products through cost-share assistance. Financial assistance under the Cooperator program will be made available on a competitive basis and applications will be reviewed against the evaluation criteria contained herein and in the Cooperator program regulations. All U.S. agricultural commodities, except tobacco, are eligible for consideration. Under the Cooperator program, the FAS enters into agreements with eligible nonprofit U.S. trade organizations to share the cost of certain overseas marketing and promotion activities.
Requirements: To participate in the Cooperator program, an applicant must: be a nonprofit U.S. agricultural trade organization; and agree to contribute resources to its proposed promotional activities.
Geographic Focus: All States
Contact: Maureen Quinn, Director; (202) 720-7115 or (202) 720-4327; fax (202) 720-1727; maureen.quinn@usda.gov or podadmin@fas.usda.gov
Sally Klusaritz, Deputy Director; (202) 720-3448 or (202) 720-4327; fax (202) 720-1727; sally.klusaritz@usda.gov or podadmin@fas.usda.gov
Internet: http://www.fas.usda.gov/mos/programs/fmdprogram.asp
Sponsor: U.S. Department of Agriculture
1400 Independence Avenue SW
Washington, DC 20250

USDA High Energy Cost Grants 4812
The High Energy Cost Grant Program provides financial assistance for the improvement of energy generation, transmission, and distribution facilities servicing eligible rural communities with home energy costs that are over 275 percent of the national average. Grants under this program may be used for the acquisition, construction, installation, repair, replacement, or improvement of energy generation, transmission, or distribution facilities in communities with extremely high energy costs. On-grid and off-grid renewable energy projects, and energy efficiency, and energy conservation projects are eligible.
Requirements: To be eligible an applicant must be: a legally-organized for-profit or nonprofit organization such as, but not limited to, a corporation, association, partnership (including a limited liability partnership), cooperative, or trust; a sole proprietorship; a State or local government, or any agency or instrumentality of a State or local government, including a municipal utility or public power authority; an Indian tribe, a tribally-owned entity, and Alaska Native Corporation; an individual or group of individuals; or any of the above entities located in a U.S. Territory or other area authorized by law to participate in programs of the Rural Utilities Service or under the Rural Electrification Act.

Geographic Focus: All States
Contact: Kristi Kubista-Hovis, Rural Development Electric Programs; (202) 720-9545; fax (202) 690-0717; Kristi.Kubista-Hovis@wdc.usda.gov
Internet: http://www.rurdev.usda.gov/UEP_Our_grant_programs.html
Sponsor: U.S. Department of Agriculture
1400 Independence Avenue, SW
Washington, DC 20250

USDA Hispanic-Serving Institutions Education Grants 4813
The Hispanic-Serving Institutions Education Grants are intended to promote and strengthen the ability of Hispanic-Serving Institutions to carry out higher education programs in the food and agricultural sciences. The programs aim is to attract outstanding students and produce graduates capable of enhancing the nation's food and agricultural scientific and professional work force. Award recipients may subcontract to organizations not eligible to apply provided such organizations are necessary for the conduct of the project. The budget for subcontractors must be included with the corresponding budget narrative. Applicants are encouraged to collaborate with a USDA agency. Regular project applications must be received by February 9, while collaborative applications are due March 8. Application information, including samples of application packages and frequently asked questions, are available at the website.
Requirements: Only public or other non-profit Hispanic-Serving Institutions are eligible to apply for this program. To qualify as an Hispanic-Serving Institution, applicants must at the time of application, have an enrollment of undergraduate full-time equivalent students that is at least 25 percent. By submitting an application, the organization certifies that it is eligible to receive funding under this program.
Geographic Focus: All States
Amount of Grant: Up to 1,100,000 USD
Contact: Irma Lawrence, National Program Leader; (202) 720-2082 or (202) 720-1793; fax (202) 720-2030; ilawrence@nifa.usda.gov
Internet: http://www.csrees.usda.gov/fo/fundview.cfm?fonum=1094
Sponsor: U.S. Department of Agriculture
1400 Independence Avenue, SW, Stop 2201
Washington, DC 20250-2201

USDA Household Water Well System Grants 4814
The Household Water Well System (HWWS) Grant Program provides grants to qualified private non-profit organizations to establish lending programs for household water wells in rural areas. Homeowners or eligible individuals may borrow money from an organization receiving a HWWS grant so they may construct or upgrade their private well systems. Rural areas are defined as locations other than cities or towns of more than 50,000 people and the contiguous and adjacent urbanized area of such towns and cities. Funds may be used to create a revolving loan fund to provide low-interest loans to eligible individuals to construct, refurbish, and service individually-owned household water well systems.
Requirements: An organization is eligible to receive a HWWS grant if it: is a private, non-profit organization; has a Dun and Bradstreet (D&B) Data Universal Numbering System (DUNS) number; has an active registration with current information in the Central Contractor Registration (CCR) database; has the legal capacity and authority to carry out the grant purpose; has sufficient expertise and experience in lending activities; has sufficient expertise and experience in promoting the safe and productive use of individually-owned HWWS and ground water; has no delinquent debt to the Federal Government or no outstanding judgments to repay a Federal debt; and demonstrates that it possesses the financial, technical, and managerial capability to comply with Federal and State laws and requirements.
Restrictions: An individual cannot receive a Household Water Well System grant. Funds may not be provided for home sewer or septic system projects.
Geographic Focus: All States
Date(s) Application is Due: Jun 4
Contact: Jacqueline M. Ponti-Lazaruk, Assistant Administrator; (202) 690-2670; fax (202) 690-0649; jacki.ponti@wdc.usda.gov
Internet: http://www.rurdev.usda.gov/UWP-individualwellsystems.htm
Sponsor: U.S. Department of Agriculture
1400 Independence Avenue, SW
Washington, DC 20250

USDA Housing Application Packaging Grants 4815
Housing Application Packaging Grants provide government funds to tax-exempt public agencies and private non-profit organizations to package applications for submission to Housing and Community Facilities Programs. Packagers assist very low- and low-income applicants with the application process by pre-screening, making preliminary eligibility determinations, ensuring the application is complete, and helping the applicant understand the program. Grants reimburse eligible organizations for part or all of the costs of conducting, administering, and coordinating an effective housing application packaging program in colonias and designated counties.
Restrictions: The following are restrictions under the housing application packaging grants: funds are available only in the areas defined in Exhibit D of RD Instruction 1944-B; the packager may not charge fees or accept compensation or gratuities directly or indirectly from the very low- and low-income families being assisted under this program; the packager may not represent or be associated with anyone else, other than the applicant, who may benefit in any way in the proposed transaction; if the packager is compensated for this service from other sources, then the packager is not eligible for compensation from this source except as permitted by RHS; grantees who are funded to do self-help housing effort; and the authorized representatives must have no pecuniary interest in the award of the architectural or construction contracts, the purchase of equipment, or the purchase of the land for the housing site.
Geographic Focus: All States

Contact: Bill Downs; (202) 720-1499 or (202) 690-1533; bill.downs@wdc.usda.gov
Internet: http://www.rurdev.usda.gov/HAD-Packaging_Grants.html
Sponsor: U.S. Department of Agriculture
1400 Independence Avenue, SW
Washington, DC 20250

USDA Housing Preservation Grants 4816
The Housing Preservation Grant (HPG) program provides grants to sponsoring organizations for the repair or rehabilitation of low- and very low-income housing. The grants are competitive and are made available in areas wherever there is a concentration of need. Those assisted must own very low- or low-income housing, either as homeowners, landlords, or members of a cooperative. Very low income is defined as below 50 percent of the area median income (AMI); low income is between 50 and 80 percent of AMI. Eligible sponsors include state agencies, units of local government, Native American tribes, and nonprofit organizations. HPG funds received by the sponsors are combined with other programs or funds and used as loans, grants, or subsidies for recipient households based on a plan contained in the sponsor's application.
Requirements: Eligible are state and local governments, nonprofit corporations, federally recognized Indian tribes, and consortia of eligible entities. Funds must be used within a two-year period. The population limit of towns served is 20,000.
Geographic Focus: All States
Contact: Bill Downs; (202) 720-1499 or (202) 690-1533; bill.downs@wdc.usda.gov
Internet: http://www.rurdev.usda.gov/HAD-HPG_Grants.html
Sponsor: U.S. Department of Agriculture
1400 Independence Avenue, SW
Washington, DC 20250

USDA Individual Water and Waste Water Grants 4817
Individual Water and Waste Water Grants provide Government funds to households residing in an area recognized as a colonia before October 1, 1989. Grant funds may be used to connect service lines to a residence, pay utility hook-up fees, install plumbing and related fixtures, i.e. a bathroom sink, bathtub or shower, commode, kitchen sink, water heater, outside spigot, or bathroom, if lacking. These grants are available to households who own and occupy the dwelling. These grants are available only in Arizona, California, New Mexico, and Texas. Applicants need not be age 62 or older. For more information about this program, or to file an application, applicants should contact the local Rural Development office in their area.
Requirements: Individual Water and Waste Water Grant applicants must meet the following *Requirements:* own a dwelling located in a colonia and must present evidence of ownership; have a total taxable income based on the latest Federal income tax form from all individuals residing in the household that is below the most recent poverty income guidelines established by the Department of Health and Human Services; and must not be delinquent on any Federal debt.
Restrictions: Maximum grant to any individual for water service lines, connections, and/or construction of a bathroom is $3,500. Maximum grant to any individual for sewer service lines, connections, and/or construction of a bathroom is $4,000. Lifetime assistance to any individual for initial or subsequent Section 306C WWD grants may not exceed a cumulative total of $5,000.
Geographic Focus: Arizona, California, New Mexico, Texas
Amount of Grant: Up to 5,000 USD
Contact: Bill Downs; (202) 720-1499 or (202) 690-1533; bill.downs@wdc.usda.gov
Internet: http://www.rurdev.usda.gov/HAD-IWWW_Grants.html
Sponsor: U.S. Department of Agriculture
1400 Independence Avenue, SW
Washington, DC 20250

USDA Market Access Program Grants 4818
The Market Access Program (MAP), formerly the Market Promotion Program, uses funds from the U.S. Department of Agriculture's (USDA) Commodity Credit Corporation (CCC) to help U.S. producers, exporters, private companies, and other trade organizations finance promotional activities for U.S. agricultural products. The MAP encourages the development, maintenance, and expansion of commercial export markets for agricultural commodities. Activities financed include consumer promotions, market research, technical assistance, and trade servicing.
Requirements: To participate in the MAP, an applicant must be a nonprofit U.S. agricultural trade organization, a nonprofit SRTG, a nonprofit U.S. agricultural cooperative, or a State government agency. A small-sized U.S. commercial entity may participate through a MAP participant.
Geographic Focus: All States
Contact: Maureen Quinn, Director; (202) 720-7115 or (202) 720-4327; fax (202) 720-1727; maureen.quinn@usda.gov or podadmin@fas.usda.gov
Internet: http://www.fas.usda.gov/mos/programs/map.asp
Sponsor: U.S. Department of Agriculture
1400 Independence Avenue SW
Washington, DC 20250

USDA Multi-Family Housing Preservation and Revitalization Grants 4819
Multi-Family Housing Programs offer Rural Rental Housing grants to provide affordable multi-family rental housing for very low-, low-, and moderate-income families; the elderly; and persons with disabilities. This is primarily a direct mortgage program, but funds may also be used to buy and improve land and to provide necessary facilities such as water and waste disposal systems. In addition, deep subsidy rental assistance is available to eligible families. The goal of the MPR program is to restructure Rural Rental Housing loans and Off-Farm Labor Housing loans and provide grants to revitalize Multi-Family Housing projects in order to extend the affordable use of these projects without displacing tenants due to increased rents.
Geographic Focus: All States
Contact: Carolyn Bell; (202) 690-1533; fax (202) 690-0500
Internet: http://www.rurdev.usda.gov/HMF_MPR.html
Sponsor: U.S. Department of Agriculture
1400 Independence Avenue, SW
Washington, DC 20250

USDA Native American Indian Tribe Utilities Program Grants 4820
Rural Development works with a wide variety of public and nonprofit organizations to provide funding options to communities throughout rural America. Organizations eligible to apply for funds include state and local governmental entities; nonprofit groups, such as community development organizations; associations, private corporations, and cooperatives operating on a not-for-profit basis; and Federally recognized Native American groups. These program areas provide a variety of financial services to communities and individuals.
Geographic Focus: All States
Contact: Jacqueline M. Ponti-Lazaruk, Assistant Administrator; (202) 690-2670; fax (202) 690-0649; jacki.ponti@wdc.usda.gov
Internet: http://www.rurdev.usda.gov/WEP_Native_American_Tribes.html
Sponsor: U.S. Department of Agriculture
1400 Independence Avenue, SW
Washington, DC 20250

USDA Predevelopment Planning Grants 4821
Predevelopment planning grants may be available, if needed, to assist in paying costs associated with developing a complete application for a proposed project. State Directors are authorized to make grants up to $15,000 or 75 percent of the project costs, whichever is less. Funding for the balance of the eligible project costs not funded by the PPG must be from applicant resources or funds from other sources. Applications are accepted at any time through our Rural Development State and Area Offices.
Requirements: The applicant must meet the eligibility requirements of Part 1780.7 of RU.S. Instruction 1780. The median household income of the proposed area to be served by the project must be either below the poverty line or below 80 percent of the statewide non-metropolitan median household income. The eligible predevelopment items funded with these grant funds must be agreed to and accepted by the Agency prior to disbursement of the predevelopment planning grant. Applicant must provide financial information to document that they do not have the resources to pay predevelopment expenses on their own. Grants are limited to projects the Agency expects to fund soon after the application is submitted. PPG costs are those necessary expenses to be incurred to develop a complete application and are limited to eligible grant purposes.
Geographic Focus: All States
Amount of Grant: Up to 15,000 USD
Contact: Jacqueline M. Ponti-Lazaruk, Assistant Administrator; (202) 690-2670; fax (202) 720-1725; jacki.ponti@wdc.usda.gov
Internet: http://www.rurdev.usda.gov/UWP-predevelopment.htm
Sponsor: U.S. Department of Agriculture
1400 Independence Avenue, SW
Washington, DC 20250

USDA Public Television Digital Transition Grants 4822
Public Television Digital Transition grants assist Public Television Stations serving substantial rural populations in transitioning to digital broadcast television transmission. Funds may be used to acquire and install facilities and software necessary for the transition. Grant funds may also be used for associated engineering and environmental studies. Applications are accepted annually, after the National Office publishes a Notice of Funds Availability (NOFA) in the Federal Register when funding has been approved by Congress and signed into law by the President. Grant funds may be used to acquire, lease, and/or install facilities and software necessary to the digital transition, including: digital transmitters, translators, and repeaters, including all facilities required to initiate DTV broadcasting; power upgrades of existing DTV equipment, including replacement of low-power digital transmitters with digital transmitters capable of delivering the final authorized power level; studio-to-transmitter links; equipment to allow local control over digital content and programming, including: Master control equipment; digital program production equipment, including cameras, editing, mixing and storage equipment; multicasting and datacasting equipment; cost of the lease of facilities, if any, for up to three years; and associated engineering and environmental studies necessary to Implementation.
Requirements: Public television stations which serve rural areas are eligible to apply. A public television station is a non-commercial educational television broadcast station that is qualified for Community Service Grants by the Corporation of Public Broadcasting under section 396(k) of the Communications Act of 1934.
Restrictions: Individuals are not eligible for this program. Grants are not renewable.
Geographic Focus: All States
Contact: Norberto Esteves, Technical Staff Branch Chief; (202) 720-0699 or (202) 690-4493; fax (202) 720-1051; norberto.esteves@wdc.usda.gov
Internet: http://www.rurdev.usda.gov/UTP_DTV.html
Sponsor: U.S. Department of Agriculture
1400 Independence Avenue, SW
Washington, DC 20250

USDA Rural Business Enterprise Grants 4823
The USDA Rural Business Enterprise Grants (RBEG) provides grants that finance and facilitate development of small and emerging rural businesses, help fund distance learning networks, and help fund employment related adult education programs. To assist with business development, RBEGs may fund a broad array of activities. Examples of eligible fund use include: acquisition or development of land, easements, or rights of way; construction, conversion, renovation of buildings, plants, machinery, equipment, access streets and roads, parking areas, and utilities; pollution control; capitalization of revolving loan funds including funds that will make loans for start ups and working capital; training and technical assistance; distance adult learning for job training and advancement; rural transportation improvement; and project planning. Any project funded under the RBEG program should benefit small and emerging private businesses in rural areas. Small and emerging private businesses are those that will employ 50 or fewer new employees and have less than $1 million in projected gross revenues. Applicants may apply through their Rural Development State Office. Additional information is available at the website.
Requirements: Rural public entities (towns, communities, state agencies, and authorities), Indian tribes and rural private non-profit corporations are eligible to apply for funding. At least fifty-one percent of the outstanding interest in any project must have membership or be owned by U.S. citizens or resident aliens.
Geographic Focus: All States
Amount of Grant: 10,000 - 500,000 USD
Contact: Suzette Agans; (202) 690-4730; fax (202) 690-4737; suzette.agans@wdc.usda.gov
Internet: http://www.rurdev.usda.gov/BCP_rbeg.html
Sponsor: U.S. Department of Agriculture
1400 Independence Avenue, SW
Washington, DC 20250

USDA Rural Business Opportunity Grants 4824
Grant funds provide for technical assistance, training, and planning activities that improve economic conditions in rural areas. Grantees may use funds to identify and analyze business opportunities, including opportunities in export markets, that will use local economic and human resources; identify, train, and provide technical assistance to existing or prospective rural entrepreneurs and managers; establish business support centers and otherwise assist in the creation of new rural businesses, the development of methods of financing local businesses, and the enhancement of the capacity of local individuals and entities to engage in sound economic activities; conduct regional, community, and local economic development planning, coordination, and leadership development; establish centers for training, technology, and trade that will aid rural businesses in the utilization of interactive communications technologies to develop international trade opportunities and markets; and pay for technical assistance and/or training. The maximum grant for a project serving a single state is $50,000. The maximum grant for a project serving two or more states is $150,000.
Requirements: Eligibility is limited to rural public bodies, rural nonprofit corporations, rural Indian tribes, and cooperatives with primarily rural members that conduct activities for the mutual benefit of the membership are eligible provided they have sufficient financial strength and expertise to carry out the activity to be funded.
Geographic Focus: All States
Date(s) Application is Due: Aug 1
Amount of Grant: Up to 50,000 USD
Contact: Tracey Kennedy, Acting Program Leader; (800) 795-3272 or (202) 690-4730; fax (202) 690-4737; tracey.kennedy@wdc.usda.gov
Internet: http://www.rurdev.usda.gov/BCP_RBOG.html
Sponsor: U.S. Department of Agriculture
1400 Independence Avenue, SW
Washington, DC 20250

USDA Rural Community Development Initiative Grants 4825
The objective of the Rural Community Development Initiative Grants is to develop the capacity and ability of private, nonprofit community-based housing and community development organizations, and low income rural communities to improve housing, community facilities, community and economic development projects in rural areas. Rural Community Development Initiative grants may be used for but are not limited to: training sub-grantees to conduct a program on home-ownership education; training sub-grantees to conduct a program for minority business entrepreneurs; providing technical assistance to sub-grantees on how to effectively prepare a strategic plan; provide technical assistance to sub-grantees on how to access alternative funding sources; building organizational capacity through board training; developing training tools, such as videos, workbooks, and reference guides to be used by the sub-grantee; providing technical assistance and training on how to develop successful child care facilities; and providing training on effective fundraising techniques.
Geographic Focus: All States
Contact: Rob Nelson, Deputy Director; (202) 720-9647 or (202) 720-0654; fax (202) 690-0500; rob.nelson@wdc.usda.gov
Internet: http://www.rurdev.usda.gov/HAD-RCDI_Grants.html
Sponsor: U.S. Department of Agriculture
1400 Independence Avenue, SW
Washington, DC 20250

USDA Rural Cooperative Development Grants 4826
The primary objective of this grant program is to improve the economic condition of rural areas through the creation or retention of jobs and development of new rural cooperatives, value-added processing, and other rural businesses. Grant funds are provided for the establishment and operation of Centers that have the expertise or who can contract out for the expertise to assist individuals or entities in the start-up, expansion or operational improvement of rural businesses, especially cooperative or mutually-owned businesses. Grant funds and matching funds may be used for, but are not limited to, providing the following to individuals, cooperatives, small businesses and other similar entities in eligible rural areas served by the Center: applied research, feasibility, environmental and other studies that may be useful for the purpose of cooperative development; collection, interpretation and dissemination of principles, facts, technical knowledge, or other information for the purpose of cooperative development; providing training and instruction for the purpose of cooperative development; providing loans and grants for the purpose of cooperative development in accordance with the annual Notice of Funding Availability and applicable regulations; and providing technical assistance, research services and advisory services for the purpose of cooperative development.
Requirements: Nonprofit corporations and institutions of higher education are eligible.
Restrictions: Public bodies and individuals are not eligible to apply for the RCDG program. Grant funds may be used to pay for 75 percent (95 percent when the applicant is a 1994 Institution) of the cost of establishing and operating centers for rural cooperative development.
Geographic Focus: All States
Amount of Grant: Up to 175,000 USD
Contact: Tracey Kennedy; (202) 690-1428 or (800) 795-3272; tracey.kennedy@wdc.usda.gov
Internet: http://www.rurdev.usda.gov/BCP-RCDG_Grants.html
Sponsor: U.S. Department of Agriculture
1400 Independence Avenue, SW
Washington, DC 20250

USDA Rural Economic Development Grants 4827
The REDLG program provides funding to rural projects through local utility organizations. Under the REDLoan program, USDA provides zero interest loans to local utilities which they, in turn, pass through to local businesses (ultimate recipients) for projects that will create and retain employment in rural areas. The ultimate recipients repay the lending utility directly. The utility is responsible for repayment to the Agency. Under the REDGrant program, USDA provides grant funds to local utility organizations which use the funding to establish revolving loan funds. Loans are made from the revolving loan fund for projects that will create or retain rural jobs. Examples of eligible projects include: capitalization of revolving loan funds; technical assistance in conjunction with projects funded under a zero interest REDLoan; business incubators; Community Development Assistance to non-profits and public bodies (particularly job creation or enhancement); facilities and equipment for education and training for rural residents to facilitate economic development; facilities and equipment for medical care to rural residents; and telecommunications/computer networks for distance learning or long distance medical care. To apply for funding for the REDLG program, applicants should contact their Rural Development State Office.
Requirements: To receive funding under the REDLG program (which will be forwarded to selected eligible projects) an entity must: have borrowed and repaid or pre-paid an insured, direct, or guaranteed loan received under the Rural Electrification Act; be a not-for-profit utility that is eligible to receive assistance from the Rural Development Electric or Telecommunication Program; or be a current Rural Development Electric or Telecommunication Programs Borrower.
Geographic Focus: All States
Contact: Tracey Kennedy, Acting Program Leader; (202) 690-1428 or (800) 795-3272; fax (202) 690-4737; tracey.kennedy@wdc.usda.gov
Internet: http://www.rurdev.usda.gov/BCP_redlg.html
Sponsor: U.S. Department of Agriculture
1400 Independence Avenue, SW
Washington, DC 20250

USDA Rural Energy for America - Energy Audit and Renewable Energy Development Assistance Grants 4828
The REAP Energy Audit and Renewable Energy Development Assistance Grant provides grant assistance to entities that will assist agriculture producers and small rural businesses by conducting energy audits and providing information on renewable energy development assistance. The maximum amount for an energy audit-renewable energy development assistance grant is $100,000. Most rural projects that reduce energy use and result in savings for the agricultural producer or small business are eligible as energy efficiency projects. These include projects such as retrofitting lighting or insulation, or purchasing or replacing equipment with more efficiency units. Eligible renewable energy projects include projects that produce energy from wind, solar, biomass, geothermal, hydro power and hydrogen-based sources. The projects can produce any form of energy including, heat, electricity, or fuel. The grants are awarded on a competitive basis and can be up to 25% of total eligible project costs. Grant requests as low as $2,500 for renewable energy systems and $1,500 for energy efficiency improvements will be considered. The grant funds for a project must be used by the grant recipient to assist agriculture producers or small rural businesses with conducting or promoting energy audits and or renewable energy development assistance.
Requirements: To be eligible for an energy audit grant or a renewable energy development assistance grant, the applicant must be one of the following: a unit of State, tribal, or local government; a land-grant college or university or other institution of higher education; a rural electric cooperative; a public power entity; or an instrumentality of a State, tribal, or local government. The applicant must have sufficient capacity to perform the energy audit or renewable energy development assistance activities that they propose in the application.
Geographic Focus: All States
Contact: Tracey Kennedy, Acting Program Leader; (202) 690-1428 or (800) 795-3272; fax (202) 690-4737; tracey.kennedy@wdc.usda.gov
Internet: http://www.rurdev.usda.gov/BCP_ReapEaReda.html
Sponsor: U.S. Department of Agriculture
1400 Independence Avenue, SW
Washington, DC 20250

USDA Rural Energy for America - Feasibility Study Grants 4829

The REAP Feasibility Study Grant program provides grants for energy audits and renewable energy development assistance. It also provides funds to agricultural producers and rural small businesses to conduct feasibility study for a renewable energy system. The grants are awarded on a competitive basis and can be up to 25% of total eligible project costs. Grants are limited to $50,000 for renewable energy feasibility studies. Eligible feasibility studies for renewable energy systems include projects that will produce energy from wind, solar, biomass, geothermal, hydro power and hydrogen-based sources. The energy to be produced includes, heat, electricity, or fuel. For all projects, the system must be located in a rural area, must be technically feasible, and must be owned by the applicant. To apply for funding for the REAP Grant Program applicants should contact their Rural Development State Office.
Requirements: The program is designed to assist farmers, ranchers and rural small businesses. All agricultural producers, including farmers and ranchers, who gain 50% or more of their gross income from the agricultural operations are eligible. Small businesses that are located in a rural area can also apply. Rural electric cooperatives may also be eligible to apply.
Geographic Focus: All States
Amount of Grant: Up to 50,000 USD
Contact: Nivin Elgohary, Assistant Administrator; (202) 720-9545 or (202) 720-9540; fax (202) 720-1725; nivin.elgohary@wdc.usda.gov
Internet: http://www.rurdev.usda.gov/BCP_ReapGrants.html
Sponsor: U.S. Department of Agriculture
1400 Independence Avenue, SW
Washington, DC 20250

USDA Rural Energy for America - Renewable Energy System and Energy Efficiency Improvement Guaranteed Grants 4830

The Rural Energy for America Program (REAP) provides financial assistance to agricultural producers and rural small businesses in rural America to purchase, install, and construct renewable energy systems; make energy efficiency improvements to non-residential buildings and facilities; use renewable technologies that reduce energy consumption; and participate in energy audits, renewable energy development assistance, and feasibility studies. REAP creates opportunities for economic development for rural businesses by supporting renewable energy and energy efficiency projects, via loan guarantees and grants. The program provides assistance to qualified applicants to finance renewable energy (renewable biomass, anaerobic digesters, geothermal for electric generation, geothermal for direct use, hydroelectric (30 megawatts or less), hydrogen, small and large wind, small and large solar and ocean (including tidal, wave, current, and thermal) and energy efficiency projects. It expands the existing private credit structure by providing a credit enhancement via a loan guarantee. The REAP Renewable Energy System Grant and Loan Guarantee provides financial assistance to agriculture producers and rural small business for the specific purpose of purchasing, installing and constructing renewable energy systems. This type of assistance may require that a business level feasibility study be completed by an independent qualified consultant as part of the application. Eligible project costs for Renewable Energy Systems and Energy Efficiency Improvements are: post-application purchase and installation of equipment (new, refurbished, or remanufactured), except agricultural tillage equipment, used equipment, and vehicles; post-application construction or improvements, except residential; energy audits or assessments; permit and license fees; professional service fees, except for application preparation; feasibility studies and technical reports; business plans and retrofitting; construction of a new energy efficient facility only when the facility is used for the same purpose, is approximately the same size, and - based on the energy audit - will provide more energy savings than improving an existing facility; only costs identified in the energy audit for energy efficiency improvements are allowed; and new equipment as long as it is of similar size to the equipment being replaced. The minimum Renewable Energy System Grant request is $2,500 up to a maximum of 25 percent of eligible project costs or $500,000, whichever is less. The minimum Energy Efficiency Improvement Grant request is $1,500 up to a maximum of 25 percent of eligible project costs or $250,000, whichever is less.
Requirements: Grant eligibility is limited to rural small businesses and agricultural producers. Grant projects must meet the following conditions: the grant must go towards the purchase of a renewable energy system or to make energy efficiency improvements; the technology is pre-commercial or commercially available, and replicable; the project must have technical merit, as specified in Rural Development Regulation 4280 subpart B; a rural small business must be located in a rural area, though an agriculture producer may be located in a rural or non-rural area; the applicant must be the owner of the project and control the revenues, expenses, operations, and maintenance of the project; sites must be controlled by the agricultural producer or small business for the financing term of any associated Federal loans or loan guarantees; and the project must have satisfactory sources of revenue, for the life of the project, that will be used for the operation, management, maintenance, and debt service of the project.
Geographic Focus: All States
Amount of Grant: 1,500 - 500,000 USD
Contact: Tracey Kennedy, Acting Program Leader; (202) 690-1428 or (800) 795-3272; fax (202) 690-4737; tracey.kennedy@wdc.usda.gov
Internet: http://www.rurdev.usda.gov/BCP_ReapResEei.html
Sponsor: U.S. Department of Agriculture
1400 Independence Avenue, SW
Washington, DC 20250

USDA Rural Housing Repair and Rehabilitation Grants 4831

The USDA Rural Repair and Rehabilitation Grants program provides loans and grants to very low-income homeowners to repair, improve, or modernize their dwellings or to remove health and safety hazards. Grant funds may be used only to pay for repairs and improvements resulting in the removal of health and safety hazards. A grant/loan combination is made if the applicant can repay part of the cost. Grants of up to $7,500 are available. Loans and grants can be combined for up to $27,500 in assistance.
Requirements: Grants are only available to homeowners who are 62 years old or older and cannot repay a Section 504 loan. Repaired properties do not need to meet other HCFP code requirements, but the installation of water and waste systems and related fixtures must meet local health department requirements. Water supply and sewage disposal systems should normally meet HCFP requirements.
Geographic Focus: All States
Amount of Grant: Up to 7,500 USD
Contact: Bill Downs, Acting Director; (202) 720-1499 or (202) 690-1533; fax (202) 690-0500; bill.downs@wdc.usda.gov
Internet: http://www.rurdev.usda.gov/HAD-RR_Loans_Grants.html
Sponsor: U.S. Department of Agriculture
1400 Independence Avenue, SW
Washington, DC 20250

USDA Rural Microentrepreneur Assistance Grants 4832

The purpose of the RMAP program is to support the development and ongoing success of rural microentrepreneurs and microenterprises. Direct loans and grants are made to selected Microenterprise Development Organizations (MDOs). RMAP funding may be used to provide fixed interest rate microloans to rural microentrepreneurs for startup and growing microenterprises. Eligible MDOs will be automatically eligible to receive microlender technical assistance grants to provide technical assistance and training to microentrepreneurs that have received or are seeking a microloan under RMAP. Technical assistance-only grants (for technical assistance and training) may be made to MDOs that have sources of funding other than RMAP funds for making or facilitating microloans. Allowable costs include provision of education, guidance, or instruction to one or more rural microentrepreneurs to: prepare them for self-employment; improve the state of their existing rural microenterprises; increase their capacity in a specific technical aspect of the subject business; and assist a rural microentrepreneur in achieving a degree of business preparedness and/or functions that will allow them to obtain or have the ability to obtain business loans independently. To apply for funding for the Rural Microentrepreneur Assistance Program, applicants should contact their Rural Development State Office.
Requirements: Non-profit entities, Indian tribes, and public institutions of higher education that, for the benefit of rural microentrepreneurs and microenterprises, provides training and technical assistance, makes microloans or facilitates access to capital or another related service, and/or has demonstrated record of delivering, or an effective plan to develop a program to deliver such services are eligible. The following entities are generally eligible to apply for grants from MDOs provided they owe no delinquent debt to the Federal Government: individual citizens or individuals who have been legally admitted to the U.S; those located in a rural area defined as an area of a State not in a city or town that has a population of more than 50,000 inhabitants and the contiguous and adjacent urbanized area; and a microentrepreneur, or microenterprise as defined is a business entity with not more than 10 full-time equivalent employees that is in need of $50,00 or less in business capital and/or in need of business based technical assistance and training.
Geographic Focus: All States
Contact: Claudette Fernandez; (202) 690-4730; claudette.fernandez@wdc.usda.gov
Internet: http://www.rurdev.usda.gov/BCP_RMAP.html
Sponsor: U.S. Department of Agriculture
1400 Independence Avenue, SW
Washington, DC 20250

USDA Rural Utilities Service Weather Radio Transmitter Grants 4833

The Rural Utilities Service Weather Radio Transmitter Grant Program provides grant funds to finance the installation of new transmitters to extend the coverage of the National Oceanic and Atmospheric Administration's Weather Radio system (NOAA Weather Radio) in rural America. Grant funds are available to facilitate the expansion of NOAA Weather Radio system coverage into rural areas that are not covered or are poorly covered. Grant funds are extremely limited. The amount of funds remaining for Weather Radio Transmitter grants likely would not finance a complete weather radio transmitter system. The grant recipient would have to supplement the grant with additional funds of its own. This program provides grant funds for use in rural areas and communities of 50,000 or less inhabitants.
Requirements: Applicants must be non-profit corporations or associations (including Rural Utilities Service electric and telecommunications borrower cooperatives), units of local or state government, or Federally-recognized Indian tribes. Grant funds must be used to purchase and install NOAA Weather Radio transmitters and antennas, plus certain associated facilities that will be combined with donated tower space and other site resources to establish new rural NOAA Weather Radio transmitter sites.
Geographic Focus: All States
Contact: Craig Wulf; (202) 720-8427; fax (202) 720-2734; craig.wulf@wdc.usda.gov
Internet: http://www.rurdev.usda.gov/UTP_WeatherRadio.html
Sponsor: U.S. Department of Agriculture
1400 Independence Avenue, SW
Washington, DC 20250

USDA Section 306C Water and Waste Disposal Grants to Alleviate Health Risks 4834

The primary purpose of the USDA Section 306C Water and Waste Disposal Grants to Alleviate Health Risks program is to provide water and waste disposal facilities and services to low income rural communities whose residents face significant health risks. Every effort is made to identify and fund the neediest projects. The use of RD loan funds, as well as funds from other sources, in conjunction with the grant funds is strongly encouraged whenever feasible to maximize the investment. Generally, applicants are expected to borrow as much as they can afford to repay, as in the regular loan program. However, water and waste disposal systems can obtain up to 100 percent grants to construct basic drinking water, sanitary sewer, solid waste disposal and storm drainage to serve the residents of Colonias. Also, under this program, the

systems can obtain funds to provide grant assistance directly to individuals to install necessary indoor plumbing like bathrooms and pay other costs of connecting to the system. Applications are accepted at any time through our Rural Development State and Area Offices.
Requirements: These funds have been set aside for eligible projects that benefit members of Federally Recognized Native American Tribes and the Colonias area. Colonias is a term used to describe subdivisions that exist outside incorporated areas located along the United States-Mexico border. Colonias are generally characterized as small communities with inadequate drinking water, poor sanitary waste disposal facilities, and substandard housing. Residents of the rural area to be served must face significant health risks due to the fact that a significant proportion of the community residents do not have access to, or are not served by, adequate, affordable, water and/or waste disposal systems. Documentation to support the poor sanitary waste disposal and health risks should be provided to USDA.
Geographic Focus: All States
Contact: Jacqueline M. Ponti-Lazaruk, Assistant Administrator; (202) 690-2670; fax (202) 690-0649; jacki.ponti@wdc.usda.gov
Internet: http://www.rurdev.usda.gov/UWP-Colonias.html
Sponsor: U.S. Department of Agriculture
1400 Independence Avenue, SW
Washington, DC 20250

USDA Section 306D Water and Waste System Grants for Alaskan Villages   4835
The primary purpose of the USDA Section 306D Water and Waste system Grants for Alaskan Villages is to fund water and waste disposal systems in rural Alaskan Villages. Funds must be used for development and construction of water and wastewater systems to correct dire health and sanitation conditions in those villages. Many communities in remote rural Alaska, where villages are accessible by plane or boat only, are essentially inaccessible during the long, hard winters. They lag far behind the lower 48 States in having safe and dependable drinking water and suitable waste disposal systems available. Construction costs are extremely high. This is due in part to the severe weather conditions, which makes laying pipe difficult, if not impossible. These conditions also require the use of insulated pipe, or in areas of permafrost, above ground utilidors, often with heat traced insulated pipe. The vast distances from the transportation hub of Anchorage to a village increases costs substantially as the material must be delivered by barge or air. This maximum grant is 75 percent of the project cost. Predevelopment planning grants are also available in conjunction with this program. Applications are accepted at any time through our Rural Development State and Area Offices.
Requirements: The applicant for these grants must be a rural Alaskan Village or the State of Alaska for the benefit of a rural Alaskan Village or hub.
Restrictions: There is a match requirement from the State of Alaska for 25 percent of the project cost.
Geographic Focus: Alaska
Contact: Jacqueline M. Ponti-Lazaruk, Assistant Administrator; (202) 690-2670; fax (202) 690-0649; jacki.ponti@wdc.usda.gov
Internet: http://www.rurdev.usda.gov/UWP-AlaskanVillage.html
Sponsor: U.S. Department of Agriculture
1400 Independence Avenue, SW
Washington, DC 20250

USDA Self-Help Technical Assistance Grants   4836
Self-Help Technical Assistance Grants provide financial assistance to qualified nonprofit organizations and public bodies in building homes in rural areas for low-income individuals and their families. Any state, political subdivision, private or public nonprofit corporation is eligible to apply. Grants are used to pay salaries, rent, and office expenses of the nonprofit organization. Pre-development grants up to $10,000 may be available to qualified organizations. Specific information and a current application are available at the applicant's local Rural Development office. State contacts are posted on the website.
Requirements: Eligible organizations may use technical assistance funds to hire the personnel to carry out a technical assistance program for self-help housing in rural areas; to pay necessary and reasonable office and administrative expenses; to purchase or rent equipment such as power tools for use by families participating in self-help housing construction; and to pay fees for training self-help group members in construction techniques or for other professional services needed.
Restrictions: Funds may not be used to hire personnel to perform any construction work, to buy real estate or building materials, or pay any debts, expenses, or costs other than outlined for participating families in self-help projects.
Geographic Focus: All States
Amount of Grant: Up to 10,000 USD
Contact: Bill Downs; (202) 720-9647 or (202) 690-1533; bill.downs@wdc.usda.gov
Internet: http://www.rurdev.usda.gov/HAD-Self-Help_Grants.html
Sponsor: U.S. Department of Agriculture
1400 Independence Avenue, SW
Washington, DC 20250

USDA Small, Socially-Disadvantaged Producer Grants   4837
Formerly known as the Small, Minority Producer Grant Program, the primary objective of the SSDPG program is to provide technical assistance to small, socially-disadvantaged agricultural producers through eligible cooperatives and associations of cooperatives. Grants are awarded on a competitive basis. The maximum award amount per grant is $175,000.
Requirements: Cooperatives and Cooperative Development Centers are eligible to apply for the SSDPG Program.
Restrictions: Grant funds shall not be used to pay for any of the following activities; duplicate current services or replace or substitute support previously provided. If the current service is inadequate, however, grant funds may be used to expand the level of effort or services beyond that which is currently being provided; pay costs of preparing the application package for funding under this program; pay costs of the project incurred prior to the date of grant approval; fund political or lobbying activities; pay for assistance to any private business enterprise that does not have at least 51 percent ownership by those who are either citizens of the United States or reside in the United States after being legally admitted for permanent residence; pay any judgment or debt owed to the United States; plan, repair, rehabilitate, acquire, or construct a building or facility, including a processing facility; purchase, rent, or install fixed equipment, including processing equipment; purchase vehicles, including boats; pay for operating costs of cooperatives or association of cooperatives; fund research and development; fund any activities prohibited by 7 CFR part 3015 or 3019; pay expenses for applicant employee training; pay expenses not directly related to the funded project; fund any direct expenses related for the production of any commodity or product to which value will be added, including seed, rootstock, labor for harvesting the crop, and delivery of the commodity to a processing facility; purchase land; or fund architectural or engineering design work for a specific physical facility.
Geographic Focus: All States
Amount of Grant: Up to 175,000 USD
Contact: Tracey Kennedy, Acting Program Leader; (800) 795-3272 or (202) 720-8460; fax (202) 690-4737; tracey.kennedy@wdc.usda.gov or cpgrants@wdc.usda.gov
Internet: http://www.rurdev.usda.gov/BCP_SSDPG.html
Sponsor: U.S. Department of Agriculture
1400 Independence Avenue, SW
Washington, DC 20250

USDA Solid Waste Management Grants   4838
The purpose of the USDA Solid Waste Management Grant program is to evaluate current landfill conditions to determine threats to water resources. Provide technical assistance and/or training to enhance operator skills in the operation and maintenance of active landfills. Provide technical assistance and/or training to help communities reduce the solid waste stream. Provide technical assistance and/or training for operators of landfills which are closed or will be closed in the near future with the development and implementation of closure plans, future land use plans, safety and maintenance planning, and closure scheduling within permit requirements. Applications will be accepted from October 1 through December 31 of each calendar year.
Requirements: Entities eligible for Solid Waste Management (SWM) grants are: private nonprofit organizations with tax exempt status designated by the Internal Revenue Service; public bodies; federally acknowledged or State recognized Native American tribe or group; and academic institutions. Organizations must be incorporated by December 31 of the year the application period occurs to be eligible for funds. Applicants must also have the proven ability; background; experience, as evidenced by the organization's satisfactory completion of project(s) similar to those proposed; legal authority; and actual capacity to provide technical assistance and/or training on a regional basis to associations as provided in 1775.63.
Restrictions: Private businesses, Federal agencies, and individuals are ineligible for these grants.
Geographic Focus: All States
Date(s) Application is Due: Dec 31
Contact: Jacqueline M. Ponti-Lazaruk, Assistant Administrator; (202) 690-2670 or (202) 690-0649; jacki.ponti@wdc.usda.gov
Internet: http://www.rurdev.usda.gov/UWP-solidwastemanagement.htm
Sponsor: U.S. Department of Agriculture
1400 Independence Avenue, SW
Washington, DC 20250

USDA Special Research Grants   4839
The program supports research to facilitate or expand promising breakthroughs in areas of the food and agricultural sciences of importance to the nation and to facilitate or expand ongoing state-federal food and agricultural research programs. Areas of basic and applied research are generally limited to high-priority problems of a regional or national scope. Areas currently considered are water quality, integrated pest management, potato breeding, and range land research. Application deadlines are announced each fiscal year in the Federal Register and may also be obtained by calling the Office of Extramural Programs.
Requirements: State agricultural experiment stations, all colleges and universities, other research institutions and organizations, federal agencies, private organizations or corporations, and individuals having a demonstrable capacity to conduct research to facilitate or expand promising breakthroughs in areas of the food and agricultural sciences of importance to the United States are eligible to apply.
Geographic Focus: All States
Amount of Grant: Up to 95,000,000 USD
Contact: Andrea L. Brandon; (202) 720-9181; abrandon@nifa.usda.gov
Internet: http://www.csrees.usda.gov/funding/rfas/pmap.html
Sponsor: U.S. Department of Agriculture
1400 Independence Avenue, SW, Stop 2201
Washington, DC 20250-2201

USDA State Bulk Fuel Revolving Fund Grants   4840
The High Energy Cost Grant Program provides financial assistance for the improvement of energy generation, transmission, and distribution facilities servicing eligible rural communities with home energy costs that are over 275 percent of the national average. Grants under this program may be used for the acquisition, construction, installation, repair, replacement, or improvement of energy generation, transmission, or distribution facilities in communities with extremely high energy costs. On-grid and off-grid renewable energy projects, and energy efficiency, and energy conservation projects are eligible. State Bulk Fuel Revolving Fund Grants (CFDA 10.858) are made to state government entities to establish and support revolving funds to provide a more cost-effective means of purchasing fuel for remote communities that are not served by surface transportation year round.

Geographic Focus: All States
Contact: Kristi Kubista-Hovis, Rural Development Electric Programs; (202) 720-9545; fax (202) 690-0717; Kristi.Kubista-Hovis@wdc.usda.gov
Internet: http://www.rurdev.usda.gov/UEP_Our_grant_programs.html
Sponsor: U.S. Department of Agriculture
1400 Independence Avenue, SW
Washington, DC 20250

USDA Technical and Supervisory Assistance Grants 4841
The Technical and Supervisory Assistance Grants fund housing delivery and counseling projects to assist low-income rural families in obtaining adequate housing and/or to provide the necessary guidance to promote their continued occupancy of already adequate housing. Uses of grant funds may include, but are not limited to: the development and implementation of a program of technical and supervisory assistance; reasonable salaries of professional, technical, and clerical staff; necessary and reasonable office expenses such as office supplies and office rental, office utilities, telephone services, and office equipment rental; administrative costs such as work compensation, liability insurance, audit reports, travel to and attendance at RD approved training sessions, and the employer's share of Social Security and health benefits; reasonable fees for necessary training of grantee personnel, including travel and per diem to attend authorized regional training sessions; and other reasonable travel and miscellaneous expenses. Specific guidelines, current applications, and state requirements are available at local Rural Development offices. All state offices and contacts are available at the website.
Requirements: Applicants must be public or private nonprofit corporations, agencies, institutions, organizations, federally recognized tribes, and other associations.
Restrictions: Grant funds may not be used for the following: acquisition construction, repair, or rehabilitation of structures or acquisition of land, vehicles, or equipment; replacement of or substitution for any financial support which would be available from any other source; duplication of current services; hiring personnel to perform construction; buying property of any kind from families receiving technical or supervisory assistance from the grantee under the terms of the TSA grant; paying for or reimbursing the grantee for any expenses or debts incurred before RHS/RD executes the grant agreement; paying any debts, expenses or costs which should be the responsibilities of the individual families receiving technical and supervisory assistance; any type of political activities, and other costs including contributions and donations, entertainment, fines and penalties, interest and other financial costs, legislative expenses and any excess of cost from other grant agreements.
Geographic Focus: All States
Contact: Bill Downs, Acting Director; (202) 720-9647 or (202) 690-1533; fax (202) 690-0500; bill.downs@wdc.usda.gov
Internet: http://www.rurdev.usda.gov/HAD-TSA_Grants.html
Sponsor: U.S. Department of Agriculture
1400 Independence Avenue, SW
Washington, DC 20250

USDA Technical Assistance and Training Grants for Rural Waste Systems 4842
The Technical Assistance and Training Grants fund technical assistance and/or training to associations (located in rural areas, cities, or towns with a population of 10,000 or less) on a wide range of issues relating to delivery of water and waste disposal service. Grants must be used to generate a Technical Assistance and Training program for the purpose of: identifying and evaluating solutions to water problems of associations in rural areas relating to source, storage, treatment, or distribution; identifying and evaluating solutions to waste problems of associations in rural areas relating to collection, treatment, or disposal; assisting associations in the preparation of water and/or waste loan and/or grant applications; providing technical assistance and/or training to association personnel that will improve the management, operation and maintenance of water and waste disposal facilities; or paying expenses associated with providing the assistance and training. Specific guidelines and current applications are available at the state regional offices. Regional office contacts are located on the website.
Requirements: Grants may be made to private non-profit corporations that have been granted tax exempt status by the Internal Revenue Service. Applicants must also have the proven ability, background, experience, legal authority, and capacity to provide technical assistance and/or training on a regional basis to associations. Grant assistance is available to qualified applicants to identify and evaluate solutions to water and waste disposal problems, to improve operation and maintenance of existing water and waste disposal facilities, and to assist associations in preparing applications for water and waste disposal facilities in rural areas. Applicants must submit their information to the appropriate agency office between October 1 and December 31 each fiscal year.
Restrictions: Grant funds may not be used for the following: duplicate current services, or replace or substitute support normally provided by other means, such as those performed by an association's consultant in developing a project, including feasibility, design, and cost estimates; fund political or lobbying activities; purchase real estate or vehicles, improve or renovate office space, or repair and maintain privately owned property; pay the costs for construction, improvement, rehabilitation, modification or operation and maintenance of water, wastewater, and solid waste disposal facilities; construct or furnish a building; intervene in the federal regulatory or adjudicatory proceedings; sue the federal government or any other government entities.
Geographic Focus: All States, Puerto Rico, U.S. Virgin Islands, American Samoa
Contact: Jacqueline Ponti-Lazaruk; (202) 690-2670 or (202) 720-9589; fax (202) 720-0718; jacki.ponti@wdc.usda.gov
Internet: http://www.rurdev.usda.gov/UWP-wwtat.htm
Sponsor: U.S. Department of Agriculture
1400 Independence Avenue, SW
Washington, DC 20250

USDA Value-Added Producer Grants 4843
The primary objective of the VAPG program is to help agricultural producers enter into value-added activities related to the processing and/or marketing of bio-based value-added products. Generating new products, creating and expanding marketing opportunities, and increasing producer income are the end goals of this program. Two types of grants are available: Planning Grants (maximum $100,000) for economic planning activities, such as feasibility studies, or development of marketing and/or business plans for a value-added venture; and Working Capital Grants (maximum $300,000) for expenses related to the marketing and/or processing of the value-added product. For more information about the program, contact your State Rural Development Office. A contact person, address, phone number, and email address for each State Office is posted on the website.
Requirements: Eligible applicants are independent producers, farmer and rancher cooperatives, agricultural producer groups, and majority-controlled producer-based business ventures. Grant amounts are limited to 50 percent of total eligible project costs. Applications require confirmation of matching funds for the balance of project costs at application submission.
Geographic Focus: All States
Amount of Grant: Up to 300,000 USD
Contact: Tracey Kennedy, Acting Program Leader; (202) 690-1428 or (202) 690-4730; fax (202) 690-4737; tracey.kennedy@wdc.usda.gov
Internet: http://www.rurdev.usda.gov/BCP_VAPG_Grants.html
Sponsor: U.S. Department of Agriculture
1400 Independence Avenue, SW
Washington, DC 20250

USDA Water and Waste Disposal Grants 4844
The purpose of the USDA Water and Waste Disposal Grant program is to develop water and waste disposal systems in rural areas and towns with a population not in excess of 10,000. Applications are accepted at any time through our Rural Development State and Area Offices.
Requirements: The funds are available to public bodies, non-profit corporations and Indian tribes. To qualify, applicants must be unable to obtain the financing from other sources at rates and terms they can afford and/or their own resources. Funds can be used for construction, land acquisition, legal fees, engineering fees, capitalized interest, equipment, initial operation and maintenance costs, project contingencies, and any other cost that is determined by the Rural Development to be necessary for the completion of the project. Projects must be primarily for the benefit of rural users.
Geographic Focus: All States
Contact: Scott Barringer; (202) 720-9583; fax (202)690-0649
Internet: http://www.rurdev.usda.gov/UWP-dispdirectloansgrants.htm
Sponsor: U.S. Department of Agriculture
1400 Independence Avenue, SW
Washington, DC 20250

USDC/NOAA American Rivers Community-Based Restoration River Grants 4845
The Community-Based Restoration Program River Grants program funds river restoration projects in the Northeast, Mid-Atlantic, Northwest, and California. NOAA, an agency of the U.S. Commerce Department, and American Rivers will jointly evaluate proposals and award grants to implement fish passage, selective dam removal, and other associated habitat restoration projects that benefit anadromous and marine resources. These grants are designed to provide support for local communities that are utilizing dam removal or fish passage to restore and protect the ecological integrity of their rivers and improve freshwater habitats important to migratory (anadromous) fish. Applications are being evaluated based upon four priority criteria: ecological merits of the project technical feasibility of the project; benefits provided to the local community; and financial clarity and strength of the application. Grants are provided for three distinct project phases: Construction, Engineering Design and Feasibility Analysis. Proposals for Construction phase funding may request a maximum award of $150,000. Proposals for Engineering Design or Feasibility Analysis phases may request a maximum award of $100,000. Eligible groups will demonstrate how their project: will successfully restore anadromous fish habitat, access to existing anadromous fish habitat, or natural riverine functions; is the correct approach, based on ecological, social, economic, and engineering considerations; will minimize any identifiable short- or long-term negative impacts to the river system as a result of the project; has had community involvement in project decision making and may have community involvement in the implementation; and will have the potential for public outreach and education. Potential applicants are strongly encouraged to contact American Rivers to discuss potential projects prior to submitting an application.
Requirements: Stream barrier removal projects in the Northeast, Mid-Atlantic, Northwest and California are eligible to apply.
Geographic Focus: All States
Date(s) Application is Due: Dec 9
Amount of Grant: 25,000 - 150,000 USD
Contact: Serena McClain, (202) 347-7550, ext. 3004; fax (202) 347-9240; smcclain@americanrivers.org or rivergrants@americanrivers.org
Internet: http://www.americanrivers.org/our-work/restoring-rivers/dams/background/noaa-grants-program.html
Sponsor: U.S. Department of Commerce
1401 Constitution Avenue, NW, Room 5128
Washington, DC 20230

USDC/NOAA National Marine Aquaculture Initiative Grants 4846
NOAA launched the National Marine Aquaculture Initiative (NMAI) in 1998 to encourage scientific research and development to support a robust, sustainable domestic marine aquaculture industry. The competition fosters dynamic partnerships that channel resources toward the development of sustainable aquaculture technologies. Projects often

involve partnerships among commercial companies, research institutions, universities, state governments, and coastal communities. Currently, NOAA Sea Grant's National Marine Aquaculture Initiative is making $3.2 million available through a Sea Grant Aquaculture Research competitive grants program. Funds will support marine aquaculture research projects as part of the overall plan to support the development of environmentally and economically sustainable ocean, coastal, and Great Lakes aquaculture. Priorities for this competition include: research to inform specific regulatory decisions; research that supports multi-use spatial planning; and socio-economic research targeted to understand aquaculture in a larger context. The deadline for receipt of preproposals via electronic mail at the National Sea Grant Office is 4:00 p.m. Eastern Time on February 7.
Requirements: Institutions of higher education, nonprofit organizations, commercial organizations, State, local and Indian tribal governments and individuals are eligible.
Restrictions: Federal agencies and their personnel are not permitted to receive federal funding under this competition; however, federal scientists can serve as uncompensated partners or co-Principal Investigators on research proposals. Directors of the state Sea Grant Programs are not eligible to compete for funds under this announcement, although for administrative purposes, they will be considered to be the Principal Investigator for all awards made to their state programs.
Geographic Focus: All States
Date(s) Application is Due: Feb 7
Amount of Grant: 50,000 - 500,000 USD
Contact: Dr. Gene Kim, (301) 734-1281; oar.hq.sg.aquaculture@noaa.gov
Internet: http://www.grants.gov/search/search.do;jsessionid=MynvQR9LnVNshhngjY2T HgjbvFLty914kZ1Fwnq4PVT5shWzCxgy!1460891328?oppId=135993&mode=VIEW
Sponsor: U.S. Department of Commerce
1401 Constitution Avenue, NW, Room 5128
Washington, DC 20230

USDC/NOAA Open Rivers Initiative Grants 4847
The NOAA Open Rivers Initiative (ORI) provides funding to catalyze the implementation of locally-driven projects to remove dams and other river barriers, in order to benefit living marine and coastal resources, particularly diadromous fish. Projects funded through the Open Rivers Initiative have strong on-the-ground habitat restoration components that foster economic, educational, and social benefits for citizens and their communities in addition to long-term ecological habitat improvements for NOAA trust resources. Through the ORI, NOAA provides funding and technical assistance for barrier removal projects. Proposals selected for funding through this solicitation will be implemented through a cooperative agreement. Funding of up to $7,000,000 is expected to be available for ORI Project Grants. The Office of Habitat Conservation will administer this grant initiative, and anticipates that typical awards will range from $200,000 to $750,000. Although a select few may fall outside of this range, project proposals requesting less than $100,000 or greater than $3,000,000 will not be accepted.
Requirements: Eligible applicants are institutions of higher education, non-profits, industry and commercial (for profit) organizations, organizations under the jurisdiction of foreign governments, international organizations, and state, local and Indian tribal governments whose projects have the potential to benefit NOAA trust resources.
Restrictions: Applications from federal agencies or employees of federal agencies will not be considered.
Geographic Focus: All States
Date(s) Application is Due: Nov 17
Contact: Cathy Bozek, (301) 713-0174, ext. 150; cathy.bozek@noaa.gov
Internet: http://www.habitat.noaa.gov/funding/ori.html
Sponsor: U.S. Department of Commerce
1401 Constitution Avenue, NW, Room 5128
Washington, DC 20230

USDC Advanced Manufacturing Jobs and Innovation Accelerator Grants 4848
The Advanced Manufacturing Jobs and Innovation Accelerator Challenge (Advanced Manufacturing Jobs Accelerator) will provide strategic, catalytic funding for competitive, high potential regional partnerships that accelerate innovation and strengthen capacity in advanced manufacturing. The objectives of the challenge are to create jobs, grow the economy, and enhance the competitiveness of U.S. manufacturers in the global marketplace. The participating agencies in the Advanced Manufacturing Jobs Accelerator intend to offer a combination of funding and technical assistance to approximately 12 projects across the United States, with individual grant awards of approximately $800,000 over an expected project period of three years. Applicants may propose projects that focus on providing education and training to unemployed workers, incumbent (employed) workers, and/or post-secondary students who are pursuing a high-skill occupation. Participants must be at least 18 years of age. Applicants should direct all technical questions regarding the EDA program to the appropriate EDA Regional Office listed in the announcement.
Requirements: Funds awarded under the 7(j) Technical Assistance Program may be used to conduct planning and research (including feasibility studies and market research); identify and develop new business opportunities; furnish centralized services with regard to public services and Federal government programs; establish and strengthen business service agencies (including trade associations and cooperatives); and, furnish business counseling, management training, and legal and other related services.
Geographic Focus: All States
Date(s) Application is Due: Jul 9
Contact: Sanchia Gomez, (215) 597-4400
Internet: http://www.eda.gov/ffo.htm
Sponsor: U.S. Department of Commerce
1401 Constitution Avenue, NW, Suite 7800
Washington, DC 20230

USDC Business Center - American Indian and Alaska Native Program Grants 4849
The Minority Business Development Agency (MBDA) is the only federal agency created specifically to foster the full participation and entrepreneurial parity of minority business enterprises (MBEs) in our national economy. MBDA actively promotes the growth and global competitiveness of U.S. businesses that are minority-owned by offering strategic deal-making and business consulting services through a nationwide network comprised of MBDA staff and the MBDA Business Center program funded by the Agency. This Federal Funding Opportunity (FFO) announces the anticipated availability of funding for the MBDA Business Center – American Indian and Alaska Native program, and solicits competitive applications for operators of MBDA Business Centers – American Indian and Alaska Native in six locations. The services provided will be implemented to generate increased financing and contract opportunities and related awards to minority business enterprises (MBEs). In addition, the services provided will assist MBEs to create and retain jobs.MBDA intends to award six (6) individual cooperative agreements pursuant to this FFO. The total award period for each of the MBDA Business Center – American Indian and Alaska Native projects is expected to be five (5) years. Specific locations and funding amounts for the MBDA Business Center – American Indian and Alaska Native projects are detailed in the table below and in Appendix A of the full text of the announcement. MBDA will fund the financial assistance awards for the projects identified in this FFO for a total of $1,575,000 in FY 2012. Funding for future years of this program has not yet been appropriated. The Agency also anticipates that $1,575,000 will be available in FY 2013 through FY 2016 to support continuation funding for this project.Note: The MBDA Business Center – American Indian and Alaska Native program is not a grant program to start or to expand an individual business. Applications under this FFO must be to operate an MBDA Business Center – American Indian and Alaska Native and to provide business consulting services to eligible minority-owned firms as set forth in this FFO. Applications that do not meet these requirements will not be considered by MBDA for funding. The award period under this solicitation is anticipated to be five (5) years, with five consecutive funding periods. Applicants must submit project plans and budgets for the entire award period and for each of the five (5) funding periods.
Requirements: For-profit entities (including but not limited to sole-proprietorships, partnerships, limited liability companies and corporations), non-profit organizations, state and local government entities, Native American Tribes and educational institutions are eligible to apply to operate MBDA Business Centers.
Geographic Focus: All States
Contact: Cynthia Rios, Program Management Unit Supervisor; (202) 482-1940
Internet: http://www.grants.gov/search/search.do;jsessionid=xcckPprcn1L1yLLSWyvJFJZ hR7BhKs69Zwxbf7Z1xG1MmhLv0qWY!64499778?oppId=170153&mode=VIEW
Sponsor: U.S. Department of Commerce
1401 Constitution Avenue, NW
Washington, DC 20230

USDC Disaster Relief Opportunity Grants 4850
Through this Disaster Relief Opportunity, EDA intends to award investments in regions experiencing severe economic distress as a result of natural disasters that were declared as major Federal disasters. The EAA program provides a wide range of technical, disaster recovery, economic recovery planning, and public works assistance. It responds adaptively to pressing economic recovery issues and is well-suited to help address challenges faced by regions affected by natural disasters. Through this program, EDA can support the development of disaster recovery strategies and recovery implementation, including infrastructure improvements and by using revolving loan funds (RLFs). Subject to the availability of funds, EDA may enter into grants or cooperative agreements with eligible applicants in order to provide funding for eligible investment activities under this Disaster Relief Opportunity.
Requirements: Pursuant to PWEDA, an eligible applicant for and eligible recipient of EDA investment assistance under this announcement include a(n): district organization; Indian Tribe or a consortium of Indian Tribes; State, city or other political subdivision of a State, including a special purpose unit of a State or local government engaged in economic or infrastructure development activities, or a consortium of political subdivisions; institution of higher education or a consortium of institutions of higher education; or public or private non-profit organization or association acting in cooperation with officials of a political subdivision of a State.
Geographic Focus: All States
Date(s) Application is Due: Mar 28
Contact: H. Philip Paradice, Jr., Regional Director; (404) 730-3002; fax (404) 730-3025
Internet: http://www.grants.gov/search/search.do;jsessionid=t2WqPzpK7yW8yGJTBLQt GftPCVhJfbpJ0n6jzsBTxfTcsw26y4gQ!1869518295?oppId=159393&mode=VIEW
Sponsor: U.S. Department of Commerce
1401 Constitution Avenue, NW, Suite 7800
Washington, DC 20230

USDC i6 Challenge Grants 4851
EDA solicits competitive applications to encourage and reward innovative, ground-breaking ideas that greatly expand innovation, commercialization and new enterprise formation across the United States. The i6 Challenge will award applicants submitting the best strategies to create Proof of Concept Centers that greatly increase innovation within their organizations, create processes to commercialize or implement innovation, and build networks that can utilize that innovation and entrepreneurship for local economic development. EDA, subject to the availability of funds, intends to award at least six winning applicants, one per EDA region, grants of up to $1,000,000 each for a project period of up to two years from date of award. In addition, Small Business Innovation Research grants that are part of or central to winning applications may be eligible to receive supplemental awards from participating agencies after the initial technical and merit review conducted by EDA. The Office of Innovation and Entrepreneurship will work with interested applicants to share their applications with the appropriate agency partners. Deadline for submission of applications is July 20.

Requirements: Under this FFO, applicants must demonstrate at the time of application a matching share which must be available and committed to the project from non-Federal sources. EDA will give preference to applications with higher matching shares to further leverage Federal funds and help ensure additional project impact. Generally, the amount of an EDA grant may not exceed 50 percent of the total cost of the project. Eligible applicants include: State governments; county governments; city or township governments; public and state controlled institutions of higher education; Native American tribal governments (Federally recognized); nonprofits having a 501(c)3 status with the IRS, other than institutions of higher education; nonprofits that do not have a 501(c)3 status with the IRS, other than institutions of higher education; private institutions of higher education; and others (defined at the website).
Geographic Focus: All States
Date(s) Application is Due: Jul 20
Amount of Grant: Up to 1,000,000 USD
Contact: Chivas Grannum, (215) 597-4603; fax (215) 597-1063
Robin Cooley, (404) 730-3002; fax (404) 730-3025
Internet: http://www.grants.gov/search/search.do;jsessionid=pt6rPXYBTqxZqv1YCLrdn YJBgkysdd2yvpqQxThnqpcgDNhpJglh!-2018416081?oppId=175993&mode=VIEW
Sponsor: U.S. Department of Commerce
1401 Constitution Avenue, NW, Suite 7800
Washington, DC 20230

USDC Low-Power Television and Translator Upgrade Grants 4852
The Low-Power Television and Translator Upgrade program reimburses the eligible costs to upgrade analog low power television broadcast stations, Class A television stations, television translator stations, and television booster stations in rural communities to digital transmission. Applications are received the first business day of each month, and the final closing date for receipt of Upgrade program applications will be July 2.
Requirements: Eligible stations must be broadcasting a licensed digital signal before applying for a grant.
Geographic Focus: All States
Date(s) Application is Due: Jul 2
Contact: Dr. Bernadette McGuire-Rivera, Associate Administrator; (202) 482-5802; fax (202) 501-8009; bmcguire-rivera@ntia.doc.gov
Internet: http://www.ntia.doc.gov/category/low-power-television-and-translator-program
Sponsor: U.S. Department of Commerce
1401 Constitution Avenue, NW
Washington, DC 20230

USDC Market Development Cooperator Program (MDCP) Grants 4853
The goal of the Market Development Cooperator Program is to develop, maintain, and expand foreign markets for non-agricultural goods and services produced in the United States. The intended beneficiaries of the program are U.S. producers of non-agricultural goods or services that seek to export such goods or services. The International Trade Administration (ITA) encourages applicants to propose activities that would be most appropriate to the market development needs of their U.S. industry or industries. Examples of activities might include: opening an overseas office or offices to perform a variety of market development services for companies joining a consortium to avail themselves of such services; detailing a private-sector representative to a US&FCS post in accordance with 15 USC 4723(c); commissioning overseas market research, participating in overseas trade exhibitions, and trade missions to promote U.S. exports, and/or hosting reverse trade missions; and conducting U.S. product demonstrations abroad. The applicant must contribute at least two dollars for each federal dollar provided. Full guidelines are available on the website or may be obtained by contacting the office listed. No award will exceed $300,000. ITA anticipates concluding seven (7) to ten (10) awards.
Requirements: U.S. trade associations; nonprofit industry organizations; state trade departments and their regional associations, including centers for international trade development; and private industry firms or groups of firms in cases where no entity described above represents that industry are eligible.
Geographic Focus: All States
Date(s) Application is Due: Feb 21
Contact: Brad Hess; (202) 482-2969; fax (202) 482-5828; Brad.Hess@trade.gov
Internet: http://ita.doc.gov/td/mdcp/
Sponsor: U.S. Department of Commerce - 1
14th Street and Constitution Avenue NW, Herbert C Hoover Building
Washington, DC 20230

USDC Planning and Local Technical Assistance Grants 4854
The Economic Development Administration announces general policies and application procedures for grant-based investments under the Planning and Local Technical Assistance Programs. These programs will help communities develop the planning and technical expertise to support communities and regions in their comprehensive, entrepreneurial, and innovation-based economic development efforts. Resulting in increased private investment and higher-skill, higher-wage jobs in areas experiencing substantial and persistent economic distress, these programs are designed to enhance the competitiveness of regions. EDA's Planning and Local Technical Assistance Programs are two of the six economic development assistance programs the agency operates. Under the Planning Program, EDA provides assistance to eligible recipients to create regional economic development plans in order to stimulate and guide the economic development efforts of a community or region. EDA's Local Technical Assistance Program helps eligible recipients fill the knowledge and information gaps that may prevent leaders in the public and nonprofit sectors in economically distressed regions from making optimal decisions on local economic development issues.
Requirements: Eligible applicants include: district organizations; Indian tribes or a consortium of Indian tribes; states, cities or other political subdivisions of a state, including special purpose units of a state or local government engaged in economic or infrastructure development activities, or a consortium of political subdivisions; institutions of higher education or a consortium of institutions of higher education; or public or private non-profit organizations or associations acting in cooperation with officials of a political subdivision of a state.
Restrictions: EDA is not authorized to provide grants directly to individuals or to for-profit entities seeking to start or expand a private business.
Geographic Focus: All States
Contact: Lindsey Pangretic, Director, Research and National Technical Assistance Division; (202) 482-4085 or (202) 482-2900; grants@eda.doc.gov
Internet: http://www.grants.gov/search/search.do;jsessionid=kDW2PsLT1zdv3HLW1Bp wx3yQyQbpJPt1XnmTfyM1yGJpBP99tt2g!-757993493?oppId=58876&mode=VIEW
Sponsor: U.S. Department of Commerce
1401 Constitution Avenue, NW, Suite 7800
Washington, DC 20230

USDC Postsecondary Grants Internships 4855
The Postsecondary Grants Internship Program (PGIP) integrates academic theory and workplace requirements. Students in the program gain increased skills and knowledge, explore Federal career options, develop professional networks, and gain a greater awareness of the role of Federal agencies. Both summer and academic-year internships are available under this program on an on-going basis. The program offers a 10-week summer term and 15-week fall and spring terms. Most internship placements are in the Washington, D.C. area, but some assignments are available at locations around the United States at Census regional and local offices. Internship selections are made from a pool of high potential college undergraduate and graduate students through Commerce's program partners. Interns receive stipends as well as paid domestic round-trip transportation expenses between their schools/homes and work location. Assistance with temporary housing arrangements is also provided.
Requirements: Basic eligibility requires a student to be a U.S. citizen enrolled as an undergraduate or graduate student at an accredited educational institution.
Geographic Focus: All States
Contact: Chris A. Cowan; (301) 480-3538; chris.cowan@hhs.gov
Internet: http://www.census.gov/hrd/www/jobs/pgip.html
Sponsor: U.S. Department of Commerce
4600 Silver Hill Road
Washington, DC 20233

USDC Public Works and Economic Adjustment Assistance Grants 4856
The Economic Development Administration (EDA) supports development in economically distressed areas of the United States by fostering job creation and attracting private investment. Specifically, under this Federal Funding Opportunity (FFO), EDA will consider construction, non-construction, and revolving loan fund investments under the Public Works and Economic Adjustment Assistance programs. Grants made under these programs will leverage regional assets to support the implementation of regional economic development strategies designed to create jobs, leverage private capital, encourage economic development, and strengthen America's ability to compete in the global marketplace. Under this FFO, EDA solicits applications from rural and urban communities to develop initiatives that advance new ideas and creative approaches to address rapidly evolving economic conditions.
Requirements: Eligible applicants for EDA investment assistance include: a state, city, county, or other political subdivision of a state, including a special purpose unit of a State or local government engaged in economic or infrastructure development activities, or a consortium of such political subdivision; an institution of higher education or a consortium of institutions of higher education; an Economic Development District organization; a private or public nonprofit organization or association, including a faith-based non-profit organization, acting in cooperation with officials of a political subdivision of a State; or an Indian Tribe, or a consortium of Indian Tribes. As used in this paragraph, 'State' includes the Commonwealth of Puerto Rico, the U.S. Virgin Islands, Guam, American Samoa, the Commonwealth of the Northern Mariana Islands, the Republic of the Marshall Islands, the Federated States of Micronesia, and the Republic of Palau.
Restrictions: Individuals, companies, corporations and associations organized for profit are not eligible.
Geographic Focus: All States, Guam, Marshall Islands, Northern Mariana Islands, Puerto Rico, U.S. Virgin Islands, American Samoa, Micronesia, Palau
Date(s) Application is Due: Mar 9; Jun 8; Sep 14; Dec 15
Contact: H. Philip Paradice, Jr.; (404) 730-3002; pparadice@eda.doc.gov
Internet: http://www.grants.gov/search/search.do;jsessionid=XfMNPyLVtKZGfvLW3JwvdS K5pPRLXhYfvGW9cMTxNhDKM5QzmZ6x!545677704?oppId=131493&mode=VIEW
Sponsor: U.S. Department of Commerce
1401 Constitution Avenue, NW, Suite 7800
Washington, DC 20230

USDC State Broadband Initiative Grants 4857
The National Telecommunications and Information Administration's State Broadband Initiative implements the purposes of both the American Recovery and Reinvestment Act and the Broadband Data Improvement Act, which envisioned a comprehensive program — led by state entities or non-profit organizations working at their direction — to help integrate broadband and information technology into state and local economies. Through the State Broadband Initiative (formerly called the State Broadband Data and Development grant program), NTIA awarded a total of $293 million to 56 grantees, one from each of the 50 states, five territories, and the District of Columbia, or their designees. Grantees are using this funding to support the efficient and creative use of broadband technology to better compete in the digital economy. These state-created efforts vary depending on local needs but include programs to assist small businesses and community institutions in using technology more effectively, conduct research on barriers to broadband adoption, implement innovative

applications that increase access to government services and information, and support state and local task forces to expand broadband access and adoption. Since accurate data is critical for broadband planning, another purpose of the State Broadband Initiative is to assist states in gathering data twice a year on the availability, speed, and location of broadband services, as well as the broadband services that community institutions use. The data will be used by NTIA to update its publicly searchable, interactive National Broadband Map.
Geographic Focus: All States
Contact: Dr. Bernadette McGuire-Rivera, Associate Administrator; (202) 482-5802; fax (202) 501-8009; bmcguire-rivera@ntia.doc.gov
Internet: http://www.ntia.doc.gov/category/state-broadband-initiative
Sponsor: U.S. Department of Commerce
1401 Constitution Avenue, NW
Washington, DC 20230

USDC Strong Cities, Strong Communities Visioning Challenge Grants   4858
The Strong Cities, Strong Communities Initiative (SC2 Initiative) is an interagency EDA pilot program that aims to enhance neighborhoods, towns, cities and regions across the country by strengthening the capacity of local governments to develop and facilitate strategic economic development. The SC2 Initiative is designed to bolster local government capacity to implement economic development strategies that address issues of persistent economic distress by providing necessary technical assistance and access to Federal agency expertise and encouraging the creation of new public-private sector partnerships. By leveraging existing assets, providing additional resources, and fostering new connections at the local and national level, the SC2 Initiative will support cities as they develop comprehensive plans for their communities, and invest in strategies that will lead to economic growth and job creation. Under this FFO, the United States Economic Development Administration (EDA) anticipates making awards of up to $1 million to six cities (each a Recipient City)—one in each of EDA's six regions. Each Recipient City will use the awarded funds to conduct a Challenge Competition, consisting of two distinct phases. In the first phase, Recipient Cities will invite Multidisciplinary Teams to compete for financial prizes that will be awarded for the three highest-ranked economic development proposals— a document offering innovative, relevant, and implementable ideas on how to address both short- and long-term economic development challenges facing the Recipient City—(Economic Development Proposals). An Economic Development Proposal will briefly identify innovative, practical ideas for supporting the economic development goals of the Recipient City and mitigating the causes of persistent distress within the community, and will describe in detail the process by which the Multidisciplinary Team submitting it will develop a more comprehensive Economic Development Plan for the Recipient City. Evaluation panels—a group of individuals formed by each Recipient City who will evaluate Economic Development Proposals—(Evaluation Panels) will evaluate and rank Economic Development Proposals to determine which Multidisciplinary Teams receive financial prizes using an established set of criteria: winners will be identified based on the degree to which their submitted Economic Development Proposals best meet the specific needs of each participating community.
Requirements: EDA can only fund proposals that benefit a Region that, on the date of application, meets one (or more) of the following economic distress criteria: an unemployment rate that is, for the most recent 24-month period for which data are available, at least one percentage point greater than the national average unemployment rate; per capita income that is, for the most recent period for which data are available, 80 percent or less of the national average per capita income; or has a Special Need, as determined by EDA pursuant to 13 C.F.R. § 301.3(a)(1)(iii).
Geographic Focus: All States
Date(s) Application is Due: Jul 23
Amount of Grant: Up to 1,000,000 USD
Contact: Thomas Pellegrino, (404) 730-3002; thomas.a.pellegrino@eda.gov
Internet: http://www07.grants.gov/search/search.do;jsessionid=6rjfPhFGqSjplhpdDYLhn FBmKt7j8xsWWx52hyQyC3mTSZyTynZJ!64499778?oppId=176893&mode=VIEW
Sponsor: U.S. Department of Commerce
1401 Constitution Avenue, NW, Suite 7800
Washington, DC 20230

USDC Supplemental Appropriations Disaster Relief Opportunity Grants   4859
EDA intends to award investments in regions experiencing severe economic distress as a result of severe storms and flooding that occurred between March and May 2010. Under this announcement, EDA solicits applications for Economic Adjustment Assistance investments under the Public Works and Economic Development Act of 1965, as amended. Through the Economic Adjustment Assistance program (CFDA No. 11.307), winning applicants will utilize EDA's flexible set of program tools to develop and implement on a regional basis long-term economic redevelopment strategies for certain disaster-impacted regions in the United States.
Requirements: Eligible applicants include: state governments; county governments; city or township governments; public and state controlled institutions of higher education; Native American tribal governments (Federally recognized); nonprofits having a 501(c)3 status with the IRS, other than institutions of higher education; nonprofits that do not have a 501(c)3 status with the IRS, other than institutions of higher education; and private institutions of higher education.
Geographic Focus: All States
Date(s) Application is Due: Feb 9
Contact: Lindsey Pangretic, (202) 482-4085; grants@eda.doc.gov
Internet: http://www.grants.gov/search/search.do;jsessionid=xcckPprcn1L1yLLSWyvJFJZ hR7BhKs69Zwxbf7Z1xG1MmhLv0qWY!64499778?oppId=69933&mode=VIEW
Sponsor: U.S. Department of Commerce
1401 Constitution Avenue, NW, Suite 7800
Washington, DC 20230

USDC Technology Opportunities Program Grants   4860
The program seeks to promote the widespread use and availability of advanced telecommunications and information technologies in the public and nonprofit sectors. The purpose of this program is to develop a nationwide, interactive, multimedia information infrastructure that is accessible to all citizens, in rural areas as well as urban areas. Grants are awarded to support projects that improve the quality of, and the public's access to, cultural, education, and training resources; reduce the cost, improve the quality, and/or increase the accessibility of health care and public health services; promote responsive public safety services; improve the effectiveness and efficiency of government services; and foster communication, resource-sharing, and economic development within communities, both rural and urban. Application kits are available on the Web site.
Requirements: State, local, and tribal governments, nonprofit health care providers, school districts, libraries, universities and colleges, public safety services, and other nonprofit entities may apply.
Geographic Focus: All States
Amount of Grant: 265,501 - 700,000 USD
Contact: Dr. Bernadette McGuire-Rivera, Associate Administrator; (202) 482-5802; fax (202) 501-8009; bmcguire-rivera@ntia.doc.gov or top@ntia.doc.gov
Internet: http://www.ntia.doc.gov/category/broadband-technology-opportunities-program
Sponsor: U.S. Department of Commerce
1401 Constitution Avenue, NW
Washington, DC 20230

USDC University Center Economic Development Program Competition   4861
The purpose of EDA's University Center Economic Development Program (also referred to as the University Center program) is to assist institutions of higher education and consortia of institutions of higher education in establishing and operating University Centers specifically focused on leveraging university assets to build regional economic ecosystems that support high-growth entrepreneurship. University Centers collaborate with other EDA partners by providing resources to develop, implement and support regional strategies that promote job creation, the development of high-skilled regional talent pools, and business expansion in a region's innovation clusters. These resources may include technology commercialization, feasibility studies, market research, economic impact analyses, training, and other technical assistance to help communities foster vibrant economic ecosystems.
Requirements: Public and State controlled institutions of higher education, as well as private institutions of higher education, are eligible to apply.
Geographic Focus: All States
Amount of Grant: 80,000 - 200,000 USD
Contact: Gloria Huang, Program Analyst; (404) 730-2827; fax (404) 730-3025
Internet: http://www.grants.gov/search/search.do;jsessionid=0k71PzTTNRrJcknhhl1pQ QTxWqT0yvKywLpB4n1LTj7XXb5LpT4g!712472910?oppId=143093&mode=VIEW
Sponsor: U.S. Department of Commerce
1401 Constitution Avenue, NW, Suite 7800
Washington, DC 20230

USDD Cultural Resources Program Assistance Announcement Grants   4862
Army facilities are rich in cultural resources such as archeological sites, archeological artifacts, Native American sacred sites, and historic buildings, structures, and districts. The Army, in recognition of its growing inventory of cultural resources and limited fiscal resources, intends to provide for the stewardship of its cultural resources through development of progressive and efficient management strategies. To meet this challenge, the Army recognizes the value of involving interested stakeholders to assist in their management efforts. Cultural resource support is needed in four areas of interest: (1) curation support for Army archeological collections; (2) development of Army Integrated Resources Management Plans (ICMPs) and historic properties components to the ICRMP under the Army alternate procedures; (3) technical support to the Army for cultural resources management needs; and (4) Native American consultation support. This is a continuously open announcement and may be revised as needed. Changes will be posted at Grants.gov (http://grants.gov/applicants/find_grant_opportunities.jsp). Applicants are encouraged to sign up on Grants.gov for "send me change notification emails" by following the link on the synopsis page for the program announcement/funding opportunity. Proposals may be submitted at any time until the final closing date, and they will be evaluated as received. Because the nature and scope of the proposals will vary, it is anticipated that the size and duration of each award will vary. There are no specified funding limitations.
Requirements: Eligible applicants include: private/public/state-controlled institutions of higher education; Hispanic-serving institutions; historically black colleges and universities/minority institutions; tribally-controlled colleges and universities; Alaska native and native Hawaiian serving institutions; nonprofits with 501(c)3 status (other than institutions of higher education; small businesses; for-profit organizations (other than small businesses); Indian/Native American tribal governments; Indian/Native American tribally designated organizations; non-domestic (non-United States) entities (foreign organizations); and federal, state, and local government agencies. Any of the above listed organizations can apply to provide all or any part of the needed cultural resources support. Joint ventures between two or more organizations can be used as a means to enhance support potential.
Geographic Focus: All States
Date(s) Application is Due: Jan 30
Contact: Blossom Widder, Grants Officer; (301) 619-7143; blossom.widder@us.army.mil
Internet: http://www.grants.gov/search/search.do;jsessionid=Q2lZP9lV4mvG5TgvVqhZ2Y cTpzV1NQypcLBss0zn38199gQ1WYBM!-2099600874?oppId=134093&mode=VIEW
Sponsor: U.S. Department of Defense
1400 Defense Pentagon
Washington, DC 20301-1400

USDJ Edward Byrne Memorial Justice Assistance Grants 4863
The Edward Byrne Memorial Justice Assistance Grant (JAG) program is the primary provider of federal criminal justice funding to state and local jurisdictions. The JAG program provides states and units of local governments with critical funding necessary to support a range of program areas including law enforcement, prosecution and court programs including indigent defense, prevention and education programs, corrections and community corrections, drug treatment and enforcement, crime victim and witness initiatives, and planning, evaluation, and technology improvement programs. Applicants must register in GMS prior to submitting an application for this funding opportunity. The deadline to register in GMS and the deadline to apply for funding under this announcement is 8:00 p.m. eastern time on June 10. JAG funds may be used for state and local initiatives, technical assistance, strategic planning, research and evaluation (including forensics), data collection, training, personnel, equipment, forensic laboratories, supplies, contractual support, and criminal justice information systems that will improve or enhance such areas as: law enforcement programs; prosecution and court programs, including indigent defense; prevention and education programs; corrections and community corrections programs; drug treatment and enforcement programs; planning, evaluation, and technology improvement programs; and crime victim and witness programs (other than compensation).
Requirements: Applicants are limited to units of local government, which includes: a town, township, village, parish, city, county, borough, or other general purpose political subdivision of a state. In addition, it may also be a federally recognized Indian tribe that performs law enforcement functions.
Geographic Focus: All States
Date(s) Application is Due: Jun 10
Contact: Sam Beamon, Justice Information Center Assistant; (202) 353-8592 or (202) 616-6500; fax (202) 305-1367; Samuel.Beamon@ojp.usdoj.gov
Internet: https://www.bja.gov/%5CFunding%5C14JAGLocalSol.pdf
Sponsor: U.S. Department of Justice - 1
810 Seventh Street NW, 4th Floor
Washington, DC 20531

USDJ National Criminal History Improvement Program Grants 4864
The goal of the NCHIP grant program is to improve the nation's safety and security by enhancing the quality, completeness, and accessibility of criminal history record information and by ensuring the nationwide implementation of criminal justice and noncriminal justice background check systems. Achieving this goal is contingent on accomplishing four objectives: providing direct financial and technical assistance to states and tribes to improve their criminal records systems and other related systems in an effort to support background checks; ensuring the infrastructure is developed to connect criminal history records systems to the state record repository or appropriate federal agency record system and ensuring records are accessible through the Federal Bureau of Investigation's (FBI) records systems; providing the training and technical assistance needed to ensure that records systems are developed and managed to conform to FBI standards and appropriate technologies, while ensuring that contributing agencies adhere to the highest standards of practice with respect to privacy and confidentiality; and using systematic evaluation and standardized performance measurement and statistics to assess progress made in improving national records holdings and background check systems. All applications are due by 11:59 p.m. eastern time on May 12.
Requirements: Eligible applicants are limited to the agency designated by the governor in each state to administer the NCHIP program, and federally recognized tribal entities. States and tribes may choose to submit applications as part of a multi-state consortium, multi-tribe consortium, or other entity. In such cases, please contact your BJS program manager for further information.
Geographic Focus: All States
Date(s) Application is Due: May 12
Contact: Devon B. Adams; (202) 307-0765; askbjs@usdoj.gov
Internet: http://www.bjs.gov/index.cfm?ty=fun#currentsolicitations
Sponsor: U.S. Department of Justice
810 Seventh Street, NW
Washington, DC 20531

USDJ NICS Act Record Improvement Program Grants 4865
The purpose of the USDJ NICS Act Record Improvement Program Grant is to announce the continuation of the National Instant Criminal Background Check System (NICS) Act Record Improvement Program (NARIP) in the current fiscal year (FY), identify the program priorities, and provide information on application requirements. All applications are due by 11:59 p.m. eastern time on May 12. NARIP was enacted to improve the completeness, automation, and transmittal of records to state and federal systems used by the NICS. Such records include criminal history records, records of felony convictions, warrants, records of protective orders, convictions for misdemeanors involving domestic violence and stalking, drug arrests and convictions, records of mental health adjudications, and others which may disqualify an individual from possessing or receiving a firearm under federal law.
Requirements: The NARIP applications must be submitted by: the agency designated by the Governor to administer the NCHIP program; the state or territory central administrative office or similar entity designated by statute or regulation to administer federal grant funds on behalf of the jurisdiction's court system; or federally recognized Indian tribal government.
Geographic Focus: All States
Date(s) Application is Due: May 12
Contact: Devon B. Adams, Chief, Criminal Justice Data Improvement Program; (202) 307-0765; askbjs@usdoj.gov
Internet: http://www.bjs.gov/index.cfm?ty=fun#currentsolicitations
Sponsor: U.S. Department of Justice
810 Seventh Street, NW
Washington, DC 20531

USFA Development Grants 4866
The USFA Development Grant Program was established to assist programs dedicated to developing young fencers from economically-deprived backgrounds and to broaden the base of American fencing by combating financial barriers that prevent potential athletes from participating in the sport. Grants are awarded in the form of cash to organizations such as fencing clubs, park and recreation departments, foundations, civic organizations and educational institutions.
Requirements: Clubs, community-based organizations (Park & Rec, YMCA, Boys & Girls Club, etc.), education-based organizations (elementary, middle, secondary school or college program), military, and disabled sports programs are eligible to apply. Priority will be given to USFA member organizations that have specific goals and programs designed to match the mission statement above.
Restrictions: Awards will not be given to individuals. Awards are subject to taxation under IRS code.
Geographic Focus: All States
Date(s) Application is Due: Jan 11
Contact: David Blake, Chair; (719) 866-4511; fax (719) 632-5737; info@usfencing.org
Internet: http://www.usfencing.org/pages/3866
Sponsor: United States Fencing Association
1 Olympic Plaza
Colorado Springs, CO 80909

USFA Equipment Subsidy Grants 4867
The USFA Equipment Subsidy Grant Program was established to assist new and existing programs that receive little financial support. Its purposes are to encourage fencing start-up programs, to assist interested eligible organizations in establishing group fencing instruction, and to introduce beginning fencers to the USFA. The grant provides a $1,000 subsidy to organizations that purchase $1,500 or more in fencing equipment.
Requirements: Clubs, community-based organizations (Park & Rec, YMCA, Boys & Girls Club, etc.), education-based organizations (elementary, middle, secondary school or college program), military, and disabled sports programs are eligible to apply. Equipment must remain the property of the program and not that of the individual participants.
Restrictions: Awards will not be given to individuals. Awards are subject to taxation under IRS code.
Geographic Focus: All States
Date(s) Application is Due: Jan 11
Amount of Grant: 1,000 USD
Contact: David Blake, Chair; (719) 866-4511; fax (719) 632-5737; info@usfencing.org
Internet: http://www.usfencing.org/pages/3866
Sponsor: United States Fencing Association
1 Olympic Plaza
Colorado Springs, CO 80909

USGA Foundation For the Good of the Game Grants 4868
The foundation awards grants to empower organizations that introduce the game to people who would otherwise not have the opportunity, specifically children from economically disadvantaged backgrounds and individuals with disabilities. Grant awards are directed to instructional programs, caddie or other work-based curriculum, and the construction of facilities that make the game more affordable and accessible as well as teach individuals the life values inherent in the game. Funding requests will be considered for golf course and practice range access; golf instruction; golf equipment, including adaptive golf equipment for individuals with disabilities; transportation; and construction costs for alternative, beginner-friendly golf courses and golf facilities in areas where there are obstacles to affordable access to the game. The amount and duration of grants awarded vary based on the type of organization, proposal, and identified needs.
Requirements: Eligible applicants must have tax-exempt status.
Restrictions: The foundation does not fund requests for clothing, tournament entry fees, travel expenses and other costs associated with competitive events, academic scholarships, research studies not related to USGA goals, vehicle purchase, construction of buildings, computer and video equipment, swing analysis equipment, awards and trophies, food and beverage, or donations for fundraising tournaments.
Geographic Focus: All States
Date(s) Application is Due: Jan 20
Contact: Judy Bell; (719) 471-4810, ext. 11; fax (719) 471-4976; grants@usga.org
Internet: http://www.usga.org/aboutus/foundation/grants/philosophies_guidelines.html
Sponsor: United States Golf Association Foundation
1631 Mesa Avenue
Colorado Springs, CO 80906

USG Foundation Grants 4869
The Foundation is committed to social responsibility and supports local and national charitable organizations that serve and educate the communities in which USG Corporation operates. The Foundation originated in 1979 to enrich the lives of families, friends, colleagues, customers and citizens where USG employees live and work. It provides financial assistance to non-profit organizations with solutions in mind for social, health and educational issues. For more information contact the Foundation.
Geographic Focus: All States
Contact: Corporate Responsibility Administrator; (312) 606-4297; usgfoundation@usg.com
Internet: http://www.usg.com/company/corporate-responsibility.html
Sponsor: USG Foundation
550 West Adams
Chicago, IL 60606

US Soccer Foundation Annual Program and Field Grants 4870
The foundation will award grants exclusively to projects and programs that develop players, coaches, and referees in economically disadvantaged urban areas encompassing populations of 50,000 or more. The one exception to this exclusive focus is the foundation's Synthetic Field Building grants. Synthetic Field Building grants support the construction of state-of-the-art synthetic grass soccer fields and will continue to be available to projects serving all types of communities, though the highest priority will be given to projects serving players in economically disadvantaged urban areas.
Requirements: Individuals or organizations are eligible to register for the foundation's annual Program and Field grants if funding is requested for: (1) a soccer-specific program or field project that benefits a not-for-profit purpose and meets the established focus for the annual grant cycle; (2) In addition to satisfying Criteria #1, a field project (including lighting) where the real property is owned at the time of registration or a minimum ten year lease/land use agreement is in place at the time of registration; (3) In addition to satisfying Criteria #1 and #2, lighting where the applicant has written authorization at the time of registration from the communitiy where the project resides to add/use lights at the field. The foundation's annual grantmaking cycle includes the following grant types: (1) PROGRAM - A project that meets the foundation's annual focus and does not contain a construction element. Program grant elements that will be considered for funding include uniforms; player equipment (shoes, shin guards, etc.); team equipment (goals, balls, cones, etc.); games and practice travel costs (excludes expenses for professional games); facility rental costs; registration costs; coaches' training and fees; referees' training and fees. (2) FIELD - A project that meets the foundation's annual focus and does contain a construction element such as field renovation, addition or improvement of irrigation equipment, addition or improvement of field equipment, or lighting. This grant type does not include upgrading an existing field with a synthetic grass surface. (3) SYNTHETIC FIELD BUILDING - A project consisting wholly of field development construction utilizing the Synthetic Field Building package consisting of four components: FieldTurf synthetic surface pitch; Kwik Goal field equipment; Musco lights; and TGI signage. Projects for upgrading existing fields with a synthetic grass surface also falls within the Synthetic Field Building grant type. Register at the website in order to submit an online application.
Restrictions: Individuals or organizations are ineligible to register for the foundation's annual Program and Field grants if support is requested for: (a) a program or project that discriminates by race, creed, color, sex, or national origin; (b) a field project (including lighting) where the real property is not owned at the time of registration or a minimum ten year lease/land use agreement is not in place at the time of registration; (c) a single individual; (d) foreign projects or individuals; (e) for-profit organizations; (f) lighting where the applicant does not have written authorization at the time of registration from the community where the project resides to add/use lights at the field; (g) pass-through-grants, i.e., grants awarded to one organization for the purpose of granting to another; (h) political campaigns.
Geographic Focus: All States
Date(s) Application is Due: Oct 30
Contact: Malcolm Granado, Grants Assistant; (202) 872-6656; fax (202) 872-6655; mgranado@ussoccerfoundation.org
Internet: http://www.ussoccerfoundation.org/site/c.ipIQKXOvFoG/b.5482625/
Sponsor: United States Soccer Foundation
1211 Connecticut Avenue NW, Suite 500
Washington, DC 20036

US Soccer Foundation Planning Grants 4871
The Planning Grants Initiative offers grants of up to $10,000 in the form of credit with Clough Harbour Sports, the foundation's Supplier for Soccer Facility Design and Planning Services. Clough Harbour Sports will produce a master plan for your project, positioning your organization to solicit support from donors and decision-makers. Priority will be given to projects in urban, economically disadvantaged areas.
Requirements: To apply, go to grants.ussoccerfoundation.org/planning online.
Restrictions: Individuals or organizations are ineligible to register for the foundation's annual Program and Field grants if support is requested for: (a) a program or project that discriminates by race, creed, color, sex, or national origin; (b) a field project (including lighting) where the real property is not owned at the time of registration or a minimum ten year lease/land use agreement is not in place at the time of registration; (c) a single individual; (d) foreign projects or individuals; (e) for-profit organizations; (f) lighting where the applicant does not have written authorization at the time of registration from the community where the project resides to add/use lights at the field; (g) pass-through-grants, i.e., grants awarded to one organization for the purpose of granting to another; (h) political campaigns.
Geographic Focus: All States
Date(s) Application is Due: Apr 1
Amount of Grant: Up to 10,000 USD
Contact: Malcolm Granado; (202) 872-6656; mgranado@ussoccerfoundation.org
Internet: http://www.ussoccerfoundation.org/site/c.ipIQKXOvFoG/b.5474501/
Sponsor: United States Soccer Foundation
1211 Connecticut Avenue NW, Suite 500
Washington, DC 20036

USTA Althea Gibson Leadership Awards 4872
The Althea Gibson Leadership Awards honor the memory, life, and achievements of an exceptional pioneer who paved the way for millions who followed. Gibson rose from a troubled childhood, overcame an impoverished upbringing, dedicated herself to excellence and succeeded in sport and in the classroom. The grants provide funding to competitive junior players aspiring to achieve national and/or international rankings. Funding will be based on the success level of the player in the previous year (e.g., end of the year USTA ranking list/performance) and recommendations/commentary about the individuals' team spirit and leadership qualities. Only two grants are awarded per year in the amount of $2,500 each.
Requirements: For consideration the player must be ranked in the Top 100 at the section or national (i.e., USTA) level, in his/her age category, or player must have an ITF, ATP / WTA Ranking. Players must be in high school between the ages of 14-18 years old and must be training and competing in tournaments year-round. Application instructions can be downloaded from the website.
Geographic Focus: All States
Date(s) Application is Due: Dec 31
Amount of Grant: 2,500 USD
Contact: Michele Kern, Diversity Assistant; (914) 696-7203; kern@usta.com
Internet: http://tinyurl.com/cb4vog
Sponsor: United States Tennis Association
70 W Red Oak Lane
White Plains, NY 10604

USTA CTA and NJTL Community Tennis Development Workshop Scholarships 4873
The scholarships provide funding for conference registration and two nights' hotel accommodations to attend the Community Tennis Development Workshop sponsored by the USTA. The number of scholarships awarded varies each year.
Requirements: The scholarships are open to all USTA-registered Community Tennis Association (CTA) and National Junior Tennis League (NJTL) Chapter/Program Leaders who have demonstrated continued excellence in community development and/or youth programming. Priority will be given to applicants from organizations that have never received a scholarship. Applications are generally available in October and are due in November. Scholarships will be awarded in December.
Restrictions: District and Section Staff are not eligible to apply.
Geographic Focus: All States
Date(s) Application is Due: Nov 15
Contact: Valerie Chin, NJTL Conact; (914) 696-7160; chin@usta.com
Internet: http://tinyurl.com/b6698q
Sponsor: United States Tennis Association
70 W Red Oak Lane
White Plains, NY 10604

USTA Excellence Grants 4874
Excellence grants are awarded to players, based purely on merit. These grants are provided by the USTA to players who have met certain results, according to the criteria chosen for their birth year (see website).
Requirements: To qualify, a player will need to satisfy at least three of the bullet points listed for their birth year (download the criteria sheet from the website). All players must be U.S. citizens or eligible to represent the U.S. in International Team Competitions.
Geographic Focus: All States
Date(s) Application is Due: Jan 15
Amount of Grant: 5,000 USD
Contact: Herlinda Lombardi; (561) 962-6428; Herlinda@usta.com
Internet: http://tinyurl.com/6mwdyq
Sponsor: United States Tennis Association
70 W Red Oak Lane
White Plains, NY 10604

USTA Junior Team Tennis Stipends 4875
USTA Jr. Team Tennis connects kids together in teams to play singles, doubles and mixed doubles against other teams within a league. It promotes social skills and important values by fostering a spirit of cooperation and unity, as well as individual self-growth. The program is designed for kids ages 6-18 who are immediately placed on teams.
Requirements: Area Coordinators are eligible for stipends to start new leagues or expand existing ones. The number of stipends available varies by Section. Applications are generally available starting in January. Completed applications must be submitted to Section by October 15. Stipends will be awarded in mid-November.
Geographic Focus: All States
Date(s) Application is Due: Oct 15
Amount of Grant: 250 - 1,000 USD
Contact: Marikate Murren, National Manager; (914) 696-7234; murren@usta.com
Internet: http://tinyurl.com/cb4vog
Sponsor: United States Tennis Association
70 W Red Oak Lane
White Plains, NY 10604

USTA Multicultural Excellence Grants 4876
The program provides funding to competitive junior development tennis programs that are training youngsters aspiring to achieve national and/or international rankings. Funding will be based on number of players with sectional and national rankings in a specific program. Grants award $5,000 plus coaching assistance
Requirements: Applicants must be a year-round program that provide a high level of on-court instruction and off-court training opportunities. Programs must also have a history of developing tournament level players.
Geographic Focus: All States
Date(s) Application is Due: Dec 31
Contact: Michele Kern, Diversity Assistant; (914) 696-7203; kern@usta.com
Internet: http://www.usta.com/?sc_itemid={C3323E2C-6F91-43EA-809B-646ADE64C212}&sc_mode=preview&sc_lang=en#MEPG
Sponsor: United States Tennis Association
70 W Red Oak Lane
White Plains, NY 10604

USTA Multicultural Individual Player Grant for National Competition & Training 4877
The award provides funding to competitive junior players aspiring to achieve national and/or international rankings. Funding will be based on the success level of the player in the previous year. Applications are due at the Section level at the end of December. Applications will then be submitted to the USTA National Headquarters for review by January 16th. Grant award decisions will be made on or before February 1st. The number of awards available varies.
Requirements: Players who are highly talented and come from a multicultural background are encouraged to apply. Junior players must be training and competing in tournaments year-round. Players must also have a history of strong national tournament results. Contact the sponsor for application instructions.
Geographic Focus: All States
Date(s) Application is Due: Dec 31
Contact: Michele Kern, Diversity Assistant; (914) 696-7203; kern@usta.com
Internet: http://tinyurl.com/cb4vog
Sponsor: United States Tennis Association
70 W Red Oak Lane
White Plains, NY 10604

USTA NJTL Arthur Ashe Essay and Art Contest 4878
Arthur Ashe was an American hero fighting battles both on and off the court. In his life, he broke barriers in the tennis world, becoming a three-time grand slam champion, and the first African American male to win a grand slam tournament. Off the court, he was a social activist taking on issues like racial prejudice, AIDS, apartheid and youth education. One of his many legacies includes the National Junior Tennis League (NJTL), a network of youth-serving organizations that provides tennis and education for all. NJTL participants write or draw about what the selected Arthur Ashe quote means to them, including examples from Ashe's life and their own. Ten winners will be chosen (five girls and five boys, ages 10, 12, 14, 16 and 18) and will receive an all-expense paid weekend trip, including a parent or guardian, to tour New York City and attend the Arthur Ashe Kids' Day.
Requirements: Participants must be 18 years of age or younger, a legal resident of the 50 United States and/or D.C., and be participating in a program sponsored by your local NJTL Program/Chapter any time between January 6 and June 26. See the sponsor's website for official contest rules.
Restrictions: Essays and artwork must be in English and will not be returned.
Geographic Focus: All States
Date(s) Application is Due: Jul 10
Contact: Valerie Chin, Outreach Coordinator; (914) 696-7160; chin@usta.com
Internet: http://tinyurl.com/bj8t5q
Sponsor: United States Tennis Association
70 W Red Oak Lane
White Plains, NY 10604

USTA NJTL Tennis and Leadership Camp Scholarships 4879
The week-long camp is designed to teach and inspire the values of civic engagement, academic excellence, and leadership. Exclusively for youth, ages 12-14, who participate in National Junior Tennis League (NJTL) programs nation-wide, attendees are selected through an application process consider- ing their tennis talent, sportsmanship, leadership skills, and financial need. The all-expense paid trip provides the campers with valuable tennis instruction plus a rewarding educational and motivational experience. Tennis is the focus of the week; however, other activities are planned such as sightseeing, cultural, sporting, and social activities.
Requirements: Players must be a current NJTL participant; 12-14 years of age; within the JNTRP's skill rating level of 3.0-4.5; and whose family demonstrates a financial need. Applications become available in late March. Completed applications must be received by your local NJTL Section by May 18. Scholarships will be awarded in June.
Geographic Focus: All States
Date(s) Application is Due: May 18
Contact: Valerie Chin, Outreach Coordinator; (914) 696-7160; chin@usta.com
Internet: http://tinyurl.com/9vxdnm
Sponsor: United States Tennis Association
70 W Red Oak Lane
White Plains, NY 10604

USTA Okechi Womeodu Scholar Athlete Grants 4880
The Okechi Womeodu Scholar Athlete Grants honor the memory, life, and achievements of an exceptional young man, who otherwise would have had a very promising future, on and off the court. The grants provide funding to competitive junior players who have achieved national and/or international rankings. Funding will be based on the success level of the player in the previous year (e.g., end of the year USTA ranking list/performance). Only two grants are awarded per year (one male recipient, one female recipient) in the amount of $5,000 each.
Requirements: For consideration the player must be ranked in the Top 100 nationally (i.e., USTA) in his/her age category, or player must have an ITF, ATP/WTA Ranking. Players must be training and competing in tournaments year-round and have a history of strong national tournament results. Players must be in high school between the ages of 14-18 years old with a grade point average of 3.0 or higher. Input from members of the USTA Elite Player Development staff will be sought. Application instructions can be downloaded from the website.
Geographic Focus: All States
Date(s) Application is Due: Dec 31
Contact: Michele Kern, Diversity Assistant; (914) 696-7203; kern@usta.com
Internet: http://tinyurl.com/cb4vog
Sponsor: United States Tennis Association
70 W Red Oak Lane
White Plains, NY 10604

USTA Player Development Grants 4881
USTA Player Development Grants are determined in February and August of each year. The overall dollar amount of grants and the allocation of services will be determined by the General Manager of Player Development, along with the Director of Coaching, Head of Men's Tennis and the Head of Women's Tennis. If awarded, grants will include travel allowances, meal and service allowances, as well as reimburse tournament fees, hotel accommodations.
Requirements: These grants are provided to players under the following scenarios: (1) Players with whom the USTA Player Development Staff is working with on a full-time basis. In return, the player will need to participate in the USTA Player Development Program, which will include spending a significant amount of time at one of the USTA designated facilities. Communication will be clear, understood and the arrangement will be mutually agreed upon by both parties prior to entering into the relationship. (2) Players who are in a coaching situation that is working well for them, but where the USTA can provide support (mutually agreed upon by both parties). In return for this support, the USTA will develop a working relationship with the player and his/her coach to assist the player in reaching his/her maximum potential. Communication will be clear, understood and the arrangement will be mutually agreed upon by both parties prior to entering into the relationship. (3) Players who are in a coaching situation that is working for them and who may not necessarily want or need support from the USTA. In these situations, USTA support will be limited. In all cases, players do not have to complete an application for this grant but must complete an agreement before receiving these grants. Once grants have been determined, letters are sent to players informing them of their grant amount. Players are expected to complete their grant agreement by the deadline date listed and disbursements will be made once that process has been completed.
Geographic Focus: All States
Contact: Herlinda Lombardi; (561) 962-6428; Herlinda@usta.com
Internet: http://tinyurl.com/6mwdyq
Sponsor: United States Tennis Association
70 W Red Oak Lane
White Plains, NY 10604

USTA Pro Circuit Community Involvement Day Grants 4882
The goals of these events are two-fold: 1) to develop community interest and support for the Pro Circuit events; 2) to introduce tennis to new players and generate interest for USTA Tennis programs in the community. The grant is applicable to funding various activities during a USTA Pro Circuit tournament, i.e. Kid's Day, Wheelchair Tennis Exhibition. Applications are available in October and April.
Requirements: It is suggested that you begin planning a year in advance in order to have everything in place to submit for the grant. Contact the sponsor for application instructions. Completed applications are due November and May. Grants will be awarded in December and June.
Geographic Focus: All States
Date(s) Application is Due: Apr 0; Oct 0
Amount of Grant: 500 - 3,000 USD
Contact: Louise Maher, Pro Circuit Coordinator; (914) 696-7032; maher@usta.com
Internet: http://tinyurl.com/b6698q
Sponsor: United States Tennis Association
70 W Red Oak Lane
White Plains, NY 10604

USTA Public Facility Assistance Grants 4883
The highly competitive Public Facility Assistance Program is intended to have a major impact on the growth of tennis in a community and the clients served by that organization. The need for new tennis facilities or improvements at existing facilities is not, in and of itself, sufficient justification for a grant. Review includes a thorough evaluation of the programmatic, administrative, financial and organizational accomplishments of the applicant. The amount of funding varies: Category I - up to $4,000 with possible Section or District match; Category II - up to $35,000 or 20% project total; Category III - up to $50,000 or 20% project total.
Requirements: The process begins with submission of a Tennis Facility Inquiry Form found online. After review of the Inquiry Form and initial follow-up conversation with a USTA representative, some applicants will qualify to submit a full USTA Public Facility Funding Application. Inquiry is open year round. Applications are accepted from March to October 1st. Grantees are notified within 60 days of submitting an application of grant status.
Geographic Focus: All States
Date(s) Application is Due: Oct 1
Contact: Shannon Hatton, Programs Coordinator; (914) 696-7291; technical@usta.com
Internet: http://tinyurl.com/cb4vog
Sponsor: United States Tennis Association
70 W Red Oak Lane
White Plains, NY 10604

USTA Recreational Tennis Grants 4884
The Recreational Tennis Division awards grants to non-profit community based organizations that support tennis programming and infrastructure in their local community. The USTA seeks applicants that are well established community based organizations or agencies committed to: increase tennis participation, support tennis programming, and foster diversity with both participation and programming. The USTA will award grants to selected organizations that present a clear vision for establishing community based partnerships to meet these objectives. Recreational Tennis Grant applicants have the option to apply for assistance in two (2) distinct areas: Program/Project Support ($2,500 - $10,000) and Community Partnership Investment ($10,000 - $50,000).
Requirements: USTA Community Tennis Associations (CTA), USTA National Junior Tennis League (NJTL) Chapters and Programs, Parks and Recreation Agencies, Schools

(K-12) / School Districts, Military Base organizations, and nonprofit community-based organizations are eligible to apply. Priority will be given to team-based play tennis programs utilizing the Quickstart format for 10 and under children and to organizations with multiple community-based partnerships to support tennis programming and infrastructure. Grant funds can be used for: advertising, marketing, and public relations; tennis equipment; tennis court fees; insurance; scholarships and registration fees; security and/or background checks; staff/officials' fees; technology; tennis uniforms; organization development training /education; general tennis program/project support.
Restrictions: The USTA Recreational Tennis Grant does not fund: Capital Projects; Tennis Facility Renovation Projects; Tennis Facility Construction Projects; Individuals; USTA Section/Districts; or, For-Profit Organizations. If declined, applicants must submit another online grant application to be considered for future funding.
Geographic Focus: All States
Date(s) Application is Due: Jan 30; May 15
Amount of Grant: 2,500 - 50,000 USD
Contact: David Slade, Program Contact; (914) 696-7241; slade@usta.com
Internet: http://tinyurl.com/bjdovw
Sponsor: United States Tennis Association
70 W Red Oak Lane
White Plains, NY 10604

USTA Serves College Education Scholarships 4885
USTA Serves awards college education scholarships annually to high school seniors who have excelled academically, demonstrated community service and participated in an organized tennis program. This scholarship is partially supported by the Ambrose Monell Foundation. A $6,000 scholarship will be awarded over four years to students entering a two or four-year college or university.
Requirements: The recipients of the USTA Serves College Education Scholarship are eligible to receive $1,500 per year for a total of up to $6,000 to cover costs of tuition, room and board and educational materials. The scholarship will be paid directly to the college or university in which the student is enrolled and is disbursed annually based on the recipient's standing with his/her college.
Restrictions: If a recipient of a USTA Serves scholarship is enrolling in a two-year community college program, he/she will be awarded $3,000 in two payments during the first and second years.
Geographic Focus: All States
Date(s) Application is Due: Feb 9
Amount of Grant: 3,000 - 6,000 USD
Contact: Jackie Materasso, Foundation Coordinator; (914) 696-7175; materasso@usta.com
Internet: http://tinyurl.com/aps2zf
Sponsor: United States Tennis Association
70 W Red Oak Lane
White Plains, NY 10604

USTA Serves College Textbook Scholarships 4886
USTA Serves has established a college textbook scholarship which provides a one-time award to assist students in purchasing textbooks or supplies. A $1,000 scholarship will be awarded to students entering a two or four-year college or university program.
Requirements: The scholarships are open to high school graduates who have excelled academically, participated extensively in USTA youth tennis programs, and have demonstrated financial need. The recipients of the College Textbook Scholarship are eligible to receive a one-time $1000 award. The scholarship will be paid directly to the college or university bookstore in which the student is enrolled at the beginning of the academic year.
Geographic Focus: All States
Date(s) Application is Due: Feb 9
Amount of Grant: 1,000 USD
Contact: Jackie Materasso, Foundation Coordinator; (914) 696-7175; materasso@usta.com
Internet: http://tinyurl.com/aps2zf
Sponsor: United States Tennis Association
70 W Red Oak Lane
White Plains, NY 10604

USTA Serves Dwight F. Davis Memorial Scholarships 4887
Dwight Filley Davis began playing tennis at the age of 15 in 1894. In 1900, the year he graduated from college, Davis purchased a 217-troy ounce silver bowl as a prize for an international lawn tennis competition. This was the birth of the Davis Cup. Davis became president of the U.S. Lawn Tennis Association in 1923. This scholarship was created by the late Dwight F. Davis, III, grandson of Dwight Filley Davis, and is now generously supported by the Davis family. It is their wish that the recipients maintain contact with them. This program awards college educational scholarships annually to two high school seniors who has excelled academically, participated extensively in USTA youth tennis programs, and who are entering a four-year college or university program to support the individual pursuit of excellence in academics and tennis.
Requirements: Each recipient of a USTA Serves scholarship is expected to enroll as a full-time undergraduate student as defined by his/her undergraduate institution, no later than the opening fall semester or term after notice of selection for the scholarship. The recipients are eligible to receive $1,875 per year for a total of up to $7,500 to cover costs of tuition, room and board and educational materials. The scholarship will be paid directly to the college or university in which the student is enrolled and is disbursed annually based on the recipient's standing with his/her college. Applications must be mailed directly to USTA Section offices. Detailed application information is available at the website.
Restrictions: Applicants receiving full grant and aid scholarships in the sport of tennis from their respective schools are not eligible for a USTA Serves scholarship.
Geographic Focus: All States
Date(s) Application is Due: Feb 9
Amount of Grant: 7,500 USD
Contact: Jackie Materasso, Foundation Coordinator; (914) 696-7175; materasso@usta.com
Internet: http://tinyurl.com/aps2zf
Sponsor: United States Tennis Association
70 W Red Oak Lane
White Plains, NY 10604

USTA Serves Dwight Mosley Scholarships 4888
This scholarship was named in memory of Dwight A. Mosley, the first African American elected to the USTA Board of Directors. The scholarship was created with input from the USTA Multicultural Participation Committee and supports the Level One Priority of Diversity within the USTA. A $10,000 scholarship will be awarded over four years to one male and one female student of diverse ethnic backgrounds who are entering a four-year college or university program.
Requirements: The scholarship is available to USTA ranked high school seniors of ethnically diverse heritage who have excelled academically and participated extensively in an organized community tennis program. Applicants must demonstrate sportsmanship on and off the court. Recipients are eligible to receive $2,500 per year for a total of up to $10,000 to cover costs of tuition, room and board and educational materials. The scholarship will be paid directly to the college or university in which the student is enrolled and is disbursed annually based on the recipient's standing with his/her college.
Geographic Focus: All States
Date(s) Application is Due: Feb 9
Amount of Grant: 10,000 USD
Contact: Jackie Materasso, Foundation Coordinator; (914) 696-7175; materasso@usta.com
Internet: http://tinyurl.com/aps2zf
Sponsor: United States Tennis Association
70 W Red Oak Lane
White Plains, NY 10604

USTA Serves Eve Kraft Scholarships 4889
This scholarship is named in memory of Eve Kraft of Princeton, New Jersey, a tennis pioneer who introduced thousands of young people to the game of tennis, particularly in disadvantaged communities. Kraft became the first-ever women's varsity tennis coach at Princeton in 1971 and led the team to an undefeated record during her three-year tenure. She later founded and was director of the USTA Center for Education and Recreational Tennis in Princeton. The scholarship is partially supported by the Kraft family. A $2,500 scholarship will be awarded to one male and one female student entering a four-year college or university program.
Requirements: The scholarships are available to two high school seniors, one male and one female, who have excelled academically, demonstrated community service, played tennis in an organized program and who reside in an economically disadvantaged community. Recipients are eligible to receive a one-time $2,500 award. The scholarship will be paid directly to the college or university in which the student is enrolled.
Geographic Focus: All States
Date(s) Application is Due: Feb 9
Amount of Grant: 2,500 USD
Contact: Jackie Materasso, Foundation Coordinator; (914) 696-7175; materasso@usta.com
Internet: http://tinyurl.com/aps2zf
Sponsor: United States Tennis Association
70 W Red Oak Lane
White Plains, NY 10604

USTA Serves Marian Wood Baird Scholarship 4890
This scholarship is named in honor of the late Marian Wood Baird, who had been recognized by the USTA for over 40 years of volunteer service. Honors bestowed on Mrs. Baird included her induction into the Western Tennis Association Hall of Fame in 1994, the 1993 USTA Seniors' Service Award, and the 1979 USTA Service Bowl. The scholarship is generously supported by the Baird Family, and it is their wish that the recipient maintain contact with them. A $15,000 scholarship will be awarded over four years to a student who is entering a four-year college or university program.
Requirements: The scholarship is available to high school seniors who have excelled academically, demonstrated achievements in leadership, and participated extensively in an organized community tennis program (such as USTA School Tennis, USTA National Junior Tennis League (NJTL), USTA Team Tennis, or USTA High Performance or other such qualified programs as determined by the Scholarship Committee). Applicants must demonstrate sportsmanship on and off the court. The recipient is eligible to receive $3,750 per year for a total of up to $15,000 to cover costs of tuition, room and board and educational materials. The scholarship will be paid directly to the college or university in which the student is enrolled and is disbursed annually based on the recipient's standing with his/her college.
Geographic Focus: All States
Date(s) Application is Due: Feb 9
Amount of Grant: 15,000 USD
Samples: 2008 - Alison Krantz, Sugar Grove, IL.
Contact: Jackie Materasso, Foundation Coordinator; (914) 696-7175; materasso@usta.com
Internet: http://tinyurl.com/aps2zf
Sponsor: United States Tennis Association
70 W Red Oak Lane
White Plains, NY 10604

USTA Serves Player Incentive Awards 4891

USTA Serves - Foundation for Academics. Character. Excellence. is a not-for-profit corporation whose mission is to support, monitor and promote programs that enhance the lives of underserved children through the integration of tennis and education. It encourages children to pursue their goals and highest dreams by succeeding in school and becoming responsible citizens, targeting youngsters from all cultural and ethnic backgrounds. The Player Incentive Award is a one time, nonrenewable grant of $500. Its purpose is to encourage the development of USTA youth tennis program participants with great potential and a commitment to academic excellence.

Requirements: The applicant must: currently be enrolled in grades 6-11; show financial need for all tennis related fees; demonstrate a strong commitment to academic achievement; be a participant in a USTA youth tennis program; and, be a middle school player with high school varsity team potential or high school varsity player. Each recipient is expected to use the award for expenses such as tournament fees, indoor/winter lessons, summer tennis programs, and/or fees for participation in USTA and other tennis organization programs. The required application form can be downloaded at the website.
Restrictions: The player incentive award will be paid directly to the USTA program (or sponsoring organization) which is to disburse funds for the recipient's approved expenses.
Geographic Focus: All States
Date(s) Application is Due: Feb 9
Contact: Jackie Materasso; (914) 696-7175; materasso@usta.com
Internet: http://tinyurl.com/at7pj8
Sponsor: United States Tennis Association
70 W Red Oak Lane
White Plains, NY 10604

USTA Tennis Block Party Grants 4892

Tennis Block Parties are an integral part of the USTA's Tennis Month promotional platform designed to kick off the outdoor tennis season in May. These events can be hosted at any public facility and should feature two to three hours of tennis instruction, interactive games, and attractions for player of all ages and abilities. Grants are available to local Tennis Block Party organizers with the goal of increasing attendance at and awareness of the events. Amounts range based on: ability to host the event in May; active USTA Member Organization; commitment to run USTA Programs and/or formats (Jr. Team Tennis, the QuickStart Format and/or USTA League); public facility; and, detailed marketing budget.

Requirements: A Block Party Site Commitment form (available at website) must be completed to be considered for a grant. Grant funds may only be used for event advertising purposes including: creation and distribution of event posters, flyers, postcards, web banners, event banners and print ads; media buys to promote the Tennis Block Party.
Restrictions: Funds may not be used for hospitality, tennis professionals, celebrities, T-Shirts, balloons, water, etc.
Geographic Focus: All States
Date(s) Application is Due: Mar 15
Contact: Virgil Christian; (914) 697-2366; christian@usta.com
Internet: http://tinyurl.com/c8ujtw
Sponsor: United States Tennis Association
70 W Red Oak Lane
White Plains, NY 10604

UUA Bennett Award for Congregational Action on Human Justice & Social Action 4893

The Bennett Award for Congregational Action on Human Justice and Social Action, instituted in 1999 by James Bennett to honor the congregation that has done exemplary work in social justice, is accompanied by a $500 cash award that is presented at General Assembly. Dr. James R. Bennett is professor emeritus of the University of Arkansas and he is the former director of the Gustavus Meyers Center of Human Rights in North America, founded in 1984.

Requirements: Nominations are due March 15 and should include: a 1-4 page report on the social justice action or program; a testimonial from partner organizations or community members where applicable; and any relevant documentation and media generated about the effort.
Geographic Focus: All States
Date(s) Application is Due: Mar 15
Contact: Audra Friend, Program Coordinator; (617) 948-4656 or (617) 742-2100; fax (617) 742-0321; afriend@uua.org or socialjustice@uua.org
Internet: http://www.uua.org/giving/awardsscholarships/bennettaward/index.shtml
Sponsor: Unitarian Universalist Association
25 Beacon Street
Boston, MA 02108

UUA Holmes-Weatherly Award 4894

The Holmes-Weatherly Award is given to an individual or organization, not necessarily a Unitarian Universalist, whose life-long commitment to faith-based social justice is reflected in societal transformation. The Unitarian Society for Social Justice established the award in 1951 to honor its founders, Revs. John Haynes Holmes and Arthur Weatherly. Awarded each year at the General Assembly Awards Breakfast, the recognition is accompanied by a $500 cash award. Nominations should include: a one-page introduction to the nominee; no more than three letters of personal testimony or reference; and any relevant media that has been generated about the nominee.

Geographic Focus: All States
Date(s) Application is Due: Mar 1
Contact: Lesley Murdock; (202) 393-2255, ext. 10; fax (202) 393-5494; lmurdock@uua.org
Internet: http://www.uua.org/giving/awardsscholarships/holmes-weatherlyaward/index.shtml
Sponsor: Unitarian Universalist Association
25 Beacon Street
Boston, MA 02108

UUA Skinner Sermon Award 4895

The Skinner Sermon Award honors Clarence Skinner, the late dean of the Tufts College School of Religion in Medford, Massachusetts. The award was established to stimulate preaching concerned with the social implications of religion. Criteria in judging sermons include: grasp of the subject, religious depth, originality, conviction, and understanding of other perspectives. Also considered are prophecy and timeliness, courage, personal involvement, strong argument, orientation to action, and inspiration. The sermon is delivered by the author in a special worship service at the General Assembly. The award carries an honorarium of $500. The sermon is delivered by the author in a special worship service at the General Assembly. Individuals may submit only one entry.

Requirements: The award is open to any Unitarian Universalist layperson, religious educator, or minister.
Geographic Focus: All States
Date(s) Application is Due: Mar 1
Amount of Grant: 500 USD
Contact: Lesley Murdock, (202) 393-2255, ext. 10; lmurdock@uua.org or socialjustice@uua.org
Internet: http://www.uua.org/action/awards/skinner/index.shtml
Sponsor: Unitarian Universalist Association
25 Beacon Street
Boston, MA 02108

V.V. Cooke Foundation Grants 4896

The foundation awards grants to nonprofits in Kentucky, with an emphasis on support of the Baptist Church and religious organizations, schools and higher education institutions, and medical education. Children and youth organizations also receive support. Types of funding include: general operating support; continuing support; annual campaigns; capital campaigns; building construction and renovation; equipment acquisition; program development; and professorships. Application deadlines are January 15, April 15, July 15, and October 15.

Requirements: Grants are awarded to nonprofit organizations in Kentucky.
Restrictions: Grants are not awarded to individuals or for general endowment funds, scholarships, fellowships, or loans.
Geographic Focus: Kentucky
Date(s) Application is Due: Jan 15; Apr 15; Jul 15; Oct 15
Amount of Grant: 100 - 50,000 USD
Contact: Theodore L. Merhoff, (502) 241-0303; merhoff@bellsouth.net
Sponsor: V.V. Cooke Foundation
P.O. Box 202
Pewee Valley, KY 40056-0202

Valentine Foundation Grants 4897

The foundation supports organizations and programs that empower women and girls to recognize and develop their full potential or that are making efforts to change established attitudes that discourage women and girls from realizing their potential. Grants are made to support effective fundamental change, including efforts to change attitudes, policies, and social patterns. Funding is generally split to offer equal support to programs for girls and programs for women. Programs for women must include advocacy for social change. A two-page descriptive letter must meet the listed application deadline date; if interested, the foundation will invite a full proposal.

Requirements: The foundation primarily funds nonprofits serving the greater Philadelphia area or that have a national focus.
Restrictions: The foundation will not fund scholarships, endowments, or capital.
Geographic Focus: All States
Date(s) Application is Due: Jun 30
Amount of Grant: 5,000 - 15,000 USD
Contact: Alexandra Frazier; (610) 642-4887; info@valentinefoundation.org
Internet: http://www.valentinefoundation.org/guidelines.html
Sponsor: Valentine Foundation
300 Quarry Lane
Haverford, PA 19041

Valerie Adams Memorial Charitable Trust Grants 4898

The Valerie Adams Memorial Charitable Trust was established in Georgia in 2001. the Fund's primary fields of interest include: elementary and secondary education; the performing arts; and religion. There are no annual deadlines, although a specific application form is required. Applicants should begin by forwarding a letter of interest to the trust manager. Though grants are given primarily in Georgia, the Trust also considers applications from outside the state. Awards have typically ranged from $2,000 to $60,000.

Geographic Focus: All States
Contact: Douglas Curling, Trustee; (678) 672-4010 or (866) 972-4708; fax (678) 672-4016; doug@newkentcap.com
Sponsor: Valerie Adams Memorial Charitable Trust
11200 Bowen Road
Roswell, GA 30075-2239

Vancouver Foundation Disability Supports for Employment Grants 4899

The purpose of the Disability Supports for Employment Fund (DSEF) is to support new approaches to employment for people with disabilities that may complement or augment existing programs in the community. The intent of the program is to support initiatives by non-profit, charitable organizations that will promote the social and economic independence of individuals with disabilities.

Requirements: Grants are available to assist eligible organizations throughout B.C. who are working to increase employment opportunities and ultimately the rate of employment for

persons with disabilities in their communities. Projects must demonstrate that they do not duplicate or replicate existing government-funded programs, supports and services for persons with disabilities. There is a two-stage application process. The first stage, submit a Letter of Inquiry, consisting of an informal proposal to determine basic suitability and eligibility. The second stage is a full application. If your Letter of Inquiry fits within the funding guidelines you will be sent a grant application form with specific instructions for completion. The deadline dates are June 18 for the Letter of Inquiry and August 13 for the grant application. Applicant will receives final decision approximately 12 weeks after deadline.
Geographic Focus: All States, Canada
Date(s) Application is Due: Jun 18
Contact: Andria Teather; (604) 688-2204; fax (604) 688-4170; info@vancouverfoundation.ca
Internet: http://www.vancouverfoundation.ca/grants/specialprograms.htm
Sponsor: Vancouver Foundation
555 West Hastings Street, Suite 1200
Vancouver, BC V6B 4N6 Canada

Vancouver Foundation Grants and Community Initiatives Program   4900
Vancouver Foundation's Grants and Community Initiatives program provides Community Impact Grants in nine fields of interest: Animal Welfare; Arts and Culture; Children, Youth and Families; Education; Environment; Health and Social Development; Health and Medical Research; Youth Homelessness; Youth Philanthropy. The Vancouver Foundation has a two-stage application process. The first stage is a letter of intent. This consists of a brief proposal to determine basic suitability. The second stage is submission of a full grant application by a specific date. The letter of intent may be submitted online. You will be notified, if you are invited to submit a full grant application. The following is a list of deadline dates for the letters of intent and applications. Animal Welfare, Arts and Culture, Children, Youth and Families, Education, Environment, and Health and Social Development grants have a deadline date of: Letter of Intent, June 18, Application, August 6. Youth Homelessness grants: Letter of Intent, August 6, Application, September 24. Youth Philanthropy grants: Letter of Intent, September 17, Application, October 1. Health and Medical Research grants deadline dates are undetermined, at this time.
Requirements: Under our Grants and Community Initiatives program, Vancouver Foundation funds eligible applicants, which include: registered charities and qualified donees under the Income Tax Act; First Nations that may be considered a public body performing a function of government.
Restrictions: The Foundation does not fund the following: 100% of a proposal's costs; an organization's ongoing operational or core expenses; retroactive funding, or for any expenses to be incurred prior to the Foundation's decision date; debt retirement or reserves; mortgage pay-downs; conferences, competitions, symposia, annual events, or travel to/attendance at such events; office equipment and furniture; activities of religious organizations that serve primarily their membership and/or their direct religious purposes, unless the community at large will benefit significantly; sabbatical leaves, student exchanges; medical facilities or equipment; league-based sports and recreation programs; library acquisitions and construction; school construction; publication of books; academic or dissertation research; research with human subjects; endowment matching grants; capital requests, with the exceptions noted above; activities previously supported through government funding; bursaries, scholarships and awards; school trips, annual events or equipment; grants to individuals or businesses; funding requests if reports on any previous grants are overdue.
Geographic Focus: All States, Canada
Contact: Mark Gifford, Director; (604) 629-5362; markg@vancouverfoundation.ca
Internet: http://www.vancouverfoundation.ca/grants/communityinitiatives.htm
Sponsor: Vancouver Foundation
555 West Hastings Street, Suite 1200
Vancouver, BC V6B 4N6 Canada

Vancouver Sun Children's Fund Grants   4901
In partnership with Vancouver Foundation, the Vancouver Sun Children's Fund provides grants twice yearly to registered charities in British Columbia that directly serve the needs of children and youth (up to18 years) with special challenges. Grants range from $100 to $5,000 and recommendations are made by Vancouver Foundation's Children, Youth and Families Advisory Committee whose members have knowledge and experience in the fields of children's physical, mental and emotional health.
Requirements: Eligible applicants are registered charities and other qualified organizations under the Income Tax Act. They must demonstrate fiscal responsibility and effective management. To apply, submit your Letter of Intent electronically.
Restrictions: Grants are not made to individuals or businesses.
Geographic Focus: All States, Canada
Contact: Mark Gifford Director, Grants and Community Initiatives; (604) 688-2204; fax (604) 688-4170; markg@vancouverfoundation.ca
Internet: http://www.vancouverfoundation.ca/grants/specialprograms.htm
Sponsor: Vancouver Sun Children's Fund c/o Vancouver Foundation
Harbour Centre, 555 West Hastings Street, Suite 1200, Box 12132
Vancouver, BC V6B 4N6 Canada

Vanderburgh Community Foundation Grants   4902
The Vanderburgh Community Foundation is a nonprofit, public charity created for the people of Vanderburgh County, Indiana. The Foundation allows nonprofits to fulfill their missions by strengthening their ability to meet community needs through grants that assist charitable programs, address community issues, support community agencies, launch community initiatives, and support leadership development. Funding priorities include arts and culture; community development; education; health; human services; environment; recreation; and youth development. The Foundation's grant cycle is announced at the end of July. The preliminary proposal form is available at the website.

Requirements: The Foundation gives primarily to 501(c)3 tax-exempt organizations in Vanderburgh County, Indiana. Organizations must first submit a preliminary proposal to determine their eligibility. Proposals will be reviewed within 30 days, then select applicants will receive a formal invitation to submit a full proposal. Grant checks are distributed the following January.
Restrictions: The following project areas are not considered for funding: religious organizations for religious purposes; political parties or campaigns; endowment creation or debt reduction; capital campaign; operating costs not directly related to the proposed project; annual appeals or membership contributions; and travel requests for groups or individuals such as bands, sports teams, or classes.
Geographic Focus: Indiana
Date(s) Application is Due: Aug 5
Amount of Grant: 1,000 - 10,000 USD
Contact: Carol Pace, Program Officer; (812) 422-1245; fax (812) 429-0840
Internet: http://www.vanderburghcommunityfoundation.org/disc-grants
Sponsor: Vanderburgh Community Foundation
401 South East 6th Street, Suite 203
Evansville, IN 47708

Vanderburgh Community Foundation Women's Fund   4903
The Vanderburgh Community Foundation Women's Fund pools gifts of all sizes from a broad base of donors to support Vanderburgh grantmaking, education and advocacy work. The Women's Fund endowment is a permanent resource created to address the changing needs and priorities of women and children in the Vanderburgh County. Project areas considered including community development; education; health; human services; capital projects; endowment creation; or other activities that improve the quality of life for women, children, or both in Vanderburgh County. The preliminary proposal form is available at the Foundation website.
Requirements: Consideration will be given to nonprofit organizations that are 501(c)3 tax exempt. Organizations not classified as tax exempt may be considered with a fiscal sponsor. A preliminary proposal is required before submitting a full proposal.
Restrictions: Project areas not considered for funding include the following: projects or programs of organizations that are not committed to gender equity; funding to reduce or retire debt of the organization; projects that focus solely on the spiritual needs and growth of a church congregation or members of other religious organizations; political parties or campaigns; operating costs not directly related to the proposed project (the organization's general operating expenses including equipment, staff salary, rent, and utilities); event sponsorships, annual appeals, and membership contributions; travel expenses for groups or individuals such as bands, sports teams, or classes; scholarships or other grants to individuals.
Geographic Focus: Indiana
Date(s) Application is Due: Jul 13
Amount of Grant: 1,000 - 55,000 USD
Contact: Carol Pace, Program Officer; (812) 422-1245; fax (812) 429-0840
Internet: http://www.womensfundvc.org/
Sponsor: Vanderburgh Community Foundation
401 South East 6th Street, Suite 203
Evansville, IN 47708

Vanguard Public Foundation Grant Funds   4904
Vanguard provides funding to groups in northern California under four categories; the Social Justice Fund, the Community Institution Building Program, the Technical Assistance and Capacity Building Program, and the Social Justice Sabbatical Fund. Types of support include seed money, technical assistance, and operating expenses. Priority is given to projects without access to traditional funding sources because they may be thought to be risky, controversial, or of low priority. Vanguard strongly encourages coalitions that emphasize joint strategies and projects. Visit the web site for application guidelines. The next deadline to submit a proposal for the Social Justice Fund is October 14 and for a Social Justice Sabbatical is December 15. Annual deadline dates may vary; contact program staff for exact dates.
Requirements: Vanguard funds new or existing organizations involved in direct organizing or advocacy that are based in northern California (i.e., all counties north of Monterey). At the time a grant is made, an organization must either be tax-exempt or have a fiscal sponsor.
Restrictions: Vanguard does not fund capital campaigns or equipment purchase; organizations involved in direct services, research, or education, unless the proposed project clearly has an organizing component and cannot be supported within the general program budget; production costs for film; out-of-state travel; one-time conferences or events not integrally related to ongoing organizing; organizations with access to traditional funding sources and budgets of over $200,000 (unless the project for which funds are requested is unlikely to attract support because of its risky or controversial character); and costs already incurred.
Geographic Focus: California
Date(s) Application is Due: Oct 14; Dec 15
Contact: Director; (415) 487-2111; fax (415) 487-2124; danielle@vanguardsf.org
Internet: http://www.vanguardsf.org
Sponsor: Vanguard Public Foundation
383 Rhode Island Street, Suite 301
San Francisco, CA 94103

Van Kampen Boyer Molinari Charitable Foundation Grants   4905
The Van Kampen Boyer Molinari Charitable Foundation primarily provides grants in the states of Illinois, Michigan, California, New Jersey, and New York (although support is sometimes given outside of these states). The Foundation's primary fields of interest include: the arts; athletics and sports (primarily equestrianism); cancer research; children and youth services; education; health organizations; specialty hospitals; and human services. Target populations include children and youth, and awards range from $5,000 to $70,000. There

is no specific application form, so applicants should provide a letter detailing their program and budgetary needs. There are no deadlines with which to adhere.
Geographic Focus: All States
Amount of Grant: 5,000 - 75,000 USD
Contact: Joan M. Mack, President; (616) 402-2238 or (561) 707-2337
Sponsor: Van Kampen Boyer Molinari Charitable Foundation
5440 East Farr Road
Fruitport, MI 49415-9751

Van Kampen Foundation Grants 4906
The Van Kampen Foundation was established in Illinois in 1996 with a primary donation from Judith Van Kampen, widow of a well-known investment banker and author of books about the end of the world. The primary interest of the Foundation is the development of public library materials, manuscripts, and artifacts for Christian educational purposes. Awards range up to $25,000. There are no specific application forms or deadlines, and interested parties should begin by contacting the Foundation in writing.
Geographic Focus: All States
Amount of Grant: Up to 25,000 USD
Contact: Kristen Wisen, Director; (630) 588 -7200
Sponsor: Van Kampen Foundation
290 S. County Farm Road, 3rd Floor
Wheaton, IL 60187-2440

Vectren Foundation Grants 4907
The foundation focuses its efforts in four major areas of giving: Education, Arts & Culture, Civic, and Health & Human Services. Priority will be given to those organizations and activities that serve to improve the quality of life in the communities Vectren serves.
Requirements: The only awards grants to organizations exempt from Federal Tax under Section 501(c)3 of the IRS code. The funding request application can be downloaded from the website. Applications should include a copy of your tax-exempt ruling from the IRS; a list of current board members and annual report, if available; and, a current operating and project budget. Applications for contributions to capital fund drives or to purchase equipment should also provide a clear description of the project, including its goals and objectives; and, a financial plan showing how the project will be funded. The plan should include other possible sources of support and funds that have been pledged or received to date.
Restrictions: The foundation will not: support programs, activities or campaigns that advance a specific religious agenda; make contributions to political, fraternal, labor or veteran's organizations, unless the activity is for direct community involvement; make contributions to issues-oriented organizations; will not award scholarships or grants that benefit individuals (This includes individuals raising funds for charitable purposes, student ambassador programs and sponsorship of individual sports or academic teams.); or, award grants involving travel outside of the Vectren Service Territory.
Geographic Focus: Indiana
Contact: Mark H. Miller; (812) 491-4176; fax (812) 491-4078; mmiller@vectren.com
Internet: http://www.vectren.com/web/holding/discover/foundation/foundation_i.jsp
Sponsor: Vectren Foundation
One Vectren Square
Evansville, IN 47708

Verizon Foundation Connecticut Grants 4908
The foundation awards grants for new or existing programs that address the issues of education, literacy, and workforce development. The foundation will entertain creative and innovative responses from nonprofit organizations and award one-time grants. Special focus is on projects that serve as best practice models and can be replicated throughout the state of Connecticut and the Northeast. The foundation seeks to support initiatives that may be used for, but are not limited to, the following areas: literacy, technology training, job retention training, preparing/coaching, and challenge/matching grants. The foundation will only accept applications submitted via the online process.
Requirements: Nonprofit 501(c)3 public charities and schools with current National Center for Education Statistics (NCES) School and District registration, involved in projects/programs benefiting Connecticut communities served by Verizon are eligible to apply.
Restrictions: The foundation will not consider requests or grants for sectarian, endowment, and/or capital campaigns.
Geographic Focus: Connecticut
Contact: John Butler; (800) 360-7955; fax (908) 630-2660; john.f.butler@verizon.com
Internet: http://foundation.verizon.com/cybergrants/plsql/vznadmin.vz_www.iyc?x_zip=06101
Sponsor: Verizon Foundation
500 Summit Lake Drive
Valhalla, NY 10595

Verizon Foundation Delaware Grants 4909
The foundation awards one-year grants to Delaware nonprofit organizations to support literacy initiatives, community technology development and workforce development programs as well as charitable and cultural events. The foundation invites proposals that: focus on basic literacy programs that build on reading skills for children and adults; proposals that focus on computer and web-based literacy programs; and strengthen the region's workforce. Grants support the implementation of a project/program and are not to be used for outside presentations, research, or travel. Awards will be made to those organizations with proposals that best meet the needs of Delaware residents. Proposals must be posted via the foundation's online application process; instructions are available online.
Requirements: Delaware 501(c)3 nonprofit whose programs benefit low-income, ethnic, minority, limited-English-speaking, and disabled communities in Delaware's various rural, urban, and inner-city regions.
Restrictions: Grants may not be used for any products, goods, or services offered by Verizon or any of its affiliates; capital improvement, furniture, etc; endowments; administrative expenses, such as salaries or grant preparation fees.
Geographic Focus: Delaware
Date(s) Application is Due: Jul 15
Amount of Grant: Up to 25,000 USD
Contact: Kay Fowler; (800) 360-7955; fax (908) 630-2660; karen.e.fowler@verizon.com
Internet: http://foundation.verizon.com/cybergrants/plsql/vznadmin.vz_www.iyc?x_zip=19801
Sponsor: Verizon Foundation
901 Tatnall Street, 2nd Floor
Wilmington, DE 19801

Verizon Foundation Domestic Violence Prevention Grants 4910
The Verizon Foundation is working to help stop the cycle of violence by providing financial, technical and human expertise to local and national organizations that focus on education, prevention, victim relief and empowerment. The Foundation only accepts electronic proposals through its online process, and reviews unsolicited proposals on a continuous calendar year basis from January 1st through October 31st.
Requirements: Proposals will be considered from eligible tax-exempt organizations in certain 501(c)3 subsections as defined by the Internal Revenue Service (IRS). Proposals will also be considered from elementary and secondary schools (public and private) that are registered with the National Center for Education Statistics (NCES). Proposals may also be considered from eligible tax-exempt organizations in the subsection 170(B)(1)(a)(i)—Church, provided that the proposal will benefit a large portion of a community without regard to religious affiliation and does not duplicate the work of other agencies in the community.
Restrictions: The Verizon Foundation does not provide funding for any of the following: individuals; private charity or foundation; organizations not exempt under Section 501(c)3 of the Internal Revenue Code, and not eligible for tax-deductible support; religious organizations, unless the particular program will benefit a large portion of a community without regard to religious affiliation and does not duplicate the work of other agencies in the community; political causes, candidates, organizations or campaigns; organizations that discriminate on the basis of age, color, citizenship, disability, disabled veteran status, gender, race, religion, national origin, marital status, sexual orientation, military service or status or Vietnam-era veteran status; organizations whose primary purpose is to influence legislation; endowments or capital campaigns; film, music, TV, video and media production projects or broadcast program underwriting; research studies, unless related to projects we are already supporting; sports sponsorships; performing arts tours; association memberships; or organizations that have received a grant from the Verizon Foundation in the last three consecutive years - organization may reapply after a one-year hiatus.
Geographic Focus: All States
Amount of Grant: 5,000 - 10,000 USD
Contact: Patrick Gaston; (800) 360-7955; fax (908) 630-2660; patrick.g.gaston@erizon.com
Internet: http://foundation.verizon.com/core/domestic.shtml
Sponsor: Verizon Foundation
1 Verizon Way
Basking Ridge, NJ 07920

Verizon Foundation Grants 4911
The foundation concentrates its venture philanthropy in five priority funding areas, with an emphasis on providing innovative technology solutions to solve problems. Areas of interest include: literacy—link basic and computer literacy experts across the nation to create a more literate America; Internet safety—partner with the nonprofit community to expand its capacity through the use of technology; education—programs that develop a prepared workforce; domestic violence prevention—financial, technical and human expertise to local and national organizations that focus on education, prevention, victim relief and empowerment; and healthcare and accessibility—technology to help underserved populations and people with disabilities access information on critical health issues. The Foundation only accepts electronic proposals through its online process, and reviews unsolicited proposals on a continuous calendar year basis from January 1st through October 31st.
Requirements: Proposals will be considered from eligible tax-exempt organizations in certain 501(c)3 subsections as defined by the Internal Revenue Service (IRS). Proposals will also be considered from elementary and secondary schools (public and private) that are registered with the National Center for Education Statistics (NCES). Proposals may also be considered from eligible tax-exempt organizations in the subsection 170(B)(1)(a)(i)—Church, provided that the proposal will benefit a large portion of a community without regard to religious affiliation and does not duplicate the work of other agencies in the community.
Restrictions: The Verizon Foundation does not provide funding for any of the following: individuals; private charity or foundation; organizations not exempt under Section 501(c)3 of the Internal Revenue Code, and not eligible for tax-deductible support; religious organizations, unless the particular program will benefit a large portion of a community without regard to religious affiliation and does not duplicate the work of other agencies in the community; political causes, candidates, organizations or campaigns; organizations that discriminate on the basis of age, color, citizenship, disability, disabled veteran status, gender, race, religion, national origin, marital status, sexual orientation, military service or status or Vietnam-era veteran status; organizations whose primary purpose is to influence legislation; endowments or capital campaigns; film, music, TV, video and media production projects or broadcast program underwriting; research studies, unless related to projects we are already supporting; sports sponsorships; performing arts tours; association memberships; or organizations that have received a grant from the Verizon Foundation in the last three consecutive years - organization may reapply after a one-year hiatus.
Geographic Focus: All States
Amount of Grant: 5,000 - 10,000 USD
Contact: Patrick Gaston; (800) 360-7955; fax (908) 630-2660; patrick.g.gaston@erizon.com

Internet: http://foundation.verizon.com/grant/guidelines.shtml
Sponsor: Verizon Foundation
1 Verizon Way
Basking Ridge, NJ 07920

Verizon Foundation Great Lakes Region Grants   4912
The foundation invites applications, in the Great Lakes Region (Illinois, Indiana, Michigan, Ohio, and Wisconsin), for grants that support education, literacy, and workforce development projects by nonprofits. Proposals are accepted for programs that provide job training for individuals including welfare-to-work, English as a separate language, and school-to-work training programs; and that assist people with disabilities in acquiring computer skills through adaptive technology that prepares them to enter the workforce. Applications are only accepted on-line.
Requirements: Applicants must be nonprofit 501(c)3 organizations whose programs benefit under served communities (low-income, ethnic, minority, limited-English-speaking, and disabled communities in various rural, urban, and inner-city regions) served by Verizon. Nonprofit organizations located outside of Verizon serving territory but assisting under served communities in Verizon-serving territory also are eligible.
Restrictions: These funds may not be used for any products, goods, or services offered by Verizon or any of its affiliates; capital renovations or furniture; or administrative expenses or grant preparation fees.
Geographic Focus: Illinois, Indiana, Michigan, Ohio, Wisconsin
Amount of Grant: 5,000 - 25,000 USD
Contact: John VanWyck; (231) 727-1246; fax (231) 727-1691; john.vanwyck@verizon.com
Internet: http://foundation.verizon.com/cybergrants/plsql/vznadmin.vz_www.iyc?x_zip=48901
Sponsor: Verizon Foundation
860 Terrace Street, MIGFIPR
Muskegon, MI 49440

Verizon Foundation Health Care and Accessibility Grants   4913
The Verizon Foundation invests in projects that provide technology to help under served populations and people with disabilities access information on critical health issues. It also supports innovative technology that helps health care providers increase their efficiency, effectiveness and reach. The Foundation only accepts electronic proposals through its online process, and reviews unsolicited proposals on a continuous calendar year basis from January 1st through October 31st.
Requirements: Proposals will be considered from eligible tax-exempt organizations in certain 501(c)3 subsections as defined by the Internal Revenue Service (IRS). Proposals will also be considered from elementary and secondary schools (public and private) that are registered with the National Center for Education Statistics (NCES). Proposals may also be considered from eligible tax-exempt organizations in the subsection 170(B)(1)(a)(i)—Church, provided that the proposal will benefit a large portion of a community without regard to religious affiliation and does not duplicate the work of other agencies in the community.
Restrictions: The Verizon Foundation does not provide funding for any of the following: individuals; private charity or foundation; organizations not exempt under Section 501(c)3 of the Internal Revenue Code, and not eligible for tax-deductible support; religious organizations, unless the particular program will benefit a large portion of a community without regard to religious affiliation and does not duplicate the work of other agencies in the community; political causes, candidates, organizations or campaigns; organizations that discriminate on the basis of age, color, citizenship, disability, disabled veteran status, gender, race, religion, national origin, marital status, sexual orientation, military service or status or Vietnam-era veteran status; organizations whose primary purpose is to influence legislation; endowments or capital campaigns; film, music, TV, video and media production projects or broadcast program underwriting; research studies, unless related to projects we are already supporting; sports sponsorships; performing arts tours; association memberships; or organizations that have received a grant from the Verizon Foundation in the last three consecutive years - organization may reapply after a one-year hiatus.
Geographic Focus: All States
Amount of Grant: 5,000 - 10,000 USD
Contact: Patrick Gaston; (800) 360-7955; fax (908) 630-2660; patrick.g.gaston@erizon.com
Internet: http://foundation.verizon.com/core/health.shtml
Sponsor: Verizon Foundation
1 Verizon Way
Basking Ridge, NJ 07920

Verizon Foundation Internet Safety Grants   4914
Through its Internet Safety program, the Verizon Foundation invests in programs and organizations that: help law enforcement officers investigate Internet-related crimes against children; educate parents and caregivers about measures they can take to help children use the Internet safely; teach teens and young children how to protect themselves and avoid putting themselves in danger or breaking the law; and warn adults about the pitfalls and dangers online. The Foundation only accepts electronic proposals through its online process, and reviews unsolicited proposals on a continuous calendar year basis from January 1st through October 31st.
Requirements: Proposals will be considered from eligible tax-exempt organizations in certain 501(c)3 subsections as defined by the Internal Revenue Service (IRS). Proposals will also be considered from elementary and secondary schools (public and private) that are registered with the National Center for Education Statistics (NCES). Proposals may also be considered from eligible tax-exempt organizations in the subsection 170(B)(1)(a)(i)—Church, provided that the proposal will benefit a large portion of a community without regard to religious affiliation and does not duplicate the work of other agencies in the community.
Restrictions: The Verizon Foundation does not provide funding for any of the following: individuals; private charity or foundation; organizations not exempt under Section 501(c)3 of the Internal Revenue Code, and not eligible for tax-deductible support; religious organizations, unless the particular program will benefit a large portion of a community without regard to religious affiliation and does not duplicate the work of other agencies in the community; political causes, candidates, organizations or campaigns; organizations that discriminate on the basis of age, color, citizenship, disability, disabled veteran status, gender, race, religion, national origin, marital status, sexual orientation, military service or status or Vietnam-era veteran status; organizations whose primary purpose is to influence legislation; endowments or capital campaigns; film, music, TV, video and media production projects or broadcast program underwriting; research studies, unless related to projects we are already supporting; sports sponsorships; performing arts tours; association memberships; or organizations that have received a grant from the Verizon Foundation in the last three consecutive years - organization may reapply after a one-year hiatus.
Geographic Focus: All States
Amount of Grant: 5,000 - 10,000 USD
Contact: Patrick Gaston; (800) 360-7955; fax (908) 630-2660; patrick.g.gaston@erizon.com
Internet: http://foundation.verizon.com/core/internet_safety.shtml
Sponsor: Verizon Foundation
1 Verizon Way
Basking Ridge, NJ 07920

Verizon Foundation Literacy Grants   4915
The Verizon Foundation is investing in online resources, community-based initiatives and national programs that teach non-readers to read and advance the complex skills necessary for educational achievement and job success in the 21st Century. Its primary goal goal is to advance student achievement through innovative technology that increases educator effectiveness at home, in the classroom or in the community. The Foundation only accepts electronic proposals through its online process, and reviews unsolicited proposals on a continuous calendar year basis from January 1st through October 31st.
Requirements: Proposals will be considered from eligible tax-exempt organizations in certain 501(c)3 subsections as defined by the Internal Revenue Service (IRS). Proposals will also be considered from elementary and secondary schools (public and private) that are registered with the National Center for Education Statistics (NCES). Proposals may also be considered from eligible tax-exempt organizations in the subsection 170(B)(1)(a)(i)—Church, provided that the proposal will benefit a large portion of a community without regard to religious affiliation and does not duplicate the work of other agencies in the community.
Restrictions: The Verizon Foundation does not provide funding for any of the following: individuals; private charity or foundation; organizations not exempt under Section 501(c)3 of the Internal Revenue Code, and not eligible for tax-deductible support; religious organizations, unless the particular program will benefit a large portion of a community without regard to religious affiliation and does not duplicate the work of other agencies in the community; political causes, candidates, organizations or campaigns; organizations that discriminate on the basis of age, color, citizenship, disability, disabled veteran status, gender, race, religion, national origin, marital status, sexual orientation, military service or status or Vietnam-era veteran status; organizations whose primary purpose is to influence legislation; endowments or capital campaigns; film, music, TV, video and media production projects or broadcast program underwriting; research studies, unless related to projects we are already supporting; sports sponsorships; performing arts tours; association memberships; or organizations that have received a grant from the Verizon Foundation in the last three consecutive years - organization may reapply after a one-year hiatus.
Geographic Focus: All States
Amount of Grant: 5,000 - 10,000 USD
Contact: Patrick Gaston; (800) 360-7955; fax (908) 630-2660; patrick.g.gaston@erizon.com
Internet: http://foundation.verizon.com/core/literacy.shtml
Sponsor: Verizon Foundation
1 Verizon Way
Basking Ridge, NJ 07920

Verizon Foundation Maine Grants   4916
The foundation invites proposals in Maine for grants that support the use of technology by Maine school systems. The program seeks proposals that demonstrate collaboration via the use of technology to enhance course offerings in Maine's K-12 education system; improve the efficiency in the operation of school systems statewide via the use of distance-learning technology; use technology applications that enable the school system to reach the community it serves more effectively; emphasize teaching and learning; have administrative support; lead to measurable cost savings as a result of collaboration; overcome challenges posed by Maine's vast geography and sparse population; demonstrate new solutions to traditional educational problems and challenges; and can be replicated throughout other school systems. The Foundation only accepts electronic proposals through its online process, and reviews unsolicited proposals on a continuous calendar year basis from January 1st through October 31st.
Requirements: Proposals will be considered from eligible tax-exempt organizations in certain 501(c)3 subsections as defined by the Internal Revenue Service (IRS). Proposals will also be considered from elementary and secondary schools (public and private) that are registered with the National Center for Education Statistics (NCES). Proposals may also be considered from eligible tax-exempt organizations in the subsection 170(B)(1)(a)(i)—Church, provided that the proposal will benefit a large portion of a community without regard to religious affiliation and does not duplicate the work of other agencies in the community.
Restrictions: The Verizon Foundation does not provide funding for any of the following: individuals; private charity or foundation; organizations not exempt under Section 501(c)3 of the Internal Revenue Code, and not eligible for tax-deductible support; religious organizations, unless the particular program will benefit a large portion of a community without regard to religious affiliation and does not duplicate the work of other agencies in the community; political causes, candidates, organizations or campaigns; organizations that discriminate on the basis of age, color, citizenship, disability, disabled veteran status, gender, race, religion, national origin, marital status, sexual orientation, military service or status or

Vietnam-era veteran status; organizations whose primary purpose is to influence legislation; endowments or capital campaigns; film, music, TV, video and media production projects or broadcast program underwriting; research studies, unless related to projects we are already supporting; sports sponsorships; performing arts tours; association memberships; or organizations that have received a grant from the Verizon Foundation in the last three consecutive years - organization may reapply after a one-year hiatus.
Geographic Focus: Maine
Amount of Grant: 5,000 - 10,000 USD
Contact: Stephanie Lee, Regional Director; (617) 743-5440; stephanie.s.lee@verizon.com
Internet: http://foundation.verizon.com/cybergrants/plsql/vznadmin.vz_www.iyc?x_zip=04330
Sponsor: Verizon Foundation
185 Franklin Street, Room 1702
Boston, MA 02110

Verizon Foundation Maryland Grants 4917

The foundation invites applications, in Maryland, to receive financial grants that support education, literacy, health care access, workforce development, and the reduction of domestic violence. Consideration will be given to proposals for programs that provide job training for individuals, including welfare-to-work and school-to-work training programs; and assist people with disabilities in acquiring computer skills through adaptive technology that prepares them to enter the workforce. The Foundation only accepts electronic proposals through its online process, and reviews unsolicited proposals on a continuous calendar year basis from January 1st through October 31st.
Requirements: Proposals will be considered from eligible tax-exempt organizations in certain 501(c)3 subsections as defined by the Internal Revenue Service (IRS). Proposals will also be considered from elementary and secondary schools (public and private) that are registered with the National Center for Education Statistics (NCES). Proposals may also be considered from eligible tax-exempt organizations in the subsection 170(B)(1)(a)(i)—Church, provided that the proposal will benefit a large portion of a community without regard to religious affiliation and does not duplicate the work of other agencies in the community.
Restrictions: The Verizon Foundation does not provide funding for any of the following: individuals; private charity or foundation; organizations not exempt under Section 501(c)3 of the Internal Revenue Code, and not eligible for tax-deductible support; religious organizations, unless the particular program will benefit a large portion of a community without regard to religious affiliation and does not duplicate the work of other agencies in the community; political causes, candidates, organizations or campaigns; organizations that discriminate on the basis of age, color, citizenship, disability, disabled veteran status, gender, race, religion, national origin, marital status, sexual orientation, military service or status or Vietnam-era veteran status; organizations whose primary purpose is to influence legislation; endowments or capital campaigns; film, music, TV, video and media production projects or broadcast program underwriting; research studies, unless related to projects we are already supporting; sports sponsorships; performing arts tours; association memberships; or organizations that have received a grant from the Verizon Foundation in the last three consecutive years - organization may reapply after a one-year hiatus.
Geographic Focus: Maryland
Amount of Grant: 5,000 - 10,000 USD
Contact: Diane Miles; (410) 393-7450 or (800) 360-7955; diane.f.miles@verizon.com
Internet: http://foundation.verizon.com/cybergrants/plsql/vznadmin.vz_www.iyc?x_zip=21202
Sponsor: Verizon Foundation
1 East Pratt Street, 10E
Baltimore, MD 21202

Verizon Foundation New Jersey Check into Literacy Program Grants 4918

The foundation awards grants in New Jersey to support literacy. Grants are awarded in the following program areas: Verizon Reads—literacy programs that build on reading skills for children and adults, and proposals that focus on computer and Web-based literacy programs; and Verizon Connects—technology grants to support nonprofits' operational efficiency through use of computers and the Internet, technology training for individuals including welfare-to-work and school-to-work training programs, and adaptive technology that prepares people with disabilities to enter the workforce.
Requirements: New Jersey 501(c)3 tax-exempt organizations that benefit under served communities in the Verizon-serving territory are eligible. Nonprofit organizations located outside of the Verizon-serving territory but assisting under served communities in the Verizon-serving territory also are eligible.
Geographic Focus: New Jersey
Date(s) Application is Due: May 15
Amount of Grant: 1,000 - 25,000 USD
Contact: Maurice Brown, Director; (973) 416-1464 or (800) 360-7955; fax (908) 630-2660; maurice.j.brown@verizon.com
Internet: http://foundation.verizon.com/cybergrants/plsql/vznadmin.vz_www.iyc?x_zip=07920
Sponsor: Verizon Foundation
540 Broad Street, 18th Floor
Newark, NJ 07102

Verizon Foundation New York Grants 4919

The Verizon Foundation—the philanthropic arm of Verizon Communications—supports a variety of programs and events in communities from Buffalo to Brooklyn. As one of the largest corporate contributors in New York, Verizon is proud to have directed more than 6,000 grants totaling more than $14 million to some 2,700 non-profits across the state. Those non-profits include school districts and universities, multicultural groups and hospitals, children's organizations and those assisting the disabled and victims of domestic violence. Through the Foundation, Verizon New York underscores the company's commitment to key funding priorities—combating literacy and domestic violence, empowering communities with technology, bridging the digital divide, creating a skilled work force, and galvanizing employees to volunteer. The Foundation only accepts electronic proposals through its online process, and reviews unsolicited proposals on a continuous calendar year basis from January 1st through October 31st.
Requirements: Proposals will be considered from eligible tax-exempt organizations in certain 501(c)3 subsections as defined by the Internal Revenue Service (IRS). Proposals will also be considered from elementary and secondary schools (public and private) that are registered with the National Center for Education Statistics (NCES). Proposals may also be considered from eligible tax-exempt organizations in the subsection 170(B)(1)(a)(i)—Church, provided that the proposal will benefit a large portion of a community without regard to religious affiliation and does not duplicate the work of other agencies in the community.
Restrictions: The Verizon Foundation does not provide funding for any of the following: individuals; private charity or foundation; organizations not exempt under Section 501(c)3 of the Internal Revenue Code, and not eligible for tax-deductible support; religious organizations, unless the particular program will benefit a large portion of a community without regard to religious affiliation and does not duplicate the work of other agencies in the community; political causes, candidates, organizations or campaigns; organizations that discriminate on the basis of age, color, citizenship, disability, disabled veteran status, gender, race, religion, national origin, marital status, sexual orientation, military service or status or Vietnam-era veteran status; organizations whose primary purpose is to influence legislation; endowments or capital campaigns; film, music, TV, video and media production projects or broadcast program underwriting; research studies, unless related to projects we are already supporting; sports sponsorships; performing arts tours; association memberships; or organizations that have received a grant from the Verizon Foundation in the last three consecutive years - organization may reapply after a one-year hiatus.
Geographic Focus: New York
Amount of Grant: 5,000 - 10,000 USD
Contact: Sandy Wilson; (800) 360-7955; fax (908) 630-2660; sandra.c.wilson@verizon.com
Internet: http://foundation.verizon.com/cybergrants/plsql/vznadmin.vz_www.iyc?x_zip=10007
Sponsor: Verizon Foundation
140 West Street, 26th Floor, Room 2621
New York, NY 10007

Verizon Foundation Northeast Region Grants 4920

The Verizon Foundation is committed to supporting programs and projects that leverage technology to improve basic computer literacy and domestic violence initiatives, seeking organizations that serve the needs of diverse communities, people with disabilities, and the economically and socially challenged. The Foundation only accepts electronic proposals through its online process, and reviews unsolicited proposals on a continuous calendar year basis from January 1st through October 31st.
Requirements: Proposals will be considered from eligible tax-exempt organizations in certain 501(c)3 subsections as defined by the Internal Revenue Service (IRS). Proposals will also be considered from elementary and secondary schools (public and private) that are registered with the National Center for Education Statistics (NCES). Proposals may also be considered from eligible tax-exempt organizations in the subsection 170(B)(1)(a)(i)—Church, provided that the proposal will benefit a large portion of a community without regard to religious affiliation and does not duplicate the work of other agencies in the community.
Restrictions: The Verizon Foundation does not provide funding for any of the following: individuals; private charity or foundation; organizations not exempt under Section 501(c)3 of the Internal Revenue Code, and not eligible for tax-deductible support; religious organizations, unless the particular program will benefit a large portion of a community without regard to religious affiliation and does not duplicate the work of other agencies in the community; political causes, candidates, organizations or campaigns; organizations that discriminate on the basis of age, color, citizenship, disability, disabled veteran status, gender, race, religion, national origin, marital status, sexual orientation, military service or status or Vietnam-era veteran status; organizations whose primary purpose is to influence legislation; endowments or capital campaigns; film, music, TV, video and media production projects or broadcast program underwriting; research studies, unless related to projects we are already supporting; sports sponsorships; performing arts tours; association memberships; or organizations that have received a grant from the Verizon Foundation in the last three consecutive years - organization may reapply after a one-year hiatus.
Geographic Focus: Massachusetts, Rhode Island
Amount of Grant: 5,000 - 10,000 USD
Contact: Rick Colon, Regional Director; (781) 849-2046; richard.b.colon@verizon.com
Internet: http://foundation.verizon.com/cybergrants/plsql/vznadmin.vz_www.iyc?x_zip=02184
Sponsor: Verizon Foundation
125 Lundquist Drive, Room 1730
Braintree, MA 02184

Verizon Foundation Pennsylvania Grants 4921

Verizon Foundation Pennsylvania is investing in online resources, community-based initiatives and state-wide programs that teach non readers to read and advance the complex skills necessary for educational achievement and job success in the 21st Century. The grants have enabled the recipient organizations to improve basic literacy skills, create new and diverse approaches to technology-based learning, and help domestic violence victims rebuild their lives. The Foundation only accepts electronic proposals through its online process, and reviews unsolicited proposals on a continuous calendar year basis from January 1st through October 31st.
Requirements: Proposals will be considered from eligible tax-exempt organizations in certain 501(c)3 subsections as defined by the Internal Revenue Service (IRS). Proposals will also be considered from elementary and secondary schools (public and private) that are registered with the National Center for Education Statistics (NCES). Proposals may also be considered from eligible tax-exempt organizations in the subsection 170(B)(1)(a)(i)—Church, provided that the proposal will benefit a large portion of a community without regard to religious affiliation and does not duplicate the work of other agencies in the community.

Restrictions: The Verizon Foundation does not provide funding for any of the following: individuals; private charity or foundation; organizations not exempt under Section 501(c)3 of the Internal Revenue Code, and not eligible for tax-deductible support; religious organizations, unless the particular program will benefit a large portion of a community without regard to religious affiliation and does not duplicate the work of other agencies in the community; political causes, candidates, organizations or campaigns; organizations that discriminate on the basis of age, color, citizenship, disability, disabled veteran status, gender, race, religion, national origin, marital status, sexual orientation, military service or status or Vietnam-era veteran status; organizations whose primary purpose is to influence legislation; endowments or capital campaigns; film, music, TV, video and media production projects or broadcast program underwriting; research studies, unless related to projects we are already supporting; sports sponsorships; performing arts tours; association memberships; or organizations that have received a grant from the Verizon Foundation in the last three consecutive years - organization may reapply after a one-year hiatus.
Geographic Focus: Pennsylvania
Amount of Grant: 5,000 - 10,000 USD
Contact: Denise Loughlin; (215) 466-3351; denise.g.loughlin@verizon.com
Internet: http://www22.verizon.com/about/community/pa/community/comm_index.html
Sponsor: Verizon Foundation
3478 Kirkwood Road
Philadelphia, PA 19114

Verizon Foundation South Carolina Literacy & Internet Safety Grants   4922
The foundation invites applications, in South Carolina, for grants that support the use of technology by nonprofits in literacy and Internet safety. A total of $45,000 will be distributed to nonprofit organizations throughout the state. Grants will range from $1,500 to $10,000, and will cover a one-year period. The Foundation only accepts electronic proposals through its online process.
Requirements: Applicants must be nonprofit 501(c)3 organizations whose programs benefit under-served South Carolina communities (low-income, ethnic, minority, limited-English-speaking, and disabled communities in various rural, urban, and inner-city regions) served by Verizon. Nonprofit organizations located outside of Verizon serving territory but assisting under-served communities in Verizon-serving territory also are eligible.
Restrictions: Grants may not be used for any products, goods, or services offered by Verizon or any of its affiliates; capital renovations or furniture; or administrative expenses or grant preparation fees.
Geographic Focus: South Carolina
Date(s) Application is Due: Aug 29
Amount of Grant: 5,000 - 10,000 USD
Contact: Chris Rutledge; (800) 360-7955; fax (908) 630-2660; chris.rutledge@verizon.com
Internet: http://foundation.verizon.com/cybergrants/plsql/vznadmin.vz_www.iyc?x_zip=33601
Sponsor: Verizon Foundation
P.O. Box 110, MC FLTC0006
Tampa, FL 33601

Verizon Foundation Southeast Region Grants   4923
The Foundation is currently inviting applications by nonprofits in the southeastern U.S. to receive financial grants to support education and workforce literacy initiatives that use technology. Of special interest are proposals that provide literacy training for individuals in welfare-to-work and school-to-work training programs, including technology and literacy training; proposals that assist people with disabilities in acquiring computer skills through adaptive technology that prepares them to enter the workforce; proposals that utilize technology to enhance workforce literacy efforts; and proposals that deliver workforce literacy training via e-learning methods. The Foundation only accepts electronic proposals through its online process, and reviews unsolicited proposals on a continuous calendar year basis from January 1st through October 31st.
Requirements: Proposals will be considered from eligible tax-exempt organizations in certain 501(c)3 subsections as defined by the Internal Revenue Service (IRS). Proposals will also be considered from elementary and secondary schools (public and private) that are registered with the National Center for Education Statistics (NCES). Proposals may also be considered from eligible tax-exempt organizations in the subsection 170(B)(1)(a)(i)—Church, provided that the proposal will benefit a large portion of a community without regard to religious affiliation and does not duplicate the work of other agencies in the community.
Restrictions: The Verizon Foundation does not provide funding for any of the following: individuals; private charity or foundation; organizations not exempt under Section 501(c)3 of the Internal Revenue Code, and not eligible for tax-deductible support; religious organizations, unless the particular program will benefit a large portion of a community without regard to religious affiliation and does not duplicate the work of other agencies in the community; political causes, candidates, organizations or campaigns; organizations that discriminate on the basis of age, color, citizenship, disability, disabled veteran status, gender, race, religion, national origin, marital status, sexual orientation, military service or status or Vietnam-era veteran status; organizations whose primary purpose is to influence legislation; endowments or capital campaigns; film, music, TV, video and media production projects or broadcast program underwriting; research studies, unless related to projects we are already supporting; sports sponsorships; performing arts tours; association memberships; or organizations that have received a grant from the Verizon Foundation in the last three consecutive years - organization may reapply after a one-year hiatus.
Geographic Focus: Alabama, Georgia, Kentucky, North Carolina, South Carolina
Contact: Julie Smith; (678) 259-2085; julie.c.smith@verizon.com
Internet: http://foundation.verizon.com/cybergrants/plsql/vznadmin.vz_www.iyc?x_zip=30022
Sponsor: Verizon Foundation
5055 North Point Parkway
Alpharetta, GA 30022

Verizon Foundation Vermont Grants   4924
The Foundation is committed to supporting programs and projects that leverage technology to improve basic computer literacy and domestic violence initiatives, seeking organizations that serve the needs of diverse communities, people with disabilities, and the economically and socially challenged. Last year, Verizon Foundation donated close to $250,000 to Vermont nonprofit organizations and our employees clocked more than 16,000 volunteer hours to community organizations. The Foundation only accepts electronic proposals through its online process, and reviews unsolicited proposals on a continuous calendar year basis from January 1st through October 31st.
Requirements: Proposals will be considered from eligible tax-exempt organizations in certain 501(c)3 subsections as defined by the Internal Revenue Service (IRS). Proposals will also be considered from elementary and secondary schools (public and private) that are registered with the National Center for Education Statistics (NCES). Proposals may also be considered from eligible tax-exempt organizations in the subsection 170(B)(1)(a)(i)—Church, provided that the proposal will benefit a large portion of a community without regard to religious affiliation and does not duplicate the work of other agencies in the community.
Restrictions: The Verizon Foundation does not provide funding for any of the following: individuals; private charity or foundation; organizations not exempt under Section 501(c)3 of the Internal Revenue Code, and not eligible for tax-deductible support; religious organizations, unless the particular program will benefit a large portion of a community without regard to religious affiliation and does not duplicate the work of other agencies in the community; political causes, candidates, organizations or campaigns; organizations that discriminate on the basis of age, color, citizenship, disability, disabled veteran status, gender, race, religion, national origin, marital status, sexual orientation, military service or status or Vietnam-era veteran status; organizations whose primary purpose is to influence legislation; endowments or capital campaigns; film, music, TV, video and media production projects or broadcast program underwriting; research studies, unless related to projects we are already supporting; sports sponsorships; performing arts tours; association memberships; or organizations that have received a grant from the Verizon Foundation in the last three consecutive years - organization may reapply after a one-year hiatus.
Geographic Focus: Vermont
Amount of Grant: 5,000 - 10,000 USD
Contact: Stephanie Lee, Regional Director; (617) 743-5440; stephanie.s.lee@verizon.com
Internet: http://foundation.verizon.com/cybergrants/plsql/vznadmin.vz_www.iyc?x_zip=05403
Sponsor: Verizon Foundation
185 Franklin Street, Room 1702
Boston, MA 02110

Verizon Foundation Virginia Grants   4925
Verizon Foundation grants have touched and will continue to affect thousands of lives in Virginia. Verizon is committed to investing in the technological, financial, and human resources necessary to build more literate communities that can prosper in the information era, and to foster domestic violence awareness, prevention, and recovery. The Foundation will continue to form strong partnerships with Virginia's non-profit community to achieve its funding priority goals and improve the quality of life for people across the Commonwealth. The Foundation only accepts electronic proposals through its online process, and reviews unsolicited proposals on a continuous calendar year basis from January 1st through October 31st.
Requirements: Proposals will be considered from eligible tax-exempt organizations in certain 501(c)3 subsections as defined by the Internal Revenue Service (IRS). Proposals will also be considered from elementary and secondary schools (public and private) that are registered with the National Center for Education Statistics (NCES). Proposals may also be considered from eligible tax-exempt organizations in the subsection 170(B)(1)(a)(i)—Church, provided that the proposal will benefit a large portion of a community without regard to religious affiliation and does not duplicate the work of other agencies in the community.
Restrictions: The Verizon Foundation does not provide funding for any of the following: individuals; private charity or foundation; organizations not exempt under Section 501(c)3 of the Internal Revenue Code, and not eligible for tax-deductible support; religious organizations, unless the particular program will benefit a large portion of a community without regard to religious affiliation and does not duplicate the work of other agencies in the community; political causes, candidates, organizations or campaigns; organizations that discriminate on the basis of age, color, citizenship, disability, disabled veteran status, gender, race, religion, national origin, marital status, sexual orientation, military service or status or Vietnam-era veteran status; organizations whose primary purpose is to influence legislation; endowments or capital campaigns; film, music, TV, video and media production projects or broadcast program underwriting; research studies, unless related to projects we are already supporting; sports sponsorships; performing arts tours; association memberships; or organizations that have received a grant from the Verizon Foundation in the last three consecutive years - organization may reapply after a one-year hiatus.
Geographic Focus: Virginia
Amount of Grant: 5,000 - 10,000 USD
Contact: Stephan Clementi, (804) 772-1673 or (800) 360-7955; steve.clementi@verizon.com
Internet: http://foundation.verizon.com/cybergrants/plsql/vznadmin.vz_www.iyc?x_zip=24012
Sponsor: Verizon Foundation
703 East Grace Street, 7th Floor
Richmond, VA 23219

Verizon Foundation West Virginia Grants   4926
The foundation awards grants in West Virginia to help the nonprofit community find technology-based solutions that improve constituent service, outreach, and programming. The program seeks proposals to improve the efficiency in the operation of a nonprofit with the use of computers and the Internet; proposals for technology applications that enable the agency to reach the community it serves more effectively; and technology-based solutions that can help improve constituent service, outreach, and programming. Grants must be used to enhance the technology-based resources and/or programming of the nonprofit organization. The Foundation

only accepts electronic proposals through its online process, and reviews unsolicited proposals on a continuous calendar year basis from January 1st through October 31st.
Requirements: Proposals will be considered from eligible tax-exempt organizations in certain 501(c)3 subsections as defined by the Internal Revenue Service (IRS). Proposals will also be considered from elementary and secondary schools (public and private) that are registered with the National Center for Education Statistics (NCES). Proposals may also be considered from eligible tax-exempt organizations in the subsection 170(B)(1)(a)(i)—Church, provided that the proposal will benefit a large portion of a community without regard to religious affiliation and does not duplicate the work of other agencies in the community.
Restrictions: The Verizon Foundation does not provide funding for any of the following: individuals; private charity or foundation; organizations not exempt under Section 501(c)3 of the Internal Revenue Code, and not eligible for tax-deductible support; religious organizations, unless the particular program will benefit a large portion of a community without regard to religious affiliation and does not duplicate the work of other agencies in the community; political causes, candidates, organizations or campaigns; organizations that discriminate on the basis of age, color, citizenship, disability, disabled veteran status, gender, race, religion, national origin, marital status, sexual orientation, military service or status or Vietnam-era veteran status; organizations whose primary purpose is to influence legislation; endowments or capital campaigns; film, music, TV, video and media production projects or broadcast program underwriting; research studies, unless related to projects we are already supporting; sports sponsorships; performing arts tours; association memberships; or organizations that have received a grant from the Verizon Foundation in the last three consecutive years - organization may reapply after a one-year hiatus.
Geographic Focus: West Virginia
Contact: Joseph Long, (304) 344-7267; joseph.b.long@verizon.com
Internet: http://foundation.verizon.com/cybergrants/plsql/vznadmin.vz_www.iyc?x_zip=25314
Sponsor: Verizon Foundation
1500 MacCorkle Avenue SE, Room 500
Charleston, WV 25314

Verizon Wireless Hopeline Program Grants 4927
Verizon Wireless is dedicated to serving the communities in which it operates throughout the country. Through its HopeLine program, the company focuses primarily on putting wireless services to work to combat domestic violence. Verizon Wireless' HopeLine program also makes financial grants to regional and national domestic violence organizations, such as the Family Violence Prevention Fund, the National Coalition Against Domestic Violence and other select community interest groups. In addition to domestic violence, Verizon Wireless' philanthropic activities extend to assisting in public safety, disaster relief, and numerous nonprofit causes close to the communities it serves.
Requirements: 501(c)3 nonprofit organizations with valid IRS tax ID are eligible.
Geographic Focus: Maine, New Hampshire, New Jersey, New York, Rhode Island, Vermont
Contact: Program Contact; (845) 365-7212 or (845) 365-7212
Internet: http://aboutus.vzw.com/communityservice/hopeLine.html
Sponsor: Verizon Wireless
2000 Corporate Drive, 4th Floor
Orangeburg, NY 10962

Vermillion County Community Foundation Grants 4928
The role of the Vermillion County Community Foundation is to offer financial assistance to projects that preserve the area's history, enrich lives, and provide for the future of Vermillion County. Grant proposal information is available at the Foundation's office.
Geographic Focus: Indiana
Contact: Larry Lynn, Board President; (765) 832-8665; lecrly72@hughes.net
Internet: http://www.thevccf.org/communit.htm
Sponsor: Vermillion County Community Foundation
407 South Main Street
Clinton, IN 47842

Vermont Community Foundation Grants 4929
The foundation has broad program interests and will consider any project that meets a clearly defined community need in Vermont. Categories of support include, but are not limited to: the arts and humanities; education; the environment; historic resources; health; public affairs and community development; and social services.
Requirements: To be eligible, an organization must: have 501(c)3 tax-exempt status and not be classified as a private foundation; be located in or serve the people of Vermont; and employ staff and provide services without discrimination on the basis of race, religion, sex, age, national origin, disability, or sexual orientation. See Foundations website for additional guidelines, including rolling deadlines, and application forms.
Restrictions: The foundation does not make grants for endowments, annual operating or capital campaigns, religious purposes, individuals, debts, or equipment unless it is an integral part of an otherwise eligible project.
Geographic Focus: Vermont
Contact: Peter Espenshade; (802) 388-3355, ext. 248; pespenshade@vermontcf.org
Internet: http://www.vermontcf.org/apply/
Sponsor: Vermont Community Foundation
3 Court Street, P.O. Box 30
Middlebury, VT 05753

Vernon K. Krieble Foundation Grants 4930
The Foundation was established in 1984 by the family of Professor Vernon K. Krieble, scientist, educator, inventor, and entrepreneur. Recognizing that the Foundation's assets are the product of a free and democratic society, the founders considered it fitting that those assets be used "to further democratic capitalism and the preserve and promote a society of free, educated, healthy and creative individuals." The Foundation offers support to non-profit charitable and educational organizations that demonstrate leadership in furthering the original objectives, so that future generations can aspire to and achieve their full potential in a free society. Awards range from $2,500 to $50,000. There are no deadlines.
Requirements: Nonprofit 501(c)3 organizations are eligible. Funding is provided only for those organizations and projects which involve public policy research and education on issues supporting the preservation, and in some cases the restoration, or freedom and democracy in the United States, according to the principles of the Founding Fathers. Written proposals should include a summary of the project, the project budget, the amount requested, the qualifications of individuals involved, and a copy of the organization's Internal Revenue Service determination letter.
Geographic Focus: All States
Contact: Helen E. Krieble, President; (303) 758-3956; fax (303) 488-0068
Internet: http://www.krieble.org/grants
Sponsor: Vernon K. Krieble Foundation
1777 S Harrison Street, Suite 807
Denver, CO 80210

VHA Health Foundation Grants 4931
The Foundation has dedicated its resources to create a legacy strategy, which will build on its vision of the last decade by focusing on two critical issues that will significantly improve the delivery of health care: patient safety and disaster relief. Programs submitted for funding consideration must represent a new and innovative approach to hospital emergency preparedness and be beyond the concept stage - ready to test, implement, expand, or diffuse. Innovations should be either transformational (i.e. involve significant change in current operations) and/or disruptive (i.e., have profound impact on services and economics) in nature.
Requirements: Unsolicited inquires may be submitted at any time during the year. The Letter of Inquiry is the required first step in the process. Eligible programs should clearly incorporate four key elements: Innovation, Impact, Replicability and Sustainability. Grants are available to U.S. health care providers, including hospitals, health care systems, clinics, and medical practices with IRS tax-exempt 501(c)3 status. Local partnerships are encouraged to apply, but, since the hospital is the foundation's primary audience, the health care provider must serve as fiduciary agent and play an integral role in the program. An organization may submit multiple inquiries for consideration. Previously funded organizations may apply. Applicants are required to financially invest in the program with cash from any source and/or through in-kind contributions specific to the grant period. The minimum level of the investment is equal to one-half of the funding requested from the foundation.
Restrictions: The foundation will not consider requests for seed money or planning grants; primary research and development of technology; construction or renovation; indirect costs or overhead; endowments; political activities or attempts to influence specific legislation; individual scholarships or tuition assistance; or programs outside the United States.
Geographic Focus: All States
Contact: Michael Regier; (877) 847-1450 or (972) 830-0422; vhahealthfoundation@vha.com
Internet: https://www.vhafoundation.org/portal/server.pt?open=512&objID=1204&PageID=0&cached=true&mode=2&userID=504686
Sponsor: VHA Health Foundation
220 Easr Las Colinas Boulevard
Irving, TX 75039-5500

Viacom Foundation Grants (Formerly CBS Foundation) 4932
The purpose of the foundation is to strengthen the communities in which Viacom employees and audiences live and work. Grants are awarded to nonprofit organizations in the areas of arts & culture, children/youth/family, diversity, education, environment, health/medical, industry, social/civic/human services. Types of support include general operating grants, matching gifts, continuing support, annual campaigns, capital campaigns, curriculum development, program grants, and scholarships to children of Viacom employees only. Grants are made through corporate contributions and employee matching gifts to selected nonprofit organizations on a one-to-one basis.
Requirements: To submit an application send a proposal outlining project and expected benefit(s), copy of IRS 501(c)3 determination letter, financial plan, list of board of directors and officers, and a copy of latest audited financial statements.
Restrictions: The program does not make loans or grants for advertising, endowments, or for capital costs including construction and renovation. Individuals are not eligible.
Geographic Focus: All States
Contact: Karen Zatorski, Vice President, Public Affairs; (212) 975-8552
Internet: http://www.viacom.com/fundingoverview.jhtml
Sponsor: Viacom Foundation
51 West 52nd Street
New York, NY 10019

Victor E. Speas Foundation Grants 4933
The Victor E. Speas Foundation was established to provide medical care for the needy, to further medical research, and to support and promote quality educational, cultural, human-services, and health-care programming. In the area of arts, culture, and humanities, the foundation supports programming that: fosters the enjoyment and appreciation of the visual and performing arts; strengthens humanities and arts-related education programs; provides affordable access; enhances artistic elements in communities; and nurtures a new generation of artists. In the area of education, the foundation supports programming that: promotes effective teaching; improves the academic achievement of, or expands educational opportunities for, disadvantaged students; improves governance and management; strengthens nonprofit organizations, school leadership, and teaching; and bolsters strategic initiatives of area colleges and universities. In the area of health, the foundation supports programming that improves the delivery of health care to the indigent, uninsured, and other vulnerable populations and addresses health and health-care problems that intersect with social factors.

In the area of human services, the foundation funds programming that: strengthens agencies that deliver critical human services and maintains the community's safety net and helps agencies respond to federal, state, and local public policy changes. In the area of community improvement, the foundation funds capacity-building and infrastructure-development projects including: assessments, planning, and implementation of technology for management and programmatic functions within an organization; technical assistance on wide-ranging topics, including grant writing, strategic planning, financial management services, business development, board and volunteer management, and marketing; and mergers, affiliations, or other restructuring efforts. Grant requests for general operating support and program support will be considered. Grants from the foundation are one year in duration. Application materials are available for download at the grant website. There are no application deadlines for the Victor E. Speas Foundation. Proposals are reviewed on an ongoing basis.
Requirements: Applicants must have 501(c)3 tax-exempt status and serve the residents of Kansas City, Missouri. Two copies of the completed application must be mailed.
Restrictions: Grant requests for capital support will not be considered. The trust does not support requests from individuals, organizations attempting to influence policy through direct lobbying, or any political campaigns.
Geographic Focus: Missouri
Contact: Spence Heddens; (816) 292-4301; Spence.heddens@baml.com
Internet: https://www.bankofamerica.com/philanthropic/fn_search.action
Sponsor: Victor E. Speas Foundation
1200 Main Street, 14th Floor, P.O. Box 219119
Kansas City, MO 64121-9119

Victoria S. and Bradley L. Geist Foundation Capacity Building Grants 4934
The Foundation wishes to support foster children, their caregivers, and transitioning foster youth. The Foundation recognizes that the strength and capacity of the nonprofit organizations and programs serving foster children, their families, and youth are key to the healthy development of foster children and transitioning youth. The Foundation offers this Request for Proposals to provide meaningful support that enables nonprofit organizations and programs to strengthen and grow their capacity to serve foster children, their caregivers and transitioning foster youth. Capacity building efforts may address: governance and leadership; strategic relationships; evaluation and impact; resource development; internal operations and management; program design, delivery and evaluation; executive and key staff transitions; and staff training. Grants generally range from $5,000 to $40,000 and may be multi-year commitments, based on submission of satisfactory progress reports.
Requirements: Tax-exempt Hawaii organizations are eligible to apply. Organizations may be either 501(c)3 or religious organizations. Units of government and public schools are not eligible under this Request for Proposals.
Restrictions: Fiscal sponsorships are not permissible. Grants will not be made for capital, endowments, re-granting activities or operating costs.
Geographic Focus: Hawaii
Date(s) Application is Due: Jan 17; May 15; Sep 14
Contact: Carrie Shoda-Sutherland; (808) 566-5524; csutherland@hcf-hawaii.org
Internet: http://www.hawaiicommunityfoundation.org/grants/grants/grant/victoria-s-and-bradley-l-geist-foundation-capacity-building
Sponsor: Victoria S. and Bradley L. Geist Foundation
827 Fort Street Mall
Honolulu, HI 96813-4317

Victoria S. and Bradley L. Geist Foundation Enhancement Grants 4935
The purpose of the Foundation's Enhancements for Foster Children program is to enhance the lives of foster children by providing items and services that allow them to enjoy a quality of life similar to that of their peers. The funds are offered in the belief that every child is special and that their growth should be nurtured and celebrated. Grants range from $5,000 to $50,000. Grantees may propose an administrative fee for administering these funds.
Requirements: Tax-exempt Hawaii organizations are eligible to apply. This includes nonprofit organizations, 501(c)3 organizations, religious organizations that are exempt from taxation, and units of government.
Restrictions: Enhancements funds are not intended for basic living expenses such as housing, groceries, medical and dental care, and ordinary tuition expenses.
Geographic Focus: Hawaii
Date(s) Application is Due: Sep 14
Contact: Christel Wuerfel; (808) 566-5524 or (888) 731-3863; cwuerfel@hcf-hawaii.org
Internet: http://www.hawaiicommunityfoundation.org/grants/grants/grant/victoria-s-and-bradley-l-geist-foundation-enhancements
Sponsor: Victoria S. and Bradley L. Geist Foundation
827 Fort Street Mall
Honolulu, HI 96813-4317

Victoria S. and Bradley L. Geist Foundation Grants Supporting Foster Care 4936
Victoria and Bradley Geist were single children who grew up in non-traditional families. They created their successes in life through their own personal efforts. The Geists were quiet philanthropists who gave anonymously and generously. During their lives, they planned to use the wealth they had accumulated to establish the Victoria S. and Bradley L. Geist Foundation. The Foundation wishes to support foster children and their caregivers. The Foundation recognizes that the appropriate resources and support for foster children and their caregivers contribute to healthier and happier lives. The Foundation offers this Request for Proposals to provide meaningful support for efforts that will result in supportive homes and experiences for Hawaii's foster children.
Requirements: Tax-exempt Hawaii organizations are eligible to apply. This includes nonprofit organizations, 501(c)3 organizations, religious organizations that are exempt from taxation, and units of government.
Restrictions: Requests are considered in relationship to the size of the organization's operating budget. Capital requests and endowments will not be funded.
Geographic Focus: Hawaii
Date(s) Application is Due: Jan 17; May 15; Sep 14
Amount of Grant: 10,000 - 100,000 USD
Contact: Christel Wuerfel; (808) 537-6333 or (888) 731-3863; cwuerfel@hcf-hawaii.org
Internet: http://www.hawaiicommunityfoundation.org/grants/grants/grant/victoria-s-and-bradley-l-geist-foundation-supporting-foster-children-and-their-c
Sponsor: Victoria S. and Bradley L. Geist Foundation
827 Fort Street Mall
Honolulu, HI 96813-4317

Victoria S. and Bradley L. Geist Foundation Grants Supporting Transitioning Foster Youth 4937
The Foundation recognizes that transitioning foster youth will succeed and give back to the community when they have positive and supportive peer and adult networks, opportunities to pursue employment and post-secondary education and training, and basic supports available in the community when needed. Preference will be given to efforts that seek youth input and engagement in initial and ongoing program development and work in one or more of the following areas: effectively connect youth with opportunities and community resources for employment and post-secondary education and training; support positive, lifelong adult connections; support positive peer networks; support youth efforts in community service and in advocacy efforts to improve the child welfare system; and support youth in meeting basic needs. Grants usually range from $10,000 to $100,000 per year.
Requirements: Tax-exempt Hawaii organizations are eligible to apply. This includes nonprofit organizations, 501(c)3 organizations, religious organizations that are exempt from taxation, and units of government.
Restrictions: Requests are considered in relationship to the size of the organization's operating budget. Capital requests and endowments will not be funded.
Geographic Focus: Hawaii
Date(s) Application is Due: Jan 17; May 15; Sep 14
Contact: Christel Wuerfel; (808) 537-6333 or (888) 731-3863; cwuerfel@hcf-hawaii.org
Internet: http://www.hawaiicommunityfoundation.org/grants/grants/grant/victoria-s-and-bradley-l-geist-foundation-supporting-transitioning-foster-youth
Sponsor: Victoria S. and Bradley L. Geist Foundation
827 Fort Street Mall
Honolulu, HI 96813-4317

Vigneron Memorial Fund Grants 4938
The Vigneron Memorial Fund was established in 1959 to support charitable organizations that work to improve the lives of physically disabled children and adults. Preference is given to charitable organizations that serve the people of the city of Providence or the town of Narragansett, Rhode Island. Capital requests that fund handicapped assistive devices (wheelchairs, walkers, etc.) or adaptive equipment (lift installation, ramp installation, etc.) are strongly encouraged. Grant requests for general operating or program support will also be considered. The majority of grants from the Vigneron Memorial Fund are one year in duration. Applicants must apply online at the grant website. Applicants are strongly encouraged to do the following before applying: review the downloadable state application procedures for additional helpful information and clarifications; review the downloadable online-application guidelines at the grant website; review the foundation's funding history (link is available from the grant website); review the online application questions in advance; and review the list of required attachments. These will generally include: a list of board members, financial statements (audited, reviewed, or compiled by independent auditor); an organization summary; a list of other funding sources; an IRS Determination letter; and other required documents. All attachments must be uploaded in the online application as PDF, Word, or Excel files. The Vigneron Memorial Fund shares a mission and grantmaking focus with the John D. & Katherine A. Johnston Foundation. Both foundations have the same proposal deadline date of 11:59 p.m. on April 1. Applicants will be notified of grant decisions before May 31.
Requirements: Applicants must have 501(c)3 tax-exempt status.
Restrictions: The fund does not support requests from individuals, organizations attempting to influence policy through direct lobbying, or any political campaigns.
Geographic Focus: Rhode Island
Date(s) Application is Due: Apr 1
Contact: Emma Greene, Director; (617) 434-0329; emma.m.greene@baml.com
Internet: https://www.bankofamerica.com/philanthropic/fn_search.action
Sponsor: Vigneron Memorial Fund
225 Franklin Street, 4th Floor, MA1-225-04-02
Boston, MA 02110

Viking Children's Fund Grants 4939
The fund supports the needs of children in Minnesota and the upper Midwest. Grants support research at the University of Minnesota Department of Pediatrics into the major diseases and disorders of childhood; and nonprofits that focus efforts in the areas of health education and family services supporting the well-being of children in the upper Midwest.
Requirements: Nonprofit organizations in Minnesota and the upper Midwest, including Iowa, North Dakota, South Dakota, and Wisconsin, are eligible.
Geographic Focus: Iowa, Minnesota, North Dakota, South Dakota, Wisconsin
Date(s) Application is Due: Apr 1
Contact: Patrick Leopold; (952) 828-6500; info@vikings.com
Internet: http://www.vikings.com/commchildfund.html
Sponsor: Minnesota Vikings Football Club
9520 Viking Drive
Eden Prairie, MN 55344

Virginia A. Hodgkinson Research Prize 4940
In partnership with the Association for Research on Nonprofit Organizations and Voluntary Action, the research prize is awarded annually in recognition of a book that informs nonprofit policy and practice. Recipients are researchers and practitioners who work in or with the voluntary sector, and through their work, have achieved local, regional, national, or international impact and recognition. Submissions from researchers and practitioners representing any discipline, nonprofit field, or organization are welcome. Multidisciplinary approaches, submissions from young scholars and practitioners working in collaboration with others, and from researchers and practitioners at the start of their careers are encouraged. Two research prizes will be awarded.
Requirements: Each submission will be judged on the contribution the research makes to policy and practice. The research article, report, or book must have been published within three calendar years prior to the year of the award. Books can be considered more than once. Entries must be published by a university press or commercial publishing house. Submissions from scholars representing any discipline are welcome. In addition, submissions are encouraged from young scholars, practitioners working in collaboration with university-based researchers, and scholars working on multi-disciplinary approaches. Self-nominations will be accepted.
Restrictions: Prior prize recipients are ineligible for a five-year period after their award.
Geographic Focus: All States
Date(s) Application is Due: Jun 30
Amount of Grant: 1,000 - 2,000 USD
Contact: Thomas Jeavons, Executive Director; (317) 684-2120; tjeavons@arnova.org
Internet: http://www.independentsector.org/programs/research/vah_research_prize.html
Sponsor: Independent Sector
1200 18th Street NW, Suite 200
Washington, DC 20036

Virginia Commission for the Arts Artists in Education Residency Grants 4941
The primary purpose of Virginia Commission for the Arts Artists in Education Residency Grants is to place professional artists of various artistic disciplines in residencies for elementary and secondary students and their teachers. Residencies must be designed to reinforce the arts instruction provided by the school/school division. This program provides elementary and secondary students, teachers, and the community at large opportunities to work with professional artists. The residencies enhance arts instruction in the school curriculum and highlight the importance of the arts as essential components of a complete education and a valued part of community life. Each residency must include workshops for a core group of students, at least one formal teacher workshop conducted by the artist, and community performances/exhibitions and activities/workshops. Residencies of ten days or more must also include studio time for the artists. If any residency activities take place outside of the regular school day, transportation should be available so that all students can participate. Generally, the Commission will award no more than 50 percent of the total cash cost of the residency program. First-time applicants, however, may request up to two-thirds (2/3) of the total eligible cash cost of the residency. Only the following residency expenses are eligible for funding: salary for the resident artist(s); consumable materials for the artist's workshops; consumable materials for the workshop participants; travel (standard rate per mile) for the residency artist(s); program documentation (audio or video tapes, slides); and honorarium and travel expenses for the artist(s) for one on-site pre-residency planning day (to take place during the fiscal year of the grant award and prior to the residency).
Requirements: Virginia elementary and secondary schools which meet the Basic Eligibility criteria are eligible to apply for funding through this program. Private, federally tax-exempt schools that are in compliance with the Civil Rights Act and the Rehabilitation Act may also submit applications. School divisions may also apply on behalf of several schools; however, they must comply with all Commission requirements regarding the minimum length of each residency, residency components, on-site coordinator, etc. Tax-exempt arts, service, and civic organizations may work in partnership with the local school(s) in planning and implementing the residency program.
Restrictions: Grant funds may not be used for teachers presently working within the school/school division or the organization/institution. Funds from other Commission programs may not be used to match any portion of residency income. Generally the Commission will not fund the same type of residency and/or the same artist(s) in the same school or school division for more than three years. Applications which involve the same discipline in the same school division with many of the same artists must include an explanation as to how this program differs substantially from past programs and why the same discipline or artist was selected.
Geographic Focus: Virginia
Contact: Cathy Welborn; (804) 225-3132; catherine.welborn@arts.virginia.gov
Internet: http://www.arts.virginia.gov/grants/strengthening/residency_grants.html
Sponsor: Virginia Commission for the Arts
223 Governor Street, 2nd Floor
Richmond, VA 23219-2010

Virginia Commission for the Arts General Operating Grants 4942
The commission awards grants for general operating support to assist organizations of artistic merit in fulfilling their missions by providing funds to maintain their stability and encourage their advancement. Funds may be awarded to cover general operating expenses, special projects, construction or renovation costs, and reserve funds. Most general operating support grants are awarded for a two-year period. Organizations may apply for 10 percent of their previous year's cash income for each year of the grant period. Application materials are available on the Web site.
Requirements: Virginia organizations whose primary purpose is the arts (excluding units of government and educational institutions and their private companion foundations), that have an independent governing board, and that are exempt from federal income tax under Section 501(c)3 of the Internal Revenue Code are eligible to apply. Organizations must be incorporated for at least a year before applying for General Operating Support and must have completed a season of programs.
Geographic Focus: Virginia
Date(s) Application is Due: Mar 1
Amount of Grant: 500 - 150,000 USD
Contact: Cathy Welborn, (804) 225-3132; catherine.welborn@arts.virginia.gov
Internet: http://www.arts.virginia.gov/grants/infrastructure/support_artorg.html
Sponsor: Virginia Commission for the Arts
223 Governor Street, 2nd Floor
Richmond, VA 23219-2010

Virginia Commission for the Arts Local Government Challenge Grants 4943
The primary purpose of Virginia Commission for the Arts Local Government Challenge Grants is to encourage local governments to support the arts. The Commission will match, up to $5,000, subject to funds available, tax monies given by independent town, city, and county governments to arts organizations. The money, which does not include school arts budgets or arts programming by parks and recreation departments, may be granted either by a local arts commission/council or directly by the governing board.
Requirements: Independent city, town, or county governments in Virginia are eligible.
Restrictions: The Commission does not match payments paid for specific performances.
Geographic Focus: Virginia
Date(s) Application is Due: Apr 1
Contact: Cathy Welborn, (804) 225-3132; catherine.welborn@arts.virginia.gov
Internet: http://www.arts.virginia.gov/grants/infrastructure/locgov_challenge.html
Sponsor: Virginia Commission for the Arts
223 Governor Street, 2nd Floor
Richmond, VA 23219-2010

Virginia Commission for the Arts Project Grants 4944
The primary purposes of Virginia Commission for the Arts Project Grants are: to increase access to high quality arts for all Virginians; to increase opportunities for artists to create and present their work; and to expand arts education opportunities for young people. This grant program supports a wide variety of arts activities and is open to any not-for-profit organization presenting the arts. It is one of the Commission's most competitive grant programs. Generally, the Commission will not support the same project for more than three years. The Commission will favor applications for the creation and/or production of new works by Virginia artists. Eligible activities include: commissions of new works of art; performances, exhibitions, film or video screenings, readings, and publication of literature; operating support for new and emerging arts organizations (organizations whose primary purpose is the arts, that are three years old or less, and that had a previous year's income of less than $50,000); artist residencies; workshops, seminars, classes; guest artists; educational programs of arts organizations; classes or other training in all disciplines of the arts; summer arts camps; scholarships for young people for arts instruction; arts festivals; architectural feasibility studies; surveys and planning; conferences; information and advisory services to artists and arts organizations; space and equipment for artists; touring events from out of state; and transportation for school children, older adults, and other special groups to attend arts events.
Requirements: Virginia not-for-profit organizations, units of government, or educational institutions that meet the basic eligibility criteria are eligible. Each department of a college or university is considered to be a separate applicant. Organizations receiving general operating support grants will not be eligible for Project Grants.
Geographic Focus: Virginia
Date(s) Application is Due: Mar 1
Contact: Cathy Welborn, (804) 225-3132; catherine.welborn@arts.virginia.gov
Internet: http://www.arts.virginia.gov/grants/accessible/project_grants.html
Sponsor: Virginia Commission for the Arts
223 Governor Street, 2nd Floor
Richmond, VA 23219-2010

Virginia Commission for the Arts Touring Assistance Grants 4945
The primary purpose of Virginia Commission for the Arts Touring Assistance Grants is to increase opportunities for Virginians to experience high-quality performing arts events. This program supports touring by Virginia performing artists and arts organizations within the state. Grants are made to the presenter for performers' fees. Touring artists apply to be listed in the tour directory with a set dollar amount reserved to support their touring. Presenters should send applications for touring support to the commission at least four weeks prior to the event and before December 1. The commission will fund up to 50% of the fee for any touring program listed in the commission's tour directory. Presenters should contact artists and negotiate contracts before submitting applications to the commission.
Requirements: Nonprofit, tax-exempt Virginia organizations and Virginia performing artists are eligible to apply for project and unrestricted grants. Programs should be open to the public, and the presenter must provide community-wide publicity. Elementary and secondary schools, senior living facilities, correctional facilities, and hospitals may be exempt from this requirement.
Geographic Focus: Virginia
Date(s) Application is Due: Dec 1
Contact: Cathy Welborn, (804) 225-3132; catherine.welborn@arts.virginia.gov
Internet: http://www.arts.virginia.gov/grants/accessible/assistance_presenters.html
Sponsor: Virginia Commission for the Arts
223 Governor Street, 2nd Floor
Richmond, VA 23219-2010

Virginia Foundation for the Humanities Discretionary Grants 4946
The Virginia Foundation for the Humanities (VFH) was established in 1974 as a nonprofit organization dedicated to promoting the humanities, and to using the humanities to address issues of broad public concern. Since 1974, the VFH has awarded more than 3,000 grants, supporting tens of thousands of separate activities, and serving audiences in every city and county in Virginia. Goals of the VFH grant program are as follows: to encourage the development

of high-quality educational programs in the humanities; to support accessible programs that reach the broadest possible audience in Virginia; to support the work of humanities institutions - museums, libraries, historical societies, colleges, and universities - as well as other non-profit organizations working within the humanities; to explore the stories that define Virginia and its people; and to address the issues that are most important to communities in Virginia. Projects supported include exhibits, public forums and discussions, media programs (film, video, radio, and digital media), publications, research, teachers' institutes and seminars, oral history projects, lectures and conferences, and other kinds of programs that draw on the resources of the humanities, address important issues, and enrich the cultural life of the state. The program names six key-priority areas of interest: Books, Reading, and Literacy; Rights and Responsibilities; Media and Culture; Violence and Community; Science, Technology, and Society; Virginia History. Other identified areas of interest are teacher education programs (especially those related to Virginia's Standards of Learning); African American history and culture; Native American history and culture; history and culture of minority communities in Virginia; Virginia's folklife and traditional culture(s); and the future of rural Virginia. The foundation's interest is not confined to only these topics. Discretionary Grants allow VFH to make smaller grants (up to $3,000) at any time of the year. These grants may be used to plan larger projects or to implement programs which require only a modest amount of funding. Decisions are normally made within four weeks following receipt of the application. Applications should be submitted via the VFH online system (available at the foundation's website) which requires as a first step, creation of an account and password. Grant guidelines are available at the website in downloadable Word format. Applicants should contact VFH staff in advance before submitting a Discretionary Grant proposal. Draft proposals are strongly encouraged and are recommended to be submitted at least three weeks prior to the deadline to allow time for a thorough staff review.
Requirements: Any incorporated non-profit organization in Virginia is eligible to apply. Incorporated non-profit organizations based outside of Virginia are also eligible if their project deals with a subject directly related to Virgina and a significant audience within the state is anticipated. All VFH grants must be matched with at least an equal amount of cost share, which can be in the form of cash or in-kind contributions from non-Federal sources. Sources and amounts of anticipated cost share should be indicated at the time of the proposal.
Restrictions: VFH Grants may not be used to support the following: advocacy or political action programs that promote a particular solution or point of view; creative or performing arts, unless they are used in a supporting role to enhance discussion of issues or interpretation; research or writing unless these are integral to programs having a direct public audience; subvention of publications; courses for credit, except those designed especially for teachers; acquisition of equipment; building construction, restoration, or preservation; meals, other than necessary travel expenses for program personnel; international travel; indirect costs; and projects whose primary audience is children or youth.
Geographic Focus: All States
Contact: David Bearinger; (434) 924-3296; fax (434) 296-4714; dab@virginia.edu
Internet: http://virginiahumanities.org/grants/
Sponsor: Virginia Foundation for the Humanities
145 Ednam Drive
Charlottesville, VA 22903-4629

Virginia Foundation for the Humanities Open Grants 4947
The Virginia Foundation for the Humanities (VFH) was established in 1974 as a nonprofit organization dedicated to promoting the humanities, and to using the humanities to address issues of broad public concern. Since 1974, the VFH has awarded more than 3,000 grants, supporting tens of thousands of separate activities, and serving audiences in every city and county in Virginia. Goals of the VFH grant program are as follows: to encourage the development of high-quality educational programs in the humanities; to support accessible programs that reach the broadest possible audience in Virginia; to support the work of humanities institutions - museums, libraries, historical societies, colleges, and universities - as well as other non-profit organizations working within the humanities; to explore the stories that define Virginia and its people; and to address the issues that are most important to communities in Virginia. Projects supported include exhibits, public forums and discussions, media programs (film, video, radio, and digital media), publications, research, teachers' institutes and seminars, oral history projects, lectures and conferences, and other kinds of programs that draw on the resources of the humanities, address important issues, and enrich the cultural life of the state. The program names six key-priority areas of interest: Books, Reading, and Literacy; Rights and Responsibilities; Media and Culture; Violence and Community; Science, Technology, and Society; and Virginia History. Other identified areas of interest are teacher-education programs (especially those related to Virginia's Standards of Learning); African-American history and culture; Native-American history and culture; history and culture of minority communities in Virginia; Virginia's folklife and traditional culture(s); and the future of rural Virginia. The foundation's interest is not confined to only these topics. Open Grant applications are usually considered in three annual grant cycles with deadlines of October 15, February 1, and May 1. Applications should be submitted via the VFH online system (available at the foundation's website) which requires as a first step, creation of an account and password. Grant guidelines are available at the website in downloadable Word format. All applicants are urged to contact the staff prior to submission of their proposals. Draft proposals are strongly encouraged and are recommended to be submitted at least three weeks prior to the deadline to allow time for a thorough staff review.
Requirements: Any incorporated non-profit organization in Virginia is eligible to apply. Incorporated non-profit organizations based outside of Virginia are also eligible if their project deals with a subject directly related to Virgina and a significant audience within the state is anticipated. All VFH grants must be matched with at least an equal amount of cost share, which can be in the form of cash or in-kind contributions from non-Federal sources. Sources and amounts of anticipated cost share should be indicated at the time of the proposal.
Restrictions: VFH Grants may not be used to support the following: advocacy or political action programs that promote a particular solution or point of view; creative or performing arts, unless they are used in a supporting role to enhance discussion of issues or interpretation; research or writing unless these are integral to programs having a direct public audience; subvention of publications; courses for credit, except those designed especially for teachers; acquisition of equipment; building construction, restoration, or preservation; meals, other than necessary travel expenses for program personnel; international travel; indirect costs; and projects whose primary audience is children or youth.
Geographic Focus: All States, Canada
Date(s) Application is Due: Feb 1; May 1; Oct 15
Amount of Grant: Up to 10,000 USD
Contact: David Bearinger; (434) 924-3296; fax (434) 296-4714; dab@virginia.edu
Internet: http://virginiahumanities.org/grants/
Sponsor: Virginia Foundation for the Humanities
145 Ednam Drive
Charlottesville, VA 22903-4629

Virginia Foundation for the Humanities Residential Fellowships 4948
The Virginia Foundation for the Humanities (VFH) supports scholarly work on the humanities and in the public interest. The foundation's residential fellowship program is located at its facility in Charlottesville, Virginia, in the foothills of the Blue Ridge Mountains. The fellowship offers time, space, and resources to scholars and writers bringing the humanities to visibility - applying the tools of history, philosophy, ethics, cultural studies, and literary criticism to matters of public concern. Fellowships are awarded for one semester or for a full year. Stipends range up to $15,000 per semester. Fellows have visiting-faculty status at the nearby University of Virginia as well as the opportunity to get to know VFH staff members and become involved, formally or informally, in a variety of public humanities projects. Fellows also appear on With Good Reason, a VFH Radio program. Candidates must apply through an online application system at the foundation website. Applicants will need to create a login account to use this system. Letters of recommendation must be mailed separately to the contact information given.
Requirements: The foundation seeks applications that are intellectually stimulating, imaginative, and accessible to the public. There are no restrictions on topic, and applications are invited from across the broad spectrum of the humanities. Candidates may be faculty members in the humanities, independent scholars, or others working on projects in the humanities and need not have advanced degrees. However, the foundation generally does not support dissertation work and strongly encourages postdoctoral applicants to apply for projects other than dissertation revisions.
Restrictions: The foundation does not support work toward a degree. Former VFH Fellows must wait three years before applying for another fellowship. Former Fellows are welcome to apply for space (without stipend) at any time.
Geographic Focus: All States, All Countries
Date(s) Application is Due: Dec 1
Amount of Grant: Up to 30,000 USD
Contact: Ann Spencer, (434) 924-3296; fax (434) 296-4714; aspencer@virginia.edu
Internet: http://virginiahumanities.org/fellowships/
Sponsor: Virginia Foundation for the Humanities
145 Ednam Drive
Charlottesville, VA 22903-4629

Virginia Historical Society Research Fellowships 4949
The society offers fellowships of up to four weeks a year to help defray travel expenses for commuting researchers who wish to conduct research using collections of the society. Awards include the Andrew W. Mellon Research Fellowships, the Betty Sams Christian Fellowships in business history, the Frances Lewis Fellowships in women's studies, and the Reese Fellowships in American Bibliography and the History of the Book in the Americas. Recipients are expected to work on a regular basis in the society's reading room. Applicants whose research promises to result in significant publication, including the Virginia Magazine of History and Biography, will receive primary consideration. Applicants should send an original and three copies of the following: cover letter, resume, two letters of recommendation (which may be sent separately), and a description of their research project not longer than two double-spaced pages that also states the length of the award requested.
Requirements: Applications are welcome from doctoral candidates who reside outside of the Richmond metropolitan area.
Restrictions: Undergraduates, master's students, and graduate students not yet admitted to PhD candidacy are not eligible.
Geographic Focus: Virginia
Date(s) Application is Due: Feb 1
Amount of Grant: 150 - 2,000 USD
Contact: Nelson Lankford, (804) 342-9672; fax (804) 355-2399; nlankford@vahistorical.org
Internet: http://www.vahistorical.org/research/fellowships.htm
Sponsor: Virginia Historical Society
428 N Boulevard
Richmond, VA 23220

Virginia W. Kettering Foundation Grants 4950
The Virginia W. Kettering Foundation, a private family foundation in Dayton, Ohio, was activated in 2003 when Virginia Kettering passed away at the age of 95. To continue her legacy of confident determination and passionate commitment to the Dayton area, Virginia Kettering directed the stewards of her foundation to support charitable organizations for charitable purposes within Montgomery, Greene, Clark, Miami, Darke, Preble, Butler and Warren Counties.
Requirements: 501(c)3 organizations located in, or that serve, the counties of Montgomery, Greene, Clark, Miami, Darke, Preble, Butler and Warren in Ohio.
Geographic Focus: Ohio
Date(s) Application is Due: Mar 1; Sep 1

Amount of Grant: 5,000 - 50,000 USD
Contact: Judith M. Thompson; (973) 228-1021; fax (973) 228-2399; info@ketteringfund.org
Internet: http://vwketteringfoundation.org/main.html
Sponsor: Virginia W. Kettering Foundation
1480 Kettering Tower
Dayton, OH 45423

Visiting Nurse Foundation Grants — 4951

The foundation awards grants in support of home- and community-based health care for the medically underserved in Cook and the collar counties of Lake, McHenry, DuPage, Kane and Will, with a focus on Chicago. Priority areas are home health care services; prevention and health promotion; and early intervention. Preference is given to programs using nurses to provide the care. Types of support include program, capital, and general operating grants. Letters of intent should be submitted by deadline dates listed, and full proposals will be by invitation only.
Requirements: Nonprofit organizations in Cook, Lake, McHenry, DuPage, Kane, and Will counties of Illinois are eligible.
Restrictions: No grants are made to individuals.
Geographic Focus: Illinois
Date(s) Application is Due: Jan 19; Apr 19; Oct 20
Amount of Grant: 15,000 - 80,000 USD
Contact: Robert N. DiLeonardi; (312) 214-1521; fax (312) 214-1529; info@vnafoundation.net
Internet: http://www.vnafoundation.net
Sponsor: Visiting Nurse Association Foundation
20 N Wacker Drive, Suite 3118
Chicago, IL 60606

Volvo Adventure Environmental Awards — 4952

The Volvo Adventure Environmental Award is for teams of between two and five young people working on a practical action project that will improve their school or community environment. The young people aged 13 to 16 should be devising action plans to help their environment under the following five headings: biodiversity - helping animals and plants in the community or school; waste - reduction, reuse, and recycle; water - conserve or improve water quality in the community or school; transport - travel (environmental impact); and energy - reduce energy use or make it more sustainable. The best entry from each country will be asked to join an international conference to present their ideas in Sweden, and where they can win: 1st place = $10,000, 2nd = $6,000, and 3rd = $4,000. All of the ideas and action plans will be published and presented to the United Nations Environment Program.
Requirements: Applicant groups must meet the following criteria: have (or have plans to start) an environmental project in the team's school or local community; team is writing and implementing a practical action plan that will improve the team's school or community environment; and team has at least one adult who can act as a referee for the group.
Restrictions: Projects must be submitted in English.
Geographic Focus: All States, All Countries
Date(s) Application is Due: Jan 31
Amount of Grant: 4,000 - 10,000 USD
Contact: Geno Effler; (949) 341-6715 or (949) 351-1495; geffler@volvocars.com
Internet: http://www.volvoadventure.org/guidelines.aspx
Sponsor: Volvo Cars of North America
One Premier Place
Irvine, CA 92618

VSA/Metlife Connect All Grants — 4953

VSA and MetLife Foundation have designed the Arts Connect All funding opportunity to encourage arts organizations to create or enhance multi-session, inclusive education programs by strengthening partnerships with local public schools. The goals of Arts Connect All are the following: enable more students with disabilities to experience social, cognitive, and cultural development through arts learning alongside their peers without disabilities; create educational access and inclusion in the arts for students with disabilities; and document the contributions that arts organizations make to inclusive education in public schools. VSA and MetLife Foundation invite proposals from arts organizations creating or enhancing inclusive educational programs that undertake all of the following: incorporate inclusive teaching practices; provide access to students with all types of disabilities; develop social, cognitive, and artistic skills; involve people with disabilities in planning and implementation; build staff, teacher, and/or artist knowledge and skill of inclusive practices; and collaborate with public schools, actively engaging students, parents, and school administrators. A maximum of 10 awards of up to $15,000 will be given to selected organizations. Examples of appropriate use of funds may include, but are not limited to: expanding existing accessibility programs into educational efforts, program development support, knowledge and skill building of inclusive practices, and promotional/outreach efforts to expand audience. Grants will be awarded based on their ability to address the following: identify, assess, and address constituent and community need; collaborate at a high level with public schools; model innovative and multi-modal approaches for inclusion of people with disabilities; involve people with disabilities in the planning and implementation of educational programming; increase access to program activities, content, and materials by everyone, including students with or without disabilities; implement evaluation strategies that investigate the relationship between program goals, program activities, and the development of participant social, cognitive, and artistic skills; and; and deliver the program as articulated in the application packet. The application and additional guidelines for the proposal are available at the website.
Requirements: Nonprofit 501(c)3 performing and/or exhibiting arts organizations, including museums, theaters, and multidisciplinary arts presenters that are creating or have an established educational program are eligible to apply. Organizations must have as their primary mission the goal of advancing the arts and/or a specific art form. All eligible programs must: have students with disabilities and without disabilities learning together at the same time and place; involve kindergarten through grade 12 public school students in the target audience; be ongoing or have multiple sessions; take place during or after school hours; receive awards in a maximum of three grant cycles (second or third year grants must expand or enhance programs funded in a previous cycle). Only certain arts organizations located in and partnering with public schools in specific metropolitan areas are eligible. A full list of specific locations is posted on the website.
Restrictions: The following entities are not eligible to apply: individuals; schools, universities, performing or visual arts departments of universities, and foundations raising funds for schools or universities; arts and/or arts education programs of disability organizations and of non-presenting/non-exhibiting arts educations organizations; programs that have received Arts Connect All grants in three consecutive grant cycles; and VSA affiliates.
Geographic Focus: Arizona, California, Colorado, Connecticut, Florida, Georgia, Maryland, Massachusetts, Michigan, Minnesota, Missouri, North Carolina, Oklahoma, Oregon, Pennsylvania, Rhode Island, Tennessee, Texas, Washington
Date(s) Application is Due: Nov 19
Contact: Stephanie Litvak; (202) 416-8898; vsainfo@kennedy-center.org
Internet: http://www.kennedy-center.org/education/vsa/programs/arts_connect_all.cfm
Sponsor: John F. Kennedy Center for the Performing Arts
2700 F Street NW
Washington, DC 20566

VSA/Volkswagen Group of America Exhibition Awards — 4954

VSA and Volkswagen Group of America team up to recognize and showcase emerging artists with disabilities, ages 16-25, who are living in the U.S. This collaboration supports these artists at a critical time when many are deciding whether to pursue the arts as a career. The award validates, and helps finance, that life-defining choice. Every year, fifteen artists are selected for the exhibition and share cash awards generously provided by Volkswagen Group of America: a $20,000 grand prize, a $10,000 first award, a $6,000 second award, and 12 awards of excellence of $2,000 each. The awards are available each year, but programs, themes, and requirements vary. Interested applicants may check the website for current programs available.
Geographic Focus: All States
Contact: Betty Siegel; (202) 416-8898; fax (202) 416-4840; vsainfo@kennedy-center.org
Internet: http://www.kennedy-center.org/education/vsa/programs/momentum.cfm
Sponsor: John F. Kennedy Center for the Performing Arts
2700 F Street NW
Washington, DC 20566

VSA International Art Program for Children with Disabilities Grants — 4955

An affiliate of the Kennedy Center for the Performing Arts, VSA was founded by Ambassador Jean Kennedy Smith. With a national and international network, it provides arts and education opportunities for youth and adults with disabilities and increases access to the arts for all. VSA presents a unique opportunity for student-artists with disabilities from around the world to display their artwork side-by-side in an online exhibition. A selection of artwork from the online entries will be chosen for a live exhibition at the U.S. Department of Education in Washington D.C. Children with disabilities are encouraged to create a family portrait that illustrates themselves among the people that provide love, support, and encouragement in their lives - their families. Portraying themselves with some of the most important people in their lives gives testament to the idea that family - no matter how big or how small - help shape who we are and provide the foundation for who we will be. Additional information about how to submit artwork is available at the website.
Requirements: Any children with a disability, ages 5-18, may submit their work. Each entry requires full information about the artist, their disability, and the work submitted.
Restrictions: Work submitted must be two dimensional, and no larger than 18x24 inches.
Geographic Focus: All States, All Countries
Date(s) Application is Due: Jul 1
Contact: Betty Siegel; (202) 416-8898; fax (202) 416-4840; vsainfo@kennedy-center.org
Internet: http://www.kennedy-center.org/education/vsa/programs/vsa_iap.cfm
Sponsor: John F. Kennedy Center for the Performing Arts
2700 F Street NW
Washington, DC 20566

Vulcan Materials Company Foundation Grants — 4956

The company foundation supports nonprofit organizations in company-operating areas. Grants support a broad array of programs and projects in the areas of health and welfare, community and economic development, education (including an employee matching grants program), the environment, law and justice, women and children, arts and humanities, minorities, and literacy. Requests will be considered for support of general operating expenses, capital and annual campaigns, scholarship funds, research, continuing support, and seed money. There are no application deadlines.
Requirements: The foundation awards grants only to public charities and units of government, such as public schools and parks. A public charity is any Section 501(c)3 charitable organization that is not a private foundation because it meets one of the three internal Revenue Code definitions: 509(a)1, 509(a)2 or 509(a)3.
Restrictions: The foundation does not fund individuals; organizations outside the United States; telephone or mass-mail appeals, political organizations; testimonial dinners; sectarian religious activities; organizations which have discriminatory practices; or athletic, labor, fraternal and veterans associations. The Foundation generally will not consider requests from organizations located in communities where Vulcan has no operations, offices or employees.
Geographic Focus: Alabama, Arizona, Arkansas, California, Florida, Georgia, Illinois, Indiana, Iowa, Kansas, Kentucky, Louisiana, Maryland, Mississippi, Missouri, New Mexico, North Carolina, Pennsylvania, South Carolina, Tennessee, Texas, Virginia, Wisconsin
Contact: Program Contact; (205) 298-3222; giving@vmcmail.com

Internet: http://www.vulcanmaterials.com/social.asp?content=guidelines
Sponsor: Vulcan Materials Company Foundation
P.O. Box 385014
Birmingham, AL 35238-5014

W.C. Griffith Foundation Grants 4957
The foundation awards grants, primarily in Indiana, to nonprofit organizations in its areas of interest, including arts and culture, cancer and medical research, children and youth services, Christian churches and organizations, community development, education, environmental programs, health organizations and hospitals, higher education, homeless services, human reproduction and fertility, library science and libraries, minorities, museums, music and performing arts, secondary education, and social services delivery. Types of support include building construction/renovation, capital campaigns, and continuing support. There are no application forms or deadlines. The board meets in June and November; proposals should be received in May and October.
Requirements: Nonprofits are eligible. Preference is given to requests from Indianapolis.
Geographic Focus: All States
Contact: Curt Farran, c/o National City Bank of Indiana; (317) 267-7262
Sponsor: W.C. Griffith Foundation
101 West Washington Street, Suite 600 East
Indianapolis, IN 46255

W. C. Griffith Foundation Grants 4958
The W. C. Griffith Foundation was established in 1959 by a donation of William C. Griffith, and Ruth Perry Griffith. The Foundation gives primarily in Indianapolis-Carmel, Indiana area. The Foundation provides support primarily for hospitals, health associations, medical and cancer research, the arts, including music and museums, community funds and development, higher, secondary, and other education, family planning services, child welfare, the homeless, the environment, libraries, and Christian religious organizations.
Requirements: Applicants should submit the following: detailed description of project and amount of funding requested; 1 Copy of the proposal.
Geographic Focus: Indiana
Contact: Trust Coordinator; fax (317) 693-2504
Sponsor: W.C. Griffith Foundation
101 West Ohio Street, Suite 1450
Indianapolis, IN 46204-1998

W.H. and Mary Ellen Cobb Charitable Trust Grants 4959
The Cobb's were originally from Kentucky, but moved to the Texas Panhandle where they owned and operated several clothing stores. Although they did not have children of their own, they were interested in the well-being of children and therefore established their charitable trust to benefit local charities in the Panhandle whose mission has a strong "emphasis on helping children." This foundation makes approximately five-seven awards each year and grants are typically between $1,000 and $25,000. Applicants must apply online at the grant website. Applicants are strongly encouraged to do the following before applying: review the downloadable state application procedures for additional helpful information and clarifications; review the downloadable online-application guidelines at the grant website; review the trust's funding history (link is available from the grant website); review the online application questions in advance; and review the list of required attachments. These will generally include: a list of board members, financial statements (audited, reviewed, or compiled by independent auditor); an organization summary; a list of other funding sources; an IRS Determination letter; and other required documents. All attachments must be uploaded in the online application as PDF, Word, or Excel files.
Requirements: The W.H. & Mary Ellen Cobb Charitable Trust considers requests from charitable organizations whose primary focus is the provision of services that benefit children. Organizations must: be geographically located within the Texas Panhandle; serve residents of the Panhandle, Amarillo, and vicinity; and have 501(c)3 tax-exempt status.
Restrictions: The trust does not support requests from individuals, organizations attempting to influence policy through direct lobbying, or any political campaigns.
Geographic Focus: Texas
Date(s) Application is Due: Sep 30
Contact: Mark J. Smith; (817) 390-6028; tx.philanthropic@baml.com
Internet: https://www.bankofamerica.com/philanthropic/fn_search.action
Sponsor: W.H. and Mary Ellen Cobb Charitable Trust
500 West 7th Street, 15th Floor, TX1-497-15-08
Fort Worth, TX 76102-4700

W.K. Kellogg Foundation Civic Engagement Grants 4960
The Foundation believes that people have the inherent capacity to solve their own problems and that social transformation is within the reach of all communities. It partners with those committed to inclusion, impact, and innovation in solving public problems. It seeks engagement through dialogue, leadership development, collaboration, and new models of organizing. The Foundation amplifies voices, and supports the civic and philanthropic infrastructures that help propel vulnerable children and communities forward. By partnering with diverse communities, it supports new solutions tailored to meet the needs of children and families who are most vulnerable.
Requirements: To be eligible for support, your organization or institution, as well as the purpose of the proposed project, must qualify under regulations of the United States Internal Revenue Service. The Kellogg Foundation does not have any submission deadlines. Grant applications are accepted throughout the year and are reviewed at its headquarters in Battle Creek, Michigan, or in its regional office in Mexico.
Restrictions: In general, the Foundation does not provide funding for: operational phases of established programs; capital requests (which includes the construction, purchase, renovation, and/or furnishing of facilities); equipment; conferences and workshops; films, television and/or radio programs; endowments; development campaigns; or research/studies (unless they are an integral part of a larger program budget being considered for funding).
Geographic Focus: All States
Contact: Deborah A. Rey, (269) 969-2133 or (269) 968-1611; fax (269) 968-0413
Internet: http://www.wkkf.org/what-we-support/civic-engagement.aspx
Sponsor: W.K. Kellogg Foundation
1 Michigan Avenue East
Battle Creek, MI 49017-4012

W.K. Kellogg Foundation Healthy Kids Grants 4961
The Foundation believes that children need nutrition, stimulation, healthy living conditions and access to quality health care. It helps many of them get all four, by funding organizations that improve birth outcomes and first food experiences, create access to healthy foods, improve health services, and educate families and communities about the inter-related factors that determine well-being. The Foundation especially focuses on children who are disadvantaged by multiple societal factors, a disproportionate percentage of whom are children of color.
Requirements: To be eligible for support, your organization or institution, as well as the purpose of the proposed project, must qualify under regulations of the United States Internal Revenue Service. The Kellogg Foundation does not have any submission deadlines. Grant applications are accepted throughout the year and are reviewed at its headquarters in Battle Creek, Michigan, or in its regional office in Mexico.
Restrictions: In general, the Foundation does not provide funding for: operational phases of established programs; capital requests (which includes the construction, purchase, renovation, and/or furnishing of facilities); equipment; conferences and workshops; films, television and/or radio programs; endowments; development campaigns; or research/studies (unless they are an integral part of a larger program budget being considered for funding).
Geographic Focus: All States
Contact: Deborah A. Rey; (269) 969-2133 or (269) 968-1611; fax (269) 968-0413
Internet: http://www.wkkf.org/what-we-support/healthy-kids.aspx
Sponsor: W.K. Kellogg Foundation
1 Michigan Avenue East
Battle Creek, MI 49017-4012

W.K. Kellogg Foundation Racial Equity Grants 4962
The Foundation believes that all children should have equal access to opportunity. To make this vision a reality, it directs its grants and resources to support racial healing and to remove systemic barriers that hold some children back. It invests in community and national organizations whose innovative and effective programs foster racial healing. And through action-oriented research and public policy work, the Foundation is helping translate insights into new strategies and sustainable solutions.
Requirements: To be eligible for support, your organization or institution, as well as the purpose of the proposed project, must qualify under regulations of the United States Internal Revenue Service. The Kellogg Foundation does not have any submission deadlines. Grant applications are accepted throughout the year and are reviewed at its headquarters in Battle Creek, Michigan, or in its regional office in Mexico.
Restrictions: In general, the Foundation does not provide funding for: operational phases of established programs; capital requests (which includes the construction, purchase, renovation, and/or furnishing of facilities); equipment; conferences and workshops; films, television and/or radio programs; endowments; development campaigns; or research/studies (unless they are an integral part of a larger program budget being considered for funding).
Geographic Focus: All States
Contact: Deborah A. Rey; (269) 969-2133 or (269) 968-1611; fax (269) 968-0413
Internet: http://www.wkkf.org/what-we-support/racial-equity.aspx
Sponsor: W.K. Kellogg Foundation
1 Michigan Avenue East
Battle Creek, MI 49017-4012

W.K. Kellogg Foundation Secure Families Grants 4963
The primary needs of the family must be addressed to create pathways out of poverty for children. The Foundation supports programs that increase family stability, foster quality jobs, careers and entrepreneurship, and promote secondary achievement and financial independence. It further supports strategies that increase income, assets, and aspirations of vulnerable children and their families and reduce disparities based on class, gender and race. The Foundation focuses on three areas, each with a direct impact on the ability of families to generate income and accumulate assets: family stability; career ladders; and financial independence.
Requirements: To be eligible for support, your organization or institution, as well as the purpose of the proposed project, must qualify under regulations of the United States Internal Revenue Service. The Kellogg Foundation does not have any submission deadlines. Grant applications are accepted throughout the year and are reviewed at its headquarters in Battle Creek, Michigan, or in its regional office in Mexico.
Restrictions: In general, the Foundation does not provide funding for: operational phases of established programs; capital requests (which includes the construction, purchase, renovation, and/or furnishing of facilities); equipment; conferences and workshops; films, television and/or radio programs; endowments; development campaigns; or research/studies (unless they are an integral part of a larger program budget being considered for funding).
Geographic Focus: All States
Contact: Deborah A. Rey; (269) 969-2133 or (269) 968-1611; fax (269) 968-0413
Internet: http://www.wkkf.org/what-we-support/secure-families.aspx
Sponsor: W.K. Kellogg Foundation
1 Michigan Avenue East
Battle Creek, MI 49017-4012

W.M. Keck Foundation Southern California Grants 4964

The Southern California program seeks to promote the education and healthy development of children and youth, strengthening families and enhancing the lives of people in the Greater Los Angeles area through its support of organizations that provide arts and cultural enrichment, civic and community services, early childhood and pre-college education, and health care. A special emphasis is placed on projects that focus on children and youth from low-income families, special needs populations, and safety-net services. Collaborative initiatives, as well as projects arising from the vision of one organization's strong leadership, are supported. Historically, grants range from $100,000 to $1 million, and typically are under $500,000. Applicants are strongly urged to contact Foundation staff well in advance of submitting a Phase I Application. The best times for these contacts are between January 1 and February 15 leading up to a May 1 submittal, or between July 1 and August 15 leading up to a November 1 submittal.
Requirements: Nonprofit organizations, including colleges and universities, pursuing relevant projects in Los Angeles County are eligible to apply.
Restrictions: Grants are not considered for: general operating expenses, endowments or deficit reduction; general and federated campaigns, including fundraising events, dinners or mass mailings; individuals; conference or seminar sponsorship; book publication and film or theater productions; public policy research; institutions that are located outside the United States; institutions that do not have at least three consecutive full, certified, audited financial statements; conduit organizations, unified funds or organizations that use grant funds from donors to support other organizations or individuals; or institutions that are subsidiaries or affiliates of larger entities that do not have a separate board of directors and independent audited financial statements.
Geographic Focus: California
Date(s) Application is Due: May 1; Nov 1
Contact: Margie Antonetti; (213) 680-3833; mantonetti@wmkeck.org
Internet: http://www.wmkeck.org/grant-programs/southern-california-program.html
Sponsor: W.M. Keck Foundation
550 S Hope Street, Suite 2500
Los Angeles, CA 90071

W.P. and Bulah Luse Foundation Grants 4965

The W.P. and Bulah Luse Foundation was established in 1947. Mr. Luse, a self-made wildcatter in the early Texas oilfields, and his wife Bulah created this foundation to support and promote quality education, human-services, and health-care programming for underserved populations. Special consideration is given to charitable organizations that serve the people of Dallas, Texas, and its surrounding communities. The majority of grants from the Luse Foundation are one year in duration. Applicants must apply online at the grant website. Applicants are strongly encouraged to do the following before applying: review the downloadable state application procedures for additional helpful information and clarifications; review the downloadable online-application guidelines at the grant website; review the foundation's funding history (link is available from the grant website); review the online application questions in advance; and review the list of required attachments. These will generally include: a list of board members, financial statements (audited, reviewed, or compiled by independent auditor); an organization summary; a list of other funding sources; an IRS Determination letter; and other required documents. All attachments must be uploaded in the online application as PDF, Word, or Excel files. The W.P. & Bulah Luse Foundation has biannual deadlines of June 30 and December 31. Applications must be submitted by 11:59 p.m. on the deadline dates. Grant applicants for the June deadline will be notified of grant decisions by October 31. Grant applicants for the December deadline will be notified of grant decisions by April 30 of the following year.
Requirements: Applicants must have 501(c)3 tax-exempt status.
Geographic Focus: Texas
Date(s) Application is Due: Jun 30; Dec 31
Contact: David Ross, Senior Vice President; tx.philanthropic@baml.com
Internet: https://www.bankofamerica.com/philanthropic/fn_search.action
Sponsor: W.P. and Bulah Luse Foundation
901 Main Street, 19th Floor, TX1-492-19-11
Dallas, TX 75202-3714

W. Paul and Lucille Caudill Little Foundation Grants 4966

The mission of the Foundation is generally to promote education and, specifically, to develop creativity mainly through the fine arts. Grants of $100,000 or more must be matched dollar for dollar with new money by other gifts within a time period specified when the grant is awarded. One of the following will be accepted as proof: a spreadsheet showing donors' names, amount of gift, and date of gift; copies of checks; or an award letter (e.g., from the Council on Postsecondary Education or from the city or county).
Requirements: Applicants must be a nonprofit agency located in Fayette, Rowan or Elliott Counties in existence at least three years and likely to continue.
Restrictions: Agencies may not apply for another grant until two years after final payment of any previous grant. In general, grant requests for salaries only and for agency survival will not be considered.
Geographic Focus: Kentucky
Contact: Barbara A. Fischer; (859) 225-3343; fax (859) 243-0770; bfischer@bgcf.org
Internet: http://www.bgcf.org/page27526.cfm
Sponsor: W. Paul and Lucille Caudill Little Foundation
250 W Main Street, Suite 1220
Lexington, KY 40507

W. Waldo and Jenny Lynn M. Bradley Foundation Grants 4967

Established in Georgia in 1997 by W. Waldo and Jenny Lynn Bradley, the Foundation's primary fields of interest include higher education, hospitals, the arts, and Protestant agencies and churches. With a geographic focus in Georgia and North Carolina, the major type of funding is general operating support. There are no specific application forms or deadlines, and applicants should forward a two- to three-page letter outlining the need and overall annual operating budget of the organization. A copy of the organization's 501(c)3 letter or church status proof should be included.
Geographic Focus: Georgia, North Carolina
Contact: W. Waldo Bradley, President; (912) 447-7000
Sponsor: W. Waldo and Jenny Lynn M. Bradley Foundation
204 Old West Lathrop Avenue, P.O. Box 1408
Savannah, GA 31402-1408

Wabash River Enhancement Corporation Agricultural Cost-Share Grants 4968

The Wabash River Enhancement Corporation (WREC) will provide up to 75% of the total cost of design and installation of specific agricultural green practices to improve water quality in the Wabash River. Additionally technical assistance and consultation is provided for free. Projects eligible for funding include buffer strips, conservation tillage, cover crops, grassed waterways, nutrient and pest management, prescribed grazing, stream-bank stabilization; turf to prairie conversion; tree planting, two-stage ditch construction, bioreactor, and drainage-water management. Interested applicants may either download a paper application or fill out an online form at the website. The corporation reviews applications on a monthly basis. WREC is a nonprofit agency formed by 3 local governments (Lafayette, West Lafayette, Tippecanoe County) and Purdue University, to lead the multi-jurisdictional effort to enhance the Wabash River Corridor. The Wabash River Enhancement Corporation was funded through a North Central Health Services grant at its formation. WREC seeks funding for planning, landacquisition, environmental work, and development projects through public and private sector funding sources.
Requirements: Agricultural landowners in critical areas of the Region of the Great Bend of the Wabash River are eligible to apply for these grants. Projects must be approved by both WREC's steering committee and funder the Indiana Department of Environmental Management before funding can be obtained. All work must be completed on a cost-reimbursement basis.
Geographic Focus: Indiana
Contact: Sara Peel, Director, (765) 337-9100 or (765) 420-8505; speel@lafayette.in.gov
Internet: http://www.wabashriver.net/costshare/
Sponsor: Wabash River Enhancement Corporation
200 N. 2nd Street
Lafayette, IN 47901

Wabash River Enhancement Corporation Urban 4969

The Wabash River Enhancement Corporation (WREC) will provide up to 75% of the total cost of design and installation of specific urban green practices to improve water quality in the Wabash River. Additionally technical assistance and consultation is provided for free. Projects eligible for funding include rain gardens, rain barrels, pervious pavement, native plants, trees, bioswales, green roofs, stream-bank stabilization, turf to prairie conversion, turf to tree conversion, and infrastructure retrofits. A brochure about the program is available for download from the grant web page. Interested applicants are encouraged to contact the Director of Watershed Projects for information on how to apply.
Requirements: Landowners in Lafayette, West Lafayette, and most of Tippecanoe County are eligible to apply. The Wabash River Enhancement Corporation and its partners will evaluate and rank applications with priority given to practices that address local concerns.
Geographic Focus: All States
Contact: Sara Peel, Director, Watershed Projects; (765) 337-9100; speel@lafayette.in.gov
Internet: http://www.wabashriver.net/costshare/
Sponsor: Wabash River Enhancement Corporation
200 N. 2nd Street
Lafayette, IN 47901

Wabash River Heritage Corridor Fund Grants 4970

The Wabash River Heritage Corridor Fund is a periodic program intended to protect and enhance the natural, recreational, and cultural resources located along the Wabash River. The corridor is defined as 'the strip of land in Indiana abutting the Wabash River, the Little River, and the portage between the Little and the Maumee Rivers.' This corridor spans almost the entire length of the state, and includes the following nineteen counties: Adams, Allen, Carroll, Cass, Fountain, Gibson, Huntington, Jay, Knox, Miami, Parke, Posey, Sullivan, Tippecanoe, Vermillion, Vigo, Wabash, Warren, and Wells. The Wabash River Heritage Corridor Commission consists of one representative from each of these counties, as well as representatives of the Department of Natural Resources and other state government agencies.
Requirements: Under the historical and cultural component of the Wabash River Heritage Corridor Fund matching grants program, grant awards are made in three project categories. One application packet covers all three project categories: Stabilization, Rehabilitation, Acquisition projects, Archaeological Investigation projects, and Educational / Interpretive Exhibits and Facilities projects. Eligible applicants include (a) private, non-profit organizations with 501(c)3 tax exempt status (including local historical societies and preservation organizations), and (b) local governmental units (including city and county agencies and commissions funded by a consortium of local governments). Applicants must be located in the geographical areas noted in the description above. A subject property must be, at a minimum, determined eligible for listing in the Indiana Register of Historic Sites and Structures. All properties assisted with Wabash funds must possess both a close geographic proximity to the river and a clear contextual connection to the river and the historical development of the Corridor.
Restrictions: Individuals and private, for-profit entities are not eligible to receive grant funds because federal regulations prohibit grant recipients from making a financial profit as a direct result of the grant-assisted project. Federal regulations do not allow grant funds to be awarded to active religious organizations, or to be used to assist buildings that are used primarily for religious functions. Note also that state and federal auditing and income tax regulations prevent the DHPA from making a grant award to an organization which is not incorporated, or which does not otherwise exist as a legal entity. Note that properties within the boundaries of historic

districts which are designated as non-contributing (NC) are not eligible to receive grant funding. Properties listed in the State Register of Historic Sites and Structures which are not also listed in the National Register of Historic Places are not eligible to receive grant funding.
Geographic Focus: Indiana
Amount of Grant: Up to 250,000 USD
Contact: James A. Glass, Division Director; (317) 232-3492; jglass@dnr.in.gov
Internet: http://www.in.gov/dnr/historic/11816.htm#wabash
Sponsor: Indiana Department of Natural Resources
402 West Washington Street, Room W274
Indianapolis, IN 46204

Wabash Valley Community Foundation Grants 4971

The Foundation's mission is to promote community investment for a better tomorrow. Giving primarily for arts and culture, education, human services, community development, and religion. Each year, the Foundation provides grants to nonprofit organizations for projects that meet the charitable needs in the Wabash Valley. With limited unrestricted funding available, the Foundation focuses its priorities on the following: the prevention of problems rather than on the symptoms; to maintain a proactive focus and an ability to respond to creative ideas from grant seekers; to assist grant seekers to better respond to the changing needs of the community; to encourage program that enhance cooperation and collaboration among institutions within the community; to leverage funds through the use of seed money, match, and challenge grants; and to fund projects that will make a significant improvement to the community.
Requirements: A letter of intent is required before submitting a grant request, along with a tax-exempt verification. Selected organizations will then be invited tot submit a full proposal.
Restrictions: Giving is restricted to Clay, Sullivan, and Vigo counties in Indiana. Funding is not available for the following: operational expenses of existing programs; endowments or deficit funding; funds for redistribution by the grantee; conferences, publications, films, television and radio programs unless integral to the project for which the grant is sought; religious purposes; travel for individuals or groups such as bands, sports teams and classes; annual appeals and membership contributions; commonly accepted community services, which are tax supported such as fire and police protection, welfare and library service, etc; or political campaigns or lobbying activities
Geographic Focus: Indiana
Date(s) Application is Due: Jun 1; Nov 1
Contact: Beth Tevlin, (812) 232-2234 or (877) 232-2230; beth@wvcf.com
Internet: http://www.wvcf.com/wvcf_index3.htm
Sponsor: Wabash Valley Community Foundation
2901 Ohio Boulevard, Suite 153
Terre Haute, IN 47803

Wabash Valley Human Services Grants 4972

The organization is committed to community development and providing services to low-income residents in southwestern Indiana. Funding seeks to help homeowners make necessary repairs to their homes. Repairs such as new roofs or gutters, or accessibility modifications such as ramps and kitchen/bath conversions are coupled with energy enhancements such as insulation and air sealing. Along with these services all electrical, mechanical and structural systems will be evaluated and if possible, made compliant to the stricter of State or local codes. Initial approach is by telephone, and deadlines generally are in May.
Requirements: Services under this program are provided to families residing in Daviess, Greene, Knox and Sullivan counties.
Geographic Focus: Indiana
Contact: Bertha Proctor, (812) 882-7927; fax (812) 882-7982; pace@pacecaa.org
Internet: http://www.wvhs.org/
Sponsor: Wabash Valley Human Services
525 N 4th Street
Vincennes, IN 47591-1444

Waitt Family Foundation Grants 4973

The Waitt Family Foundation is looking for programs with real potential to improve the lives of people in at-risk populations throughout the world. These programs, supported by the Waitt Helping Hands Fund, will encourage collaboration across various disciplines or related organizations in order to change the way people see themselves, others, and the opportunities before them. The Foundation is interested in programs that foster independence, self-help, and self-reliance, and want people to obtain the skills necessary to better themselves and their communities. Most importantly, the Foundation is looking for projects that create long-term change to help the greatest number of people. There is a $100,000 minimum for all grant requests. Multi-year proposals will be considered.
Requirements: Organizations must have a U.S. tax identification number and be able to provide a current copy of their IRS 501(c)3 determination letter. Only organizations with federal non-profit agency tax status can receive financial support.
Restrictions: The Foundation does not fund the following categories: individuals; for-profit organizations; capital campaigns; endowments; debt reduction; arts; religious organizations; public education institutions; health care organizations or hospitals; or lobbying prohibited by the Internal Revenue Code.
Geographic Focus: California, Iowa, Nebraska, South Dakota
Date(s) Application is Due: Feb 1; May 1; Aug 1; Oct 1
Contact: Cherie Jacobson, (858) 551-4400; fax (858) 551-6871; grants@waittfoundation.org
Internet: http://waittfoundation.org/grants/guidelines.html
Sponsor: Waitt Family Foundation
P.O. Box 1948
La Jolla, CA 92038-1948

Wallace Alexander Gerbode Foundation Grants 4974

The Foundation is interested in programs and projects offering potential for significant impact. The primary focus is on the California San Francisco Bay area and Hawaii. The Foundation's interests generally fall under the following categories: arts and culture, environment, reproductive rights and health, citizen participation/building communities/inclusiveness, strength of the philanthropic process and the nonprofit sector, and special projects. Letter of inquiry are accepted on an ongoing basis. Awards range from $1,600 to $75,000. The Foundation also has a Special Awards program to commission new works of art. Special Awards program announcements, including guidelines, an application and deadlines, are posted on the Foundation's website. Generally Special Award programs are announced in May, applications are due in late August and awards are announced in January.
Requirements: Eligible organizations must be 501(c)3 nonprofits. Letters of inquiry should be sent to the Administrative Manager and include a brief description of the proposed work, a description of the organization, and a budget.
Restrictions: The Foundation generally does not support direct services, deficit budgets, general operating funds, building or equipment funds, general fundraising campaigns, religious purposes, private schools, publications, scholarships, or grants to individuals.
Geographic Focus: California, Hawaii
Contact: Olivia Malabuyo Tablante; (415) 391-0911; fax (415) 391-4587; olivia@gerbode.org
Internet: http://fdncenter.org/grantmaker/gerbode
Sponsor: Wallace Alexander Gerbode Foundation
111 Pine Street, Suite 1515
San Francisco, CA 94111

Wallace Alexander Gerbode Foundation Special Award Grants 4975

The Foundation is interested in programs and projects offering potential for significant impact. For over twenty years, the Foundation has made innovative grants through its Special Award Program to San Francisco Bay Area arts institutions to commission new works by gifted individual artists: playwrights, choreographers, composers, as well as visual artists, poets, and multi-media artists. These Grants help underwrite culturally and aesthetically diverse, acclaimed new works by prominent artists and artists who are up-and-coming. The Grants support artists at critical junctures in their careers, enabled local nonprofit arts organizations to develop and premiere substantial new works, and enrich Bay Area audiences, readers, and viewers by supporting first access to ambitious, original creations. Special Award Grants announcements, including guidelines, an application and deadlines, are posted on the Foundation's website. Generally Special Award Grants are announced in May, applications are due in late August and awards are announced in January.
Requirements: Proposed commissions in any genre are accepted. Applicant organizations must be nonprofit and based in the counties of Alameda, Contra Costa, Marin, Monterey, Napa, Santa Clara, San Francisco, San Mateo, Santa Cruz, Solano, and Sonoma.
Geographic Focus: California
Date(s) Application is Due: Aug 25
Contact: Olivia Malabuyo Tablante; (415) 391-0911; fax (415) 391-4587; olivia@gerbode.org
Internet: http://foundationcenter.org/grantmaker/gerbode/index.html
Sponsor: Wallace Alexander Gerbode Foundation
111 Pine Street, Suite 1515
San Francisco, CA 94111

Wallace Foundation Grants 4976

The foundation has three current objectives: strengthen education leadership to improve student achievement; improve after-school learning opportunities; and expand participation in arts and culture. Specifically, the fund seeks to develop effective school leaders to improve student learning, create new standards for community participation in the arts, and provide high-quality informal learning opportunities in communities for children and families. Most grants are awarded as part of funds-initiated programs, and unsolicited proposals are rarely funded. Nevertheless, organizations may submit a one- to two-page letter of inquiry describing the project, the organization, the estimated total for the project, and the portion requiring funding.
Requirements: U.S. nonprofit organizations are eligible. In most cases, the foundation identifies and evaluates prospective grantees through the issuance of Requests for Proposals or other careful screening processes. This also means that unsolicited proposals are rarely funded. Nevertheless, you may submit an inquiry by email briefly describing the project, your organization, the estimated total for the project and the portion requiring funding to: The Wallace Foundation, grantrequest@wallacefoundation.org.
Restrictions: Grants do not support religious or fraternal organizations; international programs; conferences; historical restoration; health, medical, or social service programs; environmental/conservation programs; capital campaigns; emergency funds or deficit financing; private foundations; or individuals.
Geographic Focus: All States
Contact: Holly Dodge, Grants Administrator; (212) 251-9700; fax (212) 679-6990
Internet: http://www.wallacefoundation.org/GrantsPrograms/GrantApproach/Pages/FundingGuidelines.aspx
Sponsor: Wallace Foundation
5 Penn Plaza, 7th Floor
New York, NY 10001

Wallace Global Fund Grants 4977

The Wallace Global Fund is guided by the vision of the late Henry A. Wallace, former Secretary of Agriculture and Vice-President under Franklin D. Roosevelt. Committed to serving the general welfare, his life exemplified farsightedness, global vision, and receptivity to new ideas. The Fund supports activities at the global and national level, and will consider significant local or regional initiatives offering the potential to leverage broader national or global impact. It will consider proposals for either core or project-specific support. It does not fund purchase of land, capital construction, profit-making businesses, debt reduction, endowment campaigns,

fundraising drives/events, or scholarships, tuition assistance or other forms of personal financial aid. Grants are being reviewed on a quarterly basis in March, June, September and December.
Requirements: Applicants based in the United States must be registered 501(c)3 non-profit educational organizations. Applicants based outside the United States must show 501(c)3 equivalency under U.S. law and, if invited to submit a proposal, will be asked to sign an affidavit stating this equivalency. Potential grantees without 501(c)3 status will be asked for further documentation regarding the charitable purpose of the activity.
Restrictions: Grants are not made to: individuals; universities; for-profit organizations; endowments; capital fund projects; scholarships; conferences; books or magazines; building construction; or travel (not including project-related travel). The fund does not support film or video projects, the acquisition of land, or grants intended to support candidates for political office.
Geographic Focus: All States
Contact: Ellen Dorsey; (202) 452-1530; fax (202) 452-0922; contact@wgf.org
Internet: http://www.wgf.org/grants
Sponsor: Wallace Global Fund
1990 M Street NW, Suite 250
Washington, DC 20036

Walmart Foundation Facility Giving Grants 4978
Walmart's founder, Sam Walton, introduced the philosophy, "operate globally, give back locally." The Walmart Foundation supports local, state and national organizations providing opportunities in the local communities served. Areas of focus include education, workforce development/economic opportunity, health and wellness, and environmental sustainability.
Requirements: Applicants must fit within one of the Foundation's four focus areas and be one of the following: hold a current tax-exempt status under Section 501(c)3, 4, 6 or 19 of the Internal Revenue Code; be a recognized government entity that is requesting funds exclusively for public purposes; be a K-12 public/private school, charter school, community/junior college, state/private college or university; or be a church or other faith based organization with proposed projects that address and benefit the needs of the community at large.
Restrictions: Applicants must offer programs that benefit the local community. Applicants receiving sponsorship at the national level are excluded from applying. Applications are online.
Geographic Focus: All States
Date(s) Application is Due: Dec 1
Contact: Grants Administrator; (800) 966-6546
Internet: http://walmartstores.com/CommunityGiving/238.aspx
Sponsor: Walmart Foundation
702 SW 8th Street
Bentonville, AR 72716

Walmart Foundation National Giving Grants 4979
The Walmart Foundation's mission is to create opportunities so people can live better. The Grants support initiatives focused on enhancing opportunities in education, workforce development/economic opportunity, health and wellness, and environmental sustainability. The Foundation supports applicants implementing programs in multiple sites across the country or applications with innovative initiatives that are ready for replication nationally. Awards are $250,000 or higher.
Requirements: Applicants must be 501(c)3 organizations; recognized by the Internal Revenue Service as a "public charity" within the meaning of either Section 509(a)(1) or 509(a)(2) of the Internal Revenue Code; and must operate on a national scope through the existence of chapters or affiliates in a large number of states around the country; or possess a regional/local focus, but seek funding to replicate program activities nationally. In the case of proposals seeking funding for replication, organizations must demonstrate the capacity to support national expansion and be ready to begin the replication process.
Restrictions: The Foundation does not accept unsolicited proposals but does accept letters of inquiry providing a general understanding of the problem or issue, the need for the proposed solution and the applicant's capacity to carry out the work. If the applicant is selected to submit a full proposal, guidelines and additional information will be provided. The letter of intent is submitted online.
Geographic Focus: All States
Contact: Grants Administrator; (479) 273-4000
Internet: http://walmartstores.com/CommunityGiving/8782.aspx
Sponsor: Walmart Foundation
702 SW 8th Street
Bentonville, AR 72716

Walmart Foundation State Giving Grants 4980
The Walmart Foundation's mission is to create opportunities so people can live better. The Grants support initiatives aligned with their mission and having a long-lasting, positive impact within a state or region. Service areas include education, workforce development/economic opportunity, health and wellness, and environmental sustainability. The Foundation has a particular interest in supporting the following populations: veterans and military families, traditionally underserved groups, individuals with disabilities, and people impacted by natural disasters. Awards are $25,000 or higher.
Requirements: Applicants must be 501(c)3 organizations.
Restrictions: Funding awarded in a particular state must be fully allocated within that state. Applications accepted online only.
Geographic Focus: All States
Date(s) Application is Due: Apr 22; Sep 28
Contact: Grants Administrator; (479) 273-4000
Internet: http://walmartstores.com/CommunityGiving/8168.aspx?p=8979
Sponsor: Walmart Foundation
702 SW 8th Street
Bentonville, AR 72716

Walt Disney Company Foundation Grants 4981
The foundation funds medical and health services, health and welfare of children, youth activities, higher education, community funds, music, and cultural arts in Los Angeles and Orange Counties in California and Orange and Osceola Counties in Florida. Types of support include general operating support, continuing support, annual campaigns, capital campaigns, program development, scholarship funds, fellowships, and employee-related scholarships. Previous grants have supported downtown revitalization in both New York City, where Disney redeveloped an old Times Square theater, and Los Angeles, where support has been given for a new music hall that will be home to the Los Angeles Philharmonic Orchestra.
Requirements: 501(c)3 tax-exempt organizations in California and Florida may apply.
Restrictions: Disney will not make grants for scholarships, religious organizations, building campaigns, start-up campaigns, seed purposes, research, loans, conferences, general fund drives, annual charitable appeals, and political purposes.
Geographic Focus: California, Florida, New York
Amount of Grant: 1,000 USD
Contact: Tillie Baptie, Executive Director; (818) 560-1006; fax (818) 563-5271
Internet: http://disney.go.com/disneyhand/contributions/wdcfoundation.html
Sponsor: Walt Disney Company Foundation
500 S Buena Vista Street
Burbank, CA 91521-0987

Walter and Elise Haas Fund Grants 4982
The mission of the fund is to help build a healthy, just, and vibrant society in which people feel connected to and responsible for their community. The fund supports nonprofit organizations in its areas of interest, including the arts—arts education, preservation of cultural heritage, cultural commons, and the Creative Fund; economic security—incomes, assets, and economic development; Jewish life—promoting diversity, creative expression, building partnerships, and new leadership; education—youth leadership, parent organizing, community partnerships, and school partnerships with the community; and other grantmaking interests. Types of support include operating budgets, technical assistance, continuing support, seed money, land acquisition, emergency funds, capital campaigns, building funds, special projects, equipment, matching funds, and endowment funds. There are no application deadlines. Submit an application cover sheet with the proposal.
Requirements: 501(c)3 tax-exempt organizations that are not classified as 509(a) private foundations, fiscal sponsors meeting these classifications, and governmental entities are eligible. Applicant organization must be based in or managing significant activities in San Francisco or Alameda County. Within Alameda County, the fund places the highest priority on projects in Oakland and Berkeley. The Jewish Life program area's geographic focus extends to the broader Bay Area. At present, the Creative Work Fund considers applications from Alameda, Contra Costa, San Francisco, and Solano counties.
Restrictions: As a general rule, the fund does not provide grants to individuals or to for-profit entities; for general fundraising benefits and events; for endowment campaigns (Rare exceptions may be made for organizations that have a long-standing relationship to the fund's legacy or when endowment goals are incorporated into a larger capital campaign.); for the creation of a film or video, or of original creative art work, except through the Creative Work Fund; or for scholarships or fellowships.
Geographic Focus: California
Contact: Pamela David, Executive Director; (415) 398-4474
Internet: http://www.haassr.org/html/current_programs/index.cfm
Sponsor: Walter and Elise Haas Fund
1 Lombard Street, Suite 305
San Francisco, CA 94111-1130

Walter L. Gross III Family Foundation Grants 4983
The foundation awards grants to eligible Ohio and Kentucky nonprofit organizations in its areas of interest, including animals and wildlife, Christian churches and organizations, community outreach programs, education, environment, health care and medical, and social services. Grants are considered on a case-by-case basis and have been awarded to support building construction/renovation and general operating support. There are no application forms or deadlines with which to adhere, and applicants should begin by contacting the office directly.
Requirements: Ohio and Kentucky 501(c)3 nonprofit organizations are eligible to apply.
Geographic Focus: Kentucky, Ohio
Amount of Grant: 1,000 - 20,000 USD
Contact: Walter L. Gross III; (513) 785-6060 or (513) 785-6072; fax (513) 683-9467
Sponsor: Walter L. Gross III Family Foundation
9435 Waterstone Boulevard, Suite 390
Cincinnati, OH 45249-8227

Walton Family Foundation Home Region Grants 4984
The Walton Family Foundation's home region grants focus on programs that measurably improve the quality of life and enhance educational and economic opportunities for the citizens and communities of northwest Arkansas, throughout the state of Arkansas, and in the delta region. Areas of focus are education, economic development and quality of life. Three primary focus area are Arkansas Education reform, Northwest Arkansas, and Delta Region of Arkansas an Mississippi.
Requirements: An organization interested in applying for a grant must send a brief letter of inquiry succinctly describing the organization and the proposed project, specifying and briefly explaining its relevance to a particular Foundation funding area and initiative, and providing an estimate of the funds that would be requested. If, based on the letter of inquiry, the project appears to match the Foundation's funding criteria and priorities, the applicant may be invited to submit a formal grant proposal and budget.
Restrictions: An applicant should not submit a formal grant proposal until receiving an invitation following submission of a letter of inquiry. An invitation to submit a formal grant proposal does not mean that funding will be approved.

Geographic Focus: Arkansas, Mississippi
Contact: Janet Post; (479) 464-1570; fax (479) 464-1580
Internet: http://www.waltonfamilyfoundation.org/homeregion
Sponsor: Walton Family Foundation
P.O. Box 2030
Bentonville, AR 72712

Warren County Community Foundation Grants 4985
The Warren County Community Foundation Grants fund projects with focus on: innovative approaches or making significant improvements in solving Warren County problems; maintaining a proactive awareness with the ability to respond to creative ideas; and preventing problems rather than treating symptoms of problems. Grant categories include education, human services, recreation, arts and culture; citizenship, environment, and economic development.
Requirements: When applying for a Warren County Community Grant, organizations should first submit a pre-application letter, which will be reviewed by the Foundation's grant committee. The pre-application letter should be one page, provide a detailed description of the project, including the targeted group it will benefit, the amount of funding requested, and the projected time line, along with the applicant's contact information. Pre-application letters are accepted on the third Thursday in January for April funding, and the third Thursday in May for funding in August. If the project meets the guidelines and funds are likely to be available, the organization is asked to submit eleven copies of the Grant Application form and any attachments. Organizations should contact the Foundation office for a current application.
Restrictions: The Foundation will not fund any of the following: travel or expenses for individuals and groups such as clubs, sports and teams, and classes; projects outside of Warren County (unless it is significant to Warren County residents); organizations fully-funded by government; projects for day-to-day operations, endowments, or excessively long-term projects; religious activities or programs serving one denomination; political organizations or activities; nationwide and/or statewide fund raising efforts.
Geographic Focus: Indiana
Contact: Carol Clark; (765) 764-1501; fax (765) 764-1501; warrencountyfoundation@yahoo.com
Internet: http://www.warrencountyfoundation.com/Grants.html
Sponsor: Warren County Community Foundation
31 North Monroe Street
Williamsport, IN 47993

Warren County Community Foundation Mini-Grants 4986
The Warren County Community Foundation funds community projects that have the greatest impact on meeting the needs of Warren County. Projects should focus on: innovative approaches or making significant improvements in solving Warren County problems; maintaining a proactive awareness with the ability to respond to creative ideas; and preventing problems rather than treating symptoms of problems. Grant priorities include: education, human services, recreation, arts and culture, citizenship, environment, and economic development. In order for the Foundation to react in a more timely matter to needs in the community, the Board has appropriated funds to the Mini-Grant Program. The Mini-Grants Program funds requests of $250 or less with a 30 day approval process. Established grant policies and exclusions will still apply.
Requirements: Applicants should submit a pre-application letter: a one page summary of the proposed project, the targeted group it will benefit, the amount of funding requested, and the projected time frame to complete the project. The applicant will be contacted to submit a grant application if the Foundation decides that the project is appropriate for funding.
Restrictions: Grants are made on a first-come, first-served basis, until the funds have been expended for that calendar year.
Geographic Focus: Indiana
Contact: Carol Clark; (765) 764-1501; warrencountyfoundation@yahoo.com
Internet: http://www.warrencountyfoundation.com/Grants.html
Sponsor: Warren County Community Foundation
31 North Monroe Street
Williamsport, IN 47993

Warrick County Community Foundation Grants 4987
The Warrick County Community Foundation is a nonprofit, public charity created for the people of Warrick County, Indiana. The Foundation helps nonprofits fulfill their missions by strengthening their ability to meet community needs through grants that assist charitable programs, address community issues, support community agencies, launch community initiatives, and support leadership development. Program areas considered for funding including arts and culture; community development; education; health; human services; environment; recreation; and youth development. The application, supplemental forms needed, and examples of recent grants are available at the website.
Requirements: The Foundation welcomes proposals from nonprofit organizations that are deemed tax-exempt under sections 501(c)3 and 509(a) of the IRS code and from governmental agencies serving the Warrick County. Proposals from nonprofit organizations not classified as a 501(c)3 public charity may be considered if the project is charitable and supports a community need.
Restrictions: Project areas not considered for funding include religious organizations for religious purposes; political parties or campaigns; endowment creation or debt reduction; operating costs; capital campaigns; annual appeals or membership contributions; travel requests for groups or individuals such as bands, sports teams, or classes.
Geographic Focus: Indiana
Date(s) Application is Due: Sep 4
Contact: Karen Embry, Administrative Assistant; (812) 897-2030
Internet: http://www.warrickcommunityfoundation.org/disc-grants
Sponsor: Warrick County Community Foundation
224 West Main Street, P.O. Box 215
Boonville, IN 47601

Washington Area Fuel Fund Grants 4988
For more than 160 years, Washington Gas has been an integral part of the growing metropolitan region of Washington D.C. Chartered by the 30th Congress and signed into law by President James Polk in 1848, the company has developed a Charitable Giving Program that is designed to make a meaningful and lasting impact on the communities it serves. The company's signature philanthropic program is the Washington Area Fuel Fund (WAFF). An unforeseen financial crisis brought on by an accident, medical problem, or loss of income can force a family or a senior citizen to choose between food and warmth. When all other government assistance has run out or simply is not available, WAFF has paid for all types of fuel to heat homes of families in need. The Salvation Army disburses WAFF assistance through its 11 offices located throughout the Washington metropolitan area from January 1 through May 31. Once eligibility for WAFF assistance is established, The Salvation Army will issue a check for the appropriate amount and mail it directly to the applicant's utility company or supplier. A list of Salvation Army Offices with their addresses and phone numbers is available at the web site.
Requirements: Eligible applicants must be in an emergency situation and be no longer eligible for any government energy-assistance programs. Applicants must also meet WAFF income guidelines and live in one of the following geographic areas: the District of Columbia; Calvert, Charles, Montgomery, Prince George's, or St. Mary's Counties in Maryland; and Arlington, Fairfax, Loudoun, and Prince William Counties (or in the Cities of Alexandria, Fairfax, and Falls Church) in Virginia.
Restrictions: Funds should be used principally for the payment of heating bills, but may also be used for the purchase and installation of low-cost energy-conservation measures.
Geographic Focus: District of Columbia, Maryland, Virginia
Contact: Ernest R. Holz; (202) 756-2692; Ernie_Holz@uss.salvationarmy.org
Internet: http://www.washingtonareafuelfund.org/get-assistance/
Sponsor: Washington Gas Company
101 Constitution Avenue, North West, 3rd Floor
Washington, DC 20080

Washington Area Women's Foundation African American Giving Circle Grants 4989
Founded in 2004, the African American Women's Giving Circle (AAWGC) is a charitable fund established out of The Women's Foundation. The circle includes 15-25 women who have each made a financial commitment of $5,000 over a two-year period and agreed to work together as part of a shared grantmaking and learning experience. The AAWGC makes grants that support African American women-led organizations that improve the lives of African American women and girls in the Washington metropolitan region.
Requirements: Nonprofits in the Washington metropolitan area are eligible to apply.
Geographic Focus: District of Columbia
Contact: Nicole Cozier; (202) 347-7737, ext. 203; fax (202) 347-7739; ncozier@wawf.org
Internet: http://community.thewomensfoundation.org/page.aspx?pid=223
Sponsor: Washington Area Women's Foundation
1331 H Street, NW, Suite 1000
Washington, DC 20005

Washington Area Women's Foundation Early Care and Education Grants 4990
In response to the findings in "A Portrait of Women & Girls in the Washington Metropolitan Area," the Women's Foundation created Stepping Stones to help build the economic security and financial independence of low-income, women-headed families. Stepping Stones is the first multi-year initiative of its kind for the region and will be the major focus of grants and program work. One area of funding under the Stepping Stones umbrella is known as Early Care and Education Funders Collaborative Grants. The Collaborative's mission is threefold: to increase the capacity and institutional stability of early care and education programs in the region; to enable these entities to develop and manage their resources more effectively; and to improve early care and education programs through grantmaking, public education, and training and technical assistance.
Requirements: Nonprofits in the Washington metropolitan area are eligible to apply.
Geographic Focus: District of Columbia
Contact: Maya Garrett; (202) 347-7737, ext. 210; fax (202) 347-7739; mgarrett@wawf.org
Internet: http://community.thewomensfoundation.org/page.aspx?pid=415
Sponsor: Washington Area Women's Foundation
1331 H Street, NW, Suite 1000
Washington, DC 20005

Washington Area Women's Foundation Financial Education and Wealth Grants 4991
In response to the findings in "A Portrait of Women & Girls in the Washington Metropolitan Area," the Women's Foundation created Stepping Stones to help build the economic security and financial independence of low-income, women-headed families. Stepping Stones is the first multi-year initiative of its kind for the region and will be the major focus of grants and program work. One area of funding under the Stepping Stones umbrella is known as Financial Education and Wealth Creation Fund Grants. The objective of the Financial Education and Wealth Creation Fund is to help low-income, women-headed families in the Washington, D.C., Metropolitan Area obtain a base level of financial knowledge and increase their collective wealth. There are two types of grants: Planning Grants – targeting established organizations that are developing or improving an idea, approach, and/or collaborative model (Planning Grants are no longer available); and Impact Grants – targeting organizations that can demonstrate a track record in delivering results.
Requirements: Nonprofits in the Washington metropolitan area are eligible to apply.
Geographic Focus: District of Columbia
Contact: Nicole Cozier; (202) 347-7737, ext. 203; fax (202) 347-7739; ncozier@wawf.org
Internet: http://thewomensfoundation.org/our-work/financial-education-and-wealth-creation-fund/
Sponsor: Washington Area Women's Foundation
1331 H Street, NW, Suite 1000
Washington, DC 20005

Washington Area Women's Foundation Jobs Fund Grants   4992
In response to the findings in "A Portrait of Women & Girls in the Washington Metropolitan Area," the Women's Foundation created Stepping Stones to help build the economic security and financial independence of low-income, women-headed families. Stepping Stones is the first multi-year initiative of its kind for the region and will be the major focus of grants and program work. One area of funding under the Stepping Stones umbrella is known as Jobs Fund Grants. The objective of this Fund is to help build the life-long economic security of low-income women-headed families in the Washington, D.C., metropolitan area by building better pathways to self-sufficient jobs, and by increasing the percentage of single mothers being placed in, retaining, and advancing in high-growth jobs in three targeted sectors (health care, real estate, and protective services) and non-traditional occupations. The Jobs Fund targets three high-growth sectors in the region: Health Care (some examples of occupations include medical assistants, medical records/health information technicians, nurses, and dental hygienists); Real Estate (some examples of occupations include brokers, sales agents, and property managers); and Protective Services (some examples of occupations include police officers, fire fighters, security guards, and occupations related to homeland security). The Jobs Fund has two types of grant opportunities: Planning Grants – targeting established organizations that are developing or improving an idea, approach, and/or collaborative model (6-12 months); and Impact Grants – targeting organizations that can demonstrate a track record in delivering results (12 months).
Requirements: Nonprofits in the Washington metropolitan area are eligible to apply.
Geographic Focus: District of Columbia
Contact: Nicole Cozier; (202) 347-7737, ext. 203; fax (202) 347-7739; ncozier@wawf.org
Internet: http://thewomensfoundation.org/our-work/jobs-fund/
Sponsor: Washington Area Women's Foundation
1331 H Street, NW, Suite 1000
Washington, DC 20005

Washington Area Women's Foundation Leadership Awards   4993
The Leadership Awards Program invests in the work of outstanding, emerging community-based organizations that exhibit vision and impact in serving the critical needs of women and girls. Each year, the Leadership Awards recognizes innovative nonprofit organizations in the Washington metropolitan area working to positively impact the lives of women and girls in a given issue area. The embodiment of "citizen philanthropy," the Leadership Awards Program engages 40 to 60 volunteers in every level of the selection of awardees – doing telephone interviews with key staff at the organizations, visiting the organizations to see their work in action, and evaluating all they have learned to select the final winners through deliberation and consensus.
Requirements: Nonprofits in the Washington metropolitan area are eligible to apply.
Geographic Focus: District of Columbia
Contact: Nicole Cozier; (202) 347-7737, ext. 203; fax (202) 347-7739; ncozier@wawf.org
Internet: http://thewomensfoundation.org/join-us/become-a-grantee-partner/funding-opportunities/#leadership
Sponsor: Washington Area Women's Foundation
1331 H Street, NW, Suite 1000
Washington, DC 20005

Washington Area Women's Foundation Open Door Capacity Fund Grants   4994
In 2011, The Women's Foundation responded to the continuing national economic crisis and increase in local poverty by sharpening its focus on the economic security of women and girls. The Foundation wanted to ensure that our community's collective resources are focused on the intersection of where there is the most need and where we can have the most impact. The Open Door Capacity Fund helps the Foundation's Grantee Partners build their organizational capacity and strengthen their work and infrastructure. The program has funding available only from time-to-time, so potential applicants should check the website for current funding cycles.
Requirements: Nonprofits in the Washington metropolitan area are eligible to apply.
Geographic Focus: District of Columbia
Contact: Nicole Cozier; (202) 347-7737, ext. 203; fax (202) 347-7739; ncozier@wawf.org
Internet: http://thewomensfoundation.org/join-us/become-a-grantee-partner/funding-opportunities/#stepping
Sponsor: Washington Area Women's Foundation
1331 H Street, NW, Suite 1000
Washington, DC 20005

Washington Area Women's Foundation Rainmakers Giving Circle Grants   4995
Launched in 2003, The Women's Foundation's Rainmakers Giving Circle's mission is to improve the lives of young women in the Washington metropolitan area by supporting programs that foster their empowerment, self-esteem and ability to achieve their full potential. The Rainmakers Giving Circle supports programs for young women and girls (10-21) that encourage the healthy development of and prevention of risk factors among young women and girls. The Rainmakers focus on programs that empower and increase competence among young women and girls in the areas of employment, education, health, and life skills. The Rainmakers contribute to programs where the grants make a significant impact in the continuation, expansion or enhancement of the program. Rainmakers Giving Circle members commit to give $5,000 each to the giving circle over two years.
Requirements: Nonprofits in the Washington metropolitan area are eligible to apply.
Geographic Focus: District of Columbia
Date(s) Application is Due: Dec 5
Contact: Nicole Cozier; (202) 347-7737, ext. 203; fax (202) 347-7739; ncozier@wawf.org
Internet: http://community.thewomensfoundation.org/page.aspx?pid=222
Sponsor: Washington Area Women's Foundation
1331 H Street, NW, Suite 1000
Washington, DC 20005

Washington Area Women's Foundation Strategic Oppor and Partnership Grants   4996
In response to the findings in "A Portrait of Women & Girls in the Washington Metropolitan Area," the Women's Foundation created Stepping Stones to help build the economic security and financial independence of low-income, women-headed families. Stepping Stones is the first multi-year initiative of its kind for the region and will be the major focus of grants and program work. One area of funding under the Stepping Stones umbrella is known as Strategic Opportunity and Partnership Fund Grants. This Fund provides grants to nonprofit organizations engaged in research, policy advocacy, grassroots efforts, capacity building or communications and media activities that support the overall goals of Stepping Stones.
Requirements: Nonprofits in the Washington metropolitan area are eligible to apply.
Geographic Focus: District of Columbia
Contact: Nicole Cozier; (202) 347-7737, ext. 203; fax (202) 347-7739; ncozier@wawf.org
Internet: http://thewomensfoundation.org/our-work/stepping-stones/strategic-opportunity-and-partnership-fund/
Sponsor: Washington Area Women's Foundation
1331 H Street, NW, Suite 1000
Washington, DC 20005

Washington County Community Foundation Grants   4997
The Washington County Community Foundation offers grants to nonprofit organizations in Washington County. Organizations may sign up to be notified of current grant cycles and criteria. The application and examples of previously funded projects are available at the Foundation website.
Requirements: Funding will be made to nonprofit organizations whose programs benefit Washington County residents. Grants from Washington County Community Foundation must meet legal and tax requirements as to purpose and may be made only to non-profit organizations and causes. Grant recipients must show that their financial affairs are being properly administered and may be required to submit audited balance sheets and operating statements.
Restrictions: Applicants are required to attend an orientation meeting before beginning the grant writing process. Funding is not available for the following: political parties or campaigns; sectarian religious purposes that do not serve the general public; programs or equipment that was committed to prior to the grant application submission; or endowment creation or debt reduction.
Geographic Focus: Indiana
Contact: Judy Johnson, Executive Director; (812) 883-7334; info@wccf.biz
Internet: http://wccf.biz/grants/grant-criteria.html
Sponsor: Washington County Community Foundation
1707 North Shelby Street, P.O. Box 50
Salem, IN 47167

Washington County Community Foundation Youth Grants   4998
The purpose of the Washington County Youth Foundation is to improve the quality of life in Washington County. The principle consideration in a grant is its effectiveness in meeting demonstrated or perceived health, education, cultural, recreational, environmental, or social needs in the community, or in making studies to determine how best to meet such needs. The participation of other contributions by using matching, challenge, and other grant techniques is strongly encouraged. The application and examples of previously funded grants are available at the Foundation website.
Requirements: Grants from Washington County Youth Foundation must meet legal and tax requirements and may be made only to non-profit organizations and causes. Grant recipients must show that their financial affairs are being properly administered and may be required to submit audited balance sheets and operating statements. To qualify for funding, projects must address a community need, be planned and implemented by a youth group in the county, and associated with a non-profit organization.
Restrictions: Funding is not available for the following: political parties or campaigns; sectarian religious purposes that do not serve the general community; endowment creation and debt reduction; programs or equipment that was committed to prior to the grant application submission; meeting routine budgets.
Geographic Focus: Indiana
Contact: Judy Johnson, Executive Director; (812) 883-7334; info@wccf.biz
Internet: http://wccf.biz/youth_foundation/yf_grant-criteria.html
Sponsor: Washington County Community Foundation
1707 North Shelby Street, P.O. Box 50
Salem, IN 47167

Washington Families Fund Grants   4999
WFF is a public-private partnership that leverages and increases funding for targeted services in response to the significant unmet need for affordable housing and social supports that homeless families are experiencing across the state of Washington. WFF aims to benefit homeless families with children under the age of 18 and homeless pregnant women. Funds are intended both to help sustain existing support service programs and to create new service-enriched housing across Washington State. WFF funding will primarily support comprehensive and individualized case management services for homeless families. Programs may also provide a range of additional services that are tailored to address the families' needs and identified to be an important link for housing stability. These service programs must be linked to affordable housing. Guidelines and application are available online.
Requirements: WFF will select projects that are designed to fit the community and respond to local needs; urban, suburban, and rural providers are encouraged to apply. Eligible organizations are local housing authorities; nonprofit housing and/or supportive service organizations; public development authorities; and federally recognized Indian tribes in the State of Washington. Partnerships between service providers, nonprofit housing agencies, and public housing authorities are encouraged.
Restrictions: Homeless shelters and other emergency housing options are not eligible.

Geographic Focus: All States
Contact: Kelly Smith; (206) 805-6135 or (206) 805-6100; Kelly.Smith@BuildingChanges.org
Internet: http://www.buildingchanges.org/grantee-toolbox/overview
Sponsor: AIDS Housing of Washington
2014 East Madison, Suite 200
Seattle, WA 98122

Washington Gas Charitable Giving Contributions 5000
For more than 160 years, Washington Gas has been an integral part of the growing metropolitan region of Washington D.C. Chartered by the 30th Congress and signed into law by President James Polk in 1848, the company has developed a Charitable Giving Program that is designed to make a meaningful and lasting impact on the communities it serves. Washington Gas focuses on three primary areas: education, the environment, and health. Types of support offered are grants, in-kind contributions, and volunteer resources. In the area of education, emphasis is placed on the development of math, science, technology, and business skills in K-12 youth. Consideration is also given to arts-related programs. In the area of the environment, emphasis is placed on programs that promote cleaner air and water programs that protect and preserve the ecological system of the metropolitan area. In the area of health, consideration is given to health organizations that strive to improve the health and well-being of individuals within the community. Emphasis is also placed on energy assistance programs for low-income residents to heat and cool their homes, reducing illness and casualties resulting from exposure to extreme temperatures. The company accepts applications on a rolling basis. Basic guidelines are listed at the website and provided in a downloadable PDF file. Applications must be mailed to the contact information given. Notification of acceptance or rejection generally takes fifteen business days or longer.
Requirements: 501(c)3 organizations are eligible to apply. The company prefers to support specific programs over general funding.
Restrictions: Support is not provided to religious organizations for sectarian purposes, political associations, organizations with strictly a sports focus, individuals, and requests for capital or endowment campaigns.
Geographic Focus: District of Columbia, Maryland, Virginia
Contact: Tracye Funn, (703) 750-1000; tfunn@washgas.com
Internet: http://www.washgas.com/pages/CharitableGiving
Sponsor: Washington Gas Company
101 Constitution Avenue, North West, 3rd Floor
Washington, DC 20080

Waste Management Charitable Giving Grants 5001
Waste Management is a large company with facilities that span the North American continent. The company lends it's support and services to organizations that promote civic pride, economic development and revitalization. The three areas of interest are environment, environmental education, and community. There are no specific deadlines with which to adhere. Contact the Foundation for further application information and guidelines.
Requirements: Charity and public organizations that have been approved by the IRS as a 501(c)3tax-exempt status are eligible to apply, however donations requested must be used exclusively for public purposes. Nonprofit organizations interested in requesting financial, in-kind or product donations should submit requests to: Pierpont Communications, Attn: Waste Management, 1800 West Loop South, Suite 800, Houston, TX, 77027.
Restrictions: No support will be provided for: requests from organizations without a 501(c)3 tax-exempt status or do not use funds received exclusively for public purposes - please note that Waste Management rarely provides contributions to social services, arts, and health related organizations; Individuals; religious organizations regardless of faith, unless the project benefits the community, such as a soup kitchen that is housed in a church; political candidates or lobbying organizations; organizations with a limited constituency, such as fraternal, labor or veteran's groups; endowments or foundations; travel by groups or individuals; anti-business groups; organizations that discriminate on the basis of race, color, religion, or gender; operating costs; capital campaigns; or multi-year requests.
Geographic Focus: All States
Contact: Charitable Contributions Coordinator; (713) 512-6200; fax (713) 512-6299
Internet: http://www.wm.com/WM/community/Commitment.asp
Sponsor: Waste Management Corporation
1001 Fannin, Suite 4000
Houston, TX 77002

Water and Land Stewardship Fund Grants 5002
The purpose of the fund is to improve the region's environmental quality by focusing on water quality and related land use issues and to encourage grassroots efforts that raise awareness about these concerns. Areas of interest are: raising awareness of and appreciation for water and related land resources throughout Worcester County; fostering collaboration among groups who are working on these issues; supporting innovative approaches to the region's environmental issues; supporting smaller organizations who are doing this work but have little financial capacity; and providing a forum for sharing ideas about environmental issues in the region.
Requirements: Nonprofit organizations, grassroots or other community groups working to improve the environmental health of Worcester County are eligible to apply.
Restrictions: Grants may not be used for expenses already incurred by the applicant. Groups are only eligible for one grant per calendar year.
Geographic Focus: Massachusetts
Date(s) Application is Due: Jul 15
Contact: Pamela B. Kane, (508) 755-0980; pkane@greaterworcester.org
Internet: http://www.greaterworcester.org/grants/WLS.htm
Sponsor: Greater Worcester Community Foundation
370 Main Street, Suite 650
Worcester, MA 01608-1738

Wayne and Gladys Valley Foundation Grants 5003
The foundation awards grants to California nonprofits in its primary areas of interest, including education at all levels, health care and medical research, youth and families, human services, sciences and engineering, and religion. Types of support include general operating support, building construction/renovation, program development, professorships, research, and matching funds. There are no application forms or deadlines. The board meets in February, May, September, and November to consider requests.
Requirements: California nonprofits in Alameda, Contra Costa, and Santa Clara Counties are eligible.
Geographic Focus: California
Contact: Michael Desler; (510) 466-6060; fax (510) 466-6067; info@wgvalley.org
Sponsor: Wayne and Gladys Valley Foundation
1939 Harrison Street, Suite 510
Oakland, CA 94612-3532

Wayne County Foundation - Vigran Family Foundation Grants 5004
Lifelong Richmond, Indiana, resident Stanley Vigran considered forming a private foundation as a way to support causes that were important to him and his family including education, religion, and the arts. The Vigran family remains actively involved through a separate board which oversees the operations of the organization. Vigran's family continues his legacy of giving in the Whitewater Valley and remain involved in the causes that were so much a part of their father's work. Contact the Foundation for the application and further guidelines.
Requirements: Interested applicants should submit a one-page letter of inquiry.
Geographic Focus: Indiana
Date(s) Application is Due: Sep 1
Contact: Stephen C. Borchers; (765) 962-1638; steve@waynecountyfoundation.org
Internet: http://www.waynecountyfoundation.org/grant_center/vigran.html
Sponsor: Vigran Family Foundation / Wayne County Foundation
33 South 7th Street, Suite 1
Richmond, IN 47374

Wayne County Foundation Grants 5005
The Foundation seeks to serve the charitable, cultural, educational, and community needs of the citizens in Wayne County, Indiana. Areas of interest include animal welfare; agriculture; the performing arts; cancer and glaucoma research/ child abuse prevention; delinquency prevention; the environment; historic preservation; homelessness; human service needs; literacy; mental health; special needs therapy; and senior citizens. Grants will be made primarily to established organizations that serve the county. The programs of such organizations will reflect the concerns of community leadership. Types of support include equipment, program development, conferences and seminars, publication, seed money, and scholarship funds. Normally, grant commitments are for one year. Deadlines vary according to program. The application and samples of previously funded projects available at the website.
Requirements: The following information must be submitted to apply: the completed application cover; a statement of need; project description and anticipated community impact; a brief description of the applicant's history, purpose, and population served; a plan to evaluate the success or effectiveness of the proposed project; the project budget and narrative budget; the 501(c)3 determination letter; a list of Board members with contact information; evidence of the Board's approval for application; statement of financial position and operating statement; and current Form 990.
Restrictions: The Foundation will not support annual fund campaigns; operating or capital debt reduction; religious purposes; grants to individuals or for travel purposes; services commonly regarded as the responsibility of government such as fire and police protection; public school services required by state law; standard instructional or regular operating costs of nonpublic schools; or repeat funding of projects previously supported in recent grant periods.
Geographic Focus: Indiana
Date(s) Application is Due: Apr 1; Jul 30; Oct 1
Contact: Stephen C. Borchers; (765) 962-1638; steve@waynecountyfoundation.org
Internet: http://www.waynecountyfoundation.org/index.html
Sponsor: Wayne County Foundation
33 South 7th Street, Suite 1
Richmond, IN 47374

Wayne County Foundation Women's Fund Grants 5006
The Women's Fund was established through the Wayne County Foundation to support creative and innovative efforts to enhance the lives of women and girls. The Fund provides grants that give opportunities, encouragement, knowledge, and hope to women and girls. With the gifts and grants, the fund strives to empower women and girls to become strong, active citizens. The flexible structure of the Women's Fund is designed to give credibility to women's philanthropy and women's challenges, assure sustainability, maximize community impact, and ensure grantee success. Local business and community women form the Advisory Board that directs all activities, seeks funding proposals, and facilitates grant awards. Grants are limited to $1,000 per application. The application is available at the website.
Requirements: Applicants must be 501(c)3 organizations operating in Wayne County whose project serves a broad segment of the community. To be considered, applicants must submit the following: a summary of the program, conference, training or other formal experience members in the applicant's organization wishes to attend (a brochures and supplementary materials may be included to help the Foundation understand the opportunity, but they should not be used as a substitute for a written summary); a statement describing why this opportunity is important to the woman and organization; a description of the organization's history, purpose, and population served; a statement detailing how this grant will help advance the organization; a project budget; and the Women's Fund grant application cover page.
Restrictions: The following cannot be supported by grant funding: individuals; annual fund campaigns and/or operating funds or operating or capital debt reduction; religious activities;

travel expenses; services commonly regarded as the responsibility of the government, such as fire and police protection; and projects outside of Wayne County, Indiana.
Geographic Focus: Indiana
Date(s) Application is Due: Feb 13
Amount of Grant: Up to 1,000 USD
Contact: Stephen C. Borchers; (765) 962-1638; steve@waynecountyfoundation.org
Internet: http://www.waynecountyfoundation.org/grant_center/womens_fund.html
Sponsor: Wayne County Foundation
33 South 7th Street, Suite 1
Richmond, IN 47374

WCI Childcare Capacity Grants 5007
West Central Initiative (WCI) is a regional community foundation that works to strengthen the region of west central Minnesota by: encouraging business and employment opportunities; providing training and support to workers and their families; working with communities and the region to help them thrive; and promoting philanthropy. WCI serves the nine counties of Becker, Clay, Douglas, Grant, Otter Tail, Pope, Stevens, Traverse and Wilkin. WCI Childcare Capacity Grants help expand the capacity of child care centers in communities with a shortage of licensed care. Grant funding will provide no more than $750 per increased licensed slot created or per existing licensed slot saved if the center would otherwise close. Maximum awards are: $37,500 for full-day, year-round programs and $10,000 for an after-school child care center. Other types of programs will be considered on a case-by-case basis. Requests up to $7,500 are accepted any time and will usually be processed within three weeks. Requests exceeding $7,500 will usually be processed within six weeks. Requests should be made with enough lead time for WCI to make a final decision concerning funding before any costs are incurred. WCI staff generally visit applicants to discuss the proposal prior to WCI's funding decision.
Requirements: Applicants are encouraged to talk to the Program Director prior to submitting application. Applicant centers must meet the needs of working parents, be located in a community where there is a shortage of licensed child care, and be owned and run by a 501(c)3 non-profit organization or by a unit of government. Funding must be matched by cash on a dollar-for-dollar basis. Donated materials or services needed to meet licensing standards can be counted as match. Child care fees will not be counted as match. Applicants must provide evidence that their venture is likely to have a positive cash flow upon completion. Generally funds may be used as needed in a project for equipment, facilities or cash flow during a "fill-up" period after opening. If funds are used to renovate leased facilities, a five-year lease is required.
Restrictions: Organizations that incorporate religious education into their child care services are ineligible. Funding may not be used for existing operating deficits or to reduce existing operating debt. If an applicant operates both child care and preschool services, only costs associated with providing child care are eligible.
Geographic Focus: Minnesota
Contact: Wendy Merrick, (218) 739-2239 or (800) 735-2239; info@wcif.org
Internet: http://www.wcif.org/?page=Grant_Applications
Sponsor: West Central Initiative
1000 Western Avenue
Fergus Falls, MN 56537

WCI Community Leadership Fellowships 5008
West Central Initiative (WCI) is a regional community foundation that works to strengthen the region of west central Minnesota by: encouraging business and employment opportunities; providing training and support to workers and their families; working with communities and the region to help them thrive; and promoting philanthropy. WCI serves the nine counties of Becker, Clay, Douglas, Grant, Otter Tail, Pope, Stevens, Traverse and Wilkin. WCI Community Leadership Fellowships support diverse representation and inclusivity in training programs that are focused on community leadership development. The funding can be used by qualifying individuals to meet tuition and other costs, such as child care, transportation and lost wages. Requests are accepted any time and will usually be processed within three weeks. Requests should be made with enough lead time for WCI to make a final decision concerning funding before any costs are incurred. WCI staff may contact applicants to discuss their proposals.
Requirements: Applicants are encouraged to talk to the Program Director prior to submitting application. Applicants must be: participating in a community-focused leadership program that emphasizes developing, connecting and mobilizing citizens to do more and do better in addressing community issues and controlling their community's future; permanent residents of WCI's nine-county service area for at least the two previous years with intentions to remain in the region and serve as a community leader; legitimate candidates for assistance from a charitable foundation, including, but not limited to members of minority groups, recent international immigrants and refugees, disabled persons, low income individuals, and moderate income persons facing extraordinary expenses or loss of income in order to participate; and nominated for assistance by a community leadership development program operated by a non-profit or governmental organization.
Restrictions: The program must be located within 300 miles of WCI's service region. Air travel is ineligible. Programs focused on a specific business, occupation, or industries are generally a low priority for support.
Geographic Focus: Minnesota
Amount of Grant: 500 USD
Contact: Wendy Merrick, (218) 739-2239 or (800) 735-2239; info@wcif.org
Internet: http://www.wcif.org/?page=Grant_Applications
Sponsor: West Central Initiative
1000 Western Avenue
Fergus Falls, MN 56537

WCI Community Mobilization Grants 5009
West Central Initiative (WCI) is a regional community foundation that works to strengthen the region of west central Minnesota by: encouraging business and employment opportunities; providing training and support to workers and their families; working with communities and the region to help them thrive; and promoting philanthropy. WCI serves the nine counties of Becker, Clay, Douglas, Grant, Otter Tail, Pope, Stevens, Traverse and Wilkin. WCI Community Mobilization Grants provide funding to help communities develop a partnership among concerned citizens and a shared vision to address critical community concerns. Eligible projects include broad-based efforts that bring citizens together to map their community's resources and plan action that enhances their community's development and ability to address critical issues. Requests are accepted at any time and will usually be processed within three weeks. Requests must be made with enough lead time for WCI to make a final decision concerning funding before any costs are incurred. WCI staff typically contact or visit applicants to discuss their proposals.
Requirements: Applicants are encouraged to talk to the Program Director prior to submitting application. Eligible proposals generally must: spring from a need to develop a community consensus or shared vision for addressing a critical issue within the community; address a critical need within WCI's service region; be submitted by a 501(c)3 non-profit organization or unit of government willing to accept financial responsibility for the project; demonstrate commitment and interest from a broad-based group which is representative of the various stakeholders in the project; secure one dollar of cash match for each dollar requested from WCI. Matching requirements can be waived in hardship cases.
Restrictions: Grants are not intended to support the strategic planning efforts of single organizations or multi-agency collaborations, but the citizens of geographically-defined communities. WCI will not support projects for: arts, cultural activities, historic facilities, or museums; sports programs, recreational activities, and related facilities or events; religious activities; fund drives, grant writing, or fundraising programs; lobbying or political activities; routine, city, county, or township planning or zoning; event planning; feasibility studies, architectural design, or implementation planning; or strategic or long range planning focused on the needs or services of a single organization or a multi-agency collaboration.
Geographic Focus: Minnesota
Amount of Grant: 5,000 USD
Contact: Wendy Merrick, (218) 739-2239 or (800) 735-2239; info@wcif.org
Internet: http://www.wcif.org/?page=Grant_Applications
Sponsor: West Central Initiative
1000 Western Avenue
Fergus Falls, MN 56537

WCI Family Economic Success Local Impact Grants 5010
West Central Initiative (WCI) is a regional community foundation that works to strengthen the region of west central Minnesota by: encouraging business and employment opportunities; providing training and support to workers and their families; working with communities and the region to help them thrive; and promoting philanthropy. WCI serves the nine counties of Becker, Clay, Douglas, Grant, Otter Tail, Pope, Stevens, Traverse and Wilkin. WCI Family Economic Success Local Impact Grants are designed to support services that help families overcome barriers to workforce participation and self-sufficiency. Funding supports these four goals: family members building skills that qualify them to hold better jobs; job seekers and workers finding and being able to afford dependable, convenient, and appropriate child care needed to maintain a job; children of working families getting the early childhood care and education that prepares them to succeed in school and life; and families taking advantage of tax benefits and developing knowledge and skills to achieve family economic success. Grant requests are accepted at any time. Please allow at least six weeks for the review process. Requests should be made with enough lead time for WCI to make a funding decision before any project costs are incurred. WCI staff generally visit applicants to discuss the proposal prior to making a funding decision.
Requirements: Applicants are encouraged to talk to the Program Director prior to submitting application. Applicants must: be a 501(c)3 nonprofit organization or unit of government that accepts responsibility for the project; clearly define how the project will measurably impact one or more of the four goals; and incorporate a dollar-for-dollar match on the proposal. Cash match is preferred.
Restrictions: Ineligible projects include: arts, cultural activities and festivals; sports or recreation-focused events; historic facilities or museums; religious activities; fund drives or fundraising programs; lobbying or political activities; remedial programs or prevention programs targeted toward "at-risk" populations; and buildings and equipment.
Geographic Focus: Minnesota
Amount of Grant: 5,000 USD
Contact: Wendy Merrick, (218) 739-2239 or (800) 735-2239; info@wcif.org
Internet: http://www.wcif.org/?page=Grant_Applications
Sponsor: West Central Initiative
1000 Western Avenue
Fergus Falls, MN 56537

WCI Family Economic Success Regionwide Grants 5011
West Central Initiative (WCI) is a regional community foundation that works to strengthen the region of west central Minnesota by: encouraging business and employment opportunities; providing training and support to workers and their families; working with communities and the region to help them thrive; and promoting philanthropy. WCI serves the nine counties of Becker, Clay, Douglas, Grant, Otter Tail, Pope, Stevens, Traverse and Wilkin. The WCI Family Economic Success Regionwide Grants are part of the WCI Family Economic Success (FES) Program which is designed to support services that help families overcome barriers to workforce participation and self-sufficiency. The four FES goals are: family members building skills that qualify them to hold better jobs; job seekers and workers finding and affording the dependable, convenient, and appropriate child care they need to maintain a job; children of

working families getting the early childhood care and education that prepares them to succeed in school and life; and families taking advantage of tax benefits and developing knowledge and skills to achieve family economic success. Grant requests are accepted at any time. Please allow at least six weeks for the review process. Requests should be made with enough lead time for WCI to make a funding decision before any project costs are incurred. WCI staff generally visit applicants to discuss the proposal prior to making a funding decision.
Requirements: Applicants are encouraged to talk to the Program Director prior to submitting application. Grant applications must originate with one of the three FES work groups and must: be submitted on behalf of the work group by a 501(c)3 nonprofit organization or unit of government that accepts responsibility for the project; clearly define how the project will measurably impact one or more of the four FES goals on a region-wide, nine-county level; and incorporate a dollar-for-dollar match on the proposal. Cash match is preferred.
Restrictions: The following projects are ineligible: arts, cultural activities and festivals; sports or recreation-focused events; historic facilities or museums; religious activities; fund drives or fundraising programs; lobbying or political activities; remedial programs or prevention programs targeted toward "at-risk" populations; and buildings and equipment.
Geographic Focus: Minnesota
Contact: Wendy Merrick, (218) 739-2239 or (800) 735-2239; info@wcif.org
Internet: http://www.wcif.org/?page=Grant_Applications
Sponsor: West Central Initiative
1000 Western Avenue
Fergus Falls, MN 56537

WCI Leadership Development Grants 5012
West Central Initiative (WCI) is a regional community foundation that works to strengthen the region of west central Minnesota by: encouraging business and employment opportunities; providing training and support to workers and their families; working with communities and the region to help them thrive; and promoting philanthropy. WCI serves the nine counties of Becker, Clay, Douglas, Grant, Otter Tail, Pope, Stevens, Traverse and Wilkin. WCI Leadership Development Grants are designed to help create and sustain on-going community leadership programs. The purpose is to expand the base of regional leaders. Requests are accepted any time and will usually be processed within three weeks. Grant requests should be made with enough lead time for WCI to make a final decision concerning funding before any costs are incurred. WCI staff frequently contact or visit applicants to discuss their proposals. Funding awarded is a maximum of $5,000 the first year, $4,000 the second year, and $3,000 the third and subsequent years.
Requirements: Applicants are encouraged to talk to the Program Director prior to submitting application. Eligible applications must incorporate the following: emphasis on enhancing community leadership in a geographically-defined place such as a city, township or county within the nine-county region served by WCI; emphasis on developing, connecting and mobilizing citizens; a host organization committed to program development and delivery; and a non-discriminatory participant selection process. In addition, priority is given to programs with the following characteristics: programs which are ongoing; programs delivered to a cadre of twelve to twenty individuals over no fewer than four session half-day (or longer) sessions; and programs which incorporate three pieces: skill development, team-building, and information about the community that is important to being a leader.
Geographic Focus: Minnesota
Contact: Wendy Merrick, (218) 739-2239 or (800) 735-2239; info@wcif.org
Internet: http://www.wcif.org/?page=Grant_Applications
Sponsor: West Central Initiative
1000 Western Avenue
Fergus Falls, MN 56537

WCI Minnesota Beautiful Grants 5013
West Central Initiative (WCI) is a regional community foundation that works to strengthen the region of west central Minnesota by: encouraging business and employment opportunities; providing training and support to workers and their families; working with communities and the region to help them thrive; and promoting philanthropy. WCI serves the nine counties of Becker, Clay, Douglas, Grant, Otter Tail, Pope, Stevens, Traverse and Wilkin. WCI Minnesota Beautiful Grants are a partnership with Valspar Corporation to restore and beautify community structures with paint and coatings provided by Minneapolis-based Valspar Corporation to complete various restoration and beautification projects. The application process is coordinated by WCI with final decisions and overall administration provided by Valspar.
Requirements: Applicants are encouraged to talk to the Program Director prior to submitting application. The selection criteria include the following: visual impact of the project; public benefit to the community; volunteer participation and support; planning and documentation of the project; and historic or cultural significance. Some eligible projects include, but are not limited to, the following: historic buildings, structures, or landmarks; facilities for senior or disabled citizens; community centers or other public buildings; and murals or other visual impact projects. Volunteer participation from within the nine counties served by WCI is required. Submittal of commitment letters from volunteers or volunteer groups is highly recommended. Projects must be completed within the calendar year awarded.
Restrictions: Some ineligible projects include denominational churches, schools (except murals), city maintenance, or privately owned facilities that do not meet any of the above criteria. Projects using a contractor to complete the work are ineligible.
Geographic Focus: Minnesota
Date(s) Application is Due: Mar 7
Contact: Wendy Merrick, (218) 739-2239 or (800) 735-2239; info@wcif.org
Internet: http://www.wcif.org/?page=Grant_Applications
Sponsor: West Central Initiative
1000 Western Avenue
Fergus Falls, MN 56537

Weatherwax Foundation Grants 5014
The foundation awards grants in Michigan to projects that promote and support education, civic and social programs, culture, science, and the arts, primarily in the greater Jackson area and, to a lesser extent, in the adjacent counties. Types of support include building construction and renovation; matching and challenge grants; general operating grants; program development; scholarships; annual and capital campaigns; and emergency funds. The initial approach is a two-page proposal that may be submitted at any time. Granting decisions are made in January, May, and August.
Requirements: Giving primarily in Hillsdale, Lenawee, and Jackson counties, MI.
Restrictions: No grants to individuals; or for computer purchases.
Geographic Focus: Michigan
Contact: Program Contact; (517) 787-2117; fax (517) 787-2118
Internet: http://www.lib.msu.edu/harris23/grants/wfbrochu.htm
Sponsor: Weatherwax Foundation
P.O. Box 1111
Jackson, MI 49204

Weaver Foundation Grants 5015
The mission of the foundation is to help the Greater Greensboro community enhance and improve the quality of life and the economic environment for its citizens while developing a sense of philanthropy, civic education, and commitment in current and future generations of the founders' families. The focus areas include support for education; programs for children and youth; protection of the environment; efforts to reduce poverty and improve the lives of the disadvantaged and the needy; advancement of human and civil rights, racial tolerance, and diversity; enhancement of parks, recreation, and the quality of life; and economic development. Inquiries are welcomed via letter, telephone, or email; full proposals are by invitation. Grants are generally made quarterly.
Requirements: 501(c)3 nonprofits serving the greater Greensboro, North Carolina, community are eligible.
Restrictions: The foundation does not support political programs or voter registration efforts, conferences, travel, video production, fraternal groups, individuals, or religious organizations.
Geographic Focus: North Carolina
Contact: Tara Sandercock; (336) 379-9100 or (336) 378-7910; rlm@weaverfoundation.com
Internet: http://www.weaverfoundation.com/guidelines/index.php
Sponsor: Weaver Foundation
324 W. Wendover Avenue, Suite 300, P.O. Box 26040
Greensboro, NC 27408-8440

Weaver Popcorn Foundation Grants 5016
Established in Indiana in 1997, the Weaver Popcorn Foundation offers funding throughout the State of Indiana. Its primary fields of interest include: boy scouts; children and youth services; education; family services; domestic violence; health care; higher education; human services; and secondary school programs. The primary type of funding is general operating support. A formal application is not required, and interested parties should submit a brief overview/history of the organization, its mission, and an outline of budgetary needs. There are no annual deadlines specified. Typical awards range from $250 to $20,000, though some grants have reached as much as $125,000.
Requirements: Any Indiana non-profit is eligible to apply.
Geographic Focus: Indiana
Contact: Brian Hamilton, (317) 915-4050
Sponsor: Weaver Popcorn Foundation
14470 Bergen Boulevard, Suite 100
Noblesville, IN 46060-3377

Wege Foundation Grants 5017
The Wege Foundation awards grants in Michigan in five specific categories: education, environment, arts and culture, health care, and human services. Areas of interest include children and youth services; Christian agencies and churches; community development; elementary and secondary education; environmental resources; higher education; hospitals (general); human services; museums; and performing arts. The Foundation strives to be an inspiration for other communities. According to the Foundation's vision, "Grand Rapids inspires others to create communities that forge a balance in the environment, health, education, and arts to encourage healthier lives in mind, body, and spirit."
Requirements: Grants are awarded to nonprofit organizations in the greater Kent County, MI, area, with emphasis on the Grand Rapids area. The applicant may access the application after an online quiz.
Restrictions: The Foundation only funds organizations classified as tax-exempt under section 501(c)3 of the Internal Revenue Code. Grants are not awarded for operating budgets.
Geographic Focus: Michigan
Date(s) Application is Due: Feb 15; Sep 15
Contact: Jody Price; (616) 957-0480; fax (616) 957-0616; jprice@wegefoundation.org
Internet: http://www.wegefoundation.com/seekingagrant/seekingagrant.html
Sponsor: Wege Foundation
P.O. Box 6388
Grand Rapids, MI 49516-6388

Weingart Foundation Grants 5018
Weingart Foundation makes grants to assist organizations that work in the areas of health, human services, and education. The Foundation gives highest priority to activities that provide greater access to people who are economically disadvantaged and underserved. Of particular interest to the Foundation are applications that specifically address the needs of low-income children and youth, older adults, and people affected by disabilities and homelessness. The Foundation also funds activities that benefit the general community and improve the quality of

life for all individuals in Southern California. Weingart Foundation offers the following types of grants: core support; capital; capacity building; program; and a small grant program. See website for a description of each grant type: http://www.weingartfnd.org/default.asp?PID=5
Requirements: An organization that is certified as tax exempt under Section 501(c)3 of the U.S. Internal Revenue Code and is not a private foundation as defined in section 509(a) of that Code is eligible for consideration. Preference is given to organizations providing services in the following six Southern California counties: Los Angeles, Orange, Riverside, Santa Barbara, San Bernardino, and Ventura.
Restrictions: Grants are not made: for propagandizing, influencing legislation and/or elections, promoting voter registration; for political candidates, political campaigns; for litigation; to institutions limiting their services to persons of a single religious sect or denomination; for social or political issues outside the United States of America; to individuals; to federated appeals or for the collection of funds for redistribution to other nonprofit groups; for conferences, workshops, temporary exhibits, travel, surveys, films or publishing activities; for endowment funds; for contingencies, deficits or debt reduction; for fundraising dinners or events; for research. Grants generally are not approved for: national organizations that do not have local chapters operating in the geographic area of grant focus; projects or programs normally financed by government sources; refugee or religious programs, consumer interest or environmental advocacy; feasibility studies. The Foundation does not fund Section 509(a)(3) Type III non-functionally integrated supporting organizations.
Geographic Focus: California
Contact: Administrator; (213) 688-7799; fax (213) 688-1515; info@weingartfnd.org
Internet: http://www.weingartfnd.org
Sponsor: Weingart Foundation
1055 W Seventh Street, Suite 3050
Los Angeles, CA 90017-2305

Welborn Baptist Foundation Faith-Based Initiatives Grants **5019**
The Welborn Baptist Foundation is seeking to fund lasting change in the communities it serves. Towards that end, the Foundation will assess grant proposals based on: demonstrated long-term results, or exceptional potential for such results based on well-established research; addressing root causes rather than symptoms; fit with the Foundation's target areas of emphasis; deep, established collaborations with (not just referrals from) other like-minded organizations; excellent prospects for long-term sustainability without Foundation resources; and a clear implementation plan that enables successes to be replicated elsewhere. The Foundation's Baptist heritage has led it to designate grants each year to Christian faith-based entities and organizations that exemplify its mission: to apply Christian principles in support of improved community health, well-being, and quality of life. Though broad in scope, historical funding has focused on messaging initiatives (such as evangelism and discipleship) of youth-oriented faith-based organizations, as well as ministry outreaches of both churches and faith-based organizations. Messaging initiatives provide the spiritual direction which fosters health in body, soul, and spirit; ministry outreaches typically are those that involve ongoing relationships with those served, as opposed to those providing daily needs. Typically, projects designed to meet urgent human needs such as food pantries, soup kitchens, direct shelter services, rental and utility assistance programs and the like are not considered to be within the purview of the Foundation.
Requirements: Giving is limited to: Gallatin, Saline, Wabash, Wayne and White counties in Illinous; Dubois, Gibson, Perry, Pike, Posey, Spencer, Vanderburgh, and Warrick counties in Indiana; and Henderson County, Kentucky. Applicants must submit a Letter of Interest (LOI). All secular, church and other faith-based not-for-profit organizations that are tax exempt under section 501(c)3 of the IRS Code are eligible. Participation beyond the Letter of Interest stage is by invitation only.
Restrictions: The following program and project areas will not be considered for funding: scholarships, loans, grants or fellowship support directly to or for the benefit of specific and known individuals; establishment of, or contributions to, a permanent endowment, foundation, trust or permanent interest-bearing account; carrying on of propaganda or attempt to influence legislation or public elections; restricting the services, facilities or employment provided by the grant to individuals based on race, creed, color, sex, or national origin; any governmental agencies reporting to an elected or appointed official (except for schools governed by citizens boards); any requests for funding for deficits or retirement of debt; fundraising events; annual fund drives; venture capital for competitive profit making ventures; or basic scientific research. Additionally, it should be noted that the Foundation does not fund applications seeking replacement dollars (i.e., funding to substitute for dollars lost from another grantor).
Geographic Focus: Illinois, Indiana, Kentucky
Contact: Kevin Bain; (812) 437-8260 or (877) 437-8260; info@welbornfdn.org
Internet: http://www.welbornfdn.org/grant-process/funding-targets
Sponsor: Welborn Baptist Foundation
Twenty-One Southeast Third Street, Suite 610
Evansville, IN 47708

Welborn Baptist Foundation General Opportunity Grants **5020**
The Welborn Baptist Foundation is seeking to fund lasting change in the communities it serves. Towards that end, the Foundation will assess grant proposals based on: demonstrated long-term results, or exceptional potential for such results based on well-established research; addressing root causes rather than symptoms; fit with the Foundation's target areas of emphasis; deep, established collaborations with (not just referrals from) other like-minded organizations; excellent prospects for long-term sustainability without Foundation resources; and a clear implementation plan that enables successes to be replicated elsewhere. To meet needs that do not naturally fit into the other priority target areas, but which are consistent with the Foundation's mission, the General Opportunity target area has been established. In the past, General Opportunity grants have focused on opportunities that enhance the general health and/or the health educational status of the community. Ideal opportunities for consideration in this category are those which address both health and health education. Proposals which have only a peripheral relationship to health or health education are not likely to be funded.
Requirements: Giving is limited to: Gallatin, Saline, Wabash, Wayne and White counties in Illinous; Dubois, Gibson, Perry, Pike, Posey, Spencer, Vanderburgh, and Warrick counties in Indiana; and Henderson County, Kentucky. Applicants must submit a Letter of Interest (LOI). All secular, church and other faith-based not-for-profit organizations that are tax exempt under section 501(c)3 of the IRS Code are eligible. Participation beyond the Letter of Interest stage is by invitation only.
Restrictions: The following program and project areas will not be considered for funding: scholarships, loans, grants or fellowship support directly to or for the benefit of specific and known individuals; establishment of, or contributions to, a permanent endowment, foundation, trust or permanent interest-bearing account; carrying on of propaganda or attempt to influence legislation or public elections; restricting the services, facilities or employment provided by the grant to individuals based on race, creed, color, sex, or national origin; any governmental agencies reporting to an elected or appointed official (except for schools governed by citizens boards); any requests for funding for deficits or retirement of debt; fundraising events; annual fund drives; venture capital for competitive profit making ventures; or basic scientific research. Additionally, it should be noted that the Foundation does not fund applications seeking replacement dollars (i.e., funding to substitute for dollars lost from another grantor).
Geographic Focus: All States
Contact: Kevin Bain; (812) 437-8260 or (877) 437-8260; info@welbornfdn.org
Internet: http://www.welbornfdn.org/grant-process/funding-targets
Sponsor: Welborn Baptist Foundation
Twenty-One Southeast Third Street, Suite 610
Evansville, IN 47708

Welborn Baptist Foundation Improvements to Community Health Status Grants **5021**
The Welborn Baptist Foundation is seeking to fund lasting change in the communities it serves. Towards that end, the Foundation will assess grant proposals based on: demonstrated long-term results, or exceptional potential for such results based on well-established research; addressing root causes rather than symptoms; fit with the Foundation's target areas of emphasis; deep, established collaborations with (not just referrals from) other like-minded organizations; excellent prospects for long-term sustainability without Foundation resources; and a clear implementation plan that enables successes to be replicated elsewhere. in the area of Improvements to Community Health Status, the Foundation has initiated a community-wide coalition designed to achieve long-term reduction in the proportion of residents that are either overweight or obese, through increased physical activity and healthier eating. Beyond this, the Foundation's funding objective in this target area is for all community residents to proactively take the appropriate steps that can lead to lower levels of chronic illness. The primary focus is therefore on: programs that increase the access of high-risk populations to health care services; and programs that address the prevention and successful management of chronic disease states.
Requirements: Giving is limited to: Gallatin, Saline, Wabash, Wayne and White counties in Illinous; Dubois, Gibson, Perry, Pike, Posey, Spencer, Vanderburgh, and Warrick counties in Indiana; and Henderson County, Kentucky. Applicants must submit a Letter of Interest (LOI). All secular, church and other faith-based not-for-profit organizations that are tax exempt under section 501(c)3 of the IRS Code are eligible. Participation beyond the Letter of Interest stage is by invitation only.
Restrictions: The following program and project areas will not be considered for funding: scholarships, loans, grants or fellowship support directly to or for the benefit of specific and known individuals; establishment of, or contributions to, a permanent endowment, foundation, trust or permanent interest-bearing account; carrying on of propaganda or attempt to influence legislation or public elections; restricting the services, facilities or employment provided by the grant to individuals based on race, creed, color, sex, or national origin; any governmental agencies reporting to an elected or appointed official (except for schools governed by citizens boards); any requests for funding for deficits or retirement of debt; fundraising events; annual fund drives; venture capital for competitive profit making ventures; or basic scientific research. Additionally, it should be noted that the Foundation does not fund applications seeking replacement dollars (i.e., funding to substitute for dollars lost from another grantor).
Geographic Focus: Illinois, Indiana, Kentucky
Contact: Kevin Bain; (812) 437-8260 or (877) 437-8260; info@welbornfdn.org
Internet: http://www.welbornfdn.org/grant-process/funding-targets
Sponsor: Welborn Baptist Foundation
Twenty-One Southeast Third Street, Suite 610
Evansville, IN 47708

Wells County Foundation Grants **5022**
The Wells County Foundation Grants give priority to programs having a positive effect on the Wells County community. Grant making fields of interest include arts and culture, education, civic affairs, youth, environment, community development, animal welfare, recreation, and health and human services. In reviewing grant proposals, the Foundation gives careful consideration to: the potential impact of the request and the number of people benefited; an innovative approach; the degree to which the applicant works with or complements the services of other community organizations; the extent of local involvement and support for the project; the organization's demonstrated fiscal responsibility and management qualification; and the organization's ability to obtain necessary additional and future funding.
Requirements: Applicants are encouraged to contact the Foundation to discuss their project. They should be prepared to give a brief discussion to enable the Foundation to determine whether the request falls within the grant-making guidelines. In addition, the staff will inform the applicant of the deadline for the most current grant cycle. Grant proposals for projects should include the following: a title page with the organization's contact information, the project's title and amount requested; a proposal narrative, summarizing what issues the project will address, its expectations, how many will benefit, the role of volunteers, its planned evaluation, and a signed endorsement by the Board of Directors; financial information, with the project budget, two pricing quotes for equipment requested, a list of other funding sources, and the project's funding for the future; and organizational

information, including a brief history with mission and purpose, list of officers, financial statement or audit, and a copy of the tax exemption the IRS.
Restrictions: No grants will be made to any political organization or to support attempts to influence the legislation of any governing body other than through making available to the community at large the results of non-partisan analysis, study and/or research.
Geographic Focus: Indiana
Date(s) Application is Due: Feb 15; Jun 15; Oct 17
Contact: Tammy Slater; (260) 824-8620; wellscountyfound@wellscountyfound.org
Internet: http://www.wellscountyfound.org/Grants.html
Sponsor: Wells County Foundation
360 North Main Street, Suite C
Bluffton, IN 46714

Wells Fargo Housing Foundation Grants 5023
The Wells Fargo Housing Foundation provide sustainable homeownership opportunities for low-to moderate-income people by providing volunteer and financial resources to local and national nonprofit housing organizations. To accomplish this mission, the Foundation works with established local and national nonprofit housing organizations that have demonstrated the ability to create homeownership opportunities for low- to moderate-income families. It also supports nonprofit housing organizations that help low- to moderate-income homeowners make necessary repairs and upgrades. Home ownership grant areas of interest include: development and pre-development of construction or rehab of owner-occupied homes; home buyer education, as well as pre- and post-purchase counseling; counseling and prevention activities to avoid foreclosure and may include modification assistance; down payment and closing cost subsidies, interest rate buy downs and other subsidies that assist home buyers and homeowners to purchase or retain their homes; and essential home repairs, purchases and modifications (e.g. repair or replacement of a furnace or to build a ramp for handicap accessibility). Submission periods are January 2 through January 31 and July 1 through July 31.
Requirements: 501(c)3 nonprofits with organizations in Wells Fargo communities are eligible.
Restrictions: The foundation does not fund individuals; club memberships; endowment campaigns; video or film production; start-up funding for new organizations; political campaigns; sports, athletics; fundraising dinners; purchase of advertising; health/single disease issues; recreation programs; religious organizations for religious purposes; or organizations designed primarily for lobbying.
Geographic Focus: Alabama, Alaska, Arizona, Arkansas, California, Colorado, Connecticut, Delaware, District of Columbia, Florida, Georgia, Idaho, Illinois, Indiana, Iowa, Kansas, Maryland, Michigan, Minnesota, Mississippi, Montana, Nebraska, Nevada, New Jersey, New Mexico, New York, North Carolina, North Dakota, Ohio, Oregon, Pennsylvania, South Carolina, South Dakota, Tennessee, Texas, Utah, Virginia, Washington, Wisconsin, Wyoming
Date(s) Application is Due: Jan 31; Jul 31
Amount of Grant: 5,000 - 10,000 USD
Contact: Contact; (612) 667-5131; fax (612) 316-0417; wfhf@wellsfargo.com
Internet: https://www.wellsfargo.com/about/wfhf/about_wfhf
Sponsor: Wells Fargo Housing Foundation
90 S 7th Street, 4th Floor, MAC N9305-043
Minneapolis, MN 55479

Western Indiana Community Foundation Grants 5024
The Western Indiana Community Foundation focuses its attention on local needs within the geographical boundaries as set by the Board of Directors. Primary fields of interest include: health, charitable service, education, cultural affairs, and community improvement. The Foundation is especially interested in learning of plans for: start-up costs for new programs; one-time projects or needs; and capital needs beyond an applicant's capabilities and needs. Grant applications may be submitted throughout the year. Applicants will be notified immediately following the Board of Directors decision.
Requirements: Organizations must fill out the online application and include the following information: their full contact information, description of the project, and grant request amount; other funding sources for the project, an itemized expenses list and project timeline; the organization's IRS tax exempt status, how they plan to evaluate the project, and a description of public relations plans/foundation funding. The application packet should then be mailed to the Foundation,
Restrictions: The Foundation will not consider: grants for individuals; organizations for political or religious purposes; support for regular operating budgets; contributions to endowments; providing for long term funding; post-event situations; or apparel such as school/sport uniforms.
Geographic Focus: Indiana
Contact: Dale White; (765)-793-0702; fax (765)-793-0703; dwhite@wicf-inc.org
Internet: http://www.wicf-inc.org/grant_guidelines.asp
Sponsor: Western Indiana Community Foundation
135 South Stringtown Road
Covington, IN 47932-0175

Western New York Foundation Grants 5025
The Foundation supports sustainable organizations that improve the quality of life in Western New York. The Foundation makes investments that build on nonprofits' proven strengths in order to improve their effectiveness and their ability to fulfill their missions. Funding is provided in these categories: human services; education; urban and rural development; arts, culture, and humanities; and housing, park and land use.
Requirements: Western New York State 501(c)3 organizations located within one of the following counties are eligible: Allegany, Cattaraugus, Chautauqua, Erie, Genesee, Niagara, and Wyoming.
Restrictions: Only one application may be submitted at a time. Funded organizations may reapply two years following the final payment of an award. The following are ineligible: religious organizations for religious purposes; political organizations, campaigns, and candidates; municipal and government entities; grants or loans to individuals; fund-raising events, i.e. sponsorships, tables, dinners, and telethons; endowments; scholarships; operating expenses; hospital capital campaigns; and general capital campaigns.
Geographic Focus: New York
Date(s) Application is Due: Jun 30; Nov 30
Contact: Beth Kinsman Gosch; (716) 839-4225; bgosch@wnyfoundation.org
Internet: http://www.wnyfoundation.org
Sponsor: Western New York Foundation
11 Summer Street, Fourth Floor
Buffalo, NY 14209

Western Pennsylvania Environmental Awards 5026
The Western Pennsylvania Environmental Awards recognize and honor the outstanding achievements of organizations, businesses, and individuals in a wide range of environmental initiatives throughout the western Pennsylvania region. The Pennsylvania Environmental Council sponsors these environmental efforts to enhance the quality of life in western Pennsylvania. Awardees receive a $5,000 cash award designated to the nonprofit organization of their choice; a custom framed commemorative photograph; two complimentary tickets to the awards dinner; media recognition of the program and award; commemorative poster of the awardee's project; and recognition and a full description of the winning project in the dinner program.
Requirements: Awards are open to any group, individual, program, or organization located in western Pennsylvania. Nominations are submitted online. Applicants should refer to the website for the current deadline.
Geographic Focus: Pennsylvania
Amount of Grant: 5,000 USD
Contact: Sally Tarhi; (412) 481-9400; fax (412) 481-9401; wpea@pecpa.org
Internet: http://www.pecpa.org/wpea
Sponsor: Pennsylvania Environmental Council
22 Terminal Way
Pittsburgh, PA 15219

West Hawai'i Fund for Nonprofit Organizations 5027
The Fund makes grants for projects/programs that improve the quality of life for the residents of West Hawai'i (North Kohala through Hawaiian Ocean View Estates). The Fund especially welcomes proposals that involve people and organizations from different sectors of the community who are working together to address an issue of concern to the community. The Fund encourages collaboration that increases networking and the levels of involvement and trustworthiness between people in the community. Proposal submission information is available online.
Geographic Focus: Hawaii
Amount of Grant: 10,000 USD
Contact: Program Contact; (808) 885-2174
Internet: http://www.hawaiicommunityfoundation.org/index.php?id=71&categoryID=22
Sponsor: Hawai'i Community Foundation
1164 Bishop Street, Suite 800
Honolulu, HI 96813

Westinghouse Charitable Giving Grants 5028
The foundation makes charitable contributions to community priorities primarily where Westinghouse has a presence. Areas of emphasis include education—elementary, secondary, and high school programs that emphasize math and science (some non-fine arts programs); health and welfare—to improve quality of life in the community; and civic and social affairs—to support economic development, environmental quality, and the preservation of public safety. Within each area, the foundation actively encourages programs that meet the needs of special populations, such as the disadvantaged, the young, the elderly, the gifted, people with disabilities, minorities, and women. Because of the foundation's approach to funding in Westinghouse plant locations, all organizations, except colleges and universities, should submit their requests for support to the nearest Westinghouse location. Applications are accepted on an ongoing basis.
Requirements: 501(c)3 tax-exempt organizations are eligible.
Restrictions: The following organizations and activities are ineligible: individuals; political contributions; religious organizations; highly specialized health, medical, or welfare programs; fine arts organizations/programs; organizations that discriminate by race, color, creed, gender, or national origin; hospitals; colleges, universities, and two-year institutions; capital improvement or building projects; medical education; chairs or professorships; liberal arts, fine arts, or similar educational programs; educational research programs, regardless of academic discipline; graduate education; general endowment; equipment purchases at universities; United Way-affiliated agencies; tickets; or memberships.
Geographic Focus: All States
Contact: Program Officer; (412) 374-6824; fax (412) 642-4874
Internet: http://www.westinghousenuclear.com/E2.asp
Sponsor: Westinghouse Electric Corporation
P.O. Box 355, ECE 575C
Pittsburgh, PA 15230-0355

West Virginia Commission on the Arts Accessibility Services Grants 5029
The purpose of the West Virginia Commission on the Arts Accessibility Services Grants is to support accessibility services that give all citizens an opportunity to participate in arts programs. Activities and requests could include: leasing or renting of ramps; leasing or renting assisted listening equipment; and creating alternate formats for materials such as large print programs, Braille, printed materials, cassette tapes, and captioning. Funding is limited to 50% of eligible items up to $500.
Requirements: West Virginia schools, non-profit arts organizations or other community organizations with an arts mission are eligible. A 50% cash match is required.

Restrictions: Capital expenditures or purchase of equipment is ineligible.
Geographic Focus: West Virginia
Date(s) Application is Due: Feb 1; Mar 1; Jul 1
Amount of Grant: 500 USD
Contact: Barbara Anderson; (304) 558-0240; Barbie.J.Anderson@wv.gov
Internet: http://www.wvculture.org/arts/grantbook/generalcats.htm#access
Sponsor: West Virginia Commission on the Arts
1900 Kanawha Boulevard E
Charleston, WV 25305-0300

West Virginia Commission on the Arts Artist Visit Grants   5030
The purpose of the West Virginia Commission on the Arts Artist Visit Grants is to provide funding to schools and other sponsors to present touring state, regional, or national performing, literary, and visual artists. Funding supports arts exposure experiences (one to four days with no more than four hours per day) that should be a component of an ongoing curriculum-based arts education program and not a substitute for hands on learning. Applicants may request up to 50% of artist's or company's contract fee and expenses.
Requirements: West Virginia schools, non-profit arts organizations or other community organizations incorporating the arts into their mission are eligible. Projects should be developed using the West Virginia Department of Education Fine Arts Content Standards and Objectives. A 50% match is required.
Geographic Focus: West Virginia
Date(s) Application is Due: Mar 1
Contact: Barbara Anderson; (304) 558-0240; Barbie.J.Anderson@wv.gov
Internet: http://www.wvculture.org/arts/grantbook/artsined.htm#visit
Sponsor: West Virginia Commission on the Arts
1900 Kanawha Boulevard E
Charleston, WV 25305-0300

West Virginia Commission on the Arts Challenge America Partnership Grants   5031
The primary purpose of the West Virginia Commission on the Arts Challenge America Partnership Grants is to strengthen America's communities through the unique power of the arts. The focus of the program is on arts education and outreach documentation and evaluation, with funds available for projects in the areas of arts education, access to the arts, positive alternatives for youth, cultural heritage/preservation, and community arts development. All applicants must submit a letter of intent by December 1.
Requirements: Nonprofit West Virginia arts organizations with current West Virginia Division of Culture and History or West Virginia Commission on the Arts grants or past successful grant administration track records with proven success of incorporating artists and arts projects in community development, health or social improvement, and economic development programs are eligible. College and university arts faculty and departments that present community outreach and arts in education opportunities to the region surrounding their institution are also eligible. Applicants must provide 50% cash match.
Geographic Focus: West Virginia
Date(s) Application is Due: Feb 1
Contact: Barbara Anderson; (304) 558-0240; Barbie.J.Anderson@wv.gov
Internet: http://www.wvculture.org/arts/grantbook/tech.htm#challenge
Sponsor: West Virginia Commission on the Arts
1900 Kanawha Boulevard E
Charleston, WV 25305-0300

West Virginia Commission on the Arts Community Connections Grants   5032
The purpose of the West Virginia Commission on the Arts Community Connections Grants is to: assist communities in assessing their cultural needs and resources; develop dialogue between all facets of the community; and develop a structure for the efficient use of resources and the provision of a stable cultural environment. Grants are one to two years designed to help communities develop a cultural plan by promoting communication between existing arts organizations, artists, citizens, local government, business, chambers of commerce, tourism, educators and others. A community cultural plan assesses community resources, develops dialogue, and identifies the most efficient ways to use existing resources while developing new resources to provide a rich cultural environment in the community. Applicants to the first year may apply for funding to coordinate the community cultural planning process. Second year applicants may apply for funding to implement the goals outlined in the cultural plan.
Requirements: West Virginia non-profit arts organizations, city or county governments or similar organizations are eligible. Paid, professional staff is not a requirement. A 50% cash match is required.
Geographic Focus: West Virginia
Date(s) Application is Due: Mar 1
Contact: Barbara Anderson; (304) 558-0240; Barbie.J.Anderson@wv.gov
Internet: http://www.wvculture.org/arts/grantbook/community.htm#comm
Sponsor: West Virginia Commission on the Arts
1900 Kanawha Boulevard E
Charleston, WV 25305-0300

West Virginia Commission on the Arts Cultural Facilities and Capital Resources   5033
The primary purpose of the West Virginia Commission on the Arts Cultural Facilities and Capital Resources Grants is to provide financial support for acquisition of real property, renovations to existing facilities, and capital equipment that provides infrastructure for arts organizations (primary purpose) and history museums (secondary opportunity). The goal is to increase or assure public access to the arts; encourage collaborations and partnerships that leverage public and private investment; serve more than one county; contribute to economic development; further cultural development in rural, underserved, or minority communities; address known health and safety deficiencies; create or improve access to facilities for working artists with disabilities; improve, expand, or rehabilitate existing buildings to provide for handicapped accessibility; or reduce an organization's operating costs. Applications may request up to 50% of eligible expenses for acquisition of real property, renovation of existing property, and purchase of durable equipment. Applicants must submit a letter of intent by April 1.
Requirements: Primary eligibility is for arts organizations with three years of successful arts administration of grants approved by the West Virginia Council for the Arts, and a secondary opportunity for history museums. Agencies of municipal or county governments, including county school boards and not-for profit, tax-exempt 501(c)3 or 501(c)4 West Virginia corporations are eligible. A 50% cash match is required.
Restrictions: Colleges and universities are not eligible.
Geographic Focus: West Virginia
Date(s) Application is Due: Jul 1
Amount of Grant: 2,500 - 500,000 USD
Contact: Barbara Anderson; (304) 558-0240; Barbie.J.Anderson@wv.gov
Internet: http://www.wvculture.org/arts/grantbook/cultfac.htm
Sponsor: West Virginia Commission on the Arts
1900 Kanawha Boulevard E
Charleston, WV 25305-0300

West Virginia Commission on the Arts Fast Track ADA and Emergency Grants   5034
The purpose of the West Virginia Commission on the Arts Fast Track Americans with Disabilities Act (ADA) and Emergency Grants provide rapid access to funding for emergencies and resolution of ADA and health and safety deficiencies. Funding provides for smaller renovation and construction projects to comply with ADA and regulations concerning access to public buildings for people with disabilities, and to answer emergency needs when damage to museum infra-structure or sudden failure of equipment may result in harm to arts and history collections and public safety. Applicants may request up to 50% of eligible expenses for acquisition of real property, renovation of existing property, and purchase of durable equipment. Applications are received throughout the year.
Requirements: Primary eligibility is for arts organizations with three years of successful administration of grants. A secondary eligibility is for history museums. Agencies of municipal or county governments, including county school boards and not-for profit 501(c)3 West Virginia corporations may apply. A 50% cash match is required.
Restrictions: Colleges and universities are not eligible.
Geographic Focus: West Virginia
Amount of Grant: 2,000 - 10,000 USD
Contact: Barbara Anderson; (304) 558-0240; Barbie.J.Anderson@wv.gov
Internet: http://www.wvculture.org/arts/grantbook/cultfac.htm#fast
Sponsor: West Virginia Commission on the Arts
1900 Kanawha Boulevard E
Charleston, WV 25305-0300

West Virginia Commission on the Arts Initiative/Opportunity Grants   5035
The West Virginia Commission on the Arts has allocated limited funds to respond to special grant requests outside of the regularly scheduled application deadlines. The purpose of the Initiative/Opportunity Grants is to present new or extended arts experiences for the public. Projects that support innovative approaches and serve special audiences are encouraged.
Requirements: West Virginia non-profit arts organizations and communities are eligible. A 50% cash match is required. To request information and discuss proposals, contact the Director of Arts.
Geographic Focus: West Virginia
Contact: Barbara Anderson; (304) 558-0240; Barbie.J.Anderson@wv.gov
Director of Arts; (304) 558-0240, ext. 721.
Internet: http://www.wvculture.org/arts/grantbook/tech.htm#new
Sponsor: West Virginia Commission on the Arts
1900 Kanawha Boulevard E
Charleston, WV 25305-0300

West Virginia Commission on the Arts Long-Range Planning Grants   5036
The purpose of the West Virginia Commission on the Arts Long-Range Planning Grants is to strengthen arts organizations and prepare them for success in fundraising and efficiency in providing arts experiences. Support is available for outside consultants and planners to analyze the applicant organization's administrative, artistic, programmatic and financial management; marketing; and fundraising and incorporate those findings into a long range plan through facilitated meetings with the board of directors and community members. Funding is limited to 50% of the consultant's fee and expenses not to exceed $10,000.
Requirements: West Virginia non-profit arts organizations and institutions with professional staff, or those organizations that have been in existence for a minimum of two years, are eligible to apply. A 50% cash match is required.
Geographic Focus: West Virginia
Date(s) Application is Due: Mar 1
Contact: Barbara Anderson; (304) 558-0240; Barbie.J.Anderson@wv.gov
Internet: http://www.wvculture.org/arts/grantbook/community.htm#plan
Sponsor: West Virginia Commission on the Arts
1900 Kanawha Boulevard E
Charleston, WV 25305-0300

West Virginia Commission on the Arts Long-Term Artist Residencies   5037
The primary purpose of the West Virginia Commission on the Arts Long-Term Artist Residencies is to provide funding for curriculum-based hands-on projects that involve an identified group of students and teachers in the creative process and integrate the arts into daily instruction. Projects must provide teachers with the tools that will enable them to continue to utilize the arts after the residency is completed and the artist leaves. Residency projects (5 weeks or longer, up to one year)

present an artist in a series of programs that demonstrate his/her artistry and skills. Residencies are a partnership between the sponsor, whether a school or community, and the artist. The residency should be organized to meet specific goals developed by a residency committee and should stress the creative aspects of the artist's work including interpretation of the training and skills required to be an artist. A residency committee comprising community leaders, artists, educators, and other appropriate persons must be organized and must select an artist who meets the commission's criteria and who will also best suit the structure of the project in terms of talent, personality, working methods, medium, etc. Applications should include a description of program sites, equipment, curriculum objectives, artist selection procedure, schedule, budget, evaluation procedures, housing and travel arrangements for the artist, and plans for professional development workshops for teachers and administrators. Financial assistance for the long-term residency is limited to two years unless the sponsor can justify the need to continue the support because of the rural or underserved audience involved in the project. Sponsors of long-term residencies may request 50 percent artist contract fee as well as expenses, and supplies needed for the residency, up to a maximum request of $12,000. A letter of intent is requested by December 1; full application is due by March 1.
Requirements: Residency sponsors may be West Virginia schools, community arts organizations, arts institutions, or libraries. The eligibility of other types of organizations will be considered case by case.
Geographic Focus: West Virginia
Date(s) Application is Due: Mar 1
Amount of Grant: Up to 12,000 USD
Contact: Barbara Anderson; (304) 558-0240; Barbie.J.Anderson@wv.gov
Internet: http://www.wvculture.org/arts/grantbook/artsined.htm#long
Sponsor: West Virginia Commission on the Arts
1900 Kanawha Boulevard E
Charleston, WV 25305-0300

West Virginia Commission on the Arts Major Institutions Support Grants **5038**
The purpose of the West Virginia Commission on the Arts Major Institutions Support Grants is to support and stabilize organizations by providing financial assistance toward their overall budgets for arts programming. Selection criteria include artistic excellence, effective management, community impact and year-round programming and accessibility to audiences and artists. Funding awarded is between 2% and 6% of the organization's operating budget. Match is achieved through the organization's operating budget.
Requirements: Applicant organizations must: have a minimum operating budget of at least $1,000,000 or more; have been in existence for five years as a West Virginia nonprofit during which time a permanent, paid, professional staff, including a business manager and artistic director, have administered the organization's programming on an annual basis; have received Grants for at least three previous grant cycles; serve a large audience that represents a broad cross section of citizens, including people who are disabled or institutionalized, senior citizens, lower income groups, and culturally diverse audiences; demonstrate compliance with Section 504 of the Rehabilitation Act and the Americans with Disabilities Act; and provide longstanding local arts service and welcome and outreach to state and regional audiences.
Restrictions: The following institutions are ineligible: organizations whose primary thrust is education and which award academic credits; organizations receiving operating funds from other state agencies; organizations whose main purpose is not the arts; divisions or departments of larger institutions; and national service organizations.
Geographic Focus: West Virginia
Date(s) Application is Due: Mar 1
Contact: Barbara Anderson; (304) 558-0240; Barbie.J.Anderson@wv.gov
Internet: http://www.wvculture.org/arts/grantbook/generalcats.htm#major
Sponsor: West Virginia Commission on the Arts
1900 Kanawha Boulevard E
Charleston, WV 25305-0300

West Virginia Commission on the Arts Media Arts Grants **5039**
The purpose of the West Virginia Commission on the Arts Media Arts Grants is provide financial assistance to arts organizations for media projects (film, video and audio). Priority is given to projects that reflect a relevance to West Virginia by celebrating its artistic resources or documenting the culture of a particular community, ethnic group or artistic asset of the state. Support is available for artist's fees, production and post-production (editing) costs, and presentation costs for media projects. First time applicants must submit a letter of intent by December 1.
Requirements: West Virginia non-profit arts organizations and other not-for-profit organizations with an arts-related mission, media presenters or media arts groups are eligible. Applicants must provide a 50% cash match.
Restrictions: Organizations may not request support for current professional staff for media projects. The proposed project must be out of the regular scope of work for the organization.
Geographic Focus: West Virginia
Date(s) Application is Due: Mar 1
Contact: Barbara Anderson; (304) 558-0240; Barbie.J.Anderson@wv.gov
Internet: http://www.wvculture.org/arts/grantbook/community.htm#media
Sponsor: West Virginia Commission on the Arts
1900 Kanawha Boulevard E
Charleston, WV 25305-0300

West Virginia Commission on the Arts Mid-Size Institutions Support Grants **5040**
The purpose of the West Virginia Commission on the Arts Mid-Size Institutions Support Grants is to support and stabilize organizations by providing financial assistance toward their overall budgets for arts programming. Mid-size institutions are eligible for one operating support grant. The selection criteria include artistic excellence, effective management, community impact and year-round programming and accessibility to audiences and artists. Funding is between 2% and 15% of the organization's operating budget. Match is achieved through the organization's operating budget. New applicants must submit a letter of intent by December 1.
Requirements: Eligible applicant organizations must: have an operating budget of $150,000 to $1,000,000; have been incorporated as a non-profit for five years and have been a successful applicant to the West Virginia Commission on the Arts for three grant cycles; serve a broad cross-section of citizens, including but not be limited to citizens of varying ages, ethnicities, abilities, gender, income and educational level, with reasonable outreach to be inclusive; demonstrate compliance with Section 504 of the Rehabilitation Act and the Americans with Disabilities Act; and provide longstanding arts service, welcome and outreach to state and regional audiences.
Restrictions: Ineligible applicants include the following: organizations whose primary thrust is education and which award academic credits, i.e., colleges, universities and other degree-granting institutions; organizations receiving operating funds from other state agencies; organizations whose main purpose is not the arts; divisions or departments of larger institutions; and national service organizations.
Geographic Focus: West Virginia
Date(s) Application is Due: Mar 1
Contact: Barbara Anderson; (304) 558-0240; Barbie.J.Anderson@wv.gov
Internet: http://www.wvculture.org/arts/grantbook/generalcats.htm#mid
Sponsor: West Virginia Commission on the Arts
1900 Kanawha Boulevard E
Charleston, WV 25305-0300

West Virginia Commission on the Arts Mini Grants **5041**
The West Virginia Commission on the Arts Mini Grants are designed for individual West Virginia schools or other sponsors that do not present a season of events. Sponsors may request funding to assist with the presentation of West Virginia artists in performances, workshops, and other projects. The program has limited funds that are available on a first-come, first-served basis. Applications from schools that have not already received a mini-grant for the fiscal year will receive funding priority. The applicant may request up to 50% of artist fees and travel expenses up to $1,000.
Requirements: Schools, non-profit arts organizations or other community organizations incorporating the arts into their mission are eligible. Organizations must be exempt from federal income tax under Section 501(c)3 of the Internal Revenue Code and be chartered in West Virginia as a nonprofit organization for at least one year prior to application. Applications must be received at least six weeks prior to the starting date of the project and include artist contracts and resumes.
Restrictions: Sponsors that have already received a grant through a general grant program are not eligible for mini grants in the same fiscal year.
Geographic Focus: West Virginia
Date(s) Application is Due: Mar 1
Contact: Barbara Anderson; (304) 558-0240; Barbie.J.Anderson@wv.gov
Internet: http://www.wvculture.org/arts/grantbook/community.htm#mini
Sponsor: West Virginia Commission on the Arts
1900 Kanawha Boulevard E
Charleston, WV 25305-0300

West Virginia Commission on the Arts Peer Assistance Network Grants **5042**
The purpose of the West Virginia Commission on the Arts Peer Assistance Network Grants is to increase the stability and capacity of West Virginia arts organizations. By exchanging advice among peers who manage similar programs and projects, the Peer Assistance Network provides a support structure and communication network for arts organizations. Highly skilled arts leaders share their expertise and strengthen the overall arts community in West Virginia. Applicants may request up to two free advisory sessions with arts educators, arts administrators, and artists who have received facilitation training and have areas of expertise to share. The advisors can be scheduled to come to local communities to meet with board of directors to facilitate and advise. Areas of assistance include audience development, fundraising, budgeting, strategic planning, board development, marketing, arts in education projects, technical theater needs, diversity and accessibility training, organizational assessment, artist cooperatives and computer uses among others. Advisors are provided a stipend and travel costs. There are no application deadlines.
Requirements: Non-profit arts and community organizations that provide arts experiences for community members are eligible. Non-profit organizations may also apply on the behalf of artists in their community. Application forms are available online or by contacting staff.
Geographic Focus: West Virginia
Contact: Barbara Anderson; (304) 558-0240; Barbie.J.Anderson@wv.gov
Internet: http://www.wvculture.org/arts/grantbook/tech.htm#peer
Sponsor: West Virginia Commission on the Arts
1900 Kanawha Boulevard E
Charleston, WV 25305-0300

West Virginia Commission on the Arts Performing Arts Grants **5043**
The primary purpose of the West Virginia Commission on the Arts Performing Arts Grants is to provide funding for West Virginia arts organizations and communities in the creation and presentation of new works and the production of existing works in the performing arts. Applicants should contact arts staff to discuss proposals before applying. Music, theater, and dance groups, who are self-presenters and produce existing works in the performing arts, may request assistance to support up to 50% or performing and technical artist fees. These costs may include choreographers, directors, and music directors or scenic, costume, lighting, sound and set designers. First time applicants must submit a letter of intent by December 1.
Requirements: West Virginia non-profit arts organizations and communities are eligible. Applicant must provide a 50% cash match.
Restrictions: Permanent company artists and full-time employees are not eligible.
Geographic Focus: West Virginia

Date(s) Application is Due: Mar 1
Contact: Barbara Anderson; (304) 558-0240; Barbie.J.Anderson@wv.gov
Internet: http://www.wvculture.org/arts/grantbook/community.htm#presenting
Sponsor: West Virginia Commission on the Arts
1900 Kanawha Boulevard E
Charleston, WV 25305-0300

West Virginia Commission on the Arts Presenting Artists Grants — 5044

The primary purpose of the West Virginia Commission on the Arts Presenting Artists Grants is to enable West Virginia sponsors to present national, regional and in-state touring groups as performing, literary, visual, and media artists or exhibitions in their communities, arts facilities and schools. A second sites program offers sponsors and presenters support to present West Virginia artist(s) in a run-out performance. A run-out performance is the presentation of a touring West Virginia theater company, dance company, or orchestra at a second location for a performance that originates in the home community of the touring group. Each applicant is eligible for support for no more than three run-out performances per fiscal year. Run-out assistance is available for up to 50% of the company's contract fee and travel costs up to a maximum of $4,000 per event. First-time applicants are required to submit a letter of intent by December 1.
Requirements: West Virginia nonprofit arts organizations and communities are eligible. A 50% match is required.
Geographic Focus: West Virginia
Date(s) Application is Due: Mar 1
Contact: Barbara Anderson; (304) 558-0240; Barbie.J.Anderson@wv.gov
Internet: http://www.wvculture.org/arts/grantbook/community.htm#presenting
Sponsor: West Virginia Commission on the Arts
1900 Kanawha Boulevard E
Charleston, WV 25305-0300

West Virginia Commission on the Arts Professional Development Grants — 5045

The purpose of the West Virginia Commission on the Arts Professional Development for Artists Grants is to acknowledge the significant contribution that artists make to the quality of life in local communities and the region by supporting the ability of artists to enhance, expand, or improve their own work and advancing that work to a higher creative and professional level. Emerging and professional artists are eligible to apply for support to expand or improve their own work or to share their expertise with others. Organizations are eligible to apply for support to create, expand, or improve programs that support individual artists. This can include the following: self-designed apprenticeships (joint application must be filed by master and apprentice); collaborations with peers or community organizations; new equipment (excluding computers except where it is the primary tool used); materials to pursue new departures in artists' work; costs of professional development workshops (travel, registration fees, meals and lodging); and materials used for educational and community settings. Funding is limited to 75% for the first year and 50% for subsequent years. The maximum is $2,500 for individual artist projects and $5,000 for arts organization projects.
Requirements: Individual artists who are at least eighteen years old and legal residents of West Virginia for at least one year before the application deadline are eligible. Emerging and professional artists are eligible. Applicants creating work under the supervision of a master artist or instructor will be reviewed on a case-by-case basis. Non-profit West Virginia arts organizations that are expanding their services to better meet the needs of artists are eligible. A 25% match is required for the first year and a 50% match is required for subsequent years.
Geographic Focus: West Virginia
Date(s) Application is Due: Feb 1
Contact: Barbara Anderson; (304) 558-0240; Barbie.J.Anderson@wv.gov
Internet: http://www.wvculture.org/arts/grantbook/direct.htm#individ
Sponsor: West Virginia Commission on the Arts
1900 Kanawha Boulevard E
Charleston, WV 25305-0300

West Virginia Commission on the Arts Re-Granting Grants — 5046

The purpose of the West Virginia Commission on the Arts Re-Granting Grants is to allow arts organizations with a mission of community arts support to designate funds for re-granting according to community need. First time applicants must submit a letter of intent by December 1.
Requirements: West Virginia non-profit arts organizations and other not-for-profit organizations with an arts-related mission, which are interested in re-granting funds for arts activities based on community identified need are eligible. Applications must include a copy of their current or proposed re-granting guidelines in addition to a narrative that answers the following: what organizations/individuals within the community have been identified as possible recipients of re-granting funds; what application process will be used; are grants to be project oriented and if not, how will awards be determined; what funding levels will be set for grant awards. If the applicant organization does not currently have a re-granting program in place, the Arts staff can provide samples guidelines for successful re-granting programs. A 50% cash match is required.
Geographic Focus: West Virginia
Date(s) Application is Due: Mar 1
Amount of Grant: 6,000 USD
Contact: Barbara Anderson; (304) 558-0240; Barbie.J.Anderson@wv.gov
Internet: http://www.wvculture.org/arts/grantbook/community.htm#regrant
Sponsor: West Virginia Commission on the Arts
1900 Kanawha Boulevard E
Charleston, WV 25305-0300

West Virginia Commission on the Arts Short-Term Artist Residencies — 5047

The West Virginia Commission on the Arts Short-Term Artist Residencies primary purpose is to provide funding for curriculum-based, hands-on projects that involve an identified group of students and teachers in the creative process and integrate the arts into daily instruction. Projects must provide teachers with the tools that will enable them to continue to utilize the arts after the residency is completed. Residency projects (1 - 4 weeks or total of 5 - 20 days over a longer period of time) present an artist in a series of programs that demonstrate his/her artistry and skills. Residencies are a partnership between the sponsor, whether a school or community, and the artist. The residency should be organized to meet specific goals developed by a residency committee and should stress the creative aspects of the artist's work including interpretation of the training and skills required to be an artist. All residencies should be developed using the West Virginia Department of Education Fine Arts Content Standards and Objectives.
Requirements: Residency sponsors may be West Virginia schools, community arts organizations, arts institutions, or libraries. The eligibility of other types of organizations will be considered case-by-case. Applicant must provide a 50% cash match.
Geographic Focus: West Virginia
Date(s) Application is Due: Mar 1
Contact: Barbara Anderson; (304) 558-0240; Barbie.J.Anderson@wv.gov
Internet: http://www.wvculture.org/arts/grantbook/artsined.htm#short
Sponsor: West Virginia Commission on the Arts
1900 Kanawha Boulevard E
Charleston, WV 25305-0300

West Virginia Commission on the Arts Special Projects Grants — 5048

The purpose of the West Virginia Commission on the Arts Special Projects Grants is to provide funding for new and ongoing projects that establish, expand or advance both school curriculum and arts education programming. Funding supports projects that actively engage students or educators beyond arts "exposure" experiences. These projects typically occur in classroom or school settings but support is also available for projects benefiting students, teachers, or artists occurring outside of school. Proposals might include, but are not limited to: teacher or student hands-on arts workshops, development of education programs by artists or arts organizations that will tour the schools; summer or after-school programs; creation of educational materials in conjunction with arts programs; projects that strengthen a current school arts program by adding unavailable components; and innovative partnerships between schools and community arts organizations. Funding is limited to 50% of the fees for artists, specialists, consultants; equipment/materials required to develop the project is limited to $150.
Requirements: West Virginia schools, non-profit arts organizations or other community organizations incorporating the arts into their mission. Projects should be developed using the West Virginia Department of Education Fine Arts Content Standards and Objectives. A 50% cash match is required.
Geographic Focus: West Virginia
Date(s) Application is Due: Mar 1
Contact: Barbara Anderson; (304) 558-0240; Barbie.J.Anderson@wv.gov
Internet: http://www.wvculture.org/arts/grantbook/artsined.htm#special
Sponsor: West Virginia Commission on the Arts
1900 Kanawha Boulevard E
Charleston, WV 25305-0300

West Virginia Commission on the Arts Staffing Support Grants — 5049

The purpose of the West Virginia Commission on the Arts Staffing Support Grants is to provide support for staff positions. The process creates the optimum environment and support for success for each applicant organization and furthers the goal of strengthening arts organizations and expanding capacity. Funding provides support and technical assistance for full- or part-time non-profit arts management staff positions and management interns. Phased support for arts management staff is provided: 75% in year one; 50% in year two; and 25% in year three. Organizations with paid managers may apply for assistance of 50% of the salary for an arts management intern not to exceed $3,000. A letter of intent must be submitted by December 1.
Requirements: West Virginia non-profit arts organizations currently with or without staff, which have been in existence for a minimum of two years are eligible. The organization must have an operating budget of not less than $25,000. A long-range plan indicating the need for and responsibilities of staff position must accompany the application.
Geographic Focus: West Virginia
Date(s) Application is Due: Mar 1
Contact: Barbara Anderson; (304) 558-0240; Barbie.J.Anderson@wv.gov
Internet: http://www.wvculture.org/arts/grantbook/community.htm#staff
Sponsor: West Virginia Commission on the Arts
1900 Kanawha Boulevard E
Charleston, WV 25305-0300

West Virginia Commission on the Arts Travel and Training Grants — 5050

The primary purpose of the West Virginia Commission on the Arts Travel and Training Grants is to provide support for professional development travel costs. The program encourages artistic exposure to new works, especially experimental or avant-garde works, and work by rural and culturally diverse artists. Funding supports artists, arts administrators and arts educators of all-volunteer or professionally staffed non-profit arts organizations to attend seminars, conferences, workshops, and showcases of national significance or importance to their field of expertise outside of the state of West Virginia. Events of a national scope that are scheduled within the state of West Virginia will be considered for funding. Funding is for 50% of eligible expenses (excluding registration fees) with the following limits: first time attendance up to $300; second time attendance up to $200; and third time attendance up to $100. Application should be made no later than six weeks prior to the event.

Requirements: Any West Virginia working artist, arts administrator and or arts educator is eligible. A 50% cash match is required.
Restrictions: Individual applicants may receive only one Grant per fiscal year. No more than three staff members from one organization may receive a Grant during a fiscal year.
Geographic Focus: West Virginia
Amount of Grant: 100 - 300 USD
Contact: Barbara Anderson; (304) 558-0240; Barbie.J.Anderson@wv.gov
Internet: http://www.wvculture.org/arts/grantbook/tech.htm#training
Sponsor: West Virginia Commission on the Arts
1900 Kanawha Boulevard E
Charleston, WV 25305-0300

West Virginia Commission on the Arts Visual Arts Grants 5051
The purpose of the West Virginia Commission on the Arts Visual Arts Grants is to support performances and exhibitions, conservation and care of art collections, artist residencies and production of catalogs for West Virginia artists. Funding opportunities include artist fees for guest lecturers, performances, and curators. Other costs eligible for up to 50% support include exhibition rental, one-way shipping and special installation costs, insurance and security. The maximum funding per exhibit is $10,000. First time applicants must submit a letter of intent by December 1.
Requirements: West Virginia non-profit museums and galleries, art centers and alternative spaces are eligible. A 50% cash match is required.
Geographic Focus: West Virginia
Date(s) Application is Due: Mar 1
Contact: Barbara Anderson; (304) 558-0240; Barbie.J.Anderson@wv.gov
Internet: http://www.wvculture.org/arts/grantbook/community.htm#visual
Sponsor: West Virginia Commission on the Arts
1900 Kanawha Boulevard E
Charleston, WV 25305-0300

WestWind Foundation Environment Grants 5052
Concerned about the global loss of forest cover and biodiversity, the Trustees of the WestWind Foundation decided to create an Environment Program that would support effective NGOs that address these issues. In late 2006, WestWind formally launched its new climate initiative. The initiative supports non-profit organizations that are working throughout the Southeast United States to build public support for immediate action on climate change. The foundation will consider a range of strategies, but has prioritized organizations working to: promote state and/or regional collaborative action through creative partnerships with business; launch grassroots campaigns and educational efforts, particularly to stop the construction of new coal-fired power plants; or enable state and/or local government action by working with local leaders. Applicants should submit an online Letter of Inquiry (LOI) prior to the annual deadline. Typically, WestWind will respond to LOIs between 4 to 6 weeks after the letter has been received.
Requirements: Non-profit organizations interested in submitting an LOI for review should check the website for updates on the LOI submission process. Any environmental organization can submit a letter of inquiry to WestWind as long as the NGO has its 501(c)3 IRS determination letter.
Geographic Focus: All States
Date(s) Application is Due: Sep 1
Contact: Roxana Bonnell, (434) 977-5762, ext. 24; fax (434) 977-3176; bonnell@westwindfoundation.org or info@westwindfoundation.org
Internet: http://www.westwindfoundation.org/program-areas/environment-program/
Sponsor: WestWind Foundation
204 East High Street
Charlottesville, VA 22902

Weyerhaeuser Company Foundation Grants 5053
The foundation's mission is to improve the quality of life in communities where Weyerhaeuser has a major presence and to provide leadership that increases public understanding of issues where society's needs intersect with the interests of the forest products industry. Community service grants include awards in the fields of education and youth, health and welfare, civic and community improvement, and culture and the arts. In addition to community grants, industry-related awards are made to educational institutions, environmental groups, and professional organizations that promote further understanding of how the forest products industry responds to a changing society. Types of support include seed money, building construction/renovation, equipment acquisition, employee-related scholarships, publication, conferences and seminars, fellowships, lectureships, operating budgets, research, program development, employee matching gifts, and technical assistance. Applicants should send a short letter that introduces the project and sponsoring organization and provide tax-exempt status evidence. If further consideration is warranted, the foundation may ask for additional information or a formal proposal. Proposals may be submitted at any time.
Requirements: Applying organizations must have nonprofit, tax-exempt status. To be considered for funding, an organization must: serve a community within a 50-mile radius of a major Weyerhaeuser facility; support a state-wide issue of interest to the Foundation and Weyerhaeuser in the key states of Alabama, Arkansas, Louisiana, Mississippi, North Carolina, Oklahoma, Oregon or Washington; or support a selected, high-priority national or international initiative directly related to the sustainability and importance of working forests. A limited number of smaller awards are also made to other locales where fewer employees are based.
Restrictions: Grants are not awarded to individuals or for political campaigns, activities that influence legislation, religious organizations seeking funds for theological purposes, or funds to purchase tickets or tables at fundraising benefits.
Geographic Focus: Alabama, Arizona, Arkansas, California, Colorado, District of Columbia, Georgia, Idaho, Illinois, Kentucky, Louisiana, Maryland, Michigan, Minnesota, Mississippi, Missouri, New Hampshire, New Jersey, New Mexico, North Carolina, Ohio, Oklahoma, Oregon, Pennsylvania, South Carolina, Texas, Utah, Virginia, Washington, West Virginia, Wisconsin
Date(s) Application is Due: Aug 31
Contact: Anne Levya; (253) 924-3159; fax (253) 924-3658; foundation@weyerhaeuser.com
Internet: http://www.weyerhaeuser.com/Sustainability/Foundation
Sponsor: Weyerhaeuser Company Foundation
P.O. Box 9777
Federal Way, WA 98063-9777

Weyerhaeuser Family Environment, Conservation and Preservation Grants 5054
The Weyerhaeuser Family Foundation supports programs of national and international significance that promote the welfare of human and natural resources. These efforts will enhance the creativity, strengths and skills already possessed by those in need and reinforce the sustaining processes inherent in nature. The Foundation supports multi-site, national or international projects that preserve and protect the environment, promise better utilization of scarce resources and forestry projects. Multi-site, national and international educational projects will also be considered. The Letter of Intent is the first step in the application process and should be no more than two pages, to which you must attach a one-page budget summary and an Application Cover Sheet-General Program.
Requirements: U.S. nonprofit, tax-exempt organizations are eligible.
Restrictions: The General Program does not fund projects serving only local or regional domestic areas; to be eligible, projects must be multi-site, national or international. In addition, the Foundation will not consider proposals in the following areas: books or media projects, unless the project is connected to other areas of Foundation interest; capital projects; individuals, scholarships or fellowships; land acquisitions or trades; lobbying activity; ongoing projects or general operating support for an organization; organizations located outside the United States; or research projects.
Geographic Focus: All States
Date(s) Application is Due: Apr 1
Amount of Grant: 5,000 - 30,000 USD
Contact: Peter A. Konrad, Program Consultant; (303) 993-5385
Internet: http://www.wfamilyfoundation.org/general_program.html
Sponsor: Weyerhaeuser Family Foundation
2000 Wells Fargo Place, 30 East Seventh Street
St. Paul, MN 55101-4930

Whatcom Community Foundation Grants 5055
Whatcom Community Foundation is a nonprofit, publicly-supported philanthropic institution that manages a pool of charitable funds whose income is used to meet the changing needs of the greater Whatcom County community. The Foundation serves as a funding partner to area nonprofits that engage in community-building projects in Whatcom County. Funding is provided in the following fields: arts and culture; children with special healthcare needs; environment; mental health; and youth and family. Through the South Fork Community Fund, awards are also made to support effective educational, social and recreational programs, and services for children, youth and families to help build community in the South Fork Valley area. Additional information regarding funding available and deadlines is posted to the website as it becomes available.
Requirements: Washington tax-exempt nonprofit organizations serving Whatcom County are eligible. The Foundation is primarily interested in working with organizations and individuals to build community capacity, which is defined as the combined influence of the community's commitment, resources, and skills which can be utilized to build on community strengths and address community challenges.
Restrictions: The Foundation will not: review incomplete grant applications or those out of the requested format; make grants when the activities are not clearly described; make grants when the outcomes are not specific or realistic; make grants when the income and expense statements are incomplete or unclear; make grants for capital requests (bricks and mortar), endowment funds, debt retirement, political campaigns, religious activities, memberships in civic organizations or trade associations, courtesy advertising, tickets for benefits, and fundraising events; make grants to individuals or for-profit organizations; or make grants to organizations that discriminate on the basis of gender, religion, sexual orientation, ethnicity, national origin or physical ability. The Foundation is less likely to: fund organizational or operating support; make grants for more than one year; support one-time events; make grants that provide direct service without building community; make grants over $10,000; make grants directly or indirectly to governmental organizations; or make grants for capital equipment over $500.
Geographic Focus: Washington
Date(s) Application is Due: Jan 31
Amount of Grant: 1,000 - 10,000 USD
Contact: Pamela Jons; (360) 671-6463; fax (360) 671-6437; pjons@whatcomcf.org
Internet: http://www.whatcomcf.org/apply_for_grant.html
Sponsor: Whatcom Community Foundation
119 Grand Avenue, Suite A
Bellingham, WA 98225

Whirlpool Foundation Grants 5056
Building on its history of concern for the communities in which Whirlpool operates, the foundation gives priority to projects addressing three strategic issues: lifelong learning, comprising programs addressing basic education, job training or retraining, and continuing education; cultural diversity, which includes support of programs that enable communities to appreciate diversity and promote better understanding among people through the study of language, customs, and traditions, and innovative cultural exchanges; and quality family life, which supports innovative community-based responses designed to strengthen families, improve parenting capabilities, and address the balance between parenting and job performance.

Foundation resources are allocated across three programs—foundation grants; employee-directed programs, such as matching gifts and Dollars for Doers programs; and scholarships for employees' dependents. Additional types of support include matching funds, operating budgets, annual campaigns, emergency funds, building funds, equipment, and research. Applications are reviewed four times annually. Applicants are encouraged to contact the office for company operating areas and for additional information including where to submit applications.
Requirements: Tax-exempt organizations worldwide in Whirlpool communities are eligible.
Restrictions: Grants will not be made to individuals; for-profit organizations; political causes; religious-related organizations; social, labor, veterans, or fraternal organizations; athletic associations and events; fund-raising benefits; United Way agencies seeking general operating support; or national groups whose local chapters have already received support.
Geographic Focus: All States
Amount of Grant: 1,000 - 5,000 USD
Contact: Pamela Silcox; (269) 923-5584; fax (269) 925-0154; pamela_j_silcox@whirlpool.com
Internet: http://www.whirlpoolcorp.com/responsibility/building_communities/whirlpool_foundation.aspx
Sponsor: Whirlpool Foundation
2000 North M-63
Benton Harbor, MI 49022-2692

White County Community Foundation Grants 5057
The White County Community Foundation Grants fund projects in the following categories: education - to develop the untapped capacities of those of all ages, families, or communities; human services - to achieve a positive change in the conditions that adversely affect the elderly, disabled, or economically disadvantaged; recreation - to create or expand family-oriented leisure time opportunities; arts and culture - to encourage and stimulate the arts and historical preservation; citizenship - to generate an increased level of volunteerism, increased county-wide cooperation, and new leadership; environment - to help protect or enhance the environment that must support our life systems beyond the next century; and economic - to generate economic development activity within the area of direct job creation opportunity in White County. Priority is given to projects that: reach as many people as possible; identify and address an immediate community need; improve the ability of the organization to serve the community over the long-term; are run by non-profit organization; serve White County; and demonstrate fundraising from sources other that the Foundation as well as support from within the requesting organization.
Requirements: Before applying, organizations should contact the Foundation to verify deadlines and funding priorities, and to ensure they have the current application form. Once applicants reach this stage, they should include the following information with the online or hard copy application: a brief description of the organization; a narrative on the nature, purpose, and benefits of the project; a description of the project coordination; a project timeline with anticipated start and completion dates; a detailed budget; funding sources and future plan for funding; the impact of the project on the community; organization's most recent year-end financial statements and current operating budget; IRS determination letter; organization's board members; board member authorization for project funding.
Restrictions: The following projects are not eligible for funding: individuals; projects outside the White County area; programs normally funded by local government; projects to fund an endowment, ongoing operating budget, existing deficit, debt reduction; or multi-year, long-term funding; religious activities that predominantly serve one denomination; special events such as parades, festivals, and sporting activities; political organizations or campaigns; national and state fundraising efforts; and projects that indicate discrimination.
Geographic Focus: Indiana
Contact: Lesley Wineland Goss; (574) 583-6911; fax (574) 583-8757; director@whitecf.org
Internet: http://www.whitecf.org/CommGrant.html
Sponsor: White County Community Foundation
1001 South Main Street
Monticello, IN 47960

Whitehorse Foundation Grants 5058
The Whitehorse Foundation was established in 1990 as a supporting organization of The Seattle Foundation. The mission of The Whitehorse Foundation is to fund organizations working to improve the quality of life for residents of Snohomish County, Washington. Each grant application to the Foundation is thoughtfully considered by the Foundation's Board of Trustees. There is a two-step application process. The first step in seeking support is to submit a concise two-page letter of inquiry describing your project and request. The second step is a formal application process for those requests that are determined to meet the Foundation's funding criteria. Letters of inquiry can be submitted at any time and the board meets twice a year to consider funding requests. Grants are made to nonprofit organizations for project support or ongoing operating support. The Foundation is interested in programs in the early stages of development, which convey an achievable funding plan (demonstrating strong community commitment) or a compelling impact. The Foundation is interested in programs that: focus on prevention and root causes of problems rather than intervention; address many problems at once, rather than one problem at a time; strengthen families' capacity to support, nurture and guide their children; promote responsible parenthood to improve children's emotional, economic and social well-being; enable families to acquire the knowledge and skills needed for self-sufficiency; involve families and community residents in program design, development and management; will have a significant and ongoing impact; and offer opportunities for leveraging resources by forming partnerships with other grantmakers, other nonprofits, the government and the private sector.
Requirements: The Whitehorse Foundation supports nonprofit organizations in Snohomish County that work to improve the lives of children, youth and families. All applicant organizations must qualify as tax-exempt under section 501(c)3 of the IRS code.
Geographic Focus: Washington
Amount of Grant: Up to 250,000 USD
Contact: Ceil Erickson, Grantmaking Director; (206) 515-2131 or (206) 515-2109; fax (206) 622-7673; c.erickson@seattlefoundation.org or grantmaking@seattlefoundation.org
Internet: http://www.seattlefoundation.org/nonprofits/whitehorse/Pages/Whitehorse Foundation.aspx
Sponsor: Whitehorse Foundation
1200 Fifth Avenue, Suite 1300
Seattle, WA 98101-3151

Whiting Foundation Grants 5059
Whiting Foundation Grants award funds in the Genesee County area, including the city of Flint, Michigan, with emphasis on basic human needs, the needs of the underprivileged, and cultural activities. Awards range from $2,500 to $25,000.
Requirements: There is no application form. Applicants should submit a concise request describing the proposed activity and an explanation of the need. A current and future budget with details of administrative and salary expenses should be included.
Geographic Focus: Michigan
Date(s) Application is Due: Apr 30
Contact: Donald E. Johnson, Jr., President; (810) 767-3600
Sponsor: Whiting Foundation
718 Harrison Street
Flint, MI 48502

Whitley County Community Foundation Grants 5060
The Whitley County Community Foundation directs grants to charitable projects that will make a positive impact on Whitley County and its people, with particular interest in projects that shed new light on local needs and provide innovative, long-term solutions. Categories of support include: arts & culture, health, civic affairs, recreation, community development, welfare, and education. Grant reviews are scheduled on May 1 and December 1, but applicants are encouraged to submit proposals well in advance.
Requirements: The grant application must include a copy of the organization's IRS tax exempt letter, its annual budget and its projected budget. The cover letter should include: an introduction that establishes the organization's purpose and credibility, with background and accomplishments; a statement of need addressing why the project is necessary, documenting the need with statistics; what the organization hopes to accomplish with measurable objectives; what methods will be used to analyze results and refine the program; and how the project will be funded or maintained in the future. The packet may also include endorsement letters, a list of the board of directors, and a list of past support from other funders.
Restrictions: The Foundation is unlikely to support: annual campaigns, political activities, private schools, advertising, religious/sectarian causes, organizations outside the Whitley service area, and debt retirement.
Geographic Focus: Indiana
Date(s) Application is Due: May 1; Dec 1
Contact: September McConnell; (260) 244-5224; fax (260) 244-5724; sepwccf@gmail.com
Internet: http://whitleycountycommunityfoundation.org/grantseekers.html
Sponsor: Whitley County Community Foundation
400 North Whitley Street
Columbia City, IN 46725

Whitney Foundation Grants 5061
The Foundation awards grants to nonprofit organizations primarily in Minnesota in its areas of interest, including AIDS prevention, arts, children and youth services, education, and human services. Types of support include program development, annual campaigns, and continuing support. Application forms are not required. Awards range from $100 to $5,000.
Requirements: Eligible applicants must be 501(c)3 organizations.
Geographic Focus: Minnesota
Contact: Carol VanOrnum, (952) 835-2577
Sponsor: Whitney Foundation
601 Carlson Parkway
Minnetonka, MN 55305

WHO Foundation Education/Literacy Grants 5062
The foundation nationally supports grass-roots charities serving the overlooked needs of women and children. Grants are provided to organizations dedicated to education/literacy of children. Up to $5,000 can be requested for after-school programs, libraries, tutoring/mentoring programs, preschool or early education, shelters, child care programs, or other programs benefiting women and children.
Requirements: In order to qualify for funding, an organization must have a 501(c)3 status in their name (no affiliates accepted) and must have been incorporated for a minimum of 3 years prior to application. Funding will be considered, but not guaranteed, to charities which focus on education and meet the following criteria: total organization budget of $3 million or less; all Government funding totaling less than 30% of income; and, United Way funding of less than 30% of income. Funding requests must be made using the WHO Foundation application. Electronic and faxed submissions will not be accepted. Please note that the foundation does not wish to receive phone calls.
Restrictions: Funding will not be given to the following types of organizations: personal requests, loans or scholarships to individuals; religious organizations; building campaigns; and capital campaigns.
Geographic Focus: All States
Contact: Cindy Turek; (800) 946-4663; fax (972) 386-8736; who@beauticontrol.com
Internet: http://www.whofoundation.org/WHO_FundingEd.htm
Sponsor: WHO (Women Helping Others) Foundation
P.O. Box 816029
Dallas, TX 75381-6029

WHO Foundation General Grants 5063
The foundation nationally supports grass-roots charities serving the overlooked needs of women and children. Grants are provided to organizations serving women and/or children in the United States and Puerto Rico. Specific projects and programs addressing health, education, and social service needs are the priority. The foundation recognizes the value of new programs created to respond to changing needs and will consider funding projects of an original or pioneering nature within an existing organization. Application and guidelines are available for download at the sponsor's website.
Requirements: 501(c)3 nonprofit organizations in the United States and Puerto Rico are eligible. Organizations must have been incorporated for a minimum of three years prior to application. Preference will be given to organizations with an operating budget of $3 million or less, those not dependent upon government grants, and those with greater organizational program costs than personnel costs. Funding requests must be made using the WHO Foundation application. Electronic and faxed submissions will not be accepted.
Restrictions: The following types of organizations, activities or purposes will not be considered: personal requests, loans or scholarships to individuals; educational institutions; endowment campaigns; international programs or projects; government agencies; fiscal agents; religious organizations (including young Men's and Women's Christian Association); political causes, candidates, organizations or campaigns; foundations that are grant making institutions; advertising in charitable publications; sports organizations; labor groups; research projects; travel for individuals or groups; conferences, galas, charity balls, sponsorships, seminars, or reunions; capital campaigns; salaries; or building campaigns (i.e. Habitat for Humanity).
Geographic Focus: All States
Amount of Grant: 5,000 - 30,000 USD
Contact: Cindy Turek; (800) 946-4663; fax (972) 386-8736; who@beauticontrol.com
Internet: http://www.whofoundation.org/WHO_FundingCriteria.htm
Sponsor: WHO (Women Helping Others) Foundation
P.O. Box 816029
Dallas, TX 75381-6029

Widgeon Point Charitable Foundation Grants 5064
The foundation supports nonprofits in New York and Connecticut in its areas of interest, including secondary, higher, legal, and medical education; youth; zoos; museums; arts and culture; conservation and environment; historic preservation; family planning; libraries; and religion. Types of support include general operating budgets, capital campaigns, building funds, endowment funds, equipment acquisition, conferences and seminars, publications, and renovation projects. There are no application deadlines. Applicants should submit a two-page letter of application.
Requirements: Nonprofits in New York and Connecticut are eligible. The foundation does not accept unsolicited proposals. Interested and qualified organizations should submit a letter of inquiry prior to preparing a formal proposal. There are no specific deadlines.
Restrictions: Grants are not awarded to individuals or for endowments, capital costs, renovation, equipment, conferences, publications, and media projects.
Geographic Focus: Connecticut, New York
Contact: Jeffrey Coopersmith, (516) 483-5800 or (516) 483-5815; jcoopersmith@csvpc.com
Sponsor: Widgeon Point Charitable Foundation
50 Charles Lindbergh Boulevard, Suite 605
Uniondale, NY 11553-3650

Wieboldt Foundation Grants 5065
The Wieboldt Foundation limits its grant making to the Chicago metropolitan area. The foundation supports multi-issue community organizing groups that work in low-income neighborhoods, that are accountable to neighborhood residents, and through which people are empowered to have a major voice in shaping decisions that affect their lives.
Requirements: The Wieboldt Foundation supports organizations that: organize by enlisting and nurturing participation of a large number of neighborhood residents, organizations and institutions; recruit, develop, and formally train local leadership; enable local residents to develop an agenda, to devise strategies, and to carry out action effectively to address issues; demonstrate innovative strategies or create new local institutions that strengthen local community capacity; broaden their impact by working with other groups, whenever possible; are led by a board of directors that is representative of and accountable to community residents; show evidence of significant local fundraising. To be considered for financial support, send us a Letter of Inquiry to awards@wieboldt.org outlining the nature of your organization and rationale for funding from the Wieboldt Foundation. Letters of Inquiry will be reviewed by staff and a committee of the board who will make a determination on whether to invite your organization to submit a full proposal.
Restrictions: The Wieboldt Foundation generally does not fund individuals, studies and research, conferences, capital development, or direct or social service programs.
Geographic Focus: Illinois
Date(s) Application is Due: Jun 1; Aug 3; Oct 5; Nov 30
Contact: Regina McGraw; (312) 786-9377, ext. 1; fax (312) 786-9232; reginam@wieboldt.org
Internet: http://wieboldt.org/grant-guidelines/
Sponsor: Wieboldt Foundation
53 West Jackson Boulivard, Suite 838
Chicago, IL 60604

Wilbur and Patsy Bradley Family Foundation Grants 5066
Established in Missouri in 2000, the Wilbur and Patsy Bradley Family Foundation offers support to the arts, higher education programs, and Protestant agencies and churches throughout the State of Missouri. Since there are no application forms, applicants should forward a letter on their organization's letterhead outlining the project and budgetary needs. There are no annual deadlines, and grants range from $500 to $1,500.
Requirements: Applicants must serve the residents of Missouri. The Foundation pays particular attention to those that serve the communities of Lebanon or Springfield.
Geographic Focus: All States, Missouri
Amount of Grant: 500 - 1,500 USD
Contact: Wilbur H. Bradley, (417) 532-7784 or (417) 588-2281
Sponsor: Wilbur and Patsy Bradley Family Foundation
401 Blue Bird Lane
Lebanon, MO 65536-2079

Wilburforce Foundation Grants 5067
The foundation is dedicated to protecting nature's richness and diversity through funding programs that help preserve remaining wild places. The Foundation uses conservation science to identify specific priority regions in which it will fund. These regions correspond with the foundation focus on habitat security, focal species and wildlife linkages. Funding is focused on organizations that work to protect habitats that are critically important to sustaining abundant ecological communities in Western Canada and the Western United States. Types of support include: increasing the amount of protected critical wildlife habitat; assuring the quality and extent of key connective lands between core habitat areas; lessening immediate threats to critical wildlife habitats; improving management programs that preserve the ecological integrity of existing or proposed protected areas; increasing knowledge of wildlife populations and/or improving management plans that ensure the viability of focal species in a region; and building the capacity of grantees that are working to protect priority areas. Applicants who are interested in submitting a grant proposal must contact the appropriate regional staff member prior to developing a proposal. Guidelines are available online.
Requirements: Only applicant organizations from Alaska, Arizona, British Columbia, Nevada, New Mexico, Oregon, Utah, Washington, or Yellowstone to Yukon with tax-exempt status are eligible. For population programs, the foundation will consider funding educational or advocacy programs with a national or Pacific Northwest regional scope from organizations anywhere in the country.
Restrictions: The foundation generally will not consider any of the following types of projects: agricultural issues; air quality or other clean air programs; annual meetings, conferences, or symposia; energy-related programs; environmental education; environmental justice programs; habitat restoration; land acquisition and/or stewardship; marine or other water-only programs; pollution prevention or other pollution-related projects; salmon recovery programs; sustainable development or other economically-based programs; sprawl or growth management programs; transportation-related programs; wildlife rehabilitation programs; or youth education programs. Grants do not fund deficit financing; endowment funds; funding of individual scholarships or fellowships; individuals; schools or universities; cities, counties, or other governmental agencies; indirect costs; or loans.
Geographic Focus: Alaska, Arizona, Nevada, New Mexico, Oregon, Utah, Washington, Canada
Date(s) Application is Due: Feb 16; May 18; Aug 17; Nov 15
Contact: Tim Greyhavens; (206) 632-2325; fax (206) 632-2326; tim@wilburforce.org
Internet: http://www.wilburforce.org/grant_guidelines/index.html
Sponsor: Wilburforce Foundation
3601 Fremont Avenue N, Suite 304
Seattle, WA 98103-8753

WILD Foundation Grants 5068
Founded in 1974, WILD is the only international organization dedicated entirely and explicitly to wilderness protection around the world. WILD works to protect the planet's last wild places and the wildlife and people who depend upon them, because wilderness areas provide essential social, spiritual, biological and economic benefits. The WILD Foundation focuses on four main program areas: World Wilderness Congress, wilderness policy and research, communications and field projects. Refer to the Foundations website for more detailed information on each program of interest. There are no specific deadlines with which to adhere. Contact the Foundation for further application information and guidelines.
Geographic Focus: All States
Contact: Charlotte Baron; (303) 442-8811; fax (303) 442-8877; info@wild.org
Internet: http://www.wild.org/main/about/
Sponsor: WILD Foundation
717 Poplar Avenue
Boulder, CO 80304

Wild Rivers Community Foundation Holiday Partnership Grants 5069
The Wild Rivers Community Foundation hosts an annual Holiday Partnership to assist our community with raising resources over the holidays for those in need. Organizations in Del Norte and Curry County, who help provide emergency supplies, food, winter clothing, hygiene products and gifts to children and adults in the region during the upcoming holiday season are encouraged to link with each other during this program. The application and additional information are available at the website.
Requirements: Applicants must be nonprofit organizations serving children and adults in the counties of Del Norte or Curry.
Geographic Focus: California
Date(s) Application is Due: Nov 1
Contact: Geneva Wiki; (707) 465-1238; fax (707) 465-1209; gwiki@wildriverscf.org
Internet: http://www.wildriverscf.org/content/view/112/108/
Sponsor: Wild Rivers Community Foundation
879 J Street, Suite I
Crescent City, CA 95531

Wild Rivers Community Foundation Summer Youth Mini Grants 5070
The Wild Rivers Community Foundation is committed to supporting children and youth, and values programs that offer opportunities for them to learn, play and develop in a safe, productive setting while school is not in session. The Foundation recognizes that organizations offering summer programs for children and youth are integral to providing

those opportunities. Small grants are awarded to agencies to expand and enrich summer recreation programs for Del Norte and Curry County children operating between June and September. Grants are normally made for expenses such as sports and recreational equipment, arts and craft supplies, special events and field trips, and camperships for low-income participants. The Summer Youth Program often provides grants to help defray the costs of transportation, equipment, and scholarships. The application and additional information are available at the website.
Requirements: Applicants must be nonprofit organizations that provide summer youth programs in the counties of Del Norte or Curry.
Geographic Focus: California
Date(s) Application is Due: Apr 1
Contact: Gina Zottola; (707) 465-1238; fax (707) 465-1209; gzottola@wildriverscf.org
Internet: http://www.wildriverscf.org/content/view/106/
Sponsor: Wild Rivers Community Foundation
879 J Street, Suite I
Crescent City, CA 95531

Willary Foundation Grants 5071
The Willary Foundation supports projects that are interesting, creative, and imaginative and that benefit communities in northeastern Pennsylvania. The Foundation is particularly interested in projects that support leadership and the development of leadership in business, the economy, education, human services, government, the arts, media, and research. The Foundation gives preference to efforts that have a ripple effect in the community and those that are conducted in conjunction with other sources of funding. Willary seeks to foster both individuals and groups with unique, innovative, or unusual ideas and efforts. The application and samples of previously funded projects are available at the Foundation website.
Requirements: Individuals and nonprofits in Lackawanna and Luzerne counties, Pennsylvania, are eligible to apply.
Restrictions: Generally, Willary will not consider applications for capital campaigns and annual drives.
Geographic Focus: Pennsylvania
Date(s) Application is Due: Mar 10; Aug 27
Contact: Linda Donovan; (570) 961-6952; fax (570) 961-7269; info@willary.org
Internet: http://www.willary.org
Sponsor: Willary Foundation
P.O. Box 283
Scranton, PA 18501-0937

William A. Badger Foundation Grants 5072
The Nabors to Neighbors Foundation was created in 2007 to assist charitable organizations focusing on need based projects for direct programming, capital and operating initiatives. This is a family foundation dedicated to organizations that deliver measurable results, seek partnerships and collaborations, utilize their resources within their respective communities while working to increase equity for those most in need. The Foundation encourages nonprofit organizations to apply who specialize in, though not limited to, improving the lives of children, education and medical initiatives. The Foundation makes no geographic restrictions on distributions. However, it has been the practice of the Trustees to make grants within Whitfield County, specifically Dalton, located in north Georgia. Requests must be postmarked by February 1, July 9 or October 1 in order to be considered.
Requirements: The Nabors to Neighbors Foundation makes grants to qualified 501(c)3 organizations. All requests must include: background information on the organization, including a brief history, the organization's current address and phone number and the name and title or the primary contact; the goals, objectives, and budget for the one project or program for which funds are being requested; the amount of the grant requested; summary of how the funds will be used; supporting financial information on the organization, to include current financial status and listing of Board of Trustees; copy of organization's tax exemption letter from the Internal Revenue Service. Application form is available online and all requests must be postmarked by February 1, July 9 or October 1 in order to be considered.
Restrictions: Grants are not made to: individuals; an organization to be used as pass-through funds for an ineligible organization Faith-based organizations without a 501(c)3 exemption; organizations with political purposes, nor to organizations which discriminate on the basis of race, ethnic origin, sexual or religious preference, age or gender.
Geographic Focus: All States
Date(s) Application is Due: Feb 1; Jul 9; Oct 1
Contact: Trustee, c/o Wachovia Bank; grantinquiries8@wachovia.com
Internet: https://www.wachovia.com/foundation/v/index.jsp?vgnextoid=108bf296ac212210VgnVCM100000617d6fa2RCRD&vgnextfmt=default
Sponsor: Nabors to Neighbors Foundation
3280 Peachtree Road NE, Suite 400, MC G0141-041
Atlanta, GA 30305

William A. Miller Foundation Grants 5073
Established through a donation by Jayne Miller in Indiana in 2000, the William A. Miller Foundation gives support primarily in Hagerstown, Indiana. Its primary focus is on community and economic development, and it will consider support for the arts, community education, and general operating support for community area non-profits. There are no specific application formats or deadlines, and applicants should apply directly to the U.S. Bank office in the form of a two- to three-page letter.
Geographic Focus: Indiana
Contact: Trustee; (765) 965-2293
Sponsor: William A. Miller Foundation
P.O. Box 1118
Cincinnati, OH 45201-1118

William and Flora Hewlett Foundation Environmental Grants 5074
The William and Flora Hewlett Foundation has been making grants since 1967 to solve social and environmental problems at home and around the world. The Foundation's Environmental Grants goals are to: conserve the Western United States and Canada for wildlife and people; slow global climate change by reducing greenhouse gas emissions; ensure that the United States energy supply is clean and consumption is efficient; and address environmental problems that disproportionately affect disadvantaged communities in the San Francisco Bay Area. Support for western conservation support four key strategies: land (protecting large open spaces); water (restoring river flows and conserve areas near rivers and streams); energy (reducing fossil fuel development and increase energy efficiency and renewable energy sources; and broad-based support (building broad-based support for land, water, and energy goals among key stakeholders). Support for energy and climate pursue strategies in three areas: global climate policy; national energy policy; and sustainable transportation. Support for the San Francisco Bay Area is provided to regional organizations partnering with residents of these communities to: improve and expand urban parks; support outdoor recreation programs for youth; and improve public transportation available to these communities.
Requirements: Applicants whose project or organization aligns closely with the Foundation's goals and strategies, may submit a brief on-line letter of inquiry. Western conservation is supported in twelve states and three Canadian provinces: Alaska, Arizona, California, Colorado, Idaho, Montana, Nevada, New Mexico, Oregon, Washington, Wyoming, British Columbia, Alberta, and Yukon.
Restrictions: The Foundation does not consider requests to fund student aid, individual scholarships, construction, equipment and computer purchases, health research, or health education programs. Few, if any, letters of inquiry are funded. A full proposal should not be submitted unless expressly requested. The majority of awards are made to organizations by invitation. Due to the volume of submissions the Foundation does not respond to phone calls or emails regarding letters of inquiry. Submissions via the online letter of inquiry form receive a response within thirty days or as soon thereafter as possible.
Geographic Focus: All States, Canada
Contact: Tom Steinbach; (650) 234-4500; fax (650) 234-4501; info@hewlett.org
Internet: http://www.hewlett.org/programs/environment-program
Sponsor: William and Flora Hewlett Foundation
2121 Sand Hill Road
Menlo Park, CA 94025

William B. Dietrich Foundation Grants 5075
The Foundation awards funding to nonprofits preferably for local needs. There are no submission deadlines. Areas of interest include children, the elderly, AIDS, museums, and libraries.
Requirements: Applicants may apply in writing, outlining the nature of the organization, the intended use of funds requested. A copy of the Internal Revenue Service determination letter should be submitted.
Restrictions: No grants are provided for individuals.
Geographic Focus: All States
Contact: Frank G. Cooper, President; (215) 979-1919
Sponsor: William B. Dietrich Foundation
P.O. Box 58177
Philadelphia, PA 19102-8177

William B. Stokely Jr. Foundation Grants 5076
The Foundation participates in scholarship funding at various colleges and universities mainly in eastern Tennessee. Grants are made to the educational institutions, which then distribute funds through their scholarship programs. Consideration also is given to requests from the arts, health service, civic organizations, and youth services. The Foundation does not require completion of a formal application, nor are there established deadline dates. All proposals must be submitted in writing.
Geographic Focus: Tennessee
Amount of Grant: 250 - 100,000 USD
Contact: William Stokely III, President; (865) 966-4878
Sponsor: William B. Stokely Jr. Foundation
620 Campbell Station Road, Suite 27
Knoxville, TN 37922-1636

William Bingham Foundation Grants 5077
As a family foundation, the William Bingham Foundation furthers the philanthropic intent of its founder, Elizabeth Bingham Blossom, to support organizations in the fields of education, science, health and human services, and the arts. A current area of interest is unsolicited proposals from organizations currently addressing water quality issues related to hydraulic fracturing in the Marcellus Shale drilling areas in New York, West Virginia, Ohio, Maryland, and Virginia. Awards range from $10,000 to $35,000.
Requirements: Grants are made only to public U.S. charities and range in size depending on program budget and goals. Although there are no additional geographic restrictions, grants often reflect the needs of the communities in which Trustees reside. From time to time, the Foundation selects a particular area of interest for requests coming from organizations with which they do not currently have a relationship. Currently proposals are accepted only from organizations that have been invited to apply. Organizations that have been invited to submit a grant proposal may contact the Foundation to obtain application forms.
Restrictions: Capital grants for new construction are limited to projects that seek U.S. Green Building Council LEED (Leadership in Energy and Environmental Design) certification at least at the Silver level. Grants for renovation are limited to projects that seek LEED certification. The Foundation limits higher education grants to Colleges and Universities that have signed the American College and University Presidents Climate Commitment. No grants are made to individuals.

Geographic Focus: All States
Contact: Laura Gilbertson; (440) 331-6350; info@WBinghamFoundation.org
Internet: http://www.wbinghamfoundation.org/procedures.html
Sponsor: William Bingham Foundation
20325 Center Ridge Road, Suite 629
Rocky River, OH 44116-3554

William Blair and Company Foundation Grants 5078

Contributing to the community is an important part of the culture of William Blair and Company. The Foundation was officially established in Illinois in 1980, with giving primarily centered around metropolitan Chicago. All partners of the firm contribute part of their individual share of profits to the Foundation. Donation requests are made to the Foundation by partners and employees. The Foundation supports a broad range of causes including: civic affairs; public safety; arts and culture; higher education; youth-oriented activities; healthcare research; cultural affairs; and civic charities. Types of support include: annual campaigns; building and renovation; capital campaigns; general operating support; endowments; fellowships; internship programs; and scholarship funding. There are no specific deadlines or applications forms required. Funding typically ranges from $500 to $25,000.
Requirements: Requests can be made by sending a letter with a general description of the organization and its special purpose. Activities should have a significant impact on the Chicago metropolitan area.
Geographic Focus: Illinois
Contact: E. David Coolidge III, Vice President; (312) 236-1600
Sponsor: William Blair and Company Foundation
222 W Adams Street, 28th Floor
Chicago, IL 60606

William C. Kenney Watershed Protection Foundation Ecosystem Grants 5079

Established in California in 1994, the William C. Kenney Watershed Protection Foundation supports small, local environmental groups working to protect key threatened wild rivers in the Western United States and larger campaigns for ecosystems that contain significant wild rivers (i.e., the Arctic Refuge, southern Utah, Oregon, and California). Grants also support regional and national organizations that disseminate information and training on national policy issues that directly impact the work of local groups and projects that provide training and information in communication skills and strategies. Types of support include general operating support, technical assistance, capacity building, advocacy, and special projects. Previous grant recipients are eligible for opportunity grants.
Requirements: 501(c)3 nonprofit organizations in British Columbia or the Western United States, including Alaska, Arizona, California, Colorado, Idaho, Montana, Nevada, New Mexico, Oregon, Utah, Washington, and Wyoming, are eligible. Organizations must have annual operating budgets under $740,000, collaborate with other groups, be innovative, and produce measurable results.
Restrictions: Grants do not support watershed restoration, land acquisition, endowments, research, or legal work. The foundation does not accept unsolicited applications for its Leadership Grants.
Geographic Focus: Alaska, Arizona, California, Colorado, Idaho, Montana, Nevada, New Mexico, Oregon, Utah, Washington, Wyoming, Canada
Amount of Grant: Up to 30,000 USD
Contact: Jay P. Kenney; (303) 722-0722; fax (415) 369-9180; jay@kenneyfdn.org
Sponsor: William C. Kenney Watershed Protection Foundation
910 Gaylord Street
Denver, CO 80206-3754

William G. and Helen C. Hoffman Foundation Grants 5080

Helen C. Hoffman resided in the Village of South Orange, New Jersey. Her foundation was established in 1998 in memory of herself and her husband after the death of their daughter Corinne Blair. Her testamentary wish was to establish this foundation for charitable, religious, scientific, literary, and educational purposes. Her preference was to support blindness and its cure. Approximately 90% of the grants will provide support to the blind and, to medical research for the prevention of blindness. The remaining 10% will fund annual grants in the following areas of interest: education, the arts, environment and, social/civic causes. Requests must be received by January 15 for the March meeting and, August 22 for the October meeting. Application forms are available online. Applicants will receive notice acknowledging receipt of the grant request, and subsequently be notified of the grant declination or approval.
Requirements: Any U.S. 501(c)3 non-profit organizations may apply. Proposals should be submitted in the following format: completed Common Grant Application Form; an original Proposal Statement; an audited financial report and a current year operating budget; a copy of your official IRS Letter with your tax determination; a listing of your Board of Directors. Proposal Statements (second item in the above Format) should answer these questions: what are the objectives and expected outcomes of this program/project/request; what strategies will be used to accomplish your objective; what is the timeline for completion; if this is part of an on-going program, how long has it been in operation; what criteria will you use to measure success; if the request is not fully funded, what other sources can you engage; an Itemized budget should be included; please describe any collaborative ventures. Prior to the distribution of funds, all approved grantees must sign and return a Grant Agreement Form, stating that the funds will be used for the purpose intended. Progress reports and Completion reports must also be filed as required for your specific grant. All current grantees must be in good standing with required documentation prior to submitting new proposals to any foundation.
Restrictions: Grants are not made for political purposes, nor to organizations which discriminate on the basis of race, ethnic origin, sexual or religious preference, age or gender.
Geographic Focus: All States
Date(s) Application is Due: Jan 15; Aug 22
Amount of Grant: 5,000 - 15,000 USD
Contact: Wachovia Bank, N.A., Trustee; grantinquiries2@wachovia.com
Internet: https://www.wachovia.com/foundation/v/index.jsp?vgnextoid=522852199c0aa110VgnVCM1000004b0d1872RCRD&vgnextfmt=default
Sponsor: William G. and Helen C. Hoffman Foundation
190 River Road, NJ3132
Summit, NJ 07901

William G. Baker, Jr. Memorial Fund Grants 5081

The William G. Baker, Jr. Memorial Fund was established in 1964 by Mary S. Baker in memory of her husband. The fund continues the Baker's civic-minded philanthropic tradition, offering grants that range from $1,000 to $40,000. Its grant making program primarily benefits the residents of the greater Baltimore area. The Fund commits its resources to enhance the region's economy and quality of life through investments in a broadly defined cultural sector in which all residents may participate and thrive. Its grants will support artistic and cultural organizations and their partners that enhance an individual's sense of self and pleasure and make Baltimore a more attractive place to live, work and play.
Requirements: Organizations (or their fiscal agents) serving the Baltimore area that qualify as public charities under section 501(c)3 of the Internal Revenue Code and do not discriminate on the basis of race, creed, national origin, color, physical handicap, gender or sexual orientation are eligible to apply.
Restrictions: No grants will be made to individuals, or for religious/sectarian purposes or deficit financing.
Geographic Focus: Maryland
Date(s) Application is Due: Jan 1; Mar 3; Jul 7; Sep 26
Amount of Grant: 1,000 - 40,000 USD
Contact: Odessa Hampton, Program Assistant; (410) 332-4171; ohampton@bcf.org
Internet: http://www.bcf.org/ourgrants/ourgrantsdetail.aspx?grid=1
Sponsor: William G. Baker, Jr. Memorial Fund
2 East Read Street, 9th Floor
Baltimore, MD 21202

William G. Gilmore Foundation Grants 5082

The foundation supports nonprofits primarily in the San Francisco Bay Area, CA; some funding also in Pueblo, CO and Portland, OR. Giving primarily for the arts, health, and children, youth, and social services.
Requirements: California, Colorado, and Oregon nonprofits are eligible to apply. Contact the Foundation for additional application information.
Restrictions: No grants to individuals.
Geographic Focus: California, Colorado, Oregon
Amount of Grant: 1,000 - 50,000 USD
Contact: Faye Wilson, Executive Director; (415) 546-1400; fax (415) 391-8732
Sponsor: William G. Gilmore Foundation
120 Montgomery Street, Suite 1880
San Francisco, CA 94104-4317

William G. Kelley Foundation Grants 5083

The foundation's grants are available to help individuals and families overcome physical challenges. Grants are awarded based on physical and financial need. Priority will be given to applicants requesting assistance in the fields of assistive technology or universal design. Interested applicants are invited to send a letter of inquiry to the foundation, at the above address, describing the intended use of the funds, including estimates for materials and labor. Applicants should demonstrate financial need. One project grant will also be available to a nonprofit organization that provides support to individuals with physical challenges. Projects aiming to foster inclusion of people with challenges through accessibility and universal design will be given priority. Grant applications are accepted on a rolling basis. Application and guidelines are available online.
Requirements: Residents and nonprofit organizations of Essex and Middlesex Counties in Massachusetts may apply.
Geographic Focus: Massachusetts
Amount of Grant: Up to 2,000 USD
Contact: Grants Administrator; info@williamgkelley.org
Internet: http://www.williamgkelley.org/news_events.htm
Sponsor: William G. Kelley Foundation
1 Marlboro Road
Georgetown, MA 01833

William G. McGowan Charitable Fund Grants 5084

The fund awards grants to eligible nonprofit organizations that are devoted to three specific philanthropic goals: developing the talents and gifts of the very young, especially those who have been disenfranchised by virtue of low income status, inner-city conditions or family situations; funding for selected areas of medical research directed toward finding cures for, or relieving the pain and suffering of, those afflicted with debilitating conditions or diseases; and the McGowan Scholars program, which provides financial assistance to selected college and university students interested in pursuing an undergraduate or graduate degree at a college or university business school accredited by the International Association for Management Education or Association of Collegiate Business Schools and Programs.
Requirements: Nonprofit organizations in the following states and cities are eligible: Chicago, IL; District of Columbia and its Virginia suburbs; metropolitan Kansas City, western New York; and northeast Pennsylvania.
Restrictions: The fund does not support multiyear grants; accept requests online; or fund art or theatrical activities, building funds, church renovation campaigns, or endowments.
Geographic Focus: California, District of Columbia, Illinois, Missouri, New York, Pennsylvania, Virginia

Date(s) Application is Due: Jan 2; May 1; Sep 1
Amount of Grant: 10,000 - 100,000 USD
Contact: Bernard Goodrich; (301) 320-8570; fax (301) 320-8627; goodric@aol.com
Internet: http://www.mcgowanfund.org/guidelines.html
Sponsor: William G. McGowan Charitable Fund
P.O. Box 40515
Washington, DC 20016-0515

William G. Selby and Marie Selby Foundation Grants 5085
The purpose of the Foundation is to improve the quality of life to Sarasota County, Florida, and its bordering counties. Because of the Selby's interest in education, scholarships are also given annually to students from the local area for undergraduate study. The Foundation focuses its grant making on capital expenditures. Giving includes support of educational, human services, and arts programs.
Requirements: Giving is limited to Charlotte, DeSoto, Manatee, and Sarasota counties, Florida.
Restrictions: Generally, the foundation does not award contributions to other foundations, nor for installment grants. In addition, grants are not awarded for conferences, seminars, workshops, travel, surveys, advertising programs, fund-raising costs, seed grants, personal research, or the support of graduate study.
Geographic Focus: Florida
Date(s) Application is Due: Feb 1; Aug 1
Amount of Grant: 78,915 USD
Contact: Janet D. Noah; (941) 957-0442; fax (941) 957-3135; jnoah@selbyfdn.org
Internet: http://www.selbyfdn.org/
Sponsor: William G. Selby and Marie Selby Foundation
1800 Second Street, Suite 750
Sarasota, FL 34236

William H. Hannon Foundation Grants 5086
The foundation awards grants to eligible California nonprofit organizations in its areas of interest, including Roman Catholic education (elementary, secondary, and higher); churches; medical research; hospitals; health care and human services, especially for those least able to afford quality care; and needs of the disadvantaged, aged, sick, and the homeless. There are no application deadlines or forms. Applications should be sent at least three weeks before quarterly board meetings, in March, June, September, and December.
Requirements: California nonprofit organizations serving Los Angeles and southern California areas are eligible.
Geographic Focus: California
Contact: Kathleen Hannon Aikenhead; (310) 260-2470; williamhannonfdn@yahoo.com
Internet: http://www.hannonfoundation.org
Sponsor: William H. Hannon Foundation
729 Montana Avenue, Suite 5
Santa Monica, CA 90403

William J. and Dorothy K. O'Neill Foundation Grants 5087
Foundation grantmaking activities include family, health, arts and culture, community, animals, education, environment, employment, fatherhood, recreation, religion, law enforcement/crime, human services, and housing. Types of support include general operating support, program development, seed grants, and matching funds. The foundation has no formal application form; requests should be made in writing. Grants are awarded for capacity building activities that develop or improve the effectiveness, impact and strength of: the organization's Board of Trustees and/or its Board leadership; the organization's strategic plan; the organization's staff; and the organization's programs. Grant requests should include the amount requested; specific project including goals, objectives, approach, and methods; project budget and timeline; other sources of funding; evaluation plan; qualifications and experience of key personnel; description of organization; most recent annual report; and copy of IRS classification letter. Requests may be submitted at any time but will be considered four times each year when the grantmaking committee meets. Annual deadline dates may vary; contact program staff for exact dates.
Requirements: 501(c)3 organizations in metropolitan areas where O'Neill family members currently live are eligible, including Washington, DC; Naples, FL, area; Big Island, HI; Baltimore/Annapolis, MD; New York, NY area; Cincinnati/Cleveland, OH; Columbus and Licking County, OH; Richmond/Virginia Beach, VA; and Houston, TX.
Restrictions: The foundation does not make grants to individuals, to organizations that are wholly outside the United States, or in response to form letters for annual appeals.
Geographic Focus: District of Columbia, Florida, Hawaii, Maryland, New York, Ohio, Texas, Virginia
Date(s) Application is Due: Jan 24; Apr 25; Jul 18; Oct 10
Amount of Grant: 35,000 - 620,000 USD
Contact: Program Contact; (216) 831-4134; fax (216) 831-3779; oneillfdn@aol.com
Internet: http://www.oneillfdn.org/application.htm
Sponsor: William J. and Dorothy K. O'Neill Foundation
30195 Chagrin Boulevard, Suite 250
Cleveland, OH 44124

William J. Brace Charitable Trust 5088
The William J. Brace Charitable Trust was established in 1958 to support and promote quality educational, cultural, human-services, and health-care programming, with a preference for the following three areas: the education and health of children; the health and care of older adults; and hospitals in Kansas City, Missouri. Grant requests for general operating support and program support will be considered. Grants from the Trust are one year in duration. There are no application deadlines for the Brace Charitable Trust. Proposals are reviewed on an ongoing basis. Applicants may download the application and Missouri state guidelines at the grant website. Applicants are strongly encouraged to review the state guidelines for additional helpful information and clarifications on the three areas of interest.
Restrictions: The Brace Charitable Trust generally supports organizations that serve the residents of Kansas City, Missouri. Grant requests for capital support will not be considered.
Geographic Focus: Missouri
Contact: Spence Heddens; (816) 292-4301; Spence.heddens@baml.com
Internet: https://www.bankofamerica.com/philanthropic/fn_search.action
Sponsor: William J. Brace Charitable Trust
1200 Main Street, 14th Floor, P.O. Box 219119
Kansas City, MO 64121-9119

William L. and Victorine Q. Adams Foundation Grants 5089
Incorporated in 1984, The William L. and Victorine Q. Adams Foundation is a private, charitable organization dedicated to improving the lives of young people through consideration of funding requests from organizations whose mission is to improve education, strengthen neighborhoods and support institutions that will enhance the quality of life and general welfare of Baltimore's citizens. Primary fields of interest include: community and economic development; education; and human services. Funding comes in the form of general operating support. The annual application deadline is May 1. Recent awards have ranged from $500 to $16,000.
Requirements: Applicants must be 501(c)3 agencies serving the residents of Baltimore, Maryland, and its surrounding suburbs.
Geographic Focus: Maryland
Date(s) Application is Due: May 1
Contact: Blanche Rodgers; (410) 783-3216 or (410) 783-3208; brodgers@ar-companies.com
Internet: http://www.adamsfound.org/about/index.html
Sponsor: William L. and Victorine Q. Adams Foundation
1040 Park Avenue, Suite 300
Baltimore, MD 21201-5635

William M. Cage Library Trust Grants 5090
Established through a donation by William M. Cage in 1993, the William M. Cage Library Trust limits giving to the State of Virginia. Its primary field of interest is the support of public libraries. In lieu of a specific application form, applicants should submit an explanation of why the grant-maker is considered an appropriate donor for the project, along with a detailed description of the project and the amount of funding requested. The annual deadline is December 1.
Requirements: Only 501(c)3 organization located in, or supporting residents of, Virginia should apply.
Geographic Focus: Virginia
Date(s) Application is Due: Dec 1
Contact: John C. Cowan, Trustee; (540) 373-4331; fax (540) 371-8972
Sponsor: William M. Cage Library Trust
321 William Street
Fredericksburg, VA 22401-5831

William M. Weaver Foundation Grants 5091
Established in Texas in 2003 by the William M. Weaver Charitable Trust, the Foundation offers funding support primarily in Dawson County, Texas. Its major fields of interest include: community development; economic development; and Protestant agencies and churches. Financial support typically comes in the form of general operating costs. There are no specified application forms required, so interested parties should formulate a proposal in letter form. This two- or three-page approach should include a detailed program overview, budgetary needs, and any goals that the organization has established. There are no annual deadlines listed. Most recent grants have ranged from $5,000 to just over $100,000.
Requirements: Any 501(c)3 or Protestant agency/church serving the residents of Dawson County, Texas, are welcome to apply.
Geographic Focus: Texas
Contact: Elwood Freeman, (806) 872-5457
Sponsor: William M. Weaver Foundation
2651 JBS Parkway, Building 4, Suite E
Odessa, TX 79762

William McCaskey Chapman and Adaline Dinsmore Chapman Foundation Grants 5092
The William McCaskey & Adaline Dinsmore Chapman Foundation is a private foundation making grants for a variety of K-12 educational purposes to nonprofit organizations serving young people in the coastal communities of Monterey County, California. The foundation awards grants to California educational organizations that provide financial assistance to children under the age of 19 years who exhibit academic potential and financial need. Grants may be made to both public and private schools and other organizations offering educational opportunities. Types of support include capital campaigns, general operating support, and scholarship funds. Grants must be matched dollar for dollar. Request an application from the office.
Requirements: California K-12 educational organizations in Monterey County, including Marina, Seaside, Presidio of Monterey and Annex, Del Rey Oaks, Sand City, Monterey, Pacific Grove, Pebble Beach, Carmel-by-the-Sea, Carmel Valley, Big Sur, and unincorporated areas within the geographical area defined by these communities, are eligible.
Geographic Focus: California
Date(s) Application is Due: Mar 1
Contact: Emily Hull-Parsons; (831) 372-2100; info@thechapmanfoundation.org
Internet: http://www.thechapmanfoundation.org/applyingforfunds.html
Sponsor: William McCaskey Chapman and Adaline Dinsmore Chapman Foundation
2100 Garden Road Suite B-E
Monterey, CA 93940

William Robert Baird Charitable Trust Grants 5093

The trust awards grants to Louisiana and Mississippi nonprofits in its areas of interest, including food banks, social services, children and youth services, and economically disadvantaged. Types of support include general operating support, program development, emergency fund, capital campaigns, endowment funds, and matching funds. There are no application forms or deadlines.
Requirements: Louisiana and Mississippi nonprofits may apply.
Restrictions: Individuals are ineligible.
Geographic Focus: Louisiana, Mississippi
Amount of Grant: 2,000 - 40,000 USD
Contact: John David Barr; (601) 484-5887; jdbarr@ecitizensnationalbank.com
Sponsor: William Robert Baird Charitable Trust
512 22nd Avenue, P.O. Box 911
Meridian, MS 39302-5853

William S. Abell Foundation Grants 5094

The William S. Abell Foundation awards grants to eligible nonprofit organizations in its areas of interest, including economically disadvantaged, food distribution, homelessness, mental health services, reproductive and prenatal health, Roman Catholic services, and women. Grants have supported church-related food and shelter centers, abused women and children, the mentally disabled, and women's prenatal care. The board meets in March, June, September, and December. There are no application forms; deadlines are one month prior to board meetings.
Requirements: Nonprofit organizations in the District of Columbia and five nearby Maryland counties are eligible.
Geographic Focus: District of Columbia, Maryland
Date(s) Application is Due: Jan 15; Apr 15; Jul 15; Oct 15
Amount of Grant: 5,000 - 65,000 USD
Contact: Carol Doolan; (301) 652-2224; cdoolan@williamsabellfoundation.org
Internet: http://www.williamsabellfoundation.org
Sponsor: William S. Abell Foundation
8401 Connecticut Avenue, Suite 1204
Chevy Chase, MD 20815-5821

Williams Companies Foundation Grants 5095

The Foundation provides opportunities to improve the quality of life including but not limited to health and welfare, scholarships, and education. Applicants should submit proof of nonprofit status and a letter with an outline describing the organization, the amount and purpose of the request, and whether the request is for general operating support or for a specific program. There are no application deadlines.
Requirements: Nonprofits in Williams operating communities are eligible.
Restrictions: No grants are made to individuals.
Geographic Focus: Alabama, Louisiana, New Jersey, North Carolina, Pennsylvania, South Carolina, Texas, Virginia
Contact: Alison Anthony; (918) 573-4903; communityrelationstulsa@williams.com
Internet: http://www.williams.com/community/foundation.asp
Sponsor: Williams Companies Foundation
One Williams Center, MD 50-5
Tulsa, OK 74172

William T. Grant Foundation Youth Service Improvement Grants (YSIG) 5096

The program supports activities conducted by community-based organizations in the New York metropolitan area to improve the quality of services for young people (8-25 years of age). The program is designed to help good programs get better. Organizations should identify aspects of their current services that require improvement and propose a project with two main elements: (1) a plan of activities to improve the program services, and (2) an assessment plan to track the implementation of the improvement plan and its short-term results. Applications are accepted in the spring and the fall.
Requirements: To be eligible for consideration, organizations must have 501(c)3 tax-exemption; provide services to youth located in the New York metropolitan area, defined as the following counties: (in New York) Bronx, Kings, Nassau, New York, Putnam, Queens, Richmond, Rockland, Suffolk, and Westchester counties; (in New Jersey) Bergen, Essex, Hudson, Hunterdon, Mercer, Middlesex, Monmouth, Morris, Ocean, Passaic, Somerset, Sussex, and Union counties; and (in Connecticut) Fairfield, New Haven, and Litchfield counties; serve youth aged 8-25 years; and have an operating budget between $250,000 and $5.0 million. In the case of organizations that serve youth only, this is the total organizational budget. In the case of multipurpose organizations (i.e., those not exclusively focused on youth), the organizational operating budget must be less than $20 million, and the budget for services to youth (direct and indirect costs) must be between $250,000 and $5.0 million.
Restrictions: The program program does not award grants to organizations that do not serve youth directly; staff from applicant organizations must have direct contact with youth at the point-of-service. The program does not support ongoing service delivery, general operating support, organizational development activities not directly related to improving the quality of youth services, service expansion or program growth, building campaigns, scholarships, endowments, lobbying, or awards to individuals.
Geographic Focus: Connecticut, New Jersey, New York
Amount of Grant: Up to 25,000 USD
Contact: Sharon Brewster; (212) 752-0071; fax (212) 752-1398; sbrewster@wtgrantfdn.org
Internet: http://www.wtgrantfoundation.org/funding_opportunities/service-improvement-grants/youth_service_improvement/youth_service_improvement_grants
Sponsor: William T. Grant Foundation
570 Lexington Avenue, 18th Floor
New York, NY 10022-6837

William T. Sloper Trust for Andres J. Sloper Musical Fund Grants 5097

The Andrew J. Sloper Musical Fund was established in 1937 to "bring excellent and cultural music to New Britain, such as symphony orchestras, smaller orchestras, choral societies, bands, and musicians, either vocal or instrumental." Preference is given to organizations that offer musical performance (instrumental or vocal) of exceptional merit. Grants from the Sloper Musical Fund are one year in duration. Applicants must apply online at the grant website. Applicants are strongly encouraged to do the following before applying: review the downloadable state application procedures for additional helpful information and clarifications; review the downloadable online-application guidelines at the grant website; review the trust's funding history (link is available from the grant website); review the online application questions in advance; and review the list of required attachments. These will generally include: a list of board members, financial statements (audited, reviewed, or compiled by independent auditor); an organization summary; a list of other funding sources; an IRS Determination letter; and other required documents. All attachments must be uploaded in the online application as PDF, Word, or Excel files. The deadline for application to the Andrew J. Sloper Musical Fund is 11:59 p.m. on June 1. Applicants will be notified of grant decisions by letter within two to three months after the proposal deadline.
Requirements: Applicant organizations must serve the people of New Britain, Connecticut. Musical performances must be conducted in New Britain, Connecticut.
Restrictions: The Sloper Musical Fund specifically serves the people of New Britain, Connecticut. Grant requests for capital projects will not be considered. Applicants will not be awarded a grant for more than 3 consecutive years. The fund does not support requests from individuals, organizations attempting to influence policy through direct lobbying, or any political campaigns.
Geographic Focus: Connecticut
Date(s) Application is Due: Jun 1
Contact: Carmen Britt; (860) 657-7019; carmen.britt@baml.com
Internet: https://www.bankofamerica.com/philanthropic/fn_search.action
Sponsor: William T. Sloper Trust for Andrew J. Sloper Musical Fund
200 Glastonbury Boulevard, Suite # 200, CT2-545-02-05
Glastonbury, CT 06033-4056

Wilson-Wood Foundation Grants 5098

The Wilson-Wood Foundation established in 1983, supports organizations involved with: adult education; aging, centers/services; children/youth, services; education; health care; housing/shelter, development; human services; nutrition; women, centers/services. Giving is limited to the Manatee-Sarasota, Florida area, for for the underprivileged and the less fortunate in the community.
Requirements: Non-profits in the Manatee-Sarasota, Florida area are eligible to apply. Initial approach should be a phone call to the Foundation prior to submitting a letter of inquiry (must be received by June 1). There is no application form required. Applicants must submit two copies of the proposal. Application must include the following information: timetable for implementation and evaluation of project; qualifications of key personnel; name, address and phone number of organization; copy of IRS Determination Letter, must be dated within the past 10 years; brief history of organization and description of its mission; copy of most recent annual report/audited financial statement/990; descriptive literature about organization; listing of board of directors, trustees, officers and other key people and their affiliations; detailed description of project and amount of funding requested; copy of current year's organizational budget and/or project budget; listing of additional sources and amount of support.
Restrictions: No support for foreign organizations, supporting organizations, or private foundations. No grants to individuals, or for endowment funds, deficit financing, travel projects, research, fundraising costs, multi-year projects, conferences, emergency funding or start up costs.
Geographic Focus: Florida
Date(s) Application is Due: Jun 1
Amount of Grant: 8,000 - 30,000 USD
Contact: Susan Wood, Executive Director; (941) 966-3635
Sponsor: Wilson-Wood Foundation
930 Scherer Way
Osprey, FL 34229-6867

Windgate Charitable Foundation Grants 5099

The foundation funds national organizations, with an emphasis on those in the Midwest and Southwest, that have a positive impact on elementary and secondary education, recreation, family services, seniors, Christian religion, children, arts education, and youth services. The foundation tends to make one-time grants or to support two- to three-year projects. It prefers program support over capital funds, gives priority to matching-fund requests, and does not give grants for undesignated annual-fund gifts, debt retirement, or completed projects or to private religious schools or individuals. It prefers to fund projects of its own initiative rather than unsolicited grants. Thus, an inquiry about current initiatives will be useful. There are no application deadlines. The board meets two to three times each year.
Requirements: Nonprofit organizations are eligible.
Restrictions: No support for private religious schools. No grants to individuals, or for endowments, undesignated annual funds, debt retirement, completed projects, or group travel for performance or competition.
Geographic Focus: All States
Amount of Grant: 3,000 - 1,400,000 USD
Contact: John Brown, Executive Director; (479) 524-9829
Sponsor: Windgate Charitable Foundation
P.O. Box 826
Siloam Springs, AR 72761-0826

Windward Youth Leadership Fund Grants 5100
The Windward Youth Leadership Fund (WYLF) is a way for youth to apply for and "earn" up to $5,000 for their club or group activities by doing something positive for Windward Oahu. In addition to engaging youth in community service, one of the primary goals of this small grants program is to help youth build their leadership skills. Although parents, coaches and teachers may provide guidance, the projects must be youth-driven.
Requirements: Groups with at least three participants up to age 18 may apply including, but not limited to: school classes, teams, clubs, etc; youth activity groups, hula halau, music groups, scouts, etc; programs that serve youth; church youth groups; youth sports teams. Applicant groups must have a base in Windward Oahu, a majority of youth participants must be Windward Oahu residents and service projects should serve communities along the Windward coast from Kahuku to Waimanalo. Applicants must be a public school or a nonprofit 501(c)3 organization or have a sponsoring agency that is a 501(c)3 organization that can receive the funds. Youth groups can not use the Windward Youth Leadership Fund to raise funds for their own group by doing a service project that also benefits their own group. Youth groups are also encouraged to undertake projects that broaden their horizons beyond the scope of their everyday activities.
Restrictions: Applications that do not clearly demonstrate participation of youth in the project planning and writing of the proposal will most likely be denied.
Geographic Focus: Hawaii
Amount of Grant: 500 - 5,000 USD
Contact: Elizabeth Murph, (808) 263-7073; bmurph@castlefoundation.org
Internet: http://castlefoundation.org/windward-youth.htm
Sponsor: Harold K. L. Castle Foundation
1197 Auloa Road
Kailua, HI 96734

Winifred & Harry B. Allen Foundation Grants 5101
Established in 1963 in honor of Harry B. Allen, president of the Belvedere Land Company, and his wife, the Foundation has as its primary fields of interest: animal and wildlife preservation; education; the environmental programs; environmental education; protection of natural resources; health care; health organizations; human services; immigrants/refugees; performing arts; and visual arts. Though giving is centered around Marin County, California, the Foundation has also supported 501(c)3 organizations in Massachusetts, Georgia, New York, and the District of Columbia. Applicants should contact the Foundation in writing, stating the purpose and offering proof of tax exempt status. Though there are no specific deadlines, the Board meets four times annually, including April 15, June 15, September 15, and December 15.
Restrictions: No grants are given to individuals.
Geographic Focus: California, District of Columbia, Georgia, Massachusetts, New York
Amount of Grant: 500 - 5,000 USD
Contact: Howard B. Allen, (415) 435-2439; fax (415) 435-3166
Sponsor: Winifred and Harry B. Allen Foundation
83 Beach Road, P.O. Box 380
Belvedere, CA 94920-0380

Winston-Salem Foundation Competitive Grants 5102
The foundation makes competitive grant awards to tax-exempt, nonprofit agencies in the greater Forsyth County, North Carolina, area. Its charitable purposes include: public interest, education and recreation, health, human services, arts and culture, youth, and older adults. Grants ordinarily are made for proposals that initiate, expand, or improve direct services to people and for endowment purposes under certain conditions. Additional types of support include program development, seed grants, scholarship funds, technical assistance, employee matching gifts, scholarships to individuals, and matching funds. Except in unusual cases, grants will be approved for one year at a time. Potential applicants should contact the office for an appointment to introduce the proposed project.
Requirements: Organizations in Davidson, Davie, Forsyth, Surry, Stokes, Wilkes, and Yadkin counties in North Carolina are eligible to apply.
Restrictions: Grants for major equipment purposes and for capital campaigns in support of local community facilities are of low priority.
Geographic Focus: North Carolina
Contact: Brittney Gaspari, Grants Director; (336) 725-2382; fax (336) 727-0581; bgaspari@wsfoundation.org or info@wsfoundation.org
Internet: http://www.wsfoundation.org/grant-seekers/types-of-grants/competitive-grants/
Sponsor: Winston-Salem Foundation
860 W Fifth Street
Winston-Salem, NC 27101-2506

Winston-Salem Foundation Elkin/Tri-County Grants 5103
The Funds consist of three component trusts established by Richard T. Chatham, Lucy Hanes Chatham, and citizens of Elkin to benefit the community. Ordinarily, grants are made for projects that initiate, expand or improve direct service to people. Applicants should send a two or three page letter describing the need for the project, its goals and objectives, its cost and the portion of the cost requested.
Requirements: A list of board members is required, as well as organizational and project budgets, and evidence of non-profit 501(c)3 tax-exempt status. The chief board officer must sign the proposal or write an endorsement cover letter.
Restrictions: Grants will be made only to legally recognized non-profit organizations and educational institutions in Wilkes, Surry, and Yadkin Counties. Those that benefit residents of the Elkin-Jonesville-Dobson-Roaring River radius will be of priority interest to the advisory committee. Grants will not be made for on-going operating expenses. Foundation funds will not be granted to supplant tax or government funds for projects or institutions that would ordinarily receive public funding support.
Geographic Focus: North Carolina
Date(s) Application is Due: Jun 15
Amount of Grant: 500 - 7,000 USD
Contact: Brittney Gaspari, Grants Director; (336) 725-2382; fax (336) 727-0581; bgaspari@wsfoundation.org or info@wsfoundation.org
Internet: http://www.wsfoundation.org/grant-seekers/types-of-grants/elkintri-county-grants/
Sponsor: Winston-Salem Foundation
860 W Fifth Street
Winston-Salem, NC 27101-2506

Winston-Salem Foundation Stokes County Grants 5104
The Trust provides grants to non-profit organizations or informal groups in Stokes County for worthy public and charitable purposes with an emphasis on developing leaders and inspiring others. Leadership can be either formal and traditional, or demonstrated in less traditional ways that are creative and innovative, including leading by example. The trust is designed both to work with established organizations and to encourage new initiatives. Special attention will be given to encouraging leadership in certain focus areas: education; arts; environmental protection and recreational use; historical preservation; local government and community services; health; and organizations and issues affecting minorities and low-resource communities.
Requirements: Applicants can be informal groups of people with innovative ideas, including those that might grow into nonprofit organizations; or established organizations with 501(c)3 tax-exempt status. The Advisory Board will also consider letters from small groups of people with good ideas who need guidance about turning them into formal grant proposals in the future.
Restrictions: Grants will not be made for projects or institutions that would ordinarily receive public funding. However, public institutions such as schools or parks may submit proposals for innovative projects for which funds are not ordinarily provided.
Geographic Focus: North Carolina
Date(s) Application is Due: Sep 11
Amount of Grant: Up to 3,000 USD
Contact: Brittney Gaspari; (336) 725-2382; fax (336) 727-0581; bgaspari@wsfoundation.org
Internet: http://www.wsfoundation.org/grant-seekers/types-of-grants/stokes-county-grants/
Sponsor: Winston-Salem Foundation
860 W Fifth Street
Winston-Salem, NC 27101-2506

Winthrop Rockefeller Foundation Grants 5105
The foundation provides grants to Arkansas-based nonprofit organizations that provide service in the following areas: economic development—to empower individuals and institutions to improve the standard of living and economic viability of low-income communities; education—to enable all children and adults to develop fully their capacities to improve themselves and to contribute to the educational, cultural, economic, civic, and social vitality of their communities; and economic, racial, and social justice— to engage institutions and individuals in the struggle for pervasive justice in the lives of all Arkansans and their communities. There are no application deadlines; concept papers (three-page maximum) are accepted throughout the year. The board meets quarterly to make funding decisions.
Requirements: Arkansas nonprofit organizations are eligible.
Restrictions: The foundation does not make grants for capital purposes, basic scientific research, deficit operations, individuals, or endowments.
Geographic Focus: Arkansas
Contact: Lori E. Kindy; (501) 376-6854; fax (501) 374-4797; programstaff@wrfoundation.org
Internet: http://www.wrockefellerfoundation.org/index.php?page=grants
Sponsor: Winthrop Rockefeller Foundation
225 East Markham Street, Suite 200
Little Rock, AR 72201

Wisconsin Energy Foundation Grants 5106
The mission of the Foundation is to create brighter futures for the communities in which Wisconsin Energy Corporation does business, enhancing the growth and success of the company. The Foundation supports initiatives promoting economic health, arts and culture, education and environment.
Requirements: Applicants must be a 501(c)3 organization located in a community served by Wisconsin Energy Corporation. See the geographical funding area map on the website. Applications must be submitted online from the website.
Geographic Focus: Michigan, Wisconsin
Date(s) Application is Due: Jan 31; Apr 30; Jul 31; Oct 31
Contact: Patricia McNew; (414) 221-2107; patti.mcnew@we-energies.com
Internet: http://www.wec-foundation.com
Sponsor: Wisconsin Energy Foundation
231 West Michigan Street
Milwaukee, WI 53201

Wisconsin Humanities Council Major Grants 5107
The Wisconsin Humanities Council (WHC) considers proposals on any topic that may be addressed from the perspective of one or more of the humanities disciplines and that will respond to or engage the interest of a public audience. The audience for WHC-sponsored programs is the general public of all ages. The WHC is especially interested in making public humanities programs available to people who might not otherwise have easy access to them, and in sponsoring programs that involve the active participation of a public audience. Humanities topics include, but are not limited to: history; philosophy; languages; linguistics; literature; cultural anthropology; archaeology; jurisprudence; the history, theory, and criticism of the arts; ethics; religious studies; and those aspects of the social sciences

that employ historical or philosophical approaches. Projects supported by the WHC will ordinarily involve at least one scholar with a master's, Ph.D., or other graduate degree in an appropriate humanities discipline, or a specialist who is well qualified. Priority funding will be given to project that reach participants who have limited access to cultural programs; are built on collaboration among two or more organizations or institutions; use the humanities in innovative ways; seek to have a long term impact on participants and/or communities; and promise participants an experience that has depth and the potential to be transformative. Examples of projects that meet funding guidelines are posted on the website.
Requirements: Any non-profit organization in the state of Wisconsin, or ad hoc group that is formed for the purpose of implementing an eligible public humanities project, may apply for funding. Ad hoc groups do not need to be incorporated or have formal tax-exempt status. Eligible projects must be firmly rooted in the humanities, although the may involve the sciences, social sciences, and the arts when humanities approaches are taken to these fields; involve humanities experts as active participants in project planning; demonstrate community interest and show community support; be designed for a general audience; and encourage reflection and thoughtful conversation. Applicants must prepare letters of intent, which should outline briefly the nature of the proposed program, identify the sponsoring organization(s), and state the approximate amount of money that will be requested from the WHC.
Restrictions: Ineligible expenses include capital expenses, indirect or overhead costs, expenses related to fundraising, anything related to an archival project, museum acquisitions, or staff salaries.
Geographic Focus: Wisconsin
Date(s) Application is Due: Apr 15; Aug 15; Dec 15
Contact: Dena Wortzel; (608) 265-5593 or (608) 262-0706; dwortzel@wisc.edu
Internet: http://www.wisconsinhumanities.org/grants.html
Sponsor: Wisconsin Humanities Council
222 South Bedford Street, Suite F
Madison, WI 53703-3688

Wisconsin Humanities Council Mini-Grants for Scholarly Research 5108
The Wisconsin Humanities Council (WHC) awards mini-grants to support scholarly research that will lead to public humanities programs. Eligible project must be firmly rooted in the humanities, although they may also involve the sciences, social sciences, and the arts when humanities approaches are taken in these fields. Projects must involve humanities experts, demonstrate community interest, and show community support. They must also be designed for a general audience and encourage reflection and thoughtful conversation. The WHC strongly encourages the use of scholarships, free admission days, and other flexible admission policies that make WHC-funded projects accessible to participants for whom a fee could present an obstacle. Priority will be given to proposals with annual budgets of less than $1 million; projects that promise to reach participants who have limited access to cultural programs; and projects built on collaboration among two or more organizations or institutions. Applicants are encouraged to contact WHC staff to discuss their project. Staff can advise applicants on project design and offer advice on the preparation of a competitive proposal. First-time applicants are strongly encouraged to submit a draft of their proposal for feedback (although this must be done at least two weeks in advance of a grant deadline). Specific guidelines, including tips and samples for projects that meet the grant guidelines, are available at the Council website.
Requirements: Any non-profit organization in the state of Wisconsin, or ad hoc group that is formed for the purpose of implementing an eligible public humanities project, may apply for funding. Ad hoc groups do not need to be incorporated or have formal tax-exempt status. All grants require matching funds that are equal to or greater than the amount requested from the WHC. Matching funds may be cash or in-kind. A budget narrative must describe the cash or in-kind sources of all matching funds. Funds from the WHC may be requested for such reasonable project-related expenses as honoraria for humanities experts, per diem and travel expenses for project personnel, printing and publicity, telephone, facility rental, and materials necessary for the project. Admission or registration fees may be charged, but all anticipated income from fees must be shown in the budget as part of the matching funds and must be explained in the budget narrative.
Restrictions: Ineligible expenses include capital expenses, indirect or overhead costs, expenses related to fundraising, anything related to an archival project, museum acquisitions or salaries for staff hired specifically for the project.
Geographic Focus: Wisconsin
Date(s) Application is Due: Feb 1; May 1; Aug 1; Nov 1
Contact: Dena Wortzel; (608) 265-5593 or (608) 262-0706; dwortzel@wisc.edu
Internet: http://www.wisconsinhumanities.org
Sponsor: Wisconsin Humanities Council
222 South Bedford Street, Suite F
Madison, WI 53703-3688

Wolf Aviation Fund Grants 5109
The Foundation promotes and supports the advancement of personal air transportation by seeking out and funding the most promising individuals and worthy projects that advance the field of general aviation. The foundation awards grants, and helps individuals locate aviation scholarships and flight training. Through these programs, the Foundation hopes to: increase the public's knowledge of aviation through publications, seminars, and other information media. Electronic mail is preferred for all correspondence and applications.
Requirements: Grants are awarded to innovative individuals, groups, and projects.
Geographic Focus: All States
Date(s) Application is Due: Nov 15
Contact: Rol Murrow, Executive Director; (575) 774-0029; mail@wolf-aviation.org
Internet: http://www.wolf-aviation.org/news.htm
Sponsor: Alfred L. and Constance C. Wolf Aviation Fund
2060 State Highway 595
Lindrith, NM 87029

Wolfe Associates Grants 5110
Wolfe Associates Grants are made in the following fields: health and medicine; religion; education; culture, community service, youth skills development, and business. Awards range from $500 to $25,000.
Requirements: Applicants must be 501(c)3 organizations. Funding is primarily made to, but is not limited to, Ohio organizations. Application is made by sending a cover with a brief summary of the request, the amount requested, a copy of the organization's Internal Revenue Service determination letter and most recent form 990, and financial statements. There are no submission deadlines.
Geographic Focus: Ohio
Contact: Rita J. Wolfe, Vice President; (614) 460-3782
Sponsor: Wolfe Associates
34 S Third Street
Columbus, OH 43215

Women's Foundation Greater Kansas City Grants 5111
The Women's Foundation of Greater Kansas City is committed to improving the quality of life for women and girls in the community. Improving the lives of women and girls is central to its mission and integral in making Kansas City a better community; one in which women and girls can thrive. The Foundation funds programs, projects and activities that: provide gender-specific solutions to problems facing women and girls; effect long-term, positive changes in systems which currently prevent women and girls from reaching their potential; expand choices and opportunities for women and girls; enhance dignity and self-worth for women and girls; and are led by women and foster women's leadership. One year grants will be awarded in amounts up to $25,000.
Requirements: Applicant not for profit organizations must be tax-exempt as defined by the IRS code, section 501(c)3 and must be incorporated by the Secretary of State or be established by statue within a State and are therefore not required to be incorporated.
Restrictions: The Foundation will not fund: individuals; scholarships; religious organizations for religious activities; government agencies; organizations which restrict choices or limit options; endowments; political parties, candidates or political activities; start-up programs (less than one year old); programs inconsistent with non-discrimination policies; or capital fund drives (specific equipment/capital needs may be funded if tied to proposed program).
Geographic Focus: Missouri
Date(s) Application is Due: Aug 15
Contact: Emily Fish; (913) 831-0711, ext. 27; fax (913) 831-0881; women@wfgkc.org
Internet: http://www.wfgkc.org/grants.html
Sponsor: Women's Foundation Greater Kansas City
6950 Squibb Road, Suite 220
Mission, KS 66202

Women's Funding Alliance Grants 5112
The alliance supports nonprofits in Washington for programs and projects supporting women and children in its areas of interest, including poverty, sexual assault, discrimination, domestic violence, education, and reproductive rights. Preference will be given to organizations that have women in leadership positions and who incorporate diversity in their projects and agencies. Grants are awarded once a year in the following areas: general operating support, capacity building, project specific and population specific. Nonprofits interested in being included on the request-for-proposal list can email the alliance. All Letters of Inquiry are due on May 31st. Applicants invited to submit a full proposal will be notified the third week of June. Full proposals are due in the Women's Funding Alliance office by 5:00 PM on July 23rd.
Requirements: Washington nonprofits are eligible.
Geographic Focus: Washington
Contact: Sara Reyerson, (206) 467-6733; fax (206) 467-7537; sara@wfalliance.org
Internet: http://www.wfalliance.org/apply_for_funding.htm
Sponsor: Women's Funding Alliance
603 Stewart Street, Suite 207
Seattle, WA 98101-1229

Wood-Claeyssens Foundation Grants 5113
The Foundation awards grants to eligible California nonprofit organizations. Types of support include annual campaigns, capital campaigns, continuing support, and general operating support. An application is available on the website.
Requirements: California 501(c)3 organizations serving Santa Barbara and Ventura Counties are eligible.
Restrictions: Funding is not available to individuals or to organizations that discriminate on the basis of age, gender, race, ethnicity, sexual orientation, disability, national origin, political affiliation or religious belief.
Geographic Focus: California
Date(s) Application is Due: Jun 30
Contact: Noelle Claeyssens Burkey; (805) 966-0543; wcf0543@gmail.com
Internet: http://www.woodclaeyssensfoundation.com/Funding.htm
Sponsor: Wood-Claeyssens Foundation
P.O. Box 30586
Santa Barbara, CA 93130-0586

Woods Charitable Fund Grants 5114
This program seeks to strengthen the community by improving opportunities and life outcomes for all people in Lincoln, Nebraska. Areas of interest include human services; education; civic and community; and arts and culture. The Fund gives considerations to programs and initiatives related to the following: support to organizations that haven't traditionally served refugees and immigrants but are trying to integrate them into their client bases and work forces; expanding English language education for New

Americans; helping develop community acceptance and appreciation for New Americans; and extending research and planning concerning immigrants and refugees in Lincoln. Interested applicants are asked to contact the Fund by telephone or by sending a two page letter of intent, including budget information, by mail, facsimile or email. After reviewing the letter of intent, the Fund may request a complete application. Grants range from $1,000 to $100,000 with the average size being $21,500.
Requirements: Generally applicants should be 501(c)3 organizations serving Lincoln, Nebraska. Funding is provided in four principle ares of interest: human services; education; civic and community life; and arts and culture.
Restrictions: The following are ineligible: capital projects for health care institutions; environmental programs; funding of endowments; fundraising benefits or program advertising; individual needs; medical and scientific research; programs for individual schools; religious programs; residential care and medical clinics; scholarships and fellowships; and sponsorships. College and university proposals are reviewed only if they directly involve faculty and/or students in applied projects of benefit and concern to the community. Ineligible organizations are those that have had proposals approved or declined in the preceding twelve months or that are recipients of active, multiyear grants. This does not apply when organizations are involved in collaborative proposals.
Geographic Focus: Nebraska
Contact: Pam Baker; (402) 436-5971; fax 402) 742-0123; pbaker@woodscharitable.org
Internet: http://www.woodscharitable.org/about/index.html
Sponsor: Woods Charitable Fund
P.O. Box 81309
Lincoln, NE 68501

Woods Fund of Chicago Grants 5115

The goal of Woods Fund of Chicago is to increase opportunities for less advantaged people and communities in the metropolitan area, including the opportunity to shape decisions affecting them. The Foundation supports nonprofits in engaging people in civic life, addressing the causes of poverty and other challenges facing the region, promoting more effective public policies, reducing racism and other barriers to equal opportunity, and building a sense of community and common ground. The Foundation is particularly interested in supporting those organizations and initiatives that focus on enabling work and reducing poverty within Chicago's less-advantaged communities. Grants are concentrated in three program areas: community organizing; public policy; and the intersection of community organizing and public policy. In addition, a limited number of grants are awarded in the arts and culture program area. Applicants must submit an inquiry form. If the Foundation responds favorably, applicants will be asked to submit a full application. Inquiry forms are accepted January 1 through the last business day in January and July 1 through the last business day in July.
Requirements: Applicants must be 501(c)3 organizations in the metropolitan Chicago area.
Restrictions: Areas not eligible include: business or economic development projects; capital campaigns, capital projects, and capital acquisitions; endowments; fundraising benefits or program advertising; health care organizations; housing construction or rehabilitation; individual needs; medical or scientific research; programs in and for individual public and private schools; religious or ecumenical programs; residential care, rehabilitation, counseling, clinics and recreational programs; scholarships and fellowships; and social and welfare services, except special projects with a clear public policy strategy.
Geographic Focus: Illinois
Contact: Deborah D. Clark; (312) 782-2698; fax (312) 782-4155; dclark@woodsfund.org
Internet: http://www.woodsfund.org/site/epage/61436_735.htm
Sponsor: Woods Fund of Chicago
35 East Wacker Drive, Suite 1760
Chicago, IL 60601

Woodward Fund Grants 5116

Grants support nonprofit institutions, corporations, and associations that are located in Georgia or one of its neighboring states and are organized and operated exclusively for religious, educational, and charitable and scientific purposes. Grantmaking focuses on capital projects. The distribution committee makes its decisions based on materials provided in the grant request. The trust does not require a formal application form, but requests a proposal outlining the project or program and containing the following information: project/program description; complete itemized project budget, including project schedule; need for the project; other funding sources, including the amount received from each source; names and qualifications of those conducting the project; objectives and how they will be achieved; a brief description of the applicant organization; method and criteria for project evaluation; list of officers, board of directors, or trustees; copy of the 501(c)3 designation letter; and plans for recognition of the trust in the project. Applicants should not contact committee members personally concerning a proposal or anticipated approach to the fund.
Requirements: 501(c)3 nonprofit organizations in Georgia and its neighboring states are eligible. Government agencies to which contributions by individuals are made deductible from income by IRS laws also are eligible.
Restrictions: Grants are not awarded to individuals or for scholarships or student loans.
Geographic Focus: Alabama, Florida, Georgia, North Carolina, South Carolina, Tennessee
Date(s) Application is Due: May 1; Nov 1
Amount of Grant: 5,000 - 300,000 USD
Contact: Alice Sheets, c/o Wachovia Bank, NA Trustee; grantinquiries8@wachovia.com
Internet: https://www.wachovia.com/charitable_services/woodward_overview.asp
Sponsor: David, Helen, and Marian Woodward Fund
3280 Peachtree Road NE, Suite 400, MC G0141-041
Atlanta, GA 30305

World Bank JJ/WBGSP Partners Programs 5117

The fund supports 11 Partnership Programs with universities around the world. These programs enable scholars to receive specialized training in key areas of development, such as economic policy management or infrastructure management. The Programs seek promising candidates from the public sector in developing countries, such as central banks and ministries of finance and planning. All Partnership Programs lead to a master's degree. Participating universities include: Centre d'Etudes et de Recherches sur Le Developpement International (France); McGill University (Montreal); Columbia University (New York City); University of Tsukuba (Japan); Yokohama National University (Japan); Keio University (Japan); Saitama University (Japan); Harvard University (Cambridge, MA); Makerere University (Uganda); Universite De Cocody (Republique de Cote D'Ivoire); University of Ghana (Ghana); and Universite De Yaounde II (Cameroon). All Programs extend for 15 to 24 months, which may include a concurrent internship period of three to four months as part of the degree requirement. The number of scholars admitted in each intake varies from five to fifteen.
Geographic Focus: All States
Contact: Secretariat; (202) 473-1000; fax (202) 477-6391; opportunities@worldbank.org
Internet: http://go.worldbank.org/E061CRZP40
Sponsor: World Bank
1818 H Street NW
Washington, DC 20433

WSF Rusty Kanokogi Fund for the Advancement of U.S. Judo Grants 5118

The Rusty Kanokogi Fund for the Advancement of U.S. Judo was established in 2009 to provide direct financial assistance to aspiring athletes with successful competitive records who have the potential to achieve even higher performance levels and rankings. The goal of the fund is to relieve aspiring elite-level female athletes of the financial burden associated with competing at higher levels and to permit them to concentrate on their training. Requests for assistance are considered for coaching, specialized training, equipment, athletic clothing and/or travel.
Requirements: Female judo players in training for national and international competition are eligible to apply. Individual applicants must be U.S. citizens or legal residents and be eligible to compete for a U.S. national team. Individuals applying for this grant are evaluated based upon the following criteria: financial need; present and potential level and ranking; lack of support from traditional sources; role of award in continued participation and advancement; potential impact of grant on advancing women in sports; contribution to greater visibility of female athletes; and priority given to those who present a plan for reimbursing the grant in the future, whether financially or otherwise contributing to women's sports. Two letters of recommendation are required. One recommendation must be from USA Judo. The other recommendation may be from someone familiar with the applicant's athletic competition records.
Restrictions: An individual may be awarded only one grant per calendar year. Be aware that it is likely that, by accepting a grant, an athlete's college eligibility may be affected.
Geographic Focus: All States
Date(s) Application is Due: Nov 30
Amount of Grant: Up to 5,000 USD
Contact: Jennifer L. Eddy; (800) 227-3988 or (516) 542-4700; fax (516) 542-4716; JEddy@WomensSportsFoundation.org or Info@WomensSportsFoundation.org
Internet: http://www.womenssportsfoundation.org/sitecore/content/home/programs/grants/rusty-kanokogi-fund-for-the-advancement-of-us-judo-grant.aspx
Sponsor: Women's Sports Foundation
1899 Hempstead Turnpike, Suite 400
East Meadow, NY 11554

WSF Travel and Training Fund Grants 5119

The fund provides direct financial assistance to aspiring athletes with successful competitive records who have the potential to achieve even higher performance levels and rankings. The goal of the fund is to relieve female athletes of the financial burden associated with competing at higher levels and to permit them to concentrate on their training. Requests for assistance are considered for coaching, specialized training, equipment, attire, and/or travel.
Requirements: Female teams with regional and/or national rankings or successful competitive records who have the potential to achieve higher performance levels and rankings are eligible. Individuals must be U.S. citizens or legal residents and eligible to compete for the U.S. National Team.
Restrictions: High school and college/university varsity and/or recreation teams are not eligible.
Geographic Focus: All States
Date(s) Application is Due: Dec 31
Amount of Grant: Up to 5,000 USD
Contact: Jennifer L. Eddy, Senior Director of Programs; (800) 227-3988 or (516) 542-4700; fax (516) 542-4716; JEddy@WomensSportsFoundation.org or Info@WomensSportsFoundation.org
Internet: http://www.womenssportsfoundation.org/sitecore/content/home/programs/travel-and-training-fund.aspx
Sponsor: Women's Sports Foundation
1899 Hempstead Turnpike, Suite 400
East Meadow, NY 11554

WWF International Smart Gear Competition 5120

WWF's International Smart Gear Competition, first held in 2005, brings together the fishing industry, research institutes, universities, and government, to inspire and reward practical, innovative fishing gear designs that reduce bycatch - the accidental catch and related deaths of sea turtles, birds, marine mammals, cetaceans and non-target fish species in fishing gear such as longlines and nets. WWF offers more than $50,000 in prize money to attract innovative ideas that may prove to be a valuable solution to some of the most pressing bycatch problems in fisheries around the globe. Financial support for the competition

is provided by a number of government departments including National Oceanic and Atmospheric Administration (NOAA), Canadian Department of Fisheries and Oceans (DFO), as well as support from a number of foundations and corporations.
Requirements: The competition is open to eligible entrants from any background. The Grand Prize Winner will be awarded $30,000, and Runner-Up Winners will be awarded $10,000. A Special Tuna Prize, $7,500, may be awarded to entrants that address an issue of major concern to WWF, the bycatch associated with tuna fisheries around the world. An international panel made up of gear technologists, fisheries experts, representatives of the seafood industry, fishermen, scientists, researchers and conservationists judges the entries. The judges are guided by the following criteria: does it reduce bycatch of nontarget fish and other species, especially vulnerable and/or endangered species; is the idea innovative and original; is the idea practical and is the idea easy to use; is the idea cost-effective; will it allow fishermen to maintain or increase profitability; could the idea actually be developed?
Geographic Focus: All States, All Countries
Date(s) Application is Due: Mar 15
Contact: Mike Osmond; smartgear@smartgear.org or Michael.Osmond@wwfus.org
Internet: http://www.smartgear.org/
Sponsor: World Wildlife Fund
P.O. Box 97180
Washington, DC 20090-7180

Xcel Energy Foundation Grants 5121
The foundation awards grants in its service territory for initiatives in four program areas: environment, education, community development, and arts and culture. Deadlines are: environment, Feb 7 and Aug 1; education, Feb 7; community development, May 2; arts and culture, Aug 1. Applicants must submit a letter of inquiry online for the specific program area for which funds are being requested. (Common grant forms are not accepted.) Applicants will be notified about the results of their inquiry; full proposals are by invitation only.
Requirements: Nonprofit organizations are eligible.
Restrictions: Grants do not support individuals; political parties; national organizations; research programs; government agencies; endowment campaigns; athletic or scholarship competitions; religious, political, veteran, and fraternal organizations (except for programs that are of direct benefit to the community and not for themselves); benefits or fundraising activities; advertising or sponsorships; programs of individual organizations that receive more than 50 percent of their program budget from the United Way or other federated giving drives to which Xcel Energy contributes; disease-specific organizations; sports and athletic programs; or capital projects.
Geographic Focus: All States
Date(s) Application is Due: Feb 7; May 2; Aug 1
Contact: Program Contact; Foundation@xcelenergy.com
Internet: http://www.xcelenergy.com/XLWEB/CDA/0,2914,1-1-1_4359_4842_4846-954-0_0_0-0,00.html
Sponsor: Xcel Energy Foundation
414 Nicollet Mall
Minneapolis, MN 55401-1993

Xerox Foundation Grants 5122
Xerox Foundation Grants assist a variety of social, civic and cultural organizations that provide broad-based programs and services in cities where our employees work and live. The Foundation also remains committed to a program of grants to colleges and universities to prepare qualified men and women for careers in business, science, government, and general education. The Foundation seeks to further advance knowledge in science and technology, and to enhance learning opportunities for minorities and the disadvantaged. Worldwide, Xerox philanthropy tries to engage national leadership in addressing major social problems and to support programs in education, employability and cultural affairs. Other areas of particular focus include programs responsive to the national concern for the environment and the application of information technology. Large grants may be approved for more than one year (multi-year grants). All organizations that have previously received support on an annual basis from the Foundation, must re-submit a request each year to be evaluated for continued support.
Requirements: Grants are made only to 501(c)3 and 509(a) organizations. No specific application form is used. Requests for grants/funding should be submitted in letter form describing the project or program. This request should contain the legal name of the organization, the official contact person, its tax- exempt status, a brief description of its activities and programs, the purpose for which the grant is being requested, the benefits expected, the plans for evaluation, the projected budget, and the expected sources and amount of needed funds.
Restrictions: The foundation declines requests to support individuals; capital grants (new construction or renovation); endowments or endowed chairs; organizations supported by United Way, unless permission has been granted by United Way to a member agency to conduct a capital fund drive or a special benefit; political organizations or candidates; religious or sectarian groups; or municipal, county, state, federal, or quasi-government agencies.
Geographic Focus: All States
Contact: Joseph M. Cahalan, President; (203) 968-2453 or (203) 968-3000
Internet: http://www.xerox.com/about-xerox/citizenship/xerox-foundation/enus.html
Sponsor: Xerox Foundation
45 Glover Avenue, P.O. Box 4505
Norwalk, CT 06856-4505

Yampa Valley Community Foundation Erickson Business Week Scholarships 5123
The Foundation supports programs benefiting the Yampa Valley community. The purpose of the Erickson Business Week Scholarships is to enable a student to attend the annual Business Week conference sponsored by the Colorado Chapter of Junior Achievement.
Requirements: Applicants should complete the online Junior Acheivement Business Week application and then call the Foundation for further instructions.
Geographic Focus: Colorado
Contact: Jennifer Shea; (907) 879-8632; fax (919) 530-8852; jennifer@yvcf.org
Internet: http://www.yvcf.org/scholarship-apply.php
Sponsor: Yampa Valley Community Foundation
465 Anglers Drive, Suite 2-G
Steamboat Springs, CO 80488

Yampa Valley Community Foundation Grants 5124
The Foundation supports innovative programs benefiting the Yampa Valley community. Funding is provided for proposals that: promote the mission of the Foundation; serve either a broad or underserved population in the Yampa Valley; demonstrate the anticipated impact in the Yampa Valley; define the measurement and evaluation process to be used; effectively leverage the Foundation's resources; and exhibit sound business and financial practices. Grants may be awarded for innovative programs demonstrating progress toward achieving community goals in five focus areas: arts and culture, education, environment, health and human services, and recreation. Initially a letter of intent, providing an overview of the proposed project or program and the funding requested, should be submitted. Selected applicants will be invited to submit a full proposal.
Requirements: Eligible organizations must be a nonprofit 501(c)3 organization or fiscally sponsored by a qualifying organization in Routt or Moffat Counties that benefit the Yampa Valley. Only grant requests for charitable purposes that have a public benefit are considered.
Restrictions: The Foundation does not grant for debt reduction, endowments, political purposes or religious purposes. Proposals are typically declined for individual or professional development, team or travel expenses, retro-active grants for projects already completed or in process, or 100% of funding for a project. Funded programs and services may not include any political or religious intentions.
Geographic Focus: Colorado
Date(s) Application is Due: Jun 1
Contact: Jennifer Shea; (970) 879-8632; fax (970) 871-0431; jennifer@yvcf.org
Internet: http://www.yvcf.org/grants.php
Sponsor: Yampa Valley Community Foundation
465 Anglers Drive, Suite 2-G
Steamboat Springs, CO 80488

Yawkey Foundation Grants 5125
The Yawkey Foundation is committed to continuing the legacy of Tom and Jean Yawkey by making significant and positive impacts on the quality of life of children, families, and the underserved in the areas of New England and Georgetown County, South Carolina. Funding supports the areas of health care, education, human services, youth and amateur athletics, arts and culture, and conservation and wildlife. Request should be limited to $25,000 unless otherwise directed. Applications are currently accepted only from organizations previously funded by the Foundation. Deadlines are: arts and culture, conservation, and health care March 1; human services June 15; education September 1; and youth and amateur athletics November 15.
Requirements: Eligible applicants must be tax-exempt 501(c)3 organizations. Proposals must provide significant benefits to a broad constituency either in New England or Georgetown County, South Carolina. The Foundation has a particular concern for organizations that serve disadvantaged children and families and also considers the following: relevance of the proposed project or program to the Foundation's areas of interest; need outlined in the proposal and how the organization has and will continue to address that need; the organization's fiscal health and ability to manage its resources effectively; ability of the project or program to leverage funding and support from other sources; ability of the organization and its staff to achieve the desired results; adequacy of proposed activities, budget, and timetable to achieve the desired results; and evidence of appropriate cooperation with other organizations.
Restrictions: All final reports for prior funding must be submitted before applying for additional funding. Only one request may be submitted during a twelve-month period. Organizations that have received three or more years of consecutive funding will not be eligible to reapply for funding for a one-year period. The Foundation does not make grants to: organizations that are not tax-exempt under section 501(c)3 of the Internal Revenue Service; individuals; private foundations; 509(a)3 Type III non-functionally integrated organizations; organizations or programs that provide benefits outside of the United States; legislative lobbying; foundations created by political or governmental or for-profit organizations; political campaigns and causes; government agencies, or agencies directly benefiting public entities; public school districts and public schools (including charter schools); community and economic development corporations or programs; advocacy groups; operating deficits or retirement of debt; general endowments; general capital campaigns; events, conferences, seminars, and group travel; awards, prizes, and monuments; fraternal, trade, civic, or labor organizations; music, video, or film production; feasibility or research studies; pass-through, intermediary organizations or foundations; religious organizations for sectarian purposes; and workforce development programs.
Geographic Focus: Connecticut, Maine, Massachusetts, New Hampshire, Rhode Island, South Carolina, Vermont
Contact: Nancy Brodnicki, Grants Program Administrator; (781) 329-7470
Internet: http://www.yawkeyfoundation.org/grant_guidelines.html
Sponsor: Yawkey Foundation
990 Washington Street
Dedham, MA 02026-6716

Yellow Corporate Foundation Grants 5126
The corporate foundation supports nonprofit organizations in the Kansas City, MO, area. Categories of support include cultural programs and entertainment, education, community development, and health programs. United Way agencies in communities in which the company does business receive 80 percent of the foundation's giving. Education support

goes to colleges and universities. Community development support includes economic development, urban leagues, and chambers of commerce. Health and social service support includes programs assisting the visually impaired; disabled children, including psychological disabilities; and groups that aid battered women.
Requirements: IRS 501(c)3 tax-exempt nonprofit organizations in Missouri are eligible.
Restrictions: Grants are not made to individuals, nor to political, religious, or national health organizations.
Geographic Focus: Missouri
Contact: Daniel J. Churay, Director; (913) 696-6170
Sponsor: Yellow Corporate Foundation
10990 Roe Avenue, M.S. A515
Overland Park, KS 66211-1213

Young Family Foundation Grants (Texas) 5127
The foundation's major purpose is to: foster activities of youth by awarding funds for projects of the Boy Scouts, Girl Scouts, Schools, school organizations, and other youth programs; promote goodwill in the community by awarding funds for community projects through local government and organizations such as Volunteer Firemen, Emergency Medical Services, Helping Hands, Churches, and other charitable organizations; provide funds to other charitable organizations such as the National MPS Society, American Red Cross, American Cancer Society, and other nationally recognized charitable organizations, and; foster the benefits of higher education by awarding academic college scholarships and vocational school scholarships to worthy graduates of Ganado High School, and academic college scholarships to worthy graduates of Louise High School and Tidehaven High School who live in the Ganado Telephone Company's service area and will/are attend/attending full-time an accredited College or University located in the state of Texas;
Requirements: Priority is given to tax-exempt organizations that operate within the Ganado, Texas, area. However, grant contributions are also made to nationally recognized charitable organizations.
Geographic Focus: Texas
Samples: Hospice of South Texas; National MPS Society; Boy Scouts of America.
Contact: Barbara Larson, (361) 771-3331 or (888) 395-1499; b.larson@ykc.com
Internet: http://www.youngfamilyfoundation.com/
Sponsor: Raymond A. and Royce A. Young
P.O. Box 329
Ganado, TX 77962

Youth Action Net Fellowships 5128
Youth Action Net supports youth leadership development through its global and national Fellowship programs throughout the world. National Fellowships are currently operating in Brazil and Mexico, with future Institutes planned for Australia, Chile, Egypt, Haiti, Israel, and Spain. The Global Fellowship Program targets exceptional young social entrepreneurs anywhere in the world who have developed innovative approaches to addressing issues of international relevance. This personalized learning experience, together with a $1,000, will allow these impressive young leaders to deepen and expand their impact.
Requirements: Young people aged 18 to 29 are eligible. Both individuals and groups may apply. Individuals applying must have a leadership role in a youth-led initiative that works to create positive change in their community. Applications must be written in English.
Geographic Focus: All States
Amount of Grant: 1,000 USD
Contact: Ashok Regmi; (410) 347-1500; fax (410) 347-1188; yan@iyfnet.org
Internet: http://www.youthactionnet.org/index.php?fuse=fellowmainpage
Sponsor: International Youth Foundation
32 South Street, Suite 500
Baltimore, MD 21202

Youth Action Net Universidad Europea de Madrid (UEM) Prize 5129
The Universidad de Madrid (UEM) has launched a special prize to recognize and support the accomplishments of young social entrepreneurs in Spain. Supported by the Sylvan/Laureate Foundation and the International Youth Foundation (IYF) as part of its Youth Action Net program, the UEM Prize for Young Social Entrepreneurs is open to young people, ages 18 to 29, who have developed innovative solutions to addressing social and environmental challenges. The ten award recipients selected annually will receive: a stipend of 3,000 Euros ($4,500 USD) for their organization and/or project; two specialized training workshops focused on the successful administration of social projects; mentoring and technical support by qualified experts for their project; and recognition and exposure for their project. The deadline for applications is August 31, with an awards ceremony on September 25.
Geographic Focus: All States
Date(s) Application is Due: Aug 31
Amount of Grant: 3,000 EUR
Contact: Ashok Regmi; (410) 347-1500; fax (410) 347-1188; yan@iyfnet.org
Internet: http://www.youthactionnet.org/index.php?fuse=mediacontent&id=60
Sponsor: International Youth Foundation
32 South Street, Suite 500
Baltimore, MD 21202

Youth As Resources Grants 5130
Capitalizing on the energy, creativity and enthusiasm of Baltimore's young people, Youth As Resources makes grants for youth-designed and carried out community organizing projects. Funding is available for projects: that put the ideas and energy of young people address critical community needs; where young people think up with the idea, come up with a plan, do the work and make the decisions with the help and support of adults; that are sustainable and make change last; that can be started and finished by the same group of young people; and that have a realistic budget and a solid plan. Youth As Resources will consider youth-led business projects as long as all proceeds are used to address critical community needs. Project requests may range from $500 to $3,500. The average cost of a project is $2,000. There are two grant cycles per year.
Restrictions: Youth As Resources grants will not pay for stipends.
Geographic Focus: Maryland
Date(s) Application is Due: Nov 13
Amount of Grant: 500 - 3,500 USD
Contact: Julie Reeder, Program Director; (410) 576-9551; jreeder@bcf.org
Internet: http://www.bcf.org/ourgrants/ourgrantsdetail.aspx?grid=8
Sponsor: Baltimore Community Foundation
2 East Read Street, 9th Floor
Baltimore, MD 21202

Youth as Resources Mini-Grants 5131
Mini-grants are awarded to local youth groups who initiate and carry out a community service project or event that tackles a social problem or assists development. Project topics range from health, housing, education and the environment, to drug abuse, gangs, illiteracy and crime.
Requirements: Projects must have a governing youth-adult advisory committee. Youth and adults, ages 9 and up, can serve on the Advisory Committee. Grant applicants must consist of youth groups, affiliated with a 501(c)3 organization. The project must address a community need and must be planned and implemented by a youth group located in the community served. Deadline for applications is late spring - contact sponsor for specific date.
Restrictions: Grant money may not be used for overhead costs, salaries or wages, donations to other organizations or for the purchase of capital items.
Geographic Focus: All States
Amount of Grant: 50 - 500 USD
Contact: Gavin Mariano, (219) 938-7070, ext. 2707; gmariano@crisiscenterysb.org
Internet: http://www.crisiscenterysb.org/youthasresources/default.htm
Sponsor: Crisis Center
101 North Montgomery
Gary, IN 46403

Youth Philanthropy Project 5132
The program encourages young people from across the region to participate in community service and to develop leadership skills, and especially encourages student volunteerism and philanthropy by engaging young people in decision-making about the distribution of grant dollars.
Requirements: Any youth-run organization that impacts the City of Richmond, Henrico, Hanover and Chesterfield Counties that is in need of funding for programs that benefit the community. Applicants may include, but are not limited to, church youth groups, school clubs or volunteer organizations that involve youth in the planning, implementation and evaluation of the proposed program. Consideration is given to youth-driven organizations that provide programs or services relating to one or more of the following focus areas - [1] Creating Safe Neighborhoods: Supporting a community where neighbors share an interest in protecting their communities and providing residents with the tools to identify and address their assets and needs; [2] Strengthening Families: Encouraging families to build stronger, healthier, and more productive environments for themselves, their community and their children; and [3] Achieving Academic Success: Supporting programs that promote literacy, improve test scores, increase school attendance, and encourage parental involvement.
Restrictions: Applications sent by facsimile or email will not be accepted.
Geographic Focus: Virginia
Date(s) Application is Due: Apr 12; Oct 12
Amount of Grant: 500 - 10,000 USD
Contact: Susan Hallett; (804) 330-7400, ext. 124; shallett@tcfrichmond.org
Internet: http://www.tcfrichmond.org/page2479.cfm
Sponsor: Community Foundation Serving Richmond and Central Virginia
7501 Boulders View Drive, Suite 110
Richmond, VA 23225

YSA ABC Summer of Service Awards 5133
ABC, in partnership with Youth Service America, is calling on young change-makers to apply for an ABC Summer of Service Award. Winners receive a $1,000 award to help make a lasting, positive change in the world. Young people located in and around ABC-affiliate communities who are creating lasting, positive change through volunteer and community service projects are ideal applicants. YSA is especially interested in ongoing, youth-led projects that highlight the creativity and commitment of young people working to meet the needs of others.
Requirements: Youth ages 5-18 located in and around ABC-affiliate communities are eligible to submit their good work and be considered for an ABC Summer of Service Award. Applications are due by midnight on September 1. Applicants must have already implemented a service project in their community. The ABC Summer of Service Award is recognizing youth that have already served their community. All applicants are required to have a sponsoring organization or school. The award check will be sent to the sponsoring organization or school. The sponsoring organization or school will accept the award funds for the applicant and work with them to utilize the funds. YSA cannot send award funds to an individual. Applicants younger than 13, must have a parent or guardian prepare and submit the application for them.
Geographic Focus: All States
Date(s) Application is Due: Sep 1
Amount of Grant: 1,000 USD
Contact: Amanda McDonald; (202) 296-2992; fax (202) 296-4030; McDonald@ysa.org
Internet: http://www.ysa.org/ABC
Sponsor: Youth Service America
1101 15th Street NW, Suite 200
Washington, DC 20005

YSA Get Ur Good On Grants　5134
The Get Ur Good On Grants, a program started by Miley Cyrus and Youth Service America in 2009, offers young people around the world an opportunity to help make a lasting positive change. Youth, ages 5 to 25, worldwide are eligible to apply for a $500 Get Ur Good On Grant to support youth-led projects. Projects must address a demonstrated community need or issue and must take place during Global Youth Service Day
Geographic Focus: All States
Date(s) Application is Due: Mar 10
Amount of Grant: 500 USD
Contact: Kevin Hollander, (202) 296-2992; fax (202) 296-4030; khollander@ysa.org
Internet: http://www.gysd.org/gysd_grants
Sponsor: Youth Service America
1101 15th Street NW, Suite 200
Washington, DC 20005

YSA Global Youth Service Day Lead Agency Grants　5135
Youth Service America and State Farm will support up to 100 Global Youth Service Day (GYSD) and Semester of Service Lead Agencies for Global Youth Service Day (mid-April). Lead Agencies are local, regional, or statewide organizations across the United States, and the Canadian provinces of Alberta, Ontario, or New Brunswick that increase the scale, visibility, and impact of Global Youth Service Day by taking a lead role in their city, region, or state. These Lead Agencies convene a planning coalition of at least 10 partner organizations that collectively engage at least 600 youth volunteers in service on GYSD, engage local media and elected officials, and plan a high profile signature project or celebration of service. The Agencies receive a $2,000 GYSD planning grant sponsored by State Farm, travel support to attend the Youth Service Institute, and ongoing training and technical assistance from Youth Service America to ensure a successful Global Youth Service Day or Semester of Service. Past Lead Agencies have leveraged their position as a GYSD Lead Agency to strengthen their programs, form new partnerships, expand their volunteer base, garner media attention, gain support from local public officials, and secure additional funding.
Requirements: Lead agencies must be located in one of the 50 states, the District of Columbia, or the Canadian provinces of Alberta, Ontario, or New Brunswick; demonstrate the organizational capacity to fulfill the responsibilities of a lead agency; have the ability to engage a variety of community groups; have the ability to plan to mobilize a citywide, regional, or statewide National Youth Service Day celebration involving more than 500 youth volunteers in service over the weekend of the event; and respond to quick deadline press opportunities.
Geographic Focus: All States, Canada
Date(s) Application is Due: Jul 17
Amount of Grant: 2,000 USD
Contact: Chris Wagner; (202) 296-2992; fax (202) 296-4030; outreach@ysa.org
Internet: http://www.ysa.org/grants/leadagency
Sponsor: Youth Service America
1101 15th Street NW, Suite 200
Washington, DC 20005

YSA MLK Day Lead Organizer Grants　5136
YSA (Youth Service America) and CNCS (the Corporation for National and Community Service) will provide MLK Day Lead Organizer grants to organizations for Martin Luther King Day of Service activities. MLK Day Lead Organizers will engage youth and adult volunteers on MLK Day (especially families volunteering together), use service as a strategy to meet important community needs, and build partnerships with other organizations in their community to achieve scale, visibility, and impact on MLK Day. Grant amounts are $1,000, $2,000, $3,000 and $4,000. Each grant amount has a different minimum number of volunteers and coalition partners required. YSA will award between 16 and 64 grants, depending on how many grantees are selected for each grant amount. YSA will accept applications in two rounds: from June 6 – July 17 and from September 1 – September 30. Round one applicants will be notified by August 16 and round two applicants will be notified by October 20. Applicants declined from round 1 may edit their application and resubmit during round 2.
Requirements: The program is open to organizations from all 50 states and the District of Columbia. YSA is especially looking for applicants in the following metropolitan areas: New York City, Los Angeles, Chicago, Philadelphia, Dallas-Fort Worth, San Francisco-Oakland-San Jose, Boston, Atlanta, Washington, DC, Houston, Detroit, Phoenix, Seattle-Tacoma, Tampa-St. Petersburg-Sarasota, Minneapolis-St. Paul, Miami-Fort Lauderdale, Denver, Cleveland-Akron, Orlando-Daytona Beach-Melbourne, and Sacramento. Organizations in any location within the United States are welcome to apply. Preference will be given to the following types of organizations: Volunteer centers; K?12 schools or school districts; Colleges and universities; Youth development organizations; Nonprofits and community organizations who address one or more of the priority issue areas.
Geographic Focus: All States
Date(s) Application is Due: Sep 30
Amount of Grant: 1,000 - 4,000 USD
Contact: Chris Wagner; (202) 296-2992; fax (202) 296-4030; outreach@ysa.org
Internet: http://www.ysa.org/grants/mlkday
Sponsor: Youth Service America
1101 15th Street NW, Suite 200
Washington, DC 20005

YSA National Child Awareness Month Youth Ambassador Grants　5137
A project of YSA (Youth Service America) and Festival of Children Foundation, this year-long Ambassadorship will help youth (ages 16-22) combat critical issues facing young people today. NCAM Youth Ambassadors will serve as community leaders, raising public awareness and affecting change around their issue area. Fifty-one NCAM Youth Ambassadors will be selected – one per state & DC – creating a powerful national network of young people who raise their collective voice in service to other youth. Youth Ambassadors will receive an all-expense paid, three-day leadership training on Capitol Hill; $1,000 grant to support the development of a youth-focused service initiative; ongoing networking opportunities with other NCAM Youth Ambassadors across the country; ongoing training and mobilization resources; a platform to grow their service initiatives.
Requirements: Eligible applicants must be between ages 16-22, and reside in the United States; attend the training in Washington, D.C. (mid-September, expenses are covered); participation in Global Youth Service Day (mid-April); and, collaborate with a sponsoring organization or school.
Geographic Focus: All States
Amount of Grant: 1,000 USD
Contact: Amanda Villacorta; (202) 296-2992; fax (202) 296-4030; info@ysa.org
Internet: http://www.ysa.org/grants/NCAM
Sponsor: Youth Service America
1101 15th Street NW, Suite 200
Washington, DC 20005

YSA NEA Youth Leaders for Literacy Grants　5138
Youth Leaders for Literacy will award 30 young people from across the U.S. each with $500 grants. Successful projects will be youth-led and address an established literacy need in the applicant's school or community. The projects will launch on NEA's Read Across America Day on March 2nd and culminate on Global Youth Service Day (mid-April_.
Requirements: All 50 states and the District of Columbia are eligible to apply. Youth ages 5-25 are welcome to apply along with an adult ally (an adult ally is a non-controlling mentor who offers support and guidance in the fulfillment of the service project).
Geographic Focus: All States
Amount of Grant: 500 USD
Contact: Amanda McDonald; (202) 296-2992; fax (202) 296-4030; McDonald@ysa.org
Internet: http://www.ysa.org/grants/nea-youth-leaders-literacy
Sponsor: Youth Service America
1101 15th Street NW, Suite 200
Washington, DC 20005

YSA Radio Disney's Hero for Change Award　5139
Radio Disney is offering young change-makers the chance to be a Hero for Change. Heroes for change are young change-makers located in Radio Disney communities who are creating positive change through volunteer and service projects. Continue to be a Hero for Change through protecting the planet, providing meals to those who need them, or giving kids just like you the resources to star in their own play, be an athlete or an artist. Winners receive a $500 award to help make a lasting, positive change in the world, plus a chance to meet other amazing young people at the Radio Disney Music Awards in Los Angeles this April. The annual deadline is March 24.
Requirements: Young heroes, ages 5 to 18, that live near Radio Disney communities and are creating positive change through service are eligible to apply.
Geographic Focus: All States
Date(s) Application is Due: Mar 24
Amount of Grant: 500 USD
Contact: Amy Floryan; (202) 296-2992; fax (202) 296-4030; afloryan@ysa.org
Internet: http://www.ysa.org/RadioDisney
Sponsor: Youth Service America
1101 15th Street NW, Suite 200
Washington, DC 20005

YSA Sodexo Lead Organizer Grants　5140
Sodexo Lead Organizers will work with ten or more partner organizations to engage at least 600 youth volunteers in learning about and addressing the issue of childhood hunger in their communities, beginning during Hunger and Homelessness Awareness Week (November) and continuing through Global Youth Service Day (GYSD). Sodexo Lead Organizers will also build new partnerships in their community and increase public awareness about the issue of hunger and young people's role in solving the problem. Finally, they will report on their efforts to YSA and document effective strategies for engaging youth in addressing childhood hunger. Twelve organizations will receive $2,000 in financial assistance as well as travel and lodging expenses for the Youth Service Institute provided by Sodexo Foundation.
Requirements: The Sodexo Lead Organizer grant program is open to U.S. organizations only.
Geographic Focus: All States
Date(s) Application is Due: Jul 15
Contact: Amanda McDonald, Grants Manager; (202) 296-2992; fax (202) 296-4030; McDonald@ysa.org or info@ysa.org
Internet: http://www.ysa.org/grants/sodexoleadorganizer
Sponsor: Youth Service America
1101 15th Street NW, Suite 200
Washington, DC 20005

YSA State Farm Good Neighbor YOUth In The Driver Seat Grants　5141
Learning to drive is one of the most exciting milestones in a teen's life. To support teens and their teachers in this rite of passage, YSA and State Farm are offering YOUth in the Driver Seat, a service and learning program that includes training, ongoing support, and a $1,500 grant to implement a fourteen week project that encourages safe driving habits, service to the community, and student achievement. With help from the service-learning experts at YSA, teachers and their students will design their own academic-standards-based project. Past participants have included an English class that created public service announcements about safe driving, a Science class that studied the physics of safe driving, a Civics class that launched a town-wide good driver campaign, and more.

Requirements: Grant applicants must meet the following *Requirements:* be a resident of the 50 states or the District of Columbia; be a certified teacher or professor who currently teaches in a public, private, faith-based, charter, or higher education institution within the 50 states or the District of Columbia; or be a school-based service-learning coordinator, whose primary role is to coordinate service-learning projects in a school or university as described above, or be a youth between the ages of 5 and 25. Teachers or school-based service-learning coordinators should secure approval from the principal or other relevant leadership before submitting a service-learning project proposal.
Geographic Focus: All States
Date(s) Application is Due: Jun 23
Amount of Grant: Up to 1,500 USD
Contact: Amy Floryan; (202) 296-2992; fax (202) 296-4030; afloryan@ysa.org
Internet: http://www.ysa.org/grants/YOUthInTheDriverSeat
Sponsor: Youth Service America
1101 15th Street NW, Suite 200
Washington, DC 20005

YSA UnitedHealth HEROES Service-Learning Grants   5142
The UnitedHealth HEROES program is a service-learning, health literacy initiative developed by UnitedHealthcare and YSA. The program awards grants to help youth, ages 5-25, create and implement local, hands-on programs to fight childhood obesity through walking, running or hiking programs. Each grant engages participating youth in service-learning, an effective teaching and learning strategy that supports student learning, academic achievement, and workplace readiness. The grants encourage semester-long projects that launch on Martin Luther King, Jr. Day of Service and culminate on Global Youth Service Day.
Requirements: Schools, service-learning coordinators, non-profits, and students in the health professions located in all 50 states and the District of Columbia are eligible to apply for the $500-$1,000 grants.
Geographic Focus: All States
Amount of Grant: 1,000 USD
Contact: Amanda McDonald; (202) 296-2992; McDonald@ysa.org or info@ysa.org
Internet: http://www.ysa.org/HEROES
Sponsor: Youth Service America
1101 15th Street NW, Suite 200
Washington, DC 20005

Yves Rocher Foundation Women of the Earth Awards   5143
The awards honor women who act for the good of nature and the well-being of all humankind. The first-prize winner will be entered in the international awards with other first-prize winners from the U.S., Canada, France, Germany, Belgium, the Netherlands, and Spain, and could win additional funds for her project. Winners will be honored in an early spring awards ceremony. Guidelines and application are available online.
Requirements: Women 18 or over are eligible. Prize money will be distributed to tax-exempt organizations.
Geographic Focus: All States
Date(s) Application is Due: Sep 30
Amount of Grant: 1,500 - 6,000 USD
Contact: Christina Hane, (001) 450-442-9555, ext. 2158; rpr@yrnet.com
Internet: http://www.yves-rocher-fondation.org/ca/en/women_of_the_earth_awards/the_prize/
Sponsor: Yves Rocher Foundation
2199 Fernand Lafontaine
Longueuil, QC J4G 2V7 Canada

Z. Smith Reynolds Foundation Community Economic Development Grants   5144
The Foundation seeks to foster economic well-being for all families and to build economic vitality and sustainability for all communities. The Foundation invests in organizations and projects that achieve the following: protects and increases the incomes and assets of low-income families and individuals; and increases community control of economic assets and economic independence for the benefit of rural or low-income residents. New programs, rather than those that are well-established and well-funded, receive priority consideration. Types of support include operating budgets, continuing support, annual campaigns, seed grants, matching funds, projects/programs, conferences and seminars, and technical assistance.
Requirements: The foundation makes grants only to nonprofit, tax-exempt, charitable organizations and institutions in North Carolina.
Restrictions: The foundation does not give priority to: the arts; capital campaigns; computer hardware or software purchases; conferences, seminars, or symposiums; crisis intervention programs; fund raising events; historic preservation; local food banks; or substance abuse treatment programs.
Geographic Focus: North Carolina
Date(s) Application is Due: Feb 1; Aug 1
Amount of Grant: 5,000 - 14,000,000 USD
Contact: Mary Fant Donnan, (800) 443-8319, ext. 101 or (336) 725-7541, ext. 101; fax (336) 725-6069; maryd@zsr.org or info@zsr.org
Internet: http://www.zsr.org/community.htm
Sponsor: Z. Smith Reynolds Foundation
147 South Cherry Street, Suite 200
Winston-Salem, NC 27101-5287

Z. Smith Reynolds Foundation Democracy and Civic Engagement Grants   5145
The Foundation seeks to foster a government that is accountable to the needs of the people; a media that provides fair and substantial information on issues facing the state and its people; a citizenry that is engaged, well-informed and participates in the life of the state; and sound public policy that is built upon comprehensive and balanced research. New programs, rather than those that are well-established and well-funded, receive priority consideration. Types of support include operating budgets, continuing support, annual campaigns, seed grants, matching funds, projects/programs, conferences and seminars, and technical assistance.
Requirements: The foundation makes grants only to nonprofit, tax-exempt, charitable organizations and institutions in North Carolina.
Restrictions: The foundation does not give priority to: the arts; capital campaigns; computer hardware or software purchases; conferences, seminars, or symposiums; crisis intervention programs; fund raising events; historic preservation; local food banks; or substance abuse treatment programs.
Geographic Focus: North Carolina
Date(s) Application is Due: Feb 1; Aug 1
Amount of Grant: 5,000 - 14,000,000 USD
Contact: Joy Vermillion Heinsohn, (800) 443-8319, ext. 106 or (336) 725-7541, ext. 106; fax (336) 725-6069; joyv@zsr.org or info@zsr.org
Internet: http://www.zsr.org/democracy.htm
Sponsor: Z. Smith Reynolds Foundation
147 South Cherry Street, Suite 200
Winston-Salem, NC 27101-5287

Z. Smith Reynolds Foundation Nancy Susan Reynolds Awards   5146
The Awards recognize the uncommon leadership of North Carolinians whose vision, determination, resourcefulness and strength of character have caused them to succeed when other individuals might have failed. What is remarkable is how each recipient - usually with limited resources and in spite of the odds - has accomplished extraordinary good in his or her community. Each award is accompanied by a grant of $25,000. The recipient receives $5,000, and $20,000 is distributed to tax-exempt, charitable, North Carolina organizations selected by the award recipient. Up to three awards will be presented annually, in the following categories: advocacy; personal service; and race relations.
Requirements: Nominees for the award must be living residents of North Carolina. They should be persons not typically in the limelight who perform valuable public service, predominately at the community level. They may be volunteers or paid, full-time employees of the organizations through which their service is rendered.
Restrictions: Anonymous nominations will not be accepted.
Geographic Focus: North Carolina
Date(s) Application is Due: Jun 1
Amount of Grant: 25,000 USD
Contact: Leslie Winner, Executive Director; (800) 443-8319, ext. 105 or (336) 725-7541, ext. 105; fax (336) 725-6069; lwinner@zsr.org or info@zsr.org
Internet: http://www.zsr.org/about_awards.htm
Sponsor: Z. Smith Reynolds Foundation
147 South Cherry Street, Suite 200
Winston-Salem, NC 27101-5287

Z. Smith Reynolds Foundation Sabbatical Grants   5147
The program supports sabbaticals of three to six months during which nonprofit organization leaders in North Carolina are not working for their organization, but instead are engaged in activities that offer personal renewal and professional growth. Sabbatical participants will have an opportunity to plan, reflect, rest, read, and study or explore interests that are unrelated to their field of work. They can do something for themselves, such as travel, return to school, or read books they've never had time to read. They will decide what will give them that needed renewal. Participants should not plan to engage in organized professional development activities while on sabbatical; rather, they should focus on rest and renewal. Sabbaticals must begin before April of the year after selection and must last for one continuous period of three to six months. Sabbatical recipients will be expected to be released completely from their organizational obligations during their sabbatical and to return to their organizations for at least the same length of time as their sabbatical. Those selected will also attend one-and-one-half day pre- and post-sabbatical retreats.
Requirements: Individuals in paid, full-time leadership positions who have served their North Carolina nonprofit organizations for at least three years, two of which as leaders, are eligible. Preference is given to individuals with at least five years of experience with their organization. Individuals who work for statewide, regional, or local nonprofit organizations may apply.
Restrictions: This program is not designed for career public school, college, university, or government employees.
Geographic Focus: North Carolina
Date(s) Application is Due: Dec 1
Amount of Grant: 25,000 USD
Contact: LaRita Bell, Sabbatical Program Coordinator; (800) 443-8319, ext. 103 or (336) 725-7541, ext. 103; fax (336) 725-6069; larita@zsr.org or info@zsr.org
Internet: http://www.zsr.org/sabbatical-program
Sponsor: Z. Smith Reynolds Foundation
147 South Cherry Street, Suite 200
Winston-Salem, NC 27101-5287

Subject Index

AIDS
Abbott Fund Global AIDS Care Grants, 82
Abbott Fund Science Educ Grants, 83
AEC Grants, 175
Aid for Starving Children Int'l Grants, 212
Ann and Robert H. Lurie Family Fndn Grants, 473
Blowitz-Ridgeway Fndn Grants, 792
Bodenwein Public Benevolent Fndn Grants, 806
Boston Fndn Grants, 819
Cable Positive's Tony Cox Community Grants, 886
Charles Delmar Fndn Grants, 1039
Child's Dream Grants, 1104
Children Affected by AIDS Network Grants, 1106
Children Affected by AIDS Fndn Family Assistance Emergency Grants, 1107
Colin Higgins Fndn Grants, 1204
Comer Fndn Grants, 1236
Community Fndn AIDS Endowment Awards, 1245
Community Fndn for Southern Arizona Grants, 1261
Community Fndn of Broward Grants, 1275
Conwood Charitable Grants, 1366
Cooper Industries Fndn Grants, 1370
Coors Brewing Corp Contributions Grants, 1371
Cornerstone Fndn of NE Wisconsin Grants, 1375
Cowles Charitable Grants, 1392
Dade Community Fndn Community AIDS Partnership Grants, 1428
Dade Community Fndn Grants, 1430
Dallas Women's Fndn Grants, 1438
Danellie Fndn Grants, 1442
David Geffen Fndn Grants, 1452
DHHS AIDS Project Grants, 1525
DIFFA/Chicago Grants, 1547
Duchossois Family Fndn Grants, 1616
Dyson Mid-Hudson Valley Project Support, 1636
Eddie C. and Sylvia Brown Family Fndn Grants, 1653
Emily Davie and Joseph S. Kornfeld Fndn Grants, 1697
Ensworth Charitable Fndn Grants, 1710
Firelight Fndn Grants, 1817
Frances L. and Edwin L. Cummings Grants, 1919
Frank E. and Seba B. Payne Fndn Grants, 1927
Fund for the City of New York Grants, 1978
Gill Fndn - Gay and Lesbian Grants, 2054
Green Bay Packers Fndn Grants, 2148
Hagedorn Grants, 2207
Hasbro Children's Fund, 2256
Henry J. Kaiser Family Fndn Grants, 2310
Horizon Fndn for New Jersey Grants, 2364
Indiana AIDS Grants, 2539
IREX Small Grant Fund for Civil Society Projects in Africa and Asia, 2581
Ittleson Fndn AIDS Grants, 2589
Johnson & Johnson Corp Contributions Grants, 2718
M. Bastian Family Fndn Grants, 2951
McCarthy Family Fndn Grants, 3073
Mildred V. Horn Fndn Grants, 3176
New York Life Fndn Grants, 3341
NYCT AIDS/HIV Grants, 3542
NYCT Girls and Young Women Grants, 3548
Oppenstein Brothers Fndn Grants, 3685
Oracle Corp Contributions Grants, 3686
Paul Rapoport Fndn Grants, 3765
Pfizer Healthcare Charitable Contributions, 3863
Playboy Fndn Grants, 3913
Puerto Rico Community Fndn Grants, 3986
Quantum Corp Snap Server Grants, 3995
Questar Corp Contributions Grants, 3997
Rhode Island Fndn Grants, 4073
Rich Fndn Grants, 4090
Ruth Anderson Fndn Grants, 4176
S. Mark Taper Fndn Grants, 4201
San Diego HIV Funding Collaborative Grants, 4251
San Francisco Fndn Community Health Grants, 4263
Scherman Fndn Grants, 4305
United Methodist Committee on Relief Global AIDS Grants, 4719
USAID/Cambodia Maternal and Child Health, Tuberculosis, HIV/AIDS. and Malaria Grants, 4736

USAID Comprehensive District-Based Support for Better HIV/TB Patient Outcomes Grants, 4747
USAID Economic Prospectsfor Armenia-Turkey Normalization Grants, 4750
USAID HIV Prevention with Key Populations - Mali Grants, 4757
USAID Strengthening Through Indian Health Professional Assoc & Scaling Up Grants, 4784
USAID Systems Strengthening for Better HIV/TB Patient Outcomes Grants, 4785
USCM HIV/AIDS Prevention Grants, 4794
Victor E. Speas Fndn Grants, 4933

AIDS Counseling
Ann and Robert H. Lurie Family Fndn Grants, 473
Child's Dream Grants, 1104
Community Fndn AIDS Endowment Awards, 1245
Dade Community Fndn Community AIDS Partnership Grants, 1428
DHHS Adolescent Family Life Demo Projects, 1524
DIFFA/Chicago Grants, 1547
Dyson Mid-Hudson Valley Project Support, 1636
Eddie C. and Sylvia Brown Family Fndn Grants, 1653
IREX Small Grant Fund for Civil Society Projects in Africa and Asia, 2581
Ms. Fndn for Women Health Grants, 3225
NYCT AIDS/HIV Grants, 3542
NYCT Neighborhood Revitalization Grants, 3555
San Diego HIV Funding Collaborative Grants, 4251
Union Square Award for Social Justice, 4717
United Methodist Commiittee on Relief Global AIDS Grants, 4719
USAID/Cambodia Maternal and Child Health, Tuberculosis, HIV/AIDS. and Malaria Grants, 4736
USAID HIV Prevention Key Pop - Mali Grants, 4757
USAID Strengthening Through Indian Health Professional Assoc & Scaling Up Grants, 4784

AIDS Education
Abbott Fund Science Educ Grants, 83
African American Fund of New Jersey Grants, 192
Aid for Starving Children Int'l Grants, 212
Alfred E. Chase Charitable Fndn Grants, 366
Cable Positive's Tony Cox Community Grants, 886
CDC School Health Programs to Prevent the Spread of HIV Coop Agreements, 975
Child's Dream Grants, 1104
Colin Higgins Fndn Grants, 1204
Comer Fndn Grants, 1236
Community Fndn AIDS Endowment Awards, 1245
Dade Community Fndn Community AIDS Partnership Grants, 1428
DIFFA/Chicago Grants, 1547
Dyson Mid-Hudson Valley Project Support, 1636
Eddie C. and Sylvia Brown Family Fndn Grants, 1653
Frances L. and Edwin L. Cummings Grants, 1919
Gill Fndn - Gay and Lesbian Grants, 2054
GNOF IMPACT Kahn-Oppenheim Grants, 2084
Health Fndn of Greater Indianapolis Grants, 2282
IREX Small Grant Fund for Civil Society Projects in Africa and Asia, 2581
Ittleson Fndn AIDS Grants, 2589
McCarthy Family Fndn Grants, 3073
Morris and Gwendolyn Cafritz Fndn Grants, 3218
Ms. Fndn for Women Health Grants, 3225
NYCT AIDS/HIV Grants, 3542
Paul Rapoport Fndn Grants, 3765
Portland Fndn - Women's Giving Circle Grant, 3935
Pride Fndn Grants, 3958
San Diego HIV Funding Collaborative Grants, 4251
Sierra Health Fndn Responsive Grants, 4353
Union Square Award for Social Justice, 4717
United Methodist Committee on Relief Global AIDS Grants, 4719
USAID/Cambodia Maternal and Child Health, Tuberculosis, HIV/AIDS. and Malaria Grants, 4736
USAID HIV Prevention with Key Populations - Mali Grants, 4757

USAID Strengthening Through Indian Health Professional Assoc & Scaling Up Grants, 4784
USAID Systems Strengthening for Better HIV/TB Patient Outcomes Grants, 4785
USCM HIV/AIDS Prevention Grants, 4794

AIDS Prevention
Abbott Fund Global AIDS Care Grants, 82
Abbott Fund Science Educ Grants, 83
Aid for Starving Children Int'l Grants, 212
Cable Positive's Tony Cox Community Grants, 886
CDC School Health Programs to Prevent the Spread of HIV Coop Agreements, 975
Child's Dream Grants, 1104
Colin Higgins Fndn Grants, 1204
Community Fndn AIDS Endowment Awards, 1245
Dade Community Fndn Community AIDS Partnership Grants, 1428
DIFFA/Chicago Grants, 1547
Dyson Mid-Hudson Valley Project Support, 1636
Eddie C. and Sylvia Brown Family Fndn Grants, 1653
Frances L. and Edwin L. Cummings Grants, 1919
GNOF IMPACT Kahn-Oppenheim Grants, 2084
Ittleson Fndn AIDS Grants, 2589
Morris and Gwendolyn Cafritz Fndn Grants, 3218
Ms. Fndn for Women Health Grants, 3225
NYCT AIDS/HIV Grants, 3542
Paul Rapoport Fndn Grants, 3765
Questar Corp Contributions Grants, 3997
Rainbow Endowment Grants, 4007
RCF General Community Grants, 4032
San Diego HIV Funding Collaborative Grants, 4251
Union Square Award for Social Justice, 4717
United Methodist Committee on Relief Global AIDS Grants, 4719
USAID/Cambodia Maternal and Child Health, Tuberculosis, HIV/AIDS. and Malaria Grants, 4736
USAID HIV Prevention with Key Populations - Mali Grants, 4757
USAID Strengthening Through Indian Health Professional Assoc & Scaling Up Grants, 4784
USAID Systems Strengthening for Better HIV/TB Patient Outcomes Grants, 4785
USCM HIV/AIDS Prevention Grants, 4794

Aboriginal Studies
CDECD Historic Restoration Grants, 983
Vancouver Fndn Grants & Comm Inits, 4900
Vanderburgh Community Fndn Women's Fund, 4903

Abortion
General Service Reproductive Justice Grants, 2007
Huber Fndn Grants, 2382
Playboy Fndn Grants, 3913

Academic Achievement
3M Fndn Community Giving Grants, 15
Albertson's Charitable Giving Grants, 345
Albert W. Rice Charitable Fndn Grants, 347
Alfred E. Chase Charitable Fndn Grants, 366
Alice Tweed Tuohy Fndn Grants, 372
American Savings Fndn Grants, 445
AON Fndn Grants, 491
Aquila Corp Grants, 521
ARCO Fndn Educ Grants, 528
ASTA Academic Scholarships, 597
Atlanta Falcons Youth Fndn Grants, 607
Best Buy Children's Fndn @15 Scholarship, 750
Cargill Citizenship Fund-Corp Giving Grants, 925
Carnegie Corp of New York Grants, 940
Charles H. Pearson Fndn Grants, 1045
CICF John H. Brown & Robert Burse Grant, 1125
Citigroup Fndn Grants, 1139
Clarence E. Heller Charitable Fndn Grants, 1150
CNCS AmeriCorps State and National Grants, 1182
Community Fndn of Santa Cruz County Grants, 1305
Community Fndn Silicon Valley Grants, 1331
Community Impact Fund, 1332

800 / Academic Achievement

DB Americas Fndn Grants, 1466
Dept of Ed Even Start Grants, 1508
Dept of Ed Magnet Schools Assistance Grants, 1509
DOJ Juvenile Mentoring Grants, 1560
Dreyer's Fndn Large Grants, 1606
FEDCO Charitable Fndn Educ Grants, 1798
Fluor Fndn Grants, 1875
Fndn for Mid South Comm Development Grants, 1897
Frank Reed and Margaret Jane Peters Memorial Fund II Grants, 1934
Gamble Fndn Grants, 1983
General Mills Fndn Celebrating Communities of Color Grants, 2002
General Mills Fndn Grants, 2003
George W. Wells Fndn Grants, 2030
GNOF IMPACT Grants for Educ, 2079
Greater Milwaukee Fndn Grants, 2137
Guy I. Bromley Grants, 2180
Harold Brooks Fndn Grants, 2227
Harvest Fndn Grants, 2254
HBF Pathways Out of Poverty Grants, 2273
Helena Rubinstein Fndn Grants, 2292
J. Knox Gholston Fndn Grants, 2599
Jane's Grants, 2639
Jessie B. Cox Charitable Grants, 2670
John W. Speas and Effie E. Speas Grants, 2732
Kimball Int'l-Habig Fndn Grants, 2823
Kuki'o Community Fund, 2845
Legacy Fndn College Readiness Grant, 2874
Lewis H. Humphreys Charitable Grants, 2889
Lloyd G. Balfour Fndn Attleboro-Specific Charities Grants, 2916
Louetta M. Cowden Fndn Grants, 2922
Louis and Elizabeth Nave Flarsheim Charitable Fndn Grants, 2924
Louis R. Cappelli Fndn Grants, 2926
Lynde and Harry Bradley Fndn Grants, 2947
Lynde and Harry Bradley Fndn Prizes, 2948
Marie C. and Joseph C. Wilson Fndn Rochester Small Grants, 3006
Meyer Fndn Educ Grants, 3142
Monsanto Int'l Grants, 3207
Nellie Mae Educ Fndn District-Level Grants, 3297
Nellie Mae Educ Fndn State Level Systems Change Grants, 3299
NFWF Nature of Learning Grants, 3381
NGA Midwest School Garden Grants, 3407
Price Chopper's Golub Fndn Two-Year Health Care Scholarship, 3951
Public Educ Power Grants, 3981
Quantum Fndn Grants, 3996
RGK Fndn Grants, 4072
Roney-Fitzpatrick Fndn Grants, 4150
S. Mark Taper Fndn Grants, 4201
Saint Paul Fndn Grants, 4219
Schumann Fund for New Jersey Grants, 4311
Seybert Inst for Poor Boys and Girls Grants, 4338
Speer Grants, 4450
Subaru of America Fndn Grants, 4518
Texas Commission on Arts Educ Grants, 4579
US Airways Educ Fndn Grants, 4790
USTA Althea Gibson Leadership Awards, 4872
USTA Okechi Womeodu Scholar Athlete Grants, 4880
USTA Serves College Educ Scholarships, 4885
USTA Serves College Textbook Scholarships, 4886
USTA Serves Dwight F. Davis Scholarships, 4887
USTA Serves Dwight Mosley Scholarships, 4888
USTA Serves Eve Kraft Scholarships, 4889
USTA Serves Marian Wood Baird Scholarship, 4890
USTA Serves Player Incentive Awards, 4891
Victor E. Speas Fndn Grants, 4933
Youth Philanthropy Project, 5132

Accounting
Alaska State Council on the Arts Community Arts Development Grants, 327
Regents Professional Opportunity Scholarships, 4044

Accounting Education
Nonprofit Management Grants, 3458

Addictions
Abell Fndn Criminal Justice and Addictions Grants, 95
Boyd Gaming Corp Contributions Program, 825
Bush Fndn Health & Human Services Grants, 875
Drug Free Communities Support Program, 1608
Fndn for a Drug-Free World Classroom Tools, 1890
Griffin Fndn Grants, 2165
Johnson & Johnson Corp Contributions Grants, 2718
Lydia deForest Charitable Grants, 2946
MGM Resorts Fndn Community Grants, 3153
National Center for Responsible Gaming Conference Scholarships, 3250
National Center for Resp Gaming Travel Grants, 3251
OSF-Baltimore Tackling Drug Addiction Grants, 3698
Rainbow Grants, 4009

Adolescent Health
Agnes M. Lindsay Grants, 203
Appalachian Reg Comm Health Care Grants, 507
Benton Community Fndn - The Cookie Jar Grant, 729
Blowitz-Ridgeway Fndn Grants, 792
CDC School Health Programs to Prevent the Spread of HIV Coop Agreements, 975
CFFVR Basic Needs Giving Partnership Grants, 1002
Cigna Civic Affairs Sponsorships, 1129
Community Fndn of Bloomington and Monroe County - Precision Health Network Cycle Grants, 1270
Cone Health Fndn Grants, 1348
Crail-Johnson Fndn Grants, 1393
DHHS Emergency Med Services for Children, 1531
DTE Energy Health & Human Services Grants, 1613
Flinn Fndn Grants, 1842
Fndn for Seacoast Health Grants, 1895
Fndns of E Chicago Health Grants, 1910
General Service Fndn Human Rights and Economic Justice Grants, 2006
Gibson County Community Fndn Women's Fund, 2051
Grand Rapids Community Ionia Youth Grants, 2120
Grand Rapids Comm SE Ottawa Youth Grants, 2123
Grand Rapids Community Sparta Youth Grants, 2125
Humana Fndn Grants, 2388
John Edward Fowler Memorial Fndn Grants, 2693
Johnson & Johnson Comm Health Care Grants, 2717
Marie C. and Joseph C. Wilson Fndn Rochester Small Grants, 3006
Mary Black Fndn Community Health Grants, 3032
MetroWest Health Grants to Reduce Incidence of High Risk Behaviors Among Adolescents, 3136
MMS and Alliance Charitable Fndn Grants for Community Action and Care for the Medically Uninsured, 3194
Oakland Fund for Children and Youth Grants, 3634
Phoenix Coyotes Charities Grants, 3879
Porter County Health and Wellness Grant, 3933
RCF The Women's Grants, 4035
Robert and Joan Dircks Fndn Grants, 4104
Seattle Fndn Health and Wellness Grants, 4328
United Methodist Health Ministry Grants, 4722
USAID NGO Health Service Delivery Grants, 4771

Adolescents
AON Fndn Grants, 491
AT&T Fndn Civic and Comm Service Grants, 599
Bernard and Audre Rapoport Fndn Democracy and Civic Participation Grants, 737
Best Buy Children's Fndn @15 Community Grants, 749
Best Buy Children's Fndn National Grants, 752
Best Buy Children's Fndn Twin Cities Minnesota Capital Grants, 753
Charlotte R. Schmidlapp Grants, 1058
Connecticut Community Fndn Grants, 1350
Dell Fndn Open Grants, 1490
DHHS Comprehensive Community Mental Health Services Grants for Children with Serious Emotional Disturbances, 1530
FCD Child Development Grants, 1796
Greater Worcester Comm Discretionary Grants, 2140
MetroWest Health Grants to Reduce Incidence of High Risk Behaviors Among Adolescents, 3136
NFL Player Youth Football Camp Grants, 3353
Oakland Fund for Children and Youth Grants, 3634
Robert Bowne Fndn Fellowships, 4107
Robert Bowne Fndn Lit Grants, 4108
Robert Bowne Fndn Youth-Centered Grants, 4109
Susan A. & Donald P. Babson Charitable Grants, 4534
USAID Comprehensive District-Based Support for Better HIV/TB Patient Outcomes Grants, 4747

Adoption
Abell-Hanger Fndn Grants, 91
ACF Adoption Opportunities Project Grants, 113
A Child Waits Fndn Grants, 128
Allan C. and Leila J. Garden Fndn Grants, 374
Dade Community Fndn Safe Passage Grants, 1431
Dave Thomas Fndn for Adoption Grants, 1449
DHHS Adolescent Family Life Demo Projects, 1524
Rainbow Academy Fndn Grants, 4006
Taproot Fndn Capacity-Building Service Grants, 4560
Topeka Community Building Families Grants, 4643
Victoria S. and Bradley L. Geist Fndn Enhancement Grants, 4935

Adult Basic Education
BBF Florida Family Lit Init Grants, 697
BBF Maryland Family Lit Init Grants, 700
Bill and Melinda Gates Fndn Financial Services for the Poor Grants, 767
Charles Nelson Robinson Grants, 1052
Community Fndn Boone County Adult Lit Grant, 1272
Emma G. Harris Fndn Grants, 1701
First Lady's Family Lit Init for Texas Family Lit Trailblazer Grants, 1821
First Lady's Family Lit Init for Texas Implementation Grants, 1823
First Lady's Family Lit Init for Texas Planning, 1824
Fndns of E Chicago Financial Indep Grants, 1909
Georgia-Pacific Fndn Educ Grants, 2031
Green Fndn Educ Grants, 2153
IIE Western Union Family Scholarships, 2462
IRA Pearson Fndn-IRA-Rotary Lit Awards, 2572
Joyce Fndn Employment Grants, 2749
McCarthy Family Fndn Grants, 3073
McCune Charitable Fndn Grants, 3077
Meyer Fndn Economic Security Grants, 3141
Nationwide Insurance Fndn Grants, 3285
PacifiCare Fndn Grants, 3725
PepsiCo Fndn Grants, 3819
Reinberger Fndn Grants, 4052
USAID Reading Enhancement for Advancing Development Grants, 4778
Xerox Fndn Grants, 5122

Adult Development
Bernard and Audre Rapoport Fndn Democracy and Civic Participation Grants, 737
George Family Fndn Grants, 2017
IIE Western Union Family Scholarships, 2462

Adult and Continuing Education
Ahmanson Fndn Grants, 207
ALA Coretta Scott King Book Donation Grant, 261
ALA DEMCO New Leaders Travel Grants, 264
Albert W. Cherne Fndn Grants, 346
Allen P. and Josephine B. Green Fndn Grants, 380
Allyn Fndn Grants, 392
Appalachian Regional Commission Business Development Revolving Loan Grants, 501
Appalachian Regional Commission Educ and Training Grants, 504
Arkell Hall Fndn Grants, 562
Arlington Community Fndn Grants, 564
Atkinson Fndn Community Grants, 606
Atlanta Fndn Grants, 608
Auburn Fndn Grants, 611
Azadoutioun Fndn Grants, 631
Ball Brothers Fndn General Grants, 637
Battle Creek Community Fndn Grants, 684
BBF Florida Family Lit Init Grants, 697
BBF Maine Family Lit Init Grants, 698
BBF Maine Family Lit Init Planning Grants, 699

SUBJECT INDEX

African Americans / 801

BBF Maryland Family Lit Init Grants, 700
BBF Maryland Family Lit Init Planning Grants, 701
BBF National Grants for Family Lit, 702
Benton Community Fndn Grants, 730
Berrien Community Fndn Grants, 744
Besser Fndn Grants, 748
Blandin Fndn Invest Early Grants, 788
Blue Mountain Community Fndn Grants, 800
Blue River Community Fndn Grants, 801
Bodenwein Public Benevolent Fndn Grants, 806
Boettcher Fndn Grants, 810
Booth-Bricker Grants, 815
Booth Ferris Fndn Grants, 816
Boston Fndn Grants, 819
Brooklyn Community Fndn Educ and Youth Achievement Grants, 851
Brown County Community Fndn Grants, 853
Burton Morgan Adult Entrepreneurship Grants, 868
Carl B. and Florence E. King Fndn Grants, 928
Catherine Manley Gaylord Fndn Grants, 956
Cemala Fndn Grants, 988
CFFVR Basic Needs Giving Partnership Grants, 1002
CFFVR Schmidt Family G4 Grants, 1020
Charles Nelson Robinson Grants, 1052
Chicago Board of Trade Fndn Grants, 1079
CIGNA Fndn Grants, 1130
Cisco Systems Fndn San Jose Community Grants, 1137
Colorado Springs Community Grants, 1215
Community Fndn of Bartholomew County Heritage Grants, 1267
Community Fndn of Bartholomew County James A. Henderson Award for Fundraising, 1268
Community Fndn of Boone County - Adult Lit Init Grants, 1272
Community Fndn of Central Illinois Grants, 1276
Community Fndn of Greater Fort Wayne - Community Endowment and Clarke Endowment Grants, 1285
Community Fndn of Shreveport-Bossier Grants, 1307
Connelly Fndn Grants, 1353
Constantin Fndn Grants, 1362
Coors Brewing Corp Contributions Grants, 1371
Cornerstone Fndn of NE Wisconsin Grants, 1375
Cowles Charitable Grants, 1392
Cruise Industry Charitable Fndn Grants, 1404
Dayton Power and Light Fndn Grants, 1464
Dept of Ed Child Care Access Means Parents in School Grants, 1507
Dollar General Adult Lit Grants, 1568
Dollar General Family Lit Grants, 1569
eBay Fndn Community Grants, 1648
Emma B. Howe Memorial Fndn Grants, 1700
Emma G. Harris Fndn Grants, 1701
Essex County Community Fndn Merrimack Valley General Grants, 1756
F.R. Bigelow Fndn Grants, 1781
Family Lit and Hawaii Pizza Hut Lit Fund, 1785
Field Fndn of Illinois Grants, 1806
First Lady's Family Lit Init for Texas Family Lit Trailblazer Grants, 1821
First Lady's Family Lit Init for Texas Implementation Grants, 1823
First Lady's Family Lit Init for Texas Planning, 1824
Fisher Fndn Grants, 1831
Fndns of E Chicago Financial Indep Grants, 1909
Frances L. and Edwin L. Cummings Grants, 1919
G.N. Wilcox Grants, 1982
George Fndn Grants, 2018
Georgia-Pacific Fndn Educ Grants, 2031
Gibson County Community Fndn Women's Fund, 2051
Goodrich Corp Fndn Grants, 2104
Green Fndn Educ Grants, 2153
Guido A. and Elizabeth H. Binda Fndn Grants, 2172
Hallmark Corp Fndn Grants, 2212
Harold Simmons Fndn Grants, 2230
Helen Steiner Rice Fndn Grants, 2299
Henry and Ruth Blaustein Rosenberg Grants, 2306
Howard and Bush Fndn Grants, 2374
HRSA Nurse Educ, Practice, Quality and Retention Grants, 2381
Hundred Club of Colorado Springs Grants, 2391

Hundred Club of Connecticut Grants, 2392
Hundred Club of Denver Grants, 2394
Hundred Club of Durango Grants, 2395
Hundred Club of Pueblo Grants, 2398
IBM Adult Training and Workforce Development Grants, 2423
IIE Western Union Family Scholarships, 2462
Indiana Workforce Acceleration Grants, 2552
James A. and Faith Knight Fndn Grants, 2621
James Ford Bell Fndn Grants, 2623
John H. and Wilhelmina D. Harland Charitable Fndn Grants, 2698
Joseph H. and Florence A. Roblee Fndn Grants, 2736
JP Morgan Chase Comm Development Grants, 2753
Kansas Arts Commission Artist Fellowships, 2776
Kirkpatrick Fndn Grants, 2827
Laura Jane Musser Rural Arts Grants, 2863
Liberty Bank Fndn Grants, 2890
Liz Claiborne Fndn Grants, 2915
Lubrizol Fndn Grants, 2933
Mardag Fndn Grants, 3001
Marie C. and Joseph C. Wilson Fndn Rochester Small Grants, 3006
MARPAT Fndn Grants, 3023
McCune Charitable Fndn Grants, 3077
Middlesex Savings Charitable Fndn Ed Opportunities Grants, 3174
National Endowment for the Arts - Regional Partnership Agreement Grants, 3258
National Endowment for Arts Commun Grants, 3260
National Endowment for the Arts Presenting Grants: Art Works, 3268
National Home Library Fndn Grants, 3276
Nationwide Insurance Fndn Grants, 3285
Norcliffe Fndn Grants, 3459
Norton Fndn Grants, 3514
NYCT Workforce Development Grants, 3560
Oppenstein Brothers Fndn Grants, 3685
PacifiCare Fndn Grants, 3725
Parkersburg Area Comm Fndn Action Grants, 3738
Paul and Mary Haas Fndn Contributions and Student Scholarships, 3756
Perry County Community Fndn Grants, 3827
Peyton Anderson Fndn Grants, 3862
Pfizer Medical Educ Track One Grants, 3864
Pike County Community Fndn Grants, 3888
Piper Jaffray Fndn Communities Giving Grants, 3899
Principal Financial Group Fndn Grants, 3966
Pulaski County Community Fndn Grants, 3988
Richard and Rhoda Goldman Grants, 4077
RWJF Jobs to Careers: Promoting Work-Based Learning for Quality Care, 4185
Saint Paul Fndn Grants, 4219
Samuel S. Johnson Fndn Grants, 4239
San Antonio Area Fndn Grants, 4240
Sara Lee Fndn Grants, 4296
Schlessman Family Fndn Grants, 4307
Sioux Falls Area Community Grants, 4364
Sioux Falls Area Community Fndn Spot Grants, 4366
Sisters of Charity Fndn of Cleveland Good Samaritan Grants, 4373
Sisters of Charity Fndn of Cleveland Reducing Health and Ed Disparities in the Central Neighborhood Grants, 4374
Sisters of Saint Joseph Charitable Grants, 4376
Sonora Area Fndn Competitive Grants, 4404
Sorenson Legacy Fndn Grants, 4407
Sprint Fndn Grants, 4463
Strake Fndn Grants, 4511
TAC Arts Educ Community-Learning Grants, 4552
TAC Arts Educ Mini Grants, 4553
Talbert and Leota Abrams Fndn, 4558
Thomas Sill Fndn Grants, 4619
Tom's of Maine Grants, 4640
U.S. Department of Educ Child Care Access Means Parents in School Grants, 4689
U.S. Department of Educ Innovative Strategies in Community Colleges for Working Adults and Displaced Workers Grants, 4692
UPS Fndn Economic and Global Lit Grants, 4730

USDA Rural Business Enterprise Grants, 4823
Vanderburgh Community Fndn Grants, 4902
Warrick County Community Fndn Grants, 4987
Whirlpool Fndn Grants, 5056
Wilson-Wood Fndn Grants, 5098
Xerox Fndn Grants, 5122

Adults
ALA Writers Live at the Library Grants, 336
Carrie E. and Lena V. Glenn Fndn Grants, 944
Charles Delmar Fndn Grants, 1039
Charles Nelson Robinson Grants, 1052
Emma G. Harris Fndn Grants, 1701
Emma J. Adams Grants, 1702
Fndns of E Chicago Financial Indep Grants, 1909
GNOF Gert Community Grants, 2076
MetLife Fndn Empowering Older Adults Grants, 3130
Meyer Fndn Economic Security Grants, 3141
National Endowment for Arts Agencies Grants, 3263
National Endowment for Arts Museum Grants, 3265
National Endowment for Arts Opera Grants, 3267
Piper Trust Educ Grants, 3902
Piper Trust Older Adults Grants, 3904
Piper Trust Reglious Organizations Grants, 3905
U.S. Department of Educ Innovative Strategies in Community Colleges for Working Adults and Displaced Workers Grants, 4692
Wild Rivers Community Fndn Holiday Partnership Grants, 5069

Advertising
CDECD Historic Preser Enhancement Grants, 981
Charles Stewart Mott Fndn Anti-Poverty Grants, 1054
DogTime Technology Grant, 1553
Google Grants Beta, 2107
IREX Egypt Media Development Grants, 2575
IREX Small Grant Fund for Media Projects in Africa and Asia, 2582

Aeronautical/Astronautical Engineering
Air Force Association Junior ROTC Grants, 215

Aerospace
Air Force Association Civil Air Patrol Unit Grants, 214
Air Force Association Junior ROTC Grants, 215

African American Students
Head Start Replacement Grantee: Colorado, 2275
Head Start Replacement Grantee: Florida, 2276
Head Start Replacement Grantee: West Virginia, 2277
Miller Brewing Corp Contributions Grants, 3180
NACC David Stevenson Fellowships, 3235
NACC William Diaz Fellowships, 3236
OSF Campaign for Black Male Achievement, 3703

African American Studies
Alabama Humanities Fndn Mini Grants, 231
Alabama Humanities Planning/Consultant Grants, 232
George J. and Effie L. Seay Fndn Grants, 2024
Virginia Fndn for Humanities Discr Grants, 4946
Virginia Fndn for the Humanities Open Grants, 4947

African Americans
African American Fund of New Jersey Grants, 192
African American Heritage Grants, 193
ALA Coretta Scott King-Virginia Hamilton Award for Lifetime Achievement, 259
ALA Coretta Scott King Book Awards, 260
ALA Coretta Scott King Book Donation Grant, 261
Arkansas Community Fndn Arkansas Black Hall of Fame Grants, 559
Boston Fndn Grants, 819
Charles Delmar Fndn Grants, 1039
Charles Parker Trust for Public Music Grants, 1053
CMA Fndn Grants, 1178
Coca-Cola Fndn Grants, 1195
Community Fndn of Louisville Grants, 1299
Community Fndn of St. Joseph County African American Community Grants, 1312
Connecticut Community Fndn Grants, 1350

802 / African Americans

DHHS Maternal and Child Health Grants, 1536
Effie and Wofford Cain Fndn Grants, 1674
GNOF IMPACT Grants for Health and Human Services, 2080
Head Start Replacement Grantee: Colorado, 2275
Head Start Replacement Grantee: Florida, 2276
Head Start Replacement Grantee: West Virginia, 2277
Historic Landmarks Fndn of Indiana African American Heritage Grants, 2333
Joyce Awards, 2746
Kansas Arts Commission Artist Fellowships, 2776
North Carolina Arts Council Outreach Grants, 3479
NYSCA Special Arts Services: General Operating Support Grants, 3614
OSF Campaign for Black Male Achievement, 3703
Philadelphia Organizational Effectiveness Grants, 3872
Saint Luke's Health Inits Grants, 4216
Saint Paul Fndn SpectrumGrants, 4222
Strowd Roses Grants, 4515
Virginia Fndn for the Humanities Discr Grants, 4946
Virginia Fndn for the Humanities Open Grants, 4947
Washington Area Women's Fndn African American Women's Giving Circle Grants, 4989

African Art

Christensen Fund Regional Grants, 1112
Doris Duke Charitable Fndn Arts Grants, 1584
NYSCA Special Arts Services: General Program Support Grants, 3615

After-School Programs

Agere Corp and Community Involvement Grants, 199
ALA Coretta Scott King Book Donation Grant, 261
Arizona Commission on the Arts After-School Program Residencies, 535
Arizona Commission on the Arts Educ Grants, 536
Arizona Republic Newspaper Contributions, 547
Arkansas Arts Council AIE After School/Summer Residency Grants, 551
Baltimore Community Fndn Arts and Culture Path Grants, 641
Barr Fndn Grants (Massachusetts), 676
Boston Globe Fndn Grants, 821
Brooklyn Community Fndn Community Arts for All Grants, 849
Cal Ripken Sr. Fndn Grants, 912
Carnegie Corp of New York Grants, 940
CCF Community Priorities Fund, 961
CDECD Arts Catalyze Placemaking in Every Community Grants, 977
CDECD Arts Catalyze Placemaking Leadership Grants, 978
CDECD Arts Catalyze Placemaking Sustaining Relevance Grants, 979
CFFVR Basic Needs Giving Partnership Grants, 1002
CFFVR Mielke Family Fndn Grants, 1015
Charles Stewart Mott Fndn Anti-Poverty Grants, 1054
CICF Summer Youth Grants, 1128
CIRCLE Civic Educ at the High School Level Research Grants, 1135
CNCS AmeriCorps State and National Grants, 1182
Community Fndn of Broward Grants, 1275
Community Fndn of Greenville Hollingsworth Funds Program/Project Grants, 1296
CVS Community Grants, 1422
Delaware Community Next Generation Grants, 1485
Dermody Properties Fndn Grants, 1517
Dreyer's Fndn Large Grants, 1606
Duluth-Superior Area Community Fndn Grants, 1620
Edna McConnell Clark Fndn Grants, 1659
Edward W. and Stella C. Van Houten Grants, 1670
Emma B. Howe Memorial Fndn Grants, 1700
Fargo-Moorhead Area Fndn Woman's Grants, 1789
Foellinger Fndn Grants, 1877
Fndn for the Mid South Educ Grants, 1898
Frank B. Hazard General Charity Grants, 1926
Frank Loomis Palmer Grants, 1931
Frank M. Tait Fndn Grants, 1932
Fremont Area Community Fndn Grants, 1955
German Protestant Orphan Asylum Fndn Grants, 2044
Ginn Fndn Grants, 2056
GNOF Coastal 5 + 1 Grants, 2070
GNOF IMPACT Grants for Youth Development, 2081
Grable Fndn Grants, 2108
Grand Circle Fndn Associates Grants, 2112
GTECH After School Advantage Grants, 2170
HBF Pathways Out of Poverty Grants, 2273
Head Start Replacement Grantee: Colorado, 2275
Head Start Replacement Grantee: Florida, 2276
Head Start Replacement Grantee: West Virginia, 2277
Helen Bader Fndn Grants, 2293
Henry and Ruth Blaustein Rosenberg Grants, 2306
Indep Comm Fndn Educ, Culture & Arts Grant, 2526
J.C. Penney Company Grants, 2594
Jeffris Wood Fndn Grants, 2660
Jim Moran Fndn Grants, 2680
John Clarke Grants, 2689
Kenny's Kids Grants, 2803
Kuki'o Community Fund, 2845
LA84 Fndn Grants, 2847
Louis Calder Fndn Grants, 2925
Luella Kemper Grants, 2939
Luther I. Replogle Fndn Grants, 2945
Mabel Louise Riley Family Strengthening Grants, 2958
Marin Community Fndn Stinson Bolinas Community Grants, 3013
Meyer Fndn Educ Grants, 3142
Milton Hicks Wood and Helen Gibbs Wood Charitable Grants, 3184
Mitsubishi Electric America Fndn Grants, 3190
Monsanto Int'l Grants, 3207
Montana Community Fndn Grants, 3211
MONY Fndn Grants, 3214
National 4-H Afterschool Training Grants, 3248
National Endowment for the Arts - National Arts and Humanities Youth Program Awards, 3255
Nestle Purina PetCare Ed Grants, 3302
New York Life Fndn Grants, 3341
NFL Charities NFL Player Fndn Grants, 3347
NYSCA Literature: Public Programs, 3600
Oklahoma City Community Programs & Grants, 3666
Pacers Fndn Be Educated Grants, 3721
Paul G. Allen Family Fndn Grants, 3759
PG&E Community Vitality Grants, 3868
Phoenix Coyotes Charities Grants, 3879
Pinkerton Fndn Grants, 3892
Piper Trust Children Grants, 3901
Piper Trust Educ Grants, 3902
Priddy Fndn Grants, 3957
RCF Summertime Kids Grants, 4034
Robert Bowne Fndn Fellowships, 4107
Robert Bowne Fndn Lit Grants, 4108
Robert Bowne Fndn Youth-Centered Grants, 4109
Rohm and Haas Company Grants, 4145
Romic Environmental's Charitable Contributions, 4148
Samuel S. Fels Grants, 4238
Samuel S. Johnson Fndn Grants, 4239
Share Our Strength Grants, 4340
Skillman Fndn Good Schools Grants, 4382
SOBP A.E. Bennett Research Award, 4388
Southbury Community Trust Fund, 4409
South Carolina Arts Commission AIE Residency Plus Individual Site Grants, 4411
South Carolina Arts Commission AIE Residency Plus Multi-Site Grants, 4412
South Carolina Arts Commission Arts in Educ After School Arts Init Grants, 4418
Stark Community Fndn Grants, 4477
Susan A. & Donald P. Babson Charitable Grants, 4534
TAC Arts Educ Community-Learning Grants, 4552
TAC Arts Educ Mini Grants, 4553
Tauck Family Fndn Grants, 4563
Time Warner Diverse Voices in the Arts Grants, 4635
Tri-State Community Twenty-first Century Endowment Grants, 4666
U.S. Department of Educ 21st Century Community Learning Centers, 4687
VSA/Metlife Connect All Grants, 4953
W.H. and Mary Ellen Cobb Charitable Grants, 4959
Wallace Fndn Grants, 4976
West Virginia Comm on the Arts Special Grants, 5048
William Blair and Company Fndn Grants, 5078
William G. and Helen C. Hoffman Fndn Grants, 5080
Wisconsin Energy Fndn Grants, 5106

Age Discrimination

Allstate Corp Giving Grants, 386
Allstate Corp Hometown Commitment Grants, 387
Allstate Fndn Safe and Vital Communities Grants, 390
Allstate Fndn Tolerance, Inclusion, and Diversity Grants, 391
ANLAF Int'l Fund for Sexual Minorities Grants, 471
Meyer Fndn Economic Security Grants, 3141

Aging/Gerontology

Abington Fndn Grants, 100
Administration on Aging Senior Medicare Patrol Project Grants, 166
American Society on Aging Hall of Fame Award, 448
American Society on Aging NOMA Award for Excellence in Multicultural Aging, 449
Anne L. and George H. Clapp Charitable and Ed Grants, 476
Arlington Community Fndn Grants, 564
Austin-Bailey Health and Wellness Fndn Grants, 614
Bender Fndn Grants, 726
Brookdale Fndn Leadership in Aging Fellowships, 844
Brookdale Fndn National Group Respite Grants, 845
Caesars Fndn Grants, 891
Carl B. and Florence E. King Fndn Grants, 928
Carl W. and Carrie Mae Joslyn Grants, 938
Catherine Kennedy Home Fndn Grants, 955
Charles Delmar Fndn Grants, 1039
CHCF Grants, 1063
Claude Pepper Fndn Grants, 1160
Clay Fndn Grants, 1162
CNCS Foster Grandparent Grants, 1185
CNCS Senior Companion Grants, 1187
Community Fndn in Jacksonville Senior Roundtable Aging Adults Grants, 1263
Community Memorial Fndn Grants, 1334
Conwood Charitable Grants, 1366
Cralle Fndn Grants, 1394
Daniels Grants, 1443
Daphne Seybolt Culpeper Memorial Fndn Grants, 1445
DHHS Special Programs for the Aging: Training, Research, and DiscretionaryGrants, 1538
Dolfinger-McMahon Fndn Grants, 1565
Dr. P. Phillips Fndn Grants, 1601
Edward N. and Della L. Thome Memorial Fndn Direct Services Grants, 1666
Effie and Wofford Cain Fndn Grants, 1674
Emma J. Adams Grants, 1702
Encore Purpose Prize, 1704
Fallon OrNda Community Health Grants, 1783
Gates Family Children, Youth & Family Grants, 1989
Greater Worcester Community Jeppson Memorial Fund for Brookfield Grants, 2141
Harry Kramer Grants, 2242
Hartford Aging and Health Program Awards, 2247
Helen Bader Fndn Grants, 2293
Helen Steiner Rice Fndn Grants, 2299
Henrietta Tower Wurts Memorial Fndn Grants, 2304
Horace A. Kimball and S. Ella Kimball Grants, 2362
James H. Cummings Fndn Grants, 2626
Jerome and Mildred Paddock Fndn Grants, 2666
John G. Martin Fndn Grants, 2696
Leicester Savings Bank Fund, 2879
M.B. and Edna Zale Fndn Grants, 2950
M.D. Anderson Fndn Grants, 2952
Margaret L. Wendt Fndn Grants, 3004
Marjorie Moore Charitable Fndn Grants, 3021
Mary Jane Luick Grants, 3040
Maurice J. Masserini Charitable Grants, 3064
McLean Contributionship Grants, 3088
Mericos Fndn Grants, 3121
MetroWest Health Fndn Grants--Healthy Aging, 3135
Metzger-Price Grants, 3137
Northland Fndn Grants, 3506
Ordean Fndn Grants, 3691

SUBJECT INDEX

Paul Balint Charitable Grants, 3757
Piper Trust Healthcare & Med Research Grants, 3903
Piper Trust Older Adults Grants, 3904
Posey Community Fndn Women's Grants, 3938
Posey County Community Fndn Grants, 3939
Powell Fndn Grants, 3942
Quantum Fndn Grants, 3996
Retirement Research Fndn General Grants, 4067
Rhode Island Fndn Grants, 4073
Rose Community Fndn Aging Grants, 4152
S. Mark Taper Fndn Grants, 4201
SW Init Fndn Grants, 4446
Steelcase Fndn Grants, 4497
Strowd Roses Grants, 4515
Vigneron Grants, 4938
Wilson-Wood Fndn Grants, 5098

Agribusiness
CLIF Bar Family Fndn Grants, 1173
McCune Charitable Fndn Grants, 3077
MDARD AgD Value Added/Regional Food Systems Grants, 3091
MDARD County Fairs Cap Improvement Grants, 3092
MDARD Specialty Crop Block Grants-Farm Bill, 3093
USAID Economic Prospectsfor Armenia-Turkey Normalization Grants, 4750
USDA 1890 Land Grant Colleges and Universities Init Grants, 4797
USDA Fed-State Marketing Improvement Grants, 4810
USDA Small Disadvantaged Producer Grants, 4837

Agricultural Commodities
ADEC Agricultural Telecommunications Grants, 159
Aid for Starving Children Int'l Grants, 212
MDARD AgD Value Added/Regional Food Systems Grants, 3091
MDARD Specialty Crop Block Grants-Farm Bill, 3093
USAID Malawi Local Capacity Devel Grants, 4767
USDA Fed-State Marketing Improvement Grants, 4810

Agricultural Economics
Honeybee Health Improvement Project Grants, 2355
MDARD Specialty Crop Block Grants-Farm Bill, 3093
Social Justice Fund NW Montana Giving Project Grants, 4399
USAID African Innovation Mechanism Grants, 4738
USAID India-Africa Agriculture Innovation Bridge Grants, 4760
USAID Malawi Local Capacity Devel Grants, 4767
USAID Resilience and Economic Growth in the Sahel - Enhanced Resilience Grants, 4779
USDA Agricultural and Rural Economic Research Grants, 4798

Agricultural Extension
Heifer Ed Grants for Teachers, 2289
Phi Upsilon Omicron Florence Fallgatter Distinguished Service Award, 3877

Agricultural Management
Golden LEAF Fndn Grants, 2097
USAID India-Africa Agriculture Innovation Bridge Grants, 4760

Agricultural Planning/Policy
American Jewish World Service Grants, 441
Blue Cross Blue Shield of Minnesota Healthy Impact Assessment Demonstration Project Grants, 795
Blue Cross Blue Shield of Minnesota Fndn - Healthy Equity: Health Impact Assessment Grants, 796
Clarence E. Heller Charitable Fndn Grants, 1150
EPA Regional Agricultural IPM Grants, 1735
Farm Aid Grants, 1790
GNOF Coastal 5 + 1 Grants, 2070
Great Lakes Protection Grants, 2147
Institute for Agriculture and Trade Policy Food and Society Fellowships, 2561
Max and Anna Levinson Fndn Grants, 3066
MDARD Specialty Crop Block Grants-Farm Bill, 3093
The World Food Prize, 4606

USAID African Innovation Mechanism Grants, 4738
USAID Albania Critical Economic Growth Areas Grants, 4740
USAID India-Africa Agriculture Innovation Bridge Grants, 4760
USAID Malawi Local Capacity Devel Grants, 4767
USDA Coop Extension System Educ Grants, 4803
USDA Foreign Market Development Grants, 4811
USDA Market Access Grants, 4818

Agriculture
Abelard Fndn East Grants, 87
Abelard Fndn West Grants, 88
Agway Fndn Grants, 205
ALSAM Fndn Grants, 395
America the Beautiful Fund Operation Green Plant Grants, 451
Anderson Fndn Grants, 460
Ben & Jerry's Fndn Grants, 724
Bush Fndn Ecological Health Grants, 874
Canada-U.S. Fulbright Mid-Career Grants, 917
Chiquita Brands Int'l Grants, 1110
CLIF Bar Family Fndn Grants, 1173
Curtis and Edith Munson Fndn Grants, 1418
David Robinson Fndn Grants, 1454
EPA Regional Agricultural IPM Grants, 1735
Farm Aid Grants, 1790
Flinn Fndn Scholarships, 1843
Gamble Fndn Grants, 1983
GNOF Plaquemines Community Grants, 2091
Golden LEAF Fndn Grants, 2097
HAF Co-op Community Grants, 2192
Harry Chapin Fndn Grants, 2240
Heifer Ed Grants for Principals, 2288
Heifer Ed Grants for Teachers, 2289
Honeybee Health Improvement Project Grants, 2355
IIE New Leaders Group Award for Understanding, 2460
Indiana Corn Marketing Council Retailer Grant for Tank Cleaning, 2536
Institute for Agriculture and Trade Policy Food and Society Fellowships, 2561
John Deere Fndn Grants, 2692
Lindbergh Grants, 2907
Marriott Int'l Corp Giving Grants, 3024
Max and Anna Levinson Fndn Grants, 3066
McCune Charitable Fndn Grants, 3077
MDARD AgD Value Added Food Systems Grants, 3091
MDARD Specialty Crop Block Grants-Farm Bill, 3093
Monfort Family Fndn Grants, 3203
PepsiCo Fndn Grants, 3819
Perry County Community Fndn Grants, 3827
Posey County Community Fndn Grants, 3939
Puerto Rico Community Fndn Grants, 3986
Richland County Bank Grants, 4091
Rose Fndn for Comm & the Environment N California Environmental Grassroots Grants, 4158
Samuel S. Johnson Fndn Grants, 4239
Seneca Foods Fndn Grants, 4336
Slow Food in Schools Micro-Grants, 4384
Strolling of the Heifers Scholarships for Farmers, 4514
Trull Fndn Grants, 4673
USAID African Innovation Mechanism Grants, 4738
USAID Albania Critical Economic Growth Areas Grants, 4740
USAID Food Security, Nutrition, Biodiversity and Conservation Grants, 4752
USAID Grants for Building Disaster-Resilient Communities in Southern Africa, 4755
USAID India-Africa Agriculture Innovation Bridge Grants, 4760
USAID Int'l Food Relief Partnership Grants, 4764
USAID Malawi Local Capacity Devel Grants, 4767
USDA Agricultural & Rural Economic Research, 4798
USDA Community Food Projects Grants, 4802
USDA Farm Labor Housing Grants, 4809
USDA Foreign Market Development Grants, 4811
USDA Hispanic-Serving Insts Educ Grants, 4813
USDA Market Access Grants, 4818
USDA Special Research Grants, 4839
USDA Value-Added Producer Grants, 4843

Agriculture Education
ADEC Agricultural Telecommunications Grants, 159
Annie's Cases for Causes Product Donations, 479
Annie's Grants for Gardens, 480
California Fertilizer Fndn School Garden Grants, 905
Charles Nelson Robinson Grants, 1052
Conservation, Food, and Health Fndn Grants for Developing Countries, 1359
Dean Foods Community Involvement Grants, 1469
Fruit Tree 101, 1967
GEF Green Thumb Challenge, 1996
HAF Co-op Community Grants, 2192
Heifer Ed Grants for Principals, 2288
Heifer Ed Grants for Teachers, 2289
Lowe's Outdoor Classroom Grants, 2928
Marriott Int'l Corp Giving Grants, 3024
McCune Charitable Fndn Grants, 3077
NGA Heinz Wholesome Memories Intergenerational Garden Awards, 3404
NGA Mantis Award, 3406
NGA Midwest School Garden Grants, 3407
Posey County Community Fndn Grants, 3939
Richland County Bank Grants, 4091
Scholastic Welch's Harvest Grants, 4309
Slow Food in Schools Micro-Grants, 4384
Strolling of the Heifers Scholarships for Farmers, 4514
Subaru Adopt a School Garden Grants, 4517
USAID African Innovation Mechanism Grants, 4738
USAID India-Africa Agriculture Innovation Bridge Grants, 4760
USAID Malawi Local Capacity Devel Grants, 4767
USDA Agricultural and Rural Economic Research Grants, 4798
USDA Value-Added Producer Grants, 4843

Agriscience
Honeybee Health Improvement Project Grants, 2355

Airplanes
NW Airlines KidCares Med Travel Assistance, 3508
TSA Advanced Surveillance Grants, 4674

Alaskan Natives
ACF Native American Social and Economic Development Strategies Grants, 123
Dept of Ed Alaska Native Ed Programs, 1506
EPA State Indoor Radon Grants, 1738
IMLS Native Am Library Services Basic Grants, 2517
IMLS Native American Library Services Enhancement Grants, 2518
Kansas Arts Commission Artist Fellowships, 2776
USDA Section 306D Water and Waste System Grants for Alaskan Villages, 4835
USDC Business Center - American Indian and Alaska Native Grants, 4849

Alcohol Education
CFFVR Alcoholism and Drug Abuse Grants, 1001
Coors Brewing Corp Contributions Grants, 1371
Diageo Fndn Grants, 1546
George P. Davenport Grants, 2026
Maine State Troopers Fndn Grants, 2991
NYCT Girls and Young Women Grants, 3548
NYCT Substance Abuse Grants, 3558
Sierra Health Fndn Responsive Grants, 4353
U.S. Department of Educ Programs for Native Hawaiians, 4696

Alcohol/Alcoholism
AAA Fndn for Traffic Safety Grants, 50
ACF Native American Social and Economic Development Strategies Grants, 123
Achelis Fndn Grants, 127
African American Fund of New Jersey Grants, 192
Alex Stern Family Fndn Grants, 360
Alliance Healthcare Fndn Grants, 383
AMA Fndn Fund for Better Health Grants, 409
Atkinson Fndn Community Grants, 606
Barberton Community Fndn Grants, 666
Berks County Community Fndn Grants, 734

Alcohol/Alcoholism

Bodman Fndn Grants, 807
Bush Fndn Health & Human Services Grants, 875
California Arts Council Arts and Accessibility Technical Assistance Grants, 894
Cambridge Community Fndn Grants, 913
Carlisle Fndn Grants, 931
Carpenter Fndn Grants, 943
CFFVR Alcoholism and Drug Abuse Grants, 1001
Cleo Fndn Grants, 1164
Colorado Springs Community Grants, 1215
Community Fndn for Southern Arizona Grants, 1261
Community Fndn of Broward Grants, 1275
ConocoPhillips Grants, 1355
Constantin Fndn Grants, 1362
Coors Brewing Corp Contributions Grants, 1371
D.F. Halton Fndn Grants, 1424
Dallas Women's Fndn Grants, 1438
Daniels Grants, 1443
Dave Coy Fndn Grants, 1447
Dennis and Phyllis Washington Fndn Grants, 1498
Do Right Fndn Grants, 1581
Drug Free Communities Support Program, 1608
EIF Community Grants, 1675
Farmers Insurance Corp Giving Grants, 1791
Fndn for a Healthy Kentucky Grants, 1891
Frances and John L. Loeb Family Grants, 1917
Fuller Fndn Grants, 1974
George P. Davenport Grants, 2026
Greater Worcester Comm Discretionary Grants, 2140
Hasbro Children's Fund, 2256
Health Fndn of Greater Cincinnati Grants, 2281
Hoffberger Fndn Grants, 2342
Huffy Fndn Grants, 2384
Humanitas Fndn Grants, 2390
Jackson Fndn Grants, 2613
Johnson & Johnson Corp Contributions Grants, 2718
Joseph Drown Fndn Grants, 2735
Joseph H. and Florence A. Roblee Fndn Grants, 2736
Kuki'o Community Fund, 2845
L. W. Pierce Family Fndn Grants, 2846
Maine Community Fndn Vincent B. and Barbara G. Welch Grants, 2990
Maine State Troopers Fndn Grants, 2991
Margaret L. Wendt Fndn Grants, 3004
Mary Owen Borden Fndn Grants, 3046
Memorial Fndn Grants, 3117
Mid-Iowa Health Fndn Comm Response Grants, 3168
Musgrave Fndn Grants, 3231
Northern Trust Company Corp Giving Program, 3504
NYCT Substance Abuse Grants, 3558
Ordean Fndn Grants, 3691
Pacers Fndn Be Drug-Free Grants, 3720
PacifiCorp Fndn for Learning Grants, 3727
Pajaro Valley Community Health Health Insurance/ Coverage & Educ on Using the System Grants, 3731
Peter & Elizabeth C. Tower Mental Health Reference and Resource Materials Mini-Grants, 3837
Peter & Elizabeth Tower Substance Abuse Grants, 3842
Puerto Rico Community Fndn Grants, 3986
Quantum Corp Snap Server Grants, 3995
Questar Corp Contributions Grants, 3997
Ruth Anderson Fndn Grants, 4176
RWJF New Jersey Health Inits Grants, 4187
S.H. Cowell Fndn Grants, 4199
SAMHSA Drug Free Communities Grants, 4230
SAMHSA Strategic Prevention Framework State Incentive Grants, 4231
Sid W. Richardson Fndn Grants, 4350
Sioux Falls Area Community Fndn Spot Grants, 4366
Southbury Community Trust Fund, 4409
State Justice Institute Curriculum Adaptation and Training Grants, 4488
State Justice Institute Partner Grants, 4489
State Justice Institute Project Grants, 4490
State Justice Institute Strategic Init Grants, 4492
State Justice Institute Tech Assistance Grants, 4493
Stewart Huston Charitable Grants, 4505
Topeka Community Fndn Grants, 4644
U.S. Department of Educ Programs for Native Hawaiians, 4696
Union Bank, N.A. Fndn Grants, 4709
Victor E. Speas Fndn Grants, 4933
Whitney Fndn Grants, 5061

Allergy
AAAAI RSLAAIS Leadership Award, 49
Coca-Cola Fndn Grants, 1195

Allied Health
Mary Black Fndn Community Health Grants, 3032

Allied Health Education
Columbus Fndn Small Grants, 1232
CVS All Kids Can Grants, 1420
CVS Community Grants, 1422
Health Fndn of Greater Indianapolis Grants, 2282
J.M. Long Fndn Grants, 2603
James G.K. McClure Educ and Devel Grants, 2624
Lettie Pate Whitehead Fndn Grants, 2888
Pajaro Valley Community Health Trust Diabetes and Contributing Factors Grants, 3732
Schering-Plough Fndn Health Grants, 4304

Alternative Education
Georgia-Pacific Fndn Educ Grants, 2031
Pacers Fndn Be Educated Grants, 3721

Alternative Fuels
Colorado Bioscience Discovery Evaluation Grants, 1211
Connecticut Light & Power Corp Contributions, 1352
DOE Initial H-Prize Competition for Breakthrough Advances in Materials for Hydrogen Storage, 1551
Entergy Charitable Fndn Low-Income Inits and Solutions Grants, 1711
Hydrogen Student Design Contest, 2415
Indiana Corn Marketing Council Retailer Grant for Tank Cleaning, 2536
Max and Anna Levinson Fndn Grants, 3066
PG&E Community Vitality Grants, 3868
Progress Energy Fndn Environmental Stewardship Grants, 3970

Alternative Medicine
Blowitz-Ridgeway Fndn Grants, 792
James Hervey Johnson Charitable Ed Grants, 2627
Jenifer Altman Fndn Grants, 2662
U.S. Department of Educ Vocational Rehabilitation Services Projects for American Indians with Disabilities Grants, 4702

Alternative Modes of Education
James R. Thorpe Fndn Grants, 2636
Nellie Mae Educ Public Understanding Grants, 3298
Pentair Fndn Educ and Community Grants, 3816
RWJF Jobs to Careers: Promoting Work-Based Learning for Quality Care, 4185
Seattle Fndn Educ Grants, 4326
Teaching Tolerance Grants, 4567
U.S. Department of Educ Vocational Rehabilitation Services Projects for American Indians with Disabilities Grants, 4702

Alzheimer's Disease
Austin S. Nelson Fndn Grants, 617
Balfe Family Fndn Grants, 636
Brookdale Fndn Leadership in Aging Fellowships, 844
Brookdale Fndn National Group Respite Grants, 845
Caesars Fndn Grants, 891
CFFVR Robert and Patricia Endries Family Fndn Grants, 1018
CNCS Senior Companion Grants, 1187
Dyson Mid-Hudson Valley Project Support, 1636
Edward N. and Della L. Thome Memorial Fndn Direct Services Grants, 1666
F.M. Kirby Fndn Grants, 1780
Fremont Area Community Fndn Grants, 1955
G.N. Wilcox Grants, 1982
GNOF IMPACT Harold W. Newman, Jr. Charitable Grants, 2083
Grand Rapids Area Community Fndn Grants, 2114
Helen Bader Fndn Grants, 2293
Henrietta Lange Burk Grants, 2303
Merkel Family Fndn Grants, 3123
NW Mutual Fndn Grants, 3509
Peyton Anderson Fndn Grants, 3862
Rose Community Fndn Aging Grants, 4152

American History
ALA Gale Cengage History Research and Innovation Award, 280
NEH Family and Youth Programs in American History Grants, 3291
NEH Interpreting America's Hist Places Grants, 3292
Richard and Caroline T. Gwathmey Grants, 4075

American Indian Culture
Delta Air Lines Fndn Arts and Culture Grants, 1493
McCune Charitable Fndn Grants, 3077

American Indian History
McCune Charitable Fndn Grants, 3077
NEH Family and Youth Programs in American History Grants, 3291
NEH Interpreting America's Hist Places Grants, 3292

American Indian Language
McCune Charitable Fndn Grants, 3077

American Recovery and Reinvestment Act
DHHS American Recovery and Reinvestment Act of 2009 Head Start Expansion, 1526
DHHS ARRA Strengthening Communities Fund - Nonprofit Capacity Building Grants, 1527
DHHS ARRA Strengthening Communities Fund - State, Local, and Tribal Government Capacity Building Grants, 1528
DHHS Community Services Block Grant Training and Technical Assistance Program: Capacity-Building for Ongoing CSBG Programs and Strategic Planning and Coordination Grants, 1529
DHS ARRA Fire Station Construction Grants, 1542
DHS ARRA Port Security Grants, 1543
DHS ARRA Transit Security Grants, 1544
DHS FY 2009 Transit Security Grants, 1545
TSA Advanced Surveillance Grants, 4674

American Studies
Alabama Humanities Fndn Mini Grants, 231
Alabama Humanities Planning/Consultant Grants, 232
Canada-U.S. Fulbright Mid-Career Grants, 917
McCune Charitable Fndn Grants, 3077

Animal Care
2701 Fndn Grants, 37
Adam Richter Charitable Grants, 145
Alberto Culver Corp Contributions Grants, 343
American Humane Assoc Second Chance Grants, 440
Ann L. & Carol Green Rhodes Charitable Grants, 483
Armstrong McDonald Fndn Grants, 565
Austin Community Fndn Grants, 616
Banfield Charitable Grants, 652
Batchelor Fndn Grants, 679
Beim Fndn Grants, 718
Benton County Fndn Grants, 731
Bernice Barbour Fndn Grants, 743
Build-A-Bear Workshop Fndn Grants, 861
Champlin Fndns Grants, 1029
Charles H. Hall Fndn, 1044
Charlotte County (FL) Community Fndn Grants, 1056
Columbus Fndn Small Grants, 1232
Community Fndn of Abilene Humane Treatment of Animals Grants, 1266
Community Fndn of Broward Grants, 1275
Community Fndn of Tampa Bay Grants, 1316
Cooke-Hay Fndn Grants, 1367
Dade Community Fndn Grants, 1430
Dean Foods Community Involvement Grants, 1469
DeRoy Testamentary Fndn Grants, 1518
Doris Day Animal Fndn Grants, 1583
Ethel Frends Fndn Grants, 1759

SUBJECT INDEX

Fargo-Moorhead Area Fndn Grants, 1788
Florida Sea Turtle Grants, 1871
Fuller Fndn Grants, 1974
Gamble Fndn Grants, 1983
Green Bay Packers Fndn Grants, 2148
Green Fndn Special Project Grants, 2155
Handsel Fndn Grants, 2221
Hulman & Company Fndn Grants, 2387
Jane's Grants, 2639
Jaqua Fndn Grants, 2653
Kenneth A. Scott Charitable Grants, 2801
Kirkpatrick Fndn Grants, 2827
Letha E. House Fndn Grants, 2886
Lubbock Area Fndn Grants, 2931
Lucy Downing Nisbet Charitable Grants, 2935
Maddie's Fund Comm Collaborative Projects, 2967
Maddie's Fund Community Shelter Data Grants, 2968
Maddie's Fund Lifesaving Awards, 2969
Margaret T. Morris Fndn Grants, 3005
McCune Charitable Fndn Grants, 3077
Meacham Fndn Grants, 3102
Natalie W. Furniss Charitable Grants, 3244
Nestle Purina PetCare Emergency Response and Disaster Relief Grants, 3303
Nestle Purina PetCare Pet Related Grants, 3304
Nestle Purina PetCare Support Dog and Police K-9 Organization Grants, 3305
NFWF Bird Conservation Init Grants, 3358
NFWF National Whale Conservation Grants, 3378
NFWF Wildlife & Habitat Conservation Grants, 3399
Owen County Community Fndn Grants, 3716
Perkins Charitable Fndn Grants, 3823
Perry County Community Fndn Grants, 3827
Pet Care Trust Fish in the Classroom Grant, 3828
Pet Care Trust Sue Busch Memorial Award, 3829
Petco Fndn 4 Rs Project Support Grants, 3830
Petco Fndn Capital Grants, 3831
Petco Fndn Product Support Grants, 3832
Petco Fndn We Are Family Too Grants, 3833
PetSmart Conference Sponsorships, 3851
PetSmart Free-Roaming Cat Spay-Neuter Grants, 3852
PetSmart Grant for Canadian Agencies, 3853
PetSmart Model Volunteering Grants, 3854
PetSmart Spay/Neuter Clinic Equipment Grant, 3855
PetSmart Targeted Spay/Neuter Grants, 3856
PMI Fndn Grants, 3918
Puerto Rico Community Fndn Grants, 3986
Ralph and Virginia Mullin Fndn Grants, 4012
Ryder System Charitable Grants, 4191
San Antonio Area Fndn Grants, 4240
SanDisk Corp Community Sharing Program, 4253
Sands Memorial Fndn Grants, 4256
Santa Fe Community Fndn Seasonal Grants, 4290
Search Dog Fndn Rescue Dog Assistance, 4318
Seattle Fndn Benjamin N. Phillips Grants, 4322
Sonora Area Fndn Competitive Grants, 4404
SW Florida Community Competitive Grants, 4442
Summerlee Fndn Grants, 4523
Toby Wells Fndn Grants, 4638
Tom's of Maine Grants, 4640
Vancouver Fndn Grants & Comm Inits, 4900
Walter L. Gross III Family Fndn Grants, 4983
William J. and Dorothy K. O'Neill Fndn Grants, 5087

Animal Ecology
American Forests Global ReLeaf Grants, 434
NFWF/Exxon Save the Tiger Grants, 3354
NFWF ConocoPhillips SPIRIT of Conservation Migratory Bird Grants, 3369
NFWF Dissolved Oxygen Environmental Benefit Grants, 3372

Animal Feeds/Nutrition
Nestle Purina PetCare Emergency Response and Disaster Relief Grants, 3303
Petco Fndn 4 Rs Project Support Grants, 3830
Petco Fndn Product Support Grants, 3832
Petco Fndn We Are Family Too Grants, 3833

Animal Genetics/Breeding
Bernice Barbour Fndn Grants, 743

NFWF ConocoPhillips SPIRIT of Conservation Migratory Bird Grants, 3369
Pegasus Fndn Grants, 3810

Animal Rescue
Alfred C. and Ersa S. Arbogast Fndn Grants, 365
American Humane Assoc Second Chance Grants, 440
Ann L. & Carol Green Rhodes Charitable Grants, 483
Community Fndn of Abilene Humane Treatment of Animals Grants, 1266
DogTime Annual Grant, 1552
DogTime Technology Grant, 1553
Go Daddy Cares Charitable Contributions, 2094
Green Fndn Special Project Grants, 2155
HAF Companion Animal Welfare and Rescue, 2195
Kirkpatrick Fndn Grants, 2827
Lucy Downing Nisbet Charitable Grants, 2935
Maddie's Fund Comm Collaborative Projects, 2967
Maddie's Fund Community Shelter Data Grants, 2968
Maddie's Fund Lifesaving Awards, 2969
Maine Comm Belvedere Animal Welfare Grants, 2975
Meacham Fndn Grants, 3102
Nestle Purina PetCare Emergency Response and Disaster Relief Grants, 3303
Nestle Purina PetCare Pet Related Grants, 3304
Petco Fndn 4 Rs Project Support Grants, 3830
Petco Fndn Product Support Grants, 3832
Petco Fndn We Are Family Too Grants, 3833
PetSmart Conference Sponsorships, 3851
PetSmart Free-Roaming Cat Spay-Neuter Grants, 3852
PetSmart Grant for Canadian Agencies, 3853
PetSmart Model Volunteering Grants, 3854
PetSmart Spay/Neuter Clinic Equipment Grant, 3855
PetSmart Targeted Spay/Neuter Grants, 3856
Search Dog Fndn Rescue Dog Assistance, 4318
Sioux Falls Area Community Fndn Field-of-Interest and Donor-Advised Grants, 4365
Toby Wells Fndn Grants, 4638

Animal Research Policy
Vancouver Fndn Grants & Comm Inits, 4900

Animal Rights
Adam Richter Charitable Grants, 145
Albert and Bessie Mae Kronkosky Charitable Fndn Grants, 339
Ann L. & Carol Green Rhodes Charitable Grants, 483
Aragona Family Fndn Grants, 522
Bernice Barbour Fndn Grants, 743
Blue Mountain Community Fndn Grants, 800
Bodenwein Public Benevolent Fndn Grants, 806
Chamberlain Fndn Grants, 1027
Charles H. Hall Fndn, 1044
Clark Charitable Grants, 1155
Cleveland-Cliffs Fndn Grants, 1165
Community Fndn of Abilene Humane Treatment of Animals Grants, 1266
Community Fndn of Broward Grants, 1275
Cooke-Hay Fndn Grants, 1367
David Bohnett Fndn Grants, 1451
Frank Stanley Beveridge Fndn Grants, 1936
HAF Companion Animal Welfare and Rescue, 2195
Harrison County Community Fndn Grants, 2233
Harrison County Community Signature Grants, 2234
Helen V. Brach Fndn Grants, 2300
Horace A. Kimball and S. Ella Kimball Grants, 2362
Letha E. House Fndn Grants, 2886
Meacham Fndn Grants, 3102
Natalie W. Furniss Charitable Grants, 3244
Park Fndn Grants, 3739
Perkins Charitable Fndn Grants, 3823
Rhode Island Fndn Grants, 4073
Summerlee Fndn Grants, 4523
Thelma Doelger Charitable Grants, 4604
Vancouver Fndn Grants & Comm Inits, 4900
Walter L. Gross III Family Fndn Grants, 4983

Animal Welfare
A. J. Macdonald Fndn for Animal Welfare, 42
Alfred C. and Ersa S. Arbogast Fndn Grants, 365
American Humane Assoc Second Chance Grants, 440

Animals As Pets / 805

Annenberg Fndn Grants, 477
Arkansas Community Fndn Grants, 561
Austin S. Nelson Fndn Grants, 617
Back Home Again Fndn Grants, 633
Barbara Meyer Elsner Fndn Grants, 665
Caesar Puff Fndn Grants, 890
Central Okanagan Fndn Grants, 997
Community Fndn of Abilene Humane Treatment of Animals Grants, 1266
Community Fndn of Muncie and Delaware County Maxon Grants, 1303
Ethel Frends Fndn Grants, 1759
Go Daddy Cares Charitable Contributions, 2094
Greygates Fndn Grants, 2164
Guy I. Bromley Grants, 2180
HAF Companion Animal Welfare and Rescue, 2195
Harrison County Community Signature Grants, 2234
Herbert A. and Adrian W. Woods Fndn Grants, 2313
Illinois DNR State Furbearer Grants, 2501
J. Edwin Treakle Fndn Grants, 2596
John M. Weaver Fndn Grants, 2705
Katharine Matthies Fndn Grants, 2788
Lucy Downing Nisbet Charitable Grants, 2935
Maddie's Fund Comm Collaborative Projects, 2967
Maddie's Fund Community Shelter Data Grants, 2968
Maddie's Fund Lifesaving Awards, 2969
Maine Community Fndn Belvedere Animal Welfare Grants, 2975
McCune Charitable Fndn Grants, 3077
Meacham Fndn Grants, 3102
Nestle Purina PetCare Emergency Response and Disaster Relief Grants, 3303
Petco Fndn 4 Rs Project Support Grants, 3830
Petco Fndn Product Support Grants, 3832
Petco Fndn We Are Family Too Grants, 3833
PetSmart Conference Sponsorships, 3851
PetSmart Free-Roaming Cat Spay-Neuter Grants, 3852
PetSmart Grant for Canadian Agencies, 3853
PetSmart Model Volunteering Grants, 3854
PetSmart Spay/Neuter Clinic Equipment Grant, 3855
PetSmart Targeted Spay/Neuter Grants, 3856
PMI Fndn Grants, 3918
Robert R. Meyer Fndn Grants, 4121
Santa Fe Community Fndn Seasonal Grants, 4290
Sarkeys Fndn Grants, 4297
Seattle Fndn Benjamin N. Phillips Grants, 4322
SeaWorld & Busch Gardens Conservation Grants, 4332
Sioux Falls Area Community Fndn Field-of-Interest and Donor-Advised Grants, 4365
Wells County Fndn Grants, 5022

Animals as Pets
Ann L. & Carol Green Rhodes Charitable Grants, 483
Banfield Charitable Grants, 652
Bernice Barbour Fndn Grants, 743
Build-A-Bear Workshop Fndn Grants, 861
Charles H. Hall Fndn, 1044
DogTime Annual Grant, 1552
DogTime Technology Grant, 1553
Doris Day Animal Fndn Grants, 1583
Ethel Frends Fndn Grants, 1759
HAF Companion Animal Welfare and Rescue, 2195
Humane Society of the United States Foreclosure Pets Grants, 2389
Kenneth A. Scott Charitable Grants, 2801
Maddie's Fund Comm Collaborative Projects, 2967
Maddie's Fund Lifesaving Awards, 2969
Maine Comm Belvedere Animal Welfare Grants, 2975
Mericos Fndn Grants, 3121
Nestle Purina PetCare Emergency Response and Disaster Relief Grants, 3303
Nestle Purina PetCare Pet Related Grants, 3304
Petco Fndn 4 Rs Project Support Grants, 3830
Petco Fndn Capital Grants, 3831
Petco Fndn Product Support Grants, 3832
Petco Fndn We Are Family Too Grants, 3833
Ralph and Virginia Mullin Fndn Grants, 4012
Santa Fe Community Fndn Seasonal Grants, 4290

Animals for Assistance/Therapy
Blum-Kovler Fndn Grants, 803
Columbus Fndn Small Grants, 1232
HAF Companion Animal Welfare and Rescue, 2195
Lumpkin Family Healthy People Grants, 2942
May and Stanley Smith Charitable Grants, 3069
Nestle Purina PetCare Support Dog and Police K-9 Organization Grants, 3305
Planet Dog Fndn Grants, 3911
Reader's Digest Partners for Sight Fndn Grants, 4036
Robert R. Meyer Fndn Grants, 4121

Animation
Illinois Arts Council Media Arts Grants, 2472
National Endowment for Arts Media Grants, 3264

Anthropology
Canada-U.S. Fulbright Mid-Career Grants, 917
Horowitz Fndn for Social Policy Grants, 2370
Horowitz Fndn for Social Policy Special Awards, 2371
IMLS 21st Century Museum Pro Grants, 2512
IMLS American Heritage Preservation Grants, 2513
IMLS National Leadership Grants, 2515
Morris K. Udall and Stewart L. Udall Fndn Dissertation Fellowships, 3219
North Carolina Arts Council Folklife Internship, 3467
NYSCA Museum General Operating Support, 3602
S.E.VEN Fund WHY Prize, 4198

Anthropology, Cultural
Florida Humanities Council Mini Grants, 1869
NYHC Major and Mini Grants, 3567
Wisconsin Humanities Council Major Grants, 5107

Anthropology, Social
Natonal Endowment for the Arts Research Grants: Art Works, 3286

Appalachia
Appalachian Ministries Grants, 499
Appalachian Regional Commission Asset-Based Development Project Grants, 500
Appalachian Regional Commission Community Infrastructure Grants, 502
Appalachian Reg Distressed Counties Grants, 503
Appalachian Regional Comm Training Grants, 504
Commission on Religion in Appalachia Grants, 1238

Aquaculture/Hydroponics
NFWF Bring Back the Natives Grants, 3359
USDA Farm Labor Housing Grants, 4809
USDC/NOAA Nat Marine Aquaculture Grants, 4846

Aquariums
IMLS 21st Century Museum Pro Grants, 2512
IMLS American Heritage Preservation Grants, 2513
IMLS National Leadership Grants, 2515
NSTA Distinguished Informal Science Ed Award, 3531
Union Bank, N.A. Fndn Grants, 4709

Aquatic Ecology
GNOF Environmental Grants, 2073
GNOF Plaquemines Community Grants, 2091
SeaWorld & Busch Gardens Conservation Grants, 4332
USDC/NOAA Marine Aquaculture Grants, 4846

Arboreta
American Forests Global ReLeaf Grants, 434
IMLS 21st Century Museum Pro Grants, 2512
IMLS American Heritage Preservation Grants, 2513
IMLS National Leadership Grants, 2515
Stanley Smith Horticultural Grants, 4474

Archaeology
Alabama Humanities Fndn Mini Grants, 231
Alabama Humanities Planning/Consultant Grants, 232
Canada-U.S. Fulbright Mid-Career Grants, 917
Chamberlain Fndn Grants, 1027
Colonel Stanley R. McNeil Fndn Grants, 1210
Florida Humanities Council Mini Grants, 1869
Luther I. Replogle Fndn Grants, 2945
Montana Arts Council Cultural & Aesthetic Grants, 3209
Stewart Huston Charitable Grants, 4505
Wisconsin Humanities Council Major Grants, 5107

Archaeology Education
Joukowsky Family Fndn Grants, 2743
Luther I. Replogle Fndn Grants, 2945

Archery
Easton Fndns Archery Facility Grants, 1644
USAA – Ann Hoyt / Jim Easton JOAD Grants, 4734

Architecture
AAF Accent on Architecture Community Grants, 58
AAF Richard Riley Award, 59
Alabama State Council on the Arts Community Arts Collaborative Ventures Grants, 236
Alabama State Council on the Arts Community Arts Program Development Grants, 239
Alabama State Council on the Arts Community Planning & Design Grants, 241
Denver Fndn Community Grants, 1502
Energy Fndn Buildings Grants, 1705
Energy Fndn Power Grants, 1707
Enterprise Community Partners Rose Architectural Fellowships, 1719
Enterprise Comm Partners Terwilliger Fellowship, 1720
Florida Div of Cultural Affairs Multidisciplinary Grants, 1857
Indianapolis Preservation Grants, 2543
Indiana Preservation Grants, 2544
NHSCA Operating Grants, 3428
NYFA Gregory Millard Fellowships, 3565
NYSCA Architecture, Planning, and Design: Capital Fixtures and Equipment Purchase Grants, 3570
NYSCA Architecture, Planning, and Design: Capital Project Grants, 3571
NYSCA Architecture, Planning, and Design: Design and Planning Studies Grants, 3572
NYSCA Architecture, Planning, and Design: General Operating Support Grants, 3573
NYSCA Architecture, Planning, and Design: General Program Support Grants, 3574
NYSCA Architecture, Planning, and Design: Independent Project Grants, 3575
NYSCA Architecture, Planning, and Design: Project Support Grants, 3576
OSF-Baltimore Community Fellowships, 3695
PCA Arts Organizations & Grants for Visual Arts, 3785
PCA Entry Track Arts Organizations and Program Grants for Visual Arts, 3799
Regents Professional Opportunity Scholarships, 4044
Richard and Caroline T. Gwathmey Grants, 4075
Rudy Bruner Award for Urban Excellence, 4173
SSRC-Van Alen Fellowships, 4467

Architecture Education
Enterprise Community Partners Rose Architectural Fellowships, 1719
Enterprise Comm Partners Terwilliger Fellowship, 1720
NYSCA Architecture, Planning, and Design: Project Support Grants, 3576

Architecture History
CDECD Historic Preservation & Planning Grants, 982
Indianapolis Preservation Grants, 2543
Indiana Preservation Grants, 2544
NYSCA Architecture, Planning, and Design: Capital Fixtures and Equipment Purchase Grants, 3570
NYSCA Architecture, Planning, and Design: Capital Project Grants, 3571
NYSCA Architecture, Planning, and Design: Design and Planning Studies Grants, 3572
NYSCA Architecture, Planning, and Design: General Operating Support Grants, 3573
NYSCA Architecture, Planning, and Design: General Program Support Grants, 3574
NYSCA Architecture, Planning, and Design: Independent Project Grants, 3575
NYSCA Architecture, Planning, and Design: Project Support Grants, 3576
Richard and Caroline T. Gwathmey Grants, 4075

Archives
ALA Jan Merrill-Oldham Professional Development Grant, 291
Beerman Fndn Grants, 717
Brown Fndn Grants, 854
CE and S Fndn Grants, 985
IMLS Native Am Library Services Basic Grants, 2517
IMLS Native American Library Services Enhancement Grants, 2518
Lucy Downing Nisbet Charitable Grants, 2935
Montana Arts Council Cultural and Aesthetic Project Grants, 3209
National Endowment for Arts Music Grants, 3266
NEH Preservation Assistance Grants for Smaller Institutions, 3293
NEH Preservation Microfilming of Brittle Books and Serials Grants, 3294
Temple Univ George D. McDowell Fellowship, 4577

Area Studies
Horowitz Fndn for Social Policy Grants, 2370
Horowitz Fndn for Social Policy Special Awards, 2371

Art Appreciation
Abell Fndn Arts and Culture Grants, 92
Adobe Art and Culture Grants, 167
Akron Community Fndn Arts & Culture Grants, 218
Alliant Energy Fndn Community Grants, 384
Ann L. & Carol Green Rhodes Charitable Grants, 483
Arkansas Arts Council AIE Arts Curriculum Project Grants, 552
Arthur F. and Alice E. Adams Charitable Grants, 574
Benton County Fndn Grants, 731
Bloomington Area Arts Council Grants, 791
Boyd Gaming Corp Contributions Program, 825
California Arts Council State Networks Grants, 897
Carl B. and Florence E. King Fndn Grants, 928
Carrier Corp Contributions Grants, 946
Chicago Community Arts Assistance Grants, 1081
Chicago Cultural Outreach Grants, 1095
Chicago Neighborhood Arts Grants, 1097
Daviess County Community Fndn Arts and Culture Grants, 1455
Delaware Division of the Arts Community-Based Organizations Opportunity Grants, 1487
Delta Air Lines Fndn Arts and Culture Grants, 1493
Donald W. Reynolds Fndn Special Grants, 1577
Edward R. Godfrey Fndn Grants, 1667
Fleishhacker Fndn Small Grants in the Arts, 1839
Fleishhacker Fndn Special Arts Grants, 1840
Florida Div of Cultural Affairs Culture Builds Florida Expansion Funding, 1848
Florida Div of Cultural Affairs Culture Builds Florida Seed Funding, 1849
Georgia Council for the Arts Project Grants, 2037
Guy I. Bromley Grants, 2180
Hahl Proctor Charitable Grants, 2208
Helen Bader Fndn Grants, 2293
Helen Gertrude Sparks Charitable Grants, 2294
Honda of America Manufacturing Fndn Grants, 2354
Indianapolis Power & Light Community Grants, 2540
Japan Fndn Los Angeles Mini-Grants for Japanese Arts & Culture, 2651
Japan Fndn New York Small Grants for Arts and Culture, 2652
John Reynolds and Eleanor B. Allen Charitable Fndn Grants, 2710
John W. Speas and Effie E. Speas Grants, 2732
Kansas Arts Commission American Masterpieces Kansas Grants, 2775
Lewis H. Humphreys Charitable Grants, 2889
Louetta M. Cowden Fndn Grants, 2922
Louis and Elizabeth Nave Flarsheim Charitable Fndn Grants, 2924
Massachusetts Cultural Council Local Cultural Council Grants, 3057

SUBJECT INDEX   Art Education / 807

Massachusetts Cultural Council Traditional Arts Apprenticeships, 3058
National Endowment for the Arts - National Arts and Humanities Youth Program Awards, 3255
National Endowment for the Arts - National Partnership Agreement Grants, 3256
National Endowment for Arts Commun Grants, 3260
Nevada Arts Council Folklife Apprenticeships, 3309
North Carolina Arts Council Arts and Audiences Grants, 3466
North Carolina Arts Council Community Public Art and Design Development Grants, 3472
North Carolina Arts Council Community Public Art and Design Implementation Grants, 3473
North Dakota Council on the Arts Presenter Support Grants, 3497
NYSCA Arts Educ: Community Learning Grants, 3577
NYSCA Arts Educ: General Operating Support, 3578
NYSCA Arts Educ Program Support Grants, 3579
NYSCA Arts Educ: K-12 In-School Grants, 3580
NYSCA Arts Educ: Services to the Field Grants, 3582
NYSCA Dance: Long-Term Residency in New York State Grants, 3586
NYSCA Electronic Media and Film: General Operating Support, 3590
NYSCA Electronic Media and Film: General Program Support, 3591
NYSCA Electronic Media and Film: Screenings Grants, 3592
NYSCA Electronic Media and Film: Workspace Grants, 3593
NYSCA Folk Arts: Exhibitions Grants, 3594
NYSCA Folk Arts: Presentation Grants, 3596
NYSCA Folk Arts: Regional and County Folk Arts Grants, 3597
NYSCA Lit: General Operating Support Grants, 3598
NYSCA Museum Program Support Grants, 3603
NYSCA Museum: Project Support Grants, 3604
NYSCA Presenting: General Operating Support, 3609
NYSCA Presenting: General Program Support, 3610
NYSCA Presenting: Presenting Grants, 3611
NYSCA Presenting: Services to the Field Grants, 3612
NYSCA Special Art Services Project Support, 3613
NYSCA Special Arts Services: General Operating Support Grants, 3614
NYSCA Special Arts Services: General Program Support Grants, 3615
NYSCA Special Arts Services: Instruction Grants, 3616
NYSCA Special Arts Services: Professional Performances Grants, 3617
NYSCA State and Local Partnerships: General Operating Support Grants, 3619
NYSCA State and Local Partnerships: General Program Support Grants, 3620
NYSCA State and Local Partnerships: Services to the Field Grants, 3621
NYSCA State and Local Partnerships: Workshops Grants, 3622
NYSCA Theatre General Program Support, 3624
NYSCA Theatre Pro Performances Grants, 3625
NYSCA Theatre: Services to the Field Grants, 3626
NYSCA Visual Arts: Exhibitions and Installations Grants, 3627
NYSCA Visual Arts: General Operating Support, 3628
NYSCA Visual Arts: General Program Support, 3629
NYSCA Visual Arts: Services to the Field Grants, 3630
Paul E. and Klare N. Reinhold Fndn Grants, 3758
Perry County Community Fndn Grants, 3827
Phoenix Coyotes Charities Grants, 3879
Pike County Community Fndn Grants, 3888
PMI Fndn Grants, 3918
Progress Energy Fndn Economic Vitality Grants, 3969
Richard H. Driehaus Fndn MacArthur Fund for Arts and Culture, 4085
RISCA Project Grants for Organizations, Individuals and Educ, 4100
San Diego Fndn Arts & Culture Grants, 4243
San Diego Women's Fndn Grants, 4252
San Francisco Fndn Fund For Artists Award For Playwrights and Theatre Ensembles, 4272

San Francisco Fndn Fund for Artists Award for Visual and Media Artists, 4273
San Francisco Fndn Fund For Artists Matching Commissions Grants, 4274
San Francisco Fndn Koshland Program Arts and Culture Mini-Grants, 4280
Silicon Valley Community Fndn Donor Circle for the Arts Grants, 4354
Sorenson Legacy Fndn Grants, 4407
Stinson Fndn Grants, 4506
TAC Touring Arts and Arts Access Grants, 4557
Texas Commission on the Arts County Arts Expansion Program, 4582
Texas Instruments Corp Arts and Culture Grants, 4596
Virginia Commission for the Arts Project Grants, 4944
W. Paul and Lucille Caudill Little Fndn Grants, 4966
Warrick County Community Fndn Grants, 4987

Art Conservation
Abell Fndn Arts and Culture Grants, 92
Akron Community Fndn Arts & Culture Grants, 218
Arkansas Arts Council AIE Curriculum Grants, 552
Christensen Fund Regional Grants, 1112
CNL Corp Giving Arts & Culture Grants, 1190
Jane and Jack Fitzpatrick Grants, 2640
MacArthur Fndn Chicago Arts and Culture General Operations Grants, 2961
McCune Charitable Fndn Grants, 3077
National Endowment for the Arts - State Partnership Agreement Grants, 3259
National Endowment for Arts Commun Grants, 3260
National Endowment for Arts Museum Grants, 3265
North Carolina Arts Council Arts and Audiences Grants, 3466
NYSCA Arts Educ: Services to the Field Grants, 3582
NYSCA Electronic Media and Film: Screenings Grants, 3592
NYSCA Folk Arts: General Program Support, 3595
NYSCA Folk Arts: Presentation Grants, 3596
NYSCA Folk Arts: Regional and County Folk Arts Grants, 3597
NYSCA Museum General Operating Support, 3602
NYSCA Museum Program Support Grants, 3603
NYSCA Museum: Project Support Grants, 3604
NYSCA Presenting: Services to the Field Grants, 3612
NYSCA Special Art Services Project Support, 3613
NYSCA Special Arts Services: General Operating Support Grants, 3614
NYSCA Special Arts Services: General Program Support Grants, 3615
NYSCA Special Arts Services: Instruction and Training Grants, 3616
NYSCA Special Arts Services: Professional Performances Grants, 3617
NYSCA State and Local Partnerships: General Program Support Grants, 3620
NYSCA State and Local Partnerships: Services to the Field Grants, 3621
PCA Entry Track Arts Organizations and Program Grants for Traditional and Folk Arts, 3798
Pike County Community Fndn Grants, 3888
Rockefeller Brothers Charles E. Culpeper Arts and Culture Grants in New York City, 4129
South Carolina Arts Commission Folklife & Traditional Arts Grants, 4421
W. Paul and Lucille Caudill Little Fndn Grants, 4966

Art Criticism
Akron Community Fndn Arts & Culture Grants, 218
Alabama Humanities Fndn Mini Grants, 231
Alabama Humanities Planning/Consultant Grants, 232
California Arts Council Arts and Accessibility Technical Assistance Grants, 894
California Arts Council Public Value Grants, 895
Florida Div of Cultural Affairs Culture Builds Florida Expansion Funding, 1848
Florida Div of Cultural Affairs Culture Builds Florida Seed Funding, 1849
Florida Humanities Council Mini Grants, 1869
Jerome Fndn Grants, 2667

National Endowment for Arts Agencies Grants, 3263
NYHC Major and Mini Grants, 3567
NYSCA Visual Arts: General Operating Support, 3628
NYSCA Visual Arts: General Program Support, 3629
NYSCA Visual Arts: Services to the Field Grants, 3630
PCA Arts Organizations & Grants for Visual Arts, 3785
PCA Entry Track Arts Organizations and Program Grants for Visual Arts, 3799
Wisconsin Humanities Council Major Grants, 5107

Art Education
2 Depot Square Ipswich Charitable Fndn Grants, 4
3M Company Arts and Culture Grants, 12
3M Fndn Community Giving Grants, 15
Abbott Fund Community Grants, 81
Abell-Hanger Fndn Grants, 91
Abell Fndn Arts and Culture Grants, 92
Adobe Art and Culture Grants, 167
Adobe Youth Voices Grants, 170
Aetna Fndn Arts Grants in Connecticut, 181
Akron Community Fndn Arts & Culture Grants, 218
Alabama State Council on the Arts Collaborative Ventures Grants, 235
Alabama State Council on the Arts Community Arts Collaborative Ventures Grants, 236
Alabama State Council on the Arts Community Arts Operating Support Grants, 237
Alabama State Council on the Arts Community Arts Presenting Grants, 238
Alabama State Council on the Arts Community Arts Program Development Grants, 239
Alabama State Council on the Arts Community Planning & Design Grants, 241
Alabama State Council on the Arts in Educ Partnership Grants, 242
Alabama State Council on the Arts Multi-Discipline and Festival Grants, 243
Alabama State Council on the Arts Operating Support Grants, 244
Alabama State Council Arts Presenting Grants, 245
Alabama State Council on the Arts Program Development Grants, 246
Alabama State Council on the Arts Project Assistance Grants, 247
Alabama State Council on the Arts Projects of Individual Artists Grants, 248
Alaska Airlines Corp Giving Grants, 320
Alaska Airlines Fndn Grants, 321
ALZA Corp Contributions Grants, 405
Amer-Scandinavian Fndn Public Project Grants, 419
American Express Historic Preservation Grants, 431
Andy Warhol Fndn for the Visual Arts Grants, 464
Angels Baseball Fndn Grants, 465
Anna Fitch Ardenghi Grants, 472
Annenberg Fndn Grants, 477
Ann L. & Carol Green Rhodes Charitable Grants, 483
APS Fndn Grants, 518
Arizona Commission on the Arts Educ Grants, 536
Arizona Comm on the Arts Folklorist Residencies, 537
Arizona Commission on the Arts Visual/Media Arts Organizations Grants, 539
Arkansas Arts Council AIE After School/Summer Residency Grants, 551
Arkansas Arts Council AIE Arts Curriculum Project Grants, 552
Arkansas Arts Council AIE In-School Residency, 553
Arkansas Arts Council AIE Mini Grants, 554
Arkansas Arts Council Expansion Arts Grants, 556
Arkansas Arts Council General Operating Support, 557
Arthur F. and Alice E. Adams Charitable Grants, 574
Arts and Science Council Grants, 576
Arts Council of Winston-Salem and Forsyth County Organizational Support Grants, 577
Arts Midwest Performing Arts Grants, 579
Ashland Corp Contributions Grants, 587
Assurant Health Fndn Grants, 596
Baltimore Community Fndn Arts and Culture Path Grants, 641
Bay and Paul Fndns Grants, 693
Bayer Fndn Grants, 696

808 / Art Education

Benton County Fndn Grants, 731
Bernard & Audre Rapoport Arts & Culture Grant, 735
Beverley Taylor Sorenson Art Works for Kids, 757
Bloomington Area Arts Council Grants, 791
Boyd Gaming Corp Contributions Program, 825
British Columbia Arts Council Artists in Ed Grants, 842
Brooklyn Community Fndn Community Arts for All Grants, 849
California Arts Council Arts and Accessibility Technical Assistance Grants, 894
California Arts Council Public Value Grants, 895
California Arts Council State Networks Grants, 897
CDECD Arts Catalyze Placemaking in Every Community Grants, 977
CDECD Arts Catalyze Placemaking Leadership Grants, 978
CDECD Arts Catalyze Placemaking Sustaining Relevance Grants, 979
CE and S Fndn Grants, 985
Charlotte Martin Fndn Youth Grants, 1057
Charlotte R. Schmidlapp Grants, 1058
Chicago Community Arts Assistance Grants, 1081
Chicago Community Trust Arts and Culture Grants: Improving Access to Arts Learning Opps, 1082
Chicago Community Trust Arts and Culture Grants: SMART Growth, 1083
Chicago Cultural Outreach Grants, 1095
Chicago Neighborhood Arts Grants, 1097
Chicago Tribune Fndn Grants for Cultural Organizations, 1101
Christensen Fund Regional Grants, 1112
Cisco Systems Fndn San Jose Community Grants, 1137
City of Oakland Cultural Arts Dept Grants, 1142
Clowes Grants, 1177
CNL Corp Giving Arts & Culture Grants, 1190
Community Fndn of St. Joseph County ArtsEverywhere Grants, 1313
Connecticut Community Fndn Grants, 1350
Cooper Fndn Grants, 1369
Cooper Industries Fndn Grants, 1370
Coughlin-Saunders Fndn Grants, 1377
Crescent Porter Hale Fndn Grants, 1398
DAAD Research Grants for Doctoral Candidates and Young Academics and Scientists, 1427
Daviess County Community Fndn Arts and Culture Grants, 1455
DB Americas Fndn Grants, 1466
Delonne Anderson Family Fndn, 1492
Delta Air Lines Fndn Arts and Culture Grants, 1493
District of Columbia Commission on the Arts-Arts Educ Teacher Mini-Grants, 1549
Donald W. Reynolds Fndn Special Grants, 1577
Eisner Fndn Grants, 1678
Erie Community Fndn Grants, 1750
Ethel S. Abbott Charitable Fndn Grants, 1760
Fleishhacker Fndn Small Grants in the Arts, 1839
Fleishhacker Fndn Special Arts Grants, 1840
Florida Div of Cultural Affairs Culture Builds Florida Expansion Funding, 1848
Florida Div of Cultural Affairs Culture Builds Florida Seed Funding, 1849
Florida Div of Cultural Affairs Specific Cultural Project Grants, 1862
Florida Div of Cultural Affairs Touring Grants, 1863
Ford Motor Company Grants, 1885
Frank and Lydia Bergen Fndn Grants, 1925
George A Ohl Jr. Fndn Grants, 2012
George Gund Fndn Grants, 2020
Georgia Council for the Arts Partner Grants for Service Organizations, 2036
Georgia Council for the Arts Project Grants, 2037
Grand Rapids Area Community Fndn Grants, 2114
Grand Rapids Area Community Fndn Nashwauk Area Endowment Grants, 2115
Greater Worcester Comm Discretionary Grants, 2140
Green Fndn Arts Grants, 2152
Green Fndn Educ Grants, 2153
Greenwall Fndn Arts and Humanities Grants, 2157
Guy I. Bromley Grants, 2180
H & R Fndn Grants, 2181
H. Reimers Bechtel Charitable Grants, 2186
Harry Chapin Fndn Grants, 2240
Hearst Fndns Culture Grants, 2284
Helen Bader Fndn Grants, 2293
Helen Gertrude Sparks Charitable Grants, 2294
Herman Goldman Fndn Grants, 2317
Honda of America Manufacturing Fndn Grants, 2354
Horace Moses Charitable Fndn Grants, 2363
Horizon Fndn for New Jersey Grants, 2364
Horizon Fndn Grants, 2365
Huntington Arts Council Arts-in-Educ Grants, 2400
Huntington Arts Council JP Morgan Chase Artist Reach Out Grants, 2402
IBM Arts and Culture Grants, 2424
Illinois Arts Council Arts-in-Education Residency Grants, 2463
Illinois Arts Council Service Organization Grants, 2464
Illinois Arts Council Community Access Grants, 2466
Illinois Arts Council Ethnic & Folk Arts Grants, 2469
Illinois Arts Council Multidisciplinary Grants, 2473
Illinois Arts Council Partners in Excellence, 2475
Indiana Arts Commission American Masterpieces Grants, 2530
Indiana Arts Commission Multi-regional Major Arts Insts Grants, 2532
Iowa Arts Council Artists in Schools/Communities Residency Grants, 2571
Jacob and Hilda Blaustein Fndn Grants, 2615
Jane's Grants, 2639
Jane Bradley Pettit Fndn Arts and Culture Grants, 2641
Japan Fndn Los Angeles Mini-Grants for Japanese Arts & Culture, 2651
Japan Fndn New York Small Grants for Arts and Culture, 2652
Jayne and Leonard Abess Fndn Grants, 2657
Jewish Women's Fndn of New York Grants, 2677
John F. Kennedy Center for the Performing Arts National Rosemary Kennedy Internship, 2694
John W. Speas and Effie E. Speas Grants, 2732
Joseph S. Stackpole Charitable Grants, 2741
Jovid Fndn Grants, 2745
Judith and Jean Pape Adams Charitable Fndn Tulsa Area Grants, 2755
Kansas Arts Commission Arts-in-Educ Grants, 2779
Kansas Arts Commission Operational Support for Arts and Cultural Organizations, 2781
Kansas Arts Commission Partnership Agreement Grants, 2782
Kathryne Beynon Fndn Grants, 2791
Kennedy Center Experiential Educ Internship, 2798
Kohler Fndn Grants, 2833
Leon and Thea Koerner Fndn Grants, 2883
Lettie Pate Whitehead Fndn Grants, 2888
Lied Fndn Grants, 2900
Lincoln Financial Group Fndn Grants, 2906
Louetta M. Cowden Fndn Grants, 2922
Louis and Elizabeth Nave Flarsheim Grants, 2924
Louis R. Cappelli Fndn Grants, 2926
Lubrizol Fndn Grants, 2933
Luther I. Replogle Fndn Grants, 2945
Madison Community Fndn Grants, 2971
Manitoba Arts Council Artist in Community Residency Grants, 2994
Marie H. Bechtel Charitable Grants, 3007
Marion I. & Henry J. Knott Discretionary Grants, 3018
Marion I. and Henry J. Knott Standard Grants, 3019
Massachusetts Cultural Adams Arts Grants, 3052
Massachusetts Cultural Council Local Cultural Council Grants, 3057
Massachusetts Cultural Council Traditional Arts Apprenticeships, 3058
McCune Charitable Fndn Grants, 3077
McGregor Grants, 3082
Mead Johnson Nutritionals Evansville-Area Organizations Grants, 3103
Merkel Family Fndn Grants, 3123
Mimi and Peter Haas Grants, 3185
Morris and Gwendolyn Cafritz Grants, 3218
National Endowment for the Arts - National Arts and Humanities Youth Program Awards, 3255
National Endowment for the Arts - National Partnership Agreement Grants, 3256
National Endowment for the Arts - State Partnership Agreement Grants, 3259
National Endowment for Arts Agencies Grants, 3263
National Endowment for Arts Media Grants, 3264
National Endowment for the Arts Presenting Grants: Art Works, 3268
Nevada Arts Council Circuit Rider Grants, 3308
Nevada Arts Council Learning Grants, 3313
Nevada Arts Council Residency Express Grants, 3315
NHSCA Artist Residencies in Schools Grants, 3423
NHSCA Arts in Health Care Project Grants, 3424
NHSCA General Project Grants, 3427
NHSCA Youth Arts Project Grants: For Extended Arts Learning, 3430
NJSCA Arts Project Support, 3446
NJSCA General Program Support Grants, 3449
North Carolina Arts Council Arts in Educ Artist Residencies Grants, 3468
North Carolina Arts Council Arts in Educ Grants, 3469
North Carolina Arts Council Arts in Educ Rural Development Grants, 3470
North Carolina Arts Council Community Public Art and Design Development Grants, 3472
North Carolina Arts Council Community Public Art and Design Implementation Grants, 3473
North Carolina GlaxoSmithKline Fndn Grants, 3490
North Dakota Council on the Arts Presenter Support Grants, 3497
NYFA Artists in the School Community Planning Grants, 3562
NYSCA Arts Educ: Community-based Learning Grants, 3577
NYSCA Arts Educ: General Operating Support, 3578
NYSCA Arts Educ Program Support Grants, 3579
NYSCA Arts Educ: K-12 In-School Grants, 3580
NYSCA Arts Education: Local Capacity Building Grants, 3581
NYSCA Arts Educ: Services to the Field Grants, 3582
NYSCA Dance Gen Operating Support Grants, 3584
NYSCA Dance Gen Program Support Grants, 3585
NYSCA Dance: Long-Term Residency in New York State Grants, 3586
NYSCA Electronic Media and Film: General Program Support, 3591
NYSCA Electronic Media and Film: Workspace Grants, 3593
NYSCA Folk Arts: General Program Support, 3595
NYSCA Folk Arts: Regional and County Folk Arts Grants, 3597
NYSCA Museum: Project Support Grants, 3604
NYSCA Special Arts Services: General Operating Support Grants, 3614
NYSCA Special Arts Services: General Program Support Grants, 3615
NYSCA Special Arts Services: Instruction and Training Grants, 3616
NYSCA State and Local Partnerships: Workshops Grants, 3622
NYSCA Theatre Pro Performances Grants, 3625
Ohio Arts Council Arts Partnership Grants, 3650
Ohio Arts Council Traditional Arts Apprenticeship Grants, 3655
Ontario Arts Council Compass Grants, 3677
Ontario Arts Council Travel Assistance Grants, 3682
Paul E. and Klare N. Reinhold Fndn Grants, 3758
PCA Arts in Educ Residencies, 3772
PCA Arts Organizations and Arts Programs Grants for Arts Educ Organizations, 3776
PCA Arts Organizations & Grants for Crafts, 3778
PCA Arts Organizations & Grants for Visual Arts, 3785
PCA Entry Track Arts Organizations and Program Grants for Arts Educ Organizations, 3788
PCA Entry Track Arts Organizations and Program Grants for Crafts, 3790
Peacock Fndn Grants, 3809
Pentair Fndn Educ and Community Grants, 3816
Phoenix Coyotes Charities Grants, 3879
Pike County Community Fndn Grants, 3888

PMI Fndn Grants, 3918
Princeton Area Community Fndn Thomas George Artists Grants, 3965
Rainbow Media Holdings Corp Giving, 4010
Reynolds and Reynolds Company Fndn Grants, 4070
RISCA Project Grants for Organizations, Individuals and Educ, 4100
Robert W. Woodruff Fndn Grants, 4124
Rockwell Int'l Corp Grants, 4141
Saint Paul Companies Fndn Grants, 4217
San Diego Women's Fndn Grants, 4252
San Francisco Fndn Faith Program and Arts and Culture Program, 4267
San Francisco Fndn Fund for Artists Award for Visual and Media Artists, 4273
San Francisco Fndn Murphy and Cadogan Fellowships in the Fine Arts, 4282
Santa Barbara Fndn Towbes Fund for the Performing Arts Grants, 4288
Sid W. Richardson Fndn Grants, 4350
Silicon Valley Community Fndn Donor Circle for the Arts Grants, 4354
Sorenson Legacy Fndn Grants, 4407
South Carolina Arts Commission AIE Residency Plus Individual Site Grants, 4411
South Carolina Arts Commission AIE Residency Plus Multi-Site Grants, 4412
South Carolina Arts Commission Arts in Educ After School Arts Init Grants, 4418
Stinson Fndn Grants, 4506
Stockton Rush Bartol Fndn Grants, 4508
Sunny and Abe Rosenberg Fndn Grants, 4529
TAC Arts Educ Community-Learning Grants, 4552
TAC Arts Educ Mini Grants, 4553
TAC Touring Arts and Arts Access Grants, 4557
Target Corp Local Store Grants, 4561
Taylor S. Abernathy and Patti Harding Abernathy Charitable Grants, 4564
Teaching Tolerance Grants, 4567
Texas Commission on Arts Educ Grants, 4579
Texas Commission on the Arts Arts in Educ Team Building/Texas Music Project Grants, 4580
Texas Commission on the Arts County Arts Expansion Program, 4582
Texas Comm on the Arts Young Masters Grants, 4594
Third Millennium Fndn Grants, 4607
Tom's of Maine Grants, 4640
Vancouver Fndn Grants & Comm Inits, 4900
Virginia Commission for the Arts Artists in Educ Residency Grants, 4941
Virginia Commission for the Arts Project Grants, 4944
VSA/Metlife Connect All Grants, 4953
W. Paul and Lucille Caudill Little Fndn Grants, 4966
Walter and Elise Haas Grants, 4982
Washington Gas Charitable Contributions, 5000
Weatherwax Fndn Grants, 5014
Westinghouse Charitable Giving Grants, 5028
West Virginia Commission on the Arts Challenge America Partnership Grants, 5031
West Virginia Comm on the Arts Mini Grants, 5041
West Virginia Comm on the Arts Special Grants, 5048
William G. Baker, Jr. Grants, 5081
Windgate Charitable Fndn Grants, 5099

Art History
Akron Community Fndn Arts & Culture Grants, 218
Arkansas Arts Council AIE Arts Curriculum Project Grants, 552
CAA Millard Meiss Publication Grants, 885
California Arts Council Arts and Accessibility Technical Assistance Grants, 894
California Arts Council Public Value Grants, 895
California Arts Council State Networks Grants, 897
Chicago Neighborhood Arts Grants, 1097
CNL Corp Giving Arts & Culture Grants, 1190
Donald W. Reynolds Fndn Special Grants, 1577
Florida Div of Cultural Affairs Culture Builds Florida Expansion Funding, 1848
Florida Div of Cultural Affairs Culture Builds Florida Seed Funding, 1849

Florida Humanities Council Mini Grants, 1869
Germanistic Society of America Fellowships, 2043
HAF Community Partnerships with Native Artists Grants, 2194
Kentucky Arts Council Folk and Traditional Arts Apprenticeship Grant, 2808
Louis R. Cappelli Fndn Grants, 2926
McCune Charitable Fndn Grants, 3077
National Endowment for Arts Museum Grants, 3265
North Carolina Arts Council Arts and Audiences Grants, 3466
North Dakota Council on the Arts Presenter Support Grants, 3497
NYHC Major and Mini Grants, 3567
NYSCA Folk Arts: General Program Support, 3595
NYSCA Folk Arts: Presentation Grants, 3596
NYSCA Folk Arts: Regional and County Folk Arts Grants, 3597
NYSCA Museum: Project Support Grants, 3604
NYSCA Special Arts Services: General Operating Support Grants, 3614
NYSCA State and Local Partnerships: General Program Support Grants, 3620
Pike County Community Fndn Grants, 3888
San Francisco Fndn Faith Program and Arts and Culture Program, 4267
Texas Comm on Arts County Expansion Grants, 4582
Wisconsin Humanities Council Major Grants, 5107

Art Museums
American Express Charitable Grants, 429
Arkansas Arts Council AIE Arts Curriculum Project Grants, 552
Barbara Meyer Elsner Fndn Grants, 665
Bernard & Audre Rapoport Arts & Culture Grant, 735
Blum-Kovler Fndn Grants, 803
California Arts Council State Networks Grants, 897
Chapman Family Charitable Grants, 1034
Delta Air Lines Fndn Arts and Culture Grants, 1493
Donald W. Reynolds Fndn Children's Discovery Init Grants, 1576
Florida Div of Cultural Affairs Museum Grants, 1858
Helen Pumphrey Denit Charitable Grants, 2297
Jane and Jack Fitzpatrick Grants, 2640
Jane Bradley Pettit Fndn Arts and Culture Grants, 2641
Jerry L. and Barbara J. Burris Fndn Grants, 2669
MacArthur Fndn Chicago Arts and Culture General Operations Grants, 2961
McCune Charitable Fndn Grants, 3077
Mericos Fndn Grants, 3121
Merkel Family Fndn Grants, 3123
Meyer and Stephanie Eglin Fndn Grants, 3139
National Endowment for the Arts - State Partnership Agreement Grants, 3259
NHSCA Cultural Facilities Grants: Barrier Free Access for All, 3426
NJSCA Arts Project Support, 3446
NJSCA General Program Support Grants, 3449
NYSCA Arts Educ: General Operating Support, 3578
NYSCA Arts Educ Program Support Grants, 3579
NYSCA Electronic Media and Film: General Operating Support, 3590
NYSCA Electronic Media & Film Gen Support, 3591
NYSCA Electronic Media and Film: Screenings Grants, 3592
NYSCA Electronic Media and Film: Workspace Grants, 3593
NYSCA Museum General Operating Support, 3602
NYSCA Museum Program Support Grants, 3603
NYSCA Museum: Project Support Grants, 3604
NYSCA Presenting: General Program Support, 3610
NYSCA State and Local Partnerships: Services to the Field Grants, 3621
NYSCA Visual Arts: Exhibitions and Installations Grants, 3627
Parker Fndn (California) Grants, 3736
PCA Arts Organizations and Arts Programs Grants for Art Museums, 3775
PCA Entry Track Arts Organizations and Program Grants for Art Museums, 3787

S. Spencer Scott Grants, 4202
Seattle Fndn C. Keith Birkenfeld Grants, 4323
Texas Instruments Corp Arts and Culture Grants, 4596
Texas Instruments Fndn Arts and Culture Grants, 4599
Virginia Commission for the Arts Project Grants, 4944
West Virginia Comm on Arts Visual Arts Grants, 5051

Art Works/Artifacts
Abell Fndn Arts and Culture Grants, 92
Aetna Fndn Arts Grants in Connecticut, 181
Akron Community Fndn Arts & Culture Grants, 218
Arthur F. and Alice E. Adams Charitable Grants, 574
California Arts Council State Networks Grants, 897
Delta Air Lines Fndn Arts and Culture Grants, 1493
Fleishhacker Fndn Small Grants in the Arts, 1839
Fleishhacker Fndn Special Arts Grants, 1840
Huntington Arts Council Arts-in-Educ Grants, 2400
Huntington Arts Council JP Morgan Chase Artist Reach Out Grants, 2402
Illinois Arts Council Community Access Grants, 2466
Joyce Fndn Culture Grants, 2747
Kansas Arts Commission American Masterpieces Kansas Grants, 2775
Marie Walsh Sharpe Art Fndn Grants, 3009
McCune Charitable Fndn Grants, 3077
National Endowment for the Arts - State Partnership Agreement Grants, 3259
North Carolina Arts Facility Design Grants, 3474
NYSCA Folk Arts: Exhibitions Grants, 3594
NYSCA Museum: Project Support Grants, 3604
NYSCA Visual Arts: Operating Support Grants, 3628
NYSCA Visual Arts: Services to the Field Grants, 3630
Ohio Arts Council Individual Excellence Awards, 3648
Ohio Arts Council Building Cultural Diversity Init Grants, 3651
Ohio River Border Init Grants, 3661
Richard Florsheim Art Grants, 4083
Rockefeller Brothers Charles E. Culpeper Arts and Culture Grants in New York City, 4129

Art in Public Places
Abbott Fund Community Grants, 81
Abell Fndn Arts and Culture Grants, 92
Adobe Art and Culture Grants, 167
Aetna Fndn Arts Grants in Connecticut, 181
Akron Community Fndn Arts & Culture Grants, 218
Amador Community Fndn Grants, 408
Arthur F. and Alice E. Adams Charitable Grants, 574
Artist Trust GAP Grants, 575
Boyd Gaming Corp Contributions Program, 825
California Arts Council State Networks Grants, 897
CFFVR Fox Valley Community Arts Grants, 1011
Chicago Community Trust Arts and Culture Grants: Supporting Diverse Arts Productions and Fostering Art in Every Community, 1084
Chicago Neighborhood Arts Grants, 1097
Daviess County Comm Arts and Culture Grants, 1455
Delta Air Lines Fndn Arts and Culture Grants, 1493
Ellen Abbott Gilman Grants, 1685
Entergy Corp Open Grants for Arts and Culture, 1713
Fleishhacker Fndn Small Grants in the Arts, 1839
Fleishhacker Fndn Special Arts Grants, 1840
Georgia Council for the Arts Project Grants, 2037
Grand Rapids Area Community Fndn Grants, 2114
Grand Rapids Area Community Fndn Nashwauk Area Endowment Grants, 2115
Helen S. Boylan Fndn Grants, 2298
Huntington Arts Council Arts-in-Educ Grants, 2400
Huntington Arts Council Decentralization Community Arts Grants, 2401
Huntington Arts Council JP Morgan Chase Artist Reach Out Grants, 2402
Huntington Arts Council JP Morgan Chase Organization/Stabilization Regrants, 2403
Illinois Arts Council Service Organizations Grants, 2464
Illinois Arts Council Community Access Grants, 2466
Illinois Arts Council Local Arts Agencies Grants, 2471
Illinois Arts Council Partners in Excellence, 2475
Indiana Arts Commission Multi-regional Major Arts Insts Grants, 2532

810 / Art in Public Places

Kansas Arts Commission American Masterpieces Kansas Grants, 2775
Kohler Fndn Grants, 2833
Massachusetts Cultural Council Local Cultural Council Grants, 3057
Massachusetts Fndn for the Humanities Cultural Economic Development Grants, 3059
Minnesota State Arts Board Cultural Community Partnership Grants, 3188
National Endowment for Arts Our Town Grants, 3257
National Endowment for the Arts - State Partnership Agreement Grants, 3259
National Endowment for Arts Commun Grants, 3260
National Endowment for Arts Agencies Grants, 3263
National Endowment for Arts Museum Grants, 3265
National Endowment for Arts Music Grants, 3266
National Endowment for Arts Opera Grants, 3267
Nevada Arts Council Learning Grants, 3313
NHSCA Cultural Facilities Grants: Barrier Free Access for All, 3426
NJSCA Arts Project Support, 3446
North Carolina Arts Council Arts and Audiences Grants, 3466
North Carolina Arts Council Community Public Art and Design Development Grants, 3472
North Carolina Arts Council Community Public Art and Design Implementation Grants, 3473
North Carolina Arts Facility Design Grants, 3474
NYSCA Architecture, Planning, and Design: Project Support Grants, 3576
NYSCA Arts Educ: Community-based Learning Grants, 3577
NYSCA Arts Educ Program Support Grants, 3579
NYSCA Electronic Media & Film Grants, 3592
NYSCA Electronic Media and Film: Workspace Grants, 3593
NYSCA Folk Arts: Exhibitions Grants, 3594
NYSCA Folk Arts: Regional and County Folk Arts Grants, 3597
NYSCA Presenting: General Operating Support, 3609
NYSCA Presenting: General Program Support, 3610
NYSCA Presenting: Presenting Grants, 3611
NYSCA Presenting: Services to the Field Grants, 3612
NYSCA Special Art Services Project Support, 3613
NYSCA Special Arts Services: General Support, 3615
NYSCA State and Local Partnerships: General Operating Support Grants, 3619
NYSCA State and Local Partnerships: General Program Support Grants, 3620
NYSCA State and Local Partnerships: Services to the Field Grants, 3621
NYSCA State & Local Partner Workshops Grants, 3622
NYSCA Theatre Gen Operating Support Grants, 3623
NYSCA Theatre General Program Support, 3624
NYSCA Theatre Pro Performances Grants, 3625
NYSCA Theatre: Services to the Field Grants, 3626
NYSCA Visual Arts: Exhibitions and Installations Grants, 3627
NYSCA Visual Arts: General Operating Support, 3628
NYSCA Visual Arts: General Program Support, 3629
NYSCA Visual Arts: Services to the Field Grants, 3630
Ontario Arts Council Compass Grants, 3677
PNM Power Up Grants, 3925
Rockefeller Brothers Charles E. Culpeper Arts and Culture Grants in New York City, 4129
San Diego Fndn Arts & Culture Grants, 4243
Santa Barbara Fndn Towbes Fund for the Performing Arts Grants, 4288
Silicon Valley Community Fndn Donor Circle for the Arts Grants, 4354
TAC Arts Access Grant, 4549
TAC Arts Build Communities Grants, 4551
TAC Arts Grants, 4554
TAC Rural Arts Project Support Grants, 4555
Target Fndn Grants, 4562
Virginia Commission for the Arts Project Grants, 4944
VSA Int'l Art Program for Children with Disabilities Grants, 4955
W. Paul and Lucille Caudill Little Fndn Grants, 4966
William G. Baker, Jr. Grants, 5081

Art, Experimental
Connecticut Community Fndn Grants, 1350
Minnesota State Arts Board Cultural Community Partnership Grants, 3188
National Endowment for Arts Commun Grants, 3260
National Endowment for Arts Agencies Grants, 3263
National Endowment for Arts Media Grants, 3264
National Endowment for Arts Museum Grants, 3265
National Endowment for the Arts Presenting Grants: Art Works, 3268
NYFA Gregory Millard Fellowships, 3565
NYSCA Theatre Gen Operating Support Grants, 3623
NYSCA Theatre General Program Support, 3624
NYSCA Visual Arts: General Operating Support, 3628
NYSCA Visual Arts: General Program Support, 3629
NYSCA Visual Arts: Workspace Facilities Grants, 3631
Ohio Arts Council Arts Innovation Grants, 3649
Ohio Arts Council Building Cultural Diversity Init Grants, 3651
PCA Arts Organizations and Arts Programs Grants for Arts Educ Organizations, 3776
PCA Arts Organizations and Arts Programs Grants for Film and Electronic Media, 3780
PCA Entry Track Arts Organizations and Program Grants for Arts Educ Organizations, 3788
PCA Entry Track Arts Organizations and Program Grants for Film and Electronic Media, 3792
San Francisco Fndn James D. Phelan Award in Film, Video, and Digital Media, 4278
Texas Commission on the Arts County Arts Expansion Program, 4582

Arthritis
Adams Fndn Grants, 155
Balfe Family Fndn Grants, 636
Community Fndn of Broward Grants, 1275
Pfizer Healthcare Charitable Contributions, 3863

Artist Studios
Chicago Neighborhood Arts Grants, 1097
National Endowment for Arts Agencies Grants, 3263
National Endowment for the Arts Presenting Grants: Art Works, 3268
NYSCA Visual Arts: Workspace Facilities Grants, 3631

Artists in Residence
18th Street Arts Complex Residency Grants, 19
Andy Warhol Fndn for the Visual Arts Grants, 464
Arizona Commission on the Arts After-School Program Residencies, 535
Arizona Commission on the Arts Educ Grants, 536
Arizona Comm on the Arts Folklorist Residencies, 537
Arizona Commission on the Arts Individual Artist Residencies, 538
Arizona Commission on the Arts Visual/Media Arts Organizations Grants, 539
Arkansas Arts Council AIE After School/Summer Residency Grants, 551
Arkansas Arts Council AIE In-School Residency, 553
Arkansas Arts Council AIE Mini Grants, 554
Arts Midwest Performing Arts Grants, 579
Bay and Paul Fndns Grants, 693
British Columbia Arts Council Artists in Education Grants, 842
California Arts Council Arts and Accessibility Technical Assistance Grants, 894
California Arts Council Public Value Grants, 895
CDECD Arts Catalyze Placemaking in Every Community Grants, 977
CDECD Arts Catalyze Placemaking Leadership Grants, 978
CDECD Arts Catalyze Placemaking Sustaining Relevance Grants, 979
Chicago Cultural Outreach Grants, 1095
City of Oakland Cultural Arts Dept Grants, 1142
Community Fndn of St. Joseph County ArtsEverywhere Grants, 1313
Delaware Division of Arts Opportunity Grants, 1489
District of Columbia Commission on the Arts-Arts Educ Teacher Mini-Grants, 1549

Frank and Lydia Bergen Fndn Grants, 1925
Illinois Arts Council Arts-in-Education Residency Grants, 2463
Iowa Arts Council Artists in Schools/Communities Residency Grants, 2571
Jerome Fndn Grants, 2667
Kansas Arts Commission Artist Fellowships, 2776
Kentucky Arts Council Poetry Out Loud Grants, 2810
Kentucky Arts Council Teaching Together Grant, 2811
Manitoba Arts Council Artist in Community Residency Grants, 2994
Manitoba Arts Council Special Opps Grants, 2997
Marjorie Moore Charitable Fndn Grants, 3021
Minnesota State Arts Board Cultural Community Partnership Grants, 3188
National Endowment for Arts Commun Grants, 3260
National Endowment for the Arts Dance Grants: Art Works, 3262
National Endowment for Arts Agencies Grants, 3263
National Endowment for Arts Museum Grants, 3265
National Endowment for Arts Music Grants, 3266
National Endowment for Arts Opera Grants, 3267
National Endowment for the Arts Presenting Grants: Art Works, 3268
Nevada Arts Council Residency Express Grants, 3315
NHSCA Artist Residencies in Schools Grants, 3423
NHSCA Arts in Health Care Project Grants, 3424
NHSCA Youth Arts Project Grants: For Extended Arts Learning, 3430
North Carolina Arts Council Arts in Educ Rural Development Grants, 3470
North Carolina Arts Council Residency Grants, 3481
North Carolina Arts Council Touring/Presenting Grants, 3483
NYFA Artists in the School Community Planning Grants, 3562
NYSCA Arts Educ Program Support Grants, 3579
NYSCA Arts Educ: K-12 In-School Grants, 3580
NYSCA Arts Education: Local Capacity Building Grants, 3581
NYSCA Arts Educ: Services to the Field Grants, 3582
NYSCA Dance: Long-Term Residency in New York State Grants, 3586
NYSCA Electr Media & Film Workspace Grants, 3593
NYSCA Folk Arts: Presentation Grants, 3596
NYSCA Special Art Services Project Support, 3613
NYSCA Visual Arts: General Operating Support, 3628
NYSCA Visual Arts: General Program Support, 3629
NYSCA Visual Arts: Services to the Field Grants, 3630
NYSCA Visual Arts: Workspace Facilities Grants, 3631
Ohio Arts Council Artist Express Grants, 3643
Ohio Arts Council Artist in Residence Grants, 3644
Ohio Arts Council Artist in Residence Grants for Sponsors, 3645
PCA Arts in Educ Residencies, 3772
PCA Arts Organizations & Grants for Crafts, 3778
PCA Arts Organizations & Grants for Visual Arts, 3785
PCA Entry Track Arts Organizations and Program Grants for Crafts, 3790
PCA Entry Track Arts Organizations and Program Grants for Visual Arts, 3799
PennPAT New Directions Grants for Presenters, 3813
South Carolina Arts Commission AIE Residency Plus Individual Site Grants, 4411
South Carolina Arts Commission AIE Residency Plus Multi-Site Grants, 4412
TAC Arts Access Grant, 4549
TAC Arts Build Communities Grants, 4551
TAC Arts Educ Mini Grants, 4553
TAC Arts Grants, 4554
TAC Rural Arts Project Support Grants, 4555
Virginia Commission for the Arts Project Grants, 4944
West Virginia Commission on the Arts Long-Term Artist Residencies, 5037
West Virginia Commission on the Arts Short-Term Artist Residencies, 5047

Artists' Colonies
Appalachian Regional Commission Tourist Development Grants, 511

SUBJECT INDEX

Artists' Fellowships

Andy Warhol Fndn for the Visual Arts Grants, 464
Arts and Science Council Grants, 576
Delaware Division of the Arts Opportunity Grants--Arts Organizations, 1488
Doris Duke Charitable Fndn Arts Grants, 1584
Illinois Arts Council Visual Arts Grants, 2478
Jerome Fndn Grants, 2667
Joyce Fndn Culture Grants, 2747
Kentucky Arts Council Al Smith Fellowship, 2806
North Carolina Arts Council Regional Artist Project Grants, 3480
North Dakota Council on the Arts Individual Artist Fellowships, 3495
NYFA Deutsche Bank Americas Fellowship, 3564
NYFA Gregory Millard Fellowships, 3565
NYSCA Dance: Long-Term Residency in New York State Grants, 3586
NYSCA Visual Arts: Exhibitions and Installations Grants, 3627
Paul Green Fndn Playwrights Fellowship, 3762
Pew Fellowships in the Arts, 3860
Rasmuson Fndn Individual Artists Awards, 4022
South Carolina Arts Commission Fellowships, 4415
South Carolina Arts Commission Sub-Grants, 4426
Stockton Rush Bartol Fndn Grants, 4508

Arts Administration

Alabama State Council on the Arts Collaborative Ventures Grants, 235
Alabama State Council on the Arts Community Arts Technical Assistance Grants, 240
Alabama State Council on the Arts Operating Support Grants, 244
Alabama State Council on the Arts Program Development Grants, 246
Alabama State Council on the Arts Project Assistance Grants, 247
Alabama State Council on the Arts Technical Assistance Grants for Individuals, 249
Alabama State Council on the Arts Technical Assistance Grants for Organizations, 250
Alaska State Council on the Arts Community Arts Development Grants, 327
Alaska State Council on Arts Operating Grants, 328
Alcatel-Lucent Technologies Fndn Grants, 349
Andy Warhol Fndn for the Visual Arts Grants, 464
Arkansas Arts Council General Operating Support, 557
Arts and Science Council Grants, 576
ArtsWave Impact Grants, 580
ArtsWave Project Grants, 581
Bush Fndn Regional Arts Development Grants, 878
California Arts Council State-Local Partnership Grants, 896
California Arts Council State Networks Grants, 897
California Arts Council Tech Assistance Grants, 898
Chicago Community Trust Arts and Culture Grants: SMART Growth, 1083
Community Fndn in Jacksonville Art Ventures Small Organizations Professional Assistance Grants, 1262
Community Fndn of St. Joseph County ArtsEverywhere Grants, 1313
Connecticut Commission on the Arts Art in Public Spaces, 1349
Corning Fndn Cultural Grants, 1376
Delaware Division of the Arts Opportunity Grants--Arts Organizations, 1488
Florida Div of Cultural Affairs Culture Builds Florida Expansion Funding, 1848
Florida Div of Cultural Affairs Culture Builds Florida Seed Funding, 1849
Florida Div of Cultural Affairs Endowments, 1851
Florida Div of Cultural Affairs General Program Support Grants, 1854
Florida Div of Cultural Affairs Multidisc Grants, 1857
Florida Div of Cultural Affairs Professional Theatre Grants, 1861
Florida Div of Cultural Affairs Underserved Cultural Community Development Grants, 1864
Frey Fndn Grants, 1963
Georgia Council for the Arts Partner Grants for Organizations, 2035
Georgia Council for the Arts Partner Grants for Service Organizations, 2036
Greater Columbus Arts Council Operating Grant, 2133
Illinois Arts Council Service Organization Grants, 2464
Illinois Arts Council Artstour Grants, 2465
Illinois Arts Council Local Arts Agencies Grants, 2471
Illinois Arts Council Partners in Excellence, 2475
Illinois Arts Council Presenters Dev Grants, 2476
Illinois Arts Council Visual Arts Grants, 2478
Indiana Arts Comm Capacity Building Grants, 2531
Indiana Arts Commission Multi-regional Major Arts Insts Grants, 2532
Indiana Arts Commission Statewide Arts Service Organization Grants, 2533
J.L. Bedsole Fndn Grants, 2600
Jerome Fndn Travel and Study Grants, 2668
John F. Kennedy Center for the Performing Arts National Rosemary Kennedy Internship, 2694
Kansas Arts Commission Arts-in-Communities Project Grants, 2777
Kansas Arts Commission Arts-in-Communities Project Mini-Grants, 2778
Kansas Arts Commission Operational Support for Arts and Cultural Organizations, 2781
Kansas Arts Commission Partnership Agreement Grants, 2782
Kennedy Center Experiential Educ Internship, 2798
Microsoft Comm Affairs Puget Sound Grants, 3163
Minnesota State Arts Board Cultural Community Partnership Grants, 3188
National Endowment for the Arts - Grants for Arts Projects: Challenge America Fast-Track, 3254
National Endowment for the Arts - State Partnership Agreement Grants, 3259
National Endowment for Arts Agencies Grants, 3263
National Endowment for Arts Museum Grants, 3265
National Endowment for Arts Music Grants, 3266
National Endowment for the Arts Presenting Grants: Art Works, 3268
National Endowment for Arts Theater Grants, 3269
Nevada Arts Council Professional Dev Grants, 3314
Newfoundland and Labrador Arts Council Sustaining Grants, 3323
NHSCA General Project Grants, 3427
NHSCA Operating Grants, 3428
NJSCA Arts Project Support, 3446
NJSCA Financial and Instal Stabilization Grants, 3447
NJSCA General Program Support Grants, 3449
NJSCA Projects Serving Artists Grants, 3450
North Carolina Arts Council Arts in Educ Rural Development Grants, 3470
North Carolina Arts Council Community Arts Administration Internship, 3471
North Carolina Arts Council Folklife Grants, 3476
North Carolina Arts Council Gen Support, 3477
North Carolina Arts Council Outreach Grants, 3479
North Carolina Arts Council Technical Assistance Grants, 3482
North Dakota Council on the Arts Community Access Grants, 3494
North Dakota Council on the Arts Instal Support Grants, 3496
North Dakota Council on Arts Presenter Support, 3497
NYSCA Dance: Long-Term Residency in New York State Grants, 3586
NYSCA Literature: Services to the Field Grants, 3601
NYSCA Presenting: Services to the Field Grants, 3612
NYSCA State and Local Partnerships: Administrative Salary Support Grants, 3618
NYSCA State and Local Partnerships: General Program Support Grants, 3620
NYSCA State and Local Partnerships: Services to the Field Grants, 3621
NYSCA Theatre General Program Support, 3624
NYSCA Theatre Pro Performances Grants, 3625
NYSCA Theatre: Services to the Field Grants, 3626
NYSCA Visual Arts: Exhibitions and Installations Grants, 3627

Arts Festivals / 811

NYSCA Visual Arts: General Program Support, 3629
NYSCA Visual Arts: Services to the Field Grants, 3630
NYSCA Visual Arts: Workspace Facilities Grants, 3631
Ohio Artists on Tour Fee Support Requests, 3642
Ontario Arts Council Artists in the Community/Workplace Grants, 3676
Ontario Arts Council Compass Grants, 3677
Ontario Arts Council Integrated Arts Grants, 3678
Ontario Arts Council Presenter/Producer Grants, 3680
PCA-PCD Organizational Short-Term Professional Development and Consulting Grants, 3769
PCA Arts Management Internship, 3773
PCA Arts Organizations and Arts Programs Grants for Arts Service Organizations, 3777
PCA Arts Organizations and Arts Programs Grants for Local Arts, 3782
PCA Entry Track Arts Organizations and Program Grants for Arts Service Organizations, 3789
PCA Entry Track Arts Organizations and Program Grants for Local Arts, 3794
PCA Management/Technical Assistance Grants, 3800
PCA Pennsylvania Partners in the Arts Program Stream Grants, 3801
PCA Pennsylvania Partners in Arts Stream Grants, 3802
Procter and Gamble Grants, 3967
Prudential Fndn Arts and Culture Grants, 3975
Regional Arts and Cultural Council General Support Grants, 4045
Regional Arts and Cultural Council Opportunity Grants, 4046
Regional Arts and Cultural Council Professional Development Grants, 4047
RISCA Project Grants for Organizations, Individuals and Educ, 4100
Robert Sterling Clark Arts and Culture Grants, 4122
Rockefeller Brothers Charles E. Culpeper Arts and Culture Grants in New York City, 4129
Sid W. Richardson Fndn Grants, 4350
South Carolina Arts Commission Annual Operating Support for Organizations Grants, 4414
South Carolina Arts Commission Arts and Economic Impact Study Assistance Grants, 4416
South Carolina Arts Commission Facility Grants, 4417
South Carolina Arts Commission Cultural Tourism Init Grants, 4419
South Carolina Arts Commission Cultural Visions Grants, 4420
South Carolina Arts Commission Incentive Grants for Employer Sponsored Benefits, 4422
South Carolina Arts Commission Leadership and Organizational Development Grants, 4423
South Carolina Arts Commission Long Term Operating Support for Organizations Grants, 4424
South Carolina Arts Commission Statewide Arts Participation Init Grants, 4425
South Carolina Arts Commission Sub-Grants, 4426
Stockton Rush Bartol Fndn Grants, 4508
TAC Arts Access Grant, 4549
TAC Arts Access Technical Assistance Grants, 4550
TAC Arts Build Communities Grants, 4551
TAC Arts Grants, 4554
TAC Rural Arts Project Support Grants, 4555
TAC Technical Assistance Grants, 4556
Virginia Commission for the Arts General Operating Grants, 4942
Virginia Commission for the Arts Local Government Challenge Grants, 4943
West Virginia Commission on the Arts Long-Range Planning Grants, 5036
West Virginia Commission on the Arts Major Insts Support Grants, 5038
West Virginia Commission on the Arts Mid-Size Insts Support Grants, 5040

Arts Festivals

Abell Fndn Arts and Culture Grants, 92
Adobe Art and Culture Grants, 167
AEGON Transamerica Arts and Culture Grants, 176
Alaska State Council on the Arts Community Arts Development Grants, 327

812 / Arts Festivals

Angels Baseball Fndn Grants, 465
Appalachian Regional Commission Tourist Development Grants, 511
ArtsWave Impact Grants, 580
ArtsWave Project Grants, 581
California Arts Council State Networks Grants, 897
Con Edison Corp Arts and Culture Grants, 1344
Daviess County Community Fndn Arts and Culture Grants, 1455
Delaware Division of the Arts Community-Based Organizations Opportunity Grants, 1487
Delta Air Lines Fndn Arts and Culture Grants, 1493
Entergy Corp Open Grants for Arts and Culture, 1713
EQT Fndn Art and Culture Grants, 1743
Frank and Lydia Bergen Fndn Grants, 1925
Honda of America Manufacturing Fndn Grants, 2354
Indiana Arts Commission Multi-regional Major Arts Insts Grants, 2532
Kroger Fndn Diversity Grants, 2842
Leon and Thea Koerner Fndn Grants, 2883
Macquarie Bank Fndn Grants, 2966
Marie Walsh Sharpe Art Fndn Grants, 3009
Massachusetts Cultural Council Local Cultural Council Grants, 3057
Minnesota State Arts Board Cultural Community Partnership Grants, 3188
National Endowment for the Arts - Grants for Arts Projects: Challenge America Fast-Track, 3254
National Endowment for the Arts - State Partnership Agreement Grants, 3259
National Endowment for Arts Commun Grants, 3260
National Endowment for Arts Music Grants, 3266
National Endowment for the Arts Presenting Grants: Art Works, 3268
National Endowment for Arts Theater Grants, 3269
North Carolina Arts Council Folklife Grants, 3476
NYSCA Architecture, Planning, and Design: General Program Support Grants, 3574
NYSCA Arts Educ: Community-based Learning Grants, 3577
NYSCA Arts Educ: General Operating Support, 3578
NYSCA Arts Educ Program Support Grants, 3579
NYSCA Arts Educ: Services to the Field Grants, 3582
NYSCA Electronic Media and Film: General Exhibition Grants, 3589
NYSCA Electronic Media & Film Gen Support, 3591
NYSCA Electronic Media and Film: Screenings Grants, 3592
NYSCA Folk Arts: General Program Support, 3595
NYSCA Folk Arts: Presentation Grants, 3596
NYSCA Folk Arts: Regional and County Folk Arts Grants, 3597
NYSCA Presenting: General Operating Support, 3609
NYSCA Presenting: General Program Support, 3610
NYSCA Presenting: Presenting Grants, 3611
NYSCA Presenting: Services to the Field Grants, 3612
NYSCA Special Art Services Project Support, 3613
NYSCA Special Arts Services: General Operating Support Grants, 3614
NYSCA Special Arts Services: General Program Support Grants, 3615
NYSCA Special Arts Services: Instruction and Training Grants, 3616
NYSCA Special Arts Services: Professional Performances Grants, 3617
NYSCA State and Local Partnerships: Services to the Field Grants, 3621
NYSCA Theatre: Services to the Field Grants, 3626
Ohio Arts Council Sustainability Grants, 3654
Ohio River Border Init Grants, 3661
Ontario Arts Council Integrated Arts Grants, 3678
Ontario Arts Council Presenter/Producer Grants, 3680
PCA Art Organizations and Art Programs Grants for Presenting Organizations, 3771
PCA Entry Track Arts Organizations and Program Grants for Presenting Organizations, 3796
PCA Pennsylvania Partners in the Arts Program Stream Grants, 3801
PCA Pennsylvania Partners in the Arts Project Stream Grants, 3802

Richard Florsheim Art Grants, 4083
Rockefeller Brothers Charles E. Culpeper Arts and Culture Grants in New York City, 4129
Santa Barbara Fndn Towbes Fund for the Performing Arts Grants, 4288
South Carolina Arts Commission Cultural Tourism Init Grants, 4419
TAC Arts Access Grant, 4549
TAC Arts Build Communities Grants, 4551
TAC Arts Grants, 4554
TAC Rural Arts Project Support Grants, 4555
Texas Commission on the Arts Cultural Connections- Visual & Media Arts Touring Exhibits Grants, 4589
Texas Instruments Corp Arts and Culture Grants, 4596
Virginia Commission for the Arts Project Grants, 4944
William G. Baker, Jr. Grants, 5081

Arts and Culture
1st Source Fndn Grants, 3
3M Fndn Community Giving Grants, 15
ABS Fndn Grants, 107
Abundance Fndn Local Community Grants, 109
ACF Native American Social and Economic Development Strategies Grants, 123
Ackerman Fndn Grants, 129
Adams-Mastrovich Family Fndn Grants, 146
Adams Fndn Grants, 154
Adams Fndn Grants, 153
Adams Fndn Grants, 155
Adelaide Breed Bayrd Fndn Grants, 161
AEGON Transamerica Arts and Culture Grants, 176
Ahearn Family Fndn Grants, 206
Albert E. and Birdie W. Einstein Grants, 342
Alvah H. and Wyline P. Chapman Fndn Grants, 402
American Express Charitable Grants, 429
Annenberg Fndn Grants, 477
Anne Thorne Weaver Family Fndn Grants, 478
Appalachian Regional Commission Tourist Development Grants, 511
Arizona Republic Newspaper Contributions, 547
Arkansas Arts Council AIE Arts Curriculum Project Grants, 552
ARS Fndn Grants, 568
ArtsWave Impact Grants, 580
ArtsWave Project Grants, 581
Assisi Fndn of Memphis Capital Project Grants, 593
Assisi Fndn of Memphis General Grants, 594
Assisi Fndn of Memphis Mini Grants, 595
Ayres Fndn Grants, 630
Back Home Again Fndn Grants, 633
Bank of America Charitable Fndn Matching Gifts, 658
Bank of America Corp Sponsorships, 661
BBVA Compass Fndn Charitable Grants, 703
Benwood Fndn Focus Area Grants, 733
Bernard & Audre Rapoport Arts & Culture Grant, 735
Blackford County Community Fndn Grants, 780
Blandin Fndn Itasca County Area Vitality Grants, 789
Bloomington Area Arts Council Grants, 791
Blumenthal Fndn Grants, 804
Boeing Company Contributions Grants, 809
Bonfils-Stanton Fndn Grants, 814
Boston Globe Fndn Grants, 821
Boulder County Arts Alliance Neodata Grants, 823
Burlington Industries Fndn Grants, 865
Business Bank of Nevada Community Grants, 879
California Arts Council State Networks Grants, 897
Cardinal Health Fndn Grants, 923
CDECD Arts Catalyze Placemaking in Every Community Grants, 977
CDECD Arts Catalyze Placemaking Leadership Grants, 978
CDECD Arts Catalyze Placemaking Sustaining Relevance Grants, 979
CFFVR Chilton Area Community Fndn Grants, 1006
Charles H. Hall Fndn, 1044
Charles Parker Trust for Public Music Grants, 1053
Chicago CityArts Grants, 1080
Chicago Community Arts Assistance Grants, 1081
Chicago Community Trust Arts and Culture Grants: Improving Access to Arts Learning Opps, 1082

Chicago Community Trust Arts and Culture Grants: SMART Growth, 1083
Chicago Community Trust Arts and Culture Grants: Supporting Diverse Arts Productions and Fostering Art in Every Community, 1084
Chicago Cultural Outreach Grants, 1095
Chicago Neighborhood Arts Grants, 1097
Chicago Tribune Fndn Grants for Cultural Organizations, 1101
CICF City of Noblesville Community Grant, 1118
CICF F.R. Hensel Grant for Fine Arts, Music, and Educ, 1121
CICF J. Proctor Grant for Aged Men & Women, 1124
Cleveland Community Responsive Grants, 1168
Community Fndn for San Benito County Grants, 1258
Community Fndn for SE Michigan Grants, 1259
Community Fndn in Jacksonville Art Ventures Small Organizations Professional Assistance Grants, 1262
Community Fndn of Bloomington and Monroe County Grants, 1271
Community Fndn of Boone County Grants, 1274
Community Fndn Of Greater Lafayette Grants, 1289
Community Fndn of Jackson County Grants, 1298
Community Fndn of Muncie and Delaware County Grants, 1302
Community Fndn of Muncie and Delaware County Maxon Grants, 1303
Community Partners Lawrence County Grants, 1328
Community Partnerships Martin County Grants, 1329
Community Impact Fund, 1332
Con Edison Corp Arts and Culture Grants, 1344
Countess Moira Charitable Fndn Grants, 1381
Covenant Ed Fndn Grants, 1383
Crown Point Community Fndn Grants, 1402
CSRA Community Fndn Grants, 1407
D.V. and Ida J. McEachern Charitable Grants, 1425
Davis Family Fndn Grants, 1462
Decatur County Comm Large Project Grants, 1476
Decatur County Comm Small Project Grants, 1477
DeKalb County Community Fndn Grants, 1481
Delta Air Lines Fndn Arts and Culture Grants, 1493
Dr. P. Phillips Fndn Grants, 1601
DTE Energy Fndn Cultural Grants, 1610
Duke Energy Fndn Community Vitality Grants, 1618
Dyson Mid-Hudson Valley Project Support, 1636
E.J. Grassmann Grants, 1638
Eaton Charitable Grants, 1647
Elkhart County Comm Fund for Elkhart County, 1683
Emy-Lou Biedenharn Fndn Grants, 1703
Ensworth Charitable Fndn Grants, 1710
EQT Fndn Art and Culture Grants, 1743
Eulalie Bloedel Schneider Fndn Grants, 1767
Fifth Third Fndn Grants, 1810
Florida Div of Cultural Affairs Dance Grants, 1850
Florida Div of Cultural Affairs Endowments, 1851
Florida Div of Cultural Affairs Facilities Grants, 1852
Florida Div of Cultural Affairs Folk Arts Grants, 1853
Florida Div of Cultural Affairs Literature Grants, 1855
Florida Div of Cultural Affairs Media Grants, 1856
Florida Div of Cultural Affairs Museum Grants, 1858
Florida Div of Cultural Affairs Music Grants, 1859
Florida Div of Cultural Affairs Presenter Grants, 1860
Florida Div of Cultural Affairs Specific Cultural Project Grants, 1862
Florida Div of Cultural Affairs Underserved Cultural Community Development Grants, 1864
Florida Div of Cultural Affairs Visual Arts Grant, 1865
Franklin H. Wells and Ruth L. Wells Grants, 1930
Frank Loomis Palmer Grants, 1931
Frank M. Tait Fndn Grants, 1932
Furth Family Fndn Grants, 1938
George A. and Grace L. Long Fndn Grants, 2008
George H.C. Ensworth Grants, 2022
George J. and Effie L. Seay Fndn Grants, 2024
George Kress Fndn Grants, 2025
Georgia Council for the Arts Partner Grants for Organizations, 2035
Georgia Council for the Arts Project Grants, 2037
GNOF IMPACT Grants for Arts and Culture, 2078
Greater Des Moines Fndn Grants, 2134

SUBJECT INDEX

Arts and Culture / 813

Greene County Fndn Grants, 2150
Green Fndn Arts Grants, 2152
Grundy Fndn Grants, 2169
Halliburton Fndn Grants, 2211
Hampton Roads Community Fndn Nonprofit Facilities Improvement Grants, 2218
Hancock County Community Fndn - Field of Interest Grants, 2219
Harold and Arlene Schnitzer CARE Grants, 2226
Harrison County Community Fndn Grants, 2233
Harrison County Community Signature Grants, 2234
Harvey Randall Wickes Fndn Grants, 2255
Hearst Fndns Culture Grants, 2284
Helen Bader Fndn Grants, 2293
Hendricks County Community Fndn Grants, 2302
Herbert A. and Adrian W. Woods Fndn Grants, 2313
Huntington County Community Fndn - Hiner Family Grant, 2405
Hutton Fndn Grants, 2412
Illinois Arts Council Service Organization Grants, 2464
Illinois Arts Council Community Access Grants, 2466
Illinois Arts Council Partners in Excellence, 2475
Inasmuch Fndn Grants, 2523
Intergrys Corp Grants, 2565
James L. and Mary Jane Bowman Grants, 2632
Jane's Grants, 2639
Jane and Jack Fitzpatrick Grants, 2640
Jane Bradley Pettit Fndn Arts and Culture Grants, 2641
Jennings County Community Fndn Women's Giving Circle Grant, 2665
John P. Murphy Fndn Grants, 2708
Johnson Controls Fndn Arts and Culture Grants, 2719
John W. and Anna H. Hanes Fndn Grants, 2728
Joyce Fndn Culture Grants, 2747
Kennedy Center HSC Fndn Internship, 2799
Kennedy Center Summer HSC Fndn Internship, 2800
Kentucky Arts Council Al Smith Fellowship, 2806
Kentucky Arts Council Emerging Artist Award, 2807
Kentucky Arts Council Folk and Traditional Arts Apprenticeship Grant, 2808
Kettering Family Fndn Grants, 2817
Kohler Fndn Grants, 2833
Laclede Gas Charitable Grants, 2848
Laidlaw Fndn Youh Organizing Catalyst Grants, 2853
Laidlaw Fndn Youth Organizaing Inits Grants, 2854
Lake County Community Grants, 2856
Land O'Lakes Fndn California Region Grants, 2858
Land O'Lakes Fndn Community Grants, 2859
Laura Jane Musser Intercultural Harmony Grants, 2862
Laura Jane Musser Rural Arts Grants, 2863
Laura Jane Musser Rural Init Grants, 2864
Laurel Fndn Grants, 2867
Legler Benbough Fndn Grants, 2877
Leo Goodwin Fndn Grants, 2882
Leon and Thea Koerner Fndn Grants, 2883
Libra Fndn Grants, 2899
Lindbergh Grants, 2907
Lucy Downing Nisbet Charitable Grants, 2935
Lumpkin Family Fndn Lively Arts and Dynamic Learning Communities Grants, 2943
Lyndhurst Fndn Grants, 2949
MacArthur Fndn Chicago Arts and Culture Int'l Connections Grants, 2962
Madison County Community Fndn - City of Anderson Quality of Life Grant, 2972
Maine Community Fndn Expansion Arts Grants, 2981
Maine Comm Fndn Rines/Thompson Grants, 2987
Maine Community Fndn Vincent B. and Barbara G. Welch Grants, 2990
Marietta McNeill Morgan and Samuel Tate Morgan, Jr. Grants, 3008
Marion I. and Henry Knott Discretionary Grants, 3018
Marion I. and Henry J. Knott Standard Grants, 3019
Marjorie Moore Charitable Fndn Grants, 3021
Massachusetts Cultural Council Cultural Facilities Capital Grants, 3053
Massachusetts Cultural Council Cultural Facilities Feasibility and Technical Assistance Grants, 3054
Massachusetts Cultural Council Cultural Facilities Systems Replacement Plan Grants Grants, 3055

Massachusetts Cultural Council Cultural Investment Portfolio, 3056
Massachusetts Cultural Council Local Cultural Council Grants, 3057
Massachusetts Cultural Council Traditional Arts Apprenticeships, 3058
Maurice J. Masserini Charitable Grants, 3064
McCune Charitable Fndn Grants, 3077
McCune Fndn Humananities Grants, 3079
McGraw-Hill Companies Community Grants, 3081
McGregor Grants, 3082
MeadWestvaco Sustainable Communities Grant, 3105
Medtronic Fndn Community Link Arts, Civic, and Culture Grants, 3109
Merkel Family Fndn Grants, 3123
Meyer Memorial Trust Grassroots Grants, 3147
Meyer Memorial Trust Responsive Grants, 3148
Miller Fndn Grants, 3181
Milton and Sally Avery Arts Fndn Grants, 3183
Moline Fndn Community Grants, 3202
Monsanto Access to the Arts Grants, 3204
Montana Arts Council Cultural and Aesthetic Project Grants, 3209
Montana Community Fndn Grants, 3211
Mr. and Mrs. William Foulds Family Grants, 3222
Nathaniel and Elizabeth P. Stevens Fndn Grants, 3247
National Endowment for the Arts - National Arts and Humanities Youth Program Awards, 3255
National Endowment for Arts Our Town Grants, 3257
National Endowment for the Arts - State Partnership Agreement Grants, 3259
National Endowment for Arts Commun Grants, 3260
National Endowment for Arts Media Grants, 3264
National Endowment for the Arts Presenting Grants: Art Works, 3268
National Endowment for Arts Theater Grants, 3269
Nevada Arts Council Circuit Rider Grants, 3308
Nevada Arts Council Heritage Awards, 3311
Newfoundland and Labrador Arts Council Community Arts Grants, 3318
Newfoundland and Labrador Arts Council Labrador Cultural Travel Grants, 3319
Newfoundland and Labrador Arts Council Professional Artists Travel Fund, 3320
Newfoundland and Labrador Arts Council Professional Festivals Grants, 3321
Newfoundland and Labrador Arts Council Professional Project Grants, 3322
Newfoundland and Labrador Arts Council Sustaining Grants, 3323
Newfoundland and Labrador Arts Council Visiting Artists Grants, 3324
NHSCA Traditional Arts Apprenticeships, 3429
Nissan Neighbors Grants, 3445
NJSCA Financial and Instal Stabilization Grants, 3447
Norcliffe Fndn Grants, 3459
Nord Family Fndn Grants, 3461
Norfolk Southern Fndn Grants, 3463
North Dakota Community Fndn Grants, 3493
North Dakota Council on Arts Presenter Support, 3497
NYSCA Architecture, Planning, and Design: General Program Support Grants, 3574
NYSCA Architecture, Planning, and Design: Project Support Grants, 3576
NYSCA Arts Educ: Community-based Learning Grants, 3577
NYSCA Arts Educ: General Operating Support, 3578
NYSCA Arts Educ Program Support Grants, 3579
NYSCA Arts Educ: K-12 In-School Grants, 3580
NYSCA Arts Educ: Services to the Field Grants, 3582
NYSCA Dance: Commissions Grants, 3583
NYSCA Dance Gen Operating Support Grants, 3584
NYSCA Dance Gen Program Support Grants, 3585
NYSCA Dance: Long-Term Residency in New York State Grants, 3586
NYSCA Dance: Services to the Field Grants, 3587
NYSCA Electronic Media and Film: General Exhibition Grants, 3589
NYSCA Electronic Media and Film: General Operating Support, 3590

NYSCA Electronic Media and Film: General Program Support, 3591
NYSCA Elect Media & Film Screenings Grants, 3592
NYSCA Electronic Media and Film: Workspace Grants, 3593
NYSCA Folk Arts: Exhibitions Grants, 3594
NYSCA Folk Arts: General Program Support, 3595
NYSCA Folk Arts: Presentation Grants, 3596
NYSCA Folk Arts: Regional and County Folk Arts Grants, 3597
NYSCA Museum General Operating Support, 3602
NYSCA Museum Program Support Grants, 3603
NYSCA Museum: Project Support Grants, 3604
NYSCA Presenting: General Operating Support, 3609
NYSCA Presenting: General Program Support, 3610
NYSCA Presenting: Presenting Grants, 3611
NYSCA Presenting: Services to the Field Grants, 3612
NYSCA Special Art Services Project Support, 3613
NYSCA Special Arts Services: General Operating Support Grants, 3614
NYSCA Special Arts Services: General Program Support Grants, 3615
NYSCA Special Arts Services: Instruction and Training Grants, 3616
NYSCA Special Arts Services: Professional Performances Grants, 3617
NYSCA State and Local Partnerships: General Operating Support Grants, 3619
NYSCA State and Local Partnerships: General Program Support Grants, 3620
NYSCA State and Local Partnerships: Services to the Field Grants, 3621
NYSCA State and Local Partnerships: Workshops Grants, 3622
NYSCA Theatre Gen Operating Support Grants, 3623
NYSCA Theatre General Program Support, 3624
NYSCA Theatre Pro Performances Grants, 3625
NYSCA Theatre: Services to the Field Grants, 3626
NYSCA Visual Arts: Exhibitions and Installations Grants, 3627
NYSCA Visual Arts: General Operating Support, 3628
NYSCA Visual Arts: General Program Support, 3629
NYSCA Visual Arts: Services to the Field Grants, 3630
NYSCA Visual Arts: Workspace Facilities Grants, 3631
Orange County Community Fndn Grants, 3688
Orange County Community Fndn Grants, 3687
OSF-Baltimore Community Fellowships, 3695
Owen County Community Fndn Grants, 3716
Pacific Life Fndn Grants, 3726
Packard Fndn Local Grants, 3729
Parke County Community Fndn Grants, 3735
Paul and Edith Babson Fndn Grants, 3755
Paul G. Allen Family Fndn Grants, 3759
PCA Pennsylvania Partners in the Arts Program Stream Grants, 3801
PCA Pennsylvania Partners in the Arts Project Stream Grants, 3802
Peoples Bancorp Fndn Grants, 3817
Perkin Grants, 3821
Peyton Anderson Fndn Grants, 3862
Piedmont Natural Gas Charitable Contributions, 3883
Pier 1 Imports Grants, 3887
Pinnacle Entertainment Fndn Grants, 3893
PMI Fndn Grants, 3918
PNC Charitable Trust and Fndn Grants, 3921
PNC Ecnomic Development Grants, 3922
Portland Fndn Grants, 3936
Portland General Electric Fndn Grants, 3937
PPG Industries Fndn Grants, 3943
Price Chopper's Golub Fndn Grants, 3950
Priddy Fndn Grants, 3957
Progress Energy Fndn Economic Vitality Grants, 3969
Rasmuson Fndn Creative Ventures Grants, 4021
Rasmuson Organizational Advancement Grants, 4023
Regional Arts & Cultural Council Project Grants, 4048
Robert F. Stoico / FIRSTFED Grants, 4112
Robert Lee Blaffer Fndn Grants, 4115
Robert W. Woodruff Fndn Grants, 4124
Rohm and Haas Company Grants, 4145
Rose Hills Fndn Grants, 4162

814 / Arts and Culture

S. Spencer Scott Grants, 4202
Samuel N. and Mary Castle Fndn Grants, 4236
Sandy Hill Fndn Grants, 4257
San Francisco Fndn FAITHS Arts and Culture Mini Grants, 4268
Santa Barbara Fndn Towbes Fund for the Performing Arts Grants, 4288
Sarkeys Fndn Grants, 4297
Seattle Fndn Arts and Culture Grants, 4320
Seattle Fndn C. Keith Birkenfeld Grants, 4323
Sioux Falls Area Community Grants, 4364
Sioux Falls Area Community Fndn Field-of-Interest and Donor-Advised Grants, 4365
Sioux Falls Area Community Fndn Spot Grants, 4366
Sony Corp of America Corp Philanthropy Grants, 4405
Sosland Fndn Grants, 4408
Sprague Fndn Grants, 4461
Starke County Community Fndn Grants, 4482
Stewart Huston Charitable Grants, 4505
Stinson Fndn Grants, 4506
Sunbeam Products Grants, 4526
Sunny and Abe Rosenberg Fndn Grants, 4529
T. Rowe Price Associates Fndn Grants, 4548
Telluride Fndn Community Grants, 4573
Texas Instruments Corp Arts and Culture Grants, 4596
Texas Instruments Fndn Arts and Culture Grants, 4599
Textron Corp Contributions Grants, 4601
Thomas B. & Elizabeth M. Sheridan Grants, 4614
Thomas J. Long Fndn Community Grants, 4618
Toro Fndn Grants, 4647
Toyota Motor Engineering & Manufacturing North America Grants, 4651
Toyota Motor Manufacturing of Alabama Grants, 4652
Toyota Motor Manufacturing of Indiana Grants, 4653
Toyota Motor Manufacturing Mississippi Grants, 4655
Toyota Motor Manufacturing of Texas Grants, 4656
Toyota Motor Manufacturing W Virginia Grants, 4657
Toyota Motor N America of New York Grants, 4658
Toyota Motor Sales, USA Grants, 4659
TWS Fndn Grants, 4683
U.S. Bank Fndn Grants, 4686
Union Bank Corp Sponsorships and Donations, 4708
Union Square Awards Grants, 4718
United Technologies Corp Grants, 4725
USDD Cultural Resources Program Assistance Announcement Grants, 4862
Valerie Adams Memorial Charitable Grants, 4898
Vanderburgh Community Fndn Grants, 4902
Victor E. Speas Fndn Grants, 4933
Virginia Commission for the Arts Local Government Challenge Grants, 4943
Virginia Commission for the Arts Project Grants, 4944
Virginia Fndn for Humanities Discr Grants, 4946
Virginia Fndn for the Humanities Open Grants, 4947
Virginia Fndn for the Humanities Residential Fellowships, 4948
Virginia W. Kettering Fndn Grants, 4950
VSA/Volkswagen America Exhibition Awards, 4954
W.M. Keck Fndn Southern California Grants, 4964
Wabash Valley Community Fndn Grants, 4971
Wallace Alexander Gerbode Fndn Grants, 4974
Wallace Alexander Gerbode Fndn Special Award Grants, 4975
Warren County Community Fndn Grants, 4985
Warren County Community Fndn Mini-Grants, 4986
Washington County Community Fndn Grants, 4997
Washington County Community Youth Grants, 4998
Weatherwax Fndn Grants, 5014
Wells County Fndn Grants, 5022
West Virginia Commission on the Arts Artist Visit Grants, 5030
West Virginia Commission on the Arts Community Connections Grants, 5032
West Virginia Commission on the Arts Cultural Facilities and Capital Resources Grants, 5033
West Virginia Commission on the Arts Fast Track ADA and Emergency Grants, 5034
West Virginia Commission on the Arts Init/Opportunity Grants, 5035

West Virginia Commission on the Arts Media Arts Grants, 5039
West Virginia Commission on the Arts Peer Assistance Network Grants, 5042
West Virginia Commission on the Arts Presenting Artists Grants, 5044
West Virginia Commission on the Arts Re-Granting Grants, 5046
West Virginia Comm on the Arts Special Grants, 5048
West Virginia Commission on the Arts Staffing Support Grants, 5049
West Virginia Commission on the Arts Travel and Training Grants, 5050
White County Community Fndn Grants, 5057
Whiting Fndn Grants, 5059
Whitley County Community Fndn Grants, 5060
Wilbur and Patsy Bradley Family Fndn Grants, 5066
Willary Fndn Grants, 5071
William B. Stokely Jr. Fndn Grants, 5076
William Bingham Fndn Grants, 5077
William L. and Victorine Q. Adams Fndn Grants, 5089
Winston-Salem Fndn Competitive Grants, 5102
Wisconsin Energy Fndn Grants, 5106
Wisconsin Humanities Council Mini-Grants for Scholarly Research, 5108
Woods Charitable Grants, 5114
Yawkey Fndn Grants, 5125

Arts, Fine
Anderson Fndn Grants, 460
Anne Thorne Weaver Family Fndn Grants, 478
ArtsWave Impact Grants, 580
Ayres Fndn Grants, 630
Charles H. Hall Fndn, 1044
Chicago CityArts Grants, 1080
Crystelle Waggoner Charitable Grants, 1405
DTE Energy Fndn Cultural Grants, 1610
EQT Fndn Art and Culture Grants, 1743
GNOF IMPACT Grants for Arts and Culture, 2078
Hearst Fndns Culture Grants, 2284
Helen Bader Fndn Grants, 2293
Helen Gertrude Sparks Charitable Grants, 2294
Helen Pumphrey Denit Charitable Grants, 2297
J. Edwin Treakle Fndn Grants, 2596
Joyce Fndn Culture Grants, 2747
Katrine Menzing Deakins Charitable Grants, 2793
Lewis H. Humphreys Charitable Grants, 2889
Lumpkin Family Fndn Lively Arts and Dynamic Learning Communities Grants, 2943
Massachusetts Cultural Council Local Cultural Council Grants, 3057
NJSCA Financial and Instal Stabilization Grants, 3447
NJSCA Projects Serving Artists Grants, 3450
PCA-PCD Professional Development for Individual Artists Grants, 3770
PCA Arts Organizations and Arts Programs Grants for Arts Service Organizations, 3777
PCA Entry Track Arts Organizations and Program Grants for Arts Service Organizations, 3789
PCA Pennsylvania Partners in the Arts Program Stream Grants, 3801
PCA Pennsylvania Partners in the Arts Project Stream Grants, 3802
PCA Professional Development Grants, 3803
PCA Strategies for Success Grants - Basic Level, 3805
PCA Strategies for Success Grants - Intermediate, 3806
PennPAT Artist Technical Assistance Grants, 3811
PennPAT Strategic Opportunity Grants, 3815
Progress Energy Fndn Economic Vitality Grants, 3969
Richard and Caroline T. Gwathmey Grants, 4075
RISCA Professional Arts Development Grants, 4099
RISCA Project Grants for Organizations, Individuals and Educ, 4100
Stinson Fndn Grants, 4506
TAC Arts Access Grant, 4549
TAC Arts Build Communities Grants, 4551
Thelma Braun and Bocklett Family Fndn Grants, 4603
Virginia Commission for the Arts Project Grants, 4944

SUBJECT INDEX

Arts, General
1st Source Fndn Grants, 3
2 Depot Square Ipswich Charitable Fndn Grants, 4
3M Company Arts and Culture Grants, 12
A.C. Ratshesky Fndn Grants, 39
Aaron Fndn Grants, 73
Abbot and Dorothy H. Stevens Fndn Grants, 79
Abbott Fund Community Grants, 81
Abell Fndn Arts and Culture Grants, 92
ABIG Fndn Grants, 99
ABS Fndn Grants, 107
ACF Fndn Grants, 119
Achelis Fndn Grants, 127
ACTION Council of Monterey County Grants, 134
Acuity Charitable Fndn Grants, 140
Adam Richter Charitable Grants, 145
Adams-Mastrovich Family Fndn Grants, 146
Adams County Community Pennsylvania Grants, 149
Adams Family Fndn I Grants, 150
Adobe Art and Culture Grants, 167
Adobe Community Investment Grants, 168
AEC Grants, 175
AEGON Transamerica Arts and Culture Grants, 176
AFG Industries Grants, 191
African American Fund of New Jersey Grants, 192
A Friends' Fndn Grants, 194
Ahearn Family Fndn Grants, 206
Ahmanson Fndn Grants, 207
AHS Fndn Grants, 208
Air Products and Chemicals Grants, 216
Akzo Nobel Chemicals Grants, 219
Alabama Power Fndn Grants, 233
Alabama State Council on the Arts Collaborative Ventures Grants, 235
Alabama State Council on the Arts Community Arts Collaborative Ventures Grants, 236
Alabama State Council on the Arts Community Arts Operating Support Grants, 237
Alabama State Council on the Arts Community Arts Presenting Grants, 238
Alabama State Council on the Arts Community Arts Program Development Grants, 239
Alabama State Council on the Arts Community Arts Technical Assistance Grants, 240
Alabama State Council on the Arts Community Planning & Design Grants, 241
Alabama State Council on the Arts in Educ Partnership Grants, 242
Alabama State Council on the Arts Multi-Discipline and Festival Grants, 243
Alabama State Council on the Arts Presenting Grants, 245
Alabama State Council on the Arts Program Development Grants, 246
Alabama State Council on the Arts Project Assistance Grants, 247
Alabama State Council on the Arts Projects of Individual Artists Grants, 248
Alabama State Council on the Arts Technical Assistance Grants for Individuals, 249
Alabama State Council on the Arts Technical Assistance Grants for Organizations, 250
Aladdin Industries Fndn Grants, 263
Alaska Airlines Corp Giving Grants, 320
Alaska Airlines Fndn Grants, 321
Alberto Culver Corp Contributions Grants, 343
Albuquerque Community Fndn Grants, 348
Alcatel-Lucent Technologies Fndn Grants, 349
Alcoa Fndn Grants, 350
Alexander & Baldwin Fndn Hawaiian and Pacific Island Grants, 352
Alexander & Baldwin Fndn Mainland Grants, 353
Alex Brown and Sons Charitable Fndn Grants, 359
Alex Stern Family Fndn Grants, 360
Alice Tweed Tuohy Fndn Grants, 372
Allegheny Technologies Charitable Trust, 377
Alticor Corp Community Contributions Grants, 396
Altman Fndn Health Care Grants, 397
Altria Group Arts and Culture Grants, 399
Alvah H. and Wyline P. Chapman Fndn Grants, 402
Alvin and Fanny Blaustein Thalheimer Grants, 403

SUBJECT INDEX Arts, General / 815

Alvin and Lucy Owsley Fndn Grants, 404
Amador Community Fndn Grants, 408
Amarillo Area/Harrington Fndns Grants, 412
Ambrose and Ida Fredrickson Fndn Grants, 414
Ameren Corp Community Grants, 418
Amer-Scandinavian Fndn Public Project Grants, 419
American Express Charitable Grants, 429
American Express Historic Preservation Grants, 431
American for the Arts Emergency Relief Fund, 435
American Savings Fndn Grants, 445
American Schlafhorst Fndn Grants, 446
Amerigroup Fndn Grants, 452
Amon G. Carter Fndn Grants, 458
Anderson Fndn Grants, 460
Andrew Family Fndn Grants, 462
Angels Baseball Fndn Grants, 465
Anna Fitch Ardenghi Grants, 472
Annenberg Fndn Grants, 477
Anne Thorne Weaver Family Fndn Grants, 478
Annie Sinclair Knudsen Memorial Fund/Kaua'i Community Grants, 482
Ann L. & Carol Green Rhodes Charitable Grants, 483
AON Fndn Grants, 491
APAP Cultural Exchange Grants, 492
Appalachian Regional Commission Tourist Development Grants, 511
Applied Biosystems Grants, 514
Applied Materials Corp Philanthropy Program, 515
APS Fndn Grants, 518
AptarGroup Fndn Grants, 519
Aquila Corp Grants, 521
Aratani Fndn Grants, 523
Arizona Cardinals Grants, 534
Arizona Public Service Corp Giving Grants, 545
Arizona Republic Fndn Grants, 546
Arkansas Arts Council Collab Project Support, 555
Arkansas Community Fndn Grants, 561
Arlington Community Fndn Grants, 564
Armstrong McDonald Fndn Grants, 565
Arthur Ashley Williams Fndn Grants, 572
Arthur F. and Alice E. Adams Charitable Grants, 574
Artist Trust GAP Grants, 575
Arts Council of Winston-Salem and Forsyth County Organizational Support Grants, 577
ArtsWave Impact Grants, 580
ArtsWave Project Grants, 581
ArvinMeritor Fndn Arts and Culture Grants, 582
Assurant Health Fndn Grants, 596
Atherton Family Fndn Grants, 604
Athwin Fndn Grants, 605
Atlanta Fndn Grants, 608
Audrey and Sydney Irmas Charitable Fndn Grants, 612
Aurora Fndn Grants, 613
Austin Community Fndn Grants, 616
Autodesk Community Relations Grants, 619
AutoNation Corp Giving Grants, 620
Autzen Fndn Grants, 622
Ayres Fndn Grants, 630
Back Home Again Fndn Grants, 633
Bacon Family Fndn Grants, 634
Bailey Fndn Grants, 635
Baltimore Community Fndn Arts and Culture Path Grants, 641
BancorpSouth Fndn Grants, 651
Banfi Vintners Fndn Grants, 653
BankAtlantic Fndn Grants, 654
Bank of America Charitable Fndn Matching Gifts, 658
Barbara Meyer Elsner Fndn Grants, 665
Barberton Community Fndn Grants, 666
Baring Fndn Grants, 667
Barker Welfare Fndn Grants, 669
Barnes and Noble Local Sponsorships and Charitable Donations, 670
Barnes and Noble National Sponsorships and Charitable Donations, 671
Barnes Group Fndn Grants, 672
Barra Fndn Community Grants, 673
Barra Fndn Project Grants, 674
Barrasso Usdin Kupperman Freeman and Sarver LLC Corp Grants, 675

Batchelor Fndn Grants, 679
Baton Rouge Area Fndn Grants, 682
Battle Creek Community Fndn Grants, 684
Batts Fndn Grants, 687
Bay Area Community Fndn Grants, 694
Bayer Fndn Grants, 696
Beazley Fndn Grants, 714
Beckley Area Fndn Grants, 716
Beim Fndn Grants, 718
Belk Fndn Grants, 721
Bemis Company Fndn Grants, 723
Ben B. Cheney Fndn Grants, 725
Beneficia Fndn Grants, 727
Benton Community Fndn Grants, 730
Benton County Fndn Grants, 731
Benwood Fndn Community Grants, 732
Berks County Community Fndn Grants, 734
Bernard & Audre Rapoport Arts & Culture Grant, 735
Bernard Osher Fndn Grants, 742
Berrien Community Fndn Grants, 744
Besser Fndn Grants, 748
Biogen Corp Giving Grants, 773
Black Hills Corp Grants, 781
Blanche and Irving Laurie Fndn Grants, 784
Blanche and Julian Robertson Family Fndn Grants, 785
Bloomington Area Arts Council Grants, 791
Blue Grass Community Fndn Grants, 799
Blue Mountain Community Fndn Grants, 800
Blue River Community Fndn Grants, 801
Bodenwein Public Benevolent Fndn Grants, 806
Borkee-Hagley Fndn Grants, 817
Bosque Fndn Grants, 818
Boston Fndn Grants, 819
Boston Fndn Init to Strengthen Arts and Cultural Service Organizations, 820
Boulder County Arts Alliance Neodata Grants, 823
Bradley-Turner Fndn Grants, 828
Bridgestone/Firestone Grants, 836
Bright Family Fndn Grants, 837
Brooklyn Community Fndn Community Arts for All Grants, 849
Brown County Community Fndn Grants, 853
Brown Fndn Grants, 854
Bunbury Company Grants, 863
Burlington Northern Santa Fe Fndn Grants, 866
Bush Fndn Regional Arts Development Grants, 878
Butler Manufacturing Company Fndn Grants, 881
Bydale Fndn Grants, 882
CAA Millard Meiss Publication Grants, 885
Cabot Corp Fndn Grants, 887
Caleb C. and Julia W. Dula Ed and Charitable Fndn Grants, 893
California Arts Council State-Local Partnerships, 896
California Arts Council State Networks Grants, 897
California Coastal Art and Poetry Contest, 899
California Community Fndn Art Grants, 900
Callaway Fndn Grants, 909
Cambridge Community Fndn Grants, 913
Campbell Soup Fndn Grants, 916
Canada-U.S. Fulbright Mid-Career Grants, 917
Capital City Bank Group Fndn Grants, 920
Carl and Eloise Pohlad Family Fndn Grants, 927
Carl B. and Florence E. King Fndn Grants, 928
Carl C. Icahn Fndn Grants, 929
Carl M. Freeman Fndn FACES Grants, 932
Carolyn Fndn Grants, 942
Carpenter Fndn Grants, 943
Carrie E. and Lena V. Glenn Fndn Grants, 944
CCH California Story Grants, 965
Ceil & Michael E. Pulitzer Fndn Grants, 987
Cemala Fndn Grants, 988
Central Okanagan Fndn Grants, 997
Cessna Fndn Grants, 1000
CFFVR Clintonville Area Fndn Grants, 1008
CFFVR Fox Valley Community Arts Grants, 1011
CFFVR Frank C. Shattuck Community Grants, 1012
CFFVR Project Grants, 1017
CFFVR Robert & Patricia Endries Family Grant, 1018
CFFVR Shawano Area Community Fndn Grants, 1021
CFFVR Waupaca Area Community Fndn Grants, 1023

CFFVR Women's Fund for the Fox Valley Grants, 1025
Chamberlain Fndn Grants, 1027
Champlin Fndns Grants, 1029
Charles H. Dater Fndn Grants, 1042
Charles H. Hall Fndn, 1044
Charles Lafitte Fndn Grants, 1049
Charles M. Bair Family Grants, 1051
Charlotte County (FL) Community Fndn Grants, 1056
Chautauqua Region Community Fndn Grants, 1062
Chicago Board of Trade Fndn Grants, 1079
Chicago CityArts Grants, 1080
Chicago Community Arts Assistance Grants, 1081
Chicago Cultural Outreach Grants, 1095
Chicago Neighborhood Arts Grants, 1097
Chicago Sun Times Charity Grants, 1098
Chiles Fndn Grants, 1108
Christy-Houston Fndn Grants, 1115
Chula Vista Charitable Fndn Grants, 1116
CICF Legacy Grants, 1126
CIGNA Fndn Grants, 1130
Cincinnati Bell Fndn Grants, 1131
Cincinnati Milacron Fndn Grants, 1132
Cinergy Fndn Grants, 1133
CIT Corp Giving Grants, 1138
Citigroup Fndn Grants, 1139
Citizens Bank Mid-Atlantic Charitable Grants, 1140
City of Oakland Cultural Arts Dept Grants, 1142
Claneil Fndn Grants, 1145
Clarcor Fndn Grants, 1148
Clark-Winchcole Fndn Grants, 1152
Clark County Community Fndn Grants, 1156
Claude Worthington Benedum Fndn Grants, 1161
Cleveland-Cliffs Fndn Grants, 1165
Cleveland Browns Fndn Grants, 1166
Clorox Company Fndn Grants, 1176
Clowes Grants, 1177
CNA Fndn Grants, 1179
CNL Corp Giving Arts & Culture Grants, 1190
Coastal Community Fndn of S Carolina Grants, 1193
Coca-Cola Fndn Grants, 1195
Cockrell Fndn Grants, 1196
Coeta and Donald Barker Fndn Grants, 1197
Colgate-Palmolive Company Grants, 1202
Collins Fndn Grants, 1209
Columbus Fndn Competitive Grants, 1220
Columbus Fndn Mary Eleanor Morris Grants, 1225
Columbus Fndn Paul G. Duke Grants, 1227
Columbus Fndn Siemer Family Grants, 1231
Columbus Fndn Small Grants, 1232
Comer Fndn Grants, 1236
Communities Fndn of Texas Grants, 1243
Community Fndn Alliance City of Evansville Endowment Grants, 1246
Community Fndn for Greater Buffalo Grants, 1247
Community Fndn for Monterey County Grants, 1255
Community Fndn for Muskegon County Grants, 1256
Community Fndn for NE Michigan Grants, 1257
Community Fndn for Southern Arizona Grants, 1261
Community Fndn in Jacksonville Art Ventures Small Organizations Professional Assistance Grants, 1262
Community Fndn of Bartholomew County Heritage Grants, 1267
Community Fndn of Bartholomew County James A. Henderson Award for Fundraising, 1268
Community Fndn of Broward Grants, 1275
Community Fndn of Central Illinois Grants, 1276
Community Fndn of East Central Illinois Grants, 1278
Community Fndn of Greater Birmingham Grants, 1280
Community Fndn of Greater Flint Grants, 1282
Community Fndn of Greater Fort Wayne - Community Endowment and Clarke Endowment Grants, 1285
Community Fndn of Greater Fort Wayne - Edna Fndn Grants, 1286
Community Fndn of Greater Greensboro Grants, 1288
Community Fndn of Greater New Britain Grants, 1291
Community Fndn of Greater Tampa Grants, 1292
Community Fndn of Greenville-Greenville Women Giving Grants, 1293
Community Fndn of Greenville Community Enrichment Grants, 1294

Arts, General

Community Fndn of Greenville Hollingsworth Funds Program/Project Grants, 1296
Community Fndn of Middle Tennessee Grants, 1300
Community Fndn of Mount Vernon and Knox County Grants, 1301
Community Fndn of Riverside County Grants, 1304
Community Fndn of Santa Cruz County Grants, 1305
Community Fndn of Sarasota County Grants, 1306
Community Fndn of Shreveport-Bossier Grants, 1307
Community Fndn of South Alabama Grants, 1308
Community Fndn of SE Connecticut Grants, 1309
Community Fndn of South Puget Sound Grants, 1311
Community Fndn of St. Joseph County African American Community Grants, 1312
Community Fndn of Switzerland County Grants, 1315
Community Fndn of Tampa Bay Grants, 1316
Community Fndn of the Eastern Shore Community Needs Grants, 1317
Community Fndn of the Ozarks Grants, 1320
Community Fndn of the Verdugos Ed Endowment Grants, 1321
Community Fndn of the Verdugos Grants, 1322
Community Fndn of Wabash County Grants, 1326
Community Fndn of Western N Carolina Grants, 1327
Community Fndn Silicon Valley Advancing Arts, 1330
Community Fndn Silicon Valley Grants, 1331
Compton Fndn Grants, 1338
Con Edison Corp Arts and Culture Grants, 1344
Connecticut Community Fndn Grants, 1350
Connelly Fndn Grants, 1353
ConocoPhillips Fndn Grants, 1354
ConocoPhillips Grants, 1355
CONSOL Coal Group Grants, 1360
Constantin Fndn Grants, 1362
Consumers Energy Fndn, 1365
Cooke Fndn Grants, 1368
Cooper Fndn Grants, 1369
Cooper Industries Fndn Grants, 1370
Cord Fndn Grants, 1372
Corina Higginson Grants, 1373
Cornerstone Fndn of NE Wisconsin Grants, 1375
Coughlin-Saunders Fndn Grants, 1377
Cowles Charitable Grants, 1392
Cralle Fndn Grants, 1394
Cranston Fndn Grants, 1395
Crossroads Fund Seed Grants, 1400
CSX Corp Contributions Grants, 1408
Cudd Fndn Grants, 1410
Cumberland Community Fndn Grants, 1413
Cumberland Community Fndn Summertime Kids Grants, 1414
Cummins Fndn Grants, 1415
CUNA Mutual Group Fndn, 1416
Curtis Fndn Grants, 1419
Cyrus Eaton Fndn Grants, 1423
Dade Community Fndn GLBT Grants, 1429
Dade Community Fndn Grants, 1430
DaimlerChrysler Corp Grants, 1432
Dairy Queen Corp Contributions Grants, 1433
Dale and Edna Walsh Fndn Grants, 1435
Dallas Fndn Grants, 1436
Dana Corp Fndn Grants, 1440
Dance Advance Grants, 1441
Darden Restaurants Fndn Grants, 1446
David Geffen Fndn Grants, 1452
Daviess County Community Fndn Arts and Culture Grants, 1455
Dayton Fndn Grants, 1463
Daywood Fndn Grants, 1465
DB Americas Fndn Grants, 1466
Deaconess Community Fndn Grants, 1467
Dearborn Community Fndn City of Lawrenceburg Community Grants, 1471
Dearborn Community County Progress Grants, 1473
Dell Fndn Open Grants, 1490
Delonne Anderson Family Fndn, 1492
Delta Air Lines Fndn Arts and Culture Grants, 1493
DeMatteis Family Fndn Grants, 1497
Denver Fndn Community Grants, 1502
Dept of Ed Recreational Services for Individuals with Disabilities, 1512
Dermody Properties Fndn Grants, 1517
DeRoy Testamentary Fndn Grants, 1518
Dolfinger-McMahon Fndn Grants, 1565
Donald and Sylvia Robinson Family Fndn Grants, 1573
Doris Duke Charitable Fndn Arts Grants, 1584
Dorothy Rider Pool Health Care Grants, 1589
Douty Fndn Grants, 1595
Drs. Bruce and Lee Fndn Grants, 1607
DTE Energy Fndn Cultural Grants, 1610
Dubois County Community Fndn Grants, 1615
Duluth-Superior Area Community Fndn Grants, 1620
DuPage Community Fndn Grants, 1624
Durfee Fndn Sabbatical Grants, 1625
Dyson Mid-Hudson Valley Project Support, 1636
E.J. Grassmann Grants, 1638
E.L. Wiegand Fndn Grants, 1639
Eastman Chemical Company Fndn Grants, 1643
East Tennessee Fndn Grants, 1646
Eberly Fndn Grants, 1649
Eddie C. and Sylvia Brown Family Fndn Grants, 1653
Eddy Knight Family Fndn Grants, 1654
EDS Fndn Grants, 1661
Edward W. and Stella C. Van Houten Grants, 1670
Edwin W. and Catherine M. Davis Fndn Grants, 1672
Eisner Fndn Grants, 1678
Elizabeth Morse Genius Charitable Grants, 1682
Elkhart County Community Fndn Grants, 1684
Ellen Abbott Gilman Grants, 1685
El Paso Community Fndn Grants, 1688
El Paso Corp Fndn Grants, 1689
El Pomar Fndn Awards and Grants, 1690
Elsie H. Wilcox Fndn Grants, 1691
Elsie Lee Garthwaite Memorial Fndn Grants, 1692
EMC Corp Grants, 1693
Emerson Electric Company Contributions Grants, 1695
Emily Hall Tremaine Fndn Grants, 1698
Ensworth Charitable Fndn Grants, 1710
Entergy Corp Micro Grants, 1712
Entergy Corp Open Grants for Arts and Culture, 1713
EQT Fndn Art and Culture Grants, 1743
Erie Community Fndn Grants, 1750
Essex County Community Discretionary Grants, 1752
Essex County Community Fndn Merrimack Valley General Grants, 1756
Esther M. and Freeman E. Everett Grants, 1757
Ethel and Raymond F. Rice Fndn Grants, 1758
Ethel S. Abbott Charitable Fndn Grants, 1760
Ethel Sergeant Clark Smith Fndn Grants, 1761
Eugene M. Lang Fndn Grants, 1764
Evanston Community Fndn Grants, 1771
F.M. Kirby Fndn Grants, 1780
F.R. Bigelow Fndn Grants, 1781
Fairfield County Community Fndn Grants, 1782
Fargo-Moorhead Area Fndn Grants, 1788
Farmers Insurance Corp Giving Grants, 1791
Faye McBeath Fndn Grants, 1794
Fayette County Fndn Grants, 1795
Ferree Fndn Grants, 1804
Fidelity Fndn Grants, 1805
Fieldstone Fndn Grants, 1808
First People's Fund Community Spirit Awards, 1825
Fishman Family Fndn Grants, 1835
Fleishhacker Fndn Small Grants in the Arts, 1839
Fleishhacker Fndn Special Arts Grants, 1840
Florida Div of Cultural Affairs Endowments, 1851
Florida Div of Cultural Affairs Facilities Grants, 1852
Florida Div of Cultural Affairs Folk Arts Grants, 1853
Florida Div of Cultural Affairs Literature Grants, 1855
Florida Div of Cultural Affairs Media Grants, 1856
Florida Div of Cultural Affairs Multidisciplinary Grants, 1857
Florida Div of Cultural Affairs Museum Grants, 1858
Florida Div of Cultural Affairs Music Grants, 1859
Florida Div of Cultural Affairs Presenter Grants, 1860
Florida Div of Cultural Affairs Specific Cultural Project Grants, 1862
Florida Div of Cultural Affairs Underserved Cultural Community Development Grants, 1864
Florida Div of Cultural Affairs Visual Arts Grant, 1865
Florida Humanities Council Major Grants, 1868
Florida Humanities Council Partnership Grants, 1870
Foellinger Fndn Grants, 1877
Fondren Fndn Grants, 1878
Ford Motor Company Grants, 1885
Forrest C. Lattner Fndn Grants, 1887
Fndn for Enhancing Communities Grants, 1893
Fndn for the Carolinas Grants, 1896
Frances and John L. Loeb Family Grants, 1917
Francis L. Abreu Charitable Grants, 1922
Franklin County Community Fndn Grants, 1929
Frank Stanley Beveridge Fndn Grants, 1936
Fred Baldwin Memorial Fndn Grants, 1941
Fred C. and Katherine B. Andersen Fndn Grants, 1942
Frederick S. Upton Fndn Grants, 1947
Fred L. Emerson Fndn Grants, 1949
Fremont Area Community Amazing X Grants, 1953
Fremont Area Community Fndn Grants, 1955
Fuller Fndn Grants, 1974
Fulton County Community Fndn Grants, 1975
Fund for Southern Communities Grants, 1977
Garland and Agnes Taylor Gray Fndn Grants, 1988
Gateway Fndn Grants, 1992
Gaylord and Dorothy Donnelley Fndn Grants, 1993
Gebbie Fndn Grants, 1995
GenCorp Fndn Grants, 1998
General Dynamics Corp Grants, 2001
General Mills Fndn Celebrating Communities of Color Grants, 2002
General Mills Fndn Grants, 2003
General Motors Fndn Grants Support Program, 2004
George A. and Grace L. Long Fndn Grants, 2008
George and Ruth Bradford Fndn Grants, 2010
George A Ohl Jr. Fndn Grants, 2012
George Frederick Jewett Fndn Grants, 2019
George Gund Fndn Grants, 2020
George H.C. Ensworth Grants, 2022
George S. and Dolores Dore Eccles Fndn Grants, 2027
George W. Brackenridge Fndn Grants, 2028
George W. Codrington Charitable Fndn Grants, 2029
Georgia Council for the Arts Partner Grants for Organizations, 2035
Georgia Council for the Arts Project Grants, 2037
Geraldine R. Dodge Fndn Arts Grants, 2040
Gheens Fndn Grants, 2048
Gibson Fndn Grants, 2052
Gill Fndn - Gay and Lesbian Grants, 2054
Ginger and Barry Ackerley Fndn Grants, 2055
Ginn Fndn Grants, 2056
Giving Sum Annual Grant, 2058
Gladys Brooks Fndn Grants, 2059
GlaxoSmithKline Corp Grants, 2060
GNOF Exxon-Mobil Grants, 2074
GNOF Freeman Challenge Grants, 2075
GNOF IMPACT Grants for Arts and Culture, 2078
GNOF Norco Community Grants, 2089
Goizueta Fndn Grants, 2096
Golden Rule Fndn Grants, 2098
Goodrich Corp Fndn Grants, 2104
Good Works Fndn Grants, 2105
Goodyear Tire Grants, 2106
Grace and Franklin Bernsen Fndn Grants, 2109
Grand Haven Area Community Fndn Grants, 2113
Grand Rapids Area Community Fndn Grants, 2114
Grand Rapids Area Community Fndn Nashwauk Area Endowment Grants, 2115
Grand Rapids Area Community Wyoming Grants, 2116
Grand Rapids Area Community Fndn Wyoming Youth Grants, 2117
Grand Rapids Community Ionia County Grants, 2119
Grand Rapids Community Fndn Lowell Grants, 2121
Grand Rapids Community SE Ottawa Grants, 2122
Grand Rapids Community Sparta Grants, 2124
Greater Cincinnati Fndn Priority and Small Projects/Capacity-Building Grants, 2132
Greater Green Bay Community Fndn Grants, 2135
Greater Kanawha Valley Fndn Grants, 2136
Greater Milwaukee Fndn Grants, 2137
Greater Saint Louis Community Fndn Grants, 2138

SUBJECT INDEX

Arts, General / 817

Greater Tacoma Community Fndn Grants, 2139
Greater Worcester Community Jeppson Memorial Fund for Brookfield Grants, 2141
Greater Worcester Community Youth for Community Improvement Grants, 2144
Green Diamond Charitable Contributions, 2149
Green Fndn Arts Grants, 2152
Greenwall Fndn Arts and Humanities Grants, 2157
Gregory C. Carr Fndn Grants, 2161
Griffin Fndn Grants, 2165
Guido A. and Elizabeth H. Binda Fndn Grants, 2172
Gulf Coast Community Fndn Grants, 2174
H & R Fndn Grants, 2181
H.A. and Mary K. Chapman Charitable Grants, 2182
H.B. Fuller Company Fndn Grants, 2183
H.J. Heinz Company Fndn Grants, 2184
H. Leslie Hoffman & Elaine Hoffman Grants, 2185
H. Reimers Bechtel Charitable Grants, 2186
HAF Community Partnerships with Native Artists Grants, 2194
Hall Family Fndn Grants, 2210
Hallmark Corp Fndn Grants, 2212
Hamilton Family Fndn Grants, 2213
Harley Davidson Fndn Grants, 2224
Harold Alfond Fndn Grants, 2225
Harold K. L. Castle Fndn Grants, 2228
Harold Simmons Fndn Grants, 2230
Harris and Eliza Kempner Grants, 2231
Harrison County Community Signature Grants, 2234
Harry Bramhall Gilbert Charitable Grants, 2238
Harry C. Trexler Grants, 2239
Harry Kramer Grants, 2242
Harry W. Bass, Jr. Fndn Grants, 2246
Hartford Courant Fndn Grants, 2248
Hartford Fndn Regular Grants, 2253
Hawaii Community Fndn West Hawaii Grants, 2266
HCA Fndn Grants, 2274
Hearst Fndns Culture Grants, 2284
Heinz Endowments Grants, 2291
Helena Rubinstein Fndn Grants, 2292
Helen Bader Fndn Grants, 2293
Helen Gertrude Sparks Charitable Grants, 2294
Helen S. Boylan Fndn Grants, 2298
Henrietta Tower Wurts Memorial Fndn Grants, 2304
Henry and Ruth Blaustein Rosenberg Grants, 2306
Henry W. Bull Fndn Grants, 2312
Herbert H. and Grace A. Dow Fndn Grants, 2315
Herman Abbott Family Fndn Grants, 2316
Herman Goldman Fndn Grants, 2317
Hershey Company Grants, 2318
High Meadow Fndn Grants, 2321
Hill Crest Fndn Grants, 2324
Hillman Fndn Grants, 2327
Hillsdale County Community Gen Adult Grants, 2328
Hillsdale Grants, 2329
Hilton Head Island Fndn Grants, 2330
Hoglund Fndn Grants, 2344
Holland/Zeeland Community Fndn Grants, 2345
Homer A. Scott and Mildred S. Scott Grants, 2350
Honda of America Manufacturing Fndn Grants, 2354
Horace A. Kimball and S. Ella Kimball Grants, 2362
Horizons Community Issues Grants, 2366
Houston Endowment Grants, 2373
Howard and Bush Fndn Grants, 2374
Howard County Community Fndn Grants, 2375
Howe Fndn of North Carolina Grants, 2377
Hudson Webber Fndn Grants, 2383
Huffy Fndn Grants, 2384
Hugh J. Andersen Fndn Grants, 2385
Humana Fndn Grants, 2388
Huntington Arts Council Arts-in-Educ Grants, 2400
Huntington Arts Council Decentralization Community Arts Grants, 2401
Huntington Arts Council JP Morgan Chase Organization/Stabilization Regrants, 2403
Huntington County Community Fndn - Make a Difference Grants, 2406
Huntington Fndn Grants, 2408
Huntington National Bank Comm Affairs Grant, 2409
Hutchinson Community Fndn Grants, 2410
Hut Fndn Grants, 2411
Hyde Family Fndns Grants, 2414
I.A. O'Shaughnessy Fndn Grants, 2416
IBM Arts and Culture Grants, 2424
Idaho Community Fndn Eastern Region Competitive Grants, 2432
Idaho Power Company Corp Contributions, 2433
IIE Freeman Fndn Indonesia Internships, 2456
IIE Japan-U.S. Teacher Exchange for Educ for Sustainable Development, 2457
Illinois Arts Council Service Organization Grants, 2464
Illinois Arts Council Community Access Grants, 2466
Illinois Arts Council Dance Grants, 2467
Illinois Arts Council Ethnic & Folk Arts Grants, 2469
Illinois Arts Council Local Arts Agencies Grants, 2471
Illinois Arts Council Multidisciplinary Grants, 2473
Illinois Arts Council Partners in Excellence, 2475
Illinois Tool Works Fndn Grants, 2511
Indep Comm Fndn Educ, Culture & Arts Grant, 2526
Indiana Arts Comm American Masterpieces Grants, 2530
Indiana Arts Commission Multi-regional Major Arts Insts Grants, 2532
Indianapolis Power & Light Community Grants, 2540
Irving S. Gilmore Fndn Grants, 2584
Irvin Stern Fndn Grants, 2585
J.B. Reynolds Fndn Grants, 2592
J. Bulow Campbell Fndn Grants, 2593
J. Edwin Treakle Fndn Grants, 2596
J. F. Maddox Fndn Grants, 2597
J.M. Long Fndn Grants, 2603
J. Mack Robinson Fndn Grants, 2604
J. Walton Bissell Fndn Grants, 2608
Jackson County Community Fndn Grants, 2611
Jackson Fndn Grants, 2613
Jacob and Hilda Blaustein Fndn Grants, 2615
Jacobs Family Spirit of the Diamond Grants, 2618
Jacobs Family Village Neighborhoods Grants, 2619
James & Abigail Campbell Family Fndn Grants, 2620
James A. and Faith Knight Fndn Grants, 2621
James F. and Marion L. Miller Fndn Grants, 2622
James Ford Bell Fndn Grants, 2623
James Graham Brown Quality of Life Grants, 2625
James Irvine Fndn Creative Connections Grants, 2628
James M. Collins Fndn Grants, 2633
James R. Thorpe Fndn Grants, 2636
James S. Copley Fndn Grants, 2637
Jane Bradley Pettit Fndn Arts and Culture Grants, 2641
Janus Fndn Grants, 2647
Japan Fndn Los Angeles Mini-Grants for Japanese Arts & Culture, 2651
Japan Fndn New York Small Grants for Arts and Culture, 2652
Jasper Fndn Grants, 2655
Jay and Rose Phillips Family Fndn Grants, 2656
Jean and Louis Dreyfus Fndn Grants, 2658
JELD-WEN Fndn Grants, 2661
Jennings County Community Fndn Grants, 2664
Jerome Fndn Grants, 2667
Jerome Fndn Travel and Study Grants, 2668
Jerry L. and Barbara J. Burris Fndn Grants, 2669
Jessie Ball Dupont Grants, 2671
John Ben Snow Grants, 2687
John Deere Fndn Grants, 2692
John F. Kennedy Center for the Performing Arts National Rosemary Kennedy Internship, 2694
John G. Duncan Grants, 2695
John H. and Wilhelmina D. Harland Charitable Fndn Grants, 2698
John I. Smith Charities Grants, 2700
John J. Leidy Fndn Grants, 2701
John Jewett & Helen Chandler Garland Grants, 2702
John Lord Knight Fndn Grants, 2703
John M. Ross Fndn Grants, 2704
John S. and James L. Knight Fndn Communities Grants, 2711
John S. and James L. Knight Fndn Donor Advised Grants, 2712
Johns Manville Grants, 2716
Johnson Controls Fndn Arts and Culture Grants, 2719
John W. Alden Grants, 2727
John W. Anderson Fndn Grants, 2729
John W. Speas and Effie E. Speas Grants, 2732
Joseph Alexander Fndn Grants, 2734
Joseph Drown Fndn Grants, 2735
Josephine S. Gumbiner Fndn Grants, 2739
Josiah W. and Bessie H. Kline Fndn Grants, 2742
JP Morgan Chase Arts and Culture Grants, 2752
Judith and Jean Pape Adams Charitable Fndn Tulsa Area Grants, 2755
Judith Clark-Morrill Fndn Grants, 2756
Kahuku Community Fund, 2762
Kansas Arts Commission American Masterpieces Kansas Grants, 2775
Kansas Arts Commission Arts-in-Communities Project Grants, 2777
Kansas Arts Commission Arts-in-Communities Project Mini-Grants, 2778
Kansas Arts Commission Partnership Agreement Grants, 2782
Kansas Arts Commission Visual Arts Grants, 2783
Katharine Matthies Fndn Grants, 2788
Katherine John Murphy Fndn Grants, 2790
Kathryne Beynon Fndn Grants, 2791
Kenneth T. and Eileen L. Norris Fndn Grants, 2802
KeySpan Fndn Grants, 2821
Kimball Int'l-Habig Fndn Grants, 2823
Kirkpatrick Fndn Grants, 2827
Kohler Fndn Grants, 2833
Kosciusko County Community Fndn Grants, 2838
Kovler Family Fndn Grants, 2840
Laila Twigg-Smith Art Scholarship, 2855
Leeway Fndn Art and Change Grants, 2872
Leeway Fndn Transformation Award, 2873
Leicester Savings Bank Fund, 2879
Leo Niessen Jr., Charitable Grants, 2885
Lewis H. Humphreys Charitable Grants, 2889
Liberty Bank Fndn Grants, 2890
Lied Fndn Grants, 2900
Lillian S. Wells Fndn Grants, 2901
Lincoln Financial Group Fndn Grants, 2906
Lotus 88 Fndn for Women and Children Grants, 2921
Louie M. and Betty M. Phillips Fndn Grants, 2923
Louis and Elizabeth Nave Flarsheim Charitable Fndn Grants, 2924
Louis Calder Fndn Grants, 2925
Lowe Fndn Grants, 2929
Lowell Berry Fndn Grants, 2930
Lubbock Area Fndn Grants, 2931
Lubrizol Fndn Grants, 2933
Lucile Horton Howe & Mitchell B. Howe Grants, 2934
Lucy Downing Nisbet Charitable Grants, 2935
Lucy Gooding Charitable Fndn Grants, 2937
Ludwick Family Fndn Grants, 2938
Lumpkin Family Fndn Lively Arts and Dynamic Learning Communities Grants, 2943
Luther I. Replogle Fndn Grants, 2945
M. Bastian Family Fndn Grants, 2951
M.J. Murdock Charitable Trust General Grants, 2954
MacArthur Fndn Chicago Arts and Culture Int'l Connections Grants, 2962
Macquarie Bank Fndn Grants, 2966
Madison County Community General Grants, 2973
Manitoba Arts Council Community Connections and Access Grants, 2995
Manitoba Arts Council Special Opps Grants, 2997
Marathon Petroleum Corp Grants, 2999
Marcia and Otto Koehler Fndn Grants, 3000
Mardag Fndn Grants, 3001
Margaret L. Wendt Fndn Grants, 3004
Margaret T. Morris Fndn Grants, 3005
Marie H. Bechtel Charitable Grants, 3007
Marietta McNeill Morgan and Samuel Tate Morgan, Jr. Grants, 3008
Mars Fndn Grants, 3025
Marsh Corp Grants, 3027
Mary C. & Perry F. Spencer Fndn Grants, 3034
Mary Duke Biddle Fndn Grants, 3036
Mary K. Chapman Fndn Grants, 3042
Mary Owen Borden Fndn Grants, 3046
Mary S. and David C. Corbin Fndn Grants, 3048

Arts, General

Massachusetts Cultural Adams Arts Grants, 3052
Massachusetts Cultural Council Cultural Facilities Capital Grants, 3053
Massachusetts Cultural Council Cultural Facilities Feasibility and Technical Assistance Grants, 3054
Massachusetts Cultural Council Cultural Facilities Systems Replacement Plan Grants Grants, 3055
Massachusetts Cultural Council Local Cultural Council Grants, 3057
Massachusetts Fndn for the Humanities Cultural Economic Development Grants, 3059
Max A. Adler Charitable Fndn Grants, 3065
Maximilian E. and Marion O. Hoffman Fndn, 3067
McColl Fndn Grants, 3074
McCombs Fndn Grants, 3075
McConnell Fndn Grants, 3076
McInerny Fndn Grants, 3083
McKesson Fndn Grants, 3084
Mead Johnson Nutritionals Evansville-Area Organizations Grants, 3103
Mead Witter Fndn Grants, 3106
Mericos Fndn Grants, 3121
Meriden Fndn Grants, 3122
Merkel Family Fndn Grants, 3123
Mervin Bovaird Fndn Grants, 3128
Meyer and Pepa Gold Family Fndn Grants, 3138
Meyer Memorial Trust Special Grants, 3149
MGN Family Fndn Grants, 3154
Microsoft Comm Affairs Puget Sound Grants, 3163
Mid-America Arts Regional Touring Grants, 3167
Miguel Aleman Fndn Grants, 3175
Miller, Canfield, Paddock and Stone, P.L.C. Corp Giving Grants, 3179
Mimi and Peter Haas Grants, 3185
Minnesota State Arts Board Cultural Community Partnership Grants, 3188
Moline Fndn Community Grants, 3202
Monfort Family Fndn Grants, 3203
Morris and Gwendolyn Cafritz Fndn Grants, 3218
Motorola Fndn Grants, 3221
Nathan Cummings Fndn Grants, 3246
National Endowment for the Arts - Grants for Arts Projects: Challenge America Fast-Track, 3254
National Endowment for the Arts - National Arts and Humanities Youth Program Awards, 3255
National Endowment for the Arts - State Partnership Agreement Grants, 3259
National Endowment for Arts Commun Grants, 3260
NEH Family and Youth Programs in American History Grants, 3291
NEH Preservation Assistance Grants for Smaller Institutions, 3293
Nelda C. and H.J. Lutcher Stark Fndn Grants, 3296
Nevada Arts Council Folklife Apprenticeships, 3309
Nevada Arts Council Heritage Awards, 3311
Nevada Arts Council Jackpot Grants, 3312
New Earth Fndn Grants, 3317
Newfoundland and Labrador Arts Council Professional Project Grants, 3322
New Hampshire Charitable Fndn Grants, 3325
Newton County Community Fndn Grants, 3336
New York Life Fndn Grants, 3341
NHSCA Arts in Health Care Project Grants, 3424
NHSCA Conservation License Plate Grants, 3425
NHSCA Cultural Facilities Grants: Barrier Free Access for All, 3426
Nicholas H. Noyes Jr. Memorial Fndn Grants, 3434
Nina Mason Pulliam Charitable Grants, 3443
NJSCA Financial and Instal Stabilization Grants, 3447
NJSCA Projects Serving Artists Grants, 3450
Noble County Community Fndn Grants, 3456
Nordson Corp Fndn Grants, 3462
North Carolina Arts Facility Design Grants, 3474
North Carolina Community Fndn Grants, 3489
North Dakota Council on the Arts Community Access Grants, 3494
North Dakota Council on Arts Presenter Support, 3497
Northern Trust Company Corp Giving Program, 3504
North Georgia Community Fndn Grants, 3505
NW Mutual Fndn Grants, 3509

Norton Fndn Grants, 3514
Norwin S. and Elizabeth N. Bean Fndn Grants, 3515
NYHC Major and Mini Grants, 3567
NYHC Reading and Discussion Grants, 3568
Oceanside Charitable Fndn Grants, 3637
Ohio Artists on Tour Fee Support Requests, 3642
Ohio Arts Council Artist Express Grants, 3643
Ohio Arts Council Artist in Residence Grants for Artists, 3644
Ohio Arts Council Artist in Residence Grants for Sponsors, 3645
Ohio Arts Council Artists with Disabilities Access Grants, 3646
Ohio Arts Council Arts Access Grants, 3647
Ohio Arts Council Individual Excellence Awards, 3648
Ohio Arts Council Arts Innovation Grants, 3649
Ohio Arts Council Arts Partnership Grants, 3650
Ohio Arts Council Building Cultural Diversity Init Grants, 3651
Ohio Arts Council Capacity Building Grants for Organizations and Communities, 3652
Ohio Arts Council Int'l Partnership Grants, 3653
Ohio Arts Council Sustainability Grants, 3654
Ohio River Border Init Grants, 3661
Ohio Valley Fndn Grants, 3662
Oklahoma City Community Programs & Grants, 3666
Oleonda Jameson Grants, 3667
Olive Smith Browning Charitable Grants, 3671
Ontario Arts Council Aboriginal Project Grants, 3675
Ontario Arts Council Compass Grants, 3677
Ontario Arts Council Travel Assistance Grants, 3682
Oppenstein Brothers Fndn Grants, 3685
ORBI Artist Fast Track Grants, 3689
Oscar Rennebohm Fndn Grants, 3694
PacifiCorp Fndn for Learning Grants, 3727
Palm Beach and Martin Counties Grants, 3733
Parkersburg Area Comm Fndn Action Grants, 3738
Patrick and Aimee Butler Family Fndn Community Arts and Humanities Grants, 3747
Patrick and Anna M. Cudahy Grants, 3751
Paul and Mary Haas Fndn Contributions and Student Scholarships, 3756
PCA-PCD Professional Development for Individual Artists Grants, 3770
PCA Art Organizations and Art Programs Grants for Presenting Organizations, 3771
PCA Arts Organizations and Arts Programs Grants for Arts Service Organizations, 3777
PCA Arts Organizations & Grants for Crafts, 3778
PCA Arts Organizations and Arts Programs Grants for Local Arts, 3782
PCA Entry Track Arts Organizations and Program Grants for Arts Service Organizations, 3789
PCA Entry Track Arts Organizations and Program Grants for Crafts, 3790
PCA Entry Track Arts Organizations and Program Grants for Presenting Organizations, 3796
PCA Entry Track Arts Organizations and Program Grants for Theatre, 3797
PCA Pennsylvania Partners in the Arts Program Stream Grants, 3801
PCA Pennsylvania Partners in the Arts Project Stream Grants, 3802
PCA Professional Development Grants, 3803
PCA Strategies for Success Grants - Basic Level, 3805
PCA Strategies for Success Grants - Intermediate, 3806
Peacock Fndn Grants, 3809
PennPAT Artist Technical Assistance Grants, 3811
PennPAT Strategic Opportunity Grants, 3815
Perpetual Trust for Charitable Giving Grants, 3826
Perry County Community Fndn Grants, 3827
Peter Kiewit Fndn General Grants, 3845
Peter Kiewit Fndn Small Grants, 3847
Peter Norton Family Fndn Grants, 3849
Pew Charitable Trusts Arts and Culture Grants, 3857
Peyton Anderson Fndn Grants, 3862
PGE Fndn Grants, 3869
Phil Hardin Fndn Grants, 3875
Philip L. Graham Grants, 3876
Phoenix Coyotes Charities Grants, 3879

Phoenix Suns Charities Grants, 3881
Pike County Community Fndn Grants, 3888
Pinellas County Grants, 3891
Pinkerton Fndn Grants, 3892
Pinnacle Entertainment Fndn Grants, 3893
Piper Jaffray Fndn Communities Giving Grants, 3899
Piper Trust Arts and Culture Grants, 3900
Pittsburgh Fndn Community Grants, 3910
Plough Fndn Grants, 3915
PMI Fndn Grants, 3918
PMP Professional Development Grants, 3919
PMP Project Grants, 3920
PNC Fndn Grow Up Great Grants, 3924
Polk Bros. Fndn Grants, 3929
Posey Community Fndn Women's Grants, 3938
Posey County Community Fndn Grants, 3939
Powell Family Fndn Grants, 3941
Powell Fndn Grants, 3942
Price Chopper's Golub Fndn Grants, 3950
Price Family Charitable Grants, 3952
Pride Fndn Grants, 3958
Prince Charitable Trusts Chicago Grants, 3959
Prince Charitable Trusts D.C. Grants, 3960
Prince Charitable Trusts Rhode Island Grants, 3961
Princeton Area Comm Greater Mercer Grants, 3963
Princeton Area Community Fndn Thomas George Artists Grants, 3965
Principal Financial Group Fndn Grants, 3966
Prudential Fndn Arts and Culture Grants, 3975
PSEG Corp Contributions Grants, 3979
Puerto Rico Community Fndn Grants, 3986
Pulaski County Community Fndn Grants, 3988
Putnam County Community Fndn Grants, 3990
Rainbow Media Holdings Corp Giving, 4010
Rajiv Gandhi Fndn Grants, 4011
Ralphs Food 4 Less Fndn Grants, 4014
Rancho Bernardo Community Fndn Grants, 4015
Rasmuson Fndn Capital Grants, 4020
Rasmuson Fndn Individual Artists Awards, 4022
Rathmann Family Fndn Grants, 4026
RBC Dain Rauscher Fndn Grants, 4031
Regional Arts and Cultural Council Grants, 4046
Regional Arts & Cultural Council Project Grants, 4048
Reynolds American Fndn Grants, 4068
Rhode Island Fndn Grants, 4073
Richard and Caroline T. Gwathmey Grants, 4075
Richard and Helen DeVos Fndn Grants, 4076
Richard and Susan Smith Family Fndn Grants, 4078
Richard D. Bass Fndn Grants, 4079
Richard H. Driehaus Fndn MacArthur Fund for Arts and Culture, 4085
Righteous Persons Fndn Grants, 4093
Ripley County Community Fndn Grants, 4095
Ripley County Community Small Project Grants, 4096
RISCA Professional Arts Development Grants, 4099
RISCA Project Grants for Organizations, Individuals and Educ, 4100
Robert and Helen Haddad Fndn Grants, 4103
Robert B McMillen Fndn Grants, 4106
Robert G. Cabell III and Maude Cabell Grants, 4113
Robert Lee Blaffer Fndn Grants, 4115
Robert R. Meyer Fndn Grants, 4121
Rochester Area Community Fndn Grants, 4127
Rochester Area Fndn Grants, 4128
Rockefeller Brothers Charles E. Culpeper Arts and Culture Grants in New York City, 4129
Rockefeller Fndn Partnerships Affirming Community Transformation Grants, 4139
Rockwell Int'l Corp Grants, 4141
Roger L. and Agnes C. Dell Charitable Grants, 4143
Rogers Family Fndn Grants, 4144
Rollin M. Gerstacker Fndn Grants, 4146
Ronald McDonald House Charities Grants, 4149
Rosie's For All Kids Fndn Grants, 4163
Ross Fndn Grants, 4164
Roy and Christine Sturgis Charitable Grants, 4166
Rucker & Margaret Agee Grants, 4171
Rucker-Donnell Fndn Grants, 4172
Rush County Community Fndn Grants, 4174
Ruth and Vernon Taylor Fndn Grants, 4177

SUBJECT INDEX

Ruth H. and Warren A. Ellsworth Fndn Grants, 4179
Ruth Mott Fndn Grants, 4180
S. Livingston Mather Charitable Grants, 4200
S. Mark Taper Fndn Grants, 4201
S. Spencer Scott Grants, 4202
Sage Fndn Grants, 4204
Saint Louis Rams Fndn Community Donations, 4214
Saint Paul Companies Fndn Grants, 4217
Salem Fndn Charitable Grants, 4223
Salisbury Community Fndn Grants, 4224
Samuel N. and Mary Castle Fndn Grants, 4236
Samuel S. Fels Grants, 4238
Samuel S. Johnson Fndn Grants, 4239
San Antonio Area Fndn Grants, 4240
SanDisk Corp Community Sharing Program, 4253
San Francisco Fndn Faith Program and Arts and Culture Program, 4267
San Francisco Fndn Fund for Artists Award for Visual and Media Artists, 4273
San Francisco Fndn Fund For Artists Matching Commissions Grants, 4274
San Francisco Fndn Koshland Program Arts and Culture Mini-Grants, 4280
San Juan Island Community Fndn Grants, 4283
Santa Barbara Fndn Towbes Fund for the Performing Arts Grants, 4288
Santa Fe Community Fndn Seasonal Grants, 4290
Sara Lee Fndn Grants, 4296
Sartain Lanier Family Fndn Grants, 4298
Schering-Plough Fndn Community Inits Grants, 4303
Scherman Fndn Grants, 4305
Schramm Fndn Grants, 4310
Schurz Communications Fndn Grants, 4312
Scott County Community Fndn Grants, 4314
Seabury Fndn Grants, 4316
Seagate Tech Corp Capacity to Care Grants, 4317
Seattle Fndn Arts and Culture Grants, 4320
Seattle Fndn C. Keith Birkenfeld Grants, 4323
Seaver Institute Grants, 4331
Self Fndn Grants, 4335
Sensient Technologies Fndn Grants, 4337
Shopko Fndn Community Charitable Grants, 4346
Simmons Fndn Grants, 4360
Sioux Falls Area Community Grants, 4364
Sioux Falls Area Community Fndn Spot Grants, 4366
Siragusa Fndn Arts & Culture Grants, 4367
Social Justice Fund NW General Grants, 4397
Sonoco Fndn Grants, 4403
Sonora Area Fndn Competitive Grants, 4404
Sony Corp of America Corp Philanthropy Grants, 4405
Sosland Fndn Grants, 4408
Southbury Community Trust Fund, 4409
South Carolina Arts Comm Accessibility Grants, 4410
South Carolina Arts Commission AIE Residency Plus Individual Site Grants, 4411
South Carolina Arts Commission AIE Residency Plus Multi-Site Grants, 4412
South Carolina Arts Commission American Masterpieces in South Carolina Grants, 4413
South Carolina Arts Commission Annual Operating Support for Organizations Grants, 4414
South Carolina Arts Commission Fellowships, 4415
South Carolina Arts Commission Arts and Economic Impact Study Assistance Grants, 4416
South Carolina Arts Commission Facility Grants, 4417
South Carolina Arts Commission Arts in Educ After School Arts Init Grants, 4418
South Carolina Arts Commission Cultural Tourism Init Grants, 4419
South Carolina Arts Commission Cultural Visions Grants, 4420
South Carolina Arts Commission Incentive Grants for Employer Sponsored Benefits, 4422
South Carolina Arts Commission Leadership and Organizational Development Grants, 4423
South Carolina Arts Commission Long Term Operating Support for Organizations Grants, 4424
South Carolina Arts Commission Statewide Arts Participation Init Grants, 4425
South Carolina Arts Commission Sub-Grants, 4426

South Carolina Arts Commission Traditional Arts Apprenticeship Grants, 4427
South Madison Community Fndn Grants, 4440
SW Florida Community Fndn Arts & Attractions Grants, 4441
SW Florida Community Competitive Grants, 4442
SW Gas Corp Fndn Grants, 4445
Spencer County Community Fndn Grants, 4451
Sprint Fndn Grants, 4463
Square D Fndn Grants, 4464
Stackpole-Hall Fndn Grants, 4472
Stark Community Fndn Women's Grants, 4481
Steelcase Fndn Grants, 4497
Stettinius Fund for Nonprofit Leadership Awards, 4500
Steuben County Community Fndn Grants, 4501
Stinson Fndn Grants, 4506
Stowe Family Fndn Grants, 4510
Strake Fndn Grants, 4511
Stranahan Fndn Grants, 4512
Strowd Roses Grants, 4515
Subaru of Indiana Automotive Fndn Grants, 4519
Suffolk County Office of Film and Cultural Affairs Cultural Arts Grants, 4521
Sulzberger Fndn Grants, 4522
Summit Fndn Grants, 4524
Sunderland Fndn Grants, 4527
Sunoco Fndn Grants, 4530
Susan Mott Webb Charitable Grants, 4536
Susan Vaughan Fndn Grants, 4537
TAC Arts Access Grant, 4549
TAC Arts Build Communities Grants, 4551
Target Corp Local Store Grants, 4561
Target Fndn Grants, 4562
Tauck Family Fndn Grants, 4563
Taylor S. Abernathy and Patti Harding Abernathy Charitable Grants, 4564
TCF Bank Fndn Grants, 4565
TE Fndn Grants, 4572
Telluride Fndn Community Grants, 4573
Tension Envelope Fndn Grants, 4578
Texas Commission on the Arts Create-4 Grants, 4586
Texas Commission on the Arts Cultural Connections-Visual & Media Arts Touring Exhibits Grants, 4589
Texas Commission on Arts Special Opps Grants, 4593
Texas Comm on the Arts Young Masters Grants, 4594
Thanks Be to Grandmother Winifred Grants, 4602
Thelma Braun and Bocklett Family Fndn Grants, 4603
Thomas C. Ackerman Fndn Grants, 4615
Thomas W. Briggs Fndn Grants, 4621
Thornton Fndn Grants, 4624
Tides Fndn Grants, 4632
Tom's of Maine Grants, 4640
Topeka Community Fndn Grants, 4644
Toyota Motor Manufacturing of Alabama Grants, 4652
Toyota Motor Manufacturing of Indiana Grants, 4653
Toyota Motor Manufacturing Mississippi Grants, 4655
Toyota Motor Manufacturing of Texas Grants, 4656
Toyota Motor Manufacturing W Virginia Grants, 4657
Toyota Motor Sales, USA Grants, 4659
Triangle Community Fndn Donor Grants, 4668
Trinity Fndn Grants, 4669
Trull Fndn Grants, 4673
Tull Charitable Fndn Grants, 4679
Turner Fndn Grants, 4681
Turner Voices Corp Contributions, 4682
Union Benevolent Association Grants, 4710
United Technologies Corp Grants, 4725
Unity Fndn Of LaPorte County Grants, 4726
US Airways Community Contributions, 4788
US Airways Community Fndn Grants, 4789
Vancouver Fndn Grants & Comm Inits, 4900
Vectren Fndn Grants, 4907
Vermont Community Fndn Grants, 4929
Virginia Commission for the Arts Artists in Educ Residency Grants, 4941
Virginia Commission for the Arts Local Government Challenge Grants, 4943
Virginia Commission for the Arts Project Grants, 4944
VSA/Volkswagen Group of America Exhibition Awards, 4954

Assisted-Living Programs / 819

VSA Int'l Art Program for Children with Disabilities Grants, 4955
Vulcan Materials Company Fndn Grants, 4956
W.C. Griffith Fndn Grants, 4957
W. C. Griffith Fndn Grants, 4958
W. Paul and Lucille Caudill Little Fndn Grants, 4966
W. Waldo and Jenny Lynn M. Bradley Grants, 4967
Wallace Alexander Gerbode Fndn Grants, 4974
Wallace Alexander Gerbode Special Grants, 4975
Wallace Fndn Grants, 4976
Walt Disney Company Fndn Grants, 4981
Walter and Elise Haas Grants, 4982
Walter L. Gross III Family Fndn Grants, 4983
Warrick County Community Fndn Grants, 4987
Wayne County Fndn Vigran Family Grants, 5004
Wayne County Fndn Grants, 5005
Weingart Fndn Grants, 5018
West Virginia Commission on the Arts Accessibility Services Grants, 5029
West Virginia Commission on the Arts Challenge America Partnership Grants, 5031
West Virginia Commission on the Arts Major Insts Support Grants, 5038
West Virginia Commission on the Arts Mid-Size Insts Support Grants, 5040
West Virginia Commission on the Arts Professional Development for Artists Grants, 5045
West Virginia Commission on the Arts Re-Granting Grants, 5046
West Virginia Comm on Arts Visual Arts Grants, 5051
Weyerhaeuser Company Fndn Grants, 5053
Widgeon Point Charitable Fndn Grants, 5064
Wilbur and Patsy Bradley Family Fndn Grants, 5066
WILD Fndn Grants, 5068
William A. Miller Fndn Grants, 5073
William G. and Helen C. Hoffman Fndn Grants, 5080
William G. Baker, Jr. Grants, 5081
William G. Gilmore Fndn Grants, 5082
William G. Selby and Marie Selby Fndn Grants, 5085
William J. and Dorothy K. O'Neill Fndn Grants, 5087
William L. and Victorine Q. Adams Fndn Grants, 5089
Winston-Salem Fndn Stokes County Grants, 5104
Xcel Energy Fndn Grants, 5121
Xerox Fndn Grants, 5122
Yellow Corp Fndn Grants, 5126

Asian Americans
Ben B. Cheney Fndn Grants, 725
John R. Oishei Fndn Grants, 2709
Kansas Arts Commission Artist Fellowships, 2776
North Carolina Arts Council Outreach Grants, 3479
NYSCA Special Arts Services: General Operating Support Grants, 3614
Philadelphia Organizational Effectiveness Grants, 3872
Saint Paul Fndn SpectrumGrants, 4222

Asian Arts
Christensen Fund Regional Grants, 1112
E. Rhodes and Leona B. Carpenter Fndn Grants, 1640

Assisted-Living Programs
Adelaide Breed Bayrd Fndn Grants, 161
Arizona Republic Newspaper Contributions, 547
California Endowment Innovative Ideas Challenge Grants, 904
CFFVR Basic Needs Giving Partnership Grants, 1002
Christine and Katharina Pauly Charitable Grants, 1114
CICF Senior Grants, 1127
Clark and Ruby Baker Fndn Grants, 1154
CNCS AmeriCorps State and National Grants, 1182
CNCS Senior Corps Retired and Senior Volunteer Grants, 1188
David Lane Grants for Aged & Indigent Women, 1453
Edward N. and Della L. Thome Memorial Fndn Direct Services Grants, 1666
Frank B. Hazard General Charity Grants, 1926
GNOF Maison Hospitaliere Grants, 2086
James R. Thorpe Fndn Grants, 2636
Jenkins Fndn: Improving the Health of Greater Richmond Grants, 2663

Assistive Technology
Appalachian Regional Commission Telecommunications Grants, 510
John D. and Katherine A. Johnston Fndn Grants, 2691
May and Stanley Smith Charitable Grants, 3069
NYSCA Dance: Services to the Field Grants, 3587
Reader's Digest Partners for Sight Fndn Grants, 4036
U.S. Department of Educ Rehabilitation Engineering Research Centers Grants, 4698
Vigneron Grants, 4938

Asthma
AAAAI RSLAAIS Leadership Award, 49
GNOF IMPACT Kahn-Oppenheim Grants, 2084
Kathryne Beynon Fndn Grants, 2791
Quantum Fndn Grants, 3996

Astronomy
Perkin Grants, 3821

At-Risk Students
Alfred E. Chase Charitable Fndn Grants, 366
Bernard & Audre Rapoport Arts & Culture Grant, 735
Bernard and Audre Rapoport Fndn University of Texas at Austin Scholarship Programs, 739
Best Buy Children's Fndn @15 Community Grants, 749
Charles H. Pearson Fndn Grants, 1045
CNCS AmeriCorps State and National Grants, 1182
DOL Youthbuild Grants, 1571
Elizabeth Morse Genius Charitable Grants, 1682
Fndn for the Mid South Educ Grants, 1898
GTECH After School Advantage Grants, 2170
GTECH Community Involvement Grants, 2171
Guy I. Bromley Grants, 2180
Helen Irwin Littauer Ed Grants, 2295
Henry E. Niles Fndn Grants, 2309
Hilda and Preston Davis Fndn Grants, 2322
John W. Speas and Effie E. Speas Grants, 2732
LEGO Children's Grants, 2878
Lewis H. Humphreys Charitable Grants, 2889
Louetta M. Cowden Fndn Grants, 2922
Louis and Elizabeth Nave Flarsheim Charitable Fndn Grants, 2924
Mardag Fndn Grants, 3001
MetroWest Health Grants to Reduce Incidence of High Risk Behaviors Among Adolescents, 3136
Meyer Fndn Educ Grants, 3142
Michael Reese Health Trust Responsive Grants, 3160
National Home Library Fndn Grants, 3276
Pacers Fndn Be Educated Grants, 3721
Piper Trust Educ Grants, 3902
Portland General Electric Fndn Grants, 3937
Public Educ Power Grants, 3981
Sidgmore Family Fndn Grants, 4348
Sioux Falls Area Community Fndn Field-of-Interest and Donor-Advised Grants, 4365
Stocker Fndn Grants, 4507
Tauck Family Fndn Grants, 4563
Thomas Sill Fndn Grants, 4619
Union Bank, N.A. Fndn Grants, 4709
Victor E. Speas Fndn Grants, 4933

At-Risk Youth
ABC Charities Grants, 85
Abundance Fndn Local Community Grants, 109
ACF Mentoring Children of Prisoners Grants, 121
Acushnet Fndn Grants, 143
Adam Reineman Charitable Grants, 144
Adelaide Christian Home For Children Grants, 162
Adobe Youth Voices Grants, 170
Aid for Starving Children African American Indep Single Mother's Grants, 210
Aid for Starving Children Emergency Assistance Grants, 211
Albert W. Cherne Fndn Grants, 346
Alfred E. Chase Charitable Fndn Grants, 366
Alliance Healthcare Fndn Grants, 383
Allstate Fndn Tolerance, Inclusion, and Diversity Grants, 391
Amelia Sillman Rockwell and Carlos Perry Rockwell Charities Grants, 417
Andre Agassi Charitable Fndn Grants, 461
ATA Local Community Relations Grants, 600
Baton Rouge Area Fndn Every Kid a King Grants, 681
Batters Up USA Equipment Grants, 683
Bay Area Community Fndn Grants, 694
Ben & Jerry's Fndn Grants, 724
Bernard & Audre Rapoport Arts & Culture Grant, 735
Bernard and Audre Rapoport Fndn Community Building and Social Service Grants, 736
Bernard and Audre Rapoport Fndn Democracy and Civic Participation Grants, 737
Bernard and Audre Rapoport Fndn Health Grants, 738
Best Buy Children's Fndn @15 Community Grants, 749
Boston Fndn Grants, 819
Bright Promises Fndn Grants, 838
CCF Community Priorities Fund, 961
CFFVR Basic Needs Giving Partnership Grants, 1002
CFFVR Robert and Patricia Endries Family Fndn Grants, 1018
CFFVR Schmidt Family G4 Grants, 1020
Charles H. Pearson Fndn Grants, 1045
Charles Lafitte Fndn Grants, 1049
Chicago Community Trust Arts and Culture Grants: Improving Access to Arts Learning Opps, 1082
Christine and Katharina Pauly Charitable Grants, 1114
CIT Corp Giving Grants, 1138
Citizens Bank Mid-Atlantic Charitable Grants, 1140
CMA Fndn Grants, 1178
CNCS AmeriCorps State and National Grants, 1182
CNCS Foster Grandparent Grants, 1185
Collective Brands Fndn Payless Gives Shoes 4 Kids Grants, 1207
Columbus Fndn Traditional Grants, 1233
Commonweal Community Assistance Grants, 1239
Community Fndn of Greater Greensboro Grants, 1288
ConocoPhillips Grants, 1355
Constellation Energy Corp Grants, 1364
Corina Higginson Grants, 1373
Countess Moira Charitable Fndn Grants, 1381
Covenant to Care for Children Grants, 1389
Cruise Industry Charitable Fndn Grants, 1404
CTCNet/Youth Visions for Stronger Neighborhoods Grants, 1409
Dallas Women's Fndn Grants, 1438
Deaconess Fndn Advocacy Grants, 1468
Deborah Munroe Noonan Grants, 1475
Denver Broncos Charities Grants, 1501
DHHS Maternal and Child Health Grants, 1536
DOJ Juvenile Mentoring Grants, 1560
DOL Youthbuild Grants, 1571
Do Right Fndn Grants, 1581
Duke Endowment Child Care Grants, 1617
Eckerd Family Fndn Grants, 1651
Elizabeth Morse Genius Charitable Grants, 1682
EPA Children's Health Protection Grants, 1728
Eulalie Bloedel Schneider Fndn Grants, 1767
Ford Family Fndn Grants - Positive Youth Development, 1880
Fndn for the Mid South Wealth Building Grants, 1900
Fndns of E Chicago Youth Development Grants, 1912
Frank Reed and Margaret Jane Peters Memorial Fund II Grants, 1934
Frederick W. Marzahl Grants, 1948
Fuller Fndn Grants, 1974
German Protestant Orphan Asylum Fndn Grants, 2044
Go Daddy Cares Charitable Contributions, 2094
Grace and Franklin Bernsen Fndn Grants, 2109
Grand Circle Fndn Associates Grants, 2112
GTECH After School Advantage Grants, 2170
Guy I. Bromley Grants, 2180
Hasbro Children's Fund, 2256
Hawai'i Children's Trust Fund Community Awareness Events Grants, 2258
Hazen Fndn Youth Organizing Grants, 2270
Health Fndn of Greater Cincinnati Grants, 2281
Hearst Fndns Social Service Grants, 2285
Helen Irwin Littauer Ed Grants, 2295
Henry E. Niles Fndn Grants, 2309
Herbert A. and Adrian W. Woods Fndn Grants, 2313
Hilda and Preston Davis Fndn Grants, 2322
Horace Moses Charitable Fndn Grants, 2363
Indep Comm Fndn Educ, Culture & Arts Grant, 2526
Initiaive Fndn Inside-Out Connections Grants, 2556
IYI Responsible Fatherhood Grants, 2591
Janus Fndn Grants, 2647
Jenifer Altman Fndn Grants, 2662
Jim Moran Fndn Grants, 2680
John Edward Fowler Memorial Fndn Grants, 2693
Jovid Fndn Grants, 2745
Kansas Arts Commission Artist Fellowships, 2776
Kansas Arts Commission Arts-in-Educ Grants, 2779
Legacy Fndn College Readiness Grant, 2874
LEGO Children's Grants, 2878
Leo Goodwin Fndn Grants, 2882
Leon and Thea Koerner Fndn Grants, 2883
Lillian S. Wells Fndn Grants, 2901
Lily Palmer Fry Grants, 2905
Louis R. Cappelli Fndn Grants, 2926
Lumpkin Family Fndn Strong Community Leadership Grants, 2944
Luther I. Replogle Fndn Grants, 2945
Mabel A. Horne Grants, 2956
Mardag Fndn Grants, 3001
Marion and Miriam Rose Grants, 3015
MARPAT Fndn Grants, 3023
Mary Black Early Childhood Devel Grants, 3033
Mary Owen Borden Fndn Grants, 3046
Mathile Family Fndn Grants, 3062
McKesson Fndn Grants, 3084
MetroWest Health Grants to Reduce Incidence of High Risk Behaviors Among Adolescents, 3136
Meyer Fndn Educ Grants, 3142
MGM Resorts Fndn Community Grants, 3153
Michael Reese Health Trust Responsive Grants, 3160
Mid-Iowa Health Fndn Comm Response Grants, 3168
Monsanto Int'l Grants, 3207
Monsanto Kids Garden Fresh Grants, 3208
MONY Fndn Grants, 3214
Moran Family Fndn Grants, 3216
National 4-H Afterschool Training Grants, 3248
Nationwide Insurance Fndn Grants, 3285
Nestle Purina PetCare Ed Grants, 3302
Nestle Purina PetCare Youth Grants, 3306
New Jersey Center for Hispanic Policy, Research and Development Innovative Inits Grants, 3329
New York Life Fndn Grants, 3341
NFL Charities NFL Player Fndn Grants, 3347
Nike Giving - Cash and Product Grants, 3442
NYFA Artists in the School Community Planning Grants, 3562
Ober Kaler Community Grants, 3635
OneFamily Fndn Grants, 3673
Pacers Fndn Be Drug-Free Grants, 3720
Pacers Fndn Be Educated Grants, 3721
PacifiCorp Fndn for Learning Grants, 3727
Paul G. Allen Family Fndn Grants, 3759
Peter and Elizabeth C. Tower Fndn Annual Intellectual Disabilities Grants, 3834
Peter and Elizabeth C. Tower Fndn Annual Mental Health Grants, 3835
Peter & Elizabeth C. Tower Mental Health Reference and Resource Materials Mini-Grants, 3837
Peter and Elizabeth C. Tower Fndn Social and Emotional Preschool Curriculum Grants, 3841
PeyBack Fndn Grants, 3861
Pinkerton Fndn Grants, 3892

Assisted-Living Programs
Marjorie Moore Charitable Fndn Grants, 3021
Mary Black Fndn Active Living Grants, 3031
May and Stanley Smith Charitable Grants, 3069
McLean Contributionship Grants, 3088
MetroWest Health Fndn Grants--Healthy Aging, 3135
Perkins-Ponder Fndn Grants, 3822
Priddy Fndn Grants, 3957
Reinberger Fndn Grants, 4052
Sheltering Arms Grants, 4344
Sophia Romero Grants, 4406
Union Bank Corp Sponsorships and Donations, 4708
Union Bank, N.A. Fndn Grants, 4709

SUBJECT INDEX

Piper Trust Children Grants, 3901
Piper Trust Educ Grants, 3902
Plum Creek Fndn Grants, 3917
Porter County Health and Wellness Grant, 3933
Portland General Electric Fndn Grants, 3937
Public Educ Power Grants, 3981
Raymond John Wean Fndn Grants, 4028
Richard Davoud Donchian Fndn Grants, 4080
Robert R. McCormick Tribune Civics Grants, 4118
Robins Fndn Grants, 4126
Romic Environmental's Charitable Contributions, 4148
Ronald McDonald House Charities Grants, 4149
RWJF Local Funding Partnerships Grants, 4186
Saginaw County Community Fndn Youth FORCE Grants, 4208
Santa Barbara Strategy Core Suupport Grants, 4286
SAS Institute Community Relations Donations, 4300
Schlessman Family Fndn Grants, 4307
Sidgmore Family Fndn Grants, 4348
Sioux Falls Area Community Fndn Field-of-Interest and Donor-Advised Grants, 4365
Skillman Fndn Good Schools Grants, 4382
Sobrato Family Fndn Grants, 4389
Sobrato Family Fndn Meeting Space Grants, 4390
Sobrato Family Fndn Office Space Grants, 4391
Southwire Company Grants, 4447
Staples Fndn for Learning Grants, 4475
Starbucks Shared Planet Youth Action Grants, 4476
Stewart Huston Charitable Grants, 4505
Stocker Fndn Grants, 4507
Strengthening Families - Strengthening Communities Grants, 4513
Sunny and Abe Rosenberg Fndn Grants, 4529
TAC Arts Educ Community-Learning Grants, 4552
TAC Arts Educ Mini Grants, 4553
Target Fndn Grants, 4562
Tauck Family Fndn Grants, 4563
Thomas Sill Fndn Grants, 4619
Threshold Fndn Justice and Democracy Grants, 4626
Topfer Family Fndn Grants, 4646
Tri-State Comm 21st Century Endowment Grants, 4666
Trinity Trust Summer Youth Mini Grants, 4672
TSYSF Individual Scholarships, 4675
TSYSF Team Grants, 4676
Turner Voices Corp Contributions, 4682
U.S. Bank Fndn Grants, 4686
Union Bank, N.A. Fndn Grants, 4709
Victor E. Speas Fndn Grants, 4933
W.K. Kellogg Fndn Healthy Kids Grants, 4961
Whiting Fndn Grants, 5059
Wood-Claeyssens Fndn Grants, 5113
YSA National Child Awareness Month Youth Ambassador Grants, 5137

Athletics
Adler-Clark Electric Comm Commitment Grants, 164
Bank of America Corp Sponsorships, 661
Batters Up USA Equipment Grants, 683
Charlotte Martin Fndn Youth Grants, 1057
Chatham Athletic Fndn Grants, 1060
Finish Line Youth Fndn Founder's Grants, 1812
Finish Line Youth Fndn Grants, 1813
Finish Line Youth Fndn Legacy Grants, 1814
George B. Page Fndn Grants, 2013
NFL Charities NFL Player Fndn Grants, 3347
NFL Charities Pro Bowl Comm Grants in Hawaii, 3348
ODKF Athletic Grants, 3638
Olive Smith Browning Charitable Grants, 3671
Regents Professional Opportunity Scholarships, 4044
Telluride Fndn Community Grants, 4573
Textron Corp Contributions Grants, 4601
Todd Brock Family Fndn Grants, 4639
TSYSF Individual Scholarships, 4675
TSYSF Team Grants, 4676
Van Kampen Boyer Molinari Charitable Grants, 4905
Yawkey Fndn Grants, 5125

Audience Development
Aaron Copland Fund for Music Recording Program, 71
Air Products and Chemicals Grants, 216
Alvin and Fanny Blaustein Thalheimer Grants, 403
ALZA Corp Contributions Grants, 405
American Express Historic Preservation Grants, 431
Andy Warhol Fndn for the Visual Arts Grants, 464
ArtsWave Impact Grants, 580
ArtsWave Project Grants, 581
Chicago Community Trust Arts and Culture Grants: Supporting Diverse Arts Productions and Fostering Art in Every Community, 1084
Community Fndn of St. Joseph County ArtsEverywhere Grants, 1313
Connecticut Community Fndn Grants, 1350
Florida Div of Cultural Affairs Culture Builds Florida Seed Funding, 1849
Florida Div of Cultural Affairs Professional Theatre Grants, 1861
Joyce Fndn Culture Grants, 2747
Kansas Arts Commission Arts-in-Communities Project Grants, 2777
Kansas Arts Commission Arts-in-Communities Project Mini-Grants, 2778
McKesson Fndn Grants, 3084
National Endowment for Arts Agencies Grants, 3263
Nevada Arts Council Professional Devel Grants, 3314
NHSCA General Project Grants, 3427
NHSCA Operating Grants, 3428
North Carolina Arts Council Tech Assistance, 3482
North Dakota Council on the Arts Community Access Grants, 3494
North Dakota Council on Arts Support Grants, 3496
NYSCA Dance: Commissions Grants, 3583
NYSCA Museum General Operating Support, 3602
NYSCA Museum Program Support Grants, 3603
NYSCA Museum: Project Support Grants, 3604
NYSCA Presenting: General Operating Grants, 3609
Ohio River Border Init Grants, 3661
PCA Art Organizations and Art Programs Grants for Presenting Organizations, 3771
PCA Arts Organizations & Grants for Dance, 3779
PCA Arts Organizations and Arts Programs Grants for Film and Electronic Media, 3780
PCA Arts Organizations & Grants for Lit, 3781
PCA Arts Organizations and Arts Programs Grants for Local Arts, 3782
PCA Arts Organizations & Grants for Theatre, 3783
PCA Arts Organizations and Arts Programs Grants for Traditional and Folk Arts, 3784
PCA Entry Track Arts Organizations and Program Grants for Dance, 3791
PCA Entry Track Arts Organizations and Program Grants for Film and Electronic Media, 3792
PCA Entry Track Arts Organizations and Program Grants for Local Arts, 3794
PCA Entry Track Arts Organizations and Program Grants for Presenting Organizations, 3796
PCA Entry Track Arts Organizations and Program Grants for Theatre, 3797
PCA Entry Track Arts Organizations and Program Grants for Traditional and Folk Arts, 3798
PCA Management/Technical Assistance Grants, 3800
PCA Pennsylvania Partners in the Arts Program Stream Grants, 3801
PCA Pennsylvania Partners in the Arts Project Stream Grants, 3802
PennPAT Fee-Support Grants for Presenters, 3812
PennPAT New Directions Grants for Presenters, 3813
PennPAT Presenter Travel Grants, 3814
Piper Trust Arts and Culture Grants, 3900
RISCA Professional Arts Development Grants, 4099
RISCA Project Grants for Organizations, Individuals and Educ, 4100
South Carolina Arts Commission American Masterpieces in South Carolina Grants, 4413
South Carolina Arts Comm Cultural Tourism, 4419
South Carolina Arts Commission Statewide Arts Participation Init Grants, 4425
SW Florida Community Fndn Arts & Attractions Grants, 4441
Stockton Rush Bartol Fndn Grants, 4508
TAC Arts Grants, 4554

TAC Rural Arts Project Support Grants, 4555
Wallace Fndn Grants, 4976
West Virginia Commission on the Arts Long-Term Artist Residencies, 5037
Wisconsin Humanities Council Major Grants, 5107

Audio Production
Historic Landmarks Fndn of Indiana Historic Preservation Educ Grants, 2334
Illinois Arts Council Media Arts Grants, 2472
Kentucky Arts Council Al Smith Fellowship, 2806
Kentucky Arts Council Emerging Artist Award, 2807
National Endowment for Arts Opera Grants, 3267
North Carolina Arts Council Folklife Documentary Project Grants, 3475
North Carolina Arts Council Folklife Grants, 3476
NYSCA Electronic Media and Film: General Exhibition Grants, 3589
NYSCA Elect Media & Film Workspace Grants, 3593
PAS Internship, 3742
PCA Arts Organizations and Arts Programs Grants for Film and Electronic Media, 3780
PCA Entry Track Arts Organizations and Program Grants for Film and Electronic Media, 3792
West Virginia Comm on Arts Media Grants, 5039

Audiovisual Materials
ALA ALSC Bookapalooza Grants, 222
ALA Baker and Taylor Entertainment Audio Music/ Video Product Award, 229
ALA BWI Collection Development Grant, 252
ALA Gale Cengage Learning Award for Excellence in Reference and Adult Library Services, 281
Cincinnati Bell Fndn Grants, 1131
Historic Landmarks Fndn of Indiana Historic Preservation Educ Grants, 2334
Maine Community Fndn Rose and Samuel Rudman Library Grants, 2988
Vermont Community Fndn Grants, 4929

Autism
CFFVR Wisconsin Daughters and Sons Grants, 1024
Horizon Fndn for New Jersey Grants, 2364
Ireland Family Fndn Grants, 2574
Rainbow Academy Fndn Grants, 4006
Thompson Charitable Fndn Grants, 4622

Automotive Engineering
ArvinMeritor Grants, 585
AutoZone Community Relations Grants, 621

Aviation
Air Force Association Civil Air Patrol Unit Grants, 214
Lindbergh Grants, 2907
PAMA Awards Program, 3734
Ray Fndn Grants, 4027
Wolf Aviation Grants, 5109

Band Music
Florida Div of Cultural Affairs Music Grants, 1859
Illinois Arts Council Music Grants, 2474
NYSCA Music Community Schools Grants, 3605
NYSCA Music Gen Operating Support, 3606
NYSCA Music Gen Program Support Grants, 3607
PennPAT Artist Technical Assistance Grants, 3811
PennPAT Strategic Opportunity Grants, 3815
William T. Sloper Trust Musical Grants, 5097

Banking
Bill and Melinda Gates Fndn Financial Services for the Poor Grants, 767
Germanistic Society of America Fellowships, 2043

Bankruptcy
American College of Bankruptcy Grants, 426
Telluride Fndn Emergency/Out of Cycle Grants, 4574

Baptist Church
AHS Fndn Grants, 208
Alvah H. and Wyline P. Chapman Fndn Grants, 402

Beerman Fndn Grants, 717
Booth-Bricker Grants, 815
Bosque Fndn Grants, 818
Bradley-Turner Fndn Grants, 828
Effie and Wofford Cain Fndn Grants, 1674
MacDonald-Peterson Fndn Grants, 2965
V.V. Cooke Fndn Grants, 4896
Welborn Baptist Fndn Faith-Based Inits Grants, 5019

Basic Living Expenses
ACFEF Disaster Relief Fund Member Assistance, 117
AGMA Relief Grants, 201
Ben B. Cheney Fndn Grants, 725
Carl R. Hendrickson Family Fndn Grants, 935
CICF City of Noblesville Community Grant, 1118
Kessler Fndn Hurricane Emergency Grants, 2815
SAG Motion Picture Players Welfare Grants, 4209
Swindells Charitable Fndn, 4542

Basic Skills Education
Ahmanson Fndn Grants, 207
Albert W. Cherne Fndn Grants, 346
Allen P. and Josephine B. Green Fndn Grants, 380
Allyn Fndn Grants, 392
Arkell Hall Fndn Grants, 562
Atkinson Fndn Community Grants, 606
Atlanta Fndn Grants, 608
Auburn Fndn Grants, 611
Azadoutioun Fndn Grants, 631
Ball Brothers Fndn General Grants, 637
Baptist Community Ministries Grants, 664
Battle Creek Community Fndn Grants, 684
Benton Community Fndn Grants, 730
Berrien Community Fndn Grants, 744
Blue Mountain Community Fndn Grants, 800
Blue River Community Fndn Grants, 801
Bodenwein Public Benevolent Fndn Grants, 806
Boettcher Fndn Grants, 810
Booth-Bricker Grants, 815
Booth Ferris Fndn Grants, 816
Boston Fndn Grants, 819
Brown County Community Fndn Grants, 853
Carl B. and Florence E. King Fndn Grants, 928
Catherine Manley Gaylord Fndn Grants, 956
Cemala Fndn Grants, 988
CenturyLink Clarke M. Williams Fndn Grants, 998
Chicago Board of Trade Fndn Grants, 1079
CICF City of Noblesville Community Grant, 1118
CIGNA Fndn Grants, 1130
Colorado Springs Community Grants, 1215
Community Fndn of Bartholomew County Heritage Grants, 1267
Community Fndn of Bartholomew County James A. Henderson Award for Fundraising, 1268
Community Fndn of Central Illinois Grants, 1276
Community Fndn of Greater Fort Wayne - Community Endowment and Clarke Endowment Grants, 1285
Community Fndn of Shreveport-Bossier Grants, 1307
Corina Higginson Grants, 1373
Cornerstone Fndn of NE Wisconsin Grants, 1375
Cowles Charitable Grants, 1392
Cruise Industry Charitable Fndn Grants, 1404
Dayton Power and Light Fndn Grants, 1464
Dept of Ed Even Start Grants, 1508
DOL Youthbuild Grants, 1571
F.R. Bigelow Fndn Grants, 1781
Field Fndn of Illinois Grants, 1806
Frances L. and Edwin L. Cummings Grants, 1919
G.N. Wilcox Grants, 1982
George Fndn Grants, 2018
George W. Wells Fndn Grants, 2030
Georgia-Pacific Fndn Educ Grants, 2031
Guido A. and Elizabeth H. Binda Fndn Grants, 2172
Hallmark Corp Fndn Grants, 2212
Harold Simmons Fndn Grants, 2230
Helen Steiner Rice Fndn Grants, 2299
Household Int'l Corp Giving Grants, 2372
Howard and Bush Fndn Grants, 2374
John H. and Wilhelmina D. Harland Grants, 2698
John I. Smith Charities Grants, 2700

Joseph H. and Florence A. Roblee Fndn Grants, 2736
Joyce Fndn Employment Grants, 2749
JP Morgan Chase Comm Development Grants, 2753
Kirkpatrick Fndn Grants, 2827
Mardag Fndn Grants, 3001
Mary Wilmer Covey Charitable Grants, 3049
May and Stanley Smith Charitable Grants, 3069
Michael and Susan Dell Fndn Grants, 3158
Middlesex Savings Ed Opportunities Grants, 3174
Norcliffe Fndn Grants, 3459
Norton Fndn Grants, 3514
Oppenstein Brothers Fndn Grants, 3685
PacifiCare Fndn Grants, 3725
Parkersburg Area Comm Fndn Action Grants, 3738
Paul and Mary Haas Fndn Contributions, 3756
PepsiCo Fndn Grants, 3819
Peyton Anderson Fndn Grants, 3862
Principal Financial Group Fndn Grants, 3966
Richard and Rhoda Goldman Grants, 4077
Robert Bowne Fndn Fellowships, 4107
Robert Bowne Fndn Lit Grants, 4108
Robert Bowne Fndn Youth-Centered Grants, 4109
Saint Paul Fndn Grants, 4219
San Antonio Area Fndn Grants, 4240
Sara Lee Fndn Grants, 4296
Seattle Fndn Educ Grants, 4326
Sony Corp of America Corp Philanthropy Grants, 4405
Sprint Fndn Grants, 4463
Sterling-Turner Charitable Fndn Grants, 4499
Strake Fndn Grants, 4511
Talbert and Leota Abrams Fndn, 4558
U.S. Dept of Ed Centers for Independent Living, 4688
U.S. Department of Educ Rehabilitation Training-- Rehabilitation Continuing Educ Programs, 4700
USAID Reading Enhancement for Advancing Development Grants, 4778
Whirlpool Fndn Grants, 5056
Wilson-Wood Fndn Grants, 5098

Beautification
Columbus Fndn Joseph A. Jeffrey Grants, 1224
GNOF Gert Community Grants, 2076
Mertz Gilmore Fndn NYC Communities Grants, 3126
Telluride Fndn Community Grants, 4573
WCI Minnesota Beautiful Grants, 5013

Behavioral Medicine
Allen P. and Josephine B. Green Fndn Grants, 380
NHLBI Ruth L. Kirschstein National Research Service Awards for Individual Postdoctoral Fellows, 3418
NHLBI Ruth L. Kirschstein National Research Service Awards for Individual Predoctoral Fellowships to Promote Diversity in Health-Related Research, 3419
Premera Blue Cross CARES Grants, 3945

Behavioral Sciences
ALA Distinguished Educ and Behavioral Sciences Librarian Award, 265
Arizona Diamondbacks Charities Grants, 542
Health Fndn of Greater Cincinnati Grants, 2281
National Center for Resp Gaming Travel Grants, 3251

Bilingual/Bicultural Education
Kroger Fndn Diversity Grants, 2842
National Home Library Fndn Grants, 3276
USAID Development Assistance Grants, 4748

Biochemistry
Greater Milwaukee Fndn Grants, 2137
Millipore Fndn Grants, 3182

Biodiversity
Bay and Paul Fndns, Inc Grants, 692
BP Conservation Programme Future Conservationist Awards, 826
Household Int'l Corp Giving Grants, 2372
Illinois DNR Youth Recreation Corps Grants, 2508
Jenifer Altman Fndn Grants, 2662
MacArthur Fndn Conservation and Sustainable Development Grants, 2963

Max and Anna Levinson Fndn Grants, 3066
NE Utilities Fndn Grants, 3498
NW Fund for the Environment Grants, 3510
Orchard Fndn Grants, 3690
Overbrook Fndn Grants, 3715
Rohm and Haas Company Grants, 4145
Shared Earth Fndn Grants, 4339
Threshold Fndn Sustainable Planet Grants, 4627
Tom's of Maine Grants, 4640
USAID Food Security, Nutrition, Biodiversity and Conservation Grants, 4752
Volvo Adventure Environmental Awards, 4952
WestWind Fndn Environment Grants, 5052

Bioengineering
NHLBI Bioengineering and Obesity Grants, 3411

Biographies
ALA Schneider Family Book Award, 317
ALA Stonewall Book Awards - Israel Fishman Nonfiction Award, 330
Virginia Historical Society Research Fellowships, 4949

Biological Resources
Colorado Bioscience Discovery Evaluation Grants, 1211
Indianapolis Power & Light Company Environmentalist of the Year Award, 2541
Indianapolis Power & Light Company Golden Eagle Environmental Grants, 2542

Biological Sciences
Brookdale Fndn Leadership in Aging Fellowships, 844
Flinn Fndn Grants, 1842
James Ford Bell Fndn Grants, 2623
Margaret and James A. Elkins Jr. Fndn Grants, 3003
NHLBI Ruth L. Kirschstein National Research Service Awards for Individual Senior Fellows, 3421
Richard King Mellon Fndn Grants, 4087

Biology
Canada-U.S. Fulbright Mid-Career Grants, 917
Collins Fndn Grants, 1209
Marion I. and Henry J. Knott Standard Grants, 3019
North Carolina GlaxoSmithKline Fndn Grants, 3490

Biology, Cellular
NHLBI Research on the Role of Cardiomyocyte Mitochondria in Heart Disease: An Integrated Approach, 3417

Biology, Conservation
Christensen Fund Regional Grants, 1112

Biology, Molecular
Bay and Paul Fndns Grants, 693

Biology, Reproductive
USAID Implementation Science for Strengthening Use of Evidence in Family Planning/Reproductive Health Programming Grants, 4758

Biomass Fuels
Colorado Bioscience Discovery Evaluation Grants, 1211
Illinois Clean Energy Community Fndn Energy Efficiency Grants, 2479
Illinois Clean Energy Community Fndn Renewable Energy Grants, 2481
Illinois Clean Energy Community Fndn Solar Thermal Installation Grants, 2482
McCune Charitable Fndn Grants, 3077
USDA Bioenergy Program for Advanced Biofuel Payments to Advanced Biofuel Producers, 4799

Biomedical Education
Bristol-Myers Squibb Clinical Outcomes and Research Grants, 839
Komen Greater NYC Small Grants, 2836
Piper Trust Healthcare & Med Research Grants, 3903
Sierra Health Fndn Responsive Grants, 4353

SUBJECT INDEX

Biomedical Research
100 Mile Man Fndn Grants, 27
A.O. Smith Community Grants, 46
Achelis Fndn Grants, 127
Alcoa Fndn Grants, 350
Allyn Fndn Grants, 392
ALSAM Fndn Grants, 395
American Foodservice Charitable Grants, 433
Amgen Fndn Grants, 456
Annenberg Fndn Grants, 477
Anthony R. Abraham Fndn Grants, 489
Arizona Cardinals Grants, 534
Armstrong McDonald Fndn Grants, 565
Arthur F. and Alice E. Adams Charitable Grants, 574
Batchelor Fndn Grants, 679
BCBSNC Fndn Grants, 712
Beim Fndn Grants, 718
Blue Shield of California Grants, 802
Blum-Kovler Fndn Grants, 803
Bodman Fndn Grants, 807
Booth-Bricker Grants, 815
Bosque Fndn Grants, 818
Bright Family Fndn Grants, 837
Bristol-Myers Squibb Clinical Research Grants, 839
Brookdale Fndn Leadership in Aging Fellowships, 844
Burden Grants, 864
Callaway Golf Company Fndn Grants, 910
Campbell Soup Fndn Grants, 916
Carl C. Icahn Fndn Grants, 929
Carrie Estelle Doheny Fndn Grants, 945
Chapin Hall Int'l Fellowships in Children's Policy Research, 1032
Charles H. Revson Fndn Grants, 1047
Charles Lafitte Fndn Grants, 1049
Chiles Fndn Grants, 1108
Chiron Fndn Community Grants, 1111
Claude Pepper Fndn Grants, 1160
CMA Fndn Grants, 1178
Columbus Fndn Competitive Grants, 1220
Community Fndn of Broward Grants, 1275
Connecticut Health Fndn Health Init Grants, 1351
Countess Moira Charitable Fndn Grants, 1381
DAAD Research Grants for Doctoral Candidates and Young Academics and Scientists, 1427
DeMatteis Family Fndn Grants, 1497
Denton A. Cooley Fndn Grants, 1500
Dorothea Haus Ross Fndn Grants, 1587
Dr. Scholl Fndn Grants, 1602
Edwin S. Webster Fndn Grants, 1671
Effie and Wofford Cain Fndn Grants, 1674
Emerson Charitable Grants, 1694
Emma B. Howe Memorial Fndn Grants, 1700
Eugene M. Lang Fndn Grants, 1764
Eugene McDermott Fndn Grants, 1765
Feldman Fndn Grants, 1801
Fidelity Fndn Grants, 1805
Fishman Family Fndn Grants, 1835
Flinn Fndn Grants, 1842
Forrest C. Lattner Fndn Grants, 1887
Frank Stanley Beveridge Fndn Grants, 1936
Fritz B. Burns Fndn Grants, 1965
Gebbie Fndn Grants, 1995
George Fndn Grants, 2018
George W. Brackenridge Fndn Grants, 2028
Gheens Fndn Grants, 2048
Gil and Dody Weaver Fndn Grants, 2053
Greenspun Family Fndn Grants, 2156
H.A. and Mary K. Chapman Charitable Grants, 2182
Harry A. and Margaret D. Towsley Fndn Grants, 2236
Harry Edison Fndn, 2241
Healthcare Fndn of New Jersey Grants, 2280
Hilda and Preston Davis Fndn Grants, 2322
HomeBanc Fndn Grants, 2347
J.B. Reynolds Fndn Grants, 2592
J.W. Kieckhefer Fndn Grants, 2607
James H. Cummings Fndn Grants, 2626
Joe W. and Dorothy Dorsett Brown Fndn Grants, 2684
John R. Oishei Fndn Grants, 2709
John S. Dunn Research Fndn Grants and Chairs, 2715
Johnson & Johnson Corp Contributions Grants, 2718
Joseph Alexander Fndn Grants, 2734
Joseph Drown Fndn Grants, 2735
Josiah W. and Bessie H. Kline Fndn Grants, 2742
Kenneth T. and Eileen L. Norris Fndn Grants, 2802
Kettering Grants, 2818
Komen Greater NYC Clinical Research Enrollment Grants, 2834
Komen Greater NYC Breast Health Grants, 2835
Lillian S. Wells Fndn Grants, 2901
Lindbergh Grants, 2907
Lucile Horton Howe & Mitchell B. Howe Grants, 2934
Lumpkin Family Healthy People Grants, 2942
M.J. Murdock Charitable Trust General Grants, 2954
Margaret L. Wendt Fndn Grants, 3004
Margaret T. Morris Fndn Grants, 3005
Mary K. Chapman Fndn Grants, 3042
Mary S. and David C. Corbin Fndn Grants, 3048
McCarthy Family Fndn Grants, 3073
McCombs Fndn Grants, 3075
McLean Contributionship Grants, 3088
Mericos Fndn Grants, 3121
Meyer and Pepa Gold Family Fndn Grants, 3138
MGN Family Fndn Grants, 3154
Monfort Family Fndn Grants, 3203
National Lottery Community Grants, 3279
NHLBI Ancillary Studies in Clinical Trials, 3410
NHLBI Investigator Multi-Site Clinical Trials, 3413
NHLBI Lymphatics in Health & Disease in Digestive, Urinary, Cardio & Pulmonary Systems, 3415
NHLBI Ruth L. Kirschstein National Research Service Awards for Individual Postdoctoral Fellows, 3418
NHLBI Ruth L. Kirschstein National Research Service Awards for Individual Predoctoral Fellowships to Promote Diversity in Health-Related Research, 3419
NHLBI Ruth L. Kirschstein National Research Service Awards for Individual Predoctoral MD/PhD Fellows and Other Dual Degree Fellows, 3420
NHLBI Ruth L. Kirschstein National Research Service Awards for Individual Senior Fellows, 3421
NHLBI Ruth L. Kirschstein National Research Service Award Short-Term Research Training Grants, 3422
NIEHS Hazardous Materials Worker Health and Safety Training Grants, 3438
Norcliffe Fndn Grants, 3459
Notsew Orm Sands Fndn Grants, 3516
NSF Accelerating Innovation Research, 3520
Nuffield Fndn Africa Grants, 3532
Nuffield Fndn Small Grants, 3535
Pasadena Fndn Average Grants, 3741
Patron Saints Fndn Grants, 3753
Perkin Grants, 3821
Perpetual Trust for Charitable Giving Grants, 3826
Piper Trust Healthcare & Med Research Grants, 3903
Presbyterian Health Fndn Bridge, Seed and Equipment Grants, 3947
Price Family Charitable Grants, 3952
Rajiv Gandhi Fndn Grants, 4011
Reinberger Fndn Grants, 4052
RGK Fndn Grants, 4072
Richard and Susan Smith Family Fndn Grants, 4078
Robert E. and Evelyn McKee Fndn Grants, 4110
Ronald McDonald House Charities Grants, 4149
Russell Berrie Fndn Grants, 4175
Saint Luke's Fndn Grants, 4215
Salisbury Community Fndn Grants, 4224
San Antonio Area Fndn Grants, 4240
Sarah Scaife Fndn Grants, 4295
Sarkeys Fndn Grants, 4297
Schering-Plough Fndn Health Grants, 4304
Sensient Technologies Fndn Grants, 4337
Sidgmore Family Fndn Grants, 4348
Starr Fndn Grants, 4483
Thomas and Dorothy Leavey Fndn Grants, 4612
Thomas Austin Finch, Sr. Fndn Grants, 4613
Victor E. Speas Fndn Grants, 4933
W.C. Griffith Fndn Grants, 4957
Wayne and Gladys Valley Fndn Grants, 5003
William G. and Helen C. Hoffman Fndn Grants, 5080
William G. McGowan Charitable Grants, 5084
William H. Hannon Fndn Grants, 5086

Biomedical Research Resources
Nestle Fndn Training Grant, 3301
NHLBI Ruth L. Kirschstein National Research Service Award Short-Term Research Training Grants, 3422
NSF Accelerating Innovation Research, 3520

Biomedical Research Training
NHLBI Ruth L. Kirschstein National Research Service Awards for Individual Postdoctoral Fellows, 3418
NHLBI Ruth L. Kirschstein National Research Service Awards for Individual Predoctoral Fellowships to Promote Diversity in Health-Related Research, 3419
NHLBI Ruth L. Kirschstein National Research Service Award Short-Term Research Training Grants, 3422
Piper Trust Healthcare & Med Research Grants, 3903

Biomedicine
Komen Greater NYC Small Grants, 2836
Lumpkin Family Healthy People Grants, 2942
Mary K. Chapman Fndn Grants, 3042
Prudential Fndn Educ Grants, 3977

Biotechnology
Lumpkin Family Healthy People Grants, 2942
North Carolina Biotech Event Sponsorships, 3485
North Carolina Biotech Center Meeting Grants, 3486
North Carolina Biotech Center Multidisciplinary Research Grants, 3487
North Carolina Biotech Center Regional Development Grants, 3488

Bipolar Disorder
Peter and Elizabeth C. Tower Fndn Annual Mental Health Grants, 3835

Birth/Congenital Defects
TJX Fndn Grants, 4637

Bisexuals
ALA Diversity and Outreach Fair, 267
ALFJ Astraea U.S. General Fund, 362
Community Fndn SE Michigan HOPE Grants, 1260
Kalamazoo Community LBGT Equality Grants, 2771
Ms. Fndn for Women Ending Violence Grants, 3224
Ms. Fndn for Women Health Grants, 3225
New York Fndn Grants, 3338
Philanthrofund Fndn Grants, 3874

Book Awards
ALA Coretta Scott King Book Awards, 260
ALA Dartmouth Medal, 262
ALA Schneider Family Book Award, 317
ALA Stonewall Book Awards - Barbara Gittings Literature Award, 329
ALA Stonewall Book Awards - Israel Fishman Nonfiction Award, 330

Books
ALA Allie Beth Martin Award, 221
ALA Clarence Day Award, 258
ALA Coretta Scott King Book Donation Grant, 261
ALA Dartmouth Medal, 262
ALA Donald G. Davis Article Award, 269
ALA John Phillip Immroth Memorial Award, 293
ALA Schneider Family Book Award, 317
ALA Stonewall Book Awards - Barbara Gittings Literature Award, 329
ALA Stonewall Book Awards - Israel Fishman Nonfiction Award, 330
Arizona State Library LSTA Collections Grants, 548
Better World Books LEAP Grants for Libraries, 755
Better World Books LEAP Grants for Nonprofits, 756
Covenant to Care for Children Grants, 1389
Maine Community Fndn Rose and Samuel Rudman Library Grants, 2988
National Home Library Fndn Grants, 3276
NYSCA Literature: Public Programs, 3600
Virginia Fndn for Humanities Discr Grants, 4946
Virginia Fndn for the Humanities Open Grants, 4947

824 / Botanical Gardens

Botanical Gardens
America the Beautiful Fund Operation Green Plant Grants, 451
Annie's Cases for Causes Product Donations, 479
Annie's Grants for Gardens, 480
Auburn Fndn Grants, 611
Bay and Paul Fndns, Inc Grants, 692
Bayer Advanced Grow Together with Roses School Garden Awards, 695
Ethel S. Abbott Charitable Fndn Grants, 1760
GEF Green Thumb Challenge, 1996
GreenWorks! Butterfly Garden Grants, 2159
H. Reimers Bechtel Charitable Grants, 2186
Hampton Roads Community Fndn Horticulture Educ Grants, 2217
Herbert A. and Adrian W. Woods Fndn Grants, 2313
IMLS 21st Century Museum Pro Grants, 2512
IMLS American Heritage Preservation Grants, 2513
IMLS National Leadership Grants, 2515
Kelvin and Eleanor Smith Fndn Grants, 2796
Nature Hills Nursery Green America Awards, 3287
NGA Midwest School Garden Grants, 3407
Perry County Community Fndn Grants, 3827
PMI Fndn Grants, 3918
Posey County Community Fndn Grants, 3939
Project Orange Thumb Grants, 3972
Spencer County Community Fndn Grants, 4451
Stanley Smith Horticultural Grants, 4474
Union Bank, N.A. Fndn Grants, 4709
Union Pacific Fndn Community and Civic Grants, 4714
Warrick County Community Fndn Grants, 4987
Widgeon Point Charitable Fndn Grants, 5064
William Bingham Fndn Grants, 5077

Bowling
USBC Annual Zeb Scholarship, 4792
USBC Earl Anthony Scholarships, 4793

Breast Cancer
Acuity Charitable Fndn Grants, 140
Avon Products Fndn Grants, 625
Campbell Soup Fndn Grants, 916
CFFVR Women's Fund for Fox Valley Grants, 1025
CMA Fndn Grants, 1178
GNOF IMPACT Harold W. Newman, Jr. Grants, 2083
Henry and Ruth Blaustein Rosenberg Grants, 2306
IBCAT Screening Mammography Grants, 2422
Komen Greater NYC Clinical Research Enrollment Grants, 2834
Komen Greater NYC Breast Health Grants, 2835
Komen Greater NYC Small Grants, 2836
Mary Kay Ash Charitable Fndn Grants, 3043
Meyer and Stephanie Eglin Fndn Grants, 3139
Pfizer Healthcare Charitable Contributions, 3863
Premera Blue Cross CARES Grants, 3945
Seattle Fndn Medical Funds Grants, 4329
Susan G. Komen Breast Cancer Fndn Challege Grants: Breast Cancer and the Environment, 4535

Broadcast Media
Akron Community Fndn Arts & Culture Grants, 218
Appalachian Community Media Justice Grants, 495
Boeckmann Charitable Fndn Grants, 808
Broadcasting Board of Governors David Burke Distinguished Journalism Award, 843
Florida Div of Cultural Affairs Media Grants, 1856
Geraldine R. Dodge Fndn Media Grants, 2042
Henry J. Kaiser Family Fndn Grants, 2310
National Endowment for Arts Agencies Grants, 3263
Reinberger Fndn Grants, 4052
USAID Strengthening Free and Independent Media in South Sudan Grants, 4783

Building/Construction
African American Heritage Grants, 193
Ahearn Family Fndn Grants, 206
Appalachian Regional Comm Housing Grants, 508
Baton Rouge Area Fndn Credit Bureau Grants, 680
Best Buy Children's Fndn Twin Cities Minnesota Capital Grants, 753

Bush Fndn Arts & Humanities Capital Projects, 872
CDECD Endangered Properties Grants, 980
CFFVR Sikora Family Grants, 1022
Charles H. Farnsworth Grants, 1043
Clark and Ruby Baker Fndn Grants, 1154
Cleveland Capital Grants, 1167
Community Fndn of Abilene Community Grants, 1264
Coughlin-Saunders Fndn Grants, 1377
DeKalb County Community Fndn - Immediate Response Grant, 1479
DHS ARRA Fire Station Construction Grants, 1542
Dwight Stuart Youth Capacity-Building Grants, 1627
Eugene Straus Charitable Trust, 1766
Florida Div of Cultural Affairs Facilities Grants, 1852
Ford Family Grants Public Convening Spaces, 1881
Gladys Brooks Fndn Grants, 2059
GNOF Albert N. & Hattie M. McClure Grants, 2068
GNOF Coastal 5 + 1 Grants, 2070
GNOF Community Revitalization Grants, 2071
GNOF Exxon-Mobil Grants, 2074
GNOF Jefferson Community Grants, 2085
GNOF Norco Community Grants, 2089
Hillcrest Fndn Grants, 2325
Home Building Industry Disaster Relief Fund, 2348
Hometown Indiana Grants, 2353
HRF Hudson River Improvement Grants, 2378
IDOT Economic Development Grants, 2436
IDOT Truck Access Route Grants, 2438
IDPH Hosptial Capital Investment Grants, 2441
IEDC Industrial Development Grant Fund, 2443
Illinois DCEO Business Development Public Infrastructure Grants, 2483
Illinois DCEO Community Development Assistance For Economic Development Grants, 2488
Illinois DNR Park and Recreational Facility Construction Grants, 2499
Indiana Historic Preservation Grants, 2537
Janson Fndn Grants, 2646
Jean and Price Daniel Fndn Grants, 2659
Jennings County Community Fndn Grants, 2664
John C. Lasko Fndn Grants, 2688
Katharine Matthies Grants, 2788
Kosciusko County Community Fndn REMC Operation Round Up Grants, 2839
Lotus 88 Fndn for Women and Children Grants, 2921
Lowe's Outdoor Classroom Grants, 2928
Marietta McNeill Morgan and Samuel Tate Morgan, Jr. Grants, 3008
Marion County Historic Preservation Grants, 3016
Massachusetts Cultural Council Cultural Facilities Capital Grants, 3053
Massachusetts Cultural Council Cultural Facilities Feasibility and Technical Assistance Grants, 3054
Massachusetts Cultural Council Cultural Facilities Systems Replacement Plan Grants Grants, 3055
MDARD County Fairs Cap Improvement Grants, 3092
MetroWest Health Fndn Capital Grants for Health-Related Facilities, 3134
National Trust for Historic Preservation Diversity Scholarship, 3280
Nicor Corp Contributions, 3435
Norcliffe Fndn Grants, 3459
Paul Ogle Fndn Grants, 3764
Petco Fndn Capital Grants, 3831
Porter County Community Fndn Grants, 3931
Priddy Fndn Capital Grants, 3954
Pulte Homes Corp Contributions, 3989
Retirement Research Accessible Faith Grants, 4066
Robert R. Meyer Fndn Grants, 4121
Rosie's For All Kids Fndn Grants, 4163
Ross Fndn Grants, 4164
South Carolina Arts Commission Facility Grants, 4417
Suntrust Bank Atlanta Fndn Grants, 4531
USDA Farm Labor Housing Grants, 4809
USDA Self-Help Technical Assistance Grants, 4836
US Soccer Annual Program & Field Grants, 4870
USTA Public Facility Assistance Grants, 4883
Vermillion County Community Fndn Grants, 4928
Vigneron Grants, 4938

SUBJECT INDEX

Buildings, Residential
GNOF Community Revitalization Grants, 2071
GNOF Jefferson Community Grants, 2085
Pulte Homes Corp Contributions, 3989
Wells Fargo Housing Fndn Grants, 5023

Bullying
Pacers Fndn Be Tolerant Grants, 3723

Burial Services
Homer C. and Martha W. Gutchess Fndn Grants, 2351

Burns
Austin S. Nelson Fndn Grants, 617
John S. Dunn Research Fndn Grants and Chairs, 2715

Business
100 Women in Hedge Funds Fndn Grants, 28
Aladdin Industries Fndn Grants, 263
ALA Morningstar Pub Librarian Support Award, 302
AmerUs Group Charitable Fndn, 455
Appalachian Regional Commission Business Development Revolving Loan Grants, 501
Appalachian Regional Commission Leadership Development and Capacity Building Grants, 509
Archer Daniels Midland Fndn Grants, 527
ARCO Fndn Educ Grants, 528
Arizona Comm on Arts After-School Residencies, 535
AT&T Fndn Civic and Comm Service Grants, 599
Beldon Grants, 720
Boyd Gaming Corp Contributions Program, 825
Burton Morgan Youth Entrepreneurship Grants, 870
Charles G. Koch Charitable Fndn Grants, 1041
Chesapeake Bay Trust Mini Grants, 1072
Collins C. Diboll Private Fndn Grants, 1208
Community Memorial Fndn Grants, 1334
ConocoPhillips Grants, 1355
Constellation Energy Corp Grants, 1364
Dow Chemical Company Grants, 1596
Duke Energy Economic Development Grants, 1619
E.L. Wiegand Fndn Grants, 1639
Fitzpatrick and Francis Family Business Continuity Fndn Grants, 1837
Ford Motor Company Grants, 1885
Fulbright Binational Business Grants in Mexico, 1969
Fulbright Business Grants in Spain, 1970
GMFUS Marshall Memorial Fellowships, 2066
Graco Fndn Grants, 2111
Herbert B. Jones Fndn Grants, 2314
Hitachi Fndn Business and Work Grants, 2339
Hormel Family Fndn Business Plan Award, 2367
John Ben Snow Grants, 2687
JP Morgan Chase Comm Development Grants, 2753
Kenny's Kids Grants, 2803
Lincoln Financial Group Fndn Grants, 2906
Nevada Arts Council Learning Grants, 3313
New Jersey Office of Faith Based Inits Creating Wealth Through Asset Building Grants, 3331
New York Life Fndn Grants, 3341
NHSCA Arts in Health Care Project Grants, 3424
OSF-Baltimore Community Fellowships, 3695
Phoenix Suns Charities Grants, 3881
Princeton Area Community Fndn Fund for Women and Girls Grants, 3962
Procter and Gamble Grants, 3967
Prudential Fndn Educ Grants, 3977
Southern Minnesota Init Grants, 4437
Texas Instruments Civic and Business Grants, 4597
United Technologies Corp Grants, 4725
USAID Economic Prospectsfor Armenia-Turkey Normalization Grants, 4750
USAID India Partnership Grants, 4761
USAID Pakistan Private Investment Init Grants, 4772
USDA 1890 Land Grant Colleges and Universities Init Grants, 4797
USDA Rural Economic Development Grants, 4827
USDA Rural Energy for America - Energy Audit and Renewable Energy Devel Assistance Grants, 4828
USDA Rural Energy for America - Feasibility Study Grants, 4829

SUBJECT INDEX

USDA Rural Microentrepreneur Assist Grants, 4832
USDA Small Disadvantaged Producer Grants, 4837
Willary Fndn Grants, 5071
Wolfe Associates Grants, 5110
Xerox Fndn Grants, 5122
Yampa Valley Community Fndn Erickson Business Week Scholarships, 5123
Yellow Corp Fndn Grants, 5126

Business Administration
Canada-U.S. Fulbright Mid-Career Grants, 917
Cargill Citizenship Fund-Corp Giving Grants, 925
Nonprofit Management Grants, 3458
Richard Davoud Donchian Fndn Grants, 4080
William G. McGowan Charitable Grants, 5084

Business Cycles/Crises
Community Fndn of Greater Fort Wayne - Collaborative Efforts Grants, 1284

Business Development
100 Women in Hedge Funds Fndn Grants, 28
ACF Native American Social and Economic Development Strategies Grants, 123
ALA President's Award for Advocacy, 310
Amber Grants, 413
American Chemical Society Chemical Technology Partnership Mini Grants, 424
Appalachian Regional Commission Business Development Revolving Loan Grants, 501
Appalachian Regional Commission Export and Trade Development Grants, 506
Appalachian Regional Commission Leadership Development and Capacity Building Grants, 509
Aquila Corp Grants, 521
Arkansas Arts Council Sally A. Williams Grants, 558
Arkansas Community Fndn Arkansas Black Hall of Fame Grants, 559
Bailey Fndn Grants, 635
Boyd Gaming Corp Contributions Program, 825
CCHD Economic Development Grants, 967
CDECD Tourism Product Development Grants, 984
ChevronTexaco Contributions Program, 1078
Chicago Tribune Fndn Civic Grants, 1100
Community Fndn in Jacksonville Art Ventures Small Organizations Professional Assistance Grants, 1262
Connecticut Light & Power Corp Contributions, 1352
Courage Center Judd Jacobson Memorial Award, 1382
Draper Richards Kaplan Fndn Grants, 1603
Ewing Marion Kauffman Fndn Grants and Inits, 1777
Fitzpatrick and Francis Family Business Continuity Fndn Grants, 1837
Four Times Fndn Grants, 1914
Frey Fndn Grants, 1963
Fulbright Binational Business Grants in Mexico, 1969
Fulbright Business Grants in Spain, 1970
General Motors Fndn Grants Support Program, 2004
Grand Haven Area Community Fndn Grants, 2113
HAF Technical Assistance Grants, 2206
Harold Alfond Fndn Grants, 2225
Helen Bader Fndn Grants, 2293
Hormel Family Fndn Business Plan Award, 2367
IEDC Industrial Development Grant Fund, 2443
IEDC Int'l Trade Show Assistance Program, 2444
Illinois DCEO Community Development Assistance For Economic Development Grants, 2488
Indiana 21st Century Research and Tech Awards, 2528
Indiana Corn Marketing Council Retailer Grant for Tank Cleaning, 2536
Indiana SBIR/STTR Commercialization Enhancement Program, 2548
Indiana Waste Tire Grants, 2551
ING Fndn Grants, 2555
Jacobs Family Village Neighborhoods Grants, 2619
JP Morgan Chase Arts and Culture Grants, 2752
Kalamazoo Community Fndn Capacity Building Grants, 2764
Kalamazoo Community Fndn Economic and Community Development Grants, 2765
Lewis H. Humphreys Charitable Grants, 2889

Louis and Elizabeth Nave Flarsheim Charitable Fndn Grants, 2924
MDEQ Brownfield Redevelopment and Site Reclamation Grants, 3095
NASE Fndn Future Entrepreneur Scholarship, 3241
NASE Growth Grants, 3242
NASE Succeed Scholarships, 3243
National Endowment for Arts Our Town Grants, 3257
National Endowment for Arts Agencies Grants, 3263
National Endowment for the Arts Presenting Grants: Art Works, 3268
Natonal Endowment for the Arts Research Grants: Art Works, 3286
New Jersey Center for Hispanic Policy, Research and Development Entrepreneurship Grants, 3326
New Jersey Office of Faith Based Inits Creating Wealth Through Asset Building Grants, 3331
New Mexico Women's Fndn Grants, 3335
Nonprofit Management Grants, 3458
NE Utilities Fndn Grants, 3498
Northern Trust Company Corp Giving Program, 3504
Packard Fndn Organizational Effectiveness and Philanthropy Grants, 3730
Priddy Fndn Organizational Development Grants, 3956
Prudential Fndn Economic Development Grants, 3976
Pulaski County Community Fndn Grants, 3988
RISCA Professional Arts Development Grants, 4099
Southbury Community Trust Fund, 4409
South Carolina Arts Commission Cultural Tourism Init Grants, 4419
South Carolina Arts Commission Cultural Visions Grants, 4420
South Carolina Arts Commission Incentive Grants for Employer Sponsored Benefits, 4422
South Carolina Arts Commission Leadership and Organizational Development Grants, 4423
South Carolina Arts Commission Long Term Operating Support for Organizations Grants, 4424
Tech Enhancement Certification for Hoosiers, 4571
Texas Instruments Corp Arts and Culture Grants, 4596
Texas Instruments Civic and Business Grants, 4597
Texas Instruments Fndn Arts and Culture Grants, 4599
Thomas Austin Finch, Sr. Fndn Grants, 4613
U.S. Department of Educ Vocational Rehabilitation Services Projects for American Indians with Disabilities Grants, 4702
USAID Economic Prospectsfor Armenia-Turkey Normalization Grants, 4750
USAID India Partnership Grants, 4761
USAID Pakistan Private Investment Init Grants, 4772
US CRDF Science & Tech Entrepreneurship Business Partnership Grants in Armenia, 4795
US CRDF STEP Business Partnership Grant Competition Ukraine, 4796
USDA 1890 Land Grant Colleges and Universities Init Grants, 4797
USDA Rural Business Enterprise Grants, 4823
USDA Rural Business Opportunity Grants, 4824
USDA Rural Economic Development Grants, 4827
USDA Rural Energy for America - Energy Audit and Renewable Energy Devel Assistance Grants, 4828
USDA Rural Energy for America Feasibility Grants, 4829
USDA Rural Microentrepreneur Assist Grants, 4832
USDA Small Disadvantaged Producer Grants, 4837
USDC Public Works and Economic Adjustment Assistance Grants, 4856

Business Education
3M Fndn Community Giving Grants, 15
Abell-Hanger Fndn Grants, 91
Alcoa Fndn Grants, 350
Allstate Corp Giving Grants, 386
Allstate Corp Hometown Commitment Grants, 387
Allstate Fndn Safe and Vital Communities Grants, 390
AMI Semiconductors Corp Grants, 457
Appalachian Regional Commission Business Development Revolving Loan Grants, 501
Aquila Corp Grants, 521
Benton Community Fndn Grants, 730
Blue River Community Fndn Grants, 801

Canadian Studies / 825

Boettcher Fndn Grants, 810
Bright Family Fndn Grants, 837
Brown County Community Fndn Grants, 853
Citigroup Fndn Grants, 1139
Coca-Cola Fndn Grants, 1195
Coleman Fndn Entrepreneurship Educ Grants, 1201
Community Fndn of Bartholomew County Heritage Grants, 1267
Community Fndn of Bartholomew County James A. Henderson Award for Fundraising, 1268
Community Fndn of Greater Fort Wayne - Community Endowment and Clarke Endowment Grants, 1285
Consumers Energy Fndn, 1365
Cummins Fndn Grants, 1415
D.F. Halton Fndn Grants, 1424
DaimlerChrysler Corp Grants, 1432
Essex County Community Fndn First Jobs Grant, 1754
F.M. Kirby Fndn Grants, 1780
Fitzpatrick and Francis Family Business Grants, 1837
FMC Fndn Grants, 1876
Fulbright Binational Business Grants in Mexico, 1969
Fulbright Business Grants in Spain, 1970
GenCorp Fndn Grants, 1998
General Motors Fndn Grants Support Program, 2004
Herbert B. Jones Fndn Grants, 2314
James M. Collins Fndn Grants, 2633
JP Morgan Chase Comm Development Grants, 2753
McCune Charitable Fndn Grants, 3077
Monfort Family Fndn Grants, 3203
New Jersey Office of Faith Based Inits Creating Wealth Through Asset Building Grants, 3331
Olin Corp Charitable Grants, 3669
Richard and Helen DeVos Fndn Grants, 4076
Robert W. Woodruff Fndn Grants, 4124
Sid W. Richardson Fndn Grants, 4350
Sprint Fndn Grants, 4463
Target Corp Local Store Grants, 4561
Union Bank, N.A. Fndn Grants, 4709
USAID Economic Prospectsfor Armenia-Turkey Normalization Grants, 4750
USAID India Partnership Grants, 4761
Virginia Historical Society Research Fellowships, 4949
Washington Gas Charitable Contributions, 5000
Wayne and Gladys Valley Fndn Grants, 5003
William G. McGowan Charitable Grants, 5084
William L. and Victorine Q. Adams Fndn Grants, 5089
Yampa Valley Community Fndn Erickson Business Week Scholarships, 5123

Business Ethics
Richard Davoud Donchian Fndn Grants, 4080

Business History
Natonal Endowment for the Arts Research Grants: Art Works, 3286
Virginia Historical Society Research Fellowships, 4949

Business and Commerce
Bikes Belong Fndn Research Grants, 762
CDECD Tourism Product Development Grants, 984
GNOF New Orleans Works Grants, 2088
Illinois DCEO Coal Development Grants, 2486
NE Utilities Fndn Grants, 3498
Texas Instruments Civic and Business Grants, 4597
USAID Economic Prospectsfor Armenia-Turkey Normalization Grants, 4750
USAID India Partnership Grants, 4761
USAID Pakistan Private Investment Init Grants, 4772

Campaign Finance Reform
Arca Fndn Grants, 526
Joyce Fndn Democracy Grants, 2748
Orchard Fndn Grants, 3690
State Strategies Grants, 4494

Canadian History
ALA Donald G. Davis Article Award, 269

Canadian Studies
Canada-U.S. Fulbright Mid-Career Grants, 917

Cancer Detection
2COBS Private Charitable Fndn Grants, 6
A/H Fndn Grants, 48
Angels Baseball Fndn Grants, 465
Ann and Robert H. Lurie Family Fndn Grants, 473
Austin S. Nelson Fndn Grants, 617
Avon Products Fndn Grants, 625
Balfe Family Fndn Grants, 636
CFFVR Jewelers Mutual Charitable Giving, 1014
CMA Fndn Grants, 1178
Coleman Fndn Cancer Care Grants, 1199
General Motors Fndn Grants Support Program, 2004
Gil and Dody Weaver Fndn Grants, 2053
GNOF IMPACT Harold W. Newman, Jr. Charitable Grants, 2083
Mary Kay Ash Charitable Fndn Grants, 3043
Seattle Fndn Medical Funds Grants, 4329
Susan G. Komen Breast Cancer Fndn Challege Grants: Breast Cancer and the Environment, 4535
TD4HIM Fndn Grants, 4566
W. C. Griffith Fndn Grants, 4958

Cancer Prevention
2COBS Private Charitable Fndn Grants, 6
A/H Fndn Grants, 48
Acuity Charitable Fndn Grants, 140
Angels Baseball Fndn Grants, 465
Ann and Robert H. Lurie Family Fndn Grants, 473
Austin S. Nelson Fndn Grants, 617
Balfe Family Fndn Grants, 636
CFFVR Jewelers Mutual Charitable Giving, 1014
Coleman Fndn Cancer Care Grants, 1199
Community Fndn of Broward Grants, 1275
Cowles Charitable Grants, 1392
Georgia Power Fndn Grants, 2039
Gil and Dody Weaver Fndn Grants, 2053
GNOF IMPACT Harold W. Newman, Jr. Charitable Grants, 2083
GNOF IMPACT Kahn-Oppenheim Grants, 2084
Greenwall Fndn Bioethics Grants, 2158
IDPH Carolyn Adams Ticket for the Cure Community Grants, 2439
Mary Kay Ash Charitable Fndn Grants, 3043
RCF General Community Grants, 4032
Susan G. Komen Breast Cancer Fndn Challege Grants: Breast Cancer and the Environment, 4535
TD4HIM Fndn Grants, 4566
W. C. Griffith Fndn Grants, 4958

Cancer/Carcinogenesis
2COBS Private Charitable Fndn Grants, 6
Alexander and Margaret Stewart Grants, 354
Alex Stern Family Fndn Grants, 360
Angels Baseball Fndn Grants, 465
Annunziata Sanguinetti Fndn Grants, 485
Aragona Family Fndn Grants, 522
Bodenwein Public Benevolent Fndn Grants, 806
Booth-Bricker Grants, 815
Callaway Golf Company Fndn Grants, 910
CFFVR Robert and Patricia Endries Family Fndn Grants, 1018
Charles Lafitte Fndn Grants, 1049
Chicago Board of Trade Fndn Grants, 1079
Chicago White Metal Charitable Fndn Grants, 1102
Chiron Fndn Community Grants, 1111
Coleman Fndn Cancer Care Grants, 1199
Community Fndn of Broward Grants, 1275
Cooper Industries Fndn Grants, 1370
Coors Brewing Corp Contributions Grants, 1371
D.F. Halton Fndn Grants, 1424
DeRoy Testamentary Fndn Grants, 1518
Duchossois Family Fndn Grants, 1616
E.L. Wiegand Fndn Grants, 1639
Emerson Charitable Grants, 1694
Emma B. Howe Memorial Fndn Grants, 1700
Farmers Insurance Corp Giving Grants, 1791
Fondren Fndn Grants, 1878
Fred C. and Katherine B. Andersen Fndn Grants, 1942
General Motors Fndn Grants Support Program, 2004
Georgia Power Fndn Grants, 2039

GNOF IMPACT Harold W. Newman, Jr. Charitable Grants, 2083
Greenspun Family Fndn Grants, 2156
Greenwall Fndn Bioethics Grants, 2158
Hagedorn Fndn Grants, 2207
Hillman Fndn Grants, 2327
HomeBanc Fndn Grants, 2347
Horizon Fndn for New Jersey Grants, 2364
Janus Fndn Grants, 2647
Jenifer Altman Fndn Grants, 2662
John S. Dunn Research Fndn Grants and Chairs, 2715
K21 Health Fndn Cancer Care Grants, 2759
Komen Greater NYC Clinical Research Enrollment Grants, 2834
Komen Greater NYC Com Breast Health Grants, 2835
Lillian S. Wells Fndn Grants, 2901
Louis R. Cappelli Fndn Grants, 2926
Mary Kay Ash Charitable Fndn Grants, 3043
Nell Warren Elkin and William Simpson Elkin, 3300
Oracle Corp Contributions Grants, 3686
Premera Blue Cross CARES Grants, 3945
Robert R. Meyer Fndn Grants, 4121
Russell Berrie Fndn Grants, 4175
Seattle Fndn Medical Funds Grants, 4329
Susan G. Komen Breast Cancer Fndn Challege Grants: Breast Cancer and the Environment, 4535
Thompson Charitable Fndn Grants, 4622
Union Bank, N.A. Fndn Grants, 4709
Victor E. Speas Fndn Grants, 4933
Visiting Nurse Fndn Grants, 4951
W.C. Griffith Fndn Grants, 4957
W. C. Griffith Fndn Grants, 4958
Whirlpool Fndn Grants, 5056
William G. McGowan Charitable Grants, 5084

Canoeing
ODKF Athletic Grants, 3638

Cardiology
Abbott Fund Science Educ Grants, 83
Genentech Corp Charitable Contributions, 2000
Harold R. Bechtel Charitable Remainder Grants, 2229
Horizon Fndn for New Jersey Grants, 2364
Joseph Drown Fndn Grants, 2735
Nell Warren Elkin and William Simpson Elkin, 3300
NHLBI Ancillary Studies in Clinical Trials, 3410
NHLBI Research on the Role of Cardiomyocyte Mitochondria in Heart Disease: An Integrated Approach, 3417

Cardiomyocyte Mitochondria
NHLBI Research on the Role of Cardiomyocyte Mitochondria in Heart Disease: An Integrated Approach, 3417

Cardiovascular Diseases
Abbott Fund Science Educ Grants, 83
Balfe Family Fndn Grants, 636
Bristol-Myers Squibb Clinical Research Grants, 839
CVS All Kids Can Grants, 1420
D.F. Halton Fndn Grants, 1424
E.L. Wiegand Fndn Grants, 1639
Emma B. Howe Memorial Fndn Grants, 1700
GNOF IMPACT Harold W. Newman, Jr. Charitable Grants, 2083
GNOF IMPACT Kahn-Oppenheim Grants, 2084
Harold R. Bechtel Charitable Remainder Grants, 2229
Henrietta Lange Burk Grants, 2303
Johnson & Johnson Comm Health Care Grants, 2717
Lucy Downing Nisbet Charitable Grants, 2935
Nell Warren Elkin and William Simpson Elkin, 3300
NHLBI Ancillary Studies in Clinical Trials, 3410
NHLBI Career Transition Awards, 3412
NHLBI Lymphatics in Health & Disease in Digestive, Urinary, Cardio & Pulmonary Systems, 3415
NHLBI Research on the Role of Cardiomyocyte Mitochondria in Heart Disease, 3417
Pfizer Healthcare Charitable Contributions, 3863
Premera Blue Cross CARES Grants, 3945
Rich Fndn Grants, 4090

Saint Luke's Health Inits Grants, 4216
Seattle Fndn Medical Funds Grants, 4329

Cardiovascular Health
DTE Energy Health & Human Services Grants, 1613
GNOF IMPACT Kahn-Oppenheim Grants, 2084
Mary Black Fndn Community Health Grants, 3032
Premera Blue Cross CARES Grants, 3945

Cardiovascular System
NHLBI Lymphatics in Health & Disease in Digestive, Cardiovascular and Pulmonary Systems, 3414
NHLBI Research on the Role of Cardiomyocyte Mitochondria in Heart Disease: An Integrated Approach, 3417
NHLBI Ruth L. Kirschstein National Research Service Awards for Individual Postdoctoral Fellows, 3418

Care Givers
Brookdale Fndn National Group Respite Grants, 845
CNCS Senior Corps Retired & Volunteer Grants, 1188
Rosalynn Carter Institute Georgia Caregiver of the Year Awards, 4151

Career Education and Planning
Actors Fund Social Services and Financial Assist, 139
AMD Corp Contributions Grants, 416
Asian American Institute Impact Fellowships, 588
Burton Morgan Youth Entrepreneurship Grants, 870
Canada-U.S. Fulbright Mid-Career Grants, 917
Chiron Fndn Community Grants, 1111
Cisco Systems Fndn San Jose Community Grants, 1137
Cleveland Browns Fndn Grants, 1166
Cleveland Fenn Ed Grants, 1169
Comer Fndn Grants, 1236
Community Fndn of Boone Cty Women's Grants, 1273
Community Fndn of Greater Flint Grants, 1282
DaimlerChrysler Corp Grants, 1432
Dept of Ed Projects with Industry Grants, 1511
Dwight Stuart Youth Fndn Grants, 1628
Ewing Marion Kauffman Fndn Grants and Inits, 1777
Ford Motor Company Grants, 1885
Fndns of E Chicago Financial Indep Grants, 1909
Girl's Best Friend Fndn Grants, 2057
HAF Educ Grants, 2196
Hartford Aging and Health Program Awards, 2247
Highmark Corp Giving Grants, 2319
Int'l Paper Company Fndn Grants, 2568
KeyBank Fndn Grants, 2820
Lincoln Financial Group Fndn Grants, 2906
McCarthy Family Fndn Grants, 3073
Meyer Fndn Educ Grants, 3142
New York Life Fndn Grants, 3341
NYCT Workforce Development Grants, 3560
NYCT Youth Development Grants, 3561
Pentair Fndn Educ and Community Grants, 3816
Piper Jaffray Fndn Communities Giving Grants, 3899
Saint Paul Fndn Grants, 4219
TE Fndn Grants, 4572
U.S. Department of Educ 21st Century Community Learning Centers, 4687
USDC Advanced Manufacturing Jobs and Innovation Accelerator Challenge Grants, 4848
USDC Business Center - American Indian and Alaska Native Grants, 4849
USDC i6 Challenge Grants, 4851
USDC Postsecondary Grants Internships, 4855

Cataloging and Classification
ALA Esther J. Piercy Award, 275
ALA Margaret Mann Citation, 297
National Endowment for Arts Museum Grants, 3265
NEH Preservation Assistance Grants for Smaller Institutions, 3293

Catholic Church
Adams-Mastrovich Family Fndn Grants, 146
AHS Fndn Grants, 208
Alvah H. and Wyline P. Chapman Fndn Grants, 402
Anthony R. Abraham Fndn Grants, 489

SUBJECT INDEX

Archer Daniels Midland Fndn Grants, 527
Better Way Fndn Grants, 754
Blanche M. Walsh Charity Grants, 786
Booth-Bricker Grants, 815
Carrie Estelle Doheny Fndn Grants, 945
CCF Community Priorities Fund, 961
CCHD Economic Development Grants, 967
Charity Incorporated Grants, 1035
Charles Delmar Fndn Grants, 1039
Claude A. and Blanche McCubbin Abbott Grants, 1158
Collins C. Diboll Private Fndn Grants, 1208
Connelly Fndn Grants, 1353
Crescent Porter Hale Fndn Grants, 1398
Dorothea Haus Ross Fndn Grants, 1587
Edward and Ellen Roche Relief Fndn Grants, 1663
Eugene B. Casey Fndn Grants, 1762
Fred and Sherry Abernethy Fndn Grants, 1940
Furth Family Fndn Grants, 1980
G.A. Ackermann Grants, 1981
Hackett Fndn Grants, 2188
Helen V. Brach Fndn Grants, 2300
Humanitas Fndn Grants, 2390
I.A. O'Shaughnessy Fndn Grants, 2416
Ida Alice Ryan Charitable Grants, 2431
Kevin P. & Sydney B. Knight Family Grants, 2819
MacDonald-Peterson Fndn Grants, 2965
Marion I. and Henry J. Knott Fndn Discretionary Grants, 3018
Marion I. and Henry J. Knott Standard Grants, 3019
Mary's Pence Ministry Grants, 3029
Mary's Pence Study Grants, 3030
Mary E. and Michael Blevins Charitable Grants, 3037
Moran Family Fndn Grants, 3216
Pauline E. Fitzpatrick Charitable Trust, 3763
Peter and Georgia Angelos Fndn Grants, 3843
Piper Trust Reglious Organizations Grants, 3905
Raskob Fndn for Catholic Activities Grants, 4019
Richard D. Bass Fndn Grants, 4079
Sage Fndn Grants, 4204
Shirley W. & William L. Griffin Grants, 4345
Strake Fndn Grants, 4511
T. James Kavanagh Fndn Grants, 4545
Thomas and Dorothy Leavey Fndn Grants, 4612
Tyler Aaron Bookman Memorial Fndn Grants, 4684
William H. Hannon Fndn Grants, 5086
William S. Abell Fndn Grants, 5094

Cerebral Palsy
Austin S. Nelson Fndn Grants, 617
CFFVR Robert and Patricia Endries Family Fndn Grants, 1018
Circle K Corp Contributions Grants, 1136
F.M. Kirby Fndn Grants, 1780
Robert R. Meyer Fndn Grants, 4121

Cervical Cancer
GNOF IMPACT Harold W. Newman, Jr. Charitable Grants, 2083
Seattle Fndn Medical Funds Grants, 4329

Chamber Music
ACMP Fndn Community Music Grants, 130
Ann Arbor Area Community Fndn Grants, 474
Bay and Paul Fndns Grants, 693
Clarence E. Heller Charitable Fndn Grants, 1150
Columbus Fndn Small Grants, 1232
Florida Div of Cultural Affairs Music Grants, 1859
Illinois Arts Council Music Grants, 2474
Massachusetts Cultural Adams Arts Grants, 3052
National Endowment for Arts Music Grants, 3266
NYSCA Music Community Schools Grants, 3605
NYSCA Music Gen Program Support Grants, 3607
PennPAT Strategic Opportunity Grants, 3815

Charter Schools
Achelis Fndn Grants, 127
ALA Coretta Scott King Book Donation Grant, 261
Bodman Fndn Grants, 807
GNOF IMPACT Grants for Educ, 2079
GNOF Jefferson Community Grants, 2085

Luther I. Replogle Fndn Grants, 2945
Meyer Fndn Educ Grants, 3142
NYSCA Arts Educ: K-12 In-School Grants, 3580
VSA/Metlife Connect All Grants, 4953

Chemical Engineering
AIChE Women's Committee Mentorship Excellence Award, 209
American Chemical Society Award for Team Innovation, 423
Dorr Fndn Grants, 1591
James T. Grady-James H. Stack Award for Interpreting Chemistry for the Public, 2638
Lubrizol Fndn Grants, 2933

Chemical Physics
American Chemical Society Award for Team Innovation, 423

Chemical Sciences
ACS Award for Encouraging Disadvantaged Students into Careers in the Chemical Sciences, 132
ACS Award for Encouraging Women into Careers in the Chemical Sciences, 133
American Chemical Society Award for Team Innovation, 423

Chemistry
American Chemical Society Award for Team Innovation, 423
American Chemical Society Chemical Technology Partnership Mini Grants, 424
American Chemical Society Corp Associates Seed Grants, 425
Award for Volunteer Service to the American Chemical Society, 626
Canada-U.S. Fulbright Mid-Career Grants, 917
James T. Grady-James H. Stack Award for Interpreting Chemistry for the Public, 2638
Lubrizol Fndn Grants, 2933
Marion I. and Henry J. Knott Standard Grants, 3019
Millipore Fndn Grants, 3182
North Carolina GlaxoSmithKline Fndn Grants, 3490

Chemistry Education
American Chemical Society Assoc Seed Grants, 425
Dorr Fndn Grants, 1591
FMC Fndn Grants, 1876
George I. Alden Grants, 2023
North Carolina GlaxoSmithKline Fndn Grants, 3490

Child Abuse
ACF Native American Social and Economic Development Strategies Grants, 123
A Glimmer of Hope Fndn Grants, 200
Albert and Bessie Mae Kronkosky Grants, 339
Arizona Republic Fndn Grants, 546
Arizona Republic Newspaper Contributions, 547
Austin S. Nelson Fndn Grants, 617
Baxter Int'l Fndn Grants, 691
Burton G. Bettingen Grants, 871
Carl B. and Florence E. King Fndn Grants, 928
Carl C. Icahn Fndn Grants, 929
CFFVR Schmidt Family G4 Grants, 1020
Charles H. Hall Fndn, 1044
Charles Lafitte Fndn Grants, 1049
Cleveland-Cliffs Fndn Grants, 1165
Community Fndn for Greater New Haven Women & Girls Grants, 1254
ConocoPhillips Fndn Grants, 1354
Covenant to Care for Children Grants, 1389
Dade Community Fndn Grants, 1430
Delaware Community Fndn-Youth Philanthropy Board for Kent County, 1483
Detroit Lions Charities Grants, 1520
DHHS Promoting Safe & Stable Families Grants, 1537
DOJ Children's Justice Act Partnership for Indian Communities, 1555
DOJ Internet Crimes against Children Task Force Grants, 1558

Child Development / 827

DOJ Rural Domestic Violence and Child Victimization Enforcement Grants, 1562
Doris and Victor Day Fndn Grants, 1582
Doris Duke Charitable Fndn Child Abuse Prevention Grants, 1585
Duke Endowment Child Care Grants, 1617
Elkhart County Comm Elkhart County Grants, 1683
Elliot Fndn Inc Grants, 1686
Fassino Fndn Grants, 1793
Faye McBeath Fndn Grants, 1794
Green Bay Packers Fndn Grants, 2148
Hasbro Children's Fund, 2256
Hawai'i Children's Trust Fund Community Awareness Events Grants, 2258
Hearst Fndns Social Service Grants, 2285
Herbert A. and Adrian W. Woods Fndn Grants, 2313
Hoglund Fndn Grants, 2344
Huie-Dellmon Grants, 2386
Initiaive Fndn Inside-Out Connections Grants, 2556
James R. Thorpe Fndn Grants, 2636
Jane Bradley Pettit Fndn Community and Social Development Grants, 2642
Jim Moran Fndn Grants, 2680
John W. Speas and Effie E. Speas Grants, 2732
Katharine Matthies Fndn Grants, 2788
Kenny's Kids Grants, 2803
Linford and Mildred White Charitable Grants, 2909
Maine State Troopers Fndn Grants, 2991
McCarthy Family Fndn Grants, 3073
McGregor Grants, 3082
Meyer Fndn Healthy Communities Grants, 3143
Oak Fndn Child Abuse Grants, 3632
Olga Sipolin Children's Grants, 3668
Patrick and Aimee Butler Family Fndn Community Human Services Grants, 3749
Peacock Fndn Grants, 3809
Questar Corp Contributions Grants, 3997
RadioShack StreetSentz Community Grants, 4005
Reynolds and Reynolds Associate Fndn Grants, 4069
Richard and Caroline T. Gwathmey Grants, 4075
Robert R. McCormick Tribune Comm Grants, 4119
Robert R. Meyer Fndn Grants, 4121
Seybert Inst for Poor Boys and Girls Grants, 4338
Southbury Community Trust Fund, 4409
Target Corp Local Store Grants, 4561
Topfer Family Fndn Grants, 4646

Child Care
Alexander and Margaret Stewart Grants, 354
Allan C. and Leila J. Garden Fndn Grants, 374
Arizona Republic Newspaper Contributions, 547
Child Care Center Enhancement Grants, 1105
Collective Brands Fndn Payless Gives Shoes 4 Kids Grants, 1207
Frank Loomis Palmer Grants, 1931
GNOF Stand Up For Our Children Grants, 2093
Init Fndn Minnesota Early Childhood Grants, 2560
Leo Goodwin Fndn Grants, 2882
Linden Fndn Grants, 2908
Marion and Miriam Rose Grants, 3015
Medtronic Fndn Community Link Human Services Grants, 3112
Perkins-Ponder Fndn Grants, 3822
Phi Upsilon Omicron Frances Morton Holbrook Alumni Award, 3878
Piper Trust Children Grants, 3901
Saint Paul Fndn Community Sharing Grants, 4218
Seattle Fndn C. Keith Birkenfeld Grants, 4323
U.S. Bank Fndn Grants, 4686
Union Bank, N.A. Fndn Grants, 4709
WCI Childcare Capacity Grants, 5007
WCI Family Econ Success Local Impact Grants, 5010
WCI Family Econ Success Regionwide Grants, 5011

Child Development
Bernard and Audre Rapoport Fndn Health Grants, 738
Frank M. Tait Fndn Grants, 1932
Init Fndn Minnesota Early Childhood Grants, 2560
Kalamazoo Community Fndn Youth Development Grants, 2773

Mericos Fndn Grants, 3121
Peter and Elizabeth C. Tower Fndn Social and Emotional Preschool Curriculum Grants, 3841
Piper Trust Healthcare & Med Research Grants, 3903
Southern Minnesota Init Fndn AmeriCorps Leap Grants, 4431
Southern Minnesota Init Fndn Incentive Grants, 4435
Vanderburgh Community Fndn Grants, 4902
WCI Childcare Capacity Grants, 5007

Child Psychology/Development
ACF Head Start and Early Head Start Grants, 120
AON Fndn Grants, 491
Carnegie Corp of New York Grants, 940
Charles Hayden Fndn Grants, 1048
Chicago Board of Trade Fndn Grants, 1079
Colorado Interstate Gas Grants, 1213
Community Fndn of Greater New Britain Grants, 1291
Community Fnd Virgin Isls Kimelman Grants, 1324
Connecticut Community Fndn Grants, 1350
CUNA Mutual Group Fndn Grants, 1417
CVS All Kids Can Grants, 1420
Dept of Ed Parental Info and Resource Centers, 1510
DHHS Emergency Med Services for Children, 1531
Effie and Wofford Cain Fndn Grants, 1674
FCD Child Development Grants, 1796
Fndn for Seacoast Health Grants, 1895
George Family Fndn Grants, 2017
Harold Simmons Fndn Grants, 2230
Helen Bader Fndn Grants, 2293
Henrietta Tower Wurts Memorial Fndn Grants, 2304
Hoglund Fndn Grants, 2344
Lawrence J. and Anne Rubenstein Charitable Fndn Grants, 2868
Mericos Fndn Grants, 3121
Mimi and Peter Haas Grants, 3185
Pasadena Fndn Average Grants, 3741
Philip L. Graham Grants, 3876
Piper Jaffray Fndn Communities Giving Grants, 3899
Robert and Polly Dunn Fndn Grants, 4105
Saint Paul Companies Fndn Grants, 4217
Salem Fndn Charitable Grants, 4223
Sara Lee Fndn Grants, 4296
Seabury Fndn Grants, 4316

Child Sexual Abuse
A Glimmer of Hope Fndn Grants, 200
Austin S. Nelson Fndn Grants, 617
CFFVR Schmidt Family G4 Grants, 1020
DOJ Children's Justice Act Partnership for Indian Communities, 1555
DOJ Internet Crimes against Children Task Force Grants, 1558
Doris Duke Charitable Fndn Child Abuse Prevention Grants, 1585
Hawai'i Children's Trust Fund Community Awareness Events Grants, 2258
Hearst Fndns Social Service Grants, 2285
Ms. Fndn for Women Ending Violence Grants, 3224
Oak Fndn Child Abuse Grants, 3632
Patrick and Aimee Butler Family Fndn Community Human Services Grants, 3749
Reynolds and Reynolds Associate Fndn Grants, 4069
Robert R. Meyer Fndn Grants, 4121

Child Welfare
3 Roots Fndn Grants, 10
1104 Fndn Grants, 34
ACF Adoption Opportunities Project Grants, 113
Agnes M. Lindsay Grants, 203
A Good Neighbor Fndn Grants, 204
Albert and Bessie Mae Kronkosky Charitable Fndn Grants, 339
Alex Stern Family Fndn Grants, 360
Allen P. and Josephine B. Green Fndn Grants, 380
Alliance Healthcare Fndn Grants, 383
Anne L. and George H. Clapp Ed Grants, 476
Annie E. Casey Fndn Grants, 481
Baltimore Community Fndn Youth Path Grants, 649
Baton Rouge Area Fndn Every Kid a King Grants, 681
Bernard and Audre Rapoport Fndn Health Grants, 738
Blum-Kovler Fndn Grants, 803
Bodenwein Public Benevolent Fndn Grants, 806
Bodman Fndn Grants, 807
Brett Family Fndn Grants, 833
Brookdale Fndn Relatives as Parents Grants, 846
Brooklyn Benevolent Society Grants, 847
Burton G. Bettingen Grants, 871
Caleb C. and Julia W. Dula Ed and Charitable Fndn Grants, 893
Carl B. and Florence E. King Fndn Grants, 928
Carl C. Icahn Fndn Grants, 929
Carls Fndn Grants, 937
Carolyn Fndn Grants, 942
Carrie Estelle Doheny Fndn Grants, 945
Chapin Hall Int'l Fellowships in Children's Policy Research, 1032
Charles Lafitte Fndn Grants, 1049
CICF Christmas Fund, 1117
Clara Abbott Fndn Need-Based Grants, 1146
Colonel Stanley R. McNeil Fndn Grants, 1210
Colorado Springs Community Grants, 1215
Columbus Fndn Siemer Family Grants, 1231
Community Fndn for Muskegon County Grants, 1256
ConocoPhillips Grants, 1355
Corina Higginson Grants, 1373
Cumberland Community Fndn Grants, 1413
D. W. McMillan Fndn Grants, 1426
Dade Community Fndn Safe Passage Grants, 1431
Daniels Grants, 1443
Dave Thomas Fndn for Adoption Grants, 1449
Detlef Schrempf Fndn Grants, 1519
DHHS Abandoned Infants Assistance Grants, 1523
DHHS Welfare Reform Research, Evaluations, and National Studies Grants, 1540
Dorothea Haus Ross Fndn Grants, 1587
Dr. P. Phillips Fndn Grants, 1601
Duke Endowment Child Care Grants, 1617
Edward and Ellen Roche Relief Fndn Grants, 1663
Greygates Fndn Grants, 2164
Hawaii Community Fndn Reverend Takie Okumura Family Grants, 2264
Helen V. Brach Fndn Grants, 2300
Hoblitzelle Fndn Grants, 2341
Huffy Fndn Grants, 2384
IREX Small Grant Fund for Civil Society Projects in Africa and Asia, 2581
J.W. Kieckhefer Fndn Grants, 2607
Janirve Fndn Grants, 2645
John H. and Wilhelmina D. Harland Grants, 2698
John I. Smith Charities Grants, 2700
Josephine Goodyear Fndn Grants, 2738
Kaneta Fndn Grants, 2774
Katherine John Murphy Fndn Grants, 2790
Kathryne Beynon Fndn Grants, 2791
Kenny's Kids Grants, 2803
L. W. Pierce Family Fndn Grants, 2846
Lettie Pate Evans Fndn Grants, 2887
Lucile Horton Howe & Mitchell B. Howe Grants, 2934
Lucy Gooding Charitable Fndn Trust, 2936
Nuffield Fndn Children and Families Grants, 3533
Oak Fndn Child Abuse Grants, 3632
Oakland Fund for Children and Youth Grants, 3634
Ober Kaler Community Grants, 3635
Olga Sipolin Children's Grants, 3668
OneFamily Fndn Grants, 3673
Orchard Fndn Grants, 3690
Piper Trust Children Grants, 3901
RadioShack StreetSentz Community Grants, 4005
Robert R. McCormick Tribune Comm Grants, 4119
Ruth Eleanor Bamberger and John Ernest Bamberger Memorial Fndn Grants, 4178
Scott B. and Annie P. Appleby Charitable Grants, 4313
Stackpole-Hall Fndn Grants, 4472
Stuart Fndn Grants, 4516
Victoria and Bradley Geist Enhancement Grants, 4935
W. C. Griffith Fndn Grants, 4958
W.H. and Mary Ellen Cobb Charitable Grants, 4959
W.K. Kellogg Fndn Secure Families Grants, 4963
Walt Disney Company Fndn Grants, 4981

Child/Maternal Health
AAP Community Access To Child Health Advocacy Training Grants, 62
AAP Community Access to Child Health Planning Grants, 64
AAP Community Access To Child Health Residency Training Grants, 65
AAP Community Access To Child Health Resident Grants, 66
AAP Leonard P. Rome Community Access to Child Health Visiting Professorships, 67
Abbott Fund Access to Health Care Grants, 80
AEGON Transamerica Health & Welfare Grants, 179
Albert and Bessie Mae Kronkosky Charitable Fndn Grants, 339
Alcatel-Lucent Technologies Fndn Grants, 349
Batchelor Fndn Grants, 679
BCBSNC Fndn Grants, 712
Bernard and Audre Rapoport Fndn Health Grants, 738
Blackford County Community WOW Grants, 779
Blowitz-Ridgeway Fndn Grants, 792
California Endowment Innovative Ideas Grants, 904
CDC State and Local Childhood Lead Poisoning Prevention Grants, 976
CFFVR Schmidt Family G4 Grants, 1020
Chapin Hall Int'l Fellowships in Children's Policy Research, 1032
Charles H. Dater Fndn Grants, 1042
Cleveland Browns Fndn Grants, 1166
Community Fndn for Greater New Haven Women & Girls Grants, 1254
Community Fndn of Bloomington and Monroe County - Precision Health Network Cycle Grants, 1270
Community Fndn of Boone Cty Women's Grants, 1273
Connecticut Health Fndn Health Init Grants, 1351
Dallas Women's Fndn Grants, 1438
DHHS Emergency Med Services for Children, 1531
DHHS Health Centers Grants for Residents of Public Housing, 1533
DHHS Healthy Tomorrows Partnerships for Children Grants, 1534
DHHS Maternal and Child Health Grants, 1536
DHHS Technical and Non-Financial Assistance to Health Centers, 1539
DOI Urban Park & Rec Recovery Grants, 1554
DTE Energy Health & Human Services Grants, 1613
Edwards Grants, 1669
Edward W. and Stella C. Van Houten Grants, 1670
El Paso Community Fndn Grants, 1688
EPA Children's Health Protection Grants, 1728
F.M. Kirby Fndn Grants, 1780
Flinn Fndn Grants, 1842
Fndn for Seacoast Health Grants, 1895
Frances and John L. Loeb Family Grants, 1917
Gibson County Community Fndn Women's Fund, 2051
GlaxoSmithKline Corp Grants, 2060
GNOF Stand Up For Our Children Grants, 2093
Healthcare Fndn of New Jersey Grants, 2280
Health Fndn of Greater Cincinnati Grants, 2281
Health Fndn of Greater Indianapolis Grants, 2282
Hoglund Fndn Grants, 2344
Jane Bradley Pettit Fndn Health Grants, 2643
Jewish Grants, 2675
Johnson & Johnson Comm Health Care Grants, 2717
Johnson & Johnson Corp Contributions Grants, 2718
Kaiser Permanente Cares for Comm Grants, 2763
Kansas Health Fndn Recognition Grants, 2784
Ken W. Davis Fndn Grants, 2813
Long Island Community Fndn Grants, 2920
Lowe Fndn Grants, 2929
Mary Black Fndn Active Living Grants, 3031
Medicaid/SCHIP Eligibility Pilots, 3107
Medtronic Fndn Patient Link Grants, 3113
Michael Reese Health Trust Responsive Grants, 3160
Mid-Iowa Health Fndn Comm Response Grants, 3168
Nestle Health Training Grant, 3301
Oakland Fund for Children and Youth Grants, 3634
PACCAR Fndn Grants, 3719
Pajaro Valley Community Health Trust Insurance/ Coverage & Educ on Using the System Grants, 3731

SUBJECT INDEX

Children and Youth / 829

Porter County Health and Wellness Grant, 3933
Porter County Women's Grant, 3934
Premera Blue Cross CARES Grants, 3945
Prince Charitable Trusts Chicago Grants, 3959
Quantum Corp Snap Server Grants, 3995
Quantum Fndn Grants, 3996
RGK Fndn Grants, 4072
Robert R. Meyer Fndn Grants, 4121
Ronald McDonald House Charities Grants, 4149
Saigh Fndn Grants, 4210
Seattle Fndn Health and Wellness Grants, 4328
Sidgmore Family Fndn Grants, 4348
Sisters of Charity Fndn of Canton Grants, 4372
Stewart Huston Charitable Grants, 4505
TJX Fndn Grants, 4637
Topfer Family Fndn Grants, 4646
USAID/Cambodia Maternal and Child Health, Tuberculosis, HIV/AIDS. and Malaria Grants, 4736
USAID Family Health Plus Project Grants, 4751
USAID Implementation Science for Strengthening Use of Evidence in Family Planning/Reproductive Health Programming Grants, 4758
Walt Disney Company Fndn Grants, 4981
WHO Fndn General Grants, 5063

Children and Youth
1st and 10 Fndn Grants, 1
2 Depot Square Ipswich Charitable Fndn Grants, 4
3 Roots Fndn Grants, 10
3M Company Health and Human Services Grants, 14
3M Fndn Community Giving Grants, 15
21st Century Threshold Project Gifts, 21
118 Fndn Grants, 29
1104 Fndn Grants, 34
A.C. Ratshesky Fndn Grants, 39
A.V. Hunter Grants, 47
AAF Accent on Architecture Community Grants, 58
AAP Anne E. Dyson Child Advocacy Awards, 61
Aaron Fndn Grants, 72
Abbot and Dorothy H. Stevens Fndn Grants, 79
Abbott Fund Community Grants, 81
ABC Charities Grants, 85
Abeles Fndn Grants, 89
Able To Play Challenge Grants, 101
ABS Fndn Grants, 107
Abundance Fndn Local Community Grants, 109
ACE Charitable Fndn Grants, 111
ACF ACYF Runaway and Homeless Youth Basic Center Grants, 112
ACF Adoption Opportunities Project Grants, 113
ACF Community-Based Abstinence Educ Grants, 116
ACF Fndn Grants, 119
ACF Head Start and Early Head Start Grants, 120
ACF Mentoring Children of Prisoners Grants, 121
ACF Native American Social and Economic Development Strategies Grants, 123
ACF Preferred Communities Grants, 124
ACF Supplemental Services for Recently Arrived Refugees Grants, 125
Achelis Fndn Grants, 127
A Child Waits Fndn Grants, 128
ACTION Council of Monterey County Grants, 134
Acuity Charitable Fndn Grants, 140
Adams and Reese LLP Corp Giving Grants, 147
Adams Family Fndn I Grants, 150
Adams Family Fndn of Ohio Grants, 151
Adams Rotary Memorial Fund A Grants, 157
Adelaide Breed Bayrd Fndn Grants, 161
Adelaide Christian Home For Children Grants, 162
Administaff Community Affairs Grants, 165
AEGON Transamerica Health & Welfare Grants, 179
Aetna Fndn Obesity Grants, 185
Aetna Fndn Regional Health Grants, 187
Aetna Summer Academic Enrichment Grants, 189
A Friends' Fndn Grants, 194
A Glimmer of Hope Fndn Grants, 200
Agnes M. Lindsay Grants, 203
A Good Neighbor Fndn Grants, 204
Agway Fndn Grants, 205
Ahearn Family Fndn Grants, 206

Akonadi Fndn Anti-Racism Grants, 217
Akzo Nobel Chemicals Grants, 219
ALA Baker and Taylor Conference Grants, 228
ALA Coretta Scott King Book Donation Grant, 261
ALA MAE Award for Best Teen Lit, 296
ALA Sara Jaffarian School Library Award for Exemplary Humanities Programming, 316
ALA Schneider Family Book Award, 317
ALA Scholastic Library Publishing Award, 318
ALA Sullivan Award for Administrators Supporting Services to Children, 332
Albert E. and Birdie W. Einstein Grants, 342
Albert W. Cherne Fndn Grants, 346
Albert W. Rice Charitable Fndn Grants, 347
Alcatel-Lucent Technologies Fndn Grants, 349
Alexander H. Bright Charitable Grants, 358
Alfred and Tillie Shemanski Testamentary Grants, 363
Alfred E. Chase Charitable Fndn Grants, 366
Alfred J Mcallister and Dorothy N Mcallister Fndn Grants, 367
Alice Tweed Tuohy Fndn Grants, 372
A Little Hope Grants, 373
Allan C. and Leila J. Garden Fndn Grants, 374
Alliance Healthcare Fndn Grants, 383
Alliant Energy Fndn Hometown Challenge Grants, 385
Allstate Tolerance, Inclusion, and Diversity Grants, 391
Altria Group Positive Youth Development Grants, 401
Alvah H. and Wyline P. Chapman Fndn Grants, 402
Alvin and Lucy Owsley Fndn Grants, 404
Amelia Sillman Rockwell and Carlos Perry Rockwell Charities Grants, 417
Ameren Corp Community Grants, 418
American Foodservice Charitable Grants, 433
American Savings Fndn Grants, 445
American Schlafhorst Fndn Grants, 446
Amerigroup Fndn Grants, 452
AMERIND Community Service Project Grants, 453
AmerUs Group Charitable Fndn, 455
Anderson Fndn Grants, 460
Andre Agassi Charitable Fndn Grants, 461
Andrew Family Fndn Grants, 462
Angels Baseball Fndn Grants, 465
Angels for Kids Fndn Grants, 466
Anheuser-Busch Fndn Grants, 470
ANLAF Int'l Fund for Sexual Minorities Grants, 471
Anna Fitch Ardenghi Grants, 472
Ann and Robert H. Lurie Family Fndn Grants, 473
Anne J. Caudal Fndn Grants, 475
Anne L. and George H. Clapp Charitable Grants, 476
Annenberg Fndn Grants, 477
Annie's Grants for Gardens, 480
Annie E. Casey Fndn Grants, 481
Annunziata Sanguinetti Fndn Grants, 485
Anthony R. Abraham Fndn Grants, 489
Antone & Edene Vidinha Charitable Grants, 490
Appalachian Reg Comm Health Care Grants, 507
APS Fndn Grants, 518
Aquila Corp Grants, 521
Aragona Family Fndn Grants, 522
Aratani Fndn Grants, 523
Arcadia Fndn Grants, 525
Arizona Cardinals Grants, 534
Arizona Commission on the Arts After-School Program Residencies, 535
Arizona Community Fndn Grants, 540
Arizona Diamondbacks Charities Grants, 542
Arizona Public Service Corp Giving Grants, 545
Arizona Republic Fndn Grants, 546
Arizona Republic Newspaper Contributions, 547
Arizona State Library LSTA Learning Grants, 550
Arlington Community Fndn Grants, 564
Asian American Institute Impact Fellowships, 588
Aspen Community Fndn Grants, 592
AT&T Fndn Civic and Comm Service Grants, 599
ATA Local Community Relations Grants, 600
Athwin Fndn Grants, 605
Atkinson Fndn Community Grants, 606
Atlanta Falcons Youth Fndn Grants, 607
Austin-Bailey Health and Wellness Fndn Grants, 614
Austin College Leadership Award, 615

Austin S. Nelson Fndn Grants, 617
Avon Products Fndn Grants, 625
Babcock Charitable Grants, 632
Back Home Again Fndn Grants, 633
Bailey Fndn Grants, 635
Baltimore Community Fndn Arts and Culture Path Grants, 641
Baltimore Community Fndn Children's Fresh Air Society Grants, 642
Baltimore Community Fndn Youth Path Grants, 649
BancorpSouth Fndn Grants, 651
Banfield Charitable Grants, 652
BankAtlantic Fndn Grants, 654
Bank of America Charitable Fndn Critical Needs Grants, 656
Bank of America Charitable Fndn Matching Gifts, 658
Bank of America Corp Sponsorships, 661
Baptist Community Ministries Grants, 664
Barberton Community Fndn Grants, 666
Barker Fndn Grants, 668
Barrasso Usdin Kupperman Freeman and Sarver LLC Corp Grants, 675
Barr Fndn Grants, 677
Barr Grants, 678
Batchelor Fndn Grants, 679
Baton Rouge Area Fndn Every Kid a King Grants, 681
Batters Up USA Equipment Grants, 683
Batts Fndn Grants, 687
Baxter Int'l Fndn Grants, 691
Bay and Paul Fndns, Inc Grants, 692
BBF Florida Family Lit Init Grants, 697
BBF Maryland Family Lit Init Grants, 700
BBF Maryland Family Lit Init Planning Grants, 701
BCBSM Building Healthy Communities Elementary Schools and Community Partners Grants, 704
BCBSM Children Angel Awards, 705
BCBSM Corp Contributions Grants, 706
Bella Vista Fndn Grants, 722
Ben & Jerry's Fndn Grants, 724
Bender Fndn Grants, 726
Benton County Fndn Grants, 731
Bernard & Audre Rapoport Arts & Culture Grant, 735
Bernard and Audre Rapoport Fndn Health Grants, 738
Bernard F. Reynolds Charitable Grants, 741
Berrien Community Fndn Grants, 744
Bikes Belong Fndn Paul David Clark Bicycling Safety Grants, 760
Bikes Belong Fndn REI Grants, 761
Bill and Melinda Gates Fndn Water, Sanitation and Hygiene Grants, 770
Birmingham Fndn Grants, 774
Bitha Godfrey & Maude J. Thomas Charitable Fndn Grants, 776
BJ's Charitable Fndn Grants, 777
BJ's Wholesale Clubs Local Charitable Giving, 778
Blackford County Community WOW Grants, 779
Blackford County Community Fndn Grants, 780
Blanche and Irving Laurie Fndn Grants, 784
Blandin Fndn Invest Early Grants, 788
Blowitz-Ridgeway Fndn Grants, 792
Blue Cross Blue Shield of Minnesota Fndn - Healthy Children: Growing Up Healthy Grants, 794
Bodenwein Public Benevolent Fndn Grants, 806
Bodman Fndn Grants, 807
Bohemian Fndn Pharos Grants, 811
Booth-Bricker Grants, 815
Borkee-Hagley Fndn Grants, 817
Boston Globe Fndn Grants, 821
Bradley-Turner Fndn Grants, 828
Brett Family Fndn Grants, 833
Brian G. Dyson Fndn Grants, 834
Bright Family Fndn Grants, 837
Brookdale Fndn Relatives as Parents Grants, 846
Brooklyn Community Caring Neighbors Grants, 848
Brooklyn Community Fndn Community Arts for All Grants, 849
Brooklyn Community Fndn Educ and Youth Achievement Grants, 851
Brooklyn Community Green Communities Grants, 852
Brown Fndn Grants, 854

Bryan Adams Fndn Grants, 858
Build-A-Bear Workshop Bear Hugs Fndn Lit and Educ Grants, 860
Build-A-Bear Workshop Fndn Grants, 861
Bunbury Company Grants, 863
Burden Grants, 864
Burlington Industries Fndn Grants, 865
Burning Fndn Grants, 867
Burton G. Bettingen Grants, 871
Business Wire Lit Init, 880
C.F. Adams Charitable Grants, 884
Caesars Fndn Grants, 891
Cailloux Fndn Grants, 892
California Arts Council Arts and Accessibility Technical Assistance Grants, 894
California Arts Council Public Value Grants, 895
California Community Fndn Art Grants, 900
California Pizza Kitchen Fndn Grants, 907
Callaway Golf Company Fndn Grants, 910
Cal Ripken Sr. Fndn Grants, 912
Cambridge Community Fndn Grants, 913
Campbell Soup Fndn Grants, 916
Capital City Bank Group Fndn Grants, 920
Captain Planet Fndn Grants, 922
Caring Fndn Grants, 926
Carl B. and Florence E. King Fndn Grants, 928
Carlisle Fndn Grants, 931
Carlos and Marguerite Mason Grants, 934
Carls Fndn Grants, 937
Carl W. and Carrie Mae Joslyn Grants, 938
Carolyn Fndn Grants, 942
Carpenter Fndn Grants, 943
Carrie E. and Lena V. Glenn Fndn Grants, 944
Carrie Estelle Doheny Grants, 945
Carroll County Community Fndn Grants, 947
Case Fndn Grants, 950
Castle and Cooke California Corp Giving Grants, 953
CCF Community Priorities Fund, 961
CDC Grants for Violence-Related Injury Prevention Research, 974
Cemala Fndn Grants, 988
Central Okanagan Fndn Grants, 997
Cessna Fndn Grants, 1000
CFFVR Basic Needs Giving Partnership Grants, 1002
CFFVR Clintonville Area Fndn Grants, 1007
CFFVR Frank C. Shattuck Community Grants, 1012
CFFVR Infant Welfare Circle of Kings Daughters Grants, 1013
CFFVR Mielke Family Fndn Grants, 1015
CFFVR Myra M. and Robert L. Vandehey Fndn Grants, 1016
CFFVR Project Grants, 1017
CFFVR Robert and Patricia Endries Family Fndn Grants, 1018
CFFVR Schmidt Family G4 Grants, 1020
CFFVR Shawano Area Community Fndn Grants, 1021
CFFVR Women's Fund for the Fox Valley Region Grants, 1025
Chamberlain Fndn Grants, 1027
Champ-A Champion Fur Kids Grants, 1028
Chapin Hall Int'l Fellowships in Children's Policy Research, 1032
Chapman Charitable Fndn Grants, 1033
Chapman Family Charitable Grants, 1034
Charity Incorporated Grants, 1035
CharityWorks Grants, 1036
Charles and Lynn Schusterman Family Grants, 1038
Charles Delmar Fndn Grants, 1039
Charles H. Dater Fndn Grants, 1042
Charles H. Hall Fndn, 1044
Charles H. Pearson Fndn Grants, 1045
Charles Hayden Fndn Grants, 1048
Charles Lafitte Fndn Grants, 1049
Charles Stewart Mott Fndn Grants, 1055
Charlotte R. Schmidlapp Grants, 1058
Chautauqua Region Community Fndn Grants, 1062
CHC Fndn Grants, 1065
Chesapeake Bay Environmental Ed Grants, 1069
Chicago Board of Trade Fndn Grants, 1079
Chicago Tribune Fndn Grants for Cultural Organizations, 1101
Chick and Sophie Major Memorial Duck Calling Contest Scholarships, 1103
Child's Dream Grants, 1104
Children Affected by AIDS Network Grants, 1106
Children Affected by AIDS Fndn Family Assistance Emergency Grants, 1107
Christine and Katharina Pauly Charitable Grants, 1114
Chula Vista Charitable Fndn Grants, 1116
CICF Howard Intermill and Marion Intermill Fenstermaker Grants, 1122
CICF Indianapolis Fndn Community Grants, 1123
CICF John H. Brown & Robert Burse Grant, 1125
CICF Summer Youth Grants, 1128
Cingular Wireless Charitable Contributions, 1134
Circle K Corp Contributions Grants, 1136
CIT Corp Giving Grants, 1138
Citizens Bank Mid-Atlantic Charitable Grants, 1140
Citizens Savings Fndn Grants, 1141
Clara Abbott Fndn Need-Based Grants, 1146
Claremont Community Fndn Grants, 1149
Clark-Winchcole Fndn Grants, 1152
Clark Fndn Grants, 1157
Clayton Baker Grants, 1163
Cleo Fndn Grants, 1164
Cleveland Browns Fndn Grants, 1166
CLIF Bar Family Fndn Grants, 1173
Clipper Ship Fndn Grants, 1175
Clorox Company Fndn Grants, 1176
CNA Fndn Grants, 1179
CNCS AmeriCorps State and National Grants, 1182
CNCS Foster Grandparent Grants, 1185
CNCS Social Innovation Grants, 1189
Coeta and Donald Barker Fndn Grants, 1197
Collective Brands Fndn Grants, 1206
Collective Brands Fndn Payless Gives Shoes 4 Kids Grants, 1207
Colonel Stanley R. McNeil Fndn Grants, 1210
Columbus Fndn Paul G. Duke Grants, 1227
Columbus Fndn Siemer Family Grants, 1231
Columbus Fndn Traditional Grants, 1233
Comer Fndn Grants, 1236
Commonweal Community Assistance Grants, 1239
Commonwealth Fund Harkness Fellowships in Health Care Policy and Practice, 1242
Communities Fndn of Texas Grants, 1243
Community Fndn for Greater Buffalo Grants, 1247
Community Fndn for Greater New Haven Women & Girls Grants, 1254
Community Fndn for Muskegon County Grants, 1256
Community Fndn for San Benito County Grants, 1258
Community Fndn for Southern Arizona Grants, 1261
Community Fndn of Abilene Future Grants, 1265
Community Fndn of Bloomington and Monroe County Grants, 1271
Community Fndn of Broward Grants, 1275
Community Fndn of Grant County Grants, 1279
Community Fndn Greater Chattanooga Grants, 1281
Community Fndn of Greater Flint Grants, 1282
Community Fndn of Greater Fort Wayne - Edna Fndn Grants, 1286
Community Fndn Of Greater Lafayette Grants, 1289
Community Fndn of Greater Memphis Grants, 1290
Community Fndn of Greater New Britain Grants, 1291
Community Fndn of Greater Tampa Grants, 1292
Community Fndn of Louisville Grants, 1299
Community Fndn of Mount Vernon and Knox County Grants, 1301
Community Fndn of Muncie and Delaware County Maxon Grants, 1303
Community Fndn of Riverside County Grants, 1304
Community Fndn of Santa Cruz County Grants, 1305
Community Fndn of Shreveport-Bossier Grants, 1307
Community Fndn of SE Connecticut Grants, 1309
Community Fndn of the Eastern Shore Youth Fndn Grants, 1319
Community Fndn of the Verdugos Ed Endowment Grants, 1321
Community Fndn of Virgin Islands Anderson Family Teacher Grants, 1323
Community Fnd Virgin Isls Kimelman Grants, 1324
Community Fndn of Virgin Islands Mini Grants, 1325
Community Fndn of Western N Carolina Grants, 1327
Community Partners Lawrence County Grants, 1328
Community Impact Fund, 1332
Comprehensive Health Educ Fndn Grants, 1337
ConAgra Foods Community Impact Grants, 1342
ConAgra Foods Nourish Our Comm Grants, 1343
Con Edison Corp Giving Civic Grants, 1345
Constellation Energy Corp Grants, 1364
Conwood Charitable Grants, 1366
Corina Higginson Grants, 1373
Covenant to Care for Children Critical Grants, 1388
Covenant to Care for Children Grants, 1389
Crail-Johnson Fndn Grants, 1393
Cralle Fndn Grants, 1394
Credit Suisse First Boston Fndn Grants, 1397
CSRA Community Fndn Grants, 1407
CSX Corp Contributions Grants, 1408
CTCNet/Youth Visions for Stronger Neighborhoods Grants, 1409
Cudd Fndn Grants, 1410
Cumberland Community Fndn Grants, 1413
Cumberland Community Fndn Summertime Kids Grants, 1414
CVS Community Grants, 1422
Cyrus Eaton Fndn Grants, 1423
D.V. and Ida J. McEachern Charitable Grants, 1425
D. W. McMillan Fndn Grants, 1426
Dade Community Fndn GLBT Grants, 1429
Dade Community Fndn Grants, 1430
Dade Community Fndn Safe Passage Grants, 1431
Dairy Queen Corp Contributions Grants, 1433
Daisy Marquis Jones Fndn Grants, 1434
Dallas Mavericks Fndn Grants, 1437
Dammann Grants, 1439
Danellie Fndn Grants, 1442
Daphne Seybolt Culpeper Memorial Fndn Grants, 1445
Darden Restaurants Fndn Grants, 1446
Dave Coy Fndn Grants, 1447
Dave Thomas Fndn for Adoption Grants, 1449
David and Barbara B. Hirschhorn Fndn Grants, 1450
Daviess County Community Fndn Youth Development Grants, 1460
Daywood Fndn Grants, 1465
DB Americas Fndn Grants, 1466
Deaconess Community Fndn Grants, 1467
Deaconess Fndn Advocacy Grants, 1468
Dearborn Community Fndn City of Lawrenceburg Youth Grants, 1472
Deborah Munroe Noonan Grants, 1475
Decatur County Community Fndn Small Project Grants, 1477
Dekko Fndn Grants, 1482
Delaware Community Fndn-Youth Philanthropy Board for Kent County, 1483
Delaware Community Fund For Women Grants, 1484
Delaware Community Next Generation Grants, 1485
Delaware Community Fndn Youth Philanthropy Board for New Castle County Grants, 1486
Dell Fndn Open Grants, 1490
Dennis and Phyllis Washington Fndn Grants, 1498
Denver Fndn Community Grants, 1502
Denver Fndn Social Venture Partners Grants, 1503
Dept of Ed Safe and Drug-Free Schools and Communities State Grants, 1513
Dept of Ed Workplace & Comm Transition Training for Incarcerated Youth Offenders, 1515
Dermody Properties Fndn Capstone Award, 1516
Dermody Properties Fndn Grants, 1517
Detlef Schrempf Fndn Grants, 1519
Deuce McAllister Catch 22 Fndn Grants, 1521
DHHS Abandoned Infants Assistance Grants, 1523
DHHS American Recovery and Reinvestment Act of 2009 Head Start Expansion, 1526
DHHS Community Services Block Grant Training and Technical Assistance Program: Capacity-Building

for Ongoing CSBG Programs and Strategic Planning and Coordination Grants, 1529
DHHS Comprehensive Community Mental Health Services Grants for Children with Serious Emotional Disturbances, 1530
DHHS Emergency Med Services for Children, 1531
DHHS Healthy Tomorrows Partnerships for Children Grants, 1534
DOI Urban Park & Rec Recovery Grants, 1554
Dole Food Company Charitable Contributions, 1564
Dolfinger-McMahon Fndn Grants, 1565
DOL Youthbuild Grants, 1571
Donald W. Reynolds Fndn Children's Discovery Init Grants, 1576
Donald W. Reynolds Fndn Special Grants, 1577
Donnie Avery Catches for Kids Fndn, 1578
Dora Roberts Fndn Grants, 1579
Dorothea Haus Ross Fndn Grants, 1587
Douty Fndn Grants, 1595
Dr. John T. Macdonald Fndn Grants, 1600
Dr. P. Phillips Fndn Grants, 1601
Dr. Scholl Fndn Grants, 1602
Dreyer's Fndn Large Grants, 1606
DTE Energy Fndn Leadership Grants, 1614
Duke Endowment Child Care Grants, 1617
Dwight Stuart Youth Capacity-Building Grants, 1627
Dwight Stuart Youth Fndn Grants, 1628
Dyson Mid-Hudson Valley Project Support, 1636
E.L. Wiegand Fndn Grants, 1639
East Tennessee Fndn Grants, 1646
eBay Fndn Community Grants, 1648
Eckerd Family Fndn Grants, 1651
Eddy Knight Family Fndn Grants, 1654
Edina Realty Fndn Grants, 1656
Edna McConnell Clark Fndn Grants, 1659
Edna Wardlaw Charitable Grants, 1660
Edward and Ellen Roche Relief Fndn Grants, 1663
Edward and Helen Bartlett Fndn Grants, 1664
Edward S. Moore Fndn Grants, 1668
Edwards Grants, 1669
Edward W. and Stella C. Van Houten Grants, 1670
Edyth Bush Charitable Fndn Grants, 1673
Eisner Fndn Grants, 1678
Elizabeth Carse Fndn Grants, 1681
Elizabeth Morse Genius Charitable Grants, 1682
Ellen Abbott Gilman Grants, 1685
Elliot Fndn Inc Grants, 1686
El Paso Community Fndn Grants, 1688
Elsie H. Wilcox Fndn Grants, 1691
Elsie Lee Garthwaite Memorial Fndn Grants, 1692
EMC Corp Grants, 1693
Emerson Kampen Fndn Grants, 1696
Emma B. Howe Memorial Fndn Grants, 1700
Entergy Corp Micro Grants, 1712
Entergy Corp Open Grants for Healthy Families, 1715
EQT Fndn Educ Grants, 1745
Essex County Community Fndn Greater Lawrence Summer Grants, 1755
Essex County Community Fndn Merrimack Valley General Grants, 1756
Esther M. and Freeman E. Everett Charitable Fndn Grants, 1757
Ethel Sergeant Clark Smith Fndn Grants, 1761
Eugene McDermott Fndn Grants, 1765
Eulalie Bloedel Schneider Fndn Grants, 1767
Evanston Community Fndn Grants, 1771
Ezra M. Cutting Grants, 1779
F.R. Bigelow Fndn Grants, 1781
Fairfield County Community Fndn Grants, 1782
Fallon OrNda Community Health Grants, 1783
FAR Grants, 1787
Fargo-Moorhead Area Fndn Grants, 1788
Fargo-Moorhead Area Fndn Woman's Grants, 1789
Fassino Fndn Grants, 1793
Faye McBeath Fndn Grants, 1794
Fayette County Community Fndn Grants, 1795
FCD Child Development Grants, 1796
Federal Express Corp Contributions Program, 1799
Ferree Fndn Grants, 1804
Finish Line Youth Fndn Founder's Grants, 1812

Finish Line Youth Fndn Grants, 1813
Finish Line Youth Fndn Legacy Grants, 1814
Firelight Fndn Grants, 1817
Florence Hunt Maxwell Fndn Grants, 1844
Florida BRAIVE Fund of Dade Community, 1846
Florida Sports Fndn Junior Golf Grants, 1872
Floyd A. and Kathleen C. Cailloux Fndn Grants, 1874
Foellinger Fndn Grants, 1877
Ford Family Fndn Grants - Positive Youth Development, 1880
Ford Family Fndn Grants - Technical Assistance, 1882
Forest Fndn Grants, 1886
Foster Fndn Grants, 1888
Fndn for Appalachian Ohio Access to Environmental Educ Mini-Grants, 1892
Foundation for Young Australians Indigenous Small Grants, 1901
Foundation for Young Australians Spark Grants, 1902
Foundation for Young Australians Your Eyes Only Awards, 1903
Foundation for Young Australians Change Grants, 1904
Foundation for Young Australians Youth Led Futures Grants, 1905
Fndns of E Chicago Family Support Grants, 1908
Fndns of E Chicago Youth Development Grants, 1912
Fourjay Fndn Grants, 1913
Four Times Fndn Grants, 1914
Frances L. and Edwin L. Cummings Grants, 1919
Francis Beidler Fndn Grants, 1921
Francis L. Abreu Charitable Grants, 1922
Francis T. & Louise T. Nichols Fndn Grants, 1923
Frank B. Hazard General Charity Grants, 1926
Frank E. and Seba B. Payne Fndn Grants, 1927
Frank M. Tait Fndn Grants, 1932
Frank Reed and Margaret Jane Peters Memorial Fund I Grants, 1933
Frank Reed and Margaret Jane Peters Memorial Fund II Grants, 1934
Frank S. Flowers Fndn Grants, 1935
Frank Stanley Beveridge Fndn Grants, 1936
Fred Baldwin Memorial Fndn Grants, 1941
Fred C. and Katherine B. Andersen Fndn Grants, 1942
Freddie Mac Fndn Grants, 1944
Frederick McDonald Grants, 1946
Frederick S. Upton Fndn Grants, 1947
Frederick W. Marzahl Grants, 1948
Fred L. Emerson Fndn Grants, 1949
Fred Meyer Fndn Grants, 1950
Fremont Area Community Amazing X Grants, 1953
Fremont Area Community Fndn Grants, 1955
Fremont Area Comm Summer Youth Grants, 1956
Frey Fndn Grants, 1963
Fund for the City of New York Grants, 1978
Furth Family Fndn Grants, 1980
G.A. Ackermann Grants, 1981
Gamble Fndn Grants, 1983
Gardiner Savings Inst Charitable Fndn Grants, 1987
Gates Family Children, Youth & Family Grants, 1989
GCI Corp Contributions Grants, 1994
Gebbie Fndn Grants, 1995
GEF Green Thumb Challenge, 1996
Gene Haas Fndn, 1999
General Mills Fndn Celebrating Communities of Color Grants, 2002
General Mills Fndn Grants, 2003
George A. Hormel Testamentary Grants, 2009
George and Ruth Bradford Fndn Grants, 2010
George A Ohl Jr. Fndn Grants, 2012
George B. Page Fndn Grants, 2013
George Fndn Grants, 2018
George H.C. Ensworth Grants, 2022
George J. and Effie L. Seay Fndn Grants, 2024
George Kress Fndn Grants, 2025
George P. Davenport Grants, 2026
George S. and Dolores Dore Eccles Fndn Grants, 2027
George W. Brackenridge Fndn Grants, 2028
George W. Codrington Charitable Fndn Grants, 2029
George W. Wells Fndn Grants, 2030
German Protestant Orphan Asylum Fndn Grants, 2044
Giant Food Charitable Grants, 2050

Gil and Dody Weaver Fndn Grants, 2053
Ginger and Barry Ackerley Fndn Grants, 2055
Ginn Fndn Grants, 2056
Gloria Barron Prize for Young Heroes, 2064
GNOF Coastal 5 + 1 Grants, 2070
GNOF Cox Charities of New Orleans Grants, 2072
GNOF Exxon-Mobil Grants, 2074
GNOF Gert Community Grants, 2076
GNOF IMPACT Grants for Youth Development, 2081
GNOF Norco Community Grants, 2089
Go Daddy Cares Charitable Contributions, 2094
Godfrey Fndn Grants, 2095
Goizueta Fndn Grants, 2096
Golden State Warriors Fndn Grants, 2099
Grable Fndn Grants, 2108
Grace and Franklin Bernsen Fndn Grants, 2109
Grace Bersted Fndn Grants, 2110
Graco Fndn Grants, 2111
Grand Circle Fndn Associates Grants, 2112
Grand Haven Area Community Fndn Grants, 2113
Grand Rapids Area Community Fndn Grants, 2114
Grand Rapids Area Community Fndn Nashwauk Area Endowment Grants, 2115
Grand Rapids Area Community Fndn Wyoming Grants, 2116
Grand Rapids Area Community Fndn Wyoming Youth Grants, 2117
Grand Rapids Community Fndn Grants, 2118
Grand Rapids Community Ionia County Grants, 2119
Grand Rapids Community SE Ottawa Grants, 2122
Grand Rapids Comm SE Ottawa Youth Grants, 2123
Grand Rapids Community Sparta Grants, 2124
Grand Rapids Community Sparta Youth Grants, 2125
Granger Fndn Grants, 2127
Greater Des Moines Fndn Grants, 2134
Greater Worcester Comm Discretionary Grants, 2140
Greater Worcester Community Jeppson Memorial Fund for Brookfield Grants, 2141
Greater Worcester Community Youth for Community Improvement Grants, 2144
Green Bay Packers Fndn Grants, 2148
Green Fndn Special Project Grants, 2155
Greenspun Family Fndn Grants, 2156
GreenWorks! Butterfly Garden Grants, 2159
Gregory L. Gibson Charitable Fndn Grants, 2163
Greygates Fndn Grants, 2164
Grotto Fndn Project Grants, 2166
Gulf Coast Community Operating Grants, 2176
Gulf Coast Fndn of Community Grants, 2177
Guy I. Bromley Grants, 2180
H.B. Fuller Company Fndn Grants, 2183
H.J. Heinz Company Fndn Grants, 2184
H. Leslie Hoffman & Elaine Hoffman Grants, 2185
Haddad Fndn Grants, 2189
HAF Community Grants, 2193
HAF Mada Huggins Caldwell Grants, 2200
HAF Summer Youth Funding Partnerships, 2205
Hagedorn Grants, 2207
Hahl Proctor Charitable Grants, 2208
Hall-Perrine Fndn Grants, 2209
Hall Family Fndn Grants, 2210
Hampton Roads Community Fndn Beach Grants, 2214
Hancock County Community Fndn - Field of Interest Grants, 2219
Harold and Arlene Schnitzer CARE Grants, 2226
Harold Brooks Fndn Grants, 2227
Harold R. Bechtel Charitable Remainder Grants, 2229
Harris and Eliza Kempner Grants, 2231
Harry B. and Jane H. Brock Fndn Grants, 2237
Harry C. Trexler Grants, 2239
Harry W. Bass, Jr. Fndn Grants, 2246
Hartford Courant Fndn Grants, 2248
Hartford Fndn Regular Grants, 2253
Harvey Randall Wickes Fndn Grants, 2255
Hasbro Children's Fund, 2256
Hawai'i Children's Trust Fund Community Awareness Events Grants, 2258
Hawaii Community Human Services Grants, 2262
Hawaii Community Fndn Reverend Takie Okumura Family Grants, 2264

832 / Children and Youth

Hazen Fndn Youth Organizing Grants, 2270
HBF Pathways Out of Poverty Grants, 2273
HCA Fndn Grants, 2274
Head Start Replacement Grantee: Colorado, 2275
Head Start Replacement Grantee: Florida, 2276
Head Start Replacement Grantee: West Virginia, 2277
Hedco Fndn Grants, 2287
Heineman Fndn for Research, Educ, Charitable and Scientific Purposes, 2290
Heinz Endowments Grants, 2291
Helena Rubinstein Fndn Grants, 2292
Helen Bader Fndn Grants, 2293
Helen Gertrude Sparks Charitable Grants, 2294
Helen S. Boylan Fndn Grants, 2298
Helen V. Brach Fndn Grants, 2300
Henrietta Tower Wurts Memorial Fndn Grants, 2304
Henry and Ruth Blaustein Rosenberg Grants, 2306
Henry County Community Fndn - TASC Youth Grants, 2307
Henry County Community Fndn Grants, 2308
Herbert A. and Adrian W. Woods Fndn Grants, 2313
Herbert H. and Grace A. Dow Fndn Grants, 2315
Herman Goldman Fndn Grants, 2317
Hershey Company Grants, 2318
Hilda and Preston Davis Fndn Grants, 2322
Hilfiger Family Fndn Grants, 2323
Hill Fndn Grants, 2326
Hillman Fndn Grants, 2327
Hilton Head Island Fndn Grants, 2330
Hilton Hotels Corp Giving Grants, 2331
Hoglund Fndn Grants, 2344
Holland/Zeeland Community Fndn Grants, 2345
Homer A. Scott and Mildred S. Scott Grants, 2350
Honeywell Family Safety and Security Grants, 2356
Horace A. Kimball and S. Ella Kimball Grants, 2362
Horizons Community Issues Grants, 2366
Household Int'l Corp Giving Grants, 2372
Howard and Bush Fndn Grants, 2374
Howard County Community Fndn Grants, 2375
Hugh J. Andersen Fndn Grants, 2385
Humana Fndn Grants, 2388
Hundred Club of Colorado Springs Grants, 2391
Hundred Club of Connecticut Grants, 2392
Hundred Club of Denver Grants, 2394
Hundred Club of Durango Grants, 2395
Hundred Club of Pueblo Grants, 2398
Huntington Fndn Grants, 2408
Huntington National Bank Comm Affairs Grant, 2409
Hutchinson Community Fndn Grants, 2410
Hut Fndn Grants, 2411
Hutton Fndn Grants, 2412
Hyams Fndn Grants, 2413
Illinois Tool Works Fndn Grants, 2511
Impact 100 Grants, 2522
Independent Community Fndn Neighborhood Renewal Grants, 2527
ING Fndn Grants, 2555
Initaive Fndn Inside-Out Connections Grants, 2556
Init Fndn Innovation Grants, 2559
Init Fndn Minnesota Early Childhood Grants, 2560
Institute for Agriculture and Trade Policy Food and Society Fellowships, 2561
Intel Int'l Community Grants, 2564
Int'l Paper Company Fndn Grants, 2568
IRC Community Collaboratives for Refugee Women and Youth Grants, 2573
IREX Small Grant Fund for Civil Society Projects in Africa and Asia, 2581
Irving S. Gilmore Fndn Grants, 2584
Isabel Allende Fndn Esperanza Grants, 2586
IYI Responsible Fatherhood Grants, 2591
J. Bulow Campbell Fndn Grants, 2593
J.C. Penney Company Grants, 2594
J. Edwin Treakle Fndn Grants, 2596
J. F. Maddox Fndn Grants, 2597
J. Willard and Alice S. Marriott Fndn Grants, 2609
Jackson Fndn Grants, 2613
Jacob and Hilda Blaustein Fndn Grants, 2615
Jacob G. Schmidlapp Grants, 2616
Jacobs Family Village Neighborhoods Grants, 2619

James & Abigail Campbell Family Fndn Grants, 2620
James Ford Bell Fndn Grants, 2623
James H. Cummings Fndn Grants, 2626
James J. and Angelia M. Harris Fndn Grants, 2630
James M. Cox Fndn of Georgia Grants, 2634
James R. Thorpe Fndn Grants, 2636
James S. Copley Fndn Grants, 2637
Jane Bradley Pettit Fndn Community and Social Development Grants, 2642
Janirve Fndn Grants, 2645
Janus Fndn Grants, 2647
Jaquelin Hume Fndn Grants, 2654
Jay and Rose Phillips Family Fndn Grants, 2656
JELD-WEN Fndn Grants, 2661
Jerome and Mildred Paddock Fndn Grants, 2666
Jim Blevins Fndn Grants, 2678
Jim Moran Fndn Grants, 2680
JM Fndn Grants, 2681
Joan Bentinck-Smith Charitable Fndn Grants, 2682
John Clarke Grants, 2689
John Edward Fowler Memorial Fndn Grants, 2693
John Gogian Family Fndn Grants, 2697
John Jewett & Helen Chandler Garland Grants, 2702
John M. Ross Fndn Grants, 2704
John P. McGovern Fndn Grants, 2707
John S. and James L. Knight Fndn Communities Grants, 2711
Johnson Controls Fndn Arts and Culture Grants, 2719
John W. Alden Grants, 2727
John W. and Anna H. Hanes Fndn Grants, 2728
John W. Anderson Fndn Grants, 2729
John W. Speas and Effie E. Speas Grants, 2732
Joseph H. and Florence A. Roblee Fndn Grants, 2736
Josephine G. Russell Grants, 2737
Josephine Goodyear Fndn Grants, 2738
Josephine S. Gumbiner Fndn Grants, 2739
Joseph S. Stackpole Charitable Grants, 2741
Josiah W. and Bessie H. Kline Fndn Grants, 2742
JP Morgan Chase Arts and Culture Grants, 2752
Judith Clark-Morrill Fndn Grants, 2756
Kaiser Permanente Cares for Comm Grants, 2763
Kalamazoo Community Good Neighbor Grants, 2768
Kalamazoo Community Fndn Individuals and Families Grants, 2769
Kalamazoo Community Fndn Youth Development Grants, 2773
Kaneta Fndn Grants, 2774
Kansas Arts Commission Arts-in-Educ Grants, 2779
Katharine Matthies Fndn Grants, 2788
Kathryne Beynon Fndn Grants, 2791
Katie's Krops Grants, 2792
Katrine Menzing Deakins Charitable Grants, 2793
Kawabe Grants, 2794
Kenny's Kids Grants, 2803
Ken W. Davis Fndn Grants, 2813
Kevin P. & Sydney B. Knight Family Grants, 2819
Kiki Madazine Grow Strong Girls through Leadership Grants, 2822
Kimberly-Clark Community Grants, 2824
Kirkpatrick Fndn Grants, 2827
Knight Fndn Donor Advised Grants, 2828
Knight Fndn Grants - Georgia, 2829
Kosciusko County Community Fndn Grants, 2838
Kovler Family Fndn Grants, 2840
Kroger Fndn Hunger Relief Grants, 2844
L. W. Pierce Family Fndn Grants, 2846
LaGrange Independent Fndn for Endowments, 2851
Laidlaw Fndn Youh Organizing Catalyst Grants, 2853
Laidlaw Fndn Youth Organizaing Inits Grants, 2854
Land O'Lakes Fndn Community Grants, 2859
Lands' End Corp Giving Program, 2861
Laura Jane Musser Intercultural Harmony Grants, 2862
Laura Jane Musser Rural Arts Grants, 2863
Laura Moore Cunningham Fndn Grants, 2866
Lawrence J. and Anne Rubenstein Charitable Fndn Grants, 2868
LEGO Children's Grants, 2878
Leicester Savings Bank Fund, 2879
Leo Goodwin Fndn Grants, 2882
Leon and Thea Koerner Fndn Grants, 2883

Leo Niessen Jr., Charitable Grants, 2885
Lily Palmer Fry Grants, 2905
Lisa and Douglas Goldman Grants, 2910
LISC NFL Grassroots Grants, 2913
Lloyd G. Balfour Fndn Attleboro-Specific Charities Grants, 2916
Long Island Community Fndn Grants, 2920
Lotus 88 Fndn for Women and Children Grants, 2921
Louetta M. Cowden Fndn Grants, 2922
Louis Calder Fndn Grants, 2925
Louis R. Cappelli Fndn Grants, 2926
Lowell Berry Fndn Grants, 2930
Lucile Horton Howe & Mitchell B. Howe Grants, 2934
Lucy Gooding Charitable Fndn Trust, 2936
Lucy Gooding Charitable Fndn Grants, 2937
Ludwick Family Fndn Grants, 2938
Luther I. Replogle Fndn Grants, 2945
Lyndhurst Fndn Grants, 2949
M.E. Raker Fndn Grants, 2953
Mabel A. Horne Grants, 2956
Mabel Louise Riley Fndn Family Strengthening Small Grants, 2958
Mabel Louise Riley Fndn Grants, 2959
MacDonald-Peterson Fndn Grants, 2965
Madison Community Fndn Grants, 2971
Maine Community Fndn Edward H. Daveis Benevolent Grants, 2979
Maine Community Fndn Peaks Island Grants, 2984
Maine Community Fndn People of Color Grants, 2985
Maine Community Fndn Vincent B. and Barbara G. Welch Grants, 2990
Maine Women's Fund Girls' Grantmaking Init, 2993
Marathon Petroleum Corp Grants, 2999
Mardag Fndn Grants, 3001
Margaret L. Wendt Fndn Grants, 3004
Margaret T. Morris Fndn Grants, 3005
Marie H. Bechtel Charitable Grants, 3007
Marion and Miriam Rose Grants, 3015
Mark Wahlberg Youth Fndn Grants, 3022
MARPAT Fndn Grants, 3023
Marsh Corp Grants, 3027
Mary's Pence Ministry Grants, 3029
Mary Black Early Childhood Devel Grants, 3033
Mary C. & Perry F. Spencer Fndn Grants, 3034
Mary E. Ober Fndn Grants, 3039
Mary Jennings Sport Camp Scholarship, 3041
Mary Wilmer Covey Charitable Grants, 3049
Mathile Family Fndn Grants, 3062
Maurice J. Masserini Charitable Grants, 3064
Max A. Adler Charitable Fndn Grants, 3065
Maximilian E. and Marion O. Hoffman Fndn, 3067
Maxon Charitable Fndn Grants, 3068
May and Stanley Smith Charitable Grants, 3069
McCarthy Family Fndn Grants, 3073
McCombs Fndn Grants, 3075
McConnell Fndn Grants, 3076
McKesson Fndn Grants, 3084
McLean Contributionship Grants, 3088
McLean Fndn Grants, 3089
McMillen Fndn Grants, 3090
Mead Johnson Nutritionals Evansville-Area Organizations Grants, 3103
Medtronic Fndn Community Link Human Services Grants, 3112
Medtronic Fndn Patient Link Grants, 3113
Memorial Fndn for Children Grants, 3116
Memorial Fndn Grants, 3117
Mercedes-Benz USA Corp Contributions Grants, 3118
Merck Family Fund Urban Farming and Youth Leadership Grants, 3119
Merck Family Fund Youth Transforming Urban Communities Grants, 3120
Mericos Fndn Grants, 3121
Meriden Fndn Grants, 3122
Merkel Family Fndn Grants, 3123
Metro Health Fndn Grants, 3133
Metzger-Price Grants, 3137
Meyer Fndn Educ Grants, 3142
Meyer Memorial Trust Special Grants, 3149
MGM Resorts Fndn Community Grants, 3153

SUBJECT INDEX   Children and Youth / 833

MGN Family Fndn Grants, 3154
Michael and Susan Dell Fndn Grants, 3158
Mid-Iowa Health Fndn Comm Response Grants, 3168
Milken Family Fndn Grants, 3178
Milton Hicks Wood and Helen Gibbs Wood Charitable Grants, 3184
Minneapolis Fndn Community Grants, 3186
Mix It Up Grants, 3191
MLB Tomorrow Grants, 3193
Mockingbird Fndn Grants, 3196
Monsanto Access to the Arts Grants, 3204
Monsanto America's Farmers Grow Rural Grants, 3205
Monsanto Int'l Grants, 3207
Monsanto Kids Garden Fresh Grants, 3208
Montana Arts Council Cultural and Aesthetic Project Grants, 3209
MONY Fndn Grants, 3214
Moody Fndn Grants, 3215
Morris and Gwendolyn Cafritz Fndn Grants, 3218
Musgrave Fndn Grants, 3231
NASE Fndn Future Entrepreneur Scholarship, 3241
Nathan B. and Florence R. Burt Fndn Grants, 3245
Nathan Cummings Fndn Grants, 3246
National 4-H Afterschool Training Grants, 3248
National Endowment for the Arts - National Arts and Humanities Youth Program Awards, 3255
National Endowment for the Arts Dance Grants: Art Works, 3262
National Endowment for Arts Agencies Grants, 3263
National Endowment for Arts Museum Grants, 3265
National Endowment for Arts Opera Grants, 3267
National Endowment for the Arts Presenting Grants: Art Works, 3268
National Endowment for Arts Theater Grants, 3269
NCFL/Better World Books Libraries and Families Award, 3288
Nelda C. and H.J. Lutcher Stark Fndn Grants, 3296
Nestle Purina PetCare Ed Grants, 3302
Nestle Purina PetCare Youth Grants, 3306
Nestle Very Best in Youth Competition, 3307
Nevada Community Fndn Grants, 3316
New Earth Fndn Grants, 3317
Newfoundland and Labrador Arts Council Visiting Artists Grants, 3324
New Hampshire Charitable Fndn Grants, 3325
New Jersey Center for Hispanic Policy, Research and Development Innovative Inits Grants, 3329
New York Life Fndn Grants, 3341
NFL Charities NFL Player Fndn Grants, 3347
NFL Charities Pro Bowl Comm Grants in Hawaii, 3348
NFL Club Matching Youth Football Field/Stadium Grants, 3349
NFL Grassroots Field Grants, 3350
NFL High School Coach of the Week Grant, 3351
NFL High School Football Coach of the Year, 3352
NFL Player Youth Football Camp Grants, 3353
NGA Healthy Sprouts Awards, 3403
NGA Heinz Wholesome Memories Intergenerational Garden Awards, 3404
NGA Youth Garden Grants, 3409
Nicholas H. Noyes Jr. Memorial Fndn Grants, 3434
Nike and Ashoka GameChangers: Change the Game for Women in Sport, 3439
Nike Bowerman Track Renovation Grants, 3440
Nike Fndn Grants, 3441
Nike Giving - Cash and Product Grants, 3442
Nina Mason Pulliam Charitable Grants, 3443
Nordson Corp Fndn Grants, 3462
North Dakota Community Fndn Grants, 3493
Northland Fndn Grants, 3506
NW Airlines KidCares Med Travel Assistance, 3508
NW Mutual Fndn Grants, 3509
NW Minnesota Fndn Asset Building Grants, 3511
NRA Fndn Grants, 3517
Nuffield Fndn Children and Families Grants, 3533
Nu Skin Force for Good Fndn Grants, 3536
NYCH Together Grants, 3541
NYCT Children & Youth with Disabilities Grant, 3544
NYCT Girls and Young Women Grants, 3548
NYCT Mental Health and Retardation Grants, 3554

NYCT Social Services and Welfare Grants, 3557
NYCT Youth Development Grants, 3561
Oak Fndn Child Abuse Grants, 3632
Oakland Fund for Children and Youth Grants, 3634
Ober Kaler Community Grants, 3635
Oceanside Charitable Fndn Grants, 3637
Ohio County Community Fndn Grants, 3658
Ohio County Community Fndn Mini-Grants, 3660
Ohio Valley Fndn Grants, 3662
OJJDP National Mentoring Grants, 3664
OJJDP Tribal Juvenile Accountability Discretionary Grants, 3665
Oleonda Jameson Grants, 3667
Olga Sipolin Children's Grants, 3668
Olive B. Cole Fndn Grants, 3670
Olive Smith Browning Charitable Grants, 3671
OneFamily Fndn Grants, 3673
Orchard Fndn Grants, 3690
Ordean Fndn Grants, 3691
Oregon Youth Soccer Fndn Grants, 3692
OSF-Baltimore Ed & Youth Devel Grants, 3697
OUT Fund for Lesbian & Gay Liberation Grants, 3714
Overbrook Fndn Grants, 3715
Pacers Fndn Be Drug-Free Grants, 3720
Pacers Fndn Be Educated Grants, 3721
Pacers Fndn Be Healthy and Fit Grants, 3722
Pacers Fndn Be Tolerant Grants, 3723
Pacers Fndn Indiana Fever's Be Younique Grants, 3724
Packard Fndn Local Grants, 3729
Pajaro Valley Community Health Insurance/Coverage & Educ on Using the System Grants, 3731
Parker Fndn (California) Grants, 3736
Pasadena Fndn Average Grants, 3741
Patrick and Aimee Butler Family Fndn Community Human Services Grants, 3749
Patrick and Anna M. Cudahy Grants, 3751
Paul and Edith Babson Fndn Grants, 3755
Paul E. and Klare N. Reinhold Fndn Grants, 3758
Paul G. Allen Family Fndn Grants, 3759
Pay It Forward Fndn Mini Grants, 3768
Peoples Bancorp Fndn Grants, 3817
PepsiCo Fndn Grants, 3819
Perkins-Ponder Fndn Grants, 3822
Perkins Charitable Fndn Grants, 3823
Perpetual Trust for Charitable Giving Grants, 3826
Peter and Elizabeth C. Tower Fndn Annual Mental Health Grants, 3835
Peter and Elizabeth C. Tower Fndn Learning Disability Grants, 3836
Peter & Elizabeth C. Tower Mental Health Reference and Resource Materials Mini-Grants, 3837
Peter and Elizabeth C. Tower Fndn Phase II Technology Init Grants, 3839
Peter and Elizabeth C. Tower Fndn Phase I Technology Init Grants, 3840
Peter and Elizabeth C. Tower Fndn Social and Emotional Preschool Curriculum Grants, 3841
Peter and Elizabeth C. Tower Fndn Substance Abuse Grants, 3842
Peter M. Putnam Fndn Grants, 3848
Pew Trusts Children and Youth Grants, 3858
PeyBack Fndn Grants, 3861
Peyton Anderson Fndn Grants, 3862
Philadelphia Organizational Effectiveness Grants, 3872
Philadelphia Fndn YOUThadelphia Grants, 3873
Phil Hardin Fndn Grants, 3875
Philip L. Graham Grants, 3876
Phoenix Coyotes Charities Grants, 3879
Phoenix Suns Charities Grants, 3881
Piedmont Health Fndn Grants, 3882
Pier 1 Imports Grants, 3887
Pike County Community Fndn Grants, 3888
Pinellas County Grants, 3891
Pinkerton Fndn Grants, 3892
Pinnacle Entertainment Fndn Grants, 3893
Pinnacle Fndn Grants, 3894
Piper Trust Arts and Culture Grants, 3900
Piper Trust Children Grants, 3901
Pittsburgh Fndn Community Grants, 3910
Plough Fndn Grants, 3915

Plum Creek Fndn Grants, 3917
PNC Fndn Grow Up Great Grants, 3924
Pohlad Family Fndn, 3928
Polk Bros. Fndn Grants, 3929
Pollock Fndn Grants, 3930
Porter County Health and Wellness Grant, 3933
Portland Fndn - Women's Giving Circle Grant, 3935
Portland Fndn Grants, 3936
Posey Community Fndn Women's Grants, 3938
Posey County Community Fndn Grants, 3939
Pott Fndn Grants, 3940
Powell Family Fndn Grants, 3941
Powell Fndn Grants, 3942
Price Chopper's Golub Fndn Grants, 3950
Price Family Charitable Grants, 3952
Prince Charitable Trusts Chicago Grants, 3959
Princeton Area Community Fndn Fund for Women and Girls Grants, 3962
Princeton Area Community Fndn Rebecca Annitto Service Opportunities for Students Award, 3964
Prudential Fndn Educ Grants, 3977
PSEG Corp Contributions Grants, 3979
Public Educ Power Grants, 3981
Public Welfare Fndn Grants, 3984
Pulaski County Community Fndn Grants, 3988
Putnam County Community Fndn Grants, 3990
Quaker Oats Company Kids Care Clubs Grants, 3992
Qualcomm Grants, 3993
Quantum Fndn Grants, 3996
QuikTrip Corp Contributions Grants, 3998
R.J. McElroy Grants, 4001
RadioShack StreetSentz Community Grants, 4005
Rainbow Academy Fndn Grants, 4006
Rainbow Endowment Grants, 4007
Rajiv Gandhi Fndn Grants, 4011
Ralph M. Parsons Fndn Grants, 4013
Rathmann Family Fndn Grants, 4026
Raymond John Wean Fndn Grants, 4028
RCF General Community Grants, 4032
RCF Summertime Kids Grants, 4034
Rehab Therapy Fndn Grants, 4050
Reinberger Fndn Grants, 4052
Reynolds and Reynolds Associate Fndn Grants, 4069
RGK Fndn Grants, 4072
Rhode Island Fndn Grants, 4073
Richard and Rhoda Goldman Grants, 4077
Richard and Susan Smith Family Fndn Grants, 4078
Richard Davoud Donchian Fndn Grants, 4080
Richard King Mellon Fndn Grants, 4087
Richland County Bank Grants, 4091
Roberta Leventhal Sudakoff Fndn Grants, 4102
Robert and Joan Dircks Fndn Grants, 4104
Robert B McMillen Fndn Grants, 4106
Robert Bowne Fndn Fellowships, 4107
Robert Bowne Fndn Lit Grants, 4108
Robert Bowne Fndn Youth-Centered Grants, 4109
Robert R. McCormick Tribune Civics Grants, 4118
Robert R. McCormick Tribune Comm Grants, 4119
Robert R. Meyer Fndn Grants, 4121
Robert W. Woodruff Fndn Grants, 4124
Robins Fndn Grants, 4126
Rochester Area Community Fndn Grants, 4127
Rochester Area Fndn Grants, 4128
Roger L. and Agnes C. Dell Charitable Grants, 4143
Romic Environmental's Charitable Contributions, 4148
Ronald McDonald House Charities Grants, 4149
Roney-Fitzpatrick Fndn Grants, 4150
Rose Community Fndn Child and Family Development Grants, 4153
Rosie's For All Kids Fndn Grants, 4163
Ross Fndn Grants, 4164
Roy and Christine Sturgis Charitable Grants, 4166
Roy J. Carver Charitable Trust Youth Grants, 4167
Rush County Community Fndn Grants, 4174
Ruth Anderson Fndn Grants, 4176
Ruth H. and Warren A. Ellsworth Fndn Grants, 4179
Rutter's Children's Charities Grants, 4181
RWJF Local Funding Partnerships Grants, 4186
S.H. Cowell Fndn Grants, 4199
S. Livingston Mather Charitable Grants, 4200

Children and Youth

S. Mark Taper Fndn Grants, 4201
Saginaw Community Fndn Discretionary Grants, 4205
Saginaw Community Fndn YWCA Fund for Women and Girls Grants, 4207
Saginaw County Community Fndn Youth FORCE Grants, 4208
Saigh Fndn Grants, 4210
Salmon Fndn Grants, 4225
Salt River Health and Human Services Grants, 4228
SAMHSA Strategic Prevention Framework State Incentive Grants, 4231
Samueli Fndn Youth Services Grants, 4234
Samuel N. and Mary Castle Fndn Grants, 4236
Samuel S. Johnson Fndn Grants, 4239
San Diego Fndn for Change Grants, 4247
Sands Fndn Grants, 4255
San Juan Island Community Fndn Grants, 4283
Sarkeys Fndn Grants, 4297
Saucony Run for Good Fndn Grants, 4301
Scheumann Fndn Grants, 4306
Scholastic Book Grants, 4308
Scholastic Welch's Harvest Grants, 4309
Schramm Fndn Grants, 4310
Schumann Fund for New Jersey Grants, 4311
Schurz Communications Fndn Grants, 4312
Scott County Community Fndn Grants, 4314
Seabury Fndn Grants, 4316
Seattle Fndn Arts and Culture Grants, 4320
Seattle Fndn Benjamin N. Phillips Grants, 4322
Seattle Fndn C. Keith Birkenfeld Grants, 4323
Seattle Fndn Economy Grants, 4325
Self Fndn Grants, 4335
Seneca Foods Fndn Grants, 4336
Shopko Fndn Community Charitable Grants, 4346
Sidgmore Family Fndn Grants, 4348
Sidney Stern Grants, 4349
Sid W. Richardson Fndn Grants, 4350
Siebert Lutheran Fndn Grants, 4351
Sierra Health Fndn Responsive Grants, 4353
Simmons Fndn Grants, 4360
Singing for Change Fndn Grants, 4363
Sioux Falls Area Community Grants, 4364
Sioux Falls Area Community Fndn Field-of-Interest and Donor-Advised Grants, 4365
Sioux Falls Area Community Fndn Spot Grants, 4366
Siragusa Fndn Human Services Grants, 4369
Sisters of Charity Fndn of Canton Grants, 4372
Sisters of Mercy of North Carolina Fndn Grants, 4375
Sisters of Saint Joseph Charitable Grants, 4376
Sisters of St. Joseph Healthcare Fndn Grants, 4377
Skaggs Fndn Grants, 4378
Skillman Community Connections Small Grants, 4379
Skillman Fndn Good Opportunities Grants, 4381
Skillman Fndn Good Schools Grants, 4382
Smith Richardson Fndn Direct Service Grants, 4385
SOBP A.E. Bennett Research Award, 4388
Sobrato Family Fndn Grants, 4389
Sobrato Family Fndn Meeting Space Grants, 4390
Sobrato Family Fndn Office Space Grants, 4391
Sodexo Fndn STOP Hunger Scholarships, 4400
Sonoco Fndn Grants, 4403
Sorenson Legacy Fndn Grants, 4407
Southbury Community Trust Fund, 4409
South Carolina Arts Commission AIE Residency Plus Individual Site Grants, 4411
South Carolina Arts Commission AIE Residency Plus Multi-Site Grants, 4412
Southern Minnesota Init Fndn AmeriCorps Leap Grants, 4431
Southern Minnesota Init Fndn BookStart Grants, 4432
Southern Minnesota Init Fndn Community Growth Init Grants, 4433
Southern Minnesota Home Visiting Grants, 4434
Southern Minnesota Init Fndn Incentive Grants, 4435
Southern Minnesota Youth Explorer Grants, 4436
Special Olympics Project UNIFY Grants, 4449
Spencer County Community Fndn Grants, 4451
Sport Manitoba Women to Watch Grants, 4460
Sprague Fndn Grants, 4461
Staples Fndn for Learning Grants, 4475

Starbucks Shared Planet Youth Action Grants, 4476
Stark Community SummerTime Kid Grants, 4480
Stark Community Fndn Women's Grants, 4481
State Justice Institute Curriculum Adaptation and Training Grants, 4488
State Justice Institute Partner Grants, 4489
State Justice Institute Project Grants, 4490
State Justice Institute Strategic Init Grants, 4492
State Justice Institute Tech Assistance Grants, 4493
Steelcase Fndn Grants, 4497
Steven B. Achelis Fndn Grants, 4502
Stinson Fndn Grants, 4506
Stockton Rush Bartol Fndn Grants, 4508
Stowe Family Fndn Grants, 4510
Strengthening Families - Strengthening Communities Grants, 4513
Strowd Roses Grants, 4515
Stuart Fndn Grants, 4516
Subaru of America Fndn Grants, 4518
Sunderland Fndn Grants, 4527
Sunny and Abe Rosenberg Fndn Grants, 4529
Susan A. & Donald P. Babson Charitable Grants, 4534
Susan Mott Webb Charitable Grants, 4536
SVP Early Childhood Development and Parenting Grants, 4538
Swindells Charitable Fndn, 4542
Sylvia Adams Charitable Grants, 4543
Symantec Community Relations and Corp Philanthropy Grants, 4544
T. Raymond Gregory Family Fndn Grants, 4547
TAC Arts Access Grant, 4549
TAC Arts Build Communities Grants, 4551
Taproot Fndn Capacity-Building Service Grants, 4560
Tauck Family Fndn Grants, 4563
Telluride Fndn Community Grants, 4573
Textron Corp Contributions Grants, 4601
Thelma Braun and Bocklett Family Fndn Grants, 4603
Theodore Edson Parker Fndn Grants, 4605
Thomas Austin Finch, Sr. Fndn Grants, 4613
Thomas Sill Fndn Grants, 4619
Thomas W. Briggs Fndn Grants, 4621
Thompson Charitable Fndn Grants, 4622
Time Warner Diverse Voices in the Arts Grants, 4635
Time Warner Youth Media & Creative Grants, 4636
TJX Fndn Grants, 4637
Toby Wells Fndn Grants, 4638
Todd Brock Family Fndn Grants, 4639
Tom's of Maine Grants, 4640
Tony Hawk Fndn Grants, 4641
Topeka Community Fndn Boss Hawg's Charitable Giving Grants, 4642
Topeka Community Building Families Grants, 4643
Topeka Community Fndn Grants, 4644
Topeka West Rotary Youth Enrichment Grants, 4645
Topfer Family Fndn Grants, 4646
Toyota Motor Manufacturing of Indiana Grants, 4653
Toyota Motor of Kentucky Grants, 4654
Toyota Motor Manufacturing Mississippi Grants, 4655
Toyota Motor Manufacturing of Texas Grants, 4656
Toyota Technical Center Grants, 4660
Triangle Community Fndn Community Grants, 4667
Triangle Community Fndn Donor Grants, 4668
Trinity Fndn Grants, 4669
Trull Fndn Grants, 4673
TSYSF Individual Scholarships, 4675
TSYSF Team Grants, 4676
Turner B. Bunn, Jr. & Catherine E. Bunn Grants, 4680
Tyler Aaron Bookman Memorial Fndn Grants, 4684
U.S. Department of Ed Early Reading 1st Grants, 4691
U.S. Lacrosse Emerging Groups Grants, 4703
U.S. Lacrosse Equipment Grants, 4704
Union Bank Corp Sponsorships and Donations, 4708
Union Bank, N.A. Fndn Grants, 4709
Union Benevolent Association Grants, 4710
Union Pacific Fndn Community and Civic Grants, 4714
Union Square Award for Social Justice, 4717
Union Square Awards Grants, 4718
United Methodist Child Mental Health Grants, 4721
United Methodist Health Ministry Grants, 4722
UPS Fndn Economic and Global Lit Grants, 4730

USA Football Equipment Grants, 4735
USAID Global Development Alliance Grants, 4753
USAID National Governance Project Grant, 4770
USAID Service Delivery & Support for Families Caring For Orphans and Vulnerable Childrens, 4781
USAID Unsolicited Proposal Grants, 4786
USDA Child and Adult Care Food Program, 4800
USFA Development Grants, 4866
USFA Equipment Subsidy Grants, 4867
US Soccer Annual Program & Field Grants, 4870
USTA Althea Gibson Leadership Awards, 4872
USTA CTA and NJTL Community Tennis Development Workshop Scholarships, 4873
USTA Excellence Grants, 4874
USTA Junior Team Tennis Stipends, 4875
USTA Multicultural Excellence Grants, 4876
USTA Multicultural Individual Player Grant for National Competition and Training, 4877
USTA NJTL Arthur Ashe Essay and Art Contest, 4878
USTA NJTL Tennis and Leadership Camp Scholarships, 4879
USTA Okechi Womeodu Scholar Athlete Grants, 4880
USTA Player Development Grants, 4881
USTA Pro Circuit Community Involvement Day Grants, 4882
USTA Public Facility Assistance Grants, 4883
USTA Recreational Tennis Grants, 4884
USTA Serves Player Incentive Awards, 4891
USTA Tennis Block Party Grants, 4892
V.V. Cooke Fndn Grants, 4896
Vancouver Fndn Grants & Comm Inits, 4900
Vancouver Sun Children's Grants, 4901
Vanderburgh Community Fndn Grants, 4902
Van Kampen Boyer Molinari Charitable Grants, 4905
Victor E. Speas Fndn Grants, 4933
Victoria S. and Bradley L. Geist Fndn Enhancement Grants, 4935
Victoria S. and Bradley L. Geist Fndn Grants Supporting Foster Care and Their Caregivers, 4936
Victoria S. and Bradley L. Geist Fndn Grants Supporting Transitioning Foster Youth, 4937
Vigneron Grants, 4938
Viking Children's Grants, 4939
VSA/Metlife Connect All Grants, 4953
VSA/Volkswagen Group of America Exhibition Awards, 4954
VSA Int'l Art Program for Children with Disabilities Grants, 4955
Vulcan Materials Company Fndn Grants, 4956
W.C. Griffith Fndn Grants, 4957
W. C. Griffith Fndn Grants, 4958
W.H. and Mary Ellen Cobb Charitable Grants, 4959
W.K. Kellogg Fndn Secure Families Grants, 4963
W.M. Keck Fndn Southern California Grants, 4964
Waitt Family Fndn Grants, 4973
Warrick County Community Fndn Grants, 4987
Wayne County Fndn Women's Grants, 5006
WCI Childcare Capacity Grants, 5007
Weaver Fndn Grants, 5015
Weaver Popcorn Fndn Grants, 5016
Weingart Fndn Grants, 5018
Wells County Fndn Grants, 5022
Westinghouse Charitable Giving Grants, 5028
Whitehorse Fndn Grants, 5058
Whiting Fndn Grants, 5059
Whitney Fndn Grants, 5061
WHO Fndn Educ/Lit Grants, 5062
Widgeon Point Charitable Fndn Grants, 5064
Wild Rivers Community Fndn Holiday Partnership Grants, 5069
Wild Rivers Community Fndn Summer Youth Mini Grants, 5070
William A. Badger Fndn Grants, 5072
William B. Stokely Jr. Fndn Grants, 5076
William Bingham Fndn Grants, 5077
William G. and Helen C. Hoffman Fndn Grants, 5080
William G. McGowan Charitable Grants, 5084
William J. and Dorothy K. O'Neill Fndn Grants, 5087
William J. Brace Charitable Trust, 5088
William Robert Baird Charitable Grants, 5093

SUBJECT INDEX

Williams Companies Fndn Grants, 5095
William T. Grant Fndn Youth Service Improvement Grants, 5096
Wilson-Wood Fndn Grants, 5098
Windgate Charitable Fndn Grants, 5099
Windward Youth Leadership Grants, 5100
Winston-Salem Fndn Competitive Grants, 5102
Winston-Salem Fndn Elkin/Tri-County Grants, 5103
Wisconsin Energy Fndn Grants, 5106
Wolfe Associates Grants, 5110
Women's Funding Alliance Grants, 5112
Wood-Claeyssens Fndn Grants, 5113
WSF Rusty Kanokogi Fund for the Advancement of U.S. Judo Grants, 5118
WSF Travel and Training Grants, 5119
Yampa Valley Community Fndn Erickson Business Week Scholarships, 5123
Yawkey Fndn Grants, 5125
Yellow Corp Fndn Grants, 5126
Young Family Fndn Grants, 5127
Youth Action Net Fellowships, 5128
Youth As Resources Grants, 5130
Youth as Resources Mini-Grants, 5131
YSA National Child Awareness Month Youth Ambassador Grants, 5137
YSA NEA Youth Leaders for Lit Grants, 5138
YSA Radio Disney's Hero for Change Award, 5139
YSA Sodexo Lead Organizer Grants, 5140
YSA UnitedHealth HEROES Service-Learning, 5142

Children's Literature
Akonadi Fndn Anti-Racism Grants, 217
ALA Coretta Scott King-Virginia Hamilton Award for Lifetime Achievement, 259
ALA Coretta Scott King Book Awards, 260
ALA May Hill Arbuthnot Honor Lecture Award, 300
ALA Schneider Family Book Award, 317
ALA Scholastic Library Publishing Award, 318
Arizona State Library LSTA Learning Grants, 550
Bernard & Audre Rapoport Arts & Culture Grant, 735
Chicago Tribune Fndn Grants for Cultural Organizations, 1101
Florida Div of Cultural Affairs Literature Grants, 1855
NYCH Together Grants, 3541
PCA Arts Organizations & Grants for Lit, 3781
SCBWI Don Freeman Memorial Grant, 4302

Children's Museums
American Express Charitable Grants, 429
Angels Baseball Fndn Grants, 465
Anschutz Family Fndn Grants, 486
Back Home Again Fndn Grants, 633
Ben B. Cheney Fndn Grants, 725
Cabot Corp Fndn Grants, 887
Chapman Family Charitable Grants, 1034
Chicago Tribune Fndn Grants for Cultural Organizations, 1101
Donald W. Reynolds Children's Discovery Grants, 1576
Florida Div of Cultural Affairs Museum Grants, 1858
Francis Beidler Fndn Grants, 1921
IMLS 21st Century Museum Pro Grants, 2512
IMLS American Heritage Preservation Grants, 2513
IMLS National Leadership Grants, 2515
Jerry L. and Barbara J. Burris Fndn Grants, 2669
LEGO Children's Grants, 2878
Lewis H. Humphreys Charitable Grants, 2889
Lied Fndn Grants, 2900
MacArthur Fndn Chicago Arts and Culture General Operations Grants, 2961
Maurice Amado Fndn Grants, 3063
Merkel Family Fndn Grants, 3123
Phoenix Suns Charities Grants, 3881
S. Spencer Scott Grants, 4202
Seattle Fndn C. Keith Birkenfeld Grants, 4323
Union Pacific Fndn Community and Civic Grants, 4714

Children's Theater
Bernard & Audre Rapoport Arts & Culture Grant, 735
Chicago Tribune Fndn Grants for Cultural Organizations, 1101
Florida Div of Cultural Affairs Community Theatre Grants, 1847
Florida Div of Cultural Affairs Professional Theatre Grants, 1861
Illinois Arts Council Theater Grants, 2477
LEGO Children's Grants, 2878
MacArthur Fndn Chicago Arts and Culture General Operations Grants, 2961
National Endowment for Arts Theater Grants, 3269
NYSCA Arts Educ: General Operating Support, 3578
NYSCA Theatre Gen Operating Support Grants, 3623
NYSCA Theatre General Program Support, 3624
NYSCA Theatre Pro Performances Grants, 3625
Parker Fndn (California) Grants, 3736
PCA Arts Organizations & Grants for Theatre, 3783
PCA Entry Track Arts Organizations and Program Grants for Theatre, 3797
Santa Barbara Fndn Towbes Fund for the Performing Arts Grants, 4288

Chiropractic
Regents Professional Opportunity Scholarships, 4044

Choreography
Andy Warhol Fndn for the Visual Arts Grants, 464
Bush Fndn Arts & Humanities Grants: Short-Term Organizational Support, 873
Creative Work Grants, 1396
Dance Advance Grants, 1441
Jerome Fndn Grants, 2667
Kentucky Arts Council Al Smith Fellowship, 2806
Minnesota State Arts Board Cultural Community Partnership Grants, 3188
National Endowment for the Arts Dance Grants: Art Works, 3262
North Carolina Arts Cncl New Realities Grants, 3478
NYFA Gregory Millard Fellowships, 3565
NYSCA Dance: Commissions Grants, 3583
NYSCA Dance Gen Operating Support Grants, 3584
NYSCA Dance: Long-Term Residency in New York State Grants, 3586
PCA Arts Organizations and Grants for Dance, 3779
PCA Entry Track Arts Organizations and Program Grants for Dance, 3791
PCA Strategies for Success Grants - Advanced, 3804
PCA Strategies for Success Grants - Basic Level, 3805
PCA Strategies for Success Grants - Intermediate, 3806
PennPAT Artist Technical Assistance Grants, 3811
PennPAT Strategic Opportunity Grants, 3815
Rasmuson Fndn Individual Artists Awards, 4022
San Francisco Fndn Fund For Artists Award For Choreographers, 4270
South Carolina Arts Commission American Masterpieces in South Carolina Grants, 4413
South Carolina Arts Commission Fellowships, 4415
Wallace Alexander Gerbode Fndn Special Award Grants, 4975

Chronic Illness
Aetna Fndn Health Grants in Connecticut, 184
Atkinson Fndn Community Grants, 606
Community Fndn of Greater Memphis Grants, 1290
Emma B. Howe Memorial Fndn Grants, 1700
Health Fndn of Greater Cincinnati Grants, 2281
Herbert A. and Adrian W. Woods Fndn Grants, 2313
Kaiser Permanente Cares for Comm Grants, 2763
Kenny's Kids Grants, 2803
Mary Wilmer Covey Charitable Grants, 3049
Medtronic Fndn Patient Link Grants, 3113
Mid-Iowa Health Fndn Comm Response Grants, 3168
RWJF New Jersey Health Inits Grants, 4187
TJX Fndn Grants, 4637
Welborn Baptist Fndn Improvements to Community Health Status Grants, 5021

Churches
A.H.K. Fndn Grants, 40
ABC Charities Grants, 85
Abel Fndn Grants, 90
Adam Richter Charitable Grants, 145

Churches / 835

Adams County Community Fndn of Pennsylvania Grants, 149
Adelaide Christian Home For Children Grants, 162
AHS Fndn Grants, 208
ALA Coretta Scott King Book Donation Grant, 261
Alavi Fndn Grants, 335
Albert B. Cuppage Charitable Fndn Grants, 341
Albert E. and Birdie W. Einstein Grants, 342
ALSAM Fndn Grants, 395
Alvah H. and Wyline P. Chapman Fndn Grants, 402
American Foodservice Charitable Grants, 433
Anthony R. Abraham Fndn Grants, 489
Antone & Edene Vidinha Charitable Grants, 490
A Quiet Place Grants, 520
Aragona Family Fndn Grants, 522
Archer Daniels Midland Fndn Grants, 527
Arkansas Arts Council Collab Project Support, 555
Arronson Fndn Grants, 567
Austin S. Nelson Fndn Grants, 617
Beerman Fndn Grants, 717
Blue Cross Blue Shield of Minnesota Healthy Neighborhoods: Connect Grants, 798
Bolthouse Fndn Grants, 813
Booth-Bricker Grants, 815
Bosque Fndn Grants, 818
Boston Fndn Grants, 819
Brad Brock Family Fndn Grants, 827
Bradley Family Fndn (California) Grants, 829
Caddock Fndn Grants, 888
Caesar Puff Fndn Grants, 890
Callaway Fndn Grants, 909
Carnahan-Jackson Fndn Grants, 939
Caterpillar Fndn Grants, 954
Catherine Kennedy Home Fndn Grants, 955
CCCF Alpha Grants, 959
CCCF Dora Maclellan Brown Christian Priority Grants, 960
CE and S Fndn Grants, 985
Champlin Fndns Grants, 1029
Chapman Family Charitable Grants, 1034
Charity Incorporated Grants, 1035
Charles Parker Trust for Public Music Grants, 1053
Chiles Fndn Grants, 1108
Clark-Winchcole Fndn Grants, 1152
Commission on Religion in Appalachia Grants, 1238
Community Fndn of East Central Illinois Grants, 1278
Community Fndn of Greenville Community Enrichment Grants, 1294
Community Fndn of Greenville Hollingsworth Funds Program/Project Grants, 1296
Conwood Charitable Grants, 1366
Covenant Fndn of Atlanta Grants, 1384
Covenant Mountain Ministries Grants, 1387
Danellie Fndn Grants, 1442
Dan Murphy Fndn Grants, 1444
Emerson Kampen Fndn Grants, 1696
Fred and Sherry Abernethy Fndn Grants, 1940
General Mills Fndn Grants, 2003
George Kress Fndn Grants, 2025
George W. Brackenridge Fndn Grants, 2028
H. Reimers Bechtel Charitable Grants, 2186
HAF Hansen Family Trust Christian Endowment Grants, 2197
HAF Mada Huggins Caldwell Grants, 2200
Helen Steiner Rice Fndn Grants, 2299
High Meadow Fndn Grants, 2321
Howe Fndn of North Carolina Grants, 2377
I.A. O'Shaughnessy Fndn Grants, 2416
J. Mack Robinson Fndn Grants, 2604
James M. Collins Fndn Grants, 2633
Jessie Ball Dupont Grants, 2671
Jim Blevins Fndn Grants, 2678
John H. and Wilhelmina D. Harland Grants, 2698
John I. Smith Charities Grants, 2700
Kathryne Beynon Fndn Grants, 2791
Kawabe Grants, 2794
MacDonald-Peterson Fndn Grants, 2965
Maine Community Fndn Steeples Grants, 2989
Mary Duke Biddle Fndn Grants, 3036
Maxon Charitable Fndn Grants, 3068

836 / Churches

Mervin Bovaird Fndn Grants, 3128
Missouri United Methodist Ministry Grants, 3189
Needmor Grants, 3289
North Carolina Arts Council Arts in Educ Rural Development Grants, 3470
Parker Fndn Grants to Support Chr Evangelism, 3737
Perkins Charitable Fndn Grants, 3823
Presbyterian Church USA Sam and Helen R. Walton Award, 3946
Retirement Research Accessible Faith Grants, 4066
Richard and Helen DeVos Fndn Grants, 4076
Rollin M. Gerstacker Fndn Grants, 4146
RRF Accessible Faith Grants, 4169
Selby and Richard McRae Fndn Grants, 4334
Sioux Falls Area Community Grants, 4364
Sioux Falls Area Community Fndn Field-of-Interest and Donor-Advised Grants, 4365
Sioux Falls Area Community Fndn Spot Grants, 4366
Sunderland Fndn Grants, 4527
Susan Mott Webb Charitable Grants, 4536
Temple-Inland Fndn Grants, 4576
W.C. Griffith Fndn Grants, 4957
W. C. Griffith Fndn Grants, 4958
W. Waldo and Jenny Lynn M. Bradley Grants, 4967
Walter L. Gross III Family Fndn Grants, 4983
Wege Fndn Grants, 5017
William H. Hannon Fndn Grants, 5086
William T. Sloper Trust for Andres J. Sloper Musical Grants, 5097

Citizenship
ArvinMeritor Fndn Civic Grants, 583
Aspen Community Fndn Grants, 592
Battle Creek Community Fndn Grants, 684
Bay and Paul Fndns Grants, 693
Bernard and Audre Rapoport Fndn Democracy and Civic Participation Grants, 737
Carnegie Corp of New York Grants, 940
Chesapeake Bay Trust Forestry Mini Grants, 1071
Chesapeake Bay Trust Mini Grants, 1072
Citizens Bank Mid-Atlantic Charitable Grants, 1140
Community Fndn of Abilene Community Grants, 1264
FAS Project Schools Grants, 1792
Harvest Fndn Grants, 2254
HBF Encouraging Citizen Involvement Grants, 2272
John Edward Fowler Memorial Fndn Grants, 2693
Kenneth T. and Eileen L. Norris Fndn Grants, 2802
Lubrizol Fndn Grants, 2933
Marsh Corp Grants, 3027
Mary & Walter Frear Eleemosynary Grants, 3035
New Jersey Center for Hispanic Policy, Research and Development Immigration Integration Grants, 3328
NYCT Civic Affairs Grants, 3545
NYCT Fund for New Citizens Grants, 3547
Ottinger Fndn Grants, 3712
Piper Jaffray Fndn Communities Giving Grants, 3899
PIP Fulfilling the Dream Fund, 3907
PIP Racial Justice Collaborative Grants, 3908
PIP U.S. Human Rights Grants, 3909
Puffin/Nation Prize for Creative Citizenship, 3987
Richard King Mellon Fndn Grants, 4087
Stuart Fndn Grants, 4516
Surdna Fndn Sustainable Environments Grants, 4533
USAID Civic Participation Grants, 4743
Wallace Alexander Gerbode Fndn Grants, 4974
Warren County Community Fndn Grants, 4985
Warren County Community Fndn Mini-Grants, 4986
White County Community Fndn Grants, 5057

Civic Affairs
A.O. Smith Community Grants, 46
Abbott Fund Global AIDS Care Grants, 82
Acushnet Fndn Grants, 143
Adams Fndn Grants, 155
Advanced Micro Devices Comm Affairs Grants, 172
AEGON Transamerica Fndn Civic and Community Grants, 177
AEP Corp Giving Grants, 180
AFG Industries Grants, 191
Akonadi Fndn Anti-Racism Grants, 217

Akzo Nobel Chemicals Grants, 219
Alabama Power Fndn Grants, 233
Alaska Airlines Corp Giving Grants, 320
Alaska Airlines Fndn Grants, 321
Alberto Culver Corp Contributions Grants, 343
Albert Pick Jr. Grants, 344
Alcatel-Lucent Technologies Fndn Grants, 349
Alcoa Fndn Grants, 350
Alex Brown and Sons Charitable Fndn Grants, 359
Alfred P. Sloan Fndn Civic Inits Grants, 368
Alice Tweed Tuohy Fndn Grants, 372
Allegheny Fndn Grants, 376
Allegheny Technologies Charitable Trust, 377
Alliant Energy Fndn Community Grants, 384
ALZA Corp Contributions Grants, 405
American Express Historic Preservation Grants, 431
Amon G. Carter Fndn Grants, 458
Annenberg Fndn Grants, 477
Applied Biosystems Grants, 514
Arie and Ida Crown Grants, 533
Arizona Cardinals Grants, 534
Arizona Republic Fndn Grants, 546
Arizona Republic Newspaper Contributions, 547
Arkansas Community Fndn Grants, 561
Armstrong McDonald Fndn Grants, 565
ArvinMeritor Fndn Civic Grants, 583
ArvinMeritor Grants, 585
Ashland Corp Contributions Grants, 587
Asian American Institute Impact Fellowships, 588
ATA Political Engagement Grant, 601
ATF Gang Resistance Educ and Training Program Coop Agreements, 603
Atkinson Fndn Community Grants, 606
Autodesk Community Relations Grants, 619
AutoZone Community Relations Grants, 621
Avery Dennison Fndn Grants, 623
Banfi Vintners Grants, 653
Barker Welfare Fndn Grants, 669
Baughman Fndn Grants, 688
Bay Area Community Fndn Grants, 694
Bayer Fndn Grants, 696
Bechtel Group Fndn Building Positive Community Relationships Grants, 715
Bemis Company Fndn Grants, 723
Bernard and Audre Rapoport Fndn Democracy and Civic Participation Grants, 737
Bertha Russ Lytel Fndn Grants, 745
Bertha Wolf-Rosenthal Fndn for Community Service Stipend, 746
Besser Fndn Grants, 748
Bicknell Grants, 759
Black Hills Corp Grants, 781
Blum-Kovler Fndn Grants, 803
Blumenthal Fndn Grants, 804
Boeing Company Contributions Grants, 809
Boston Globe Fndn Grants, 821
Brainerd Fndn Grants, 831
Bridgestone/Firestone Grants, 836
Brown Fndn Grants, 854
Burlington Industries Fndn Grants, 865
Burlington Northern Santa Fe Fndn Grants, 866
Cailloux Fndn Grants, 892
Central Carolina Community Fndn Community Impact Grants, 994
CFFVR Basic Needs Giving Partnership Grants, 1002
Charles M. Bair Family Grants, 1051
Charles Stewart Mott Fndn Grants, 1055
Chatlos Fndn Grants, 1061
Chesapeake Corp Fndn Grants, 1076
Chicago Tribune Fndn Civic Grants, 1100
Chicago White Metal Charitable Fndn Grants, 1102
CICF Indianapolis Fndn Community Grants, 1123
CICF Legacy Grants, 1126
CIGNA Fndn Grants, 1130
Cincinnati Bell Fndn Grants, 1131
CIRCLE Civic Educ at the High School Level Research Grants, 1135
Civic Change Award, 1143
Clarcor Fndn Grants, 1148
Cleveland-Cliffs Fndn Grants, 1165

Cleveland Community Responsive Grants, 1168
Clinton County Community Fndn Grants, 1174
Clorox Company Fndn Grants, 1176
CNA Fndn Grants, 1179
CNCS AmeriCorps NCCC Project Grants, 1181
Cockrell Fndn Grants, 1196
Colgate-Palmolive Company Grants, 1202
Colorado Interstate Gas Grants, 1213
Columbus Fndn Mary Eleanor Morris Grants, 1225
Columbus Fndn Small Grants, 1232
Comerica Charitable Fndn Grants, 1237
Commonwealth Edison Grants, 1240
Community Fndn for Greater Buffalo Grants, 1247
Community Fndn for Greater New Haven Neighborhood Small Grants, 1249
Community Fndn for Greater New Haven Valley Neighborhood Grants, 1253
Community Fndn for NE Michigan Grants, 1257
Community Fndn for SE Michigan Grants, 1259
Community Fndn of Greater Greensboro Grants, 1288
Community Fndn of Howard County Grants, 1297
Community Fndn of Middle Tennessee Grants, 1300
Community Fndn of Muncie and Delaware County Maxon Grants, 1303
Community Fndn of Santa Cruz County Grants, 1305
Community Fndn of Sarasota County Grants, 1306
Community Fndn of South Alabama Grants, 1308
Community Fndn of SE Connecticut Grants, 1309
Community Fndn of St. Joseph County Special Project Challenge Grants, 1314
Community Fndn of the Verdugos Grants, 1322
Community Partners Lawrence County Grants, 1328
Community Partnerships Martin County Grants, 1329
Community Impact Fund, 1332
Community in the Connecting AAPIs To Advocate and Lead Grants, 1333
Con Edison Corp Giving Civic Grants, 1345
Connecticut Light & Power Corp Contributions, 1352
Connelly Fndn Grants, 1353
ConocoPhillips Grants, 1355
Consumers Energy Fndn, 1365
Cooper Industries Fndn Grants, 1370
Cranston Fndn Grants, 1395
Crown Point Community Fndn Grants, 1402
Cruise Industry Charitable Fndn Grants, 1404
CSRA Community Fndn Grants, 1407
CSX Corp Contributions Grants, 1408
Cumberland Community Fndn Grants, 1413
DaimlerChrysler Corp Grants, 1432
Dana Corp Fndn Grants, 1440
Dayton Fndn Grants, 1463
Dayton Power and Light Fndn Grants, 1464
Decatur County Comm Large Project Grants, 1476
Dell Fndn Open Grants, 1490
Delta Air Lines Community Enrichment Grants, 1494
Denver Fndn Community Grants, 1502
Detroit Lions Charities Grants, 1520
Dr. Scholl Fndn Grants, 1602
Duluth-Superior Area Community Fndn Grants, 1620
Dunspaugh-Dalton Fndn Grants, 1623
Eastman Chemical Company Fndn Grants, 1643
eBay Fndn Community Grants, 1648
Elmer L. and Eleanor J. Andersen Fndn Grants, 1687
El Paso Community Fndn Grants, 1688
El Pomar Fndn Awards and Grants, 1690
Ethel Sergeant Clark Smith Fndn Grants, 1761
Evan and Susan Bayh Fndn Grants, 1769
F.M. Kirby Fndn Grants, 1780
Fargo-Moorhead Area Fndn Woman's Grants, 1789
Farmers Insurance Corp Giving Grants, 1791
Faye McBeath Fndn Grants, 1794
Ferree Fndn Grants, 1804
Fifth Third Fndn Grants, 1810
FirstEnergy Fndn Community Grants, 1819
Florida Humanities Civic Reflection Grants, 1867
Floyd A. and Kathleen C. Cailloux Fndn Grants, 1874
Fluor Fndn Grants, 1875
Ford Fndn Peace and Social Justice Grants, 1884
Ford Motor Company Grants, 1885
Fndn for the Carolinas Grants, 1896

SUBJECT INDEX

Civic Engagement / 837

Fndn NW Grants, 1906
France-Merrick Fndns Grants, 1915
Frank S. Flowers Fndn Grants, 1935
Frey Fndn Grants, 1963
Fulton County Community Fndn Grants, 1975
Fund for the City of New York Grants, 1978
GenCorp Fndn Grants, 1998
General Dynamics Corp Grants, 2001
George Gund Fndn Grants, 2020
Georgia-Pacific Fndn Entrepreneurship Grants, 2033
Gibson County Community Fndn Women's Fund, 2051
GMFUS Black Sea Trust for Regional Grants, 2065
GNOF IMPACT Grants for Youth Development, 2081
Goldseker Fndn Community Affairs Grants, 2100
Goodrich Corp Fndn Grants, 2104
Goodyear Tire Grants, 2106
Grace and Franklin Bernsen Fndn Grants, 2109
Grand Haven Area Community Fndn Grants, 2113
Greater Tacoma Community Fndn Grants, 2139
Greater Worcester Comm Discretionary Grants, 2140
Green Bay Packers Fndn Grants, 2148
Gulf Coast Community Fndn Grants, 2174
H.A. and Mary K. Chapman Charitable Grants, 2182
Halliburton Fndn Grants, 2211
Hallmark Corp Fndn Grants, 2212
Hancock County Community Fndn - Field of Interest Grants, 2219
HBF Encouraging Citizen Involvement Grants, 2272
Helen K. and Arthur E. Johnson Fndn Grants, 2296
Helen S. Boylan Fndn Grants, 2298
Hillman Fndn Grants, 2327
Hilton Hotels Corp Giving Grants, 2331
Hoblitzelle Fndn Grants, 2341
Household Int'l Corp Giving Grants, 2372
Howard and Bush Fndn Grants, 2374
Howard County Community Fndn Grants, 2375
Hugh J. Andersen Fndn Grants, 2385
Huntington County Community Fndn - Make a Difference Grants, 2406
Hutton Fndn Grants, 2412
Hyams Fndn Grants, 2413
IMLS 21st Century Museum Pro Grants, 2512
IMLS American Heritage Preservation Grants, 2513
IMLS National Leadership Grants, 2515
ING Fndn Grants, 2555
Intergrys Corp Grants, 2565
IREX Kosovo Civil Society Project Grants, 2576
IREX Russia Civil Society Support Grants, 2580
IREX Small Grant Fund for Civil Society Projects in Africa and Asia, 2581
ISI William Simon Fellows for Noble Purpose, 2588
J.L. Bedsole Fndn Grants, 2600
James L. and Mary Jane Bowman Grants, 2632
John Deere Fndn Grants, 2692
John J. Leidy Fndn Grants, 2701
John Merck Grants, 2706
John S. and James L. Knight Fndn Communities Grants, 2711
John S. and James L. Knight Fndn National and New Inits Grants, 2714
Johnson Controls Fndn Civic Activities Grants, 2720
Katharine Matthies Fndn Grants, 2788
Kosciusko County Community Fndn Grants, 2838
Laclede Gas Charitable Grants, 2848
Lake County Community Fndn Grants, 2856
Land O'Lakes Fndn California Region Grants, 2858
Laura Jane Musser Rural Init Grants, 2864
Liberty Hill Fndn Environmental Justice Grants, 2891
Liberty Hill Fndn Fund for Change Grants, 2893
Liberty Hill Fndn Seed Grants, 2896
Liberty Hill Fndn Special Opportunity Grants, 2897
Lisa and Douglas Goldman Grants, 2910
Lockheed Martin Philanthropic Grants, 2918
Louie M. and Betty M. Phillips Fndn Grants, 2923
Lubbock Area Fndn Grants, 2931
Lubrizol Fndn Grants, 2933
Lynde and Harry Bradley Fndn Grants, 2947
Lynde and Harry Bradley Fndn Prizes, 2948
Madison County Community Fndn - City of Anderson Quality of Life Grant, 2972

Madison County Community General Grants, 2973
Mars Fndn Grants, 3025
Marsh Corp Grants, 3027
Mary & Walter Frear Eleemosynary Grants, 3035
Mary K. Chapman Fndn Grants, 3042
McCombs Fndn Grants, 3075
McCune Fndn Civic Grants, 3078
Meadows Fndn Grants, 3104
MeadWestvaco Sustainable Communities Grant, 3105
Meriden Fndn Grants, 3122
Mertz Gilmore Climate Change Grants, 3125
Mertz Gilmore Fndn NYC Communities Grants, 3126
MGM Resorts Fndn Community Grants, 3153
Microsoft Comm Affairs Puget Sound Grants, 3163
Morris and Gwendolyn Cafritz Fndn Grants, 3218
Motorola Fndn Grants, 3221
Ms. Fndn Women Building Democracy Grants, 3223
Musgrave Fndn Grants, 3231
National Endowment for Arts Our Town Grants, 3257
National Endowment for the Arts - Regional Partnership Agreement Grants, 3258
NHSCA Arts in Health Care Project Grants, 3424
NHSCA General Project Grants, 3427
Nina Mason Pulliam Charitable Grants, 3443
Noble County Community Fndn Grants, 3456
Norcliffe Fndn Grants, 3459
Nord Family Fndn Grants, 3461
Nordson Corp Fndn Grants, 3462
Northern Trust Company Corp Giving Program, 3504
NYCT Civic Affairs Grants, 3545
NYCT Hunger and Homelessnes Grants, 3553
Onan Family Fndn Grants, 3672
Orange County Community Fndn Grants, 3687
Owens Corning Fndn Grants, 3717
PACCAR Fndn Grants, 3719
Pacific Life Fndn Grants, 3726
PacifiCorp Fndn for Learning Grants, 3727
Paul and Mary Haas Fndn Contributions and Student Scholarships, 3756
Paul Ogle Fndn Grants, 3764
Percy B. Ferebee Endowment Grants, 3820
Pew Charitable Trusts Civic Project Grants, 3859
Philip L. Graham Grants, 3876
Piedmont Natural Gas Corp and Charitable Contributions, 3883
Piper Jaffray Fndn Communities Giving Grants, 3899
Plum Creek Fndn Grants, 3917
PMI Fndn Grants, 3918
Powell Family Fndn Grants, 3941
Princeton Area Community Fndn Greater Mercer Grants, 3963
Procter and Gamble Grants, 3967
Puerto Rico Community Fndn Grants, 3986
Putnam Fndn Grants, 3991
Rainbow Endowment Grants, 4007
Ralph M. Parsons Fndn Grants, 4013
RCF General Community Grants, 4032
RGK Fndn Grants, 4072
Rice Fndn Grants, 4074
Richard and Rhoda Goldman Grants, 4077
Richard King Mellon Fndn Grants, 4087
Robert R. McCormick Tribune Civics Grants, 4118
Robert W. Woodruff Fndn Grants, 4124
Rochester Area Community Fndn Grants, 4127
Rockefeller Brothers Democratic Practice Grants, 4131
Rockefeller Brothers Peace and Security Grants, 4133
Rockefeller Brothers Pivotal Places Grants: New York City, 4134
Rockefeller Brothers Pivotal Places Grants: Serbia, Montenegro, and Kosova, 4135
Rockefeller Brothers Sustainable Devel Grants, 4136
Rockefeller Family Grants, 4137
Rohm and Haas Company Grants, 4145
Ronald McDonald House Charities Grants, 4149
Rose Hills Fndn Grants, 4162
Ruth and Vernon Taylor Fndn Grants, 4177
Sage Fndn Grants, 4204
Salisbury Community Fndn Grants, 4224
San Diego Fndn Civil Society Grants, 4244
San Diego Women's Fndn Grants, 4252

Schramm Fndn Grants, 4310
Seagate Tech Corp Capacity to Care Grants, 4317
Shell Oil Company Fndn Grants, 4343
Sony Corp of America Corp Philanthropy Grants, 4405
Sosland Fndn Grants, 4408
Spencer County Community Fndn Grants, 4451
Sprague Fndn Grants, 4461
Square D Fndn Grants, 4464
Stackpole-Hall Fndn Grants, 4472
Stark Comm Neighborhood Partnership Grants, 4479
State Strategies Grants, 4494
State Street Fndn Grants, 4495
Stewart Huston Charitable Grants, 4505
Sunderland Fndn Grants, 4527
Sunoco Fndn Grants, 4530
Surdna Fndn Sustainable Environments Grants, 4533
T. Rowe Price Associates Fndn Grants, 4548
TE Fndn Grants, 4572
Tension Envelope Fndn Grants, 4578
Texas Instruments Civic and Business Grants, 4597
Thomas W. Briggs Fndn Grants, 4621
Threshold Fndn Election Integrity Grants, 4625
Tides Fndn Grants, 4632
TJX Fndn Grants, 4637
Toro Fndn Grants, 4647
Town Creek Fndn Grants, 4650
Toyota Motor Engineering & Manufacturing North America Grants, 4651
Toyota Motor Manufacturing Mississippi Grants, 4655
Toyota Motor Manufacturing W Virginia Grants, 4657
Toyota Motor N America of New York Grants, 4658
Toyota Motor Sales, USA Grants, 4659
Triangle Community Fndn Community Grants, 4667
United Technologies Corp Grants, 4725
USAID Civic Participation Grants, 4743
USAID Civil Society Sustainability Project Grants in Bosnia and Herzegovina, 4744
US Airways Educ Fndn Grants, 4790
Vectren Fndn Grants, 4907
Vernon K. Krieble Fndn Grants, 4930
Viacom Fndn Grants (Formerly CBS Fndn), 4932
W.K. Kellogg Fndn Civic Engagement Grants, 4960
Waste Management Charitable Giving Grants, 5001
Weatherwax Fndn Grants, 5014
Weaver Fndn Grants, 5015
Wells County Fndn Grants, 5022
Westinghouse Charitable Giving Grants, 5028
Whitley County Community Fndn Grants, 5060
William Blair and Company Fndn Grants, 5078
William G. and Helen C. Hoffman Fndn Grants, 5080
Woods Charitable Grants, 5114
Xerox Fndn Grants, 5122
Z. Smith Reynolds Fndn Democracy and Civic Engagement Grants, 5145

Civic Engagement

AEGON Transamerica Fndn Civic and Community Grants, 177
ALA President's Award for Advocacy, 310
ATA Political Engagement Grant, 601
Ben B. Cheney Fndn Grants, 725
Bernard and Audre Rapoport Fndn Democracy and Civic Participation Grants, 737
CDECD Arts Catalyze Placemaking in Every Community Grants, 977
CDECD Arts Catalyze Placemaking Leadership Grants, 978
CDECD Arts Catalyze Placemaking Sustaining Relevance Grants, 979
Community Fndn of Greater Fort Wayne - John S. and James L. Knight Fndn Donor-Advised Grants, 1287
Con Edison Corp Giving Civic Grants, 1345
Decatur County Comm Small Project Grants, 1477
Ford Family Grants Public Convening Spaces, 1881
GNOF Coastal 5 + 1 Grants, 2070
GNOF IMPACT Grants for Educ, 2079
GNOF IMPACT Grants for Youth Development, 2081
GNOF Stand Up For Our Children Grants, 2093
Goldseker Fndn Community Affairs Grants, 2100
Johnson Controls Fndn Civic Activities Grants, 2720

838 / Civic Engagement

Mabel Louise Riley Family Strengthening Grants, 2958
Maine Community Fndn People of Color Grants, 2985
McCune Fndn Civic Grants, 3078
Medtronic Fndn Community Link Arts, Civic, and Culture Grants, 3109
Mertz Gilmore Fndn NYC Communities Grants, 3126
Ms. Fndn Women Building Democracy Grants, 3223
National 4-H Afterschool Training Grants, 3248
National Endowment for Arts Commun Grants, 3260
National Endowment for the Arts Dance Grants: Art Works, 3262
Nokomis Fndn Grants, 3457
OSF Documentary Photography Project Audience Engagement Grant, 3706
Philanthrofund Fndn Grants, 3874
Piper Trust Older Adults Grants, 3904
PMI Fndn Grants, 3918
Robert R. McCormick Tribune Civics Grants, 4118
Rockefeller Brothers Democratic Practice Grants, 4131
Rockefeller Brothers Peace and Security Grants, 4133
Rockefeller Brothers Pivotal Places Grants: Serbia, Montenegro, and Kosova, 4135
Rockefeller Brothers Sustainable Devel Grants, 4136
Sioux Falls Area Community Fundn Grants, 4364
Sioux Falls Area Community Fndn Spot Grants, 4366
Texas Instruments Civic and Business Grants, 4597
Threshold Fndn Justice and Democracy Grants, 4626
Union Bank, N.A. Fndn Grants, 4709
USAID Civic Participation Grants, 4743
USAID Community Livelihoods Project in Yemen Grant, 4746
YSA MLK Day Lead Organizer Grants, 5136

Civics

Ben B. Cheney Fndn Grants, 725
Bernard and Audre Rapoport Fndn Democracy and Civic Participation Grants, 737
Con Edison Corp Giving Civic Grants, 1345
Gill Fndn - Gay and Lesbian Grants, 2054
Hershey Company Grants, 2318
Johnson Controls Fndn Civic Activities Grants, 2720
McCune Fndn Civic Grants, 3078
Toyota Motor Engineering & Manufacturing North America Grants, 4651
Toyota Motor Manufacturing of Texas Grants, 4656
Toyota Motor Manufacturing W Virginia Grants, 4657
Toyota Motor N America of New York Grants, 4658
Toyota Motor Sales, USA Grants, 4659

Civics Education

ACF Ethnic Community Self-Help Grants, 118
Asian American Institute Impact Fellowships, 588
Ben B. Cheney Fndn Grants, 725
Bernard and Audre Rapoport Fndn Democracy and Civic Participation Grants, 737
CIRCLE Civic Educ at the High School Level Research Grants, 1135
Civic Educ Consortium Grants, 1144
Community in the Connecting AAPIs To Advocate and Lead Grants, 1333
Con Edison Corp Giving Civic Grants, 1345
FAS Project Schools Grants, 1792
Hatton W. Sumners Fndn for the Study and Teaching of Self Government Grants, 2257
HBF Encouraging Citizen Involvement Grants, 2272
Johnson Controls Fndn Civic Activities Grants, 2720
McCune Fndn Civic Grants, 3078
NYCT Civic Affairs Grants, 3545
Pew Charitable Trusts Civic Project Grants, 3859
Richard King Mellon Fndn Grants, 4087
Robert R. McCormick Tribune Civics Grants, 4118
Threshold Fndn Election Integrity Grants, 4625
United States Institute of Peace - National Peace Essay Contest for High School Students, 4724
USAID Civic Participation Grants, 4743
W.K. Kellogg Fndn Civic Engagement Grants, 4960

Civil Law

IREX Kosovo Civil Society Project Grants, 2576
IREX Moldova Citizen Participation Grants, 2578
IREX Russia Civil Society Support Grants, 2580
IREX Small Grant Fund for Civil Society Projects in Africa and Asia, 2581
John Merck Grants, 2706
Nation Institute Robert Masur Fellowship in Civil Liberties, 3284
Threshold Fndn Election Integrity Grants, 4625
USAID Economic Prospectsfor Armenia-Turkey Normalization Grants, 4750

Civil Service

CNCS AmeriCorps NCCC Project Grants, 1181
IREX Moldova Citizen Participation Grants, 2578
IREX Small Grant Fund for Civil Society Projects in Africa and Asia, 2581
John Merck Grants, 2706
OSF Civil Service Awards, 3705
USAID Civil Society Sustainability Project Grants in Bosnia and Herzegovina, 4744

Civil Society

Cowles Charitable Grants, 1392
David Bohnett Fndn Grants, 1451
Ford Fndn Peace and Social Justice Grants, 1884
Joel L. Fleishman Civil Society Fellowships, 2683
OSF Burma Project/SE Asia Init Grants, 3702
Proteus Grants, 3973
USAID Civil Society Sustainability Project Grants in Bosnia and Herzegovina, 4744
USAID Economic Prospectsfor Armenia-Turkey Normalization Grants, 4750

Civil War

ALA Coretta Scott King Book Awards, 260
Richard and Caroline T. Gwathmey Grants, 4075

Civil/Human Rights

A.J. Muste Memorial Institute General Grants, 44
Abelard Fndn East Grants, 87
Abelard Fndn West Grants, 88
Agape Fndn for Nonviolent Social Change Board of Trustees Grants, 197
Agape for Nonviolent Social Change Peace Prizes, 198
Akonadi Fndn Anti-Racism Grants, 217
ALA Coretta Scott King Book Awards, 260
ALA Paul Howard Award for Courage, 307
Allstate Corp Giving Grants, 386
Allstate Corp Hometown Commitment Grants, 387
Allstate Fndn Safe and Vital Communities Grants, 390
Alvah H. and Wyline P. Chapman Fndn Grants, 402
American Jewish World Service Grants, 441
AmerUs Group Charitable Fndn, 455
Andrew Goodman Fndn Grants, 463
Arca Fndn Grants, 526
Arizona Community Fndn Grants, 540
Assisi Fndn of Memphis Capital Project Grants, 593
Assisi Fndn of Memphis General Grants, 594
Assisi Fndn of Memphis Mini Grants, 595
Atlanta Women's Fndn Grants, 609
Bernard and Audre Rapoport Fndn Democracy and Civic Participation Grants, 737
Blumenthal Fndn Grants, 804
Brico Grants, 835
Bydale Fndn Grants, 882
CarEth Fndn Grants, 924
Carrier Corp Contributions Grants, 946
CCF Social and Economic Justice Grants, 964
Coastal Community Fndn of S Carolina Grants, 1193
Commission on Religion in Appalachia Grants, 1238
Community Fndn Greater Chattanooga Grants, 1281
Community Fndn of Greater Greensboro Grants, 1288
Community Fndn of Western N Carolina Grants, 1327
Compton Fndn Grants, 1338
Conrad N. Hilton Humanitarian Prize, 1356
Corina Higginson Grants, 1373
Cowles Charitable Grants, 1392
Crossroads Fund Seed Grants, 1400
Cummins Fndn Grants, 1415
David and Barbara B. Hirschhorn Fndn Grants, 1450
David Bohnett Fndn Grants, 1451

SUBJECT INDEX

David Geffen Fndn Grants, 1452
Dept of Ed Magnet Schools Assistance Grants, 1509
Eugene McDermott Fndn Grants, 1765
Evelyn and Walter Haas, Jr. Fund Gay and Lesbian Rights Grants, 1772
Evelyn and Walter Haas, Jr. Fund Immigrant Rights Grants, 1773
Fargo-Moorhead Area Fndn Grants, 1788
FCYO Youth Organizing Grants, 1797
Fitzpatrick, Cella, Harper & Scinto Pro Bono, 1836
Ford Fndn Peace and Social Justice Grants, 1884
Ford Motor Company Grants, 1885
Frank Stanley Beveridge Fndn Grants, 1936
Fred C. and Mary R. Koch Fndn Grants, 1943
Fund for Southern Communities Grants, 1977
Gill Fndn - Gay and Lesbian Grants, 2054
Gregory C. Carr Fndn Grants, 2161
H.J. Heinz Company Fndn Grants, 2184
Harold Simmons Fndn Grants, 2230
Harry Chapin Fndn Grants, 2240
HBF Defending Freedoms Grants, 2271
Henry J. Kaiser Family Fndn Grants, 2310
Herman Goldman Fndn Grants, 2317
Horizons Community Issues Grants, 2366
Int'l Human Rights Funders Grants, 2567
IREX Kosovo Civil Society Project Grants, 2576
IREX Moldova Citizen Participation Grants, 2578
IREX Russia Civil Society Support Grants, 2580
IREX Small Grant Fund for Civil Society Projects in Africa and Asia, 2581
ISI William Simon Fellows for Noble Purpose, 2588
Jacob and Hilda Blaustein Fndn Grants, 2615
Jay and Rose Phillips Family Fndn Grants, 2656
Jenifer Altman Fndn Grants, 2662
Jewish Funds for Justice Grants, 2676
John D. and Catherine T. MacArthur Fndn Global Challenges Grants, 2690
John Merck Grants, 2706
Joyce Fndn Democracy Grants, 2748
Knox County Community Fndn Grants, 2831
Liberty Hill Fndn Environmental Justice Grants, 2891
Liberty Hill Fndn Fund for Change Grants, 2893
Liberty Hill Fndn Seed Grants, 2896
Liberty Hill Fndn Special Opportunity Grants, 2897
Lisa and Douglas Goldman Grants, 2910
Margaret L. Wendt Fndn Grants, 3004
Marriott Int'l Corp Giving Grants, 3024
Max and Anna Levinson Fndn Grants, 3066
Maytree Fndn Refugee and Immigrant Grants, 3071
Mertz Gilmore Fndn NYC Communities Grants, 3126
Minneapolis Fndn Community Grants, 3186
Nation Institute Robert Masur Fellowship in Civil Liberties, 3284
Needmor Grants, 3289
New York Fndn Grants, 3338
NLADA Kutak-Dodds Prizes, 3451
Norman Fndn Grants, 3464
NRA Fndn Grants, 3517
NYCT Fund for New Citizens Grants, 3547
OSF Advancing the Rights and Integration of Roma Grants, 3699
OSF Arab Regional Office Grants, 3701
OSF Burma Project/SE Asia Init Grants, 3702
OSF Central Eurasia Project Grants, 3704
OSF Documentary Photography Project Audience Engagement Grant, 3706
OSF Human Rights and Governance Grants, 3708
OSI Sentencing and Incarceration Alternatives Project Grants, 3711
Ottinger Fndn Grants, 3712
Otto Bremer Fndn Grants, 3713
OUT Fund for Lesbian & Gay Liberation Grants, 3714
Overbrook Fndn Grants, 3715
Paul Green Fndn Human Rights Project Grants, 3761
PDF Community Organizing Grants, 3807
PDF Fiscal Sponsorship Grant, 3808
Petra Fndn Fellows Awards, 3850
Philadelphia Organizational Effectiveness Grants, 3872
Philanthrofund Fndn Grants, 3874
Playboy Fndn Grants, 3913

SUBJECT INDEX

Proteus Grants, 3973
Rainbow Endowment Grants, 4007
Rajiv Gandhi Fndn Grants, 4011
Righteous Persons Fndn Grants, 4093
Robert F. Kennedy Human Rights Award, 4111
Samuel Rubin Fndn Grants, 4237
Samuel S. Johnson Fndn Grants, 4239
San Diego Fndn for Change Grants, 4247
Scherman Fndn Grants, 4305
Sidney Stern Grants, 4349
Sir Dorabji Tata Grants for NGOs or Voluntary Organizations, 4370
Sister Grants for Women's Organizations, 4371
Skoll Fndn Awards for Social Entrepreneurship, 4383
Social Justice Fund NW Criminal Justice Giving Project Grants, 4394
Social Justice Fund NW Economic Justice Giving Project Grants, 4395
Social Justice Fund NW General Grants, 4397
Social Justice Fund NW LGBTQ Giving Project Grants, 4398
Social Justice Fund NW Montana Project Grants, 4399
Southern Poverty Law Center Strategic Litigation Grants, 4439
Steelcase Fndn Grants, 4497
Teaching Tolerance Grants, 4567
Teaching Tolerance Mix-it-Up Grants, 4568
Third Wave Fndn Lela Breitbart Grants, 4609
Third Wave Organizing & Advocacy Grants, 4610
Third Wave Reproductive Health & Justice Grants, 4611
Tides Fndn Grants, 4632
Tifa Fndn Grants, 4633
United Methodist Women Brighter Future for Children and Youth Grants, 4723
United States Institute of Peace - National Peace Essay Contest for High School Students, 4724
USAID Civil Society Sustainability Project Grants in Bosnia and Herzegovina, 4744
Vanguard Public Fndn Grant Funds, 4904
Vernon K. Krieble Fndn Grants, 4930
Warrick County Community Fndn Grants, 4987
Weaver Fndn Grants, 5015
Women's Funding Alliance Grants, 5112
YSA MLK Day Lead Organizer Grants, 5136

Classroom Instruction
Air Force Association Junior ROTC Grants, 215
Arkema Fndn Science Teachers Program, 563
Charles Stewart Mott Fndn Grants, 1055
Civic Educ Consortium Grants, 1144
Clowes Grants, 1177
Coca-Cola Fndn Grants, 1195
EDS Technology Grants, 1662
FEDCO Charitable Fndn Educ Grants, 1798
Fndn for the Mid South Educ Grants, 1898
IIE Toyota Int'l Teacher Professional Dev Grants, 2461
J. Knox Gholston Fndn Grants, 2599
J. Marion Sims Fndn Teachers' Pet Grant, 2605
Kettering Grants, 2818
KeySpan Fndn Grants, 2821
Long Island Community Fndn Grants, 2920
Melinda Gray Ardia Environmental Fndn Grants, 3114
National Endowment for Arts Theater Grants, 3269
Public Educ Power Grants, 3981
Randall L. Tobias Fndn Grants, 4017
Robert R. McCormick Tribune Civics Grants, 4118
Sprint Fndn Grants, 4463
Stuart Fndn Grants, 4516
UPS Fndn Economic and Global Lit Grants, 4730
Vectren Fndn Grants, 4907

Climatology
Bullitt Fndn Grants, 862
Energy Fndn Buildings Grants, 1705
Energy Fndn Climate Grants, 1706
Freshwater Future Climate Grants, 1958
Jenifer Altman Fndn Grants, 2662
NFWF Marine & Coastal Conservation Grants, 3377
Threshold Fndn Sustainable Planet Grants, 4627
USAID Global Development Alliance Grants, 4753

Clinical Medicine, General
Bristol-Myers Squibb Clinical Outcomes and Research Grants, 839
CVS All Kids Can Grants, 1420
Henry and Ruth Blaustein Rosenberg Grants, 2306
MMS and Alliance Charitable Fndn Int'l Health Studies Grants, 3195
Piper Trust Healthcare & Med Research Grants, 3903

Clinical Research
Meyer and Pepa Gold Family Fndn Grants, 3138
MMS and Alliance Charitable Fndn Int'l Health Studies Grants, 3195
NHLBI Ancillary Studies in Clinical Trials, 3410
NHLBI Ruth L. Kirschstein National Research Service Awards for Individual Postdoctoral Fellows, 3418
NHLBI Ruth L. Kirschstein National Research Service Awards for Individual Predoctoral MD/PhD Fellows and Other Dual Degree Fellows, 3420
NSF Accelerating Innovation Research, 3520
Perpetual Trust for Charitable Giving Grants, 3826
Victor E. Speas Fndn Grants, 4933

Clinical Trials
Bristol-Myers Squibb Clinical Outcomes and Research Grants, 839
NHLBI Investigator Initiated Multi-Site Clinical Trials, 3413

Clinics
Ann Arbor Area Community Fndn Grants, 474
California Community Fndn Health Care Grants, 901
Clark and Ruby Baker Fndn Grants, 1154
Covidien Medical Product Donations, 1390
Crystelle Waggoner Charitable Grants, 1405
Deborah Munroe Noonan Grants, 1475
E. Rhodes and Leona B. Carpenter Fndn Grants, 1640
Fondren Fndn Grants, 1878
Fndn for Health Enhancement Grants, 1894
George E. Hatcher, Jr. and Ann Williams Hatcher Fndn Grants, 2015
George W. Wells Fndn Grants, 2030
Gladys Brooks Fndn Grants, 2059
GNOF IMPACT Gulf States Eye Surgery Fund, 2082
Helen Irwin Littauer Ed Grants, 2295
Lumpkin Family Healthy People Grants, 2942
Lydia deForest Charitable Grants, 2946
Marietta McNeill Morgan and Samuel Tate Morgan, Jr. Grants, 3008
Meyer Fndn Healthy Communities Grants, 3143
Mt. Sinai Health Care Fndn Health of the Urban Community Grants, 3227
Norfolk Southern Fndn Grants, 3463
Piper Trust Healthcare & Med Research Grants, 3903
RCF General Community Grants, 4032
Reinberger Fndn Grants, 4052
Sheltering Arms Grants, 4344
Union Square Awards Grants, 4718

Coal Processing
Illinois DCEO Coal Competitiveness Grants, 2484
Illinois DCEO Coal Demonstration Grants, 2485
Illinois DCEO Coal Revival Grants, 2487

Coastal Processes
California Coastal Art and Poetry Contest, 899
GNOF Bayou Communities Grants, 2069
MDEQ Beach Monitoring Grants - Inland Lakes, 3094
MDEQ Coastal Management Planning and Construction Grants, 3097
MDEQ Great Lakes Areas of Concern Land Acquisition Grants, 3099
NFWF Columbia River Estuarine Coastal Grant, 3367
NFWF Community Salmon Fund Partnerships, 3368
NFWF King County Community Salmon Grants, 3375
NFWF Marine & Coastal Conservation Grants, 3377
NFWF Oregon Governor's Fund for the Environment Grants, 3383
NFWF Pacific Grassroots Salmonid Init Grants, 3384
NFWF Pierce Community Salmon Grant, 3385

NFWF Pioneers in Conservation Grants, 3386
NFWF Radical Salmon Design Contest, 3388
NFWF Salmon Recovery Funding Board Community Salmon Grants, 3389
NW Fund for the Environment Grants, 3510
Park Fndn Grants, 3739
Richard and Rhoda Goldman Grants, 4077

Cognitive Development/Processes
ACF Head Start and Early Head Start Grants, 120
Charlotte R. Schmidlapp Grants, 1058
CVS Community Grants, 1422
Dekko Fndn Grants, 1482
Dwight Stuart Youth Fndn Grants, 1628
Head Start Replacement Grantee: Colorado, 2275
Head Start Replacement Grantee: Florida, 2276
Head Start Replacement Grantee: West Virginia, 2277
National Center for Resp Gaming Travel Grants, 3251
Peter and Elizabeth C. Tower Fndn Phase II Technology Init Grants, 3839
Peter and Elizabeth C. Tower Fndn Phase I Technology Init Grants, 3840

Collaboration
ALA Sara Jaffarian School Library Award for Exemplary Humanities Programming, 316
Arkansas Arts Council Collab Project Support, 555
Bill and Melinda Gates Fndn Agricultural Development Grants, 765
California Endowment Innovative Ideas Challenge Grants, 904
Chicago Community Trust Arts and Culture Grants: Supporting Diverse Arts Productions and Fostering Art in Every Community, 1084
Chicago Community Trust Health Grants, 1087
Chicago Community Trust Preventing and Eliminating Hunger Grants, 1092
Chicago Community Trust Public Safety and Justice Grants, 1093
CNCS Social Innovation Grants, 1189
GNOF Coastal 5 + 1 Grants, 2070
GNOF Community Revitalization Grants, 2071
GNOF Environmental Grants, 2073
GNOF Gulf Coast Oil Spill Grants, 2077
GNOF IMPACT Grants for Health and Human Services, 2080
GNOF IMPACT Grants for Youth Development, 2081
GNOF Norco Community Grants, 2089
GNOF Organizational Effectiveness Grants and Workshops, 2090
GNOF Stand Up For Our Children Grants, 2093
Helen Bader Fndn Grants, 2293
IRA Pearson Fndn-IRA-Rotary Lit Awards, 2572
Maine Community Fndn Edward H. Daveis Benevolent Grants, 2979
National Endowment for the Arts Dance Grants: Art Works, 3262
National Endowment for Arts Theater Grants, 3269
Nonprofit Management Grants, 3458
NW Minnesota Fndn Asset Building Grants, 3511
Piper Trust Arts and Culture Grants, 3900
Rasmuson Fndn Creative Ventures Grants, 4021
Santa Barbara Fndn Monthly Express Grants, 4284
Teagle Fndn Grants, 4569
Trinity Trust Community Response Grants, 4671
Union Square Arts Award, 4716
WCI Community Mobilization Grants, 5009

College-Preparatory Education
3M Fndn Community Giving Grants, 15
CenturyLink Clarke M. Williams Fndn Grants, 998
Chicago Community Trust Arts and Culture Grants: Improving Access to Arts Learning Opps, 1082
Chicago Community Trust Educ Grants, 1085
CNCS AmeriCorps State and National Grants, 1182
Dwight Stuart Youth Fndn Grants, 1628
Florida High School/High Tech Project Grants, 1866
Fndn for the Mid South Educ Grants, 1898
Georgia-Pacific Fndn Educ Grants, 2031
Goizueta Fndn Grants, 2096

840 / College-Preparatory Education

GTECH Community Involvement Grants, 2171
Legacy Fndn College Readiness Grant, 2874
Mary Wilmer Covey Charitable Grants, 3049
McCune Charitable Fndn Grants, 3077
Meyer Fndn Educ Grants, 3142
Piper Trust Educ Grants, 3902
Teagle Fndn Grants, 4569
Time Warner Diverse Voices in the Arts Grants, 4635

Comedic Artists
HAF Arts and Culture: Lynne and Bob Wells Grant for Performing Artists, 2190

Communications
Abell-Hanger Fndn Grants, 91
American Express Historic Preservation Grants, 431
Brainerd Fndn Grants, 831
Canada-U.S. Fulbright Mid-Career Grants, 917
Chicago Board of Trade Fndn Grants, 1079
Citigroup Fndn Grants, 1139
Dekko Fndn Grants, 1482
EPA Children's Health Protection Grants, 1728
EQT Fndn Educ Grants, 1745
Heineman Fndn for Research, Educ, Charitable and Scientific Purposes, 2290
Henry J. Kaiser Family Fndn Grants, 2310
Homer A. Scott and Mildred S. Scott Grants, 2350
Kalamazoo Community Fndn Front Porch Grants, 2767
Microsoft Software Donation Grants, 3164
Motorola Fndn Grants, 3221
NSF CISE Communicating Research to Public Audiences Grants, 3522
NSF CISE Community-Based Data Interoperability Networks Grants, 3523
NSF CISE Computing and Communication Fndns: Core Programs Grants, 3525
OSF Affordable Access to Digital Communications Init, 3700
Philip L. Graham Grants, 3876
Rainbow Media Holdings Corp Giving, 4010
Sprint Fndn Grants, 4463
USDA Rural Utilities Service Weather Radio Transmitter Grants, 4833
USDC Technology Opportunities Grants, 4860
Viacom Fndn Grants (Formerly CBS Fndn), 4932
Washington Area Women's Fndn Strategic Opportunity and Partnership Grants, 4996
William C. Kenney Watershed Protection Fndn Ecosystem Grants, 5079

Communicative Disorders, Hearing
Reinberger Fndn Grants, 4052

Community Colleges
AACC Building Better Communities Through Regional Economic Development Partnerships, 54
Bank of America Charitable Fndn Educ and Workforce Development Grants, 657
Chicago Community Trust Workforce Grants, 1094
Delaware Division of the Arts Community-Based Organizations Opportunity Grants, 1487
Edna Haddad Welfare Trust Fund Scholarships, 1658
Emma G. Harris Fndn Grants, 1701
GNOF New Orleans Works Grants, 2088
Guy I. Bromley Grants, 2180
Kentucky Arts Council Access Assistance Grants, 2805
Louetta M. Cowden Fndn Grants, 2922
Marion Gardner Jackson Charitable Grants, 3017
Norfolk Southern Fndn Grants, 3463
Olive Smith Browning Charitable Grants, 3671
Reinberger Fndn Grants, 4052

Community Development
1st and 10 Fndn Grants, 1
2 Depot Square Ipswich Charitable Fndn Grants, 4
3M Company Arts and Culture Grants, 12
3M Company Health and Human Services Grants, 14
4S Ranch~Del Sur Community Fndn Grants, 17
7-Eleven Coorporate Giving Grants, 18
41 Washington Street Fndn Grants, 22

118 Fndn Grants, 29
300th Quincy Block Association Grants, 31
A.J. Fletcher Fndn Grants, 41
A/H Fndn Grants, 48
AACC Building Better Communities Through Regional Economic Development Partnerships, 54
AAP Resident Init Grants, 69
AAUW Int'l Project Grants, 76
Abbey Charitable Grants, 78
Abbot and Dorothy H. Stevens Fndn Grants, 79
Abbott Fund Access to Health Care Grants, 80
Abbott Fund Community Grants, 81
Abelard Fndn East Grants, 87
Abelard Fndn West Grants, 88
Abell Fndn Community Development Grants, 93
Abell Fndn Workforce Development Grants, 97
Abernethy Family Fndn Grants, 98
Able To Serve Grants, 102
Able Trust Voc Rehab Grants for Agencies, 103
ACF Assets for Indep Demonstration Grants, 114
ACF Assets for Indep Individual Development Account Grants, 115
ACF Ethnic Community Self-Help Grants, 118
ACF Fndn Grants, 119
ACF Native American Social and Economic Development Strategies Grants, 123
Ackerman Fndn Grants, 129
ACTION Council of Monterey County Grants, 134
Active Awareness Grants, 136
Adam Reineman Charitable Grants, 144
Adams County Comm Fndn of Indiana Grants, 148
Adams Family Fndn of Ohio Grants, 151
Adams Fndn Grants, 154
Adams Fndn Grants, 155
Adobe Community Investment Grants, 168
AEC Grants, 175
Aetna Fndn Arts Grants in Connecticut, 181
Aetna Fndn Strengthening Neighborhhods Grants in Connecticut, 188
Agnes M. Lindsay Grants, 203
AIChE Women's Inits Committee Mentorship Excellence Award, 209
Air Products and Chemicals Grants, 216
ALA ALSC Bookapalooza Grants, 222
ALA Baker and Taylor Entertainment Audio Music/Video Product Award, 229
ALA Baker and Taylor Summer Reading Grants, 230
ALA Charlie Robinson Award, 256
ALA Highsmith Library Innovation Award, 285
ALA Loleta D. Fyan Grant, 295
ALA Maureen Hayes Author/Illustrator Award, 299
ALA National Friends of Libraries Week Awards, 303
ALA Scholastic Library Publishing National Library Week Grant, 319
Alberto Culver Corp Contributions Grants, 343
Albert Pick Jr. Grants, 344
Alexander & Baldwin Fndn Hawaiian and Pacific Island Grants, 352
Alexander & Baldwin Fndn Mainland Grants, 353
Alexander Eastman Fndn Grants, 355
Alex Stern Family Fndn Grants, 360
Alfred J Mcallister and Dorothy N Mcallister Fndn Grants, 367
Alice Tweed Tuohy Fndn Grants, 372
All for the Earth Grants, 381
Alliance for Community Trees Home Depot Fndn NeighborWoods Grants, 382
Alliant Energy Fndn Community Grants, 384
Alliant Energy Fndn Hometown Challenge Grants, 385
Allstate Agency Hands in the Community Grants, 388
Allyn Fndn Grants, 392
Alpha Kappa Alpha Ed Advancement Fndn Community Assistance Awards, 393
Alticor Corp Community Contributions Grants, 396
Altman Fndn Health Care Grants, 397
Altman Fndn Strengthening Communities Grants, 398
AMA-MSS Chapter Involvement Grants, 406
AMA-MSS Chapter of the Year Award, 407
Amador Community Fndn Grants, 408
AMA Fndn Fund for Better Health Grants, 409

AMA Fndn Healthy Communities/Healthy America Grants, 410
AMA Fndn Jack B. McConnell, MD Awards for Excellence in Volunteerism, 411
AMD Corp Contributions Grants, 416
Ameren Corp Community Grants, 418
Amer-Scandinavian Fndn Public Project Grants, 419
American Express Charitable Grants, 429
American Express Community Service Grants, 430
American Foodservice Charitable Grants, 433
American Jewish World Service Grants, 441
American Savings Fndn Grants, 445
America the Beautiful Fund Operation Green Plant Grants, 451
Amerigroup Fndn Grants, 452
AMERIND Community Service Project Grants, 453
AmerUs Group Charitable Fndn, 455
Anderson Fndn Grants, 460
Angels Baseball Fndn Grants, 465
Anheuser-Busch Fndn Grants, 470
Ann and Robert H. Lurie Family Fndn Grants, 473
Ann Arbor Area Community Fndn Grants, 474
Anne Thorne Weaver Family Fndn Grants, 478
Annie Sinclair Knudsen Memorial Fund/Kaua'i Community Grants, 482
Appalachian Community Fund General Grants, 493
Appalachian Community Fund GLBTQ Grants, 494
Appalachian Community Media Justice Grants, 495
Appalachian Community Fund Seize the Moment Grants, 496
Appalachian Community Fund Special Opportunities Grants, 497
Appalachian Community Fund Technical Assistance Grants, 498
Appalachian Regional Commission Asset-Based Development Project Grants, 500
Appalachian Regional Commission Community Infrastructure Grants, 502
Appalachian Regional Commission Distressed Counties Grants, 503
Appalachian Regional Commission Educ and Training Grants, 504
Appalachian Regional Commission Leadership Development and Capacity Building Grants, 509
Applied Materials Corp Philanthropy Program, 515
APS Fndn Grants, 518
Aragona Family Fndn Grants, 522
Aratani Fndn Grants, 523
Arizona Public Service Corp Giving Grants, 545
Arizona State Library LSTA Community Grants, 549
Arkansas Community Fndn Giving Tree Grants, 560
Arkansas Community Fndn Grants, 561
Arlington Community Fndn Grants, 564
Armstrong McDonald Fndn Grants, 565
A Rocha USA Grants, 566
Artist Trust GAP Grants, 575
ArvinMeritor Fndn Civic Grants, 583
ATA Political Engagement Grant, 601
Autauga Area Community Fndn Grants, 618
Autodesk Community Relations Grants, 619
AutoZone Community Relations Grants, 621
Ayres Fndn Grants, 630
Babcock Charitable Grants, 632
Bacon Family Fndn Grants, 634
Bailey Fndn Grants, 635
Ball Brothers Fndn General Grants, 637
Ball Brothers Fndn Organizational Effectiveness/Executive Mentoring Grants, 638
Ball Brothers Fndn Rapid Grants, 639
Baltimore Community Fndn Arts and Culture Path Grants, 641
Baltimore Community Fndn Human Services Path Grants, 644
Baltimore Community Neighborhood Grants, 646
Baltimore Comm Neighborhoods Path Grants, 647
Baltimore Community Fndn Transportation Path Grants, 648
Baltimore Community Fndn Youth Path Grants, 649
Baltimore Women's Giving Circle Grants, 650
BancorpSouth Fndn Grants, 651

BankAtlantic Fndn Grants, 654
Bank of America Charitable Fndn Community Development Grants, 655
Bank of America Charitable Fndn Educ and Workforce Development Grants, 657
Bank of America Charitable Fndn Matching Gifts, 658
Bank of America Charitable Student Leaders Grants, 659
Bank of America Corp Sponsorships, 661
Barberton Community Fndn Grants, 666
Barnes Group Fndn Grants, 672
Barrasso Usdin Kupperman Freeman and Sarver LLC Corp Grants, 675
Baton Rouge Area Fndn Grants, 682
Battle Creek Community Fndn Grants, 684
Battle Creek Community Neighborhood Grants, 686
Batts Fndn Grants, 687
Baughman Fndn Grants, 688
Bayer Advanced Grow Together with Roses School Garden Awards, 695
BCBSM Building Healthy Communities Elementary Schools and Community Partners Grants, 704
BCBSM Community Health Matching Grants, 707
BCBSM Fndn Proposal Development Awards, 709
Beazley Fndn Grants, 714
Beckley Area Fndn Grants, 716
Ben B. Cheney Fndn Grants, 725
Bennett Family Fndn of Texas Grants, 728
Benwood Fndn Community Grants, 732
Benwood Fndn Focus Area Grants, 733
Bernard & Audre Rapoport Arts & Culture Grant, 735
Bernard and Audre Rapoport Fndn Democracy and Civic Participation Grants, 737
Bernard and Audre Rapoport Fndn Health Grants, 738
Bertha Wolf-Rosenthal Fndn for Community Service Stipend, 746
Best Buy Children's Fndn @15 Community Grants, 749
Best Buy Children's Fndn Twin Cities Minnesota Capital Grants, 753
Bikes Belong Fndn Paul David Clark Bicycling Safety Grants, 760
Bikes Belong Fndn Research Grants, 762
Bikes Belong Grants, 763
Bill and Katie Weaver Charitable Grants, 764
Bill and Melinda Gates Fndn Agricultural Development Grants, 765
Bill and Melinda Gates Fndn Financial Services for the Poor Grants, 767
Biogen Corp Giving Grants, 773
Birmingham Fndn Grants, 774
Bitha Godfrey & Maude J. Thomas Charitable Fndn Grants, 776
BJ's Wholesale Clubs Local Charitable Giving, 778
Blackford County Community Fndn Grants, 780
Black Hills Corp Grants, 781
Black River Falls Area Fndn Grants, 782
Blanche and Julian Robertson Family Fndn Grants, 785
Blandin Fndn Invest Early Grants, 788
Blandin Rural Community Leadership Grants, 790
Blue Cross Blue Shield of Minnesota Fndn - Healthy Children: Growing Up Healthy Grants, 794
Blue Cross Blue Shield of Minnesota Healthy Neighborhoods: Connect Grants, 798
Blumenthal Fndn Grants, 804
Bodenwein Public Benevolent Fndn Grants, 806
Boeing Company Contributions Grants, 809
Bohemian Fndn Pharos Grants, 811
Bollinger Fndn Grants, 812
Bonfils-Stanton Fndn Grants, 814
Bosque Fndn Grants, 818
Boulder County Arts Alliance Neodata Endowment Grants, 823
Bowling Green Community Fndn Grants, 824
Boyd Gaming Corp Contributions Program, 825
Bradley Family Fndn (California) Grants, 829
Brett Family Fndn Grants, 833
Brian G. Dyson Fndn Grants, 834
Bridgestone/Firestone Grants, 836
Brooklyn Community Caring Neighbors Grants, 848
Brooklyn Community Fndn Community Arts for All Grants, 849

Brooklyn Community Fndn Community Development Grants, 850
Brooklyn Community Fndn Educ and Youth Achievement Grants, 851
Brooklyn Community Green Communities Grants, 852
Brunswick Fndn Dollars for Doers Grants, 856
Bryan Adams Fndn Grants, 858
Burlington Industries Fndn Grants, 865
Burton D. Morgan Hudson Community Grants, 869
Business Bank of Nevada Community Grants, 879
C.F. Adams Charitable Grants, 884
Caleb C. and Julia W. Dula Ed and Charitable Fndn Grants, 893
California Arts Council State-Local Partnership Grants, 896
California Community Fndn Art Grants, 900
California Community Fndn Health Care Grants, 901
California Community Fndn Human Development Grants, 902
California Community Fndn Neighborhood Revitalization Grants, 903
California Endowment Innovative Ideas Challenge Grants, 904
California Fertilizer Fndn School Garden Grants, 905
Callaway Fndn Grants, 909
Cal Ripken Sr. Fndn Grants, 912
Cambridge Community Fndn Grants, 913
Campbell Soup Fndn Grants, 916
Capital City Bank Group Fndn Grants, 920
CarEth Fndn Grants, 924
Caring Fndn Grants, 926
Carl B. and Florence E. King Fndn Grants, 928
Carl M. Freeman Fndn FACES Grants, 932
Carl M. Freeman Fndn Grants, 933
Carnahan-Jackson Fndn Grants, 939
Carrie E. and Lena V. Glenn Fndn Grants, 944
Carrie Estelle Doheny Fndn Grants, 945
Carrier Corp Contributions Grants, 946
Carroll County Community Fndn Grants, 947
Case Fndn Grants, 950
Cash 4 Clubs Sports Grants, 951
Cass County Community Fndn Grants, 952
Castle and Cooke California Corp Giving Grants, 953
Catherine Kennedy Home Fndn Grants, 955
Catherine Manley Gaylord Fndn Grants, 956
CCFF Community Grant, 962
CCHD Community Development Grants, 966
Center for Venture Philanthropy, 991
Central New York Community Fndn Grants, 996
Central Okanagan Fndn Grants, 997
Cessna Fndn Grants, 1000
CFFVR Basic Needs Giving Partnership Grants, 1002
CFFVR Bridge Grants, 1003
CFFVR Capacity Building Grants, 1004
CFFVR Capital Credit Union Charitable Giving, 1005
CFFVR Chilton Area Community Fndn Grants, 1006
CFFVR Clintonville Area Fndn Grants, 1007
CFFVR Clintonville Area Fndn Grants, 1008
CFFVR Doug and Carla Salmon Fndn Grants, 1009
CFFVR Environmental Stewardship Grants, 1010
CFFVR Frank C. Shattuck Community Grants, 1012
CFFVR Infant Welfare Circle of Kings Daughters Grants, 1013
CFFVR Mielke Family Fndn Grants, 1015
CFFVR Myra M. and Robert L. Vandehey Fndn Grants, 1016
CFFVR Project Grants, 1017
CFFVR Robert and Patricia Endries Family Fndn Grants, 1018
CFFVR Schmidt Family G4 Grants, 1020
CFFVR Shawano Area Community Fndn Grants, 1021
CFFVR Sikora Family Grants, 1022
CFFVR Waupaca Area Community Fndn Grants, 1023
CFFVR Wisconsin Daughters and Sons Grants, 1024
CFFVR Women's Fund for the Fox Valley Region Grants, 1025
CFNCR Starbucks Memorial Fund, 1026
Champlin Fndns Grants, 1029
Charity Incorporated Grants, 1035
Charles Delmar Fndn Grants, 1039

Charles H. Farnsworth Grants, 1043
Charles H. Price II Family Fndn Grants, 1046
Charles M. and Mary D. Grant Fndn Grants, 1050
Charlotte County (FL) Community Fndn Grants, 1056
CHC Fndn Grants, 1065
Chemtura Corp Contributions Grants, 1067
Chesapeake Bay Trust Capacity Building Grants, 1068
Chesapeake Bay Environmental Ed Grants, 1069
Chesapeake Bay Fisheries & Headwaters Grants, 1070
Chesapeake Bay Trust Outreach and Community Engagement Grants, 1073
Chesapeake Corp Fndn Grants, 1076
Chicago Community Trust Arts and Culture Grants: SMART Growth, 1083
Chicago Community Trust Fellowships, 1086
Chicago Community Trust Health Grants, 1087
Chicago Tribune Fndn Civic Grants, 1100
Chiquita Brands Int'l Grants, 1110
Christian Science Society of Boonville Irrevocable Trust, 1113
Christy-Houston Fndn Grants, 1115
Chula Vista Charitable Fndn Grants, 1116
CICF City of Noblesville Community Grant, 1118
CICF Senior Grants, 1127
CICF Summer Youth Grants, 1128
Cincinnati Milacron Fndn Grants, 1132
Cinergy Fndn Grants, 1133
Circle K Corp Contributions Grants, 1136
Citigroup Fndn Grants, 1139
Citizens Savings Fndn Grants, 1141
Claneil Fndn Grants, 1145
Clarence T.C. Ching Fndn Grants, 1151
Clark and Carolyn Adams Fndn Grants, 1153
Claude Worthington Benedum Fndn Grants, 1161
Cleveland Community Responsive Grants, 1168
Cleveland Lake-Geauga Grants, 1170
Cleveland Neighborhood Connections Grants, 1171
Clinton County Community Fndn Grants, 1174
Clipper Ship Fndn Grants, 1175
Clorox Company Fndn Grants, 1176
CNA Fndn Grants, 1179
CNCS AmeriCorps Indian Planning Grants, 1180
CNCS AmeriCorps State and National Grants, 1182
CNCS AmeriCorps VISTA Project Grants, 1184
CNCS Social Innovation Grants, 1189
Coastal Bend Community Fndn Grants, 1192
Cobb Family Fndn Grants, 1194
Coeta and Donald Barker Fndn Grants, 1197
Coleman Fndn Cancer Care Grants, 1199
Collaboration Prize, 1205
Colorado Clean Energy Solar Innovation Grants, 1212
Colorado Springs Community Grants, 1215
Columbus Fndn Joseph A. Jeffrey Grants, 1224
Columbus Fndn Siemer Family Grants, 1231
Columbus Fndn Small Grants, 1232
Comerica Charitable Fndn Grants, 1237
Communities Fndn of Texas Grants, 1243
Community Development Financial Inst Bank Enterprise Awards, 1244
Community Fndn Alliance City of Evansville Endowment Grants, 1246
Community Fndn for Greater Buffalo Grants, 1247
Community Fndn for Greater New Haven $5,000 and Under Grants, 1248
Community Fndn for Greater New Haven Neighborhood Small Grants, 1249
Community Fndn for Greater New Haven Quinnipiac River Grants, 1250
Community Fndn for Greater New Haven Responsive New Grants, 1251
Community Fndn for Greater New Haven Sponsorship Grants, 1252
Community Fndn for Greater New Haven Valley Neighborhood Grants, 1253
Community Fndn for Greater New Haven Women & Girls Grants, 1254
Community Fndn for Muskegon County Grants, 1256
Community Fndn for San Benito County Grants, 1258
Community Fndn in Jacksonville Senior Roundtable Aging Adults Grants, 1263

842 / Community Development

Community Fndn of Abilene Community Grants, 1264
Community Fndn of Bloomington and Monroe County - Precision Health Network Cycle Grants, 1270
Community Fndn of Bloomington and Monroe County Grants, 1271
Community Fndn of Boone County Grants, 1274
Community Fndn of Collier County Capacity Building Grants, 1277
Community Fndn of East Central Illinois Grants, 1278
Community Fndn of Grant County Grants, 1279
Community Fndn of Greater Birmingham Grants, 1280
Community Fndn of Greater Fort Wayne - John S. and James L. Knight Fndn Donor-Advised Grants, 1287
Community Fndn of Greater Greensboro Grants, 1288
Community Fndn of Greater Memphis Grants, 1290
Community Fndn of Greater New Britain Grants, 1291
Community Fndn of Greater Tampa Grants, 1292
Community Fndn of Greenville-Greenville Women Giving Grants, 1293
Community Fndn of Greenville Community Enrichment Grants, 1294
Community Fndn of Greenville Hollingsworth Funds Capital Grants, 1295
Community Fndn of Greenville Hollingsworth Funds Program/Project Grants, 1296
Community Fndn of Howard County Grants, 1297
Community Fndn of Louisville Grants, 1299
Community Fndn of Middle Tennessee Grants, 1300
Community Fndn of Mount Vernon and Knox County Grants, 1301
Community Fndn of Muncie and Delaware County Grants, 1302
Community Fndn of Muncie and Delaware County Maxon Grants, 1303
Community Fndn of Santa Cruz County Grants, 1305
Community Fndn of Southern Indiana Grants, 1310
Community Fndn of St. Joseph County Special Project Challenge Grants, 1314
Community Fndn of Switzerland County Grants, 1315
Community Fndn of Tampa Bay Grants, 1316
Community Fndn of the Eastern Shore Community Needs Grants, 1317
Community Fndn of the Eastern Shore Field of Interest Grants, 1318
Community Fndn of the Ozarks Grants, 1320
Community Fndn of the Verdugos Ed Grants, 1321
Community Fndn of the Verdugos Grants, 1322
Community Fndn of Virgin Islands Anderson Family Teacher Grants, 1323
Community Fndn of Virgin Islands Mini Grants, 1325
Community Fndn of Wabash County Grants, 1326
Community Fndn of Western N Carolina Grants, 1327
Community Partnerships Martin County Grants, 1329
Community POWER (Partners On Waste Educ and Reduction), 1335
Community Technology Fndn of California Building Communities Through Technology Grants, 1336
Compton Fndn Grants, 1338
ConAgra Foods Community Impact Grants, 1342
ConAgra Foods Nourish Our Comm Grants, 1343
Con Edison Corp Giving Community Grants, 1346
Con Edison Corp Giving Environmental Grants, 1347
Connecticut Light & Power Corp Contributions, 1352
Connelly Fndn Grants, 1353
ConocoPhillips Fndn Grants, 1354
CONSOL Coal Group Grants, 1360
Constantin Fndn Grants, 1362
Constellation Energy Corp EcoStar Grants, 1363
Constellation Energy Corp Grants, 1364
Cornerstone Fndn of NE Wisconsin Grants, 1375
Covidien Partnership for Neighborhood Wellness Grants, 1391
Cralle Fndn Grants, 1394
Crestlea Fndn Grants, 1399
Cruise Industry Charitable Fndn Grants, 1404
CSL Behring Local Empowerment for Advocacy Development Grants, 1406
CSRA Community Fndn Grants, 1407
CSX Corp Contributions Grants, 1408
Cumberland Community Fndn Grants, 1413

Cummins Fndn Grants, 1415
Curtis and Edith Munson Fndn Grants, 1418
Curtis Fndn Grants, 1419
CVS All Kids Can Grants, 1420
D.F. Halton Fndn Grants, 1424
D. W. McMillan Fndn Grants, 1426
Dade Community Fndn Community AIDS Partnership Grants, 1428
Dade Community Fndn GLBT Grants, 1429
Dade Community Fndn Grants, 1430
Dade Community Fndn Safe Passage Grants, 1431
Daisy Marquis Jones Fndn Grants, 1434
Dallas Fndn Grants, 1436
Danellie Fndn Grants, 1442
Daviess County Community Fndn Health Grants, 1457
Daviess County Community Fndn Human Services Grants, 1458
Daviess County Community Recreation Grants, 1459
Daywood Fndn Grants, 1465
DB Americas Fndn Grants, 1466
Deaconess Fndn Advocacy Grants, 1468
Dearborn Community Fndn City of Lawrenceburg Community Grants, 1471
Dearborn Community Fndn City of Lawrenceburg Youth Grants, 1472
Dearborn Community Fndn Sprint Ed Excellence Grants, 1474
Decatur County Comm Large Project Grants, 1476
Decatur County Community Fndn Small Project Grants, 1477
DeKalb County Community Fndn Grants, 1481
Delaware Community Fund For Women Grants, 1484
Delaware Community Next Generation Grants, 1485
Delta Air Lines Community Enrichment Grants, 1494
Denver Strengthening Neighborhoods Grants, 1504
Denver Fndn Technical Assistance Grants, 1505
Dept of Ed Safe and Drug-Free Schools and Communities State Grants, 1513
Dermody Properties Fndn Capstone Award, 1516
DeRoy Testamentary Fndn Grants, 1518
DHHS American Recovery and Reinvestment Act of 2009 Head Start Expansion, 1526
DHHS ARRA Strengthening Communities Fund - Nonprofit Capacity Building Grants, 1527
DHHS ARRA Strengthening Communities Fund - State, Local, and Tribal Government Capacity Building Grants, 1528
DHHS Community Services Block Grant Training and Technical Assistance Program: Capacity-Building for Ongoing CSBG Programs and Strategic Planning and Coordination Grants, 1529
DHS ARRA Fire Station Construction Grants, 1542
Diageo Fndn Grants, 1546
Dole Food Company Charitable Contributions, 1564
Donald W. Reynolds Fndn Charitable Food Distribution Grants, 1575
Dorothy G. Griffin Charitable Fndn Grants, 1588
Doug and Carla Salmon Fndn Grants, 1594
Douty Fndn Grants, 1595
Dow Chemical Company Grants, 1596
Dow Corning Corp Contributions Grants, 1597
Dr. P. Phillips Fndn Grants, 1601
Drug Free Communities Support Program, 1608
DTE Energy Community Development Grants, 1609
DTE Energy Fndn Diversity Grants, 1611
DTE Energy Fndn Leadership Grants, 1614
Duke Energy Economic Development Grants, 1619
Duneland Health Council Incorporated Grants, 1621
Durfee Fndn Sabbatical Grants, 1625
Dynegy Fndn Grants, 1630
Dyson Fndn Mid-Hudson Valley General Operating Support Grants, 1635
Dyson Mid-Hudson Valley Project Support, 1636
East Tennessee Fndn Affordable Housing Fund, 1645
East Tennessee Fndn Grants, 1646
Eaton Charitable Grants, 1647
Eberly Fndn Grants, 1649
Eddie C. and Sylvia Brown Family Fndn Grants, 1653
Eddy Knight Family Fndn Grants, 1654
Edina Realty Fndn Grants, 1656

SUBJECT INDEX

Edward and Ellen Roche Relief Fndn Grants, 1663
Edward R. Godfrey Fndn Grants, 1667
Edward W. and Stella C. Van Houten Grants, 1670
Edwin S. Webster Fndn Grants, 1671
Edyth Bush Charitable Fndn Grants, 1673
Elizabeth & Avola W. Callaway Fndn Grants, 1680
Elkhart County Community Fndn Fund for Elkhart County, 1683
Elkhart County Community Fndn Grants, 1684
Ellen Abbott Gilman Grants, 1685
Elliot Fndn Inc Grants, 1686
El Paso Community Fndn Grants, 1688
El Paso Corp Fndn Grants, 1689
El Pomar Fndn Awards and Grants, 1690
Elsie H. Wilcox Fndn Grants, 1691
Encore Purpose Prize, 1704
Ensign-Bickford Fndn Grants, 1709
Ensworth Charitable Fndn Grants, 1710
Entergy Corp Micro Grants, 1712
Entergy Corp Open Grants for Arts and Culture, 1713
Entergy Corp Open Grants for Community Improvement & Enrichment, 1714
Entergy Corp Open Grants for Healthy Families, 1715
Enterprise Community Partners Green Charrette Grants, 1716
Enterprise Community Partners Pre-Development Design Grants, 1718
Enterprise Community Partners Rose Architectural Fellowships, 1719
EPA Environmental Educ Grants, 1729
EPA Environmental Justice Collaborative Problem-Solving Coop Agreements Program, 1730
EQT Fndn Community Grants, 1744
Essex County Community Fndn First Jobs Grant, 1754
Essex County Community Fndn Greater Lawrence Summer Grants, 1755
Essex County Community Fndn Merrimack Valley General Grants, 1756
Ethel S. Abbott Charitable Fndn Grants, 1760
Ethel Sergeant Clark Smith Fndn Grants, 1761
Eugene McDermott Fndn Grants, 1765
Eugene Straus Charitable Trust, 1766
Evanston Community Fndn Grants, 1771
Evelyn and Walter Haas, Jr. Fund Nonprofit Leadership Grants, 1774
Ewa Beach Community Trust Fund, 1775
Fairfield County Community Fndn Grants, 1782
Fargo-Moorhead Area Fndn Grants, 1788
Fayette County Fndn Grants, 1795
Fel-Pro Mecklenburger Fndn Grants, 1800
Feldman Fndn Grants, 1801
Ferree Fndn Grants, 1804
Fidelity Fndn Grants, 1805
Fieldstone Fndn Grants, 1808
Fifth Third Bank Corp Giving, 1809
Fifth Third Fndn Grants, 1810
FINRA Investor Educ Fndn Financial Educ in Your Community Grants, 1815
Fireman's Fund Insurance Heritage Grants, 1818
FirstEnergy Fndn Community Grants, 1819
Fisher Fndn Grants, 1831
Fishman Family Fndn Grants, 1835
Flextronics Fndn Disaster Relief Grants, 1841
Florida BRAIVE Fund of Dade Community, 1846
Florida Humanities Civic Reflection Grants, 1867
FMC Fndn Grants, 1876
Foellinger Fndn Grants, 1877
Fondren Fndn Grants, 1878
Ford Family Fndn Grants - Critical Needs, 1879
Ford Family Fndn Grants - Positive Youth Development, 1880
Ford Family Grants Public Convening Spaces, 1881
Ford Family Fndn Grants - Technical Assistance, 1882
Ford Motor Company Grants, 1885
Forest Fndn Grants, 1886
Foster G. McGaw Prize, 1889
Fndn for a Drug-Free World Classroom Tools, 1890
Fndn for Appalachian Ohio Access to Environmental Educ Mini-Grants, 1892
Fndn for Enhancing Communities Grants, 1893

SUBJECT INDEX

Community Development / 843

Foundation for Young Australians Indigenous Small Grants, 1901
Foundation for Young Australians Spark Grants, 1902
Foundation for Young Australians Your Eyes Only Awards, 1903
Foundation for Young Australians Youth Change Grants, 1904
Foundation for Young Australians Youth Led Futures Grants, 1905
Fndn NW Grants, 1906
Fndns of E Chicago Community Economic Development Grants, 1907
Fndns of E Chicago Financial Indep Grants, 1909
Fourjay Fndn Grants, 1913
France-Merrick Fndns Grants, 1915
Frances L. and Edwin L. Cummings Grants, 1919
Frances W. Emerson Fndn Grants, 1920
Frank & Larue Reynolds Charitable Grants, 1924
Frank and Lydia Bergen Fndn Grants, 1925
Franklin County Community Fndn Grants, 1929
Franklin H. Wells and Ruth L. Wells Grants, 1930
Frank Stanley Beveridge Fndn Grants, 1936
Fred Baldwin Memorial Fndn Grants, 1941
Freddie Mac Fndn Grants, 1944
Frederick McDonald Grants, 1946
Fremont Area Community Amazing X Grants, 1953
Fremont Area Community Elderly Needs Grants, 1954
Fremont Area Community Fndn Grants, 1955
Freshwater Future Climate Grants, 1958
Fuller Fndn Grants, 1974
Fund for the City of New York Grants, 1978
Gamble Fndn Grants, 1983
Gannett Fndn Community Action Grants, 1984
Gates Family Fndn Community Development & Revitalization Grants, 1990
GCI Corp Contributions Grants, 1994
Gebbie Fndn Grants, 1995
Gene Haas Fndn, 1999
Genentech Corp Charitable Contributions, 2000
George A. and Grace L. Long Fndn Grants, 2008
George A. Hormel Testamentary Grants, 2009
George and Sarah Buchanan Fndn Grants, 2011
George A Ohl Jr. Fndn Grants, 2012
George B. Page Fndn Grants, 2013
George Gund Fndn Grants, 2020
George Kress Fndn Grants, 2025
Georgia Council for the Arts Partner Grants for Service Organizations, 2036
Georgiana Goddard Eaton Grants, 2038
Geraldine R. Dodge Fndn Arts Grants, 2040
Gertrude and William C. Wardlaw Grants, 2045
Gertrude E. Skelly Charitable Fndn Grants, 2046
Gheens Fndn Grants, 2048
Giant Eagle Fndn Grants, 2049
Gibson County Community Fndn Women's Fund, 2051
Ginger and Barry Ackerley Fndn Grants, 2055
Ginn Fndn Grants, 2056
Giving Sum Annual Grant, 2058
Gladys Brooks Fndn Grants, 2059
GlaxoSmithKline Corp Grants, 2060
GNOF Bayou Communities Grants, 2069
GNOF Community Revitalization Grants, 2071
GNOF Cox Charities of New Orleans Grants, 2072
GNOF Environmental Grants, 2073
GNOF Exxon-Mobil Grants, 2074
GNOF Gert Community Grants, 2076
GNOF IMPACT Grants for Arts and Culture, 2078
GNOF IMPACT Grants for Health and Human Services, 2080
GNOF Jefferson Community Grants, 2085
GNOF New Orleans Works Grants, 2088
GNOF Norco Community Grants, 2089
GNOF St. Bernard Community Grants, 2092
Godfrey Fndn Grants, 2095
Golden Rule Fndn Grants, 2098
Goldseker Fndn Community Affairs Grants, 2100
Goldseker Fndn Community Grants, 2101
Good Works Fndn Grants, 2105
Grace and Franklin Bernsen Fndn Grants, 2109
Graco Fndn Grants, 2111

Grand Rapids Area Community Fndn Wyoming Grants, 2116
Grand Rapids Area Community Fndn Wyoming Youth Grants, 2117
Grand Rapids Community Fndn Grants, 2118
Grand Rapids Community Ionia County Grants, 2119
Grand Rapids Community Ionia Youth Grants, 2120
Grand Rapids Community Fndn Lowell Grants, 2121
Grand Rapids Community SE Ottawa Grants, 2122
Grand Rapids Comm SE Ottawa Youth Grants, 2123
Grand Rapids Community Sparta Grants, 2124
Grand Rapids Community Sparta Youth Grants, 2125
Grassroots Exchange Grants, 2128
Greater Cincinnati Fndn Priority and Small Projects/ Capacity-Building Grants, 2132
Greater Des Moines Fndn Grants, 2134
Greater Green Bay Community Fndn Grants, 2135
Greater Milwaukee Fndn Grants, 2137
Greater Saint Louis Community Fndn Grants, 2138
Greater Worcester Community Jeppson Memorial Fund for Brookfield Grants, 2141
Green Diamond Charitable Contributions, 2149
Greene County Fndn Grants, 2150
Green Fndn Special Project Grants, 2155
Greenwall Fndn Arts and Humanities Grants, 2157
GreenWorks! Grants, 2160
Gregory L. Gibson Charitable Fndn Grants, 2163
Group 70 Fndn Fund, 2167
Grover Hermann Fndn Grants, 2168
Grundy Fndn Grants, 2169
Guido A. and Elizabeth H. Binda Fndn Grants, 2172
Gulf Coast Community Fndn Grants, 2174
Gulf Coast Community Operating Grants, 2176
Gulf Coast Fndn of Community Grants, 2177
Guy I. Bromley Grants, 2180
H & R Fndn Grants, 2181
H.B. Fuller Company Fndn Grants, 2183
H. Leslie Hoffman & Elaine Hoffman Grants, 2185
H. Reimers Bechtel Charitable Grants, 2186
HAF Community Grants, 2193
HAF Justin Keele Make a Difference Award, 2198
HAF Southern Humboldt Grants, 2204
HAF Technical Assistance Grants, 2206
Hagedorn Grants, 2207
Hall Family Fndn Grants, 2210
Hamilton Family Fndn Grants, 2213
Hampton Roads Community Fndn Beach Grants, 2214
Hampton Roads Community Fndn Community Leadership Partners Grants, 2215
Hancock County Community Fndn - Programming Mini-Grants, 2220
Harley Davidson Fndn Grants, 2224
Harold Alfond Fndn Grants, 2225
Harold and Arlene Schnitzer CARE Grants, 2226
Harold R. Bechtel Charitable Remainder Grants, 2229
Harris and Eliza Kempner Grants, 2231
Harrison County Community Signature Grants, 2234
Harry B. and Jane H. Brock Fndn Grants, 2237
Harry Bramhall Gilbert Charitable Grants, 2238
Harry C. Trexler Grants, 2239
Harry Kramer Grants, 2242
Harry S. Black and Allon Fuller Grants, 2243
Harry W. Bass, Jr. Fndn Grants, 2246
Hartford Courant Fndn Grants, 2248
Hartford Fndn Application Planning Grants, 2249
Hartford Fndn Evaluation Grants, 2250
Hartford Fndn Regular Grants, 2253
Harvest Fndn Grants, 2254
Hawai'i Children's Trust Fund Community Awareness Events Grants, 2258
Hawaiian Electric Industries Charitable Grants, 2259
Hawaii Community Fndn Community Capacity Building Grants, 2260
Hawaii Community Geographic-Specific Grants, 2261
Hawaii Community Human Services Grants, 2262
Hawaii Community Fndn Organizational Capacity Building Grants, 2263
Hawaii Community Fndn Reverend Takie Okumura Family Grants, 2264
Hawaii Community Fndn Social Change Grants, 2265

Hawaii Community Fndn West Hawaii Grants, 2266
Health Fndn of Greater Cincinnati Grants, 2281
Hedco Fndn Grants, 2287
Heifer Ed Grants for Teachers, 2289
Helen Bader Fndn Grants, 2293
Helen S. Boylan Fndn Grants, 2298
Hendricks County Community Fndn Grants, 2302
Henrietta Tower Wurts Memorial Fndn Grants, 2304
Henry A. and Mary J. MacDonald Fndn, 2305
Henry County Community Fndn Grants, 2308
Henry M. Jackson Fndn Grants, 2311
Herbert H. and Grace A. Dow Fndn Grants, 2315
Hershey Company Grants, 2318
Highmark Corp Giving Grants, 2319
High Meadow Fndn Grants, 2321
Hill Crest Fndn Grants, 2324
Hillman Fndn Grants, 2327
Hillsdale County Community Gen Adult Grants, 2328
Hilton Head Island Fndn Grants, 2330
Hirtzel Memorial Fndn Grants, 2332
Hoglund Fndn Grants, 2344
Holland/Zeeland Community Fndn Grants, 2345
Hollie and Anna Oakley Fndn Grants, 2346
Homer Fndn Grants, 2352
Honda of America Manufacturing Fndn Grants, 2354
Honor the Earth Grants, 2361
Horace A. Kimball and S. Ella Kimball Grants, 2362
Horizon Fndn for New Jersey Grants, 2364
Horizon Fndn Grants, 2365
Hormel Fndn Grants, 2369
Houston Endowment Grants, 2373
Howard and Bush Fndn Grants, 2374
Howard County Community Fndn Grants, 2375
Howard H. Callaway Fndn Grants, 2376
Howe Fndn of North Carolina Grants, 2377
Hudson Webber Fndn Grants, 2383
Hugh J. Andersen Fndn Grants, 2385
Hulman & Company Fndn Grants, 2387
Humana Fndn Grants, 2388
Huntington Arts Council Arts-in-Educ Grants, 2400
Huntington Arts Council Decentralization Community Arts Grants, 2401
Huntington Arts Council JP Morgan Chase Artist Reach Out Grants, 2402
Huntington Arts Council JP Morgan Chase Organization/Stabilization Regrants, 2403
Huntington Clinical Fndn Grants, 2404
Huntington County Community Fndn - Make a Difference Grants, 2406
Huntington County Community Fndn - Stephanie Pyle Grant, 2407
Hutchinson Community Fndn Grants, 2410
Hut Fndn Grants, 2411
Hutton Fndn Grants, 2412
Hyams Fndn Grants, 2413
Hyde Family Fndns Grants, 2414
I.A. O'Shaughnessy Fndn Grants, 2416
IBM Community Development Grants, 2425
ICC Faculty Fellowships, 2428
ICC Listening to Communities Grants, 2429
ICC Scholarship of Engagement Faculty Grants, 2430
Idaho Community Fndn Eastern Region Competitive Grants, 2432
Idaho Power Company Corp Contributions, 2433
IIE Eurobank EFG Scholarships, 2455
Illinois DCEO Community Development Assistance For Economic Development Grants, 2488
Illinois DCEO Employer Training Investment Grants - Competitive Component, 2491
Illinois DCEO Employer Training Investment Grants - Incentive Component, 2492
Illinois DCEO Employer Training Investment Program Multi-Company Training Grants, 2493
Illinois DCEO Employer Training Investment Program Single Company Training Grants, 2494
Illinois DCEO Large Business Dev Grants, 2495
Illinois DNR Biodiversity Field Trip Grants, 2496
Illinois Tool Works Fndn Grants, 2511
Impact 100 Grants, 2522
Inasmuch Fndn Grants, 2523

844 / Community Development

Indep Blue Cross Charitable Med Care Grants, 2524
Indep Community Fndn Community Quality of Life Grant, 2525
Indep Comm Fndn Educ, Culture & Arts Grant, 2526
Indiana Household Hazardous Waste Grants, 2538
Indiana Humanities Council Init Grants, 2539
Indianapolis Power & Light Company Community Grants, 2540
Indiana Regional Economic Development Partnership Grants, 2546
ING Fndn Grants, 2555
Init Fndn Healthy Lakes and Rivers Partnerships, 2558
Init Fndn Innovation Grants, 2559
Init Fndn Minnesota Early Childhood Grants, 2560
Intel Community Grants, 2562
Intel Int'l Community Grants, 2564
Intergrys Corp Grants, 2565
Int'l Paper Company Fndn Grants, 2568
Ireland Family Fndn Grants, 2574
IREX Project Smile Grants, 2579
Irving S. Gilmore Fndn Grants, 2584
Irvin Stern Fndn Grants, 2585
Isabel Allende Fndn Esperanza Grants, 2586
J.B. Reynolds Fndn Grants, 2592
J. Bulow Campbell Fndn Grants, 2593
J.C. Penney Company Grants, 2594
J.E. and L.E. Mabee Fndn Grants, 2595
J. Edwin Treakle Fndn Grants, 2596
J. F. Maddox Fndn Grants, 2597
J. Knox Gholston Fndn Grants, 2599
J.L. Bedsole Fndn Grants, 2600
J.M. Kaplan Fund Migrations Grants, 2602
J. Marion Sims Fndn Teachers' Pet Grant, 2605
J.W. Kieckhefer Fndn Grants, 2607
J. Willard and Alice S. Marriott Fndn Grants, 2609
Jackson County Community Fndn Grants, 2611
Jackson County Community Fndn Youth Advisory Committee Grants, 2612
Jacksonville Jaguars Fndn Grants, 2614
Jacob and Hilda Blaustein Fndn Grants, 2615
Jacob G. Schmidlapp Grants, 2616
Jacobs Family Jabara Learning Opps Grants, 2617
Jacobs Family Spirit of the Diamond Grants, 2618
Jacobs Family Village Neighborhoods Grants, 2619
James & Abigail Campbell Family Fndn Grants, 2620
James A. and Faith Knight Fndn Grants, 2621
James F. and Marion L. Miller Fndn Grants, 2622
James Ford Bell Fndn Grants, 2623
James Graham Brown Quality of Life Grants, 2625
James Irvine Fndn Creative Connections Grants, 2628
James Irvine Fndn Leadership Awards, 2629
James J. and Angelia M. Harris Fndn Grants, 2630
James J. McCann Charitable Trust and McCann Fndn, Inc Grants, 2631
James R. Dougherty Jr. Fndn Grants, 2635
James S. Copley Fndn Grants, 2637
Jane Bradley Pettit Fndn Community and Social Development Grants, 2642
Janesville Fndn Grants, 2644
Janirve Fndn Grants, 2645
Janus Fndn Grants, 2647
Jasper Fndn Grants, 2655
JELD-WEN Fndn Grants, 2661
Jennings County Community Fndn Grants, 2664
Jewish Community Fndn of LA Israel Grants, 2674
Jewish Funds for Justice Grants, 2676
Joan Bentinck-Smith Charitable Fndn Grants, 2682
Joe W. and Dorothy Dorsett Brown Fndn Grants, 2684
John and Elizabeth Whiteley Fndn Grants, 2685
John and Margaret Post Fndn Grants, 2686
John Ben Snow Grants, 2687
John Deere Fndn Grants, 2692
John G. Duncan Grants, 2695
John H. and Wilhelmina D. Harland Charitable Fndn Grants, 2698
John H. Wellons Fndn Grants, 2699
John Jewett & Helen Chandler Garland Grants, 2702
John M. Ross Fndn Grants, 2704
John P. McGovern Fndn Grants, 2707

John Reynolds and Eleanor B. Allen Charitable Fndn Grants, 2710
John S. and James L. Knight Comm Grants, 2711
John S. and James L. Knight Fndn Grants, 2713
John S. and James L. Knight Fndn National and New Inits Grants, 2714
John S. Dunn Research Fndn Grants and Chairs, 2715
Johnson Controls Fndn Civic Activities Grants, 2720
Johnson Controls Fndn Educ and Arts Matching Gift Grants, 2721
Johnson County Community Fndn Grants, 2723
Johnson County Community Fndn Youth Philanthropy Init Grants, 2724
John W. Alden Grants, 2727
John W. Anderson Fndn Grants, 2729
John W. Speas and Effie E. Speas Grants, 2732
Josephine G. Russell Grants, 2737
Josephine Goodyear Fndn Grants, 2738
Joseph S. Stackpole Charitable Grants, 2741
Joyce Fdn Employment Grants, 2749
JP Morgan Chase Arts and Culture Grants, 2752
Judith Clark-Morrill Fndn Grants, 2756
K.S. Adams Fndn Grants, 2758
K21 Health Fndn Cancer Care Grants, 2759
K21 Health Fndn Grants, 2760
Kahuku Community Fund, 2762
Kalamazoo Community Fndn Economic and Community Development Grants, 2765
Kalamazoo Community Fndn Front Porch Grants, 2767
Kalamazoo Community Fndn John E. Fetzer Institute Grants, 2770
Kalamazoo Community Fndn Mini-Grants, 2772
Ka Papa O Kakuhihewa Fund, 2785
Katharine Matthies Fndn Grants, 2788
Katie's Krops Grants, 2792
Kent D. Steadley and Mary L. Steadley Trust, 2804
KeySpan Fndn Grants, 2821
Knight Fndn Donor Advised Grants, 2828
Knox County Community Fndn Grants, 2831
Kosciusko County Community Fndn Grants, 2838
Kosciusko County Community Fndn REMC Operation Round Up Grants, 2839
Kroger Grassroots Community Support Grants, 2843
L. W. Pierce Family Fndn Grants, 2846
Laclede Gas Charitable Grants, 2848
LaGrange Independent Fndn for Endowments, 2851
Laidlaw Fndn Youh Organizing Catalyst Grants, 2853
Laidlaw Fndn Youth Organizaing Inits Grants, 2854
Lake County Community Grants, 2856
Lana'i Community Benefit Fund, 2857
Land O'Lakes Fndn California Region Grants, 2858
Land O'Lakes Fndn Community Grants, 2859
Lands' End Corp Giving Program, 2861
Laura Jane Musser Intercultural Harmony Grants, 2862
Lee and Ramona Bass Fndn Grants, 2871
Legacy Partners in Environmental Ed Grants, 2876
Legler Benbough Fndn Grants, 2877
Leicester Savings Bank Fund, 2879
Leo Niessen Jr., Charitable Grants, 2885
Lewis H. Humphreys Charitable Grants, 2889
Liberty Bank Fndn Grants, 2890
Liberty Hill Fndn Environmental Justice Grants, 2891
Liberty Hill Fndn Fund for a New LA Grants, 2892
Liberty Hill Fndn Fund for Change Grants, 2893
Liberty Hill Lesbian & Gay Community Grants, 2894
Liberty Hill Fndn Seed Grants, 2896
Liberty Hill Fndn Special Opportunity Grants, 2897
Libra Fndn Future Grants, 2898
Lillian S. Wells Fndn Grants, 2901
Lilly Endowment Giving Indiana Funds for Tomorrow Grants, 2903
LISC Financial Opportunity Center Social Innovation Grants, 2911
LISC NFL Grassroots Grants, 2913
Liz Claiborne Fndn Grants, 2915
Local Inits Support Corp Grants, 2917
Long Island Community Fndn Grants, 2920
Lotus 88 Fndn for Women and Children Grants, 2921
Louetta M. Cowden Grants, 2922
Louie M. and Betty M. Phillips Fndn Grants, 2923

Louis and Elizabeth Nave Flarsheim Charitable Fndn Grants, 2924
Louis Calder Fndn Grants, 2925
Lowell Berry Fndn Grants, 2930
Lubbock Area Fndn Grants, 2931
Lubrizol Corp Community Grants, 2932
Lucy Downing Nisbet Charitable Grants, 2935
Lucy Gooding Charitable Fndn Grants, 2937
Lumpkin Family Fndn Lively Arts and Dynamic Learning Communities Grants, 2943
Lumpkin Family Fndn Strong Community Leadership Grants, 2944
M.B. and Edna Zale Fndn Grants, 2950
M3C Fellowships, 2955
Mabel F. Hoffman Charitable Grants, 2957
Mabel Louise Riley Fndn Family Strengthening Small Grants, 2958
Mabel Louise Riley Fndn Grants, 2959
Mabel Y. Hughes Charitable Grants, 2960
MacArthur Fndn Policy Research Grants, 2964
MacDonald-Peterson Fndn Grants, 2965
Maddie's Fund Lifesaving Awards, 2969
Madison Community Fndn Grants, 2971
Madison County Community General Grants, 2973
Maine Community Fndn Baldwin Area Grants, 2974
Maine Community Fndn Belvedere Historic Preservation Grants, 2976
Maine Community Fndn Building Grants, 2978
Maine Community Fndn Edward H. Daveis Benevolent Grants, 2979
Maine Community Fndn Gracie Grants, 2982
Maine Community Fndn Peaks Island Grants, 2984
Maine Community Fndn Ram Island Conservation Challenge Grants, 2986
Maine Community Fndn Rose and Samuel Rudman Library Grants, 2988
Maine Community Fndn Steeples Grants, 2989
Manitoba Arts Council Artist in Community Residency Grants, 2994
Manitoba Arts Council Community Connections and Access Grants, 2995
Manitoba Arts Council Special Opps Grants, 2997
Marathon Petroleum Corp Grants, 2999
Margaret L. Wendt Fndn Grants, 3004
Marie C. and Joseph C. Wilson Fndn Rochester Small Grants, 3006
Marie H. Bechtel Charitable Grants, 3007
Marin Community Affordable Housing Grants, 3010
Marin Community Fndn Ending the Cycle of Poverty Grants, 3011
Marin Community Fndn Social Justice and Interfaith Understanding Grants, 3012
Marin Community Fndn Stinson Bolinas Community Grants, 3013
Marion Gardner Jackson Charitable Grants, 3017
Marshall County Community Fndn Grants, 3026
Marsh Corp Grants, 3027
Mary C. & Perry F. Spencer Fndn Grants, 3034
Mary Duke Biddle Fndn Grants, 3036
Mary E. Babcock Fndn, 3038
Mary Reynolds Babcock Fndn Grants, 3047
Massachusetts Cultural Council Cultural Investment Portfolio, 3056
Massachusetts Fndn for the Humanities Cultural Economic Development Grants, 3059
Massage Therapy Community Service Grants, 3061
Max and Anna Levinson Fndn Grants, 3066
Maximilian E. and Marion O. Hoffman Fndn, 3067
Maxon Charitable Fndn Grants, 3068
Maytree Fndn Assisting Local Leaders with Immigrant Employment Strategies Grants, 3070
McCallum Family Fndn Grants, 3072
McColl Fndn Grants, 3074
McConnell Fndn Grants, 3076
McCune Charitable Fndn Grants, 3077
McKnight Fndn Virginia McKnight Binger Awards in Human Service, 3087
McMillen Fndn Grants, 3090
MDARD County Fairs Cap Improvement Grants, 3092

SUBJECT INDEX

Community Development / 845

MDEQ Brownfield Redevelopment and Site Reclamation Grants, 3095
Mead Johnson Nutritionals Evansville-Area Organizations Grants, 3103
MeadWestvaco Sustainable Communities Grant, 3105
Medtronic Fndn Community Link Arts, Civic, and Culture Grants, 3109
Melville Charitable Grants, 3115
Merck Family Fund Youth Transforming Urban Communities Grants, 3120
Mertz Gilmore Climate Change Grants, 3125
Mertz Gilmore Fndn NYC Communities Grants, 3126
Mervin Bovaird Fndn Grants, 3128
MetLife Building Livable Communities Grants, 3129
MetLife Fndn Empowering Older Adults Grants, 3130
MetLife Fndn Promoting Employee Volunteerism, 3132
Metzger-Price Grants, 3137
Meyer Fndn Management Assistance Grants, 3144
Meyer Fndn Strong Nonprofit Sector Grants, 3145
Meyer Memorial Trust Responsive Grants, 3148
Meyer Memorial Trust Special Grants, 3149
MFRI Operation Diploma Small Grants for Indiana Family Readiness Groups, 3152
MGM Resorts Fndn Community Grants, 3153
Miami County Community Fndn - Boomerang Sisterhood Grant, 3155
Miami County Community Fndn - Operation Round Up Grants, 3156
Miami County Community Fndn Grants, 3157
Micron Technology Fndn Community Grants, 3161
Microsoft Unlimited Potential (UP) - Community Technology Skills Grants, 3165
Mid-Iowa Health Fndn Comm Response Grants, 3168
Middlesex Savings Charitable Fndn Community Development Grants, 3173
Middlesex Savings Charitable Fndn Ed Opportunities Grants, 3174
Minnesota Small Cities Development Grants, 3187
MLB Tomorrow Grants, 3193
Monsanto Civic Partnership Grants, 3206
Montgomery County Community Fndn Grants, 3213
Moody Fndn Grants, 3215
Morris and Gwendolyn Cafritz Fndn Grants, 3218
Motorola Fndn Grants, 3221
Mr. and Mrs. William Foulds Family Grants, 3222
Ms. Fndn Women Building Democracy Grants, 3223
Natalie W. Furniss Charitable Grants, 3244
National Endowment for the Arts - National Arts and Humanities Youth Program Awards, 3255
National Endowment for Arts Our Town Grants, 3257
National Endowment for the Arts - Regional Partnership Agreement Grants, 3258
National Endowment for Arts Commun Grants, 3260
National Endowment for Arts Agencies Grants, 3263
National Endowment for Arts Music Grants, 3266
National Endowment for Arts Opera Grants, 3267
National Endowment for the Arts Presenting Grants: Art Works, 3268
National Endowment for Arts Theater Grants, 3269
National Environmental Educ Fndn - Department of Defense Legacy Award, 3270
National Lottery Community Grants, 3279
National Trust for Historic Preservation Diversity Scholarship, 3280
Natonal Endowment for the Arts Research Grants: Art Works, 3286
Nature Hills Nursery Green America Awards, 3287
Nelda C. and H.J. Lutcher Stark Fndn Grants, 3296
Nestle Purina PetCare Ed Grants, 3302
Nevada Arts Council Learning Grants, 3313
Nevada Community Fndn Grants, 3316
New Earth Fndn Grants, 3317
New Jersey Office of Faith Based Inits Service to Seniors Grants, 3333
Newman W. Benson Fndn Grants, 3334
Newton County Community Fndn Grants, 3336
New York Fndn Grants, 3338
New York Landmarks Conservancy City Ventures Grants, 3339
NFL Charities NFL Player Fndn Grants, 3347
NGA 'Remember Me' Rose Garden Awards, 3401
NICHD Academic-Community Partnership Conference Series Grants, 3433
Nissan Neighbors Grants, 3445
NJSCA Projects Serving Artists Grants, 3450
Noble County Community Fndn Celebrate Diversity Project Grants, 3455
Noble County Community Fndn Grants, 3456
Nonprofit Management Grants, 3458
Norfolk Southern Fndn Grants, 3463
North Carolina Arts Council Community Public Art and Design Development Grants, 3472
North Carolina Arts Council Community Public Art and Design Implementation Grants, 3473
North Carolina Biotech Center Meeting Grants, 3486
North Carolina Biotech Center Regional Development Grants, 3488
North Carolina Community Fndn Grants, 3489
North Central Health Services Grants, 3491
North Central Health Services Grants, 3492
Northern Chautauqua Community Grants, 3499
Northern Chautauqua DFT Communications Community Betterment Grants, 3500
Northern Chautauqua Lake Shore Savings and Loan Community Reinvestment Grants, 3502
Northern New York Community Fndn Grants, 3503
Northern Trust Company Corp Giving Program, 3504
North Georgia Community Fndn Grants, 3505
NW Mutual Fndn Grants, 3509
NW Minnesota Fndn Asset Building Grants, 3511
NW Minnesota Fndn Women's Grants, 3512
Norwin S. and Elizabeth N. Bean Fndn Grants, 3515
NSERC Michael Smith Awards, 3519
NSF CISE Communicating Research to Public Audiences Grants, 3522
NSF CISE Community-Based Data Interoperability Networks Grants, 3523
NSF CISE Computing and Communication Fndns: Core Programs Grants, 3525
NWHF Kaiser Permanente Community Grants, 3538
NYCT Community Development Grants, 3546
NYCT Fund for New Citizens Grants, 3547
NYCT Girls and Young Women Grants, 3548
NYCT Grants for the Elderly, 3549
NYCT Historic Preservation Grants, 3551
NYCT Human Justice Grants, 3552
NYCT Neighborhood Revitalization Grants, 3555
NYCT Technical Assistance Grants, 3559
NYHC Reading and Discussion Grants, 3568
NYHC Speakers in the Humanities Grants, 3569
NYSCA Arts Educ: Community-based Learning Grants, 3577
NYSCA Arts Ed Local Capacity Building Grants, 3581
Oceanside Charitable Fndn Grants, 3637
Office Depot Fndn Caring is Sharing Grants, 3639
Ohio Arts Council Arts Innovation Grants, 3649
Ohio Arts Council Sustainability Grants, 3654
Ohio County Community Fndn Board of Directors Grants, 3656
Ohio County Community Fndn Grants, 3658
Ohio County Community Fndn Junior Grants, 3659
Ohio County Community Fndn Mini-Grants, 3660
Ohio Valley Fndn Grants, 3662
Oleonda Jameson Grants, 3667
OneStar Fndn AmeriCorps Grants, 3674
Ontario Arts Council Aboriginal Project Grants, 3675
Open Spaces Sacred Places National Awards, 3684
Oscar Rennebohm Fndn Grants, 3694
OSF-Baltimore Community Fellowships, 3695
OSI After Prison Init Grants, 3710
Otto Bremer Fndn Grants, 3713
Owen County Community Fndn Grants, 3716
Owens Fndn Grants, 3718
Packard Fndn Local Grants, 3729
Packard Fndn Organizational Effectiveness and Philanthropy Grants, 3730
Palm Beach and Martin Counties Grants, 3733
Parke County Community Fndn Grants, 3735
Parker Fndn (California) Grants, 3736
Parkersburg Area Comm Fndn Action Grants, 3738
Patrick and Anna M. Cudahy Grants, 3751
Paul and Edith Babson Fndn Grants, 3755
Paul G. Allen Family Fndn Grants, 3759
Paul Ogle Fndn Grants, 3764
Pay It Forward Fndn Mini Grants, 3768
PCA Arts Organizations and Arts Programs Grants for Local Arts, 3782
PCA Entry Track Arts Organizations and Program Grants for Local Arts, 3794
Peacock Fndn Grants, 3809
Pentair Fndn Educ and Community Grants, 3816
Peoples Bancorp Fndn Grants, 3817
Percy B. Ferebee Endowment Grants, 3820
Perkins Charitable Fndn Grants, 3823
Perpetual Trust for Charitable Giving Grants, 3826
Perry County Community Fndn Grants, 3827
Pet Care Trust Fish in the Classroom Grant, 3828
Pet Care Trust Sue Busch Memorial Award, 3829
Peter and Elizabeth C. Tower Fndn Organizational Scholarships, 3838
Peter and Elizabeth C. Tower Fndn Social and Emotional Preschool Curriculum Grants, 3841
Peter Kiewit Fndn General Grants, 3845
Peter Kiewit Fndn Small Grants, 3847
Petra Fndn Fellows Awards, 3850
PG&E Community Investment Grants, 3867
PG&E Community Vitality Grants, 3868
Phelps County Community Fndn Grants, 3870
Philadelphia Organizational Effectiveness Grants, 3872
Philadelphia Fndn YOUTHadelphia Grants, 3873
Piedmont Health Fndn Grants, 3882
Piedmont Natural Gas Corp and Charitable Contributions, 3883
Pike County Community Fndn Grants, 3888
Pi Lambda Theta Anna Tracey Memorial Award, 3889
Pi Lambda Theta Lillian and Henry Barry Award in Human Relations, 3890
Pinellas County Grants, 3891
Pinnacle Entertainment Fndn Grants, 3893
Piper Trust Older Adults Grants, 3904
Piper Trust Reglous Organizations Grants, 3905
Pittsburgh Fndn Community Grants, 3910
Plough Fndn Grants, 3915
Plum Creek Fndn Grants, 3917
PMP Professional Development Grants, 3919
PMP Project Grants, 3920
PNC Charitable Trust and Fndn Grants, 3921
PNC Ecnomic Development Grants, 3922
PNC Fndn Grow Up Great Grants, 3924
PNM Power Up Grants, 3925
Polk Bros. Fndn Grants, 3929
Porter County Community Fndn Grants, 3931
Portland Fndn Grants, 3936
Portland General Electric Fndn Grants, 3937
Posey Community Fndn Women's Grants, 3938
Posey County Community Fndn Grants, 3939
Pott Fndn Grants, 3940
PPG Industries Fndn Grants, 3943
Price Family Charitable Grants, 3952
Price Gilbert, Jr. Charitable Grants, 3953
Priddy Fndn Operating Grants, 3955
Priddy Fndn Organizational Development Grants, 3956
Priddy Fndn Grants, 3957
Prince Charitable Trusts D.C. Grants, 3960
Prince Charitable Trusts Rhode Island Grants, 3961
Princeton Area Community Fndn Fund for Women and Girls Grants, 3962
Princeton Area Community Fndn Greater Mercer Grants, 3963
Progress Energy Corp Contributions Grants, 3968
Progress Energy Fndn Economic Vitality Grants, 3969
Project Orange Thumb Grants, 3972
Prudential Fndn Arts and Culture Grants, 3975
Prudential Fndn Economic Development Grants, 3976
PSEG Corp Contributions Grants, 3979
Public Welfare Fndn Grants, 3984
Puerto Rico Community Fndn Grants, 3986
Pulaski County Community Fndn Grants, 3988
Putnam County Community Fndn Grants, 3990
Quantum Fndn Grants, 3996

846 / Community Development

QuikTrip Corp Contributions Grants, 3998
R.E.B. Awards for Distinguished Ed Leadership, 4000
Ralph and Virginia Mullin Fndn Grants, 4012
Rancho Santa Fe Fndn Grants, 4016
Raskob Fndn for Catholic Activities Grants, 4019
Rasmuson Fndn Capital Grants, 4020
Rasmuson Fndn Special Project Grants, 4025
RCF General Community Grants, 4032
RCF Individual Assistance Grants, 4033
Regence Fndn Access to Health Care Grants, 4039
Regence Fndn Health Care Community Awareness and Engagement Grants, 4040
Regence Fndn Health Care Connections Grants, 4041
Regence Fndn Improving End-of-Life Grants, 4042
Regence Fndn Tools and Technology Grants, 4043
Retirement Research Accessible Faith Grants, 4066
Retirement Research Fndn General Grants, 4067
Reynolds American Fndn Grants, 4068
Reynolds and Reynolds Associate Fndn Grants, 4069
Rhode Island Fndn Grants, 4073
Richard D. Bass Fndn Grants, 4079
Richard M. Fairbanks Fndn Grants, 4088
Rich Fndn Grants, 4090
Richland County Bank Grants, 4091
Ripley County Community Fndn Grants, 4095
Ripley County Community Small Project Grants, 4096
RISCA Professional Arts Development Grants, 4099
RISCA Project Grants for Organizations, Individuals and Educ, 4100
Rite Aid Corp Grants, 4101
Roberta Leventhal Sudakoff Fndn Grants, 4102
Robert and Joan Dircks Fndn Grants, 4104
Robert B McMillen Fndn Grants, 4106
Robert G. Cabell III and Maude Morgan Cabell Fndn Grants, 4113
Robert Lee Blaffer Fndn Grants, 4115
Robert R. Meyer Fndn Grants, 4121
Rochester Area Community Fndn Grants, 4127
Rochester Area Fndn Grants, 4128
Rockefeller Brothers Pivotal Places Grants: New York City, 4134
Rockefeller Fndn Grants, 4138
Rockwell Fund, Inc. Grants, 4140
Rockwell Int'l Corp Grants, 4141
Rollin M. Gerstacker Fndn Grants, 4146
Rose Fndn For Communities and the Environment Consumer Privacy Rights Grants, 4156
Rose Fndn For Communities and the Environment Kern County Air Pollution Mitigation Grants, 4157
Rose Fndn for Comm & the Environment N California Environmental Grassroots Grants, 4158
Rose Fndn For Communities and the Environment SE Madera County Responsible Growth Grants, 4159
Rosie's For All Kids Fndn Grants, 4163
Ross Fndn Grants, 4164
Roy J. Carver Charitable Trust Youth Grants, 4167
RR Donnelley Community Grants, 4168
Rucker-Donnell Fndn Grants, 4172
Rush County Community Fndn Grants, 4174
Ruth Anderson Fndn Grants, 4176
Ruth H. and Warren A. Ellsworth Fndn Grants, 4179
Rutter's Children's Charities Grants, 4181
RWJF Vulnerable Populations Portfolio Grants, 4190
Ryder System Charitable Fndn Grants, 4191
S.E.VEN Fund 'In The River They Swim' Essay Competition, 4194
S.E.VEN Fund Annual Grants, 4195
S.E.VEN Fund Mini-Grants, 4196
S.E.VEN Fund Open Enterprise Solutions to Poverty RFP Grants, 4197
S.E.VEN Fund WHY Prize, 4198
S. Livingston Mather Charitable Grants, 4200
S. Spencer Scott Grants, 4202
Safeco Insurance Community Grants, 4203
Sage Fndn Grants, 4204
Saginaw Community Fndn Discretionary Grants, 4205
Saginaw Community Fndn Senior Citizen Enrichment Fund, 4206
Saginaw County Community Fndn Youth FORCE Grants, 4208

Saint Paul Companies Fndn Grants, 4217
Saint Paul Fndn Lowertown Future Grants, 4220
Saint Paul Management Improvement Grants, 4221
Salt River Project Civic Leadership Grants, 4226
Samuel L. Phillips Family Fndn Grants, 4235
Samuel S. Johnson Fndn Grants, 4239
San Diego Fndn Civil Society Grants, 4244
San Diego Fndn Environment Blasker Grants, 4245
San Diego Environment Community Grants, 4246
San Diego Fndn Paradise Valley Hospital Community Grants, 4249
San Diego Science & Tech Blasker Grants, 4250
San Diego Women's Fndn Grants, 4252
San Francisco Fndn Art Awards James Duval Phelan Literary Award, 4258
San Francisco Fndn Environment Grants, 4266
San Francisco Fndn Faith Program and Arts and Culture Program, 4267
San Francisco Fndn Fund For Artists Award For Choreographers, 4270
San Francisco Fndn Fund For Artists Award For Playwrights and Theatre Ensembles, 4272
San Francisco Fndn Fund for Artists Award for Visual and Media Artists, 4273
San Francisco Fndn John Gutmann Photography Fellowship Award, 4279
San Francisco Fndn Koshland Program Arts and Culture Mini-Grants, 4280
San Francisco Fndn Murphy and Cadogan Fellowships in the Fine Arts, 4282
Santa Barbara Fndn Monthly Express Grants, 4284
Santa Barbara Strategy Grants Capital Support, 4285
Santa Barbara Fndn Strategy Grants - Innovation, 4287
Sarkeys Fndn Grants, 4297
Sartain Lanier Family Fndn Grants, 4298
Schering-Plough Fndn Community Inits Grants, 4303
Schramm Fndn Grants, 4310
Schumann Fund for New Jersey Grants, 4311
Schurz Communications Fndn Grants, 4312
Scott County Community Fndn Grants, 4314
Seattle Fndn Annual Neighborhoods and Communities Grants, 4319
Seattle Fndn Benjamin N. Phillips Grants, 4322
Seattle Fndn C. Keith Birkenfeld Grants, 4323
Seattle Fndn Economy Grants, 4325
Seattle Fndn Health and Wellness Grants, 4328
Seattle Fndn Neighbor to Neighbor Small Grants, 4330
Self Fndn Grants, 4335
Sensient Technologies Fndn Grants, 4337
Shaw's Supermarkets Donations, 4342
Shell Oil Company Fndn Grants, 4343
Shopko Fndn Green Bay Community Grants, 4347
Sidgmore Family Fndn Grants, 4348
Sidney Stern Grants, 4349
Siebert Lutheran Fndn Grants, 4351
Sierra Grants, 4352
Sierra Health Fndn Responsive Grants, 4353
Silicon Valley Community Fndn Elizabeth Anabo BRICC Awards, 4357
Silicon Valley Community Fndn Immigrant Integration Grants, 4358
Silicon Valley Community Fndn Regional Planning Grants, 4359
Simple Advise Educ Center Grants, 4361
Simpson Lumber Charitable Contributions, 4362
Sioux Falls Area Community Grants, 4364
Sioux Falls Area Community Fndn Spot Grants, 4366
Sir Dorabji Tata Grants for NGOs or Voluntary Organizations, 4370
Sisters of Charity Fndn of Cleveland Good Samaritan Grants, 4373
Sisters of Charity Fndn of Cleveland Reducing Health and Ed Disparities in the Central Neighborhood Grants, 4374
Skillman Community Connections Small Grants, 4379
Skillman Fndn Good Neighborhoods Grants, 4380
Skillman Fndn Good Opportunities Grants, 4381
Skillman Fndn Good Schools Grants, 4382
Slow Food in Schools Micro-Grants, 4384
Smith Richardson Fndn Direct Service Grants, 4385

SUBJECT INDEX

SOBP A.E. Bennett Research Award, 4388
Sobrato Family Fndn Grants, 4389
Sobrato Family Fndn Meeting Space Grants, 4390
Sobrato Family Fndn Office Space Grants, 4391
SOCFOC Catholic Ministries Grants, 4392
SOCFOC Community Collaborations Grants, 4393
Sodexo Fndn STOP Hunger Scholarships, 4400
Solutia Grants, 4402
Sonoco Fndn Grants, 4403
Sorenson Legacy Fndn Grants, 4407
Southbury Community Trust Fund, 4409
South Carolina Arts Commission Arts and Economic Impact Study Assistance Grants, 4416
South Carolina Arts Commission Cultural Tourism Init Grants, 4419
South Carolina Arts Commission Cultural Visions Grants, 4420
South Carolina Arts Commission Leadership and Organizational Development Grants, 4423
South Carolina Arts Commission Statewide Arts Participation Init Grants, 4425
South Carolina Arts Commission Sub-Grants, 4426
Southern Minnesota Init Fndn AmeriCorps Leap Grants, 4431
Southern Minnesota Init Fndn Community Growth Init Grants, 4433
Southern Minnesota Home Visiting Grants, 4434
Southern Minnesota Init Fndn Incentive Grants, 4435
South Madison Community Fndn Grants, 4440
SW Florida Community Competitive Grants, 4442
SW Florida Community Good Samaritan Grants, 4443
SW Gas Corp Fndn Grants, 4445
SW Init Fndn Grants, 4446
Southwire Company Grants, 4447
Speer Grants, 4450
Spencer County Community Fndn Grants, 4451
Sprague Fndn Grants, 4461
Springs Close Fndn Grants, 4462
St. Joseph Community Health Fndn Catherine Kasper Award, 4468
St. Joseph Community Health Fndn Improving Healthcare Access Grants, 4469
St. Louis-Jefferson Solid Waste Management Waste Reduction and Recycling Grants, 4470
Stackner Family Fndn Grants, 4471
Stackpole-Hall Fndn Grants, 4472
Stark Community Fndn Grants, 4477
Stark Community Fndn Neighborhood Community & Economic Devel Tech Assistance Grants, 4478
Stark Community Fndn Neighborhood Partnership Grants, 4479
Stark Community SummerTime Kid Grants, 4480
Starke County Community Fndn Grants, 4482
State Farm Strong Neighborhoods Grants, 4485
State Farm Project Ignition Grants, 4487
Steelcase Fndn Grants, 4497
Steuben County Community Fndn Grants, 4501
Stocker Fndn Grants, 4507
Stowe Family Fndn Grants, 4510
Stranahan Fndn Grants, 4512
Strengthening Families - Strengthening Communities Grants, 4513
Strowd Roses Grants, 4515
Summit Fndn Grants, 4524
Sunderland Fndn Grants, 4527
Suntrust Bank Atlanta Fndn Grants, 4531
Surdna Fndn Sustainable Environments Grants, 4533
Susan Mott Webb Charitable Grants, 4536
Susan Vaughan Fndn Grants, 4537
Sweet Water Grants, 4541
T. Raymond Gregory Family Fndn Grants, 4547
T. Rowe Price Associates Fndn Grants, 4548
TAC Arts Access Grant, 4549
TAC Arts Build Communities Grants, 4551
TAC Arts Educ Community-Learning Grants, 4552
TAC Arts Grants, 4554
TAC Rural Arts Project Support Grants, 4555
Taylor S. Abernathy and Patti Harding Abernathy Charitable Grants, 4564
TCF Bank Fndn Grants, 4565

SUBJECT INDEX

Community Education / 847

TE Fndn Grants, 4572
Telluride Fndn Community Grants, 4573
Temple-Inland Fndn Grants, 4576
Tension Envelope Fndn Grants, 4578
Texas Commission on Arts Educ Grants, 4579
Texas Commission on the Arts Create-1 Grants, 4583
Texas Commission on the Arts Create-3 Grants, 4585
Texas Commission on the Arts Create-4 Grants, 4586
Texas Commission on the Arts Create-5 Grants, 4587
Texas Commission On The Arts Cultural Connections Consultant/Simply Solutions Grants, 4590
Texas Commission On The Arts GPA1, 4592
Texas Commission on the Arts Special Opportunities Grants, 4593
Texas Instruments Fndn Arts and Culture Grants, 4599
Thelma Braun and Bocklett Family Fndn Grants, 4603
Theodore Edson Parker Fndn Grants, 4605
Third Sector New England Inclusion Init Grants, 4608
Thomas and Dorothy Leavey Fndn Grants, 4612
Thomas Austin Finch, Sr. Fndn Grants, 4613
Thomas C. Ackerman Fndn Grants, 4615
Thompson Charitable Fndn Grants, 4622
Threshold Fndn Justice and Democracy Grants, 4626
Threshold Fndn Thriving Resilient Communities Funding Circle, 4628
Topeka Community Fndn Grants, 4644
Toyota Motor Engineering & Manufacturing North America Grants, 4651
Toyota Motor Manufacturing of Alabama Grants, 4652
Toyota Motor Manufacturing of Indiana Grants, 4653
Toyota Motor of Kentucky Grants, 4654
Toyota Motor Manufacturing Mississippi Grants, 4655
Toyota Motor Manufacturing W Virginia Grants, 4657
Toyota Motor N America of New York Grants, 4658
Toyota Motor Sales, USA Grants, 4659
Toyota Technical Center Grants, 4660
Triangle Community Fndn Community Grants, 4667
Triangle Community Fndn Donor Grants, 4668
Trinity Fndn Grants, 4669
Trinity Fndn Grants, 4670
Trinity Trust Community Response Grants, 4671
Trull Fndn Grants, 4673
Tulane University Community Service Scholars, 4677
Tulane University Public Service Fellows, 4678
Turner Fndn Grants, 4681
TWS Fndn Grants, 4683
U.S. Department of Educ 21st Century Community Learning Centers, 4687
UniBank 911 Emergency Personnel Educ Fund, 4707
Union Bank Corp Sponsorships and Donations, 4708
Union Bank, N.A. Fndn Grants, 4709
Union Benevolent Association Grants, 4710
Union County Community Fndn Grants, 4711
Union County Fndn Grants, 4712
Union Square Award for Social Justice, 4717
Union Square Awards Grants, 4718
Unity Fndn Of LaPorte County Grants, 4726
UPS Corp Giving Grants, 4727
UPS Fndn Community Safety Grants, 4728
USAID Albania Critical Economic Growth Areas Grants, 4740
USAID Community Infrastructure Dev Grants, 4745
USAID Development Assistance Grants, 4748
USAID Palestinian Comm Assistance Grants, 4773
USAID Resilience and Economic Growth in the Sahel - Enhanced Resilience Grants, 4779
US Airways Educ Fndn Grants, 4790
USA Volleyball Fndn Ed Grants, 4791
USBC Earl Anthony Scholarships, 4793
USCM HIV/AIDS Prevention Grants, 4794
USDA Community Food Projects Grants, 4802
USDA Coop Extension System Educ Grants, 4803
USDA Denali Comm High Energy Cost Grants, 4805
USDA High Energy Cost Grants, 4812
USDA Rural Community Development Grants, 4825
USDA State Bulk Fuel Revolving Grants, 4840
USDC Public Works and Economic Adjustment Assistance Grants, 4856
USDC Strong Cities, Strong Communities Visioning Challenge Grants, 4858

US Soccer Annual Program & Field Grants, 4870
USTA Junior Team Tennis Stipends, 4875
USTA Pro Circuit Community Involvement Day Grants, 4882
USTA Public Facility Assistance Grants, 4883
USTA Recreational Tennis Grants, 4884
USTA Tennis Block Party Grants, 4892
Vancouver Fndn Disability Supports for Employment Grants, 4899
Vancouver Fndn Grants & Comm Inits, 4900
Vancouver Sun Children's Grants, 4901
Vanderburgh Community Fndn Grants, 4902
Vanguard Public Fndn Grant Funds, 4904
Vermillion County Community Fndn Grants, 4928
Vermont Community Fndn Grants, 4929
Victoria S. and Bradley L. Geist Fndn Capacity Building Grants, 4934
Victoria S. and Bradley L. Geist Fndn Enhancement Grants, 4935
Victoria S. and Bradley L. Geist Fndn Grants Supporting Foster Care and Their Caregivers, 4936
Vulcan Materials Company Fndn Grants, 4956
W.C. Griffith Fndn Grants, 4957
W. C. Griffith Fndn Grants, 4958
W.K. Kellogg Fndn Secure Families Grants, 4963
Wabash Valley Community Fndn Grants, 4971
Wallace Alexander Gerbode Fndn Grants, 4974
Wallace Fndn Grants, 4976
Walter L. Gross III Family Fndn Grants, 4983
Warrick County Community Fndn Grants, 4987
Waste Management Charitable Giving Grants, 5001
Water and Land Stewardship Grants, 5002
Wayne County Fndn Vigran Family Grants, 5004
Wayne County Fndn Grants, 5005
Wayne County Fndn Women's Grants, 5006
WCI Community Leadership Fellowships, 5008
WCI Community Mobilization Grants, 5009
WCI Family Econ Success Local Impact Grants, 5010
WCI Leadership Development Grants, 5012
Wells County Fndn Grants, 5022
Western Indiana Community Fndn Grants, 5024
West Hawai'i Fund for Nonprofit Organizations, 5027
West Virginia Commission on the Arts Challenge America Partnership Grants, 5031
West Virginia Commission on the Arts Init/Opportunity Grants, 5035
West Virginia Commission on the Arts Major Insts Support Grants, 5038
West Virginia Commission on the Arts Mid-Size Insts Support Grants, 5040
West Virginia Commission on the Arts Re-Granting Grants, 5046
Weyerhaeuser Company Fndn Grants, 5053
Whitley County Community Fndn Grants, 5060
WHO Fndn Educ/Lit Grants, 5062
Wieboldt Fndn Grants, 5065
Willary Fndn Grants, 5071
William A. Badger Fndn Grants, 5072
William A. Miller Fndn Grants, 5073
William Blair and Company Fndn Grants, 5078
William G. and Helen C. Hoffman Fndn Grants, 5080
William G. Baker, Jr. Grants, 5081
William G. Gilmore Fndn Grants, 5082
William J. and Dorothy K. O'Neill Fndn Grants, 5087
William L. and Victorine Q. Adams Fndn Grants, 5089
William M. Weaver Fndn Grants, 5091
William S. Abell Fndn Grants, 5094
Wilson-Wood Fndn Grants, 5098
Winston-Salem Fndn Elkin/Tri-County Grants, 5103
Winthrop Rockefeller Fndn Grants, 5105
Wisconsin Humanities Council Mini-Grants for Scholarly Research, 5108
Women's Fndn Greater Kansas City Grants, 5111
Woods Charitable Grants, 5114
World Bank JJ/WBGSP Partners Programs, 5117
Xcel Energy Fndn Grants, 5121
Xerox Fndn Grants, 5122
Yampa Valley Community Fndn Grants, 5124
Yellow Corp Fndn Grants, 5126
Young Family Fndn Grants, 5127

Youth As Resources Grants, 5130
YSA MLK Day Lead Organizer Grants, 5136
Z. Smith Reynolds Fndn Community Economic Development Grants, 5144

Community Education
ACF Native American Social and Economic Development Strategies Grants, 123
Adams Fndn Grants, 154
ALA Charlie Robinson Award, 256
ALA Highsmith Library Innovation Award, 285
ALA John Cotton Dana Library Public Relations Award, 292
ALA National Friends of Libraries Week Awards, 303
ALA Polaris Innovation in Tech John Iliff Award, 309
ALA Sara Jaffarian School Library Award for Exemplary Humanities Programming, 316
Appalachian Community Fund Special Opportunities Grants, 497
Appalachian Regional Commission Leadership Development and Capacity Building Grants, 509
Arkansas Arts Council Collab Project Support, 555
ATA Local Community Relations Grants, 600
Autauga Area Community Fndn Grants, 618
Ben B. Cheney Fndn Grants, 725
Benwood Fndn Focus Area Grants, 733
Bernard and Audre Rapoport Fndn Democracy and Civic Participation Grants, 737
Best Buy Children's Fndn @15 Community Grants, 749
Better World Books LEAP Grants for Libraries, 755
Better World Books LEAP Grants for Nonprofits, 756
Bill and Melinda Gates Fndn Agricultural Development Grants, 765
Bill and Melinda Gates Fndn Financial Services for the Poor Grants, 767
Blackford County Community Fndn Grants, 780
Blue Cross Blue Shield of Minnesota Fndn - Health Equity: Building Health Together Grants, 793
Blue Cross Blue Shield of Minnesota Fndn - Healthy Equity: Health Impact Assessment Demonstration Project Grants, 795
Bright Promises Fndn Grants, 838
Brunswick Fndn Dollars for Doers Grants, 856
California Endowment Innovative Ideas Grants, 904
CarEth Fndn Grants, 924
CCFF Community Grant, 962
Charles H. Farnsworth Grants, 1043
Charles H. Price II Family Fndn Grants, 1046
Charles Parker Trust for Public Music Grants, 1053
Citizens Savings Fndn Grants, 1141
Clark and Carolyn Adams Fndn Grants, 1153
Community Fndn of Bloomington and Monroe County - Precision Health Network Cycle Grants, 1270
Community Fndn of Greater Fort Wayne - Barbara Burt Leadership Development Grants, 1283
Community Fndn of Greater Fort Wayne - John S. and James L. Knight Fndn Donor-Advised Grants, 1287
Con Edison Corp Giving Community Grants, 1346
Deaconess Fndn Advocacy Grants, 1468
Delta Air Lines Community Enrichment Grants, 1494
Doug and Carla Salmon Fndn Grants, 1594
EQT Fndn Community Grants, 1744
Evelyn & Walter Haas Nonprofit Leader Grants, 1774
Fifth Third Bank Corp Giving, 1809
Fndns of E Chicago Financial Indep Grants, 1909
General Service Fndn Colorado Grants, 2005
Georgia-Pacific Fndn Educ Grants, 2031
Green Fndn Educ Grants, 2153
Guy I. Bromley Grants, 2180
Helen Bader Fndn Grants, 2293
Init Fndn Minnesota Early Childhood Grants, 2560
John S. and James L. Knight Fndn Grants, 2713
Kalamazoo Community Fndn John E. Fetzer Institute Grants, 2770
Kalamazoo Community Fndn Mini-Grants, 2772
Laura Jane Musser Intercultural Harmony Grants, 2862
LEGO Children's Grants, 2878
Louetta M. Cowden Fndn Grants, 2922
Lucy Downing Nisbet Charitable Grants, 2935
Marion Gardner Jackson Charitable Grants, 3017

848 / Community Education

Mary E. Babcock Fndn, 3038
McCune Charitable Fndn Grants, 3077
Medtronic Fndn Community Link Arts, Civic, and Culture Grants, 3109
Mertz Gilmore Fndn NYC Communities Grants, 3126
MetLife Building Livable Communities Grants, 3129
Michael and Susan Dell Fndn Grants, 3158
Michael Reese Health Trust Core Grants, 3159
Michael Reese Health Trust Responsive Grants, 3160
MMS and Alliance Charitable Fndn Grants for Community Action and Care for the Medically Uninsured, 3194
Mt. Sinai Health Care Fndn Health of the Urban Community Grants, 3227
National Endowment for Arts Museum Grants, 3265
National Endowment for Arts Opera Grants, 3267
National Home Library Fndn Grants, 3276
Nellie Mae Educ Public Understanding Grants, 3298
NFL Charities NFL Player Fndn Grants, 3347
Norfolk Southern Fndn Grants, 3463
North Central Health Services Grants, 3491
NSTA Distinguished Informal Science Ed Award, 3531
NYSCA Arts Educ: Community-based Learning Grants, 3577
NYSCA Arts Ed Local Capacity Building Grants, 3581
NYSCA Museum: Project Support Grants, 3604
Ohio County Community Fndn Board of Directors Grants, 3656
Ohio County Community Fndn Junior Grants, 3659
Parker Fndn (California) Grants, 3736
Pay It Forward Fndn Mini Grants, 3768
Peter and Elizabeth C. Tower Fndn Social and Emotional Preschool Curriculum Grants, 3841
Peter Kiewit Fndn Small Grants, 3847
PG&E Community Investment Grants, 3867
Piper Trust Educ Grants, 3902
Portland Fndn - Women's Giving Circle Grant, 3935
PPG Industries Fndn Grants, 3943
RCF General Community Grants, 4032
RCF Individual Assistance Grants, 4033
Red Robin Fndn U-ACT Grants, 4038
Richland County Bank Grants, 4091
Robert Lee Blaffer Fndn Grants, 4115
Saginaw Community Fndn Discretionary Grants, 4205
Saginaw County Community Fndn Youth FORCE Grants, 4208
Santa Barbara Fndn Strategy Grants - Innovation, 4287
Seattle Fndn Benjamin N. Phillips Grants, 4322
Seattle Fndn C. Keith Birkenfeld Grants, 4323
Seattle Fndn Educ Grants, 4326
Threshold Fndn Thriving Resilient Communities Funding Circle, 4628
Trinity Trust Community Response Grants, 4671
USAID Reading Enhancement for Advancing Development Grants, 4778
VSA/Metlife Connect All Grants, 4953
W.K. Kellogg Fndn Civic Engagement Grants, 4960
WCI Community Leadership Fellowships, 5008
William A. Miller Fndn Grants, 5073

Community Outreach
3M Fndn Community Giving Grants, 15
118 Fndn Grants, 29
AAAAI RSLAAIS Leadership Award, 49
Abell Fndn Community Development Grants, 93
Abell Fndn Workforce Development Grants, 97
Able To Serve Grants, 102
Adams County Comm Fndn of Indiana Grants, 148
ALA Charlie Robinson Award, 256
ALA Highsmith Library Innovation Award, 285
ALA John Cotton Dana Library Public Relations Award, 292
ALA Loleta D. Fyan Grant, 295
ALA National Friends of Libraries Week Awards, 303
ALA Sara Jaffarian School Library Award for Exemplary Humanities Programming, 316
Allstate Corp Giving Grants, 386
Allstate Corp Hometown Commitment Grants, 387
Allstate Fndn Safe and Vital Communities Grants, 390
Altman Fndn Strengthening Communities Grants, 398

American Chemical Society Corp Associates Seed Grants, 425
American Express Community Service Grants, 430
American Express Historic Preservation Grants, 431
American Foodservice Charitable Grants, 433
Anderson Fndn Grants, 460
Angels Baseball Fndn Grants, 465
Ann L. & Carol Green Rhodes Charitable Grants, 483
Antone & Edene Vidinha Charitable Grants, 490
Appalachian Community Fund General Grants, 493
Appalachian Community Fund GLBTQ Grants, 494
Appalachian Community Media Justice Grants, 495
Appalachian Community Fund Seize the Moment Grants, 496
Appalachian Community Fund Special Opportunities Grants, 497
Aragona Family Fndn Grants, 522
Arbor Day Fndn Grants, 524
Arkansas Arts Council Collab Project Support, 555
ATA School-Community Relations Awards, 602
Autauga Area Community Fndn Grants, 618
Ayres Fndn Grants, 630
BancorpSouth Fndn Grants, 651
Batchelor Fndn Grants, 679
Ben B. Cheney Fndn Grants, 725
Bernard & Audre Rapoport Arts & Culture Grant, 735
Bernard and Audre Rapoport Fndn Democracy and Civic Participation Grants, 737
Bernard and Audre Rapoport Fndn Health Grants, 738
Bill and Katie Weaver Charitable Grants, 764
Bill and Melinda Gates Fndn Agricultural Development Grants, 765
Blandin Fndn Itasca County Area Vitality Grants, 789
Blandin Rural Community Leadership Grants, 790
Blue Cross Blue Shield of Minnesota Fndn - Healthy Equity: Public Libraries for Health Grants, 797
Blue Cross Blue Shield of Minnesota Healthy Neighborhoods: Connect Grants, 798
Bohemian Fndn Pharos Grants, 811
Boston Fndn Grants, 819
Bright Promises Fndn Grants, 838
Brookdale Fndn National Group Respite Grants, 845
Brooklyn Community Fndn Educ and Youth Achievement Grants, 851
Brunswick Fndn Dollars for Doers Grants, 856
Burton D. Morgan Hudson Community Grants, 869
Cable Positive's Tony Cox Community Grants, 886
California Community Fndn Human Development Grants, 902
California Endowment Innovative Ideas Challenge Grants, 904
Cambridge Community Fndn Grants, 913
Campbell Soup Fndn Grants, 916
Caring Fndn Grants, 926
Carl B. and Florence E. King Fndn Grants, 928
Carrie E. and Lena V. Glenn Fndn Grants, 944
Carrier Corp Contributions Grants, 946
Catherine Kennedy Home Fndn Grants, 955
CCHD Community Development Grants, 966
Center for Venture Philanthropy, 991
Ceres Fndn Grants, 999
Cessna Fndn Grants, 1000
CFFVR Alcoholism and Drug Abuse Grants, 1001
CFFVR Basic Needs Giving Partnership Grants, 1002
CFFVR Capacity Building Grants, 1004
CFFVR Capital Credit Union Charitable Giving, 1005
CFFVR Chilton Area Community Fndn Grants, 1006
CFFVR Clintonville Area Fndn Grants, 1008
CFFVR Fox Valley Community Arts Grants, 1011
CFFVR Frank C. Shattuck Community Grants, 1012
CFFVR SAC Developmental Disabilities Grants, 1019
CFFVR Schmidt Family G4 Grants, 1020
CFFVR Shawano Area Community Fndn Grants, 1021
CFFVR Waupaca Area Community Fndn Grants, 1023
CFFVR Wisconsin Daughters and Sons Grants, 1024
CFFVR Women's Fund for the Fox Valley Region Grants, 1025
Charles Delmar Fndn Grants, 1039
Chesapeake Bay Trust Outreach and Community Engagement Grants, 1073

CICF City of Noblesville Community Grant, 1118
Citizens Savings Fndn Grants, 1141
Clark-Winchcole Fndn Grants, 1152
Clipper Ship Fndn Grants, 1175
Clorox Company Fndn Grants, 1176
Colonel Stanley R. McNeil Fndn Grants, 1210
Columbus Fndn Traditional Grants, 1233
Community Fndn for Greater New Haven Women & Girls Grants, 1254
Community Fndn for San Benito County Grants, 1258
Community Fndn in Jacksonville Senior Roundtable Aging Adults Grants, 1263
Community Fndn of Abilene Community Grants, 1264
Community Fndn of Bloomington and Monroe County - Precision Health Network Cycle Grants, 1270
Community Fndn of Greater Fort Wayne - John S. and James L. Knight Fndn Donor-Advised Grants, 1287
Community Fndn of Greater New Britain Grants, 1291
Community Fndn of Greenville Community Enrichment Grants, 1294
Community Fndn of Greenville Hollingsworth Funds Program/Project Grants, 1296
Community Fndn of St. Joseph County African American Community Grants, 1312
Community Fndn of Switzerland County Grants, 1315
Community Fndn of the Eastern Shore Youth Fndn Grants, 1319
Community Fndn of Virgin Islands Mini Grants, 1325
ConAgra Foods Nourish Our Comm Grants, 1343
Cowles Charitable Grants, 1392
Cralle Fndn Grants, 1394
Curtis and Edith Munson Fndn Grants, 1418
Curtis Fndn Grants, 1419
D. W. McMillan Fndn Grants, 1426
Dade Community Fndn Community AIDS Partnership Grants, 1428
Dade Community Fndn GLBT Grants, 1429
Dade Community Fndn Safe Passage Grants, 1431
Danellie Fndn Grants, 1442
Deaconess Fndn Advocacy Grants, 1468
Delaware Community Fndn-Youth Philanthropy Board for Kent County, 1483
Delaware Division of the Arts Community-Based Organizations Opportunity Grants, 1487
Delta Air Lines Community Enrichment Grants, 1494
DHHS ARRA Strengthening Communities Fund - Nonprofit Capacity Building Grants, 1527
DHHS ARRA Strengthening Communities Fund - State, Local, and Tribal Government Capacity Building Grants, 1528
DHHS Healthy Tomorrows Partnerships for Children Grants, 1534
East Tennessee Fndn Grants, 1646
Edina Realty Fndn Grants, 1656
Edward and Ellen Roche Relief Fndn Grants, 1663
Edward W. and Stella C. Van Houten Grants, 1670
Eisner Fndn Grants, 1678
Elden and Mary Lee Gutwein Family Grants, 1679
Elizabeth & Avola W. Callaway Fndn Grants, 1680
Elkhart County Community Fndn Fund for Elkhart County, 1683
Elsie H. Wilcox Fndn Grants, 1691
EPA Children's Health Protection Grants, 1728
EQT Fndn Community Grants, 1744
Essex County Community Emergency Grants, 1753
Ethel Sergeant Clark Smith Fndn Grants, 1761
Evan and Susan Bayh Fndn Grants, 1769
Family Lit and Hawaii Pizza Hut Lit Fund, 1785
FAR Grants, 1787
Fargo-Moorhead Area Fndn Woman's Grants, 1789
Fifth Third Bank Corp Giving, 1809
Florida BRAIVE Fund of Dade Community, 1846
Florida Div of Cultural Affairs Media Grants, 1856
Florida Div of Cultural Affairs Multidisciplinary Grants, 1857
Florida Div of Cultural Affairs Touring Grants, 1863
Ford Family Fndn Grants - Technical Assistance, 1882
Fndn for Mid South Comm Development Grants, 1897
Frank & Larue Reynolds Charitable Grants, 1924
Frank and Lydia Bergen Fndn Grants, 1925

SUBJECT INDEX   Community Outreach / 849

Frederick W. Marzahl Grants, 1948
Fremont Area Community Amazing X Grants, 1953
Fremont Area Community Elderly Needs Grants, 1954
Fremont Area Comm Summer Youth Grants, 1956
General Service Fndn Colorado Grants, 2005
George and Sarah Buchanan Fndn Grants, 2011
George A Ohl Jr. Fndn Grants, 2012
George Family Fndn Grants, 2017
Georgiana Goddard Eaton Grants, 2038
Giant Eagle Fndn Grants, 2049
Giving Sum Annual Grant, 2058
GNOF IMPACT Grants for Health and Human Services, 2080
Goldseker Fndn Community Affairs Grants, 2100
Goldseker Fndn Human Services Grants, 2102
Grand Rapids Area Community Fndn Wyoming Youth Grants, 2117
Grand Rapids Community Ionia County Grants, 2119
Grand Rapids Community Ionia Youth Grants, 2120
Grand Rapids Comm SE Ottawa Youth Grants, 2123
Grand Rapids Community Sparta Youth Grants, 2125
GTECH Community Involvement Grants, 2171
Gulf Coast Community Operating Grants, 2176
Gulf Coast Fndn of Community Grants, 2177
Guy I. Bromley Grants, 2180
Hahl Proctor Charitable Grants, 2208
Harley Davidson Fndn Grants, 2224
Harry Kramer Grants, 2242
Hartford Courant Fndn Grants, 2248
Hawai'i Children's Trust Fund Community Awareness Events Grants, 2258
Hawaii Community Fndn Community Capacity Building Grants, 2260
Hawaii Community Geographic-Specific Grants, 2261
Hawaii Community Human Services Grants, 2262
Hawaii Community Fndn Organizational Capacity Building Grants, 2263
HCA Fndn Grants, 2274
Head Start Replacement Grantee: Colorado, 2275
Head Start Replacement Grantee: Florida, 2276
Head Start Replacement Grantee: West Virginia, 2277
Health Fndn of Greater Cincinnati Grants, 2281
Heartland Arts Fund, 2286
Helen Bader Fndn Grants, 2293
Henrietta Tower Wurts Memorial Fndn Grants, 2304
Henry County Community Fndn - TASC Youth Grants, 2307
High Meadow Fndn Grants, 2321
Hilton Head Island Fndn Grants, 2330
Hitachi Fndn Business and Work Grants, 2339
Hitachi Fndn Yoshiyama Awards, 2340
Hollie and Anna Oakley Fndn Grants, 2346
Horace A. Kimball and S. Ella Kimball Grants, 2362
Howard H. Callaway Fndn Grants, 2376
Hulman & Company Fndn Grants, 2387
Humanitas Fndn Grants, 2390
IBM Community Development Grants, 2425
Illinois Arts Council Partners in Excellence, 2475
IMLS Native Am Library Services Basic Grants, 2517
IMLS Native American Library Services Enhancement Grants, 2518
Indiana Household Hazardous Waste Grants, 2538
Indianapolis Power & Light Company Grants, 2540
Ireland Family Fndn Grants, 2574
Jacobs Family Spirit of the Diamond Grants, 2618
James & Abigail Campbell Family Fndn Grants, 2620
Janirve Fndn Grants, 2645
Jennings County Community Fndn Grants, 2664
John H. Wellons Fndn Grants, 2699
John S. and James L. Knight Fndn Grants, 2713
Johnson County Community Fndn Grants, 2723
Johnson Fndn Wingspread Conference Support, 2725
John W. Anderson Fndn Grants, 2729
John W. Speas and Effie E. Speas Grants, 2732
Judith Clark-Morrill Fndn Grants, 2756
K21 Health Fndn Cancer Care Grants, 2759
K21 Health Fndn Grants, 2760
Kalamazoo Community Fndn Front Porch Grants, 2767
Kalamazoo Community Fndn John E. Fetzer Institute Grants, 2770

Kalamazoo Community Fndn Mini-Grants, 2772
Kaneta Fndn Grants, 2774
Kentucky Arts Council Access Assistance Grants, 2805
Kosciusko County Community Fndn Grants, 2838
L. W. Pierce Family Fndn Grants, 2846
Laclede Gas Charitable Grants, 2848
Land O'Lakes Fndn Community Grants, 2859
Land O'Lakes Fndn Dollars for Doers, 2860
Laura Jane Musser Intercultural Harmony Grants, 2862
Lee and Ramona Bass Fndn Grants, 2871
Leo Niessen Jr., Charitable Grants, 2885
Lewis H. Humphreys Charitable Grants, 2889
Lily Auchincloss Fndn Grants, 2904
Liz Claiborne Fndn Grants, 2915
Lois and Richard England Family Fndn Jewish Community Life Grants, 2919
Lotus 88 Fndn for Women and Children Grants, 2921
Louetta M. Cowden Fndn Grants, 2922
Louis and Elizabeth Nave Flarsheim Charitable Fndn Grants, 2924
Lowe's Outdoor Classroom Grants, 2928
Lucy Downing Nisbet Charitable Grants, 2935
Lucy Gooding Charitable Fndn Grants, 2937
M.B. and Edna Zale Fndn Grants, 2950
Mabel F. Hoffman Charitable Grants, 2957
Mabel Louise Riley Fndn Family Strengthening Small Grants, 2958
Madison County Community General Grants, 2973
Maine Community Fndn Baldwin Area Grants, 2974
Maine Community Fndn Belvedere Animal Welfare Grants, 2975
Maine Community Fndn Peaks Island Grants, 2984
Manitoba Arts Council Special Opps Grants, 2997
Marion Gardner Jackson Charitable Grants, 3017
Mary Reynolds Babcock Fndn Grants, 3047
Maxon Charitable Fndn Grants, 3068
McKnight Fndn Multiservice Grants, 3085
McKnight Fndn Virginia McKnight Binger Awards in Human Service, 3087
MDARD AgD Value Added/Regional Food Systems Grants, 3091
MDEQ Community Pollution Prevention (P2) Grants: Household Drug Collections, 3098
Mead Johnson Nutritionals Evansville-Area Organizations Grants, 3103
MedImmune Charitable Grants, 3108
Medtronic Fndn Community Link Arts, Civic, and Culture Grants, 3109
Melville Charitable Grants, 3115
MetLife Building Livable Communities Grants, 3129
MetLife Fndn Promoting Employee Volunteerism, 3132
MFRI Operation Diploma Small Grants for Indiana Family Readiness Groups, 3152
Michael Reese Health Trust Responsive Grants, 3160
Mid-Iowa Health Fndn Comm Response Grants, 3168
Military Ex-Prisoners of War Fndn Grants, 3177
Mr. and Mrs. William Foulds Family Grants, 3222
Ms. Fndn Women Building Democracy Grants, 3223
Mt. Sinai Health Care Fndn Health of the Urban Community Grants, 3227
NAR Realtor Magazine Good Neighbor Awards, 3240
National Endowment for the Arts - Regional Partnership Agreement Grants, 3258
National Endowment for Arts Commun Grants, 3260
National Endowment for Arts Agencies Grants, 3263
National Endowment for Arts Museum Grants, 3265
National Endowment for Arts Music Grants, 3266
National Endowment for Arts Opera Grants, 3267
National Endowment for the Arts Presenting Grants: Art Works, 3268
National Endowment for Arts Theater Grants, 3269
NEI Innovative Patient Outreach Programs And Ocular Screening Technologies To Improve Detection Of Diabetic Retinopathy Grants, 3295
Nellie Mae Educ Public Understanding Grants, 3298
Newton County Community Fndn Grants, 3336
NFF Community Assistance Grants, 3343
NFL Charities NFL Player Fndn Grants, 3347
Nissan Fndn Grants, 3444
NNEDVF/Altria Doors of Hope Program, 3452

Norfolk Southern Fndn Grants, 3463
North Central Health Services Grants, 3492
NW Mutual Fndn Grants, 3509
NW Minnesota Fndn Asset Building Grants, 3511
NSF CISE Community-Based Data Interoperability Networks Grants, 3523
NSF CISE Computing and Communication Fndns: Core Programs Grants, 3525
NYCH Together Grants, 3541
NYCT Fund for New Citizens Grants, 3547
NYCT Human Justice Grants, 3552
NYCT Neighborhood Revitalization Grants, 3555
Ohio Arts Council Arts Access Grants, 3647
Ohio Arts Council Int'l Partnership Grants, 3653
Ohio County Community Fndn Board of Directors Grants, 3656
Ohio County Community Fndn Junior Grants, 3659
Ontario Arts Council Aboriginal Project Grants, 3675
Owens Fndn Grants, 3718
Parke County Community Fndn Grants, 3735
Parker Fndn (California) Grants, 3736
Patrick and Anna M. Cudahy Grants, 3751
Pay It Forward Fndn Mini Grants, 3768
PCA Arts Organizations and Arts Programs Grants for Arts Educ Organizations, 3776
PCA Arts Organizations & Grants for Crafts, 3778
PCA Arts Organizations & Grants for Dance, 3779
PCA Arts Organizations & Grants for Lit, 3781
PCA Arts Organizations & Grants for Theatre, 3783
PCA Arts Organizations and Arts Programs Grants for Traditional and Folk Arts, 3784
PCA Arts Organizations & Grants for Visual Arts, 3785
PCA Entry Track Arts Organizations and Program Grants for Arts Educ Organizations, 3788
PCA Entry Track Arts Organizations and Program Grants for Crafts, 3790
PCA Entry Track Arts Organizations and Program Grants for Dance, 3791
PCA Entry Track Arts Organizations and Program Grants for Theatre, 3797
PCA Entry Track Arts Organizations and Program Grants for Traditional and Folk Arts, 3798
PCA Entry Track Arts Organizations and Program Grants for Visual Arts, 3799
PCA Pennsylvania Partners in the Arts Program Stream Grants, 3801
PCA Pennsylvania Partners in the Arts Project Stream Grants, 3802
Peacock Fndn Grants, 3809
PepsiCo Fndn Grants, 3819
Percy B. Ferebee Endowment Grants, 3820
Perpetual Trust for Charitable Giving Grants, 3826
Perry County Community Fndn Grants, 3827
PG&E Community Investment Grants, 3867
Phoenix Coyotes Charities Grants, 3879
Pike County Community Fndn Grants, 3888
Pi Lambda Theta Lillian and Henry Barry Award in Human Relations, 3890
Pinellas County Grants, 3891
Piper Trust Older Adults Grants, 3904
Piper Trust Reglious Organizations Grants, 3905
Planet Dog Fndn Grants, 3911
Plough Fndn Grants, 3915
PNM Power Up Grants, 3925
Polk Bros. Fndn Grants, 3929
Posey Community Fndn Women's Grants, 3938
Posey County Community Fndn Grants, 3939
Pott Fndn Grants, 3940
Powell Fndn Grants, 3942
PPG Industries Fndn Grants, 3943
Price Family Charitable Grants, 3952
Prince Charitable Trusts D.C. Grants, 3960
Prince Charitable Trusts Rhode Island Grants, 3961
Princeton Area Community Fndn Greater Mercer Grants, 3963
Prudential Fndn Arts and Culture Grants, 3975
Pulaski County Community Fndn Grants, 3988
Qualcomm Grants, 3993
Rainbow Families Fndn Grants, 4008
Rasmuson Fndn Capital Grants, 4020

850 / Community Outreach

RCF General Community Grants, 4032
RCF Individual Assistance Grants, 4033
Rhode Island Fndn Grants, 4073
Richard and Helen DeVos Fndn Grants, 4076
Richard D. Bass Fndn Grants, 4079
Rite Aid Corp Grants, 4101
Rockefeller Brothers Pivotal Places Grants NY City, 4134
Ross Fndn Grants, 4164
Rush County Community Fndn Grants, 4174
Saginaw Community Fndn Discretionary Grants, 4205
Saginaw County Community Fndn Youth FORCE Grants, 4208
Saint Luke's Fndn Grants, 4215
Saint Luke's Health Inits Grants, 4216
Salt River Project Civic Leadership Grants, 4226
San Diego Women's Fndn Grants, 4252
Santa Barbara Strategy Grants Capital Support, 4285
Santa Barbara Fndn Strategy Grants - Innovation, 4287
Schurz Communications Fndn Grants, 4312
Scott County Community Fndn Grants, 4314
Shopko Fndn Green Bay Community Grants, 4347
Siebert Lutheran Fndn Grants, 4351
Simple Advise Educ Center Grants, 4361
Sisters of Charity Fndn of Cleveland Good Samaritan Grants, 4373
SOCFOC Catholic Ministries Grants, 4392
Social Justice Fund NW Criminal Justice Giving Project Grants, 4394
Sonoco Fndn Grants, 4403
Sony Corp of America Corp Philanthropy Grants, 4405
Sorenson Legacy Fndn Grants, 4407
South Carolina Arts Commission Statewide Arts Participation Init Grants, 4425
Spencer County Community Fndn Grants, 4451
St. Joseph Community Health Fndn Improving Healthcare Access Grants, 4469
State Farm Project Ignition Grants, 4487
Stocker Fndn Grants, 4507
Strowd Roses Grants, 4515
Susan Mott Webb Charitable Grants, 4536
Susan Vaughan Fndn Grants, 4537
TAC Arts Educ Community-Learning Grants, 4552
TAC Arts Educ Mini Grants, 4553
Telluride Fndn Community Grants, 4573
Thomas Austin Finch, Sr. Fndn Grants, 4613
Thompson Charitable Fndn Grants, 4622
Topeka Community Fndn Grants, 4644
Toyota Motor N America of New York Grants, 4658
Triangle Community Fndn Community Grants, 4667
Trinity Fndn Grants, 4669
Trinity Fndn Grants, 4670
U.S. Department of Educ Programs for Native Hawaiians, 4696
UNCFSP TIEAD Internship, 4705
Union Benevolent Association Grants, 4710
Union Square Awards Grants, 4718
Unity Fndn Of LaPorte County Grants, 4726
USAID Palestinian Comm Assistance Grants, 4773
USCM HIV/AIDS Prevention Grants, 4794
USTA Pro Circuit Community Involvement Day Grants, 4882
USTA Recreational Tennis Grants, 4884
USTA Tennis Block Party Grants, 4892
Vancouver Fndn Disability Supports for Employment Grants, 4899
Vancouver Fndn Grants & Comm Inits, 4900
Vancouver Sun Children's Grants, 4901
VHA Health Fndn Grants, 4931
W. C. Griffith Fndn Grants, 4958
Walter L. Gross III Family Fndn Grants, 4983
Warrick County Community Fndn Grants, 4987
WCI Childcare Capacity Grants, 5007
WCI Community Mobilization Grants, 5009
WCI Family Econ Success Local Impact Grants, 5010
WCI Family Econ Success Regionwide Grants, 5011
WCI Leadership Development Grants, 5012
West Virginia Commission on the Arts Community Connections Grants, 5032
West Virginia Commission on the Arts Major Insts Support Grants, 5038
West Virginia Commission on the Arts Mid-Size Insts Support Grants, 5040
West Virginia Commission on the Arts Re-Granting Grants, 5046
Wieboldt Fndn Grants, 5065
William G. and Helen C. Hoffman Fndn Grants, 5080
William G. Gilmore Fndn Grants, 5082
Wilson-Wood Fndn Grants, 5098
Woods Charitable Grants, 5114
Woods Fund of Chicago Grants, 5115

Community Services

2COBS Private Charitable Fndn Grants, 6
3M Company Health and Human Services Grants, 14
49ers Fndn Grants, 23
100 Angels Charitable Fndn Grants, 24
A/H Fndn Grants, 48
AACC Project Reach Grants, 56
AACC Service Learning Mini-Grants, 57
Abbot and Dorothy H. Stevens Fndn Grants, 79
Abbott Fund Community Grants, 81
Abell Fndn Community Development Grants, 93
Abernethy Family Fndn Grants, 98
ABIG Fndn Grants, 99
Able To Serve Grants, 102
Able Trust Voc Rehab Grants for Agencies, 103
ACF Assets for Indep Individual Development Account Grants, 115
ACF Ethnic Community Self-Help Grants, 118
ACF Native American Social and Economic Development Strategies Grants, 123
ACF Preferred Communities Grants, 124
Ackerman Fndn Grants, 129
Active Awareness Grants, 136
Adams County Comm Fndn of Indiana Grants, 148
Adams Family Fndn of Ohio Grants, 151
Adelaide Breed Bayrd Fndn Grants, 161
Agnes M. Lindsay Grants, 203
Agway Fndn Grants, 205
Aid for Starving Children Emergency Grants, 211
Alabama State Council on the Arts Operating Support Grants, 244
ALA Exceptional Service Award, 278
ALA Highsmith Library Innovation Award, 285
ALA Joseph W. Lippincott Award, 294
ALA National Friends of Libraries Week Awards, 303
Albert B. Cuppage Charitable Fndn Grants, 341
Allyn Fndn Grants, 392
Alpha Kappa Alpha Ed Advancement Fndn Community Assistance Awards, 393
Altman Fndn Strengthening Communities Grants, 398
AMA Fndn Fund for Better Health Grants, 409
American Express Community Service Grants, 430
American Psychiatric Fndn Helping Hands Grants, 443
Andersen Corp Fndn, 459
Angels Baseball Fndn Grants, 465
Anheuser-Busch Fndn Grants, 470
Ann and Robert H. Lurie Family Fndn Grants, 473
Anne Thorne Weaver Family Fndn Grants, 478
Anthem Blue Cross and Blue Shield Grants, 488
Appalachian Community Fund General Grants, 493
Appalachian Community Fund GLBTQ Grants, 494
Appalachian Community Media Justice Grants, 495
Appalachian Community Fund Seize the Moment Grants, 496
Appalachian Community Fund Special Opportunities Grants, 497
Appalachian Community Fund Technical Assistance Grants, 498
Aragona Family Fndn Grants, 522
ArvinMeritor Fndn Civic Grants, 583
ArvinMeritor Fndn Human Services Grants, 584
Ashland Corp Contributions Grants, 587
ASME Charles T. Main Awards, 590
AT&T Fndn Civic and Comm Service Grants, 599
Austin College Leadership Award, 615
Austin Community Fndn Grants, 616
Autauga Area Community Fndn Grants, 618
Avery Dennison Fndn Grants, 623
Ayres Fndn Grants, 630

Bailey Fndn Grants, 635
Baltimore Community Fndn Human Services Path Grants, 644
BancorpSouth Fndn Grants, 651
Bank of America Charitable Fndn Matching Gifts, 658
Bay and Paul Fndns Grants, 693
Bayer Advanced Grow Together with Roses School Garden Awards, 695
Beerman Fndn Grants, 717
Ben B. Cheney Fndn Grants, 725
Benwood Fndn Community Grants, 732
Bernard and Audre Rapoport Fndn Democracy and Civic Participation Grants, 737
Bernard and Audre Rapoport Fndn Health Grants, 738
Bernard and Audre Rapoport Fndn University of Texas at Austin Scholarship Programs, 739
Bertha Wolf-Rosenthal Fndn for Community Service Stipend, 746
Best Buy Children's Fndn @15 Community Grants, 749
Best Buy Children's Fndn @15 Scholarship, 750
Best Buy Children's Fndn National Grants, 752
Bill and Katie Weaver Charitable Grants, 764
Biogen Corp Giving Grants, 773
Birmingham Fndn Grants, 774
Bitha Godfrey & Maude J. Thomas Charitable Fndn Grants, 776
BJ's Charitable Fndn Grants, 777
BJ's Wholesale Clubs Local Charitable Giving, 778
Blackford County Community Fndn Grants, 780
Black River Falls Area Fndn Grants, 782
Blandin Fndn Expand Opportunity Grants, 787
Blandin Fndn Invest Early Grants, 788
Blandin Fndn Itasca County Area Vitality Grants, 789
Blue Cross Blue Shield of Minnesota Fndn - Health Equity: Building Health Together Grants, 793
Blue Cross Blue Shield of Minnesota Fndn - Healthy Children: Growing Up Healthy Grants, 794
Blue Cross Blue Shield of Minnesota Fndn - Healthy Equity: Health Impact Assessment Demonstration Project Grants, 795
Blue Mountain Community Fndn Grants, 800
Blumenthal Fndn Grants, 804
Boeckmann Charitable Fndn Grants, 808
Bohemian Fndn Pharos Grants, 811
Bonfils-Stanton Fndn Grants, 814
Boston Globe Fndn Grants, 821
Bowling Green Community Fndn Grants, 824
Bright Promises Fndn Grants, 838
Brooklyn Benevolent Society Grants, 847
Brown Fndn Grants, 854
Brunswick Fndn Dollars for Doers Grants, 856
Burton D. Morgan Hudson Community Grants, 869
Byerly Fndn Grants, 883
Caddock Fndn Grants, 888
Cailloux Fndn Grants, 892
California Community Fndn Health Care Grants, 901
California Comm Human Development Grants, 902
California Endowment Innovative Ideas Challenge Grants, 904
California Fertilizer Fndn School Garden Grants, 905
Callaway Fndn Grants, 909
Caring Fndn Grants, 926
Carl R. Hendrickson Family Fndn Grants, 935
Carrie E. and Lena V. Glenn Fndn Grants, 944
Cartis Creative Services Grants, 948
Castle and Cooke California Corp Giving Grants, 953
Catholic Health Communities Grants, 957
CCHD Community Development Grants, 966
CE and S Fndn Grants, 985
Center for Venture Philanthropy, 991
Central Okanagan Fndn Grants, 997
Ceres Fndn Grants, 999
CFFVR Capacity Building Grants, 1004
CFFVR Chilton Area Community Fndn Grants, 1006
CFFVR Waupaca Area Community Fndn Grants, 1023
CFNCR Starbucks Memorial Fund, 1026
Charles and Lynn Schusterman Family Grants, 1038
Charles Delmar Fndn Grants, 1039
Charles H. Dater Fndn Grants, 1042
Charles H. Farnsworth Grants, 1043

SUBJECT INDEX

Community Services / 851

Charlotte County (FL) Community Fndn Grants, 1056
Chicago Community Trust Fellowships, 1086
Chicago Community Poverty Alleviation Grants, 1091
Christian Science Society of Boonville Irrevocable Trust, 1113
Cingular Wireless Charitable Contributions, 1134
Cisco Systems Fndn San Jose Community Grants, 1137
Citizens Savings Fndn Grants, 1141
Clara Abbott Fndn Need-Based Grants, 1146
Cleveland Lake-Geauga Grants, 1170
Cleveland Neighborhood Connections Grants, 1171
CNCS AmeriCorps NCCC Project Grants, 1181
CNCS AmeriCorps State and National Grants, 1182
CNCS AmeriCorps State and National Planning Grants, 1183
Coleman Fndn Cancer Care Grants, 1199
Colonel Stanley R. McNeil Fndn Grants, 1210
Community Fndn for Greater New Haven Women & Girls Grants, 1254
Community Fndn for San Benito County Grants, 1258
Community Fndn in Jacksonville Senior Roundtable Aging Adults Grants, 1263
Community Fndn of Abilene Community Grants, 1264
Community Fndn of Boone Cty Women's Grants, 1273
Community Fndn of Central Illinois Grants, 1276
Community Fndn of Greater Flint Grants, 1282
Community Fndn of Muncie and Delaware County Maxon Grants, 1303
Community Fndn of Riverside County Grants, 1304
Community Fndn of St. Joseph County African American Community Grants, 1312
Community Fndn of St. Joseph County Special Project Challenge Grants, 1314
Community Fndn of Switzerland County Grants, 1315
Community Fndn of Virgin Islands Mini Grants, 1325
Community Fndn Silicon Valley Grants, 1331
Community POWER (Partners On Waste Educ and Reduction), 1335
Community Technology Fndn of California Building Communities Through Technology Grants, 1336
ConAgra Foods Nourish Our Comm Grants, 1343
Con Edison Corp Giving Community Grants, 1346
Con Edison Corp Giving Environmental Grants, 1347
Connecticut Commission on the Arts Art in Public Spaces, 1349
ConocoPhillips Fndn Grants, 1354
Cord Fndn Grants, 1372
Covenant Fndn of Atlanta Grants, 1384
Cralle Fndn Grants, 1394
Cruise Industry Charitable Fndn Grants, 1404
CTCNet/Youth Visions for Stronger Neighborhoods Grants, 1409
Cullen Fndn Grants, 1411
CVS Caremark Charitable Grants, 1421
CVS Community Grants, 1422
D. W. McMillan Fndn Grants, 1426
Dade Community Fndn Community AIDS Partnership Grants, 1428
Dade Community Fndn Safe Passage Grants, 1431
Dairy Queen Corp Contributions Grants, 1433
Dale and Edna Walsh Fndn Grants, 1435
Dallas Mavericks Fndn Grants, 1437
Daviess County Community Fndn Health Grants, 1457
Daviess County Comm Human Services Grants, 1458
Deaconess Fndn Advocacy Grants, 1468
Dearborn Community County Progress Grants, 1473
Delta Air Lines Community Enrichment Grants, 1494
Dennis and Phyllis Washington Fndn Grants, 1498
DHHS American Recovery and Reinvestment Act of 2009 Head Start Expansion, 1526
DHHS ARRA Strengthening Communities Fund - Nonprofit Capacity Building Grants, 1527
DHHS ARRA Strengthening Communities Fund - State, Local, and Tribal Government Capacity Building Grants, 1528
DHHS Community Services Block Grant Training and Technical Assistance Program: Capacity-Building for Ongoing CSBG Programs and Strategic Planning and Coordination Grants, 1529
DHS ARRA Fire Station Construction Grants, 1542

Dominion Fndn Human Needs Grants, 1572
Donald W. Reynolds Fndn Charitable Food Distribution Grants, 1575
Do Something BR!CK Awards, 1592
Do Something Plum Youth Grants, 1593
Doug and Carla Salmon Fndn Grants, 1594
Drug Free Communities Support Program, 1608
DTE Energy Fndn Leadership Grants, 1614
Dynegy Fndn Grants, 1630
Eastman Chemical Company Fndn Grants, 1643
East Tennessee Fndn Grants, 1646
Edina Realty Fndn Grants, 1656
Edward and Ellen Roche Relief Fndn Grants, 1663
Effie and Wofford Cain Fndn Grants, 1674
Elden and Mary Lee Gutwein Family Grants, 1679
Elizabeth & Avola W. Callaway Fndn Grants, 1680
Elkhart County Community Fndn Fund for Elkhart County, 1683
Ellen Abbott Gilman Grants, 1685
Emerson Charitable Grants, 1694
Emma G. Harris Fndn Grants, 1701
Encore Purpose Prize, 1704
Ensworth Charitable Fndn Grants, 1710
Entergy Corp Micro Grants, 1712
Enterprise Community Partners Rose Architectural Fellowships, 1719
Essex County Community Discretionary Grants, 1752
Esther M. and Freeman E. Everett Charitable Fndn Grants, 1757
Ethel Frends Fndn Grants, 1759
Ethel S. Abbott Charitable Fndn Grants, 1760
Ethel Sergeant Clark Smith Grants, 1761
Eugene B. Casey Fndn Grants, 1762
Evan and Susan Bayh Fndn Grants, 1769
Evelyn and Walter Haas, Jr. Fund Nonprofit Leadership Grants, 1774
Faye McBeath Fndn Grants, 1794
FEDCO Charitable Fndn Educ Grants, 1798
FEMA Assistance to Firefighters Grants, 1802
Fifth Third Bank Corp Giving, 1809
Fireman's Fund Insurance Heritage Grants, 1818
Florida BRAIVE Fund of Dade Community, 1846
Florida Humanities Civic Reflection Grants, 1867
Floyd A. and Kathleen C. Cailloux Fndn Grants, 1874
Ford Family Fndn Grants - Critical Needs, 1879
Foster Fndn Grants, 1888
Fndn for a Drug-Free World Classroom Tools, 1890
Fndn for Mid South Comm Development Grants, 1897
Frances and Benjamin Benenson Fndn Grants, 1916
Frank & Larue Reynolds Charitable Grants, 1924
Frank G. and Freida K. Brotz Family Grants, 1928
Fred Meyer Fndn Grants, 1950
Frist Fndn Grants, 1964
Gardiner Savings Inst Charitable Fndn Grants, 1987
Gene Haas Fndn, 1999
General Dynamics Corp Grants, 2001
George A. and Grace L. Long Fndn Grants, 2008
George A Ohl Jr. Fndn Grants, 2012
George B. Page Fndn Grants, 2013
Georgiana Goddard Eaton Grants, 2038
Gil and Dody Weaver Fndn Grants, 2053
Giving Sum Annual Grant, 2058
Gloria Barron Prize for Young Heroes, 2064
GNOF IMPACT Grants for Health and Human Services, 2080
GNOF Maison Hospitaliere Grants, 2086
Godfrey Fndn Grants, 2095
Goldseker Fndn Community Affairs Grants, 2100
Goldseker Fndn Community Grants, 2101
Goldseker Fndn Human Services Grants, 2102
Goodrich Corp Fndn Grants, 2104
Goodyear Tire Grants, 2106
Grand Rapids Community Ionia County Grants, 2119
Green Bay Packers Fndn Grants, 2148
Green Diamond Charitable Contributions, 2149
GreenWorks! Butterfly Garden Grants, 2159
GreenWorks! Grants, 2160
GTECH Community Involvement Grants, 2171
Gulf Coast Community Operating Grants, 2176
Gulf Coast Fndn of Community Grants, 2177

Gumdrop Books Librarian Scholarships, 2179
H. Reimers Bechtel Charitable Grants, 2186
HAF Community Grants, 2193
HAF Justin Keele Make a Difference Award, 2198
HAF Southern Humboldt Grants, 2204
Hagedorn Grants, 2207
Hahl Proctor Charitable Grants, 2208
Harold R. Bechtel Charitable Remainder Grants, 2229
Harold Simmons Fndn Grants, 2230
Harrison County Community Fndn Grants, 2233
Harrison County Community Signature Grants, 2234
Harris Teeter Corp Contributions Grants, 2235
Harry S. Truman Scholarships, 2244
Harvest Fndn Grants, 2254
Hawai'i Children's Trust Fund Community Awareness Events Grants, 2258
Hawaii Community Geographic-Specific Grants, 2261
Hawaii Community Human Services Grants, 2262
Hazen Fndn Public Educ Grants, 2269
Hazen Fndn Youth Organizing Grants, 2270
Head Start Replacement Grantee: Colorado, 2275
Head Start Replacement Grantee: Florida, 2276
Head Start Replacement Grantee: West Virginia, 2277
Healthcare Fndn for Orange County Grants, 2279
Health Fndn of Greater Cincinnati Grants, 2281
Helena Rubinstein Fndn Grants, 2292
Helen Bader Fndn Grants, 2293
Helen K. and Arthur E. Johnson Fndn Grants, 2296
Henrietta Tower Wurts Memorial Fndn Grants, 2304
Henry A. and Mary J. MacDonald Fndn, 2305
Henry County Community Fndn - TASC Youth Grants, 2307
Herbert A. and Adrian W. Woods Fndn Grants, 2313
Hitachi Fndn Yoshiyama Awards, 2340
Hollie and Anna Oakley Fndn Grants, 2346
Horace A. Kimball and S. Ella Kimball Grants, 2362
Horizons Community Issues Grants, 2366
Howard H. Callaway Fndn Grants, 2376
Hulman & Company Fndn Grants, 2387
IBM Community Development Grants, 2425
ICC Community Service Mini-Grant, 2426
ICC Day of Service Action Grants, 2427
ICC Faculty Fellowships, 2428
ICC Listening to Communities Grants, 2429
ICC Scholarship of Engagement Faculty Grants, 2430
Ida Alice Ryan Charitable Grants, 2431
Independent Community Fndn Neighborhood Renewal Grants, 2527
Indiana Recycling Grants, 2545
ING Fndn Grants, 2555
Init Fndn Innovation Grants, 2559
Ireland Family Fndn Grants, 2574
IREX Project Smile Grants, 2579
J. Knox Gholston Fndn Grants, 2599
Jacob and Hilda Blaustein Fndn Grants, 2615
Jacobs Family Spirit of the Diamond Grants, 2618
James A. and Faith Knight Fndn Grants, 2621
James L. and Mary Jane Bowman Grants, 2632
James M. Cox Fndn of Georgia Grants, 2634
Janus Fndn Grants, 2647
Jennings County Community Fndn Grants, 2664
Jennings County Community Fndn Women's Giving Circle Grant, 2665
Jewish Funds for Justice Grants, 2676
Joan Bentinck-Smith Charitable Fndn Grants, 2682
John Clarke Grants, 2689
John S. and James L. Knight Fndn Grants, 2713
Johnson County Community Fndn Grants, 2723
John W. Anderson Fndn Grants, 2729
John W. Speas and Effie E. Speas Grants, 2732
Join Hands Day Excellence Awards, 2733
Joseph Drown Fndn Grants, 2735
Joyce Fndn Employment Grants, 2749
Judith Clark-Morrill Fndn Grants, 2756
K21 Health Fndn Grants, 2760
KaBOOM-CA Playground Challenge Grants, 2761
Kalamazoo Community Fndn John E. Fetzer Institute Grants, 2770
Kalamazoo Community Fndn Mini-Grants, 2772
Kaneta Fndn Grants, 2774

Community Services

Kentucky Arts Council Access Assistance Grants, 2805
Knight Fndn Donor Advised Grants, 2828
Knox County Community Fndn Grants, 2831
Koret Fndn Grants, 2837
L. W. Pierce Family Fndn Grants, 2846
Laclede Gas Charitable Grants, 2848
LaGrange Independent Fndn for Endowments, 2851
Land O'Lakes Fndn Dollars for Doers, 2860
Laura Jane Musser Intercultural Harmony Grants, 2862
Lee and Ramona Bass Fndn Grants, 2871
LEGO Children's Grants, 2878
Leo Niessen Jr., Charitable Grants, 2885
Lewis H. Humphreys Charitable Grants, 2889
Liberty Bank Fndn Grants, 2890
Louie M. and Betty M. Phillips Fndn Grants, 2923
Louis and Elizabeth Nave Flarsheim Charitable Fndn Grants, 2924
Lowe's Charitable and Ed Fndn Grants, 2927
Lucy Gooding Charitable Fndn Grants, 2937
Lyndhurst Fndn Grants, 2949
M3C Fellowships, 2955
Mabel Louise Riley Fndn Family Strengthening Small Grants, 2958
Maddie's Fund Comm Collaborative Projects, 2967
Maddie's Fund Lifesaving Awards, 2969
Madison County Community General Grants, 2973
Maine Community Fndn Baldwin Area Grants, 2974
Marathon Petroleum Corp Grants, 2999
Marion Gardner Jackson Charitable Grants, 3017
Marsh Corp Grants, 3027
Mary E. and Michael Blevins Charitable Grants, 3037
McCallum Family Fndn Grants, 3072
McCune Charitable Fndn Grants, 3077
McCune Fndn Human Services Grants, 3080
McGregor Grants, 3082
McKnight Fndn Multiservice Grants, 3085
McKnight Fndn Virginia McKnight Binger Awards in Human Service, 3087
MDEQ Community Pollution Prevention (P2) Grants: Household Drug Collections, 3098
Mead Johnson Nutritionals Evansville-Area Organizations Grants, 3103
MedImmune Charitable Grants, 3108
Melville Charitable Grants, 3115
Mertz Gilmore Fndn NYC Communities Grants, 3126
MetLife Building Livable Communities Grants, 3129
Metzger-Price Grants, 3137
Meyer and Stephanie Eglin Fndn Grants, 3139
MFRI Operation Diploma Small Grants for Indiana Family Readiness Groups, 3152
Michael Reese Health Trust Core Grants, 3159
Michael Reese Health Trust Responsive Grants, 3160
Microsoft Software Donation Grants, 3164
Middlesex Savings Charitable Fndn Capacity Building Grants, 3172
Middlesex Savings Charitable Fndn Community Development Grants, 3173
Minnesota Small Cities Development Grants, 3187
MMS and Alliance Charitable Fndn Grants for Community Action and Care for the Medically Uninsured, 3194
MONY Fndn Grants, 3214
MTV Think Venturer Comm Service Grants, 3229
NAGC Masters and Specialists Award, 3237
NAR Realtor Magazine Good Neighbor Awards, 3240
Nathaniel and Elizabeth P. Stevens Fndn Grants, 3247
National Endowment for the Arts - National Arts and Humanities Youth Program Awards, 3255
National Inclusion Grants, 3278
New Hampshire Charitable Fndn Grants, 3325
New Jersey Office of Faith Based Inits Service to Seniors Grants, 3333
Newman W. Benson Fndn Grants, 3334
Newton County Community Fndn Grants, 3336
New Voices J-Lab Journalism Grants, 3337
New York Life Fndn Grants, 3341
NFL Charities NFL Player Fndn Grants, 3347
NGA 'Remember Me' Rose Garden Awards, 3401
Nike Fndn Grants, 3441
Nissan Fndn Grants, 3444
Nissan Neighbors Grants, 3445
Norcross Wildlife Fndn Grants, 3460
Norfolk Southern Fndn Grants, 3463
North Central Health Services Grants, 3492
North Central Health Services Grants, 3491
NW Mutual Fndn Grants, 3509
NYCT Grants for the Elderly, 3549
NYCT Neighborhood Revitalization Grants, 3555
NYCT Technical Assistance Grants, 3559
NYSCA Arts Educ: Community-based Learning Grants, 3577
OceanFirst Fndn Grants, 3636
Ohio Artists on Tour Fee Support Requests, 3642
Ohio Arts Council Arts Access Grants, 3647
Ohio County Community Fndn Board of Directors Grants, 3656
Ohio County Community Fndn Grants, 3658
Ohio County Community Fndn Junior Grants, 3659
Ohio County Community Fndn Mini-Grants, 3660
Ohio Valley Fndn Grants, 3662
Olga Sipolin Children's Grants, 3668
Olive Smith Browning Charitable Grants, 3671
OSF-Baltimore Community Fellowships, 3695
Owens Fndn Grants, 3718
PacifiCorp Fndn for Learning Grants, 3727
Parker Fndn (California) Grants, 3736
Patrick and Aimee Butler Family Fndn Community Arts and Humanities Grants, 3747
Patrick and Anna M. Cudahy Grants, 3751
Paul and Edith Babson Fndn Grants, 3755
Pay It Forward Fndn Mini Grants, 3768
Peacock Fndn Grants, 3809
Percy B. Ferebee Endowment Grants, 3820
Perpetual Trust for Charitable Giving Grants, 3826
Pfizer Healthcare Charitable Contributions, 3863
Phi Kappa Phi Scholar Award, 3871
Pier 1 Imports Grants, 3887
Pike County Community Fndn Grants, 3888
Pinnacle Entertainment Fndn Grants, 3893
Pinnacle Fndn Grants, 3894
Piper Trust Healthcare & Med Research Grants, 3903
Piper Trust Older Adults Grants, 3904
Piper Trust Reglous Organizations Grants, 3905
Planet Dog Fndn Grants, 3911
PNC Ecnomic Development Grants, 3922
Polk Bros. Fndn Grants, 3929
Pott Fndn Grants, 3940
Powell Fndn Grants, 3942
PPG Industries Fndn Grants, 3943
Praxair Fndn Grants, 3944
President's Student Service Scholarships, 3949
Price Family Charitable Grants, 3952
Princeton Area Community Fndn Greater Mercer Grants, 3963
Princeton Area Community Fndn Rebecca Annitto Service Opportunities for Students Award, 3964
Progress Energy Corp Contributions Grants, 3968
Project Orange Thumb Grants, 3972
Prudential CARES Volunteer Grants, 3974
Prudential Spirit of Community Awards, 3978
Public Interest Law Fndn Community Grants, 3982
Putnam County Community Fndn Grants, 3990
Quality Health Fndn Grants, 3994
Ralph and Virginia Mullin Fndn Grants, 4012
Rasmuson Fndn Special Project Grants, 4025
RCF General Community Grants, 4032
RCF Individual Assistance Grants, 4033
Regence Fndn Access to Health Care Grants, 4039
Regence Fndn Health Care Community Awareness and Engagement Grants, 4040
Regence Fndn Health Care Connections Grants, 4041
Regence Fndn Improving End-of-Life Grants, 4042
Regence Fndn Tools and Technology Grants, 4043
Richland County Bank Grants, 4091
Robert R. McCormick Tribune Veterans Grants, 4120
Rochester Area Fndn Grants, 4128
Rose Hills Fndn Grants, 4162
Rucker-Donnell Fndn Grants, 4172
Rutter's Children's Charities Grants, 4181
RWJF Community Health Leaders Awards, 4183
RWJF Jobs to Careers: Promoting Work-Based Learning for Quality Care, 4185
RWJF Local Funding Partnerships Grants, 4186
RWJF Vulnerable Populations Portfolio Grants, 4190
Safeco Insurance Community Grants, 4203
Saginaw Community Fndn Discretionary Grants, 4205
Saginaw County Community Fndn Youth FORCE Grants, 4208
Salem Fndn Charitable Grants, 4223
SAMHSA Strategic Prevention Framework State Incentive Grants, 4231
Samuel Huntington Public Service Award, 4232
Samuel S. Fels Grants, 4238
San Antonio Area Fndn Grants, 4240
San Diego Women's Fndn Grants, 4252
Sandy Hill Fndn Grants, 4257
San Juan Island Community Fndn Grants, 4283
Santa Barbara Strategy Grants Capital Support, 4285
Santa Barbara Fndn Strategy Grants - Innovation, 4287
Santa Fe Community Fndn root2fruit Santa Fe, 4289
Sarkeys Fndn Grants, 4297
Schering-Plough Fndn Community Inits Grants, 4303
Scherman Fndn Grants, 4305
Seattle Fndn Annual Neighborhoods and Communities Grants, 4319
Seattle Fndn Basic Needs Grants, 4321
Seattle Fndn Benjamin N. Phillips Grants, 4322
Seattle Fndn C. Keith Birkenfeld Grants, 4323
Shaw's Supermarkets Donations, 4342
Shopko Fndn Green Bay Community Grants, 4347
Sidgmore Family Fndn Grants, 4348
Sierra Health Fndn Responsive Grants, 4353
Silicon Valley Community Fndn Elizabeth Anabo BRICC Awards, 4357
Sir Dorabji Tata Grants for NGOs or Voluntary Organizations, 4370
Slow Food in Schools Micro-Grants, 4384
Smith Richardson Fndn Direct Service Grants, 4385
Sobrato Family Fndn Grants, 4389
Sobrato Family Fndn Meeting Space Grants, 4390
Sobrato Family Fndn Office Space Grants, 4391
SOCFOC Catholic Ministries Grants, 4392
Sodexo Fndn STOP Hunger Scholarships, 4400
Sorenson Legacy Fndn Grants, 4407
Southern Minnesota Init Fndn Community Growth Init Grants, 4433
Southern Minnesota Home Visiting Grants, 4434
SW Gas Corp Fndn Grants, 4445
SW Init Fndn Grants, 4446
Special Olympics Project UNIFY Grants, 4449
Sport Manitoba Intro of a New Sport Grants, 4457
Sport Manitoba Sport Special Inits Grants, 4459
Sprint Fndn Grants, 4463
St. Joseph Community Health Fndn Improving Healthcare Access Grants, 4469
Stan and Sandy Checketts Fndn, 4473
Starbucks Shared Planet Youth Action Grants, 4476
Stark Community Fndn Grants, 4477
Stark Community Fndn Neighborhood Partnership Grants, 4479
Stark Community SummerTime Kid Grants, 4480
State Farm Project Ignition Grants, 4487
Stocker Fndn Grants, 4507
Swaim-Gause-Rucker Fndn Grants, 4540
T. Raymond Gregory Family Fndn Grants, 4547
Tauck Family Fndn Grants, 4563
TD4HIM Fndn Grants, 4566
Teaching Tolerance Grants, 4567
Telluride Fndn Community Grants, 4573
Thelma Braun and Bocklett Family Fndn Grants, 4603
Thomas Austin Finch, Sr. Fndn Grants, 4613
Thompson Charitable Fndn Grants, 4622
Tiger Woods Fndn Grants, 4634
Tom's of Maine Grants, 4640
Topeka Community Fndn Boss Hawg's Charitable Giving Grants, 4642
Topeka Community Building Families Grants, 4643
Toyota Motor Engineering & Manufacturing North America Grants, 4651
Toyota Motor Manufacturing of Alabama Grants, 4652

SUBJECT INDEX

Toyota Motor Manufacturing of Indiana Grants, 4653
Toyota Motor of Kentucky Grants, 4654
Toyota Motor Manufacturing Mississippi Grants, 4655
Toyota Motor Manufacturing W Virginia Grants, 4657
Toyota Motor N America of New York Grants, 4658
Toyota Motor Sales, USA Grants, 4659
TRDRP Participatory Research Awards, 4663
Tri-County Electric People Grants, 4665
Triangle Community Fndn Donor Grants, 4668
Trinity Fndn Grants, 4670
Trinity Trust Community Response Grants, 4671
Tulane University Community Service Scholars, 4677
Tull Charitable Fndn Grants, 4679
U.S. Department of Educ Programs for Native Hawaiians, 4696
U.S. Department of Educ Special Educ--National Activities--Parent Information Centers, 4701
Union Pacific Health & Human Services Grants, 4715
UPS Fndn Community Safety Grants, 4728
USAID Community Infrastructure Dev Grants, 4745
USAID Palestinian Comm Assistance Grants, 4773
US Airways Community Fndn Grants, 4789
US Airways Educ Fndn Grants, 4790
USA Volleyball Fndn Ed Grants, 4791
USBC Annual Zeb Scholarship, 4792
USFA Development Grants, 4866
USFA Equipment Subsidy Grants, 4867
USTA CTA and NJTL Community Tennis Development Workshop Scholarships, 4873
USTA Junior Team Tennis Stipends, 4875
USTA Pro Circuit Community Involvement Day Grants, 4882
USTA Public Facility Assistance Grants, 4883
USTA Recreational Tennis Grants, 4884
USTA Tennis Block Party Grants, 4892
Vigneron Grants, 4938
Visiting Nurse Fndn Grants, 4951
W.K. Kellogg Fndn Healthy Kids Grants, 4961
Walton Family Fndn Home Region Grants, 4984
Warrick County Community Fndn Grants, 4987
WCI Childcare Capacity Grants, 5007
WCI Community Leadership Fellowships, 5008
WCI Community Mobilization Grants, 5009
WCI Family Econ Success Local Impact Grants, 5010
WCI Leadership Development Grants, 5012
Weaver Popcorn Fndn Grants, 5016
WHO Fndn Educ/Lit Grants, 5062
Widgeon Point Charitable Fndn Grants, 5064
Wieboldt Fndn Grants, 5065
William A. Miller Fndn Grants, 5073
William G. and Helen C. Hoffman Fndn Grants, 5080
William M. Weaver Fndn Grants, 5091
Wilson-Wood Fndn Grants, 5098
Windward Youth Leadership Grants, 5100
Winston-Salem Fndn Competitive Grants, 5102
Winston-Salem Fndn Stokes County Grants, 5104
Wolfe Associates Grants, 5110
Woods Charitable Grants, 5114
Xcel Energy Fndn Grants, 5121
Youth Action Net Fellowships, 5128
Youth As Resources Grants, 5130
YSA ABC Summer of Service Awards, 5133
YSA Get Ur Good On Grants, 5134
YSA Global Youth Service Lead Agency Grants, 5135
YSA NEA Youth Leaders for Lit Grants, 5138
YSA Radio Disney's Hero for Change Award, 5139
YSA Sodexo Lead Organizer Grants, 5140
YSA State Farm Good Neighbor YOUth In The Driver Seat Grants, 5141
YSA UnitedHealth HEROES Service-Learning Grants, 5142

Community and School Relations
AAF Richard Riley Award, 59
Altman Fndn Strengthening Communities Grants, 398
American Express Community Service Grants, 430
ArvinMeritor Fndn Civic Grants, 583
ATA School-Community Relations Awards, 602
Charles Stewart Mott Fndn Grants, 1055
Columbia Gas of Virginia Grants, 1218
Con Edison Corp Giving Community Grants, 1346
ConocoPhillips Grants, 1355
Delta Air Lines Community Enrichment Grants, 1494
DOJ Gang-Free Schools and Communities Intervention Grants, 1557
Evanston Community Fndn Grants, 1771
F.R. Bigelow Fndn Grants, 1781
Farmers Insurance Corp Giving Grants, 1791
Fndn for a Drug-Free World Classroom Tools, 1890
GreenWorks! Butterfly Garden Grants, 2159
GreenWorks! Grants, 2160
Hawaii Community Geographic-Specific Grants, 2261
HBF Pathways Out of Poverty Grants, 2273
Heifer Ed Grants for Teachers, 2289
ICC Community Service Mini-Grant, 2426
ICC Day of Service Action Grants, 2427
ICC Faculty Fellowships, 2428
ICC Listening to Communities Grants, 2429
ICC Scholarship of Engagement Faculty Grants, 2430
Jackson County Community Fndn Youth Advisory Committee Grants, 2612
Joe W. and Dorothy Dorsett Brown Fndn Grants, 2684
M3C Fellowships, 2955
Mead Johnson Nutritionals Evansville-Area Organizations Grants, 3103
MetLife Building Livable Communities Grants, 3129
Mt. Sinai Health Care Fndn Health of the Urban Community Grants, 3227
National Inclusion Grants, 3278
Nellie Mae Educ Public Understanding Grants, 3298
NGA 'Remember Me' Rose Garden Awards, 3401
NYSCA Arts Educ: K-12 In-School Grants, 3580
NYSCA Arts Ed Local Capacity Building Grants, 3581
OneFamily Fndn Grants, 3673
Princeton Area Community Fndn Greater Mercer Grants, 3963
Prudential CARES Volunteer Grants, 3974
R.E.B. Awards for Distinguished Ed Leadership, 4000
Red Robin Fndn U-ACT Grants, 4038
Rockefeller Brothers Pivotal Places Grants: New York City, 4134
RWJF Jobs to Careers: Promoting Work-Based Learning for Quality Care, 4185
Saginaw Community Fndn Discretionary Grants, 4205
Self Fndn Grants, 4335
Slow Food in Schools Micro-Grants, 4384
State Farm Fndn Grants, 4486
State Farm Project Ignition Grants, 4487
TRDRP Participatory Research Awards, 4663
U.S. Department of Educ Programs for Native Hawaiians, 4696
Vancouver Fndn Grants & Comm Inits, 4900
W.K. Kellogg Fndn Racial Equity Grants, 4962
Walter and Elise Haas Grants, 4982
West Virginia Comm on the Arts Special Grants, 5048

Compensatory Education
Cincinnati Bell Fndn Grants, 1131
Community Fndn Silicon Valley Grants, 1331
Do Right Fndn Grants, 1581
Romic Environmental's Charitable Contributions, 4148
Teaching Tolerance Grants, 4567

Compulsive Behavior
Peter and Elizabeth C. Tower Fndn Annual Mental Health Grants, 3835

Computer Applications
Apple Worldwide Developers Conference Student Scholarships, 513
Ian Hague Perl 6 Development Grants, 2421
Perl 6 Microgrants, 3824
Perl Fndn Grants, 3825
SAS Institute Community Relations Donations, 4300

Computer Education/Literacy
Achelis Fndn Grants, 127
Adobe Youth Voices Grants, 170
ALA Info Today Library of the Future Award, 287
Benton Community Fndn - The Cookie Jar Grant, 729

Blue Cross Blue Shield of Minnesota Fndn - Healthy Equity: Public Libraries for Health Grants, 797
Bodman Fndn Grants, 807
Comcast Fndn Grants, 1235
Community Fndn Boone Cnty Adult Lit Grants, 1272
DeKalb County Community Fndn - Lit Grant, 1480
Farmers Insurance Corp Giving Grants, 1791
HAF Community Grants, 2193
Hearst Fndns Social Service Grants, 2285
IIE Western Union Family Scholarships, 2462
IMLS Native Am Library Services Basic Grants, 2517
IMLS Native American Library Services Enhancement Grants, 2518
Kroger Fndn Diversity Grants, 2842
Robert R. McCormick Tribune Comm Grants, 4119
Romic Environmental's Charitable Contributions, 4148
TAC Arts Grants, 4554
TAC Rural Arts Project Support Grants, 4555
Union Bank, N.A. Fndn Grants, 4709
USDC State Broadband Init Grants, 4857
Verizon Fndn Grants, 4911
Verizon Fndn Maryland Grants, 4917
Verizon Fndn New York Grants, 4919
Verizon Fndn NE Region Grants, 4920
Verizon Fndn Pennsylvania Grants, 4921
Verizon Fndn SE Region Grants, 4923
Verizon Fndn Vermont Grants, 4924
Verizon Fndn Virginia Grants, 4925
Verizon Fndn West Virginia Grants, 4926

Computer Engineering
Claude Worthington Benedum Fndn Grants, 1161
NSF CISE Computing Infrastructure Grants, 3526

Computer Graphics
Adobe Youth Voices Grants, 170

Computer Music
Apple Worldwide Developers Conference Student Scholarships, 513
Florida Div of Cultural Affairs Music Grants, 1859
National Endowment for Arts Music Grants, 3266
NYSCA Music Gen Program Support Grants, 3607
NYSCA Music: New Music Facilities, 3608

Computer Programming
Ian Hague Perl 6 Development Grants, 2421
Perl 6 Microgrants, 3824
Perl Fndn Grants, 3825

Computer Science
ConocoPhillips Grants, 1355
Microsoft Authorized Refurbisher Donations, 3162
North Carolina GlaxoSmithKline Fndn Grants, 3490
NSF CISE Computer and Network Systems: Core Programs Grants, 3524
NSF CISE Computing Infrastructure Grants, 3526
Rockwell Int'l Corp Grants, 4141

Computer Science Education
NSF CISE Computing Infrastructure Grants, 3526
PSEG Environmental Educ Grants, 3980

Computer Software
Adobe Youth Voices Grants, 170
Alice Tweed Tuohy Fndn Grants, 372
EDS Technology Grants, 1662
Ian Hague Perl 6 Development Grants, 2421
McLean Contributionship Grants, 3088
Microsoft Comm Affairs Puget Sound Grants, 3163
Microsoft Software Donation Grants, 3164
Perl Fndn Grants, 3825
SAS Institute Community Relations Donations, 4300
TAC Arts Access Grant, 4549
TAC Arts Access Technical Assistance Grants, 4550
TAC Arts Build Communities Grants, 4551
TAC Arts Grants, 4554
TAC Rural Arts Project Support Grants, 4555
TAC Technical Assistance Grants, 4556

854 / Computer Systems Analysis

Computer Systems Analysis
NSF Atmospheric Sciences Mid-Size Infrastructure Opportunity Grants, 3521
USDC State Broadband Init Grants, 4857

Computer Technology
ADC Fndn Technology Access Grants, 158
Apple Worldwide Developers Conference Student Scholarships, 513
Best Buy Children's Fndn @15 Community Grants, 749
Ian Hague Perl 6 Development Grants, 2421
Illinois DCEO Eliminate Dig Divide Grants, 2489
Illinois DCEO Emerging Technological Enterprises Grants, 2490
John R. Oishei Fndn Grants, 2709
Meyer Fndn Economic Security Grants, 3141
Microsoft Authorized Refurbisher Donations, 3162
National Endowment for Arts Media Grants, 3264
NEH Family and Youth Programs in American History Grants, 3291
NSF CISE Computer and Network Systems: Core Programs Grants, 3524
Olin Corp Charitable Grants, 3669
OSF Affordable Access to Digital Comm, 3700
Perl 6 Microgrants, 3824
Perl Fndn Grants, 3825
Peter and Elizabeth C. Tower Fndn Phase II Technology Init Grants, 3839
Peter and Elizabeth C. Tower Fndn Phase I Technology Init Grants, 3840
PSEG Environmental Educ Grants, 3980
USDC State Broadband Init Grants, 4857
Verizon Fndn Great Lakes Region Grants, 4912
Verizon Fndn Internet Safety Grants, 4914
Verizon Fndn Maryland Grants, 4917
Verizon Fndn New York Grants, 4919
Verizon Fndn NE Region Grants, 4920
Verizon Fndn Pennsylvania Grants, 4921
Verizon Fndn SE Region Grants, 4923
Verizon Fndn Vermont Grants, 4924
Verizon Fndn Virginia Grants, 4925
Verizon Fndn West Virginia Grants, 4926

Computer-Aided Instruction
ALA Information Technology Pathfinder Award, 286
Blue Cross Blue Shield of Minnesota Fndn - Healthy Equity: Public Libraries for Health Grants, 797
PeopleSoft Community Relations Grants, 3818
Verizon Fndn Great Lakes Region Grants, 4912

Conferences
4imprint One by One Charitable Giving, 16
ALA Adelaide Del Frate Conference Sponsorship Award, 220
ALA Annual Conference Professional Development Attendance Award, 225
ALA Bogle Pratt Int'l Library Travel Fund Grant, 251
ALA Jan Merrill-Oldham Professional Development Grant, 291
ALA Supporting Diversity Stipend, 333
ALA Young Adult Literature Symposium Stipend, 337
Apple Worldwide Developers Conference Student Scholarships, 513
ARTBA Transportation Development Grants, 569
AWDF Solidarity Grants, 628
CCF Grassroots Exchange Grants, 963
Community Fndn of St. Joseph County ArtsEverywhere Grants, 1313
Delaware Division of the Arts Opportunity Grants-- Arts Organizations, 1488
Family Lit and Hawaii Pizza Hut Lit Fund, 1785
Florida Humanities Civic Reflection Grants, 1867
Greater Worcester Community Mini-Grants, 2142
Hatton W. Sumners Fndn for the Study and Teaching of Self Government Grants, 2257
Historic Landmarks Fndn of Indiana Historic Preservation Educ Grants, 2334
ICC Listening to Communities Grants, 2429
IEDC Int'l Trade Show Assistance Program, 2444
Ka Papa O Kakuhihewa Fund, 2785

NASE Succeed Scholarships, 3243
National Center for Responsible Gaming Conference Scholarships, 3250
National Endowment for Arts Agencies Grants, 3263
National Endowment for Arts Music Grants, 3266
NICHD Academic-Community Partnership Conference Series Grants, 3433
Nicor Corp Contributions, 3435
NYSCA Architecture, Planning, and Design: Project Support Grants, 3576
Ohio County Community Fndn Conference/Training Grants, 3657
Oppenstein Brothers Fndn Grants, 3685
PAS PASIC Scholarships, 3744
PCA Professional Development Grants, 3803
Pioneer Hi-Bred Conferences & Meetings Grants, 3896
South Madison Community Fndn Grants, 4440
TAC Arts Access Grant, 4549
TAC Arts Build Communities Grants, 4551
TAC Arts Grants, 4554
TAC Rural Arts Project Support Grants, 4555
Virginia Fndn for Humanities Discr Grants, 4946
Virginia Fndn for the Humanities Open Grants, 4947

Conferences, Travel to
Acumen East Africa Fellowship, 141
ALA ALTAFF/GALE Outstanding Trustee Conference Grant, 224
ALA Atlas Systems Mentoring Award, 227
ALA Bogle Pratt Int'l Library Travel Fund Grant, 251
ALA EBSCO Midwinter Meeting Sponsorship, 274
ALA Jan Merrill-Oldham Professional Development Grant, 291
ALA Morningstar Pub Librarian Support Award, 302
ALA NMRT Professional Development Grant, 305
ALA Penguin Young Readers Group Award, 308
ALA Routledge Distance Learning Librarianship Conference Sponsorship Award, 315
ALA Supporting Diversity Stipend, 333
ALA Young Adult Literature Symposium Stipend, 337
ALFJ Astraea U.S. and Int'l Movement Fund, 361
Arkansas Arts Council Sally A. Williams Grants, 558
ARTBA Transportation Development Grants, 569
AWDF Solidarity Grants, 628
GNOF Organizational Effectiveness Grants and Workshops, 2090
NAA Fndn Teacher Fellowships, 3234
NACC David Stevenson Fellowships, 3235
NACC William Diaz Fellowships, 3236
National Center for Responsible Gaming Conference Scholarships, 3250
NICHD Academic-Community Partnership Conference Series Grants, 3433
Ohio County Community Fndn Conference/Training Grants, 3657
PAS PASIC Scholarships, 3744
PCA Professional Development Grants, 3803
Phi Upsilon Omicron Florence Fallgatter Distinguished Service Award, 3877
Phi Upsilon Omicron Frances Morton Holbrook Alumni Award, 3878
Pioneer Hi-Bred Conferences & Meetings Grants, 3896
Texas Commission on the Arts Cultural Connections Grants, 4591
TSYSF Team Grants, 4676

Conflict/Dispute Resolution
A.J. Muste Memorial Institute Counter Recruitment Grants, 43
A.J. Muste Memorial Institute General Grants, 44
A.J. Muste Memorial Institute Int'l Nonviolence Training Grants, 45
Agape Fndn for Nonviolent Social Change Board of Trustees Grants, 197
Agape Fndn for Nonviolent Social Change Prizes, 198
Allen Lane Fndn Grants, 379
Allstate Corp Giving Grants, 386
Allstate Corp Hometown Commitment Grants, 387
Arthur B. Schultz Fndn Grants, 573
Bay and Paul Fndns Grants, 693

Chicago Community Trust Arts and Culture Grants: Improving Access to Arts Learning Opps, 1082
Compton Fndn Grants, 1338
Ford Fndn Peace and Social Justice Grants, 1884
Honor the Earth Grants, 2361
Laura Jane Musser Intercultural Harmony Grants, 2862
Mary Owen Borden Fndn Grants, 3046
Max and Anna Levinson Fndn Grants, 3066
Morris K. Udall and Stewart L. Udall Fndn Dissertation Fellowships, 3219
NGA 'Remember Me' Rose Garden Awards, 3401
Ploughshares Grants, 3916
Sioux Falls Area Community Fndn Spot Grants, 4366
State Justice Institute Curriculum Adaptation and Training Grants, 4488
State Justice Institute Partner Grants, 4489
State Justice Institute Project Grants, 4490
State Justice Institute Strategic Init Grants, 4492
State Justice Institute Tech Assistance Grants, 4493
Stuart Fndn Grants, 4516
Surdna Fndn Sustainable Environments Grants, 4533
Union Square Award for Social Justice, 4717
United Methodist Women Brighter Future for Children and Youth Grants, 4723
United States Institute of Peace - National Peace Essay Contest for High School Students, 4724

Conservation
America the Beautiful Fund Operation Green Plant Grants, 451
Chingos Fndn Grants, 1109
Columbus Fndn Competitive Grants, 1220
ConocoPhillips Fndn Grants, 1354
HRF New York City Environmental Grants for Newton Creek, 2379
Illinois Clean Energy Community Fndn K-12 Wind Schools Pilot Grants, 2480
Illinois Clean Energy Community Fndn Renewable Energy Grants, 2481
Illinois Clean Energy Community Fndn Solar Thermal Installation Grants, 2482
Lee and Ramona Bass Fndn Grants, 2871
Maine Community Fndn Maine Land Conservation Grants, 2983
NFF Collaboration Support Grants, 3342
NFF Mid-Capacity Assistance Grants, 3345
NFWF Alaska Fish and Wildlife Grants, 3356
NFWF Freshwater Fish Conservation Init Grants, 3374
NFWF Native Plant Conservation Init Grants, 3380
NHSCA Conservation License Plate Grants, 3425
Packard Fndn Local Grants, 3729
USAID Food Security, Nutrition, Biodiversity and Conservation Grants, 4752
William B. Stokely Jr. Fndn Grants, 5076

Conservation Education
Illinois Clean Energy Community Fndn K-12 Wind Schools Pilot Grants, 2480
Kirkpatrick Fndn Grants, 2827
McCune Charitable Fndn Grants, 3077
NFF Collaboration Support Grants, 3342
NFWF Native Plant Conservation Init Grants, 3380
NHSCA Conservation License Plate Grants, 3425
UNESCO World Heritage Grants, 4706

Conservation, Agriculture
Abell Fndn Conservation and Environment Grants, 94
Alabama Power Plant a Tree Grants, 234
Americana Fndn Grants, 422
Bullitt Fndn Grants, 862
Clarence E. Heller Charitable Fndn Grants, 1150
CLIF Bar Family Fndn Grants, 1173
Conservation, Food, and Health Fndn Grants for Developing Countries, 1359
Dean Foods Community Involvement Grants, 1469
Farm Aid Grants, 1790
Fndn for Appalachian Ohio Access to Environmental Educ Mini-Grants, 1892
Freeman Fndn Grants, 1952
Fruit Tree 101, 1967

SUBJECT INDEX

Gates Family Fndn Parks, Conservation & Recreation Grants, 1991
Honeybee Health Improvement Project Grants, 2355
Jessie Smith Noyes Fndn Grants, 2672
Norman Fndn Grants, 3464
Organic Farming Research Fndn Grants, 3693
PepsiCo Fndn Grants, 3819
Steward of the Land Award, 4504
UNESCO World Heritage Grants, 4706
USAID India-Africa Agriculture Innovation Bridge Grants, 4760
Wabash River Enhancement Corp Agricultural Cost-Share Grants, 4968
Weyerhaeuser Family Fndn Environment, Conservation and Preservation Grants, 5054

Conservation, Natural Resources
Abel Fndn Grants, 90
Abell Fndn Conservation and Environment Grants, 94
Access Fund Climbing Preservation Grants, 110
ACF Native American Social and Economic Development Strategies Grants, 123
Acorn Fndn Grants, 131
Alabama Power Plant a Tree Grants, 234
Alaska Conservation Fndn Awards, 322
Alaska Conservation Fndn Opportunity Grants, 324
Alaska Conservation Fndn Rapid Response Grants, 325
Alaska Conservation Fndn Watchable Wildlife Conservation Grants, 326
Alberto Culver Corp Contributions Grants, 343
Allen P. and Josephine B. Green Fndn Grants, 380
Alliant Energy Fndn Community Grants, 384
Altria Group Environment Grants, 400
Ambrose and Ida Fredrickson Fndn Grants, 414
Americana Fndn Grants, 422
AmerUs Group Charitable Fndn, 455
Amgen Fndn Grants, 456
Anne L. and George H. Clapp Ed Grants, 476
Appalachian Regional Commission Transportation and Highways Grants, 512
Arbor Day Fndn Grants, 524
Archer Daniels Midland Fndn Grants, 527
Arthur B. Schultz Fndn Grants, 573
Ashland Corp Contributions Grants, 587
Atkinson Fndn Community Grants, 606
Banrock Station Wines Wetlands Grants, 662
Batchelor Fndn Grants, 679
Beim Fndn Grants, 718
Bella Vista Fndn Grants, 722
Beneficia Fndn Grants, 727
Blue Cross Blue Shield of Minnesota Fndn - Healthy Equity: Health Impact Assessment Demonstration Project Grants, 795
Boeing Company Contributions Grants, 809
BP Conservation Programme Future Conservationist Awards, 826
Brico Grants, 835
Brunswick Fndn Grants, 857
Bullitt Fndn Grants, 862
Burning Fndn Grants, 867
Bydale Fndn Grants, 882
Cape Branch Fndn Grants, 919
Carls Fndn Grants, 937
Carpenter Fndn Grants, 943
Central Okanagan Fndn Grants, 997
CFFVR Environmental Stewardship Grants, 1010
Champlin Fndns Grants, 1029
CHC Fndn Grants, 1065
Chesapeake Bay Environmental Ed Grants, 1069
Chesapeake Bay Trust Forestry Mini Grants, 1071
Chesapeake Bay Trust Mini Grants, 1072
Chesapeake Bay Trust Outreach and Community Engagement Grants, 1073
Chesapeake Bay Trust Pioneer Grants, 1074
Chevron Hawaii Educ Fund, 1077
Clarence E. Heller Charitable Fndn Grants, 1150
Clark Charitable Grants, 1155
CLIF Bar Family Fndn Grants, 1173
Coeta and Donald Barker Fndn Grants, 1197
Collins Fndn Grants, 1209

Columbia Gas of Virginia Grants, 1218
Columbus Fndn Mary Eleanor Morris Grants, 1225
Columbus Fndn Small Grants, 1232
Community Fndn for Greater New Haven Quinnipiac River Grants, 1250
Community Fndn of Middle Tennessee Grants, 1300
Community Fndn of Santa Cruz County Grants, 1305
Conservation, Food, and Health Fndn Grants for Developing Countries, 1359
Constellation Energy Corp EcoStar Grants, 1363
Constellation Energy Corp Grants, 1364
Cooper Fndn Grants, 1369
Crestlea Fndn Grants, 1399
Cumberland Community Fndn Grants, 1413
Cyrus Eaton Fndn Grants, 1423
David Bohnett Fndn Grants, 1451
Davis Conservation Fndn Grants, 1461
Donald and Sylvia Robinson Family Fndn Grants, 1573
Dorrance Family Fndn Grants, 1590
Dorr Fndn Grants, 1591
Earth Island Institute Brower Youth Awards, 1641
Edna Wardlaw Charitable Grants, 1660
ESRI Conservation Grants, 1751
Evan and Susan Bayh Fndn Grants, 1769
Field Fndn of Illinois Grants, 1806
Fields Pond Fndn Grants, 1807
FishAmerica Fndn Chesapeake Bay Grants, 1827
FishAmerica Fndn Conservation Grants, 1828
FishAmerica Fndn Marine and Anadromous Fish Habitat Restoration Grants, 1829
FishAmerica Fndn Research Grants, 1830
Florida Sea Turtle Grants, 1871
Ford Motor Company Grants, 1885
France-Merrick Fndns Grants, 1915
Frank Stanley Beveridge Fndn Grants, 1936
Freeman Fndn Grants, 1952
Frey Fndn Grants, 1963
Gannett Fndn Community Action Grants, 1984
Gates Family Fndn Parks, Conservation & Recreation Grants, 1991
Gaylord and Dorothy Donnelley Fndn Grants, 1993
George B. Storer Fndn Grants, 2014
George Frederick Jewett Fndn Grants, 2019
George Gund Fndn Grants, 2020
George H. and Jane A. Mifflin Grants, 2021
Giving Sum Annual Grant, 2058
Grand Victoria Fndn Illinois Core Grants, 2126
Greater Milwaukee Fndn Grants, 2137
Great Lakes Protection Grants, 2147
Green Diamond Charitable Contributions, 2149
Harry A. and Margaret D. Towsley Fndn Grants, 2236
Henry J. Kaiser Family Fndn Grants, 2310
Horizon Fndn Grants, 2365
Illinois Clean Energy Community Fndn Energy Efficiency Grants, 2479
Illinois Clean Energy Community Fndn K-12 Wind Schools Pilot Grants, 2480
Illinois Clean Energy Community Fndn Renewable Energy Grants, 2481
Illinois Clean Energy Community Fndn Solar Thermal Installation Grants, 2482
Illinois DNR Youth Recreation Corps Grants, 2508
J.W. Kieckhefer Fndn Grants, 2607
Jane's Grants, 2639
Jessie B. Cox Charitable Grants, 2670
Jessie Ball Dupont Grants, 2671
John D. and Catherine T. MacArthur Fndn Global Challenges Grants, 2690
KeySpan Fndn Grants, 2821
Lindbergh Grants, 2907
Liz Claiborne and Art Ortenberg Fndn Grants, 2914
Lyndhurst Fndn Grants, 2949
M.E. Raker Fndn Grants, 2953
MacArthur Fndn Conservation and Sustainable Development Grants, 2963
Margaret L. Wendt Fndn Grants, 3004
Mary C. & Perry F. Spencer Fndn Grants, 3034
Mary Owen Borden Fndn Grants, 3046
McLean Contributionship Grants, 3088
MDEQ Local Water Quality Monitoring Grants, 3100

Conservation, Natural Resources / 855

Miguel Aleman Fndn Grants, 3175
Montana Community Fndn Grants, 3211
National Geographic All Roads Seed Grants, 3272
National Geographic Conservation Grants, 3273
National Geographic Genographic Legacy Grants, 3274
National Geographic Young Explorers Grants, 3275
National Wetlands Awards, 3282
Nelda C. and H.J. Lutcher Stark Fndn Grants, 3296
New Earth Fndn Grants, 3317
New Hampshire Charitable Fndn Grants, 3325
NFF Collaboration Support Grants, 3342
NFF Community Assistance Grants, 3343
NFF Matching Grants, 3344
NFF Mid-Capacity Assistance Grants, 3345
NFF Wilderness Stewardship Grants, 3346
NFWF/Exxon Save the Tiger Grants, 3354
NFWF Acres for America Grants, 3355
NFWF Alaska Fish and Wildlife Grants, 3356
NFWF Aleutian Islands Risk Assessment Grants, 3357
NFWF Bird Conservation Init Grants, 3358
NFWF Bronx River Watershed Init Grants, 3360
NFWF Budweiser Conservationist of the Year, 3361
NFWF California Coastal Restoration Grants, 3362
NFWF Chesapeake Bay Conservation Innovation Grants, 3363
NFWF Chesapeake Bay Stewardship Fund Small Watershed Grants, 3364
NFWF Chesapeake Targeted Watershed Grants, 3365
NFWF Columbia Basin Water Trans Grants, 3366
NFWF Columbia River Estuarine Coastal Grant, 3367
NFWF Community Salmon Fund Partnerships, 3368
NFWF ConocoPhillips SPIRIT of Conservation Migratory Bird Grants, 3369
NFWF Coral Reef Conservation Project Grants, 3370
NFWF Dissolved Oxygen Environmental Benefit Grants, 3372
NFWF Freshwater Fish Conservation Init Grants, 3374
NFWF King County Community Salmon Grants, 3375
NFWF Long Island Sound Futures Grants, 3376
NFWF Marine & Coastal Conservation Grants, 3377
NFWF National Whale Conservation Grants, 3378
NFWF National Wildlife Refuge Friends Group Grants, 3379
NFWF Native Plant Conservation Init Grants, 3380
NFWF Nature of Learning Grants, 3381
NFWF One Fly Conservation Partnerships, 3382
NFWF Oregon Governor's Fund for the Environment Grants, 3383
NFWF Pacific Grassroots Salmonid Init Grants, 3384
NFWF Pierce Community Salmon Grant, 3385
NFWF Pioneers in Conservation Grants, 3386
NFWF Radical Salmon Design Contest, 3388
NFWF Salmon Recovery Funding Board Community Salmon Grants, 3389
NFWF Seafarer's Environmental Educ Grants, 3390
NFWF Shell Marine Habitat Grants, 3391
NFWF Southern Co Longleaf Legacy Grants, 3392
NFWF Southern Company Power of Flight Bird Conservation Grants, 3393
NFWF State Comprehensive Wildlife Conservation Support Grants, 3395
NFWF Sustain Our Great Lakes Grants, 3396
NFWF Tampa Bay Environmental Grants, 3397
NFWF Upper Mississippi Riv Watershed Grants, 3398
NFWF Wildlife & Habitat Conservation Grants, 3399
NFWF Wildlife Links Grants, 3400
NHSCA Conservation License Plate Grants, 3425
Nina Mason Pulliam Charitable Grants, 3443
Norcliffe Fndn Grants, 3459
Norman Fndn Grants, 3464
North American Wetlands Conservation Grants, 3465
NW Fund for the Environment Grants, 3510
NRA Fndn Grants, 3517
Ogden Codman Grants, 3641
Olin Corp Charitable Grants, 3669
Oscar Rennebohm Fndn Grants, 3694
Overbrook Fndn Grants, 3715
Palm Beach and Martin Counties Grants, 3733
Patricia Price Peterson Fndn Grants, 3746
PG&E Bright Ideas Grants, 3866

Conservation, Natural Resources

PG&E Community Vitality Grants, 3868
Piedmont Natural Gas Fndn Environmental Stewardship and Energy Sustainability Grant, 3884
Plum Creek Fndn Grants, 3917
PNM Reduce Your Use Grants, 3926
Posey County Community Fndn Grants, 3939
Project AWARE Fndn Grants, 3971
Pulte Homes Corp Contributions, 3989
Putnam Fndn Grants, 3991
Rajiv Gandhi Fndn Grants, 4011
REI Conservation and Outdoor Rec Grants, 4051
Richard and Rhoda Goldman Grants, 4077
Robert W. Woodruff Fndn Grants, 4124
Rohm and Haas Company Grants, 4145
Ross Fndn Grants, 4164
Royal Caribbean Cruises Ocean Fund, 4165
San Juan Island Community Fndn Grants, 4283
Schumann Fund for New Jersey Grants, 4311
SeaWorld & Busch Gardens Conservation Grants, 4332
Shared Earth Fndn Grants, 4339
Singing for Change Fndn Grants, 4363
Skaggs Fndn Grants, 4378
Solutia Grants, 4402
Stonyfield Farm Profits for the Planet Grants, 4509
Stowe Family Fndn Grants, 4510
Sulzberger Fndn Grants, 4522
Susan Vaughan Fndn Grants, 4537
Sweet Water Grants, 4541
Tides California Wildlands Grassroots Fund, 4630
Tides Fndn Grants, 4632
Tom's of Maine Grants, 4640
Tourism Cares Worldwide Grants, 4649
UNESCO World Heritage Grants, 4706
USDC/NOAA American Rivers Community-Based Restoration Program River Grants, 4845
Volvo Adventure Environmental Awards, 4952
Waste Management Charitable Giving Grants, 5001
Wege Fndn Grants, 5017
WestWind Fndn Environment Grants, 5052
Weyerhaeuser Family Fndn Environment, Conservation and Preservation Grants, 5054
Widgeon Point Charitable Fndn Grants, 5064
Wilburforce Fndn Grants, 5067
WILD Fndn Grants, 5068

Construction Engineering
Barrasso Usdin Kupperman Freeman and Sarver LLC Corp Grants, 675
GNOF Coastal 5 + 1 Grants, 2070
Massachusetts Cultural Council Cultural Facilities Feasibility and Technical Assistance Grants, 3054
USDA Rural Business Enterprise Grants, 4823

Construction Management
Girl's Best Friend Fndn Grants, 2057
Massachusetts Cultural Council Cultural Facilities Capital Grants, 3053
Massachusetts Cultural Council Cultural Facilities Systems Replacement Plan Grants Grants, 3055

Consumer Behavior
Bodman Fndn Grants, 807
Citigroup Fndn Grants, 1139
Wallace Global Grants, 4977

Consumer Education/Information
ACF Assets for Indep Individual Development Account Grants, 115
Achelis Fndn Grants, 127
American College of Bankruptcy Grants, 426
Bodman Fndn Grants, 807
Citigroup Fndn Grants, 1139
CNCS Senior Corps Retired and Senior Volunteer Grants, 1188
Covidien Partnership for Neighborhood Wellness Grants, 1391
HAF Natural Environment Grants, 2202
Phi Upsilon Omicron Florence Fallgatter Distinguished Service Award, 3877

Consumer Law
Rose Fndn For Communities and the Environment Consumer Privacy Rights Grants, 4156

Consumer Sciences
Phi Upsilon Omicron Florence Fallgatter Distinguished Service Award, 3877
Phi Upsilon Omicron Frances Morton Holbrook Alumni Award, 3878

Consumer Services
EPA Children's Health Protection Grants, 1728
IIE New Leaders Group Award for Mutual Understanding, 2460

Contraceptives
NFL Player Youth Football Camp Grants, 3353

Conventional Warfare
Conrad N. Hilton Humanitarian Prize, 1356
Town Creek Fndn Grants, 4650

Cooperative Agreements
National Endowment for the Arts - Regional Partnership Agreement Grants, 3258
National Endowment for the Arts - State Partnership Agreement Grants, 3259
NYSCA Dance: Services to the Field Grants, 3587
RISCA Professional Arts Development Grants, 4099

Cooperative Education
Cleveland Fenn Ed Grants, 1169
Head Start Replacement Grantee: Colorado, 2275
Head Start Replacement Grantee: Florida, 2276
Head Start Replacement Grantee: West Virginia, 2277

Cooperatives
Collaboration Prize, 1205
Head Start Replacement Grantee: Colorado, 2275
Head Start Replacement Grantee: West Virginia, 2277
ICC Listening to Communities Grants, 2429
Indiana Regional Economic Development Partnership Grants, 2546
Kentucky Arts Council Access Assistance Grants, 2805
NYSCA Dance: Services to the Field Grants, 3587
USDA Rural Coop Development Grants, 4826

Copyright Law
ALA Robert L. Oakley Scholarship, 313

Coral Reefs
NOAA Projects to Improve or Amend Coral Reef Fishery Management Plans, 3453

Corporate/Strategic Planning
Blue Cross Blue Shield of Minnesota Fndn - Healthy Equity: Health Impact Assessment Grants, 796
CNCS AmeriCorps State and National Grants, 1182
Community Fndn of St. Joseph County ArtsEverywhere Grants, 1313
GNOF Organizational Effectiveness Grants and Workshops, 2090
Middlesex Savings Charitable Fndn Capacity Building Grants, 3172
NASE Growth Grants, 3242
Nonprofit Management Grants, 3458
PCA Strategies for Success Grants - Advanced, 3804
Peter and Elizabeth C. Tower Fndn Phase II Technology Init Grants, 3839
Peter and Elizabeth C. Tower Fndn Phase I Technology Init Grants, 3840
RISCA Professional Arts Development Grants, 4099

Counseling/Guidance
A.V. Hunter Grants, 47
Arizona Republic Newspaper Contributions, 547
Atkinson Fndn Community Grants, 606
Bollinger Fndn Grants, 812
Chicago Community Trust Housing Grants: Preserving Home Ownership and Preventing Foreclosure, 1089
Community Fndn for Southern Arizona Grants, 1261
DHHS Health Centers Grants for Residents of Public Housing, 1533
DOJ Rural Domestic Violence and Child Victimization Enforcement Grants, 1562
DOL Youthbuild Grants, 1571
Edina Realty Fndn Grants, 1656
Financial Capability Innovation Fund II Grants, 1811
Ford Fndn Peace and Social Justice Grants, 1884
Greater Worcester Comm Discretionary Grants, 2140
Gulf Coast Community Operating Grants, 2176
Gulf Coast Fndn of Community Grants, 2177
Hudson Webber Fndn Grants, 2383
Humanitas Fndn Grants, 2390
Indep Community Fndn Quality of Life Grant, 2525
James R. Thorpe Fndn Grants, 2636
Legacy Fndn College Readiness Grant, 2874
Leo Niessen Jr., Charitable Grants, 2885
Mary Owen Borden Fndn Grants, 3046
MGM Resorts Fndn Community Grants, 3153
MGN Family Fndn Grants, 3154
OneFamily Fndn Grants, 3673
Robert R. Meyer Fndn Grants, 4121
Ruth H. and Warren A. Ellsworth Fndn Grants, 4179
Seabury Fndn Grants, 4316
Seybert Inst for Poor Boys and Girls Grants, 4338
SVP Early Childhood Development and Parenting Grants, 4538
Target Corp Local Store Grants, 4561
TE Fndn Grants, 4572
Textron Corp Contributions Grants, 4601
U.S. Department of Educ Innovative Strategies in Community Colleges for Working Adults and Displaced Workers Grants, 4692
USDA Tech and Supervisory Assistance Grants, 4841
Vermont Community Fndn Grants, 4929
Whirlpool Fndn Grants, 5056

Counseling/Guidance Education
Medtronic Fndn Community Link Human Services Grants, 3112
Robert R. McCormick Tribune Comm Grants, 4119

Craft Arts
Alabama State Council on the Arts Community Arts Collaborative Ventures Grants, 236
Alabama State Council on the Arts Community Arts Operating Support Grants, 237
Alabama State Council on the Arts Community Arts Presenting Grants, 238
Alabama State Council on the Arts Community Arts Program Development Grants, 239
Alabama State Council on the Arts Community Planning & Design Grants, 241
Alabama State Council on the Arts in Educ Partnership Grants, 242
Alabama State Council on the Arts Multi-Discipline and Festival Grants, 243
Arkansas Arts Council AIE After School/Summer Residency Grants, 551
Arkansas Arts Council AIE In-School Residency, 553
Dept of Ed Recreational Services for Individuals with Disabilities, 1512
Florida Div of Cultural Affairs Multidisciplinary Grants, 1857
Illinois Arts Council Visual Arts Grants, 2478
Iowa Arts Council Artists in Schools/Communities Residency Grants, 2571
Kentucky Arts Council Al Smith Fellowship, 2806
Kentucky Arts Council Emerging Artist Award, 2807
Minnesota State Arts Board Cultural Community Partnership Grants, 3188
Nevada Arts Council Folklife Opps Grants, 3310
NHSCA Artist Residencies in Schools Grants, 3423
NHSCA Youth Arts Project Grants: For Extended Arts Learning, 3430
NJSCA Arts Project Support, 3446
NJSCA Folk Arts Apprenticeships, 3448
NJSCA General Program Support Grants, 3449
NYFA Gregory Millard Fellowships, 3565

SUBJECT INDEX

ORBI Artist Fast Track Grants, 3689
PCA-PCD Professional Development for Individual Artists Grants, 3770
PCA Arts in Educ Residencies, 3772
PCA Arts Organizations & Grants for Crafts, 3778
PCA Busing Grants, 3786
PCA Entry Track Arts Organizations and Program Grants for Crafts, 3790
PCA Pennsylvania Partners in the Arts Program Stream Grants, 3801
PCA Pennsylvania Partners in the Arts Project Stream Grants, 3802
PCA Professional Development Grants, 3803
PCA Strategies for Success Grants - Basic Level, 3805
PCA Strategies for Success Grants - Intermediate, 3806
Rasmuson Fndn Individual Artists Awards, 4022
Ruth Mott Fndn Grants, 4180
South Carolina Arts Commission Fellowships, 4415
TAC Arts Access Grant, 4549
Trinity Trust Summer Youth Mini Grants, 4672
Wild Rivers Community Fndn Summer Youth Mini Grants, 5070

Craniofacial Anomalies
Ronald McDonald House Charities Grants, 4149

Creative Writing
A.J. Fletcher Fndn Grants, 41
Bush Fndn Arts & Humanities Grants: Short-Term Organizational Support, 873
Constance Saltonstall Fndn for the Arts Grants, 1361
Dwight Stuart Youth Fndn Grants, 1628
Emma A. Sheafer Charitable Grants, 1699
Florida Div of Cultural Affairs Multidisciplinary Grants, 1857
Illinois Arts Council Literature Grants, 2470
Jerome Fndn Travel and Study Grants, 2668
Kentucky Arts Council Al Smith Fellowship, 2806
Kentucky Arts Council Emerging Artist Award, 2807
Leon and Thea Koerner Fndn Grants, 2883
McKesson Fndn Grants, 3084
NHSCA Artist Residencies in Schools Grants, 3423
NHSCA Youth Arts Project Grants: For Extended Arts Learning, 3430
NYFA Gregory Millard Fellowships, 3565
NYSCA Lit: General Operating Support Grants, 3598
NYSCA Literature: General Support Grants, 3599
Ohio Arts Council Individual Excellence Awards, 3648
PCA Arts Organizations & Grants for Lit, 3781
PCA Strategies for Success Grants - Advanced, 3804
PCA Strategies for Success Grants - Intermediate, 3806
Union Square Arts Award, 4716
Wallace Alexander Gerbode Fndn Special Award Grants, 4975

Creativity
ALA Excellence in Academic Libraries Award, 276
ALA Innovation Award, 288
ALA Isadore Gilbert Mudge Award, 290
ALA John Cotton Dana Library Public Relations Award, 292
Charlotte R. Schmidlapp Grants, 1058
Meyer Fndn Educ Grants, 3142
Phoenix Coyotes Charities Grants, 3879
Puffin/Nation Prize for Creative Citizenship, 3987

Credit
Baton Rouge Area Fndn Credit Bureau Grants, 680
Financial Capability Innovation Fund II Grants, 1811
NAR Partners in Housing Awards, 3239

Crime Control
Cemala Fndn Grants, 988
Colorado Springs Community Grants, 1215
DOJ Gang-Free Schools and Communities Intervention Grants, 1557
DOJ Juvenile Justice and Delinquency Prevention Special Emphasis Grants, 1559
DOJ National Institute of Justice Visiting Fellows, 1561
Do Right Fndn Grants, 1581

Gardiner Howland Shaw Fndn Grants, 1986
George H. and Jane A. Mifflin Grants, 2021
Sonora Area Fndn Competitive Grants, 4404

Crime Prevention
1st and 10 Fndn Grants, 1
Abbot and Dorothy H. Stevens Fndn Grants, 79
Abell Fndn Criminal Justice and Addictions Grants, 95
Austin S. Nelson Fndn Grants, 617
Baptist Community Ministries Grants, 664
Beazley Fndn Grants, 714
BJ's Charitable Fndn Grants, 777
CFNCR Starbucks Memorial Fund, 1026
Clarcor Fndn Grants, 1148
Columbus Neighborhood Partnership Grants, 1226
ConocoPhillips Fndn Grants, 1354
Constantin Fndn Grants, 1362
Cornerstone Fndn of NE Wisconsin Grants, 1375
Daphne Seybolt Culpeper Memorial Fndn Grants, 1445
DOJ Community-Based Delinquency Prevention Grants, 1556
DOJ Internet Crimes against Children Task Force Grants, 1558
DOJ Juvenile Justice and Delinquency Prevention Special Emphasis Grants, 1559
DOJ National Institute of Justice Visiting Fellows, 1561
Elliot Fndn Inc Grants, 1686
Farmers Insurance Corp Giving Grants, 1791
Frank Stanley Beveridge Fndn Grants, 1936
G.N. Wilcox Grants, 1982
George H. and Jane A. Mifflin Grants, 2021
Heinz Endowments Grants, 2291
Herman Goldman Fndn Grants, 2317
Hudson Webber Fndn Grants, 2383
Initiaive Fndn Inside-Out Connections Grants, 2556
Jacobs Family Spirit of the Diamond Grants, 2618
Joseph H. and Florence A. Roblee Fndn Grants, 2736
Kahuku Community Fund, 2762
Knox County Community Fndn Grants, 2831
Lyndhurst Fndn Grants, 2949
OJJDP Tribal Juvenile Accountability Discretionary Grants, 3665
Ordean Fndn Grants, 3691
OSI Sentencing and Incarceration Alternatives Project Grants, 3711
Perry County Community Fndn Grants, 3827
Pike County Community Fndn Grants, 3888
Plough Fndn Grants, 3915
Plum Creek Fndn Grants, 3917
Posey County Community Fndn Grants, 3939
R.C. Baker Fndn Grants, 3999
RCF General Community Grants, 4032
Reynolds American Fndn Grants, 4068
Romic Environmental's Charitable Contributions, 4148
Sid W. Richardson Fndn Grants, 4350
Sonoco Fndn Grants, 4403
Thomas W. Briggs Fndn Grants, 4621
Threshold Fndn Election Integrity Grants, 4625
Union Bank, N.A. Fndn Grants, 4709
USDJ Edward Byrne Justice Assistance Grants, 4863

Crime Victims
Austin S. Nelson Fndn Grants, 617
Burton G. Bettingen Grants, 871
Carrie E. and Lena V. Glenn Fndn Grants, 944
CFNCR Starbucks Memorial Fund, 1026
Cralle Fndn Grants, 1394
Edward and Ellen Roche Relief Fndn Grants, 1663
Initiaive Fndn Inside-Out Connections Grants, 2556
John W. Speas and Effie E. Speas Grants, 2732
Linford and Mildred White Charitable Grants, 2909
Olga Sipolin Children's Grants, 3668
USDJ Edward Byrne Justice Assistance Grants, 4863

Criminal Behavior
Abell Fndn Criminal Justice and Addictions Grants, 95
Do Right Fndn Grants, 1581
John R. Oishei Fndn Grants, 2709
Ordean Fndn Grants, 3691
OSF-Baltimore Criminal & Juv Justice Grants, 3696

Crisis Counseling / 857

OSI Sentencing and Incarceration Alternatives Project Grants, 3711
William J. and Dorothy K. O'Neill Fndn Grants, 5087

Criminal Information Systems
USDJ Nat Criminal History Improvement Grants, 4864
USDJ NICS Act Record Improvement Grants, 4865

Criminal Justice
Abelard Fndn East Grants, 87
Abelard Fndn West Grants, 88
Abell Fndn Criminal Justice and Addictions Grants, 95
Baptist Community Ministries Grants, 664
Bernard F. and Alva B. Gimbel Fndn Grants, 740
Bread and Roses Community Grants, 832
Carroll County Community Fndn Grants, 947
CDC Grants for Violence-Related Injury Prevention Research, 974
Chicago Community Trust Public Safety and Justice Grants, 1093
Coastal Community Fndn of S Carolina Grants, 1193
Daisy Marquis Jones Fndn Grants, 1434
DOJ Juvenile Justice and Delinquency Prevention Special Emphasis Grants, 1559
DOJ National Institute of Justice Visiting Fellows, 1561
Gardiner Howland Shaw Fndn Grants, 1986
Henry County Community Fndn Grants, 2308
Margaret L. Wendt Fndn Grants, 3004
Marion I. and Henry J. Knott Standard Grants, 3019
Motorola Fndn Grants, 3221
Ms. Fndn Women Building Democracy Grants, 3223
OSF-Baltimore Criminal & Juv Justice Grants, 3696
OSF Burma Project/SE Asia Init Grants, 3702
OSI After Prison Init Grants, 3710
OSI Sentencing and Incarceration Alternatives Project Grants, 3711
Overbrook Fndn Grants, 3715
PIP Fulfilling the Dream Fund, 3907
PIP Racial Justice Collaborative Grants, 3908
PIP U.S. Human Rights Grants, 3909
Public Interest Law Fndn Community Grants, 3982
Public Welfare Fndn Grants, 3984
Puerto Rico Community Fndn Grants, 3986
San Diego County Bar Fndn Grants, 4241
Sioux Falls Area Community Grants, 4364
Sioux Falls Area Community Fndn Spot Grants, 4366
Social Justice Fund NW Criminal Justice Giving Project Grants, 4394
State Justice Institute Curriculum Adaptation and Training Grants, 4488
State Justice Institute Partner Grants, 4489
State Justice Institute Project Grants, 4490
State Justice Institute Scholarships, 4491
State Justice Institute Strategic Init Grants, 4492
State Justice Institute Tech Assistance Grants, 4493
Texas Commission on the Arts Arts Respond Project Grants, 4581
Threshold Fndn Justice and Democracy Grants, 4626
Vulcan Materials Company Fndn Grants, 4956

Crisis Counseling
ACF ACYF Runaway and Homeless Youth Basic Center Grants, 112
Actors Fund Social Services and Financial Assist, 139
Adams Fndn Grants, 155
Austin S. Nelson Fndn Grants, 617
Barr Grants, 678
Charles H. Pearson Fndn Grants, 1045
CICF Christmas Fund, 1117
Community Fndn of Bartholomew County Women's Giving Circle, 1269
D. W. McMillan Fndn Grants, 1426
Duchossois Family Fndn Grants, 1616
Duluth-Superior Area Community Fndn Grants, 1620
Edwards Grants, 1669
Farm Aid Grants, 1790
GNOF Plaquemines Community Grants, 2091
Medtronic Fndn Community Link Human Services Grants, 3112
Nationwide Insurance Fndn Grants, 3285

858 / Crisis Counseling

Ordean Fndn Grants, 3691
Pentair Fndn Educ and Community Grants, 3816
Perry County Community Fndn Grants, 3827
Pike County Community Fndn Grants, 3888
SAG Motion Picture Players Welfare Grants, 4209
Sands Fndn Crisis Grants, 4254
Sensient Technologies Fndn Grants, 4337
Sierra Health Fndn Responsive Grants, 4353
Spencer County Community Fndn Grants, 4451
Warrick County Community Fndn Grants, 4987

Critical Care Medicine
Baptist Community Ministries Grants, 664
Caterpillar Fndn Grants, 954
E.L. Wiegand Fndn Grants, 1639
Herman Goldman Fndn Grants, 2317
Lowe Fndn Grants, 2929
Piper Trust Healthcare & Med Research Grants, 3903
Questar Corp Contributions Grants, 3997
Stewart Huston Charitable Grants, 4505

Cross-Cultural Studies
eBay Fndn Community Grants, 1648
Nellie Mae Educ Fndn District-Level Grants, 3297
NYSCA Arts Educ: Services to the Field Grants, 3582
NYSCA Folk Arts: Presentation Grants, 3596

Culinary Arts
Adolph Coors Fndn Grants, 171
Carl B. and Florence E. King Fndn Grants, 928

Cultural Activities/Programs
2 Depot Square Ipswich Charitable Fndn Grants, 4
3M Company Arts and Culture Grants, 12
49ers Fndn Grants, 23
A.C. Ratshesky Fndn Grants, 39
A.J. Fletcher Fndn Grants, 41
A.O. Smith Community Grants, 46
Aaron Fndn Grants, 73
Abell-Hanger Fndn Grants, 91
ABIG Fndn Grants, 99
Abington Fndn Grants, 100
Achelis Fndn Grants, 127
Adelaide Breed Bayrd Fndn Grants, 161
Adobe Art and Culture Grants, 167
Adobe Community Investment Grants, 168
AEC Grants, 175
AEGON Transamerica Fndn Civic and Community Grants, 177
AEP Corp Giving Grants, 180
Aetna Fndn Arts Grants in Connecticut, 181
African American Fund of New Jersey Grants, 192
Ahmanson Fndn Grants, 207
Air Products and Chemicals Grants, 216
Alabama Power Fndn Grants, 233
Aladdin Industries Fndn Grants, 263
ALA National Friends of Libraries Week Awards, 303
Alaska Airlines Corp Giving Grants, 320
Alaska Airlines Fndn Grants, 321
ALA Writers Live at the Library Grants, 336
Albert and Bessie Mae Kronkosky Charitable Fndn Grants, 339
Alberto Culver Corp Contributions Grants, 343
Albert Pick Jr. Grants, 344
Albuquerque Community Fndn Grants, 348
Alcatel-Lucent Technologies Fndn Grants, 349
Alcoa Fndn Grants, 350
Alex Stern Family Fndn Grants, 360
ALFJ Astraea U.S. General Fund, 362
Allegheny Technologies Charitable Trust, 377
Allen P. and Josephine B. Green Fndn Grants, 380
Alliant Energy Fndn Community Grants, 384
Alticor Corp Community Contributions Grants, 396
Alvin and Fanny Blaustein Thalheimer Grants, 403
ALZA Corp Contributions Grants, 405
Amarillo Area/Harrington Fndns Grants, 412
Ambrose Monell Fndn Grants, 415
Ameren Corp Community Grants, 418
Amer-Scandinavian Fndn Public Project Grants, 419
American Savings Fndn Grants, 445

Anheuser-Busch Fndn Grants, 470
ANLAF Int'l Fund for Sexual Minorities Grants, 471
Anna Fitch Ardenghi Grants, 472
Ann Arbor Area Community Fndn Grants, 474
Anne L. and George H. Clapp Charitable and Ed Grants, 476
Ann Peppers Fndn Grants, 484
AON Fndn Grants, 491
Appalachian Regional Commission Tourist Development Grants, 511
Applied Biosystems Grants, 514
AptarGroup Fndn Grants, 519
Aquila Corp Grants, 521
Aratani Fndn Grants, 523
Archer Daniels Midland Fndn Grants, 527
Arcus Fndn Grants, 529
Arcus Fndn Gay and Lesbian Grants, 530
Arcus Fndn National Grants, 531
Argyros Fndn Grants, 532
Arie and Ida Crown Grants, 533
Arizona Cardinals Grants, 534
Arizona Public Service Corp Giving Grants, 545
Arizona Republic Fndn Grants, 546
Arizona Republic Newspaper Contributions, 547
Arkansas Community Fndn Grants, 561
Armstrong McDonald Fndn Grants, 565
ArtsWave Impact Grants, 580
ArtsWave Project Grants, 581
ArvinMeritor Fndn Arts and Culture Grants, 582
ArvinMeritor Grants, 585
Ashland Corp Contributions Grants, 587
Atherton Family Fndn Grants, 604
Atlanta Fndn Grants, 608
Audrey and Sydney Irmas Charitable Fndn Grants, 612
Austin Community Fndn Grants, 616
Avery Dennison Fndn Grants, 623
Avista Fndn Grants, 624
Bacon Family Fndn Grants, 634
Ball Brothers Fndn General Grants, 637
Baltimore Community Fndn Arts and Culture Path Grants, 641
Barberton Community Fndn Grants, 666
Barker Welfare Fndn Grants, 669
Barra Fndn Project Grants, 674
Barr Fndn Grants (Massachusetts), 676
Batts Fndn Grants, 687
Bay Area Community Fndn Grants, 694
BCBSNC Fndn Grants, 712
Bechtel Group Fndn Building Positive Community Relationships Grants, 715
Beckley Area Fndn Grants, 716
Beim Fndn Grants, 718
Belk Fndn Grants, 721
Benton Community Fndn Grants, 730
Benton County Fndn Grants, 731
Benwood Fndn Focus Area Grants, 733
Berks County Community Fndn Grants, 734
Berrien Community Fndn Grants, 744
Bertha Russ Lytel Fndn Grants, 745
Besser Fndn Grants, 748
Black Hills Corp Grants, 781
Blade Fndn Grants, 783
Blandin Fndn Itasca County Area Vitality Grants, 789
Blue Cross Blue Shield of Minnesota Healthy Neighborhoods: Connect Grants, 798
Blue Grass Community Fndn Grants, 799
Blue River Community Fndn Grants, 801
Blum-Kovler Fndn Grants, 803
Bodenwein Public Benevolent Fndn Grants, 806
Bodman Fndn Grants, 807
Boeing Company Contributions Grants, 809
Boettcher Fndn Grants, 810
Booth Ferris Fndn Grants, 816
Boston Fndn Grants, 819
Bradley-Turner Fndn Grants, 828
Brown County Community Fndn Grants, 853
Burlington Northern Santa Fe Fndn Grants, 866
Bydale Fndn Grants, 882
Cailloux Fndn Grants, 892
California Community Fndn Art Grants, 900

Cambridge Community Fndn Grants, 913
Carl and Eloise Pohlad Family Fndn Grants, 927
Carl B. and Florence E. King Fndn Grants, 928
Carl C. Icahn Fndn Grants, 929
Carolyn Fndn Grants, 942
Carroll County Community Fndn Grants, 947
CDECD Arts Catalyze Placemaking in Every Community Grants, 977
CDECD Arts Catalyze Placemaking Leadership Grants, 978
CDECD Arts Catalyze Placemaking Sustaining Relevance Grants, 979
Cemala Fndn Grants, 988
Central Carolina Community Fndn Community Impact Grants, 994
Central Minnesota Community Fndn Grants, 995
Central Okanagan Community Fndn Grants, 997
Cessna Fndn Grants, 1000
Chamberlain Fndn Grants, 1027
Charles H. Dater Fndn Grants, 1042
Charles H. Price II Family Fndn Grants, 1046
Charles M. Bair Family Grants, 1051
Charles Parker Trust for Public Music Grants, 1053
Charlotte County (FL) Community Fndn Grants, 1056
Charlotte Martin Fndn Youth Grants, 1057
Chautauqua Region Community Fndn Grants, 1062
Chesapeake Corp Fndn Grants, 1076
Chicago Board of Trade Fndn Grants, 1079
Chicago Community Arts Assistance Grants, 1081
Chicago Community Trust Arts and Culture Grants: Supporting Diverse Arts Productions and Fostering Art in Every Community, 1084
Chicago Sun Times Charity Grants, 1098
Chicago Title and Trust Company Fndn Grants, 1099
Chiles Fndn Grants, 1108
Christy-Houston Fndn Grants, 1115
CICF Clare Noyes Grant, 1119
CICF Efroymson Grants, 1120
CICF Indianapolis Fndn Community Grants, 1123
CICF Legacy Grants, 1126
CIGNA Fndn Grants, 1130
Cincinnati Bell Fndn Grants, 1131
Cinergy Fndn Grants, 1133
Cingular Wireless Charitable Contributions, 1134
Citigroup Fndn Grants, 1139
Citizens Bank Mid-Atlantic Charitable Grants, 1140
Claneil Fndn Grants, 1145
Clarcor Fndn Grants, 1148
Claremont Community Fndn Grants, 1149
Clark County Community Fndn Grants, 1156
Clark Fndn Grants, 1157
Cleveland-Cliffs Fndn Grants, 1165
Cleveland Browns Fndn Grants, 1166
Cleveland Community Responsive Grants, 1168
Clinton County Community Fndn Grants, 1174
CNA Fndn Grants, 1185
CNL Corp Giving Arts & Culture Grants, 1190
Coastal Community Fndn of S Carolina Grants, 1193
Cockrell Fndn Grants, 1196
Colgate-Palmolive Company Grants, 1202
Collins Fndn Grants, 1209
Colorado Interstate Gas Grants, 1213
Columbus Fndn John W. and Edna McManus Shepard Grants, 1223
Columbus Fndn Robert E. and Genevieve B. Schaefer Grants, 1229
Comcast Fndn Grants, 1235
Comer Fndn Grants, 1236
Comerica Charitable Fndn Grants, 1237
Commonwealth Edison Grants, 1240
Communities Fndn of Texas Grants, 1243
Community Fndn Alliance City of Evansville Endowment Grants, 1246
Community Fndn for NE Michigan Grants, 1257
Community Fndn of Bartholomew County Heritage Grants, 1267
Community Fndn of Bartholomew County James A. Henderson Award for Fundraising, 1268
Community Fndn of Bloomington and Monroe County Grants, 1271

SUBJECT INDEX

Cultural Activities/Programs / 859

Community Fndn of Greater Birmingham Grants, 1280
Community Fndn of Greater Fort Wayne - Community Endowment and Clarke Endowment Grants, 1285
Community Fndn of Greater Fort Wayne - John S. and James L. Knight Fndn Donor-Advised Grants, 1287
Community Fndn of Greater Greensboro Grants, 1288
Community Fndn of Greater Tampa Grants, 1292
Community Fndn of Howard County Grants, 1297
Community Fndn of Mount Vernon and Knox County Grants, 1301
Community Fndn of Riverside County Grants, 1304
Community Fndn of Shreveport-Bossier Grants, 1307
Community Fndn of SE Connecticut Grants, 1309
Community Fndn of South Puget Sound Grants, 1311
Community Fndn of St. Joseph County ArtsEverywhere Grants, 1313
Community Fndn of the Verdugos Grants, 1322
Community Fndn of Western N Carolina Grants, 1327
Community Impact Fund, 1332
Compton Fndn Grants, 1338
Connecticut Community Fndn Grants, 1350
Connelly Fndn Grants, 1353
ConocoPhillips Grants, 1355
CONSOL Coal Group Grants, 1360
Constantin Fndn Grants, 1362
Consumers Energy Fndn, 1365
Cooke Fndn Grants, 1368
Cooper Industries Fndn Grants, 1370
Cornerstone Fndn of NE Wisconsin Grants, 1375
Cowles Charitable Grants, 1392
Cranston Fndn Grants, 1395
CSX Corp Contributions Grants, 1408
Cudd Fndn Grants, 1410
Cullen Fndn Grants, 1411
Cultural Society of Filipino Americans Grants, 1412
Cumberland Community Fndn Grants, 1413
Cyrus Eaton Fndn Grants, 1423
DaimlerChrysler Corp Grants, 1432
Dairy Queen Corp Contributions Grants, 1433
Dana Corp Fndn Grants, 1440
Darden Restaurants Fndn Grants, 1446
Daviess County Community Fndn Arts and Culture Grants, 1455
Dayton Fndn Grants, 1463
Dayton Power and Light Fndn Grants, 1464
DB Americas Fndn Grants, 1466
Deluxe Corp Fndn Grants, 1496
Denver Fndn Community Grants, 1502
Dolfinger-McMahon Fndn Grants, 1565
Dorot Fndn Grants, 1586
Dr. Scholl Fndn Grants, 1602
Dunspaugh-Dalton Fndn Grants, 1623
DuPage Community Fndn Grants, 1624
Durfee Fndn Sabbatical Grants, 1625
Dyer-Ives Fndn Small Grants, 1629
Eastman Chemical Company Fndn Grants, 1643
Eberly Fndn Grants, 1649
Edna Wardlaw Charitable Grants, 1660
Edward S. Moore Fndn Grants, 1668
Edwin S. Webster Fndn Grants, 1671
Elkhart County Community Fndn Grants, 1684
Elmer L. and Eleanor J. Andersen Fndn Grants, 1687
Emerson Charitable Grants, 1694
Ensign-Bickford Fndn Grants, 1709
Entergy Corp Micro Grants, 1712
Erie Community Fndn Grants, 1750
Essex County Community Discretionary Grants, 1752
Ethel and Raymond F. Rice Fndn Grants, 1758
Ethel Sergeant Clark Smith Fndn Grants, 1761
Fargo-Moorhead Area Fndn Grants, 1788
Farmers Insurance Corp Giving Grants, 1791
FEDCO Charitable Fndn Educ Grants, 1798
Ferree Fndn Grants, 1804
Fidelity Fndn Grants, 1805
Field Fndn of Illinois Grants, 1806
Fieldstone Fndn Grants, 1808
FirstEnergy Fndn Community Grants, 1819
First People's Fund Community Spirit Awards, 1825
Fishman Family Fndn Grants, 1835
Florida Div of Cultural Affairs Endowments, 1851
Florida Div of Cultural Affairs Facilities Grants, 1852
Florida Div of Cultural Affairs Specific Cultural Project Grants, 1862
Floyd A. and Kathleen C. Cailloux Fndn Grants, 1874
Fluor Fndn Grants, 1875
Fondren Fndn Grants, 1878
Fndn for Enhancing Communities Grants, 1893
Fndn NW Grants, 1906
France-Merrick Fndns Grants, 1915
Francis L. Abreu Charitable Grants, 1922
Frank and Lydia Bergen Fndn Grants, 1925
Frank E. and Seba B. Payne Fndn Grants, 1927
Fred C. and Katherine B. Andersen Fndn Grants, 1942
Frederick S. Upton Fndn Grants, 1947
Fred L. Emerson Fndn Grants, 1949
Fremont Area Community Fndn Grants, 1955
Fulton County Community Fndn Grants, 1975
G.N. Wilcox Grants, 1982
Garland and Agnes Taylor Gray Fndn Grants, 1988
Gateway Grants, 1992
Gaylord and Dorothy Donnelley Fndn Grants, 1993
Gebbie Fndn Grants, 1995
General Dynamics Corp Grants, 2001
General Mills Fndn Celebrating Communities of Color Grants, 2002
General Mills Fndn Grants, 2003
General Motors Fndn Grants Support Program, 2004
George Frederick Jewett Fndn Grants, 2019
George W. Codrington Charitable Fndn Grants, 2029
Georgia Power Fndn Grants, 2039
Gertrude and William C. Wardlaw Grants, 2045
Giving Sum Annual Grant, 2058
GlaxoSmithKline Corp Grants, 2060
GNOF Exxon-Mobil Grants, 2074
Goizueta Fndn Grants, 2096
Golden State Warriors Fndn Grants, 2099
Goodrich Corp Fndn Grants, 2104
Goodyear Tire Grants, 2106
Grand Haven Area Community Fndn Grants, 2113
Grand Rapids Community Fndn Grants, 2118
Greater Cincinnati Fndn Priority and Small Projects/ Capacity-Building Grants, 2132
Greater Green Bay Community Fndn Grants, 2135
Greater Milwaukee Fndn Grants, 2137
Greater Tacoma Community Fndn Grants, 2139
Greater Worcester Comm Discretionary Grants, 2140
Greater Worcester Community Youth for Community Improvement Grants, 2144
Guido A. and Elizabeth H. Binda Fndn Grants, 2172
Gulf Coast Community Fndn Grants, 2174
Guy I. Bromley Grants, 2180
H.B. Fuller Company Fndn Grants, 2183
H.J. Heinz Company Fndn Grants, 2184
HAF Mada Huggins Caldwell Grants, 2200
Hahl Proctor Charitable Grants, 2208
Harley Davidson Fndn Grants, 2224
Harold K. L. Castle Fndn Grants, 2228
Harry W. Bass, Jr. Fndn Grants, 2246
Hearst Fndns Culture Grants, 2284
Helen K. and Arthur E. Johnson Fndn Grants, 2296
Henry and Ruth Blaustein Rosenberg Grants, 2306
High Meadow Fndn Grants, 2321
Hill Crest Fndn Grants, 2324
Hill Fndn Grants, 2326
Hillman Fndn Grants, 2327
Hillsdale Grants, 2329
Historic Landmarks Fndn of Indiana Historic Preservation Educ Grants, 2334
Hoblitzelle Fndn Grants, 2341
Holland/Zeeland Community Fndn Grants, 2345
Homer Fndn Grants, 2352
Houston Endowment Grants, 2373
Howard and Bush Fndn Grants, 2374
Hudson Webber Fndn Grants, 2383
Huffy Fndn Grants, 2384
Hugh J. Andersen Fndn Grants, 2385
Humana Fndn Grants, 2388
Huntington County Community Fndn - Make a Difference Grants, 2406
Hyde Family Fndns Grants, 2414
I.A. O'Shaughnessy Fndn Grants, 2416
IBM Arts and Culture Grants, 2424
Idaho Community Fndn Eastern Region Competitive Grants, 2432
Idaho Power Company Corp Contributions, 2433
IMLS Native Hawaiian Library Services Grants, 2519
Impact 100 Grants, 2522
Indiana Arts Commission American Masterpieces Grants, 2530
Indiana Humanities Council Init Grants, 2539
Indianapolis Power & Light Company Community Grants, 2540
Intergrys Corp Grants, 2565
J.M. Long Fndn Grants, 2603
J.W. Kieckhefer Fndn Grants, 2607
Jacobs Family Spirit of the Diamond Grants, 2618
James L. and Mary Jane Bowman Grants, 2632
Jane's Grants, 2639
Janus Fndn Grants, 2647
Jessie Ball Dupont Grants, 2671
John Ben Snow Grants, 2687
John Deere Fndn Grants, 2692
John H. and Wilhelmina D. Harland Charitable Fndn Grants, 2698
John J. Leidy Fndn Grants, 2701
John R. Oishei Fndn Grants, 2709
John S. and James L. Knight Fndn Communities Grants, 2711
John S. and James L. Knight Fndn Donor Advised Grants, 2712
Johnson Controls Fndn Arts and Culture Grants, 2719
Joukowsky Family Fndn Grants, 2743
Joyce Fndn Culture Grants, 2747
JP Morgan Chase Arts and Culture Grants, 2752
Judith and Jean Pape Adams Charitable Fndn Tulsa Area Grants, 2755
Katharine Matthies Fndn Grants, 2788
Katherine John Murphy Fndn Grants, 2790
Kennedy Center HSC Fndn Internship, 2799
Kennedy Center Summer HSC Fndn Internship, 2800
Kenneth T. and Eileen L. Norris Fndn Grants, 2802
Kimball Int'l-Habig Fndn Grants, 2823
Kirkpatrick Fndn Grants, 2827
Knight Fndn Donor Advised Grants, 2828
Koret Fndn Grants, 2837
Land O'Lakes Fndn Community Grants, 2859
Liberty Bank Fndn Grants, 2890
Lied Fndn Grants, 2900
Lincoln Financial Group Fndn Grants, 2906
Lockheed Martin Philanthropic Grants, 2918
Lotus 88 Fndn for Women and Children Grants, 2921
Lowell Berry Fndn Grants, 2930
Lubbock Area Fndn Grants, 2931
Luther I. Replogle Fndn Grants, 2945
Lynde and Harry Bradley Fndn Grants, 2947
Lynde and Harry Bradley Fndn Prizes, 2948
Lyndhurst Fndn Grants, 2949
Mabel Louise Riley Fndn Grants, 2959
Mabel Y. Hughes Charitable Grants, 2960
Madison County Community General Grants, 2973
Maine Community Fndn Rose and Samuel Rudman Library Grants, 2988
Marcia and Otto Koehler Fndn Grants, 3000
Margaret and James A. Elkins Jr. Fndn Grants, 3003
Margaret T. Morris Fndn Grants, 3005
Marion I. & Henry J. Knott Discretionary Grants, 3018
Marion I. and Henry J. Knott Standard Grants, 3019
MARPAT Fndn Grants, 3023
Mars Fndn Grants, 3025
Marsh Corp Grants, 3027
Mary K. Chapman Fndn Grants, 3042
Mary Owen Borden Fndn Grants, 3046
Mary S. and David C. Corbin Fndn Grants, 3048
Massachusetts Cultural Council Cultural Investment Portfolio, 3056
Massachusetts Cultural Council Local Cultural Council Grants, 3057
Massachusetts Fndn for the Humanities Cultural Economic Development Grants, 3059
Massachusetts Fndn for Humanities Grants, 3060

860 / Cultural Activities/Programs

Maurice Amado Fndn Grants, 3063
Maurice J. Masserini Charitable Grants, 3064
Maxon Charitable Fndn Grants, 3068
McConnell Fndn Grants, 3076
McInerny Fndn Grants, 3083
McKesson Fndn Grants, 3084
Meadows Fndn Grants, 3104
Mertz Gilmore Fndn NYC Dance Grants, 3127
Miami County Community Fndn - Operation Round Up Grants, 3156
Microsoft Comm Affairs Puget Sound Grants, 3163
Millipore Fndn Grants, 3182
Minnesota State Arts Board Cultural Community Partnership Grants, 3188
Monfort Family Fndn Grants, 3203
Montana Arts Council Cultural and Aesthetic Project Grants, 3209
Montana Community Fndn Grants, 3211
Motorola Fndn Grants, 3221
Mr. and Mrs. William Foulds Family Grants, 3222
Nathaniel and Elizabeth P. Stevens Fndn Grants, 3247
National Endowment for the Arts - Grants for Arts Projects: Challenge America Fast-Track, 3254
National Endowment for the Arts - National Arts and Humanities Youth Program Awards, 3255
National Endowment for Arts Our Town Grants, 3257
National Endowment for the Arts - Regional Partnership Agreement Grants, 3258
National Endowment for Arts Agencies Grants, 3263
New York Life Fndn Grants, 3341
Nicholas H. Noyes Jr. Memorial Fndn Grants, 3434
Nina Mason Pulliam Charitable Grants, 3443
Noble County Community Fndn Celebrate Diversity Project Grants, 3455
Noble County Community Fndn Grants, 3456
Norcliffe Fndn Grants, 3459
Nordson Corp Fndn Grants, 3462
Norfolk Southern Fndn Grants, 3463
North Carolina Arts Council Technical Assistance Grants, 3482
North Dakota Council on Arts Support Grants, 3496
Northern New York Community Fndn Grants, 3503
Northern Trust Company Corp Giving Program, 3504
NYSCA Arts Educ Program Support Grants, 3579
NYSCA Arts Educ: K-12 In-School Grants, 3580
NYSCA Arts Education: Local Capacity Building Grants, 3581
NYSCA Arts Educ: Services to the Field Grants, 3582
NYSCA Dance Gen Program Support Grants, 3585
NYSCA Folk Arts: Exhibitions Grants, 3594
NYSCA Folk Arts: General Program Support, 3595
NYSCA Folk Arts: Presentation Grants, 3596
NYSCA Folk Arts: Regional and County Folk Arts Grants, 3597
NYSCA Museum Program Support Grants, 3603
NYSCA Special Arts Services: General Program Support Grants, 3615
NYSCA Special Arts Services: Instruction and Training Grants, 3616
NYSCA State and Local Partnerships: General Program Support Grants, 3620
NYSCA State and Local Partnerships: Services to the Field Grants, 3621
NYSCA State and Local Partnerships: Workshops Grants, 3622
NYSCA Theatre General Program Support, 3624
NYSCA Theatre: Services to the Field Grants, 3626
NYSCA Visual Arts: Exhibitions and Installations Grants, 3627
NYSCA Visual Arts: General Operating Support, 3628
NYSCA Visual Arts: General Program Support, 3629
NYSCA Visual Arts: Services to the Field Grants, 3630
Ogden Codman Grants, 3641
Ohio Arts Council Capacity Building Grants for Organizations and Communities, 3652
Oklahoma City Community Programs & Grants, 3666
Oleonda Jameson Grants, 3667
Onan Family Fndn Grants, 3672
Oppenstein Brothers Fndn Grants, 3685
Owens Corning Fndn Grants, 3717
PACCAR Fndn Grants, 3719
Palm Beach and Martin Counties Grants, 3733
Parkersburg Area Comm Fndn Action Grants, 3738
Patrick and Aimee Butler Family Fndn Community Arts and Humanities Grants, 3747
Paul V. Sherlock Center on Disabilities Access for All Abilities Mini Grants, 3767
PCA Arts Organizations and Arts Programs Grants for Arts Service Organizations, 3777
PCA Arts Organizations and Arts Programs Grants for Local Arts, 3782
PCA Busing Grants, 3786
PCA Entry Track Arts Organizations and Program Grants for Arts Service Organizations, 3789
PCA Entry Track Arts Organizations and Program Grants for Local Arts, 3794
PCA Entry Track Arts Organizations and Program Grants for Theatre, 3797
Percy B. Ferebee Endowment Grants, 3820
Perkins Charitable Fndn Grants, 3823
Peter Kiewit Fndn General Grants, 3845
Peter Kiewit Fndn Small Grants, 3847
Pew Charitable Trusts Arts and Culture Grants, 3857
Peyton Anderson Fndn Grants, 3862
PGE Fndn Grants, 3869
Phelps County Community Fndn Grants, 3870
Philadelphia Organizational Effectiveness Grants, 3872
Philip L. Graham Grants, 3876
Phoenix Suns Charities Grants, 3881
Piper Jaffray Fndn Communities Giving Grants, 3899
Piper Trust Arts and Culture Grants, 3900
Pittsburgh Fndn Community Grants, 3910
Plum Creek Fndn Grants, 3917
PNC Fndn Grow Up Great Grants, 3924
Polk Bros. Fndn Grants, 3929
Pollock Fndn Grants, 3930
Porter County Community Fndn Grants, 3931
Prince Charitable Trusts Chicago Grants, 3959
Prince Charitable Trusts D.C. Grants, 3960
Prince Charitable Trusts Rhode Island Grants, 3961
Principal Financial Group Fndn Grants, 3966
Procter and Gamble Grants, 3967
Puerto Rico Community Fndn Grants, 3986
Putnam Fndn Grants, 3991
Qualcomm Grants, 3993
R.C. Baker Fndn Grants, 3999
Rainbow Endowment Grants, 4007
Ralph M. Parsons Fndn Grants, 4013
Ralphs Food 4 Less Fndn Grants, 4014
Rancho Bernardo Community Fndn Grants, 4015
Rasmuson Fndn Capital Grants, 4020
RCF General Community Grants, 4032
Reinberger Fndn Grants, 4052
Richard and Rhoda Goldman Grants, 4077
Richard and Susan Smith Family Fndn Grants, 4078
Richard H. Driehaus Fndn Grants, 4084
Richard H. Driehaus Fndn MacArthur Fund for Arts and Culture, 4085
Richard King Mellon Fndn Grants, 4087
Rich Fndn Grants, 4090
Riley Fndn Grants, 4094
Robert B McMillen Fndn Grants, 4106
Robert G. Cabell III and Maude Morgan Cabell Fndn Grants, 4113
Robert W. Woodruff Fndn Grants, 4124
Robins Fndn Grants, 4126
Rochester Area Community Fndn Grants, 4127
Rochester Area Fndn Grants, 4128
Rockefeller Brothers Charles E. Culpeper Arts and Culture Grants in New York City, 4129
Rockefeller Brothers Democratic Practice Grants, 4131
Rockefeller Brothers Peace and Security Grants, 4133
Rockefeller Brothers Pivotal Places Grants: Serbia, Montenegro, and Kosova, 4135
Rockefeller Brothers Sustainable Devel Grants, 4136
Rockefeller Fndn Grants, 4138
Rockwell Int'l Corp Grants, 4141
Roger L. and Agnes C. Dell Charitable Grants, 4143
Rollin M. Gerstacker Fndn Grants, 4146
Ross Fndn Grants, 4164
Roy and Christine Sturgis Charitable Grants, 4166
Ruth Anderson Fndn Grants, 4176
Ryder System Charitable Fndn Grants, 4191
S. Livingston Mather Charitable Grants, 4200
S. Spencer Scott Grants, 4202
Sage Fndn Grants, 4204
Saint Paul Companies Fndn Grants, 4217
Saint Paul Fndn Grants, 4219
San Antonio Area Fndn Grants, 4240
San Diego Fndn Arts & Culture Grants, 4243
San Francisco Fndn Faith Program and Arts and Culture Program, 4267
Santa Barbara Fndn Towbes Fund for the Performing Arts Grants, 4288
Sarah Scaife Fndn Grants, 4295
Sara Lee Fndn Grants, 4296
Sarkeys Fndn Grants, 4297
Schering-Plough Fndn Community Inits Grants, 4303
Schlessman Family Fndn Grants, 4307
Schurz Communications Fndn Grants, 4312
Scott B. and Annie P. Appleby Charitable Grants, 4313
Scott County Community Fndn Grants, 4314
Seabury Fndn Grants, 4316
Seagate Tech Corp Capacity to Care Grants, 4317
Seattle Fndn Arts and Culture Grants, 4320
Seaver Institute Grants, 4331
Self Fndn Grants, 4335
Shell Oil Company Fndn Grants, 4343
Siragusa Fndn Arts & Culture Grants, 4367
Skaggs Fndn Grants, 4378
Social Justice Fund NW General Grants, 4397
Sonoco Fndn Grants, 4403
Sonora Area Fndn Competitive Grants, 4404
Sony Corp of America Corp Philanthropy Grants, 4405
Sosland Fndn Grants, 4408
South Carolina Arts Commission Annual Operating Support for Organizations Grants, 4414
South Carolina Arts Commission Cultural Tourism Init Grants, 4419
South Carolina Arts Commission Cultural Visions Grants, 4420
South Carolina Arts Commission Folklife & Traditional Arts Grants, 4421
South Carolina Arts Commission Traditional Arts Apprenticeship Grants, 4427
SW Florida Community Competitive Grants, 4442
SW Gas Corp Fndn Grants, 4445
Spencer County Community Fndn Grants, 4451
Sprague Fndn Grants, 4461
Sprint Fndn Grants, 4463
Square D Fndn Grants, 4464
Stackpole-Hall Fndn Grants, 4472
Starr Fndn Grants, 4483
Stewart Huston Charitable Grants, 4505
Stockton Rush Bartol Fndn Grants, 4508
Strake Fndn Grants, 4511
Stranahan Fndn Grants, 4512
Summit Fndn Grants, 4524
Sunderland Fndn Grants, 4527
Sunoco Fndn Grants, 4530
Target Fndn Grants, 4562
Tauck Family Fndn Grants, 4563
Taylor S. Abernathy and Patti Harding Abernathy Charitable Grants, 4564
TCF Bank Fndn Grants, 4565
TE Fndn Grants, 4572
Telluride Fndn Community Grants, 4573
Tension Envelope Fndn Grants, 4578
Texas Instruments Corp Arts and Culture Grants, 4596
Texas Instruments Fndn Arts and Culture Grants, 4599
Theodore Edson Parker Fndn Grants, 4605
Third Millennium Fndn Grants, 4607
Thomas B. & Elizabeth M. Sheridan Grants, 4614
Thomas C. Ackerman Fndn Grants, 4615
Thomas J. Long Fndn Community Grants, 4618
Thomas W. Briggs Fndn Grants, 4621
Thornton Fndn Grants, 4624
Tides Fndn Grants, 4632
TJX Fndn Grants, 4637
Tom's of Maine Grants, 4640

SUBJECT INDEX   Cultural Heritage / 861

Topeka Community Fndn Grants, 4644
Topeka West Rotary Youth Enrichment Grants, 4645
Tri-State Community Twenty-first Century Endowment Grants, 4666
Triangle Community Fndn Community Grants, 4667
Turner Voices Corp Contributions, 4682
U.S. Bank Fndn Grants, 4686
U.S. Department of Educ 21st Century Community Learning Centers, 4687
Union Bank, N.A. Fndn Grants, 4709
Union Pacific Fndn Community and Civic Grants, 4714
United Technologies Corp Grants, 4725
US Airways Community Contributions, 4788
US Airways Community Fndn Grants, 4789
USDC Technology Opportunities Grants, 4860
Valerie Adams Memorial Charitable Grants, 4898
Vancouver Fndn Grants & Comm Inits, 4900
Vectren Fndn Grants, 4907
Viacom Fndn Grants (Formerly CBS Fndn), 4932
Virginia Fndn for Humanities Discr Grants, 4946
Virginia Fndn for the Humanities Open Grants, 4947
Virginia Historical Society Research Fellowships, 4949
Wallace Alexander Gerbode Fndn Grants, 4974
Walt Disney Company Fndn Grants, 4981
Washington County Community Youth Grants, 4998
Wayne County Fndn Vigran Family Grants, 5004
Wayne County Fndn Grants, 5005
Western Indiana Community Fndn Grants, 5024
Weyerhaeuser Company Fndn Grants, 5053
Widgeon Point Charitable Fndn Grants, 5064
William B. Stokely Jr. Fndn Grants, 5076
William Blair and Company Fndn Grants, 5078
William G. Baker, Jr. Grants, 5081
William J. and Dorothy K. O'Neill Fndn Grants, 5087
Winston-Salem Fndn Competitive Grants, 5102
Xcel Energy Fndn Grants, 5121
Xerox Fndn Grants, 5122
Yellow Corp Fndn Grants, 5126

Cultural Diversity
ACF Preferred Communities Grants, 124
Ackerman Fndn Grants, 129
Aetna Fndn Diversity Grants in Connecticut, 182
Akonadi Fndn Anti-Racism Grants, 217
ALA Supporting Diversity Stipend, 333
Alcoa Fndn Grants, 350
ALFJ Astraea U.S. General Fund, 362
American Express Historic Preservation Grants, 431
American Society on Aging NOMA Award for Excellence in Multicultural Aging, 449
Andy Warhol Fndn for the Visual Arts Grants, 464
Arcus Fndn Grants, 529
Arcus Fndn Gay and Lesbian Grants, 530
Arcus Fndn National Grants, 531
Aspen Community Fndn Grants, 592
AT&T Fndn Civic and Comm Service Grants, 599
Blue Cross Blue Shield of Minnesota Healthy Neighborhoods: Connect Grants, 798
California Arts Council State Networks Grants, 897
California Arts Council Tech Assistance Grants, 898
California Endowment Innovative Ideas Challenge Grants, 904
Cargill Citizenship Fund-Corp Giving Grants, 925
Central Minnesota Community Fndn Grants, 995
Charles Parker Trust for Public Music Grants, 1053
Chicago Community Trust Arts and Culture Grants: Improving Access to Arts Learning Opps, 1082
Chicago Community Trust Arts and Culture Grants: Supporting Diverse Arts Productions and Fostering Art in Every Community, 1084
Chicago Tribune Fndn Grants for Cultural Organizations, 1101
Comcast Fndn Grants, 1235
Community Fndn of Greater Fort Wayne - John S. and James L. Knight Fndn Donor-Advised Grants, 1287
Community Fndn of Greater Greensboro Grants, 1288
Con Edison Corp Arts and Culture Grants, 1344
Connecticut Commission on the Arts Art in Public Spaces, 1349
Cultural Society of Filipino Americans Grants, 1412

Delta Air Lines Prize for Global Understanding, 1495
EQT Fndn Art and Culture Grants, 1743
EQT Fndn Community Grants, 1744
First People's Fund Community Spirit Awards, 1825
Fndn for the Carolinas Grants, 1896
George Fndn Grants, 2018
Girl's Best Friend Fndn Grants, 2057
Henry County Community Fndn Grants, 2308
Indianapolis Power & Light Company Community Grants, 2540
John S. and James L. Knight Fndn Grants, 2713
Kalamazoo Community Good Neighbor Grants, 2768
Kansas Arts Commission Artist Fellowships, 2776
Koret Fndn Grants, 2837
Kroger Fndn Diversity Grants, 2842
Laidlaw Fndn Youth Organizaing Inits Grants, 2854
Laura Jane Musser Intercultural Harmony Grants, 2862
Lillian S. Wells Fndn Grants, 2901
Massachusetts Cultural Adams Arts Grants, 3052
Minnesota State Arts Board Cultural Community Partnership Grants, 3188
Mix It Up Grants, 3191
Motorola Fndn Grants, 3221
Nathan Cummings Fndn Grants, 3246
National Endowment for Arts Our Town Grants, 3257
National Endowment for the Arts - Regional Partnership Agreement Grants, 3258
National Endowment for Arts Big Read Grants, 3261
Nellie Mae Educ Fndn District-Level Grants, 3297
NJSCA Folk Arts Apprenticeships, 3448
Noble County Community Fndn Celebrate Diversity Project Grants, 3455
Noble County Community Fndn Grants, 3456
North Carolina Arts Council Outreach Grants, 3479
NYSCA Museum General Operating Support, 3602
NYSCA Presenting: General Operating Support, 3609
NYSCA Special Arts Services: General Operating Support Grants, 3614
NYSCA Theatre General Program Support, 3624
NYSCA Visual Arts: General Operating Support, 3628
Open Meadows Fndn Grants, 3683
PCA Arts Organizations and Arts Programs Grants for Arts Educ Organizations, 3776
PCA Arts Organizations & Grants for Lit, 3781
PCA Entry Track Arts Organizations and Program Grants for Arts Educ Organizations, 3788
Philadelphia Organizational Effectiveness Grants, 3872
Piper Trust Arts and Culture Grants, 3900
Pittsburgh Fndn Community Grants, 3910
Portland General Electric Fndn Grants, 3937
Prudential Fndn Arts and Culture Grants, 3975
Reynolds American Fndn Grants, 4068
RISCA Project Grants for Organizations, Individuals and Educ, 4100
Rockefeller Fndn Partnerships Affirming Community Transformation Grants, 4139
Seabury Fndn Grants, 4316
Sioux Falls Area Community Grants, 4364
Sioux Falls Area Community Fndn Spot Grants, 4366
Social Justice Fund NW Criminal Justice Giving Project Grants, 4394
South Carolina Arts Commission Folklife & Traditional Arts Grants, 4421
Southern Minnesota Init Grants, 4437
Subaru of America Fndn Grants, 4518
Teaching Tolerance Grants, 4567
Third Millennium Fndn Grants, 4607
USTA Althea Gibson Leadership Awards, 4872
USTA Multicultural Excellence Grants, 4876
USTA Okechi Womeodu Scholar Athlete Grants, 4880
Vancouver Fndn Grants & Comm Inits, 4900
Wallace Fndn Grants, 4976
Washington County Community Youth Grants, 4998
Whirlpool Fndn Grants, 5056
Women's Funding Alliance Grants, 5112

Cultural Heritage
Abell Fndn Arts and Culture Grants, 92
Adobe Art and Culture Grants, 167
Adolph Coors Fndn Grants, 171

Aetna Fndn Arts Grants in Connecticut, 181
African American Heritage Grants, 193
Alaska State Council on Arts Operating Support, 328
Amer-Scandinavian Fndn Public Project Grants, 419
Americana Fndn Grants, 422
Appalachian Regional Commission Tourist Development Grants, 511
Arts and Science Council Grants, 576
Bay and Paul Fndns, Inc Grants, 692
Central Minnesota Community Fndn Grants, 995
Central Okanagan Fndn Grants, 997
Charlotte County (FL) Community Fndn Grants, 1056
Chicago Community Arts Assistance Grants, 1081
CICF Efroymson Grants, 1120
Columbus Fndn John W. and Edna McManus Shepard Grants, 1223
Con Edison Corp Arts and Culture Grants, 1344
Cultural Society of Filipino Americans Grants, 1412
Daviess County Community Fndn Arts and Culture Grants, 1455
Dayton Fndn Grants, 1463
Delta Air Lines Prize for Global Understanding, 1495
Dorot Fndn Grants, 1586
DTE Energy Fndn Diversity Grants, 1611
EQT Fndn Art and Culture Grants, 1743
First People's Fund Community Spirit Awards, 1825
Garland and Agnes Taylor Gray Fndn Grants, 1988
Giving Sum Annual Grant, 2058
GNOF IMPACT Grants for Arts and Culture, 2078
Hawaii Community Fndn Reverend Takie Okumura Family Grants, 2264
Historic Landmarks Fndn of Indiana Historic Preservation Educ Grants, 2334
Historic Landmarks Legal Defense Grants, 2338
Homer Fndn Grants, 2352
Huntington County Community Fndn - Hiner Family Grant, 2405
Infinity Fndn Grants, 2553
Jane Bradley Pettit Fndn Arts and Culture Grants, 2641
Japan Fndn Los Angeles Mini-Grants for Japanese Arts & Culture, 2651
Japan Fndn New York Grants for Arts & Culture, 2652
Jewish Funds for Justice Grants, 2676
Judith and Jean Pape Adams Charitable Fndn Tulsa Area Grants, 2755
Kansas Arts Commission Artist Fellowships, 2776
Leon and Thea Koerner Fndn Grants, 2883
Lotus 88 Fndn for Women and Children Grants, 2921
Lubrizol Corp Community Grants, 2932
Marion County Historic Preservation Grants, 3016
MARPAT Fndn Grants, 3023
Mary K. Chapman Fndn Grants, 3042
Massachusetts Cultural Adams Arts Grants, 3052
Massachusetts Cultural Council Local Cultural Council Grants, 3057
Maurice Amado Fndn Grants, 3063
Minnesota State Arts Board Cultural Community Partnership Grants, 3188
NEH Preservation Assistance Grants for Smaller Institutions, 3293
Nellie Mae Educ Fndn District-Level Grants, 3297
Nevada Arts Council Folklife Opps Grants, 3310
NIAF Italian Culture and Heritage Grants, 3432
NJSCA Folk Arts Apprenticeships, 3448
North Carolina Arts Council Folklife Documentary Project Grants, 3475
Nu Skin Force for Good Fndn Grants, 3536
NYSCA Folk Arts: Exhibitions Grants, 3594
NYSCA Folk Arts: General Program Support, 3595
NYSCA Folk Arts: Presentation Grants, 3596
NYSCA Folk Arts: Regional and County Folk Arts Grants, 3597
NYSCA Museum General Operating Support, 3602
NYSCA Museum Program Support Grants, 3603
NYSCA Special Arts Services: General Program Support Grants, 3615
NYSCA Special Arts Services: Instruction and Training Grants, 3616
NYSCA State and Local Partnerships: General Program Support Grants, 3620

862 / Cultural Heritage

NYSCA Visual Arts: Services to the Field Grants, 3630
PCA Arts Organizations and Arts Programs Grants for Art Museums, 3775
PCA Entry Track Arts Organizations and Program Grants for Art Museums, 3787
Righteous Persons Fndn Grants, 4093
Rockefeller Brothers Charles E. Culpeper Arts and Culture Grants in New York City, 4129
Schering-Plough Fndn Community Inits Grants, 4303
South Carolina Arts Commission Folklife & Traditional Arts Grants, 4421
South Carolina Arts Commission Traditional Arts Apprenticeship Grants, 4427
Suffolk County Office of Film and Cultural Affairs Cultural Arts Grants, 4521
Virginia Fndn for Humanities Discr Grants, 4946
Virginia Fndn for the Humanities Open Grants, 4947
Virginia Historical Society Research Fellowships, 4949
W.M. Keck Fndn Southern California Grants, 4964
Wabash River Heritage Corridor Grants, 4970
Walter and Elise Haas Grants, 4982
West Virginia Commission on the Arts Challenge America Partnership Grants, 5031
William G. Baker, Jr. Grants, 5081
Winston-Salem Fndn Stokes County Grants, 5104

Cultural Identity
CICF Efroymson Grants, 1120
Columbus John W. & Edna Shepard Grants, 1223
Con Edison Corp Arts and Culture Grants, 1344
Cultural Society of Filipino Americans Grants, 1412
Delta Air Lines Prize for Global Understanding, 1495
DTE Energy Fndn Diversity Grants, 1611
EQT Fndn Art and Culture Grants, 1743
First People's Fund Community Spirit Awards, 1825
Homer Fndn Grants, 2352
James & Abigail Campbell Family Fndn Grants, 2620
Jewish Community Fndn of LA Israel Grants, 2674
Laura Jane Musser Intercultural Harmony Grants, 2862
Lois and Richard England Family Fndn Jewish Community Life Grants, 2919
NJSCA Folk Arts Apprenticeships, 3448
NYSCA Folk Arts: General Program Support, 3595
NYSCA Special Arts Services: General Program Support Grants, 3615
NYSCA Special Arts Services: Instruction and Training Grants, 3616
NYSCA State and Local Partnerships: General Program Support Grants, 3620
NYSCA State and Local Partnerships: Services to the Field Grants, 3621
NYSCA Visual Arts: Services to the Field Grants, 3630
Triangle Community Fndn Community Grants, 4667
Virginia Fndn for Humanities Discr Grants, 4946
Virginia Fndn for the Humanities Open Grants, 4947
Virginia Historical Society Research Fellowships, 4949
W.M. Keck Fndn Southern California Grants, 4964
WILD Fndn Grants, 5068

Cultural Outreach
2 Depot Square Ipswich Charitable Fndn Grants, 4
3M Company Arts and Culture Grants, 12
3M Fndn Community Giving Grants, 15
Abell Fndn Arts and Culture Grants, 92
Abney Fndn Grants, 105
Adobe Art and Culture Grants, 167
Akonadi Fndn Anti-Racism Grants, 217
Alabama State Council on the Arts Collaborative Ventures Grants, 235
Alabama State Council on the Arts Operating Support Grants, 244
Alabama State Council on the Arts Program Development Grants, 246
Alabama State Council on Arts Project Assistance, 247
Alabama State Council on the Arts Projects of Individual Artists Grants, 248
ALA Donald G. Davis Article Award, 269
ALA Writers Live at the Library Grants, 336
Alexander & Baldwin Fndn Hawaiian and Pacific Island Grants, 352

Alexander & Baldwin Fndn Mainland Grants, 353
ALFJ Astraea U.S. General Fund, 362
Altria Group Arts and Culture Grants, 399
Andrew Goodman Fndn Grants, 463
Anheuser-Busch Fndn Grants, 470
Anna Fitch Ardenghi Grants, 472
Annie Sinclair Knudsen Memorial Fund/Kaua'i Community Grants, 482
Appalachian Regional Commission Tourist Development Grants, 511
Arcus Fndn Grants, 529
Arcus Fndn Gay and Lesbian Grants, 530
Arcus Fndn National Grants, 531
ArtsWave Impact Grants, 580
ArtsWave Project Grants, 581
Avista Fndn Grants, 624
Avon Products Fndn Grants, 625
Ball Brothers Fndn General Grants, 637
Barnes Group Fndn Grants, 672
Baxter Int'l Fndn Grants, 691
Bayer Fndn Grants, 696
Benton County Fndn Grants, 731
Bernard & Audre Rapoport Arts & Culture Grant, 735
Biogen Corp Giving Grants, 773
Blandin Fndn Itasca County Area Vitality Grants, 789
Blue Cross Blue Shield of Minnesota Healthy Neighborhoods: Connect Grants, 798
Bridgestone/Firestone Grants, 836
Brooklyn Community Fndn Community Arts for All Grants, 849
Carl B. and Florence E. King Fndn Grants, 928
CFFVR Clintonville Area Fndn Grants, 1008
Charles H. Price II Family Fndn Grants, 1046
Charles Parker Trust for Public Music Grants, 1053
Chicago Community Arts Assistance Grants, 1081
Chicago Community Trust Arts and Culture Grants: Supporting Diverse Arts Productions and Fostering Art in Every Community, 1084
Chicago Tribune Fndn Grants for Cultural Organizations, 1101
CICF Efroymson Grants, 1120
Cingular Wireless Charitable Contributions, 1134
Clinton County Community Fndn Grants, 1174
CNL Corp Giving Arts & Culture Grants, 1190
Columbus Fndn John W. and Edna McManus Shepard Grants, 1223
Columbus Fndn Robert E. and Genevieve B. Schaefer Grants, 1229
Columbus Fndn Siemer Family Grants, 1231
Comer Fndn Grants, 1236
Community Fndn of Greater Fort Wayne - John S. and James L. Knight Fndn Donor-Advised Grants, 1287
Community Fndn of Greater New Britain Grants, 1291
Community Fndn of Greenville-Greenville Women Giving Grants, 1293
Community Fndn of Howard County Grants, 1297
Community Fndn of the Eastern Shore Community Needs Grants, 1317
Con Edison Corp Arts and Culture Grants, 1344
Corning Fndn Cultural Grants, 1376
Cullen Fndn Grants, 1411
Cultural Society of Filipino Americans Grants, 1412
Cumberland Community Fndn Summertime Kids Grants, 1414
Dade Community Fndn Grants, 1430
Delonne Anderson Family Fndn, 1492
Deluxe Corp Fndn Grants, 1496
Dr. P. Phillips Fndn Grants, 1601
DTE Energy Fndn Diversity Grants, 1611
Edward Bangs Kelley and Elza Kelley Grants, 1665
Eisner Fndn Grants, 1678
El Paso Corp Fndn Grants, 1689
Essex County Community Fndn Merrimack Valley General Grants, 1756
Fairfield County Community Fndn Grants, 1782
Fallon OrNda Community Health Grants, 1783
Family Lit and Hawaii Pizza Hut Lit Fund, 1785
Federal Express Corp Contributions Program, 1799
Fel-Pro Mecklenburger Fndn Grants, 1800
First People's Fund Community Spirit Awards, 1825

Fishman Family Fndn Grants, 1835
Florida Div of Cultural Affairs Media Grants, 1856
Florida Div of Cultural Affairs Touring Grants, 1863
Ford Fndn Diversity Fellowships, 1883
Fred Baldwin Memorial Fndn Grants, 1941
Gannett Fndn Community Action Grants, 1984
Geraldine R. Dodge Fndn Arts Grants, 2040
Good Works Fndn Grants, 2105
Greater Worcester Community Jeppson Memorial Fund for Brookfield Grants, 2141
Group 70 Fndn Fund, 2167
Guy I. Bromley Grants, 2180
H.A. and Mary K. Chapman Charitable Grants, 2182
H.J. Heinz Company Fndn Grants, 2184
Harry Bramhall Gilbert Charitable Grants, 2238
Hartford Fndn Regular Grants, 2253
Hawaii Community Fndn West Hawaii Grants, 2266
Hearst Fndns Culture Grants, 2284
Heartland Arts Fund, 2286
Helen Bader Fndn Grants, 2293
Henry and Ruth Blaustein Rosenberg Grants, 2306
Henry M. Jackson Fndn Grants, 2311
Hershey Company Grants, 2318
Highmark Corp Giving Grants, 2319
Hilton Head Island Fndn Grants, 2330
Homer Fndn Grants, 2352
Horizons Community Issues Grants, 2366
Humana Fndn Grants, 2388
Hutchinson Community Fndn Grants, 2410
Hut Fndn Grants, 2411
IBM Arts and Culture Grants, 2424
Indep Comm Fndn Educ, Culture & Arts Grant, 2526
Indiana Arts Commission American Masterpieces Grants, 2530
Indiana Humanities Council Init Grants, 2539
Infinity Fndn Grants, 2553
Irving S. Gilmore Fndn Grants, 2584
Irvin Stern Fndn Grants, 2585
J. Bulow Campbell Fndn Grants, 2593
Jackson County Community Fndn Grants, 2611
Jacob G. Schmidlapp Grants, 2616
Jacobs Family Village Neighborhoods Grants, 2619
James Ford Bell Fndn Grants, 2623
James Irvine Fndn Creative Connections Grants, 2628
James S. Copley Fndn Grants, 2637
Jane Bradley Pettit Fndn Arts and Culture Grants, 2641
Japan Fndn Center for Global Partnership Grants, 2649
JELD-WEN Fndn Grants, 2661
Jewish Women's Fndn of New York Grants, 2677
Joseph H. and Florence A. Roblee Fndn Grants, 2736
Judith and Jean Pape Adams Charitable Fndn Tulsa Area Grants, 2755
Kahuku Community Fund, 2762
Katrine Menzing Deakins Charitable Grants, 2793
Laidlaw Fndn Youh Organizing Catalyst Grants, 2853
Lana'i Community Benefit Fund, 2857
Land O'Lakes Fndn Community Grants, 2859
Lubrizol Corp Community Grants, 2932
Ludwick Family Fndn Grants, 2938
M.B. and Edna Zale Fndn Grants, 2950
M.J. Murdock Charitable Trust General Grants, 2954
Maine Community Fndn Charity Grants, 2977
Mary Duke Biddle Fndn Grants, 3036
Mary K. Chapman Fndn Grants, 3042
Massachusetts Cultural Council Local Grants, 3057
Massachusetts Fndn for the Humanities Cultural Economic Development Grants, 3059
Max and Anna Levinson Fndn Grants, 3066
Mertz Gilmore Fndn NYC Dance Grants, 3127
Minnesota State Arts Board Cultural Community Partnership Grants, 3188
Montana Arts Council Cultural and Aesthetic Project Grants, 3209
Nathan Cummings Fndn Grants, 3246
National Endowment for the Arts - National Arts and Humanities Youth Program Awards, 3255
National Endowment for Arts Our Town Grants, 3257
National Endowment for Arts Agencies Grants, 3263
National Endowment for Arts Museum Grants, 3265
National Endowment for the Arts Music Grants, 3266

SUBJECT INDEX

Dance / 863

New Earth Fndn Grants, 3317
NJSCA Folk Arts Apprenticeships, 3448
NJSCA Projects Serving Artists Grants, 3450
NYSCA Arts Educ Program Support Grants, 3579
NYSCA Arts Educ: K-12 In-School Grants, 3580
NYSCA Arts Education: Capacity Building Grants, 3581
NYSCA Arts Educ: Services to the Field Grants, 3582
NYSCA Folk Arts: Exhibitions Grants, 3594
NYSCA Folk Arts: General Program Support, 3595
NYSCA Folk Arts: Presentation Grants, 3596
NYSCA Folk Arts: Regional and County Folk Arts Grants, 3597
NYSCA Museum Program Support Grants, 3603
NYSCA Special Arts Services: General Program Support Grants, 3615
NYSCA Special Arts Services: Instruction and Training Grants, 3616
NYSCA State and Local Partnerships: General Program Support Grants, 3620
NYSCA State and Local Partnerships: Services to the Field Grants, 3621
NYSCA State and Local Partnerships: Workshops Grants, 3622
NYSCA Theatre: Services to the Field Grants, 3626
NYSCA Visual Arts: Exhibitions and Installations Grants, 3627
NYSCA Visual Arts: General Program Support, 3629
NYSCA Visual Arts: Services to the Field Grants, 3630
PCA Art Organizations and Art Programs Grants for Presenting Organizations, 3771
PCA Arts Organizations and Arts Programs Grants for Arts Educ Organizations, 3776
PCA Arts Organizations & Grants for Crafts, 3778
PCA Arts Organizations & Grants for Dance, 3779
PCA Arts Organizations & Grants for Lit, 3781
PCA Arts Organizations and Arts Programs Grants for Local Arts, 3782
PCA Arts Organizations & Grants for Theatre, 3783
PCA Arts Organizations and Arts Programs Grants for Traditional and Folk Arts, 3784
PCA Arts Organizations & Grants for Visual Arts, 3785
PCA Entry Track Arts Organizations and Program Grants for Arts Educ Organizations, 3788
PCA Entry Track Arts Organizations and Program Grants for Crafts, 3790
PCA Entry Track Arts Organizations and Program Grants for Dance, 3791
PCA Entry Track Arts Organizations and Program Grants for Local Arts, 3794
PCA Entry Track Arts Organizations and Program Grants for Presenting Organizations, 3796
PCA Entry Track Arts Organizations and Program Grants for Theatre, 3797
PCA Entry Track Arts Organizations and Program Grants for Traditional and Folk Arts, 3798
PCA Entry Track Arts Organizations and Program Grants for Visual Arts, 3799
Phoenix Coyotes Charities Grants, 3879
Pinellas County Grants, 3891
Piper Trust Arts and Culture Grants, 3900
Progress Energy Corp Contributions Grants, 3968
Qualcomm Grants, 3993
Rancho Bernardo Community Fndn Grants, 4015
Rasmuson Fndn Creative Ventures Grants, 4021
Rasmuson Organizational Advancement Grants, 4023
Richard and Susan Smith Family Fndn Grants, 4078
Rockefeller Brothers Charles E. Culpeper Arts and Culture Grants in New York City, 4129
Salem Fndn Charitable Grants, 4223
Samuel N. and Mary Castle Fndn Grants, 4236
Santa Barbara Fndn Towbes Fund for the Performing Arts Grants, 4288
Sorenson Legacy Fndn Grants, 4407
Southbury Community Trust Fund, 4409
Sprint Fndn Grants, 4463
Suffolk County Office of Film and Cultural Affairs Cultural Arts Grants, 4521
TAC Touring Arts and Arts Access Grants, 4557
Teaching Tolerance Grants, 4567
Textron Corp Contributions Grants, 4601

Thomas J. Long Fndn Community Grants, 4618
Trull Fndn Grants, 4673
Union Benevolent Association Grants, 4710
Valerie Adams Memorial Charitable Grants, 4898
Virginia Fndn for Humanities Discr Grants, 4946
Virginia Fndn for the Humanities Open Grants, 4947
W.C. Griffith Fndn Grants, 4957
Wallace Alexander Gerbode Fndn Grants, 4974
Washington County Community Youth Grants, 4998
Whirlpool Fndn Grants, 5056

Curriculum Development
A.O. Smith Community Grants, 46
Adobe Art and Culture Grants, 167
Adobe Community Investment Grants, 168
ALA Information Technology Pathfinder Award, 286
ALA Sara Jaffarian School Library Award for Exemplary Humanities Programming, 316
ALZA Corp Contributions Grants, 405
Amgen Fndn Grants, 456
Arizona Commission on the Arts Educ Grants, 536
Arkansas Arts Council AIE Mini Grants, 554
Bayer Fndn Grants, 696
Bernard F. and Alva B. Gimbel Fndn Grants, 740
Best Buy Children's Fndn @15 Teach Awards, 751
Beverley Taylor Sorenson Art Works for Kids, 757
Booth Ferris Fndn Grants, 816
Bowling Green Community Fndn Grants, 824
Cambridge Community Fndn Grants, 913
Carnahan-Jackson Fndn Grants, 939
Caroline Lawson Ivey Memorial Fndn Grants, 941
CenterPointEnergy Minnegasco Grants, 993
Christensen Fund Regional Grants, 1112
Citigroup Fndn Grants, 1139
Crail-Johnson Fndn Grants, 1393
CTCNet/Youth Visions for Stronger Neighborhoods Grants, 1409
Delonne Anderson Family Fndn, 1492
District of Columbia Commission on the Arts-Arts Educ Teacher Mini-Grants, 1549
Dorr Fndn Grants, 1591
EDS Technology Grants, 1662
EPA Environmental Educ Grants, 1729
Family Lit and Hawaii Pizza Hut Lit Fund, 1785
Ford Motor Company Grants, 1885
Fndn for the Mid South Educ Grants, 1898
George I. Alden Grants, 2023
GlaxoSmithKline Corp Grants, 2060
Huntington Arts Council Arts-in-Educ Grants, 2400
ICC Faculty Fellowships, 2428
ICC Scholarship of Engagement Faculty Grants, 2430
Indiana Rural Capacity Grants, 2547
Jennings County Community Fndn Grants, 2664
Ka Papa O Kakuhihewa Fund, 2785
Kiki Madazine Grow Strong Girls through Leadership Grants, 2822
Leave No Trace Master Educator Scholarships, 2870
Louis R. Cappelli Fndn Grants, 2926
Lowe's Outdoor Classroom Grants, 2928
Lynde and Harry Bradley Fndn Grants, 2947
Lynde and Harry Bradley Fndn Prizes, 2948
M3C Fellowships, 2955
Meadows Fndn Grants, 3104
Melinda Gray Ardia Environmental Fndn Grants, 3114
Meyer Fndn Educ Grants, 3142
Microsoft Comm Affairs Puget Sound Grants, 3163
NACC William Diaz Fellowships, 3236
NAGC Masters and Specialists Award, 3237
National Home Library Fndn Grants, 3276
New Jersey Office of Faith Based Inits English as a Second Language Grants, 3332
NGA Hansen's Natural and Native School Garden Grants, 3402
NGA Midwest School Garden Grants, 3407
North Carolina Arts Council Arts in Educ Artist Residencies Grants, 3468
North Carolina Arts Council Ed Grants, 3469
North Carolina Arts Council Arts in Educ Rural Development Grants, 3470
NRA Fndn Grants, 3517

NYSCA Arts Educ: Community-based Learning Grants, 3577
NYSCA Arts Educ: General Operating Support, 3578
NYSCA Arts Educ Program Support Grants, 3579
NYSCA Arts Educ: K-12 In-School Grants, 3580
NYSCA Arts Ed Local Capacity Building Grants, 3581
NYSCA Arts Educ: Services to the Field Grants, 3582
Ohio Arts Council Artist Express Grants, 3643
Ohio Arts Council Arts Partnership Grants, 3650
Paul and Mary Haas Fndn Contributions and Student Scholarships, 3756
Pew Charitable Trusts Arts and Culture Grants, 3857
Piedmont Natural Gas Fndn Environmental Stewardship and Energy Sustainability Grant, 3884
Polk Bros. Fndn Grants, 3929
Procter and Gamble Grants, 3967
Public Educ Power Grants, 3981
Pulte Homes Corp Contributions, 3989
Randall L. Tobias Fndn Grants, 4017
Rathmann Family Fndn Grants, 4026
Righteous Persons Fndn Grants, 4093
Samuel S. Fels Grants, 4238
SAS Institute Community Relations Donations, 4300
Silicon Valley Community Fndn Educ Grants, 4356
Sorenson Legacy Fndn Grants, 4407
South Madison Community Fndn Grants, 4440
State Justice Institute Curriculum Adaptation and Training Grants, 4488
State Justice Institute Partner Grants, 4489
State Justice Institute Project Grants, 4490
State Justice Institute Strategic Init Grants, 4492
State Justice Institute Tech Assistance Grants, 4493
Stuart Fndn Grants, 4516
Subaru Adopt a School Garden Grants, 4517
Sun Academic Excellence Grants, 4525
SVP Early Childhood Development and Parenting Grants, 4538
Target Corp Local Store Grants, 4561
Teaching Tolerance Grants, 4567
USDA Hispanic-Serving Insts Educ Grants, 4813
USGA Fndn For the Good of the Game Grants, 4868
Vancouver Fndn Grants & Comm Inits, 4900
Vectren Fndn Grants, 4907
Verizon Fndn Maine Grants, 4916
Wege Fndn Grants, 5017
Western Indiana Community Fndn Grants, 5024
West Virginia Commission on the Arts Long-Term Artist Residencies, 5037
Weyerhaeuser Company Fndn Grants, 5053
William McCaskey Chapman and Adaline Dinsmore Chapman Fndn Grants, 5092
YSA State Farm Good Neighbor YOUth In The Driver Seat Grants, 5141

Cystic Fibrosis
Robert R. Meyer Fndn Grants, 4121
Ryder System Charitable Fndn Grants, 4191

DNA
Motorola Fndn Grants, 3221

Dance
Achelis Fndn Grants, 127
Actors Fund Dancers' Resource, 137
Alabama State Council on the Arts Collaborative Ventures Grants, 235
Alabama State Council on the Arts Community Arts Collaborative Ventures Grants, 236
Alabama State Council on the Arts Community Arts Operating Support Grants, 237
Alabama State Council on the Arts Community Arts Presenting Grants, 238
Alabama State Council on the Arts Community Arts Program Development Grants, 239
Alabama State Council on the Arts Community Arts Planning & Design Grants, 241
Alabama State Council on the Arts in Educ Partnership Grants, 242
Alabama State Council on the Arts Multi-Discipline and Festival Grants, 243

Dance

Alabama State Council Arts Presenting Grants, 245
Alabama State Council on the Arts Program Development Grants, 246
Alabama State Council on the Arts Project Assistance Grants, 247
Alabama State Council on the Arts Projects of Individual Artists Grants, 248
Alaska State Council on the Arts Community Arts Development Grants, 327
Alaska State Council on the Arts Operating Support Grants, 328
Altria Group Arts and Culture Grants, 399
Alvin and Lucy Owsley Fndn Grants, 404
Arkansas Arts Council AIE After School/Summer Residency Grants, 551
Arkansas Arts Council AIE In-School Residency, 553
Arts Midwest Performing Arts Grants, 579
Bodman Fndn Grants, 807
Carnahan-Jackson Fndn Grants, 939
Chicago Tribune Fndn Grants for Cultural Organizations, 1101
CICF Clare Noyes Grant, 1119
City of Oakland Cultural Arts Dept Grants, 1142
Community Fndn of Western N Carolina Grants, 1327
Conseil des arts de Montreal Touring Grants, 1358
CONSOL Coal Group Grants, 1360
Cooke Fndn Grants, 1368
Creative Work Grants, 1396
Crystelle Waggoner Charitable Grants, 1405
Dance Advance Grants, 1441
Dept of Ed Recreational Services for Individuals with Disabilities, 1512
Doris Duke Charitable Fndn Arts Grants, 1584
Emma A. Sheafer Charitable Grants, 1699
Flinn Fndn Grants, 1842
Florida Div of Cultural Affairs Dance Grants, 1850
Florida Div of Cultural Affairs General Program Support Grants, 1854
Florida Div of Cultural Affairs Multidisciplinary Grants, 1857
Gateway Fndn Grants, 1992
Georgia Council for the Arts Partner Grants for Organizations, 2035
Georgia Council for the Arts Partner Grants for Service Organizations, 2036
HAF Arts and Culture: Lynne and Bob Wells Grant for Performing Artists, 2190
Hahl Proctor Charitable Grants, 2208
Hyde Family Fndns Grants, 2414
Illinois Arts Council Dance Grants, 2467
Iowa Arts Council Artists in Schools/Communities Residency Grants, 2571
Jerome Fndn Grants, 2667
Jerome Fndn Travel and Study Grants, 2668
Joyce Awards, 2746
Kansas Arts Commission Artist Fellowships, 2776
Kenneth T. and Eileen L. Norris Fndn Grants, 2802
Leon and Thea Koerner Fndn Grants, 2883
MacArthur Fndn Chicago Arts and Culture General Operations Grants, 2961
Mary Duke Biddle Fndn Grants, 3036
Massachusetts Cultural Adams Arts Grants, 3052
Mertz Gilmore Fndn NYC Dance Grants, 3127
Minnesota State Arts Board Cultural Community Partnership Grants, 3188
National Endowment for the Arts - National Arts and Humanities Youth Program Awards, 3255
National Endowment for the Arts Dance Grants: Art Works, 3262
National Endowment for Arts Media Grants, 3264
National Endowment for the Arts Presenting Grants: Art Works, 3268
Nevada Arts Council Folklife Opps Grants, 3310
NHSCA Artist Residencies in Schools Grants, 3423
NHSCA Youth Arts Project Grants: For Extended Arts Learning, 3430
NJSCA Arts Project Support, 3446
NJSCA Folk Arts Apprenticeships, 3448
NJSCA General Program Support Grants, 3449
North Carolina Arts Council Gen Support, 3477
NYFA Building Up Infrastructure Levels for Dance Grants, 3563
NYSCA Dance: Commissions Grants, 3583
NYSCA Dance Gen Operating Support Grants, 3584
NYSCA Dance Gen Program Support Grants, 3585
NYSCA Dance: Long-Term Residency in New York State Grants, 3586
NYSCA Dance: Services to the Field Grants, 3587
NYSCA Presenting: Operating Support Grants, 3609
NYSCA Special Art Services Project Support, 3613
NYSCA Special Arts Services: Professional Performances Grants, 3617
Ontario Arts Council Integrated Arts Grants, 3678
Paul and Edith Babson Fndn Grants, 3755
PCA Arts in Educ Residencies, 3772
PCA Arts Organizations & Grants for Dance, 3779
PCA Entry Track Arts Organizations and Program Grants for Dance, 3791
PCA Strategies for Success Grants - Advanced, 3804
PCA Strategies for Success Grants - Basic Level, 3805
PCA Strategies for Success Grants - Intermediate, 3806
PennPAT Artist Technical Assistance Grants, 3811
PennPAT Strategic Opportunity Grants, 3815
Procter and Gamble Grants, 3967
Puerto Rico Community Fndn Grants, 3986
Richard D. Bass Fndn Grants, 4079
Richard H. Driehaus Fndn Grants, 4084
Richard H. Driehaus Fndn Small Theater and Dance Grants, 4086
Roberta Leventhal Sudakoff Fndn Grants, 4102
Robert R. Meyer Fndn Grants, 4121
Ruth Mott Fndn Grants, 4180
San Francisco Fndn Fund For Artists Award For Choreographers, 4270
Sid W. Richardson Fndn Grants, 4350
Sioux Falls Area Community Grants, 4364
Sioux Falls Area Community Fndn Spot Grants, 4366
Southbury Community Trust Fund, 4409
South Carolina Arts Comm Accessibility Grants, 4410
South Carolina Arts Commission American Masterpieces in South Carolina Grants, 4413
South Carolina Arts Commission Fellowships, 4415
Third Millennium Fndn Grants, 4607
Union Square Arts Award, 4716
Wallace Alexander Gerbode Fndn Special Grants, 4975
Wallace Fndn Grants, 4976

Dance Education

CICF Clare Noyes Grant, 1119
Florida Div of Cultural Affairs Dance Grants, 1850
Green Fndn Educ Grants, 2153
Leon and Thea Koerner Fndn Grants, 2883
National Endowment for the Arts Dance Grants: Art Works, 3262
NHSCA Youth Arts Project Grants: For Extended Arts Learning, 3430
NYSCA Dance Gen Operating Support Grants, 3584
NYSCA Dance Gen Program Support Grants, 3585
NYSCA State & Partnerships: Workshops Grants, 3622
Third Millennium Fndn Grants, 4607

Data Analysis

Maddie's Fund Community Shelter Data Grants, 2968
Natonal Endowment for the Arts Research Grants: Art Works, 3286

Databases

ALA Information Technology Pathfinder Award, 286
Chicago Community Poverty Alleviation Grants, 1091
IMLS Native Am Library Services Basic Grants, 2517
IMLS Native American Library Services Enhancement Grants, 2518
Natonal Endowment for the Arts Research Grants: Art Works, 3286
NYSCA Literature: Services to the Field Grants, 3601
Public Safety Fndn of America Grants, 3983
USDJ Nat Criminal History Improvement Grants, 4864
USDJ NICS Act Record Improvement Grants, 4865

Day Care

A.V. Hunter Grants, 47
Atkinson Fndn Community Grants, 606
Bernard F. and Alva B. Gimbel Fndn Grants, 740
Carnegie Corp of New York Grants, 940
CFFVR Basic Needs Giving Partnership Grants, 1002
Community Fndn of the Verdugos Ed Grants, 1321
Corina Higginson Grants, 1373
Daviess County Community Fndn Youth Development Grants, 1460
Dekko Fndn Grants, 1482
Dept of Ed Child Care Access Means Parents in School Grants, 1507
Dermody Properties Fndn Grants, 1517
District of Columbia Commission on the Arts-Arts Educ Teacher Mini-Grants, 1549
Fargo-Moorhead Area Fndn Woman's Grants, 1789
FCD Child Development Grants, 1796
Florida BRAIVE Fund of Dade Community, 1846
Fred & Gretel Biel Charitable Grants, 1939
Grable Fndn Grants, 2108
Gulf Coast Community Operating Grants, 2176
Gulf Coast Fndn of Community Grants, 2177
Hasbro Children's Fund, 2256
Jenifer Altman Fndn Grants, 2662
John Gogian Family Fndn Grants, 2697
Josephine S. Gumbiner Grants, 2739
Kathryne Beynon Fndn Grants, 2791
Ken W. Davis Fndn Grants, 2813
Knox County Community Fndn Grants, 2831
Kosciusko County Community Fndn REMC Operation Round Up Grants, 2839
Mary Owen Borden Fndn Grants, 3046
North Carolina Arts Council Arts in Educ Rural Development Grants, 3470
OneFamily Fndn Grants, 3673
Perry County Community Fndn Grants, 3827
Pike County Community Fndn Grants, 3888
PMI Fndn Grants, 3918
Porter County Women's Grant, 3934
Posey County Community Fndn Grants, 3939
RCF Summertime Kids Grants, 4034
Skillman Fndn Good Schools Grants, 4382
Spencer County Community Fndn Grants, 4451
Strengthening Families - Strengthening Communities Grants, 4513
Thomas Sill Fndn Grants, 4619
U.S. Department of Educ 21st Century Community Learning Centers, 4687
U.S. Department of Educ Child Care Access Means Parents in School Grants, 4689
U.S. Department of Educ Innovative Strategies in Community Colleges for Working Adults and Displaced Workers Grants, 4692
Union Bank, N.A. Fndn Grants, 4709
USDA Child and Adult Care Food Program, 4800
W.H. and Mary Ellen Cobb Charitable Grants, 4959
WCI Childcare Capacity Grants, 5007

Death Penalty

Paul Green Fndn Efforts to Abolish the Death Penalty in North Carolina Grants, 3760
Tides Fndn Death Penalty Mobilization Grants, 4631
Tides Fndn Grants, 4632

Death/Mortality

Actors Fund Funeral and Burial Assistance, 138
CIGNA Fndn Grants, 1130
DHHS Health Centers Grants for Residents of Public Housing, 1533
DHHS Maternal and Child Health Grants, 1536
George E. Hatcher, Jr. and Ann Williams Hatcher Fndn Grants, 2015
Greenwall Fndn Bioethics Grants, 2158
Liz Claiborne and Art Ortenberg Fndn Grants, 2914
Quantum Corp Snap Server Grants, 3995

Dementia

Brookdale Fndn National Group Respite Grants, 845
Helen Bader Fndn Grants, 2293

SUBJECT INDEX

Henrietta Lange Burk Grants, 2303
Pfizer Healthcare Charitable Contributions, 3863

Democracy
Arizona Republic Newspaper Contributions, 547
HBF Encouraging Citizen Involvement Grants, 2272
National Endowment for Democracy Reagan-Fascell Democracy Fellowships, 3252
National Endowment for Democracy Visiting Fellows Program, 3253
Proteus Grants, 3973
Robert R. McCormick Tribune Civics Grants, 4118
Susan A. & Donald P. Babson Charitable Grants, 4534
Threshold Fndn Election Integrity Grants, 4625
Vernon K. Krieble Fndn Grants, 4930

Dental Education
Baxter Int'l Fndn Grants, 691
DeKalb County Community Fndn - Garrett Hospital Aid Fndn Grants, 1478
NHLBI Ruth L. Kirschstein National Research Service Award Short-Term Research Training Grants, 3422
Pajaro Valley Community Health Trust Insurance/Coverage & Educ on Using the System Grants, 3731
Pollock Fndn Grants, 3930

Dental Health and Hygiene
Aetna Fndn Regional Health Grants, 187
Alexander Eastman Fndn Grants, 355
Campbell Hoffman Fndn Grants, 915
Elkhart County Community Fndn Fund for Elkhart County, 1683
Health Fndn of Greater Indianapolis Grants, 2282
Henrietta Tower Wurts Memorial Fndn Grants, 2304
Jenkins Fndn: Improving the Health of Greater Richmond Grants, 2663
Nelda C. and H.J. Lutcher Stark Fndn Grants, 3296
Pajaro Valley Community Health Trust Insurance/Coverage & Educ on Using the System Grants, 3731
Pew Trusts Children and Youth Grants, 3858
Regents Professional Opportunity Scholarships, 4044
Ruth Eleanor Bamberger and John Ernest Bamberger Memorial Fndn Grants, 4178
Saint Luke's Health Inits Grants, 4216
St. Joseph Community Health Fndn Improving Healthcare Access Grants, 4469

Dentistry, Preventive
Fndn for Health Enhancement Grants, 1894

Depression
Aetna Fndn Regional Health Grants, 187
George Fndn Grants, 2018
Grand Rapids Comm SE Ottawa Youth Grants, 2123
Horizon Fndn for New Jersey Grants, 2364
Peter and Elizabeth C. Tower Fndn Annual Mental Health Grants, 3835
Pfizer Healthcare Charitable Contributions, 3863

Design Arts
AAF Accent on Architecture Community Grants, 58
Alabama State Council on the Arts Community Arts Collaborative Ventures Grants, 236
Alabama State Council on the Arts Community Arts Operating Support Grants, 237
Alabama State Council on the Arts Community Arts Presenting Grants, 238
Alabama State Council on the Arts Community Arts Program Development Grants, 239
Alabama State Council on the Arts Community Planning & Design Grants, 241
Alabama State Council on the Arts in Educ Partnership Grants, 242
Alabama State Council on the Arts Multi-Discipline and Festival Grants, 243
Arkansas Arts Council AIE After School/Summer Residency Grants, 551
Arkansas Arts Council AIE In-School Residency, 553
Emily Hall Tremaine Fndn Grants, 1698
Group 70 Fndn Fund, 2167

Illinois Arts Council Visual Arts Grants, 2478
Iowa Arts Council Artists in Schools/Communities Residency Grants, 2571
Jayne and Leonard Abess Fndn Grants, 2657
Minnesota State Arts Board Cultural Community Partnership Grants, 3188
National Endowment for the Arts - National Arts and Humanities Youth Program Awards, 3255
National Endowment for Arts Commun Grants, 3260
National Endowment for Arts Media Grants, 3264
National Endowment for Arts Presenting Grants, 3268
Nevada Arts Council Learning Grants, 3313
NYSCA Architecture, Planning, and Design: Capital Fixtures and Equipment Purchase Grants, 3570
NYSCA Architecture, Planning, and Design: Capital Project Grants, 3571
NYSCA Architecture, Planning, and Design: Design and Planning Studies Grants, 3572
NYSCA Architecture, Planning, and Design: General Operating Support Grants, 3573
NYSCA Architecture, Planning, and Design: General Program Support Grants, 3574
NYSCA Architecture, Planning, and Design: Independent Project Grants, 3575
NYSCA Architecture, Planning, and Design: Project Support Grants, 3576
RISCA Design Innovation Grant, 4097
South Carolina Arts Comm Accessibility Grants, 4410

Developing/Underdeveloped Nations
American Jewish World Service Grants, 441
Arthur B. Schultz Fndn Grants, 573
Bill and Melinda Gates Fndn Agricultural Development Grants, 765
Bill & Melinda Gates Emergency Response Grants, 766
Bill and Melinda Gates Fndn Water, Sanitation and Hygiene Grants, 770
Conrad N. Hilton Humanitarian Prize, 1356
Conservation, Food, and Health Fndn Grants for Developing Countries, 1359
Covidien Medical Product Donations, 1390
Harold Simmons Fndn Grants, 2230
IRA Pearson Fndn-IRA-Rotary Lit Awards, 2572
John Deere Fndn Grants, 2692
King Baudouin Int'l Development Prize, 2825
Liz Claiborne and Art Ortenberg Fndn Grants, 2914
Nestle Fndn Training Grant, 3301
Nike Fndn Grants, 3441
OSF Burma Project/SE Asia Init Grants, 3702
S.E.VEN Fund $50k VINE Project Prizes, 4193
S.E.VEN Fund 'In The River They Swim' Essay Competition, 4194
S.E.VEN Fund Open Enterprise Solutions to Poverty RFP Grants, 4197
Sir Dorabji Tata Grants for NGOs or Voluntary Organizations, 4370
UNESCO World Heritage Grants, 4706
USDA Foreign Market Development Grants, 4811
USDA Market Access Grants, 4818

Developmentally Disabled
Ayres Fndn Grants, 630
Caesars Fndn Grants, 891
Catherine Kennedy Home Fndn Grants, 955
CNCS Foster Grandparent Grants, 1185
Coleman Developmental Disabilities Grants, 1200
Columbus Fndn Traditional Grants, 1233
Community Fndn of Riverside County Grants, 1304
Conwood Charitable Grants, 1366
CVS Community Grants, 1422
Dr. Scholl Fndn Grants, 1602
Emma G. Harris Fndn Grants, 1701
George W. Wells Fndn Grants, 2030
Grace Bersted Fndn Grants, 2110
H & R Fndn Grants, 2181
J. Willard and Alice S. Marriott Fndn Grants, 2609
John D. and Katherine A. Johnston Fndn Grants, 2691
John Gogian Family Fndn Grants, 2697
John Merck Grants, 2706
John W. Anderson Fndn Grants, 2729

Kessler Fndn Community Employment Grants, 2814
LA84 Fndn Grants, 2847
Leon and Thea Koerner Fndn Grants, 2883
Lewis H. Humphreys Charitable Grants, 2889
Lucy Gooding Charitable Fndn Grants, 2937
Marjorie Moore Charitable Fndn Grants, 3021
Moody Fndn Grants, 3215
National Endowment for the Arts - Grants for Arts Projects: Challenge America Fast-Track, 3254
North Carolina GlaxoSmithKline Fndn Grants, 3490
Paul V. Sherlock Center on Disabilities Access for All Abilities Mini Grants, 3767
Peter and Elizabeth C. Tower Fndn Annual Intellectual Disabilities Grants, 3834
Peter & Elizabeth C. Tower Mental Health Reference and Resource Materials Mini-Grants, 3837
Peter and Elizabeth C. Tower Fndn Phase II Technology Init Grants, 3839
Peter and Elizabeth C. Tower Fndn Phase I Technology Init Grants, 3840
Peter and Elizabeth C. Tower Fndn Social and Emotional Preschool Curriculum Grants, 3841
Robert and Joan Dircks Fndn Grants, 4104
Ross Fndn Grants, 4164
Simple Advise Educ Center Grants, 4361
Spencer County Community Fndn Grants, 4451
Strowd Roses Grants, 4515
VSA/Metlife Connect All Grants, 4953

Diabetes
Abbott Fund Access to Health Care Grants, 80
Abbott Fund Science Educ Grants, 83
Aetna Fndn Regional Health Grants, 187
Austin S. Nelson Fndn Grants, 617
Balfe Family Fndn Grants, 636
Campbell Soup Fndn Grants, 916
CFFVR Basic Needs Giving Partnership Grants, 1002
CFFVR Jewelers Mutual Charitable Giving, 1014
CFFVR Robert and Patricia Endries Grants, 1018
CNCS Senior Companion Grants, 1187
Dorothy Rider Pool Health Care Grants, 1589
Florence Hunt Maxwell Fndn Grants, 1844
Fndn for Mid South Health & Wellness Grants, 1899
Gheens Fndn Grants, 2048
GNOF IMPACT Kahn-Oppenheim Grants, 2084
Greenwall Fndn Bioethics Grants, 2158
Henry and Ruth Blaustein Rosenberg Grants, 2306
Horizon Fndn for New Jersey Grants, 2364
J. Spencer Barnes Memorial Fndn Grants, 2606
Johnson & Johnson Comm Health Care Grants, 2717
Kovler Family Fndn Grants, 2840
M. Bastian Family Fndn Grants, 2951
NEI Innovative Patient Outreach Programs And Ocular Screening Technologies To Improve Detection Of Diabetic Retinopathy Grants, 3295
Pajaro Valley Community Health Trust Diabetes and Contributing Factors Grants, 3732
Pfizer Healthcare Charitable Contributions, 3863
Premera Blue Cross CARES Grants, 3945
Richard and Susan Smith Family Fndn Grants, 4078
Seattle Fndn Medical Funds Grants, 4329
William G. and Helen C. Hoffman Fndn Grants, 5080

Diabetic Retinopathy
NEI Innovative Patient Outreach Programs And Ocular Screening Technologies To Improve Detection Of Diabetic Retinopathy Grants, 3295

Diagnosis, Medical
Alexander and Margaret Stewart Grants, 354
Community Fndn of Riverside County Grants, 1304
Covidien Partnership for Neighborhood Wellness Grants, 1391
Emma B. Howe Memorial Fndn Grants, 1700
NEI Innovative Patient Outreach Programs And Ocular Screening Technologies To Improve Detection Of Diabetic Retinopathy Grants, 3295
NHLBI Investigator Initiated Multi-Site Clinical Trials, 3413
Piper Trust Healthcare & Med Research Grants, 3903

Dietary Foods
Institute for Agriculture and Trade Policy Food and Society Fellowships, 2561
Slow Food in Schools Micro-Grants, 4384

Dietetics/Nutrition
Chefs Move to Schools Grants, 1066
GNOF IMPACT Kahn-Oppenheim Grants, 2084
PepsiCo Fndn Grants, 3819
Phi Upsilon Omicron Frances Morton Holbrook Alumni Award, 3878
Union Bank, N.A. Fndn Grants, 4709
USAID Food Security, Nutrition, Biodiversity and Conservation Grants, 4752
USAID Grants for Building Disaster-Resilient Communities in Southern Africa, 4755

Digestive Diseases and Disorders
NHLBI Lymphatics in Health & Disease in Digestive, Urinary, Cardio & Pulmonary Systems, 3415

Disabled
Abbot and Dorothy H. Stevens Fndn Grants, 79
Abell-Hanger Fndn Grants, 91
Able To Serve Grants, 102
Able Trust Voc Rehab Grants for Agencies, 103
Able Trust Vocational Rehabilitation Grants for Individuals, 104
ACF Adoption Opportunities Project Grants, 113
Adams Rotary Memorial Fund A Grants, 157
Aetna Fndn Health Grants in Connecticut, 184
Albert and Bessie Mae Kronkosky Charitable Fndn Grants, 339
Alberto Culver Corp Contributions Grants, 343
Albert W. Cherne Fndn Grants, 346
Albert W. Rice Charitable Fndn Grants, 347
Albuquerque Community Fndn Grants, 348
Alexander and Margaret Stewart Grants, 354
Alfred E. Chase Charitable Fndn Grants, 366
Alticor Corp Community Contributions Grants, 396
Amelia Sillman Rockwell and Carlos Perry Rockwell Charities Grants, 417
Amerigroup Fndn Grants, 452
ANLAF Int'l Fund for Sexual Minorities Grants, 471
Anne J. Caudal Fndn Grants, 475
Ann Peppers Fndn Grants, 484
Annunziata Sanguinetti Fndn Grants, 485
Arizona Community Fndn Grants, 540
Armstrong McDonald Fndn Grants, 565
Arthur Ashley Williams Fndn Grants, 572
Atkinson Fndn Community Grants, 606
Austin S. Nelson Fndn Grants, 617
Ayres Fndn Grants, 630
BancorpSouth Fndn Grants, 651
Baxter Int'l Fndn Grants, 691
Berrien Community Fndn Grants, 744
Bodenwein Public Benevolent Fndn Grants, 806
Boston Fndn Grants, 819
Boston Globe Fndn Grants, 821
Callaway Golf Company Fndn Public Grants, 910
Carl R. Hendrickson Family Fndn Grants, 935
Carls Fndn Grants, 937
Carl W. and Carrie Mae Joslyn Grants, 938
Carnahan-Jackson Fndn Grants, 939
Carrie E. and Lena V. Glenn Fndn Grants, 944
Carrie Estelle Doheny Fndn Grants, 945
Caterpillar Fndn Grants, 954
Catherine Kennedy Home Fndn Grants, 955
CDC Grants for Violence-Related Injury Prevention Research, 974
Cessna Fndn Grants, 1000
CFFVR Robert and Patricia Endries Family Fndn Grants, 1018
CFFVR SAC Developmental Disabilities Grants, 1019
Champ-A Champion Fur Kids Grants, 1028
Charles Delmar Fndn Grants, 1039
Charles H. Hall Fndn, 1044
Charles Nelson Robinson Grants, 1052
Chatlos Fndn Grants, 1061
CHCF Grants, 1063
CICF Indianapolis Fndn Community Grants, 1123
Clara Blackford Smith and W. Aubrey Smith Charitable Fndn Grants, 1147
Clark-Winchcole Fndn Grants, 1152
Clipper Ship Fndn Grants, 1175
CNA Fndn Grants, 1179
CNCS Foster Grandparent Grants, 1185
CNCS Senior Companion Grants, 1187
Coleman Developmental Disabilities Grants, 1200
Colgate-Palmolive Company Grants, 1202
Collins Fndn Grants, 1209
Columbus Fndn Traditional Grants, 1233
Community Fndn of Greater Birmingham Grants, 1280
Community Fndn of Shreveport-Bossier Grants, 1307
Community Fndn of the Verdugos Ed Endowment Grants, 1321
Community Fndn of the Verdugos Grants, 1322
Cooper Industries Fndn Grants, 1370
Cornerstone Fndn of NE Wisconsin Grants, 1375
Cralle Fndn Grants, 1394
Crescent Porter Hale Fndn Grants, 1398
Cumberland Community Fndn Summertime Kids Grants, 1414
D. W. McMillan Fndn Grants, 1426
Dammann Grants, 1439
Daniels Grants, 1443
Daphne Seybolt Culpeper Memorial Fndn Grants, 1445
Delaware Community Fndn Youth Philanthropy Board for New Castle County Grants, 1486
Denver Broncos Charities Grants, 1501
Dept of Ed Projects with Industry Grants, 1511
Dept of Ed Recreational Services for Individuals with Disabilities, 1512
DFN Hurricane Katrina and Disability Rapid Response Grants, 1522
Dolan Fndn Grants, 1563
Doree Taylor Charitable Fndn, 1580
Dorothea Haus Ross Fndn Grants, 1587
Edwards Grants, 1669
Effie and Wofford Cain Fndn Grants, 1674
Eisner Grants, 1678
El Paso Community Fndn Grants, 1688
Elsie H. Wilcox Fndn Grants, 1691
Emma B. Howe Memorial Fndn Grants, 1700
Enterprise Rent-A-Car Fndn Grants, 1721
Eva L. and Joseph M. Bruening Fndn Grants, 1768
Fassino Fndn Grants, 1793
Fisa Fndn Grants, 1826
Florence Hunt Maxwell Fndn Grants, 1844
Foellinger Fndn Grants, 1877
Fourjay Fndn Grants, 1913
Fremont Area Community Amazing X Grants, 1953
Gannett Fndn Community Action Grants, 1984
George A Ohl Jr. Fndn Grants, 2012
Gertrude M. Conduff Fndn Grants, 2047
Gheens Fndn Grants, 2048
GNOF IMPACT Grants for Health and Human Services, 2080
Goizueta Fndn Grants, 2096
Grace and Franklin Bernsen Fndn Grants, 2109
Grace Bersted Fndn Grants, 2110
Greater Milwaukee Fndn Grants, 2137
Green Bay Packers Fndn Grants, 2148
Greygates Fndn Grants, 2164
Gulf Coast Community Fndn Grants, 2174
Hackett Fndn Grants, 2188
Harold Brooks Fndn Grants, 2227
Harry C. Trexler Grants, 2239
Harry Kramer Grants, 2242
Harry S. Black and Allon Fuller Grants, 2243
Hasbro Children's Fund, 2256
Helen Gertrude Sparks Charitable Grants, 2294
Helen Irwin Littauer Ed Grants, 2295
Helen Steiner Rice Fndn Grants, 2299
Henrietta Lange Burk Grants, 2303
Henry E. Niles Fndn Grants, 2309
Henry W. Bull Fndn Grants, 2312
Herbert A. and Adrian W. Woods Fndn Grants, 2313
Hilda and Preston Davis Fndn Grants, 2322
Hill Fndn Grants, 2326
Hoblitzelle Fndn Grants, 2341
Horace A. Kimball and S. Ella Kimball Grants, 2362
Household Int'l Corp Giving Grants, 2372
Howe Fndn of North Carolina Grants, 2377
Ireland Family Fndn Grants, 2574
J.W. Kieckhefer Fndn Grants, 2607
J. Walton Bissell Fndn Grants, 2608
J. Willard and Alice S. Marriott Fndn Grants, 2609
Jackson Fndn Grants, 2613
James Ford Bell Fndn Grants, 2623
Janirve Fndn Grants, 2645
Jay and Rose Phillips Family Fndn Grants, 2656
John D. and Katherine A. Johnston Fndn Grants, 2691
John Gogian Family Fndn Grants, 2697
John H. and Wilhelmina D. Harland Charitable Fndn Grants, 2698
John H. Wellons Fndn Grants, 2699
John I. Smith Charities Grants, 2700
John J. Leidy Fndn Grants, 2701
Johnson Scholarship Fndn Grants, 2726
John W. Alden Grants, 2727
Joseph P. Kennedy Jr. Fndn Grants, 2740
Josiah W. and Bessie H. Kline Fndn Grants, 2742
Kansas Arts Commission Artist Fellowships, 2776
Kennedy Center Summer HSC Fndn Internship, 2800
Kenneth T. and Eileen L. Norris Fndn Grants, 2802
Kentucky Arts Council Access Assistance Grants, 2805
Ken W. Davis Fndn Grants, 2813
Kessler Fndn Community Employment Grants, 2814
Kessler Fndn Hurricane Emergency Grants, 2815
Kessler Fndn Signature Employment Grants, 2816
LA84 Fndn Grants, 2847
Lands' End Corp Giving Program, 2861
Lucy Gooding Charitable Fndn Trust, 2936
Ludwick Family Fndn Grants, 2938
Luella Kemper Grants, 2939
Lydia deForest Charitable Grants, 2946
M.E. Raker Fndn Grants, 2953
M.J. Murdock Charitable Trust General Grants, 2954
Maine Community Fndn Charity Grants, 2977
Manitoba Arts Council Community Connections and Access Grants, 2995
Margaret L. Wendt Fndn Grants, 3004
Marie C. and Joseph C. Wilson Rochester Grants, 3006
Marion Isabell Coe Grants, 3020
Marjorie Moore Charitable Fndn Grants, 3021
Marriott Int'l Corp Giving Grants, 3024
Mary Duke Biddle Fndn Grants, 3036
Mary Wilmer Covey Charitable Grants, 3049
May and Stanley Smith Charitable Grants, 3069
Medtronic Fndn Patient Link Grants, 3113
MGM Resorts Fndn Community Grants, 3153
Mid-Iowa Health Fndn Comm Response Grants, 3168
Military Ex-Prisoners of War Fndn Grants, 3177
Mitsubishi Electric America Fndn Grants, 3190
Mockingbird Fndn Grants, 3196
Montana Arts Council Cultural & Aesthetic Grants, 3209
Mt. Sinai Health Care Fndn Health of the Jewish Community Grants, 3226
Nicor Gas Sharing Grants, 3436
Nina Mason Pulliam Charitable Grants, 3443
North Carolina Arts Council Outreach Grants, 3479
NYCT Children & Youth with Disabilities Grant, 3544
Oppenstein Brothers Fndn Grants, 3685
Ordean Fndn Grants, 3691
OUT Fund for Lesbian & Gay Liberation Grants, 3714
Pasadena Fndn Average Grants, 3741
Patrick John Bennett, Jr. Memorial Fndn Grants, 3752
Paul Balint Charitable Grants, 3757
Paul V. Sherlock Center on Disabilities Access for All Abilities Mini Grants, 3767
Peacock Fndn Grants, 3809
Pentair Fndn Educ and Community Grants, 3816
Perkins-Ponder Fndn Grants, 3822
Pi Lambda Theta Lillian and Henry Barry Award in Human Relations, 3890
Piper Trust Children Grants, 3901
Pittsburgh Fndn Community Grants, 3910
R.C. Baker Fndn Grants, 3999
R.S. Gernon Grants, 4002

SUBJECT INDEX

Rajiv Gandhi Fndn Grants, 4011
Reader's Digest Partners for Sight Fndn Grants, 4036
Rehab Therapy Fndn Grants, 4050
Robert R. Meyer Fndn Grants, 4121
Rockwell Int'l Corp Grants, 4141
Roeher Institute Research Grants, 4142
Roy and Christine Sturgis Charitable Grants, 4166
S. Mark Taper Fndn Grants, 4201
San Francisco Fndn Disability Rights Advocate Fund Emergency Grants, 4265
Sara Lee Fndn Grants, 4296
Schlessman Family Fndn Grants, 4307
Schurz Communications Fndn Grants, 4312
Seabury Fndn Grants, 4316
Sheltering Arms Grants, 4344
Shopko Fndn Community Charitable Grants, 4346
Sidney Stern Grants, 4349
Sid W. Richardson Fndn Grants, 4350
Simple Advise Educ Center Grants, 4361
Sioux Falls Area Community Grants, 4364
Sioux Falls Area Community Fndn Spot Grants, 4366
Siragusa Fndn Human Services Grants, 4369
Sophia Romero Grants, 4406
South Carolina Arts Comm Accessibility Grants, 4410
Sprint Fndn Grants, 4463
Starr Fndn Grants, 4483
Steelcase Fndn Grants, 4497
Strowd Roses Grants, 4515
Sylvia Adams Charitable Grants, 4543
TAC Touring Arts and Arts Access Grants, 4557
Taproot Fndn Capacity-Building Service Grants, 4560
Third Wave Fndn Lela Breitbart Grants, 4609
Third Wave Organizing & Advocacy Grants, 4610
Third Wave Fndn Reproductive Health and Justice Grants, 4611
Thomas Austin Finch, Sr. Fndn Grants, 4613
Thomas Sill Fndn Grants, 4619
TJX Fndn Grants, 4637
Toby Wells Fndn Grants, 4638
Tom's of Maine Grants, 4640
Trinity Trust Summer Youth Mini Grants, 4672
U.S. Department of Educ 21st Century Community Learning Centers, 4687
U.S. Department of Educ Centers for Independent Living, 4688
U.S. Department of Educ Disability and Rehabilitation Research and Related Projects, 4690
U.S. Department of Educ Migrant and Seasonal Farmworkers Grants, 4693
U.S. Department of Educ Parent Information and Training, 4695
U.S. Department of Educ Rehabilitation Engineering Research Centers Grants, 4698
U.S. Department of Educ Rehabilitation Research Training Centers, 4699
U.S. Department of Educ Rehabilitation Training--Rehabilitation Continuing Educ Programs--Institute on Rehabilitation Issues, 4700
U.S. Department of Educ Special Educ--National Activities--Parent Information Centers, 4701
U.S. Department of Educ Vocational Rehabilitation Services Projects for American Indians with Disabilities Grants, 4702
Union Benevolent Association Grants, 4710
Union County Community Fndn Grants, 4711
USAID Economic Prospectsfor Armenia-Turkey Normalization Grants, 4750
US Airways Educ Fndn Grants, 4790
USFA Development Grants, 4866
USFA Equipment Subsidy Grants, 4867
USGA Fndn For the Good of the Game Grants, 4868
Vancouver Fndn Disability Supports for Employment Grants, 4899
Vancouver Sun Children's Grants, 4901
Verizon Fndn Great Lakes Region Grants, 4912
Victor E. Speas Fndn Grants, 4933
Vigneron Grants, 4938
VSA/Metlife Connect All Grants, 4953
VSA/Volkswagen Group of America Exhibition Awards, 4954

VSA Int'l Art Program for Children with Disabilities Grants, 4955
W.P. and Bulah Luse Fndn Grants, 4965
Weingart Fndn Grants, 5018
Wells Fargo Housing Fndn Grants, 5023
Westinghouse Charitable Giving Grants, 5028
William J. and Dorothy K. O'Neill Fndn Grants, 5087
Wilson-Wood Fndn Grants, 5098
Yellow Corp Fndn Grants, 5126

Disabled (Target Groups)
ALA Diversity and Outreach Fair, 267
ALA Schneider Family Book Award, 317
Anne J. Caudal Fndn Grants, 475
Autodesk Community Relations Grants, 619
Chiron Fndn Community Grants, 1111
Community Fndn of Boone County - Adult Lit Init Grants, 1272
Courage Center Judd Jacobson Memorial Award, 1382
Kessler Fndn Community Employment Grants, 2814
Kessler Fndn Hurricane Emergency Grants, 2815
Kessler Fndn Signature Employment Grants, 2816
Singing for Change Fndn Grants, 4363
USAID Economic Prospectsfor Armenia-Turkey Normalization Grants, 4750
Verizon Fndn Maryland Grants, 4917
Verizon Fndn New York Grants, 4919
Verizon Fndn NE Region Grants, 4920
Verizon Fndn Pennsylvania Grants, 4921
Verizon Fndn SE Region Grants, 4923
Verizon Fndn Vermont Grants, 4924
Verizon Fndn Virginia Grants, 4925
Verizon Fndn West Virginia Grants, 4926
William G. Kelley Fndn Grants, 5083

Disabled Student Support
Able Trust Vocational Rehabilitation Grants for Individuals, 104
Allan C. and Leila J. Garden Fndn Grants, 374
American Council of the Blind Scholarships, 427
Champ-A Champion Fur Kids Grants, 1028
CVS All Kids Can Grants, 1420
CVS Community Grants, 1422
Florida High School/High Tech Project Grants, 1866
Guy I. Bromley Grants, 2180
Johnson Scholarship Fndn Grants, 2726
Lettie Pate Whitehead Fndn Grants, 2888
Lewis H. Humphreys Charitable Grants, 2889
Louetta M. Cowden Fndn Grants, 2922
Mitsubishi Electric America Fndn Grants, 3190
Ohio Arts Council Artists with Disabilities Access Grants, 3646
Peacock Fndn Grants, 3809
Peter and Elizabeth C. Tower Fndn Annual Intellectual Disabilities Grants, 3834
Roy and Christine Sturgis Charitable Grants, 4166
SW Florida Community Fndn Undergraduate and Graduate Scholarships, 4444
William G. and Helen C. Hoffman Fndn Grants, 5080

Disabled, Accessibility for
Able To Play Challenge Grants, 101
Able Trust Voc Rehabilitation Grants for Agencies, 103
Adolph Coors Fndn Grants, 171
Anne J. Caudal Fndn Grants, 475
Arthur B. Schultz Fndn Grants, 573
CNCS AmeriCorps State and National Planning Grants, 1183
Coleman Developmental Disabilities Grants, 1200
CVS Community Grants, 1422
GNOF Community Revitalization Grants, 2071
Harry S. Black and Allon Fuller Grants, 2243
HRF Hudson River Improvement Grants, 2378
Hugh J. Andersen Fndn Grants, 2385
Jay and Rose Phillips Family Fndn Grants, 2656
John F. Kennedy Center for the Performing Arts National Rosemary Kennedy Internship, 2694
Johnson Scholarship Fndn Grants, 2726
John W. Speas and Effie E. Speas Grants, 2732
Kennedy Center Experiential Educ Internship, 2798

Disabled, Accessibility for / 867

Kennedy Center HSC Fndn Internship, 2799
Kessler Fndn Community Employment Grants, 2814
Kessler Fndn Hurricane Emergency Grants, 2815
Kessler Fndn Signature Employment Grants, 2816
Lewis H. Humphreys Charitable Grants, 2889
Louis and Elizabeth Nave Flarsheim Charitable Fndn Grants, 2924
Marietta McNeill Morgan and Samuel Tate Morgan, Jr. Grants, 3008
Mary Wilmer Covey Charitable Grants, 3049
Mitsubishi Electric America Fndn Grants, 3190
National Endowment for Arts Commun Grants, 3260
NIDRR Field-Initiated Projects, 3437
NYCT Children & Youth with Disabilities Grant, 3544
NYSCA Architecture, Planning, and Design: Capital Project Grants, 3571
Ohio Arts Council Artists with Disabilities Access Grants, 3646
Ohio Arts Council Arts Partnership Grants, 3650
Paul V. Sherlock Center on Disabilities Access for All Abilities Mini Grants, 3767
PCA Art Organizations and Art Programs Grants for Presenting Organizations, 3771
PCA Arts Organizations Grants for Music, 3774
PCA Arts Organizations and Arts Programs Grants for Art Museums, 3775
PCA Arts Organizations and Arts Programs Grants for Arts Educ Organizations, 3776
PCA Arts Organizations and Arts Programs Grants for Arts Service Organizations, 3777
PCA Arts Organizations & Grants for Crafts, 3778
PCA Arts Organizations & Grants for Dance, 3779
PCA Arts Organizations and Arts Programs Grants for Film and Electronic Media, 3780
PCA Arts Organizations & Grants for Lit, 3781
PCA Arts Organizations and Arts Programs Grants for Local Arts, 3782
PCA Arts Organizations & Grants for Theatre, 3783
PCA Arts Organizations and Arts Programs Grants for Traditional and Folk Arts, 3784
PCA Arts Organizations & Grants for Visual Arts, 3785
PCA Busing Grants, 3786
PCA Entry Track Arts Organizations and Program Grants for Art Museums, 3787
PCA Entry Track Arts Organizations and Program Grants for Arts Educ Organizations, 3788
PCA Entry Track Arts Organizations and Program Grants for Arts Service Organizations, 3789
PCA Entry Track Arts Organizations and Program Grants for Crafts, 3790
PCA Entry Track Arts Organizations and Program Grants for Dance, 3791
PCA Entry Track Arts Organizations and Program Grants for Film and Electronic Media, 3792
PCA Entry Track Arts Organizations and Program Grants for Local Arts, 3794
PCA Entry Track Arts Organizations and Program Grants for Music, 3795
PCA Entry Track Arts Organizations and Program Grants for Presenting Organizations, 3796
PCA Entry Track Arts Organizations and Program Grants for Theatre, 3797
PCA Entry Track Arts Organizations and Program Grants for Traditional and Folk Arts, 3798
PCA Entry Track Arts Organizations and Program Grants for Visual Arts, 3799
PCA Management/Technical Assistance Grants, 3800
PCA Pennsylvania Partners in the Arts Program Stream Grants, 3801
PCA Pennsylvania Partners in the Arts Project Stream Grants, 3802
Pi Lambda Theta Lillian and Henry Barry Award in Human Relations, 3890
Piper Trust Children Grants, 3901
Robins Fndn Grants, 4126
RRF Accessible Faith Grants, 4169
Sheltering Arms Grants, 4344
Sioux Falls Area Community Fndn Field-of-Interest and Donor-Advised Grants, 4365
South Carolina Arts Comm Accessibility Grants, 4410

South Carolina Arts Commission Facility Grants, 4417
Stanley Smith Horticultural Grants, 4474
TAC Arts Access Grant, 4549
TAC Arts Build Communities Grants, 4551
TAC Arts Grants, 4554
TAC Rural Arts Project Support Grants, 4555
U.S. Department of Educ Disability and Rehabilitation Research and Related Projects, 4690
U.S. Department of Educ Rehabilitation Engineering Research Centers Grants, 4698
USAID Economic Prospectsfor Armenia-Turkey Normalization Grants, 4750
US Airways Educ Fndn Grants, 4790
Verizon Fndn Great Lakes Region Grants, 4912
Vigneron Grants, 4938
VSA/Metlife Connect All Grants, 4953
West Virginia Commission on the Arts Accessibility Services Grants, 5029
William G. and Helen C. Hoffman Fndn Grants, 5080

Disabled, Education
AACC Project Reach Grants, 56
ALA Schneider Family Book Award, 317
Charles Lafitte Fndn Grants, 1049
DeKalb County Community Fndn - Garrett Hospital Aid Grants, 1478
Jay and Rose Phillips Family Fndn Grants, 2656
Johnson Scholarship Fndn Grants, 2726
Kessler Fndn Community Employment Grants, 2814
Marion I. & Henry J. Knott Discretionary Grants, 3018
Marion I. and Henry J. Knott Standard Grants, 3019
Marjorie Moore Charitable Fndn Grants, 3021
Mary Wilmer Covey Charitable Grants, 3049
Patrick John Bennett, Jr. Memorial Fndn Grants, 3752
Roy and Christine Sturgis Charitable Grants, 4166
Singing for Change Fndn Grants, 4363
Toby Wells Fndn Grants, 4638
VSA/Metlife Connect All Grants, 4953

Disabled, Higher Education
Greenspun Family Fndn Grants, 2156
Kessler Fndn Community Employment Grants, 2814

Disadvantaged, Economically
A.C. Ratshesky Fndn Grants, 39
Abbot and Dorothy H. Stevens Fndn Grants, 79
ACF Assets for Indep Demonstration Grants, 114
ACF Assets for Indep Individual Development Account Grants, 115
Achelis Fndn Grants, 127
ACS Award for Encouraging Disadvantaged Students into Careers in the Chemical Sciences, 132
Adelaide Dawson Lynch Grants, 163
Ahmanson Fndn Grants, 207
Aid for Starving Children African American Indep Single Mother's Grants, 210
Aid for Starving Children Emergency Assistance Grants, 211
ALA Coretta Scott King Book Donation Grant, 261
ALA Diversity and Outreach Fair, 267
ALA Supporting Diversity Stipend, 333
Alberto Culver Corp Contributions Grants, 343
Albert W. Rice Charitable Fndn Grants, 347
Albuquerque Community Fndn Grants, 348
Alfred and Tillie Shemanski Testamentary Grants, 363
Alfred E. Chase Charitable Fndn Grants, 366
Allan C. and Leila J. Garden Fndn Grants, 374
Allen Hilles Grants, 378
Alticor Corp Community Contributions Grants, 396
Amelia Sillman Rockwell and Carlos Perry Rockwell Charities Grants, 417
Amerigroup Fndn Grants, 452
Andrew Family Fndn Grants, 462
Anschutz Family Fndn Grants, 486
Ansell, Zaro, Grimm & Aaron Fndn Grants, 487
ARCO Fndn Educ Grants, 528
Arkansas Arts Council Collab Project Support, 555
Arthur and Sara Jo Kobacker, Alfred and Ida Kobacker Fndn Grants, 571
Atkinson Fndn Community Grants, 606

Austin-Bailey Health and Wellness Fndn Grants, 614
Avista Fndn Grants, 624
Ayres Fndn Grants, 630
Batchelor Fndn Grants, 679
BBVA Compass Fndn Charitable Grants, 703
BCBSM Community Health Matching Grants, 707
Bicknell Grants, 759
Bill & Melinda Gates Emergency Response Grants, 766
Blue Cross Blue Shield of Minnesota Fndn - Health Equity: Building Health Together Grants, 793
Blue Cross Blue Shield of Minnesota Fndn - Healthy Equity: Public Libraries for Health Grants, 797
Bodenwein Public Benevolent Fndn Grants, 806
Bodman Fndn Grants, 807
Boston Globe Fndn Grants, 821
Brett Family Fndn Grants, 833
Bright Promises Fndn Grants, 838
Buhl Fndn - Frick Ed Fund, 859
Bunbury Company Grants, 863
Burning Fndn Grants, 867
Business Wire Lit Init, 880
Butler Manufacturing Company Fndn Grants, 881
Callaway Golf Company Fndn Grants, 910
CarEth Fndn Grants, 924
Carl B. and Florence E. King Fndn Grants, 928
Carl R. Hendrickson Family Fndn Grants, 935
Carls Fndn Grants, 937
Carolyn Fndn Grants, 942
Carrie E. and Lena V. Glenn Fndn Grants, 944
CCHD Community Development Grants, 966
Ceres Fndn Grants, 999
Cessna Fndn Grants, 1000
CFFVR Basic Needs Giving Partnership Grants, 1002
CFFVR Jewelers Mutual Charitable Giving, 1014
CFFVR Robert and Patricia Endries Family Fndn Grants, 1018
CFFVR Schmidt Family G4 Grants, 1020
CFFVR Waupaca Area Community Fndn Grants, 1023
Charles Delmar Fndn Grants, 1039
Charles H. Dater Fndn Grants, 1042
Charles H. Hall Fndn, 1044
Charles H. Pearson Fndn Grants, 1045
Charles Nelson Robinson Grants, 1052
Charles Parker Trust for Public Music Grants, 1053
Chicago Community Poverty Alleviation Grants, 1091
Chicago Community Trust Workforce Grants, 1094
Chicago Tribune Fndn Grants for Cultural Organizations, 1101
Child's Dream Grants, 1104
CICF Efroymson Grants, 1120
CICF Senior Grants, 1127
CIT Corp Giving Grants, 1138
Clara Blackford Smith and W. Aubrey Smith Charitable Fndn Grants, 1147
Clark and Ruby Baker Fndn Grants, 1154
Claude Pepper Fndn Grants, 1160
Clayton Baker Grants, 1163
Cleveland Community Responsive Grants, 1168
Clipper Ship Fndn Grants, 1175
CNA Fndn Grants, 1179
CNCS AmeriCorps State and National Grants, 1182
CNCS AmeriCorps VISTA Project Grants, 1184
CNCS Foster Grandparent Grants, 1185
CNCS Senior Companion Grants, 1187
Colonel Stanley R. McNeil Grants, 1210
Commonweal Community Assistance Grants, 1239
Community Fndn for Greater Buffalo Grants, 1247
Community Fndn of Boone Cty Women's Grants, 1273
Community Fndn of Broward Grants, 1275
Community Fndn of Greater Birmingham Grants, 1280
Community Fndn of Greenville Hollingsworth Funds Program/Project Grants, 1296
Community Fndn of SE Connecticut Grants, 1309
Community Fndn of Virgin Islands Anderson Family Teacher Grants, 1323
Cone Health Fndn Grants, 1348
Constantin Fndn Grants, 1362
Constellation Energy Corp Grants, 1364
Cooper Industries Fndn Grants, 1370
Corina Higginson Grants, 1373

Cornerstone Fndn of NE Wisconsin Grants, 1375
Covidien Medical Product Donations, 1390
Crail-Johnson Fndn Grants, 1393
Cralle Fndn Grants, 1394
Cumberland Community Fndn Summertime Kids Grants, 1414
CVS All Kids Can Grants, 1420
CVS Community Grants, 1422
D. W. McMillan Fndn Grants, 1426
Danellie Fndn Grants, 1442
Daniels Grants, 1443
Daphne Seybolt Culpeper Memorial Fndn Grants, 1445
David Lane Grants for Aged & Indigent Women, 1453
Decatur County Community Fndn Small Project Grants, 1477
Delaware Division of the Arts Community-Based Organizations Opportunity Grants, 1487
Dennis and Phyllis Washington Fndn Grants, 1498
DHHS American Recovery and Reinvestment Act of 2009 Head Start Expansion, 1526
DHHS ARRA Strengthening Communities Fund - Nonprofit Capacity Building Grants, 1527
DHHS Community Services Block Grant Training and Technical Assistance Program: Capacity-Building for Ongoing CSBG Programs and Strategic Planning and Coordination Grants, 1529
DOL Youthbuild Grants, 1571
Doree Taylor Charitable Fndn, 1580
Dorothea Haus Ross Fndn Grants, 1587
Douty Fndn Grants, 1595
Dr. and Mrs. Paul Pierce Memorial Fndn Grants, 1599
Dresher Fndn Grants, 1605
Dwight Stuart Youth Fndn Grants, 1628
East Tennessee Fndn Affordable Housing Fund, 1645
Eaton Charitable Grants, 1647
Edina Realty Fndn Grants, 1656
Edward and Ellen Roche Relief Fndn Grants, 1663
Edward W. and Stella C. Van Houten Grants, 1670
Eisner Fndn Grants, 1678
Elizabeth Carse Fndn Grants, 1681
El Paso Community Fndn Grants, 1688
Elsie Lee Garthwaite Memorial Fndn Grants, 1692
EMC Corp Grants, 1693
Ensworth Charitable Fndn Grants, 1710
Faye McBeath Fndn Grants, 1794
Financial Capability Innovation Fund II Grants, 1811
Fitzpatrick, Cella, Harper & Scinto Pro Bono, 1836
Flinn Fndn Grants, 1842
Florence Hunt Maxwell Fndn Grants, 1844
Florida Sports Fndn Junior Golf Grants, 1872
Fndn for Mid South Comm Development Grants, 1897
Fndn for the Mid South Wealth Building Grants, 1900
Fourjay Fndn Grants, 1913
Frank Loomis Palmer Grants, 1931
Frank Reed and Margaret Jane Peters Memorial Fund I Grants, 1933
Frank Reed and Margaret Jane Peters Memorial Fund II Grants, 1934
Fred & Gretel Biel Charitable Grants, 1939
Frederick McDonald Grants, 1946
Frederick W. Marzahl Grants, 1948
Gamble Fndn Grants, 1983
General Service Fndn Colorado Grants, 2005
George A. and Grace L. Long Fndn Grants, 2008
George A Ohl Jr. Fndn Grants, 2012
George W. Wells Fndn Grants, 2030
Georgiana Goddard Eaton Grants, 2038
German Protestant Orphan Asylum Fndn Grants, 2044
Ginger and Barry Ackerley Fndn Grants, 2055
GNOF IMPACT Grants for Health and Human Services, 2080
GNOF IMPACT Gulf States Eye Surgery Fund, 2082
GNOF Maison Hospitaliere Grants, 2086
Goizueta Fndn Grants, 2096
Goldseker Fndn Human Services Grants, 2102
Grable Fndn Grants, 2108
Grassroots Exchange Grants, 2128
Greygates Fndn Grants, 2164
Grover Hermann Fndn Grants, 2168
Guy I. Bromley Grants, 2180

SUBJECT INDEX   Disadvantaged, Economically / 869

H.A. and Mary K. Chapman Charitable Grants, 2182
H.J. Heinz Company Fndn Grants, 2184
HAF Community Grants, 2193
HAF Kayla Wood Girls Grants, 2199
Harold and Arlene Schnitzer CARE Grants, 2226
Harold Brooks Fndn Grants, 2227
Harry C. Trexler Grants, 2239
Harry S. Black and Allon Fuller Grants, 2243
Hasbro Children's Fund, 2256
Hazen Fndn Youth Organizing Grants, 2270
HBF Pathways Out of Poverty Grants, 2273
Hearst Fndns Social Service Grants, 2285
Helen Gertrude Sparks Charitable Grants, 2294
Helen Irwin Littauer Ed Grants, 2295
Help America Fndn Grants, 2301
Henrietta Lange Burk Grants, 2303
Henrietta Tower Wurts Memorial Fndn Grants, 2304
Henry E. Niles Fndn Grants, 2309
Herbert A. and Adrian W. Woods Fndn Grants, 2313
Herman Goldman Fndn Grants, 2317
Hillcrest Fndn Grants, 2325
Horace A. Kimball and S. Ella Kimball Grants, 2362
Horace Moses Charitable Fndn Grants, 2363
Howard and Bush Fndn Grants, 2374
Humane Society of the United States Foreclosure Pets Grants, 2389
Hyams Fndn Grants, 2413
IBCAT Screening Mammography Grants, 2422
IIE David L. Boren Fellowships, 2454
Init Fndn Innovation Grants, 2559
Ittleson Fndn AIDS Grants, 2589
J. Jill Compassion Grants, 2598
Jacksonville Jaguars Fndn Grants, 2614
James Ford Bell Fndn Grants, 2623
James H. Cummings Fndn Grants, 2626
James R. Thorpe Fndn Grants, 2636
Jane's Grants, 2639
Jane Bradley Pettit Fndn Community and Social Development Grants, 2642
Janirve Fndn Grants, 2645
Jaquelin Hume Fndn Grants, 2654
Jeffris Wood Fndn Grants, 2660
Jerome and Mildred Paddock Fndn Grants, 2666
Jessie B. Cox Charitable Grants, 2670
Jewish Funds for Justice Grants, 2676
Jim Moran Fndn Grants, 2680
John Clarke Grants, 2689
John D. and Katherine A. Johnston Fndn Grants, 2691
John P. Murphy Fndn Grants, 2708
Johnson Scholarship Fndn Grants, 2726
John W. Boynton Grants, 2730
John W. Speas and Effie E. Speas Grants, 2732
Joseph H. and Florence A. Roblee Fndn Grants, 2736
Josephine G. Russell Grants, 2737
Josephine Goodyear Fndn Grants, 2738
Joseph S. Stackpole Charitable Grants, 2741
Kahuku Community Fund, 2762
Kawabe Grants, 2794
Kentucky Arts Council Access Assistance Grants, 2805
KeyBank Fndn Grants, 2820
Kimball Int'l-Habig Fndn Grants, 2823
Kroger Fndn Hunger Relief Grants, 2844
Lands' End Corp Giving Program, 2861
Legler Benbough Fndn Grants, 2877
LEGO Children's Grants, 2878
Leo Niessen Jr., Charitable Grants, 2885
Lewis H. Humphreys Charitable Grants, 2889
Liberty Bank Fndn Grants, 2890
Lily Palmer Fry Grants, 2905
Linden Fndn Grants, 2908
Linford and Mildred White Charitable Grants, 2909
LISC Financial Opportunity Center Social Innovation Grants, 2911
Liz Claiborne Fndn Grants, 2915
Local Inits Support Corp Grants, 2917
Long Island Community Fndn Grants, 2920
Louetta M. Cowden Fndn Grants, 2922
Louis and Elizabeth Nave Flarsheim Charitable Fndn Grants, 2924
Lucy Downing Nisbet Charitable Grants, 2935

Lucy Gooding Charitable Fndn Trust, 2936
Lucy Gooding Charitable Fndn Grants, 2937
Luella Kemper Grants, 2939
Lydia deForest Charitable Grants, 2946
M.D. Anderson Fndn Grants, 2952
Mabel A. Horne Grants, 2956
Mabel F. Hoffman Charitable Grants, 2957
Maine Comm Belvedere Animal Welfare Grants, 2975
Maine Community Fndn Charity Grants, 2977
Maine Community Fndn People of Color Grants, 2985
Manitoba Arts Council Community Connections and Access Grants, 2995
Marathon Petroleum Corp Grants, 2999
Margaret L. Wendt Fndn Grants, 3004
Marietta McNeill Morgan and Samuel Tate Morgan, Jr. Grants, 3008
Marin Community Affordable Housing Grants, 3010
Marin Community Fndn Ending the Cycle of Poverty Grants, 3011
Marin Community Fndn Social Justice and Interfaith Understanding Grants, 3012
Marin Community Successful Aging Grants, 3014
Marion Isabell Coe Grants, 3020
Mark Wahlberg Youth Fndn Grants, 3022
MARPAT Fndn Grants, 3023
Marsh Corp Grants, 3027
Mary's Pence Ministry Grants, 3029
Mary E. Ober Fndn Grants, 3039
Mary Jane Luick Grants, 3040
Mary K. Chapman Fndn Grants, 3042
Mary Owen Borden Fndn Grants, 3046
Massachusetts Bar Fndn IOLTA Grants, 3050
May and Stanley Smith Charitable Grants, 3069
Medtronic Fndn Community Link Arts, Civic, and Culture Grants, 3109
Medtronic Fndn CommunityLink Educ Grants, 3110
Medtronic Fndn CommunityLink Health Grants, 3111
Medtronic Fndn Community Link Human Services Grants, 3112
Melville Charitable Grants, 3115
Mercedes-Benz USA Corp Contributions Grants, 3118
Mertz Gilmore Climate Change Grants, 3125
Meyer Fndn Economic Security Grants, 3141
Meyer Fndn Healthy Communities Grants, 3143
Meyer Fndn Strong Nonprofit Sector Grants, 3145
MGM Resorts Fndn Community Grants, 3153
MGN Family Fndn Grants, 3154
Michael and Susan Dell Fndn Grants, 3158
Middlesex Savings Charitable Fndn Community Development Grants, 3173
Middlesex Savings Charitable Fndn Ed Opportunities Grants, 3174
Minneapolis Fndn Community Grants, 3186
Minnesota Small Cities Development Grants, 3187
Mizuho USA Fndn Grants, 3192
MMS and Alliance Charitable Fndn Grants for Community Action and Care for the Medically Uninsured, 3194
Modest Needs Bridge Grants, 3197
Modest Needs Hurricane Sandy Relief Grants, 3198
Modest Needs New Employment Grants, 3199
Monsanto Int'l Grants, 3207
Moody Fndn Grants, 3215
Moran Family Fndn Grants, 3216
Mr. and Mrs. William Foulds Family Grants, 3222
National Endowment for the Arts - National Arts and Humanities Youth Program Awards, 3255
National Endowment for the Arts - Regional Partnership Agreement Grants, 3258
National Endowment for Arts Commun Grants, 3260
National Endowment for Arts Agencies Grants, 3263
National Endowment for Arts Media Grants, 3264
National Endowment for Arts Museum Grants, 3265
National Endowment for Arts Music Grants, 3266
National Endowment for Arts Opera Grants, 3267
National Endowment for Arts Theater Grants, 3269
National Home Library Fndn Grants, 3276
Nationwide Insurance Fndn Grants, 3285
Nelda C. and H.J. Lutcher Stark Fndn Grants, 3296
Nellie Mae Educ Fndn District-Level Grants, 3297

New York Fndn Grants, 3338
NGA Midwest School Garden Grants, 3407
Nicholas H. Noyes Jr. Memorial Fndn Grants, 3434
Nike Fndn Grants, 3441
NLADA Kutak-Dodds Prizes, 3451
Norman Fndn Grants, 3464
Northern Trust Company Corp Giving Program, 3504
NW Mutual Fndn Grants, 3509
Norton Fndn Grants, 3514
NYCT Workforce Development Grants, 3560
Ober Kaler Community Grants, 3635
Oleonda Jameson Grants, 3667
Olga Sipolin Children's Grants, 3668
Olive B. Cole Fndn Grants, 3670
Oppenstein Brothers Fndn Grants, 3685
Ordean Fndn Grants, 3691
OSF-Baltimore Community Fellowships, 3695
OSF Campaign for Black Male Achievement, 3703
Owens Fndn Grants, 3718
PCA Art Organizations and Art Programs Grants for Presenting Organizations, 3771
PCA Arts Organizations Grants for Music, 3774
PCA Arts Organizations and Arts Programs Grants for Art Museums, 3775
PCA Arts Organizations and Arts Programs Grants for Arts Educ Organizations, 3776
PCA Arts Organizations and Arts Programs Grants for Arts Service Organizations, 3777
PCA Arts Organizations & Grants for Crafts, 3778
PCA Arts Organizations & Grants for Dance, 3779
PCA Arts Organizations and Arts Programs Grants for Film and Electronic Media, 3780
PCA Arts Organizations & Grants for Lit, 3781
PCA Arts Organizations and Arts Programs Grants for Local Arts, 3782
PCA Arts Organizations & Grants for Theatre, 3783
PCA Arts Organizations and Arts Programs Grants for Traditional and Folk Arts, 3784
PCA Arts Organizations & Grants for Visual Arts, 3785
PCA Busing Grants, 3786
PCA Entry Track Arts Organizations and Program Grants for Art Museums, 3787
PCA Entry Track Arts Organizations and Program Grants for Arts Educ Organizations, 3788
PCA Entry Track Arts Organizations and Program Grants for Arts Service Organizations, 3789
PCA Entry Track Arts Organizations and Program Grants for Crafts, 3790
PCA Entry Track Arts Organizations and Program Grants for Dance, 3791
PCA Entry Track Arts Organizations and Program Grants for Film and Electronic Media, 3792
PCA Entry Track Arts Organizations and Program Grants for Local Arts, 3794
PCA Entry Track Arts Organizations and Program Grants for Music, 3795
PCA Entry Track Arts Organizations and Program Grants for Presenting Organizations, 3796
PCA Entry Track Arts Organizations and Program Grants for Theatre, 3797
PCA Entry Track Arts Organizations and Program Grants for Traditional and Folk Arts, 3798
PCA Entry Track Arts Organizations and Program Grants for Visual Arts, 3799
PCA Pennsylvania Partners in the Arts Program Stream Grants, 3801
PCA Pennsylvania Partners in the Arts Project Stream Grants, 3802
Peacock Fndn Grants, 3809
PepsiCo Fndn Grants, 3819
Perkins-Ponder Fndn Grants, 3822
Perpetual Trust for Charitable Giving Grants, 3826
Peter M. Putnam Fndn Grants, 3848
PeyBack Fndn Grants, 3861
Pfizer Healthcare Charitable Contributions, 3863
Piper Trust Educ Grants, 3902
Piper Trust Healthcare & Med Research Grants, 3903
Plum Creek Fndn Grants, 3917
PMI Fndn Grants, 3918
PNC Ecnomic Development Grants, 3922

870 / Disadvantaged, Economically

Pohlad Family Fndn, 3928
Porter County Women's Grant, 3934
Powell Fndn Grants, 3942
Premera Blue Cross CARES Grants, 3945
Prince Charitable Trusts D.C. Grants, 3960
Prudential Fndn Arts and Culture Grants, 3975
Prudential Fndn Economic Development Grants, 3976
Prudential Fndn Educ Grants, 3977
Public Educ Power Grants, 3981
Public Welfare Fndn Grants, 3984
R.S. Gernon Grants, 4002
Ralph M. Parsons Fndn Grants, 4013
Raskob Fndn for Catholic Activities Grants, 4019
RBC Dain Rauscher Fndn Grants, 4031
RealNetworks Fndn Grants, 4037
Reynolds American Fndn Grants, 4068
Rhode Island Fndn Grants, 4073
Richard and Susan Smith Family Fndn Grants, 4078
Richard H. Driehaus Fndn Grants, 4084
Richards Fndn Grants, 4089
Robert and Joan Dircks Fndn Grants, 4104
Robert B McMillen Fndn Grants, 4106
Robert R. McCormick Tribune Veterans Grants, 4120
Robert R. Meyer Fndn Grants, 4121
Robin Hood Fndn Grants, 4125
Rockefeller Fndn Grants, 4138
Roney-Fitzpatrick Fndn Grants, 4150
Rosie's For All Kids Fndn Grants, 4163
RWJF Vulnerable Populations Portfolio Grants, 4190
Ryder System Charitable Fndn Grants, 4191
S.E.VEN Fund 'In The River They Swim' Essay Competition, 4194
S.E.VEN Fund Annual Grants, 4195
S.E.VEN Fund Mini-Grants, 4196
S.E.VEN Fund Open Enterprise Solutions to Poverty RFP Grants, 4197
S.E.VEN Fund WHY Prize, 4198
S. Mark Taper Fndn Grants, 4201
Saigh Fndn Grants, 4210
Saint Paul Companies Fndn Grants, 4217
Salt River Health and Human Services Grants, 4228
Sands Fndn Grants, 4255
Santa Fe Community Fndn Seasonal Grants-Spring Cycle, 4291
Schlessman Family Fndn Grants, 4307
Schumann Fund for New Jersey Grants, 4311
Seybert Inst for Poor Boys and Girls Grants, 4338
Sheltering Arms Grants, 4344
Shopko Fndn Community Charitable Grants, 4346
Singing for Change Fndn Grants, 4363
Sioux Falls Area Community Grants, 4364
Sioux Falls Area Community Fndn Field-of-Interest and Donor-Advised Grants, 4365
Sioux Falls Area Community Fndn Spot Grants, 4366
Sir Dorabji Tata Grants for NGOs or Voluntary Organizations, 4370
Sister Grants for Women's Organizations, 4371
Sisters of Charity Fndn of Canton Grants, 4372
Sisters of Mercy of North Carolina Fndn Grants, 4375
Sisters of St. Joseph Healthcare Fndn Grants, 4377
Social Justice Fund NW Economic Justice Giving Project Grants, 4395
Social Justice Fund NW Environmental Justice Giving Project Grants, 4396
Sophia Romero Grants, 4406
Southwire Company Grants, 4447
Speer Grants, 4450
Sport Manitoba KidSport Athlete Grants, 4458
Staples Fndn for Learning Grants, 4475
Stark Community Fndn Women's Grants, 4481
Starr Fndn Grants, 4483
State Strategies Grants, 4494
Steelcase Fndn Grants, 4497
Steven B. Achelis Fndn Grants, 4502
Stewart Huston Charitable Grants, 4505
Strowd Roses Grants, 4515
Subaru Adopt a School Garden Grants, 4517
Sunny and Abe Rosenberg Fndn Grants, 4529
Swindells Charitable Fndn, 4542
TAC Touring Arts and Arts Access Grants, 4557
Tauck Family Fndn Grants, 4563
Teagle Fndn Grants, 4569
Textron Corp Contributions Grants, 4601
Thelma Braun and Bocklett Family Fndn Grants, 4603
Theodore Edson Parker Fndn Grants, 4605
Thompson Charitable Fndn Grants, 4622
Thompson Fndn Grants, 4623
Threshold Fndn Justice and Democracy Grants, 4626
Time Warner Diverse Voices in the Arts Grants, 4635
Trinity Trust Summer Youth Mini Grants, 4672
Trull Fndn Grants, 4673
TSYSF Individual Scholarships, 4675
TSYSF Team Grants, 4676
U.S. Bank Fndn Grants, 4686
U.S. Department of Educ Child Care Access Means Parents in School Grants, 4689
UNESCO World Heritage Grants, 4706
Union Bank, N.A. Fndn Grants, 4709
Union Benevolent Association Grants, 4710
Union Labor Health Fndn Community Grants, 4713
US Airways Educ Fndn Grants, 4790
USDA Denali Comm High Energy Cost Grants, 4805
USDA Housing Application Packaging Grants, 4815
USDA Housing Preservation Grants, 4816
USDA Self-Help Technical Assistance Grants, 4836
USDA Tech and Supervisory Assistance Grants, 4841
USFA Development Grants, 4866
USFA Equipment Subsidy Grants, 4867
USGA Fndn For the Good of the Game Grants, 4868
US Soccer Annual Program & Field Grants, 4870
US Soccer Fndn Planning Grants, 4871
USTA NJTL Tennis and Leadership Camp Scholarships, 4879
USTA Serves College Textbook Scholarships, 4886
USTA Serves Eve Kraft Scholarships, 4889
USTA Serves Player Incentive Awards, 4891
Verizon Fndn Delaware Grants, 4909
Verizon Fndn Great Lakes Region Grants, 4912
Walter and Elise Haas Grants, 4982
Washington Area Fuel Grants, 4988
Washington Gas Charitable Contributions, 5000
Weaver Fndn Grants, 5015
Westinghouse Charitable Giving Grants, 5028
Wild Rivers Community Fndn Holiday Partnership Grants, 5069
Wild Rivers Community Fndn Summer Youth Mini Grants, 5070
William G. and Helen C. Hoffman Fndn Grants, 5080
William H. Hannon Fndn Grants, 5086
William J. Brace Charitable Trust, 5088
William Robert Baird Charitable Grants, 5093
William S. Abell Fndn Grants, 5094
Wilson-Wood Fndn Grants, 5098

Disaster Preparedness

3M Company Health and Human Services Grants, 14
AEGON Transamerica Disaster Relief Grants, 178
Baxter Int'l Corp Giving Grants, 689
Bill & Melinda Gates Emergency Response Grants, 766
CDC Fndn Emergency Response Grants, 972
CDC Fndn Global Disaster Response Grants, 973
CNCS AmeriCorps Indian Planning Grants, 1180
CNCS AmeriCorps NCCC Project Grants, 1181
CNCS AmeriCorps State and National Grants, 1182
Elizabeth Morse Genius Charitable Grants, 1682
GNOF Bayou Communities Grants, 2069
GNOF Gulf Coast Oil Spill Grants, 2077
GNOF Plaquemines Community Grants, 2091
GNOF St. Bernard Community Grants, 2092
Honeywell Corp Humanitarian Relief Grants, 2358
Nationwide Insurance Fndn Grants, 3285
Office Depot Fndn Disaster Relief Grants, 3640
Safeco Insurance Community Grants, 4203
USAID Grant for Operationalizing a Neighborhood Approach to Reduce Urban Disaster Risk in Latin America and the Caribbean, 4754
USAID Haiti Disaster Risk Reduction Capacity Building Grants, 4756
USAID Public-Private Alliance Proposals in Burma, Thailand, and Vietnam, 4775
USAID Rapid Response for Sudan Grants, 4776
USAID Rapid Response to Pakistanis Affected by Disasters - Phase Two Grants, 4777
USDC Disaster Relief Opportunity Grants, 4850
USDC Supplemental Appropriations Disaster Relief Opportunity Grants, 4859

Disaster Relief

2 Life 18 Fndn Grants, 5
3M Company Health and Human Services Grants, 14
Adler-Clark Electric Community Commitment Fndn Grants, 164
AEGON Transamerica Disaster Relief Grants, 178
Aid for Starving Children Int'l Grants, 212
AIG Disaster Relief Grants, 213
Albert and Bessie Mae Kronkosky Charitable Fndn Grants, 339
Albertson's Charitable Giving Grants, 345
Alice Tweed Tuohy Fndn Grants, 372
Allstate Corp Giving Grants, 386
Allstate Corp Hometown Commitment Grants, 387
Allstate Fndn Safe and Vital Communities Grants, 390
American for the Arts Emergency Relief Fund, 435
Angels Wings Fndn Int'l Grants, 469
Anheuser-Busch Fndn Grants, 470
Applied Materials Corp Philanthropy Program, 515
AT&T Fndn Civic and Comm Service Grants, 599
Avon Products Fndn Grants, 625
Barr Fndn Grants, 677
Baxter Int'l Corp Giving Grants, 689
Beazley Fndn Grants, 714
Bill & Melinda Gates Emergency Response Grants, 766
BJ's Charitable Fndn Grants, 777
Boeing Company Contributions Grants, 809
California Endowment Innovative Ideas Grants, 904
Callaway Golf Company Fndn Grants, 910
Campbell Soup Fndn Grants, 916
Cargill Citizenship Fund-Corp Giving Grants, 925
Carnegie Corp of New York Grants, 940
CDC Fndn Emergency Response Grants, 972
CDC Fndn Global Disaster Response Grants, 973
CE and S Fndn Grants, 985
Citigroup Fndn Grants, 1139
CNCS AmeriCorps Indian Planning Grants, 1180
CNCS AmeriCorps NCCC Project Grants, 1181
CNCS AmeriCorps State and National Grants, 1182
CNCS AmeriCorps State and National Planning Grants, 1183
CNCS AmeriCorps VISTA Project Grants, 1184
Coca-Cola Fndn Grants, 1195
Computer Associates Community Grants, 1341
Covidien Medical Product Donations, 1390
Cultural Society of Filipino Americans Grants, 1412
DENSO North America Fndn Grants, 1499
DFN Hurricane Katrina and Disability Rapid Response Grants, 1522
Diageo Fndn Grants, 1546
Elizabeth Morse Genius Charitable Grants, 1682
Essex County Community Emergency Grants, 1753
Farm Aid Grants, 1790
Farmers Insurance Corp Giving Grants, 1791
Federal Express Corp Contributions Program, 1799
Flextronics Fndn Disaster Relief Grants, 1841
Ford Fndn Peace and Social Justice Grants, 1884
Freeman Fndn Grants, 1952
GNOF Bayou Communities Grants, 2069
GNOF Gulf Coast Oil Spill Grants, 2077
GNOF Plaquemines Community Grants, 2091
GNOF St. Bernard Community Grants, 2092
Gulf Coast Community Fndn Grants, 2174
H. Schaffer Fndn Grants, 2187
Harry Kramer Grants, 2242
Home Building Industry Disaster Relief Fund, 2348
Honeywell Corp Humanitarian Relief Grants, 2358
Humana Fndn Grants, 2388
Int'l Assoc of Emergency Managers Scholarships, 2566
Jessie Ball Dupont Grants, 2671
John Deere Fndn Grants, 2692
John S. and James L. Knight Fndn Communities Grants, 2711

SUBJECT INDEX

Kessler Fndn Hurricane Emergency Grants, 2815
Kimberly-Clark Community Grants, 2824
Knight Fndn Grants - Montana, 2830
Kroger Grassroots Community Support Grants, 2843
M.J. Murdock Charitable Trust General Grants, 2954
Merkel Fndn Grants, 3124
Modest Needs Hurricane Sandy Relief Grants, 3198
Nationwide Insurance Fndn Grants, 3285
Nestle Purina PetCare Emergency Response and Disaster Relief Grants, 3303
Noble County Community Fndn Grants, 3456
Office Depot Fndn Disaster Relief Grants, 3640
Perry County Community Fndn Grants, 3827
Pike County Community Fndn Grants, 3888
Posey County Community Fndn Grants, 3939
Procter and Gamble Grants, 3967
Public Welfare Fndn Grants, 3984
Ralphs Food 4 Less Fndn Grants, 4014
Richard and Rhoda Goldman Grants, 4077
Robert R. Meyer Fndn Grants, 4121
Rockefeller Fndn Grants, 4138
San Diego Fndn After-the-Fires Grants, 4242
Schering-Plough Fndn Health Grants, 4304
Seneca Foods Fndn Grants, 4336
Sony Corp of America Corp Philanthropy Grants, 4405
Spencer County Community Fndn Grants, 4451
State Farm Companies Safe Neighbors Grants, 4484
Sunoco Fndn Grants, 4530
Thompson Charitable Fndn Grants, 4622
Union Bank, N.A. Fndn Grants, 4709
USAID Grant for Operationalizing a Neighborhood Approach to Reduce Urban Disaster Risk in Latin America and the Caribbean, 4754
USAID Haiti Disaster Risk Reduction Capacity Building Grants, 4756
USAID Public-Private Alliance Proposals in Burma, Thailand, and Vietnam, 4775
USAID Rapid Response for Sudan Grants, 4776
USAID Rapid Response to Pakistanis Affected by Disasters - Phase Two Grants, 4777
USDC Disaster Relief Opportunity Grants, 4850
USDC Supplemental Appropriations Disaster Relief Opportunity Grants, 4859
Verizon Wireless Hopeline Grants, 4927
VHA Health Fndn Grants, 4931
Warrick County Community Fndn Grants, 4987

Disasters
2 Life 18 Fndn Grants, 5
3M Company Health and Human Services Grants, 14
Adler-Clark Electric Community Commitment Fndn Grants, 164
AEGON Transamerica Disaster Relief Grants, 178
AIG Disaster Relief Grants, 213
American Express Charitable Grants, 429
American Foodservice Charitable Grants, 433
American Forests Global ReLeaf Grants, 434
Baxter Int'l Corp Giving Grants, 689
Bill & Melinda Gates Emergency Response Grants, 766
CDC Fndn Emergency Response Grants, 972
CDC Fndn Global Disaster Response Grants, 973
CNCS AmeriCorps Indian Planning Grants, 1180
CNCS AmeriCorps NCCC Project Grants, 1181
CNCS AmeriCorps State and National Grants, 1182
Community Fndn of Greater Memphis Grants, 1290
Elizabeth Morse Genius Charitable Grants, 1682
FAR Grants, 1787
Flextronics Fndn Disaster Relief Grants, 1841
Francis T. & Louise T. Nichols Fndn Grants, 1923
GNOF Bayou Communities Grants, 2069
GNOF Gulf Coast Oil Spill Grants, 2077
GNOF Plaquemines Community Grants, 2091
GNOF St. Bernard Community Grants, 2092
Harry Kramer Grants, 2242
Honeywell Corp Humanitarian Relief Grants, 2358
Hormel Foods Charitable Grants, 2368
J. Edwin Treakle Fndn Grants, 2596
Knight Fndn Grants - Montana, 2830
Nestle Purina PetCare Emergency Response and Disaster Relief Grants, 3303

Office Depot Fndn Disaster Relief Grants, 3640
Rohm and Haas Company Grants, 4145
State Farm Companies Safe Neighbors Grants, 4484
USAID Grant for Operationalizing a Neighborhood Approach to Reduce Urban Disaster Risk in Latin America and the Caribbean, 4754
USAID Haiti Disaster Risk Reduction Capacity Building Grants, 4756
USAID Public-Private Alliance Proposals in Burma, Thailand, and Vietnam, 4775
USAID Rapid Response for Sudan Grants, 4776
USAID Rapid Response to Pakistanis Affected by Disasters - Phase Two Grants, 4777
USDC Disaster Relief Opportunity Grants, 4850
USDC Supplemental Appropriations Disaster Relief Opportunity Grants, 4859

Disciples of Christ Church
AHS Fndn Grants, 208
Alvah H. and Wyline P. Chapman Fndn Grants, 402
MacDonald-Peterson Fndn Grants, 2965

Discrimination
AAUW Breaking through Barriers Award, 74
Allstate Corp Giving Grants, 386
Allstate Corp Hometown Commitment Grants, 387
Allstate Fndn Safe and Vital Communities Grants, 390
Allstate Fndn Tolerance, Inclusion, and Diversity Grants, 391
Colin Higgins Fndn Courage Awards, 1203
Community Fndn Greater Chattanooga Grants, 1281
Georgia Power Fndn Grants, 2039
HBF Defending Freedoms Grants, 2271
Hitachi Fndn Yoshiyama Awards, 2340
Otto Bremer Fndn Grants, 3713
Philanthrofund Fndn Grants, 3874
San Diego Fndn for Change Grants, 4247
Sioux Falls Area Community Fndn Spot Grants, 4366
Social Justice Fund NW Criminal Justice Giving Project Grants, 4394
Threshold Fndn Justice and Democracy Grants, 4626
Waitt Family Fndn Grants, 4973
Women's Funding Alliance Grants, 5112

Disease, Chronic
George E. Hatcher, Jr. and Ann Williams Hatcher Fndn Grants, 2015
Marin Community Successful Aging Grants, 3014
Mary Wilmer Covey Charitable Grants, 3049
TJX Fndn Grants, 4637

Diseases
Albertson's Charitable Giving Grants, 345
Batchelor Fndn Grants, 679
Bill and Melinda Gates Fndn Water, Sanitation and Hygiene Grants, 770
George E. Hatcher, Jr. and Ann Williams Hatcher Fndn Grants, 2015
Henry and Ruth Blaustein Rosenberg Grants, 2306
Mary Wilmer Covey Charitable Grants, 3049
Premera Blue Cross CARES Grants, 3945
Robert R. Meyer Fndn Grants, 4121

Distance Learning
ALA e-Learning Scholarships, 270
ALA Information Technology Pathfinder Award, 286
ALA Routledge Distance Learning Librarianship Conference Sponsorship Award, 315
ALA Sara Jaffarian School Library Award for Exemplary Humanities Programming, 316
Alfred P. Sloan Fndn Civic Inits Grants, 368
Chatlos Fndn Grants, 1061
Hillsdale Grants, 2329
National Endowment for Arts Commun Grants, 3260
USDA Distance Learning and Telemed Grants, 4806
USDA Rural Business Enterprise Grants, 4823

Diversity
Aetna Fndn Diversity Grants in Connecticut, 182
ALA Diversity and Outreach Fair, 267

Domestic Violence / 871

ALA Diversity Research Grant, 268
ALA Supporting Diversity Stipend, 333
BBVA Compass Fndn Charitable Grants, 703
Benton Community Fndn - The Cookie Jar Grant, 729
Boeing Company Contributions Grants, 809
Community Fndn of Boone Cty Women's Grants, 1273
Community Fndn Of Greater Lafayette Grants, 1289
Diversity Leadership Academy Grants, 1550
EQT Fndn Community Grants, 1744
Johnson County Community Fndn Youth Philanthropy Init Grants, 2724
Kalamazoo Community Good Neighbor Grants, 2768
KeyBank Fndn Grants, 2820
Maine Community Fndn People of Color Grants, 2985
NAA Fndn Diversity PowerMind Fellowships, 3232
NAA Fndn Minority Fellowships, 3233
NHLBI Ruth L. Kirschstein National Research Service Awards for Individual Senior Fellows, 3421
PepsiCo Fndn Grants, 3819
Seagate Tech Corp Capacity to Care Grants, 4317
Sisters of Mercy of North Carolina Fndn Grants, 4375
Stewart Huston Charitable Grants, 4505
USAID Unsolicited Proposal Grants, 4786
USTA Multicultural Individual Player Grant for National Competition and Training, 4877

Documentaries
Andy Warhol Fndn for the Visual Arts Grants, 464
CCH California Story Grants, 965
CCH Documentary Project Production Grants, 969
CCH Documentary Public Engagement Grants, 970
CCH Documentary Project Research and Development Grants, 971
Connecticut Community Fndn Grants, 1350
Illinois Arts Council Media Arts Grants, 2472
North Carolina Arts Council Folklife Documentary Project Grants, 3475
OSF Documentary Photography Project Audience Engagement Grant, 3706
PCA Arts Organizations and Arts Programs Grants for Film and Electronic Media, 3780
PCA Entry Track Arts Organizations and Program Grants for Film and Electronic Media, 3792
Pi Lambda Theta Anna Tracey Memorial Award, 3889
San Francisco Bay Area Documentary Grants, 4261
Texas Commission on the Arts Cultural Connections- Visual & Media Arts Touring Exhibits Grants, 4589
Texas Filmmakers Production Grants, 4595

Domestic Violence
A.V. Hunter Grants, 47
Abbot and Dorothy H. Stevens Fndn Grants, 79
Abelard Fndn East Grants, 87
Abelard Fndn West Grants, 88
Advocate Safehouse Project Grants, 174
Alberto Culver Corp Contributions Grants, 343
Allstate Fndn Economic Empowerment Grants, 389
Amelia Sillman Rockwell and Carlos Perry Rockwell Charities Grants, 417
Arizona Republic Newspaper Contributions, 547
Atherton Family Fndn Grants, 604
Atkinson Fndn Community Grants, 606
Austin-Bailey Health and Wellness Fndn Grants, 614
Austin S. Nelson Fndn Grants, 617
Baxter Int'l Fndn Grants, 691
Bemis Company Fndn Grants, 723
Blue Shield of California Grants, 802
Boston Jewish Community Women's Grants, 822
Bush Fndn Health & Human Services Grants, 875
Callaway Golf Company Fndn Violence Prevention Grants, 911
Cambridge Community Fndn Grants, 913
Carlisle Fndn Grants, 931
Carl M. Freeman Fndn FACES Grants, 932
Carrie E. and Lena V. Glenn Fndn Grants, 944
Catherine Kennedy Home Fndn Grants, 955
CDC Grants for Violence-Related Injury Prevention Research, 974
Charity Incorporated Grants, 1035
Charles Nelson Robinson Grants, 1052

872 / Domestic Violence

Chicago Community Trust Public Safety and Justice Grants, 1093
Claneil Fndn Grants, 1145
Colorado Springs Community Grants, 1215
Columbus Fndn Small Grants, 1232
Commission on Religion in Appalachia Grants, 1238
Community Fndn of Broward Grants, 1275
Community Fndn of Middle Tennessee Grants, 1300
Covenant Mountain Ministries Grants, 1387
Covenant to Care for Children Critical Grants, 1388
Crail-Johnson Fndn Grants, 1393
Dade Community Fndn GLBT Grants, 1429
Dallas Women's Fndn Grants, 1438
Dammann Grants, 1439
Deluxe Corp Fndn Grants, 1496
Dennis and Phyllis Washington Fndn Grants, 1498
Detroit Lions Charities Grants, 1520
DOJ Rural Domestic Violence and Child Victimization Enforcement Grants, 1562
Duke Endowment Child Care Grants, 1617
Duluth-Superior Area Community Fndn Grants, 1620
Edina Realty Fndn Grants, 1656
Edward and Ellen Roche Relief Fndn Grants, 1663
Faye McBeath Fndn Grants, 1794
Fisa Fndn Grants, 1826
Frank B. Hazard General Charity Grants, 1926
Fremont Area Community Fndn Grants, 1955
Gardiner Howland Shaw Fndn Grants, 1986
Go Daddy Cares Charitable Contributions, 2094
Greater Worcester Comm Discretionary Grants, 2140
Hawai'i Children's Trust Fund Community Awareness Events Grants, 2258
Health Fndn of Greater Indianapolis Grants, 2282
Henry and Ruth Blaustein Rosenberg Grants, 2306
Herbert A. and Adrian W. Woods Fndn Grants, 2313
Hilton Head Island Fndn Grants, 2330
Hugh J. Andersen Fndn Grants, 2385
James R. Dougherty Jr. Fndn Grants, 2635
Jane Bradley Pettit Fndn Community and Social Development Grants, 2642
Jeffris Wood Fndn Grants, 2660
Jim Moran Fndn Grants, 2680
John Gogian Family Fndn Grants, 2697
John W. Speas and Effie E. Speas Grants, 2732
Kahuku Community Fund, 2762
Lucy Downing Nisbet Charitable Grants, 2935
Mabel A. Horne Grants, 2956
Maine State Troopers Fndn Grants, 2991
Mardag Fndn Grants, 3001
Mary Kay Ash Charitable Fndn Grants, 3043
Mertz Gilmore Fndn NYC Communities Grants, 3126
Meyer Fndn Healthy Communities Grants, 3143
Morris and Gwendolyn Cafritz Fndn Grants, 3218
NNEDVF/Altria Doors of Hope Program, 3452
Northern Trust Company Corp Giving Program, 3504
Northland Fndn Grants, 3506
OneFamily Fndn Grants, 3673
PacifiCorp Fndn for Learning Grants, 3727
Piper Jaffray Fndn Communities Giving Grants, 3899
Portland General Electric Fndn Grants, 3937
Posey Community Fndn Women's Grants, 3938
Quantum Fndn Grants, 3996
R.S. Gernon Grants, 4002
RadioShack StreetSentz Community Grants, 4005
Reinberger Fndn Grants, 4052
Reynolds and Reynolds Associate Fndn Grants, 4069
ROSE Grants, 4161
S. Mark Taper Fndn Grants, 4201
Scherman Fndn Grants, 4305
State Justice Institute Curriculum Adaptation and Training Grants, 4488
State Justice Institute Partner Grants, 4489
State Justice Institute Project Grants, 4490
State Justice Institute Strategic Init Grants, 4492
State Justice Institute Tech Assistance Grants, 4493
Target Corp Local Store Grants, 4561
TJX Fndn Grants, 4637
Verizon Domestic Violence Prevention Grants, 4910
Verizon Fndn Grants, 4911
Verizon Fndn Maryland Grants, 4917

Verizon Fndn New York Grants, 4919
Verizon Fndn NE Region Grants, 4920
Verizon Fndn Pennsylvania Grants, 4921
Verizon Fndn Vermont Grants, 4924
Verizon Fndn Virginia Grants, 4925
Verizon Fndn West Virginia Grants, 4926
Verizon Wireless Hopeline Grants, 4927
Women's Funding Alliance Grants, 5112
Yellow Corp Fndn Grants, 5126

Drama
ALA Stonewall Book Awards - Barbara Gittings Literature Award, 329
ArtsWave Impact Grants, 580
Bush Fndn Arts & Humanities Grants: Short-Term Organizational Support, 873
Herman Goldman Fndn Grants, 2317
Illinois Arts Council Media Arts Grants, 2472
North Carolina Arts Cncl New Realities Grants, 3478
North Carolina Arts Council Residency Grants, 3481
NYFA Gregory Millard Fellowships, 3565
NYSCA Lit: General Operating Support Grants, 3598
NYSCA Literature: General Support Grants, 3599
Ontario Arts Council Theatre Creators' Grants, 3681
PCA Arts Organizations & Grants for Theatre, 3783
PCA Entry Track Arts Organizations and Program Grants for Theatre, 3797
PCA Strategies for Success Grants - Basic Level, 3805
PCA Strategies for Success Grants - Intermediate, 3806

Dramatic/Theater Arts
Alaska State Council on the Arts Community Arts Development Grants, 327
Alaska State Council on the Arts Operating Support Grants, 328
Alcatel-Lucent Technologies Fndn Grants, 349
Ann L. & Carol Green Rhodes Charitable Grants, 483
Arts Midwest Performing Arts Grants, 579
ArtsWave Impact Grants, 580
ArtsWave Project Grants, 581
Blanche and Irving Laurie Fndn Grants, 784
Butler Manufacturing Company Fndn Grants, 881
CCH California Story Grants, 965
Clarcor Fndn Grants, 1148
Community Fndn of Sarasota County Grants, 1306
Community Fndn of St. Joseph County ArtsEverywhere Grants, 1313
Con Edison Corp Arts and Culture Grants, 1344
Emma A. Sheafer Charitable Grants, 1699
F.M. Kirby Fndn Grants, 1780
Florida Div of Cultural Affairs Theatre Grants, 1847
Florida Div of Cultural Affairs General Program Support Grants, 1854
Florida Div of Cultural Affairs Professional Theatre Grants, 1861
Florida Div of Cultural Affairs Specific Cultural Project Grants, 1862
Florida Div of Cultural Affairs Underserved Cultural Community Development Grants, 1864
Fndn NW Grants, 1906
Gateway Fndn Grants, 1992
Georgia Council for the Arts Partner Grants for Service Organizations, 2036
Greater Columbus Arts Council Operating Grant, 2133
Hearst Fndns Culture Grants, 2284
High Meadow Fndn Grants, 2321
Huffy Fndn Grants, 2384
IFP Minnesota McKnight Screenwriters Fellows, 2449
Illinois Arts Council Theater Grants, 2477
Iowa Arts Council Artists in Schools/Communities Residency Grants, 2571
Jerome Fndn Grants, 2667
Jerome Fndn Travel and Study Grants, 2668
Joyce Fndn Culture Grants, 2747
Kansas Arts Commission Artist Fellowships, 2776
Kenneth T. and Eileen L. Norris Fndn Grants, 2802
Leon and Thea Koerner Fndn Grants, 2883
Lettie Pate Evans Fndn Grants, 2887
MacArthur Fndn Chicago Arts and Culture General Operations Grants, 2961

MacArthur Fndn Chicago Arts and Culture Int'l Connections Grants, 2962
Mary & Walter Frear Eleemosynary Grants, 3035
Meyer Memorial Trust Special Grants, 3149
National Endowment for the Arts - National Arts and Humanities Youth Program Awards, 3255
National Endowment for Arts Media Grants, 3264
NHSCA Artist Residencies in Schools Grants, 3423
NHSCA Youth Arts Project Grants: For Extended Arts Learning, 3430
NJSCA Arts Project Support, 3446
NJSCA Financial and Instal Stabilization Grants, 3447
NJSCA General Program Support Grants, 3449
Norcliffe Fndn Grants, 3459
North Carolina Arts Council Gen Support, 3477
NYFA Gregory Millard Fellowships, 3565
NYSCA Architecture, Planning, and Design: Capital Fixtures and Equipment Purchase Grants, 3570
NYSCA Architecture, Planning, and Design: General Program Support Grants, 3574
NYSCA Arts Educ: General Operating Support, 3578
NYSCA Arts Educ Program Support Grants, 3579
NYSCA Arts Educ: Services to the Field Grants, 3582
NYSCA Presenting: General Operating Support, 3609
NYSCA Presenting: Presenting Grants, 3611
NYSCA Presenting: Services to the Field Grants, 3612
NYSCA Special Art Services Project Support, 3613
NYSCA Special Arts Services: General Program Support Grants, 3615
NYSCA Special Arts Services: Instruction and Training Grants, 3616
NYSCA Special Arts Services: Professional Performances Grants, 3617
NYSCA State and Local Partnerships: General Operating Support Grants, 3619
NYSCA State and Local Partnerships: General Program Support Grants, 3620
NYSCA State and Local Partnerships: Services to the Field Grants, 3621
NYSCA State and Local Partnerships: Workshops Grants, 3622
NYSCA Theatre Gen Operating Support Grants, 3623
NYSCA Theatre General Program Support, 3624
NYSCA Theatre Pro Performances Grants, 3625
NYSCA Theatre: Services to the Field Grants, 3626
Ontario Arts Council Theatre Creators' Grants, 3681
Parker Fndn (California) Grants, 3736
PCA-PCD Professional Development for Individual Artists Grants, 3770
PCA Arts in Educ Residencies, 3772
PCA Arts Organizations & Grants for Theatre, 3783
PCA Busing Grants, 3786
PCA Entry Track Arts Organizations and Program Grants for Theatre, 3797
PCA Pennsylvania Partners in the Arts Program Stream Grants, 3801
PCA Pennsylvania Partners in the Arts Project Stream Grants, 3802
PCA Professional Development Grants, 3803
PCA Strategies for Success Grants - Advanced, 3804
PCA Strategies for Success Grants - Basic Level, 3805
PCA Strategies for Success Grants - Intermediate, 3806
PennPAT Artist Technical Assistance Grants, 3811
PennPAT Strategic Opportunity Grants, 3815
Peyton Anderson Fndn Grants, 3862
Philip L. Graham Grants, 3876
Procter and Gamble Grants, 3967
Rich Fndn Grants, 4090
Robert Sterling Clark Arts and Culture Grants, 4122
Robert W. Woodruff Fndn Grants, 4124
Santa Barbara Fndn Towbes Fund for the Performing Arts Grants, 4288
South Carolina Arts Comm Accessibility Grants, 4410
TAC Arts Access Grant, 4549
Virginia Commission for the Arts Project Grants, 4944
VSA/Volkswagen Group of America Exhibition Awards, 4954
Wallace Fndn Grants, 4976
Walt Disney Company Fndn Grants, 4981

SUBJECT INDEX

Drawing
Constance Saltonstall Fndn for the Arts Grants, 1361
SCBWI Don Freeman Memorial Grant, 4302
Third Millennium Fndn Grants, 4607

Driver Education
AAA Fndn for Traffic Safety Grants, 50
State Farm Companies Safe Neighbors Grants, 4484
State Farm Project Ignition Grants, 4487
Toyota USA Fndn Safety Grants, 4662
YSA State Farm Good Neighbor YOUth In The Driver Seat Grants, 5141

Dropouts
CNCS AmeriCorps State and National Grants, 1182
CNCS Senior Corps Retired and Senior Volunteer Grants, 1188
Coca-Cola Fndn Grants, 1195
DOJ Juvenile Mentoring Grants, 1560
Joseph Drown Fndn Grants, 2735
Meyer Fndn Educ Grants, 3142
Pacers Fndn Be Educated Grants, 3721
PepsiCo Fndn Grants, 3819
Rockwell Fund, Inc. Grants, 4140
Romic Environmental's Charitable Contributions, 4148

Drug Education
Alcatel-Lucent Technologies Fndn Grants, 349
Appalachian Regional Commission Educ and Training Grants, 504
CFFVR Alcoholism and Drug Abuse Grants, 1001
Comer Fndn Grants, 1236
Dept of Ed Safe and Drug-Free Schools and Communities State Grants, 1513
Drug Free Communities Support Program, 1608
Fndn for a Drug-Free World Classroom Tools, 1890
GNOF IMPACT Kahn-Oppenheim Grants, 2084
Grand Rapids Area Community Fndn Wyoming Youth Grants, 2117
Grand Rapids Community Ionia Youth Grants, 2120
Grand Rapids Comm SE Ottawa Youth Grants, 2123
Grand Rapids Community Sparta Youth Grants, 2125
Green Fndn Educ Grants, 2153
MetroWest Health Grants to Reduce Incidence of High Risk Behaviors Among Adolescents, 3136
NYCT Girls and Young Women Grants, 3548
NYCT Substance Abuse Grants, 3558
OSF-Baltimore Tackling Drug Addiction Grants, 3698
Sprint Fndn Grants, 4463
U.S. Department of Educ Programs for Native Hawaiians, 4696

Drug Testing
Drug Free Communities Support Program, 1608

Drugs/Drug Abuse
Achelis Fndn Grants, 127
African American Fund of New Jersey Grants, 192
Aladdin Industries Fndn Grants, 263
Alfred P. Sloan Fndn Civic Inits Grants, 368
Alliance Healthcare Fndn Grants, 383
Appalachian Regional Commission Educ and Training Grants, 504
Arizona Commission on the Arts After-School Program Residencies, 535
Atkinson Fndn Community Grants, 606
Audrey and Sydney Irmas Charitable Fndn Grants, 612
Austin S. Nelson Fndn Grants, 617
Barberton Community Fndn Grants, 666
Battle Creek Community Fndn Grants, 684
Benton Community Fndn Grants, 730
Berks County Community Fndn Grants, 734
Blue River Community Fndn Grants, 801
Bodman Fndn Grants, 807
Brown County Community Fndn Grants, 853
Cambridge Community Fndn Grants, 913
Carnahan-Jackson Fndn Grants, 939
Carpenter Fndn Grants, 943
Carrie E. and Lena V. Glenn Fndn Grants, 944
CFFVR Alcoholism and Drug Abuse Grants, 1001
Cleo Fndn Grants, 1164
Colorado Springs Community Grants, 1215
Columbus Fndn Small Grants, 1232
Comer Fndn Grants, 1236
Community Fndn for Southern Arizona Grants, 1261
Community Fndn of Bartholomew County Heritage Grants, 1267
Community Fndn of Bartholomew County James A. Henderson Award for Fundraising, 1268
Community Fndn of Broward Grants, 1275
Community Fndn of Greater Birmingham Grants, 1280
Community Fndn of Greater Fort Wayne - Community Endowment and Clarke Endowment Grants, 1285
ConocoPhillips Fndn Grants, 1354
ConocoPhillips Grants, 1355
Constantin Fndn Grants, 1362
Cornerstone Fndn of NE Wisconsin Grants, 1375
D.F. Halton Fndn Grants, 1424
Danellie Fndn Grants, 1442
Daniels Grants, 1443
Dave Coy Fndn Grants, 1447
Delaware Community Fndn-Youth Philanthropy Board for Kent County, 1483
Delaware Community Next Generation Grants, 1485
Dennis and Phyllis Washington Fndn Grants, 1498
Dept of Ed Safe and Drug-Free Schools and Communities State Grants, 1513
DeRoy Testamentary Fndn Grants, 1518
Do Right Fndn Grants, 1581
DPA Promoting Policy Change Advocacy Grants, 1598
Drug Free Communities Support Program, 1608
eBay Fndn Community Grants, 1648
EIF Community Grants, 1675
Eva L. and Joseph M. Bruening Fndn Grants, 1768
Farmers Insurance Corp Giving Grants, 1791
Florida BRAIVE Fund of Dade Community, 1846
Fndn for a Drug-Free World Classroom Tools, 1890
Fndn for a Healthy Kentucky Grants, 1891
Fourjay Fndn Grants, 1913
Frances and John L. Loeb Family Grants, 1917
Fuller Fndn Grants, 1974
GEICO Public Service Awards, 1997
GNOF IMPACT Kahn-Oppenheim Grants, 2084
Grand Rapids Comm SE Ottawa Youth Grants, 2123
Greater Worcester Comm Discretionary Grants, 2140
Gulf Coast Community Operating Grants, 2176
Gulf Coast Fndn of Community Grants, 2177
Hasbro Children's Fund, 2256
Health Fndn of Greater Cincinnati Grants, 2281
Hearst Fndns Social Service Grants, 2285
Hoffberger Fndn Grants, 2342
Huffy Fndn Grants, 2384
Humanitas Fndn Grants, 2390
Jackson Fndn Grants, 2613
Johnson & Johnson Corp Contributions Grants, 2718
Joseph Drown Fndn Grants, 2735
Joseph H. and Florence A. Roblee Fndn Grants, 2736
Kahuku Community Fund, 2762
Kuki'o Community Fund, 2845
L. W. Pierce Family Fndn Grants, 2846
Lillian S. Wells Fndn Grants, 2901
Lucile Horton Howe and Mitchell B. Howe Fndn Grants, 2934
Margaret L. Wendt Fndn Grants, 3004
Mary Owen Borden Fndn Grants, 3046
MDEQ Community Pollution Prevention (P2) Grants: Household Drug Collections, 3098
Memorial Fndn Grants, 3117
MetroWest Health Grants to Reduce Incidence of High Risk Behaviors Among Adolescents, 3136
Mid-Iowa Health Fndn Comm Response Grants, 3168
Musgrave Fndn Grants, 3231
Northern Trust Company Corp Giving Program, 3504
NYCT Substance Abuse Grants, 3558
Oakland Fund for Children and Youth Grants, 3634
Olin Corp Charitable Grants, 3669
Ordean Fndn Grants, 3691
Pacers Fndn Be Drug-Free Grants, 3720
PacifiCorp Fndn for Learning Grants, 3727
Pasadena Fndn Average Grants, 3741

Early Childhood Education / 873

Patrick and Aimee Butler Family Fndn Community Human Services Grants, 3749
Patrick and Anna M. Cudahy Grants, 3751
Peter & Elizabeth C. Tower Mental Health Reference and Resource Materials Mini-Grants, 3837
Peter and Elizabeth C. Tower Fndn Substance Abuse Grants, 3842
Phoenix Suns Charities Grants, 3881
Piedmont Natural Gas Fndn Health and Human Services Grants, 3885
Puerto Rico Community Fndn Grants, 3986
Quantum Corp Snap Server Grants, 3995
Questar Corp Contributions Grants, 3997
Romic Environmental's Charitable Contributions, 4148
Ruth Anderson Fndn Grants, 4176
RWJF New Jersey Health Inits Grants, 4187
SAMHSA Campus Suicide Prevention Grants, 4229
SAMHSA Drug Free Communities Grants, 4230
SAMHSA Strategic Prevention Framework State Incentive Grants, 4231
Seabury Fndn Grants, 4316
Sid W. Richardson Fndn Grants, 4350
Sioux Falls Area Community Grants, 4364
Sioux Falls Area Community Fndn Spot Grants, 4366
Southbury Community Trust Fund, 4409
Stackpole-Hall Fndn Grants, 4472
State Justice Institute Curriculum Adaptation and Training Grants, 4488
State Justice Institute Partner Grants, 4489
State Justice Institute Project Grants, 4490
State Justice Institute Strategic Init Grants, 4492
State Justice Institute Tech Assistance Grants, 4493
Stewart Huston Charitable Grants, 4505
Tides Fndn Grants, 4632
Topeka Community Fndn Grants, 4644
Trull Fndn Grants, 4673
U.S. Department of Educ Programs for Native Hawaiians, 4696
Union Bank, N.A. Fndn Grants, 4709
USDJ Edward Byrne Justice Assistance Grants, 4863
Victor E. Speas Fndn Grants, 4933
Whitney Fndn Grants, 5061

Dyslexia
Claremont Community Fndn Grants, 1149
Talbert and Leota Abrams Fndn, 4558

Early Childhood Development
ACF Native American Social and Economic Development Strategies Grants, 123
Bernard & Audre Rapoport Arts & Culture Grant, 735
Bernard and Audre Rapoport Fndn Community Building and Social Service Grants, 736
Bernard and Audre Rapoport Fndn Health Grants, 738
Better Way Fndn Grants, 754
Blue Cross Blue Shield of Minnesota Fndn - Healthy Children: Growing Up Healthy Grants, 794
Linden Fndn Grants, 2908
Lyndhurst Fndn Grants, 2949
Piper Trust Children Grants, 3901
Piper Trust Educ Grants, 3902
Piper Trust Healthcare & Med Research Grants, 3903
TJX Fndn Grants, 4637
Vanderburgh Community Fndn Grants, 4902
WCI Family Econ Success Regionwide Grants, 5011

Early Childhood Education
ACF Native American Social and Economic Development Strategies Grants, 123
Aetna Summer Academic Enrichment Grants, 189
ALA Coretta Scott King Book Donation Grant, 261
Barr Fndn Grants (Massachusetts), 676
Bernard & Audre Rapoport Arts & Culture Grant, 735
Better Way Fndn Grants, 754
Community Fndn of Bartholomew County Women's Giving Circle, 1269
Fndn for the Carolinas Grants, 1896
Georgia-Pacific Fndn Educ Grants, 2031
German Protestant Orphan Asylum Fndn Grants, 2044
GNOF Stand Up For Our Children Grants, 2093

Harry A. and Margaret D. Towsley Fndn Grants, 2236
LEGO Children's Grants, 2878
Leon and Thea Koerner Fndn Grants, 2883
Linden Fndn Grants, 2908
Luella Kemper Grants, 2939
Marsh Corp Grants, 3027
McCune Charitable Fndn Grants, 3077
McGregor Grants, 3082
Meyer Fndn Educ Grants, 3142
Moody Fndn Grants, 3215
PacifiCorp Fndn for Learning Grants, 3727
Packard Fndn Local Grants, 3729
Paul G. Allen Family Fndn Grants, 3759
Phi Upsilon Omicron Florence Fallgatter Distinguished Service Award, 3877
Pier 1 Imports Grants, 3887
Piper Trust Children Grants, 3901
Piper Trust Educ Grants, 3902
Reinberger Fndn Grants, 4052
Robert R. McCormick Tribune Comm Grants, 4119
Robert R. Meyer Fndn Grants, 4121
Rollins-Luetkemeyer Fndn Grants, 4147
Samuel N. and Mary Castle Fndn Grants, 4236
Seattle Fndn Educ Grants, 4326
Skillman Fndn Good Schools Grants, 4382
Stocker Fndn Grants, 4507
Taproot Fndn Capacity-Building Service Grants, 4560
TJX Fndn Grants, 4637
USAID Reading Enhancement for Advancing Development Grants, 4778
VSA/Metlife Connect All Grants, 4953
WCI Family Econ Success Regionwide Grants, 5011

Earth Science Education
GreenWorks! Butterfly Garden Grants, 2159
Scholastic Welch's Harvest Grants, 4309

Earth Sciences
PG&E Bright Ideas Grants, 3866
Research Program at Earthwatch Grants, 4053

Earthquake Engineering
AEGON Transamerica Disaster Relief Grants, 178
Honeywell Corp Humanitarian Relief Grants, 2358
Office Depot Fndn Disaster Relief Grants, 3640

Eating Disorders
Hilda and Preston Davis Fndn Grants, 2322

Ecology
Alaska Conservation Operating Grants, 323
Alaska Conservation Fndn Opportunity Grants, 324
Alaska Conservation Fndn Rapid Response Grants, 325
Alaska Conservation Fndn Watchable Wildlife Conservation Grants, 326
Beirne Carter Fndn Grants, 719
Beneficia Fndn Grants, 727
Brainerd Fndn Grants, 831
Bunbury Company Grants, 863
Bush Fndn Ecological Health Grants, 874
Carnahan-Jackson Fndn Grants, 939
Clarence E. Heller Charitable Fndn Grants, 1150
Coastal Community Fndn of S Carolina Grants, 1193
Conservation, Food, and Health Fndn Grants for Developing Countries, 1359
EPA Environmental Educ Grants, 1729
GNOF Community Revitalization Grants, 2071
HRF Hudson River Improvement Grants, 2378
HRF New York City Environmental Grants for Newton Creek, 2379
Illinois DNR Youth Recreation Corps Grants, 2508
Jenifer Altman Fndn Grants, 2662
John D. and Catherine T. MacArthur Fndn Global Challenges Grants, 2690
MacArthur Fndn Conservation and Sustainable Development Grants, 2963
NFWF Bronx River Watershed Init Grants, 3360
NFWF Pulling Together Init Grants, 3387
NW Fund for the Environment Grants, 3510
Piedmont Natural Gas Corp Contributions, 3883

Putnam Fndn Grants, 3991
St. Louis-Jefferson Solid Waste Management Waste Reduction and Recycling Grants, 4470
Sweet Water Grants, 4541
Union Bank, N.A. Fndn Grants, 4709
UPS Fndn Environmental Sustainability Grants, 4731
William C. Kenney Watershed Protection Fndn Ecosystem Grants, 5079

Ecology, Aquatic
Alaska Conservation Fndn Opportunity Grants, 324
Alaska Conservation Fndn Rapid Response Grants, 325
Alaska Conservation Fndn Watchable Wildlife Conservation Grants, 326
Great Lakes Protection Grants, 2147
HRF New York City Environmental Grants for Newton Creek, 2379
NFWF Shell Marine Habitat Grants, 3391
NFWF Southern Co Longleaf Legacy Grants, 3392
NFWF Upper Mississippi Riv Watershed Grants, 3398
USDC/NOAA Open Rivers Init Grants, 4847

Ecology, Environmental Education
EPA State Senior Environ Employment Grants, 1739
GNOF Plaquemines Community Grants, 2091
Illinois DNR Biodiversity Field Trip Grants, 2496
NFWF Southern Company Power of Flight Bird Conservation Grants, 3393
Norfolk Southern Fndn Grants, 3463
Northern Chautauqua Environmental Grants, 3501
Piedmont Natural Gas Fndn Environmental Stewardship and Energy Sustainability Grant, 3884
Tri-State Community Twenty-first Century Endowment Grants, 4666
USAID Palestinian Community Infrastructure Development Grants, 4774

Ecology, Terrestrial
Alaska Conservation Fndn Opportunity Grants, 324
Alaska Conservation Fndn Rapid Response Grants, 325
Alaska Conservation Fndn Watchable Wildlife Conservation Grants, 326

Econometrics/Forecasting
S.E.VEN Fund $50k VINE Project Prizes, 4193

Economic Development
A/H Fndn Grants, 48
AACC Building Better Communities Through Regional Economic Development Partnerships, 54
Abbey Charitable Grants, 78
ACF Native American Social and Economic Development Strategies Grants, 123
Achelis Fndn Grants, 127
ACTION Council of Monterey County Grants, 134
Air Products and Chemicals Grants, 216
Alabama Power Fndn Grants, 233
Alcatel-Lucent Technologies Fndn Grants, 349
Allen Hilles Grants, 378
Alliant Energy Fndn Community Grants, 384
Allstate Corp Giving Grants, 386
Allstate Corp Hometown Commitment Grants, 387
Allstate Fndn Safe and Vital Communities Grants, 390
Alticor Corp Community Contributions Grants, 396
Alvin and Fanny Blaustein Thalheimer Grants, 403
Amador Community Fndn Grants, 408
American Express Charitable Grants, 429
American Jewish World Service Grants, 441
American Savings Fndn Grants, 445
AMI Semiconductors Corp Grants, 457
Anderson Fndn Grants, 460
Anne Thorne Weaver Family Fndn Grants, 478
Appalachian Regional Commission Asset-Based Development Project Grants, 500
Appalachian Regional Commission Community Infrastructure Grants, 502
Appalachian Regional Commission Distressed Counties Grants, 503
Appalachian Regional Commission Educ and Training Grants, 504

Appalachian Regional Commission Leadership Development and Capacity Building Grants, 509
Aquila Corp Grants, 521
Aragona Family Fndn Grants, 522
Arizona Community Fndn Grants, 540
Arizona Republic Newspaper Contributions, 547
Arkansas Community Fndn Arkansas Black Hall of Fame Grants, 559
Arkansas Community Fndn Giving Tree Grants, 560
Arthur B. Schultz Fndn Grants, 573
Avista Fndn Grants, 624
Ayres Fndn Grants, 630
Azadoutioun Fndn Grants, 631
Bacon Family Fndn Grants, 634
BankAtlantic Fndn Grants, 654
Barberton Community Fndn Grants, 666
Bay and Paul Fndns, Inc Grants, 692
Bayer Fndn Grants, 696
Berks County Community Fndn Grants, 734
Bikes Belong Fndn Research Grants, 762
Bill and Katie Weaver Charitable Grants, 764
Bitha Godfrey & Maude J. Thomas Charitable Fndn Grants, 776
Blandin Fndn Expand Opportunity Grants, 787
Blue Cross Blue Shield of Minnesota Healthy Neighborhoods: Connect Grants, 798
Bodman Fndn Grants, 807
Boeing Company Contributions Grants, 809
Bollinger Fndn Grants, 812
Brico Grants, 835
Brooklyn Fndn Community Development Grants, 850
Byerly Fndn Grants, 883
C.F. Adams Charitable Grants, 884
California Endowment Innovative Ideas Challenge Grants, 904
Campbell Soup Fndn Grants, 916
Carl and Eloise Pohlad Family Fndn Grants, 927
Carlisle Fndn Grants, 931
Carnegie Corp of New York Grants, 940
CCHD Economic Development Grants, 967
CDECD Tourism Product Development Grants, 984
CenterPointEnergy Minnegasco Grants, 993
CharityWorks Grants, 1036
Charles M. and Mary D. Grant Fndn Grants, 1050
Charles Stewart Mott Fndn Anti-Poverty Grants, 1054
Charles Stewart Mott Fndn Grants, 1055
Chemtura Corp Contributions Grants, 1067
ChevronTexaco Contributions Program, 1078
Chicago Community Poverty Alleviation Grants, 1091
Chicago Community Trust Workforce Grants, 1094
Chicago Title and Trust Company Fndn Grants, 1099
Circle K Corp Contributions Grants, 1136
CIT Corp Giving Grants, 1138
Citigroup Fndn Grants, 1139
Citizens Savings Fndn Grants, 1141
Claude Worthington Benedum Fndn Grants, 1161
Cleveland Community Responsive Grants, 1168
Cleveland Fenn Ed Grants, 1169
Cleveland Lake-Geauga Grants, 1170
CNCS AmeriCorps Indian Planning Grants, 1180
CNCS Social Innovation Grants, 1189
Columbus Fndn John W. and Edna McManus Shepard Grants, 1223
Columbus Neighborhood Partnership Grants, 1226
Columbus Fndn Robert E. and Genevieve B. Schaefer Grants, 1229
Comerica Charitable Fndn Grants, 1237
Commonwealth Edison Grants, 1240
Community Development Financial Inst Bank Enterprise Awards, 1244
Community Fndn for San Benito County Grants, 1258
Community Fndn for SE Michigan Grants, 1259
Community Fndn of Greater New Britain Grants, 1291
Community Fndn of Jackson County Grants, 1298
Community Fndn of Muncie and Delaware County Grants, 1302
Community Fndn of Santa Cruz County Grants, 1305
Community Fndn of Wabash County Grants, 1326
Community Technology Fndn of California Building Communities Through Technology Grants, 1336

SUBJECT INDEX

Economic Development / 875

Connecticut Light & Power Corp Contributions, 1352
Constellation Energy Corp Grants, 1364
CSRA Community Fndn Grants, 1407
Curtis Fndn Grants, 1419
Dade Community Fndn Grants, 1430
Daywood Fndn Grants, 1465
DB Americas Fndn Grants, 1466
Dearborn Community City of Aurora Grants, 1470
Denver Fndn Community Grants, 1502
DHHS Community Services Block Grant Training and Technical Assistance Program: Capacity-Building for Ongoing CSBG Programs and Strategic Planning and Coordination Grants, 1529
DHHS Indep Demonstration Program, 1535
Dorothy G. Griffin Charitable Fndn Grants, 1588
DTE Energy Fndn Environmental Grants, 1612
Duke Energy Economic Development Grants, 1619
East Tennessee Fndn Grants, 1646
eBay Fndn Community Grants, 1648
Eddy Knight Family Fndn Grants, 1654
El Paso Community Fndn Grants, 1688
EPA Brownfields Assessment Pilot Grants, 1724
EPA Brownfields Cleanup Grants, 1725
Erie Community Fndn Grants, 1750
Ezra M. Cutting Grants, 1779
Farm Aid Grants, 1790
Fayette County Fndn Grants, 1795
FCYO Youth Organizing Grants, 1797
Ferree Fndn Grants, 1804
Fndn for Appalachian Ohio Access to Environmental Educ Mini-Grants, 1892
Fndn for Mid South Comm Development Grants, 1897
Four Times Fndn Grants, 1914
France-Merrick Fndns Grants, 1915
Frances W. Emerson Fndn Grants, 1920
Franklin H. Wells and Ruth L. Wells Grants, 1930
Frederick McDonald Grants, 1946
Frist Fndn Grants, 1964
Fund for Southern Communities Grants, 1977
Gannett Fndn Community Action Grants, 1984
Gebbie Fndn Grants, 1995
George B. Page Fndn Grants, 2013
George Gund Fndn Grants, 2020
Georgia-Pacific Fndn Enrichment Grants, 2032
Gheens Fndn Grants, 2048
GNOF Bayou Communities Grants, 2069
GNOF Environmental Grants, 2073
GNOF Gert Community Grants, 2076
GNOF Jefferson Community Grants, 2085
GNOF Metropolitan Opportunities Grants, 2087
GNOF New Orleans Works Grants, 2088
Golden LEAF Fndn Grants, 2097
Grand Victoria Fndn Illinois Core Grants, 2126
Grassroots Government Leadership Award, 2129
Greater Columbus Arts Council Operating Grant, 2133
Greater Tacoma Community Fndn Grants, 2139
Green Diamond Charitable Contributions, 2149
Grotto Fndn Project Grants, 2166
Grover Hermann Fndn Grants, 2168
Gulf Coast Fndn of Community Capacity Building Grants, 2175
HAF Technical Assistance Grants, 2206
Harry B. and Jane H. Brock Fndn Grants, 2237
Harvest Fndn Grants, 2254
Hawaii Community Fndn West Hawaii Grants, 2266
Haymarket People's Fund Sustaining Grants, 2267
Hearst Fndns Social Service Grants, 2285
Heinz Endowments Grants, 2291
Helen Bader Fndn Grants, 2293
Helen S. Boylan Fndn Grants, 2298
Holland/Zeeland Community Fndn Grants, 2345
Hormel Fndn Grants, 2369
Household Int'l Corp Giving Grants, 2372
Howard and Bush Fndn Grants, 2374
Hudson Webber Fndn Grants, 2383
Huntington National Bank Comm Affairs Grant, 2409
Hutchinson Community Fndn Grants, 2410
Hut Fndn Grants, 2411
IIE David L. Boren Fellowships, 2454
IIE Freeman Fndn Indonesia Internships, 2456

Illinois DCEO Coal Competitiveness Grants, 2484
Illinois DCEO Coal Revival Grants, 2487
Illinois DCEO Community Development Assistance For Economic Development Grants, 2488
Illinois DNR Youth Recreation Corps Grants, 2508
Indep Comm Fndn Educ, Culture & Arts Grant, 2526
Indianapolis Power & Light Company Community Grants, 2540
Indiana Regional Economic Development Partnership Grants, 2546
ING Fndn Grants, 2555
Init Fndn Innovation Grants, 2559
J. Edwin Treakle Fndn Grants, 2596
J. F. Maddox Fndn Grants, 2597
J.L. Bedsole Fndn Grants, 2600
Jackson County Community Fndn Grants, 2611
Jackson Fndn Grants, 2613
Jacobs Family Village Neighborhoods Grants, 2619
Jane and Jack Fitzpatrick Grants, 2640
Janesville Fndn Grants, 2644
Janirve Fndn Grants, 2645
Jennings County Community Fndn Grants, 2664
Jewish Community Fndn of LA Israel Grants, 2674
Jewish Women's Fndn of New York Grants, 2677
John D. and Catherine T. MacArthur Fndn Global Challenges Grants, 2690
John Deere Fndn Grants, 2692
John S. and James L. Knight Fndn Communities Grants, 2711
Judith Clark-Morrill Fndn Grants, 2756
K.S. Adams Fndn Grants, 2758
Kalamazoo Community Fndn Economic and Community Development Grants, 2765
Kent D. Steadley and Mary L. Steadley Trust, 2804
Knight Fndn Donor Advised Grants, 2828
Koret Fndn Grants, 2837
Laura Jane Musser Rural Init Grants, 2864
Liberty Bank Fndn Grants, 2890
Liberty Hill Fndn Fund for a New LA Grants, 2892
Libra Fndn Future Grants, 2898
Lincoln Financial Group Fndn Grants, 2906
LISC Financial Opportunity Center Social Innovation Grants, 2911
Local Inits Support Corp Grants, 2917
Long Island Community Fndn Grants, 2920
Lynde and Harry Bradley Fndn Grants, 2947
Lynde and Harry Bradley Fndn Prizes, 2948
Lyndhurst Fndn Grants, 2949
M.J. Murdock Charitable Trust General Grants, 2954
MacArthur Fndn Conservation and Sustainable Development Grants, 2963
MacDonald-Peterson Fndn Grants, 2965
Madison County Community Fndn - City of Anderson Quality of Life Grant, 2972
Madison County Community General Grants, 2973
Marathon Petroleum Corp Grants, 2999
Marie H. Bechtel Charitable Grants, 3007
Marin Community Affordable Housing Grants, 3010
Marin Community Fndn Ending the Cycle of Poverty Grants, 3011
Mary E. Babcock Fndn, 3038
Massachusetts Cultural Adams Arts Grants, 3052
Max and Anna Levinson Fndn Grants, 3066
Maxon Charitable Fndn Grants, 3068
McCune Charitable Fndn Grants, 3077
MDEQ Brownfield Redevelopment and Site Reclamation Grants, 3095
Melville Charitable Grants, 3115
Metzger-Price Grants, 3137
MGM Resorts Fndn Community Grants, 3153
Microsoft Comm Affairs Puget Sound Grants, 3163
Miguel Aleman Fndn Grants, 3175
Miller Fndn Grants, 3181
Minneapolis Fndn Community Grants, 3186
Minnesota Small Cities Development Grants, 3187
Mizuho USA Fndn Grants, 3192
Montana Community Fndn Grants, 3211
Morris and Gwendolyn Cafritz Fndn Grants, 3218
NASE Succeed Scholarships, 3243
National Endowment for Arts Our Town Grants, 3257

National Endowment for Arts Agencies Grants, 3263
National Endowment for Arts Theater Grants, 3269
Natonal Endowment for the Arts Research Grants: Art Works, 3286
NHSCA General Project Grants, 3427
Nonprofit Management Grants, 3458
Norman Fndn Grants, 3464
NE Utilities Fndn Grants, 3498
NW Minnesota Fndn Asset Building Grants, 3511
NW Minnesota Fndn Women's Grants, 3512
NYCT Community Development Grants, 3546
NYCT Girls and Young Women Grants, 3548
Owen County Community Fndn Grants, 3716
Paul and Edith Babson Fndn Grants, 3755
Paul Ogle Fndn Grants, 3764
PDF Community Organizing Grants, 3807
Percy B. Ferebee Endowment Grants, 3820
Philadelphia Organizational Effectiveness Grants, 3872
Phil Hardin Fndn Grants, 3875
Piedmont Natural Gas Corp and Charitable Contributions, 3883
Piedmont Natural Gas Fndn Workforce Development Grant, 3886
Pittsburgh Fndn Community Grants, 3910
Plough Fndn Grants, 3915
PMI Fndn Grants, 3918
PNC Ecnomic Development Grants, 3922
Priddy Fndn Organizational Development Grants, 3956
Prince Charitable Trusts D.C. Grants, 3960
Princeton Area Community Fndn Fund for Women and Girls Grants, 3962
Princeton Area Comm Greater Mercer Grants, 3963
Procter and Gamble Grants, 3967
Progress Energy Fndn Economic Vitality Grants, 3969
Prudential Fndn Economic Development Grants, 3976
PSEG Corp Contributions Grants, 3979
Public Welfare Fndn Grants, 3984
Puerto Rico Community Fndn Grants, 3986
Pulaski County Community Fndn Grants, 3988
Putnam County Community Fndn Grants, 3990
RCF General Community Grants, 4032
Reynolds American Fndn Grants, 4068
Reynolds and Reynolds Company Fndn Grants, 4070
Rhode Island Fndn Grants, 4073
Richard D. Bass Fndn Grants, 4079
Richard H. Driehaus Fndn Grants, 4084
Richard King Mellon Fndn Grants, 4087
Riley Fndn Grants, 4094
Roberta Leventhal Sudakoff Fndn Grants, 4102
Robert F. Stoico / FIRSTFED Grants, 4112
Robert Sterling Clark Arts and Culture Grants, 4122
Robert W. Woodruff Fndn Grants, 4124
Rockefeller Fndn Grants, 4138
Ross Fndn Grants, 4164
Ryder System Charitable Fndn Grants, 4191
S.E.VEN Fund $50k VINE Project Prizes, 4193
S. Mark Taper Fndn Grants, 4201
San Diego Fndn for Change Grants, 4247
Sandy Hill Fndn Grants, 4257
Santa Fe Community Fndn Seasonal Grants-Spring Cycle, 4291
Schumann Fund for New Jersey Grants, 4311
Seattle Fndn Economy Grants, 4325
Shastri Indo-Canadian Institute Action Research Project Grants, 4341
Sioux Falls Area Community Grants, 4364
Sioux Falls Area Community Fndn Spot Grants, 4366
Sister Grants for Women's Organizations, 4371
Sisters of Saint Joseph Charitable Grants, 4376
Sobrato Family Fndn Grants, 4389
Sobrato Family Fndn Meeting Space Grants, 4390
Sobrato Family Fndn Office Space Grants, 4391
Sonoco Fndn Grants, 4403
Southbury Community Trust Fund, 4409
South Carolina Arts Commission Arts and Economic Impact Study Assistance Grants, 4416
South Carolina Arts Commission Cultural Tourism Init Grants, 4419
South Carolina Arts Commission Cultural Visions Grants, 4420

876 / Economic Development

Southern Minnesota Init Fndn Community Growth Init Grants, 4433
Southern Minnesota Home Visiting Grants, 4434
Southern Minnesota Init Fndn Incentive Grants, 4435
Speer Grants, 4450
Stark Community Fndn Grants, 4477
Sunoco Fndn Grants, 4530
Suntrust Bank Atlanta Fndn Grants, 4531
TCF Bank Fndn Grants, 4565
Texas Commission on the Arts Arts Respond Project Grants, 4581
Texas Instruments Corp Arts and Culture Grants, 4596
Texas Instruments Fndn Arts and Culture Grants, 4599
Textron Corp Contributions Grants, 4601
Thomas and Dorothy Leavey Fndn Grants, 4612
Threshold Fndn Thriving Resilient Communities Funding Circle, 4628
U.S. Bank Fndn Grants, 4686
Union Bank Corp Sponsorships and Donations, 4708
Union Bank, N.A. Fndn Grants, 4709
Union County Community Fndn Grants, 4711
USAID Albania Critical Economic Growth Areas Grants, 4740
USAID Call for Public-Private Alliance Proposals in Serbia, 4742
USAID Development Assistance Grants, 4748
USAID Global Development Alliance Grants, 4753
USAID Resilience and Economic Growth in the Sahel - Enhanced Resilience Grants, 4779
USAID Unsolicited Proposal Grants, 4786
US CRDF Science & Tech Entrepreneurship Business Partnership Grants in Armenia, 4795
US CRDF STEP Business Partnership Grant Competition Ukraine, 4796
USDA Coop Extension System Educ Grants, 4803
USDA Denali Comm High Energy Cost Grants, 4805
USDA Housing Application Packaging Grants, 4815
USDA Rural Business Opportunity Grants, 4824
USDA Rural Coop Development Grants, 4826
USDA Rural Economic Development Grants, 4827
USDA Rural Energy for America - Energy Audit and Renewable Energy Devel Assistance Grants, 4828
USDA Rural Energy for America - Feasibility Study Grants, 4829
USDA Small Disadvantaged Producer Grants, 4837
USDA Value-Added Producer Grants, 4843
USDC Planning and Local Technical Assistance Grants, 4854
USDC Public Works and Economic Adjustment Assistance Grants, 4856
USDC Technology Opportunities Grants, 4860
USDC University Center Economic Development Program Competition, 4861
Vulcan Materials Company Fndn Grants, 4956
W.K. Kellogg Fndn Healthy Kids Grants, 4961
Waitt Family Fndn Grants, 4973
Wallace Global Grants, 4977
Walmart Fndn National Giving Grants, 4979
Walter and Elise Haas Grants, 4982
Walton Family Fndn Home Region Grants, 4984
Warren County Community Fndn Grants, 4985
Warren County Community Fndn Mini-Grants, 4986
Waste Management Charitable Giving Grants, 5001
Weaver Fndn Grants, 5015
Westinghouse Charitable Giving Grants, 5028
White County Community Fndn Grants, 5057
William L. and Victorine Q. Adams Fndn Grants, 5089
William M. Weaver Fndn Grants, 5091
Winthrop Rockefeller Fndn Grants, 5105
World Bank JJ/WBGSP Partners Programs, 5117
Yellow Corp Fndn Grants, 5126
Z. Smith Reynolds Fndn Community Economic Development Grants, 5144

Economic Justice
Agape Fndn for Nonviolent Social Change Board of Trustees Grants, 197
Andrew Goodman Fndn Grants, 463
GNOF Coastal 5 + 1 Grants, 2070
GNOF Community Revitalization Grants, 2071
GNOF Environmental Grants, 2073
GNOF New Orleans Works Grants, 2088
Maine Women's Fund Economic Security Grants, 2992
Mertz Gilmore Fndn NYC Communities Grants, 3126
New York Fndn Grants, 3338
OSF-Baltimore Community Fellowships, 3695
OSF Burma Project/SE Asia Init Grants, 3702
Otto Bremer Fndn Grants, 3713
Sapelo Fndn Social Justice Grants, 4294
Skoll Fndn Awards for Social Entrepreneurship, 4383
Social Justice Fund NW Economic Justice Giving Project Grants, 4395

Economic Opportunities
ACF Native American Social and Economic Development Strategies Grants, 123
Arizona Women Deborah G. Carstens Grants, 543
Bill and Katie Weaver Charitable Grants, 764
Chicago Community Poverty Alleviation Grants, 1091
CNCS AmeriCorps Indian Planning Grants, 1180
CNCS AmeriCorps VISTA Project Grants, 1184
CNCS Social Innovation Grants, 1189
Edward and Ellen Roche Relief Fndn Grants, 1663
Ezra M. Cutting Grants, 1779
GNOF Environmental Grants, 2073
GNOF IMPACT Grants for Arts and Culture, 2078
GNOF Metropolitan Opportunities Grants, 2087
GNOF New Orleans Works Grants, 2088
Hearst Fndns Social Service Grants, 2285
Illinois DCEO Coal Competitiveness Grants, 2484
Legler Benbough Fndn Grants, 2877
Libra Fndn Future Grants, 2898
Maine Women's Fund Economic Security Grants, 2992
Mary E. Babcock Fndn, 3038
Minnesota Small Cities Development Grants, 3187
National Endowment for Arts Our Town Grants, 3257
New York Fndn Grants, 3338
Piedmont Natural Gas Fndn Workforce Development Grant, 3886
Robin Hood Fndn Grants, 4125
Saint Paul Companies Fndn Grants, 4217
Santa Fe Community Fndn Seasonal Grants-Spring Cycle, 4291
Seattle Fndn Economy Grants, 4325
Sobrato Family Fndn Grants, 4389
Sobrato Family Fndn Meeting Space Grants, 4390
Sobrato Family Fndn Office Space Grants, 4391
Threshold Fndn Thriving Resilient Communities Funding Circle, 4628
U.S. Bank Fndn Grants, 4686
USAID Call for Public-Private Alliance Proposals in Serbia, 4742
USAID Global Development Alliance Grants, 4753
USAID Unsolicited Proposal Grants, 4786
Walmart Fndn Facility Giving Grants, 4978
Walmart Fndn National Giving Grants, 4979
Walmart Fndn State Giving Grants, 4980
Washington Area Women's Fndn Early Care and Educ Funders Collaborative Grants, 4990
Washington Area Women's Fndn Financial Educ and Wealth Creation Grants, 4991
Washington Area Women's Fndn Jobs Grants, 4992
Washington Area Women's Fndn Open Door Capacity Grants, 4994
Washington Area Women's Fndn Strategic Opportunity and Partnership Grants, 4996

Economic Self-Sufficiency
Abington Fndn Grants, 100
ACF Assets for Indep Demonstration Grants, 114
ACF Assets for Indep Individual Development Account Grants, 115
ACF Ethnic Community Self-Help Grants, 118
ACF Preferred Communities Grants, 124
Adolph Coors Fndn Grants, 171
Arizona Women Deborah G. Carstens Grants, 543
Aspen Community Fndn Grants, 592
Atkinson Fndn Community Grants, 606
Battle Creek Community Fndn Grants, 684
BBVA Compass Fndn Charitable Grants, 703
Boeing Company Contributions Grants, 809
CFFVR Waupaca Area Community Fndn Grants, 1023
Charles Stewart Mott Fndn Anti-Poverty Grants, 1054
Chicago Community Poverty Alleviation Grants, 1091
Chicago Community Trust Workforce Grants, 1094
Citizens Bank Mid-Atlantic Charitable Grants, 1140
Columbus Fndn John W. and Edna McManus Shepard Grants, 1223
Community Fndn of Bartholomew County Women's Giving Circle, 1269
Community Fndn of Boone Cty Women's Grants, 1273
Community Fndn Greater Chattanooga Grants, 1281
Community Fndn Silicon Valley Grants, 1331
Dining for Women Grants, 1548
Dollar General Adult Lit Grants, 1568
Dollar General Family Lit Grants, 1569
Eaton Charitable Grants, 1647
Edward and Ellen Roche Relief Fndn Grants, 1663
Eileen Fisher Activating Leadership Grants for Women and Girls, 1676
Emma B. Howe Memorial Fndn Grants, 1700
Eulalie Bloedel Schneider Fndn Grants, 1767
Ewing Marion Kauffman Fndn Grants and Inits, 1777
Ezra M. Cutting Grants, 1779
FCD Child Development Grants, 1796
Fndn for the Carolinas Grants, 1896
Fndn for Mid South Comm Development Grants, 1897
Graco Fndn Grants, 2111
Hearst Fndns Social Service Grants, 2285
Henry E. Niles Fndn Grants, 2309
Independent Community Fndn Neighborhood Renewal Grants, 2527
Jewish Community Fndn of LA Israel Grants, 2674
Johnson Scholarship Fndn Grants, 2726
Jovid Fndn Grants, 2745
Kahuku Community Fund, 2762
KeyBank Fndn Grants, 2820
Legler Benbough Fndn Grants, 2877
Libra Fndn Future Grants, 2898
Liz Claiborne Fndn Grants, 2915
Madison Community Fndn Altrusa Int'l of Madison Grants, 2970
Maine Community Fndn Baldwin Area Grants, 2974
Maine Women's Fund Economic Security Grants, 2992
Mary & Walter Frear Eleemosynary Grants, 3035
May and Stanley Smith Charitable Grants, 3069
Medtronic Fndn Community Link Human Services Grants, 3112
Mizuho USA Fndn Grants, 3192
Modest Needs Bridge Grants, 3197
Modest Needs Hurricane Sandy Relief Grants, 3198
Modest Needs New Employment Grants, 3199
Modest Needs Self-Sufficiency Grants, 3201
Montana Community Fndn Women's Grants, 3212
Nehemiah Community Fndn Grants, 3290
New Mexico Women's Fndn Grants, 3335
New York Fndn Grants, 3338
Nokomis Fndn Grants, 3457
Northland Fndn Grants, 3506
Olive B. Cole Fndn Grants, 3670
Piedmont Natural Gas Fndn Workforce Development Grant, 3886
Pinellas County Grants, 3891
Porter County Women's Grant, 3934
Princeton Area Community Fndn Fund for Women and Girls Grants, 3962
RBC Dain Rauscher Fndn Grants, 4031
Retirement Research Fndn General Grants, 4067
Robin Hood Fndn Grants, 4125
Robins Fndn Grants, 4126
Rockwell Fund, Inc. Grants, 4140
Sailors' Snug Harbor of Boston Fishing Communities Init Grants, 4212
Salt River Health and Human Services Grants, 4228
Samuel S. Johnson Fndn Grants, 4239
Santa Fe Community Fndn Seasonal Grants-Spring Cycle, 4291
Seabury Fndn Grants, 4316
Sobrato Family Fndn Grants, 4389
Sobrato Family Fndn Meeting Space Grants, 4390

SUBJECT INDEX

Education / 877

Sobrato Family Fndn Office Space Grants, 4391
Speer Grants, 4450
Strengthening Families - Strengthening Communities Grants, 4513
Surdna Fndn Sustainable Environments Grants, 4533
TE Fndn Grants, 4572
Threshold Fndn Thriving Resilient Communities Funding Circle, 4628
Thrivent Financial for Lutherans Fndn Grants, 4629
U.S. Bank Fndn Grants, 4686
U.S. Department of Educ Rehabilitation Research Training Centers, 4699
Union Bank, N.A. Fndn Grants, 4709
Union Square Award for Social Justice, 4717
Union Square Awards Grants, 4718
USAID Call for Public-Private Alliance Proposals in Serbia, 4742
USAID Development Assistance Grants, 4748
Washington Area Women's Fndn Early Care and Educ Funders Collaborative Grants, 4990
Washington Area Women's Fndn Financial Educ and Wealth Creation Grants, 4991
Washington Area Women's Fndn Jobs Grants, 4992
Washington Area Women's Leadership Awards, 4993
Washington Area Women's Fndn Open Door Capacity Grants, 4994
Washington Area Women's Fndn Strategic Opportunity and Partnership Grants, 4996
World Bank JJ/WBGSP Partners Programs, 5117

Economic Stimulus
CDECD Tourism Product Development Grants, 984
DHHS ARRA Strengthening Communities Fund - Nonprofit Capacity Building Grants, 1527
DHHS ARRA Strengthening Communities Fund - State, Local, and Tribal Government Capacity Building Grants, 1528
DHHS Community Services Block Grant Training and Technical Assistance Program: Capacity-Building for Ongoing CSBG Programs and Strategic Planning and Coordination Grants, 1529
DHS ARRA Fire Station Construction Grants, 1542
DHS ARRA Port Security Grants, 1543
DHS ARRA Transit Security Grants, 1544
DHS FY 2009 Transit Security Grants, 1545
Ezra M. Cutting Grants, 1779
Libra Fndn Future Grants, 2898
TSA Advanced Surveillance Grants, 4674

Economics
Alfred P. Sloan Fndn Civic Inits Grants, 368
ANLAF Int'l Fund for Sexual Minorities Grants, 471
Appalachian Regional Commission Business Development Revolving Loan Grants, 501
AT&T Fndn Civic and Comm Service Grants, 599
Atkinson Fndn Community Grants, 606
Atlanta Women's Fndn Grants, 609
Burton Morgan Youth Entrepreneurship Grants, 870
Canada-U.S. Fulbright Mid-Career Grants, 917
Carnegie Corp of New York Grants, 940
Chapin Hall Int'l Fellowships in Children's Policy Research, 1032
Charles G. Koch Charitable Fndn Grants, 1041
Crossroads Fund Seed Grants, 1400
Dr. Scholl Fndn Grants, 1602
ESRI Conservation Grants, 1751
Fairfield County Community Fndn Grants, 1782
Flinn Fndn Scholarships, 1843
Ford Motor Company Grants, 1885
Freeman Fndn Grants, 1952
George S. and Dolores Dore Eccles Fndn Grants, 2027
Germanistic Society of America Fellowships, 2043
Harry Chapin Fndn Grants, 2240
Horowitz Fndn for Social Policy Grants, 2370
Horowitz Fndn for Social Policy Special Awards, 2371
IIE Leonora Lindsley Memorial Fellowships, 2458
IIE Nancy Petry Scholarship, 2459
IIE New Leaders Group Award for Mutual Understanding, 2460
IIE Western Union Family Scholarships, 2462
IMLS Nat Medal for Museum & Library Service, 2516
IREX Small Grant Fund for Civil Society Projects in Africa and Asia, 2581
Jovid Fndn Grants, 2745
JP Morgan Chase Comm Development Grants, 2753
New York Life Fndn Grants, 3341
Ottinger Fndn Grants, 3712
Rajiv Gandhi Fndn Grants, 4011
RAND Corp Graduate Summer Associateships, 4018
Samuel Rubin Fndn Grants, 4237
Seattle Fndn Economy Grants, 4325
Silicon Valley Community Fndn Economic Security Grants, 4355
Third Wave Fndn Lela Breitbart Grants, 4609
Third Wave Organizing & Advocacy Grants, 4610
Third Wave Fndn Reproductive Health and Justice Grants, 4611
Tides Fndn Grants, 4632
Town Creek Fndn Grants, 4650
USAID Resilience and Economic Growth in the Sahel - Enhanced Resilience Grants, 4779
USDC Market Development Cooperator Grants, 4853

Economics Education
3M Fndn Community Giving Grants, 15
Air Products and Chemicals Grants, 216
Alcoa Fndn Grants, 350
Allstate Corp Giving Grants, 386
Allstate Corp Hometown Commitment Grants, 387
Allstate Fndn Safe and Vital Communities Grants, 390
Coca-Cola Fndn Grants, 1195
FMC Fndn Grants, 1876
George W. Codrington Charitable Fndn Grants, 2029
Household Int'l Corp Giving Grants, 2372
IREX Small Grant Fund for Civil Society Projects in Africa and Asia, 2581
J.L. Bedsole Fndn Grants, 2600
McCune Charitable Fndn Grants, 3077
Michael and Susan Dell Fndn Grants, 3158
PACCAR Fndn Grants, 3719
Procter and Gamble Grants, 3967
RBC Dain Rauscher Fndn Grants, 4031
Sid W. Richardson Fndn Grants, 4350
Sprint Fndn Grants, 4463
USDA Agricultural and Rural Economic Research Grants, 4798
Washington Area Women's Fndn Early Care and Educ Funders Collaborative Grants, 4990

Ecosystems
Alaska Conservation Fndn Awards, 322
Arthur B. Schultz Fndn Grants, 573
Beneficia Fndn Grants, 727
Blue Cross Blue Shield of Minnesota Fndn - Healthy Equity: Health Impact Assessment Demonstration Project Grants, 795
Brainerd Fndn Grants, 831
CNCS AmeriCorps State and National Grants, 1182
Conservation, Food, and Health Fndn Grants for Developing Countries, 1359
GNOF Gulf Coast Oil Spill Grants, 2077
Illinois DNR Youth Recreation Corps Grants, 2508
MacArthur Fndn Conservation and Sustainable Development Grants, 2963
Threshold Fndn Sustainable Planet Grants, 4627
Washington Gas Charitable Contributions, 5000
WestWind Fndn Environment Grants, 5052
William C. Kenney Watershed Protection Fndn Ecosystem Grants, 5079

Education
1st Source Fndn Grants, 3
2 Depot Square Ipswich Charitable Fndn Grants, 4
7-Eleven Coorporate Giving Grants, 18
21st Century ILGWU Heritage Grants, 20
21st Century Threshold Project Gifts, 21
41 Washington Street Fndn Grants, 22
49ers Fndn Grants, 23
360 Degrees of Giving Grants, 32
786 Fndn Grants, 33
1104 Fndn Grants, 34
1675 Fndn Grants, 35
A.C. Ratshesky Fndn Grants, 39
A.J. Fletcher Fndn Grants, 41
A.J. Muste Memorial Institute Counter Recruitment Grants, 43
AAAS Science and Technology Policy Fellowships: Health, Educ and Human Services, 53
AACC Plus 50 Init Grants, 55
AACC Project Reach Grants, 56
AAF Accent on Architecture Community Grants, 58
AAP Resident Init Grants, 69
AAUW Community Action Grants, 75
AAUW Int'l Project Grants, 76
Abbey Charitable Grants, 78
Abbot and Dorothy H. Stevens Fndn Grants, 79
Abbott Fund Community Grants, 81
Abbott Fund Global AIDS Care Grants, 82
Abeles Fndn Grants, 89
Abernethy Family Fndn Grants, 98
ABIG Fndn Grants, 99
Abington Fndn Grants, 100
Able To Serve Grants, 102
Abney Fndn Grants, 105
Aboudane Family Fndn Grants, 106
ABS Fndn Grants, 107
Abundance Fndn Int'l Grants, 108
Abundance Fndn Local Community Grants, 109
ACE Charitable Fndn Grants, 111
ACF Ethnic Community Self-Help Grants, 118
ACF Fndn Grants, 119
A Charitable Fndn Grants, 126
Achelis Fndn Grants, 127
Ackerman Fndn Grants, 129
Acuity Charitable Fndn Grants, 140
Adams County Comm Fndn of Indiana Grants, 148
Adams County Comm Fndn of Penn Grants, 149
Adams Fndn Grants, 153
Adams Fndn Grants, 155
Adelaide Breed Bayrd Fndn Grants, 161
Adelaide Christian Home For Children Grants, 162
Adler-Clark Electric Community Commitment Fndn Grants, 164
Administaff Community Affairs Grants, 165
Administration on Aging Senior Medicare Patrol Project Grants, 166
Adobe Art and Culture Grants, 167
Adobe Community Investment Grants, 168
Advanced Micro Devices Comm Affairs Grants, 172
Advocate Safehouse Project Grants, 174
AEGON Transamerica Fndn Civic and Community Grants, 177
AEP Corp Giving Grants, 180
Aetna Fndn Educ Grants in Connecticut, 183
Aetna Summer Academic Enrichment Grants, 189
AFG Industries Grants, 191
African American Fund of New Jersey Grants, 192
A Friends' Fndn Grants, 194
A Fund for Women Grants, 195
Agere Corp and Community Involvement Grants, 199
Agnes B. Hunt Grants, 202
Agnes M. Lindsay Grants, 203
Air Force Association Civil Air Patrol Unit Grants, 214
Air Products and Chemicals Grants, 216
Akonadi Fndn Anti-Racism Grants, 217
ALA ALSC Bookapalooza Grants, 222
Alabama State Council on the Arts Community Arts Collaborative Ventures Grants, 236
Alabama State Council on the Arts Community Arts Operating Support Grants, 237
Alabama State Council on the Arts Community Arts Presenting Grants, 238
Alabama State Council on the Arts Community Arts Program Development Grants, 239
Alabama State Council on the Arts Community Planning & Design Grants, 241
Alabama State Council on the Arts in Educ Partnership Grants, 242
Alabama State Council on the Arts Multi-Discipline and Festival Grants, 243

Education

Aladdin Industries Fndn Grants, 263
ALA Distinguished Educ and Behavioral Sciences Librarian Award, 265
Alaska Airlines Corp Giving Grants, 320
Alaska Airlines Fndn Grants, 321
Albert and Margaret Alkek Fndn Grants, 340
Albert B. Cuppage Charitable Fndn Grants, 341
Albert E. and Birdie W. Einstein Grants, 342
Albert Pick Jr. Grants, 344
Albertson's Charitable Giving Grants, 345
Albert W. Rice Charitable Fndn Grants, 347
Albuquerque Community Fndn Grants, 348
Alcoa Fndn Grants, 350
Alcon Fndn Grants, 351
Alexander & Baldwin Fndn Hawaiian and Pacific Island Grants, 352
Alexander & Baldwin Fndn Mainland Grants, 353
Alexander H. Bright Charitable Grants, 358
Alex Brown and Sons Charitable Fndn Grants, 359
Alex Stern Family Fndn Grants, 360
Alfred and Tillie Shemanski Testamentary Grants, 363
Alfred Bersted Fndn Grants, 364
Alfred E. Chase Charitable Fndn Grants, 366
Alfred J Mcallister and Dorothy N Mcallister Fndn Grants, 367
Alice Tweed Tuohy Fndn Grants, 372
Allan C. and Leila J. Garden Fndn Grants, 374
Allegan County Community Fndn Grants, 375
Allegheny Fndn Grants, 376
Allegheny Technologies Charitable Trust, 377
Allen Hilles Grants, 378
Allen P. and Josephine B. Green Fndn Grants, 380
All for the Earth Fndn Grants, 381
Allstate Corp Giving Grants, 386
Allstate Corp Hometown Commitment Grants, 387
Allstate Fndn Safe and Vital Communities Grants, 390
Alpha Kappa Alpha Ed Advancement Fndn Community Assistance Awards, 393
Alticor Corp Community Contributions Grants, 396
Altman Fndn Health Care Grants, 397
Altria Group Positive Youth Development Grants, 401
Alvah H. and Wyline P. Chapman Fndn Grants, 402
Alvin and Fanny Blaustein Thalheimer Grants, 403
ALZA Corp Contributions Grants, 405
AMA-MSS Chapter Involvement Grants, 406
Amador Community Fndn Grants, 408
Amarillo Area/Harrington Fndns Grants, 412
Ambrose and Ida Fredrickson Fndn Grants, 414
Ambrose Monell Fndn Grants, 415
AMD Corp Contributions Grants, 416
Americana Fndn Grants, 422
American Chemical Society Corp Associates Seed Grants, 425
American Electric Power Grants, 428
American Express Charitable Grants, 429
American Express Leaders for Tomorrow Grants, 432
American Foodservice Charitable Grants, 433
American Gas Fndn Grants, 437
American Honda Fndn Grants, 439
American Jewish World Service Grants, 441
American Savings Fndn Grants, 445
American Schlafhorst Grants, 446
AMERIND Community Service Project Grants, 453
Amgen Fndn Grants, 456
Amon G. Carter Fndn Grants, 458
Andersen Corp Fndn, 459
Anderson Fndn Grants, 460
Andre Agassi Charitable Fndn Grants, 461
Andrew Family Fndn Grants, 462
Angels Baseball Fndn Grants, 465
Angels On Track Fndn Grants, 468
Angels Wings Fndn Int'l Grants, 469
Anheuser-Busch Fndn Grants, 470
ANLAF Int'l Fund for Sexual Minorities Grants, 471
Anna Fitch Ardenghi Grants, 472
Ann Arbor Area Community Fndn Grants, 474
Anne L. and George H. Clapp Charitable and Ed Grants, 476
Annenberg Fndn Grants, 477
Annie E. Casey Fndn Grants, 481

Annie Sinclair Knudsen Memorial Fund/Kaua'i Community Grants, 482
Ann L. & Carol Green Rhodes Charitable Grants, 483
Ann Peppers Fndn Grants, 484
Annunziata Sanguinetti Fndn Grants, 485
Anthony R. Abraham Fndn Grants, 489
Antone & Edene Vidinha Charitable Grants, 490
AON Fndn Grants, 491
Appalachian Regional Commission Educ and Training Grants, 504
Applied Biosystems Grants, 514
Applied Materials Corp Philanthropy Program, 515
APS Fndn Grants, 518
AptarGroup Fndn Grants, 519
Aragona Family Fndn Grants, 522
Aratani Fndn Grants, 523
Arcadia Fndn Grants, 525
ARCO Fndn Educ Grants, 528
Arie and Ida Crown Grants, 533
Arizona Cardinals Grants, 534
Arizona Community Fndn Grants, 540
Arizona Diamondbacks Charities Grants, 542
Arizona Public Service Corp Giving Grants, 545
Arizona Republic Fndn Grants, 546
Arizona Republic Newspaper Contributions, 547
Arkansas Community Fndn Arkansas Black Hall of Fame Grants, 559
Arkansas Community Fndn Grants, 561
ARS Fndn Grants, 568
ARTBA Transportation Development Grants, 569
Arthur and Rochelle Belfer Fndn Grants, 570
Arthur and Sara Jo Kobacker, Alfred and Ida Kobacker Fndn Grants, 571
Arthur Ashley Williams Fndn Grants, 572
Arthur B. Schultz Fndn Grants, 573
ArvinMeritor Grants, 585
Ashland Corp Contributions Grants, 587
Aspen Community Fndn Grants, 592
Assisi Fndn of Memphis Capital Project Grants, 593
Assisi Fndn of Memphis General Grants, 594
Assisi Fndn of Memphis Mini Grants, 595
Assurant Health Fndn Grants, 596
AT&T Fndn Civic and Comm Service Grants, 599
Atherton Family Fndn Grants, 604
Athwin Fndn Grants, 605
Atlanta Fndn Grants, 608
Aurora Fndn Grants, 613
Austin College Leadership Award, 615
Austin Community Fndn Grants, 616
Autodesk Community Relations Grants, 619
AutoNation Corp Giving Grants, 620
AutoZone Community Relations Grants, 621
Avery Dennison Fndn Grants, 623
Avista Fndn Grants, 624
Babcock Charitable Grants, 632
Bacon Family Fndn Grants, 634
Balfe Family Fndn Grants, 636
Ball Brothers Fndn Organizational Effectiveness/Executive Mentoring Grants, 638
Baltimore Community Fndn Children's Fresh Air Society Grants, 642
Baltimore Community Fndn Youth Path Grants, 649
BancorpSouth Fndn Grants, 651
BankAtlantic Fndn Grants, 654
Bank of America Charitable Fndn Matching Gifts, 658
Bank of America Charitable Fndn Student Leaders Grants, 659
Bank of America Corp Sponsorships, 661
Baptist Community Ministries Grants, 664
Barberton Community Fndn Grants, 666
Barker Fndn Grants, 668
Barker Welfare Fndn Grants, 669
Barnes and Noble Local Sponsorships and Charitable Donations, 670
Barnes and Noble National Sponsorships and Charitable Donations, 671
Barra Fndn Community Grants, 673
Barra Fndn Project Grants, 674
Barrasso Usdin Kupperman Freeman and Sarver LLC Corp Grants, 675

Barr Fndn Grants, 677
Batchelor Fndn Grants, 679
Baton Rouge Area Fndn Every Kid a King Grants, 681
Baton Rouge Area Fndn Grants, 682
Batts Fndn Grants, 687
Baxter Int'l Corp Giving Grants, 689
Bay Area Community Fndn Grants, 694
Bayer Advanced Grow Together with Roses School Garden Awards, 695
Bayer Fndn Grants, 696
BBVA Compass Fndn Charitable Grants, 703
BCBSM Fndn Student Award Program, 710
Beazley Fndn Grants, 714
Bechtel Group Fndn Building Positive Community Relationships Grants, 715
Beckley Area Fndn Grants, 716
Beim Fndn Grants, 718
Beirne Carter Fndn Grants, 719
Bemis Company Fndn Grants, 723
Ben B. Cheney Fndn Grants, 725
Bennett Family Fndn of Texas Grants, 728
Benton County Community Fndn Grants, 731
Berks County Community Fndn Grants, 734
Bernard F. and Alva B. Gimbel Fndn Grants, 740
Bernard Osher Fndn Grants, 742
Berrien Community Fndn Grants, 744
Besser Fndn Grants, 748
Best Buy Children's Fndn @15 Teach Awards, 751
Beverley Taylor Sorenson Art Works for Kids, 757
BHHS Legacy Fndn Grants, 758
Bicknell Fndn Grants, 759
Bill Hannon Fndn Grants, 771
Biogen Corp Giving Grants, 773
Bitha Godfrey & Maude J. Thomas Charitable Fndn Grants, 776
BJ's Charitable Fndn Grants, 777
Blackford County Community Fndn Grants, 780
Black Hills Corp Grants, 781
Blade Fndn Grants, 783
Blanche and Irving Laurie Fndn Grants, 784
Blanche and Julian Robertson Family Fndn Grants, 785
Blanche M. Walsh Charity Grants, 786
Blandin Fndn Expand Opportunity Grants, 787
Blowitz-Ridgeway Fndn Grants, 792
Blue Cross Blue Shield of Minnesota Fndn - Health Equity: Building Health Together Grants, 793
Blue Grass Community Fndn Grants, 799
Blumenthal Fndn Grants, 804
BoatUS Fndn Grassroots Grants, 805
Boettcher Fndn Grants, 810
Bohemian Fndn Pharos Grants, 811
Bollinger Fndn Grants, 812
Booth-Bricker Grants, 815
Boston Globe Fndn Grants, 821
Boston Jewish Community Women's Grants, 822
Boulder County Arts Alliance Neodata Endowment Grants, 823
Bowling Green Community Fndn Grants, 824
Bradley-Turner Fndn Grants, 828
Bradley Family Fndn (California) Grants, 829
Bridgestone/Firestone Grants, 836
Bright Family Fndn Grants, 837
Bristol-Myers Squibb Fndn Community Grants, 840
Brooklyn Community Fndn Community Arts for All Grants, 849
Brooklyn Community Fndn Educ and Youth Achievement Grants, 851
Brooklyn Community Fndn Green Communities Grants, 852
Brown Fndn Grants, 854
Brown Rudnick Charitable Relationship Grants, 855
Bryan Adams Fndn Grants, 858
Build-A-Bear Workshop Bear Hugs Fndn Lit and Educ Grants, 860
Build-A-Bear Workshop Fndn Grants, 861
Burden Grants, 864
Burton Morgan Adult Entrepreneurship Grants, 868
Burton Morgan Youth Entrepreneurship Grants, 870
Burton G. Bettinger Grants, 871
Business Bank of Nevada Community Grants, 879

SUBJECT INDEX

Education / 879

Business Wire Lit Init, 880
Butler Manufacturing Company Fndn Grants, 881
Byerly Fndn Grants, 883
Cabot Corp Fndn Grants, 887
Cailloux Fndn Grants, 892
California Community Fndn Art Grants, 900
Callaway Fndn Grants, 909
Callaway Golf Company Fndn Grants, 910
Cambridge Community Fndn Grants, 913
Campbell Soup Fndn Grants, 916
Canada-U.S. Fulbright Mid-Career Grants, 917
Cape Branch Fndn Grants, 919
Capital City Bank Group Fndn Grants, 920
Capital Region Community Fndn Grants, 921
Cardinal Health Fndn Grants, 923
Cargill Citizenship Fund-Corp Giving Grants, 925
Caring Fndn Grants, 926
Carl and Eloise Pohlad Family Fndn Grants, 927
Carl B. and Florence E. King Fndn Grants, 928
Carl C. Icahn Fndn Grants, 929
Carl Gellert and Celia Berta Gellert Fndn Grants, 930
Carl M. Freeman Fndn FACES Grants, 932
Carl R. Hendrickson Family Fndn Grants, 935
Carl W. and Carrie Mae Joslyn Grants, 938
Carnahan-Jackson Fndn Grants, 939
Carolyn Fndn Grants, 942
Carpenter Fndn Grants, 943
Carrie E. and Lena V. Glenn Fndn Grants, 944
Carrier Corp Contributions Grants, 946
Carroll County Community Fndn Grants, 947
Cass County Community Fndn Grants, 952
Catherine Manley Gaylord Fndn Grants, 956
CCFF Community Grant, 962
CDC Grants for Violence-Related Injury Prevention Research, 974
Center for the Study of Philanthropy Senior Int'l Fellowships, 990
CenterPointEnergy Minnegasco Grants, 993
Central Carolina Community Fndn Community Impact Grants, 994
Central Okanagan Fndn Grants, 997
CenturyLink Clarke M. Williams Fndn Grants, 998
Cessna Fndn Grants, 1000
CFFVR Basic Needs Giving Partnership Grants, 1002
CFFVR Chilton Area Community Fndn Grants, 1006
CFFVR Clintonville Area Fndn Grants, 1007
CFFVR Clintonville Area Fndn Grants, 1008
CFFVR Doug and Carla Salmon Fndn Grants, 1009
CFFVR Frank C. Shattuck Community Grants, 1012
CFFVR Jewelers Mutual Charitable Giving, 1014
CFFVR Mielke Family Fndn Grants, 1015
CFFVR Myra M. and Robert L. Vandehey Fndn Grants, 1016
CFFVR Project Grants, 1017
CFFVR SAC Developmental Disabilities Grants, 1019
CFFVR Shawano Area Community Fndn Grants, 1021
CFFVR Waupaca Area Community Fndn Grants, 1023
CFFVR Wisconsin Daughters and Sons Grants, 1024
Chamberlain Fndn Grants, 1027
Champlin Fndns Grants, 1029
Chapin Hall Int'l Fellowships in Children's Policy Research, 1032
Chapman Charitable Fndn Grants, 1033
Charity Incorporated Grants, 1035
CharityWorks Grants, 1036
Charles and Lynn Schusterman Family Grants, 1038
Charles Delmar Fndn Grants, 1039
Charles F. Bacon Grants, 1040
Charles H. Dater Fndn Grants, 1042
Charles H. Hall Fndn, 1044
Charles H. Pearson Fndn Grants, 1045
Charles H. Price II Family Fndn Grants, 1046
Charles H. Revson Fndn Grants, 1047
Charles Lafitte Fndn Grants, 1049
Charles Stewart Mott Fndn Anti-Poverty Grants, 1054
Charles Stewart Mott Fndn Grants, 1055
Charlotte County (FL) Community Fndn Grants, 1056
Charlotte Martin Fndn Youth Grants, 1057
Chase Paymentech Corp Giving Grants, 1059
Chautauqua Region Community Fndn Grants, 1062

Chemtura Corp Contributions Grants, 1067
Chesapeake Bay Trust Capacity Building Grants, 1068
Chesapeake Corp Fndn Grants, 1076
Chevron Hawaii Educ Fund, 1077
ChevronTexaco Contributions Program, 1078
Chicago Community Trust Educ Grants, 1085
Chicago Sun Times Charity Grants, 1098
Chiron Fndn Community Grants, 1111
Christensen Fund Regional Grants, 1112
Christy-Houston Fndn Grants, 1115
Chula Vista Charitable Fndn Grants, 1116
CICF F.R. Hensel Grant for Fine Arts, Music, and Educ, 1121
CICF Indianapolis Fndn Community Grants, 1123
CICF Legacy Grants, 1126
Cingular Wireless Charitable Contributions, 1134
Circle K Corp Contributions Grants, 1136
Cisco Systems Fndn San Jose Community Grants, 1137
CIT Corp Giving Grants, 1138
Citigroup Fndn Grants, 1139
Citizens Bank Mid-Atlantic Charitable Grants, 1140
Citizens Savings Fndn Grants, 1141
Claneil Fndn Grants, 1145
Clara Blackford Smith and W. Aubrey Smith Charitable Fndn Grants, 1147
Clarcor Fndn Grants, 1148
Clarence E. Heller Charitable Fndn Grants, 1150
Clarence T.C. Ching Fndn Grants, 1151
Clark and Carolyn Adams Fndn Grants, 1153
Clark County Community Fndn Grants, 1156
Clark Fndn Grants, 1157
Claude Worthington Benedum Fndn Grants, 1161
Clay Fndn Grants, 1162
Cleveland-Cliffs Fndn Grants, 1165
Cleveland Lake-Geauga Grants, 1170
Cleveland H. Dodge Fndn Grants, 1172
Clinton County Community Fndn Grants, 1174
Clorox Company Fndn Grants, 1176
Clowes Grants, 1177
CNA Fndn Grants, 1179
CNCS AmeriCorps NCCC Project Grants, 1181
CNCS AmeriCorps VISTA Project Grants, 1184
CNCS School Turnaround AmeriCorps Grants, 1186
CNL Corp Giving Entrepreneurship & Leadership Grants, 1191
Coastal Bend Community Fndn Grants, 1192
Coastal Community Fndn of S Carolina Grants, 1193
Coca-Cola Fndn Grants, 1195
Cogswell Benevolent Grants, 1198
Coleman Fndn Entrepreneurship Educ Grants, 1201
Colgate-Palmolive Company Grants, 1202
Collins C. Diboll Private Fndn Grants, 1208
Collins Fndn Grants, 1209
Colonel Stanley R. McNeil Fndn Grants, 1210
Columbia Gas of Virginia Grants, 1218
Columbus Fndn Competitive Grants, 1220
Columbus Fndn Mary Eleanor Morris Grants, 1225
Columbus Neighborhood Partnership Grants, 1226
Columbus Fndn Paul G. Duke Grants, 1227
Columbus Fndn Siemer Family Grants, 1231
Columbus Fndn Small Grants, 1232
Columbus Fndn Traditional Grants, 1233
Comcast Fndn Grants, 1235
Comerica Charitable Fndn Grants, 1237
Commonwealth Edison Grants, 1240
Communities Fndn of Texas Grants, 1243
Community Fndn Alliance City of Evansville Endowment Grants, 1246
Community Fndn for Greater Buffalo Grants, 1247
Community Fndn for Monterey County Grants, 1255
Community Fndn for Muskegon County Grants, 1256
Community Fndn for NE Michigan Grants, 1257
Community Fndn for San Benito County Grants, 1258
Community Fndn for Southern Arizona Grants, 1261
Community Fndn of Boone County Grants, 1274
Community Fndn of Broward Grants, 1275
Community Fndn of East Central Illinois Grants, 1278
Community Fndn of Grant County Grants, 1279
Community Fndn of Greater Birmingham Grants, 1280
Community Fndn of Greater Flint Grants, 1282

Community Fndn Of Greater Lafayette Grants, 1289
Community Fndn of Greater New Britain Grants, 1291
Community Fndn of Greater Tampa Grants, 1292
Community Fndn of Greenville-Greenville Women Giving Grants, 1293
Community Fndn of Greenville Community Enrichment Grants, 1294
Community Fndn of Greenville Hollingsworth Funds Program/Project Grants, 1296
Community Fndn of Howard County Grants, 1297
Community Fndn of Jackson County Grants, 1298
Community Fndn of Middle Tennessee Grants, 1300
Community Fndn of Mount Vernon and Knox County Grants, 1301
Community Fndn of Muncie and Delaware County Grants, 1302
Community Fndn of Muncie and Delaware County Maxon Grants, 1303
Community Fndn of Riverside County Grants, 1304
Community Fndn of Santa Cruz County Grants, 1305
Community Fndn of Sarasota County Grants, 1306
Community Fndn of South Alabama Grants, 1308
Community Fndn of SE Connecticut Grants, 1309
Community Fndn of Southern Indiana Grants, 1310
Community Fndn of South Puget Sound Grants, 1311
Community Fndn of St. Joseph County African American Community Grants, 1312
Community Fndn of St. Joseph County Special Project Challenge Grants, 1314
Community Fndn of Switzerland County Grants, 1315
Community Fndn of Tampa Bay Grants, 1316
Community Fndn of the Ozarks Grants, 1320
Community Fndn of the Verdugos Ed Endowment Grants, 1321
Community Fndn of the Verdugos Grants, 1322
Community Fndn of Virgin Islands Anderson Family Teacher Grants, 1323
Community Fnd Virgin Isls Kimelman Grants, 1324
Community Fndn of Virgin Islands Mini Grants, 1325
Community Fndn of Wabash County Grants, 1326
Community Fndn of Western N Carolina Grants, 1327
Community Partners Lawrence County Grants, 1328
Community Partnerships Martin County Grants, 1329
Community Memorial Fndn Grants, 1334
Compton Fndn Int'l Fellowships, 1339
Compton Fndn Mentor Fellowships, 1340
Connecticut Commission on the Arts Art in Public Spaces, 1349
Connecticut Community Fndn Grants, 1350
Connecticut Light & Power Corp Contributions, 1352
Consumers Energy Fndn, 1365
Conwood Charitable Grants, 1366
Cooke Fndn Grants, 1368
Cooper Fndn Grants, 1369
Cooper Industries Fndn Grants, 1370
Cord Fndn Grants, 1372
Corina Higginson Grants, 1373
Cornerstone Fndn of NE Wisconsin Grants, 1375
Corning Fndn Cultural Grants, 1376
Coughlin-Saunders Fndn Grants, 1377
Covenant Fndn of New York Ignition Grants, 1385
Cowles Charitable Grants, 1392
Cralle Fndn Grants, 1394
Cranston Fndn Grants, 1395
Credit Suisse First Boston Fndn Grants, 1397
Crown Point Community Fndn Grants, 1402
Cruise Industry Charitable Fndn Grants, 1404
CSRA Community Fndn Grants, 1407
CSX Corp Contributions Grants, 1408
Cudd Fndn Grants, 1410
Cullen Fndn Grants, 1411
Cultural Society of Filipino Americans Grants, 1412
Cumberland Community Fndn Grants, 1413
Cummins Fndn Grants, 1415
CUNA Mutual Group Fndn, 1416
CVS Caremark Charitable Grants, 1421
CVS Community Grants, 1422
Cyrus Eaton Fndn Grants, 1423
D.F. Halton Fndn Grants, 1424
D.V. and Ida J. McEachern Charitable Grants, 1425

880 / Education

DAAD Research Grants for Doctoral Candidates and Young Academics and Scientists, 1427
Dade Community Fndn GLBT Grants, 1429
Dade Community Fndn Grants, 1430
DaimlerChrysler Corp Grants, 1432
Dairy Queen Corp Contributions Grants, 1433
Dallas Fndn Grants, 1436
Dallas Mavericks Fndn Grants, 1437
Dammann Grants, 1439
Dana Corp Fndn Grants, 1440
Danellie Fndn Grants, 1442
Daniels Grants, 1443
Dan Murphy Fndn Grants, 1444
Daphne Seybolt Culpeper Memorial Fndn Grants, 1445
Darden Restaurants Fndn Grants, 1446
Davenport-Hatch Fndn Grants, 1448
David and Barbara B. Hirschhorn Fndn Grants, 1450
David Robinson Fndn Grants, 1454
Davis Family Fndn Grants, 1462
Dayton Fndn Grants, 1463
DB Americas Fndn Grants, 1466
Deaconess Community Fndn Grants, 1467
Dean Foods Community Involvement Grants, 1469
Dearborn Community Fndn City of Lawrenceburg Community Grants, 1471
Dearborn Community Fndn City of Lawrenceburg Youth Grants, 1472
Dearborn Community County Progress Grants, 1473
Dearborn Community Fndn Sprint Ed Excellence Grants, 1474
Deborah Munroe Noonan Grants, 1475
Decatur County Comm Large Project Grants, 1476
DeKalb County Community Fndn Grants, 1481
Dekko Fndn Grants, 1482
Delaware Community Fndn-Youth Philanthropy Board for Kent County, 1483
Dell Fndn Open Grants, 1490
Delonne Anderson Family Fndn, 1492
Delta Air Lines Community Enrichment Grants, 1494
Deluxe Corp Fndn Grants, 1496
DeMatteis Family Fndn Grants, 1497
Denver Broncos Charities Grants, 1501
Denver Fndn Community Grants, 1502
Denver Fndn Social Venture Partners Grants, 1503
Dept of Ed Even Start Grants, 1508
Dept of Ed Magnet Schools Assistance Grants, 1509
Dept of Ed Safe and Drug-Free Schools and Communities State Grants, 1513
Dermody Properties Fndn Capstone Award, 1516
Dermody Properties Fndn Grants, 1517
DeRoy Testamentary Fndn Grants, 1518
Detroit Lions Charities Grants, 1520
DHHS American Recovery and Reinvestment Act of 2009 Head Start Expansion, 1526
DHHS Health Centers Grants for Residents of Public Housing, 1533
Dining for Women Grants, 1548
DOJ Community-Based Delinquency Prevention Grants, 1556
DOJ Gang-Free Schools and Communities Intervention Grants, 1557
Dolan Fndn Grants, 1563
Dole Food Company Charitable Contributions, 1564
Dolfinger-McMahon Fndn Grants, 1565
Dollar General Adult Lit Grants, 1568
Dollar General Family Lit Grants, 1569
Dollar General Youth Lit Grants, 1570
Donaldson Fndn Grants, 1574
Donnie Avery Catches for Kids Fndn, 1578
Dora Roberts Fndn Grants, 1579
Doris and Victor Day Fndn Grants, 1582
Dorothy G. Griffin Charitable Fndn Grants, 1588
Dorrance Family Fndn Grants, 1590
Douty Fndn Grants, 1595
Dr. and Mrs. Paul Pierce Memorial Fndn Grants, 1599
Dr. P. Phillips Fndn Grants, 1601
Dream Weaver Fndn, 1604
Dresher Fndn Grants, 1605
Drs. Bruce and Lee Fndn Grants, 1607
DTE Energy Community Development Grants, 1609

DTE Energy Fndn Diversity Grants, 1611
DTE Energy Fndn Environmental Grants, 1612
DTE Energy Fndn Leadership Grants, 1614
Dubois County Community Fndn Grants, 1615
Duke Endowment Child Care Grants, 1617
Duke Energy Economic Development Grants, 1619
Duluth-Superior Area Community Fndn Grants, 1620
Duneland Health Council Incorporated Grants, 1621
DuPage Community Fndn Grants, 1624
Durfee Fndn Sabbatical Grants, 1625
Dyer-Ives Fndn Small Grants, 1629
Dynegy Fndn Grants, 1630
Dyson Fndn Mid-Hudson Valley General Operating Support Grants, 1635
Dyson Mid-Hudson Valley Project Support, 1636
E.L. Wiegand Fndn Grants, 1639
Eastman Chemical Company Fndn Grants, 1643
East Tennessee Fndn Grants, 1646
Eaton Charitable Grants, 1647
eBay Fndn Community Grants, 1648
Eberly Fndn Grants, 1649
Eddie C. and Sylvia Brown Family Fndn Grants, 1653
Eddy Knight Family Fndn Grants, 1654
Eden Hall Fndn Grants, 1655
Edith and Francis Mulhall Achilles Grants, 1657
Edna McConnell Clark Fndn Grants, 1659
EDS Fndn Grants, 1661
Edward and Helen Bartlett Fndn Grants, 1664
Edward Bangs Kelley and Elza Kelley Grants, 1665
Edward S. Moore Fndn Grants, 1668
Edward W. and Stella C. Van Houten Grants, 1670
Edwin S. Webster Fndn Grants, 1671
Edyth Bush Charitable Fndn Grants, 1673
EIF Community Grants, 1675
Elizabeth & Avola W. Callaway Fndn Grants, 1680
Elizabeth Morse Genius Charitable Grants, 1682
Elkhart County Community Fndn Grants, 1684
Ellen Abbott Gilman Grants, 1685
Elmer L. and Eleanor J. Andersen Fndn Grants, 1687
El Paso Community Fndn Grants, 1688
El Paso Corp Fndn Grants, 1689
El Pomar Fndn Awards and Grants, 1690
Elsie H. Wilcox Fndn Grants, 1691
Elsie Lee Garthwaite Memorial Fndn Grants, 1692
Emerson Electric Company Contributions Grants, 1695
Emma B. Howe Memorial Fndn Grants, 1700
Ensign-Bickford Fndn Grants, 1709
Ensworth Charitable Fndn Grants, 1710
Entergy Corp Micro Grants, 1712
Enterprise Rent-A-Car Fndn Grants, 1721
EQT Fndn Educ Grants, 1745
Erie Community Fndn Grants, 1750
Essex County Community Discretionary Grants, 1752
Essex County Community Fndn Greater Lawrence Summer Grants, 1755
Essex County Community Fndn Merrimack Valley General Grants, 1756
Esther M. and Freeman E. Everett Charitable Fndn Grants, 1757
Ethel Sergeant Clark Smith Fndn Grants, 1761
Eugene G. & Margaret M. Blackford Grants, 1763
Eugene M. Lang Fndn Grants, 1764
Eugene McDermott Fndn Grants, 1765
Evan and Susan Bayh Fndn Grants, 1769
Evanston Community Fndn Grants, 1771
Ewing Halsell Fndn Grants, 1776
F.M. Kirby Fndn Grants, 1780
F.R. Bigelow Fndn Grants, 1781
Fairfield County Community Fndn Grants, 1782
Families Count: The National Honors Program, 1784
Family Lit and Hawaii Pizza Hut Lit Fund, 1785
Fargo-Moorhead Area Fndn Grants, 1788
Fargo-Moorhead Area Fndn Woman's Grants, 1789
Farm Aid Grants, 1790
Farmers Insurance Corp Giving Grants, 1791
Faye McBeath Fndn Grants, 1794
Fayette County Fndn Grants, 1795
FCD Child Development Grants, 1796
FCYO Youth Organizing Grants, 1797
FEDCO Charitable Fndn Educ Grants, 1798

Federal Express Corp Contributions Program, 1799
Ferree Fndn Grants, 1804
Fidelity Fndn Grants, 1805
Fieldstone Fndn Grants, 1808
Fifth Third Fndn Grants, 1810
FirstEnergy Fndn Community Grants, 1819
Fishman Family Fndn Grants, 1835
Florian O. Bartlett Grants, 1845
Florida BRAIVE Fund of Dade Community, 1846
Floyd A. and Kathleen C. Cailloux Fndn Grants, 1874
Fluor Fndn Grants, 1875
FMC Fndn Grants, 1876
Foellinger Fndn Grants, 1877
Fondren Fndn Grants, 1878
Ford Motor Company Grants, 1885
Forrest C. Lattner Fndn Grants, 1887
Foster Fndn Grants, 1888
Fndn for a Drug-Free World Classroom Tools, 1890
Fndn for Enhancing Communities Grants, 1893
Fndn for the Mid South Educ Grants, 1898
Foundation for Young Australians Indigenous Small Grants, 1901
Foundation for Young Australians Spark Grants, 1902
Foundation for Young Australians Your Eyes Only Awards, 1903
Foundation for Young Australians Youth Change Grants, 1904
Foundation for Young Australians Youth Led Futures Grants, 1905
Fndn NW Grants, 1906
Fourjay Fndn Grants, 1913
Frances and John L. Loeb Family Grants, 1917
Frances C. & William P. Smallwood Grants, 1918
Frances W. Emerson Fndn Grants, 1920
Francis Beidler Fndn Grants, 1921
Francis T. & Louise T. Nichols Fndn Grants, 1923
Frank B. Hazard General Charity Grants, 1926
Frank E. and Seba B. Payne Fndn Grants, 1927
Franklin County Community Fndn Grants, 1929
Franklin H. Wells and Ruth L. Wells Grants, 1930
Frank Loomis Palmer Grants, 1931
Frank Reed and Margaret Jane Peters Memorial Fund I Grants, 1933
Frank Reed and Margaret Jane Peters Memorial Fund II Grants, 1934
Frank Stanley Beveridge Fndn Grants, 1936
Frank W. and Carl S. Adams Grants, 1937
Fraser-Parker Fndn Grants, 1938
Fred and Sherry Abernethy Fndn Grants, 1940
Fred Baldwin Memorial Fndn Grants, 1941
Fred C. and Mary R. Koch Fndn Grants, 1943
Freddie Mac Fndn Grants, 1944
FRED Ed Ethyl Grants, 1945
Frederick S. Upton Fndn Grants, 1947
Frederick W. Marzahl Grants, 1948
Fred Meyer Fndn Grants, 1950
FRED Technology Grants for Rural Schools, 1951
Fremont Area Community Amazing X Grants, 1953
Fremont Area Community Fndn Grants, 1955
Fremont Area Comm Summer Youth Grants, 1956
Fritz B. Burns Fndn Grants, 1965
Frost Fndn Grants, 1966
Fruit Tree 101, 1967
Fuller E. Callaway Fndn Grants, 1973
Furth Family Fndn Grants, 1980
G.N. Wilcox Grants, 1982
Gannett Fndn Community Action Grants, 1984
Garden Crusader Award, 1985
Gardiner Howland Shaw Fndn Grants, 1986
Gardiner Savings Inst Charitable Fndn Grants, 1987
Garland and Agnes Taylor Gray Fndn Grants, 1988
Gateway Fndn Grants, 1992
Gebbie Fndn Grants, 1995
GEICO Public Service Awards, 1997
Gene Haas Fndn, 1999
Genentech Corp Charitable Contributions, 2000
General Mills Fndn Celebrating Communities of Color Grants, 2002
General Mills Fndn Grants, 2003
General Motors Fndn Grants Support Program, 2004

SUBJECT INDEX

Education / 881

George A. and Grace L. Long Fndn Grants, 2008
George A. Hormel Testamentary Grants, 2009
George and Ruth Bradford Fndn Grants, 2010
George A Ohl Jr. Fndn Grants, 2012
George B. Storer Fndn Grants, 2014
George Family Fndn Grants, 2017
George Frederick Jewett Fndn Grants, 2019
George Gund Fndn Grants, 2020
George H. and Jane A. Mifflin Grants, 2021
George H.C. Ensworth Grants, 2022
George I. Alden Grants, 2023
George J. and Effie L. Seay Fndn Grants, 2024
George Kress Fndn Grants, 2025
George P. Davenport Grants, 2026
George W. Brackenridge Fndn Grants, 2028
George W. Codrington Charitable Fndn Grants, 2029
George W. Wells Fndn Grants, 2030
Georgia-Pacific Fndn Educ Grants, 2031
Georgia-Pacific Fndn Entrepreneurship Grants, 2033
Georgiana Goddard Eaton Grants, 2038
Georgia Power Fndn Grants, 2039
Gertrude and William C. Wardlaw Grants, 2045
Gheens Fndn Grants, 2048
Gibson Fndn Grants, 2052
Gil and Dody Weaver Fndn Grants, 2053
Ginger and Barry Ackerley Fndn Grants, 2055
Ginn Fndn Grants, 2056
Giving Sum Annual Grant, 2058
GlaxoSmithKline Corp Grants, 2060
Glazer Family Fndn Grants, 2062
GNOF Bayou Communities Grants, 2069
GNOF Exxon-Mobil Grants, 2074
GNOF Freeman Challenge Grants, 2075
GNOF Gert Community Grants, 2076
GNOF IMPACT Kahn-Oppenheim Grants, 2084
Godfrey Fndn Grants, 2095
Goizueta Fndn Grants, 2096
Golden LEAF Fndn Grants, 2097
Golden State Warriors Fndn Grants, 2099
Goodrich Corp Fndn Grants, 2104
Good Works Fndn Grants, 2105
Goodyear Tire Grants, 2106
Grable Fndn Grants, 2108
Grace and Franklin Bernsen Fndn Grants, 2109
Grace Bersted Fndn Grants, 2110
Graco Fndn Grants, 2111
Grand Haven Area Community Fndn Grants, 2113
Grand Rapids Area Community Fndn Wyoming Grants, 2116
Grand Rapids Area Community Fndn Wyoming Youth Grants, 2117
Grand Rapids Community Fndn Grants, 2118
Grand Rapids Community Ionia County Grants, 2119
Grand Rapids Community Ionia Youth Grants, 2120
Grand Rapids Community Fndn Lowell Grants, 2121
Grand Rapids Community SE Ottawa Grants, 2122
Grand Rapids Comm SE Ottawa Youth Grants, 2123
Grand Rapids Community Sparta Grants, 2124
Grand Rapids Community Sparta Youth Grants, 2125
Grand Victoria Fndn Illinois Core Grants, 2126
Great-West Life Grants, 2130
Greater Cincinnati Fndn Priority and Small Projects/Capacity-Building Grants, 2132
Greater Green Bay Community Fndn Grants, 2135
Greater Kanawha Valley Fndn Grants, 2136
Greater Milwaukee Fndn Grants, 2137
Greater Saint Louis Community Fndn Grants, 2138
Greater Tacoma Community Fndn Grants, 2139
Greater Worcester Comm Discretionary Grants, 2140
Greater Worcester Community Jeppson Memorial Fund for Brookfield Grants, 2141
Green Bay Packers Fndn Grants, 2148
Green Diamond Charitable Contributions, 2149
Greene County Fndn Grants, 2150
Green Fndn Arts Grants, 2152
Green Fndn Educ Grants, 2153
Gregory Family Fndn Grants (Massachusetts), 2162
Gregory L. Gibson Charitable Fndn Grants, 2163
Group 70 Fndn Fund, 2167
GTECH After School Advantage Grants, 2170

GTECH Community Involvement Grants, 2171
Guido A. and Elizabeth H. Binda Fndn Grants, 2172
Gulf Coast Community Fndn Grants, 2174
Gulf Coast Community Operating Grants, 2176
Gulf Coast Fndn of Community Grants, 2177
Guy I. Bromley Grants, 2180
H & R Fndn Grants, 2181
H.A. and Mary K. Chapman Charitable Grants, 2182
H.B. Fuller Company Fndn Grants, 2183
H.J. Heinz Company Fndn Grants, 2184
H. Leslie Hoffman & Elaine Hoffman Grants, 2185
H. Reimers Bechtel Charitable Grants, 2186
HAF Summer Youth Funding Partnerships, 2205
Hagedorn Grants, 2207
Hahl Proctor Charitable Grants, 2208
Hall-Perrine Fndn Grants, 2209
Hall Family Fndn Grants, 2210
Halliburton Fndn Grants, 2211
Hallmark Corp Fndn Grants, 2212
Hamilton Family Fndn Grants, 2213
Hampton Roads Community Fndn Nonprofit Facilities Improvement Grants, 2218
Hancock County Community Fndn - Field of Interest Grants, 2219
Harbus Fndn Grants, 2223
Harold Alfond Fndn Grants, 2225
Harold and Arlene Schnitzer CARE Grants, 2226
Harold R. Bechtel Charitable Remainder Grants, 2229
Harris and Eliza Kempner Grants, 2231
Harris Teeter Corp Contributions Grants, 2235
Harry A. and Margaret D. Towsley Fndn Grants, 2236
Harry B. and Jane H. Brock Fndn Grants, 2237
Harry Bramhall Gilbert Charitable Grants, 2238
Harry C. Trexler Grants, 2239
Harry Chapin Fndn Grants, 2240
Harry W. Bass, Jr. Fndn Grants, 2246
Hartford Courant Fndn Grants, 2248
Hartford Fndn Regular Grants, 2253
Harvest Fndn Grants, 2254
Hawai'i Children's Trust Fund Community Awareness Events Grants, 2258
Hawaiian Electric Industries Charitable Grants, 2259
Hawaii Community Fndn West Hawaii Grants, 2266
HBF Pathways Out of Poverty Grants, 2273
Heartland Arts Fund, 2286
Hedco Fndn Grants, 2287
Heifer Ed Grants for Principals, 2288
Heinz Endowments Grants, 2291
Helena Rubinstein Fndn Grants, 2292
Helen Bader Fndn Grants, 2293
Helen Gertrude Sparks Charitable Grants, 2294
Helen K. and Arthur E. Johnson Fndn Grants, 2296
Helen Pumphrey Denit Charitable Grants, 2297
Helen S. Boylan Fndn Grants, 2298
Helen V. Brach Fndn Grants, 2300
Hendricks County Community Fndn Grants, 2302
Henrietta Tower Wurts Memorial Fndn Grants, 2304
Henry and Ruth Blaustein Rosenberg Grants, 2306
Henry County Community Fndn - TASC Youth Grants, 2307
Henry County Community Fndn Grants, 2308
Herbert H. and Grace A. Dow Fndn Grants, 2315
Highmark Corp Giving Grants, 2319
Hilda and Preston Davis Fndn Grants, 2322
Hillcrest Fndn Grants, 2325
Hillman Fndn Grants, 2327
Hillsdale County Community General Adult Fndn Grants, 2328
Hillsdale Grants, 2329
Hilton Head Island Fndn Grants, 2330
Hilton Hotels Corp Giving Grants, 2331
Hirtzel Memorial Fndn Grants, 2332
Historic Landmarks Fndn of Indiana Historic Preservation Educ Grants, 2334
Hoblitzelle Fndn Grants, 2341
Hoffberger Fndn Grants, 2342
Hoglund Fndn Grants, 2344
Holland/Zeeland Community Fndn Grants, 2345
Hollie and Anna Oakley Fndn Grants, 2346
HomeBanc Fndn Grants, 2347

Homer Fndn Grants, 2352
Honda of America Manufacturing Fndn Grants, 2354
Horace A. Kimball and S. Ella Kimball Grants, 2362
Horace Moses Charitable Fndn Grants, 2363
Horizon Fndn Grants, 2365
Hormel Foods Charitable Grants, 2368
Hormel Fndn Grants, 2369
Household Int'l Corp Giving Grants, 2372
Howard and Bush Fndn Grants, 2374
Howard County Community Fndn Grants, 2375
Howard H. Callaway Fndn Grants, 2376
Howe Fndn of North Carolina Grants, 2377
Hudson Webber Fndn Grants, 2383
Huffy Fndn Grants, 2384
Hulman & Company Fndn Grants, 2387
Hundred Club of Colorado Springs Grants, 2391
Hundred Club of Connecticut Grants, 2392
Hundred Club of Denver Grants, 2394
Hundred Club of Durango Grants, 2395
Hundred Club of Pueblo Grants, 2398
Huntington Clinical Fndn Grants, 2404
Huntington County Community Fndn - Make a Difference Grants, 2406
Huntington National Bank Comm Affairs Grant, 2409
Hutchinson Community Fndn Grants, 2410
Hut Fndn Grants, 2411
Hyams Fndn Grants, 2413
Hyde Family Fndns Grants, 2414
I.A. O'Shaughnessy Fndn Grants, 2416
Idaho Community Fndn Eastern Region Competitive Grants, 2432
Idaho Power Company Corp Contributions, 2433
IIE Freeman Fndn Indonesia Internships, 2456
Illinois Arts Council Artstour Grants, 2465
Illinois DNR Schoolyard Habitat Action Grants, 2500
Illinois Tool Works Fndn Grants, 2511
Impact 100 Grants, 2522
Inasmuch Fndn Grants, 2523
Indep Comm Fndn Educ, Culture & Arts Grant, 2526
Indiana Humanities Council Init Grants, 2539
Indianapolis Power & Light Company Community Grants, 2540
Indiana Rural Capacity Grants, 2547
Intergrys Corp Grants, 2565
Ireland Family Fndn Grants, 2574
IREX Egypt Media Development Grants, 2575
Irving S. Gilmore Fndn Grants, 2584
Irvin Stern Fndn Grants, 2585
Isabel Allende Fndn Esperanza Grants, 2586
Ittleson Fndn Mental Health Grants, 2590
J. Bulow Campbell Fndn Grants, 2593
J.E. and L.E. Mabee Fndn Grants, 2595
J. Edwin Treakle Fndn Grants, 2596
J. F. Maddox Fndn Grants, 2597
J. Jill Compassion Grants, 2598
J. Mack Robinson Fndn Grants, 2604
J.W. Kieckhefer Fndn Grants, 2607
J. Willard and Alice S. Marriott Fndn Grants, 2609
J. Willard Marriott, Jr. Fndn Grants, 2610
Jackson County Community Fndn Grants, 2611
Jackson Fndn Grants, 2613
Jacob and Hilda Blaustein Fndn Grants, 2615
Jacob G. Schmidlapp Grants, 2616
Jacobs Family Village Neighborhoods Grants, 2619
James & Abigail Campbell Family Fndn Grants, 2620
James A. and Faith Knight Fndn Grants, 2621
James F. and Marion L. Miller Fndn Grants, 2622
James Ford Bell Fndn Grants, 2623
James G.K. McClure Educ and Devel Grants, 2624
James J. and Angelia M. Harris Fndn Grants, 2630
James J. McCann Charitable Trust and McCann Fndn, Inc Grants, 2631
James L. and Mary Jane Bowman Grants, 2632
James M. Cox Fndn of Georgia Grants, 2634
James R. Thorpe Fndn Grants, 2636
James S. Copley Fndn Grants, 2637
Jane's Grants, 2639
Janesville Fndn Grants, 2644
Janus Fndn Grants, 2647
Jasper Fndn Grants, 2655

882 / Education

Jay and Rose Phillips Family Fndn Grants, 2656
Jean and Louis Dreyfus Fndn Grants, 2658
JELD-WEN Fndn Grants, 2661
Jennings County Community Fndn Grants, 2664
Jennings County Community Fndn Women's Giving Circle Grant, 2665
Jessie B. Cox Charitable Grants, 2670
Jessie Ball Dupont Grants, 2671
Jewish Women's Fndn of New York Grants, 2677
Jim Moran Fndn Grants, 2680
JM Fndn Grants, 2681
Joan Bentinck-Smith Charitable Fndn Grants, 2682
Joe W. and Dorothy Dorsett Brown Fndn Grants, 2684
John and Elizabeth Whiteley Fndn Grants, 2685
John Clarke Grants, 2689
John Deere Fndn Grants, 2692
John G. Duncan Grants, 2695
John G. Martin Fndn Grants, 2696
John Jewett & Helen Chandler Garland Grants, 2702
John Lord Knight Fndn Grants, 2703
John M. Ross Fndn Grants, 2704
John M. Weaver Fndn Grants, 2705
John P. McGovern Fndn Grants, 2707
John R. Oishei Fndn Grants, 2709
John S. and James L. Knight Fndn Communities Grants, 2711
John S. and James L. Knight Fndn Donor Advised Grants, 2712
John S. and James L. Knight Fndn Grants, 2713
Johns Manville Grants, 2716
Johnson & Johnson Corp Contributions Grants, 2718
John W. Alden Grants, 2727
John W. and Anna H. Hanes Fndn Grants, 2728
Joseph Drown Fndn Grants, 2735
Josephine G. Russell Grants, 2737
Josephine S. Gumbiner Fndn Grants, 2739
Joseph S. Stackpole Charitable Grants, 2741
Josiah W. and Bessie H. Kline Fndn Grants, 2742
Journal Gazette Fndn Grants, 2744
JP Morgan Chase Arts and Culture Grants, 2752
Judith and Jean Pape Adams Charitable Fndn Tulsa Area Grants, 2755
Judith Clark-Morrill Fndn Grants, 2756
Kahuku Community Fund, 2762
Kaneta Fndn Grants, 2774
Ka Papa O Kakuhihewa Fund, 2785
Kathryne Beynon Fndn Grants, 2791
Katrine Menzing Deakins Charitable Grants, 2793
Kelvin and Eleanor Smith Fndn Grants, 2796
Kenneth A. Scott Charitable Grants, 2801
Kenny's Kids Grants, 2803
Kettering Family Fndn Grants, 2817
Kevin P. & Sydney B. Knight Family Grants, 2819
KeySpan Fndn Grants, 2821
Kiki Madazine Grow Strong Girls through Leadership Grants, 2822
Knight Fndn Donor Advised Grants, 2828
Knox County Community Fndn Grants, 2831
Kohler Fndn Grants, 2833
Koret Fndn Grants, 2837
Kosciusko County Community Fndn Grants, 2838
Kovler Family Fndn Grants, 2840
Laclede Gas Charitable Grants, 2848
LaGrange Independent Fndn for Endowments, 2851
Laidlaw Fndn Multi-Year Grants, 2852
Laidlaw Fndn Youh Organizing Catalyst Grants, 2853
Laidlaw Fndn Youth Organizaing Inits Grants, 2854
Laila Twigg-Smith Art Scholarship, 2855
Lake County Community Grants, 2856
Lana'i Community Benefit Fund, 2857
Lands' End Corp Giving Program, 2861
Laura Moore Cunningham Fndn Grants, 2866
Laurel Fndn Grants, 2867
Leave No Trace Master Educator Scholarships, 2870
Lee and Ramona Bass Fndn Grants, 2871
Legler Benbough Fndn Grants, 2877
Leicester Savings Bank Fund, 2879
Leonard L. and Bertha U. Abess Fndn Grants, 2884
Leo Niessen Jr., Charitable Grants, 2885
Liberty Bank Fndn Grants, 2890

Lincoln Financial Group Fndn Grants, 2906
Lisa and Douglas Goldman Grants, 2910
Lloyd G. Balfour Fndn Attleboro-Specific Charities Grants, 2916
Long Island Community Fndn Grants, 2920
Lotus 88 Fndn for Women and Children Grants, 2921
Louie M. and Betty M. Phillips Fndn Grants, 2923
Louis Calder Fndn Grants, 2925
Lowell Berry Fndn Grants, 2930
Lubrizol Corp Community Grants, 2932
Lucile Horton Howe & Mitchell B. Howe Grants, 2934
Lucy Gooding Charitable Fndn Grants, 2937
Ludwick Family Fndn Grants, 2938
Luella Kemper Grants, 2939
Lumpkin Family Fndn Strong Community Leadership Grants, 2944
Luther I. Replogle Fndn Grants, 2945
Lydia deForest Charitable Grants, 2946
Lynde and Harry Bradley Fndn Grants, 2947
Lynde and Harry Bradley Fndn Prizes, 2948
M.B. and Edna Zale Fndn Grants, 2950
M.E. Raker Fndn Grants, 2953
M.J. Murdock Charitable Trust General Grants, 2954
Mabel A. Horne Grants, 2956
Mabel F. Hoffman Charitable Grants, 2957
Mabel Louise Riley Fndn Grants, 2959
Mabel Y. Hughes Charitable Grants, 2960
Macquarie Bank Fndn Grants, 2966
Madison County Community Fndn - City of Anderson Quality of Life Grant, 2972
Maine Community Fndn Baldwin Area Grants, 2974
Maine Community Fndn Vincent B. and Barbara G. Welch Grants, 2990
Mann T. Lowry Fndn Grants, 2998
Marathon Petroleum Corp Grants, 2999
Marcia and Otto Koehler Fndn Grants, 3000
Mardag Fndn Grants, 3001
Margaret Abell Powell Grants, 3002
Margaret L. Wendt Fndn Grants, 3004
Marie H. Bechtel Charitable Grants, 3007
Marion Gardner Jackson Charitable Grants, 3017
Mars Fndn Grants, 3025
Marshall County Community Fndn Grants, 3026
Marsh Corp Grants, 3027
Mary C. & Perry F. Spencer Fndn Grants, 3034
Mary & Walter Frear Eleemosynary Grants, 3035
Mary E. Babcock Fndn, 3038
Mary E. Ober Fndn Grants, 3039
Mary K. Chapman Fndn Grants, 3042
Mary Owen Borden Fndn Grants, 3046
Mary Wilmer Covey Charitable Grants, 3049
Maurice Amado Fndn Grants, 3063
Maximilian E. and Marion O. Hoffman Fndn, 3067
Maytree Fndn Refugee and Immigrant Grants, 3071
McCarthy Family Fndn Grants, 3073
McColl Fndn Grants, 3074
McCombs Fndn Grants, 3075
McCune Charitable Fndn Grants, 3077
McGregor Grants, 3082
McInerny Fndn Grants, 3083
McKesson Fndn Grants, 3084
McLean Contributionship Grants, 3088
McMillen Fndn Grants, 3090
Mead Johnson Nutritionals Evansville-Area Organizations Grants, 3103
Meadows Fndn Grants, 3104
Mead Witter Fndn Grants, 3106
Melville Charitable Grants, 3115
Memorial Fndn Grants, 3117
Mercedes-Benz USA Corp Contributions Grants, 3118
Mericos Fndn Grants, 3121
Merkel Family Fndn Grants, 3123
Merkel Fndn Grants, 3124
Mervin Bovaird Fndn Grants, 3128
Metzger-Price Grants, 3137
Meyer Memorial Trust Special Grants, 3149
MGM Resorts Fndn Community Grants, 3153
MGN Family Fndn Grants, 3154
Miami County Community Fndn - Operation Round Up Grants, 3156

Miami County Community Fndn Grants, 3157
Micron Technology Fndn Community Grants, 3161
Microsoft Comm Affairs Puget Sound Grants, 3163
Middlesex Savings Charitable Fndn Ed Opportunities Grants, 3174
Miguel Aleman Fndn Grants, 3175
Milken Family Fndn Grants, 3178
Miller Brewing Corp Contributions Grants, 3180
Mimi and Peter Haas Grants, 3185
Moline Fndn Community Grants, 3202
Monfort Family Fndn Grants, 3203
Montana Community Fndn Grants, 3211
Morris and Gwendolyn Cafritz Fndn Grants, 3218
Morris K. Udall and Stewart L. Udall Fndn Native American Congressional Internships, 3220
Mr. and Mrs. William Foulds Family Grants, 3222
Musgrave Fndn Grants, 3231
NAGC Masters and Specialists Award, 3237
NAR HOPE Awards for Minority Owners, 3238
Natalie W. Furniss Charitable Grants, 3244
Nathaniel and Elizabeth P. Stevens Fndn Grants, 3247
National Housing Endowment Challenge/Build/Grow Grant, 3277
National Inclusion Grants, 3278
Needmor Grants, 3289
Nehemiah Community Fndn Grants, 3290
NEH Preservation Assistance Grants for Smaller Institutions, 3293
Nelda C. and H.J. Lutcher Stark Fndn Grants, 3296
Nestle Purina PetCare Ed Grants, 3302
Nestle Purina PetCare Pet Related Grants, 3304
Nestle Purina PetCare Youth Grants, 3306
New Earth Fndn Grants, 3317
Newton County Community Fndn Grants, 3336
New York Fndn Grants, 3338
NFWF Columbia River Estuarine Coastal Grant, 3367
NFWF Community Salmon Fund Partnerships, 3368
NFWF King County Community Salmon Grants, 3375
NFWF National Whale Conservation Grants, 3378
NFWF Nature of Learning Grants, 3381
NFWF One Fly Conservation Partnerships, 3382
NFWF Oregon Governor's Fund for the Environment Grants, 3383
NFWF Pacific Grassroots Salmonid Init Grants, 3384
NFWF Pierce Community Salmon Grant, 3385
NFWF Pioneers in Conservation Grants, 3386
NFWF Radical Salmon Design Contest, 3388
NFWF Salmon Recovery Funding Board Community Salmon Grants, 3389
NGA Hooked on Hydroponics Awards, 3405
NGA Midwest School Garden Grants, 3407
NGA Wuzzleburg Preschool Garden Awards, 3408
NHSCA General Project Grants, 3427
Nicor Corp Contributions, 3435
Nike Fndn Grants, 3441
Nina Mason Pulliam Charitable Grants, 3443
Nissan Fndn Grants, 3444
Nissan Neighbors Grants, 3445
Noble County Community Fndn Celebrate Diversity Project Grants, 3455
Noble County Community Fndn Grants, 3456
Norcliffe Fndn Grants, 3459
Nordson Corp Fndn Grants, 3462
Norfolk Southern Fndn Grants, 3463
Norman Fndn Grants, 3464
North Carolina Community Fndn Grants, 3489
North Carolina GlaxoSmithKline Fndn Grants, 3490
North Central Health Services Grants, 3492
NE Utilities Fndn Grants, 3498
Northern New York Community Fndn Grants, 3503
Northern Trust Company Corp Giving Program, 3504
North Georgia Community Fndn Grants, 3505
NW Mutual Fndn Grants, 3509
NW Minnesota Fndn Women's Grants, 3512
NW Minnesota Fndn Women's Scholarships, 3513
Norwin S. and Elizabeth N. Bean Fndn Grants, 3515
NRA Fndn Grants, 3517
NYCT AIDS/HIV Grants, 3542
NYCT Community Development Grants, 3546
NYCT Girls and Young Women Grants, 3548

SUBJECT INDEX

Education / 883

NYCT Hunger and Homelessnes Grants, 3553
NYCT Social Services and Welfare Grants, 3557
NYCT Substance Abuse Grants, 3558
NYSCA Museum General Operating Support, 3602
NYSCA Museum: Project Support Grants, 3604
Ober Kaler Community Grants, 3635
OceanFirst Fndn Grants, 3636
Oceanside Charitable Fndn Grants, 3637
Ohio County Community Fndn Grants, 3658
Ohio County Community Fndn Mini-Grants, 3660
OJJDP National Mentoring Grants, 3664
Oklahoma City Community Programs & Grants, 3666
Oleonda Jameson Grants, 3667
Olga Sipolin Children's Grants, 3668
Onan Family Fndn Grants, 3672
OneFamily Fndn Grants, 3673
OneStar Fndn AmeriCorps Grants, 3674
Ontario Arts Council Compass Grants, 3677
Ontario Arts Council Travel Assistance Grants, 3682
Orange County Community Fndn Grants, 3688
Orange County Community Fndn Grants, 3687
Ordean Fndn Grants, 3691
Organic Farming Research Fndn Grants, 3693
OSF-Baltimore Community Fellowships, 3695
OSF-Baltimore Ed & Youth Devel Grants, 3697
OSF-Baltimore Tackling Drug Addiction Grants, 3698
OSF Arab Regional Office Grants, 3701
OSF European Commission Internships for Young Roma Graduates, 3707
OSI After Prison Init Grants, 3710
Owen County Community Fndn Grants, 3716
PacifiCare Fndn Grants, 3725
Pacific Life Fndn Grants, 3726
PacifiCorp Fndn for Learning Grants, 3727
Pacific Rainbow Fndn Grants, 3728
Palm Beach and Martin Counties Grants, 3733
Parker Fndn (California) Grants, 3736
Parkersburg Area Comm Fndn Action Grants, 3738
Park Fndn Grants, 3739
Partnership Enhancement Grants, 3740
Patrick and Anna M. Cudahy Grants, 3751
Patrick John Bennett, Jr. Memorial Fndn Grants, 3752
Paul and Edith Babson Fndn Grants, 3755
Paul and Mary Haas Fndn Contributions and Student Scholarships, 3756
Paul G. Allen Family Fndn Grants, 3759
Paul Ogle Fndn Grants, 3764
PDF Community Organizing Grants, 3807
Peacock Fndn Grants, 3809
Pentair Fndn Educ and Community Grants, 3816
Peoples Bancorp Fndn Grants, 3817
Percy B. Ferebee Endowment Grants, 3820
Perkin Grants, 3821
Perkins Charitable Fndn Grants, 3823
Perpetual Trust for Charitable Giving Grants, 3826
Perry County Community Fndn Grants, 3827
Peter Kiewit Fndn General Grants, 3845
Peter Kiewit Fndn Small Grants, 3847
Pew Charitable Trusts Arts and Culture Grants, 3857
Pew Trusts Children and Youth Grants, 3858
Pfizer Healthcare Charitable Contributions, 3863
PG&E Community Vitality Grants, 3868
PGE Fndn Grants, 3869
Phelps County Community Fndn Grants, 3870
Philadelphia Organizational Effectiveness Grants, 3872
Philadelphia Fndn YOUTHadelphia Grants, 3873
Phil Hardin Fndn Grants, 3875
Philip L. Graham Grants, 3876
Piedmont Health Fndn Grants, 3882
Piedmont Natural Gas Charitable Contributions, 3883
Pike County Community Fndn Grants, 3888
Pinellas County Grants, 3891
Pinkerton Fndn Grants, 3892
Pinnacle Fndn Grants, 3894
Pioneer Hi-Bred Community Grants, 3895
PIP Communities for Public Ed Reform Grants, 3898
Piper Trust Arts and Culture Grants, 3900
Pittsburgh Fndn Community Grants, 3910
Playboy Fndn Grants, 3913
Plough Fndn Grants, 3915

PMI Fndn Grants, 3918
PNC Charitable Trust and Fndn Grants, 3921
Pohlad Family Fndn, 3928
Polk Bros. Fndn Grants, 3929
Portland Fndn Grants, 3936
Portland General Electric Fndn Grants, 3937
Posey County Community Fndn Grants, 3939
Powell Fndn Grants, 3942
PPG Industries Fndn Grants, 3943
Praxair Fndn Grants, 3944
Presbyterian Health Fndn Bridge, Seed and Equipment Grants, 3947
Price Chopper's Golub Fndn Grants, 3950
Price Family Charitable Grants, 3952
Price Gilbert, Jr. Charitable Grants, 3953
Pride Fndn Grants, 3958
Prince Charitable Trusts Chicago Grants, 3959
Princeton Area Community Fndn Fund for Women and Girls Grants, 3962
Princeton Area Community Fndn Greater Mercer Grants, 3963
Principal Financial Group Fndn Grants, 3966
Progress Energy Corp Contributions Grants, 3968
Project Orange Thumb Grants, 3972
Prudential Fndn Educ Grants, 3977
PSEG Corp Contributions Grants, 3979
PSEG Environmental Educ Grants, 3980
Public Educ Power Grants, 3981
Puerto Rico Community Fndn Grants, 3986
Pulaski County Community Fndn Grants, 3988
Putnam County Community Fndn Grants, 3990
Putnam Fndn Grants, 3991
Qualcomm Grants, 3993
Quantum Fndn Grants, 3996
Questar Corp Contributions Grants, 3997
QuikTrip Corp Contributions Grants, 3998
R.C. Baker Fndn Grants, 3999
R.E.B. Awards for Distinguished Ed Leadership, 4000
R.J. McElroy Grants, 4001
R.S. Gernon Grants, 4002
Rachel Alexandra Girls Grants, 4003
Rajiv Gandhi Fndn Grants, 4011
Ralphs Food 4 Less Fndn Grants, 4014
Randall L. Tobias Fndn Grants, 4017
Rasmuson Fndn Capital Grants, 4020
Rathmann Family Fndn Grants, 4026
Ray Fndn Grants, 4027
Raymond John Wean Fndn Grants, 4028
RBC Dain Rauscher Fndn Grants, 4031
RCF General Community Grants, 4032
RCF Summertime Kids Grants, 4034
Retirement Research Fndn General Grants, 4067
Reynolds Family Fndn Grants, 4071
RGK Fndn Grants, 4072
Rhode Island Fndn Grants, 4073
Richard and Caroline T. Gwathmey Grants, 4075
Richard and Helen DeVos Fndn Grants, 4076
Richard and Rhoda Goldman Grants, 4077
Richard and Susan Smith Family Fndn Grants, 4078
Richard D. Bass Fndn Grants, 4079
Richard Davoud Donchian Fndn Grants, 4080
Richard King Mellon Fndn Grants, 4087
Richland County Bank Grants, 4091
Riley Fndn Grants, 4094
Ripley County Community Fndn Grants, 4095
Ripley County Community Small Project Grants, 4096
Roberta Leventhal Sudakoff Fndn Grants, 4102
Robert and Helen Haddad Fndn Grants, 4103
Robert and Joan Dircks Fndn Grants, 4104
Robert Bowne Fndn Fellowships, 4107
Robert Bowne Fndn Lit Grants, 4108
Robert Bowne Fndn Youth-Centered Grants, 4109
Robert F. Stoico / FIRSTFED Grants, 4112
Robert Lee Blaffer Fndn Grants, 4115
Robert W. Woodruff Fndn Grants, 4124
Robins Fndn Grants, 4126
Rochester Area Community Fndn Grants, 4127
Rochester Area Fndn Grants, 4128
Rockefeller Brothers Democratic Practice Grants, 4131
Rockefeller Brothers Peace and Security Grants, 4133

Rockefeller Brothers Pivotal Places Grants: Serbia, Montenegro, and Kosova, 4135
Rockefeller Brothers Sustainable Devel Grants, 4136
Rockwell Int'l Corp Grants, 4141
Roger L. and Agnes C. Dell Charitable Grants, 4143
Rogers Family Fndn Grants, 4144
Rohm and Haas Company Grants, 4145
Rollin M. Gerstacker Fndn Grants, 4146
Romic Environmental's Charitable Contributions, 4148
Ronald McDonald House Charities Grants, 4149
Roney-Fitzpatrick Fndn Grants, 4150
Rose Hills Fndn Grants, 4162
Ross Fndn Grants, 4164
Royal Caribbean Cruises Ocean Fund, 4165
Roy and Christine Sturgis Charitable Grants, 4166
RR Donnelley Community Grants, 4168
RRF General Grants, 4170
Rucker & Margaret Agee Grants, 4171
Rush County Community Fndn Grants, 4174
Ruth Anderson Fndn Grants, 4176
Ruth and Vernon Taylor Fndn Grants, 4177
Ruth H. and Warren A. Ellsworth Fndn Grants, 4179
Rutter's Children's Charities Grants, 4181
RWJF Jobs to Careers: Promoting Work-Based Learning for Quality Care, 4185
S.H. Cowell Fndn Grants, 4199
S. Livingston Mather Charitable Grants, 4200
S. Mark Taper Fndn Grants, 4201
S. Spencer Scott Grants, 4202
Saigh Fndn Grants, 4210
Saint Louis Rams Fndn Community Donations, 4214
Saint Paul Companies Fndn Grants, 4217
Saint Paul Fndn Grants, 4219
Salem Fndn Charitable Grants, 4223
Salisbury Community Fndn Grants, 4224
Salmon Fndn Grants, 4225
Samueli Fndn Youth Services Grants, 4234
Samuel N. and Mary Castle Fndn Grants, 4236
Samuel S. Fels Grants, 4238
Samuel S. Johnson Fndn Grants, 4239
San Diego Fndn for Change Grants, 4247
San Diego Women's Fndn Grants, 4252
SanDisk Corp Community Sharing Program, 4253
San Francisco Fndn Community Health Grants, 4263
San Francisco Fndn Multicultural Fellowship, 4281
San Juan Island Community Fndn Grants, 4283
Santa Fe Community Fndn Seasonal Grants-Spring Cycle, 4291
Sarah Scaife Fndn Grants, 4295
Sara Lee Fndn Grants, 4296
Sarkeys Fndn Grants, 4297
SAS Institute Community Relations Donations, 4300
Schering-Plough Fndn Health Grants, 4304
Schlessman Family Fndn Grants, 4307
Scholastic Book Grants, 4308
Schumann Fund for New Jersey Grants, 4311
Schurz Communications Fndn Grants, 4312
Scott County Community Fndn Grants, 4314
Seabury Fndn Grants, 4316
Seagate Tech Corp Capacity to Care Grants, 4317
Seattle Fndn Arts and Culture Grants, 4320
Seattle Fndn Benjamin N. Phillips Grants, 4322
Seattle Fndn Educ Grants, 4326
Selby and Richard McRae Fndn Grants, 4334
Self Fndn Grants, 4335
Seneca Foods Fndn Grants, 4336
Sensient Technologies Fndn Grants, 4337
Shell Oil Company Fndn Grants, 4343
Shopko Fndn Community Charitable Grants, 4346
Sidgmore Family Fndn Grants, 4348
Sidney Stern Grants, 4349
Siebert Lutheran Fndn Grants, 4351
Sierra Grants, 4352
Silicon Valley Community Fndn Educ Grants, 4356
Simmons Fndn Grants, 4360
Simpson Lumber Charitable Contributions, 4362
Sir Dorabji Tata Grants for NGOs or Voluntary Organizations, 4370
Sister Grants for Women's Organizations, 4371
Sisters of Charity Fndn of Canton Grants, 4372

Sisters of Charity Fndn of Cleveland Reducing Health Disparities in Central Neighborhood Grants, 4374
Sisters of Mercy of North Carolina Fndn Grants, 4375
Skillman Community Connections Small Grants, 4379
Skillman Fndn Good Opportunities Grants, 4381
Skillman Fndn Good Schools Grants, 4382
Snee Reinhardt Charitable Fndn Grants, 4387
SOBP A.E. Bennett Research Award, 4388
Sobrato Family Fndn Grants, 4389
Sobrato Family Fndn Meeting Space Grants, 4390
Sobrato Family Fndn Office Space Grants, 4391
Solutia Grants, 4402
Sorenson Legacy Fndn Grants, 4407
Sosland Fndn Grants, 4408
Southbury Community Trust Fund, 4409
South Carolina Arts Commission AIE Residency Plus Individual Site Grants, 4411
Southern Minnesota Init Fndn BookStart Grants, 4432
Southern Minnesota Youth Explorer Grants, 4436
South Madison Community Fndn Grants, 4440
SW Florida Community Competitive Grants, 4442
SW Florida Community Fndn Undergraduate and Graduate Scholarships, 4444
SW Gas Corp Fndn Grants, 4445
Southwire Company Grants, 4447
Spencer County Community Fndn Grants, 4451
Sprague Fndn Grants, 4461
Springs Close Fndn Grants, 4462
Sprint Fndn Grants, 4463
Square D Fndn Grants, 4464
St. Joseph Community Health Fndn Catherine Kasper Award, 4468
St. Joseph Community Health Fndn Improving Healthcare Access Grants, 4469
St. Louis-Jefferson Solid Waste Management Waste Reduction and Recycling Grants, 4470
Stark Community Fndn Women's Grants, 4481
State Farm Strong Neighborhoods Grants, 4485
State Farm Fndn Grants, 4486
State Justice Institute Scholarships, 4491
State Street Fndn Grants, 4495
Steelcase Fndn Grants, 4497
Steele-Reese Fndn Grants, 4498
Stettinius Fund for Nonprofit Leadership Awards, 4500
Steuben County Community Fndn Grants, 4501
Stewart Huston Charitable Grants, 4505
Stinson Fndn Grants, 4506
Stocker Fndn Grants, 4507
Stowe Family Fndn Grants, 4510
Stranahan Fndn Grants, 4512
Strowd Roses Grants, 4515
Stuart Fndn Grants, 4516
Subaru of America Fndn Grants, 4518
Subaru of Indiana Automotive Fndn Grants, 4519
Sulzberger Fndn Grants, 4522
Sun Academic Excellence Grants, 4525
Sunoco Fndn Grants, 4530
Susan A. & Donald P. Babson Charitable Grants, 4534
Susan Mott Webb Charitable Grants, 4536
Susan Vaughan Fndn Grants, 4537
SVP Early Childhood Dev and Parenting Grants, 4538
Symantec Community Relations and Corp Philanthropy Grants, 4544
T. James Kavanagh Fndn Grants, 4545
T. Rowe Price Associates Fndn Grants, 4548
Taproot Fndn Capacity-Building Service Grants, 4560
Tauck Family Fndn Grants, 4563
Taylor S. Abernathy and Patti Harding Abernathy Charitable Grants, 4564
TCF Bank Fndn Grants, 4565
Teaching Tolerance Grants, 4567
TE Fndn Grants, 4572
Telluride Fndn Community Grants, 4573
Texas Commission on Arts Project Grants, 4581
Thelma Braun and Bocklett Family Fndn Grants, 4603
Theodore Edson Parker Fndn Grants, 4605
Thomas Austin Finch, Sr. Fndn Grants, 4613
Thomas B. & Elizabeth M. Sheridan Grants, 4614
Thomas C. Ackerman Fndn Grants, 4615
Thomas J. Atkins Grants, 4617

Thomas J. Long Fndn Community Grants, 4618
Thomas Thompson Grants, 4620
Thomas W. Briggs Fndn Grants, 4621
Thompson Charitable Fndn Grants, 4622
Thompson Fndn Grants, 4623
Tifa Fndn Grants, 4633
Tiger Woods Fndn Grants, 4634
TJX Fndn Grants, 4637
Tom's of Maine Grants, 4640
Topeka Community Fndn Grants, 4644
Toro Fndn Grants, 4647
Toyota Motor Engineering & Manufacturing North America Grants, 4651
Toyota Motor Manufacturing of Alabama Grants, 4652
Toyota Motor Manufacturing of Indiana Grants, 4653
Toyota Motor of Kentucky Grants, 4654
Toyota Motor Manufacturing Mississippi Grants, 4655
Toyota Motor Manufacturing of Texas Grants, 4656
Toyota Motor Manufacturing W Virginia Grants, 4657
Toyota Motor N America of New York Grants, 4658
Toyota Motor Sales, USA Grants, 4659
Toyota Technical Center Grants, 4660
Tri-State Community 21st Century Endowment, 4666
Triangle Community Fndn Donor Grants, 4668
Trinity Fndn Grants, 4669
Trull Fndn Grants, 4673
Tulane University Community Service Scholars, 4677
Tulane University Public Service Fellows, 4678
Tull Charitable Fndn Grants, 4679
Turner Fndn Grants, 4681
Turner Voices Corp Contributions, 4682
TWS Fndn Grants, 4683
U.S. Bank Fndn Grants, 4686
U.S. Department of Educ Rehabilitation Training--Rehabilitation Continuing Educ Programs--Institute on Rehabilitation Issues, 4700
UniBank 911 Emergency Personnel Educ Fund, 4707
Union Bank Corp Sponsorships and Donations, 4708
Union Benevolent Association Grants, 4710
United Technologies Corp Grants, 4725
Unity Fndn Of LaPorte County Grants, 4726
UPS Fndn Economic and Global Lit Grants, 4730
Ursula Thrush Peace Seed Grants, 4733
USAID Development Assistance Grants, 4748
USAID Economic Prospectsfor Armenia-Turkey Normalization Grants, 4750
USAID HIV Prevention with Key Populations - Mali Grants, 4757
USAID Palestinian Comm Assistance Grants, 4773
USAID Palestinian Community Infrastructure Development Grants, 4774
USAID Reading Enhancement for Advancing Development Grants, 4778
US Airways Community Fndn Grants, 4789
USA Volleyball Fndn Ed Grants, 4791
USDC Technology Opportunities Grants, 4860
USG Fndn Grants, 4869
V.V. Cooke Fndn Grants, 4896
Valerie Adams Memorial Charitable Grants, 4898
Vancouver Fndn Grants & Comm Inits, 4900
Vanderburgh Community Fndn Grants, 4902
Vanguard Public Fndn Grant Funds, 4904
Verizon Fndn Connecticut Grants, 4908
Verizon Fndn Maine Grants, 4916
Verizon Fndn Maryland Grants, 4917
Verizon Fndn New York Grants, 4919
Verizon Fndn NE Region Grants, 4920
Verizon Fndn Pennsylvania Grants, 4921
Verizon Fndn Vermont Grants, 4924
Verizon Fndn Virginia Grants, 4925
Verizon Fndn West Virginia Grants, 4926
Vermont Community Fndn Grants, 4929
Viacom Fndn Grants (Formerly CBS Fndn), 4932
Virginia W. Kettering Fndn Grants, 4950
Vulcan Materials Company Fndn Grants, 4956
W. C. Griffith Fndn Grants, 4957
W.C. Griffith Fndn Grants, 4958
W.H. and Mary Ellen Cobb Charitable Grants, 4959
W.K. Kellogg Fndn Secure Families Grants, 4963
W.P. and Bulah Luse Fndn Grants, 4965

Wabash Valley Community Fndn Grants, 4971
Wallace Fndn Grants, 4976
Walmart Fndn Facility Giving Grants, 4978
Walmart Fndn National Giving Grants, 4979
Walter and Elise Haas Grants, 4982
Walter L. Gross III Family Fndn Grants, 4983
Walton Family Fndn Home Region Grants, 4984
Warren County Community Fndn Grants, 4985
Warren County Community Fndn Mini-Grants, 4986
Warrick County Community Fndn Grants, 4987
Washington Area Women's Fndn Early Care and Educ Funders Collaborative Grants, 4990
Washington County Community Fndn Grants, 4997
Washington County Community Youth Grants, 4998
Washington Gas Charitable Contributions, 5000
Water and Land Stewardship Grants, 5002
Wayne and Gladys Valley Fndn Grants, 5003
Wayne County Fndn Vigran Family Grants, 5004
Wayne County Fndn Grants, 5005
Weatherwax Fndn Grants, 5014
Weaver Fndn Grants, 5015
Weaver Popcorn Fndn Grants, 5016
Wege Fndn Grants, 5017
Welborn Baptist General Opportunity Grants, 5020
Wells County Fndn Grants, 5022
Western Indiana Community Fndn Grants, 5024
Westinghouse Charitable Giving Grants, 5028
West Virginia Commission on the Arts Artist Visit Grants, 5030
Weyerhaeuser Company Fndn Grants, 5053
White County Community Fndn Grants, 5057
Whitley County Community Fndn Grants, 5060
Whitney Fndn Grants, 5061
WHO Fndn Educ/Lit Grants, 5062
WHO Fndn General Grants, 5063
Wieboldt Fndn Grants, 5065
Willary Fndn Grants, 5071
William A. Badger Fndn Grants, 5072
William Bingham Fndn Grants, 5077
William G. and Helen C. Hoffman Fndn Grants, 5080
William G. McGowan Charitable Grants, 5084
William G. Selby and Marie Selby Fndn Grants, 5085
William H. Hannon Fndn Grants, 5086
William J. and Dorothy K. O'Neill Fndn Grants, 5087
William L. and Victorine Q. Adams Fndn Grants, 5089
William McCaskey Chapman and Adaline Dinsmore Chapman Fndn Grants, 5092
Williams Companies Fndn Grants, 5095
Wilson-Wood Fndn Grants, 5098
Winifred & Harry B. Allen Fndn Grants, 5101
Winston-Salem Fndn Competitive Grants, 5102
Winston-Salem Fndn Elkin/Tri-County Grants, 5103
Winston-Salem Fndn Stokes County Grants, 5104
Winthrop Rockefeller Fndn Grants, 5105
Wolf Aviation Grants, 5109
Women's Fndn Greater Kansas City Grants, 5111
Women's Funding Alliance Grants, 5112
Wood-Claeyssens Fndn Grants, 5113
Woodward Grants, 5116
World Bank JJ/WBGSP Partners Programs, 5117
Xcel Energy Fndn Grants, 5121
Xerox Fndn Grants, 5122
Yawkey Fndn Grants, 5125
Young Family Fndn Grants, 5127
Youth Philanthropy Project, 5132
YSA ABC Summer of Service Awards, 5133
YSA Get Ur Good On Grants, 5134
YSA NEA Youth Leaders for Lit Grants, 5138
YSA Sodexo Lead Organizer Grants, 5140
YSA State Farm Good Neighbor YOUth In The Driver Seat Grants, 5141

Education Reform
AACC Plus 50 Init Grants, 55
Achelis Fndn Grants, 127
American Express Historic Preservation Grants, 431
Anheuser-Busch Fndn Grants, 470
Bay and Paul Fndns Grants, 693
Bernard F. and Alva B. Gimbel Fndn Grants, 740
Bill & Melinda Gates Policy & Advocacy Grants, 769

SUBJECT INDEX

Bodman Fndn Grants, 807
Boeing Company Contributions Grants, 809
Buhl Fndn - Frick Ed Fund, 859
Carnegie Corp of New York Grants, 940
Charles Hayden Fndn Grants, 1048
Charles Stewart Mott Fndn Grants, 1055
CNCS School Turnaround AmeriCorps Grants, 1186
Dow Corning Corp Contributions Grants, 1597
FAS Project Schools Grants, 1792
Fndn for the Mid South Educ Grants, 1898
Frances and John L. Loeb Family Grants, 1917
GNOF IMPACT Grants for Educ, 2079
Hazen Fndn Public Educ Grants, 2269
J.C. Penney Company Grants, 2594
J. F. Maddox Fndn Grants, 2597
John W. Speas and Effie E. Speas Grants, 2732
Joseph Drown Fndn Grants, 2735
Joseph H. and Florence A. Roblee Fndn Grants, 2736
Lewis H. Humphreys Charitable Grants, 2889
Louis and Elizabeth Nave Flarsheim Charitable Fndn Grants, 2924
Minneapolis Fndn Community Grants, 3186
North Carolina Arts Council Arts in Educ Rural Development Grants, 3470
Phil Hardin Fndn Grants, 3875
PIP Communities for Public Ed Reform Grants, 3898
Portland General Electric Fndn Grants, 3937
Prince Charitable Trusts Chicago Grants, 3959
Randall L. Tobias Fndn Grants, 4017
Richard Davoud Donchian Fndn Grants, 4080
Sapelo Fndn Environmental Protection Grants, 4293
Sprint Fndn Grants, 4463
William J. Brace Charitable Trust, 5088

Education and Work
AEGON Transamerica Fndn Civic and Community Grants, 177
Appalachian Regional Commission Educ and Training Grants, 504
Brooklyn Community Fndn Green Communities Grants, 852
Cleveland Fenn Ed Grants, 1169
Indiana Workforce Acceleration Grants, 2552
New Jersey Center for Hispanic Policy, Research and Development Workforce Grants, 3330
NYCT Workforce Development Grants, 3560
PepsiCo Fndn Grants, 3819
Santa Fe Community Fndn Seasonal Grants-Spring Cycle, 4291
Sobrato Family Fndn Grants, 4389
Sobrato Family Fndn Meeting Space Grants, 4390
Sobrato Family Fndn Office Space Grants, 4391
Toyota Motor Engineering & Manufacturing North America Grants, 4651
Toyota Motor Manufacturing W Virginia Grants, 4657
USAID Call for Public-Private Alliance Proposals in Serbia, 4742
USAID Workforce Development Program in Mexico Grants, 4787
Vectren Fndn Grants, 4907
Xerox Fndn Grants, 5122

Educational Administration
ALA May Hill Arbuthnot Honor Lecture Award, 300
CNCS School Turnaround AmeriCorps Grants, 1186
George I. Alden Grants, 2023
Guy I. Bromley Grants, 2180
John W. Speas and Effie E. Speas Grants, 2732
Lewis H. Humphreys Charitable Grants, 2889
Louetta M. Cowden Fndn Grants, 2922
Louis and Elizabeth Nave Flarsheim Charitable Fndn Grants, 2924
Meadows Fndn Grants, 3104
Meyer Fndn Educ Grants, 3142
Nellie Mae Educ Fndn District-Level Grants, 3297
Nellie Mae Educ Fndn State Level Systems Change Grants, 3299
R.E.B. Awards for Distinguished Ed Leadership, 4000
Time Warner Diverse Voices in the Arts Grants, 4635
Wallace Fndn Grants, 4976

Educational Evaluation/Assessment
A.O. Smith Community Grants, 46
ALA John Cotton Dana Library Public Relations Award, 292
Blue Cross Blue Shield of Minnesota Fndn - Healthy Equity: Health Impact Assessment Demonstration Project Grants, 795
First Lady's Family Lit Init for Texas Grants, 1822
Nellie Mae Educ Public Understanding Grants, 3298
Nellie Mae Educ Fndn State Level Systems Change Grants, 3299
North Carolina Arts Council Arts in Educ Rural Development Grants, 3470
PacifiCare Fndn Grants, 3725
Stuart Fndn Grants, 4516
Teagle Fndn Grants, 4569
UNESCO World Heritage Grants, 4706
UPS Fndn Economic and Global Lit Grants, 4730
William J. Brace Charitable Trust, 5088

Educational Finance
Allstate Corp Giving Grants, 386
Allstate Corp Hometown Commitment Grants, 387
Allstate Fndn Safe and Vital Communities Grants, 390

Educational Instruction
A.J. Muste Memorial Institute Counter Recruitment Grants, 43
AACC Plus 50 Init Grants, 55
Adobe Youth Voices Grants, 170
ALA May Hill Arbuthnot Honor Lecture Award, 300
BCBSM Fndn Student Award Program, 710
Bill & Melinda Gates Policy & Advocacy Grants, 769
Blue Cross Blue Shield of Minnesota Fndn - Healthy Equity: Public Libraries for Health Grants, 797
Carroll County Community Fndn Grants, 947
Charles H. Dater Fndn Grants, 1042
Charlotte Martin Fndn Youth Grants, 1057
Columbus Fndn Siemer Family Grants, 1231
Delonne Anderson Family Fndn, 1492
Georgia-Pacific Fndn Educ Grants, 2031
Harry S. Truman Scholarships, 2244
Head Start Replacement Grantee: Colorado, 2275
Head Start Replacement Grantee: Florida, 2276
Head Start Replacement Grantee: West Virginia, 2277
Heifer Ed Grants for Principals, 2288
IIE Toyota Int'l Teacher Professional Development Grants, 2461
Kaneta Fndn Grants, 2774
Leave No Trace Master Educator Scholarships, 2870
Leonard L. and Bertha U. Abess Fndn Grants, 2884
Mary Wilmer Covey Charitable Grants, 3049
National Endowment for the Arts Dance Grants: Art Works, 3262
Nellie Mae Educ Public Understanding Grants, 3298
Nellie Mae Educ Fndn State Level Systems Change Grants, 3299
San Diego Women's Fndn Grants, 4252
Southern Minnesota Init Fndn BookStart Grants, 4432
Ursula Thrush Peace Seed Grants, 4733
USGA Fndn For the Good of the Game Grants, 4868
Warrick County Community Fndn Grants, 4987

Educational Planning/Policy
Achelis Fndn Grants, 127
Bill & Melinda Gates Policy & Advocacy Grants, 769
Blue Cross Blue Shield of Minnesota Fndn - Healthy Equity: Health Impact Assessment Demonstration Project Grants, 795
Blue Cross Blue Shield of Minnesota Fndn - Healthy Equity: Health Impact Assessment Grants, 796
Bodman Fndn Grants, 807
Charles G. Koch Charitable Fndn Grants, 1041
Chicago Tribune Fndn Civic Grants, 1100
Georgia-Pacific Fndn Educ Grants, 2031
GNOF IMPACT Grants for Educ, 2079
GTECH Community Involvement Grants, 2171
Guy I. Bromley Grants, 2180
Hazen Fndn Public Educ Grants, 2269
Japan Center for Global Partnership Grants, 2650
John W. Speas and Effie E. Speas Grants, 2732
Kaneta Fndn Grants, 2774
Leonard L. and Bertha U. Abess Fndn Grants, 2884
Lewis H. Humphreys Charitable Grants, 2889
Louetta M. Cowden Fndn Grants, 2922
Louis and Elizabeth Nave Flarsheim Charitable Fndn Grants, 2924
Meyer Fndn Educ Grants, 3142
Michael and Susan Dell Fndn Grants, 3158
Nellie Mae Educ Fndn District-Level Grants, 3297
Nellie Mae Educ Fndn State Level Systems Change Grants, 3299
NYCT Hunger and Homelessnes Grants, 3553
OSF-Baltimore Ed & Youth Devel Grants, 3697
Phil Hardin Fndn Grants, 3875
Robert R. McCormick Tribune Civics Grants, 4118
Schumann Fund for New Jersey Grants, 4311
Seattle Fndn Educ Grants, 4326
Stuart Fndn Grants, 4516
USAID Development Assistance Grants, 4748
Wallace Fndn Grants, 4976

Educational Psychology
Ittleson Fndn Mental Health Grants, 2590

Educational Technology
ALA Information Technology Pathfinder Award, 286
Alcatel-Lucent Technologies Fndn Grants, 349
Arizona Commission on the Arts Educ Grants, 536
Bay and Paul Fndns, Inc Grants, 692
Buhl Fndn - Frick Ed Fund, 859
EDS Technology Grants, 1662
FRED Ed Ethyl Grants, 1945
FRED Technology Grants for Rural Schools, 1951
Hilda and Preston Davis Fndn Grants, 2322
Illinois DCEO Eliminate Dig Divide Grants, 2489
Illinois DCEO Emerging Technological Enterprises Grants, 2490
Jessie Ball Dupont Grants, 2671
Mitsubishi Electric America Fndn Grants, 3190
Nellie Mae Educ Fndn State Level Systems Change Grants, 3299
PeopleSoft Community Relations Grants, 3818
Thomas J. Long Fndn Community Grants, 4618
USDA Distance Learning and Telemed Grants, 4806
Verizon Fndn Grants, 4911

Educational Testing/Measurement
Legacy Fndn College Readiness Grant, 2874

Educational Theory
Guy I. Bromley Grants, 2180
John W. Speas and Effie E. Speas Grants, 2732
Lewis H. Humphreys Charitable Grants, 2889
Louetta M. Cowden Fndn Grants, 2922
Louis and Elizabeth Nave Flarsheim Charitable Fndn Grants, 2924

Elder Abuse
Administration on Aging Senior Medicare Patrol Project Grants, 166
A Glimmer of Hope Fndn Grants, 200
Arizona Republic Newspaper Contributions, 547
Austin S. Nelson Fndn Grants, 617
CICF Senior Grants, 1127
Hearst Fndns Social Service Grants, 2285
Peacock Fndn Grants, 3809
Reynolds and Reynolds Associate Fndn Grants, 4069

Elderly
A.V. Hunter Grants, 47
AAA Fndn for Traffic Safety Grants, 50
Abbot and Dorothy H. Stevens Fndn Grants, 79
Administration on Aging Senior Medicare Patrol Project Grants, 166
A Glimmer of Hope Fndn Grants, 200
Agnes M. Lindsay Grants, 203
Aladdin Industries Fndn Grants, 263
ALA Diversity and Outreach Fair, 267
ALA Exceptional Service Award, 278

Elderly

Albert and Bessie Mae Kronkosky Charitable Fndn Grants, 339
Albert W. Rice Charitable Fndn Grants, 347
Alex Stern Family Fndn Grants, 360
Alfred E. Chase Charitable Fndn Grants, 366
Allen P. and Josephine B. Green Fndn Grants, 380
Amelia Sillman Rockwell and Carlos Perry Rockwell Charities Grants, 417
Ameren Corp Community Grants, 418
American Schlafhorst Fndn Grants, 446
AMI Semiconductors Corp Grants, 457
Amon G. Carter Fndn Grants, 458
Ann Arbor Area Community Fndn Grants, 474
Ann Peppers Fndn Grants, 484
Anschutz Family Fndn Grants, 486
Arizona Community Fndn Grants, 540
Arizona Republic Fndn Grants, 546
Arizona Republic Newspaper Contributions, 547
Arkell Hall Fndn Grants, 562
Arthur and Rochelle Belfer Fndn Grants, 570
Atkinson Fndn Community Grants, 606
Avon Products Fndn Grants, 625
Bailey Fndn Grants, 635
Barberton Community Fndn Grants, 666
BCBSM Corp Contributions Grants, 706
BCBSNC Fndn Grants, 712
Ben B. Cheney Fndn Grants, 725
Bender Fndn Grants, 726
Berrien Community Fndn Grants, 744
Bertha Russ Lytel Fndn Grants, 745
Birmingham Fndn Grants, 774
Blackford County Community Fndn Grants, 780
Blanche and Irving Laurie Fndn Grants, 784
Bodenwein Public Benevolent Fndn Grants, 806
Boston Fndn Grants, 819
Brookdale Fndn National Group Respite Grants, 845
Brookdale Fndn Relatives as Parents Grants, 846
Bryan Adams Fndn Grants, 858
Burden Grants, 864
Caleb C. and Julia W. Dula Ed and Charitable Fndn Grants, 893
California Endowment Innovative Ideas Challenge Grants, 904
Callaway Fndn Grants, 909
Callaway Golf Company Fndn Grants, 910
Cambridge Community Fndn Grants, 913
Carl R. Hendrickson Family Fndn Grants, 935
Carl W. and Carrie Mae Joslyn Grants, 938
Carrie E. and Lena V. Glenn Fndn Grants, 944
Carrie Estelle Doheny Fndn Grants, 945
Carroll County Community Fndn Grants, 947
Caterpillar Fndn Grants, 954
Catherine Kennedy Home Fndn Grants, 955
CCF Community Priorities Fund, 961
CFFVR Basic Needs Giving Partnership Grants, 1002
CFFVR Frank C. Shattuck Community Grants, 1012
Charles F. Bacon Grants, 1040
Charles H. Farnsworth Grants, 1043
Charles Nelson Robinson Grants, 1052
Chatlos Fndn Grants, 1061
Christine and Katharina Pauly Charitable Grants, 1114
CICF Indianapolis Fndn Community Grants, 1123
CICF Senior Grants, 1127
Clipper Ship Fndn Grants, 1175
CNA Fndn Grants, 1179
CNCS Foster Grandparent Grants, 1185
CNCS Senior Companion Grants, 1187
CNCS Senior Corps Retired and Senior Volunteer Grants, 1188
Columbus Fndn Allen Eiry Grants, 1219
Columbus Fndn J. Floyd Dixon Grants, 1222
Columbus Fndn Small Grants, 1232
Commonwealth Fund Harkness Fellowships in Health Care Policy and Practice, 1242
Community Fndn in Jacksonville Senior Roundtable Aging Adults Grants, 1263
Community Fndn of Riverside County Grants, 1304
Community Fndn of Santa Cruz County Grants, 1305
Community Fndn of Shreveport-Bossier Grants, 1307
Community Fndn of the Ozarks Grants, 1320
Comprehensive Health Educ Fndn Grants, 1337
ConocoPhillips Grants, 1355
Cooke Fndn Grants, 1368
Crescent Porter Hale Fndn Grants, 1398
Dade Community Fndn GLBT Grants, 1429
Daisy Marquis Jones Fndn Grants, 1434
Danellie Fndn Grants, 1442
Daniels Grants, 1443
David Lane Grants for Aged & Indigent Women, 1453
Deluxe Corp Fndn Grants, 1496
Dennis and Phyllis Washington Fndn Grants, 1498
Dermody Properties Fndn Capstone Award, 1516
DHHS Special Programs for the Aging: Training, Research, and Discretionary Grants, 1538
Doree Taylor Charitable Fndn, 1580
Dr. Scholl Fndn Grants, 1602
Edward N. and Della L. Thome Memorial Fndn Direct Services Grants, 1666
Edward W. and Stella C. Van Houten Grants, 1670
Edwin W. and Catherine M. Davis Fndn Grants, 1672
Eisner Fndn Grants, 1678
Elizabeth Morse Genius Charitable Grants, 1682
Ellen Abbott Gilman Grants, 1685
Encore Purpose Prize, 1704
EPA Senior Environmental Employment Grants, 1736
EPA State Senior Environ Employment Grants, 1739
Essex County Community Fndn Merrimack Valley General Grants, 1756
Ethel and Raymond F. Rice Fndn Grants, 1758
Eva L. and Joseph M. Bruening Fndn Grants, 1768
Ewa Beach Community Trust Fund, 1775
Fan Fox and Leslie R. Samuels Fndn Grants, 1786
Faye McBeath Fndn Grants, 1794
Florence Hunt Maxwell Fndn Grants, 1844
Foellinger Fndn Grants, 1877
Fndn for the Carolinas, 1896
Fourjay Fndn Grants, 1913
Frances and John L. Loeb Family Grants, 1917
Frank Reed and Margaret Jane Peters Memorial Fund I Grants, 1933
Frederick McDonald Grants, 1946
Fremont Area Community Elderly Needs Grants, 1954
Fremont Area Community Fndn Grants, 1955
G.N. Wilcox Grants, 1982
George A Ohl Jr. Fndn Grants, 2012
George Fndn Grants, 2018
George P. Davenport Grants, 2026
George W. Wells Fndn Grants, 2030
Gertrude M. Conduff Fndn Grants, 2047
GNOF Gert Community Grants, 2076
GNOF IMPACT Grants for Health and Human Services, 2080
GNOF Maison Hospitaliere Grants, 2086
Goldseker Fndn Human Services Grants, 2102
Greygates Fndn Grants, 2164
Grover Hermann Fndn Grants, 2168
H. Leslie Hoffman & Elaine Hoffman Grants, 2185
Hackett Fndn Grants, 2188
HAF Senior Opportunities Grants, 2203
Hagedorn Grants, 2207
Harold Brooks Fndn Grants, 2227
Harry C. Trexler Grants, 2239
Harry Kramer Grants, 2242
Health Canada National Seniors Indep Grants, 2278
Health Fndn of Greater Indianapolis Grants, 2282
Helen Gertrude Sparks Charitable Grants, 2294
Helen Steiner Rice Fndn Grants, 2299
Henrietta Lange Burk Grants, 2303
Henry County Community Fndn Grants, 2308
Henry E. Niles Fndn Grants, 2309
Herbert H. and Grace A. Dow Fndn Grants, 2315
Hilda and Preston Davis Fndn Grants, 2322
Hill Fndn Grants, 2326
Hoglund Fndn Grants, 2344
Holland/Zeeland Community Fndn Grants, 2345
Hugh J. Andersen Fndn Grants, 2385
J. F. Maddox Fndn Grants, 2597
J. Walton Bissell Fndn Grants, 2608
Jacob G. Schmidlapp Grants, 2616
James & Abigail Campbell Family Fndn Grants, 2620
James R. Thorpe Fndn Grants, 2636
Jane Bradley Pettit Fndn Community and Social Development Grants, 2642
Janirve Fndn Grants, 2645
Jay and Rose Phillips Family Fndn Grants, 2656
Jean and Louis Dreyfus Fndn Grants, 2658
Jewish Grants, 2675
Jim Moran Fndn Grants, 2680
John Edward Fowler Memorial Fndn Grants, 2693
John G. Martin Fndn Grants, 2696
John H. Wellons Fndn Grants, 2699
John W. Anderson Fndn Grants, 2729
John W. Boynton Grants, 2730
Kaiser Permanente Cares for Comm Grants, 2763
Kansas Arts Commission Artist Fellowships, 2776
Katharine Matthies Fndn Grants, 2788
Kawabe Grants, 2794
Kentucky Arts Council Access Assistance Grants, 2805
Kimberly-Clark Community Grants, 2824
Leon and Thea Koerner Fndn Grants, 2883
Leo Niessen Jr., Charitable Grants, 2885
Lettie Pate Whitehead Fndn Grants, 2888
Long Island Community Fndn Grants, 2920
Lowell Berry Fndn Grants, 2930
Madison Community Fndn Grants, 2971
Maine Comm Belvedere Animal Welfare Grants, 2975
Mardag Fndn Grants, 3001
Marie C. and Joseph C. Wilson Fndn Rochester Small Grants, 3006
Marin Community Successful Aging Grants, 3014
Marion Isabell Coe Grants, 3020
Marjorie Moore Charitable Fndn Grants, 3021
Mary Black Fndn Active Living Grants, 3031
May and Stanley Smith Charitable Grants, 3069
McLean Fndn Grants, 3089
Medtronic Fndn Patient Link Grants, 3113
Memorial Fndn Grants, 3117
Mericos Fndn Grants, 3121
Metro Health Fndn Grants, 3133
MetroWest Health Fndn Grants--Healthy Aging, 3135
MGM Resorts Fndn Community Grants, 3153
Michael Reese Health Trust Responsive Grants, 3160
Mid-Iowa Health Fndn Comm Response Grants, 3168
Military Ex-Prisoners of War Fndn Grants, 3177
Montana Arts Council Cultural and Aesthetic Project Grants, 3209
Montana Community Fndn Grants, 3211
Mr. and Mrs. William Foulds Family Grants, 3222
Mt. Sinai Health Care Fndn Health of the Jewish Community Grants, 3226
Musgrave Fndn Grants, 3231
Nathan B. and Florence R. Burt Fndn Grants, 3245
National Endowment for the Arts Presenting Grants: Art Works, 3268
NGA Heinz Wholesome Memories Intergenerational Garden Awards, 3404
NIAF Anthony Campitelli Endowed Grants, 3431
Nicor Gas Sharing Grants, 3436
Nina Mason Pulliam Charitable Grants, 3443
Norcliffe Fndn Grants, 3459
Northland Fndn Grants, 3506
NW Minnesota Fndn Asset Building Grants, 3511
Nuffield Fndn Africa Grants, 3532
Nuffield Fndn Open Door Grants, 3534
Nuffield Fndn Small Grants, 3535
Oppenstein Brothers Fndn Grants, 3685
OUT Fund for Lesbian & Gay Liberation Grants, 3714
PacifiCorp Fndn for Learning Grants, 3727
Pasadena Fndn Average Grants, 3741
Paul and Mary Haas Fndn Contributions and Student Scholarships, 3756
Paul Balint Charitable Grants, 3757
Pauline E. Fitzpatrick Charitable Trust, 3763
PCA Art Organizations and Art Programs Grants for Presenting Organizations, 3771
PCA Arts Organizations Grants for Music, 3774
PCA Arts Organizations and Arts Programs Grants for Art Museums, 3775
PCA Arts Organizations and Arts Programs Grants for Arts Educ Organizations, 3776

SUBJECT INDEX

PCA Arts Organizations and Arts Programs Grants for Arts Service Organizations, 3777
PCA Arts Organizations & Grants for Crafts, 3778
PCA Arts Organizations & Grants for Dance, 3779
PCA Arts Organizations and Arts Programs Grants for Film and Electronic Media, 3780
PCA Arts Organizations & Grants for Lit, 3781
PCA Arts Organizations and Arts Programs Grants for Local Arts, 3782
PCA Arts Organizations & Grants for Theatre, 3783
PCA Arts Organizations and Arts Programs Grants for Traditional and Folk Arts, 3784
PCA Arts Organizations & Grants for Visual Arts, 3785
PCA Busing Grants, 3786
PCA Entry Track Arts Organizations and Program Grants for Art Museums, 3787
PCA Entry Track Arts Organizations and Program Grants for Arts Educ Organizations, 3788
PCA Entry Track Arts Organizations and Program Grants for Arts Service Organizations, 3789
PCA Entry Track Arts Organizations and Program Grants for Crafts, 3790
PCA Entry Track Arts Organizations and Program Grants for Dance, 3791
PCA Entry Track Arts Organizations and Program Grants for Film and Electronic Media, 3792
PCA Entry Track Arts Organizations and Program Grants for Local Arts, 3794
PCA Entry Track Arts Organizations and Program Grants for Music, 3795
PCA Entry Track Arts Organizations and Program Grants for Presenting Organizations, 3796
PCA Entry Track Arts Organizations and Program Grants for Theatre, 3797
PCA Entry Track Arts Organizations and Program Grants for Traditional and Folk Arts, 3798
PCA Entry Track Arts Organizations and Program Grants for Visual Arts, 3799
PCA Pennsylvania Partners in the Arts Program Stream Grants, 3801
PCA Pennsylvania Partners in the Arts Project Stream Grants, 3802
Perkins-Ponder Fndn Grants, 3822
Phelps County Community Fndn Grants, 3870
Pi Lambda Theta Anna Tracey Memorial Award, 3889
Pinellas County Grants, 3891
Piper Trust Educ Grants, 3902
Piper Trust Older Adults Grants, 3904
Piper Trust Reglious Organizations Grants, 3905
Plum Creek Fndn Grants, 3917
Portland Fndn - Women's Giving Circle Grant, 3935
Powell Fndn Grants, 3942
Public Welfare Fndn Grants, 3984
Puerto Rico Community Fndn Grants, 3986
Quantum Fndn Grants, 3996
R.C. Baker Fndn Grants, 3999
R.S. Gernon Grants, 4002
Ralph M. Parsons Fndn Grants, 4013
Retirement Research Accessible Faith Grants, 4066
Retirement Research Fndn General Grants, 4067
Reynolds and Reynolds Associate Fndn Grants, 4069
Richard and Rhoda Goldman Grants, 4077
Robert & Clara Milton Fund for Senior Housing, 4117
Rochester Area Community Fndn Grants, 4127
Rollin M. Gerstacker Fndn Grants, 4146
Rose Community Fndn Aging Grants, 4152
RRF Accessible Faith Grants, 4169
RRF General Grants, 4170
Ruth Anderson Fndn Grants, 4176
Saginaw Community Fndn Senior Citizen Enrichment Fund, 4206
Sailors' Snug Harbor of Boston Elder Grants, 4211
Sailors' Snug Harbor of Boston Fishing Communities Init Grants, 4212
Saint George's Society of New York Scholarships, 4213
Salisbury Community Fndn Grants, 4224
Schramm Fndn Grants, 4310
Sid W. Richardson Fndn Grants, 4350
Siragusa Fndn Human Services Grants, 4369
Sisters of Mercy of North Carolina Fndn Grants, 4375

Sisters of Saint Joseph Charitable Grants, 4376
Sophia Romero Grants, 4406
SW Gas Corp Fndn Grants, 4445
Stewart Huston Charitable Grants, 4505
Susan A. & Donald P. Babson Charitable Grants, 4534
Swindells Charitable Fndn, 4542
TAC Touring Arts and Arts Access Grants, 4557
Taproot Fndn Capacity-Building Service Grants, 4560
Thelma Braun and Bocklett Family Fndn Grants, 4603
Thelma Doelger Charitable Grants, 4604
Theodore Edson Parker Fndn Grants, 4605
Thomas Austin Finch, Sr. Fndn Grants, 4613
Topfer Family Fndn Grants, 4646
Trull Fndn Grants, 4673
Union Benevolent Association Grants, 4710
Victor E. Speas Fndn Grants, 4933
Westinghouse Charitable Giving Grants, 5028
Wild Rivers Community Holiday Partnership, 5069
William H. Hannon Fndn Grants, 5086
William J. Brace Charitable Trust, 5088
Windgate Charitable Fndn Grants, 5099
Winston-Salem Fndn Competitive Grants, 5102
Wood-Claeyssens Fndn Grants, 5113

Electoral Systems
Baptist Community Ministries Grants, 664
Carnegie Corp of New York Grants, 940
Ford Fndn Peace and Social Justice Grants, 1884
Joyce Fndn Democracy Grants, 2748
Threshold Fndn Election Integrity Grants, 4625

Electric Power
PNM Reduce Your Use Grants, 3926
PSEG Environmental Educ Grants, 3980

Electronic Media
ALA Dartmouth Medal, 262
ALA e-Learning Scholarships, 270
Appalachian Community Media Justice Grants, 495
Florida Div of Cultural Affairs Media Grants, 1856
Geraldine R. Dodge Fndn Media Grants, 2042
IFP New York State Council on the Arts Electronic Media and Film Program Distribution Grants, 2451
NYSCA Electronic Media and Film: Film Festivals Grants, 3588
NYSCA Electronic Media and Film: General Exhibition Grants, 3589
NYSCA Electronic Media and Film: General Operating Support, 3590
NYSCA Electronic Media and Film: General Program Support, 3591
NYSCA Electronic Media and Film: Screenings Grants, 3592
NYSCA Electronic Media and Film: Workspace Grants, 3593
PCA Arts Organizations and Arts Programs Grants for Film and Electronic Media, 3780
PCA Arts Organizations & Grants for Visual Arts, 3785
PCA Entry Track Arts Organizations and Program Grants for Visual Arts, 3799
Reinberger Fndn Grants, 4052
USAID Strengthening Free and Independent Media in South Sudan Grants, 4783

Electronics/Electrical Engineering
Motorola Fndn Grants, 3221

Elementary Education
3M Fndn Community Giving Grants, 15
21st Century Threshold Project Gifts, 21
A.O. Smith Community Grants, 46
AAF Richard Riley Award, 59
Abeles Fndn Grants, 89
Abernethy Family Fndn Grants, 98
Acuity Charitable Fndn Grants, 140
Adams Family Fndn I Grants, 150
AEC Grants, 175
AEP Corp Giving Grants, 180
Aetna Fndn Educ Grants in Connecticut, 183
Aetna Summer Academic Enrichment Grants, 189

Agere Corp and Community Involvement Grants, 199
Ahmanson Fndn Grants, 207
Alabama Power Fndn Grants, 233
ALA Coretta Scott King Book Donation Grant, 261
ALA Information Technology Pathfinder Award, 286
Alcatel-Lucent Technologies Fndn Grants, 349
AMD Corp Contributions Grants, 416
American Electric Power Grants, 428
American Honda Fndn Grants, 439
AmerUs Group Charitable Fndn, 455
Archer Daniels Midland Fndn Grants, 527
Arkansas Arts Council AIE Arts Curriculum Project Grants, 552
Arkansas Arts Council AIE Mini Grants, 554
Arkema Fndn Science Teachers Program, 563
Armstrong McDonald Fndn Grants, 565
ArvinMeritor Fndn Arts and Culture Grants, 582
ATF Gang Resistance Educ and Training Program Coop Agreements, 603
AutoNation Corp Giving Grants, 620
Avista Fndn Grants, 624
Ball Brothers Fndn General Grants, 637
Barnes and Noble Local Sponsorships and Charitable Donations, 670
Barnes and Noble National Sponsorships and Charitable Donations, 671
Baxter Int'l Corp Giving Grants, 689
Bay and Paul Fndns, Inc Grants, 692
Benton Community Fndn - The Cookie Jar Grant, 729
Benton County Fndn Grants, 731
Bernard & Audre Rapoport Arts & Culture Grant, 735
Berrien Community Fndn Grants, 744
Bertha Russ Lytel Fndn Grants, 745
Blackford County Community Fndn Grants, 780
Boeing Company Contributions Grants, 809
Bohemian Fndn Pharos Grants, 811
Booth-Bricker Grants, 815
Booth Ferris Fndn Grants, 816
Boston Fndn Grants, 819
British Columbia Arts Council Artists in Education Grants, 842
Brown Fndn Grants, 854
Buhl Fndn - Frick Ed Fund, 859
Burlington Industries Fndn Grants, 865
Burton Morgan Youth Entrepreneurship Grants, 870
Cadence Design Systems Grants, 889
California Arts Council Public Value Grants, 895
Callaway Fndn Grants, 909
Carnegie Corp of New York Grants, 940
Caroline Lawson Ivey Memorial Fndn Grants, 941
Carrie E. and Lena V. Glenn Fndn Grants, 944
Carrie Estelle Doheny Fndn Grants, 945
Carroll County Community Fndn Grants, 947
CDC School Health Programs to Prevent the Spread of HIV Coop Agreements, 975
CenturyLink Clarke M. Williams Fndn Grants, 998
CFFVR Mielke Family Fndn Grants, 1015
CFFVR Shawano Area Community Fndn Grants, 1021
Chapman Charitable Fndn Grants, 1033
Charity Incorporated Grants, 1035
Charles H. Price II Family Fndn Grants, 1046
Charles Lafitte Fndn Grants, 1049
Chesapeake Bay Trust Mini Grants, 1072
Chesapeake Corp Fndn Grants, 1076
Christensen Fund Regional Grants, 1112
Cincinnati Bell Fndn Grants, 1131
Cinergy Fndn Grants, 1133
Cisco Systems Fndn San Jose Community Grants, 1137
Citigroup Fndn Grants, 1139
Clara Blackford Smith and W. Aubrey Smith Charitable Fndn Grants, 1147
Clarence E. Heller Charitable Fndn Grants, 1150
Clinton County Community Fndn Grants, 1174
CNCS AmeriCorps Indian Planning Grants, 1180
CNCS AmeriCorps State and National Grants, 1182
CNCS Foster Grandparent Grants, 1185
CNCS Senior Corps Retired and Senior Volunteer Grants, 1188
Coca-Cola Fndn Grants, 1195
Colonel Stanley R. McNeil Fndn Grants, 1210

888 / Elementary Education

Colorado Interstate Gas Grants, 1213
Colorado Springs Community Grants, 1215
Columbus Fndn J. Floyd Dixon Grants, 1222
Columbus Fndn Siemer Family Grants, 1231
Comcast Fndn Grants, 1235
Commonweal Community Assistance Grants, 1239
Community Fndn of Central Illinois Grants, 1276
Community Fndn Silicon Valley Grants, 1331
Connelly Fndn Grants, 1353
ConocoPhillips Grants, 1355
Cooper Fndn Grants, 1369
Credit Suisse First Boston Fndn Grants, 1397
Crescent Porter Hale Fndn Grants, 1398
Cullen Fndn Grants, 1411
CVS All Kids Can Grants, 1420
CVS Community Grants, 1422
DaimlerChrysler Corp Grants, 1432
Daniels Grants, 1443
Dean Foods Community Involvement Grants, 1469
Decatur County Comm Large Project Grants, 1476
Dekko Fndn Grants, 1482
Dennis and Phyllis Washington Fndn Grants, 1498
District of Columbia Commission on the Arts-Arts Educ Teacher Mini-Grants, 1549
Dorr Fndn Grants, 1591
Douty Fndn Grants, 1595
Dow Corning Corp Contributions Grants, 1597
Dr. and Mrs. Paul Pierce Memorial Fndn Grants, 1599
Dr. Scholl Fndn Grants, 1602
Dresher Fndn Grants, 1605
Dreyer's Fndn Large Grants, 1606
Duke Energy Economic Development Grants, 1619
Dunn Fndn K-12 Grants, 1622
Dunspaugh-Dalton Fndn Grants, 1623
Dynegy Fndn Grants, 1630
E.J. Grassmann Grants, 1638
Eaton Charitable Grants, 1647
Effie and Wofford Cain Fndn Grants, 1674
Eisner Fndn Grants, 1678
Elizabeth Carse Fndn Grants, 1681
Emily Hall Tremaine Fndn Grants, 1698
Entergy Corp Micro Grants, 1712
EQT Fndn Educ Grants, 1745
Ethel and Raymond F. Rice Fndn Grants, 1758
Eugene McDermott Fndn Grants, 1765
FAS Project Schools Grants, 1792
Ferree Fndn Grants, 1804
Field Fndn of Illinois Grants, 1806
Firelight Fndn Grants, 1817
FirstEnergy Fndn Math, Science, and Technology Educ Grants, 1820
Fisher Fndn Grants, 1831
Fleishhacker Fndn Educ Grants, 1838
Floyd A. and Kathleen C. Cailloux Fndn Grants, 1874
France-Merrick Fndns Grants, 1915
Frances and John L. Loeb Family Grants, 1917
Frances L. and Edwin L. Cummings Grants, 1919
Francis T. & Louise T. Nichols Fndn Grants, 1923
Frank B. Hazard General Charity Grants, 1926
Frank Loomis Palmer Grants, 1931
Frank M. Tait Fndn Grants, 1932
Frank Reed and Margaret Jane Peters Memorial Fund II Grants, 1934
Fred & Gretel Biel Charitable Grants, 1939
Fred Meyer Fndn Grants, 1950
Gardiner Savings Inst Charitable Fndn Grants, 1987
GenCorp Fndn Grants, 1998
General Mills Fndn Grants, 2003
General Service Fndn Colorado Grants, 2005
George F. Baker Grants, 2016
George Fndn Grants, 2018
George Frederick Jewett Fndn Grants, 2019
George J. and Effie L. Seay Fndn Grants, 2024
Georgia-Pacific Fndn Educ Grants, 2031
GNOF Cox Charities of New Orleans Grants, 2072
GNOF Exxon-Mobil Grants, 2074
GNOF IMPACT Grants for Educ, 2079
GNOF Jefferson Community Grants, 2085
GNOF Norco Community Grants, 2089
GNOF Plaquemines Community Grants, 2091

Goodrich Corp Fndn Grants, 2104
Grace and Franklin Bernsen Fndn Grants, 2109
Green Fndn Educ Grants, 2153
Greenspun Family Fndn Grants, 2156
Grundy Fndn Grants, 2169
HAF Educ Grants, 2196
Halliburton Fndn Grants, 2211
Harold Alfond Fndn Grants, 2225
Harrison County Community Fndn Grants, 2233
Harrison County Community Signature Grants, 2234
Hearst Fndns Culture Grants, 2284
Helen Bader Fndn Grants, 2293
Herman Goldman Fndn Grants, 2317
Horizon Fndn Grants, 2365
Household Int'l Corp Giving Grants, 2372
Houston Endowment Grants, 2373
Hutchinson Community Fndn Grants, 2410
Hutton Fndn Grants, 2412
Illinois Arts Council Arts-in-Education Residency Grants, 2463
Intel Community Grants, 2562
Intel Int'l Community Grants, 2564
J.C. Penney Company Grants, 2594
J. Knox Gholston Fndn Grants, 2599
J.L. Bedsole Fndn Grants, 2600
J. Marion Sims Fndn Teachers' Pet Grant, 2605
Janus Fndn Grants, 2647
Jaquelin Hume Fndn Grants, 2654
John Clarke Grants, 2689
John P. Murphy Fndn Grants, 2708
Joseph S. Stackpole Charitable Grants, 2741
JP Morgan Chase Arts and Culture Grants, 2752
Katharine Matthies Fndn Grants, 2788
Katrine Menzing Deakins Charitable Grants, 2793
Kent D. Steadley and Mary L. Steadley Trust, 2804
Kentucky Arts Council TranspARTation Grant, 2812
KeySpan Fndn Grants, 2821
Kohler Fndn Grants, 2833
Koret Fndn Grants, 2837
Laura Jane Musser Rural Init Grants, 2864
Lawrence J. and Anne Rubenstein Charitable Fndn Grants, 2868
LEGO Children's Grants, 2878
Linford and Mildred White Charitable Grants, 2909
Lloyd G. Balfour Fndn Attleboro-Specific Charities Grants, 2916
Lockheed Martin Philanthropic Grants, 2918
Lowe's Charitable and Ed Fndn Grants, 2927
Lubbock Area Fndn Grants, 2931
Lubrizol Corp Community Grants, 2932
Luella Kemper Grants, 2939
Luther I. Replogle Grants, 2945
Lyndhurst Fndn Grants, 2949
Mardag Fndn Grants, 3001
Margaret and James A. Elkins Jr. Fndn Grants, 3003
Marion I. and Henry J. Knott Fndn Discretionary Grants, 3018
Marion I. and Henry J. Knott Standard Grants, 3019
Marjorie Moore Charitable Fndn Grants, 3021
Marsh Corp Grants, 3027
Mathile Family Fndn Grants, 3062
McColl Fndn Grants, 3074
McConnell Fndn Grants, 3076
McGraw-Hill Companies Community Grants, 3081
Mead Johnson Nutritionals Evansville-Area Organizations Grants, 3103
Meadows Fndn Grants, 3104
Medtronic Fndn Patient Link Grants, 3113
Memorial Fndn for Children Grants, 3116
Mericos Fndn Grants, 3121
Meyer Fndn Educ Grants, 3142
Meyer Memorial Trust Grassroots Grants, 3147
Meyer Memorial Trust Responsive Grants, 3148
MGM Resorts Fndn Community Grants, 3153
Micron Technology Fndn Community Grants, 3161
Mildred V. Horn Fndn Grants, 3176
Miller Fndn Grants, 3181
Milton and Sally Avery Arts Fndn Grants, 3183
Moody Fndn Grants, 3215
Motorola Fndn Grants, 3221

Musgrave Fndn Grants, 3231
National 4-H Afterschool Training Grants, 3248
National Endowment for the Arts - National Arts and Humanities Youth Program Awards, 3255
National Home Library Fndn Grants, 3276
Nellie Mae Educ Fndn District-Level Grants, 3297
Nellie Mae Educ Public Understanding Grants, 3298
Nellie Mae Educ Fndn State Level Systems Change Grants, 3299
NFL Club Matching Youth Football Field/Stadium Grants, 3349
NFL Grassroots Field Grants, 3350
NFL High School Coach of the Week Grant, 3351
NFL High School Football Coach of the Year, 3352
NFL Player Youth Football Camp Grants, 3353
NGA Hooked on Hydroponics Awards, 3405
NGA Wuzzleburg Preschool Garden Awards, 3408
NHSCA Artist Residencies in Schools Grants, 3423
NHSCA Youth Arts Project Grants: For Extended Arts Learning, 3430
Nicholas H. Noyes Jr. Memorial Fndn Grants, 3434
Nordson Corp Fndn Grants, 3462
North Carolina Arts Council Arts in Educ Rural Development Grants, 3470
Norton Fndn Grants, 3514
NYFA Artists in the School Community Planning Grants, 3562
NYSCA Arts Edu Community Learning Grants, 3577
NYSCA Arts Educ: General Operating Support, 3578
NYSCA Arts Educ: K-12 In-School Grants, 3580
NYSCA Arts Education Capacity Building Grants, 3581
NYSCA Arts Educ: Services to the Field Grants, 3582
Ober Kaler Community Grants, 3635
Olga Sipolin Children's Grants, 3668
Oppenstein Brothers Fndn Grants, 3685
Oracle Corp Contributions Grants, 3686
Owens Corning Fndn Grants, 3717
Pew Trusts Children and Youth Grants, 3858
Peyton Anderson Fndn Grants, 3862
PG&E Bright Ideas Grants, 3866
PGE Fndn Grants, 3869
Phil Hardin Fndn Grants, 3875
Phoenix Coyotes Charities Grants, 3879
Phoenix Suns Charities Grants, 3881
Pier 1 Imports Grants, 3887
Pioneer Hi-Bred Community Grants, 3895
Piper Jaffray Fndn Communities Giving Grants, 3899
Plough Fndn Grants, 3915
PMI Fndn Grants, 3918
Powell Fndn Grants, 3942
Procter and Gamble Grants, 3967
Public Educ Power Grants, 3981
Quantum Fndn Grants, 3996
R.S. Gernon Grants, 4002
Rajiv Gandhi Fndn Grants, 4011
Randall L. Tobias Fndn Grants, 4017
Raskob Fndn for Catholic Activities Grants, 4019
RBC Dain Rauscher Fndn Grants, 4031
Reinberger Fndn Grants, 4052
Reynolds American Fndn Grants, 4068
Reynolds and Reynolds Company Fndn Grants, 4070
Richard and Susan Smith Family Fndn Grants, 4078
Richland County Bank Grants, 4091
Robert R. McCormick Tribune Comm Grants, 4119
Robert R. Meyer Fndn Grants, 4121
Robert W. Woodruff Fndn Grants, 4124
Rollins-Luetkemeyer Fndn Grants, 4147
Ronald McDonald House Charities Grants, 4149
Ruth Eleanor Bamberger and John Ernest Bamberger Memorial Fndn Grants, 4178
Sage Fndn Grants, 4204
Saigh Fndn Grants, 4210
San Francisco Fndn Community Health Grants, 4263
San Juan Island Community Fndn Grants, 4283
Sartain Lanier Family Fndn Grants, 4298
Scholastic Welch's Harvest Grants, 4309
Schramm Fndn Grants, 4310
Seagate Tech Corp Capacity to Care Grants, 4317
Seattle Fndn Educ Grants, 4326
Seneca Foods Fndn Grants, 4336

SUBJECT INDEX

Emergency Services / 889

Shopko Fndn Community Charitable Grants, 4346
Sid W. Richardson Fndn Grants, 4350
Silicon Valley Community Fndn Educ Grants, 4356
Sioux Falls Area Community Grants, 4364
Sioux Falls Area Community Fndn Spot Grants, 4366
Sisters of Charity Fndn of Canton Grants, 4372
SOBP A.E. Bennett Research Award, 4388
Social Justice Fund NW General Grants, 4397
Sonora Area Fndn Competitive Grants, 4404
Sony Corp of America Corp Philanthropy Grants, 4405
SW Gas Corp Fndn Grants, 4445
Staples Fndn for Learning Grants, 4475
State Farm Fndn Grants, 4486
Stocker Fndn Grants, 4507
Strowd Roses Grants, 4515
Subaru Adopt a School Garden Grants, 4517
Sun Academic Excellence Grants, 4525
Sunny and Abe Rosenberg Fndn Grants, 4529
Sunoco Fndn Grants, 4530
T. James Kavanagh Fndn Grants, 4545
Taproot Fndn Capacity-Building Service Grants, 4560
Target Corp Local Store Grants, 4561
Teaching Tolerance Grants, 4567
Temple-Inland Fndn Grants, 4576
Thelma Braun and Bocklett Family Fndn Grants, 4603
Trull Fndn Grants, 4673
U.S. Department of Educ 21st Century Community Learning Centers, 4687
Union Bank Corp Sponsorships and Donations, 4708
Union Bank, N.A. Fndn Grants, 4709
Union County Community Fndn Grants, 4711
UPS Fndn Economic and Global Lit Grants, 4730
USA Football Equipment Grants, 4735
USAID Reading Enhancement for Advancing Development Grants, 4778
Valerie Adams Memorial Charitable Grants, 4898
Verizon Fndn Maine Grants, 4916
Victor E. Speas Fndn Grants, 4933
W.H. and Mary Ellen Cobb Charitable Grants, 4959
W.K. Kellogg Fndn Racial Equity Grants, 4962
Washington Gas Charitable Contributions, 5000
Wege Fndn Grants, 5017
Westinghouse Charitable Giving Grants, 5028
WHO Fndn General Grants, 5063
William Blair and Company Fndn Grants, 5078
William J. Brace Charitable Trust, 5088
William McCaskey Chapman and Adaline Dinsmore Chapman Fndn Grants, 5092
Windgate Charitable Fndn Grants, 5099
Winthrop Rockefeller Fndn Grants, 5105

Emergency Preparedness
AEGON Transamerica Disaster Relief Grants, 178
AIG Disaster Relief Grants, 213
ArvinMeritor Fndn Human Services Grants, 584
Bill & Melinda Gates Emergency Response Grants, 766
CNCS AmeriCorps State and National Grants, 1182
Dyson Fndn Emergency Grants, 1631
Elizabeth Morse Genius Charitable Grants, 1682
FEMA Staffing for Adequate Fire and Emergency Response Grants, 1803
GNOF Gulf Coast Oil Spill Grants, 2077
IAFF Harvard Univ Trade Union Scholarships, 2417
IAFF Labour College of Canada Residential Scholarship, 2418
IAFF National Labor College Scholarships, 2419
IDPH Emergency Med Serv Assistance Grants, 2440
Int'l Assoc of Emergency Managers Scholarships, 2566
Knight Fndn Grants - Montana, 2830
Nationwide Insurance Fndn Grants, 3285
Office Depot Fndn Disaster Relief Grants, 3640
Piedmont Natural Gas Fndn Health and Human Services Grants, 3885
Search Dog Fndn Rescue Dog Assistance, 4318
Seattle Fndn Benjamin N. Phillips Grants, 4322
Southern California Edison Public Safety and Preparedness Grants, 4430
South Madison Community Fndn Grants, 4440
USDC Supplemental Appropriations Disaster Relief Opportunity Grants, 4859

Emergency Programs
2 Life 18 Fndn Grants, 5
100 Club of Arizona Benefit Grants, 25
100 Club of Arizona Safety Enhancement Stipends, 26
200 Club of Mercer County Grants, 30
ACFEF Disaster Relief Fund Member Assistance, 117
AEGON Transamerica Disaster Relief Grants, 178
Agape Fndn for Nonviolent Social Change Alice Hamburg Emergency Grants, 196
Aid for Starving Children Emergency Assistance Grants, 211
AIG Disaster Relief Grants, 213
Alcatel-Lucent Technologies Fndn Grants, 349
Alexander Fndn Emergency Grants, 356
American for the Arts Emergency Relief Fund, 435
Appalachian Regional Commission Distressed Counties Grants, 503
ArvinMeritor Fndn Human Services Grants, 584
ATA Local Community Relations Grants, 600
Baltimore Community Fndn Kelly People's Emergency Grants, 645
Bank of America Critical Needs Grants, 656
Bill & Melinda Gates Emergency Response Grants, 766
BJ's Charitable Fndn Grants, 777
Blowitz-Ridgeway Fndn Grants, 792
Carl R. Hendrickson Family Fndn Grants, 935
Charles H. Hall Fndn, 1044
Children Affected by AIDS Fndn Family Assistance Emergency Grants, 1107
CICF Senior Grants, 1127
CNCS AmeriCorps State and National Grants, 1182
Community Fndn of Mount Vernon and Knox County Grants, 1301
Cooper Industries Fndn Grants, 1370
Coughlin-Saunders Fndn Grants, 1377
Covidien Medical Product Donations, 1390
DeKalb County Community Fndn - Immediate Response Grant, 1479
DFN Hurricane Katrina and Disability Rapid Response Grants, 1522
DHHS Emergency Med Services for Children, 1531
Doree Taylor Charitable Fndn, 1580
Dyson Fndn Emergency Grants, 1631
Elizabeth Morse Genius Charitable Grants, 1682
Ethel Frends Fndn Grants, 1759
Flextronics Fndn Disaster Relief Grants, 1841
Florence Hunt Maxwell Fndn Grants, 1844
Ford Family Fndn Grants - Critical Needs, 1879
Fndns of E Chicago Public Safety Grants, 1911
Frank B. Hazard General Charity Grants, 1926
Frank Loomis Palmer Grants, 1931
GNOF Albert N. & Hattie M. McClure Grants, 2068
GNOF Gulf Coast Oil Spill Grants, 2077
Harold Brooks Fndn Grants, 2227
Haymarket Urgent Response Grants, 2268
Helen Irwin Littauer Ed Grants, 2295
Helen V. Brach Fndn Grants, 2300
Henrietta Lange Burk Grants, 2303
Hundred Club of Colorado Springs Grants, 2391
Hundred Club of Connecticut Grants, 2392
Hundred Club of Contra Costa County Survivor Benefits Grants, 2393
Hundred Club of Denver Grants, 2394
Hundred Club of Durango Grants, 2395
Hundred Club of Los Angeles Grants, 2396
Hundred Club of Palm Springs Grants, 2397
Hundred Club of Pueblo Grants, 2398
Hundred Club of Santa Clara County Grants, 2399
Idaho Community Fndn Eastern Region Competitive Grants, 2432
James R. Thorpe Fndn Grants, 2636
Jane's Grants, 2639
Kalamazoo Community Fndn Individuals and Families Grants, 2769
Knight Fndn Grants - Montana, 2830
Kosciusko County Community Fndn REMC Operation Round Up Grants, 2839
Martin C. Kauffman 100 Club of Alameda County Survivor Benefits Grants, 3028
McGregor Grants, 3082

McKesson Fndn Grants, 3084
Meyer Memorial Trust Emergency Grants, 3146
Middlesex Savings Charitable Fndn Capacity Building Grants, 3172
Middlesex Savings Charitable Fndn Community Development Grants, 3173
Montana Community Big Sky LIFT Grants, 3210
Montana Community Fndn Grants, 3211
Nationwide Insurance Fndn Grants, 3285
Nicor Gas Sharing Grants, 3436
Office Depot Fndn Disaster Relief Grants, 3640
Oklahoma City Community Programs & Grants, 3666
Olga Sipolin Children's Grants, 3668
Packard Fndn Local Grants, 3729
PG&E Community Vitality Grants, 3868
Piedmont Natural Gas Fndn Health and Human Services Grants, 3885
Porter County Emergency Grants, 3932
Porter County Women's Grant, 3934
Prince Charitable Trusts D.C. Grants, 3960
RCF Individual Assistance Grants, 4033
Reinberger Fndn Grants, 4052
RESIST Emergency Grants, 4056
Salt River Health and Human Services Grants, 4228
San Diego Fndn After-the-Fires Grants, 4242
Sands Fndn Crisis Grants, 4254
Search Dog Fndn Rescue Dog Assistance, 4318
Seattle Fndn Benjamin N. Phillips Grants, 4322
Sobrato Family Fndn Meeting Space Grants, 4390
Sobrato Family Fndn Office Space Grants, 4391
Southern California Edison Civic Affairs Grants, 4428
Southern California Edison Public Safety and Preparedness Grants, 4430
Telluride Fndn Emergency/Out of Cycle Grants, 4574
UniBank 911 Emergency Personnel Educ Fund, 4707
Union Bank, N.A. Fndn Grants, 4709
USAID Int'l Emergency Food Assistance Grants, 4763
USAID Palestinian Comm Assistance Grants, 4773
USDA Emergency Community Water Assistance Grants, 4807
USDC Supplemental Appropriations Disaster Relief Opportunity Grants, 4859
W.H. and Mary Ellen Cobb Charitable Grants, 4959
Washington Area Fuel Grants, 4988
Widgeon Point Charitable Fndn Grants, 5064

Emergency Services
100 Club of Arizona Benefit Grants, 25
100 Club of Arizona Safety Enhancement Stipends, 26
A & B Family Fndn Grants, 38
ACF ACYF Runaway and Homeless Youth Basic Center Grants, 112
Actors Fund Dancers' Resource, 137
Actors Fund Social Services and Financial Assist, 139
Adams Family Fndn of Tennessee Grants, 152
AEGON Transamerica Disaster Relief Grants, 178
Agape Fndn for Nonviolent Social Change Alice Hamburg Emergency Grants, 196
AGMA Relief Grants, 201
Aid for Starving Children Emergency Assistance Grants, 211
AIG Disaster Relief Grants, 213
Alexander Fndn Emergency Grants, 356
Alexander Fndn Holiday Grants, 357
ArvinMeritor Fndn Human Services Grants, 584
Austin S. Nelson Fndn Grants, 617
Baltimore Community Fndn Kelly People's Emergency Grants, 645
Bank of America Charitable Fndn Critical Needs Grants, 656
Barberton Community Fndn Grants, 666
Bill & Melinda Gates Emergency Response Grants, 766
Bread and Roses Community Grants, 832
Burlington Industries Fndn Grants, 865
Campbell Soup Fndn Grants, 916
Carpenter Fndn Grants, 943
Carrier Corp Contributions Grants, 946
CE and S Fndn Grants, 985
Charles H. Hall Fndn, 1044
CICF Senior Grants, 1127

890 / Emergency Services

Clara Abbott Fndn Need-Based Grants, 1146
CNCS AmeriCorps State and National Grants, 1182
Community Fndn of Greater Birmingham Grants, 1280
Dearborn Community City of Aurora Grants, 1470
DeKalb County Community Fndn - Immediate Response Grant, 1479
DHHS Emergency Med Services for Children, 1531
DHS ARRA Fire Station Construction Grants, 1542
Dyson Fndn Emergency Grants, 1631
Elizabeth Morse Genius Charitable Grants, 1682
Essex County Community Emergency Grants, 1753
Farm Aid Grants, 1790
Fayette County Fndn Grants, 1795
FEMA Staffing for Adequate Fire and Emergency Response Grants, 1803
Florida BRAIVE Fund of Dade Community, 1846
Ford Family Fndn Grants - Critical Needs, 1879
Fndns of E Chicago Public Safety Grants, 1911
Frank B. Hazard General Charity Grants, 1926
Fred & Gretel Biel Charitable Grants, 1939
General Mills Fndn Grants, 2003
GNOF Gulf Coast Oil Spill Grants, 2077
Goldseker Fndn Community Affairs Grants, 2100
Gulf Coast Community Operating Grants, 2176
Gulf Coast Fndn of Community Grants, 2177
Harold Brooks Fndn Grants, 2227
Humanitas Fndn Grants, 2390
Hundred Club of Colorado Springs Grants, 2391
Hundred Club of Connecticut Grants, 2392
Hundred Club of Contra Costa County Survivor Benefits Grants, 2393
Hundred Club of Denver Grants, 2394
Hundred Club of Durango Grants, 2395
Hundred Club of Los Angeles Grants, 2396
Hundred Club of Palm Springs Grants, 2397
Hundred Club of Pueblo Grants, 2398
Hundred Club of Santa Clara County Grants, 2399
IAFF Labour College of Canada Residential Scholarship, 2418
IAFF National Labor College Scholarships, 2419
IAFF W. H. McClennan Scholarship, 2420
IDPH Emergency Med Serv Assistance Grants, 2440
IDPH Local Health Department Public Health Emergency Response Grants, 2442
Indiana AIDS Grants, 2529
Int'l Assoc of Emergency Managers Scholarships, 2566
John W. Boynton Grants, 2730
John W. Speas and Effie E. Speas Grants, 2732
Kalamazoo Community Fndn Individuals and Families Grants, 2769
Kessler Fndn Hurricane Emergency Grants, 2815
Knight Fndn Grants - Montana, 2830
Lewis H. Humphreys Charitable Grants, 2889
Louis and Elizabeth Nave Flarsheim Grants, 2924
Martin C. Kauffman 100 Club of Alameda County Survivor Benefits Grants, 3028
Mary E. Ober Fndn Grants, 3039
McCune Fndn Human Services Grants, 3080
Meyer Memorial Trust Emergency Grants, 3146
Middlesex Savings Charitable Fndn Community Development Grants, 3173
Montana Community Big Sky LIFT Grants, 3210
Montana Community Fndn Grants, 3211
Morris and Gwendolyn Cafritz Fndn Grants, 3218
Nationwide Insurance Fndn Grants, 3285
Nestle Purina PetCare Emergency Response and Disaster Relief Grants, 3303
Office Depot Fndn Disaster Relief Grants, 3640
Olga Sipolin Children's Grants, 3668
Owens Fndn Grants, 3718
Piedmont Natural Gas Fndn Health and Human Services Grants, 3885
Piper Trust Healthcare & Med Research Grants, 3903
Porter County Community Fndn Grants, 3931
Prince Charitable Trusts Chicago Grants, 3959
Raskob Fndn for Catholic Activities Grants, 4019
RCF Individual Assistance Grants, 4033
Reinberger Fndn Grants, 4052
Rhode Island Fndn Grants, 4073
Robert R. Meyer Fndn Grants, 4121

SAG Motion Picture Players Welfare Grants, 4209
Saint George's Society of New York Scholarships, 4213
Saint Paul Fndn Community Sharing Grants, 4218
Salt River Health and Human Services Grants, 4228
San Diego Fndn After-the-Fires Grants, 4242
Sands Fndn Crisis Grants, 4254
San Francisco Fndn Disability Rights Advocate Fund Emergency Grants, 4265
Search Dog Fndn Rescue Dog Assistance, 4318
Seattle Fndn Basic Needs Grants, 4321
Sioux Falls Area Community Fndn Field-of-Interest and Donor-Advised Grants, 4365
Sisters of Charity Cleveland Good Samaritan Grants, 4373
Southern California Edison Civic Affairs Grants, 4428
Southern California Edison Public Safety and Preparedness Grants, 4430
SW Florida Community Good Samaritan Grants, 4443
UNESCO World Heritage Grants, 4706
UniBank 911 Emergency Personnel Educ Fund, 4707
Union Bank Corp Sponsorships and Donations, 4708
Union Bank, N.A. Fndn Grants, 4709
Union Pacific Health & Human Services Grants, 4715
USAID Int'l Emergency Food Assistance Grants, 4763
USDC Supplemental Appropriations Disaster Relief Opportunity Grants, 4859

Emission Control
Energy Fndn Power Grants, 1707
MDEQ Clean Diesel Grants, 3096
United Technologies Corp Grants, 4725

Emotional/Mental Health
ACFEF Disaster Relief Fund Member Assistance, 117
Adolph Coors Fndn Grants, 171
Advancing Colorado's Mental Health Care Grants, 173
ATA Local Community Relations Grants, 600
Bella Vista Fndn Grants, 722
Charles H. Pearson Fndn Grants, 1045
CICF Christmas Fund, 1117
Cigna Civic Affairs Sponsorships, 1129
Community Fndn of Boone Cty Women's Grants, 1273
Cone Health Fndn Grants, 1348
DTE Energy Health & Human Services Grants, 1613
Elizabeth Morse Genius Charitable Grants, 1682
Fndn for Mid South Health & Wellness Grants, 1899
George W. Wells Fndn Grants, 2030
Gibson County Community Fndn Women's Fund, 2051
GNOF Gulf Coast Oil Spill Grants, 2077
HAF Mada Huggins Caldwell Grants, 2200
Hasbro Children's Fund, 2256
Herbert A. and Adrian W. Woods Fndn Grants, 2313
Long Island Community Fndn Grants, 2920
Lydia deForest Charitable Grants, 2946
Mary Black Fndn Community Health Grants, 3032
Moran Family Fndn Grants, 3216
New Jersey Center for Hispanic Policy, Research and Development Innovative Inits Grants, 3329
NFL Charities Pro Bowl Comm Grants in Hawaii, 3348
Peter and Elizabeth C. Tower Fndn Phase II Technology Init Grants, 3839
Peter and Elizabeth C. Tower Fndn Phase I Technology Init Grants, 3840
Peter and Elizabeth C. Tower Fndn Social and Emotional Preschool Curriculum Grants, 3841
Phoenix Coyotes Charities Grants, 3879
Piedmont Natural Gas Fndn Health and Human Services Grants, 3885
Porter County Women's Grant, 3934
Premera Blue Cross CARES Grants, 3945
Robert R. McCormick Tribune Veterans Grants, 4120
Schlessman Family Fndn Grants, 4307
Sophia Romero Grants, 4406
Taproot Fndn Capacity-Building Service Grants, 4560

Emotionally Disturbed
DHHS Comprehensive Community Mental Health Services Grants for Children with Serious Emotional Disturbances, 1530
Herbert A. and Adrian W. Woods Fndn Grants, 2313
Marion and Miriam Rose Grants, 3015

SUBJECT INDEX

Employee Benefits
IEDC Skills Enhancement Fund, 2445
South Carolina Arts Commission Incentive Grants for Employer Sponsored Benefits, 4422

Employment Opportunity Programs
21st Century ILGWU Heritage Grants, 20
Able Trust Vocational Rehabilitation Grants for Individuals, 104
Achelis Fndn Grants, 127
A Fund for Women Grants, 195
Albert W. Rice Charitable Fndn Grants, 347
Alfred E. Chase Charitable Fndn Grants, 366
Annie E. Casey Fndn Grants, 481
AT&T Fndn Civic and Comm Service Grants, 599
Baxter Int'l Corp Giving Grants, 689
BBF Maine Family Lit Init Grants, 698
BBF Maine Family Lit Init Planning Grants, 699
Bernard and Audre Rapoport Fndn Community Building and Social Service Grants, 736
Bernard F. and Alva B. Gimbel Fndn Grants, 740
Blue Cross Blue Shield of Minnesota Fndn - Health Equity: Building Health Together Grants, 793
Bodman Fndn Grants, 807
Boston Fndn Grants, 819
Bush Fndn Health & Human Services Grants, 875
CarEth Fndn Grants, 924
CCHD Economic Development Grants, 967
Charles H. Pearson Fndn Grants, 1045
Charles Hayden Fndn Grants, 1048
Chicago Community Poverty Alleviation Grants, 1091
Chiron Fndn Community Grants, 1111
CICF Efroymson Grants, 1120
Cleveland Fenn Ed Grants, 1169
CNCS AmeriCorps State and National Grants, 1182
Coleman Developmental Disabilities Grants, 1200
Community Fndn of Middle Tennessee Grants, 1300
Connecticut Community Fndn Grants, 1350
Crail-Johnson Fndn Grants, 1393
Cruise Industry Charitable Fndn Grants, 1404
Dept of Ed Projects with Industry Grants, 1511
Dept of Ed Recreational Services for Individuals with Disabilities, 1512
DHHS ARRA Strengthening Communities Fund - Nonprofit Capacity Building Grants, 1527
Diageo Fndn Grants, 1546
DOL Homeless Veterans Reintegration Grants, 1566
Do Right Fndn Grants, 1581
Duke Energy Economic Development Grants, 1619
Edward N. and Della L. Thome Memorial Fndn Direct Services Grants, 1666
EPA Brownfields Assessment Pilot Grants, 1724
Essex County Community Fndn Merrimack Valley General Grants, 1756
Ewing Marion Kauffman Fndn Grants and Inits, 1777
Families Count: The National Honors Program, 1784
Fisa Fndn Grants, 1826
Frank B. Hazard General Charity Grants, 1926
Frank Reed and Margaret Jane Peters Memorial Fund II Grants, 1934
Frank Stanley Beveridge Fndn Grants, 1936
Frederick W. Marzahl Grants, 1948
Gardiner Howland Shaw Fndn Grants, 1986
George W. Wells Fndn Grants, 2030
Georgiana Goddard Eaton Grants, 2038
GNOF Metropolitan Opportunities Grants, 2087
GNOF New Orleans Works Grants, 2088
Golden LEAF Fndn Grants, 2097
Graco Fndn Grants, 2111
Hampton Roads Community Fndn Health and Human Service Grants, 2216
Harold Brooks Fndn Grants, 2227
Helen Bader Fndn Grants, 2293
Henry County Community Fndn Grants, 2308
Henry E. Niles Fndn Grants, 2309
IBM Adult Training and Workforce Dev Grants, 2423
Illinois DCEO Employer Training Investment Grants - Competitive Component, 2491
Illinois DCEO Employer Training Investment Grants - Incentive Component, 2492

SUBJECT INDEX

Illinois DCEO Employer Training Investment Program Multi-Company Training Grants, 2493
Illinois DCEO Employer Training Investment Program Single Company Training Grants, 2494
Illinois DCEO Large Business Dev Grants, 2495
Illinois DNR Youth Recreation Corps Grants, 2508
Init Fndn Innovation Grants, 2559
John Gogian Family Fndn Grants, 2697
Johnson & Johnson Corp Contributions Grants, 2718
Jovid Fndn Grants, 2745
Joyce Fndn Employment Grants, 2749
Kessler Fndn Community Employment Grants, 2814
Kessler Fndn Signature Employment Grants, 2816
Kimball Int'l-Habig Fndn Grants, 2823
M.D. Anderson Fndn Grants, 2952
Mabel Louise Riley Fndn Family Strengthening Small Grants, 2958
Mabel Louise Riley Fndn Grants, 2959
Madison Community Fndn Grants, 2971
Marriott Int'l Corp Giving Grants, 3024
Maytree Fndn Assisting Local Leaders with Immigrant Employment Strategies Grants, 3070
Meyer Fndn Economic Security Grants, 3141
Meyer Fndn Educ Grants, 3142
Minnesota Small Cities Development Grants, 3187
Mizuho USA Fndn Grants, 3192
Modest Needs New Employment Grants, 3199
Nathaniel and Elizabeth P. Stevens Fndn Grants, 3247
National Endowment for the Arts - Regional Partnership Agreement Grants, 3258
Needmor Grants, 3289
Nehemiah Community Fndn Grants, 3290
New Mexico Women's Fndn Grants, 3335
NIDRR Field-Initiated Projects, 3437
Northern Trust Company Corp Giving Program, 3504
Northland Fndn Grants, 3506
NYCT Workforce Development Grants, 3560
Perry County Community Fndn Grants, 3827
Piedmont Natural Gas Fndn Workforce Development Grant, 3886
Pinkerton Fndn Grants, 3892
Priddy Fndn Grants, 3957
Princeton Area Community Fndn Fund for Women and Girls Grants, 3962
Richard King Mellon Fndn Grants, 4087
Richard M. Fairbanks Fndn Grants, 4088
Robert F. Stoico / FIRSTFED Grants, 4112
Robert R. McCormick Tribune Veterans Grants, 4120
Rockwell Fund, Inc. Grants, 4140
Romic Environmental's Charitable Contributions, 4148
S. Mark Taper Fndn Grants, 4201
Santa Fe Community Fndn Seasonal Grants-Spring Cycle, 4291
Sara Lee Fndn Grants, 4296
Sioux Falls Area Community Grants, 4364
Sioux Falls Area Community Fndn Spot Grants, 4366
Siragusa Fndn Human Services Grants, 4369
Sobrato Family Fndn Grants, 4389
Starr Fndn Grants, 4483
State Street Fndn Grants, 4495
Textron Corp Contributions Grants, 4601
U.S. Department of Educ Vocational Rehabilitation Services Projects for American Indians with Disabilities Grants, 4702
USAID Economic Prospectsfor Armenia-Turkey Normalization Grants, 4750
USDC Planning & Local Tech Assistance Grants, 4854
USDC Public Works and Economic Adjustment Assistance Grants, 4856
Vancouver Fndn Disability Supports for Employment Grants, 4899
Verizon Fndn Connecticut Grants, 4908
Verizon Fndn Maryland Grants, 4917
Verizon Fndn New York Grants, 4919
Verizon Fndn NE Region Grants, 4920
Verizon Fndn Pennsylvania Grants, 4921
Verizon Fndn SE Region Grants, 4923
Verizon Fndn Vermont Grants, 4924
Verizon Fndn Virginia Grants, 4925
Verizon Fndn West Virginia Grants, 4926

Warrick County Community Fndn Grants, 4987
WCI Family Econ Success Local Impact Grants, 5010
William J. and Dorothy K. O'Neill Fndn Grants, 5087
Women's Funding Alliance Grants, 5112

Employment/Unemployment Studies
DHHS Welfare Reform Research, Evaluations, and National Studies Grants, 1540
Joyce Fndn Employment Grants, 2749

Endocrinology
Genentech Corp Charitable Contributions, 2000
Jenifer Altman Fndn Grants, 2662

Endowments
Doug and Carla Salmon Fndn Grants, 1594
Florida Div of Cultural Affairs Endowments, 1851
Gertrude M. Conduff Fndn Grants, 2047
GNOF Freeman Challenge Grants, 2075
Hearst Fndns Culture Grants, 2284
Joukowsky Family Fndn Grants, 2743
Margaret T. Morris Fndn Grants, 3005
Roy and Christine Sturgis Charitable Grants, 4166
W.P. and Bulah Luse Fndn Grants, 4965

Energy
Appalachian Regional Commission Energy Grants, 505
Clarence E. Heller Charitable Fndn Grants, 1150
Colorado Clean Energy Solar Innovation Grants, 1212
Colorado Renewables in Performance Contracting Grants, 1214
Conservation, Food, and Health Fndn Grants for Developing Countries, 1359
Dollar Energy Grants, 1567
Energy Fndn Climate Grants, 1706
Entergy Charitable Fndn Low-Income Inits and Solutions Grants, 1711
General Motors Fndn Grants Support Program, 2004
Grand Victoria Fndn Illinois Core Grants, 2126
Honor the Earth Grants, 2361
Illinois Clean Energy Community Fndn Energy Efficiency Grants, 2479
Illinois Clean Energy Community Fndn K-12 Wind Schools Pilot Grants, 2480
Illinois Clean Energy Community Fndn Renewable Energy Grants, 2481
Illinois Clean Energy Community Fndn Solar Thermal Installation Grants, 2482
Indiana Corn Marketing Council Retailer Grant for Tank Cleaning, 2536
McCune Charitable Fndn Grants, 3077
Nicor Gas Sharing Grants, 3436
Rockefeller Bro Cross-Program Energy Grants, 4130
SW Init Fndn Grants, 4446
Surdna Fndn Sustainable Environments Grants, 4533
USAID Global Development Alliance Grants, 4753
USDA Denali Comm High Energy Cost Grants, 4805
USDA High Energy Cost Grants, 4812
USDA Rural Energy for America Renewable System & Efficiency Improvement Guaranteed Grants, 4830
USDA State Bulk Fuel Revolving Grants, 4840
William & Flora Hewlett Environmental Grants, 5074

Energy Assistance
Kessler Fndn Hurricane Emergency Grants, 2815
Washington Area Fuel Grants, 4988
Washington Gas Charitable Contributions, 5000

Energy Conservation
Appalachian Regional Commission Energy Grants, 505
Bullitt Fndn Grants, 862
CenterPointEnergy Minnegasco Grants, 993
CNCS AmeriCorps NCCC Project Grants, 1181
CNCS AmeriCorps State and National Grants, 1182
CNCS Senior Corps Retired & Volunteer Grants, 1188
Columbia Gas of Virginia Grants, 1218
Connecticut Light & Power Corp Contributions, 1352
Constellation Energy Corp EcoStar Grants, 1363
Constellation Energy Corp Grants, 1364
Energy Fndn Buildings Grants, 1705

Energy Fndn Climate Grants, 1706
Energy Fndn Power Grants, 1707
Energy Fndn Transportation Grants, 1708
Entergy Charitable Fndn Low-Income Inits and Solutions Grants, 1711
Illinois Clean Energy Community Fndn K-12 Wind Schools Pilot Grants, 2480
Illinois Clean Energy Community Fndn Renewable Energy Grants, 2481
Illinois Clean Energy Community Fndn Solar Thermal Installation Grants, 2482
Ka Papa O Kakuhihewa Fund, 2785
Mertz Gilmore Climate Change Grants, 3125
NE Utilities Fndn Grants, 3498
NSF Partnership for Advancing Technologies in Housing Grants, 3529
PG&E Bright Ideas Grants, 3866
PG&E Community Vitality Grants, 3868
PNM Reduce Your Use Grants, 3926
Rockefeller Bro Cross-Program Energy Grants, 4130
Rohm and Haas Company Grants, 4145
Rose Fndn For Communities and the Environment Kern County Air Pollution Mitigation Grants, 4157
Sioux Falls Area Community Grants, 4364
Sioux Falls Area Community Fndn Spot Grants, 4366
Union Bank, N.A. Fndn Grants, 4709
USDA Denali Comm High Energy Cost Grants, 4805
USDA High Energy Cost Grants, 4812
USDA State Bulk Fuel Revolving Grants, 4840
Volvo Adventure Environmental Awards, 4952

Energy Conversion
CNCS AmeriCorps NCCC Project Grants, 1181
Colorado Renewables in Performance Contracting Grants, 1214
Illinois DCEO Coal Competitiveness Grants, 2484
Illinois DCEO Coal Demonstration Grants, 2485
Illinois DCEO Coal Development Grants, 2486
Illinois DCEO Coal Revival Grants, 2487
Rockefeller Bro Cross-Program Energy Grants, 4130

Energy Economics
Colorado Clean Energy Solar Innovation Grants, 1212
Energy Fndn Power Grants, 1707
Energy Fndn Transportation Grants, 1708
GNOF Coastal 5 + 1 Grants, 2070
McCune Charitable Fndn Grants, 3077

Energy Education
Appalachian Regional Commission Energy Grants, 505
CenterPointEnergy Minnegasco Grants, 993
McCune Charitable Fndn Grants, 3077
NE Utilities Fndn Grants, 3498
PNM Reduce Your Use Grants, 3926
Rockefeller Bro Cross-Program Energy Grants, 4130

Energy Engineering
McCune Charitable Fndn Grants, 3077
Micron Technology Fndn Community Grants, 3161

Energy Planning/Policy
AAAS Science and Technology Policy Fellowships: Energy, Environment, and Agriculture, 52
Appalachian Regional Commission Asset-Based Development Project Grants, 500
Appalachian Regional Commission Community Infrastructure Grants, 502
Appalachian Regional Commission Distressed Counties Grants, 503
Appalachian Regional Commission Energy Grants, 505
Blue Cross Blue Shield of Minnesota Fndn - Healthy Equity: Health Impact Assessment Demonstration Project Grants, 795
Blue Cross Blue Shield of Minnesota Fndn - Healthy Equity: Health Impact Assessment Grants, 796
Energy Fndn Climate Grants, 1706
Energy Fndn Power Grants, 1707
Energy Fndn Transportation Grants, 1708
Illinois Clean Energy Community Fndn Energy Efficiency Grants, 2479

Illinois Clean Energy Community Fndn Renewable Energy Grants, 2481
Illinois Clean Energy Community Fndn Solar Thermal Installation Grants, 2482
Japan Center for Global Partnership Grants, 2650
Rockefeller Bro Cross-Program Energy Grants, 4130
USDA Predevelopment Planning Grants, 4821
USDA Rural Energy for America - Renewable Energy System and Energy Efficiency Improvement Guaranteed Grants, 4830

Energy Utilization
Columbia Gas of Virginia Grants, 1218
Illinois DCEO Coal Competitiveness Grants, 2484
Illinois DCEO Coal Demonstration Grants, 2485
Illinois DCEO Coal Development Grants, 2486
McCune Charitable Fndn Grants, 3077
Rockefeller Bro Cross-Program Energy Grants, 4130
USDA Rural Energy for America - Energy Audit and Renewable Energy Devel Assistance Grants, 4828
USDA Rural Energy for America - Feasibility Study Grants, 4829
USDA Rural Energy for America - Renewable Energy System and Energy Efficiency Improvement Guaranteed Grants, 4830
USDA Value-Added Producer Grants, 4843

Energy, Fossil
Energy Fndn Climate Grants, 1706
GNOF Coastal 5 + 1 Grants, 2070
Illinois DCEO Coal Demonstration Grants, 2485
Illinois DCEO Coal Development Grants, 2486
Illinois DCEO Coal Revival Grants, 2487
McCune Charitable Fndn Grants, 3077
USDA Rural Energy for America - Renewable Energy System and Energy Efficiency Improvement Guaranteed Grants, 4830

Energy, Geothermal
Illinois Clean Energy Community Fndn Renewable Energy Grants, 2481
McCune Charitable Fndn Grants, 3077
USDA Rural Energy for America Renewable System & Efficiency Improvement Guaranteed Grants, 4830

Energy, Hydro
DOE Initial H-Prize Competition for Breakthrough Advances in Materials for Hydrogen Storage, 1551
Honor the Earth Grants, 2361
Hydrogen Student Design Contest, 2415

Energy, Solar
Colorado Clean Energy Solar Innovation Grants, 1212
Colorado Renewables in Performance Contracting Grants, 1214
Illinois Clean Energy Community Fndn Energy Efficiency Grants, 2479
Illinois Clean Energy Community Fndn Renewable Energy Grants, 2481
Illinois Clean Energy Community Fndn Solar Thermal Installation Grants, 2482
McCune Charitable Fndn Grants, 3077
PG&E Bright Ideas Grants, 3866
PG&E Community Vitality Grants, 3868
Progress Energy Fndn Environmental Stewardship Grants, 3970
USDA Rural Energy for America - Renewable Energy System and Energy Efficiency Improvement Guaranteed Grants, 4830

Energy, Wind
Illinois Clean Energy Community Fndn Energy Efficiency Grants, 2479
Illinois Clean Energy Community Fndn K-12 Wind Schools Pilot Grants, 2480
Illinois Clean Energy Community Fndn Renewable Energy Grants, 2481
Illinois Clean Energy Community Fndn Solar Thermal Installation Grants, 2482
McCune Charitable Fndn Grants, 3077

Progress Energy Fndn Environmental Stewardship Grants, 3970
USDA Rural Energy for America - Renewable Energy System and Energy Efficiency Improvement Guaranteed Grants, 4830

Engineering
Acuity Charitable Fndn Grants, 140
Applied Biosystems Grants, 514
ARCO Fndn Educ Grants, 528
ArvinMeritor Grants, 585
Canada-U.S. Fulbright Mid-Career Grants, 917
Community Fndn of Greater Flint Grants, 1282
ConocoPhillips Grants, 1355
Cummins Fndn Grants, 1415
DAAD Research Grants for Doctoral Candidates and Young Academics and Scientists, 1427
Flinn Fndn Scholarships, 1843
Fluor Fndn Grants, 1875
Fulbright Binational Business Grants in Mexico, 1969
Fulbright Business Grants in Spain, 1970
Hearst Fndns Culture Grants, 2284
Honeywell Corp Leadership Challenge Academy, 2359
IIE AmCham Charitable Fndn U.S. Studies Scholarship, 2453
IIE David L. Boren Fellowships, 2454
IIE Japan-U.S. Teacher Exchange for Educ for Sustainable Development, 2457
IIE Leonora Lindsley Memorial Fellowships, 2458
IIE New Leaders Group Award for Mutual Understanding, 2460
IIE Western Union Family Scholarships, 2462
Indiana Space Grant Consortium Grants for Informal Educ Partnerships, 2549
Indiana Space Grant Consortium Workforce Development Grants, 2550
Meadows Fndn Grants, 3104
Medtronic Fndn CommunityLink Educ Grants, 3110
Millipore Fndn Grants, 3182
NSERC Brockhouse Canada Prize for Interdisciplinary Research in Science and Engineering Grant, 3518
OSF-Baltimore Community Fellowships, 3695
Regents Professional Opportunity Scholarships, 4044
Rockwell Int'l Corp Grants, 4141
Wayne and Gladys Valley Fndn Grants, 5003

Engineering Design
Indianapolis Preservation Grants, 2543
Indiana Preservation Grants, 2544
RISCA Design Innovation Grant, 4097

Engineering Education
3M Fndn Community Giving Grants, 15
Acuity Charitable Fndn Grants, 140
Advanced Micro Devices Comm Affairs Grants, 172
Alcatel-Lucent Technologies Fndn Grants, 349
Alcoa Fndn Grants, 350
AMD Corp Contributions Grants, 416
Applied Biosystems Grants, 514
ArvinMeritor Grants, 585
DaimlerChrysler Corp Grants, 1432
Dayton Power and Light Fndn Grants, 1464
DENSO North America Fndn Grants, 1499
Emerson Charitable Grants, 1694
FMC Fndn Grants, 1876
Ford Motor Company Grants, 1885
Goodrich Corp Fndn Grants, 2104
Hulman & Company Fndn Grants, 2387
Indiana Space Grant Consortium Grants for Informal Educ Partnerships, 2549
Indiana Space Grant Consortium Workforce Development Grants, 2550
Praxair Fndn Grants, 3944
Qualcomm Grants, 3993
Ralph M. Parsons Fndn Grants, 4013
Rollin M. Gerstacker Fndn Grants, 4146
Roy and Christine Sturgis Charitable Grants, 4166
SAS Institute Community Relations Donations, 4300
United Technologies Corp Grants, 4725
Washington Gas Charitable Contributions, 5000

English Education
Bay Area Community Fndn Grants, 694
Beerman Fndn Grants, 717
CE and S Fndn Grants, 985
Essex County Community Fndn Greater Lawrence Summer Grants, 1755
New Jersey Office of Faith Based Inits English as a Second Language Grants, 3332

English as a Second Language
ACF Supplemental Services for Recently Arrived Refugees Grants, 125
Blue Cross Blue Shield of Minnesota Fndn - Healthy Equity: Public Libraries for Health Grants, 797
Dollar General Adult Lit Grants, 1568
Dollar General Family Lit Grants, 1569
Emma G. Harris Fndn Grants, 1701
Essex County Community Fndn Greater Lawrence Summer Grants, 1755
IIE Western Union Family Scholarships, 2462
Int'l Paper Company Fndn Grants, 2568
Luella Kemper Grants, 2939
Meyer Fndn Economic Security Grants, 3141
Middlesex Savings Ed Opportunities Grants, 3174
National Book Scholarship Fund, 3249
New Jersey Office of Faith Based Inits English as a Second Language Grants, 3332
Ray Solem Fndn Grants to Help Immigrants Learn English in Innovative Ways, 4029
Robert R. McCormick Tribune Comm Grants, 4119
Sophia Romero Grants, 4406
Teaching Tolerance Grants, 4567
Textron Corp Contributions Grants, 4601
Verizon Fndn Great Lakes Region Grants, 4912
Woods Charitable Grants, 5114

Entertainment Industry
Actors Fund Dancers' Resource, 137
Actors Fund Funeral and Burial Assistance, 138
Actors Fund Social Services and Financial Assist, 139
AGMA Relief Grants, 201
SAG Motion Picture Players Welfare Grants, 4209

Entomology
GreenWorks! Butterfly Garden Grants, 2159
Honeybee Health Improvement Project Grants, 2355

Entrepreneurship
Achelis Fndn Grants, 127
Adolph Coors Fndn Grants, 171
Allstate Corp Giving Grants, 386
Allstate Corp Hometown Commitment Grants, 387
Allstate Fndn Safe and Vital Communities Grants, 390
Alvin and Fanny Blaustein Thalheimer Grants, 403
Amber Grants, 413
Appalachian Regional Commission Business Development Revolving Loan Grants, 501
AutoZone Community Relations Grants, 621
Bodman Fndn Grants, 807
Burton Morgan Adult Entrepreneurship Grants, 868
California Endowment Ideas Challenge Grants, 904
Carl R. Hendrickson Family Fndn Grants, 935
ChevronTexaco Contributions Program, 1078
CNL Corp Giving Entrepreneurship & Leadership Grants, 1191
Coleman Fndn Entrepreneurship Educ Grants, 1201
Connecticut Light & Power Corp Contributions, 1352
Courage Center Judd Jacobson Memorial Award, 1382
Diageo Fndn Grants, 1546
Draper Richards Kaplan Fndn Grants, 1603
Echoing Green Fellowships, 1650
Eileen Fisher Women-Owned Business Grants, 1677
Ewing Marion Kauffman Fndn Grants and Inits, 1777
Georgia-Pacific Fndn Entrepreneurship Grants, 2033
GNOF New Orleans Works Grants, 2088
Herbert B. Jones Fndn Grants, 2314
JM Fndn Grants, 2681
Johnson Scholarship Fndn Grants, 2726
Libra Fndn Future Grants, 2898
Linden Fndn Grants, 2908

SUBJECT INDEX

Environmental Conservation / 893

Maine Women's Fund Economic Security Grants, 2992
Minneapolis Fndn Community Grants, 3186
Monfort Family Fndn Grants, 3203
NASE Fndn Future Entrepreneur Scholarship, 3241
National Endowment for Arts Our Town Grants, 3257
New Jersey Center for Hispanic Policy, Research and Development Entrepreneurship Grants, 3326
Olive B. Cole Fndn Grants, 3670
OSF-Baltimore Community Fellowships, 3695
Paul and Edith Babson Fndn Grants, 3755
PepsiCo Fndn Grants, 3819
RISCA Professional Arts Development Grants, 4099
S.E.VEN Fund $50k VINE Project Prizes, 4193
S.E.VEN Fund 'In The River They Swim' Essay Competition, 4194
S.E.VEN Fund Annual Grants, 4195
S.E.VEN Fund Mini-Grants, 4196
S.E.VEN Fund Open Enterprise Solutions to Poverty RFP Grants, 4197
Skoll Fndn Awards for Social Entrepreneurship, 4383
SW Init Fndn Grants, 4446
Union Bank, N.A. Fndn Grants, 4709
USAID Unsolicited Proposal Grants, 4786
USDA 1890 Land Grant Colleges and Universities Init Grants, 4797
USDA Rural Business Opportunity Grants, 4824
USDA Rural Microentrepreneur Assist Grants, 4832
USDC i6 Challenge Grants, 4851
USDC University Center Economic Development Program Competition, 4861
Vancouver Fndn Disability Supports for Employment Grants, 4899
W.K. Kellogg Fndn Civic Engagement Grants, 4960
Youth Action Net Universidad Europea de Madrid Prize, 5129

Environment
3 Rivers Wet Weather Demonstration Grants, 9
A Charitable Fndn Grants, 126
American Rivers Community-Based Restoration Program River Grants, 444
Anderson Fndn Grants, 460
As You Sow, 598
Baxter Int'l Corp Giving Grants, 689
BBVA Compass Fndn Charitable Grants, 703
Benwood Fndn Focus Area Grants, 733
Bertha Wolf-Rosenthal Fndn for Community Service Stipend, 746
Bridgestone/Firestone Grants, 836
Bristol-Myers Squibb Fndn Community Grants, 840
C.F. Adams Charitable Grants, 884
Caesars Fndn Grants, 891
Charles M. and Mary D. Grant Fndn Grants, 1050
Chesapeake Bay Trust Restoration Grants, 1075
CICF City of Noblesville Community Grant, 1118
Cleveland Community Responsive Grants, 1168
Collective Brands Fndn Grants, 1206
Columbus Fndn Joseph A. Jeffrey Grants, 1224
Community Fndn for SE Michigan Grants, 1259
Community Fndn of Boone County Grants, 1274
Community Fndn Of Greater Lafayette Grants, 1289
Con Edison Corp Giving Environmental Grants, 1347
Cornell Lab of Ornithology Mini-Grants, 1374
Crystelle Waggoner Charitable Grants, 1405
DeKalb County Community Fndn Grants, 1481
DuPage Community Fndn Grants, 1624
Earth Island Institute Community Wetland Restoration Grants, 1642
El Paso Corp Fndn Grants, 1689
El Pomar Fndn Awards and Grants, 1690
Energy Fndn Transportation Grants, 1708
EPA Air Pollution Control Support Grants, 1722
EPA Brownfields Area-Wide Planning Grants, 1723
EPA Brownfields Environmental Workforce Development and Job Training Grants, 1726
EPA Environmental Justice Collaborative Problem-Solving Coop Agreements Program, 1730
EPA Environmental Justice Small Grants, 1731
EPA Pestwise Registration Improvement Act Partnership Grants, 1734

EPA Source Reduction Assistance Grants, 1737
EQT Fndn Environment Grants, 1746
Erie Community Fndn Grants, 1750
Evan Frankel Fndn Grants, 1770
Fairfield County Community Fndn Grants, 1782
Freshwater Future Advocate Mentor Program, 1957
Freshwater Future Climate Grants, 1958
Freshwater Future Healing Our Waters Grants, 1959
Freshwater Future Insight Services Grants, 1960
Freshwater Future Project Grants, 1961
Freshwater Future Special Opportunity Grants, 1962
Georgia-Pacific Fndn Environment Grants, 2034
GNOF Norco Community Grants, 2089
Grand Haven Area Community Fndn Grants, 2113
Greater Cincinnati Fndn Priority and Small Projects/Capacity-Building Grants, 2132
Great Lakes Fishery Trust Habitat Protection and Restoration Grants, 2146
Green Fndn Special Project Grants, 2155
Gregory C. Carr Fndn Grants, 2161
Grundy Fndn Grants, 2169
HAF Natural Environment Grants, 2202
Hampton Roads Community Fndn Nonprofit Facilities Improvement Grants, 2218
Harry A. and Margaret D. Towsley Fndn Grants, 2236
Heinz Endowments Grants, 2291
Hendricks County Community Fndn Grants, 2302
Henry M. Jackson Fndn Grants, 2311
Honeywell Sustainable Opportunities Grants, 2360
Household Int'l Corp Giving Grants, 2372
Illinois DNR Biodiversity Field Trip Grants, 2496
Illinois DNR Habitat Grants, 2497
Illinois DNR Migratory Waterfowl Stamp Grants, 2498
Illinois DNR Park and Recreational Facility Construction Grants, 2499
Illinois DNR State Furbearer Grants, 2501
Illinois DNR State Pheasant Grants, 2502
Illinois DNR Wildlife Preservation Fund Large Project Grants, 2505
Illinois DNR Wildlife Preservation Fund Small Project Grants, 2506
Illinois DNR Wildlife Preservation Maintenance of Wildlife Rehabilitation Facilities Grants, 2507
Init Fndn Healthy Lakes and Rivers Partnerships, 2558
Intergrys Corp Grants, 2565
Jasper Fndn Grants, 2655
Jennings County Community Fndn Women's Giving Circle Grant, 2665
John W. and Anna H. Hanes Fndn Grants, 2728
Kalamazoo Community Environment Grants, 2766
Laidlaw Fndn Youh Organizing Catalyst Grants, 2853
Lake County Community Grants, 2856
Laurel Fndn Grants, 2867
Liberty Hill Fndn Environmental Justice Grants, 2891
Liberty Hill Fndn Fund for Change Grants, 2893
Liberty Hill Fndn Seed Grants, 2896
Liberty Hill Fndn Special Opportunity Grants, 2897
Lily Palmer Fry Grants, 2905
Lumpkin Family Healthy Environments Grants, 2941
Madison Community Fndn Grants, 2971
Maine Community Fndn Maine Land Conservation Grants, 2983
Marathon Petroleum Corp Grants, 2999
Marriott Int'l Corp Giving Grants, 3024
Meadows Fndn Grants, 3104
Mericos Fndn Grants, 3121
NFF Mid-Capacity Assistance Grants, 3345
NFWF Alaska Fish and Wildlife Grants, 3356
NFWF Aleutian Islands Risk Assessment Grants, 3357
Nissan Fndn Grants, 3444
Norcliffe Fndn Grants, 3459
North Dakota Community Fndn Grants, 3493
Northrop Grumman Corp Grants, 3507
Orange County Community Fndn Grants, 3688
Pacific Life Fndn Grants, 3726
Parke County Community Fndn Grants, 3735
Parker Fndn (California) Grants, 3736
Pathways to Nature Conservation Grants, 3745
Patrick and Aimee Butler Family Fndn Community Environment Grants, 3748

Paul and Edith Babson Fndn Grants, 3755
PepsiCo Fndn Grants, 3819
Peter Kiewit Fndn Neighborhood Grants, 3846
Piedmont Natural Gas Fndn Environmental Stewardship and Energy Sustainability Grant, 3884
PMI Fndn Grants, 3918
PNC Fndn Green Building Grants, 3923
Progress Energy Environmental Stewardship Grants, 3970
PSEG Corp Contributions Grants, 3979
Putnam County Community Fndn Grants, 3990
RCF General Community Grants, 4032
Rohm and Haas Company Grants, 4145
Salt River Project Environmental Quality Grants, 4227
Santa Fe Community Fndn Seasonal Grants, 4291
Sartain Lanier Family Fndn Grants, 4298
Scherman Fndn Grants, 4305
Seattle Fndn Environment Grants, 4327
Social Justice Fund NW Environmental Justice Giving Project Grants, 4396
Sony Corp of America Corp Philanthropy Grants, 4405
Southern Cal Edison Environmental Grants, 4429
Starke County Community Fndn Grants, 4482
Susan G. Komen Breast Cancer Fndn Challenge Grants: Breast Cancer and the Environment, 4535
Toyota Motor Engineering & Manufacturing North America Grants, 4651
Toyota Motor Manufacturing of Alabama Grants, 4652
Toyota Motor Manufacturing of Indiana Grants, 4653
Toyota Motor of Kentucky Grants, 4654
Toyota Motor Manufacturing Mississippi Grants, 4655
Toyota Motor Manufacturing W Virginia Grants, 4657
Toyota Motor N America of New York Grants, 4658
Toyota Motor Sales, USA Grants, 4659
Toyota Technical Center Grants, 4660
Toyota USA Fndn Environmental Grants, 4661
Tri-State Community Twenty-first Century Endowment Grants, 4666
Union Bank Corp Sponsorships and Donations, 4708
USAID Bengal Tiger Conservation Grants, 4741
USAID Mekong Partnership for the Environment Project Grants, 4769
Vanderburgh Community Fndn Grants, 4902
Wabash River Enhancement Corp Urban, 4969
Walmart Fndn Facility Giving Grants, 4978
Warren County Community Fndn Grants, 4985
Warren County Community Fndn Mini-Grants, 4986
Wells County Fndn Grants, 5022
WestWind Fndn Environment Grants, 5052
White County Community Fndn Grants, 5057
William & Flora Hewlett Environmental Grants, 5074
William B. Stokely Jr. Fndn Grants, 5076
Wisconsin Energy Fndn Grants, 5106
Xerox Fndn Grants, 5122

Environmental Biology
Geraldine R. Dodge Fndn Environment Grants, 2041
Northrop Grumman Corp Grants, 3507
Susan G. Komen Breast Cancer Fndn Challenge Grants: Breast Cancer and the Environment, 4535

Environmental Conservation
As You Sow, 598
Chesapeake Bay Fisheries & Headwaters Grants, 1070
Chesapeake Bay Trust Restoration Grants, 1075
CNCS AmeriCorps NCCC Project Grants, 1181
CNCS AmeriCorps State and National Grants, 1182
CNCS AmeriCorps VISTA Project Grants, 1184
Collective Brands Fndn Grants, 1206
Crown Point Community Fndn Grants, 1402
Dean Foods Community Involvement Grants, 1469
Earth Island Institute Brower Youth Awards, 1641
George H.C. Ensworth Grants, 2022
GNOF Coastal 5 + 1 Grants, 2070
GNOF Environmental Grants, 2073
GNOF Gulf Coast Oil Spill Grants, 2077
HAF Natural Environment Grants, 2202
Honeywell Sustainable Opportunities Grants, 2360
HRF Hudson River Improvement Grants, 2378
HRF New York City Environmental Grants for Newton Creek, 2379

894 / Environmental Conservation

Illinois Clean Energy Community Fndn K-12 Wind Schools Pilot Grants, 2480
Illinois DNR Wildlife Preservation Fund Large Project Grants, 2505
Joyce Fndn Environment Grants, 2750
Kalamazoo Community Environment Grants, 2766
Kirkpatrick Fndn Grants, 2827
Lucy Downing Nisbet Charitable Grants, 2935
Lumpkin Family Healthy Environments Grants, 2941
Maine Community Fndn Maine Land Conservation Grants, 2983
Maine Comm Fndn Rines/Thompson Grants, 2987
MDEQ Local Water Quality Monitoring Grants, 3100
Meadows Fndn Grants, 3104
Meyer Memorial Trust Grassroots Grants, 3147
Meyer Memorial Trust Responsive Grants, 3148
National Environmental Educ Fndn - Department of Defense Legacy Award, 3270
National Environmental Ed Every Day Grants, 3271
NFF Mid-Capacity Assistance Grants, 3345
NFWF Alaska Fish and Wildlife Grants, 3356
NFWF Native Plant Conservation Init Grants, 3380
NHSCA Conservation License Plate Grants, 3425
Northrop Grumman Corp Grants, 3507
Packard Fndn Local Grants, 3729
Pathways to Nature Conservation Grants, 3745
Piedmont Natural Gas Corp and Charitable Contributions, 3883
Piedmont Natural Gas Fndn Environmental Stewardship and Energy Sustainability Grant, 3884
Progress Energy Fndn Environmental Stewardship Grants, 3970
Rohm and Haas Company Grants, 4145
Seattle Fndn Environment Grants, 4327
Social Justice Fund NW Environmental Justice Giving Project Grants, 4396
Sony Corp of America Corp Philanthropy Grants, 4405
Sunbeam Products Grants, 4526
Threshold Fndn Sustainable Planet Grants, 4627
Tides California Wildlands Grassroots Fund, 4630
Toyota USA Fndn Environmental Grants, 4661
Union Bank, N.A. Fndn Grants, 4709
USAID Bengal Tiger Conservation Grants, 4741
Wabash River Enhancement Corp Urban, 4969
Western Pennsylvania Environmental Awards, 5026
WestWind Fndn Environment Grants, 5052

Environmental Design
Baltimore Community Environment Path Grants, 643
CICF Efroymson Grants, 1120
EQT Fndn Environment Grants, 1746
GNOF Gulf Coast Oil Spill Grants, 2077
Marin Community Affordable Housing Grants, 3010
Morris K. Udall and Stewart L. Udall Fndn Dissertation Fellowships, 3219
National Endowment for Arts Commun Grants, 3260
NHSCA Artist Residencies in Schools Grants, 3423
NHSCA Youth Arts Project Grants: For Extended Arts Learning, 3430
Northrop Grumman Corp Grants, 3507
PNC Fndn Green Building Grants, 3923
San Francisco Fndn Environment Grants, 4266
Vancouver Fndn Grants & Comm Inits, 4900
Western Pennsylvania Environmental Awards, 5026

Environmental Economics
Brainerd Fndn Grants, 831
Geraldine R. Dodge Fndn Environment Grants, 2041
GNOF Environmental Grants, 2073
GNOF Gulf Coast Oil Spill Grants, 2077
GNOF New Orleans Works Grants, 2088
Jenifer Altman Fndn Grants, 2662
Rockefeller Brothers Sustainable Devel Grants, 4136
Threshold Fndn Thriving Resilient Communities Funding Circle, 4628
Wallace Global Grants, 4977

Environmental Education
3M Company Environmental Giving Grants, 13
786 Fndn Grants, 33

2701 Fndn Grants, 37
Abbott Fund Community Grants, 81
Abelard Fndn East Grants, 87
Abelard Fndn West Grants, 88
Abell Fndn Conservation and Environment Grants, 94
ACF Native American Environmental Regulatory Enhancement Grants, 122
ACTION Council of Monterey County Grants, 134
Adams Fndn Grants, 154
Administaff Community Affairs Grants, 165
AEC Grants, 175
A Friends' Fndn Grants, 194
Alaska Airlines Corp Giving Grants, 320
Alaska Airlines Fndn Grants, 321
Alexander & Baldwin Fndn Hawaiian and Pacific Island Grants, 352
Alexander & Baldwin Fndn Mainland Grants, 353
All for the Earth Fndn Grants, 381
Alpine Winter Fndn Grants, 394
Amador Community Fndn Grants, 408
American Bank Fndn Grants, 437
America the Beautiful Fund Operation Green Plant Grants, 451
Annie's Grants for Gardens, 480
Arbor Day Fndn Grants, 524
A Rocha USA Grants, 566
As You Sow, 598
AutoNation Corp Giving Grants, 620
Baltimore Community Fndn Children's Fresh Air Society Grants, 642
Baltimore Community Environment Path Grants, 643
Banrock Station Wines Wetlands Grants, 662
Barker Welfare Fndn Grants, 669
Beldon Grants, 720
Bennett Family Fndn of Texas Grants, 728
Blumenthal Fndn Grants, 804
Boeing Company Contributions Grants, 809
Brooklyn Community Fndn Green Communities Grants, 852
Bullitt Fndn Grants, 862
Cabot Corp Fndn Grants, 887
California Fertilizer Fndn School Garden Grants, 905
California Green Trees for Golden State Grant, 906
Captain Planet Fndn Grants, 922
Cargill Citizenship Fund-Corp Giving Grants, 925
Carls Fndn Grants, 937
Carrier Corp Contributions Grants, 946
CenterPointEnergy Minnegasco Grants, 993
CFFVR Environmental Stewardship Grants, 1010
Chesapeake Bay Environmental Ed Grants, 1069
Chesapeake Bay Trust Forestry Mini Grants, 1071
Chesapeake Bay Trust Mini Grants, 1072
Chesapeake Bay Trust Outreach and Community Engagement Grants, 1073
Clarence E. Heller Charitable Fndn Grants, 1150
CNCS AmeriCorps State and National Grants, 1182
Columbia Gas of Virginia Grants, 1218
Columbus Fndn Scotts Miracle-Gro Community Garden Academy Grants, 1230
Community Fndn for Greater New Haven Quinnipiac River Grants, 1250
Community Fndn of Sarasota County Grants, 1306
Community POWER (Partners On Waste Educ and Reduction), 1335
Con Edison Corp Giving Environmental Grants, 1347
Constellation Energy Corp EcoStar Grants, 1363
CSX Corp Contributions Grants, 1408
Curtis and Edith Munson Fndn Grants, 1418
Daviess County Community Environment Grants, 1456
Dean Foods Community Involvement Grants, 1469
Dorr Fndn Grants, 1591
DTE Energy Fndn Environmental Grants, 1612
Dyson Mid-Hudson Valley Project Support, 1636
Earth Island Institute Community Wetland Restoration Grants, 1642
EPA Brownfields Environmental Workforce Development and Job Training Grants, 1726
EPA Environmental Educ Grants, 1729
EPA Environmental Justice Small Grants, 1731
EPA Environmental Justice Small Grants, 1732

SUBJECT INDEX

EPA Source Reduction Assistance Grants, 1737
EREF Solid Waste Research Grants, 1747
EREF Sustainability Research Grants, 1748
EREF Unsolicited Proposal Grants, 1749
Eulalie Bloedel Schneider Fndn Grants, 1767
Fargo-Moorhead Area Fndn Grants, 1788
Fndn for Appalachian Ohio Access to Environmental Educ Mini-Grants, 1892
Frederick W. Marzahl Grants, 1948
Frost Fndn Grants, 1966
Fruit Tree 101, 1967
Fuller Fndn Grants, 1974
Gamble Fndn Grants, 1983
Gannett Fndn Community Action Grants, 1984
Gates Family Fndn Parks, Conservation & Recreation Grants, 1991
GEF Green Thumb Challenge, 1996
George and Ruth Bradford Fndn Grants, 2010
Georgia-Pacific Fndn Environment Grants, 2034
Geraldine R. Dodge Fndn Environment Grants, 2041
GNOF Environmental Grants, 2073
GNOF Gulf Coast Oil Spill Grants, 2077
Grand Victoria Fndn Illinois Core Grants, 2126
GreenWorks! Butterfly Garden Grants, 2159
GreenWorks! Grants, 2160
HAF Educ Grants, 2196
HAF Natural Environment Grants, 2202
Heifer Ed Grants for Principals, 2288
Hilton Head Island Fndn Grants, 2330
Honda of America Manufacturing Fndn Grants, 2354
Honeywell Sustainable Opportunities Grants, 2360
Horizon Fndn Grants, 2365
Household Int'l Corp Giving Grants, 2372
HRF Hudson River Improvement Grants, 2378
HRF New York City Environmental Grants for Newton Creek, 2379
Illinois DNR Schoolyard Habitat Action Grants, 2500
Illinois DNR Wildlife Preservation Fund Small Project Grants, 2506
Illinois DNR Youth Recreation Corps Grants, 2508
Indiana Recycling Grants, 2545
Int'l Paper Company Fndn Grants, 2568
Int'l Paper Environmental Awards, 2569
Jessie Ball Dupont Grants, 2671
John D. and Catherine T. MacArthur Fndn Global Challenges Grants, 2690
Johnson Fndn Wingspread Conference Support, 2725
Kalamazoo Community Environment Grants, 2766
KEEN Effect Grants, 2795
KeySpan Fndn Grants, 2821
Kimball Int'l-Habig Fndn Grants, 2823
Knox County Community Fndn Grants, 2831
Leave No Trace Master Educator Scholarships, 2870
Legacy Partners in Environmental Educ Grants, 2875
Legacy Partners in Environmental Ed Grants, 2876
Lowe's Outdoor Classroom Grants, 2928
MacArthur Fndn Conservation and Sustainable Development Grants, 2963
McCune Charitable Fndn Grants, 3077
MDEQ Community Pollution Prevention (P2) Grants: Household Drug Collections, 3098
Meadows Fndn Grants, 3104
Melinda Gray Ardia Environmental Fndn Grants, 3114
Morris K. Udall and Stewart L. Udall Fndn Dissertation Fellowships, 3219
National Wetlands Awards, 3282
NFWF Acres for America Grants, 3355
NFWF Alaska Fish and Wildlife Grants, 3356
NFWF Aleutian Islands Risk Assessment Grants, 3357
NFWF Budweiser Conservationist of the Year, 3361
NFWF Five-Star Restoration Challenge Grants, 3373
NFWF Native Plant Conservation Init Grants, 3380
NFWF Nature of Learning Grants, 3381
NFWF Pacific Grassroots Salmonid Init Grants, 3384
NFWF Shell Marine Habitat Grants, 3391
NFWF Southern Co Longleaf Legacy Grants, 3392
NFWF So Company Power of Flight Grants, 3394
NFWF Upper Mississippi Riv Watershed Grants, 3398
NGA Hansen's Natural and Native School Garden Grants, 3402

SUBJECT INDEX

NGA Midwest School Garden Grants, 3407
NGA Youth Garden Grants, 3409
Northern Chautauqua Environmental Grants, 3501
Northrop Grumman Corp Grants, 3507
NYCT New York City Environment Grants, 3556
Olin Corp Charitable Grants, 3669
Oracle Corp Contributions Grants, 3686
Partnership Enhancement Grants, 3740
Pathways to Nature Conservation Grants, 3745
Patrick and Aimee Butler Family Fndn Community Environment Grants, 3748
Perry County Community Fndn Grants, 3827
Peter Kiewit Fndn Neighborhood Grants, 3846
PG&E Community Investment Grants, 3867
Piedmont Natural Gas Corp and Charitable Contributions, 3883
Piedmont Natural Gas Fndn Environmental Stewardship and Energy Sustainability Grant, 3884
Pike County Community Fndn Grants, 3888
Project AWARE Fndn Grants, 3971
Project Orange Thumb Grants, 3972
PSEG Environmental Educ Grants, 3980
Rockefeller Brothers Sustainable Devel Grants, 4136
Rohm and Haas Company Grants, 4145
Rose Fndn for Comm & the Environment N California Environmental Grassroots Grants, 4158
S. D. Bechtel, Jr. Fndn / Stephen Bechtel Fund Environmental Educ Grants, 4192
Schering-Plough Fndn Community Inits Grants, 4303
Scott County Community Fndn Grants, 4314
Seabury Fndn Grants, 4316
Seattle Fndn Environment Grants, 4327
SeaWorld & Busch Gardens Conservation Grants, 4332
Skaggs Fndn Grants, 4378
Social Justice Fund NW Environmental Justice Giving Project Grants, 4396
Social Justice Fund NW General Grants, 4397
Sorenson Legacy Fndn Grants, 4407
Southern Cal Edison Environmental Grants, 4429
Spencer County Community Fndn Grants, 4451
Subaru Adopt a School Garden Grants, 4517
TE Fndn Grants, 4572
Telluride Fndn Community Grants, 4573
Toyota USA Fndn Environmental Grants, 4661
Union Bank, N.A. Fndn Grants, 4709
UPS Fndn Environmental Sustainability Grants, 4731
USAID Bengal Tiger Conservation Grants, 4741
USAID Mekong Partnership for the Environment Project Grants, 4769
Vancouver Fndn Grants & Comm Inits, 4900
Volvo Adventure Environmental Awards, 4952
Vulcan Materials Company Fndn Grants, 4956
Waste Management Charitable Giving Grants, 5001
Water and Land Stewardship Grants, 5002
Western Pennsylvania Environmental Awards, 5026
WestWind Fndn Environment Grants, 5052
Weyerhaeuser Family Fndn Environment, Conservation and Preservation Grants, 5054
Winifred & Harry B. Allen Fndn Grants, 5101

Environmental Effects

3M Company Environmental Giving Grants, 13
A Rocha USA Grants, 566
Brainerd Fndn Grants, 831
Bydale Fndn Grants, 882
Carrier Corp Contributions Grants, 946
Clarence E. Heller Charitable Fndn Grants, 1150
Community Fndn for Greater New Haven Quinnipiac River Grants, 1250
Daviess County Comm Environment Grants, 1456
EPA Brownfields Area-Wide Planning Grants, 1723
EPA Brownfields Assessment Pilot Grants, 1724
EPA Brownfields Cleanup Grants, 1725
EPA Children's Health Protection Grants, 1728
Georgia-Pacific Fndn Environment Grants, 2034
Geraldine R. Dodge Fndn Environment Grants, 2041
Great Lakes Protection Grants, 2147
Jenifer Altman Fndn Grants, 2662
John D. and Catherine T. MacArthur Fndn Global Challenges Grants, 2690

Kalamazoo Community Environment Grants, 2766
Northrop Grumman Corp Grants, 3507
Pathways to Nature Conservation Grants, 3745
PG&E Community Investment Grants, 3867
Piedmont Natural Gas Corp and Charitable Contributions, 3883
Progress Energy Fndn Environmental Stewardship Grants, 3970
Rockefeller Brothers Sustainable Devel Grants, 4136
Rose Fndn for Comm & the Environment N California Environmental Grassroots Grants, 4158
San Francisco Fndn Environment Grants, 4266
Toyota USA Fndn Environmental Grants, 4661
UPS Fndn Environmental Sustainability Grants, 4731
USAID Bengal Tiger Conservation Grants, 4741
USDC/NOAA Open Rivers Init Grants, 4847
Western Pennsylvania Environmental Awards, 5026

Environmental Effects, Fossil Fuels

Energy Fndn Transportation Grants, 1708
GNOF Coastal 5 + 1 Grants, 2070
GNOF Gulf Coast Oil Spill Grants, 2077
Indiana Corn Marketing Council Retailer Grant for Tank Cleaning, 2536
Progress Energy Fndn Environmental Stewardship Grants, 3970

Environmental Health

AAAS Science and Technology Policy Fellowships: Energy, Environment, and Agriculture, 52
AAAS Science and Technology Policy Fellowships: Health, Educ and Human Services, 53
Abelard Fndn East Grants, 87
Abelard Fndn West Grants, 88
Abell Fndn Conservation and Environment Grants, 94
Acorn Fndn Grants, 131
ACTION Council of Monterey County Grants, 134
Acumen Global Fellowships, 142
Adams Fndn Grants, 154
Administaff Community Affairs Grants, 165
Adolph Coors Fndn Grants, 171
AEC Grants, 175
Akonadi Fndn Anti-Racism Grants, 217
Alaska Airlines Corp Giving Grants, 320
Alaska Airlines Fndn Grants, 321
Alaska Conservation Fndn Opportunity Grants, 324
Alaska Conservation Fndn Rapid Response Grants, 325
Alaska Conservation Fndn Watchable Wildlife Conservation Grants, 326
Alexander & Baldwin Fndn Hawaiian and Pacific Island Grants, 352
Alexander & Baldwin Fndn Mainland Grants, 353
Alliance Healthcare Fndn Grants, 383
American Gas Fndn Grants, 437
American Hiking Society National Trails Grants, 438
America the Beautiful Fund Operation Green Plant Grants, 451
Applied Biosystems Grants, 514
A Rocha USA Grants, 566
Ashland Corp Contributions Grants, 587
Baltimore Community Environment Path Grants, 643
Beldon Grants, 720
Bennett Family Fndn of Texas Grants, 728
Blue Cross Blue Shield of Minnesota Fndn - Healthy Children: Growing Up Healthy Grants, 794
Blue Cross Blue Shield of Minnesota Fndn - Healthy Equity: Health Impact Assessment Demonstration Project Grants, 795
Bunbury Company Grants, 863
Burning Fndn Grants, 867
California State Parks Restore & Cleanup Grants, 908
CDC State and Local Childhood Lead Poisoning Prevention Grants, 976
Chesapeake Bay Trust Outreach and Community Engagement Grants, 1073
Columbus Fndn Small Grants, 1232
Community Fndn for Greater New Haven Quinnipiac River Grants, 1250
Community Fndn of Santa Cruz County Grants, 1305
Community Fndn of Switzerland County Grants, 1315

Environmental Health / 895

Daviess County Comm Environment Grants, 1456
Donald and Sylvia Robinson Family Fndn Grants, 1573
DTE Energy Fndn Environmental Grants, 1612
Edna Wardlaw Charitable Grants, 1660
EPA Brownfields Assessment Pilot Grants, 1724
EPA Children's Health Protection Grants, 1728
Fields Pond Fndn Grants, 1807
Fremont Area Community Fndn Grants, 1955
Frost Fndn Grants, 1966
Gates Family Fndn Parks, Conservation & Recreation Grants, 1991
GNOF Gulf Coast Oil Spill Grants, 2077
Health Fndn of Greater Cincinnati Grants, 2281
Heineman Fndn for Research, Educ, Charitable and Scientific Purposes, 2290
Honeywell Sustainable Opportunities Grants, 2360
Houston Endowment Grants, 2373
IIE David L. Boren Fellowships, 2454
Illinois Clean Energy Community Fndn Energy Efficiency Grants, 2479
Illinois Clean Energy Community Fndn Renewable Energy Grants, 2481
Illinois Clean Energy Community Fndn Solar Thermal Installation Grants, 2482
Indianapolis Power & Light Company Community Grants, 2540
Int'l Paper Environmental Awards, 2569
Jessie B. Cox Charitable Grants, 2670
Legacy Partners in Environmental Educ Grants, 2875
Max and Anna Levinson Fndn Grants, 3066
National Geographic All Roads Seed Grants, 3272
National Geographic Conservation Grants, 3273
National Geographic Genographic Legacy Grants, 3274
National Geographic Young Explorers Grants, 3275
Natonal Endowment for the Arts Research Grants: Art Works, 3286
NFF Wilderness Stewardship Grants, 3346
NFWF Acres for America Grants, 3355
NFWF Aleutian Islands Risk Assessment Grants, 3357
NFWF Budweiser Conservationist of the Year, 3361
NFWF Columbia Basin Water Trans Grants, 3366
NFWF Coral Reef Conservation Project Grants, 3370
NFWF Delaware Estuary Watershed Grants, 3371
NFWF Five-Star Restoration Challenge Grants, 3373
NFWF Pacific Grassroots Salmonid Init Grants, 3384
NFWF Seafarer's Environmental Educ Grants, 3390
NOAA Projects to Improve or Amend Coral Reef Fishery Management Plans, 3453
NW Fund for the Environment Grants, 3510
NYCT New York City Environment Grants, 3556
Open Spaces Sacred Places National Awards, 3684
Pathways to Nature Conservation Grants, 3745
Patrick and Aimee Butler Family Fndn Community Environment Grants, 3748
Piedmont Natural Gas Fndn Environmental Stewardship and Energy Sustainability Grant, 3884
Pioneer Hi-Bred Community Grants, 3895
Powell Fndn Grants, 3942
Prince Charitable Trusts D.C. Grants, 3960
Rose Fndn For Communities and the Environment Kern County Air Pollution Mitigation Grants, 4157
Rose Fndn for Comm & the Environment N California Environmental Grassroots Grants, 4158
S. D. Bechtel, Jr. Fndn / Stephen Bechtel Fund Environmental Educ Grants, 4192
San Diego Fndn for Change Grants, 4247
San Francisco Fndn Community Health Grants, 4263
San Francisco Fndn Environment Grants, 4266
Sapelo Fndn Environmental Protection Grants, 4293
Schering-Plough Fndn Community Inits Grants, 4303
SeaWorld & Busch Gardens Conservation Grants, 4332
Solutia Grants, 4402
Taproot Fndn Capacity-Building Service Grants, 4560
Threshold Fndn Thriving Resilient Communities Funding Circle, 4628
Toyota Motor Manufacturing of Texas Grants, 4656
USDC/NOAA American Rivers Community-Based Restoration Program River Grants, 4845
Vancouver Fndn Grants & Comm Inits, 4900
Washington Gas Charitable Contributions, 5000

Environmental Health

Weaver Fndn Grants, 5015
WILD Fndn Grants, 5068
Winifred & Harry B. Allen Fndn Grants, 5101

Environmental Issues

Acumen Global Fellowships, 142
Collective Brands Fndn Grants, 1206
Con Edison Corp Giving Environmental Grants, 1347
EPA Brownfields Environmental Workforce Development and Job Training Grants, 1726
GNOF Environmental Grants, 2073
GNOF Gulf Coast Oil Spill Grants, 2077
HAF Natural Environment Grants, 2202
Hillsdale County Community Gen Adult Grants, 2328
Illinois DNR Migratory Waterfowl Stamp Grants, 2498
Lumpkin Family Healthy Environments Grants, 2941
Morris K. Udall and Stewart L. Udall Fndn Dissertation Fellowships, 3219
PG&E Community Investment Grants, 3867
Salt River Project Environmental Quality Grants, 4227
Seattle Fndn Environment Grants, 4327
Southern Cal Edison Environmental Grants, 4429
Toyota USA Fndn Environmental Grants, 4661
Western Pennsylvania Environmental Awards, 5026
White County Community Fndn Grants, 5057

Environmental Law

ACF Native American Environmental Regulatory Enhancement Grants, 122
Alaska Conservation Fndn Opportunity Grants, 324
Alaska Conservation Fndn Rapid Response Grants, 325
Alaska Conservation Fndn Watchable Wildlife Conservation Grants, 326
Alexander H. Bright Charitable Grants, 358
Brainerd Fndn Grants, 831
Bullitt Fndn Grants, 862
EPA Environmental Justice Small Grants, 1732
Geraldine R. Dodge Fndn Environment Grants, 2041
GNOF Environmental Grants, 2073
GNOF Gulf Coast Oil Spill Grants, 2077
Honor the Earth Grants, 2361
Jessie Smith Noyes Fndn Grants, 2672
Letha E. House Fndn Grants, 2886
MacArthur Fndn Conservation and Sustainable Development Grants, 2963
Norman Fndn Grants, 3464
Rockefeller Brothers Sustainable Devel Grants, 4136
Rose Fndn for Comm & the Environment N California Environmental Grassroots Grants, 4158
Town Creek Fndn Grants, 4650
Wallace Global Grants, 4977
WILD Fndn Grants, 5068

Environmental Planning/Policy

3M Company Environmental Giving Grants, 13
2701 Fndn Grants, 37
Abell Fndn Conservation and Environment Grants, 94
ACF Native American Environmental Regulatory Enhancement Grants, 122
Achelis Fndn Grants, 127
A Friends' Fndn Grants, 194
Alaska Conservation Fndn Opportunity Grants, 324
Alaska Conservation Fndn Rapid Response Grants, 325
Alaska Conservation Fndn Watchable Wildlife Conservation Grants, 326
Altria Group Environment Grants, 400
As You Sow, 598
Baltimore Community Environment Path Grants, 643
Beldon Grants, 720
Blue Cross Blue Shield of Minnesota Fndn - Healthy Equity: Health Impact Assessment Demonstration Project Grants, 795
Blue Cross Blue Shield of Minnesota Fndn - Healthy Equity: Health Impact Assessment Grants, 796
Bodman Fndn Grants, 807
CFFVR Environmental Stewardship Grants, 1010
Clarence E. Heller Charitable Fndn Grants, 1150
CLIF Bar Family Fndn Grants, 1173
Community Fndn for Greater New Haven Quinnipiac River Grants, 1250

Con Edison Corp Giving Environmental Grants, 1347
Curtis and Edith Munson Fndn Grants, 1418
Daviess County Comm Environment Grants, 1456
Dyson Mid-Hudson Valley Project Support, 1636
Earth Island Institute Community Wetland Restoration Grants, 1642
EPA Air Pollution Control Support Grants, 1722
EPA Brownfields Area-Wide Planning Grants, 1723
EPA Brownfields Environmental Workforce Development and Job Training Grants, 1726
EPA Regional Agricultural IPM Grants, 1735
EPA State Senior Environ Employment Grants, 1739
EPA Tribal Support for the National Environmental Information Exchange Network, 1742
EQT Fndn Environment Grants, 1746
Fields Pond Fndn Grants, 1807
Freshwater Future Climate Grants, 1958
Freshwater Future Healing Our Waters Grants, 1959
Freshwater Future Insight Services Grants, 1960
Freshwater Future Project Grants, 1961
Georgia-Pacific Fndn Environment Grants, 2034
Geraldine R. Dodge Fndn Environment Grants, 2041
GNOF Coastal 5 + 1 Grants, 2070
GNOF Community Revitalization Grants, 2071
GNOF Environmental Grants, 2073
GNOF Gulf Coast Oil Spill Grants, 2077
Harrison County Community Signature Grants, 2234
Hilfiger Family Fndn Grants, 2323
Honda of America Manufacturing Fndn Grants, 2354
Honeywell Sustainable Opportunities Grants, 2360
HRF Hudson River Improvement Grants, 2378
HRF New York City Environmental Grants for Newton Creek, 2379
Illinois Clean Energy Community Fndn Renewable Energy Grants, 2481
Illinois Clean Energy Community Fndn Solar Thermal Installation Grants, 2482
Illinois DNR Migratory Waterfowl Stamp Grants, 2498
Illinois DNR Park and Recreational Facility Construction Grants, 2499
Illinois DNR State Furbearer Grants, 2501
Illinois DNR State Pheasant Grants, 2502
Illinois DNR Wildlife Preservation Fund Large Project Grants, 2505
Japan Center for Global Partnership Grants, 2650
John D. and Catherine T. MacArthur Fndn Global Challenges Grants, 2690
Joyce Fndn Environment Grants, 2750
Kalamazoo Community Environment Grants, 2766
Lumpkin Family Healthy Environments Grants, 2941
MacArthur Fndn Conservation and Sustainable Development Grants, 2963
MDEQ Brownfield Redevelopment and Site Reclamation Grants, 3095
Morris K. Udall and Stewart L. Udall Fndn Dissertation Fellowships, 3219
NFWF Shell Marine Habitat Grants, 3391
NFWF Southern Co Longleaf Legacy Grants, 3392
NFWF Southern Company Power of Flight Bird Conservation Grants, 3393
NFWF Upper Mississippi Riv Watershed Grants, 3398
NYCT New York City Environment Grants, 3556
Pathways to Nature Conservation Grants, 3745
Patrick and Aimee Butler Family Fndn Community Environment Grants, 3748
Praxair Fndn Grants, 3944
Prince Charitable Trusts Chicago Grants, 3959
Prince Charitable Trusts Rhode Island Grants, 3961
Rockefeller Brothers Sustainable Devel Grants, 4136
Rose Fndn for Comm & the Environment N California Environmental Grassroots Grants, 4158
Rose Fndn For Communities and the Environment SE Madera County Responsible Growth Grants, 4159
S. D. Bechtel, Jr. Fndn / Stephen Bechtel Fund Environmental Educ Grants, 4192
Seattle Fndn Environment Grants, 4327
Social Justice Fund NW Environmental Justice Giving Project Grants, 4396
Southern Cal Edison Environmental Grants, 4429
Toyota USA Fndn Environmental Grants, 4661

UPS Fndn Environmental Sustainability Grants, 4731
USAID Bengal Tiger Conservation Grants, 4741
USAID Mekong Partnership for the Environment Project Grants, 4769
USDA Coop Extension System Educ Grants, 4803
USDA State Bulk Fuel Revolving Grants, 4840
USDC/NOAA Open Rivers Init Grants, 4847
Wallace Global Grants, 4977
Water and Land Stewardship Grants, 5002
WestWind Fndn Environment Grants, 5052
Weyerhaeuser Family Fndn Environment, Conservation and Preservation Grants, 5054
WILD Fndn Grants, 5068
William C. Kenney Watershed Protection Fndn Ecosystem Grants, 5079

Environmental Programs

3M Company Environmental Giving Grants, 13
3M Fndn Community Giving Grants, 15
786 Fndn Grants, 33
1675 Fndn Grants, 35
2701 Fndn Grants, 37
AAAS Science and Technology Policy Fellowships: Energy, Environment, and Agriculture, 52
Abbot and Dorothy H. Stevens Fndn Grants, 79
Abbott Fund Community Grants, 81
Abelard Fndn East Grants, 87
Abelard Fndn West Grants, 88
Abel Fndn Grants, 90
Abell-Hanger Fndn Grants, 91
Abell Fndn Conservation and Environment Grants, 94
Access Fund Climbing Preservation Grants, 110
ACE Charitable Fndn Grants, 111
Acorn Fndn Grants, 131
ACTION Council of Monterey County Grants, 134
Adam Richter Charitable Grants, 145
Adams Fndn Grants, 154
Administaff Community Affairs Grants, 165
AEC Grants, 175
AEP Corp Giving Grants, 180
Agape Fndn for Nonviolent Social Change Alice Hamburg Emergency Grants, 196
Agape Fndn for Nonviolent Social Change Grants, 197
Air Products and Chemicals Grants, 216
Akonadi Fndn Anti-Racism Grants, 217
Akzo Nobel Chemicals Grants, 219
Alaska Airlines Corp Giving Grants, 320
Alaska Airlines Fndn Grants, 321
Alaska Conservation Fndn Awards, 322
Alaska Conservation Operating Grants, 323
Alaska Conservation Fndn Opportunity Grants, 324
Alaska Conservation Fndn Rapid Response Grants, 325
Alaska Conservation Fndn Watchable Wildlife Conservation Grants, 326
Alberto Culver Corp Contributions Grants, 343
Albuquerque Community Fndn Grants, 348
Alcoa Fndn Grants, 350
Alexander & Baldwin Fndn Hawaiian and Pacific Island Grants, 352
Alexander & Baldwin Fndn Mainland Grants, 353
Alexander H. Bright Charitable Grants, 358
Alfred P. Sloan Fndn Civic Inits Grants, 368
Allegan County Community Fndn Grants, 375
Allen P. and Josephine B. Green Fndn Grants, 380
All for the Earth Fndn Grants, 381
Alliance for Community Trees Home Depot Fndn NeighborWoods Grants, 382
Alliant Energy Fndn Community Grants, 384
Alpine Winter Fndn Grants, 394
Altria Group Environment Grants, 400
Amador Community Fndn Grants, 408
Ameren Corp Community Grants, 418
American Electric Power Grants, 428
American Express Historic Preservation Grants, 431
American Forests Global ReLeaf Grants, 434
American Gas Fndn Grants, 437
American Hiking Society National Trails Grants, 438
American Honda Fndn Grants, 439
America the Beautiful Fund Operation Green Plant Grants, 451

SUBJECT INDEX / Environmental Programs / 897

Amgen Fndn Grants, 456
Andrew Family Fndn Grants, 462
Anheuser-Busch Fndn Grants, 470
Ann Arbor Area Community Fndn Grants, 474
Annie's Grants for Gardens, 480
Appalachian Regional Commission Transportation and Highways Grants, 512
Applied Biosystems Grants, 514
APS Fndn Grants, 518
Arbor Day Fndn Grants, 524
Archer Daniels Midland Fndn Grants, 527
Arizona Community Fndn Grants, 540
Arizona Public Service Corp Giving Grants, 545
Arkansas Community Fndn Grants, 561
Armstrong McDonald Fndn Grants, 565
A Rocha USA Grants, 566
Arthur Ashley Williams Fndn Grants, 572
Arthur B. Schultz Fndn Grants, 573
Ashland Corp Contributions Grants, 587
As You Sow, 598
AT&T Fndn Civic and Comm Service Grants, 599
Atherton Family Fndn Grants, 604
Athwin Fndn Grants, 605
Austin Community Fndn Grants, 616
Autodesk Community Relations Grants, 619
AutoNation Corp Giving Grants, 620
Autzen Fndn Grants, 622
Azadoutioun Fndn Grants, 631
Bacon Family Fndn Grants, 634
Baltimore Community Environment Path Grants, 643
Banrock Station Wines Wetlands Grants, 662
Barr Fndn Grants (Massachusetts), 676
Batchelor Fndn Grants, 679
Baton Rouge Area Fndn Grants, 682
Baxter Int'l Corp Giving Grants, 689
Bay and Paul Fndns Grants, 693
Beazley Fndn Grants, 714
Beim Fndn Grants, 718
Beldon Grants, 720
Bella Vista Fndn Grants, 722
Ben & Jerry's Fndn Grants, 724
Bender Fndn Grants, 726
Beneficia Fndn Grants, 727
Bennett Family Fndn of Texas Grants, 728
Benwood Fndn Focus Area Grants, 733
Berks County Community Fndn Grants, 734
Bernard F. and Alva B. Gimbel Fndn Grants, 740
Berrien Community Fndn Grants, 744
Bertha Wolf-Rosenthal Fndn for Community Service Stipend, 746
Bikes Belong Fndn Paul David Clark Bicycling Safety Grants, 760
Bikes Belong Fndn REI Grants, 761
Bikes Belong Grants, 763
Black Hills Corp Grants, 781
Blanche and Julian Robertson Family Fndn Grants, 785
Bodenwein Public Benevolent Fndn Grants, 806
Boeing Company Contributions Grants, 809
Booth Ferris Fndn Grants, 816
Borkee-Hagley Fndn Grants, 817
Boston Fndn Grants, 819
Boston Globe Fndn Grants, 821
Brainerd Fndn Grants, 831
Brian G. Dyson Fndn Grants, 834
Brico Grants, 835
Brooklyn Community Fndn Green Communities Grants, 852
Brunswick Fndn Grants, 857
Build-A-Bear Workshop Fndn Grants, 861
Bullitt Fndn Grants, 862
Bunbury Company Grants, 863
Burning Fndn Grants, 867
Burton G. Bettingen Grants, 871
Bydale Fndn Grants, 882
Caesars Fndn Grants, 891
California Coastal Art and Poetry Contest, 899
California Green Trees for Golden State Grant, 906
California State Parks Restore & Cleanup Grants, 908
Callaway Fndn Grants, 909
Callaway Golf Company Fndn Grants, 910

Cambridge Community Fndn Grants, 913
Capital Region Community Fndn Grants, 921
Captain Planet Fndn Grants, 922
Carl and Eloise Pohlad Family Fndn Grants, 927
Carl M. Freeman Fndn FACES Grants, 932
Carolyn Fndn Grants, 942
Carrie E. and Lena V. Glenn Fndn Grants, 944
Carrier Corp Contributions Grants, 946
Caterpillar Fndn Grants, 954
Cemala Fndn Grants, 988
CenterPointEnergy Minnegasco Grants, 993
Cessna Fndn Grants, 1000
CFFVR Environmental Stewardship Grants, 1010
CFFVR Project Grants, 1017
CFFVR Shawano Area Community Fndn Grants, 1021
Charles Delmar Fndn Grants, 1039
Charles Stewart Mott Fndn Grants, 1055
Charlotte County (FL) Community Fndn Grants, 1056
Chesapeake Bay Trust Capacity Building Grants, 1068
Chesapeake Bay Environmental Ed Grants, 1069
Chesapeake Bay Fisheries & Headwaters Grants, 1070
Chesapeake Bay Trust Outreach and Community Engagement Grants, 1073
Chesapeake Bay Trust Pioneer Grants, 1074
Chevron Hawaii Educ Fund, 1077
CICF Indianapolis Fndn Community Grants, 1123
Cinergy Fndn Grants, 1133
Citigroup Fndn Grants, 1139
Citizens Bank Mid-Atlantic Charitable Grants, 1140
Claneil Fndn Grants, 1145
Clarence E. Heller Charitable Fndn Grants, 1150
Clark Fndn Grants, 1157
Claude Worthington Benedum Fndn Grants, 1161
Clayton Baker Grants, 1163
Cleveland-Cliffs Fndn Grants, 1165
CLIF Bar Family Fndn Grants, 1173
CNCS AmeriCorps NCCC Project Grants, 1181
Coastal Community Fndn of S Carolina Grants, 1193
Collective Brands Fndn Grants, 1206
Colorado Interstate Gas Grants, 1213
Columbia Gas of Virginia Grants, 1218
Columbus Fndn Scotts Miracle-Gro Community Garden Academy Grants, 1230
Community Fndn for Greater Buffalo Grants, 1247
Community Fndn for Greater New Haven Quinnipiac River Grants, 1250
Community Fndn for Monterey County Grants, 1255
Community Fndn for Muskegon County Grants, 1256
Community Fndn for NE Michigan Grants, 1257
Community Fndn for Southern Arizona Grants, 1261
Community Fndn for East Central Illinois Grants, 1278
Community Fndn of Greater Birmingham Grants, 1280
Community Fndn of Greater Flint Grants, 1282
Community Fndn of Greater Greensboro Grants, 1288
Community Fndn of Greater Memphis Grants, 1290
Community Fndn of Greater Tampa Grants, 1292
Community Fndn of Greenville-Greenville Women Giving Grants, 1293
Community Fndn of Greenville Community Enrichment Grants, 1294
Community Fndn of Middle Tennessee Grants, 1300
Community Fndn of Mount Vernon and Knox County Grants, 1301
Community Fndn of Santa Cruz County Grants, 1305
Community Fndn of SE Connecticut Grants, 1309
Community Fndn of Southern Indiana Grants, 1310
Community Fndn of South Puget Sound Grants, 1311
Community Fndn of St. Joseph County Special Project Challenge Grants, 1314
Community Fndn of Tampa Bay Grants, 1316
Community Fndn of the Eastern Shore Community Needs Grants, 1317
Community Fndn of the Verdugos Grants, 1322
Community Fndn of Wabash County Grants, 1326
Community Fndn of Western N Carolina Grants, 1327
Community POWER (Partners On Waste Educ and Reduction), 1335
Compton Fndn Grants, 1338
Con Edison Corp Giving Environmental Grants, 1347
Connecticut Community Fndn Grants, 1350

Connecticut Light & Power Corp Contributions, 1352
ConocoPhillips Grants, 1355
Constellation Energy Corp EcoStar Grants, 1363
Constellation Energy Corp Grants, 1364
Consumers Energy Fndn, 1365
Cooke Fndn Grants, 1368
Cooper Fndn Grants, 1369
Cooper Industries Fndn Grants, 1370
Coors Brewing Corp Contributions Grants, 1371
Corina Higginson Grants, 1373
Cornell Lab of Ornithology Mini-Grants, 1374
Cowles Charitable Grants, 1392
Cruise Industry Charitable Fndn Grants, 1404
Crystelle Waggoner Charitable Grants, 1405
CSRA Community Fndn Grants, 1407
Cumberland Community Fndn Grants, 1413
Curtis and Edith Munson Fndn Grants, 1418
Cyrus Eaton Fndn Grants, 1423
Dade Community Fndn Grants, 1430
DaimlerChrysler Corp Grants, 1432
Dana Corp Fndn Grants, 1440
Darden Restaurants Fndn Grants, 1446
David Bohnett Fndn Grants, 1451
Daviess County Comm Environment Grants, 1456
Davis Conservation Fndn Grants, 1461
Dayton Fndn Grants, 1463
Dearborn Community County Progress Grants, 1473
Dole Food Company Charitable Contributions, 1564
Dolfinger-McMahon Fndn Grants, 1565
Donald and Sylvia Robinson Family Fndn Grants, 1573
Dorot Fndn Grants, 1586
Dorrance Family Fndn Grants, 1590
Do Something BR!CK Awards, 1592
Dow Chemical Company Grants, 1596
Dow Corning Corp Contributions Grants, 1597
Dr. Scholl Fndn Grants, 1602
Drs. Bruce and Lee Fndn Grants, 1607
DTE Energy Community Development Grants, 1609
DTE Energy Fndn Environmental Grants, 1612
Dubois County Community Fndn Grants, 1615
Duluth-Superior Area Community Fndn Grants, 1620
Dyer-Ives Fndn Small Grants, 1629
Dyson Mid-Hudson Valley Project Support, 1636
E.J. Grassmann Grants, 1638
Earth Island Institute Brower Youth Awards, 1641
Earth Island Institute Community Wetland Restoration Grants, 1642
eBay Fndn Community Grants, 1648
Edward and Helen Bartlett Fndn Grants, 1664
Edward Bangs Kelley and Elza Kelley Grants, 1665
Edward R. Godfrey Fndn Grants, 1667
Edwin W. and Catherine M. Davis Fndn Grants, 1672
EIF Community Grants, 1675
Elliot Fndn Inc Grants, 1686
Elmer L. and Eleanor J. Andersen Fndn Grants, 1687
El Paso Community Fndn Grants, 1688
Emily Hall Tremaine Fndn Grants, 1698
Energy Fndn Buildings Grants, 1705
Energy Fndn Power Grants, 1707
Ensworth Charitable Fndn Grants, 1710
EPA Air Pollution Control Support Grants, 1722
EPA Brownfields Area-Wide Planning Grants, 1723
EPA Brownfields Assessment Pilot Grants, 1724
EPA Brownfields Cleanup Grants, 1725
EPA Brownfields Environmental Workforce Development and Job Training Grants, 1726
EPA Children's Health Protection Grants, 1728
EPA Environmental Justice Small Grants, 1731
EPA Regional Agricultural IPM Grants, 1735
EPA Senior Environmental Employment Grants, 1736
EPA Source Reduction Assistance Grants, 1737
EPA State Senior Environ Employment Grants, 1739
EPA Tribal Support for the National Environmental Information Exchange Network, 1742
EQT Fndn Environment Grants, 1746
EREF Solid Waste Research Grants, 1747
EREF Sustainability Research Grants, 1748
EREF Unsolicited Proposal Grants, 1749
ESRI Conservation Grants, 1751
Essex County Community Discretionary Grants, 1752

898 / Environmental Programs

Ethel and Raymond F. Rice Fndn Grants, 1758
Ewing Halsell Fndn Grants, 1776
FEDCO Charitable Fndn Educ Grants, 1798
Ferree Fndn Grants, 1804
Field Fndn of Illinois Grants, 1806
Fields Pond Fndn Grants, 1807
FirstEnergy Fndn Community Grants, 1819
Florida Sea Turtle Grants, 1871
Ford Fndn Peace and Social Justice Grants, 1884
Forest Fndn Grants, 1886
Forrest C. Lattner Fndn Grants, 1887
Foster Fndn Grants, 1888
Frances and John L. Loeb Family Grants, 1917
Franklin County Community Fndn Grants, 1929
Fred C. and Mary R. Koch Fndn Grants, 1943
Freeman Fndn Grants, 1952
Fremont Area Community Fndn Grants, 1955
Freshwater Future Climate Grants, 1958
Freshwater Future Healing Our Waters Grants, 1959
Freshwater Future Project Grants, 1961
Freshwater Future Special Opportunity Grants, 1962
Frost Fndn Grants, 1966
Fuller Fndn Grants, 1974
Fulton County Community Fndn Grants, 1975
Fund for Southern Communities Grants, 1977
G.N. Wilcox Grants, 1982
Gamble Fndn Grants, 1983
Gannett Fndn Community Action Grants, 1984
Garden Crusader Award, 1985
Gates Family Fndn Parks, Conservation & Recreation Grants, 1991
Gaylord and Dorothy Donnelley Fndn Grants, 1993
Gebbie Fndn Grants, 1995
GenCorp Fndn Grants, 1998
General Motors Fndn Grants Support Program, 2004
George and Ruth Bradford Fndn Grants, 2010
George A Ohl Jr. Fndn Grants, 2012
George Gund Fndn Grants, 2020
George H. and Jane A. Mifflin Grants, 2021
George H.C. Ensworth Grants, 2022
Georgia-Pacific Fndn Environment Grants, 2034
Georgia Power Fndn Grants, 2039
Geraldine R. Dodge Fndn Environment Grants, 2041
Gibson Fndn Grants, 2052
Giving Sum Annual Grant, 2058
GNOF Bayou Communities Grants, 2069
GNOF Coastal 5 + 1 Grants, 2070
GNOF Environmental Grants, 2073
GNOF Exxon-Mobil Grants, 2074
GNOF Gert Community Grants, 2076
GNOF Gulf Coast Oil Spill Grants, 2077
Good Works Fndn Grants, 2105
Grace and Franklin Bernsen Fndn Grants, 2109
Grand Rapids Area Community Wyoming Grants, 2116
Grand Rapids Community Fndn Grants, 2118
Grand Rapids Community Ionia County Grants, 2119
Grand Rapids Community Fndn Lowell Grants, 2121
Grand Rapids Community SE Ottawa Grants, 2122
Grand Rapids Community Sparta Grants, 2124
Grand Victoria Fndn Illinois Core Grants, 2126
Grassroots Exchange Grants, 2128
Greater Green Bay Community Fndn Grants, 2135
Greater Saint Louis Community Fndn Grants, 2138
Greater Tacoma Community Fndn Grants, 2139
Greater Worcester Comm Discretionary Grants, 2140
Greater Worcester Community Youth for Community Improvement Grants, 2144
Great Lakes Fishery Trust Access Grants, 2145
Green Diamond Charitable Contributions, 2149
GreenWorks! Grants, 2160
Guido A. and Elizabeth H. Binda Fndn Grants, 2172
H.A. and Mary K. Chapman Charitable Grants, 2182
Hagedorn Grants, 2207
Harley Davidson Fndn Grants, 2224
Harold K. L. Castle Fndn Grants, 2228
Harrison County Community Fndn Grants, 2233
Harrison County Community Signature Grants, 2234
Harry C. Trexler Grants, 2239
Harry Chapin Fndn Grants, 2240
Hawaiian Electric Industries Charitable Grants, 2259

Hawaii Community Fndn West Hawaii Grants, 2266
Heineman Fndn for Research, Educ, Charitable and Scientific Purposes, 2290
Helen S. Boylan Fndn Grants, 2298
Henry J. Kaiser Family Fndn Grants, 2310
Hershey Company Grants, 2318
High Meadow Fndn Grants, 2321
Hilfiger Family Fndn Grants, 2323
Hillman Fndn Grants, 2327
Hoblitzelle Fndn Grants, 2341
Holland/Zeeland Community Fndn Grants, 2345
Homer Fndn Grants, 2352
Honda of America Manufacturing Fndn Grants, 2354
Honeywell Sustainable Opportunities Grants, 2360
Honor the Earth Grants, 2361
Horace A. Kimball and S. Ella Kimball Grants, 2362
Houston Endowment Grants, 2373
HRF Tibor T. Polgar Fellowships, 2380
Hudson Webber Fndn Grants, 2383
Huntington County Community Fndn - Make a Difference Grants, 2406
Idaho Power Company Corp Contributions, 2433
Illinois Clean Energy Community Fndn Energy Efficiency Grants, 2479
Illinois Clean Energy Community Fndn Renewable Energy Grants, 2481
Illinois Clean Energy Community Fndn Solar Thermal Installation Grants, 2482
Illinois DNR Biodiversity Field Trip Grants, 2496
Illinois DNR Migratory Waterfowl Stamp Grants, 2498
Illinois DNR Park and Recreational Facility Construction Grants, 2499
Illinois DNR Schoolyard Habitat Action Grants, 2500
Illinois DNR State Furbearer Grants, 2501
Illinois DNR State Pheasant Grants, 2502
Illinois DNR Wildlife Preservation Fund Large Project Grants, 2505
Illinois DNR Wildlife Preservation Maintenance of Wildlife Rehabilitation Facilities Grants, 2507
Illinois DNR Youth Recreation Corps Grants, 2508
Illinois Tool Works Fndn Grants, 2511
IMLS Nat Medal for Museum & Library Service, 2516
Impact 100 Grants, 2522
Inasmuch Fndn Grants, 2523
Indianapolis Power & Light Company Community Grants, 2540
Indianapolis Power & Light Company Environmentalist of the Year Award, 2541
Indianapolis Power & Light Company Golden Eagle Environmental Grants, 2542
Indiana Recycling Grants, 2545
Intel Community Grants, 2562
Intel Int'l Community Grants, 2564
Int'l Paper Company Fndn Grants, 2568
Int'l Paper Environmental Awards, 2569
Jackson County Community Fndn Grants, 2611
Jackson Fndn Grants, 2613
Jacobs Family Spirit of the Diamond Grants, 2618
Jacobs Family Village Neighborhoods Grants, 2619
James & Abigail Campbell Family Fndn Grants, 2620
James A. and Faith Knight Fndn Grants, 2621
James Ford Bell Fndn Grants, 2623
James M. Cox Fndn of Georgia Grants, 2634
Jane's Grants, 2639
Janirve Fndn Grants, 2645
Jenifer Altman Fndn Grants, 2662
Jennings County Community Fndn Grants, 2664
Jessie B. Cox Charitable Grants, 2670
Jessie Smith Noyes Fndn Grants, 2672
John Merck Grants, 2706
John W. and Anna H. Hanes Grants, 2728
Kalamazoo Community Environment Grants, 2766
Ka Papa O Kakuhihewa Fund, 2785
Katharine Matthies Fndn Grants, 2788
KEEN Effect Grants, 2795
Kelvin and Eleanor Smith Fndn Grants, 2796
Kenneth T. and Eileen L. Norris Fndn Grants, 2802
Kettering Family Fndn Grants, 2817
Kettering Grants, 2818
KeySpan Fndn Grants, 2821

Knox County Community Fndn Grants, 2831
Kosciusko County Community Fndn Grants, 2838
Laidlaw Fndn Youth Organizaing Inits Grants, 2854
Lands' End Corp Giving Program, 2861
Leave No Trace Master Educator Scholarships, 2870
Lee and Ramona Bass Fndn Grants, 2871
Legacy Partners in Environmental Educ Grants, 2875
Legacy Partners in Environmental Ed Grants, 2876
Letha E. House Fndn Grants, 2886
Liberty Hill Fndn Environmental Justice Grants, 2891
Liberty Hill Fndn Fund for Change Grants, 2893
Liberty Hill Fndn Seed Grants, 2896
Liberty Hill Fndn Special Opportunity Grants, 2897
Libra Fndn Grants, 2899
Lisa and Douglas Goldman Grants, 2910
Long Island Community Fndn Grants, 2920
Lotus 88 Fndn for Women and Children Grants, 2921
Lubrizol Fndn Grants, 2933
Lumpkin Family Healthy Environments Grants, 2941
Lumpkin Family Fndn Strong Community Leadership Grants, 2944
Lyndhurst Fndn Grants, 2949
M.E. Raker Fndn Grants, 2953
Macquarie Bank Fndn Grants, 2966
Margaret T. Morris Fndn Grants, 3005
Marie C. and Joseph C. Wilson Fndn Rochester Small Grants, 3006
Marie H. Bechtel Charitable Grants, 3007
Mars Fndn Grants, 3025
Marshall County Community Fndn Grants, 3026
Mary C. & Perry F. Spencer Fndn Grants, 3034
Mary K. Chapman Fndn Grants, 3042
Mary Owen Borden Fndn Grants, 3046
Max and Anna Levinson Fndn Grants, 3066
Maxon Charitable Fndn Grants, 3068
McConnell Fndn Grants, 3076
McGraw-Hill Companies Community Grants, 3081
McInerny Fndn Grants, 3083
McKesson Fndn Grants, 3084
McLean Contributionship Grants, 3088
MDEQ Brownfield Redevelopment and Site Reclamation Grants, 3095
MDEQ Community Pollution Prevention (P2) Grants: Household Drug Collections, 3098
Mead Witter Fndn Grants, 3106
Melinda Gray Ardia Environmental Fndn Grants, 3114
Mertz Gilmore Climate Change Grants, 3125
Mervin Bovaird Fndn Grants, 3128
Meyer Memorial Trust Special Grants, 3149
Miami County Community Fndn - Operation Round Up Grants, 3156
Microsoft Comm Affairs Puget Sound Grants, 3163
Miguel Aleman Fndn Grants, 3175
Mimi and Peter Haas Grants, 3185
Morris and Gwendolyn Cafritz Fndn Grants, 3218
Motorola Fndn Grants, 3221
Natalie W. Furniss Charitable Grants, 3244
Nathan Cummings Fndn Grants, 3246
National Environmental Educ Fndn - Department of Defense Legacy Award, 3270
National Environmental Ed Every Day Grants, 3271
National Geographic All Roads Seed Grants, 3272
National Geographic Conservation Grants, 3273
National Geographic Genographic Legacy Grants, 3274
National Geographic Young Explorers Grants, 3275
Nelda C. and H.J. Lutcher Stark Fndn Grants, 3296
New Earth Fndn Grants, 3317
New Hampshire Charitable Fndn Grants, 3325
NFF Collaboration Support Grants, 3342
NFF Community Assistance Grants, 3343
NFF Matching Grants, 3344
NFF Mid-Capacity Assistance Grants, 3345
NFWF Acres for America Grants, 3355
NFWF Alaska Fish and Wildlife Grants, 3356
NFWF Aleutian Islands Risk Assessment Grants, 3357
NFWF Bring Back the Natives Grants, 3359
NFWF Budweiser Conservationist of the Year, 3361
NFWF Columbia Basin Water Trans Grants, 3366
NFWF Columbia River Estuarine Coastal Grant, 3367
NFWF Community Salmon Fund Partnerships, 3368

SUBJECT INDEX

Environmental Programs / 899

NFWF Coral Reef Conservation Project Grants, 3370
NFWF Delaware Estuary Watershed Grants, 3371
NFWF Five-Star Restoration Challenge Grants, 3373
NFWF King County Community Salmon Grants, 3375
NFWF Native Plant Conservation Init Grants, 3380
NFWF Nature of Learning Grants, 3381
NFWF One Fly Conservation Partnerships, 3382
NFWF Oregon Governor's Fund for the Environment Grants, 3383
NFWF Pacific Grassroots Salmonid Init Grants, 3384
NFWF Pierce Community Salmon Grant, 3385
NFWF Pioneers in Conservation Grants, 3386
NFWF Radical Salmon Design Contest, 3388
NFWF Salmon Recovery Funding Board Community Salmon Grants, 3389
NFWF Seafarer's Environmental Educ Grants, 3390
NFWF State Comprehensive Wildlife Conservation Support Grants, 3395
NGA Midwest School Garden Grants, 3407
Nina Mason Pulliam Charitable Grants, 3443
Nissan Neighbors Grants, 3445
NOAA Projects to Improve or Amend Coral Reef Fishery Management Plans, 3453
Norcross Wildlife Fndn Grants, 3460
Norfolk Southern Fndn Grants, 3463
Norman Fndn Grants, 3464
North Carolina Community Fndn Grants, 3489
NE Utilities Fndn Grants, 3498
Northern Chautauqua Environmental Grants, 3501
North Georgia Community Fndn Grants, 3505
Northrop Grumman Corp Grants, 3507
NW Fund for the Environment Grants, 3510
NRA Fndn Grants, 3517
NSF Partnership for Advancing Technologies in Housing Grants, 3529
Nu Skin Force for Good Fndn Grants, 3536
NYCT New York City Environment Grants, 3556
Ogden Codman Grants, 3641
Oracle Corp Contributions Grants, 3686
Orchard Fndn Grants, 3690
Oscar Rennebohm Fndn Grants, 3694
OSF Central Eurasia Project Grants, 3704
Ottinger Fndn Grants, 3712
Overbrook Fndn Grants, 3715
Owen County Community Fndn Grants, 3716
Owens Corning Fndn Grants, 3717
PacifiCorp Fndn for Learning Grants, 3727
Palm Beach and Martin Counties Grants, 3733
Park Fndn Grants, 3739
Partnership Enhancement Grants, 3740
Pathways to Nature Conservation Grants, 3745
Patricia Price Peterson Fndn Grants, 3746
Patrick and Aimee Butler Family Fndn Community Arts and Humanities Grants, 3747
Patrick and Aimee Butler Family Fndn Community Environment Grants, 3748
Patrick and Anna M. Cudahy Grants, 3751
Paul G. Allen Family Fndn Grants, 3759
Peacock Fndn Grants, 3809
Perkins Charitable Fndn Grants, 3823
Perry County Community Fndn Grants, 3827
Peter Kiewit Fndn Neighborhood Grants, 3846
PG&E Bright Ideas Grants, 3866
PG&E Community Vitality Grants, 3868
PGE Fndn Grants, 3869
Philadelphia Organizational Effectiveness Grants, 3872
Piedmont Natural Gas Corp and Charitable Contributions, 3883
Piedmont Natural Gas Fndn Environmental Stewardship and Energy Sustainability Grant, 3884
Pinellas County Grants, 3891
Pioneer Hi-Bred Community Grants, 3895
Pittsburgh Fndn Community Grants, 3910
Plum Creek Fndn Grants, 3917
Porter County Community Fndn Grants, 3931
Posey County Community Fndn Grants, 3939
Powell Family Fndn Grants, 3941
Powell Fndn Grants, 3942
Praxair Fndn Grants, 3944
Prince Charitable Trusts Chicago Grants, 3959

Prince Charitable Trusts D.C. Grants, 3960
Prince Charitable Trusts Rhode Island Grants, 3961
Princeton Area Community Fndn Greater Mercer Grants, 3963
Principal Financial Group Fndn Grants, 3966
Procter and Gamble Grants, 3967
Progress Energy Corp Contributions Grants, 3968
Project AWARE Fndn Grants, 3971
Project Orange Thumb Grants, 3972
Public Welfare Fndn Grants, 3984
Pulaski County Community Fndn Grants, 3988
Putnam Fndn Grants, 3991
Rajiv Gandhi Fndn Grants, 4011
Rathmann Family Fndn Grants, 4026
RCF General Community Grants, 4032
REI Conservation and Outdoor Rec Grants, 4051
Reinberger Fndn Grants, 4052
Rhode Island Fndn Grants, 4073
Rice Fndn Grants, 4074
Richard and Rhoda Goldman Grants, 4077
Richard King Mellon Fndn Grants, 4087
Riley Fndn Grants, 4094
Ripley County Community Fndn Grants, 4095
Ripley County Community Small Project Grants, 4096
Robert R. Meyer Fndn Grants, 4121
Robert W. Woodruff Fndn Grants, 4124
Robins Fndn Grants, 4126
Rochester Area Community Fndn Grants, 4127
Rockefeller Brothers Sustainable Devel Grants, 4136
Rockefeller Family Grants, 4137
Rollin M. Gerstacker Fndn Grants, 4146
Romic Environmental's Charitable Contributions, 4148
Rose Fndn For Communities and the Environment Consumer Privacy Rights Grants, 4156
Rose Fndn For Communities and the Environment Kern County Air Pollution Mitigation Grants, 4157
Rose Fndn for Comm & the Environment N California Environmental Grassroots Grants, 4158
Rose Fndn For Communities and the Environment SE Madera County Responsible Growth Grants, 4159
Rose Fndn For Communities and the Environment Watershed Protection Grants, 4160
Ross Fndn Grants, 4164
Royal Caribbean Cruises Ocean Fund, 4165
Rucker & Margaret Agee Grants, 4171
Ruth Anderson Fndn Grants, 4176
Ruth and Vernon Taylor Fndn Grants, 4177
S. D. Bechtel, Jr. Fndn / Stephen Bechtel Fund Environmental Educ Grants, 4192
S.H. Cowell Fndn Grants, 4199
S. Livingston Mather Charitable Grants, 4200
S. Mark Taper Fndn Grants, 4201
Salisbury Community Fndn Grants, 4224
Samuel S. Johnson Fndn Grants, 4239
San Diego Fndn Environment Blasker Grants, 4245
San Diego Environment Community Grants, 4246
San Diego Fndn for Change Grants, 4247
San Diego Women's Fndn Grants, 4252
SanDisk Corp Community Sharing Program, 4253
San Francisco Fndn Community Health Grants, 4263
San Francisco Fndn Environment Grants, 4266
San Juan Island Community Fndn Grants, 4283
Santa Fe Community Fndn Seasonal Grants-Spring Cycle, 4291
Sapelo Fndn Environmental Protection Grants, 4293
Schering-Plough Fndn Community Inits Grants, 4303
Schumann Fund for New Jersey Grants, 4311
Scott County Community Fndn Grants, 4314
Seabury Fndn Grants, 4316
Seagate Tech Corp Capacity to Care Grants, 4317
Seattle Fndn Environment Grants, 4327
SeaWorld & Busch Gardens Conservation Grants, 4332
SEJ An Awards for Reporting on Environment, 4333
Shared Earth Fndn Grants, 4339
Shaw's Supermarkets Donations, 4342
Shell Oil Company Fndn Grants, 4343
Sierra Grants, 4352
Singing for Change Fndn Grants, 4363
Sioux Falls Area Community Fndn Spot Grants, 4366
Siragusa Fndn Arts & Culture Grants, 4367

Sisters of Saint Joseph Charitable Grants, 4376
Skaggs Fndn Grants, 4378
Snee Reinhardt Charitable Fndn Grants, 4387
Social Justice Fund NW Environmental Justice Giving Project Grants, 4396
Solutia Grants, 4402
Sonora Area Fndn Competitive Grants, 4404
Sony Corp of America Corp Philanthropy Grants, 4405
Sorenson Legacy Fndn Grants, 4407
Southern Cal Edison Environmental Grants, 4429
SW Florida Community Competitive Grants, 4442
SW Gas Corp Fndn Grants, 4445
Spencer County Community Fndn Grants, 4451
St. Louis-Jefferson Solid Waste Management Waste Reduction and Recycling Grants, 4470
Stackpole-Hall Fndn Grants, 4472
Steelcase Fndn Grants, 4497
Steuben County Community Fndn Grants, 4501
Stewart Huston Charitable Grants, 4505
Stonyfield Farm Profits for the Planet Grants, 4509
Strowd Roses Grants, 4515
Sulzberger Fndn Grants, 4522
Summit Fndn Grants, 4524
Surdna Fndn Sustainable Environments Grants, 4533
Susan Vaughan Fndn Grants, 4537
SVP Environment Grants, 4539
Sweet Water Grants, 4541
Taproot Fndn Capacity-Building Service Grants, 4560
Telluride Fndn Community Grants, 4573
Theodore Edson Parker Fndn Grants, 4605
Thomas Sill Fndn Grants, 4619
Thompson Charitable Fndn Grants, 4622
Tides California Wildlands Grassroots Fund, 4630
Tides Fndn Grants, 4632
Tom's of Maine Grants, 4640
Topeka Community Fndn Grants, 4644
Toro Fndn Grants, 4647
Tourism Cares Worldwide Grants, 4649
Town Creek Fndn Grants, 4650
Toyota Motor Manufacturing of Alabama Grants, 4652
Toyota Motor Manufacturing Mississippi Grants, 4655
Toyota Motor Manufacturing W Virginia Grants, 4657
Toyota USA Fndn Environmental Grants, 4661
Triangle Community Fndn Donor Grants, 4668
Trinity Fndn Grants, 4669
Trull Fndn Grants, 4673
Turner Fndn Grants, 4681
Union Bank Corp Sponsorships and Donations, 4708
Union Benevolent Association Grants, 4710
Union Pacific Fndn Community and Civic Grants, 4714
United Technologies Corp Grants, 4725
Unity Fndn Of LaPorte County Grants, 4726
UPS Fndn Environmental Sustainability Grants, 4731
USAID Bengal Tiger Conservation Grants, 4741
USAID Mekong Partnership for the Environment Project Grants, 4769
USDA Denali Comm High Energy Cost Grants, 4805
USDA High Energy Cost Grants, 4812
USDA State Bulk Fuel Revolving Grants, 4840
USDC/NOAA American Rivers Community-Based Restoration Program River Grants, 4845
USDC/NOAA Open Rivers Init Grants, 4847
Vancouver Fndn Grants & Comm Inits, 4900
Vermont Community Fndn Grants, 4929
Virginia W. Kettering Fndn Grants, 4950
Volvo Adventure Environmental Awards, 4952
Vulcan Materials Company Fndn Grants, 4956
W. C. Griffith Fndn Grants, 4958
Wallace Alexander Gerbode Fndn Grants, 4974
Wallace Global Grants, 4977
Walmart Fndn National Giving Grants, 4979
Walter L. Gross III Family Fndn Grants, 4983
Warrick County Community Fndn Grants, 4987
Washington County Community Fndn Grants, 4997
Washington County Community Youth Grants, 4998
Washington Gas Charitable Contributions, 5000
Waste Management Charitable Giving Grants, 5001
Weaver Fndn Grants, 5015
Wege Fndn Grants, 5017
Western Pennsylvania Environmental Awards, 5026

900 / Environmental Programs   SUBJECT INDEX

Westinghouse Charitable Giving Grants, 5028
Weyerhaeuser Company Fndn Grants, 5053
Weyerhaeuser Family Fndn Environment, Conservation and Preservation Grants, 5054
Widgeon Point Charitable Fndn Grants, 5064
Wilburforce Fndn Grants, 5067
William C. Kenney Watershed Protection Fndn Ecosystem Grants, 5079
William G. and Helen C. Hoffman Fndn Grants, 5080
William J. and Dorothy K. O'Neill Fndn Grants, 5087
Winifred & Harry B. Allen Fndn Grants, 5101
Winston-Salem Fndn Stokes County Grants, 5104
YSA Radio Disney's Hero for Change Award, 5139
YSA Sodexo Lead Organizer Grants, 5140
Yves Rocher Fndn Women of the Earth Awards, 5143

Environmental Protection
American Rivers Community-Based Restoration Program River Grants, 444
Caesars Fndn Grants, 891
Collective Brands Fndn Grants, 1206
Con Edison Corp Giving Environmental Grants, 1347
Earth Island Institute Community Wetland Restoration Grants, 1642
EPA Air Pollution Control Support Grants, 1722
EPA Source Reduction Assistance Grants, 1737
Freshwater Future Healing Our Waters Grants, 1959
Freshwater Future Project Grants, 1961
Freshwater Future Special Opportunity Grants, 1962
Georgia-Pacific Fndn Environment Grants, 2034
GNOF Coastal 5 + 1 Grants, 2070
GNOF Community Revitalization Grants, 2071
GNOF Environmental Grants, 2073
Great Lakes Fishery Trust Habitat Protection and Restoration Grants, 2146
HAF Natural Environment Grants, 2202
Honeywell Sustainable Opportunities Grants, 2360
IIE Freeman Fndn Indonesia Internships, 2456
Illinois DNR Migratory Waterfowl Stamp Grants, 2498
Illinois DNR Park and Recreational Facility Construction Grants, 2499
Illinois DNR State Furbearer Grants, 2501
Illinois DNR Wildlife Preservation Fund Large Project Grants, 2505
Illinois DNR Wildlife Preservation Maintenance of Wildlife Rehabilitation Facilities Grants, 2507
Kalamazoo Community Environment Grants, 2766
Lucy Downing Nisbet Charitable Grants, 2935
Lumpkin Family Healthy Environments Grants, 2941
MDEQ Clean Diesel Grants, 3096
Meadows Fndn Grants, 3104
National Environmental Ed Every Day Grants, 3271
NFF Collaboration Support Grants, 3342
NFF Mid-Capacity Assistance Grants, 3345
NFWF Alaska Fish and Wildlife Grants, 3356
Northern Chautauqua Environmental Grants, 3501
Pathways to Nature Conservation Grants, 3745
Piedmont Natural Gas Corp and Charitable Contributions, 3883
Piedmont Natural Gas Fndn Environmental Stewardship and Energy Sustainability Grant, 3884
RCF General Community Grants, 4032
Seattle Fndn Environment Grants, 4327
Sioux Falls Area Community Grants, 4364
Sioux Falls Area Community Fndn Spot Grants, 4366
Social Justice Fund NW Environmental Justice Giving Project Grants, 4396
Southern Cal Edison Environmental Grants, 4429
Toyota USA Fndn Environmental Grants, 4661
USAID Bengal Tiger Conservation Grants, 4741
USAID Mekong Partnership for the Environment Project Grants, 4769
WestWind Fndn Environment Grants, 5052

Environmental Research
A Charitable Fndn Grants, 126
Acumen Global Fellowships, 142
EPA Brownfields Area-Wide Planning Grants, 1723
EPA Brownfields Environmental Workforce Development and Job Training Grants, 1726
EPA Surveys, Studies, Research, Investigations, Demonstrations, and Special Purpose Activities Relating to the Clean Air Act, 1740
Georgia-Pacific Fndn Environment Grants, 2034
GNOF Gulf Coast Oil Spill Grants, 2077
Honeywell Sustainable Opportunities Grants, 2360
Western Pennsylvania Environmental Awards, 5026
WILD Fndn Grants, 5068

Environmental Services
Baxter Int'l Corp Giving Grants, 689
Bill & Melinda Gates Emergency Response Grants, 766
Carl C. Icahn Fndn Grants, 929
Con Edison Corp Giving Environmental Grants, 1347
Elkhart County Community Fndn Fund for Elkhart County, 1683
Freshwater Future Insight Services Grants, 1960
Georgia-Pacific Fndn Environment Grants, 2034
Green Fndn Special Project Grants, 2155
Kalamazoo Community Environment Grants, 2766
KEEN Effect Grants, 2795
Lumpkin Family Healthy Environments Grants, 2941
Patrick and Aimee Butler Family Fndn Community Environment Grants, 3748
Seattle Fndn Environment Grants, 4327
Toyota USA Fndn Environmental Grants, 4661
WestWind Fndn Environment Grants, 5052

Environmental Studies
Abell Fndn Conservation and Environment Grants, 94
Annie Sinclair Knudsen Memorial Fund/Kaua'i Community Grants, 482
Brainerd Fndn Grants, 831
Canada-U.S. Fulbright Mid-Career Grants, 917
Collins Fndn Grants, 1209
Con Edison Corp Giving Environmental Grants, 1347
Curtis and Edith Munson Fndn Grants, 1418
Daviess County Comm Environment Grants, 1456
EPA Surveys, Studies, Research, Investigations, Demonstrations, and Special Purpose Activities Relating to the Clean Air Act, 1740
EREF Sustainability Research Grants, 1748
Fred Baldwin Memorial Fndn Grants, 1941
Georgia-Pacific Fndn Environment Grants, 2034
Group 70 Fndn Fund, 2167
HRF Hudson River Improvement Grants, 2378
HRF New York City Environmental Grants for Newton Creek, 2379
IDEM Section 205(j) Water Quality Management Planning Grants, 2434
IIE Nancy Petry Scholarship, 2459
Indianapolis Power & Light Company Grants, 2540
Kalamazoo Community Environment Grants, 2766
NFWF Community Salmon Fund Partnerships, 3368
NFWF King County Community Salmon Grants, 3375
NFWF Pierce Community Salmon Grant, 3385
NFWF Radical Salmon Design Contest, 3388
NFWF Salmon Recovery Funding Board Community Salmon Grants, 3389
Norwin S. and Elizabeth N. Bean Fndn Grants, 3515
NYCT New York City Environment Grants, 3556
NYSCA Arts Educ: Community Learning Grants, 3577
NYSCA Arts Educ: General Operating Support, 3578
NYSCA Arts Educ: K-12 In-School Grants, 3580
NYSCA Arts Education: Local Capacity Building Grants, 3581
NYSCA Arts Educ: Services to the Field Grants, 3582
Olin Corp Charitable Grants, 3669
Piedmont Natural Gas Fndn Environmental Stewardship and Energy Sustainability Grant, 3884
Richard and Rhoda Goldman Grants, 4077
S. D. Bechtel, Jr. Fndn / Stephen Bechtel Fund Environmental Educ Grants, 4192
Southbury Community Trust Fund, 4409
Starr Fndn Grants, 4483
Trull Fndn Grants, 4673
UPS Fndn Environmental Sustainability Grants, 4731
Weingart Fndn Grants, 5018
Wilburforce Fndn Grants, 5067
WILD Fndn Grants, 5068

Enzymes/Enzymology
NHLBI Career Transition Awards, 3412

Epidemiology
DHHS AIDS Project Grants, 1525

Epilepsy
F.M. Kirby Fndn Grants, 1780

Episcopal Church
AHS Fndn Grants, 208
Alavi Fndn Grants, 335
Alvah H. and Wyline P. Chapman Fndn Grants, 402
Barra Fndn Project Grants, 674
Bishop Robert Paddock Grants, 775
Booth-Bricker Grants, 815
Effie and Wofford Cain Fndn Grants, 1674
Herbert A. and Adrian W. Woods Fndn Grants, 2313
John and Elizabeth Whiteley Fndn Grants, 2685
MacDonald-Peterson Fndn Grants, 2965
Robert E. and Evelyn McKee Fndn Grants, 4110

Equal Opportunity
Air Products and Chemicals Grants, 216
ALFJ Astraea U.S. General Fund, 362
Allstate Corp Giving Grants, 386
Allstate Corp Hometown Commitment Grants, 387
Allstate Fndn Safe and Vital Communities Grants, 390
Benton Community Fndn - The Cookie Jar Grant, 729
Compton Fndn Grants, 1338
DaimlerChrysler Corp Grants, 1432
Evelyn and Walter Haas, Jr. Fund Immigrant Rights Grants, 1773
Frances and John L. Loeb Family Grants, 1917
GNOF Community Revitalization Grants, 2071
HAF Community Grants, 2193
Liberty Hill Fndn Fund for a New LA Grants, 2892
Manitoba Arts Council Community Connections and Access Grants, 2995
PIP Fulfilling the Dream Fund, 3907
PIP Racial Justice Collaborative Grants, 3908
PIP U.S. Human Rights Grants, 3909
Playboy Fndn Freedom of Expression Award, 3912
Playboy Fndn Social Change Documentary Film Grants, 3914
Sapelo Fndn Social Justice Grants, 4294
Singing for Change Fndn Grants, 4363
UPS Fndn Diversity Grants, 4729
Vanguard Public Fndn Grant Funds, 4904

Equine Studies
Bay Area Community Fndn Grants, 694

Equipment/Instrumentation
Ball Brothers Fndn Rapid Grants, 639
Bally's Total Fitness Equipment Grants, 640
Ben B. Cheney Fndn Grants, 725
Boeing Company Contributions Grants, 809
Campbell Soup Fndn Grants, 916
Catherine Manley Gaylord Fndn Grants, 956
Charles Hayden Fndn Grants, 1048
Chatlos Fndn Grants, 1061
Claremont Community Fndn Grants, 1149
Collins Fndn Grants, 1209
Community Fndn of Abilene Community Grants, 1264
Community Fndn of Abilene Future Grants, 1265
Community Fndn of the Verdugos Ed Endowment Grants, 1321
Coughlin-Saunders Fndn Grants, 1377
Delaware Division of the Arts Opportunity Grants-Artists, 1479
DHS ARRA Transit Security Grants, 1544
DHS FY 2009 Transit Security Grants, 1545
Dr. Scholl Fndn Grants, 1602
E.L. Wiegand Fndn Grants, 1639
EDS Technology Grants, 1662
Fireman's Fund Insurance Heritage Grants, 1818
FRED Ed Ethyl Grants, 1945
Fritz B. Burns Fndn Grants, 1965
Gladys Brooks Fndn Grants, 2059

SUBJECT INDEX

GNOF Albert N. & Hattie M. McClure Grants, 2068
Greater Worcester Community Mini-Grants, 2142
Hartford Fndn Implementation Support Grants, 2251
Hartford Fndn Nonprofit Support Grants, 2252
Hillcrest Fndn Grants, 2325
Hill Fndn Grants, 2326
Homer Fndn Grants, 2352
IDPH Hosptial Capital Investment Grants, 2441
Illinois DCEO Community Development Assistance For Economic Development Grants, 2488
Indep Comm Fndn Educ, Culture & Arts Grant, 2526
Janson Fndn Grants, 2646
Jennings County Community Fndn Grants, 2664
Katharine Matthies Fndn Grants, 2788
Ludwick Family Fndn Grants, 2938
Marion I. and Henry J. Knott Fndn Discretionary Grants, 3018
Marion I. and Henry J. Knott Standard Grants, 3019
Meacham Fndn Grants, 3102
Nevada Arts Council Residency Express Grants, 3315
Nicor Corp Contributions, 3435
Norcliffe Fndn Grants, 3459
Norcross Wildlife Fndn Grants, 3460
Norwin S. and Elizabeth N. Bean Fndn Grants, 3515
NSF Atmospheric Sciences Mid-Size Infrastructure Opportunity Grants, 3521
NYSCA Architecture, Planning, and Design: Capital Fixtures and Equipment Purchase Grants, 3570
NYSCA Music: New Music Facilities, 3608
NYSCA Visual Arts: Workspace Facilities Grants, 3631
Piper Trust Arts and Culture Grants, 3900
Porter County Community Fndn Grants, 3931
Priddy Fndn Capital Grants, 3954
Ralph M. Parsons Fndn Grants, 4013
Ryder System Charitable Fndn Grants, 4191
Saint Luke's Health Inits Grants, 4216
Santa Barbara Strategy Grants Capital Support, 4285
Schering-Plough Fndn Health Grants, 4304
Scholastic Welch's Harvest Grants, 4309
Seattle Fndn Medical Funds Grants, 4329
South Madison Community Fndn Grants, 4440
Square D Fndn Grants, 4464
St. Joseph Community Health Fndn Catherine Kasper Award, 4468
St. Joseph Community Health Fndn Improving Healthcare Access Grants, 4469
Stanley Smith Horticultural Grants, 4474
SVP Early Childhood Development and Parenting Grants, 4538
Tri-State Community Twenty-first Century Endowment Grants, 4666
TSA Advanced Surveillance Grants, 4674
USDJ Edward Byrne Justice Assistance Grants, 4863
West Virginia Commission on the Arts Cultural Facilities and Capital Resources Grants, 5033

Estuarine Sciences
FishAmerica Fndn Chesapeake Bay Grants, 1827
FishAmerica Fndn Conservation Grants, 1828
HRF Hudson River Improvement Grants, 2378
HRF Tibor T. Polgar Fellowships, 2380
NFWF Delaware Estuary Watershed Grants, 3371

Ethics
Alabama Humanities Fndn Mini Grants, 231
Alabama Humanities Planning/Consultant Grants, 232
ALA Paul Howard Award for Courage, 307
Alice Tweed Tuohy Fndn Grants, 372
Bay and Paul Fndns Grants, 693
Cargill Citizenship Fund-Corp Giving Grants, 925
Community Fndn of Greater Flint Grants, 1282
ConocoPhillips Grants, 1355
Cooper Fndn Grants, 1369
Elizabeth Morse Genius Charitable Grants, 1682
Graco Fndn Grants, 2111
James Hervey Johnson Charitable Ed Grants, 2627
Marion Gardner Jackson Charitable Grants, 3017
Morris K. Udall and Stewart L. Udall Fndn Native American Congressional Internships, 3220
NYHC Major and Mini Grants, 3567

Richard Davoud Donchian Fndn Grants, 4080
Sarah Scaife Fndn Grants, 4295
Virginia Fndn for the Humanities Residential Fellowships, 4948
Wisconsin Humanities Council Major Grants, 5107

Ethnicity
ALA Supporting Diversity Stipend, 333

Evolutionary Biology
Bay and Paul Fndns Grants, 693

Exchange Programs, Student
Delaware Division of the Arts Opportunity Grants-Artists, 1489

Exercise
Air Products and Chemicals Grants, 216
BCBSNC Fndn Grants, 712
Bikes Belong Paul Clark Bicycling Safety Grants, 760
Bikes Belong Fndn REI Grants, 761
Bikes Belong Grants, 763
Bright Promises Fndn Grants, 838
Dekko Fndn Grants, 1482
Elizabeth Morse Genius Charitable Grants, 1682
Finish Line Youth Fndn Founder's Grants, 1812
Finish Line Youth Fndn Grants, 1813
Gebbie Fndn Grants, 1995
GNOF IMPACT Kahn-Oppenheim Grants, 2084
Healthcare Fndn for Orange County Grants, 2279
Linford and Mildred White Charitable Grants, 2909
Paso del Norte Health Fndn Grants, 3743
PepsiCo Fndn Grants, 3819
Phoenix Coyotes Charities Grants, 3879
Saucony Run for Good Fndn Grants, 4301
United Methodist Child Mental Health Grants, 4721

Exhibitions, Collections, Performances
Alaska State Council on the Arts Community Arts Development Grants, 327
Andy Warhol Fndn for the Visual Arts Grants, 464
APAP Cultural Exchange Grants, 492
Arizona Commission on the Arts After-School Program Residencies, 535
Arizona Commission on the Arts Visual/Media Arts Organizations Grants, 539
Arkansas Arts Council AIE Mini Grants, 554
Boulder County Arts Alliance Neodata Endowment Grants, 823
CCH California Story Grants, 965
CCH Documentary Project Production Grants, 969
CCH Documentary Public Engagement Grants, 970
CCH Documentary Project Research and Development Grants, 971
Chicago Community Trust Arts and Culture Grants: Supporting Diverse Arts Productions and Fostering Art in Every Community, 1084
Christensen Fund Regional Grants, 1112
Community Fndn of St. Joseph County ArtsEverywhere Grants, 1313
Corning Fndn Cultural Grants, 1376
Crystelle Waggoner Charitable Grants, 1405
Delaware Div of Arts Opportunity Grants, 1489
Fieldstone Fndn Grants, 1808
Florida Humanities Council Major Grants, 1868
Frank and Lydia Bergen Fndn Grants, 1925
Greater Worcester Community Jeppson Memorial Fund for Brookfield Grants, 2141
Greater Worcester Community Mini-Grants, 2142
Illinois Arts Council Presenters Dev Grants, 2476
Illinois Arts Council Visual Arts Grants, 2478
Japan Fndn Los Angeles Mini-Grants for Japanese Arts & Culture, 2651
Japan Fndn New York Small Grants for Arts and Culture, 2652
Jerome Fndn Grants, 2667
Kentucky Arts Council TranspARTation Grant, 2812
Massachusetts Fndn for the Humanities Cultural Economic Development Grants, 3059
Massachusetts Fndn for Humanities Grants, 3060

MDARD County Fairs Cap Improvement Grants, 3092
Montana Arts Council Cultural and Aesthetic Project Grants, 3209
Musgrave Fndn Grants, 3231
National Endowment for the Arts - Grants for Arts Projects: Challenge America Fast-Track, 3254
National Endowment for Arts Commun Grants, 3260
National Endowment for Arts Agencies Grants, 3263
National Endowment for Arts Museum Grants, 3265
National Endowment for the Arts Presenting Grants: Art Works, 3268
Nevada Arts Council Folklife Apprenticeships, 3309
Nevada Arts Council Jackpot Grants, 3312
Nevada Arts Council Residency Express Grants, 3315
North Carolina Arts Cncl New Realities Grants, 3478
North Dakota Council on Arts Support Grants, 3496
NYFA Building Up Infrastructure Dance Grants, 3563
NYSCA Architecture, Planning, and Design: Project Support Grants, 3576
NYSCA Arts Educ Program Support Grants, 3579
NYSCA Dance: Commissions Grants, 3583
NYSCA Dance Gen Operating Support Grants, 3584
NYSCA Folk Arts: Exhibitions Grants, 3594
NYSCA Folk Arts: Regional and County Folk Arts Grants, 3597
NYSCA Museum General Operating Support, 3602
NYSCA Museum Program Support Grants, 3603
NYSCA Museum: Project Support Grants, 3604
NYSCA Music Gen Operating Support Grants, 3606
NYSCA Music Gen Program Support Grants, 3607
NYSCA Presenting: General Program Support, 3610
NYSCA Presenting: Presenting Grants, 3611
NYSCA Visual Arts: Exhibitions and Installations Grants, 3627
Ohio Arts Council Arts Access Grants, 3647
PCA Arts Organizations Grants for Music, 3774
PCA Arts Organizations and Arts Programs Grants for Art Museums, 3775
PCA Arts Organizations Grants for Dance, 3779
PCA Arts Organizations and Arts Programs Grants for Film and Electronic Media, 3780
PCA Arts Organizations & Grants for Lit, 3781
PCA Arts Organizations & Grants for Visual Arts, 3785
PCA Entry Track Arts Organizations and Program Grants for Art Museums, 3787
PCA Entry Track Arts Organizations and Program Grants for Film and Electronic Media, 3792
PCA Entry Track Arts Organizations and Program Grants for Literature, 3793
PCA Entry Track Arts Organizations and Program Grants for Music, 3795
PCA Entry Track Arts Organizations and Program Grants for Visual Arts, 3799
PCA Strategies for Success Grants - Advanced, 3804
PCA Strategies for Success Grants - Intermediate, 3806
Principal Financial Group Fndn Grants, 3966
Rasmuson Fndn Creative Ventures Grants, 4021
Rasmuson Fndn Individual Artists Awards, 4022
RISCA Project Grants for Organizations, Individuals and Educ, 4100
Seaver Institute Grants, 4331
South Carolina Arts Commission Folklife & Traditional Arts Grants, 4421
Stockton Rush Bartol Fndn Grants, 4508
TAC Arts Access Grant, 4549
TAC Arts Build Communities Grants, 4551
TAC Arts Grants, 4554
TAC Rural Arts Project Support Grants, 4555
TAC Touring Arts and Arts Access Grants, 4557
Target Fndn Grants, 4562
Texas Commission on the Arts Cultural Connections-Visual & Media Arts Touring Exhibits Grants, 4589
Texas Instruments Fndn Arts and Culture Grants, 4599
Virginia Fndn for Humanities Discr Grants, 4946
Virginia Fndn for the Humanities Open Grants, 4947
VSA/Metlife Connect All Grants, 4953
VSA/Volkswagen Group of America Exhibition Awards, 4954
VSA Int'l Art Program for Children with Disabilities Grants, 4955

902 / Exhibitions, Collections, Performances

Wabash River Heritage Corridor Grants, 4970
West Virginia Commission on the Arts Long-Term Artist Residencies, 5037
West Virginia Commission on the Arts Presenting Artists Grants, 5044
West Virginia Commission on the Arts Short-Term Artist Residencies, 5047
West Virginia Commission on the Arts Visual Arts Grants, 5051
Wisconsin Humanities Council Mini-Grants for Scholarly Research, 5108

Eye Diseases
Alice C. A. Sibley Grants, 371
Austin S. Nelson Fndn Grants, 617
Columbus Fndn Competitive Grants, 1220
Donald and Sylvia Robinson Family Fndn Grants, 1573
E.L. Wiegand Fndn Grants, 1639
George Gund Fndn Grants, 2020
GNOF IMPACT Gulf States Eye Surgery Fund, 2082
NEI Innovative Patient Outreach Programs And Ocular Screening Technologies To Improve Detection Of Diabetic Retinopathy Grants, 3295

Facility Support
Easton Fndns Archery Facility Grants, 1644
Florida Div of Cultural Affairs Facilities Grants, 1852
GNOF Albert N. & Hattie M. McClure Grants, 2068
HRF Hudson River Improvement Grants, 2378
Marion and Miriam Rose Grants, 3015
Mertz Gilmore Fndn NYC Dance Grants, 3127
Michael Reese Health Trust Core Grants, 3159
NHSCA Cultural Facilities Grants: Barrier Free Access for All, 3426
NYSCA Music: New Music Facilities, 3608
NYSCA Visual Arts: Workspace Facilities Grants, 3631
Texas Commission on the Arts Create-3 Grants, 4585
Texas Commission on the Arts Create-5 Grants, 4587
Texas Commission On The Arts GPA1, 4592
West Virginia Commission on the Arts Cultural Facilities and Capital Resources Grants, 5033

Faculty Development
American Chemical Society Chemical Technology Partnership Mini Grants, 424
Aspen Community Fndn Grants, 592
Carpenter Fndn Grants, 943
EPA Environmental Educ Grants, 1729
HAF Technical Assistance Grants, 2206
Lee and Ramona Bass Fndn Grants, 2871
Manitoba Arts Council Special Opps Grants, 2997
McGregor Grants, 3082
Pi Lambda Theta Anna Tracey Memorial Award, 3889
Richard M. Fairbanks Fndn Grants, 4088
Robert M. Hearin Fndn Grants, 4116
Texas Commission on the Arts Create-1 Grants, 4583

Faculty Support
ALA Excellence in Academic Libraries Award, 276
NHLBI Ruth L. Kirschstein National Research Service Awards for Individual Predoctoral Fellowships to Promote Diversity in Health-Related Research, 3419
Texas Commission on the Arts Create-2 Grants, 4584

Familial Abuse
A Glimmer of Hope Fndn Grants, 200
Ahmanson Fndn Grants, 207
Austin S. Nelson Fndn Grants, 617
California Endowment Innovative Ideas Challenge Grants, 904
CDC Grants for Violence-Related Injury Prevention Research, 974
Community Fndn of Broward Grants, 1275
Covenant Mountain Ministries Grants, 1387
Covenant to Care for Children Critical Grants, 1388
Elkhart County Community Fndn Fund for Elkhart County, 1683
Hawai'i Children's Trust Fund Community Awareness Events Grants, 2258
Hearst Fndns Social Service Grants, 2285

Herbert A. and Adrian W. Woods Fndn Grants, 2313
Initiaive Fndn Inside-Out Connections Grants, 2556
John W. Speas and Effie E. Speas Grants, 2732
Ms. Fndn for Women Ending Violence Grants, 3224
Patrick and Aimee Butler Family Fndn Community Human Services Grants, 3749
Quantum Fndn Grants, 3996
RadioShack StreetSentz Community Grants, 4005
Verizon Wireless Hopeline Grants, 4927

Family
3M Fndn Community Giving Grants, 15
200 Club of Mercer County Grants, 30
A & B Family Fndn Grants, 38
ACF ACYF Runaway and Homeless Youth Basic Center Grants, 112
ACF Adoption Opportunities Project Grants, 113
ACF Assets for Indep Demonstration Grants, 114
ACF Assets for Indep Individual Development Account Grants, 115
ACF Ethnic Community Self-Help Grants, 118
ACF Head Start and Early Head Start Grants, 120
ACF Mentoring Children of Prisoners Grants, 121
ACF Native American Social and Economic Development Strategies Grants, 123
ACF Preferred Communities Grants, 124
Achelis Fndn Grants, 127
ACTION Council of Monterey County Grants, 134
Actors Fund Social Services and Financial Assist, 139
Acushnet Fndn Grants, 143
Adams Family Fndn of Ohio Grants, 151
AEGON Transamerica Health & Welfare Grants, 179
African American Fund of New Jersey Grants, 192
A Glimmer of Hope Fndn Grants, 200
Agnes M. Lindsay Grants, 203
Akzo Nobel Chemicals Grants, 219
ALA Writers Live at the Library Grants, 336
Alcatel-Lucent Technologies Fndn Grants, 349
Alexander Eastman Fndn Grants, 355
Alex Stern Family Fndn Grants, 360
Alfred and Tillie Shemanski Testamentary Grants, 363
Alvah H. and Wyline P. Chapman Fndn Grants, 402
Alvin and Fanny Blaustein Thalheimer Grants, 403
Amelia Sillman Rockwell and Carlos Perry Rockwell Charities Grants, 417
Ameren Corp Community Grants, 418
American Savings Fndn Grants, 445
Amerigroup Fndn Grants, 452
AmerUs Group Charitable Fndn, 455
Andrew Family Fndn Grants, 462
Angels for Kids Fndn Grants, 466
Anne J. Caudal Fndn Grants, 475
Annie E. Casey Fndn Grants, 481
Anschutz Family Fndn Grants, 486
Appalachian Regional Comm Housing Grants, 508
AptarGroup Fndn Grants, 519
Arizona Cardinals Grants, 534
Arizona Commission on the Arts After-School Program Residencies, 535
Arizona Community Fndn Grants, 540
Arizona Diamondbacks Charities Grants, 542
Arizona Republic Fndn Grants, 546
Aspen Community Fndn Grants, 592
AT&T Fndn Civic and Comm Service Grants, 599
Atkinson Fndn Community Grants, 606
Atlanta Fndn Grants, 608
Auburn Fndn Grants, 611
AutoNation Corp Giving Grants, 620
Bank of America Charitable Fndn Critical Needs Grants, 656
Barberton Community Fndn Grants, 666
Barker Welfare Fndn Grants, 669
Battle Creek Community Fndn Grants, 684
BBF Florida Family Lit Init Grants, 697
BBF Maine Family Lit Init Grants, 698
BBF Maine Family Lit Init Planning Grants, 699
BBF Maryland Family Lit Init Grants, 700
BBF Maryland Family Lit Init Planning Grants, 701
BBF National Grants for Family Lit, 702
Ben & Jerry's Fndn Grants, 724

SUBJECT INDEX

Benton Community Fndn Grants, 730
Bernard F. Reynolds Charitable Grants, 741
Berrien Community Fndn Grants, 744
Better Way Fndn Grants, 754
BJ's Charitable Fndn Grants, 777
BJ's Wholesale Clubs Local Charitable Giving, 778
Blanche and Julian Robertson Family Fndn Grants, 785
Blue Cross Blue Shield of Minnesota Fndn - Health Equity: Building Health Together Grants, 793
Blue River Community Fndn Grants, 801
Blumenthal Fndn Grants, 804
Bodenwein Public Benevolent Fndn Grants, 806
Bodman Fndn Grants, 807
Boeckmann Charitable Fndn Grants, 808
Bohemian Fndn Pharos Grants, 811
Booth-Bricker Grants, 815
Borkee-Hagley Fndn Grants, 817
Boston Fndn Grants, 819
Boston Globe Fndn Grants, 821
Bradley-Turner Fndn Grants, 828
Brookdale Fndn Leadership in Aging Fellowships, 844
Brookdale Fndn National Group Respite Grants, 845
Brooklyn Community Fndn Community Development Grants, 850
Brown County Community Fndn Grants, 853
Brown Fndn Grants, 854
Bunbury Company Grants, 863
Burlington Industries Fndn Grants, 865
Bush Fndn Health & Human Services Grants, 875
Cailloux Fndn Grants, 892
California Endowment Innovative Ideas Challenge Grants, 904
Callaway Golf Company Fndn Violence Prevention Grants, 911
Campbell Soup Fndn Grants, 916
Cargill Citizenship Fund-Corp Giving Grants, 925
Carlisle Fndn Grants, 931
Carolyn Fndn Grants, 942
Carpenter Fndn Grants, 943
Catherine Kennedy Home Fndn Grants, 955
Cemala Fndn Grants, 988
Central Carolina Community Fndn Community Impact Grants, 994
Central Okanagan Fndn Grants, 997
CFFVR Basic Needs Giving Partnership Grants, 1002
CFFVR Myra M. and Robert L. Vandehey Fndn Grants, 1016
CFFVR Waupaca Area Community Fndn Grants, 1023
Chapin Hall Int'l Fellowships in Children's Policy Research, 1032
Charity Incorporated Grants, 1035
CharityWorks Grants, 1036
Charles Stewart Mott Fndn Grants, 1055
CICF Indianapolis Fndn Community Grants, 1123
Citizens Bank Mid-Atlantic Charitable Grants, 1140
Clara Abbott Fndn Need-Based Grants, 1146
Claude Worthington Benedum Fndn Grants, 1161
Clay Fndn Grants, 1162
Cleo Fndn Grants, 1164
Columbus Fndn Paul G. Duke Grants, 1227
Columbus Fndn Traditional Grants, 1233
Comer Fndn Grants, 1236
Community Fndn for Greater Buffalo Grants, 1247
Community Fndn of Bartholomew County Heritage Grants, 1267
Community Fndn of Bartholomew County James A. Henderson Award for Fundraising, 1268
Community Fndn of Broward Grants, 1275
Community Fndn of Central Illinois Grants, 1276
Community Fndn Greater Chattanooga Grants, 1281
Community Fndn of Greater Fort Wayne - Community Endowment and Clarke Endowment Grants, 1285
Community Fndn of Greenville Community Enrichment Grants, 1294
Community Fndn of Greenville Hollingsworth Funds Program/Project Grants, 1296
Community Fndn of Louisville Grants, 1299
Community Fndn of Riverside County Grants, 1304
Community Fndn of Sarasota County Grants, 1306
Community Fndn of SE Connecticut Grants, 1309

SUBJECT INDEX

Family

Community Fndn of Southern Indiana Grants, 1310
Community Fndn of Virgin Islands Mini Grants, 1325
Community Impact Fund, 1332
Community Memorial Fndn Grants, 1334
Connecticut Community Fndn Grants, 1350
Constantin Fndn Grants, 1362
Constellation Energy Corp Grants, 1364
Covenant Mountain Ministries Grants, 1387
Covenant to Care for Children Critical Grants, 1388
Crail-Johnson Fndn Grants, 1393
Credit Suisse First Boston Fndn Grants, 1397
CSRA Community Fndn Grants, 1407
CSX Corp Contributions Grants, 1408
D.F. Halton Fndn Grants, 1424
Dade Community Fndn GLBT Grants, 1429
Dairy Queen Corp Contributions Grants, 1433
Dammann Grants, 1439
Darden Restaurants Fndn Grants, 1446
Daviess County Community Fndn Youth Development Grants, 1460
Daywood Fndn Grants, 1465
Dekko Fndn Grants, 1482
Delaware Community Next Generation Grants, 1485
Delta Air Lines Community Enrichment Grants, 1494
Dennis and Phyllis Washington Fndn Grants, 1498
Dept of Ed Alaska Native Ed Programs, 1506
Dept of Ed Even Start Grants, 1508
Dermody Properties Fndn Capstone Award, 1516
Dermody Properties Fndn Grants, 1517
DHHS Abandoned Infants Assistance Grants, 1523
DHHS Adolescent Family Life Demo Projects, 1524
DHHS Comprehensive Community Mental Health Services Grants for Children with Serious Emotional Disturbances, 1530
DHHS Indep Demonstration Program, 1535
DOJ Juvenile Justice and Delinquency Prevention Special Emphasis Grants, 1559
Dolfinger-McMahon Fndn Grants, 1565
Dominion Fndn Human Needs Grants, 1572
Donald and Sylvia Robinson Family Fndn Grants, 1573
Donaldson Fndn Grants, 1574
Dorothy G. Griffin Charitable Fndn Grants, 1588
Dr. P. Phillips Fndn Grants, 1601
Eckerd Family Fndn Grants, 1651
Edina Realty Fndn Grants, 1656
EIF Community Grants, 1675
Eisner Fndn Grants, 1678
El Paso Community Fndn Grants, 1688
Elsie Lee Garthwaite Memorial Fndn Grants, 1692
EMC Corp Grants, 1693
Emma B. Howe Memorial Fndn Grants, 1700
Entergy Charitable Fndn Low-Income Inits and Solutions Grants, 1711
Entergy Corp Micro Grants, 1712
Entergy Corp Open Grants for Healthy Families, 1715
EPA Children's Health Protection Grants, 1728
Eulalie Bloedel Schneider Fndn Grants, 1767
Evanston Community Fndn Grants, 1771
Fairfield County Community Fndn Grants, 1782
Families Count: The National Honors Program, 1784
Family Lit and Hawaii Pizza Hut Lit Fund, 1785
FAR Grants, 1787
Farm Aid Grants, 1790
Farmers Insurance Corp Giving Grants, 1791
Fassino Fndn Grants, 1793
Faye McBeath Fndn Grants, 1794
FCD Child Development Grants, 1796
Fidelity Fndn Grants, 1805
Fifth Third Fndn Grants, 1810
First Lady's Family Lit Init for Texas Family Lit Trailblazer Grants, 1821
First Lady's Family Lit Init for Texas Grants, 1822
First Lady's Family Lit Init for Texas Implementation Grants, 1823
First Lady's Family Lit Init for Texas Planning, 1824
Fisher House Fndn Newman's Own Awards, 1833
Fitzpatrick and Francis Family Business Continuity Fndn Grants, 1837
Florida BRAIVE Fund of Dade Community, 1846
Floyd A. and Kathleen C. Cailloux Fndn Grants, 1874

Foellinger Fndn Grants, 1877
Fndn for Seacoast Health Grants, 1895
Fndn for the Carolinas Grants, 1896
Fndn for the Mid South Wealth Building Grants, 1900
Fndns of E Chicago Family Support Grants, 1908
Fred C. and Katherine B. Andersen Fndn Grants, 1942
Fred C. and Mary R. Koch Fndn Grants, 1943
Fremont Area Community Fndn Grants, 1955
Frey Fndn Grants, 1963
G.N. Wilcox Fndn Grants, 1982
Gardiner Savings Inst Charitable Fndn Grants, 1987
Gates Family Children, Youth & Family Grants, 1989
Gebbie Fndn Grants, 1995
General Mills Fndn Celebrating Communities of Color Grants, 2002
General Mills Fndn Grants, 2003
George A. Hormel Testamentary Grants, 2009
George and Ruth Bradford Fndn Grants, 2010
George Fndn Grants, 2018
George Gund Fndn Grants, 2020
George Kress Fndn Grants, 2025
George W. Wells Fndn Grants, 2030
Georgia Council for the Arts Partner Grants for Service Organizations, 2036
Georgiana Goddard Eaton Grants, 2038
Glazer Family Fndn Grants, 2062
GNOF Gert Community Grants, 2076
GNOF Stand Up For Our Children Grants, 2093
Goizueta Fndn Grants, 2096
Grable Fndn Grants, 2108
Grand Rapids Community Fndn Grants, 2118
Grand Rapids Comm SE Ottawa Youth Grants, 2123
Grand Rapids Community Sparta Youth Grants, 2125
Gulf Coast Community Operating Grants, 2176
Gulf Coast Fndn of Community Grants, 2177
H.J. Heinz Company Fndn Grants, 2184
Hagedorn Grants, 2207
Hahl Proctor Charitable Grants, 2208
Hall Family Fndn Grants, 2210
Harold and Arlene Schnitzer CARE Grants, 2226
Harold R. Bechtel Charitable Remainder Grants, 2229
Hartford Courant Fndn Grants, 2248
Hasbro Children's Fund, 2256
Hawai'i Children's Trust Fund Community Awareness Events Grants, 2258
Hawaiian Electric Industries Charitable Grants, 2259
Health Fndn of Greater Indianapolis Grants, 2282
Heinz Endowments Grants, 2291
Helen Bader Fndn Grants, 2293
Helen Steiner Rice Fndn Grants, 2299
Help America Fndn Grants, 2301
Henrietta Tower Wurts Memorial Fndn Grants, 2304
Hoffberger Fndn Grants, 2342
Horizons Community Issues Grants, 2366
Household Int'l Corp Giving Grants, 2372
Howard and Bush Fndn Grants, 2374
Hugh J. Andersen Fndn Grants, 2385
Humanitas Fndn Grants, 2390
Hutchinson Community Fndn Grants, 2410
Hut Fndn Grants, 2411
Hutton Fndn Grants, 2412
Hyams Fndn Grants, 2413
Illinois Arts Council Ethnic & Folk Arts Master Apprentice Grants, 2468
Illinois Tool Works Fndn Grants, 2511
Impact 100 Grants, 2522
Init Fndn Innovation Grants, 2559
IYI Responsible Fatherhood Grants, 2591
J.C. Penney Company Grants, 2594
J. F. Maddox Fndn Grants, 2597
Jacksonville Jaguars Fndn Grants, 2614
Jacob and Hilda Blaustein Fndn Grants, 2615
Jacob G. Schmidlapp Grants, 2616
Jacobs Family Village Neighborhoods Grants, 2619
James & Abigail Campbell Family Fndn Grants, 2620
James A. and Faith Knight Fndn Grants, 2621
James M. Cox Fndn of Georgia Grants, 2634
James R. Dougherty Jr. Fndn Grants, 2635
Jane Bradley Pettit Fndn Community and Social Development Grants, 2642

Janirve Fndn Grants, 2645
Jay and Rose Phillips Family Fndn Grants, 2656
Jim Moran Fndn Grants, 2680
John P. McGovern Fndn Grants, 2707
John S. and James L. Knight Fndn Communities Grants, 2711
Johnson & Johnson Corp Contributions Grants, 2718
Joseph S. Stackpole Charitable Grants, 2741
Kahuku Community Fund, 2762
Kalamazoo Community Fndn Individuals and Families Grants, 2769
Kalamazoo Community LBGT Equality Grants, 2771
Kansas Health Fndn Recognition Grants, 2784
Kimberly-Clark Community Grants, 2824
Kuki'o Community Fund, 2845
Lands' End Corp Giving Program, 2861
Leon and Thea Koerner Fndn Grants, 2883
Leo Niessen Jr., Charitable Grants, 2885
Lettie Pate Evans Fndn Grants, 2887
Linden Fndn Grants, 2908
Liz Claiborne Fndn Grants, 2915
Lotus 88 Fndn for Women and Children Grants, 2921
Lucile Horton Howe and Mitchell B. Howe Fndn Grants, 2934
Lyndhurst Fndn Grants, 2949
M.B. and Edna Zale Fndn Grants, 2950
Margaret T. Morris Fndn Grants, 3005
Marie & Joseph Wilson Rochester Small Grants, 3006
Marsh Corp Grants, 3027
Mary C. & Perry F. Spencer Fndn Grants, 3034
Mary E. Ober Fndn Grants, 3039
Mary Owen Borden Fndn Grants, 3046
McCarthy Family Fndn Grants, 3073
McGregor Grants, 3082
McKesson Fndn Grants, 3084
McKnight Fndn Region & Communities Grants, 3086
Mervin Bovaird Fndn Grants, 3128
MFRI Operation Diploma Small Grants for Indiana Family Readiness Groups, 3152
Microsoft Comm Affairs Puget Sound Grants, 3163
Miller Brewing Corp Contributions Grants, 3180
Milton Hicks Wood and Helen Gibbs Wood Charitable Grants, 3184
Mimi and Peter Haas Grants, 3185
Minneapolis Fndn Community Grants, 3186
Montana Community Big Sky LIFT Grants, 3210
Moran Family Fndn Grants, 3216
Morris and Gwendolyn Cafritz Fndn Grants, 3218
National Book Scholarship Fund, 3249
Nationwide Insurance Fndn Grants, 3285
NCFL/Better World Books Libraries and Families Award, 3288
NGA Heinz Wholesome Memories Intergenerational Garden Awards, 3404
Nicholas H. Noyes Jr. Memorial Fndn Grants, 3434
NIDRR Field-Initiated Projects, 3437
Nina Mason Pulliam Charitable Grants, 3443
Northland Fndn Grants, 3506
NW Mutual Fndn Grants, 3509
NW Minnesota Fndn Asset Building Grants, 3511
Norton Fndn Grants, 3514
Nuffield Fndn Children and Families Grants, 3533
NYCT Girls and Young Women Grants, 3548
NYCT Substance Abuse Grants, 3558
Ohio County Community Fndn Grants, 3658
Ohio County Community Fndn Mini-Grants, 3660
Oleonda Jameson Grants, 3667
Orchard Fndn Grants, 3690
Ordean Fndn Grants, 3691
Parkersburg Area Comm Fndn Action Grants, 3738
Paul and Mary Haas Fndn Contributions and Student Scholarships, 3756
Perpetual Trust for Charitable Giving Grants, 3826
Peter & Elizabeth C. Tower Mental Health Reference and Resource Materials Mini-Grants, 3837
PGE Fndn Grants, 3869
Philadelphia Organizational Effectiveness Grants, 3872
Philadelphia Fndn YOUTHadelphia Grants, 3873
Philip L. Graham Grants, 3876
Phoenix Suns Charities Grants, 3881

904 / Family

Pinkerton Fndn Grants, 3892
Pinnacle Fndn Grants, 3894
Piper Jaffray Fndn Communities Giving Grants, 3899
Piper Trust Educ Grants, 3902
Pittsburgh Fndn Community Grants, 3910
Plough Fndn Grants, 3915
PNC Fndn Grow Up Great Grants, 3924
Polk Bros. Fndn Grants, 3929
Portland General Electric Fndn Grants, 3937
Posey Community Fndn Women's Grants, 3938
Pride Fndn Grants, 3958
Prince Charitable Trusts D.C. Grants, 3960
PSEG Corp Contributions Grants, 3979
Rainbow Academy Fndn Grants, 4006
Rainbow Endowment Grants, 4007
Rainbow Families Fndn Grants, 4008
Ralph M. Parsons Fndn Grants, 4013
Raymond John Wean Fndn Grants, 4028
RBC Dain Rauscher Fndn Grants, 4031
Rhode Island Fndn Grants, 4073
Richard and Helen DeVos Fndn Grants, 4076
Richard King Mellon Fndn Grants, 4087
Rite Aid Corp Grants, 4101
Robert Bowne Fndn Fellowships, 4107
Robert Bowne Fndn Lit Grants, 4108
Robert Bowne Fndn Youth-Centered Grants, 4109
Robins Fndn Grants, 4126
Rochester Area Community Fndn Grants, 4127
Rosalynn Carter Institute Georgia Caregiver of the Year Awards, 4151
Rose Community Fndn Child and Family Development Grants, 4153
Rosie's For All Kids Fndn Grants, 4163
Ruth H. and Warren A. Ellsworth Fndn Grants, 4179
S.H. Cowell Fndn Grants, 4199
S. Livingston Mather Charitable Grants, 4200
S. Mark Taper Fndn Grants, 4201
Saginaw Community Fndn YWCA Fund for Women and Girls Grants, 4207
SanDisk Corp Community Sharing Program, 4253
Sarkeys Fndn Grants, 4297
Schumann Fund for New Jersey Grants, 4311
Scott County Community Fndn Grants, 4314
Seabury Fndn Grants, 4316
Seattle Fndn Benjamin N. Phillips Grants, 4322
Sensient Technologies Fndn Grants, 4337
Shopko Fndn Community Charitable Grants, 4346
Simmons Fndn Grants, 4360
Singing for Change Fndn Grants, 4363
Sisters of Charity Fndn of Canton Grants, 4372
Sisters of Saint Joseph Charitable Grants, 4376
Smith Richardson Fndn Direct Service Grants, 4385
Sobrato Family Fndn Grants, 4389
Sobrato Family Fndn Meeting Space Grants, 4390
Sobrato Family Fndn Office Space Grants, 4391
Sophia Romero Grants, 4406
Sorenson Legacy Fndn Grants, 4407
Southwire Company Grants, 4447
Starbucks Shared Planet Youth Action Grants, 4476
Stark Community Fndn Neighborhood Partnership Grants, 4479
State Justice Institute Curriculum Adaptation and Training Grants, 4488
State Justice Institute Partner Grants, 4489
State Justice Institute Project Grants, 4490
State Justice Institute Scholarships, 4491
State Justice Institute Strategic Init Grants, 4492
State Justice Institute Tech Assistance Grants, 4493
Steven B. Achelis Fndn Grants, 4502
Stinson Fndn Grants, 4506
Strengthening Families - Strengthening Communities Grants, 4513
Stuart Fndn Grants, 4516
Sunderland Fndn Grants, 4527
Susan A. & Donald P. Babson Charitable Grants, 4534
Taproot Fndn Capacity-Building Service Grants, 4560
Target Corp Local Store Grants, 4561
Target Fndn Grants, 4562
Thompson Charitable Fndn Grants, 4622
TJX Fndn Grants, 4637

Topeka Community Building Families Grants, 4643
Topeka Community Fndn Grants, 4644
Toyota Motor Manufacturing of Indiana Grants, 4653
Toyota Motor of Kentucky Grants, 4654
Toyota Technical Center Grants, 4660
Turner Fndn Grants, 4681
U.S. Department of Ed Early Reading 1st Grants, 4691
U.S. Department of Educ Migrant and Seasonal Farmworkers Grants, 4693
U.S. Department of Educ Parent Information and Training, 4695
U.S. Department of Educ Special Educ--National Activities--Parent Information Centers, 4701
USAID Family Health Plus Project Grants, 4751
USAID Service Delivery & Support for Families Caring For Orphans and Vulnerable Childrens, 4781
USDA Multi-Family Housing Preservation and Revitalization Grants, 4819
USDA Tech and Supervisory Assistance Grants, 4841
Vancouver Fndn Grants & Comm Inits, 4900
Verizon Wireless Hopeline Grants, 4927
Viacom Fndn Grants (Formerly CBS Fndn), 4932
Victoria S. and Bradley L. Geist Fndn Grants Supporting Foster Care and Their Caregivers, 4936
Viking Children's Grants, 4939
VSA Int'l Art Program for Children with Disabilities Grants, 4955
Vulcan Materials Company Fndn Grants, 4956
W.K. Kellogg Fndn Secure Families Grants, 4963
Wabash Valley Human Services Grants, 4972
Waitt Family Fndn Grants, 4973
Wallace Fndn Grants, 4976
Wayne and Gladys Valley Fndn Grants, 5003
Whirlpool Fndn Grants, 5056
Whitehorse Fndn Grants, 5058
William G. Gilmore Fndn Grants, 5082
William J. and Dorothy K. O'Neill Fndn Grants, 5087
Windgate Charitable Fndn Grants, 5099
Youth Philanthropy Project, 5132

Family Planning

Albert W. Cherne Fndn Grants, 346
Allyn Fndn Grants, 392
Columbus Fndn Small Grants, 1232
Conservation, Food, and Health Fndn Grants for Developing Countries, 1359
Cowles Charitable Grants, 1392
David Robinson Fndn Grants, 1454
DHHS Adolescent Family Life Demo Projects, 1524
Donald and Sylvia Robinson Family Fndn Grants, 1573
Frances and John L. Loeb Family Grants, 1917
General Service Reproductive Justice Grants, 2007
Health Fndn of Greater Indianapolis Grants, 2282
Huber Fndn Grants, 2382
J.W. Kieckhefer Fndn Grants, 2607
Jacob and Hilda Blaustein Fndn Grants, 2615
James Ford Bell Fndn Grants, 2623
MARPAT Fndn Grants, 3023
Mary Owen Borden Fndn Grants, 3046
Oppenstein Brothers Fndn Grants, 3685
Pasadena Fndn Average Grants, 3741
Perkins Charitable Fndn Grants, 3823
Portland Fndn - Women's Giving Circle Grant, 3935
Radcliffe Inst Individual Residential Fellowships, 4004
Richard and Rhoda Goldman Grants, 4077
Rose Community Child and Family Devel Grants, 4153
S.H. Cowell Fndn Grants, 4199
S. Livingston Mather Charitable Grants, 4200
Saint Luke's Health Inits Grants, 4216
Samuel S. Johnson Fndn Grants, 4239
Scherman Fndn Grants, 4305
Seabury Fndn Grants, 4316
Susan Vaughan Fndn Grants, 4537
Union Benevolent Association Grants, 4710
W. C. Griffith Fndn Grants, 4958
Widgeon Point Charitable Fndn Grants, 5064

Family Practice

Dorothy Rider Pool Health Care Grants, 1589
IYI Responsible Fatherhood Grants, 2591

Family/Marriage Counseling

Adams Family Fndn of Tennessee Grants, 152
Amelia Sillman Rockwell and Carlos Perry Rockwell Charities Grants, 417
Callaway Golf Company Fndn Violence Prevention Grants, 911
Charles H. Pearson Fndn Grants, 1045
Decatur County Community Fndn Small Project Grants, 1477
DHHS Promoting Safe & Stable Families Grants, 1537
Florida BRAIVE Fund of Dade Community, 1846
George W. Wells Fndn Grants, 2030
Gulf Coast Community Operating Grants, 2176
Gulf Coast Fndn of Community Grants, 2177
Olga Sipolin Children's Grants, 3668
Robert R. McCormick Tribune Comm Grants, 4119
Sophia Romero Grants, 4406

Farm and Ranch Management

Bill and Melinda Gates Fndn Agricultural Development Grants, 765
Organic Farming Research Fndn Grants, 3693
Pioneer Hi-Bred Community Grants, 3895
Steward of the Land Award, 4504
USDA Farm Labor Housing Grants, 4809

Farming

Bill and Melinda Gates Fndn Agricultural Development Grants, 765
Chicago Community Trust Health Grants, 1087
MDARD AgD Value Added/Regional Food Systems Grants, 3091
MDARD Specialty Crop Block Grants-Farm Bill, 3093
Merck Family Fund Urban Farming and Youth Leadership Grants, 3119
Monsanto Int'l Grants, 3207
Steward of the Land Award, 4504
Union Bank, N.A. Fndn Grants, 4709
USAID Int'l Food Relief Partnership Grants, 4764
USDA Farmers Market Promotion Grants, 4808

Fashion/Textiles Design

Minnesota State Arts Board Cultural Community Partnership Grants, 3188
Phi Upsilon Omicron Florence Fallgatter Distinguished Service Award, 3877
RISCA Design Innovation Grant, 4097

Fellowship Programs, General

AAAS Science and Technology Policy Fellowships: Energy, Environment, and Agriculture, 52
AAAS Science and Technology Policy Fellowships: Health, Educ and Human Services, 53
Acumen Global Fellowships, 142
APSA Minority Fellowships, 517
ASM Congressional Science Fellowships, 589
Brookdale Fndn Leadership in Aging Fellowships, 844
Carrier Corp Contributions Grants, 946
Charles H. Revson Fndn Grants, 1047
Compton Fndn Int'l Fellowships, 1339
Compton Fndn Mentor Fellowships, 1340
Council on Fndns Emerging Philanthropic Leaders Fellowships, 1378
Durfee Fndn Stanton Fellowship, 1626
Edward W. and Stella C. Van Houten Grants, 1670
Enterprise Comm Partners Terwilliger Fellowship, 1720
Ford Fndn Diversity Fellowships, 1883
Fritz B. Burns Fndn Grants, 1965
Grover Hermann Fndn Grants, 2168
IREX MENA Media TV Production Grants, 2577
Joukowsky Family Fndn Grants, 2743
Lubrizol Fndn Grants, 2933
Lynde and Harry Bradley Fndn Grants, 2947
Lynde and Harry Bradley Fndn Prizes, 2948
MedImmune Charitable Grants, 3108
Mericos Fndn Grants, 3121
NACC David Stevenson Fellowships, 3235
NACC William Diaz Fellowships, 3236
National Endowment for Democracy Visiting Fellows Program, 3253

SUBJECT INDEX

NHLBI Ruth L. Kirschstein National Research Service Awards for Individual Predoctoral Fellowships to Promote Diversity in Health-Related Research, 3419
NHLBI Ruth L. Kirschstein National Research Service Awards for Individual Predoctoral MD/PhD Fellows and Other Dual Degree Fellows, 3420
NHLBI Ruth L. Kirschstein National Research Service Awards for Individual Senior Fellows, 3421
Paul & Daisy Soros Fellows for New Americans, 3754
Phil Hardin Fndn Grants, 3875
Price Family Charitable Grants, 3952
Radcliffe Inst Individual Residential Fellowships, 4004
Rhode Island Fndn Grants, 4073
San Francisco Fndn John Gutmann Photography Fellowship Award, 4279
San Francisco Fndn Multicultural Fellowship, 4281
Siragusa Fndn Health Services & Med Grants, 4368
SSRC-Van Alen Fellowships, 4467
Tulane University Public Service Fellows, 4678
Virginia Humanities Residential Fellowships, 4948
Youth Action Net Fellowships, 5128

Feminism
ALFJ Astraea U.S. General Fund, 362
ANLAF Int'l Fund for Sexual Minorities Grants, 471
Radcliffe Inst Individual Residential Fellowships, 4004

Fencing
USFA Development Grants, 4866
USFA Equipment Subsidy Grants, 4867

Fiction
ALA Romance Writers of America Library Grant, 314
ALA Schneider Family Book Award, 317
Illinois Arts Council Literature Grants, 2470
Kentucky Arts Council Al Smith Fellowship, 2806
Kentucky Arts Council Emerging Artist Award, 2807
Minnesota State Arts Board Cultural Community Partnership Grants, 3188
North Carolina Arts Council Residency Grants, 3481
NYFA Gregory Millard Fellowships, 3565
NYSCA Lit: General Operating Support Grants, 3598
NYSCA Literature: General Support Grants, 3599
PCA Arts Organizations & Grants for Lit, 3781
PCA Entry Track Arts Organizations and Program Grants for Literature, 3793
PCA Strategies for Success Grants - Advanced, 3804
PCA Strategies for Success Grants - Basic Level, 3805
PCA Strategies for Success Grants - Intermediate, 3806

Film Libraries
MacArthur Fndn Chicago Arts and Culture General Operations Grants, 2961

Film Production
ALFJ Astraea U.S. General Fund, 362
Bush Fndn Arts & Humanities Grants: Short-Term Organizational Support, 873
IFP Chicago Production Fund In-Kind Grant, 2446
IFP Minnesota Fresh Filmmakers Grants, 2447
IFP Minnesota McKnight Screenwriters Fellows, 2449
IFP Minnesota TV Grants, 2450
IFP New York State Council on the Arts Electronic Media and Film Program Distribution Grants, 2451
Illinois Arts Council Media Arts Grants, 2472
Jerome Fndn Grants, 2667
Ka Papa O Kakuhihewa Fund, 2785
North Carolina Arts Council Folklife Documentary Project Grants, 3475
North Carolina Arts Council Folklife Grants, 3476
NYFA Gregory Millard Fellowships, 3565
NYSCA Electronic Media and Film: General Exhibition Grants, 3589
NYSCA Electronic Media and Film: General Operating Support, 3590
NYSCA Electronic Media and Film: General Program Support, 3591
NYSCA Electronic Media and Film: Screenings Grants, 3592
NYSCA Elect Media and Film Workspace Grants, 3593

PCA Arts Organizations and Arts Programs Grants for Film and Electronic Media, 3780
PCA Entry Track Arts Organizations and Program Grants for Film and Electronic Media, 3792
Playboy Fndn Grants, 3913
Playboy Fndn Social Change Documentary Film Grants, 3914
San Francisco Bay Area Documentary Grants, 4261
San Francisco Fndn James D. Phelan Award in Film, Video, and Digital Media, 4278
Texas Filmmakers Production Grants, 4595
West Virginia Commission on the Arts Media Arts Grants, 5039

Film Scoring
IFP Chicago Production Fund In-Kind Grant, 2446
IFP Minnesota TV Grants, 2450
Kentucky Arts Council Al Smith Fellowship, 2806
Kentucky Arts Council Emerging Artist Award, 2807

Films
Canada-U.S. Fulbright Mid-Career Grants, 917
CCH Documentary Project Production Grants, 969
CCH Documentary Public Engagement Grants, 970
CCH Documentary Project Research and Development Grants, 971
Community Fndn of Greater Greensboro Grants, 1288
Conseil des arts de Montreal Touring Grants, 1358
IFP Chicago Production Fund In-Kind Grant, 2446
IFP Minnesota Fresh Filmmakers Grants, 2447
IFP Minnesota McKnight Film Fellowships, 2448
IFP Minnesota TV Grants, 2450
MacArthur Fndn Chicago Arts and Culture General Operations Grants, 2961
Massachusetts Fndn for Humanities Grants, 3060
National Endowment for Arts Media Grants, 3264
NYSCA Electronic Media and Film: Film Festivals Grants, 3588
NYSCA Electronic Media and Film: General Exhibition Grants, 3589
NYSCA Electronic Media and Film: General Operating Support, 3590
NYSCA Electronic Media and Film: General Program Support, 3591
NYSCA Electronic Media and Film: Screenings Grants, 3592
NYSCA Electronic Media and Film: Workspace Grants, 3593
Pi Lambda Theta Anna Tracey Memorial Award, 3889
Playboy Fndn Social Change Documentary Film Grants, 3914
San Francisco Bay Area Documentary Grants, 4261
Texas Commission on the Arts Cultural Connections-Visual & Media Arts Touring Exhibits Grants, 4589
Texas Filmmakers Production Grants, 4595
Third Millennium Fndn Grants, 4607
Time Warner Youth Media & Creative Grants, 4636

Finance
Bill and Melinda Gates Fndn Financial Services for the Poor Grants, 767
Colgate-Palmolive Company Grants, 1202
Community Development Financial Inst Bank Enterprise Awards, 1244
CUNA Mutual Group Fndn Grants, 1417
Enterprise Community Partners MetLife Fndn Awards for Excellence in Affordable Housing, 1717
FINRA Investor Educ Fndn Financial Educ in Your Community Grants, 1815
FINRA Smart Investing@Your Library Grants, 1816
Fndn for the Mid South Wealth Building Grants, 1900
Hartford Fndn Nonprofit Support Grants, 2252
Intel Finance Internships, 2563
John R. Oishei Fndn Grants, 2709
Lincoln Financial Group Fndn Grants, 2906
Lumity Technology Leadership Award, 2940
NAR HOPE Awards for Minority Owners, 3238
NASE Growth Grants, 3242
Nevada Arts Council Residency Express Grants, 3315
Nonprofit Management Grants, 3458

North Carolina Arts Council Community Arts Administration Internship, 3471
North Dakota Council on the Arts Instal Support Grants, 3496
Paul and Mary Haas Fndn Contributions and Student Scholarships, 3756
Social Justice Fund NW Criminal Justice Giving Project Grants, 4394

Financial Aid (Scholarships and Loans)
Alfred and Tillie Shemanski Testamentary Grants, 363
Barrasso Usdin Kupperman Freeman and Sarver LLC Corp Grants, 675
Brooklyn Community Fndn Community Development Grants, 850
Crown Point Community Fndn Scholarships, 1403
Edward W. and Stella C. Van Houten Grants, 1670
Frank and Lydia Bergen Fndn Grants, 1925
Greygates Fndn Grants, 2164
Gulf Coast Fndn of Community Scholarships, 2178
J. Willard Marriott, Jr. Fndn Grants, 2610
Jim Blevins Fndn Scholarships, 2679
John H. Wellons Fndn Grants, 2699
Judge Isaac Anderson, Jr. Scholarship, 2754
K21 Health Fndn Cancer Care Grants, 2759
Marathon Petroleum Corp Grants, 2999
Morgan Babcock Scholarships, 3217
Seattle Fndn Doyne M. Green Scholarships, 4324
Sioux Falls Area Community Fndn Field-of-Interest and Donor-Advised Grants, 4365
Thomas B. & Elizabeth M. Sheridan Grants, 4614
W.P. and Bulah Luse Fndn Grants, 4965

Financial Education
Abbey Charitable Grants, 78
ACF Assets for Indep Individual Development Account Grants, 115
Arizona Women Deborah G. Carstens Grants, 543
Bill and Melinda Gates Fndn Financial Services for the Poor Grants, 767
Citigroup Fndn Grants, 1139
Financial Capability Innovation Fund II Grants, 1811
FINRA Investor Educ Fndn Financial Educ in Your Community Grants, 1815
FINRA Smart Investing@Your Library Grants, 1816
Greater Worcester Community Youth for Community Improvement Grants, 2144
Hampton Roads Community Fndn Health and Human Service Grants, 2216
ING Fndn Grants, 2555
Johnson Scholarship Fndn Grants, 2726
Joseph S. Stackpole Charitable Grants, 2741
KeyBank Fndn Grants, 2820
McCune Charitable Fndn Grants, 3077
McGraw-Hill Companies Community Grants, 3081
Meyer Fndn Economic Security Grants, 3141
Montana Community Fndn Women's Grants, 3212
New York Life Fndn Grants, 3341
State Farm Companies Safe Neighbors Grants, 4484
TCF Bank Fndn Grants, 4565

Financial Literature
African American Fund of New Jersey Grants, 192
Allstate Fndn Economic Empowerment Grants, 389
Alvin and Fanny Blaustein Thalheimer Grants, 403
Arizona Women Deborah G. Carstens Grants, 543
BBVA Compass Fndn Charitable Grants, 703
Benton Community Fndn - The Cookie Jar Grant, 729
Bill and Melinda Gates Fndn Financial Services for the Poor Grants, 767
Blue Cross Blue Shield of Minnesota Fndn - Healthy Equity: Public Libraries for Health Grants, 797
Chicago Community Trust Housing Grants: Advancing Affordable Rental Housing, 1088
Chicago Community Trust Housing Grants: Preserving Home Ownership and Preventing Foreclosure, 1089
Chicago Community Trust Housing Grants: Preventing and Ending Homelessness, 1090
CNCS AmeriCorps State and National Grants, 1182
CNCS AmeriCorps VISTA Project Grants, 1184

906 / Financial Literature

Community Fndn of Boone Cty Adult Lit Grants, 1272
Financial Capability Innovation Fund II Grants, 1811
FINRA Investor Educ Fndn Financial Educ in Your Community Grants, 1815
FINRA Smart Investing@Your Library Grants, 1816
Fndn for the Mid South Wealth Building Grants, 1900
GNOF Coastal 5 + 1 Grants, 2070
Hampton Roads Community Fndn Health and Human Service Grants, 2216
Hearst Fndns Social Service Grants, 2285
Household Int'l Corp Giving Grants, 2372
IIE Western Union Family Scholarships, 2462
Johnson Scholarship Fndn Grants, 2726
Joseph S. Stackpole Charitable Grants, 2741
KeyBank Fndn Grants, 2820
Maine Women's Fund Economic Security Grants, 2992
Marin Community Fndn Ending the Cycle of Poverty Grants, 3011
McGraw-Hill Companies Community Grants, 3081
Medtronic Fndn Community Link Human Services Grants, 3112
Meyer Fndn Economic Security Grants, 3141
Middlesex Savings Charitable Fndn Ed Opportunities Grants, 3174
Robin Hood Fndn Grants, 4125
Union Bank, N.A. Fndn Grants, 4709

Fine Arts
Abel and Sophia Sheng Charitable Fndn Grants, 86
Abell-Hanger Fndn Grants, 91
Achelis Fndn Grants, 127
ALA Stonewall Book Awards - Israel Fishman Nonfiction Award, 330
Alliant Energy Fndn Community Grants, 384
ArtsWave Impact Grants, 580
ArtsWave Project Grants, 581
Berks County Community Fndn Grants, 734
Bodenwein Public Benevolent Fndn Grants, 806
Bodman Fndn Grants, 807
Charles H. Hall Fndn, 1044
CICF Clare Noyes Grant, 1119
CICF F.R. Hensel Grant for Fine Arts, Music, and Educ, 1121
Claremont Community Fndn Grants, 1149
Clowes Grants, 1177
Con Edison Corp Arts and Culture Grants, 1344
Crystelle Waggoner Charitable Grants, 1405
E.L. Wiegand Fndn Grants, 1639
Elizabeth Morse Genius Charitable Grants, 1682
Fleishhacker Fndn Educ Grants, 1838
George A. and Grace L. Long Fndn Grants, 2008
George H.C. Ensworth Grants, 2022
Hahl Proctor Charitable Grants, 2208
Hall Family Fndn Grants, 2210
Helen Gertrude Sparks Charitable Grants, 2294
Helen Pumphrey Denit Charitable Grants, 2297
Henrietta Lange Burk Grants, 2303
Jerry L. and Barbara J. Burris Fndn Grants, 2669
John W. Speas and Effie E. Speas Grants, 2732
Joyce Fndn Culture Grants, 2747
Katrine Menzing Deakins Charitable Grants, 2793
Leon and Thea Koerner Fndn Grants, 2883
Lewis H. Humphreys Charitable Grants, 2889
Lied Fndn Grants, 2900
Louis and Elizabeth Nave Flarsheim Charitable Fndn Grants, 2924
Lumpkin Family Healthy People Grants, 2942
MacArthur Fndn Chicago Arts and Culture Int'l Connections Grants, 2962
Marietta McNeill Morgan and Samuel Tate Morgan, Jr. Grants, 3008
Marion Gardner Jackson Charitable Grants, 3017
NHSCA Cultural Facilities Grants: Barrier Free Access for All, 3426
NJSCA Arts Project Support, 3446
NJSCA General Program Support Grants, 3449
NYSCA Architecture, Planning, and Design: General Program Support Grants, 3574
NYSCA Architecture, Planning, and Design: Project Support Grants, 3576

NYSCA Arts Educ: Community-based Learning Grants, 3577
NYSCA Arts Educ: General Operating Support, 3578
NYSCA Arts Educ Program Support Grants, 3579
NYSCA Arts Educ: K-12 In-School Grants, 3580
NYSCA Arts Educ: Services to the Field Grants, 3582
NYSCA Dance Gen Operating Support Grants, 3584
NYSCA Dance Gen Program Support Grants, 3585
NYSCA Dance: Long-Term Residency in New York State Grants, 3586
NYSCA Dance: Services to the Field Grants, 3587
NYSCA Special Art Services Project Support, 3613
NYSCA State and Local Partnerships: General Operating Support Grants, 3619
NYSCA State and Local Partnerships: General Program Support Grants, 3620
NYSCA State and Local Partnerships: Services to the Field Grants, 3621
Owens Corning Fndn Grants, 3717
PCA-PCD Professional Development for Individual Artists Grants, 3770
PCA Busing Grants, 3786
PCA Pennsylvania Partners in the Arts Program Stream Grants, 3801
PCA Pennsylvania Partners in the Arts Project Stream Grants, 3802
PCA Strategies for Success Grants - Basic Level, 3805
PCA Strategies for Success Grants - Intermediate, 3806
PennPAT Artist Technical Assistance Grants, 3811
PennPAT Strategic Opportunity Grants, 3815
Phoenix Coyotes Charities Grants, 3879
Puerto Rico Community Fndn Grants, 3986
R.C. Baker Fndn Grants, 3999
RISCA Professional Arts Development Grants, 4099
Robert R. Meyer Fndn Grants, 4121
Stinson Fndn Grants, 4506
Texas Commission on the Arts Cultural Connections- Visual & Media Arts Touring Exhibits Grants, 4589
Time Warner Youth Media & Creative Grants, 4636
Viacom Fndn Grants (Formerly CBS Fndn), 4932
Virginia Commission for the Arts Project Grants, 4944
VSA/Volkswagen of America Exhibition Awards, 4954
W. Paul and Lucille Caudill Little Fndn Grants, 4966

Fire
AMERIND Poster Contest, 454
Fireman's Fund Insurance Heritage Grants, 1818
Illinois DNR Volunteer Fire Assistance Grants, 2504
NFF Matching Grants, 3344

Fire Prevention
100 Club of Arizona Benefit Grants, 25
100 Club of Arizona Safety Enhancement Stipends, 26
Adler-Clark Electric Comm Commitment Grants, 164
AMERIND Poster Contest, 454
Burlington Northern Santa Fe Fndn Grants, 866
ConocoPhillips Grants, 1355
DHS ARRA Fire Station Construction Grants, 1542
FEMA Assistance to Firefighters Grants, 1802
FEMA Staffing for Adequate Fire and Emergency Response Grants, 1803
Fireman's Fund Insurance Heritage Grants, 1818
Francis T. & Louise T. Nichols Fndn Grants, 1923
GEICO Public Service Awards, 1997
Hundred Club of Palm Springs Grants, 2397
Hundred Club of Santa Clara County Grants, 2399
Illinois DNR Volunteer Fire Assistance Grants, 2504
Martin C. Kauffman 100 Club of Alameda County Survivor Benefits Grants, 3028
NFF Collaboration Support Grants, 3342
RCF General Community Grants, 4032
Seneca Foods Fndn Grants, 4336
Thompson Charitable Fndn Grants, 4622

Firearms
Joyce Fndn Gun Violence Prevention Grants, 2751
NRA Fndn Grants, 3517

Fish and Fisheries
Chesapeake Bay Fisheries & Headwaters Grants, 1070
Curtis and Edith Munson Fndn Grants, 1418

SUBJECT INDEX

FishAmerica Fndn Chesapeake Bay Grants, 1827
FishAmerica Fndn Conservation Grants, 1828
FishAmerica Fndn Marine and Anadromous Fish Habitat Restoration Grants, 1829
FishAmerica Fndn Research Grants, 1830
Fisheries and Habitat Partnership Grants, 1834
GNOF Bayou Communities Grants, 2069
GNOF Coastal 5 + 1 Grants, 2070
GNOF Gulf Coast Oil Spill Grants, 2077
GNOF Plaquemines Community Grants, 2091
GNOF St. Bernard Community Grants, 2092
Great Lakes Fishery Trust Access Grants, 2145
HRF Hudson River Improvement Grants, 2378
Indiana Clean Vessel Act Grants, 2535
MDEQ Coastal Management Planning and Construction Grants, 3097
MDEQ Great Lakes Areas of Concern Land Acquisition Grants, 3099
NFWF Bring Back the Natives Grants, 3359
NFWF California Coastal Restoration Grants, 3362
NFWF Chesapeake Bay Conservation Grants, 3363
NFWF Chesapeake Bay Stewardship Fund Small Watershed Grants, 3364
NFWF Chesapeake Targeted Watershed Grants, 3365
NFWF Columbia Basin Water Trans Grants, 3366
NFWF Columbia River Estuarine Coastal Grant, 3367
NFWF Community Salmon Fund Partnerships, 3368
NFWF Freshwater Fish Conservation Init Grants, 3374
NFWF King County Community Salmon Grants, 3375
NFWF One Fly Conservation Partnerships, 3382
NFWF Oregon Governor's Environment Grants, 3383
NFWF Pacific Grassroots Salmonid Init Grants, 3384
NFWF Pierce Community Salmon Grant, 3385
NFWF Pioneers in Conservation Grants, 3386
NFWF Radical Salmon Design Contest, 3388
NFWF Salmon Recovery Funding Board Community Salmon Grants, 3389
NFWF Seafarer's Environmental Educ Grants, 3390
NFWF Shell Marine Habitat Grants, 3391
NFWF Southern Co Longleaf Legacy Grants, 3392
NFWF State Comprehensive Wildlife Conservation Support Grants, 3395
NFWF Sustain Our Great Lakes Grants, 3396
NFWF Tampa Bay Environmental Grants, 3397
NFWF Upper Mississippi Riv Watershed Grants, 3398
North American Wetlands Conservation Grants, 3465
NW Fund for the Environment Grants, 3510
Royal Caribbean Cruises Ocean Fund, 4165
Sailors' Snug Harbor of Boston Fishing Communities Init Grants, 4212
USDC/NOAA American Rivers Community-Based Restoration Program River Grants, 4845
USDC/NOAA Open Rivers Init Grants, 4847
WWF Int'l Smart Gear Competition, 5120

Fitness
ACF Native American Social and Economic Development Strategies Grants, 123
BCBSNC Fndn Fit Together Grants, 711
BCBSNC Fndn Grants, 712
Boeing Company Contributions Grants, 809
Collective Brands Fndn Grants, 1206
Fndn for a Healthy Kentucky Grants, 1891
General Mills Fndn Celebrating Communities of Color Grants, 2002
GNOF IMPACT Kahn-Oppenheim Grants, 2084
Mary Black Fndn Active Living Grants, 3031
Medtronic Fndn CommunityLink Health Grants, 3111
PepsiCo Fndn Grants, 3819
RCF Summertime Kids Grants, 4034
Robert R. Meyer Fndn Grants, 4121
Ruth Mott Fndn Grants, 4180
Special Olympics Project UNIFY Grants, 4449

Folk Medicine
North Carolina Arts Council Folklife Documentary Project Grants, 3475
North Carolina Arts Council Folklife Grants, 3476
Virginia Fndn for Humanities Discr Grants, 4946
Virginia Fndn for the Humanities Open Grants, 4947

Folk Music

ArtsWave Impact Grants, 580
Charles Parker Trust for Public Music Grants, 1053
Florida Div of Cultural Affairs Folk Arts Grants, 1853
Florida Div of Cultural Affairs Music Grants, 1859
Nevada Arts Council Folklife Opps Grants, 3310
NJSCA Folk Arts Apprenticeships, 3448
North Carolina Arts Council Folklife Internship, 3467
North Carolina Arts Council Folklife Documentary Project Grants, 3475
North Carolina Arts Council Folklife Grants, 3476
NYSCA Folk Arts: General Program Support, 3595
NYSCA Folk Arts: Presentation Grants, 3596
NYSCA Special Art Services Project Support, 3613
NYSCA Special Arts Services: Professional Performances Grants, 3617
PennPAT Strategic Opportunity Grants, 3815
Richard and Caroline T. Gwathmey Grants, 4075
Virginia Fndn for Humanities Discr Grants, 4946
Virginia Fndn for the Humanities Open Grants, 4947

Folk/Ethnic Arts

AEGON Transamerica Arts and Culture Grants, 176
Alaska State Council on the Arts Operating Support Grants, 328
Arizona Comm on the Arts Folklorist Residencies, 537
Arizona Commission on the Arts Individual Artist Residencies, 538
Arkansas Arts Council AIE After School/Summer Residency Grants, 551
Arkansas Arts Council AIE In-School Residency, 553
ArtsWave Impact Grants, 580
ArtsWave Project Grants, 581
Community Fndn of Western N Carolina Grants, 1327
Delaware Division of the Arts Opportunity Grants-Artists, 1489
Florida Div of Cultural Affairs Folk Arts Grants, 1853
Florida Div of Cultural Affairs General Program Support Grants, 1854
Florida Div of Cultural Affairs Multidisciplinary Grants, 1857
George J. and Effie L. Seay Fndn Grants, 2024
Georgia Council for the Arts Project Grants, 2037
Illinois Arts Council Arts-in-Education Residency Grants, 2463
Illinois Arts Council Ethnic & Folk Arts Master Apprentice Grants, 2468
Illinois Arts Council Ethnic & Folk Arts Grants, 2469
Iowa Arts Council Artists in Schools/Communities Residency Grants, 2571
Kentucky Arts Council Folk and Traditional Arts Apprenticeship Grant, 2808
Massachusetts Cultural Adams Arts Grants, 3052
Minnesota State Arts Board Cultural Community Partnership Grants, 3188
Montana Arts Council Cultural and Aesthetic Project Grants, 3209
National Endowment for the Arts - National Arts and Humanities Youth Program Awards, 3255
National Endowment for the Arts - Regional Partnership Agreement Grants, 3258
National Endowment for Arts Media Grants, 3264
National Endowment for the Arts Presenting Grants: Art Works, 3268
Nevada Arts Council Folklife Apprenticeships, 3309
Nevada Arts Council Folklife Opps Grants, 3310
NHSCA Artist Residencies in Schools Grants, 3423
NHSCA Traditional Arts Apprenticeships, 3429
NHSCA Youth Arts Project Grants: For Extended Arts Learning, 3430
NJSCA Arts Project Support, 3446
NJSCA Financial and Instal Stabilization Grants, 3447
NJSCA Folk Arts Apprenticeships, 3448
NJSCA General Program Support Grants, 3449
North Carolina Arts Council Folklife Internship, 3467
North Carolina Arts Council Folklife Documentary Project Grants, 3475
North Carolina Arts Council Folklife Grants, 3476
NYSCA Folk Arts: Exhibitions Grants, 3594
NYSCA Folk Arts: General Program Support, 3595
NYSCA Folk Arts: Presentation Grants, 3596
NYSCA Folk Arts: Regional and County Folk Arts Grants, 3597
NYSCA Special Art Services Project Support, 3613
NYSCA Special Arts Services: General Operating Support Grants, 3614
NYSCA Special Arts Services: General Program Support Grants, 3615
NYSCA Special Arts Services: Instruction and Training Grants, 3616
NYSCA Special Arts Services: Professional Performances Grants, 3617
NYSCA State and Local Partnerships: General Operating Support Grants, 3619
NYSCA State and Local Partnerships: Services to the Field Grants, 3621
Ohio Arts Council Traditional Arts Apprenticeship Grants, 3655
PCA-PCD Professional Development for Individual Artists Grants, 3770
PCA Arts in Educ Residencies, 3772
PCA Arts Organizations and Arts Programs Grants for Arts Service Organizations, 3777
PCA Arts Organizations and Arts Programs Grants for Traditional and Folk Arts, 3784
PCA Busing Grants, 3786
PCA Entry Track Arts Organizations and Program Grants for Arts Service Organizations, 3789
PCA Entry Track Arts Organizations and Program Grants for Traditional and Folk Arts, 3798
PCA Pennsylvania Partners in the Arts Program Stream Grants, 3801
PCA Pennsylvania Partners in the Arts Project Stream Grants, 3802
PCA Professional Development Grants, 3803
PCA Strategies for Success Grants - Basic Level, 3805
PCA Strategies for Success Grants - Intermediate, 3806
PennPAT Artist Technical Assistance Grants, 3811
PennPAT Strategic Opportunity Grants, 3815
Phoenix Coyotes Charities Grants, 3879
Rasmuson Fndn Individual Artists Awards, 4022
RISCA Folk Arts Apprenticeships, 4098
South Carolina Arts Comm Accessibility Grants, 4410
South Carolina Arts Commission Folklife & Traditional Arts Grants, 4421
South Carolina Arts Commission Traditional Arts Apprenticeship Grants, 4427
Southern New England Folk and Traditional Arts Apprenticeship Grants, 4438
TAC Arts Access Grant, 4549
Virginia Commission for the Arts Project Grants, 4944
Virginia Fndn for Humanities Discr Grants, 4946
Virginia Fndn for the Humanities Open Grants, 4947

Folklore and Mythology

Alabama Humanities Fndn Mini Grants, 231
Alabama Humanities Planning/Consultant Grants, 232
Canada-U.S. Fulbright Mid-Career Grants, 917
Florida Div of Cultural Affairs Folk Arts Grants, 1853
Florida Humanities Council Mini Grants, 1869
Montana Arts Council Cultural and Aesthetic Project Grants, 3209
North Carolina Arts Council Folklife Documentary Project Grants, 3475
NYHC Major and Mini Grants, 3567
Virginia Fndn for Humanities Discr Grants, 4946
Virginia Fndn for the Humanities Open Grants, 4947

Food Banks

A Charitable Fndn Grants, 126
Adams Family Fndn of Tennessee Grants, 152
Adams Fndn Grants, 155
Adelaide Dawson Lynch Grants, 163
Adler-Clark Electric Community Commitment Fndn Grants, 164
Albert W. Rice Charitable Fndn Grants, 347
Alfred E. Chase Charitable Fndn Grants, 366
Anthony R. Abraham Fndn Grants, 489
Aragona Family Fndn Grants, 522
Arizona Community Fndn Grants, 540
Arthur Ashley Williams Fndn Grants, 572
Back Home Again Fndn Grants, 633
Batchelor Fndn Grants, 679
Caesar Puff Fndn Grants, 890
Caesars Fndn Grants, 891
Callaway Golf Company Fndn Grants, 910
Campbell Soup Fndn Grants, 916
Carl M. Freeman Fndn FACES Grants, 932
Carrie Estelle Doheny Fndn Grants, 945
Catherine Kennedy Home Fndn Grants, 955
Cessna Fndn Grants, 1000
CFFVR Capital Credit Union Charitable Giving, 1005
CFFVR Jewelers Mutual Charitable Giving, 1014
Charles H. Farnsworth Grants, 1043
Charles H. Pearson Fndn Grants, 1045
Charles Nelson Robinson Grants, 1052
Chicago Community Trust Preventing and Eliminating Hunger Grants, 1092
CICF Christmas Fund, 1117
CICF Senior Grants, 1127
Corina Higginson Grants, 1373
Daphne Seybolt Culpeper Memorial Fndn Grants, 1445
Delaware Community Fndn Youth Philanthropy Board for New Castle County Grants, 1486
Denver Fndn Community Grants, 1502
Donald W. Reynolds Fndn Charitable Food Distribution Grants, 1575
Doree Taylor Charitable Fndn, 1580
Dr. and Mrs. Paul Pierce Memorial Fndn Grants, 1599
Edina Realty Fndn Grants, 1656
Frank B. Hazard General Charity Grants, 1926
Frank Reed and Margaret Jane Peters Memorial Fund II Grants, 1934
Frank Stanley Beveridge Fndn Grants, 1936
George W. Wells Fndn Grants, 2030
GNOF Gulf Coast Oil Spill Grants, 2077
Green Bay Packers Fndn Grants, 2148
H.J. Heinz Company Fndn Grants, 2184
Harold Brooks Fndn Grants, 2227
Hearst Fndns Social Service Grants, 2285
Helen Gertrude Sparks Charitable Grants, 2294
Indep Community Fndn Community Quality of Life Grant, 2525
Kathryne Beynon Fndn Grants, 2791
Kenneth T. and Eileen L. Norris Fndn Grants, 2802
Kroger Fndn Hunger Relief Grants, 2844
Land O'Lakes Fndn Community Grants, 2859
Lincoln Financial Group Fndn Grants, 2906
Lydia deForest Charitable Grants, 2946
MacDonald-Peterson Fndn Grants, 2965
Marsh Corp Grants, 3027
Maurice J. Masserini Charitable Grants, 3064
McCarthy Family Fndn Grants, 3073
Merck Family Fund Urban Farming and Youth Leadership Grants, 3119
Middlesex Savings Charitable Fndn Community Development Grants, 3173
Monsanto Int'l Grants, 3207
Norfolk Southern Fndn Grants, 3463
NW Mutual Fndn Grants, 3509
Olga Sipolin Children's Grants, 3668
Ordean Fndn Grants, 3691
Packard Fndn Local Grants, 3729
Pinnacle Entertainment Fndn Grants, 3893
Pott Fndn Grants, 3940
Procter and Gamble Grants, 3967
Project Orange Thumb Grants, 3972
Reinberger Fndn Grants, 4052
Samuel S. Johnson Fndn Grants, 4239
Shaw's Supermarkets Donations, 4342
Sierra Health Fndn Responsive Grants, 4353
Sisters of Charity Fndn of Cleveland Good Samaritan Grants, 4373
Sobrato Family Fndn Grants, 4389
Sobrato Family Fndn Meeting Space Grants, 4390
Sobrato Family Fndn Office Space Grants, 4391
Stewart Huston Charitable Grants, 4505
Swindells Charitable Fndn, 4542
Textron Corp Contributions Grants, 4601
USAID Int'l Food Relief Partnership Grants, 4764

Vancouver Fndn Grants & Comm Inits, 4900
William Blair and Company Fndn Grants, 5078
William Robert Baird Charitable Grants, 5093
Wood-Claeyssens Fndn Grants, 5113

Food Consumption
Aetna Fndn Regional Health Grants, 187
Charles H. Hall Fndn, 1044
Coca-Cola Fndn Grants, 1195
Johnson Controls Fndn Health and Social Services Grants, 2722

Food Distribution
Albertson's Charitable Giving Grants, 345
Albert W. Rice Charitable Fndn Grants, 347
Amon G. Carter Fndn Grants, 458
Arizona Republic Newspaper Contributions, 547
Bacon Family Fndn Grants, 634
Benton Community Fndn Grants, 730
Blue River Community Fndn Grants, 801
Brown County Community Fndn Grants, 853
Caesars Fndn Grants, 891
Catherine Kennedy Home Fndn Grants, 955
Charles H. Pearson Fndn Grants, 1045
Chicago Community Trust Health Grants, 1087
Chicago Community Trust Preventing and Eliminating Hunger Grants, 1092
Christine and Katharina Pauly Charitable Grants, 1114
Cisco Systems Fndn San Jose Community Grants, 1137
Clark Fndn Grants, 1157
Commission on Religion in Appalachia Grants, 1238
Community Fndn of Bartholomew County Heritage Grants, 1267
Community Fndn of Bartholomew County James A. Henderson Award for Fundraising, 1268
Community Fndn of Greater Fort Wayne - Community Endowment and Clarke Endowment Grants, 1285
Community Fndn of Middle Tennessee Grants, 1300
Conservation, Food, and Health Fndn Grants for Developing Countries, 1359
Darden Restaurants Fndn Grants, 1446
David Lane Grants for Aged & Indigent Women, 1453
DeKalb County Community Fndn - Immediate Response Grant, 1479
DeRoy Testamentary Fndn Grants, 1518
Donald and Sylvia Robinson Family Fndn Grants, 1573
Donald W. Reynolds Fndn Charitable Food Distribution Grants, 1575
Doris and Victor Day Fndn Grants, 1582
Florence Hunt Maxwell Health Grants, 1844
Frank Reed and Margaret Jane Peters Memorial Fund II Grants, 1934
Garden Crusader Award, 1985
General Mills Fndn Grants, 2003
George W. Wells Fndn Grants, 2030
Giant Food Charitable Grants, 2050
GNOF Gulf Coast Oil Spill Grants, 2077
Harris Graduate School of Public Policy Studies Research Development Grants, 2232
Harris Teeter Corp Contributions Grants, 2235
Harry Chapin Fndn Grants, 2240
Helen Gertrude Sparks Charitable Grants, 2294
Horace Moses Charitable Fndn Grants, 2363
John Edward Fowler Memorial Fndn Grants, 2693
John G. Martin Fndn Grants, 2696
Johnson Controls Fndn Health and Social Services Grants, 2722
Ken W. Davis Fndn Grants, 2813
Land O'Lakes Fndn Community Grants, 2859
Lucy Downing Nisbet Charitable Grants, 2935
Marsh Corp Grants, 3027
McGregor Grants, 3082
Merck Family Fund Urban Farming and Youth Leadership Grants, 3119
Microsoft Comm Affairs Puget Sound Grants, 3163
Needmor Grants, 3289
NYCT Grants for the Elderly, 3549
Olga Sipolin Children's Grants, 3668
OneFamily Fndn Grants, 3673
PepsiCo Fndn Grants, 3819

Prince Charitable Trusts D.C. Grants, 3960
Robert R. Meyer Fndn Grants, 4121
Rockefeller Fndn Grants, 4138
Seagate Tech Corp Capacity to Care Grants, 4317
Sensient Technologies Fndn Grants, 4337
Share Our Strength Grants, 4340
Sid W. Richardson Fndn Grants, 4350
Sioux Falls Area Community Fndn Field-of-Interest and Donor-Advised Grants, 4365
Starr Fndn Grants, 4483
The World Food Prize, 4606
Thomas C. Ackerman Fndn Grants, 4615
Tri-County Electric People Grants, 4665
USAID African Innovation Mechanism Grants, 4739
USAID Int'l Food Relief Partnership Grants, 4764
USAID Palestinian Comm Assistance Grants, 4773
USDA Child and Adult Care Food Program, 4800
USDA Community Food Projects Grants, 4802
USDA Fed-State Marketing Improvement Grants, 4810
USDA Foreign Market Development Grants, 4811
USDA Market Access Grants, 4818
W.K. Kellogg Fndn Healthy Kids Grants, 4961
William S. Abell Fndn Grants, 5094

Food Engineering
USAID Int'l Food Relief Partnership Grants, 4764

Food Labeling
HAF Co-op Community Grants, 2192

Food Management
Adolph Coors Fndn Grants, 171
USAID Grants for Building Disaster-Resilient Communities in Southern Africa, 4755

Food Processing
HAF Co-op Community Grants, 2192
Institute for Agriculture and Trade Policy Food and Society Fellowships, 2561

Food Production
MDARD AgD Value Added/Regional Food Systems Grants, 3091
USAID Grants for Building Disaster-Resilient Communities in Southern Africa, 4755

Food Safety
AAAS Science and Technology Policy Fellowships: Health, Educ and Human Services, 53
Aetna Fndn Regional Health Grants, 187
Chefs Move to Schools Grants, 1066
Dean Foods Community Involvement Grants, 1469
GNOF Gulf Coast Oil Spill Grants, 2077
HAF Co-op Community Grants, 2192
MDARD AgD Value Added/Regional Food Systems Grants, 3091
PepsiCo Fndn Grants, 3819
Sara Lee Fndn Grants, 4296
The World Food Prize, 4606
USDA Hispanic-Serving Insts Educ Grants, 4813

Food Sciences
Chefs Move to Schools Grants, 1066
Coca-Cola Fndn Grants, 1195
Harry Chapin Fndn Grants, 2240
Phi Upsilon Omicron Florence Fallgatter Distinguished Service Award, 3877
Phi Upsilon Omicron Frances Morton Holbrook Alumni Award, 3878
The World Food Prize, 4606
USDA Hispanic-Serving Insts Educ Grants, 4813
USDA Special Research Grants, 4839

Food Service Industry
Adler-Clark Electric Community Commitment Fndn Grants, 164
American Express Charitable Grants, 429
Chefs Move to Schools Grants, 1066
Circle K Corp Contributions Grants, 1136

Food Stamps
Chicago Community Trust Health Grants, 1087
Chicago Community Trust Preventing and Eliminating Hunger Grants, 1092

Food Technology
CLIF Bar Family Fndn Grants, 1173
USAID Grants for Building Disaster-Resilient Communities in Southern Africa, 4755

Foods
ACFEF Disaster Relief Fund Member Assistance, 117
Annie's Cases for Causes Product Donations, 479
Chefs Move to Schools Grants, 1066
CLIF Bar Family Fndn Grants, 1173
Columbus Fndn Traditional Grants, 1233
ConAgra Foods Community Impact Grants, 1342
ConAgra Foods Nourish Our Comm Grants, 1343
Dean Foods Community Involvement Grants, 1469
Essex County Community Fndn Merrimack Valley General Grants, 1756
Institute for Agriculture and Trade Policy Food and Society Fellowships, 2561
Marriott Int'l Corp Giving Grants, 3024
Seneca Foods Fndn Grants, 4336
Simmons Fndn Grants, 4360
Slow Food in Schools Micro-Grants, 4384
USAID African Innovation Mechanism Grants, 4739
USAID Food Security, Nutrition, Biodiversity and Conservation Grants, 4752
USAID Grants for Building Disaster-Resilient Communities in Southern Africa, 4755
USAID Int'l Emergency Food Assistance Grants, 4763
USAID Int'l Food Relief Partnership Grants, 4764
USDA Special Research Grants, 4839

Football
Arizona Cardinals Grants, 534
Atlanta Falcons Youth Fndn Grants, 607
Green Bay Packers Fndn Grants, 2148
LISC NFL Grassroots Grants, 2913
Viking Children's Grants, 4939

Foreign Languages
Alabama Humanities Fndn Mini Grants, 231
Alabama Humanities Planning/Consultant Grants, 232
IIE Eurobank EFG Scholarships, 2455
IIE Leonora Lindsley Memorial Fellowships, 2458
Wisconsin Humanities Council Major Grants, 5107

Foreign Languages Education
Alavi Fndn Grants, 335
IIE David L. Boren Fellowships, 2454
IIE Leonora Lindsley Memorial Fellowships, 2458
Whirlpool Fndn Grants, 5056

Forest Ecology
American Forests Global ReLeaf Grants, 434
EPA Environmental Justice Small Grants, 1732
GNOF Plaquemines Community Grants, 2091
Illinois DNR Urban & Comm Forestry Grants, 2503
ISA John Z. Duling Grants, 2587
NFWF Upper Mississippi Riv Watershed Grants, 3398
Orchard Fndn Grants, 3690
Ross Fndn Grants, 4164

Forest Economics
Illinois DNR Urban & Comm Forestry Grants, 2503
ISA John Z. Duling Grants, 2587

Forest Products Industry
Green Diamond Charitable Contributions, 2149
USDA Fed-State Marketing Improvement Grants, 4810
Weyerhaeuser Company Fndn Grants, 5053

Forestry
Illinois DNR Urban & Comm Forestry Grants, 2503
Int'l Paper Company Fndn Grants, 2568
Maine Community Fndn Baldwin Area Grants, 2974
USAID Global Development Alliance Grants, 4753

SUBJECT INDEX

Forestry Management
Community Fndn of Western N Carolina Grants, 1327
Great Lakes Protection Grants, 2147
Illinois DNR Urban & Comm Forestry Grants, 2503
ISA John Z. Duling Grants, 2587
NFWF Upper Mississippi Riv Watershed Grants, 3398
Rose Fndn for Comm & the Environment N California Environmental Grassroots Grants, 4158
Wallace Global Grants, 4977

Forestry/Forest Sciences
NFF Community Assistance Grants, 3343

Forests and Woodlands
Ambrose and Ida Fredrickson Fndn Grants, 414
American Forests Global ReLeaf Grants, 434
Callaway Fndn Grants, 909
Eugene B. Casey Fndn Grants, 1762
Freeman Fndn Grants, 1952
Green Diamond Charitable Contributions, 2149
Illinois DNR Urban & Comm Forestry Grants, 2503
Jenifer Altman Fndn Grants, 2662
John D. and Catherine T. MacArthur Fndn Global Challenges Grants, 2690
MacArthur Fndn Conservation and Sustainable Development Grants, 2963
NFF Collaboration Support Grants, 3342
NFF Community Assistance Grants, 3343
NFF Matching Grants, 3344
NFF Mid-Capacity Assistance Grants, 3345
NFF Wilderness Stewardship Grants, 3346
NFWF Upper Mississippi Riv Watershed Grants, 3398
NW Fund for the Environment Grants, 3510
Partnership Enhancement Grants, 3740
Rose Fndn for Comm & the Environment N California Environmental Grassroots Grants, 4158
WestWind Fndn Environment Grants, 5052
Weyerhaeuser Company Fndn Grants, 5053
Wilburforce Fndn Grants, 5067

Fossil Fuels
David Bohnett Fndn Grants, 1451
NFF Collaboration Support Grants, 3342
NFF Matching Grants, 3344
William & Flora Hewlett Environmental Grants, 5074

Fossil Fuels, Coal
Illinois DCEO Coal Revival Grants, 2487

Fossil Fuels, Natural Gas
PSEG Environmental Educ Grants, 3980

Foster Care
ABC Charities Grants, 85
Alfred and Tillie Shemanski Testamentary Grants, 363
Allan C. and Leila J. Garden Fndn Grants, 374
Annie E. Casey Fndn Grants, 481
Brookdale Fndn Relatives as Parents Grants, 846
CNCS Foster Grandparent Grants, 1185
Community Fndn of Broward Grants, 1275
Covenant to Care for Children Critical Grants, 1388
Dade Community Fndn Safe Passage Grants, 1431
Dyson Mid-Hudson Valley Project Support, 1636
Eisner Fndn Grants, 1678
Marion and Miriam Rose Grants, 3015
Mockingbird Fndn Grants, 3196
NYCT Youth Development Grants, 3561
Parker Fndn (California) Grants, 3736
Pew Trusts Children and Youth Grants, 3858
Peyton Anderson Fndn Grants, 3862
Samueli Fndn Youth Services Grants, 4234
Stuart Fndn Grants, 4516
Sunny and Abe Rosenberg Fndn Grants, 4529
Taproot Fndn Capacity-Building Service Grants, 4560
Victoria S. and Bradley L. Geist Fndn Enhancement Grants, 4935
Victoria S. and Bradley L. Geist Fndn Grants Supporting Foster Care and Their Caregivers, 4936
Victoria S. and Bradley L. Geist Fndn Grants Supporting Transitioning Foster Youth, 4937

Fruits
Fruit Tree 101, 1967

Fuel Cells
Illinois Clean Energy Community Fndn Energy Efficiency Grants, 2479
Illinois Clean Energy Community Fndn Renewable Energy Grants, 2481
Illinois Clean Energy Community Fndn Solar Thermal Installation Grants, 2482

Fund-Raising
ALA President's Award for Advocacy, 310
Ball Brothers Fndn Organizational Effectiveness/ Executive Mentoring Grants, 638
Barnes and Noble National Sponsorships and Charitable Donations, 671
Beim Fndn Grants, 718
BJ's Wholesale Clubs Local Charitable Giving, 778
Community Fndn of Collier County Capacity Building Grants, 1277
Dyson Fndn Management Assistance Program Mini-Grants, 1632
Dyson Fndn Nonprofit Strategic Restructuring Init Grants, 1637
GNOF Organizational Effectiveness Grants and Workshops, 2090
Goldseker Fndn Non-Profit Management Assistance Grants, 2103
Indianapolis Preservation Grants, 2543
Indiana Preservation Grants, 2544
Maine Community Fndn Belvedere Animal Welfare Grants, 2975
Meyer Fndn Benevon Grants, 3140
Middlesex Savings Charitable Fndn Capacity Building Grants, 3172
Nestle Purina PetCare Pet Related Grants, 3304
Nonprofit Management Grants, 3458
North Carolina Arts Council Community Arts Administration Internship, 3471
PCA Management/Technical Assistance Grants, 3800
PCA Strategies for Success Grants - Advanced, 3804
Pfizer Special Events Grants, 3865
Princeton Area Community Fndn Fund for Women and Girls Grants, 3962
Saint Louis Rams Fndn Community Donations, 4214
Santa Fe Community Fndn Special and Urgent Needs Grants, 4292
Social Justice Fund NW Criminal Justice Giving Project Grants, 4394
South Carolina Arts Commission Leadership and Organizational Development Grants, 4423
Sport Manitoba Bingo Allocations Grants, 4454
TAC Arts Access Technical Assistance Grants, 4550
TAC Technical Assistance Grants, 4556
Victor E. Speas Fndn Grants, 4933
Wilburforce Fndn Grants, 5067

Gambling
Boyd Gaming Corp Contributions Program, 825
National Center for Responsible Gaming Conference Scholarships, 3250
National Center for Resp Gaming Travel Grants, 3251

Gangs
A.V. Hunter Grants, 47
ATF Gang Resistance Educ and Training Program Coop Agreements, 603
Callaway Golf Company Fndn Violence Prevention Grants, 911
Chicago Community Trust Arts and Culture Grants: Improving Access to Arts Learning Opps, 1082
DOJ Gang-Free Schools and Communities Intervention Grants, 1557
DOJ Juvenile Mentoring Grants, 1560
eBay Fndn Community Grants, 1648
Piedmont Natural Gas Fndn Health and Human Services Grants, 3885
Union Bank, N.A. Fndn Grants, 4709

Gifted/Talented Education / 909

Gardening
Bayer Advanced Grow Together with Roses School Garden Awards, 695
Chicago Community Trust Health Grants, 1087
Columbus Fndn Scotts Miracle-Gro Community Garden Academy Grants, 1230
Garden Crusader Award, 1985
Katie's Krops Grants, 2792
NGA Healthy Sprouts Awards, 3403
NGA Midwest School Garden Grants, 3407
NGA Youth Garden Grants, 3409
PNM Power Up Grants, 3925
Robert R. Meyer Fndn Grants, 4121
Scotts Company Give Back to Grow Awards, 4315
Subaru Adopt a School Garden Grants, 4517
Wabash River Enhancement Corp Urban, 4969

Gender Equity
A.J. Muste Memorial Institute General Grants, 44
AAUW Community Action Grants, 75
AAUW Int'l Project Grants, 76
Cambridge Community Fndn Grants, 913
Dallas Women's Fndn Grants, 1438
Eileen Fisher Activating Leadership Grants for Women and Girls, 1676
Ms. Fndn for Women Ending Violence Grants, 3224
OUT Fund for Lesbian & Gay Liberation Grants, 3714
United States Institute of Peace - National Peace Essay Contest for High School Students, 4724

Genetics
Dr. John T. Macdonald Fndn Grants, 1600
Dr. Scholl Fndn Grants, 1602
Libra Fndn Grants, 2899
NHLBI Career Transition Awards, 3412
Starr Fndn Grants, 4483

Geography
AAG Meredith F. Burrill Award, 60
Canada-U.S. Fulbright Mid-Career Grants, 917
Detroit Lions Charities Grants, 1520
ESRI Conservation Grants, 1751
Luther I. Replogle Fndn Grants, 2945
Morris K. Udall and Stewart L. Udall Fndn Dissertation Fellowships, 3219

Geography Education
AAG Meredith F. Burrill Award, 60
Luther I. Replogle Fndn Grants, 2945

Geology
ConocoPhillips Grants, 1355
Weingart Fndn Grants, 5018

Geophysics
ConocoPhillips Grants, 1355

Geriatrics
CICF Senior Grants, 1127
Columbus Jewish Fndn Grants, 1234
Ellen Abbott Gilman Grants, 1685
Greenwall Fndn Bioethics Grants, 2158
Hartford Aging and Health Program Awards, 2247
Healthcare Fndn of New Jersey Grants, 2280
Jenkins Fndn: Improving the Health of Greater Richmond Grants, 2663
Mt. Sinai Health Care Fndn Health of the Jewish Community Grants, 3226
Piper Trust Older Adults Grants, 3904

German Language/Literature
Germanistic Society of America Fellowships, 2043

Gifted/Talented Education
Ford Motor Company Grants, 1885
Hearst Fndns Culture Grants, 2284
J. Knox Gholston Fndn Grants, 2599
Lynde and Harry Bradley Fndn Grants, 2947
Lynde and Harry Bradley Fndn Prizes, 2948
Mary Wilmer Covey Charitable Grants, 3049

910 / Gifted/Talented Education

Meyer Fndn Educ Grants, 3142
NAGC Masters and Specialists Award, 3237

Girls
AAUW Int'l Project Grants, 76
Arizona Fndn for Women Carstens Grants, 543
Arizona Fndn for Women General Grants, 544
Barr Fndn Grants, 677
Benton Community Fndn - The Cookie Jar Grant, 729
Dallas Women's Fndn Grants, 1438
Dining for Women Grants, 1548
Eileen Fisher Activating Leadership Grants for Women and Girls, 1676
Fisa Fndn Grants, 1826
Frederick McDonald Grants, 1946
HAF Kayla Wood Girls Grants, 2199
Jewish Women's Fndn of New York Grants, 2677
Maine Women's Fund Economic Security Grants, 2992
Maine Women's Fund Girls' Grantmaking Init, 2993
Mary Jennings Sport Camp Scholarship, 3041
Montana Community Fndn Women's Grants, 3212
New Mexico Women's Fndn Grants, 3335
Nike Fndn Grants, 3441
Open Meadows Fndn Grants, 3683
Pacers Fndn Indiana Fever's Be Younique Grants, 3724
RCF The Women's Grants, 4035
Valentine Fndn Grants, 4897
Washington Area Women's Fndn African American Women's Giving Circle Grants, 4989
Washington Area Women's Fndn Early Care and Educ Funders Collaborative Grants, 4990
Washington Area Women's Fndn Financial Educ and Wealth Creation Grants, 4991
Washington Area Women's Fndn Jobs Grants, 4992
Washington Area Women's Leadership Awards, 4993
Washington Area Women's Fndn Open Door Capacity Grants, 4994
Washington Area Women's Fndn Rainmakers Giving Circle Grants, 4995
WSF Rusty Kanokogi Fund for the Advancement of U.S. Judo Grants, 5118

Glaucoma
Columbus Fndn Competitive Grants, 1220
GNOF IMPACT Gulf States Eye Surgery Fund, 2082

Global Change
Acumen East Africa Fellowship, 141
Bill and Melinda Gates Fndn Agricultural Development Grants, 765
Bill & Melinda Gates Emergency Response Grants, 766
Bill & Melinda Gates Policy & Advocacy Grants, 769
Bill and Melinda Gates Fndn Water, Sanitation and Hygiene Grants, 770

Global Issues
Acumen Global Fellowships, 142
Bill and Melinda Gates Fndn Agricultural Development Grants, 765
Bill & Melinda Gates Emergency Response Grants, 766
Bill & Melinda Gates Policy & Advocacy Grants, 769
Bill and Melinda Gates Fndn Water, Sanitation and Hygiene Grants, 770
CDC Fndn Global Disaster Response Grants, 973
IIE David L. Boren Fellowships, 2454
United States Institute of Peace - National Peace Essay Contest for High School Students, 4724
USDA Hispanic-Serving Insts Educ Grants, 4813

Global Warming
PepsiCo Fndn Grants, 3819

Globalization
Boeing Company Contributions Grants, 809
Public Welfare Fndn Grants, 3984
Wallace Global Grants, 4977

Golf
Florida Sports Fndn Junior Golf Grants, 1872

Government
ACF Native American Social and Economic Development Strategies Grants, 123
ALA NewsBank/Readex C. J. Reynolds Award, 304
Anderson Fndn Grants, 460
Arca Fndn Grants, 526
Arlington Community Fndn Grants, 564
ASM Congressional Science Fellowships, 589
AT&T Fndn Civic and Comm Service Grants, 599
Baptist Community Ministries Grants, 664
Beim Fndn Grants, 718
California Arts Council Public Value Grants, 895
Carnegie Corp of New York Grants, 940
Chautauqua Region Community Fndn Grants, 1062
Chesapeake Bay Trust Forestry Mini Grants, 1071
Chesapeake Bay Trust Mini Grants, 1072
Community Memorial Fndn Grants, 1334
Do Right Fndn Grants, 1581
Effie and Wofford Cain Fndn Grants, 1674
Eugene B. Casey Fndn Grants, 1762
Ford Fndn Diversity Fellowships, 1883
Ford Fndn Peace and Social Justice Grants, 1884
GMFUS Marshall Memorial Fellowships, 2066
Hatton W. Sumners Fndn for the Study and Teaching of Self Government Grants, 2257
Japan Fndn Center for Global Partnership Grants, 2649
Margaret L. Wendt Fndn Grants, 3004
Microsoft Comm Affairs Puget Sound Grants, 3163
Morris K. Udall and Stewart L. Udall Fndn Native American Congressional Internships, 3220
Nathan Cummings Fndn Grants, 3246
NYCT Civic Affairs Grants, 3545
OSF Central Eurasia Project Grants, 3704
OSF Human Rights and Governance Grants, 3708
Playboy Fndn Grants, 3913
Rajiv Gandhi Fndn Grants, 4011
Richard and Caroline T. Gwathmey Grants, 4075
Rockefeller Brothers Democratic Practice Grants, 4131
Rockefeller Brothers Peace and Security Grants, 4133
Rockefeller Brothers Pivotal Places Grants: Serbia, Montenegro, and Kosova, 4135
Rockefeller Brothers Sustainable Devel Grants, 4136
Sapelo Fndn Social Justice Grants, 4294
Sprague Fndn Grants, 4461
USAID Economic Prospectsfor Armenia-Turkey Normalization Grants, 4750
USAID Leadership Init for Good Governance in Africa Grants, 4766
USAID National Governance Project Grant, 4770
USAID Strengthening Democratic Local Governance in South Sudan Grants, 4782
USDJ Nat Criminal History Improvement Grants, 4864
USDJ NICS Act Record Improvement Grants, 4865
Virginia Commission for the Arts Local Government Challenge Grants, 4943
Willary Fndn Grants, 5071

Government Documents
ALA Margaret T. Lane/Virginia F. Saunders Memorial Research Award, 298
ALA ProQuest Documents to the People Award, 311
HBF Defending Freedoms Grants, 2271

Government Regulations
DPA Promoting Policy Change Advocacy Grants, 1598

Government Studies
Henry M. Jackson Fndn Grants, 2311

Government, Comparative
Canada-U.S. Fulbright Mid-Career Grants, 917

Government, Federal
Arkansas Arts Council Collab Project Support, 555
DHHS Emerging Leaders Program Internships, 1532
GEICO Public Service Awards, 1997
IIE David L. Boren Fellowships, 2454
Ms. Fndn Women Building Democracy Grants, 3223
Mt. Sinai Health Care Fndn Policy Grants, 3228
Pittsburgh Fndn Community Grants, 3910
Supreme Court Fellows Commission Fellowships, 4532
USDC Postsecondary Grants Internships, 4855
USDJ Nat Criminal History Improvement Grants, 4864
USDJ NICS Act Record Improvement Grants, 4865

Government, Local
Alfred P. Sloan Selected National Issues Grants, 370
Arkansas Arts Council Collab Project Support, 555
Blue Cross Blue Shield of Minnesota Fndn - Health Equity: Building Health Together Grants, 793
CDECD Historic Preser Enhancement Grants, 981
CDECD Historic Preservation Survey and Planning Grants, 982
Community Fndn of Greater Fort Wayne - John S. and James L. Knight Fndn Donor-Advised Grants, 1287
Cone Health Fndn Grants, 1348
DOJ Community-Based Delinquency Prevention Grants, 1556
DPA Promoting Policy Change Advocacy Grants, 1598
EPA Brownfields Cleanup Grants, 1725
Ford Fndn Peace and Social Justice Grants, 1884
Grassroots Government Leadership Award, 2129
HAF Community Grants, 2193
Illinois DCEO Community Development Assistance For Economic Development Grants, 2488
Katharine Matthies Fndn Grants, 2788
Lynde and Harry Bradley Fndn Grants, 2947
Lynde and Harry Bradley Fndn Prizes, 2948
Marjorie Moore Charitable Fndn Grants, 3021
Ms. Fndn Women Building Democracy Grants, 3223
National Endowment for Arts Our Town Grants, 3257
Nevada Arts Council Learning Grants, 3313
NHSCA Arts in Health Care Project Grants, 3424
NHSCA General Project Grants, 3427
Parke County Community Fndn Grants, 3735
PCA Arts Organizations and Arts Programs Grants for Local Arts, 3782
PCA Entry Track Arts Organizations and Program Grants for Local Arts, 3794
Robert R. McCormick Tribune Civics Grants, 4118
Robert Sterling Clark Fndn Government Accountability Grants, 4123
USAID Strengthening Democratic Local Governance in South Sudan Grants, 4782
Virginia Commission for the Arts Local Government Challenge Grants, 4943

Government, Municipal
Ben & Jerry's Fndn Grants, 724
Bikes Belong Fndn REI Grants, 761
Bikes Belong Grants, 763
CDECD Historic Preser Enhancement Grants, 981
CDECD Historic Preservation Survey and Planning Grants, 982
DHS ARRA Fire Station Construction Grants, 1542
FEMA Assistance to Firefighters Grants, 1802
Grassroots Government Leadership Award, 2129
IDEM Section 205(j) Water Quality Management Planning Grants, 2434
IDEM Section 319(h) Nonpoint Source Grants, 2435
IEDC Industrial Development Grant Fund, 2443
Indiana Household Hazardous Waste Grants, 2538
Indiana Recycling Grants, 2545
Katharine Matthies Fndn Grants, 2788
Virginia Commission for the Arts Local Government Challenge Grants, 4943
Widgeon Point Charitable Fndn Grants, 5064

Government, State
Arkansas Arts Council Collab Project Support, 555
Cone Health Fndn Grants, 1348
DOJ Community-Based Delinquency Prevention Grants, 1556
DPA Promoting Policy Change Advocacy Grants, 1598
EPA Brownfields Cleanup Grants, 1725
Ford Fndn Peace and Social Justice Grants, 1884
HAF Community Grants, 2193
Kentucky Arts Council Access Assistance Grants, 2805
Lynde and Harry Bradley Fndn Grants, 2947
Lynde and Harry Bradley Fndn Prizes, 2948

Ms. Fndn Women Building Democracy Grants, 3223
Mt. Sinai Health Care Fndn Policy Grants, 3228
Robert Sterling Clark Fndn Government Accountability Grants, 4123

Governmental Functions
Alfred P. Sloan Selected National Issues Grants, 370
ConocoPhillips Fndn Grants, 1354
Fund for the City of New York Grants, 1978
HBF Encouraging Citizen Involvement Grants, 2272
Henry J. Kaiser Family Fndn Grants, 2310
Jacob and Hilda Blaustein Fndn Grants, 2615
Ms. Fndn Women Building Democracy Grants, 3223
NYCT Civic Affairs Grants, 3545
Rockefeller Family Grants, 4137
Sosland Fndn Grants, 4408
Town Creek Fndn Grants, 4650
USAID Leadership Init for Good Governance in Africa Grants, 4766
USAID Strengthening Democratic Local Governance in South Sudan Grants, 4782
USDC Technology Opportunities Grants, 4860
USDJ Nat Criminal History Improvement Grants, 4864
USDJ NICS Act Record Improvement Grants, 4865

Graduate Education
ALA Jan Merrill-Oldham Professional Development Grant, 291
OSF Civil Service Awards, 3705

Graphic Design
Illinois Arts Council Visual Arts Grants, 2478
Minnesota State Arts Board Cultural Community Partnership Grants, 3188
NYFA Gregory Millard Fellowships, 3565
NYSCA Architecture, Planning, and Design: Capital Fixtures and Equipment Purchase Grants, 3570
NYSCA Architecture, Planning, and Design: Capital Project Grants, 3571
NYSCA Architecture, Planning, and Design: Design and Planning Studies Grants, 3572
NYSCA Architecture, Planning, and Design: General Operating Support Grants, 3573
NYSCA Architecture, Planning, and Design: General Program Support Grants, 3574
NYSCA Architecture, Planning, and Design: Independent Project Grants, 3575
PCA Arts Organizations & Grants for Visual Arts, 3785
PCA Entry Track Arts Organizations and Program Grants for Visual Arts, 3799
RISCA Design Innovation Grant, 4097
Ruth Mott Fndn Grants, 4180

Grassroots Leadership
1st Source Fndn Ernestine M. Raclin Community Leadership Award, 2
3M Community Volunteer Award, 11
Abelard Fndn East Grants, 87
Abelard Fndn West Grants, 88
AEGON Transamerica Fndn Civic and Community Grants, 177
Aetna Fndn Volunteer Grants, 190
Agape Fndn for Nonviolent Social Change Board of Trustees Grants, 197
Akonadi Fndn Anti-Racism Grants, 217
American Express Charitable Grants, 429
American Express Leaders for Tomorrow Grants, 432
Bank of America Charitable Volunteer Grants, 660
Ben & Jerry's Fndn Grants, 724
Bernard and Audre Rapoport Fndn Community Building and Social Service Grants, 736
Blandin Rural Community Leadership Grants, 790
Brainerd Fndn Grants, 831
Community Fndn of Greater Fort Wayne - John S. and James L. Knight Fndn Donor-Advised Grants, 1287
Crossroads Fund Seed Grants, 1400
DTE Energy Fndn Leadership Grants, 1614
Dyson Fndn Mid-Hudson Philanthropy Grants, 1633
Eileen Fisher Activating Leadership Grants for Women and Girls, 1676
EPA Environmental Justice Small Grants, 1732
Eulalie Bloedel Schneider Fndn Grants, 1767
Evelyn and Walter Haas, Jr. Fund Nonprofit Leadership Grants, 1774
Freshwater Future Advocate Mentor Program, 1957
Freshwater Future Insight Services Grants, 1960
Fund for Southern Communities Grants, 1977
Girl's Best Friend Fndn Grants, 2057
GNOF Coastal 5 + 1 Grants, 2070
GNOF Community Revitalization Grants, 2071
GNOF Environmental Grants, 2073
GNOF Gulf Coast Oil Spill Grants, 2077
GNOF St. Bernard Community Grants, 2092
GNOF Stand Up For Our Children Grants, 2093
Grassroots Exchange Grants, 2128
Great Clips Corp Giving, 2131
GreenWorks! Grants, 2160
Haymarket People's Fund Sustaining Grants, 2267
Haymarket Urgent Response Grants, 2268
Hazen Fndn Youth Organizing Grants, 2270
Hyams Fndn Grants, 2413
Init Fndn Healthy Communities Partnerships, 2557
Japan Fndn Center for Global Partnership Grants, 2649
John Edward Fowler Memorial Fndn Grants, 2693
Kalamazoo Community Good Neighbor Grants, 2768
LISC NFL Grassroots Grants, 2913
Lumpkin Family Strong Comm Leadership Grants, 2944
Mary Reynolds Babcock Fndn Grants, 3047
Merck Family Fund Urban Farming and Youth Leadership Grants, 3119
Mertz Gilmore Fndn NYC Communities Grants, 3126
Mertz Gilmore Fndn NYC Dance Grants, 3127
MetLife Fndn Promoting Employee Volunteerism, 3132
Miller Fndn Grants, 3181
Needmor Grants, 3289
Nike Giving - Cash and Product Grants, 3442
Norman Fndn Grants, 3464
Open Meadows Fndn Grants, 3683
Ottinger Fndn Grants, 3712
Paul and Edith Babson Fndn Grants, 3755
PDF Community Organizing Grants, 3807
Philanthrofund Grants, 3874
Salt River Project Civic Leadership Grants, 4226
San Francisco Fndn Koshland Program Arts and Culture Mini-Grants, 4280
Sisters of Saint Joseph Charitable Grants, 4376
Southern Minnesota Init Grants, 4437
SW Init Fndn Grants, 4446
State Strategies Grants, 4494
Union Square Awards Grants, 4718
United Methodist Committee on Relief Hunger and Poverty Grants, 4720
United Methodist Women Brighter Future for Children and Youth Grants, 4723
Washington Area Women's Fndn Strategic Opportunity and Partnership Grants, 4996
WCI Community Leadership Fellowships, 5008
WCI Leadership Development Grants, 5012

Great Lakes
Freshwater Future Healing Our Waters Grants, 1959
George Gund Fndn Grants, 2020
Great Lakes Protection Grants, 2147
Joyce Fndn Environment Grants, 2750
MDEQ Coastal Management Planning and Construction Grants, 3097
MDEQ Local Water Quality Monitoring Grants, 3100
NFWF Sustain Our Great Lakes Grants, 3396

Grief
A Little Hope Grants, 373
Dell Fndn Open Grants, 1490
Robert R. Meyer Fndn Grants, 4121

Gun Control
Clayton Baker Grants, 1163
David Bohnett Fndn Grants, 1451
Joyce Fndn Gun Violence Prevention Grants, 2751
Overbrook Fndn Grants, 3715
Richard and Rhoda Goldman Grants, 4077

HIV
Abbott Fund Science Educ Grants, 83
Alfred E. Chase Charitable Fndn Grants, 366
Alliance Healthcare Fndn Grants, 383
Blowitz-Ridgeway Fndn Grants, 792
Bodenwein Public Benevolent Fndn Grants, 806
Cable Positive's Tony Cox Community Grants, 886
CDC School Health Programs to Prevent the Spread of HIV Coop Agreements, 975
Child's Dream Grants, 1104
Children Affected by AIDS Network Grants, 1106
Children Affected by AIDS Fndn Family Assistance Emergency Grants, 1107
Colin Higgins Fndn Grants, 1204
Community Fndn for Southern Arizona Grants, 1261
Community Fndn of Broward Grants, 1275
Dallas Women's Fndn Grants, 1438
DHHS Abandoned Infants Assistance Grants, 1523
DIFFA/Chicago Grants, 1547
El Paso Community Fndn Grants, 1688
Firelight Fndn Grants, 1817
Frances L. and Edwin L. Cummings Grants, 1919
Gill Fndn - Gay and Lesbian Grants, 2054
Hagedorn Grants, 2207
Health Fndn of Greater Indianapolis Grants, 2282
Henry J. Kaiser Family Fndn Grants, 2310
Horizon Fndn for New Jersey Grants, 2364
Indiana AIDS Grants, 2529
IREX Small Grant Fund for Civil Society Projects in Africa and Asia, 2581
Jessie Smith Noyes Fndn Grants, 2672
Johnson & Johnson Corp Contributions Grants, 2718
McCarthy Family Fndn Grants, 3073
NHLBI Microbiome of the Lung and Respiratory Tract in HIV-Infected Individuals and HIV-Uninfected Controls, 3416
NYCT AIDS/HIV Grants, 3542
NYCT Girls and Young Women Grants, 3548
OUT Fund for Lesbian & Gay Liberation Grants, 3714
Paul Rapoport Fndn Grants, 3765
Playboy Fndn Grants, 3913
Questar Corp Contributions Grants, 3997
Rainbow Endowment Grants, 4007
San Diego HIV Funding Collaborative Grants, 4251
Scherman Grants, 4305
Sister Grants for Women's Organizations, 4371
United Methodist Committee on Relief Global AIDS Grants, 4719
USAID/Cambodia Maternal and Child Health, Tuberculosis, HIV/AIDS. and Malaria Grants, 4736
USAID Comprehensive District-Based Support for Better HIV/TB Patient Outcomes Grants, 4747
USAID Economic Prospectsfor Armenia-Turkey Normalization Grants, 4750
USAID HIV Prevention with Key Populations - Mali Grants, 4757
USAID Strengthening Through Indian Health Professional Assoc & Scaling Up Grants, 4784
USAID Systems Strengthening for Better HIV/TB Patient Outcomes Grants, 4785
USCM HIV/AIDS Prevention Grants, 4794

Habitat Preservation
1772 Fndn Fellowships, 36
Chesapeake Bay Fisheries & Headwaters Grants, 1070
George H.C. Ensworth Grants, 2022
Great Lakes Fishery Trust Habitat Protection and Restoration Grants, 2146
Green Diamond Charitable Contributions, 2149
Greygates Fndn Grants, 2164
HRF Hudson River Improvement Grants, 2378
Huntington County Comm Hiner Family Grant, 2405
Illinois DNR Habitat Grants, 2497
Illinois DNR Migratory Waterfowl Stamp Grants, 2498
Illinois DNR State Furbearer Grants, 2501
Illinois DNR State Pheasant Grants, 2502
Illinois DNR Wildlife Preservation Fund Large Project Grants, 2505
Illinois DNR Wildlife Preservation Fund Small Project Grants, 2506

912 / Habitat Preservation — SUBJECT INDEX

Illinois DNR Wildlife Preservation Maintenance of Wildlife Rehabilitation Facilities Grants, 2507
NFWF Shell Marine Habitat Grants, 3391
NFWF Southern Co Longleaf Legacy Grants, 3392
NFWF Southern Company Power of Flight Bird Conservation Grants, 3393
NFWF Upper Mississippi Riv Watershed Grants, 3398
NFWF Wildlife & Habitat Conservation Grants, 3399
NE Utilities Fndn Grants, 3498
Shared Earth Fndn Grants, 4339
Sioux Falls Area Community Grants, 4364
Sioux Falls Area Community Fndn Spot Grants, 4366
Union Bank, N.A. Fndn Grants, 4709
United Technologies Corp Grants, 4725
USAID Bengal Tiger Conservation Grants, 4741

Habitats
Arthur B. Schultz Fndn Grants, 573
Banrock Station Wines Wetlands Grants, 662
Davis Conservation Fndn Grants, 1461
FishAmerica Fndn Chesapeake Bay Grants, 1827
FishAmerica Fndn Conservation Grants, 1828
FishAmerica Fndn Marine and Anadromous Fish Habitat Restoration Grants, 1829
FishAmerica Fndn Research Grants, 1830
Fisheries and Habitat Partnership Grants, 1834
Florida Sea Turtle Grants, 1871
Great Lakes Fishery Trust Habitat Protection and Restoration Grants, 2146
Illinois DNR Habitat Grants, 2497
Illinois DNR Migratory Waterfowl Stamp Grants, 2498
Illinois DNR Schoolyard Habitat Action Grants, 2500
Illinois DNR State Furbearer Grants, 2501
Illinois DNR State Pheasant Grants, 2502
Illinois DNR Wildlife Preservation Fund Large Project Grants, 2505
Illinois DNR Wildlife Preservation Fund Small Project Grants, 2506
Illinois DNR Wildlife Preservation Maintenance of Wildlife Rehabilitation Facilities Grants, 2507
Illinois DNR Youth Recreation Corps Grants, 2508
MDEQ Great Lakes Areas of Concern Land Acquisition Grants, 3099
NFWF Acres for America Grants, 3355
NFWF Alaska Fish and Wildlife Grants, 3356
NFWF Aleutian Islands Risk Assessment Grants, 3357
NFWF Bring Back the Natives Grants, 3359
NFWF California Coastal Restoration Grants, 3362
NFWF Columbia River Estuarine Coastal Grant, 3367
NFWF Community Salmon Fund Partnerships, 3368
NFWF ConocoPhillips SPIRIT of Conservation Migratory Bird Grants, 3369
NFWF Dissolved Oxygen Environmental Benefit Grants, 3372
NFWF King County Community Salmon Grants, 3375
NFWF One Fly Conservation Partnerships, 3382
NFWF Oregon Governor's Fund for the Environment Grants, 3383
NFWF Pacific Grassroots Salmonid Init Grants, 3384
NFWF Pierce Community Salmon Grant, 3385
NFWF Pioneers in Conservation Grants, 3386
NFWF Radical Salmon Design Contest, 3388
NFWF Salmon Recovery Funding Board Community Salmon Grants, 3389
NFWF State Comprehensive Wildlife Conservation Support Grants, 3395
NFWF Sustain Our Great Lakes Grants, 3396
NFWF Tampa Bay Environmental Grants, 3397
NFWF Wildlife & Habitat Conservation Grants, 3399
PG&E Community Vitality Grants, 3868
SeaWorld & Busch Gardens Conservation Grants, 4332
USAID Bengal Tiger Conservation Grants, 4741
USDC/NOAA American Rivers Community-Based Restoration Program River Grants, 4845
Wilburforce Fndn Grants, 5067

Hawaiian Natives
Antone & Edene Vidinha Charitable Grants, 490
EPA State Indoor Radon Grants, 1738
IMLS Native Hawaiian Library Services Grants, 2519
U.S. Department of Educ Native Hawaiian Educ Grants, 4694
U.S. Department of Educ Programs for Native Hawaiians, 4696

Hazardous Waste
Acorn Fndn Grants, 131
EPA Hazardous Waste Grants for Tribes, 1733
Honor the Earth Grants, 2361
HRF Hudson River Improvement Grants, 2378
Indiana Household Hazardous Waste Grants, 2538
Jessie Smith Noyes Fndn Grants, 2672
NIEHS Hazardous Materials Worker Health and Safety Training Grants, 3438
San Diego Fndn for Change Grants, 4247
Sioux Falls Area Community Grants, 4364
Sioux Falls Area Community Fndn Spot Grants, 4366

Hazardous Waste, Disposal/Clean-Up
EPA Brownfields Assessment Pilot Grants, 1724
EPA Brownfields Cleanup Grants, 1725
EPA Environmental Justice Small Grants, 1732
EPA Hazardous Waste Grants for Tribes, 1733
Great Lakes Protection Grants, 2147
Indiana Household Hazardous Waste Grants, 2538
MDEQ Brownfield Redevelopment and Site Reclamation Grants, 3095
NIEHS Hazardous Materials Worker Health and Safety Training Grants, 3438

Health
3M Fndn Community Giving Grants, 15
7-Eleven Coorporate Giving Grants, 18
1675 Fndn Grants, 35
Abundance Fndn Int'l Grants, 108
Ackerman Fndn Grants, 129
Adams and Reese LLP Corp Giving Grants, 147
Adams Fndn Grants, 153
AEGON Transamerica Health & Welfare Grants, 179
Aetna Fndn Obesity Grants, 185
Albert and Margaret Alkek Fndn Grants, 340
American Electric Power Grants, 428
Appalachian Reg Comm Health Care Grants, 507
Arkansas Community Fndn Arkansas Black Hall of Fame Grants, 559
Austin College Leadership Award, 615
Autodesk Community Relations Grants, 619
Back Home Again Fndn Grants, 633
Bernard and Audre Rapoport Fndn Health Grants, 738
Bright Promises Fndn Grants, 838
Bristol-Myers Squibb Fndn Community Grants, 840
Caesars Fndn Grants, 891
Cailloux Fndn Grants, 892
Capital City Bank Group Fndn Grants, 920
CFFVR Chilton Area Community Fndn Grants, 1006
CFFVR Jewelers Mutual Charitable Giving, 1014
CFFVR Project Grants, 1017
Chapman Charitable Fndn Grants, 1033
Charles M. and Mary D. Grant Fndn Grants, 1050
CICF J. Proctor Grant for Aged Men & Women, 1124
Cigna Civic Affairs Sponsorships, 1129
Cleveland Community Responsive Grants, 1168
Columbus Fndn Competitive Grants, 1220
Community Fndn for San Benito County Grants, 1258
Community Fndn for SE Michigan Grants, 1259
Community Fndn Of Greater Lafayette Grants, 1289
Community Fndn of South Puget Sound Grants, 1311
CSX Corp Contributions Grants, 1408
D.V. and Ida J. McEachern Charitable Grants, 1425
Daisy Marquis Jones Fndn Grants, 1434
Dale and Edna Walsh Fndn Grants, 1435
Decatur County Community Fndn Small Project Grants, 1477
Dining for Women Grants, 1548
DTE Energy Health & Human Services Grants, 1613
Dyson Mid-Hudson Valley Project Support, 1636
Edward and Helen Bartlett Fndn Grants, 1664
Edyth Bush Charitable Fndn Grants, 1673
El Paso Corp Fndn Grants, 1689
El Pomar Fndn Awards and Grants, 1690
Federal Express Corp Contributions Program, 1799
Fidelity Fndn Grants, 1805
Fifth Third Fndn Grants, 1810
Fndn for the Carolinas Grants, 1896
Fndns of E Chicago Health Grants, 1910
Freddie Mac Fndn Grants, 1944
Fremont Area Community Amazing X Grants, 1953
Genentech Corp Charitable Contributions, 2000
George H.C. Ensworth Grants, 2022
Gil and Dody Weaver Fndn Grants, 2053
GNOF Bayou Communities Grants, 2069
GNOF IMPACT Grants for Health and Human Services, 2080
Grand Haven Area Community Fndn Grants, 2113
Halliburton Fndn Grants, 2211
Hampton Roads Community Fndn Nonprofit Facilities Improvement Grants, 2218
Hancock County Community Fndn - Field of Interest Grants, 2219
Harold and Arlene Schnitzer CARE Grants, 2226
Harrison County Community Fndn Grants, 2233
Harrison County Community Signature Grants, 2234
Harry Edison Fndn, 2241
Harry S. Black and Allon Fuller Grants, 2243
Harry W. Bass, Jr. Fndn Grants, 2246
Herbert A. and Adrian W. Woods Fndn Grants, 2313
Hilda and Preston Davis Fndn Grants, 2322
Hill Crest Fndn Grants, 2324
Hillsdale County Community General Adult Fndn Grants, 2328
Hoffberger Fndn Grants, 2342
Intergrys Corp Grants, 2565
J.E. and L.E. Mabee Fndn Grants, 2595
J. Willard Marriott, Jr. Fndn Grants, 2610
Jane Bradley Pettit Fndn Health Grants, 2643
Jasper Fndn Grants, 2655
Jennings County Community Fndn Women's Giving Circle Grant, 2665
Jim Blevins Fndn Grants, 2678
Johnson Controls Fndn Health and Social Services Grants, 2722
Lake County Community Grants, 2856
Legler Benbough Fndn Grants, 2877
Libra Fndn Grants, 2899
Lindbergh Grants, 2907
Lisa and Douglas Goldman Grants, 2910
Lucy Downing Nisbet Charitable Grants, 2935
Lumpkin Family Healthy People Grants, 2942
Lydia deForest Charitable Grants, 2946
Mann T. Lowry Fndn Grants, 2998
Mary Black Fndn Community Health Grants, 3032
Mary Wilmer Covey Charitable Grants, 3049
Medtronic Fndn CommunityLink Health Grants, 3111
Mercedes-Benz USA Corp Contributions Grants, 3118
Meyer Memorial Trust Grassroots Grants, 3147
Meyer Memorial Trust Responsive Grants, 3148
MGM Resorts Fndn Community Grants, 3153
Moran Family Fndn Grants, 3216
Nelda C. and H.J. Lutcher Stark Fndn Grants, 3296
New Jersey Center for Hispanic Policy, Research and Development Innovative Inits Grants, 3329
Norcliffe Fndn Grants, 3459
Northrop Grumman Corp Grants, 3507
OneStar Fndn AmeriCorps Grants, 3674
Orange County Community Fndn Grants, 3688
Pacific Life Fndn Grants, 3726
Pajaro Valley Community Health Trust Diabetes and Contributing Factors Grants, 3732
Peyton Anderson Fndn Grants, 3862
PMI Fndn Grants, 3918
Porter County Health and Wellness Grant, 3933
PPG Industries Fndn Grants, 3943
Public Welfare Fndn Grants, 3984
Pulte Homes Corp Contributions, 3989
Qualcomm Grants, 3993
Ripley County Community Small Project Grants, 4096
Rockwell Fund, Inc. Grants, 4140
Rogers Family Fndn Grants, 4144
Rohm and Haas Company Grants, 4145
Salt River Health and Human Services Grants, 4228

SUBJECT INDEX   Health Care / 913

Samuel N. and Mary Castle Fndn Grants, 4236
Seattle Fndn Benjamin N. Phillips Grants, 4322
Seattle Fndn Health and Wellness Grants, 4328
Simpson Lumber Charitable Contributions, 4362
Skoll Fndn Awards for Social Entrepreneurship, 4383
Snee Reinhardt Charitable Fndn Grants, 4387
Sobrato Family Fndn Grants, 4389
Sobrato Family Fndn Meeting Space Grants, 4390
Sobrato Family Fndn Office Space Grants, 4391
Sony Corp of America Corp Philanthropy Grants, 4405
Special Olympics Project UNIFY Grants, 4449
Taproot Fndn Capacity-Building Service Grants, 4560
Textron Corp Contributions Grants, 4601
Tifa Fndn Grants, 4633
Toro Fndn Grants, 4647
Toyota Motor Manufacturing of Alabama Grants, 4652
Toyota Motor Manufacturing Mississippi Grants, 4655
Toyota Motor Manufacturing of Texas Grants, 4656
Toyota Motor Manufacturing W Virginia Grants, 4657
United Methodist Health Ministry Grants, 4722
USAID Accelerating Progress Against Tuberculosis in Kenya Grants, 4737
USAID Economic Prospectsfor Armenia-Turkey Normalization Grants, 4750
USAID Family Health Plus Project Grants, 4751
USAID HIV Prevention with Key Populations - Mali Grants, 4757
USAID Implementation Science for Strengthening Use of Evidence in Family Planning/Reproductive Health Programming Grants, 4758
USAID Integration of Care and Support within the Health System to Support Better Patient Outcomes Grants, 4762
USAID Knowledge for Health II Grants, 4765
USAID Mekong Partnership for the Environment Project Grants, 4769
USAID NGO Health Service Delivery Grants, 4771
USAID Palestinian Comm Assistance Grants, 4773
USAID Strengthening Through Indian Health Professional Assoc & Scaling Up Grants, 4784
USG Fndn Grants, 4869
Walmart Fndn Facility Giving Grants, 4978
Walmart Fndn National Giving Grants, 4979
Wege Fndn Grants, 5017
Welborn Baptist General Opportunity Grants, 5020
Welborn Baptist Fndn Improvements to Community Health Status Grants, 5021
Whitley County Community Fndn Grants, 5060
William Bingham Fndn Grants, 5077
Williams Companies Fndn Grants, 5095
Wolfe Associates Grants, 5110

Health Care
2 Depot Square Ipswich Charitable Fndn Grants, 4
3M Company Health and Human Services Grants, 14
49ers Fndn Grants, 23
100 Mile Man Fndn Grants, 27
118 Fndn Grants, 29
1104 Fndn Grants, 34
A/H Fndn Grants, 48
AAP Community Access To Child Health Implementation Grants, 63
AAP Resident Init Grants, 69
Aaron Fndn Grants, 72
Aaron Fndn Grants, 73
Abbott Fund Access to Health Care Grants, 80
Abbott Fund Community Grants, 81
Abbott Fund Global AIDS Care Grants, 82
Abbott Fund Science Educ Grants, 83
Abell Fndn Health and Human Services Grants, 96
Abernethy Family Fndn Grants, 98
Abington Fndn Grants, 100
Able To Serve Grants, 102
Abney Fndn Grants, 105
Aboudane Family Fndn Grants, 106
ACFEF Disaster Relief Fund Member Assistance, 117
ACF Fndn Grants, 119
Achelis Fndn Grants, 127
Acuity Charitable Fndn Grants, 140
Acushnet Fndn Grants, 143

Adam Reineman Charitable Grants, 144
Adam Richter Charitable Grants, 145
Adams and Reese LLP Corp Giving Grants, 147
Adams County Community Fndn of Pennsylvania Grants, 149
Adams Family Fndn I Grants, 150
Adelaide Breed Bayrd Fndn Grants, 161
Adler-Clark Electric Community Commitment Fndn Grants, 164
Administaff Community Affairs Grants, 165
Adolph Coors Fndn Grants, 171
Advanced Micro Devices Comm Affairs Grants, 172
AEC Grants, 175
AEGON Transamerica Health & Welfare Grants, 179
AEP Corp Giving Grants, 180
Aetna Fndn Health Grants in Connecticut, 184
Aetna Fndn Obesity Grants, 185
Aetna Fndn Racial and Ethnic Health Care Equity Grants, 186
AFG Industries Grants, 191
African American Fund of New Jersey Grants, 192
A Friends' Fndn Grants, 194
Agnes M. Lindsay Grants, 203
A Good Neighbor Fndn Grants, 204
Ahmanson Fndn Grants, 207
Aid for Starving Children African American Indep Single Mother's Grants, 210
Aid for Starving Children Int'l Grants, 212
Air Products and Chemicals Grants, 216
Akzo Nobel Chemicals Grants, 219
Alabama Power Fndn Grants, 233
Aladdin Industries Fndn Grants, 263
Alberto Culver Corp Contributions Grants, 343
Albert Pick Jr. Grants, 344
Albertson's Charitable Giving Grants, 345
Albert W. Rice Charitable Fndn Grants, 347
Albuquerque Community Fndn Grants, 348
Alcatel-Lucent Technologies Fndn Grants, 349
Alcoa Fndn Grants, 350
Alfred and Tillie Shemanski Testamentary Grants, 363
Alfred Bersted Fndn Grants, 364
Alfred E. Chase Charitable Fndn Grants, 366
Alice C. A. Sibley Grants, 371
Alice Tweed Tuohy Fndn Grants, 372
Allegan County Community Fndn Grants, 375
Allegheny Technologies Charitable Trust, 377
Alpha Kappa Alpha Ed Advancement Fndn Community Assistance Awards, 393
ALSAM Fndn Grants, 395
Alticor Corp Community Contributions Grants, 396
Altman Fndn Health Care Grants, 397
Alvin and Lucy Owsley Fndn Grants, 404
ALZA Corp Contributions Grants, 405
AMA-MSS Chapter Involvement Grants, 406
AMA-MSS Chapter of the Year Award, 407
Amador Community Fndn Grants, 408
AMA Fndn Healthy Communities/Healthy America Grants, 410
AMA Fndn Jack B. McConnell, MD Awards for Excellence in Volunteerism, 411
Amarillo Area/Harrington Fndns Grants, 412
Amelia Sillman Rockwell and Carlos Perry Rockwell Charities Grants, 417
American Express Community Service Grants, 430
American Foodservice Charitable Grants, 433
American Jewish World Service Grants, 441
American Schlafhorst Fndn Grants, 446
Andersen Corp Fndn, 459
Angels Baseball Fndn Grants, 465
Angels Wings Fndn Int'l Grants, 469
Anheuser-Busch Fndn Grants, 470
Anna Fitch Ardenghi Grants, 472
Ann and Robert H. Lurie Family Fndn Grants, 473
Annie E. Casey Fndn Grants, 481
Annie Sinclair Knudsen Memorial Fund/Kaua'i Community Grants, 482
Ann Peppers Fndn Grants, 484
Annunziata Sanguinetti Fndn Grants, 485
Anschutz Family Fndn Grants, 486
Anthem Blue Cross and Blue Shield Grants, 488

Antone & Edene Vidinha Charitable Grants, 490
Appalachian Reg Comm Health Care Grants, 507
APS Fndn Grants, 518
AptarGroup Fndn Grants, 519
Aragona Family Fndn Grants, 522
Aratani Fndn Grants, 523
Arcadia Fndn Grants, 525
Argyros Fndn Grants, 532
Arie and Ida Crown Grants, 533
Arizona Cardinals Grants, 534
Arizona Community Fndn Grants, 540
Arizona Diamondbacks Charities Grants, 542
Arizona Public Service Corp Giving Grants, 545
Arkell Hall Fndn Grants, 562
Arlington Community Fndn Grants, 564
Armstrong McDonald Fndn Grants, 565
Arronson Fndn Grants, 567
ARS Fndn Grants, 568
ArvinMeritor Grants, 585
Aspen Community Fndn Grants, 592
Assisi Fndn of Memphis Capital Project Grants, 593
Assisi Fndn of Memphis General Grants, 594
Assisi Fndn of Memphis Mini Grants, 595
Assurant Health Fndn Grants, 596
AT&T Fndn Civic and Comm Service Grants, 599
Atherton Family Fndn Grants, 604
Athwin Fndn Grants, 605
Atlanta Fndn Grants, 608
Aurora Fndn Grants, 613
Austin-Bailey Health and Wellness Fndn Grants, 614
Austin Community Fndn Grants, 616
Autzen Fndn Grants, 622
Babcock Charitable Grants, 632
Bacon Family Fndn Grants, 634
Bailey Fndn Grants, 635
Balfe Family Fndn Grants, 636
Ball Brothers Fndn General Grants, 637
Banfi Vintners Fndn Grants, 653
Baptist-Trinity Lutheran Legacy Fndn Grants, 663
Barberton Community Fndn Grants, 666
Barker Fndn Grants, 668
Barker Welfare Fndn Grants, 669
Barra Fndn Community Grants, 673
Barra Fndn Project Grants, 674
Barrasso Usdin Kupperman Freeman and Sarver LLC Corp Grants, 675
Batchelor Fndn Grants, 679
Baton Rouge Area Fndn Grants, 682
Battle Creek Community Fndn Grants, 684
Baxter Int'l Corp Giving Grants, 689
Baxter Int'l Fndn Foster G. McGaw Prize, 690
Baxter Int'l Fndn Grants, 691
BCBSM Corp Contributions Grants, 706
BCBSM Community Health Matching Grants, 707
BCBSM Fndn Investigator Research Grants, 708
BCBSM Fndn Proposal Development Awards, 709
BCBSM Fndn Student Award Program, 710
BCBS of Massachusetts Fndn Grants, 713
Beazley Fndn Grants, 714
Bechtel Group Fndn Building Positive Community Relationships Grants, 715
Beckley Area Fndn Grants, 716
Beerman Fndn Grants, 717
Beirne Carter Fndn Grants, 719
Ben B. Cheney Fndn Grants, 725
Bender Fndn Grants, 726
Benton County Fndn Grants, 731
Berks County Community Fndn Grants, 734
Berrien Community Fndn Grants, 744
Bert W. Martin Fndn Grants, 747
Besser Fndn Grants, 748
Better Way Fndn Grants, 754
BHHS Legacy Fndn Grants, 758
Biogen Corp Giving Grants, 773
Birmingham Fndn Grants, 774
Blanche and Irving Laurie Fndn Grants, 784
Blanche and Julian Robertson Family Fndn Grants, 785
Blowitz-Ridgeway Fndn Grants, 792
Blue Grass Community Fndn Grants, 799
Blue Mountain Community Fndn Grants, 800

Health Care

Blue Shield of California Grants, 802
Blum-Kovler Fndn Grants, 803
Bodenwein Public Benevolent Fndn Grants, 806
Bodman Fndn Grants, 807
Boeing Company Contributions Grants, 809
Boettcher Fndn Grants, 810
Booth-Bricker Grants, 815
Bosque Fndn Grants, 818
Boston Fndn Grants, 819
Boston Globe Fndn Grants, 821
Boston Jewish Community Women's Grants, 822
Boyd Gaming Corp Contributions Program, 825
Bradley-Turner Fndn Grants, 828
Brian G. Dyson Fndn Grants, 834
Bridgestone/Firestone Grants, 836
Bright Family Fndn Grants, 837
Bristol-Myers Squibb Patient Assistance Grants, 841
Brooklyn Community Caring Neighbors Grants, 848
Burlington Industries Fndn Grants, 865
Burlington Northern Santa Fe Fndn Grants, 866
Bush Fndn Health & Human Services Grants, 875
Bush Fndn Medical Fellowships, 877
Butler Manufacturing Company Fndn Grants, 881
Caesars Fndn Grants, 891
Caleb C. and Julia W. Dula Ed and Charitable Fndn Grants, 893
California Community Fndn Health Care Grants, 901
Callaway Fndn Grants, 909
Callaway Golf Company Fndn Grants, 910
Cambridge Community Fndn Grants, 913
Camp-Younts Fndn Grants, 914
Campbell Hoffman Fndn Grants, 915
Campbell Soup Fndn Grants, 916
Capital City Bank Group Fndn Grants, 920
Capital Region Community Fndn Grants, 921
Cardinal Health Fndn Grants, 923
Caring Fndn Grants, 926
Carl and Eloise Pohlad Family Fndn Grants, 927
Carl C. Icahn Fndn Grants, 929
Carl Gellert and Celia Berta Gellert Fndn Grants, 930
Carl M. Freeman Fndn FACES Grants, 932
Carl R. Hendrickson Family Fndn Grants, 935
Carlsbad Charitable Fndn Grants, 936
Carls Fndn Grants, 937
Carl W. and Carrie Mae Joslyn Grants, 938
Carolyn Fndn Grants, 942
Carpenter Fndn Grants, 943
Carrie Estelle Doheny Fndn Grants, 945
Carrier Corp Contributions Grants, 946
Carroll County Community Fndn Grants, 947
Carylon Fndn Grants, 949
Catherine Kennedy Home Fndn Grants, 955
CDC Grants for Violence-Related Injury Prevention Research, 974
CE and S Fndn Grants, 985
Cemala Fndn Grants, 988
Central Carolina Community Fndn Community Impact Grants, 994
Central New York Community Fndn Grants, 996
Central Okanagan Fndn Grants, 997
CFFVR Capital Credit Union Charitable Giving, 1005
CFFVR Clintonville Area Fndn Grants, 1008
CFFVR Clintonville Area Fndn Grants, 1007
CFFVR Frank C. Shattuck Community Grants, 1012
CFFVR Jewelers Mutual Charitable Giving, 1014
CFFVR Myra M. and Robert L. Vandehey Fndn Grants, 1016
CFFVR Robert and Patricia Endries Family Fndn Grants, 1018
CFFVR Shawano Area Community Fndn Grants, 1021
CFFVR Women's Fund for the Fox Valley Region Grants, 1025
Chamberlain Fndn Grants, 1027
Champlin Fndns Grants, 1029
Chapman Charitable Fndn Grants, 1033
CharityWorks Grants, 1036
Charles A. Frueauff Fndn Grants, 1037
Charles Delmar Fndn Grants, 1039
Charles F. Bacon Grants, 1040
Charles H. Dater Fndn Grants, 1042

Charles H. Farnsworth Grants, 1043
Charles H. Hall Fndn, 1044
Charles H. Pearson Fndn Grants, 1045
Charles Lafitte Fndn Grants, 1049
Charles Nelson Robinson Grants, 1052
Charles Stewart Mott Fndn Grants, 1055
Charlotte County (FL) Community Fndn Grants, 1056
Chase Paymentech Corp Giving Grants, 1059
Chatlos Fndn Grants, 1061
Chemtura Corp Contributions Grants, 1067
Chesapeake Corp Fndn Grants, 1076
Chicago Board of Trade Fndn Grants, 1079
Chicago White Metal Charitable Fndn Grants, 1102
Children Affected by AIDS Fndn Family Assistance Emergency Grants, 1107
Christine and Katharina Pauly Charitable Grants, 1114
Christy-Houston Fndn Grants, 1115
Chula Vista Charitable Fndn Grants, 1116
CICF Indianapolis Fndn Community Grants, 1123
CICF Legacy Grants, 1126
CICF Senior Grants, 1127
Cigna Civic Affairs Sponsorships, 1129
CIGNA Fndn Grants, 1130
Cinergy Fndn Grants, 1133
Cisco Systems Fndn San Jose Community Grants, 1137
CIT Corp Giving Grants, 1138
Citigroup Fndn Grants, 1139
Citizens Bank Mid-Atlantic Charitable Grants, 1140
Claneil Fndn Grants, 1145
Clara Blackford Smith and W. Aubrey Smith Charitable Fndn Grants, 1147
Clarcor Fndn Grants, 1148
Clarence E. Heller Charitable Fndn Grants, 1150
Clarence T.C. Ching Fndn Grants, 1151
Clark-Winchcole Fndn Grants, 1152
Clark and Ruby Baker Fndn Grants, 1154
Clark County Community Fndn Grants, 1156
Clark Fndn Grants, 1157
Claude Bennett Family Fndn Grants, 1159
Claude Worthington Benedum Fndn Grants, 1161
Clay Fndn Grants, 1162
Cleo Fndn Grants, 1164
Cleveland-Cliffs Fndn Grants, 1165
CLIF Bar Family Fndn Grants, 1173
CNA Fndn Grants, 1179
Coastal Community Fndn of S Carolina Grants, 1193
Coca-Cola Fndn Grants, 1195
Cockrell Fndn Grants, 1196
Coeta and Donald Barker Fndn Grants, 1197
Coleman Fndn Cancer Care Grants, 1199
Colgate-Palmolive Company Grants, 1202
Colin Higgins Fndn Grants, 1204
Collins C. Diboll Private Fndn Grants, 1208
Collins Fndn Grants, 1209
Colonel Stanley R. McNeil Fndn Grants, 1210
Colorado Interstate Gas Grants, 1213
Colorado Springs Community Grants, 1215
Colorado Grants, 1216
Columbus Fndn Allen Eiry Grants, 1219
Columbus Fndn J. Floyd Dixon Grants, 1222
Columbus Fndn Mary Eleanor Morris Grants, 1225
Columbus Fndn Robert E. and Genevieve B. Schaefer Grants, 1229
Columbus Fndn Traditional Grants, 1233
Comer Fndn Grants, 1236
Comerica Charitable Fndn Grants, 1237
Commission on Religion in Appalachia Grants, 1238
Commonweal Community Assistance Grants, 1239
Commonwealth Fund Australian-American Health Policy Fellowships, 1241
Communities Fndn of Texas Grants, 1243
Community Fndn Alliance City of Evansville Endowment Grants, 1246
Community Fndn for Greater Buffalo Grants, 1247
Community Fndn for Monterey County Grants, 1255
Community Fndn for Muskegon County Grants, 1256
Community Fndn for Southern Arizona Grants, 1261
Community Fndn of Bloomington and Monroe County Grants, 1271
Community Fndn of Broward Grants, 1275

Community Fndn of Central Illinois Grants, 1276
Community Fndn of East Central Illinois Grants, 1278
Community Fndn of Greater Birmingham Grants, 1280
Community Fndn of Greater Flint Grants, 1282
Community Fndn of Greater Greensboro Grants, 1288
Community Fndn of Greater New Britain Grants, 1291
Community Fndn of Greater Tampa Grants, 1292
Community Fndn of Greenville-Greenville Women Giving Grants, 1293
Community Fndn of Greenville Community Enrichment Grants, 1294
Community Fndn of Greenville Hollingsworth Funds Program/Project Grants, 1296
Community Fndn of Middle Tennessee Grants, 1300
Community Fndn of Mount Vernon and Knox County Grants, 1301
Community Fndn of Sarasota County Grants, 1306
Community Fndn of Shreveport-Bossier Grants, 1307
Community Fndn of South Alabama Grants, 1308
Community Fndn of SE Connecticut Grants, 1309
Community Fndn of Tampa Bay Grants, 1316
Community Fndn of the Eastern Shore Community Needs Grants, 1317
Community Fndn of the Ozarks Grants, 1320
Community Fndn of the Verdugos Grants, 1322
Community Fndn of Wabash North County Grants, 1326
Community Fndn of Western N Carolina Grants, 1327
Community Partners Lawrence County Grants, 1328
Community Fndn Silicon Valley Grants, 1331
Community Technology Fndn of California Building Communities Through Technology Grants, 1336
Comprehensive Health Educ Fndn Grants, 1337
ConAgra Foods Community Impact Grants, 1342
ConAgra Foods Nourish Our Comm Grants, 1343
Connecticut Health Fndn Health Init Grants, 1351
Connelly Fndn Grants, 1353
ConocoPhillips Grants, 1355
Conrad N. Hilton Humanitarian Prize, 1356
Constantin Fndn Grants, 1362
Conwood Charitable Grants, 1366
Cooke Fndn Grants, 1368
Cooper Industries Fndn Grants, 1370
Cornerstone Fndn of NE Wisconsin Grants, 1375
Crail-Johnson Fndn Grants, 1393
Cranston Fndn Grants, 1395
Crestlea Fndn Grants, 1399
Crystelle Waggoner Charitable Grants, 1405
CSRA Community Fndn Grants, 1407
Cudd Fndn Grants, 1410
Cullen Fndn Grants, 1411
Cumberland Community Fndn Grants, 1413
Curtis Fndn Grants, 1419
CVS Caremark Charitable Grants, 1421
Cyrus Eaton Fndn Grants, 1423
D. W. McMillan Fndn Grants, 1426
Dade Community Fndn Grants, 1430
DaimlerChrysler Corp Grants, 1432
Dairy Queen Corp Contributions Grants, 1433
Dallas Fndn Grants, 1436
Dallas Mavericks Fndn Grants, 1437
Dana Corp Fndn Grants, 1440
Danellie Fndn Grants, 1442
Dan Murphy Fndn Grants, 1444
Daphne Seybolt Culpeper Memorial Fndn Grants, 1445
David and Barbara B. Hirschhorn Fndn Grants, 1450
David Geffen Fndn Grants, 1452
David Lane Grants for Aged & Indigent Women, 1453
Daviess County Community Fndn Health Grants, 1457
Davis Family Fndn Grants, 1462
Dayton Fndn Grants, 1463
Dayton Power and Light Fndn Grants, 1464
Daywood Fndn Grants, 1465
Deaconess Community Fndn Grants, 1467
Dean Foods Community Involvement Grants, 1469
Dearborn Community County Progress Grants, 1473
Deborah Munroe Noonan Grants, 1475
Delaware Community Fndn-Youth Philanthropy Board for Kent County, 1483
Dell Fndn Open Grants, 1490
DeMatteis Family Fndn Grants, 1497

SUBJECT INDEX

Health Care / 915

Dennis and Phyllis Washington Fndn Grants, 1498
Denton A. Cooley Fndn Grants, 1500
Denver Fndn Community Grants, 1502
DeRoy Testamentary Fndn Grants, 1518
Detroit Lions Charities Grants, 1520
DHHS Adolescent Family Life Demo Projects, 1524
DHHS Emergency Med Services for Children, 1531
DHHS Health Centers Grants for Residents of Public Housing, 1533
DHHS Healthy Tomorrows Partnerships for Children Grants, 1534
DHHS Technical and Non-Financial Assistance to Health Centers, 1539
Dolan Fndn Grants, 1563
Dole Food Company Charitable Contributions, 1564
Dolfinger-McMahon Fndn Grants, 1565
Dominion Fndn Human Needs Grants, 1572
Dora Roberts Fndn Grants, 1579
Doree Taylor Charitable Fndn, 1580
Doris and Victor Day Fndn Grants, 1582
Dorothea Haus Ross Fndn Grants, 1587
Dorothy Rider Pool Health Care Grants, 1589
Do Something BR!CK Awards, 1592
Dr. and Mrs. Paul Pierce Memorial Fndn Grants, 1599
Dr. John T. Macdonald Fndn Grants, 1600
DTE Energy Health & Human Services Grants, 1613
Dubois County Community Fndn Grants, 1615
Duneland Health Council Incorporated Grants, 1621
Dunspaugh-Dalton Fndn Grants, 1623
DuPage Community Fndn Grants, 1624
Dyson Fndn Mid-Hudson Valley General Operating Support Grants, 1635
Dyson Mid-Hudson Valley Project Support, 1636
E.J. Grassmann Grants, 1638
Eddie C. and Sylvia Brown Family Fndn Grants, 1653
Eden Hall Fndn Grants, 1655
Edna Wardlaw Charitable Grants, 1660
EDS Fndn Grants, 1661
Edward and Ellen Roche Relief Fndn Grants, 1663
Edward Bangs Kelley and Elza Kelley Grants, 1665
Edward N. and Della L. Thome Memorial Fndn Direct Services Grants, 1666
Edwards Grants, 1669
Edward W. and Stella C. Van Houten Grants, 1670
Effie and Wofford Cain Fndn Grants, 1674
Elizabeth Morse Genius Charitable Grants, 1682
Elkhart County Community Fndn Grants, 1684
El Paso Community Fndn Grants, 1688
Elsie H. Wilcox Fndn Grants, 1691
Elsie Lee Garthwaite Memorial Fndn Grants, 1692
Emerson Electric Company Contributions Grants, 1695
Ensworth Charitable Fndn Grants, 1710
Entergy Corp Open Grants for Healthy Families, 1715
Erie Community Fndn Grants, 1750
Ethel S. Abbott Charitable Fndn Grants, 1760
Ethel Sergeant Clark Smith Fndn Grants, 1761
Eugene M. Lang Fndn Grants, 1764
Eugene McDermott Grants, 1765
Evanston Community Fndn Grants, 1771
Ewing Halsell Fndn Grants, 1776
F.M. Kirby Fndn Grants, 1780
F.R. Bigelow Fndn Grants, 1781
Fairfield County Community Fndn Grants, 1782
Fan Fox and Leslie R. Samuels Fndn Grants, 1786
FAR Grants, 1787
Fargo-Moorhead Area Fndn Grants, 1788
Fargo-Moorhead Area Fndn Woman's Grants, 1789
Farmers Insurance Corp Giving Grants, 1791
Faye McBeath Fndn Grants, 1794
Fayette County Fndn Grants, 1795
Ferree Fndn Grants, 1804
Fidelity Fndn Grants, 1805
Field Fndn of Illinois Grants, 1806
FirstEnergy Fndn Community Grants, 1819
Fisa Fndn Grants, 1826
Fisher Fndn Grants, 1831
Fisher House Fndn Newman's Own Awards, 1833
Flextronics Fndn Disaster Relief Grants, 1841
Flinn Fndn Grants, 1842
Florence Hunt Maxwell Fndn Grants, 1844

Florian O. Bartlett Grants, 1845
Floyd A. and Kathleen C. Cailloux Fndn Grants, 1874
Fluor Fndn Grants, 1875
FMC Fndn Grants, 1876
Foellinger Fndn Grants, 1877
Fondren Fndn Grants, 1878
Ford Motor Company Grants, 1885
Forrest C. Lattner Fndn Grants, 1887
Foster Fndn Grants, 1888
Fndn for Enhancing Communities Grants, 1893
Fndn for Health Enhancement Grants, 1894
Fndn for Seacoast Health Grants, 1895
Fndns of E Chicago Health Grants, 1910
Fourjay Fndn Grants, 1913
Frances and John L. Loeb Family Grants, 1917
Frances L. and Edwin L. Cummings Grants, 1919
Frances W. Emerson Fndn Grants, 1920
Francis L. Abreu Charitable Grants, 1922
Francis T. & Louise T. Nichols Fndn Grants, 1923
Frank B. Hazard General Charity Grants, 1926
Franklin County Community Fndn Grants, 1929
Franklin H. Wells and Ruth L. Wells Grants, 1930
Frank Reed and Margaret Jane Peters Memorial Fund I Grants, 1933
Frank Reed and Margaret Jane Peters Memorial Fund II Grants, 1934
Frank S. Flowers Fndn Grants, 1935
Frank Stanley Beveridge Fndn Grants, 1936
Frank W. and Carl S. Adams Grants, 1937
Fred & Gretel Biel Charitable Grants, 1939
Fred C. and Katherine B. Andersen Fndn Grants, 1942
Frederick McDonald Grants, 1946
Frederick W. Marzahl Grants, 1948
Fremont Area Community Elderly Needs Grants, 1954
Fremont Area Community Fndn Grants, 1955
Frist Fndn Grants, 1964
Fuller E. Callaway Fndn Grants, 1973
Fulton County Community Fndn Grants, 1975
G.N. Wilcox Grants, 1982
Gates Family Children, Youth & Family Grants, 1989
Gebbie Fndn Grants, 1995
GenCorp Fndn Grants, 1998
General Mills Fndn Grants, 2003
General Motors Fndn Grants Support Program, 2004
General Service Fndn Human Rights and Economic Justice Grants, 2006
George A. and Grace L. Long Fndn Grants, 2008
George and Ruth Bradford Fndn Grants, 2010
George A Ohl Jr. Fndn Grants, 2012
George E. Hatcher, Jr. and Ann Williams Hatcher Fndn Grants, 2015
George Family Fndn Grants, 2017
George Fndn Grants, 2018
George Frederick Jewett Fndn Grants, 2019
George Kress Fndn Grants, 2025
George P. Davenport Grants, 2026
George W. Wells Fndn Grants, 2030
Georgia Power Fndn Grants, 2039
Gertrude and William C. Wardlaw Grants, 2045
Gertrude E. Skelly Charitable Fndn Grants, 2046
Gheens Fndn Grants, 2048
Giant Eagle Fndn Grants, 2049
Gibson Fndn Grants, 2052
Gill Fndn - Gay and Lesbian Grants, 2054
Ginn Fndn Grants, 2056
GlaxoSmithKline Corp Grants, 2060
GNOF IMPACT Grants for Health and Human Services, 2080
GNOF IMPACT Harold W. Newman, Jr. Charitable Grants, 2083
GNOF Norco Community Grants, 2089
Godfrey Fndn Grants, 2095
Golden State Warriors Fndn Grants, 2099
Goodrich Corp Fndn Grants, 2104
Grace and Franklin Bernsen Grants, 2109
Grace Bersted Fndn Grants, 2110
Grand Rapids Area Community Fndn Wyoming Grants, 2116
Grand Rapids Community Fndn Grants, 2118
Grand Rapids Community Ionia County Grants, 2119

Grand Rapids Community Fndn Lowell Grants, 2121
Grand Rapids Community SE Ottawa Grants, 2122
Grand Rapids Community Sparta Grants, 2124
Greater Cincinnati Fndn Priority and Small Projects/ Capacity-Building Grants, 2132
Greater Green Bay Community Fndn Grants, 2135
Greater Kanawha Valley Fndn Grants, 2136
Greater Milwaukee Fndn Grants, 2137
Greater Saint Louis Community Fndn Grants, 2138
Greater Tacoma Community Fndn Grants, 2139
Greater Worcester Comm Discretionary Grants, 2140
Green Bay Packers Fndn Grants, 2148
Green Diamond Charitable Contributions, 2149
Greene County Fndn Grants, 2150
Green Fndn Human Services Grants, 2154
Gregory L. Gibson Charitable Fndn Grants, 2163
Griffin Fndn Grants, 2165
Grotto Fndn Project Grants, 2166
Grover Hermann Fndn Grants, 2168
Guido A. and Elizabeth H. Binda Fndn Grants, 2172
Gulf Coast Community Fndn Grants, 2174
Guy I. Bromley Grants, 2180
H & R Fndn Grants, 2181
H.A. and Mary K. Chapman Charitable Grants, 2182
H. Leslie Hoffman & Elaine Hoffman Grants, 2185
H. Schaffer Fndn Grants, 2187
Hagedorn Grants, 2207
Hall-Perrine Fndn Grants, 2209
Hallmark Corp Fndn Grants, 2212
Harley Davidson Fndn Grants, 2224
Harold Alfond Fndn Grants, 2225
Harold R. Bechtel Charitable Remainder Grants, 2229
Harold Simmons Fndn Grants, 2230
Harris and Eliza Kempner Grants, 2231
Harrison County Community Signature Grants, 2234
Harry S. Black and Allon Fuller Grants, 2243
Harry Sudakoff Fndn Grants, 2245
Hartford Courant Fndn Grants, 2248
Hartford Fndn Regular Grants, 2253
Harvest Fndn Grants, 2254
Hawaii Community Fndn Reverend Takie Okumura Family Grants, 2264
Hawaii Community Fndn West Hawaii Grants, 2266
HCA Fndn Grants, 2274
Healthcare Fndn of New Jersey Grants, 2280
Health Fndn of Greater Indianapolis Grants, 2282
Health Fndn of So Florida Responsive Grants, 2283
Hedco Fndn Grants, 2287
Heineman Fndn for Research, Educ, Charitable and Scientific Purposes, 2290
Helena Rubinstein Fndn Grants, 2292
Helen Gertrude Sparks Charitable Grants, 2294
Helen Irwin Littauer Ed Grants, 2295
Helen K. and Arthur E. Johnson Fndn Grants, 2296
Helen Pumphrey Denit Charitable Grants, 2297
Helen S. Boylan Fndn Grants, 2298
Helen Steiner Rice Fndn Grants, 2299
Helen V. Brach Fndn Grants, 2300
Henrietta Lange Burk Grants, 2303
Henry A. and Mary J. MacDonald Fndn, 2305
Henry County Community Fndn Grants, 2308
Henry W. Bull Fndn Grants, 2312
Herman Goldman Fndn Grants, 2317
Hershey Company Grants, 2318
Highmark Corp Giving Grants, 2319
High Meadow Fndn Grants, 2321
Hill Fndn Grants, 2326
Hillman Fndn Grants, 2327
Hillsdale Grants, 2329
Hilton Head Island Fndn Grants, 2330
Hilton Hotels Corp Giving Grants, 2331
Hirtzel Memorial Fndn Grants, 2332
Hoblitzelle Fndn Grants, 2341
Holland/Zeeland Community Fndn Grants, 2345
Hollie and Anna Oakley Fndn Grants, 2346
Homer Fndn Grants, 2352
Honda of America Manufacturing Fndn Grants, 2354
Horace A. Kimball and S. Ella Kimball Grants, 2362
Horace Moses Charitable Fndn Grants, 2363
Horizon Fndn for New Jersey Grants, 2364

Health Care

Horizons Community Issues Grants, 2366
Hormel Foods Charitable Grants, 2368
Hormel Fndn Grants, 2369
Household Int'l Corp Giving Grants, 2372
Houston Endowment Grants, 2373
Howard and Bush Fndn Grants, 2374
Huffy Fndn Grants, 2384
Hugh J. Andersen Fndn Grants, 2385
Humanitas Fndn Grants, 2390
Huntington Clinical Fndn Grants, 2404
Huntington County Community Fndn - Make a Difference Grants, 2406
Huntington National Bank Comm Affairs Grant, 2409
Hutchinson Community Fndn Grants, 2410
Hut Fndn Grants, 2411
Hutton Fndn Grants, 2412
I.A. O'Shaughnessy Fndn Grants, 2416
Idaho Community Fndn Eastern Region Competitive Grants, 2432
Idaho Power Company Corp Contributions, 2433
IDPH Emergency Med Serv Assistance Grants, 2440
Illinois Tool Works Fndn Grants, 2511
Inasmuch Fndn Grants, 2523
Indep Blue Cross Charitable Med Care Grants, 2524
Intergrys Corp Grants, 2565
Irving S. Gilmore Fndn Grants, 2584
Irvin Stern Fndn Grants, 2585
Isabel Allende Fndn Esperanza Grants, 2586
J.C. Penney Company Grants, 2594
J. Edwin Treakle Fndn Grants, 2596
J.L. Bedsole Fndn Grants, 2600
J.W. Kieckhefer Fndn Grants, 2607
J. Willard Marriott, Jr. Fndn Grants, 2610
Jackson County Community Fndn Grants, 2611
Jackson Fndn Grants, 2613
Jacob and Hilda Blaustein Fndn Grants, 2615
Jacob G. Schmidlapp Grants, 2616
Jacobs Family Village Neighborhoods Grants, 2619
James & Abigail Campbell Family Fndn Grants, 2620
James Ford Bell Fndn Grants, 2623
James Graham Brown Quality of Life Grants, 2625
James J. and Angelia M. Harris Fndn Grants, 2630
James J. McCann Charitable Trust and McCann Fndn, Inc Grants, 2631
James L. and Mary Jane Bowman Grants, 2632
James M. Collins Fndn Grants, 2633
James M. Cox Fndn of Georgia Grants, 2634
James R. Dougherty Jr. Fndn Grants, 2635
James S. Copley Fndn Grants, 2637
Jane Bradley Pettit Fndn Health Grants, 2643
Janirve Fndn Grants, 2645
Janus Fndn Grants, 2647
Jay and Rose Phillips Family Fndn Grants, 2656
Jean and Louis Dreyfus Fndn Grants, 2658
JELD-WEN Fndn Grants, 2661
Jenkins Fndn: Improving the Health of Greater Richmond Grants, 2663
Jennings County Community Fndn Grants, 2664
Jerome and Mildred Paddock Fndn Grants, 2666
Jessie B. Cox Charitable Grants, 2670
Jessie Ball Dupont Grants, 2671
Jewish Grants, 2675
Jim Blevins Fndn Grants, 2678
John Clarke Grants, 2689
John Deere Fndn Grants, 2692
John Edward Fowler Memorial Fndn Grants, 2693
John G. Duncan Grants, 2695
John G. Martin Fndn Grants, 2696
John H. Wellons Fndn Grants, 2699
John J. Leidy Fndn Grants, 2701
John Jewett & Helen Chandler Garland Grants, 2702
John Lord Knight Fndn Grants, 2703
John P. McGovern Fndn Grants, 2707
John P. Murphy Fndn Grants, 2708
John R. Oishei Fndn Grants, 2709
John S. and James L. Knight Fndn Donor Advised Grants, 2712
John S. Dunn Research Fndn Grants and Chairs, 2715
Johns Manville Grants, 2716
Johnson & Johnson Corp Contributions Grants, 2718
Johnson Controls Fndn Health and Social Services Grants, 2722
Johnson County Community Fndn Grants, 2723
John W. Alden Grants, 2727
John W. and Anna H. Hanes Fndn Grants, 2728
John W. Anderson Fndn Grants, 2729
Joseph Drown Fndn Grants, 2735
Josephine G. Russell Grants, 2737
Josephine S. Gumbiner Fndn Grants, 2739
K. M. Hunter Fndn Social Welfare Grants, 2757
K21 Health Fndn Grants, 2760
Kahuku Community Fund, 2762
Kaiser Permanente Cares for Comm Grants, 2763
Kate B. Reynolds Charitable Health Care Grants, 2786
Kate B. Reynolds Charitable Trust Poor and Needy Grants, 2787
Katharine Matthies Grants, 2788
Katherine John Murphy Fndn Grants, 2790
Katrine Menzing Deakins Charitable Grants, 2793
Kelvin and Eleanor Smith Fndn Grants, 2796
Kendrick Fndn Grants, 2797
Ken W. Davis Fndn Grants, 2813
Kettering Family Fndn Grants, 2817
KeySpan Fndn Grants, 2821
L. W. Pierce Family Fndn Grants, 2846
Laidlaw Fndn Youth Organizaing Inits Grants, 2854
Lands' End Corp Giving Program, 2861
Laura Moore Cunningham Fndn Grants, 2866
Lee and Ramona Bass Fndn Grants, 2871
Lena Benas Grants, 2881
Leo Niessen Jr., Charitable Grants, 2885
Liberty Bank Fndn Grants, 2890
Lisa and Douglas Goldman Grants, 2910
Lockheed Martin Philanthropic Grants, 2918
Louetta M. Cowden Fndn Grants, 2922
Louie M. and Betty M. Phillips Fndn Grants, 2923
Louis R. Cappelli Fndn Grants, 2926
Lowe Fndn Grants, 2929
Lowell Berry Fndn Grants, 2930
Lubrizol Fndn Grants, 2933
Ludwick Family Fndn Grants, 2938
Lumpkin Family Healthy People Grants, 2942
M.B. and Edna Zale Fndn Grants, 2950
M. Bastian Family Fndn Grants, 2951
Mabel A. Horne Grants, 2956
Mabel F. Hoffman Charitable Grants, 2957
Mabel Y. Hughes Charitable Grants, 2960
Macquarie Bank Fndn Grants, 2966
Maine Community Fndn Vincent B. and Barbara G. Welch Grants, 2990
Marathon Petroleum Corp Grants, 2999
Margaret L. Wendt Fndn Grants, 3004
Marie C. and Joseph C. Wilson Fndn Rochester Small Grants, 3006
Marietta McNeill Morgan and Samuel Tate Morgan, Jr. Grants, 3008
Marion I. and Henry J. Knott Fndn Discretionary Grants, 3018
Marion I. and Henry J. Knott Standard Grants, 3019
Marjorie Moore Charitable Fndn Grants, 3021
Mars Fndn Grants, 3025
Mary Black Fndn Community Health Grants, 3032
Mary K. Chapman Fndn Grants, 3042
Mary Owen Borden Fndn Grants, 3046
Mary S. and David C. Corbin Fndn Grants, 3048
Mary Wilmer Covey Charitable Grants, 3049
Max A. Adler Charitable Fndn Grants, 3065
Max and Anna Levinson Fndn Grants, 3066
Maxon Charitable Fndn Grants, 3068
McColl Fndn Grants, 3074
McConnell Fndn Grants, 3076
McGregor Grants, 3082
McInerny Fndn Grants, 3083
McLean Contributionship Grants, 3088
McMillen Fndn Grants, 3090
Meadows Fndn Grants, 3104
MeadWestvaco Sustainable Communities Grant, 3105
Mead Witter Fndn Grants, 3106
Mericos Fndn Grants, 3121
Meriden Fndn Grants, 3122
Mervin Bovaird Fndn Grants, 3128
Metro Health Fndn Grants, 3133
MetroWest Health Fndn Capital Grants for Health-Related Facilities, 3134
MetroWest Health Fndn Grants--Healthy Aging, 3135
Metzger-Price Grants, 3137
Meyer Fndn Healthy Communities Grants, 3143
Meyer Memorial Trust Special Grants, 3149
MGN Family Fndn Grants, 3154
Michael Reese Health Trust Core Grants, 3159
Miguel Aleman Fndn Grants, 3175
Military Ex-Prisoners of War Fndn Grants, 3177
Millipore Fndn Grants, 3182
Milton Hicks Wood and Helen Gibbs Wood Charitable Grants, 3184
Mimi and Peter Haas Grants, 3185
MMS and Alliance Charitable Fndn Grants for Community Action and Care for the Medically Uninsured, 3194
Moline Fndn Community Grants, 3202
Monfort Family Fndn Grants, 3203
Mt. Sinai Health Care Fndn Health of the Jewish Community Grants, 3226
Nathan Cummings Fndn Grants, 3246
Needmor Grants, 3289
Nell Warren Elkin and William Simpson Elkin, 3300
New Hampshire Charitable Fndn Grants, 3325
NHSCA Arts in Health Care Project Grants, 3424
Nicholas H. Noyes Jr. Memorial Fndn Grants, 3434
Nina Mason Pulliam Charitable Grants, 3443
Noble County Community Fndn Grants, 3456
Nordson Corp Fndn Grants, 3462
North Carolina Arts Council Outreach Grants, 3479
North Carolina Community Fndn Grants, 3489
North Carolina GlaxoSmithKline Fndn Grants, 3490
North Central Health Services Grants, 3492
Northern New York Community Fndn Grants, 3503
Northern Trust Company Corp Giving Program, 3504
Northrop Grumman Corp Grants, 3507
NW Mutual Fndn Grants, 3509
Norwin S. and Elizabeth N. Bean Fndn Grants, 3515
Nuffield Fndn Africa Grants, 3532
Nuffield Fndn Small Grants, 3535
NWHF Health Advocacy Small Grants, 3537
NWHF Kaiser Permanente Community Grants, 3538
NYCT AIDS/HIV Grants, 3542
NYCT Blindness and Visual Disabilities Grants, 3543
NYCT Children & Youth with Disabilities Grant, 3544
NYCT Girls and Young Women Grants, 3548
NYCT Grants for the Elderly, 3549
NYCT Health Serv, Systems, & Policies Grants, 3550
NYCT Mental Health and Retardation Grants, 3554
Oceanside Charitable Fndn Grants, 3637
Ogden Codman Grants, 3641
Ohio County Community Fndn Grants, 3658
Ohio County Community Fndn Mini-Grants, 3660
Oklahoma City Community Programs & Grants, 3666
Oleonda Jameson Grants, 3667
Olga Sipolin Children's Grants, 3668
Olin Corp Charitable Grants, 3669
Oppenstein Brothers Fndn Grants, 3685
Ordean Fndn Grants, 3691
Oscar Rennebohm Fndn Grants, 3694
OSF Mental Health Init Grants, 3709
Owen County Community Fndn Grants, 3716
PacifiCorp Fndn for Learning Grants, 3727
Pacific Rainbow Fndn Grants, 3728
Pajaro Valley Community Health Trust Insurance/Coverage & Educ on Using the System Grants, 3731
Palm Beach and Martin Counties Grants, 3733
Parkersburg Area Comm Fndn Action Grants, 3738
Patrick and Anna M. Cudahy Grants, 3751
Patron Saints Fndn Grants, 3753
Paul and Mary Haas Fndn Contributions and Student Scholarships, 3756
Paul E. and Klare N. Reinhold Fndn Grants, 3758
Paul Ogle Fndn Grants, 3764
Peacock Fndn Grants, 3809
Percy B. Ferebee Endowment Grants, 3820
Perkins Charitable Fndn Grants, 3823

Health Care

Perpetual Trust for Charitable Giving Grants, 3826
Perry County Community Fndn Grants, 3827
Peter Kiewit Fndn General Grants, 3845
Peter Kiewit Fndn Small Grants, 3847
Peyton Anderson Fndn Grants, 3862
Pfizer Healthcare Charitable Contributions, 3863
Pfizer Special Events Grants, 3865
Phelps County Community Fndn Grants, 3870
Philadelphia Organizational Effectiveness Grants, 3872
Philadelphia Fndn YOUTHadelphia Grants, 3873
Phoenix Coyotes Charities Grants, 3879
Piedmont Health Fndn Grants, 3882
Piedmont Natural Gas Fndn Health and Human Services Grants, 3885
Pike County Community Fndn Grants, 3888
Pinnacle Entertainment Fndn Grants, 3893
Pinnacle Fndn Grants, 3894
Pittsburgh Fndn Community Grants, 3910
Plough Fndn Grants, 3915
Polk Bros. Fndn Grants, 3929
Pollock Fndn Grants, 3930
Posey Community Fndn Women's Grants, 3938
Posey County Community Fndn Grants, 3939
Powell Fndn Grants, 3942
Presbyterian Health Fndn Bridge, Seed and Equipment Grants, 3947
Price Chopper's Golub Fndn Grants, 3950
Price Chopper's Golub Fndn Two-Year Health Care Scholarship, 3951
Price Family Charitable Grants, 3952
Priddy Fndn Grants, 3957
Pride Fndn Grants, 3958
Prince Charitable Trusts Chicago Grants, 3959
Principal Financial Group Fndn Grants, 3966
Procter and Gamble Grants, 3967
Puerto Rico Community Fndn Grants, 3986
Pulaski County Community Fndn Grants, 3988
Putnam County Community Fndn Grants, 3990
Qualcomm Grants, 3993
Quality Health Fndn Grants, 3994
Quantum Fndn Grants, 3996
Questar Corp Contributions Grants, 3997
R.C. Baker Fndn Grants, 3999
R.S. Gernon Grants, 4002
Rainbow Academy Fndn Grants, 4006
Rainbow Endowment Grants, 4007
Rajiv Gandhi Fndn Grants, 4011
Ralph M. Parsons Fndn Grants, 4013
Ralphs Food 4 Less Fndn Grants, 4014
Raskob Fndn for Catholic Activities Grants, 4019
Rasmuson Fndn Capital Grants, 4020
Rathmann Family Fndn Grants, 4026
Regence Fndn Access to Health Care Grants, 4039
Regence Fndn Health Care Community Awareness and Engagement Grants, 4040
Regence Fndn Health Care Connections Grants, 4041
Regence Fndn Improving End-of-Life Grants, 4042
Regence Fndn Tools and Technology Grants, 4043
Retirement Research Fndn General Grants, 4067
Reynolds and Reynolds Associate Fndn Grants, 4069
Rhode Island Fndn Grants, 4073
Richard and Helen DeVos Fndn Grants, 4076
Richard and Rhoda Goldman Grants, 4077
Richard and Susan Smith Family Fndn Grants, 4078
Richard D. Bass Fndn Grants, 4079
Richard E. Griffin Family Fndn Grants, 4081
Richard King Mellon Fndn Grants, 4087
Richard M. Fairbanks Fndn Grants, 4088
Richmond Eye and Ear Grants, 4092
Riley Fndn Grants, 4094
Ripley County Community Fndn Grants, 4095
Ripley County Community Small Project Grants, 4096
Rite Aid Corp Grants, 4101
Robert and Helen Haddad Fndn Grants, 4103
Robert and Joan Dircks Fndn Grants, 4104
Robert E. and Evelyn McKee Fndn Grants, 4110
Robert W. Woodruff Fndn Grants, 4124
Rochester Area Community Fndn Grants, 4127
Rochester Area Fndn Grants, 4128
Rockefeller Brothers Peace and Security Grants, 4133

Rockefeller Brothers Pivotal Places Grants: Serbia, Montenegro, and Kosova, 4135
Rockefeller Fndn Grants, 4138
Rockwell Int'l Corp Grants, 4141
Rollin M. Gerstacker Fndn Grants, 4146
Rollins-Luetkemeyer Fndn Grants, 4147
Ronald McDonald House Charities Grants, 4149
Rose Community Fndn Health Grants, 4154
Rose Hills Fndn Grants, 4162
Rosie's For All Kids Fndn Grants, 4163
Roy and Christine Sturgis Charitable Grants, 4166
Rush County Community Fndn Grants, 4174
Russell Berrie Fndn Grants, 4175
Ruth Anderson Fndn Grants, 4176
Ruth and Vernon Taylor Fndn Grants, 4177
Ruth Eleanor Bamberger and John Ernest Bamberger Memorial Fndn Grants, 4178
Ruth H. and Warren A. Ellsworth Fndn Grants, 4179
RWJF Changes in Health Care Financing and Organization Grants, 4182
RWJF Community Health Leaders Awards, 4183
RWJF Jobs to Careers: Promoting Work-Based Learning for Quality Care, 4185
RWJF Local Funding Partnerships Grants, 4186
RWJF Pioneer Portfolio Grants, 4189
RWJF Vulnerable Populations Portfolio Grants, 4190
Ryder System Charitable Fndn Grants, 4191
S. Livingston Mather Charitable Grants, 4200
S. Mark Taper Fndn Grants, 4201
Saigh Fndn Grants, 4210
Sailors' Snug Harbor of Boston Elder Grants, 4211
Saint Louis Rams Fndn Community Donations, 4214
Saint Luke's Fndn Grants, 4215
Samuel S. Johnson Fndn Grants, 4239
San Antonio Area Fndn Grants, 4240
San Diego Health & Human Services Grants, 4248
San Diego Fndn Paradise Valley Hospital Community Grants, 4249
Sands Fndn Grants, 4255
San Francisco Fndn Community Health Grants, 4263
San Juan Island Community Fndn Grants, 4283
Santa Barbara Strategy Core Suupport Grants, 4286
Sarah Scaife Fndn Grants, 4295
Sarkeys Fndn Grants, 4297
Schering-Plough Fndn Health Grants, 4304
Schramm Fndn Grants, 4310
Schurz Communications Fndn Grants, 4312
Scott County Community Fndn Grants, 4314
Seagate Tech Corp Capacity to Care Grants, 4317
Seattle Fndn Benjamin N. Phillips Grants, 4322
Seattle Fndn Health and Wellness Grants, 4328
Self Fndn Grants, 4335
Seneca Foods Fndn Grants, 4336
Shell Oil Company Fndn Grants, 4343
Sheltering Arms Grants, 4344
Sidney Stern Grants, 4349
Siebert Lutheran Fndn Grants, 4351
Simmons Fndn Grants, 4360
Simple Advise Educ Center Grants, 4361
Singing for Change Fndn Grants, 4363
Sioux Falls Area Community Grants, 4364
Sioux Falls Area Community Fndn Field-of-Interest and Donor-Advised Grants, 4365
Sioux Falls Area Community Fndn Spot Grants, 4366
Siragusa Fndn Arts & Culture Grants, 4367
Siragusa Fndn Health Services & Medical Research Grants, 4368
Sir Dorabji Tata Grants for NGOs or Voluntary Organizations, 4370
Sisters of Charity Fndn of Canton Grants, 4372
Sisters of Mercy of North Carolina Fndn Grants, 4375
Sisters of Saint Joseph Charitable Grants, 4376
SOCFOC Catholic Ministries Grants, 4392
Solo Cup Fndn Grants, 4401
Sonoco Fndn Grants, 4403
Sonora Area Fndn Competitive Grants, 4404
Sophia Romero Grants, 4406
Sosland Fndn Grants, 4408
Southbury Community Trust Fund, 4409
South Madison Community Fndn Grants, 4440

SW Florida Community Competitive Grants, 4442
SW Gas Corp Fndn Grants, 4445
Southwire Company Grants, 4447
Spencer County Community Fndn Grants, 4451
Sprague Fndn Grants, 4461
Springs Close Fndn Grants, 4462
Stackpole-Hall Fndn Grants, 4472
Stan and Sandy Checketts Fndn, 4473
Starr Fndn Grants, 4483
State Street Fndn Grants, 4495
Steelcase Fndn Grants, 4497
Steele-Reese Fndn Grants, 4498
Steuben County Community Fndn Grants, 4501
Stewart Huston Charitable Grants, 4505
Strowd Roses Grants, 4515
Subaru of Indiana Automotive Fndn Grants, 4519
Sulzberger Fndn Grants, 4522
Summit Fndn Grants, 4524
Sunderland Fndn Grants, 4527
Sunflower Fndn Bridge Grants, 4528
Sunoco Fndn Grants, 4530
Susan Mott Webb Charitable Grants, 4536
Susan Vaughan Fndn Grants, 4537
Swindells Charitable Fndn, 4542
Taylor S. Abernathy and Patti Harding Abernathy Charitable Grants, 4564
Telluride Fndn Community Grants, 4573
Temple-Inland Fndn Grants, 4576
Tension Envelope Fndn Grants, 4578
Texas Instruments Corp Health and Human Services Grants, 4598
Textron Corp Contributions Grants, 4601
Thelma Braun and Bocklett Family Fndn Grants, 4603
Theodore Edson Parker Fndn Grants, 4605
Thomas and Dorothy Leavey Fndn Grants, 4612
Thomas Austin Finch, Sr. Fndn Grants, 4613
Thomas C. Ackerman Fndn Grants, 4615
Thomas J. Atkins Grants, 4617
Thomas J. Long Fndn Community Grants, 4618
Thomas Sill Fndn Grants, 4619
Thomas Thompson Grants, 4620
Thompson Charitable Fndn Grants, 4622
TJX Fndn Grants, 4637
Todd Brock Family Fndn Grants, 4639
Toyota Motor Engineering & Manufacturing North America Grants, 4651
Toyota Motor Manufacturing of Alabama Grants, 4652
Toyota Motor Manufacturing Mississippi Grants, 4655
Toyota Motor Manufacturing of Texas Grants, 4656
Toyota Motor Manufacturing W Virginia Grants, 4657
Triangle Community Fndn Donor Grants, 4668
Tull Charitable Fndn Grants, 4679
Turner Fndn Grants, 4681
TWS Fndn Grants, 4683
U.S. Department of Educ 21st Century Community Learning Centers, 4687
Union Bank Corp Sponsorships and Donations, 4708
Union Bank, N.A. Fndn Grants, 4709
Union Benevolent Association Grants, 4710
Union County Community Fndn Grants, 4711
United Methodist Committee on Relief Global AIDS Grants, 4719
United Methodist Child Mental Health Grants, 4721
United Technologies Corp Grants, 4725
USAID Family Health Plus Project Grants, 4751
USAID HIV Prevention with Key Populations - Mali Grants, 4757
USAID Integration of Care and Support within the Health System to Support Better Patient Outcomes Grants, 4762
USAID NGO Health Service Delivery Grants, 4771
US Airways Community Fndn Grants, 4789
USDA Delta Health Care Services Grants, 4804
Vancouver Fndn Grants & Comm Inits, 4900
Vancouver Sun Children's Grants, 4901
Verizon Fndn Grants, 4911
Verizon Health Care and Accessibility Grants, 4913
Vermont Community Fndn Grants, 4929
VHA Health Fndn Grants, 4931
Victor E. Speas Fndn Grants, 4933

/ Health Care

Vigneron Grants, 4938
Virginia W. Kettering Fndn Grants, 4950
Vulcan Materials Company Fndn Grants, 4956
W. C. Griffith Fndn Grants, 4958
W.C. Griffith Fndn Grants, 4957
W.H. and Mary Ellen Cobb Charitable Grants, 4959
W.K. Kellogg Fndn Secure Families Grants, 4963
W.M. Keck Fndn Southern California Grants, 4964
W.P. and Bulah Luse Fndn Grants, 4965
Wabash Valley Community Fndn Grants, 4971
Waitt Family Fndn Grants, 4973
Walter L. Gross III Family Fndn Grants, 4983
Warrick County Community Fndn Grants, 4987
Washington Gas Charitable Contributions, 5000
Wayne and Gladys Valley Fndn Grants, 5003
Wayne County Fndn Grants, 5005
Weatherwax Fndn Grants, 5014
Weaver Popcorn Fndn Grants, 5016
Weingart Fndn Grants, 5018
Welborn Baptist General Opportunity Grants, 5020
Welborn Baptist Fndn Improvements to Community Health Status Grants, 5021
Western Indiana Community Fndn Grants, 5024
Weyerhaeuser Company Fndn Grants, 5053
WHO Fndn General Grants, 5063
William A. Badger Fndn Grants, 5072
William B. Stokely Jr. Fndn Grants, 5076
William Blair and Company Fndn Grants, 5078
William G. and Helen C. Hoffman Fndn Grants, 5080
William G. Gilmore Fndn Grants, 5082
William G. McGowan Charitable Grants, 5084
William H. Hannon Fndn Grants, 5086
William J. and Dorothy K. O'Neill Fndn Grants, 5087
William J. Brace Charitable Trust, 5088
Wilson-Wood Fndn Grants, 5098
Winifred & Harry B. Allen Fndn Grants, 5101
Winston-Salem Fndn Competitive Grants, 5102
Winston-Salem Fndn Elkin/Tri-County Grants, 5103
Winston-Salem Fndn Stokes County Grants, 5104
Wolfe Associates Grants, 5110
Wood-Claeyssens Fndn Grants, 5113
Yawkey Fndn Grants, 5125
Yellow Corp Fndn Grants, 5126

Health Care Access
2 Depot Square Ipswich Charitable Fndn Grants, 4
3M Company Health and Human Services Grants, 14
1104 Fndn Grants, 34
AAP Community Access To Child Health Advocacy Training Grants, 62
AAP Community Access To Child Health Implementation Grants, 63
AAP Community Access to Child Health Planning Grants, 64
AAP Community Access To Child Health Residency Training Grants, 65
AAP Community Access To Child Health Resident Grants, 66
AAP Leonard P. Rome Community Access to Child Health Visiting Professorships, 67
AAP Resident Init Grants, 69
Abbott Fund Community Grants, 81
Abell Fndn Health and Human Services Grants, 96
Abernethy Family Fndn Grants, 98
Abundance Fndn Int'l Grants, 108
ACF Supplemental Services for Recently Arrived Refugees Grants, 125
Achelis Fndn Grants, 127
Actors Fund Dancers' Resource, 137
Adam Richter Charitable Grants, 145
Adams and Reese LLP Corp Giving Grants, 147
Adler-Clark Electric Community Commitment Fndn Grants, 164
Administration on Aging Senior Medicare Patrol Project Grants, 166
AEGON Transamerica Health & Welfare Grants, 179
Aetna Fndn Health Grants in Connecticut, 184
Aetna Fndn Obesity Grants, 185
Aetna Fndn Racial and Ethnic Health Care Equity Grants, 186

A Friends' Fndn Grants, 194
Agnes M. Lindsay Grants, 203
Aid for Starving Children African American Indep Single Mother's Grants, 210
Aid for Starving Children Emergency Assistance Grants, 211
Albert W. Rice Charitable Fndn Grants, 347
Alexander Eastman Fndn Grants, 355
Alfred and Tillie Shemanski Testamentary Grants, 363
Alfred Bersted Fndn Grants, 364
Alfred E. Chase Charitable Fndn Grants, 366
Alice C. A. Sibley Grants, 371
Allan C. and Leila J. Garden Fndn Grants, 374
Allen Hilles Grants, 378
Alliance Healthcare Fndn Grants, 383
AMA Fndn Fund for Better Health Grants, 409
AMA Fndn Healthy Communities/Healthy America Grants, 410
Amelia Sillman Rockwell and Carlos Perry Rockwell Charities Grants, 417
American Express Community Service Grants, 430
Angels Baseball Fndn Grants, 465
Anheuser-Busch Fndn Grants, 470
Appalachian Reg Comm Health Care Grants, 507
Assurant Health Fndn Grants, 596
AT&T Fndn Civic and Comm Service Grants, 599
Autzen Fndn Grants, 622
Babcock Charitable Grants, 632
Balfe Family Fndn Grants, 636
Baptist-Trinity Lutheran Legacy Fndn Grants, 663
Baptist Community Ministries Grants, 664
Barra Fndn Community Grants, 673
Barrasso Usdin Kupperman Freeman and Sarver LLC Corp Grants, 675
Baxter Int'l Corp Giving Grants, 689
Baxter Int'l Fndn Foster G. McGaw Prize, 690
Baxter Int'l Fndn Grants, 691
BBVA Compass Fndn Charitable Grants, 703
BCBSM Community Health Matching Grants, 707
BCBSM Fndn Investigator Research Grants, 708
BCBSNC Fndn Grants, 712
BCBS of Massachusetts Fndn Grants, 713
Benton Community Fndn - The Cookie Jar Grant, 729
Benton County Fndn Grants, 731
Bernard and Audre Rapoport Fndn Health Grants, 738
Better Way Fndn Grants, 754
BHHS Legacy Fndn Grants, 758
Blue Cross Blue Shield of Minnesota Fndn - Healthy Children: Growing Up Healthy Grants, 794
Blue Shield of California Grants, 802
Bodman Fndn Grants, 807
Brian G. Dyson Fndn Grants, 834
Bristol-Myers Squibb Patient Assistance Grants, 841
Bush Fndn Health & Human Services Grants, 875
Caesars Fndn Grants, 891
California Community Fndn Health Care Grants, 901
California Endowment Innovative Ideas Challenge Grants, 904
Cardinal Health Fndn Grants, 923
Cargill Citizenship Fund-Corp Giving Grants, 925
Carl B. and Florence E. King Fndn Grants, 928
Carl R. Hendrickson Family Fndn Grants, 935
CFFVR Jewelers Mutual Charitable Giving, 1014
Chapman Charitable Fndn Grants, 1033
Charles H. Hall Fndn, 1044
Charles H. Pearson Fndn Grants, 1045
Charles Nelson Robinson Grants, 1052
Charlotte County (FL) Community Fndn Grants, 1056
CHCF Grants, 1063
Chemtura Corp Contributions Grants, 1067
CICF City of Noblesville Community Grant, 1118
CICF Senior Grants, 1127
Cigna Civic Affairs Sponsorships, 1129
Clark and Ruby Baker Fndn Grants, 1154
Claude Worthington Benedum Fndn Grants, 1161
Cleveland Community Responsive Grants, 1168
CNCS AmeriCorps Indian Planning Grants, 1180
CNCS Social Innovation Grants, 1189
Colorado Grants, 1216
Columbus Fndn Allen Eiry Grants, 1219

SUBJECT INDEX

Columbus Fndn J. Floyd Dixon Grants, 1222
Columbus Fndn Mary Eleanor Morris Grants, 1225
Comerica Charitable Fndn Grants, 1237
Community Fndn of Boone Cty Women's Grants, 1273
Community Fndn of Greater Birmingham Grants, 1280
Community Fndn of Howard County Grants, 1297
Community Fndn of Southern Indiana Grants, 1310
Community Fndn of Switzerland County Grants, 1315
Community Partners Lawrence County Grants, 1328
Community Impact Fund, 1332
Connecticut Health Fndn Health Init Grants, 1351
Covidien Medical Product Donations, 1390
Covidien Partnership for Neighborhood Wellness Grants, 1391
CVS Community Grants, 1422
D. W. McMillan Fndn Grants, 1426
David Lane Grants for Aged & Indigent Women, 1453
Daviess County Community Fndn Health Grants, 1457
Deborah Munroe Noonan Grants, 1475
DIFFA/Chicago Grants, 1547
Dining for Women Grants, 1548
Dominion Fndn Human Needs Grants, 1572
Doree Taylor Charitable Fndn, 1580
Dr. and Mrs. Paul Pierce Memorial Fndn Grants, 1599
DTE Energy Health & Human Services Grants, 1613
Dyson Mid-Hudson Valley Project Support, 1636
Edina Realty Fndn Grants, 1656
Edward and Ellen Roche Relief Fndn Grants, 1663
Edward N. and Della L. Thome Memorial Fndn Direct Services Grants, 1666
Eisner Fndn Grants, 1678
Elkhart County Community Fndn Fund for Elkhart County, 1683
Emerson Electric Company Contributions Grants, 1695
Ensworth Charitable Fndn Grants, 1710
Essex County Community Fndn Merrimack Valley General Grants, 1756
Eugene G. & Margaret M. Blackford Grants, 1763
Families Count: The National Honors Program, 1784
Faye McBeath Fndn Grants, 1794
FCD Child Development Grants, 1796
Flinn Fndn Grants, 1842
Florian O. Bartlett Grants, 1845
Fndn for a Healthy Kentucky Grants, 1891
Fndn for Mid South Comm Development Grants, 1897
Fndn for Mid South Health & Wellness Grants, 1899
Fndns of E Chicago Health Grants, 1910
Frances W. Emerson Fndn Grants, 1920
Frank B. Hazard General Charity Grants, 1926
Frank Reed and Margaret Jane Peters Memorial Fund II Grants, 1934
Frederick McDonald Grants, 1946
Frederick W. Marzahl Grants, 1948
Fulton County Community Fndn Women's Giving Circle Grants, 1976
General Service Fndn Human Rights and Economic Justice Grants, 2006
George A. and Grace L. Long Fndn Grants, 2008
George E. Hatcher, Jr. and Ann Williams Hatcher Fndn Grants, 2015
George W. Wells Fndn Grants, 2030
German Protestant Orphan Asylum Fndn Grants, 2044
Gibson County Community Fndn Women's Fund, 2051
Gibson Fndn Grants, 2052
GlaxoSmithKline Corp Grants, 2060
GNOF Bayou Communities Grants, 2069
GNOF IMPACT Grants for Health and Human Services, 2080
GNOF IMPACT Gulf States Eye Surgery Fund, 2082
GNOF IMPACT Harold W. Newman, Jr. Charitable Grants, 2083
GNOF Norco Community Grants, 2089
Grace Bersted Fndn Grants, 2110
Great-West Life Grants, 2130
Green Fndn Human Services Grants, 2154
Gregory L. Gibson Charitable Fndn Grants, 2163
Guy I. Bromley Grants, 2180
Harold and Arlene Schnitzer CARE Grants, 2226
Harold Brooks Fndn Grants, 2227
Harrison County Community Signature Grants, 2234

SUBJECT INDEX Health Care Economics / 919

Harry Edison Fndn, 2241
Harry S. Black and Allon Fuller Grants, 2243
Harry Sudakoff Fndn Grants, 2245
Harvest Fndn Grants, 2254
Healthcare Fndn for Orange County Grants, 2279
Healthcare Fndn of New Jersey Grants, 2280
Health Fndn of So Florida Responsive Grants, 2283
Helen Irwin Littauer Ed Grants, 2295
Henrietta Lange Burk Grants, 2303
Henry A. and Mary J. MacDonald Fndn, 2305
Henry E. Niles Fndn Grants, 2309
Henry J. Kaiser Family Fndn Grants, 2310
Hill Crest Fndn Grants, 2324
Horace Moses Charitable Fndn Grants, 2363
HRSA Nurse Educ, Practice, Quality and Retention Grants, 2381
Huntington Clinical Fndn Grants, 2404
Huntington County Community Fndn - Make a Difference Grants, 2406
IBCAT Screening Mammography Grants, 2422
IDPH Hosptial Capital Investment Grants, 2441
Indep Blue Cross Charitable Med Care Grants, 2524
J. Edwin Treakle Fndn Grants, 2596
James M. Cox Fndn of Georgia Grants, 2634
Jane Bradley Pettit Fndn Health Grants, 2643
Jerome and Mildred Paddock Fndn Grants, 2666
Jewish Grants, 2675
John Clarke Grants, 2689
Johnson & Johnson Comm Health Care Grants, 2717
Johnson & Johnson Corp Contributions Grants, 2718
Johnson Controls Fndn Health and Social Services Grants, 2722
Joseph Drown Fndn Grants, 2735
Kaiser Permanente Cares for Comm Grants, 2763
Kate B. Reynolds Charitable Trust Poor and Needy Grants, 2787
Kendrick Fndn Grants, 2797
Kenneth T. and Eileen L. Norris Fndn Grants, 2802
Lena Benas Grants, 2881
Louetta M. Cowden Fndn Grants, 2922
Louie M. and Betty M. Phillips Fndn Grants, 2923
Lumpkin Family Healthy People Grants, 2942
Macquarie Bank Fndn Grants, 2966
Marathon Petroleum Corp Grants, 2999
Marietta McNeill Morgan and Samuel Tate Morgan, Jr. Grants, 3008
Marion Gardner Jackson Charitable Grants, 3017
Marshall County Community Fndn Grants, 3026
Mary Black Fndn Community Health Grants, 3032
Mary K. Chapman Fndn Grants, 3042
Mary Wilmer Covey Charitable Grants, 3049
Medtronic Fndn CommunityLink Health Grants, 3111
MetroWest Health Fndn Capital Grants for Health-Related Facilities, 3134
MetroWest Health Fndn Grants--Healthy Aging, 3135
Metzger-Price Grants, 3137
Meyer Fndn Healthy Communities Grants, 3143
MGM Resorts Fndn Community Grants, 3153
Michael and Susan Dell Fndn Grants, 3158
Michael Reese Health Trust Responsive Grants, 3160
Mid-Iowa Health Fndn Comm Response Grants, 3168
MMS and Alliance Charitable Fndn Grants for Community Action and Care for the Medically Uninsured, 3194
Moline Fndn Community Grants, 3202
Morris and Gwendolyn Cafritz Fndn Grants, 3218
Ms. Fndn for Women Health Grants, 3225
Mt. Sinai Health Care Fndn Health of the Jewish Community Grants, 3226
Mt. Sinai Health Care Fndn Health of the Urban Community Grants, 3227
Mt. Sinai Health Care Fndn Policy Grants, 3228
Northern Trust Company Corp Giving Program, 3504
NW Airlines KidCares Med Travel Assistance, 3508
NYCT AIDS/HIV Grants, 3542
NYCT Blindness and Visual Disabilities Grants, 3543
NYCT Children & Youth with Disabilities Grant, 3544
NYCT Grants for the Elderly, 3549
NYCT Health Serv, Systems, & Policies Grants, 3550
NYCT Mental Health and Retardation Grants, 3554

Ohio County Community Fndn Grants, 3658
Ohio County Community Fndn Mini-Grants, 3660
Olga Sipolin Children's Grants, 3668
Orange County Community Fndn Grants, 3687
OSF-Baltimore Tackling Drug Addiction Grants, 3698
OSF Mental Health Init Grants, 3709
Otto Bremer Fndn Grants, 3713
Pajaro Valley Community Health Trust Insurance/Coverage & Educ on Using the System Grants, 3731
Paul G. Allen Family Fndn Grants, 3759
Peyton Anderson Fndn Grants, 3862
Pfizer Healthcare Charitable Contributions, 3863
Pfizer Special Events Grants, 3865
Philanthrofund Fndn Grants, 3874
Piedmont Natural Gas Fndn Health and Human Services Grants, 3885
Pinnacle Entertainment Fndn Grants, 3893
Piper Trust Healthcare & Med Research Grants, 3903
Piper Trust Older Adults Grants, 3904
Piper Trust Reglious Organizations Grants, 3905
Porter County Health and Wellness Grant, 3933
Portland Fndn - Women's Giving Circle Grant, 3935
Portland Fndn Grants, 3936
Price Chopper's Golub Fndn Grants, 3950
Qualcomm Grants, 3993
Quality Health Fndn Grants, 3994
Quantum Corp Snap Server Grants, 3995
Rainbow Endowment Grants, 4007
Ralph M. Parsons Fndn Grants, 4013
Raymond John Wean Fndn Grants, 4028
Regence Fndn Access to Health Care Grants, 4039
Regence Fndn Health Care Community Awareness and Engagement Grants, 4040
Regence Fndn Health Care Connections Grants, 4041
Regence Fndn Improving End-of-Life Grants, 4042
Regence Fndn Tools and Technology Grants, 4043
Reynolds and Reynolds Associate Fndn Grants, 4069
Robert F. Stoico / FIRSTFED Grants, 4112
Robert R. Meyer Fndn Grants, 4121
Rockefeller Fndn Grants, 4138
Rose Community Fndn Health Grants, 4154
RWJF Changes in Health Care Financing and Organization Grants, 4182
RWJF Local Funding Partnerships Grants, 4186
RWJF New Jersey Health Inits Grants, 4187
RWJF Partners Investing in Nursing's Future, 4188
RWJF Pioneer Portfolio Grants, 4189
RWJF Vulnerable Populations Portfolio Grants, 4190
SAG Motion Picture Players Welfare Grants, 4209
Sailors' Snug Harbor of Boston Elder Grants, 4211
Saint Luke's Fndn Grants, 4215
San Diego Fndn Paradise Valley Hospital Community Grants, 4249
Sands Fndn Grants, 4255
San Francisco Fndn Community Health Grants, 4263
Santa Barbara Strategy Core Suupport Grants, 4286
Santa Fe Community Fndn Seasonal Grants, 4290
Seattle Fndn Benjamin N. Phillips Grants, 4322
Seattle Fndn Health and Wellness Grants, 4328
Sheltering Arms Grants, 4344
Sierra Health Fndn Responsive Grants, 4353
Siragusa Fndn Health Services & Medical Research Grants, 4368
Sir Dorabji Tata Grants for NGOs or Voluntary Organizations, 4370
Sisters of St. Joseph Healthcare Fndn Grants, 4377
Solo Cup Fndn Grants, 4401
Sophia Romero Grants, 4406
Texas Instruments Corp Health and Human Services Grants, 4598
Thelma Braun and Bocklett Family Fndn Grants, 4603
Thomas J. Long Fndn Community Grants, 4618
Topfer Family Fndn Grants, 4646
Toyota Motor Manufacturing W Virginia Grants, 4657
Union Labor Health Fndn Community Grants, 4713
Union Square Awards Grants, 4718
United Methodist Child Mental Health Grants, 4721
USAID Accelerating Progress Against Tuberculosis in Kenya Grants, 4737
USAID Family Health Plus Project Grants, 4751

USAID HIV Prevention with Key Populations - Mali Grants, 4757
USAID Integration of Care and Support within the Health System to Support Better Patient Outcomes Grants, 4762
USAID Knowledge for Health II Grants, 4765
USAID NGO Health Service Delivery Grants, 4771
USDA Delta Health Care Services Grants, 4804
USDC Technology Opportunities Grants, 4860
Vanderburgh Community Fndn Grants, 4902
Verizon Health Care and Accessibility Grants, 4913
Visiting Nurse Fndn Grants, 4951
W.H. and Mary Ellen Cobb Charitable Grants, 4959
W.K. Kellogg Fndn Secure Families Grants, 4963
W.M. Keck Fndn Southern California Grants, 4964
W.P. and Bulah Luse Fndn Grants, 4965
Washington County Community Youth Grants, 4998
Weaver Popcorn Fndn Grants, 5016
Welborn Baptist Fndn Improvements to Community Health Status Grants, 5021
WHO Fndn General Grants, 5063
William J. Brace Charitable Trust, 5088
Wolfe Associates Grants, 5110

Health Care Administration
Bush Fndn Medical Fellowships, 877
Canada-U.S. Fulbright Mid-Career Grants, 917
Covenant Ed Fndn Grants, 1383
Deborah Munroe Noonan Grants, 1475
DHHS Technical and Non-Financial Assistance to Health Centers, 1539
E. Rhodes and Leona B. Carpenter Fndn Grants, 1640
Hartford Aging and Health Program Awards, 2247
Henry J. Kaiser Family Fndn Grants, 2310
Michael Reese Health Trust Core Grants, 3159
Mt. Sinai Health Care Fndn Policy Grants, 3228
NYCT Health Serv, Systems, & Policies Grants, 3550
OSF-Baltimore Tackling Drug Addiction Grants, 3698
RWJF Health Policy Fellowships, 4184
USAID Knowledge for Health II Grants, 4765

Health Care Assessment
Alexander Eastman Fndn Grants, 355
Blue Cross Blue Shield of Minnesota Healthy Equity: Impact Assessment Demonstration Grants, 795
Blue Cross Blue Shield of Minnesota Fndn - Healthy Equity: Health Impact Assessment Grants, 796
CHCF Grants, 1063
Commonwealth Fund Harkness Fellowships in Health Care Policy and Practice, 1242
Covidien Partnership for Neighborhood Wellness Grants, 1391
Hartford Aging and Health Program Awards, 2247
Johnson & Johnson Comm Health Care Grants, 2717
Kansas Health Fndn Recognition Grants, 2784
NYCT Children & Youth with Disabilities Grant, 3544
NYCT Health Serv, Systems, & Policies Grants, 3550
Piedmont Natural Gas Fndn Health and Human Services Grants, 3885
USAID NGO Health Service Delivery Grants, 4771
USDC Technology Opportunities Grants, 4860

Health Care Economics
AMI Semiconductors Corp Grants, 457
CDC Grants for Violence-Related Injury Prevention Research, 974
CHCF Grants, 1063
Fndn for Seacoast Health Grants, 1895
GNOF IMPACT Grants for Health and Human Services, 2080
Hartford Aging and Health Program Awards, 2247
Kendrick Fndn Grants, 2797
Mt. Sinai Health Care Fndn Policy Grants, 3228
Northern Trust Company Corp Giving Program, 3504
Percy B. Ferebee Endowment Grants, 3820
RWJF Changes in Health Care Financing and Organization Grants, 4182
Sisters of Charity Fndn of Cleveland Reducing Health Disparities in Central Neighborhood Grants, 4374
USDC Technology Opportunities Grants, 4860

Health Care Financing

Alliance Healthcare Fndn Grants, 383
Baptist-Trinity Lutheran Legacy Fndn Grants, 663
BCBSM Fndn Investigator Research Grants, 708
California Community Fndn Health Care Grants, 901
Covidien Partnership for Neighborhood Wellness Grants, 1391
Hartford Aging and Health Program Awards, 2247
Mt. Sinai Health Care Fndn Policy Grants, 3228
NYCT AIDS/HIV Grants, 3542

Health Care Personnel

Connecticut Health Fndn Health Init Grants, 1351
Covidien Partnership for Neighborhood Wellness Grants, 1391
Pfizer Medical Educ Track One Grants, 3864

Health Care Promotion

Albert W. Rice Charitable Fndn Grants, 347
Baxter Int'l Fndn Foster G. McGaw Prize, 690
Blue Cross Blue Shield of Minnesota Fndn - Healthy Equity: Public Libraries for Health Grants, 797
Cigna Civic Affairs Sponsorships, 1129
CNCS AmeriCorps Indian Planning Grants, 1180
Community Fndn of Bloomington and Monroe County - Precision Health Network Cycle Grants, 1270
Covidien Partnership for Neighborhood Wellness Grants, 1391
Fndn for Mid South Comm Development Grants, 1897
George E. Hatcher, Jr. and Ann Williams Hatcher Fndn Grants, 2015
George W. Wells Fndn Grants, 2030
Gibson County Community Fndn Women's Fund, 2051
GNOF IMPACT Grants for Health and Human Services, 2080
GNOF IMPACT Kahn-Oppenheim Grants, 2084
Hill Crest Fndn Grants, 2324
Meyer Fndn Healthy Communities Grants, 3143
Michael Reese Health Trust Responsive Grants, 3160
Moline Fndn Community Grants, 3202
Mt. Sinai Health Care Fndn Health of the Urban Community Grants, 3227
Mt. Sinai Health Care Fndn Policy Grants, 3228
Nestle Fndn Training Grant, 3301
Porter County Health and Wellness Grant, 3933
Saint Luke's Fndn Grants, 4215
Union Labor Health Fndn Community Grants, 4713
USAID Development Assistance Grants, 4748
USAID Family Health Plus Project Grants, 4751
USAID NGO Health Service Delivery Grants, 4771
USDA Delta Health Care Services Grants, 4804

Health Disparities

Aetna Fndn Racial and Ethnic Health Care Equity Grants, 186
Appalachian Reg Comm Health Care Grants, 507
California Endowment Innovative Ideas Challenge Grants, 904
GNOF IMPACT Grants for Health and Human Services, 2080
Guy I. Bromley Grants, 2180
Louetta M. Cowden Fndn Grants, 2922
Medtronic Fndn CommunityLink Health Grants, 3111
Michael and Susan Dell Fndn Grants, 3158
Porter County Health and Wellness Grant, 3933
Union Labor Health Fndn Community Grants, 4713

Health Insurance

AAP Community Access To Child Health Advocacy Training Grants, 62
AAP Community Access to Child Health Planning Grants, 64
AAP Community Access To Child Health Residency Training Grants, 65
AAP Community Access To Child Health Resident Grants, 66
AAP Leonard P. Rome Community Access to Child Health Visiting Professorships, 67
Alliance Healthcare Fndn Grants, 383
AMA Fndn Fund for Better Health Grants, 409
Austin-Bailey Health and Wellness Fndn Grants, 614
BCBSNC Fndn Grants, 712
BCBS of Massachusetts Fndn Grants, 713
Blue Shield of California Grants, 802
CHCF Grants, 1063
CHCF Local Coverage Expansion Init, 1064
Edwards Grants, 1669
Fndn for a Healthy Kentucky Grants, 1891
Guy I. Bromley Grants, 2180
Health Fndn of Greater Cincinnati Grants, 2281
Kaiser Permanente Cares for Comm Grants, 2763
Louetta M. Cowden Fndn Grants, 2922
Medicaid/SCHIP Eligibility Pilots, 3107
Michael Reese Health Trust Responsive Grants, 3160
Mid-Iowa Health Fndn Comm Response Grants, 3168
MMS and Alliance Charitable Fndn Grants for Community Action and Care for the Medically Uninsured, 3194
Mt. Sinai Health Care Fndn Policy Grants, 3228
Prince Charitable Trusts Chicago Grants, 3959
Quantum Corp Snap Server Grants, 3995
Quantum Fndn Grants, 3996
Rehab Therapy Fndn Grants, 4050
RWJF Changes in Health Care Financing and Organization Grants, 4182
South Carolina Arts Commission Incentive Grants for Employer Sponsored Benefits, 4422

Health Personnel/Professions

ALA Exceptional Service Award, 278
BCBSM Fndn Student Award Program, 710
MMS and Alliance Charitable Fndn Int'l Health Studies Grants, 3195
Prince Charitable Trusts Chicago Grants, 3959

Health Planning/Policy

3M Company Health and Human Services Grants, 14
AAAS Science and Technology Policy Fellowships: Health, Educ and Human Services, 53
AAP Community Access To Child Health Advocacy Training Grants, 62
AAP Community Access to Child Health Planning Grants, 64
AAP Community Access To Child Health Residency Training Grants, 65
AAP Community Access To Child Health Resident Grants, 66
AAP Leonard P. Rome Community Access to Child Health Visiting Professorships, 67
Acumen Global Fellowships, 142
Alvin and Fanny Blaustein Thalheimer Grants, 403
Appalachian Reg Comm Health Care Grants, 507
Baxter Int'l Corp Giving Grants, 689
BCBSM Fndn Student Award Program, 710
BCBS of Massachusetts Fndn Grants, 713
Blue Cross Blue Shield of Minnesota Fndn - Healthy Equity: Health Impact Assessment Demonstration Project Grants, 795
Blue Cross Blue Shield of Minnesota Fndn - Healthy Equity: Health Impact Assessment Grants, 796
Blue Shield of California Grants, 802
CHCF Grants, 1063
Chiron Fndn Community Grants, 1111
Cigna Civic Affairs Sponsorships, 1129
Colorado Grants, 1216
Commonwealth Fund Australian-American Health Policy Fellowships, 1241
Commonwealth Fund Harkness Fellowships in Health Care Policy and Practice, 1242
DHHS Community Services Block Grant Training and Technical Assistance Program: Capacity-Building for Ongoing CSBG Programs and Strategic Planning and Coordination Grants, 1529
Entergy Corp Open Grants for Healthy Families, 1715
Fndn for a Healthy Kentucky Grants, 1891
General Service Fndn Human Rights and Economic Justice Grants, 2006
GNOF IMPACT Grants for Health and Human Services, 2080
Greenwall Fndn Bioethics Grants, 2158
Harry S. Black and Allon Fuller Grants, 2243
Henry J. Kaiser Family Fndn Grants, 2310
Hogg Fndn for Mental Health Grants, 2343
Jane Bradley Pettit Fndn Health Grants, 2643
Japan Fndn Center for Global Partnership Grants, 2650
Kansas Health Fndn Recognition Grants, 2784
Mary Black Fndn Community Health Grants, 3032
Meyer and Pepa Gold Family Fndn Grants, 3138
Meyer Fndn Healthy Communities Grants, 3143
Mt. Sinai Health Care Fndn Policy Grants, 3228
New York Life Fndn Grants, 3341
NYCT Girls and Young Women Grants, 3548
NYCT Health Serv, Systems, & Policies Grants, 3550
NYCT Mental Health and Retardation Grants, 3554
OSF-Baltimore Tackling Drug Addiction Grants, 3698
OUT Fund for Lesbian & Gay Liberation Grants, 3714
Rainbow Endowment Grants, 4007
RAND Corp Graduate Summer Associateships, 4018
Rose Community Fndn Health Grants, 4154
RWJF Health Policy Fellowships, 4184
RWJF Partners Investing in Nursing's Future, 4188
Seattle Fndn Health and Wellness Grants, 4328
USAID Implementation Science for Strengthening Use of Evidence in Family Planning/Reproductive Health Programming Grants, 4758
USAID Knowledge for Health II Grants, 4765
USAID NGO Health Service Delivery Grants, 4771
USAID Strengthening Through Indian Health Professional Assoc & Scaling Up Grants, 4784

Health Promotion

49ers Fndn Grants, 23
Abington Fndn Grants, 100
Adolph Coors Fndn Grants, 171
AEGON Transamerica Health & Welfare Grants, 179
Air Products and Chemicals Grants, 216
Albertson's Charitable Giving Grants, 345
Alexander Eastman Fndn Grants, 355
Allen P. and Josephine B. Green Fndn Grants, 380
Alvin and Fanny Blaustein Thalheimer Grants, 403
American Academy of Dermatology Shade Structure Grants, 420
Anheuser-Busch Fndn Grants, 470
Ann Arbor Area Community Fndn Grants, 474
Ann Peppers Fndn Grants, 484
AON Fndn Grants, 491
Appalachian Reg Comm Health Care Grants, 507
AptarGroup Fndn Grants, 519
Assurant Health Fndn Grants, 596
Atkinson Fndn Community Grants, 606
Autzen Fndn Grants, 622
BCBSM Fndn Investigator Research Grants, 708
BCBSNC Fndn Fit Together Grants, 711
BCBSNC Fndn Grants, 712
Beldon Grants, 720
Bikes Belong Fndn Paul David Clark Bicycling Safety Grants, 760
Bikes Belong Fndn REI Grants, 761
Bikes Belong Fndn Research Grants, 762
Bikes Belong Grants, 763
Bright Promises Fndn Grants, 838
Bullitt Fndn Grants, 862
California Endowment Innovative Ideas Challenge Grants, 904
Caterpillar Fndn Grants, 954
CDC State and Local Childhood Lead Poisoning Prevention Grants, 976
Champ-A Champion Fur Kids Grants, 1028
Charles H. Pearson Fndn Grants, 1045
Chase Paymentech Corp Giving Grants, 1059
CHCF Grants, 1063
Chefs Move to Schools Grants, 1066
Chiquita Brands Int'l Grants, 1110
CICF Senior Grants, 1127
Cigna Civic Affairs Sponsorships, 1129
CMA Fndn Grants, 1178
CNCS AmeriCorps Indian Planning Grants, 1180
CNCS AmeriCorps State and National Grants, 1182
CNCS AmeriCorps VISTA Project Grants, 1184
CNCS Social Innovation Grants, 1189

SUBJECT INDEX

Colonel Stanley R. McNeil Fndn Grants, 1210
Colorado Grants, 1216
Colorado Trust Partnerships for Health Init, 1217
Community Fndn of Bloomington and Monroe County - Precision Health Network Cycle Grants, 1270
Community Fndn of Louisville Grants, 1299
Comprehensive Health Educ Fndn Grants, 1337
Connecticut Community Fndn Grants, 1350
Connecticut Health Fndn Health Init Grants, 1351
Conservation, Food, and Health Fndn Grants for Developing Countries, 1359
DHHS AIDS Project Grants, 1525
Dorothy Rider Pool Health Care Grants, 1589
Edward N. and Della L. Thome Memorial Fndn Direct Services Grants, 1666
Essex County Community Discretionary Grants, 1752
Ewing Halsell Fndn Grants, 1776
Finish Line Youth Fndn Founder's Grants, 1812
Finish Line Youth Fndn Grants, 1813
Finish Line Youth Fndn Legacy Grants, 1814
Floyd A. and Kathleen C. Cailloux Fndn Grants, 1874
Fndn for a Healthy Kentucky Grants, 1891
Frank Reed and Margaret Jane Peters Memorial Fund II Grants, 1934
General Mills Fndn Grants, 2003
George E. Hatcher, Jr. and Ann Williams Hatcher Fndn Grants, 2015
Glazer Family Fndn Grants, 2062
GNOF IMPACT Kahn-Oppenheim Grants, 2084
GNOF Norco Community Grants, 2089
GNOF Stand Up For Our Children Grants, 2093
Great-West Life Grants, 2130
Harry S. Black and Allon Fuller Grants, 2243
Harvest Fndn Grants, 2254
Hasbro Children's Fund, 2256
HCA Fndn Grants, 2274
Health Canada National Seniors Indep Grants, 2278
Healthcare Fndn for Orange County Grants, 2279
Health Fndn of Greater Cincinnati Grants, 2281
Health Fndn of Greater Indianapolis Grants, 2282
Health Fndn of So Florida Responsive Grants, 2283
Henry and Ruth Blaustein Rosenberg Grants, 2306
Hillcrest Fndn Grants, 2325
Hirtzel Memorial Fndn Grants, 2332
Hogg Fndn for Mental Health Grants, 2343
HomeBanc Fndn Grants, 2347
Homer Fndn Grants, 2352
Horizon Fndn for New Jersey Grants, 2364
Institute for Agriculture and Trade Policy Food and Society Fellowships, 2561
Jacob and Hilda Blaustein Fndn Grants, 2615
James Hervey Johnson Charitable Ed Grants, 2627
Jane's Grants, 2639
Jenifer Altman Fndn Grants, 2662
Jessie B. Cox Charitable Grants, 2670
Jewish Grants, 2675
Jewish Women's Fndn of New York Grants, 2677
Joe W. and Dorothy Dorsett Brown Fndn Grants, 2684
John P. McGovern Fndn Grants, 2707
Josephine S. Gumbiner Fndn Grants, 2739
Kaiser Permanente Cares for Comm Grants, 2763
Kansas Health Fndn Recognition Grants, 2784
Linford and Mildred White Charitable Grants, 2909
Louie M. and Betty M. Phillips Fndn Grants, 2923
Louis R. Cappelli Fndn Grants, 2926
Mary Black Fndn Active Living Grants, 3031
Mary Wilmer Covey Charitable Grants, 3049
McCarthy Family Fndn Grants, 3073
MedImmune Charitable Grants, 3108
Medtronic Fndn CommunityLink Health Grants, 3111
Medtronic Fndn Patient Link Grants, 3113
MetroWest Health Fndn Grants--Healthy Aging, 3135
Michael Reese Health Trust Responsive Grants, 3160
MMS and Alliance Charitable Fndn Grants for Community Action and Care for the Medically Uninsured, 3194
Nuffield Fndn Africa Grants, 3532
Nuffield Fndn Small Grants, 3535
Open Spaces Sacred Places National Awards, 3684
Paso del Norte Health Fndn Grants, 3743

PepsiCo Fndn Grants, 3819
Pfizer Healthcare Charitable Contributions, 3863
Phoenix Coyotes Charities Grants, 3879
Piedmont Health Fndn Grants, 3882
Pinnacle Fndn Grants, 3894
Premera Blue Cross CARES Grants, 3945
Prince Charitable Trusts D.C. Grants, 3960
Princeton Area Community Fndn Fund for Women and Girls Grants, 3962
Quantum Fndn Grants, 3996
Rainbow Endowment Grants, 4007
RGK Fndn Grants, 4072
Robert R. McCormick Tribune Comm Grants, 4119
Robert R. Meyer Fndn Grants, 4121
Roney-Fitzpatrick Fndn Grants, 4150
Ruth Mott Fndn Grants, 4180
Saigh Fndn Grants, 4210
San Juan Island Community Fndn Grants, 4283
Scott County Community Fndn Grants, 4314
Seagate Tech Corp Capacity to Care Grants, 4317
Sisters of Charity Fndn of Canton Grants, 4372
Sisters of Saint Joseph Charitable Grants, 4376
Sisters of St. Joseph Healthcare Fndn Grants, 4377
Sunflower Fndn Bridge Grants, 4528
Sunoco Fndn Grants, 4530
Texas Instruments Corp Health and Human Services Grants, 4598
Textron Corp Contributions Grants, 4601
Theodore Edson Parker Fndn Grants, 4605
TJX Fndn Grants, 4637
Tri-State Community Twenty-first Century Endowment Grants, 4666
United Methodist Child Mental Health Grants, 4721
USAID Implementation Science for Strengthening Use of Evidence in Family Planning/Reproductive Health Programming Grants, 4758
USAID Knowledge for Health II Grants, 4765
USAID NGO Health Service Delivery Grants, 4771
USDA Individual Water and Waste Water Grants, 4817
VHA Health Fndn Grants, 4931
Visiting Nurse Fndn Grants, 4951
Washington Gas Charitable Contributions, 5000
Whitney Fndn Grants, 5061

Health Research
Harry Edison Fndn, 2241
Meyer and Pepa Gold Family Fndn Grants, 3138
NHLBI Ruth L. Kirschstein National Research Service Awards for Individual Predoctoral MD/PhD Fellows and Other Dual Degree Fellows, 3420
Perpetual Trust for Charitable Giving Grants, 3826
Seattle Fndn Medical Funds Grants, 4329
USAID Family Health Plus Project Grants, 4751

Health Sciences
AAAS Science and Technology Policy Fellowships: Health, Educ and Human Services, 53
CFFVR Jewelers Mutual Charitable Giving, 1014
Harry A. and Margaret D. Towsley Fndn Grants, 2236
Hoglund Fndn Grants, 2344
IIE AmCham Charitable Fndn U.S. Studies Scholarship, 2453
IIE New Leaders Group Award for Mutual Understanding, 2460
Medtronic Fndn CommunityLink Educ Grants, 3110
NHLBI Lymphatics in Health & Disease in Digestive, Cardiovascular and Pulmonary Systems, 3414
North Carolina GlaxoSmithKline Fndn Grants, 3490
NYCT Blindness and Visual Disabilities Grants, 3543
San Diego Women's Fndn Grants, 4252
Siragusa Fndn Health Services & Medical Research Grants, 4368
Texas Instruments Community Services Grants, 4600
Vanderburgh Community Fndn Grants, 4902

Health Services Delivery
3M Company Health and Human Services Grants, 14
A.O. Smith Community Grants, 46
Abbott Fund Access to Health Care Grants, 80
Abell-Hanger Fndn Grants, 91

Abell Fndn Health and Human Services Grants, 96
Abington Fndn Grants, 100
Able To Serve Grants, 102
Ackerman Fndn Grants, 129
Administration on Aging Senior Medicare Patrol Project Grants, 166
Advancing Colorado's Mental Health Care Project Grants, 173
Aetna Fndn Racial and Ethnic Health Care Equity Grants, 186
Agnes B. Hunt Grants, 202
Albertson's Charitable Giving Grants, 345
Allan C. and Leila J. Garden Fndn Grants, 374
Allen P. and Josephine B. Green Fndn Grants, 380
Alticor Corp Community Contributions Grants, 396
Alvin and Fanny Blaustein Thalheimer Grants, 403
AMA Fndn Fund for Better Health Grants, 409
American Psychiatric Fndn Helping Hands Grants, 443
Amgen Fndn Grants, 456
Amon G. Carter Fndn Grants, 458
Anthem Blue Cross and Blue Shield Grants, 488
Appalachian Reg Comm Health Care Grants, 507
ArvinMeritor Grants, 585
Auburn Fndn Grants, 611
Back Home Again Fndn Grants, 633
BCBSM Fndn Investigator Research Grants, 708
BCBSM Fndn Proposal Development Awards, 709
BCBSM Fndn Student Award Program, 710
BCBSNC Fndn Grants, 712
BCBS of Massachusetts Fndn Grants, 713
BJ's Charitable Fndn Grants, 777
Blackford County Community Fndn Grants, 780
Blue Shield of California Grants, 802
Burlington Industries Fndn Grants, 865
Business Bank of Nevada Community Grants, 879
California Endowment Innovative Ideas Challenge Grants, 904
Cardinal Health Fndn Grants, 923
Carl B. and Florence E. King Fndn Grants, 928
Champ-A Champion Fur Kids Grants, 1028
Charles H. Pearson Fndn Grants, 1045
Charlotte County (FL) Community Fndn Grants, 1056
Chase Paymentech Corp Giving Grants, 1059
Christine and Katharina Pauly Charitable Grants, 1114
CICF City of Noblesville Community Grant, 1118
CICF J. Proctor Grant for Aged Men & Women, 1124
Citigroup Fndn Grants, 1139
Claude Worthington Benedum Fndn Grants, 1161
Clinton County Community Fndn Grants, 1174
CMA Fndn Grants, 1178
Colorado Grants, 1216
Colorado Trust Partnerships for Health Init, 1217
Columbus Fndn Paul G. Duke Grants, 1227
Commonwealth Fund Harkness Fellowships in Health Care Policy and Practice, 1242
Community Fndn of Boone County Grants, 1274
Community Fndn of Grant County Grants, 1279
Community Fndn of Greenville Hollingsworth Funds Program/Project Grants, 1296
Community Fndn of St. Joseph County Special Project Challenge Grants, 1314
Community Impact Fund, 1332
Cone Health Fndn Grants, 1348
Connecticut Health Fndn Health Init Grants, 1351
Consumers Energy Fndn, 1365
Crown Point Community Fndn Grants, 1402
CVS Community Grants, 1422
Daviess County Community Fndn Health Grants, 1457
Dearborn Community Fndn City of Lawrenceburg Community Grants, 1471
Decatur County Comm Large Project Grants, 1476
DeKalb County Community Fndn Grants, 1481
DeMatteis Family Fndn Grants, 1497
Dennis and Phyllis Washington Fndn Grants, 1498
DHHS Technical and Non-Financial Assistance to Health Centers, 1539
DIFFA/Chicago Grants, 1547
Dorothy Rider Pool Health Care Grants, 1589
DTE Energy Health & Human Services Grants, 1613
Eastman Chemical Company Fndn Grants, 1643

922 / Health Services Delivery

Edina Realty Fndn Grants, 1656
Emma B. Howe Memorial Fndn Grants, 1700
Entergy Corp Open Grants for Healthy Families, 1715
Ewing Halsell Fndn Grants, 1776
Fallon OrNda Community Health Grants, 1783
Flinn Fndn Grants, 1842
Fndn for a Healthy Kentucky Grants, 1891
Fndn for Health Enhancement Grants, 1894
Fndn for Mid South Health & Wellness Grants, 1899
Fndns of E Chicago Health Grants, 1910
Frances and John L. Loeb Family Grants, 1917
Fulton County Community Fndn Women's Giving Circle Grants, 1976
General Dynamics Corp Grants, 2001
George E. Hatcher, Jr. and Ann Williams Hatcher Fndn Grants, 2015
George Frederick Jewett Fndn Grants, 2019
Gil and Dody Weaver Fndn Grants, 2053
Giving Sum Annual Grant, 2058
GlaxoSmithKline Fndn IMPACT Awards, 2061
GNOF IMPACT Grants for Health and Human Services, 2080
Goodyear Tire Grants, 2106
Greater Cincinnati Fndn Priority and Small Projects/Capacity-Building Grants, 2132
Green Bay Packers Fndn Grants, 2148
Green Diamond Charitable Contributions, 2149
Grundy Fndn Grants, 2169
Hall-Perrine Fndn Grants, 2209
Hartford Aging and Health Program Awards, 2247
Hasbro Children's Fund, 2256
Health Fndn of Greater Cincinnati Grants, 2281
Hedco Fndn Grants, 2287
Helen Pumphrey Denit Charitable Grants, 2297
Helen Steiner Rice Fndn Grants, 2299
Hendricks County Community Fndn Grants, 2302
Highmark Physician eHealth Collab Grants, 2320
Hill Crest Fndn Grants, 2324
Hirtzel Memorial Fndn Grants, 2332
Hoglund Fndn Grants, 2344
HomeBanc Fndn Grants, 2347
Honda of America Manufacturing Fndn Grants, 2354
Horace A. Kimball and S. Ella Kimball Grants, 2362
IBCAT Screening Mammography Grants, 2422
Idaho Community Fndn Eastern Region Grants, 2432
James L. and Mary Jane Bowman Grants, 2632
Jane Bradley Pettit Fndn Health Grants, 2643
Jay and Rose Phillips Family Fndn Grants, 2656
Jessie B. Cox Charitable Grants, 2670
Jewish Grants, 2675
Joe W. and Dorothy Dorsett Brown Fndn Grants, 2684
Johnson & Johnson Corp Contributions Grants, 2718
Johnson County Community Fndn Grants, 2723
Josephine S. Gumbiner Fndn Grants, 2739
K. M. Hunter Fndn Social Welfare Grants, 2757
K21 Health Fndn Grants, 2760
Kaiser Permanente Cares for Comm Grants, 2763
Kendrick Fndn Grants, 2797
Ken W. Davis Fndn Grants, 2813
LaGrange County Community Fndn Grants, 2850
Liberty Bank Fndn Grants, 2890
Lynde and Harry Bradley Fndn Grants, 2947
Lynde and Harry Bradley Fndn Prizes, 2948
M.D. Anderson Fndn Grants, 2952
M.J. Murdock Charitable Trust General Grants, 2954
Madison County Community Fndn - City of Anderson Quality of Life Grant, 2972
Marie C. and Joseph C. Wilson Fndn Rochester Small Grants, 3006
Mary E. Ober Fndn Grants, 3039
McCallum Family Fndn Grants, 3072
McCune Fndn Human Services Grants, 3080
McGraw-Hill Companies Community Grants, 3081
McKesson Fndn Grants, 3084
McLean Fndn Grants, 3089
Medtronic Fndn CommunityLink Health Grants, 3111
Medtronic Fndn Patient Link Grants, 3113
Memorial Fndn Grants, 3117
MetroWest Health Fndn Capital Grants for Health-Related Facilities, 3134

MetroWest Health Fndn Grants--Healthy Aging, 3135
Michael Reese Health Trust Core Grants, 3159
Michael Reese Health Trust Responsive Grants, 3160
Mid-Iowa Health Fndn Comm Response Grants, 3168
Miller Fndn Grants, 3181
Minneapolis Fndn Community Grants, 3186
MMS and Alliance Charitable Fndn Grants for Community Action and Care for the Medically Uninsured, 3194
MMS and Alliance Charitable Fndn Int'l Health Studies Grants, 3195
Ms. Fndn for Women Health Grants, 3225
North Central Health Services Grants, 3492
Northern Trust Company Corp Giving Program, 3504
North Georgia Community Fndn Grants, 3505
Northrop Grumman Corp Grants, 3507
NYCT Children & Youth with Disabilities Grant, 3544
NYCT Girls and Young Women Grants, 3548
PACCAR Fndn Grants, 3719
PacifiCorp Fndn for Learning Grants, 3727
Pasadena Fndn Average Grants, 3741
Perry County Community Fndn Grants, 3827
Pfizer Medical Educ Track One Grants, 3864
Pfizer Special Events Grants, 3865
Piedmont Natural Gas Fndn Health and Human Services Grants, 3885
Piper Trust Older Adults Grants, 3904
Pohlad Family Fndn, 3928
Porter County Health and Wellness Grant, 3933
Premera Blue Cross Fndn CARES Grants, 3945
Priddy Fndn Grants, 3957
Prince Charitable Trusts D.C. Grants, 3960
Qualcomm Grants, 3993
Quality Health Fndn Grants, 3994
Quantum Corp Snap Server Grants, 3995
Quantum Grants, 3996
RCF General Community Grants, 4032
Robert R. McCormick Tribune Comm Grants, 4119
Robert R. Meyer Fndn Grants, 4121
Robert W. Woodruff Fndn Grants, 4124
Rochester Area Community Fndn Grants, 4127
Rockwell Int'l Corp Grants, 4141
Ruth Eleanor Bamberger and John Ernest Bamberger Memorial Fndn Grants, 4178
RWJF Changes in Health Care Financing and Organization Grants, 4182
RWJF Jobs to Careers: Promoting Work-Based Learning for Quality Care, 4185
RWJF New Jersey Health Inits Grants, 4187
Saigh Fndn Grants, 4210
Salem Fndn Charitable Grants, 4223
Samuel S. Johnson Fndn Grants, 4239
San Diego Health & Human Services Grants, 4248
San Diego Fndn Paradise Valley Hospital Community Grants, 4249
San Diego Women's Fndn Grants, 4252
San Francisco Fndn Community Health Grants, 4263
Santa Fe Community Fndn Seasonal Grants, 4290
Sartain Lanier Family Fndn Grants, 4298
Schering-Plough Fndn Health Grants, 4304
Seattle Fndn Benjamin N. Phillips Grants, 4322
Shell Oil Company Fndn Grants, 4343
Sierra Health Fndn Responsive Grants, 4353
Sisters of Charity Fndn of Canton Grants, 4372
Sisters of St. Joseph Healthcare Fndn Grants, 4377
SOCFOC Catholic Ministries Grants, 4392
Sonoco Fndn Grants, 4403
Sony Corp of America Corp Philanthropy Grants, 4405
Square D Fndn Grants, 4464
Starke County Community Fndn Grants, 4482
Starr Fndn Grants, 4483
Stewart Huston Charitable Grants, 4505
Sulzberger Fndn Grants, 4522
Sunbeam Products Grants, 4526
Sunflower Fndn Bridge Grants, 4528
Sunoco Fndn Grants, 4530
TE Fndn Grants, 4572
Temple-Inland Fndn Grants, 4576
Textron Corp Contributions Grants, 4601
Thomas J. Long Fndn Community Grants, 4618

SUBJECT INDEX

Tri-County Electric People Grants, 4665
TWS Fndn Grants, 4683
Union Bank Corp Sponsorships and Donations, 4708
Union Labor Health Fndn Community Grants, 4713
Union Pacific Health & Human Services Grants, 4715
United Methodist Committee on Relief Global AIDS Grants, 4719
United Methodist Child Mental Health Grants, 4721
Unity Fndn Of LaPorte County Grants, 4726
USAID Integration of Care and Support within the Health System to Support Better Patient Outcomes Grants, 4762
USAID Knowledge for Health II Grants, 4765
USAID NGO Health Service Delivery Grants, 4771
USAID Strengthening Through Indian Health Professional Assoc & Scaling Up Grants, 4784
US Airways Community Contributions, 4788
Vancouver Fndn Grants & Comm Inits, 4900
VHA Health Fndn Grants, 4931
Visiting Nurse Fndn Grants, 4951
W.K. Kellogg Fndn Healthy Kids Grants, 4961
Walt Disney Company Fndn Grants, 4981
Warrick County Community Fndn Grants, 4987
Washington County Community Fndn Grants, 4997
Wells County Fndn Grants, 5022
William B. Stokely Jr. Fndn Grants, 5076

Health and Safety Education

7-Eleven Coorporate Giving Grants, 18
ACE Charitable Fndn Grants, 111
Aetna Fndn Regional Health Grants, 187
Alexander and Margaret Stewart Grants, 354
Anthem Blue Cross and Blue Shield Grants, 488
Atkinson Fndn Community Grants, 606
Austin-Bailey Health and Wellness Fndn Grants, 614
Baxter Int'l Fndn Grants, 691
BCBSNC Fndn Grants, 712
BJ's Charitable Fndn Grants, 777
Blue Cross Blue Shield of Minnesota Fndn - Health Equity: Building Health Together Grants, 793
Blue Cross Blue Shield of Minnesota Fndn - Healthy Equity: Health Impact Assessment Demonstration Project Grants, 795
Carlos and Marguerite Mason Grants, 934
Caterpillar Fndn Grants, 954
CDC School Health Programs to Prevent the Spread of HIV Coop Agreements, 975
Champ-A Champion Fur Kids Grants, 1028
Charles Lafitte Fndn Grants, 1049
Chiron Fndn Community Grants, 1111
Cigna Civic Affairs Sponsorships, 1129
CLIF Bar Family Fndn Grants, 1173
Community Fndn of Louisville Grants, 1299
Comprehensive Health Educ Fndn Grants, 1337
Daviess County Community Fndn Health Grants, 1457
Dearborn Community Fndn City of Lawrenceburg Community Grants, 1471
DIFFA/Chicago Grants, 1547
Dorothy Rider Pool Health Care Grants, 1589
Dr. John T. Macdonald Fndn Grants, 1600
Edina Realty Fndn Grants, 1656
Fndn for a Healthy Kentucky Grants, 1891
Fndn for Seacoast Health Grants, 1895
Fndns of E Chicago Health Grants, 1910
Frances and John L. Loeb Family Grants, 1917
Fremont Area Comm Summer Youth Grants, 1956
GNOF IMPACT Kahn-Oppenheim Grants, 2084
Great-West Life Grants, 2130
Healthcare Fndn of New Jersey Grants, 2280
Health Fndn of Greater Cincinnati Grants, 2281
Health Fndn of So Florida Responsive Grants, 2283
Hogg Fndn for Mental Health Grants, 2343
HomeBanc Fndn Grants, 2347
Honeywell Family Safety and Security Grants, 2356
Horizon Fndn for New Jersey Grants, 2364
Indiana AIDS Grants, 2529
John P. McGovern Fndn Grants, 2707
John S. Dunn Research Fndn Grants and Chairs, 2715
Johnson & Johnson Corp Contributions Grants, 2718
Johnson County Community Fndn Grants, 2723

SUBJECT INDEX   Higher Education / 923

Kansas Health Fndn Recognition Grants, 2784
Mary Black Fndn Active Living Grants, 3031
McCarthy Family Fndn Grants, 3073
MedImmune Charitable Grants, 3108
Medtronic Fndn Patient Link Grants, 3113
MMS and Alliance Charitable Fndn Grants for Community Action and Care for the Medically Uninsured, 3194
New Jersey Center for Hispanic Policy, Research and Development Innovative Inits Grants, 3329
Northrop Grumman Corp Grants, 3507
NRA Fndn Grants, 3517
OUT Fund for Lesbian & Gay Liberation Grants, 3714
Pajaro Valley Community Health Trust Diabetes and Contributing Factors Grants, 3732
Phoenix Suns Charities Grants, 3881
Piper Trust Older Adults Grants, 3904
PMI Fndn Grants, 3918
Posey Community Fndn Women's Grants, 3938
PPG Industries Fndn Grants, 3943
Richmond Eye and Ear Grants, 4092
Robert W. Woodruff Fndn Grants, 4124
Saint Luke's Health Inits Grants, 4216
Salt River Health and Human Services Grants, 4228
Shaw's Supermarkets Donations, 4342
Sisters of Charity Fndn of Cleveland Reducing Health and Ed Disparities in Central Neighborhoods, 4374
Sisters of St. Joseph Healthcare Fndn Grants, 4377
U.S. Department of Educ 21st Century Community Learning Centers, 4687
USAID Knowledge for Health II Grants, 4765
USDA Coop Extension System Educ Grants, 4803
Viking Children's Grants, 4939
Warrick County Community Fndn Grants, 4987
Welborn Baptist General Opportunity Grants, 5020

Hearing
Columbus Fndn Dorothy E. Ann Fund (D.E.A.F.) Traditional Grants, 1221
Reinberger Fndn Grants, 4052

Hearing Impairments
Arizona Community Fndn Grants, 540
Batchelor Fndn Grants, 679
Carls Fndn Grants, 937
Carl W. and Carrie Mae Joslyn Grants, 938
Charles Delmar Fndn Grants, 1039
Columbus Fndn Competitive Grants, 1220
Columbus Fndn Dorothy E. Ann Fund Traditional Grants, 1221
Columbus Fndn Small Grants, 1232
Cralle Fndn Grants, 1394
Danellie Fndn Grants, 1442
Herbert A. and Adrian W. Woods Fndn Grants, 2313
Johnson Scholarship Fndn Grants, 2726
Kenny's Kids Grants, 2803
Lettie Pate Whitehead Fndn Grants, 2888
U.S. Department of Educ Rehabilitation Training-- Rehabilitation Continuing Educ Programs--Institute on Rehabilitation Issues, 4700
Union County Community Fndn Grants, 4711

Heating, Ventilation, and Air Conditioning
DeKalb County Community Fndn - Immediate Response Grant, 1479

Hematology
Chiron Fndn Community Grants, 1111
CSL Behring Local Empowerment for Advocacy Development Grants, 1406
NHLBI Ancillary Studies in Clinical Trials, 3410
NHLBI Ruth L. Kirschstein National Research Service Awards for Individual Postdoctoral Fellows, 3418
Victor E. Speas Fndn Grants, 4933

Hemophilia
Baxter Int'l Corp Giving Grants, 689
CSL Behring Local Empowerment for Advocacy Development Grants, 1406
Pfizer Healthcare Charitable Contributions, 3863

Higher Education
3M Fndn Community Giving Grants, 15
41 Washington Street Fndn Grants, 22
A/H Fndn Grants, 48
Aaron Fndn Grants, 73
Abbott Fund Global AIDS Care Grants, 82
Abel and Sophia Sheng Charitable Fndn Grants, 86
Abeles Fndn Grants, 89
Abel Fndn Grants, 90
Abell-Hanger Fndn Grants, 91
Abney Fndn Grants, 105
Achelis Fndn Grants, 127
Adam Richter Charitable Grants, 145
Adams-Mastrovich Family Fndn Grants, 146
Adams Fndn Grants, 155
Adams Fndn Grants, 153
Adolph Coors Fndn Grants, 171
Advanced Micro Devices Comm Affairs Grants, 172
AEC Grants, 175
Agnes M. Lindsay Grants, 203
Ahmanson Fndn Grants, 207
Air Products and Chemicals Grants, 216
Akzo Nobel Chemicals Grants, 219
Alabama Power Fndn Grants, 233
ALA Carnegie Corp of New York/New York Times I Love My Librarian Award, 254
ALA Coretta Scott King Book Donation Grant, 261
ALA Routledge Distance Learning Librarianship Conference Sponsorship Award, 315
Alavi Fndn Grants, 335
Alberto Culver Corp Contributions Grants, 343
Albertson's Charitable Giving Grants, 345
Alexander Eastman Fndn Grants, 355
Alfred and Tillie Shemanski Testamentary Grants, 363
Alfred Bersted Fndn Grants, 364
Alfred P. Sloan Fndn Civic Inits Grants, 368
Alfred P. Sloan Selected National Issues Grants, 370
Allyn Fndn Grants, 392
ALSAM Fndn Grants, 395
Amarillo Area/Harrington Fndns Grants, 412
AMD Corp Contributions Grants, 416
American Council of the Blind Scholarships, 427
American Express Charitable Grants, 429
American Foodservice Charitable Grants, 433
American Honda Fndn Grants, 439
AmerUs Group Charitable Fndn, 455
Anderson Fndn Grants, 460
Andrew Family Fndn Grants, 462
Annenberg Fndn Grants, 477
Anne Thorne Weaver Family Fndn Grants, 478
Ann Peppers Fndn Grants, 484
Antone & Edene Vidinha Charitable Grants, 490
Applied Biosystems Grants, 514
AptarGroup Fndn Grants, 519
Archer Daniels Midland Fndn Grants, 527
ARCO Fndn Educ Grants, 528
Argyros Fndn Grants, 532
Arizona Republic Newspaper Contributions, 547
Arkansas Arts Council Collab Project Support, 555
Arkell Hall Fndn Grants, 562
Armstrong McDonald Fndn Grants, 565
Aronson Fndn Grants, 567
ARS Fndn Grants, 568
Arthur and Rochelle Belfer Fndn Grants, 570
Arthur F. and Alice E. Adams Charitable Grants, 574
Ashland Corp Contributions Grants, 587
Athwin Fndn Grants, 605
Atkinson Fndn Community Grants, 606
Atlanta Fndn Grants, 608
Atran Fndn Grants, 610
Auburn Fndn Grants, 611
Autzen Fndn Grants, 622
Avista Fndn Grants, 624
Ayres Fndn Grants, 630
Babcock Charitable Grants, 632
Back Home Again Fndn Grants, 633
Bailey Fndn Grants, 635
Balfe Family Fndn Grants, 636
Ball Brothers Fndn General Grants, 637
BancorpSouth Fndn Grants, 651

Banfi Vintners Fndn Grants, 653
Bank of America Charitable Fndn Educ and Workforce Development Grants, 657
Barnes Group Fndn Grants, 672
Barr Grants, 678
Batchelor Fndn Grants, 679
Batts Fndn Grants, 687
Baughman Fndn Grants, 688
Beazley Fndn Grants, 714
Beerman Fndn Grants, 717
Belk Fndn Grants, 721
Bender Fndn Grants, 726
Bertha Russ Lytel Fndn Grants, 745
Bert W. Martin Fndn Grants, 747
Better Way Fndn Grants, 754
Bill and Katie Weaver Charitable Grants, 764
Bill Hannon Fndn Grants, 771
Blue Mountain Community Fndn Grants, 800
Blum-Kovler Fndn Grants, 803
Blumenthal Fndn Grants, 804
Bodman Fndn Grants, 807
Boeckmann Charitable Fndn Grants, 808
Boeing Company Contributions Grants, 809
Boettcher Fndn Grants, 810
Booth-Bricker Grants, 815
Bosque Fndn Grants, 818
Boston Globe Fndn Grants, 821
Bradley-Turner Fndn Grants, 828
Bradley Family Fndn (South Carolina) Grants, 830
Brian G. Dyson Fndn Grants, 834
Bright Family Fndn Grants, 837
Brooklyn Benevolent Society Grants, 847
Brown Fndn Grants, 854
Brunswick Fndn Grants, 857
Burlington Industries Fndn Grants, 865
Burlington Northern Santa Fe Fndn Grants, 866
Butler Manufacturing Company Fndn Grants, 881
Bydale Fndn Grants, 882
Cadence Design Systems Grants, 889
Caesar Puff Fndn Grants, 890
Caesars Fndn Grants, 891
Callaway Fndn Grants, 909
Callaway Golf Company Fndn Grants, 910
Camp-Younts Fndn Grants, 914
Campbell Soup Fndn Grants, 916
Capital City Bank Group Fndn Grants, 920
Cargill Citizenship Fund-Corp Giving Grants, 925
Caring Fndn Grants, 926
Carl B. and Florence E. King Fndn Grants, 928
Carnahan-Jackson Fndn Grants, 939
Carnegie Corp of New York Grants, 940
Carylon Fndn Grants, 949
CDC School Health Programs to Prevent the Spread of HIV Coop Agreements, 975
CE and S Fndn Grants, 985
Ceil & Michael E. Pulitzer Fndn Grants, 987
Cemala Fndn Grants, 988
Cessna Fndn Grants, 1000
CFFVR Clintonville Area Fndn Grants, 1008
CFFVR Clintonville Area Fndn Grants, 1007
CFFVR Doug and Carla Salmon Fndn Grants, 1009
CFFVR Shawano Area Community Fndn Grants, 1021
Champlin Fndns Grants, 1029
Chapman Charitable Fndn Grants, 1033
Charity Incorporated Grants, 1035
Charles Delmar Fndn Grants, 1039
Charles H. Revson Fndn Grants, 1047
Charles M. Bair Family Grants, 1051
Chesapeake Corp Fndn Grants, 1076
Chicago Board of Trade Fndn Grants, 1079
Chicago Community Trust Arts and Culture Grants: Improving Access to Arts Learning Opps, 1082
Chicago Community Trust Educ Grants, 1085
Chicago Title and Trust Company Fndn Grants, 1099
Chiles Fndn Grants, 1108
Chiron Fndn Community Grants, 1111
Christensen Fund Regional Grants, 1112
CIGNA Fndn Grants, 1130
Cincinnati Bell Fndn Grants, 1131
Cincinnati Milacron Fndn Grants, 1132

Cinergy Fndn Grants, 1133
Citizens Savings Fndn Grants, 1141
Clark-Winchcole Fndn Grants, 1152
Clark and Ruby Baker Fndn Grants, 1154
Clark Charitable Grants, 1155
Claude Bennett Family Fndn Grants, 1159
Claude Worthington Benedum Fndn Grants, 1161
Clay Fndn Grants, 1162
Cleveland-Cliffs Fndn Grants, 1165
Cleveland Fenn Ed Grants, 1169
Clowes Grants, 1177
CNCS AmeriCorps State and National Grants, 1182
Cobb Family Fndn Grants, 1194
Coca-Cola Fndn Grants, 1195
Cockrell Fndn Grants, 1196
Coeta and Donald Barker Fndn Grants, 1197
Collins C. Diboll Private Fndn Grants, 1208
Collins Fndn Grants, 1209
Colonel Stanley R. McNeil Fndn Grants, 1210
Colorado Interstate Gas Grants, 1213
Colorado Springs Community Grants, 1215
Columbus Fndn Small Grants, 1232
Community Fndn of Greater Birmingham Grants, 1280
Community Fndn of Greater New Britain Grants, 1291
Community Fndn of Shreveport-Bossier Grants, 1307
Community Fndn of the Verdugos Ed Endowment Grants, 1321
Community Fndn of Wabash County Grants, 1326
Connecticut Light & Power Corp Contributions, 1352
Connelly Fndn Grants, 1353
ConocoPhillips Fndn Grants, 1354
ConocoPhillips Grants, 1355
CONSOL Coal Group Grants, 1360
Constantin Fndn Grants, 1362
Constellation Energy Corp Grants, 1364
Consumers Energy Fndn, 1365
Conwood Charitable Grants, 1366
Cooper Industries Fndn Grants, 1370
Coors Brewing Corp Contributions Grants, 1371
Cord Fndn Grants, 1372
Cowles Charitable Grants, 1392
Cralle Fndn Grants, 1394
Crescent Porter Hale Fndn Grants, 1398
Crestlea Fndn Grants, 1399
CSRA Community Fndn Grants, 1407
Cullen Fndn Grants, 1411
DaimlerChrysler Corp Grants, 1432
Daniels Grants, 1443
Daphne Seybolt Culpeper Memorial Fndn Grants, 1445
Davis Family Fndn Grants, 1462
Daywood Fndn Grants, 1465
Decatur County Comm Large Project Grants, 1476
Dennis and Phyllis Washington Fndn Grants, 1498
DENSO North America Fndn Grants, 1499
DeRoy Testamentary Fndn Grants, 1518
Dolan Fndn Grants, 1563
Dora Roberts Fndn Grants, 1579
Doree Taylor Charitable Fndn, 1580
Dorot Fndn Grants, 1586
Dorr Fndn Grants, 1591
Dow Chemical Company Grants, 1596
Dow Corning Corp Contributions Grants, 1597
DTE Energy Fndn Environmental Grants, 1612
Duke Energy Economic Development Grants, 1619
Dunspaugh-Dalton Fndn Grants, 1623
Dynegy Fndn Grants, 1630
Dyson Fndn Mid-Hudson Valley General Operating Support Grants, 1635
E.J. Grassmann Grants, 1638
E.L. Wiegand Fndn Grants, 1639
E. Rhodes and Leona B. Carpenter Fndn Grants, 1640
Eberly Fndn Grants, 1649
Eden Hall Fndn Grants, 1655
Edna Haddad Welfare Trust Fund Scholarships, 1658
EDS Fndn Grants, 1661
Edward and Helen Bartlett Fndn Grants, 1664
Edwin W. and Catherine M. Davis Fndn Grants, 1672
Elizabeth & Avola W. Callaway Fndn Grants, 1680
Elsie H. Wilcox Fndn Grants, 1691
Elsie Lee Garthwaite Memorial Fndn Grants, 1692

Emerson Charitable Grants, 1694
Emerson Kampen Fndn Grants, 1696
Ethel and Raymond F. Rice Fndn Grants, 1758
Ethel S. Abbott Charitable Fndn Grants, 1760
Eugene B. Casey Fndn Grants, 1762
Eugene M. Lang Fndn Grants, 1764
Eugene McDermott Fndn Grants, 1765
Eva L. and Joseph M. Bruening Fndn Grants, 1768
Feldman Fndn Grants, 1801
Ferree Fndn Grants, 1804
FirstEnergy Fndn Community Grants, 1819
Fluor Fndn Grants, 1875
FMC Fndn Grants, 1876
Foellinger Fndn Grants, 1877
Fondren Fndn Grants, 1878
Ford Fndn Diversity Fellowships, 1883
Foster Fndn Grants, 1888
Fndn for Enhancing Communities Grants, 1893
France-Merrick Fndns Grants, 1915
Frances C. & William P. Smallwood Grants, 1918
Frances L. and Edwin L. Cummings Grants, 1919
Francis Beidler Fndn Grants, 1921
Francis L. Abreu Charitable Grants, 1922
Frank G. and Freida K. Brotz Family Grants, 1928
Fraser-Parker Fndn Grants, 1938
Fred C. and Katherine B. Andersen Fndn Grants, 1942
Frederick S. Upton Fndn Grants, 1947
Fred L. Emerson Fndn Grants, 1949
Freeman Fndn Grants, 1952
Fritz B. Burns Fndn Grants, 1965
Fuller E. Callaway Fndn Grants, 1973
Gateway Fndn Grants, 1992
Gebbie Fndn Grants, 1995
GenCorp Fndn Grants, 1998
General Service Fndn Colorado Grants, 2005
George and Ruth Bradford Fndn Grants, 2010
George B. Storer Fndn Grants, 2014
George F. Baker Grants, 2016
George Family Fndn Grants, 2017
George Frederick Jewett Fndn Grants, 2019
George I. Alden Grants, 2023
George Kress Fndn Grants, 2025
George P. Davenport Grants, 2026
George S. and Dolores Dore Eccles Fndn Grants, 2027
George W. Brackenridge Fndn Grants, 2028
George W. Codrington Charitable Fndn Grants, 2029
Georgia-Pacific Fndn Educ Grants, 2031
Georgia-Pacific Fndn Entrepreneurship Grants, 2033
Georgia Power Fndn Grants, 2039
Gertrude and William C. Wardlaw Grants, 2045
Gertrude E. Skelly Charitable Fndn Grants, 2046
Gheens Fndn Grants, 2048
GNOF Exxon-Mobil Grants, 2074
GNOF New Orleans Works Grants, 2088
GNOF Norco Community Grants, 2089
Goizueta Fndn Grants, 2096
Golden Rule Fndn Grants, 2098
Goodrich Corp Fndn Grants, 2104
Goodyear Tire Grants, 2106
Grace and Franklin Bernsen Fndn Grants, 2109
Grand Rapids Community Ionia Youth Grants, 2120
Grand Rapids Community Sparta Youth Grants, 2125
Greater Cincinnati Fndn Priority and Small Projects/ Capacity-Building Grants, 2132
Greater Milwaukee Fndn Grants, 2137
Greenspun Family Fndn Grants, 2156
Griffin Fndn Grants, 2165
Grover Hermann Fndn Grants, 2168
Guy I. Bromley Grants, 2180
H & R Fndn Grants, 2181
H. Leslie Hoffman & Elaine Hoffman Grants, 2185
H. Reimers Bechtel Charitable Grants, 2186
H. Schaffer Fndn Grants, 2187
Haddad Fndn Grants, 2189
Hall-Perrine Fndn Grants, 2209
Hall Family Fndn Grants, 2210
Halliburton Fndn Grants, 2211
Hamilton Family Fndn Grants, 2213
Harold Alfond Grants, 2225
Harold R. Bechtel Charitable Remainder Grants, 2229

Harold Simmons Fndn Grants, 2230
Harris Teeter Corp Contributions Grants, 2235
Harry B. and Jane H. Brock Fndn Grants, 2237
Harry C. Trexler Grants, 2239
Harry Kramer Grants, 2242
Harry Sudakoff Fndn Grants, 2245
Harvey Randall Wickes Fndn Grants, 2255
Hedco Fndn Grants, 2287
Helen Irwin Littauer Ed Grants, 2295
Helen Pumphrey Denit Charitable Grants, 2297
Helen S. Boylan Fndn Grants, 2298
Henry W. Bull Fndn Grants, 2312
High Meadow Fndn Grants, 2321
Hill Crest Fndn Grants, 2324
Hillcrest Fndn Grants, 2325
Hill Fndn Grants, 2326
Hirtzel Memorial Fndn Grants, 2332
Homer A. Scott and Mildred S. Scott Grants, 2350
Homer Fndn Grants, 2352
Hormel Fndn Grants, 2369
Houston Endowment Grants, 2373
Howard H. Callaway Fndn Grants, 2376
Howe Fndn of North Carolina Grants, 2377
Huffy Fndn Grants, 2384
Huie-Dellmon Grants, 2386
Humana Fndn Grants, 2388
Huntington Fndn Grants, 2408
Hutton Fndn Grants, 2412
I.A. O'Shaughnessy Fndn Grants, 2416
Idaho Power Company Corp Contributions, 2433
IDEM Section 319(h) Nonpoint Source Grants, 2435
Illinois Tool Works Fndn Grants, 2511
Indep Comm Fndn Educ, Culture & Arts Grant, 2526
Indianapolis Power & Light Company Community Grants, 2540
Indiana Workforce Acceleration Grants, 2552
Intel Community Grants, 2562
Intel Finance Internships, 2563
Intergrys Corp Grants, 2565
J.B. Reynolds Fndn Grants, 2592
J.C. Penney Company Grants, 2594
J.M. Long Fndn Grants, 2603
J. Mack Robinson Fndn Grants, 2604
J.W. Kieckhefer Fndn Grants, 2607
J. Walton Bissell Fndn Grants, 2608
J. Willard and Alice S. Marriott Fndn Grants, 2609
Jacob and Hilda Blaustein Fndn Grants, 2615
James F. and Marion L. Miller Fndn Grants, 2622
James Ford Bell Fndn Grants, 2623
James G.K. McClure Educ and Devel Grants, 2624
James Hervey Johnson Charitable Ed Grants, 2627
James J. and Angelia M. Harris Fndn Grants, 2630
James M. Collins Fndn Grants, 2633
James R. Dougherty Jr. Fndn Grants, 2635
Jane and Jack Fitzpatrick Grants, 2640
Janirve Fndn Grants, 2645
Jaqua Fndn Grants, 2653
JELD-WEN Fndn Grants, 2661
Jennings County Community Fndn Grants, 2664
Jim Blevins Fndn Grants, 2678
Joe W. and Dorothy Dorsett Brown Fndn Grants, 2684
John Ben Snow Grants, 2687
John Deere Fndn Grants, 2692
John H. and Wilhelmina D. Harland Charitable Fndn Grants, 2698
John I. Smith Charities Grants, 2700
John J. Leidy Fndn Grants, 2701
John Lord Knight Fndn Grants, 2703
John P. Murphy Fndn Grants, 2708
John R. Oishei Fndn Grants, 2709
Johnson & Johnson Corp Contributions Grants, 2718
John W. Anderson Fndn Grants, 2729
John W. Speas and Effie E. Speas Grants, 2732
Joseph Alexander Fndn Grants, 2734
Josiah W. and Bessie H. Kline Fndn Grants, 2742
Joukowsky Family Fndn Grants, 2743
Journal Gazette Fndn Grants, 2744
Katherine Baxter Memorial Fndn Grants, 2789
Katherine John Murphy Fndn Grants, 2790
Kathryne Beynon Fndn Grants, 2791

SUBJECT INDEX — Higher Education / 925

Kentucky Arts Council Access Assistance Grants, 2805
KeySpan Fndn Grants, 2821
Koret Fndn Grants, 2837
Kovler Family Fndn Grants, 2840
L. W. Pierce Family Fndn Grants, 2846
Laura Jane Musser Rural Init Grants, 2864
Lee and Ramona Bass Fndn Grants, 2871
Leo Niessen Jr., Charitable Grants, 2885
Lewis H. Humphreys Charitable Grants, 2889
Libra Fndn Grants, 2899
Lied Fndn Grants, 2900
Lillian S. Wells Fndn Grants, 2901
Lloyd G. Balfour Fndn Attleboro-Specific Charities Grants, 2916
Lockheed Martin Philanthropic Grants, 2918
Long Island Community Fndn Grants, 2920
Louetta M. Cowden Fndn Grants, 2922
Louis and Elizabeth Nave Flarsheim Charitable Fndn Grants, 2924
Lowe Fndn Grants, 2929
Lubbock Area Fndn Grants, 2931
Lubrizol Fndn Grants, 2933
Lumpkin Family Healthy People Grants, 2942
Lynde and Harry Bradley Fndn Grants, 2947
Lynde and Harry Bradley Fndn Prizes, 2948
M. Bastian Family Fndn Grants, 2951
M.E. Raker Fndn Grants, 2953
M.J. Murdock Charitable Trust General Grants, 2954
MacDonald-Peterson Fndn Grants, 2965
Madison County Community General Grants, 2973
Margaret and James A. Elkins Jr. Fndn Grants, 3003
Margaret L. Wendt Fndn Grants, 3004
Margaret T. Morris Fndn Grants, 3005
Marie H. Bechtel Charitable Grants, 3007
Marion Gardner Jackson Charitable Grants, 3017
Mary Duke Biddle Fndn Grants, 3036
Mary S. and David C. Corbin Fndn Grants, 3048
Maurice J. Masserini Charitable Grants, 3064
Max A. Adler Charitable Fndn Grants, 3065
Maxon Charitable Fndn Grants, 3068
McCallum Family Fndn Grants, 3072
McColl Fndn Grants, 3074
McCombs Fndn Grants, 3075
McCune Fndn Civic Grants, 3078
McGraw-Hill Companies Community Grants, 3081
McGregor Grants, 3082
Mead Witter Fndn Grants, 3106
Melville Charitable Grants, 3115
Mericos Fndn Grants, 3121
Meriden Fndn Grants, 3122
Merkel Family Fndn Grants, 3123
Merkel Fndn Grants, 3124
Metro Health Fndn Grants, 3133
Meyer and Stephanie Eglin Fndn Grants, 3139
Meyer Fndn Educ Grants, 3142
Meyer Memorial Trust Grassroots Grants, 3147
Meyer Memorial Trust Responsive Grants, 3148
Meyer Memorial Trust Special Grants, 3149
MFRI Operation Diploma Grants for Higher Ed, 3150
MFRI Operation Diploma Grants for Student Veterans Organizations, 3151
MGM Resorts Fndn Community Grants, 3153
MGN Family Fndn Grants, 3154
Microsoft Comm Affairs Puget Sound Grants, 3163
Mildred V. Horn Fndn Grants, 3176
Military Ex-Prisoners of War Fndn Grants, 3177
Milton and Sally Avery Arts Fndn Grants, 3183
Motorola Fndn Grants, 3221
Musgrave Fndn Grants, 3231
NEH Preservation Assistance Grants for Smaller Institutions, 3293
Nellie Mae Educ Fndn District-Level Grants, 3297
Nellie Mae Educ Public Understanding Grants, 3298
Nellie Mae Educ Fndn State Level Systems Change Grants, 3299
Nell Warren Elkin and William Simpson Elkin, 3300
New Jersey Office of Faith Based Inits Creating Wealth Through Asset Building Grants, 3331
NFL Charities Pro Bowl Comm Grants in Hawaii, 3348
Nicholas H. Noyes Jr. Memorial Fndn Grants, 3434

Nina Mason Pulliam Charitable Grants, 3443
Norcliffe Fndn Grants, 3459
Nordson Corp Fndn Grants, 3462
NW Mutual Fndn Grants, 3509
Notsew Orm Sands Fndn Grants, 3516
Ohio Arts Council Sustainability Grants, 3654
Oleonda Jameson Grants, 3667
Olin Corp Charitable Grants, 3669
Oppenstein Brothers Fndn Grants, 3685
Oscar Rennebohm Fndn Grants, 3694
Otto Bremer Fndn Grants, 3713
Owens Corning Fndn Grants, 3717
PACCAR Fndn Grants, 3719
Parkersburg Area Comm Fndn Action Grants, 3738
Park Fndn Grants, 3739
Patrick and Aimee Butler Family Fndn Community Arts and Humanities Grants, 3747
Patrick and Anna M. Cudahy Grants, 3751
Paul & Daisy Soros Fellows for New Americans, 3754
Paul Ogle Fndn Grants, 3764
Paul Stock Fndn Grants, 3766
PepsiCo Fndn Grants, 3819
Percy B. Ferebee Endowment Grants, 3820
Perkins Charitable Fndn Grants, 3823
Perpetual Trust for Charitable Giving Grants, 3826
Perry County Community Fndn Grants, 3827
Peter and Georgia Angelos Fndn Grants, 3843
Peter Kiewit Fndn General Grants, 3845
Peter Kiewit Fndn Small Grants, 3847
Peyton Anderson Fndn Grants, 3862
PGE Fndn Grants, 3869
Phil Hardin Fndn Grants, 3875
Pike County Community Fndn Grants, 3888
Pinnacle Entertainment Fndn Grants, 3893
Pioneer Hi-Bred Community Grants, 3895
Piper Jaffray Fndn Communities Giving Grants, 3899
PMI Fndn Grants, 3918
Posey County Community Fndn Grants, 3939
Pott Fndn Grants, 3940
Powell Fndn Grants, 3942
Praxair Fndn Grants, 3944
Price Chopper's Golub Fndn Grants, 3950
Price Family Charitable Grants, 3952
Price Gilbert, Jr. Charitable Grants, 3953
Princeton Area Community Fndn Greater Mercer Grants, 3963
Pulaski County Community Fndn Grants, 3988
Pulte Homes Corp Contributions, 3989
R.C. Baker Fndn Grants, 3999
Ralph M. Parsons Fndn Grants, 4013
RCF General Community Grants, 4032
Reinberger Fndn Grants, 4052
Reynolds and Reynolds Company Fndn Grants, 4070
RGK Fndn Grants, 4072
Rice Fndn Grants, 4074
Richard and Susan Smith Family Fndn Grants, 4078
Richard D. Bass Fndn Grants, 4079
Richard E. Griffin Family Fndn Grants, 4081
Richard F. and Janice F. Weaver Ed Grants, 4082
Richard King Mellon Fndn Grants, 4087
Rich Fndn Grants, 4090
Richland County Bank Grants, 4091
Ripley County Community Fndn Grants, 4095
Ripley County Community Small Project Grants, 4096
Robert and Polly Dunn Fndn Grants, 4105
Robert G. Cabell III and Maude Morgan Cabell Fndn Grants, 4113
Robert M. Hearin Fndn Grants, 4116
Robert W. Woodruff Fndn Grants, 4124
Robins Fndn Grants, 4126
Rockwell Int'l Corp Grants, 4141
Rollin M. Gerstacker Fndn Grants, 4146
Rollins-Luetkemeyer Fndn Grants, 4147
Roney-Fitzpatrick Fndn Grants, 4150
Ross Fndn Grants, 4164
Roy and Christine Sturgis Charitable Grants, 4166
Rush County Community Fndn Grants, 4174
Russell Berrie Fndn Grants, 4175
Ruth H. and Warren A. Ellsworth Fndn Grants, 4179
Ryder System Charitable Fndn Grants, 4191

SAMHSA Campus Suicide Prevention Grants, 4229
San Antonio Area Fndn Grants, 4240
Sandy Hill Fndn Grants, 4257
Sarkeys Fndn Grants, 4297
Sartain Lanier Family Fndn Grants, 4298
Schering-Plough Fndn Health Grants, 4304
Schramm Fndn Grants, 4310
Schurz Communications Fndn Grants, 4312
Scott B. and Annie P. Appleby Charitable Grants, 4313
Scott County Community Fndn Grants, 4314
Seattle Fndn Educ Grants, 4326
Selby and Richard McRae Fndn Grants, 4334
Sensient Technologies Fndn Grants, 4337
Shell Oil Company Fndn Grants, 4343
Sid W. Richardson Fndn Grants, 4350
Simmons Fndn Grants, 4360
Sioux Falls Area Community Grants, 4364
Sioux Falls Area Community Fndn Spot Grants, 4366
Sisters of Charity Fndn of Cleveland Reducing Health and Ed Disparities in the Central Neighborhood Grants, 4374
Solo Cup Fndn Grants, 4401
Sonoco Fndn Grants, 4403
Sonora Area Fndn Competitive Grants, 4404
Sony Corp of America Corp Philanthropy Grants, 4405
Sosland Fndn Grants, 4408
SW Gas Corp Fndn Grants, 4445
Sprint Fndn Grants, 4463
Square D Fndn Grants, 4464
Stackpole-Hall Fndn Grants, 4472
Starr Fndn Grants, 4483
Steelcase Fndn Grants, 4497
Steele-Reese Fndn Grants, 4498
Stowe Family Fndn Grants, 4510
Stranahan Fndn Grants, 4512
Strowd Roses Grants, 4515
Sun Academic Excellence Grants, 4525
Sunderland Fndn Grants, 4527
Sunoco Fndn Grants, 4530
Susan Mott Webb Charitable Grants, 4536
Susan Vaughan Fndn Grants, 4537
T. Rowe Price Associates Fndn Grants, 4548
Talbert and Leota Abrams Fndn, 4558
Tanner Humanities Center Research Fellowships, 4559
Teagle Fndn Grants, 4569
TE Fndn Grants, 4572
Temple-Inland Fndn Grants, 4576
Tension Envelope Fndn Grants, 4578
Textron Corp Contributions Grants, 4601
Thomas and Dorothy Leavey Fndn Grants, 4612
Thomas Austin Finch, Sr. Fndn Grants, 4613
Thomas J. Long Fndn Community Grants, 4618
Thomas Sill Fndn Grants, 4619
Thomas W. Briggs Fndn Grants, 4621
Thompson Charitable Fndn Grants, 4622
Thompson Fndn Grants, 4623
Thornton Fndn Grants, 4624
Trinity Fndn Grants, 4669
TWS Fndn Grants, 4683
U.S. Department of Educ Child Care Access Means Parents in School Grants, 4689
U.S. Department of Educ Innovative Strategies in Community Colleges for Working Adults and Displaced Workers Grants, 4692
U.S. Department of Educ Native Hawaiian Educ Grants, 4694
U.S. Department of Educ Promoting Postbaccalaureate Opportunities for Hispanic Americans Grants, 4697
Union Bank Corp Sponsorships and Donations, 4708
Union Bank, N.A. Fndn Grants, 4709
United Technologies Corp Grants, 4725
USDC Planning and Local Technical Assistance Grants, 4854
V.V. Cooke Fndn Grants, 4896
Vermillion County Community Fndn Grants, 4928
Viacom Fndn Grants (Formerly CBS Fndn), 4932
Victor E. Speas Fndn Grants, 4933
Virginia Fndn for Humanities Discr Grants, 4946
Virginia Fndn for the Humanities Open Grants, 4947
Vulcan Materials Company Fndn Grants, 4956

Higher Education

W.C. Griffith Fndn Grants, 4957
W. C. Griffith Fndn Grants, 4958
W.K. Kellogg Fndn Healthy Kids Grants, 4961
W.K. Kellogg Fndn Racial Equity Grants, 4962
W.P. and Bulah Luse Fndn Grants, 4965
W. Waldo and Jenny Lynn M. Bradley Grants, 4967
Wallace Fndn Grants, 4976
Walt Disney Company Fndn Grants, 4981
Walter L. Gross III Family Fndn Grants, 4983
Wayne and Gladys Valley Fndn Grants, 5003
Weatherwax Fndn Grants, 5014
Weaver Popcorn Fndn Grants, 5016
Wege Fndn Grants, 5017
Weingart Fndn Grants, 5018
Whitney Fndn Grants, 5061
Widgeon Point Charitable Fndn Grants, 5064
Wilbur and Patsy Bradley Family Fndn Grants, 5066
William B. Stokely Jr. Fndn Grants, 5076
William Blair and Company Fndn Grants, 5078
William G. and Helen C. Hoffman Fndn Grants, 5080
William G. Gilmore Fndn Grants, 5082
William G. Selby and Marie Selby Fndn Grants, 5085
Winthrop Rockefeller Fndn Grants, 5105
Yawkey Fndn Grants, 5125
Yellow Corp Fndn Grants, 5126

Higher Education Administration
John W. Speas and Effie E. Speas Grants, 2732
Lewis H. Humphreys Charitable Grants, 2889
Louis and Elizabeth Nave Flarsheim Charitable Fndn Grants, 2924

Higher Education Studies
ALA Young Adult Literature Symposium Stipend, 337

Higher Education, Private
A/H Fndn Grants, 48
Abell-Hanger Fndn Grants, 91
Bill and Katie Weaver Charitable Grants, 764
Booth Ferris Fndn Grants, 816
Bradley Family Fndn (South Carolina) Grants, 830
Burlington Northern Santa Fe Fndn Grants, 866
Charles A. Frueauff Fndn Grants, 1037
Coca-Cola Fndn Grants, 1195
DB Americas Fndn Grants, 1466
Dr. Scholl Fndn Grants, 1602
Dyson Fndn Mid-Hudson Valley General Operating Support Grants, 1635
Francis Beidler Fndn Grants, 1921
Georgia-Pacific Fndn Educ Grants, 2031
Goodyear Tire Grants, 2106
Haddad Fndn Grants, 2189
Hall-Perrine Fndn Grants, 2209
Huntington Fndn Grants, 2408
Jane and Jack Fitzpatrick Grants, 2640
Katherine Baxter Memorial Fndn Grants, 2789
Kenneth T. and Eileen L. Norris Fndn Grants, 2802
Lettie Pate Evans Fndn Grants, 2887
Marion I. and Henry J. Knott Fndn Grants, 3018
Marion I. and Henry J. Knott Standard Grants, 3019
Mary Duke Biddle Fndn Grants, 3036
McGregor Grants, 3082
Medtronic Fndn CommunityLink Educ Grants, 3110
Nordson Corp Fndn Grants, 3462
Plum Creek Fndn Grants, 3917
Richard F. and Janice F. Weaver Ed Grants, 4082
Sandy Hill Fndn Grants, 4257
Strake Fndn Grants, 4511
Wilbur and Patsy Bradley Family Fndn Grants, 5066

Higher Education, Public
A/H Fndn Grants, 48
Bill and Katie Weaver Charitable Grants, 764
Bradley Family Fndn (South Carolina) Grants, 830
DB Americas Fndn Grants, 1466
Dyson Fndn Mid-Hudson Valley General Operating Support Grants, 1635
Francis Beidler Fndn Grants, 1921
Georgia-Pacific Fndn Educ Grants, 2031
Goodyear Tire Grants, 2106
Huntington Fndn Grants, 2408
Jane and Jack Fitzpatrick Grants, 2640
Katherine Baxter Memorial Fndn Grants, 2789
Medtronic Fndn CommunityLink Educ Grants, 3110
Plum Creek Fndn Grants, 3917
Richard F. and Janice F. Weaver Ed Grants, 4082
Sandy Hill Fndn Grants, 4257
Wilbur and Patsy Bradley Family Fndn Grants, 5066

Hispanic Education
General Motors Fndn Grants Support Program, 2004
John R. Oishei Fndn Grants, 2709
McCune Charitable Fndn Grants, 3077
Miller Brewing Corp Contributions Grants, 3180
NACC David Stevenson Fellowships, 3235
NACC William Diaz Fellowships, 3236
New Jersey Center for Hispanic Policy, Research and Development Entrepreneurship Grants, 3326
New Jersey Center for Hispanic Policy, Research and Development Governor's Hispanic Fellows, 3327
New Jersey Center for Hispanic Policy, Research and Development Immigration Integration Grants, 3328
New Jersey Center for Hispanic Policy, Research and Development Innovative Inits Grants, 3329
New Jersey Center for Hispanic Policy, Research and Development Workforce Grants, 3330
S.H. Cowell Fndn Grants, 4199
Target Corp Local Store Grants, 4561
U.S. Department of Educ Promoting Postbaccalaureate Opportunities for Hispanic Americans Grants, 4697
USDA Hispanic-Serving Insts Educ Grants, 4813
W.K. Kellogg Fndn Racial Equity Grants, 4962

Hispanic Studies
New Jersey Center for Hispanic Policy, Research and Development Entrepreneurship Grants, 3326
New Jersey Center for Hispanic Policy, Research and Development Governor's Hispanic Fellows, 3327
New Jersey Center for Hispanic Policy, Research and Development Immigration Integration Grants, 3328
New Jersey Center for Hispanic Policy, Research and Development Workforce Grants, 3330

Hispanics
Abelard Fndn East Grants, 87
Abelard Fndn West Grants, 88
Aetna Fndn Diversity Grants in Connecticut, 182
American Express Historic Preservation Grants, 431
AT&T Fndn Civic and Comm Service Grants, 599
BBF Florida Family Lit Init Grants, 697
BBF Maine Family Lit Init Grants, 698
BBF Maine Family Lit Init Planning Grants, 699
Boeckmann Charitable Fndn Grants, 808
Charles Delmar Fndn Grants, 1039
DHHS Maternal and Child Health Grants, 1536
Effie and Wofford Cain Fndn Grants, 1674
Fndn for the Carolinas Grants, 1896
Healthcare Fndn for Orange County Grants, 2279
Henry J. Kaiser Family Fndn Grants, 2310
Joyce Awards, 2746
Kansas Arts Commission Artist Fellowships, 2776
NAR Partners in Housing Awards, 3239
New Jersey Center for Hispanic Policy, Research and Development Entrepreneurship Grants, 3326
New Jersey Center for Hispanic Policy, Research and Development Governor's Hispanic Fellows, 3327
New Jersey Center for Hispanic Policy, Research and Development Immigration Integration Grants, 3328
New Jersey Center for Hispanic Policy, Research and Development Innovative Inits Grants, 3329
New Jersey Center for Hispanic Policy, Research and Development Workforce Grants, 3330
North Carolina Arts Council Outreach Grants, 3479
NYSCA Special Arts Services: General Operating Support Grants, 3614
Philadelphia Organizational Effectiveness Grants, 3872
Robert R. Meyer Fndn Grants, 4121
Saint Paul Fndn SpectrumGrants, 4222
Strowd Roses Grants, 4515
Teaching Tolerance Grants, 4567

Historical Preservation
1772 Fndn Fellowships, 36
American Express Charitable Grants, 429
Arts Fndn, 578
Blum-Kovler Fndn Grants, 803
C.F. Adams Charitable Grants, 884
Carls Fndn Grants, 937
CDECD Endangered Properties Grants, 980
CDECD Historic Preser Enhancement Grants, 981
CDECD Historic Preservation Survey and Planning Grants, 982
CDECD Historic Restoration Grants, 983
Collins C. Diboll Private Fndn Grants, 1208
Community Partners Lawrence County Grants, 1328
Community Partnerships Martin County Grants, 1329
ConocoPhillips Fndn Grants, 1354
Crown Point Community Fndn Grants, 1402
Decatur County Comm Large Project Grants, 1476
Elkhart County Community Fndn Fund for Elkhart County, 1683
Ferree Fndn Grants, 1804
Forrest C. Lattner Fndn Grants, 1887
Fndn for the Carolinas Grants, 1896
Fndn for Mid South Comm Development Grants, 1897
Frank M. Tait Fndn Grants, 1932
George J. and Effie L. Seay Fndn Grants, 2024
George Kress Fndn Grants, 2025
Goldseker Fndn Community Grants, 2101
Huntington County Community Fndn - Hiner Family Grant, 2405
Inasmuch Fndn Grants, 2523
Indiana Historic Preservation Grants, 2537
Jane's Grants, 2639
Jane and Jack Fitzpatrick Grants, 2640
Jasper Fndn Grants, 2655
Jean and Price Daniel Fndn Grants, 2659
John W. and Anna H. Hanes Fndn Grants, 2728
Maine Community Fndn Steeples Grants, 2989
Margaret L. Wendt Fndn Grants, 3004
McCombs Fndn Grants, 3075
McLean Contributionship Grants, 3088
Mertz Gilmore Climate Change Grants, 3125
National Endowment for the Arts Presenting Grants: Art Works, 3268
NEH Interpreting America's Hist Places Grants, 3292
Norcliffe Fndn Grants, 3459
North Carolina Community Fndn Grants, 3489
NYCT Historic Preservation Grants, 3551
NYSCA Museum Program Support Grants, 3603
Orange County Community Fndn Grants, 3687
PacifiCorp Fndn for Learning Grants, 3727
Parke County Community Fndn Grants, 3735
Richard and Caroline T. Gwathmey Grants, 4075
Rollins-Luetkemeyer Fndn Grants, 4147
Samuel N. and Mary Castle Fndn Grants, 4236
Sioux Falls Area Community Grants, 4364
Sioux Falls Area Community Fndn Spot Grants, 4366
Tourism Cares Worldwide Grants, 4649
Turner Fndn Grants, 4681
Van Kampen Fndn Grants, 4906
Virginia Fndn for Humanities Discr Grants, 4946
Virginia Fndn for the Humanities Open Grants, 4947
Wabash River Heritage Corridor Grants, 4970
Widgeon Point Charitable Fndn Grants, 5064

History
1675 Fndn Grants, 35
1772 Fndn Fellowships, 36
Alabama Humanities Fndn Mini Grants, 231
Alabama Humanities Planning/Consultant Grants, 232
ALA Stonewall Book Awards - Israel Fishman Nonfiction Award, 330
Arts and Science Council Grants, 576
Arts Fndn, 578
ArvinMeritor Fndn Arts and Culture Grants, 582
Blanche and Irving Laurie Fndn Grants, 784
Canada-U.S. Fulbright Mid-Career Grants, 917
Chapin Hall Int'l Fellowships in Children's Policy Research, 1032
Charles G. Koch Charitable Fndn Grants, 1041

SUBJECT INDEX

CICF Efroymson Grants, 1120
Colonel Stanley R. McNeil Fndn Grants, 1210
Community Fndn of Bloomington and Monroe County Grants, 1271
Cooke Fndn Grants, 1368
Corning Fndn Cultural Grants, 1376
Dayton Fndn Grants, 1463
Dolfinger-McMahon Fndn Grants, 1565
Doris and Victor Day Fndn Grants, 1582
Durfee Fndn Sabbatical Grants, 1625
E.J. Grassmann Grants, 1638
Eugene McDermott Fndn Grants, 1765
Florida Humanities Council Major Grants, 1868
Florida Humanities Council Mini Grants, 1869
Garland and Agnes Taylor Gray Fndn Grants, 1988
George I. Alden Grants, 2023
Germanistic Society of America Fellowships, 2043
Henry M. Jackson Fndn Grants, 2311
Illinois Humanities Council Community Project Grants, 2510
IMLS 21st Century Museum Pro Grants, 2512
IMLS American Heritage Preservation Grants, 2513
IMLS National Leadership Grants, 2515
Margaret L. Wendt Fndn Grants, 3004
Montana Arts Council Cultural and Aesthetic Project Grants, 3209
NEH Family and Youth Programs in American History Grants, 3291
NEH Interpreting America's Hist Places Grants, 3292
NHSCA Arts in Health Care Project Grants, 3424
North Carolina Arts Council Folklife Internship, 3467
NYSCA Museum General Operating Support, 3602
OceanFirst Fndn Grants, 3636
Putnam Fndn Grants, 3991
Richard and Caroline T. Gwathmey Grants, 4075
Righteous Persons Fndn Grants, 4093
Self Fndn Grants, 4335
Sid W. Richardson Fndn Grants, 4350
South Carolina Arts Commission American Masterpieces in South Carolina Grants, 4413
Summerlee Fndn Grants, 4523
Turner Fndn Grants, 4681
Van Kampen Fndn Grants, 4906
Vermont Community Fndn Grants, 4929
Virginia Fndn for Humanities Discr Grants, 4946
Virginia Fndn for the Humanities Open Grants, 4947
Virginia Fndn for the Humanities Residential Fellowships, 4948
Virginia Historical Society Research Fellowships, 4949
Warrick County Community Fndn Grants, 4987
Wisconsin Humanities Council Major Grants, 5107

History Education
ALA Coretta Scott King Book Donation Grant, 261
American Society for Yad Vashem Grants, 447
CICF Efroymson Grants, 1120
Horizon Fndn Grants, 2365
NEH Family and Youth Programs in American History Grants, 3291
Robert R. McCormick Tribune Civics Grants, 4118
Virginia Historical Society Research Fellowships, 4949

Home Economics
Dept of Ed Recreational Services for Individuals with Disabilities, 1512
Phi Upsilon Omicron Florence Fallgatter Distinguished Service Award, 3877
Phi Upsilon Omicron Frances Morton Holbrook Alumni Award, 3878

Home Economics Education
Phi Upsilon Omicron Florence Fallgatter Distinguished Service Award, 3877
San Francisco Community Development Grants, 4262

Homeless Shelters
41 Washington Street Fndn Grants, 22
Adam Reineman Charitable Grants, 144
Adams Family Fndn of Tennessee Grants, 152
Adelaide Dawson Lynch Grants, 163

Adobe Hunger and Homelessness Grants, 169
AEGON Transamerica Health & Welfare Grants, 179
ALA Coretta Scott King Book Donation Grant, 261
ALA Diversity and Outreach Fair, 267
Alpha Kappa Alpha Ed Advancement Fndn Community Assistance Awards, 393
Alvah H. and Wyline P. Chapman Fndn Grants, 402
American Express Charitable Grants, 429
ATA Local Community Relations Grants, 600
BJ's Charitable Fndn Grants, 777
Carl B. and Florence E. King Fndn Grants, 928
Carl M. Freeman Fndn FACES Grants, 932
Charles H. Hall Fndn, 1044
Chicago Community Trust Housing Grants: Preventing and Ending Homelessness, 1090
CICF Christmas Fund, 1117
Circle K Corp Contributions Grants, 1136
Citizens Savings Fndn Grants, 1141
Clara Blackford Smith and W. Aubrey Smith Charitable Fndn Grants, 1147
Community Fndn of Bloomington and Monroe County Grants, 1271
Community Fndn of Muncie and Delaware County Maxon Grants, 1303
Community Fndn of Switzerland County Grants, 1315
Danellie Fndn Grants, 1442
Dominion Fndn Human Needs Grants, 1572
Edina Realty Fndn Grants, 1656
Elsie Lee Garthwaite Memorial Fndn Grants, 1692
Emma J. Adams Grants, 1702
Fitzpatrick, Cella, Harper & Scinto Pro Bono, 1836
Frank Loomis Palmer Grants, 1931
Frank Reed and Margaret Jane Peters Memorial Fund II Grants, 1934
George E. Hatcher, Jr. and Ann Williams Hatcher Fndn Grants, 2015
Georgiana Goddard Eaton Grants, 2038
GNOF Maison Hospitaliere Grants, 2086
Greater Worcester Community Youth for Community Improvement Grants, 2144
Green Fndn Human Services Grants, 2154
Harold Brooks Fndn Grants, 2227
Helen Irwin Littauer Ed Grants, 2295
Henrietta Lange Burk Grants, 2303
Henrietta Tower Wurts Memorial Fndn Grants, 2304
HomeBanc Fndn Grants, 2347
Honeywell Corp Housing and Shelter Grants, 2357
Horace A. Kimball and S. Ella Kimball Grants, 2362
Jeffris Wood Fndn Grants, 2660
John H. Wellons Fndn Grants, 2699
Kate B. Reynolds Charitable Trust Poor and Needy Grants, 2787
L. W. Pierce Family Fndn Grants, 2846
Leo Niessen Jr., Charitable Grants, 2885
Lydia deForest Charitable Grants, 2946
Marietta McNeill Morgan and Samuel Tate Morgan, Jr. Grants, 3008
Marriott Int'l Corp Giving Grants, 3024
McCarthy Family Fndn Grants, 3073
Medtronic Fndn Community Link Human Services Grants, 3112
Melville Charitable Grants, 3115
Meyer Fndn Healthy Communities Grants, 3143
Mildred V. Horn Fndn Grants, 3176
Norfolk Southern Fndn Grants, 3463
North Carolina Arts Council Arts in Educ Rural Development Grants, 3470
NW Mutual Fndn Grants, 3509
NYCT Grants for the Elderly, 3549
NYCT Hunger and Homelessnes Grants, 3553
Oak Fndn Housing and Homelessness Grants, 3633
Ordean Fndn Grants, 3691
Owens Fndn Grants, 3718
Packard Fndn Local Grants, 3729
Perkins-Ponder Fndn Grants, 3822
Perpetual Trust for Charitable Giving Grants, 3826
Pinnacle Fndn Grants, 3894
Plough Fndn Grants, 3915
Reinberger Fndn Grants, 4052
Robert R. Meyer Fndn Grants, 4121

San Francisco Community Development Grants, 4262
Santa Barbara Strategy Core Suupport Grants, 4286
Sierra Health Fndn Responsive Grants, 4353
Siragusa Fndn Human Services Grants, 4369
Sisters of St. Joseph Healthcare Fndn Grants, 4377
Stewart Huston Charitable Grants, 4505
Strowd Roses Grants, 4515
Swindells Charitable Fndn, 4542
Sylvia Adams Charitable Grants, 4543
Textron Corp Contributions Grants, 4601
Thompson Fndn Grants, 4623
Union Bank, N.A. Fndn Grants, 4709
Union Square Award for Social Justice, 4717
Union Square Awards Grants, 4718
Wells Fargo Housing Fndn Grants, 5023
Whitehorse Fndn Grants, 5058
William S. Abell Fndn Grants, 5094
Wilson-Wood Fndn Grants, 5098

Homelessness
41 Washington Street Fndn Grants, 22
ACE Charitable Fndn Grants, 111
ACF ACYF Runaway and Homeless Youth Basic Center Grants, 112
Achelis Fndn Grants, 127
Adam Reineman Charitable Grants, 144
Adobe Hunger and Homelessness Grants, 169
AEGON Transamerica Health & Welfare Grants, 179
African American Fund of New Jersey Grants, 192
Alpha Kappa Alpha Ed Advancement Fndn Community Assistance Awards, 393
Alvah H. and Wyline P. Chapman Fndn Grants, 402
Anschutz Family Fndn Grants, 486
Arizona Diamondbacks Charities Grants, 542
Arizona Republic Fndn Grants, 546
Atkinson Fndn Community Grants, 606
Atlanta Women's Fndn Grants, 609
Audrey and Sydney Irmas Charitable Fndn Grants, 612
Barker Welfare Fndn Grants, 669
Barr Fndn Grants, 677
Baxter Int'l Fndn Grants, 691
Berrien Community Fndn Grants, 744
Bicknell Grants, 759
BJ's Charitable Fndn Grants, 777
Bodman Fndn Grants, 807
Boston Fndn Grants, 819
Brooklyn Community Caring Neighbors Grants, 848
Carl B. and Florence E. King Fndn Grants, 928
Carlisle Fndn Grants, 931
Cemala Fndn Grants, 988
CFFVR Robert and Patricia Endries Family Fndn Grants, 1018
Charles Delmar Fndn Grants, 1039
Chicago Community Trust Housing Grants: Preserving Home Ownership and Preventing Foreclosure, 1089
Chicago Community Trust Housing Grants: Preventing and Ending Homelessness, 1090
Clipper Ship Fndn Grants, 1175
Comer Fndn Grants, 1236
Community Fndn of Greenville Hollingsworth Funds Program/Project Grants, 1296
Community Fndn of the Verdugos Grants, 1322
Cralle Fndn Grants, 1394
D. W. McMillan Fndn Grants, 1426
Dade Community Fndn Grants, 1430
Danellie Fndn Grants, 1442
Daniels Grants, 1443
Daphne Seybolt Culpeper Memorial Fndn Grants, 1445
David Geffen Fndn Grants, 1452
Deluxe Corp Fndn Grants, 1496
Denver Broncos Charities Grants, 1501
Denver Fndn Community Grants, 1502
DHHS American Recovery and Reinvestment Act of 2009 Head Start Expansion, 1526
DOL Homeless Veterans Reintegration Grants, 1566
Dominion Fndn Human Needs Grants, 1572
Dresher Fndn Grants, 1605
Edina Realty Fndn Grants, 1656
Edna Wardlaw Charitable Grants, 1660
Effie and Wofford Cain Fndn Grants, 1674

Homelessness

El Pomar Fndn Awards and Grants, 1690
Elsie Lee Garthwaite Memorial Fndn Grants, 1692
Emma J. Adams Grants, 1702
Ensworth Charitable Fndn Grants, 1710
Essex County Community Fndn Merrimack Valley General Grants, 1756
Eugene M. Lang Fndn Grants, 1764
Fassino Fndn Grants, 1793
Faye McBeath Fndn Grants, 1794
Fourjay Fndn Grants, 1913
Frances and John L. Loeb Family Grants, 1917
George A Ohl Jr. Fndn Grants, 2012
Georgia-Pacific Fndn Enrichment Grants, 2032
Georgiana Goddard Eaton Grants, 2038
Giant Food Charitable Grants, 2050
Great-West Life Grants, 2130
Greater Worcester Community Youth for Community Improvement Grants, 2144
Green Fndn Human Services Grants, 2154
Greenspun Family Fndn Grants, 2156
H.B. Fuller Company Fndn Grants, 2183
Hampton Roads Community Fndn Health and Human Service Grants, 2216
Hasbro Children's Fund, 2256
Helen Steiner Rice Fndn Grants, 2299
Helen V. Brach Fndn Grants, 2300
Henrietta Tower Wurts Memorial Fndn Grants, 2304
Hilton Hotels Corp Giving Grants, 2331
Hoffberger Fndn Grants, 2342
Honeywell Corp Housing and Shelter Grants, 2357
Horace A. Kimball and S. Ella Kimball Grants, 2362
Horace Moses Charitable Fndn Grants, 2363
Howard and Bush Fndn Grants, 2374
Humanitas Fndn Grants, 2390
Jacob G. Schmidlapp Grants, 2616
Joe W. and Dorothy Dorsett Brown Fndn Grants, 2684
John Edward Fowler Memorial Fndn Grants, 2693
John Gogian Family Fndn Grants, 2697
John H. and Wilhelmina D. Harland Charitable Fndn Grants, 2698
Joseph H. and Florence A. Roblee Fndn Grants, 2736
Kansas Arts Commission Artist Fellowships, 2776
Kate B. Reynolds Charitable Trust Poor and Needy Grants, 2787
L. W. Pierce Family Fndn Grants, 2846
Lands' End Corp Giving Program, 2861
Lawrence J. and Anne Rubenstein Charitable Fndn Grants, 2868
Leo Niessen Jr., Charitable Grants, 2885
Linden Fndn Grants, 2908
Lucy Gooding Charitable Fndn Trust, 2936
Lucy Gooding Charitable Fndn Grants, 2937
Luther I. Replogle Fndn Grants, 2945
M.J. Murdock Charitable Trust General Grants, 2954
Marietta McNeill Morgan and Samuel Tate Morgan, Jr. Grants, 3008
Marin Community Affordable Housing Grants, 3010
Mary E. Ober Fndn Grants, 3039
McCarthy Family Fndn Grants, 3073
Melville Charitable Grants, 3115
Mervin Bovaird Fndn Grants, 3128
Meyer Fndn Healthy Communities Grants, 3143
Mildred V. Horn Fndn Grants, 3176
Modest Needs Bridge Grants, 3197
Modest Needs Hurricane Sandy Relief Grants, 3198
Moody Fndn Grants, 3215
Morris and Gwendolyn Cafritz Fndn Grants, 3218
National Book Scholarship Fund, 3249
Norfolk Southern Fndn Grants, 3463
Northern Trust Company Corp Giving Program, 3504
Northland Fndn Grants, 3506
NYCT Girls and Young Women Grants, 3548
NYCT Grants for the Elderly, 3549
NYCT Hunger and Homelessnes Grants, 3553
Oak Fndn Housing and Homelessness Grants, 3633
Oppenstein Brothers Fndn Grants, 3685
Ordean Fndn Grants, 3691
Owens Fndn Grants, 3718
Patrick and Anna M. Cudahy Grants, 3751
Peacock Fndn Grants, 3809
Perpetual Trust for Charitable Giving Grants, 3826
Pinellas County Grants, 3891
Pinnacle Fndn Grants, 3894
Plough Fndn Grants, 3915
Portland General Electric Fndn Grants, 3937
Princeton Area Community Fndn Greater Mercer Grants, 3963
Publix Super Markets Charities Local Grants, 3985
Puerto Rico Community Fndn Grants, 3986
Quantum Fndn Grants, 3996
Reinberger Fndn Grants, 4052
Reynolds and Reynolds Associate Fndn Grants, 4069
Rhode Island Fndn Grants, 4073
Richard and Susan Smith Family Fndn Grants, 4078
Rich Fndn Grants, 4090
Robert R. McCormick Tribune Veterans Grants, 4120
Robert R. Meyer Fndn Grants, 4121
Robin Hood Fndn Grants, 4125
Ruth Anderson Fndn Grants, 4176
RWJF Local Funding Partnerships Grants, 4186
S. Mark Taper Fndn Grants, 4201
Saint Luke's Health Inits Grants, 4216
San Francisco Community Development Grants, 4262
Santa Barbara Strategy Core Suupport Grants, 4286
Sara Lee Fndn Grants, 4296
Schlessman Family Fndn Grants, 4307
Sensient Technologies Fndn Grants, 4337
Singing for Change Grants, 4363
Siragusa Fndn Human Services Grants, 4369
Sisters of St. Joseph Healthcare Fndn Grants, 4377
Strowd Roses Grants, 4515
Susan Mott Webb Charitable Grants, 4536
Swindells Charitable Fndn, 4542
Sylvia Adams Charitable Grants, 4543
Taproot Fndn Capacity-Building Service Grants, 4560
Thomas C. Ackerman Fndn Grants, 4615
Thompson Fndn Grants, 4623
Union Bank, N.A. Fndn Grants, 4709
Union Square Award for Social Justice, 4717
Union Square Awards Grants, 4718
USDA Child and Adult Care Food Program, 4800
Vancouver Fndn Grants & Comm Inits, 4900
W.C. Griffith Fndn Grants, 4957
W. C. Griffith Fndn Grants, 4958
Washington Families Grants, 4999
Whitehorse Fndn Grants, 5058
William G. and Helen C. Hoffman Fndn Grants, 5080
William S. Abell Fndn Grants, 5094
Wilson-Wood Fndn Grants, 5098
Xerox Fndn Grants, 5122

Homeownership

ACF Assets for Indep Demonstration Grants, 114
ACF Assets for Indep Individual Development Account Grants, 115
Action for Affordable Housing Grants, 135
Chicago Community Trust Housing Grants: Preserving Home Ownership and Preventing Foreclosure, 1089
Chicago Community Trust Housing Grants: Preventing and Ending Homelessness, 1090
Entergy Charitable Fndn Low-Income Inits and Solutions Grants, 1711
Faye McBeath Fndn Grants, 1794
Georgia-Pacific Fndn Enrichment Grants, 2032
GNOF Jefferson Community Grants, 2085
Grand Victoria Fndn Illinois Core Grants, 2126
Honeywell Corp Housing and Shelter Grants, 2357
Joseph S. Stackpole Charitable Grants, 2741
Middlesex Savings Charitable Fndn Ed Opportunities Grants, 3174
Mizuho USA Fndn Grants, 3192
Modest Needs Hurricane Sandy Relief Grants, 3198
NAR HOPE Awards for Minority Owners, 3238
NAR Partners in Housing Awards, 3239
New Jersey Office of Faith Based Inits Creating Wealth Through Asset Building Grants, 3331
OceanFirst Fndn Grants, 3636
PMI Fndn Grants, 3918
Safeco Insurance Community Grants, 4203
San Francisco Community Development Grants, 4262
Silicon Valley Community Fndn Economic Security Grants, 4355
Speer Grants, 4450
Union Bank, N.A. Fndn Grants, 4709
Wabash Valley Human Services Grants, 4972

Homosexuals, Female

Agape Fndn for Nonviolent Social Change Board of Trustees Grants, 197
ALA Diversity and Outreach Fair, 267
ALA Stonewall Book Awards - Barbara Gittings Literature Award, 329
ALA Stonewall Book Awards - Israel Fishman Nonfiction Award, 330
Alexander Fndn Emergency Grants, 356
Alexander Fndn Holiday Grants, 357
ALFJ Astraea U.S. General Fund, 362
ANLAF Int'l Fund for Sexual Minorities Grants, 471
Appalachian Community Fund GLBTQ Grants, 494
Arcus Fndn Grants, 529
Arcus Fndn Gay and Lesbian Grants, 530
Arcus Fndn National Grants, 531
Boston Globe Fndn Grants, 821
California Endowment Innovative Ideas Challenge Grants, 904
CDC Grants for Violence-Related Injury Prevention Research, 974
Colin Higgins Fndn Courage Awards, 1203
Colin Higgins Fndn Grants, 1204
Community Fndn SE Michigan HOPE Grants, 1260
Community Fndn of Santa Cruz County Grants, 1305
Dade Community Fndn GLBT Grants, 1429
David Bohnett Fndn Grants, 1451
Evelyn and Walter Haas, Jr. Fund Gay and Lesbian Rights Grants, 1772
FCYO Youth Organizing Grants, 1797
Gill Fndn - Gay and Lesbian Grants, 2054
Henry J. Kaiser Family Fndn Grants, 2310
Horizons Community Issues Grants, 2366
Kalamazoo Community LBGT Equality Grants, 2771
Liberty Hill Fndn Environmental Justice Grants, 2891
Liberty Hill Fndn Fund for Change Grants, 2893
Liberty Hill Lesbian & Gay Community Grants, 2894
Liberty Hill Fndn Queer Youth Grants, 2895
Liberty Hill Fndn Seed Grants, 2896
Liberty Hill Fndn Special Opportunity Grants, 2897
Maine Community Fndn Equity Grants, 2980
Marin Community Successful Aging Grants, 3014
Ms. Fndn Women Building Democracy Grants, 3223
Ms. Fndn for Women Ending Violence Grants, 3224
Ms. Fndn for Women Health Grants, 3225
Needmor Grants, 3289
New York Fndn Grants, 3338
OUT Fund for Lesbian & Gay Liberation Grants, 3714
Overbrook Fndn Grants, 3715
Paul Rapoport Fndn Grants, 3765
Philanthrofund Fndn Grants, 3874
Playboy Fndn Grants, 3913
Pride Fndn Grants, 3958
Proteus Grants, 3973
Rainbow Endowment Grants, 4007
Sister Grants for Women's Organizations, 4371
Subaru Rainbow Leadership Award, 4520
Susan A. & Donald P. Babson Charitable Grants, 4534
Third Wave Fndn Lela Breitbart Grants, 4609
Third Wave Organizing & Advocacy Grants, 4610
Third Wave Fndn Reproductive Health and Justice Grants, 4611
Tides Fndn Grants, 4632
Vanguard Public Fndn Grant Funds, 4904
Xerox Fndn Grants, 5122

Homosexuals, Male

Agape Fndn for Nonviolent Social Change Board of Trustees Grants, 197
ALA Diversity and Outreach Fair, 267
ALA Stonewall Book Awards - Barbara Gittings Literature Award, 329
ALA Stonewall Book Awards - Israel Fishman Nonfiction Award, 330

SUBJECT INDEX

Alexander Fndn Emergency Grants, 356
Alexander Fndn Holiday Grants, 357
ALFJ Astraea U.S. General Fund, 362
ANLAF Int'l Fund for Sexual Minorities Grants, 471
Appalachian Community Fund GLBTQ Grants, 494
Arcus Fndn Grants, 529
Arcus Fndn Gay and Lesbian Grants, 530
Arcus Fndn National Grants, 531
Boston Globe Fndn Grants, 821
Bread and Roses Community Grants, 832
California Endowment Innovative Ideas Challenge Grants, 904
CDC Grants for Violence-Related Injury Prevention Research, 974
Colin Higgins Fndn Courage Awards, 1203
Colin Higgins Fndn Grants, 1204
Community Fndn SE Michigan HOPE Grants, 1260
Community Fndn of Santa Cruz County Grants, 1305
Dade Community Fndn GLBT Grants, 1429
David Bohnett Fndn Grants, 1451
David Geffen Fndn Grants, 1452
Evelyn and Walter Haas, Jr. Fund Gay and Lesbian Rights Grants, 1772
FCYO Youth Organizing Grants, 1797
Gill Fndn - Gay and Lesbian Grants, 2054
Henry J. Kaiser Family Fndn Grants, 2310
Horizons Community Issues Grants, 2366
Kalamazoo Community LBGT Equality Grants, 2771
Liberty Hill Fndn Environmental Justice Grants, 2891
Liberty Hill Fndn Fund for Change Grants, 2893
Liberty Hill Fndn Lesbian & Gay Community Grants, 2894
Liberty Hill Fndn Queer Youth Grants, 2895
Liberty Hill Fndn Seed Grants, 2896
Liberty Hill Fndn Special Opportunity Grants, 2897
Maine Community Fndn Equity Grants, 2980
Marin Community Successful Aging Grants, 3014
Ms. Fndn Women Building Democracy Grants, 3223
Ms. Fndn for Women Ending Violence Grants, 3224
Ms. Fndn for Women Health Grants, 3225
Needmor Grants, 3289
New York Fndn Grants, 3338
OUT Fund for Lesbian & Gay Liberation Grants, 3714
Overbrook Fndn Grants, 3715
Paul Rapoport Fndn Grants, 3765
Philanthrofund Fndn Grants, 3874
Playboy Fndn Grants, 3913
Pride Fndn Grants, 3958
Proteus Grants, 3973
Rainbow Endowment Grants, 4007
San Diego Fndn for Change Grants, 4247
Subaru Rainbow Leadership Award, 4520
Susan A. & Donald P. Babson Charitable Grants, 4534
Third Wave Fndn Lela Breitbart Grants, 4609
Third Wave Organizing & Advocacy Grants, 4610
Third Wave Fndn Reproductive Health and Justice Grants, 4611
Tides Fndn Grants, 4632
USAID Comprehensive District-Based Support for Better HIV/TB Patient Outcomes Grants, 4747
Vanguard Public Fndn Grant Funds, 4904
Xerox Fndn Grants, 5122

Horticulture

Alabama Power Plant a Tree Grants, 234
Community Fndn of Western N Carolina Grants, 1327
Frederick W. Marzahl Grants, 1948
Garden Crusader Award, 1985
Grable Fndn Grants, 2108
Hagedorn Grants, 2207
Hampton Roads Community Fndn Horticulture Educ Grants, 2217
NGA 'Remember Me' Rose Garden Awards, 3401
NGA Hansen's Natural and Native School Garden Grants, 3402
NGA Heinz Wholesome Memories Intergenerational Garden Awards, 3404
NGA Mantis Award, 3406
Nina Mason Pulliam Charitable Grants, 3443
Open Spaces Sacred Places National Awards, 3684
Posey County Community Fndn Grants, 3939

Project Orange Thumb Grants, 3972
Scotts Company Give Back to Grow Awards, 4315
Stanley Smith Horticultural Grants, 4474
USDA Fed-State Marketing Improvement Grants, 4810

Hospice Care

1st and 10 Fndn Grants, 1
Adelaide Breed Bayrd Fndn Grants, 161
Alex Stern Family Fndn Grants, 360
AmerUs Group Charitable Fndn, 455
Arizona Public Service Corp Giving Grants, 545
Arronson Fndn Grants, 567
Bailey Fndn Grants, 635
Bertha Russ Lytel Fndn Grants, 745
Borkee-Hagley Fndn Grants, 817
Burlington Industries Fndn Grants, 865
Caesar Puff Fndn Grants, 890
Carl B. and Florence E. King Fndn Grants, 928
Carl W. and Carrie Mae Joslyn Grants, 938
Cemala Fndn Grants, 988
Christy-Houston Fndn Grants, 1115
Citizens Savings Fndn Grants, 1141
D. W. McMillan Fndn Grants, 1426
Danellie Fndn Grants, 1442
Dell Fndn Open Grants, 1490
Dunspaugh-Dalton Fndn Grants, 1623
E. Rhodes and Leona B. Carpenter Fndn Grants, 1640
Edward W. and Stella C. Van Houten Grants, 1670
George E. Hatcher, Jr. and Ann Williams Hatcher Fndn Grants, 2015
Gregory L. Gibson Charitable Fndn Grants, 2163
J.W. Kieckhefer Fndn Grants, 2607
L. W. Pierce Family Fndn Grants, 2846
Lucy Gooding Charitable Fndn Trust, 2936
Lucy Gooding Charitable Fndn Grants, 2937
Maine Community Fndn Charity Grants, 2977
Margaret L. Wendt Fndn Grants, 3004
Margaret T. Morris Fndn Grants, 3005
MGN Family Fndn Grants, 3154
Olin Corp Charitable Grants, 3669
Pauline E. Fitzpatrick Charitable Trust, 3763
Samuel S. Johnson Fndn Grants, 4239
Sensient Technologies Fndn Grants, 4337
Stewart Huston Charitable Grants, 4505
Thompson Charitable Fndn Grants, 4622
Visiting Nurse Fndn Grants, 4951
Young Family Fndn Grants, 5127

Hospitals

1st Source Fndn Grants, 3
Abel and Sophia Sheng Charitable Fndn Grants, 86
Acushnet Fndn Grants, 143
Adam Richter Charitable Grants, 145
Adams-Mastrovich Family Fndn Grants, 146
Adelaide Breed Bayrd Fndn Grants, 161
Akzo Nobel Chemicals Grants, 219
ALA Exceptional Service Award, 278
Alavi Fndn Grants, 335
Alcoa Fndn Grants, 350
Allyn Fndn Grants, 392
American Foodservice Charitable Grants, 433
Andrew Family Fndn Grants, 462
Annunziata Sanguinetti Fndn Grants, 485
Anthony R. Abraham Fndn Grants, 489
Antone & Edene Vidinha Charitable Grants, 490
Aragona Family Fndn Grants, 522
Archer Daniels Midland Fndn Grants, 527
Arkansas Arts Council Collab Project Support, 555
Arthur and Rochelle Belfer Fndn Grants, 570
Atran Fndn Grants, 610
Auburn Fndn Grants, 611
Audrey and Sydney Irmas Charitable Fndn Grants, 612
Bacon Family Fndn Grants, 634
Banfi Vintners Fndn Grants, 653
Barker Fndn Grants, 668
Batchelor Fndn Grants, 679
Beerman Fndn Grants, 717
Belk Fndn Grants, 721
Bertha Russ Lytel Fndn Grants, 745
Bert W. Martin Fndn Grants, 747

Blum-Kovler Fndn Grants, 803
Blumenthal Fndn Grants, 804
Boettcher Fndn Grants, 810
Burden Grants, 864
Burlington Industries Fndn Grants, 865
Burlington Northern Santa Fe Fndn Grants, 866
Caddock Fndn Grants, 888
Caesars Fndn Grants, 891
California Arts Council Public Value Grants, 895
Callaway Fndn Grants, 909
Camp-Younts Fndn Grants, 914
Capital City Bank Group Fndn Grants, 920
Caring Fndn Grants, 926
Carl B. and Florence E. King Fndn Grants, 928
Carl Gellert and Celia Berta Gellert Fndn Grants, 930
Carls Fndn Grants, 937
Carnahan-Jackson Fndn Grants, 939
Carrie Estelle Doheny Fndn Grants, 945
Carylon Fndn Grants, 949
CE and S Fndn Grants, 985
Cessna Fndn Grants, 1000
Champlin Fndns Grants, 1029
Charles Delmar Fndn Grants, 1039
Charles M. Bair Family Grants, 1051
Christy-Houston Fndn Grants, 1115
Clark-Winchcole Fndn Grants, 1152
Clark and Ruby Baker Fndn Grants, 1154
Clark Fndn Grants, 1157
CMA Fndn Grants, 1178
Cockrell Fndn Grants, 1196
Coeta and Donald Barker Fndn Grants, 1197
Commonwealth Edison Grants, 1240
Communities Fndn of Texas Grants, 1243
Community Fndn of Mount Vernon and Knox County Grants, 1301
Community Fndn of the Verdugos Ed Endowment Grants, 1321
Connelly Fndn Grants, 1353
ConocoPhillips Fndn Grants, 1354
Constantin Fndn Grants, 1362
Cowles Charitable Grants, 1392
Crystelle Waggoner Charitable Grants, 1405
Dairy Queen Corp Contributions Grants, 1433
Daphne Seybolt Culpeper Memorial Fndn Grants, 1445
Davis Family Fndn Grants, 1462
Dennis and Phyllis Washington Fndn Grants, 1498
Denton A. Cooley Fndn Grants, 1500
DeRoy Testamentary Fndn Grants, 1518
Detroit Lions Charities Grants, 1520
Dolan Fndn Grants, 1563
Dora Roberts Fndn Grants, 1579
Dr. Scholl Fndn Grants, 1602
Dunspaugh-Dalton Fndn Grants, 1623
E.J. Grassmann Grants, 1638
Eberly Fndn Grants, 1649
Eden Hall Fndn Grants, 1655
Edward S. Moore Fndn Grants, 1668
Edwards Grants, 1669
Edwin S. Webster Fndn Grants, 1671
Effie and Wofford Cain Fndn Grants, 1674
Elsie H. Wilcox Fndn Grants, 1691
Eugene B. Casey Fndn Grants, 1762
Eugene McDermott Fndn Grants, 1765
F.M. Kirby Fndn Grants, 1780
FirstEnergy Fndn Community Grants, 1819
FMC Fndn Grants, 1876
Ford Motor Company Grants, 1885
Foster Fndn Grants, 1888
Foster G. McGaw Prize, 1889
Fndn for Health Enhancement Grants, 1894
Frances L. and Edwin L. Cummings Grants, 1919
Francis T. & Louise T. Nichols Fndn Grants, 1923
Frank E. and Seba B. Payne Fndn Grants, 1927
Frank G. and Freida K. Brotz Family Grants, 1928
Frank S. Flowers Fndn Grants, 1935
Fraser-Parker Fndn Grants, 1938
Fritz B. Burns Fndn Grants, 1965
G.A. Ackermann Grants, 1981
G.N. Wilcox Grants, 1982
Gebbie Fndn Grants, 1995

930 / Hospitals

George B. Storer Fndn Grants, 2014
George E. Hatcher, Jr. and Ann Williams Hatcher Fndn Grants, 2015
George F. Baker Grants, 2016
George Kress Fndn Grants, 2025
George S. and Dolores Dore Eccles Fndn Grants, 2027
George W. Codrington Charitable Fndn Grants, 2029
Gertrude and William C. Wardlaw Grants, 2045
Gladys Brooks Fndn Grants, 2059
GNOF IMPACT Gulf States Eye Surgery Fund, 2082
Goodrich Corp Fndn Grants, 2104
Greenwall Fndn Bioethics Grants, 2158
H. Leslie Hoffman & Elaine Hoffman Grants, 2185
Harold Alfond Fndn Grants, 2225
Harry Bramhall Gilbert Charitable Grants, 2238
Harry Edison Fndn, 2241
Hartford Aging and Health Program Awards, 2247
Harvey Randall Wickes Fndn Grants, 2255
Healthcare Fndn for Orange County Grants, 2279
Hedco Fndn Grants, 2287
Helen Irwin Littauer Ed Grants, 2295
Helen Pumphrey Denit Charitable Grants, 2297
Henry County Community Fndn Grants, 2308
Hilda and Preston Davis Fndn Grants, 2322
Hoblitzelle Fndn Grants, 2341
Hudson Webber Fndn Grants, 2383
Huffy Fndn Grants, 2384
Huie-Dellmon Grants, 2386
Illinois Arts Council Artstour Grants, 2465
J.L. Bedsole Fndn Grants, 2600
J. Walton Bissell Fndn Grants, 2608
Jacob and Hilda Blaustein Fndn Grants, 2615
James G.K. McClure Educ and Devel Grants, 2624
James H. Cummings Fndn Grants, 2626
James J. and Angelia M. Harris Fndn Grants, 2630
Janirve Fndn Grants, 2645
Joe W. and Dorothy Dorsett Brown Fndn Grants, 2684
John Clarke Grants, 2689
John Jewett & Helen Chandler Garland Grants, 2702
John Lord Knight Fndn Grants, 2703
John S. Dunn Research Fndn Grants and Chairs, 2715
Joseph Alexander Fndn Grants, 2734
Josephine Goodyear Fndn Grants, 2738
Josiah W. and Bessie H. Kline Fndn Grants, 2742
Journal Gazette Fndn Grants, 2744
Katharine Matthies Fndn Grants, 2788
Katherine John Murphy Fndn Grants, 2790
Kathryne Beynon Fndn Grants, 2791
Kent D. Steadley and Mary L. Steadley Trust, 2804
Lettie Pate Evans Fndn Grants, 2887
Lillian S. Wells Fndn Grants, 2901
Lubbock Area Fndn Grants, 2931
Lucile Horton Howe and Mitchell B. Howe Fndn Grants, 2934
Lumpkin Family Healthy People Grants, 2942
Lydia deForest Charitable Grants, 2946
Mabel Y. Hughes Charitable Grants, 2960
MacDonald-Peterson Fndn Grants, 2965
Margaret and James A. Elkins Jr. Fndn Grants, 3003
Margaret L. Wendt Fndn Grants, 3004
Mary S. and David C. Corbin Fndn Grants, 3048
Maximilian E. and Marion O. Hoffman Fndn, 3067
Maxon Charitable Fndn Grants, 3068
McGregor Grants, 3082
McLean Contributionship Grants, 3088
Meadows Fndn Grants, 3104
Mericos Fndn Grants, 3121
Meriden Fndn Grants, 3122
Mervin Bovaird Fndn Grants, 3128
Meyer and Stephanie Eglin Fndn Grants, 3139
Mockingbird Fndn Grants, 3196
Nicholas H. Noyes Jr. Memorial Fndn Grants, 3434
NNEDVF/Altria Doors of Hope Program, 3452
Norcliffe Fndn Grants, 3459
North Carolina Arts Council Arts in Educ Rural Development Grants, 3470
North Central Health Services Grants, 3492
Notsew Orm Sands Fndn Grants, 3516
OceanFirst Fndn Grants, 3636
Olin Corp Charitable Grants, 3669

Oppenstein Brothers Fndn Grants, 3685
Pasadena Fndn Average Grants, 3741
Peacock Fndn Grants, 3809
Pinnacle Entertainment Fndn Grants, 3893
Piper Jaffray Fndn Communities Giving Grants, 3899
Plum Creek Fndn Grants, 3917
Pott Fndn Grants, 3940
Procter and Gamble Grants, 3967
Questar Corp Contributions Grants, 3997
R.C. Baker Fndn Grants, 3999
Ralphs Food 4 Less Fndn Grants, 4014
Raskob Fndn for Catholic Activities Grants, 4019
Reinberger Fndn Grants, 4052
Rice Fndn Grants, 4074
Richard and Susan Smith Family Fndn Grants, 4078
Rich Fndn Grants, 4090
Robert E. and Evelyn McKee Fndn Grants, 4110
Robert R. Meyer Fndn Grants, 4121
Robins Fndn Grants, 4126
Rockwell Int'l Corp Grants, 4141
Russell Berrie Fndn Grants, 4175
Ruth Eleanor Bamberger and John Ernest Bamberger Memorial Fndn Grants, 4178
Ruth H. and Warren A. Ellsworth Fndn Grants, 4179
RWJF New Jersey Health Inits Grants, 4187
Saint Luke's Health Inits Grants, 4216
Schering-Plough Fndn Health Grants, 4304
Scott County Community Fndn Grants, 4314
Seabury Fndn Grants, 4316
Sensient Technologies Fndn Grants, 4337
Shell Oil Company Fndn Grants, 4343
Sid W. Richardson Fndn Grants, 4350
Solo Cup Fndn Grants, 4401
Sonora Area Fndn Competitive Grants, 4404
Sosland Fndn Grants, 4408
Sprague Fndn Grants, 4461
Starr Fndn Grants, 4483
Strake Fndn Grants, 4511
Sulzberger Fndn Grants, 4522
Sunderland Fndn Grants, 4527
Swindells Charitable Fndn, 4542
Temple-Inland Fndn Grants, 4576
Thelma Doelger Charitable Grants, 4604
Thomas and Dorothy Leavey Fndn Grants, 4612
Thomas Austin Finch, Sr. Fndn Grants, 4613
Thompson Charitable Fndn Grants, 4622
Tri-State Community Twenty-first Century Endowment Grants, 4666
Victor E. Speas Fndn Grants, 4933
W.C. Griffith Fndn Grants, 4957
W. C. Griffith Fndn Grants, 4958
Wege Fndn Grants, 5017
Weingart Fndn Grants, 5018
William B. Stokely Jr. Fndn Grants, 5076
William H. Hannon Fndn Grants, 5086
Winifred & Harry B. Allen Fndn Grants, 5101

Hotel and Restaurant Management
Coors Brewing Corp Contributions Grants, 1371
Phi Upsilon Omicron Florence Fallgatter Distinguished Service Award, 3877

Housing
3 B's Fndn Grants, 7
786 Fndn Grants, 33
2701 Fndn Grants, 37
ACTION Council of Monterey County Grants, 134
Adelaide Benevolent Society Grants, 160
Adobe Hunger and Homelessness Grants, 169
African American Fund of New Jersey Grants, 192
Agnes M. Lindsay Grants, 203
Alexander Fndn Emergency Grants, 356
Alliant Energy Fndn Community Grants, 384
Alvin and Fanny Blaustein Thalheimer Grants, 403
AMD Corp Contributions Grants, 416
American Electric Power Grants, 428
American Express Charitable Grants, 429
AMERIND Community Service Project Grants, 453
Angels Wings Fndn Int'l Grants, 469
Ann Arbor Area Community Fndn Grants, 474

Ann Peppers Fndn Grants, 484
Appalachian Regional Comm Housing Grants, 508
Arizona Cardinals Grants, 534
Arizona Community Fndn Grants, 540
Arizona Diamondbacks Charities Grants, 542
Armstrong McDonald Fndn Grants, 565
Arthur Ashley Williams Fndn Grants, 572
Atkinson Fndn Community Grants, 606
Atlanta Fndn Grants, 608
Audrey and Sydney Irmas Charitable Fndn Grants, 612
Bacon Family Fndn Grants, 634
BancorpSouth Fndn Grants, 651
Bank of America Charitable Fndn Critical Needs Grants, 656
Batchelor Fndn Grants, 679
Beazley Fndn Grants, 714
Blue Cross Blue Shield of Minnesota Fndn - Healthy Equity: Health Impact Assessment Demonstration Project Grants, 795
Bollinger Fndn Grants, 812
Boston Fndn Grants, 819
Brooklyn Community Caring Neighbors Grants, 848
Brooklyn Community Fndn Community Development Grants, 850
Cambridge Community Fndn Grants, 913
Campbell Soup Fndn Grants, 916
Carl and Eloise Pohlad Family Fndn Grants, 927
Carl B. and Florence E. King Fndn Grants, 928
Carlisle Fndn Grants, 931
Carl M. Freeman Fndn FACES Grants, 932
Carnahan-Jackson Fndn Grants, 939
Carpenter Fndn Grants, 943
Caterpillar Fndn Grants, 954
Cemala Fndn Grants, 988
CenterPointEnergy Minnegasco Grants, 993
Cessna Fndn Grants, 1000
CFFVR Robert and Patricia Endries Family Fndn Grants, 1018
Chautauqua Region Community Fndn Grants, 1062
Chicago Community Trust Housing Grants: Advancing Affordable Rental Housing, 1088
Chicago Community Trust Housing Grants: Preserving Home Ownership and Preventing Foreclosure, 1089
Chicago Community Trust Housing Grants: Preventing and Ending Homelessness, 1090
Children Affected by AIDS Fndn Family Assistance Emergency Grants, 1107
CICF Senior Grants, 1127
Circle K Corp Contributions Grants, 1136
Citigroup Fndn Grants, 1139
Citizens Bank Mid-Atlantic Charitable Grants, 1140
Citizens Savings Fndn Grants, 1141
Claude Worthington Benedum Fndn Grants, 1161
Cleo Fndn Grants, 1164
CNCS AmeriCorps State and National Grants, 1182
CNCS AmeriCorps VISTA Project Grants, 1184
Comerica Charitable Fndn Grants, 1237
Commission on Religion in Appalachia Grants, 1238
Community Fndn AIDS Endowment Awards, 1245
Community Fndn Alliance City of Evansville Endowment Grants, 1246
Community Fndn of Greater Birmingham Grants, 1280
Community Fndn of Middle Tennessee Grants, 1300
Community Fndn of Western N Carolina Grants, 1327
Constantin Fndn Grants, 1362
Conwood Charitable Grants, 1366
Crestlea Fndn Grants, 1399
CUNA Mutual Group Fndn Grants, 1417
Danellie Fndn Grants, 1442
Darden Restaurants Fndn Grants, 1446
Dave Coy Fndn Grants, 1447
DB Americas Fndn Grants, 1466
Dearborn Community City of Aurora Grants, 1470
Dennis and Phyllis Washington Fndn Grants, 1498
Denver Fndn Community Grants, 1502
DHHS Health Centers Grants for Residents of Public Housing, 1533
DOL Youthbuild Grants, 1571
Dominion Fndn Human Needs Grants, 1572
Doree Taylor Charitable Fndn, 1580

SUBJECT INDEX   Human Reproduction/Fertility / 931

DTE Energy Community Development Grants, 1609
East Tennessee Fndn Affordable Housing Fund, 1645
East Tennessee Fndn Grants, 1646
Edward and Ellen Roche Relief Fndn Grants, 1663
Edward N. and Della L. Thome Memorial Fndn Direct Services Grants, 1666
Edwin W. and Catherine M. Davis Fndn Grants, 1672
Ensworth Charitable Fndn Grants, 1710
Entergy Charitable Fndn Low-Income Inits and Solutions Grants, 1711
Entergy Corp Open Grants for Community Improvement & Enrichment, 1714
Enterprise Community Partners Green Charrette Grants, 1716
Enterprise Community Partners MetLife Fndn Awards for Excellence in Affordable Housing, 1717
Enterprise Community Partners Pre-Development Design Grants, 1718
Enterprise Community Partners Rose Architectural Fellowships, 1719
Evanston Community Fndn Grants, 1771
Fairfield County Community Fndn Grants, 1782
Fisa Fndn Grants, 1826
Fisher Fndn Grants, 1831
Fitzpatrick, Cella, Harper & Scinto Pro Bono, 1836
Fndns of E Chicago Community Economic Development Grants, 1907
Fndns of E Chicago Family Support Grants, 1908
Fourjay Fndn Grants, 1913
Frank Reed and Margaret Jane Peters Memorial Fund II Grants, 1934
Frank Stanley Beveridge Fndn Grants, 1936
Frist Fndn Grants, 1964
Fund for the City of New York Grants, 1978
George and Ruth Bradford Fndn Grants, 2010
George A Ohl Jr. Fndn Grants, 2012
George Gund Fndn Grants, 2020
Georgia-Pacific Fndn Enrichment Grants, 2032
Georgiana Goddard Eaton Grants, 2038
Ginn Fndn Grants, 2056
GNOF Coastal 5 + 1 Grants, 2070
GNOF Community Revitalization Grants, 2071
GNOF Gert Community Grants, 2076
GNOF Jefferson Community Grants, 2085
GNOF Metropolitan Opportunities Grants, 2087
Grand Victoria Fndn Illinois Core Grants, 2126
Greater Worcester Comm Discretionary Grants, 2140
Group 70 Fndn Fund, 2167
Gulf Coast Community Fndn Grants, 2174
Hagedorn Grants, 2207
HCA Fndn Grants, 2274
Hearst Fndns Social Service Grants, 2285
Holland/Zeeland Community Fndn Grants, 2345
HomeBanc Fndn Grants, 2347
Home Building Industry Disaster Relief Fund, 2348
Honeywell Corp Housing and Shelter Grants, 2357
Household Int'l Corp Giving Grants, 2372
Huntington National Bank Comm Affairs Grant, 2409
Hutchinson Community Fndn Grants, 2410
Hyams Fndn Grants, 2413
Idaho Power Company Corp Contributions, 2433
Illinois Tool Works Fndn Grants, 2511
Independent Community Fndn Neighborhood Renewal Grants, 2527
J. Jill Compassion Grants, 2598
Jackson Fndn Grants, 2613
Jacob G. Schmidlapp Grants, 2616
James J. McCann Charitable Trust and McCann Fndn, Inc Grants, 2631
James R. Thorpe Fndn Grants, 2636
Janirve Fndn Grants, 2645
Jewish Funds for Justice Grants, 2676
Joan Bentinck-Smith Charitable Fndn Grants, 2682
Joe W. and Dorothy Dorsett Brown Fndn Grants, 2684
John H. Wellons Fndn Grants, 2699
John S. and James L. Knight Fndn Communities Grants, 2711
John W. Speas and Effie E. Speas Grants, 2732
Joseph H. and Florence A. Roblee Fndn Grants, 2736
Josephine S. Gumbiner Fndn Grants, 2739

Kahuku Community Fund, 2762
Kalamazoo Community Fndn Individuals and Families Grants, 2769
Kate B. Reynolds Charitable Trust Poor and Needy Grants, 2787
Katharine Matthies Fndn Grants, 2788
Kathryne Beynon Fndn Grants, 2791
Knox County Community Fndn Grants, 2831
Lena Benas Grants, 2881
Liberty Bank Fndn Grants, 2890
Linden Fndn Grants, 2908
Luther I. Replogle Fndn Grants, 2945
Lydia deForest Charitable Grants, 2946
Lyndhurst Fndn Grants, 2949
Mabel Louise Riley Fndn Grants, 2959
Madison Community Fndn Grants, 2971
Marietta McNeill Morgan and Samuel Tate Morgan, Jr. Grants, 3008
Marion Isabell Coe Grants, 3020
Marriott Int'l Corp Giving Grants, 3024
Mary Owen Borden Fndn Grants, 3046
Mary S. and David C. Corbin Fndn Grants, 3048
McGregor Grants, 3082
McKnight Fndn Region & Communities Grants, 3086
Mericos Fndn Grants, 3121
Meyer Fndn Healthy Communities Grants, 3143
Minneapolis Fndn Community Grants, 3186
Minnesota Small Cities Development Grants, 3187
Mizuho USA Fndn Grants, 3192
Modest Needs Bridge Grants, 3197
Morris and Gwendolyn Cafritz Fndn Grants, 3218
Musgrave Fndn Grants, 3231
NAR HOPE Awards for Minority Owners, 3238
NAR Partners in Housing Awards, 3239
National Endowment for the Arts - Grants for Arts Projects: Challenge America Fast-Track, 3254
National Endowment for the Arts - Regional Partnership Agreement Grants, 3258
Nehemiah Community Fndn Grants, 3290
New York Landmarks Conservancy City Ventures Grants, 3339
North Carolina Arts Council Arts in Educ Rural Development Grants, 3470
NW Mutual Fndn Grants, 3509
NW Minnesota Fndn Women's Grants, 3512
NSF Partnership for Advancing Technologies in Housing Grants, 3529
NYCT Community Development Grants, 3546
NYCT Girls and Young Women Grants, 3548
Oak Fndn Housing and Homelessness Grants, 3633
OceanFirst Fndn Grants, 3636
Oleonda Jameson Grants, 3667
Olga Sipolin Children's Grants, 3668
Olin Corp Charitable Grants, 3669
Ordean Fndn Grants, 3691
Owens Corning Fndn Grants, 3717
Owens Fndn Grants, 3718
Parker Fndn (California) Grants, 3736
Patrick and Aimee Butler Family Fndn Community Human Services Grants, 3749
Patrick and Anna M. Cudahy Grants, 3751
Paul G. Allen Family Fndn Grants, 3759
Peacock Fndn Grants, 3809
Perkins-Ponder Fndn Grants, 3822
Perpetual Trust for Charitable Giving Grants, 3826
Perry County Community Fndn Grants, 3827
Peyton Anderson Fndn Grants, 3862
Philadelphia Organizational Effectiveness Grants, 3872
Pike County Community Fndn Grants, 3888
Pinellas County Grants, 3891
Pinkerton Fndn Grants, 3892
Piper Jaffray Fndn Communities Giving Grants, 3899
Piper Trust Reglious Organizations Grants, 3905
Pittsburgh Fndn Community Grants, 3910
Plough Fndn Grants, 3915
PMI Fndn Grants, 3918
PNC Ecnomic Development Grants, 3922
Polk Bros. Fndn Grants, 3929
Posey County Community Fndn Grants, 3939
Prince Charitable Trusts D.C. Grants, 3960

Princeton Area Community Fndn Greater Mercer Grants, 3963
Puerto Rico Community Fndn Grants, 3986
Ralphs Food 4 Less Fndn Grants, 4014
Reinberger Fndn Grants, 4052
Reynolds American Fndn Grants, 4068
Rhode Island Fndn Grants, 4073
Robert F. Stoico / FIRSTFED Grants, 4112
Robert & Clara Milton Fund for Senior Housing, 4117
Rockwell Fund, Inc. Grants, 4140
Ruth Anderson Fndn Grants, 4176
S.H. Cowell Fndn Grants, 4199
S. Mark Taper Fndn Grants, 4201
Sailors' Snug Harbor of Boston Elder Grants, 4211
Saint Paul Fndn Community Sharing Grants, 4218
Salem Fndn Charitable Grants, 4223
Sara Lee Fndn Grants, 4296
Scherman Fndn Grants, 4305
Schramm Fndn Grants, 4310
Seagate Tech Corp Capacity to Care Grants, 4317
Sid W. Richardson Fndn Grants, 4350
Sobrato Family Fndn Grants, 4389
Southbury Community Trust Fund, 4409
Spencer County Community Fndn Grants, 4451
Stark Community Fndn Grants, 4477
Starr Fndn Grants, 4483
State Street Fndn Grants, 4495
Strengthening Families - Strengthening Communities Grants, 4513
Taproot Fndn Capacity-Building Service Grants, 4560
TCF Bank Fndn Grants, 4565
Textron Corp Contributions Grants, 4601
Thompson Charitable Fndn Grants, 4622
Thompson Fndn Grants, 4623
TJX Fndn Grants, 4637
U.S. Bank Fndn Grants, 4686
Union Bank Corp Sponsorships and Donations, 4708
Union Bank, N.A. Fndn Grants, 4709
Union Benevolent Association Grants, 4710
USDA Community Facility Grants, 4801
USDA Farm Labor Housing Grants, 4809
USDA Housing Application Packaging Grants, 4815
USDA Housing Preservation Grants, 4816
USDA Multi-Family Housing Preservation and Revitalization Grants, 4819
USDA Rural Community Development Grants, 4825
USDA Rural Housing Repair and Rehabilitation Grants, 4831
USDA Self-Help Technical Assistance Grants, 4836
USDA Tech and Supervisory Assistance Grants, 4841
Vancouver Fndn Grants & Comm Inits, 4900
Warrick County Community Fndn Grants, 4987
Washington Families Grants, 4999
Wayne County Fndn Vigran Family Grants, 5004
Wayne County Fndn Grants, 5005
Wells Fargo Housing Fndn Grants, 5023
Whitehorse Fndn Grants, 5058
William J. and Dorothy K. O'Neill Fndn Grants, 5087
Wilson-Wood Fndn Grants, 5098

Human Development
California Community Fndn Human Development Grants, 902
CCHD Economic Development Grants, 967
Chapin Hall Int'l Fellowships in Children's Policy Research, 1032
Jane and Jack Fitzpatrick Grants, 2640
Vanderburgh Community Fndn Grants, 4902

Human Learning and Memory
Coca-Cola Fndn Grants, 1195
Helen Bader Fndn Grants, 2293
Wallace Fndn Grants, 4976

Human Reproduction/Fertility
Bernard F. and Alva B. Gimbel Fndn Grants, 740
Donald and Sylvia Robinson Family Fndn Grants, 1573
Edna Wardlaw Charitable Grants, 1660
General Service Fndn Human Rights and Economic Justice Grants, 2006

Henry J. Kaiser Family Fndn Grants, 2310
Huber Fndn Grants, 2382
Jessie Smith Noyes Fndn Grants, 2672
Overbrook Fndn Grants, 3715
Packard Fndn Local Grants, 3729
Playboy Fndn Grants, 3913
Sister Grants for Women's Organizations, 4371
Susan Vaughan Fndn Grants, 4537
Third Wave Fndn Lela Breitbart Grants, 4609
Third Wave Organizing & Advocacy Grants, 4610
Third Wave Fndn Reproductive Health and Justice Grants, 4611
USAID Implementation Science for Strengthening Use of Evidence in Family Planning/Reproductive Health Programming Grants, 4758
W.C. Griffith Fndn Grants, 4957
Wallace Alexander Gerbode Fndn Grants, 4974
Wallace Global Grants, 4977
William S. Abell Fndn Grants, 5094
Women's Funding Alliance Grants, 5112

Human Resources

Bill & Melinda Gates Emergency Response Grants, 766
Bill and Melinda Gates Fndn Financial Services for the Poor Grants, 767
Bill and Melinda Gates Fndn Water, Sanitation and Hygiene Grants, 770
Kalamazoo Community Fndn Capacity Building Grants, 2764
Mann T. Lowry Fndn Grants, 2998
Middlesex Savings Charitable Fndn Capacity Building Grants, 3172

Human Services

3M Company Health and Human Services Grants, 14
3M Fndn Community Giving Grants, 15
100 Angels Charitable Fndn Grants, 24
1675 Fndn Grants, 35
Abbott Fund Global AIDS Care Grants, 82
Abell Fndn Health and Human Services Grants, 96
ABS Fndn Grants, 107
ACF Native American Social and Economic Development Strategies Grants, 123
A Charitable Fndn Grants, 126
Ackerman Fndn Grants, 129
Adams-Mastrovich Family Fndn Grants, 146
Adams and Reese LLP Corp Giving Grants, 147
Adams Family Fndn of Ohio Grants, 151
Adams Fndn Grants, 154
Adelaide Breed Bayrd Fndn Grants, 161
Adelaide Christian Home For Children Grants, 162
Adler-Clark Electric Community Commitment Fndn Grants, 164
AEGON Transamerica Civic & Community Grants, 177
AHS Fndn Grants, 208
Albert E. and Birdie W. Einstein Grants, 342
Albert W. Rice Charitable Fndn Grants, 347
Alfred and Tillie Shemanski Testamentary Grants, 363
Alfred Bersted Fndn Grants, 364
Alfred C. and Ersa S. Arbogast Fndn Grants, 365
Alfred E. Chase Charitable Fndn Grants, 366
Alfred J Mcallister and Dorothy N Mcallister Fndn Grants, 367
Allan C. and Leila J. Garden Fndn Grants, 374
Alvin and Fanny Blaustein Thalheimer Grants, 403
Amelia Sillman Rockwell and Carlos Perry Rockwell Charities Grants, 417
American Electric Power Grants, 428
American Express Charitable Grants, 429
Anderson Fndn Grants, 460
Anna Fitch Ardenghi Grants, 472
Anne J. Caudal Fndn Grants, 475
Ann L. & Carol Green Rhodes Charitable Grants, 483
Arkansas Community Fndn Grants, 561
Assisi Fndn of Memphis Capital Project Grants, 593
Assisi Fndn of Memphis General Grants, 594
Assisi Fndn of Memphis Mini Grants, 595
Autodesk Community Relations Grants, 619
AutoZone Community Relations Grants, 621
Ayres Fndn Grants, 630

Back Home Again Fndn Grants, 633
Batchelor Fndn Grants, 679
Benwood Fndn Community Grants, 732
Better Way Fndn Grants, 754
Blackford County Community Fndn Grants, 780
Blanche and Julian Robertson Family Fndn Grants, 785
Blandin Fndn Itasca County Area Vitality Grants, 789
Boeing Company Contributions Grants, 809
Brown Fndn Grants, 854
Burton D. Morgan Hudson Community Grants, 869
Business Bank of Nevada Community Grants, 879
C.F. Adams Charitable Grants, 884
Caesars Fndn Grants, 891
Carl R. Hendrickson Family Fndn Grants, 935
Cass County Community Fndn Grants, 952
CFFVR Project Grants, 1017
Charles H. Hall Fndn, 1044
Charles H. Pearson Fndn Grants, 1045
Charles M. and Mary D. Grant Fndn Grants, 1050
Charles M. Bair Family Grants, 1051
Charles Nelson Robinson Grants, 1052
Chemtura Corp Contributions Grants, 1067
ChevronTexaco Contributions Program, 1078
Chicago Community Poverty Alleviation Grants, 1091
Christine and Katharina Pauly Charitable Grants, 1114
Citizens Savings Fndn Grants, 1141
Clara Blackford Smith and W. Aubrey Smith Charitable Fndn Grants, 1147
Clark and Carolyn Adams Fndn Grants, 1153
Claude A. and Blanche McCubbin Abbott Charitable Grants, 1158
Clinton County Community Fndn Grants, 1174
CNCS Foster Grandparent Grants, 1185
CNCS Senior Companion Grants, 1187
Colonel Stanley R. McNeil Fndn Grants, 1210
Community Fndn for SE Michigan Grants, 1259
Community Fndn of Boone County Grants, 1274
Community Fndn of Grant County Grants, 1279
Community Fndn of Jackson County Grants, 1298
Community Fndn of Muncie and Delaware County Grants, 1302
Community Fndn of Muncie and Delaware County Maxon Grants, 1303
Community Fndn of Southern Indiana Grants, 1310
Community Fndn of St. Joseph County Special Project Challenge Grants, 1314
Community Partners Lawrence County Grants, 1328
Community Impact Fund, 1332
Connelly Fndn Grants, 1353
ConocoPhillips Fndn Grants, 1354
Cooper Fndn Grants, 1369
Covenant Ed Fndn Grants, 1383
Crown Point Community Fndn Grants, 1402
CSRA Community Fndn Grants, 1407
CSX Corp Contributions Grants, 1408
D.V. and Ida J. McEachern Charitable Grants, 1425
David Lane Grants for Aged & Indigent Women, 1453
David Robinson Fndn Grants, 1454
Deborah Munroe Noonan Grants, 1475
Decatur County Comm Large Project Grants, 1476
DeKalb County Community Fndn Grants, 1481
Denver Fndn Community Grants, 1502
DHHS Emerging Leaders Program Internships, 1532
Dominion Fndn Human Needs Grants, 1572
Dr. and Mrs. Paul Pierce Memorial Fndn Grants, 1599
Dr. P. Phillips Fndn Grants, 1601
Dream Weaver Fndn, 1604
Drs. Bruce and Lee Fndn Grants, 1607
DTE Energy Health & Human Services Grants, 1613
Dyson Fndn Mid-Hudson Valley Faith-Based Organization Grants, 1634
Edward and Ellen Roche Relief Fndn Grants, 1663
Edward and Helen Bartlett Fndn Grants, 1664
Edward N. and Della L. Thome Memorial Fndn Direct Services Grants, 1666
Elizabeth Morse Genius Charitable Grants, 1682
Emy-Lou Biedenharn Fndn Grants, 1703
Ensworth Charitable Fndn Grants, 1710
Esther M. and Freeman E. Everett Charitable Fndn Grants, 1757

Eugene G. & Margaret M. Blackford Grants, 1763
Eugene Straus Charitable Trust, 1766
Federal Express Corp Contributions Program, 1799
Ferree Fndn Grants, 1804
Fifth Third Fndn Grants, 1810
Fitzpatrick, Cella, Harper & Scinto Pro Bono, 1836
Flextronics Fndn Disaster Relief Grants, 1841
Florian O. Bartlett Grants, 1845
Foster Fndn Grants, 1888
Francis Beidler Fndn Grants, 1921
Frank B. Hazard General Charity Grants, 1926
Franklin H. Wells and Ruth L. Wells Grants, 1930
Frank Loomis Palmer Grants, 1931
Frank Reed and Margaret Jane Peters Memorial Fund I Grants, 1933
Frank Reed and Margaret Jane Peters Memorial Fund II Grants, 1934
Frank W. and Carl S. Adams Grants, 1937
Fred & Gretel Biel Charitable Grants, 1939
Frederick McDonald Grants, 1946
Frederick W. Marzahl Grants, 1948
Frost Fndn Grants, 1966
Furth Family Fndn Grants, 1980
G.A. Ackermann Grants, 1981
Gene Haas Fndn, 1999
George A. and Grace L. Long Fndn Grants, 2008
George B. Page Fndn Grants, 2013
George F. Baker Grants, 2016
George H.C. Ensworth Grants, 2022
George J. and Effie L. Seay Fndn Grants, 2024
George Kress Fndn Grants, 2025
George W. Wells Fndn Grants, 2030
Gertrude M. Conduff Fndn Grants, 2047
Gibson County Community Fndn Women's Fund, 2051
Gil and Dody Weaver Fndn Grants, 2053
GNOF Bayou Communities Grants, 2069
GNOF Freeman Challenge Grants, 2075
GNOF IMPACT Grants for Health and Human Services, 2080
GNOF Maison Hospitaliere Grants, 2086
GNOF Norco Community Grants, 2089
Goldseker Fndn Human Services Grants, 2102
Grace Bersted Fndn Grants, 2110
Grand Rapids Community Fndn Lowell Grants, 2121
Great-West Life Grants, 2130
Greater Des Moines Fndn Grants, 2134
Green Fndn Human Services Grants, 2154
Grover Hermann Fndn Grants, 2168
Grundy Fndn Grants, 2169
Guy I. Bromley Grants, 2180
Hackett Fndn Grants, 2188
Haddad Fndn Grants, 2189
Hahl Proctor Charitable Grants, 2208
Hampton Roads Community Fndn Health and Human Service Grants, 2216
Hampton Roads Community Fndn Nonprofit Facilities Improvement Grants, 2218
Hancock County Community Fndn - Field of Interest Grants, 2219
Harold and Arlene Schnitzer CARE Grants, 2226
Harry B. and Jane H. Brock Fndn Grants, 2237
Harry Edison Fndn, 2241
Harvey Randall Wickes Fndn Grants, 2255
HCA Fndn Grants, 2274
Helen Irwin Littauer Ed Grants, 2295
Helen Pumphrey Denit Charitable Grants, 2297
Hendricks County Community Fndn Grants, 2302
Henrietta Lange Burk Grants, 2303
Herbert A. and Adrian W. Woods Fndn Grants, 2313
Hilda and Preston Davis Fndn Grants, 2322
Hill Crest Fndn Grants, 2324
Hirtzel Memorial Fndn Grants, 2332
Horace Moses Charitable Fndn Grants, 2363
Hormel Fndn Grants, 2369
Huntington County Community Fndn - Make a Difference Grants, 2406
Hutton Fndn Grants, 2412
IDPH Emergency Med Serv Assistance Grants, 2440
IIE New Leaders Group Award for Mutual Understanding, 2460

SUBJECT INDEX

Intergrys Corp Grants, 2565
Irving S. Gilmore Fndn Grants, 2584
J. Edwin Treakle Fndn Grants, 2596
Jackson County Community Fndn Grants, 2611
Jacob G. Schmidlapp Grants, 2616
James Ford Bell Fndn Grants, 2623
James J. and Angelia M. Harris Fndn Grants, 2630
Jane's Grants, 2639
Jasper Fndn Grants, 2655
Jim Blevins Fndn Grants, 2678
Joan Bentinck-Smith Charitable Fndn Grants, 2682
John M. Weaver Fndn Grants, 2705
Johnson Controls Fndn Health and Social Services Grants, 2722
John W. and Anna H. Hanes Fndn Grants, 2728
John W. Speas and Effie E. Speas Grants, 2732
Josephine Goodyear Fndn Grants, 2738
Joseph S. Stackpole Charitable Grants, 2741
Katharine Matthies Fndn Grants, 2788
Katrine Menzing Deakins Charitable Grants, 2793
Kawabe Grants, 2794
Kent D. Steadley and Mary L. Steadley Trust, 2804
Kettering Family Fndn Grants, 2817
Kovler Family Fndn Grants, 2840
Laclede Gas Charitable Grants, 2848
Lake County Community Grants, 2856
Land O'Lakes Fndn Community Grants, 2859
Lena Benas Grants, 2881
Lewis H. Humphreys Charitable Grants, 2889
Liberty Bank Fndn Grants, 2890
Libra Fndn Grants, 2899
Linford and Mildred White Charitable Grants, 2909
Lisa and Douglas Goldman Grants, 2910
Louetta M. Cowden Fndn Grants, 2922
Louis and Elizabeth Nave Flarsheim Charitable Fndn Grants, 2924
Lucy Downing Nisbet Charitable Grants, 2935
Luella Kemper Grants, 2939
Lydia deForest Charitable Grants, 2946
M.D. Anderson Fndn Grants, 2952
Mabel A. Horne Grants, 2956
Mabel F. Hoffman Charitable Grants, 2957
MacDonald-Peterson Fndn Grants, 2965
Madison County Community Fndn - City of Anderson Quality of Life Grant, 2972
Mann T. Lowry Fndn Grants, 2998
Marathon Petroleum Corp Grants, 2999
Margaret L. Wendt Fndn Grants, 3004
Marie H. Bechtel Charitable Grants, 3007
Marietta McNeill Morgan and Samuel Tate Morgan, Jr. Grants, 3008
Marion and Miriam Rose Grants, 3015
Marion Gardner Jackson Charitable Grants, 3017
Marion I. and Henry J. Knott Fndn Discretionary Grants, 3018
Marion I. and Henry J. Knott Standard Grants, 3019
Marion Isabell Coe Grants, 3020
Marjorie Moore Charitable Fndn Grants, 3021
Marshall County Community Fndn Grants, 3026
Marsh Corp Grants, 3027
Mary E. and Michael Blevins Charitable Grants, 3037
Mary Wilmer Covey Charitable Grants, 3049
McCallum Family Fndn Grants, 3072
McCune Fndn Human Services Grants, 3080
McGraw-Hill Companies Community Grants, 3081
McKnight Fndn Virginia McKnight Binger Awards in Human Service, 3087
Memorial Fndn Grants, 3117
Mercedes-Benz USA Corp Contributions Grants, 3118
Metzger-Price Grants, 3137
Meyer Memorial Trust Grassroots Grants, 3147
Meyer Memorial Trust Responsive Grants, 3148
Middlesex Savings Charitable Fndn Community Development Grants, 3173
Miller Fndn Grants, 3181
Milton Hicks Wood and Helen Gibbs Wood Charitable Grants, 3184
MMS and Alliance Charitable Fndn Grants for Community Action and Care for the Medically Uninsured, 3194

Norfolk Southern Fndn Grants, 3463
Northrop Grumman Corp Grants, 3507
NW Minnesota Fndn Asset Building Grants, 3511
Notsew Orm Sands Fndn Grants, 3516
Olga Sipolin Children's Grants, 3668
Oppenstein Brothers Fndn Grants, 3685
Orange County Community Fndn Grants, 3688
Orange County Community Fndn Grants, 3687
Oscar Rennebohm Fndn Grants, 3694
OSI Sentencing and Incarceration Alternatives Project Grants, 3711
Pacific Life Fndn Grants, 3726
Patrick John Bennett, Jr. Memorial Fndn Grants, 3752
Paul G. Allen Family Fndn Grants, 3759
PDF Fiscal Sponsorship Grant, 3808
Perkins-Ponder Fndn Grants, 3822
Perpetual Trust for Charitable Giving Grants, 3826
Piedmont Natural Gas Corp and Charitable Contributions, 3883
PMI Fndn Grants, 3918
Pohlad Family Fndn, 3928
Portland Fndn Grants, 3936
PPG Industries Fndn Grants, 3943
Priddy Fndn Grants, 3957
Pulte Homes Corp Contributions, 3989
Putnam County Community Fndn Grants, 3990
R.S. Gernon Grants, 4002
RCF General Community Grants, 4032
Reinberger Fndn Grants, 4052
Robert Lee Adams Fndn Grants, 4114
Robert R. Meyer Fndn Grants, 4121
Robert W. Woodruff Fndn Grants, 4124
Roger L. and Agnes C. Dell Charitable Grants, 4143
Rohm and Haas Company Grants, 4145
Rollins-Luetkemeyer Fndn Grants, 4147
Sandy Hill Fndn Grants, 4257
San Juan Island Community Fndn Grants, 4283
Santa Fe Community Fndn root2fruit Santa Fe, 4289
Santa Fe Community Fndn Seasonal Grants, 4290
Sarkeys Fndn Grants, 4297
Sartain Lanier Family Fndn Grants, 4298
Scherman Fndn Grants, 4305
Schlessman Family Fndn Grants, 4307
Seattle Fndn Basic Needs Grants, 4321
Shell Oil Company Fndn Grants, 4343
Simpson Lumber Charitable Contributions, 4362
Sioux Falls Area Community Grants, 4364
Sioux Falls Area Community Fndn Field-of-Interest and Donor-Advised Grants, 4365
Sioux Falls Area Community Fndn Spot Grants, 4366
Solo Cup Fndn Grants, 4401
Sony Corp of America Corp Philanthropy Grants, 4405
Sophia Romero Grants, 4406
Sosland Fndn Grants, 4408
Sprague Fndn Grants, 4461
Stan and Sandy Checketts Fndn, 4473
Starke County Community Fndn Grants, 4482
Steelcase Fndn Grants, 4497
Stewart Huston Charitable Grants, 4505
Sunoco Fndn Grants, 4530
Swindells Charitable Grants, 4542
T. Rowe Price Associates Fndn Grants, 4548
TCF Bank Fndn Grants, 4565
Texas Instruments Corp Health and Human Services Grants, 4598
Texas Instruments Community Services Grants, 4600
Textron Corp Contributions Grants, 4601
Thelma Braun and Bocklett Family Fndn Grants, 4603
Thomas J. Long Fndn Community Grants, 4618
Toro Fndn Grants, 4647
Toyota Motor Engineering & Manufacturing North America Grants, 4651
Toyota Motor Manufacturing of Alabama Grants, 4652
Toyota Motor Manufacturing of Indiana Grants, 4653
Toyota Motor Manufacturing Mississippi Grants, 4655
Toyota Motor Manufacturing of Texas Grants, 4656
Toyota Motor Manufacturing W Virginia Grants, 4657
Turner B. Bunn, Jr. & Catherine E. Bunn Grants, 4680
TWS Fndn Grants, 4683
U.S. Bank Fndn Grants, 4686

Union Bank Corp Sponsorships and Donations, 4708
Union Pacific Health & Human Services Grants, 4715
United Technologies Corp Grants, 4725
Unity Fndn Of LaPorte County Grants, 4726
US Airways Community Fndn Grants, 4789
Vanderburgh Community Fndn Grants, 4902
Victor E. Speas Fndn Grants, 4933
Vigneron Grants, 4938
Virginia W. Kettering Fndn Grants, 4950
W.H. and Mary Ellen Cobb Charitable Grants, 4959
W.P. and Bulah Luse Fndn Grants, 4965
Walter L. Gross III Family Fndn Grants, 4983
Warren County Community Fndn Grants, 4985
Warren County Community Fndn Mini-Grants, 4986
Washington County Community Fndn Grants, 4997
Weatherwax Fndn Grants, 5014
Weaver Popcorn Fndn Grants, 5016
Wege Fndn Grants, 5017
Wells County Fndn Grants, 5022
White County Community Fndn Grants, 5057
Wieboldt Fndn Grants, 5065
Willary Fndn Grants, 5071
William Bingham Fndn Grants, 5077
William L. and Victorine Q. Adams Fndn Grants, 5089
William Robert Baird Charitable Grants, 5093
Winston-Salem Fndn Competitive Grants, 5102
Woods Charitable Grants, 5114
Yawkey Fndn Grants, 5125

Humanitarianism
Bill & Melinda Gates Emergency Response Grants, 766
Nissan Fndn Grants, 3444
Yves Rocher Fndn Women of the Earth Awards, 5143

Humanities
AFG Industries Grants, 191
Ahmanson Fndn Grants, 207
Akzo Nobel Chemicals Grants, 219
Alabama Humanities Fndn Mini Grants, 231
Alabama Humanities Planning/Consultant Grants, 232
Alex Brown and Sons Charitable Fndn Grants, 359
Amon G. Carter Fndn Grants, 458
Arkansas Community Fndn Grants, 561
Armstrong McDonald Fndn Grants, 565
Atherton Family Fndn Grants, 604
Athwin Fndn Grants, 605
Aurora Fndn Grants, 613
Avon Products Fndn Grants, 625
Banfi Vintners Fndn Grants, 653
Barra Fndn Community Grants, 673
Baton Rouge Area Fndn Grants, 682
Benton County Fndn Grants, 731
Bernard and Audre Rapoport Fndn University of Texas at Austin Scholarship Programs, 739
Bernard Osher Fndn Grants, 742
Berrien Community Fndn Grants, 744
Bicknell Grants, 759
Blue Grass Community Fndn Grants, 799
Boston Globe Fndn Grants, 821
Brookdale Fndn Leadership in Aging Fellowships, 844
Buhl Fndn - Frick Ed Fund, 859
Bush Fndn Health & Human Services Grants, 875
Caleb C. and Julia W. Dula Ed and Charitable Fndn Grants, 893
Callaway Fndn Grants, 909
Canada-U.S. Fulbright Mid-Career Grants, 917
CCH California Story Grants, 965
CCH Documentary California Reads Grants, 968
CCH Documentary Project Production Grants, 969
CCH Documentary Public Engagement Grants, 970
CCH Documentary Project Research and Development Grants, 971
Chula Vista Charitable Fndn Grants, 1116
Clark County Community Fndn Grants, 1156
Collins Fndn Grants, 1209
Columbus Fndn Competitive Grants, 1220
Comer Fndn Grants, 1236
Community Fndn for Southern Arizona Grants, 1261
Community Fndn of Central Illinois Grants, 1276
Community Fndn of East Central Illinois Grants, 1278

934 / Humanities

Community Fndn of Greater Birmingham Grants, 1280
Community Fndn of Greater Flint Grants, 1282
Community Fndn of Middle Tennessee Grants, 1300
Community Fndn of Santa Cruz County Grants, 1305
Community Fndn Silicon Valley Grants, 1331
Connecticut Community Fndn Grants, 1350
ConocoPhillips Grants, 1355
Cooke Fndn Grants, 1368
Cooper Fndn Grants, 1369
DAAD Research Grants for Doctoral Candidates and Young Academics and Scientists, 1427
Delaware Community Fund For Women Grants, 1484
Delaware Community Next Generation Grants, 1485
Delaware Community Fndn Youth Philanthropy Board for New Castle County Grants, 1486
Donald W. Reynolds Fndn Special Grants, 1577
Dubois County Community Fndn Grants, 1615
El Paso Community Fndn Grants, 1688
El Pomar Fndn Awards and Grants, 1690
Evan Frankel Fndn Grants, 1770
F.M. Kirby Fndn Grants, 1780
F.R. Bigelow Fndn Grants, 1781
Fairfield County Community Fndn Grants, 1782
Flinn Fndn Scholarships, 1843
Florida Humanities Council Major Grants, 1868
Florida Humanities Council Mini Grants, 1869
Florida Humanities Council Partnership Grants, 1870
Foellinger Fndn Grants, 1877
Ford Fndn Diversity Fellowships, 1883
Ford Motor Company Grants, 1885
Forrest C. Lattner Fndn Grants, 1887
Garland and Agnes Taylor Gray Fndn Grants, 1988
George Frederick Jewett Fndn Grants, 2019
George J. and Effie L. Seay Fndn Grants, 2024
GNOF Freeman Challenge Grants, 2075
GNOF Norco Community Grants, 2089
Grand Rapids Community Ionia Youth Grants, 2120
Grand Rapids Community Sparta Youth Grants, 2125
Greenwall Fndn Arts and Humanities Grants, 2157
Greenwall Fndn Bioethics Grants, 2158
Gregory C. Carr Fndn Grants, 2161
Hallmark Corp Fndn Grants, 2212
Harold and Arlene Schnitzer CARE Grants, 2226
Hollie and Anna Oakley Fndn Grants, 2346
Honda of America Manufacturing Fndn Grants, 2354
Idaho Power Company Corp Contributions, 2433
IIE AmCham U.S. Studies Scholarship, 2453
IIE Japan-U.S. Teacher Exchange for Educ for Sustainable Development, 2457
IIE Leonora Lindsley Memorial Fellowships, 2458
IIE New Leaders Group Award for Mutual Understanding, 2460
IIE Western Union Family Scholarships, 2462
Illinois Humanities Council Community General Support Grants, 2509
Illinois Humanities Council Community Grants, 2510
Indiana Humanities Council Init Grants, 2539
J.B. Reynolds Fndn Grants, 2592
Japan Fndn Los Angeles Mini-Grants for Japanese Arts & Culture, 2651
JELD-WEN Fndn Grants, 2661
Jerome Fndn Grants, 2667
John S. and James L. Knight Fndn Donor Advised Grants, 2712
Johnson County Community Fndn Grants, 2723
John W. Anderson Fndn Grants, 2729
Joseph Drown Fndn Grants, 2735
Katharine Matthies Fndn Grants, 2788
Knox County Community Fndn Grants, 2831
Libra Fndn Grants, 2899
Lowell Berry Fndn Grants, 2930
Marietta McNeill Morgan and Samuel Tate Morgan, Jr. Grants, 3008
Marion I. and Henry J. Knott Fndn Discretionary Grants, 3018
Marion I. and Henry J. Knott Standard Grants, 3019
Mary C. & Perry F. Spencer Fndn Grants, 3034
Massachusetts Cultural Adams Arts Grants, 3052
Massachusetts Fndn for the Humanities Cultural Economic Development Grants, 3059

Massachusetts Fndn for Humanities Grants, 3060
Maxon Charitable Fndn Grants, 3068
McCune Fndn Humananities Grants, 3079
McGregor Grants, 3082
Miami County Community Operation Round Up, 3156
Miguel Aleman Fndn Grants, 3175
Mimi and Peter Haas Grants, 3185
Moline Fndn Community Grants, 3202
Morris and Gwendolyn Cafritz Fndn Grants, 3218
NEH Family and Youth Programs in American History Grants, 3291
NEH Interpreting America's Hist Places Grants, 3292
NEH Preservation Assistance Grants for Smaller Institutions, 3293
NEH Preservation Microfilming of Brittle Books and Serials Grants, 3294
Nelda C. and H.J. Lutcher Stark Fndn Grants, 3296
New Hampshire Charitable Fndn Grants, 3325
Noble County Community Fndn Grants, 3456
Norwin S. and Elizabeth N. Bean Fndn Grants, 3515
NYHC Major and Mini Grants, 3567
NYHC Speakers in the Humanities Grants, 3569
Oceanside Charitable Fndn Grants, 3637
Owen County Community Fndn Grants, 3716
Paul Ogle Fndn Grants, 3764
Perry County Community Fndn Grants, 3827
Pew Charitable Trusts Arts and Culture Grants, 3857
Pike County Community Fndn Grants, 3888
Pinnacle Entertainment Fndn Grants, 3893
Pittsburgh Fndn Community Grants, 3910
Porter County Community Fndn Grants, 3931
Powell Family Fndn Grants, 3941
Pulaski County Community Fndn Grants, 3988
Rajiv Gandhi Fndn Grants, 4011
Ripley County Community Fndn Grants, 4095
Ripley County Community Small Project Grants, 4096
Robert R. Meyer Fndn Grants, 4121
Rush County Community Fndn Grants, 4174
Ruth and Vernon Taylor Fndn Grants, 4177
Schramm Fndn Grants, 4310
Snee Reinhardt Charitable Fndn Grants, 4387
South Madison Community Fndn Grants, 4440
Spencer County Community Fndn Grants, 4451
SSHRC Therese F. Casgrain Fellowship, 4466
Steele-Reese Fndn Grants, 4498
Steuben County Community Fndn Grants, 4501
Tanner Humanities Center Research Fellowships, 4559
Taylor S. Abernathy and Patti Harding Abernathy Charitable Grants, 4564
Vermont Community Fndn Grants, 4929
Virginia Fndn for Humanities Discr Grants, 4946
Virginia Fndn for the Humanities Fellowships, 4948
Vulcan Materials Company Fndn Grants, 4956
Warrick County Community Fndn Grants, 4987
Wisconsin Humanities Council Major Grants, 5107
Wisconsin Humanities Council Mini-Grants for Scholarly Research, 5108

Humanities Education
ALA Sara Jaffarian School Library Award for Exemplary Humanities Programming, 316
Chatlos Fndn Grants, 1061
Donald W. Reynolds Fndn Special Grants, 1577
Guy I. Bromley Grants, 2180
Honda of America Manufacturing Fndn Grants, 2354
John W. Speas and Effie E. Speas Grants, 2732
Lewis H. Humphreys Charitable Grants, 2889
Louetta M. Cowden Fndn Grants, 2922
Louis and Elizabeth Nave Flarsheim Grants, 2924
McCune Fndn Humananities Grants, 3079
Natalie W. Furniss Charitable Grants, 3244
National Endowment for the Arts - National Arts and Humanities Youth Program Awards, 3255
NEH Family and Youth Programs in American History Grants, 3291
NEH Interpreting America's Hist Places Grants, 3292
NEH Preservation Assistance Grants for Smaller Institutions, 3293
Virginia Fndn for Humanities Discr Grants, 4946
Virginia Fndn for the Humanities Open Grants, 4947

Hunger
ACE Charitable Fndn Grants, 111
Adobe Hunger and Homelessness Grants, 169
Albertson's Charitable Giving Grants, 345
American Electric Power Grants, 428
American Express Community Service Grants, 430
Arizona Republic Fndn Grants, 546
Bank of America Critical Needs Grants, 656
Bill & Melinda Gates Emergency Response Grants, 766
Bill and Melinda Gates Fndn Financial Services for the Poor Grants, 767
Bill & Melinda Gates Policy & Advocacy Grants, 769
BJ's Charitable Fndn Grants, 777
Boston Jewish Community Women's Grants, 822
Campbell Soup Fndn Grants, 916
Chicago Community Trust Preventing and Eliminating Hunger Grants, 1092
CICF Christmas Fund, 1117
Cisco Systems Fndn San Jose Community Grants, 1137
ConAgra Foods Community Impact Grants, 1342
ConAgra Foods Nourish Our Comm Grants, 1343
Conrad N. Hilton Humanitarian Prize, 1356
Coors Brewing Corp Contributions Grants, 1371
Denver Broncos Charities Grants, 1501
Dominion Fndn Human Needs Grants, 1572
Farmers Insurance Corp Giving Grants, 1791
Fourjay Fndn Grants, 1913
Fred Meyer Fndn Grants, 1950
Giant Food Charitable Grants, 2050
Greater Worcester Community Youth for Community Improvement Grants, 2144
Green Fndn Human Services Grants, 2154
HAF Hansen Family Trust Christian Grants, 2197
Harris Teeter Corp Contributions Grants, 2235
Hoffberger Fndn Grants, 2342
Humanitas Fndn Grants, 2390
John Deere Fndn Grants, 2692
John Edward Fowler Memorial Fndn Grants, 2693
Johnson Controls Fndn Health and Social Services Grants, 2722
Katie's Krops Grants, 2792
Kroger Company Donations, 2841
Kroger Fndn Hunger Relief Grants, 2844
Land O'Lakes Fndn California Region Grants, 2858
Land O'Lakes Fndn Community Grants, 2859
Meyer Fndn Healthy Communities Grants, 3143
NGA Healthy Sprouts Awards, 3403
Northern Trust Company Corp Giving Program, 3504
NYCT Girls and Young Women Grants, 3548
NYCT Hunger and Homelessnes Grants, 3553
Peacock Fndn Grants, 3809
PepsiCo Fndn Grants, 3819
Publix Super Markets Charities Local Grants, 3985
Quaker Oats Company Kids Care Clubs Grants, 3992
Quantum Fndn Grants, 3996
R.C. Baker Fndn Grants, 3999
Rainbow Families Fndn Grants, 4008
Robert R. McCormick Tribune Comm Grants, 4119
Rockefeller Fndn Grants, 4138
S. Mark Taper Fndn Grants, 4201
Santa Barbara Strategy Core Suupport Grants, 4286
Sara Lee Fndn Grants, 4296
Share Our Strength Grants, 4340
Shaw's Supermarkets Donations, 4342
Siragusa Fndn Human Services Grants, 4369
Sodexo Fndn STOP Hunger Scholarships, 4400
Southbury Community Trust Fund, 4409
United Methodist Committee on Relief Hunger and Poverty Grants, 4720
USAID Int'l Emergency Food Assistance Grants, 4763
USAID Int'l Food Relief Partnership Grants, 4764
USAID Malawi Local Capacity Devel Grants, 4767
USDA Hispanic-Serving Insts Educ Grants, 4813
YSA Sodexo Lead Organizer Grants, 5140

Hurricanes
AEGON Transamerica Disaster Relief Grants, 178
GNOF Coastal 5 + 1 Grants, 2070
Honeywell Corp Humanitarian Relief Grants, 2358
Office Depot Fndn Disaster Relief Grants, 3640

SUBJECT INDEX

Hydrodynamics
DOE Initial H-Prize Competition for Breakthrough Advances in Materials for Hydrogen Storage, 1551
HRF Hudson River Improvement Grants, 2378
Hydrogen Student Design Contest, 2415

Hydrogen and Synthetic Fuels
DOE Initial H-Prize Competition for Breakthrough Advances in Materials for Hydrogen Storage, 1551
Hydrogen Student Design Contest, 2415

Hydroponics
NGA Hooked on Hydroponics Awards, 3405
NGA Wuzzleburg Preschool Garden Awards, 3408

Hypertension
Premera Blue Cross CARES Grants, 3945

Illegal Aliens
San Diego Fndn for Change Grants, 4247

Illustration
ALA Coretta Scott King-Virginia Hamilton Award for Lifetime Achievement, 259
ALA Coretta Scott King Book Awards, 260
ALA Schneider Family Book Award, 317
CAA Millard Meiss Publication Grants, 885
SCBWI Don Freeman Memorial Grant, 4302

Immigrants
Abell Fndn Community Development Grants, 93
ACF Preferred Communities Grants, 124
ACF Supplemental Services for Recently Arrived Refugees Grants, 125
Alfred and Tillie Shemanski Testamentary Grants, 363
Atkinson Fndn Community Grants, 606
BBF Florida Family Lit Init Grants, 697
BBF Maine Family Lit Init Grants, 698
BBF Maine Family Lit Init Planning Grants, 699
Blue Cross Blue Shield of Minnesota Healthy Neighborhoods: Connect Grants, 798
Boston Fndn Grants, 819
CCF Social and Economic Justice Grants, 964
Clipper Ship Fndn Grants, 1175
Clowes Grants, 1177
Cralle Fndn Grants, 1394
Dallas Women's Fndn Grants, 1438
Deborah Munroe Noonan Grants, 1475
Edward and Ellen Roche Relief Fndn Grants, 1663
Eulalie Bloedel Schneider Fndn Grants, 1767
Evelyn and Walter Haas, Jr. Fund Immigrant Rights Grants, 1773
Fel-Pro Mecklenburger Fndn Grants, 1800
General Service Fndn Colorado Grants, 2005
Goizueta Fndn Grants, 2096
Grotto Fndn Project Grants, 2166
Henry J. Kaiser Family Fndn Grants, 2310
Hyams Fndn Grants, 2413
IIE Western Union Family Scholarships, 2462
J.M. Kaplan Fund Migrations Grants, 2602
Jaquelin Hume Fndn Grants, 2654
Margaret L. Wendt Fndn Grants, 3004
Marie C. and Joseph C. Wilson Fndn Rochester Small Grants, 3006
Maytree Fndn Assisting Local Leaders with Immigrant Employment Strategies Grants, 3070
Maytree Fndn Refugee and Immigrant Grants, 3071
Meyer Fndn Economic Security Grants, 3141
Michael Reese Health Trust Responsive Grants, 3160
Minneapolis Fndn Community Grants, 3186
New Jersey Center for Hispanic Policy, Research and Development Immigration Integration Grants, 3328
New York Fndn Grants, 3338
Norman Fndn Grants, 3464
Norton Fndn Grants, 3514
NYCT Fund for New Citizens Grants, 3547
NYCT Human Justice Grants, 3552
NYCT Youth Development Grants, 3561
Paul & Daisy Soros Fellows for New Americans, 3754
PIP American Dream Grants, 3897

PIP Four Freedoms Grants, 3906
PIP Fulfilling the Dream Fund, 3907
PIP Racial Justice Collaborative Grants, 3908
PIP U.S. Human Rights Grants, 3909
Ray Solem Fndn Grants to Help Immigrants Learn English in Innovative Ways, 4029
RWJF Local Funding Partnerships Grants, 4186
San Diego Fndn for Change Grants, 4247
San Francisco Fndn Faith Program and Arts and Culture Program, 4267
Silicon Valley Community Fndn Immigrant Integration Grants, 4358
Sophia Romero Grants, 4406
Strowd Roses Grants, 4515
Taproot Fndn Capacity-Building Service Grants, 4560
Theodore Edson Parker Fndn Grants, 4605
Woods Charitable Grants, 5114

Immigration Law
General Service Fndn Colorado Grants, 2005
J.M. Kaplan Fund Migrations Grants, 2602
Meyer Fndn Economic Security Grants, 3141
Ms. Fndn Women Building Democracy Grants, 3223
NYCT Fund for New Citizens Grants, 3547
NYCT Human Justice Grants, 3552
Silicon Valley Community Fndn Immigrant Integration Grants, 4358

Immunization Programs
Bernard and Audre Rapoport Fndn Health Grants, 738
Chiron Fndn Community Grants, 1111
German Protestant Orphan Asylum Fndn Grants, 2044
Henrietta Lange Burk Grants, 2303
New Hampshire Charitable Fndn Grants, 3325
Premera Blue Cross CARES Grants, 3945

Immunology
AAAAI RSLAAIS Leadership Award, 49
Baxter Int'l Corp Giving Grants, 689
Bristol-Myers Squibb Clinical Outcomes and Research Grants, 839

Incarceration
ALA Diversity and Outreach Fair, 267
Initiaive Fndn Inside-Out Connections Grants, 2556
Mabel Louise Riley Fndn Family Strengthening Small Grants, 2958
Meyer Fndn Economic Security Grants, 3141
New York Fndn Grants, 3338
OSF-Baltimore Criminal & Juv Justice Grants, 3696
OSI After Prison Init Grants, 3710
Threshold Fndn Justice and Democracy Grants, 4626

Independent Living Programs
Arizona Public Service Corp Giving Grants, 545
BBVA Compass Fndn Charitable Grants, 703
Charles H. Farnsworth Grants, 1043
Clark and Ruby Baker Fndn Grants, 1154
CNCS AmeriCorps State and National Grants, 1182
CNCS Senior Companion Grants, 1187
CNCS Senior Corps Retired and Senior Volunteer Grants, 1188
Coleman Developmental Disabilities Grants, 1200
Florence Hunt Maxwell Fndn Grants, 1844
Gertrude M. Conduff Fndn Grants, 2047
HAF Senior Opportunities Grants, 2203
John Edward Fowler Memorial Fndn Grants, 2693
Kessler Fndn Community Employment Grants, 2814
Lydia deForest Charitable Grants, 2946
Marietta McNeill Morgan and Samuel Tate Morgan, Jr. Grants, 3008
May and Stanley Smith Charitable Grants, 3069
McLean Contributionship Grants, 3088
Mericos Fndn Grants, 3121
MetroWest Health Fndn Grants--Healthy Aging, 3135
Peter and Elizabeth C. Tower Fndn Annual Intellectual Disabilities Grants, 3834
Piper Trust Older Adults Grants, 3904
Piper Trust Reglous Organizations Grants, 3905
Priddy Fndn Grants, 3957

Reinberger Fndn Grants, 4052
Robert & Clara Milton Fund for Senior Housing, 4117
S. Mark Taper Fndn Grants, 4201
Saginaw Community Fndn Senior Citizen Enrichment Fund, 4206
Sisters of Saint Joseph Charitable Grants, 4376
U.S. Department of Educ Centers for Independent Living, 4688
U.S. Department of Educ Parent Information and Training, 4695
U.S. Department of Educ Rehabilitation Research Training Centers, 4699
Union Bank, N.A. Fndn Grants, 4709
W.P. and Bulah Luse Fndn Grants, 4965

Indigenous Cultures
Honor the Earth Grants, 2361
North Carolina Arts Council Folklife Grants, 3476
Threshold Fndn Sustainable Planet Grants, 4627
Tom's of Maine Grants, 4640

Industrial Design
Minnesota State Arts Board Cultural Community Partnership Grants, 3188
National Endowment for Arts Commun Grants, 3260
NYSCA Architecture, Planning, and Design: Capital Fixtures and Equipment Purchase Grants, 3570
NYSCA Architecture, Planning, and Design: Capital Project Grants, 3571
NYSCA Architecture, Planning, and Design: Design and Planning Studies Grants, 3572
NYSCA Architecture, Planning, and Design: General Operating Support Grants, 3573
NYSCA Architecture, Planning, and Design: General Program Support Grants, 3574
NYSCA Architecture, Planning, and Design: Independent Project Grants, 3575
NYSCA Architecture, Planning, and Design: Project Support Grants, 3576
RISCA Design Innovation Grant, 4097

Industrial Hygiene
USAID Grants for Building Disaster-Resilient Communities in Southern Africa, 4755

Industrial Production
IEDC Industrial Development Grant Fund, 2443

Industrial Relations
PAS Internship, 3742

Industry
ACF Native American Social and Economic Development Strategies Grants, 123
ALZA Corp Contributions Grants, 405
Collective Brands Fndn Grants, 1206
Dept of Ed Projects with Industry Grants, 1511
Duke Energy Economic Development Grants, 1619
IDOT Economic Development Grants, 2436
Illinois DCEO Coal Demonstration Grants, 2485
Millipore Fndn Grants, 3182
North Carolina Biotech Center Multidisciplinary Research Grants, 3487
Northern Trust Company Corp Giving Program, 3504
USDA Rural Coop Development Grants, 4826
USDC Public Works and Economic Adjustment Assistance Grants, 4856

Infants
Bernard and Audre Rapoport Fndn Health Grants, 738
Chautauqua Region Community Fndn Grants, 1062
CIGNA Fndn Grants, 1130
CNCS Foster Grandparent Grants, 1185
DHHS Abandoned Infants Assistance Grants, 1523
DHHS Health Centers Grants for Residents of Public Housing, 1533
DHHS Maternal and Child Health Grants, 1536
Fndn for Seacoast Health Grants, 1895
George W. Wells Fndn Grants, 2030
Head Start Replacement Grantee: Colorado, 2275

Infectious Diseases/Agents

Head Start Replacement Grantee: Florida, 2276
Head Start Replacement Grantee: West Virginia, 2277
Health Fndn of Greater Indianapolis Grants, 2282
Init Fndn Minnesota Early Childhood Grants, 2560
Johnson & Johnson Comm Health Care Grants, 2717
Liz Claiborne and Art Ortenberg Fndn Grants, 2914
Milton Hicks Wood and Helen Gibbs Wood Charitable Grants, 3184
Oakland Fund for Children and Youth Grants, 3634
RWJF Local Funding Partnerships Grants, 4186
USAID Comprehensive District-Based Support for Better HIV/TB Patient Outcomes Grants, 4747

Infectious Diseases/Agents
Alliance Healthcare Fndn Grants, 383
Bristol-Myers Squibb Clinical Outcomes and Research Grants, 839
Chiron Fndn Community Grants, 1111
Pfizer Healthcare Charitable Contributions, 3863
Pfizer Medical Educ Track One Grants, 3864
Robert W. Woodruff Fndn Grants, 4124

Inflammation
Pfizer Medical Educ Track One Grants, 3864

Information Dissemination
ALA Allie Beth Martin Award, 221
ALA Arthur Curley Memorial Lecture, 226
ALA Carnegie Corp of New York/New York Times I Love My Librarian Award, 254
ALA Information Technology Pathfinder Award, 286
ALA Innovation Award, 288
ALA Melvil Dewey Medal, 301
Community Fndn of Greater Fort Wayne - John S. and James L. Knight Fndn Donor-Advised Grants, 1287
ESRI Conservation Grants, 1751
Fndn for Seacoast Health Grants, 1895
GNOF Environmental Grants, 2073
Healthcare Fndn for Orange County Grants, 2279
Nellie Mae Educ Fndn State Level Systems Change Grants, 3299
NSF Communicating Res to Public Audiences, 3527
OSF Arab Regional Office Grants, 3701
OSF Burma Project/SE Asia Init Grants, 3702
U.S. Department of Educ Disability and Rehabilitation Research and Related Projects, 4690
William C. Kenney Watershed Protection Fndn Ecosystem Grants, 5079

Information Science Education
ALA Carnegie Corp of New York/New York Times I Love My Librarian Award, 254
Information Society Innovation Grants, 2554
Regional Fund for Digital Innovation in Latin America and the Caribbean Grants, 4049

Information Science/Systems
ALA Diversity Research Grant, 268
Cisco Systems Fndn San Jose Community Grants, 1137
DaimlerChrysler Corp Grants, 1432
Frances C. & William P. Smallwood Grants, 1918
GNOF Gulf Coast Oil Spill Grants, 2077
McLean Contributionship Grants, 3088
Microsoft Comm Affairs Puget Sound Grants, 3163
Microsoft Unlimited Potential (UP) - Community Technology Skills Grants, 3165
NSF CISE Computing Infrastructure Grants, 3526
Sarah Scaife Fndn Grants, 4295
USDC Technology Opportunities Grants, 4860
USDJ Edward Byrne Justice Assistance Grants, 4863
Xerox Fndn Grants, 5122

Information Technology
ALA Carnegie Corp of New York/New York Times I Love My Librarian Award, 254
ALA Information Technology Pathfinder Award, 286
ALA Innovation Award, 288
ALA Melvil Dewey Medal, 301
Bill and Melinda Gates Fndn Library Grants, 768
DogTime Annual Grant, 1552

Fndn for Mid South Health & Wellness Grants, 1899
Go Daddy Cares Charitable Contributions, 2094
Goldseker Fndn Non-Profit Management Assistance Grants, 2103
GTECH After School Advantage Grants, 2170
IDPH Hosptial Capital Investment Grants, 2441
Illinois DCEO Eliminate Dig Divide Grants, 2489
Illinois DCEO Emerging Technological Enterprises Grants, 2490
OSF Affordable Access to Digital Communications Init, 3700
Peter and Elizabeth C. Tower Fndn Phase II Technology Init Grants, 3839
Peter and Elizabeth C. Tower Fndn Phase I Technology Init Grants, 3840

Information Theory
NSF Decision, Risk, and Management Science Research Grants, 3528

Infrastructure
IDOT Economic Development Grants, 2436
IDOT Rail Freight Program Loans and Grants, 2437
IDOT Truck Access Route Grants, 2438
Illinois DCEO Business Development Public Infrastructure Grants, 2483
Illinois DCEO Coal Competitiveness Grants, 2484
San Juan Island Community Fndn Grants, 4283
USAID Community Infrastructure Dev Grants, 4745
USAID Palestinian Comm Assistance Grants, 4773
USAID Palestinian Community Infrastructure Development Grants, 4774

Injury
CDC Grants for Violence-Related Injury Prevention Research, 974
Dorothea Haus Ross Fndn Grants, 1587
George E. Hatcher, Jr. and Ann Williams Hatcher Fndn Grants, 2015
Quantum Fndn Grants, 3996

Injury, Spinal Cord
Detroit Lions Charities Grants, 1520
Toby Wells Fndn Grants, 4638

Inner Cities
Adolph Coors Fndn Grants, 171
Arie and Ida Crown Grants, 533
Brown Rudnick Charitable Relationship Grants, 855
Central New York Community Fndn Grants, 996
Credit Suisse First Boston Fndn Grants, 1397
Detroit Lions Charities Grants, 1520
GTECH After School Advantage Grants, 2170
J. Willard and Alice S. Marriott Fndn Grants, 2609
Luther I. Replogle Fndn Grants, 2945
Marie C. and Joseph C. Wilson Fndn Rochester Small Grants, 3006
Mark Wahlberg Youth Fndn Grants, 3022
Mercedes-Benz USA Corp Contributions Grants, 3118
Millipore Fndn Grants, 3182
National Endowment for Arts Media Grants, 3264
National Endowment for Arts Opera Grants, 3267
Nina Mason Pulliam Charitable Grants, 3443
Northern Trust Company Corp Giving Program, 3504
OSF-Baltimore Community Fellowships, 3695
Saint Luke's Fndn Grants, 4215
Saint Paul Companies Fndn Grants, 4217
USDC Strong Cities, Strong Communities Visioning Challenge Grants, 4858
Verizon Fndn Great Lakes Region Grants, 4912

Instruction/Curriculum Development
ALA Sara Jaffarian School Library Award for Exemplary Humanities Programming, 316
Arkansas Arts Council AIE Arts Curriculum Project Grants, 552
Head Start Replacement Grantee: Colorado, 2275
Head Start Replacement Grantee: Florida, 2276
Head Start Replacement Grantee: West Virginia, 2277
ICC Faculty Fellowships, 2428

ICC Scholarship of Engagement Faculty Grants, 2430
IIE Toyota Int'l Teacher Professional Development Grants, 2461
J. Knox Gholston Fndn Grants, 2599
Leave No Trace Master Educator Scholarships, 2870
Meyer Fndn Educ Grants, 3142
NACC William Diaz Fellowships, 3236
New Jersey Office of Faith Based Inits English as a Second Language Grants, 3332
Ohio Arts Council Artist Express Grants, 3643
Piper Trust Reglous Organizations Grants, 3905
RISCA Project Grants for Organizations, Individuals and Educ, 4100
Robert R. McCormick Tribune Civics Grants, 4118
Scholastic Welch's Harvest Grants, 4309

Instructional Materials and Practices
Blue Cross Blue Shield of Minnesota Fndn - Healthy Equity: Public Libraries for Health Grants, 797
Caroline Lawson Ivey Memorial Fndn Grants, 941
Dept of Ed Magnet Schools Assistance Grants, 1509
EPA Environmental Educ Grants, 1729
Hatton W. Sumners Fndn for the Study and Teaching of Self Government Grants, 2257
North Carolina Arts Council Arts in Educ Artist Residencies Grants, 3468
North Carolina Arts Council Ed Grants, 3469
SVP Early Childhood Development and Parenting Grants, 4538
Tri-State Community Twenty-first Century Endowment Grants, 4666

Instrumentation, Medical
Covidien Partnership for Neighborhood Wellness Grants, 1391
IDPH Hosptial Capital Investment Grants, 2441

Instrumentation, Scientific
NSF Atmospheric Sciences Mid-Size Infrastructure Opportunity Grants, 3521

Insurance/Actuarial Science
New York Life Fndn Grants, 3341
Starr Fndn Grants, 4483

Intellectual Freedom
ALA Arthur Curley Memorial Lecture, 226
ALA Intellectual Freedom Award, 289
ALA John Phillip Immroth Memorial Award, 293
ALA Margaret T. Lane/Virginia F. Saunders Memorial Research Award, 298
ALA Paul Howard Award for Courage, 307
HBF Defending Freedoms Grants, 2271
Philip L. Graham Grants, 3876
Playboy Fndn Freedom of Expression Award, 3912
Playboy Fndn Grants, 3913

Interdisciplinary Arts
Arizona Comm on Arts Folklorist Residencies, 537
Arizona Commission on the Arts Individual Artist Residencies, 538
Arkansas Arts Council AIE After School/Summer Residency Grants, 551
Arkansas Arts Council AIE In-School Residency, 553
Florida Div of Cultural Affairs Culture Builds Florida Expansion Funding, 1848
Florida Div of Cultural Affairs Culture Builds Florida Seed Funding, 1849
Florida Div of Cultural Affairs Presenter Grants, 1860
Iowa Arts Council Artists in Schools/Communities Residency Grants, 2571
Jerome Fndn Grants, 2667
MacArthur Fndn Chicago Arts and Culture Int'l Connections Grants, 2962
North Carolina Arts Council Residency Grants, 3481
NYSCA Electronic Media and Film: Screenings Grants, 3592
NYSCA State and Local Partnerships: General Operating Support Grants, 3619
Ohio Arts Council Individual Excellence Awards, 3648

SUBJECT INDEX

PCA-PCD Professional Development for Individual Artists Grants, 3770
PCA Arts in Educ Residencies, 3772
PCA Arts Organizations and Arts Programs Grants for Arts Educ Residencies, 3776
PCA Arts Organizations & Grants for Visual Arts, 3785
PCA Busing Grants, 3786
PCA Entry Track Arts Organizations and Program Grants for Arts Educ Organizations, 3788
PCA Entry Track Arts Organizations and Program Grants for Visual Arts, 3799
PCA Pennsylvania Partners in the Arts Program Stream Grants, 3801
PCA Pennsylvania Partners in the Arts Project Stream Grants, 3802
PCA Professional Development Grants, 3803
PCA Strategies for Success Grants - Basic Level, 3805
PCA Strategies for Success Grants - Intermediate, 3806
PennPAT Artist Technical Assistance Grants, 3811
PennPAT Strategic Opportunity Grants, 3815
Richard H. Driehaus Fndn MacArthur Fund for Arts and Culture, 4085

Interior Design
Alabama State Council on the Arts Community Arts Collaborative Ventures Grants, 236
Alabama State Council on the Arts Community Arts Program Development Grants, 239
Alabama State Council on the Arts Community Planning & Design Grants, 241
NYSCA Architecture, Planning, and Design: Capital Fixtures and Equipment Purchase Grants, 3570
NYSCA Architecture, Planning, and Design: Capital Project Grants, 3571
NYSCA Architecture, Planning, and Design: Design and Planning Studies Grants, 3572
NYSCA Architecture, Planning, and Design: General Operating Support Grants, 3573
NYSCA Architecture, Planning, and Design: General Program Support Grants, 3574
NYSCA Architecture, Planning, and Design: Independent Project Grants, 3575
Phi Upsilon Omicron Frances Morton Holbrook Alumni Award, 3878
RISCA Design Innovation Grant, 4097

International Affairs
Bill & Melinda Gates Policy & Advocacy Grants, 769
GMFUS Black Sea Trust for Regional Grants, 2065
USAID African Innovation Mechanism Grants, 4739
USAID Development Innov Ventures Grants, 4749
USAID India Partnership Grants, 4761

International Agriculture
Bill and Melinda Gates Fndn Agricultural Development Grants, 765
Bill & Melinda Gates Policy & Advocacy Grants, 769
Michael and Susan Dell Fndn Grants, 3158
PepsiCo Fndn Grants, 3819
USAID African Innovation Mechanism Grants, 4738
USAID Malawi Local Capacity Devel Grants, 4767

International Economics
Bill & Melinda Gates Policy & Advocacy Grants, 769
Citigroup Fndn Grants, 1139
ConocoPhillips Grants, 1355
IIE Nancy Petry Scholarship, 2459
Jenifer Altman Fndn Grants, 2662
Michael and Susan Dell Fndn Grants, 3158
USAID African Innovation Mechanism Grants, 4739

International Education/Training
AAUW Int'l Project Grants, 76
Abundance Fndn Int'l Grants, 108
Acumen East Africa Fellowship, 141
Acumen Global Fellowships, 142
ALA ALTAFF/GALE Outstanding Trustee Conference Grant, 224
ALA Bogle Pratt Int'l Library Travel Fund Grant, 251
Amarillo Area/Harrington Fndns Grants, 412

Arthur B. Schultz Fndn Grants, 573
Bill and Melinda Gates Fndn Agricultural Development Grants, 765
Bill & Melinda Gates Policy & Advocacy Grants, 769
Center for the Study of Philanthropy Fellowships, 989
Center for the Study of Philanthropy Senior Int'l Fellowships, 990
Coca-Cola Fndn Grants, 1195
Compton Fndn Grants, 1338
DAAD Research Grants for Doctoral Candidates and Young Academics and Scientists, 1427
Dorot Fndn Grants, 1586
EDS Technology Grants, 1662
H.B. Fuller Company Fndn Grants, 2183
IREX Russia Civil Society Support Grants, 2580
IREX Small Grant Fund for Civil Society Projects in Africa and Asia, 2581
Michael and Susan Dell Fndn Grants, 3158
MMS and Alliance Charitable Fndn Int'l Health Studies Grants, 3195
OSF Civil Service Awards, 3705
OSF European Commission Internships for Young Roma Graduates, 3707
Regional Fund for Digital Innovation in Latin America and the Caribbean Grants, 4049
UNCFSP TIEAD Internship, 4705
UNESCO World Heritage Grants, 4706
USAID African Innovation Mechanism Grants, 4739
USAID India Partnership Grants, 4761

International Exchange Programs
Akzo Nobel Chemicals Grants, 219
Albuquerque Community Fndn Grants, 348
APAP Cultural Exchange Grants, 492
Coca-Cola Fndn Grants, 1195
Freeman Fndn Grants, 1952
GMFUS Black Sea Trust for Regional Grants, 2065
Japan Fndn Center for Global Partnership Grants, 2649
Mertz Gilmore Fndn NYC Dance Grants, 3127
National Endowment for the Arts - National Partnership Agreement Grants, 3256
UNCFSP TIEAD Internship, 4705

International Justice
Abundance Fndn Int'l Grants, 108
Bill & Melinda Gates Policy & Advocacy Grants, 769
OSF Burma Project/SE Asia Init Grants, 3702
PDF Fiscal Sponsorship Grant, 3808

International Organizations
Bill & Melinda Gates Policy & Advocacy Grants, 769
Gannett Fndn Community Action Grants, 1984
Harry Kramer Grants, 2242
IREX Russia Civil Society Support Grants, 2580
Medtronic Fndn CommunityLink Health Grants, 3111
OSF Civil Service Awards, 3705
Raskob Fndn for Catholic Activities Grants, 4019

International Planning/Policy
Bill & Melinda Gates Policy & Advocacy Grants, 769
GMFUS Black Sea Trust for Regional Grants, 2065
GMFUS Urban and Regional Policy Fellowships, 2067
Henry M. Jackson Fndn Grants, 2311
IREX Kosovo Civil Society Project Grants, 2576
IREX Russia Civil Society Support Grants, 2580
IREX Small Grant Fund for Civil Society Projects in Africa and Asia, 2581
Japan Fndn Center for Global Partnership Grants, 2649
Japan Center for Global Partnership Grants, 2650
Jenifer Altman Fndn Grants, 2662
John Merck Grants, 2706
Lynde and Harry Bradley Fndn Grants, 2947
Lynde and Harry Bradley Fndn Prizes, 2948
RAND Corp Graduate Summer Associateships, 4018
Samuel Rubin Fndn Grants, 4237
UNCFSP TIEAD Internship, 4705
USAID African Innovation Mechanism Grants, 4739
USAID India Partnership Grants, 4761
USAID Strengthening Democratic Local Governance in South Sudan Grants, 4782

International Programs
AAUW Int'l Project Grants, 76
Abundance Fndn Int'l Grants, 108
A Charitable Fndn Grants, 126
Acorn Fndn Grants, 131
Acumen Global Fellowships, 142
ADC Fndn Technology Access Grants, 158
ALA Carnegie-Whitney Awards, 253
ALA May Hill Arbuthnot Honor Lecture Award, 300
Alcoa Fndn Grants, 350
Allen Lane Fndn Grants, 379
American Jewish World Service Grants, 441
Archer Daniels Midland Fndn Grants, 527
Arronson Fndn Grants, 567
Atkinson Fndn Community Grants, 606
Atran Fndn Grants, 610
Azadoutioun Fndn Grants, 631
Banfi Vintners Fndn Grants, 653
Bank of America Charitable Fndn Educ and Workforce Development Grants, 657
Baring Fndn Grants, 667
Baxter Int'l Fndn Grants, 691
Bechtel Group Fndn Building Positive Community Relationships Grants, 715
Beerman Fndn Grants, 717
Besser Fndn Grants, 748
Bill and Melinda Gates Fndn Agricultural Development Grants, 765
Bill & Melinda Gates Emergency Response Grants, 766
Bill and Melinda Gates Fndn Financial Services for the Poor Grants, 767
Bill and Melinda Gates Fndn Library Grants, 768
Bill & Melinda Gates Policy & Advocacy Grants, 769
Bill and Melinda Gates Fndn Water, Sanitation and Hygiene Grants, 770
Boeckmann Charitable Fndn Grants, 808
Boston Jewish Community Women's Grants, 822
Burden Grants, 864
Caddock Fndn Grants, 888
Cargill Citizenship Fund-Corp Giving Grants, 925
Carylon Fndn Grants, 949
CE and S Fndn Grants, 985
Center for the Study of Philanthropy Fellowships, 989
Center for the Study of Philanthropy Senior Int'l Fellowships, 990
Charles and Lynn Schusterman Family Grants, 1038
Charles Delmar Fndn Grants, 1039
Charles Stewart Mott Fndn Grants, 1055
Chase Paymentech Corp Giving Grants, 1059
Chatlos Fndn Grants, 1061
Chesapeake Corp Fndn Grants, 1076
Chiquita Brands Int'l Grants, 1110
CIGNA Fndn Grants, 1130
Citigroup Fndn Grants, 1139
CNA Fndn Grants, 1179
Commonwealth Fund Australian-American Health Policy Fellowships, 1241
Compton Fndn Grants, 1338
Computer Associates Community Grants, 1341
ConocoPhillips Fndn Grants, 1354
ConocoPhillips Grants, 1355
Danellie Fndn Grants, 1442
Diageo Fndn Grants, 1546
Elden and Mary Lee Gutwein Family Grants, 1679
Foundation for Young Australians Indigenous Small Grants, 1901
Foundation for Young Australians Spark Grants, 1902
Foundation for Young Australians Youth Change Grants, 1904
Foundation for Young Australians Youth Led Futures Grants, 1905
Frances and Benjamin Benenson Fndn Grants, 1916
Gleitsman Fndn Activist Awards, 2063
H.J. Heinz Company Fndn Grants, 2184
Harold Simmons Fndn Grants, 2230
Helen Bader Fndn Grants, 2293
Henry J. Kaiser Family Fndn Grants, 2310
Hershey Company Grants, 2318
Information Society Innovation Grants, 2554
Int'l Human Rights Funders Grants, 2567

IREX Russia Civil Society Support Grants, 2580
Jacob and Hilda Blaustein Fndn Grants, 2615
James H. Cummings Fndn Grants, 2626
Japan-US Community Ed & Exchange Grants, 2648
Japan Fndn Los Angeles Mini-Grants for Japanese Arts & Culture, 2651
Jenifer Altman Fndn Grants, 2662
John Deere Fndn Grants, 2692
Ludwick Family Fndn Grants, 2938
MacArthur Fndn Chicago Arts and Culture Int'l Connections Grants, 2962
Max and Anna Levinson Fndn Grants, 3066
National Endowment for the Arts - National Arts and Humanities Youth Program Awards, 3255
National Lottery Community Grants, 3279
NFWF/Exxon Save the Tiger Grants, 3354
NFWF Coral Reef Conservation Project Grants, 3370
Nuffield Fndn Africa Grants, 3532
Nuffield Fndn Small Grants, 3535
Ohio Arts Council Int'l Partnership Grants, 3653
OSF Advancing the Rights and Integration of Roma Grants, 3699
OSF Human Rights and Governance Grants, 3708
OSF Mental Health Init Grants, 3709
Patrick and Anna M. Cudahy Grants, 3751
Paul Balint Charitable Grants, 3757
PDF Fiscal Sponsorship Grant, 3808
Petra Fndn Fellows Awards, 3850
Pfizer Healthcare Charitable Contributions, 3863
Praxair Fndn Grants, 3944
Procter and Gamble Grants, 3967
Regional Fund for Digital Innovation in Latin America and the Caribbean Grants, 4049
Reynolds Family Fndn Grants, 4071
Rockefeller Fndn Grants, 4138
Russell Berrie Fndn Grants, 4175
SanDisk Corp Community Sharing Program, 4253
Sweet Water Grants, 4541
Trull Fndn Grants, 4673
United Technologies Corp Grants, 4725
USAID African Innovation Mechanism Grants, 4739
USAID India Partnership Grants, 4761
USAID Strengthening Democratic Local Governance in South Sudan Grants, 4782
USDA Foreign Market Development Grants, 4811
USDA Market Access Grants, 4818
Volvo Adventure Environmental Awards, 4952
W.K. Kellogg Fndn Healthy Kids Grants, 4961
Wallace Global Grants, 4977
WILD Fndn Grants, 5068

International Relations
Agape Fndn for Nonviolent Social Change Prizes, 198
Arca Fndn Grants, 526
Archer Daniels Midland Fndn Grants, 527
Arie and Ida Crown Grants, 533
Bydale Fndn Grants, 882
Coca-Cola Fndn Grants, 1195
Compton Fndn Grants, 1338
ConocoPhillips Grants, 1355
Cooper Fndn Grants, 1369
Donald and Sylvia Robinson Family Fndn Grants, 1573
Eugene McDermott Fndn Grants, 1765
Ford Fndn Peace and Social Justice Grants, 1884
Freeman Fndn Grants, 1952
Fund for Southern Communities Grants, 1977
GMFUS Marshall Memorial Fellowships, 2066
GMFUS Urban and Regional Policy Fellowships, 2067
Harry Kramer Grants, 2242
Japan Fndn Los Angeles Mini-Grants for Japanese Arts & Culture, 2651
Jenifer Altman Fndn Grants, 2662
King Baudouin Int'l Development Prize, 2825
MARPAT Fndn Grants, 3023
Miguel Aleman Fndn Grants, 3175
OSF Advancing the Rights and Integration of Roma Grants, 3699
OSF Central Eurasia Project Grants, 3704
PDF Community Organizing Grants, 3807
PDF Fiscal Sponsorship Grant, 3808

Rajiv Gandhi Fndn Grants, 4011
Reynolds Family Fndn Grants, 4071
Sasakawa Peace Fndn Grants, 4299
Starr Fndn Grants, 4483
Tides Fndn Grants, 4632
UNCFSP TIEAD Internship, 4705
USDA Foreign Market Development Grants, 4811
USDA Market Access Grants, 4818

International Students
Acumen East Africa Fellowship, 141
IIE Adell and Hancock Scholarships, 2452
IIE Eurobank EFG Scholarships, 2455
IIE Freeman Fndn Indonesia Internships, 2456
National Endowment for the Arts - National Arts and Humanities Youth Program Awards, 3255
OSF Advancing the Rights and Integration of Roma Grants, 3699
OSF Civil Service Awards, 3705
OSF European Commission Internships for Young Roma Graduates, 3707
UNCFSP TIEAD Internship, 4705
VSA Int'l Art Program for Children with Disabilities Grants, 4955

International Studies
Acumen East Africa Fellowship, 141
Coca-Cola Fndn Grants, 1195
DAAD Research Grants for Doctoral Candidates and Young Academics and Scientists, 1427
IIE Adell and Hancock Scholarships, 2452
OSF European Commission Internships for Young Roma Graduates, 3707
UNCFSP TIEAD Internship, 4705

International Trade and Finance
Appalachian Regional Commission Export and Trade Development Grants, 506
Archer Daniels Midland Fndn Grants, 527
Freeman Fndn Grants, 1952
GMFUS Urban and Regional Policy Fellowships, 2067
IEDC Int'l Trade Show Assistance Program, 2444
Japan Fndn Center for Global Partnership Grants, 2649
Ploughshares Grants, 3916
Starr Fndn Grants, 4483
USAID Albania Critical Economic Growth Areas Grants, 4740
USDA Market Access Grants, 4818
USDA Rural Business Opportunity Grants, 4824
USDC Market Development Cooperator Grants, 4853

International and Comparative Law
Bill & Melinda Gates Policy & Advocacy Grants, 769
Ford Fndn Peace and Social Justice Grants, 1884
Germanistic Society of America Fellowships, 2043

Internet
ALA Information Technology Pathfinder Award, 286
Bill and Melinda Gates Fndn Library Grants, 768
DogTime Technology Grant, 1553
DOJ Internet Crimes against Children Task Force Grants, 1558
Dow Chemical Company Grants, 1596
EDS Fndn Grants, 1661
EDS Technology Grants, 1662
ESRI Conservation Grants, 1751
Illinois Arts Council Media Arts Grants, 2472
IMLS 21st Century Museum Pro Grants, 2512
IMLS National Leadership Grants, 2515
IMLS Native Am Library Services Basic Grants, 2517
IMLS Native American Library Services Enhancement Grants, 2518
Information Society Innovation Grants, 2554
Internet Society Fellowships, 2570
Microsoft Software Donation Grants, 3164
National Endowment for Arts Media Grants, 3264
OJJDP Tribal Juvenile Accountability Grants, 3665
RealNetworks Fndn Grants, 4037
Regional Fund for Digital Innovation in Latin America and the Caribbean Grants, 4049

Verizon Fndn Grants, 4911
Verizon Fndn Internet Safety Grants, 4914
Verizon Fndn Maryland Grants, 4917
Verizon Fndn New York Grants, 4919
Verizon Fndn NE Region Grants, 4920
Verizon Fndn Pennsylvania Grants, 4921
Verizon Fndn South Carolina Lit & Internet Safety Grants, 4922
Verizon Fndn SE Region Grants, 4923
Verizon Fndn Vermont Grants, 4924
Verizon Fndn Virginia Grants, 4925
Verizon Fndn West Virginia Grants, 4926
VSA Int'l Art Program for Children with Disabilities Grants, 4955

Internship Programs
Bank of America Charitable Fndn Student Leaders Grants, 659
DHHS Emerging Leaders Program Internships, 1532
George A. and Grace L. Long Fndn Grants, 2008
Kennedy Center Experiential Educ Internship, 2798
Kennedy Center HSC Fndn Internship, 2799
Kennedy Center Summer HSC Fndn Internship, 2800
Morris K. Udall and Stewart L. Udall Fndn Native American Congressional Internships, 3220
Murphy Institute Judith Kelleher Schafer Summer Internship Grants, 3230
New Jersey Center for Hispanic Policy, Research and Development Governor's Hispanic Fellows, 3327
NJSCA Folk Arts Apprenticeships, 3448
PAS Internship, 3742
PCA Arts Management Internship, 3773
Skaggs Fndn Grants, 4378
Strowd Roses Grants, 4515
Susan Mott Webb Charitable Grants, 4536
TAC Arts Access Grant, 4549
TAC Arts Build Communities Grants, 4551
USDC Postsecondary Grants Internships, 4855
West Virginia Commission on the Arts Staffing Support Grants, 5049
William Blair and Company Fndn Grants, 5078

Intervention Programs
Bodman Fndn Grants, 807
Cambridge Community Fndn Grants, 913
Ceres Fndn Grants, 999
Community Fndn Silicon Valley Grants, 1331
DOJ Gang-Free Schools and Communities Intervention Grants, 1557
Hasbro Children's Fund, 2256
Peter and Elizabeth C. Tower Fndn Annual Mental Health Grants, 3835
Priddy Fndn Grants, 3957
Union Bank, N.A. Fndn Grants, 4709
Visiting Nurse Fndn Grants, 4951

Invention and Innovation
ALA Charlie Robinson Award, 256
ALA EBSCO Community College Learning Resources Leadership Awards, 271
ALA EBSCO Community College Library Program Achievement Award, 272
ALA Excellence in Academic Libraries Award, 276
ALA Exceptional Service Award, 278
ALA Highsmith Library Innovation Award, 285
ALA Innovation Award, 288
ALA Isadore Gilbert Mudge Award, 290
ALA Polaris Innovation in Tech John Iliff Award, 309
Coleman Fndn Entrepreneurship Educ Grants, 1201
Covenant Fndn of New York Ignition Grants, 1385
GNOF Coastal 5 + 1 Grants, 2070
GNOF Metropolitan Opportunities Grants, 2087
GNOF New Orleans Works Grants, 2088
MDARD AgD Value Added/Regional Food Systems Grants, 3091
Santa Barbara Fndn Strategy Grants - Innovation, 4287

Investments and Securities
Bill & Melinda Gates Policy & Advocacy Grants, 769
S.E.VEN Fund $50k VINE Project Prizes, 4193

SUBJECT INDEX

Israel
American Society for Yad Vashem Grants, 447
Atran Fndn Grants, 610
Boston Jewish Community Women's Grants, 822
Donald and Sylvia Robinson Family Fndn Grants, 1573
Dorot Fndn Grants, 1586
Fel-Pro Mecklenburger Fndn Grants, 1800
Feldman Fndn Grants, 1801
Fishman Family Fndn Grants, 1835
Harry Kramer Grants, 2242
Helen Bader Fndn Grants, 2293
Jacob and Hilda Blaustein Fndn Grants, 2615
Jewish Community Fndn of LA Israel Grants, 2674
Koret Fndn Grants, 2837
Max and Anna Levinson Fndn Grants, 3066
Russell Berrie Fndn Grants, 4175

Japanese Americans
California Endowment Innovative Ideas Challenge Grants, 904

Japanese Art
Japan Fndn Los Angeles Mini-Grants for Japanese Arts & Culture, 2651
Japan Fndn New York Small Grants for Arts and Culture, 2652

Japanese Language/Literature
Japan Fndn Center for Global Partnership Grants, 2649

Jazz
Arts Midwest Performing Arts Grants, 579
Illinois Arts Council Music Grants, 2474
NYSCA Music Community Schools Grants, 3605
PAS PASIC Scholarships, 3744

Jewish Culture
Delta Air Lines Fndn Arts and Culture Grants, 1493
Harry Edison Fndn, 2241
Jewish Community Fndn of Los Angeles Cutting Edge Grants, 2673
Jewish Community Fndn of LA Israel Grants, 2674
Lois and Richard England Family Fndn Jewish Community Life Grants, 2919
Maurice Amado Fndn Grants, 3063
Meyer and Stephanie Eglin Fndn Grants, 3139

Jewish Services
100 Mile Man Fndn Grants, 27
A.C. Ratshesky Fndn Grants, 39
A/H Fndn Grants, 48
Aaron Catzen Fndn Grants, 70
Aaron Fndn Grants, 73
Adam Shikiar Fndn Grants, 156
Adolph Coors Fndn Grants, 171
Albert E. and Birdie W. Einstein Grants, 342
Albuquerque Community Fndn Grants, 348
Alfred and Tillie Shemanski Testamentary Grants, 363
Alvin and Fanny Blaustein Thalheimer Grants, 403
Ameren Corp Community Grants, 418
Ansell, Zaro, Grimm & Aaron Fndn Grants, 487
Archer Daniels Midland Fndn Grants, 527
Arie and Ida Crown Grants, 533
A Rocha USA Grants, 566
Arronson Fndn Grants, 567
Arthur and Rochelle Belfer Fndn Grants, 570
Atran Fndn Grants, 610
Audrey and Sydney Irmas Charitable Fndn Grants, 612
Barr Grants, 678
Beerman Fndn Grants, 717
Bender Fndn Grants, 726
Blanche and Irving Laurie Fndn Grants, 784
Blumenthal Fndn Grants, 804
Boettcher Fndn Grants, 810
Boston Jewish Community Women's Grants, 822
Caddock Fndn Grants, 888
Carl C. Icahn Fndn Grants, 929
Charles and Lynn Schusterman Family Grants, 1038
Charles H. Revson Fndn Grants, 1047
CICF Efroymson Grants, 1120

Columbus Jewish Fndn Grants, 1234
Covenant Fndn of New York Ignition Grants, 1385
Covenant Fndn of New York Signature Grants, 1386
Dave Coy Fndn Grants, 1447
David and Barbara B. Hirschhorn Fndn Grants, 1450
David Geffen Fndn Grants, 1452
Donald and Sylvia Robinson Family Fndn Grants, 1573
Dorot Fndn Grants, 1586
Fel-Pro Mecklenburger Fndn Grants, 1800
Feldman Fndn Grants, 1801
Fishman Family Fndn Grants, 1835
Frances and Benjamin Benenson Fndn Grants, 1916
Frank M. Tait Fndn Grants, 1932
George B. Page Fndn Grants, 2013
Giant Eagle Fndn Grants, 2049
Girl's Best Friend Fndn Grants, 2057
Goldseker Fndn Human Services Grants, 2102
Greenspun Family Fndn Grants, 2156
H. Schaffer Fndn Grants, 2187
Harold and Arlene Schnitzer CARE Grants, 2226
Harry Edison Fndn, 2241
Harry Kramer Grants, 2242
Healthcare Fndn of New Jersey Grants, 2280
Herman Abbott Family Fndn Grants, 2316
Hoffberger Fndn Grants, 2342
Howard and Bush Fndn Grants, 2374
Irvin Stern Fndn Grants, 2585
Jacob and Hilda Blaustein Fndn Grants, 2615
Jewish Community Fndn of Los Angeles Cutting Edge Grants, 2673
Jewish Community Fndn of LA Israel Grants, 2674
Jewish Grants, 2675
Jewish Funds for Justice Grants, 2676
Jewish Women's Fndn of New York Grants, 2677
John J. Leidy Fndn Grants, 2701
John S. and James L. Knight Fndn Communities Grants, 2711
Joseph Alexander Fndn Grants, 2734
Koret Fndn Grants, 2837
Kovler Family Fndn Grants, 2840
Lisa and Douglas Goldman Grants, 2910
Lois and Richard England Family Fndn Jewish Community Life Grants, 2919
Max A. Adler Charitable Fndn Grants, 3065
Max and Anna Levinson Fndn Grants, 3066
Meyer and Stephanie Eglin Fndn Grants, 3139
Michael Reese Health Trust Responsive Grants, 3160
Mt. Sinai Health Care Fndn Health of the Jewish Community Grants, 3226
Oppenstein Brothers Fndn Grants, 3685
Paul Balint Charitable Grants, 3757
Pollock Fndn Grants, 3930
Righteous Persons Fndn Grants, 4093
Roger L. and Agnes C. Dell Charitable Grants, 4143
Rose Community Fndn Jewish Life Grants, 4155
Sosland Fndn Grants, 4408
Tension Envelope Fndn Grants, 4578
Walter and Elise Haas Grants, 4982

Jewish Studies
Adam Shikiar Fndn Grants, 156
Ansell, Zaro, Grimm & Aaron Fndn Grants, 487
Arthur and Rochelle Belfer Fndn Grants, 570
Atran Fndn Grants, 610
Barr Grants, 678
Blanche and Irving Laurie Fndn Grants, 784
Blumenthal Fndn Grants, 804
Covenant Fndn of New York Ignition Grants, 1385
Covenant Fndn of New York Signature Grants, 1386
Dorot Fndn Grants, 1586
Fishman Family Fndn Grants, 1835
Frances and Benjamin Benenson Fndn Grants, 1916
Harry Edison Fndn, 2241
Helen Bader Fndn Grants, 2293
Herman Abbott Family Fndn Grants, 2316
Howard and Bush Fndn Grants, 2374
Irvin Stern Fndn Grants, 2585
Jewish Women's Fndn of New York Grants, 2677
Lois and Richard England Family Fndn Jewish Community Life Grants, 2919

M.B. and Edna Zale Fndn Grants, 2950
Maurice Amado Fndn Grants, 3063
Nathan Cummings Fndn Grants, 3246
Oppenstein Brothers Fndn Grants, 3685
Richard and Rhoda Goldman Grants, 4077
Righteous Persons Fndn Grants, 4093
Rose Community Fndn Jewish Life Grants, 4155
Russell Berrie Fndn Grants, 4175
Teaching Tolerance Grants, 4567

Job Training Programs
3M Fndn Community Giving Grants, 15
Abell Fndn Workforce Development Grants, 97
Able Trust Voc Rehab Grants for Agencies, 103
ACF Native American Social and Economic Development Strategies Grants, 123
ACF Supplemental Services for Recently Arrived Refugees Grants, 125
Achelis Fndn Grants, 127
Alfred E. Chase Charitable Fndn Grants, 366
Allen Lane Fndn Grants, 379
Alliant Energy Fndn Community Grants, 384
AMD Corp Contributions Grants, 416
Anschutz Family Fndn Grants, 486
Arizona Republic Newspaper Contributions, 547
Atkinson Fndn Community Grants, 606
Bank of America Charitable Fndn Educ and Workforce Development Grants, 657
Bank of America Charitable Fndn Student Leaders Grants, 659
Bayer Fndn Grants, 696
Bernard and Audre Rapoport Fndn Community Building and Social Service Grants, 736
Bodman Fndn Grants, 807
Boeing Company Contributions Grants, 809
Brooklyn Community Fndn Community Development Grants, 850
Butler Manufacturing Company Fndn Grants, 881
CFFVR Jewelers Mutual Charitable Giving, 1014
CFFVR Schmidt Family G4 Grants, 1020
Chicago Community Trust Workforce Grants, 1094
Chicago Title and Trust Company Fndn Grants, 1099
Chiron Fndn Community Grants, 1111
CICF Efroymson Grants, 1120
Citizens Bank Mid-Atlantic Charitable Grants, 1140
Cleveland Fenn Ed Grants, 1169
CNCS AmeriCorps State and National Grants, 1182
Coleman Developmental Disabilities Grants, 1200
Coleman Fndn Entrepreneurship Educ Grants, 1201
Comer Fndn Grants, 1236
Coors Brewing Corp Contributions Grants, 1371
CUNA Mutual Group Fndn Grants, 1417
DaimlerChrysler Corp Grants, 1432
Dallas Women's Fndn Grants, 1438
DB Americas Fndn Grants, 1466
DeKalb County Community Fndn - Garrett Hospital Aid Fund, 1478
Dept of Ed Projects with Industry Grants, 1511
Dept of Ed Recreational Services for Individuals with Disabilities, 1512
DHHS ARRA Strengthening Communities Fund - Nonprofit Capacity Building Grants, 1527
DHHS Emerging Leaders Program Internships, 1532
DOL Homeless Veterans Reintegration Grants, 1566
DOL Youthbuild Grants, 1571
eBay Fndn Community Grants, 1648
Edward and Ellen Roche Relief Fndn Grants, 1663
Emma G. Harris Fndn Grants, 1701
EPA Brownfields Assessment Pilot Grants, 1724
EPA Brownfields Training, Research, and Technical Assistance Grants, 1727
Essex County Community Fndn First Jobs Grant, 1754
Fairfield County Community Fndn Grants, 1782
Fel-Pro Mecklenburger Fndn Grants, 1800
Fndn for the Carolinas Grants, 1896
Frank B. Hazard General Charity Grants, 1926
General Mills Fndn Grants, 2003
GNOF Gulf Coast Oil Spill Grants, 2077
GNOF Metropolitan Opportunities Grants, 2087
GNOF New Orleans Works Grants, 2088

Job Training Programs (continued)

Golden LEAF Fndn Grants, 2097
Grand Rapids Area Community Fndn Wyoming Youth Grants, 2117
Hampton Roads Community Fndn Health and Human Service Grants, 2216
Harold Brooks Fndn Grants, 2227
HBF Pathways Out of Poverty Grants, 2273
Hearst Fndns Social Service Grants, 2285
Heineman Fndn for Research, Educ, Charitable and Scientific Purposes, 2290
Helen Bader Fndn Grants, 2293
Helen V. Brach Fndn Grants, 2300
Henry and Ruth Blaustein Rosenberg Grants, 2306
Henry E. Niles Fndn Grants, 2309
Highmark Corp Giving Grants, 2319
Hoffberger Fndn Grants, 2342
Household Int'l Corp Giving Grants, 2372
Houston Endowment Grants, 2373
Humanitas Fndn Grants, 2390
Illinois DCEO Employer Training Investment Grants - Competitive Component, 2491
Illinois DCEO Employer Training Investment Grants - Incentive Component, 2492
Illinois DCEO Employer Training Investment Program Multi-Company Training Grants, 2493
Illinois DCEO Employer Training Investment Program Single Company Training Grants, 2494
Illinois DCEO Large Business Dev Grants, 2495
Independent Community Fndn Neighborhood Renewal Grants, 2527
Indiana Regional Economic Development Partnership Grants, 2546
Init Fndn Innovation Grants, 2559
J. Jill Compassion Grants, 2598
Janus Fndn Grants, 2647
John Edward Fowler Memorial Fndn Grants, 2693
John Merck Grants, 2706
Johnson & Johnson Corp Contributions Grants, 2718
Joyce Fndn Employment Grants, 2749
Katharine Matthies Fndn Grants, 2788
Kenny's Kids Grants, 2803
Kessler Fndn Community Employment Grants, 2814
Liberty Bank Fndn Grants, 2890
Linden Fndn Grants, 2908
Liz Claiborne Fndn Grants, 2915
M.B. and Edna Zale Fndn Grants, 2950
May and Stanley Smith Charitable Grants, 3069
McGregor Grants, 3082
Meyer Fndn Economic Security Grants, 3141
MGM Resorts Fndn Community Grants, 3153
Microsoft Comm Affairs Puget Sound Grants, 3163
Middlesex Savings Charitable Fndn Ed Opportunities Grants, 3174
Miller Brewing Corp Contributions Grants, 3180
Minneapolis Fndn Community Grants, 3186
Modest Needs New Employment Grants, 3199
National Endowment for the Arts - Grants for Arts Projects: Challenge America Fast-Track, 3254
NE Utilities Fndn Grants, 3498
Northern Trust Company Corp Giving Program, 3504
Northland Fndn Grants, 3506
NYCT Community Development Grants, 3546
NYCT Social Services and Welfare Grants, 3557
NYCT Workforce Development Grants, 3560
OceanFirst Fndn Grants, 3636
Olive B. Cole Fndn Grants, 3670
OneFamily Fndn Grants, 3673
Owens Fndn Grants, 3718
Paul and Edith Babson Fndn Grants, 3755
Pentair Fndn Educ and Community Grants, 3816
Piedmont Natural Gas Fndn Workforce Development Grant, 3886
Pinellas County Grants, 3891
Piper Jaffray Fndn Communities Giving Grants, 3899
PMI Fndn Grants, 3918
Polk Bros. Fndn Grants, 3929
Portland General Electric Fndn Grants, 3937
Priddy Fndn Grants, 3957
Procter and Gamble Grants, 3967
Reynolds American Fndn Grants, 4068
Richard King Mellon Fndn Grants, 4087
Robin Hood Fndn Grants, 4125
Rockefeller Fndn Grants, 4138
Rockwell Fund, Inc. Grants, 4140
Romic Environmental's Charitable Contributions, 4148
S.H. Cowell Fndn Grants, 4199
Santa Fe Community Fndn Seasonal Grants-Spring Cycle, 4291
Sierra Health Fndn Responsive Grants, 4353
Sioux Falls Area Community Grants, 4364
Sioux Falls Area Community Fndn Spot Grants, 4366
Sobrato Family Fndn Grants, 4389
Sobrato Family Fndn Meeting Space Grants, 4390
Sobrato Family Fndn Office Space Grants, 4391
Staples Fndn for Learning Grants, 4475
Starr Fndn Grants, 4483
State Street Fndn Grants, 4495
Strolling of the Heifers Scholarships for Farmers, 4514
Taproot Fndn Capacity-Building Service Grants, 4560
Textron Corp Contributions Grants, 4601
TJX Fndn Grants, 4637
Topfer Family Fndn Grants, 4646
Tourism Cares Professional Dev Scholarships, 4648
U.S. Department of Educ 21st Century Community Learning Centers, 4687
U.S. Department of Educ Innovative Strategies in Community Colleges for Working Adults and Displaced Workers Grants, 4692
Union Bank, N.A. Fndn Grants, 4709
USAID Albania Critical Economic Growth Areas Grants, 4740
USDC Advanced Manufacturing Jobs and Innovation Accelerator Challenge Grants, 4848
USDC Business Center - American Indian and Alaska Native Grants, 4849
USDC i6 Challenge Grants, 4851
Verizon Fndn Connecticut Grants, 4908
Verizon Fndn Great Lakes Region Grants, 4912
Verizon Fndn Lit Grants, 4915
Verizon Fndn Maryland Grants, 4917
Verizon Fndn New York Grants, 4919
Verizon Fndn NE Region Grants, 4920
Verizon Fndn Pennsylvania Grants, 4921
Verizon Fndn SE Region Grants, 4923
Verizon Fndn Vermont Grants, 4924
Verizon Fndn Virginia Grants, 4925
Verizon Fndn West Virginia Grants, 4926
Waitt Family Fndn Grants, 4973
Washington Area Women's Fndn Jobs Grants, 4992
WCI Family Econ Success Local Impact Grants, 5010
WCI Family Econ Success Regionwide Grants, 5011
Whirlpool Fndn Grants, 5056
Wieboldt Fndn Grants, 5065
WILD Fndn Grants, 5068

Journalism

Akron Community Fndn Arts & Culture Grants, 218
Broadcasting Board of Governors David Burke Distinguished Journalism Award, 843
Canada-U.S. Fulbright Mid-Career Grants, 917
Dow Chemical Company Grants, 1596
GMFUS Marshall Memorial Fellowships, 2066
Harbus Fndn Grants, 2223
Helen Irwin Littauer Ed Grants, 2295
Illinois Arts Council Media Arts Grants, 2472
IREX Egypt Media Development Grants, 2575
James M. Cox Fndn of Georgia Grants, 2634
John Ben Snow Grants, 2687
John S. and James L. Knight Fndn National and New Inits Grants, 2714
Kiplinger Program in Public Affairs Journalism Fellowships, 2826
Nation Institute Ridenhour Prizes, 3283
New Voices J-Lab Journalism Grants, 3337
PCA Arts Organizations and Arts Programs Grants for Film and Electronic Media, 3780
PCA Entry Track Arts Organizations and Program Grants for Film and Electronic Media, 3792
Perl 6 Microgrants, 3824
Philip L. Graham Grants, 3876
Playboy Fndn Grants, 3913
Prudential Fndn Educ Grants, 3977
SEJ An Awards for Reporting on Environment, 4333
Town Creek Fndn Grants, 4650

Journalism Education

Helen Irwin Littauer Ed Grants, 2295
John S. and James L. Knight Fndn National and New Inits Grants, 2714
Viacom Fndn Grants (Formerly CBS Fndn), 4932

Judicial/Law Administration

Joyce Fndn Democracy Grants, 2748
Massachusetts Bar Fndn IOLTA Grants, 3050
State Justice Institute Curriculum Adaptation and Training Grants, 4488
State Justice Institute Partner Grants, 4489
State Justice Institute Project Grants, 4490
State Justice Institute Scholarships, 4491
State Justice Institute Strategic Init Grants, 4492
State Justice Institute Tech Assistance Grants, 4493
Supreme Court Fellows Commission Fellowships, 4532

Jurisprudence

NYHC Major and Mini Grants, 3567
Wisconsin Humanities Council Major Grants, 5107

Justice

Abell Fndn Criminal Justice and Addictions Grants, 95
Johnson Controls Fndn Civic Activities Grants, 2720
Morris K. Udall and Stewart L. Udall Fndn Native American Congressional Internships, 3220
Nuffield Fndn Africa Grants, 3532
Sapelo Fndn Social Justice Grants, 4294
Tifa Fndn Grants, 4633
United States Institute of Peace - National Peace Essay Contest for High School Students, 4724

Juvenile Correctional Facilities

Abell Fndn Criminal Justice and Addictions Grants, 95
CNCS Foster Grandparent Grants, 1185
Countess Moira Charitable Fndn Grants, 1381
Gardiner Howland Shaw Fndn Grants, 1986

Juvenile Delinquency

Abell Fndn Criminal Justice and Addictions Grants, 95
Annie E. Casey Fndn Grants, 481
Barker Welfare Fndn Grants, 669
Beazley Fndn Grants, 714
Boston Fndn Grants, 819
Cambridge Community Fndn Grants, 913
Connecticut Community Fndn Grants, 1350
DOJ Community-Based Delinquency Prevention Grants, 1556
DOJ Gang-Free Schools and Communities Intervention Grants, 1557
DOJ Juvenile Justice and Delinquency Prevention Special Emphasis Grants, 1559
DOJ Juvenile Mentoring Grants, 1560
DOJ National Institute of Justice Visiting Fellows, 1561
G.N. Wilcox Grants, 1982
Gardiner Howland Shaw Fndn Grants, 1986
Girl's Best Friend Fndn Grants, 2057
LA84 Fndn Grants, 2847
Maine State Troopers Fndn Grants, 2991
Mary Owen Borden Fndn Grants, 3046
McKesson Fndn Grants, 3084
OJJDP Gang Prevention Coord Assistance Grants, 3663
Oppenstein Brothers Fndn Grants, 3685
U.S. Department of Educ Programs for Native Hawaiians, 4696

Juvenile Law

DOJ Community-Based Delinquency Prevention Grants, 1556
DOJ Juvenile Justice and Delinquency Prevention Special Emphasis Grants, 1559
NYCT Girls and Young Women Grants, 3548
OJJDP Gang Prevention Coordination Assistance Grants, 3663

SUBJECT INDEX

Kayaking
ODKF Athletic Grants, 3638

Kidney Diseases and Disorders
Austin S. Nelson Fndn Grants, 617
Baxter Int'l Corp Giving Grants, 689
CFFVR Robert & Patricia Endries Family Grants, 1018
Collins C. Diboll Private Fndn Grants, 1208
Henry and Ruth Blaustein Rosenberg Grants, 2306
Pfizer Healthcare Charitable Contributions, 3863

Knowledge Acceleration
OSF Arab Regional Office Grants, 3701

Labor Economics
Libra Fndn Future Grants, 2898
National Endowment for Arts Our Town Grants, 3257
National Housing Endowment Challenge/Build/Grow Grant, 3277
Natonal Endowment for the Arts Research Grants: Art Works, 3286
Seattle Fndn Economy Grants, 4325

Labor Law
ABA Labor Lawyer Student Writing Contest, 77
Blue Cross Blue Shield of Minnesota Fndn - Healthy Equity: Health Impact Assessment Demonstration Project Grants, 795
IREX Small Grant Fund for Civil Society Projects in Africa and Asia, 2581

Labor Relations
A.J. Muste Memorial Institute General Grants, 44
CCHD Economic Development Grants, 967
IAFF Harvard Univ Trade Union Scholarships, 2417
Ontario Arts Council Artists in the Community/Workplace Grants, 3676

Land Management
Bella Vista Fndn Grants, 722
Champlin Fndns Grants, 1029
Community Fndn for SE Michigan Grants, 1259
Fremont Area Community Fndn Grants, 1955
Illinois DNR Youth Recreation Corps Grants, 2508
Maine Community Fndn Ram Island Conservation Challenge Grants, 2986
National Housing Endowment Challenge/Build/Grow Grant, 3277
NFWF Pulling Together Init Grants, 3387
NW Fund for the Environment Grants, 3510
Richard King Mellon Fndn Grants, 4087
Samuel S. Johnson Fndn Grants, 4239
Sweet Water Grants, 4541
Union Pacific Fndn Community and Civic Grants, 4714
Washington Gas Charitable Contributions, 5000
Weyerhaeuser Company Fndn Grants, 5053
William & Flora Hewlett Environmental Grants, 5074

Land Use Planning/Policy
Access Fund Climbing Preservation Grants, 110
ACF Native American Social and Economic Development Strategies Grants, 123
Blue Cross Blue Shield of Minnesota Fndn - Healthy Equity: Health Impact Assessment Demonstration Project Grants, 795
Blue Cross Blue Shield of Minnesota Fndn - Healthy Equity: Health Impact Assessment Grants, 796
Emma B. Howe Memorial Fndn Grants, 1700
Freeman Fndn Grants, 1952
GNOF Coastal 5 + 1 Grants, 2070
GNOF Community Revitalization Grants, 2071
GNOF Metropolitan Opportunities Grants, 2087
Grand Victoria Fndn Illinois Core Grants, 2126
Greater Kanawha Valley Fndn Grants, 2136
Illinois DNR Park and Recreational Facility Construction Grants, 2499
KeySpan Fndn Grants, 2821
National Environmental Ed Every Day Grants, 3271
National Housing Endowment Challenge/Build/Grow Grant, 3277

NFWF Acres for America Grants, 3355
NFWF Alaska Fish and Wildlife Grants, 3356
NFWF Aleutian Islands Risk Assessment Grants, 3357
NFWF California Coastal Restoration Grants, 3362
NFWF Sustain Our Great Lakes Grants, 3396
NFWF Tampa Bay Environmental Grants, 3397
Norcross Wildlife Fndn Grants, 3460
Patrick and Aimee Butler Family Fndn Community Arts and Humanities Grants, 3747
Pioneer Hi-Bred Community Grants, 3895
Schumann Fund for New Jersey Grants, 4311
Surdna Fndn Sustainable Environments Grants, 4533
Washington Gas Charitable Contributions, 5000
Water and Land Stewardship Grants, 5002

Landscape Architecture/Design
America the Beautiful Fund Operation Green Plant Grants, 451
Andy Warhol Fndn for the Visual Arts Grants, 464
CICF Efroymson Grants, 1120
GNOF Gert Community Grants, 2076
National Endowment for the Arts - Grants for Arts Projects: Challenge America Fast-Track, 3254
National Endowment for Arts Commun Grants, 3260
NGA Hansen's Natural and Native School Garden Grants, 3402
NYSCA Architecture, Planning, and Design: Capital Project Grants, 3571
NYSCA Architecture, Planning, and Design: Design and Planning Studies Grants, 3572
NYSCA Architecture, Planning, and Design: General Operating Support Grants, 3573
NYSCA Architecture, Planning, and Design: General Program Support Grants, 3574
NYSCA Architecture, Planning, and Design: Independent Project Grants, 3575
NYSCA Architecture, Planning, and Design: Project Support Grants, 3576
Regents Professional Opportunity Scholarships, 4044

Language
Akron Community Fndn Arts & Culture Grants, 218
Alabama Humanities Fndn Mini Grants, 231
Alabama Humanities Planning/Consultant Grants, 232
Community Memorial Fndn Grants, 1334
Dekko Fndn Grants, 1482
Florida Humanities Council Mini Grants, 1869
George Fndn Grants, 2018
Henry M. Jackson Fndn Grants, 2311
Illinois Humanities Council Community Grants, 2510
Pew Charitable Trusts Arts and Culture Grants, 3857
Ray Solem Fndn Grants to Help Immigrants Learn English in Innovative Ways, 4029

Language Acquisition and Development
Dwight Stuart Youth Fndn Grants, 1628
Ray Solem Fndn Grants to Help Immigrants Learn English in Innovative Ways, 4029
Robert Bowne Fndn Lit Grants, 4108
Robert Bowne Fndn Youth-Centered Grants, 4109

Language Arts Education
McCune Charitable Fndn Grants, 3077

Latin Language/Literature
Aetna Fndn Diversity Grants in Connecticut, 182

Law
21st Century ILGWU Heritage Grants, 20
Alabama Humanities Fndn Mini Grants, 231
Alabama Humanities Planning/Consultant Grants, 232
Bush Fndn Health & Human Services Grants, 875
Canada-U.S. Fulbright Mid-Career Grants, 917
Chapin Hall Int'l Fellowships in Children's Policy Research, 1032
Charles Stewart Mott Fndn Anti-Poverty Grants, 1054
Dave Thomas Fndn for Adoption Grants, 1449
Do Right Fndn Grants, 1581
E.L. Wiegand Fndn Grants, 1639
Florida Humanities Council Mini Grants, 1869

Fulbright Binational Business Grants in Mexico, 1969
Fulbright Business Grants in Spain, 1970
IIE AmCham Charitable Fndn U.S. Studies Scholarship, 2453
IREX Kosovo Civil Society Project Grants, 2576
IREX Small Grant Fund for Civil Society Projects in Africa and Asia, 2581
John Ben Snow Grants, 2687
Johnson Controls Fndn Civic Activities Grants, 2720
NLADA Kutak-Dodds Prizes, 3451
OSF-Baltimore Community Fellowships, 3695
Prudential Fndn Educ Grants, 3977
Rajiv Gandhi Fndn Grants, 4011
Regents Professional Opportunity Scholarships, 4044
Rockefeller Brothers Fellowship in Nonprofit Law, 4132
Seattle Fndn Doyne M. Green Scholarships, 4324
Tifa Fndn Grants, 4633
USAID Economic Prospectsfor Armenia-Turkey Normalization Grants, 4750
Vulcan Materials Company Fndn Grants, 4956
Wallace Fndn Grants, 4976

Law Enforcement
Alberta Law Fndn Grants, 338
Arizona Commission on the Arts After-School Program Residencies, 535
ATF Gang Resistance Educ and Training Program Coop Agreements, 603
Athwin Fndn Grants, 605
Baptist Community Ministries Grants, 664
Burlington Northern Santa Fe Fndn Grants, 866
Cemala Fndn Grants, 988
Colorado Springs Community Grants, 1215
Community Fndn of Louisville Grants, 1299
DOJ Internet Crimes Against Children Task Force Grants, 1558
DOJ National Institute of Justice Visiting Fellows, 1561
DOJ Rural Domestic Violence and Child Victimization Enforcement Grants, 1562
Hudson Webber Fndn Grants, 2383
Kenneth T. and Eileen L. Norris Fndn Grants, 2802
LISC Financial Opportunity Center Social Innovation Grants, 2911
LISC MetLife Fndn Community-Police Partnership Awards, 2912
Local Inits Support Corp Grants, 2917
NRA Fndn Grants, 3517
Robert R. Meyer Fndn Grants, 4121
Sonora Area Fndn Competitive Grants, 4404
USDJ Edward Byrne Justice Assistance Grants, 4863
William J. and Dorothy K. O'Neill Fndn Grants, 5087

Law and Social Change
ALA Coretta Scott King Book Awards, 260
ALFJ Astraea U.S. General Fund, 362
NLADA Kutak-Dodds Prizes, 3451
Southern Poverty Law Center Strategic Litigation Grants, 4439
Union Square Awards Grants, 4718

Law and Society
Hatton W. Sumners Fndn for the Study and Teaching of Self Government Grants, 2257
IREX Small Grant Fund for Civil Society Projects in Africa and Asia, 2581
ISI William Simon Fellows for Noble Purpose, 2588
San Diego County Bar Fndn Grants, 4241
Supreme Court Fellows Commission Fellowships, 4532
Triangle Community Fndn Donor Grants, 4668

Law, History of
Bernard and Audre Rapoport Fndn Democracy and Civic Participation Grants, 737

Leadership
1st Source Fndn Ernestine M. Raclin Community Leadership Award, 2
3M Community Volunteer Award, 11
AAAAI RSLAAIS Leadership Award, 49
Acumen East Africa Fellowship, 141

942 / Leadership

AEGON Transamerica Fndn Civic and Community Grants, 177
African American Fund of New Jersey Grants, 192
ALA Carnegie Corp of New York/New York Times I Love My Librarian Award, 254
ALA DEMCO New Leaders Travel Grants, 264
ALA EBSCO Community College Learning Resources Leadership Awards, 271
ALA EBSCO Community College Library Program Achievement Award, 272
ALA Excellence in Academic Libraries Award, 276
ALA Exceptional Service Award, 278
ALA Isadore Gilbert Mudge Award, 290
ALA Student Chapter of the Year Award, 331
Albert and Bessie Mae Kronkosky Grants, 339
American Express Charitable Grants, 429
American Express Leaders for Tomorrow Grants, 432
American Society on Aging Hall of Fame Award, 448
Annie E. Casey Fndn Grants, 481
Appalachian Regional Commission Leadership Development and Capacity Building Grants, 509
Arca Fndn Grants, 526
Asian American Institute Impact Fellowships, 588
ASM Gen-Probe Joseph Public Health Award, 591
Atlanta Falcons Youth Fndn Grants, 607
Austin College Leadership Award, 615
Bank of America Charitable Fndn Community Development Grants, 655
Bank of America Charitable Fndn Educ and Workforce Development Grants, 657
Bank of America Charitable Volunteer Grants, 660
Ben & Jerry's Fndn Grants, 724
Bernard and Audre Rapoport Fndn Democracy and Civic Participation Grants, 737
Best Buy Children's Fndn National Grants, 752
Blandin Rural Community Leadership Grants, 790
Bodman Fndn Grants, 807
Boeing Company Contributions Grants, 809
BP Conservation Programme Future Conservationist Awards, 826
Brooklyn Community Fndn Educ and Youth Achievement Grants, 851
Bullitt Fndn Grants, 862
Burton Morgan Adult Entrepreneurship Grants, 868
Bush Fndn Leadership Fellowships, 876
Carroll County Community Fndn Grants, 947
Central Carolina Community Fndn Community Impact Grants, 994
Chapin Hall Int'l Fellowships in Children's Policy Research, 1032
Charles Lafitte Fndn Grants, 1049
Charles Stewart Mott Fndn Anti-Poverty Grants, 1054
Charles Stewart Mott Fndn Grants, 1055
Charlotte R. Schmidlapp Grants, 1058
Chicago Community Trust Fellowships, 1086
CNL Corp Giving Entrepreneurship & Leadership Grants, 1191
Comcast Fndn Grants, 1235
Community Fndn of Greater Fort Wayne - Barbara Burt Leadership Development Grants, 1283
Community Fndn of Greater Fort Wayne - Collaborative Efforts Grants, 1284
Community Fndn of St. Joseph County African American Community Grants, 1312
Community Fndn of St. Joseph County ArtsEverywhere Grants, 1313
Community Fndn of the Verdugos Ed Endowment Grants, 1321
ConocoPhillips Grants, 1355
Cowles Charitable Grants, 1392
Cummins Fndn Grants, 1415
Dallas Mavericks Fndn Grants, 1437
Diversity Leadership Academy Grants, 1550
DOL Youthbuild Grants, 1571
Dorothy Rider Pool Health Care Grants, 1589
DTE Energy Fndn Leadership Grants, 1614
Duke Energy Economic Development Grants, 1619
Dyson Fndn Mid-Hudson Philanthropy Grants, 1633
Eileen Fisher Activating Leadership Grants for Women and Girls, 1676

Energy Fndn Climate Grants, 1706
Evelyn and Walter Haas, Jr. Fund Nonprofit Leadership Grants, 1774
Ewing Marion Kauffman Fndn Grants and Inits, 1777
FCD Child Development Grants, 1796
FCYO Youth Organizing Grants, 1797
Finish Line Youth Fndn Founder's Grants, 1812
Finish Line Youth Fndn Grants, 1813
Finish Line Youth Fndn Legacy Grants, 1814
Ford Family Fndn Grants - Technical Assistance, 1882
Frank Reed and Margaret Jane Peters Memorial Fund II Grants, 1934
Frist Fndn Grants, 1964
Fuller Fndn Grants, 1974
George Family Fndn Grants, 2017
GMFUS Marshall Memorial Fellowships, 2066
GNOF St. Bernard Community Grants, 2092
Grassroots Government Leadership Award, 2129
Guy I. Bromley Grants, 2180
HAF Community Grants, 2193
Hazen Fndn Public Educ Grants, 2269
Hazen Fndn Youth Organizing Grants, 2270
Heineman Fndn for Research, Educ, Charitable and Scientific Purposes, 2290
Homer A. Scott and Mildred S. Scott Grants, 2350
Horizon Fndn Grants, 2365
Humanitas Fndn Grants, 2390
Hutton Fndn Grants, 2412
IIE Eurobank EFG Scholarships, 2455
IMLS 21st Century Museum Pro Grants, 2512
IMLS National Leadership Grants, 2515
Indiana Humanities Council Init Grants, 2539
ING Fndn Grants, 2555
IREX Yemen Women's Leadership Grants, 2583
James Irvine Fndn Leadership Awards, 2629
Japan Fndn Center for Global Partnership Grants, 2649
Jewish Funds for Justice Grants, 2676
Jewish Women's Fndn of New York Grants, 2677
John D. and Catherine T. MacArthur Fndn Global Challenges Grants, 2690
John Edward Fowler Memorial Fndn Grants, 2693
Johnson & Johnson Corp Contributions Grants, 2718
Johnson Controls Fndn Educ and Arts Matching Gift Grants, 2721
John W. Gardner Leadership Award, 2731
Kalamazoo Community Good Neighbor Grants, 2768
Kalamazoo Community LBGT Equality Grants, 2771
Kiki Madazine Grow Strong Girls through Leadership Grants, 2822
Kimball Int'l-Habig Fndn Grants, 2823
Leadership IS Award, 2869
Leighton Award for Nonprofit Excellence, 2880
Louetta M. Cowden Fndn Grants, 2922
Lumpkin Family Fndn Strong Community Leadership Grants, 2944
Lyndhurst Fndn Grants, 2949
Maine Community Fndn Edward H. Daveis Benevolent Grants, 2979
Maine Community Fndn People of Color Grants, 2985
Maine Women's Fund Economic Security Grants, 2992
Maine Women's Fund Girls' Grantmaking Init, 2993
Mary E. Ober Fndn Grants, 3039
Mary Reynolds Babcock Fndn Grants, 3047
Maytree Fndn Refugee and Immigrant Grants, 3071
Merck Family Fund Urban Farming and Youth Leadership Grants, 3119
MetLife Fndn Empowering Older Adults Grants, 3130
MetLife Fndn Preparing Young People Grants, 3131
MetLife Fndn Promoting Employee Volunteerism, 3132
Meyer Fndn Management Assistance Grants, 3144
Meyer Fndn Strong Nonprofit Sector Grants, 3145
Miller Fndn Grants, 3181
Mix It Up Grants, 3191
Morgan Babcock Scholarships, 3217
NASE Fndn Future Entrepreneur Scholarship, 3241
National Endowment for the Arts - Grants for Arts Projects: Challenge America Fast-Track, 3254
National Endowment for the Arts - National Partnership Agreement Grants, 3256
National Endowment for Arts Our Town Grants, 3257

SUBJECT INDEX

National Urban Fellows Program, 3281
Nestle Very Best in Youth Competition, 3307
Nordson Corp Fndn Grants, 3462
NW Minnesota Fndn Women's Grants, 3512
NW Minnesota Fndn Women's Scholarships, 3513
NYCT Youth Development Grants, 3561
NYSCA State and Local Partnerships: Administrative Salary Support Grants, 3618
OSF Burma Project/SE Asia Init Grants, 3702
Paso del Norte Health Fndn Grants, 3743
Paul and Edith Babson Fndn Grants, 3755
PepsiCo Fndn Grants, 3819
Peter and Elizabeth C. Tower Fndn Organizational Scholarships, 3838
PeyBack Fndn Grants, 3861
Philadelphia Organizational Effectiveness Grants, 3872
Philadelphia Fndn YOUTHadelphia Grants, 3873
Philanthrofund Fndn Grants, 3874
Phil Hardin Fndn Grants, 3875
Playboy Fndn Freedom of Expression Award, 3912
Portland General Electric Fndn Grants, 3937
Princeton Area Community Fndn Rebecca Annitto Service Opportunities for Students Award, 3964
Prudential Fndn Educ Grants, 3977
Prudential Spirit of Community Awards, 3978
Quaker Oats Company Kids Care Clubs Grants, 3992
R.E.B. Awards for Distinguished Ed Leadership, 4000
Rhode Island Fndn Grants, 4073
Richard Davoud Donchian Fndn Grants, 4080
Robert R. McCormick Tribune Civics Grants, 4118
Robert R. Meyer Fndn Grants, 4121
Rockefeller Brothers Charles E. Culpeper Arts and Culture Grants in New York City, 4129
Rockefeller Brothers Democratic Practice Grants, 4131
Rockefeller Brothers Peace and Security Grants, 4133
Rockefeller Brothers Pivotal Places Grants: Serbia, Montenegro, and Kosova, 4135
Rockefeller Brothers Sustainable Devel Grants, 4136
Roney-Fitzpatrick Fndn Grants, 4150
RWJF Community Health Leaders Awards, 4183
RWJF Health Policy Fellowships, 4184
Saint Louis Rams Fndn Community Donations, 4214
Saint Paul Companies Fndn Grants, 4217
Salt River Project Civic Leadership Grants, 4226
San Francisco Community Leader Awards, 4264
Santa Barbara Fndn Monthly Express Grants, 4284
Santa Barbara Strategy Core Suupport Grants, 4286
Santa Fe Community Fndn Special and Urgent Needs Grants, 4292
Sara Lee Fndn Grants, 4296
Seybert Inst for Poor Boys and Girls Grants, 4338
Social Justice Fund NW Criminal Justice Giving Project Grants, 4394
South Carolina Arts Commission Leadership and Organizational Development Grants, 4423
Southern Minnesota Init Grants, 4437
SW Init Fndn Grants, 4446
Sprint Fndn Grants, 4463
Stettinius Fund for Nonprofit Leadership Awards, 4500
Subaru Rainbow Leadership Award, 4520
Surdna Fndn Sustainable Environments Grants, 4533
Teaching Tolerance Mix-it-Up Grants, 4568
The World Food Prize, 4606
Tifa Fndn Grants, 4633
Time Warner Diverse Voices in the Arts Grants, 4635
Tulane University Community Service Scholars, 4677
Tulane University Public Service Fellows, 4678
U.S. Army ROTC Scholarships, 4685
UPS Fndn Nonprofit Effectiveness Grants, 4732
USAID Community Livelihoods Project in Yemen Grant, 4746
USAID Economic Prospectsfor Armenia-Turkey Normalization Grants, 4750
USAID Global Development Alliance Grants, 4753
USAID Leadership Init for Good Governance in Africa Grants, 4766
USDA Rural Business Opportunity Grants, 4824
USTA NJTL Tennis and Leadership Camp Scholarships, 4879
USTA Serves Marian Wood Baird Scholarship, 4890

SUBJECT INDEX

UUA Bennett Award for Congregational Action on Human Justice and Social Action, 4893
Verizon Fndn Grants, 4911
W.K. Kellogg Fndn Civic Engagement Grants, 4960
W.K. Kellogg Fndn Healthy Kids Grants, 4961
Wallace Fndn Grants, 4976
WCI Community Leadership Fellowships, 5008
WCI Leadership Development Grants, 5012
Wieboldt Fndn Grants, 5065
Willary Fndn Grants, 5071
Windward Youth Leadership Grants, 5100
Women's Funding Alliance Grants, 5112
Xerox Fndn Grants, 5122
Youth Action Net Fellowships, 5128
YSA NEA Youth Leaders for Lit Grants, 5138
Z. Smith Reynolds Fndn Nancy Susan Reynolds Awards, 5146
Z. Smith Reynolds Fndn Sabbatical Grants, 5147

Learning Disabilities

Adams Rotary Memorial Fund A Grants, 157
CICF Howard Intermill and Marion Intermill Fenstermaker Grants, 1122
CVS All Kids Can Grants, 1420
Elsie H. Wilcox Fndn Grants, 1691
Emily Hall Tremaine Fndn Grants, 1698
Grace and Franklin Bernsen Fndn Grants, 2109
Johnson Scholarship Fndn Grants, 2726
Kimball Int'l-Habig Fndn Grants, 2823
NIAF Anthony Campitelli Endowed Grants, 3431
NYFA Artists in the School Community Planning Grants, 3562
Peter and Elizabeth C. Tower Fndn Annual Intellectual Disabilities Grants, 3834
Peter and Elizabeth C. Tower Fndn Annual Mental Health Grants, 3835
Peter and Elizabeth C. Tower Fndn Learning Disability Grants, 3836
Peter and Elizabeth C. Tower Fndn Phase II Technology Init Grants, 3839
Peter and Elizabeth C. Tower Fndn Phase I Technology Init Grants, 3840
Pinkerton Fndn Grants, 3892
Roy and Christine Sturgis Charitable Grants, 4166
Thomas Sill Fndn Grants, 4619
VSA/Metlife Connect All Grants, 4953

Learning Disabled, Education for

DeKalb County Community Fndn - Garrett Hospital Aid Fndn Grants, 1478
Johnson Scholarship Fndn Grants, 2726
Peter and Elizabeth C. Tower Fndn Annual Intellectual Disabilities Grants, 3834
VSA/Metlife Connect All Grants, 4953

Learning Motivation

Head Start Replacement Grantee: Colorado, 2275
Head Start Replacement Grantee: Florida, 2276
Head Start Replacement Grantee: West Virginia, 2277
Meyer Fndn Educ Grants, 3142
Nellie Mae Educ Fndn District-Level Grants, 3297
Subaru of America Fndn Grants, 4518

Lectureships

ALA Arthur Curley Memorial Lecture, 226
ALA May Hill Arbuthnot Honor Lecture Award, 300
ALA Romance Writers of America Library Grant, 314
NYSCA Literature: Public Programs, 3600

Legal Education

Alberta Law Fndn Grants, 338
CICF Indianapolis Fndn Community Grants, 1123
Cord Fndn Grants, 1372
Massachusetts Bar Legal Intern Fellowships, 3051
Miller Brewing Corp Contributions Grants, 3180
State Justice Institute Curriculum Adaptation and Training Grants, 4488
State Justice Institute Partner Grants, 4489
State Justice Institute Project Grants, 4490
State Justice Institute Scholarships, 4491

State Justice Institute Strategic Init Grants, 4492
State Justice Institute Tech Assistance Grants, 4493
Widgeon Point Charitable Fndn Grants, 5064

Legal Procedure

Alberta Law Fndn Grants, 338
Historic Landmarks Fndn of Indiana Legal Defense Grants, 2335

Legal Profession

Alberta Law Fndn Grants, 338

Legal Reform

Alberta Law Fndn Grants, 338
Chicago Community Trust Public Safety and Justice Grants, 1093
DPA Promoting Policy Change Advocacy Grants, 1598
J.M. Kaplan Fund Migrations Grants, 2602
Threshold Fndn Justice and Democracy Grants, 4626

Legal Services

Alberta Law Fndn Grants, 338
Altria Group Positive Youth Development Grants, 401
American College of Bankruptcy Grants, 426
BancorpSouth Fndn Grants, 651
Barrasso Usdin Kupperman Freeman and Sarver LLC Corp Grants, 675
Bingham McHale LLP Pro Bono Services, 772
Bodenwein Public Benevolent Fndn Grants, 806
Charles H. Pearson Fndn Grants, 1045
ConocoPhillips Grants, 1355
David Geffen Fndn Grants, 1452
Farm Aid Grants, 1790
Fitzpatrick, Cella, Harper & Scinto Pro Bono, 1836
Fred & Gretel Biel Charitable Grants, 1939
George H. and Jane A. Mifflin Grants, 2021
Georgiana Goddard Eaton Grants, 2038
GNOF Gulf Coast Oil Spill Grants, 2077
Historic Landmarks Fndn of Indiana Legal Defense Grants, 2335
Historic Landmarks Legal Defense Grants, 2338
Howard and Bush Fndn Grants, 2374
Lettie Pate Evans Fndn Grants, 2887
Margaret L. Wendt Fndn Grants, 3004
Marie C. and Joseph C. Wilson Fndn Rochester Small Grants, 3006
Massachusetts Bar Fndn IOLTA Grants, 3050
Massachusetts Bar Legal Intern Fellowships, 3051
McCune Fndn Human Services Grants, 3080
Meyer Fndn Economic Security Grants, 3141
Morris and Gwendolyn Cafritz Fndn Grants, 3218
NLADA Kutak-Dodds Prizes, 3451
NNEDVF/Altria Doors of Hope Program, 3452
Otto Bremer Fndn Grants, 3713
Paul Rapoport Fndn Grants, 3765
Perry County Community Fndn Grants, 3827
Public Interest Law Fndn Community Grants, 3982
Rhode Island Fndn Grants, 4073
SAG Motion Picture Players Welfare Grants, 4209
San Diego County Bar Fndn Grants, 4241
Sobrato Family Fndn Grants, 4389
Sonora Area Fndn Competitive Grants, 4404
Southbury Community Trust Fund, 4409
Southern Poverty Law Center Strategic Litigation Grants, 4439
Wieboldt Fndn Grants, 5065

Legal Systems

Carrier Corp Contributions Grants, 946

Leukemia

Austin S. Nelson Fndn Grants, 617
Louis R. Cappelli Fndn Grants, 2926
Pfizer Healthcare Charitable Contributions, 3863

Liberal Arts Education

Lee and Ramona Bass Fndn Grants, 2871
McCune Charitable Fndn Grants, 3077

Libraries / 943

Liberty

Playboy Fndn Freedom of Expression Award, 3912
Scherman Fndn Grants, 4305

Libraries

3M Company Arts and Culture Grants, 12
ABC-CLIO Award for Best Book in Library Lit, 84
Adam Shikiar Fndn Grants, 156
Ahmanson Fndn Grants, 207
Air Products and Chemicals Grants, 216
ALA Adelaide Del Frate Conference Sponsorship Award, 220
ALA ALSC Bookapalooza Grants, 222
ALA Annual Conference Professional Development Attendance Award, 225
ALA Baker and Taylor Summer Reading Grants, 230
ALA Carnegie-Whitney Awards, 253
ALA Carroll Preston Baber Research Grant, 255
ALA Citizens-Save-Libraries Grants, 257
ALA Clarence Day Award, 258
ALA Coretta Scott King-Virginia Hamilton Award for Lifetime Achievement, 259
ALA EBSCO Midwinter Meeting Sponsorship, 274
ALA Esther J. Piercy Award, 275
ALA Excellence in Library Programming Award, 277
ALA First Step Award/Wiley Professional Development Grant, 279
ALA Gale Cengage Learning Award for Excellence in Reference and Adult Library Services, 281
ALA Great Books Giveaway Competition, 282
ALA Harrassowitz Award for Leadership in Library Acquisitions Award, 284
ALA Intellectual Freedom Award, 289
ALA Isadore Gilbert Mudge Award, 290
ALA John Cotton Dana Library Public Relations Award, 292
ALA John Phillip Immroth Memorial Award, 293
ALA Loleta D. Fyan Grant, 295
ALA Margaret Mann Citation, 297
ALA Maureen Hayes Author/Illustrator Award, 299
ALA May Hill Arbuthnot Honor Lecture Award, 300
ALA Morningstar Pub Librarian Support Award, 302
ALA National Friends of Libraries Week Awards, 303
ALA NewsBank/Readex C. J. Reynolds Award, 304
ALA Pat Carterette Professional Devel Grant, 306
ALA Paul Howard Award for Courage, 307
ALA President's Award for Advocacy, 310
ALA Reference Service Press Award, 312
ALA Robert L. Oakley Scholarship, 313
ALA Scholastic Library Publishing National Library Week Grant, 319
ALA Student Chapter of the Year Award, 331
ALA Writers Live at the Library Grants, 336
Albert and Bessie Mae Kronkosky Charitable Fndn Grants, 339
Alcatel-Lucent Technologies Fndn Grants, 349
Arizona State Library LSTA Collections Grants, 548
Arizona State Library LSTA Community Grants, 549
Arizona State Library LSTA Learning Grants, 550
ATA Local Community Relations Grants, 600
Auburn Fndn Grants, 611
Barnes and Noble Local Sponsorships and Charitable Donations, 670
Bay and Paul Fndns, Inc Grants, 692
Bertha Russ Lytel Fndn Grants, 745
Better World Books LEAP Grants for Libraries, 755
Bill and Melinda Gates Fndn Library Grants, 768
Blue Cross Blue Shield of Minnesota Fndn - Healthy Equity: Public Libraries for Health Grants, 797
Bodenwein Public Benevolent Fndn Grants, 806
Boettcher Fndn Grants, 810
Booth-Bricker Grants, 815
Burlington Northern Santa Fe Fndn Grants, 866
Caleb C. and Julia W. Dula Ed and Charitable Fndn Grants, 893
Callaway Fndn Grants, 909
Carnahan-Jackson Fndn Grants, 939
CCH Documentary California Reads Grants, 968
Champlin Fndns Grants, 1029
Chautauqua Region Community Fndn Grants, 1062

944 / Libraries

Chicago Board of Trade Fndn Grants, 1079
Clarcor Fndn Grants, 1148
Clark and Ruby Baker Fndn Grants, 1154
Cobb Family Fndn Grants, 1194
Comcast Fndn Grants, 1235
Community Fndn of SE Connecticut Grants, 1309
Community Fndn of the Verdugos Ed Endowment Grants, 1321
Constantin Fndn Grants, 1362
Cooper Industries Fndn Grants, 1370
Corning Fndn Cultural Grants, 1376
Delaware Division of the Arts Community-Based Organizations Opportunity Grants, 1487
Edith and Francis Mulhall Achilles Grants, 1657
Faye McBeath Fndn Grants, 1794
FINRA Smart Investing@Your Library Grants, 1816
Frances C. & William P. Smallwood Grants, 1918
Fred C. and Katherine B. Andersen Fndn Grants, 1942
George I. Alden Grants, 2023
George Kress Fndn Grants, 2025
Gladys Brooks Fndn Grants, 2059
Green Bay Packers Fndn Grants, 2148
GUITS Library Acquisitions Grants, 2173
Gumdrop Books Librarian Scholarships, 2179
H. Schaffer Fndn Grants, 2187
Hall-Perrine Fndn Grants, 2209
Harry Bramhall Gilbert Charitable Grants, 2238
Harvey Randall Wickes Fndn Grants, 2255
Hatton W. Sumners Fndn for the Study and Teaching of Self Government Grants, 2257
Hearst Fndns Culture Grants, 2284
High Meadow Fndn Grants, 2321
Huie-Dellmon Grants, 2386
Idaho Community Fndn Eastern Region Competitive Grants, 2432
Illinois Arts Council Artstour Grants, 2465
IMLS 21st Century Museum Pro Grants, 2512
IMLS American Heritage Preservation Grants, 2513
IMLS Grants to State Library Admin Agencies, 2514
IMLS National Leadership Grants, 2515
IMLS Native Am Library Services Basic Grants, 2517
IMLS Native American Library Services Enhancement Grants, 2518
IMLS Partnership for a Nation of Learners Community Collaboration Grants, 2520
J.L. Bedsole Fndn Grants, 2600
James F. and Marion L. Miller Fndn Grants, 2622
James G.K. McClure Educ and Devel Grants, 2624
James L. and Mary Jane Bowman Grants, 2632
Janus Fndn Grants, 2647
John Ben Snow Grants, 2687
Leon and Thea Koerner Fndn Grants, 2883
Lettie Pate Evans Fndn Grants, 2887
Lucy Downing Nisbet Charitable Grants, 2935
MacArthur Fndn Chicago Arts and Culture General Operations Grants, 2961
Maine Community Fndn Charity Grants, 2977
Margaret L. Wendt Fndn Grants, 3004
McLean Contributionship Grants, 3088
Motorola Fndn Grants, 3221
National Endowment for the Arts - National Arts and Humanities Youth Program Awards, 3255
National Endowment for Arts Agencies Grants, 3263
NCFL/Better World Books Libraries and Families Award, 3288
NEH Preservation Assistance Grants for Smaller Institutions, 3293
NHSCA Arts in Health Care Project Grants, 3424
NHSCA General Project Grants, 3427
North Carolina Arts Council Arts in Educ Rural Development Grants, 3470
NYCH Together Grants, 3541
Parkersburg Area Comm Fndn Action Grants, 3738
PCA Art Organizations and Art Programs Grants for Presenting Organizations, 3771
PCA Entry Track Arts Organizations and Program Grants for Presenting Organizations, 3796
Pew Charitable Trusts Arts and Culture Grants, 3857
Phelps County Community Fndn Grants, 3870
Pollock Fndn Grants, 3930

Portland General Electric Fndn Grants, 3937
Posey County Community Fndn Grants, 3939
Procter and Gamble Grants, 3967
Reinberger Fndn Grants, 4052
Rice Fndn Grants, 4074
Rochester Area Community Fndn Grants, 4127
Rutter's Children's Charities Grants, 4181
Sara Lee Fndn Grants, 4296
Schlessman Family Fndn Grants, 4307
Sioux Falls Area Community Grants, 4364
Sioux Falls Area Community Fndn Spot Grants, 4366
Spartan Fndn Grants, 4448
Susan Vaughan Fndn Grants, 4537
Talbert and Leota Abrams Fndn, 4558
Thomas J. Long Fndn Community Grants, 4618
Thomas Sill Fndn Grants, 4619
Union Pacific Fndn Community and Civic Grants, 4714
USDA Hispanic-Serving Insts Educ Grants, 4813
USDC Technology Opportunities Grants, 4860
Van Kampen Fndn Grants, 4906
Virginia Fndn for Humanities Discr Grants, 4946
Virginia Fndn for the Humanities Open Grants, 4947
W. C. Griffith Fndn Grants, 4958
W.C. Griffith Fndn Grants, 4957
Widgeon Point Charitable Fndn Grants, 5064
William H. Hannon Fndn Grants, 5086

Libraries, Academic
ABC-CLIO Award for Best Book in Library Lit, 84
ALA Baker and Taylor Conference Grants, 228
ALA Carnegie Corp of New York/New York Times I Love My Librarian Award, 254
ALA Distinguished Educ and Behavioral Sciences Librarian Award, 265
ALA EBSCO Community College Learning Resources Leadership Awards, 271
ALA EBSCO Community College Library Program Achievement Award, 272
ALA Excellence in Academic Libraries Award, 276
ALA Excellence in Library Programming Award, 277
ALA Innovation Award, 288
ALA Isadore Gilbert Mudge Award, 290
ALA John Cotton Dana Library Public Relations Award, 292
ALA ProQuest Documents to the People Award, 311
ALA Routledge Distance Learning Librarianship Conference Sponsorship Award, 315
Arizona State Library LSTA Collections Grants, 548
Arizona State Library LSTA Community Grants, 549
Arizona State Library LSTA Learning Grants, 550
Humana Fndn Grants, 2388
IMLS Grants to State Library Admin Agencies, 2514
IMLS Native Am Library Services Basic Grants, 2517
IMLS Native American Library Services Enhancement Grants, 2518
John Deere Fndn Grants, 2692
Kelvin and Eleanor Smith Fndn Grants, 2796
Richard King Mellon Fndn Grants, 4087
Starr Fndn Grants, 4483
Wayne and Gladys Valley Fndn Grants, 5003

Libraries, Art
IMLS Grants to State Library Admin Agencies, 2514
MacArthur Fndn Chicago Arts and Culture General Operations Grants, 2961

Libraries, Law
Alberta Law Fndn Grants, 338
IMLS Grants to State Library Admin Agencies, 2514

Libraries, Medical
IMLS Grants to State Library Admin Agencies, 2514

Libraries, Public
ABC-CLIO Award for Best Book in Library Lit, 84
Adam Shikiar Fndn Grants, 156
Adelaide Breed Bayrd Fndn Grants, 161
Adler-Clark Electric Community Commitment Fndn Grants, 164
ALA Allie Beth Martin Award, 221

ALA ALTAFF/GALE Outstanding Trustee Conference Grant, 224
ALA Baker and Taylor Conference Grants, 228
ALA Baker and Taylor Entertainment Audio Music/Video Product Award, 229
ALA BWI Collection Development Grant, 252
ALA Carnegie Corp of New York/New York Times I Love My Librarian Award, 254
ALA Charlie Robinson Award, 256
ALA Citizens-Save-Libraries Grants, 257
ALA Clarence Day Award, 258
ALA DEMCO New Leaders Travel Grants, 264
ALA Diversity and Outreach Fair, 267
ALA EBSCO Excellence in Small and/or Rural Public Library Service Award, 273
ALA Excellence in Library Programming Award, 277
ALA Highsmith Library Innovation Award, 285
ALA John Cotton Dana Library Public Relations Award, 292
ALA Loleta D. Fyan Grant, 295
ALA Penguin Young Readers Group Award, 308
ALA Polaris Innovation in Tech John Iliff Award, 309
ALA ProQuest Documents to the People Award, 311
ALA Romance Writers of America Library Grant, 314
ALA Scholastic Library Publishing Award, 318
ALA Sullivan Award for Administrators Supporting Services to Children, 332
AmerUs Group Charitable Fndn, 455
Arizona State Library LSTA Collections Grants, 548
Arizona State Library LSTA Community Grants, 549
Arizona State Library LSTA Learning Grants, 550
Blue Cross Blue Shield of Minnesota Fndn - Healthy Equity: Public Libraries for Health Grants, 797
Caesar Puff Fndn Grants, 890
CCH Documentary California Reads Grants, 968
Champlin Fndns Grants, 1029
FINRA Smart Investing@Your Library Grants, 1816
Ford Family Grants Public Convening Spaces, 1881
GUITS Library Acquisitions Grants, 2173
Harry C. Trexler Grants, 2239
Hulman & Company Fndn Grants, 2387
IMLS Grants to State Library Admin Agencies, 2514
IMLS Native Am Library Services Basic Grants, 2517
IMLS Native American Library Services Enhancement Grants, 2518
J. Edwin Treakle Fndn Grants, 2596
James L. and Mary Jane Bowman Grants, 2632
John G. Martin Fndn Grants, 2696
Kent D. Steadley and Mary L. Steadley Trust, 2804
Kentucky Arts Council Access Assistance Grants, 2805
Louis R. Cappelli Fndn Grants, 2926
Maine Community Fndn Rose and Samuel Rudman Library Grants, 2988
Microsoft Comm Affairs Puget Sound Grants, 3163
Piedmont Natural Gas Corp and Charitable Contributions, 3883
Praxair Fndn Grants, 3944
Spartan Fndn Grants, 4448
Union Pacific Fndn Community and Civic Grants, 4714
William M. Cage Library Grants, 5090

Libraries, Research
ALA Excellence in Academic Libraries Award, 276
ALA Exceptional Service Award, 278
ALA Innovation Award, 288
ALA ProQuest Documents to the People Award, 311
ALA Routledge Distance Learning Librarianship Conference Sponsorship Award, 315
Alberta Law Fndn Grants, 338
GUITS Library Acquisitions Grants, 2173
IMLS Grants to State Library Admin Agencies, 2514

Libraries, School
ABC-CLIO Award for Best Book in Library Lit, 84
ALA ALSC Distinguished Service Award, 223
ALA Baker and Taylor Conference Grants, 228
ALA Carnegie Corp of New York/New York Times I Love My Librarian Award, 254
ALA Distinguished School Administrator Award, 266
ALA Excellence in Library Programming Award, 277

SUBJECT INDEX

ALA Information Technology Pathfinder Award, 286
ALA John Cotton Dana Library Public Relations Award, 292
ALA Loleta D. Fyan Grant, 295
ALA Penguin Young Readers Group Award, 308
ALA ProQuest Documents to the People Award, 311
ALA Sara Jaffarian School Library Award for Exemplary Humanities Programming, 316
ALA Scholastic Library Publishing Award, 318
Arizona State Library LSTA Community Grants, 549
Arizona State Library LSTA Learning Grants, 550
GUITS Library Acquisitions Grants, 2173
IMLS Grants to State Library Admin Agencies, 2514
National Home Library Fndn Grants, 3276
William M. Cage Library Grants, 5090

Libraries, Special
Arizona State Library LSTA Collections Grants, 548
Arizona State Library LSTA Learning Grants, 550
IMLS Grants to State Library Admin Agencies, 2514

Libraries, State
ALA Carnegie-Whitney Awards, 253
ALA Loleta D. Fyan Grant, 295
ALA ProQuest Documents to the People Award, 311
Arizona State Library LSTA Community Grants, 549
Arizona State Library LSTA Learning Grants, 550
IMLS Grants to State Library Admin Agencies, 2514

Library Administration
ABC-CLIO Award for Best Book in Library Lit, 84
ALA ALSC Distinguished Service Award, 223
ALA ALTAFF/GALE Outstanding Trustee Conference Grant, 224
ALA Charlie Robinson Award, 256
ALA Distinguished School Administrator Award, 266
ALA EBSCO Community College Learning Resources Leadership Awards, 271
ALA EBSCO Community College Library Program Achievement Award, 272
ALA Excellence in Academic Libraries Award, 276
ALA Excellence in Library Programming Award, 277
ALA Information Technology Pathfinder Award, 286
ALA Melvil Dewey Medal, 301
ALA National Friends of Libraries Week Awards, 303
ALA President's Award for Advocacy, 310
ALA Sullivan Award for Administrators Supporting Services to Children, 332
IIE Toyota Int'l Teacher Professional Development Grants, 2461
IMLS Grants to State Library Admin Agencies, 2514
Maine Community Fndn Rose and Samuel Rudman Library Grants, 2988

Library Automation
ALA Atlas Systems Mentoring Award, 227
ALA Diversity and Outreach Fair, 267
ALA Esther J. Piercy Award, 275
ALA Excellence in Academic Libraries Award, 276
ALA Gale Cengage Learning Award for Excellence in Reference and Adult Library Services, 281
ALA Harrassowitz Award for Leadership in Library Acquisitions Award, 284
ALA Innovation Award, 288
ALA Jan Merrill-Oldham Professional Development Grant, 291
ALA Melvil Dewey Medal, 301
ALA Polaris Innovation in Tech John Iliff Award, 309
ALA ProQuest Documents to the People Award, 311
ALA Romance Writers of America Library Grant, 314
Arizona State Library LSTA Collections Grants, 548
Clarcor Fndn Grants, 1148
IMLS Grants to State Library Admin Agencies, 2514
IMLS Native Am Library Services Basic Grants, 2517
IMLS Native American Library Services Grants, 2518
Richard and Caroline T. Gwathmey Grants, 4075

Library History
ALA ALSC Distinguished Service Award, 223
ALA Clarence Day Award, 258

ALA Donald G. Davis Article Award, 269
ALA Gale Cengage History Research and Innovation Award, 280
ALA Harrassowitz Award for Leadership in Library Acquisitions Award, 284
ALA John Phillip Immroth Memorial Award, 293
IMLS Grants to State Library Admin Agencies, 2514

Library Science
ALA Allie Beth Martin Award, 221
ALA ALSC Distinguished Service Award, 223
ALA Bogle Pratt Int'l Library Travel Fund Grant, 251
ALA Carnegie-Whitney Awards, 253
ALA Carnegie Corp of New York/New York Times I Love My Librarian Award, 254
ALA Coretta Scott King-Virginia Hamilton Award for Lifetime Achievement, 259
ALA DEMCO New Leaders Travel Grants, 264
ALA Diversity Research Grant, 268
ALA e-Learning Scholarships, 270
ALA EBSCO Community College Learning Resources Leadership Awards, 271
ALA EBSCO Community College Library Program Achievement Award, 272
ALA EBSCO Midwinter Meeting Sponsorship, 274
ALA Excellence in Academic Libraries Award, 276
ALA Excellence in Library Programming Award, 277
ALA First Step Award/Wiley Professional Development Grant, 279
ALA Gale Cengage History Research and Innovation Award, 280
ALA H.W. Wilson Library Staff Devel Grant, 283
ALA Harrassowitz Award for Leadership in Library Acquisitions Award, 284
ALA Info Today Library of the Future Award, 287
ALA Innovation Award, 288
ALA John Phillip Immroth Memorial Award, 293
ALA Joseph W. Lippincott Award, 294
ALA NMRT Professional Development Grant, 305
ALA Penguin Young Readers Group Award, 308
ALA ProQuest Documents to the People Award, 311
ALA Robert L. Oakley Scholarship, 313
ALA Routledge Distance Learning Librarianship Conference Sponsorship Award, 315
ALA Sara Jaffarian School Library Award for Exemplary Humanities Programming, 316
ALA Student Chapter of the Year Award, 331
ALA Sullivan Award for Administrators Supporting Services to Children, 332
ALA Ulrich's Serials Librarianship Award, 334
ALA Young Adult Literature Symposium Stipend, 337
Arizona State Library LSTA Collections Grants, 548
Canada-U.S. Fulbright Mid-Career Grants, 917
Frances C. & William P. Smallwood Grants, 1918
Margaret L. Wendt Fndn Grants, 3004
Pollock Fndn Grants, 3930
Thomas J. Long Fndn Community Grants, 4618
W. C. Griffith Fndn Grants, 4958
W.C. Griffith Fndn Grants, 4957

Library Science Education
ALA Atlas Systems Mentoring Award, 227
ALA Jan Merrill-Oldham Professional Development Grant, 291
ALA Ulrich's Serials Librarianship Award, 334
ALA Young Adult Literature Symposium Stipend, 337
Gumdrop Books Librarian Scholarships, 2179

Life Sciences
Applied Biosystems Grants, 514
Homer Fndn Grants, 2352
Research Program at Earthwatch Grants, 4053

Life Skills Training
Aid for Starving Children African American Indep Single Mother's Grants, 210
Albert W. Rice Charitable Fndn Grants, 347
Alfred E. Chase Charitable Fndn Grants, 366
Cargill Citizenship Fund-Corp Giving Grants, 925
CICF Efroymson Grants, 1120

Literacy / 945

Coleman Developmental Disabilities Grants, 1200
Coors Brewing Corp Contributions Grants, 1371
Countess Moira Charitable Fndn Grants, 1381
Cruise Industry Charitable Fndn Grants, 1404
Diageo Fndn Grants, 1546
Frank Reed and Margaret Jane Peters Memorial Fund II Grants, 1934
George W. Wells Fndn Grants, 2030
Head Start Replacement Grantee: Colorado, 2275
Head Start Replacement Grantee: Florida, 2276
Head Start Replacement Grantee: West Virginia, 2277
John Gogian Family Fndn Grants, 2697
May and Stanley Smith Charitable Grants, 3069
Middlesex Savings Charitable Fndn Ed Opportunities Grants, 3174
NGA Midwest School Garden Grants, 3407
Pinkerton Fndn Grants, 3892
Robert R. Meyer Fndn Grants, 4121
Union Bank, N.A. Fndn Grants, 4709

Linguistics/Philology
Alabama Humanities Fndn Mini Grants, 231
Alabama Humanities Planning/Consultant Grants, 232
Canada-U.S. Fulbright Mid-Career Grants, 917
Florida Humanities Council Mini Grants, 1869
George Fndn Grants, 2018
Illinois Humanities Council Community Project Grants, 2510
Wisconsin Humanities Council Major Grants, 5107

Lipids
Robert B McMillen Fndn Grants, 4106

Literacy
7-Eleven Corporate Giving Grants, 18
Adams County Comm Fndn of Indiana Grants, 148
Ahmanson Fndn Grants, 207
ALA Innovation Award, 288
Albert W. Cherne Fndn Grants, 346
Alcatel-Lucent Technologies Fndn Grants, 349
Allen P. and Josephine B. Green Fndn Grants, 380
Allyn Fndn Grants, 392
AMD Corp Contributions Grants, 416
American Savings Fndn Grants, 445
Amgen Fndn Grants, 456
Anschutz Family Fndn Grants, 486
Arizona Cardinals Grants, 534
Arizona Diamondbacks Charities Grants, 542
Arizona Republic Fndn Grants, 546
Arizona Republic Newspaper Contributions, 547
Arizona State Library LSTA Learning Grants, 550
Arkell Hall Fndn Grants, 562
Arlington Community Fndn Grants, 564
Ashland Corp Contributions Grants, 587
Assisi Fndn of Memphis Capital Project Grants, 593
Assisi Fndn of Memphis General Grants, 594
Atkinson Fndn Community Grants, 606
Atlanta Fndn Grants, 608
Auburn Fndn Grants, 611
AutoZone Community Relations Grants, 621
Azadoutioun Fndn Grants, 631
Bacon Family Fndn Grants, 634
Ball Brothers Fndn General Grants, 637
Barker Welfare Fndn Grants, 669
Barnes and Noble Local Sponsorships and Charitable Donations, 670
Barnes and Noble National Sponsorships and Charitable Donations, 671
Battle Creek Community Fndn Grants, 684
Bayer Fndn Grants, 696
BBF Florida Family Lit Init Grants, 697
BBF Maine Family Lit Init Grants, 698
BBF Maine Family Lit Init Planning Grants, 699
BBF Maryland Family Lit Init Grants, 700
BBF Maryland Family Lit Init Planning Grants, 701
BBF National Grants for Family Lit, 702
BBVA Compass Fndn Charitable Grants, 703
Benton Community Fndn Grants, 730
Berrien Community Fndn Grants, 744
Better World Books LEAP Grants for Libraries, 755

946 / Literacy — SUBJECT INDEX

Better World Books LEAP Grants for Nonprofits, 756
Blue Cross Blue Shield of Minnesota Fndn - Healthy Equity: Public Libraries for Health Grants, 797
Blue Mountain Community Fndn Grants, 800
Blue River Community Fndn Grants, 801
Bodenwein Public Benevolent Fndn Grants, 806
Bodman Fndn Grants, 807
Boettcher Fndn Grants, 810
Booth-Bricker Grants, 815
Boston Fndn Grants, 819
Boston Globe Fndn Grants, 821
Brooklyn Community Fndn Educ and Youth Achievement Grants, 851
Brown County Community Fndn Grants, 853
Build-A-Bear Workshop Bear Hugs Fndn Lit and Educ Grants, 860
Business Wire Lit Init, 880
Cabot Corp Fndn Grants, 887
Carrie Estelle Doheny Fndn Grants, 945
Cemala Fndn Grants, 988
CFFVR Jewelers Mutual Charitable Giving, 1014
CFFVR Schmidt Family G4 Grants, 1020
CFFVR Wisconsin Daughters and Sons Grants, 1024
Charles Lafitte Fndn Grants, 1049
Chicago Board of Trade Fndn Grants, 1079
Chicago Sun Times Charity Grants, 1098
Chicago Title and Trust Company Fndn Grants, 1099
CIGNA Fndn Grants, 1130
Citigroup Fndn Grants, 1139
Colorado Springs Community Grants, 1215
Comcast Fndn Grants, 1235
Comerica Charitable Fndn Grants, 1237
Community Fndn Alliance City of Evansville Endowment Grants, 1246
Community Fndn of Bartholomew County Heritage Grants, 1267
Community Fndn of Bartholomew County James A. Henderson Award for Fundraising, 1268
Community Fndn of Boone County - Adult Lit Init Grants, 1272
Community Fndn of Broward Grants, 1275
Community Fndn of Central Illinois Grants, 1276
Community Fndn of Greater Birmingham Grants, 1280
Community Fndn Greater Chattanooga Grants, 1281
Community Fndn of Greater Fort Wayne - Community Endowment and Clarke Endowment Grants, 1285
Community Fndn of Greenville Hollingsworth Funds Program/Project Grants, 1296
Community Fndn of Shreveport-Bossier Grants, 1307
Community Fndn of the Verdugos Grants, 1322
Community Fndn of Western N Carolina Grants, 1327
Community Partners Lawrence County Grants, 1328
Cooper Industries Fndn Grants, 1370
Coors Brewing Corp Contributions Grants, 1371
Cornerstone Fndn of NE Wisconsin Grants, 1375
Covenant Ed Fndn Grants, 1383
Cowles Charitable Grants, 1392
Crail-Johnson Fndn Grants, 1393
Cruise Industry Charitable Fndn Grants, 1404
CVS All Kids Can Grants, 1420
Darden Restaurants Fndn Grants, 1446
Dayton Power and Light Fndn Grants, 1464
Deaconess Community Fndn Grants, 1467
Deborah Munroe Noonan Grants, 1475
Decatur County Comm Large Project Grants, 1476
DeKalb County Community Fndn - Lit Grant, 1480
Delta Air Lines Community Enrichment Grants, 1494
Deluxe Corp Fndn Grants, 1496
Dept of Ed Even Start Grants, 1508
Dollar General Adult Lit Grants, 1568
Dollar General Family Lit Grants, 1569
Dollar General Youth Lit Grants, 1570
Donaldson Fndn Grants, 1574
Edyth Bush Charitable Grants, 1673
EIF Community Grants, 1675
El Paso Community Fndn Grants, 1688
Entergy Corp Micro Grants, 1712
Essex County Community Fndn Merrimack Valley General Grants, 1756
F.R. Bigelow Fndn Grants, 1781

Family Lit and Hawaii Pizza Hut Lit Fund, 1785
Farmers Insurance Corp Giving Grants, 1791
Faye McBeath Fndn Grants, 1794
Field Fndn of Illinois Grants, 1806
First Lady's Family Lit Init for Texas Family Lit Trailblazer Grants, 1821
First Lady's Family Lit Init for Texas Grants, 1822
First Lady's Family Lit Init for Texas Implementation Grants, 1823
First Lady's Family Lit Init for Texas Planning, 1824
Fourjay Fndn Grants, 1913
Frances L. and Edwin L. Cummings Grants, 1919
Fremont Area Community Amazing X Grants, 1953
G.N. Wilcox Grants, 1982
GenCorp Fndn Grants, 1998
General Mills Fndn Grants, 2003
George I. Alden Grants, 2023
German Protestant Orphan Asylum Fndn Grants, 2044
GlaxoSmithKline Corp Grants, 2060
Grace and Franklin Bernsen Fndn Grants, 2109
Grand Rapids Community Ionia Youth Grants, 2120
Green Bay Packers Fndn Grants, 2148
Guido A. and Elizabeth H. Binda Fndn Grants, 2172
H.B. Fuller Company Fndn Grants, 2183
Hall-Perrine Fndn Grants, 2209
Hallmark Corp Fndn Grants, 2212
Harbus Fndn Grants, 2223
Harold Simmons Fndn Grants, 2230
Harvest Fndn Grants, 2254
Hasbro Children's Fund, 2256
HBF Pathways Out of Poverty Grants, 2273
Hearst Fndns Social Service Grants, 2285
Helen Steiner Rice Fndn Grants, 2299
Henry and Ruth Blaustein Rosenberg Grants, 2306
Henry E. Niles Fndn Grants, 2309
Herbert A. and Adrian W. Woods Fndn Grants, 2313
Highmark Corp Giving Grants, 2319
Hilda and Preston Davis Fndn Grants, 2322
Houston Endowment Grants, 2373
Howard and Bush Fndn Grants, 2374
Hugh J. Andersen Fndn Grants, 2385
Humana Fndn Grants, 2388
IIE Western Union Family Scholarships, 2462
Indiana Rural Capacity Grants, 2547
Init Fndn Minnesota Early Childhood Grants, 2560
Int'l Paper Company Fndn Grants, 2568
IRA Pearson Fndn-IRA-Rotary Lit Awards, 2572
Irvin Stern Fndn Grants, 2585
James A. and Faith Knight Fndn Grants, 2621
James S. Copley Fndn Grants, 2637
Jean and Louis Dreyfus Fndn Grants, 2658
Jim Moran Fndn Grants, 2680
John Edward Fowler Memorial Fndn Grants, 2693
John H. and Wilhelmina D. Harland Charitable Fndn Grants, 2698
John I. Smith Charities Grants, 2700
John P. McGovern Fndn Grants, 2707
Joseph H. and Florence A. Roblee Fndn Grants, 2736
Kirkpatrick Fndn Grants, 2827
Kosciusko County Community Fndn REMC Operation Round Up Grants, 2839
Leo Goodwin Fndn Grants, 2882
Leo Niessen Jr., Charitable Grants, 2885
Lincoln Financial Group Fndn Grants, 2906
Lisa and Douglas Goldman Grants, 2910
Louis Calder Fndn Grants, 2925
Lubrizol Fndn Grants, 2933
Mardag Fndn Grants, 3001
Marie C. and Joseph C. Wilson Fndn Rochester Small Grants, 3006
Marin Community Fndn Stinson Bolinas Community Grants, 3013
Meyer Fndn Economic Security Grants, 3141
National Book Scholarship Fund, 3249
National Endowment for Arts Big Read Grants, 3261
National Home Library Service Grants, 3276
NCFL/Better World Books Libraries and Families Award, 3288
New York Life Fndn Grants, 3341
NFL Charities Pro Bowl Comm Grants in Hawaii, 3348

Norcliffe Fndn Grants, 3459
Nordson Corp Fndn Grants, 3462
Northern Trust Company Corp Giving Program, 3504
Norton Fndn Grants, 3514
NYSCA Lit: General Operating Support Grants, 3598
NYSCA Literature: Public Programs, 3600
OceanFirst Fndn Grants, 3636
Orchard Fndn Grants, 3690
Parkersburg Area Comm Fndn Action Grants, 3738
Paul and Mary Haas Fndn Contributions and Student Scholarships, 3756
PepsiCo Fndn Grants, 3819
Percy B. Ferebee Endowment Grants, 3820
Pew Charitable Trusts Arts and Culture Grants, 3857
Peyton Anderson Fndn Grants, 3862
Pinkerton Fndn Grants, 3892
PMI Fndn Grants, 3918
Portland General Electric Fndn Grants, 3937
Public Educ Power Grants, 3981
Publix Super Markets Charities Local Grants, 3985
Quaker Oats Company Kids Care Clubs Grants, 3992
Rajiv Gandhi Fndn Grants, 4011
Reinberger Fndn Grants, 4052
Reynolds and Reynolds Associate Fndn Grants, 4069
RGK Fndn Grants, 4072
Richard and Rhoda Goldman Grants, 4077
Richard Davoud Donchian Fndn Grants, 4080
Robert Bowne Fndn Fellowships, 4107
Robert Bowne Fndn Lit Grants, 4108
Robert Bowne Fndn Youth-Centered Grants, 4109
Robert R. Meyer Fndn Grants, 4121
Robert W. Woodruff Fndn Grants, 4124
Rosie's For All Kids Fndn Grants, 4163
RR Donnelley Community Grants, 4168
Saint Louis Rams Fndn Community Donations, 4214
Saint Paul Fndn Grants, 4219
Samuel S. Johnson Fndn Grants, 4239
San Antonio Area Fndn Grants, 4240
Sara Lee Fndn Grants, 4296
Scholastic Book Grants, 4308
Self Fndn Grants, 4335
Skillman Fndn Good Schools Grants, 4382
Sony Corp of America Corp Philanthropy Grants, 4405
Southbury Community Trust Fund, 4409
Southern Minnesota Init Fndn BookStart Grants, 4432
Sprint Fndn Grants, 4463
Stackpole-Hall Fndn Grants, 4472
Starr Fndn Grants, 4483
Stocker Fndn Grants, 4507
Strake Fndn Grants, 4511
Talbert and Leota Abrams Fndn, 4558
Textron Corp Contributions Grants, 4601
Thomas Sill Fndn Grants, 4619
U.S. Department of Educ 21st Century Community Learning Centers, 4687
U.S. Department of Ed Early Reading 1st Grants, 4691
Union Bank, N.A. Fndn Grants, 4709
UPS Fndn Economic and Global Lit Grants, 4730
USAID Reading Enhancement for Advancing Development Grants, 4778
Verizon Fndn Connecticut Grants, 4908
Verizon Fndn Delaware Grants, 4909
Verizon Fndn Grants, 4911
Verizon Fndn Great Lakes Region Grants, 4912
Verizon Fndn Lit Grants, 4915
Verizon Fndn Maryland Grants, 4917
Verizon Fndn New Jersey Check into Lit Grants, 4918
Verizon Fndn New York Grants, 4919
Verizon Fndn NE Region Grants, 4920
Verizon Fndn Pennsylvania Grants, 4921
Verizon Fndn South Carolina Lit & Internet Safety Grants, 4922
Verizon Fndn Vermont Grants, 4924
Verizon Fndn Virginia Grants, 4925
Verizon Fndn West Virginia Grants, 4926
Virginia Fndn for Humanities Discr Grants, 4946
Virginia Fndn for the Humanities Open Grants, 4947
Vulcan Materials Company Fndn Grants, 4956
Wayne County Fndn Vigran Family Grants, 5004
Wayne County Fndn Grants, 5005

SUBJECT INDEX

WHO Fndn Educ/Lit Grants, 5062
William G. and Helen C. Hoffman Fndn Grants, 5080
Wilson-Wood Fndn Grants, 5098
YSA NEA Youth Leaders for Lit Grants, 5138

Literary Arts
ALA Romance Writers of America Library Grant, 314
ALA Writers Live at the Library Grants, 336
Arkansas Arts Council Sally A. Williams Grants, 558
Florida Div of Cultural Affairs Literature Grants, 1855
Florida Div of Cultural Affairs Multidisciplinary Grants, 1857
HAF Arts and Culture: Project Grants to Artists, 2191
Kentucky Arts Council Emerging Artist Award, 2807
Laura Jane Musser Rural Arts Grants, 2863
Marion Gardner Jackson Charitable Grants, 3017
NYFA Strategic Opportunity Stipends, 3566
NYSCA Lit: General Operating Support Grants, 3598
NYSCA Literature: General Support Grants, 3599
NYSCA Literature: Public Programs, 3600
NYSCA Literature: Services to the Field Grants, 3601
NYSCA Special Arts Services: General Program Support Grants, 3615
PCA-PCD Professional Development for Individual Artists Grants, 3770
PCA Arts in Educ Residencies, 3772
PCA Arts Organizations & Grants for Lit, 3781
PCA Busing Grants, 3786
PCA Entry Track Arts Organizations and Program Grants for Literature, 3793
PCA Pennsylvania Partners in the Arts Program Stream Grants, 3801
PCA Pennsylvania Partners in the Arts Project Stream Grants, 3802
PCA Professional Development Grants, 3803
PCA Strategies for Success Grants - Basic Level, 3805
PCA Strategies for Success Grants - Intermediate, 3806
PennPAT Artist Technical Assistance Grants, 3811
PennPAT Strategic Opportunity Grants, 3815
Rasmuson Fndn Individual Artists Awards, 4022
Strowd Roses Grants, 4515
TAC Arts Access Grant, 4549
TAC Arts Build Communities Grants, 4551
TAC Arts Grants, 4554
TAC Rural Arts Project Support Grants, 4555
West Virginia Commission on the Arts Presenting Artists Grants, 5044

Literary Criticism
ALA Stonewall Book Awards - Israel Fishman Nonfiction Award, 330
Virginia Fndn for the Humanities Residential Fellowships, 4948

Literary Magazines
Illinois Arts Council Literature Grants, 2470
Manitoba Arts Council Literary Arts Publishers Project Grants, 2996
NYSCA Lit: General Operating Support Grants, 3598
NYSCA Literature: General Support Grants, 3599
NYSCA Literature: Public Programs, 3600
NYSCA Literature: Services to the Field Grants, 3601
PCA Arts Organizations & Grants for Lit, 3781
PCA Entry Track Arts Organizations and Program Grants for Literature, 3793
Poets & Writers Readings/Workshops Grants, 3927

Literature
A.J. Fletcher Fndn Grants, 41
ALA ALSC Bookapalooza Grants, 222
Alabama Humanities Fndn Mini Grants, 231
Alabama Humanities Planning/Consultant Grants, 232
Alabama State Council on the Arts Community Arts Collaborative Ventures Grants, 236
Alabama State Council on the Arts Community Arts Operating Support Grants, 237
Alabama State Council on the Arts Community Arts Presenting Grants, 238
Alabama State Council on the Arts Community Arts Program Development Grants, 239

Alabama State Council on the Arts Community Planning & Design Grants, 241
Alabama State Council on the Arts in Educ Partnership Grants, 242
Alabama State Council on the Arts Multi-Discipline and Festival Grants, 243
ALA MAE Award for Best Teen Lit, 296
Alaska State Council on the Arts Community Arts Development Grants, 327
Alaska State Council on the Arts Operating Support Grants, 328
Albert and Margaret Alkek Fndn Grants, 340
Alvah H. and Wyline P. Chapman Fndn Grants, 402
Arizona Commission on the Arts After-School Program Residencies, 535
Arkansas Arts Council AIE After School/Summer Residency Grants, 551
Arkansas Arts Council AIE In-School Residency, 553
Arthur Ashley Williams Fndn Grants, 572
Assisi Fndn of Memphis Mini Grants, 595
Bush Fndn Arts & Humanities Grants: Short-Term Organizational Support, 873
Canada-U.S. Fulbright Mid-Career Grants, 917
Cleveland-Cliffs Fndn Grants, 1165
Conseil des arts de Montreal Touring Grants, 1358
Davenport-Hatch Fndn Grants, 1448
Delaware Division of the Arts Opportunity Grants- Artists, 1489
Florida Div of Cultural Affairs General Program Support Grants, 1854
Florida Div of Cultural Affairs Literature Grants, 1855
Florida Div of Cultural Affairs Multidisciplinary Grants, 1857
Florida Humanities Council Mini Grants, 1869
George Fndn Grants, 2018
Heineman Fndn for Research, Educ, Charitable and Scientific Purposes, 2290
Helen V. Brach Fndn Grants, 2300
Hoblitzelle Fndn Grants, 2341
Illinois Arts Council Literature Grants, 2470
Illinois Arts Council Media Arts Grants, 2472
Illinois Arts Council Presenters Dev Grants, 2476
Illinois Humanities Council Community Project Grants, 2510
Iowa Arts Council Artists in Schools/Communities Residency Grants, 2571
Josiah W. and Bessie H. Kline Fndn Grants, 2742
Kansas Arts Commission Artist Fellowships, 2776
Manitoba Arts Council Literary Arts Publishers Project Grants, 2996
Mary & Walter Frear Eleemosynary Grants, 3035
McKesson Fndn Grants, 3084
Mercedes-Benz USA Corp Contributions Grants, 3118
Minnesota State Arts Board Cultural Community Partnership Grants, 3188
Montana Arts Council Cultural and Aesthetic Project Grants, 3209
National Endowment for the Arts - National Arts and Humanities Youth Program Awards, 3255
National Endowment for Arts Big Read Grants, 3261
National Endowment for the Arts Presenting Grants: Art Works, 3268
NEH Family and Youth Programs in American History Grants, 3291
NJSCA Arts Project Support, 3446
NJSCA General Program Support Grants, 3449
North Carolina Arts Council Gen Support, 3477
North Carolina Arts Council Outreach Grants, 3479
NYFA Gregory Millard Fellowships, 3565
NYHC Major and Mini Grants, 3567
NYHC Reading and Discussion Grants, 3568
NYSCA Lit: General Operating Support Grants, 3598
NYSCA Literature: General Support Grants, 3599
NYSCA Literature: Public Programs, 3600
NYSCA Literature: Services to the Field Grants, 3601
Ontario Arts Council Integrated Arts Grants, 3678
Paul G. Allen Family Fndn Grants, 3759
PCA Arts Organizations & Grants for Lit, 3781
PCA Entry Track Arts Organizations and Program Grants for Literature, 3793

PCA Strategies for Success Grants - Basic Level, 3805
Poets & Writers Readings/Workshops Grants, 3927
Richard and Caroline T. Gwathmey Grants, 4075
San Francisco Fndn Art Awards James Duval Phelan Literary Award, 4258
San Francisco Fndn Art Awards Joseph Henry Jackson Literary Award, 4259
San Francisco Fndn Art Awards Mary Tanenbaum Literary Award, 4260
South Carolina Arts Commission Annual Operating Support for Organizations Grants, 4414
South Carolina Arts Commission Fellowships, 4415
TAC Arts Grants, 4554
Thanks Be to Grandmother Winifred Grants, 4602
Wisconsin Humanities Council Major Grants, 5107
Wisconsin Humanities Council Mini-Grants for Scholarly Research, 5108

Literature, Comparative
NYSCA Literature: Public Programs, 3600

Literature, Media Arts
Florida Div of Cultural Affairs General Program Support Grants, 1854
Florida Div of Cultural Affairs Literature Grants, 1855
Geraldine R. Dodge Fndn Media Grants, 2042
National Endowment for Arts Media Grants, 3264
NYSCA Lit: General Operating Support Grants, 3598
NYSCA Literature: Public Programs, 3600
PCA-PCD Professional Development for Individual Artists Grants, 3770
PCA Arts in Educ Residencies, 3772
PCA Arts Organizations and Arts Programs Grants for Film and Electronic Media, 3780
PCA Busing Grants, 3786
PCA Entry Track Arts Organizations and Program Grants for Film and Electronic Media, 3792
PCA Pennsylvania Partners in the Arts Program Stream Grants, 3801
PCA Pennsylvania Partners in the Arts Project Stream Grants, 3802
PCA Professional Development Grants, 3803
PCA Strategies for Success Grants - Basic Level, 3805
PCA Strategies for Success Grants - Intermediate, 3806
PennPAT Artist Technical Assistance Grants, 3811
PennPAT Strategic Opportunity Grants, 3815

Literature, Modern
ALA Romance Writers of America Library Grant, 314
ALA Stonewall Book Awards - Barbara Gittings Literature Award, 329
Florida Div of Cultural Affairs Literature Grants, 1855
NYSCA Literature: General Support Grants, 3599
NYSCA Literature: Public Programs, 3600
NYSCA Literature: Services to the Field Grants, 3601

Livestock
Farm Aid Grants, 1790
USDA Fed-State Marketing Improvement Grants, 4810

Local History
ALA Gale Cengage History Research and Innovation Award, 280
Arts Fndn, 578
Beirne Carter Fndn Grants, 719
Goldseker Fndn Community Grants, 2101
Jane and Jack Fitzpatrick Grants, 2640
Massachusetts Fndn for Humanities Grants, 3060
Natonal Endowment for the Arts Research Grants: Art Works, 3286
Parke County Community Fndn Grants, 3735
Sarkeys Fndn Grants, 4297
South Carolina Arts Commission American Masterpieces in South Carolina Grants, 4413
South Carolina Arts Commission Folklife & Traditional Arts Grants, 4421
Turner Fndn Grants, 4681
Virginia Fndn for Humanities Discr Grants, 4946
Virginia Fndn for the Humanities Open Grants, 4947

Logistics
IDOT Rail Freight Program Loans and Grants, 2437
MDARD AgD Value Added/Regional Food Systems Grants, 3091

Long-Term Care
Blanche and Irving Laurie Fndn Grants, 784
Brookdale Fndn National Group Respite Grants, 845
George E. Hatcher, Jr. and Ann Williams Hatcher Fndn Grants, 2015
HRSA Nurse Educ, Practice, Quality and Retention Grants, 2381
Retirement Research Fndn General Grants, 4067
Russell Berrie Fndn Grants, 4175
Sensient Technologies Fndn Grants, 4337

Loss-Prevention Programs
Priddy Fndn Grants, 3957
RCF General Community Grants, 4032
Safeco Insurance Community Grants, 4203

Lung Disease
Austin S. Nelson Fndn Grants, 617
NHLBI Ancillary Studies in Clinical Trials, 3410
NHLBI Career Transition Awards, 3412
NHLBI Microbiome of the Lung and Respiratory Tract in HIV-Infected Individuals and HIV-Uninfected Controls, 3416

Lutheran Church
AHS Fndn Grants, 208
Alvah H. and Wyline P. Chapman Fndn Grants, 402
HAF Hansen Family Trust Christian Endowment Grants, 2197
MacDonald-Peterson Fndn Grants, 2965
Thrivent Financial for Lutherans Fndn Grants, 4629

Lymphatic System
NHLBI Lymphatics in Health & Disease in Digestive, Cardiovascular and Pulmonary Systems, 3414
NHLBI Lymphatics in Health & Disease in Digestive, Urinary, Cardio & Pulmonary Systems, 3415

Lymphoma
Pfizer Healthcare Charitable Contributions, 3863

Macroeconomics
Harris Graduate School of Public Policy Studies Research Development Grants, 2232
S.E.VEN Fund WHY Prize, 4198

Malaria
USAID/Cambodia Maternal and Child Health, Tuberculosis, HIV/AIDS. and Malaria Grants, 4736

Managed Care
Bush Fndn Medical Fellowships, 877
CHCF Grants, 1063
Fallon OrNda Community Health Grants, 1783
Piper Trust Reglious Organizations Grants, 3905

Management
Benton Community Fndn Grants, 730
Blue River Community Fndn Grants, 801
Brown County Community Fndn Grants, 853
Cause Populi Worthy Cause Grants, 958
Community Fndn of Bartholomew County Heritage Grants, 1267
Community Fndn of Bartholomew County James A. Henderson Award for Fundraising, 1268
Community Fndn of Greater Fort Wayne - Community Endowment and Clarke Endowment Grants, 1285
Dyson Fndn Management Assistance Program Mini-Grants, 1632
Dyson Fndn Nonprofit Strategic Restructuring Init Grants, 1637
GNOF Organizational Effectiveness Grants, 2090
Goldseker Fndn Non-Profit Management Assistance Grants, 2103
Hartford Fndn Nonprofit Support Grants, 2252
IIE New Leaders Group Award for Mutual Understanding, 2460
Lumity Technology Leadership Award, 2940
OSF-Baltimore Community Fellowships, 3695
Patrick and Aimee Butler Community Philanthropy & the Non-Profit Management Grants, 3750
Richard and Helen DeVos Fndn Grants, 4076
Richard King Mellon Fndn Grants, 4087
Robert Sterling Clark Fndn Government Accountability Grants, 4123
Saint Paul Management Improvement Grants, 4221
Social Justice Fund NW Criminal Justice Giving Project Grants, 4394
TAC Arts Access Technical Assistance Grants, 4550
TAC Technical Assistance Grants, 4556
Target Corp Local Store Grants, 4561
USDC Planning and Local Technical Assistance Grants, 4854
West Virginia Commission on the Arts Staffing Support Grants, 5049
Wilburforce Fndn Grants, 5067

Management Information Systems
ALA Innovation Award, 288
ALA Melvil Dewey Medal, 301
Nonprofit Management Grants, 3458

Management Planning/Policy
Community Fndn of Santa Cruz County Grants, 1305
Dyson Fndn Nonprofit Strategic Restructuring Init Grants, 1637
John W. Speas and Effie E. Speas Grants, 2732
Lewis H. Humphreys Charitable Grants, 2889
Louis and Elizabeth Nave Flarsheim Charitable Fndn Grants, 2924
MacArthur Fndn Policy Research Grants, 2964
Nonprofit Management Grants, 3458
Patrick and Aimee Butler Community Philanthropy & the Non-Profit Management Grants, 3750
Santa Barbara Fndn Strategy Grants - Innovation, 4287
TAC Arts Access Technical Assistance Grants, 4550
Washington Area Women's Fndn Strategic Opportunity and Partnership Grants, 4996

Management Sciences
DaimlerChrysler Corp Grants, 1432
General Motors Fndn Grants Support Program, 2004
Johnson & Johnson Corp Contributions Grants, 2718
NSF Decision, Risk, and Management Science Research Grants, 3528
Xerox Fndn Grants, 5122

Management Services
Rasmuson Organizational Advancement Grants, 4023

Manufacturing
Indiana 21st Century Research and Technology Fund Awards, 2528
Indiana Waste Tire Grants, 2551
Int'l Paper Company Fndn Grants, 2568
USDC Advanced Manufacturing Jobs and Innovation Accelerator Challenge Grants, 4848

Manuscripts/Books/Music Scores
CAA Millard Meiss Publication Grants, 885
H. Schaffer Fndn Grants, 2187

Marine Resources
Beneficia Fndn Grants, 727
BoatUS Fndn Grassroots Grants, 805
Coastal Community Fndn of S Carolina Grants, 1193
DHS ARRA Port Security Grants, 1543
FishAmerica Fndn Chesapeake Bay Grants, 1827
FishAmerica Fndn Conservation Grants, 1828
FishAmerica Fndn Marine and Anadromous Fish Habitat Restoration Grants, 1829
FishAmerica Fndn Research Grants, 1830
Fisheries and Habitat Partnership Grants, 1834
Indiana Boating Infrastructure Grants (BIG P), 2534
NFWF Columbia River Estuarine Coastal Grant, 3367
NFWF Community Salmon Fund Partnerships, 3368
NFWF King County Community Salmon Grants, 3375
NFWF Marine & Coastal Conservation Grants, 3377
NFWF Oregon Governor's Fund for the Environment Grants, 3383
NFWF Pacific Grassroots Salmonid Init Grants, 3384
NFWF Pierce Community Salmon Grant, 3385
NFWF Pioneers in Conservation Grants, 3386
NFWF Radical Salmon Design Contest, 3388
NFWF Salmon Recovery Funding Board Community Salmon Grants, 3389
Richard and Rhoda Goldman Grants, 4077
Royal Caribbean Cruises Ocean Fund, 4165
USDC/NOAA American Rivers Community-Based Restoration Program River Grants, 4845
Vancouver Fndn Grants & Comm Inits, 4900

Marine Sciences
Margaret T. Morris Fndn Grants, 3005
Maurice J. Masserini Charitable Grants, 3064
NFWF Marine & Coastal Conservation Grants, 3377
Skaggs Fndn Grants, 4378

Marketing Research
Bikes Belong Fndn Research Grants, 762
CDECD Tourism Product Development Grants, 984
Charles H. Farnsworth Grants, 1043
John W. Speas and Effie E. Speas Grants, 2732
Lewis H. Humphreys Charitable Grants, 2889
Louis and Elizabeth Nave Flarsheim Charitable Fndn Grants, 2924
South Carolina Arts Commission Cultural Tourism Init Grants, 4419
USDA Fed-State Marketing Improvement Grants, 4810
USDA Foreign Market Development Grants, 4811
USDA Market Access Grants, 4818
USDC Market Development Cooperator Grants, 4853

Marketing/Public Relations
4imprint One by One Charitable Giving, 16
ALA Highsmith Library Innovation Award, 285
ALA John Cotton Dana Library Public Relations Award, 292
ALA President's Award for Advocacy, 310
ALA Scholastic Library Publishing National Library Week Grant, 319
Cause Populi Worthy Cause Grants, 958
ConocoPhillips Grants, 1355
Denver Fndn Technical Assistance Grants, 1505
Dyson Fndn Management Assistance Program Mini-Grants, 1632
Dyson Fndn Nonprofit Strategic Restructuring Init Grants, 1637
GNOF Gulf Coast Oil Spill Grants, 2077
HAF Technical Assistance Grants, 2206
John W. Speas and Effie E. Speas Grants, 2732
Lewis H. Humphreys Charitable Grants, 2889
Louis and Elizabeth Nave Flarsheim Charitable Fndn Grants, 2924
MDARD AgD Value Added/Regional Food Systems Grants, 3091
MDARD Specialty Crop Block Grants-Farm Bill, 3093
National Endowment for Arts Agencies Grants, 3263
Nonprofit Management Grants, 3458
North Carolina Arts Council Community Arts Administration Internship, 3471
NYSCA State and Local Partnerships: Services to the Field Grants, 3621
Ontario Arts Council Integrated Arts Grants, 3678
PAS Internship, 3742
PCA Arts Organizations & Grants for Lit, 3781
PCA Entry Track Arts Organizations and Program Grants for Literature, 3793
PCA Management/Technical Assistance Grants, 3800
Robert Sterling Clark Fndn Government Accountability Grants, 4123
SW Florida Community Fndn Arts & Attractions Grants, 4441
TAC Arts Access Grant, 4549
TAC Arts Access Technical Assistance Grants, 4550

SUBJECT INDEX

TAC Arts Build Communities Grants, 4551
TAC Arts Grants, 4554
TAC Rural Arts Project Support Grants, 4555
TAC Technical Assistance Grants, 4556
USDA Foreign Market Development Grants, 4811
USDA Market Access Grants, 4818

Mass Communication
IREX Egypt Media Development Grants, 2575
IREX Small Grant Fund for Media Projects in Africa and Asia, 2582
Tifa Fndn Grants, 4633
Virginia Fndn for Humanities Discr Grants, 4946
Virginia Fndn for the Humanities Open Grants, 4947

Mass Media
A.J. Fletcher Fndn Grants, 41
Akron Community Fndn Arts & Culture Grants, 218
Brainerd Fndn Grants, 831
Caesar Puff Fndn Grants, 890
Chicago Board of Trade Fndn Grants, 1079
Florida Div of Cultural Affairs Media Grants, 1856
Fund for Southern Communities Grants, 1977
Geraldine R. Dodge Fndn Media Grants, 2042
Gill Fndn - Gay and Lesbian Grants, 2054
IREX Egypt Media Development Grants, 2575
IREX MENA Media TV Production Grants, 2577
IREX Small Grant Fund for Media Projects in Africa and Asia, 2582
NYSCA Electronic Media and Film: General Exhibition Grants, 3589
NYSCA Electronic Media and Film: Screenings Grants, 3592
Ottinger Fndn Grants, 3712
Ploughshares Grants, 3916
Tifa Fndn Grants, 4633
USAID Strengthening Free and Independent Media in South Sudan Grants, 4783

Massage Therapy
Massage Therapy Community Service Grants, 3061

Materials Acquisition (Books, Tapes, etc.)
ALA Allie Beth Martin Award, 221
ALA Baker and Taylor Entertainment Audio Music/Video Product Award, 229
ALA BWI Collection Development Grant, 252
ALA Coretta Scott King Book Donation Grant, 261
ALA Gale Cengage Learning Award for Excellence in Reference and Adult Library Services, 281
ALA Great Books Giveaway Competition, 282
ALA Romance Writers of America Library Grant, 314
Arizona State Library LSTA Collections Grants, 548
Ball Brothers Fndn Rapid Grants, 639
Better World Books LEAP Grants for Libraries, 755
Better World Books LEAP Grants for Nonprofits, 756
BJ's Wholesale Clubs Local Charitable Giving, 778
Cleveland Capital Grants, 1167
Hartford Fndn Implementation Support Grants, 2251
Maine Community Fndn Rose and Samuel Rudman Library Grants, 2988
NYSCA Literature: Public Programs, 3600
Porter County Health and Wellness Grant, 3933
South Carolina Arts Commission Folklife & Traditional Arts Grants, 4421
USTA Serves College Textbook Scholarships, 4886
Vancouver Fndn Grants & Comm Inits, 4900
Vermillion County Community Fndn Grants, 4928

Mathematics
Applied Biosystems Grants, 514
Baxter Int'l Corp Giving Grants, 689
Canada-U.S. Fulbright Mid-Career Grants, 917
Chevron Hawaii Educ Fund, 1077
Community Fndn of Greater Flint Grants, 1282
EQT Fndn Educ Grants, 1745
FirstEnergy Fndn Math, Science, and Technology Educ Grants, 1820
Fluor Fndn Grants, 1875
Gladys Brooks Fndn Grants, 2059
Grand Rapids Community Fndn Grants, 2118
Hearst Fndns Culture Grants, 2284
Honeywell Corp Leadership Challenge Academy, 2359
IIE AmCham Charitable Fndn U.S. Studies Scholarship, 2453
IIE David L. Boren Fellowships, 2454
IIE Japan-U.S. Teacher Exchange for Educ for Sustainable Development, 2457
Indiana Space Grant Consortium Grants for Informal Educ Partnerships, 2549
Indiana Space Grant Consortium Workforce Development Grants, 2550
Intel Community Grants, 2562
Intel Int'l Community Grants, 2564
Micron Technology Fndn Community Grants, 3161
North Carolina GlaxoSmithKline Fndn Grants, 3490
Qualcomm Grants, 3993
Toyota Motor of Kentucky Grants, 4654
Toyota Technical Center Grants, 4660
USAID In-Support for Teacher Educ Grants, 4759

Mathematics Education
3M Fndn Community Giving Grants, 15
AAUW Community Action Grants, 75
AAUW Int'l Project Grants, 76
AEP Corp Giving Grants, 180
Agere Corp and Community Involvement Grants, 199
Alcoa Fndn Grants, 350
AMD Corp Contributions Grants, 416
American Electric Power Grants, 428
Applied Biosystems Grants, 514
ARCO Fndn Educ Grants, 528
Avista Fndn Grants, 624
Baptist Community Ministries Grants, 664
Bay and Paul Fndns, Inc Grants, 692
Bay Area Community Fndn Grants, 694
Charlotte R. Schmidlapp Grants, 1058
Chiron Fndn Community Grants, 1111
ConocoPhillips Grants, 1355
Dept of Ed Alaska Native Ed Programs, 1506
Dolfinger-McMahon Fndn Grants, 1565
Eaton Charitable Grants, 1647
EMC Corp Grants, 1693
Emily Davie and Joseph S. Kornfeld Fndn Grants, 1697
Essex County Community Fndn Greater Lawrence Summer Grants, 1755
Ewing Marion Kauffman Fndn Grants and Inits, 1777
Ford Motor Company Grants, 1885
Goodrich Corp Fndn Grants, 2104
H.B. Fuller Company Fndn Grants, 2183
Houston Endowment Grants, 2373
Indiana Space Grant Consortium Grants for Informal Educ Partnerships, 2549
Indiana Space Grant Consortium Workforce Development Grants, 2550
James L. and Mary Jane Bowman Grants, 2632
Lockheed Martin Philanthropic Grants, 2918
McCune Charitable Fndn Grants, 3077
Micron Technology Fndn Community Grants, 3161
Motorola Fndn Grants, 3221
Oracle Corp Contributions Grants, 3686
Qualcomm Grants, 3993
Rathmann Family Fndn Grants, 4026
Raytheon Grants, 4030
RGK Fndn Grants, 4072
Rohm and Haas Company Grants, 4145
SAS Institute Community Relations Donations, 4300
TE Fndn Grants, 4572
United Technologies Corp Grants, 4725
USAID In-Support for Teacher Educ Grants, 4759
Washington Gas Charitable Contributions, 5000
Westinghouse Charitable Giving Grants, 5028

Mechanical Engineering
ASME Charles T. Main Awards, 590
Lubrizol Fndn Grants, 2933

Media
ALA Carnegie Corp of New York/New York Times I Love My Librarian Award, 254
ALA John Dana Library Public Relations Award, 292
Appalachian Community Media Justice Grants, 495
Caesar Puff Fndn Grants, 890
Florida Div of Cultural Affairs Media Grants, 1856
Geraldine R. Dodge Fndn Media Grants, 2042
NJSCA Arts Project Support, 3446
NJSCA General Program Support Grants, 3449
NYSCA Electronic Media and Film: General Exhibition Grants, 3589
NYSCA Electronic Media and Film: General Operating Support, 3590
OSF Arab Regional Office Grants, 3701
OSF Burma Project/SE Asia Init Grants, 3702
Reinberger Fndn Grants, 4052
Time Warner Diverse Voices in the Arts Grants, 4635
USAID Strengthening Free and Independent Media in South Sudan Grants, 4783
Virginia Fndn for Humanities Discr Grants, 4946
Virginia Fndn for the Humanities Open Grants, 4947
Willary Fndn Grants, 5071

Media Arts
Akron Community Fndn Arts & Culture Grants, 218
Alaska State Council on Arts Operating Support, 328
ALFJ Astraea U.S. General Fund, 362
Arizona Commission on the Arts Visual/Media Arts Organizations Grants, 539
Arkansas Arts Council AIE After School/Summer Residency Grants, 551
Arkansas Arts Council AIE In-School Residency, 553
Bush Fndn Arts & Humanities Grants: Short-Term Organizational Support, 873
Conseil des arts de Montreal Touring Grants, 1358
Constance Saltonstall Fndn for the Arts Grants, 1361
David Bohnett Fndn Grants, 1451
Florida Div of Cultural Affairs General Program Support Grants, 1854
Florida Div of Cultural Affairs Literature Grants, 1855
Florida Div of Cultural Affairs Media Grants, 1856
Florida Div of Cultural Affairs Multidisciplinary Grants, 1857
Geraldine R. Dodge Fndn Media Grants, 2042
Grand Rapids Area Community Fndn Grants, 2114
Grand Rapids Area Community Fndn Nashwauk Area Endowment Grants, 2115
H. Reimers Bechtel Charitable Grants, 2186
HAF Arts and Culture: Project Grants to Artists, 2191
IFP New York State Council on the Arts Electronic Media and Film Program Distribution Grants, 2451
Illinois Arts Council Media Arts Grants, 2472
Illinois Arts Council Presenters Dev Grants, 2476
Iowa Arts Council Artists in Schools/Communities Residency Grants, 2571
Japan Fndn Los Angeles Mini-Grants for Japanese Arts & Culture, 2651
Japan Fndn New York Small Grants for Arts and Culture, 2652
Jerome Fndn Grants, 2667
Jerome Fndn Travel and Study Grants, 2668
Joyce Awards, 2746
Joyce Fndn Culture Grants, 2747
Kansas Arts Commission Artist Fellowships, 2776
Kentucky Arts Council Al Smith Fellowship, 2806
Kentucky Arts Council Emerging Artist Award, 2807
Leon and Thea Koerner Fndn Grants, 2883
Minnesota State Arts Board Cultural Community Partnership Grants, 3188
Montana Arts Council Cultural and Aesthetic Project Grants, 3209
NAR HOPE Awards for Minority Owners, 3238
National Endowment for the Arts - National Arts and Humanities Youth Program Awards, 3255
National Endowment for Arts Commun Grants, 3260
National Endowment for the Arts Dance Grants: Art Works, 3262
National Endowment for Arts Media Grants, 3264
National Endowment for the Arts Presenting Grants: Art Works, 3268
NEH Family and Youth Programs in American History Grants, 3291

950 / Media Arts

NHSCA Artist Residencies in Schools Grants, 3423
NHSCA Conservation License Plate Grants, 3425
NHSCA Youth Arts Project Grants: For Extended Arts Learning, 3430
NJSCA Financial and Instal Stabilization Grants, 3447
NYFA Gregory Millard Fellowships, 3565
NYFA Strategic Opportunity Stipends, 3566
NYSCA Electronic Media and Film: Film Festivals Grants, 3588
NYSCA Electronic Media and Film: General Exhibition Grants, 3589
NYSCA Electronic Media and Film: General Operating Support, 3590
NYSCA Electronic Media and Film: General Program Support, 3591
NYSCA Electronic Media and Film: Screenings Grants, 3592
NYSCA Electronic Media and Film: Workspace Grants, 3593
NYSCA Music: New Music Facilities, 3608
NYSCA Presenting: General Operating Support, 3609
NYSCA Special Art Services Project Support, 3613
NYSCA Special Arts Services: General Operating Support Grants, 3614
NYSCA State and Local Partnerships: General Operating Support Grants, 3619
NYSCA State and Local Partnerships: General Program Support Grants, 3620
NYSCA State and Local Partnerships: Services to the Field Grants, 3621
PCA-PCD Professional Development for Individual Artists Grants, 3770
PCA Arts in Educ Residencies, 3772
PCA Arts Organizations and Arts Programs Grants for Film and Electronic Media, 3780
PCA Arts Organizations & Grants for Visual Arts, 3785
PCA Busing Grants, 3786
PCA Entry Track Arts Organizations and Program Grants for Film and Electronic Media, 3792
PCA Entry Track Arts Organizations and Program Grants for Visual Arts, 3799
PCA Pennsylvania Partners in the Arts Program Stream Grants, 3801
PCA Pennsylvania Partners in the Arts Project Stream Grants, 3802
PCA Professional Development Grants, 3803
PCA Strategies for Success Grants - Advanced, 3804
PCA Strategies for Success Grants - Basic Level, 3805
PCA Strategies for Success Grants - Intermediate, 3806
PennPAT Artist Technical Assistance Grants, 3811
PennPAT Strategic Opportunity Grants, 3815
Pittsburgh Fndn Community Grants, 3910
Rainbow Media Holdings Corp Giving, 4010
Rasmuson Fndn Individual Artists Awards, 4022
Regional Arts and Cultural Council Opportunity Grants, 4046
Reinberger Fndn Grants, 4052
Richard H. Driehaus Fndn MacArthur Fund for Arts and Culture, 4085
Ruth Mott Fndn Grants, 4180
San Francisco Fndn James D. Phelan Award in Film, Video, and Digital Media, 4278
South Carolina Arts Commission Annual Operating Support for Organizations Grants, 4414
TAC Arts Access Grant, 4549
Texas Commission on the Arts Cultural Connections-Visual & Media Arts Touring Exhibits Grants, 4589
Time Warner Youth Media & Creative Grants, 4636
Union Square Arts Award, 4716
West Virginia Commission on the Arts Media Arts Grants, 5039
West Virginia Commission on the Arts Presenting Artists Grants, 5044
Wisconsin Humanities Council Mini-Grants for Scholarly Research, 5108

Medical Education
1st Source Fndn Grants, 3
Abbot and Dorothy H. Stevens Fndn Grants, 79
Allyn Fndn Grants, 392
American Psychiatric Fndn Helping Hands Grants, 443
AmerUs Group Charitable Fndn, 455
Arkell Hall Fndn Grants, 562
Booth-Bricker Grants, 815
Bright Family Fndn Grants, 837
Bush Fndn Medical Fellowships, 877
Clowes Grants, 1177
Cord Fndn Grants, 1372
Cowles Charitable Grants, 1392
Daphne Seybolt Culpeper Memorial Fndn Grants, 1445
Denton A. Cooley Fndn Grants, 1500
Dr. Scholl Fndn Grants, 1602
Drs. Bruce and Lee Fndn Grants, 1607
Effie and Wofford Cain Fndn Grants, 1674
Flinn Fndn Grants, 1842
FMC Fndn Grants, 1876
Freeman Fndn Grants, 1952
Harry A. and Margaret D. Towsley Fndn Grants, 2236
Healthcare Fndn of New Jersey Grants, 2280
Health Fndn of Greater Indianapolis Grants, 2282
Herman Goldman Fndn Grants, 2317
J.W. Kieckhefer Fndn Grants, 2607
James H. Cummings Fndn Grants, 2626
James M. Collins Fndn Grants, 2633
John I. Smith Charities Grants, 2700
John S. Dunn Research Fndn Grants and Chairs, 2715
Kaiser Permanente Cares for Comm Grants, 2763
Lettie Pate Whitehead Fndn Grants, 2888
Lubbock Area Fndn Grants, 2931
Margaret and James A. Elkins Jr. Fndn Grants, 3003
MMS and Alliance Charitable Fndn Grants for Community Action and Care for the Medically Uninsured, 3194
MMS and Alliance Charitable Fndn Int'l Health Studies Grants, 3195
Mt. Sinai Health Care Fndn Health of the Jewish Community Grants, 3226
New York Life Fndn Grants, 3341
NHLBI Ruth L. Kirschstein National Research Service Award Short-Term Research Training Grants, 3422
Nuffield Fndn Africa Grants, 3532
Nuffield Fndn Small Grants, 3535
Paso del Norte Health Fndn Grants, 3743
Pfizer Medical Educ Track One Grants, 3864
Piper Trust Healthcare & Med Research Grants, 3903
Presbyterian Health Fndn Bridge, Seed and Equipment Grants, 3947
Rathmann Family Fndn Grants, 4026
Rice Fndn Grants, 4074
Ruth Eleanor Bamberger and John Ernest Bamberger Memorial Fndn Grants, 4178
Saint Luke's Health Inits Grants, 4216
San Antonio Area Fndn Grants, 4240
Schering-Plough Fndn Health Grants, 4304
Seattle Fndn Doyne M. Green Scholarships, 4324
Starr Fndn Grants, 4483
V.V. Cooke Fndn Grants, 4896
Victor E. Speas Fndn Grants, 4933
Widgeon Point Charitable Fndn Grants, 5064

Medical Ethics
Greenwall Fndn Bioethics Grants, 2158

Medical Informatics
Covidien Partnership for Neighborhood Wellness Grants, 1391
Fndn for Seacoast Health Grants, 1895
Healthcare Fndn for Orange County Grants, 2279

Medical Physics
Piedmont Natural Gas Fndn Health and Human Services Grants, 3885

Medical Programs
AAP Community Access To Child Health Implementation Grants, 63
Alvah H. and Wyline P. Chapman Fndn Grants, 402
Baptist-Trinity Lutheran Legacy Fndn Grants, 663
Baton Rouge Area Fndn Grants, 682
Bernard and Audre Rapoport Fndn Health Grants, 738
Carl R. Hendrickson Family Fndn Grants, 935
Carroll County Community Fndn Grants, 947
Clark and Ruby Baker Fndn Grants, 1154
Community Fndn AIDS Endowment Awards, 1245
ConocoPhillips Fndn Grants, 1354
Cultural Society of Filipino Americans Grants, 1412
Deborah Munroe Noonan Grants, 1475
DeKalb County Community Fndn - Garrett Hospital Aid Fndn Grants, 1478
Denton A. Cooley Fndn Grants, 1500
DHHS Emergency Med Services for Children, 1531
Fisher House Fndn Hero Miles Program, 1832
Florence Hunt Maxwell Fndn Grants, 1844
Frank B. Hazard General Charity Grants, 1926
Frederick McDonald Grants, 1946
Frederick W. Marzahl Grants, 1948
George A. and Grace L. Long Fndn Grants, 2008
George S. and Dolores Dore Eccles Fndn Grants, 2027
Hampton Roads Community Fndn Health and Human Service Grants, 2216
Helen Irwin Littauer Ed Grants, 2295
Henrietta Lange Burk Grants, 2303
Horace Moses Charitable Fndn Grants, 2363
IDPH Emergency Med Serv Assistance Grants, 2440
IDPH Local Health Department Public Health Emergency Response Grants, 2442
Indep Blue Cross Charitable Med Care Grants, 2524
James M. Collins Fndn Grants, 2633
John Edward Fowler Memorial Fndn Grants, 2693
Lucy Downing Nisbet Charitable Grants, 2935
M.D. Anderson Fndn Grants, 2952
Mabel A. Horne Grants, 2956
Marcia and Otto Koehler Fndn Grants, 3000
Marjorie Moore Charitable Fndn Grants, 3021
Maximilian E. and Marion O. Hoffman Fndn, 3067
Miami County Community Fndn - Operation Round Up Grants, 3156
Milken Family Fndn Grants, 3178
MMS and Alliance Charitable Fndn Int'l Health Studies Grants, 3195
Nelda C. and H.J. Lutcher Stark Fndn Grants, 3296
Parker Fndn (California) Grants, 3736
Posey County Community Fndn Grants, 3939
Robert and Joan Dircks Fndn Grants, 4104
Robert B McMillen Fndn Grants, 4106
Saint Paul Fndn Community Sharing Grants, 4218
Seabury Fndn Grants, 4316
Sisters of Charity Fndn of Cleveland Good Samaritan Grants, 4373
SOCFOC Catholic Ministries Grants, 4392
Sorenson Legacy Fndn Grants, 4407
St. Joseph Community Health Fndn Improving Healthcare Access Grants, 4469
Tri-State Community Twenty-first Century Endowment Grants, 4666
Vancouver Fndn Grants & Comm Inits, 4900
Walter L. Gross III Family Fndn Grants, 4983

Medical Research
Arthur F. and Alice E. Adams Charitable Grants, 574
Carlos and Marguerite Mason Grants, 934
Elizabeth Morse Genius Charitable Grants, 1682
Frank Reed and Margaret Jane Peters Memorial Fund II Grants, 1934
Giant Food Charitable Grants, 2050
Grover Hermann Fndn Grants, 2168
Hirtzel Memorial Fndn Grants, 2332
Kovler Family Fndn Grants, 2840
Leo Goodwin Fndn Grants, 2882
MacDonald-Peterson Fndn Grants, 2965
Margaret and James A. Elkins Jr. Fndn Grants, 3003
Mericos Fndn Grants, 3121
Meyer and Stephanie Eglin Fndn Grants, 3139
Milken Family Fndn Grants, 3178
NHLBI Ruth L. Kirschstein National Research Service Awards for Individual Predoctoral Fellowships to Promote Diversity in Health-Related Research, 3419
NHLBI Ruth L. Kirschstein National Research Service Awards for Individual Predoctoral MD/PhD Fellows and Other Dual Degree Fellows, 3420

SUBJECT INDEX

NHLBI Ruth L. Kirschstein National Research Service Awards for Individual Senior Fellows, 3421
NHLBI Ruth L. Kirschstein National Research Service Award Short-Term Research Training Grants, 3422
Notsew Orm Sands Fndn Grants, 3516
Perpetual Trust for Charitable Giving Grants, 3826
Reinberger Fndn Grants, 4052
Schramm Fndn Grants, 4310
Sioux Falls Area Community Grants, 4364
Sioux Falls Area Community Fndn Spot Grants, 4366
Victor E. Speas Fndn Grants, 4933

Medical Sciences
IIE AmCham Charitable Fndn U.S. Studies Scholarship, 2453
Pfizer Special Events Grants, 3865

Medical Technology
Appalachian Regional Commission Telecommunications Grants, 510
Bernard and Audre Rapoport Fndn Health Grants, 738
DHHS Emergency Med Services for Children, 1531
Fndn for Mid South Health & Wellness Grants, 1899
Highmark Physician eHealth Collab Grants, 2320
Indep Blue Cross Charitable Med Care Grants, 2524
Piedmont Natural Gas Fndn Health and Human Services Grants, 3885
USDA Distance Learning and Telemed Grants, 4806

Medical/Diagnostics Imaging
IBCAT Screening Mammography Grants, 2422
Maine Comm Belvedere Animal Welfare Grants, 2975
NHLBI Career Transition Awards, 3412
Piper Trust Healthcare & Med Research Grants, 3903

Medicine
Ahmanson Fndn Grants, 207
JELD-WEN Fndn Grants, 2661
OSF-Baltimore Community Fellowships, 3695
Perkin Grants, 3821
Pfizer Healthcare Charitable Contributions, 3863
Pfizer Medical Educ Track One Grants, 3864
Piper Trust Healthcare & Med Research Grants, 3903
Seattle Fndn Doyne M. Green Scholarships, 4324
Wolfe Associates Grants, 5110

Medicine, Internal
Alex Brown and Sons Charitable Fndn Grants, 359
ARS Fndn Grants, 568
Bonfils-Stanton Fndn Grants, 814
Hartford Aging and Health Program Awards, 2247

Men
Charles Delmar Fndn Grants, 1039
Katherine Baxter Memorial Fndn Grants, 2789

Menopause
Pfizer Healthcare Charitable Contributions, 3863

Mental Disorders
Able To Serve Grants, 102
Adolph Coors Fndn Grants, 171
Alexander and Margaret Stewart Grants, 354
ANLAF Int'l Fund for Sexual Minorities Grants, 471
Annunziata Sanguinetti Fndn Grants, 485
Atkinson Fndn Community Grants, 606
Auburn Fndn Grants, 611
Ben B. Cheney Fndn Grants, 725
CNCS Senior Companion Grants, 1187
Collins Fndn Grants, 1209
Community Fndn for Southern Arizona Grants, 1261
Cralle Fndn Grants, 1394
Dammann Grants, 1439
Danellie Fndn Grants, 1442
Elizabeth Morse Genius Charitable Grants, 1682
Elkhart County Community Fndn Fund for Elkhart County, 1683
Erie Community Fndn Grants, 1750
Eva L. and Joseph M. Bruening Fndn Grants, 1768
Health Fndn of Greater Cincinnati Grants, 2281

Hogg Fndn for Mental Health Grants, 2343
Howe Fndn of North Carolina Grants, 2377
James H. Cummings Fndn Grants, 2626
John W. Alden Grants, 2727
Lincoln Financial Group Fndn Grants, 2906
Luella Kemper Grants, 2939
Nina Mason Pulliam Charitable Grants, 3443
NNEDVF/Altria Doors of Hope Program, 3452
NYCT Mental Health and Retardation Grants, 3554
Oppenstein Brothers Fndn Grants, 3685
Pentair Fndn Educ and Community Grants, 3816
Peter and Elizabeth C. Tower Fndn Annual Mental Health Grants, 3835
Peter & Elizabeth C. Tower Mental Health Reference and Resource Materials Mini-Grants, 3837
Peter and Elizabeth C. Tower Fndn Phase II Technology Init Grants, 3839
Peter and Elizabeth C. Tower Fndn Phase I Technology Init Grants, 3840
Peter and Elizabeth C. Tower Fndn Social and Emotional Preschool Curriculum Grants, 3841
Piedmont Natural Gas Fndn Health and Human Services Grants, 3885
Robert and Joan Dircks Fndn Grants, 4104
Rollin M. Gerstacker Fndn Grants, 4146
SAMHSA Campus Suicide Prevention Grants, 4229
Simple Advise Educ Center Grants, 4361
Staunton Farm Fndn Grants, 4496
Strowd Roses Grants, 4515
Union County Community Fndn Grants, 4711
Vancouver Sun Children's Grants, 4901
Yellow Corp Fndn Grants, 5126

Mental Health
Abbott Fund Science Educ Grants, 83
Able Trust Vocational Rehabilitation Grants for Individuals, 104
Adams Fndn Grants, 155
Adolph Coors Fndn Grants, 171
Advancing Colorado's Mental Health Care Project Grants, 173
Allen P. and Josephine B. Green Fndn Grants, 380
Alliance Healthcare Fndn Grants, 383
American Psychiatric Fndn Helping Hands Grants, 443
Annie E. Casey Fndn Grants, 481
AON Fndn Grants, 491
Arizona Community Fndn Grants, 540
Arizona Diamondbacks Charities Grants, 542
Atlanta Women's Fndn Grants, 609
Austin S. Nelson Fndn Grants, 617
Barr Grants, 678
Baxter Int'l Fndn Grants, 691
BCBS of Massachusetts Fndn Grants, 713
Ben B. Cheney Fndn Grants, 725
Bodenwein Public Benevolent Fndn Grants, 806
Boyd Gaming Corp Contributions Program, 825
Brookdale Fndn National Group Respite Grants, 845
Brooklyn Community Caring Neighbors Grants, 848
Burton G. Bettingen Grants, 871
Bush Fndn Health & Human Services Grants, 875
Caesars Fndn Grants, 891
California Arts Council Public Value Grants, 895
California Endowment Innovative Ideas Challenge Grants, 904
Callaway Golf Company Fndn Grants, 910
Campbell Hoffman Fndn Grants, 915
CFFVR Jewelers Mutual Charitable Giving, 1014
CFFVR Robert and Patricia Endries Family Fndn Grants, 1018
CFFVR Schmidt Family G4 Grants, 1020
Charles H. Pearson Fndn Grants, 1045
Charles Hayden Fndn Grants, 1048
Chicago Board of Trade Fndn Grants, 1079
Colorado Springs Community Grants, 1215
Columbus Fndn Small Grants, 1232
Community Fndn of Broward Grants, 1275
Comprehensive Health Educ Fndn Grants, 1337
Connecticut Community Fndn Grants, 1350
Connecticut Health Fndn Health Init Grants, 1351
Cornerstone Fndn of NE Wisconsin Grants, 1375

Mental Health / 951

D. W. McMillan Fndn Grants, 1426
Dammann Grants, 1439
Daniels Grants, 1443
Dekko Fndn Grants, 1482
DHHS Adolescent Family Life Demo Projects, 1524
DHHS Comprehensive Community Mental Health Services Grants for Children with Serious Emotional Disturbances, 1530
Dolan Fndn Grants, 1563
Duchossois Family Fndn Grants, 1616
Duke Endowment Child Care Grants, 1617
eBay Fndn Community Grants, 1648
Edwards Grants, 1669
Edwin W. and Catherine M. Davis Fndn Grants, 1672
Eisner Fndn Grants, 1678
Elizabeth Morse Genius Charitable Grants, 1682
El Paso Community Fndn Grants, 1688
FAR Grants, 1787
Faye McBeath Fndn Grants, 1794
Florida BRAIVE Fund of Dade Community, 1846
Fndn for a Healthy Kentucky Grants, 1891
Fndn for Seacoast Health Grants, 1895
Fourjay Fndn Grants, 1913
Frank Stanley Beveridge Fndn Grants, 1936
Fremont Area Community Elderly Needs Grants, 1954
Frey Fndn Grants, 1963
Funding Exchange Martin-Baro Grants, 1979
George H.C. Ensworth Grants, 2022
Gheens Fndn Grants, 2048
Girl's Best Friend Fndn Grants, 2057
GNOF IMPACT Grants for Health and Human Services, 2080
Gulf Coast Community Operating Grants, 2176
Gulf Coast Fndn of Community Grants, 2177
Harold Brooks Fndn Grants, 2227
Hasbro Children's Fund, 2256
HCA Fndn Grants, 2274
Hilton Head Island Fndn Grants, 2330
Hoffberger Fndn Grants, 2342
Hogg Fndn for Mental Health Grants, 2343
Homer A. Scott and Mildred S. Scott Grants, 2350
Irvin Stern Fndn Grants, 2585
Ittleson Fndn Mental Health Grants, 2590
Jacob and Hilda Blaustein Fndn Grants, 2615
James R. Thorpe Fndn Grants, 2636
Jewish Women's Fndn of New York Grants, 2677
Lydia deForest Charitable Grants, 2946
M.J. Murdock Charitable Trust General Grants, 2954
MacDonald-Peterson Fndn Grants, 2965
Margaret L. Wendt Fndn Grants, 3004
Margaret T. Morris Fndn Grants, 3005
McCarthy Family Fndn Grants, 3073
Meadows Fndn Grants, 3104
Medtronic Fndn Patient Link Grants, 3113
Morris and Gwendolyn Cafritz Fndn Grants, 3218
North Dakota Community Fndn Grants, 3493
Northern Trust Company Corp Giving Program, 3504
NYCT Girls and Young Women Grants, 3548
NYCT Mental Health and Retardation Grants, 3554
Ordean Fndn Grants, 3691
OSF Mental Health Init Grants, 3709
Pasadena Fndn Average Grants, 3741
Paso del Norte Health Fndn Grants, 3743
Perry County Community Fndn Grants, 3827
Peter and Elizabeth C. Tower Fndn Annual Mental Health Grants, 3835
Peter & Elizabeth C. Tower Mental Health Reference and Resource Materials Mini-Grants, 3837
Peter and Elizabeth C. Tower Fndn Phase II Technology Init Grants, 3839
Peter and Elizabeth C. Tower Fndn Phase I Technology Init Grants, 3840
Peter and Elizabeth C. Tower Fndn Social and Emotional Preschool Curriculum Grants, 3841
Piedmont Natural Gas Fndn Health and Human Services Grants, 3885
Pike County Community Fndn Grants, 3888
Posey Community Fndn Women's Grants, 3938
Posey County Community Fndn Grants, 3939
Quantum Corp Snap Server Grants, 3995

952 / Mental Health

Rainbow Endowment Grants, 4007
Retirement Research Fndn General Grants, 4067
Robert E. and Evelyn McKee Fndn Grants, 4110
Romic Environmental's Charitable Contributions, 4148
Ross Fndn Grants, 4164
SAMHSA Campus Suicide Prevention Grants, 4229
SAMHSA Drug Free Communities Grants, 4230
SAMHSA Strategic Prevention Framework State Incentive Grants, 4231
Seabury Fndn Grants, 4316
Sensient Technologies Fndn Grants, 4337
Sidgmore Family Fndn Grants, 4348
Sierra Health Fndn Responsive Grants, 4353
Sioux Falls Area Community Grants, 4364
Sioux Falls Area Community Fndn Spot Grants, 4366
Sisters of St. Joseph Healthcare Fndn Grants, 4377
Sophia Romero Grants, 4406
Southbury Community Trust Fund, 4409
Spencer County Community Fndn Grants, 4451
St. Joseph Community Health Fndn Improving Healthcare Access Grants, 4469
Stackpole-Hall Fndn Grants, 4472
Staunton Farm Fndn Grants, 4496
Thomas Thompson Grants, 4620
Topeka Community Fndn Grants, 4644
Warrick County Community Fndn Grants, 4987
Whatcom Community Fndn Grants, 5055
William S. Abell Fndn Grants, 5094

Mental Retardation

Able To Serve Grants, 102
Ben B. Cheney Fndn Grants, 725
Benton Community Fndn Grants, 730
Blue River Community Fndn Grants, 801
Brown County Community Fndn Grants, 853
Community Fndn of Bartholomew County Heritage Grants, 1267
Community Fndn of Bartholomew County James A. Henderson Award for Fundraising, 1268
Community Fndn of Greater Fort Wayne - Community Endowment and Clarke Endowment Grants, 1285
George Fndn Grants, 2018
John W. Alden Grants, 2727
Joseph P. Kennedy Jr. Fndn Grants, 2740
NYCT Mental Health and Retardation Grants, 3554
Peter and Elizabeth C. Tower Fndn Annual Mental Health Grants, 3835
Pinkerton Fndn Grants, 3892
Roeher Institute Research Grants, 4142
Saint Louis Rams Fndn Community Donations, 4214
Simple Advise Educ Center Grants, 4361
Thomas Sill Fndn Grants, 4619

Mentoring Programs

ACF Mentoring Children of Prisoners Grants, 121
AIChE Women's Inits Committee Mentorship Excellence Award, 209
Alliant Energy Fndn Community Grants, 384
American Savings Fndn Grants, 445
Andrew Family Fndn Grants, 462
Ball Brothers Fndn Organizational Effectiveness/ Executive Mentoring Grants, 638
Boeing Company Contributions Grants, 809
Brooklyn Community Fndn Educ and Youth Achievement Grants, 851
Center for the Study of Philanthropy Senior Int'l Fellowships, 990
Cincinnati Bell Fndn Grants, 1131
Citigroup Fndn Grants, 1139
CMA Fndn Grants, 1178
CNCS Foster Grandparent Grants, 1185
CNCS Senior Corps Retired and Senior Volunteer Grants, 1188
Coca-Cola Fndn Grants, 1195
Community Fndn of Louisville Grants, 1299
Constellation Energy Corp Grants, 1364
Cooper Industries Fndn Grants, 1370
Covenant to Care for Children Critical Grants, 1388
Cruise Industry Charitable Fndn Grants, 1404
Delaware Community Next Generation Grants, 1485

Delaware Division of the Arts Opportunity Grants-- Arts Organizations, 1488
DOJ Juvenile Mentoring Grants, 1560
Dollar General Family Lit Grants, 1569
Dwight Stuart Youth Fndn Grants, 1628
eBay Fndn Community Grants, 1648
Farmers Insurance Corp Giving Grants, 1791
Fisa Fndn Grants, 1826
Ford Family Fndn Grants - Positive Youth Development, 1880
Fndn for the Mid South Educ Grants, 1898
Freshwater Future Advocate Mentor Program, 1957
German Protestant Orphan Asylum Fndn Grants, 2044
GNOF IMPACT Grants for Youth Development, 2081
Greater Milwaukee Fndn Grants, 2137
HBF Pathways Out of Poverty Grants, 2273
Henry E. Niles Fndn Grants, 2309
Highmark Corp Giving Grants, 2319
Init Fndn Innovation Grants, 2559
John Edward Fowler Memorial Fndn Grants, 2693
Kansas Health Fndn Recognition Grants, 2784
Kosciusko County Community Fndn REMC Operation Round Up Grants, 2839
Kuki'o Community Fund, 2845
Legacy Fndn College Readiness Grant, 2874
Liberty Bank Fndn Grants, 2890
Luella Kemper Grants, 2939
Mark Wahlberg Youth Fndn Grants, 3022
Mericos Fndn Grants, 3121
NAGC Masters and Specialists Award, 3237
National Endowment for Arts Commun Grants, 3260
National Endowment for the Arts Dance Grants: Art Works, 3262
National Endowment for Arts Music Grants, 3266
National Endowment for Arts Theater Grants, 3269
National Home Library Grants, 3276
NFL Charities Pro Bowl Comm Grants in Hawaii, 3348
Nike Fndn Grants, 3441
North Carolina Arts Council Arts in Educ Artist Residencies Grants, 3468
North Carolina Arts Council Ed Grants, 3469
NYSCA Electronic Media and Film: Workspace Grants, 3593
OJJDP National Mentoring Grants, 3664
OneFamily Fndn Grants, 3673
Ontario Arts Council Compass Grants, 3677
OSF-Baltimore Community Fellowships, 3695
Pacers Fndn Be Educated Grants, 3721
Peyton Anderson Fndn Grants, 3862
Phoenix Coyotes Charities Grants, 3879
Piedmont Natural Gas Fndn Health and Human Services Grants, 3885
Piper Trust Educ Grants, 3902
Priddy Fndn Grants, 3957
Prudential Fndn Educ Grants, 3977
Robert R. Meyer Fndn Grants, 4121
Romic Environmental's Charitable Contributions, 4148
Saint Louis Rams Fndn Community Donations, 4214
Schlessman Family Fndn Grants, 4307
Sidgmore Family Fndn Grants, 4348
South Carolina Arts Commission Traditional Arts Apprenticeship Grants, 4427
Tiger Woods Fndn Grants, 4634
Tulane University Community Service Scholars, 4677
U.S. Bank Fndn Grants, 4686
UPS Fndn Economic and Global Lit Grants, 4730
Vancouver Fndn Grants & Comm Inits, 4900
Weingart Fndn Grants, 5018
YSA MLK Day Lead Organizer Grants, 5136

Metabolic Diseases

Bristol-Myers Squibb Clinical Outcomes and Research Grants, 839

Metabolism

NHLBI Career Transition Awards, 3412
NHLBI Research on the Role of Cardiomyocyte Mitochondria in Heart Disease: An Integrated Approach, 3417

SUBJECT INDEX

Metallurgy

Dorr Fndn Grants, 1591

Methodist Church

AHS Fndn Grants, 208
Alvah H. and Wyline P. Chapman Fndn Grants, 402
Barra Fndn Project Grants, 674
Bradley-Turner Fndn Grants, 828
Danellie Fndn Grants, 1442
Effie and Wofford Cain Fndn Grants, 1674
MacDonald-Peterson Fndn Grants, 2965
McCallum Family Fndn Grants, 3072
Missouri United Methodist Ministry Grants, 3189
United Methodist Committee on Relief Global AIDS Grants, 4719
United Methodist Committee on Relief Hunger and Poverty Grants, 4720
United Methodist Child Mental Health Grants, 4721
W. Waldo and Jenny Lynn M. Bradley Grants, 4967

Microbiology

ASM Congressional Science Fellowships, 589
ASM Gen-Probe Joseph Public Health Award, 591

Microbiome

NHLBI Microbiome of the Lung and Respiratory Tract in HIV-Infected Individuals and HIV-Uninfected Controls, 3416

Microeconomics

McCune Charitable Fndn Grants, 3077

Microenterprises

Arthur B. Schultz Fndn Grants, 573
Sapelo Fndn Environmental Protection Grants, 4293
Third Wave Fndn Lela Breitbart Grants, 4609
Third Wave Organizing & Advocacy Grants, 4610
Third Wave Fndn Reproductive Health and Justice Grants, 4611
Union Bank, N.A. Fndn Grants, 4709

Microfilming and Microforms

Claremont Community Fndn Grants, 1149
NEH Preservation Microfilming of Brittle Books and Serials Grants, 3294

Microprocessors

ALA Information Technology Pathfinder Award, 286

Middle School

ALA Coretta Scott King Book Donation Grant, 261
CNCS AmeriCorps State and National Grants, 1182
Public Educ Power Grants, 3981
Robert R. McCormick Tribune Civics Grants, 4118
VSA/Metlife Connect All Grants, 4953
W.H. and Mary Ellen Cobb Charitable Grants, 4959
West Virginia Comm on the Arts Special Grants, 5048

Middle School Education

Adobe Youth Voices Grants, 170
American Electric Power Grants, 428
ATF Gang Resistance Educ and Training Program Coop Agreements, 603
Barnes and Noble Local Sponsorships and Charitable Donations, 670
Carnegie Corp of New York Grants, 940
CNCS AmeriCorps State and National Grants, 1182
Colonel Stanley R. McNeil Fndn Grants, 1210
Cooper Fndn Grants, 1369
DaimlerChrysler Corp Grants, 1432
Dr. and Mrs. Paul Pierce Memorial Fndn Grants, 1599
Eaton Charitable Grants, 1647
Elizabeth Carse Fndn Grants, 1681
Frank B. Hazard General Charity Grants, 1926
Frank Loomis Palmer Grants, 1931
Fred & Gretel Biel Charitable Grants, 1939
Fred Meyer Fndn Grants, 1950
George J. and Effie L. Seay Fndn Grants, 2024
HAF Educ Grants, 2196
Helen Bader Fndn Grants, 2293

SUBJECT INDEX

Hutton Fndn Grants, 2412
Intel Community Grants, 2562
Intel Int'l Community Grants, 2564
J.C. Penney Company Grants, 2594
J. Knox Gholston Fndn Grants, 2599
J. Marion Sims Fndn Teachers' Pet Grant, 2605
John Clarke Grants, 2689
Joseph S. Stackpole Charitable Grants, 2741
Katrine Menzing Deakins Charitable Grants, 2793
KeySpan Fndn Grants, 2821
LEGO Children's Grants, 2878
Linford and Mildred White Charitable Grants, 2909
Lowe's Charitable and Ed Fndn Grants, 2927
Luella Kemper Grants, 2939
Marjorie Moore Charitable Fndn Grants, 3021
McCune Charitable Fndn Grants, 3077
Meyer Fndn Educ Grants, 3142
Miller Fndn Grants, 3181
National Home Library Fndn Grants, 3276
Nellie Mae Educ Fndn District-Level Grants, 3297
Nellie Mae Educ Fndn State Level Systems Change Grants, 3299
New York Life Fndn Grants, 3341
NGA Hooked on Hydroponics Awards, 3405
Ober Kaler Community Grants, 3635
PG&E Bright Ideas Grants, 3866
Public Educ Power Grants, 3981
R.S. Gernon Grants, 4002
Raskob Fndn for Catholic Activities Grants, 4019
Reinberger Fndn Grants, 4052
Scholastic Welch's Harvest Grants, 4309
South Carolina Arts Commission Arts in Educ After School Arts Init Grants, 4418
Stuart Fndn Grants, 4516
Subaru Adopt a School Garden Grants, 4517
Taproot Fndn Capacity-Building Service Grants, 4560
Thelma Braun and Bocklett Family Fndn Grants, 4603
Waste Management Charitable Giving Grants, 5001
West Virginia Comm on the Arts Special Grants, 5048
William J. Brace Charitable Trust, 5088
William McCaskey Chapman and Adaline Dinsmore Chapman Fndn Grants, 5092
Wisconsin Energy Fndn Grants, 5106

Migrant Labor
Charles Delmar Fndn Grants, 1039
Luther I. Replogle Fndn Grants, 2945
Meyer Fndn Economic Security Grants, 3141
Needmor Grants, 3289
U.S. Department of Educ Migrant and Seasonal Farmworkers Grants, 4693
Union Bank, N.A. Fndn Grants, 4709
USDA Farm Labor Housing Grants, 4809

Migrants
BBF Florida Family Lit Init Grants, 697
BBF Maine Family Lit Init Planning Grants, 699
California Endowment Innovative Ideas Challenge Grants, 904
Farmers Insurance Corp Giving Grants, 1791
IIE Western Union Family Scholarships, 2462
Luther I. Replogle Fndn Grants, 2945
Union Bank, N.A. Fndn Grants, 4709

Migratory Animals and Birds
Alexander H. Bright Charitable Grants, 358
Barbara Meyer Elsner Fndn Grants, 665
Chick and Sophie Major Memorial Duck Calling Contest Scholarships, 1103
Cornell Lab of Ornithology Mini-Grants, 1374
Illinois DNR Migratory Waterfowl Stamp Grants, 2498
Illinois DNR State Furbearer Grants, 2501
Illinois DNR State Pheasant Grants, 2502
Illinois DNR Wildlife Preservation Fund Large Project Grants, 2505
Illinois DNR Wildlife Preservation Fund Small Project Grants, 2506
Illinois DNR Wildlife Preservation Maintenance of Wildlife Rehabilitation Facilities Grants, 2507
Liz Claiborne and Art Ortenberg Fndn Grants, 2914

Lucy Downing Nisbet Charitable Grants, 2935
NFWF So Company Power of Flight Grants, 3394
NFWF Wildlife Links Grants, 3400

Military Personnel
Anne J. Caudal Fndn Grants, 475
Northrop Grumman Corp Grants, 3507

Military Sciences
Air Force Association Junior ROTC Grants, 215
Cord Fndn Grants, 1372
Fisher House Fndn Newman's Own Awards, 1833
MFRI Operation Diploma Small Grants for Indiana Family Readiness Groups, 3152
Northrop Grumman Corp Grants, 3507
USDD Cultural Resources Program Assistance Announcement Grants, 4862

Military Training
Florida BRAIVE Fund of Dade Community, 1846
Gulf Coast Community Operating Grants, 2176
Gulf Coast Fndn of Community Grants, 2177
Northrop Grumman Corp Grants, 3507
U.S. Army ROTC Scholarships, 4685

Mime
Illinois Arts Council Dance Grants, 2467
NHSCA Artist Residencies in Schools Grants, 3423
NYSCA Presenting: General Operating Support, 3609

Mining
Brainerd Fndn Grants, 831
Liz Claiborne and Art Ortenberg Fndn Grants, 2914
NW Fund for the Environment Grants, 3510

Mining Engineering
CONSOL Coal Group Grants, 1360

Ministry
Chapman Charitable Fndn Grants, 1033
Chapman Family Charitable Grants, 1034
HAF Hansen Family Trust Christian Endowment Grants, 2197
Lilly Endowment Clergy Renewal Program for Indiana Congregations, 2902

Minorities
Abbot and Dorothy H. Stevens Fndn Grants, 79
Abelard Fndn East Grants, 87
Abelard Fndn West Grants, 88
ACF Adoption Opportunities Project Grants, 113
Adolph Coors Fndn Grants, 171
Akonadi Fndn Anti-Racism Grants, 217
Alberto Culver Corp Contributions Grants, 343
Alex Stern Family Fndn Grants, 360
Alliant Energy Fndn Community Grants, 384
ALSAM Fndn Grants, 395
AmerUs Group Charitable Fndn, 455
Anheuser-Busch Fndn Grants, 470
ANLAF Int'l Fund for Sexual Minorities Grants, 471
Archer Daniels Midland Grants, 527
Arlington Community Fndn Grants, 564
Armstrong McDonald Grants, 565
Arthur and Sara Jo Kobacker, Alfred and Ida Kobacker Fndn Grants, 571
Avon Products Fndn Grants, 625
Ben & Jerry's Fndn Grants, 724
Benton Community Fndn Grants, 730
Blue River Community Fndn Grants, 801
Bodenwein Public Benevolent Fndn Grants, 806
Boston Fndn Grants, 819
Boston Globe Fndn Grants, 821
Boyd Gaming Corp Contributions Program, 825
Brown County Community Fndn Grants, 853
Butler Manufacturing Company Fndn Grants, 881
California Arts Council Arts and Accessibility Technical Assistance Grants, 894
California Arts Council Tech Assistance Grants, 898
Carnegie Corp of New York Grants, 940
Charles Delmar Fndn Grants, 1039

Chesapeake Bay Trust Outreach and Community Engagement Grants, 1073
Chicago Board of Trade Fndn Grants, 1079
Colgate-Palmolive Company Grants, 1202
Colorado Interstate Gas Grants, 1213
Community Fndn of Bartholomew County Heritage Grants, 1267
Community Fndn of Bartholomew County James A. Henderson Award for Fundraising, 1268
Community Fndn of Greater Fort Wayne - Community Endowment and Clarke Endowment Grants, 1285
Community Fndn of St. Joseph County African American Community Grants, 1312
Community in the Connecting AAPIs To Advocate and Lead Grants, 1333
ConocoPhillips Fndn Grants, 1354
ConocoPhillips Grants, 1355
Cralle Fndn Grants, 1394
Crossroads Fund Seed Grants, 1400
Cummins Fndn Grants, 1415
Daphne Seybolt Culpeper Memorial Fndn Grants, 1445
Dave Thomas Fndn for Adoption Grants, 1449
DHHS Health Centers Grants for Residents of Public Housing, 1533
DHHS Maternal and Child Health Grants, 1536
Dreyer's Fndn Large Grants, 1606
Edward W. and Stella C. Van Houten Grants, 1670
Edwin S. Webster Fndn Grants, 1671
Eugene M. Lang Fndn Grants, 1764
Eugene McDermott Fndn Grants, 1765
Farm Aid Grants, 1790
Farmers Insurance Corp Giving Grants, 1791
Fel-Pro Mecklenburger Fndn Grants, 1800
Florida Div of Cultural Affairs Underserved Cultural Community Development Grants, 1864
Ford Motor Company Grants, 1885
Frederick McDonald Grants, 1946
General Mills Fndn Celebrating Communities of Color Grants, 2002
General Service Fndn Human Rights and Economic Justice Grants, 2006
George A. and Grace L. Long Fndn Grants, 2008
George W. Brackenridge Fndn Grants, 2028
George W. Wells Fndn Grants, 2030
Georgia-Pacific Fndn Entrepreneurship Grants, 2033
Grassroots Exchange Grants, 2128
Grotto Fndn Project Grants, 2166
H.J. Heinz Company Fndn Grants, 2184
HAF Community Grants, 2193
Harold Brooks Fndn Grants, 2227
Health Fndn of Greater Indianapolis Grants, 2282
Helen Steiner Rice Fndn Grants, 2299
Home Ownership Part for Everyone Awards, 2349
Humanitas Fndn Grants, 2390
ING Fndn Grants, 2555
Iowa Arts Council Artists in Schools/Communities Residency Grants, 2571
Jackson Fndn Grants, 2613
Jacksonville Jaguars Fndn Grants, 2614
Jacob G. Schmidlapp Grants, 2616
James Ford Bell Fndn Grants, 2623
Janirve Fndn Grants, 2645
John Clarke Grants, 2689
John P. Murphy Fndn Grants, 2708
Joseph H. and Florence A. Roblee Fndn Grants, 2736
Joseph S. Stackpole Charitable Grants, 2741
Joyce Awards, 2746
Katharine Matthies Fndn Grants, 2788
Kroger Fndn Diversity Grants, 2842
LA84 Fndn Grants, 2847
Marin Community Successful Aging Grants, 3014
Marriott Int'l Corp Giving Grants, 3024
Montana Arts Council Cultural and Aesthetic Project Grants, 3209
MONY Fndn Grants, 3214
NAR HOPE Awards for Minority Owners, 3238
Nellie Mae Educ Fndn State Level Systems Change Grants, 3299
NHLBI Lymphatics in Health & Disease in Digestive, Cardiovascular and Pulmonary Systems, 3414

954 / Minorities

NHLBI Ruth L. Kirschstein National Research Service Awards for Individual Predoctoral Fellowships to Promote Diversity in Health-Related Research, 3419
NNEDVF/Altria Doors of Hope Program, 3452
North Dakota Council on the Arts Community Access Grants, 3494
Norton Fndn Grants, 3514
Open Meadows Fndn Grants, 3683
Oppenstein Brothers Fndn Grants, 3685
OSF Campaign for Black Male Achievement, 3703
PCA-PCD Organizational Short-Term Professional Development and Consulting Grants, 3769
PCA Arts Management Internship, 3773
PCA Arts Organizations & Grants for Dance, 3779
PCA Entry Track Arts Organizations and Program Grants for Dance, 3791
PCA Strategies for Success Grants - Advanced, 3804
PDF Community Organizing Grants, 3807
Playboy Fndn Grants, 3913
Portland General Electric Fndn Grants, 3937
Powell Fndn Grants, 3942
Prudential Fndn Educ Grants, 3977
Rhode Island Fndn Grants, 4073
Richard and Susan Smith Family Fndn Grants, 4078
Robert R. Meyer Fndn Grants, 4121
San Francisco Fndn Multicultural Fellowship, 4281
Scherman Fndn Grants, 4305
Sensient Technologies Fndn Grants, 4337
Shell Oil Company Fndn Grants, 4343
Sister Grants for Women's Organizations, 4371
Sony Corp of America Corp Philanthropy Grants, 4405
Sophia Romero Grants, 4406
Steelcase Fndn Grants, 4497
Texas Commission on the Arts Create-2 Grants, 4584
Textron Corp Contributions Grants, 4601
Thelma Braun and Bocklett Family Fndn Grants, 4603
Third Wave Fndn Lela Breitbart Grants, 4609
Third Wave Organizing & Advocacy Grants, 4610
Third Wave Fndn Reproductive Health and Justice Grants, 4611
UNCFSP TIEAD Internship, 4705
Union Bank, N.A. Fndn Grants, 4709
UPS Fndn Diversity Grants, 4729
USTA Multicultural Excellence Grants, 4876
USTA Multicultural Individual Player Grant for National Competition and Training, 4877
USTA Okechi Womeodu Scholar Athlete Grants, 4880
USTA Serves Dwight Mosley Scholarships, 4888
Verizon Fndn Delaware Grants, 4909
Verizon Fndn Great Lakes Region Grants, 4912
Virginia Fndn for Humanities Discr Grants, 4946
Virginia Fndn for the Humanities Open Grants, 4947
Vulcan Materials Company Fndn Grants, 4956
W. C. Griffith Fndn Grants, 4958
W.C. Griffith Fndn Grants, 4957
W.K. Kellogg Fndn Civic Engagement Grants, 4960
Westinghouse Charitable Giving Grants, 5028
WILD Fndn Grants, 5068
Wilson-Wood Fndn Grants, 5098
Winston-Salem Fndn Stokes County Grants, 5104

Minorities, Ethnic
ALA Diversity and Outreach Fair, 267
California Arts Council Tech Assistance Grants, 898
Charles Parker Trust for Public Music Grants, 1053
Kentucky Arts Council Access Assistance Grants, 2805
Maine Community Fndn People of Color Grants, 2985
National Endowment for Arts Commun Grants, 3260
Prudential Fndn Arts and Culture Grants, 3975
Robert R. Meyer Fndn Grants, 4121
TAC Touring Arts and Arts Access Grants, 4557

Minority Education
3M Fndn Community Giving Grants, 15
Air Products and Chemicals Grants, 216
Akonadi Fndn Anti-Racism Grants, 217
Akzo Nobel Chemicals Grants, 219
ALA Coretta Scott King Book Donation Grant, 261
Alcoa Fndn Grants, 350
Anheuser-Busch Fndn Grants, 470

APSA Minority Fellowships, 517
ARCO Fndn Educ Grants, 528
BBVA Compass Fndn Charitable Grants, 703
Beerman Fndn Grants, 717
California Arts Council Arts and Accessibility Technical Assistance Grants, 894
California Arts Council Tech Assistance Grants, 898
CE and S Fndn Grants, 985
Charlotte R. Schmidlapp Grants, 1058
Chiron Fndn Community Grants, 1111
CIGNA Fndn Grants, 1130
Citigroup Fndn Grants, 1139
Coca-Cola Fndn Grants, 1195
Colgate-Palmolive Company Grants, 1202
Cruise Industry Charitable Fndn Grants, 1404
DaimlerChrysler Corp Grants, 1432
Dept of Ed Magnet Schools Assistance Grants, 1509
Dynegy Fndn Grants, 1630
Edward W. and Stella C. Van Houten Grants, 1670
EMC Corp Grants, 1693
FMC Fndn Grants, 1876
Graco Fndn Grants, 2111
Grand Circle Fndn Associates Grants, 2112
HAF Community Grants, 2193
Head Start Replacement Grantee: Colorado, 2275
Int'l Paper Company Fndn Grants, 2568
Johnson & Johnson Corp Contributions Grants, 2718
Kroger Fndn Diversity Grants, 2842
Lloyd G. Balfour Fndn Attleboro-Specific Charities Grants, 2916
McCune Charitable Fndn Grants, 3077
Michael and Susan Dell Fndn Grants, 3158
Miller Brewing Corp Contributions Grants, 3180
Millipore Fndn Grants, 3182
NAA Fndn Diversity PowerMind Fellowships, 3232
NAA Fndn Minority Fellowships, 3233
NACC David Stevenson Fellowships, 3235
NACC William Diaz Fellowships, 3236
NAR HOPE Awards for Minority Owners, 3238
National Home Library Fndn Grants, 3276
National Urban Fellows Program, 3281
Nellie Mae Educ Fndn State Level Systems Change Grants, 3299
Northern Trust Company Corp Giving Program, 3504
Oracle Corp Contributions Grants, 3686
OSF Campaign for Black Male Achievement, 3703
Praxair Fndn Grants, 3944
RBC Dain Rauscher Fndn Grants, 4031
RGK Fndn Grants, 4072
Sprint Fndn Grants, 4463
Union Labor Health Fndn Community Grants, 4713
Viacom Fndn Grants (Formerly CBS Fndn), 4932
William J. Brace Charitable Trust, 5088
Xerox Fndn Grants, 5122

Minority Employment
Aid for Starving Children African American Indep Single Mother's Grants, 210
Akonadi Fndn Anti-Racism Grants, 217
Albert W. Rice Charitable Fndn Grants, 347
Charles H. Pearson Fndn Grants, 1045
George W. Wells Fndn Grants, 2030
GNOF New Orleans Works Grants, 2088
Illinois DCEO Employer Training Investment Grants - Competitive Component, 2491
Illinois DCEO Employer Training Investment Grants - Incentive Component, 2492
Illinois DCEO Employer Training Investment Program Multi-Company Training Grants, 2493
Illinois DCEO Employer Training Investment Program Single Company Training Grants, 2494
Illinois DCEO Large Business Dev Grants, 2495
M.D. Anderson Fndn Grants, 2952
Mabel Louise Riley Fndn Family Strengthening Small Grants, 2958
Marriott Int'l Corp Giving Grants, 3024
Meyer Fndn Economic Security Grants, 3141
Meyer Fndn Educ Grants, 3142
OSF Campaign for Black Male Achievement, 3703
Textron Corp Contributions Grants, 4601

USAID Albania Critical Economic Growth Areas Grants, 4740
USAID Economic Prospectsfor Armenia-Turkey Normalization Grants, 4750

Minority Health
Aetna Fndn Racial and Ethnic Health Care Equity Grants, 186
Aid for Starving Children Emergency Grants, 211
Akonadi Fndn Anti-Racism Grants, 217
Anheuser-Busch Fndn Grants, 470
BCBSNC Fndn Grants, 712
BCBS of Massachusetts Fndn Grants, 713
California Endowment Innovative Ideas Challenge Grants, 904
Cigna Civic Affairs Sponsorships, 1129
Commonwealth Fund Harkness Fellowships in Health Care Policy and Practice, 1242
Connecticut Health Fndn Health Init Grants, 1351
Fndns of E Chicago Health Grants, 1910
Frank W. and Carl S. Adams Grants, 1937
GNOF IMPACT Grants for Health and Human Services, 2080
Henry J. Kaiser Family Fndn Grants, 2310
Ms. Fndn for Women Health Grants, 3225
OSF Campaign for Black Male Achievement, 3703
Portland General Electric Fndn Grants, 3937
Seattle Fndn Health and Wellness Grants, 4328
Union Labor Health Fndn Community Grants, 4713

Minority Schools
Akonadi Fndn Anti-Racism Grants, 217
Alcoa Fndn Grants, 350
Allyn Fndn Grants, 392
California Arts Council Tech Assistance Grants, 898
Coca-Cola Fndn Grants, 1195
DHHS Maternal and Child Health Grants, 1536
Head Start Replacement Grantee: Florida, 2276
Head Start Replacement Grantee: West Virginia, 2277
Meyer Fndn Educ Grants, 3142
National Home Library Fndn Grants, 3276
Nellie Mae Educ Fndn District-Level Grants, 3297
OSF Campaign for Black Male Achievement, 3703
Procter and Gamble Grants, 3967
VSA/Metlife Connect All Grants, 4953
W.K. Kellogg Fndn Racial Equity Grants, 4962

Minority/Woman-Owned Business
Akonadi Fndn Anti-Racism Grants, 217
Amber Grants, 413
Dining for Women Grants, 1548
Eileen Fisher Women-Owned Business Grants, 1677
ExxonMobil Fndn Women's Economic Opportunity Grants, 1778
Fitzpatrick and Francis Family Business Continuity Fndn Grants, 1837
ING Fndn Grants, 2555
New Jersey Center for Hispanic Policy, Research and Development Entrepreneurship Grants, 3326
New Mexico Women's Fndn Grants, 3335
UPS Fndn Diversity Grants, 4729

Multiculturalism
ALA Supporting Diversity Stipend, 333
Laura Jane Musser Intercultural Harmony Grants, 2862
Minnesota State Arts Board Cultural Community Partnership Grants, 3188
NYSCA Special Arts Services: Instruction and Training Grants, 3616
NYSCA State and Local Partnerships: General Program Support Grants, 3620

Multidisciplinary Arts
Arkansas Arts Council AIE After School/Summer Residency Grants, 551
Arkansas Arts Council AIE In-School Residency, 553
Florida Div of Cultural Affairs General Program Support Grants, 1854
National Endowment for the Arts Presenting Grants: Art Works, 3268

SUBJECT INDEX

Museums / 955

NJSCA Arts Project Support, 3446
NJSCA Financial and Instal Stabilization Grants, 3447
NJSCA General Program Support Grants, 3449
NYSCA Architecture, Planning, and Design: General Program Support Grants, 3574
NYSCA Electronic Media and Film: General Operating Support, 3590
NYSCA Electronic Media and Film: Workspace Grants, 3593
NYSCA Folk Arts: Exhibitions Grants, 3594
NYSCA Presenting: Services to the Field Grants, 3612
NYSCA Special Art Services Project Support, 3613
NYSCA State and Local Partnerships: General Program Support Grants, 3620
NYSCA State and Local Partnerships: Services to the Field Grants, 3621
NYSCA State and Local Partnerships: Workshops Grants, 3622
NYSCA Visual Arts: General Operating Support, 3628
NYSCA Visual Arts: Workspace Facilities Grants, 3631
PCA-PCD Professional Development for Individual Artists Grants, 3770
PCA Arts in Educ Residencies, 3772
PCA Arts Organizations and Arts Programs Grants for Local Arts, 3782
PCA Busing Grants, 3786
PCA Entry Track Arts Organizations and Program Grants for Local Arts, 3794
PCA Pennsylvania Partners in the Arts Program Stream Grants, 3801
PCA Pennsylvania Partners in the Arts Project Stream Grants, 3802
PCA Professional Development Grants, 3803
PCA Strategies for Success Grants - Basic Level, 3805
PCA Strategies for Success Grants - Intermediate, 3806
PennPAT Artist Technical Assistance Grants, 3811
PennPAT Strategic Opportunity Grants, 3815
Rasmuson Fndn Individual Artists Awards, 4022
Wallace Alexander Gerbode Fndn Special Award Grants, 4975

Multiple Sclerosis
Austin S. Nelson Fndn Grants, 617
Henry and Ruth Blaustein Rosenberg Grants, 2306
Pfizer Healthcare Charitable Contributions, 3863
Seattle Fndn Medical Funds Grants, 4329

Muscular Dystrophy
Doris and Victor Day Fndn Grants, 1582

Museum Education
3 Dog Garage Museum Tours, 8
Colonel Stanley R. McNeil Fndn Grants, 1210
Florida Div of Cultural Affairs Museum Grants, 1858
George J. and Effie L. Seay Fndn Grants, 2024
McCune Charitable Fndn Grants, 3077
NSTA Distinguished Informal Science Ed Award, 3531
NYSCA Museum General Operating Support, 3602
NYSCA Museum Program Support Grants, 3603
NYSCA Museum: Project Support Grants, 3604

Museums
1st Source Fndn Grants, 3
3M Company Arts and Culture Grants, 12
3M Fndn Community Giving Grants, 15
Abbot and Dorothy H. Stevens Fndn Grants, 79
Abel and Sophia Sheng Charitable Fndn Grants, 86
Air Products and Chemicals Grants, 216
Akron Community Fndn Arts & Culture Grants, 218
Albert and Bessie Mae Kronkosky Charitable Fndn Grants, 339
Albuquerque Community Fndn Grants, 348
Altria Group Arts and Culture Grants, 399
American Express Charitable Grants, 429
Amon G. Carter Fndn Grants, 458
Andrew Family Fndn Grants, 462
Andy Warhol Fndn for the Visual Arts Grants, 464
Ann L. & Carol Green Rhodes Charitable Grants, 483
Aratani Fndn Grants, 523
Arthur and Rochelle Belfer Fndn Grants, 570

Arthur Ashley Williams Fndn Grants, 572
ArvinMeritor Fndn Arts and Culture Grants, 582
Auburn Fndn Grants, 611
Back Home Again Fndn Grants, 633
Ball Brothers Fndn General Grants, 637
Barra Fndn Project Grants, 674
Batchelor Fndn Grants, 679
Bay and Paul Fndns, Inc Grants, 692
Bemis Company Fndn Grants, 723
Ben B. Cheney Fndn Grants, 725
Bender Fndn Grants, 726
Berrien Community Fndn Grants, 744
Bertha Russ Lytel Fndn Grants, 745
Booth-Bricker Grants, 815
Burlington Industries Fndn Grants, 865
Burlington Northern Santa Fe Fndn Grants, 866
Caleb C. and Julia W. Dula Ed and Charitable Fndn Grants, 893
Cape Branch Fndn Grants, 919
Carl Gellert and Celia Berta Gellert Fndn Grants, 930
Carylon Fndn Grants, 949
Ceil & Michael E. Pulitzer Fndn Grants, 987
Cessna Fndn Grants, 1000
Chamberlain Fndn Grants, 1027
Chapman Family Charitable Grants, 1034
Charles M. Bair Family Grants, 1051
Chicago Board of Trade Fndn Grants, 1079
Christensen Fund Regional Grants, 1112
Cleveland-Cliffs Fndn Grants, 1165
Cockrell Fndn Grants, 1196
Collins C. Diboll Private Fndn Grants, 1208
Colonel Stanley R. McNeil Fndn Grants, 1210
Colorado Springs Community Grants, 1215
Community Fndn Alliance City of Evansville Endowment Grants, 1246
Community Fndn of SE Connecticut Grants, 1309
Compton Fndn Grants, 1338
Connecticut Community Fndn Grants, 1350
Constantin Fndn Grants, 1362
Conwood Charitable Grants, 1366
Cooper Industries Fndn Grants, 1370
Corning Fndn Cultural Grants, 1376
Coughlin-Saunders Fndn Grants, 1377
Cowles Charitable Grants, 1392
Cralle Fndn Grants, 1394
Crystelle Waggoner Charitable Grants, 1405
David Geffen Fndn Grants, 1452
Daywood Fndn Grants, 1465
DeRoy Testamentary Fndn Grants, 1518
Donald W. Reynolds Fndn Children's Discovery Init Grants, 1576
Donald W. Reynolds Fndn Special Grants, 1577
Doris and Victor Day Fndn Grants, 1582
Dr. Scholl Fndn Grants, 1602
Duluth-Superior Area Community Fndn Grants, 1620
E. Rhodes and Leona B. Carpenter Fndn Grants, 1640
Edith and Francis Mulhall Achilles Grants, 1657
Edward S. Moore Fndn Grants, 1668
Ellen Abbott Gilman Grants, 1685
Eugene McDermott Fndn Grants, 1765
Fieldstone Fndn Grants, 1808
FirstEnergy Fndn Community Grants, 1819
Florida Div of Cultural Affairs General Program Support Grants, 1854
Florida Div of Cultural Affairs Museum Grants, 1858
George and Ruth Bradford Fndn Grants, 2010
George Fndn Grants, 2018
George I. Alden Grants, 2023
George J. and Effie L. Seay Fndn Grants, 2024
George W. Codrington Charitable Grants, 2029
Georgia Council for the Arts Partner Grants for Organizations, 2035
Greater Green Bay Community Fndn Grants, 2135
Greater Worcester Comm Discretionary Grants, 2140
Greenspun Family Fndn Grants, 2156
H. Leslie Hoffman & Elaine Hoffman Grants, 2185
Hall Family Fndn Grants, 2210
Harold and Arlene Schnitzer CARE Grants, 2226
Harold R. Bechtel Charitable Remainder Grants, 2229
High Meadow Fndn Grants, 2321

Hillman Fndn Grants, 2327
Hudson Webber Fndn Grants, 2383
Huffy Fndn Grants, 2384
Hugh J. Andersen Fndn Grants, 2385
Huie-Dellmon Grants, 2386
Idaho Power Company Corp Contributions, 2433
Illinois Arts Council Visual Arts Grants, 2478
IMLS 21st Century Museum Pro Grants, 2512
IMLS American Heritage Preservation Grants, 2513
IMLS National Leadership Grants, 2515
IMLS Nat Medal for Museum & Library Service, 2516
IMLS Native Hawaiian Library Services Grants, 2519
IMLS Partnership for a Nation of Learners Community Collaboration Grants, 2520
James F. and Marion L. Miller Fndn Grants, 2622
Jerry L. and Barbara J. Burris Fndn Grants, 2669
Jessie Ball Dupont Grants, 2671
John H. and Wilhelmina D. Harland Charitable Fndn Grants, 2698
Joseph Alexander Fndn Grants, 2734
JP Morgan Chase Arts and Culture Grants, 2752
Kenneth T. and Eileen L. Norris Fndn Grants, 2802
Kirkpatrick Fndn Grants, 2827
Lee and Ramona Bass Fndn Grants, 2871
Lettie Pate Evans Fndn Grants, 2887
Lubbock Area Fndn Grants, 2931
Mabel Y. Hughes Charitable Grants, 2960
MacArthur Fndn Chicago Arts and Culture General Operations Grants, 2961
Marcia and Otto Koehler Fndn Grants, 3000
Margaret L. Wendt Fndn Grants, 3004
Marie H. Bechtel Charitable Grants, 3007
Marin Community Fndn Stinson Bolinas Community Grants, 3013
Maurice Amado Fndn Grants, 3063
Maurice J. Masserini Charitable Grants, 3064
Maxon Charitable Fndn Grants, 3068
McConnell Fndn Grants, 3076
McLean Contributionship Grants, 3088
Mericos Fndn Grants, 3121
Merkel Family Fndn Grants, 3123
Mildred V. Horn Fndn Grants, 3176
Morris and Gwendolyn Cafritz Fndn Grants, 3218
Motorola Fndn Grants, 3221
National Endowment for the Arts - National Arts and Humanities Youth Program Awards, 3255
National Endowment for Arts Museum Grants, 3265
National Endowment for the Arts Presenting Grants: Art Works, 3268
Nicholas H. Noyes Jr. Memorial Fndn Grants, 3434
NYSCA Museum General Operating Support, 3602
NYSCA Museum Program Support Grants, 3603
OceanFirst Fndn Grants, 3636
Oppenstein Brothers Fndn Grants, 3685
Parker Fndn (California) Grants, 3736
Parkersburg Area Comm Fndn Action Grants, 3738
PCA Art Organizations and Art Programs Grants for Presenting Organizations, 3771
PCA Arts Organizations and Arts Programs Grants for Art Museums, 3775
PCA Entry Track Arts Organizations and Program Grants for Art Museums, 3787
PCA Entry Track Arts Organizations and Program Grants for Presenting Organizations, 3796
Perkins Charitable Fndn Grants, 3823
Piedmont Natural Gas Corp and Charitable Contributions, 3883
PMI Fndn Grants, 3918
Price Family Charitable Grants, 3952
R.C. Baker Fndn Grants, 3999
Reinberger Fndn Grants, 4052
Richard and Susan Smith Family Fndn Grants, 4078
Richard H. Driehaus Fndn Grants, 4084
Richard H. Driehaus Fndn MacArthur Fund for Arts and Culture, 4085
Robert W. Woodruff Fndn Grants, 4124
S. Spencer Scott Grants, 4202
Samuel S. Johnson Fndn Grants, 4239
Schlessman Family Fndn Grants, 4307
Schurz Communications Fndn Grants, 4312

956 / Museums

Seattle Fndn C. Keith Birkenfeld Grants, 4323
Sid W. Richardson Fndn Grants, 4350
Sioux Falls Area Community Grants, 4364
Sioux Falls Area Community Fndn Spot Grants, 4366
Sprint Fndn Grants, 4463
Strake Fndn Grants, 4511
Stranahan Fndn Grants, 4512
Sunderland Fndn Grants, 4527
Susan Vaughan Fndn Grants, 4537
Taylor S. Abernathy and Patti Harding Abernathy Charitable Grants, 4564
Temple-Inland Fndn Grants, 4576
Textron Corp Contributions Grants, 4601
Thelma Doelger Charitable Grants, 4604
Thomas Sill Fndn Grants, 4619
Thomas W. Briggs Fndn Grants, 4621
Tri-State Community Twenty-first Century Endowment Grants, 4666
Union Bank, N.A. Fndn Grants, 4709
Union Pacific Fndn Community and Civic Grants, 4714
Vermont Community Fndn Grants, 4929
Virginia Fndn for Humanities Discr Grants, 4946
Virginia Fndn for the Humanities Open Grants, 4947
VSA/Metlife Connect All Grants, 4953
W. C. Griffith Fndn Grants, 4958
W.C. Griffith Fndn Grants, 4957
Wabash River Heritage Corridor Grants, 4970
Wayne County Fndn Vigran Family Grants, 5004
Wayne County Fndn Grants, 5005
Weatherwax Fndn Grants, 5014
Wege Fndn Grants, 5017
West Virginia Comm on the Arts Visual Grants, 5051
Widgeon Point Charitable Fndn Grants, 5064
William B. Dietrich Fndn Grants, 5075
William B. Stokely Jr. Fndn Grants, 5076
William G. Gilmore Fndn Grants, 5082

Music
A.J. Fletcher Fndn Grants, 41
Adams-Mastrovich Family Fndn Grants, 146
Alabama State Council on the Arts Collaborative Ventures Grants, 235
Alabama State Council on the Arts Community Arts Collaborative Ventures Grants, 236
Alabama State Council on the Arts Community Arts Operating Support Grants, 237
Alabama State Council on the Arts Community Arts Presenting Grants, 238
Alabama State Council on the Arts Community Arts Program Development Grants, 239
Alabama State Council on the Arts Community Planning & Design Grants, 241
Alabama State Council on the Arts in Educ Partnership Grants, 242
Alabama State Council on the Arts Multi-Discipline and Festival Grants, 243
Alabama State Council Arts Presenting Grants, 245
Alabama State Council on the Arts Program Development Grants, 246
Alabama State Council on the Arts Project Assistance Grants, 247
Alabama State Council on the Arts Projects of Individual Artists Grants, 248
Alaska State Council on the Arts Operating Support Grants, 328
Arkansas Arts Council AIE After School/Summer Residency Grants, 551
Arkansas Arts Council AIE In-School Residency, 553
Arts Midwest Performing Arts Grants, 579
Auburn Fndn Grants, 611
Barberton Community Fndn Grants, 666
Berks County Community Fndn Grants, 734
Blanche and Irving Laurie Fndn Grants, 784
Canada-U.S. Fulbright Mid-Career Grants, 917
Charles Parker Trust for Public Music Grants, 1053
Chicago Tribune Fndn Grants for Cultural Organizations, 1101
CICF F.R. Hensel Grant for Fine Arts, Music, and Educ, 1121
City of Oakland Cultural Arts Dept Grants, 1142

Clarence E. Heller Charitable Fndn Grants, 1150
Clark Charitable Grants, 1155
Community Fndn of Bloomington and Monroe County Grants, 1271
Community Fndn of Mount Vernon and Knox County Grants, 1301
Community Fndn of Sarasota County Grants, 1306
Conseil des arts de Montreal Touring Grants, 1358
Corning Fndn Cultural Grants, 1376
Covenant to Care for Children Grants, 1389
Creative Work Grants, 1396
Cudd Fndn Grants, 1410
DAAD Research Grants for Doctoral Candidates and Young Academics and Scientists, 1427
Dept of Ed Recreational Services for Individuals with Disabilities, 1512
Durfee Fndn Sabbatical Grants, 1625
Edward R. Godfrey Fndn Grants, 1667
Edwin W. and Catherine M. Davis Fndn Grants, 1672
Ensworth Charitable Fndn Grants, 1710
FirstEnergy Fndn Community Grants, 1819
Florida Div of Cultural Affairs General Program Support Grants, 1854
Florida Div of Cultural Affairs Multidisciplinary Grants, 1857
Florida Div of Cultural Affairs Music Grants, 1859
Fndn NW Grants, 1906
Frist Fndn Grants, 1964
Georgia Council for the Arts Partner Grants for Service Organizations, 2036
Gibson Fndn Grants, 2052
Grand Rapids Area Community Fndn Grants, 2114
Grand Rapids Area Community Fndn Nashwauk Area Endowment Grants, 2115
Greater Milwaukee Fndn Grants, 2137
Hahl Proctor Charitable Grants, 2208
Harold R. Bechtel Charitable Remainder Grants, 2229
High Meadow Fndn Grants, 2321
Hyde Family Fndns Grants, 2414
I.A. O'Shaughnessy Fndn Grants, 2416
Idaho Community Fndn Eastern Region Competitive Grants, 2432
Illinois Arts Council Media Arts Grants, 2472
Illinois Arts Council Music Grants, 2474
Iowa Arts Council Artists in Schools/Communities Residency Grants, 2571
Jerome Fndn Grants, 2667
Jerome Fndn Travel and Study Grants, 2668
John Ben Snow Grants, 2687
John Reynolds and Eleanor B. Allen Charitable Fndn Grants, 2710
Joyce Awards, 2746
Kansas Arts Commission Artist Fellowships, 2776
Katharine Matthies Fndn Grants, 2788
Laura Jane Musser Rural Arts Grants, 2863
Leon and Thea Koerner Fndn Grants, 2883
Long Island Community Fndn Grants, 2920
M. Bastian Family Fndn Grants, 2951
MacArthur Fndn Chicago Arts and Culture General Operations Grants, 2961
Margaret T. Morris Fndn Grants, 3005
Mary & Walter Frear Eleemosynary Grants, 3035
Mary Duke Biddle Fndn Grants, 3036
Massachusetts Cultural Adams Arts Grants, 3052
Maurice Amado Fndn Grants, 3063
Maurice J. Masserini Charitable Grants, 3064
National Endowment for the Arts - National Arts and Humanities Youth Program Awards, 3255
National Endowment for Arts Music Grants, 3266
National Endowment for the Arts Presenting Grants: Art Works, 3268
NHSCA Artist Residencies in Schools Grants, 3423
NHSCA Youth Arts Project Grants: For Extended Arts Learning, 3430
NJSCA Arts Project Support, 3446
NJSCA Financial and Instal Stabilization Grants, 3447
NJSCA General Program Support Grants, 3449
North Carolina Arts Council Gen Support, 3477
NYFA Strategic Opportunity Stipends, 3566
NYSCA Music Community Schools Grants, 3605

SUBJECT INDEX

NYSCA Music Gen Operating Support Grants, 3606
NYSCA Music Gen Program Support Grants, 3607
NYSCA Music: New Music Facilities, 3608
NYSCA Presenting: General Operating Support, 3609
NYSCA Special Art Services Project Support, 3613
NYSCA Special Arts Services: Professional Performances Grants, 3617
Ontario Arts Council Integrated Arts Grants, 3678
Ontario Arts Council Orchestras Grants, 3679
Ontario Arts Council Presenter/Producer Grants, 3680
PAS Internship, 3742
PAS PASIC Scholarships, 3744
Paul and Edith Babson Fndn Grants, 3755
PCA-PCD Professional Development for Individual Artists Grants, 3770
PCA Arts in Educ Residencies, 3772
PCA Arts Organizations Grants for Music, 3774
PCA Entry Track Arts Organizations and Program Grants for Music, 3795
PCA Professional Development Grants, 3803
PCA Strategies for Success Grants - Advanced, 3804
PCA Strategies for Success Grants - Basic Level, 3805
PCA Strategies for Success Grants - Intermediate, 3806
PennPAT Artist Technical Assistance Grants, 3811
PennPAT Strategic Opportunity Grants, 3815
Philip L. Graham Grants, 3876
PMP Professional Development Grants, 3919
PMP Project Grants, 3920
Procter and Gamble Grants, 3967
Richard and Caroline T. Gwathmey Grants, 4075
Richard D. Bass Fndn Grants, 4079
Rollin M. Gerstacker Fndn Grants, 4146
Ruth Mott Fndn Grants, 4180
San Francisco Fndn Fund for Artists Award for Composers and Music Ensembles, 4271
Seattle Fndn C. Keith Birkenfeld Grants, 4323
Sosland Fndn Grants, 4408
South Carolina Arts Commission American Masterpieces in South Carolina Grants, 4413
South Carolina Arts Commission Fellowships, 4415
T. James Kavanagh Fndn Grants, 4545
TAC Arts Access Grant, 4549
Texas Commission on the Arts Cultural Connections- Visual & Media Arts Touring Exhibits Grants, 4589
Thelma Braun and Bocklett Family Fndn Grants, 4603
Union Square Arts Award, 4716
W.C. Griffith Fndn Grants, 4957
Walt Disney Company Fndn Grants, 4981
Whiting Fndn Grants, 5059
William T. Sloper Trust for Andres J. Sloper Musical Grants, 5097
Young Family Fndn Grants, 5127

Music Appreciation
Charles Parker Trust for Public Music Grants, 1053
Edward R. Godfrey Fndn Grants, 1667
Florida Div of Cultural Affairs Music Grants, 1859
Frank and Lydia Bergen Fndn Grants, 1925
John Reynolds and Eleanor B. Allen Charitable Fndn Grants, 2710
National Endowment for Arts Music Grants, 3266
National Endowment for Arts Opera Grants, 3267
NYSCA Music Gen Operating Support Grants, 3606
NYSCA Music Gen Program Support Grants, 3607
NYSCA Music: New Music Facilities, 3608
Paul E. and Klare N. Reinhold Fndn Grants, 3758
Progress Energy Fndn Economic Vitality Grants, 3969
Tri-State Community Twenty-first Century Endowment Grants, 4666
William T. Sloper Trust for Andres J. Sloper Musical Grants, 5097

Music Composition
A.J. Fletcher Fndn Grants, 41
Aaron Copland Fund for Music Recording Program, 71
Bush Fndn Arts & Humanities Grants: Short-Term Organizational Support, 873
Emma A. Sheafer Charitable Grants, 1699
Florida Div of Cultural Affairs Music Grants, 1859
Kentucky Arts Council Al Smith Fellowship, 2806

SUBJECT INDEX

Mockingbird Fndn Grants, 3196
National Endowment for Arts Music Grants, 3266
North Carolina Arts Cncl New Realities Grants, 3478
NYFA Gregory Millard Fellowships, 3565
NYSCA Music Gen Operating Support Grants, 3606
NYSCA Music Gen Program Support Grants, 3607
NYSCA Music: New Music Facilities, 3608
PCA-PCD Professional Development for Individual Artists Grants, 3770
PCA Strategies for Success Grants - Advanced, 3804
PCA Strategies for Success Grants - Basic Level, 3805
PCA Strategies for Success Grants - Intermediate, 3806
San Francisco Fndn Fund for Artists Award for Composers and Music Ensembles, 4271
Seattle Fndn C. Keith Birkenfeld Grants, 4323
Wallace Alexander Gerbode Fndn Special Award Grants, 4975

Music Conducting
Leon and Thea Koerner Fndn Grants, 2883
National Endowment for Arts Music Grants, 3266

Music Education
Cemala Fndn Grants, 988
Clarence E. Heller Charitable Fndn Grants, 1150
Crescent Porter Hale Fndn Grants, 1398
Deborah Munroe Noonan Grants, 1475
Florida Div of Cultural Affairs Music Grants, 1859
Frank and Lydia Bergen Fndn Grants, 1925
George A. and Grace L. Long Fndn Grants, 2008
Gibson Fndn Grants, 2052
Grand Rapids Area Community Fndn Grants, 2114
Grand Rapids Area Community Fndn Nashwauk Area Endowment Grants, 2115
Heineman Fndn for Research, Educ, Charitable and Scientific Purposes, 2290
Mockingbird Fndn Grants, 3196
National Endowment for Arts Music Grants, 3266
National Endowment for Arts Opera Grants, 3267
NYSCA Music Community Schools Grants, 3605
NYSCA Music Gen Operating Support Grants, 3606
NYSCA Music Gen Program Support Grants, 3607
NYSCA Music: New Music Facilities, 3608
Paul E. and Klare N. Reinhold Fndn Grants, 3758
Philip L. Graham Grants, 3876
Piper Trust Arts and Culture Grants, 3900
Portland General Electric Fndn Grants, 3937
Southbury Community Trust Fund, 4409
Teaching Tolerance Grants, 4567
Texas Commission on the Arts Arts in Educ Team Building/Texas Music Project Grants, 4580

Music History
ALA Coretta Scott King Book Awards, 260
National Endowment for Arts Music Grants, 3266
Richard and Caroline T. Gwathmey Grants, 4075
South Carolina Arts Commission American Masterpieces in South Carolina Grants, 4413

Music Recording
Aaron Copland Fund for Music Recording Program, 71
National Endowment for Arts Opera Grants, 3267
NYSCA Music Gen Operating Support Grants, 3606
NYSCA Music Gen Program Support Grants, 3607
NYSCA Music: New Music Facilities, 3608

Music Video Industry
National Endowment for Arts Music Grants, 3266
PAS Internship, 3742

Music, Composition
Florida Div of Cultural Affairs Music Grants, 1859
Minnesota State Arts Board Cultural Community Partnership Grants, 3188
NYSCA Music Gen Operating Support Grants, 3606
NYSCA Music Gen Program Support Grants, 3607
PCA Professional Development Grants, 3803

Music, Experimental
Arts Midwest Performing Arts Grants, 579
Conseil des arts de Montreal Diversity Award, 1357
Minnesota State Arts Board Cultural Community Partnership Grants, 3188
National Endowment for Arts Media Grants, 3264
National Endowment for Arts Music Grants, 3266
National Endowment for Arts Opera Grants, 3267
National Endowment for the Arts Presenting Grants: Art Works, 3268
National Endowment for Arts Theater Grants, 3269
NYSCA Music Community Schools Grants, 3605
NYSCA Music Gen Program Support Grants, 3607

Music, Instrumental
ACMP Fndn Community Music Grants, 130
Conseil des arts de Montreal Diversity Award, 1357
Creative Work Grants, 1396
Frank and Lydia Bergen Fndn Grants, 1925
Mockingbird Fndn Grants, 3196
NYSCA Music Gen Operating Support Grants, 3606
NYSCA Music Gen Program Support Grants, 3607
PAS PASIC Scholarships, 3744
William T. Sloper Trust for Andres J. Sloper Musical Grants, 5097

Music, Vocal
A.J. Fletcher Fndn Grants, 41
ACMP Fndn Community Music Grants, 130
Bonfils-Stanton Fndn Grants, 814
Community Fndn of Louisville Grants, 1299
Creative Work Grants, 1396
Florida Div of Cultural Affairs Music Grants, 1859
Illinois Arts Council Music Grants, 2474
Mockingbird Fndn Grants, 3196
NYSCA Music Community Schools Grants, 3605
NYSCA Music Gen Operating Support Grants, 3606
Pasadena Fndn Average Grants, 3741
Peyton Anderson Fndn Grants, 3862
San Francisco Fndn Fund for Artists Award for Composers and Music Ensembles, 4271
South Carolina Arts Commission American Masterpieces in South Carolina Grants, 4413
William T. Sloper Trust for Andres J. Sloper Musical Grants, 5097

Musical Instruments
Covenant to Care for Children Grants, 1389
Frank and Lydia Bergen Fndn Grants, 1925
Gibson Fndn Grants, 2052
John Reynolds and Eleanor B. Allen Charitable Fndn Grants, 2710
PAS Internship, 3742
Philip L. Graham Grants, 3876

Musicians in Residence
Arkansas Arts Council AIE After School/Summer Residency Grants, 551
Arkansas Arts Council AIE In-School Residency, 553
CDECD Arts Catalyze Placemaking in Every Community Grants, 977
CDECD Arts Catalyze Placemaking Leadership Grants, 978
CDECD Arts Catalyze Placemaking Sustaining Relevance Grants, 979
Frank and Lydia Bergen Fndn Grants, 1925
Minnesota State Arts Board Cultural Community Partnership Grants, 3188
National Endowment for Arts Music Grants, 3266
National Endowment for Arts Opera Grants, 3267
National Endowment for the Arts Presenting Grants: Art Works, 3268
National Endowment for Arts Theater Grants, 3269
NYSCA Music Community Schools Grants, 3605
NYSCA Music Gen Operating Support Grants, 3606
NYSCA Music Gen Program Support Grants, 3607
NYSCA Music: New Music Facilities, 3608
TAC Arts Access Grant, 4549
TAC Arts Build Communities Grants, 4551
TAC Arts Grants, 4554
TAC Rural Arts Project Support Grants, 4555

Musicology/Music Theory
Florida Div of Cultural Affairs Music Grants, 1859
North Carolina Arts Council Folklife Internship, 3467

National Disease Organizations
Alcatel-Lucent Technologies Fndn Grants, 349
Archer Daniels Midland Fndn Grants, 527
Lockheed Martin Philanthropic Grants, 2918

National Planning/Policy
J.M. Kaplan Fund Migrations Grants, 2602
National Endowment for the Arts - National Partnership Agreement Grants, 3256
Smith Richardson Fndn Domestic Public Research Fellowship, 4386

National Security
Carnegie Corp of New York Grants, 940
DHS ARRA Port Security Grants, 1543
DHS ARRA Transit Security Grants, 1544
DHS FY 2009 Transit Security Grants, 1545
Florida BRAIVE Fund of Dade Community, 1846
Gulf Coast Community Operating Grants, 2176
Gulf Coast Fndn of Community Grants, 2177
Henry M. Jackson Fndn Grants, 2311
RAND Corp Graduate Summer Associateships, 4018
TSA Advanced Surveillance Grants, 4674

Native American Education
AMERIND Community Service Project Grants, 453
Burlington Northern Santa Fe Fndn Grants, 866
Dorothea Haus Ross Fndn Grants, 1587
EPA Tribal Support for the National Environmental Information Exchange Network, 1742
First People's Fund Community Spirit Awards, 1825
General Motors Fndn Grants Support Program, 2004
HAF Community Grants, 2193
HAF Community Partnerships with Native Artists Grants, 2194
HAF Native Cultures Grants, 2201
John R. Oishei Fndn Grants, 2709
NACC David Stevenson Fellowships, 3235
NACC William Diaz Fellowships, 3236
Target Corp Local Store Grants, 4561
U.S. Department of Educ Rehabilitation Training-- Rehabilitation Continuing Educ Programs--Institute on Rehabilitation Issues, 4700
USDC Business Center - American Indian and Alaska Native Grants, 4849

Native American Languages
First People's Fund Community Spirit Awards, 1825
HAF Native Cultures Grants, 2201
U.S. Department of Educ Native Hawaiian Educ Grants, 4694

Native American Studies
Bay and Paul Fndns, Inc Grants, 692
First People's Fund Community Spirit Awards, 1825
HAF Community Partnerships with Native Artists Grants, 2194
HAF Native Cultures Grants, 2201

Native Americans
ACF Native American Environmental Regulatory Enhancement Grants, 122
Administration on Aging Senior Medicare Patrol Project Grants, 166
Alaska State Council on the Arts Operating Support Grants, 328
AMERIND Community Service Project Grants, 453
AMERIND Poster Contest, 454
California Arts Council Arts and Accessibility Technical Assistance Grants, 894
California Arts Council Public Value Grants, 895
Charles Delmar Fndn Grants, 1039
CNCS AmeriCorps State and National Grants, 1182
DHHS ARRA Strengthening Communities Fund - State, Local, and Tribal Government Capacity Building Grants, 1528

958 / Native Americans

DHHS Emergency Med Services for Children, 1531
DHHS Maternal and Child Health Grants, 1536
DOJ Children's Justice Act Partnership for Indian Communities, 1555
EPA Environmental Justice Small Grants, 1732
EPA State Indoor Radon Grants, 1738
EPA Tribal Support for the National Environmental Information Exchange Network, 1742
First People's Fund Community Spirit Awards, 1825
Four Times Fndn Grants, 1914
GNOF Bayou Communities Grants, 2069
Grotto Fndn Project Grants, 2166
HAF Community Partnerships with Native Artists Grants, 2194
HAF Native Cultures Grants, 2201
Honor the Earth Grants, 2361
IMLS Native Am Library Services Basic Grants, 2517
IMLS Native American Library Services Enhancement Grants, 2518
IMLS Native Hawaiian Library Services Grants, 2519
Kansas Arts Commission Artist Fellowships, 2776
Lotus 88 Fndn for Women and Children Grants, 2921
Morris K. Udall and Stewart L. Udall Fndn Native American Congressional Internships, 3220
National Endowment for the Arts - Grants for Arts Projects: Challenge America Fast-Track, 3254
North Carolina Arts Council Outreach Grants, 3479
NYSCA Special Arts Services: General Operating Support Grants, 3614
Percy B. Ferebee Endowment Grants, 3820
Saint Paul Fndn SpectrumGrants, 4222
Sioux Falls Area Community Fndn Field-of-Interest and Donor-Advised Grants, 4365
Susan A. & Donald P. Babson Charitable Grants, 4534
Teaching Tolerance Grants, 4567
Tides Fndn Grants, 4632
Tom's of Maine Grants, 4640
U.S. Department of Educ Vocational Rehabilitation Services Projects for American Indians with Disabilities Grants, 4702
USDA Farm Labor Housing Grants, 4809
USDA Native American Indian Utilities Grants, 4820
USDA Section 306C Water and Waste Disposal Grants to Alleviate Health Risks, 4834
USDC Business Center - American Indian and Alaska Native Grants, 4849
USDD Cultural Resources Program Assistance Announcement Grants, 4862

Natural History
Bay and Paul Fndns, Inc Grants, 692
Illinois DNR Biodiversity Field Trip Grants, 2496
IMLS 21st Century Museum Pro Grants, 2512
IMLS American Heritage Preservation Grants, 2513
IMLS National Leadership Grants, 2515

Natural Resources
786 Fndn Grants, 33
Abbot and Dorothy H. Stevens Fndn Grants, 79
BBVA Compass Fndn Charitable Grants, 703
Beirne Carter Fndn Grants, 719
Cessna Fndn Grants, 1000
CFFVR Environmental Stewardship Grants, 1010
Charles Delmar Fndn Grants, 1039
Chingos Fndn Grants, 1109
CICF Efroymson Grants, 1120
Columbus Fndn Small Grants, 1232
Community Fndn for Greater Buffalo Grants, 1247
Community Fndn of Greater Birmingham Grants, 1280
Connecticut Light & Power Corp Contributions, 1352
Constellation Energy Corp EcoStar Grants, 1363
Constellation Energy Corp Grants, 1364
Curtis and Edith Munson Fndn Grants, 1418
Dorrance Family Fndn Grants, 1590
Edward R. Godfrey Fndn Grants, 1667
Elliot Fndn Inc Grants, 1686
Fremont Area Community Fndn Grants, 1955
George and Ruth Bradford Fndn Grants, 2010
H.A. and Mary K. Chapman Charitable Grants, 2182
High Meadow Fndn Grants, 2321

Hoblitzelle Fndn Grants, 2341
Horace A. Kimball and S. Ella Kimball Grants, 2362
James Ford Bell Fndn Grants, 2623
Janirve Fndn Grants, 2645
John W. and Anna H. Hanes Fndn Grants, 2728
Knox County Community Fndn Grants, 2831
Kosciusko County Community Fndn Grants, 2838
Maine Community Fndn Baldwin Area Grants, 2974
Mary C. & Perry F. Spencer Fndn Grants, 3034
Mary K. Chapman Fndn Grants, 3042
Maxon Charitable Fndn Grants, 3068
MDEQ Brownfield Redevelopment and Site Reclamation Grants, 3095
Morris K. Udall and Stewart L. Udall Fndn Dissertation Fellowships, 3219
NFWF Acres for America Grants, 3355
NFWF Alaska Fish and Wildlife Grants, 3356
NFWF Aleutian Islands Risk Assessment Grants, 3357
NW Minnesota Fndn Asset Building Grants, 3511
Owen County Community Fndn Grants, 3716
Perkins Charitable Fndn Grants, 3823
Piedmont Natural Gas Fndn Environmental Stewardship and Energy Sustainability Grant, 3884
Pinellas County Grants, 3891
Posey County Community Fndn Grants, 3939
Pulaski County Community Fndn Grants, 3988
Rhode Island Fndn Grants, 4073
Ripley County Community Fndn Grants, 4095
Ripley County Community Small Project Grants, 4096
Rose Fndn for Comm & the Environment N California Environmental Grassroots Grants, 4158
Rose Fndn For Communities and the Environment Watershed Protection Grants, 4160
Samuel S. Johnson Fndn Grants, 4239
Scherman Fndn Grants, 4305
Seabury Fndn Grants, 4316
Sierra Grants, 4352
Sir Dorabji Tata Grants for NGOs or Voluntary Organizations, 4370
Spencer County Community Fndn Grants, 4451
St. Louis-Jefferson Solid Waste Management Waste Reduction and Recycling Grants, 4470
Texas Commission on the Arts Arts Respond Project Grants, 4581
Triangle Community Fndn Donor Grants, 4668
USAID Development Assistance Grants, 4748
USDA Hispanic-Serving Insts Educ Grants, 4813
Vancouver Fndn Grants & Comm Inits, 4900
Waste Management Charitable Giving Grants, 5001

Natural Sciences
Charles A. Frueauff Fndn Grants, 1037
Cockrell Fndn Grants, 1196
DAAD Research Grants for Doctoral Candidates and Young Academics and Scientists, 1427
HRF Hudson River Improvement Grants, 2378
Illinois DNR Biodiversity Field Trip Grants, 2496
NSERC Michael Smith Awards, 3519
Reinberger Fndn Grants, 4052

Nature Centers
Alaska Conservation Operating Grants, 323
Boston Fndn Grants, 819
CICF Efroymson Grants, 1120
Freeman Fndn Grants, 1952
Illinois DNR Biodiversity Field Trip Grants, 2496
IMLS 21st Century Museum Pro Grants, 2512
IMLS American Heritage Preservation Grants, 2513
IMLS National Leadership Grants, 2515
Union Bank, N.A. Fndn Grants, 4709

Neighborhood Revitalization
7-Eleven Coorporate Giving Grants, 18
Abell Fndn Community Development Grants, 93
Aetna Fndn Strengthening Neighborhhods Grants in Connecticut, 188
Appalachian Regional Comm Housing Grants, 508
Bank of America Charitable Fndn Community Development Grants, 655
Blackford County Community Fndn Grants, 780

Blue Cross Blue Shield of Minnesota Fndn - Healthy Children: Growing Up Healthy Grants, 794
Blue Cross Blue Shield of Minnesota Healthy Neighborhoods: Connect Grants, 798
Con Edison Corp Giving Environmental Grants, 1347
Entergy Corp Open Grants for Community Improvement & Enrichment, 1714
Fndns of E Chicago Community Economic Development Grants, 1907
George A. and Grace L. Long Fndn Grants, 2008
Georgia-Pacific Fndn Enrichment Grants, 2032
GNOF Community Revitalization Grants, 2071
GNOF Gert Community Grants, 2076
GNOF Jefferson Community Grants, 2085
GNOF St. Bernard Community Grants, 2092
Goldseker Fndn Community Grants, 2101
Honeywell Corp Housing and Shelter Grants, 2357
Intergrys Corp Grants, 2565
Leon and Thea Koerner Fndn Grants, 2883
LISC Financial Opportunity Center Social Innovation Grants, 2911
LISC MetLife Fndn Community-Police Partnership Awards, 2912
Mabel F. Hoffman Charitable Grants, 2957
Mabel Louise Riley Fndn Family Strengthening Small Grants, 2958
McKnight Fndn Region & Communities Grants, 3086
Mertz Gilmore Fndn NYC Communities Grants, 3126
MGM Resorts Fndn Community Grants, 3153
Miller Fndn Grants, 3181
National Endowment for Arts Our Town Grants, 3257
Northern Chautauqua DFT Communications Community Betterment Grants, 3500
Northern Chautauqua Lake Shore Savings and Loan Community Reinvestment Grants, 3502
Northland Fndn Grants, 3506
NYCT Historic Preservation Grants, 3551
Peter Kiewit Fndn Neighborhood Grants, 3846
PNC Ecnomic Development Grants, 3922
PNM Power Up Grants, 3925
Salt River Project Environmental Quality Grants, 4227
Seattle Fndn Annual Neighborhoods and Communities Grants, 4319
Seattle Fndn Neighbor to Neighbor Small Grants, 4330
Textron Corp Contributions Grants, 4601

Neighborhoods
Abell Fndn Community Development Grants, 93
Aetna Fndn Strengthening Neighborhhods Grants in Connecticut, 188
Alliance for Community Trees Home Depot Fndn NeighborWoods Grants, 382
Allstate Corp Giving Grants, 386
Allstate Corp Hometown Commitment Grants, 387
Allstate Fndn Safe and Vital Communities Grants, 390
America the Beautiful Fund Operation Green Plant Grants, 451
Amerigroup Fndn Grants, 452
Annie E. Casey Fndn Grants, 481
Appalachian Regional Comm Housing Grants, 508
Aquila Corp Grants, 521
Arizona Community Fndn Grants, 540
Arizona Republic Fndn Grants, 546
Arizona Republic Newspaper Contributions, 547
Baltimore Community Neighborhood Grants, 646
Baltimore Comm Neighborhoods Path Grants, 647
Bank of America Charitable Fndn Community Development Grants, 655
Battle Creek Community Neighborhood Grants, 686
Bayer Fndn Grants, 696
Beckley Area Fndn Grants, 716
Benwood Fndn Focus Area Grants, 733
Blue Cross Blue Shield of Minnesota Healthy Neighborhoods: Connect Grants, 798
Brooklyn Community Caring Neighbors Grants, 848
Brooklyn Community Fndn Community Development Grants, 850
Brooklyn Community Fndn Green Communities Grants, 852
Butler Manufacturing Company Fndn Grants, 881

SUBJECT INDEX

California Community Fndn Neighborhood Revitalization Grants, 903
Carnegie Corp of New York Grants, 940
Center for Venture Philanthropy, 991
Chicago Title and Trust Company Fndn Grants, 1099
CIT Corp Giving Grants, 1138
Citigroup Fndn Grants, 1139
Citizens Bank Mid-Atlantic Charitable Grants, 1140
Cleveland Neighborhood Connections Grants, 1171
Columbus Fndn Competitive Grants, 1220
Community Fndn for Greater New Haven Neighborhood Small Grants, 1249
Community Fndn for Greater New Haven Valley Neighborhood Grants, 1253
Community Fndn for Monterey County Grants, 1255
Community Fndn of Greater Memphis Grants, 1290
Community Fndn Silicon Valley Grants, 1331
Con Edison Corp Giving Environmental Grants, 1347
Connecticut Commission on the Arts Art in Public Spaces, 1349
Cooper Industries Fndn Grants, 1370
Crail-Johnson Fndn Grants, 1393
CSRA Community Fndn Grants, 1407
CTCNet/Youth Visions for Stronger Neighborhoods Grants, 1409
DB Americas Fndn Grants, 1466
Delaware Community Next Generation Grants, 1485
Denver Strengthening Neighborhoods Grants, 1504
Deuce McAllister Catch 22 Fndn Grants, 1521
DOI Urban Park & Rec Recovery Grants, 1554
DOJ Gang-Free Schools and Communities Intervention Grants, 1557
Dyson Fndn Mid-Hudson Valley Faith-Based Organization Grants, 1634
Edward N. and Della L. Thome Memorial Fndn Direct Services Grants, 1666
Entergy Corp Open Grants for Community Improvement & Enrichment, 1714
Enterprise Community Partners Rose Architectural Fellowships, 1719
EQT Fndn Community Grants, 1744
Erie Community Fndn Grants, 1750
F.R. Bigelow Fndn Grants, 1781
Farmers Insurance Corp Giving Grants, 1791
Fndns of E Chicago Community Economic Development Grants, 1907
Frances L. and Edwin L. Cummings Grants, 1919
Gannett Fndn Community Action Grants, 1984
George A. and Grace L. Long Fndn Grants, 2008
George Fndn Grants, 2018
George Gund Fndn Grants, 2020
Georgia-Pacific Fndn Enrichment Grants, 2032
Giant Food Charitable Grants, 2050
GNOF St. Bernard Community Grants, 2092
Goldseker Fndn Community Grants, 2101
Graco Fndn Grants, 2111
Greater Milwaukee Fndn Grants, 2137
Greater Worcester Comm Discretionary Grants, 2140
Hasbro Children's Fund, 2256
Helen Bader Fndn Grants, 2293
Herbert A. and Adrian W. Woods Fndn Grants, 2313
Hirtzel Memorial Fndn Grants, 2332
Honeywell Corp Housing and Shelter Grants, 2357
Indep Community Fndn Community Quality of Life Grant, 2525
Independent Community Fndn Neighborhood Renewal Grants, 2527
ING Fndn Grants, 2555
Intergrys Corp Grants, 2565
Johnson Controls Fndn Civic Activities Grants, 2720
JP Morgan Chase Comm Development Grants, 2753
Kalamazoo Community Fndn Front Porch Grants, 2767
Kalamazoo Community Good Neighbor Grants, 2768
Liberty Bank Fndn Grants, 2890
LISC Financial Opportunity Center Social Innovation Grants, 2911
LISC MetLife Fndn Community-Police Partnership Awards, 2912
Local Inits Support Corp Grants, 2917
Lynde and Harry Bradley Fndn Grants, 2947

Lynde and Harry Bradley Fndn Prizes, 2948
Lyndhurst Fndn Grants, 2949
Mabel Louise Riley Fndn Grants, 2959
Marion County Historic Preservation Grants, 3016
Marsh Corp Grants, 3027
McKnight Fndn Region & Communities Grants, 3086
Mertz Gilmore Fndn NYC Communities Grants, 3126
MGM Resorts Fndn Community Grants, 3153
Mizuho USA Fndn Grants, 3192
National Trust for Historic Preservation Diversity Scholarship, 3280
Nehemiah Community Fndn Grants, 3290
New York Landmarks Conservancy City Ventures Grants, 3339
Nordson Corp Fndn Grants, 3462
Northern Chautauqua DFT Communications Community Betterment Grants, 3500
Northern Chautauqua Lake Shore Savings and Loan Community Reinvestment Grants, 3502
Northern Trust Company Corp Giving Program, 3504
NYCT Social Services and Welfare Grants, 3557
Oklahoma City Community Programs & Grants, 3666
OSF-Baltimore Community Fellowships, 3695
Paul and Mary Haas Fndn Contributions and Student Scholarships, 3756
Peter Kiewit Fndn Neighborhood Grants, 3846
Piper Trust Educ Grants, 3902
PNM Power Up Grants, 3925
Powell Family Fndn Grants, 3941
Princeton Area Community Fndn Fund for Women and Girls Grants, 3962
Project Orange Thumb Grants, 3972
Ralphs Food 4 Less Fndn Grants, 4014
Ruth Mott Fndn Grants, 4180
RWJF New Jersey Health Inits Grants, 4187
Safeco Insurance Community Grants, 4203
Saint Paul Companies Fndn Grants, 4217
Saint Paul Fndn Lowertown Future Grants, 4220
Salt River Project Environmental Quality Grants, 4227
San Diego Fndn for Change Grants, 4247
Seattle Fndn Annual Neighborhoods and Communities Grants, 4319
Seattle Fndn Neighbor to Neighbor Small Grants, 4330
Skillman Community Connections Small Grants, 4379
Skillman Fndn Good Neighborhoods Grants, 4380
Skillman Fndn Good Opportunities Grants, 4381
Speer Grants, 4450
Stark Community Fndn Neighborhood Partnership Grants, 4479
State Street Fndn Grants, 4495
Stockton Rush Bartol Fndn Grants, 4508
Strengthening Families - Strengthening Communities Grants, 4513
U.S. Bank Fndn Grants, 4686
UPS Corp Giving Grants, 4727
Wieboldt Fndn Grants, 5065
Youth Philanthropy Project, 5132

Networking
ALA Information Technology Pathfinder Award, 286
Cause Populi Worthy Cause Grants, 958
NSF CISE Community-Based Data Interoperability Networks Grants, 3523
NSF CISE Computer and Network Systems: Core Programs Grants, 3524
NSF CISE Computing and Communication Fndns: Core Programs Grants, 3525
USDC State Broadband Init Grants, 4857

Neuroscience
Bristol-Myers Squibb Clinical Outcomes and Research Grants, 839
Dorothy Rider Pool Health Care Grants, 1589
National Center for Resp Gaming Travel Grants, 3251
Oracle Corp Contributions Grants, 3686

New Independent States
Charles Stewart Mott Fndn Grants, 1055
Ploughshares Grants, 3916

Nonfiction
ALA Schneider Family Book Award, 317
ALA Stonewall Book Awards - Israel Fishman Nonfiction Award, 330
CAA Millard Meiss Publication Grants, 885
Constance Saltonstall Fndn for the Arts Grants, 1361
Illinois Arts Council Literature Grants, 2470
Kentucky Arts Council Emerging Artist Award, 2807
Minnesota State Arts Board Cultural Community Partnership Grants, 3188
NYFA Gregory Millard Fellowships, 3565
NYSCA Lit: General Operating Support Grants, 3598
NYSCA Literature: General Support Grants, 3599
PCA Arts Organizations & Grants for Lit, 3781
PCA Entry Track Arts Organizations and Program Grants for Literature, 3793
PCA Strategies for Success Grants - Advanced, 3804
PCA Strategies for Success Grants - Basic Level, 3805
PCA Strategies for Success Grants - Intermediate, 3806
Quantum Corp Snap Server Grants, 3995

Nonprofit Organizations
4imprint One by One Charitable Giving, 16
ALA Loleta D. Fyan Grant, 295
Albert and Bessie Mae Kronkosky Charitable Fndn Grants, 339
Alfred P. Sloan Fndn Civic Inits Grants, 368
Allegheny Fndn Grants, 376
Altman Fndn Health Care Grants, 397
Antone & Edene Vidinha Charitable Grants, 490
Arkansas Arts Council AIE Arts Curriculum Project Grants, 552
Arkansas Arts Council Collab Project Support, 555
Arkansas Arts Council Expansion Arts Grants, 556
Arkansas Arts Council General Operating Support, 557
Arthur and Sara Jo Kobacker, Alfred and Ida Kobacker Fndn Grants, 571
Barnes and Noble National Sponsorships and Charitable Donations, 671
Battle Creek Community Fndn Grants, 684
Bayer Fndn Grants, 696
Bikes Belong Grants, 763
BJ's Wholesale Clubs Local Charitable Giving, 778
Blue Cross Blue Shield of Minnesota Fndn - Health Equity: Building Health Together Grants, 793
Blue Cross Blue Shield of Minnesota Fndn - Healthy Children: Growing Up Healthy Grants, 794
Blue Cross Blue Shield of Minnesota Fndn - Healthy Equity: Health Impact Assessment Demonstration Project Grants, 795
Blue Cross Blue Shield of Minnesota Healthy Neighborhoods: Connect Grants, 798
Blumenthal Fndn Grants, 804
Bohemian Fndn Pharos Grants, 811
Boulder County Arts Alliance Neodata Endowment Grants, 823
Brookdale Fndn National Group Respite Grants, 845
Bush Fndn Arts & Humanities Capital Projects, 872
Bush Fndn Arts & Humanities Grants: Short-Term Organizational Support, 873
Bush Fndn Regional Arts Development Grants, 878
Callaway Golf Company Fndn Grants, 910
Carl M. Freeman Fndn Grants, 933
CDECD Endangered Properties Grants, 980
CDECD Historic Preservation Survey and Planning Grants, 982
CDECD Historic Restoration Grants, 983
CDECD Tourism Product Development Grants, 984
CECP Directors' Award, 986
Center on Philanthropy and Civil Society's Emerging Leaders Int'l Fellows Program, 992
CFFVR Bridge Grants, 1003
CFFVR Capital Credit Union Charitable Giving, 1005
CFFVR Clintonville Area Fndn Grants, 1008
CFFVR Doug and Carla Salmon Fndn Grants, 1009
CFFVR Frank C. Shattuck Community Grants, 1012
CFFVR Infant Welfare Circle of Kings Daughters Grants, 1013
CFFVR Shawano Area Community Fndn Grants, 1021
CFFVR Sikora Family Grants, 1022

960 / Nonprofit Organizations — SUBJECT INDEX

CFFVR Waupaca Area Community Fndn Grants, 1023
CFFVR Wisconsin Daughters and Sons Grants, 1024
CFFVR Women's Fund for the Fox Valley Region Grants, 1025
Chicago Community Trust Fellowships, 1086
Chicago Tribune Fndn Civic Grants, 1100
CICF Christmas Fund, 1117
CICF Summer Youth Grants, 1128
Clarence T.C. Ching Fndn Grants, 1151
Cleveland Community Responsive Grants, 1168
CNCS AmeriCorps NCCC Project Grants, 1181
CNCS Social Innovation Grants, 1189
Community Fndn for Greater New Haven $5,000 and Under Grants, 1248
Community Fndn for Greater New Haven Responsive New Grants, 1251
Community Fndn for Greater New Haven Sponsorship Grants, 1252
Community Fndn of Abilene Future Grants, 1265
Community Fndn of Abilene Humane Treatment of Animals Grants, 1266
Community Fndn of Bartholomew County Women's Giving Circle, 1269
Community Fndn of Bloomington and Monroe County - Precision Health Network Cycle Grants, 1270
Community Fndn of Broward Grants, 1275
Community Fndn of Collier County Capacity Building Grants, 1277
Community Fndn of Greater Fort Wayne - Barbara Burt Leadership Development Grants, 1283
Community Fndn of Greater Fort Wayne - Collaborative Efforts Grants, 1284
Community Fndn of Muncie and Delaware County Maxon Grants, 1303
Community Fndn of St. Joseph County Special Project Challenge Grants, 1314
Community Fndn of the Eastern Shore Field of Interest Grants, 1318
Community Partners Lawrence County Grants, 1328
Community Memorial Fndn Grants, 1334
Cone Health Fndn Grants, 1348
Conseil des arts de Montreal Touring Grants, 1358
Constellation Energy Corp EcoStar Grants, 1363
Constellation Energy Corp Grants, 1364
Covenant Fndn of New York Ignition Grants, 1385
Covenant Fndn of New York Signature Grants, 1386
Covenant to Care for Children Grants, 1389
Covidien Medical Product Donations, 1390
Davenport-Hatch Fndn Grants, 1448
Daviess County Community Fndn Human Services Grants, 1458
Daviess County Community Recreation Grants, 1459
Daviess County Community Fndn Youth Development Grants, 1460
Dearborn Community Fndn Sprint Ed Excellence Grants, 1474
Deborah Munroe Noonan Grants, 1475
Decatur County Community Small Project Grants, 1477
DeKalb County Community Fndn - Immediate Response Grant, 1479
Delaware Division of the Arts Community-Based Organizations Opportunity Grants, 1487
Denver Fndn Community Grants, 1502
DHHS ARRA Strengthening Communities Fund - State, Local, and Tribal Government Capacity Building Grants, 1528
Draper Richards Kaplan Fndn Grants, 1603
DTE Energy Fndn Leadership Grants, 1614
Dubois County Community Fndn Grants, 1615
Dyson Fndn Management Assistance Program Mini-Grants, 1632
Dyson Fndn Mid-Hudson Valley General Operating Support Grants, 1635
Dyson Mid-Hudson Valley Project Support, 1636
Dyson Fndn Nonprofit Strategic Restructuring Init Grants, 1637
Elizabeth & Avola W. Callaway Fndn Grants, 1680
Enterprise Community Partners MetLife Fndn Awards for Excellence in Affordable Housing, 1717
Eugene Straus Charitable Trust, 1766

F.R. Bigelow Fndn Grants, 1781
FCYO Youth Organizing Grants, 1797
Financial Capability Innovation Fund II Grants, 1811
Forest Fndn Grants, 1886
Franklin H. Wells and Ruth L. Wells Grants, 1930
Frey Fndn Grants, 1963
Frist Fndn Grants, 1964
Fund for the City of New York Grants, 1978
Furth Family Fndn Grants, 1980
George Fndn Grants, 2018
George Gund Fndn Grants, 2020
Geraldine R. Dodge Fndn Environment Grants, 2041
Geraldine R. Dodge Fndn Media Grants, 2042
Gibson County Community Fndn Women's Fund, 2051
Ginger and Barry Ackerley Fndn Grants, 2055
GNOF Exxon-Mobil Grants, 2074
GNOF Freeman Challenge Grants, 2075
GNOF IMPACT Grants for Youth Development, 2081
GNOF New Orleans Works Grants, 2088
GNOF Norco Community Grants, 2089
GNOF Organizational Effectiveness Grants and Workshops, 2090
GNOF Stand Up For Our Children Grants, 2093
Goldseker Fndn Community Affairs Grants, 2100
Goldseker Fndn Human Services Grants, 2102
Goldseker Fndn Non-Profit Management Assistance Grants, 2103
Grand Circle Fndn Associates Grants, 2112
Grand Rapids Area Community Fndn Wyoming Grants, 2116
Grand Rapids Community SE Ottawa Grants, 2122
Grand Rapids Community Sparta Grants, 2124
Great-West Life Grants, 2130
Great Clips Corp Giving, 2131
Greater Green Bay Community Fndn Grants, 2135
Grundy Fndn Grants, 2169
Guy I. Bromley Grants, 2180
HAF Arts and Culture: Project Grants to Artists, 2191
HAF Co-op Community Grants, 2192
HAF Community Grants, 2193
HAF Educ Grants, 2196
HAF Southern Humboldt Grants, 2204
Hahl Proctor Charitable Grants, 2208
Hancock County Community Fndn - Programming Mini-Grants, 2220
Harvey Randall Wickes Fndn Grants, 2255
Helen Bader Fndn Grants, 2293
Hilton Head Island Fndn Grants, 2330
Howard H. Callaway Fndn Grants, 2376
IDEM Section 319(h) Nonpoint Source Grants, 2435
Illinois DCEO Community Development Assistance For Economic Development Grants, 2488
Illinois Humanities Council Community General Support Grants, 2509
Jacobs Family Village Neighborhoods Grants, 2619
Janesville Fndn Grants, 2644
Janson Fndn Grants, 2646
Japan-US Community Ed & Exchange Grants, 2648
Jaquelin Hume Fndn Grants, 2654
Jeffris Wood Fndn Grants, 2660
Jessie Smith Noyes Fndn Grants, 2672
Jewish Community Fndn of Los Angeles Cutting Edge Grants, 2673
Jewish Community Fndn of LA Israel Grants, 2674
John and Margaret Post Fndn Grants, 2686
John F. Kennedy Center for the Performing Arts National Rosemary Kennedy Internship, 2694
John M. Ross Fndn Grants, 2704
Johnson County Community Fndn Youth Philanthropy Init Grants, 2724
Johnson Fndn Wingspread Conference Support, 2725
John W. Gardner Leadership Award, 2731
John W. Speas and Effie E. Speas Grants, 2732
Joukowsky Family Fndn Grants, 2743
Jovid Fndn Grants, 2745
Kent D. Steadley and Mary L. Steadley Trust, 2804
Kentucky Arts Council Partnership Grants, 2809
Land O'Lakes Fndn California Region Grants, 2858
Land O'Lakes Fndn Dollars for Doers, 2860
Laura Jane Musser Rural Arts Grants, 2863

Leadership IS Award, 2869
Legacy Partners in Environmental Educ Grants, 2875
Legacy Partners in Environmental Ed Grants, 2876
Leighton Award for Nonprofit Excellence, 2880
Lewis H. Humphreys Charitable Grants, 2889
Libra Fndn Grants, 2899
Louetta M. Cowden Fndn Grants, 2922
Louis and Elizabeth Nave Flarsheim Charitable Fndn Grants, 2924
Lumity Technology Leadership Award, 2940
M.J. Murdock Charitable Trust General Grants, 2954
Maddie's Fund Lifesaving Awards, 2969
Maine Women's Fund Girls' Grantmaking Init, 2993
Marin Community Fndn Ending the Cycle of Poverty Grants, 3011
Marin Community Fndn Social Justice and Interfaith Understanding Grants, 3012
Marin Community Fndn Stinson Bolinas Community Grants, 3013
Marin Community Successful Aging Grants, 3014
Mary S. and David C. Corbin Fndn Grants, 3048
Mathile Family Fndn Grants, 3062
McCallum Family Fndn Grants, 3072
McConnell Fndn Grants, 3076
McLean Fndn Grants, 3089
Medtronic Fndn Community Link Arts, Civic, and Culture Grants, 3109
Medtronic Fndn CommunityLink Educ Grants, 3110
Medtronic Fndn CommunityLink Health Grants, 3111
Memorial Fndn for Children Grants, 3116
Meyer Fndn Benevon Grants, 3140
Meyer Fndn Management Assistance Grants, 3144
Meyer Fndn Strong Nonprofit Sector Grants, 3145
MGN Family Fndn Grants, 3154
Michael and Susan Dell Fndn Grants, 3158
Microsoft Software Donation Grants, 3164
Middlesex Savings Charitable Fndn Capacity Building Grants, 3172
Miller Fndn Grants, 3181
Modest Needs Non-Profit Grants, 3200
Montgomery County Community Fndn Grants, 3213
Morris and Gwendolyn Cafritz Fndn Grants, 3218
Ms. Fndn Women Building Democracy Grants, 3223
Ms. Fndn for Women Ending Violence Grants, 3224
NACC David Stevenson Fellowships, 3235
NACC William Diaz Fellowships, 3236
National Endowment for the Arts - National Partnership Agreement Grants, 3256
National Endowment for Arts Our Town Grants, 3257
National Endowment for the Arts - State Partnership Agreement Grants, 3259
National Endowment for Arts Commun Grants, 3260
National Endowment for the Arts Dance Grants, 3262
National Endowment for Arts Agencies Grants, 3263
National Endowment for Arts Media Grants, 3264
National Endowment for Arts Opera Grants, 3267
National Endowment for the Arts Presenting Grants: Art Works, 3268
National Endowment for Arts Theater Grants, 3269
National Environmental Ed Every Day Grants, 3271
Natonal Endowment for the Arts Research Grants: Art Works, 3286
Nehemiah Community Fndn Grants, 3290
Nellie Mae Educ Fndn District-Level Grants, 3297
Nellie Mae Educ Public Understanding Grants, 3298
New Earth Fndn Grants, 3317
New Voices J-Lab Journalism Grants, 3337
Nicor Corp Contributions, 3435
Nina Mason Pulliam Charitable Grants, 3443
Nonprofit Management Grants, 3458
Norfolk Southern Fndn Grants, 3463
Northern Chautauqua Community Grants, 3499
NWHF Health Advocacy Small Grants, 3537
NWHF Kaiser Permanente Community Grants, 3538
Ohio Arts Council Artist in Residence Grants for Sponsors, 3645
Ohio Arts Council Capacity Building Grants for Organizations and Communities, 3652
OSF-Baltimore Criminal & Juv Justice Grants, 3696
OSF-Baltimore Tackling Drug Addiction Grants, 3698

SUBJECT INDEX

Otto Bremer Fndn Grants, 3713
PCA-PCD Organizational Short-Term Professional Development and Consulting Grants, 3769
PCA Management/Technical Assistance Grants, 3800
PCA Strategies for Success Grants - Advanced, 3804
Percy B. Ferebee Endowment Grants, 3820
Peter and Elizabeth C. Tower Fndn Organizational Scholarships, 3838
Peter and Elizabeth C. Tower Fndn Phase II Technology Init Grants, 3839
Peter and Elizabeth C. Tower Fndn Phase I Technology Init Grants, 3840
Peter F. Drucker Award for Canadian Nonprofit Innovation, 3844
Pfizer Special Events Grants, 3865
Phoenix Suns Charities Grants, 3881
Piedmont Health Fndn Grants, 3882
Pier 1 Imports Grants, 3887
Planet Dog Fndn Grants, 3911
PNM Reduce Your Use Grants, 3926
Pohlad Family Fndn, 3928
Price Family Charitable Grants, 3952
Price Gilbert, Jr. Charitable Grants, 3953
Priddy Fndn Grants, 3957
Rasmuson Organizational Advancement Grants, 4023
Rasmuson Fndn Sabbatical Grants, 4024
Rhode Island Fndn Grants, 4073
Richard King Mellon Fndn Grants, 4087
Robert R. McCormick Tribune Civics Grants, 4118
Robert R. McCormick Tribune Veterans Grants, 4120
Rockefeller Brothers Fellowship in Nonprofit Law, 4132
Rose Hills Fndn Grants, 4162
Saint Paul Companies Fndn Grants, 4217
Samuel L. Phillips Family Fndn Grants, 4235
San Francisco Fndn Community Health Grants, 4263
Santa Barbara Fndn Monthly Express Grants, 4284
Santa Barbara Strategy Grants Capital Support, 4285
Santa Barbara Strategy Core Suupport Grants, 4286
Santa Barbara Fndn Strategy Grants - Innovation, 4287
Santa Fe Community Fndn root2fruit Santa Fe, 4289
Santa Fe Community Fndn Special and Urgent Needs Grants, 4292
Sasakawa Peace Fndn Grants, 4299
Share Our Strength Grants, 4340
Shaw's Supermarkets Donations, 4342
Skoll Fndn Awards for Social Entrepreneurship, 4383
Sodexo Fndn STOP Hunger Scholarships, 4400
State Street Fndn Grants, 4495
Stettinius Fund for Nonprofit Leadership Awards, 4500
Stranahan Fndn Grants, 4512
Surdna Fndn Sustainable Environments Grants, 4533
Telluride Fndn Emergency/Out of Cycle Grants, 4574
Texas Instruments Community Services Grants, 4600
Threshold Fndn Sustainable Planet Grants, 4627
Toby Wells Fndn Grants, 4638
Tri-State Community Twenty-first Century Endowment Grants, 4666
Trinity Trust Community Response Grants, 4671
Trinity Trust Summer Youth Mini Grants, 4672
Union County Fndn Grants, 4712
Union Square Arts Award, 4716
Union Square Award for Social Justice, 4717
Union Square Awards Grants, 4718
UPS Fndn Nonprofit Effectiveness Grants, 4732
USDA Self-Help Technical Assistance Grants, 4836
Verizon Fndn South Carolina Lit & Internet Safety Grants, 4922
Verizon Fndn Virginia Grants, 4925
Verizon Fndn West Virginia Grants, 4926
Virginia A. Hodgkinson Research Prize, 4940
VSA/Metlife Connect All Grants, 4953
Wallace Alexander Gerbode Fndn Grants, 4974
Wayne County Fndn Women's Grants, 5006
Wege Fndn Grants, 5017
Wild Rivers Community Fndn Holiday Partnership Grants, 5069
William A. Badger Fndn Grants, 5072
William T. Grant Fndn Youth Service Improvement Grants, 5096
Z. Smith Reynolds Fndn Sabbatical Grants, 5147

Nonviolence
Arthur B. Schultz Fndn Grants, 573

Norwegian Language/Literature
Amer-Scandinavian Fndn Public Project Grants, 419

Nuclear Science Education
Ploughshares Grants, 3916

Nuclear/Radioactive Waste Disposal
Honor the Earth Grants, 2361

Nursing
Abington Fndn Grants, 100
Brookdale Fndn Leadership in Aging Fellowships, 844
Christy-Houston Fndn Grants, 1115
Fndn for Health Enhancement Grants, 1894
Jenkins Fndn: Improving the Health of Greater Richmond Grants, 2663
Kaiser Permanente Cares for Comm Grants, 2763
NWHF Partners Investing in Nursing's Future, 3539
Pfizer Medical Educ Track One Grants, 3864
Pollock Fndn Grants, 3930
Regents Professional Opportunity Scholarships, 4044
RWJF Partners Investing in Nursing's Future, 4188
Sid W. Richardson Fndn Grants, 4350
Visiting Nurse Fndn Grants, 4951

Nursing Education
Abell-Hanger Fndn Grants, 91
Ahmanson Fndn Grants, 207
Bernard Osher Fndn Grants, 742
Bertha Russ Lytel Fndn Grants, 745
Burlington Industries Fndn Grants, 865
Daphne Seybolt Culpeper Memorial Fndn Grants, 1445
Dr. Scholl Fndn Grants, 1602
E. Rhodes and Leona B. Carpenter Fndn Grants, 1640
Edward W. and Stella C. Van Houten Grants, 1670
Effie and Wofford Cain Fndn Grants, 1674
Health Fndn of Greater Indianapolis Grants, 2282
HRSA Nurse Educ, Practice, Quality and Retention Grants, 2381
Lettie Pate Whitehead Fndn Grants, 2888
Lubbock Area Fndn Grants, 2931
Lucy Downing Nisbet Charitable Grants, 2935
Ruth Eleanor Bamberger and John Ernest Bamberger Memorial Fndn Grants, 4178
RWJF Partners Investing in Nursing's Future, 4188
Saint Luke's Health Inits Grants, 4216
Samuel S. Johnson Fndn Grants, 4239
San Antonio Area Fndn Grants, 4240
T. Raymond Gregory Family Fndn Grants, 4547

Nursing Homes
ALA Diversity and Outreach Fair, 267
ALA Exceptional Service Award, 278
Arkell Hall Fndn Grants, 562
Burden Grants, 864
CHCF Grants, 1063
CICF Senior Grants, 1127
David Lane Grants for Aged & Indigent Women, 1453
Kentucky Arts Council Access Assistance Grants, 2805
Lydia deForest Charitable Grants, 2946
McLean Contributionship Grants, 3088
Mervin Bovaird Fndn Grants, 3128
MetroWest Health Fndn Grants--Healthy Aging, 3135
Reinberger Fndn Grants, 4052
Robert & Clara Milton Fund for Senior Housing, 4117
Union Bank, N.A. Fndn Grants, 4709

Nutrition Education
Abbott Fund Access to Health Care Grants, 80
Abbott Fund Science Educ Grants, 83
ACF Native American Social and Economic Development Strategies Grants, 123
ACTION Council of Monterey County Grants, 134
Aid for Starving Children Int'l Grants, 212
BCBSM Building Healthy Communities Elementary Schools and Community Partners Grants, 704
Caesars Fndn Grants, 891

Campbell Soup Fndn Grants, 916
Chefs Move to Schools Grants, 1066
Chiquita Brands Int'l Grants, 1110
CNCS AmeriCorps State and National Grants, 1182
Coca-Cola Fndn Grants, 1195
Colonel Stanley R. McNeil Fndn Grants, 1210
Fargo-Moorhead Area Fndn Grants, 1788
Fndn for Seacoast Health Grants, 1895
Fremont Area Comm Summer Youth Grants, 1956
Great-West Life Grants, 2130
HAF Co-op Community Grants, 2192
Heifer Ed Grants for Teachers, 2289
James R. Thorpe Fndn Grants, 2636
Medtronic Fndn CommunityLink Health Grants, 3111
Milton Hicks Wood and Helen Gibbs Wood Charitable Grants, 3184
Mt. Sinai Health Care Fndn Health of the Jewish Community Grants, 3226
Mt. Sinai Health Care Fndn Health of the Urban Community Grants, 3227
Nestle Fndn Training Grant, 3301
NFL Charities Pro Bowl Comm Grants in Hawaii, 3348
NGA Healthy Sprouts Awards, 3403
Paso del Norte Health Fndn Grants, 3743
PepsiCo Fndn Grants, 3819
Perry County Community Fndn Grants, 3827
Phi Upsilon Omicron Florence Fallgatter Distinguished Service Award, 3877
Posey Community Fndn Women's Grants, 3938
Posey County Community Fndn Grants, 3939
Robert R. Meyer Fndn Grants, 4121
Shaw's Supermarkets Donations, 4342
Sierra Health Fndn Responsive Grants, 4353
U.S. Department of Educ 21st Century Community Learning Centers, 4687
USAID Food Security, Nutrition, Biodiversity and Conservation Grants, 4752
USAID Grants for Building Disaster-Resilient Communities in Southern Africa, 4755
Vancouver Fndn Grants & Comm Inits, 4900
Wilson-Wood Fndn Grants, 5098

Nutrition/Dietetics
Abbott Fund Science Educ Grants, 83
ACTION Council of Monterey County Grants, 134
Administration on Aging Senior Medicare Patrol Project Grants, 166
Albertson's Charitable Giving Grants, 345
Atkinson Fndn Community Grants, 606
Beazley Fndn Grants, 714
Better Way Fndn Grants, 754
Boeing Company Contributions Grants, 809
Boston Fndn Grants, 819
Caesars Fndn Grants, 891
Charles H. Farnsworth Grants, 1043
Chautauqua Region Community Fndn Grants, 1062
Christy-Houston Fndn Grants, 1115
ConAgra Foods Community Impact Grants, 1342
Connecticut Health Fndn Health Init Grants, 1351
Denver Fndn Community Grants, 1502
DHHS Adolescent Family Life Demo Projects, 1524
Dole Food Company Charitable Contributions, 1564
Fndn for a Healthy Kentucky Grants, 1891
General Mills Fndn Celebrating Communities of Color Grants, 2002
General Mills Fndn Grants, 2003
Grand Rapids Community Ionia Youth Grants, 2120
Grand Rapids Community Sparta Youth Grants, 2125
H.J. Heinz Company Fndn Grants, 2184
HAF Co-op Community Grants, 2192
Healthcare Fndn for Orange County Grants, 2279
Health Fndn of Greater Indianapolis Grants, 2282
Meyer Fndn Healthy Communities Grants, 3143
NFL Charities Pro Bowl Comm Grants in Hawaii, 3348
NWHF Physical Activity and Nutrition Grants, 3540
Paso del Norte Health Fndn Grants, 3743
Paul G. Allen Family Fndn Grants, 3759
Ruth Mott Fndn Grants, 4180
Sensient Technologies Fndn Grants, 4337
Sheltering Arms Grants, 4344

962 / Nutrition/Dietetics

The World Food Prize, 4606
United Methodist Child Mental Health Grants, 4721
USAID Food Security, Nutrition, Biodiversity and Conservation Grants, 4752
USAID Grants for Building Disaster-Resilient Communities in Southern Africa, 4755
USDA Child and Adult Care Food Program, 4800
USDA Community Food Projects Grants, 4802

Obesity
Aetna Fndn Obesity Grants, 185
Bright Promises Fndn Grants, 838
Campbell Soup Fndn Grants, 916
Chefs Move to Schools Grants, 1066
Chicago Community Trust Health Grants, 1087
CNCS AmeriCorps State and National Grants, 1182
Colonel Stanley R. McNeil Fndn Grants, 1210
Fndn for Mid South Health & Wellness Grants, 1899
GNOF IMPACT Kahn-Oppenheim Grants, 2084
Grand Rapids Community Ionia Youth Grants, 2120
Healthcare Fndn for Orange County Grants, 2279
Horizon Fndn for New Jersey Grants, 2364
Institute for Agriculture and Trade Policy Food and Society Fellowships, 2561
Johnson & Johnson Comm Health Care Grants, 2717
Mt. Sinai Health Care Fndn Health of the Jewish Community Grants, 3226
NHLBI Bioengineering and Obesity Grants, 3411
NW Mutual Fndn Grants, 3509
NWHF Physical Activity and Nutrition Grants, 3540
Pacers Fndn Be Healthy and Fit Grants, 3722
Pajaro Valley Community Health Trust Diabetes and Contributing Factors Grants, 3732
PepsiCo Fndn Grants, 3819
Piedmont Health Fndn Grants, 3882
RCF The Women's Grants, 4035
USDA Hispanic-Serving Insts Educ Grants, 4813
YSA UnitedHealth HEROES Service-Learning Grants, 5142

Obstetrics-Gynecology
Blanche and Irving Laurie Fndn Grants, 784
John S. Dunn Research Fndn Grants and Chairs, 2715

Occupational Health and Safety
American Chemical Society Corp Associates Seed Grants, 425
Illinois DCEO Coal Competitiveness Grants, 2484
Pioneer Hi-Bred Community Grants, 3895

Oceanography
Bay and Paul Fndns Grants, 693
Lindbergh Grants, 2907
NOAA Undersea Research Project Grants, 3454
Richard and Rhoda Goldman Grants, 4077

Oceans and Seas
NFWF Seafarer's Environmental Educ Grants, 3390
NOAA Projects to Improve or Amend Coral Reef Fishery Management Plans, 3453
NOAA Undersea Research Project Grants, 3454
Royal Caribbean Cruises Ocean Fund, 4165

Oncology
Abbott Fund Science Educ Grants, 83
Ann and Robert H. Lurie Family Fndn Grants, 473
Bristol-Myers Squibb Clinical Outcomes and Research Grants, 839
Genentech Corp Charitable Contributions, 2000
Pfizer Healthcare Charitable Contributions, 3863
Pfizer Medical Educ Track One Grants, 3864

Opera/Musical Theater
A.J. Fletcher Fndn Grants, 41
American Express Historic Preservation Grants, 431
Arkansas Arts Council AIE After School/Summer Residency Grants, 551
Arkansas Arts Council AIE In-School Residency, 553
Arthur F. and Alice E. Adams Charitable Grants, 574
Arts Midwest Performing Arts Grants, 579
ArvinMeritor Fndn Arts and Culture Grants, 582
Beneficia Fndn Grants, 727
Bonfils-Stanton Fndn Grants, 814
Boston Fndn Grants, 819
Central New York Community Fndn Grants, 996
Community Fndn of Middle Tennessee Grants, 1300
Community Fndn of Riverside County Grants, 1304
CONSOL Coal Group Grants, 1360
Corning Fndn Cultural Grants, 1376
Creative Work Grants, 1396
Edward S. Moore Fndn Grants, 1668
Florida Div of Cultural Affairs Community Theatre Grants, 1847
Florida Div of Cultural Affairs Professional Theatre Grants, 1861
George Frederick Jewett Fndn Grants, 2019
Hahl Proctor Charitable Grants, 2208
Henrietta Lange Burk Grants, 2303
Illinois Arts Council Music Grants, 2474
Iowa Arts Council Artists in Schools/Communities Residency Grants, 2571
Mabel Y. Hughes Charitable Grants, 2960
MacArthur Fndn Chicago Arts and Culture General Operations Grants, 2961
Minnesota State Arts Board Cultural Community Partnership Grants, 3188
National Endowment for the Arts - National Arts and Humanities Youth Program Awards, 3255
National Endowment for Arts Media Grants, 3264
National Endowment for Arts Opera Grants, 3267
National Endowment for the Arts Presenting Grants: Art Works, 3268
National Endowment for Arts Theater Grants, 3269
NJSCA Arts Project Support, 3446
NJSCA Financial and Instal Stabilization Grants, 3447
NJSCA General Program Support Grants, 3449
NYSCA Architecture, Planning, and Design: Capital Fixtures and Equipment Purchase Grants, 3570
NYSCA Arts Educ: General Operating Support, 3578
NYSCA Music Community Schools Grants, 3605
NYSCA Theatre Gen Operating Support Grants, 3623
NYSCA Theatre General Program Support, 3624
NYSCA Theatre Pro Performances Grants, 3625
PennPAT Artist Technical Assistance Grants, 3811
PennPAT Strategic Opportunity Grants, 3815
Piper Trust Arts and Culture Grants, 3900
Rollin M. Gerstacker Fndn Grants, 4146
Saint Paul Fndn Grants, 4219
Santa Barbara Fndn Towbes Fund for the Performing Arts Grants, 4288
Seaver Institute Grants, 4331
South Carolina Arts Commission American Masterpieces in South Carolina Grants, 4413
T. James Kavanagh Fndn Grants, 4545
Texas Instruments Fndn Arts and Culture Grants, 4599
Yellow Corp Fndn Grants, 5126

Operating Support
100 Angels Charitable Fndn Grants, 24
118 Fndn Grants, 29
Adams Family Fndn I Grants, 150
Alfred C. and Ersa S. Arbogast Fndn Grants, 365
Alfred E. Chase Charitable Fndn Grants, 366
Anne J. Caudal Fndn Grants, 475
Bennett Family Fndn of Texas Grants, 728
Blumenthal Fndn Grants, 804
Carl R. Hendrickson Family Fndn Grants, 935
Charles H. Farnsworth Grants, 1043
Chicago Community Trust Arts and Culture Grants: SMART Growth, 1083
Claude Bennett Family Fndn Grants, 1159
Dream Weaver Fndn, 1604
Emy-Lou Biedenharn Fndn Grants, 1703
Esther M. and Freeman E. Everett Charitable Fndn Grants, 1757
Ethel Frends Fndn Grants, 1759
Ford Family Fndn Grants - Technical Assistance, 1882
Frank B. Hazard General Charity Grants, 1926
Fred & Gretel Biel Charitable Grants, 1939
Frederick McDonald Grants, 1946
George and Sarah Buchanan Fndn Grants, 2011
George E. Hatcher, Jr. and Ann Williams Hatcher Fndn Grants, 2015
GNOF IMPACT Grants for Arts and Culture, 2078
GNOF IMPACT Grants for Health and Human Services, 2080
GNOF IMPACT Grants for Youth Development, 2081
GNOF Maison Hospitaliere Grants, 2086
Gulf Coast Fndn of Community Capacity Building Grants, 2175
Harry S. Black and Allon Fuller Grants, 2243
Hearst Fndns Culture Grants, 2284
Hearst Fndns Social Service Grants, 2285
Helen Pumphrey Denit Charitable Grants, 2297
Illinois Humanities Council Community General Support Grants, 2509
John D. and Katherine A. Johnston Fndn Grants, 2691
John W. Boynton Grants, 2730
Joukowsky Family Fndn Grants, 2743
K.S. Adams Fndn Grants, 2758
Katherine Baxter Memorial Fndn Grants, 2789
Kentucky Arts Council Partnership Grants, 2809
Laclede Gas Charitable Grants, 2848
Laura L. Adams Fndn Grants, 2865
Mabel A. Horne Grants, 2956
Marion I. and Henry J. Knott Fndn Discretionary Grants, 3018
Marion I. and Henry J. Knott Standard Grants, 3019
Massachusetts Cultural Council Cultural Investment Portfolio, 3056
May and Stanley Smith Charitable Grants, 3069
Meyer Fndn Economic Security Grants, 3141
Meyer Fndn Educ Grants, 3142
Michael Reese Health Trust Core Grants, 3159
Montana Community Fndn Grants, 3211
Newfoundland and Labrador Arts Council Sustaining Grants, 3323
NYSCA Architecture, Planning, and Design: General Operating Support Grants, 3573
NYSCA Arts Educ: General Operating Support, 3578
NYSCA Dance Gen Operating Support Grants, 3584
Priddy Fndn Operating Grants, 3955
Regional Arts and Cultural Council General Support Grants, 4045
Richard F. and Janice F. Weaver Ed Grants, 4082
Robert Lee Adams Fndn Grants, 4114
Robert Lee Blaffer Fndn Grants, 4115
Robert R. Meyer Fndn Grants, 4121
TAC Arts Grants, 4554
TAC Rural Arts Project Support Grants, 4555
Virginia Commission for the Arts General Operating Grants, 4942

Ophthalmology
Alcon Fndn Grants, 351
Alice C. A. Sibley Grants, 371
Joseph Alexander Fndn Grants, 2734
Regents Professional Opportunity Scholarships, 4044
Richmond Eye and Ear Grants, 4092

Optometry
Alice C. A. Sibley Grants, 371
Canadian Optometric Educ Grants, 918
Regents Professional Opportunity Scholarships, 4044

Oral Health and Hygiene
Aetna Fndn Regional Health Grants, 187
Connecticut Health Fndn Health Init Grants, 1351
Mary Black Fndn Community Health Grants, 3032
United Methodist Child Mental Health Grants, 4721

Oral History
American Society for Yad Vashem Grants, 447
Arts Fndn, 578
Massachusetts Fndn for Humanities Grants, 3060
NYSCA Folk Arts: Presentation Grants, 3596
Turner Fndn Grants, 4681
Virginia Fndn for Humanities Discr Grants, 4946
Virginia Fndn for the Humanities Open Grants, 4947

SUBJECT INDEX

Orchestras
Aaron Copland Fund for Music Recording Program, 71
Ahmanson Fndn Grants, 207
Alabama State Council on the Arts Operating Support Grants, 244
Alcatel-Lucent Technologies Fndn Grants, 349
Barr Grants, 678
Bill and Katie Weaver Charitable Grants, 764
Clarence E. Heller Charitable Fndn Grants, 1150
Claude Worthington Benedum Fndn Grants, 1161
Community Fndn Alliance City of Evansville Endowment Grants, 1246
Community Fndn of the Ozarks Grants, 1320
CONSOL Coal Group Grants, 1360
Constantin Fndn Grants, 1362
El Paso Community Fndn Grants, 1688
Emma A. Sheafer Charitable Grants, 1699
Fremont Area Community Fndn Grants, 1955
George W. Codrington Charitable Fndn Grants, 2029
Greater Columbus Arts Council Operating Grant, 2133
Griffin Fndn Grants, 2165
Henrietta Lange Burk Grants, 2303
Howard and Bush Fndn Grants, 2374
Illinois Arts Council Music Grants, 2474
Katrine Menzing Deakins Charitable Grants, 2793
Kenneth T. and Eileen L. Norris Fndn Grants, 2802
Kirkpatrick Fndn Grants, 2827
Lubbock Area Fndn Grants, 2931
MacDonald-Peterson Fndn Grants, 2965
Massachusetts Cultural Adams Arts Grants, 3052
Mr. and Mrs. William Foulds Family Grants, 3222
NJSCA Arts Project Support, 3446
NJSCA General Program Support Grants, 3449
NYSCA Music Community Schools Grants, 3605
Ontario Arts Council Orchestras Grants, 3679
Robert W. Woodruff Fndn Grants, 4124
Salisbury Community Fndn Grants, 4224
San Antonio Area Fndn Grants, 4240
Sid W. Richardson Fndn Grants, 4350
Sioux Falls Area Community Fndn Field-of-Interest and Donor-Advised Grants, 4365
Walt Disney Company Fndn Grants, 4981
Wayne County Fndn Vigran Family Grants, 5004
Wayne County Fndn Grants, 5005
William T. Sloper Trust for Andres J. Sloper Musical Grants, 5097

Organ Transplants
Carlos and Marguerite Mason Grants, 934
Pfizer Healthcare Charitable Contributions, 3863
Robert B McMillen Fndn Grants, 4106
Sid W. Richardson Fndn Grants, 4350

Organic Farming
Merck Family Fund Urban Farming and Youth Leadership Grants, 3119
Steward of the Land Award, 4504
USDA Farmers Market Promotion Grants, 4808

Organizational Development
APAP Cultural Exchange Grants, 492
California Endowment Innovative Ideas Challenge Grants, 904
Center on Philanthropy and Civil Society's Emerging Leaders Int'l Fellows Program, 992
CNCS AmeriCorps Indian Planning Grants, 1180
CNCS AmeriCorps State and National Grants, 1182
CNCS Social Innovation Grants, 1189
Community Fndn in Jacksonville Art Ventures Small Organizations Professional Assistance Grants, 1262
Deborah Munroe Noonan Grants, 1475
Easton Fndns Archery Facility Grants, 1644
GNOF Organizational Effectiveness Grants and Workshops, 2090
Goldseker Fndn Non-Profit Management Assistance Grants, 2103
Kalamazoo Community Fndn Capacity Building Grants, 2764
Kalamazoo Community Fndn Economic and Community Development Grants, 2765
Lisa and Douglas Goldman Grants, 2910
Maine Community Fndn Belvedere Animal Welfare Grants, 2975
Meyer Fndn Benevon Grants, 3140
Meyer Fndn Educ Grants, 3142
Meyer Fndn Management Assistance Grants, 3144
Meyer Fndn Strong Nonprofit Sector Grants, 3145
Middlesex Savings Charitable Fndn Capacity Building Grants, 3172
NASE Succeed Scholarships, 3243
Nonprofit Management Grants, 3458
NWHF Health Advocacy Small Grants, 3537
NWHF Kaiser Permanente Community Grants, 3538
Otto Bremer Fndn Grants, 3713
Packard Fndn Organizational Effectiveness and Philanthropy Grants, 3730
PCA-PCD Organizational Short-Term Professional Development and Consulting Grants, 3769
PCA Arts Management Internship, 3773
PCA Management/Technical Assistance Grants, 3800
PCA Strategies for Success Grants - Advanced, 3804
PCA Strategies for Success Grants - Basic Level, 3805
PCA Strategies for Success Grants - Intermediate, 3806
Peter and Elizabeth C. Tower Fndn Organizational Scholarships, 3838
Priddy Fndn Organizational Development Grants, 3956
Prudential Fndn Economic Development Grants, 3976
Rasmuson Organizational Advancement Grants, 4023
Saginaw Community Fndn Discretionary Grants, 4205
Santa Barbara Fndn Monthly Express Grants, 4284
Santa Barbara Fndn Strategy Grants - Innovation, 4287
Santa Fe Community Fndn root2fruit Santa Fe, 4289
TAC Arts Access Technical Assistance Grants, 4550
TAC Technical Assistance Grants, 4556
Telluride Fndn Technical Assistance Grants, 4575
Union Bank, N.A. Fndn Grants, 4709
Union Square Award for Social Justice, 4717
USAID Economic Prospectsfor Armenia-Turkey Normalization Grants, 4750

Organizational Theory and Behavior
Brainerd Fndn Grants, 831
Charles G. Koch Charitable Fndn Grants, 1041
North Carolina Arts Council Community Arts Administration Internship, 3471
NSF Decision, Risk, and Management Science Research Grants, 3528
PDF Community Organizing Grants, 3807
PDF Fiscal Sponsorship Grant, 3808
Santa Barbara Fndn Strategy Grants - Innovation, 4287
Social Justice Fund NW Criminal Justice Giving Project Grants, 4394

Ornithology
Cornell Lab of Ornithology Mini-Grants, 1374

Orthopedics
El Paso Community Fndn Grants, 1688
John S. Dunn Research Fndn Grants and Chairs, 2715

Osteoporosis
Premera Blue Cross CARES Grants, 3945

Otolaryngology
Richmond Eye and Ear Grants, 4092

Outpatient Care
Erie Community Fndn Grants, 1750
George A. and Grace L. Long Fndn Grants, 2008
Pinnacle Entertainment Fndn Grants, 3893

Ovarian Cancer
GNOF IMPACT Harold W. Newman Grants, 2083
Seattle Fndn Medical Funds Grants, 4329

Pain
Pfizer Healthcare Charitable Contributions, 3863
Pfizer Medical Educ Track One Grants, 3864

Painting
Constance Saltonstall Fndn for the Arts Grants, 1361
Creative Work Grants, 1396
Florida Div of Culture Multidisciplinary Grants, 1857
NYFA Gregory Millard Fellowships, 3565
PCA Arts Organizations & Grants for Visual Arts, 3785
PCA Entry Track Arts Organizations and Program Grants for Visual Arts, 3799

Palliative Care
Aetna Fndn Regional Health Grants, 187
Austin S. Nelson Fndn Grants, 617
Piper Trust Healthcare & Med Research Grants, 3903

Pancreatic Cancer
GNOF IMPACT Harold W. Newman, Jr. Charitable Grants, 2083
Pfizer Healthcare Charitable Contributions, 3863
Seattle Fndn Medical Funds Grants, 4329

Parent Education
3M Fndn Community Giving Grants, 15
ACF Head Start and Early Head Start Grants, 120
A Fund for Women Grants, 195
BBF Florida Family Lit Init Grants, 697
BBF Maine Family Lit Init Grants, 698
BBF Maine Family Lit Init Planning Grants, 699
BBF Maryland Family Lit Init Grants, 700
BBF National Grants for Family Lit, 702
Bender Fndn Grants, 726
Bodman Fndn Grants, 807
CDC School Health Programs to Prevent the Spread of HIV Coop Agreements, 975
Community Fndn for Southern Arizona Grants, 1261
Community Fndn of Bartholomew County Women's Giving Circle, 1269
Comprehensive Health Educ Fndn Grants, 1337
Connecticut Community Fndn Grants, 1350
Cooper Fndn Grants, 1369
Dave Thomas Fndn for Adoption Grants, 1449
Dept of Ed Even Start Grants, 1508
Dept of Ed Parental Info and Resource Centers, 1510
DHHS Adolescent Family Life Demo Projects, 1524
Dolfinger-McMahon Fndn Grants, 1565
Do Right Fndn Grants, 1581
FCD Child Development Grants, 1796
First Lady's Family Lit Init for Texas Family Lit Trailblazer Grants, 1821
First Lady's Family Lit Init for Texas Grants, 1822
First Lady's Family Lit Init for Texas Implementation Grants, 1823
First Lady's Family Lit Init for Texas Planning, 1824
George W. Wells Fndn Grants, 2030
German Protestant Orphan Asylum Fndn Grants, 2044
Grand Rapids Community Ionia Youth Grants, 2120
Helen V. Brach Fndn Grants, 2300
Init Fndn Minnesota Early Childhood Grants, 2560
Linden Fndn Grants, 2908
Marin Community Fndn Stinson Bolinas Community Grants, 3013
Mary Black Early Childhood Devel Grants, 3033
Medtronic Comm Link Human Services Grants, 3112
MFRI Operation Diploma Small Grants for Indiana Family Readiness Groups, 3152
MGM Resorts Fndn Community Grants, 3153
Nellie Mae Educ Fndn District-Level Grants, 3297
Olga Sipolin Children's Grants, 3668
OneFamily Fndn Grants, 3673
Philadelphia Organizational Effectiveness Grants, 3872
Philadelphia Fndn YOUTHadelphia Grants, 3873
Piper Jaffray Fndn Communities Giving Grants, 3899
San Diego Fndn for Change Grants, 4247
Seattle Fndn Benjamin N. Phillips Grants, 4322
Skillman Fndn Good Schools Grants, 4382
Southbury Community Trust Fund, 4409
Strengthening Families - Strengthening Communities Grants, 4513
Target Corp Local Store Grants, 4561
U.S. Department of Educ 21st Century Community Learning Centers, 4687

964 / Parent Education

U.S. Department of Educ Parent Information and Training, 4695
U.S. Department of Educ Special Educ--National Activities--Parent Information Centers, 4701
Union Bank, N.A. Fndn Grants, 4709
Whirlpool Fndn Grants, 5056
Wood-Claeyssens Fndn Grants, 5113

Parent Involvement
Agere Corp and Community Involvement Grants, 199
ATF Gang Resistance Educ and Training Program Coop Agreements, 603
BBF Florida Family Lit Init Grants, 697
BBF Maine Family Lit Init Grants, 698
BBF Maine Family Lit Init Planning Grants, 699
BBF Maryland Family Lit Init Grants, 700
BBF Maryland Family Lit Init Planning Grants, 701
BBF National Grants for Family Lit, 702
Bella Vista Fndn Grants, 722
Bernard F. and Alva B. Gimbel Fndn Grants, 740
Bodman Fndn Grants, 807
Community Fndn of Broward Grants, 1275
Community Fnd Virgin Isls Kimelman Grants, 1324
DB Americas Fndn Grants, 1466
Dept of Ed Even Start Grants, 1508
Dept of Ed Parental Info and Resource Centers, 1510
First Lady's Family Lit Init for Texas Family Lit Trailblazer Grants, 1821
First Lady's Family Lit Init for Texas Implementation Grants, 1823
First Lady's Family Lit Init for Texas Planning, 1824
Fndn for the Carolinas Grants, 1896
GenCorp Fndn Grants, 1998
GNOF Stand Up For Our Children Grants, 2093
Healthcare Fndn for Orange County Grants, 2279
Kimberly-Clark Community Grants, 2824
Mary Black Early Childhood Devel Grants, 3033
NCFL/Better World Books Libraries and Families Award, 3288
Northern Trust Company Corp Giving Program, 3504
Northland Fndn Grants, 3506
NYCH Together Grants, 3541
Prince Charitable Trusts Chicago Grants, 3959
Pulaski County Community Fndn Grants, 3988
Randall L. Tobias Fndn Grants, 4017
SVP Early Childhood Development and Parenting Grants, 4538
U.S. Department of Educ Programs for Native Hawaiians, 4696
United Methodist Women Brighter Future for Children and Youth Grants, 4723
Vancouver Fndn Grants & Comm Inits, 4900
Walter and Elise Haas Grants, 4982

Parks
Albert and Bessie Mae Kronkosky Grants, 339
Bacon Family Fndn Grants, 634
Bikes Belong Grants, 763
Blackford County Community Fndn Grants, 780
Brooklyn Community Fndn Green Communities Grants, 852
Brunswick Fndn Grants, 857
California State Parks Restore & Cleanup Grants, 908
Christian Science Society of Boonville Irrevocable Trust, 1113
CICF Efroymson Grants, 1120
Cinergy Fndn Grants, 1133
Clara Blackford Smith and W. Aubrey Smith Charitable Fndn Grants, 1147
Community Fndn of Bloomington and Monroe County Grants, 1271
Community Fndn of St. Joseph County Special Project Challenge Grants, 1314
Community Fndn of the Ozarks Grants, 1320
Community Partnerships Martin County Grants, 1329
ConocoPhillips Fndn Grants, 1354
Cumberland Community Fndn Grants, 1413
Dayton Fndn Grants, 1463
Delaware Division of the Arts Community-Based Organizations Opportunity Grants, 1487

DOI Urban Park & Rec Recovery Grants, 1554
Fndn for Mid South Comm Development Grants, 1897
Fred C. and Mary R. Koch Fndn Grants, 1943
Gates Family Fndn Parks, Conservation & Recreation Grants, 1991
Gateway Fndn Grants, 1992
Harry C. Trexler Grants, 2239
HRF Hudson River Improvement Grants, 2378
Illinois Arts Council Artstour Grants, 2465
Illinois DNR Park and Recreational Facility Construction Grants, 2499
Jacobs Family Spirit of the Diamond Grants, 2618
Knox County Community Fndn Grants, 2831
Lincoln Financial Group Fndn Grants, 2906
Lyndhurst Fndn Grants, 2949
Mary & Walter Frear Eleemosynary Grants, 3035
MDEQ Great Lakes Areas of Concern Land Acquisition Grants, 3099
National Endowment for Arts Agencies Grants, 3263
NW Minnesota Fndn Asset Building Grants, 3511
Open Spaces Sacred Places National Awards, 3684
Perry County Community Fndn Grants, 3827
Pike County Community Fndn Grants, 3888
PNM Power Up Grants, 3925
Prince Charitable Trusts Chicago Grants, 3959
Prince Charitable Trusts Rhode Island Grants, 3961
Pulaski County Community Fndn Grants, 3988
Safeco Insurance Community Grants, 4203
Schumann Fund for New Jersey Grants, 4311
Sioux Falls Area Community Grants, 4364
Sioux Falls Area Community Fndn Spot Grants, 4366
Tony Hawk Fndn Grants, 4641
Union Bank, N.A. Fndn Grants, 4709
Weaver Fndn Grants, 5015
William & Flora Hewlett Environmental Grants, 5074

Patents, Copyrights, Trademarks
ALA Robert L. Oakley Scholarship, 313

Pathology
Joseph Drown Fndn Grants, 2735

Pathophysiology
NHLBI Lymphatics in Health & Disease in Digestive, Urinary, Cardio & Pulmonary Systems, 3415

Patient Care and Education
Carlos and Marguerite Mason Grants, 934
Central New York Community Fndn Grants, 996
Greenwall Fndn Bioethics Grants, 2158
Healthcare Fndn of New Jersey Grants, 2280
Mary Wilmer Covey Charitable Grants, 3049
McCarthy Family Fndn Grants, 3073
Medtronic Fndn Patient Link Grants, 3113
MMS and Alliance Charitable Fndn Grants for Community Action and Care for the Medically Uninsured, 3194
Mt. Sinai Health Care Fndn Health of the Jewish Community Grants, 3226
Pfizer Healthcare Charitable Contributions, 3863
Pfizer Special Events Grants, 3865
Pinnacle Entertainment Fndn Grants, 3893
Piper Trust Reglious Organizations Grants, 3905
Rathmann Family Fndn Grants, 4026

Peace/Disarmament
A.J. Muste Memorial Institute Counter Recruitment Grants, 43
A.J. Muste Memorial Institute General Grants, 44
A.J. Muste Memorial Institute Int'l Nonviolence Training Grants, 45
Agape Fndn for Nonviolent Social Change Board of Trustees Grants, 197
Agape Fndn for Nonviolent Social Change Prizes, 198
ALA Coretta Scott King Book Awards, 260
Compton Fndn Grants, 1338
Donald and Sylvia Robinson Family Fndn Grants, 1573
Edna Wardlaw Charitable Grants, 1660
Elizabeth Morse Genius Charitable Grants, 1682
Ford Fndn Peace and Social Justice Grants, 1884

Fund for Southern Communities Grants, 1977
Haymarket People's Fund Sustaining Grants, 2267
PDF Community Organizing Grants, 3807
PDF Fiscal Sponsorship Grant, 3808
Ploughshares Grants, 3916
S.H. Cowell Fndn Grants, 4199
Samuel Rubin Fndn Grants, 4237
Sasakawa Peace Fndn Grants, 4299
Scherman Fndn Grants, 4305
Teaching Tolerance Grants, 4567
Town Creek Fndn Grants, 4650
United States Institute of Peace - National Peace Essay Contest for High School Students, 4724
Ursula Thrush Peace Seed Grants, 4733
UUA Holmes-Weatherly Award, 4894

Pedagogy
Chicago Community Trust Educ Grants, 1085

Pediatric Cancer
GNOF IMPACT Harold W. Newman, Jr. Charitable Grants, 2083
Seattle Fndn Medical Funds Grants, 4329
Victor E. Speas Fndn Grants, 4933

Pediatrics
AAP Anne E. Dyson Child Advocacy Awards, 61
AAP Community Access To Child Health Advocacy Training Grants, 62
AAP Community Access To Child Health Implementation Grants, 63
AAP Community Access to Child Health Planning Grants, 64
AAP Community Access To Child Health Residency Training Grants, 65
AAP Community Access To Child Health Resident Grants, 66
AAP Leonard P. Rome Community Access to Child Health Visiting Professorships, 67
AAP Resident Init Grants, 69
Alexander and Margaret Stewart Grants, 354
Austin S. Nelson Fndn Grants, 617
Blowitz-Ridgeway Fndn Grants, 792
DHHS Adolescent Family Life Demo Projects, 1524
Health Fndn of Greater Indianapolis Grants, 2282
Lowe Fndn Grants, 2929
M. Bastian Family Fndn Grants, 2951
Mary S. and David C. Corbin Fndn Grants, 3048
MedImmune Charitable Grants, 3108
Piper Trust Healthcare & Med Research Grants, 3903
Ralph M. Parsons Fndn Grants, 4013
Saint Luke's Health Inits Grants, 4216
Victor E. Speas Fndn Grants, 4933

Penology/Correctional Insts and Procedures
Baptist Community Ministries Grants, 664
Caddock Fndn Grants, 888
Cambridge Community Fndn Grants, 913
DOJ Juvenile Justice and Delinquency Prevention Special Emphasis Grants, 1559
Fndn for the Carolinas Grants, 1896
Gardiner Howland Shaw Fndn Grants, 1986

Performance Art
Bush Fndn Arts & Humanities Grants: Short-Term Organizational Support, 873
CFFVR Fox Valley Community Arts Grants, 1011
Crystelle Waggoner Charitable Grants, 1405
George S. and Dolores Dore Eccles Fndn Grants, 2027
Illinois Arts Council Visual Arts Grants, 2478
Jerome Fndn Grants, 2667
Katharine Matthies Fndn Grants, 2788
NYSCA Arts Educ: General Operating Support, 3578
NYSCA Arts Educ Program Support Grants, 3579
NYSCA Arts Educ: K-12 In-School Grants, 3580
NYSCA Arts Educ: Services to the Field Grants, 3582
NYSCA Dance Gen Program Support Grants, 3585
NYSCA Folk Arts: Presentation Grants, 3596
NYSCA Folk Arts: Regional and County Folk Arts Grants, 3597

SUBJECT INDEX — Performing Arts / 965

NYSCA Presenting: General Operating Support, 3609
NYSCA Presenting: General Program Support, 3610
NYSCA Presenting: Presenting Grants, 3611
NYSCA Presenting: Services to the Field Grants, 3612
NYSCA Special Art Services Project Support, 3613
NYSCA Special Arts Services: General Program Support Grants, 3615
NYSCA Special Arts Services: Instruction and Training Grants, 3616
NYSCA Special Arts Services: Professional Performances Grants, 3617
NYSCA State and Local Partnerships: General Operating Support Grants, 3619
NYSCA State and Local Partnerships: Services to the Field Grants, 3621
NYSCA Theatre Gen Operating Support Grants, 3623
NYSCA Theatre General Program Support, 3624
NYSCA Theatre Pro Performances Grants, 3625
NYSCA Theatre: Services to the Field Grants, 3626
NYSCA Visual Arts: General Operating Support, 3628
NYSCA Visual Arts: General Program Support, 3629
NYSCA Visual Arts: Services to the Field Grants, 3630
PCA Arts Organizations & Grants for Lit, 3781
PCA Entry Track Arts Organizations and Program Grants for Literature, 3793
PCA Strategies for Success Grants - Advanced, 3804
PCA Strategies for Success Grants - Basic Level, 3805
Pew Fellowships in the Arts, 3860
Progress Energy Fndn Economic Vitality Grants, 3969
Rasmuson Fndn Creative Ventures Grants, 4021
Rasmuson Fndn Individual Artists Awards, 4022
San Francisco Fndn Fund Shenson Performing Arts Fellowships, 4275
Southbury Community Trust Fund, 4409
Texas Commission on the Arts Cultural Connections-Performance Support Grants, 4588

Performing Arts
Adams-Mastrovich Family Fndn Grants, 146
Adams Fndn Grants, 153
Adams Fndn Grants, 155
AEGON Transamerica Arts and Culture Grants, 176
AHS Fndn Grants, 208
Akron Community Fndn Arts & Culture Grants, 218
Aladdin Industries Fndn Grants, 263
ALA Writers Live at the Library Grants, 336
Alcatel-Lucent Technologies Fndn Grants, 349
Alvah H. and Wyline P. Chapman Fndn Grants, 402
American Express Charitable Grants, 429
Amgen Fndn Grants, 456
AMI Semiconductors Corp Grants, 457
Amon G. Carter Fndn Grants, 458
Andrew Goodman Fndn Grants, 463
Andy Warhol Fndn for the Visual Arts Grants, 464
Ann L. & Carol Green Rhodes Charitable Grants, 483
APAP Cultural Exchange Grants, 492
Arizona Commission on the Arts After-School Program Residencies, 535
Arizona Comm on the Arts Folklorist Residencies, 537
Arizona Commission on the Arts Individual Artist Residencies, 538
Arizona Community Fndn Grants, 540
Arizona Public Service Corp Giving Grants, 545
Arkansas Arts Council Sally A. Williams Grants, 558
Arlington Community Fndn Grants, 564
Arthur F. and Alice E. Adams Charitable Grants, 574
Arts Midwest Performing Arts Grants, 579
ArvinMeritor Fndn Arts and Culture Grants, 582
Athwin Fndn Grants, 605
Atlanta Fndn Grants, 608
Autzen Fndn Grants, 622
Avon Products Fndn Grants, 625
Back Home Again Fndn Grants, 633
BancorpSouth Fndn Grants, 651
Bill and Katie Weaver Charitable Grants, 764
Blanche and Irving Laurie Fndn Grants, 784
Blue Mountain Community Fndn Grants, 800
Bodenwein Public Benevolent Fndn Grants, 806
Boeing Company Contributions Grants, 809
Booth-Bricker Grants, 815

Boulder County Arts Alliance Neodata Endowment Grants, 823
Brown Fndn Grants, 854
Burlington Northern Santa Fe Fndn Grants, 866
Carnahan-Jackson Fndn Grants, 939
CDECD Arts Catalyze Placemaking in Every Community Grants, 977
CDECD Arts Catalyze Placemaking Leadership Grants, 978
CDECD Arts Catalyze Placemaking Sustaining Relevance Grants, 979
Cemala Fndn Grants, 988
CFFVR Fox Valley Community Arts Grants, 1011
Charles Delmar Fndn Grants, 1039
Charles M. Bair Family Grants, 1051
Charles Parker Trust for Public Music Grants, 1053
City of Oakland Cultural Arts Dept Grants, 1142
Clowes Grants, 1177
Colonel Stanley R. McNeil Fndn Grants, 1210
Colorado Springs Community Grants, 1215
Con Edison Corp Arts and Culture Grants, 1344
Connecticut Community Fndn Grants, 1350
ConocoPhillips Fndn Grants, 1354
Cord Fndn Grants, 1372
Cowles Charitable Grants, 1392
Creative Work Grants, 1396
Cudd Fndn Grants, 1410
Cullen Fndn Grants, 1411
D.F. Halton Fndn Grants, 1424
Dance Advance Grants, 1441
Davis Family Fndn Grants, 1462
Deborah Munroe Noonan Grants, 1475
Delaware Division of the Arts Opportunity Grants-Artists, 1489
Delta Air Lines Community Enrichment Grants, 1494
DeMatteis Family Fndn Grants, 1497
DeRoy Testamentary Fndn Grants, 1518
District of Columbia Commission on the Arts-Arts Educ Teacher Mini-Grants, 1549
Donald and Sylvia Robinson Family Fndn Grants, 1573
Doris Duke Charitable Fndn Arts Grants, 1584
DTE Energy Fndn Cultural Grants, 1610
Dwight Stuart Youth Fndn Grants, 1628
E. Rhodes and Leona B. Carpenter Fndn Grants, 1640
Edward R. Godfrey Fndn Grants, 1667
EIF Community Grants, 1675
Elizabeth Morse Genius Charitable Grants, 1682
Elsie H. Wilcox Fndn Grants, 1691
Emma A. Sheafer Charitable Grants, 1699
Entergy Corp Open Grants for Arts and Culture, 1713
Eugene B. Casey Fndn Grants, 1762
Eugene M. Lang Fndn Grants, 1764
Fan Fox and Leslie R. Samuels Fndn Grants, 1786
FirstEnergy Fndn Community Grants, 1819
Flinn Fndn Grants, 1842
Florida Div of Cultural Affairs Culture Builds Florida Expansion Funding, 1848
Florida Div of Cultural Affairs Culture Builds Florida Seed Funding, 1849
Florida Div of Cultural Affairs Underserved Cultural Community Development Grants, 1864
Frank Loomis Palmer Grants, 1931
G.N. Wilcox Grants, 1982
General Mills Fndn Grants, 2003
George A. and Grace L. Long Fndn Grants, 2008
George Gund Fndn Grants, 2020
George W. Brackenridge Fndn Grants, 2028
George W. Codrington Charitable Fndn Grants, 2029
Georgia Power Fndn Grants, 2039
Giant Eagle Fndn Grants, 2049
GNOF IMPACT Grants for Arts and Culture, 2078
Grand Rapids Area Community Fndn Grants, 2114
Grand Rapids Area Community Fndn Nashwauk Area Endowment Grants, 2115
Green Fndn Arts Grants, 2152
Griffin Fndn Grants, 2165
Guy I. Bromley Grants, 2180
HAF Arts and Culture: Lynne and Bob Wells Grant for Performing Artists, 2190
HAF Arts and Culture: Project Grants to Artists, 2191

Hahl Proctor Charitable Grants, 2208
Harold R. Bechtel Charitable Remainder Grants, 2229
Harry C. Trexler Grants, 2239
Heartland Arts Fund, 2286
Helen Gertrude Sparks Charitable Grants, 2294
Helen S. Boylan Fndn Grants, 2298
Henrietta Lange Burk Grants, 2303
Herman Abbott Family Fndn Grants, 2316
Herman Goldman Fndn Grants, 2317
High Meadow Fndn Grants, 2321
Horace Moses Charitable Fndn Grants, 2363
Howard and Bush Fndn Grants, 2374
Illinois Arts Council Arts-in-Education Residency Grants, 2463
Illinois Arts Council Presenters Dev Grants, 2476
James M. Cox Fndn of Georgia Grants, 2634
James S. Copley Fndn Grants, 2637
Janus Fndn Grants, 2647
Japan Fndn Los Angeles Mini-Grants for Japanese Arts & Culture, 2651
Japan Fndn New York Small Grants for Arts and Culture, 2652
Jaqua Fndn Grants, 2653
Jerome Fndn Travel and Study Grants, 2668
John F. Kennedy Center for the Performing Arts National Rosemary Kennedy Internship, 2694
John I. Smith Charities Grants, 2700
John W. Speas and Effie E. Speas Grants, 2732
Joyce Awards, 2746
Joyce Fndn Culture Grants, 2747
Kansas Arts Commission Arts on Tour Grants, 2780
Kansas Arts Commission Operational Support for Arts and Cultural Organizations, 2781
Katharine Matthies Fndn Grants, 2788
Kelvin and Eleanor Smith Fndn Grants, 2796
Kennedy Center Experiential Educ Internship, 2798
Kirkpatrick Fndn Grants, 2827
Laidlaw Fndn Youth Organizaing Inits Grants, 2854
Laura Jane Musser Rural Arts Grants, 2863
Leo Goodwin Fndn Grants, 2882
Lettie Pate Evans Fndn Grants, 2887
Lewis H. Humphreys Charitable Grants, 2889
Lied Fndn Grants, 2900
Linford and Mildred White Charitable Grants, 2909
Louetta M. Cowden Fndn Grants, 2922
Louis and Elizabeth Nave Flarsheim Charitable Fndn Grants, 2924
Lubrizol Fndn Grants, 2933
Lucile Horton Howe and Mitchell B. Howe Fndn Grants, 2934
Mabel Y. Hughes Charitable Grants, 2960
MacArthur Fndn Chicago Arts and Culture Int'l Connections Grants, 2962
MacDonald-Peterson Fndn Grants, 2965
Margaret Abell Powell Grants, 3002
Margaret L. Wendt Fndn Grants, 3004
Margaret T. Morris Fndn Grants, 3005
Marie H. Bechtel Charitable Grants, 3007
Marjorie Moore Charitable Fndn Grants, 3021
MARPAT Fndn Grants, 3023
Mary Duke Biddle Fndn Grants, 3036
McColl Fndn Grants, 3074
McKesson Fndn Grants, 3084
McLean Contributionship Grants, 3088
Merkel Family Fndn Grants, 3123
Mertz Gilmore Fndn NYC Dance Grants, 3127
Meyer and Stephanie Eglin Fndn Grants, 3139
Mid-America Arts Regional Touring Grants, 3167
Mid Atlantic Arts American Masterpieces Grants, 3169
Mid Atlantic Arts Fndn ArtsConnect Grants, 3170
Mid Atlantic Arts Fndn Folk Arts Outreach Project Grants, 3171
Montana Arts Council Cultural and Aesthetic Project Grants, 3209
Morris and Gwendolyn Cafritz Fndn Grants, 3218
National Endowment for Arts Agencies Grants, 3263
National Endowment for the Arts Presenting Grants: Art Works, 3268
National Endowment for Arts Theater Grants, 3269
Nicholas H. Noyes Jr. Memorial Fndn Grants, 3434

966 / Performing Arts

NJSCA Arts Project Support, 3446
NJSCA Financial and Instal Stabilization Grants, 3447
NJSCA General Program Support Grants, 3449
North Carolina Arts Council Arts in Educ Artist Residencies Grants, 3468
North Carolina Arts Council Ed Grants, 3469
North Carolina Arts Council Outreach Grants, 3479
North Carolina Arts Council Touring/Presenting Grants, 3483
North Carolina Arts Council Visual Arts Program Support Grants, 3484
NW Mutual Fndn Grants, 3509
NYFA Building Up Infrastructure Levels for Dance Grants, 3563
NYFA Strategic Opportunity Stipends, 3566
NYSCA Architecture, Planning, and Design: General Program Support Grants, 3574
NYSCA Architecture, Planning, and Design: Project Support Grants, 3576
NYSCA Arts Educ: CommunityLearning Grants, 3577
NYSCA Arts Educ: General Operating Support, 3578
NYSCA Arts Educ Program Support Grants, 3579
NYSCA Arts Educ: K-12 In-School Grants, 3580
NYSCA Arts Educ: Services to the Field Grants, 3582
NYSCA Dance: Commissions Grants, 3583
NYSCA Dance Gen Operating Support Grants, 3584
NYSCA Dance Gen Program Support Grants, 3585
NYSCA Dance: Long-Term Residency in New York State Grants, 3586
NYSCA Dance: Services to the Field Grants, 3587
NYSCA Folk Arts: General Program Support, 3595
NYSCA Folk Arts: Presentation Grants, 3596
NYSCA Folk Arts: Regional and County Folk Arts Grants, 3597
NYSCA Music Gen Operating Support Grants, 3606
NYSCA Music Gen Program Support Grants, 3607
NYSCA Presenting: General Operating Support, 3609
NYSCA Presenting: General Program Support, 3610
NYSCA Presenting: Presenting Grants, 3611
NYSCA Presenting: Services to the Field Grants, 3612
NYSCA Special Art Services Project Support, 3613
NYSCA Special Arts Services: General Operating Support Grants, 3614
NYSCA Special Arts Services: General Program Support Grants, 3615
NYSCA Special Arts Services: Instruction and Training Grants, 3616
NYSCA Special Arts Services: Professional Performances Grants, 3617
NYSCA State and Local Partnerships: General Operating Support Grants, 3619
NYSCA State and Local Partnerships: General Program Support Grants, 3620
NYSCA State and Local Partnerships: Services to the Field Grants, 3621
NYSCA State and Local Partnerships: Workshops Grants, 3622
NYSCA Theatre Gen Operating Support Grants, 3623
NYSCA Theatre General Program Support, 3624
NYSCA Theatre Pro Performances Grants, 3625
NYSCA Theatre: Services to the Field Grants, 3626
NYSCA Visual Arts: General Operating Support, 3628
NYSCA Visual Arts: General Program Support, 3629
NYSCA Visual Arts: Services to the Field Grants, 3630
Ohio Arts Council Arts Innovation Grants, 3649
Ontario Arts Council Presenter/Producer Grants, 3680
Oppenstein Brothers Fndn Grants, 3685
Owens Corning Fndn Grants, 3717
PacifiCorp Fndn for Learning Grants, 3727
PAS PASIC Scholarships, 3744
Paul G. Allen Family Fndn Grants, 3759
Paul Green Fndn Playwrights Fellowship, 3762
PCA-PCD Professional Development for Individual Artists Grants, 3770
PCA Art Organizations and Art Programs Grants for Presenting Organizations, 3771
PCA Arts in Educ Residencies, 3772
PCA Arts Organizations Grants for Music, 3774
PCA Arts Organizations and Arts Programs Grants for Arts Service Organizations, 3777

PCA Arts Organizations & Grants for Dance, 3779
PCA Busing Grants, 3786
PCA Entry Track Arts Organizations and Program Grants for Arts Service Organizations, 3789
PCA Entry Track Arts Organizations and Program Grants for Music, 3795
PCA Entry Track Arts Organizations and Program Grants for Presenting Organizations, 3796
PCA Pennsylvania Partners in the Arts Program Stream Grants, 3801
PCA Pennsylvania Partners in the Arts Project Stream Grants, 3802
PCA Professional Development Grants, 3803
PCA Strategies for Success Grants - Advanced, 3804
PCA Strategies for Success Grants - Basic Level, 3805
PCA Strategies for Success Grants - Intermediate, 3806
PennPAT Artist Technical Assistance Grants, 3811
PennPAT Fee-Support Grants for Presenters, 3812
PennPAT New Directions Grants for Presenters, 3813
PennPAT Presenter Travel Grants, 3814
PennPAT Strategic Opportunity Grants, 3815
Pew Charitable Trusts Arts and Culture Grants, 3857
Phil Hardin Fndn Grants, 3875
Piedmont Natural Gas Corp Contributions, 3883
Pinnacle Entertainment Fndn Grants, 3893
Piper Trust Arts and Culture Grants, 3900
PMP Project Grants, 3920
Powell Fndn Grants, 3942
Principal Financial Group Fndn Grants, 3966
Progress Energy Fndn Economic Vitality Grants, 3969
Rainbow Grants, 4009
Rasmuson Fndn Creative Ventures Grants, 4021
Regional Arts and Cultural Council Opportunity Grants, 4046
Reinberger Fndn Grants, 4052
Rhode Island Fndn Grants, 4073
Richard D. Bass Fndn Grants, 4079
Richard H. Driehaus Fndn MacArthur Fund for Arts and Culture, 4085
Richard H. Driehaus Fndn Small Theater and Dance Grants, 4086
Rich Fndn Grants, 4090
Roberta Leventhal Sudakoff Fndn Grants, 4102
Ryder System Charitable Fndn Grants, 4191
San Francisco Fndn Fund Shenson Performing Arts Fellowships, 4275
San Juan Island Community Fndn Grants, 4283
Santa Barbara Fndn Towbes Fund for the Performing Arts Grants, 4288
Schurz Communications Fndn Grants, 4312
Seattle Fndn Arts and Culture Grants, 4320
Sensient Technologies Fndn Grants, 4337
Sid W. Richardson Fndn Grants, 4350
Sosland Fndn Grants, 4408
South Carolina Arts Commission American Masterpieces in South Carolina Grants, 4413
South Carolina Arts Commission Annual Operating Support for Organizations Grants, 4414
South Carolina Arts Commission Fellowships, 4415
Sprague Fndn Grants, 4461
Sprint Fndn Grants, 4463
TAC Arts Grants, 4554
TAC Rural Arts Project Support Grants, 4555
TAC Touring Arts and Arts Access Grants, 4557
Temple-Inland Fndn Grants, 4576
Texas Commission on the Arts Cultural Connections-Performance Support Grants, 4588
Textron Corp Contributions Grants, 4601
Thomas Sill Fndn Grants, 4619
Tom's of Maine Fndn Grants, 4640
Union Bank, N.A. Fndn Grants, 4709
Viacom Fndn Grants (Formerly CBS Fndn), 4932
Virginia Commission for the Arts Artists in Educ Residency Grants, 4941
Virginia Commission for the Arts Project Grants, 4944
Virginia Commission for the Arts Touring Assistance Grants, 4945
VSA/Metlife Connect All Grants, 4953
VSA/Volkswagen Group of America Exhibition Awards, 4954

W. C. Griffith Fndn Grants, 4958
W.C. Griffith Fndn Grants, 4957
Wege Fndn Grants, 5017
West Virginia Comm on the Arts Mini Grants, 5041
West Virginia Commission on the Arts Presenting Artists Grants, 5044
Wilbur and Patsy Bradley Family Fndn Grants, 5066
William G. Gilmore Fndn Grants, 5082
William T. Sloper Trust for Andres J. Sloper Musical Grants, 5097
Winifred & Harry B. Allen Fndn Grants, 5101
Xerox Fndn Grants, 5122

Periodicals
ALA Ulrich's Serials Librarianship Award, 334
NEH Preservation Microfilming of Brittle Books and Serials Grants, 3294
TAC Arts Grants, 4554

Personnel Training and Development
ALA e-Learning Scholarships, 270
ALA Excellence in Academic Libraries Award, 276
ALA H.W. Wilson Library Staff Devel Grant, 283
Bemis Company Fndn Grants, 723
Charlotte County (FL) Community Fndn Grants, 1056
Children Affected by AIDS Network Grants, 1106
Claude Worthington Benedum Fndn Grants, 1161
Community Fndn in Jacksonville Art Ventures Small Organizations Professional Assistance Grants, 1262
Community Fndn of Greater Fort Wayne - Barbara Burt Leadership Development Grants, 1283
Community Fndn of St. Joseph County ArtsEverywhere Grants, 1313
Dwight Stuart Youth Capacity-Building Grants, 1627
Dyson Fndn Management Assistance Program Mini-Grants, 1632
Dyson Fndn Nonprofit Strategic Restructuring Init Grants, 1637
FEMA Staffing for Adequate Fire and Emergency Response Grants, 1803
IEDC Skills Enhancement Fund, 2445
Jacobs Family Jabara Learning Opps Grants, 2617
Kalamazoo Community Fndn Capacity Building Grants, 2764
Maine Community Fndn Belvedere Animal Welfare Grants, 2975
NASE Succeed Scholarships, 3243
National Endowment for Arts Agencies Grants, 3263
National Endowment for Arts Theater Grants, 3269
Nonprofit Management Grants, 3458
Ohio County Community Conference Grants, 3657
Piper Trust Healthcare & Med Research Grants, 3903
Priddy Fndn Organizational Development Grants, 3956
Prudential Fndn Economic Development Grants, 3976
TAC Arts Access Technical Assistance Grants, 4550
TAC Technical Assistance Grants, 4556
Tech Enhancement Certification for Hoosiers, 4571
Texas Comm on the Arts Young Masters Grants, 4594
UNESCO World Heritage Grants, 4706
Union Bank, N.A. Fndn Grants, 4709
USDA Self-Help Technical Assistance Grants, 4836

Pest Control
Conservation, Food, and Health Fndn Grants for Developing Countries, 1359
EPA Pestwise Registration Improvement Act Partnership Grants, 1734
EPA Regional Agricultural IPM Grants, 1735
USDA Special Research Grants, 4839

Pharmaceuticals
Campbell Hoffman Fndn Grants, 915
MDEQ Community Pollution Prevention (P2) Grants: Household Drug Collections, 3098
Pfizer Healthcare Charitable Contributions, 3863
Pfizer Medical Educ Track One Grants, 3864

Pharmacology
AAA Fndn for Traffic Safety Grants, 50
Hartford Aging and Health Program Awards, 2247

SUBJECT INDEX

National Center for Resp Gaming Travel Grants, 3251
NHLBI Ruth L. Kirschstein National Research Service Awards for Individual Senior Fellows, 3421
Victor E. Speas Fndn Grants, 4933

Pharmacy
IIE New Leaders Group Award for Mutual Understanding, 2460
J.M. Long Fndn Grants, 2603
Regents Professional Opportunity Scholarships, 4044
Schering-Plough Fndn Health Grants, 4304

Pharmacy Education
Amarillo Area/Harrington Fndns Grants, 412
North Carolina GlaxoSmithKline Fndn Grants, 3490
Pfizer Healthcare Charitable Contributions, 3863
Pfizer Medical Educ Track One Grants, 3864
Schering-Plough Fndn Health Grants, 4304

Philanthropy
A.J. Fletcher Fndn Grants, 41
Alfred P. Sloan Fndn Civic Inits Grants, 368
American Fndn Grants, 436
Annunziata Sanguinetti Fndn Grants, 485
Aragona Family Fndn Grants, 522
Ashland Corp Contributions Grants, 587
Beazley Fndn Grants, 714
Berrien Community Fndn Grants, 744
Butler Manufacturing Company Fndn Grants, 881
C.F. Adams Charitable Grants, 884
Carl Gellert and Celia Berta Gellert Fndn Grants, 930
Catherine Manley Gaylord Fndn Grants, 956
CECP Directors' Award, 986
Center for the Study of Philanthropy Fellowships, 989
Center for the Study of Philanthropy Senior Int'l Fellowships, 990
CFFVR Bridge Grants, 1003
Changemakers Community-Based Grants, 1030
Chautauqua Region Community Fndn Grants, 1062
CICF Indianapolis Fndn Community Grants, 1123
Clark Fndn Grants, 1157
Cleveland-Cliffs Fndn Grants, 1165
Cogswell Benevolent Grants, 1198
Columbus Fndn Competitive Grants, 1220
Community Fndn for Monterey County Grants, 1255
Community Fndn of Greater Flint Grants, 1282
Community Fndn of SE Connecticut Grants, 1309
Community Fndn Silicon Valley Grants, 1331
Council on Fndns Emerging Philanthropic Leaders Fellowships, 1378
Council on Fndns Paul Ylvisaker Award for Public Policy Engagement, 1379
Council on Fndns Robert W. Scrivner Award for Creative Grantmaking, 1380
DaimlerChrysler Corp Grants, 1432
Davenport-Hatch Fndn Grants, 1448
Durfee Fndn Sabbatical Grants, 1625
Dyson Fndn Mid-Hudson Philanthropy Grants, 1633
Essex County Community Fndn First Jobs Grant, 1754
Ewing Marion Kauffman Fndn Grants and Inits, 1777
Fargo-Moorhead Area Fndn Grants, 1788
Fndn NW Grants, 1906
Frey Fndn Grants, 1963
George Fndn Grants, 2018
George W. Codrington Charitable Fndn Grants, 2029
Giant Eagle Fndn Grants, 2049
HAF Justin Keele Make a Difference Award, 2198
Helen V. Brach Fndn Grants, 2300
Hillsdale County Community General Adult Fndn Grants, 2328
Hoblitzelle Fndn Grants, 2341
Huffy Fndn Grants, 2384
Jackson County Community Fndn Youth Advisory Committee Grants, 2612
Jackson Fndn Grants, 2613
Janesville Fndn Grants, 2644
Joel L. Fleishman Civil Society Fellowships, 2683
Johnson County Community Fndn Youth Philanthropy Init Grants, 2724
Josiah W. and Bessie H. Kline Fndn Grants, 2742

Leo Goodwin Fndn Grants, 2882
Libra Fndn Grants, 2899
Maine Women's Fund Girls' Grantmaking Init, 2993
Mary & Walter Frear Eleemosynary Grants, 3035
McCombs Fndn Grants, 3075
Meyer Fndn Strong Nonprofit Sector Grants, 3145
NACC David Stevenson Fellowships, 3235
NACC William Diaz Fellowships, 3236
National Endowment for Arts Our Town Grants, 3257
National Lottery Community Grants, 3279
Nonprofit Management Grants, 3458
OneFamily Fndn Grants, 3673
Packard Fndn Organizational Effectiveness and Philanthropy Grants, 3730
Parkersburg Area Comm Fndn Action Grants, 3738
Park Fndn Grants, 3739
Patrick and Aimee Butler Community Philanthropy & the Non-Profit Management Grants, 3750
Paul and Mary Haas Fndn Contributions and Student Scholarships, 3756
Pay It Forward Fndn Mini Grants, 3768
Peter and Georgia Angelos Fndn Grants, 3843
PGE Fndn Grants, 3869
Philanthrofund Fndn Grants, 3874
Pittsburgh Fndn Community Grants, 3910
Richard and Caroline T. Gwathmey Grants, 4075
Rochester Area Community Fndn Grants, 4127
Ruth Anderson Fndn Grants, 4176
Saginaw Community Fndn Discretionary Grants, 4205
Saint Paul Fndn Grants, 4219
Sioux Falls Area Community Fndn Spot Grants, 4366
State Street Fndn Grants, 4495
Steve Young Family Fndn Grants, 4503
Stewart Huston Charitable Grants, 4505
UPS Fndn Nonprofit Effectiveness Grants, 4732
Virginia A. Hodgkinson Research Prize, 4940
W.K. Kellogg Fndn Civic Engagement Grants, 4960
Wallace Alexander Gerbode Grants, 4974
Wayne County Fndn Women's Grants, 5006
Youth as Resources Mini-Grants, 5131

Philosophy
Alabama Humanities Fndn Mini Grants, 231
Alabama Humanities Planning/Consultant Grants, 232
Charles G. Koch Charitable Fndn Grants, 1041
Florida Humanities Council Major Grants, 1868
Florida Humanities Council Mini Grants, 1869
Germanistic Society of America Fellowships, 2043
Illinois Humanities Council Community Project Grants, 2510
James Hervey Johnson Charitable Ed Grants, 2627
NEH Family and Youth Programs in American History Grants, 3291
NYHC Major and Mini Grants, 3567
Virginia Fndn for the Humanities Residential Fellowships, 4948
Wisconsin Humanities Council Major Grants, 5107

Photography
Alabama State Council on the Arts Community Arts Collaborative Ventures Grants, 236
Alabama State Council on the Arts Community Arts Operating Support Grants, 237
Alabama State Council on the Arts Community Arts Presenting Grants, 238
Alabama State Council on the Arts Community Arts Program Development Grants, 239
Alabama State Council on the Arts Community Planning & Design Grants, 241
Alabama State Council on the Arts in Educ Partnership Grants, 242
Alabama State Council on the Arts Multi-Discipline and Festival Grants, 243
Arkansas Arts Council AIE After School/Summer Residency Grants, 551
Arkansas Arts Council AIE In-School Residency, 553
CCH California Story Grants, 965
CCH Documentary Project Production Grants, 969
CCH Documentary Public Engagement Grants, 970

Physics Education / 967

CCH Documentary Project Research and Development Grants, 971
Constance Saltonstall Fndn for the Arts Grants, 1361
Creative Work Grants, 1396
Florida Div of Cultural Affairs Multidisciplinary Grants, 1857
Illinois Arts Council Visual Arts Grants, 2478
Iowa Arts Council Artists in Schools/Communities Residency Grants, 2571
Minnesota State Arts Board Cultural Community Partnership Grants, 3188
North Carolina Arts Council Folklife Documentary Project Grants, 3475
NYFA Gregory Millard Fellowships, 3565
OSF Documentary Photography Project Audience Engagement Grant, 3706
PCA Arts Organizations & Grants for Visual Arts, 3785
PCA Entry Track Arts Organizations and Program Grants for Visual Arts, 3799
Ruth Mott Fndn Grants, 4180
San Francisco Fndn James D. Phelan Art Award in Photography, 4276
San Francisco Fndn John Gutmann Photography Fellowship Award, 4279
Third Millennium Fndn Grants, 4607

Physical Activity
CNCS AmeriCorps State and National Grants, 1182
Collective Brands Fndn Grants, 1206
HAF Mada Huggins Caldwell Grants, 2200
Phoenix Coyotes Charities Grants, 3879

Physical Disability
Adams Rotary Memorial Fund A Grants, 157
Allan C. and Leila J. Garden Fndn Grants, 374
Ayres Fndn Grants, 630
CICF Howard Intermill and Marion Intermill Fenstermaker Grants, 1122
Elkhart County Community Fndn Fund for Elkhart County, 1683
George E. Hatcher, Jr. and Ann Williams Hatcher Fndn Grants, 2015
Grace Bersted Fndn Grants, 2110
John D. and Katherine A. Johnston Fndn Grants, 2691
Johnson Scholarship Fndn Grants, 2726
NIAF Anthony Campitelli Endowed Grants, 3431
Northland Fndn Grants, 3506
Reader's Digest Partners for Sight Fndn Grants, 4036
Sobrato Family Fndn Grants, 4389
Sobrato Family Fndn Meeting Space Grants, 4390
Sobrato Family Fndn Office Space Grants, 4391
Sylvia Adams Charitable Grants, 4543

Physical Education
BCBSM Building Healthy Communities Elementary Schools and Community Partners Grants, 704
CNCS AmeriCorps State and National Grants, 1182
Dept of Ed Recreational Services for Individuals with Disabilities, 1512
Fremont Area Comm Summer Youth Grants, 1956
Homer Fndn Grants, 2352
Mary Jennings Sport Camp Scholarship, 3041

Physical Medicine and Rehabilitation
Annunziata Sanguinetti Fndn Grants, 485
GEICO Public Service Awards, 1997
Regents Professional Opportunity Scholarships, 4044

Physical Sciences
Canada-U.S. Fulbright Mid-Career Grants, 917
Marion I. and Henry J. Knott Standard Grants, 3019
North Carolina GlaxoSmithKline Fndn Grants, 3490

Physics
Canada-U.S. Fulbright Mid-Career Grants, 917
Marion I. and Henry J. Knott Standard Grants, 3019
Weingart Fndn Grants, 5018

Physics Education
George I. Alden Grants, 2023

Physics, High Energy
USDA High Energy Cost Grants, 4812
USDA State Bulk Fuel Revolving Grants, 4840

Physiology, Human
NHLBI Lymphatics in Health & Disease in Digestive, Urinary, Cardio & Pulmonary Systems, 3415

Piano
Thelma Braun and Bocklett Family Fndn Grants, 4603

Planetariums
IMLS 21st Century Museum Pro Grants, 2512
IMLS American Heritage Preservation Grants, 2513
IMLS National Leadership Grants, 2515

Planning/Policy Studies
Ball Brothers Fndn Organizational Effectiveness/Executive Mentoring Grants, 638
GNOF IMPACT Grants for Educ, 2079
GNOF St. Bernard Community Grants, 2092
IMLS 21st Century Museum Pro Grants, 2512
IMLS National Leadership Grants, 2515
Indiana Arts Comm Capacity Building Grants, 2531
MacArthur Fndn Policy Research Grants, 2964
Meyer Fndn Healthy Communities Grants, 3143
NHSCA Operating Grants, 3428
Ohio Arts Council Capacity Building Grants for Organizations and Communities, 3652
Princeton Area Community Fndn Fund for Women and Girls Grants, 3962
TAC Arts Access Technical Assistance Grants, 4550
TAC Technical Assistance Grants, 4556
USAID Grant for Operationalizing a Neighborhood Approach to Reduce Urban Disaster Risk in Latin America and the Caribbean, 4754

Plant Genetics
John D. and Catherine T. MacArthur Fndn Global Challenges Grants, 2690
Pioneer Hi-Bred Conferences & Meetings Grants, 3896

Plant Sciences
Janirve Fndn Grants, 2645
NFWF Native Plant Conservation Init Grants, 3380
NFWF Pulling Together Init Grants, 3387
NGA Hooked on Hydroponics Awards, 3405
NGA Wuzzleburg Preschool Garden Awards, 3408
Pioneer Hi-Bred Conferences & Meetings Grants, 3896

Playgrounds
Able To Play Challenge Grants, 101
American Academy of Dermatology Shade Structure Grants, 420
Clara Blackford Smith and W. Aubrey Smith Charitable Fndn Grants, 1147
Gateway Fndn Grants, 1992
Hasbro Children's Fund, 2256
Head Start Replacement Grantee: West Virginia, 2277
KaBOOM-CA Playground Challenge Grants, 2761
Paul E. and Klare N. Reinhold Fndn Grants, 3758
William Blair and Company Fndn Grants, 5078

Podiatry
Regents Professional Opportunity Scholarships, 4044

Poetry
ALA Stonewall Book Awards - Barbara Gittings Literature Award, 329
California Coastal Art and Poetry Contest, 899
Constance Saltonstall Fndn for the Arts Grants, 1361
Illinois Arts Council Literature Grants, 2470
Kentucky Arts Council Al Smith Fellowship, 2806
Kentucky Arts Council Emerging Artist Award, 2807
Kentucky Arts Council Poetry Out Loud Grants, 2810
Minnesota State Arts Board Cultural Community Partnership Grants, 3188
National Endowment for Arts Big Read Grants, 3261
NJSCA Arts Project Support, 3446
NJSCA General Program Support Grants, 3449
North Carolina Arts Council Residency Grants, 3481
NYFA Gregory Millard Fellowships, 3565
NYSCA Lit: General Operating Support Grants, 3598
NYSCA Literature: General Support Grants, 3599
PCA Arts Organizations & Grants for Lit, 3781
PCA Entry Track Arts Organizations and Program Grants for Literature, 3793
PCA Strategies for Success Grants - Advanced, 3804
PCA Strategies for Success Grants - Basic Level, 3805
PCA Strategies for Success Grants - Intermediate, 3806
Pew Fellowships in the Arts, 3860
Poets & Writers Readings/Workshops Grants, 3927
San Francisco Fndn Art Awards Joseph Henry Jackson Literary Award, 4259
South Carolina Arts Commission Fellowships, 4415
Wallace Alexander Gerbode Fndn Special Award Grants, 4975

Poison Control
CDC State and Local Childhood Lead Poisoning Prevention Grants, 976
Community Fndn of Middle Tennessee Grants, 1300

Political Behavior
Carnegie Corp of New York Grants, 940
Fund for Southern Communities Grants, 1977
IREX Small Grant Fund for Civil Society Projects in Africa and Asia, 2581
Joyce Fndn Democracy Grants, 2748
Needmor Grants, 3289
PDF Community Organizing Grants, 3807
PDF Fiscal Sponsorship Grant, 3808
Proteus Grants, 3973
Robert Sterling Clark Fndn Government Accountability Grants, 4123
Sister Grants for Women's Organizations, 4371
State Strategies Grants, 4494
USAID Community Livelihoods Project in Yemen Grant, 4746
USAID Media and Elections Rwanda Grants, 4768
Z. Smith Reynolds Fndn Democracy and Civic Engagement Grants, 5145

Political Economics
Charles G. Koch Charitable Fndn Grants, 1041
Murphy Institute Judith Kelleher Schafer Summer Internship Grants, 3230

Political Parties
USAID Grant for Operationalizing a Neighborhood Approach to Reduce Urban Disaster Risk in Latin America and the Caribbean, 4754

Political Science
ANLAF Int'l Fund for Sexual Minorities Grants, 471
APSA Minority Fellowships, 517
Canada-U.S. Fulbright Mid-Career Grants, 917
Charles G. Koch Charitable Fndn Grants, 1041
Germanistic Society of America Fellowships, 2043
GMFUS Marshall Memorial Fellowships, 2066
Horowitz Fndn for Social Policy Grants, 2370
Horowitz Fndn for Social Policy Special Awards, 2371
Margaret L. Wendt Fndn Grants, 3004
Morris K. Udall and Stewart L. Udall Fndn Dissertation Fellowships, 3219
NYHC Major and Mini Grants, 3567
Samuel Rubin Fndn Grants, 4237

Political Science Education
Coca-Cola Fndn Grants, 1195
Hatton W. Sumners Fndn for the Study and Teaching of Self Government Grants, 2257

Political Theory
Bernard and Audre Rapoport Fndn Democracy and Civic Participation Grants, 737
Morris K. Udall and Stewart L. Udall Fndn Native American Congressional Internships, 3220
Z. Smith Reynolds Fndn Democracy and Civic Engagement Grants, 5145

Politics
Bernard and Audre Rapoport Fndn Democracy and Civic Participation Grants, 737
Energy Fndn Climate Grants, 1706
USAID Community Livelihoods Project in Yemen Grant, 4746
USAID Grant for Operationalizing a Neighborhood Approach to Reduce Urban Disaster Risk in Latin America and the Caribbean, 4754
USAID Media and Elections Program in Rwanda Grants, 4768

Pollution
3 Rivers Wet Weather Demonstration Grants, 9
EPA Air Pollution Control Support Grants, 1722
EPA Environmental Educ Grants, 1729
EPA Regional Agricultural IPM Grants, 1735
EPA Senior Environmental Employment Grants, 1736
EPA State Indoor Radon Grants, 1738
EPA State Senior Environ Employment Grants, 1739
EPA Surveys, Studies, Research, Investigations, Demonstrations, and Special Purpose Activities Relating to the Clean Air Act, 1740
Gamble Fndn Grants, 1983
Illinois Clean Energy Community Fndn Energy Efficiency Grants, 2479
Illinois Clean Energy Community Fndn Renewable Energy Grants, 2481
Rose Fndn For Communities and the Environment Kern County Air Pollution Mitigation Grants, 4157
Sapelo Fndn Environmental Protection Grants, 4293

Pollution Control
EPA Air Pollution Control Support Grants, 1722
EPA Senior Environmental Employment Grants, 1736
EPA Source Reduction Assistance Grants, 1737
EPA State Indoor Radon Grants, 1738
EPA State Senior Environ Employment Grants, 1739
EPA Surveys, Studies, Research, Investigations, Demonstrations, and Special Purpose Activities Relating to the Clean Air Act, 1740
Grand Victoria Fndn Illinois Core Grants, 2126
Illinois Clean Energy Community Fndn Energy Efficiency Grants, 2479
Illinois Clean Energy Community Fndn Renewable Energy Grants, 2481
MDEQ Clean Diesel Grants, 3096
Orchard Fndn Grants, 3690
Rose Fndn For Communities and the Environment Kern County Air Pollution Mitigation Grants, 4157
Rose Fndn for Comm & the Environment N California Environmental Grassroots Grants, 4158
Sapelo Fndn Environmental Protection Grants, 4293
Sioux Falls Area Community Fndn Spot Grants, 4366
USDA Rural Business Enterprise Grants, 4823

Pollution, Air
Bullitt Fndn Grants, 862
Bush Fndn Ecological Health Grants, 874
Carrier Corp Contributions Grants, 946
Colorado Interstate Gas Grants, 1213
EPA Air Pollution Control Support Grants, 1722
EPA Senior Environmental Employment Grants, 1736
EPA State Indoor Radon Grants, 1738
EPA State Senior Environ Employment Grants, 1739
EPA Surveys, Studies, Research, Investigations, Demonstrations, and Special Purpose Activities Relating to the Clean Air Act, 1740
MDEQ Clean Diesel Grants, 3096
Orchard Fndn Grants, 3690
Rose Fndn For Communities and the Environment Kern County Air Pollution Mitigation Grants, 4157
San Diego Fndn for Change Grants, 4247
Washington Gas Charitable Contributions, 5000

Pollution, Land
EPA Senior Environmental Employment Grants, 1736
EPA State Senior Environ Employment Grants, 1739
San Diego Fndn for Change Grants, 4247

SUBJECT INDEX

Poverty and the Poor / 969

Pollution, Noise
EPA Senior Environmental Employment Grants, 1736
EPA State Senior Environ Employment Grants, 1739
San Diego Fndn for Change Grants, 4247

Pollution, Water
American Rivers Community-Based Restoration Program River Grants, 444
Beldon Grants, 720
Chesapeake Bay Trust Capacity Building Grants, 1068
Chesapeake Bay Trust Environmental Ed Grants, 1069
Chesapeake Bay Trust Outreach and Community Engagement Grants, 1073
Chesapeake Bay Trust Pioneer Grants, 1074
Community Fndn for Greater New Haven Quinnipiac River Grants, 1250
EPA Senior Environmental Employment Grants, 1736
EPA State Senior Environ Employment Grants, 1739
Freshwater Future Insight Services Grants, 1960
Freshwater Future Project Grants, 1961
Freshwater Future Special Opportunity Grants, 1962
Great Lakes Protection Grants, 2147
Heineman Fndn for Research, Educ, Charitable and Scientific Purposes, 2290
IDEM Section 205(j) Water Quality Management Planning Grants, 2434
IDEM Section 319(h) Nonpoint Source Grants, 2435
Indiana Clean Vessel Act Grants, 2535
Joyce Fndn Environment Grants, 2750
MDEQ Beach Monitoring Grants - Inland Lakes, 3094
MDEQ Local Water Quality Monitoring Grants, 3100
MDEQ Wellhead Protection Grants, 3101
NFWF Wildlife Links Grants, 3400
Orchard Fndn Grants, 3690
PepsiCo Fndn Grants, 3819
Rohm and Haas Company Grants, 4145
Rose Fndn For Communities and the Environment Watershed Protection Grants, 4160
San Diego Fndn for Change Grants, 4247
Sapelo Fndn Environmental Protection Grants, 4293
USAID Palestinian Community Infrastructure Development Grants, 4774
USDA Section 306C Water and Waste Disposal Grants to Alleviate Health Risks, 4834
USDA Special Research Grants, 4839
Wabash River Enhancement Corp Agricultural Cost-Share Grants, 4968
Wabash River Enhancement Corp Urban, 4969
Washington Gas Charitable Contributions, 5000
William Bingham Fndn Grants, 5077

Population Control
Burning Fndn Grants, 867
Clayton Baker Grants, 1163
Cleveland H. Dodge Fndn Grants, 1172
General Service Fndn Human Rights and Economic Justice Grants, 2006
Huber Fndn Grants, 2382
Liz Claiborne and Art Ortenberg Fndn Grants, 2914
Lumpkin Family Healthy People Grants, 2942
Maine Community Fndn Belvedere Animal Welfare Grants, 2975
Packard Fndn Local Grants, 3729
S.H. Cowell Fndn Grants, 4199
Wallace Global Grants, 4977
Wilburforce Fndn Grants, 5067

Population Studies
Compton Fndn Grants, 1338
George Frederick Jewett Fndn Grants, 2019
Richard and Rhoda Goldman Grants, 4077
Wallace Global Grants, 4977

Poverty and the Poor
A.V. Hunter Grants, 47
Abelard Fndn East Grants, 87
Abelard Fndn West Grants, 88
ACE Charitable Fndn Grants, 111
ACF Assets for Indep Demonstration Grants, 114
Achelis Fndn Grants, 127

Agape Fndn for Nonviolent Social Change Board of Trustees Grants, 197
Aid for Starving Children African American Indep Single Mother's Grants, 210
Alice Tweed Tuohy Fndn Grants, 372
Alliance Healthcare Fndn Grants, 383
American Express Community Service Grants, 430
Angels in Motion Fndn Grants, 467
Ann Arbor Area Community Fndn Grants, 474
Arizona Community Fndn Grants, 540
Arizona Diamondbacks Charities Grants, 542
Arizona Republic Newspaper Contributions, 547
Atlanta Women's Fndn Grants, 609
Austin S. Nelson Fndn Grants, 617
Barberton Community Fndn Grants, 666
Barr Fndn Grants, 677
Ben & Jerry's Fndn Grants, 724
Bernard & Audre Rapoport Arts & Culture Grant, 735
Bernard and Audre Rapoport Fndn Community Building and Social Service Grants, 736
Bernard and Audre Rapoport Fndn Democracy and Civic Participation Grants, 737
Bernard and Audre Rapoport Fndn Health Grants, 738
Bernard and Audre Rapoport Fndn University of Texas at Austin Scholarship Programs, 739
Bill and Melinda Gates Fndn Agricultural Development Grants, 765
Bill & Melinda Gates Emergency Response Grants, 766
Bill and Melinda Gates Fndn Financial Services for the Poor Grants, 767
Bill and Melinda Gates Fndn Library Grants, 768
Bill & Melinda Gates Policy & Advocacy Grants, 769
Bill and Melinda Gates Fndn Water, Sanitation and Hygiene Grants, 770
Birmingham Fndn Grants, 774
Bodman Fndn Grants, 807
Burden Grants, 864
Carnegie Corp of New York Grants, 940
Carrie Estelle Doheny Fndn Grants, 945
CCF Social and Economic Justice Grants, 964
CCHD Community Development Grants, 966
CCHD Economic Development Grants, 967
CFFVR Basic Needs Giving Partnership Grants, 1002
CFFVR Jewelers Mutual Charitable Giving, 1014
CharityWorks Grants, 1036
Charles Stewart Mott Fndn Anti-Poverty Grants, 1054
Charles Stewart Mott Fndn Grants, 1055
CICF Christmas Fund, 1117
CICF Indianapolis Fndn Community Grants, 1123
CNCS AmeriCorps VISTA Project Grants, 1184
CNCS Senior Companion Grants, 1187
Community Fndn of Greater Flint Grants, 1282
Community Fndn of Greater Memphis Grants, 1290
Community Fndn of Greenville Hollingsworth Funds Program/Project Grants, 1296
Community Fndn of Louisville Grants, 1299
Community Fndn of Middle Tennessee Grants, 1300
Connelly Fndn Grants, 1353
Cummins Fndn Grants, 1415
Danellie Fndn Grants, 1442
Dept of Ed Child Care Access Means Parents in School Grants, 1507
Dept of Ed Even Start Grants, 1508
Dept of Ed Upward Bound Program, 1514
DHHS Indep Demonstration Program, 1535
Dreyer's Fndn Large Grants, 1606
Eden Hall Fndn Grants, 1655
Edyth Bush Charitable Fndn Grants, 1673
Emma B. Howe Memorial Fndn Grants, 1700
Energy Fndn Power Grants, 1707
Farmers Insurance Corp Giving Grants, 1791
Fitzpatrick, Cella, Harper & Scinto Pro Bono, 1836
Foster G. McGaw Prize, 1889
Fund for Southern Communities Grants, 1977
General Service Fndn Colorado Grants, 2005
General Service Fndn Human Rights and Economic Justice Grants, 2006
George Gund Fndn Grants, 2020
George P. Davenport Grants, 2026
Gertrude E. Skelly Charitable Fndn Grants, 2046

Ginn Fndn Grants, 2056
GNOF IMPACT Grants for Health and Human Services, 2080
GNOF Maison Hospitaliere Grants, 2086
GNOF Stand Up For Our Children Grants, 2093
Goldseker Fndn Human Services Grants, 2102
Greater Milwaukee Fndn Grants, 2137
Greater Worcester Comm Discretionary Grants, 2140
GTECH Community Involvement Grants, 2171
H.B. Fuller Company Fndn Grants, 2183
HAF Hansen Family Trust Christian Endowment Grants, 2197
Hasbro Children's Fund, 2256
HBF Pathways Out of Poverty Grants, 2273
Healthcare Fndn for Orange County Grants, 2279
Health Fndn of Greater Cincinnati Grants, 2281
Hearst Fndns Social Service Grants, 2285
Help America Fndn Grants, 2301
Henry E. Niles Fndn Grants, 2309
Henry J. Kaiser Family Fndn Grants, 2310
Hilda and Preston Davis Fndn Grants, 2322
Hillcrest Fndn Grants, 2325
Hoffberger Fndn Grants, 2342
Humanitas Fndn Grants, 2390
IBCAT Screening Mammography Grants, 2422
IIE David L. Boren Fellowships, 2454
Indep Blue Cross Charitable Med Care Grants, 2524
Irvin Stern Fndn Grants, 2585
J.L. Bedsole Fndn Grants, 2600
Jacob G. Schmidlapp Grants, 2616
Jenkins Fndn: Improving the Health of Greater Richmond Grants, 2663
Jessie Ball Dupont Grants, 2671
John Edward Fowler Memorial Fndn Grants, 2693
Josephine Goodyear Fndn Grants, 2738
Jovid Fndn Grants, 2745
Kahuku Community Fund, 2762
Kate B. Reynolds Charitable Trust Poor and Needy Grants, 2787
Kroger Company Donations, 2841
LA84 Fndn Grants, 2847
Linden Fndn Grants, 2908
Liz Claiborne and Art Ortenberg Fndn Grants, 2914
Luther I. Replogle Fndn Grants, 2945
Lynde and Harry Bradley Fndn Grants, 2947
Lynde and Harry Bradley Fndn Prizes, 2948
Marie C. and Joseph C. Wilson Fndn Rochester Small Grants, 3006
Marin Community Fndn Ending the Cycle of Poverty Grants, 3011
Mary E. Ober Fndn Grants, 3039
May and Stanley Smith Charitable Grants, 3069
Medtronic Fndn Patient Link Grants, 3113
Meyer Fndn Economic Security Grants, 3141
Meyer Fndn Healthy Communities Grants, 3143
Meyer Fndn Strong Nonprofit Sector Grants, 3145
Michael Reese Health Trust Core Grants, 3159
Michael Reese Health Trust Responsive Grants, 3160
Mid-Iowa Health Fndn Comm Response Grants, 3168
Mizuho USA Fndn Grants, 3192
Mockingbird Fndn Grants, 3196
Modest Needs Bridge Grants, 3197
Moran Family Fndn Grants, 3216
NAR Partners in Housing Awards, 3239
Nathan Cummings Fndn Grants, 3246
National Lottery Community Grants, 3279
Nationwide Insurance Fndn Grants, 3285
Needmor Grants, 3289
Northern Trust Company Corp Giving Program, 3504
OneFamily Fndn Grants, 3673
OUT Fund for Lesbian & Gay Liberation Grants, 3714
Paso del Norte Health Fndn Grants, 3743
PepsiCo Fndn Grants, 3819
Piper Trust Children Grants, 3901
Pittsburgh Fndn Community Grants, 3910
Playboy Fndn Grants, 3913
Quaker Oats Company Kids Care Clubs Grants, 3992
Robin Hood Fndn Grants, 4125
S.E.VEN Fund 'In The River They Swim' Essay Competition, 4194

970 / Poverty and the Poor

S.E.VEN Fund Annual Grants, 4195
S.E.VEN Fund Mini-Grants, 4196
S.E.VEN Fund Open Enterprise Solutions to Poverty RFP Grants, 4197
S.E.VEN Fund WHY Prize, 4198
S.H. Cowell Fndn Grants, 4199
SanDisk Corp Community Sharing Program, 4253
Santa Barbara Strategy Core Suupport Grants, 4286
Schumann Fund for New Jersey Grants, 4311
Seattle Fndn Economy Grants, 4325
Shastri Indo-Canadian Institute Action Research Project Grants, 4341
Sidgmore Family Fndn Grants, 4348
Sioux Falls Area Community Fndn Spot Grants, 4366
Siragusa Fndn Human Services Grants, 4369
Sir Dorabji Tata Grants for NGOs or Voluntary Organizations, 4370
Sisters of Charity Fndn of Canton Grants, 4372
Skillman Fndn Good Schools Grants, 4382
Speer Grants, 4450
St. Joseph Community Health Fndn Catherine Kasper Award, 4468
Starr Fndn Grants, 4483
Stewart Huston Charitable Grants, 4505
Strengthening Families - Strengthening Communities Grants, 4513
Surdna Fndn Sustainable Environments Grants, 4533
Susan A. & Donald P. Babson Charitable Grants, 4534
Sylvia Adams Charitable Grants, 4543
The World Food Prize, 4606
Third Wave Fndn Lela Breitbart Grants, 4609
Third Wave Organizing & Advocacy Grants, 4610
Third Wave Fndn Reproductive Health and Justice Grants, 4611
Thomas D. McGrain Cedar Glade Fndn Grants, 4616
Thomas Sill Fndn Grants, 4619
Thompson Fndn Grants, 4623
TJX Fndn Grants, 4637
U.S. Department of Educ Promoting Postbaccalaureate Opportunities for Hispanic Americans Grants, 4697
United Methodist Committee on Relief Hunger and Poverty Grants, 4720
USAID Albania Critical Economic Growth Areas Grants, 4740
USDA Community Food Projects Grants, 4802
USDA Self-Help Technical Assistance Grants, 4836
Vanguard Public Fndn Grant Funds, 4904
W.K. Kellogg Fndn Healthy Kids Grants, 4961
W.K. Kellogg Fndn Racial Equity Grants, 4962
W.K. Kellogg Fndn Secure Families Grants, 4963
Weaver Fndn Grants, 5015
Wieboldt Fndn Grants, 5065
William G. McGowan Charitable Grants, 5084
William J. and Dorothy K. O'Neill Fndn Grants, 5087
William Robert Baird Charitable Grants, 5093
Women's Funding Alliance Grants, 5112

Pregnancy
ACF Head Start and Early Head Start Grants, 120
Adams Family Fndn of Tennessee Grants, 152
Alliance Healthcare Fndn Grants, 383
DHHS Health Centers Grants for Residents of Public Housing, 1533
General Service Fndn Human Rights and Economic Justice Grants, 2006
Orchard Fndn Grants, 3690
Portland Fndn - Women's Giving Circle Grant, 3935
USAID Comprehensive District-Based Support for Better HIV/TB Patient Outcomes Grants, 4747
USAID Family Health Plus Project Grants, 4751
USAID HIV Prevention with Key Populations - Mali Grants, 4757
W.P. and Bulah Luse Fndn Grants, 4965

Presbyterian Church
AHS Fndn Grants, 208
Alvah H. and Wyline P. Chapman Fndn Grants, 402
Barra Fndn Project Grants, 674
Beerman Fndn Grants, 717
Booth-Bricker Grants, 815
Bradley-Turner Fndn Grants, 828
Effie and Wofford Cain Fndn Grants, 1674
MacDonald-Peterson Fndn Grants, 2965
Presbyterian Church USA Sam and Helen R. Walton Award, 3946
Speer Grants, 4450

Preschool Education
Alabama Power Fndn Grants, 233
ALA Coretta Scott King Book Donation Grant, 261
American Electric Power Grants, 428
Arizona Diamondbacks Charities Grants, 542
Arizona Republic Newspaper Contributions, 547
Arkansas Arts Council AIE Arts Curriculum Project Grants, 552
Barnes and Noble National Sponsorships and Charitable Donations, 671
Benton Community Fndn Grants, 730
Blackford County Community Fndn Grants, 780
Blue River Community Fndn Grants, 801
Bodenwein Public Benevolent Fndn Grants, 806
Booth-Bricker Grants, 815
Boston Fndn Grants, 819
Brown County Community Fndn Grants, 853
Carnegie Corp of New York Grants, 940
CFFVR Basic Needs Giving Partnership Grants, 1002
Clinton County Community Fndn Grants, 1174
CNCS Foster Grandparent Grants, 1185
Community Fndn Alliance City of Evansville Endowment Grants, 1246
Community Fndn of Bartholomew County Heritage Grants, 1267
Community Fndn of Bartholomew County James A. Henderson Award for Fundraising, 1268
Community Fndn of Greater Fort Wayne - Community Endowment and Clarke Endowment Grants, 1285
Community Fndn of Greenville Community Enrichment Grants, 1294
Community Fndn of Greenville Hollingsworth Funds Program/Project Grants, 1296
Community Fndn of Southern Indiana Grants, 1310
Community Fnd Virgin Isls Kimelman Grants, 1324
Cowles Charitable Grants, 1392
Dekko Fndn Grants, 1482
Dept of Ed Even Start Grants, 1508
Dept of Ed Parental Info and Resource Centers, 1510
DHHS American Recovery and Reinvestment Act of 2009 Head Start Expansion, 1526
District of Columbia Commission on the Arts-Arts Educ Teacher Mini-Grants, 1549
Dreyer's Fndn Large Grants, 1606
Effie and Wofford Cain Fndn Grants, 1674
Eugene M. Lang Fndn Grants, 1764
FCD Child Development Grants, 1796
Fisher Fndn Grants, 1831
Fndn for the Carolinas Grants, 1896
France-Merrick Fndns Grants, 1915
Frances and John L. Loeb Family Grants, 1917
General Service Fndn Colorado Grants, 2005
George Fndn Grants, 2018
Grable Fndn Grants, 2108
Grand Victoria Fndn Illinois Core Grants, 2126
Head Start Replacement Grantee: Colorado, 2275
Head Start Replacement Grantee: Florida, 2276
Head Start Replacement Grantee: West Virginia, 2277
Helen Steiner Rice Fndn Grants, 2299
Hutchinson Community Fndn Grants, 2410
J.C. Penney Company Grants, 2594
John Edward Fowler Memorial Fndn Grants, 2693
Johnson & Johnson Corp Contributions Grants, 2718
Kentucky Arts Council TranspARTation Grant, 2812
Lyndhurst Fndn Grants, 2949
Marie C. and Joseph C. Wilson Fndn Rochester Small Grants, 3006
Marin Community Fndn Stinson Bolinas Community Grants, 3013
Medtronic Fndn CommunityLink Educ Grants, 3110
Meyer Fndn Educ Grants, 3142
Miller Fndn Grants, 3181
Mimi and Peter Haas Grants, 3185
National Endowment for the Arts - National Arts and Humanities Youth Program Awards, 3255
National Home Library Fndn Grants, 3276
North Carolina Arts Council Arts in Educ Rural Development Grants, 3470
Norton Fndn Grants, 3514
NYSCA Arts Educ: Community-based Learning Grants, 3577
NYSCA Arts Educ: K-12 In-School Grants, 3580
NYSCA Arts Education: Local Capacity Building Grants, 3581
NYSCA Arts Educ: Services to the Field Grants, 3582
Oppenstein Brothers Fndn Grants, 3685
Peter and Elizabeth C. Tower Fndn Social and Emotional Preschool Curriculum Grants, 3841
Phoenix Suns Charities Grants, 3881
Piper Trust Arts and Culture Grants, 3900
Piper Trust Children Grants, 3901
Piper Trust Educ Grants, 3902
Piper Trust Reglious Organizations Grants, 3905
PNC Fndn Grow Up Great Grants, 3924
Portland General Electric Fndn Grants, 3937
Quantum Fndn Grants, 3996
Reynolds American Fndn Grants, 4068
Rosie's For All Kids Fndn Grants, 4163
San Antonio Area Fndn Grants, 4240
Schumann Fund for New Jersey Grants, 4311
Sid W. Richardson Fndn Grants, 4350
Topeka Community Fndn Grants, 4644
U.S. Department of Ed Early Reading 1st Grants, 4691
Union Bank, N.A. Fndn Grants, 4709
Wayne County Fndn Vigran Family Grants, 5004
Wayne County Fndn Grants, 5005
William McCaskey Chapman and Adaline Dinsmore Chapman Fndn Grants, 5092

Preventive Medicine
Alexander and Margaret Stewart Grants, 354
Banfi Vintners Fndn Grants, 653
Baptist Community Ministries Grants, 664
Battle Creek Community Fndn Grants, 684
California Endowment Innovative Ideas Challenge Grants, 904
Caterpillar Fndn Grants, 954
CDC Grants for Violence-Related Injury Prevention Research, 974
CMA Fndn Grants, 1178
Community Fndn AIDS Endowment Awards, 1245
DHHS Adolescent Family Life Demo Projects, 1524
Dr. John T. Macdonald Fndn Grants, 1600
Eden Hall Fndn Grants, 1655
Edwards Grants, 1669
Emma B. Howe Memorial Fndn Grants, 1700
Fndn for Health Enhancement Grants, 1894
Fndn for Seacoast Health Grants, 1895
Frances and John L. Loeb Family Grants, 1917
General Mills Fndn Grants, 2003
Healthcare Fndn for Orange County Grants, 2279
Health Fndn of So Florida Responsive Grants, 2283
Indep Community Fndn Community Quality of Life Grant, 2525
Johnson & Johnson Corp Contributions Grants, 2718
Kansas Health Fndn Recognition Grants, 2784
Marin Community Successful Aging Grants, 3014
Mary Black Fndn Active Living Grants, 3031
Medtronic Fndn Patient Link Grants, 3113
Michael Reese Health Trust Responsive Grants, 3160
OUT Fund for Lesbian & Gay Liberation Grants, 3714
Paso del Norte Health Fndn Grants, 3743
Pfizer Healthcare Charitable Contributions, 3863
Premera Blue Cross CARES Grants, 3945
Robert W. Woodruff Fndn Grants, 4124
Self Fndn Grants, 4335
Sid W. Richardson Fndn Grants, 4350
Sisters of Saint Joseph Charitable Grants, 4376
USAID HIV Prevention with Key Populations - Mali Grants, 4757
USCM HIV/AIDS Prevention Grants, 4794
Visiting Nurse Fndn Grants, 4951

SUBJECT INDEX

Professional Development / 971

Primary Care Services
CVS Community Grants, 1422
DHHS Adolescent Family Life Demo Projects, 1524
DHHS Health Centers Grants for Residents of Public Housing, 1533
DHHS Technical and Non-Financial Assistance to Health Centers, 1539
George Fndn Grants, 2018
Health Fndn of Greater Cincinnati Grants, 2281
Health Fndn of So Florida Responsive Grants, 2283
Kansas Health Fndn Recognition Grants, 2784
RWJF New Jersey Health Inits Grants, 4187
Union Pacific Health & Human Services Grants, 4715
W.K. Kellogg Fndn Healthy Kids Grants, 4961

Print Media
Akron Community Fndn Arts & Culture Grants, 218
Appalachian Community Media Justice Grants, 495
Florida Div of Cultural Affairs Media Grants, 1856
Geraldine R. Dodge Fndn Media Grants, 2042
Henry J. Kaiser Family Fndn Grants, 2310

Printmaking
Constance Saltonstall Fndn for the Arts Grants, 1361
San Francisco Fndn James D. Phelan Art Award in Printmaking, 4277

Prison Reform
Bernard F. and Alva B. Gimbel Fndn Grants, 740
Gardiner Howland Shaw Fndn Grants, 1986
OSI After Prison Init Grants, 3710
Threshold Fndn Justice and Democracy Grants, 4626

Prisoners
ACF Mentoring Children of Prisoners Grants, 121
Achelis Fndn Grants, 127
ALA Exceptional Service Award, 278
Arizona Community Fndn Grants, 540
Bodman Fndn Grants, 807
John Gogian Family Fndn Grants, 2697
Kansas Arts Commission Artist Fellowships, 2776
Mockingbird Fndn Grants, 3196
Valentine Fndn Grants, 4897

Prisons
ALA Coretta Scott King Book Donation Grant, 261
Kentucky Arts Council Access Assistance Grants, 2805

Private and Parochial Education
Bailey Fndn Grants, 635
Boeckmann Charitable Fndn Grants, 808
Boettcher Fndn Grants, 810
Brown Fndn Grants, 854
California Arts Council Arts and Accessibility Technical Assistance Grants, 894
California Arts Council Public Value Grants, 895
Coca-Cola Fndn Grants, 1195
Commission on Religion in Appalachia Grants, 1238
ConocoPhillips Fndn Grants, 1354
Dr. Scholl Fndn Grants, 1602
Eugene B. Casey Fndn Grants, 1762
Fleishhacker Fndn Educ Grants, 1838
Frank G. and Freida K. Brotz Family Grants, 1928
Frank Reed and Margaret Jane Peters Memorial Fund II Grants, 1934
Kenneth T. and Eileen L. Norris Fndn Grants, 2802
Kentucky Arts Council TranspARTation Grant, 2812
Lettie Pate Evans Fndn Grants, 2887
Lubbock Area Fndn Grants, 2931
Lubrizol Fndn Grants, 2933
Lynde and Harry Bradley Fndn Grants, 2947
Lynde and Harry Bradley Fndn Prizes, 2948
Marion I. and Henry J. Knott Fndn Discretionary Grants, 3018
Marion I. and Henry J. Knott Standard Grants, 3019
Mathile Family Fndn Grants, 3062
Medtronic Fndn CommunityLink Educ Grants, 3110
Mervin Bovaird Fndn Grants, 3128
MGN Family Fndn Grants, 3154
Ober Kaler Community Grants, 3635

PacifiCorp Fndn for Learning Grants, 3727
Piper Jaffray Fndn Communities Giving Grants, 3899
Piper Trust Reglous Organizations Grants, 3905
Richard King Mellon Fndn Grants, 4087
Roy and Christine Sturgis Charitable Grants, 4166
Russell Berrie Fndn Grants, 4175
S.H. Cowell Fndn Grants, 4199
Strake Fndn Grants, 4511
Sunderland Fndn Grants, 4527
T. James Kavanagh Fndn Grants, 4545
Target Corp Local Store Grants, 4561
Thomas B. & Elizabeth M. Sheridan Grants, 4614
Turner B. Bunn, Jr. & Catherine E. Bunn Grants, 4680
Ursula Thrush Peace Seed Grants, 4733

Problem Solving
Aspen Community Fndn Grants, 592
Captain Planet Fndn Grants, 922
CCHD Economic Development Grants, 967
Charles Stewart Mott Fndn Grants, 1055
Durfee Fndn Stanton Fellowship, 1626
Fred C. and Mary R. Koch Fndn Grants, 1943
Land O'Lakes Fndn Community Grants, 2859
NSF Decision, Risk, and Management Science Research Grants, 3528
RISCA Design Innovation Grant, 4097
Surdna Fndn Sustainable Environments Grants, 4533

Process Development Engineering
RISCA Design Innovation Grant, 4097

Production/Operations Management
Bush Fndn Regional Arts Development Grants, 878
Nonprofit Management Grants, 3458
NYSCA Theatre General Program Support, 3624
NYSCA Theatre: Services to the Field Grants, 3626

Professional Associations
ALA Allie Beth Martin Award, 221
ALA ALTAFF/GALE Outstanding Trustee Conference Grant, 224
ALA Annual Conference Professional Development Attendance Award, 225
ALA Atlas Systems Mentoring Award, 227
ALA Charlie Robinson Award, 256
ALA Distinguished School Administrator Award, 266
ALA EBSCO Community College Learning Resources Leadership Awards, 271
ALA EBSCO Community College Library Program Achievement Award, 272
ALA EBSCO Midwinter Meeting Sponsorship, 274
ALA Esther J. Piercy Award, 275
ALA Exceptional Service Award, 278
ALA First Step Award/Wiley Professional Development Grant, 279
ALA Gale Cengage History Research and Innovation Award, 280
ALA Harrassowitz Award for Leadership in Library Acquisitions Award, 284
ALA Intellectual Freedom Award, 289
ALA Isadore Gilbert Mudge Award, 290
ALA Jan Merrill-Oldham Professional Development Grant, 291
ALA John Phillip Immroth Memorial Award, 293
ALA Joseph W. Lippincott Award, 294
ALA MAE Award for Best Teen Lit, 296
ALA Margaret Mann Citation, 297
ALA Margaret T. Lane/Virginia F. Saunders Memorial Research Award, 298
ALA Morningstar Pub Librarian Support Award, 302
ALA NewsBank/Readex C. J. Reynolds Award, 304
ALA NMRT Professional Development Grant, 305
ALA Paul Howard Award for Courage, 307
ALA Routledge Distance Learning Librarianship Conference Sponsorship Award, 315
ALA Scholastic Library Publishing Award, 318
ALA Student Chapter of the Year Award, 331
ALA Sullivan Award for Administrators Supporting Services to Children, 332
ALA Supporting Diversity Stipend, 333

ALA Ulrich's Serials Librarianship Award, 334
ALA Young Adult Literature Symposium Stipend, 337
ASME Charles T. Main Awards, 590
ATA School-Community Relations Awards, 602
Cemala Fndn Grants, 988
IRA Pearson Fndn-IRA-Rotary Lit Awards, 2572
PCA Art Organizations and Art Programs Grants for Presenting Organizations, 3771
PCA Entry Track Arts Organizations and Program Grants for Presenting Organizations, 3796
Pfizer Special Events Grants, 3865
Phi Upsilon Omicron Florence Fallgatter Distinguished Service Award, 3877
Phi Upsilon Omicron Frances Morton Holbrook Alumni Award, 3878

Professional Development
ALA ALSC Distinguished Service Award, 223
ALA ALTAFF/GALE Outstanding Trustee Conference Grant, 224
ALA Annual Conference Professional Development Attendance Award, 225
ALA Atlas Systems Mentoring Award, 227
ALA Distinguished School Administrator Award, 266
ALA EBSCO Community College Library Program Achievement Award, 272
ALA EBSCO Midwinter Meeting Sponsorship, 274
ALA Exceptional Service Award, 278
ALA First Step Award/Wiley Professional Development Grant, 279
ALA Harrassowitz Award for Leadership in Library Acquisitions Award, 284
ALA Isadore Gilbert Mudge Award, 290
ALA Jan Merrill-Oldham Professional Development Grant, 291
ALA Joseph W. Lippincott Award, 294
ALA Margaret Mann Citation, 297
ALA NewsBank/Readex C. J. Reynolds Award, 304
ALA NMRT Professional Development Grant, 305
ALA Pat Carterette Professional Devel Grant, 306
ALA Supporting Diversity Stipend, 333
ALA Young Adult Literature Symposium Stipend, 337
BBVA Compass Fndn Charitable Grants, 703
ChevronTexaco Contributions Program, 1078
Chicago Community Trust Fellowships, 1086
CICF Summer Youth Grants, 1128
DHHS Emerging Leaders Program Internships, 1532
GNOF IMPACT Grants for Youth Development, 2081
IIE Toyota Int'l Teacher Professional Development Grants, 2461
Illinois Arts Council Service Organization Grants, 2464
John F. Kennedy Center for the Performing Arts National Rosemary Kennedy Internship, 2694
Kennedy Center HSC Fndn Internship, 2799
Kennedy Center Summer HSC Fndn Internship, 2800
Libra Fndn Future Grants, 2898
Meyer Fndn Strong Nonprofit Sector Grants, 3145
NAA Fndn Diversity PowerMind Fellowships, 3232
NAA Fndn Minority Fellowships, 3233
NAA Fndn Teacher Fellowships, 3234
NASE Succeed Scholarships, 3243
National Endowment for the Arts - Regional Partnership Agreement Grants, 3258
National Endowment for Arts Music Grants, 3266
National Endowment for Arts Opera Grants, 3267
National Endowment for the Arts Presenting Grants: Art Works, 3268
National Endowment for Arts Theater Grants, 3269
Nevada Arts Council Professional Dev Grants, 3314
NYSCA Arts Education: Local Capacity Building Grants, 3581
NYSCA Music Gen Operating Support Grants, 3606
NYSCA Presenting: Services to the Field Grants, 3612
NYSCA Special Arts Services: Instruction and Training Grants, 3616
NYSCA State and Local Partnerships: Services to the Field Grants, 3621
NYSCA State and Local Partnerships: Workshops Grants, 3622
NYSCA Visual Arts: Workspace Facilities Grants, 3631

972 / Professional Development

PAS Internship, 3742
PCA-PCD Professional Development for Individual Artists Grants, 3770
PCA Arts Organizations & Grants for Crafts, 3778
PCA Entry Track Arts Organizations and Program Grants for Crafts, 3790
PCA Professional Development Grants, 3803
PennPAT New Directions Grants for Presenters, 3813
Phi Upsilon Omicron Florence Fallgatter Distinguished Service Award, 3877
Phi Upsilon Omicron Frances Morton Holbrook Alumni Award, 3878
Piedmont Natural Gas Fndn Environmental Stewardship and Energy Sustainability Grant, 3884
Piedmont Natural Gas Fndn Workforce Development Grant, 3886
Priddy Fndn Organizational Development Grants, 3956
Prudential Fndn Economic Development Grants, 3976
Public Educ Power Grants, 3981
Regional Arts and Cultural Council Professional Development Grants, 4047
RISCA Professional Arts Development Grants, 4099
RISCA Project Grants for Organizations, Individuals and Educ, 4100
Robert R. McCormick Tribune Civics Grants, 4118
VSA/Volkswagen Group of America Exhibition Awards, 4954
West Virginia Commission on the Arts Professional Development for Artists Grants, 5045

Professorship
Cabot Corp Fndn Grants, 887
Roy and Christine Sturgis Charitable Grants, 4166

Program Evaluation
Baton Rouge Area Fndn Credit Bureau Grants, 680
Goldseker Fndn Non-Profit Management Assistance Grants, 2103
Greater Worcester Community Mini-Grants, 2142
Hartford Fndn Evaluation Grants, 2250
Indiana Arts Comm Capacity Building Grants, 2531
Marin Community Successful Aging Grants, 3014
Priddy Fndn Grants, 3957
Santa Barbara Fndn Monthly Express Grants, 4284
South Carolina Arts Commission Arts and Economic Impact Study Assistance Grants, 4416
South Carolina Arts Commission Cultural Tourism Init Grants, 4419
South Carolina Arts Commission Statewide Arts Participation Init Grants, 4425
South Madison Community Fndn Grants, 4440
SVP Early Childhood Development and Parenting Grants, 4538

Project Management
Cause Populi Worthy Cause Grants, 958
Hartford Fndn Evaluation Grants, 2250
Hartford Fndn Implementation Support Grants, 2251
Nonprofit Management Grants, 3458
Patrick and Aimee Butler Community Philanthropy & the Non-Profit Management Grants, 3750
USAID Development Innov Ventures Grants, 4749
USDA Rural Business Enterprise Grants, 4823

Prostate Gland
William G. McGowan Charitable Grants, 5084

Prosthetic Devices
U.S. Department of Educ Rehabilitation Engineering Research Centers Grants, 4698

Proteins and Macromolecules
NHLBI Career Transition Awards, 3412

Protestant Church
ABC Charities Grants, 85
AHS Fndn Grants, 208
Alvah H. and Wyline P. Chapman Fndn Grants, 402
Aragona Family Fndn Grants, 522
Atherton Family Fndn Grants, 604

Bitha Godfrey & Maude J. Thomas Charitable Fndn Grants, 776
Camp-Younts Fndn Grants, 914
Charles Delmar Fndn Grants, 1039
Clark and Ruby Baker Fndn Grants, 1154
Cobb Family Fndn Grants, 1194
Collins C. Diboll Private Fndn Grants, 1208
Cooke-Hay Fndn Grants, 1367
Dora Roberts Fndn Grants, 1579
Dresher Fndn Grants, 1605
E. Rhodes and Leona B. Carpenter Fndn Grants, 1640
Fred and Sherry Abernethy Fndn Grants, 1940
G.A. Ackermann Grants, 1981
G.N. Wilcox Grants, 1982
Huie-Dellmon Grants, 2386
J. Edwin Treakle Fndn Grants, 2596
Jim Blevins Fndn Grants, 2678
Knight Fndn Grants - Georgia, 2829
Notsew Orm Sands Fndn Grants, 3516
Stewart Huston Charitable Grants, 4505
Wilbur and Patsy Bradley Family Fndn Grants, 5066
William M. Weaver Fndn Grants, 5091

Psychiatry
APSAA Fndn Grants, 516
Blowitz-Ridgeway Fndn Grants, 792

Psychology
APSAA Fndn Grants, 516
Blowitz-Ridgeway Fndn Grants, 792
Canada-U.S. Fulbright Mid-Career Grants, 917
Chapin Hall Int'l Fellowships in Children's Policy Research, 1032
Edward Bangs Kelley and Elza Kelley Grants, 1665
George I. Alden Grants, 2023
Horowitz Fndn for Social Policy Grants, 2370
Horowitz Fndn for Social Policy Special Awards, 2371
National Center for Resp Gaming Travel Grants, 3251
Regents Professional Opportunity Scholarships, 4044

Psychology of Aging
Edward N. and Della L. Thome Memorial Fndn Direct Services Grants, 1666

Psychotherapy
APSAA Fndn Grants, 516

Public Administration
Anderson Fndn Grants, 460
Arlington Community Fndn Grants, 564
Canada-U.S. Fulbright Mid-Career Grants, 917
Carpenter Fndn Grants, 943
Chautauqua Region Community Fndn Grants, 1062
Effie and Wofford Cain Fndn Grants, 1674
Fulbright/Garcia Robles Grants, 1968
Fulbright Graduate Degree Grants in Mexico, 1971
Huffy Fndn Grants, 2384
Illinois DCEO Business Development Public Infrastructure Grants, 2483
M.D. Anderson Fndn Grants, 2952
National Urban Fellows Program, 3281
Peter Kiewit Fndn General Grants, 3845
Peter Kiewit Fndn Small Grants, 3847
S. Mark Taper Fndn Grants, 4201
Sonora Area Fndn Competitive Grants, 4404
Sosland Fndn Grants, 4408
Sprague Fndn Grants, 4461

Public Affairs
1st Source Fndn Grants, 3
AFG Industries Grants, 191
Akzo Nobel Chemicals Grants, 219
Alfred P. Sloan Fndn Public Service Awards, 369
Allegheny Fndn Grants, 376
Allegheny Technologies Charitable Trust, 377
American Express Charitable Grants, 429
Armstrong McDonald Fndn Grants, 565
AutoNation Corp Giving Grants, 620
Banfi Vintners Fndn Grants, 653
Battle Creek Community Fndn Grants, 684

Bernard and Audre Rapoport Fndn Democracy and Civic Participation Grants, 737
Berrien Community Fndn Grants, 744
Bicknell Grants, 759
Blue Grass Community Fndn Grants, 799
Bohemian Fndn Pharos Grants, 811
Brown Fndn Grants, 854
Burlington Northern Santa Fe Fndn Grants, 866
Caesars Fndn Grants, 891
Carpenter Fndn Grants, 943
Clark County Community Fndn Grants, 1156
Columbus Fndn Small Grants, 1232
Commonwealth Edison Grants, 1240
Crestlea Fndn Grants, 1399
Crossroads Fund Seed Grants, 1400
CSRA Community Fndn Grants, 1407
Cullen Fndn Grants, 1411
Cyrus Eaton Fndn Grants, 1423
Daisy Marquis Jones Fndn Grants, 1434
Emerson Electric Company Contributions Grants, 1695
Eugene McDermott Fndn Grants, 1765
F.M. Kirby Fndn Grants, 1780
Field Fndn of Illinois Grants, 1806
FirstEnergy Fndn Community Grants, 1819
Fluor Fndn Grants, 1875
FMC Fndn Grants, 1876
Francis Beidler Fndn Grants, 1921
Fulbright/Garcia Robles Grants, 1968
Fulbright Graduate Degree Grants in Mexico, 1971
Fulbright Public Policy Init Grants in Mexico, 1972
Furth Family Fndn Grants, 1980
General Dynamics Corp Grants, 2001
Germanistic Society of America Fellowships, 2043
Harry S. Truman Scholarships, 2244
HBF Encouraging Citizen Involvement Grants, 2272
Howard and Bush Fndn Grants, 2374
Howard H. Callaway Fndn Grants, 2376
Idaho Community Fndn Eastern Region Competitive Grants, 2432
IMLS Nat Medal for Museum & Library Service, 2516
IREX Kosovo Civil Society Project Grants, 2576
John Merck Grants, 2706
John S. and James L. Knight Fndn Donor Advised Grants, 2712
Katharine Matthies Fndn Grants, 2788
Kiplinger Program in Public Affairs Journalism Fellowships, 2826
Libra Fndn Grants, 2899
Lockheed Martin Philanthropic Grants, 2918
Lynde and Harry Bradley Fndn Grants, 2947
Lynde and Harry Bradley Fndn Prizes, 2948
Marathon Petroleum Corp Grants, 2999
Margaret L. Wendt Fndn Grants, 3004
Marjorie Moore Charitable Fndn Grants, 3021
Meadows Fndn Grants, 3104
Meyer Memorial Trust Grassroots Grants, 3147
Meyer Memorial Trust Responsive Grants, 3148
Mimi and Peter Haas Grants, 3185
Morris K. Udall and Stewart L. Udall Fndn Native American Congressional Internships, 3220
Musgrave Fndn Grants, 3231
New York Fndn Grants, 3338
New York Life Fndn Grants, 3341
Noble County Community Fndn Grants, 3456
OSI Sentencing and Incarceration Alternatives Project Grants, 3711
Paul E. and Klare N. Reinhold Fndn Grants, 3758
Pike County Community Fndn Grants, 3888
Putnam County Community Fndn Grants, 3990
Putnam Fndn Grants, 3991
Rajiv Gandhi Fndn Grants, 4011
Robert R. Meyer Fndn Grants, 4121
Ruth and Vernon Taylor Fndn Grants, 4177
Sage Fndn Grants, 4204
Salisbury Community Fndn Grants, 4224
Sarah Scaife Fndn Grants, 4295
Schramm Fndn Grants, 4310
Seattle Fndn Doyne M. Green Scholarships, 4324
Seaver Institute Grants, 4331
Shell Oil Company Fndn Grants, 4343

SUBJECT INDEX

Social Justice Fund NW Economic Justice Giving Project Grants, 4395
Social Justice Fund NW LGBTQ Giving Project Grants, 4398
Social Justice Fund NW Montana Giving Project Grants, 4399
Starr Fndn Grants, 4483
State Strategies Grants, 4494
Steelcase Fndn Grants, 4497
Surdna Fndn Sustainable Environments Grants, 4533
Vermont Community Fndn Grants, 4929
Vernon K. Krieble Fndn Grants, 4930
Warrick County Community Fndn Grants, 4987
Weyerhaeuser Company Fndn Grants, 5053
Wieboldt Fndn Grants, 5065
William B. Stokely Jr. Fndn Grants, 5076
William Blair and Company Fndn Grants, 5078
Winston-Salem Fndn Competitive Grants, 5102
Winthrop Rockefeller Fndn Grants, 5105

Public Broadcasting

Air Products and Chemicals Grants, 216
Broadcasting Board of Governors David Burke Distinguished Journalism Award, 843
Community Fndn of Western N Carolina Grants, 1327
ConocoPhillips Fndn Grants, 1354
Cooper Industries Fndn Grants, 1370
Corning Fndn Cultural Grants, 1376
Doree Taylor Charitable Fndn, 1580
Duluth-Superior Area Community Fndn Grants, 1620
Foellinger Fndn Grants, 1877
G.N. Wilcox Grants, 1982
IMLS Partnership for a Nation of Learners Community Collaboration Grants, 2520
Motorola Fndn Grants, 3221
Musgrave Fndn Grants, 3231
New Voices J-Lab Journalism Grants, 3337
PMI Fndn Grants, 3918
Rasmuson Fndn Capital Grants, 4020
Robert Sterling Clark Fndn Government Accountability Grants, 4123
Textron Corp Contributions Grants, 4601
Town Creek Fndn Grants, 4650

Public Education

AAF Accent on Architecture Community Grants, 58
ALA Arthur Curley Memorial Lecture, 226
Appalachian Regional Commission Transportation and Highways Grants, 512
Arkansas Arts Council Collab Project Support, 555
Barr Fndn Grants (Massachusetts), 676
Benwood Fndn Focus Area Grants, 733
Brown Fndn Grants, 854
Community Fndn of Greater Fort Wayne - John S. and James L. Knight Fndn Donor-Advised Grants, 1287
ConocoPhillips Fndn Grants, 1354
DB Americas Fndn Grants, 1466
DPA Promoting Policy Change Advocacy Grants, 1598
FEDCO Charitable Fndn Educ Grants, 1798
Geraldine R. Dodge Fndn Arts Grants, 2040
HAF Community Grants, 2193
HomeBanc Fndn Grants, 2347
Int'l Human Rights Funders Grants, 2567
John P. Murphy Fndn Grants, 2708
JP Morgan Chase Arts and Culture Grants, 2752
Kentucky Arts Council TranspARTation Grant, 2812
Komen Greater NYC Clinical Research Enrollment Grants, 2834
Komen Greater NYC Community Breast Health Grants, 2835
Lowe's Charitable and Ed Fndn Grants, 2927
Lyndhurst Fndn Grants, 2949
Melinda Gray Ardia Environmental Fndn Grants, 3114
Minneapolis Fndn Community Grants, 3186
NFWF Acres for America Grants, 3355
NFWF Alaska Fish and Wildlife Grants, 3356
NFWF Aleutian Islands Risk Assessment Grants, 3357
Ober Kaler Community Grants, 3635
PacifiCorp Fndn for Learning Grants, 3727
PG&E Community Vitality Grants, 3868

Reynolds American Fndn Grants, 4068
Stewart Huston Charitable Grants, 4505
Sunny and Abe Rosenberg Fndn Grants, 4529
Taproot Fndn Capacity-Building Service Grants, 4560
Time Warner Diverse Voices in the Arts Grants, 4635

Public Finance

ACF Assets for Indep Individual Development Account Grants, 115

Public Health

ACF Community-Based Abstinence Educ Grants, 116
Aetna Fndn Racial and Ethnic Health Care Equity Grants, 186
AMA Fndn Fund for Better Health Grants, 409
American Chemical Society Corp Associates Seed Grants, 425
Appalachian Reg Comm Health Care Grants, 507
Arca Fndn Grants, 526
ASM Congressional Science Fellowships, 589
ASM Gen-Probe Joseph Public Health Award, 591
Baxter Int'l Fndn Grants, 691
BCBSNC Fndn Fit Together Grants, 711
Blue Cross Blue Shield of Minnesota Fndn - Healthy Equity: Health Impact Assessment Demonstration Project Grants, 795
Canada-U.S. Fulbright Mid-Career Grants, 917
Caterpillar Fndn Grants, 954
CDC Fndn Global Disaster Response Grants, 973
CHCF Grants, 1063
Chicago Community Trust Health Grants, 1087
Chicago Community Poverty Alleviation Grants, 1091
Chicago Community Trust Preventing and Eliminating Hunger Grants, 1092
Cigna Civic Affairs Sponsorships, 1129
Colgate-Palmolive Company Grants, 1202
Colonel Stanley R. McNeil Fndn Grants, 1210
Colorado Trust Partnerships for Health Init, 1217
Community Fndn of Bloomington and Monroe County - Precision Health Network Cycle Grants, 1270
Conservation, Food, and Health Fndn Grants for Developing Countries, 1359
Covidien Medical Product Donations, 1390
Cruise Industry Charitable Fndn Grants, 1404
Deaconess Community Fndn Grants, 1467
DeRoy Testamentary Fndn Grants, 1518
DHHS Emerging Leaders Program Internships, 1532
E. Rhodes and Leona B. Carpenter Fndn Grants, 1640
Edward and Helen Bartlett Fndn Grants, 1664
Fndn for Seacoast Health Grants, 1895
Frances and John L. Loeb Family Grants, 1917
Frank W. and Carl S. Adams Grants, 1937
Fred L. Emerson Fndn Grants, 1949
George W. Wells Fndn Grants, 2030
GNOF IMPACT Grants for Health and Human Services, 2080
GNOF IMPACT Kahn-Oppenheim Grants, 2084
Greater Worcester Community Jeppson Memorial Fund for Brookfield Grants, 2141
Henry J. Kaiser Family Fndn Grants, 2310
IDPH Emergency Med Serv Assistance Grants, 2440
IDPH Local Health Department Public Health Emergency Response Grants, 2442
IIE Freeman Fndn Indonesia Internships, 2456
Jane's Grants, 2639
Johnson & Johnson Comm Health Care Grants, 2717
John W. Speas and Effie E. Speas Grants, 2732
Kaiser Permanente Cares for Comm Grants, 2763
Kansas Health Fndn Recognition Grants, 2784
Knox County Community Fndn Grants, 2831
Mary Black Fndn Community Health Grants, 3032
McCarthy Family Fndn Grants, 3073
Michael Reese Health Trust Responsive Grants, 3160
Morris and Gwendolyn Cafritz Fndn Grants, 3218
Nestle Fndn Training Grant, 3301
Norman Fndn Grants, 3464
NW Mutual Fndn Grants, 3509
Open Spaces Sacred Places National Awards, 3684
Pfizer Healthcare Charitable Contributions, 3863
Pfizer Medical Educ Track One Grants, 3864

Piedmont Natural Gas Fndn Health and Human Services Grants, 3885
Pollock Fndn Grants, 3930
Premera Blue Cross CARES Grants, 3945
Quality Health Fndn Grants, 3994
Rose Community Fndn Aging Grants, 4152
Rose Fndn For Communities and the Environment Kern County Air Pollution Mitigation Grants, 4157
RWJF Community Health Leaders Awards, 4183
RWJF Pioneer Portfolio Grants, 4189
Saint Luke's Health Inits Grants, 4216
San Francisco Fndn Community Health Grants, 4263
Seattle Fndn Health and Wellness Grants, 4328
Siragusa Fndn Health Services & Medical Research Grants, 4368
Solutia Grants, 4402
Sophia Romero Grants, 4406
Steelcase Fndn Grants, 4497
Texas Commission on the Arts Arts Respond Project Grants, 4581
Theodore Edson Parker Fndn Grants, 4605
USAID Family Health Plus Project Grants, 4751
USAID Knowledge for Health II Grants, 4765
USAID NGO Health Service Delivery Grants, 4771
USDC Technology Opportunities Grants, 4860

Public Planning/Policy

Able Trust Vocational Rehabilitation Grants for Individuals, 104
Achelis Fndn Grants, 127
Adolph Coors Fndn Grants, 171
ALA Highsmith Library Innovation Award, 285
ALA President's Award for Advocacy, 310
ALA Robert L. Oakley Scholarship, 313
Allegheny Fndn Grants, 376
Allen Lane Fndn Grants, 379
American Sociological Assoc Sydney S. Spivack Applied Social Research and Social Policy, 450
Amerigroup Fndn Grants, 452
AmerUs Group Charitable Fndn, 455
Arca Fndn Grants, 526
Assurant Health Fndn Grants, 596
AT&T Fndn Civic and Comm Service Grants, 599
Austin College Leadership Award, 615
Bernard F. and Alva B. Gimbel Fndn Grants, 740
Blue Cross Blue Shield of Minnesota Fndn - Healthy Equity: Health Impact Assessment Demonstration Project Grants, 795
Blue Cross Blue Shield of Minnesota Fndn - Healthy Equity: Health Impact Assessment Grants, 796
Bodman Fndn Grants, 807
Bohemian Fndn Pharos Grants, 811
Bydale Fndn Grants, 882
Carnegie Corp of New York Grants, 940
CDC State and Local Childhood Lead Poisoning Prevention Grants, 976
CDECD Tourism Product Development Grants, 984
Central Minnesota Community Fndn Grants, 995
Chapin Hall Int'l Fellowships in Children's Policy Research, 1032
Charles G. Koch Charitable Fndn Grants, 1041
Charles H. Revson Fndn Grants, 1047
Charles Stewart Mott Fndn Grants, 1055
CIGNA Fndn Grants, 1130
Civic Educ Consortium Grants, 1144
Claude Pepper Fndn Grants, 1160
Community Fndn of Mount Vernon and Knox County Grants, 1301
Community Fndn of SE Connecticut Grants, 1309
ConocoPhillips Grants, 1355
Conservation, Food, and Health Fndn Grants for Developing Countries, 1359
Crossroads Fund Seed Grants, 1400
DPA Promoting Policy Change Advocacy Grants, 1598
Duluth-Superior Area Community Fndn Grants, 1620
E.L. Wiegand Fndn Grants, 1639
Eberly Fndn Grants, 1649
Emma B. Howe Memorial Fndn Grants, 1700
Enterprise Community Partners Rose Architectural Fellowships, 1719

974 / Public Planning/Policy

Ewing Marion Kauffman Fndn Grants and Inits, 1777
F.M. Kirby Fndn Grants, 1780
FCD Child Development Grants, 1796
Ferree Fndn Grants, 1804
Ford Fndn Peace and Social Justice Grants, 1884
Frances and John L. Loeb Family Grants, 1917
Fulbright/Garcia Robles Grants, 1968
Fulbright Graduate Degree Grants in Mexico, 1971
Fulbright Public Policy Init Grants in Mexico, 1972
Gardiner Howland Shaw Fndn Grants, 1986
General Motors Fndn Grants Support Program, 2004
General Service Fndn Colorado Grants, 2005
George Gund Fndn Grants, 2020
Gill Fndn - Gay and Lesbian Grants, 2054
Girl's Best Friend Fndn Grants, 2057
GMFUS Marshall Memorial Fellowships, 2066
GNOF Community Revitalization Grants, 2071
GNOF St. Bernard Community Grants, 2092
Greenspun Family Fndn Grants, 2156
Grover Hermann Fndn Grants, 2168
Hatton W. Sumners Fndn for the Study and Teaching of Self Government Grants, 2257
Hilton Hotels Corp Giving Grants, 2331
Horowitz Fndn for Social Policy Grants, 2370
Horowitz Fndn for Social Policy Special Awards, 2371
HRF Tibor T. Polgar Fellowships, 2380
Hyams Fndn Grants, 2413
Hyde Family Fndns Grants, 2414
Illinois Tool Works Fndn Grants, 2511
J.W. Kieckhefer Fndn Grants, 2607
Jacob and Hilda Blaustein Fndn Grants, 2615
Japan Center for Global Partnership Grants, 2650
Jaquelin Hume Fndn Grants, 2654
JM Fndn Grants, 2681
Joel L. Fleishman Civil Society Fellowships, 2683
Joseph P. Kennedy Jr. Fndn Grants, 2740
Kaiser Permanente Cares for Comm Grants, 2763
Koret Fndn Grants, 2837
Laurel Fndn Grants, 2867
Lynde and Harry Bradley Fndn Grants, 2947
Lynde and Harry Bradley Fndn Prizes, 2948
M.D. Anderson Fndn Grants, 2952
MacArthur Fndn Policy Research Grants, 2964
Marin Community Affordable Housing Grants, 3010
Massachusetts Fndn for Humanities Grants, 3060
Maytree Fndn Refugee and Immigrant Grants, 3071
Mertz Gilmore Climate Change Grants, 3125
Meyer Fndn Healthy Communities Grants, 3143
Millipore Fndn Grants, 3182
Mimi and Peter Haas Grants, 3185
Minneapolis Fndn Community Grants, 3186
Morris K. Udall and Stewart L. Udall Fndn Native American Congressional Internships, 3220
Motorola Fndn Grants, 3221
Murphy Institute Judith Kelleher Schafer Summer Internship Grants, 3230
NAR HOPE Awards for Minority Owners, 3238
National Endowment for Arts Our Town Grants, 3257
National Endowment for Arts Agencies Grants, 3263
Nordson Corp Fndn Grants, 3462
Norman Fndn Grants, 3464
NSF Decision, Risk, and Management Science Research Grants, 3528
Oleonda Jameson Grants, 3667
OSF Human Rights and Governance Grants, 3708
Pittsburgh Fndn Community Grants, 3910
Playboy Fndn Grants, 3913
Ploughshares Grants, 3916
PMI Fndn Grants, 3918
Praxair Fndn Grants, 3944
Procter and Gamble Grants, 3967
RAND Corp Graduate Summer Associateships, 4018
Richard and Helen DeVos Fndn Grants, 4076
Robert Sterling Clark Fndn Government Accountability Grants, 4123
Rockefeller Family Grants, 4137
RRF General Grants, 4170
Sapelo Fndn Social Justice Grants, 4294
Sarah Scaife Fndn Grants, 4295
Schumann Fund for New Jersey Grants, 4311

Seaver Institute Grants, 4331
Sensient Technologies Fndn Grants, 4337
Sister Grants for Women's Organizations, 4371
Smith Richardson Fndn Domestic Public Research Fellowship, 4386
Social Justice Fund NW Criminal Justice Giving Project Grants, 4394
Social Justice Fund NW Montana Giving Project Grants, 4399
Tides Fndn Grants, 4632
TWS Fndn Grants, 4683
USAID Grant for Operationalizing a Neighborhood Approach to Reduce Urban Disaster Risk in Latin America and the Caribbean, 4754
USDC Public Works and Economic Adjustment Assistance Grants, 4856
US Soccer Fndn Planning Grants, 4871
Vernon K. Krieble Fndn Grants, 4930
Wallace Global Grants, 4977
Weyerhaeuser Company Fndn Grants, 5053
Wieboldt Fndn Grants, 5065

Public Policy Systems Analysis

ALA Robert L. Oakley Scholarship, 313
Grover Hermann Fndn Grants, 2168
Marin Community Affordable Housing Grants, 3010
National Endowment for Arts Our Town Grants, 3257
Smith Richardson Fndn Domestic Public Research Fellowship, 4386
USAID National Governance Project Grant, 4770

Public Relations

AAAS Early Career Award for Public Engagement with Science, 51
ALA John Cotton Dana Library Public Relations Award, 292
Alfred P. Sloan Fndn Public Service Awards, 369
ATA School-Community Relations Awards, 602
Carrier Corp Contributions Grants, 946
CDECD Historic Preser Enhancement Grants, 981
San Francisco Fndn Fund For Artists Award For Playwrights and Theatre Ensembles, 4272

Public Safety

ACF Native American Social and Economic Development Strategies Grants, 123
Ameren Corp Community Grants, 418
American Express Charitable Grants, 429
Bikes Belong Fndn Paul David Clark Bicycling Safety Grants, 760
Bikes Belong Fndn Research Grants, 762
Caesars Fndn Grants, 891
California Endowment Innovative Ideas Challenge Grants, 904
Chicago Community Trust Public Safety and Justice Grants, 1093
CNCS AmeriCorps NCCC Project Grants, 1181
EMC Corp Grants, 1693
Fndns of E Chicago Public Safety Grants, 1911
Francis Beidler Fndn Grants, 1921
Goldseker Fndn Community Affairs Grants, 2100
Harrison County Community Signature Grants, 2234
Honeywell Family Safety and Security Grants, 2356
IDPH Local Health Department Public Health Emergency Response Grants, 2442
Illinois DCEO Business Development Public Infrastructure Grants, 2483
LISC Financial Opportunity Center Social Innovation Grants, 2911
LISC MetLife Fndn Community-Police Partnership Awards, 2912
Local Inits Support Corp Grants, 2917
Meyer Fndn Healthy Communities Grants, 3143
OneStar Fndn AmeriCorps Grants, 3674
Surdna Fndn Sustainable Environments Grants, 4533
Toyota Motor Manufacturing of Indiana Grants, 4653
Toyota Motor of Kentucky Grants, 4654
Toyota USA Fndn Safety Grants, 4662
Verizon Wireless Hopeline Grants, 4927
Westinghouse Charitable Giving Grants, 5028

Public Safety Law

AMA Fndn Fund for Better Health Grants, 409
Baptist Community Ministries Grants, 664
Fndns of E Chicago Public Safety Grants, 1911
LISC MetLife Fndn Community-Police Partnership Awards, 2912
Maine State Troopers Fndn Grants, 2991
Perry County Community Fndn Grants, 3827
Pike County Community Fndn Grants, 3888
Posey County Community Fndn Grants, 3939
State Farm Project Ignition Grants, 4487
Texas Commission on the Arts Arts Respond Project Grants, 4581

Publication

AAAS Early Career Award for Public Engagement with Science, 51
ALA Isadore Gilbert Mudge Award, 290
ALA Reference Service Press Award, 312
Delaware Division of the Arts Opportunity Grants-Artists, 1489
George A Ohl Jr. Fndn Grants, 2012
Lynde and Harry Bradley Fndn Grants, 2947
Lynde and Harry Bradley Fndn Prizes, 2948
Manitoba Arts Council Literary Arts Publishers Project Grants, 2996
Manitoba Arts Council Special Opps Grants, 2997
Maurice Amado Fndn Grants, 3063
NAGC Masters and Specialists Award, 3237
National Endowment for Arts Opera Grants, 3267
NEH Family and Youth Programs in American History Grants, 3291
North Carolina Arts Council Folklife Grants, 3476
North Dakota Council on the Arts Instal Support Grants, 3496
NYSCA Architecture, Planning, and Design: Project Support Grants, 3576
NYSCA Lit: General Operating Support Grants, 3598
NYSCA Literature: General Support Grants, 3599
South Madison Community Fndn Grants, 4440

Publication Education

Bullitt Fndn Grants, 862
Seattle Fndn Educ Grants, 4326

Publishing Industry

Nation Institute Ridenhour Prizes, 3283
PCA Arts Organizations & Grants for Lit, 3781
PCA Entry Track Arts Organizations and Program Grants for Literature, 3793
SCBWI Don Freeman Memorial Grant, 4302

Publishing, Electronic

NYSCA Literature: General Support Grants, 3599
Perl 6 Microgrants, 3824

Pulmonary Diseases

Genentech Corp Charitable Contributions, 2000
M. Bastian Family Fndn Grants, 2951
NHLBI Ancillary Studies in Clinical Trials, 3410
NHLBI Lymphatics in Health & Disease in Digestive, Cardiovascular and Pulmonary Systems, 3414
NHLBI Lymphatics in Health & Disease in Digestive, Urinary, Cardio & Pulmonary Systems, 3415
NHLBI Ruth L. Kirschstein National Research Service Awards for Individual Postdoctoral Fellows, 3418
NHLBI Ruth L. Kirschstein National Research Service Awards for Individual Predoctoral MD/PhD Fellows and Other Dual Degree Fellows, 3420
Pfizer Healthcare Charitable Contributions, 3863

Puppetry

NHSCA Artist Residencies in Schools Grants, 3423

Quality of Life

Allen P. and Josephine B. Green Fndn Grants, 380
Alliant Energy Fndn Community Grants, 384
AutoZone Community Relations Grants, 621
AXA Fndn Scholarships, 629
Barr Fndn Grants (Massachusetts), 676

SUBJECT INDEX

Bernard & Audre Rapoport Arts & Culture Grant, 735
Bernard and Audre Rapoport Fndn Community Building and Social Service Grants, 736
Bernard and Audre Rapoport Fndn Democracy and Civic Participation Grants, 737
Bernard and Audre Rapoport Fndn Health Grants, 738
Bikes Belong Fndn Paul David Clark Bicycling Safety Grants, 760
Bikes Belong Fndn REI Grants, 761
Bikes Belong Fndn Research Grants, 762
Bikes Belong Grants, 763
Business Bank of Nevada Community Grants, 879
California Pizza Kitchen Fndn Grants, 907
CCF Community Priorities Fund, 961
CharityWorks Grants, 1036
Cleveland Neighborhood Connections Grants, 1171
Coleman Developmental Disabilities Grants, 1200
Collective Brands Fndn Payless Gives Shoes 4 Kids Grants, 1207
Countess Moira Charitable Fndn Grants, 1381
CSL Behring Local Empowerment for Advocacy Development Grants, 1406
Dennis and Phyllis Washington Fndn Grants, 1498
DIFFA/Chicago Grants, 1547
Elizabeth Carse Fndn Grants, 1681
Ezra M. Cutting Grants, 1779
Fifth Third Fndn Grants, 1810
Foster Fndn Grants, 1888
GNOF IMPACT Grants for Arts and Culture, 2078
Granger Fndn Grants, 2127
HAF Senior Opportunities Grants, 2203
Hall-Perrine Fndn Grants, 2209
Harry S. Black and Allon Fuller Grants, 2243
Hilton Head Island Fndn Grants, 2330
Horizon Fndn for New Jersey Grants, 2364
Jim Moran Fndn Grants, 2680
John S. and James L. Knight Fndn Communities Grants, 2711
Johnson Scholarship Fndn Grants, 2726
Ken W. Davis Fndn Grants, 2813
Kessler Fndn Community Employment Grants, 2814
Kessler Fndn Signature Employment Grants, 2816
KeyBank Fndn Grants, 2820
Lilly Endowment Giving Indiana Funds for Tomorrow Grants, 2903
Mary Wilmer Covey Charitable Grants, 3049
May and Stanley Smith Charitable Grants, 3069
Middlesex Savings Charitable Fndn Community Development Grants, 3173
NAR Realtor Magazine Good Neighbor Awards, 3240
National Endowment for Arts Our Town Grants, 3257
Nu Skin Force for Good Fndn Grants, 3536
Ruth Mott Fndn Grants, 4180
Schlessman Family Fndn Grants, 4307
Simpson Lumber Charitable Contributions, 4362
Singing for Change Fndn Grants, 4363
Theodore Edson Parker Fndn Grants, 4605
Turner Fndn Grants, 4681
Weaver Fndn Grants, 5015
Westinghouse Charitable Giving Grants, 5028

Racial Equality
ALFJ Astraea U.S. General Fund, 362
Evelyn and Walter Haas, Jr. Fund Immigrant Rights Grants, 1773
GNOF Community Revitalization Grants, 2071
HAF Community Grants, 2193
Haymarket People's Fund Sustaining Grants, 2267
Liberty Hill Fndn Fund for a New LA Grants, 2892
Maine Community Fndn People of Color Grants, 2985
PDF Fiscal Sponsorship Grant, 3808

Racism
A.J. Muste Memorial Institute General Grants, 44
Akonadi Fndn Anti-Racism Grants, 217
Allstate Corp Giving Grants, 386
Allstate Corp Hometown Commitment Grants, 387
Allstate Fndn Safe and Vital Communities Grants, 390
ANLAF Int'l Fund for Sexual Minorities Grants, 471
Central New York Community Fndn Grants, 996
Community Fndn Greater Chattanooga Grants, 1281
Cowles Charitable Grants, 1392
Crossroads Fund Seed Grants, 1400
David and Barbara B. Hirschhorn Fndn Grants, 1450
FCYO Youth Organizing Grants, 1797
Fndn for the Carolinas Grants, 1896
Georgia Power Fndn Grants, 2039
Joseph H. and Florence A. Roblee Fndn Grants, 2736
Mabel Louise Riley Fndn Grants, 2959
Meadows Fndn Grants, 3104
OUT Fund for Lesbian & Gay Liberation Grants, 3714
Palm Beach and Martin Counties Grants, 3733
PDF Community Organizing Grants, 3807
PDF Fiscal Sponsorship Grant, 3808
PIP Fulfilling the Dream Fund, 3907
PIP Racial Justice Collaborative Grants, 3908
PIP U.S. Human Rights Grants, 3909
Pittsburgh Fndn Community Grants, 3910
Saginaw Community Fndn YWCA Fund for Women and Girls Grants, 4207
Saint Paul Fndn Grants, 4219
San Diego Fndn for Change Grants, 4247
Sioux Falls Area Community Fndn Spot Grants, 4366
Teaching Tolerance Grants, 4567
Teaching Tolerance Mix-it-Up Grants, 4568
Third Wave Fndn Lela Breitbart Grants, 4609
Third Wave Organizing & Advocacy Grants, 4610
Third Wave Fndn Reproductive Health and Justice Grants, 4611
Vanguard Public Fndn Grant Funds, 4904
W.K. Kellogg Fndn Racial Equity Grants, 4962
Wieboldt Fndn Grants, 5065
Winthrop Rockefeller Fndn Grants, 5105

Radiation Effects
American Academy of Dermatology Shade Structure Grants, 420
EPA Surveys, Studies, Research, Investigations, Demonstrations, and Special Purpose Activities Relating to the Clean Air Act, 1740

Radio
Albert Pick Jr. Grants, 344
CCH Documentary Project Production Grants, 969
CCH Documentary Public Engagement Grants, 970
CCH Documentary Project Research and Development Grants, 971
Corning Fndn Cultural Grants, 1376
Doree Taylor Charitable Fndn, 1580
Duluth-Superior Area Community Fndn Grants, 1620
G.N. Wilcox Grants, 1982
Gill Fndn - Gay and Lesbian Grants, 2054
Illinois Arts Council Media Arts Grants, 2472
National Endowment for Arts Media Grants, 3264
NEH Family and Youth Programs in American History Grants, 3291
North Carolina Arts Council Folklife Grants, 3476
PCA Arts Organizations and Arts Programs Grants for Film and Electronic Media, 3780
PCA Entry Track Arts Organizations and Program Grants for Film and Electronic Media, 3792
Ploughshares Grants, 3916
TE Fndn Grants, 4572
Town Creek Fndn Grants, 4650
Union Pacific Fndn Community and Civic Grants, 4714
USAID Strengthening Free and Independent Media in South Sudan Grants, 4783
USDA Rural Utilities Service Weather Radio Transmitter Grants, 4833

Rape/Sexual Assault
Atlanta Women's Fndn Grants, 609
Meyer Fndn Healthy Communities Grants, 3143
Pacers Fndn Indiana Fever's Be Younique Grants, 3724

Reading
7-Eleven Coorporate Giving Grants, 18
ALA Baker and Taylor Summer Reading Grants, 230
ALA Clarence Day Award, 258
ALA John Phillip Immroth Memorial Award, 293
ALA MAE Award for Best Teen Lit, 296
ALA Scholastic Library Publishing Award, 318
American Savings Fndn Grants, 445
Azadoutioun Fndn Grants, 631
Barker Welfare Fndn Grants, 669
BBF Florida Family Lit Init Grants, 697
BBF Maine Family Lit Init Grants, 698
BBF Maine Family Lit Init Planning Grants, 699
BBF Maryland Family Lit Init Grants, 700
BBF Maryland Family Lit Init Planning Grants, 701
BBF National Grants for Family Lit, 702
Better World Books LEAP Grants for Libraries, 755
Better World Books LEAP Grants for Nonprofits, 756
Bodenwein Public Benevolent Fndn Grants, 806
Boettcher Fndn Grants, 810
Boston Fndn Grants, 819
CCH Documentary California Reads Grants, 968
Colorado Springs Community Grants, 1215
DeKalb County Community Fndn - Lit Grant, 1480
EQT Fndn Educ Grants, 1745
First Lady's Family Lit Init for Texas Family Lit Trailblazer Grants, 1821
First Lady's Family Lit for Texas Implementation, 1823
First Lady's Family Lit Init for Texas Planning, 1824
Howard and Bush Fndn Grants, 2374
Illinois Arts Council Presenters Dev Grants, 2476
Louis Calder Fndn Grants, 2925
Madison Community Fndn Grants, 2971
Mary & Walter Frear Eleemosynary Grants, 3035
National Endowment for the Arts - Grants for Arts Projects: Challenge America Fast-Track, 3254
National Endowment for Arts Big Read Grants, 3261
National Home Library Fndn Grants, 3276
NYCH Together Grants, 3541
NYHC Reading and Discussion Grants, 3568
NYSCA Literature: Public Programs, 3600
Piper Trust Children Grants, 3901
Poets & Writers Readings/Workshops Grants, 3927
Robert Bowne Fndn Fellowships, 4107
Robert Bowne Fndn Lit Grants, 4108
Robert Bowne Fndn Youth-Centered Grants, 4109
Robert R. Meyer Fndn Grants, 4121
Rosie's For All Kids Fndn Grants, 4163
Scholastic Book Grants, 4308
Stocker Fndn Grants, 4507
Talbert and Leota Abrams Fndn, 4558
Target Corp Local Store Grants, 4561
Teaching Tolerance Grants, 4567
USAID Reading Enhancement for Advancing Development Grants, 4778
Verizon Fndn Delaware Grants, 4909
Verizon Fndn New Jersey Check into Lit Grants, 4918
Wisconsin Humanities Council Mini-Grants for Scholarly Research, 5108

Reading Education
ALA Coretta Scott King Book Donation Grant, 261
Arizona Republic Newspaper Contributions, 547
Arlington Community Fndn Grants, 564
Baptist Community Ministries Grants, 664
BBF Florida Family Lit Init Grants, 697
BBF Maine Family Lit Init Grants, 698
BBF Maine Family Lit Init Planning Grants, 699
BBF Maryland Family Lit Init Grants, 700
BBF Maryland Family Lit Init Planning Grants, 701
BBF National Grants for Family Lit, 702
Better World Books LEAP Grants for Libraries, 755
Better World Books LEAP Grants for Nonprofits, 756
CCH Documentary California Reads Grants, 968
DaimlerChrysler Corp Grants, 1432
DeKalb County Community Fndn - Lit Grant, 1480
Emily Davie and Joseph S. Kornfeld Fndn Grants, 1697
EQT Fndn Educ Grants, 1745
Essex County Community Fndn Greater Lawrence Summer Grants, 1755
First Lady's Family Lit Init for Texas Family Lit Trailblazer Grants, 1821
First Lady's Family Lit Init for Texas Grants, 1822
First Lady's Family Lit Init for Texas Implementation Grants, 1823

976 / Reading Education

First Lady's Family Lit Init for Texas Planning, 1824
HBF Pathways Out of Poverty Grants, 2273
Head Start Replacement Grantee: Colorado, 2275
Head Start Replacement Grantee: Florida, 2276
Head Start Replacement Grantee: West Virginia, 2277
Int'l Paper Company Fndn Grants, 2568
IRA Pearson Fndn-IRA-Rotary Lit Awards, 2572
National Endowment for Arts Big Read Grants, 3261
National Home Library Fndn Grants, 3276
NCFL/Better World Books Libraries and Families Award, 3288
NYSCA Literature: Public Programs, 3600
Piper Trust Children Grants, 3901
Public Educ Power Grants, 3981
Rosie's For All Kids Fndn Grants, 4163
Stocker Fndn Grants, 4507
Stuart Fndn Grants, 4516
Target Corp Local Store Grants, 4561
U.S. Department of Ed Early Reading 1st Grants, 4691
USAID Reading Enhancement for Advancing Development Grants, 4778
Verizon Fndn Delaware Grants, 4909

Real Estate
Cleveland Capital Grants, 1167
Enterprise Community Partners Rose Architectural Fellowships, 1719
Home Ownership Part for Everyone Awards, 2349
IEDC Industrial Development Grant Fund, 2443
NAR Realtor Magazine Good Neighbor Awards, 3240
National Endowment for Arts Our Town Grants, 3257

Recidivism
OSF-Baltimore Criminal & Juv Justice Grants, 3696

Reconstructive Surgery
Ronald McDonald House Charities Grants, 4149

Recreation and Leisure
Adler-Clark Electric Community Commitment Fndn Grants, 164
African American Fund of New Jersey Grants, 192
Agnes M. Lindsay Grants, 203
Alice Tweed Tuohy Fndn Grants, 372
Amador Community Fndn Grants, 408
Andre Agassi Charitable Fndn Grants, 461
Aratani Fndn Grants, 523
Argyros Fndn Grants, 532
Arizona Republic Newspaper Contributions, 547
Armstrong McDonald Fndn Grants, 565
Arthur B. Schultz Fndn Grants, 573
Atlanta Grants, 608
Austin Community Fndn Grants, 616
Back Home Again Fndn Grants, 633
Bacon Family Fndn Grants, 634
Batters Up USA Equipment Grants, 683
Beazley Fndn Grants, 714
Beckley Area Fndn Grants, 716
Ben B. Cheney Fndn Grants, 725
Bikes Belong Fndn Paul David Clark Bicycling Safety Grants, 760
Bikes Belong Fndn REI Grants, 761
Bikes Belong Grants, 763
Blanche and Julian Robertson Family Fndn Grants, 785
BoatUS Fndn Grassroots Grants, 805
Boston Fndn Grants, 819
Brooklyn Community Fndn Green Communities Grants, 852
Brunswick Fndn Grants, 857
Campbell Soup Fndn Grants, 916
Carl C. Icahn Fndn Grants, 929
Carls Fndn Grants, 937
Carrie Estelle Doheny Fndn Grants, 945
Carrier Corp Contributions Grants, 946
CFFVR SAC Developmental Disabilities Grants, 1019
CFFVR Shawano Area Community Fndn Grants, 1021
Charity Incorporated Grants, 1035
Charlotte R. Schmidlapp Grants, 1058
Christian Science Society of Boonville Irrevocable Trust, 1113

Clara Blackford Smith and W. Aubrey Smith Charitable Fndn Grants, 1147
Cobb Family Fndn Grants, 1194
Community Fndn for NE Michigan Grants, 1257
Community Fndn for Southern Arizona Grants, 1261
Community Fndn of Boone County Grants, 1274
Community Fndn of Mount Vernon and Knox County Grants, 1301
Community Fndn of South Alabama Grants, 1308
Community Fndn of Southern Indiana Grants, 1310
Community Fndn of St. Joseph County Special Project Challenge Grants, 1314
Community Fndn of Wabash County Grants, 1326
Community Partners Lawrence County Grants, 1328
Community Partnerships Martin County Grants, 1329
Cumberland Community Fndn Summertime Kids Grants, 1414
Daviess County Community Recreation Grants, 1459
Decatur County Comm Large Project Grants, 1476
Decatur County Community Fndn Small Project Grants, 1477
Delaware Division of the Arts Community-Based Organizations Opportunity Grants, 1487
Dept of Ed Recreational Services for Individuals with Disabilities, 1512
DOI Urban Park & Rec Recovery Grants, 1554
Donnie Avery Catches for Kids Fndn, 1578
Dubois County Community Fndn Grants, 1615
Dwight Stuart Youth Fndn Grants, 1628
Emma B. Howe Memorial Fndn Grants, 1700
Fargo-Moorhead Area Fndn Grants, 1788
Florence Hunt Maxwell Fndn Grants, 1844
Foellinger Fndn Grants, 1877
Ford Family Grants Public Convening Spaces, 1881
Frank Stanley Beveridge Fndn Grants, 1936
Frederick W. Marzahl Grants, 1948
Fremont Area Community Fndn Grants, 1955
Fremont Area Comm Summer Youth Grants, 1956
Fuller Fndn Grants, 1974
Fulton County Community Fndn Grants, 1975
Gates Family Children, Youth & Family Grants, 1989
Gates Family Fndn Parks, Conservation & Recreation Grants, 1991
George A. and Grace L. Long Fndn Grants, 2008
George and Ruth Bradford Fndn Grants, 2010
George A Ohl Jr. Fndn Grants, 2012
George Fndn Grants, 2018
George Kress Fndn Grants, 2025
Gil and Dody Weaver Fndn Grants, 2053
Glazer Family Fndn Grants, 2062
Grand Haven Area Community Fndn Grants, 2113
Grand Rapids Area Community Fndn Wyoming Youth Grants, 2117
Grand Rapids Community Fndn Grants, 2118
Grand Rapids Community Fndn Lowell Grants, 2121
Greater Kanawha Valley Fndn Grants, 2136
Greater Worcester Community Jeppson Memorial Fund for Brookfield Grants, 2141
Greenspun Family Fndn Grants, 2156
HAF Summer Youth Funding Partnerships, 2205
Harrison County Community Fndn Grants, 2233
Harrison County Community Signature Grants, 2234
Harry C. Trexler Grants, 2239
Harvey Randall Wickes Fndn Grants, 2255
Hasbro Children's Fund, 2256
Helen S. Boylan Fndn Grants, 2298
Herbert H. and Grace A. Dow Fndn Grants, 2315
Holland/Zeeland Community Fndn Grants, 2345
HRF Hudson River Improvement Grants, 2378
Idaho Community Fndn Eastern Region Competitive Grants, 2432
Illinois DNR Park and Recreational Facility Construction Grants, 2499
Illinois DNR Youth Recreation Corps Grants, 2508
Impact 100 Grants, 2522
Indiana Boating Infrastructure Grants (BIG P), 2534
Indiana Clean Vessel Act Grants, 2535
James J. McCann Charitable Trust and McCann Fndn, Inc Grants, 2631
James S. Copley Fndn Grants, 2637

Josephine S. Gumbiner Fndn Grants, 2739
Kahuku Community Fund, 2762
KEEN Effect Grants, 2795
Knox County Community Fndn Grants, 2831
Kosciusko County Community Fndn Grants, 2838
LA84 Fndn Grants, 2847
LaGrange Independent Fndn for Endowments, 2851
Lana'i Community Benefit Fund, 2857
Leicester Savings Bank Fund, 2879
Lisa and Douglas Goldman Grants, 2910
Lubrizol Fndn Grants, 2933
Marie H. Bechtel Charitable Grants, 3007
Marjorie Moore Charitable Fndn Grants, 3021
Mark Wahlberg Youth Fndn Grants, 3022
Marshall County Community Fndn Grants, 3026
Maxon Charitable Fndn Grants, 3068
McCombs Fndn Grants, 3075
McConnell Fndn Grants, 3076
McKesson Fndn Grants, 3084
McMillen Fndn Grants, 3090
MDEQ Great Lakes Areas of Concern Land Acquisition Grants, 3099
Miami County Community Fndn - Operation Round Up Grants, 3156
Miller Fndn Grants, 3181
Mr. and Mrs. William Foulds Family Grants, 3222
NFF Collaboration Support Grants, 3342
NFF Community Assistance Grants, 3343
NFF Matching Grants, 3344
NFF Mid-Capacity Assistance Grants, 3345
North Dakota Community Fndn Grants, 3493
NW Minnesota Fndn Asset Building Grants, 3511
Oklahoma City Community Programs & Grants, 3666
Orange County Community Fndn Grants, 3687
Owen County Community Fndn Grants, 3716
Paul Rapoport Fndn Grants, 3765
Paul V. Sherlock Center on Disabilities Access for All Abilities Mini Grants, 3767
Perry County Community Fndn Grants, 3827
Phoenix Suns Charities Grants, 3881
Pike County Community Fndn Grants, 3888
Pinnacle Entertainment Fndn Grants, 3893
Pohlad Family Fndn, 3928
Posey County Community Fndn Grants, 3939
Pride Fndn Grants, 3958
Principal Financial Group Fndn Grants, 3966
Putnam County Community Fndn Grants, 3990
Ralphs Food 4 Less Fndn Grants, 4014
REI Conservation and Outdoor Rec Grants, 4051
Reinberger Fndn Grants, 4052
Rochester Area Fndn Grants, 4128
Roney-Fitzpatrick Fndn Grants, 4150
Saint Louis Rams Fndn Community Donations, 4214
Sarah Scaife Fndn Grants, 4295
Saucony Run for Good Fndn Grants, 4301
Scheumann Fndn Grants, 4306
Scott County Community Fndn Grants, 4314
Seabury Fndn Grants, 4316
Seneca Foods Fndn Grants, 4336
Sidgmore Family Fndn Grants, 4348
Sioux Falls Area Community Grants, 4364
Sioux Falls Area Community Fndn Field-of-Interest and Donor-Advised Grants, 4365
Sioux Falls Area Community Fndn Spot Grants, 4366
Southbury Community Trust Fund, 4409
Spencer County Community Fndn Grants, 4451
Sport Manitoba Intro of a New Sport Grants, 4457
Springs Close Fndn Grants, 4462
Starke County Community Fndn Grants, 4482
Steuben County Community Fndn Grants, 4501
Steve Young Family Fndn Grants, 4503
Strowd Roses Grants, 4515
Thomas Austin Finch, Sr. Fndn Grants, 4613
Tony Hawk Fndn Grants, 4641
Topeka West Rotary Youth Enrichment Grants, 4645
Turner B. Bunn, Jr. & Catherine E. Bunn Grants, 4680
Turner Fndn Grants, 4681
U.S. Department of Educ 21st Century Community Learning Centers, 4687
USA Volleyball Fndn Ed Grants, 4791

SUBJECT INDEX

USFA Development Grants, 4866
USFA Equipment Subsidy Grants, 4867
Vanderburgh Community Fndn Grants, 4902
Warren County Community Fndn Grants, 4985
Warren County Community Fndn Mini-Grants, 4986
Warrick County Community Fndn Grants, 4987
Washington County Community Fndn Grants, 4997
Washington County Community Youth Grants, 4998
Weaver Fndn Grants, 5015
Wells County Fndn Grants, 5022
White County Community Fndn Grants, 5057
Whitley County Community Fndn Grants, 5060
Windgate Charitable Fndn Grants, 5099
Winston-Salem Fndn Competitive Grants, 5102
Winston-Salem Fndn Stokes County Grants, 5104
Yawkey Fndn Grants, 5125

Recreation and Leisure Studies
Huntington County Community Fndn - Make a Difference Grants, 2406
MDEQ Beach Monitoring Grants - Inland Lakes, 3094

Recycling
Giant Food Charitable Grants, 2050
Union Bank, N.A. Fndn Grants, 4709

Reference Materials
ALA BWI Collection Development Grant, 252
ALA Carnegie-Whitney Awards, 253
ALA Gale Cengage Learning Award for Excellence in Reference and Adult Library Services, 281
ALA Isadore Gilbert Mudge Award, 290
ALA Morningstar Pub Librarian Support Award, 302
ALA Reference Service Press Award, 312
NEH Preservation Assistance Grants for Smaller Institutions, 3293
Virginia Historical Society Research Fellowships, 4949

Refugees
ACF Ethnic Community Self-Help Grants, 118
ACF Preferred Communities Grants, 124
ACF Supplemental Services for Recently Arrived Refugees Grants, 125
Allen Lane Fndn Grants, 379
Blumenthal Fndn Grants, 804
Clowes Grants, 1177
Dallas Women's Fndn Grants, 1438
Deborah Munroe Noonan Grants, 1475
Edward and Ellen Roche Relief Fndn Grants, 1663
General Service Fndn Colorado Grants, 2005
Goizueta Fndn Grants, 2096
IRC Community Collaboratives for Refugee Women and Youth Grants, 2573
Jaquelin Hume Fndn Grants, 2654
Laura Jane Musser Intercultural Harmony Grants, 2862
Maytree Fndn Refugee and Immigrant Grants, 3071
Michael Reese Health Trust Responsive Grants, 3160
Minneapolis Fndn Community Grants, 3186
Nathan Cummings Fndn Grants, 3246
National Book Scholarship Fund, 3249
New York Fndn Grants, 3338
PIP Four Freedoms Grants, 3906
Robert W. Woodruff Fndn Grants, 4124
San Diego Fndn for Change Grants, 4247
San Francisco Fndn Faith Program and Arts and Culture Program, 4267
Sister Grants for Women's Organizations, 4371
Theodore Edson Parker Fndn Grants, 4605
Woods Charitable Grants, 5114

Regional Economics
GNOF Coastal 5 + 1 Grants, 2070
GNOF Environmental Grants, 2073
GNOF Metropolitan Opportunities Grants, 2087
Indiana Regional Economic Development Partnership Grants, 2546
National Endowment for Arts Our Town Grants, 3257
Seattle Fndn Economy Grants, 4325
Threshold Fndn Thriving Resilient Communities Funding Circle, 4628

Regional Planning/Policy
Barr Fndn Grants (Massachusetts), 676
Blue Cross Blue Shield of Minnesota Healthy Equity: Health Impact Assessment Demon Grants, 795
Blue Cross Blue Shield of Minnesota Fndn - Healthy Equity: Health Impact Assessment Grants, 796
Canada-U.S. Fulbright Mid-Career Grants, 917
Carpenter Fndn Grants, 943
Compton Fndn Grants, 1338
Dorothy Rider Pool Health Care Grants, 1589
Fndn for the Carolinas Grants, 1896
GNOF Coastal 5 + 1 Grants, 2070
GNOF Community Revitalization Grants, 2071
GNOF Environmental Grants, 2073
GNOF Metropolitan Opportunities Grants, 2087
Indiana Regional Economic Development Partnership Grants, 2546
Lockheed Martin Philanthropic Grants, 2918
MacArthur Fndn Policy Research Grants, 2964
Morris K. Udall and Stewart L. Udall Fndn Dissertation Fellowships, 3219
National Endowment for the Arts - Regional Partnership Agreement Grants, 3258
Princeton Area Community Fndn Fund for Women and Girls Grants, 3962
Sarkeys Fndn Grants, 4297
Smith Richardson Fndn Domestic Public Research Fellowship, 4386
Southern Minnesota Init Grants, 4437
USDA Rural Business Opportunity Grants, 4824
William C. Kenney Watershed Protection Fndn Ecosystem Grants, 5079

Regional/Urban Design
Alliance for Community Trees Home Depot Fndn NeighborWoods Grants, 382
GNOF Community Revitalization Grants, 2071
GNOF Environmental Grants, 2073
GNOF Jefferson Community Grants, 2085
GNOF Metropolitan Opportunities Grants, 2087
Grand Victoria Fndn Illinois Core Grants, 2126
National Endowment for Arts Our Town Grants, 3257
National Endowment for Arts Commun Grants, 3260
National Endowment for Arts Agencies Grants, 3263
Natonal Endowment for the Arts Research Grants: Art Works, 3286
NYSCA Architecture, Planning, and Design: Capital Fixtures and Equipment Purchase Grants, 3570
NYSCA Architecture, Planning, and Design: Capital Project Grants, 3571
NYSCA Architecture, Planning, and Design: Design and Planning Studies Grants, 3572
NYSCA Architecture, Planning, and Design: General Operating Support Grants, 3573
NYSCA Architecture, Planning, and Design: General Program Support Grants, 3574
NYSCA Architecture, Planning, and Design: Independent Project Grants, 3575
NYSCA Architecture, Planning, and Design: Project Support Grants, 3576
Rudy Bruner Award for Urban Excellence, 4173
United Technologies Corp Grants, 4725

Rehabilitation/Therapy
Alberto Culver Corp Contributions Grants, 343
Alvah H. and Wyline P. Chapman Fndn Grants, 402
Cailloux Fndn Grants, 892
Carl W. and Carrie Mae Joslyn Grants, 938
Chicago Board of Trade Fndn Grants, 1079
Community Fndn for Southern Arizona Grants, 1261
Community Fndn of Sarasota County Grants, 1306
Dammann Grants, 1439
Dept of Ed Recreational Services for Individuals with Disabilities, 1512
DOJ Community-Based Delinquency Prevention Grants, 1556
Dolan Fndn Grants, 1563
Donaldson Fndn Grants, 1574
Dr. John T. Macdonald Fndn Grants, 1600
Edward W. and Stella C. Van Houten Grants, 1670

Religion / 977

Fremont Area Community Amazing X Grants, 1953
Gardiner Howland Shaw Fndn Grants, 1986
Henry County Community Fndn Grants, 2308
John W. Alden Grants, 2727
Lubrizol Fndn Grants, 2933
NIDRR Field-Initiated Projects, 3437
NYCT Girls and Young Women Grants, 3548
Ordean Fndn Grants, 3691
Paul Rapoport Fndn Grants, 3765
Phoenix Suns Charities Grants, 3881
Robert B McMillen Fndn Grants, 4106
Robert E. and Evelyn McKee Fndn Grants, 4110
Robert R. Meyer Fndn Grants, 4121
Russell Berrie Fndn Grants, 4175
U.S. Department of Educ Centers for Independent Living, 4688
U.S. Department of Educ Disability and Rehabilitation Research and Related Projects, 4690
U.S. Department of Educ Parent Information and Training, 4695
U.S. Department of Educ Rehabilitation Engineering Research Centers Grants, 4698

Rehabilitation/Therapy, Emotional/Social
Fourjay Fndn Grants, 1913
Lincoln Financial Group Fndn Grants, 2906
Military Ex-Prisoners of War Fndn Grants, 3177
NFL Charities Pro Bowl Comm Grants in Hawaii, 3348
Perry County Community Fndn Grants, 3827
Posey County Community Fndn Grants, 3939
Robert B McMillen Fndn Grants, 4106
Robert E. and Evelyn McKee Fndn Grants, 4110
Robert R. McCormick Tribune Veterans Grants, 4120
Seabury Fndn Grants, 4316
Sobrato Family Fndn Grants, 4389
Sobrato Family Fndn Meeting Space Grants, 4390
Sobrato Family Fndn Office Space Grants, 4391
Threshold Fndn Justice and Democracy Grants, 4626

Rehabilitation/Therapy, Occupational/Vocational
Able Trust Vocational Rehabilitation Grants for Individuals, 104
Achelis Fndn Grants, 127
Atkinson Fndn Community Grants, 606
Bodman Fndn Grants, 807
Lincoln Financial Group Fndn Grants, 2906
Regents Professional Opportunity Scholarships, 4044
Robert R. Meyer Fndn Grants, 4121
U.S. Department of Educ Migrant and Seasonal Farmworkers Grants, 4693
U.S. Department of Educ Rehabilitation Research Training Centers, 4699
U.S. Department of Educ Vocational Rehabilitation Services Projects for American Indians with Disabilities Grants, 4702

Rehabilitation/Therapy, Physical
Alvah H. and Wyline P. Chapman Fndn Grants, 402
Regents Professional Opportunity Scholarships, 4044
Robert B McMillen Fndn Grants, 4106
Robert R. Meyer Fndn Grants, 4121
Seabury Fndn Grants, 4316

Religion
41 Washington Street Fndn Grants, 22
1104 Fndn Grants, 34
A.C. Ratshesky Fndn Grants, 39
A.H.K. Fndn Grants, 40
A.J. Fletcher Fndn Grants, 41
Aaron Fndn Grants, 73
ABC Charities Grants, 85
Abel Fndn Grants, 90
Abell-Hanger Fndn Grants, 91
Able To Serve Grants, 102
Adams-Mastrovich Family Fndn Grants, 146
Adams County Community Fndn of Pennsylvania Grants, 149
Adams Family Fndn I Grants, 150
Adelaide Christian Home For Children Grants, 162
A Friends' Fndn Grants, 194

Religion

Ahmanson Fndn Grants, 207
Albert and Margaret Alkek Fndn Grants, 340
Albert B. Cuppage Charitable Fndn Grants, 341
Alcoa Fndn Grants, 350
Alfred and Tillie Shemanski Testamentary Grants, 363
Allen Hilles Grants, 378
ALSAM Fndn Grants, 395
Ambrose Monell Fndn Grants, 415
Amelia Sillman Rockwell and Carlos Perry Rockwell Charities Grants, 417
American Academy of Religion Regional Development Grants, 421
American Foodservice Charitable Grants, 433
Amerigroup Fndn Grants, 452
Amon G. Carter Fndn Grants, 458
Anderson Fndn Grants, 460
Anschutz Family Fndn Grants, 486
Anthony R. Abraham Fndn Grants, 489
Antone & Edene Vidinha Charitable Grants, 490
Appalachian Ministries Grants, 499
A Quiet Place Grants, 520
Aragona Family Fndn Grants, 522
Aratani Fndn Grants, 523
Archer Daniels Midland Fndn Grants, 527
Argyros Fndn Grants, 532
Arkansas Community Fndn Grants, 561
Arkell Hall Fndn Grants, 562
Armstrong McDonald Fndn Grants, 565
Arronson Fndn Grants, 567
Arthur Ashley Williams Fndn Grants, 572
Atherton Family Fndn Grants, 604
Athwin Fndn Grants, 605
Atkinson Fndn Community Grants, 606
Audrey and Sydney Irmas Charitable Fndn Grants, 612
Babcock Charitable Grants, 632
Bacon Family Fndn Grants, 634
Bailey Fndn Grants, 635
Banfi Vintners Fndn Grants, 653
Barra Fndn Project Grants, 674
Baton Rouge Area Fndn Grants, 682
Beazley Fndn Grants, 714
Beerman Fndn Grants, 717
Belk Fndn Grants, 721
Bender Fndn Grants, 726
Bernard F. Reynolds Charitable Grants, 741
Besser Fndn Grants, 748
Bill and Katie Weaver Charitable Grants, 764
Bill Hannon Fndn Grants, 771
Blumenthal Fndn Grants, 804
Bodenwein Public Benevolent Fndn Grants, 806
Bodman Fndn Grants, 807
Bolthouse Fndn Grants, 813
Borkee-Hagley Fndn Grants, 817
Brad Brock Family Fndn Grants, 827
Bradley-Turner Fndn Grants, 828
Bradley Family Fndn (California) Grants, 829
Bradley Family Fndn (South Carolina) Grants, 830
Bright Family Fndn Grants, 837
Brooklyn Benevolent Society Grants, 847
Burden Grants, 864
Burton G. Bettingen Grants, 871
Caddock Fndn Grants, 888
Caleb C. and Julia W. Dula Ed and Charitable Fndn Grants, 893
Callaway Fndn Grants, 909
Carl Gellert and Celia Berta Gellert Fndn Grants, 930
Carl R. Hendrickson Family Fndn Grants, 935
Carrie Estelle Doheny Fndn Grants, 945
Carylon Fndn Grants, 949
Catherine Manley Gaylord Fndn Grants, 956
CCCF Alpha Grants, 959
CCCF Dora Maclellan Brown Christian Priority Grants, 960
CCHD Economic Development Grants, 967
CE and S Fndn Grants, 985
CFFVR Robert and Patricia Endries Family Fndn Grants, 1018
Chamberlain Fndn Grants, 1027
Chapman Charitable Fndn Grants, 1033
Chapman Family Charitable Grants, 1034
Charles and Lynn Schusterman Family Grants, 1038
Charles Stewart Mott Fndn Anti-Poverty Grants, 1054
Chatlos Fndn Grants, 1061
Chiles Fndn Grants, 1108
Cincinnati Milacron Fndn Grants, 1132
Citizens Bank Mid-Atlantic Charitable Grants, 1140
Clark-Winchcole Fndn Grants, 1152
Clark and Carolyn Adams Fndn Grants, 1153
Clark and Ruby Baker Fndn Grants, 1154
Claude Bennett Family Fndn Grants, 1159
Cleveland-Cliffs Fndn Grants, 1165
Coastal Community Fndn of S Carolina Grants, 1193
Cogswell Benevolent Grants, 1198
Collins Fndn Grants, 1209
Commission on Religion in Appalachia Grants, 1238
Community Fndn of Greenville Community Enrichment Grants, 1294
Community Fndn of Greenville Hollingsworth Funds Program/Project Grants, 1296
Community Fndn of Mount Vernon and Knox County Grants, 1301
Connelly Fndn Grants, 1353
Conwood Charitable Grants, 1366
Cooke-Hay Fndn Grants, 1367
Cord Fndn Grants, 1372
Coughlin-Saunders Fndn Grants, 1377
Covenant Fndn of Atlanta Grants, 1384
Covenant Mountain Ministries Grants, 1387
Crowell Grants, 1401
Dade Community Fndn Grants, 1430
DaimlerChrysler Corp Grants, 1432
Dale and Edna Walsh Grants, 1435
Danellie Fndn Grants, 1442
Dan Murphy Fndn Grants, 1444
Dave Coy Fndn Grants, 1447
Davenport-Hatch Fndn Grants, 1448
David and Barbara B. Hirschhorn Fndn Grants, 1450
David Robinson Fndn Grants, 1454
Daywood Fndn Grants, 1465
Deaconess Community Fndn Grants, 1467
Delonne Anderson Family Fndn, 1492
Donald and Sylvia Robinson Family Fndn Grants, 1573
Dora Roberts Fndn Grants, 1579
Dorot Fndn Grants, 1586
Dr. Scholl Fndn Grants, 1602
Dyson Fndn Mid-Hudson Valley Faith-Based Organization Grants, 1634
Ed and Carole Abel Grants, 1652
Edward R. Godfrey Fndn Grants, 1667
Edward S. Moore Fndn Grants, 1668
Edwin W. and Catherine M. Davis Fndn Grants, 1672
Effie and Wofford Cain Fndn Grants, 1674
Elden and Mary Lee Gutwein Family Grants, 1679
Elizabeth & Avola W. Callaway Fndn Grants, 1680
Elliot Fndn Inc Grants, 1686
Elsie H. Wilcox Fndn Grants, 1691
Emily Davie and Joseph S. Kornfeld Fndn Grants, 1697
Ensworth Charitable Fndn Grants, 1710
Eugene B. Casey Fndn Grants, 1762
F.M. Kirby Fndn Grants, 1780
Fieldstone Fndn Grants, 1808
Florida Humanities Council Mini Grants, 1869
Fndn for the Carolinas Grants, 1896
Frances and Benjamin Benenson Fndn Grants, 1916
Frank G. and Freida K. Brotz Family Grants, 1928
Franklin County Community Fndn Grants, 1929
Frank S. Flowers Fndn Grants, 1935
Frank Stanley Beveridge Fndn Grants, 1936
Fraser-Parker Fndn Grants, 1938
Fred C. and Katherine B. Andersen Fndn Grants, 1942
Frederick S. Upton Fndn Grants, 1947
Frist Fndn Grants, 1964
Fritz B. Burns Fndn Grants, 1965
Fuller E. Callaway Fndn Grants, 1973
G.N. Wilcox Fndn Grants, 1985
George and Sarah Buchanan Fndn Grants, 2011
George Family Fndn Grants, 2017
George Frederick Jewett Fndn Grants, 2019
George H.C. Ensworth Grants, 2022
George I. Alden Grants, 2023
George Kress Fndn Grants, 2025
George P. Davenport Grants, 2026
Gheens Fndn Grants, 2048
Giant Eagle Fndn Grants, 2049
Grace and Franklin Bernsen Fndn Grants, 2109
Granger Fndn Grants, 2127
Great-West Life Grants, 2130
Greater Saint Louis Community Fndn Grants, 2138
Greater Worcester Comm Discretionary Grants, 2140
Greater Worcester Community Ministries Grants, 2143
Grover Hermann Fndn Grants, 2168
Guido A. and Elizabeth H. Binda Fndn Grants, 2172
H. Leslie Hoffman & Elaine Hoffman Grants, 2185
Hackett Fndn Grants, 2188
Hagedorn Fndn Grants, 2207
Harold Simmons Fndn Grants, 2230
Harry C. Trexler Grants, 2239
Harry W. Bass, Jr. Fndn Grants, 2246
Helen Bader Fndn Grants, 2293
Helen V. Brach Fndn Grants, 2300
Henry W. Bull Fndn Grants, 2312
Hillsdale Grants, 2329
Hollie and Anna Oakley Fndn Grants, 2346
Huntington Fndn Grants, 2408
I.A. O'Shaughnessy Fndn Grants, 2416
Ida Alice Ryan Charitable Grants, 2431
Illinois Humanities Council Community Project Grants, 2510
Irvin Stern Fndn Grants, 2585
J. Bulow Campbell Fndn Grants, 2593
J.C. Penney Company Grants, 2594
J.E. and L.E. Mabee Fndn Grants, 2595
J. Mack Robinson Fndn Grants, 2604
Jacob and Hilda Blaustein Fndn Grants, 2615
James Hervey Johnson Charitable Ed Grants, 2627
James J. and Angelia M. Harris Fndn Grants, 2630
James J. McCann Charitable Trust and McCann Fndn, Inc Grants, 2631
James M. Collins Fndn Grants, 2633
Janus Fndn Grants, 2647
Jayne and Leonard Abess Fndn Grants, 2657
Jenifer Altman Fndn Grants, 2662
Jessie Ball Dupont Grants, 2671
Jewish Women's Fndn of New York Grants, 2677
Joe W. and Dorothy Dorsett Brown Fndn Grants, 2684
John and Elizabeth Whiteley Fndn Grants, 2685
John C. Lasko Fndn Grants, 2688
John G. Duncan Grants, 2695
John H. and Wilhelmina D. Harland Charitable Fndn Grants, 2698
John J. Leidy Fndn Grants, 2701
John P. Murphy Fndn Grants, 2708
Joseph H. and Florence A. Roblee Fndn Grants, 2736
Kaneta Fndn Grants, 2774
Katharine Matthies Fndn Grants, 2788
Kathryne Beynon Fndn Grants, 2791
Koret Fndn Grants, 2837
Leo Niessen Jr., Charitable Grants, 2885
Libra Fndn Grants, 2899
Lotus 88 Fndn for Women and Children Grants, 2921
Louis Calder Fndn Grants, 2925
Lowell Berry Fndn Grants, 2930
Lubbock Area Fndn Grants, 2931
Lucile Horton Howe and Mitchell B. Howe Fndn Grants, 2934
Lumpkin Family Healthy People Grants, 2942
Lydia deForest Charitable Grants, 2946
M. Bastian Family Fndn Grants, 2951
Margaret L. Wendt Fndn Grants, 3004
Marion I. and Henry J. Knott Fndn Discretionary Grants, 3018
Marion I. and Henry J. Knott Standard Grants, 3019
Mary & Walter Frear Eleemosynary Grants, 3035
Mary Duke Biddle Fndn Grants, 3036
Maximilian E. and Marion O. Hoffman Fndn, 3067
Maxon Charitable Grants, 3068
McCallum Family Fndn Grants, 3072
McCombs Fndn Grants, 3075
Meriden Fndn Grants, 3122
Merkel Fndn Grants, 3124

SUBJECT INDEX

Mervin Bovaird Fndn Grants, 3128
MGN Family Fndn Grants, 3154
Missouri United Methodist Ministry Grants, 3189
Musgrave Fndn Grants, 3231
Nathan Cummings Fndn Grants, 3246
Nell Warren Elkin and William Simpson Elkin, 3300
Newman W. Benson Fndn Grants, 3334
Norcliffe Fndn Grants, 3459
North Carolina Community Fndn Grants, 3489
North Georgia Community Fndn Grants, 3505
Onan Family Fndn Grants, 3672
Parker Fndn Grants to Support Chr Evangelism, 3737
Patrick and Anna M. Cudahy Grants, 3751
Paul and Mary Haas Fndn Contributions and Student Scholarships, 3756
Paul E. and Klare N. Reinhold Fndn Grants, 3758
Perkins Charitable Fndn Grants, 3823
Peter and Georgia Angelos Fndn Grants, 3843
Pittsburgh Fndn Community Grants, 3910
PNC Charitable Trust and Fndn Grants, 3921
Polk Bros. Fndn Grants, 3929
Presbyterian Church USA Sam and Helen R. Walton Award, 3946
R.C. Baker Fndn Grants, 3999
Rainbow Grants, 4009
Retirement Research Accessible Faith Grants, 4066
Richard and Caroline T. Gwathmey Grants, 4075
Richard and Helen DeVos Fndn Grants, 4076
Richard D. Bass Fndn Grants, 4079
Righteous Persons Fndn Grants, 4093
Robert and Helen Haddad Fndn Grants, 4103
Robert E. and Evelyn McKee Fndn Grants, 4110
Robert G. Cabell III and Maude Morgan Cabell Fndn Grants, 4113
Robins Fndn Grants, 4126
Rose Community Fndn Jewish Life Grants, 4155
Rush County Community Fndn Grants, 4174
Russell Berrie Fndn Grants, 4175
S.H. Cowell Fndn Grants, 4199
Saint Paul Fndn Grants, 4219
Salisbury Community Fndn Grants, 4224
Siebert Lutheran Fndn Grants, 4351
Sioux Falls Area Community Grants, 4364
Sioux Falls Area Community Fndn Spot Grants, 4366
Sister Grants for Women's Organizations, 4371
Sisters of St. Joseph Healthcare Fndn Grants, 4377
SOCFOC Catholic Ministries Grants, 4392
SOCFOC Community Collaborations Grants, 4393
Solo Cup Fndn Grants, 4401
Southwire Company Grants, 4447
Stewart Huston Charitable Grants, 4505
Stowe Family Fndn Grants, 4510
Sunderland Fndn Grants, 4527
Susan Mott Webb Charitable Grants, 4536
T. James Kavanagh Fndn Grants, 4545
TD4HIM Fndn Grants, 4566
Thomas and Dorothy Leavey Fndn Grants, 4612
Thomas Austin Finch, Sr. Fndn Grants, 4613
Thompson Charitable Fndn Grants, 4622
Thrivent Financial for Lutherans Fndn Grants, 4629
Todd Brock Family Fndn Grants, 4639
Topeka West Rotary Youth Enrichment Grants, 4645
Trinity Fndn Grants, 4670
Trull Fndn Grants, 4673
Turner B. Bunn, Jr. & Catherine E. Bunn Grants, 4680
UUA Holmes-Weatherly Award, 4894
UUA Skinner Sermon Award, 4895
V.V. Cooke Fndn Grants, 4896
Vancouver Fndn Grants & Comm Inits, 4900
Victoria S. and Bradley L. Geist Fndn Grants Supporting Foster Care and Their Caregivers, 4936
Victoria S. and Bradley L. Geist Fndn Grants Supporting Transitioning Foster Youth, 4937
W. C. Griffith Fndn Grants, 4958
W.C. Griffith Fndn Grants, 4957
W. Waldo and Jenny Lynn M. Bradley Grants, 4967
Wabash Valley Community Fndn Grants, 4971
Walter L. Gross III Family Fndn Grants, 4983
Wayne and Gladys Valley Fndn Grants, 5003
Weingart Fndn Grants, 5018

Welborn Baptist Fndn Faith-Based Inits Grants, 5019
Widgeon Point Charitable Fndn Grants, 5064
Wilbur and Patsy Bradley Family Fndn Grants, 5066
William B. Stokely Jr. Fndn Grants, 5076
William G. and Helen C. Hoffman Fndn Grants, 5080
William H. Hannon Fndn Grants, 5086
William S. Abell Fndn Grants, 5094
Windgate Charitable Fndn Grants, 5099
Woodward Grants, 5116
Young Family Fndn Grants, 5127

Religious Studies
41 Washington Street Fndn Grants, 22
Able To Serve Grants, 102
Alabama Humanities Fndn Mini Grants, 231
Alabama Humanities Planning/Consultant Grants, 232
Alavi Fndn Grants, 335
American Academy of Religion Regional Development Grants, 421
AmerUs Group Charitable Fndn, 455
Appalachian Ministries Grants, 499
Arronson Fndn Grants, 567
Bailey Fndn Grants, 635
Beerman Fndn Grants, 717
Blumenthal Fndn Grants, 804
Boeckmann Charitable Fndn Grants, 808
Boettcher Fndn Grants, 810
Booth-Bricker Grants, 815
Booth Ferris Fndn Grants, 816
Brooklyn Benevolent Society Grants, 847
CE and S Fndn Grants, 985
Chatlos Fndn Grants, 1061
Cockrell Fndn Grants, 1196
Dave Coy Fndn Grants, 1447
Dyson Fndn Mid-Hudson Valley Faith-Based Organization Grants, 1634
E. Rhodes and Leona B. Carpenter Fndn Grants, 1640
FirstEnergy Fndn Community Grants, 1819
Frank G. and Freida K. Brotz Family Grants, 1928
George W. Brackenridge Fndn Grants, 2028
Humanitas Fndn Grants, 2390
Jayne and Leonard Abess Fndn Grants, 2657
Jewish Community Fndn of LA Israel Grants, 2674
John I. Smith Charities Grants, 2700
Kawabe Grants, 2794
Mary's Pence Study Grants, 3030
Maurice Amado Fndn Grants, 3063
Nathan Cummings Fndn Grants, 3246
Nell Warren Elkin and William Simpson Elkin, 3300
Rainbow Grants, 4009
Richard and Helen DeVos Fndn Grants, 4076
Rose Community Fndn Jewish Life Grants, 4155
Russell Berrie Fndn Grants, 4175
Siebert Lutheran Fndn Grants, 4351
Turner B. Bunn, Jr. & Catherine E. Bunn Grants, 4680
Welborn Baptist Fndn Faith-Based Inits Grants, 5019
Wisconsin Humanities Council Major Grants, 5107

Religious Welfare Programs
41 Washington Street Fndn Grants, 22
A.C. Ratshesky Fndn Grants, 39
A.H.K. Fndn Grants, 40
Able To Serve Grants, 102
Adams County Community Fndn of Pennsylvania Grants, 149
Adelaide Christian Home For Children Grants, 162
Alavi Fndn Grants, 335
American Foodservice Charitable Grants, 433
A Quiet Place Grants, 520
Babcock Charitable Grants, 632
Baton Rouge Area Fndn Every Kid a King Grants, 681
Bernard F. Reynolds Charitable Grants, 741
Bill and Katie Weaver Charitable Grants, 764
Blue Cross Blue Shield of Minnesota Fndn - Healthy Children: Growing Up Healthy Grants, 794
Blue Cross Blue Shield of Minnesota Healthy Neighborhoods: Connect Grants, 798
Brad Brock Family Fndn Grants, 827
Caesar Puff Fndn Grants, 890
Carl R. Hendrickson Family Fndn Grants, 935

Carrie E. and Lena V. Glenn Fndn Grants, 944
CCF Community Priorities Fund, 961
Charles H. Hall Fndn, 1044
Clark and Carolyn Adams Fndn Grants, 1153
Clark and Ruby Baker Fndn Grants, 1154
Claude Bennett Family Fndn Grants, 1159
Cooke-Hay Fndn Grants, 1367
Covenant Fndn of Atlanta Grants, 1384
Covenant Mountain Ministries Grants, 1387
Dan Murphy Fndn Grants, 1444
Dresher Fndn Grants, 1605
Dyson Fndn Mid-Hudson Valley Faith-Based Organization Grants, 1634
Ed and Carole Abel Fndn Grants, 1652
Edward and Ellen Roche Relief Fndn Grants, 1663
Edward R. Godfrey Grants, 1667
Ensworth Charitable Fndn Grants, 1710
Frederick W. Marzahl Grants, 1948
George A. and Grace L. Long Fndn Grants, 2008
George E. Hatcher, Jr. and Ann Williams Hatcher Fndn Grants, 2015
Greater Worcester Community Ministries Grants, 2143
Greenspun Family Fndn Grants, 2156
Grover Hermann Fndn Grants, 2168
HAF Hansen Family Trust Christian Endowment Grants, 2197
Harry Kramer Grants, 2242
Harvey Randall Wickes Fndn Grants, 2255
Helen Irwin Littauer Ed Grants, 2295
Henrietta Lange Burk Grants, 2303
Herbert A. and Adrian W. Woods Fndn Grants, 2313
Hollie and Anna Oakley Fndn Grants, 2346
Horace Moses Charitable Fndn Grants, 2363
Huntington Fndn Grants, 2408
Ida Alice Ryan Charitable Grants, 2431
Jayne and Leonard Abess Fndn Grants, 2657
Kaneta Fndn Grants, 2774
Laura Jane Musser Intercultural Harmony Grants, 2862
Lilly Endowment Clergy Renewal Program for Indiana Congregations, 2902
Margaret and James A. Elkins Jr. Fndn Grants, 3003
Mary's Pence Ministry Grants, 3029
Mary E. and Michael Blevins Charitable Grants, 3037
Mathile Family Fndn Grants, 3062
Meriden Fndn Grants, 3122
New Jersey Office of Faith Based Inits Service to Seniors Grants, 3333
Newman W. Benson Fndn Grants, 3334
NIAF Anthony Campitelli Endowed Grants, 3431
Parke County Community Fndn Grants, 3735
Perkins-Ponder Fndn Grants, 3822
Priddy Fndn Grants, 3957
Richard and Helen DeVos Fndn Grants, 4076
Robert R. McCormick Tribune Comm Grants, 4119
Rose Community Fndn Jewish Life Grants, 4155
Sierra Health Fndn Responsive Grants, 4353
Sioux Falls Area Community Fndn Field-of-Interest and Donor-Advised Grants, 4365
Sisters of Charity Fndn of Canton Grants, 4372
Sisters of Charity Fndn of Cleveland Good Samaritan Grants, 4373
Solo Cup Fndn Grants, 4401
St. Joseph Community Health Fndn Improving Healthcare Access Grants, 4469
Swindells Charitable Fndn, 4542
Todd Brock Family Fndn Grants, 4639
Triangle Community Fndn Donor Grants, 4668
Vancouver Fndn Grants & Comm Inits, 4900
W. C. Griffith Fndn Grants, 4958

Remedial Education
Albert W. Rice Charitable Fndn Grants, 347
Alfred E. Chase Charitable Fndn Grants, 366
Amgen Fndn Grants, 456
Charles H. Pearson Fndn Grants, 1045
Fndn for the Mid South Educ Grants, 1898
Frank Reed and Margaret Jane Peters Memorial Fund II Grants, 1934
George W. Wells Fndn Grants, 2030
GNOF IMPACT Grants for Youth Development, 2081

980 / Remedial Education

Harold Brooks Fndn Grants, 2227
J. Knox Gholston Fndn Grants, 2599
Lewis H. Humphreys Charitable Grants, 2889
Luella Kemper Grants, 2939
Mary Wilmer Covey Charitable Grants, 3049
National Home Library Fndn Grants, 3276
Piper Trust Educ Grants, 3902
U.S. Department of Educ Innovative Strategies in Community Colleges for Working Adults and Displaced Workers Grants, 4692

Renewable Energy Sources
Appalachian Regional Commission Energy Grants, 505
Bush Fndn Ecological Health Grants, 874
Carolyn Fndn Grants, 942
Colorado Clean Energy Solar Innovation Grants, 1212
Colorado Renewables in Performance Contracting Grants, 1214
Energy Fndn Power Grants, 1707
GNOF Coastal 5 + 1 Grants, 2070
Grand Victoria Fndn Illinois Core Grants, 2126
Illinois Clean Energy Community Fndn Solar Thermal Installation Grants, 2482
Mertz Gilmore Climate Change Grants, 3125
NE Utilities Fndn Grants, 3498
Progress Energy Environmental StewardGrants, 3970
SW Init Fndn Grants, 4446
Union Bank, N.A. Fndn Grants, 4709
USDA Rural Energy for America - Energy Audit and Renewable Energy Devel Assistance Grants, 4828
USDA Rural Energy America Feasibility Grants, 4829
USDA Rural Energy for America - Renewable Energy System and Energy Efficiency Improvement Guaranteed Grants, 4830
USDA Value-Added Producer Grants, 4843
William & Flora Hewlett Environmental Grants, 5074

Renovation
Charles H. Farnsworth Grants, 1043
Chatham Athletic Fndn Grants, 1060
Chicago Community Trust Housing Grants: Advancing Affordable Rental Housing, 1088
Eugene Straus Charitable Trust, 1766
Ford Family Grants Public Convening Spaces, 1881
GNOF Albert N. & Hattie M. McClure Grants, 2068
GNOF Exxon-Mobil Grants, 2074
GNOF Jefferson Community Grants, 2085
GNOF Norco Community Grants, 2089
GNOF St. Bernard Community Grants, 2092
Hillcrest Fndn Grants, 2325
HRF Hudson River Improvement Grants, 2378
IDPH Hosptial Capital Investment Grants, 2441
Illinois DCEO Community Development Assistance For Economic Development Grants, 2488
Janson Fndn Grants, 2646
Katharine Matthies Fndn Grants, 2788
Marietta McNeill Morgan and Samuel Tate Morgan, Jr. Grants, 3008
Montana Community Fndn Grants, 3211
NYCT Historic Preservation Grants, 3551
Perkins-Ponder Fndn Grants, 3822
Priddy Fndn Capital Grants, 3954
USDA Farm Labor Housing Grants, 4809
Vigneron Grants, 4938
West Virginia Commission on the Arts Fast Track ADA and Emergency Grants, 5034

Reproduction
Orchard Fndn Grants, 3690
Packard Fndn Local Grants, 3729
Public Welfare Fndn Grants, 3984
Scherman Fndn Grants, 4305
USAID Implementation Science for Strengthening Use of Evidence in Family Planning/Reproductive Health Programming Grants, 4758

Reproductive Rights
Baxter Int'l Corp Giving Grants, 689
General Service Reproductive Justice Grants, 2007
Ms. Fndn for Women Health Grants, 3225

USAID Implementation Science for Strengthening Use of Evidence in Family Planning/Reproductive Health Programming Grants, 4758

Research Participation
ALA Carroll Preston Baber Research Grant, 255
Alexander Eastman Fndn Grants, 355
Ball Brothers Fndn Rapid Grants, 639
Carrier Corp Contributions Grants, 946
Community Fndn for Greater New Haven Quinnipiac River Grants, 1250
Cruise Industry Charitable Fndn Grants, 1404
Edward W. and Stella C. Van Houten Grants, 1670
FAR Grants, 1787
George A Ohl Jr. Fndn Grants, 2012
Gill Fndn - Gay and Lesbian Grants, 2054
Harry W. Bass, Jr. Fndn Grants, 2246
Henry W. Bull Fndn Grants, 2312
Herbert H. and Grace A. Dow Fndn Grants, 2315
Hilton Hotels Corp Giving Grants, 2331
Hoglund Fndn Grants, 2344
HomeBanc Fndn Grants, 2347
Ireland Family Fndn Grants, 2574
John G. Duncan Grants, 2695
John W. Anderson Fndn Grants, 2729
McCarthy Family Fndn Grants, 3073
Melville Charitable Grants, 3115
NAGC Masters and Specialists Award, 3237
Nelda C. and H.J. Lutcher Stark Fndn Grants, 3296
NRA Fndn Grants, 3517
NSF Accelerating Innovation Research, 3520
Peacock Fndn Grants, 3809
Percy B. Ferebee Endowment Grants, 3820
Pet Care Trust Fish in the Classroom Grant, 3828
Pinkerton Fndn Grants, 3892
Pittsburgh Fndn Community Grants, 3910
Pott Fndn Grants, 3940
R.C. Baker Fndn Grants, 3999
Retirement Research Fndn General Grants, 4067
Robert B McMillen Fndn Grants, 4106
Robert M. Hearin Fndn Grants, 4116
Ross Fndn Grants, 4164
Skaggs Fndn Grants, 4378
Smith Richardson Fndn Domestic Public Research Fellowship, 4386
Vancouver Fndn Grants & Comm Inits, 4900
W. C. Griffith Fndn Grants, 4958
WILD Fndn Grants, 5068

Research Resources (Health/Safety/Medical)
John W. Anderson Fndn Grants, 2729
NSERC Brockhouse Canada Prize for Interdisciplinary Research in Science and Engineering Grant, 3518
Sorenson Legacy Fndn Grants, 4407

Respiratory Diseases
NHLBI Ancillary Studies in Clinical Trials, 3410
NHLBI Microbiome of the Lung and Respiratory Tract in HIV-Infected Individuals and HIV-Uninfected Controls, 3416
NHLBI Ruth L. Kirschstein National Research Service Awards for Individual Predoctoral MD/PhD Fellows and Other Dual Degree Fellows, 3420
Pfizer Healthcare Charitable Contributions, 3863

Restoration and Preservation
1772 Fndn Fellowships, 36
ALA Jan Merrill-Oldham Professional Development Grant, 291
Albuquerque Community Fndn Grants, 348
Allegheny Fndn Grants, 376
Ambrose and Ida Fredrickson Grants, 414
American Express Historic Preservation Grants, 431
Anne L. and George H. Clapp Charitable and Ed Grants, 476
Auburn Fndn Grants, 611
Barberton Community Fndn Grants, 666
Berrien Community Fndn Grants, 744
Blue Mountain Community Fndn Grants, 800
Boeing Company Contributions Grants, 809

Booth-Bricker Grants, 815
Bradley Family Fndn (South Carolina) Grants, 830
Callaway Fndn Grants, 909
Carls Fndn Grants, 937
Champlin Fndns Grants, 1029
Charlotte County (FL) Community Fndn Grants, 1056
Chesapeake Bay Fisheries & Headwaters Grants, 1070
Chesapeake Bay Trust Restoration Grants, 1075
Cleveland Capital Grants, 1167
CLIF Bar Family Fndn Grants, 1173
Community Fndn Alliance City of Evansville Endowment Grants, 1246
Community Fndn for Monterey County Grants, 1255
Community Fndn of Middle Tennessee Grants, 1300
Community Fndn of Sarasota County Grants, 1306
Corning Fndn Cultural Grants, 1376
Crown Point Community Fndn Grants, 1402
Cudd Fndn Grants, 1410
D.F. Halton Fndn Grants, 1424
East Tennessee Fndn Affordable Housing Fund, 1645
Fayette County Fndn Grants, 1795
FirstEnergy Fndn Community Grants, 1819
FishAmerica Fndn Chesapeake Bay Grants, 1827
FishAmerica Fndn Conservation Grants, 1828
Fndn for Mid South Comm Development Grants, 1897
France-Merrick Fndns Grants, 1915
Fred C. and Katherine B. Andersen Fndn Grants, 1942
Gates Family Fndn Community Development & Revitalization Grants, 1990
George Fndn Grants, 2018
George Frederick Jewett Fndn Grants, 2019
GNOF Bayou Communities Grants, 2069
GNOF Exxon-Mobil Grants, 2074
Goldseker Fndn Community Grants, 2101
Greater Green Bay Community Fndn Grants, 2135
Greater Milwaukee Fndn Grants, 2137
Great Lakes Fishery Trust Habitat Protection and Restoration Grants, 2146
HAF Natural Environment Grants, 2202
High Meadow Fndn Grants, 2321
Historic Landmarks Fndn of Indiana African American Heritage Grants, 2333
Historic Landmarks Fndn of Indiana Legal Defense Grants, 2335
Historic Landmarks Fndn of Indiana Marion County Historic Preservation Funds, 2336
Historic Landmarks Fndn of Indiana Preservation Grants, 2337
Hoblitzelle Fndn Grants, 2341
Holland/Zeeland Community Fndn Grants, 2345
Hometown Indiana Grants, 2353
HRF Hudson River Improvement Grants, 2378
Huntington County Community Fndn - Hiner Family Grant, 2405
Illinois DNR Youth Recreation Corps Grants, 2508
Illinois Tool Works Fndn Grants, 2511
IMLS 21st Century Museum Pro Grants, 2512
IMLS American Heritage Preservation Grants, 2513
IMLS Save America's Treasures Grants, 2521
Indiana Historic Preservation Grants, 2537
Jane's Grants, 2639
Jasper Fndn Grants, 2655
Jean and Price Daniel Fndn Grants, 2659
Jennings County Community Fndn Grants, 2664
Jessie Ball Dupont Grants, 2671
Kirkpatrick Fndn Grants, 2827
Lettie Pate Evans Fndn Grants, 2887
Lily Auchincloss Fndn Grants, 2904
Lumpkin Family Fndn Strong Community Leadership Grants, 2944
M.E. Raker Fndn Grants, 2953
Maine Community Fndn Belvedere Historic Preservation Grants, 2976
Mars Fndn Grants, 3025
Mary Black Fndn Active Living Grants, 3031
McLean Contributionship Grants, 3088
Mildred V. Horn Fndn Grants, 3176
Montana Arts Council Cultural and Aesthetic Project Grants, 3209
National Endowment for Arts Commun Grants, 3260

SUBJECT INDEX

National Trust for Historic Preservation Diversity Scholarship, 3280
New York Landmarks Conservancy City Ventures Grants, 3339
NFWF Bring Back the Natives Grants, 3359
Norcliffe Fndn Grants, 3459
North Carolina Community Fndn Grants, 3489
Norwin S. and Elizabeth N. Bean Fndn Grants, 3515
NYCT Historic Preservation Grants, 3551
NYSCA Media & Film: Festivals Grants, 3588
Ogden Codman Grants, 3641
Palm Beach and Martin Counties Grants, 3733
Parkersburg Area Comm Fndn Action Grants, 3738
Perkins Charitable Fndn Grants, 3823
Preservation Maryland Heritage Grants, 3948
Richard and Caroline T. Gwathmey Grants, 4075
Ripley County Community Small Project Grants, 4096
Robert G. Cabell III and Maude Morgan Cabell Fndn Grants, 4113
Rose Fndn for Comm & the Environment N California Environmental Grassroots Grants, 4158
Ross Fndn Grants, 4164
Roy and Christine Sturgis Charitable Grants, 4166
S.H. Cowell Fndn Grants, 4199
Saginaw Community Fndn Discretionary Grants, 4205
Salisbury Community Fndn Health Grants, 4224
Sosland Fndn Grants, 4408
SW Florida Community Competitive Grants, 4442
Stewart Huston Charitable Grants, 4505
Sweet Water Grants, 4541
Tourism Cares Worldwide Grants, 4649
Union Bank, N.A. Fndn Grants, 4709
USDA Housing Preservation Grants, 4816
Wabash River Heritage Corridor Grants, 4970
Wayne County Fndn Vigran Family Grants, 5004
Wayne County Fndn Grants, 5005
WCI Minnesota Beautiful Grants, 5013
Wells Fargo Housing Fndn Grants, 5023
Widgeon Point Charitable Fndn Grants, 5064

Restoration and Preservation, Art Works/Artifacts
1772 Fndn Fellowships, 36
Andy Warhol Fndn for the Visual Arts Grants, 464
E. Rhodes and Leona B. Carpenter Fndn Grants, 1640
IMLS Save America's Treasures Grants, 2521
Jane and Jack Fitzpatrick Grants, 2640
Maine Community Fndn Rose and Samuel Rudman Library Grants, 2988
National Endowment for Arts Museum Grants, 3265
National Endowment for the Arts Presenting Grants: Art Works, 3268
NEH Preservation Assistance Grants for Smaller Institutions, 3293
NYSCA Folk Arts: Exhibitions Grants, 3594
PCA Arts Organizations and Arts Programs Grants for Art Museums, 3775
PCA Entry Track Arts Organizations and Program Grants for Art Museums, 3787
Robert R. Meyer Fndn Grants, 4121
West Virginia Commission on the Arts Cultural Facilities and Capital Resources Grants, 5033

Restoration and Preservation, Manuscripts/Books/Music Scores
1772 Fndn Fellowships, 36
IMLS Save America's Treasures Grants, 2521
Maine Community Fndn Rose and Samuel Rudman Library Grants, 2988
National Endowment for Arts Theater Grants, 3269
NEH Preservation Assistance Grants for Smaller Institutions, 3293
NEH Preservation Microfilming of Brittle Books and Serials Grants, 3294
PCA Arts Organizations and Arts Programs Grants for Art Museums, 3775
PCA Entry Track Arts Organizations and Program Grants for Art Museums, 3787

Restoration and Preservation, Structural/Architectural
1772 Fndn Fellowships, 36
American Express Historic Preservation Grants, 431
Andy Warhol Fndn for the Visual Arts Grants, 464
Benton Community Fndn Grants, 730
Blue River Community Fndn Grants, 801
Brown County Community Fndn Grants, 853
Caleb C. and Julia W. Dula Ed and Charitable Fndn Grants, 893
CDECD Endangered Properties Grants, 980
CDECD Historic Preser Enhancement Grants, 981
CDECD Historic Preservation Survey and Planning Grants, 982
CDECD Historic Restoration Grants, 983
Cleveland Capital Grants, 1167
Community Fndn of Bartholomew Heritage Grants, 1267
Community Fndn of Bartholomew County James A. Henderson Award for Fundraising, 1268
Community Fndn of Greater Fort Wayne - Community Endowment and Clarke Endowment Grants, 1285
Gates Family Fndn Community Development & Revitalization Grants, 1990
GNOF Exxon-Mobil Grants, 2074
GNOF Jefferson Community Grants, 2085
GNOF St. Bernard Community Grants, 2092
Grand Rapids Community Fndn Grants, 2118
Harold K. L. Castle Fndn Grants, 2228
Historic Landmarks Fndn of Indiana African American Heritage Grants, 2333
Historic Landmarks Indiana Legal Defense Grant, 2335
Historic Landmarks Fndn of Indiana Marion County Historic Preservation Funds, 2336
Hometown Indiana Grants, 2353
HRF Hudson River Improvement Grants, 2378
IMLS National Leadership Grants, 2515
IMLS Save America's Treasures Grants, 2521
Indiana Historic Preservation Grants, 2537
Jane and Jack Fitzpatrick Grants, 2640
Kosciusko County Community Fndn REMC Operation Round Up Grants, 2839
Laura Jane Musser Rural Init Grants, 2864
Maine Community Fndn Belvedere Historic Preservation Grants, 2976
Maine Community Fndn Steeples Grants, 2989
MDEQ Brownfield Redevelopment and Site Reclamation Grants, 3095
NAR Partners in Housing Awards, 3239
NYSCA Architecture, Planning, and Design: Capital Fixtures and Equipment Purchase Grants, 3570
NYSCA Architecture, Planning, and Design: Capital Project Grants, 3571
NYSCA Architecture, Planning, and Design: Design and Planning Studies Grants, 3572
NYSCA Architecture, Planning, and Design: General Operating Support Grants, 3573
NYSCA Architecture, Planning, and Design: General Program Support Grants, 3574
NYSCA Architecture, Planning, and Design: Independent Project Grants, 3575
Preservation Maryland Heritage Grants, 3948
Rhode Island Fndn Grants, 4073
Ripley County Community Fndn Grants, 4095
Ripley County Community Small Project Grants, 4096
Robert R. Meyer Fndn Grants, 4121
Textron Corp Contributions Grants, 4601
Trull Fndn Grants, 4673
Wabash River Heritage Corridor Grants, 4970

Retirement
CNCS Senior Corps Retired Volunteer Grants, 1188
David Lane Grants for Aged & Indigent Women, 1453
Robert & Clara Milton Fund for Senior Housing, 4117
RRF General Grants, 4170

Risk Factors/Analysis
AAAS Science and Technology Policy Fellowships: Health, Educ and Human Services, 53
NSF Decision, Risk, and Management Science Research Grants, 3528

Roman Catholic Church
Adams-Mastrovich Family Fndn Grants, 146
AHS Fndn Grants, 208
Alvah H. and Wyline P. Chapman Fndn Grants, 402
Claude A. and Blanche McCubbin Abbott Charitable Grants, 1158
Fred and Sherry Abernethy Fndn Grants, 1940
G.A. Ackermann Grants, 1981
MacDonald-Peterson Fndn Grants, 2965
Merkel Fndn Grants, 3124
Pauline E. Fitzpatrick Charitable Trust, 3763

Runaway Youth
ACF ACYF Runaway and Homeless Youth Basic Center Grants, 112
Burton G. Bettingen Grants, 871
Christine and Katharina Pauly Charitable Grants, 1114
ConocoPhillips Fndn Grants, 1354
Denver Fndn Community Grants, 1502
Fndns of E Chicago Youth Development Grants, 1912

Rural Areas
Agnes M. Lindsay Grants, 203
Agway Fndn Grants, 205
ALA Diversity and Outreach Fair, 267
ALA EBSCO Excellence in Small and/or Rural Public Library Service Award, 273
ANLAF Int'l Fund for Sexual Minorities Grants, 471
Appalachian Ministries Grants, 499
Blandin Fndn Expand Opportunity Grants, 787
CNCS AmeriCorps NCCC Project Grants, 1181
Colin Higgins Fndn Grants, 1204
Dean Foods Community Involvement Grants, 1469
Dept of Ed Alaska Native Ed Programs, 1506
Dept of Ed Parental Info and Resource Centers, 1510
DOJ Rural Domestic Violence and Child Victimization Enforcement Grants, 1562
Donald W. Reynolds Fndn Children's Discovery Init Grants, 1576
Farm Aid Grants, 1790
Florida Div of Cultural Affairs Underserved Cultural Community Development Grants, 1864
FRED Ed Ethyl Grants, 1945
FRED Technology Grants for Rural Schools, 1951
Golden LEAF Fndn Grants, 2097
Greenwall Fndn Bioethics Grants, 2158
Health Canada National Seniors Indep Grants, 2278
J.L. Bedsole Fndn Grants, 2600
James G.K. McClure Educ and Devel Grants, 2624
Kansas Arts Commission Artist Fellowships, 2776
Laura Jane Musser Rural Init Grants, 2864
Montana Arts Council Cultural and Aesthetic Project Grants, 3209
National Book Scholarship Fund, 3249
National Endowment for the Arts - National Arts and Humanities Youth Program Awards, 3255
National Endowment for Arts Media Grants, 3264
National Endowment for Arts Museum Grants, 3265
National Endowment for Arts Music Grants, 3266
National Endowment for Arts Opera Grants, 3267
National Endowment for Arts Theater Grants, 3269
Nevada Arts Council Professional Dev Grants, 3314
NHSCA Conservation License Plate Grants, 3425
North Dakota Council on the Arts Community Access Grants, 3494
OUT Fund for Lesbian & Gay Liberation Grants, 3714
PCA Art Organizations and Art Programs Grants for Presenting Organizations, 3771
PCA Arts in Educ Residencies, 3772
PCA Arts Organizations Grants for Music, 3774
PCA Arts Organizations and Arts Programs Grants for Art Museums, 3775
PCA Arts Organizations and Arts Programs Grants for Arts Educ Organizations, 3776
PCA Arts Organizations and Arts Programs Grants for Arts Service Organizations, 3777
PCA Arts Organizations & Grants for Crafts, 3778
PCA Arts Organizations & Grants for Dance, 3779
PCA Arts Organizations and Arts Programs Grants for Film and Electronic Media, 3780

982 / Rural Areas

PCA Arts Organizations & Grants for Lit, 3781
PCA Arts Organizations and Arts Programs Grants for Local Arts, 3782
PCA Arts Organizations & Grants for Theatre, 3783
PCA Arts Organizations and Arts Programs Grants for Traditional and Folk Arts, 3784
PCA Arts Organizations & Grants for Visual Arts, 3785
PCA Busing Grants, 3786
PCA Entry Track Arts Organizations and Program Grants for Art Museums, 3787
PCA Entry Track Arts Organizations and Program Grants for Arts Educ Organizations, 3788
PCA Entry Track Arts Organizations and Program Grants for Arts Service Organizations, 3789
PCA Entry Track Arts Organizations and Program Grants for Crafts, 3790
PCA Entry Track Arts Organizations and Program Grants for Dance, 3791
PCA Entry Track Arts Organizations and Program Grants for Film and Electronic Media, 3792
PCA Entry Track Arts Organizations and Program Grants for Literature, 3793
PCA Entry Track Arts Organizations and Program Grants for Local Arts, 3794
PCA Entry Track Arts Organizations and Program Grants for Music, 3795
PCA Entry Track Arts Organizations and Program Grants for Presenting Organizations, 3796
PCA Entry Track Arts Organizations and Program Grants for Theatre, 3797
PCA Entry Track Arts Organizations and Program Grants for Traditional and Folk Arts, 3798
PCA Entry Track Arts Organizations and Program Grants for Visual Arts, 3799
Peter Kiewit Fndn General Grants, 3845
Peter Kiewit Fndn Small Grants, 3847
Rochester Area Community Fndn Grants, 4127
Samuel S. Johnson Fndn Grants, 4239
Sapelo Fndn Environmental Protection Grants, 4293
Social Justice Fund NW Montana Giving Project Grants, 4399
Steele-Reese Fndn Grants, 4498
TAC Rural Arts Project Support Grants, 4555
USDA 1890 Land Grant Colleges and Universities Init Grants, 4797
USDA Community Facility Grants, 4801
USDA Delta Health Care Services Grants, 4804
USDA Denali Comm High Energy Cost Grants, 4805
USDA Emergency Community Water Assistance Grants, 4807
USDA High Energy Cost Grants, 4812
USDA Household Water Well System Grants, 4814
USDA Housing Preservation Grants, 4816
USDA Individual Water and Waste Water Grants, 4817
USDA Native American Indian Utilities Grants, 4820
USDA Predevelopment Planning Grants, 4821
USDA Public TV Digital Transition Grants, 4822
USDA Rural Business Enterprise Grants, 4823
USDA Rural Business Opportunity Grants, 4824
USDA Rural Community Development Grants, 4825
USDA Rural Coop Development Grants, 4826
USDA Rural Economic Development Grants, 4827
USDA Rural Energy for America - Energy Audit and Renewable Energy Devel Assistance Grants, 4828
USDA Rural Energy for America - Feasibility Study Grants, 4829
USDA Rural Energy for America - Renewable Energy System and Energy Efficiency Improvement Guaranteed Grants, 4830
USDA Rural Housing Repair and Rehabilitation Grants, 4831
USDA Rural Utilities Service Weather Radio Transmitter Grants, 4833
USDA Section 306C Water and Waste Disposal Grants to Alleviate Health Risks, 4834
USDA Self-Help Technical Assistance Grants, 4836
USDA Small Disadvantaged Producer Grants, 4837
USDA Solid Waste Management Grants, 4838
USDA State Bulk Fuel Revolving Grants, 4840
USDA Tech and Supervisory Assistance Grants, 4841
USDA Technical Assistance and Training Grants for Rural Waste Systems, 4842
USDA Value-Added Producer Grants, 4843
USDA Water and Waste Disposal Grants, 4844
USDC Technology Opportunities Grants, 4860
Verizon Fndn Great Lakes Region Grants, 4912
Virginia Fndn for Humanities Discr Grants, 4946
Virginia Fndn for the Humanities Open Grants, 4947
W.K. Kellogg Fndn Healthy Kids Grants, 4961
West Virginia Commission on the Arts Long-Term Artist Residencies, 5037

Rural Development
Cleveland Lake-Geauga Grants, 1170
CNCS AmeriCorps NCCC Project Grants, 1181
Donald W. Reynolds Fndn Children's Discovery Init Grants, 1576
Florida Div of Cultural Affairs Underserved Cultural Community Development Grants, 1864
Illinois DCEO Community Development Assistance For Economic Development Grants, 2488
Indiana Rural Capacity Grants, 2547
Laura Jane Musser Rural Init Grants, 2864
MDARD County Fairs Cap Improvement Grants, 3092
National Endowment for Arts Our Town Grants, 3257
North Carolina Arts Council Arts in Educ Rural Development Grants, 3470
Peter Kiewit Fndn Small Grants, 3847
Priddy Fndn Organizational Development Grants, 3956
TAC Rural Arts Project Support Grants, 4555
USAID Unsolicited Proposal Grants, 4786
USDA 1890 Land Grant Colleges and Universities Init Grants, 4797
USDA Community Facility Grants, 4801
USDA Delta Health Care Services Grants, 4804
USDA Household Water Well System Grants, 4814
USDA Multi-Family Housing Preservation and Revitalization Grants, 4819
USDA Native American Indian Utilities Grants, 4820
USDA Predevelopment Planning Grants, 4821
USDA Public TV Digital Transition Grants, 4822
USDA Rural Business Enterprise Grants, 4823
USDA Rural Community Development Grants, 4825
USDA Rural Energy for America - Renewable Energy System and Energy Efficiency Improvement Guaranteed Grants, 4830
USDA Rural Housing Repair and Rehab Grants, 4831
USDA Rural Microentrepreneur Assist Grants, 4832
USDA Rural Utilities Service Weather Radio Transmitter Grants, 4833
USDA Section 306C Water and Waste Disposal Grants to Alleviate Health Risks, 4834
USDA Small Disadvantaged Producer Grants, 4837
USDA Solid Waste Management Grants, 4838
USDA State Bulk Fuel Revolving Grants, 4840
USDA Water and Waste Disposal Grants, 4844

Rural Education
BBF Florida Family Lit Init Grants, 697
BBF Maine Family Lit Init Grants, 698
BBF Maine Family Lit Init Planning Grants, 699
Coastal Community Fndn of S Carolina Grants, 1193
Dept of Ed Parental Info and Resource Centers, 1510
Florida Div of Cultural Affairs Facilities Grants, 1852
FRED Ed Ethyl Grants, 1945
FRED Technology Grants for Rural Schools, 1951
Golden LEAF Fndn Grants, 2097
Indiana Rural Capacity Grants, 2547
U.S. Department of Educ 21st Century Community Learning Centers, 4687
USDA Distance Learning and Telemed Grants, 4806

Rural Health Care
Agway Fndn Grants, 205
Appalachian Reg Comm Health Care Grants, 507
Claude Worthington Benedum Fndn Grants, 1161
Fndn for Mid South Health & Wellness Grants, 1899
IBCAT Screening Mammography Grants, 2422
Jenkins Fndn: Improving the Health of Greater Richmond Grants, 2663

SUBJECT INDEX

Kansas Health Fndn Recognition Grants, 2784
Marathon Petroleum Corp Grants, 2999
Marin Community Successful Aging Grants, 3014
Mary Black Fndn Community Health Grants, 3032
Moline Fndn Community Grants, 3202
Pioneer Hi-Bred Community Grants, 3895
Rajiv Gandhi Fndn Grants, 4011
RWJF Local Funding Partnerships Grants, 4186
USDA Delta Health Care Services Grants, 4804
USDA Distance Learning and Telemed Grants, 4806

Rural Planning/Policy
Blue Cross Blue Shield of Minnesota Fndn - Healthy Equity: Health Impact Assessment Grants, 796
GNOF St. Bernard Community Grants, 2092
Indiana Rural Capacity Grants, 2547
Laura Jane Musser Rural Init Grants, 2864
National Endowment for Arts Our Town Grants, 3257
National Endowment for Arts Museum Grants, 3265
National Urban Fellows Program, 3281
NYSCA Architecture, Planning, and Design: Capital Project Grants, 3571
NYSCA Architecture, Planning, and Design: Design and Planning Studies Grants, 3572
NYSCA Architecture, Planning, and Design: General Operating Support Grants, 3573
NYSCA Architecture, Planning, and Design: General Program Support Grants, 3574
NYSCA Architecture, Planning, and Design: Independent Project Grants, 3575
USDA 1890 Land Grant Colleges and Universities Init Grants, 4797
USDA Community Facility Grants, 4801
USDA Denali Comm High Energy Cost Grants, 4805
USDA Predevelopment Planning Grants, 4821
USDA Rural Community Development Grants, 4825
USDA Rural Coop Development Grants, 4826
USDA Rural Energy for America - Energy Audit and Renewable Energy Devel Assistance Grants, 4828
USDA Rural Energy for America - Feasibility Study Grants, 4829
USDA Rural Energy for America - Renewable Energy System and Energy Efficiency Improvement Guaranteed Grants, 4830
USDA Small Disadvantaged Producer Grants, 4837
USDA Tech and Supervisory Assistance Grants, 4841
USDA Technical Assistance and Training Grants for Rural Waste Systems, 4842
USDA Value-Added Producer Grants, 4843
Virginia Fndn for Humanities Discr Grants, 4946
Virginia Fndn for the Humanities Open Grants, 4947

Safety
7-Eleven Coorporate Giving Grants, 18
100 Club of Arizona Benefit Grants, 25
100 Club of Arizona Safety Enhancement Stipends, 26
AAA Fndn for Traffic Safety Grants, 50
ACF Native American Social and Economic Development Strategies Grants, 123
Air Products and Chemicals Grants, 216
Alcatel-Lucent Technologies Fndn Grants, 349
Allstate Corp Giving Grants, 386
Allstate Corp Hometown Commitment Grants, 387
Allstate Fndn Safe and Vital Communities Grants, 390
Alpine Winter Fndn Grants, 394
AMD Corp Contributions Grants, 416
American Academy of Dermatology Shade Structure Grants, 420
American Electric Power Grants, 428
AMERIND Poster Contest, 454
Angels On Track Fndn Grants, 468
AutoNation Corp Giving Grants, 620
AutoZone Community Relations Grants, 621
Beazley Fndn Grants, 714
Bikes Belong Fndn Paul David Clark Bicycling Safety Grants, 760
Bikes Belong Fndn REI Grants, 761
Bikes Belong Fndn Research Grants, 762
Bikes Belong Grants, 763
BJ's Charitable Fndn Grants, 777

SUBJECT INDEX

Blue Cross Blue Shield of Minnesota Fndn - Health Equity: Building Health Together Grants, 793
BoatUS Fndn Grassroots Grants, 805
Caring Fndn Grants, 926
Columbus Neighborhood Partnership Grants, 1226
Cooper Industries Fndn Grants, 1370
DaimlerChrysler Corp Grants, 1432
Decatur County Comm Large Project Grants, 1476
Detroit Lions Charities Grants, 1520
DOI Urban Park & Rec Recovery Grants, 1554
EPA Children's Health Protection Grants, 1728
Farmers Insurance Corp Giving Grants, 1791
Faye McBeath Fndn Grants, 1794
Federal Express Corp Contributions Program, 1799
FEMA Assistance to Firefighters Grants, 1802
Ford Motor Company Grants, 1885
France-Merrick Fndns Grants, 1915
Frank Stanley Beveridge Fndn Grants, 1936
GEICO Public Service Awards, 1997
General Mills Fndn Grants, 2003
Glazer Family Fndn Grants, 2062
Goodyear Tire Grants, 2106
Greater Worcester Community Jeppson Memorial Fund for Brookfield Grants, 2141
Harrison County Community Fndn Grants, 2233
Harrison County Community Signature Grants, 2234
Harvest Fndn Grants, 2254
Helen V. Brach Fndn Grants, 2300
Honeywell Family Safety and Security Grants, 2356
Hundred Club of Palm Springs Grants, 2397
Hundred Club of Santa Clara County Grants, 2399
John Deere Fndn Grants, 2692
LISC Financial Opportunity Center Social Innovation Grants, 2911
LISC MetLife Fndn Community-Police Partnership Awards, 2912
Local Inits Support Corp Grants, 2917
Lowe's Charitable and Ed Fndn Grants, 2927
Mabel Louise Riley Fndn Grants, 2959
Martin C. Kauffman 100 Club of Alameda County Survivor Benefits Grants, 3028
Monsanto Int'l Grants, 3207
Needmor Grants, 3289
NNEDVF/Altria Doors of Hope Program, 3452
Noble County Community Fndn Grants, 3456
NRA Fndn Grants, 3517
Olin Corp Charitable Grants, 3669
PacifiCorp Fndn for Learning Grants, 3727
PG&E Community Vitality Grants, 3868
Philanthrofund Fndn Grants, 3874
Pioneer Hi-Bred Community Grants, 3895
PPG Industries Fndn Grants, 3943
Public Safety Fndn of America Grants, 3983
REI Conservation and Outdoor Rec Grants, 4051
Robert R. Meyer Fndn Grants, 4121
Rohm and Haas Company Grants, 4145
Safeco Insurance Community Grants, 4203
Salt River Health and Human Services Grants, 4228
Samueli Fndn Human Security Grants, 4233
State Farm Companies Safe Neighbors Grants, 4484
Toyota Motor Engineering & Manufacturing North America Grants, 4651
Toyota Motor Manufacturing of Alabama Grants, 4652
Toyota Motor Manufacturing of Indiana Grants, 4653
Toyota Motor of Kentucky Grants, 4654
Toyota Motor N America of New York Grants, 4658
Toyota Motor Sales, USA Grants, 4659
Toyota Technical Center Grants, 4660
Toyota USA Fndn Safety Grants, 4662
UPS Fndn Community Safety Grants, 4728
USDC Technology Opportunities Grants, 4860
Verizon Fndn Internet Safety Grants, 4914
Verizon Fndn South Carolina Lit & Internet Safety Grants, 4922
William G. McGowan Charitable Grants, 5084

Sanitary Engineering
Bill and Melinda Gates Fndn Water, Sanitation and Hygiene Grants, 770
Dorr Fndn Grants, 1591

USAID Palestinian Community Infrastructure Development Grants, 4774

Satellite Communication
National Endowment for Arts Media Grants, 3264

Schizophrenia
Peter and Elizabeth C. Tower Fndn Annual Mental Health Grants, 3835
Peter & Elizabeth C. Tower Mental Health Reference and Resource Materials Mini-Grants, 3837

Scholarship Programs, General
Abell-Hanger Fndn Grants, 91
Abney Fndn Grants, 105
Achelis Fndn Grants, 127
Agnes M. Lindsay Grants, 203
Alabama State Council on the Arts Community Arts Collaborative Ventures Grants, 236
Alabama State Council on the Arts Community Arts Operating Support Grants, 237
Alabama State Council on the Arts Community Arts Presenting Grants, 238
Alabama State Council on the Arts Community Arts Program Development Grants, 239
Alabama State Council on the Arts Community Planning & Design Grants, 241
Alabama State Council on the Arts Multi-Discipline and Festival Grants, 243
Aladdin Industries Fndn Grants, 263
Albert B. Cuppage Charitable Fndn Grants, 341
Albuquerque Community Fndn Grants, 348
Amarillo Area/Harrington Fndns Grants, 412
American Council of the Blind Scholarships, 427
American Foodservice Charitable Grants, 433
Andrew Family Fndn Grants, 462
Angels Wings Fndn Int'l Grants, 469
Antone & Edene Vidinha Charitable Grants, 490
Apple Worldwide Developers Conference Student Scholarships, 513
Aratani Fndn Grants, 523
Archer Daniels Midland Fndn Grants, 527
Arizona Community Fndn Scholarships, 541
Arkansas Community Fndn Grants, 561
Arlington Community Fndn Grants, 564
ASM Gen-Probe Joseph Public Health Award, 591
ASTA Academic Scholarships, 597
AXA Fndn Scholarships, 629
Bailey Fndn Grants, 635
Barberton Community Fndn Grants, 666
Batts Fndn Grants, 687
Ben B. Cheney Fndn Grants, 725
Bernard and Audre Rapoport Fndn University of Texas at Austin Scholarship Programs, 739
Best Buy Children's Fndn @15 Scholarship, 750
Blade Fndn Grants, 783
Blue Mountain Community Fndn Grants, 800
Bodman Fndn Grants, 807
Boettcher Fndn Grants, 810
Bradley Family Fndn (South Carolina) Grants, 830
Bright Family Fndn Grants, 837
Burlington Industries Fndn Grants, 865
Burlington Northern Santa Fe Fndn Grants, 866
Butler Manufacturing Company Fndn Grants, 881
Campbell Soup Fndn Grants, 916
Carnahan-Jackson Fndn Grants, 939
Carpenter Fndn Grants, 943
Carrier Corp Contributions Grants, 946
Catherine Manley Gaylord Fndn Grants, 956
CFFVR Doug and Carla Salmon Fndn Grants, 1009
CFFVR Shawano Area Community Fndn Grants, 1021
CFFVR Women's Fund for the Fox Valley Region Grants, 1025
Champlin Fndns Grants, 1029
Chautauqua Region Community Fndn Grants, 1062
Chick and Sophie Major Memorial Duck Calling Contest Scholarships, 1103
Chiles Fndn Grants, 1108
Christy-Houston Fndn Grants, 1115
Clarence T.C. Ching Fndn Grants, 1151

Scholarship Programs, General / 983

Clark-Winchcole Fndn Grants, 1152
Cleveland-Cliffs Fndn Grants, 1165
Cleveland Lake-Geauga Grants, 1170
Clinton County Community Fndn Grants, 1174
Coca-Cola Fndn Grants, 1195
Collins Fndn Grants, 1209
Comerica Charitable Fndn Grants, 1237
Community Fndn for Greater Buffalo Grants, 1247
Community Fndn for Muskegon County Grants, 1256
Community Fndn of Bloomington and Monroe County Grants, 1271
Community Fndn of Greater Greensboro Grants, 1288
Community Fndn of Greater New Britain Grants, 1291
Community Fndn of Mount Vernon and Knox County Grants, 1301
Community Fndn of South Puget Sound Grants, 1311
Community Fndn of the Verdugos Grants, 1322
Community Fndn Silicon Valley Grants, 1331
Constellation Energy Corp Grants, 1364
Cooper Industries Fndn Grants, 1370
Cord Fndn Grants, 1372
Crescent Porter Hale Fndn Grants, 1398
Crown Point Community Fndn Scholarships, 1403
CSRA Community Fndn Grants, 1407
DAAD Research Grants for Doctoral Candidates and Young Academics and Scientists, 1427
Danellie Fndn Grants, 1442
Daphne Seybolt Culpeper Memorial Fndn Grants, 1445
Dell Scholars Program Scholarships, 1491
Dorr Fndn Grants, 1591
Dubois County Community Fndn Grants, 1615
Edna Haddad Welfare Trust Fund Scholarships, 1658
Edward W. and Stella C. Van Houten Grants, 1670
El Paso Community Fndn Grants, 1688
Elsie H. Wilcox Fndn Grants, 1691
Ensign-Bickford Fndn Grants, 1709
Fairfield County Community Fndn Grants, 1782
Fargo-Moorhead Area Fndn Woman's Grants, 1789
Flinn Fndn Grants, 1842
FMC Fndn Grants, 1876
Fourjay Fndn Grants, 1913
Frances and John L. Loeb Family Grants, 1917
Frank & Larue Reynolds Charitable Grants, 1924
Franklin County Community Fndn Grants, 1929
Frank S. Flowers Fndn Grants, 1935
Fritz B. Burns Fndn Grants, 1965
Gebbie Fndn Grants, 1995
General Mills Fndn Grants, 2003
George and Ruth Bradford Fndn Grants, 2010
George Family Fndn Grants, 2017
George Fndn Grants, 2018
George I. Alden Grants, 2023
George W. Brackenridge Fndn Grants, 2028
Georgia-Pacific Fndn Entrepreneurship Grants, 2033
Gertrude E. Skelly Charitable Fndn Grants, 2046
Gil and Dody Weaver Fndn Grants, 2053
Gladys Brooks Fndn Grants, 2059
Goizueta Fndn Grants, 2096
Golden Rule Fndn Grants, 2098
Greater Saint Louis Community Fndn Grants, 2138
Green Bay Packers Fndn Grants, 2148
Griffin Fndn Grants, 2165
Grover Hermann Fndn Grants, 2168
Gulf Coast Community Fndn Grants, 2174
Gulf Coast Fndn of Community Scholarships, 2178
Gumdrop Books Librarian Scholarships, 2179
Harold Simmons Fndn Grants, 2230
Harry Bramhall Gilbert Charitable Grants, 2238
Harry Kramer Grants, 2242
Helen V. Brach Fndn Grants, 2300
Henry County Community Fndn Grants, 2308
High Meadow Fndn Grants, 2321
Hilton Hotels Corp Giving Grants, 2331
Hirtzel Memorial Fndn Grants, 2332
Hoglund Fndn Grants, 2344
Holland/Zeeland Community Fndn Grants, 2345
HomeBanc Fndn Grants, 2347
Homer Fndn Grants, 2352
Hormel Foods Charitable Grants, 2368
Huie-Dellmon Grants, 2386

984 / Scholarship Programs, General

Humana Fndn Grants, 2388
Hundred Club of Colorado Springs Grants, 2391
Hundred Club of Connecticut Grants, 2392
Hundred Club of Denver Grants, 2394
Hundred Club of Durango Grants, 2395
Hundred Club of Pueblo Grants, 2398
Huntington Arts Council Arts-in-Educ Grants, 2400
IAFF Harvard Univ Trade Union Scholarships, 2417
IAFF Labour College of Canada Residential Scholarship, 2418
IAFF National Labor College Scholarships, 2419
IAFF W. H. McClennan Scholarship, 2420
Idaho Power Company Corp Contributions, 2433
IIE Adell and Hancock Scholarships, 2452
Indiana Workforce Acceleration Grants, 2552
Intel Community Grants, 2562
Intel Int'l Community Grants, 2564
Int'l Assoc of Emergency Managers Scholarships, 2566
Isabel Allende Fndn Esperanza Grants, 2586
J.E. and L.E. Mabee Fndn Grants, 2595
J.L. Bedsole Fndn Grants, 2600
J. Willard and Alice S. Marriott Fndn Grants, 2609
J. Willard Marriott, Jr. Fndn Grants, 2610
Jacob G. Schmidlapp Grants, 2616
James & Abigail Campbell Family Fndn Grants, 2620
James G.K. McClure Educ and Devel Grants, 2624
James J. McCann Charitable Trust and McCann Fndn, Inc Grants, 2631
James R. Thorpe Fndn Grants, 2636
Janus Fndn Grants, 2647
JELD-WEN Fndn Grants, 2661
Jim Blevins Fndn Scholarships, 2679
John and Elizabeth Whiteley Fndn Grants, 2685
John J. Leidy Fndn Grants, 2701
John Jewett & Helen Chandler Garland Grants, 2702
John M. Ross Fndn Grants, 2704
John R. Oishei Fndn Grants, 2709
John W. Anderson Fndn Grants, 2729
Joseph Alexander Fndn Grants, 2734
Josephine G. Russell Grants, 2737
Joukowsky Family Fndn Grants, 2743
Judge Isaac Anderson, Jr. Scholarship, 2754
Kathryne Beynon Fndn Grants, 2791
Kawabe Grants, 2794
Kettering Grants, 2818
Kohl's Cares Scholarships, 2832
Laura L. Adams Fndn Grants, 2865
Lawrence J. and Anne Rubenstein Charitable Fndn Grants, 2868
Leo Goodwin Fndn Grants, 2882
Lillian S. Wells Fndn Grants, 2901
Louis Calder Fndn Grants, 2925
Lowell Berry Fndn Grants, 2930
Lubbock Area Fndn Grants, 2931
Lubrizol Fndn Grants, 2933
Lumpkin Family Healthy People Grants, 2942
Lynde and Harry Bradley Fndn Grants, 2947
Lynde and Harry Bradley Fndn Prizes, 2948
M. Bastian Family Fndn Grants, 2951
Mary Jennings Sport Camp Scholarship, 3041
Mary M. Aaron Memorial Trust Scholarships, 3045
Maxon Charitable Fndn Grants, 3068
McInerny Fndn Grants, 3083
Mead Witter Fndn Grants, 3106
MGN Family Fndn Grants, 3154
Military Ex-Prisoners of War Fndn Grants, 3177
Morgan Babcock Scholarships, 3217
NAGC Masters and Specialists Award, 3237
NASE Fndn Future Entrepreneur Scholarship, 3241
Nelda C. and H.J. Lutcher Stark Fndn Grants, 3296
New Hampshire Charitable Fndn Grants, 3325
New York Life Fndn Grants, 3341
NHSCA Operating Grants, 3428
North Carolina Community Fndn Grants, 3489
NW Minnesota Fndn Women's Scholarships, 3513
Oklahoma City Community Programs & Grants, 3666
Oleonda Jameson Grants, 3667
Ordean Fndn Grants, 3691
Owens Fndn Grants, 3718
Parkersburg Area Comm Fndn Action Grants, 3738

Park Fndn Grants, 3739
Patrick and Anna M. Cudahy Grants, 3751
Paul and Mary Haas Fndn Contributions and Student Scholarships, 3756
Percy B. Ferebee Endowment Grants, 3820
Pott Fndn Grants, 3940
Price Chopper's Golub Fndn Two-Year Health Care Scholarship, 3951
Price Family Charitable Grants, 3952
Puerto Rico Community Fndn Grants, 3986
Randall L. Tobias Fndn Grants, 4017
Rathmann Family Fndn Grants, 4026
Rhode Island Fndn Grants, 4073
Robert M. Hearin Fndn Grants, 4116
Ruth Eleanor Bamberger and John Ernest Bamberger Memorial Fndn Grants, 4178
Ryder System Charitable Fndn Grants, 4191
S. Livingston Mather Charitable Grants, 4200
Saint George's Society of New York Scholarships, 4213
Saint Paul Companies Fndn Grants, 4217
Samuel S. Johnson Fndn Grants, 4239
Sara Lee Fndn Grants, 4296
Seabury Fndn Grants, 4316
Seattle Fndn Doyne M. Green Scholarships, 4324
Seneca Foods Fndn Grants, 4336
Simmons Fndn Grants, 4360
Sodexo Fndn STOP Hunger Scholarships, 4400
SW Florida Community Fndn Undergraduate and Graduate Scholarships, 4444
Square D Fndn Grants, 4464
Starr Fndn Grants, 4483
State Justice Institute Scholarships, 4491
Strengthening Families - Strengthening Communities Grants, 4513
Strolling of the Heifers Scholarships for Farmers, 4514
Strowd Roses Grants, 4515
Stuart Fndn Grants, 4516
T. James Kavanagh Fndn Grants, 4545
Target Corp Local Store Grants, 4561
Temple-Inland Fndn Grants, 4576
Third Wave Fndn Lela Breitbart Grants, 4609
Third Wave Organizing & Advocacy Grants, 4610
Third Wave Fndn Reproductive Health and Justice Grants, 4611
Thomas and Dorothy Leavey Fndn Grants, 4612
Thomas Austin Finch, Sr. Fndn Grants, 4613
Thomas B. & Elizabeth M. Sheridan Grants, 4614
Thompson Charitable Fndn Grants, 4622
Tourism Cares Professional Dev Scholarships, 4648
Trinity Fndn Grants, 4669
Trull Fndn Grants, 4673
Tulane University Community Service Scholars, 4677
U.S. Army ROTC Scholarships, 4685
United States Institute of Peace - National Peace Essay Contest for High School Students, 4724
USAID Scholarships for Youth and Teachers, 4780
USBC Annual Zeb Scholarship, 4792
USBC Earl Anthony Scholarships, 4793
USTA NJTL Tennis and Leadership Camp Scholarships, 4879
USTA Serves College Educ Scholarships, 4885
USTA Serves College Textbook Scholarships, 4886
USTA Serves Dwight F. Davis Scholarships, 4887
USTA Serves Dwight Mosley Scholarships, 4888
USTA Serves Eve Kraft Scholarships, 4889
USTA Serves Marian Wood Baird Scholarship, 4890
USTA Serves Player Incentive Awards, 4891
Vulcan Materials Company Fndn Grants, 4956
Walt Disney Company Fndn Grants, 4981
Whirlpool Fndn Grants, 5056
William B. Stokely Jr. Fndn Grants, 5076
William G. and Helen C. Hoffman Fndn Grants, 5080
William G. Gilmore Fndn Grants, 5082
William G. McGowan Charitable Grants, 5084
William G. Selby and Marie Selby Fndn Grants, 5085
Williams Companies Fndn Grants, 5095
Wood-Claeyssens Fndn Grants, 5113
Xerox Fndn Grants, 5122
Young Family Fndn Grants, 5127

School Dental Programs
Healthcare Fndn of New Jersey Grants, 2280
Pollock Fndn Grants, 3930

School Food Programs
Annie's Cases for Causes Product Donations, 479
Chefs Move to Schools Grants, 1066
Chicago Community Trust Health Grants, 1087
ConAgra Foods Community Impact Grants, 1342
ConAgra Foods Nourish Our Comm Grants, 1343
DeKalb County Community Fndn - Immediate Response Grant, 1479
HAF Co-op Community Grants, 2192
Share Our Strength Grants, 4340
Slow Food in Schools Micro-Grants, 4384

School Health Programs
Appalachian Reg Comm Health Care Grants, 507
Chefs Move to Schools Grants, 1066
Cigna Civic Affairs Sponsorships, 1129
Circle K Corp Contributions Grants, 1136
Colonel Stanley R. McNeil Fndn Grants, 1210
Cone Health Fndn Grants, 1348
Dr. John T. Macdonald Fndn Grants, 1600
Fndns of E Chicago Health Grants, 1910
Gibson County Community Fndn Women's Fund, 2051
Healthcare Fndn of New Jersey Grants, 2280
Health Fndn of Greater Cincinnati Grants, 2281
McKesson Fndn Grants, 3084
Mt. Sinai Health Care Fndn Health of the Urban Community Grants, 3227
Piedmont Health Fndn Grants, 3882
Seattle Fndn Health and Wellness Grants, 4328
Union Labor Health Fndn Community Grants, 4713
United Methodist Health Ministry Grants, 4722
Visiting Nurse Fndn Grants, 4951

School-to-Work Transition
AACC Project Reach Grants, 56
Abell Fndn Workforce Development Grants, 97
Able Trust Voc Rehab Grants for Agencies, 103
AEGON Transamerica Fndn Community Grants, 177
Alliant Energy Fndn Community Grants, 384
American Honda Fndn Grants, 439
Cleveland Fenn Ed Grants, 1169
Crail-Johnson Fndn Grants, 1393
Denver Fndn Community Grants, 1502
Edna McConnell Clark Fndn Grants, 1659
Ewing Marion Kauffman Fndn Grants and Inits, 1777
Georgia-Pacific Fndn Entrepreneurship Grants, 2033
Hawaiian Electric Industries Charitable Grants, 2259
J. Willard and Alice S. Marriott Fndn Grants, 2609
KeyBank Fndn Grants, 2820
Liberty Bank Fndn Grants, 2890
Meyer Fndn Economic Security Grants, 3141
Meyer Fndn Educ Grants, 3142
Nevada Community Fndn Grants, 3316
New Jersey Center for Hispanic Policy, Research and Development Workforce Grants, 3330
Pentair Fndn Educ and Community Grants, 3816
Peter and Elizabeth C. Tower Fndn Annual Intellectual Disabilities Grants, 3834
Piedmont Natural Gas Workforce Devel Grant, 3886
Reynolds American Fndn Grants, 4068
Rohm and Haas Company Grants, 4145
S.H. Cowell Fndn Grants, 4199
Textron Corp Contributions Grants, 4601
USAID Workforce Development Program in Mexico Grants, 4787
Vectren Fndn Grants, 4907
Verizon Fndn Great Lakes Region Grants, 4912
Verizon Fndn Maryland Grants, 4917
Verizon Fndn New Jersey Check into Lit Grants, 4918
Verizon Fndn New York Grants, 4919
Verizon Fndn NE Region Grants, 4920
Verizon Fndn Pennsylvania Grants, 4921
Verizon Fndn SE Region Grants, 4923
Verizon Fndn Vermont Grants, 4924
Verizon Fndn Virginia Grants, 4925
Verizon Fndn West Virginia Grants, 4926

SUBJECT INDEX

Science

AAAS Early Career Award for Public Engagement with Science, 51
Albert and Margaret Alkek Fndn Grants, 340
Alcoa Fndn Grants, 350
Alex Brown and Sons Charitable Fndn Grants, 359
Alfred P. Sloan Fndn Civic Inits Grants, 368
Alvah H. and Wyline P. Chapman Fndn Grants, 402
ALZA Corp Contributions Grants, 405
American Schlafhorst Fndn Grants, 446
Angels Baseball Fndn Grants, 465
Applied Biosystems Grants, 514
ARCO Fndn Educ Grants, 528
Arizona Cardinals Grants, 534
Arkema Fndn Science Teachers Program, 563
Armstrong McDonald Fndn Grants, 565
Arthur Ashley Williams Fndn Grants, 572
Arts and Science Council Grants, 576
ArvinMeritor Grants, 585
Banfi Vintners Fndn Grants, 653
Baxter Int'l Corp Giving Grants, 689
Bay Area Community Fndn Grants, 694
Bemis Company Fndn Grants, 723
Blumenthal Fndn Grants, 804
Bonfils-Stanton Fndn Grants, 814
Bristol-Myers Squibb Fndn Community Grants, 840
Cabot Corp Fndn Grants, 887
Canada-U.S. Fulbright Mid-Career Grants, 917
Carl Gellert and Celia Berta Gellert Fndn Grants, 930
Carylon Fndn Grants, 949
Chamberlain Fndn Grants, 1027
Chevron Hawaii Educ Fund, 1077
Cleveland-Cliffs Fndn Grants, 1165
Community Fndn of Greater Flint Grants, 1282
Cyrus Eaton Fndn Grants, 1423
DAAD Research Grants for Doctoral Candidates and Young Academics and Scientists, 1427
DaimlerChrysler Corp Grants, 1432
Davenport-Hatch Fndn Grants, 1448
Dolan Fndn Grants, 1563
Dow Chemical Company Grants, 1596
E.L. Wiegand Fndn Grants, 1639
EQT Fndn Educ Grants, 1745
Fieldstone Fndn Grants, 1808
FirstEnergy Fndn Math, Science, and Technology Educ Grants, 1820
Flinn Fndn Scholarships, 1843
Fluor Fndn Grants, 1875
Frank Stanley Beveridge Fndn Grants, 1936
Fred C. and Mary R. Koch Fndn Grants, 1943
Genentech Corp Charitable Contributions, 2000
George A Ohl Jr. Fndn Grants, 2012
George Fndn Grants, 2018
Gladys Brooks Fndn Grants, 2059
Grace and Franklin Bernsen Fndn Grants, 2109
Grand Rapids Community Fndn Grants, 2118
H.B. Fuller Company Fndn Grants, 2183
Harry W. Bass, Jr. Fndn Grants, 2246
Hearst Fndns Culture Grants, 2284
Heineman Fndn for Research, Educ, Charitable and Scientific Purposes, 2290
Helen V. Brach Fndn Grants, 2300
Herbert H. and Grace A. Dow Fndn Grants, 2315
Hoblitzelle Fndn Grants, 2341
Honeywell Corp Leadership Challenge Academy, 2359
Idaho Community Fndn Eastern Region Competitive Grants, 2432
IIE AmCham Charitable Fndn U.S. Studies Scholarship, 2453
IIE Japan-U.S. Teacher Exchange for Educ for Sustainable Development, 2457
IIE Leonora Lindsley Memorial Fellowships, 2458
IIE New Leaders Group Award for Mutual Understanding, 2460
IIE Western Union Family Scholarships, 2462
IMLS 21st Century Museum Pro Grants, 2512
IMLS American Heritage Preservation Grants, 2513
IMLS National Leadership Grants, 2515
Indiana Space Grant Consortium Grants for Informal Educ Partnerships, 2549
Indiana Space Grant Consortium Workforce Development Grants, 2550
Intel Community Grants, 2562
Intel Int'l Community Grants, 2564
Josiah W. and Bessie H. Kline Fndn Grants, 2742
Kenneth T. and Eileen L. Norris Fndn Grants, 2802
M.J. Murdock Charitable Trust General Grants, 2954
Marion Gardner Jackson Charitable Grants, 3017
Mary & Walter Frear Eleemosynary Grants, 3035
Massachusetts Cultural Adams Arts Grants, 3052
McCarthy Family Fndn Grants, 3073
McGregor Grants, 3082
Meadows Fndn Grants, 3104
Medtronic Fndn CommunityLink Educ Grants, 3110
Mercedes-Benz USA Corp Contributions Grants, 3118
Micron Technology Fndn Community Grants, 3161
Miguel Aleman Fndn Grants, 3175
National Wetlands Awards, 3282
NEH Family and Youth Programs in American History Grants, 3291
North Carolina GlaxoSmithKline Fndn Grants, 3490
NSERC Brockhouse Canada Prize for Interdisciplinary Research in Science and Engineering Grant, 3518
NSF Communicating Res to Public Audiences, 3527
Nuffield Fndn Africa Grants, 3532
Nuffield Fndn Small Grants, 3535
Phoenix Suns Charities Grants, 3881
Puerto Rico Community Fndn Grants, 3986
Qualcomm Grants, 3993
R.C. Baker Fndn Grants, 3999
Rajiv Gandhi Fndn Grants, 4011
Richard and Caroline T. Gwathmey Grants, 4075
Richard and Rhoda Goldman Grants, 4077
Roberta Leventhal Sudakoff Fndn Grants, 4102
Robins Fndn Grants, 4126
Rockefeller Fndn Grants, 4138
Russell Berrie Fndn Grants, 4175
Saint Louis Rams Fndn Community Donations, 4214
San Diego Science & Tech Blasker Grants, 4250
San Diego Women's Fndn Grants, 4252
Sarah Scaife Fndn Grants, 4295
Schramm Fndn Grants, 4310
Seaver Institute Grants, 4331
Sidney Stern Grants, 4349
Sid W. Richardson Fndn Grants, 4350
Solutia Grants, 4402
Sorenson Legacy Fndn Grants, 4407
Thanks Be to Grandmother Winifred Grants, 4602
Toyota Technical Center Grants, 4660
Tri-State Community Twenty-first Century Endowment Grants, 4666
USAID In-Support for Teacher Educ Grants, 4759
USDA Coop Extension System Educ Grants, 4803
Wayne and Gladys Valley Fndn Grants, 5003
Xerox Fndn Grants, 5122

Science Education

3M Fndn Community Giving Grants, 15
AAUW Community Action Grants, 75
AAUW Int'l Project Grants, 76
Abbott Fund Global AIDS Care Grants, 82
Abell-Hanger Fndn Grants, 91
AEP Corp Giving Grants, 180
Aetna Fndn Educ Grants in Connecticut, 183
Agere Corp and Community Involvement Grants, 199
Alcoa Fndn Grants, 350
Alfred P. Sloan Fndn Civic Inits Grants, 368
AMD Corp Contributions Grants, 416
American Electric Power Grants, 428
American Honda Fndn Grants, 439
Amgen Fndn Grants, 456
Applied Biosystems Grants, 514
Arizona Community Fndn Grants, 540
Arkema Fndn Science Teachers Program, 563
ArvinMeritor Grants, 585
Avista Fndn Grants, 624
Baptist Community Ministries Grants, 664
Bay and Paul Fndns, Inc Grants, 692
Bayer Fndn Grants, 696
Bill and Melinda Gates Ag Development Grants, 765
Bodman Fndn Grants, 807
Cabot Corp Fndn Grants, 887
Charlotte R. Schmidlapp Grants, 1058
Chicago Board of Trade Fndn Grants, 1079
Chiron Fndn Community Grants, 1111
ConocoPhillips Grants, 1355
DaimlerChrysler Corp Grants, 1432
DENSO North America Fndn Grants, 1499
Dept of Ed Alaska Native Ed Programs, 1506
Dorr Fndn Grants, 1591
Dow Chemical Company Grants, 1596
Eaton Charitable Grants, 1647
EMC Corp Grants, 1693
Emily Davie and Joseph S. Kornfeld Fndn Grants, 1697
Essex County Community Fndn Greater Lawrence Summer Grants, 1755
Ewing Marion Kauffman Fndn Grants and Inits, 1777
Ford Motor Company Grants, 1885
Fred C. and Mary R. Koch Fndn Grants, 1943
Genentech Corp Charitable Contributions, 2000
Goodrich Corp Fndn Grants, 2104
Heineman Fndn for Research, Educ, Charitable and Scientific Purposes, 2290
Houston Endowment Grants, 2373
Indiana Space Grant Consortium Grants for Informal Educ Partnerships, 2549
Indiana Space Grant Consortium Workforce Development Grants, 2550
James L. and Mary Jane Bowman Grants, 2632
Lockheed Martin Philanthropic Grants, 2918
Luther I. Replogle Fndn Grants, 2945
McCarthy Family Fndn Grants, 3073
McCune Charitable Fndn Grants, 3077
MedImmune Charitable Grants, 3108
Medtronic Fndn Patient Link Grants, 3113
Mercedes-Benz USA Corp Contributions Grants, 3118
Micron Technology Fndn Community Grants, 3161
Motorola Fndn Grants, 3221
NSF Communicating Res to Public Audiences, 3527
NSTA Distinguished Informal Science Ed Award, 3531
Olin Corp Charitable Grants, 3669
Oracle Corp Contributions Grants, 3686
Patricia Price Peterson Fndn Grants, 3746
PG&E Bright Ideas Grants, 3866
Pittsburgh Fndn Community Grants, 3910
Praxair Fndn Grants, 3944
PSEG Environmental Educ Grants, 3980
Qualcomm Grants, 3993
Rathmann Family Fndn Grants, 4026
Raytheon Grants, 4030
RGK Fndn Grants, 4072
Rohm and Haas Company Grants, 4145
Roy and Christine Sturgis Charitable Grants, 4166
SAS Institute Community Relations Donations, 4300
Schering-Plough Fndn Health Grants, 4304
Seagate Tech Corp Capacity to Care Grants, 4317
Solutia Grants, 4402
TE Fndn Grants, 4572
United Technologies Corp Grants, 4725
USAID In-Support for Teacher Educ Grants, 4759
Washington Gas Charitable Contributions, 5000
Weatherwax Fndn Grants, 5014
Westinghouse Charitable Giving Grants, 5028
Xerox Fndn Grants, 5122

Science and Technology

ADC Fndn Technology Access Grants, 158
Ameren Corp Community Grants, 418
American Gas Fndn Grants, 437
ASM Congressional Science Fellowships, 589
Autodesk Community Relations Grants, 619
Bill and Melinda Gates Fndn Agricultural Development Grants, 765
DENSO North America Fndn Grants, 1499
Duke Energy Economic Development Grants, 1619
Hearst Fndns Culture Grants, 2284
IIE David L. Boren Fellowships, 2454
Illinois DCEO Eliminate Dig Divide Grants, 2489
Meyer Fndn Economic Security Grants, 3141
Paul G. Allen Family Fndn Grants, 3759

986 / Science and Technology

Rohm and Haas Company Grants, 4145
San Diego Science & Tech Blasker Grants, 4250
SAS Institute Community Relations Donations, 4300
US CRDF Science & Tech Entrepreneurship Business Partnership Grants in Armenia, 4795
US CRDF STEP Business Partnership Grant Competition Ukraine, 4796
William Bingham Fndn Grants, 5077

Science and Technology Centers
Illinois DCEO Emerging Technological Enterprises Grants, 2490
Marion Gardner Jackson Charitable Grants, 3017
NSTA Distinguished Informal Science Ed Award, 3531
USDC i6 Challenge Grants, 4851

Scriptwriting
Bush Fndn Arts & Humanities Grants: Short-Term Organizational Support, 873
IFP Minnesota McKnight Screenwriters Fellows, 2449
Kentucky Arts Council Al Smith Fellowship, 2806
Kentucky Arts Council Emerging Artist Award, 2807
PCA Arts Organizations & Grants for Lit, 3781
PCA Entry Track Arts Organizations and Program Grants for Literature, 3793
PCA Strategies for Success Grants - Advanced, 3804
PCA Strategies for Success Grants - Basic Level, 3805
PCA Strategies for Success Grants - Intermediate, 3806
Rasmuson Fndn Individual Artists Awards, 4022

Sculpture
Florida Div of Cultural Affairs Multidiscip Grants, 1857
Hall Family Fndn Grants, 2210
NYFA Gregory Millard Fellowships, 3565
PCA Arts Organizations & Grants for Visual Arts, 3785
PCA Entry Track Arts Organizations and Program Grants for Visual Arts, 3799
Pew Fellowships in the Arts, 3860

Sea Turtles
Florida Sea Turtle Grants, 1871

Seafood
GNOF Gulf Coast Oil Spill Grants, 2077
USDA Fed-State Marketing Improvement Grants, 4810

Secondary Education
3M Fndn Community Giving Grants, 15
21st Century Threshold Project Gifts, 21
A.O. Smith Community Grants, 46
AAF Richard Riley Award, 59
AAUW Community Action Grants, 75
AAUW Int'l Project Grants, 76
Abel and Sophia Sheng Charitable Fndn Grants, 86
Abeles Fndn Grants, 89
Abernethy Family Fndn Grants, 98
Acuity Charitable Fndn Grants, 140
Adams Family Fndn I Grants, 150
Adolph Coors Fndn Grants, 171
AEP Corp Giving Grants, 180
Aetna Fndn Educ Grants in Connecticut, 183
Aetna Summer Academic Enrichment Grants, 189
A Fund for Women Grants, 195
Agere Corp and Community Involvement Grants, 199
Ahmanson Fndn Grants, 207
Alabama Power Fndn Grants, 233
ALA Information Technology Pathfinder Award, 286
Alcatel-Lucent Technologies Fndn Grants, 349
Alcoa Fndn Grants, 350
AMD Corp Contributions Grants, 416
American Electric Power Grants, 428
American Honda Fndn Grants, 439
AmerUs Group Charitable Fndn, 455
Anderson Fndn Grants, 460
Andrew Family Fndn Grants, 462
Applied Biosystems Grants, 514
Archer Daniels Midland Fndn Grants, 527
ARCO Fndn Educ Grants, 528
Arkansas Arts Council AIE Arts Curriculum Project Grants, 552

Arkansas Arts Council AIE Mini Grants, 554
Armstrong McDonald Fndn Grants, 565
Atkinson Fndn Community Grants, 606
Auburn Fndn Grants, 611
AutoNation Corp Giving Grants, 620
Avista Fndn Grants, 624
Ayres Fndn Grants, 630
Ball Brothers Fndn General Grants, 637
Bank of America Charitable Fndn Educ and Workforce Development Grants, 657
Barnes and Noble Local Sponsorships and Charitable Donations, 670
Baxter Int'l Corp Giving Grants, 689
Bay and Paul Fndns, Inc Grants, 692
Benton County Fndn Grants, 731
Berrien Community Fndn Grants, 744
Blackford County Community Fndn Grants, 780
Boeckmann Charitable Fndn Grants, 808
Boeing Company Contributions Grants, 809
Boettcher Fndn Grants, 810
Bohemian Fndn Pharos Grants, 811
Booth-Bricker Grants, 815
Booth Ferris Fndn Grants, 816
Boston Fndn Grants, 819
British Columbia Arts Council Artists in Education Grants, 842
Brooklyn Benevolent Society Grants, 847
Brown Fndn Grants, 854
Buhl Fndn - Frick Ed Fund, 859
Burlington Industries Fndn Grants, 865
Burton Morgan Youth Entrepreneurship Grants, 870
Cadence Design Systems Grants, 889
California Arts Council Arts and Accessibility Technical Assistance Grants, 894
California Arts Council Public Value Grants, 895
Callaway Fndn Grants, 909
Camp-Younts Fndn Grants, 914
Cape Branch Fndn Grants, 919
Carnegie Corp of New York Grants, 940
Caroline Lawson Ivey Memorial Fndn Grants, 941
Carrie E. and Lena V. Glenn Fndn Grants, 944
Carrie Estelle Doheny Fndn Grants, 945
Carroll County Community Fndn Grants, 947
CDC School Health Programs to Prevent the Spread of HIV Coop Agreements, 975
CenturyLink Clarke M. Williams Fndn Grants, 998
CFFVR Mielke Family Fndn Grants, 1015
Chapman Charitable Fndn Grants, 1033
Charity Incorporated Grants, 1035
Charles H. Pearson Fndn Grants, 1045
Charles H. Price II Family Fndn Grants, 1046
Charles Nelson Robinson Grants, 1052
Chesapeake Bay Trust Mini Grants, 1072
Chesapeake Corp Fndn Grants, 1076
Chick and Sophie Major Memorial Duck Calling Contest Scholarships, 1103
CIGNA Fndn Grants, 1130
Cincinnati Bell Fndn Grants, 1131
Cinergy Fndn Grants, 1133
CIRCLE Civic Educ at the High School Level Research Grants, 1135
Cisco Systems Fndn San Jose Community Grants, 1137
Citigroup Fndn Grants, 1139
Citizens Savings Fndn Grants, 1141
Clara Blackford Smith and W. Aubrey Smith Charitable Fndn Grants, 1147
Clarence E. Heller Charitable Fndn Grants, 1150
Clinton County Community Fndn Grants, 1174
Clowes Grants, 1177
CNCS AmeriCorps Indian Planning Grants, 1180
CNCS AmeriCorps State and National Grants, 1182
CNCS Foster Grandparent Grants, 1185
CNCS Senior Corps Retired Volunteer Grants, 1188
Cobb Family Fndn Grants, 1194
Coca-Cola Fndn Grants, 1195
Coeta and Donald Barker Fndn Grants, 1197
Colonel Stanley R. McNeil Fndn Grants, 1210
Colorado Interstate Gas Grants, 1213
Columbus Fndn Siemer Family Grants, 1231
Commonweal Community Assistance Grants, 1239

SUBJECT INDEX

Community Fndn of Central Illinois Grants, 1276
Community Fndn of Southern Indiana Grants, 1310
Community Fndn Silicon Valley Grants, 1331
Connelly Fndn Grants, 1353
ConocoPhillips Grants, 1355
Constantin Fndn Grants, 1362
Cooper Fndn Grants, 1369
Cowles Charitable Grants, 1392
Crail-Johnson Fndn Grants, 1393
Credit Suisse First Boston Fndn Grants, 1397
Crescent Porter Hale Fndn Grants, 1398
Crestlea Fndn Grants, 1399
Cullen Fndn Grants, 1411
Cummins Fndn Grants, 1415
CVS All Kids Can Grants, 1420
DaimlerChrysler Corp Grants, 1432
Dean Foods Community Involvement Grants, 1469
Decatur County Comm Large Project Grants, 1476
Dekko Fndn Grants, 1482
Dennis and Phyllis Washington Fndn Grants, 1498
Dept of Ed Alaska Native Ed Programs, 1506
Dept of Ed Upward Bound Program, 1514
District of Columbia Commission on the Arts-Arts Educ Teacher Mini-Grants, 1549
Dorr Fndn Grants, 1591
Dow Corning Corp Contributions Grants, 1597
Dr. and Mrs. Paul Pierce Memorial Fndn Grants, 1599
Dr. Scholl Fndn Grants, 1602
Dresher Fndn Grants, 1605
Dreyer's Fndn Large Grants, 1606
Duke Energy Economic Development Grants, 1619
Dunn Fndn K-12 Grants, 1622
Dunspaugh-Dalton Fndn Grants, 1623
Dynegy Fndn Grants, 1630
E.J. Grassmann Grants, 1638
Eaton Charitable Grants, 1647
Effie and Wofford Cain Fndn Grants, 1674
Eisner Fndn Grants, 1678
Elizabeth Carse Fndn Grants, 1681
Emily Hall Tremaine Fndn Grants, 1698
EQT Fndn Educ Grants, 1745
Ethel and Raymond F. Rice Fndn Grants, 1758
Eugene McDermott Fndn Grants, 1765
Eva L. and Joseph M. Bruening Fndn Grants, 1768
FAS Project Schools Grants, 1792
Ferree Fndn Grants, 1804
Field Fndn of Illinois Grants, 1806
Firelight Fndn Grants, 1817
FirstEnergy Fndn Community Grants, 1819
FirstEnergy Fndn Math, Science, and Technology Educ Grants, 1820
Fleishhacker Fndn Educ Grants, 1838
Florida High School/High Tech Project Grants, 1866
Fondren Fndn Grants, 1878
France-Merrick Fndns Grants, 1915
Frances and John L. Loeb Family Grants, 1917
Frances L. and Edwin L. Cummings Grants, 1919
Francis L. Abreu Charitable Grants, 1922
Francis T. & Louise T. Nichols Fndn Grants, 1923
Frank B. Hazard General Charity Grants, 1926
Frank Loomis Palmer Grants, 1931
Frank M. Tait Fndn Grants, 1932
Frank Reed and Margaret Jane Peters Memorial Fund II Grants, 1934
Fred & Gretel Biel Charitable Grants, 1939
Fred C. and Katherine B. Andersen Fndn Grants, 1942
Fred Meyer Fndn Grants, 1950
Gardiner Savings Inst Charitable Fndn Grants, 1987
GenCorp Fndn Grants, 1998
General Mills Fndn Grants, 2003
General Service Fndn Colorado Grants, 2005
George A Ohl Jr. Fndn Grants, 2012
George F. Baker Grants, 2016
George Fndn Grants, 2018
George Frederick Jewett Fndn Grants, 2019
George I. Alden Grants, 2023
George J. and Effie L. Seay Fndn Grants, 2024
Georgia-Pacific Fndn Educ Grants, 2031
GNOF Cox Charities of New Orleans Grants, 2072
GNOF Exxon-Mobil Grants, 2074

SUBJECT INDEX

Secondary Education / 987

GNOF IMPACT Grants for Educ, 2079
GNOF Jefferson Community Grants, 2085
GNOF New Orleans Works Grants, 2088
GNOF Norco Community Grants, 2089
GNOF Plaquemines Community Grants, 2091
Goizueta Fndn Grants, 2096
Golden Rule Fndn Grants, 2098
Goodrich Corp Fndn Grants, 2104
Grace and Franklin Bernsen Fndn Grants, 2109
Greater Milwaukee Fndn Grants, 2137
Green Fndn Educ Grants, 2153
Greenspun Family Fndn Grants, 2156
Greenwall Fndn Bioethics Grants, 2158
Grundy Fndn Grants, 2169
HAF Educ Grants, 2196
Halliburton Fndn Grants, 2211
Harold Alfond Fndn Grants, 2225
Harrison County Community Fndn Grants, 2233
Harrison County Community Signature Grants, 2234
HBF Pathways Out of Poverty Grants, 2273
Hearst Fndns Culture Grants, 2284
Helen Bader Fndn Grants, 2293
Helen Gertrude Sparks Charitable Grants, 2294
Honeywell Corp Leadership Challenge Academy, 2359
Horace A. Kimball and S. Ella Kimball Grants, 2362
Horizon Fndn Grants, 2365
Household Int'l Corp Giving Grants, 2372
Houston Endowment Grants, 2373
Howe Fndn of North Carolina Grants, 2377
Huie-Dellmon Grants, 2386
Hutchinson Community Fndn Grants, 2410
Hutton Fndn Grants, 2412
I.A. O'Shaughnessy Fndn Grants, 2416
Idaho Power Company Corp Contributions, 2433
IIE Japan-U.S. Teacher Exchange for Educ for Sustainable Development, 2457
IIE Toyota Int'l Teacher Professional Development Grants, 2461
Illinois Arts Council Arts-in-Education Residency Grants, 2463
Indiana Space Grant Consortium Grants for Informal Educ Partnerships, 2549
Indiana Space Grant Consortium Workforce Development Grants, 2550
Intel Community Grants, 2562
Intel Int'l Community Grants, 2564
J.C. Penney Company Grants, 2594
J. Knox Gholston Fndn Grants, 2599
J.L. Bedsole Fndn Grants, 2600
J. Mack Robinson Fndn Grants, 2604
J. Marion Sims Fndn Teachers' Pet Grant, 2605
J. Walton Bissell Fndn Grants, 2608
Janirve Fndn Grants, 2645
Janus Fndn Grants, 2647
John Clarke Grants, 2689
John H. Wellons Fndn Grants, 2699
John P. Murphy Fndn Grants, 2708
Joseph S. Stackpole Charitable Grants, 2741
JP Morgan Chase Arts and Culture Grants, 2752
JP Morgan Chase Comm Development Grants, 2753
Katharine Matthies Fndn Grants, 2788
Katrine Menzing Deakins Charitable Grants, 2793
Kenneth T. and Eileen L. Norris Fndn Grants, 2802
Kent D. Steadley and Mary L. Steadley Trust, 2804
Kentucky Arts Council TranspARTation Grant, 2812
KeySpan Fndn Grants, 2821
Kohler Fndn Grants, 2833
Koret Fndn Grants, 2837
Laura Jane Musser Rural Init Grants, 2864
Lawrence J. and Anne Rubenstein Charitable Fndn Grants, 2868
Lee and Ramona Bass Fndn Grants, 2871
Legacy Fndn College Readiness Grant, 2874
Lettie Pate Evans Fndn Grants, 2887
Linford and Mildred White Charitable Grants, 2909
Lloyd G. Balfour Fndn Attleboro-Specific Charities Grants, 2916
Lockheed Martin Philanthropic Grants, 2918
Louis R. Cappelli Fndn Grants, 2926
Lowe's Charitable and Ed Fndn Grants, 2927

Lubbock Area Fndn Grants, 2931
Lubrizol Corp Community Grants, 2932
Lubrizol Fndn Grants, 2933
Luella Kemper Grants, 2939
Lumpkin Family Healthy People Grants, 2942
Luther I. Replogle Fndn Grants, 2945
Lyndhurst Fndn Grants, 2949
Maine Women's Fund Girls' Grantmaking Init, 2993
Margaret and James A. Elkins Jr. Fndn Grants, 3003
Marion I. and Henry J. Knott Fndn Discretionary Grants, 3018
Marion I. and Henry J. Knott Standard Grants, 3019
Marjorie Moore Charitable Fndn Grants, 3021
Mary Duke Biddle Fndn Grants, 3036
Mathile Family Fndn Grants, 3062
McCarthy Family Fndn Grants, 3073
McColl Fndn Grants, 3074
McConnell Fndn Grants, 3076
McCune Charitable Fndn Grants, 3077
McGraw-Hill Companies Community Grants, 3081
Mead Johnson Nutritionals Evansville-Area Organizations Grants, 3103
Mead Witter Fndn Grants, 3106
Medtronic Fndn CommunityLink Educ Grants, 3110
Medtronic Fndn Patient Link Grants, 3113
Mericos Fndn Grants, 3121
Meyer Fndn Educ Grants, 3142
Meyer Memorial Trust Grassroots Grants, 3147
Meyer Memorial Trust Responsive Grants, 3148
MGM Resorts Fndn Community Grants, 3153
Micron Technology Fndn Community Grants, 3161
Mildred V. Horn Fndn Grants, 3176
Military Ex-Prisoners of War Fndn Grants, 3177
Milton and Sally Avery Arts Fndn Grants, 3183
Moody Fndn Grants, 3215
Motorola Fndn Grants, 3221
Musgrave Fndn Grants, 3231
National 4-H Afterschool Training Grants, 3248
National Endowment for the Arts - National Arts and Humanities Youth Program Awards, 3255
Nellie Mae Educ Fndn District-Level Grants, 3297
Nellie Mae Educ Public Understanding Grants, 3298
Nellie Mae Educ Fndn State Level Systems Change Grants, 3299
NFL Club Matching Youth Football Field/Stadium Grants, 3349
NFL Grassroots Field Grants, 3350
NFL High School Coach of the Week Grant, 3351
NFL High School Football Coach of the Year, 3352
NFL Player Youth Football Camp Grants, 3353
NGA Hooked on Hydroponics Awards, 3405
NHSCA Artist Residencies in Schools Grants, 3423
NHSCA Youth Arts Project Grants: For Extended Arts Learning, 3430
Nicholas H. Noyes Jr. Memorial Fndn Grants, 3434
Nina Mason Pulliam Charitable Grants, 3443
Norcliffe Fndn Grants, 3459
Nordson Corp Fndn Grants, 3462
North Carolina Arts Council Arts in Educ Rural Development Grants, 3470
Norton Fndn Grants, 3514
NYFA Artists in the School Community Planning Grants, 3562
NYSCA Arts Educ: Community-based Learning Grants, 3577
NYSCA Arts Educ: K-12 In-School Grants, 3580
NYSCA Arts Ed Local Capacity Building Grants, 3581
NYSCA Arts Educ: Services to the Field Grants, 3582
Ober Kaler Community Grants, 3635
Olga Sipolin Children's Grants, 3668
Oppenstein Brothers Fndn Grants, 3685
Oracle Corp Contributions Grants, 3686
Owens Corning Fndn Grants, 3717
Owens Fndn Grants, 3718
Parkersburg Area Comm Fndn Action Grants, 3738
Perpetual Trust for Charitable Giving Grants, 3826
Pew Trusts Children and Youth Grants, 3858
PG&E Bright Ideas Grants, 3866
PGE Fndn Grants, 3869
Phil Hardin Fndn Grants, 3875

Phoenix Coyotes Charities Grants, 3879
Phoenix Suns Charities Grants, 3881
Pioneer Hi-Bred Community Grants, 3895
Piper Jaffray Fndn Communities Giving Grants, 3899
PMI Fndn Grants, 3918
Price Family Charitable Grants, 3952
Procter and Gamble Grants, 3967
Public Educ Power Grants, 3981
Quantum Fndn Grants, 3996
R.S. Gernon Grants, 4002
Randall L. Tobias Fndn Grants, 4017
Raskob Fndn for Catholic Activities Grants, 4019
RBC Dain Rauscher Fndn Grants, 4031
Reinberger Fndn Grants, 4052
Reynolds American Fndn Grants, 4068
Reynolds and Reynolds Company Fndn Grants, 4070
Richard and Susan Smith Family Fndn Grants, 4078
Richland County Bank Grants, 4091
Robert R. McCormick Tribune Civics Grants, 4118
Robert R. McCormick Tribune Comm Grants, 4119
Robert F. Meyer Fndn Grants, 4121
Robert W. Woodruff Fndn Grants, 4124
Rollins-Luetkemeyer Fndn Grants, 4147
Roy and Christine Sturgis Charitable Grants, 4166
Ruth Eleanor Bamberger and John Ernest Bamberger Memorial Fndn Grants, 4178
Sage Fndn Grants, 4204
Saigh Fndn Grants, 4210
San Juan Island Community Fndn Grants, 4283
Sartain Lanier Family Fndn Grants, 4298
Schering-Plough Fndn Health Grants, 4304
Scott County Community Fndn Grants, 4314
Seabury Fndn Grants, 4316
Seagate Tech Corp Capacity to Care Grants, 4317
Seattle Fndn Educ Grants, 4326
Seneca Foods Fndn Grants, 4336
Shopko Fndn Community Charitable Grants, 4346
Sid W. Richardson Fndn Grants, 4350
Silicon Valley Community Fndn Educ Grants, 4356
Sioux Falls Area Community Grants, 4364
Sioux Falls Area Community Fndn Spot Grants, 4366
Sisters of Charity Fndn of Canton Grants, 4372
SOBP A.E. Bennett Research Award, 4388
Social Justice Fund NW General Grants, 4397
Sonoco Fndn Grants, 4403
Sony Corp of America Corp Philanthropy Grants, 4405
Sosland Fndn Grants, 4408
South Carolina Arts Commission Arts in Educ After School Arts Init Grants, 4418
SW Gas Corp Fndn Grants, 4445
Sprague Fndn Grants, 4461
Stackpole-Hall Fndn Grants, 4472
Staples Fndn for Learning Grants, 4475
State Farm Fndn Grants, 4486
Strake Fndn Grants, 4511
Strowd Roses Grants, 4515
Stuart Fndn Grants, 4516
Subaru Adopt a School Garden Grants, 4517
Sun Academic Excellence Grants, 4525
Sunoco Fndn Grants, 4530
Susan Vaughan Fndn Grants, 4537
T. James Kavanagh Fndn Grants, 4545
T. Rowe Price Associates Fndn Grants, 4548
Tanner Humanities Center Research Fellowships, 4559
Taproot Fndn Capacity-Building Service Grants, 4560
TE Fndn Grants, 4572
Temple-Inland Fndn Grants, 4576
Thelma Braun and Bocklett Family Fndn Grants, 4603
Thomas and Dorothy Leavey Fndn Grants, 4612
Thomas B. & Elizabeth M. Sheridan Grants, 4614
Thornton Fndn Grants, 4624
Trull Fndn Grants, 4673
Turner Voices Corp Contributions, 4682
U.S. Department of Educ 21st Century Community Learning Centers, 4687
Union Bank Corp Sponsorships and Donations, 4708
Union Bank, N.A. Fndn Grants, 4709
Union County Community Fndn Grants, 4711
United States Institute of Peace - National Peace Essay Contest for High School Students, 4724

988 / Secondary Education

UPS Fndn Economic and Global Lit Grants, 4730
USA Football Equipment Grants, 4735
USAID Reading Enhancement for Advancing Development Grants, 4778
USBC Earl Anthony Scholarships, 4793
Valerie Adams Memorial Charitable Grants, 4898
Verizon Fndn Maine Grants, 4916
Victor E. Speas Fndn Grants, 4933
W.C. Griffith Fndn Grants, 4957
W. C. Griffith Fndn Grants, 4958
W.H. and Mary Ellen Cobb Charitable Grants, 4959
W.K. Kellogg Fndn Racial Equity Grants, 4962
Washington Gas Charitable Contributions, 5000
Weaver Popcorn Fndn Grants, 5016
Wege Fndn Grants, 5017
Weingart Fndn Grants, 5018
Westinghouse Charitable Giving Grants, 5028
Widgeon Point Charitable Fndn Grants, 5064
William J. Brace Charitable Trust, 5088
William McCaskey Chapman and Adaline Dinsmore Chapman Fndn Grants, 5092
Windgate Charitable Fndn Grants, 5099
Winthrop Rockefeller Fndn Grants, 5105

Security
Henry J. Kaiser Family Fndn Grants, 2310
Honeywell Family Safety and Security Grants, 2356
Koret Fndn Grants, 2837
Otto Bremer Fndn Grants, 3713
Philanthrofund Fndn Grants, 3874
Public Welfare Fndn Grants, 3984
Rockefeller Brothers Peace and Security Grants, 4133
Rockefeller Brothers Pivotal Places Grants: Serbia, Montenegro, and Kosova, 4135
Scherman Fndn Grants, 4305
Skoll Fndn Awards for Social Entrepreneurship, 4383

Sedimentology
HRF Hudson River Improvement Grants, 2378

Seminars
Acumen East Africa Fellowship, 141
Alaska Airlines Fndn Grants, 321
Alavi Fndn Grants, 335
Arkansas Arts Council AIE Mini Grants, 554
ARTBA Transportation Development Grants, 569
Blue Cross Blue Shield of Minnesota Fndn - Healthy Equity: Public Libraries for Health Grants, 797
GNOF Environmental Grants, 2073
GNOF Organizational Effectiveness Grants and Workshops, 2090
Greater Worcester Community Jeppson Memorial Fund for Brookfield Grants, 2141
Greater Worcester Community Mini-Grants, 2142
Ka Papa O Kakuhihewa Fund, 2785
Meyer Fndn Benevon Grants, 3140
Nevada Arts Council Jackpot Grants, 3312
Oppenstein Brothers Fndn Grants, 3685
Stark Community Fndn Neighborhood Community & Economic Devel Tech Assistance Grants, 4478
Virginia Fndn for Humanities Discr Grants, 4946
Virginia Fndn for the Humanities Open Grants, 4947

Senile Dementia
Helen Bader Fndn Grants, 2293
Henrietta Lange Burk Grants, 2303
Pfizer Healthcare Charitable Contributions, 3863

Senior Citizen Programs and Services
Adelaide Breed Bayrd Fndn Grants, 161
Amelia Sillman Rockwell and Carlos Perry Rockwell Charities Grants, 417
Arkell Hall Fndn Grants, 562
California Endowment Innovative Ideas Challenge Grants, 904
Carlsbad Charitable Fndn Grants, 936
Christine and Katharina Pauly Charitable Grants, 1114
Citizens Savings Fndn Grants, 1141
Clark and Ruby Baker Fndn Grants, 1154
CNCS AmeriCorps Indian Planning Grants, 1180

CNCS Foster Grandparent Grants, 1185
CNCS Senior Companion Grants, 1187
CNCS Senior Corps Retired & Volunteer Grants, 1188
Community Fndn in Jacksonville Senior Roundtable Aging Adults Grants, 1263
Community Fndn of Boone County Grants, 1274
Community Fndn of the Verdugos Grants, 1322
ConocoPhillips Fndn Grants, 1354
Corina Higginson Grants, 1373
Dave Coy Fndn Grants, 1447
David Lane Grants for Aged & Indigent Women, 1453
Dermody Properties Fndn Grants, 1517
Edward N. and Della L. Thome Memorial Fndn Direct Services Grants, 1666
Eisner Fndn Grants, 1678
Florence Hunt Maxwell Fndn Grants, 1844
Frank B. Hazard General Charity Grants, 1926
Frank Reed and Margaret Jane Peters Memorial Fund I Grants, 1933
Frederick McDonald Grants, 1946
Fulton County Community Fndn Women's Giving Circle Grants, 1976
GNOF Gert Community Grants, 2076
GNOF IMPACT Grants for Health and Human Services, 2080
GNOF Maison Hospitaliere Grants, 2086
HAF Hansen Family Trust Christian Endowment Grants, 2197
HAF Senior Opportunities Grants, 2203
Helen Bader Fndn Grants, 2293
Helen K. and Arthur E. Johnson Fndn Grants, 2296
Henrietta Lange Burk Grants, 2303
Illinois Arts Council Artstour Grants, 2465
Illinois Tool Works Fndn Grants, 2511
IMLS Native Am Library Services Basic Grants, 2517
IMLS Native American Library Services Enhancement Grants, 2518
Jim Moran Fndn Grants, 2680
Kansas Health Fndn Recognition Grants, 2784
Kroger Fndn Hunger Relief Grants, 2844
Lana'i Community Benefit Fund, 2857
M.D. Anderson Fndn Grants, 2952
Marin Community Fndn Stinson Bolinas Community Grants, 3013
Marin Community Successful Aging Grants, 3014
Marjorie Moore Charitable Fndn Grants, 3021
McLean Fndn Grants, 3089
Mericos Fndn Grants, 3121
Morris and Gwendolyn Cafritz Fndn Grants, 3218
New Jersey Center for Hispanic Policy, Research and Development Innovative Inits Grants, 3329
New Jersey Office of Faith Based Inits Service to Seniors Grants, 3333
NHSCA General Project Grants, 3427
PCA Busing Grants, 3786
PCA Pennsylvania Partners in the Arts Program Stream Grants, 3801
PCA Pennsylvania Partners in the Arts Project Stream Grants, 3802
Piper Trust Reglious Organizations Grants, 3905
PMI Fndn Grants, 3918
Portland General Electric Fndn Grants, 3937
Priddy Fndn Grants, 3957
Rancho Bernardo Community Fndn Grants, 4015
Robert & Clara Milton Fund for Senior Housing, 4117
Saginaw Community Fndn Senior Citizen Enrichment Fund, 4206
Scott County Community Fndn Grants, 4314
Seattle Fndn Basic Needs Grants, 4321
Sierra Health Fndn Responsive Grants, 4353
Sophia Romero Grants, 4406
South Carolina Arts Comm Accessibility Grants, 4410
Union Bank, N.A. Fndn Grants, 4709
Vigneron Grants, 4938
White County Community Fndn Grants, 5057

Service Delivery Programs
Able To Serve Grants, 102
Administration on Aging Senior Medicare Patrol Project Grants, 166

Alfred P. Sloan Fndn Public Service Awards, 369
Ambrose Monell Fndn Grants, 415
AMD Corp Contributions Grants, 416
Bohemian Fndn Pharos Grants, 811
Brad Brock Family Fndn Grants, 827
Brett Family Fndn Grants, 833
Carl R. Hendrickson Family Fndn Grants, 935
Chase Paymentech Corp Giving Grants, 1059
Citigroup Fndn Grants, 1139
Clark and Ruby Baker Fndn Grants, 1154
CNCS Senior Companion Grants, 1187
Community Fndn of Broward Grants, 1275
Community Fndn of Santa Cruz County Grants, 1305
Community Memorial Fndn Grants, 1334
Consumers Energy Fndn, 1365
DOL Youthbuild Grants, 1571
Ethel Frends Fndn Grants, 1759
Eugene McDermott Fndn Grants, 1765
Fallon OrNda Community Health Grants, 1783
Fel-Pro Mecklenburger Fndn Grants, 1800
Ferree Fndn Grants, 1804
Florence Hunt Maxwell Fndn Grants, 1844
Gertrude E. Skelly Charitable Fndn Grants, 2046
Goldseker Fndn Non-Profit Management Assistance Grants, 2103
Goodrich Corp Fndn Grants, 2104
GreenWorks! Butterfly Garden Grants, 2159
Harry C. Trexler Grants, 2239
Hasbro Children's Fund, 2256
Hawai'i Children's Trust Fund Community Awareness Events Grants, 2258
Health Fndn of So Florida Responsive Grants, 2283
Hearst Fndns Social Service Grants, 2285
Hoffberger Fndn Grants, 2342
Hogg Fndn for Mental Health Grants, 2343
Howard and Bush Fndn Grants, 2374
Hyde Family Fndns Grants, 2414
ICC Community Service Mini-Grant, 2426
ICC Scholarship of Engagement Faculty Grants, 2430
IRC Community Collaboratives for Refugee Women and Youth Grants, 2573
Ittleson Fndn AIDS Grants, 2589
Jenkins Fndn: Improving the Health of Greater Richmond Grants, 2663
Jerome and Mildred Paddock Fndn Grants, 2666
JM Fndn Grants, 2681
Louis R. Cappelli Fndn Grants, 2926
Luther I. Replogle Fndn Grants, 2945
Marin Community Fndn Stinson Bolinas Community Grants, 3013
Mary's Pence Ministry Grants, 3029
Maytree Fndn Refugee and Immigrant Grants, 3071
Mericos Fndn Grants, 3121
Middlesex Savings Charitable Fndn Capacity Building Grants, 3172
Middlesex Savings Charitable Fndn Community Development Grants, 3173
Modest Needs Non-Profit Grants, 3200
PCA Arts Organizations and Arts Programs Grants for Arts Service Organizations, 3777
PCA Entry Track Arts Organizations and Program Grants for Arts Service Organizations, 3789
Qualcomm Grants, 3993
Rancho Bernardo Community Fndn Grants, 4015
Richard and Susan Smith Family Fndn Grants, 4078
Robert and Joan Dircks Fndn Grants, 4104
Robert E. and Evelyn McKee Fndn Grants, 4110
Robert R. McCormick Tribune Veterans Grants, 4120
Saint George's Society of New York Scholarships, 4213
Santa Barbara Fndn Strategy Grants - Innovation, 4287
Seagate Tech Corp Capacity to Care Grants, 4317
Seattle Fndn Basic Needs Grants, 4321
Shirley W. & William L. Griffin Charitable Fndn Grants, 4345
Singing for Change Fndn Grants, 4363
Sisters of Charity Fndn of Canton Grants, 4372
State Farm Fndn Grants, 4486
Sunoco Fndn Grants, 4530
SVP Early Childhood Development and Parenting Grants, 4538

SUBJECT INDEX

Symantec Community Relations and Corp Philanthropy Grants, 4544
Tri-County Electric People Grants, 4665
Union Pacific Health & Human Services Grants, 4715
United Methodist Women Brighter Future for Children and Youth Grants, 4723
USAID Strengthening Democratic Local Governance in South Sudan Grants, 4782
William T. Grant Fndn Youth Service Improvement Grants, 5096
Youth as Resources Mini-Grants, 5131
YSA UnitedHealth HEROES Service-Learning Grants, 5142

Service Learning
AACC Service Learning Mini-Grants, 57
ALA Atlas Systems Mentoring Award, 227
Countess Moira Charitable Fndn Grants, 1381
GreenWorks! Butterfly Garden Grants, 2159
GreenWorks! Grants, 2160
HAF Justin Keele Make a Difference Award, 2198
Maine Community Fndn Gracie Grants, 2982
Robert R. McCormick Tribune Civics Grants, 4118
TAC Arts Educ Mini Grants, 4553
Windward Youth Leadership Grants, 5100
YSA ABC Summer of Service Awards, 5133
YSA NEA Youth Leaders for Lit Grants, 5138
YSA Sodexo Lead Organizer Grants, 5140

Set Design/Theater Decoration
Florida Div of Cultural Affairs Community Theatre Grants, 1847
Florida Div of Cultural Affairs Professional Theatre Grants, 1861
NYSCA Architecture, Planning, and Design: Capital Fixtures and Equipment Purchase Grants, 3570
NYSCA Theatre General Program Support, 3624

Sex Education
ACF Community-Based Abstinence Educ Grants, 116
DHHS Adolescent Family Life Demo Projects, 1524
General Service Reproductive Justice Grants, 2007
Ittleson Fndn AIDS Grants, 2589
Ms. Fndn for Women Ending Violence Grants, 3224
Ms. Fndn for Women Health Grants, 3225
Susan A. & Donald P. Babson Charitable Grants, 4534

Sex Roles
FCYO Youth Organizing Grants, 1797
Ford Fndn Peace and Social Justice Grants, 1884
State Justice Institute Curriculum Adaptation and Training Grants, 4488
State Justice Institute Partner Grants, 4489
State Justice Institute Project Grants, 4490
State Justice Institute Strategic Init Grants, 4492
State Justice Institute Tech Assistance Grants, 4493
Susan A. & Donald P. Babson Charitable Grants, 4534

Sexism
ANLAF Int'l Fund for Sexual Minorities Grants, 471
Ms. Fndn for Women Ending Violence Grants, 3224
PDF Community Organizing Grants, 3807
Saginaw Community Fndn YWCA Fund for Women and Girls Grants, 4207
Sioux Falls Area Community Fndn Spot Grants, 4366
Teaching Tolerance Mix-it-Up Grants, 4568
Third Wave Fndn Lela Breitbart Grants, 4609
Third Wave Organizing & Advocacy Grants, 4610
Third Wave Fndn Reproductive Health and Justice Grants, 4611
Vanguard Public Fndn Grant Funds, 4904

Sexual Abuse
A Glimmer of Hope Fndn Grants, 200
Arizona Republic Fndn Grants, 546
Austin S. Nelson Fndn Grants, 617
Baxter Int'l Fndn Grants, 691
Burton G. Bettingen Grants, 871
CFFVR Schmidt Family G4 Grants, 1020
Community Fndn for Southern Arizona Grants, 1261

Fassino Fndn Grants, 1793
Ford Fndn Peace and Social Justice Grants, 1884
Grand Rapids Area Community Fndn Wyoming Youth Grants, 2117
Hearst Fndns Social Service Grants, 2285
Initiaive Fndn Inside-Out Connections Grants, 2556
OJJDP Tribal Juvenile Accountability Discretionary Grants, 3665
OneFamily Fndn Grants, 3673
Women's Funding Alliance Grants, 5112

Sexual Behavior
ACF Community-Based Abstinence Educ Grants, 116
DHHS Adolescent Family Life Demo Projects, 1524
Playboy Fndn Grants, 3913
Pride Fndn Grants, 3958
Ruth Mott Fndn Grants, 4180

Sexuality
Ms. Fndn for Women Health Grants, 3225
Overbrook Fndn Grants, 3715

Sexually Transmitted Diseases
Cone Health Fndn Grants, 1348
DHHS Adolescent Family Life Demo Projects, 1524
Ittleson Fndn AIDS Grants, 2589
Kate B. Reynolds Charitable Health Care Grants, 2786
Pfizer Healthcare Charitable Contributions, 3863
USAID Comprehensive District-Based Support for Better HIV/TB Patient Outcomes Grants, 4747

Shade
American Academy of Dermatology Shade Structure Grants, 420

Shelters
3 B's Fndn Grants, 7
Adelaide Dawson Lynch Grants, 163
Alberto Culver Corp Contributions Grants, 343
Amelia Sillman Rockwell and Carlos Perry Rockwell Charities Grants, 417
American Express Charitable Grants, 429
American Humane Assoc Second Chance Grants, 440
Arizona Republic Fndn Grants, 546
Arizona Republic Newspaper Contributions, 547
Aspen Community Fndn Grants, 592
Atkinson Fndn Community Grants, 606
BancorpSouth Fndn Grants, 651
Blowitz-Ridgeway Fndn Grants, 792
Brooklyn Community Caring Neighbors Grants, 848
Campbell Soup Fndn Grants, 916
Cemala Fndn Grants, 988
CFFVR Capital Credit Union Charitable Giving, 1005
CFFVR Jewelers Mutual Charitable Giving, 1014
CFFVR Schmidt Family G4 Grants, 1020
Charles H. Hall Fndn, 1044
Charles Nelson Robinson Grants, 1052
Chautauqua Region Community Fndn Grants, 1062
Christian Science Society of Boonville Irrevocable Trust, 1113
CICF Senior Grants, 1127
Cisco Systems Fndn San Jose Community Grants, 1137
Clara Blackford Smith and W. Aubrey Smith Charitable Fndn Grants, 1147
Columbus Fndn Traditional Grants, 1233
Comer Fndn Grants, 1236
Constantin Fndn Grants, 1362
Dallas Women's Fndn Grants, 1438
David Lane Grants for Aged & Indigent Women, 1453
Dennis and Phyllis Washington Fndn Grants, 1498
Doree Taylor Charitable Fndn, 1580
Doris and Victor Day Fndn Grants, 1582
East Tennessee Fndn Grants, 1646
Edina Realty Fndn Grants, 1656
EPA Environmental Justice Small Grants, 1732
Frank B. Hazard General Charity Grants, 1926
Frank Loomis Palmer Grants, 1931
Frank Reed and Margaret Jane Peters Memorial Fund II Grants, 1934
George and Ruth Bradford Fndn Grants, 2010

Single-Parent Families / 989

George E. Hatcher, Jr. and Ann Williams Hatcher Fndn Grants, 2015
GNOF Maison Hospitaliere Grants, 2086
HAF Community Grants, 2193
Hahl Proctor Charitable Grants, 2208
Harold Brooks Fndn Grants, 2227
Helen Irwin Littauer Ed Grants, 2295
Helen V. Brach Fndn Grants, 2300
HomeBanc Fndn Grants, 2347
Household Int'l Corp Giving Grants, 2372
Humane Society of the United States Foreclosure Pets Grants, 2389
Humanitas Fndn Grants, 2390
Jacob G. Schmidlapp Grants, 2616
Jeffris Wood Fndn Grants, 2660
John W. Speas and Effie E. Speas Grants, 2732
Joseph S. Stackpole Charitable Grants, 2741
Kenneth A. Scott Charitable Grants, 2801
Ken W. Davis Fndn Grants, 2813
Lied Fndn Grants, 2900
Lincoln Financial Group Fndn Grants, 2906
Luther I. Replogle Fndn Grants, 2945
Lydia deForest Charitable Grants, 2946
Mardag Fndn Grants, 3001
Marietta McNeill Morgan and Samuel Tate Morgan, Jr. Grants, 3008
Marriott Int'l Corp Giving Grants, 3024
Mary Kay Domestic Violence Shelter Grants, 3044
Maurice J. Masserini Charitable Grants, 3064
Meacham Fndn Grants, 3102
Melville Charitable Grants, 3115
Mericos Fndn Grants, 3121
Mervin Bovaird Fndn Grants, 3128
MGN Family Fndn Grants, 3154
Middlesex Savings Charitable Fndn Community Development Grants, 3173
Needmor Grants, 3289
NNEDVF/Altria Doors of Hope Program, 3452
Oleonda Jameson Grants, 3667
Olga Sipolin Children's Grants, 3668
OneFamily Fndn Grants, 3673
Otto Bremer Fndn Grants, 3713
Packard Fndn Local Grants, 3729
Perkins-Ponder Grants, 3822
Perpetual Trust for Charitable Giving Grants, 3826
Pinkerton Fndn Grants, 3892
Porter County Women's Grant, 3934
Posey County Community Fndn Grants, 3939
R.S. Gernon Grants, 4002
Ralph and Virginia Mullin Fndn Grants, 4012
S. Mark Taper Fndn Grants, 4201
Samuel S. Johnson Fndn Grants, 4239
Santa Barbara Strategy Core Suupport Grants, 4286
Spencer County Community Fndn Grants, 4451
Swindells Charitable Fndn, 4542
Target Corp Local Store Grants, 4561
Textron Corp Contributions Grants, 4601
Thomas Sill Fndn Grants, 4619
Thompson Charitable Fndn Grants, 4622
TJX Fndn Grants, 4637
Tri-County Electric People Grants, 4665
USDA Child and Adult Care Food Program, 4800
Vancouver Fndn Grants & Comm Inits, 4900
Warrick County Community Fndn Grants, 4987

Short Stories
ALA Stonewall Book Awards - Barbara Gittings Literature Award, 329

Singing
HAF Arts and Culture: Lynne and Bob Wells Grant for Performing Artists, 2190

Single-Parent Families
Arkell Hall Fndn Grants, 562
Austin-Bailey Health and Wellness Fndn Grants, 614
CFFVR Robert and Patricia Endries Family Fndn Grants, 1018
Community Fndn of Bartholomew County Women's Giving Circle, 1269

990 / Single-Parent Families

Crail-Johnson Fndn Grants, 1393
Cralle Fndn Grants, 1394
David Robinson Fndn Grants, 1454
Eugene M. Lang Fndn Grants, 1764
Fndns of E Chicago Family Support Grants, 1908
Kalamazoo Community Fndn Individuals and Families Grants, 2769
Mabel Louise Riley Family Strengthening Grants, 2958
Mary Black Early Childhood Devel Grants, 3033
Medtronic Fndn Community Link Human Services Grants, 3112
OSF Campaign for Black Male Achievement, 3703
Robin Hood Fndn Grants, 4125
Seattle Fndn Benjamin N. Phillips Grants, 4322
Smith Richardson Fndn Direct Service Grants, 4385
Topeka Community Building Families Grants, 4643
USAID Service Delivery & Support for Families Caring For Orphans and Vulnerable Childrens, 4781
Whitehorse Fndn Grants, 5058

Sleep Disorders
NHLBI Ancillary Studies in Clinical Trials, 3410
NHLBI Ruth L. Kirschstein National Research Service Awards for Individual Postdoctoral Fellows, 3418

Small Businesses
Appalachian Regional Commission Business Development Revolving Loan Grants, 501
Appalachian Regional Commission Leadership Development and Capacity Building Grants, 509
CCHD Economic Development Grants, 967
Chautauqua Region Community Fndn Grants, 1062
Draper Richards Kaplan Fndn Grants, 1603
Eileen Fisher Women-Owned Business Grants, 1677
Fitzpatrick and Francis Family Business Continuity Fndn Grants, 1837
Frederick McDonald Grants, 1946
IEDC Int'l Trade Show Assistance Program, 2444
Indiana 21st Century Research and Technology Fund Awards, 2528
Indiana SBIR/STTR Commercialization Enhancement Program, 2548
KeyBank Fndn Grants, 2820
Maine Community Fndn Charity Grants, 2977
McCune Charitable Fndn Grants, 3077
NASE Growth Grants, 3242
New Jersey Center for Hispanic Policy, Research and Development Entrepreneurship Grants, 3326
New Jersey Office of Faith Based Inits Creating Wealth Through Asset Building Grants, 3331
NE Utilities Fndn Grants, 3498
RISCA Professional Arts Development Grants, 4099
S.E.VEN Fund $50k VINE Project Prizes, 4193
Safeco Insurance Community Grants, 4203
Tech Enhancement Certification for Hoosiers, 4571
Union Bank, N.A. Fndn Grants, 4709
USAID Economic Prospectsfor Armenia-Turkey Normalization Grants, 4750
USAID India Partnership Grants, 4761
USAID Pakistan Private Investment Init Grants, 4772
USDA 1890 Land Grant Colleges and Universities Init Grants, 4797
USDA Farmers Market Promotion Grants, 4808
USDA Foreign Market Development Grants, 4811
USDA Market Access Grants, 4818
USDA Rural Business Enterprise Grants, 4823
USDA Rural Coop Development Grants, 4826
USDA Rural Microentrepreneur Assist Grants, 4832

Smoking Behavior
American Legacy Fndn Small Innovative Grants, 442
Fndn for a Healthy Kentucky Grants, 1891
GNOF IMPACT Kahn-Oppenheim Grants, 2084
Grand Rapids Area Community Fndn Wyoming Youth Grants, 2117
Health Fndn of Greater Indianapolis Grants, 2282
Pfizer Healthcare Charitable Contributions, 3863
Pfizer Medical Educ Track One Grants, 3864
Premera Blue Cross CARES Grants, 3945
TRDRP Research Grants, 4664

Soccer
HAF Kayla Wood Girls Grants, 2199
Oregon Youth Soccer Fndn Grants, 3692
Susan A. & Donald P. Babson Charitable Grants, 4534
US Soccer Annual Program & Field Grants, 4870
US Soccer Fndn Planning Grants, 4871

Social Change
A.J. Muste Memorial Institute Counter Recruitment Grants, 43
A.J. Muste Memorial Institute General Grants, 44
A.J. Muste Memorial Institute Int'l Nonviolence Training Grants, 45
Abelard Fndn East Grants, 87
Abelard Fndn West Grants, 88
Acumen East Africa Fellowship, 141
Agape Fndn for Nonviolent Social Change Board of Trustees Grants, 197
Agape Fndn for Nonviolent Social Change Prizes, 198
Akonadi Fndn Anti-Racism Grants, 217
ALFJ Astraea U.S. General Fund, 362
Appalachian Community Fund General Grants, 493
Appalachian Community Fund GLBTQ Grants, 494
Appalachian Community Media Justice Grants, 495
Appalachian Comm Seize the Moment Grants, 496
Arcus Fndn Grants, 529
Arcus Fndn Gay and Lesbian Grants, 530
Arcus Fndn National Grants, 531
Ben & Jerry's Fndn Grants, 724
Blue Cross Blue Shield of Minnesota Healthy Neighborhoods: Connect Grants, 798
Bread and Roses Community Grants, 832
Brett Family Fndn Grants, 833
Changemakers Community-Based Grants, 1030
Changemakers Innovation Awards, 1031
Colin Higgins Fndn Grants, 1204
Community Fndn of Broward Grants, 1275
Community Fndn of Greater Fort Wayne - John S. and James L. Knight Fndn Donor-Advised Grants, 1287
Community Technology Fndn of California Building Communities Through Technology Grants, 1336
Crossroads Fund Seed Grants, 1400
Do Something Plum Youth Grants, 1593
Earth Island Institute Brower Youth Awards, 1641
Echoing Green Fellowships, 1650
Encore Purpose Prize, 1704
FCYO Youth Organizing Grants, 1797
Frey Fndn Grants, 1963
Fund for Southern Communities Grants, 1977
Gleitsman Fndn Activist Awards, 2063
Hawaii Community Fndn Social Change Grants, 2265
Haymarket People's Fund Sustaining Grants, 2267
Haymarket Urgent Response Grants, 2268
Ittleson Fndn Mental Health Grants, 2590
Jay and Rose Phillips Family Fndn Grants, 2656
Jenifer Altman Fndn Grants, 2662
Jewish Funds for Justice Grants, 2676
Joel L. Fleishman Civil Society Fellowships, 2683
Leeway Fndn Art and Change Grants, 2872
Leeway Fndn Transformation Award, 2873
Liberty Hill Fndn Environmental Justice Grants, 2891
Liberty Hill Fndn Fund for Change Grants, 2893
Liberty Hill Fndn Seed Grants, 2896
Liberty Hill Fndn Special Opportunity Grants, 2897
Maine Women's Fund Economic Security Grants, 2992
Mary E. Ober Fndn Grants, 3039
McCune Charitable Fndn Grants, 3077
Minneapolis Fndn Community Grants, 3186
Mix It Up Grants, 3191
National Endowment for Democracy Reagan-Fascell Democracy Fellowships, 3252
National Endowment for Democracy Visiting Fellows Program, 3253
Nike and Ashoka GameChangers: Change the Game for Women in Sport, 3439
Nike Giving - Cash and Product Grants, 3442
Norman Fndn Grants, 3464
Open Meadows Fndn Grants, 3683
OSF Documentary Photography Project Audience Engagement Grant, 3706
Paul G. Allen Family Fndn Grants, 3759
PDF Community Organizing Grants, 3807
PDF Fiscal Sponsorship Grant, 3808
Philanthrofund Fndn Grants, 3874
Playboy Fndn Grants, 3913
RESIST Accessibility Grants, 4054
RESIST Arthur Raymond Cohen Grants, 4055
RESIST Emergency Grants, 4056
RESIST Freda Friedman Salzman Grants, 4057
RESIST General Support Grants, 4058
RESIST Hell Yes! Award, 4059
RESIST Ken Hale Tribute Grants, 4060
RESIST Leslie D'Cora Holmes Grants, 4061
RESIST Mike Riegle Tribute Grants, 4062
RESIST Multi-Year Grants, 4063
RESIST Sharon Kurtz Grants, 4064
RESIST Technical Assistance Grants, 4065
Robert F. Kennedy Human Rights Award, 4111
S.E.VEN Fund 'In The River They Swim' Essay Competition, 4194
S.E.VEN Fund Open Enterprise Solutions to Poverty RFP Grants, 4197
Samuel Rubin Fndn Grants, 4237
San Diego Fndn for Change Grants, 4247
Singing for Change Fndn Grants, 4363
Sister Grants for Women's Organizations, 4371
Skoll Fndn Awards for Social Entrepreneurship, 4383
Social Justice Fund NW Criminal Justice Giving Project Grants, 4394
Social Justice Fund NW Economic Justice Giving Project Grants, 4395
Social Justice Fund NW General Grants, 4397
Social Justice Fund NW LGBTQ Giving Project Grants, 4398
Social Justice Fund NW Montana Giving Project Grants, 4399
SSHRC Therese F. Casgrain Fellowship, 4466
Teaching Tolerance Mix-it-Up Grants, 4568
Union Square Arts Award, 4716
United Methodist Women Brighter Future for Children and Youth Grants, 4723
USAID Global Development Alliance Grants, 4753
UUA Bennett Award for Congregational Action on Human Justice and Social Action, 4893
UUA Holmes-Weatherly Award, 4894
Valentine Fndn Grants, 4897
Vanguard Public Fndn Grant Funds, 4904
Winthrop Rockefeller Fndn Grants, 5105
Youth Action Net Fellowships, 5128

Social History
American Society for Yad Vashem Grants, 447
Arts Fndn, 578
Illinois Humanities Council Community Project Grants, 2510
Natonal Endowment for the Arts Research Grants: Art Works, 3286
NEH Interpreting America's Hist Places Grants, 3292
Turner Fndn Grants, 4681

Social Justice
ALA Coretta Scott King Book Awards, 260
ALFJ Astraea U.S. General Fund, 362
CCF Grassroots Exchange Grants, 963
CCF Social and Economic Justice Grants, 964
GNOF Community Revitalization Grants, 2071
Grassroots Exchange Grants, 2128
Haymarket People's Fund Sustaining Grants, 2267
Johnson Controls Fndn Civic Activities Grants, 2720
Marin Community Fndn Social Justice and Interfaith Understanding Grants, 3012
McCune Charitable Fndn Grants, 3077
Mertz Gilmore Fndn NYC Communities Grants, 3126
Meyer Fndn Healthy Communities Grants, 3143
Northland Fndn Grants, 3506
OSF-Baltimore Community Fellowships, 3695
OSF Burma Project/SE Asia Init Grants, 3702
PDF Fiscal Sponsorship Grant, 3808
RESIST Accessibility Grants, 4054
RESIST Arthur Raymond Cohen Grants, 4055

SUBJECT INDEX

RESIST Emergency Grants, 4056
RESIST Freda Friedman Salzman Grants, 4057
RESIST General Support Grants, 4058
RESIST Hell Yes! Award, 4059
RESIST Ken Hale Tribute Grants, 4060
RESIST Leslie D'Cora Holmes Grants, 4061
RESIST Mike Riegle Tribute Grants, 4062
RESIST Multi-Year Grants, 4063
RESIST Sharon Kurtz Grants, 4064
RESIST Technical Assistance Grants, 4065
Sapelo Fndn Social Justice Grants, 4294
Skoll Fndn Awards for Social Entrepreneurship, 4383
SSHRC Therese F. Casgrain Fellowship, 4466
Union Square Awards Grants, 4718

Social Measurement and Indicators
Asian American Institute Impact Fellowships, 588
Wallace Global Grants, 4977

Social Movements
Akonadi Fndn Anti-Racism Grants, 217
ALA Coretta Scott King Book Awards, 260
ALFJ Astraea U.S. General Fund, 362
Arcus Fndn Grants, 529
Arcus Fndn Gay and Lesbian Grants, 530
Arcus Fndn National Grants, 531
Crossroads Fund Seed Grants, 1400
Mix It Up Grants, 3191
PDF Fiscal Sponsorship Grant, 3808
Teaching Tolerance Mix-it-Up Grants, 4568
Third Sector New England Inclusion Init Grants, 4608

Social Science Education
Caroline Lawson Ivey Memorial Fndn Grants, 941
Lettie Pate Evans Fndn Grants, 2887
McCune Charitable Fndn Grants, 3077
Radcliffe Inst Individual Residential Fellowships, 4004

Social Sciences
Alabama Humanities Fndn Mini Grants, 231
Alabama Humanities Planning/Consultant Grants, 232
American Sociological Assoc Sydney S. Spivack Applied Social Research and Social Policy, 450
Banfi Vintners Fndn Grants, 653
Blowitz-Ridgeway Fndn Grants, 792
Brookdale Fndn Leadership in Aging Fellowships, 844
Canada-U.S. Fulbright Mid-Career Grants, 917
Community Fndn of Wabash County Grants, 1326
DAAD Research Grants for Doctoral Candidates and Young Academics and Scientists, 1427
Health Fndn of Greater Cincinnati Grants, 2281
Horowitz Fndn for Social Policy Grants, 2370
Horowitz Fndn for Social Policy Special Awards, 2371
HRF Hudson River Improvement Grants, 2378
IIE AmCham Charitable Fndn U.S. Studies Scholarship, 2453
IIE Japan-U.S. Teacher Exchange for Educ for Sustainable Development, 2457
IIE New Leaders Group Award for Mutual Understanding, 2460
IIE Western Union Family Scholarships, 2462
John Ben Snow Grants, 2687
John Lord Knight Fndn Grants, 2703
Leicester Savings Bank Fund, 2879
McGregor Grants, 3082
National Center for Resp Gaming Travel Grants, 3251
National Lottery Community Grants, 3279
Nuffield Fndn Africa Grants, 3532
Nuffield Fndn Small Grants, 3535
NYHC Major and Mini Grants, 3567
Oleonda Jameson Grants, 3667
Radcliffe Inst Individual Residential Fellowships, 4004
RAND Corp Graduate Summer Associateships, 4018
Research Program at Earthwatch Grants, 4053
SSHRC Therese F. Casgrain Fellowship, 4466
SSRC-Van Alen Fellowships, 4467
The World Food Prize, 4606
Thomas Sill Fndn Grants, 4619
Wisconsin Humanities Council Major Grants, 5107

Social Security
SSA Work Incentives Planning & Assistance, 4465

Social Services
1st Source Fndn Grants, 3
21st Century ILGWU Heritage Grants, 20
100 Mile Man Fndn Grants, 27
786 Fndn Grants, 33
2701 Fndn Grants, 37
A.O. Smith Community Grants, 46
A/H Fndn Grants, 48
AAAS Science and Technology Policy Fellowships: Health, Educ and Human Services, 53
Aaron Catzen Fndn Grants, 70
Aaron Fndn Grants, 73
Aaron Fndn Grants, 72
Abbot and Dorothy H. Stevens Fndn Grants, 79
Abbott Fund Community Grants, 81
ABC Charities Grants, 85
Abel Fndn Grants, 90
Abell Fndn Health and Human Services Grants, 96
Able To Serve Grants, 102
Abney Fndn Grants, 105
ACF Assets for Indep Demonstration Grants, 114
ACF Ethnic Community Self-Help Grants, 118
ACF Head Start and Early Head Start Grants, 120
ACF Mentoring Children of Prisoners Grants, 121
ACF Preferred Communities Grants, 124
ACF Supplemental Services for Recently Arrived Refugees Grants, 125
Adams and Reese LLP Corp Giving Grants, 147
Adams Family Fndn I Grants, 150
Administaff Community Affairs Grants, 165
Advanced Micro Devices Comm Affairs Grants, 172
AEC Grants, 175
AEGON Transamerica Fndn Civic and Community Grants, 177
AEP Corp Giving Grants, 180
AFG Industries Grants, 191
A Friends' Fndn Grants, 194
A Glimmer of Hope Fndn Grants, 200
AGMA Relief Grants, 201
A Good Neighbor Fndn Grants, 204
Ahmanson Fndn Grants, 207
Air Products and Chemicals Grants, 216
Akzo Nobel Chemicals Grants, 219
Alabama Power Fndn Grants, 233
ALA Coretta Scott King Book Donation Grant, 261
Aladdin Industries Fndn Grants, 263
Alberto Culver Corp Contributions Grants, 343
Albert Pick Jr. Grants, 344
Albertson's Charitable Giving Grants, 345
Albert W. Cherne Fndn Grants, 346
Albuquerque Community Fndn Grants, 348
Alcatel-Lucent Technologies Fndn Grants, 349
Alcoa Fndn Grants, 350
Alexander & Baldwin Fndn Hawaiian and Pacific Island Grants, 352
Alexander & Baldwin Fndn Mainland Grants, 353
Alexander Eastman Fndn Grants, 355
Alexander H. Bright Charitable Grants, 358
Alex Stern Family Fndn Grants, 360
Allegheny Technologies Charitable Trust, 377
Allen Lane Fndn Grants, 379
Alliant Energy Fndn Community Grants, 384
Allyn Fndn Grants, 392
ALSAM Fndn Grants, 395
ALZA Corp Contributions Grants, 405
Amador Community Fndn Grants, 408
Amarillo Area/Harrington Fndns Grants, 412
Ambrose and Ida Fredrickson Fndn Grants, 414
American Foodservice Charitable Grants, 433
Amerigroup Fndn Grants, 452
Amgen Fndn Grants, 456
AMI Semiconductors Corp Grants, 457
Amon G. Carter Fndn Grants, 458
Andrew Family Fndn Grants, 462
Anheuser-Busch Fndn Grants, 470
Anna Fitch Ardenghi Grants, 472
Ann Arbor Area Community Fndn Grants, 474

Social Services / 991

Anne L. and George H. Clapp Charitable and Ed Grants, 476
Ann Peppers Fndn Grants, 484
Annunziata Sanguinetti Fndn Grants, 485
Anthony R. Abraham Fndn Grants, 489
Aragona Family Fndn Grants, 522
Archer Daniels Midland Fndn Grants, 527
Argyros Fndn Grants, 532
Arizona Cardinals Grants, 534
Arizona Public Service Corp Giving Grants, 545
Arkansas Community Fndn Grants, 561
Armstrong McDonald Fndn Grants, 565
ARS Fndn Grants, 568
Arthur and Sara Jo Kobacker, Alfred and Ida Kobacker Fndn Grants, 571
Arthur Ashley Williams Fndn Grants, 572
Aspen Community Fndn Grants, 592
AT&T Fndn Civic and Comm Service Grants, 599
Atherton Family Fndn Grants, 604
Athwin Fndn Grants, 605
Atkinson Fndn Community Grants, 606
Atlanta Fndn Grants, 608
Auburn Fndn Grants, 611
Aurora Fndn Grants, 613
Austin Community Fndn Grants, 616
Autzen Fndn Grants, 622
Avery Dennison Fndn Grants, 623
Azadoutioun Fndn Grants, 631
Bailey Fndn Grants, 635
Balfe Family Fndn Grants, 636
Ball Brothers Fndn General Grants, 637
Baltimore Community Fndn Human Services Path Grants, 644
BancorpSouth Fndn Grants, 651
BankAtlantic Fndn Grants, 654
Barberton Community Fndn Grants, 666
Barker Fndn Grants, 668
Barker Welfare Fndn Grants, 669
Barra Fndn Community Grants, 673
Barra Fndn Project Grants, 674
Barr Grants, 678
Batchelor Fndn Grants, 679
Baton Rouge Area Fndn Grants, 682
Battle Creek Community Fndn Grants, 684
Batts Fndn Grants, 687
Baxter Int'l Fndn Grants, 691
Bayer Fndn Grants, 696
Beazley Fndn Grants, 714
Bechtel Group Fndn Building Positive Community Relationships Grants, 715
Beim Fndn Grants, 718
Ben B. Cheney Fndn Grants, 725
Bender Fndn Grants, 726
Benton Community Fndn Grants, 730
Benwood Fndn Community Grants, 732
Berks County Community Fndn Grants, 734
Bernard F. and Alva B. Gimbel Fndn Grants, 740
Bernard Osher Fndn Grants, 742
Besser Fndn Grants, 748
Bishop Robert Paddock Grants, 775
Blade Fndn Grants, 783
Blanche and Irving Laurie Fndn Grants, 784
Blandin Fndn Itasca County Area Vitality Grants, 789
Blue Grass Community Fndn Grants, 799
Blue Mountain Community Fndn Grants, 800
Blue River Community Fndn Grants, 801
Blum-Kovler Fndn Grants, 803
Blumenthal Fndn Grants, 804
Bodenwein Public Benevolent Fndn Grants, 806
Bodman Fndn Grants, 807
Boeckmann Charitable Fndn Grants, 808
Boeing Company Contributions Grants, 809
Boettcher Fndn Grants, 810
Booth-Bricker Grants, 815
Booth Ferris Fndn Grants, 816
Borkee-Hagley Fndn Grants, 817
Bosque Fndn Grants, 818
Boston Fndn Grants, 819
Bridgestone/Firestone Grants, 836
Bright Family Fndn Grants, 837

992 / Social Services

Brookdale Fndn National Group Respite Grants, 845
Brooklyn Benevolent Society Grants, 847
Brooklyn Community Caring Neighbors Grants, 848
Brooklyn Community Fndn Community Development Grants, 850
Brooklyn Community Fndn Educ and Youth Achievement Grants, 851
Brown County Community Fndn Grants, 853
Burlington Industries Fndn Grants, 865
Burlington Northern Santa Fe Fndn Grants, 866
Burton G. Bettingen Grants, 871
Butler Manufacturing Company Fndn Grants, 881
Bydale Fndn Grants, 882
California Arts Council Public Value Grants, 895
Cambridge Community Fndn Grants, 913
Camp-Younts Fndn Grants, 914
Campbell Soup Fndn Grants, 916
Capital City Bank Group Fndn Grants, 920
Carl and Eloise Pohlad Family Fndn Grants, 927
Carl B. and Florence E. King Fndn Grants, 928
Carl M. Freeman Fndn FACES Grants, 932
Carl R. Hendrickson Family Fndn Grants, 935
Carolyn Fndn Grants, 942
Carpenter Fndn Grants, 943
Carrie E. and Lena V. Glenn Fndn Grants, 944
Carrie Estelle Doheny Fndn Grants, 945
Catherine Kennedy Home Fndn Grants, 955
Cemala Fndn Grants, 988
Central Carolina Community Fndn Community Impact Grants, 994
Cessna Fndn Grants, 1000
CFFVR Clintonville Area Fndn Grants, 1007
CFFVR Frank C. Shattuck Community Grants, 1012
CFFVR Project Grants, 1017
CFFVR Robert and Patricia Endries Family Fndn Grants, 1018
CFFVR Shawano Area Community Fndn Grants, 1021
CFFVR Waupaca Area Community Fndn Grants, 1023
Chamberlain Fndn Grants, 1027
Champlin Fndns Grants, 1029
Charles A. Frueauff Fndn Grants, 1037
Charles Delmar Fndn Grants, 1039
Charles F. Bacon Grants, 1040
Charles M. Bair Family Grants, 1051
Charlotte County (FL) Community Fndn Grants, 1056
Chase Paymentech Corp Giving Grants, 1059
Chatlos Fndn Grants, 1061
Chautauqua Region Community Fndn Grants, 1062
CHC Fndn Grants, 1065
Chicago Sun Times Charity Grants, 1098
CICF Christmas Fund, 1117
CICF Indianapolis Fndn Community Grants, 1123
CICF J. Proctor Grant for Aged Men & Women, 1124
CIGNA Fndn Grants, 1130
Cincinnati Bell Fndn Grants, 1131
Cinergy Fndn Grants, 1133
Cingular Wireless Charitable Contributions, 1134
Citigroup Fndn Grants, 1139
Claneil Fndn Grants, 1145
Clarcor Fndn Grants, 1148
Claremont Community Fndn Grants, 1149
Clark-Winchcole Fndn Grants, 1152
Clark Charitable Grants, 1155
Clark County Community Fndn Grants, 1156
Claude Worthington Benedum Fndn Grants, 1161
Cleveland-Cliffs Fndn Grants, 1165
Cleveland Community Responsive Grants, 1168
Clipper Ship Fndn Grants, 1175
Clowes Grants, 1177
CNA Fndn Grants, 1179
Coastal Community Fndn of S Carolina Grants, 1193
Cockrell Fndn Grants, 1196
Coeta and Donald Barker Fndn Grants, 1197
Colgate-Palmolive Company Grants, 1202
Collins Fndn Grants, 1209
Colorado Interstate Gas Grants, 1213
Colorado Springs Community Grants, 1215
Columbus Fndn Competitive Grants, 1220
Columbus Fndn J. Floyd Dixon Grants, 1222
Columbus Fndn Mary Eleanor Morris Grants, 1225

Columbus Fndn Paul G. Duke Grants, 1227
Columbus Fndn R. Alvin Stevenson Grants, 1228
Columbus Fndn Small Grants, 1232
Columbus Fndn Traditional Grants, 1233
Columbus Jewish Fndn Grants, 1234
Comer Fndn Grants, 1236
Comerica Charitable Fndn Grants, 1237
Commission on Religion in Appalachia Grants, 1238
Commonwealth Edison Grants, 1240
Communities Fndn of Texas Grants, 1243
Community Fndn Alliance City of Evansville Endowment Grants, 1246
Community Fndn for Monterey County Grants, 1255
Community Fndn for Muskegon County Grants, 1256
Community Fndn for NE Michigan Grants, 1257
Community Fndn for San Benito County Grants, 1258
Community Fndn for Southern Arizona Grants, 1261
Community Fndn of Bartholomew County Heritage Grants, 1267
Community Fndn of Bartholomew County James A. Henderson Award for Fundraising, 1268
Community Fndn of Bloomington and Monroe County Grants, 1271
Community Fndn of Central Illinois Grants, 1276
Community Fndn of East Central Illinois Grants, 1278
Community Fndn of Greater Birmingham Grants, 1280
Community Fndn of Greater Flint Grants, 1282
Community Fndn of Greater Fort Wayne - Community Endowment and Clarke Endowment Grants, 1285
Community Fndn of Greater Fort Wayne - Edna Fndn Grants, 1286
Community Fndn of Greater Greensboro Grants, 1288
Community Fndn of Greater New Britain Grants, 1291
Community Fndn of Greater Tampa Grants, 1292
Community Fndn of Greenville-Greenville Women Giving Grants, 1293
Community Fndn of Greenville Community Enrichment Grants, 1294
Community Fndn of Greenville Hollingsworth Funds Program/Project Grants, 1296
Community Fndn of Howard County Grants, 1297
Community Fndn of Middle Tennessee Grants, 1300
Community Fndn of Mount Vernon and Knox County Grants, 1301
Community Fndn of Riverside County Grants, 1304
Community Fndn of Santa Cruz County Grants, 1305
Community Fndn of Sarasota County Grants, 1306
Community Fndn of Shreveport-Bossier Grants, 1307
Community Fndn of South Alabama Grants, 1308
Community Fndn of SE Connecticut Grants, 1309
Community Fndn of Tampa Bay Grants, 1316
Community Fndn of the Verdugos Grants, 1322
Community Fndn of Wabash County Grants, 1326
Community Fndn of Western N Carolina Grants, 1327
Community Fndn Silicon Valley Grants, 1331
Compton Fndn Grants, 1338
ConAgra Foods Community Impact Grants, 1342
ConAgra Foods Nourish Our Comm Grants, 1343
Connecticut Commission on the Arts Art in Public Spaces, 1349
Connelly Fndn Grants, 1353
ConocoPhillips Fndn Grants, 1354
ConocoPhillips Grants, 1355
Constantin Fndn Grants, 1362
Constellation Energy Corp Grants, 1364
Consumers Energy Fndn, 1365
Cooke Fndn Grants, 1368
Cooper Industries Fndn Grants, 1370
Cord Fndn Grants, 1372
Corina Higginson Grants, 1373
Cornerstone Fndn of NE Wisconsin Grants, 1375
Coughlin-Saunders Fndn Grants, 1377
Cowles Charitable Grants, 1392
Crail-Johnson Fndn Grants, 1393
Cralle Fndn Grants, 1394
Cranston Fndn Grants, 1395
Crescent Porter Hale Fndn Grants, 1398
Crestlea Fndn Grants, 1399
Crossroads Fund Seed Grants, 1400
Crystelle Waggoner Charitable Grants, 1405

CSX Corp Contributions Grants, 1408
Cultural Society of Filipino Americans Grants, 1412
Cumberland Community Fndn Grants, 1413
Cumberland Community Fndn Summertime Kids Grants, 1414
CUNA Mutual Group Fndn, 1416
Curtis Fndn Grants, 1419
Cyrus Eaton Fndn Grants, 1423
D.F. Halton Fndn Grants, 1424
D. W. McMillan Fndn Grants, 1426
Dade Community Fndn Grants, 1430
DaimlerChrysler Corp Grants, 1432
Dallas Fndn Grants, 1436
Dana Corp Fndn Grants, 1440
Danellie Fndn Grants, 1442
Daphne Seybolt Culpeper Memorial Fndn Grants, 1445
Darden Restaurants Fndn Grants, 1446
Dave Coy Fndn Grants, 1447
Daviess County Community Fndn Human Services Grants, 1458
Dayton Fndn Grants, 1463
Dayton Power and Light Fndn Grants, 1464
Daywood Fndn Grants, 1465
Dearborn Community County Progress Grants, 1473
Delaware Community Fndn-Youth Philanthropy Board for Kent County, 1483
Delaware Community Fund For Women Grants, 1484
Delaware Community Next Generation Grants, 1485
Delaware Community Fndn Youth Philanthropy Board for New Castle County Grants, 1486
Dell Fndn Open Grants, 1490
Delta Air Lines Community Enrichment Grants, 1494
Deluxe Corp Fndn Grants, 1496
DeMatteis Family Fndn Grants, 1497
Denver Fndn Community Grants, 1502
DeRoy Testamentary Fndn Grants, 1518
Detroit Lions Charities Grants, 1520
DHHS Adolescent Family Life Demo Projects, 1524
DHHS ARRA Strengthening Communities Fund - Nonprofit Capacity Building Grants, 1527
DHHS ARRA Strengthening Communities Fund - State, Local, and Tribal Government Capacity Building Grants, 1528
DHHS Health Centers Grants for Residents of Public Housing, 1533
Dolfinger-McMahon Fndn Grants, 1565
Donald and Sylvia Robinson Family Fndn Grants, 1573
Donaldson Fndn Grants, 1574
Dorothy G. Griffin Charitable Fndn Grants, 1588
Dr. P. Phillips Fndn Grants, 1601
Dr. Scholl Fndn Grants, 1602
Duchossois Family Fndn Grants, 1616
Duluth-Superior Area Community Fndn Grants, 1620
Dunspaugh-Dalton Fndn Grants, 1623
Dyer-Ives Fndn Small Grants, 1629
Dyson Fndn Mid-Hudson Valley Faith-Based Organization Grants, 1634
E.J. Grassmann Grants, 1638
Eden Hall Fndn Grants, 1655
Edina Realty Fndn Grants, 1656
Edna Wardlaw Charitable Grants, 1660
Edwards Grants, 1669
Edwin W. and Catherine M. Davis Fndn Grants, 1672
EIF Community Grants, 1675
Eisner Fndn Grants, 1678
Elizabeth & Avola W. Callaway Fndn Grants, 1680
Elizabeth Carse Fndn Grants, 1681
Elizabeth Morse Genius Charitable Grants, 1682
Elkhart County Community Fndn Grants, 1684
El Paso Community Fndn Grants, 1688
Elsie H. Wilcox Fndn Grants, 1691
Emerson Charitable Grants, 1694
Ensign-Bickford Fndn Grants, 1709
Ensworth Charitable Fndn Grants, 1710
Enterprise Rent-A-Car Fndn Grants, 1721
EPA Environmental Justice Small Grants, 1732
Erie Community Fndn Grants, 1750
Esther M. and Freeman E. Everett Charitable Fndn Grants, 1757
Ethel and Raymond F. Rice Fndn Grants, 1758

SUBJECT INDEX

Social Services / 993

Ethel Sergeant Clark Smith Fndn Grants, 1761
Eugene M. Lang Fndn Grants, 1764
Evan and Susan Bayh Fndn Grants, 1769
F.M. Kirby Fndn Grants, 1780
F.R. Bigelow Fndn Grants, 1781
Families Count: The National Honors Program, 1784
Fargo-Moorhead Area Fndn Grants, 1788
Fargo-Moorhead Area Fndn Woman's Grants, 1789
Farmers Insurance Corp Giving Grants, 1791
Feldman Fndn Grants, 1801
Field Fndn of Illinois Grants, 1806
Fieldstone Fndn Grants, 1808
FirstEnergy Fndn Community Grants, 1819
Fisher Fndn Grants, 1831
Flextronics Fndn Disaster Relief Grants, 1841
Flinn Fndn Grants, 1842
Fluor Fndn Grants, 1875
FMC Fndn Grants, 1876
Foellinger Fndn Grants, 1877
Fondren Grants, 1878
Ford Motor Company Grants, 1885
Forrest C. Lattner Fndn Grants, 1887
Fndn for Enhancing Communities Grants, 1893
Fndn NW Grants, 1906
Fourjay Fndn Grants, 1913
Frances C. & William P. Smallwood Grants, 1918
Frances L. and Edwin L. Cummings Grants, 1919
Frank B. Hazard General Charity Grants, 1926
Frank S. Flowers Fndn Grants, 1935
Frank Stanley Beveridge Fndn Grants, 1936
Frank W. and Carl S. Adams Grants, 1937
Fred C. and Katherine B. Andersen Fndn Grants, 1942
Fred C. and Mary R. Koch Fndn Grants, 1943
Fred L. Emerson Fndn Grants, 1949
Fremont Area Community Elderly Needs Grants, 1954
Fremont Area Community Fndn Grants, 1955
Frist Fndn Grants, 1964
Fritz B. Burns Fndn Grants, 1965
Fuller E. Callaway Fndn Grants, 1973
G.A. Ackermann Grants, 1981
G.N. Wilcox Grants, 1982
Gebbie Fndn Grants, 1995
GenCorp Fndn Grants, 1998
George and Ruth Bradford Fndn Grants, 2010
George A Ohl Jr. Fndn Grants, 2012
George Frederick Jewett Fndn Grants, 2019
George Gund Fndn Grants, 2020
George H. and Jane A. Mifflin Grants, 2021
George W. Brackenridge Fndn Grants, 2028
Georgiana Goddard Eaton Grants, 2038
Gill Fndn - Gay and Lesbian Grants, 2054
Giving Sum Annual Grant, 2058
GNOF IMPACT Grants for Health and Human Services, 2080
GNOF IMPACT Grants for Youth Development, 2081
GNOF Maison Hospitaliere Grants, 2086
GNOF Norco Community Grants, 2089
Goizueta Fndn Grants, 2096
Goldseker Fndn Human Services Grants, 2102
Grace and Franklin Bernsen Fndn Grants, 2109
Graco Fndn Grants, 2111
Grand Haven Area Community Fndn Grants, 2113
Grand Rapids Area Community Fndn Wyoming Grants, 2116
Grand Rapids Community Fndn Grants, 2118
Grand Rapids Community Ionia County Grants, 2119
Grand Rapids Community Fndn Lowell Grants, 2121
Grand Rapids Community SE Ottawa Grants, 2122
Grand Rapids Community Sparta Grants, 2124
Greater Cincinnati Fndn Priority and Small Projects/ Capacity-Building Grants, 2132
Greater Green Bay Community Fndn Grants, 2135
Greater Kanawha Valley Fndn Grants, 2136
Greater Milwaukee Fndn Grants, 2137
Greater Saint Louis Community Fndn Grants, 2138
Greater Tacoma Community Fndn Grants, 2139
Greater Worcester Comm Discretionary Grants, 2140
Green Bay Packers Fndn Grants, 2148
Green Fndn Human Services Grants, 2154
Gregory Family Fndn Grants (Massachusetts), 2162
Grotto Fndn Project Grants, 2166
Guido A. and Elizabeth H. Binda Fndn Grants, 2172
Gulf Coast Community Fndn Grants, 2174
H & R Fndn Grants, 2181
H.A. and Mary K. Chapman Charitable Grants, 2182
H.B. Fuller Company Fndn Grants, 2183
H.J. Heinz Company Fndn Grants, 2184
H. Leslie Hoffman & Elaine Hoffman Grants, 2185
H. Schaffer Fndn Grants, 2187
Hagedorn Grants, 2207
Hall-Perrine Fndn Grants, 2209
Halliburton Fndn Grants, 2211
Hallmark Corp Fndn Grants, 2212
Hampton Roads Community Fndn Health and Human Service Grants, 2216
Hannaford Charitable Fndn Grants, 2222
Harold and Arlene Schnitzer CARE Grants, 2226
Harold K. L. Castle Fndn Grants, 2228
Harold R. Bechtel Charitable Remainder Grants, 2229
Harold Simmons Fndn Grants, 2230
Harris and Eliza Kempner Grants, 2231
Harrison County Community Fndn Grants, 2233
Harrison County Community Signature Grants, 2234
Harry A. and Margaret D. Towsley Fndn Grants, 2236
Harry C. Trexler Grants, 2239
Harry Kramer Grants, 2242
Harry Sudakoff Fndn Grants, 2245
Hartford Aging and Health Program Awards, 2247
Hartford Courant Fndn Grants, 2248
Hartford Fndn Regular Grants, 2253
Hawaii Community Human Services Grants, 2262
Health Fndn of Greater Indianapolis Grants, 2282
Hearst Fndns Social Service Grants, 2285
Hedco Fndn Grants, 2287
Helen K. and Arthur E. Johnson Fndn Grants, 2296
Helen S. Boylan Fndn Grants, 2298
Henrietta Tower Wurts Memorial Fndn Grants, 2304
Henry W. Bull Fndn Grants, 2312
Hershey Company Grants, 2318
Highmark Corp Giving Grants, 2319
High Meadow Fndn Grants, 2321
Hilfiger Family Fndn Grants, 2323
Hill Fndn Grants, 2326
Hillman Fndn Grants, 2327
Hoblitzelle Fndn Grants, 2341
Hoglund Fndn Grants, 2344
Holland/Zeeland Community Fndn Grants, 2345
Homer A. Scott and Mildred S. Scott Grants, 2350
Homer Fndn Grants, 2352
Horace A. Kimball and S. Ella Kimball Grants, 2362
Horizons Community Issues Grants, 2366
Household Int'l Corp Giving Grants, 2372
Houston Endowment Grants, 2373
Howard and Bush Fndn Grants, 2374
Howard County Community Fndn Grants, 2375
Howard H. Callaway Fndn Grants, 2376
Howe Fndn of North Carolina Grants, 2377
Huffy Fndn Grants, 2384
Huie-Dellmon Grants, 2386
Humana Fndn Grants, 2388
Huntington Fndn Grants, 2408
Huntington National Bank Comm Affairs Grant, 2409
Hutchinson Community Fndn Grants, 2410
Hutton Fndn Grants, 2412
Hyde Family Fndns Grants, 2414
Illinois Tool Works Fndn Grants, 2511
Intergrys Corp Grants, 2565
Ireland Family Fndn Grants, 2574
J.B. Reynolds Fndn Grants, 2592
J.C. Penney Company Grants, 2594
J.E. and L.E. Mabee Fndn Grants, 2595
J.L. Bedsole Fndn Grants, 2600
J.M. Long Fndn Grants, 2603
J.W. Kieckhefer Fndn Grants, 2607
Jacob G. Schmidlapp Grants, 2616
James Graham Brown Quality of Life Grants, 2625
James H. Cummings Fndn Grants, 2626
James J. and Angelia M. Harris Fndn Grants, 2630
James M. Collins Fndn Grants, 2633
James R. Dougherty Jr. Fndn Grants, 2635
James S. Copley Fndn Grants, 2637
Janirve Fndn Grants, 2645
Janus Fndn Grants, 2647
Jean and Louis Dreyfus Fndn Grants, 2658
Jerome and Mildred Paddock Fndn Grants, 2666
Jessie Ball Dupont Grants, 2671
Jewish Funds for Justice Grants, 2676
John Deere Fndn Grants, 2692
John Edward Fowler Memorial Fndn Grants, 2693
John G. Duncan Grants, 2695
John G. Martin Fndn Grants, 2696
John H. and Wilhelmina D. Harland Charitable Fndn Grants, 2698
John I. Smith Charities Grants, 2700
John J. Leidy Fndn Grants, 2701
John Jewett & Helen Chandler Garland Grants, 2702
John P. McGovern Fndn Grants, 2707
John P. Murphy Fndn Grants, 2708
John R. Oishei Fndn Grants, 2709
John S. and James L. Knight Fndn Donor Advised Grants, 2712
Johns Manville Grants, 2716
John W. Boynton Grants, 2730
Joseph Alexander Fndn Grants, 2734
Joseph Drown Fndn Grants, 2735
Josephine G. Russell Grants, 2737
Josiah W. and Bessie H. Kline Fndn Grants, 2742
Journal Gazette Fndn Grants, 2744
JP Morgan Chase Comm Development Grants, 2753
K. M. Hunter Fndn Social Welfare Grants, 2757
Kahuku Community Fund, 2762
Kansas Arts Commission Artist Fellowships, 2776
Katharine Matthies Fndn Grants, 2788
Kathryne Beynon Fndn Grants, 2791
Kentucky Arts Council Access Assistance Grants, 2805
Knight Fndn Grants - Georgia, 2829
L. W. Pierce Family Fndn Grants, 2846
Laclede Gas Charitable Grants, 2848
Lana'i Community Benefit Fund, 2857
Lands' End Corp Giving Program, 2861
Laura Moore Cunningham Fndn Grants, 2866
Lawrence J. and Anne Rubenstein Charitable Fndn Grants, 2868
Leon and Thea Koerner Fndn Grants, 2883
Lillian S. Wells Fndn Grants, 2901
Lincoln Financial Group Fndn Grants, 2906
Lisa and Douglas Goldman Grants, 2910
Lockheed Martin Philanthropic Grants, 2918
Lotus 88 Fndn for Women and Children Grants, 2921
Louie M. and Betty M. Phillips Fndn Grants, 2923
Lowell Berry Fndn Grants, 2930
Lubbock Area Fndn Grants, 2931
Lubrizol Fndn Grants, 2933
Lucile Horton Howe and Mitchell B. Howe Fndn Grants, 2934
Lucy Gooding Charitable Fndn Grants, 2937
Lynde and Harry Bradley Fndn Grants, 2947
Lynde and Harry Bradley Fndn Prizes, 2948
M.B. and Edna Zale Fndn Grants, 2950
M. Bastian Family Fndn Grants, 2951
M.E. Raker Fndn Grants, 2953
Mabel Louise Riley Fndn Grants, 2959
Mabel Y. Hughes Charitable Grants, 2960
Mann T. Lowry Fndn Grants, 2998
Marcia and Otto Koehler Fndn Grants, 3000
Margaret and James A. Elkins Jr. Fndn Grants, 3003
Margaret T. Morris Fndn Grants, 3005
Mars Fndn Grants, 3025
Mary K. Chapman Fndn Grants, 3042
Mary S. and David C. Corbin Fndn Grants, 3048
McCallum Family Fndn Grants, 3072
McCarthy Family Fndn Grants, 3073
McConnell Fndn Grants, 3076
McCune Charitable Fndn Grants, 3077
McCune Fndn Human Services Grants, 3080
McInerny Fndn Grants, 3083
McKesson Fndn Grants, 3084
McKnight Fndn Multiservice Grants, 3085
McKnight Fndn Virginia McKnight Binger Awards in Human Service, 3087

994 / Social Services

McLean Fndn Grants, 3089
Mead Johnson Nutritionals Evansville-Area Organizations Grants, 3103
Meadows Fndn Grants, 3104
Mead Witter Fndn Grants, 3106
Melville Charitable Grants, 3115
Meriden Fndn Grants, 3122
Mervin Bovaird Fndn Grants, 3128
Metro Health Fndn Grants, 3133
Meyer Fndn Healthy Communities Grants, 3143
Meyer Memorial Trust Special Grants, 3149
MGN Family Fndn Grants, 3154
Microsoft Comm Affairs Puget Sound Grants, 3163
Miguel Aleman Fndn Grants, 3175
Mildred V. Horn Fndn Grants, 3176
Miller, Canfield, Paddock and Stone, P.L.C. Corp Giving Grants, 3179
Millipore Fndn Grants, 3182
Mimi and Peter Haas Grants, 3185
Moline Fndn Community Grants, 3202
Monsanto Int'l Grants, 3207
Montana Community Fndn Grants, 3211
Motorola Fndn Grants, 3221
Needmor Grants, 3289
Nelda C. and H.J. Lutcher Stark Fndn Grants, 3296
New Earth Fndn Grants, 3317
New Hampshire Charitable Fndn Grants, 3325
Nicholas H. Noyes Jr. Memorial Fndn Grants, 3434
Norcliffe Fndn Grants, 3459
Nord Family Fndn Grants, 3461
Nordson Corp Fndn Grants, 3462
North Carolina Community Fndn Grants, 3489
Northern New York Community Fndn Grants, 3503
Northern Trust Company Corp Giving Program, 3504
NW Mutual Fndn Grants, 3509
NW Minnesota Fndn Asset Building Grants, 3511
Norton Fndn Grants, 3514
Norwin S. and Elizabeth N. Bean Fndn Grants, 3515
Nuffield Fndn Africa Grants, 3532
Nuffield Fndn Open Door Grants, 3534
Nuffield Fndn Small Grants, 3535
NYCT Girls and Young Women Grants, 3548
NYCT Social Services and Welfare Grants, 3557
Ogden Codman Grants, 3641
Oklahoma City Community Programs & Grants, 3666
Oleonda Jameson Grants, 3667
Onan Family Fndn Grants, 3672
Oppenstein Brothers Fndn Grants, 3685
Ordean Fndn Grants, 3691
Owen County Community Fndn Grants, 3716
Owens Fndn Grants, 3718
Pacific Life Fndn Grants, 3726
PacifiCorp Fndn for Learning Grants, 3727
Parkersburg Area Comm Fndn Action Grants, 3738
Patrick and Anna M. Cudahy Grants, 3751
Paul Balint Charitable Grants, 3757
PCA Arts Organizations and Arts Programs Grants for Local Arts, 3782
PCA Entry Track Arts Organizations and Program Grants for Local Arts, 3794
Peacock Fndn Grants, 3809
Percy B. Ferebee Endowment Grants, 3820
Perkin Grants, 3821
Perpetual Trust for Charitable Giving Grants, 3826
Peter Kiewit Fndn General Grants, 3845
Peter Kiewit Fndn Small Grants, 3847
Pew Trusts Children and Youth Grants, 3858
Peyton Anderson Fndn Grants, 3862
Phelps County Community Fndn Grants, 3870
Philadelphia Organizational Effectiveness Grants, 3872
Philadelphia Fndn YOUTHadelphia Grants, 3873
Philip L. Graham Grants, 3876
Phi Upsilon Omicron Florence Fallgatter Distinguished Service Award, 3877
Phoenix Suns Charities Grants, 3881
Pinellas County Grants, 3891
Pittsburgh Fndn Community Grants, 3910
Plough Fndn Grants, 3915
PNC Charitable Trust and Fndn Grants, 3921
Polk Bros. Fndn Grants, 3929

Pollock Fndn Grants, 3930
Pott Fndn Grants, 3940
Powell Fndn Grants, 3942
Pride Fndn Grants, 3958
Prince Charitable Trusts Rhode Island Grants, 3961
Principal Financial Group Fndn Grants, 3966
Procter and Gamble Grants, 3967
Puerto Rico Community Fndn Grants, 3986
Questar Corp Contributions Grants, 3997
R.C. Baker Fndn Grants, 3999
Rajiv Gandhi Fndn Grants, 4011
Rancho Bernardo Community Fndn Grants, 4015
Raskob Fndn for Catholic Activities Grants, 4019
Rasmuson Fndn Capital Grants, 4020
Rasmuson Fndn Special Project Grants, 4025
RBC Dain Rauscher Fndn Grants, 4031
RCF General Community Grants, 4032
RCF Individual Assistance Grants, 4033
Regence Fndn Access to Health Care Grants, 4039
Regence Fndn Health Care Community Awareness and Engagement Grants, 4040
Regence Fndn Health Care Connections Grants, 4041
Regence Fndn Improving End-of-Life Grants, 4042
Regence Fndn Tools and Technology Grants, 4043
Reinberger Fndn Grants, 4052
Reynolds American Fndn Grants, 4068
Reynolds Family Fndn Grants, 4071
Rhode Island Fndn Grants, 4073
Richard and Helen DeVos Fndn Grants, 4076
Richard E. Griffin Family Fndn Grants, 4081
Richard King Mellon Fndn Grants, 4087
Richards Fndn Grants, 4089
Rich Fndn Grants, 4090
Ripley County Community Fndn Grants, 4095
Ripley County Community Small Project Grants, 4096
Rite Aid Corp Grants, 4101
Robert and Joan Dircks Fndn Grants, 4104
Robert G. Cabell III and Maude Morgan Cabell Fndn Grants, 4113
Robert R. McCormick Tribune Veterans Grants, 4120
Robert R. Meyer Fndn Grants, 4121
Robert W. Woodruff Fndn Grants, 4124
Robins Fndn Grants, 4126
Rochester Area Community Fndn Grants, 4127
Rochester Area Fndn Grants, 4128
Rockwell Int'l Corp Grants, 4141
Roeher Institute Research Grants, 4142
Rogers Family Fndn Grants, 4144
Rollin M. Gerstacker Fndn Grants, 4146
Ronald McDonald House Charities Grants, 4149
Roy and Christine Sturgis Charitable Grants, 4166
RRF General Grants, 4170
Rucker & Margaret Agee Grants, 4171
Russell Berrie Fndn Grants, 4175
Ruth Anderson Fndn Grants, 4176
Ruth and Vernon Taylor Fndn Grants, 4177
S.H. Cowell Fndn Grants, 4199
S. Livingston Mather Charitable Grants, 4200
Sailors' Snug Harbor of Boston Elder Grants, 4211
Saint Paul Fndn Community Sharing Grants, 4218
Salisbury Community Fndn Grants, 4224
Samuel S. Johnson Fndn Grants, 4239
San Antonio Area Fndn Grants, 4240
San Diego Health & Human Services Grants, 4248
Sandy Hill Fndn Grants, 4257
Santa Fe Community Fndn Seasonal Grants, 4290
Sarkeys Fndn Grants, 4297
Scherman Fndn Grants, 4305
Schlessman Family Fndn Grants, 4307
Schumann Fund for New Jersey Grants, 4311
Seagate Tech Corp Capacity to Care Grants, 4317
Seattle Fndn Basic Needs Grants, 4321
Seattle Fndn Doyne M. Green Scholarships, 4324
Selby and Richard McRae Fndn Grants, 4334
Self Fndn Grants, 4335
Sensient Technologies Fndn Grants, 4337
Sidney Stern Grants, 4349
Sid W. Richardson Fndn Grants, 4350
Siebert Lutheran Fndn Grants, 4351
Sioux Falls Area Community Grants, 4364

Sioux Falls Area Community Fndn Spot Grants, 4366
Sisters of Charity Fndn of Canton Grants, 4372
Sisters of Mercy of North Carolina Fndn Grants, 4375
Sisters of Saint Joseph Charitable Grants, 4376
Sobrato Family Fndn Grants, 4389
Sobrato Family Fndn Meeting Space Grants, 4390
Sobrato Family Fndn Office Space Grants, 4391
Sonora Area Fndn Competitive Grants, 4404
Sosland Fndn Grants, 4408
Southern Minnesota Init Fndn AmeriCorps Leap Grants, 4431
SW Florida Community Competitive Grants, 4442
SW Gas Corp Fndn Grants, 4445
Sprague Fndn Grants, 4461
Stackpole-Hall Fndn Grants, 4472
Starr Fndn Grants, 4483
State Street Fndn Grants, 4495
Steele-Reese Fndn Grants, 4498
Stewart Huston Charitable Grants, 4505
Stowe Family Fndn Grants, 4510
Sunoco Fndn Grants, 4530
Susan Mott Webb Charitable Grants, 4536
Sylvia Adams Charitable Grants, 4543
T. Rowe Price Associates Fndn Grants, 4548
Target Corp Local Store Grants, 4561
Tauck Family Fndn Grants, 4563
Taylor S. Abernathy and Patti Harding Abernathy Charitable Grants, 4564
Textron Corp Contributions Grants, 4601
Theodore Edson Parker Fndn Grants, 4605
Thomas and Dorothy Leavey Fndn Grants, 4612
Thomas C. Ackerman Fndn Grants, 4615
Thomas J. Atkins Grants, 4617
Thomas J. Long Fndn Community Grants, 4618
Thomas Thompson Grants, 4620
Thomas W. Briggs Fndn Grants, 4621
Thompson Charitable Fndn Grants, 4622
TJX Fndn Grants, 4637
Tom's of Maine Grants, 4640
Topeka Community Building Families Grants, 4643
Topfer Family Fndn Grants, 4646
Triangle Community Fndn Donor Grants, 4668
Trinity Fndn Grants, 4670
Trull Fndn Grants, 4673
Tull Charitable Fndn Grants, 4679
TWS Fndn Grants, 4683
U.S. Department of Educ 21st Century Community Learning Centers, 4687
Union Bank, N.A. Fndn Grants, 4709
Union Benevolent Association Grants, 4710
Union Pacific Fndn Community and Civic Grants, 4714
Union Pacific Health & Human Services Grants, 4715
United Technologies Corp Grants, 4725
US Airways Community Contributions, 4788
USG Fndn Grants, 4869
Vancouver Fndn Grants & Comm Inits, 4900
Vermont Community Fndn Grants, 4929
Victoria S. and Bradley L. Geist Fndn Grants Supporting Foster Care and Their Caregivers, 4936
Victoria S. and Bradley L. Geist Fndn Grants Supporting Transitioning Foster Youth, 4937
Vulcan Materials Company Fndn Grants, 4956
W.H. and Mary Ellen Cobb Charitable Grants, 4959
Wabash Valley Community Fndn Grants, 4971
Walter L. Gross III Family Fndn Grants, 4983
Washington County Community Fndn Grants, 4997
Washington County Community Youth Grants, 4998
Wayne and Gladys Valley Fndn Grants, 5003
Wayne County Fndn Vigran Family Grants, 5004
Wayne County Fndn Grants, 5005
Weatherwax Fndn Grants, 5014
Weingart Fndn Grants, 5018
Weyerhaeuser Company Fndn Grants, 5053
Whiting Fndn Grants, 5059
WHO Fndn General Grants, 5063
William G. and Helen C. Hoffman Fndn Grants, 5080
William G. Gilmore Fndn Grants, 5082
William G. Selby and Marie Selby Fndn Grants, 5085
William Robert Baird Charitable Grants, 5093
Wilson-Wood Fndn Grants, 5098

SUBJECT INDEX

Winston-Salem Fndn Competitive Grants, 5102
Wood-Claeyssens Fndn Grants, 5113
Yellow Corp Fndn Grants, 5126

Social Services Delivery

A.C. Ratshesky Fndn Grants, 39
Aaron Fndn Grants, 73
Abbott Fund Community Grants, 81
Abel Fndn Grants, 90
ABIG Fndn Grants, 99
Able To Serve Grants, 102
ACF Native American Social and Economic Development Strategies Grants, 123
African American Fund of New Jersey Grants, 192
Agnes B. Hunt Grants, 202
Albert and Margaret Alkek Fndn Grants, 340
Albert E. and Birdie W. Einstein Grants, 342
Alexander & Baldwin Fndn Hawaiian and Pacific Island Grants, 352
Alexander & Baldwin Fndn Mainland Grants, 353
Allegan County Community Fndn Grants, 375
Alliant Energy Fndn Community Grants, 384
Alticor Corp Community Contributions Grants, 396
Ameren Corp Community Grants, 418
American Savings Fndn Grants, 445
American Schlafhorst Fndn Grants, 446
Andersen Corp Fndn, 459
Anheuser-Busch Fndn Grants, 470
Ann Peppers Fndn Grants, 484
AptarGroup Fndn Grants, 519
Arlington Community Fndn Grants, 564
ArvinMeritor Grants, 585
Aurora Fndn Grants, 613
Autzen Fndn Grants, 622
Bacon Family Fndn Grants, 634
Balfe Family Fndn Grants, 636
Barra Fndn Community Grants, 673
Barr Fndn Grants, 677
Bayer Fndn Grants, 696
Bernard F. and Alva B. Gimbel Fndn Grants, 740
Bicknell Grants, 759
Bill Hannon Fndn Grants, 771
Blackford County Community Fndn Grants, 780
Blanche and Julian Robertson Family Fndn Grants, 785
Blanche M. Walsh Charity Grants, 786
Boston Jewish Community Women's Grants, 822
Capital City Bank Group Fndn Grants, 920
Charity Incorporated Grants, 1035
Charles H. Hall Fndn, 1044
Charles Lafitte Fndn Grants, 1049
Charlotte County (FL) Community Fndn Grants, 1056
Chase Paymentech Corp Giving Grants, 1059
Chicago Community Trust Housing Grants: Preventing and Ending Homelessness, 1090
Chiron Fndn Community Grants, 1111
CICF Legacy Grants, 1126
Cingular Wireless Charitable Contributions, 1134
CIT Corp Giving Grants, 1138
Cleveland Community Responsive Grants, 1168
Clinton County Community Fndn Grants, 1174
CNCS AmeriCorps NCCC Project Grants, 1181
Columbus Fndn Mary Eleanor Morris Grants, 1225
Columbus Fndn R. Alvin Stevenson Grants, 1228
Community Fndn of South Puget Sound Grants, 1311
Community Fndn of St. Joseph County Special Project Challenge Grants, 1314
Crystelle Waggoner Charitable Grants, 1405
CSRA Community Fndn Grants, 1407
Cudd Fndn Grants, 1410
Cultural Society of Filipino Americans Grants, 1412
Dairy Queen Corp Contributions Grants, 1433
David Robinson Fndn Grants, 1454
Deaconess Community Fndn Grants, 1467
Deluxe Corp Fndn Grants, 1496
DeMatteis Family Fndn Grants, 1497
Dennis and Phyllis Washington Fndn Grants, 1498
DeRoy Testamentary Fndn Grants, 1518
DHHS ARRA Strengthening Communities Fund - Nonprofit Capacity Building Grants, 1527
DHL Charitable Shipment Support, 1541

Donald and Sylvia Robinson Family Fndn Grants, 1573
Dora Roberts Fndn Grants, 1579
Dresher Fndn Grants, 1605
Drs. Bruce and Lee Fndn Grants, 1607
DuPage Community Fndn Grants, 1624
Eastman Chemical Company Fndn Grants, 1643
Edna Wardlaw Charitable Grants, 1660
EDS Fndn Grants, 1661
Eva L. and Joseph M. Bruening Fndn Grants, 1768
Evan and Susan Bayh Fndn Grants, 1769
Ewing Halsell Fndn Grants, 1776
Foster Fndn Grants, 1888
Fndn for the Carolinas Grants, 1896
Francis L. Abreu Charitable Grants, 1922
Frank B. Hazard General Charity Grants, 1926
Fraser-Parker Fndn Grants, 1938
G.A. Ackermann Grants, 1981
General Dynamics Corp Grants, 2001
George B. Storer Fndn Grants, 2014
George Fndn Grants, 2018
GNOF IMPACT Grants for Health and Human Services, 2080
GNOF Maison Hospitaliere Grants, 2086
Goldseker Fndn Human Services Grants, 2102
Goldseker Fndn Non-Profit Management Assistance Grants, 2103
Goodyear Tire Grants, 2106
Greater Cincinnati Fndn Priority and Small Projects/ Capacity-Building Grants, 2132
Green Fndn Human Services Grants, 2154
Gregory Family Fndn Grants (Massachusetts), 2162
Hall-Perrine Fndn Grants, 2209
Hampton Roads Community Fndn Health and Human Service Grants, 2216
Hampton Roads Community Fndn Nonprofit Facilities Improvement Grants, 2218
Harold Alfond Fndn Grants, 2225
Harrison County Community Fndn Grants, 2233
Harrison County Community Signature Grants, 2234
Harry W. Bass, Jr. Fndn Grants, 2246
Harvest Fndn Grants, 2254
Hasbro Children's Fund, 2256
Hawaii Community Human Services Grants, 2262
Hearst Fndns Social Service Grants, 2285
Hillsdale Grants, 2329
Hirtzel Memorial Fndn Grants, 2332
Homer Fndn Grants, 2352
Howard and Bush Fndn Grants, 2374
Hugh J. Andersen Fndn Grants, 2385
Ida Alice Ryan Charitable Grants, 2431
Ittleson Fndn Mental Health Grants, 2590
J. F. Maddox Fndn Grants, 2597
James M. Collins Fndn Grants, 2633
Jane Bradley Pettit Fndn Community and Social Development Grants, 2642
Jay and Rose Phillips Family Fndn Grants, 2656
Jennings County Community Fndn Women's Giving Circle Grant, 2665
Jerome and Mildred Paddock Fndn Grants, 2666
Joe W. and Dorothy Dorsett Brown Fndn Grants, 2684
K. M. Hunter Fndn Social Welfare Grants, 2757
Ken W. Davis Fndn Grants, 2813
Kettering Family Fndn Grants, 2817
KeyBank Fndn Grants, 2820
KeySpan Fndn Grants, 2821
Laclede Gas Charitable Grants, 2848
Laura Moore Cunningham Fndn Grants, 2866
Louie M. and Betty M. Phillips Fndn Grants, 2923
Ludwick Family Fndn Grants, 2938
Mabel Louise Riley Fndn Family Strengthening Small Grants, 2958
Mann T. Lowry Fndn Grants, 2998
Marie C. and Joseph C. Wilson Fndn Rochester Small Grants, 3006
Marin Community Successful Aging Grants, 3014
Marion I. and Henry J. Knott Fndn Discretionary Grants, 3018
Marion I. and Henry J. Knott Standard Grants, 3019
Mary E. Ober Fndn Grants, 3039
Mary K. Chapman Fndn Grants, 3042

McCune Charitable Fndn Grants, 3077
McCune Fndn Human Services Grants, 3080
MeadWestvaco Sustainable Communities Grant, 3105
Memorial Fndn Grants, 3117
Meriden Fndn Grants, 3122
Miller, Canfield, Paddock and Stone, P.L.C. Corp Giving Grants, 3179
Moline Fndn Community Grants, 3202
Monsanto Int'l Grants, 3207
Musgrave Fndn Grants, 3231
North Georgia Community Fndn Grants, 3505
NYCT Social Services and Welfare Grants, 3557
Ohio Valley Fndn Grants, 3662
Oscar Rennebohm Fndn Grants, 3694
Palm Beach and Martin Counties Grants, 3733
Parke County Community Fndn Grants, 3735
Peoples Bancorp Fndn Grants, 3817
Peter Kiewit Fndn Small Grants, 3847
Pew Trusts Children and Youth Grants, 3858
Polk Bros. Fndn Grants, 3929
Pollock Fndn Grants, 3930
Portland Fndn - Women's Giving Circle Grant, 3935
Powell Fndn Grants, 3942
Priddy Fndn Grants, 3957
Prince Charitable Trusts Chicago Grants, 3959
Rasmuson Fndn Capital Grants, 4020
Rasmuson Fndn Special Project Grants, 4025
Regence Fndn Access to Health Care Grants, 4039
Regence Fndn Health Care Community Awareness and Engagement Grants, 4040
Regence Fndn Health Care Connections Grants, 4041
Regence Fndn Improving End-of-Life Grants, 4042
Regence Fndn Tools and Technology Grants, 4043
Reynolds Family Fndn Grants, 4071
Richard and Susan Smith Family Fndn Grants, 4078
Ripley County Community Small Project Grants, 4096
Robert R. Meyer Fndn Grants, 4121
Rollins-Luetkemeyer Fndn Grants, 4147
Ronald McDonald House Charities Grants, 4149
Ryder System Charitable Fndn Grants, 4191
San Diego Health & Human Services Grants, 4248
Sandy Hill Fndn Grants, 4257
San Francisco Fndn Community Health Grants, 4263
San Juan Island Community Fndn Grants, 4283
Santa Barbara Fndn Strategy Grants - Innovation, 4287
Santa Fe Community Fndn Seasonal Grants, 4290
Sarkeys Fndn Grants, 4297
Sartain Lanier Family Fndn Grants, 4298
Schramm Fndn Grants, 4310
Seagate Tech Corp Capacity to Care Grants, 4317
Seattle Fndn Basic Needs Grants, 4321
Shell Oil Company Fndn Grants, 4343
Sierra Health Fndn Responsive Grants, 4353
Sisters of Charity Fndn of Canton Grants, 4372
Sisters of Mercy of North Carolina Fndn Grants, 4375
Sisters of St. Joseph Healthcare Fndn Grants, 4377
Sonoco Fndn Grants, 4403
Sony Corp of America Corp Philanthropy Grants, 4405
Southern Minnesota Init Fndn AmeriCorps Leap Grants, 4431
SW Gas Corp Fndn Grants, 4445
Square D Fndn Grants, 4464
Sulzberger Fndn Grants, 4522
Summit Fndn Grants, 4524
Taproot Fndn Capacity-Building Service Grants, 4560
Target Fndn Grants, 4562
Thomas J. Atkins Grants, 4617
Thomas J. Long Fndn Community Grants, 4618
Trull Fndn Grants, 4673
TWS Fndn Grants, 4683
U.S. Bank Fndn Grants, 4686
United Methodist Child Mental Health Grants, 4721
USAID Community Infrastructure Dev Grants, 4745
US Airways Community Contributions, 4788
Virginia W. Kettering Fndn Grants, 4950
W.C. Griffith Fndn Grants, 4957
Walter L. Gross III Family Fndn Grants, 4983
Westinghouse Charitable Giving Grants, 5028
Whiting Fndn Grants, 5059
Whitney Fndn Grants, 5061

Social Services Delivery

WHO Fndn General Grants, 5063
Wild Rivers Community Fndn Holiday Partnership Grants, 5069
William H. Hannon Fndn Grants, 5086
William J. and Dorothy K. O'Neill Fndn Grants, 5087
William S. Abell Fndn Grants, 5094
Winthrop Rockefeller Fndn Grants, 5105
Woodward Grants, 5116

Social Stratification/Mobility
ANLAF Int'l Fund for Sexual Minorities Grants, 471
FCYO Youth Organizing Grants, 1797
Meyer Fndn Economic Security Grants, 3141
National Endowment for the Arts - Regional Partnership Agreement Grants, 3258
Natonal Endowment for the Arts Research Grants: Art Works, 3286
OUT Fund for Lesbian & Gay Liberation Grants, 3714
PDF Fiscal Sponsorship Grant, 3808
Threshold Fndn Thriving Resilient Communities Funding Circle, 4628

Social Work
Canada-U.S. Fulbright Mid-Career Grants, 917
Chapin Hall Int'l Fellowships in Children's Policy Research, 1032
Chicago Community Trust Housing Grants: Preventing and Ending Homelessness, 1090
Elizabeth Morse Genius Charitable Grants, 1682
GNOF IMPACT Grants for Youth Development, 2081
NW Minnesota Fndn Asset Building Grants, 3511
Regents Professional Opportunity Scholarships, 4044

Sociology
Canada-U.S. Fulbright Mid-Career Grants, 917
Chapin Hall Int'l Fellowships in Children's Policy Research, 1032
Edward Bangs Kelley and Elza Kelley Grants, 1665
Horowitz Fndn for Social Policy Grants, 2370
Horowitz Fndn for Social Policy Special Awards, 2371

Sociology, Applied
American Sociological Assoc Sydney S. Spivack Applied Social Research and Social Policy, 450

Software
Microsoft Authorized Refurbisher Donations, 3162

Soil Sciences
Organic Farming Research Fndn Grants, 3693

Solid Waste Disposal
EPA Tribal Solid Waste Management Assistance Grants, 1741
EREF Solid Waste Research Grants, 1747
EREF Sustainability Research Grants, 1748
EREF Unsolicited Proposal Grants, 1749
Fremont Area Community Fndn Grants, 1955
Indiana Recycling Grants, 2545
USDA Individual Water and Waste Water Grants, 4817
USDA Technical Assistance and Training Grants for Rural Waste Systems, 4842

Space Sciences
GenCorp Fndn Grants, 1998

Special Education
Air Products and Chemicals Grants, 216
Akzo Nobel Chemicals Grants, 219
Annunziata Sanguinetti Fndn Grants, 485
Blackford County Community Fndn Grants, 780
Carroll County Community Fndn Grants, 947
Clinton County Community Fndn Grants, 1174
CVS Community Grants, 1422
Dorr Fndn Grants, 1591
Hasbro Children's Fund, 2256
Henry County Community Fndn Grants, 2308
Henry E. Niles Fndn Grants, 2309
Herbert A. and Adrian W. Woods Fndn Grants, 2313
Marjorie Moore Charitable Fndn Grants, 3021
Parke County Community Fndn Grants, 3735
Peter and Elizabeth C. Tower Fndn Annual Intellectual Disabilities Grants, 3834
Roy and Christine Sturgis Charitable Grants, 4166
Scott County Community Fndn Grants, 4314
Skaggs Fndn Grants, 4378
Stewart Huston Charitable Grants, 4505
Thomas Sill Fndn Grants, 4619
U.S. Department of Educ Centers for Independent Living, 4688
U.S. Department of Educ Rehabilitation Training--Rehabilitation Continuing Educ Programs--Institute on Rehabilitation Issues, 4700
U.S. Department of Educ Special Educ--National Activities--Parent Information Centers, 4701

Special Populations
Alfred E. Chase Charitable Fndn Grants, 366
Bill & Melinda Gates Policy & Advocacy Grants, 769
Carl R. Hendrickson Family Fndn Grants, 935
Charles H. Hall Fndn, 1044
Emma G. Harris Fndn Grants, 1701
Florence Hunt Maxwell Fndn Grants, 1844
Guy I. Bromley Grants, 2180
Helen Irwin Littauer Ed Grants, 2295
Henrietta Lange Burk Grants, 2303
Herbert A. and Adrian W. Woods Fndn Grants, 2313
IIE AmCham Fndn U.S. Studies Scholarship, 2453
John Clarke Grants, 2689
Louetta M. Cowden Fndn Grants, 2922
Marin Community Successful Aging Grants, 3014
Ms. Fndn Women Building Democracy Grants, 3223
NYSCA Special Arts Services: Instruction and Training Grants, 3616
PCA Pennsylvania Partners in the Arts Program Stream Grants, 3801
PCA Pennsylvania Partners in the Arts Project Stream Grants, 3802
Piper Trust Children Grants, 3901
Roy and Christine Sturgis Charitable Grants, 4166
TAC Arts Access Grant, 4549
TAC Arts Access Technical Assistance Grants, 4550
TAC Arts Build Communities Grants, 4551
Texas Commission On The Arts Cultural Connections Consultant/Simply Solutions Grants, 4590
Vigneron Grants, 4938

Specialized Museums
American Express Charitable Grants, 429
Donald W. Reynolds Fndn Children's Discovery Init Grants, 1576
Florida Div of Cultural Affairs Museum Grants, 1858
George J. and Effie L. Seay Fndn Grants, 2024
Jerry L. and Barbara J. Burris Fndn Grants, 2669
MacArthur Fndn Chicago Arts and Culture General Operations Grants, 2961
NYSCA Museum Program Support Grants, 3603
S. Spencer Scott Grants, 4202
Seattle Fndn C. Keith Birkenfeld Grants, 4323
Union Pacific Fndn Community and Civic Grants, 4714

Speech
Claude Pepper Fndn Grants, 1160
Playboy Fndn Freedom of Expression Award, 3912
Reinberger Fndn Grants, 4052

Speech Pathology
Community Memorial Fndn Grants, 1334
Edward W. and Stella C. Van Houten Grants, 1670
German Protestant Orphan Asylum Fndn Grants, 2044
Regents Professional Opportunity Scholarships, 4044

Sports
Active Awareness Grants, 136
Angels Baseball Fndn Grants, 465
Bank of America Corp Sponsorships, 661
Barberton Community Fndn Grants, 666
Barrasso Usdin Kupperman Freeman and Sarver LLC Corp Grants, 675
Batters Up USA Equipment Grants, 683
Bert W. Martin Fndn Grants, 747
Bikes Belong Fndn REI Grants, 761
BoatUS Fndn Grassroots Grants, 805
Callaway Golf Company Fndn Grants, 910
Cal Ripken Sr. Fndn Grants, 912
Carl and Eloise Pohlad Family Fndn Grants, 927
Carl C. Icahn Fndn Grants, 929
CFFVR Robert and Patricia Endries Family Fndn Grants, 1018
Charlotte Martin Fndn Youth Grants, 1057
Chatham Athletic Fndn Grants, 1060
Chiles Fndn Grants, 1108
Cleveland Browns Fndn Grants, 1166
Collins C. Diboll Private Fndn Grants, 1208
Community Fndn of the Ozarks Grants, 1320
CONSOL Coal Group Grants, 1360
Daniels Grants, 1443
Daviess County Community Recreation Grants, 1459
Daviess County Community Fndn Youth Development Grants, 1460
Dearborn Community City of Aurora Grants, 1470
Dearborn Community Fndn City of Lawrenceburg Youth Grants, 1472
Denver Broncos Charities Grants, 1501
Dept of Ed Recreational Services for Individuals with Disabilities, 1512
Detroit Lions Charities Grants, 1520
Dwight Stuart Youth Fndn Grants, 1628
Easton Fndns Archery Facility Grants, 1644
Elizabeth Morse Genius Charitable Grants, 1682
El Pomar Fndn Awards and Grants, 1690
Finish Line Youth Fndn Founder's Grants, 1812
Finish Line Youth Fndn Grants, 1813
Finish Line Youth Fndn Legacy Grants, 1814
FishAmerica Fndn Marine and Anadromous Fish Habitat Restoration Grants, 1829
FishAmerica Fndn Research Grants, 1830
Florida Sports Fndn Junior Golf Grants, 1872
Florida Sports Fndn Major and Regional Programs Grants, 1873
George Kress Fndn Grants, 2025
GNOF IMPACT Grants for Youth Development, 2081
Grand Rapids Area Community Fndn Wyoming Youth Grants, 2117
Greater Worcester Community Jeppson Memorial Fund for Brookfield Grants, 2141
Gregory L. Gibson Charitable Fndn Grants, 2163
Helen Bader Fndn Grants, 2293
Henrietta Tower Wurts Memorial Fndn Grants, 2304
Homer Fndn Grants, 2352
Howard H. Callaway Fndn Grants, 2376
Jacksonville Jaguars Fndn Grants, 2614
Jewish Women's Fndn of New York Grants, 2677
Kalamazoo Community Fndn Youth Development Grants, 2773
Kenny's Kids Grants, 2803
Kevin P. & Sydney B. Knight Family Grants, 2819
Kimball Int'l-Habig Fndn Grants, 2823
Knox County Community Fndn Grants, 2831
LA84 Fndn Grants, 2847
Laura L. Adams Fndn Grants, 2865
Lisa and Douglas Goldman Grants, 2910
Louis R. Cappelli Fndn Grants, 2926
Marion I. and Henry J. Knott Standard Grants, 3019
Mary Jennings Sport Camp Scholarship, 3041
McCombs Fndn Grants, 3075
MLB Tomorrow Grants, 3193
NFL Club Matching Youth Football Field/Stadium Grants, 3349
NFL Grassroots Field Grants, 3350
NFL High School Coach of the Week Grant, 3351
NFL High School Football Coach of the Year, 3352
NFL Player Youth Football Camp Grants, 3353
NFWF Wildlife Links Grants, 3400
Nike and Ashoka GameChangers: Change the Game for Women in Sport, 3439
Nike Bowerman Track Renovation Grants, 3440
Nike Giving - Cash and Product Grants, 3442
NRA Fndn Grants, 3517
NSS Fndn Hunting Heritage Partnership Grants, 3530

SUBJECT INDEX

Substance Abuse / 997

ODKF Athletic Grants, 3638
Oregon Youth Soccer Fndn Grants, 3692
Paul and Edith Babson Fndn Grants, 3755
Paul E. and Klare N. Reinhold Fndn Grants, 3758
Paul Stock Fndn Grants, 3766
Perry County Community Fndn Grants, 3827
Peter M. Putnam Fndn Grants, 3848
Phoenix Coyotes Charities Grants, 3879
Posey County Community Fndn Grants, 3939
PSEG Corp Contributions Grants, 3979
REI Conservation and Outdoor Rec Grants, 4051
Richard and Helen DeVos Fndn Grants, 4076
Robert R. Meyer Fndn Grants, 4121
Roney-Fitzpatrick Fndn Grants, 4150
Saint Louis Rams Fndn Community Donations, 4214
SanDisk Corp Community Sharing Program, 4253
Saucony Run for Good Fndn Grants, 4301
Scheumann Fndn Grants, 4306
Seneca Foods Fndn Grants, 4336
Sidgmore Family Fndn Grants, 4348
Sport Manitoba Athlete/Team Travel Assistance Grants, 4452
Sport Manitoba Athlete Skill Development Clinics Grants, 4453
Sport Manitoba Bingo Allocations Grants, 4454
Sport Manitoba Coaches/Officials Travel Assistance Grants, 4455
Sport Manitoba Hosting Regional Championships Grants, 4456
Sport Manitoba Intro of a New Sport Grants, 4457
Sport Manitoba KidSport Athlete Grants, 4458
Sport Manitoba Sport Special Inits Grants, 4459
Sport Manitoba Women to Watch Grants, 4460
Summit Fndn Grants, 4524
Susan A. & Donald P. Babson Charitable Grants, 4534
Telluride Fndn Community Grants, 4573
Topeka West Rotary Youth Enrichment Grants, 4645
TSYSF Individual Scholarships, 4675
TSYSF Team Grants, 4676
U.S. Lacrosse Emerging Groups Grants, 4703
U.S. Lacrosse Equipment Grants, 4704
UPS Corp Giving Grants, 4727
USAA – Ann Hoyt / Jim Easton JOAD Grants, 4734
USA Football Equipment Grants, 4735
USA Volleyball Fndn Ed Grants, 4791
USBC Annual Zeb Scholarship, 4792
USBC Earl Anthony Scholarships, 4793
USFA Development Grants, 4866
USFA Equipment Subsidy Grants, 4867
USGA Fndn For the Good of the Game Grants, 4868
US Soccer Annual Program & Field Grants, 4870
US Soccer Fndn Planning Grants, 4871
USTA Althea Gibson Leadership Awards, 4872
USTA CTA and NJTL Community Tennis Development Workshop Scholarships, 4873
USTA Excellence Grants, 4874
USTA Junior Team Tennis Stipends, 4875
USTA Multicultural Excellence Grants, 4876
USTA Multicultural Individual Player Grant for National Competition and Training, 4877
USTA NJTL Arthur Ashe Essay and Art Contest, 4878
USTA NJTL Tennis and Leadership Camp Scholarships, 4879
USTA Okechi Womeodu Scholar Athlete Grants, 4880
USTA Player Development Grants, 4881
USTA Pro Circuit Comm Involvement Day Grants, 4882
USTA Public Facility Assistance Grants, 4883
USTA Recreational Tennis Grants, 4884
USTA Serves College Educ Scholarships, 4885
USTA Serves College Textbook Scholarships, 4886
USTA Serves Dwight F. Davis Scholarships, 4887
USTA Serves Dwight Mosley Scholarships, 4888
USTA Serves Eve Kraft Scholarships, 4889
USTA Serves Marian Wood Baird Scholarship, 4890
USTA Serves Player Incentive Awards, 4891
USTA Tennis Block Party Grants, 4892
WSF Rusty Kanokogi Fund for the Advancement of U.S. Judo Grants, 5118
WSF Travel and Training Grants, 5119
Young Family Fndn Grants, 5127

Sports Equipment
Bank of America Corp Sponsorships, 661
Batters Up USA Equipment Grants, 683
Chatham Athletic Fndn Grants, 1060
Covenant to Care for Children Grants, 1389
Easton Fndns Archery Facility Grants, 1644
Finish Line Youth Fndn Founder's Grants, 1812
Finish Line Youth Fndn Legacy Grants, 1814
Kalamazoo Community Fndn Youth Development Grants, 2773
Kroger Grassroots Community Support Grants, 2843
Nike Bowerman Track Renovation Grants, 3440
Scheumann Fndn Grants, 4306
Sioux Falls Area Community Fndn Field-of-Interest and Donor-Advised Grants, 4365
Trinity Trust Summer Youth Mini Grants, 4672
TSYSF Individual Scholarships, 4675
TSYSF Team Grants, 4676
USAA – Ann Hoyt / Jim Easton JOAD Grants, 4734
Van Kampen Boyer Molinari Charitable Grants, 4905
Wild Rivers Community Fndn Summer Youth Mini Grants, 5070

Sports Medicine
Active Awareness Grants, 136
Angels Baseball Fndn Grants, 465

Sports, Amateur
Bank of America Corp Sponsorships, 661
Batters Up USA Equipment Grants, 683
Chatham Athletic Fndn Grants, 1060
Easton Fndns Archery Facility Grants, 1644
Laura L. Adams Fndn Grants, 2865
Telluride Fndn Community Grants, 4573
TSYSF Individual Scholarships, 4675
TSYSF Team Grants, 4676
USAA – Ann Hoyt / Jim Easton JOAD Grants, 4734
WSF Rusty Kanokogi Fund for the Advancement of U.S. Judo Grants, 5118

Statistics
Alfred P. Sloan Selected National Issues Grants, 370
ASA Deming Lecturer Award, 586
Maddie's Fund Community Shelter Data Grants, 2968
Natonal Endowment for the Arts Research Grants: Art Works, 3286

Storytelling
Head Start Replacement Grantee: Colorado, 2275
Head Start Replacement Grantee: Florida, 2276
Head Start Replacement Grantee: West Virginia, 2277
National Endowment for Arts Media Grants, 3264
Nevada Arts Council Folklife Opps Grants, 3310
NHSCA Artist Residencies in Schools Grants, 3423
North Carolina Arts Council Residency Grants, 3481
Ruth Mott Fndn Grants, 4180

Strategic Planning
ALA John Cotton Dana Library Public Relations Award, 292
Blue Cross Blue Shield of Minnesota Fndn - Healthy Equity: Health Impact Assessment Grants, 796
CNCS AmeriCorps State and National Grants, 1182
Community Fndn of Greater Fort Wayne - Collaborative Efforts Grants, 1284
GNOF Organizational Effectiveness Grants and Workshops, 2090
Goldseker Fndn Non-Profit Management Grants, 2103
Guy I. Bromley Grants, 2180
HAF Technical Assistance Grants, 2206
John W. Speas and Effie E. Speas Grants, 2732
Lewis H. Humphreys Charitable Grants, 2889
Louetta M. Cowden Fndn Grants, 2922
Louis and Elizabeth Nave Flarsheim Charitable Fndn Grants, 2924
Meyer Fndn Management Assistance Grants, 3144
Middlesex Savings Charitable Fndn Capacity Building Grants, 3172
Packard Fndn Organizational Effectiveness and Philanthropy Grants, 3730
PCA-PCD Organizational Short-Term Professional Development and Consulting Grants, 3769
PCA Management/Technical Assistance Grants, 3800
Peter and Elizabeth C. Tower Fndn Phase II Technology Init Grants, 3839
Peter and Elizabeth C. Tower Fndn Phase I Technology Init Grants, 3840
Salt River Project Civic Leadership Grants, 4226
Santa Barbara Fndn Monthly Express Grants, 4284
Santa Fe Community Fndn root2fruit Santa Fe, 4289
Santa Fe Community Fndn Special and Urgent Needs Grants, 4292
TAC Arts Access Grant, 4549
TAC Arts Build Communities Grants, 4551
West Virginia Commission on the Arts Long-Range Planning Grants, 5036

Stress
Grand Rapids Area Community Fndn Wyoming Youth Grants, 2117
Peter and Elizabeth C. Tower Fndn Annual Mental Health Grants, 3835
Premera Blue Cross CARES Grants, 3945

Stroke
CNCS Senior Companion Grants, 1187
Henrietta Lange Burk Grants, 2303
Premera Blue Cross CARES Grants, 3945

Student Personnel Services
MFRI Operation Diploma Grants for Higher Ed, 3150
MFRI Operation Diploma Grants for Student Veterans Organizations, 3151
U.S. Department of Educ Innovative Strategies in Community Colleges for Working Adults and Displaced Workers Grants, 4692

Student Support (incl. Dissertation Support)
ALA Excellence in Academic Libraries Award, 276
U.S. Department of Educ Child Care Access Means Parents in School Grants, 4689

Substance Abuse
Altria Group Positive Youth Development Grants, 401
Alvah H. and Wyline P. Chapman Fndn Grants, 402
Austin S. Nelson Fndn Grants, 617
Chicago Community Trust Housing Grants: Preventing and Ending Homelessness, 1090
Cone Health Fndn Grants, 1348
Cralle Fndn Grants, 1394
DPA Promoting Policy Change Advocacy Grants, 1598
Gamble Fndn Grants, 1983
George H.C. Ensworth Grants, 2022
George W. Wells Fndn Grants, 2030
Hearst Fndns Social Service Grants, 2285
Hoblitzelle Fndn Grants, 2341
Initiaive Fndn Inside-Out Connections Grants, 2556
Lydia deForest Charitable Grants, 2946
May and Stanley Smith Charitable Grants, 3069
Memorial Fndn Grants, 3117
MetroWest Health Grants to Reduce Incidence of High Risk Behaviors Among Adolescents, 3136
Pacers Fndn Be Drug-Free Grants, 3720
Paso del Norte Health Fndn Grants, 3743
Patrick and Aimee Butler Family Fndn Community Human Services Grants, 3749
Peter & Elizabeth C. Tower Mental Health Reference and Resource Materials Mini-Grants, 3837
Peter and Elizabeth C. Tower Fndn Phase II Technology Init Grants, 3839
Peter and Elizabeth C. Tower Fndn Phase I Technology Init Grants, 3840
Peter and Elizabeth C. Tower Fndn Substance Abuse Grants, 3842
Piedmont Natural Gas Fndn Health and Human Services Grants, 3885
Reinberger Fndn Grants, 4052
Sierra Health Fndn Responsive Grants, 4353
Sioux Falls Area Community Grants, 4364
Sioux Falls Area Community Fndn Spot Grants, 4366

Steelcase Fndn Grants, 4497
T.L.L. Temple Fndn Grants, 4546
Union Bank, N.A. Fndn Grants, 4709

Suicide
CDC Grants for Violence-Related Injury Prevention Research, 974
SAMHSA Campus Suicide Prevention Grants, 4229

Suicide Prevention
ACF Native American Social and Economic Development Strategies Grants, 123
Florida BRAIVE Fund of Dade Community, 1846
Gulf Coast Community Operating Grants, 2176
Gulf Coast Fndn of Community Grants, 2177
RCF General Community Grants, 4032

Summer Camp
Back Home Again Fndn Grants, 633
Covenant to Care for Children Grants, 1389
Florence Hunt Maxwell Fndn Grants, 1844
Frederick W. Marzahl Grants, 1948
German Protestant Orphan Asylum Fndn Grants, 2044
Gil and Dody Weaver Fndn Grants, 2053
HAF Mada Huggins Caldwell Grants, 2200
Lily Palmer Fry Grants, 2905
Marin Community Fndn Stinson Bolinas Community Grants, 3013
RCF Summertime Kids Grants, 4034
Robert Lee Adams Fndn Grants, 4114
Wild Rivers Community Fndn Summer Youth Mini Grants, 5070

Supportive Housing Programs
ACF Assets for Indep Individual Development Account Grants, 115
Adelaide Benevolent Society Grants, 160
Adelaide Breed Bayrd Fndn Grants, 161
AGMA Relief Grants, 201
Bank of America Charitable Fndn Critical Needs Grants, 656
Bill & Melinda Gates Emergency Response Grants, 766
Blue Cross Blue Shield of Minnesota Fndn - Healthy Children: Growing Up Healthy Grants, 794
Charles H. Farnsworth Grants, 1043
Chicago Community Trust Housing Grants: Advancing Affordable Rental Housing, 1088
Chicago Community Trust Housing Grants: Preventing and Ending Homelessness, 1090
Citizens Savings Fndn Grants, 1141
David Lane Grants for Aged & Indigent Women, 1453
DHHS Community Services Block Grant Training and Technical Assistance Program: Capacity-Building for Ongoing CSBG Programs and Strategic Planning and Coordination Grants, 1529
Dominion Fndn Human Needs Grants, 1572
Edward N. and Della L. Thome Memorial Fndn Direct Services Grants, 1666
Fitzpatrick, Cella, Harper & Scinto Pro Bono, 1836
Fndns of E Chicago Family Support Grants, 1908
GNOF Community Revitalization Grants, 2071
GNOF Maison Hospitaliere Grants, 2086
Goldseker Fndn Human Services Grants, 2102
Hearst Fndns Social Service Grants, 2285
Home Building Industry Disaster Relief Fund, 2348
Lena Benas Grants, 2881
Linden Fndn Grants, 2908
Lydia deForest Charitable Grants, 2946
Madison Community Fndn Grants, 2971
Marin Community Affordable Housing Grants, 3010
Marin Community Successful Aging Grants, 3014
Marion Isabell Coe Grants, 3020
May and Stanley Smith Charitable Grants, 3069
McKnight Fndn Region & Communities Grants, 3086
Mericos Fndn Grants, 3121
Mertz Gilmore Fndn NYC Communities Grants, 3126
Meyer Memorial Trust Responsive Grants, 3148
MGM Resorts Fndn Community Grants, 3153
Mizuho USA Fndn Grants, 3192
Nathaniel and Elizabeth P. Stevens Fndn Grants, 3247
Northland Fndn Grants, 3506
Parker Fndn (California) Grants, 3736
Perkins-Ponder Fndn Grants, 3822
Piedmont Natural Gas Fndn Health and Human Services Grants, 3885
Piper Trust Reglious Organizations Grants, 3905
PNC Ecnomic Development Grants, 3922
Priddy Fndn Grants, 3957
Reinberger Fndn Grants, 4052
Robert R. McCormick Tribune Comm Grants, 4119
Rockwell Fund, Inc. Grants, 4140
SAG Motion Picture Players Welfare Grants, 4209
U.S. Bank Fndn Grants, 4686
Union Bank Corp Sponsorships and Donations, 4708
Union Bank, N.A. Fndn Grants, 4709
USDA Community Facility Grants, 4801
USDA Farm Labor Housing Grants, 4809
USDA Housing Application Packaging Grants, 4815
Whitehorse Fndn Grants, 5058

Surfing
ODKF Athletic Grants, 3638

Surgery
Carlos and Marguerite Mason Grants, 934
Clark Fndn Grants, 1157
Denton A. Cooley Fndn Grants, 1500
E.L. Wiegand Fndn Grants, 1639
Fndn for Health Enhancement Grants, 1894
Pfizer Healthcare Charitable Contributions, 3863
Richmond Eye and Ear Grants, 4092

Surrogate Parenting
Brookdale Fndn Relatives as Parents Grants, 846

Surveying and Mapping
CDECD Historic Preservation Survey and Planning Grants, 982

Sustainable Development
ALA ALSC Distinguished Service Award, 223
ALA Highsmith Library Innovation Award, 285
ALA Loleta D. Fyan Grant, 295
ALA President's Award for Advocacy, 310
Alaska Conservation Operating Grants, 323
American Jewish World Service Grants, 441
Annie's Cases for Causes Product Donations, 479
Appalachian Regional Commission Transportation and Highways Grants, 512
Bill and Melinda Gates Fndn Agricultural Development Grants, 765
Boeing Company Contributions Grants, 809
BP Conservation Programme Future Conservationist Awards, 826
Bush Fndn Ecological Health Grants, 874
Charlotte County (FL) Community Fndn Grants, 1056
Clarence E. Heller Charitable Grants, 1150
CLIF Bar Family Fndn Grants, 1173
Community Fndn in Jacksonville Art Ventures Small Organizations Professional Assistance Grants, 1262
Community Fndn of Abilene Community Grants, 1264
Conservation, Food, and Health Fndn Grants for Developing Countries, 1359
DB Americas Fndn Grants, 1466
Doris Duke Charitable Fndn Arts Grants, 1584
Draper Richards Kaplan Fndn Grants, 1603
ESRI Conservation Grants, 1751
GNOF Coastal 5 + 1 Grants, 2070
GNOF Community Revitalization Grants, 2071
GNOF Environmental Grants, 2073
HAF Co-op Community Grants, 2192
HAF Community Grants, 2193
Honor the Earth Grants, 2361
IIE David L. Boren Fellowships, 2454
IIE Japan-U.S. Teacher Exchange for Educ for Sustainable Development, 2457
Jenifer Altman Fndn Grants, 2662
Jessie Smith Noyes Fndn Grants, 2672
John D. and Catherine T. MacArthur Fndn Global Challenges Grants, 2690
Kalamazoo Community Fndn Economic and Community Development Grants, 2765
KEEN Effect Grants, 2795
MacArthur Fndn Conservation and Sustainable Development Grants, 2963
Mary E. Ober Fndn Grants, 3039
McCune Charitable Fndn Grants, 3077
McGraw-Hill Companies Community Grants, 3081
Michael Reese Health Trust Core Grants, 3159
NASE Succeed Scholarships, 3243
National Endowment for Arts Our Town Grants, 3257
National Endowment for the Arts - Regional Partnership Agreement Grants, 3258
National Endowment for Arts Commun Grants, 3260
National Endowment for the Arts Dance Grants: Art Works, 3262
National Endowment for Arts Agencies Grants, 3263
National Endowment for Arts Theater Grants, 3269
National Geographic All Roads Seed Grants, 3272
National Geographic Conservation Grants, 3273
National Geographic Genographic Legacy Grants, 3274
National Geographic Young Explorers Grants, 3275
Nellie Mae Educ Fndn District-Level Grants, 3297
Nellie Mae Educ Fndn State Level Systems Change Grants, 3299
PepsiCo Fndn Grants, 3819
Priddy Fndn Organizational Development Grants, 3956
Pulte Homes Corp Contributions, 3989
Rockefeller Brothers Democratic Practice Grants, 4131
Rockefeller Brothers Peace and Security Grants, 4133
Rockefeller Brothers Pivotal Places Grants: Serbia, Montenegro, and Kosova, 4135
Rockefeller Brothers Sustainable Devel Grants, 4136
Santa Barbara Strategy Grants Capital Support, 4285
Shaw's Supermarkets Donations, 4342
Skoll Fndn Awards for Social Entrepreneurship, 4383
Threshold Fndn Justice and Democracy Grants, 4626
Threshold Fndn Sustainable Planet Grants, 4627
Threshold Fndn Thriving Resilient Communities Funding Circle, 4628
United Technologies Corp Grants, 4725
Wallace Global Grants, 4977

Swimming
ODKF Athletic Grants, 3638

Symposiums
National Endowment for Arts Museum Grants, 3265
NYSCA Presenting: Services to the Field Grants, 3612

Systems Engineering
RISCA Design Innovation Grant, 4097

Taxes and Taxation
Fndn for the Mid South Wealth Building Grants, 1900
State Strategies Grants, 4494

Teacher Attitudes
Elizabeth Carse Fndn Grants, 1681
Meyer Fndn Educ Grants, 3142

Teacher Certification
Chicago Community Trust Educ Grants, 1085
DaimlerChrysler Corp Grants, 1432
Nellie Mae Educ Fndn State Level Systems Change Grants, 3299
Piper Trust Reglious Organizations Grants, 3905

Teacher Education
AAF Accent on Architecture Community Grants, 58
Abell-Hanger Fndn Grants, 91
Agere Corp and Community Involvement Grants, 199
AMD Corp Contributions Grants, 416
ATA Local Community Relations Grants, 600
Baxter Int'l Corp Giving Grants, 689
Benton County Fndn Grants, 731
Booth Ferris Fndn Grants, 816
Carnegie Corp of New York Grants, 940
ChevronTexaco Contributions Program, 1078
Chicago Community Trust Educ Grants, 1085

SUBJECT INDEX

Citigroup Fndn Grants, 1139
Clarence E. Heller Charitable Fndn Grants, 1150
Claude Worthington Benedum Fndn Grants, 1161
DB Americas Fndn Grants, 1466
Elizabeth Carse Fndn Grants, 1681
EPA Environmental Educ Grants, 1729
Fndn for the Mid South Educ Grants, 1898
Fritz B. Burns Fndn Grants, 1965
GenCorp Fndn Grants, 1998
Golden LEAF Fndn Grants, 2097
Grand Victoria Fndn Illinois Core Grants, 2126
Guy I. Bromley Grants, 2180
Hatton W. Sumners Fndn for the Study and Teaching of Self Government Grants, 2257
Houston Endowment Grants, 2373
IIE Japan-U.S. Teacher Exchange for Educ for Sustainable Development, 2457
IIE Toyota Int'l Teacher Professional Development Grants, 2461
Jewish Women's Fndn of New York Grants, 2677
Johnson & Johnson Corp Contributions Grants, 2718
John W. Speas and Effie E. Speas Grants, 2732
Joseph H. and Florence A. Roblee Fndn Grants, 2736
Kawabe Grants, 2794
Kentucky Arts Council Teaching Together Grant, 2811
Leave No Trace Master Educator Scholarships, 2870
Lewis H. Humphreys Charitable Grants, 2889
Lied Fndn Grants, 2900
Louetta M. Cowden Fndn Grants, 2922
Louis and Elizabeth Nave Flarsheim Charitable Fndn Grants, 2924
Meadows Fndn Grants, 3104
Micron Technology Fndn Community Grants, 3161
NYSCA Arts Educ: Community-based Learning Grants, 3577
NYSCA Arts Educ: K-12 In-School Grants, 3580
NYSCA Arts Education: Local Capacity Building Grants, 3581
NYSCA Arts Educ: Services to the Field Grants, 3582
Piper Trust Reglious Organizations Grants, 3905
Procter and Gamble Grants, 3967
SAS Institute Community Relations Donations, 4300
Seagate Tech Corp Capacity to Care Grants, 4317
Stuart Fndn Grants, 4516
Subaru of America Fndn Grants, 4518
Texas Commission on Arts Educ Grants, 4579
Union County Community Fndn Grants, 4711
USAID Scholarships for Youth and Teachers, 4780
Virginia Fndn for Humanities Discr Grants, 4946
Virginia Fndn for the Humanities Open Grants, 4947
Wallace Fndn Grants, 4976

Teacher Education, Inservice
Arizona Commission on the Arts Educ Grants, 536
Arizona Comm on the Arts Folklorist Residencies, 537
Baxter Int'l Corp Giving Grants, 689
BBVA Compass Fndn Charitable Grants, 703
Benton County Fndn Grants, 731
Caroline Lawson Ivey Memorial Fndn Grants, 941
Charles Hayden Fndn Grants, 1048
Coca-Cola Fndn Grants, 1195
District of Columbia Commission on the Arts-Arts Educ Teacher Mini-Grants, 1549
eBay Fndn Community Grants, 1648
EDS Technology Grants, 1662
Elizabeth Carse Fndn Grants, 1681
Fleishhacker Fndn Educ Grants, 1838
Flinn Fndn Grants, 1842
Fndn for the Mid South Educ Grants, 1898
Guy I. Bromley Grants, 2180
John W. Speas and Effie E. Speas Grants, 2732
Lafayette - West Lafayette Convention and Visitors Bureau Tourist Promotion Grants, 2849
Lewis H. Humphreys Charitable Grants, 2889
Louetta M. Cowden Fndn Grants, 2922
Louis and Elizabeth Nave Flarsheim Charitable Fndn Grants, 2924
Meyer Fndn Educ Grants, 3142
Micron Technology Fndn Community Grants, 3161
PCA Arts in Educ Residencies, 3772

Public Educ Power Grants, 3981
SVP Early Childhood Development and Parenting Grants, 4538
TAC Arts Educ Mini Grants, 4553
Verizon Fndn Grants, 4911
West Virginia Commission on the Arts Long-Term Artist Residencies, 5037

Teacher Training
Baxter Int'l Corp Giving Grants, 689
BBVA Compass Fndn Charitable Grants, 703
Chicago Community Trust Educ Grants, 1085
Chiron Fndn Community Grants, 1111
Elizabeth Carse Fndn Grants, 1681
George J. and Effie L. Seay Fndn Grants, 2024
Guy I. Bromley Grants, 2180
IIE Japan-U.S. Teacher Exchange for Educ for Sustainable Development, 2457
IIE Toyota Int'l Teacher Professional Development Grants, 2461
John W. Speas and Effie E. Speas Grants, 2732
Kawabe Grants, 2794
Kentucky Arts Council Teaching Together Grant, 2811
Louetta M. Cowden Fndn Grants, 2922
Louis and Elizabeth Nave Flarsheim Charitable Fndn Grants, 2924
Meyer Fndn Educ Grants, 3142
NAA Fndn Teacher Fellowships, 3234
Nellie Mae Educ Fndn District-Level Grants, 3297
Piedmont Natural Gas Fndn Environmental Stewardship and Energy Sustainability Grant, 3884
Piper Trust Reglious Organizations Grants, 3905
Public Educ Power Grants, 3981
Robert R. McCormick Tribune Civics Grants, 4118
Sidgmore Family Fndn Grants, 4348
TAC Arts Educ Mini Grants, 4553
USAID Scholarships for Youth and Teachers, 4780
Virginia Fndn for Humanities Discr Grants, 4946
Virginia Fndn for the Humanities Open Grants, 4947
W.H. and Mary Ellen Cobb Charitable Grants, 4959

Technological Change
Best Buy Children's Fndn National Grants, 752
Best Buy Children's Fndn Twin Cities Minnesota Capital Grants, 753
Bill and Melinda Gates Fndn Agricultural Development Grants, 765
Bill and Melinda Gates Fndn Library Grants, 768
USAID Grants for Building Disaster-Resilient Communities in Southern Africa, 4755

Technology
A.J. Fletcher Fndn Grants, 41
ADC Fndn Technology Access Grants, 158
Adobe Youth Voices Grants, 170
ALA Info Today Library of the Future Award, 287
Alfred P. Sloan Fndn Civic Inits Grants, 368
American Honda Fndn Grants, 439
Appalachian Regional Commission Telecommunications Grants, 510
Applied Biosystems Grants, 514
ArvinMeritor Grants, 585
AT&T Fndn Civic and Comm Service Grants, 599
Barberton Community Fndn Grants, 666
Best Buy Children's Fndn @15 Community Grants, 749
Best Buy Children's Fndn @15 Teach Awards, 751
Best Buy Children's Fndn National Grants, 752
Best Buy Children's Fndn Twin Cities Minnesota Capital Grants, 753
Bill and Melinda Gates Fndn Financial Services for the Poor Grants, 767
Bill and Melinda Gates Fndn Library Grants, 768
Cabot Corp Fndn Grants, 887
Cause Populi Worthy Cause Grants, 958
Cleveland-Cliffs Fndn Grants, 1165
Community Fndn of Broward Grants, 1275
Community Fndn of St. Joseph County ArtsEverywhere Grants, 1313
Community Technology Fndn of California Building Communities Through Technology Grants, 1336

Crail-Johnson Fndn Grants, 1393
Dolan Fndn Grants, 1563
Dwight Stuart Youth Capacity-Building Grants, 1627
EDS Fndn Grants, 1661
EQT Fndn Educ Grants, 1745
ESRI Conservation Grants, 1751
Family Lit and Hawaii Pizza Hut Lit Fund, 1785
FirstEnergy Fndn Math, Science, and Technology Educ Grants, 1820
Ford Motor Company Grants, 1885
FRED Ed Ethyl Grants, 1945
FRED Technology Grants for Rural Schools, 1951
Frist Fndn Grants, 1964
GNOF Coastal 5 + 1 Grants, 2070
GNOF Gulf Coast Oil Spill Grants, 2077
GNOF New Orleans Works Grants, 2088
Go Daddy Cares Charitable Contributions, 2094
Greater Worcester Community Mini-Grants, 2142
GTECH After School Advantage Grants, 2170
H.B. Fuller Company Fndn Grants, 2183
Hartford Fndn Nonprofit Support Grants, 2252
Honeywell Corp Leadership Challenge Academy, 2359
IDPH Hosptial Capital Investment Grants, 2441
IIE Japan-U.S. Teacher Exchange for Educ for Sustainable Development, 2457
Illinois DCEO Eliminate Dig Divide Grants, 2489
Illinois DCEO Emerging Technological Enterprises Grants, 2490
IMLS 21st Century Museum Pro Grants, 2512
IMLS American Heritage Preservation Grants, 2513
IMLS National Leadership Grants, 2515
IMLS Native Am Library Services Basic Grants, 2517
IMLS Native American Library Services Enhancement Grants, 2518
Indiana 21st Century Research and Technology Fund Awards, 2528
Indiana SBIR/STTR Commercialization Enhancement Program, 2548
Indiana Space Grant Consortium Grants for Informal Educ Partnerships, 2549
Indiana Space Grant Consortium Workforce Development Grants, 2550
Indiana Waste Tire Grants, 2551
Intel Community Grants, 2562
Intel Finance Internships, 2563
Intel Int'l Community Grants, 2564
Jessie Ball Dupont Grants, 2671
John R. Oishei Fndn Grants, 2709
Lindbergh Grants, 2907
Lumity Technology Leadership Award, 2940
Marion I. and Henry J. Knott Fndn Discretionary Grants, 3018
Marion I. and Henry J. Knott Standard Grants, 3019
Meadows Fndn Grants, 3104
Mericos Fndn Grants, 3121
Mertz Gilmore Climate Change Grants, 3125
Meyer Fndn Economic Security Grants, 3141
Micron Technology Fndn Community Grants, 3161
Microsoft Authorized Refurbisher Donations, 3162
Microsoft Comm Affairs Puget Sound Grants, 3163
Microsoft Software Donation Grants, 3164
Microsoft Unlimited Potential (UP) - Community Technology Skills Grants, 3165
Miguel Aleman Fndn Grants, 3175
Monfort Family Fndn Grants, 3203
NEH Family and Youth Programs in American History Grants, 3291
NEH Preservation Assistance Grants for Smaller Institutions, 3293
North Carolina Arts Council Arts in Educ Artist Residencies Grants, 3468
North Carolina Arts Council Ed Grants, 3469
NSF Partnership for Advancing Technologies in Housing Grants, 3529
NYSCA Literature: Services to the Field Grants, 3601
PCA Arts Organizations and Arts Programs Grants for Arts Educ Organizations, 3776
PCA Entry Track Arts Organizations and Program Grants for Arts Educ Organizations, 3788
Pittsburgh Fndn Community Grants, 3910

1000 / Technology

Praxair Fndn Grants, 3944
Princeton Area Community Fndn Fund for Women and Girls Grants, 3962
Public Safety Fndn of America Grants, 3983
Puerto Rico Community Fndn Grants, 3986
Rajiv Gandhi Fndn Grants, 4011
RAND Corp Graduate Summer Associateships, 4018
RealNetworks Fndn Grants, 4037
Regional Fund for Digital Innovation in Latin America and the Caribbean Grants, 4049
Rockefeller Fndn Grants, 4138
Rockwell Int'l Corp Grants, 4141
Roney-Fitzpatrick Fndn Grants, 4150
San Diego Women's Fndn Grants, 4252
SAS Institute Community Relations Donations, 4300
Schramm Fndn Grants, 4310
Seaver Institute Grants, 4331
Southern Minnesota Youth Explorer Grants, 4436
Sprint Fndn Grants, 4463
State Justice Institute Curriculum Adaptation and Training Grants, 4488
State Justice Institute Partner Grants, 4489
State Justice Institute Project Grants, 4490
State Justice Institute Strategic Init Grants, 4492
State Justice Institute Tech Assistance Grants, 4493
Stuart Fndn Grants, 4516
TAC Arts Grants, 4554
TAC Rural Arts Project Support Grants, 4555
TechFndn TechGrants, 4570
Tech Enhancement Certification for Hoosiers, 4571
USDA Rural Business Opportunity Grants, 4824
USDC Low-Power Television and Translator Upgrade Grants, 4852
Verizon Fndn Connecticut Grants, 4908
Verizon Fndn Grants, 4911
Verizon Fndn Lit Grants, 4915
Verizon Fndn Maine Grants, 4916
Verizon Fndn Maryland Grants, 4917
Verizon Fndn New York Grants, 4919
Verizon Fndn NE Region Grants, 4920
Verizon Fndn Pennsylvania Grants, 4921
Verizon Fndn South Carolina Lit & Internet Safety Grants, 4922
Verizon Fndn SE Region Grants, 4923
Verizon Fndn Vermont Grants, 4924
Verizon Fndn Virginia Grants, 4925
Verizon Fndn West Virginia Grants, 4926
Waitt Family Fndn Grants, 4973
Xerox Fndn Grants, 5122

Technology Education
AAUW Community Action Grants, 75
AAUW Int'l Project Grants, 76
ADC Fndn Technology Access Grants, 158
Adobe Youth Voices Grants, 170
AEP Corp Giving Grants, 180
ALA Polaris Innovation in Tech John Iliff Award, 309
Alfred P. Sloan Fndn Civic Inits Grants, 368
American Council of the Blind Scholarships, 427
American Electric Power Grants, 428
Appalachian Regional Commission Telecommunications Grants, 510
ArvinMeritor Grants, 585
Avista Fndn Grants, 624
Best Buy Children's Fndn @15 Community Grants, 749
Best Buy Children's Fndn @15 Teach Awards, 751
Best Buy Children's Fndn National Grants, 752
Best Buy Children's Fndn Twin Cities Minnesota Capital Grants, 753
Bill and Melinda Gates Fndn Agricultural Development Grants, 765
Bill and Melinda Gates Fndn Library Grants, 768
Boeing Company Contributions Grants, 809
Buhl Fndn - Frick Ed Fund, 859
CenterPointEnergy Minnegasco Grants, 993
Charles Lafitte Fndn Grants, 1049
Chicago Board of Trade Fndn Grants, 1079
Citigroup Fndn Grants, 1139
Community Technology Fndn of California Building Communities Through Technology Grants, 1336

Eaton Charitable Grants, 1647
EDS Technology Grants, 1662
Ewing Marion Kauffman Fndn Grants and Inits, 1777
Illinois DCEO Eliminate Dig Divide Grants, 2489
Indiana Space Grant Consortium Grants for Informal Educ Partnerships, 2549
Indiana Space Grant Consortium Workforce Development Grants, 2550
Intel Finance Internships, 2563
Kenny's Kids Grants, 2803
Marie C. and Joseph C. Wilson Rochester Grants, 3006
Meyer Fndn Economic Security Grants, 3141
Micron Technology Fndn Community Grants, 3161
Olin Corp Charitable Grants, 3669
Oracle Corp Contributions Grants, 3686
Procter and Gamble Grants, 3967
PSEG Environmental Educ Grants, 3980
Qualcomm Grants, 3993
RGK Fndn Grants, 4072
Roney-Fitzpatrick Fndn Grants, 4150
Roy and Christine Sturgis Charitable Grants, 4166
SAS Institute Community Relations Donations, 4300
Sony Corp of America Corp Philanthropy Grants, 4405
Southern Minnesota Youth Explorer Grants, 4436
Sun Academic Excellence Grants, 4525
Tech Enhancement Certification for Hoosiers, 4571
United Technologies Corp Grants, 4725
Verizon Fndn Maryland Grants, 4917
Verizon Fndn New York Grants, 4919
Verizon Fndn NE Region Grants, 4920
Verizon Fndn Pennsylvania Grants, 4921
Verizon Fndn SE Region Grants, 4923
Verizon Fndn Vermont Grants, 4924
Verizon Fndn Virginia Grants, 4925
Verizon Fndn West Virginia Grants, 4926
Washington Gas Charitable Contributions, 5000
Wayne and Gladys Valley Fndn Grants, 5003
Whirlpool Fndn Grants, 5056
Xerox Fndn Grants, 5122

Technology Education Translation
Bill and Melinda Gates Fndn Library Grants, 768
NEH Family and Youth Programs in American History Grants, 3291

Technology Planning/Policy
ALFJ Astraea U.S. and Int'l Movement Fund, 361
Bill and Melinda Gates Fndn Financial Services for the Poor Grants, 767
Bill and Melinda Gates Fndn Library Grants, 768
Cause Populi Worthy Cause Grants, 958
Community Fndn of Collier County Capacity Building Grants, 1277
Dyson Fndn Management Assistance Program Mini-Grants, 1632
Dyson Fndn Nonprofit Strategic Restructuring Init Grants, 1637
Gill Fndn - Gay and Lesbian Grants, 2054
Illinois DCEO Eliminate Dig Divide Grants, 2489
Illinois DCEO Emerging Technological Enterprises Grants, 2490
Nonprofit Management Grants, 3458
Peter and Elizabeth C. Tower Fndn Phase II Technology Init Grants, 3839
Peter and Elizabeth C. Tower Fndn Phase I Technology Init Grants, 3840

Technology Transfer
Bill and Melinda Gates Fndn Library Grants, 768
Boeing Company Contributions Grants, 809
Colorado Bioscience Discovery Evaluation Grants, 1211
Ian Hague Perl 6 Development Grants, 2421
Illinois DCEO Coal Development Grants, 2486
Illinois DCEO Eliminate Dig Divide Grants, 2489
Illinois DCEO Emerging Technological Enterprises Grants, 2490
Indiana 21st Century Research and Technology Fund Awards, 2528
Indiana SBIR/STTR Commercialization Enhancement Program, 2548

Indiana Waste Tire Grants, 2551
NSF CISE Computing Infrastructure Grants, 3526
Perl Fndn Grants, 3825
U.S. Department of Educ Rehabilitation Engineering Research Centers Grants, 4698
USAID Unsolicited Proposal Grants, 4786
US CRDF Science & Tech Entrepreneurship Business Partnership Grants in Armenia, 4795
US CRDF STEP Business Partnership Grant Competition Ukraine, 4796

Technology, Hardware and Software
Albert and Bessie Mae Kronkosky Charitable Fndn Grants, 339
Alice Tweed Tuohy Fndn Grants, 372
Armstrong McDonald Fndn Grants, 565
Atherton Family Fndn Grants, 604
Bill and Melinda Gates Fndn Library Grants, 768
Central Carolina Community Fndn Community Impact Grants, 994
Central New York Community Fndn Grants, 996
Chatlos Fndn Grants, 1061
Chicago Community Poverty Alleviation Grants, 1091
Citigroup Fndn Grants, 1139
DaimlerChrysler Corp Grants, 1432
Dave Thomas Fndn for Adoption Grants, 1449
Dow Chemical Company Grants, 1596
Dwight Stuart Youth Capacity-Building Grants, 1627
E.L. Wiegand Fndn Grants, 1639
EDS Technology Grants, 1662
Grand Haven Area Community Fndn Grants, 2113
GTECH After School Advantage Grants, 2170
Illinois DCEO Eliminate Dig Divide Grants, 2489
Illinois DCEO Emerging Technological Enterprises Grants, 2490
Microsoft Comm Affairs Puget Sound Grants, 3163
Nonprofit Management Grants, 3458
NYSCA Literature: Services to the Field Grants, 3601
Oklahoma City Community Programs & Grants, 3666
Pasadena Fndn Average Grants, 3741
Paul E. and Klare N. Reinhold Fndn Grants, 3758
Peter and Elizabeth C. Tower Fndn Phase II Technology Init Grants, 3839
Peter and Elizabeth C. Tower Fndn Phase I Technology Init Grants, 3840
Puerto Rico Community Fndn Grants, 3986
Robert G. Cabell III and Maude Morgan Cabell Fndn Grants, 4113
TechFndn TechGrants, 4570
Weingart Fndn Grants, 5018

Teen Pregnancy
Adams Family Fndn of Tennessee Grants, 152
African American Fund of New Jersey Grants, 192
Aid for Starving Children African American Indep Single Mother's Grants, 210
Burning Fndn Grants, 867
Caterpillar Fndn Grants, 954
Community Fndn of Western N Carolina Grants, 1327
Cone Health Fndn Grants, 1348
Delaware Community Next Generation Grants, 1485
DHHS Adolescent Family Life Demo Projects, 1524
DHHS Welfare Reform Research, Evaluations, and National Studies Grants, 1540
Fisa Fndn Grants, 1826
Grand Rapids Area Community Fndn Wyoming Youth Grants, 2117
Grand Rapids Community Ionia Youth Grants, 2120
Grand Rapids Comm SE Ottawa Youth Grants, 2123
Grand Rapids Community Sparta Youth Grants, 2125
Health Fndn of Greater Indianapolis Grants, 2282
Helen V. Brach Fndn Grants, 2300
Henry and Ruth Blaustein Rosenberg Grants, 2306
Hoffberger Fndn Grants, 2342
Joseph Drown Fndn Grants, 2735
Mary Black Early Childhood Devel Grants, 3033
MetroWest Health Grants to Reduce Incidence of High Risk Behaviors Among Adolescents, 3136
Northern Trust Company Corp Giving Program, 3504
OneFamily Fndn Grants, 3673

SUBJECT INDEX

Philadelphia Organizational Effectiveness Grants, 3872
Prince Charitable Trusts Chicago Grants, 3959
Puerto Rico Community Fndn Grants, 3986
Thompson Charitable Fndn Grants, 4622

Telecommunications
ADC Fndn Technology Access Grants, 158
ADEC Agricultural Telecommunications Grants, 159
ALA Information Technology Pathfinder Award, 286
Appalachian Regional Commission Telecommunications Grants, 510
Dow Chemical Company Grants, 1596
FRED Technology Grants for Rural Schools, 1951
John W. Speas and Effie E. Speas Grants, 2732
USDA Distance Learning and Telemed Grants, 4806
USDA Rural Business Opportunity Grants, 4824
USDC Technology Opportunities Grants, 4860

Telemedicine
Appalachian Regional Commission Telecommunications Grants, 510
USDA Distance Learning and Telemed Grants, 4806

Television
1st Source Fndn Grants, 3
H. Reimers Bechtel Charitable Grants, 2186
National Endowment for Arts Media Grants, 3264
NEH Family and Youth Programs in American History Grants, 3291
Park Fndn Grants, 3739
PCA Arts Organizations and Arts Programs Grants for Film and Electronic Media, 3780
PCA Entry Track Arts Organizations and Program Grants for Film and Electronic Media, 3792
Righteous Persons Fndn Grants, 4093
Time Warner Youth Media & Creative Grants, 4636
USDA Public TV Digital Transition Grants, 4822
USDC Low-Power Television and Translator Upgrade Grants, 4852

Television, Cable
Cable Positive's Tony Cox Community Grants, 886

Television, Children's
Farmers Insurance Corp Giving Grants, 1791
Union Pacific Fndn Community and Civic Grants, 4714

Television, Public
Air Products and Chemicals Grants, 216
ConocoPhillips Fndn Grants, 1354
Corning Fndn Cultural Grants, 1376
Doree Taylor Charitable Fndn, 1580
Farmers Insurance Corp Giving Grants, 1791
George W. Codrington Charitable Fndn Grants, 2029
Hawaiian Electric Industries Charitable Grants, 2259
James J. McCann Charitable Trust and McCann Fndn, Inc Grants, 2631
John Ben Snow Grants, 2687
North Carolina Arts Council Visual Arts Program Support Grants, 3484
Onan Family Fndn Grants, 3672
PMI Fndn Grants, 3918
Robert Sterling Clark Arts and Culture Grants, 4122
TE Fndn Grants, 4572
Town Creek Fndn Grants, 4650
Union Pacific Fndn Community and Civic Grants, 4714
USDA Public TV Digital Transition Grants, 4822
USDC Low-Power Television and Translator Upgrade Grants, 4852

Tennis
USTA CTA and NJTL Community Tennis Development Workshop Scholarships, 4873
USTA Multicultural Excellence Grants, 4876
USTA Multicultural Individual Player Grant for National Competition and Training, 4877
USTA NJTL Tennis and Leadership Camp Scholarships, 4879
USTA Okechi Womeodu Scholar Athlete Grants, 4880
USTA Pro Circuit Comm Involvement Day Grants, 4882

USTA Recreational Tennis Grants, 4884
USTA Serves College Educ Scholarships, 4885
USTA Serves College Textbook Scholarships, 4886
USTA Serves Dwight Mosley Scholarships, 4888
USTA Serves Eve Kraft Scholarships, 4889
USTA Serves Player Incentive Awards, 4891
USTA Tennis Block Party Grants, 4892

Terminally Ill
Cralle Fndn Grants, 1394
Florence Hunt Maxwell Fndn Grants, 1844
Herbert A. and Adrian W. Woods Fndn Grants, 2313
May and Stanley Smith Charitable Grants, 3069

Terrorism
Alfred P. Sloan Selected National Issues Grants, 370
DHS ARRA Port Security Grants, 1543
DHS ARRA Transit Security Grants, 1544
DHS FY 2009 Transit Security Grants, 1545
Harry Kramer Grants, 2242
Public Safety Fndn of America Grants, 3983
TSA Advanced Surveillance Grants, 4674

Textile/Weaving Arts
Florida Div of Cultural Affairs Presenter Grants, 1860
HAF Arts and Culture: Project Grants to Artists, 2191

Theater
Adams Fndn Grants, 153
Adams Fndn Grants, 155
Alabama State Council on the Arts Community Arts Collaborative Ventures Grants, 236
Alabama State Council on the Arts Community Arts Operating Support Grants, 237
Alabama State Council on the Arts Community Arts Presenting Grants, 238
Alabama State Council on the Arts Community Arts Program Development Grants, 239
Alabama State Council on the Arts Community Planning & Design Grants, 241
Alabama State Council on the Arts in Educ Partnership Grants, 242
Alabama State Council on the Arts Multi-Discipline and Festival Grants, 243
Altria Group Arts and Culture Grants, 399
American Express Charitable Grants, 429
Ann L. & Carol Green Rhodes Charitable Grants, 483
Arkansas Arts Council AIE After School/Summer Residency Grants, 551
Arkansas Arts Council AIE In-School Residency, 553
City of Oakland Cultural Arts Dept Grants, 1142
Colonel Stanley R. McNeil Fndn Grants, 1210
Conseil des arts de Montreal Touring Grants, 1358
Florida Div of Cultural Affairs Community Theatre Grants, 1847
Florida Div of Cultural Affairs General Program Support Grants, 1854
Florida Div of Cultural Affairs Multidisciplinary Grants, 1857
Florida Div of Cultural Affairs Professional Theatre Grants, 1861
Frank Loomis Palmer Grants, 1931
Horace Moses Charitable Grants, 2363
Idaho Power Company Corp Contributions, 2433
Leon and Thea Koerner Fndn Grants, 2883
MacArthur Fndn Chicago Arts and Culture General Operations Grants, 2961
Minnesota State Arts Board Cultural Community Partnership Grants, 3188
National Endowment for the Arts Presenting Grants: Art Works, 3268
National Endowment for Arts Theater Grants, 3269
NJSCA Arts Project Support, 3446
NJSCA General Program Support Grants, 3449
NYSCA Architecture, Planning, and Design: Capital Fixtures and Equipment Purchase Grants, 3570
NYSCA Special Arts Services: Professional Performances Grants, 3617
NYSCA Theatre General Program Support, 3624
NYSCA Theatre Pro Performances Grants, 3625

Ontario Arts Council Integrated Arts Grants, 3678
Parker Fndn (California) Grants, 3736
Paul and Edith Babson Fndn Grants, 3755
Richard H. Driehaus Fndn Small Theater and Dance Grants, 4086
Robert R. Meyer Fndn Grants, 4121
Ruth Mott Fndn Grants, 4180
Santa Barbara Fndn Towbes Fund for the Performing Arts Grants, 4288
Sioux Falls Area Community Fndn Field-of-Interest and Donor-Advised Grants, 4365
Sioux Falls Area Community Fndn Spot Grants, 4366
Union Square Arts Award, 4716
West Virginia Commission on the Arts Performing Arts Grants, 5043
Whitney Fndn Grants, 5061

Theater/Film Criticism
Florida Div of Cultural Affairs Community Theatre Grants, 1847
Florida Div of Cultural Affairs Professional Theatre Grants, 1861
Joyce Awards, 2746
Paul Green Fndn Playwrights Fellowship, 3762
Richard H. Driehaus Fndn Grants, 4084
San Francisco Fndn Fund For Artists Award For Playwrights and Theatre Ensembles, 4272

Theology
AmerUs Group Charitable Fndn, 455
Appalachian Ministries Grants, 499
Atherton Family Fndn Grants, 604
Beerman Fndn Grants, 717
Bishop Robert Paddock Grants, 775
Boettcher Fndn Grants, 810
Booth-Bricker Grants, 815
Booth Ferris Fndn Grants, 816
CE and S Fndn Grants, 985
E. Rhodes and Leona B. Carpenter Fndn Grants, 1640
FirstEnergy Fndn Community Grants, 1819
Jewish Funds for Justice Grants, 2676
John I. Smith Charities Grants, 2700
Mary's Pence Ministry Grants, 3029
Mary's Pence Study Grants, 3030
Rainbow Grants, 4009
Sister Grants for Women's Organizations, 4371

Third World Nations
Carl R. Hendrickson Family Fndn Grants, 935
Conservation, Food, and Health Fndn Grants for Developing Countries, 1359
Dorothea Haus Ross Fndn Grants, 1587
HAF Hansen Family Trust Christian Endowment Grants, 2197
PepsiCo Fndn Grants, 3819

Tobacco
Altria Group Positive Youth Development Grants, 401
American Legacy Fndn Small Innovative Grants, 442
Fuller Fndn Grants, 1974
Health Fndn of Greater Indianapolis Grants, 2282
Paso del Norte Health Fndn Grants, 3743
TRDRP Participatory Research Awards, 4663
TRDRP Research Grants, 4664
U.S. Department of Ed Programs for Hawaiians, 4696

Tolerance
Allstate Fndn Tolerance, Inclusion, and Diversity Grants, 391
Elizabeth Morse Genius Charitable Grants, 1682
Pacers Fndn Be Tolerant Grants, 3723
Playboy Fndn Freedom of Expression Award, 3912

Tolerance, Ethnic
Allstate Fndn Tolerance, Inclusion, and Diversity Grants, 391
Charles Parker Trust for Public Music Grants, 1053
Elizabeth Morse Genius Charitable Grants, 1682
Pacers Fndn Be Tolerant Grants, 3723
Skoll Fndn Awards for Social Entrepreneurship, 4383

1002 / Tolerance, Religious

Tolerance, Religious
Alfred and Tillie Shemanski Testamentary Grants, 363
Allstate Fndn Tolerance, Inclusion, and Diversity Grants, 391
Elizabeth Morse Genius Charitable Grants, 1682
Kawabe Grants, 2794
Laura Jane Musser Intercultural Harmony Grants, 2862
Marin Community Fndn Social Justice and Interfaith Understanding Grants, 3012
Pacers Fndn Be Tolerant Grants, 3723
Playboy Fndn Freedom of Expression Award, 3912
Skoll Fndn Awards for Social Entrepreneurship, 4383

Touring Arts Programs
APAP Cultural Exchange Grants, 492
EQT Fndn Art and Culture Grants, 1743
Georgia Council for the Arts Partner Grants for Organizations, 2035
Illinois Arts Council Artstour Grants, 2465
Illinois Arts Council Presenters Dev Grants, 2476
Japan Fndn Los Angeles Mini-Grants for Japanese Arts & Culture, 2651
Japan Fndn New York Small Grants for Arts and Culture, 2652
Kansas Arts Commission Arts on Tour Grants, 2780
Kansas Arts Commission Operational Support for Arts and Cultural Organizations, 2781
Mid Atlantic Arts Fndn American Masterpieces Grants, 3169
Mid Atlantic Arts Fndn ArtsConnect Grants, 3170
Mid Atlantic Arts Fndn Folk Arts Outreach Project Grants, 3171
National Endowment for Arts Commun Grants, 3260
National Endowment for the Arts Dance Grants: Art Works, 3262
National Endowment for Arts Music Grants, 3266
National Endowment for Arts Opera Grants, 3267
National Endowment for the Arts Presenting Grants: Art Works, 3268
National Endowment for Arts Theater Grants, 3269
NHSCA General Project Grants, 3427
NYSCA Arts Educ: Services to the Field Grants, 3582
NYSCA Dance: Long-Term Residency in New York State Grants, 3586
NYSCA Electronic Media and Film: Film Festivals Grants, 3588
NYSCA Electronic Media and Film: General Operating Support, 3590
NYSCA Electronic Media and Film: Screenings Grants, 3592
NYSCA Literature: Public Programs, 3600
NYSCA Presenting: General Operating Support, 3609
NYSCA Presenting: Services to the Field Grants, 3612
NYSCA Special Art Services Project Support, 3613
NYSCA Special Arts Services: General Operating Support Grants, 3614
NYSCA Special Arts Services: Professional Performances Grants, 3617
NYSCA State and Local Partnerships: General Operating Support Grants, 3619
NYSCA State and Local Partnerships: General Program Support Grants, 3620
NYSCA State and Local Partnerships: Services to the Field Grants, 3621
PCA-PCD Professional Development for Individual Artists Grants, 3770
PCA Art Organizations and Art Programs Grants for Presenting Organizations, 3771
PCA Arts Organizations and Arts Programs Grants for Art Museums, 3775
PCA Arts Organizations and Arts Programs Grants for Arts Service Organizations, 3777
PCA Arts Organizations & Grants for Dance, 3779
PCA Arts Organizations and Arts Programs Grants for Local Arts, 3782
PCA Arts Organizations & Grants for Theatre, 3783
PCA Arts Organizations and Arts Programs Grants for Traditional and Folk Arts, 3784
PCA Arts Organizations & Grants for Visual Arts, 3785
PCA Busing Grants, 3786
PCA Entry Track Arts Organizations and Program Grants for Art Museums, 3787
PCA Entry Track Arts Organizations and Program Grants for Arts Service Organizations, 3789
PCA Entry Track Arts Organizations and Program Grants for Dance, 3791
PCA Entry Track Arts Organizations and Program Grants for Local Arts, 3794
PCA Entry Track Arts Organizations and Program Grants for Presenting Organizations, 3796
PCA Entry Track Arts Organizations and Program Grants for Theatre, 3797
PCA Entry Track Arts Organizations and Program Grants for Traditional and Folk Arts, 3798
PCA Entry Track Arts Organizations and Program Grants for Visual Arts, 3799
PCA Pennsylvania Partners in the Arts Program Stream Grants, 3801
PCA Pennsylvania Partners in the Arts Project Stream Grants, 3802
PCA Strategies for Success Grants - Basic Level, 3805
PCA Strategies for Success Grants - Intermediate, 3806
PennPAT Artist Technical Assistance Grants, 3811
PennPAT Fee-Support Grants for Presenters, 3812
PennPAT New Directions Grants for Presenters, 3813
PennPAT Presenter Travel Grants, 3814
PennPAT Strategic Opportunity Grants, 3815
Pew Charitable Trusts Arts and Culture Grants, 3857
TAC Arts Access Grant, 4549
TAC Arts Build Communities Grants, 4551
TAC Arts Grants, 4554
TAC Rural Arts Project Support Grants, 4555
TAC Touring Arts and Arts Access Grants, 4557
Virginia Commission for the Arts Touring Assistance Grants, 4945

Tourism
Abell Fndn Community Development Grants, 93
Appalachian Regional Commission Tourist Development Grants, 511
ASTA Academic Scholarships, 597
Bikes Belong Fndn Research Grants, 762
CDECD Historic Preservation Survey and Planning Grants, 982
CDECD Tourism Product Development Grants, 984
Connecticut Commission on the Arts Art in Public Spaces, 1349
Florida Sports Fndn Major and Regional Programs Grants, 1873
Greater Columbus Arts Council Operating Grant, 2133
Historic Landmarks Fndn of Indiana Historic Preservation Educ Grants, 2334
IDOT Economic Development Grants, 2436
Lafayette - West Lafayette Convention and Visitors Bureau Tourist Promotion Grants, 2849
Massachusetts Cultural Adams Arts Grants, 3052
Miller Fndn Grants, 3181
NFWF So Company Power of Flight Grants, 3394
Pathways to Nature Conservation Grants, 3745
Principal Financial Group Fndn Grants, 3966
South Carolina Arts Commission Cultural Tourism Init Grants, 4419
SW Florida Community Fndn Arts & Attractions Grants, 4441
Tourism Cares Professional Dev Scholarships, 4648
Tourism Cares Worldwide Grants, 4649

Toxic Substances
African American Fund of New Jersey Grants, 192
Beldon Grants, 720
Bullitt Fndn Grants, 862
Clarence E. Heller Charitable Fndn Grants, 1150
Orchard Fndn Grants, 3690

Training and Development
Able Trust Vocational Rehabilitation Grants for Individuals, 104
ACF Native American Social and Economic Development Strategies Grants, 123
ALA Melvil Dewey Medal, 301
Alberto Culver Corp Contributions Grants, 343
Boeing Company Contributions Grants, 809
Buhl Fndn - Frick Ed Fund, 859
Burden Grants, 864
CCF Grassroots Exchange Grants, 963
CCHD Economic Development Grants, 967
Chesapeake Bay Trust Capacity Building Grants, 1068
Cleveland H. Dodge Fndn Grants, 1172
Community Fndn in Jacksonville Art Ventures Small Organizations Professional Assistance Grants, 1262
Community Fndn of Greater Fort Wayne - Barbara Burt Leadership Development Grants, 1283
Community Fndn of Middle Tennessee Grants, 1300
Community Fndn of the Verdugos Ed Endowment Grants, 1321
ConocoPhillips Grants, 1355
Conservation, Food, and Health Fndn Grants for Developing Countries, 1359
Cruise Industry Charitable Fndn Grants, 1404
Darden Restaurants Fndn Grants, 1446
Delaware Division of the Arts Opportunity Grants--Arts Organizations, 1488
DHHS Emerging Leaders Program Internships, 1532
DHHS Special Programs for the Aging: Training, Research, and DiscretionaryGrants, 1538
DHHS Technical and Non-Financial Assistance to Health Centers, 1539
DOJ Community-Based Delinquency Prevention Grants, 1556
DOJ Juvenile Mentoring Grants, 1560
DOL Youthbuild Grants, 1571
Dwight Stuart Youth Capacity-Building Grants, 1627
Dyson Fndn Management Assistance Program Mini-Grants, 1632
Dyson Fndn Nonprofit Strategic Restructuring Init Grants, 1637
Entergy Charitable Fndn Low-Income Inits and Solutions Grants, 1711
Fremont Area Community Amazing X Grants, 1953
Gardiner Howland Shaw Fndn Grants, 1986
GNOF Organizational Effectiveness Grants, 2090
Greater Milwaukee Fndn Grants, 2137
Greater Worcester Community Mini-Grants, 2142
Hartford Aging and Health Program Awards, 2247
Hartford Fndn Nonprofit Support Grants, 2252
IMLS 21st Century Museum Pro Grants, 2512
IMLS American Heritage Preservation Grants, 2513
IMLS National Leadership Grants, 2515
IMLS Native Am Library Services Basic Grants, 2517
IMLS Native American Library Services Enhancement Grants, 2518
Indep Comm Fndn Educ, Culture & Arts Grant, 2526
Indiana Arts Comm Capacity Building Grants, 2531
Indiana Arts Commission Statewide Arts Service Organization Grants, 2533
Indiana Rural Capacity Grants, 2547
Int'l Assoc of Emergency Managers Scholarships, 2566
Jacob and Hilda Blaustein Fndn Grants, 2615
Jacobs Family Village Neighborhoods Grants, 2619
John D. and Catherine T. MacArthur Fndn Global Challenges Grants, 2690
Jovid Fndn Grants, 2745
Kalamazoo Community Fndn Economic and Community Development Grants, 2765
Koret Fndn Grants, 2837
Lafayette - West Lafayette Convention and Visitors Bureau Tourist Promotion Grants, 2849
Mary Wilmer Covey Charitable Grants, 3049
Microsoft Comm Affairs Puget Sound Grants, 3163
MMS and Alliance Charitable Fndn Int'l Health Studies Grants, 3195
NASE Succeed Scholarships, 3243
National Endowment for the Arts - National Partnership Agreement Grants, 3256
National Endowment for the Arts Presenting Grants: Art Works, 3268
National Housing Endowment Challenge/Build/Grow Grant, 3277
NEH Preservation Assistance Grants for Smaller Institutions, 3293

SUBJECT INDEX

Nevada Arts Council Jackpot Grants, 3312
New Hampshire Charitable Fndn Grants, 3325
NHLBI Ruth L. Kirschstein National Research Service Award Short-Term Research Training Grants, 3422
NHSCA Operating Grants, 3428
NNEDVF/Altria Doors of Hope Program, 3452
Nonprofit Management Grants, 3458
North Carolina Arts Council Arts in Educ Artist Residencies Grants, 3468
North Carolina Arts Council Ed Grants, 3469
North Carolina Arts Council Arts in Educ Rural Development Grants, 3470
North Carolina Arts Council Community Arts Administration Internship, 3471
NYSCA Special Arts Services: General Operating Support Grants, 3614
Ohio County Community Fndn Conference/Training Grants, 3657
OJJDP National Mentoring Grants, 3664
OJJDP Tribal Juvenile Accountability Discretionary Grants, 3665
OneFamily Fndn Grants, 3673
Ottinger Fndn Grants, 3712
Partnership Enhancement Grants, 3740
Peter and Elizabeth C. Tower Fndn Social and Emotional Preschool Curriculum Grants, 3841
Piedmont Natural Gas Fndn Workforce Development Grant, 3886
PNC Fndn Grow Up Great Grants, 3924
Porter County Community Fndn Grants, 3931
Priddy Fndn Organizational Development Grants, 3956
Princeton Area Community Fndn Fund for Women and Girls Grants, 3962
Prudential Fndn Economic Development Grants, 3976
Prudential Fndn Educ Grants, 3977
Raskob Fndn for Catholic Activities Grants, 4019
RISCA Folk Arts Apprenticeships, 4098
RRF General Grants, 4170
Saint Luke's Health Inits Grants, 4216
San Francisco Fndn Fund Shenson Performing Arts Fellowships, 4275
Scott County Community Fndn Grants, 4314
Sioux Falls Area Community Grants, 4364
Sioux Falls Area Community Fndn Spot Grants, 4366
Social Justice Fund NW Criminal Justice Giving Project Grants, 4394
South Carolina Arts Commission Leadership and Organizational Development Grants, 4423
Southern New England Folk and Traditional Arts Apprenticeship Grants, 4438
South Madison Community Fndn Grants, 4440
Sport Manitoba Athlete Skill Development Clinics Grants, 4453
Sport Manitoba Women to Watch Grants, 4460
Stark Community Fndn Neighborhood Community & Economic Devel Tech Assistance Grants, 4478
State Justice Institute Curriculum Adaptation and Training Grants, 4488
State Justice Institute Partner Grants, 4489
State Justice Institute Project Grants, 4490
State Justice Institute Strategic Init Grants, 4492
State Justice Institute Tech Assistance Grants, 4493
Stuart Fndn Grants, 4516
Symantec Community Relations and Corp Philanthropy Grants, 4544
TAC Arts Grants, 4554
TAC Rural Arts Project Support Grants, 4555
TechFndn TechGrants, 4570
Texas Comm on the Arts Young Masters Grants, 4594
U.S. Department of Educ Disability and Rehabilitation Research and Related Projects, 4690
U.S. Department of Educ Parent Information and Training, 4695
U.S. Department of Educ Rehabilitation Research Training Centers, 4699
Union Bank, N.A. Fndn Grants, 4709
USDA Rural Business Enterprise Grants, 4823
USDA Rural Business Opportunity Grants, 4824
USDC Technology Opportunities Grants, 4860
USDJ Edward Byrne Justice Assistance Grants, 4863
USTA Althea Gibson Leadership Awards, 4872
USTA CTA and NJTL Community Tennis Development Workshop Scholarships, 4873
USTA Multicultural Individual Player Grant for National Competition and Training, 4877
USTA Player Development Grants, 4881
Vancouver Fndn Disability Supports for Employment Grants, 4899
Victoria S. and Bradley L. Geist Fndn Grants Supporting Foster Care and Their Caregivers, 4936
Victoria S. and Bradley L. Geist Fndn Grants Supporting Transitioning Foster Youth, 4937
Wilburforce Fndn Grants, 5067
William C. Kenney Watershed Protection Fndn Ecosystem Grants, 5079

Transexuals
ALA Diversity and Outreach Fair, 267
ALFJ Astraea U.S. General Fund, 362
Community Fndn SE Michigan HOPE Grants, 1260
Maine Community Fndn Equity Grants, 2980
Ms. Fndn for Women Ending Violence Grants, 3224
Ms. Fndn for Women Health Grants, 3225
New York Fndn Grants, 3338
Philanthrofund Fndn Grants, 3874

Transitional Students
Guy I. Bromley Grants, 2180
Lewis H. Humphreys Charitable Grants, 2889
Louetta M. Cowden Fndn Grants, 2922
Meyer Fndn Educ Grants, 3142

Translation
National Endowment for Arts Commun Grants, 3260

Transportation
A.V. Hunter Grants, 47
AAA Fndn for Traffic Safety Grants, 50
Able To Serve Grants, 102
Able Trust Voc Rehab Grants for Agencies, 103
ACFEF Disaster Relief Fund Member Assistance, 117
Appalachian Regional Commission Transportation and Highways Grants, 512
ARTBA Transportation Development Grants, 569
Baltimore Community Fndn Transportation Path Grants, 648
Barberton Community Fndn Grants, 666
Bullitt Fndn Grants, 862
CICF Senior Grants, 1127
Community Fndn of Greater Birmingham Grants, 1280
Dave Coy Fndn Grants, 1447
David Bohnett Fndn Grants, 1451
Dearborn Community City of Aurora Grants, 1470
DHS ARRA Port Security Grants, 1543
DHS ARRA Transit Security Grants, 1544
DHS FY 2009 Transit Security Grants, 1545
Elizabeth Morse Genius Charitable Grants, 1682
Energy Fndn Power Grants, 1707
Energy Fndn Transportation Grants, 1708
Fallon OrNda Community Health Grants, 1783
Farmers Insurance Corp Giving Grants, 1791
Foellinger Fndn Grants, 1877
Fremont Area Community Amazing X Grants, 1953
Gateway Fndn Grants, 1992
Helen Steiner Rice Fndn Grants, 2299
Hillcrest Fndn Grants, 2325
IDOT Rail Freight Program Loans and Grants, 2437
IDOT Truck Access Route Grants, 2438
Illinois DCEO Business Development Public Infrastructure Grants, 2483
Illinois DCEO Coal Competitiveness Grants, 2484
J.M. Kaplan Fund City Life Grants, 2601
Kentucky Arts Council TranspARTation Grant, 2812
McKnight Fndn Region & Communities Grants, 3086
MDEQ Clean Diesel Grants, 3096
National Endowment for the Arts - Regional Partnership Agreement Grants, 3258
Oklahoma City Community Programs & Grants, 3666
Rochester Area Community Fndn Grants, 4127
Saint Paul Fndn Community Sharing Grants, 4218
Sisters of Charity Fndn of Cleveland Good Samaritan Grants, 4373
Surdna Fndn Sustainable Environments Grants, 4533
TSA Advanced Surveillance Grants, 4674
US Airways Community Contributions, 4788
USDC Public Works and Economic Adjustment Assistance Grants, 4856
Vigneron Grants, 4938
Yellow Corp Fndn Grants, 5126

Transportation Engineering
Appalachian Regional Commission Transportation and Highways Grants, 512
ARTBA Transportation Development Grants, 569
Elizabeth Morse Genius Charitable Grants, 1682

Transportation Planning/Policy
Appalachian Regional Commission Transportation and Highways Grants, 512
ARTBA Transportation Development Grants, 569
Baltimore Community Fndn Transportation Path Grants, 648
Bikes Belong Fndn Paul David Clark Bicycling Safety Grants, 760
Bikes Belong Fndn REI Grants, 761
Bikes Belong Fndn Research Grants, 762
Bikes Belong Grants, 763
Blue Cross Blue Shield of Minnesota Fndn - Healthy Equity: Health Impact Assessment Demonstration Project Grants, 795
Blue Cross Blue Shield of Minnesota Fndn - Healthy Equity: Health Impact Assessment Grants, 796
Elizabeth Morse Genius Charitable Grants, 1682
Energy Fndn Transportation Grants, 1708
GNOF Metropolitan Opportunities Grants, 2087
USDA Fed-State Marketing Improvement Grants, 4810
USDA Rural Business Enterprise Grants, 4823
Volvo Adventure Environmental Awards, 4952
William & Flora Hewlett Environmental Grants, 5074

Trauma
Peter and Elizabeth C. Tower Fndn Annual Mental Health Grants, 3835
Quantum Fndn Grants, 3996
Robert R. McCormick Tribune Veterans Grants, 4120

Travel
AAP Program Delegate Awards, 68
ALA Adelaide Del Frate Conference Sponsorship Award, 220
ALA DEMCO New Leaders Travel Grants, 264
ALA First Step Award/Wiley Professional Development Grant, 279
ALA Maureen Hayes Author/Illustrator Award, 299
ALA NewsBank/Readex C. J. Reynolds Award, 304
ALFJ Astraea U.S. and Int'l Movement Fund, 361
APAP Cultural Exchange Grants, 492
ASTA Academic Scholarships, 597
CCF Grassroots Exchange Grants, 963
Durfee Fndn Stanton Fellowship, 1626
Fisher House Fndn Hero Miles Program, 1832
Internet Society Fellowships, 2570
Kentucky Arts Council TranspARTation Grant, 2812
Lafayette - West Lafayette Convention and Visitors Bureau Tourist Promotion Grants, 2849
MMS and Alliance Charitable Fndn Int'l Health Studies Grants, 3195
National Center for Resp Gaming Travel Grants, 3251
Newfoundland and Labrador Arts Council Community Arts Grants, 3318
Newfoundland and Labrador Arts Council Labrador Cultural Travel Grants, 3319
Newfoundland and Labrador Arts Council Professional Artists Travel Fund, 3320
Newfoundland and Labrador Arts Council Professional Festivals Grants, 3321
Newfoundland and Labrador Arts Council Professional Project Grants, 3322
Newfoundland and Labrador Arts Council Visiting Artists Grants, 3324

NW Airlines KidCares Med Travel Assistance, 3508
Ontario Arts Council Travel Assistance Grants, 3682
PCA Busing Grants, 3786
PennPAT Presenter Travel Grants, 3814
Pinellas County Grants, 3891
PMP Professional Development Grants, 3919
Robert R. Meyer Fndn Grants, 4121
South Carolina Arts Commission Cultural Tourism Init Grants, 4419
Sport Manitoba Athlete/Team Travel Assistance Grants, 4452
Sport Manitoba Coaches/Officials Travel Assistance Grants, 4455
Sport Manitoba Women to Watch Grants, 4460
Stark Community Fndn Neighborhood Community & Economic Devel Tech Assistance Grants, 4478
Texas Commission on the Arts Cultural Connections Grants, 4591
Tourism Cares Professional Dev Scholarships, 4648
Tourism Cares Worldwide Grants, 4649
West Virginia Commission on the Arts Professional Development for Artists Grants, 5045
West Virginia Commission on the Arts Travel and Training Grants, 5050

Trees
Arbor Day Fndn Grants, 524
California Green Trees for Golden State Grant, 906
Chesapeake Bay Trust Forestry Mini Grants, 1071
GNOF Gert Community Grants, 2076
Illinois DNR Urban & Comm Forestry Grants, 2503

Tropical Zones
Beneficia Fndn Grants, 727
John D. and Catherine T. MacArthur Fndn Global Challenges Grants, 2690
MacArthur Fndn Conservation and Sustainable Development Grants, 2963

Tuberculosis
Alliance Healthcare Fndn Grants, 383
USAID/Cambodia Maternal and Child Health, Tuberculosis, HIV/AIDS. and Malaria Grants, 4736
USAID Accelerating Progress Against Tuberculosis in Kenya Grants, 4737
USAID Comprehensive District-Based Support for Better HIV/TB Patient Outcomes Grants, 4747
USAID Systems Strengthening for Better HIV/TB Patient Outcomes Grants, 4785

Undergraduate Education
Flinn Fndn Grants, 1842
IIE AmCham Charitable Fndn U.S. Studies Scholarship, 2453
North Carolina GlaxoSmithKline Fndn Grants, 3490
Sprint Fndn Grants, 4463

Unitarian Church
AHS Fndn Grants, 208
Alvah H. and Wyline P. Chapman Fndn Grants, 402
MacDonald-Peterson Fndn Grants, 2965
UUA Skinner Sermon Award, 4895

United States History
ALA Coretta Scott King Book Awards, 260
ALA Donald G. Davis Article Award, 269
MARPAT Fndn Grants, 3023
NEH Family & Youth Grants in American History, 3291
NEH Interpreting America's Hist Places Grants, 3292
Richard and Caroline T. Gwathmey Grants, 4075
Virginia Fndn for Humanities Discr Grants, 4946
Virginia Fndn for the Humanities Open Grants, 4947

Urban Affairs
Audrey and Sydney Irmas Charitable Fndn Grants, 612
Charles H. Revson Fndn Grants, 1047
Chicago Community Trust Housing Grants: Advancing Affordable Rental Housing, 1088
Columbus Fndn Competitive Grants, 1220
Community Fndn for Muskegon County Grants, 1256

Community Fndn of East Central Illinois Grants, 1278
Community Fndn of St. Joseph County Special Project Challenge Grants, 1314
Horowitz Fndn for Social Policy Grants, 2370
Horowitz Fndn for Social Policy Special Awards, 2371
Howard and Bush Fndn Grants, 2374
National Endowment for the Arts - National Arts and Humanities Youth Program Awards, 3255
Nellie Mae Educ Fndn District-Level Grants, 3297
Nordson Corp Fndn Grants, 3462
Paul and Edith Babson Fndn Grants, 3755
Pittsburgh Fndn Community Grants, 3910
Yellow Corp Fndn Grants, 5126

Urban Areas
Abelard Fndn East Grants, 87
Abelard Fndn West Grants, 88
Achelis Fndn Grants, 127
Annie E. Casey Fndn Grants, 481
Barr Fndn Grants (Massachusetts), 676
Bodman Fndn Grants, 807
Booth Ferris Fndn Grants, 816
California Green Trees for Golden State Grant, 906
CE and S Fndn Grants, 985
CNCS AmeriCorps NCCC Project Grants, 1181
Commonwealth Fund Harkness Fellowships in Health Care Policy and Practice, 1242
CUNA Mutual Group Fndn, 1416
DB Americas Fndn Grants, 1466
Dept of Ed Parental Info and Resource Centers, 1510
E.L. Wiegand Fndn Grants, 1639
Elmer L. and Eleanor J. Andersen Fndn Grants, 1687
Fund for the City of New York Grants, 1978
GNOF Community Revitalization Grants, 2071
GNOF Jefferson Community Grants, 2085
Hasbro Children's Fund, 2256
Hudson Webber Fndn Grants, 2383
Illinois DNR Urban & Comm Forestry Grants, 2503
Irvin Stern Fndn Grants, 2585
ISA John Z. Duling Grants, 2587
Lynde and Harry Bradley Fndn Grants, 2947
Lynde and Harry Bradley Fndn Prizes, 2948
Lyndhurst Fndn Grants, 2949
MacArthur Fndn Policy Research Grants, 2964
Mark Wahlberg Youth Fndn Grants, 3022
Massachusetts Cultural Adams Arts Grants, 3052
Merck Family Fund Urban Farming and Youth Leadership Grants, 3119
Merck Family Fund Youth Transforming Urban Communities Grants, 3120
National Book Scholarship Fund, 3249
National Endowment for Arts Media Grants, 3264
National Endowment for Arts Museum Grants, 3265
National Endowment for Arts Music Grants, 3266
National Endowment for Arts Opera Grants, 3267
National Endowment for Arts Theater Grants, 3269
Nevada Arts Council Professional Dev Grants, 3314
NFWF So Company Power of Flight Grants, 3394
NW Fund for the Environment Grants, 3510
Paul and Edith Babson Fndn Grants, 3755
Rajiv Gandhi Fndn Grants, 4011
Richard King Mellon Fndn Grants, 4087
Rudy Bruner Award for Urban Excellence, 4173
Schumann Fund for New Jersey Grants, 4311
Surdna Fndn Sustainable Environments Grants, 4533
TAC Arts Grants, 4554
USDA Farm Labor Housing Grants, 4809
USDC Technology Opportunities Grants, 4860
US Soccer Fndn Planning Grants, 4871
Walt Disney Company Fndn Grants, 4981
William & Flora Hewlett Environmental Grants, 5074
William G. McGowan Charitable Grants, 5084

Urban Education
ALA Coretta Scott King Book Donation Grant, 261
Carnegie Corp of New York Grants, 940
Dept of Ed Parental Info and Resource Centers, 1510
Frances and John L. Loeb Family Grants, 1917
Merck Family Fund Youth Transforming Urban Communities Grants, 3120

Michael and Susan Dell Fndn Grants, 3158
National Home Library Fndn Grants, 3276
Nellie Mae Educ Fndn District-Level Grants, 3297
U.S. Department of Educ 21st Century Community Learning Centers, 4687

Urban Geography
Arbor Day Fndn Grants, 524
California Green Trees for Golden State Grant, 906
Open Spaces Sacred Places National Awards, 3684

Urban History
Goldseker Fndn Community Grants, 2101
Natonal Endowment for the Arts Research Grants: Art Works, 3286

Urban Planning/Policy
Air Products and Chemicals Grants, 216
Andy Warhol Fndn for the Visual Arts Grants, 464
Blue Cross Blue Shield of Minnesota Fndn - Healthy Equity: Health Impact Assessment Grants, 796
Canada-U.S. Fulbright Mid-Career Grants, 917
CE and S Fndn Grants, 985
Community Fndn for Muskegon County Grants, 1256
Enterprise Community Partners Green Charrette Grants, 1716
Enterprise Community Partners Pre-Development Design Grants, 1718
FMC Fndn Grants, 1876
GNOF Community Revitalization Grants, 2071
GNOF Jefferson Community Grants, 2085
GNOF St. Bernard Community Grants, 2092
Illinois DNR Urban & Comm Forestry Grants, 2503
MacArthur Fndn Policy Research Grants, 2964
Merck Family Fund Youth Transforming Urban Communities Grants, 3120
Meyer Fndn Healthy Communities Grants, 3143
Michael and Susan Dell Fndn Grants, 3158
National Endowment for Arts Our Town Grants, 3257
National Endowment for Arts Museum Grants, 3265
National Urban Fellows Program, 3281
Natonal Endowment for the Arts Research Grants: Art Works, 3286
NYSCA Architecture, Planning, and Design: Capital Project Grants, 3571
NYSCA Architecture, Planning, and Design: Design and Planning Studies Grants, 3572
NYSCA Architecture, Planning, and Design: General Operating Support Grants, 3573
NYSCA Architecture, Planning, and Design: General Program Support Grants, 3574
NYSCA Architecture, Planning, and Design: Independent Project Grants, 3575
Open Spaces Sacred Places National Awards, 3684
Paul and Edith Babson Fndn Grants, 3755
Price Family Charitable Grants, 3952
Sensient Technologies Fndn Grants, 4337
Western New York Fndn Grants, 5025

Urban Sociology
Michael and Susan Dell Fndn Grants, 3158
Open Spaces Sacred Places National Awards, 3684

Urinary Tract
NHLBI Lymphatics in Health & Disease in Digestive, Urinary, Cardio & Pulmonary Systems, 3415

Urologic Diseases
NHLBI Lymphatics in Health & Disease in Digestive, Urinary, Cardio & Pulmonary Systems, 3415
Pfizer Healthcare Charitable Contributions, 3863

Urology
Pfizer Healthcare Charitable Contributions, 3863

Utilities
Actors Fund Social Services and Financial Assist, 139
AGMA Relief Grants, 201
Alexander Fndn Emergency Grants, 356
Barberton Community Fndn Grants, 666

SUBJECT INDEX

Children Affected by AIDS Fndn Family Assistance Emergency Grants, 1107
Colorado Clean Energy Solar Innovation Grants, 1212
Dollar Energy Grants, 1567
Energy Fndn Power Grants, 1707
Entergy Charitable Fndn Low-Income Inits and Solutions Grants, 1711
Illinois DCEO Business Development Public Infrastructure Grants, 2483
Illinois DCEO Coal Demonstration Grants, 2485
Illinois DCEO Coal Development Grants, 2486
Kessler Fndn Hurricane Emergency Grants, 2815
MGM Resorts Fndn Community Grants, 3153
Modest Needs Self-Sufficiency Grants, 3201
Nicor Gas Sharing Grants, 3436
Saint Paul Fndn Community Sharing Grants, 4218
Southern California Edison Civic Affairs Grants, 4428
USDA Native American Indian Utilities Grants, 4820
USDA Predevelopment Planning Grants, 4821

Vaccines
Chiron Fndn Community Grants, 1111
Pfizer Medical Educ Track One Grants, 3864

Values/Moral Education
Albert and Bessie Mae Kronkosky Charitable Fndn Grants, 339
Cargill Citizenship Fund-Corp Giving Grants, 925
CICF John H. Brown & Robert Burse Grant, 1125
ConocoPhillips Grants, 1355
Fndn for a Drug-Free World Classroom Tools, 1890
Mary E. Ober Fndn Grants, 3039
McCune Fndn Humananities Grants, 3079
Moran Family Fndn Grants, 3216
Quaker Oats Company Kids Care Clubs Grants, 3992
Red Robin Fndn U-ACT Grants, 4038

Venereal Diseases
DHHS Adolescent Family Life Demo Projects, 1524

Venture Capital
Draper Richards Kaplan Fndn Grants, 1603
NASE Growth Grants, 3242
Union Bank, N.A. Fndn Grants, 4709
USAID Development Innov Ventures Grants, 4749
Washington Area Women's Fndn Strategic Opportunity and Partnership Grants, 4996

Veterans
Anne J. Caudal Fndn Grants, 475
Balfe Family Fndn Grants, 636
Charles Delmar Fndn Grants, 1039
CNCS AmeriCorps Indian Planning Grants, 1180
CNCS AmeriCorps State and National Grants, 1182
CNCS AmeriCorps VISTA Project Grants, 1184
CNCS Senior Corps Retired Volunteer Grants, 1188
David Robinson Fndn Grants, 1454
DOL Homeless Veterans Reintegration Grants, 1566
Fitzpatrick, Cella, Harper & Scinto Pro Bono, 1836
Help America Fndn Grants, 2301
MFRI Operation Diploma Grants for Higher Ed, 3150
MFRI Operation Diploma Grants for Student Veterans Organizations, 3151
MGN Family Fndn Grants, 3154
Military Ex-Prisoners of War Fndn Grants, 3177
Northrop Grumman Corp Grants, 3507
Robert R. McCormick Tribune Veterans Grants, 4120

Veterinary Medicine
Albert and Bessie Mae Kronkosky Charitable Fndn Grants, 339
Bernice Barbour Fndn Grants, 743
Bodman Fndn Grants, 807
Fuller Fndn Grants, 1974
IIE AmCham U.S. Studies Scholarship, 2453
IIE New Leaders Group Award for Mutual Understanding, 2460
Kenneth A. Scott Charitable Grants, 2801
Maddie's Fund Community Shelter Data Grants, 2968
Natalie W. Furniss Charitable Grants, 3244

NHLBI Ruth L. Kirschstein National Research Service Awards for Individual Senior Fellows, 3421
Petco Fndn 4 Rs Project Support Grants, 3830
Petco Fndn We Are Family Too Grants, 3833
Posey County Community Fndn Grants, 3939
Regents Professional Opportunity Scholarships, 4044

Veterinary Medicine Education
Banfield Charitable Grants, 652
Maddie's Fund Comm Collaborative Projects, 2967
Maddie's Fund Community Shelter Data Grants, 2968
Meacham Fndn Grants, 3102
NHLBI Ruth L. Kirschstein National Research Service Award Short-Term Research Training Grants, 3422
Pet Care Trust Sue Busch Memorial Award, 3829

Video Production
Bush Fndn Arts & Humanities Grants: Short-Term Organizational Support, 873
CCH Documentary Public Engagement Grants, 970
CCH Documentary Project Research and Development Grants, 971
Illinois Arts Council Media Arts Grants, 2472
Jerome Fndn Grants, 2667
National Endowment for Arts Opera Grants, 3267
North Carolina Arts Council Folklife Documentary Project Grants, 3475
North Carolina Arts Council Folklife Grants, 3476
NYFA Gregory Millard Fellowships, 3565
NYSCA Electronic Media and Film: General Exhibition Grants, 3589
PCA Arts Organizations and Arts Programs Grants for Film and Electronic Media, 3780
PCA Entry Track Arts Organizations and Program Grants for Film and Electronic Media, 3792
San Francisco Fndn James D. Phelan Award in Film, Video, and Digital Media, 4278
West Virginia Commission on the Arts Media Arts Grants, 5039

Videos
ALA ALSC Bookapalooza Grants, 222
ALA Information Technology Pathfinder Award, 286
ALFJ Astraea U.S. General Fund, 362
CCH Documentary Project Production Grants, 969
CCH Documentary Public Engagement Grants, 970
CCH Documentary Project Research and Development Grants, 971
Cincinnati Bell Fndn Grants, 1131
Creative Work Grants, 1396
National Endowment for Arts Media Grants, 3264
San Francisco Fndn James D. Phelan Award in Film, Video, and Digital Media, 4278

Violence
49ers Fndn Grants, 23
A.J. Muste Institute Counter Recruitment Grants, 43
A.J. Muste Memorial Institute Int'l Nonviolence Training Grants, 45
Abelard Fndn East Grants, 87
Abelard Fndn West Grants, 88
Advocate Safehouse Project Grants, 174
Agape Fndn for Nonviolent Social Change Board of Trustees Grants, 197
Ahmanson Fndn Grants, 207
Allen Lane Fndn Grants, 379
Alliance Healthcare Fndn Grants, 383
Allstate Corp Giving Grants, 386
Allstate Corp Hometown Commitment Grants, 387
Atkinson Fndn Community Grants, 606
Atlanta Women's Fndn Grants, 609
California Endowment Innovative Ideas Grants, 904
Carlisle Fndn Grants, 931
Caterpillar Fndn Grants, 954
CDC Grants for Violence-Related Injury Prevention Research, 974
David Bohnett Fndn Grants, 1451
DOJ Rural Domestic Violence and Child Victimization Enforcement Grants, 1562
Do Right Fndn Grants, 1581

Violent Crime/ 1005

Hasbro Children's Fund, 2256
Hitachi Fndn Yoshiyama Awards, 2340
Initiaive Fndn Inside-Out Connections Grants, 2556
Isabel Allende Fndn Esperanza Grants, 2586
Jewish Women's Fndn of New York Grants, 2677
Joseph Drown Fndn Grants, 2735
Joseph H. and Florence A. Roblee Fndn Grants, 2736
Joyce Fndn Gun Violence Prevention Grants, 2751
Liberty Hill Fndn Environmental Justice Grants, 2891
Liberty Hill Fndn Fund for Change Grants, 2893
Liberty Hill Fndn Seed Grants, 2896
Liberty Hill Fndn Special Opportunity Grants, 2897
Oakland Fund for Children and Youth Grants, 3634
Overbrook Fndn Grants, 3715
Quantum Fndn Grants, 3996
Reynolds American Fndn Grants, 4068
Richard and Rhoda Goldman Grants, 4077
San Diego Fndn for Change Grants, 4247
Sister Grants for Women's Organizations, 4371
Sisters of St. Joseph Healthcare Fndn Grants, 4377
Sonoco Fndn Grants, 4403
Target Corp Local Store Grants, 4561
Teaching Tolerance Grants, 4567
United Methodist Women Brighter Future for Children and Youth Grants, 4723
Verizon Wireless Hopeline Grants, 4927
Virginia Fndn for Humanities Discr Grants, 4946
Virginia Fndn for the Humanities Open Grants, 4947
Waitt Family Fndn Grants, 4973
Youth Philanthropy Project, 5132

Violence Prevention
Albert W. Rice Charitable Fndn Grants, 347
Alfred E. Chase Charitable Fndn Grants, 366
AMA Fndn Fund for Better Health Grants, 409
Atlanta Women's Fndn Grants, 609
Charles H. Pearson Fndn Grants, 1045
Chicago Community Trust Public Safety and Justice Grants, 1093
Edward and Ellen Roche Relief Fndn Grants, 1663
Frank Reed and Margaret Jane Peters Memorial Fund II Grants, 1934
George W. Wells Fndn Grants, 2030
Go Daddy Cares Charitable Contributions, 2094
Initiaive Fndn Inside-Out Connections Grants, 2556
Joyce Fndn Gun Violence Prevention Grants, 2751
Linford and Mildred White Charitable Grants, 2909
Maine Women's Fund Economic Security Grants, 2992
Meyer Fndn Healthy Communities Grants, 3143
Moody Fndn Grants, 3215
Ms. Fndn for Women Ending Violence Grants, 3224
Philanthrofund Fndn Grants, 3874
RCF General Community Grants, 4032
Robert R. McCormick Tribune Comm Grants, 4119
Union Bank, N.A. Fndn Grants, 4709
Virginia Fndn for Humanities Discr Grants, 4946
Virginia Fndn for the Humanities Open Grants, 4947

Violence in Schools
49ers Fndn Grants, 23
Allen Hilles Grants, 378
DOJ Gang-Free Schools and Communities Intervention Grants, 1557
U.S. Department of Educ Programs for Native Hawaiians, 4696

Violent Crime
Advocate Safehouse Project Grants, 174
Allstate Corp Giving Grants, 386
Allstate Corp Hometown Commitment Grants, 387
ATF Gang Resistance Educ and Training Program Coop Agreements, 603
CFNCR Starbucks Memorial Fund, 1026
HAF Mada Huggins Caldwell Grants, 2200
Initiaive Fndn Inside-Out Connections Grants, 2556
Joyce Fndn Gun Violence Prevention Grants, 2751
Max and Anna Levinson Fndn Grants, 3066
Plough Fndn Grants, 3915
State Justice Institute Curriculum Adaptation and Training Grants, 4488

1006 / Violent Crime

State Justice Institute Partner Grants, 4489
State Justice Institute Project Grants, 4490
State Justice Institute Strategic Init Grants, 4492
State Justice Institute Tech Assistance Grants, 4493
USDJ Edward Byrne Justice Assistance Grants, 4863

Vision
Alcon Fndn Grants, 351
Canadian Optometric Educ Grants, 918
Meyer Fndn Management Assistance Grants, 3144
Meyer Fndn Strong Nonprofit Sector Grants, 3145
Nina Mason Pulliam Charitable Grants, 3443
NYCT Blindness and Visual Disabilities Grants, 3543

Visual Arts
18th Street Arts Complex Residency Grants, 19
Alabama State Council on the Arts Community Arts Collaborative Ventures Grants, 236
Alabama State Council on the Arts Community Arts Operating Support Grants, 237
Alabama State Council on the Arts Community Arts Presenting Grants, 238
Alabama State Council on the Arts Community Arts Program Development Grants, 239
Alabama State Council on the Arts Community Planning & Design Grants, 241
Alabama State Council on the Arts in Educ Partnership Grants, 242
Alabama State Council on the Arts Multi-Discipline and Festival Grants, 243
ALA Coretta Scott King Book Awards, 260
Alaska State Council on the Arts Operating Support Grants, 328
ALA Writers Live at the Library Grants, 336
Altria Group Arts and Culture Grants, 399
AmerUs Group Charitable Fndn, 455
Amgen Fndn Grants, 456
Amon G. Carter Fndn Grants, 458
Andy Warhol Fndn for the Visual Arts Grants, 464
Arizona Commission on the Arts Visual/Media Arts Organizations Grants, 539
Arkansas Arts Council AIE After School/Summer Residency Grants, 551
Arkansas Arts Council Sally A. Williams Grants, 558
ArvinMeritor Fndn Arts and Culture Grants, 582
Athwin Fndn Grants, 605
Booth-Bricker Grants, 815
Brown Fndn Grants, 854
Bush Fndn Arts & Humanities Grants: Short-Term Organizational Support, 873
CAA Millard Meiss Publication Grants, 885
California Community Fndn Art Grants, 900
Christensen Fund Regional Grants, 1112
Colorado Springs Community Grants, 1215
ConocoPhillips Fndn Grants, 1354
Constance Saltonstall Fndn for the Arts Grants, 1361
Cord Fndn Grants, 1372
Creative Work Grants, 1396
DAAD Research Grants for Doctoral Candidates and Young Academics and Scientists, 1427
Delaware Division of the Arts Opportunity Grants-Artists, 1489
Delta Air Lines Community Enrichment Grants, 1494
DTE Energy Fndn Cultural Grants, 1610
Dwight Stuart Youth Fndn Grants, 1628
Entergy Corp Open Grants for Arts and Culture, 1713
Flinn Fndn Grants, 1842
Florida Div of Cultural Affairs General Program Support Grants, 1854
Florida Div of Cultural Affairs Multidisciplinary Grants, 1857
Florida Div of Cultural Affairs Visual Arts Grant, 1865
General Mills Fndn Grants, 2003
George Gund Fndn Grants, 2020
George S. and Dolores Dore Eccles Fndn Grants, 2027
Georgia Council for the Arts Partner Grants for Organizations, 2035
Georgia Council for the Arts Partner Grants for Service Organizations, 2036
Georgia Power Fndn Grants, 2039
Geraldine R. Dodge Fndn Arts Grants, 2040
GNOF IMPACT Grants for Arts and Culture, 2078
Grand Rapids Area Community Fndn Grants, 2114
Grand Rapids Area Community Fndn Nashwauk Area Endowment Grants, 2115
Green Fndn Arts Grants, 2152
Guy I. Bromley Grants, 2180
HAF Arts and Culture: Project Grants to Artists, 2191
Helen Gertrude Sparks Charitable Grants, 2294
Illinois Arts Council Presenters Dev Grants, 2476
Illinois Arts Council Visual Arts Grants, 2478
Iowa Arts Council Artists in Schools/Communities Residency Grants, 2571
James M. Cox Fndn of Georgia Grants, 2634
Jerome Fndn Grants, 2667
Jerome Fndn Travel and Study Grants, 2668
John W. Speas and Effie E. Speas Grants, 2732
Joyce Awards, 2746
JP Morgan Chase Arts and Culture Grants, 2752
Kansas Arts Commission Artist Fellowships, 2776
Kansas Arts Commission Visual Arts Grants, 2783
Kelvin and Eleanor Smith Fndn Grants, 2796
Kentucky Arts Council Al Smith Fellowship, 2806
Kentucky Arts Council Emerging Artist Award, 2807
Kirkpatrick Fndn Grants, 2827
Laura Jane Musser Rural Arts Grants, 2863
Leon and Thea Koerner Fndn Grants, 2883
Lewis H. Humphreys Charitable Grants, 2889
Lily Auchincloss Fndn Grants, 2904
Louetta M. Cowden Fndn Grants, 2922
Louis and Elizabeth Nave Flarsheim Charitable Fndn Grants, 2924
Margaret L. Wendt Fndn Grants, 3004
Marie Walsh Sharpe Art Fndn Grants, 3009
MARPAT Fndn Grants, 3023
Massachusetts Cultural Adams Arts Grants, 3052
Mid Atlantic Arts Fndn American Masterpieces Grants, 3169
Mid Atlantic Arts Fndn ArtsConnect Grants, 3170
Mid Atlantic Arts Fndn Folk Arts Outreach Project Grants, 3171
Milton and Sally Avery Arts Fndn Grants, 3183
Minnesota State Arts Board Cultural Community Partnership Grants, 3188
Montana Arts Council Cultural and Aesthetic Project Grants, 3209
National Endowment for Arts Media Grants, 3264
National Endowment for the Arts Presenting Grants: Art Works, 3268
NHSCA Artist Residencies in Schools Grants, 3423
NHSCA Conservation License Plate Grants, 3425
NHSCA Youth Arts Project Grants: For Extended Arts Learning, 3430
NJSCA Arts Project Support, 3446
NJSCA Financial and Instal Stabilization Grants, 3447
NJSCA General Program Support Grants, 3449
North Carolina Arts Council Gen Support, 3477
North Carolina Arts Cncl New Realities Grants, 3478
North Carolina Arts Council Outreach Grants, 3479
North Carolina Arts Council Residency Grants, 3481
North Carolina Arts Council Visual Arts Program Support Grants, 3484
NYFA Deutsche Bank Americas Fellowship, 3564
NYFA Strategic Opportunity Stipends, 3566
NYSCA Architecture, Planning, and Design: General Program Support Grants, 3574
NYSCA Architecture, Planning, and Design: Project Support Grants, 3576
NYSCA Arts Educ: Community-based Learning Grants, 3577
NYSCA Arts Educ: General Operating Support, 3578
NYSCA Arts Educ Program Support Grants, 3579
NYSCA Arts Educ: Services to the Field Grants, 3582
NYSCA Dance Gen Operating Support Grants, 3584
NYSCA Dance Gen Program Support Grants, 3585
NYSCA Dance: Long-Term Residency in New York State Grants, 3586
NYSCA Dance: Services to the Field Grants, 3587
NYSCA Electronic Media and Film: Film Festivals Grants, 3588
NYSCA Electronic Media and Film: General Exhibition Grants, 3589
NYSCA Electronic Media and Film: General Operating Support, 3590
NYSCA Electronic Media and Film: General Program Support, 3591
NYSCA Electronic Media and Film: Screenings Grants, 3592
NYSCA Electronic Media and Film: Workspace Grants, 3593
NYSCA Folk Arts: Exhibitions Grants, 3594
NYSCA Folk Arts: Presentation Grants, 3596
NYSCA Folk Arts: Regional and County Folk Arts Grants, 3597
NYSCA Presenting: General Operating Support, 3609
NYSCA Presenting: General Program Support, 3610
NYSCA Presenting: Presenting Grants, 3611
NYSCA Presenting: Services to the Field Grants, 3612
NYSCA Special Art Services Project Support, 3613
NYSCA Special Arts Services: General Operating Support Grants, 3614
NYSCA Special Arts Services: General Program Support Grants, 3615
NYSCA Special Arts Services: Instruction and Training Grants, 3616
NYSCA Special Arts Services: Professional Performances Grants, 3617
NYSCA State and Local Partnerships: General Operating Support Grants, 3619
NYSCA State and Local Partnerships: General Program Support Grants, 3620
NYSCA State and Local Partnerships: Services to the Field Grants, 3621
NYSCA State and Local Partnerships: Workshops Grants, 3622
NYSCA Theatre Gen Operating Support Grants, 3623
NYSCA Theatre General Program Support, 3624
NYSCA Theatre Pro Performances Grants, 3625
NYSCA Theatre: Services to the Field Grants, 3626
NYSCA Visual Arts: Exhibitions and Installations Grants, 3627
NYSCA Visual Arts: General Operating Support, 3628
NYSCA Visual Arts: General Program Support, 3629
NYSCA Visual Arts: Services to the Field Grants, 3630
NYSCA Visual Arts: Workspace Facilities Grants, 3631
Ohio Arts Council Individual Excellence Awards, 3648
Ohio Arts Council Arts Innovation Grants, 3649
Ontario Arts Council Integrated Arts Grants, 3678
PacifiCorp Fndn for Learning Grants, 3727
Parker Fndn (California) Grants, 3736
Paul G. Allen Family Fndn Grants, 3759
PCA-PCD Professional Development for Individual Artists Grants, 3770
PCA Arts in Educ Residencies, 3772
PCA Arts Organizations and Arts Programs Grants for Arts Service Organizations, 3777
PCA Arts Organizations & Grants for Visual Arts, 3785
PCA Busing Grants, 3786
PCA Entry Track Arts Organizations and Program Grants for Arts Service Organizations, 3789
PCA Entry Track Arts Organizations and Program Grants for Visual Arts, 3799
PCA Pennsylvania Partners in the Arts Program Stream Grants, 3801
PCA Pennsylvania Partners in the Arts Project Stream Grants, 3802
PCA Professional Development Grants, 3803
PCA Strategies for Success Grants - Advanced, 3804
PCA Strategies for Success Grants - Basic Level, 3805
PCA Strategies for Success Grants - Intermediate, 3806
Peter Norton Family Fndn Grants, 3849
Philip L. Graham Grants, 3876
Phoenix Coyotes Charities Grants, 3879
Piedmont Natural Gas Corp and Charitable Contributions, 3883
Powell Fndn Grants, 3942
Procter and Gamble Grants, 3967
Progress Energy Fndn Economic Vitality Grants, 3969
Rasmuson Fndn Individual Artists Awards, 4022

SUBJECT INDEX

Regional Arts and Cultural Council Opportunity Grants, 4046
Reinberger Fndn Grants, 4052
Richard and Caroline T. Gwathmey Grants, 4075
Richard Florsheim Art Grants, 4083
Richard H. Driehaus Fndn MacArthur Fund for Arts and Culture, 4085
Santa Barbara Fndn Towbes Fund for the Performing Arts Grants, 4288
Sid W. Richardson Fndn Grants, 4350
South Carolina Arts Comm Accessibility Grants, 4410
South Carolina Arts Commission Annual Operating Support for Organizations Grants, 4414
South Carolina Arts Commission Fellowships, 4415
Sprint Fndn Grants, 4463
TAC Arts Access Grant, 4549
Textron Corp Contributions Grants, 4601
Thomas Sill Fndn Grants, 4619
Tom's of Maine Grants, 4640
Union Square Arts Award, 4716
Vigneron Grants, 4938
Wallace Alexander Gerbode Fndn Special Award Grants, 4975
West Virginia Commission on the Arts Presenting Artists Grants, 5044
West Virginia Commission on the Arts Visual Arts Grants, 5051
Winifred & Harry B. Allen Fndn Grants, 5101
Wood-Claeyssens Fndn Grants, 5113

Visual Impairments
Agnes M. Lindsay Grants, 203
American Council of the Blind Scholarships, 427
Annunziata Sanguinetti Fndn Grants, 485
Armstrong McDonald Fndn Grants, 565
Atran Fndn Grants, 610
Carl W. and Carrie Mae Joslyn Grants, 938
Charles Delmar Fndn Grants, 1039
Chicago Board of Trade Fndn Grants, 1079
Claremont Community Fndn Grants, 1149
Columbus Fndn Small Grants, 1232
Cornerstone Fndn of NE Wisconsin Grants, 1375
Cralle Fndn Grants, 1394
Donald and Sylvia Robinson Family Fndn Grants, 1573
El Paso Community Fndn Grants, 1688
Eugene G. & Margaret M. Blackford Grants, 1763
Florence Hunt Maxwell Fndn Grants, 1844
George Gund Fndn Grants, 2020
Hagedorn Grants, 2207
J. Walton Bissell Fndn Grants, 2608
John W. Alden Grants, 2727
Josiah W. and Bessie H. Kline Fndn Grants, 2742
Lettie Pate Whitehead Fndn Grants, 2888
Lydia deForest Charitable Grants, 2946
Mericos Fndn Grants, 3121
Mitsubishi Electric America Fndn Grants, 3190
Nina Mason Pulliam Charitable Grants, 3443
NYCT Blindness and Visual Disabilities Grants, 3543
Pfizer Healthcare Charitable Contributions, 3863
Philadelphia Organizational Effectiveness Grants, 3872
Reader's Digest Partners for Sight Fndn Grants, 4036
S. Mark Taper Fndn Grants, 4201
Starr Fndn Grants, 4483
Thomas Sill Fndn Grants, 4619
U.S. Department of Educ Rehabilitation Training--Rehabilitation Continuing Educ Programs--Institute on Rehabilitation Issues, 4700
Union County Community Fndn Grants, 4711
W.P. and Bulah Luse Fndn Grants, 4965
William G. and Helen C. Hoffman Fndn Grants, 5080
Yellow Corp Fndn Grants, 5126

Vocational Counseling
Able Trust Voc Rehab Grants for Agencies, 103
Achelis Fndn Grants, 127
Bodman Fndn Grants, 807
DHHS Adolescent Family Life Demo Projects, 1524
GNOF Gulf Coast Oil Spill Grants, 2077
GNOF New Orleans Works Grants, 2088
Graco Fndn Grants, 2111

Legacy Fndn College Readiness Grant, 2874
U.S. Department of Educ Parent Information and Training, 4695

Vocational Services
Bernard and Audre Rapoport Fndn Community Building and Social Service Grants, 736
GNOF Gulf Coast Oil Spill Grants, 2077
GNOF New Orleans Works Grants, 2088

Vocational Training
Alfred E. Chase Charitable Fndn Grants, 366
Bernard and Audre Rapoport Fndn Community Building and Social Service Grants, 736
Charles Nelson Robinson Grants, 1052
DOL Youthbuild Grants, 1571
Emma G. Harris Fndn Grants, 1701
Gamble Fndn Grants, 1983
George W. Wells Fndn Grants, 2030
GNOF Gulf Coast Oil Spill Grants, 2077
GNOF Metropolitan Opportunities Grants, 2087
GNOF New Orleans Works Grants, 2088
IIE Japan-U.S. Teacher Exchange for Educ for Sustainable Development, 2457
KeyBank Fndn Grants, 2820
MGM Resorts Fndn Community Grants, 3153
Middlesex Savings Ed Opportunities Grants, 3174
NE Utilities Fndn Grants, 3498
Piedmont Natural Gas Fndn Workforce Development Grant, 3886
PMI Fndn Grants, 3918
Sioux Falls Area Community Grants, 4364
Sioux Falls Area Community Fndn Spot Grants, 4366
Tourism Cares Professional Dev Scholarships, 4648
Union Bank, N.A. Fndn Grants, 4709

Vocational/Technical Education
Able Trust Voc Rehab Grants for Agencies, 103
Agere Corp and Community Involvement Grants, 199
Akzo Nobel Chemicals Grants, 219
ALA EBSCO Community College Learning Resources Leadership Awards, 271
ALA EBSCO Community College Library Program Achievement Award, 272
American Council of the Blind Scholarships, 427
Appalachian Regional Commission Telecommunications Grants, 510
Atkinson Fndn Community Grants, 606
Bernard Osher Fndn Grants, 742
Besser Fndn Grants, 748
Burlington Industries Fndn Grants, 865
Charles Nelson Robinson Grants, 1052
Clay Fndn Grants, 1162
Connecticut Light & Power Corp Contributions, 1352
Constantin Fndn Grants, 1362
Cooper Industries Fndn Grants, 1370
Crail-Johnson Fndn Grants, 1393
D.F. Halton Fndn Grants, 1424
DaimlerChrysler Corp Grants, 1432
Duke Energy Economic Development Grants, 1619
Emma G. Harris Fndn Grants, 1701
FirstEnergy Fndn Community Grants, 1819
Frances L. and Edwin L. Cummings Grants, 1919
Georgia-Pacific Fndn Entrepreneurship Grants, 2033
GNOF Gulf Coast Oil Spill Grants, 2077
GNOF New Orleans Works Grants, 2088
Golden Rule Fndn Grants, 2098
Graco Fndn Grants, 2111
IIE Western Union Family Scholarships, 2462
Indiana Workforce Acceleration Grants, 2552
Irvin Stern Fndn Grants, 2585
Janus Fndn Grants, 2647
Kimball Int'l-Habig Fndn Grants, 2823
Mabel Louise Riley Fndn Grants, 2959
McCune Charitable Fndn Grants, 3077
Miller Brewing Corp Contributions Grants, 3180
National Housing Endowment Challenge/Build/Grow Grant, 3277
Norcliffe Fndn Grants, 3459
Oppenstein Brothers Fndn Grants, 3685

Paul and Mary Haas Fndn Contributions and Student Scholarships, 3756
Principal Financial Group Fndn Grants, 3966
Samuel S. Johnson Fndn Grants, 4239
Seabury Fndn Grants, 4316
Stackpole-Hall Fndn Grants, 4472
U.S. Department of Educ Innovative Strategies in Community Colleges for Working Adults and Displaced Workers Grants, 4692
U.S. Department of Educ Rehabilitation Research Training Centers, 4699
United Technologies Corp Grants, 4725
USDC Public Works and Economic Adjustment Assistance Grants, 4856
WILD Fndn Grants, 5068

Volleyball
ODKF Athletic Grants, 3638

Volunteers
3M Community Volunteer Award, 11
ACE Charitable Fndn Grants, 111
Aetna Fndn Volunteer Grants, 190
Agway Fndn Grants, 205
Allstate Agency Hands in the Community Grants, 388
ALZA Corp Contributions Grants, 405
AMA Fndn Jack B. McConnell, MD Awards for Excellence in Volunteerism, 411
Ann Arbor Area Community Fndn Grants, 474
Anschutz Family Fndn Grants, 486
Aragona Family Fndn Grants, 522
Aspen Community Fndn Grants, 592
ATA Local Community Relations Grants, 600
Award for Volunteer Service to the American Chemical Society, 626
Ball Brothers Fndn Organizational Effectiveness/ Executive Mentoring Grants, 638
Bank of America Charitable Volunteer Grants, 660
Baring Fndn Grants, 667
BCBSM Children Angel Awards, 705
Benton Community Fndn Grants, 730
Blue River Community Fndn Grants, 801
Bodman Fndn Grants, 807
Brown County Community Fndn Grants, 853
Brunswick Fndn Dollars for Doers Grants, 856
Brunswick Fndn Grants, 857
C.F. Adams Charitable Grants, 884
Cadence Design Systems Grants, 889
Cambridge Community Fndn Grants, 913
Campbell Soup Fndn Grants, 916
Caterpillar Fndn Grants, 954
Central Minnesota Community Fndn Grants, 995
Central New York Community Fndn Grants, 996
CFFVR Waupaca Area Community Fndn Grants, 1023
CharityWorks Grants, 1036
Charles G. Koch Charitable Fndn Grants, 1041
Charles Stewart Mott Fndn Grants, 1055
Chemtura Corp Contributions Grants, 1067
Chesapeake Bay Trust Forestry Mini Grants, 1071
Chesapeake Bay Trust Mini Grants, 1072
CNCS AmeriCorps Indian Planning Grants, 1180
CNCS AmeriCorps NCCC Project Grants, 1181
CNCS AmeriCorps State and National Grants, 1182
CNCS Foster Grandparent Grants, 1185
CNCS Senior Companion Grants, 1187
CNCS Senior Corps Retired and Senior Volunteer Grants, 1188
CNCS Social Innovation Grants, 1189
Colorado Interstate Gas Grants, 1213
Comcast Fndn Grants, 1235
Comerica Charitable Fndn Grants, 1237
Commonwealth Edison Grants, 1240
Community Fndn of Bartholomew County Heritage Grants, 1267
Community Fndn of Bartholomew County James A. Henderson Award for Fundraising, 1268
Community Fndn of Greater Fort Wayne - Community Endowment and Clarke Endowment Grants, 1285
Community Fndn of Greenville Community Enrichment Grants, 1294

1008 / Volunteerism

ConocoPhillips Grants, 1355
Constellation Energy Corp Grants, 1364
Cooper Industries Fndn Grants, 1370
Coors Brewing Corp Contributions Grants, 1371
Davis Conservation Fndn Grants, 1461
Dell Fndn Open Grants, 1490
Dynegy Fndn Grants, 1630
eBay Fndn Community Grants, 1648
Fargo-Moorhead Area Fndn Grants, 1788
FCYO Youth Organizing Grants, 1797
Fidelity Fndn Grants, 1805
G.N. Wilcox Grants, 1982
Giant Eagle Fndn Grants, 2049
Great-West Life Grants, 2130
Harry B. and Jane H. Brock Fndn Grants, 2237
Helen Steiner Rice Fndn Grants, 2299
Help America Fndn Grants, 2301
Hilton Hotels Corp Giving Grants, 2331
Hormel Foods Charitable Grants, 2368
Huntington County Community Fndn - Stephanie Pyle Grant, 2407
ICC Community Service Mini-Grant, 2426
ICC Day of Service Action Grants, 2427
ICC Faculty Fellowships, 2428
ICC Listening to Communities Grants, 2429
ICC Scholarship of Engagement Faculty Grants, 2430
Illinois DNR Volunteer Fire Assistance Grants, 2504
Int'l Paper Company Fndn Grants, 2568
J.C. Penney Company Grants, 2594
Janus Fndn Grants, 2647
Jessie Ball Dupont Grants, 2671
John Ben Snow Grants, 2687
Johns Manville Grants, 2716
Johnson Controls Fndn Educ and Arts Matching Gift Grants, 2721
John W. Gardner Leadership Award, 2731
John W. Speas and Effie E. Speas Grants, 2732
Join Hands Day Excellence Awards, 2733
Katie's Krops Grants, 2792
Land O'Lakes Fndn Dollars for Doers, 2860
Lewis H. Humphreys Charitable Grants, 2889
Lillian S. Wells Fndn Grants, 2901
Lockheed Martin Philanthropic Grants, 2918
Louis and Elizabeth Nave Flarsheim Charitable Fndn Grants, 2924
M3C Fellowships, 2955
Maine Community Fndn Baldwin Area Grants, 2974
McCombs Fndn Grants, 3075
MetLife Fndn Empowering Older Adults Grants, 3130
MetLife Fndn Preparing Young People Grants, 3131
MetLife Fndn Promoting Employee Volunteerism, 3132
MMS and Alliance Charitable Fndn Grants for Community Action and Care for the Medically Uninsured, 3194
MONY Fndn Grants, 3214
Morgan Babcock Scholarships, 3217
Nordson Corp Fndn Grants, 3462
North Carolina GlaxoSmithKline Fndn Grants, 3490
Oklahoma City Community Programs & Grants, 3666
Olin Corp Charitable Grants, 3669
Oppenstein Brothers Fndn Grants, 3685
PepsiCo Fndn Grants, 3819
PetSmart Model Volunteering Grants, 3854
PGE Fndn Grants, 3869
Phi Upsilon Omicron Florence Fallgatter Distinguished Service Award, 3877
PNM Reduce Your Use Grants, 3926
Praxair Fndn Grants, 3944
Princeton Area Community Fndn Greater Mercer Grants, 3963
Procter and Gamble Grants, 3967
Prudential CARES Volunteer Grants, 3974
Prudential Fndn Educ Grants, 3977
Prudential Spirit of Community Awards, 3978
Quaker Oats Company Kids Care Clubs Grants, 3992
Research Program at Earthwatch Grants, 4053
Rhode Island Fndn Grants, 4073
RISCA Project Grants for Organizations, Individuals and Educ, 4100
Rohm and Haas Company Grants, 4145

Sensient Technologies Fndn Grants, 4337
Sisters of Mercy of North Carolina Fndn Grants, 4375
Sisters of Saint Joseph Charitable Grants, 4376
Sodexo Fndn STOP Hunger Scholarships, 4400
Sony Corp of America Corp Philanthropy Grants, 4405
Stackpole-Hall Fndn Grants, 4472
State Farm Project Ignition Grants, 4487
Steve Young Family Fndn Grants, 4503
SVP Early Childhood Dev and Parenting Grants, 4538
Symantec Community Relations and Corp Philanthropy Grants, 4544
Taproot Fndn Capacity-Building Service Grants, 4560
Tiger Woods Fndn Grants, 4634
Tri-State Community Twenty-first Century Endowment Grants, 4666
Triangle Community Fndn Community Grants, 4667
Triangle Community Fndn Donor Grants, 4668
Union Benevolent Association Grants, 4710
United Technologies Corp Grants, 4725
UPS Fndn Economic and Global Lit Grants, 4730
Virginia A. Hodgkinson Research Prize, 4940
W.K. Kellogg Fndn Civic Engagement Grants, 4960
W.K. Kellogg Fndn Healthy Kids Grants, 4961
Wilburforce Fndn Grants, 5067
WILD Fndn Grants, 5068
Xerox Fndn Grants, 5122
Youth Philanthropy Project, 5132
YSA ABC Summer of Service Awards, 5133
YSA MLK Day Lead Organizer Grants, 5136
YSA National Child Awareness Month Youth Ambassador Grants, 5137
YSA Sodexo Lead Organizer Grants, 5140
YSA UnitedHealth HEROES Service-Learning Grants, 5142

Voter Educational Programs
Farmers Insurance Corp Giving Grants, 1791
HBF Encouraging Citizen Involvement Grants, 2272
NYCT Civic Affairs Grants, 3545
Ottinger Fndn Grants, 3712
Threshold Fndn Election Integrity Grants, 4625

Voter Registration Programs
HBF Encouraging Citizen Involvement Grants, 2272
Joyce Fndn Democracy Grants, 2748

Wage and Salary Administration
NYSCA Architecture, Planning, and Design: Project Support Grants, 3576
NYSCA Museum: Project Support Grants, 3604
NYSCA State and Local Partnerships: Administrative Salary Support Grants, 3618
NYSCA Theatre Pro Performances Grants, 3625

Waste Management
Bill and Melinda Gates Fndn Water, Sanitation and Hygiene Grants, 770
EPA Hazardous Waste Grants for Tribes, 1733
EPA Tribal Solid Waste Management Assistance Grants, 1741
EREF Sustainability Research Grants, 1748
EREF Unsolicited Proposal Grants, 1749
Volvo Adventure Environmental Awards, 4952

Waste Management (Agriculture)
EPA Hazardous Waste Grants for Tribes, 1733
Indiana Waste Tire Grants, 2551
USDA Fed-State Marketing Improvement Grants, 4810

Waste Management/Fossil Energy
Honor the Earth Grants, 2361
Indiana Waste Tire Grants, 2551
Lindbergh Grants, 2907
NYCT New York City Environment Grants, 3556
Rohm and Haas Company Grants, 4145
USDA Bioenergy Program for Advanced Biofuel Payments to Advanced Biofuel Producers, 4799

SUBJECT INDEX

Wastewater Treatment
Bill and Melinda Gates Fndn Water, Sanitation and Hygiene Grants, 770
EPA Hazardous Waste Grants for Tribes, 1733
Illinois DCEO Business Development Public Infrastructure Grants, 2483
USDA Native American Indian Utilities Grants, 4820
USDA Section 306C Water and Waste Disposal Grants to Alleviate Health Risks, 4834
USDA Section 306D Water and Waste System Grants for Alaskan Villages, 4835
USDA Solid Waste Management Grants, 4838
USDA Water and Waste Disposal Grants, 4844

Water Polo
ODKF Athletic Grants, 3638

Water Resources
3 Rivers Wet Weather Demonstration Grants, 9
1675 Fndn Grants, 35
Alaska Conservation Operating Grants, 323
Altria Group Environment Grants, 400
Appalachian Regional Commission Transportation and Highways Grants, 512
Barr Fndn Grants (Massachusetts), 676
Beldon Grants, 720
Bill and Melinda Gates Fndn Water, Sanitation and Hygiene Grants, 770
Brunswick Fndn Grants, 857
Bullitt Fndn Grants, 862
Bydale Fndn Grants, 882
Cape Branch Fndn Grants, 919
Carolyn Fndn Grants, 942
Chesapeake Bay Trust Capacity Building Grants, 1068
Chesapeake Bay Environmental Ed Grants, 1069
Chesapeake Bay Trust Forestry Mini Grants, 1071
Chesapeake Bay Trust Mini Grants, 1072
Chesapeake Bay Trust Outreach and Community Engagement Grants, 1073
Chesapeake Bay Trust Pioneer Grants, 1074
CNCS AmeriCorps State and National Grants, 1182
Community Fndn for Muskegon County Grants, 1256
Diageo Fndn Grants, 1546
FishAmerica Fndn Marine and Anadromous Fish Habitat Restoration Grants, 1829
FishAmerica Fndn Research Grants, 1830
Fremont Area Community Fndn Grants, 1955
Freshwater Future Insight Services Grants, 1960
Freshwater Future Project Grants, 1961
Gebbie Fndn Grants, 1995
GNOF Coastal 5 + 1 Grants, 2070
Greater Milwaukee Fndn Grants, 2137
HRF Hudson River Improvement Grants, 2378
Joyce Fndn Environment Grants, 2750
MDEQ Beach Monitoring Grants - Inland Lakes, 3094
MDEQ Coastal Management Planning and Construction Grants, 3097
MDEQ Great Lakes Areas of Concern Land Acquisition Grants, 3099
MDEQ Local Water Quality Monitoring Grants, 3100
MDEQ Wellhead Protection Grants, 3101
NFF Collaboration Support Grants, 3342
NFF Community Assistance Grants, 3343
NFF Matching Grants, 3344
NFF Mid-Capacity Assistance Grants, 3345
NFWF Bronx River Watershed Init Grants, 3360
NFWF Chesapeake Bay Conservation Innovation Grants, 3363
NFWF Chesapeake Bay Stewardship Fund Small Watershed Grants, 3364
NFWF Chesapeake Targeted Watershed Grants, 3365
NFWF Long Island Sound Futures Grants, 3376
NFWF Shell Marine Habitat Grants, 3391
NFWF Southern Co Longleaf Legacy Grants, 3392
NFWF Upper Mississippi Riv Watershed Grants, 3398
NW Fund for the Environment Grants, 3510
PepsiCo Fndn Grants, 3819
Pioneer Hi-Bred Community Grants, 3895
Rose Fndn For Communities and the Environment Watershed Protection Grants, 4160

SUBJECT INDEX

Sweet Water Grants, 4541
Thompson Charitable Fndn Grants, 4622
Union Bank, N.A. Fndn Grants, 4709
USAID Grants for Building Disaster-Resilient Communities in Southern Africa, 4755
USAID Palestinian Community Infrastructure Development Grants, 4774
USDA Native American Indian Utilities Grants, 4820
USDA Section 306D Water and Waste System Grants for Alaskan Villages, 4835
USDA Solid Waste Management Grants, 4838
W.K. Kellogg Fndn Healthy Kids Grants, 4961
Wabash River Enhancement Corp Agricultural Cost-Share Grants, 4968
William Bingham Fndn Grants, 5077
William C. Kenney Watershed Protection Fndn Ecosystem Grants, 5079

Water Resources, Environmental Impacts
American Rivers Community-Based Restoration Program River Grants, 444
Appalachian Regional Commission Transportation and Highways Grants, 512
Bella Vista Fndn Grants, 722
Bill and Melinda Gates Fndn Water, Sanitation and Hygiene Grants, 770
Chesapeake Bay Environmental Ed Grants, 1069
Chesapeake Bay Fisheries & Headwaters Grants, 1070
Chesapeake Bay Trust Outreach and Community Engagement Grants, 1073
Community Fndn for Greater New Haven Quinnipiac River Grants, 1250
Freshwater Future Insight Services Grants, 1960
GNOF Bayou Communities Grants, 2069
GNOF Coastal 5 + 1 Grants, 2070
GNOF Environmental Grants, 2073
GNOF Gulf Coast Oil Spill Grants, 2077
HAF Natural Environment Grants, 2202
Household Int'l Corp Giving Grants, 2372
IDEM Section 205(j) Water Quality Management Planning Grants, 2434
IDEM Section 319(h) Nonpoint Source Grants, 2435
Illinois DNR Migratory Waterfowl Stamp Grants, 2498
Indiana Clean Vessel Act Grants, 2535
Init Fndn Healthy Lakes and Rivers Partnerships, 2558
Joyce Fndn Environment Grants, 2750
Lumpkin Family Healthy Environments Grants, 2941
MDEQ Beach Monitoring Grants - Inland Lakes, 3094
MDEQ Community Pollution Prevention (P2) Grants: Household Drug Collections, 3098
MDEQ Wellhead Protection Grants, 3101
Meadows Fndn Grants, 3104
NFF Community Assistance Grants, 3343
NFF Mid-Capacity Assistance Grants, 3345
NFWF Bronx River Watershed Init Grants, 3360
NFWF Chesapeake Bay Stewardship Fund Small Watershed Grants, 3364
NFWF Long Island Sound Futures Grants, 3376
NFWF Sustain Our Great Lakes Grants, 3396
Northern Chautauqua Environmental Grants, 3501
Pathways to Nature Conservation Grants, 3745
PepsiCo Fndn Grants, 3819
Rose Fndn for Comm & the Environment N California Environmental Grassroots Grants, 4158
Rose Fndn For Communities and the Environment Watershed Protection Grants, 4160
Sioux Falls Area Community Grants, 4364
Sioux Falls Area Community Fndn Spot Grants, 4366
USDC/NOAA Open Rivers Init Grants, 4847
Wabash River Enhancement Corp Agricultural Cost-Share Grants, 4968
Wabash River Enhancement Corp Urban, 4969
Water and Land Stewardship Grants, 5002
White County Community Fndn Grants, 5057

Water Resources, Management/Planning
Appalachian Regional Commission Transportation and Highways Grants, 512
Bill and Melinda Gates Fndn Water, Sanitation and Hygiene Grants, 770

Blue Cross Blue Shield of Minnesota Fndn - Healthy Equity: Health Impact Assessment Demonstration Project Grants, 795
Blue Cross Blue Shield of Minnesota Fndn - Healthy Equity: Health Impact Assessment Grants, 796
Chesapeake Bay Trust Capacity Building Grants, 1068
GNOF Coastal 5 + 1 Grants, 2070
GNOF Community Revitalization Grants, 2071
IDEM Section 205(j) Water Quality Management Planning Grants, 2434
IEDC Industrial Development Grant Fund, 2443
Illinois DNR Youth Recreation Corps Grants, 2508
Joyce Fndn Environment Grants, 2750
Lindbergh Grants, 2907
NFWF Chesapeake Bay Stewardship Fund Small Watershed Grants, 3364
PepsiCo Fndn Grants, 3819
Rose Fndn For Communities and the Environment Watershed Protection Grants, 4160
Union Pacific Fndn Community and Civic Grants, 4714
Volvo Adventure Environmental Awards, 4952
Wabash River Enhancement Corp Agricultural Cost-Share Grants, 4968

Water Supply
Aid for Starving Children Int'l Grants, 212
Altria Group Environment Grants, 400
Appalachian Regional Commission Transportation and Highways Grants, 512
Bill and Melinda Gates Fndn Water, Sanitation and Hygiene Grants, 770
Bush Fndn Ecological Health Grants, 874
Diageo Fndn Grants, 1546
GNOF Gulf Coast Oil Spill Grants, 2077
IDEM Section 205(j) Water Quality Management Planning Grants, 2434
IDEM Section 319(h) Nonpoint Source Grants, 2435
MDEQ Wellhead Protection Grants, 3101
Monsanto Int'l Grants, 3207
NFWF Chesapeake Bay Stewardship Fund Small Watershed Grants, 3364
PepsiCo Fndn Grants, 3819
Rose Fndn For Communities and the Environment Watershed Protection Grants, 4160
USAID Grants for Building Disaster-Resilient Communities in Southern Africa, 4755
USAID Mekong Partnership for the Environment Project Grants, 4769
USAID Palestinian Community Infrastructure Development Grants, 4774
USDA Emergency Community Water Assistance Grants, 4807
USDA Household Water Well System Grants, 4814
USDA Individual Water and Waste Water Grants, 4817
USDA Native American Indian Utilities Grants, 4820
USDA Section 306C Water and Waste Disposal Grants to Alleviate Health Risks, 4834
USDA Technical Assistance and Training Grants for Rural Waste Systems, 4842
USDA Water and Waste Disposal Grants, 4844
William & Flora Hewlett Environmental Grants, 5074
William Bingham Fndn Grants, 5077

Water Treatment
Bill and Melinda Gates Fndn Water, Sanitation and Hygiene Grants, 770
IDEM Section 205(j) Water Quality Management Planning Grants, 2434
Illinois DCEO Business Development Public Infrastructure Grants, 2483
NFWF Chesapeake Bay Stewardship Fund Small Watershed Grants, 3364
Rose Fndn For Communities and the Environment Watershed Protection Grants, 4160
USAID Grants for Building Disaster-Resilient Communities in Southern Africa, 4755
USAID Palestinian Community Infrastructure Development Grants, 4774
USDA Emergency Community Water Assistance Grants, 4807

USDA Section 306C Water and Waste Disposal Grants to Alleviate Health Risks, 4834
USDA Section 306D Water and Waste System Grants for Alaskan Villages, 4835
USDA Solid Waste Management Grants, 4838
USDA Water and Waste Disposal Grants, 4844
USDC Public Works and Economic Adjustment Assistance Grants, 4856

Waterways and Harbors
American Rivers Community-Based Restoration Program River Grants, 444
Chesapeake Bay Fisheries & Headwaters Grants, 1070
Chesapeake Bay Trust Restoration Grants, 1075
Freshwater Future Healing Our Waters Grants, 1959
Freshwater Future Insight Services Grants, 1960
Freshwater Future Project Grants, 1961
Freshwater Future Special Opportunity Grants, 1962
GNOF Coastal 5 + 1 Grants, 2070
Grand Victoria Fndn Illinois Core Grants, 2126
HRF Hudson River Improvement Grants, 2378
Indiana Boating Infrastructure Grants (BIG P), 2534
MDEQ Coastal Management Planning and Construction Grants, 3097
MDEQ Local Water Quality Monitoring Grants, 3100
NFF Community Assistance Grants, 3343
NFWF Chesapeake Bay Stewardship Fund Small Watershed Grants, 3364
Patrick and Aimee Butler Family Fndn Community Environment Grants, 3748
Wabash River Enhancement Corp Agricultural Cost-Share Grants, 4968
Wabash River Enhancement Corp Urban, 4969

Welfare Reform
Baton Rouge Area Fndn Every Kid a King Grants, 681
DHHS Welfare Reform Research, Evaluations, and National Studies Grants, 1540
Harris Graduate School of Public Policy Studies Research Development Grants, 2232
Legler Benbough Fndn Grants, 2877
Macquarie Bank Fndn Grants, 2966
NYCT Social Services and Welfare Grants, 3557
Public Welfare Fndn Grants, 3984
Whitley County Community Fndn Grants, 5060

Welfare-to-Work Programs
Abell Fndn Workforce Development Grants, 97
AEGON Transamerica Fndn Civic and Community Grants, 177
Benton County Fndn Grants, 731
Bishop Robert Paddock Grants, 775
Carl R. Hendrickson Family Fndn Grants, 935
Cessna Fndn Grants, 1000
Chicago Community Poverty Alleviation Grants, 1091
CICF Efroymson Grants, 1120
Citigroup Fndn Grants, 1139
Cleveland Fenn Ed Grants, 1169
CNCS AmeriCorps State and National Grants, 1182
D. W. McMillan Fndn Grants, 1426
Do Right Fndn Grants, 1581
Edward and Ellen Roche Relief Fndn Grants, 1663
Elizabeth Carse Fndn Grants, 1681
Elizabeth Morse Genius Charitable Grants, 1682
Frank B. Hazard General Charity Grants, 1926
Helen Bader Fndn Grants, 2293
Mabel Louise Riley Fndn Family Strengthening Small Grants, 2958
Marin Community Fndn Ending the Cycle of Poverty Grants, 3011
Meyer Fndn Economic Security Grants, 3141
New Jersey Center for Hispanic Policy, Research and Development Workforce Grants, 3330
NYCT Social Services and Welfare Grants, 3557
Priddy Fndn Grants, 3957
Prudential Fndn Educ Grants, 3977
Robert R. McCormick Tribune Comm Grants, 4119
Robert R. McCormick Tribune Veterans Grants, 4120
SSA Work Incentives Planning & Assistance, 4465
Textron Corp Contributions Grants, 4601

U.S. Bank Fndn Grants, 4686
Union Bank, N.A. Fndn Grants, 4709
USAID Workforce Development Program in Mexico Grants, 4787
Verizon Fndn Great Lakes Region Grants, 4912
Verizon Fndn Maryland Grants, 4917
Verizon Fndn New York Grants, 4919
Verizon Fndn NE Region Grants, 4920
Verizon Fndn Pennsylvania Grants, 4921
Verizon Fndn SE Region Grants, 4923
Verizon Fndn Vermont Grants, 4924
Verizon Fndn Virginia Grants, 4925
Verizon Fndn West Virginia Grants, 4926
Whitley County Community Fndn Grants, 5060

Wellness
7-Eleven Coorporate Giving Grants, 18
CFFVR Jewelers Mutual Charitable Giving, 1014
Chefs Move to Schools Grants, 1066
CICF City of Noblesville Community Grant, 1118
CICF J. Proctor Grant for Aged Men & Women, 1124
Cigna Civic Affairs Sponsorships, 1129
Finish Line Youth Fndn Founder's Grants, 1812
Finish Line Youth Fndn Grants, 1813
Finish Line Youth Fndn Legacy Grants, 1814
Fndn for Mid South Health & Wellness Grants, 1899
Giant Food Charitable Grants, 2050
Hillsdale County Comm General Adult Grants, 2328
Mary Wilmer Covey Charitable Grants, 3049
Mt. Sinai Health Care Fndn Health of the Urban Community Grants, 3227
Robert R. McCormick Tribune Comm Grants, 4119
Seattle Fndn Health and Wellness Grants, 4328
Walmart Fndn Facility Giving Grants, 4978
Walmart Fndn National Giving Grants, 4979
Washington Gas Charitable Contributions, 5000

Wetlands
2701 Fndn Grants, 37
Banrock Station Wines Wetlands Grants, 662
Bella Vista Fndn Grants, 722
Cape Branch Fndn Grants, 919
Chesapeake Bay Environmental Ed Grants, 1069
Chesapeake Bay Trust Mini Grants, 1072
CICF Efroymson Grants, 1120
Earth Island Institute Community Wetland Restoration Grants, 1642
Freshwater Future Special Opportunity Grants, 1962
GNOF Coastal 5 + 1 Grants, 2070
HAF Natural Environment Grants, 2202
National Wetlands Awards, 3282
NFWF Columbia River Estuarine Coastal Grant, 3367
NFWF Community Salmon Fund Partnerships, 3368
NFWF Five-Star Restoration Challenge Grants, 3373
NFWF Oregon Governor's Fund for the Environment Grants, 3383
NFWF Pioneers in Conservation Grants, 3386
NFWF Shell Marine Habitat Grants, 3391
NFWF Southern Co Longleaf Legacy Grants, 3392
NFWF Upper Mississippi Riv Watershed Grants, 3398
North American Wetlands Conservation Grants, 3465
NW Fund for the Environment Grants, 3510
NYCT New York City Environment Grants, 3556
Rose Fndn for Comm & the Environment N California Environmental Grassroots Grants, 4158
Sweet Water Grants, 4541
Tides California Wildlands Grassroots Fund, 4630
Waste Management Charitable Giving Grants, 5001

Wilderness
Illinois DNR State Furbearer Grants, 2501
NFF Collaboration Support Grants, 3342
NFF Mid-Capacity Assistance Grants, 3345

Wildlife
2701 Fndn Grants, 37
Acorn Fndn Grants, 131
Alaska Conservation Operating Grants, 323
Albert and Bessie Mae Kronkosky Charitable Fndn Grants, 339
Alexander H. Bright Charitable Grants, 358
Alfred C. and Ersa S. Arbogast Fndn Grants, 365
Alfred J Mcallister and Dorothy N Mcallister Fndn Grants, 367
Ann L. & Carol Green Rhodes Charitable Grants, 483
Aragona Family Fndn Grants, 522
Arthur Ashley Williams Fndn Grants, 572
Arthur B. Schultz Fndn Grants, 573
Banfi Vintners Fndn Grants, 653
Barbara Meyer Elsner Fndn Grants, 665
Batchelor Fndn Grants, 679
Beim Fndn Grants, 718
Bullitt Fndn Grants, 862
Cambridge Community Fndn Grants, 913
Carl C. Icahn Fndn Grants, 929
Chesapeake Bay Fisheries & Headwaters Grants, 1070
Chevron Hawaii Educ Fund, 1077
Chicago Board of Trade Fndn Grants, 1079
Chicago White Metal Charitable Fndn Grants, 1102
Chingos Fndn Grants, 1109
CICF Efroymson Grants, 1120
Collins Fndn Grants, 1209
Community Fndn of Greater Tampa Grants, 1292
Community Fndn of the Verdugos Grants, 1322
Constellation Energy Corp EcoStar Grants, 1363
Cruise Industry Charitable Fndn Grants, 1404
Davis Conservation Fndn Grants, 1461
Dolfinger-McMahon Fndn Grants, 1565
Donald and Sylvia Robinson Family Fndn Grants, 1573
Dream Weaver Fndn, 1604
Elkhart County Community Fndn Fund for Elkhart County, 1683
El Paso Community Fndn Grants, 1688
FishAmerica Fndn Chesapeake Bay Grants, 1827
FishAmerica Fndn Conservation Grants, 1828
FishAmerica Fndn Marine and Anadromous Fish Habitat Restoration Grants, 1829
FishAmerica Fndn Research Grants, 1830
Fuller Fndn Grants, 1974
George and Ruth Bradford Fndn Grants, 2010
GNOF Gulf Coast Oil Spill Grants, 2077
Great Lakes Fishery Trust Access Grants, 2145
Great Lakes Protection Grants, 2147
GreenWorks! Butterfly Garden Grants, 2159
Greygates Fndn Grants, 2164
H.A. and Mary K. Chapman Charitable Grants, 2182
HAF Natural Environment Grants, 2202
Illinois DNR Habitat Grants, 2497
Illinois DNR Migratory Waterfowl Stamp Grants, 2498
Illinois DNR Schoolyard Habitat Action Grants, 2500
Illinois DNR State Furbearer Grants, 2501
Illinois DNR State Pheasant Grants, 2502
Illinois DNR Wildlife Preservation Fund Large Project Grants, 2505
Illinois DNR Wildlife Preservation Fund Small Project Grants, 2506
Illinois DNR Wildlife Preservation Maintenance of Wildlife Rehabilitation Facilities Grants, 2507
J.M. Long Fndn Grants, 2603
James Ford Bell Fndn Grants, 2623
James M. Cox Fndn of Georgia Grants, 2634
James S. Copley Fndn Grants, 2637
John M. Weaver Fndn Grants, 2705
Kenneth A. Scott Charitable Grants, 2801
Knox County Community Fndn Grants, 2831
Lindbergh Grants, 2907
Liz Claiborne and Art Ortenberg Fndn Grants, 2914
Lucy Downing Nisbet Charitable Grants, 2935
M. Bastian Family Fndn Grants, 2951
Mars Fndn Grants, 3025
Mary K. Chapman Fndn Grants, 3042
MDEQ Coastal Management Planning and Construction Grants, 3097
MDEQ Great Lakes Areas of Concern Land Acquisition Grants, 3099
Mericos Fndn Grants, 3121
Natalie W. Furniss Charitable Grants, 3244
Nature Hills Nursery Green America Awards, 3287
NFF Collaboration Support Grants, 3342
NFF Community Assistance Grants, 3343
NFF Matching Grants, 3344
NFF Mid-Capacity Assistance Grants, 3345
NFWF/Exxon Save the Tiger Grants, 3354
NFWF Acres for America Grants, 3355
NFWF Alaska Fish and Wildlife Grants, 3356
NFWF Aleutian Islands Risk Assessment Grants, 3357
NFWF Bird Conservation Init Grants, 3358
NFWF Budweiser Conservationist of the Year, 3361
NFWF California Coastal Restoration Grants, 3362
NFWF Columbia Basin Water Trans Grants, 3366
NFWF ConocoPhillips SPIRIT of Conservation Migratory Bird Grants, 3369
NFWF Dissolved Oxygen Environmental Benefit Grants, 3372
NFWF Long Island Sound Futures Grants, 3376
NFWF Marine & Coastal Conservation Grants, 3377
NFWF National Whale Conservation Grants, 3378
NFWF National Wildlife Refuge Friends Group Grants, 3379
NFWF Pulling Together Init Grants, 3387
NFWF Seafarer's Environmental Educ Grants, 3390
NFWF State Comprehensive Wildlife Conservation Support Grants, 3395
NFWF Sustain Our Great Lakes Grants, 3396
NFWF Tampa Bay Environmental Grants, 3397
NFWF Wildlife & Habitat Conservation Grants, 3399
NFWF Wildlife Links Grants, 3400
Nina Mason Pulliam Charitable Grants, 3443
Norcross Wildlife Fndn Grants, 3460
North American Wetlands Conservation Grants, 3465
North Dakota Community Fndn Grants, 3493
NW Fund for the Environment Grants, 3510
NSS Fndn Hunting Heritage Partnership Grants, 3530
Olin Corp Charitable Grants, 3669
Oracle Corp Contributions Grants, 3686
Pathways to Nature Conservation Grants, 3745
Perkins Charitable Fndn Grants, 3823
Perry County Community Fndn Grants, 3827
Pike County Community Fndn Grants, 3888
Posey County Community Fndn Grants, 3939
Richard King Mellon Fndn Grants, 4087
Rose Fndn for Comm & the Environment N California Environmental Grassroots Grants, 4158
Royal Caribbean Cruises Ocean Fund, 4165
Schumann Fund for New Jersey Grants, 4311
SeaWorld & Busch Gardens Conservation Grants, 4332
Shared Earth Fndn Grants, 4339
Sioux Falls Area Community Grants, 4364
Sioux Falls Area Community Fndn Spot Grants, 4366
Skaggs Fndn Grants, 4378
Spencer County Community Fndn Grants, 4451
Susan Mott Webb Charitable Grants, 4536
Sweet Water Grants, 4541
Tom's of Maine Grants, 4640
Trull Fndn Grants, 4673
Union Bank, N.A. Fndn Grants, 4709
Warrick County Community Fndn Grants, 4987
Waste Management Charitable Giving Grants, 5001
Wilburforce Fndn Grants, 5067
WILD Fndn Grants, 5068
William & Flora Hewlett Environmental Grants, 5074
Winifred & Harry B. Allen Fndn Grants, 5101
WWF Int'l Smart Gear Competition, 5120
Yawkey Fndn Grants, 5125

Wine and Grape Industry
USDA Fed-State Marketing Improvement Grants, 4810

Women
100 Women in Hedge Funds Fndn Grants, 28
360 Degrees of Giving Grants, 32
AAUW Breaking through Barriers Award, 74
ACE Charitable Fndn Grants, 111
ACF Head Start and Early Head Start Grants, 120
ACS Award for Encouraging Women into Careers in the Chemical Sciences, 133
AEC Grants, 175
A Fund for Women Grants, 195
AIChE Women's Inits Committee Mentorship Excellence Award, 209

SUBJECT INDEX

Women / 1011

Alberto Culver Corp Contributions Grants, 343
Allen Hilles Grants, 378
Allstate Corp Giving Grants, 386
Allstate Corp Hometown Commitment Grants, 387
Amber Grants, 413
American Jewish World Service Grants, 441
ANLAF Int'l Fund for Sexual Minorities Grants, 471
Archer Daniels Midland Fndn Grants, 527
Arizona Women Deborah G. Carstens Grants, 543
Arizona Fndn for Women General Grants, 544
Arkell Hall Fndn Grants, 562
Armstrong McDonald Grants, 565
Arthur and Rochelle Belfer Fndn Grants, 570
Atlanta Women's Fndn Grants, 609
Atran Fndn Grants, 610
Avon Products Fndn Grants, 625
AWDF Main Grants, 627
AWDF Solidarity Grants, 628
Baltimore Women's Giving Circle Grants, 650
Beim Fndn Grants, 718
Benton Community Fndn - The Cookie Jar Grant, 729
Bill and Melinda Gates Fndn Agricultural Development Grants, 765
Bodenwein Public Benevolent Fndn Grants, 806
Boston Fndn Grants, 819
Boston Globe Fndn Grants, 821
Boston Jewish Community Women's Grants, 822
Brico Grants, 835
Bristol-Myers Squibb Fndn Community Grants, 840
Brooklyn Benevolent Society Grants, 847
Cambridge Community Fndn Grants, 913
Carnegie Corp of New York Grants, 940
Carrie E. and Lena V. Glenn Fndn Grants, 944
CDC Grants for Violence-Related Injury Prevention Research, 974
Cemala Fndn Grants, 988
CFFVR Schmidt Family G4 Grants, 1020
CFFVR Women's Fund for the Fox Valley Region Grants, 1025
Charles Delmar Fndn Grants, 1039
Charlotte R. Schmidlapp Grants, 1058
Chicago Fndn for Women Grants, 1096
Claneil Fndn Grants, 1145
Colgate-Palmolive Company Grants, 1202
Commission on Religion in Appalachia Grants, 1238
Community Fndn for Greater New Haven Women & Girls Grants, 1254
Community Fndn of Bartholomew County Women's Giving Circle, 1269
Community Fndn of Riverside County Grants, 1304
ConocoPhillips Fndn Grants, 1354
ConocoPhillips Grants, 1355
Corina Higginson Grants, 1373
Cowles Charitable Grants, 1392
Cralle Fndn Grants, 1394
Cummins Fndn Grants, 1415
Daisy Marquis Jones Fndn Grants, 1434
Dallas Women's Fndn Grants, 1438
Daphne Seybolt Culpeper Memorial Fndn Grants, 1445
David Lane Grants for Aged & Indigent Women, 1453
Delaware Community Fund For Women Grants, 1484
Dennis and Phyllis Washington Fndn Grants, 1498
Dining for Women Grants, 1548
Do Right Fndn Grants, 1581
Edward and Ellen Roche Relief Fndn Grants, 1663
Eileen Fisher Activating Leadership Grants for Women and Girls, 1676
Eileen Fisher Women-Owned Business Grants, 1677
El Paso Community Fndn Grants, 1688
Eulalie Bloedel Schneider Fndn Grants, 1767
ExxonMobil Fndn Women's Economic Grants, 1778
Fargo-Moorhead Area Fndn Woman's Grants, 1789
Fassino Fndn Grants, 1793
Ford Fndn Peace and Social Justice Grants, 1884
Fndn for the Carolinas Grants, 1896
Fourjay Fndn Grants, 1913
Frederick McDonald Grants, 1946
Fremont Area Community Fndn Grants, 1955
Gardiner Howland Shaw Fndn Grants, 1986
General Service Fndn Colorado Grants, 2005

General Service Fndn Human Rights and Economic Justice Grants, 2006
George Family Fndn Grants, 2017
Georgia-Pacific Fndn Entrepreneurship Grants, 2033
Georgia Power Fndn Grants, 2039
Girl's Best Friend Fndn Grants, 2057
GNOF Maison Hospitaliere Grants, 2086
Go Daddy Cares Charitable Contributions, 2094
Grassroots Exchange Grants, 2128
Greater Worcester Comm Discretionary Grants, 2140
H.J. Heinz Company Fndn Grants, 2184
Harry B. and Jane H. Brock Fndn Grants, 2237
Health Canada National Seniors Indep Grants, 2278
Health Fndn of Greater Indianapolis Grants, 2282
Heineman Fndn for Research, Educ, Charitable and Scientific Purposes, 2290
Helena Rubinstein Fndn Grants, 2292
Helen Steiner Rice Fndn Grants, 2299
Helen V. Brach Fndn Grants, 2300
Henrietta Tower Wurts Memorial Fndn Grants, 2304
Huffy Fndn Grants, 2384
ING Fndn Grants, 2555
Intel Community Grants, 2562
Intel Int'l Community Grants, 2564
IRC Community Collaboratives for Refugee Women and Youth Grants, 2573
IREX Small Grant Fund for Civil Society Projects in Africa and Asia, 2581
IREX Yemen Women's Leadership Grants, 2583
Isabel Allende Fndn Esperanza Grants, 2586
J. Jill Compassion Grants, 2598
Jackson Fndn Grants, 2613
James A. and Faith Knight Fndn Grants, 2621
James Ford Bell Fndn Grants, 2623
James R. Dougherty Jr. Fndn Grants, 2635
Jean and Louis Dreyfus Fndn Grants, 2658
Jewish Women's Fndn of New York Grants, 2677
Joseph H. and Florence A. Roblee Fndn Grants, 2736
Josephine Goodyear Fndn Grants, 2738
Josephine S. Gumbiner Fndn Grants, 2739
Katharine Matthies Fndn Grants, 2788
Katherine Baxter Memorial Fndn Grants, 2789
Kosciusko County Community Fndn Grants, 2838
Kroger Fndn Diversity Grants, 2842
LA84 Fndn Grants, 2847
Leeway Fndn Art and Change Grants, 2872
Leeway Fndn Transformation Award, 2873
Liz Claiborne and Art Ortenberg Fndn Grants, 2914
Liz Claiborne Fndn Grants, 2915
Long Island Community Fndn Grants, 2920
Lotus 88 Fndn for Women and Children Grants, 2921
Maine Women's Fund Economic Security Grants, 2992
Maine Women's Fund Girls' Grantmaking Init, 2993
Mardag Fndn Grants, 3001
Mary's Pence Ministry Grants, 3029
Mary's Pence Study Grants, 3030
Mary Jane Luick Grants, 3040
Mary Kay Ash Charitable Grants, 3043
Mary Kay Domestic Violence Shelter Grants, 3044
Mercedes-Benz USA Corp Contributions Grants, 3118
Metro Health Fndn Grants, 3133
Miami County Community Fndn - Boomerang Sisterhood Grant, 3155
Montana Arts Council Cultural and Aesthetic Project Grants, 3209
Montana Community Fndn Women's Grants, 3212
National Book Scholarship Fund, 3249
New Mexico Women's Fndn Grants, 3335
New York Fndn Grants, 3338
Nike and Ashoka GameChangers: Change the Game for Women in Sport, 3439
Nike Fndn Grants, 3441
Nina Mason Pulliam Charitable Grants, 3443
Nokomis Fndn Grants, 3457
North Carolina Community Fndn Grants, 3489
NRA Fndn Grants, 3517
NYCT Girls and Young Women Grants, 3548
Olin Corp Charitable Grants, 3669
OneFamily Fndn Grants, 3673
Open Meadows Fndn Grants, 3683

Overbrook Fndn Grants, 3715
Patrick and Aimee Butler Family Fndn Community Human Services Grants, 3749
PDF Community Organizing Grants, 3807
PDF Fiscal Sponsorship Grant, 3808
Peacock Fndn Grants, 3809
Perpetual Trust for Charitable Giving Grants, 3826
Playboy Fndn Grants, 3913
Posey Community Fndn Women's Grants, 3938
Pott Fndn Grants, 3940
Princeton Area Community Fndn Women and Girls Grants, 3962
R.S. Gernon Grants, 4002
Rachel Alexandra Girls Grants, 4003
Rajiv Gandhi Fndn Grants, 4011
RCF The Women's Grants, 4035
Robert R. Meyer Fndn Grants, 4121
Rochester Area Community Fndn Grants, 4127
Rochester Area Fndn Grants, 4128
Rockefeller Family Grants, 4137
ROSE Grants, 4161
S. Mark Taper Fndn Grants, 4201
Saginaw Community Fndn YWCA Fund for Women and Girls Grants, 4207
San Diego Fndn for Change Grants, 4247
Sara Lee Fndn Grants, 4296
Schramm Fndn Grants, 4310
Simmons Fndn Grants, 4360
Siragusa Fndn Human Services Grants, 4369
Sister Grants for Women's Organizations, 4371
Sisters of Mercy of North Carolina Fndn Grants, 4375
Sophia Romero Grants, 4406
SW Gas Corp Fndn Grants, 4445
Sport Manitoba Women to Watch Grants, 4460
SSHRC Therese F. Casgrain Fellowship, 4466
Stark Community Fndn Women's Grants, 4481
Strowd Roses Grants, 4515
Textron Corp Contributions Grants, 4601
Thanks Be to Grandmother Winifred Grants, 4602
Theodore Edson Parker Fndn Grants, 4605
Third Wave Fndn Lela Breitbart Grants, 4609
Third Wave Organizing & Advocacy Grants, 4610
Third Wave Reproductive Health & Justice Grants, 4611
Thomas Sill Fndn Grants, 4619
Tides Fndn Grants, 4632
United Methodist Women Brighter Future for Children and Youth Grants, 4723
USAID Comprehensive District-Based Support for Better HIV/TB Patient Outcomes Grants, 4747
USAID Global Development Alliance Grants, 4753
Valentine Fndn Grants, 4897
Vanguard Public Fndn Grant Funds, 4904
Victor E. Speas Fndn Grants, 4933
Vulcan Materials Company Fndn Grants, 4956
W.K. Kellogg Fndn Civic Engagement Grants, 4960
Washington Area Women's Fndn African American Women's Giving Circle Grants, 4989
Washington Area Women's Fndn Early Care and Educ Funders Collaborative Grants, 4990
Washington Area Women's Fndn Financial Educ and Wealth Creation Grants, 4991
Washington Area Women's Fndn Jobs Grants, 4992
Washington Area Women's Leadership Awards, 4993
Washington Area Women's Fndn Open Door Capacity Grants, 4994
Washington Area Women's Fndn Rainmakers Giving Circle Grants, 4995
Washington Area Women's Fndn Strategic Opportunity and Partnership Grants, 4996
Wayne County Fndn Women's Grants, 5006
Weingart Fndn Grants, 5018
WHO Fndn Educ/Lit Grants, 5062
WHO Fndn General Grants, 5063
Wieboldt Fndn Grants, 5065
William S. Abell Fndn Grants, 5094
Wilson-Wood Fndn Grants, 5098
Women's Fndn Greater Kansas City Grants, 5111
Women's Funding Alliance Grants, 5112
WSF Travel and Training Grants, 5119
Yellow Corp Fndn Grants, 5126

1012 / Women's Education — SUBJECT INDEX

Women's Education
360 Degrees of Giving Grants, 32
AAUW Community Action Grants, 75
AAUW Int'l Project Grants, 76
ACS Award for Encouraging Women into Careers in the Chemical Sciences, 133
A Fund for Women Grants, 195
Arizona Women Deborah G. Carstens Grants, 543
Arizona Fndn for Women General Grants, 544
Avon Products Fndn Grants, 625
AWDF Main Grants, 627
AWDF Solidarity Grants, 628
Baltimore Women's Giving Circle Grants, 650
Barr Fndn Grants, 677
Benton Community Fndn - The Cookie Jar Grant, 729
Blackford County Community WOW Grants, 779
Boston Jewish Community Women's Grants, 822
CFFVR Schmidt Family G4 Grants, 1020
Chicago Fndn for Women Grants, 1096
Citigroup Fndn Grants, 1139
Community Fndn for Greater New Haven Women & Girls Grants, 1254
Community Fndn of Bartholomew County Women's Giving Circle, 1269
Community Fndn of Boone Cty Women's Grants, 1273
Dining for Women Grants, 1548
ExxonMobil Fndn Women's Econ Opp Grants, 1778
Gibson County Community Fndn Women's Fund, 2051
Heineman Fndn for Research, Educ, Charitable and Scientific Purposes, 2290
Int'l Paper Company Fndn Grants, 2568
IREX Small Grant Fund for Civil Society Projects in Africa and Asia, 2581
IREX Yemen Women's Leadership Grants, 2583
James A. and Faith Knight Fndn Grants, 2621
Jewish Women's Fndn of New York Grants, 2677
Lettie Pate Whitehead Fndn Grants, 2888
Liz Claiborne Fndn Grants, 2915
Nike Fndn Grants, 3441
PepsiCo Fndn Grants, 3819
Porter County Women's Grant, 3934
Posey Community Fndn Women's Grants, 3938
Rachel Alexandra Girls Grants, 4003
Radcliffe Inst Individual Residential Fellowships, 4004
RCF The Women's Grants, 4035
RGK Fndn Grants, 4072
Saginaw Community Fndn YWCA Fund for Women and Girls Grants, 4207
Samuel S. Fels Grants, 4238
Siragusa Fndn Human Services Grants, 4369
Sister Grants for Women's Organizations, 4371
Stark Community Fndn Women's Grants, 4481
USAID Global Development Alliance Grants, 4753
Washington Area Women's Fndn African American Women's Giving Circle Grants, 4989
Washington Area Women's Fndn Financial Educ and Wealth Creation Grants, 4991
Washington Area Women's Fndn Jobs Grants, 4992
Washington Area Women's Open Door Grants, 4994
Washington Area Women's Fndn Rainmakers Giving Circle Grants, 4995
Washington Area Women's Fndn Strategic Opportunity and Partnership Grants, 4996
Wayne County Fndn Women's Grants, 5006
WHO Fndn General Grants, 5063
Women's Fndn Greater Kansas City Grants, 5111

Women's Employment
Aid for Starving Children African American Indep Single Mother's Grants, 210
Albert W. Rice Charitable Fndn Grants, 347
Anschutz Family Fndn Grants, 486
Arizona Fndn for Women Deb Carstens Grants, 543
Arizona Fndn for Women General Grants, 544
Atlanta Women's Fndn Grants, 609
Avon Products Fndn Grants, 625
Baltimore Women's Giving Circle Grants, 650
Benton Community Fndn - The Cookie Jar Grant, 729
Bernard and Audre Rapoport Fndn Community Building and Social Service Grants, 736
Bill and Melinda Gates Fndn Agricultural Development Grants, 765
CFFVR Schmidt Family G4 Grants, 1020
Charles H. Pearson Fndn Grants, 1045
Chicago Fndn for Women Grants, 1096
Community Fndn for Greater New Haven Women & Girls Grants, 1254
Community Fndn of Bartholomew County Women's Giving Circle, 1269
Community Fndn of Greater Flint Grants, 1282
ExxonMobil Fndn Women's Economic Opportunity Grants, 1778
George W. Wells Fndn Grants, 2030
Girl's Best Friend Fndn Grants, 2057
Illinois DCEO Employer Training Investment Grants - Competitive Component, 2491
Illinois DCEO Employer Training Investment Grants - Incentive Component, 2492
Illinois DCEO Employer Training Investment Program Multi-Company Training Grants, 2493
Illinois DCEO Employer Training Investment Program Single Company Training Grants, 2494
Illinois DCEO Large Business Dev Grants, 2495
IREX Yemen Women's Leadership Grants, 2583
Liz Claiborne Fndn Grants, 2915
M.D. Anderson Fndn Grants, 2952
Maine Women's Fund Economic Security Grants, 2992
Meyer Fndn Economic Security Grants, 3141
Pasadena Fndn Average Grants, 3741
Posey Community Fndn Women's Grants, 3938
Radcliffe Inst Individual Residential Fellowships, 4004
RCF The Women's Grants, 4035
Rockefeller Family Grants, 4137
Sister Grants for Women's Organizations, 4371
Stark Community Fndn Women's Grants, 4481
Textron Corp Contributions Grants, 4601
USAID Global Development Alliance Grants, 4753
USAID Unsolicited Proposal Grants, 4786
Washington Area Women's Fndn African American Women's Giving Circle Grants, 4989
Washington Area Women's Fndn Early Care and Educ Funders Collaborative Grants, 4990
Washington Area Women's Fndn Open Door Capacity Grants, 4994
Washington Area Women's Fndn Rainmakers Giving Circle Grants, 4995

Women's Health
A Fund for Women Grants, 195
Agape Fndn for Nonviolent Social Change Board of Trustees Grants, 197
Allen Hilles Grants, 378
Alliance Healthcare Fndn Grants, 383
Appalachian Reg Comm Health Care Grants, 507
Arizona Fndn for Women General Grants, 544
Atlanta Women's Fndn Grants, 609
Avon Products Fndn Grants, 625
AWDF Main Grants, 627
AWDF Solidarity Grants, 628
Baltimore Women's Giving Circle Grants, 650
Benton Community Fndn - The Cookie Jar Grant, 729
Bernard and Audre Rapoport Fndn Health Grants, 738
Blackford County Community WOW Grants, 779
Blanche and Irving Laurie Fndn Grants, 784
Boston Jewish Community Women's Grants, 822
California Endowment Innovative Ideas Challenge Grants, 904
CFFVR Schmidt Family G4 Grants, 1020
Charles F. Bacon Grants, 1040
Chicago Fndn for Women Grants, 1096
Collective Brands Fndn Grants, 1206
Community Fndn for Greater New Haven Women & Girls Grants, 1254
Community Fndn of Bloomington and Monroe County - Precision Health Network Cycle Grants, 1270
Community Fndn of Boone Cty Women's Grants, 1273
David Lane Grants for Aged & Indigent Women, 1453
Dining for Women Grants, 1548
ExxonMobil Fndn Women's Economic Opportunity Grants, 1778
Fisa Fndn Grants, 1826
Fndn for Seacoast Health Grants, 1895
Fndns of E Chicago Health Grants, 1910
General Service Reproductive Justice Grants, 2007
Gibson County Community Fndn Women's Fund, 2051
GNOF Maison Hospitaliere Grants, 2086
Harry B. and Jane H. Brock Fndn Grants, 2237
IBCAT Screening Mammography Grants, 2422
James A. and Faith Knight Fndn Grants, 2621
Jennings County Community Fndn Women's Giving Circle Grant, 2665
Jewish Women's Fndn of New York Grants, 2677
Johnson & Johnson Comm Health Care Grants, 2717
Kate B. Reynolds Charitable Health Care Grants, 2786
Kosciusko County Community Fndn REMC Operation Round Up Grants, 2839
Lillian S. Wells Fndn Grants, 2901
Lowe Fndn Grants, 2929
Maine Women's Fund Economic Security Grants, 2992
Mary Kay Ash Charitable Fndn Grants, 3043
Ms. Fndn for Women Health Grants, 3225
Nike Fndn Grants, 3441
Pfizer Healthcare Charitable Contributions, 3863
Pfizer Medical Educ Track One Grants, 3864
Porter County Health and Wellness Grant, 3933
Porter County Women's Grant, 3934
Posey Community Fndn Women's Grants, 3938
Pride Fndn Grants, 3958
Radcliffe Inst Individual Residential Fellowships, 4004
Ralph M. Parsons Fndn Grants, 4013
RCF The Women's Grants, 4035
Robert R. Meyer Fndn Grants, 4121
Saginaw Community Fndn YWCA Fund for Women and Girls Grants, 4207
Seattle Fndn Health and Wellness Grants, 4328
Siragusa Fndn Human Services Grants, 4369
Sister Grants for Women's Organizations, 4371
Stark Community Fndn Women's Grants, 4481
USAID Comprehensive District-Based Support for Better HIV/TB Patient Outcomes Grants, 4747
USAID Family Health Plus Project Grants, 4751
USAID NGO Health Service Delivery Grants, 4771
W.P. and Bulah Luse Fndn Grants, 4965
Washington Area Women's Fndn African American Women's Giving Circle Grants, 4989
Washington Area Women's Fndn Rainmakers Giving Circle Grants, 4995
WHO Fndn General Grants, 5063
William S. Abell Fndn Grants, 5094

Women's Rights
AAUW Breaking through Barriers Award, 74
Arizona Fndn for Women General Grants, 544
AWDF Main Grants, 627
AWDF Solidarity Grants, 628
Baxter Int'l Corp Giving Grants, 689
Benton Community Fndn - The Cookie Jar Grant, 729
Bernard and Audre Rapoport Fndn Democracy and Civic Participation Grants, 737
Bill and Melinda Gates Fndn Agricultural Development Grants, 765
Blackford County Community WOW Grants, 779
Community Fndn of Bartholomew County Women's Giving Circle, 1269
Community Fndn of Boone Cty Women's Grants, 1273
Dining for Women Grants, 1548
Elkhart County Community Fndn Fund for Elkhart County, 1683
ExxonMobil Fndn Women's Economic Opportunity Grants, 1778
General Service Reproductive Justice Grants, 2007
HBF Defending Freedoms Grants, 2271
Mary Kay Domestic Violence Shelter Grants, 3044
New York Fndn Grants, 3338
OSF Advancing the Rights and Integration of Roma Grants, 3699
OSF Arab Regional Office Grants, 3701
Patrick and Aimee Butler Family Fndn Community Human Services Grants, 3749
PDF Fiscal Sponsorship Grant, 3808

SUBJECT INDEX

Porter County Women's Grant, 3934
Radcliffe Inst Individual Residential Fellowships, 4004
RCF The Women's Grants, 4035
Saginaw Community Fndn YWCA Fund for Women and Girls Grants, 4207
Sister Grants for Women's Organizations, 4371
Washington Area Women's Fndn African American Women's Giving Circle Grants, 4989
Washington Area Women's Fndn Rainmakers Giving Circle Grants, 4995

Women's Studies
Alabama Humanities Fndn Mini Grants, 231
Alabama Humanities Planning/Consultant Grants, 232
NYHC Major and Mini Grants, 3567
Radcliffe Inst Individual Residential Fellowships, 4004
Saginaw Community Fndn YWCA Fund for Women and Girls Grants, 4207
Sister Grants for Women's Organizations, 4371
Stark Community Fndn Women's Grants, 4481
Virginia Historical Society Research Fellowships, 4949

Work Motivation
Abell Fndn Workforce Development Grants, 97
Elizabeth Morse Genius Charitable Grants, 1682
USAID Workforce Development Program in Mexico Grants, 4787

Workforce Development
Abell Fndn Workforce Development Grants, 97
AEGON Transamerica Fndn Civic and Community Grants, 177
Alfred E. Chase Charitable Fndn Grants, 366
AutoZone Community Relations Grants, 621
Bernard and Audre Rapoport Fndn Community Building and Social Service Grants, 736
Boeing Company Contributions Grants, 809
Charles Stewart Mott Fndn Anti-Poverty Grants, 1054
Chicago Community Trust Workforce Grants, 1094
Cleveland Fenn Ed Grants, 1169
Clowes Grants, 1177
CNCS AmeriCorps State and National Grants, 1182
Community Fndn for SE Michigan Grants, 1259
Elizabeth Morse Genius Charitable Grants, 1682
Emma G. Harris Fndn Grants, 1701
Fndn for Mid South Comm Development Grants, 1897
Frederick W. Marzahl Grants, 1948
GNOF Coastal 5 + 1 Grants, 2070
GNOF Metropolitan Opportunities Grants, 2087
GNOF New Orleans Works Grants, 2088
Grand Victoria Fndn Illinois Core Grants, 2126
Harold Brooks Fndn Grants, 2227
Harry S. Black and Allon Fuller Grants, 2243
Helen Bader Fndn Grants, 2293
IDOT Economic Development Grants, 2436
Illinois DCEO Business Development Public Infrastructure Grants, 2483
Illinois DCEO Coal Revival Grants, 2487
Illinois DCEO Community Development Assistance For Economic Development Grants, 2488
Indiana Rural Capacity Grants, 2547
KeyBank Fndn Grants, 2820
Libra Fndn Future Grants, 2898
Linden Fndn Grants, 2908
Marin Community Fndn Ending the Cycle of Poverty Grants, 3011
Mertz Gilmore Fndn NYC Communities Grants, 3126
Meyer Fndn Economic Security Grants, 3141
Meyer Fndn Educ Grants, 3142
Middlesex Savings Charitable Fndn Ed Opportunities Grants, 3174
Nellie Mae Educ Fndn State Level Systems Change Grants, 3299
Nevada Community Fndn Grants, 3316
New Jersey Center for Hispanic Policy, Research and Development Workforce Grants, 3330
New York Fndn Grants, 3338
NWHF Partners Investing in Nursing's Future, 3539
PG&E Community Investment Grants, 3867
PG&E Community Vitality Grants, 3868

Piedmont Natural Gas Fndn Workforce Development Grant, 3886
Piper Trust Older Adults Grants, 3904
PMI Fndn Grants, 3918
Priddy Fndn Organizational Development Grants, 3956
Prudential Fndn Economic Development Grants, 3976
RCF General Community Grants, 4032
Reinberger Fndn Grants, 4052
Robert R. McCormick Tribune Comm Grants, 4119
Robert R. McCormick Tribune Veterans Grants, 4120
U.S. Bank Fndn Grants, 4686
Union Bank, N.A. Fndn Grants, 4709
USAID Call for Public-Private Alliance Proposals in Serbia, 4742
USAID Global Development Alliance Grants, 4753
USAID Unsolicited Proposal Grants, 4786
USAID Workforce Development Program in Mexico Grants, 4787
Verizon Fndn Grants, 4911
Verizon Fndn Lit Grants, 4915
Walmart Fndn Facility Giving Grants, 4978
Walmart Fndn National Giving Grants, 4979

Workshops
Alaska State Council on the Arts Community Arts Development Grants, 327
Arkansas Arts Council AIE Arts Curriculum Project Grants, 552
Arkansas Arts Council AIE Mini Grants, 554
Blue Cross Blue Shield of Minnesota Fndn - Healthy Equity: Public Libraries for Health Grants, 797
CDECD Arts Catalyze Placemaking in Every Community Grants, 977
CDECD Arts Catalyze Placemaking Leadership Grants, 978
CDECD Arts Catalyze Placemaking Sustaining Relevance Grants, 979
District of Columbia Commission on the Arts-Arts Educ Teacher Mini-Grants, 1549
Family Lit and Hawaii Pizza Hut Lit Fund, 1785
GNOF Organizational Effectiveness Grants and Workshops, 2090
HAF Educ Grants, 2196
Hartford Fndn Nonprofit Support Grants, 2252
Heartland Arts Fund, 2286
Ka Papa O Kakuhihewa Fund, 2785
Mabel Louise Riley Fndn Family Strengthening Small Grants, 2958
Meyer Fndn Benevon Grants, 3140
Middlesex Savings Charitable Fndn Ed Opportunities Grants, 3174
NAA Fndn Teacher Fellowships, 3234
NAGC Masters and Specialists Award, 3237
NASE Succeed Scholarships, 3243
National Endowment for the Arts - Grants for Arts Projects: Challenge America Fast-Track, 3254
National Endowment for Arts Our Town Grants, 3257
National Endowment for the Arts - Regional Partnership Agreement Grants, 3258
National Endowment for Arts Commun Grants, 3260
National Endowment for Arts Agencies Grants, 3263
National Endowment for Arts Music Grants, 3266
National Endowment for Arts Opera Grants, 3267
National Endowment for the Arts Presenting Grants: Art Works, 3268
National Endowment for Arts Theater Grants, 3269
North Carolina Arts Council Folklife Grants, 3476
NYSCA Architecture, Planning, and Design: Project Support Grants, 3576
NYSCA Electronic Media and Film: Workspace Grants, 3593
NYSCA Presenting: Services to the Field Grants, 3612
NYSCA State and Local Partnerships: Workshops Grants, 3622
NYSCA Theatre: Services to the Field Grants, 3626
PCA Arts Organizations and Arts Programs Grants for Arts Educ Organizations, 3776
PCA Entry Track Arts Organizations and Program Grants for Arts Educ Organizations, 3788
PCA Professional Development Grants, 3803

PMP Professional Development Grants, 3919
Poets & Writers Readings/Workshops Grants, 3927
RISCA Project Grants for Organizations, Individuals and Educ, 4100
TAC Arts Access Grant, 4549
TAC Arts Build Communities Grants, 4551
TAC Arts Educ Community-Learning Grants, 4552
TAC Arts Grants, 4554
TAC Rural Arts Project Support Grants, 4555
Texas Commission on the Arts Cultural Connections Grants, 4591
Union Square Awards Grants, 4718
Virginia Fndn for Humanities Discr Grants, 4946
Virginia Fndn for the Humanities Open Grants, 4947
West Virginia Commission on the Arts Professional Development for Artists Grants, 5045

Writers in Residence
Arkansas Arts Council AIE After School/Summer Residency Grants, 551
Arkansas Arts Council AIE In-School Residency, 553
CDECD Arts Catalyze Placemaking in Every Community Grants, 977
CDECD Arts Catalyze Placemaking Leadership Grants, 978
CDECD Arts Catalyze Placemaking Sustaining Relevance Grants, 979
National Endowment for Arts Commun Grants, 3260
National Endowment for the Arts Presenting Grants: Art Works, 3268
San Francisco Fndn Art Awards James Duval Phelan Literary Award, 4258
San Francisco Fndn Art Awards Joseph Henry Jackson Literary Award, 4259
San Francisco Fndn Art Awards Mary Tanenbaum Literary Award, 4260
TAC Arts Access Grant, 4549
TAC Arts Build Communities Grants, 4551
TAC Arts Grants, 4554
TAC Rural Arts Project Support Grants, 4555

Writing
ALA Coretta Scott King-Virginia Hamilton Award for Lifetime Achievement, 259
ALA Joseph W. Lippincott Award, 294
ALA Romance Writers of America Library Grant, 314
BCBSM Fndn Proposal Development Awards, 709
EQT Fndn Educ Grants, 1745
Gulf Coast Fndn of Community Capacity Building Grants, 2175
Jayne and Leonard Abess Fndn Grants, 2657
Kentucky Arts Council Al Smith Fellowship, 2806
Kentucky Arts Council Emerging Artist Award, 2807
NYSCA Lit: General Operating Support Grants, 3598
NYSCA Literature: General Support Grants, 3599
NYSCA Literature: Public Programs, 3600
NYSCA Literature: Services to the Field Grants, 3601
PCA Arts Organizations & Grants for Lit, 3781
PCA Entry Track Arts Organizations and Program Grants for Literature, 3793
Robert Bowne Fndn Fellowships, 4107
United States Institute of Peace - National Peace Essay Contest for High School Students, 4724
Wallace Alexander Gerbode Special Awards, 4975

Writing/Composition Education
Baptist Community Ministries Grants, 664
Bay and Paul Fndns, Inc Grants, 692
Emily Davie and Joseph S. Kornfeld Fndn Grants, 1697
Entergy Charitable Fndn Low-Income Inits and Solutions Grants, 1711
Houston Endowment Grants, 2373
NAGC Masters and Specialists Award, 3237
NYSCA Literature: General Support Grants, 3599
NYSCA Literature: Public Programs, 3600
Poets & Writers Readings/Workshops Grants, 3927
Robert Bowne Fndn Lit Grants, 4108
Robert Bowne Fndn Youth-Centered Grants, 4109

1014 / Young Adult Literature

Young Adult Literature
ALA Baker and Taylor Conference Grants, 228
ALA BWI Collection Development Grant, 252
ALA Coretta Scott King-Virginia Hamilton Award for Lifetime Achievement, 259
ALA Coretta Scott King Book Awards, 260
ALA MAE Award for Best Teen Lit, 296
ALA Schneider Family Book Award, 317
ALA Scholastic Library Publishing Award, 318
ALA Supporting Diversity Stipend, 333
ALA Young Adult Literature Symposium Stipend, 337
Florida Div of Cultural Affairs Literature Grants, 1855
SCBWI Don Freeman Memorial Grant, 4302

Youth Programs
3M Fndn Community Giving Grants, 15
AAA Fndn for Traffic Safety Grants, 50
Aaron Fndn Grants, 73
Abbot and Dorothy H. Stevens Fndn Grants, 79
ABC Charities Grants, 85
Abell-Hanger Fndn Grants, 91
ABS Fndn Grants, 107
Abundance Fndn Local Community Grants, 109
ACF Community-Based Abstinence Educ Grants, 116
ACF Mentoring Children of Prisoners Grants, 121
ACF Native American Social and Economic Development Strategies Grants, 123
ACMP Fndn Community Music Grants, 130
Acuity Charitable Fndn Grants, 140
Acushnet Fndn Grants, 143
Adams and Reese LLP Corp Giving Grants, 147
Adams County Comm Fndn of Indiana Grants, 148
Adelaide Breed Bayrd Fndn Grants, 161
Adelaide Christian Home For Children Grants, 162
Adolph Coors Fndn Grants, 171
African American Fund of New Jersey Grants, 192
Agnes M. Lindsay Grants, 203
Agway Fndn Grants, 205
Ahmanson Fndn Grants, 207
Aladdin Industries Fndn Grants, 263
ALA MAE Award for Best Teen Lit, 296
ALA Scholastic Library Publishing Award, 318
ALA Supporting Diversity Stipend, 333
Albert and Bessie Mae Kronkosky Charitable Fndn Grants, 339
Albert B. Cuppage Charitable Fndn Grants, 341
Alberto Culver Corp Contributions Grants, 343
Albert Pick Jr. Grants, 344
Albertson's Charitable Giving Grants, 345
Albert W. Rice Charitable Fndn Grants, 347
Alcatel-Lucent Technologies Fndn Grants, 349
Alice Tweed Tuohy Fndn Grants, 372
Allegan County Community Fndn Grants, 375
Alliance Healthcare Fndn Grants, 383
Alliant Energy Fndn Community Grants, 384
Allyn Fndn Grants, 392
Alvin and Lucy Owsley Fndn Grants, 404
Amelia Sillman Rockwell and Carlos Perry Rockwell Charities Grants, 417
American Express Historic Preservation Grants, 431
American Foodservice Charitable Grants, 433
American Honda Fndn Grants, 439
AmerUs Group Charitable Fndn, 455
Amon G. Carter Fndn Grants, 458
Andersen Corp Fndn, 459
Anderson Fndn Grants, 460
Andre Agassi Charitable Fndn Grants, 461
Andrew Family Fndn Grants, 462
Andrew Goodman Fndn Grants, 463
Ann and Robert H. Lurie Family Fndn Grants, 473
Ann Arbor Area Community Fndn Grants, 474
Annenberg Fndn Grants, 477
Annie's Grants for Gardens, 480
Ann L. & Carol Green Rhodes Charitable Grants, 483
Anschutz Family Fndn Grants, 486
Anthony R. Abraham Fndn Grants, 489
Antone & Edene Vidinha Charitable Grants, 490
Appalachian Regional Commission Business Development Revolving Loan Grants, 501
Aquila Corp Grants, 521

Aragona Family Fndn Grants, 522
Archer Daniels Midland Fndn Grants, 527
Arizona Community Fndn Grants, 540
Arizona Diamondbacks Charities Grants, 542
Arkansas Community Fndn Arkansas Black Hall of Fame Grants, 559
Arkema Fndn Science Teachers Program, 563
Armstrong McDonald Fndn Grants, 565
Arronson Fndn Grants, 567
ArvinMeritor Fndn Arts and Culture Grants, 582
AT&T Fndn Civic and Comm Service Grants, 599
ATA Local Community Relations Grants, 600
ATF Gang Resistance Educ and Training Program Coop Agreements, 603
Athwin Fndn Grants, 605
Atlanta Falcons Youth Fndn Grants, 607
Atlanta Fndn Grants, 608
Autzen Fndn Grants, 622
AXA Fndn Scholarships, 629
Back Home Again Fndn Grants, 633
Bacon Family Fndn Grants, 634
Bailey Fndn Grants, 635
Ball Brothers Fndn Organizational Effectiveness/Executive Mentoring Grants, 638
BancorpSouth Fndn Grants, 651
Barker Welfare Fndn Grants, 669
Batchelor Fndn Grants, 679
Baton Rouge Area Fndn Every Kid a King Grants, 681
Batters Up USA Equipment Grants, 683
Baughman Fndn Grants, 688
Bay Area Community Fndn Grants, 694
Beazley Fndn Grants, 714
Beirne Carter Fndn Grants, 719
Belk Fndn Grants, 721
Ben & Jerry's Fndn Grants, 724
Ben B. Cheney Fndn Grants, 725
Bender Fndn Grants, 726
Benton Community Fndn Grants, 730
Benton County Fndn Grants, 731
Berks County Community Fndn Grants, 734
Bernard & Audre Rapoport Arts & Culture Grant, 735
Bernard and Audre Rapoport Fndn Community Building and Social Service Grants, 736
Bernard and Audre Rapoport Fndn Democracy and Civic Participation Grants, 737
Berrien Community Fndn Grants, 744
Best Buy Children's Fndn @15 Community Grants, 749
Best Buy Children's Fndn @15 Teach Awards, 751
Birmingham Fndn Grants, 774
Blanche and Julian Robertson Family Fndn Grants, 785
Blue River Community Fndn Grants, 801
Blumenthal Fndn Grants, 804
Bodenwein Public Benevolent Fndn Grants, 806
Bodman Fndn Grants, 807
Boeckmann Charitable Fndn Grants, 808
Bohemian Fndn Pharos Grants, 811
Boston Fndn Grants, 819
Boston Globe Fndn Grants, 821
Bright Family Fndn Grants, 837
Brooklyn Benevolent Society Grants, 847
Brooklyn Community Fndn Community Arts for All Grants, 849
Brooklyn Community Fndn Educ and Youth Achievement Grants, 851
Brown County Community Fndn Grants, 853
Buhl Fndn - Frick Ed Fund, 859
Bullitt Fndn Grants, 862
Burlington Industries Fndn Grants, 865
Bush Fndn Health & Human Services Grants, 875
Butler Manufacturing Company Fndn Grants, 881
C.F. Adams Charitable Grants, 884
Caddock Fndn Grants, 888
Callaway Golf Company Fndn Grants, 910
Camp-Younts Fndn Grants, 914
Captain Planet Fndn Grants, 922
Cardinal Health Fndn Grants, 923
Cargill Citizenship Fund-Corp Giving Grants, 925
Carl and Eloise Pohlad Family Fndn Grants, 927
Carl B. and Florence E. King Fndn Grants, 928
Carl R. Hendrickson Family Fndn Grants, 935

Carnahan-Jackson Fndn Grants, 939
Carnegie Corp of New York Grants, 940
Carrie E. and Lena V. Glenn Fndn Grants, 944
Carrie Estelle Doheny Fndn Grants, 945
Carrier Corp Contributions Grants, 946
Carroll County Community Fndn Grants, 947
Caterpillar Fndn Grants, 954
CCF Social and Economic Justice Grants, 964
Cemala Fndn Grants, 988
Cessna Fndn Grants, 1000
CFFVR Clintonville Area Fndn Grants, 1007
CFFVR Infant Welfare Circle of Kings Daughters Grants, 1013
CFFVR Jewelers Mutual Charitable Giving, 1014
CFFVR Myra M. and Robert L. Vandehey Fndn Grants, 1016
CFFVR Robert and Patricia Endries Family Fndn Grants, 1018
CFFVR Schmidt Family G4 Grants, 1020
CFFVR Shawano Area Community Fndn Grants, 1021
Champlin Fndns Grants, 1029
Chapin Hall Int'l Fellowships in Children's Policy Research, 1032
Charles Hayden Fndn Grants, 1048
Charles M. Bair Family Grants, 1051
Charlotte Martin Fndn Youth Grants, 1057
Chesapeake Bay Environmental Ed Grants, 1069
Chicago Tribune Fndn Grants for Cultural Organizations, 1101
Chicago White Metal Charitable Fndn Grants, 1102
Chiquita Brands Int'l Grants, 1110
Christine and Katharina Pauly Charitable Grants, 1114
CICF Clare Noyes Grant, 1119
CICF Howard Intermill and Marion Intermill Fenstermaker Grants, 1122
CICF Summer Youth Grants, 1128
Cincinnati Bell Fndn Grants, 1131
Cincinnati Milacron Fndn Grants, 1132
Cinergy Fndn Grants, 1133
Circle K Corp Contributions Grants, 1136
Citizens Savings Fndn Grants, 1141
Clarcor Fndn Grants, 1148
Claremont Community Fndn Grants, 1149
Clark-Winchcole Fndn Grants, 1152
Clark and Ruby Baker Fndn Grants, 1154
Clark Fndn Grants, 1157
Clay Fndn Grants, 1162
Cleveland H. Dodge Fndn Grants, 1172
CLIF Bar Family Fndn Grants, 1173
CNCS Foster Grandparent Grants, 1185
CNCS Senior Corps Retired and Senior Volunteer Grants, 1188
Coca-Cola Fndn Grants, 1195
Cockrell Fndn Grants, 1196
Coleman Fndn Entrepreneurship Educ Grants, 1201
Colgate-Palmolive Company Grants, 1202
Collective Brands Fndn Payless Gives Shoes 4 Kids Grants, 1207
Collins C. Diboll Private Fndn Grants, 1208
Collins Fndn Grants, 1209
Colonel Stanley R. McNeil Fndn Grants, 1210
Colorado Interstate Gas Grants, 1213
Colorado Springs Community Grants, 1215
Columbus Fndn Small Grants, 1232
Comcast Fndn Grants, 1235
Communities Fndn of Texas Grants, 1243
Community Fndn for Greater New Haven Women & Girls Grants, 1254
Community Fndn for NE Michigan Grants, 1257
Community Fndn for San Benito County Grants, 1258
Community Fndn of Abilene Future Grants, 1265
Community Fndn of Bartholomew County Heritage Grants, 1267
Community Fndn of Bartholomew County James A. Henderson Award for Fundraising, 1268
Community Fndn of Boone County Grants, 1274
Community Fndn of East Central Illinois Grants, 1278
Community Fndn of Greater Fort Wayne - Community Endowment and Clarke Endowment Grants, 1285
Community Fndn of Greater Tampa Grants, 1292

SUBJECT INDEX

Youth Programs/ 1015

Community Fndn of Mount Vernon and Knox County Grants, 1301
Community Fndn of Santa Cruz County Grants, 1305
Community Fndn of Sarasota County Grants, 1306
Community Fndn of SE Connecticut Grants, 1309
Community Fndn of Southern Indiana Grants, 1310
Community Fndn of St. Joseph County Special Project Challenge Grants, 1314
Community Fndn of Switzerland County Grants, 1315
Community Fndn of Eastern Shore Youth Grants, 1319
Community Fndn of the Ozarks Grants, 1320
Community Fndn of the Verdugos Ed Endowment Grants, 1321
Community Fndn of the Verdugos Grants, 1322
Community Fndn of Virgin Islands Mini Grants, 1325
Community Fndn Silicon Valley Grants, 1331
Community Impact Fund, 1332
Community Memorial Fndn Grants, 1334
ConAgra Foods Nourish Our Comm Grants, 1343
Connecticut Community Fndn Grants, 1350
ConocoPhillips Fndn Grants, 1354
ConocoPhillips Grants, 1355
Constantin Fndn Grants, 1362
Constellation Energy Corp Grants, 1364
Cooke Fndn Grants, 1368
Cooper Industries Fndn Grants, 1370
Cord Fndn Grants, 1372
Cornerstone Fndn of NE Wisconsin Grants, 1375
Countess Moira Charitable Fndn Grants, 1381
Covenant to Care for Children Grants, 1389
Cowles Charitable Grants, 1392
Cralle Fndn Grants, 1394
Crescent Porter Hale Fndn Grants, 1398
Cruise Industry Charitable Fndn Grants, 1404
CTCNet/Youth Visions for Stronger Neighborhoods Grants, 1409
Cudd Fndn Grants, 1410
Cumberland Community Fndn Summertime Kids Grants, 1414
Cummins Fndn Grants, 1415
Cyrus Eaton Fndn Grants, 1423
D.F. Halton Fndn Grants, 1424
D. W. McMillan Fndn Grants, 1426
Dade Community Fndn Grants, 1430
Dairy Queen Corp Contributions Grants, 1433
Dallas Women's Fndn Grants, 1438
Dana Corp Fndn Grants, 1440
Daniels Grants, 1443
Daphne Seybolt Culpeper Memorial Fndn Grants, 1445
Dayton Fndn Grants, 1463
Daywood Fndn Grants, 1465
Deaconess Fndn Advocacy Grants, 1468
Dearborn Community City of Aurora Grants, 1470
Dearborn Community Fndn City of Lawrenceburg Community Grants, 1471
Dearborn Community Fndn City of Lawrenceburg Youth Grants, 1472
Deborah Munroe Noonan Grants, 1475
Decatur County Comm Large Project Grants, 1476
Decatur County Community Fndn Small Project Grants, 1477
DeKalb County Community Fndn - Garrett Hospital Aid Fndn Grants, 1478
DeKalb County Community Fndn Grants, 1481
Dekko Fndn Grants, 1482
Delaware Community Fndn-Youth Philanthropy Board for Kent County, 1483
Delaware Community Fndn Youth Philanthropy Board for New Castle County Grants, 1486
Dennis and Phyllis Washington Fndn Grants, 1498
Denver Broncos Charities Grants, 1501
Dept of Ed Workplace & Comm Transition Training for Incarcerated Youth Offenders, 1515
DeRoy Testamentary Fndn Grants, 1518
Detroit Lions Charities Grants, 1520
Deuce McAllister Catch 22 Fndn Grants, 1521
District of Columbia Commission on the Arts-Arts Educ Teacher Mini-Grants, 1549
DOJ Juvenile Justice and Delinquency Prevention Special Emphasis Grants, 1559

Dollar General Family Lit Grants, 1569
Dollar General Youth Lit Grants, 1570
DOL Youthbuild Grants, 1571
Donaldson Fndn Grants, 1574
Dorr Fndn Grants, 1591
Do Something BR!CK Awards, 1592
Do Something Plum Youth Grants, 1593
Dresher Fndn Grants, 1605
Dubois County Community Fndn Grants, 1615
Dunspaugh-Dalton Fndn Grants, 1623
Dwight Stuart Youth Capacity-Building Grants, 1627
Dwight Stuart Youth Fndn Grants, 1628
Earth Island Institute Brower Youth Awards, 1641
Easton Fndns Archery Facility Grants, 1644
East Tennessee Fndn Grants, 1646
Eberly Fndn Grants, 1649
Eddy Knight Family Fndn Grants, 1654
Edna McConnell Clark Fndn Grants, 1659
Edna Wardlaw Charitable Grants, 1660
Edward S. Moore Fndn Grants, 1668
Edwin S. Webster Fndn Grants, 1671
Edwin W. and Catherine M. Davis Fndn Grants, 1672
EIF Community Grants, 1675
Eisner Fndn Grants, 1678
El Paso Community Fndn Grants, 1688
Elsie Lee Garthwaite Memorial Fndn Grants, 1692
Emerson Charitable Grants, 1694
Emerson Kampen Grants, 1696
Ensworth Charitable Fndn Grants, 1710
Enterprise Rent-A-Car Fndn Grants, 1721
Essex County Community Discretionary Grants, 1752
Essex County Community Fndn First Jobs Grant, 1754
Essex County Community Fndn Greater Lawrence Summer Grants, 1755
Esther M. and Freeman E. Everett Charitable Fndn Grants, 1757
Ethel and Raymond F. Rice Fndn Grants, 1758
Ewa Beach Community Trust Fund, 1775
Ewing Halsell Fndn Grants, 1776
F.M. Kirby Fndn Grants, 1780
Fargo-Moorhead Area Fndn Grants, 1788
Fargo-Moorhead Area Fndn Woman's Grants, 1789
Farmers Insurance Corp Giving Grants, 1791
Fayette County Fndn Grants, 1795
FCYO Youth Organizing Grants, 1797
Ferree Fndn Grants, 1804
Field Fndn of Illinois Grants, 1806
Finish Line Youth Fndn Founder's Grants, 1812
Finish Line Youth Fndn Legacy Grants, 1814
FINRA Smart Investing@Your Library Grants, 1816
FirstEnergy Fndn Community Grants, 1819
Florence Hunt Maxwell Fndn Grants, 1844
Foellinger Fndn Grants, 1877
Fondren Fndn Grants, 1878
Ford Family Fndn Grants - Positive Youth Development, 1880
Ford Family Fndn Grants - Technical Assistance, 1882
Ford Motor Company Grants, 1885
Fndn for a Drug-Free World Classroom Tools, 1890
Fndn for Appalachian Ohio Access to Environmental Educ Mini-Grants, 1892
Fndn for the Carolinas Grants, 1896
Fndns of E Chicago Youth Development Grants, 1912
Francis T. & Louise T. Nichols Fndn Grants, 1923
Frank B. Hazard General Charity Grants, 1926
Frank G. and Freida K. Brotz Family Grants, 1928
Frank Reed and Margaret Jane Peters Memorial Fund I Grants, 1933
Frank Stanley Beveridge Fndn Grants, 1936
Frederick S. Upton Fndn Grants, 1947
Frederick W. Marzahl Grants, 1948
Fremont Area Community Amazing X Grants, 1953
Fremont Area Community Fndn Grants, 1955
Fremont Area Comm Summer Youth Grants, 1956
Frist Fndn Grants, 1964
Fuller E. Callaway Fndn Grants, 1973
G.N. Wilcox Grants, 1982
Gamble Fndn Grants, 1983
Gannett Fndn Community Action Grants, 1984
GEF Green Thumb Challenge, 1996

General Service Fndn Colorado Grants, 2005
George A. and Grace L. Long Fndn Grants, 2008
George and Ruth Bradford Fndn Grants, 2010
George B. Storer Fndn Grants, 2014
George Fndn Grants, 2018
George I. Alden Grants, 2023
George W. Brackenridge Fndn Grants, 2028
George W. Wells Fndn Grants, 2030
Georgia-Pacific Fndn Entrepreneurship Grants, 2033
Gertrude and William C. Wardlaw Grants, 2045
Gil and Dody Weaver Fndn Grants, 2053
Glazer Family Fndn Grants, 2062
GNOF Coastal 5 + 1 Grants, 2070
GNOF Cox Charities of New Orleans Grants, 2072
GNOF Gert Community Grants, 2076
GNOF IMPACT Grants for Youth Development, 2081
GNOF Norco Community Grants, 2089
Go Daddy Cares Charitable Contributions, 2094
Godfrey Fndn Grants, 2095
Goizueta Fndn Grants, 2096
Grace and Franklin Bernsen Fndn Grants, 2109
Graco Fndn Grants, 2111
Grand Haven Area Community Fndn Grants, 2113
Grand Rapids Area Community Fndn Wyoming Youth Grants, 2117
Grand Rapids Community Fndn Grants, 2118
Grand Rapids Community Ionia Youth Grants, 2120
Grand Rapids Comm SE Ottawa Youth Grants, 2123
Grand Rapids Community Sparta Youth Grants, 2125
Grand Victoria Fndn Illinois Core Grants, 2126
Greater Milwaukee Fndn Grants, 2137
Greater Tacoma Community Fndn Grants, 2139
Greater Worcester Comm Discretionary Grants, 2140
Green Bay Packers Fndn Grants, 2148
Grover Hermann Fndn Grants, 2168
H.B. Fuller Company Fndn Grants, 2183
H.J. Heinz Company Fndn Grants, 2184
H. Leslie Hoffman & Elaine Hoffman Grants, 2185
HAF Community Grants, 2193
HAF Hansen Family Trust Christian Endowment Grants, 2197
HAF Natural Environment Grants, 2202
Hagedorn Grants, 2207
Hahl Proctor Charitable Grants, 2208
Hall Family Fndn Grants, 2210
Harold and Arlene Schnitzer CARE Grants, 2226
Harold K. L. Castle Fndn Grants, 2228
Harold Simmons Fndn Grants, 2230
Harris and Eliza Kempner Grants, 2231
Harry Bramhall Gilbert Charitable Grants, 2238
Hartford Courant Fndn Grants, 2248
Hatton W. Sumners Fndn for the Study and Teaching of Self Government Grants, 2257
Hawaii Community Fndn Reverend Takie Okumura Family Grants, 2264
Hazen Fndn Youth Organizing Grants, 2270
HCA Fndn Grants, 2274
Healthcare Fndn for Orange County Grants, 2279
Hearst Fndns Social Service Grants, 2285
Helena Rubinstein Fndn Grants, 2292
Helen Irwin Littauer Ed Grants, 2295
Helen K. and Arthur E. Johnson Fndn Grants, 2296
Helen S. Boylan Fndn Grants, 2298
Hendricks County Community Fndn Grants, 2302
Henrietta Tower Wurts Memorial Fndn Grants, 2304
Henry and Ruth Blaustein Rosenberg Grants, 2306
Henry County Community Fndn - TASC Youth Grants, 2307
Henry M. Jackson Fndn Grants, 2311
Hill Crest Fndn Grants, 2324
Hill Fndn Grants, 2326
Hillman Fndn Grants, 2327
Hilton Hotels Corp Giving Grants, 2331
Hoglund Fndn Grants, 2344
Holland/Zeeland Community Fndn Grants, 2345
Horace A. Kimball and S. Ella Kimball Grants, 2362
Horace Moses Charitable Fndn Grants, 2363
Howard and Bush Fndn Grants, 2374
Huffy Fndn Grants, 2384
Hulman & Company Fndn Grants, 2387

Youth Programs

Humana Fndn Grants, 2388
Hut Fndn Grants, 2411
Hutton Fndn Grants, 2412
Hyams Fndn Grants, 2413
Illinois Tool Works Fndn Grants, 2511
Initiaive Fndn Inside-Out Connections Grants, 2556
J. F. Maddox Fndn Grants, 2597
J.M. Long Fndn Grants, 2603
J.W. Kieckhefer Fndn Grants, 2607
J. Walton Bissell Fndn Grants, 2608
J. Willard and Alice S. Marriott Fndn Grants, 2609
Jackson County Community Fndn Youth Advisory Committee Grants, 2612
Jacksonville Jaguars Fndn Grants, 2614
Jacobs Family Village Neighborhoods Grants, 2619
James & Abigail Campbell Family Fndn Grants, 2620
James Graham Brown Quality of Life Grants, 2625
James J. and Angelia M. Harris Fndn Grants, 2630
James R. Thorpe Fndn Grants, 2636
James S. Copley Fndn Grants, 2637
Janirve Fndn Grants, 2645
Janus Fndn Grants, 2647
Jean and Louis Dreyfus Fndn Grants, 2658
Jeffris Wood Fndn Grants, 2660
JELD-WEN Fndn Grants, 2661
Jim Blevins Fndn Grants, 2678
John Edward Fowler Memorial Fndn Grants, 2693
John F. Kennedy Center for the Performing Arts National Rosemary Kennedy Internship, 2694
John G. Martin Fndn Grants, 2696
John H. and Wilhelmina D. Harland Charitable Fndn Grants, 2698
John Jewett & Helen Chandler Garland Grants, 2702
John M. Ross Fndn Grants, 2704
Johnson County Community Fndn Youth Philanthropy Init Grants, 2724
John W. and Anna H. Hanes Fndn Grants, 2728
John W. Anderson Fndn Grants, 2729
Join Hands Day Excellence Awards, 2733
Joseph H. and Florence A. Roblee Fndn Grants, 2736
Josephine G. Russell Grants, 2737
Josephine Goodyear Fndn Grants, 2738
Josiah W. and Bessie H. Kline Fndn Grants, 2742
JP Morgan Chase Arts and Culture Grants, 2752
Judith Clark-Morrill Fndn Grants, 2756
Kalamazoo Community LBGT Equality Grants, 2771
Kansas Arts Commission Arts on Tour Grants, 2780
Katharine Matthies Fndn Grants, 2788
Katherine John Murphy Fndn Grants, 2790
Kathryne Beynon Fndn Grants, 2791
Kenneth T. and Eileen L. Norris Fndn Grants, 2802
Knox County Community Fndn Grants, 2831
Koret Fndn Grants, 2837
Kosciusko County Community Fndn Grants, 2838
Kosciusko County Community Fndn REMC Operation Round Up Grants, 2839
Kroger Grassroots Community Support Grants, 2843
Kuki'o Community Fund, 2845
L. W. Pierce Family Fndn Grants, 2846
LA84 Fndn Grants, 2847
Lana'i Community Benefit Fund, 2857
Land O'Lakes Fndn California Region Grants, 2858
Land O'Lakes Fndn Community Grants, 2859
Lawrence J. and Anne Rubenstein Charitable Fndn Grants, 2868
Legacy Fndn College Readiness Grant, 2874
LEGO Children's Grants, 2878
Leo Goodwin Fndn Grants, 2882
Liberty Bank Fndn Grants, 2890
Libra Fndn Grants, 2899
Lied Fndn Grants, 2900
Lillian S. Wells Fndn Grants, 2901
Lily Palmer Fry Grants, 2905
Linden Fndn Grants, 2908
Linford and Mildred White Charitable Grants, 2909
Lloyd G. Balfour Fndn Attleboro-Specific Charities Grants, 2916
Louis Calder Fndn Grants, 2925
Louis R. Cappelli Fndn Grants, 2926
Lubrizol Fndn Grants, 2933
Lucile Horton Howe & Mitchell B. Howe Grants, 2934
Lucy Gooding Charitable Fndn Grants, 2937
Luella Kemper Grants, 2939
Lumpkin Family Healthy People Grants, 2942
Luther I. Replogle Fndn Grants, 2945
Lyndhurst Fndn Grants, 2949
M.E. Raker Fndn Grants, 2953
M.J. Murdock Charitable Trust General Grants, 2954
Mabel A. Horne Grants, 2956
Mabel F. Hoffman Charitable Grants, 2957
Mabel Y. Hughes Charitable Grants, 2960
MacDonald-Peterson Fndn Grants, 2965
Madison Community Fndn Grants, 2971
Maine Community Fndn Edward H. Daveis Benevolent Grants, 2979
Maine Comm Fndn Rines/Thompson Grants, 2987
Maine Community Fndn Vincent B. and Barbara G. Welch Grants, 2990
Mardag Fndn Grants, 3001
Margaret and James A. Elkins Jr. Fndn Grants, 3003
Marie C. and Joseph C. Wilson Fndn Rochester Small Grants, 3006
Marie H. Bechtel Charitable Grants, 3007
Mark Wahlberg Youth Fndn Grants, 3022
MARPAT Fndn Grants, 3023
Marsh Corp Grants, 3027
Mary Black Early Childhood Devel Grants, 3033
Mary & Walter Frear Eleemosynary Grants, 3035
Mary E. Ober Fndn Grants, 3039
Mary Owen Borden Fndn Grants, 3046
Mary S. and David C. Corbin Fndn Grants, 3048
Mathile Family Fndn Grants, 3062
Max and Anna Levinson Fndn Grants, 3066
Maxon Charitable Fndn Grants, 3068
McCombs Fndn Grants, 3075
McGregor Grants, 3082
McInerny Fndn Grants, 3083
McKesson Fndn Grants, 3084
McLean Contributionship Grants, 3088
McMillen Fndn Grants, 3090
Mead Witter Fndn Grants, 3106
Merck Family Fund Urban Farming and Youth Leadership Grants, 3119
Merck Family Fund Youth Transforming Urban Communities Grants, 3120
Mericos Fndn Grants, 3121
Meriden Fndn Grants, 3122
Merkel Family Fndn Grants, 3123
Mervin Bovaird Fndn Grants, 3128
MetLife Fndn Preparing Young People Grants, 3131
Meyer Memorial Trust Special Grants, 3149
MGN Family Fndn Grants, 3154
Microsoft Comm Affairs Puget Sound Grants, 3163
Microsoft Software Donation Grants, 3164
Mid-Iowa Health Fndn Comm Response Grants, 3168
Middlesex Savings Charitable Fndn Capacity Building Grants, 3172
Middlesex Savings Charitable Fndn Ed Opportunities Grants, 3174
Millipore Fndn Grants, 3182
Minneapolis Fndn Community Grants, 3186
Monsanto Access to the Arts Grants, 3204
Monsanto Int'l Grants, 3207
Monsanto Kids Garden Fresh Grants, 3208
Montana Community Fndn Grants, 3211
MONY Fndn Grants, 3214
Moody Fndn Grants, 3215
Nathaniel and Elizabeth P. Stevens Fndn Grants, 3247
National 4-H Afterschool Training Grants, 3248
National Endowment for the Arts - Grants for Arts Projects: Challenge America Fast-Track, 3254
National Endowment for the Arts - National Arts and Humanities Youth Program Awards, 3255
Nestle Purina PetCare Ed Grants, 3302
Nestle Purina PetCare Youth Grants, 3306
Nevada Community Fndn Grants, 3316
New York Fndn Grants, 3338
New York Life Fndn Grants, 3341
NFL Charities NFL Player Fndn Grants, 3347
NFL Charities Pro Bowl Comm Grants in Hawaii, 3348
NFL Grassroots Field Grants, 3350
NFL Player Youth Football Camp Grants, 3353
Nicholas H. Noyes Jr. Memorial Fndn Grants, 3434
Nike and Ashoka GameChangers: Change the Game for Women in Sport, 3439
Nike Fndn Grants, 3441
Noble County Community Fndn Grants, 3456
Norcliffe Fndn Grants, 3459
North Carolina Community Fndn Grants, 3489
North Dakota Community Fndn Grants, 3493
Northland Fndn Grants, 3506
NW Mutual Fndn Grants, 3509
Norton Fndn Grants, 3514
NRA Fndn Grants, 3517
NYCT Girls and Young Women Grants, 3548
NYCT Youth Development Grants, 3561
Oakland Fund for Children and Youth Grants, 3634
OceanFirst Fndn Grants, 3636
Ohio Valley Fndn Grants, 3662
Oleonda Jameson Grants, 3667
Olin Corp Charitable Grants, 3669
Olive B. Cole Fndn Grants, 3670
Onan Family Fndn Grants, 3672
OneFamily Fndn Grants, 3673
Oppenstein Brothers Fndn Grants, 3685
Orange County Community Fndn Grants, 3687
Ordean Grants, 3691
Pacers Fndn Be Drug-Free Grants, 3720
Pacers Fndn Be Educated Grants, 3721
Pacers Fndn Be Healthy and Fit Grants, 3722
Pacers Fndn Be Tolerant Grants, 3723
Pacers Fndn Indiana Fever's Be Younique Grants, 3724
PacifiCorp Fndn for Learning Grants, 3727
Parke County Community Fndn Grants, 3735
Parker Fndn (California) Grants, 3736
Pasadena Fndn Average Grants, 3741
Patrick and Anna M. Cudahy Grants, 3751
Paul and Edith Babson Fndn Grants, 3755
Paul G. Allen Family Fndn Grants, 3759
Paul Rapoport Fndn Grants, 3765
PCA Arts Organizations and Arts Programs Grants for Arts Educ Organizations, 3776
PCA Busing Grants, 3786
PCA Entry Track Arts Organizations and Program Grants for Arts Educ Organizations, 3788
PCA Pennsylvania Partners in the Arts Program Stream Grants, 3801
PCA Pennsylvania Partners in the Arts Project Stream Grants, 3802
PDF Community Organizing Grants, 3807
Peacock Fndn Grants, 3809
Pentair Fndn Educ and Community Grants, 3816
Perkins-Ponder Fndn Grants, 3822
Perkins Charitable Fndn Grants, 3823
Perpetual Trust for Charitable Giving Grants, 3826
Perry County Community Fndn Grants, 3827
Peter and Elizabeth C. Tower Fndn Annual Intellectual Disabilities Grants, 3834
Peter and Elizabeth C. Tower Fndn Annual Mental Health Grants, 3835
Peter and Elizabeth C. Tower Fndn Learning Disability Grants, 3836
Peter & Elizabeth C. Tower Mental Health Reference and Resource Materials Mini-Grants, 3837
Peter and Elizabeth C. Tower Fndn Phase II Technology Init Grants, 3839
Peter and Elizabeth C. Tower Fndn Phase I Technology Init Grants, 3840
Peter and Elizabeth C. Tower Fndn Social and Emotional Preschool Curriculum Grants, 3841
Peter and Elizabeth C. Tower Fndn Substance Abuse Grants, 3842
Peter Kiewit Fndn General Grants, 3845
Peter Kiewit Fndn Small Grants, 3847
PeyBack Fndn Grants, 3861
Phoenix Coyotes Charities Grants, 3879
Piedmont Natural Gas Corp and Charitable Contributions, 3883
Piedmont Natural Gas Fndn Health and Human Services Grants, 3885

SUBJECT INDEX

Youth Services/ 1017

Pike County Community Fndn Grants, 3888
Pinkerton Fndn Grants, 3892
Pinnacle Entertainment Fndn Grants, 3893
Pinnacle Fndn Grants, 3894
Piper Jaffray Fndn Communities Giving Grants, 3899
Plough Fndn Grants, 3915
Plum Creek Fndn Grants, 3917
PMI Fndn Grants, 3918
PNC Fndn Grow Up Great Grants, 3924
Pohlad Family Fndn, 3928
Polk Bros. Fndn Grants, 3929
Pollock Fndn Grants, 3930
Porter County Health and Wellness Grant, 3933
Portland Fndn - Women's Giving Circle Grant, 3935
Posey Community Fndn Women's Grants, 3938
Posey County Community Fndn Grants, 3939
Pott Fndn Grants, 3940
Price Chopper's Golub Fndn Grants, 3950
Priddy Fndn Grants, 3957
Pride Fndn Grants, 3958
Prince Charitable Trusts D.C. Grants, 3960
Procter and Gamble Grants, 3967
Prudential Fndn Educ Grants, 3977
Prudential Spirit of Community Awards, 3978
Publix Super Markets Charities Local Grants, 3985
R.C. Baker Fndn Grants, 3999
Ralph M. Parsons Fndn Grants, 4013
Ralphs Food 4 Less Fndn Grants, 4014
Raskob Fndn for Catholic Activities Grants, 4019
Ray Fndn Grants, 4027
Rhode Island Fndn Grants, 4073
Rice Fndn Grants, 4074
Richard and Rhoda Goldman Grants, 4077
Richard King Mellon Fndn Grants, 4087
Rich Fndn Grants, 4090
Righteous Persons Fndn Grants, 4093
Robert and Polly Dunn Fndn Grants, 4105
Robert B McMillen Fndn Grants, 4106
Robert Bowne Fndn Fellowships, 4107
Robert Bowne Fndn Lit Grants, 4108
Robert Bowne Fndn Youth-Centered Grants, 4109
Robert E. and Evelyn McKee Fndn Grants, 4110
Robert R. McCormick Tribune Civics Grants, 4118
Robert R. McCormick Tribune Comm Grants, 4119
Rochester Area Fndn Grants, 4128
Rockwell Int'l Corp Grants, 4141
Roger L. and Agnes C. Dell Charitable Grants, 4143
Rohm and Haas Company Grants, 4145
Rollin M. Gerstacker Fndn Grants, 4146
Ronald McDonald House Charities Grants, 4149
Rose Hills Fndn Grants, 4162
Roy and Christine Sturgis Charitable Grants, 4166
Rush County Community Fndn Grants, 4174
Russell Berrie Fndn Grants, 4175
Ruth Eleanor Bamberger and John Ernest Bamberger Memorial Fndn Grants, 4178
S. Livingston Mather Charitable Grants, 4200
Saginaw County Community Fndn Youth FORCE Grants, 4208
Saint Louis Rams Fndn Community Donations, 4214
Salisbury Community Fndn Grants, 4224
Salmon Fndn Grants, 4225
SAMHSA Strategic Prevention Framework State Incentive Grants, 4231
Samuel S. Johnson Fndn Grants, 4239
San Diego Fndn for Change Grants, 4247
SanDisk Corp Community Sharing Program, 4253
Sands Fndn Grants, 4255
Sara Lee Fndn Grants, 4296
Saucony Run for Good Fndn Grants, 4301
Scheumann Fndn Grants, 4306
Schlessman Family Fndn Grants, 4307
Schurz Communications Fndn Grants, 4312
Scott County Community Fndn Grants, 4314
Seabury Fndn Grants, 4316
Seattle Fndn Benjamin N. Phillips Grants, 4322
Self Fndn Grants, 4335
Seneca Foods Fndn Grants, 4336
Seybert Inst for Poor Boys and Girls Grants, 4338
Sid W. Richardson Fndn Grants, 4350

Sierra Health Fndn Responsive Grants, 4353
Skaggs Fndn Grants, 4378
Snee Reinhardt Charitable Fndn Grants, 4387
Sobrato Family Fndn Grants, 4389
Sobrato Family Fndn Meeting Space Grants, 4390
Sobrato Family Fndn Office Space Grants, 4391
Sonoco Fndn Grants, 4403
Sorenson Legacy Fndn Grants, 4407
Southbury Community Trust Fund, 4409
South Carolina Arts Commission AIE Residency Plus Individual Site Grants, 4411
South Carolina Arts Commission AIE Residency Plus Multi-Site Grants, 4412
SW Gas Corp Fndn Grants, 4445
Special Olympics Project UNIFY Grants, 4449
Spencer County Community Fndn Grants, 4451
Sport Manitoba Athlete/Team Travel Assistance Grants, 4452
Sport Manitoba Athlete Skill Development Clinics Grants, 4453
Sport Manitoba Bingo Allocations Grants, 4454
Sport Manitoba Coaches/Officials Travel Assistance Grants, 4455
Sport Manitoba Hosting Regional Championships Grants, 4456
Sport Manitoba Intro of a New Sport Grants, 4457
Sport Manitoba KidSport Athlete Grants, 4458
Sport Manitoba Sport Special Inits Grants, 4459
Sport Manitoba Women to Watch Grants, 4460
Sprint Fndn Grants, 4463
Stackpole-Hall Grants, 4472
Staples Fndn for Learning Grants, 4475
Stark Community SummerTime Kid Grants, 4480
State Street Fndn Grants, 4495
Strowd Roses Grants, 4515
Sunbeam Products Grants, 4526
Sunderland Fndn Grants, 4527
Sunny and Abe Rosenberg Fndn Grants, 4529
Susan A. & Donald P. Babson Charitable Grants, 4534
Susan Mott Webb Charitable Grants, 4536
Talbert and Leota Abrams Fndn, 4558
Tauck Family Fndn Grants, 4563
TCF Bank Fndn Grants, 4565
TD4HIM Fndn Grants, 4566
Teaching Tolerance Mix-it-Up Grants, 4568
Teagle Fndn Grants, 4569
Tension Envelope Fndn Grants, 4578
Thomas and Dorothy Leavey Fndn Grants, 4612
Thomas Austin Finch, Sr. Fndn Grants, 4613
Thomas C. Ackerman Fndn Grants, 4615
Thomas J. Long Fndn Community Grants, 4618
Thomas W. Briggs Fndn Grants, 4621
Thompson Charitable Fndn Grants, 4622
Threshold Fndn Justice and Democracy Grants, 4626
Tiger Woods Fndn Grants, 4634
Time Warner Diverse Voices in the Arts Grants, 4635
Time Warner Youth Media & Creative Grants, 4636
Toby Wells Fndn Grants, 4638
Topeka Community Fndn Boss Hawg's Charitable Giving Grants, 4642
Topeka West Rotary Youth Enrichment Grants, 4645
Toyota Motor Manufacturing Mississippi Grants, 4655
Toyota USA Fndn Safety Grants, 4662
Triangle Community Fndn Community Grants, 4667
Trinity Trust Community Response Grants, 4671
Trinity Trust Summer Youth Mini Grants, 4672
Trull Fndn Grants, 4673
TSYSF Team Grants, 4676
Tull Charitable Fndn Grants, 4679
U.S. Lacrosse Emerging Groups Grants, 4703
U.S. Lacrosse Equipment Grants, 4704
Union Bank, N.A. Fndn Grants, 4709
Union Benevolent Association Grants, 4710
Union Pacific Fndn Community and Civic Grants, 4714
USAA – Ann Hoyt / Jim Easton JOAD Grants, 4734
USFA Development Grants, 4866
USFA Equipment Subsidy Grants, 4867
USGA Fndn For the Good of the Game Grants, 4868
USTA Althea Gibson Leadership Awards, 4872

USTA CTA and NJTL Community Tennis Development Workshop Scholarships, 4873
USTA Excellence Grants, 4874
USTA Junior Team Tennis Stipends, 4875
USTA Multicultural Individual Player Grant for National Competition and Training, 4877
USTA NJTL Arthur Ashe Essay and Art Contest, 4878
USTA NJTL Tennis and Leadership Camp Scholarships, 4879
USTA Okechi Womeodu Scholar Athlete Grants, 4880
USTA Player Development Grants, 4881
USTA Pro Circuit Community Involvement Day Grants, 4882
USTA Public Facility Assistance Grants, 4883
USTA Recreational Tennis Grants, 4884
USTA Serves Player Incentive Awards, 4891
USTA Tennis Block Party Grants, 4892
Vancouver Fndn Grants & Comm Inits, 4900
Vanderburgh Community Fndn Grants, 4902
Van Kampen Boyer Molinari Charitable Grants, 4905
Viacom Fndn Grants (Formerly CBS Fndn), 4932
Victor E. Speas Fndn Grants, 4933
Victoria S. and Bradley L. Geist Fndn Grants Supporting Foster Care and Their Caregivers, 4936
Victoria S. and Bradley L. Geist Fndn Grants Supporting Transitioning Foster Youth, 4937
Volvo Adventure Environmental Awards, 4952
Vulcan Materials Company Fndn Grants, 4956
W.K. Kellogg Fndn Civic Engagement Grants, 4960
W.K. Kellogg Fndn Healthy Kids Grants, 4961
Walt Disney Company Fndn Grants, 4981
Warrick County Community Fndn Grants, 4987
Washington County Community Fndn Grants, 4997
Wayne and Gladys Valley Fndn Grants, 5003
Weaver Popcorn Fndn Grants, 5016
Wege Fndn Grants, 5017
West Virginia Commission on the Arts Challenge America Partnership Grants, 5031
Weyerhaeuser Company Fndn Grants, 5053
Widgeon Point Charitable Fndn Grants, 5064
William B. Stokely Jr. Fndn Grants, 5076
William Blair and Company Fndn Grants, 5078
William G. Gilmore Fndn Grants, 5082
William T. Grant Fndn Youth Service Improvement Grants, 5096
Wilson-Wood Fndn Grants, 5098
Windgate Charitable Fndn Grants, 5099
Windward Youth Leadership Grants, 5100
Wisconsin Energy Fndn Grants, 5106
Wood-Claeyssens Fndn Grants, 5113
Yawkey Fndn Grants, 5125
Youth Action Net Universidad Europea de Madrid Prize, 5129
Youth as Resources Mini-Grants, 5131
Youth Philanthropy Project, 5132
YSA Get Ur Good On Grants, 5134
YSA Global Youth Service Lead Agency Grants, 5135
YSA MLK Day Lead Organizer Grants, 5136
YSA National Child Awareness Month Youth Ambassador Grants, 5137
YSA NEA Youth Leaders for Lit Grants, 5138
YSA Radio Disney's Hero for Change Award, 5139
YSA State Farm Good Neighbor YOUth In The Driver Seat Grants, 5141

Youth Services
ABS Fndn Grants, 107
Abundance Fndn Local Community Grants, 109
ACF Native American Social and Economic Development Strategies Grants, 123
Acuity Charitable Fndn Grants, 140
Adams and Reese LLP Corp Giving Grants, 147
Adelaide Christian Home For Children Grants, 162
ALA Penguin Young Readers Group Award, 308
ALA Supporting Diversity Stipend, 333
Alfred and Tillie Shemanski Testamentary Grants, 363
Allan C. and Leila J. Garden Fndn Grants, 374
Amelia Sillman Rockwell and Carlos Perry Rockwell Charities Grants, 417
Anderson Fndn Grants, 460

1018 /Youth Services

ATA Local Community Relations Grants, 600
Back Home Again Fndn Grants, 633
Baton Rouge Area Fndn Every Kid a King Grants, 681
Baxter Int'l Corp Giving Grants, 689
Ben B. Cheney Fndn Grants, 725
Bernard & Audre Rapoport Arts & Culture Grant, 735
Bernard and Audre Rapoport Fndn Community Building and Social Service Grants, 736
Bernard and Audre Rapoport Fndn Democracy and Civic Participation Grants, 737
Best Buy Children's Fndn @15 Community Grants, 749
C.F. Adams Charitable Grants, 884
Caesars Fndn Grants, 891
CFFVR Jewelers Mutual Charitable Giving, 1014
Charles H. Pearson Fndn Grants, 1045
Christine and Katharina Pauly Charitable Grants, 1114
CICF Howard Intermill and Marion Intermill Fenstermaker Grants, 1122
Citizens Savings Fndn Grants, 1141
CNCS AmeriCorps State and National Grants, 1182
CNCS Foster Grandparent Grants, 1185
Collective Brands Fndn Payless Gives Shoes 4 Kids Grants, 1207
Community Fndn for San Benito County Grants, 1258
Community Fndn of Abilene Future Grants, 1265
Community Fndn of Southern Indiana Grants, 1310
Countess Moira Charitable Fndn Grants, 1381
Covenant to Care for Children Grants, 1389
Deaconess Fndn Advocacy Grants, 1468
Deborah Munroe Noonan Grants, 1475
Decatur County Comm Large Project Grants, 1476
Decatur County Community Fndn Small Project Grants, 1477
Deuce McAllister Catch 22 Fndn Grants, 1521
Emerson Kampen Fndn Grants, 1696
Esther M. and Freeman E. Everett Charitable Fndn Grants, 1757
Eugene Straus Charitable Trust, 1766
Ezra M. Cutting Grants, 1779
Finish Line Youth Fndn Legacy Grants, 1814
Fndn for the Mid South Wealth Building Grants, 1900
Fndns of E Chicago Youth Development Grants, 1912
Frederick McDonald Grants, 1946
George B. Page Fndn Grants, 2013
George H.C. Ensworth Grants, 2022
George W. Wells Fndn Grants, 2030
Gil and Dody Weaver Fndn Grants, 2053
GNOF Norco Community Grants, 2089
Go Daddy Cares Charitable Contributions, 2094
Greenspun Family Fndn Grants, 2156
Grover Hermann Fndn Grants, 2168
Haddad Fndn Grants, 2189
HAF Hansen Family Trust Christian Endowment Grants, 2197
Hazen Fndn Youth Organizing Grants, 2270
Hearst Fndns Social Service Grants, 2285
Initiaive Fndn Inside-Out Connections Grants, 2556
Jim Blevins Fndn Grants, 2678
Johnson County Community Fndn Youth Philanthropy Init Grants, 2724
John W. Speas and Effie E. Speas Grants, 2732
Joseph S. Stackpole Charitable Grants, 2741
Judith Clark-Morrill Fndn Grants, 2756
Kovler Family Fndn Grants, 2840
Kroger Grassroots Community Support Grants, 2843
Lake County Community Grants, 2856
Land O'Lakes Fndn California Region Grants, 2858
Land O'Lakes Fndn Community Grants, 2859
Legacy Fndn College Readiness Grant, 2874
LEGO Children's Grants, 2878
Lily Palmer Fry Grants, 2905
M.D. Anderson Fndn Grants, 2952
MacDonald-Peterson Fndn Grants, 2965
Madison Community Fndn Grants, 2971
Marion and Miriam Rose Grants, 3015
Mary Black Early Childhood Devel Grants, 3033
Mathile Family Fndn Grants, 3062
McCune Fndn Human Services Grants, 3080
MetLife Fndn Preparing Young People Grants, 3131
Middlesex Savings Charitable Fndn Capacity Building Grants, 3172
Milton Hicks Wood and Helen Gibbs Wood Charitable Grants, 3184
Monsanto Int'l Grants, 3207
Monsanto Kids Garden Fresh Grants, 3208
Moody Fndn Grants, 3215
NFL Charities NFL Player Fndn Grants, 3347
Olga Sipolin Children's Grants, 3668
Olive B. Cole Fndn Grants, 3670
Oppenstein Brothers Fndn Grants, 3685
Orange County Community Fndn Grants, 3687
Pacers Fndn Be Drug-Free Grants, 3720
Pacers Fndn Be Educated Grants, 3721
Pacers Fndn Be Tolerant Grants, 3723
Pacers Fndn Indiana Fever's Be Younique Grants, 3724
Parker Fndn (California) Grants, 3736
Paul and Edith Babson Fndn Grants, 3755
Peter and Elizabeth C. Tower Fndn Annual Intellectual Disabilities Grants, 3834
Peter and Elizabeth C. Tower Fndn Annual Mental Health Grants, 3835
Peter and Elizabeth C. Tower Fndn Learning Disability Grants, 3836
Peter & Elizabeth C. Tower Mental Health Reference and Resource Materials Mini-Grants, 3837
Peter and Elizabeth C. Tower Fndn Phase II Technology Init Grants, 3839
Peter and Elizabeth C. Tower Fndn Phase I Technology Init Grants, 3840
Peter and Elizabeth C. Tower Fndn Social and Emotional Preschool Curriculum Grants, 3841
Peter and Elizabeth C. Tower Fndn Substance Abuse Grants, 3842
PG&E Community Investment Grants, 3867
Piedmont Natural Gas Fndn Health and Human Services Grants, 3885
Pinnacle Entertainment Fndn Grants, 3893
Piper Trust Educ Grants, 3902
PMI Fndn Grants, 3918
Porter County Health and Wellness Grant, 3933
Portland Fndn - Women's Giving Circle Grant, 3935
Price Chopper's Golub Fndn Grants, 3950
Reinberger Fndn Grants, 4052
Richard Davoud Donchian Fndn Grants, 4080
Saginaw County Community Fndn Youth FORCE Grants, 4208
Sandy Hill Fndn Grants, 4257
Scheumann Fndn Grants, 4306
Seattle Fndn Basic Needs Grants, 4321
Seattle Fndn Benjamin N. Phillips Grants, 4322
Sobrato Family Fndn Grants, 4389
Sobrato Family Fndn Meeting Space Grants, 4390
Sobrato Family Fndn Office Space Grants, 4391
SW Init Fndn Grants, 4446
Sunny and Abe Rosenberg Fndn Grants, 4529
Toyota Motor Manufacturing Mississippi Grants, 4655
Toyota Motor Manufacturing of Texas Grants, 4656
Toyota USA Fndn Safety Grants, 4662
Trinity Trust Community Response Grants, 4671
Trinity Trust Summer Youth Mini Grants, 4672
Union Pacific Health & Human Services Grants, 4715
Vanderburgh Community Fndn Grants, 4902
Washington County Community Fndn Grants, 4997
Weaver Popcorn Fndn Grants, 5016
Wolfe Associates Grants, 5110
Wood-Claeyssens Fndn Grants, 5113

Youth Violence
Alliance Healthcare Fndn Grants, 383
Allstate Fndn Tolerance, Inclusion, and Diversity Grants, 391
ATF Gang Resistance Educ and Training Program Coop Agreements, 603
Bernard and Audre Rapoport Fndn Community Building and Social Service Grants, 736
Callaway Golf Company Fndn Violence Prevention Grants, 911
Chicago Community Trust Public Safety and Justice Grants, 1093

SUBJECT INDEX

Dept of Ed Workplace & Comm Transition Training for Incarcerated Youth Offenders, 1515
Deuce McAllister Catch 22 Fndn Grants, 1521
Fndns of E Chicago Youth Development Grants, 1912
Gamble Fndn Grants, 1983
Girl's Best Friend Fndn Grants, 2057
Go Daddy Cares Charitable Contributions, 2094
Kansas Health Fndn Recognition Grants, 2784
Kuki'o Community Fund, 2845
Ms. Fndn for Women Ending Violence Grants, 3224
NFL Charities Pro Bowl Comm Grants in Hawaii, 3348
OJJDP Gang Prevention Coordination Assistance Grants, 3663
Ordean Fndn Grants, 3691
Phoenix Neighborhood Block Watch Grants, 3880
Piedmont Natural Gas Fndn Health and Human Services Grants, 3885
Sorenson Legacy Fndn Grants, 4407
Trinity Fndn Grants, 4669
U.S. Department of Educ Programs for Native Hawaiians, 4696
United Methodist Women Brighter Future for Children and Youth Grants, 4723
William G. McGowan Charitable Grants, 5084

Zoology
DeRoy Testamentary Fndn Grants, 1518
Jerry L. and Barbara J. Burris Fndn Grants, 2669

Zoos
Albert and Bessie Mae Kronkosky Charitable Fndn Grants, 339
Bay and Paul Fndns, Inc Grants, 692
Blum-Kovler Fndn Grants, 803
Cessna Fndn Grants, 1000
Chamberlain Fndn Grants, 1027
Chesapeake Bay Trust Mini Grants, 1072
Chingos Fndn Grants, 1109
Cobb Family Fndn Grants, 1194
DeRoy Testamentary Fndn Grants, 1518
FirstEnergy Fndn Community Grants, 1819
George F. Baker Grants, 2016
Hampton Roads Community Fndn Horticulture Educ Grants, 2217
IMLS 21st Century Museum Pro Grants, 2512
IMLS National Leadership Grants, 2515
Jerry L. and Barbara J. Burris Fndn Grants, 2669
Katherine John Murphy Fndn Grants, 2790
Lee and Ramona Bass Fndn Grants, 2871
Oscar Rennebohm Fndn Grants, 3694
Parker Fndn (California) Grants, 3736
Perry County Community Fndn Grants, 3827
Pike County Community Fndn Grants, 3888
PMI Fndn Grants, 3918
Posey County Community Fndn Grants, 3939
Procter and Gamble Grants, 3967
Reinberger Fndn Grants, 4052
Ryder System Charitable Fndn Grants, 4191
Saint Louis Rams Fndn Community Donations, 4214
San Diego Environment Community Grants, 4246
Schlessman Family Fndn Grants, 4307
Sioux Falls Area Community Fndn Field-of-Interest and Donor-Advised Grants, 4365
Spencer County Community Fndn Grants, 4451
Thelma Doelger Charitable Grants, 4604
Union Pacific Fndn Community and Civic Grants, 4714
Warrick County Community Fndn Grants, 4987
Widgeon Point Charitable Fndn Grants, 5064

Program Type Index

NOTE: Numbers refer to entry numbers

Adult Basic Education
7-Eleven Coorporate Giving Grants, 18
A.C. Ratshesky Fnd Grants, 39
Able Trust Voc Rehab Grants for Agencies, 103
ACE Charitable Fnd Grants, 111
Achelis Fnd Grants, 127
Adolph Coors Fnd Grants, 171
Ahmanson Fnd Grants, 207
Aid for Starving Children African American Independence Single Mother's Grants, 210
ALA Writers Live at the Library Grants, 336
Albert W. Cherne Fnd Grants, 346
Albert W. Rice Charitable Fnd Grants, 347
Allyn Fnd Grants, 392
Arkell Hall Fnd Grants, 562
Arlington Comm Fnd Grants, 564
Atkinson Fnd Comm Grants, 606
Atlanta Fnd Grants, 608
Auburn Fnd Grants, 611
Autauga Area Comm Fnd Grants, 618
Azadoutioun Fnd Grants, 631
Ball Brothers Fnd General Grants, 637
Battle Creek Comm Fnd Grants, 684
Battle Creek Comm Fdn Mini-Grants, 685
BBF Maine Fam Lit Initiative Plng Grants, 699
Benton Comm Fnd Grants, 730
Benton County Fnd Grants, 731
Blandin Fnd Invest Early Grants, 788
Blue Cross Blue Shield of Minnesota Fdn - Healthy Equity: Public Libraries for Health Grants, 797
Blue Mountain Comm Fnd Grants, 800
Blue River Comm Fnd Grants, 801
Bodenwein Public Benevolent Fdn Grants, 806
Bodman Fnd Grants, 807
Boettcher Fnd Grants, 810
Booth-Bricker Fund Grants, 815
Boston Fnd Grants, 819
Boston Globe Fnd Grants, 821
Bowling Green Comm Fnd Grants, 824
Bridgestone/Firestone Trust Fund Grants, 836
Brooklyn Comm Fnd Educ and Youth Achievement Grants, 851
Brown County Comm Fnd Grants, 853
Carl R. Hendrickson Family Fnd Grants, 935
Carrie Estelle Doheny Fnd Grants, 945
Cass County Comm Fnd Grants, 952
CCHD Comm Dev Grants, 966
Cemala Fnd Grants, 988
Charles Nelson Robinson Fund Grants, 1052
Charlotte County Comm Fdn Grts, 1056
Chicago Board of Trade Fnd Grants, 1079
CICF Efroymson Grants, 1120
CIGNA Fnd Grants, 1130
Clinton County Comm Fnd Grants, 1174
CNCS AmeriCorps State and National Grants, 1182
CNCS AmeriCorps VISTA Project Grants, 1184
Coastal Bend Comm Fnd Grants, 1192
Colorado Springs Cmty Trust Fund Grants, 1215
Columbus Fnd Competitive Grants, 1220
Columbus Fnd Small Grants, 1232
Comm Fnd of Bartholomew County Heritage Fund Grants, 1267
Comm Fdn of Boone County Grants, 1274
Comm Fdn of Central Illinois Grants, 1276
Comm Fdn of Greater Fort Wayne - Cmty Endowment and Clarke Endowment Grants, 1285
Comm Fdn of Grtr New Britain Grants, 1291
Comm Fdn of Shreveport-Bossier Grants, 1307
Comm Fdn of SE Connecticut Grants, 1309
Constantin Fnd Grants, 1362
Coors Brewing Corporate Contributions Grants, 1371
Cornerstone Fnd of NE Wisconsin Grts, 1375
Cowles Charitable Trust Grants, 1392
Daisy Marquis Jones Fnd Grants, 1434
Dayton Power and Light Fnd Grants, 1464
Dean Foods Comm Involvement Grants, 1469
DeKalb Cty Comm Fdn - Lit Grant, 1480
Dollar General Adult Lit Grants, 1568

Dollar General Family Lit Grants, 1569
DOL Youthbuild Grants, 1571
Dr. Scholl Fnd Grants, 1602
Eaton Charitable Fund Grants, 1647
Edward & Ellen Roche Relief Fdn Grants, 1663
Edward W & Stella C Van Houten Grants, 1670
Elizabeth Morse Genius Char Trust Grants, 1682
El Pomar Fnd Awards and Grants, 1690
Emma G. Harris Fnd Grants, 1701
Eulalie Bloedel Schneider Fnd Grants, 1767
F.R. Bigelow Fnd Grants, 1781
Field Fnd of Illinois Grants, 1806
First Lady's Family Lit Initiative for Texas Family Lit Trailblazer Grants, 1821
First Lady's Family Lit Initiative for Texas, 1822
First Lady's Family Lit Initiative for Texas Implementation Grants, 1823
First Lady's Family Lit Initiative for Texas Planning Grants, 1824
Fnds of E Chgo Fin Independence Grts, 1909
Frances L & Edwin L Cummings Mem Fund, 1919
Frank Reed and Margaret Jane Peters Memorial Fund II Grants, 1934
G.N. Wilcox Trust Grants, 1982
Gannett Fdn Comm Action Grants, 1984
Gardiner Howland Shaw Fnd Grants, 1986
George Fnd Grants, 2018
George W. Wells Fnd Grants, 2030
Goldseker Fnd Human Services Grants, 2102
Goodrich Corporation Fnd Grants, 2104
Grand Victoria Fnd Illinois Core Grants, 2126
Green Fnd Educ Grants, 2153
Greygates Fnd Grants, 2164
Guido A & Elizabeth H Binda Fdn Grants, 2172
H.B. Fuller Company Fnd Grants, 2183
HAF Comm Grants, 2193
Hallmark Corporate Fnd Grants, 2212
Harold Brooks Fnd Grants, 2227
Harold Simmons Fnd Grants, 2230
HBF Pathways Out of Poverty Grants, 2273
Helen Steiner Rice Fnd Grants, 2299
Hoblitzelle Fnd Grants, 2341
Howard and Bush Fnd Grants, 2374
Humanitas Fnd Grants, 2390
Hyams Fnd Grants, 2413
Idaho Power Company Corp Contributions, 2433
James A. and Faith Knight Fnd Grants, 2621
James Ford Bell Fnd Grants, 2623
James S. Copley Fnd Grants, 2637
John H. and Wilhelmina D. Harland Charitable Fnd Grants, 2698
John I. Smith Charities Grants, 2700
John S & James L Knight Fdn Dnr Adv Fd Grts, 2712
Joseph H & Florence A Roblee Fdn Grants, 2736
Joseph S. Stackpole Charitable Trust Grants, 2741
Joyce Fnd Employment Grants, 2749
Kentucky Arts Cncl Teaching Art Together, 2811
KeySpan Fnd Grants, 2821
Laura Jane Musser Rural Initiative Grants, 2864
Leo Niessen Jr., Charitable Trust Grants, 2885
Liberty Bank Fnd Grants, 2890
Lubrizol Fnd Grants, 2933
Lydia deForest Charitable Trust Grants, 2946
Mabel Louise Riley Fnd Family Strengthening Small Grants, 2958
Mardag Fnd Grants, 3001
Marin Comm Fnd Social Justice and Interfaith Understanding Grants, 3012
Mary Wilmer Covey Charitable Trust Grants, 3049
May and Stanley Smith Char Trust Grants, 3069
McCarthy Family Fnd Grants, 3073
McCune Charitable Fnd Grants, 3077
Meyer Fnd Economic Security Grants, 3141
Middlesex Savings Charitable Fnd Educational Opportunities Grants, 3174
National Book Scholarship Fund, 3249
Nina Mason Pulliam Charitable Trust Grants, 3443
Norcliffe Fnd Grants, 3459

NYCT Fund for New Citizens Grants, 3547
NYCT Hunger and Homelessnes Grants, 3553
Oak Fdn Housing & Homelessness Grants, 3633
Oppenstein Brothers Fnd Grants, 3685
Palm Beach and Martin Counties Grants, 3733
Parkersburg Area Cmty Fdn Action Grants, 3738
Paul and Mary Haas Fnd Contributions and Student Scholarships, 3756
PepsiCo Fnd Grants, 3819
Peyton Anderson Fnd Grants, 3862
Piper Jaffray Fdn Communities Giving Grants, 3899
PMI Fnd Grants, 3918
Portland General Electric Fnd Grants, 3937
Princeton Comm Fnd Greater Mercer Grants, 3963
Principal Financial Group Fnd Grants, 3966
Putnam County Comm Fdn Grants, 3990
RCF Individual Assistance Grants, 4033
Reinberger Fnd Grants, 4052
Richard and Rhoda Goldman Fund Grants, 4077
Robert R. McCormick Tribune Comm Grants, 4119
Robert R. McCormick Tribune Veterans Grants, 4120
Robert R. Meyer Fnd Grants, 4121
Rose Comm Fnd Child and Family Dev Grants, 4153
Rose Hills Fnd Grants, 4162
Saint Paul Fnd Grants, 4219
San Antonio Area Fnd Grants, 4240
San Francisco Fnd Koshland Program Arts and Culture Mini-Grants, 4280
Santa Fe Comm Fnd Seasonal Grants-Spring, 4291
Sara Lee Fnd Grants, 4296
Sisters of Charity Cleveland Reducing Health & Educational Disparities Grants, 4374
Sony Corporation of America Corp Philan Grts, 4405
Sorenson Legacy Fnd Grants, 4407
Sprint Fnd Grants, 4463
Talbert and Leota Abrams Fnd, 4558
Texas Cmsn on the Arts Arts Respond Prj Grts, 4581
Texas Comsn on the Arts Create-2 Pgm Grants, 4584
Thomas Sill Fnd Grants, 4619
TJX Fnd Grants, 4637
Tri-State Comm Twenty-first Century Endowment Fund Grants, 4666
US Dept of Educ Rehab Trng--Rehabilitation Continuing Educ Programs --Institute on Rehabilitation Issues , 4700
Union Square Awards Grants, 4718
UPS Fnd Economic & Global Lit Grts, 4730
US Airways Educ Fnd Grants, 4790
Vanderburgh Comm Fdn Women's Fund, 4903
Vectren Fnd Grants, 4907
Verizon Fnd Great Lakes Region Grants, 4912
Verizon Fnd New York Grants, 4919
Verizon Fnd Virginia Grants, 4925
Wayne County Fnd - Vigran Family Fnd Grants, 5004
Wayne County Fnd Grants, 5005
Whirlpool Fnd Grants, 5056
WHO Fnd General Grants, 5063
Wilson-Wood Fnd Grants, 5098
Xerox Fnd Grants, 5122

Adult/Family Literacy Training
7-Eleven Coorporate Giving Grants, 18
A.C. Ratshesky Fnd Grants, 39
Abell Fnd Workforce Dev Grants, 97
Able Trust Voc Rehab Grants for Agencies, 103
Able Trust Vocational Rehabilitation Grants for Individuals, 104
ACE Charitable Fnd Grants, 111
Achelis Fnd Grants, 127
Adams Cty Comm Fdn of Indiana Grts, 148
Adolph Coors Fnd Grants, 171
Ahmanson Fnd Grants, 207
Aid for Starving Children African American Independence Single Mother's Grants, 210
Albert W. Cherne Fnd Grants, 346
Albert W. Rice Charitable Fnd Grants, 347
Alcatel-Lucent Technologies Fnd Grants, 349
Alliant Energy Fnd Comm Grants, 384

Adult/Family Literacy Training

Allyn Fnd Grants, 392
Altman Fnd Health Care Grants, 397
Amador Comm Fnd Grants, 408
American Savings Fnd Grants, 445
Amgen Fnd Grants, 456
Andersen Corporate Fnd, 459
Annenberg Fnd Grants, 477
Anschutz Family Fnd Grants, 486
Arizona Cardinals Grants, 534
Arizona Republic Fnd Grants, 546
Arizona Republic Newspaper Corp Contribs, 547
Arkell Hall Fnd Grants, 562
Arlington Comm Fnd Grants, 564
Assisi Fnd of Memphis General Grants, 594
Assisi Fdn of Memphis Mini Grants, 595
Atkinson Fnd Comm Grants, 606
Atlanta Fnd Grants, 608
Auburn Fnd Grants, 611
Autauga Area Comm Fnd Grants, 618
Azadoutioun Fnd Grants, 631
Bacon Family Fnd Grants, 634
Ball Brothers Fnd General Grants, 637
Barnes and Noble Local Sponsorships and Charitable Donations, 670
Barnes and Noble National Sponsorships and Charitable Donations, 671
Barra Fnd Comm Fund Grants, 673
Battle Creek Comm Fnd Grants, 684
Battle Creek Comm Fdn Mini-Grants, 685
Bayer Fnd Grants, 696
BBF Florida Family Lit Initiative Grants, 697
BBF Maine Fam Lit Init Implementation Grants, 698
BBF Maine Fam Lit Init Planning Grants, 699
BBF Maryland Fam Lit Init Implement Grants, 700
BBF Maryland Fam Lit Init Planning Grants, 701
BBF National Grants for Family Lit, 702
BBVA Compass Fnd Charitable Grants, 703
Beazley Fnd Grants, 714
Benton Comm Fnd Grants, 730
Best Buy Children's Fdn @15 Teach Awards, 751
Better World Books LEAP Grants for Libraries, 755
Better World Books LEAP Grts for Nonprofits, 756
Blue Cross Blue Shield of Minnesota Fdn - Healthy Equity: Public Libraries for Health Grants, 797
Blue Mountain Comm Fnd Grants, 800
Blue River Comm Fnd Grants, 801
Bodenwein Public Benevolent Fdn Grants, 806
Bodman Fnd Grants, 807
Boettcher Fnd Grants, 810
Booth-Bricker Fund Grants, 815
Boston Fnd Grants, 819
Boston Globe Fnd Grants, 821
Bowling Green Comm Fnd Grants, 824
Brooklyn Comm Fnd Educ and Youth Achievement Grants, 851
Brown County Comm Fnd Grants, 853
Build-A-Bear Workshop Bear Hugs Fnd Lit and Educ Grants, 860
Business Wire Lit Initiative, 880
Cabot Corporation Fnd Grants, 887
Caesars Fnd Grants, 891
Carl B. and Florence E. King Fnd Grants, 928
Carl R. Hendrickson Family Fnd Grants, 935
Carrie Estelle Doheny Fnd Grants, 945
Cass County Comm Fnd Grants, 952
Catherine Manley Gaylord Fnd Grants, 956
Cemala Fnd Grants, 988
Central Okanagan Fnd Grants, 997
CFFVR Basic Needs Giving Partnership Grts, 1002
CFFVR Schmidt Family G4 Grants, 1020
CFFVR Wisc King's Daughters & Sons Grants, 1024
Charles Delmar Fnd Grants, 1039
Charles Nelson Robinson Fund Grants, 1052
Charlotte County Comm Fdn Grts, 1056
Chicago Board of Trade Fnd Grants, 1079
Chicago Title & Trust Co Fnd Grants, 1099
CICF Efroymson Grants, 1120
CIGNA Fnd Grants, 1130
Cleveland-Cliffs Fnd Grants, 1165
Clinton County Comm Fnd Grants, 1174

CNA Fnd Grants, 1179
CNCS AmeriCorps State and National Grants, 1182
CNCS AmeriCorps VISTA Project Grants, 1184
Coastal Bend Comm Fnd Grants, 1192
Coca-Cola Fnd Grants, 1195
Colorado Springs Cmty Trust Fund Grants, 1215
Columbus Fnd Competitive Grants, 1220
Columbus Fnd Small Grants, 1232
Comcast Fnd Grants, 1235
Comerica Charitable Fnd Grants, 1237
Comm Fnd of Bartholomew County Heritage Fund Grants, 1267
Comm Fnd of Boone County - Adult Lit Initiative Grants, 1272
Comm Fdn of Boone County Grants, 1274
Comm Fnd of Broward Grants, 1275
Comm Fdn of Central Illinois Grants, 1276
Comm Fdn of Grtr Birmingham Grants, 1280
Comm Fdn of Greater Chattanooga Grants, 1281
Comm Fnd of Greater Fort Wayne - Cmty Endwt & Clarke Endwt Grants, 1285
Comm Fdn of Greenville Hollingsworth Funds Program/Project Grants, 1296
Comm Fnd of Mdl Tennessee Grants, 1300
Comm Fnd of Muncie and Delaware County Maxon Grants, 1303
Comm Fdn of Shreveport-Bossier Grts, 1307
Comm Fdn of SE Connecticut Grants, 1309
Comm Fnd of the Verdugos Educational Endowment Fund Grants, 1321
Comm Fnd of the Verdugos Grants, 1322
Comm Fnd Silicon Valley Grants, 1331
Cooper Industries Fnd Grants, 1370
Coors Brewing Corporate Contributions Grants, 1371
Cornerstone Fdn of NE Wisconsin Grants, 1375
Cowles Charitable Trust Grants, 1392
Crail-Johnson Fnd Grants, 1393
Cruise Industry Charitable Fnd Grants, 1404
Cumberland Comm Fnd Grants, 1413
Daisy Marquis Jones Fnd Grants, 1434
Dallas Women's Fnd Grants, 1438
Danellie Fnd Grants, 1442
Darden Restaurants Fnd Grants, 1446
Dayton Power and Light Fnd Grants, 1464
Deaconess Comm Fnd Grants, 1467
Delonne Anderson Family Fnd, 1492
Delta Air Lines Fdn Cmty Enrichment Grants, 1494
Deluxe Corporation Fnd Grants, 1496
Denver Fnd Comm Grants, 1502
Dept of Ed Alaska Native Ed Pgms, 1506
Dept of Ed Even Start Grants, 1508
DHHS ARRA Strengthening Communities Fund - Nonprofit Capacity Building Grants, 1527
Diageo Fnd Grants, 1546
Dolfinger-McMahon Fnd Grants, 1565
Dollar General Adult Lit Grants, 1568
Dollar General Family Lit Grants, 1569
Donaldson Fnd Grants, 1574
Dr. Scholl Fnd Grants, 1602
Duke Energy Fdn Econ Dev Grants, 1619
Edward & Ellen Roche Relief Fdn Grants, 1663
Edward W & Stella C Van Houten Mem Fund, 1670
EIF Comm Grants, 1675
Elizabeth Morse Genius Char Trust Grants, 1682
El Paso Comm Fnd Grants, 1688
Emma G. Harris Fnd Grants, 1701
Entergy Charitable Fnd Low-Income Initiatives and Solutions Grants, 1711
Entergy Corporation Micro Grants, 1712
Essex County Comm Fnd Merrimack Valley General Fund Grants, 1756
F.R. Bigelow Fnd Grants, 1781
Fam Lit & HI Pizza Hut Lit Fund, 1785
Farmers Insurance Corporate Giving Grants, 1791
Faye McBeath Fnd Grants, 1794
Field Fnd of Illinois Grants, 1806
Financial Capability Innovation Fund II Grants, 1811
First Lady's Family Lit Initiative for Texas Family Lit Trailblazer Grants, 1821
First Lady's Fam Lit Init for Texas Grants, 1822

PROGRAM TYPE INDEX

First Lady's Family Lit Initiative for Texas Implementation Grants, 1823
First Lady's Family Lit Initiative for Texas Planning Grants, 1824
Fisher Fnd Grants, 1831
Fnd for the MidSouth Wlth Bldg Grts, 1900
Fnds of E Chgo Fin Independence Grts, 1909
Fourjay Fnd Grants, 1913
Frances L & Edwin L Cummings Mem Fund, 1919
Frank Reed and Margaret Jane Peters Memorial Fund II Grants, 1934
Fred & Gretel Biel Charitable Trust Grants, 1939
Fremont Area Cmty Fdn Amazing X Grants, 1953
G.N. Wilcox Trust Grants, 1982
Gannett Fdn Comm Action Grants, 1984
GenCorp Fnd Grants, 1998
George Fnd Grants, 2018
George I. Alden Trust Grants, 2023
George W. Wells Fnd Grants, 2030
Gibson Fnd Grants, 2052
Goldseker Fnd Human Services Grants, 2102
Grand Rapids Comm Fnd Ionia County Youth Fund Grants, 2120
Grand Victoria Fnd Illinois Core Grants, 2126
Green Bay Packers Fnd Grants, 2148
Green Fnd Educ Grants, 2153
Guido A & Elizabeth H Binda Fdn Grants, 2172
H.B. Fuller Company Fnd Grants, 2183
HAF Comm Grants, 2193
Hallmark Corporate Fnd Grants, 2212
Hamilton Family Fnd Grants, 2213
Hancock County Fnd - Field of Interest Grants, 2219
Harbus Fnd Grants, 2223
Harold Brooks Fnd Grants, 2227
Harold Simmons Fnd Grants, 2230
Harry S. Black and Allon Fuller Fund Grants, 2243
Harvest Fnd Grants, 2254
Hasbro Children's Fund, 2256
Hawaii Comm Fnd Geographic-Specific Grants, 2261
HBF Pathways Out of Poverty Grants, 2273
Hearst Fnds Social Service Grants, 2285
Helen Bader Fnd Grants, 2293
Helen Steiner Rice Fnd Grants, 2299
Henry & Ruth Blaustein Rosenberg Fdn Grants, 2306
Henry E. Niles Fnd Grants, 2309
Highmark Corporate Giving Grants, 2319
Hilda and Preston Davis Fnd Grants, 2322
Hoblitzelle Fnd Grants, 2341
Hoglund Fnd Grants, 2344
Howard and Bush Fnd Grants, 2374
Humana Fnd Grants, 2388
Hundred Club of Durango Grants, 2395
IBM Adult Trng & Workforce Dev Grts, 2423
Illinois DCEO Eliminate the Digital Divide, 2489
Independence Comm Fnd Education, Culture & Arts Grant, 2526
Int'l Paper Co Fnd Grants, 2568
Irvin Stern Fnd Grants, 2585
IYI Responsible Fatherhood Grants, 2591
Jacobs Family Fdn Vlg Neighborhoods Grants, 2619
James & Abigail Campbell Fam Fdn Grts, 2620
James A. and Faith Knight Fnd Grants, 2621
James S. Copley Fnd Grants, 2637
Jean and Louis Dreyfus Fnd Grants, 2658
Jessie Ball Dupont Fund Grants, 2671
Jim Moran Fnd Grants, 2680
John Edward Fowler Mem Fdn Grants, 2693
John H. and Wilhelmina D. Harland Charitable Fnd Grants, 2698
John I. Smith Charities Grants, 2700
John Merck Fnd Grants, 2706
John P. McGovern Fnd Grants, 2707
John S & James L Knight Fdn Dnr Adv Fd Grts, 2712
Johnson Scholarship Fnd Grants, 2726
Joseph H & Florence A Roblee Fdn Grants, 2736
Joseph S. Stackpole Charitable Trust Grants, 2741
Joyce Fnd Employment Grants, 2749
Leo Goodwin Fnd Grants, 2882
Leo Niessen Jr., Charitable Trust Grants, 2885
Linden Fnd Grants, 2908

PROGRAM TYPE INDEX

Louis Calder Fnd Grants, 2925
Lubrizol Fnd Grants, 2933
Lydia deForest Charitable Trust Grants, 2946
Mabel Louise Riley Fnd Family Strengthening Small Grants, 2958
Macquarie Bank Fnd Grants, 2966
Mardag Fnd Grants, 3001
Marie C. and Joseph C. Wilson Fnd Rochester Small Grants, 3006
Marin Comm Fnd Social Justice and Interfaith Understanding Grants, 3012
MARPAT Fnd Grants, 3023
Mary D. & Walter F Frear Eleemosynary Trust, 3035
Mary Wilmer Covey Charitable Trust Grants, 3049
Maximilian E & Marion O Hoffman Fdn, 3067
May & Stanley Smith Char Trust Grants, 3069
Maytree Fdn Refugee & Immigrant Grants, 3071
McCune Charitable Fnd Grants, 3077
McGraw-Hill Companies Comm Grants, 3081
Melville Charitable Trust Grants, 3115
Meyer Fnd Economic Security Grants, 3141
MFRI Operation Diploma Small Grants for Indiana Family Readiness Groups, 3152
Middlesex Savings Charitable Fnd Educational Opportunities Grants, 3174
Mizuho USA Fnd Grants, 3192
Montgomery Cty Comm Fdn Grants, 3213
Morris & Gwendolyn Cafritz Fdn Grants, 3218
National Book Scholarship Fund, 3249
Nat'l Endowment for the Arts Big Read, 3261
National Home Library Fnd Grants, 3276
Nationwide Insurance Fnd Grants, 3285
NCFL/Better World Bks Libs & Families Awd, 3288
New York Life Fnd Grants, 3341
Norcliffe Fnd Grants, 3459
Nordson Corporation Fnd Grants, 3462
Northern Chautauqua Comm Fnd Comm Grants, 3499
Northern Trust Company Charitable Trust and Corporate Giving Program, 3504
Norton Fnd Grants, 3514
NYCT Workforce Dev Grants, 3560
PacifiCare Fnd Grants, 3725
Palm Beach and Martin Counties Grants, 3733
Parkersburg Area Comm Fdn Action Grts, 3738
Paul and Mary Haas Fnd Contributions and Student Scholarships, 3756
PepsiCo Fnd Grants, 3819
Percy B. Ferebee Endowment Grants, 3820
Pew Charitable Trusts Children & Youth Grts, 3858
Peyton Anderson Fnd Grants, 3862
Pinkerton Fnd Grants, 3892
Piper Trust Children Grants, 3901
Piper Trust Educ Grants, 3902
PMI Fnd Grants, 3918
Price Chopper's Golub Fnd Grants, 3950
Principal Financial Group Fnd Grants, 3966
RCF Individual Assistance Grants, 4033
Reinberger Fnd Grants, 4052
Reynolds & Reynolds Assoc Fdn Grants, 4069
RGK Fnd Grants, 4072
Richard and Rhoda Goldman Fund Grants, 4077
Richard Davoud Donchian Fnd Grants, 4080
Robert Bowne Fnd Fellowships, 4107
Robert Bowne Fnd Lit Grants, 4108
Robert Bowne Fdn Youth-Centered Grants, 4109
Robert R. McCormick Tribune Comm Grants, 4119
Robert R. Meyer Fnd Grants, 4121
Rochester Area Comm Fnd Grants, 4127
Rose Hills Fnd Grants, 4162
RR Donnelley Comm Grants, 4168
Saint Louis Rams Fdn Comm Donations, 4214
Saint Paul Fnd Grants, 4219
Samuel S. Johnson Fnd Grants, 4239
San Antonio Area Fnd Grants, 4240
San Diego Women's Fnd Grants, 4252
Santa Fe Comm Fnd Seasonal Grants-Spring, 4291
Sara Lee Fnd Grants, 4296
Seattle Fnd Benjamin N. Phillips Grants, 4322
Seaver Institute Grants, 4331
Sidney Stern Memorial Trust Grants, 4349

Sierra Health Fnd Responsive Grants, 4353
Sisters of Charity Cleveland Reducing Health & Educational Disparities Grants, 4374
Skillman Fnd Good Schools Grants, 4382
Sony Corp of America Corp Philant Grants, 4405
Sorenson Legacy Fnd Grants, 4407
Southbury Comm Trust Fund, 4409
Sprint Fnd Grants, 4463
Stackpole-Hall Fnd Grants, 4472
Starbucks Fdn Shared Planet Youth Action, 4476
Stark Comm Fdn Women's Fund Grants, 4481
Sterling-Turner Charitable Fnd Grants, 4499
Stocker Fnd Grants, 4507
Strowd Roses Grants, 4515
Stuart Fnd Grants, 4516
Talbert and Leota Abrams Fnd, 4558
Target Corporation Local Store Grants, 4561
Textron Corporate Contributions Grants, 4601
Thomas Sill Fnd Grants, 4619
TJX Fnd Grants, 4637
Todd Brock Family Fnd Grants, 4639
Tri-State Comm Twenty-first Century Endowment Fund Grants, 4666
U.S. Bank Fnd Grants, 4686
Union Bank, N.A. Fnd Grants, 4709
UPS Fnd Economic and Global Lit Grants, 4730
US Airways Comm Contributions, 4788
US Airways Educ Fnd Grants, 4790
Vanderburgh Comm Fdn Women's Fund, 4903
Vectren Fnd Grants, 4907
Verizon Fnd Delaware Grants, 4909
Verizon Fnd Grants, 4911
Verizon Fnd Great Lakes Region Grants, 4912
Verizon Fnd Maryland Grants, 4917
Verizon Fnd New Jersey Check into Lit Grants, 4918
Verizon Fnd New York Grants, 4919
Verizon Fnd NE Region Grants, 4920
Verizon Fnd Pennsylvania Grants, 4921
Verizon Fnd South Carolina Lit & Internet Safety Grants, 4922
Verizon Fnd Vermont Grants, 4924
Verizon Fnd Virginia Grants, 4925
Verizon Fnd West Virginia Grants, 4926
Vulcan Materials Company Fnd Grants, 4956
Wallace Fnd Grants, 4976
Wayne County Fnd - Vigran Family Fnd Grants, 5004
Wayne County Fnd Grants, 5005
WCI Comm Leadership Fellowships, 5008
Western New York Fnd Grants, 5025
WHO Fnd Education/Lit Grants, 5062
WHO Fnd General Grants, 5063
Wilson-Wood Fnd Grants, 5098
Winston-Salem Fdn Stokes County Grants, 5104
Woods Charitable Fund Grants, 5114
Xerox Fnd Grants, 5122
Young Family Fnd Grants, 5127
YSA NEA Youth Leaders for Lit Grants, 5138

Awards/Prizes
1st Source Fnd Ernestine M. Raclin Comm Leadership Award, 2
3M Comm Volunteer Award, 11
AAAAI RSLAAIS Leadership Award, 49
AAAS Early Career Award for Public Engagement with Science, 51
AAF Richard Riley Award, 59
AAG Meredith F. Burrill Award, 60
AAP Anne E. Dyson Child Advocacy Awards, 61
AAUW Breaking through Barriers Award, 74
ABA Labor Lawyer Student Writing Contest, 77
ABC-CLIO Award for Best Book in Library Lit, 84
ACS Award for Encouraging Disadvantaged Students into Careers in the Chemical Sciences, 132
ACS Award for Encouraging Women into Careers in the Chemical Sciences, 133
Agape Fnd for Nonviolent Social Change Prizes, 198
AIChE Women's Initiatives Committee Mentorship Excellence Award, 209
ALA Allie Beth Martin Award, 221
ALA ALSC Distinguished Service Award, 223

ALA Annual Conference Professional Dev Attendance Award, 225
ALA Atlas Systems Mentoring Award, 227
ALA Baker and Taylor Entertainment Audio Music/Video Product Award, 229
ALA Carnegie Corporation of New York/New York Times I Love My Librarian Award, 254
ALA Charlie Robinson Award, 256
ALA Clarence Day Award, 258
ALA Coretta Scott King-Virginia Hamilton Award for Lifetime Achievement, 259
ALA Coretta Scott King Book Awards, 260
ALA Coretta Scott King Book Donation Grant, 261
ALA Dartmouth Medal, 262
ALA Distinguished Educ and Behavioral Sciences Librarian Award, 265
ALA Distinguished School Admin Award, 266
ALA Diversity and Outreach Fair, 267
ALA Diversity Research Grant, 268
ALA Donald G. Davis Article Award, 269
ALA EBSCO Comm College Learning Resources Leadership Awards, 271
ALA EBSCO Comm College Library Program Achievement Award, 272
ALA EBSCO Excellence in Small and/or Rural Public Library Service Award, 273
ALA Esther J. Piercy Award, 275
ALA Excellence in Academic Libraries Award, 276
ALA Excellence in Library Programming Award, 277
ALA Exceptional Service Award, 278
ALA Gale Cengage History Research and Innovation Award, 280
ALA Gale Cengage Learning Award for Excellence in Reference and Adult Library Services, 281
ALA Great Books Giveaway Competition, 282
ALA Harrassowitz Award for Leadership in Library Acquisitions Award, 284
ALA Highsmith Library Innovation Award, 285
ALA Information Tech Pathfinder Award, 286
ALA Info Today Library of the Future Awd, 287
ALA Innovation Award, 288
ALA Intellectual Freedom Award, 289
ALA Isadore Gilbert Mudge Award, 290
ALA John Cotton Dana Library Pub Rel Awd, 292
ALA John Phillip Immroth Memorial Award, 293
ALA Joseph W. Lippincott Award, 294
ALA MAE Award for Best Teen Lit Pgm, 296
ALA Margaret Mann Citation, 297
ALA Maureen Hayes Author/Illustrator Award, 299
ALA May Hill Arbuthnot Honor Lecture Awd, 300
ALA Melvil Dewey Medal, 301
ALA Morningstar Pub Librarian Support Awd, 302
ALA National Friends of Libraries Wk Awds, 303
ALA NewsBank/Rdx Catharine J Reynolds Awd, 304
ALA Paul Howard Award for Courage, 307
ALA Penguin Young Readers Group Award, 308
ALA Polaris Innovation in Tech John Iliff Award, 309
ALA President's Award for Advocacy, 310
ALA ProQuest Documents to the People Award, 311
ALA Reference Service Press Award, 312
ALA Routledge Distance Learning Librarianship Conference Sponsorship Award, 315
ALA Sara Jaffarian School Library Award for Exemplary Humanities Programming, 316
ALA Schneider Family Book Award, 317
ALA Scholastic Library Publishing Award, 318
ALA Scholastic Library Publishing National Library Week Grant, 319
Alaska Conservation Fnd Awards, 322
ALA Stonewall Book Awards - Barbara Gittings Lit Award, 329
ALA Stonewall Book Awards - Israel Fishman Nonfiction Award, 330
ALA Student Chapter of the Year Award, 331
ALA Sullivan Award for Administrators Supporting Services to Children, 332
ALA Ulrich's Serials Librarianship Award, 334
ALA Young Adult Lit Symposium Stipend, 337
Alfred & Tillie Shemanski Testamentary Grants, 363
Alfred P. Sloan Fdn Public Service Awds, 369

Awards/Prizes

AMA-MSS Chapter of the Year Award, 407
American Chem Society Award for Team Innov, 423
American Society on Aging Hall of Fame Award, 448
American Society on Aging NOMA Award for Excellence in Multicultural Aging, 449
AMERIND Poster Contest, 454
Anne J. Caudal Fnd Grants, 475
Annie E. Casey Fnd Grants, 481
Apple Worldwide Developers Conference Student Scholarships, 513
ASA Deming Lecturer Award, 586
ASME Charles T. Main Awards, 590
ASM Gen-Probe Joseph Public Health Award, 591
ATA School-Comm Relations Awards, 602
Austin College Leadership Award, 615
Award for Volunteer Service to the American Chemical Society, 626
Baxter Int'l Fnd Foster G. McGaw Prize, 690
Bayer Advanced Grow Together with Roses School Garden Awards, 695
BCBSM Children Angel Awards, 705
BCBSM Fdn Proposal Dev Awds, 709
BP Conservation Programme Future Conservationist Awards, 826
Broadcasting Board of Governors David Burke Distinguished Journalism Award, 843
California Coastal Art and Poetry Contest, 899
CECP Directors' Award, 986
Changemakers Innovation Awards, 1031
Chick and Sophie Major Memorial Duck Calling Contest Scholarships, 1103
Civic Change Award, 1143
Claude Pepper Fnd Grants, 1160
Colin Higgins Fnd Courage Awards, 1203
Collaboration Prize, 1205
Comm Fnd AIDS Endwt Awds, 1245
Comm Fnd of Bartholomew County James A. Henderson Award for Fundraising, 1268
Conrad N. Hilton Humanitarian Prize, 1356
Conseil des arts de Montreal Diversity Award, 1357
Council on Fnds Paul Ylvisaker Award for Public Policy Engagement, 1379
Council on Fnds Robert W. Scrivner Award for Creative Grantmaking, 1380
Courage Center Judd Jacobson Mem Awd, 1382
Delta Air Lines Prize for Global Understanding, 1495
DOE Initial H-Prize Competition for Breakthrough Advances in Materials for Hydrogen Storage, 1551
Do Something BR!CK Awards, 1592
El Pomar Fnd Awards and Grants, 1690
Encore Purpose Prize, 1704
Enterprise Comm Partners MetLife Fnd Awards for Excellence in Affordable Housing, 1717
First People's Fund Comm Spirit Awards, 1825
Foster G. McGaw Prize, 1889
Fnd for Young Ausies Your Eyes Only Awards, 1903
Garden Crusader Award, 1985
GEF Green Thumb Challenge, 1996
GEICO Public Service Awards, 1997
General Mills Fnd Celebrating Communities of Color Grants, 2002
GlaxoSmithKline Corporate Grants, 2060
GlaxoSmithKline Fdn IMPACT Awds, 2061
Gleitsman Fnd Activist Awards, 2063
Gloria Barron Prize for Young Heroes, 2064
Google Grants Beta, 2107
Grassroots Government Leadership Award, 2129
Great Clips Corporate Giving, 2131
Heifer Educational Fund Grants for Principals, 2288
Hitachi Fnd Yoshiyama Awards, 2340
Home Ownership Participation for All Awards, 2349
Hormel Family Fdn Business Plan Awd, 2367
Hydrogen Student Design Contest, 2415
IMLS Nat Medal for Museum & Library Service, 2516
Int'l Paper Environmental Awards, 2569
IRA Pearson Fdn-IRA-Rotary Lit Awds, 2572
J. Marion Sims Fnd Teachers' Pet Grant, 2605
James Irvine Fnd Leadership Awards, 2629
James T. Grady-James H. Stack Award for Interpreting Chemistry for the Public, 2638

John W. Gardner Leadership Award, 2731
Joyce Awards, 2746
Kentucky Arts Council Emerging Artist Award, 2807
King Baudouin Int'l Dev Prize, 2825
Kohl's Cares Scholarships, 2832
Koret Fnd Grants, 2837
Leadership IS Award, 2869
Leighton Award for Nonprofit Excellence, 2880
LISC MetLife Police Partnership Awards, 2912
Lumity Tech Leadership Award, 2940
Lynde and Harry Bradley Fnd Prizes, 2948
Maddie's Fund Lifesaving Awards, 2969
McKnight Fnd Virginia McKnight Binger Awards in Human Service, 3087
Miguel Aleman Fnd Grants, 3175
NAGC Masters and Specialists Award, 3237
NAR Realtor Mag Good Neighbor Awds, 3240
National Wetlands Awards, 3282
Nation Institute Ridenhour Prizes, 3283
Nation Institute Robert Masur Fellowship in Civil Liberties, 3284
Nature Hills Nursery Green America Awards, 3287
Nestle Very Best in Youth Competition, 3307
Nevada Arts Council Heritage Awards, 3311
NFL High Schl Football Coach of the Yr Awd, 3352
NFWF Budweiser Conservationist of the Yr Awd, 3361
NFWF Radical Salmon Design Contest, 3388
NGA 'Remember Me' Rose Schl Garden Awds, 3401
NGA Heinz Wholesome Memories Intergenerational Garden Awards, 3404
NGA Hooked on Hydroponics Awards, 3405
NGA Mantis Award, 3406
NGA Wuzzleburg Preschool Garden Awards, 3408
NHLBI Career Transition Awards, 3412
Nike and Ashoka GameChangers: Change the Game for Women in Sport, 3439
NLADA Kutak-Dodds Prizes, 3451
NSERC Brockhouse Canada Prize for Interdisciplinary Research in Science and Engineering Grant, 3518
NSERC Michael Smith Awards, 3519
NSTA Distinguished Informal Science Award, 3531
Ohio Arts Council Arts Indiv Excellence Awds, 3648
PAMA Awards Program, 3734
Pet Care Trust Sue Busch Memorial Award, 3829
Peter F. Drucker Award for Canadian Nonprofit Innovation, 3844
Petra Fnd Fellows Awards, 3850
Pfizer Special Events Grants, 3865
Phi Kappa Phi Scholar Award, 3871
Phi Upsilon Omicron Florence Fallgatter Distinguished Service Award, 3877
Phi Upsilon Omicron Frances Morton Holbrook Alumni Award, 3878
Pi Lambda Theta Anna Tracey Mem Awd, 3889
Pi Lambda Theta Lillian and Henry Barry Award in Human Relations, 3890
Playboy Fnd Freedom of Expression Award, 3912
Portland General Electric Fnd Grants, 3937
Presbyterian Church USA Sam and Helen R. Walton Award, 3946
Prince Charitable Trusts Chicago Grants, 3959
Princeton Area Comm Fdn Rebecca Annitto Service Opportunities for Students Awd, 3964
Prudential CARES Volunteer Grants, 3974
Prudential Spirit of Comm Awards, 3978
Puffin/Nation Prize for Creative Citizenship, 3987
R.E.B. Awards for Distinguished Educational Leadership, 4000
Rajiv Gandhi Fnd Grants, 4011
Robert F. Kennedy Human Rights Award, 4111
Rosalynn Carter Institute Georgia Caregiver of the Year Awards, 4151
Rudy Bruner Award for Urban Excellence, 4173
RWJF Comm Health Leaders Awards, 4183
S.E.VEN Fund $50k VINE Project Prizes, 4193
S.E.VEN Fund 'In The River They Swim' Essay Competition, 4194
S.E.VEN Fund Open Enterprise Solutions to Poverty RFP Grants, 4197
S.E.VEN Fund WHY Prize, 4198

San Francisco Fnd Art Awards James Duval Phelan Literary Award, 4258
San Francisco Fnd Art Awards Joseph Henry Jackson Literary Award, 4259
San Francisco Fnd Art Awards Mary Tanenbaum Literary Award, 4260
San Francisco Fnd Comm Leadership Awards, 4264
San Francisco Fnd Fund For Artists Award For Choreographers, 4270
San Francisco Fnd Fund for Artists Award for Composers and Music Ensembles, 4271
San Francisco Fnd Fund for Artists Award for Visual and Media Artists, 4273
San Francisco Fnd James D. Phelan Art Award in Photography, 4276
San Francisco Fnd James D. Phelan Art Award in Printmaking, 4277
San Francisco Fnd James D. Phelan Award in Film, Video, and Digital Media, 4278
San Francisco Fnd John Gutmann Photography Fellowship Award, 4279
San Francisco Fnd Koshland Program Arts and Culture Mini-Grants, 4280
Scotts Company Give Back to Grow Awards, 4315
SeaWorld & Busch Gardens Conservation Grants, 4332
SEJ Annual Awds for Rptg on the Environment, 4333
Silicon Valley Comm Fnd Elizabeth Anabo BRICC Awards, 4357
Skoll Fdn Awds for Social Entrepreneurship, 4383
South Carolina Arts Comsn Artists Fwsps, 4415
State Farm Project Ignition Grants, 4487
Stettinius Fund for Nonprofit Ldrsp Awds, 4500
Steward of the Land Award, 4504
Subaru Rainbow Leadership Award, 4520
The World Food Prize, 4606
TRDRP Participatory Research Awards, 4663
Union Square Arts Award, 4716
Union Square Award for Social Justice, 4717
United States Institute of Peace - National Peace Essay Contest for High School Students, 4724
USBC Annual Zeb Scholarship, 4792
USTA Althea Gibson Leadership Awards, 4872
USTA Excellence Grants, 4874
USTA NJTL Arthur Ashe Essay & Art Cnst, 4878
USTA Okechi Womeodu Scholar Athlete Grts, 4880
USTA Player Dev Grants, 4881
UUA Bennett Award for Congregational Action on Human Justice and Social Action, 4893
UUA Holmes-Weatherly Award, 4894
UUA Skinner Sermon Award, 4895
Virginia A. Hodgkinson Research Prize, 4940
Volvo Adventure Environmental Awards, 4952
VSA/Volkswagen Grp of America Exhib Awds, 4954
Wallace Alexander Gerbode Fdn Spcl Awd Grts, 4975
Washington Area Women's Fdn Ldrsp Awds, 4993
Washington Cty Comm Fdn Youth Grts, 4998
Western Pennsylvania Environmental Awards, 5026
WWF Int'l Smart Gear Competition, 5120
Youth Action Net Universidad Europea de Madrid Prize, 5129
YSA Get Ur Good On Grants, 5134
Yves Rocher Fnd Women of the Earth Awards, 5143
Z. Smith Reynolds Nancy Susan Reynolds Award, 5146

Basic Research

100 Mile Man Fnd Grants, 27
A.O. Smith Comm Grants, 46
AAA Fnd for Traffic Safety Grants, 50
AAAS Science and Tech Policy Fellowships: Health, Educ and Human Services, 53
Abbott Fund Access to Health Care Grants, 80
Abbott Fund Science Educ Grants, 83
Abell-Hanger Fnd Grants, 91
Abington Fnd Grants, 100
A Charitable Fnd Grants, 126
Achelis Fnd Grants, 127
Adams County Comm Fnd of Pennsylvania Grants, 149
ADEC Agricultural Telecommunications Grants, 159
Administration on Aging Senior Medicare Patrol Project Grants, 166

PROGRAM TYPE INDEX

Basic Research / 1023

AEC Trust Grants, 175
African American Heritage Grants, 193
Akonadi Fnd Anti-Racism Grants, 217
ALA Carroll Preston Baber Research Grant, 255
ALA Innovation Award, 288
ALA Margaret T. Lane/Virginia F. Saunders Memorial Research Award, 298
ALA ProQuest Documents to the People Award, 311
Alaska Conservation Fnd Watchable Wildlife Conservation Trust Grants, 326
Alberta Law Fnd Grants, 338
Albert and Margaret Alkek Fnd Grants, 340
Alcoa Fnd Grants, 350
Alexander and Margaret Stewart Trust Grants, 354
Alex Stern Family Fnd Grants, 360
Alfred P Sloan Fdn Selected Nat'l Issues Grts, 370
Allen Lane Fnd Grants, 379
Allyn Fnd Grants, 392
ALSAM Fnd Grants, 395
Alvin and Lucy Owsley Fnd Grants, 404
ALZA Corporate Contributions Grants, 405
Amarillo Area/Harrington Fnds Grants, 412
Ameren Corporation Comm Grants, 418
American Chemical Society Award for Team Innovation, 423
American Chemical Society Chemical Tech Partnership Mini Grants, 424
American College of Bankruptcy Grants, 426
American Legacy Fdn Small Innovative Grants, 442
American Schlafhorst Fnd Grants, 446
American Sociological Assoc Sydney S Spivack Pgm in Applied Social Rsch & Social Policy, 450
AMERIND Comm Service Project Grants, 453
Amgen Fnd Grants, 456
AMI Semiconductors Corporate Grants, 457
Amon G. Carter Fnd Grants, 458
Andrew Family Fnd Grants, 462
Angels Baseball Fnd Grants, 465
Ann & Robert H Lurie Family Fdn Grants, 473
Ann Arbor Area Comm Fnd Grants, 474
Ann Peppers Fnd Grants, 484
Anthony R. Abraham Fnd Grants, 489
Applied Biosystems Grants, 514
Arcadia Fnd Grants, 525
Arcus Fnd National Fund Grants, 531
Arie and Ida Crown Memorial Grants, 533
Arizona Cardinals Grants, 534
Arizona Comm Fnd Grants, 540
Arizona Public Service Corp Gvg Pgm Grts, 545
A Rocha USA Grants, 566
Arronson Fnd Grants, 567
Arthur Ashley Williams Fnd Grants, 572
Arthur F & Alice E Adams Charitable Fdn Grts, 574
Assisi Fnd of Memphis General Grants, 594
Assurant Health Fnd Grants, 596
ASTA Academic Scholarships, 597
Atran Fnd Grants, 610
Ball Brothers Fnd General Grants, 637
Ball Brothers Fnd Rapid Grants, 639
Banfield Charitable Trust Grants, 652
Barra Fnd Project Grants, 674
Batchelor Fnd Grants, 679
Batts Fnd Grants, 687
Baxter Int'l Fnd Grants, 691
Bay and Paul Fnds Grants, 693
Bayer Fnd Grants, 696
BCBSM Fodn Investigator Initiated Rsch Grts, 708
BCBSM Fnd Student Award Program, 710
BCBSNC Fnd Grants, 712
BCBS of Massachusetts Fnd Grants, 713
Beim Fnd Grants, 718
Benton Comm Fnd Grants, 730
Berks County Comm Fnd Grants, 734
Better Way Fnd Grants, 754
Bikes Belong Fnd Research Grants, 762
Bill and Melinda Gates Ag Dev Grants, 765
Bill and Melinda Gates Fnd Financial Services for the Poor Grants, 767
Bill and Melinda Gates Fnd Policy and Advocacy Grants, 769

Bill and Melinda Gates Fnd Water, Sanitation and Hygiene Grants, 770
Bishop Robert Paddock Trust Grants, 775
Blandin Fnd Expand Opportunity Grants, 787
Blowitz-Ridgeway Fnd Grants, 792
Blue Shield of California Grants, 802
Blum-Kovler Fnd Grants, 803
Bodenwein Public Benevolent Fdn Grants, 806
Bodman Fnd Grants, 807
Booth-Bricker Fund Grants, 815
Bosque Fnd Grants, 818
Brainerd Fnd Grants, 831
Brico Fund Grants, 835
Bridgestone/Firestone Trust Fund Grants, 836
Bristol-Myers Squibb Clinical Outcomes and Research Grants, 839
Brookdale Fnd Leadership in Aging Fellowships, 844
Bryan Adams Fnd Grants, 858
Burden Trust Grants, 864
Burlington Industries Fnd Grants, 865
Burton G. Bettingen Grants, 871
Bydale Fnd Grants, 882
Cabot Corporation Fnd Grants, 887
Caesars Fnd Grants, 891
Callaway Golf Company Fnd Grants, 910
Campbell Soup Fnd Grants, 916
Canadian Optometric Ed Trust Fund Grts, 918
Cape Branch Fnd Grants, 919
Cargill Citizenship Fund-Corp Gvg Grants, 925
Carl & Eloise Pohlad Family Fnd Grants, 927
Carl Gellert and Celia Berta Gellert Fdn Grts, 930
Carl M. Freeman Fnd Grants, 933
Carl W. and Carrie Mae Joslyn Trust Grants, 938
Carnegie Corporation of New York Grants, 940
Carrier Corporation Contributions Grants, 946
CDC Grants for Violence-Related Injury Prevention Research, 974
CDECD Historic Preservation Survey and Planning Grants, 982
Center on Philanthropy and Civil Society's Emerging Leaders Int'l Fellows Program, 992
Champ-A Champion Fur Kids Grants, 1028
Chapman Charitable Fnd Grants, 1033
Charles G. Koch Charitable Fnd Grants, 1041
Charles H. Farnsworth Trust Grants, 1043
Charles H. Price II Family Fnd Grants, 1046
Charles H. Revson Fnd Grants, 1047
Charles Lafitte Fnd Grants, 1049
Charles Stewart Mott Fdn Anti-Poverty Grts, 1054
CHCF Grants, 1063
Chicago Board of Trade Fnd Grants, 1079
Chicago Comm Trust Housing Grants: Advancing Affordable Rental Housing, 1088
Chiles Fnd Grants, 1108
Chiron Fnd Comm Grants, 1111
CICF Indianapolis Fdn Comm Grants, 1123
Cincinnati Milacron Fnd Grants, 1132
CIRCLE Civic Educ at the High School Level Research Grants, 1135
Claneil Fnd Grants, 1145
Clarence E Heller Charitable Fdn Grants, 1150
Clark Fnd Grants, 1157
Claude Pepper Fnd Grants, 1160
Cleveland-Cliffs Fnd Grants, 1165
CMA Fnd Grants, 1178
Coeta and Donald Barker Fnd Grants, 1197
Coleman Fnd Cancer Care Grants, 1199
Colonel Stanley R. McNeil Fnd Grants, 1210
Colorado Bioscience Discovery Eval Grts, 1211
Colorado Clean Enrg Fd Solar Innovation Grts, 1212
Commonweal Fnd Comm Assistance Grants, 1239
Commonwealth Fund Australian-American Health Policy Fellowships, 1241
Commonwealth Fund Harkness Fellowships in Health Care Policy and Practice, 1242
Communities Fnd of Texas Grants, 1243
Comm Fnd AIDS Endwt Awds, 1245
Comm Fdn for Grtr Buffalo Grants, 1247
Comm Fdn for Muskegon Cty Grants, 1256
Comm Fdn for NE Michigan Grants, 1257

Comm Fdn for Southern Arizona Grants, 1261
Comm Fdn of Boone County Grants, 1274
Comm Fdn of Broward Grants, 1275
Comm Fdn of Greater Fort Wayne - Cmty Endwt & Clarke Endwt Grants, 1285
Comm Fnd of Mt Vernon & Knox County Grants, 1301
Comm Fnd of Muncie & Delaware County Grant, 1302
Comm Fdn of S Alabama Grants, 1308
Comm Fdn of St. Joseph County African American Comm Grants, 1312
Comm Fdn of Wabash Cty Grants, 1326
Conservation, Food, and Health Fnd Grants for Developing Countries, 1359
Coors Brewing Corporate Contributions Grants, 1371
Cord Fnd Grants, 1372
Corina Higginson Trust Grants, 1373
Cowles Charitable Trust Grants, 1392
Cudd Fnd Grants, 1410
D.F. Halton Fnd Grants, 1424
DAAD Research Grants for Doctoral Candidates and Young Academics and Scientists, 1427
Dance Advance Grants, 1441
Dave Thomas Fnd for Adoption Grants, 1449
Davis Family Fnd Grants, 1462
Daywood Fnd Grants, 1465
DeMatteis Family Fnd Grants, 1497
Denton A. Cooley Fnd Grants, 1500
Detroit Lions Charities Grants, 1520
DHHS Emergency Medical Svcs for Children, 1531
DHHS Independence Demonstration Program, 1535
DHHS Promoting Safe & Stable Families Grts, 1537
DHHS Spcl Pgms for the Aging Trng, Rsch, and Discretionary Projects and Pgms Grts, 1538
DHHS Welfare Reform Research, Evaluations, and National Studies Grants, 1540
DOE Initial H-Prize Competition for Breakthrough Advances in Materials for Hydrogen Storage, 1551
DOJ Juvenile Justice and Delinquency Prevention Special Emphasis Grants, 1559
Dolfinger-McMahon Fnd Grants, 1565
Donald & Sylvia Robinson Family Fdn Grts, 1573
Dorothea Haus Ross Fnd Grants, 1587
Dorothy Rider Pool Health Care Grants, 1589
Dorr Fnd Grants, 1591
Dresher Fnd Grants, 1605
Drs. Bruce and Lee Fnd Grants, 1607
Duchossois Family Fnd Grants, 1616
Eberly Fnd Grants, 1649
Edward Bangs Kelley & Elza Kelley Fdn Grts, 1665
Edward S. Moore Fnd Grants, 1668
Edward W & Stella C Van Houten Mem Fund, 1670
Edwin S. Webster Fnd Grants, 1671
Edwin W & Catherine M Davis Fdn Grants, 1672
EIF Comm Grants, 1675
Elizabeth Morse Genius Char Trust Grants, 1682
Elmer L & Eleanor J Andersen Fdn Grnts, 1687
Emerson Charitable Trust Grants, 1694
Energy Fnd Power Grants, 1707
Ensign-Bickford Fnd Grants, 1709
Enterprise Comm Partners Rose Architectural Fellowships, 1719
EPA Surveys, Studies, Research, Investigations, Demonstrations, and Special Purpose Activities Relating to the Clean Air Act, 1740
EREF Solid Waste Research Grants, 1747
EREF Sustainability Research Grants, 1748
Eugene McDermott Fnd Grants, 1765
Ewing Halsell Fnd Grants, 1776
F.M. Kirby Fnd Grants, 1780
FAR Fund Grants, 1787
Farmers Insurance Corporate Giving Grants, 1791
FCD Child Dev Grants, 1796
Feldman Fnd Grants, 1801
Fidelity Fnd Grants, 1805
FirstEnergy Fnd Comm Grants, 1819
FishAmerica Fnd Marine and Anadromous Fish Habitat Restoration Grants, 1829
FishAmerica Fnd Research Grants, 1830
Fishman Family Fnd Grants, 1835
Flinn Fnd Grants, 1842

Basic Research

Florida Sea Turtle Grants, 1871
Ford Fdn Peace & Social Justice Grts, 1884
Forest Fnd Grants, 1886
Forrest C. Lattner Fnd Grants, 1887
Fdn for Enhancing Communities Grts, 1893
Fnd for Seacoast Health Grants, 1895
Fnd for the Carolinas Grants, 1896
Frances C & William P Smallwood Fdn Grts, 1918
Francis L. Abreu Charitable Trust Grants, 1922
Frank G & Freida K Brotz Fam Fdn Grts, 1928
Frank M. Tait Fnd Grants, 1932
Frank Reed and Margaret Jane Peters Memorial Fund II Grants, 1934
Frank Stanley Beveridge Fnd Grants, 1936
Freeman Fnd Grants, 1952
Freshwater Future Project Grants, 1961
Fritz B. Burns Fnd Grants, 1965
Fulbright/Garcia Robles Grants, 1968
Fulbright Binational Business Grants in Mexico, 1969
Fulbright Business Grants in Spain, 1970
Fulbright Grad Degree Pgm Grants in Mexico, 1971
Fulbright Public Policy Grants in Mexico, 1972
Gebbie Fnd Grants, 1995
General Motors Fnd Grants, 2004
George B. Storer Fnd Grants, 2014
George Fnd Grants, 2018
George Frederick Jewett Fnd Grants, 2019
George Gund Fnd Grants, 2020
George S & Dolores Dore Eccles Fdn Grants, 2027
George W. Brackenridge Fnd Grants, 2028
George W Codrington Charitable Fdn Grts, 2029
Georgia-Pacific Fdn Environment Grts, 2034
Georgia Power Fnd Grants, 2039
Gil and Dody Weaver Fnd Grants, 2053
Gill Fnd Gay & Lesbian Fund, 2054
Girl's Best Friend Fnd Grants, 2057
GMFUS Urban & Regnl Policy Fwsps, 2067
GNOF IMPACT Grants for Education, 2079
Great Lakes Fishery Trust Access Grants, 2145
Great Lakes Protection Fund Grants, 2147
Green Diamond Charitable Contributions, 2149
Greenwall Fnd Bioethics Grants, 2158
HA & Mary K Chapman Char Trust Grts, 2182
H. Leslie Hoffman & Elaine S. Hoffman Grants, 2185
Harold R. Bechtel Charitable Remainder Uni-Trust Grants, 2229
Harold Simmons Fnd Grants, 2230
Harris Graduate School of Public Policy Studies Research Dev Grants, 2232
Harry A & Margaret D Towsley Fdn Grts, 2236
Harry Edison Fnd, 2241
Hartford Aging and Health Program Awards, 2247
Healthcare Fnd of New Jersey Grants, 2280
Health Fnd of South Florida Responsive Grants, 2283
Heineman Fnd for Research, Education, Charitable and Scientific Purposes, 2290
Helen Bader Fnd Grants, 2293
Helen V. Brach Fnd Grants, 2300
Henrietta Lange Burk Fund Grants, 2303
Henry W. Bull Fnd Grants, 2312
Herbert A & Adrian W Woods Fdn Grts, 2313
Herbert H & Grace A Dow Fdn Grts, 2315
Herman Goldman Fnd Grants, 2317
Hilda and Preston Davis Fnd Grants, 2322
Hill Crest Fnd Grants, 2324
Hilton Hotels Corporate Giving, 2331
Hirtzel Memorial Fnd Grants, 2332
Hoglund Fnd Grants, 2344
HomeBanc Fnd Grants, 2347
Honeybee Health Improvement Project Grants, 2355
Honeywell Corp Sustainable Opportunities, 2360
Hormel Fnd Grants, 2369
Horowitz Fnd for Social Policy Grants, 2370
Horowitz Fdn for Social Policy Spcl Awds, 2371
Household Int'l Corp Giving Grants, 2372
HRF New York City Environmental Grants for Newton Creek, 2379
HRSA Nurse Education, Practice, Quality and Retention Grants, 2381
Huffy Fnd Grants, 2384
Huie-Dellmon Trust Grants, 2386
Huntington County Comm Fnd - Make a Difference Grants, 2406
Hutchinson Comm Fnd Grants, 2410
Hydrogen Student Design Contest, 2415
ICC Faculty Fellowships, 2428
IDEM Section 319(h) Nonpoint Source Grants, 2435
Illinois DCEO Coal Demonstration Grants, 2485
Illinois DCEO Coal Dev Grants, 2486
Illinois DCEO Coal Revival Grants, 2487
IMLS Grants to State Library Adm Agencies, 2514
IMLS National Leadership Grants, 2515
Impact 100 Grants, 2522
Indiana 21st Century Research & Tech Awards, 2528
Indiana SBIR/STTR Commercialization Enhancement Program, 2548
Infinity Fnd Grants, 2553
Intergrys Corporation Grants, 2565
Int'l Human Rights Funders Grants, 2567
Ireland Family Fnd Grants, 2574
Ittleson Fnd AIDS Grants, 2589
Ittleson Fnd Mental Health Grants, 2590
J.B. Reynolds Fnd Grants, 2592
J.W. Kieckhefer Fnd Grants, 2607
Jackson Fnd Grants, 2613
Jacob and Hilda Blaustein Fnd Grants, 2615
James H. Cummings Fnd Grants, 2626
James L & Mary Jane Bowman Char Trust, 2632
James M. Collins Fnd Grants, 2633
James R. Dougherty Jr. Fnd Grants, 2635
James S. Copley Fnd Grants, 2637
Jane Bradley Pettit Fnd Health Grants, 2643
Japan Fnd Center for Global Partnership Grants, 2649
Japan Fnd Center for Global Partnership Institutional Grants, 2650
Jaquelin Hume Fnd Grants, 2654
Jenifer Altman Fnd Grants, 2662
Jessie Ball Dupont Fund Grants, 2671
Jewish Women's Fdn of New York Grants, 2677
JM Fnd Grants, 2681
Joel L. Fleishman Civil Society Fellowships, 2683
Joe W & Dorothy Dorsett Brown Fdn Grants, 2684
John D. and Catherine T. MacArthur Fnd Global Challenges Grants, 2690
John Deere Fnd Grants, 2692
John P. McGovern Fnd Grants, 2707
John S Dunn Research Fdn Grants & Chairs, 2715
Johnson & Johnson Corp Contribs Grants, 2718
John W. Alden Trust Grants, 2727
Joseph Alexander Fnd Grants, 2734
Josephine Goodyear Fnd Grants, 2738
Josiah W & Bessie H Kline Fdn Grants, 2742
Joyce Fnd Employment Grants, 2749
JP Morgan Chase Comm Dev Grts, 2753
Kathryne Beynon Fnd Grants, 2791
Kenneth T & Eileen L Norris Fdn Grants, 2802
Kettering Fund Grants, 2818
Kevin P & Sydney B Knight Family Fdn Grts, 2819
Komen Grtr NYC Clin Rsch Enrollment Grts, 2834
Komen Grtr NYC Comty Breast Health Grts, 2835
Koret Fnd Grants, 2837
Kovler Family Fnd Grants, 2840
Land O'Lakes Fdn California Region Grts, 2858
Laurel Fnd Grants, 2867
Leo Goodwin Fnd Grants, 2882
Libra Fnd Grants, 2899
Lillian S. Wells Fnd Grants, 2901
Lindbergh Grants, 2907
Lotus 88 Fnd for Women and Children, 2921
Louis Calder Fnd Grants, 2925
Lubbock Area Fnd Grants, 2931
Lubrizol Fnd Grants, 2933
Lucile Horton Howe & Mitchell B. Howe Grants, 2934
Lumpkin Family Fdn Healthy People Grts, 2942
Luther I. Replogle Fnd Grants, 2945
Lynde and Harry Bradley Fnd Grants, 2947
M. Bastian Family Fnd Grants, 2951
M.J. Murdock Charitable Trust General Grants, 2954
Mabel Louise Riley Fnd Grants, 2959
Mabel Y. Hughes Charitable Trust Grants, 2960
MacArthur Fnd Conservation and Sustainable Dev Grants, 2963
MacArthur Fnd Policy Research Grants, 2964
Marcia and Otto Koehler Fnd Grants, 3000
Margaret & James A Elkins Jr Fdn Grts, 3003
Margaret L. Wendt Fnd Grants, 3004
Margaret T. Morris Fnd Grants, 3005
Mary K. Chapman Fnd Grants, 3042
Mary Kay Ash Charitable Fnd Grants, 3043
Mary S & David C Corbin Fdn Grants, 3048
Maximilian E & Marion O Hoffman Fdn, 3067
McCarthy Family Fnd Grants, 3073
McCombs Fnd Grants, 3075
McCune Charitable Fnd Grants, 3077
McCune Fnd Civic Grants, 3078
McGraw-Hill Companies Comm Grants, 3081
McGregor Fund Grants, 3082
McLean Contributionship Grants, 3088
MDARD Spclty Crop Block Grant-Farm Bill, 3093
MDEQ Beach Monitoring - Inland Lakes, 3094
MDEQ Local Water Qlty Monitoring Grants, 3100
Meadows Fnd Grants, 3104
Mead Witter Fnd Grants, 3106
MedImmune Charitable Grants, 3108
Melville Charitable Trust Grants, 3115
Mericos Fnd Grants, 3121
Merkel Fnd Grants, 3124
Mertz Gilmore Climate Change Solutions Grants, 3125
Mervin Bovaird Fnd Grants, 3128
Meyer & Pepa Gold Family Fnd Grants, 3138
Meyer and Stephanie Eglin Fnd Grants, 3139
Meyer Memorial Trust Responsive Grants, 3148
Meyer Memorial Trust Special Grants, 3149
MGM Resorts Fnd Comm Grants, 3153
MGN Family Fnd Grants, 3154
Miguel Aleman Fnd Grants, 3175
Milken Family Fnd Grants, 3178
Millipore Fnd Grants, 3182
Mimi and Peter Haas Fund Grants, 3185
MMS and Alliance Charitable Fnd Int'l Health Studies Grants, 3195
Monfort Family Fnd Grants, 3203
Montgomery Cty Comm Fnd Grants, 3213
Motorola Fnd Grants, 3221
Musgrave Fnd Grants, 3231
NACC David Stevenson Fellowships, 3235
NACC William Diaz Fellowships, 3236
National Book Scholarship Fund, 3249
Nat'l Cntr for Responsible Gaming Travel Grts, 3251
National Lottery Comm Fund Grants, 3279
National Wetlands Awards, 3282
Natonal Endowment for the Arts Research Grants, 3286
Nellie Mae Educ Fnd District Change Grants, 3297
Nellie Mae Educ Public Understanding Grants, 3298
Nellie Mae Educ Fnd State Level Systems Change Grants, 3299
Nell Warren Elkin and William Simpson Elkin Fnd Grants, 3300
Nestle Fnd Training Grant, 3301
NFWF Acres for America Grants, 3355
NFWF Chesapeake Bay Conservation Innovation Grants, 3363
NFWF Chesapeake Bay Tgtd Watershed Grts, 3365
NFWF National Whale Conservation Fund, 3378
NFWF Southern Co Longleaf Legacy Grts, 3392
NFWF Wildlife and Habitat Conservation Initiative Grants, 3399
NHLBI Ancillary Studies in Clinical Trials, 3410
NHLBI Bioengineering and Obesity Grants, 3411
NHLBI Career Transition Awards, 3412
NHLBI Investigator Initiated Multi-Site Clinical Trials, 3413
NHLBI Lymphatics in Health & Disease in the Dgstv, Cardiov & Pulmonary Systems, 3414
NHLBI Lymphatics in Health and Disease in the Digestive, Urinary, Cardiovascular and Pulmonary Systems, 3415
NHLBI Microbiome of the Lung and Respiratory Tract in HIV-Infected Individuals and HIV-Uninfected Controls, 3416

NHLBI Research on the Role of Cardiomyocyte
    Mitochondria in Heart Disease: An Integrated
    Approach, 3417
NHLBI Ruth L Kirschstein Nat'l Rsch Svc Awards for
    Individual Postdoc Fellows, 3418
NHLBI Ruth L Kirschstein Nat'l Rsch Svc Awds for
    Indiv Predoc Fellowships to Promote Diversity in
    Health-Related Research, 3419
NHLBI Ruth L. Kirschstein National Research Service
    Awards for Individual Senior Fellows, 3421
NHLBI Ruth L. Kirschstein National Research Service
    Award Short-Term Institutional Research Training
    Grants, 3422
NIDRR Field-Initiated Projects, 3437
NIEHS Hazardous Materials Worker Health and Safety
    Training Grants, 3438
NOAA Undersea Rsch Pgm Project Grts, 3454
Noble County Comm Fnd Grants, 3456
Norcliffe Fnd Grants, 3459
Norfolk Southern Fnd Grants, 3463
NW Mutual Fnd Grants, 3509
NW Fund for the Environment Grants, 3510
Notsew Orm Sands Fnd Grants, 3516
NRA Fnd Grants, 3517
NSF Accelerating Innovation Research, 3520
NSF Atmospheric Sciences Mid-Size Infrastructure
    Opportunity Grants, 3521
NSF CISE Communicating Research to Public
    Audiences Grants, 3522
NSF CISE Comm-Based Data Interoperability
    Networks Grants, 3523
NSF CISE Computer & Network Systems Grants, 3524
NSF CISE Computing and Communication Fnds : Core
    Grants, 3525
NSF CISE Computing Rsch Infrastructure, 3526
NSF Communicating Rsch to Public Audiences, 3527
NSF Decision, Risk, and Management Science Research
    Grants, 3528
Nuffield Fdn Children and Families Grants, 3533
Nuffield Fnd Open Door Grants, 3534
Nuffield Fnd Small Grants, 3535
NYCT New York City Environment Grants, 3556
NYSCA Architecture, Planning, and Design:
    Independent Project Grants, 3575
NYSCA Architecture, Planning, and Design: Project
    Support Grants, 3576
NYSCA Museum: Project Support Grants, 3604
Ohio Arts Council Capacity Building Grants for
    Organizations and Communities, 3652
OJJDP Gang Prevention Coordination Assistance
    Grants, 3663
Oklahoma City Comm Pgms & Grts, 3666
Olin Corporation Charitable Trust Grants, 3669
OneFamily Fnd Grants, 3673
Ontario Arts Council Integrated Arts Grants, 3678
Open Spaces Sacred Places National Awards, 3684
Oppenstein Brothers Fnd Grants, 3685
Oracle Corporate Contributions Grants, 3686
Orchard Fnd Grants, 3690
Organic Farming Research Fnd Grants, 3693
Oscar Rennebohm Fnd Grants, 3694
PacifiCorp Fnd for Learning Grants, 3727
Park Fnd Grants, 3739
Patron Saints Fnd Grants, 3753
Paul G. Allen Family Fnd Grants, 3759
Paul Rapoport Fnd Grants, 3765
Paul Stock Fnd Grants, 3766
Peacock Fnd Grants, 3809
Percy B. Ferebee Endowment Grants, 3820
Perkin Fund Grants, 3821
Perl 6 Microgrants, 3824
Perpetual Trust for Charitable Giving Grants, 3826
Pet Care Trust Fish in the Classroom Grant, 3828
Peter Kiewit Fnd General Grants, 3845
Peter Kiewit Fnd Small Grants, 3847
Peyton Anderson Fnd Grants, 3862
Phelps County Comm Fnd Grants, 3870
Phi Kappa Phi Scholar Award, 3871
Phil Hardin Fnd Grants, 3875
Philip L. Graham Fund Grants, 3876

Phoenix Suns Charities Grants, 3881
Pinkerton Fnd Grants, 3892
Piper Jaffray Fdn Communities Giving Grts, 3899
Piper Trust Healthcare & Med Rsch Grts, 3903
Porter County Comm Fnd Grants, 3931
Powell Family Fnd Grants, 3941
PPG Industries Fnd Grants, 3943
Presbyterian Health Fnd Bridge, Seed and Equipment
    Grants, 3947
Price Family Charitable Fund Grants, 3952
Price Gilbert, Jr. Charitable Fund Grants, 3953
Project AWARE Fnd Grants, 3971
Prudential Fnd Educ Grants, 3977
R.C. Baker Fnd Grants, 3999
Rajiv Gandhi Fnd Grants, 4011
Ralph M. Parsons Fnd Grants, 4013
Reinberger Fnd Grants, 4052
Research Program at Earthwatch Grants, 4053
RGK Fnd Grants, 4072
Richard & Susan Smith Family Fdn Grts, 4078
Richard Davoud Donchian Fnd Grants, 4080
Rich Fnd Grants, 4090
Robert B McMillen Fnd Grants, 4106
Robert E & Evelyn McKee Fdn Grants, 4110
Robert G. Cabell III and Maude Morgan Cabell Fnd
    Grants, 4113
Robert M. Hearin Fnd Grants, 4116
Robert P & Clara I Milton Fund for Sr Housing, 4117
Rockefeller Fnd Grants, 4138
Rockwell Int'l Corporate Trust Grants, 4141
Roeher Institute Research Grants, 4142
Rohm and Haas Company Grants, 4145
Rollins-Luetkemeyer Fnd Grants, 4147
Ronald McDonald House Charities Grants, 4149
Ross Fnd Grants, 4164
Royal Caribbean Cruises Ocean Fund, 4165
Roy & Christine Sturgis Charitable Trust Grts, 4166
RRF General Grants, 4170
Russell Berrie Fnd Grants, 4175
RWJF Changes in Health Care Financing and
    Organization Grants, 4182
RWJF Health Policy Fellowships, 4184
RWJF Partners Investing in Nursing's Future, 4188
RWJF Pioneer Portfolio Grants, 4189
S.E.VEN Fund Annual Grants, 4195
S.E.VEN Fund Mini-Grants, 4196
S.E.VEN Fund Open Enterprise Solutions to Poverty
    RFP Grants, 4197
S.E.VEN Fund WHY Prize, 4198
S. Mark Taper Fnd Grants, 4201
Sage Fnd Grants, 4204
Saint Luke's Fnd Grants, 4215
San Antonio Area Fnd Grants, 4240
Sands Memorial Fnd Grants, 4256
Sarah Scaife Fnd Grants, 4295
Sarkeys Fnd Grants, 4297
Schramm Fnd Grants, 4310
Seattle Fnd Medical Funds Grants, 4329
Seaver Institute Grants, 4331
SeaWorld & Busch Gardens Conservation Grants, 4332
Self Fnd Grants, 4335
Sensient Technologies Fnd Grants, 4337
Sidgmore Family Fnd Grants, 4348
Sid W. Richardson Fnd Grants, 4350
Sioux Falls Area Comm Fnd Comm Fund Grants, 4364
Sioux Falls Area Comm Fnd Spot Grants, 4366
Siragusa Fnd Arts & Culture Grants, 4367
Siragusa Fnd Health & Med Research Grants, 4368
Skaggs Fnd Grants, 4378
Smith Richardson Fnd Domestic Public Research
    Fellowship, 4386
Sony Corp of America Corp Philant Grants, 4405
Sorenson Legacy Fnd Grants, 4407
South Carolina Arts Commission Arts and Economic
    Impact Study Assistance Grants, 4416
Southwest Gas Corporation Fnd Grants, 4445
SSRC-Van Alen Fellowships, 4467
Stackner Family Fnd Grants, 4471
Stanley Smith Horticultural Trust Grants, 4474
Starr Fnd Grants, 4483

State Farm Companies Safe Neighbors Grants, 4484
Steuben County Comm Fdn Grants, 4501
Strake Fnd Grants, 4511
Surdna Fdn Sustainable Environments Grants, 4533
Susan G. Komen Breast Cancer Fnd Challege Grants:
    Breast Cancer and the Environment, 4535
T. James Kavanagh Fnd Grants, 4545
TD4HIM Fnd Grants, 4566
Temple-Inland Fnd Grants, 4576
Temple Univ George D McDowell Fellowship, 4577
Theodore Edson Parker Fnd Grants, 4605
Thomas & Dorothy Leavey Fdn Grants, 4612
Thomas Austin Finch, Sr. Fnd Grants, 4613
Thomas Thompson Trust Grants, 4620
Thompson Charitable Fnd Grants, 4622
Thornton Fnd Grants, 4624
Tides Fdn Calif Wildlands Grassroots Fund, 4630
TRDRP Participatory Research Awards: CARA/
    SARA, 4663
TRDRP Research Grants, 4664
Tri-State Comm Twenty-first Century Endowment
    Fund Grants, 4666
TWS Fnd Grants, 4683
US Dept of Educ Disability and Rehabilitation Research
    and Related Projects, 4690
US Dept of Educ Rehabilitation Engineering Research
    Centers Grants, 4698
US Dept of Educ Rehabilitation Research Training
    Centers , 4699
Union Pacific Fdn Comm & Civic Grts, 4714
Union Pacific Fdn Health & Human Svcs Grts, 4715
USAID/Cambodia Maternal and Child Health,
    Tuberculosis, HIV/AIDS. and Malaria Grants, 4736
USAID Comprehensive District-Based Support for
    Better HIV/TB Patient Outcomes Grants, 4747
USAID Dev Innov Ventures Grts, 4749
USAID Implementation Science for Strengthening Use
    of Evidence in Family Planning/Reproductive Health
    Programming Grants, 4758
USAID Palestinian Comm Infrastructure Grants, 4774
USAID Strengthening RMNCH Through Indian
    Health Professional Associations and Scaling Up
    Uptake Grants, 4784
US CRDF Science and Tech Entrepreneurship Program
    Business Partnership Grant - Armenia, 4795
USDA Hispanic-Serving Institutions Grants, 4813
USDC/NOAA National Marine Aquaculture Initiative
    Grants, 4846
USDC Planning and Local Tech Assistance, 4854
Vancouver Fnd Grants and Comm Initiatives, 4900
Victor E. Speas Fnd Grants, 4933
Viking Children's Fund Grants, 4939
Virginia A. Hodgkinson Research Prize, 4940
Virginia Fnd for Humanities Discretionary Grants, 4946
Virginia Fdn for the Humanities Open Grants, 4947
Virginia Fnd for the Humanities Residential
    Fellowships, 4948
Virginia W. Kettering Fnd Grants, 4950
Visiting Nurse Fnd Grants, 4951
Vulcan Materials Company Fnd Grants, 4956
Washington Area Women's Fnd Early Care and Educ
    Funders Collaborative Grants, 4990
Washington Area Women's Fnd Strategic Opportunity
    and Partnership Fund Grants, 4996
Wayne and Gladys Valley Fnd Grants, 5003
Weyerhaeuser Company Fnd Grants, 5053
Whirlpool Fnd Grants, 5056
WILD Fnd Grants, 5068
Willary Fnd Grants, 5071
William Blair and Company Fnd Grants, 5078
William G & Helen C Hoffman Fdn Grants, 5080
William G. McGowan Charitable Fund Grants, 5084
William H. Hannon Fnd Grants, 5086
William S. Abell Fnd Grants, 5094
Wolf Aviation Fund Grants, 5109
Xerox Fnd Grants, 5122

Building Construction and/or Renovation
2 Life 18 Fnd Grants, 5
1772 Fnd Fellowships, 36

Building Construction and/or Renovation

A.C. Ratshesky Fnd Grants, 39
A.J. Fletcher Fnd Grants, 41
A.O. Smith Comm Grants, 46
Abbot & Dorothy H Stevens Fdn Grants, 79
Abbott Fund Global AIDS Care Grants, 82
Abel & Sophia Sheng Charitable Fdn Grts, 86
Abel Fnd Grants, 90
Abell Fdn Comm Dev Grts, 93
A Charitable Fnd Grants, 126
Achelis Fnd Grants, 127
Acushnet Fnd Grants, 143
Adam Reineman Charitable Trust Grants, 144
Adam Richter Charitable Trust Grants, 145
Adams County Comm Fnd of Pennsylvania Grants, 149
ADC Fnd Tech Access Grants, 158
Adelaide Benevolent Society Grants, 160
Adelaide Breed Bayrd Fnd Grants, 161
Adolph Coors Fnd Grants, 171
AEGON Transamerica Fdn Arts & Culture Grts, 176
AEGON Transamerica Fdn Disaster Rlf Grts, 178
AEP Corporate Giving Grants, 180
African American Heritage Grants, 193
Agnes M. Lindsay Trust Grants, 203
Ahmanson Fnd Grants, 207
Air Products and Chemicals Grants, 216
Akzo Nobel Chemicals Grants, 219
Alabama Power Fnd Grants, 233
Albert and Bessie Mae Kronkosky Charitable Fnd Grants, 339
Albertson's Charitable Giving Grants, 345
Albert W. Cherne Fnd Grants, 346
Alcoa Fnd Grants, 350
Alexander & Baldwin Fnd Hawaiian and Pacific Island Grants, 352
Alexander & Baldwin Fdn Mainland Grants, 353
Alex Brown & Sons Charitable Fdn Grants, 359
Alex Stern Family Fnd Grants, 360
Alice Tweed Tuohy Fnd Grants, 372
Allegan County Comm Fnd Grants, 375
Allegheny Technologies Charitable Trust, 377
Allen P & Josephine B Green Fdn Grts, 380
Allyn Fnd Grants, 392
Alvah H & Wyline P Chapman Fnd Grts, 402
Alvin & Fanny Blaustein Thalheimer Fdn Grts, 403
Ambrose and Ida Fredrickson Fnd Grants, 414
Ameren Corporation Comm Grants, 418
Americana Fnd Grants, 422
American Express Historic Preservation Grants, 431
American Savings Fnd Grants, 445
American Schlafhorst Fnd Grants, 446
Amerigroup Fnd Grants, 452
Amon G. Carter Fnd Grants, 458
Anderson Fnd Grants, 460
Andre Agassi Charitable Fnd Grants, 461
Angels Wings Fnd Int'l Grants, 469
Anheuser-Busch Fnd Grants, 470
Anne L. and George H. Clapp Charitable and Educational Trust Grants, 476
Annenberg Fnd Grants, 477
Ann Peppers Fnd Grants, 484
Anthony R. Abraham Fnd Grants, 489
Antone & Edene Vidinha Char Trust Grts, 490
Appalachian Reg'l Commission Housing Grts, 508
Appalachian Regional Commission Transportation and Highways Grants, 512
Aratani Fnd Grants, 523
Arcadia Fnd Grants, 525
Arcus Fnd Fund Grants, 529
Arie and Ida Crown Memorial Grants, 533
Arizona Comm Fnd Grants, 540
Arkell Hall Fnd Grants, 562
Armstrong McDonald Fnd Grants, 565
Arronson Fnd Grants, 567
ArvinMeritor Fnd Arts & Culture Grts, 582
Aspen Comm Fnd Grants, 592
Assisi Fnd of Memphis General Grants, 594
Atherton Family Fnd Grants, 604
Atkinson Fnd Comm Grants, 606
Atlanta Fnd Grants, 608
Auburn Fnd Grants, 611

Autzen Fnd Grants, 622
Ayres Fnd Grants, 630
Babcock Charitable Trust Grants, 632
Bacon Family Fnd Grants, 634
Bailey Fnd Grants, 635
Ball Brothers Fnd General Grants, 637
Baltimore Comm Fnd Arts and Culture Grants, 641
Bank of America Charitable Fnd Volunteer Grants, 660
Barker Fnd Grants, 668
Barker Welfare Fnd Grants, 669
Barra Fnd Project Grants, 674
Barrasso Usdin Kupperman Freeman and Sarver LLC Corporate Grants, 675
Baton Rouge Area Fdn Credit Bureau Grts, 680
Battle Creek Comm Fnd Grants, 684
Baughman Fnd Grants, 688
Beazley Fnd Grants, 714
Beckley Area Fnd Grants, 716
Belk Fnd Grants, 721
Bemis Company Fnd Grants, 723
Ben B. Cheney Fnd Grants, 725
Bender Fnd Grants, 726
Berrien Comm Fnd Grants, 744
Bertha Russ Lytel Fnd Grants, 745
Besser Fnd Grants, 748
Best Buy Children's Fnd Twin Cities Minnesota Capital Grants, 753
Bicknell Fund Grants, 759
Bikes Belong Fnd Paul David Clark Bicycling Safety Grants, 760
Bikes Belong Fnd REI Grants, 761
Bikes Belong Grants, 763
Bill and Melinda Gates Fnd Emergency Response Grants, 766
Bill & Melinda Gates Fdn Library Grts, 768
Bill and Melinda Gates Fnd Water, Sanitation and Hygiene Grants, 770
Bill Hannon Fnd Grants, 771
Blanche and Irving Laurie Fnd Grants, 784
Blanche & Julian Robertson Family Fdn Grants, 785
Blue Cross Blue Shield of Minnesota Fdn-Healthy Equity: Public Libraries for Health Grts, 797
Blue Grass Comm Fnd Grants, 799
Blue Mountain Comm Fnd Grants, 800
Blue River Comm Fnd Grants, 801
Blumenthal Fnd Grants, 804
Bodenwein Public Benevolent Fdn Grants, 806
Bodman Fnd Grants, 807
Boeing Company Contributions Grants, 809
Boettcher Fnd Grants, 810
Bohemian Fnd Pharos Fund Grants, 811
Booth-Bricker Fund Grants, 815
Booth Ferris Fnd Grants, 816
Borkee-Hagley Fnd Grants, 817
Bosque Fnd Grants, 818
Boston Globe Fnd Grants, 821
Bradley Family Fdn Grants, 830
Brico Fund Grants, 835
Bright Family Fnd Grants, 837
Brooklyn Comm Fnd Comm Dev Grants, 850
Brooklyn Comm Fnd Green Communities Grants, 852
Brunswick Fnd Grants, 857
Bryan Adams Fnd Grants, 858
Bunbury Company Grants, 863
Burlington Northern Santa Fe Fdn Grants, 866
Burton G. Bettinger Grants, 871
Bush Fnd Arts & Humanities Cap Projects Grants, 872
Cabot Corporation Fnd Grants, 887
Cailloux Fnd Grants, 892
California Comm Fnd Neighborhood Revitalization Grants, 903
Callaway Fnd Grants, 909
Cambridge Comm Fnd Grants, 913
Campbell Soup Fnd Grants, 916
Cape Branch Fnd Grants, 919
Capital Region Comm Fnd Grants, 921
Cargill Citizenship Fund-Corp Gvg Grants, 925
Carl & Eloise Pohlad Family Fdn Grants, 927
Carl C. Icahn Fnd Grants, 929
Carl Gellert and Celia Berta Gellert Fdn Grts, 930

Carl M. Freeman Fnd FACES Grants, 932
Carl M. Freeman Fnd Grants, 933
Carlos and Marguerite Mason Trust Grants, 934
Carls Fnd Grants, 937
Carnahan-Jackson Fnd Grants, 939
Carolyn Fnd Grants, 942
Carrie E. and Lena V. Glenn Fnd Grants, 944
Carrie Estelle Doheny Fnd Grants, 945
Caterpillar Fnd Grants, 954
CDECD Endangered Properties Grants, 980
CDECD Historic Preserv Enhancement Grts, 981
CDECD Historic Restoration Grants, 983
CE and S Fnd Grants, 985
Cemala Fnd Grants, 988
CenterPointEnergy Minnegasco Grants, 993
Central Minnesota Comm Fdn Grants, 995
Central New York Comm Fdn Grants, 996
Cessna Fnd Grants, 1000
Champlin Fnds Grants, 1029
Charles A. Frueauff Fnd Grants, 1037
Charles & Lynn Schusterman Fam Fdn Grants, 1038
Charles Delmar Fnd Grants, 1039
Charles H. Farnsworth Trust Grants, 1043
Charles Hayden Fnd Grants, 1048
Charles M & Mary D Grant Fdn Grants, 1050
Charlotte R. Schmidlapp Fund Grants, 1058
Chatham Athletic Fnd Grants, 1060
Chatlos Fnd Grants, 1061
Chautauqua Region Comm Fdn Grts, 1062
CHC Fnd Grants, 1065
Chemtura Corporation Contributions Grants, 1067
Chicago Comm Trust Hsg Grants: Preserving Hm Ownership & Preventing Foreclosure, 1089
Chicago Sun Times Charity Trust Grants, 1098
Chicago Title & Trust Co Fdn Grants, 1099
Chiles Fnd Grants, 1108
Christensen Fund Regional Grants, 1112
Christy-Houston Fnd Grants, 1115
Cincinnati Bell Fnd Grants, 1131
Citigroup Fnd Grants, 1139
Citizens Bank Mid-Atlantic Char Fdn Grts, 1140
Citizens Savings Fnd Grants, 1141
Claneil Fnd Grants, 1145
Clara Blackford Smith and W. Aubrey Smith Charitable Fnd Grants, 1147
Clarence T.C. Ching Fnd Grants, 1151
Clark-Winchcole Fnd Grants, 1152
Clark and Ruby Baker Fnd Grants, 1154
Clark Charitable Trust Grants, 1155
Clark County Comm Fnd Grants, 1156
Clark Fnd Grants, 1157
Claude Worthington Benedum Fdn Grants, 1161
Clay Fnd Grants, 1162
Clayton Baker Trust Grants, 1163
Cleveland-Cliffs Fnd Grants, 1165
Cleveland Fnd Capital Grants, 1167
Cleveland H. Dodge Fnd Grants, 1172
Clipper Ship Fnd Grants, 1175
Clowes Fund Grants, 1177
Coastal Comm Fdn of SC Grants, 1193
Cockrell Fnd Grants, 1196
Coeta and Donald Barker Fnd Grants, 1197
Collins C. Diboll Private Fnd Grants, 1208
Collins Fnd Grants, 1209
Colonel Stanley R. McNeil Fnd Grants, 1210
Colorado Renewables in Performance Contracting Grants, 1214
Colorado Springs Cmty Trust Fund Grants, 1215
Columbus Fnd Competitive Grants, 1220
Columbus Fnd Joseph A. Jeffrey Endowment Fund Grants, 1224
Columbus Fdn Neighborhood Partnership Grts, 1226
Communities Fnd of Texas Grants, 1243
Comm Fnd Alliance City of Evansville Endowment Fund Grants, 1246
Comm Fdn for Grtr Buffalo Grants, 1247
Comm Fdn for Monterey Cty Grants, 1255
Comm Fdn for Muskegon Cty Grants, 1256
Comm Fdn for Southern Arizona Grants, 1261
Comm Fdn of Abilene Comm Grts, 1264

PROGRAM TYPE INDEX

Building Construction and/or Renovation / 1027

Comm Fnd of Bartholomew County Heritage Fund Grants, 1267
Comm Fnd of Bloomington and Monroe County Grants, 1271
Comm Fnd of Broward Grants, 1275
Comm Fdn of E Ctrl Illinois Grts, 1278
Comm Fdn of Grtr Birmingham Grants, 1280
Comm Fdn of Greater Flint Grants, 1282
Comm Fdn of Grtr New Britain Grts, 1291
Comm Fnd of Greenville Hollingsworth Funds Capital Projects Grants, 1295
Comm Fnd of Mt Vernon & Knox County Grants, 1301
Comm Fdn of Shreveport-Bossier Grts, 1307
Comm Fdn of SE Connecticut Grants, 1309
Comm Fnd of the Verdugos Educational Endowment Fund Grants, 1321
Comm Memorial Fnd Grants, 1334
Connecticut Comm Fnd Grants, 1350
Connecticut Light & Power Corp Contribs, 1352
ConocoPhillips Fnd Grants, 1354
Constantin Fnd Grants, 1362
Constellation Energy Corporate Grants, 1364
Consumers Energy Fnd, 1365
Cooke Fnd Grants, 1368
Cooper Fnd Grants, 1369
Cooper Industries Fnd Grants, 1370
Cord Fnd Grants, 1372
Cornerstone Fdn of NE Wisconsin Grants, 1375
Corning Fnd Cultural Grants, 1376
Coughlin-Saunders Fnd Grants, 1377
Cowles Charitable Trust Grants, 1392
Crail-Johnson Fnd Grants, 1393
Crestlea Fnd Grants, 1399
Crowell Trust Grants, 1401
Cudd Fnd Grants, 1410
Cullen Fnd Grants, 1411
Cumberland Comm Fnd Grants, 1413
CVS Comm Grants, 1422
DV & Ida J McEachern Char Trust Grts, 1425
Dade Comm Fnd GLBT Comm Projects Grants, 1429
DaimlerChrysler Corporation Fund Grants, 1432
Daisy Marquis Jones Fnd Grants, 1434
Dallas Fnd Grants, 1436
Dana Corporation Fnd Grants, 1440
Danellie Fnd Grants, 1442
Daphne Seybolt Culpeper Mem Fdn Grts, 1445
Dave Coy Fnd Grants, 1447
Davenport-Hatch Fnd Grants, 1448
Dayton Fnd Grants, 1463
Daywood Fnd Grants, 1465
DeKalb County Comm Fnd - Immediate Response Grant, 1479
Deluxe Corporation Fnd Grants, 1496
DeMatteis Family Fnd Grants, 1497
Dennis & Phyllis Washington Fdn Grants, 1498
DENSO North America Fnd Grants, 1499
Denver Fnd Comm Grants, 1502
DeRoy Testamentary Fnd Grants, 1518
DHS ARRA Fire Station Const Grants, 1542
DHS FY 2009 Transit Security Grants, 1545
Dolan Fnd Grants, 1563
DOL Youthbuild Grants, 1571
Donald & Sylvia Robinson Family Fdn Grts, 1573
Donald W Reynolds Fdn Spcl Projects Grts, 1577
Doris and Victor Day Fnd Grants, 1582
Dorothea Haus Ross Fnd Grants, 1587
Dr. John T. Macdonald Fnd Grants, 1600
Dr. P. Phillips Fnd Grants, 1601
Dresher Fnd Grants, 1605
Drs. Bruce and Lee Fnd Grants, 1607
DTE Energy Fdn Comm Dev Grants, 1609
Duke Energy Fdn Comm Vitality Grants, 1618
Dwight Stuart Youth Fnd Capacity-Building Initiative Grants, 1627
Dyson Fnd Emergency Fund Grants, 1631
E.J. Grassmann Trust Grants, 1638
E.L. Wiegand Fnd Grants, 1639
Eastman Chemical Co Fdn Grants, 1643
Easton Fnds Archery Facility Grants, 1644
East Tennessee Fdn Afrdbl Housing Trust Fund, 1645

East Tennessee Fnd Grants, 1646
Eaton Charitable Fund Grants, 1647
Eberly Fnd Grants, 1649
Edward S. Moore Fnd Grants, 1668
Edwards Memorial Trust Grants, 1669
Edward W & Stella C Van Houten Mem Fund, 1670
Edwin S. Webster Fnd Grants, 1671
Edyth Bush Charitable Fnd Grants, 1673
Effie and Wofford Cain Fnd Grants, 1674
Eisner Fnd Grants, 1678
Elmer L & Eleanor J Andersen Fdn Grnts, 1687
El Paso Corporate Fnd Grants, 1689
El Pomar Fnd Awards and Grants, 1690
Elsie H. Wilcox Fnd Grants, 1691
Energy Fnd Buildings Grants, 1705
Ensign-Bickford Fnd Grants, 1709
Enterprise Comm Partners Pre-Dev Grants, 1718
Enterprise Rent-A-Car Fnd Grants, 1721
Erie Comm Fnd Grants, 1750
Ethel and Raymond F. Rice Fnd Grants, 1758
Ethel S. Abbott Charitable Fnd Grants, 1760
Eugene B. Casey Fnd Grants, 1762
Eugene McDermott Fnd Grants, 1765
Eugene Straus Charitable Trust, 1766
Eva L & Joseph M Bruening Fdn Grants, 1768
Evan Frankel Fnd Grants, 1770
Ewing Halsell Fnd Grants, 1776
F.R. Bigelow Fnd Grants, 1781
Fairfield County Comm Fdn Grts, 1782
Fallon OrNda Comm Health Fund Grants, 1783
Fan Fox & Leslie R Samuels Fdn Grants, 1786
Fargo-Moorhead Area Fnd Grants, 1788
Faye McBeath Fnd Grants, 1794
Fayette County Fnd Grants, 1795
Feldman Fnd Grants, 1801
Fidelity Fnd Grants, 1805
Field Fnd of Illinois Grants, 1806
Fifth Third Fnd Grants, 1810
Finish Line Youth Fnd Legacy Grants, 1814
Fisa Fnd Grants, 1826
Florida Div of Cultural Affrs Facilities Grts, 1852
Fluor Fnd Grants, 1875
FMC Fnd Grants, 1876
Foellinger Fnd Grants, 1877
Ford Motor Company Fund Grants, 1885
Foster Fnd Grants, 1888
Fnd for the Carolinas Grants, 1896
Fnd NW Grants, 1906
France-Merrick Fnds Grants, 1915
Francis Beidler Fnd Grants, 1921
Frank E. and Seba B. Payne Fnd Grants, 1927
Frank Loomis Palmer Fund Grants, 1931
Frederick S. Upton Fnd Grants, 1947
Fred L. Emerson Fnd Grants, 1949
Fremont Area Cmty Fdn Amazing X Grants, 1953
Fremont Area Comm Fnd Grants, 1955
Frey Fnd Grants, 1963
Fritz B. Burns Fnd Grants, 1965
Fuller E. Callaway Fnd Grants, 1973
G.N. Wilcox Trust Grants, 1982
Gates Family Comm Dev & Revitalization Grants, 1990
Gateway Fnd Grants, 1992
Gaylord & Dorothy Donnelley Fdn Grants, 1993
Gebbie Fnd Grants, 1995
GenCorp Fnd Grants, 1998
General Dynamics Corporation Grants, 2001
General Motors Fnd Grants, 2004
George A. Hormel Testamentary Trust Grants, 2009
George and Ruth Bradford Fnd Grants, 2010
George B. Storer Fnd Grants, 2014
George Fnd Grants, 2018
George Frederick Jewett Fnd Grants, 2019
George Gund Fnd Grants, 2020
George H & Jane A Mifflin Mem Fund Grts, 2021
George I. Alden Trust Grants, 2023
George Kress Fnd Grants, 2025
George S & Dolores Dore Eccles Fnd Grants, 2027
George W Codrington Charitable Fdn Grts, 2029
Georgia-Pacific Fnd Enrichment Grants, 2032
Gheens Fnd Grants, 2048

Ginger and Barry Ackerley Fnd Grants, 2055
Gladys Brooks Fnd Grants, 2059
GNOF Albert N & Hattie M McClure Grts, 2068
GNOF Bayou Communities Grants, 2069
GNOF Coastal 5 + 1 Grants, 2070
GNOF Comm Revitalization Grants, 2071
GNOF Environmental Fund Grants, 2073
GNOF Exxon-Mobil Grants, 2074
GNOF Gert Comm Fund Grants, 2076
GNOF Jefferson Comm Grants, 2085
GNOF Norco Comm Grants, 2089
GNOF Plaquemines Comm Grants, 2091
GNOF St. Bernard Comm Grants, 2092
Goodrich Corporation Fnd Grants, 2104
Grace and Franklin Bernsen Fnd Grants, 2109
Graco Fnd Grants, 2111
Grand Rapids Area Comm Fnd Wyoming Grants, 2116
Grand Rapids Comm Fdn Ionia Cty Grts, 2119
Grand Rapids Comm Fnd Lowell Area Grants, 2121
Grand Rapids Comm Fnd SE Ottawa Grants, 2122
Grand Rapids Comm Fdn Sparta Grants, 2124
Grand Victoria Fnd Illinois Core Grants, 2126
Greater Saint Louis Comm Fdn Grants, 2138
Greater Tacoma Comm Fdn Grts, 2139
Greater Worcester Comm Fnd Jeppson Memorial Fund for Brookfield Grants, 2141
Green Diamond Charitable Contributions, 2149
Greenspun Family Fnd Grants, 2156
GreenWorks! Butterfly Garden Grants, 2159
GreenWorks! Grants, 2160
Grover Hermann Fnd Grants, 2168
Guido A & Elizabeth H Binda Fdn Grants, 2172
H & R Fnd Grants, 2181
HA & Mary K Chapman Char Trust Grts, 2182
H.J. Heinz Company Fnd Grants, 2184
Hall Family Fnd Grants, 2210
Harold Alfond Fnd Grants, 2225
Harold & Arlene Schnitzer CARE Fdn Grts, 2226
Harold K. L. Castle Fnd Grants, 2228
Harold Simmons Fnd Grants, 2230
Harris and Eliza Kempner Fund Grants, 2231
Harry A & Margaret D Towsley Fdn Grts, 2236
Harry Bramhall Gilbert Char Trust Grts, 2238
Harry C. Trexler Trust Grants, 2239
Harry Edison Fnd, 2241
Harry Kramer Grants, 2242
Harry W. Bass, Jr. Fnd Grants, 2246
Hartford Fnd Regular Grants, 2253
Harvest Fnd Grants, 2254
Harvey Randall Wickes Fnd Grants, 2255
Hawaii Comm Fnd Geographic-Specific Grants, 2261
Health Fnd of Grtr Indianapolis Grts, 2282
Hedco Fnd Grants, 2287
Helen Bader Fnd Grants, 2293
Helen S. Boylan Fnd Grants, 2298
Helen V. Brach Fnd Grants, 2300
Henry & Ruth Blaustein Rosenberg Fdn Grants, 2306
Henry W. Bull Fnd Grants, 2312
High Meadow Fnd Grants, 2321
Hillcrest Fnd Grants, 2325
Hill Crest Fnd Grants, 2324
Hillman Fnd Grants, 2327
Hilton Hotels Corporate Giving, 2331
Hirtzel Memorial Fnd Grants, 2332
Hoblitzelle Fnd Grants, 2341
Hoglund Fnd Grants, 2344
Home Building Industry Disaster Relief Fund, 2348
Homer A Scott & Mildred S Scott Fdn Grants, 2350
Hometown Indiana Grants, 2353
Honeywell Corp Family Safety & Security Grts, 2356
Honeywell Corp Housing & Shelter Grts, 2357
Honeywell Corp Humanitarian Relief Grts, 2358
Horace A Kimball & S Ella Kimball Fdn Grts, 2362
Horizon Fnd Grants, 2365
Hormel Fnd Grants, 2369
Household Int'l Corp Giving Grants, 2372
Howard and Bush Fnd Grants, 2374
Howard County Comm Fnd Grts, 2375
HRF Hudson River Improvement Grants, 2378
Hudson Webber Fnd Grants, 2383

Building Construction and/or Renovation

Huie-Dellmon Trust Grants, 2386
Hyams Fnd Grants, 2413
Hyde Family Fnds Grants, 2414
I.A. O'Shaughnessy Fnd Grants, 2416
Idaho Power Co Corp Contributions, 2433
IDOT Economic Dev Pgm Grts, 2436
IDOT Rail Freight Pgm Loans & Grants, 2437
IDOT Truck Access Route Pgm Grts, 2438
IDPH Hosptial Capital Investment Grants, 2441
IEDC Industrial Dev Grant Fund, 2443
Illinois DCEO Business Dev Public Infrastructure Grants, 2483
Illinois DCEO Coal Competitiveness Grants, 2484
Illinois DCEO Coal Demonstration Grants, 2485
Illinois DCEO Comm Dev Assistance Pgm for Economic Dev (CDAP-ED) Grants, 2488
Illinois DCEO Emerging Technological Enterprises Grants, 2490
Illinois DNR Park and Recreational Facility Construction Grants, 2499
Illinois Tool Works Fnd Grants, 2511
IMLS 21st Cent Museum Pros Grts, 2512
Inasmuch Fnd Grants, 2523
Independence Comm Fnd Quality of Life Grant, 2525
Independence Comm Fnd Education, Culture & Arts Grant, 2526
Independence Comm Fnd Neighborhood Renewal Grants, 2527
Indiana Boating Infrastructure Grants (BIG P), 2534
Indiana Corn Marketing Council Retailer Grant for Tank Cleaning, 2536
Indiana Historic Preservation Fund Grants, 2537
Indianapolis Preservation Grants, 2543
Indiana Preservation Grants, 2544
J.B. Reynolds Fnd Grants, 2592
J. Bulow Campbell Fnd Grants, 2593
J.E. and L.E. Mabee Fnd Grants, 2595
J. Edwin Treakle Fnd Grants, 2596
J. F. Maddox Fnd Grants, 2597
J. Knox Gholston Fnd Grants, 2599
J.M. Kaplan Fund City Life Grants, 2601
J.W. Kieckhefer Fnd Grants, 2607
Jackson Fnd Grants, 2613
Jacob and Hilda Blaustein Fnd Grants, 2615
Jacobs Family Fnd Jabara Learning Opportunities Grants, 2617
Jacobs Family Fdn Vlg Neighborhoods Grants, 2619
James & Abigail Campbell Fam Fdn Grts, 2620
James A. and Faith Knight Fnd Grants, 2621
James Graham Brown Fdn Qlty of Life Grts, 2625
James H. Cummings Fnd Grants, 2626
James J & Angelia M Harris Fdn Grts, 2630
James J. McCann Charitable Trust and McCann Fnd, Inc Grants, 2631
James M. Cox Fnd of Georgia Grants, 2634
James R. Dougherty Jr. Fnd Grants, 2635
Jane's Trust Grants, 2639
Jane and Jack Fitzpatrick Fund Grants, 2640
Janesville Fnd Grants, 2644
Janirve Fnd Grants, 2645
Janson Fnd Grants, 2646
Jay & Rose Phillips Fam Fdn Grts, 2656
Jean and Price Daniel Fnd Grants, 2659
JELD-WEN Fnd Grants, 2661
Jenkins Fnd: Improving the Health of Greater Richmond Grants, 2663
Jennings County Comm Fdn Grts, 2664
Jessie Ball Dupont Fund Grants, 2671
John Ben Snow Memorial Trust Grants, 2687
John C. Lasko Fnd Trust Grants, 2688
John D & Katherine A Johnston Fdn Grants, 2691
John Deere Fnd Grants, 2692
John Edward Fowler Mem Fdn Grants, 2693
John G. Duncan Trust Grants, 2695
John G. Martin Fnd Grants, 2696
John H. and Wilhelmina D. Harland Charitable Fnd Grants, 2698
John J. Leidy Fnd Grants, 2701
John Jewett & Helen Chandler Garland Fdn, 2702
John W & Anna H Hanes Fdn Grants, 2728
Joseph Alexander Fnd Grants, 2734
Joseph H & Florence A Roblee Fdn Grants, 2736
Josephine Goodyear Fnd Grants, 2738
Josiah W & Bessie H Kline Fdn Grants, 2742
Katharine Matthies Fnd Grants, 2788
Katherine John Murphy Fnd Grants, 2790
Kelvin and Eleanor Smith Fnd Grants, 2796
Kenneth T & Eileen L Norris Fdn Grants, 2802
Kenny's Kids Grants, 2803
Kessler Fdn Hurricane Sandy Emergency Grts, 2815
KeyBank Fnd Grants, 2820
L. W. Pierce Family Fnd Grants, 2846
Leicester Savings Bank Fund, 2879
Lettie Pate Evans Fnd Grants, 2887
Lewis H. Humphreys Charitable Trust Grants, 2889
Lied Fnd Trust Grants, 2900
Lillian S. Wells Fnd Grants, 2901
Louie M & Betty M Phillips Fdn Grants, 2923
Lowe's Outdoor Classroom Grants, 2928
Lowe Fnd Grants, 2929
Lubbock Area Fnd Grants, 2931
Lubrizol Fnd Grants, 2933
Lucy Gooding Charitable Fnd Trust, 2936
Lucy Gooding Charitable Fdn Trust Grts, 2937
Ludwick Family Fnd Grants, 2938
Luther I. Replogle Fnd Grants, 2945
M.D. Anderson Fnd Grants, 2952
M.E. Raker Fnd Grants, 2953
M.J. Murdock Charitable Trust General Grants, 2954
Mabel Y. Hughes Charitable Trust Grants, 2960
Macquarie Bank Fnd Grants, 2966
Marcia and Otto Koehler Fnd Grants, 3000
Margaret & James A Elkins Jr Fdn Grts, 3003
Margaret T. Morris Fnd Grants, 3005
Marietta McNeill Morgan and Samuel Tate Morgan, Jr. Trust Grants, 3008
Marin Comty Fdn Affordable Housing Grts, 3010
Marion Cty Historic Preservn Fund Grts, 3016
Marion I & Henry J Knott Fdn Discret Grants, 3018
Marion I & Henry J Knott Fdn Std Grants, 3019
Marjorie Moore Charitable Fnd Grants, 3021
Mars Fnd Grants, 3025
Marsh Corporate Grants, 3027
Mary Black Fnd Active Living Grants, 3031
Mary D. & Walter F Frear Eleemosynary Trust, 3035
Mary K. Chapman Fnd Grants, 3042
Mary S & David C Corbin Fdn Grants, 3048
Massachusetts Cultural Council Cultural Facilities Capital Grants, 3053
Massachusetts Cultural Council Cultural Facilities Feasibility and Tech Assistance Grants, 3054
Massachusetts Cultural Council Cultural Facilities Systems Replacement Plan Grants Grants, 3055
Mathile Family Fnd Grants, 3062
Maurice J. Masserini Charitable Trust Grants, 3064
Max A. Adler Charitable Fnd Grants, 3065
Maximilian E & Marion O Hoffman Fdn, 3067
McGregor Fund Grants, 3082
McInerny Fnd Grants, 3083
McLean Contributionship Grants, 3088
McMillen Fnd Grants, 3090
MDARD County Fairs Cap Imprvmt Grts, 3092
MDEQ Brownfield ReDev and Site Reclamation Grants, 3095
Meacham Fnd Memorial Grants, 3102
Melville Charitable Trust Grants, 3115
Mericos Fnd Grants, 3121
Mervin Bovaird Fnd Grants, 3128
MetroWest Health Fnd Capital Grants for Health-Related Facilities, 3134
Meyer Memorial Trust Grassroots Grants, 3147
Meyer Memorial Trust Responsive Grants, 3148
Meyer Memorial Trust Special Grants, 3149
Microsoft Comty Affairs Puget Sound Grts, 3163
Mildred V. Horn Fnd Grants, 3176
Miller, Canfield, Paddock and Stone, P.L.C. Corporate Giving Grants, 3179
Minneapolis Fnd Comm Grants, 3186
Minnesota Small Cities Dev Grants, 3187
MLB Tomorrow Fund Grants, 3193
Montana Arts Cncl Cltrl & Aesthetic Proj Grts, 3209
Mt. Sinai Health Care Fnd Health of the Jewish Comm Grants, 3226
Mt. Sinai Health Care Fnd Health of the Urban Comm Grants, 3227
Musgrave Fnd Grants, 3231
National Lottery Comm Fund Grants, 3279
National Trust for Historic Preservation Diversity Scholarship, 3280
NEH Interpreting America's Historic Places, 3292
New York Landmarks Conservancy City Ventures Grants, 3339
New York Life Fnd Grants, 3341
NFL Club Matching Youth Football Field/Stadium Grants, 3349
NFL Grassroots Field Grants, 3350
NFWF Bronx Rvr Watershed Init Grts, 3360
NHSCA Cultural Facilities Grants: Barrier Free Access for All, 3426
NIAF Anthony Campitelli Endwd Fund Grts, 3431
Nicor Corporate Contributions, 3435
Nike Bowerman Track Renovation Grants, 3440
Nina Mason Pulliam Charitable Trust Grants, 3443
Norcliffe Fnd Grants, 3459
Nordson Corporation Fnd Grants, 3462
North Carolina Arts Cncl Facility Dsgn Grts, 3474
North Central Health Services Grants, 3491
Northern New York Comm Fdn Grants, 3503
Northern Trust Company Charitable Trust and Corporate Giving Program, 3504
NW Mutual Fnd Grants, 3509
Norwin S & Elizabeth N Bean Fdn Grts, 3515
NYCT Historic Preservation Grants, 3551
NYSCA Architecture, Planning, and Design: Capital Fixtures and Equipment Purchase Grants, 3570
NYSCA Architecture, Planning, and Design: Capital Project Grants, 3571
NYSCA Architecture, Planning, and Design: Design and Planning Studies Grants, 3572
Ohio Valley Fnd Grants, 3662
Oklahoma City Comm Pgms & Grts, 3666
Oleonda Jameson Trust Grants, 3667
Olin Corporation Charitable Trust Grants, 3669
Oppenstein Brothers Fnd Grants, 3685
Oscar Rennebohm Fnd Grants, 3694
Otto Bremer Fnd Grants, 3713
Overbrook Fnd Grants, 3715
PACCAR Fnd Grants, 3719
Parkersburg Area Comm Fdn Action Grts, 3738
Pasadena Fnd Average Grants, 3741
Patrick and Anna M. Cudahy Fund Grants, 3751
Patron Saints Fnd Grants, 3753
Paul and Mary Haas Fnd Contributions and Student Scholarships, 3756
Paul E & Klare N Reinhold Fdn Grts, 3758
Paul Ogle Fnd Grants, 3764
Paul Stock Fnd Grants, 3766
PCA Entry Track Arts Organizations and Arts Grants for Dance, 3791
Perkin Fund Grants, 3821
Petco Fnd 4 Rs Project Support Grants, 3830
Petco Fnd Capital Grants, 3831
Peter and Elizabeth C. Tower Fnd Phase II Tech Initiative Grants, 3839
Peter Norton Family Fnd Grants, 3849
Phil Hardin Fnd Grants, 3875
Pioneer Hi-Bred Comm Grants, 3895
Piper Trust Healthcare & Med Rsch Grts, 3903
Piper Trust Reglious Organizations Grants, 3905
Pittsburgh Fdn Comm Fund Grts, 3910
Plough Fnd Grants, 3915
PNC Ecnomic Dev Grants, 3922
Pohlad Family Fnd, 3928
Porter County Emergency Grants, 3932
Porter County Health and Wellness Grant, 3933
PPG Industries Fnd Grants, 3943
Preservation Maryland Heritage Fund Grants, 3948
Price Chopper's Golub Fnd Grants, 3950
Price Family Charitable Fund Grants, 3952
Priddy Fnd Capital Grants, 3954

PROGRAM TYPE INDEX

Capital Campaigns / 1029

Prince Charitable Trusts Chicago Grants, 3959
Prince Char Trusts Dist of Columbia Grts, 3960
Prince Charitable Trusts Rhode Island Grants, 3961
Principal Financial Group Fnd Grants, 3966
Procter and Gamble Fund Grants, 3967
Project Orange Thumb Grants, 3972
Prudential Fdn Econ Dev Grants, 3976
Public Welfare Fnd Grants, 3984
Puerto Rico Comm Fnd Grants, 3986
Pulte Homes Corporate Contributions, 3989
Quantum Corporation Snap Server Grants, 3995
Quantum Fnd Grants, 3996
R.C. Baker Fnd Grants, 3999
Radcliffe Inst Indiv Residential Fellowships, 4004
Ralph M. Parsons Fnd Grants, 4013
Rathmann Family Fnd Grants, 4026
RBC Dain Rauscher Fnd Grants, 4031
RCF General Comm Grants, 4032
Reinberger Fnd Grants, 4052
Retirement Rsch Fdn Accessible Faith Grants, 4066
Rhode Island Fnd Grants, 4073
Richard and Helen DeVos Fnd Grants, 4076
Richard D. Bass Fnd Grants, 4079
Richard King Mellon Fnd Grants, 4087
Rich Fnd Grants, 4090
Riley Fnd Grants, 4094
Robert G. Cabell III and Maude Morgan Cabell Fnd Grants, 4113
Robert Lee Blaffer Fnd Grants, 4115
Robert R. Meyer Fnd Grants, 4121
Robert W. Woodruff Fnd Grants, 4124
Robin Hood Fnd Grants, 4125
Robins Fnd Grants, 4126
Rochester Area Comm Fnd Grants, 4127
Rockefeller Brothers Fund Charles E. Culpeper Arts and Culture Grants in New York City, 4129
Rockefeller Brothers Fund Pivotal Places Grants: New York City, 4134
Rockwell Int'l Corporate Trust Grants, 4141
Rollin M. Gerstacker Fnd Grants, 4146
Ronald McDonald House Charities Grants, 4149
Rose Comm Fnd Health Grants, 4154
Rose Hills Fnd Grants, 4162
Ross Fnd Grants, 4164
Roy & Christine Sturgis Charitable Trust Grts, 4166
Roy J Carver Char Trust Youth Pgm Grts, 4167
RRF Accessible Faith Grants, 4169
Rush County Comm Fnd Grants, 4174
Russell Berrie Fnd Grants, 4175
Ruth Anderson Fnd Grants, 4176
Ruth H & Warren A Ellsworth Fdn Grts, 4179
S.H. Cowell Fnd Grants, 4199
S. Livingston Mather Charitable Trust Grants, 4200
S. Mark Taper Fnd Grants, 4201
Safeco Insurance Comm Grants, 4203
Sage Fnd Grants, 4204
Saginaw Comm Fdn Discretionary Grts, 4205
Saint Paul Companies Fnd Grants, 4217
Saint Paul Fnd Grants, 4219
Saint Paul Fdn Lowertown Future Fund Grts, 4220
Samuel S. Johnson Fnd Grants, 4239
San Antonio Area Fnd Grants, 4240
San Juan Island Comm Fnd Grants, 4283
Santa Barbara Strategy Capital Support, 4285
Sarkeys Fnd Grants, 4297
Sartain Lanier Family Fnd Grants, 4298
Schering-Plough Fdn Comm Initvs Grts, 4303
Schramm Fnd Grants, 4310
Scott B & Annie P Appleby Char Trust Grts, 4313
Seabury Fnd Grants, 4316
Seattle Fnd Arts and Culture Grants, 4320
Seattle Fdn C Keith Birkenfeld Mem Tr Grts, 4323
Seneca Foods Fnd Grants, 4336
Sensient Technologies Fnd Grants, 4337
Sidney Stern Memorial Trust Grants, 4349
Sid W. Richardson Fnd Grants, 4350
Siebert Lutheran Fnd Grants, 4351
Simmons Fnd Grants, 4360
Sisters of Mercy of North Carolina Fdn Grts, 4375
Skillman Fnd Good Schools Grants, 4382

Solo Cup Fnd Grants, 4401
Sonora Area Fnd Competitive Grants, 4404
Sony Corp of America Corp Philant Grants, 4405
Sorenson Legacy Fnd Grants, 4407
Sosland Fnd Grants, 4408
Southbury Comm Trust Fund, 4409
South Carolina Arts Comsn Accessibility Grts, 4410
South Carolina Arts Commission Arts Facility Projects Grants, 4417
Southwest Florida Comm Fnd Arts & Attractions Grants, 4441
Southwest Gas Corporation Fnd Grants, 4445
Spencer Cty Comm Fdn Grants, 4451
Stackner Family Fnd Grants, 4471
Stackpole-Hall Fnd Grants, 4472
Stanley Smith Horticultural Trust Grants, 4474
Starr Fnd Grants, 4483
State Farm Companies Strong Neighborhoods, 4485
Stewart Huston Charitable Trust Grants, 4505
Strake Fnd Grants, 4511
Stranahan Fnd Grants, 4512
Strengthening Families - Strengthening Communities Grants, 4513
Strowd Roses Grants, 4515
Subaru of Indiana Automotive Fdn Grts, 4519
Sulzberger Fnd Grants, 4522
Summit Fnd Grants, 4524
Sunderland Fnd Grants, 4527
Sunoco Fnd Grants, 4530
Suntrust Bank Atlanta Fnd Grants, 4531
Susan Mott Webb Charitable Trust Grants, 4536
Susan Vaughan Fnd Grants, 4537
T. James Kavanagh Fnd Grants, 4545
T.L.L. Temple Fnd Grants, 4546
Target Fnd Grants, 4562
TE Fnd Grants, 4572
Texas Instruments Corp Arts & Culture Grts, 4596
Textron Corporate Contributions Grants, 4601
Thomas Austin Finch, Sr. Fnd Grants, 4613
Thomas B & Elizabeth M Sheridan Fdn Grts, 4614
Thomas W. Briggs Fnd Grants, 4621
Thompson Charitable Fnd Grants, 4622
Thornton Fnd Grants, 4624
Tony Hawk Fnd Grants, 4641
Topeka Comm Fnd Grants, 4644
Tourism Cares Worldwide Grants, 4649
Triangle Comm Fdn Donor-Advised Grts, 4668
Tull Charitable Fnd Grants, 4679
Turner Fnd Grants, 4681
Union Bank, N.A. Fnd Grants, 4709
Union Pacific Fdn Health & Human Svcs Grts, 4715
United Technologies Corporation Grants, 4725
US Airways Comm Fnd Grants, 4789
USDA Farm Labor Housing Grants, 4809
USDA Housing Preservation Grants, 4816
USDA Public Telev Digital Transition Grts, 4822
USDA Rural Economic Dev Grants, 4827
USDA Rural Utilities Service Weather Radio Transmitter Grants, 4833
USDA Self-Help Tech Assistance Grants, 4836
USDA Special Research Grants, 4841
USDC Public Works and Economic Adjustment Assistance Grants, 4856
USDC University Center Economic Dev Program Competition, 4861
USGA Fdn for the Good of the Game Grts, 4868
US Soccer Fdn Annual Pgm & Field Grts, 4870
USTA Public Facility Assistance Grants, 4883
V.V. Cooke Fnd Grants, 4896
Victor E. Speas Fnd Grants, 4933
Vigneron Fnd Grants, 4938
Virginia Commission for the Arts General Operating Grants, 4942
W. C. Griffith Fnd Grants, 4958
W.C. Griffith Fnd Grants, 4957
Wabash River Heritage Corridor Fund Grants, 4970
Wabash Valley Human Services Grants, 4972
Walter and Elise Haas Fund Grants, 4982
Walter L. Gross III Family Fnd Grants, 4983
Warrick Cty Comm Fdn Grants, 4987

Wayne and Gladys Valley Fnd Grants, 5003
WCI Minnesota Beautiful Grants, 5013
Weatherwax Fnd Grants, 5014
Weingart Fnd Grants, 5018
Wells Fargo Housing Fnd Grants, 5023
West Virginia Commission on the Arts Fast Track ADA and Emergency Grants, 5034
Weyerhaeuser Company Fnd Grants, 5053
Whirlpool Fnd Grants, 5056
Widgeon Point Charitable Fnd Grants, 5064
William Blair and Company Fnd Grants, 5078
William G. Gilmore Fnd Grants, 5082
William G. McGowan Charitable Fund Grants, 5084
William G Selby & Marie Selby Fdn Grts, 5085
William H. Hannon Fnd Grants, 5086
Wilson-Wood Fnd Grants, 5098
Winston-Salem Fdn Competitive Grts, 5102
Winthrop Rockefeller Fnd Grants, 5105
Woodward Fund Grants, 5116
Xcel Energy Fnd Grants, 5121
Xerox Fnd Grants, 5122

Capital Campaigns

41 Washington Street Fnd Grants, 22
100 Women in Hedge Funds Fnd Grants, 28
A.J. Fletcher Fnd Grants, 41
Aaron Fnd Grants, 73
Abbot & Dorothy H Stevens Fdn Grants, 79
Abbott Fund Global AIDS Care Grants, 82
Abel Fnd Grants, 90
Abell-Hanger Fnd Grants, 91
Achelis Fnd Grants, 127
Ackerman Fnd Grants, 129
Acushnet Fnd Grants, 143
Adams County Comm Fnd of Pennsylvania Grants, 149
ADC Fnd Tech Access Grants, 158
Adelaide Breed Bayrd Fnd Grants, 161
Adolph Coors Fnd Grants, 171
AEC Trust Grants, 175
AEP Corporate Giving Grants, 180
Agnes M. Lindsay Trust Grants, 203
Ahmanson Fnd Grants, 207
Air Products and Chemicals Grants, 216
Alabama Power Fnd Grants, 233
Alavi Fnd Grants, 335
Albert and Bessie Mae Kronkosky Charitable Fnd Grants, 339
Albert B Cuppage Charitable Fdn Grts, 341
Alberto Culver Corporate Contributions Grants, 343
Albert W. Cherne Fnd Grants, 346
Albert W. Rice Charitable Fnd Grants, 347
Alcoa Fnd Grants, 350
Alexander & Baldwin Fnd Hawaiian and Pacific Island Grants, 352
Alexander & Baldwin Fdn Mainland Grants, 353
Alexander Eastman Fnd Grants, 355
Alex Brown & Sons Charitable Fdn Grants, 359
Alex Stern Family Fnd Grants, 360
Alice Tweed Tuohy Fnd Grants, 372
Allen P & Josephine B Green Fdn Grts, 380
Alliant Energy Fnd Comm Grants, 384
Allyn Fnd Grants, 392
Alvah H & Wyline P Chapman Fdn Grts, 402
Alvin & Fanny Blaustein Thalheimer Fdn Grts, 403
Ameren Corporation Comm Grants, 418
Americana Fnd Grants, 422
American Electric Power Grants, 428
American Schlafhorst Grants, 446
Amgen Fnd Grants, 456
Amon G. Carter Fnd Grants, 458
Anderson Fnd Grants, 460
Andrew Family Fnd Grants, 462
Angels Baseball Fnd Grants, 465
Anheuser-Busch Fnd Grants, 470
Anne L. and George H. Clapp Charitable and Educational Trust Grants, 476
Anne Thorne Weaver Family Fnd Grants, 478
Ann Peppers Fnd Grants, 484
Aratani Fnd Grants, 523
Arcadia Fnd Grants, 525

1030 / Capital Campaigns

Arie and Ida Crown Memorial Grants, 533
Arizona Public Service Corp Gvg Pgm Grts, 545
Arkell Hall Fnd Grants, 562
Armstrong McDonald Fnd Grants, 565
Arronson Fnd Grants, 567
Arthur Ashley Williams Fnd Grants, 572
Assisi Fdn of Memphis Capital Project Grants, 593
Assurant Health Fnd Grants, 596
Atherton Family Fnd Grants, 604
Athwin Fnd Grants, 605
Atran Fnd Grants, 610
Auburn Fnd Grants, 611
Avon Products Fnd Grants, 625
Ayres Fnd Grants, 630
Bacon Family Fnd Grants, 634
Bailey Fnd Grants, 635
Ball Brothers Fnd General Grants, 637
Barker Fnd Grants, 668
Barker Welfare Fnd Grants, 669
Barra Fnd Project Grants, 674
Barrasso Usdin Kupperman Freeman and Sarver LLC Corporate Grants, 675
Batchelor Fnd Grants, 679
Baton Rouge Area Fnd Grants, 682
Batts Fnd Grants, 687
Baughman Fnd Grants, 688
Beazley Fnd Grants, 714
Bemis Company Fnd Grants, 723
Ben B. Cheney Fnd Grants, 725
Bender Fnd Grants, 726
Benton Comm Fnd Grants, 730
Benwood Fnd Comm Grants, 732
Benwood Fnd Focus Area Grants, 733
Berks County Comm Fnd Grants, 734
Berrien Comm Fnd Grants, 744
Besser Fnd Grants, 748
Bill and Melinda Gates Fnd Emergency Response Grants, 766
Bill & Melinda Gates Fdn Library Grts, 768
Bill and Melinda Gates Fnd Water, Sanitation and Hygiene Grants, 770
Bill Hannon Fnd Grants, 771
Blanche and Irving Laurie Fnd Grants, 784
Blanche & Julian Robertson Family Fdn Grants, 785
Blowitz-Ridgeway Fnd Grants, 792
Blue Mountain Comm Fnd Grants, 800
Blue River Comm Fnd Grants, 801
Blumenthal Fnd Grants, 804
Bodenwein Public Benevolent Fdn Grants, 806
Bodman Fnd Grants, 807
Boeing Company Contributions Grants, 809
Boettcher Fnd Grants, 810
Bonfils-Stanton Fnd Grants, 814
Booth-Bricker Fund Grants, 815
Booth Ferris Fnd Grants, 816
Borkee-Hagley Fnd Grants, 817
Bosque Fnd Grants, 818
Bradley-Turner Fnd Grants, 828
Brooklyn Comty Fdn Caring Neighbors Grts, 848
Brooklyn Comm Fnd Comm Arts for All Grants, 849
Brooklyn Comm Fnd Comm Dev Grants, 850
Brooklyn Comm Fnd Educ and Youth Achievement Grants, 851
Brooklyn Comm Fnd Green Communities Grants, 852
Brown County Comm Fnd Grants, 853
Brunswick Fnd Grants, 857
Bunbury Company Grants, 863
Burlington Industries Fnd Grants, 865
Burlington Northern Santa Fe Fdn Grants, 866
Burton D Morgan Fdn Hudson Comty Grts, 869
Burton D Morgan Youth Entrepreneurship Grants, 870
Burton G. Bettengen Grants, 871
Bush Arts & Humanities Capital Projects Grants, 872
Cabot Corporation Fnd Grants, 887
Cailloux Fnd Grants, 892
Callaway Fnd Grants, 909
Cargill Citizenship Fund-Corp Gvg Grants, 925
Carl & Eloise Pohlad Family Fdn Grants, 927
Carl B. and Florence E. King Fnd Grants, 928
Carl C. Icahn Fnd Grants, 929

Carl Gellert and Celia Berta Gellert Fdn Grts, 930
Carlisle Fnd Grants, 931
Carl M. Freeman Fnd Grants, 933
Carls Fnd Grants, 937
Carl W. and Carrie Mae Joslyn Trust Grants, 938
Carnahan-Jackson Fnd Grants, 939
Carpenter Fnd Grants, 943
Carrie Estelle Doheny Fnd Grants, 945
Carrier Corporation Contributions Grants, 946
Caterpillar Fnd Grants, 954
CE and S Fnd Grants, 985
Cemala Fnd Grants, 988
Central Minnesota Comm Fdn Grants, 995
Central New York Comm Fdn Grants, 996
Cessna Fnd Grants, 1000
CFFVR Basic Needs Gvg Partnership Grts, 1002
CFFVR Clintonville Area Fnd Grants, 1008
CFFVR Clintonville Area Fnd Grants, 1007
CFFVR Doug & Carla Salmon Fdn Grts, 1009
CFFVR Frank C. Shattuck Comm Grants, 1012
CFFVR Robert & Patricia Endries Family Grants, 1018
CFFVR Schmidt Family G4 Grants, 1020
CFFVR Sikora Family Memorial Grants, 1022
Champlin Fnds Grants, 1029
Chapman Charitable Fnd Grants, 1033
Chapman Family Charitable Trust Grants, 1034
Charles A. Frueauff Fnd Grants, 1037
Charles & Lynn Schusterman Fam Fdn Grants, 1038
Charles Delmar Fnd Grants, 1039
Charles H. Revson Fnd Grants, 1047
Charles Hayden Fnd Grants, 1048
Charles M & Mary D Grant Fdn Grants, 1050
Charles Stewart Mott Fnd Grants, 1055
Chatlos Fnd Grants, 1061
CHC Fnd Grants, 1065
Chesapeake Corporation Fnd Grants, 1076
Chicago Board of Trade Fnd Grants, 1079
Chicago Sun Times Charity Trust Grants, 1098
CICF Indianapolis Fdn Comm Grants, 1123
Cincinnati Milacron Fnd Grants, 1132
Citigroup Fnd Grants, 1139
Claneil Fnd Grants, 1145
Clarcor Fnd Grants, 1148
Clark and Ruby Baker Fnd Grants, 1154
Clark Charitable Trust Grants, 1155
Clark Fnd Grants, 1157
Claude Worthington Benedum Fdn Grants, 1161
Cleveland-Cliffs Fnd Grants, 1165
Cleveland Fnd Capital Grants, 1167
Clipper Ship Fnd Grants, 1175
Clowes Fund Grants, 1177
Coastal Comm Fdn of SC Grants, 1193
Cockrell Fnd Grants, 1196
Collins C. Diboll Private Fnd Grants, 1208
Colonel Stanley R. McNeil Fnd Grants, 1210
Colorado Interstate Gas Grants, 1213
Colorado Springs Cmty Trust Fund Grants, 1215
Columbus Fnd Competitive Grants, 1220
Commonwealth Edison Grants, 1240
Communities Fnd of Texas Grants, 1243
Comm Fdn for Grtr Buffalo Grants, 1247
Comm Fdn for Monterey Cty Grants, 1255
Comm Fdn for Muskegon Cty Grants, 1256
Comm Fnd of Bartholomew Cnty Heritage Grants, 1267
Comm Fnd of Boone County Grants, 1274
Comm Fdn of Central Illinois Grants, 1276
Comm Fnd of Grtr Birmingham Grants, 1280
Comm Fnd of Greater Flint Grants, 1282
Comm Fnd of Greater Fort Wayne - Cmty Endwt & Clarke Endwt Grants, 1285
Comm Fnd of Grtr Lafayette Grts, 1289
Comm Fnd of Grtr New Britain Grts, 1291
Comm Fnd of Greenville Hollingsworth Funds Capital Projects Grants, 1295
Comm Fnd of Greenville Hollingsworth Funds Program/Project Grants, 1296
Comm Fnd of Mt Vernon & Knox County Grants, 1301
Comm Fnd of S Alabama Grants, 1308
Comm Fnd of St. Joseph County ArtsEverywhere Grants, 1313

PROGRAM TYPE INDEX

Comm Fnd of St. Joseph County Special Project Challenge Grants, 1314
Comm Fnd of the Verdugos Educational Endowment Fund Grants, 1321
Connecticut Comm Fnd Grants, 1350
Connelly Fnd Grants, 1353
ConocoPhillips Grants, 1355
Constantin Fnd Grants, 1362
Constellation Energy Corporate Grants, 1364
Consumers Energy Fnd, 1365
Cooke Fnd Grants, 1368
Cooper Fnd Grants, 1369
Cooper Industries Fnd Grants, 1370
Cornerstone Fdn of NE Wisconsin Grants, 1375
Corning Fnd Cultural Grants, 1376
Coughlin-Saunders Fnd Grants, 1377
Countess Moira Charitable Fnd Grants, 1381
Covidien Partnership for Neighborhood Wellness, 1391
Cowles Charitable Trust Grants, 1392
Crail-Johnson Fnd Grants, 1393
Cralle Fnd Grants, 1394
Crescent Porter Hale Fnd Grants, 1398
Crestlea Fnd Grants, 1399
CSRA Comm Fnd Grants, 1407
Cudd Fnd Grants, 1410
Cullen Fnd Grants, 1411
Cumberland Comm Fnd Grants, 1413
D.F. Halton Fnd Grants, 1424
Dale and Edna Walsh Fnd Grants, 1435
Dallas Fnd Grants, 1436
Dana Corporation Fnd Grants, 1440
Danellie Fnd Grants, 1442
Daphne Seybolt Culpeper Mem Fnd Grts, 1445
Dave Coy Fnd Grants, 1447
Davenport-Hatch Fnd Grants, 1448
David & Barbara B. Hirschhorn Fdn Grt, 1450
David Geffen Fnd Grants, 1452
Daywood Fnd Grants, 1465
Deaconess Comm Fnd Grants, 1467
Delonne Anderson Family Fnd, 1492
DeMatteis Family Fnd Grants, 1497
DENSO North America Fnd Grants, 1499
Denton A. Cooley Fnd Grants, 1500
Dermody Properties Fnd Grants, 1517
DHHS ARRA Strengthening Communities Fund - Nonprofit Capacity Building Grants, 1527
DHHS ARRA Strengthening Communities Fund - State, Local, and Tribal Government Capacity Building Grants, 1528
DHHS Comm Svcs Blk Grant Trng & Techn Assistance: Capacity-Bldg for Ongoing CSBG Pgms and Strat Plng & Coordination, 1529
Dolan Fnd Grants, 1563
Donald & Sylvia Robinson Family Fdn Grts, 1573
Donald W. Reynolds Fnd Charitable Food Distribution Grants, 1575
Dorrance Family Fnd Grants, 1590
Doug and Carla Salmon Fnd Grants, 1594
Dr. P. Phillips Fnd Grants, 1601
Dresher Fnd Grants, 1605
Dreyer's Fnd Large Grants, 1606
Drs. Bruce and Lee Fnd Grants, 1607
Duchossois Family Fnd Grants, 1616
Duke Endowment Child Care Grants, 1617
Duluth-Superior Area Comm Fdn Grts, 1620
Dunspaugh-Dalton Fnd Grants, 1623
DuPage Comm Fnd Grants, 1624
Dwight Stuart Youth Fnd Capacity-Building Initiative Grants, 1627
Dyson Fnd Mid-Hudson Valley Project Grants, 1636
E.J. Grassmann Trust Grants, 1638
E Rhodes & Leona B Carpenter Fdn Grts, 1640
Eastman Chemical Co Fnd Grants, 1643
Easton Fnds Archery Facility Grants, 1644
Eaton Charitable Fund Grants, 1647
Eden Hall Fnd Grants, 1655
Edward S. Moore Fnd Grants, 1668
Edwards Memorial Trust Grants, 1669
Edward W & Stella C Van Houten Mem Fund, 1670
Edwin S. Webster Fnd Grants, 1671

PROGRAM TYPE INDEX

Capital Campaigns / 1031

Edwin W & Catherine M Davis Fdn Grants, 1672
Edyth Bush Charitable Fnd Grants, 1673
Effie and Wofford Cain Fnd Grants, 1674
Eisner Fnd Grants, 1678
Elmer L & Eleanor J Andersen Fdn Grnts, 1687
Emma A. Sheafer Charitable Trust Grants, 1699
Ensign-Bickford Fnd Grants, 1709
Enterprise Rent-A-Car Fnd Grants, 1721
Erie Comm Fnd Grants, 1750
Ethel and Raymond F. Rice Fnd Grants, 1758
Ethel S. Abbott Charitable Fnd Grants, 1760
Ethel Sergeant Clark Smith Fnd Grants, 1761
Eugene McDermott Fnd Grants, 1765
Eugene Straus Charitable Trust, 1766
Eva L & Joseph M Bruening Fdn Grants, 1768
Evelyn and Walter Haas, Jr. Fund Gay and Lesbian Rights Grants, 1772
Ewing Halsell Fnd Grants, 1776
Ewing Marion Kauffman Fnd Grants, 1777
F.R. Bigelow Fnd Grants, 1781
Fallon OrNda Comm Health Fund Grants, 1783
Fargo-Moorhead Area Fnd Grants, 1788
Faye McBeath Fnd Grants, 1794
Ferree Fnd Grants, 1804
Fidelity Fnd Grants, 1805
Field Fnd of Illinois Grants, 1806
Fields Pond Fnd Grants, 1807
FirstEnergy Fnd Comm Grants, 1819
Fisa Fnd Grants, 1826
Fleishhacker Fnd Educ Grants, 1838
Fluor Fnd Grants, 1875
FMC Fnd Grants, 1876
Foellinger Fnd Grants, 1877
Forest Fnd Grants, 1886
Fnd for Mid South Health & Wellness Grants, 1899
Fnd NW Grants, 1906
Fourjay Fnd Grants, 1913
France-Merrick Fnds Grants, 1915
Francis L. Abreu Charitable Trust Grants, 1922
Frank and Lydia Bergen Fnd Grants, 1925
Franklin County Comm Fdn Grts, 1929
Frank M. Tait Fnd Grants, 1932
Frank Stanley Beveridge Fnd Grants, 1936
Frank W & Carl S Adams Mem Fund Grts, 1937
Fred Baldwin Memorial Fnd Grants, 1941
Fred C & Katherine B Andersen Fdn Grts, 1942
Freddie Mac Fnd Grants, 1944
Frederick McDonald Trust Grants, 1946
Frederick S. Upton Fnd Grants, 1947
Fred L. Emerson Fnd Grants, 1949
Frist Fnd Grants, 1964
Fritz B. Burns Fnd Grants, 1965
Fuller E. Callaway Fnd Grants, 1973
G.N. Wilcox Trust Grants, 1982
Gaylord & Dorothy Donnelley Fdn Grants, 1993
Gebbie Fnd Grants, 1995
GenCorp Fnd Grants, 1998
General Dynamics Corporation Grants, 2001
General Mills Fnd Grants, 2003
George B. Page Fnd Grants, 2013
George B. Storer Fnd Grants, 2014
George Fnd Grants, 2018
George Gund Fnd Grants, 2020
George H & Jane A Mifflin Mem Fund Grts, 2021
George I. Alden Trust Grants, 2023
George Kress Fnd Grants, 2025
George S & Dolores Dore Eccles Fdn Grants, 2027
George W. Brackenridge Fnd Grants, 2028
George W Codrington Charitable Fdn Grts, 2029
George W. Wells Fnd Grants, 2030
Georgia-Pacific Fdn Entrepreneurship Grts, 2033
Georgia Power Fnd Grants, 2039
Gheens Fnd Grants, 2048
Gil and Dody Weaver Fnd Grants, 2053
Gill Fnd Gay & Lesbian Fund, 2054
Ginger and Barry Ackerley Fnd Grants, 2055
Gladys Brooks Fnd Grants, 2059
GNOF Exxon-Mobil Grants, 2074
GNOF Norco Comm Grants, 2089
Goodrich Corporation Fnd Grants, 2104

Good Works Fnd Grants, 2105
Grace and Franklin Bernsen Fnd Grants, 2109
Graco Fnd Grants, 2111
Grand Haven Area Comm Fdn Grants, 2113
Grand Rapids Area Comm Fdn Wyoming Grants, 2116
Grand Rapids Comm Fnd Grants, 2118
Grand Rapids Comm Fdn Ionia Cty Grts, 2119
Grand Rapids Comm Fnd SE Ottawa Grants, 2122
Grand Rapids Comm Fdn Sparta Grts, 2124
Greater Tacoma Comm Fdn Grts, 2139
Greater Worcester Comm Fnd Jeppson Memorial Fund for Brookfield Grants, 2141
Grover Hermann Fnd Grants, 2168
Grundy Fnd Grants, 2169
Guido A & Elizabeth H Binda Fdn Grants, 2172
H & R Fnd Grants, 2181
HA & Mary K Chapman Char Trust Grts, 2182
H.J. Heinz Company Fnd Grants, 2184
H. Schaffer Fnd Grants, 2187
Hagedorn Fund Grants, 2207
Hall Family Fnd Grants, 2210
Hallmark Corporate Fnd Grants, 2212
Hamilton Family Fnd Grants, 2213
Hampton Roads Comm Fnd Nonprofit Facilities Improvement Grants, 2218
Hannaford Charitable Fnd Grants, 2222
Harold & Arlene Schnitzer CARE Fdn Grts, 2226
Harold K. L. Castle Fnd Grants, 2228
Harold Simmons Fnd Grants, 2230
Harris and Eliza Kempner Fund Grants, 2231
Harry A & Margaret D Towsley Fdn Grts, 2236
Harry B. and Jane H. Brock Fnd Grants, 2237
Harry Bramhall Gilbert Char Trust Grts, 2238
Harry C. Trexler Trust Grants, 2239
Harry Edison Fnd, 2241
Harry Kramer Grants, 2242
Harry S. Thorpe Fnd Grants, 2244
Harry W. Bass, Jr. Fnd Grants, 2246
Hartford Courant Fnd Grants, 2248
Hartford Fdn Implementation Sppt Grts, 2251
Hartford Fdn Nonprofit Support Grants, 2252
Hartford Fnd Regular Grants, 2253
HCA Fnd Grants, 2274
Hearst Fnds Culture Grants, 2284
Hearst Fnds Social Service Grants, 2285
Hedco Fnd Grants, 2287
Helen Bader Fnd Grants, 2293
Helen K & Arthur E Johnson Fdn Grts, 2296
Helen S. Boylan Fnd Grants, 2298
Henry & Ruth Blaustein Rosenberg Fdn Grants, 2306
Henry W. Bull Fnd Grants, 2312
Herbert A & Adrian W Woods Fdn Grts, 2313
Hershey Company Grants, 2318
High Meadow Fnd Grants, 2321
Hillcrest Fnd Grants, 2325
Hill Crest Fnd Grants, 2324
Hillman Fnd Grants, 2327
Hirtzel Memorial Fnd Grants, 2332
Hoglund Fnd Grants, 2344
Holland/Zeeland Comm Fdn Grts, 2345
Homer A Scott & Mildred S Scott Fdn Grants, 2350
Honor the Earth Grants, 2361
Horace A Kimball & S Ella Kimball Fdn Grts, 2362
Hormel Fnd Grants, 2369
Houston Endowment Grants, 2373
Hudson Webber Fnd Grants, 2383
Huffy Fnd Grants, 2384
Hugh J. Andersen Fnd Grants, 2385
Huie-Dellmon Trust Grants, 2386
Huntington County Comm Fnd - Make a Difference Grants, 2406
Hyams Fnd Grants, 2413
Hyde Family Fnds Grants, 2414
Ida Alice Ryan Charitable Trust Grants, 2431
Idaho Power Co Corp Contributions, 2433
IDOT Rail Freight Pgm Loans & Grants, 2437
IDOT Truck Access Route Pgm Grts, 2438
IEDC Industrial Dev Grant Fund, 2443
Illinois DCEO Coal Competitiveness Grants, 2484
Illinois DCEO Coal Demonstration Grants, 2485
Illinois Tool Works Fnd Grants, 2511

Impact 100 Grants, 2522
Inasmuch Fnd Grants, 2523
Independence Comm Fnd Quality of Life Grant, 2525
Independence Comm Fnd Education, Culture & Arts Grant, 2526
Independence Comm Fnd Neighborhood Renewal Grants, 2527
Indiana Arts Commission Cap Bldg Grts, 2531
Indiana Reg'l Econ Dev Partnership Grts, 2546
Intergrys Corporation Grants, 2565
Irving S. Gilmore Fnd Grants, 2584
J.B. Reynolds Fnd Grants, 2592
J. Bulow Campbell Fnd Grants, 2593
J. Edwin Treakle Fnd Grants, 2596
J. F. Maddox Fnd Grants, 2597
Jackson Cty Comm Fdn Unrestricted Grts, 2611
Jackson Fnd Grants, 2613
Jacob G. Schmidlapp Trust Grants, 2616
James A. and Faith Knight Fnd Grants, 2621
James F & Marion L Miller Fdn Grts, 2622
James Graham Brown Fdn Qlty of Life Grts, 2625
James H. Cummings Fnd Grants, 2626
James J & Angelia M Harris Fdn Grts, 2630
James M. Cox Fnd of Georgia Grants, 2634
James R. Dougherty Jr. Fnd Grants, 2635
James R. Thorpe Fnd Grants, 2636
James S. Copley Fnd Grants, 2637
Jane's Trust Grants, 2639
Janesville Fnd Grants, 2644
Janirve Fnd Grants, 2645
Janson Fnd Grants, 2646
Jay & Rose Phillips Fam Fdn Grts, 2656
JELD-WEN Fnd Grants, 2661
Jenkins Fnd: Improving the Health of Greater Richmond Grants, 2663
Jessie Ball Dupont Fund Grants, 2671
Jewish Funds for Justice Grants, 2676
John and Margaret Post Fnd Grants, 2686
John G. Martin Fnd Grants, 2696
John H. and Wilhelmina D. Harland Charitable Fnd Grants, 2698
John I. Smith Charities Grants, 2700
John Jewett & Helen Chandler Garland Fdn, 2702
John R. Oishei Fnd Grants, 2709
JohnS & JamesL Knight Fdn Communities Grts, 2711
John S & James L Knight Fdn Dnr Adv Fd Grts, 2712
John W & Anna H Hanes Fdn Grants, 2728
John W. Anderson Fnd Grants, 2729
Joseph Alexander Fnd Grants, 2734
Joseph H & Florence A Roblee Fdn Grants, 2736
Josephine Goodyear Fnd Grants, 2738
Josiah W & Bessie H Kline Fdn Grants, 2742
Journal Gazette Fnd Grants, 2744
JP Morgan Chase Arts and Culture Grants, 2752
Judith and Jean Pape Adams Charitable Fnd Tulsa Area Grants, 2755
K.S. Adams Fnd Grants, 2758
Kansas Health Fnd Recognition Grants, 2784
Katharine Matthies Fnd Grants, 2788
Katherine John Murphy Fnd Grants, 2790
Kathryne Beynon Fnd Grants, 2791
Kawabe Grants, 2794
Kelvin and Eleanor Smith Fnd Grants, 2796
Kenneth T & Eileen L Norris Fdn Grants, 2802
Kenny's Kids Grants, 2803
Kettering Fund Grants, 2818
Kroger Fdn Diversity Grants, 2842
Kroger Fdn Grassroots Comty Support Grants, 2843
Kroger Fnd Hunger Relief Grants, 2844
L. W. Pierce Family Fnd Grants, 2846
Laurel Fnd Grants, 2867
Leicester Savings Bank Fund, 2879
Leighton Award for Nonprofit Excellence, 2880
Leo Goodwin Fnd Grants, 2882
Lettie Pate Evans Fnd Grants, 2887
Lewis H. Humphreys Charitable Trust Grants, 2889
Liberty Hill Fdn Enviro Justice Fund Grts, 2891
Lied Fnd Trust Grants, 2900
Lillian S. Wells Fnd Grants, 2901
Louie M & Betty M Phillips Fdn Grants, 2923

Capital Campaigns

Louis and Elizabeth Nave Flarsheim Charitable Fnd Grants, 2924
Louis Calder Fnd Grants, 2925
Lowe Fnd Grants, 2929
Lubbock Area Fnd Grants, 2931
Lubrizol Corporation Comm Grants, 2932
Lubrizol Fnd Grants, 2933
Lucy Gooding Charitable Fnd Trust, 2936
Lucy Gooding Charitable Fdn Trust Grts, 2937
Lumpkin Family Fdn Healthy People Grts, 2942
Luther I. Replogle Fnd Grants, 2945
Lynde and Harry Bradley Fnd Grants, 2947
M.E. Raker Fnd Grants, 2953
Mabel Y. Hughes Charitable Trust Grants, 2960
Macquarie Bank Fnd Grants, 2966
Mardag Fnd Grants, 3001
Margaret & James A Elkins Jr Fdn Grts, 3003
Margaret T. Morris Fnd Grants, 3005
Marietta McNeill Morgan and Samuel Tate Morgan, Jr. Trust Grants, 3008
Marion Gardner Jackson Char Trust Grts, 3017
Marion I & Henry J Knott Fdn Discret Grants, 3018
Marion I & Henry J Knott Fdn Std Grants, 3019
Marjorie Moore Charitable Fnd Grants, 3021
Mars Fnd Grants, 3025
Marsh Corporate Grants, 3027
Mary D. & Walter F Frear Eleemosynary Trust, 3035
Mary K. Chapman Fnd Grants, 3042
Mary Owen Borden Fnd Grants, 3046
Massachusetts Cultural Facilities Capital Grants, 3053
Massachusetts Cultural Council Cultural Facilities Systems Replacement Plan Grants Grants, 3055
Mathile Family Fnd Grants, 3062
Max A. Adler Charitable Fnd Grants, 3065
Maximilian E & Marion O Hoffman Fdn, 3067
McCune Fnd Human Services Grants, 3080
McGregor Fund Grants, 3082
McInerny Fnd Grants, 3083
McLean Contributionship Grants, 3088
McMillen Fnd Grants, 3090
Meacham Fnd Memorial Grants, 3102
Mead Witter Fnd Grants, 3106
MetroWest Health Fnd Capital Grants for Health-Related Facilities, 3134
Meyer Fnd Economic Security Grants, 3141
Meyer Fnd Educ Grants, 3142
Meyer Fdn Healthy Communities Grts, 3143
Microsoft Comty Affairs Puget Sound Grts, 3163
Miller, Canfield, Paddock and Stone, P.L.C. Corporate Giving Grants, 3179
Mimi and Peter Haas Fund Grants, 3185
Minneapolis Fnd Comm Grants, 3186
Montana Arts Cncl Cltrl & Aesthetic Proj Grts, 3209
Musgrave Fnd Grants, 3231
Nathaniel & Elizabeth P Stevens Fdn Grants, 3247
Nationwide Insurance Fnd Grants, 3285
Nestle Purina PetCare Pet Related Grants, 3304
New Hampshire Charitable Fnd Grants, 3325
New York Landmarks Cons Sacred Sites Grants, 3340
Nicholas H Noyes Jr Mem Fdn Grants, 3434
Nicor Corporate Contributions, 3435
Nina Mason Pulliam Charitable Trust Grants, 3443
Noble County Comm Fnd Grants, 3456
Norcliffe Fnd Grants, 3459
Nordson Corporation Fnd Grants, 3462
Norfolk Southern Fnd Grants, 3463
North Carolina Arts Council Tech Assistance, 3482
North Carolina Comm Fnd Grants, 3489
North Central Health Services Grants, 3491
North Central Health Services Grants, 3492
Northern Chautauqua Comm Fnd Comm Grants, 3499
Northern New York Comm Fdn Grts, 3503
Northern Trust Company Corporate Giving, 3504
NW Mutual Fnd Grants, 3509
Norton Fnd Grants, 3514
Norwin S & Elizabeth N Bean Fdn Grts, 3515
Notsew Orm Sands Fnd Grants, 3516
NYCT Historic Preservation Grants, 3551
NYSCA Architecture, Planning, and Design: Capital Fixtures and Equipment Purchase Grants, 3570
NYSCA Architecture, Planning, and Design: Capital Project Grants, 3571
Oak Fnd Child Abuse Grants, 3632
Ohio Valley Fnd Grants, 3662
Oleonda Jameson Trust Grants, 3667
OneFamily Fnd Grants, 3673
Oppenstein Brothers Fnd Grants, 3685
Otto Bremer Fnd Grants, 3713
Overbrook Fnd Grants, 3715
Owen County Comm Fnd Grants, 3716
PACCAR Fnd Grants, 3719
Pacific Life Fnd Grants, 3726
Parkersburg Area Comm Fdn Action Grts, 3738
Patrick and Anna M. Cudahy Fund Grants, 3751
Paul E & Klare N Reinhold Fdn Grts, 3758
Perkin Fund Grants, 3821
Petco Fnd 4 Rs Project Support Grants, 3830
Petco Fnd Capital Grants, 3831
Peter and Elizabeth C. Tower Fnd Phase II Tech Initiative Grants, 3839
Peter Kiewit Fnd General Grants, 3845
Peter Kiewit Fnd Small Grants, 3847
Pfizer Special Events Grants, 3865
Phil Hardin Fnd Grants, 3875
Phoenix Suns Charities Grants, 3881
Pinellas County Grants, 3891
Piper Jaffray Fdn Communities Giving Grts, 3899
Piper Trust Arts and Culture Grants, 3900
Piper Trust Healthcare & Med Rsch Grts, 3903
Plough Fnd Grants, 3915
Pohlad Family Fnd, 3928
Porter County Comm Fnd Grants, 3931
Powell Family Fnd Grants, 3941
Powell Fnd Grants, 3942
PPG Industries Fnd Grants, 3943
Presbyterian Health Fnd Bridge, Seed and Equipment Grants, 3947
Price Chopper's Golub Fnd Grants, 3950
Price Gilbert, Jr. Charitable Fund Grants, 3953
Priddy Fnd Capital Grants, 3954
Principal Financial Group Fnd Grants, 3966
Prudential Fnd Educ Grants, 3977
Pulte Homes Corporate Contributions, 3989
Putnam Fnd Grants, 3991
R.C. Baker Fnd Grants, 3999
Raskob Fdn for Catholic Activities Grts, 4019
Rasmuson Fnd Capital Grants, 4020
Rasmuson Fnd Special Project Grants, 4025
Rathmann Family Fnd Grants, 4026
RCF General Comm Grants, 4032
Reinberger Fnd Grants, 4052
Reynolds American Fnd Grants, 4068
Reynolds and Reynolds Co Fdn Grants, 4070
Rhode Island Fnd Grants, 4073
Richard and Helen DeVos Fnd Grants, 4076
Richard and Rhoda Goldman Fund Grants, 4077
Richard & Susan Smith Family Fdn Grts, 4078
Richard D. Bass Fnd Grants, 4079
Richard H. Driehaus Fnd Grants, 4084
Roberta Leventhal Sudakoff Fnd Grants, 4102
Robert and Polly Dunn Fnd Grants, 4105
Robert F Stoico/FIRSTFED Char Fdn Grts, 4112
Robert W. Woodruff Fnd Grants, 4124
Robins Fnd Grants, 4126
Rockefeller Brothers Fund Charles E. Culpeper Arts and Culture Grants in New York City, 4129
Rockwell Int'l Corporate Trust Grants, 4141
Rosie's For All Kids Fnd Grants, 4163
Roy & Christine Sturgis Charitable Trust Grts, 4166
Ruth and Vernon Taylor Fnd Grants, 4177
Ruth Eleanor Bamberger and John Ernest Bamberger Memorial Fnd Grants, 4178
Rutter's Children's Charities Grants, 4181
Ryder System Charitable Fnd Grants, 4191
S. Livingston Mather Charitable Trust Grants, 4200
S. Mark Taper Fnd Grants, 4201
Safeco Insurance Comm Grants, 4203
Sage Fnd Grants, 4204
Saint Paul Companies Fnd Grants, 4217
Saint Paul Fnd Grants, 4219
Salmon Fnd Grants, 4225
San Juan Island Comm Fnd Grants, 4283
Santa Barbara Strategy Capital Support, 4285
Santa Fe Comm Fdn root2fruit Santa Fe, 4289
Sara Lee Fnd Grants, 4296
Sarkeys Fnd Grants, 4297
Sartain Lanier Family Fnd Grants, 4298
Schering-Plough Fdn Comm Initvs Grts, 4303
Schering-Plough Fnd Health Grants, 4304
Schlessman Family Fnd Grants, 4307
Schurz Communications Fnd Grants, 4312
Scott B & Annie P Appleby Char Trust Grts, 4313
Seattle Fdn C Keith Birkenfeld Mem Tr Grts, 4323
Seattle Fnd Economy Grants, 4325
Selby and Richard McRae Fnd Grants, 4334
Self Fnd Grants, 4335
Sensient Technologies Fnd Grants, 4337
Sid W. Richardson Fnd Grants, 4350
Simpson Lumber Charitable Contributions, 4362
Sister Fund Grants for Women's Organizations, 4371
Sisters of Charity Cleveland Reducing Health & Educ Disparities in the Central Neighborhood Grants, 4374
Sisters of Mercy of North Carolina Fdn Grts, 4375
Solo Cup Fnd Grants, 4401
Sonora Area Fnd Competitive Grants, 4404
Sony Corp of America Corp Philant Grants, 4405
Sosland Fnd Grants, 4408
South Carolina Arts Comsn Accessibility Grts, 4410
South Carolina Arts Commission Arts Facility Projects Grants, 4417
Southwest Florida Arts & Attractions Grants, 4441
Southwest Gas Corporation Fnd Grants, 4445
Square D Fnd Grants, 4464
Stackner Family Fnd Grants, 4471
Stackpole-Hall Fnd Grants, 4472
Starr Fnd Grants, 4483
Steelcase Fnd Grants, 4497
Steele-Reese Fnd Grants, 4498
Steve Young Family Fnd Grants, 4503
Stewart Huston Charitable Trust Grants, 4505
Stowe Family Fnd Grants, 4510
Strake Fnd Grants, 4511
Stranahan Fnd Grants, 4512
Strowd Roses Grants, 4515
Subaru of Indiana Automotive Fdn Grts, 4519
Summit Fnd Grants, 4524
Sunderland Fnd Grants, 4527
Suntrust Bank Atlanta Fnd Grants, 4531
Susan Mott Webb Charitable Trust Grants, 4536
Susan Vaughan Fnd Grants, 4537
T. James Kavanagh Fnd Grants, 4545
T.L.L. Temple Fnd Grants, 4546
T. Rowe Price Associates Fnd Grants, 4548
TD4HIM Fnd Grants, 4566
TE Fnd Grants, 4572
Tension Envelope Fnd Grants, 4578
Texas Instruments Fnd Comm Services Grants, 4600
Textron Corporate Contributions Grants, 4601
Thomas B & Elizabeth M Sheridan Fdn Grts, 4614
Thomas Sill Fnd Grants, 4619
Thomas W. Briggs Fnd Grants, 4621
Thompson Charitable Fnd Grants, 4622
Topeka Comm Fnd Grants, 4644
Tourism Cares Worldwide Grants, 4649
Tull Charitable Fnd Grants, 4679
U.S. Bank Fnd Grants, 4686
Union Bank, N.A. Fnd Grants, 4709
Union Pacific Fdn Comm & Civic Grts, 4714
Union Pacific Fdn Health & Human Svcs Grts, 4715
US Airways Comm Fnd Grants, 4789
USTA Public Facility Assistance Grants, 4883
V.V. Cooke Fnd Grants, 4896
Vanderburgh Comm Fdn Women's Fund, 4903
Viacom Fnd Grants (Formerly CBS Fnd), 4932
Visiting Nurse Fnd Grants, 4951
Vulcan Materials Company Fnd Grants, 4956
W. C. Griffith Fnd Grants, 4958
W.C. Griffith Fnd Grants, 4957
WK Kellogg Fdn Healthy Kids Grants, 4961
Walt Disney Company Fnd Grants, 4981

PROGRAM TYPE INDEX

Walter and Elise Haas Fund Grants, 4982
Washington Area Women's Fnd Strategic Opportunity and Partnership Fund Grants, 4996
Wayne and Gladys Valley Fnd Grants, 5003
Weatherwax Fnd Grants, 5014
Weingart Fnd Grants, 5018
West Virginia Commission on the Arts Cultural Facilities and Capital Resources Grants, 5033
Widgeon Point Charitable Fnd Grants, 5064
Wilbur & Patsy Bradley Family Fdn Grts, 5066
William A. Badger Fnd Grants, 5072
William G & Helen C Hoffman Fdn Grants, 5080
William G. Gilmore Fnd Grants, 5082
William G Selby & Marie Selby Fdn Grts, 5085
William McCaskey Chapman and Adaline Dinsmore Chapman Fnd Grants, 5092
Wilson-Wood Fnd Grants, 5098
Winston-Salem Fdn Competitive Grts, 5102
Winston-Salem Fdn Elkin/Tri-County Grants, 5103
Woodward Fund Grants, 5116
Yellow Corporate Fnd Grants, 5126

Centers: Research/Demonstration/Service
AACC Building Better Communities Through Regional Economic Dev Partnerships, 54
Able Trust Vocational Rehab Grants for Agencies, 103
ACF ACYF Runaway and Homeless Youth Basic Center Grants, 112
ACF Adoption Opportunities Project Grants, 113
ACF Assets for Independence Individual Dev Account Grants, 115
ACF Ethnic Comm Self-Help Grants, 118
ACF Head Start and Early Head Start Grants, 120
ACF Preferred Communities Grants, 124
ACF Supplemental Services for Recently Arrived Refugees Grants, 125
Administration on Aging Senior Medicare Patrol Project Grants, 166
AMA Fdn Fund for Better Health Grts, 409
American Chemical Scty Corp Assocs Seed Grts, 425
Appalachian Regional Commission Telecommunications Grants, 510
Arizona Republic Newspaper Corp Contribs, 547
Bay and Paul Fnds Grants, 693
Blue Cross Blue Shield of Minnesota Fdn-Healthy Equity: Public Libraries for Health Grts, 797
Build-A-Bear Workshop Fnd Grants, 861
Cambridge Comm Fnd Grants, 913
CCHD Comm Dev Grants, 966
Champ-A Champion Fur Kids Grants, 1028
Charity Incorporated Grants, 1035
Chicago Comm Trust Health Grants, 1087
Chicago Comm Trust Housing Grants: Advancing Affordable Rental Housing, 1088
Chicago Comm Trust Hsg Grants: Preserving Hm Ownership & Preventing Foreclosure, 1089
Chicago Comm Trust Housing Grants: Preventing and Ending Homelessness, 1090
Chicago Comm Trust Preventing and Eliminating Hunger Grants, 1092
Chicago Comm Pub Safety & Justice Grants, 1093
Chicago Comm Trust Workforce Grants, 1094
Child Care Center Enhancement Grants, 1105
Collins C. Diboll Private Fnd Grants, 1208
Colonel Stanley R. McNeil Fnd Grants, 1210
ConocoPhillips Fnd Grants, 1354
Dallas Women's Fnd Grants, 1438
Deborah Munroe Noonan Mem Fund Grts, 1475
Dept of Ed Child Care Access Means Parents in School Grants, 1507
Dept of Ed Even Start Grants, 1508
Dept of Ed Parental Infor & Resource Cntrs, 1510
DHHS Health Centers Grants for Residents of Public Housing, 1533
DHHS Tech and Non-Financial Assistance to Health Centers, 1539
Dr. John T. Macdonald Fnd Grants, 1600
Easton Fnds Archery Facility Grants, 1644
Florida Humanities Council Major Grants, 1868
Florida Humanities Council Partnership Grants, 1870

Fnd for the Mid South Comm Dev Grants, 1897
Fnd for the Mid South Educ Grts, 1898
Fnd for the MidSouth Wlth Bldg Grts, 1900
Frank Loomis Palmer Fund Grants, 1931
Frederick McDonald Trust Grants, 1946
G.A. Ackermann Grants, 1981
George W. Wells Fnd Grants, 2030
Georgia Council for Arts Partner Grants, 2035
Goldseker Fdn Comm Affairs Grants, 2100
Goldseker Fnd Comm Grants, 2101
Goldseker Fnd Human Services Grants, 2102
Goldseker Fnd Non-Profit Management Assistance Grants, 2103
Hartford Aging and Health Program Awards, 2247
Health Fnd of Grtr Indianapolis Grts, 2282
Health Fnd of South Florida Responsive Grants, 2283
Herbert A & Adrian W Woods Fdn Grts, 2313
HRF Hudson River Improvement Grants, 2378
Hudson Webber Fnd Grants, 2383
IBCAT Screening Mammography Grants, 2422
IDPH Emergency Med Svcs Astnc Fund Grts, 2440
IDPH Hosptial Capital Investment Grants, 2441
IDPH Local Health Dept Public Health Emergency Response Grants, 2442
Illinois DCEO Emerging Tech Enterprises Grants, 2490
John Merck Fund Grants, 2706
John W & Anna H Hanes Fdn Grants, 2728
Josephine Goodyear Fnd Grants, 2738
Joseph P. Kennedy Jr. Fnd Grants, 2740
Joyce Fnd Democracy Grants, 2748
Katharine Matthies Fnd Grants, 2788
Kessler Fdn Signature Employment Grts, 2816
LEGO Children's Fund Grants, 2878
Leo Goodwin Fnd Grants, 2882
Lied Fnd Trust Grants, 2900
Lucy Gooding Charitable Fnd Trust, 2936
Margaret L. Wendt Fnd Grants, 3004
Marion Gardner Jackson Char Trust Grts, 3017
Marjorie Moore Charitable Fnd Grants, 3021
McGraw-Hill Companies Comm Grants, 3081
Mertz Gilmore Climate Change Solutions Grants, 3125
Mertz Gilmore Fnd NYC Dance Grants, 3127
MGN Family Fnd Grants, 3154
Michael Reese Health Trust Core Grants, 3159
Michael Reese Health Trust Responsive Grants, 3160
Mid-Iowa Health Fdn Comty Response Grts, 3168
MMS & Alliance Char Fdn Grts for Comm Action and Care for the Medically Uninsured, 3194
Mt. Sinai Health Care Fnd Health of the Jewish Comm Grants, 3226
Mt. Sinai Health Care Fnd Health of the Urban Comm Grants, 3227
Mt. Sinai Health Care Fnd Health Policy Grants, 3228
Nellie Mae Educ Fnd State Level Systems Change Grants, 3299
NHLBI Ancillary Studies in Clinical Trials, 3410
NHLBI Career Transition Awards, 3412
NHLBI Investigator Initiated Multi-Site Clinical Trials, 3413
NHLBI Lymphatics in Health and Disease in Digestive, Urinary, Cardio & Pulmonary Systems, 3415
NHLBI Ruth L. Kirschstein National Research Service Awards for Individual Predoctoral MD/PhD Fellows and Other Dual Degree Fellows, 3420
NNEDVF/Altria Doors of Hope Program, 3452
NSERC Brockhouse Canada Prize for Interdisciplinary Research in Science and Engineering Grant, 3518
NSF CISE Computing Rsch Infrastructure, 3526
NYSCA Dance: Services to the Field Grants, 3587
Oklahoma City Comm Pgms & Grts, 3666
OSF-Baltimore Tackling Drug Adctn Grts, 3698
OSI Sentencing and Incarceration Alternatives Project Grants, 3711
PCA Arts Organizations & Grants for Local Arts, 3782
PCA Entry Track Arts Organizations and Arts Grants for Local Arts, 3794
Piper Trust Arts and Culture Grants, 3900
Piper Trust Educ Grants, 3902
Piper Trust Healthcare & Med Rsch Grts, 3903
Piper Trust Older Adults Grants, 3904

Piper Trust Reglious Organizations Grants, 3905
Pollock Fnd Grants, 3930
Quality Health Fnd Grants, 3994
RAND Corporation Graduate Student Summer Associateships, 4018
Richard Davoud Donchian Fnd Grants, 4080
Robin Hood Fnd Grants, 4125
Rockefeller Bros Fund Peace & Security Grts, 4133
Rockwell Int'l Corporate Trust Grants, 4141
Salem Fnd Charitable Trust Grants, 4223
San Diego Women's Fnd Grants, 4252
Santa Fe Comm Fnd Seasonal Grants-Spring, 4291
Sapelo Fnd Social Justice Grants, 4294
Schering-Plough Fnd Health Grants, 4304
Scherman Fnd Grants, 4305
Sidgmore Family Fnd Grants, 4348
Sister Fund Grants for Women's Organizations, 4371
Sisters of Mercy of North Carolina Fdn Grts, 4375
Sisters of St Joseph Healthcare Fdn Grts, 4377
South Carolina Arts Commission American Masterpieces in South Carolina Grants, 4413
South Carolina Arts Comm Cultural Vis Grants, 4420
Southwest Florida Comm Competitive Grants, 4442
Sprague Fnd Grants, 4461
Stewart Huston Charitable Trust Grants, 4505
Stocker Fnd Grants, 4507
Surdna Fdn Sustainable Environments Grants, 4533
T.L.L. Temple Fnd Grants, 4546
T. Rowe Price Associates Fnd Grants, 4548
Telluride Fdn Emergency/Out of Cycle Grts, 4574
Telluride Fdn Tech Assistance Grts, 4575
TWS Fnd Grants, 4683
US Dept of Educ 21st Century Comm Learning Centers, 4687
US Dept of Educ Cntrs for Independent Lvng, 4688
US Dept of Educ Rehabilitation Engineering Research Centers Grants, 4698
US Dept of Educ Rehabilitation Research Training Centers , 4699
US Dept of Educ Special Education--National Activities--Parent Information Centers, 4701
US CRDF STEP Business Partnership Grant Competition Ukraine, 4796
USDC Business Center - American Indian and Alaska Native Grants, 4849
USDC University Center Economic Dev Program Competition, 4861
Vigneron Grants, 4938
W.P. and Bulah Luse Fnd Grants, 4965
Walter L. Gross III Family Fnd Grants, 4983
Weatherwax Fnd Grants, 5014
Weingart Fnd Grants, 5018
Wieboldt Fnd Grants, 5065
William Robert Baird Charitable Trust Grants, 5093
William T. Grant Fnd Youth Service Improvement Grants , 5096
Young Family Fnd Grants , 5127

Citizenship Instruction
Adolph Coors Fnd Grants, 171
Asian American Institute Impact Fellowships, 588
AT&T Fnd Civic and Comm Service Grants, 599
Bernard and Audre Rapoport Fnd Democracy and Civic Participation Grants, 737
Blue Cross Blue Shield of Minnesota Fdn-Healthy Equity: Public Libraries for Health Grts, 797
Brookdale Fdn Relatives as Parents Grts, 846
CCHD Comm Dev Grants, 966
CDECD Arts Catalyze Placemaking in Every Comm Grants, 977
CDECD Arts Catalyze Placemaking Leadership Grants, 978
CDECD Arts Catalyze Placemaking Sustaining Relevance Grants, 979
CIRCLE Civic Educ at the High School Level Research Grants, 1135
Civic Educ Consortium Grants, 1144
Columbus Fdn Neighborhood Partnership Grts, 1226
Dearborn Comm Fnd City of Lawrenceburg Youth Grants, 1472

1034 / Citizenship Instruction

Families Count: The National Honors Program, 1784
FAS Project Schools Grants, 1792
Fulbright Public Policy Grants in Mexico, 1972
GMFUS Black Sea Trust Regional Corp Grants, 2065
GNOF Environmental Fund Grants, 2073
HAF Comm Grants, 2193
Harvest Fnd Grants, 2254
HBF Encouraging Citizen Involvement Grants, 2272
Helen Irwin Littauer Educational Trust Grants, 2295
Henry M. Jackson Fnd Grants, 2311
John Edward Fowler Mem Fdn Grants, 2693
Joyce Fnd Democracy Grants, 2748
Koret Fnd Grants, 2837
Lynde and Harry Bradley Fnd Grants, 2947
Mardag Fnd Grants, 3001
Marin Comm Fnd Social Justice and Interfaith Understanding Grants, 3012
Marsh Corporate Grants, 3027
New Jersey Center for Hispanic Policy, Research and Dev Immigration Integration Grants, 3328
NYCT Civic Affairs Grants, 3545
NYCT Fund for New Citizens Grants, 3547
NYCT Human Justice Grants, 3552
OSF Advancing the Rights and Integration of Roma Grants, 3699
Paul & Daisy Soros Fwsps for New Americans, 3754
PIP American Dream Fund Grants, 3897
PIP Racial Justice Collaborative Grants, 3908
Saint Paul Companies Fnd Grants, 4217
Threshold Fnd Election Integrity Grants, 4625
TJX Fnd Grants, 4637
Vanderburgh Comm Fnd Women's Fund, 4903
Walter and Elise Haas Fund Grants, 4982

Community Development
1st and 10 Fnd Grants, 1
1st Source Fnd Grants, 3
2 Depot Square Ipswich Charitable Fnd Grants, 4
2 Life 18 Fnd Grants, 5
3 B's Fnd Grants, 7
3 Dog Garage Museum Tours, 8
3 Rivers Wet Weather Demonstration Program (3RWW) Grants, 9
3 Roots Fnd Grants, 10
3M Company Arts and Culture Grants, 12
3M Company Health and Human Services Grants, 14
3M Fnd Comm Giving Grants, 15
4imprint One by One Charitable Giving, 16
4S Ranch~Del Sur Comm Fdn Grts, 17
18th Street Arts Complex Residency Grants, 19
21st Century ILGWU Heritage Fund Grants, 20
21st Century Threshold Project Gifts, 21
41 Washington Street Fnd Grants, 22
100 Angels Charitable Fnd Grants, 24
100 Mile Man Fnd Grants, 27
118 Fnd Grants, 29
200 Club of Mercer County Grants, 30
300th Quincy Block Association Grants, 31
786 Fnd Grants, 33
1772 Fnd Fellowships, 36
A & B Family Fnd Grants, 38
A.C. Ratshesky Fnd Grants, 39
A.H.K. Fnd Grants, 40
A.J. Fletcher Fnd Grants, 41
A. J. Macdonald Fnd for Animal Welfare, 42
A.J. Muste Memorial Institute General Grants, 44
A.O. Smith Comm Grants, 46
A/H Fnd Grants, 48
AAAS Science and Tech Policy Fellowships: Health, Educ and Human Services, 53
AACC Building Better Communities Through Regional Economic Dev Partnerships, 54
AACC Plus 50 Initiative Grants, 55
AAF Accent on Architecture Comm Grants, 58
AAF Richard Riley Award, 59
AAP Access To Child Health Implementation, 63
AAP Resident Initiative Fund Grants, 69
Aaron Fnd Grants, 73
Aaron Fnd Grants, 72
AAUW Breaking through Barriers Award, 74

AAUW Comm Action Grants, 75
AAUW Int'l Project Grants, 76
Abbey Charitable Trust Grants, 78
Abbot & Dorothy H Stevens Fdn Grants, 79
Abbott Fund Access to Health Care Grants, 80
Abbott Fund Comm Grants, 81
Abbott Fund Global AIDS Care Grants, 82
Abbott Fund Science Educ Grants, 83
ABC Charities Grants, 85
Abel & Sophia Sheng Charitable Fdn Grts, 86
Abelard Fnd East Grants, 87
Abelard Fnd West Grants, 88
Abel Fnd Grants, 90
Abell-Hanger Fnd Grants, 91
Abell Fnd Arts and Culture Grants, 92
Abell Fdn Comm Dev Grts, 93
Abell Fdn Criminal Justice & Addictions Grts, 95
Abell Fnd Health & Human Svcs Grts, 96
Abell Fnd Workforce Dev Grants, 97
ABIG Fnd Grants, 99
Abington Fnd Grants, 100
Able To Serve Grants, 102
Able Trust Voc Rehab Grants for Agencies, 103
Able Trust Vocational Rehabilitation Grants for Individuals, 104
Abney Fnd Grants, 105
ABS Fnd Grants, 107
Abundance Fnd Int'l Grants, 108
Abundance Fdn Local Comm Grts, 109
ACE Charitable Fnd Grants, 111
ACF ACYF Runaway and Homeless Youth Basic Center Grants, 112
ACF Adoption Opportunities Project Grants, 113
ACF Assets for Indep Demo Grants, 114
ACF Assets for Independence Individual Dev Account Grants, 115
ACF Comm-Based Abstinence Educ Grants, 116
ACFEF Disaster Relief Fund Member Assistance, 117
ACF Ethnic Comm Self-Help Grants, 118
ACF Fnd Grants, 119
ACF Head Start and Early Head Start Grants, 120
ACF Mentoring Children of Prisoners Grants, 121
ACF Native American Social and Economic Dev Strategies Grants, 123
ACF Preferred Communities Grants, 124
ACF Supplemental Services for Recently Arrived Refugees Grants, 125
A Charitable Fnd Grants, 126
Achelis Fnd Grants, 127
A Child Waits Fnd Grants, 128
Ackerman Fnd Grants, 129
Acorn Fnd Grants, 131
ACS Award for Encouraging Disadvantaged Students into Careers in the Chemical Sciences, 132
ACTION Council of Monterey County Grants, 134
Action for Affordable Housing Grants, 135
Active Awareness Fund Grants, 136
Actors Fund Dancers' Resource, 137
Actors Fund Funeral and Burial Assistance, 138
Actors Fund Soc Svcs & Financial Assistance, 139
Acuity Charitable Fnd Grants, 140
Acushnet Fnd Grants, 143
Adam Reineman Charitable Trust Grants, 144
Adam Richter Charitable Trust Grants, 145
Adams-Mastrovich Family Fnd Grants, 146
Adams and Reese LLP Corporate Giving Grants, 147
Adams Cty Comm Fdn of Indiana Grts, 148
Adams Family Fnd I Grants, 150
Adams Family Fnd of Ohio Grants, 151
Adams Fnd Grants, 155
Adams Fnd Grants, 153
Adams Fnd Grants, 154
ADC Fnd Tech Access Grants, 158
ADEC Agricultural Telecommunications Grants, 159
Adelaide Benevolent Society Grants, 160
Adelaide Breed Bayrd Fnd Grants, 161
Adelaide Christian Home For Children Grants, 162
Adelaide Dawson Lynch Trust Grants, 163
Adler-Clark Electric Comm Commitment Grants, 164
Administaff Comm Affairs Grants, 165

PROGRAM TYPE INDEX

Adobe Art and Culture Grants, 167
Adobe Comm Investment Grants, 168
Adobe Hunger and Homelessness Grants, 169
Adobe Youth Voices Grants, 170
Adolph Coors Fnd Grants, 171
Advanced Micro Dvcs Comm Affairs Grts, 172
Advocate Safehouse Project Grants, 174
AEC Trust Grants, 175
AEGON Transamerica Fdn Arts & Culture Grts, 176
AEGON Transamerica Fdn Civic Grants, 177
AEGON Transamerica Health and Welfare Grants, 179
AEP Corporate Giving Grants, 180
Aetna Fnd Arts Grants in Connecticut, 181
Aetna Fdn Diversity Grants in Connecticut, 182
Aetna Fdn Educ Grts in Connecticut, 183
Aetna Fnd Health Grants in Connecticut, 184
Aetna Fnd Obesity Grants, 185
Aetna Fnd Racial and Ethnic Health Care Equity Grants, 186
Aetna Fnd Strengthening Neighborhhods Grants in Connecticut, 188
Aetna Fnd Volunteer Grants, 190
AFG Industries Grants, 191
African American Fund of New Jersey Grants, 192
African American Heritage Grants, 193
A Friends' Fnd Trust Grants, 194
A Fund for Women Grants, 195
Agape Fnd for Nonviolent Social Change Alice Hamburg Emergency Grants, 196
A Glimmer of Hope Fnd Grants, 200
AGMA Relief Fund Grants, 201
Agnes M. Lindsay Trust Grants, 203
A Good Neighbor Fnd Grants, 204
Agway Fnd Grants, 205
Ahearn Family Fnd Grants, 206
Ahmanson Fnd Grants, 207
AHS Fnd Grants, 208
AIChE Women's Initiatives Committee Mentorship Excellence Award, 209
Aid for Starving Children African American Independence Single Mother's Grants, 210
Aid for Starving Children Emergency Assistance Fund Grants, 211
Aid for Starving Children Int'l Grants, 212
AIG Disaster Relief Fund Grants, 213
Air Force Assoc Civil Air Patrol Unit Grts, 214
Air Force Association Junior ROTC Grants, 215
Air Products and Chemicals Grants, 216
Akonadi Fnd Anti-Racism Grants, 217
Akzo Nobel Chemicals Grants, 219
ALA Arthur Curley Memorial Lecture, 226
ALA Baker and Taylor Entertainment Audio Music/ Video Product Award, 229
ALA Baker and Taylor Summer Reading Grants, 230
Alabama Humanities Fnd Mini Grants, 231
Alabama Humanities Fnd Planning Grants, 232
Alabama Power Fnd Grants, 233
Alabama Power Plant a Tree Grants, 234
Alabama State Council on the Arts Collaborative Ventures Grants, 235
Alabama State Council on the Arts Comm Arts Collaborative Ventures Grants, 236
Alabama State Council on the Arts Comm Arts Presenting Grants, 238
Alabama State Council on the Arts Comm Arts Program Dev Grants, 239
Alabama State Council on the Arts Comm Arts Tech Assistance Grants, 240
Alabama State Council on the Arts Comm Planning & Design Grants, 241
Alabama State Council on the Arts in Educ Partnership Grants, 242
Alabama State Council on the Arts Multi-Discipline and Festival Grants, 243
Alabama State Council on the Arts Program Dev Grants, 246
ALA BWI Collection Dev Grant, 252
ALA Carnegie Corporation of New York/New York Times I Love My Librarian Award, 254
ALA Citizens-Save-Libraries Grants, 257

PROGRAM TYPE INDEX

Community Development / 1035

ALA Coretta Scott King Book Donation Grant, 261
ALA Diversity and Outreach Fair, 267
ALA EBSCO Excellence in Small and/or Rural Public Library Service Award, 273
ALA Excellence in Library Programming Award, 277
ALA Exceptional Service Award, 278
ALA Gale Cengage Learning Award for Excellence in Reference and Adult Library Services, 281
ALA Great Books Giveaway Competition, 282
ALA Innovation Award, 288
ALA John Cotton Dana Library Pub Rel Awd, 292
ALA Loleta D. Fyan Grant, 295
ALA MAE Award for Best Teen Lit Pgm, 296
ALA Maureen Hayes Author/Illustrator Award, 299
ALA President's Award for Advocacy, 310
ALA Scholastic Library Publishing National Library Week Grant, 319
Alaska Airlines Corporate Giving Grants, 320
Alaska Airlines Fnd Grants, 321
Alaska Conservation Fnd Operating Grants, 323
Alaska Conservation Fnd Opportunity Grants, 324
Alaska Conservation Fnd Rapid Response Grants, 325
Alaska Conservation Fnd Watchable Wildlife Conservation Trust Grants, 326
ALA Student Chapter of the Year Award, 331
ALA Writers Live at the Library Grants, 336
Alberta Law Fnd Grants, 338
Albert and Bessie Mae Kronkosky Charitable Fnd Grants, 339
Albert and Margaret Alkek Fnd Grants, 340
Albert B Cuppage Charitable Fdn Grts, 341
Alberto Culver Corporate Contributions Grants, 343
Albert Pick Jr. Fund Grants, 344
Albertson's Charitable Giving Grants, 345
Albert W. Rice Charitable Fnd Grants, 347
Albuquerque Comm Fnd Grants, 348
Alcatel-Lucent Technologies Fnd Grants, 349
Alcoa Fnd Grants, 350
Alcon Fnd Grants, 351
Alexander & Baldwin Fnd Hawaiian and Pacific Island Grants, 352
Alexander & Baldwin Fdn Mainland Grants, 353
Alexander and Margaret Stewart Trust Grants, 354
Alexander Eastman Fnd Grants, 355
Alexander Fnd Emergency Grants, 356
Alexander H. Bright Charitable Trust Grants, 358
Alex Stern Family Fnd Grants, 360
Alfred & Tillie Shemanski Testamentary Grants, 363
Alfred Bersted Fnd Grants, 364
Alfred J Mcallister and Dorothy N Mcallister Fnd Grants, 367
Alfred P Sloan Fdn Civic Initiatives Grts, 368
Alfred P Sloan Fdn Selected Nat'l Issues Grts, 370
Alice C. A. Sibley Fund Grants, 371
Alice Tweed Tuohy Fnd Grants, 372
A Little Hope Grants, 373
Allan C. and Leila J. Garden Fnd Grants, 374
Allegan County Comm Fnd Grants, 375
Allegheny Fnd Grants, 376
Allegheny Technologies Charitable Trust, 377
Allen Hilles Fund Grants, 378
Allen Lane Fnd Grants, 379
Allen P & Josephine B Green Fdn Grts, 380
All for the Earth Fnd Grants, 381
Alliance for Comm Trees Home Depot Fnd NeighborWoods Grants, 382
Alliant Energy Fnd Comm Grants, 384
Alliant Energy Fnd Hometown Challenge Grants, 385
Allstate Corporate Giving Grants, 386
Allstate Corp Hometown Commitment Grants, 387
Allstate Fnd Agency Hands in the Comm Grants, 388
Allstate Fdn Economic Empowerment Grants, 389
Allstate Fnd Safe and Vital Communities Grants, 390
Allstate Tolerance, Inclusion, & Diversity Grants, 391
Allyn Fnd Grants, 392
Alpha Kappa Alpha Educational Advancement Fnd Comm Assistance Awards, 393
ALSAM Fnd Grants, 395
Alticor Corporation Comm Contributions Grants, 396
Altman Fnd Health Care Grants, 397

Altman Fnd Strengthening Communities Grants, 398
Alvah H & Wyline P Chapman Fdn Grts, 402
Alvin & Fanny Blaustein Thalheimer Fdn Grts, 403
Alvin and Lucy Owsley Fnd Grants, 404
ALZA Corporate Contributions Grants, 405
AMA-MSS Chapter Involvement Grants, 406
Amador Comm Fnd Grants, 408
AMA Fdn Fund for Better Health Grts, 409
AMA Fnd Healthy Comm/Healthy Amer Grants, 410
AMA Fnd Jack B. McConnell, MD Awards for Excellence in Volunteerism, 411
Amarillo Area/Harrington Fnds Grants, 412
Ambrose and Ida Fredrickson Fnd Grants, 414
AMD Corporate Contributions Grants, 416
Amelia Sillman Rockwell and Carlos Perry Rockwell Charities Fund Grants, 417
Ameren Corporation Comm Grants, 418
American-Scandinavian Fnd Public Project Grants, 419
American Academy of Dermatology Shade Structure Grants, 420
Americana Fnd Grants, 422
American Chemical Society Chemical Tech Partnership Mini Grants, 424
American Chemical Scty Corp Assocs Seed Grts, 425
American Express Charitable Fund Grants, 429
American Express Fnd Comm Service Grants, 430
American Express Historic Preservation Grants, 431
American Express Leaders for Tomorrow Grants, 432
American Foodservice Charitable Trust Grants, 433
American Forests Global ReLeaf Grants, 434
American Fnd Grants, 436
American Gas Fnd Grants, 437
American Honda Fnd Grants, 439
American Humane Association 2nd Chance Grants, 440
American Jewish World Service Grants, 441
American Schlafhorst Fnd Grants, 446
American Sociological Assoc Sydney S Spivack Pgm in Applied Social Rsch & Social Policy, 450
America the Beautiful Fund Operation Green Plant Grants, 451
Amerigroup Fnd Grants, 452
AMERIND Comm Service Project Grants, 453
AmerUs Group Charitable Fnd, 455
Amgen Fnd Grants, 456
AMI Semiconductors Corporate Grants, 457
Amon G. Carter Fnd Grants, 458
Andersen Corporate Fnd, 459
Anderson Fnd Grants, 460
Andre Agassi Charitable Fnd Grants, 461
Andrew Family Fnd Grants, 462
Andrew Goodman Fnd Grants, 463
Angels Baseball Fnd Grants, 465
Angels On Track Fnd Grants, 468
Anheuser-Busch Fnd Grants, 470
ANLAF Int'l Fund for Sexual Minorities Grts, 471
Anna Fitch Ardenghi Trust Grants, 472
Ann & Robert H Lurie Family Fdn Grants, 473
Ann Arbor Area Comm Fnd Grants, 474
Anne J. Caudal Fnd Grants, 475
Anne L. and George H. Clapp Charitable and Educational Trust Grants, 476
Anne Thorne Weaver Family Fnd Grants, 478
Annie's Cases for Causes Product Donations, 479
Annie's Grants for Gardens, 480
Annie E. Casey Fnd Grants, 481
Annie Sinclair Knudsen Memorial Fund/Kaua'i Comm Grants, 482
Ann L. and Carol Green Rhodes Charitable Grants, 483
Annunziata Sanguinetti Fnd Grants, 485
Ansell, Zaro, Grimm & Aaron Fdn Grts, 487
Antone & Edene Vidinha Char Trust Grts, 490
Appalachian Comm Fund Gen Fund Grts, 493
Appalachian Comm Fund GLBTQ Grants, 494
Appalachian Comty Fund Media Justice Grts, 495
Appalachian Comm Seize the Moment Grants, 496
Appalachian Comm Fund Special Opps Grants, 497
Appalachian Comm Fund Tech Assistance Grants, 498
Appalachian Regional Commission Asset-Based Dev Project Grants, 500

Appalachian Regional Commission Business Dev Revolving Loan Fund Grants, 501
Appalachian Regional Commission Comm Infrastructure Grants, 502
Appalachian Regional Commission Distressed Counties Grants, 503
Appalachian Regional Commission Educ and Training Grants, 504
Appalachian Reg'l Commission Energy Grts, 505
Appalachian Regional Commission Export and Trade Dev Grants, 506
Appalachian Regional Comm Health Care Grants, 507
Appalachian Reg'l Commission Housing Grts, 508
Appalachian Regional Commission Leadership Dev and Capacity Building Grants, 509
Appalachian Regional Commission Telecommunications Grants, 510
Appalachian Regional Commission Tourist Grants, 511
Appalachian Regional Commission Transportation and Highways Grants, 512
Applied Biosystems Grants, 514
Applied Materials Corp Philanthropy Pgm, 515
APSAA Fnd Grants, 516
APS Fnd Grants, 518
Aquila Corporate Grants, 521
Aragona Family Fnd Grants, 522
Aratani Fnd Grants, 523
Arbor Day Fnd Grants, 524
Arcadia Fnd Grants, 525
Arca Fnd Grants, 526
Archer Daniels Midland Fnd Grants, 527
Arcus Fnd Fund Grants, 529
Arcus Fnd Gay and Lesbian Fund Grants, 530
Arcus Fnd National Fund Grants, 531
Argyros Fnd Grants, 532
Arizona Cardinals Grants, 534
Arizona Commission on the Arts After-School Program Residencies, 535
Arizona Comm on Arts Folklorist Residencies, 537
Arizona Comm Fnd Grants, 540
Arizona Diamondbacks Charities Grants, 542
Arizona Fnd for Women Deborah G. Carstens Fund Grants, 543
Arizona Fnd for Women General Grants, 544
Arizona Public Service Corp Gvg Pgm Grts, 545
Arizona Republic Fnd Grants, 546
Arizona Republic Newspaper Corp Contribs, 547
Arizona State Library LSTA Collections Grants, 548
Arizona State Library LSTA Comm Grants, 549
Arizona State Library LSTA Learning Grants, 550
Arkansas Arts Council Expansion Arts Grants, 556
Arkansas Comm Fnd Arkansas Black Hall of Fame Grants, 559
Arkansas Comm Fnd Giving Tree Grants, 560
Arkansas Comm Fnd Grants, 561
Arkell Hall Fnd Grants, 562
Arlington Comm Fnd Grants, 564
Armstrong McDonald Fnd Grants, 565
A Rocha USA Grants, 566
ARTBA Transportation Dev Fnd Grants, 569
Arthur and Sara Jo Kobacker, Alfred and Ida Kobacker Fnd Grants, 571
Arthur Ashley Williams Fnd Grants, 572
Arthur B. Schultz Fnd Grants, 573
Arthur F & Alice E Adams Charitable Fdn Grts, 574
Artist Trust GAP Grants, 575
Arts Fnd, 578
ArvinMeritor Fdn Arts & Culture Grts, 582
ArvinMeritor Fnd Civic Grants, 583
ArvinMeritor Fdn Human Svcs Grts, 584
ArvinMeritor Grants, 585
Ashland Corporate Contributions Grants, 587
Asian American Institute Impact Fellowships, 588
Aspen Comm Fnd Grants, 592
Assisi Fnd of Memphis General Grants, 594
Assisi Fnd of Memphis Mini Grants, 595
Assurant Health Fnd Grants, 596
ASTA Academic Scholarships, 597
As You Sow, 598
AT&T Fnd Civic and Comm Service Grants, 599

1036 / Community Development

ATA Local Comm Relations Grants, 600
ATA Political Engagement Grant, 601
ATF Gang Resistance Educ and Training Program Cooperative Agreements, 603
Atherton Family Fnd Grants, 604
Athwin Fnd Grants, 605
Atkinson Fnd Comm Grants, 606
Atlanta Fnd Grants, 608
Atlanta Women's Fnd Grants, 609
Auburn Fnd Grants, 611
Audrey and Sydney Irmas Charitable Fnd Grants, 612
Aurora Fnd Grants, 613
Austin Comm Fnd Grants, 616
Austin S. Nelson Fnd Grants, 617
Autauga Area Comm Fnd Grants, 618
Autodesk Comm Relations Grants, 619
AutoZone Comm Relations Grants, 621
Avery Dennison Fnd Grants, 623
Avista Fnd Grants, 624
AWDF Main Grants, 627
AWDF Solidarity Fund Grants, 628
Ayres Fnd Grants, 630
Babcock Charitable Trust Grants, 632
Back Home Again Fnd Grants, 633
Bacon Family Fnd Grants, 634
Bailey Fnd Grants, 635
Balfe Family Fnd Grants, 636
Ball Brothers Fnd General Grants, 637
Ball Brothers Fnd Organizational Effectiveness/ Executive Mentoring Grants, 638
Ball Brothers Fnd Rapid Grants, 639
Baltimore Comm Fnd Arts and Culture Grants, 641
Baltimore Comm Fnd Children's Fresh Air Society Fund Grants, 642
Baltimore Comm Fnd Environment Path Grants, 643
Baltimore Comm Fnd Human Services Grants, 644
Baltimore Comm Fnd Kelly People's Emergency Fund Grants, 645
Baltimore Comm Fnd Neighborhood Grants, 646
Baltimore Comm Fnd Neighborhoods Path Grants, 647
Baltimore Comm Fnd Transportation Path Grants, 648
Baltimore Comm Fnd Youth Path Grants, 649
Baltimore Women's Giving Circle Grants, 650
BancorpSouth Fnd Grants, 651
Banfi Vintners Fnd Grants, 653
BankAtlantic Fnd Grants, 654
Bank of America Comm Dev Grants, 655
Bank of America Critical Needs Grants, 656
Bank of America Charitable Fnd Educ and Workforce Dev Grants, 657
Bank of America Charitable Fnd Matching Gifts, 658
Bank of America Charitable Fnd Student Leaders Grants, 659
Bank of America Charitable Fnd Volunteer Grants, 660
Bank of America Corporation Sponsorships, 661
Baptist-Trinity Lutheran Legacy Fdn Grants, 663
Baptist Comm Ministries Grants, 664
Barbara Meyer Elsner Fnd Grants, 665
Barberton Comm Fnd Grants, 666
Baring Fnd Grants, 667
Barker Fnd Grants, 668
Barker Welfare Fnd Grants, 669
Barnes and Noble National Sponsorships and Charitable Donations, 671
Barnes Group Fnd Grants, 672
Barra Fnd Comm Fund Grants, 673
Barra Fnd Project Grants, 674
Barrasso Usdin Kupperman Freeman and Sarver LLC Corporate Grants, 675
Barr Fnd Grants (Massachusetts), 676
Barr Fnd Grants , 677
Barr Fund Grants, 678
Batchelor Fnd Grants, 679
Baton Rouge Area Fnd Grants, 682
Battle Creek Comm Fnd Grants, 684
Battle Creek Comm Fdn Mini-Grants, 685
Battle Creek Comm Fnd Neighborhood Grants, 686
Batts Fnd Grants, 687
Baughman Fnd Grants, 688
Baxter Int'l Corporate Giving Grants, 689

Baxter Int'l Fnd Grants, 691
Bay and Paul Fnds, Inc Grants, 692
Bayer Advanced Grow Together with Roses School Garden Awards, 695
Bayer Fnd Grants, 696
BBF Maine Family Lit Initiative Planning Grants, 699
BBF Maryland Family Lit Initiative Implementation Grants, 700
BBF Maryland Family Lit Planning Grants, 701
BBF National Grants for Family Lit, 702
BBVA Compass Fnd Charitable Grants, 703
BCBSM Building Healthy Communities Engaging Elementary Schools & Comm Partners, 704
BCBSM Corporate Contributions Grants, 706
BCBSM Fnd Comm Health Matching Grants, 707
BCBSM Fodn Investigator Initiated Rsch Grts, 708
BCBSM Fdn Proposal Dev Awds, 709
BCBSNC Fnd Grants, 712
BCBS of Massachusetts Fnd Grants, 713
Beazley Fnd Grants, 714
Bechtel Group Fnd Building Positive Comm Relationships Grants, 715
Beckley Area Fnd Grants, 716
Beerman Fnd Grants, 717
Beim Fnd Grants, 718
Beirne Carter Fnd Grants, 719
Beldon Fund Grants, 720
Bemis Company Fnd Grants, 723
Ben & Jerry's Fnd Grants, 724
Ben B. Cheney Fnd Grants, 725
Bender Fnd Grants, 726
Beneficia Fnd Grants, 727
Bennett Family Fnd of Texas Grants, 728
Benton Comm Fnd - The Cookie Jar Grant, 729
Benton Comm Fnd Grants, 730
Benton County Fnd Grants, 731
Benwood Fnd Comm Grants, 732
Benwood Fnd Focus Area Grants, 733
Berks County Comm Fnd Grants, 734
Bernard and Audre Rapoport Fnd Arts and Culture Grants, 735
Bernard and Audre Rapoport Fnd Comm Building and Social Service Grants, 736
Bernard and Audre Rapoport Fnd Democracy and Civic Participation Grants, 737
Bernard and Audre Rapoport Fnd Health Grants, 738
Bernard and Audre Rapoport Fnd University of Texas at Austin Scholarships, 739
Bernard F. Reynolds Charitable Trust Grants, 741
Bernard Osher Fnd Grants, 742
Bernice Barbour Fnd Grants, 743
Berrien Comm Fnd Grants, 744
Bertha Wolf-Rosenthal Comm Service Stipend, 746
Besser Fnd Grants, 748
Best Buy Children's Fnd @15 Comm Grants, 749
Best Buy Children's Fnd @15 Scholarship, 750
Best Buy Children's Fdn @15 Teach Awards, 751
Best Buy Children's Fnd National Grants, 752
Best Buy Children's Fnd Twin Cities Minnesota Capital Grants, 753
Better Way Fnd Grants, 754
Better World Books LEAP Grants for Libraries, 755
Better World Bks LEAP Grts for Nonprofits, 756
Beverley Taylor Sorenson Art Wks for Kids Grts, 757
BHHS Legacy Fnd Grants, 758
Bicknell Fund Grants, 759
Bikes Belong Fnd Paul David Clark Bicycling Safety Grants, 760
Bikes Belong Fnd REI Grants, 761
Bikes Belong Fnd Research Grants, 762
Bikes Belong Grants, 763
Bill and Katie Weaver Charitable Trust Grants, 764
Bill and Melinda Gates Ag Dev Grants, 765
Bill and Melinda Gates Fnd Emergency Response Grants, 766
Bill and Melinda Gates Fnd Financial Services for the Poor Grants, 767
Bill & Melinda Gates Fdn Library Grts, 768
Bill and Melinda Gates Fnd Policy and Advocacy Grants, 769

PROGRAM TYPE INDEX

Bill and Melinda Gates Fnd Water, Sanitation and Hygiene Grants, 770
Bingham McHale LLP Pro Bono Services, 772
Biogen Corporate Giving Grants, 773
Birmingham Fnd Grants, 774
Bitha Godfrey & Maude J. Thomas Charitable Fnd Grants, 776
BJ's Charitable Fnd Grants, 777
BJ's Wholesale Clubs Local Charitable Giving, 778
Blackford Cty Comm Fdn Grts, 780
Black Hills Corporation Grants, 781
Black River Falls Area Fnd Grants, 782
Blanche and Irving Laurie Fnd Grants, 784
Blanche & Julian Robertson Family Fdn Grants, 785
Blandin Fdn Expand Opportunity Grants, 787
Blandin Fnd Invest Early Grants, 788
Blandin Fnd Itasca County Area Vitality Grants, 789
Blandin Fnd Rural Comm Leadership Grants, 790
Bloomington Area Arts Council Grants, 791
Blue Cross Blue Shield of Minnesota Fdn Health Equity: Bldg Health Equity Together Grts, 793
Blue Cross Blue Shield of Minnesota Fdn Healthy Equity: Health Impact Assessment Grts, 796
Blue Cross Blue Shield of Minnesota Fdn-Healthy Equity: Public Libraries for Health Grts, 797
Blue Cross Blue Shield of Minnesota Neighborhoods: Connect for Health Challenge Grants, 798
Blue Grass Comm Fnd Grants, 799
Blue Mountain Comm Fnd Grants, 800
Blue River Comm Fnd Grants, 801
Blum-Kovler Fnd Grants, 803
Blumenthal Fnd Grants, 804
BoatUS Fnd Grassroots Grants, 805
Bodenwein Public Benevolent Fdn Grants, 806
Bodman Fnd Grants, 807
Boeing Company Contributions Grants, 809
Boettcher Fnd Grants, 810
Bohemian Fnd Pharos Fund Grants, 811
Bonfils-Stanton Fnd Grants, 814
Booth Ferris Fnd Grants, 816
Boston Fnd Grants, 819
Boston Globe Fnd Grants, 821
Boulder County Arts Alliance Neodata Endowment Grants, 823
Bowling Green Comm Fnd Grants, 824
Boyd Gaming Corporation Contributions, 825
Brad Brock Family Fnd Grants, 827
Bradley-Turner Fnd Grants, 828
Brainerd Fnd Grants, 831
Bread and Roses Comm Fund Grants, 832
Brian G. Dyson Fnd Grants, 834
Brico Fund Grants, 835
Bridgestone/Firestone Trust Fund Grants, 836
Bright Family Fnd Grants, 837
Bright Promises Fnd Grants, 838
Bristol-Myers Squibb Fnd Comm Grants, 840
Brookdale Fnd National Group Respite Grts, 845
Brookdale Fnd Relatives as Parents Grts, 846
Brooklyn Benevolent Society Grants, 847
Brooklyn Comty Fdn Caring Neighbors Grts, 848
Brooklyn Comm Fnd Comm Arts for All Grants, 849
Brooklyn Comm Fnd Comm Dev Grants, 850
Brooklyn Comm Fnd Educ and Youth Achievement Grants, 851
Brooklyn Comm Fnd Green Communities Grants, 852
Brown County Comm Fnd Grants, 853
Brown Fnd Grants, 854
Brunswick Fnd Dollars for Doers Grants, 856
Bryan Adams Fnd Grants, 858
Build-A-Bear Workshop Bear Hugs Fnd Lit and Educ Grants, 860
Build-A-Bear Workshop Fnd Grants, 861
Bunbury Company Grants, 863
Burlington Industries Fnd Grants, 865
Burlington Northern Santa Fe Fnd Grants, 866
Burning Fnd Grants, 867
Burton D. Morgan Adult Entrepreneurship Grants, 868
Burton D Morgan Fdn Hudson Comty Grts, 869
Burton D Morgan Youth Entrepreneurship Grants, 870
Burton G. Bettingen Grants, 871

PROGRAM TYPE INDEX

Community Development / 1037

Bush Fnd Arts & Humanities Grants: Short-Term Organizational Support, 873
Bush Fnd Ecological Health Grants, 874
Bush Fdn Health & Human Svcs Grts, 875
Bush Fnd Leadership Fellowships, 876
Bush Fnd Medical Fellowships, 877
Bush Fnd Regional Arts Dev Program II Grants, 878
Business Bank of Nevada Comm Grants, 879
Butler Mfg Co Fnd Grants, 881
Bydale Fnd Grants, 882
Byerly Fnd Grants, 883
Cable Positive's Tony Cox Comm Fund, 886
Cabot Corporation Fnd Grants, 887
Caddock Fnd Grants, 888
Caesars Fnd Grants, 891
Caleb C. and Julia W. Dula Educational and Charitable Fnd Grants, 893
California Arts Council State-Local Partnership Grants, 896
California Arts Council Statewide Ntwks Grts, 897
California Arts Council Tech Assistance Grts, 898
California Comm Fnd Art Grants, 900
California Comm Fnd Health Care Grants, 901
California Comm Fnd Human Dev Grants, 902
California Comm Fnd Neighborhood Revitalization Grants, 903
California Endowment Innovative Ideas Challenge Grants, 904
California Fertilizer Fnd School Garden Grants, 905
Calif Green Trees for The Golden State Grt, 906
California State Parks Restor & Cleanup Grants, 908
Callaway Fnd Grants, 909
Callaway Golf Company Fnd Grants, 910
Cal Ripken Sr. Fnd Grants, 912
Cambridge Comm Fnd Grants, 913
Camp-Younts Fnd Grants, 914
Campbell Hoffman Fnd Grants, 915
Campbell Soup Fnd Grants, 916
Canada-U.S. Fulbright Mid-Career Prof Grants, 917
Cape Branch Fnd Grants, 919
Capital City Bank Group Fnd Grants, 920
Capital Region Comm Fnd Grants, 921
CarEth Fnd Grants, 924
Cargill Citizenship Fund-Corp Gvg Grants, 925
Caring Fnd Grants, 926
Carl & Eloise Pohlad Family Fdn Grants, 927
Carl B. and Florence E. King Fnd Grants, 928
Carl C. Icahn Fnd Grants, 929
Carl Gellert and Celia Berta Gellert Fdn Grts, 930
Carlisle Fnd Grants, 931
Carl M. Freeman Fnd FACES Grants, 932
Carl M. Freeman Fnd Grants, 933
Carl R. Hendrickson Family Fnd Grants, 935
Carlsbad Charitable Fnd Grants, 936
Carl W. and Carrie Mae Joslyn Trust Grants, 938
Carnahan-Jackson Fnd Grants, 939
Carnegie Corporation of New York Grants, 940
Carolyn Fnd Grants, 942
Carpenter Fnd Grants, 943
Carrie E. and Lena V. Glenn Fnd Grants, 944
Carrie Estelle Doheny Fnd Grants, 945
Carrier Corporation Contributions Grants, 946
Carroll County Comm Fnd Grants, 947
Case Fnd Grants, 950
Cash 4 Clubs Sports Grants, 951
Cass County Comm Fnd Grants, 952
Castle and Cooke California Corp Giving, 953
Caterpillar Fnd Grants, 954
Catherine Kennedy Home Fnd Grants, 955
Catherine Manley Gaylord Fnd Grants, 956
Cause Populi Worthy Cause Grants, 958
CCF Comm Priorities Fund, 961
CCFF Comm Grant, 962
CCF Grassroots Exchange Fund Grants, 963
CCF Social and Economic Justice Fund Grants, 964
CCH California Story Fund Grants, 965
CCHD Comm Dev Grants, 966
CCHD Economic Dev Grants, 967
CCH Documentary California Reads Grants, 968
CCH Documentary Public Engagement Grants, 970

CCH Documentary Research and Dev Grants, 971
CDC Fdn Emergency Response Fund Grts, 972
CDC State and Local Childhood Lead Poisoning Prevention Grants, 976
CDECD Arts Catalyze Placemaking in Every Comm Grants, 977
CDECD Arts Catalyze Placemaking Leadership Grants, 978
CDECD Arts Catalyze Placemaking Sustaining Relevance Grants, 979
CDECD Historic Preservation Survey and Planning Grants, 982
CDECD Tourism Product Dev Grants, 984
CE and S Fnd Grants, 985
Ceil & Michael E. Pulitzer Fnd Grants, 987
Cemala Fnd Grants, 988
Center for Venture Philanthropy, 991
CenterPointEnergy Minnegasco Grants, 993
Central Carolina Comm Impact Grants, 994
Central Minnesota Comm Fdn Grants, 995
Central New York Comm Fdn Grants, 996
Central Okanagan Fnd Grants, 997
CenturyLink Clarke M Williams Fdn Grants, 998
Ceres Fnd Grants, 999
Cessna Fnd Grants, 1000
CFFVR Alcoholism and Drug Abuse Grants, 1001
CFFVR Basic Needs Gvg Partnership Grts, 1002
CFFVR Capacity Building Grants, 1004
CFFVR Capital Credit Union Charitable Giving Grants, 1005
CFFVR Chilton Area Comm Fnd Grants, 1006
CFFVR Clintonville Area Fnd Grants, 1008
CFFVR Clintonville Area Fnd Grants, 1007
CFFVR Doug & Carla Salmon Fdn Grts, 1009
CFFVR Environmental Stewardship Grants, 1010
CFFVR Fox Valley Comm Arts Grants, 1011
CFFVR Frank C. Shattuck Comm Grants, 1012
CFFVR Infant Welfare Circle of Kings Daughters Grants, 1013
CFFVR Jewelers Mutual Char Gvg Grts, 1014
CFFVR Mielke Family Fnd Grants, 1015
CFFVR Myra M. & Robert L. Vandehey Grants, 1016
CFFVR Project Grants, 1017
CFFVR Robert and Patricia Endries Family Fnd Grants, 1018
CFFVR SAC Dev Disabilities Grts, 1019
CFFVR Schmidt Family G4 Grants, 1020
CFFVR Shawano Area Comm Fnd Grants, 1021
CFFVR Sikora Family Memorial Grants, 1022
CFFVR Waupaca Area Comm Fnd Grants, 1023
CFFVR Wisconsin Daughters and Sons Grants, 1024
CFFVR Women's Fund for the Fox Valley Region Grants, 1025
CFNCR Starbucks Memorial Fund, 1026
Chamberlain Fnd Grants, 1027
Champ-A Champion Fur Kids Grants, 1028
Champlin Fnds Grants, 1029
Chapman Charitable Fnd Grants, 1033
Charity Incorporated Grants, 1035
CharityWorks Grants, 1036
Charles A. Frueauff Fnd Grants, 1037
Charles Delmar Fnd Grants, 1039
Charles F. Bacon Trust Grants, 1040
Charles G. Koch Charitable Fnd Grants, 1041
Charles H. Dater Fnd Grants, 1042
Charles H. Farnsworth Trust Grants, 1043
Charles H. Hall Fnd, 1044
Charles H. Pearson Fnd Grants, 1045
Charles H. Revson Fnd Grants, 1047
Charles Hayden Fnd Grants, 1048
Charles Lafitte Fnd Grants, 1049
Charles M & Mary D Grant Fdn Grants, 1050
Charles M. Bair Family Trust Grants, 1051
Charles Nelson Robinson Fund Grants, 1052
Chas Parker Trust for Public Music Fund Grts, 1053
Charles Stewart Mott Fdn Anti-Poverty Grts, 1054
Charles Stewart Mott Fnd Grants, 1055
Charlotte County Comm Fdn Grts, 1056
Charlotte Martin Fnd Youth Grants, 1057
Charlotte R. Schmidlapp Fund Grants, 1058

Chatham Athletic Fnd Grants, 1060
Chatlos Fnd Grants, 1061
Chautauqua Region Comm Fdn Grts, 1062
CHCF Grants, 1063
CHC Fnd Grants, 1065
Chefs Move to Schools Grants, 1066
Chemtura Corporation Contributions Grants, 1067
Chesapeake Bay Trust Capacity Bldg Grts, 1068
Chesapeake Bay Environmental Educ Grants, 1069
Chesapeake Bay Fisheries and Headwaters Grants, 1070
Chesapeake Bay Trust Forestry Mini Grants, 1071
Chesapeake Bay Trust Mini Grants, 1072
Chesapeake Bay Trust Outreach and Comm Engagement Grants, 1073
Chesapeake Bay Trust Pioneer Grants, 1074
Chesapeake Bay Trust Restoration Grants, 1075
Chesapeake Corporation Fnd Grants, 1076
Chevron Hawaii Educ Fund, 1077
Chicago Board of Trade Fnd Grants, 1079
Chicago CityArts Grants, 1080
Chicago Comm Arts Assistance Grants, 1081
Chicago Comm Trust Arts & Culture Grts: Improving Access to Arts Lrng Opportunities, 1082
Chicago Comm Trust Arts and Culture Grants: SMART Growth, 1083
Chicago Comm Trust Arts and Culture Grants: Supporting Diverse Arts Productions and Fostering Art in Every Comm, 1084
Chicago Comty Trust Educ Grts Priority 2, 1085
Chicago Comm Trust Fellowships, 1086
Chicago Comm Trust Health Grants, 1087
Chicago Comm Trust Housing Grants: Advancing Affordable Rental Housing, 1088
Chicago Comm Trust Hsg Grants: Preserving Hm Ownership & Preventing Foreclosure, 1089
Chicago Comm Trust Housing Grants: Preventing and Ending Homelessness, 1090
Chicago Comm Trust Poverty Alleviation Grants, 1091
Chicago Comm Trust Preventing and Eliminating Hunger Grants, 1092
Chicago Comm Pub Safety & Justice Grants, 1093
Chicago Comm Trust Workforce Grants, 1094
Chicago Cultural Outreach Grants, 1095
Chicago Fnd for Women Grants, 1096
Chicago Neighborhood Arts Grants, 1097
Chicago Sun Times Charity Trust Grants, 1098
Chicago Title & Trust Co Fdn Grants, 1099
Chicago Tribune Fnd Civic Grants, 1100
Chicago Tribune Grants Cultural Organizations, 1101
Chicago White Metal Charitable Fdn Grants, 1102
Child's Dream Grants, 1104
Children Affected by AIDS Fnd Camp Network Grants, 1106
Children Affected by AIDS Fnd Family Assistance Emergency Fund Grants, 1107
Chiles Fnd Grants, 1108
Chiquita Brands Int'l Grants, 1110
Christian Science Society of Boonville Irrevocable Trust, 1113
Christine and Katharina Pauly Charitable Grants, 1114
Christy-Houston Fnd Grants, 1115
Chula Vista Charitable Fnd Grants, 1116
CICF Christmas Fund, 1117
CICF City of Noblesville Comm Grant, 1118
CICF Clare Noyes Grant, 1119
CICF Efroymson Grants, 1120
CICF F.R. Hensel Grant for Fine Arts, Music, and Education, 1121
CICF Howard Intermill and Marion Intermill Fenstermaker Grants, 1122
CICF Indianapolis Fdn Comm Grants, 1123
CICF James Proctor Grant Aged Men & Women, 1124
CICF Jn Harrison Brown & Robert Burse Grt, 1125
CICF Legacy Fund Grants, 1126
CICF Senior Grants, 1127
CICF Summer Youth Grants, 1128
Cigna Civic Affairs Sponsorships, 1129
Cincinnati Bell Fnd Grants, 1131
Cincinnati Milacron Fnd Grants, 1132
Cinergy Fnd Grants, 1133

CIRCLE Civic Educ at the High School Level Research Grants, 1135
Circle K Corporation Contributions Grants, 1136
Cisco Systems Fnd San Jose Comm Grants, 1137
CIT Corporate Giving Grants, 1138
Citigroup Fnd Grants, 1139
Citizens Bank Mid-Atlantic Char Fdn Grts, 1140
Civic Educ Consortium Grants, 1144
Claneil Fnd Grants, 1145
Clara Abbott Fnd Need-Based Grants, 1146
Clara Blackford Smith and W. Aubrey Smith Charitable Fnd Grants, 1147
Clarcor Fnd Grants, 1148
Claremont Comm Fnd Grants, 1149
Clarence E Heller Charitable Fdn Grants, 1150
Clarence T.C. Ching Fnd Grants, 1151
Clark-Winchcole Fnd Grants, 1152
Clark and Carolyn Adams Fnd Grants, 1153
Clark and Ruby Baker Fnd Grants, 1154
Clark County Comm Fnd Grants, 1156
Clark Fnd Grants, 1157
Claude A. and Blanche McCubbin Abbott Charitable Trust Grants, 1158
Claude Bennett Family Fnd Grants, 1159
Claude Worthington Benedum Fdn Grants, 1161
Clay Fnd Grants, 1162
Cleo Fnd Grants, 1164
Cleveland-Cliffs Fnd Grants, 1165
Cleveland Fnd Comm Responsive Grants, 1168
Cleveland Fnd Fenn Educational Fund Grants, 1169
Cleveland Fdn Lake-Geauga Fund Grts, 1170
Cleveland Fnd Neighborhood Connections Grants, 1171
Cleveland H. Dodge Fnd Grants, 1172
CLIF Bar Family Fnd Grants, 1173
Clinton County Comm Fnd Grants, 1174
Clipper Ship Fnd Grants, 1175
Clorox Company Fnd Grants, 1176
Clowes Fund Grants, 1177
CMA Fnd Grants, 1178
CNA Fnd Grants, 1179
CNCS AmeriCorps Indian Tribes Plng Grts, 1180
CNCS AmeriCorps NCCC Project Grants, 1181
CNCS AmeriCorps State and National Grants, 1182
CNCS AmeriCorps State & Nat Planning Grants, 1183
CNCS AmeriCorps VISTA Project Grants, 1184
CNCS Foster Grandparent Projects Grants, 1185
CNCS School Turnaround AmeriCorps Grants, 1186
CNCS Senior Companion Grants, 1187
CNCS Senior Corps Retired and Senior Volunteer Grants, 1188
CNCS Social Innovation Grants, 1189
CNL Corporate Giving Arts & Culture Grants, 1190
CNL Corporate Giving Entrepreneurship & Leadership Grants, 1191
Coastal Bend Comm Fnd Grants, 1192
Coastal Comm Fdn of SC Grants, 1193
Cobb Family Fnd Grants, 1194
Coca-Cola Fnd Grants, 1195
Cockrell Fnd Grants, 1196
Coeta and Donald Barker Fnd Grants, 1197
Cogswell Benevolent Trust Grants, 1198
Coleman Fnd Cancer Care Grants, 1199
Coleman Fnd Deval Disabilities Grants, 1200
Colgate-Palmolive Company Grants, 1202
Collective Brands Fnd Grants, 1206
Collective Brands Fnd Payless Gives Shoes Grants, 1207
Collins C. Diboll Private Fnd Grants, 1208
Collins Fnd Grants, 1209
Colonel Stanley R. McNeil Fnd Grants, 1210
Colorado Bioscience Discovery Eval Grts, 1211
Colorado Clean Enrg Fd Solar Innovation Grts, 1212
Colorado Interstate Gas Grants, 1213
Colorado Renewables in Performance Contracting Grants, 1214
Colorado Springs Cmty Trust Fund Grants, 1215
Colorado Trust Grants, 1216
Columbia Gas of Virginia Grants, 1218
Columbus Fnd Competitive Grants, 1220
Columbus Fnd Dorothy E. Ann Fund (D.E.A.F.) Traditional Grants, 1221
Columbus Fnd John W. and Edna McManus Shepard Fund Grants, 1223
Columbus Fnd Joseph A. Jeffrey Endowment Fund Grants, 1224
Columbus Fdn Neighborhood Partnership Grts, 1226
Columbus Fnd Paul G. Duke Grants, 1227
Columbus Fnd R. Alvin Stevenson Fund Grants, 1228
Columbus Fnd Robert E. and Genevieve B. Schaefer Fund Grants, 1229
Columbus Fnd Scotts Miracle-Gro Comm Garden Academy Fund Grants, 1230
Columbus Fnd Siemer Family Grants, 1231
Columbus Fnd Small Grants, 1232
Columbus Fnd Traditional Grants, 1233
Columbus Jewish Fnd Grants, 1234
Comcast Fnd Grants, 1235
Comerica Charitable Fnd Grants, 1237
Commission on Religion in Appalachia Grants, 1238
Commonwealth Edison Grants, 1240
Communities Fnd of Texas Grants, 1243
Comm Dev Financial Institution Bank Enterprise Awards, 1244
Comm Fnd AIDS Endwt Awds, 1245
Comm Fnd Alliance City of Evansville Endowment Fund Grants, 1246
Comm Fdn for Grtr Buffalo Grants, 1247
Comm Fnd for Greater New Haven $5,000 and Under Grants, 1248
Comm Fnd for Greater New Haven Neighborhood Small Grants, 1249
Comm Fnd for Greater New Haven Quinnipiac River Fund Grants, 1250
Comm Fnd for Greater New Haven Responsive New Grants, 1251
Comm Fnd for Greater New Haven Grants, 1252
Comm Fnd for Greater New Haven Valley Neighborhood Grants, 1253
Comm Fnd for Greater New Haven Women & Girls Grants, 1254
Comm Fdn for Monterey Cty Grants, 1255
Comm Fdn for Muskegon Cty Grants, 1256
Comm Fdn for NE Michigan Grants, 1257
Comm Fdn for San Benito County Grants, 1258
Comm Fdn for SE Michigan Grants, 1259
Comm Fdn for SE Michigan HOPE Fund Grants, 1260
Comm Fnd for Southern Arizona Grants, 1261
Comm Fdn in Jacksonville Art Ventures Small Arts Orgs Professional Assistance Grts, 1262
Comm Fnd in Jacksonville Senior Roundtable Aging Adults Grants, 1263
Comm Fnd of Abilene Comm Grts, 1264
Comm Fnd of Abilene Future Fund Grants, 1265
Comm Fnd of Abilene Humane Treatment of Animals Grants, 1266
Comm Fnd of Bartholomew County Heritage Fund Grants, 1267
Comm Fnd of Bartholomew County Women's Giving Circle, 1269
Comm Fdn of Bloomington & Monroe Cty-Precision Health Ntwk Cycle Grts, 1270
Comm Fnd of Bloomington and Monroe County Grants, 1271
Comm Fnd of Boone County - Adult Lit Initiative Grants, 1272
Comm Fdn of Boone County Grants, 1274
Comm Fnd of Broward Grants, 1275
Comm Fdn of Central Illinois Grants, 1276
Comm Fnd of Collier County Capacity Building Grants, 1277
Comm Fdn of E Ctrl Illinois Grts, 1278
Comm Fdn of Grant Cty Grants, 1279
Comm Fdn of Grtr Birmingham Grants, 1280
Comm Fdn of Greater Chattanooga Grants, 1281
Comm Fdn of Greater Flint Grants, 1282
Comm Fnd of Greater Fort Wayne - Barbara Burt Leadership Dev Grants, 1283
Comm Fnd of Greater Fort Wayne - Collaborative Efforts Grants, 1284
Comm Fnd of Greater Fort Wayne - Cmty Endwt & Clarke Endwt Grants, 1285
Comm Fnd of Greater Fort Wayne Edna Grants, 1286
Comm Fdn of Grtr Fort Wayne - John S & James L Knight Fdn Donor-Advised Grts, 1287
Comm Fnd of Greater Greensboro Grants, 1288
Comm Fdn of Grtr Lafayette Grts, 1289
Comm Fdn of Greater Memphis Grts, 1290
Comm Fdn of Grtr New Britain Grts, 1291
Comm Fdn of Greater Tampa Grts, 1292
Comm Fnd of Greenville-Greenville Women Giving Grants, 1293
Comm Fnd of Greenville Enrichment Grants, 1294
Comm Fnd of Greenville Hollingsworth Funds Program/Project Grants, 1296
Comm Fdn of Howard County Grts, 1297
Comm Fdn of Jackson County Grts, 1298
Comm Fdn of Louisville Grants, 1299
Comm Fdn of Mdl Tennessee Grants, 1300
Comm Fnd of Mt Vernon & Knox County Grants, 1301
Comm Fnd of Muncie & Delaware County Grant, 1302
Comm Fnd of Muncie and Delaware County Maxon Grants, 1303
Comm Fdn of Riverside County Grts, 1304
Comm Fnd of Santa Cruz County Grants, 1305
Comm Fdn of Sarasota County Grts, 1306
Comm Fnd of Shreveport-Bossier Grts, 1307
Comm Fdn of S Alabama Grants, 1308
Comm Fdn of SE Connecticut Grants, 1309
Comm Fdn of Southern Indiana Grts, 1310
Comm Fnd of South Puget Sound Grants, 1311
Comm Fnd of St. Joseph County African American Comm Grants, 1312
Comm Fnd of St. Joseph County ArtsEverywhere Grants, 1313
Comm Fnd of St. Joseph County Special Project Challenge Grants, 1314
Comm Fnd of Switzerland County Grants, 1315
Comm Fnd of Tampa Bay Grants, 1316
Comm Fnd of the Eastern Shore Needs Grants, 1317
Comm Fnd of the Eastern Shore Field of Interest Grants, 1318
Comm Fnd of the Eastern Shore Youth Grants, 1319
Comm Fnd of the Ozarks Grants, 1320
Comm Fnd of the Verdugos Educational Endowment Fund Grants, 1321
Comm Fnd of the Verdugos Grants, 1322
Comm Fnd Of The Virgin Islands Anderson Family Teacher Grants, 1323
Comm Fnd of the Virgin Isl Kimelman Grants, 1324
Comm Fnd Of The Virgin Islands Mini Grants, 1325
Comm Fnd of Western North Carolina Grants, 1327
Comm Fnd Partners Lawrence County Grants, 1328
Comm Fnd Partnerships - Martin County Grants, 1329
Comm Fnd Silicon Valley Grants, 1331
Comm Impact Fund, 1332
Comm in the Connecting AAPIs To Advocate and Lead Grants, 1333
Comm Memorial Fnd Grants, 1334
Comm Partners on Waste Educ and Reduction, 1335
Comm Tech Fdn of California Building Communities Through Tech Grants, 1336
Compton Fnd Grants, 1338
Computer Associates Comm Grants, 1341
ConAgra Foods Fnd Comm Impact Grants, 1342
ConAgra Foods Fnd Nourish Our Comm Grants, 1343
Con Edison Corp Giving Arts & Culture Grants, 1344
Con Edison Corporate Giving Civic Grants, 1345
Con Edison Corp Gvg Comm Grts, 1346
Con Edison Corp Gvg Environmental Grts, 1347
Cone Health Fnd Grants, 1348
Connecticut Commission on the Arts Art in Public Spaces, 1349
Connecticut Comm Fnd Grants, 1350
Connecticut Light & Power Corp Contribs, 1352
Connelly Fnd Grants, 1353
ConocoPhillips Fnd Grants, 1354
ConocoPhillips Grants, 1355
Conseil des arts de Montreal Diversity Award, 1357
Conservation, Food, and Health Fnd Grants for Developing Countries, 1359
CONSOL Coal Group Grants, 1360

PROGRAM TYPE INDEX

Community Development / 1039

Constantin Fnd Grants, 1362
Constellation Energy Corp EcoStar Grts, 1363
Constellation Energy Corporate Grants, 1364
Consumers Energy Fnd, 1365
Conwood Charitable Trust Grants, 1366
Cooke-Hay Fnd Grants, 1367
Cooke Fnd Grants, 1368
Cooper Fnd Grants, 1369
Cooper Industries Fnd Grants, 1370
Coors Brewing Corporate Contributions Grants, 1371
Cord Fnd Grants, 1372
Corina Higginson Trust Grants, 1373
Cornell Lab of Ornithology Mini-Grants, 1374
Cornerstone Fdn of NE Wisconsin Grants, 1375
Corning Fnd Cultural Grants, 1376
Coughlin-Saunders Fnd Grants, 1377
Countess Moira Charitable Fnd Grants, 1381
Covenant Educational Fnd Grants, 1383
Covenant Fnd of Atlanta Grants, 1384
Covenant Fdn of New York Signature Grts, 1386
Covenant to Care for Children Enrichment Fund Grants, 1389
Covidien Medical Product Donations, 1390
Covidien Partnership for Neighborhood Wellness Grants, 1391
Crail-Johnson Fnd Grants, 1393
Cralle Fnd Grants, 1394
Cranston Fnd Grants, 1395
Creative Work Fund Grants, 1396
Crescent Porter Hale Fnd Grants, 1398
Crossroads Fund Seed Grants, 1400
Crown Point Comm Fnd Grants, 1402
Cruise Industry Charitable Fnd Grants, 1404
Crystelle Waggoner Charitable Trust Grants, 1405
CSL Behring Local Empowerment for Advocacy Dev Grants, 1406
CSRA Comm Fnd Grants, 1407
CSX Corporate Contributions Grants, 1408
CTCNet/Youth Visions for Stronger Neighborhoods Grants, 1409
Cullen Fnd Grants, 1411
Cultural Society of Filipino Americans Grants, 1412
Cumberland Comm Fnd Grants, 1413
Cumberland Comm Fnd Summer Kids Grants, 1414
Cummins Fnd Grants, 1415
CUNA Mutual Group Fnd, 1416
CUNA Mutual Group Fnd Grants, 1417
Curtis and Edith Munson Fnd Grants, 1418
Curtis Fnd Grants, 1419
CVS All Kids Can Grants, 1420
CVS Caremark Charitable Trust Grants, 1421
CVS Comm Grants, 1422
Cyrus Eaton Fnd Grants, 1423
D.F. Halton Fnd Grants, 1424
D. W. McMillan Fnd Grants, 1426
Dade Comm Fnd AIDS Partnership Grants, 1428
Dade Comm Fnd GLBT Comm Projects Grants, 1429
Dade Comm Fnd Grants, 1430
Dade Comm Fdn Safe Passage Grts, 1431
DaimlerChrysler Corporation Fund Grants, 1432
Daisy Marquis Jones Fnd Grants, 1434
Dale and Edna Walsh Fnd Grants, 1435
Dallas Fnd Grants, 1436
Dallas Mavericks Fnd Grants, 1437
Dallas Women's Fnd Grants, 1438
Dammann Fund Grants, 1439
Dana Corporation Fnd Grants, 1440
Danellie Fnd Grants, 1442
Daniels Fund Grants, 1443
Daphne Seybolt Culpeper Mem Fdn Grts, 1445
Darden Restaurants Fnd Grants, 1446
Dave Coy Fnd Grants, 1447
Davenport-Hatch Fnd Grants, 1448
Dave Thomas Fnd for Adoption Grants, 1449
David & Barbara B. Hirschhorn Fdn Grt, 1450
David Bohnett Fnd Grants, 1451
David Geffen Fnd Grants, 1452
David N. Lane Trust Grants for Aged and Indigent Women, 1453
Daviess County Comm Arts & Culture Grants, 1455

Daviess County Comm Fnd Environment Grants, 1456
Daviess County Comm Fnd Health Grants, 1457
Daviess County Comm Human Services Grants, 1458
Daviess County Comm Fnd Recreation Grants, 1459
Daviess County Comm Fnd Youth Dev Grants, 1460
Dayton Fnd Grants, 1463
Dayton Power and Light Fnd Grants, 1464
Daywood Fnd Grants, 1465
DB Americas Fnd Grants, 1466
Deaconess Comm Fnd Grants, 1467
Deaconess Fnd Advocacy Grants, 1468
Dean Foods Comm Involvement Grants, 1469
Dearborn Comm Fnd City of Aurora Grants, 1470
Dearborn Comm Fnd City of Lawrenceburg Comm Grants, 1471
Dearborn Comm Fnd County Progress Grants, 1473
Deborah Munroe Noonan Mem Fund Grts, 1475
Decatur County Comm Fnd Large Project Grants, 1476
Decatur County Comm Fnd Small Project Grants, 1477
DeKalb County Comm Fnd - Garrett Hospital Aid Fnd Grants, 1478
DeKalb County Comm Fnd - Lit Grant, 1480
DeKalb County Comm Fdn Grts, 1481
Dekko Fnd Grants, 1482
Delaware Comm Fnd-Youth Philanthropy Board for Kent County, 1483
Delaware Comm Fnd Fund For Women Grants, 1484
Delaware Comm Fnd Next Generation Grants, 1485
Delaware Comm Fdn Youth Philanthropy Board for New Castle County Grts, 1486
Delaware Division of the Arts Comm-Based Organizations Opportunity Grants, 1487
Dell Fnd Open Grants, 1490
Delta Air Lines Fdn Arts & Culture Grts, 1493
Delta Air Lines Fdn Cmty Enrichment Grants, 1494
DeMatteis Family Fnd Grants, 1497
Dennis & Phyllis Washington Fdn Grants, 1498
Denver Broncos Charities Fund Grants, 1501
Denver Fnd Comm Grants, 1502
Denver Fdn Social Venture Partners Grts, 1503
Denver Fnd Strengthening Neighborhoods Grants, 1504
Denver Fdn Tech Assistance Grants, 1505
Dept of Ed Even Start Grants, 1508
Dept of Ed Parental Infor & Resource Cntrs, 1510
Dept of Ed Safe and Drug-Free Schools and Communities State Grants, 1513
Dept of Ed Upwa Dermody Properties Fdn Capstone Awd rd Bound Program, 1514
Dermody Properties Fdn Capstone Awd, 1516
Dermody Properties Fnd Grants, 1517
DeRoy Testamentary Fnd Grants, 1518
Detlef Schrempf Fnd Grants, 1519
Detroit Lions Charities Grants, 1520
Deuce McAllister Catch 22 Fnd Grants, 1521
DFN Hurricane Katrina and Disability Rapid Response Grants, 1522
DHHS Abandoned Infants Assistance Grants, 1523
DHHS AIDS Project Grants, 1525
DHHS American Recovery and Reinvestment Act of 2009 Head Start Expansion, 1526
DHHS ARRA Strengthening Communities Fund - Nonprofit Capacity Building Grants, 1527
DHHS ARRA Strengthening Communities Fund - State, Local, and Tribal Government Capacity Building Grants, 1528
DHHS Comm Svcs Grant Trng & Tech Assistance Pgm: Capacity-Bldg for Ongoing CSBG Pgm, 1529
DHHS Comprehensive Comm Mental Health Services Grants for Children with Serious Emotional Disturbances, 1530
DHHS Emergency Medical Svcs for Children, 1531
DHHS Healthy Tomorrows Pshp for Children, 1534
DHHS Independence Demonstration Program, 1535
DHS ARRA Fire Station Const Grants , 1542
DHS ARRA Port Security Grants, 1543
DHS ARRA Transit Security Grants , 1544
DHS FY 2009 Transit Security Grants , 1545
Diageo Fnd Grants, 1546
DIFFA/Chicago Grants, 1547
Dining for Women Grants, 1548

District of Columbia Commission on the Arts-Arts Educ Teacher Mini-Grants, 1549
Diversity Leadership Academy Grants, 1550
DOE Initial H-Prize Competition for Breakthrough Advances in Materials for Hydrogen Storage, 1551
DogTime Annual Grant, 1552
DogTime Tech Grant, 1553
DOI Urban Park and Rec Recovery Grants, 1554
DOJ Children's Justice Act Partnership for Indian Communities, 1555
DOJ Comm-Based Delinquency Prev Grants, 1556
DOJ Gang-Free Schools and Communities Intervention Grants, 1557
DOJ Internet Crimes against Children Task Force Grants, 1558
DOJ Juvenile Mentoring Pgm Grts, 1560
DOJ Rural Domestic Violence and Child Victimization Enforcement Grants, 1562
Dole Food Company Charitable Contributions, 1564
Dolfinger-McMahon Fnd Grants, 1565
Dollar Energy Fund Grants, 1567
Dollar General Adult Lit Grants, 1568
Dollar General Family Lit Grants, 1569
Dollar General Youth Lit Grants, 1570
DOL Youthbuild Grants, 1571
Dominion Fnd Human Needs Grants, 1572
Donaldson Fnd Grants, 1574
Donald W. Reynolds Fnd Charitable Food Distribution Grants, 1575
Donald W. Reynolds Fnd Children's Discovery Initiative Grants, 1576
Donald W Reynolds Fdn Spcl Projects Grts, 1577
Donnie Avery Catches for Kids Fnd, 1578
Dora Roberts Fnd Grants, 1579
Doree Taylor Charitable Fnd, 1580
Do Right Fnd Grants, 1581
Doris and Victor Day Fnd Grants, 1582
Doris Day Animal Fnd Grants, 1583
Doris Duke Charitable Fnd Arts Grants, 1584
Doris Duke Charitable Fnd Child Abuse Prevention Grants, 1585
Dorothea Haus Ross Fnd Grants, 1587
Dorothy Rider Pool Health Care Grants, 1589
Dorrance Family Fnd Grants, 1590
Dorr Fnd Grants, 1591
Do Something BR!CK Awards, 1592
Do Something Plum Youth Grants, 1593
Doug and Carla Salmon Fnd Grants, 1594
Douty Fnd Grants, 1595
Dow Chemical Company Grants, 1596
Dow Corning Corporate Contributions Grants, 1597
DPA Promoting Policy Change Advocacy Grts, 1598
Dr. and Mrs. Paul Pierce Memorial Fnd Grants, 1599
Dr. John T. Macdonald Fnd Grants, 1600
Dr. Scholl Fnd Grants, 1602
Dream Weaver Fnd, 1604
Drs. Bruce and Lee Fnd Grants, 1607
Drug Free Communities Support Program, 1608
DTE Energy Fdn Comm Dev Grants, 1609
DTE Energy Fnd Cultural Grants, 1610
DTE Energy Fnd Diversity Grants, 1611
DTE Energy Health & Human Services Grants, 1613
DTE Energy Fnd Leadership Grants, 1614
Dubois County Comm Fnd Grants, 1615
Duke Endowment Child Care Grants, 1617
Duke Energy Fdn Comm Vitality Grants, 1618
Duke Energy Fdn Econ Dev Grants, 1619
Duluth-Superior Area Comm Fdn Grts, 1620
Duneland Health Council Incorporated Grants, 1621
Dunn Fnd K-12 Grants, 1622
Dunspaugh-Dalton Fnd Grants, 1623
DuPage Comm Fnd Grants, 1624
Durfee Fnd Sabbatical Grants, 1625
Dwight Stuart Youth Fnd Grants, 1628
Dynegy Fnd Grants, 1630
Dyson Fnd Emergency Fund Grants, 1631
Dyson Fnd Management Assistance Mini-Grants, 1632
Dyson Fnd Mid-Hudson Valley Project Grants, 1636
Dyson Fnd Nonprofit Strategic Restructuring Initiative Grants, 1637

E.J. Grassmann Trust Grants, 1638
E.L. Wiegand Fnd Grants, 1639
E Rhodes & Leona B Carpenter Fdn Grts, 1640
Earth Island Institute Comm Wetland Restoration Grants, 1642
Eastman Chemical Co Fnd Grants, 1643
Easton Fnds Archery Facility Grants, 1644
East Tennessee Fdn Afrdbl Housing Trust Fund, 1645
East Tennessee Fnd Grants, 1646
eBay Fnd Comm Grants, 1648
Eberly Fnd Grants, 1649
Ed and Carole Abel Fnd Grants, 1652
Eddie C. and Sylvia Brown Family Fnd Grants, 1653
Eden Hall Fnd Grants, 1655
Edina Realty Fnd Grants, 1656
Edna Wardlaw Charitable Trust Grants, 1660
Edward & Ellen Roche Relief Fnd Grants, 1663
Edward and Helen Bartlett Fnd Grants, 1664
Edward Bangs Kelley & Elza Kelley Fdn Grts, 1665
Edward N. and Della L. Thome Memorial Fnd Direct Services Grants, 1666
Edward R. Godfrey Fnd Grants, 1667
Edward S. Moore Fnd Grants, 1668
Edwards Memorial Trust Grants, 1669
Edward W & Stella C Van Houten Mem Fund, 1670
Edwin S. Webster Fnd Grants, 1671
Edyth Bush Charitable Fnd Grants, 1673
Effie and Wofford Cain Fnd Grants, 1674
EIF Comm Grants, 1675
Eileen Fisher Activating Leadership Grants for Women and Girls, 1676
Eileen Fisher Women-Owned Business Grants, 1677
Eisner Fnd Grants, 1678
Elden and Mary Lee Gutwein Family Fnd Grants, 1679
Elizabeth & Avola W Callaway Fdn Grants, 1680
Elizabeth Carse Fnd Grants, 1681
Elizabeth Morse Genius Char Trust Grants, 1682
Elkhart County Comm Fnd Fund, 1683
Elkhart Cty Comm Fdn Grants, 1684
Elliot Fnd Inc Grants, 1686
Elmer L & Eleanor J Andersen Fdn Grnts, 1687
El Paso Comm Fnd Grants, 1688
El Paso Corporate Fnd Grants, 1689
El Pomar Fnd Awards and Grants, 1690
Elsie H. Wilcox Fnd Grants, 1691
Elsie Lee Garthwaite Memorial Fdn Grts, 1692
Emerson Kampen Fnd Grants, 1696
Emily Davie and Joseph S. Kornfeld Fnd Grants, 1697
Emma A. Sheafer Charitable Trust Grants, 1699
Emma B. Howe Memorial Fnd Grants, 1700
Emma G. Harris Fnd Grants, 1701
Emma J. Adams Grants, 1702
Encore Purpose Prize, 1704
Energy Fnd Buildings Grants, 1705
Energy Fnd Climate Grants, 1706
Energy Fnd Power Grants, 1707
Energy Fnd Transportation Grants, 1708
Ensign-Bickford Fnd Grants, 1709
Ensworth Charitable Fnd Grants, 1710
Entergy Charitable Fnd Low-Income Initiatives and Solutions Grants, 1711
Entergy Corporation Micro Grants, 1712
Entergy Corp Open Grants for Arts and Culture, 1713
Entergy Corporation Open Grants for Comm Improvement & Enrichment, 1714
Entergy Corp Open Grants for Healthy Families, 1715
Enterprise Comm Partners Green Grants, 1716
Enterprise Comm Partners MetLife Fnd Awards for Excellence in Affordable Housing, 1717
Enterprise Comm Partners Pre-Dev Grants, 1718
Enterprise Comm Partners Rose Architectural Fellowships, 1719
Enterprise Comm Partners Terwilliger Fellowship, 1720
Enterprise Rent-A-Car Fnd Grants, 1721
EPA Air Pollution Control Pgm Support Grts, 1722
EPA Brownfields Area-Wide Planning Grants, 1723
EPA Brownfields Assessment Pilot Grants, 1724
EPA Brownfields Cleanup Grants, 1725
EPA Brownfields Environmental Workforce Dev and Job Training Grants, 1726

EPA Brownfields Training, Research, and Tech Assistance Grants, 1727
EPA Children's Health Protection Grants, 1728
EPA Environmental Educ Grants, 1729
EPA Environmental Justice Collaborative Problem-Solving Cooperative Agreements Program, 1730
EPA Environmental Justice Small Grants, 1731
EPA Environmental Justice Small Grants, 1732
EPA Hazardous Waste Manag Grants for Tribes, 1733
EPA Pestwise Registration Improvement Act Partnership Grants, 1734
EPA Regional Agricultural IPM Grants, 1735
EPA Sr Environmental Employment Gras, 1736
EPA Source Reduction Assistance Grants, 1737
EPA State Indoor Radon Grants, 1738
EPA State Senior Envir Employment Grants, 1739
EPA Surveys, Studies, Research, Investigations, Demonstrations, and Special Purpose Activities Relating to the Clean Air Act, 1740
EPA Tribal Solid Waste Management Assistance Grants, 1741
EPA Tribal Support for the National Environmental Information Exchange Network, 1742
EQT Fnd Art and Culture Grants, 1743
EQT Fnd Comm Grants, 1744
EQT Fnd Environment Grants, 1746
EREF Unsolicited Proposal Grants, 1749
Erie Comm Fnd Grants, 1750
Essex County Comm Fnd Discretionary Grants, 1752
Essex County Comm Fnd Emergency Grants, 1753
Essex County Comm Fnd First Jobs Grant, 1754
Essex County Comm Fnd Greater Lawrence Summer Fund Grants, 1755
Essex County Comm Fnd Merrimack Valley General Fund Grants, 1756
Esther M. and Freeman E. Everett Grants, 1757
Ethel and Raymond F. Rice Fnd Grants, 1758
Ethel Frends Fnd Grants, 1759
Ethel S. Abbott Charitable Fnd Grants, 1760
Ethel Sergeant Clark Smith Fnd Grants, 1761
Eugene M. Lang Fnd Grants, 1764
Eugene Straus Charitable Trust, 1766
Eva L & Joseph M Bruening Fdn Grants, 1768
Evan and Susan Bayh Fnd Grants, 1769
Evan Frankel Fnd Grants, 1770
Evanston Comm Fnd Grants, 1771
Evelyn and Walter Haas, Jr. Fund Immigrant Rights Grants, 1773
Evelyn and Walter Haas, Jr. Fund Nonprofit Leadership Grants, 1774
Ewa Beach Comm Trust Fund, 1775
Ewing Marion Kauffman Fnd Grants, 1777
Ezra M. Cutting Trust Grants, 1779
F.M. Kirby Fnd Grants, 1780
F.R. Bigelow Fnd Grants, 1781
Fairfield County Comm Fdn Grts, 1782
Fallon OrNda Comm Health Fund Grants, 1783
Families Count: The National Honors Program, 1784
Fam Lit & HI Pizza Hut Lit Fund, 1785
Fan Fox & Leslie R Samuels Fdn Grants, 1786
FAR Fund Grants, 1787
Fargo-Moorhead Area Fnd Grants, 1788
Fargo-Moorhead Area Fnd Woman's Fund Grants, 1789
Farm Aid Grants, 1790
Farmers Insurance Corporate Giving Grants, 1791
FAS Project Schools Grants, 1792
Fassino Fnd Grants, 1793
Faye McBeath Fnd Grants, 1794
Fayette County Fnd Grants, 1795
FCYO Youth Organizing Grants, 1797
FEDCO Charitable Fdn Educ Grts, 1798
Federal Express Corporate Contributions, 1799
Fel-Pro Mecklenburger Fnd Grants, 1800
Feldman Fnd Grants, 1801
FEMA Assistance to Firefighters Grants, 1802
FEMA Staffing for Adequate Fire and Emergency Response Grants, 1803
Ferree Fnd Grants, 1804
Fidelity Fnd Grants, 1805
Field Fnd of Illinois Grants, 1806

Fields Pond Fnd Grants, 1807
Fieldstone Fnd Grants, 1808
Fifth Third Bank Corporate Giving, 1809
Fifth Third Fnd Grants, 1810
Financial Capability Innovation Fund II Grants, 1811
Finish Line Youth Fnd Founder's Grants, 1812
Finish Line Youth Fnd Grants, 1813
Finish Line Youth Fnd Legacy Grants, 1814
FINRA Investor Educ Fnd Financial Educ in Your Comm Grants, 1815
FINRA Smart Investing@Your Library Grants, 1816
Fireman's Fund Ins Co Heritage Grts, 1818
FirstEnergy Fnd Comm Grants, 1819
First Lady's Fam Lit Init for Texas Grants, 1822
FishAmerica Fnd Conservation Grants, 1828
Fisher Fnd Grants, 1831
Fisher House Fdn Newman's Own Awds, 1833
Fitzpatrick and Francis Family Business Continuity Fnd Grants, 1837
Fleishhacker Fnd Educ Grants, 1838
Fleishhacker Fdn Small Grants in the Arts, 1839
Fleishhacker Fnd Special Arts Grants, 1840
Flextronics Fnd Disaster Relief Grants, 1841
Flinn Fnd Grants, 1842
Florence Hunt Maxwell Fnd Grants, 1844
Florian O. Bartlett Trust Grants, 1845
Florida BRAIVE Fund of Dade Comm Fnd, 1846
Florida Division of Cultural Affairs Comm Theatre Grants, 1847
Florida Div of Cultural Affairs Dance Grts, 1850
Florida Division of Cultural Affairs Endowment Grants, 1851
Florida Div of Cultural Affrs Facilities Grts, 1852
Florida Div of Cultural Affairs Folk Arts Grts, 1853
Florida Division of Cultural Affairs Lit Grants, 1855
Florida Div of Cultural Affairs Media Arts Grants, 1856
Florida Division of Cultural Affairs Multidisciplinary Grants, 1857
Florida Div of Cultural Affairs Museum Grts, 1858
Florida Div of Cultural Affairs Music Grts, 1859
Florida Div of Cultural Afrs Presenter Grts, 1860
Florida Division of Cultural Affairs Professional Theatre Grants, 1861
Florida Division of Cultural Affairs Specific Cultural Project Grants, 1862
Florida Div of Cultural Affairs Visual Arts Grants, 1865
Florida Humanities Cncl Civic Reflection Grts, 1867
Florida Humanities Council Mini Grants, 1869
Florida Humanities Council Partnership Grants, 1870
Florida Sports Fnd Junior Golf Grants, 1872
Florida Sports Fnd Major and Regional Grants, 1873
Floyd A. and Kathleen C. Cailloux Fnd Grants, 1874
Fluor Fnd Grants, 1875
FMC Fnd Grants, 1876
Foellinger Fnd Grants, 1877
Fondren Fnd Grants, 1878
Ford Family Fdn Grts-Critical Needs, 1879
Ford Family Fnd Grants - Positive Youth Dev, 1880
Ford Family Grants Public Convening Spaces, 1881
Ford Family Fnd Grants - Tech Assistance, 1882
Ford Fnd Diversity Fellowships, 1883
Ford Motor Company Fund Grants, 1885
Forest Fnd Grants, 1886
Forrest C. Lattner Fnd Grants, 1887
Foster Fnd Grants, 1888
Foster G. McGaw Prize, 1889
Fnd for a Drug-Free Wrld Clsrm Tools, 1890
Fnd for Appalachian Ohio Access to Environmental Educ Mini-Grants, 1892
Fdn for Enhancing Communities Grts, 1893
Fnd for Health Enhancement Grants, 1894
Fnd for Seacoast Health Grants, 1895
Fnd for the Carolinas Grants, 1896
Fnd for the Mid South Comm Dev Grants, 1897
Fnd for Mid South Health & Wellness Grants, 1899
Fnd for the MidSouth Wlth Bldg Grts, 1900
Fnd for Young Ausies Indigenous Small Grants, 1901
Fnd for Young Australians Spark Fund Grants, 1902
Fnd for Young Australians Youth Change Makers Grants, 1904

PROGRAM TYPE INDEX

Community Development / 1041

Fnd for Young Ausies Youth Led Futures Grants, 1905
Fnd NW Grants, 1906
Fnds of East Chicago Comm Economic Grants, 1907
Fnds of E Chgo Family Support Grts, 1908
Fnds of E Chgo Fin Independence Grts, 1909
Fnds of East Chicago Health Grants, 1910
Fnds of E Chgo Public Sfty Grts, 1911
Fnds of East Chicago Youth Dev Grants, 1912
Fourjay Fnd Grants, 1913
Four Times Fnd Grants, 1914
France-Merrick Fnds Grants, 1915
Frances & Benjamin Benenson Fdn Grts, 1916
Frances and John L. Loeb Family Fund Grants, 1917
Frances C & William P Smallwood Fdn Grts, 1918
Frances L & Edwin L Cummings Mem Fund, 1919
Frances W. Emerson Fnd Grants, 1920
Francis Beidler Fnd Grants, 1921
Francis L. Abreu Charitable Trust Grants, 1922
Francis T & Louise T Nichols Fdn Grts, 1923
Frank & Larue Reynolds Char Trust Grts, 1924
Frank and Lydia Bergen Fnd Grants, 1925
Frank B. Hazard General Charity Fund Grants, 1926
Frank G & Freida K Brotz Fam Fdn Grts, 1928
Franklin County Comm Fdn Grts, 1929
Franklin H. Wells and Ruth L. Wells Fnd Grants, 1930
Frank M. Tait Fnd Grants, 1932
Frank Reed and Margaret Jane Peters Memorial Fund I Grants, 1933
Frank Reed and Margaret Jane Peters Memorial Fund II Grants, 1934
Frank Stanley Beveridge Fnd Grants, 1936
Frank W & Carl S Adams Mem Fund Grts, 1937
Fred & Gretel Biel Charitable Trust Grants, 1939
Fred and Sherry Abernethy Fnd Grants, 1940
Fred Baldwin Memorial Fnd Grants, 1941
Fred C & Mary R Koch Fnd Grants, 1943
Freddie Mac Fnd Grants, 1944
FRED Educational Ethyl Grants, 1945
Frederick McDonald Trust Grants, 1946
Frederick W. Marzahl Grants, 1948
Fred L. Emerson Fnd Grants, 1949
Fred Meyer Fnd Grants, 1950
Fremont Area Cmty Fdn Amazing X Grants, 1953
Fremont Area Comm Fnd Elderly Needs Grants, 1954
Fremont Area Comm Fnd Grants, 1955
Fremont Area Comm Fnd Summer Youth Grants, 1956
Freshwater Future Advocate Mentor Program, 1957
Freshwater Future Climate Grants, 1958
Freshwater Future Healing Our Waters Grants, 1959
Freshwater Future Insight Services Grants, 1960
Freshwater Future Project Grants, 1961
Freshwater Future Special Opportunity Grants, 1962
Frey Fnd Grants, 1963
Frist Fnd Grants, 1964
Fritz B. Burns Fnd Grants, 1965
Fruit Tree 101, 1967
Fulbright/Garcia Robles Grants, 1968
Fuller E. Callaway Fnd Grants, 1973
Fuller Fnd Grants, 1974
Fulton County Comm Fnd Grants, 1975
Fulton County Comm Fnd Women's Giving Circle Grants, 1976
Fund for Southern Communities Grants, 1977
Fund for the City of New York Grants, 1978
Funding Exchange Martin-Baro Fund Grants, 1979
Furth Family Fnd Grants, 1980
G.A. Ackermann Grants, 1981
Gamble Fnd Grants, 1983
Gannett Fdn Comm Action Grants, 1984
Gardiner Howland Shaw Fnd Grants, 1986
Gardiner Savings Institution Charitable Grants, 1987
Garland & Agnes Taylor Gray Fdn Grts, 1988
Gates Fnd Children, Youth & Family Grants, 1989
Gates Family Comm Dev & Revitalization Grants, 1990
Gates Family Fnd Parks, Conservation & Recreation Grants, 1991
Gateway Fnd Grants, 1992
Gaylord & Dorothy Donnelley Fdn Grants, 1993
GCI Corporate Contributions Grants, 1994
Gebbie Fnd Grants, 1995

GEF Green Thumb Challenge, 1996
GenCorp Fnd Grants, 1998
Gene Haas Fnd, 1999
Genentech Corporate Charitable Contributions, 2000
General Dynamics Corporation Grants, 2001
General Mills Fnd Grants, 2003
General Motors Fnd Grants, 2004
General Service Fnd Colorado Grants, 2005
General Service Fnd Human Rights and Economic Justice Grants, 2006
General Service Fnd Reproductive Justice Grants, 2007
George A & Grace L Long Fdn Grts, 2008
George A. Hormel Testamentary Trust Grants, 2009
George and Ruth Bradford Fnd Grants, 2010
George and Sarah Buchanan Fnd Grants, 2011
George A Ohl Jr. Fnd Grants, 2012
George B. Page Fnd Grants, 2013
George F. Baker Trust Grants, 2016
George Family Fnd Grants, 2017
George Fnd Grants, 2018
George Frederick Jewett Fnd Grants, 2019
George Gund Fnd Grants, 2020
George H & Jane A Mifflin Mem Fund Grts, 2021
George H.C. Ensworth Grants, 2022
George I. Alden Trust Grants, 2023
George J. and Effie L. Seay Fnd Grants, 2024
George P. Davenport Trust Fund Grants, 2026
George S & Dolores Dore Eccles Fdn Grants, 2027
George W. Brackenridge Fnd Grants, 2028
George W Codrington Charitable Fdn Grts, 2029
George W. Wells Fnd Grants, 2030
Georgia-Pacific Fnd Enrichment Grants, 2032
Georgia-Pacific Fdn Entrepreneurship Grts, 2033
Georgia-Pacific Fdn Environment Grts, 2034
Georgia Council for the Arts Partner Grants for Service Organizations, 2036
Georgia Council for the Arts Project Grants, 2037
Georgiana Goddard Eaton Mem Fund Grts, 2038
Georgia Power Fnd Grants, 2039
Geraldine R. Dodge Fnd Arts Grants, 2040
Geraldine R. Dodge Fnd Media Grants, 2042
German Protestant Orphan Asylum Fnd Grants, 2044
Gertrude & William C Wardlaw Fund Grts, 2045
Gertrude E Skelly Charitable Fdn Grts, 2046
Gheens Fnd Grants, 2048
Giant Eagle Fnd Grants, 2049
Giant Food Charitable Grants, 2050
Gibson County Comm Fnd Women's Fund, 2051
Gibson Fnd Grants, 2052
Gil and Dody Weaver Fnd Grants, 2053
Gill Fnd Gay & Lesbian Fund, 2054
Ginger and Barry Ackerley Fnd Grants, 2055
Ginn Fnd Grants, 2056
Girl's Best Friend Fnd Grants, 2057
Giving Sum Annual Grant, 2058
Gladys Brooks Fnd Grants, 2059
GlaxoSmithKline Corporate Grants, 2060
Glazer Family Fnd Grants, 2062
GMFUS Black Sea Trust for Regional Corp Grants, 2065
GNOF Albert N & Hattie M McClure Grts, 2068
GNOF Bayou Communities Grants, 2069
GNOF Coastal 5 + 1 Grants, 2070
GNOF Comm Revitalization Grants, 2071
GNOF Cox Charities of New Orleans Grants, 2072
GNOF Environmental Fund Grants, 2073
GNOF Exxon-Mobil Grants, 2074
GNOF Gert Comm Fund Grants, 2076
GNOF Gulf Coast Oil Spill Grants, 2077
GNOF IMPACT Grants for Arts and Culture, 2078
GNOF IMPACT Grants for Education, 2079
GNOF IMPACT Grants for Health and Human Services, 2080
GNOF IMPACT Grts for Youth Dev't, 2081
GNOF IMPACT Gulf States Eye Surg Fund, 2082
GNOF IMPACT Harold W. Newman, Jr. Charitable Trust Grants, 2083
GNOF IMPACT Kahn-Oppenheim Trst Grts, 2084
GNOF Jefferson Comm Grants, 2085
GNOF Maison Hospitaliere Grants, 2086
GNOF Metropolitan Opportunities Grants, 2087

GNOF New Orleans Works Grants, 2088
GNOF Norco Comm Grants, 2089
GNOF Organizational Effectiveness Grants, 2090
GNOF Plaquemines Comm Grants, 2091
GNOF St. Bernard Comm Grants, 2092
GNOF Stand Up For Our Children Grants, 2093
Go Daddy Cares Charitable Contributions, 2094
Godfrey Fnd Grants, 2095
Goizueta Fnd Grants, 2096
Golden LEAF Fnd Grants, 2097
Golden Rule Fnd Grants, 2098
Golden State Warriors Fnd Grants, 2099
Goldseker Fdn Comm Affairs Grants, 2100
Goldseker Fnd Comm Grants, 2101
Goldseker Fnd Human Services Grants, 2102
Goldseker Fnd Non-Profit Management Assistance Grants, 2103
Goodrich Corporation Fnd Grants, 2104
Good Works Fnd Grants, 2105
Goodyear Tire Grants, 2106
Grable Fnd Grants, 2108
Grace and Franklin Bernsen Fnd Grants, 2109
Grace Bersted Fnd Grants, 2110
Graco Fnd Grants, 2111
Grand Circle Fnd Associates Grants, 2112
Grand Haven Area Comm Fdn Grants, 2113
Grand Rapids Area Comm Fdn Grts, 2114
Grand Rapids Area Comm Fnd Nashwauk Area Endowment Fund Grants, 2115
Grand Rapids Area Comm Fnd Wyoming Grants, 2116
Grand Rapids Area Comm Fnd Wyoming Youth Fund Grants, 2117
Grand Rapids Comm Fnd Grants, 2118
Grand Rapids Comm Fdn Ionia Cty Grts, 2119
Grand Rapids Comm Fnd Ionia County Youth Fund Grants, 2120
Grand Rapids Comm Fnd Lowell Area Grants, 2121
Grand Rapids Comm Fnd SE Ottawa Grants, 2122
Grand Rapids Comm SE Ottawa Youth Grants, 2123
Grand Rapids Comm Fdn Sparta Grts, 2124
Grand Rapids Comm Fnd Sparta Youth Grants, 2125
Grand Victoria Fnd Illinois Core Grants, 2126
Grassroots Exchange Fund Grants, 2128
Grassroots Government Leadership Award, 2129
Great-West Life Grants, 2130
Great Clips Corporate Giving, 2131
Greater Cincinnati Fnd Priority and Small Projects/Capacity-Building Grants, 2132
Grtr Columbus Arts Council Operating Grts, 2133
Greater Des Moines Fnd Grants, 2134
Grtr Green Bay Comm Fdn Grts, 2135
Greater Kanawha Valley Fnd Grants, 2136
Greater Milwaukee Fnd Grants, 2137
Greater Saint Louis Comm Fdn Grants, 2138
Greater Tacoma Comm Fdn Grts, 2139
Greater Worcester Comm Discretionary Grants, 2140
Greater Worcester Comm Fnd Jeppson Memorial Fund for Brookfield Grants, 2141
Greater Worcester Comm Fnd Mini-Grants, 2142
Greater Worcester Comm Fnd Youth for Comm Improvement Grants, 2144
Great Lakes Fishery Trust Habitat Protection and Restoration Grants, 2146
Green Bay Packers Fnd Grants, 2148
Green Diamond Charitable Contributions, 2149
Greene County Fnd Grants, 2150
Greenfield Fnd of Florida Grants, 2151
Green Fnd Arts Grants, 2152
Green Fnd Human Services Grants, 2154
Green Fnd Special Project Grants, 2155
Greenwall Fdn Arts & Humanities Grts, 2157
Greenwall Fnd Bioethics Grants, 2158
GreenWorks! Butterfly Garden Grants, 2159
GreenWorks! Grants, 2160
Gregory C. Carr Fnd Grants, 2161
Greygates Fnd Grants, 2164
Grotto Fnd Project Grants, 2166
Group 70 Fnd Fund, 2167
Grundy Fnd Grants, 2169
GTECH Comm Involvement Grants, 2171

Community Development

Guido A & Elizabeth H Binda Fdn Grants, 2172
Gulf Coast Comm Fnd Grants, 2174
Gulf Coast Fnd of Comm Operating Grants, 2176
Gulf Coast Fnd of Comm Grants, 2177
Gumdrop Books Librarian Scholarships, 2179
H & R Fnd Grants, 2181
HA & Mary K Chapman Char Trust Grts, 2182
H.B. Fuller Company Fnd Grants, 2183
H.J. Heinz Company Fnd Grants, 2184
H. Leslie Hoffman & Elaine S. Hoffman Grants, 2185
H. Reimers Bechtel Charitable Remainder Uni-Trust Grants, 2186
H. Schaffer Fnd Grants, 2187
Hackett Fnd Grants, 2188
Haddad Fnd Grants, 2189
HAF Arts and Culture: Lynne and Bob Wells Grant for Performing Artists, 2190
HAF Arts & Culture: Project Grts to Artists, 2191
HAF Co-op Comm Fund Grants, 2192
HAF Comm Grants, 2193
HAF Companion Animal Welfare and Rescue, 2195
HAF Justin Keele Make a Difference Award, 2198
HAF Mada Huggins Caldwell Fund Grants, 2200
HAF Native Cultures Fund Grants, 2201
HAF Natural Environment Grants, 2202
HAF Southern Humboldt Grants, 2204
HAF Techn Assistance Pgm Grts, 2206
Hagedorn Fund Grants, 2207
Hahl Proctor Charitable Trust Grants, 2208
Hall-Perrine Fnd Grants, 2209
Hall Family Fnd Grants, 2210
Hallmark Corporate Fnd Grants, 2212
Hamilton Family Fnd Grants, 2213
Hampton Roads Comm Fnd Beach Fund Grants, 2214
Hampton Roads Comm Fnd Comm Leadership Partners Grants, 2215
Hampton Roads Comm Fnd Health and Human Service Grants, 2216
Hampton Roads Comm Fnd Horticulture Grants, 2217
Hampton Roads Comm Fnd Nonprofit Facilities Improvement Grants, 2218
Hancock County Fnd - Field of Interest Grants, 2219
Hancock County Comm Fnd - Programming Mini-Grants, 2220
Handsel Fnd Grants, 2221
Hannaford Charitable Fnd Grants, 2222
Harbus Fnd Grants, 2223
Harley Davidson Fnd Grants, 2224
Harold Alfond Fnd Grants, 2225
Harold & Arlene Schnitzer CARE Fdn Grts, 2226
Harold Brooks Fnd Grants, 2227
Harold K. L. Castle Fnd Grants, 2228
Harold R. Bechtel Charitable Remainder Grants, 2229
Harold Simmons Fnd Grants, 2230
Harris and Eliza Kempner Fund Grants, 2231
Harris Graduate School of Public Policy Studies Research Dev Grants, 2232
Harrison Cty Comm Fdn Grts, 2233
Harrison County Comm Fnd Signature Grants, 2234
Harris Teeter Corporate Contributions Grants, 2235
Harry B. and Jane H. Brock Fnd Grants, 2237
Harry Bramhall Gilbert Char Trust Grts, 2238
Harry C. Trexler Trust Grants, 2239
Harry Chapin Fnd Grants, 2240
Harry Edison Fnd, 2241
Harry Kramer Grants, 2242
Harry S. Black and Allon Fuller Fund Grants, 2243
Harry Sudakoff Fnd Grants, 2245
Harry W. Bass, Jr. Fnd Grants, 2246
Hartford Aging and Health Program Awards, 2247
Hartford Courant Fnd Grants, 2248
Hartford Fdn Application Plng Grts, 2249
Hartford Fnd Evaluation Grants, 2250
Hartford Fdn Implementation Sppt Grts, 2251
Hartford Fnd Regular Grants, 2253
Harvest Fnd Grants, 2254
Harvey Randall Wickes Fnd Grants, 2255
Hasbro Children's Fund, 2256
Hatton W. Sumners Fnd for the Study and Teaching of Self Government Grants, 2257

Hawai'i Children's Trust Fund Comm Awareness Events Grants, 2258
Hawaiian Electric Industries Charitable Grants, 2259
Hawaii Comm Fnd Capacity Building Grants, 2260
Hawaii Comm Fnd Geographic-Specific Grants, 2261
Hawaii Comm Fnd Human Services Grants, 2262
Hawaii Comm Fnd Organizational Capacity Building Grants, 2263
Hawaii Comm Fnd Reverend Takie Okumura Family Grants, 2264
Hawaii Comm Fnd Social Change Grants, 2265
Hawaii Comm Fnd West Hawaii Fund Grants, 2266
Haymarket People's Fund Sustaining Grants, 2267
Haymarket Urgent Response Grants, 2268
Hazen Fnd Public Educ Grants, 2269
Hazen Fnd Youth Organizing Grants, 2270
HBF Defending Freedoms Grants, 2271
HBF Encouraging Citizen Involvement Grants, 2272
HBF Pathways Out of Poverty Grants, 2273
HCA Fnd Grants, 2274
Head Start Replacement Grantee: Colorado, 2275
Head Start Replacement Grantee: Florida, 2276
Health Canada National Seniors Indep Grants, 2278
Healthcare Fdn for Orange Cty Grts, 2279
Healthcare Fnd of New Jersey Grants, 2280
Health Fnd of Grtr Cincinnati Grts, 2281
Health Fnd of Grtr Indianapolis Grts, 2282
Health Fnd of South Florida Responsive Grants, 2283
Hearst Fnds Culture Grants, 2284
Hearst Fnds Social Service Grants, 2285
Heartland Arts Fund, 2286
Hedco Fnd Grants, 2287
Heifer Educational Fund Grants for Principals, 2288
Heifer Educational Fund Grants for Teachers, 2289
Heinz Endowments Grants, 2291
Helena Rubinstein Fnd Grants, 2292
Helen Bader Fnd Grants, 2293
Helen Gertrude Sparks Charitable Trust Grants, 2294
Helen Irwin Littauer Educational Trust Grants, 2295
Helen K & Arthur E Johnson Fdn Grts, 2296
Helen Pumphrey Denit Charitable Trust Grants, 2297
Helen S. Boylan Fnd Grants, 2298
Helen Steiner Rice Fnd Grants, 2299
Helen V. Brach Fnd Grants, 2300
Hendricks Cty Comm Fdn Grts, 2302
Henrietta Tower Wurts Memorial Fnd Grants, 2304
Henry A. and Mary J. MacDonald Fnd, 2305
Henry & Ruth Blaustein Rosenberg Fdn Grants, 2306
Henry County Comm Fnd - TASC Youth Grants, 2307
Henry County Comm Fnd Grants, 2308
Henry E. Niles Fnd Grants, 2309
Henry J. Kaiser Family Fnd Grants, 2310
Henry M. Jackson Fnd Grants, 2311
Henry W. Bull Fnd Grants, 2312
Herbert A & Adrian W Woods Fdn Grts, 2313
Herbert H & Grace A Dow Fdn Grants, 2315
Herman Abbott Family Fnd Grants, 2316
Herman Goldman Fnd Grants, 2317
Hershey Company Grants, 2318
Highmark Corporate Giving Grants, 2319
High Meadow Fnd Grants, 2321
Hilda and Preston Davis Fnd Grants, 2322
Hilfiger Family Fnd Grants, 2323
Hillcrest Fnd Grants, 2325
Hill Crest Fnd Grants, 2324
Hill Fnd Grants, 2326
Hillman Fnd Grants, 2327
Hillsdale County Comm General Adult Grants, 2328
Hilton Head Island Fnd Grants, 2330
Hilton Hotels Corporate Giving, 2331
Hirtzel Memorial Fnd Grants, 2332
Historic Landmarks Fnd of Indiana Historic Preservation Educ Grants, 2334
Historic Landmarks Fnd of Indiana Preservation Grants, 2337
Hitachi Fnd Business and Work Grants, 2339
Hitachi Fnd Yoshiyama Awards, 2340
Hoblitzelle Fnd Grants, 2341
Hoffberger Fnd Grants, 2342
Hogg Fnd for Mental Health Grants, 2343

Hoglund Fnd Grants, 2344
Holland/Zeeland Comm Fdn Grts, 2345
Hollie and Anna Oakley Fnd Grants, 2346
HomeBanc Fnd Grants, 2347
Home Building Industry Disaster Relief Fund, 2348
Homer A Scott & Mildred S Scott Fdn Grants, 2350
Homer C. and Martha W. Gutchess Fnd Grants, 2351
Homer Fnd Grants, 2352
Hometown Indiana Grants, 2353
Honda of America Manufacturing Fnd Grants, 2354
Honeywell Corp Family Safety & Security Grts, 2356
Honeywell Corp Leadership Challenge Academy, 2359
Honor the Earth Grants, 2361
Horace A Kimball & S Ella Kimball Fdn Grts, 2362
Horace Moses Charitable Fnd Grants, 2363
Horizon Fnd for New Jersey Grants, 2364
Horizon Fnd Grants, 2365
Horizons Comm Issues Grants, 2366
Household Int'l Corp Giving Grants, 2372
Houston Endowment Grants, 2373
Howard and Bush Fnd Grants, 2374
Howard County Comm Fdn Grts, 2375
Howard H. Callaway Fnd Grants, 2376
Howe Fnd of North Carolina Grants, 2377
HRF Hudson River Improvement Grants, 2378
Huber Fnd Grants, 2382
Hudson Webber Fnd Grants, 2383
Huffy Fnd Grants, 2384
Hugh J. Andersen Fnd Grants, 2385
Huie-Dellmon Trust Grants, 2386
Humana Fnd Grants, 2388
Humane Society of the United States Foreclosure Pets Grants, 2389
Humanitas Fnd Grants, 2390
Huntington Arts Council Arts-in-Educ Programs, 2400
Huntington Arts Council Decentralization Comm Arts Grants, 2401
Huntington Arts Council JP Morgan Chase Artist Reach Out Grants, 2402
Huntington Arts Council JP Morgan Chase Organization/Stabilization Regrants, 2403
Huntington Clinical Fnd Grants, 2404
Huntington County Comm Hiner Family Grant, 2405
Huntington County Comm Fnd - Make a Difference Grants, 2406
Huntington County Stephanie Pyle Grant, 2407
Huntington Fnd Grants, 2408
Hutchinson Comm Fnd Grants, 2410
Hut Fnd Grants, 2411
Hutton Fnd Grants, 2412
Hyams Fnd Grants, 2413
Hyde Family Fnds Grants, 2414
Hydrogen Student Design Contest, 2415
I.A. O'Shaughnessy Fnd Grants, 2416
IAFF Harvard Univ Trade Union Scholarships, 2417
IAFF Labour College of Canada Residential Scholarship, 2418
IAFF National Labor College Scholarships, 2419
IAFF W. H. McClennan Scholarship, 2420
Ian Hague Perl 6 Dev Grants, 2421
IBCAT Screening Mammography Grants, 2422
IBM Adult Trng & Workforce Dev Grts, 2423
IBM Arts and Culture Grants, 2424
IBM Comm Dev Grants, 2425
ICC Comm Service Mini-Grant, 2426
ICC Day of Service Action Grants, 2427
ICC Faculty Fellowships, 2428
ICC Listening to Communities Grants, 2429
ICC Scholarship of Engagement Faculty Grants, 2430
Ida Alice Ryan Charitable Trust Grants, 2431
Idaho Comm Eastern Region Competitive Grants, 2432
Idaho Power Co Corp Contributions, 2433
IDEM Section 205(j) Water Quality Management Planning Grants, 2434
IDEM Section 319(h) Nonpoint Source Grants, 2435
IDOT Economic Dev Pgm Grts, 2436
IDOT Rail Freight Pgm Loans & Grants, 2437
IDOT Truck Access Route Pgm Grts, 2438
IDPH Carolyn Adams Ticket for the Cure Comm Grants, 2439

PROGRAM TYPE INDEX

Community Development / 1043

IDPH Emergency Med Svcs Astnc Fund Grts, 2440
IDPH Hosptial Capital Investment Grants, 2441
IDPH Local Health Dept Public Health Emergency Response Grants, 2442
IEDC Industrial Dev Grant Fund, 2443
IEDC Int'l Trade Show Assistance Pgm, 2444
IEDC Skills Enhancement Fund, 2445
IIE David L. Boren Fellowships, 2454
IIE Freeman Fnd Indonesia Internships, 2456
Illinois Arts Council Arts Service Organizations Grants, 2464
Illinois Arts Cncl Comm Arts Access Grts, 2466
Illinois Arts Council Ethnic and Folk Arts Master Apprentice Grants, 2468
Illinois Arts Council Local Arts Agencies Grants, 2471
Illinois Arts Council Music Grants, 2474
Illinois Arts Council Presenters Dev Grants, 2476
Illinois Arts Council Vis Arts Pgm Grts, 2478
Illinois Clean Energy Comm Fnd Energy Efficiency Grants, 2479
Illinois Clean Energy Comm Fnd K-12 Wind Schools Pilot Grants, 2480
Illinois Clean Energy Comm Fnd Renewable Energy Grants, 2481
Illinois Clean Energy Comm Fnd Solar Thermal Installation Grants, 2482
Illinois DCEO Business Dev Public Infrastructure Grants, 2483
Illinois DCEO Coal Competitiveness Grants, 2484
Illinois DCEO Coal Demonstration Grants, 2485
Illinois DCEO Coal Dev Grants, 2486
Illinois DCEO Coal Revival Grants, 2487
Illinois DCEO Comm Dev Assistance Pgm for Economic Dev (CDAP-ED) Grants, 2488
Illinois DCEO Eliminate the Digital Divide, 2489
Illinois DCEO Emerging Technological Enterprises Grants, 2490
Illinois DCEO Employer Trng Investment Pgm Grts - Competitive Component, 2491
Illinois DCEO Employer Trng Investment Pgm Grts - Incentive Component, 2492
Illinois DCEO Employer Trng Investment Pgm Multi-Company Trng Grts, 2493
Illinois DCEO Employer Trng Investment Pgm Single Company Trng Grts, 2494
Illinois DCEO Large Business Dev Grants, 2495
Illinois DNR Habitat Fund Grants, 2497
Illinois DNR Migratory Waterfowl Stamp Grants, 2498
Illinois DNR Park and Recreational Facility Construction Grants, 2499
Illinois DNR Schlyd Habitat Action Grts, 2500
Illinois DNR State Furbearer Fund Grants, 2501
Illinois DNR State Pheasant Fund Grants, 2502
Illinois DNR Urban & Cmty Forestry Grts, 2503
Illinois DNR Volunteer Fire Assistance Grants, 2504
Illinois DNR Wildlife Preservation Fund Large Project Grants, 2505
Illinois DNR Wildlife Preservation Fund Small Project Grants, 2506
Illinois DNR Wildlife Preservation Maintenance of Wildlife Rehabilitation Facilities Grants, 2507
Illinois DNR Youth Recreation Corps Grants, 2508
Illinois Humanities Council Comm General Support Grants, 2509
Illinois Tool Works Fnd Grants, 2511
IMLS American Heritage Preservation Grants, 2513
IMLS Nat Medal for Museum & Library Service, 2516
IMLS Native Hawaiian Library Services Grants, 2519
IMLS Save America's Treasures Grants, 2521
Impact 100 Grants, 2522
Inasmuch Fnd Grants, 2523
Independence Blue Cross Charitable Medical Care Grants, 2524
Independence Comm Fnd Quality of Life Grant, 2525
Independence Comm Fnd Education, Culture & Arts Grant, 2526
Independence Comm Fnd Neighborhood Renewal Grants, 2527
Indiana 21st Century Research & Tech Awards, 2528
Indiana AIDS Fund Grants, 2529

Indiana Arts Commission American Masterpieces Grants, 2530
Indiana Arts Commission Cap Bldg Grts, 2531
Indiana Arts Commission Multi-regional Major Arts Institutions Grants, 2532
Indiana Arts Commission Statewide Arts Service Organization Grants, 2533
Indiana Boating Infrastructure Grants (BIG P), 2534
Indiana Clean Vessel Act Grants, 2535
Indiana Corn Marketing Council Retailer Grant for Tank Cleaning, 2536
Indiana Historic Preservation Fund Grants, 2537
Indiana Household Hazardous Waste Grants, 2538
Indiana Humanities Council Initiative Grants, 2539
Indianapolis Power & Light Company Grants, 2540
Indianapolis Preservation Grants, 2543
Indiana Preservation Grants, 2544
Indiana Recycling Grants, 2545
Indiana Reg'l Econ Dev Partnership Grts, 2546
Indiana Rural Capacity Grants, 2547
Indiana SBIR/STTR Commercialization Enhancement Program, 2548
Indiana Space Grant Consortium Grants for Informal Educ Partnerships, 2549
Indiana Space Grant Consortium Workforce Dev Grants, 2550
Indiana Waste Tire Fund Pgm Grts, 2551
Indiana Workforce Acceleration Grants, 2552
Information Soc Innovation Fund Grts, 2554
ING Fnd Grants, 2555
Initiaive Fdn Inside-Out Connections Grts, 2556
Initiative Fnd Healthy Communities Partnership Grants, 2557
Initiative Fnd Innovation Fund Grants, 2559
Initiative Fnd Minnesota Early Childhood Initiative Grants, 2560
Intel Comm Grants, 2562
Intel Int'l Comm Grants, 2564
Int'l Association of Emergency Man Scholarships, 2566
Int'l Human Rights Funders Grants, 2567
Int'l Paper Co Fnd Grants, 2568
Internet Society Fellowships, 2570
IRC Comm Collaboratives for Refugee Women and Youth Grants, 2573
Ireland Family Fnd Grants, 2574
IREX Egypt Media Dev Grants, 2575
IREX Kosovo Civil Soc Project Grts, 2576
IREX Moldova Citizen Participation Grants, 2578
IREX Project Smile Grants, 2579
IREX Russia Civil Society Support Grants, 2580
IREX Small Grant Fund for Civil Society Projects in Africa and Asia, 2581
IREX Small Grant Fund for Media Projects in Africa and Asia, 2582
IREX Yemen Women's Leadership Grants, 2583
Irving S. Gilmore Fnd Grants, 2584
Irvin Stern Fnd Grants, 2585
Isabel Allende Fnd Esperanza Grants, 2586
ISA John Z. Duling Grants, 2587
Ittleson Fnd AIDS Grants, 2589
Ittleson Fnd Mental Health Grants, 2590
IYI Responsible Fatherhood Grants, 2591
J.B. Reynolds Fnd Grants, 2592
J. Bulow Campbell Fnd Grants, 2593
J.C. Penney Company Grants, 2594
J.E. and L.E. Mabee Fnd Grants, 2595
J. Edwin Treakle Fnd Grants, 2596
J. F. Maddox Fnd Grants, 2597
J. Knox Gholston Fnd Grants, 2599
J.L. Bedsole Fnd Grants, 2600
J.M. Kaplan Fund City Life Grants, 2601
J.M. Kaplan Fund Migrations Grants, 2602
J.M. Long Fnd Grants, 2603
J. Mack Robinson Fnd Grants, 2604
J. Marion Sims Fnd Teachers' Pet Grant, 2605
J. Spencer Barnes Memorial Fnd Grants, 2606
J.W. Kieckhefer Fnd Grants, 2607
J. Walton Bissell Fnd Grants, 2608
J Willard & Alice S Marriott Fdn Grts, 2609
J. Willard Marriott, Jr. Fnd Grants, 2610

Jackson Cty Comm Fdn Unrestricted Grts, 2611
Jackson County Comm Fnd Youth Advisory Committee Grants, 2612
Jackson Fnd Grants, 2613
Jacksonville Jaguars Fnd Grants, 2614
Jacob and Hilda Blaustein Fnd Grants, 2615
Jacob G. Schmidlapp Trust Grants, 2616
Jacobs Family Fnd Jabara Learning Opportunities Grants, 2617
Jacobs Family Fnd Spirit of the Diamond Grants, 2618
Jacobs Family Fdn Vlg Neighborhoods Grants, 2619
James & Abigail Campbell Fam Fdn Grts, 2620
James A. and Faith Knight Fnd Grants, 2621
James F & Marion L Miller Fdn Grts, 2622
James Ford Bell Fnd Grants, 2623
James G.K. McClure Educational and Dev Fund Grants, 2624
James Graham Brown Fdn Qlty of Life Grts, 2625
James Irvine Fnd Creative Connections Grants, 2628
James J & Angelia M Harris Fdn Grts, 2630
James J. McCann Charitable Trust and McCann Fnd, Inc Grants, 2631
James M. Collins Fnd Grants, 2633
James M. Cox Fnd of Georgia Grants, 2634
James R. Dougherty Jr. Fnd Grants, 2635
James R. Thorpe Fnd Grants, 2636
James S. Copley Fnd Grants, 2637
Jane's Trust Grants, 2639
Jane and Jack Fitzpatrick Fund Grants, 2640
Jane Bradley Pettit Fnd Arts and Culture Grants, 2641
Jane Bradley Pettit Fnd Comm & Social Dev Grants, 2642
Jane Bradley Pettit Fnd Health Grants, 2643
Janesville Fnd Grants, 2644
Janirve Fnd Grants, 2645
Janson Fnd Grants, 2646
Janus Fnd Grants, 2647
Japan Fnd Center for Global Partnership Grants, 2649
Japan Fnd Los Angeles Mini-Grants for Japanese Arts & Culture, 2651
Japan Fnd New York Small Arts & Culture Grants, 2652
Jaquelin Hume Fnd Grants, 2654
Jasper Fnd Grants, 2655
Jean and Louis Dreyfus Fnd Grants, 2658
Jean and Price Daniel Fnd Grants, 2659
Jeffris Wood Fnd Grants, 2660
JELD-WEN Fnd Grants, 2661
Jenifer Altman Fnd Grants, 2662
Jenkins Fnd: Improving the Health of Greater Richmond Grants, 2663
Jennings County Comm Fdn Grts, 2664
Jennings County Comm Fnd Women's Giving Circle Grant, 2665
Jerome & Mildred Paddock Fdn Grts, 2666
Jerome Fnd Grants, 2667
Jerry L & Barbara J Burris Fdn Grts, 2669
Jessie B. Cox Charitable Trust Grants, 2670
Jessie Ball Dupont Fund Grants, 2671
Jessie Smith Noyes Fnd Grants, 2672
Jewish Comm Fnd of Los Angeles Cutting Edge Grants, 2673
Jewish Comm Fnd of Los Angeles Israel Grants, 2674
Jewish Fund Grants, 2675
Jewish Funds for Justice Grants, 2676
Jim Blevins Fnd Grants, 2678
Jim Moran Fnd Grants, 2680
JM Fnd Grants, 2681
Joan Bentinck-Smith Charitable Fdn Grts, 2682
Joe W & Dorothy Dorsett Brown Fdn Grts, 2684
John & Elizabeth Whiteley Fdn Grts, 2685
John and Margaret Post Fnd Grants, 2686
John Ben Snow Memorial Trust Grants, 2687
John C. Lasko Fnd Trust Grants, 2688
John Deere Fnd Grants, 2692
John Edward Fowler Mem Fdn Grants, 2693
John F. Kennedy Center for the Performing Arts National Rosemary Kennedy Internship, 2694
John G. Duncan Trust Grants, 2695
John H. and Wilhelmina D. Harland Charitable Fnd Grants, 2698
John H. Wellons Fnd Grants, 2699

John I. Smith Charities Grants, 2700
John J. Leidy Fnd Grants, 2701
John Jewett & Helen Chandler Garland Fdn, 2702
John Lord Knight Fnd Grants, 2703
John M. Ross Fnd Grants, 2704
John M. Weaver Fnd Grants, 2705
John Merck Fund Grants, 2706
John P. McGovern Fnd Grants, 2707
John R. Oishei Fnd Grants, 2709
John Reynolds and Eleanor B. Allen Charitable Fnd Grants, 2710
John S & James L Knight Fdn Dnr Adv Fd Grts, 2712
John S. and James L. Knight Fnd Grants, 2713
John S. and James L. Knight Fnd National and New Initiatives Grants, 2714
Johns Manville Fund Grants, 2716
Johnson Controls Fnd Arts and Culture Grants, 2719
Johnson Controls Fdn Civic Activities Grts, 2720
Johnson Controls Fnd Educ and Arts Matching Gift Grants, 2721
Johnson Cty Comm Fdn Grts, 2723
Johnson County Comm Fnd Youth Philanthropy Initiative Grants, 2724
Johnson Scholarship Fnd Grants, 2726
John W. Alden Trust Grants, 2727
John W & Anna H Hanes Fdn Grants, 2728
John W. Anderson Fnd Grants, 2729
John W. Boynton Fund Grants, 2730
John W. Speas and Effie E. Speas Memorial Trust Grants, 2732
Joseph Drown Fnd Grants, 2735
Joseph H & Florence A Roblee Fdn Grants, 2736
Josephine G. Russell Trust Grants, 2737
Josephine Goodyear Fnd Grants, 2738
Joseph P. Kennedy Jr. Fnd Grants, 2740
Joseph S. Stackpole Charitable Trust Grants, 2741
Josiah W & Bessie H Kline Fdn Grants, 2742
Joukowsky Family Fnd Grants, 2743
Journal Gazette Fnd Grants, 2744
Jovid Fnd Grants, 2745
Joyce Fnd Culture Grants, 2747
Joyce Fnd Democracy Grants, 2748
Joyce Fnd Employment Grants, 2749
Joyce Fnd Environment Grants, 2750
Joyce Fdn Gun Violence Prevention Grts, 2751
JP Morgan Chase Arts and Culture Grants, 2752
JP Morgan Chase Comm Dev Grts, 2753
Judge Isaac Anderson, Jr. Scholarship, 2754
Judith and Jean Pape Adams Charitable Fnd Tulsa Area Grants, 2755
Judith Clark-Morrill Fnd Grants, 2756
K. M. Hunter Charitable Social Welfare Grants, 2757
K.S. Adams Fnd Grants, 2758
K21 Health Fdn Cancer Care Fund Grts, 2759
K21 Health Fnd Grants, 2760
KaBOOM-CA Playground Challenge Grants, 2761
Kahuku Comm Fund, 2762
Kalamazoo Comm Fnd Capacity Building Grants, 2764
Kalamazoo Comm Fnd Economic and Comm Dev Grants, 2765
Kalamazoo Comm Fnd Environment Fund Grants, 2766
Kalamazoo Comm Fnd Front Porch Grants, 2767
Kalamazoo Comm Fnd Good Neighbor Grants, 2768
Kalamazoo Comm Fnd Individuals and Families Grants, 2769
Kalamazoo Comm Fnd John E. Fetzer Institute Fund Grants, 2770
Kalamazoo Comm LBGT Equality Fund Grants, 2771
Kalamazoo Comm Fdn Mini-Grts, 2772
Kalamazoo Comm Fnd Youth Dev Grants, 2773
Kaneta Fnd Grants, 2774
Kansas Health Fnd Recognition Grants, 2784
Ka Papa O Kakuhihewa Fund, 2785
Kate B. Reynolds Charitable Health Care Grants, 2786
Kate B. Reynolds Charitable Trust Poor and Needy Grants, 2787
Katharine Matthies Fnd Grants, 2788
Katherine Baxter Memorial Fnd Grants, 2789
Kathryne Beynon Fnd Grants, 2791
Katie's Krops Grants, 2792

Katrine Menzing Deakins Char Trust Grts, 2793
Kawabe Grants, 2794
KEEN Effect Grants, 2795
Kelvin and Eleanor Smith Fnd Grants, 2796
Kendrick Fnd Grants, 2797
Kenneth A. Scott Charitable Trust Grants, 2801
Kenny's Kids Grants, 2803
Kent D. Steadley and Mary L. Steadley Grants, 2804
Kentucky Arts Cncl Access Astnce Grts, 2805
Kentucky Arts Council Emerging Artist Award, 2807
Kentucky Arts Council Teaching Together Grants, 2811
Kessler Fdn Comm Employment Grts, 2814
Kessler Fdn Hurricane Sandy Emergency Grts, 2815
Kessler Fdn Signature Employment Grts, 2816
Kettering Fund Grants, 2818
Kevin P & Sydney B Knight Family Fdn Grts, 2819
KeyBank Fnd Grants, 2820
KeySpan Fnd Grants, 2821
Kiki Madazine Grow Strong Girls through Leadership Grants, 2822
Kimberly-Clark Comm Grants, 2824
Kirkpatrick Fnd Grants, 2827
Knight Fdn Donor Advised Fund Grts, 2828
Knox County Comm Fnd Grants, 2831
Kohler Fnd Grants, 2833
Komen Grtr NYC Comty Breast Health Grts, 2835
Komen Greater NYC Small Grants, 2836
Koret Fnd Grants, 2837
Kosciusko Cty Comm Fdn Grts, 2838
Kosciusko County Comm Fnd REMC Operation Round Up Grants, 2839
Kovler Family Fnd Grants, 2840
Kroger Company Donations, 2841
Kroger Fnd Diversity Grants, 2842
Kroger Fdn Grassroots Comty Support Grants, 2843
Kroger Fnd Hunger Relief Grants, 2844
L. W. Pierce Family Fnd Grants, 2846
LA84 Fnd Grants, 2847
Laclede Gas Charitable Trust Grants, 2848
Lafayette - West Lafayette Convention and Visitors Bureau Tourist Promotion Grants, 2849
LaGrange Cty Comm Fdn Grts, 2850
LaGrange Independent Fnd for Endowments, 2851
Laidlaw Fnd Multi-Year Grants, 2852
Laidlaw Fnd Youh Organizing Catalyst Grants, 2853
Laidlaw Fnd Youth Organizaing Grants, 2854
Lake County Comm Fund Grants, 2856
Lana'i Comm Benefit Fund, 2857
Land O'Lakes Fdn California Region Grts, 2858
Land O'Lakes Fnd Comm Grants, 2859
Land O'Lakes Fnd Dollars for Doers, 2860
Lands' End Corporate Giving Program, 2861
Laura Jane Musser Intrcltrl Harmony Grts, 2862
Laura Jane Musser Rural Arts Grants, 2863
Laura Jane Musser Rural Initiative Grants, 2864
Laura Moore Cunningham Fnd Grants, 2866
Laurel Fnd Grants, 2867
Lawrence J. and Anne Rubenstein Charitable Fnd Grants, 2868
Leadership IS Award, 2869
Lee and Ramona Bass Fnd Grants, 2871
Leeway Fnd Art and Change Grants, 2872
Leeway Fnd Transformation Award, 2873
Legacy Fnd College Readiness Grant, 2874
Legacy Partners in Environmental Ed Grants, 2876
Legler Benbough Fnd Grants, 2877
LEGO Children's Fund Grants, 2878
Leicester Savings Bank Fund, 2879
Leighton Award for Nonprofit Excellence, 2880
Lena Benas Grants, 2881
Leo Goodwin Fnd Grants, 2882
Leon and Thea Koerner Fnd Grants, 2883
Leo Niessen Jr., Charitable Trust Grants, 2885
Letha E. House Fnd Grants, 2886
Lettie Pate Evans Fnd Grants, 2887
Lettie Pate Whitehead Fnd Grants, 2888
Lewis H. Humphreys Charitable Trust Grants, 2889
Liberty Bank Fnd Grants, 2890
Liberty Hill Fdn Enviro Justice Fund Grts, 2891
Liberty Hill Fund for New Los Angeles Grants, 2892

Liberty Hill Fdn Fund for Change Grts, 2893
Liberty Hill Fnd Lesbian & Gay Grants, 2894
Liberty Hill Fnd Queer Youth Fund Grts, 2895
Liberty Hill Fnd Seed Fund Grants, 2896
Liberty Hill Fnd Special Opportunity Grants, 2897
Libra Fnd Future Grants, 2898
Libra Fnd Grants, 2899
Lied Fnd Trust Grants, 2900
Lillian S. Wells Fnd Grants, 2901
Lilly Endowment Giving Indiana Funds for Tomorrow Grants, 2903
Lily Auchincloss Fnd Grants, 2904
Lily Palmer Fry Memorial Trust Grants, 2905
Lincoln Financial Group Fnd Grants, 2906
Linden Fnd Grants, 2908
Lisa and Douglas Goldman Fund Grants, 2910
LISC Financial Opportunity Center Social Innovation Fund Grants, 2911
LISC MetLife Police Partnership Awards, 2912
LISC NFL Grassroots Grants, 2913
Liz Claiborne & Art Ortenberg Fdn Grts, 2914
Liz Claiborne Fnd Grants, 2915
Local Initiatives Support Corporation Grants, 2917
Lockheed Martin Philanthropic Grants, 2918
Lois and Richard England Family Fnd Jewish Comm Life Grants, 2919
Long Island Comm Fnd Grants, 2920
Lotus 88 Fnd for Women and Children, 2921
Louetta M. Cowden Fnd Grants, 2922
Louie M & Betty M Phillips Fdn Grants, 2923
Louis and Elizabeth Nave Flarsheim Charitable Fnd Grants, 2924
Louis Calder Fnd Grants, 2925
Lowe's Charitable and Educational Fnd Grants, 2927
Lowe's Outdoor Classroom Grants, 2928
Lowe Fnd Grants, 2929
Lowell Berry Fnd Grants, 2930
Lubbock Area Fnd Grants, 2931
Lubrizol Corporation Comm Grants, 2932
Lubrizol Fnd Grants, 2933
Lucile Horton Howe & Mitchell B. Howe Grants, 2934
Lucy Downing Nisbet Charitable Fund Grants, 2935
Lucy Gooding Charitable Fnd Trust, 2936
Lucy Gooding Charitable Fdn Trust Grts, 2937
Luella Kemper Trust Grants, 2939
Lumpkin Family Fdn Healthy People Grts, 2942
Lumpkin Family Fnd Strong Leadership Grants, 2944
Luther I. Replogle Fnd Grants, 2945
Lydia deForest Charitable Trust Grants, 2946
Lynde and Harry Bradley Fnd Grants, 2947
Lyndhurst Fnd Grants, 2949
M.B. and Edna Zale Fnd Grants, 2950
M. Bastian Family Fnd Grants, 2951
M.E. Raker Fnd Grants, 2953
M.J. Murdock Charitable Trust General Grants, 2954
M3C Fellowships, 2955
Mabel A. Horne Trust Grants, 2956
Mabel F. Hoffman Charitable Trust Grants, 2957
Mabel Louise Riley Fnd Family Strengthening Small Grants, 2958
Mabel Louise Riley Fnd Grants, 2959
MacArthur Fnd Chicago Arts and Culture General Operations Grants, 2961
MacArthur Fnd Chicago Arts and Culture Int'l Connections Grants, 2962
MacArthur Fnd Policy Research Grants, 2964
MacDonald-Peterson Fnd Grants, 2965
Macquarie Bank Fnd Grants, 2966
Maddie's Fund Cmty Collab Projects, 2967
Maddie's Fund Cmty Shelter Data Grts, 2968
Maddie's Fund Lifesaving Awards, 2969
Madison Comm Fnd Altrusa Int'l Grants, 2970
Madison Comm Fnd Grants, 2971
Madison County Comm Fnd - City of Anderson Quality of Life Grant, 2972
Madison County Comm Fnd General Grants, 2973
Maine Comm Fdn Baldwin Area Grts, 2974
Maine Comm Belvedere Animal Welfare Grants, 2975
Maine Comm Fnd Belvedere Historic Preservation Grants, 2976

PROGRAM TYPE INDEX

Maine Comm Fnd Charity Grants, 2977
Maine Comm Fnd Comm Building Grants, 2978
Maine Comm Fnd Ed Daveis Benevolent Grants, 2979
Maine Comm Fnd Equity Grants, 2980
Maine Comm Fnd Expansion Arts Grants, 2981
Maine Comm Fnd Gracie Grants, 2982
Maine Comm Fnd Land Conservation Grants, 2983
Maine Comm Fdn Peaks Island Grts, 2984
Maine Comm Fnd People of Color Fund Grants, 2985
Maine Comm Fnd Ram Island Conservation Challenge Grants, 2986
Maine Comm Fnd Rines/Thompson Grants, 2987
Maine Comm Fnd Rose and Samuel Rudman Library Grants, 2988
Maine Comm Fnd Steeples Grants, 2989
Maine Comm Fnd Vincent B. and Barbara G. Welch Grants, 2990
Maine Women's Fund Econ Security Grts, 2992
Maine Women's Fund Girls' Grntmkg Init, 2993
Manitoba Arts Council Artist in Comm Residency Grants, 2994
Manitoba Arts Council Comm Connections and Access Grants, 2995
Manitoba Arts Council Spcl Opps Grts, 2997
Mann T. Lowry Fnd Grants, 2998
Marathon Petroleum Corporation Grants, 2999
Marcia and Otto Koehler Fnd Grants, 3000
Mardag Fnd Grants, 3001
Margaret & James A Elkins Jr Fdn Grts, 3003
Margaret L. Wendt Fnd Grants, 3004
Margaret T. Morris Fnd Grants, 3005
Marie C. and Joseph C. Wilson Fnd Rochester Small Grants, 3006
Marie H. Bechtel Charitable Remainder Uni-Trust Grants, 3007
Marie Walsh Sharpe Art Fnd Grants, 3009
Marin Comty Fdn Affordable Housing Grts, 3010
Marin Comm Ending Cycle of Poverty Grants, 3011
Marin Comm Fnd Social Justice and Interfaith Understanding Grants, 3012
Marin Comm Fnd Stinson Bolinas Comm Grants, 3013
Marin Comm Fnd Successful Aging Grants, 3014
Marion and Miriam Rose Fund Grants, 3015
Marion Cty Historic Preservn Fund Grts, 3016
Marion Gardner Jackson Char Trust Grts, 3017
Marion I & Henry J Knott Fdn Discret Grants, 3018
Marion I & Henry J Knott Fdn Std Grants, 3019
Marjorie Moore Charitable Fnd Grants, 3021
Mark Wahlberg Youth Fnd Grants, 3022
MARPAT Fnd Grants, 3023
Marriott Int'l Corporate Giving Grts, 3024
Mars Fnd Grants, 3025
Marshall Cty Comm Fdn Grts, 3026
Marsh Corporate Grants, 3027
Mary's Pence Ministry Grants, 3029
Mary's Pence Study Grants, 3030
Mary Black Fnd Active Living Grants, 3031
Mary Black Fdn Comm Health Grts, 3032
Mary Black Fnd Early Childhood Dev Grants, 3033
Mary C. & Perry F. Spencer Fnd Grants, 3034
Mary D. & Walter F Frear Eleemosynary Trust, 3035
Mary Duke Biddle Fnd Grants, 3036
Mary E. and Michael Blevins Charitable Grants, 3037
Mary E. Babcock Fnd, 3038
Mary E. Ober Fnd Grants, 3039
Mary Jane Luick Trust Grants, 3040
Mary Jennings Sport Camp Scholarship, 3041
Mary K. Chapman Fnd Grants, 3042
Mary Kay Fnd Domestic Violence Shelter Grants, 3044
Mary Owen Borden Fnd Grants, 3046
Mary Reynolds Babcock Fnd Grants, 3047
Mary S & David C Corbin Fdn Grants, 3048
Massachusetts Bar Fnd IOLTA Grants, 3050
Massachusetts Cultural Council Adams Grants, 3052
Massachusetts Cultural Council Cultural Facilities Capital Grants, 3053
Massachusetts Cultural Council Cultural Facilities Feasibility and Tech Assistance Grants, 3054
Massachusetts Cultural Council Cultural Facilities Systems Replacement Plan Grants Grants, 3055
Massachusetts Cultural Council Cultural Investment Portfolio, 3056
Massachusetts Cultural Council Local Cultural Council Grants, 3057
Massachusetts Cultural Council Traditional Arts Apprenticeships, 3058
Massachusetts Fnd for the Humanities Cultural Economic Dev Grants, 3059
Massachusetts Fnd for Humanities Project Grants, 3060
Massage Therapy Fnd Comm Service Grants, 3061
Mathile Family Fnd Grants, 3062
Maurice Amado Fnd Grants, 3063
Maurice J. Masserini Charitable Trust Grants, 3064
Max and Anna Levinson Fnd Grants, 3066
Maximilian E & Marion O Hoffman Fdn, 3067
Maxon Charitable Fnd Grants, 3068
May & Stanley Smith Char Trust Grants, 3069
Maytree Fnd Assisting Local Leaders w/ Immigrant Employment Strategies Grts, 3070
Maytree Fnd Refugee & Immigrant Grants, 3071
McCarthy Family Fnd Grants, 3073
McColl Fnd Grants, 3074
McConnell Fnd Grants, 3076
McCune Charitable Fnd Grants, 3077
McCune Fnd Humanaties Grants, 3079
McCune Fnd Human Services Grants, 3080
McGraw-Hill Companies Comm Grants, 3081
McGregor Fund Grants, 3082
McInerny Fnd Grants, 3083
McKesson Fnd Grants, 3084
McKnight Fnd Multiservice Grants, 3085
McKnight Fnd Region and Communities Grants, 3086
McLean Contributionship Grants, 3088
McLean Fnd Grants, 3089
MDARD AgD Value Added/Regional Food Systems Grants, 3091
MDARD County Fairs Cap Imprvmt Grts, 3092
MDARD Spclty Crop Block Grant-Farm Bill, 3093
MDEQ Beach Monitoring - Inland Lakes, 3094
MDEQ Brownfield ReDev and Site Reclamation Grants, 3095
MDEQ Clean Diesel Grants, 3096
MDEQ Coastal Management Planning and Construction Grants, 3097
MDEQ Comm Pollution Prevention (P2) Grants: Household Drug Collections, 3098
MDEQ Great Lakes Areas of Concern Land Acquisition Grants, 3099
MDEQ Local Water Qlty Monitoring Grants, 3100
MDEQ Wellhead Protection Grants, 3101
Meacham Fnd Memorial Grants, 3102
Mead Johnson Nutritionals Evansville-Area Organizations Grants, 3103
Meadows Fnd Grants, 3104
Mead Witter Fnd Grants, 3106
Medicaid/SCHIP Eligibility Pilots, 3107
MedImmune Charitable Grants, 3108
Medtronic Fnd Comm Link Arts, Civic, and Culture Grants, 3109
Medtronic Fnd CommLink Health Grants, 3111
Melville Charitable Trust Grants, 3115
Memorial Fnd for Children Grants, 3116
Merck Family Fund Urban Farming and Youth Leadership Grants, 3119
Merck Family Fund Youth Transforming Urban Communities Grants, 3120
Mericos Fnd Grants, 3121
Meriden Fnd Grants, 3122
Merkel Family Fnd Grants, 3123
Mertz Gilmore Climate Change Solutions Grants, 3125
Mertz Gilmore Fnd NYC Communities Grants, 3126
Mertz Gilmore Fnd NYC Dance Grants, 3127
Mervin Bovaird Fnd Grants, 3128
MetLife Building Livable Communities Grants, 3129
MetLife Fnd Empowering Older Adults Grants, 3130
MetLife Fdn Preparing Young People Grts, 3131
MetLife Fnd Promoting Employee Volunteerism, 3132
Metro Health Fnd Grants, 3133
MetroWest Health Fnd Capital Grants for Health-Related Facilities, 3134
MetroWest Health Fnd Grants--Healthy Aging, 3135
MetroWest Health Fnd Grants to Reduce the Incidence of High Risk Behaviors Among Adolescents, 3136
Metzger-Price Fund Grants, 3137
Meyer & Pepa Gold Family Fnd Grants, 3138
Meyer and Stephanie Eglin Fnd Grants, 3139
Meyer Fnd Benevon Grants, 3140
Meyer Fnd Economic Security Grants, 3141
Meyer Fnd Educ Grants, 3142
Meyer Fdn Healthy Communities Grts, 3143
Meyer Fnd Mgmt Assistance Grts, 3144
Meyer Fdn Strong Nonprofit Sector Grts, 3145
Meyer Memorial Trust Grassroots Grants, 3147
Meyer Memorial Trust Responsive Grants, 3148
Meyer Memorial Trust Special Grants, 3149
MFRI Operation Diploma Grants for Higher Educ Institutions, 3150
MFRI Operation Diploma Grants for Student Veterans Organizations, 3151
MFRI Operation Diploma Small Grants for Indiana Family Readiness Groups, 3152
MGM Resorts Fnd Comm Grants, 3153
MGN Family Fnd Grants, 3154
Miami County Boomerang Sisterhood Grant, 3155
Miami County Operation Round Up Grants, 3156
Miami County Comm Fnd Grants, 3157
Michael and Susan Dell Fnd Grants, 3158
Michael Reese Health Trust Core Grants, 3159
Michael Reese Health Trust Responsive Grants, 3160
Microsoft Authorized Refurbisher Donations, 3162
Microsoft Comty Affairs Puget Sound Grts, 3163
Microsoft Software Donation Grants, 3164
Microsoft Unlimited Potential - Comm Tech Skills Grants, 3165
Mid-America Arts Alliance Comm Engagement with Touring Artists Grants, 3166
Mid-America Arts Alliance Reg Touring Grants, 3167
Mid-Iowa Health Fdn Comty Response Grts, 3168
Mid Atlantic Arts American Masterpieces Grants, 3169
Mid Atlantic Arts Fnd Folk Arts Outreach Project Grants, 3171
Middlesex Savings Charitable Fnd Capacity Building Grants, 3172
Middlesex Savings Charitable Comm Dev Grants, 3173
Middlesex Savings Charitable Fnd Educational Opportunities Grants, 3174
Miguel Aleman Fnd Grants, 3175
Mildred V. Horn Fnd Grants, 3176
Military Ex-Prisoners of War Fdn Grts, 3177
Milken Family Fnd Grants, 3178
Miller Brewing Corporate Contributions Grants, 3180
Miller Fnd Grants, 3181
Millipore Fnd Grants, 3182
Milton and Sally Avery Arts Fnd Grants, 3183
Milton Hicks Wood and Helen Gibbs Wood Charitable Trust Grants, 3184
Mimi and Peter Haas Fund Grants, 3185
Minneapolis Fnd Comm Grants, 3186
Minnesota Small Cities Dev Grants, 3187
Mix It Up Grants, 3191
Mizuho USA Fnd Grants, 3192
MLB Tomorrow Fund Grants, 3193
MMS & Alliance Char Fdn Grts for Comm Action and Care for the Medically Uninsured, 3194
MMS and Alliance Charitable Fnd Int'l Health Studies Grants, 3195
Modest Needs Bridge Grants, 3197
Modest Needs Hurcn Sandy Rlf Grts: Phs 2, 3198
Modest Needs New Employment Grants, 3199
Modest Needs Non-Profit Grants, 3200
Modest Needs Self-Sufficiency Grants, 3201
Moline Fnd Comm Grants, 3202
Monfort Family Fnd Grants, 3203
Monsanto America's Farmers Grow Educ Grants, 3205
Monsanto Civic Partnership Grants, 3206
Monsanto Int'l Grants, 3207
Monsanto Kids Garden Fresh Grants, 3208
Montana Arts Cncl Cltrl & Aesthetic Proj Grts, 3209
Montana Comm Fnd Grants, 3211
Montana Comm Fnd Women's Grts, 3212

1046 / Community Development

Montgomery Cty Comm Fdn Grants, 3213
MONY Fnd Grants, 3214
Moody Fnd Grants, 3215
Moran Family Fnd Grants, 3216
Morgan Babcock Scholarships, 3217
Morris & Gwendolyn Cafritz Fdn Grants, 3218
Morris K. Udall and Stewart L. Udall Fnd Native American Congressional Internships, 3220
Motorola Fnd Grants, 3221
Ms Fdn for Women Bldg Democracy Grts, 3223
Ms Fdn for Women Ending Violence Grts, 3224
Ms. Fnd for Women Health Grants, 3225
Mt. Sinai Health Care Fnd Health of the Jewish Comm Grants, 3226
Mt. Sinai Health Care Fnd Health of the Urban Comm Grants, 3227
Mt. Sinai Health Care Fnd Health Policy Grants, 3228
NAA Fdn Diversity PowerMind Fwsps, 3232
NAA Fnd Minority Fellowships, 3233
NAA Fnd Teacher Fellowships, 3234
NAR HOPE Awards for Minority Owners, 3238
NAR Partners in Housing Awards, 3239
NASE Fdn Future Entrepreneur Schlrsp, 3241
NASE Growth Grants, 3242
NASE Succeed Scholarships, 3243
Natalie W. Furniss Charitable Trust Grants, 3244
Nathaniel & Elizabeth P Stevens Fdn Grants, 3247
National Center for Responsible Gaming Conference Scholarships, 3250
Nat'l Cntr for Responsible Gaming Travel Grts, 3251
National Endowment for Democracy Reagan-Fascell Democracy Fellowships, 3252
National Endowment for Democracy Vis Fellows, 3253
National Endowment for the Arts - Grants for Arts Projects: Challenge America Fast-Track, 3254
National Endowment for the Arts - National Arts and Humanities Youth Program Awards, 3255
National Endowment for Arts Our Town Grants, 3257
National Endowment for the Arts - State Partnership Agreement Grants, 3259
National Endowment for the Arts Dance Grants, 3262
National Endowment for the Arts Local Arts Agencies Grants, 3263
National Endowment for Arts Media Grants, 3264
National Endowment for Arts Museum Grants, 3265
National Endowment for the Arts Music Grants, 3266
National Endowment for Arts Presenting Grants, 3268
National Endowment for the Arts Theater and Musical Theater Grants, 3269
National Environmental Educ Fnd - Dept of Defense Legacy Award, 3270
National Environmental Educ Every Day Grants, 3271
National Home Library Fnd Grants, 3276
National Housing Endowment Challenge/Build/Grow Grant, 3277
National Inclusion Grants, 3278
National Lottery Comm Fund Grants, 3279
National Trust for Historic Preservation Diversity Scholarship, 3280
Nationwide Insurance Fnd Grants, 3285
Natonal Endowment for the Arts Research Grants, 3286
Nature Hills Nursery Green America Awards, 3287
NCFL/Better World Bks Libs & Families Awd, 3288
Needmor Fund Grants, 3289
Nehemiah Comm Fnd Grants, 3290
NEH Interpreting America's Historic Places, 3292
NEI Innovative Patient Outreach Programs And Ocular Screening Technologies To Improve Detection Of Diabetic Retinopathy Grants, 3295
NASE Fdn Future Entrepreneur Schlrsp, 3296
Nellie Mae Educ Fnd District Change Grants, 3297
Nellie Mae Educ Public Understanding Grants, 3298
Nellie Mae Educ Fnd State Level Systems Change Grants, 3299
Nevada Arts Cncl Folklife Apprenticeship Grts, 3309
Nevada Arts Council Learning Grants, 3313
Nevada Comm Fnd Grants, 3316
New Earth Fnd Grants, 3317
Newfoundland and Labrador Arts Council Comm Arts Grants, 3318

Newfoundland and Labrador Arts Council Professional Festivals Grants, 3321
Newfoundland and Labrador Arts Council Professional Project Grants, 3322
Newfoundland and Labrador Arts Council Sustaining Grants, 3323
Newfoundland and Labrador Arts Council Visiting Artists Grants, 3324
New Hampshire Charitable Fnd Grants, 3325
New Jersey Center for Hispanic Policy, Research and Dev Entrepreneurship Grants, 3326
New Jersey Center for Hispanic Policy, Research and Dev Immigration Integration Grants, 3328
New Jersey Center for Hispanic Policy, Research and Dev Innovative Initiatives Grants, 3329
New Jersey Center for Hispanic Policy, Research and Dev Workforce Grants, 3330
New Jersey Office of Faith Based Initiatives Creating Wealth Through Asset Building Grants, 3331
New Jersey Office of Faith Based Initiatives Service to Seniors Grants, 3333
Newman W. Benson Fnd Grants, 3334
New Mexico Women's Fnd Grants, 3335
Newton Cty Comm Fdn Grts, 3336
New York Fnd Grants, 3338
New York Landmarks Cons City Ventures Grants, 3339
New York Landmarks Cons Sacred Sites Grants, 3340
New York Life Fnd Grants, 3341
NFF Collaboration Support Grants, 3342
NFF Comm Assistance Grants, 3343
NFF Matching Grants, 3344
NFF Wilderness Stewardship Grants, 3346
NFL Charities NFL Player Fnd Grants, 3347
NFL Charities Pro Bowl Comm Grants in Hawaii, 3348
NFL High School Coach of the Week Grant, 3351
NFWF Alaska Fish and Wildlife Fund Grants, 3356
NFWF California Cstl Restor Fund Grts, 3362
NFWF Chesapeake Bay Conservation Innovation Grants, 3363
NFWF Chesapeake Bay Stewardship Fund Small Watershed Grants, 3364
NFWF Chesapeake Bay Tgtd Watershed Grts, 3365
NFWF Columbia Basin Water Trans Grants, 3366
NFWF Columbia River Estuarine Coastal Grants, 3367
NFWF Comm Salmon Fund Partnerships, 3368
NFWF ConocoPhillips SPIRIT of Conservation Migratory Bird Grants, 3369
NFWF Five-Star Restoration Challenge Grants, 3373
NFWF King County Comm Salmon Grants, 3375
NFWF Native Plant Conserv Init Grts, 3380
NFWF One Fly Conserv Partnership Grts, 3382
NFWF Oregon Governor's Fund for the Environment Grants, 3383
NFWF Pacific Grassroots Salmonid Init Grts, 3384
NFWF Pierce County Comm Salmon Grants, 3385
NFWF Pioneers in Conservation Grants, 3386
NFWF Pulling Together Initiative Grants, 3387
NFWF Salmon Recovery Funding Board Comm Salmon Fund Grants, 3389
NFWF Seafarer's Environmental Educ Grants, 3390
NFWF Shell Marine Habitat Grants, 3391
NFWF Southern Company Power of Flight Bird Conservation Grants, 3393
NFWF Southern Co Power of Flight Grts, 3394
NFWF Sustain Our Great Lakes Grants, 3396
NFWF Tampa Bay Environmental Fund Grts, 3397
NFWF Upper Mississippi River Watershed Grant, 3398
NGA 'Remember Me' Rose Schl Garden Awds, 3401
NGA Hansen's Natural and Native School Garden Grants, 3402
NGA Healthy Sprouts Awards, 3403
NGA Heinz Wholesome Memories Intergenerational Garden Awards, 3404
NGA Hooked on Hydroponics Awards, 3405
NGA Midwest School Garden Grants, 3407
NGA Wuzzleburg Preschool Garden Awards, 3408
NHLBI Bioengineering and Obesity Grants, 3411
NHLBI Lymphatics in Health and Disease in the Digestive, Urinary, Cardiovascular and Pulmonary Systems, 3415

PROGRAM TYPE INDEX

NHSCA General Project Grants, 3427
NIAF Anthony Campitelli Endwd Fund Grts, 3431
NICHD Academic-Comm Partnership Conference Series Grants, 3433
Nicholas H Noyes Jr Mem Fdn Grants, 3434
Nicor Corporate Contributions, 3435
Nicor Gas Sharing Grants, 3436
Nike and Ashoka GameChangers: Change the Game for Women in Sport, 3439
Nike Bowerman Track Renovation Grants, 3440
Nike Fnd Grants, 3441
Nike Giving - Cash and Product Grants, 3442
Nina Mason Pulliam Charitable Trust Grants, 3443
Nissan Fnd Grants, 3444
Nissan Neighbors Grants, 3445
NJSCA Financial and Inst Stabilization Grants, 3447
NJSCA Folk Arts Apprenticeships, 3448
NNEDVF/Altria Doors of Hope Program, 3452
NOAA Projects to Improve or Amend Coral Reef Fishery Management Plans, 3453
Noble County Comm Fnd Celebrate Diversity Project Grants, 3455
Noble County Comm Fnd Grants, 3456
Nokomis Fnd Grants, 3457
Nonprofit Management Fund Grants, 3458
Norcliffe Fnd Grants, 3459
Norcross Wildlife Fnd Grants, 3460
Nord Family Fnd Grants, 3461
Nordson Corporation Fnd Grants, 3462
Norfolk Southern Fnd Grants, 3463
Norman Fnd Grants, 3464
North American Wetlands Conserv Grts, 3465
North Carolina Arts Council Arts and Audiences Grants, 3466
North Carolina Arts Council Arts in Educ Artist Residencies Grants, 3468
North Carolina Arts Council Arts in Educ Initiatives Grants, 3469
North Carolina Arts Council Arts in Educ Rural Dev Grants, 3470
North Carolina Arts Council Comm Public Art and Design Dev Grants, 3472
North Carolina Arts Council Comm Public Art and Design Implementation Grants, 3473
North Carolina Arts Council Folklife Grants, 3476
North Carolina Arts Council New Realities Grant, 3478
North Carolina Arts Council Visual Arts Program Support Grants, 3484
North Carolina BioTech Center Event Sponsorship Grants, 3485
North Carolina BioTech Center Meeting Grants, 3486
North Carolina BioTech Center Reg Dev Grants, 3488
North Carolina Comm Fnd Grants, 3489
North Carolina GlaxoSmithKline Fdn Grants, 3490
North Central Health Services Grants, 3491
North Central Health Services Grants, 3492
North Dakota Comm Fnd Grants, 3493
North Dakota Council on the Arts Presenter Support Grants, 3497
NE Utilities Fnd Grants, 3498
Northern Chautauqua Comm Fnd Comm Grants, 3499
Northern Chautauqua Cmty Fdn DFT Communications Cmy Betterment Grts, 3500
Northern Chautauqua Comm Fdn Lake Shore Svgs & Loan Comnty Reinvestment Grts, 3502
Northern New York Comm Fdn Grts, 3503
Northern Trust Company Charitable Trust and Corporate Giving Program, 3504
North Georgia Comm Fnd Grants, 3505
NW Airlines KidCares Medical Travel Assistance, 3508
NW Mutual Fnd Grants, 3509
NW Fund for the Environment Grants, 3510
NW Minnesota Fnd Asset Building Grants, 3511
NW Minnesota Fnd Women's Fund Grants, 3512
Norton Fnd Grants, 3514
Norwin S & Elizabeth N Bean Fdn Grts, 3515
NRA Grants, 3517
NSERC Brockhouse Canada Prize for Interdisciplinary Research in Science and Engineering Grant, 3518
NSERC Michael Smith Awards, 3519

PROGRAM TYPE INDEX

Community Development / 1047

NSF CISE Communicating Research to Public Audiences Grants, 3522
NSF CISE Comm-Based Data Interoperability Networks Grants, 3523
NSF CISE Computer and Networks Core Grants, 3524
NSF CISE Computing and Communication Fnds : Core Grants, 3525
NSF CISE Computing Rsch Infrastructure, 3526
NSF Communicating Rsch to Public Audiences, 3527
NSF Partnership for Advancing Technologies in Housing Grants, 3529
NSTA Distinguished Informal Science Award, 3531
Nuffield Fnd Africa Grants, 3532
Nuffield Fdn Children and Families Grants, 3533
Nuffield Fnd Small Grants, 3535
Nu Skin Force for Good Fnd Grants, 3536
NWHF Health Advocacy Small Grants, 3537
NWHF Kaiser Permanente Comm Fund Grants, 3538
NWHF Partners Investing in Nursing's Future, 3539
NWHF Physical Activity and Nutrition Grants, 3540
NYCH Together Grants, 3541
NYCT AIDS/HIV Grants, 3542
NYCT Children & Youth w/ Disabilities Grts, 3544
NYCT Civic Affairs Grants, 3545
NYCT Comm Dev Grants, 3546
NYCT Fund for New Citizens Grants, 3547
NYCT Girls and Young Women Grants, 3548
NYCT Grants for the Elderly, 3549
NYCT Health Svcs, Systems & Policies Grts, 3550
NYCT Historic Preservation Grants, 3551
NYCT Hunger and Homelessnes Grants, 3553
NYCT Mental Health and Retardation Grants, 3554
NYCT Neighborhood Revitalization Grants, 3555
NYCT New York City Environment Grants, 3556
NYCT Social Services and Welfare Grants, 3557
NYCT Tech Assistance Grants, 3559
NYCT Youth Dev Grants, 3561
NYFA Artists in the School Planning Grants, 3562
NYFA Strategic Opportunity Stipends, 3566
NYHC Major and Mini Grants, 3567
NYHC Reading and Discussion Grants, 3568
NYHC Speakers in the Humanities Grants, 3569
NYSCA Architecture, Planning, and Design: Capital Fixtures and Equipment Purchase Grants, 3570
NYSCA Architecture, Planning, and Design: Capital Project Grants, 3571
NYSCA Architecture, Planning, and Design: Design and Planning Studies Grants, 3572
NYSCA Architecture, Planning, and Design: General Operating Support Grants, 3573
NYSCA Architecture, Planning, and Design: General Program Support Grants, 3574
NYSCA Architecture, Planning, and Design: Project Support Grants, 3576
NYSCA Arts Education: General Operating Support Grants, 3578
NYSCA Arts Education: General Program Support Grants, 3579
NYSCA Arts Education: Local Capacity Building Grants , 3581
NYSCA Dance: Gen Operating Support Grts, 3584
NYSCA Dance: Long-Term Residency in New York State Grants, 3586
NYSCA Dance: Services to the Field Grants, 3587
NYSCA Electronic Media and Film: Film Festivals Grants, 3588
NYSCA Electronic Media and Film: General Exhibition Grants, 3589
NYSCA Electronic Media and Film: General Operating Support, 3590
NYSCA Electronic Media and Film: General Program Support, 3591
NYSCA Electronic Media & Film Grants, 3592
NYSCA Lit: General Program Support Grants, 3599
NYSCA Lit: Public Programs, 3600
NYSCA Lit: Svcs to the Field Grts, 3601
NYSCA Museum: Gen Pgm Support Grts, 3603
NYSCA Museum: Project Support Grants, 3604
NYSCA Music: Cmy Music Schools Grts, 3605
NYSCA Music: Gen Operating Support Grts, 3606

NYSCA Music: Gen Pgm Support Grts, 3607
NYSCA Music: New Music Facilities, 3608
NYSCA Presenting: General Program Support, 3610
NYSCA Presenting: Svcs to the Field Grts, 3612
NYSCA Special Art Services: Project Support, 3613
NYSCA Special Arts Services: General Operating Support Grants, 3614
NYSCA Special Arts Services: General Program Support Grants, 3615
NYSCA Special Arts Services: Instruction and Training Grants, 3616
NYSCA Special Arts Services: Professional Performances Grants, 3617
NYSCA State and Local Partnerships: General Operating Support Grants, 3619
NYSCA State and Local Partnerships: General Program Support Grants, 3620
NYSCA State and Local Partnerships: Services to the Field Grants, 3621
NYSCA State and Local Partnerships: Workshops Grants, 3622
NYSCA Theatre: Gen Pgm Support Grts, 3624
NYSCA Theatre: Pro Performances Grts, 3625
NYSCA Theatre: Services to the Field Grants, 3626
NYSCA Visual Arts: Exhibitions and Installations Grants, 3627
NYSCA Visual Arts: Operating Support Grants, 3628
NYSCA Visual Arts: General Program Support, 3629
NYSCA Visual Arts: Svcs to the Field Grts, 3630
Oak Fnd Child Abuse Grants, 3632
Oak Fdn Housing & Homelessness Grts, 3633
Oakland Fund for Children and Youth Grants, 3634
OceanFirst Fnd Grants, 3636
Oceanside Charitable Fnd Grants, 3637
ODKF Athletic Grants, 3638
Office Depot Fdn Caring is Sharing Grts, 3639
Office Depot Fnd Disaster Relief Grants, 3640
Ogden Codman Trust Grants, 3641
Ohio Artists on Tour Fee Support Requests, 3642
Ohio Arts Council Artist in Residence Grants for Artists, 3644
Ohio Arts Council Artist in Residence Grants for Sponsors, 3645
Ohio Arts Council Arts Access Grants, 3647
Ohio Arts Council Arts Innovation Pgm Grts, 3649
Ohio Arts Council Arts Partnership Grants, 3650
Ohio Arts Council Building Cultural Diversity Initiative Grants, 3651
Ohio Arts Council Capacity Building Grants for Organizations and Communities, 3652
Ohio Arts Council Int'l Partnership Grts, 3653
Ohio Arts Council Sustainability Pgm Grts, 3654
Ohio County Comm Board of Directors Grants, 3656
Ohio County Comm Fnd Conference Grants, 3657
Ohio County Comm Fnd Grants, 3658
Ohio Cty Comm Fdn Junior Grts, 3659
Ohio River Border Initiative Grants, 3661
OJJDP Gang Prevention Coordination Assistance Grants, 3663
OJJDP Tribal Juvenile Accountability Discretionary Grants, 3665
Oklahoma City Comm Pgms & Grts, 3666
Oleonda Jameson Trust Grants, 3667
Olga Sipolin Children's Fund Grants, 3668
Olin Corporation Charitable Trust Grants, 3669
Olive B. Cole Fnd Grants, 3670
Olive Smith Browning Charitable Trust Grants, 3671
Onan Family Fnd Grants, 3672
OneFamily Fnd Grants, 3673
OneStar Fnd AmeriCorps Grants, 3674
Ontario Arts Cncl Aboriginal Arts Project Grts, 3675
Ontario Arts Council Artists in the Comm/Workplace Grants, 3676
Ontario Arts Council Compass Grants, 3677
Open Meadows Fnd Grants, 3683
Open Spaces Sacred Places National Awards, 3684
Oppenstein Brothers Fnd Grants, 3685
Oracle Corporate Contributions Grants, 3686
Orange County Comm Fnd Grants, 3687
Orange County Comm Fnd Grants, 3688

ORBI Artist Fast Track Grants, 3689
Orchard Fnd Grants, 3690
Ordean Fnd Grants, 3691
Oregon Youth Soccer Fnd Grants, 3692
OSF-Baltimore Comm Fellowships, 3695
OSF-Baltimore Crim & Juv Justice Grts, 3696
OSF-Baltimore Tackling Drug Adctn Grts, 3698
OSF Affordable Access to Digital Communications Initiative, 3700
OSF Arab Regional Office Grants, 3701
OSF Burma Project/SE Asia Init Grts, 3702
OSF Central Eurasia Project Grants, 3704
OSF Human Rights and Governance Grants, 3708
OSF Mental Health Initiative Grants, 3709
OSI After Prison Initiative Grants, 3710
OSI Sentencing and Incarceration Alternatives Project Grants, 3711
Ottinger Fnd Grants, 3712
Otto Bremer Fnd Grants, 3713
Overbrook Fnd Grants, 3715
Owen County Comm Fnd Grants, 3716
Owens Corning Fnd Grants, 3717
Owens Fnd Grants, 3718
Pacers Fnd Be Drug-Free Grants, 3720
Pacers Fnd Be Educated Grants, 3721
Pacers Fnd Indiana Fever's Be Younique Grants, 3724
PacifiCare Fnd Grants, 3725
Pacific Life Fnd Grants, 3726
PacifiCorp Fnd for Learning Grants, 3727
Packard Fnd Local Grants, 3729
Packard Fnd Organizational Effectiveness and Philanthropy Grants, 3730
Pajaro Valley Comm Health Health Trust Insurance/ Coverage & Educ on Using the System Grants, 3731
Pajaro Valley Comm Health Trust Diabetes and Contributing Factors Grants, 3732
Palm Beach and Martin Counties Grants, 3733
Parke County Comm Fnd Grants, 3735
Parker Fnd (California) Grants, 3736
Parker Grants to Support Christian Evangelism, 3737
Parkersburg Area Comm Fdn Action Grts, 3738
Park Fnd Grants, 3739
Partnership Enhancement Pgm Grts, 3740
Pasadena Fnd Average Grants, 3741
PAS Internship, 3742
Paso del Norte Health Fnd Grants, 3743
Patricia Price Peterson Fnd Grants, 3746
Patrick and Aimee Butler Family Fnd Comm Arts and Humanities Grants, 3747
Patrick and Aimee Butler Family Fnd Comm Environment Grants, 3748
Patrick and Aimee Butler Family Fnd Comm Human Services Grants, 3749
Patrick and Aimee Butler Family Comm Philanthropy & the Non-Profit Management Grants, 3750
Patrick and Anna M. Cudahy Fund Grants, 3751
Patrick John Bennett, Jr. Memorial Fnd Grants, 3752
Patron Saints Fnd Grants, 3753
Paul and Edith Babson Fnd Grants, 3755
Paul and Mary Haas Fnd Contributions and Student Scholarships, 3756
Paul E & Klare N Reinhold Fdn Grts, 3758
Paul Green Fnd Efforts to Abolish the Death Penalty in North Carolina Grants, 3760
Paul Green Fnd Human Rights Project Grants, 3761
Pauline E. Fitzpatrick Charitable Trust, 3763
Paul Ogle Fnd Grants, 3764
Paul Rapoport Fnd Grants, 3765
Paul V. Sherlock Center on Disabilities Access for All Abilities Mini Grants, 3767
Pay It Forward Fnd Mini Grants, 3768
PCA-PCD Organizational Short-Term Professional Dev and Consulting Grants, 3769
PCA-PCD Professional Dev for Artists Grants, 3770
PCA Art Organizations and Art Grants for Presenting Organizations, 3771
PCA Arts Management Internship, 3773
PCA Arts Organizations and Grants for Music, 3774
PCA Arts Organizations and Arts Grants for Arts Educ Organizations, 3776

Community Development

PCA Arts Organizations and Arts Grants for Arts Service Organizations, 3777
PCA Arts Organizations and Grants for Crafts, 3778
PCA Arts Organizations & Grants for Local Arts, 3782
PCA Arts Organizations & Grants for Visual Arts, 3785
PCA Entry Track Arts Organizations and Arts Grants for Art Museums, 3787
PCA Entry Track Arts Orgs & Arts Pgms Grts for Arts Educ Orgs, 3788
PCA Entry Track Arts Orgs & Arts Pgms Grts for Arts Svc Orgs, 3789
PCA Entry Track Arts Organizations and Arts Grants for Crafts, 3790
PCA Entry Track Arts Organizations and Arts Grants for Local Arts, 3794
PCA Entry Track Arts Organizations and Arts Grants for Music, 3795
PCA Entry Track Arts Organizations and Arts Grants for Presenting Organizations, 3796
PCA Entry Track Arts Organizations and Arts Grants for Theatre, 3797
PCA Entry Track Arts Organizations and Arts Grants for Visual Arts, 3799
PCA Mgmt/Techn Assistance Grts, 3800
PCA Pennsylvania Partners in Arts Stream Grants, 3801
PCA Pennsylvania Partners in the Arts Project Stream Grants, 3802
PCA Strategies for Success Grts-Adv Level, 3804
PCA Strategies for Success Grants - Basic Level, 3805
PCA Strategies for Success Grts-Intrmd Lvl, 3806
PDF Fiscal Sponsorship Grant, 3808
Peacock Fnd Grants, 3809
PennPAT Fee-Support Grants for Presenters, 3812
Pentair Fnd Educ and Comm Grants, 3816
Peoples Bancorp Fnd Grants, 3817
PepsiCo Fnd Grants, 3819
Percy B. Ferebee Endowment Grants, 3820
Perkins-Ponder Fnd Grants, 3822
Perkins Charitable Fnd Grants, 3823
Perl Fnd Grants, 3825
Perpetual Trust for Charitable Giving Grants, 3826
Perry County Comm Fnd Grants, 3827
Pet Care Trust Fish in the Classroom Grant, 3828
Pet Care Trust Sue Busch Memorial Award, 3829
Petco Fnd 4 Rs Project Support Grants, 3830
Petco Fnd Capital Grants, 3831
Petco Fnd Product Support Grants, 3832
Petco Fnd We Are Family Too Grants, 3833
Peter and Elizabeth C. Tower Fnd Annual Intellectual Disabilities Grants, 3834
Peter and Elizabeth C. Tower Fnd Annual Mental Health Grants, 3835
Peter and Elizabeth C. Tower Fnd Learning Disability Grants, 3836
Peter and Elizabeth C. Tower Fnd Mental Health Reference and Resource Materials Mini-Grants, 3837
Peter and Elizabeth C. Tower Fnd Organizational Scholarships, 3838
Peter and Elizabeth C. Tower Fnd Tech Grants, 3839
Peter and Elizabeth C. Tower Fnd Phase I Tech Initiative Grants, 3840
Peter and Elizabeth C. Tower Fnd Social and Emotional Preschool Curriculum Grants, 3841
Peter & Elizabeth Tower Substance Abuse Grants, 3842
Peter and Georgia Angelos Fnd Grants, 3843
Peter F. Drucker Award for Canadian Nonprofit Innovation, 3844
Peter Kiewit Fnd General Grants, 3845
Peter Kiewit Fnd Neighborhood Grants, 3846
Peter Kiewit Fnd Small Grants, 3847
Peter M. Putnam Fnd Grants, 3848
Peter Norton Family Fnd Grants, 3849
Petra Fnd Fellows Awards, 3850
PetSmart Charities Conf Sponsorship Grts, 3851
PetSmart Charities Free-Roaming Cat Spay-Neuter Grants, 3852
PetSmart Charities Grts for Canadian Agncs, 3853
PetSmart Charities Model Volunteering Grants, 3854
PetSmart Charities Spay/Neuter Clinic Equipment Grant, 3855
PetSmart Charities Tgtd Spay/Neuter Grts, 3856
Pew Charitable Trusts Arts and Culture Grants, 3857
Pew Charitable Trusts Children & Youth Grts, 3858
Pew Char Trusts Spcl Civic Project Grts, 3859
Peyton Anderson Fnd Grants, 3862
Pfizer Healthcare Charitable Contributions, 3863
Pfizer Special Events Grants, 3865
PG&E Comm Investment Grants, 3867
PG&E Comm Vitality Grants, 3868
PGE Fnd Grants, 3869
Phelps County Comm Fnd Grants, 3870
Philadelphia Fdn Org'l Effectiveness Grts, 3872
Philadelphia Fdn YOUTHadelphia Grts, 3873
Philanthrofund Fnd Grants, 3874
Philip L. Graham Fund Grants, 3876
Phoenix Coyotes Charities Grants, 3879
Phoenix Neighborhood Block Watch Grants, 3880
Phoenix Suns Charities Grants, 3881
Piedmont Health Fnd Grants, 3882
Piedmont Natural Gas Corporate and Charitable Contributions, 3883
Piedmont Natural Gas Fnd Environmental Stewardship and Energy Sustainability Grant, 3884
Piedmont Natural Gas Fnd Health and Human Services Grants, 3885
Pier 1 Imports Grants, 3887
Pike County Comm Fnd Grants, 3888
Pi Lambda Theta Anna Tracey Mem Awd, 3889
Pinellas County Grants, 3891
Pinkerton Fnd Grants, 3892
Pinnacle Entertainment Fnd Grants, 3893
Pinnacle Fnd Grants, 3894
Pioneer Hi-Bred Comm Grants, 3895
PIP American Dream Fund Grants, 3897
Piper Jaffray Fdn Communities Giving Grts, 3899
Piper Trust Arts and Culture Grants, 3900
Piper Trust Children Grants, 3901
Piper Trust Educ Grants, 3902
Piper Trust Healthcare & Med Rsch Grts, 3903
Piper Trust Older Adults Grants, 3904
Piper Trust Reglious Organizations Grants, 3905
PIP Four Freedoms Fund Grants, 3906
PIP Fulfilling the Dream Fund, 3907
PIP Racial Justice Collaborative Grants, 3908
PIP U.S. Human Rights Fund Grants, 3909
Pittsburgh Fdn Comm Fund Grts, 3910
Playboy Fnd Grants, 3913
Plough Fnd Grants, 3915
Ploughshares Fund Grants, 3916
Plum Creek Fnd Grants, 3917
PMI Fnd Grants, 3918
PMP Project Grants, 3920
PNC Charitable Trust and Fnd Grants, 3921
PNC Ecnomic Dev Grants, 3922
PNC Fnd Green Building Grants, 3923
PNC Fnd Grow Up Great Grants, 3924
PNM Power Up Grants, 3925
PNM Reduce Your Use Grants, 3926
Poets & Writers Readings/Workshops Grants, 3927
Pohlad Family Fnd, 3928
Polk Bros. Fnd Grants, 3929
Pollock Fnd Grants, 3930
Porter County Comm Fnd Grants, 3931
Porter County Emergency Grants, 3932
Porter County Health and Wellness Grant, 3933
Porter County Women's Grant, 3934
Portland Fdn - Women's Giving Circle Grt, 3935
Portland Fnd Grants, 3936
Portland General Electric Fnd Grants, 3937
Posey Comm Fdn Women's Fund Grts, 3938
Posey County Comm Fnd Grants, 3939
Pott Fnd Grants, 3940
Powell Family Fnd Grants, 3941
Powell Fnd Grants, 3942
PPG Industries Fnd Grants, 3943
Praxair Fnd Grants, 3944
Premera Blue Cross CARES Grants, 3945
Presbyterian Health Fnd Bridge, Seed and Equipment Grants, 3947
Preservation Maryland Heritage Fund Grants, 3948
Price Chopper's Golub Fnd Grants, 3950
Price Family Charitable Fund Grants, 3952
Price Gilbert, Jr. Charitable Fund Grants, 3953
Priddy Fnd Organizational Dev Grants, 3956
Pride Fnd Grants, 3958
Prince Charitable Trusts Chicago Grants, 3959
Prince Char Trusts Dist of Columbia Grts, 3960
Prince Charitable Trusts Rhode Island Grants, 3961
Princeton Area Comm Fnd Fund for Women and Girls Grants, 3962
Princeton Area Comm Fnd Greater Mercer Grants, 3963
Princeton Area Comm Fnd Thomas George Artists Fund Grants, 3965
Principal Financial Group Fnd Grants, 3966
Procter and Gamble Fund Grants, 3967
Progress Energy Corp Contributions Grts, 3968
Progress Energy Fnd Economic Vitality Grants, 3969
Project Orange Thumb Grants, 3972
Proteus Fund Grants, 3973
Prudential CARES Volunteer Grants, 3974
Prudential Fnd Arts and Culture Grants, 3975
Prudential Fdn Econ Dev Grants, 3976
PSEG Corporate Contributions Grants, 3979
Public Educ Power Grants, 3981
Public Safety Fnd of America Grants, 3983
Public Welfare Fnd Grants, 3984
Publix Super Markets Charities Local Grants, 3985
Puerto Rico Comm Fnd Grants, 3986
Pulaski County Comm Fnd Grants, 3988
Pulte Homes Corporate Contributions, 3989
Putnam Cty Comm Fdn Grts, 3990
Quaker Oats Company Kids Care Clubs Grants, 3992
Quality Health Fnd Grants, 3994
Quantum Corporation Snap Server Grants, 3995
Quantum Fnd Grants, 3996
Questar Corporate Contributions Grants, 3997
QuikTrip Corporate Contributions Grants, 3998
R.C. Baker Fnd Grants, 3999
R.E.B. Awards for Distinguished Ed Leadership, 4000
R.J. McElroy Trust Grants, 4001
R.S. Gernon Trust Grants, 4002
Rachel Alexandra Girls Grants, 4003
RadioShack StreetSentz Comm Grts, 4005
Rainbow Academy Fnd Grants, 4006
Rainbow Endowment Grants, 4007
Rainbow Families Fnd Grants, 4008
Rainbow Fund Grants, 4009
Rainbow Media Holdings Corp Gvg Prgm Grts, 4010
Ralph and Virginia Mullin Fnd Grants, 4012
Ralphs Food 4 Less Fnd Grants, 4014
Rancho Bernardo Comm Fdn Grts, 4015
Rancho Santa Fe Fnd Grants, 4016
Randall L. Tobias Fnd Grants, 4017
RAND Corporation Graduate Student Summer Associateships, 4018
Raskob Fdn for Catholic Activities Grts, 4019
Rasmuson Fdn Creative Ventures Grts, 4021
Rasmuson Organizational Advancement Grants, 4023
Rasmuson Fnd Special Project Grants, 4025
Rathmann Family Fnd Grants, 4026
Ray Fnd Grants, 4027
Raymond John Wean Fnd Grants, 4028
Ray Solem Fnd Grants to Help Immigrants Learn English in Innovative Ways, 4029
Raytheon Grants, 4030
RBC Dain Rauscher Fnd Grants, 4031
RCF General Comm Grants, 4032
RCF Individual Assistance Grants, 4033
RCF Summertime Kids Grants, 4034
RCF The Women's Fund Grants, 4035
RealNetworks Fnd Grants, 4037
Red Robin Fnd U-ACT Grants, 4038
Regence Fdn Access to Health Care Grts, 4039
Regence Fnd Health Care Comm Awareness and Engagement Grants, 4040
Regence Fnd Health Care Connections Grants, 4041
Regence Fnd Improving End-of-Life Grts, 4042
Regence Fdn Tools & Tech Grts, 4043
Regional Arts and Cultural Council Opportunity Grants, 4046

PROGRAM TYPE INDEX

Community Development / 1049

Regional Arts & Cultural Council Project Grts, 4048
Regional Fund for Digital Innovation in Latin America and the Caribbean Grants, 4049
REI Conservation & Outdoor Recreation Grts, 4051
Reinberger Fnd Grants, 4052
RESIST Accessibility Grants, 4054
RESIST Arthur Raymond Cohen Grants, 4055
RESIST Emergency Grants, 4056
RESIST Freda Friedman Salzman Grants, 4057
RESIST Hell Yes! Award, 4059
RESIST Ken Hale Tribute Grants, 4060
RESIST Leslie D'Cora Holmes Grants, 4061
RESIST Mike Riegle Tribute Grants, 4062
RESIST Sharon Kurtz Grants, 4064
Retirement Rsch Fnd Accessible Faith Grants, 4066
Retirement Research Fnd Gen Pgm Grts, 4067
Reynolds American Fnd Grants, 4068
Reynolds & Reynolds Assoc Fnd Grants, 4069
Reynolds and Reynolds Co Fnd Grants, 4070
Rhode Island Fnd Grants, 4073
Rice Fnd Grants, 4074
Richard & Caroline T Gwathmey Mem Tr Grts, 4075
Richard and Helen DeVos Fnd Grants, 4076
Richard and Rhoda Goldman Fund Grants, 4077
Richard & Susan Smith Family Fdn Grts, 4078
Richard D. Bass Fnd Grants, 4079
Richard Davoud Donchian Fnd Grants, 4080
Richard Florsheim Art Fund Grants, 4083
Richard H. Driehaus Fnd MacArthur Fund for Arts and Culture, 4085
Richard M. Fairbanks Fnd Grants, 4088
Richards Fnd Grants, 4089
Rich Fnd Grants, 4090
Richland County Bank Grants, 4091
Richmond Eye and Ear Fund Grants, 4092
Righteous Persons Fnd Grants, 4093
Riley Fnd Grants, 4094
Ripley County Comm Fnd Grants, 4095
RISCA Folk Arts Apprenticeships, 4098
Rite Aid Corp Grants, 4101
Roberta Leventhal Sudakoff Fnd Grants, 4102
Robert and Helen Haddad Fnd Grants, 4103
Robert and Joan Dircks Fnd Grants, 4104
Robert and Polly Dunn Fnd Grants, 4105
Robert B McMillen Fnd Grants, 4106
Robert Bowne Fnd Fellowships, 4107
Robert Bowne Fnd Lit Grants, 4108
Robert Bowne Fdn Youth-Centered Grants, 4109
Robert F. Kennedy Human Rights Award, 4111
Robert F Stoico/FIRSTFED Char Fdn Grts, 4112
Robert G. Cabell III and Maude Morgan Cabell Fnd Grants, 4113
Robert Lee Adams Fnd Grants, 4114
Robert Lee Blaffer Fnd Grants, 4115
Robert P & Clara I Milton Fund for Sr Housing, 4117
Robert R McCormick Tribune Fdn Civics Grts, 4118
Robert R. McCormick Tribune Comm Grants, 4119
Robert R. McCormick Tribune Veterans Grants, 4120
Robert R. Meyer Fnd Grants, 4121
Robert Sterling Clark Arts & Culture Grants, 4122
Robert Sterling Clark Fnd Government Accountability Grants, 4123
Robert W. Woodruff Fnd Grants, 4124
Robin Hood Fnd Grants, 4125
Robins Fnd Grants, 4126
Rochester Area Comm Fnd Grants, 4127
Rochester Area Fnd Grants, 4128
Rockefeller Brothers Fund Charles E. Culpeper Arts and Culture Grants in New York City, 4129
Rockefeller Brothers Democratic Practice Grants, 4131
Rockefeller Bros Fund Peace & Security Grts, 4133
Rockefeller Brothers Fund Pivotal Places Grants: New York City, 4134
Rockefeller Brothers Fund Pivotal Places Grants: Serbia, Montenegro, and Kosova, 4135
Rockefeller Brothers Sustainable Dev Grants, 4136
Rockefeller Family Fund Grants, 4137
Rockefeller Fnd Grants, 4138
Rockefeller Fnd Partnerships Affirming Comm Transformation Grants, 4139

Rockwell Fund, Inc. Grants, 4140
Rockwell Int'l Corporate Trust Grants, 4141
Rohm and Haas Company Grants, 4145
Rollin M. Gerstacker Fnd Grants, 4146
Romic Environmental's Charitable Contributions, 4148
Ronald McDonald House Charities Grants, 4149
Roney-Fitzpatrick Fnd Grants, 4150
Rose Comm Fnd Aging Grants, 4152
Rose Comm Fnd Child and Family Dev Grants, 4153
Rose Comm Fnd Health Grants, 4154
Rose Comm Fdn Jewish Life Grts, 4155
Rose Fdn For Communities & the Environment Consumer Privacy Rights Grts, 4156
Rose Fdn For Communities & the Environment Kern Cty Air Pollution Mitigation Grts, 4157
Rose Communities and Environment Northern California Environmental Grassroots Grants, 4158
Rose Fnd For Communities and the Environment SE Madera County Responsible Growth Grants, 4159
Rose Hills Fnd Grants, 4162
Ross Fnd Grants, 4164
Roy & Christine Sturgis Charitable Trust Grts, 4166
Roy J Carver Char Trust Youth Pgm Grts, 4167
RR Donnelley Comm Grants, 4168
RRF General Grants, 4170
Rush County Comm Fnd Grants, 4174
Russell Berrie Fnd Grants, 4175
Ruth Anderson Fnd Grants, 4176
Ruth and Vernon Taylor Fnd Grants, 4177
Ruth Eleanor Bamberger and John Ernest Bamberger Memorial Fnd Grants, 4178
Ruth H & Warren A Ellsworth Fdn Grts, 4179
Ruth Mott Fnd Grants, 4180
Rutter's Children's Charities Grants, 4181
RWJF Changes in Health Care Financing and Organization Grants, 4182
RWJF Comm Health Leaders Awards, 4183
RWJF Health Policy Fellowships, 4184
RWJF Jobs to Careers: Promoting Work-Based Learning for Quality Care, 4185
RWJF Local Funding Partnerships Grants, 4186
RWJF New Jersey Health Initiatives Grants, 4187
RWJF Partners Investing in Nursing's Future, 4188
RWJF Pioneer Portfolio Grants, 4189
RWJF Vulnerable Populations Portfolio Grants, 4190
Ryder System Charitable Fnd Grants, 4191
S. D. Bechtel, Jr. Fnd / Stephen Bechtel Fund Environmental Educ Grants, 4192
S.E.VEN Fund $50k VINE Project Prizes, 4193
S.E.VEN Fund 'In The River They Swim' Essay Competition, 4194
S.E.VEN Fund Annual Grants, 4195
S.E.VEN Fund Mini-Grants, 4196
S.E.VEN Fund Open Enterprise Solutions to Poverty RFP Grants, 4197
S.E.VEN Fund WHY Prize, 4198
S.H. Cowell Fnd Grants, 4199
S. Mark Taper Fnd Grants, 4201
S. Spencer Scott Fund Grants, 4202
Safeco Insurance Comm Grants, 4203
Sage Fnd Grants, 4204
Saginaw Comm Fdn Discretionary Grts, 4205
Saginaw Comm Fnd Senior Citizen Enrichment, 4206
Saginaw Comm Fnd YWCA Fund for Women and Girls Grants, 4207
Saginaw County Comm Youth FORCE Grants, 4208
SAG Motion Pic Plyrs Welfare Fund Grts, 4209
Saigh Fnd Grants, 4210
Sailors' Snug Harbor of Boston Elder Grants, 4211
Sailors' Snug Harbor of Boston Fishing Communities Initiative Grants, 4212
Saint George's Society of NY Scholarships, 4213
Saint Louis Rams Fdn Comm Donations, 4214
Saint Luke's Fnd Grants, 4215
Saint Luke's Health Initiatives Grants, 4216
Saint Paul Companies Fnd Grants, 4217
Saint Paul Fdn Comm Sharing Fund Grts, 4218
Saint Paul Fnd Grants, 4219
Saint Paul Fdn Lowertown Future Fund Grts, 4220
Saint Paul Fdn Mgmt Improvement Fund Grts, 4221

Saint Paul Fnd SpectrumTrust Grants, 4222
Salem Fnd Charitable Trust Grants, 4223
Salisbury Comm Fnd Grants, 4224
Salmon Fnd Grants, 4225
Salt River Project Civic Leadership Grants, 4226
Salt River Health and Human Services Grants, 4228
SAMHSA Drug Free Communities Grants, 4230
SAMHSA Strategic Prevention Framework State Incentive Grants, 4231
Samueli Fnd Human Security Grants, 4233
Samueli Fnd Youth Services Grants, 4234
Samuel L. Phillips Family Fnd Grants, 4235
Samuel N. and Mary Castle Fnd Grants, 4236
Samuel Rubin Fnd Grants, 4237
Samuel S. Fels Fund Grants, 4238
Samuel S. Johnson Fnd Grants, 4239
San Antonio Area Fnd Grants, 4240
San Diego Fnd After-the-Fires Fund Grts, 4242
San Diego Fnd Arts & Culture Grants, 4243
San Diego Fnd Civil Society Grants, 4244
San Diego Fdn Environment Blasker Grts, 4245
San Diego Fnd Environment Comm Grants, 4246
San Diego Fnd for Change Grants, 4247
San Diego Fnd Health & Human Services Grants, 4248
San Diego Fnd Paradise Valley Hospital Comm Fund Grants, 4249
San Diego Fnd Science & Tech Blasker Grants, 4250
San Diego HIV Funding Collaborative Grants, 4251
San Diego Women's Fnd Grants, 4252
SanDisk Corp Comm Sharing Pgm, 4253
Sands Fnd Grants, 4255
Sands Memorial Fnd Grants, 4256
Sandy Hill Fnd Grants, 4257
San Francisco Fnd Art Awards James Duval Phelan Literary Award, 4258
San Francisco Fnd Art Awards Joseph Henry Jackson Literary Award, 4259
San Francisco Fnd Art Awards Mary Tanenbaum Literary Award, 4260
San Francisco Bay Area Documentary Grants, 4261
San Francisco Fnd Comm Dev Grants, 4262
San Francisco Fnd Comm Health Grants, 4263
San Francisco Faith Arts and Culture Grants, 4267
San Francisco Fnd Fund For Artists Award For Choreographers, 4270
San Francisco Fnd Fund For Artists Award For Playwrights and Theatre Ensembles, 4272
San Francisco Fnd Fund for Artists Award for Visual and Media Artists, 4273
San Francisco Fnd Fund For Artists Matching Commissions Grants, 4274
San Francisco Fnd Fund Shenson Performing Arts Fellowships, 4275
San Francisco Fnd James D. Phelan Art Award in Photography, 4276
San Francisco Fnd James D. Phelan Art Award in Printmaking, 4277
San Francisco Fnd James D. Phelan Award in Film, Video, and Digital Media, 4278
San Francisco Fnd John Gutmann Photography Fellowship Award, 4279
San Francisco Fnd Koshland Program Arts and Culture Mini-Grants, 4280
San Francisco Fnd Murphy and Cadogan Fellowships in the Fine Arts, 4282
San Juan Island Comm Fnd Grants, 4283
Santa Barbara Fdn Monthly Express Grts, 4284
Santa Barbara Strategy Capital Support, 4285
Santa Barbara Strategy Core Support Grants, 4286
Santa Barbara Fnd Strategy Grants - Innovation, 4287
Santa Barbara Fnd Towbes Fund for the Performing Arts Grants, 4288
Santa Fe Comm Fdn root2fruit Santa Fe, 4289
Santa Fe Comm Fnd Seasonal Grants-Fall Cycle, 4290
Santa Fe Comm Fnd Seasonal Grants-Spring, 4291
Santa Fe Comm Fnd Special & Urgent Needs Grants, 4292
Sapelo Fdn Environmental Protection Grts, 4293
Sapelo Fnd Social Justice Grants, 4294
Sarah Scaife Fnd Grants, 4295
Sara Lee Fnd Grants, 4296

Sarkeys Fnd Grants, 4297
Sartain Lanier Family Fnd Grants, 4298
Sasakawa Peace Fnd Grants, 4299
Saucony Run for Good Fnd Grants, 4301
SCBWI Don Freeman Memorial Grant, 4302
Schering-Plough Fdn Comm Initvs Grts, 4303
Schering-Plough Fnd Health Grants, 4304
Scherman Fnd Grants, 4305
Scheumann Fnd Grants, 4306
Schlessman Family Fnd Grants, 4307
Scholastic Book Grants, 4308
Scholastic Welch's Harvest Grants, 4309
Schramm Fnd Grants, 4310
Schumann Fund for New Jersey Grants, 4311
Schurz Communications Fnd Grants, 4312
Scott B & Annie P Appleby Char Trust Grts, 4313
Scott County Comm Fnd Grants, 4314
Scotts Company Give Back to Grow Awards, 4315
Seabury Fnd Grants, 4316
Seattle Fnd Annual Neighborhoods Grants, 4319
Seattle Fnd Arts and Culture Grants, 4320
Seattle Fnd Basic Needs Grants, 4321
Seattle Fnd Benjamin N. Phillips Grants, 4322
Seattle Fdn C Keith Birkenfeld Mem Tr Grts, 4323
Seattle Fnd Economy Grants, 4325
Seattle Fnd Educ Grants, 4326
Seattle Fnd Environment Grants, 4327
Seattle Fnd Health and Wellness Grants, 4328
Seattle Fnd Medical Funds Grants, 4329
Seattle Fdn Neighbor to Neighbor Small Grts, 4330
Seaver Institute Grants, 4331
SeaWorld & Busch Gardens Conservation Grants, 4332
Self Fnd Grants, 4335
Seneca Foods Fnd Grants, 4336
Sensient Technologies Fnd Grants, 4337
Seybert Inst for Poor Boys & Girls Grts, 4338
Share Our Strength Grants, 4340
Shastri Indo-Canadian Institute Action Research Project Grants, 4341
Shaw's Supermarkets Donations, 4342
Shell Oil Company Fnd Grants, 4343
Sheltering Arms Fund Grants, 4344
Shopko Fdn Comm Charitable Grts, 4346
Shopko Fnd Green Bay Area Comm Grants, 4347
Sidgmore Family Fnd Grants, 4348
Sidney Stern Memorial Trust Grants, 4349
Sid W. Richardson Fnd Grants, 4350
Siebert Lutheran Fnd Grants, 4351
Sierra Fund Grants, 4352
Sierra Health Fnd Responsive Grants, 4353
Silicon Valley Comm Fnd Donor Circle for the Arts Grants, 4354
Silicon Valley Comm Economic Security Grants, 4355
Silicon Valley Comm Fnd Immigrant Integration Grants, 4358
Silicon Valley Comm Regional Planning Grants, 4359
Simmons Fnd Grants, 4360
Simple Advise Educ Center Grants, 4361
Simpson Lumber Charitable Contributions, 4362
Singing for Change Fnd Grants, 4363
Sioux Falls Area Comm Fnd Comm Fund Grants, 4364
Sioux Falls Area Comm Fnd Field-of-Interest and Donor-Advised Grants, 4365
Sioux Falls Area Comm Fnd Spot Grants, 4366
Siragusa Fnd Arts & Culture Grants, 4367
Siragusa Fnd Health Services & Medical Research Grants, 4368
Siragusa Fnd Human Services Grants, 4369
Sir Dorabji Tata Trust Grants for NGOs or Voluntary Organizations, 4370
Sister Fund Grants for Women's Organizations, 4371
Sisters of Charity Fnd of Cleveland Good Samaritan Grants, 4373
Sisters of Charity Cleveland Reducing Health & Educational Disparities Grants, 4374
Sisters of Mercy of North Carolina Fdn Grts, 4375
Sisters of Saint Joseph Charitable Fund Grants, 4376
Sisters of St Joseph Healthcare Fdn Grts, 4377
Skaggs Fnd Grants, 4378
Skillman Fnd Comm Connections Small Grants, 4379
Skillman Fdn Good Neighborhoods Grts, 4380
Skillman Fdn Good Opportunities Grts, 4381
Skillman Fnd Good Schools Grants, 4382
Skoll Fdn Awds for Social Entrepreneurship, 4383
Slow Food in Schools Micro-Grants, 4384
Smith Richardson Fdn Direct Service Grts, 4385
Snee Reinhardt Charitable Fnd Grants, 4387
SOBP A.E. Bennett Research Award, 4388
Sobrato Family Fnd Grants, 4389
Sobrato Family Fdn Meeting Space Grts, 4390
Sobrato Family Fnd Office Space Grants, 4391
SOCFOC Catholic Ministries Grants, 4392
SOCFOC Comm Collaborations Grants, 4393
Social Justice Fund NW Economic Justice Giving Project Grants, 4395
Social Justice Fund NW Environmental Justice Giving Project Grants, 4396
Social Justice Fund NW General Grants, 4397
Social Justice Fund NW LGBTQ Giving Grants, 4398
Social Justice Fund NW Montana Giving Grants, 4399
Sodexo Fdn STOP Hunger Scholarships, 4400
Solo Cup Fnd Grants, 4401
Solutia Fund Grants, 4402
Sonoco Fnd Grants, 4403
Sonora Area Fnd Competitive Grants, 4404
Sony Corp of America Corp Philant Grants, 4405
Sophia Romero Trust Grants, 4406
Sorenson Legacy Fnd Grants, 4407
Sosland Fnd Grants, 4408
Southbury Comm Trust Fund, 4409
South Carolina Arts Comsn Accessibility Grts, 4410
South Carolina Arts Commission AIE Residency Plus Individual Site Grants, 4411
South Carolina Arts Commission AIE Residency Plus Multi-Site Grants, 4412
South Carolina Arts Commission American Masterpieces in South Carolina Grants, 4413
South Carolina Arts Commission Annual Operating Support for Organizations Grants, 4414
South Carolina Arts Comsn Artists Fwsps, 4415
South Carolina Arts Commission Arts and Economic Impact Study Assistance Grants, 4416
South Carolina Arts Commission Arts Facility Projects Grants, 4417
South Carolina Arts Commission Arts in Educ After School Arts Initiative Grants, 4418
South Carolina Arts Commission Cultural Tourism Initiative Grants, 4419
South Carolina Arts Commission Cultural Visions Grants, 4420
South Carolina Arts Commission Folklife & Traditional Arts Grants, 4421
South Carolina Arts Commission Incentive Grants for Employer Sponsored Benefits, 4422
South Carolina Arts Commission Leadership and Organizational Dev Grants, 4423
South Carolina Arts Commission Long Term Operating Support for Organizations Grants, 4424
South Carolina Arts Commission Statewide Arts Participation Initiative Grants, 4425
South Carolina Arts Commission Subgrants, 4426
South Carolina Arts Commission Traditional Arts Apprenticeship Grants, 4427
Southern Calif Edison Environmental Grts, 4429
Southern California Edison Public Safety and Preparedness Grants, 4430
Southern Minnesota Initiative Fnd AmeriCorps Leap Grants, 4431
Southern Minnesota Initiative BookStart Grants, 4432
Southern Minnesota Initiative Fnd Comm Growth Initiative Grants, 4433
Southern Minnesota Initiative Incentive Grants, 4435
Southern Minnesota Initiative Fund Grants, 4437
Southern New England Folk and Traditional Arts Apprenticeship Grants, 4438
Southern Poverty Law Center Strategic Litigation Grants, 4439
South Madison Comm Fnd Grants, 4440
Southwest Florida Comm Fnd Arts & Attractions Grants, 4441
Southwest Florida Comm Competitive Grants, 4442
Southwest Florida Good Samaritan Grants, 4443
Southwest Gas Corporation Fnd Grants, 4445
Southwest Initiative Fnd Grants, 4446
Southwire Company Grants, 4447
Spartan Fnd Grants, 4448
Special Olympics Project UNIFY Grants, 4449
Speer Trust Grants, 4450
Spencer Cty Comm Fdn Grants, 4451
Sport Manitoba Athlete/Team Travel Assistance Grants, 4452
Sport Manitoba Athlete Skill Dev Clinics Grants, 4453
Sport Manitoba Bingo Allocations Grants, 4454
Sport Manitoba Coaches/Officials Travel Assistance Grants, 4455
Sport Manitoba Hosting Regional Championships Grants, 4456
Sport Manitoba Intro of a New Sport Grts, 4457
Sport Manitoba KidSport Athlete Grants, 4458
Sport Manitoba Sport Special Initiatives Grants, 4459
Sport Manitoba Women to Watch Grants, 4460
Sprague Fnd Grants, 4461
Springs Close Fnd Grants, 4462
Sprint Fnd Grants, 4463
Square D Fnd Grants, 4464
SSA Work Incentives Planning and Assistance, 4465
SSRC-Van Alen Fellowships, 4467
St. Joseph Comm Health Cath Kasper Award, 4468
St. Joseph Comm Health Fnd Improving Healthcare Access Grants, 4469
St. Louis-Jefferson Solid Waste Management Waste Reduction and Recycling Grants, 4470
Stackpole-Hall Fnd Grants, 4472
Stanley Smith Horticultural Trust Grants, 4474
Staples Fnd for Learning Grants, 4475
Starbucks Fdn Shared Planet Youth Action, 4476
Stark Comm Fnd Grants, 4477
Stark Comm Fnd Neighborhood Comm and Economic Dev Tech Assistance Grants, 4478
Stark Comm Fnd Neighborhood Partnerships, 4479
Stark Comm Fnd SummerTime Kid Grants, 4480
Stark Comm Fdn Women's Fund Grants, 4481
Starke County Comm Fnd Grants, 4482
Starr Fnd Grants, 4483
State Farm Companies Safe Neighbors Grants, 4484
State Farm Companies Strong Neighborhoods, 4485
State Farm Fnd Grants, 4486
State Farm Project Ignition Grants, 4487
State Justice Institute Partner Grants, 4489
State Justice Institute Strategic Initiative Grants, 4492
State Justice Inst Tech Assistance Grts, 4493
State Strategies Fund Grants, 4494
State Street Fnd Grants, 4495
Steelcase Fnd Grants, 4497
Steele-Reese Fnd Grants, 4498
Sterling-Turner Charitable Fnd Grants, 4499
Stettinius Fund for Nonprofit Ldrsp Awds, 4500
Steuben County Comm Fdn Grants, 4501
Steven B. Achelis Fnd Grants, 4502
Steve Young Family Fnd Grants, 4503
Steward of the Land Award, 4504
Stewart Huston Charitable Trust Grants, 4505
Stinson Fnd Grants, 4506
Stocker Fnd Grants, 4507
Stockton Rush Bartol Fnd Grants, 4508
Stonyfield Farm Profits for the Planet Grants, 4509
Stowe Family Fnd Grants, 4510
Strake Fnd Grants, 4511
Stranahan Fnd Grants, 4512
Strengthening Families - Strengthening Communities Grants, 4513
Strolling of the Heifers Schlrsps for Farmers, 4514
Strowd Roses Grants, 4515
Stuart Fnd Grants, 4516
Subaru Adopt a School Garden Grants, 4517
Subaru of Indiana Automotive Fdn Grts, 4519
Suffolk County Office of Film and Cultural Affairs Cultural Arts Grants, 4521
Sulzberger Fnd Grants, 4522
Summerlee Fnd Grants, 4523

PROGRAM TYPE INDEX

Community Development / 1051

Summit Fnd Grants, 4524
Sun Academic Excellence Grants, 4525
Sunbeam Products Grants, 4526
Sunderland Fnd Grants, 4527
Sunny and Abe Rosenberg Fnd Grants, 4529
Sunoco Fnd Grants, 4530
Suntrust Bank Atlanta Fnd Grants, 4531
Supreme Ct Fellows Commission Fwsps, 4532
Surdna Fdn Sustainable Environments Grants, 4533
Susan A. and Donald P. Babson Grants, 4534
Susan Mott Webb Charitable Trust Grants, 4536
Susan Vaughan Fnd Grants, 4537
SVP Environment Grants, 4539
Swaim-Gause-Rucker Fnd Grants, 4540
Sweet Water Trust Grants, 4541
Swindells Charitable Fnd, 4542
Sylvia Adams Charitable Trust Grants, 4543
T. James Kavanagh Fnd Grants, 4545
T.L.L. Temple Fnd Grants, 4546
T. Rowe Price Associates Fnd Grants, 4548
TAC Arts Access Grant, 4549
TAC Arts Access Tech Assistance Grants, 4550
TAC Arts Build Communities Grants, 4551
TAC Arts Educ Comm-Learning Grts, 4552
TAC Arts Projects Grants, 4554
TAC Rural Arts Project Support Grants, 4555
TAC Tech Assistance Grants, 4556
TAC Touring Arts and Arts Access Touring Arts Grants, 4557
Talbert and Leota Abrams Fnd, 4558
Taproot Fnd Capacity-Building Service Grants, 4560
Target Corporation Local Store Grants, 4561
Tauck Family Fnd Grants, 4563
Taylor S. Abernathy and Patti Harding Abernathy Charitable Trust Grants, 4564
TCF Bank Fnd Grants, 4565
Teaching Tolerance Grants, 4567
Tech Enhancement Certification for Hoosiers, 4571
TE Fnd Grants, 4572
Telluride Fnd Comm Grants, 4573
Telluride Fdn Emergency/Out of Cycle Grts, 4574
Telluride Fdn Tech Assistance Grts, 4575
Temple-Inland Fnd Grants, 4576
Tension Envelope Fnd Grants, 4578
Texas Comm on the Arts Educ Project 1 Grants, 4579
Texas Comm on the Arts Arts in Educ Team Building/Texas Music Project Grants, 4580
Texas Cmsn on the Arts Arts Respond Prj Grts, 4581
Texas Comsn on the Arts County Arts Expansion Program, 4582
Texas Comsn on the Arts Create-1 Pgm Grts, 4583
Texas Comsn on the Arts Create-3 Pgm Grts, 4585
Texas Comsn on the Arts Create-4 Pgm Grts, 4586
Texas Comsn on the Arts Create-5 Pgm Grts, 4587
Texas Comsn on the Arts Cultural Connections-Performance Support Grants, 4588
Texas Comsn on the Arts Cultural Connections-Visual & Media Arts Touring Exhibits Grants, 4589
Texas Comsn on the Arts GPA1, 4592
Texas Comsn on the Arts Young Masters Grants, 4594
Texas Filmmakers Production Grants, 4595
Texas Instruments Corp Arts & Culture Grts, 4596
Texas Instruments Corporation Civic and Business Grants, 4597
Texas Instruments Corporation Health and Human Services Grants, 4598
Texas Instruments Fnd Arts and Culture Grants, 4599
Texas Instruments Fnd Comm Services Grants, 4600
Textron Corporate Contributions Grants, 4601
Thanks Be to Grandmother Winifred Fnd Grants, 4602
Thelma Braun and Bocklett Family Fnd Grants, 4603
Thelma Doelger Charitable Trust Grants, 4604
Theodore Edson Parker Fnd Grants, 4605
Third Millennium Fnd Grants, 4607
Third Sector New England Inclusion Grants, 4608
Third Wave Fnd Lela Breitbart Grants, 4609
Thomas Austin Finch, Sr. Fnd Grants, 4613
Thomas B & Elizabeth M Sheridan Fdn Grts, 4614
Thomas C. Ackerman Fnd Grants, 4615
Thomas D. McGrain Cedar Glade Fnd Grants, 4616

Thomas J. Atkins Memorial Trust Fund Grants, 4617
Thomas J. Long Fnd Comm Grants, 4618
Thomas Sill Fnd Grants, 4619
Thomas Thompson Trust Grants, 4620
Thomas W. Briggs Fnd Grants, 4621
Thompson Charitable Fnd Grants, 4622
Thompson Fnd Grants, 4623
Thornton Fnd Grants, 4624
Threshold Fnd Election Integrity Grants, 4625
Threshold Fdn Justice & Democracy Grts, 4626
Threshold Fdn Sustainable Planet Grts, 4627
Threshold Fnd Thriving Resilient Communities Funding Circle, 4628
Tides Fnd Death Penalty Mobilization Grants, 4631
Tides Fnd Grants, 4632
Tifa Fnd Grants, 4633
Tiger Woods Fnd Grants, 4634
Time Warner Yth Media & Creative Arts Grts, 4636
TJX Fnd Grants, 4637
Toby Wells Fnd Grants, 4638
Todd Brock Family Fnd Grants, 4639
Topeka Comm Fnd Boss Hawg's Grants, 4642
Topeka Comm Fnd Building Families Grants, 4643
Topeka Comm Fnd Grants, 4644
Topeka West Rotary Youth Enrichment Grants, 4645
Toro Fnd Grants, 4647
Tourism Cares Professional Dev Scholarships, 4648
Tourism Cares Worldwide Grants, 4649
Town Creek Fnd Grants, 4650
Toyota Motor Engineering & Manufacturing North America Grants, 4651
Toyota Motor Mfg of Alabama Grts, 4652
Toyota Motor Manufacturing of Indiana Grants, 4653
Toyota Motor Mfg of Kentucky Grts, 4654
Toyota Motor Mfg of Mississippi Grts, 4655
Toyota Motor Manufacturing of Texas Grants, 4656
Toyota Motor Manuf of West Virginia Grants, 4657
Toyota Motor North America of NY Grts, 4658
Toyota Motor Sales, USA Grants, 4659
Toyota Tech Center Grants, 4660
Toyota USA Fnd Environmental Grants, 4661
TRDRP Participatory Research Awards:, 4663
Tri-State Comm Twenty-first Century Endowment Fund Grants, 4666
Triangle Comm Fdn Comm Grts, 4667
Triangle Comm Fdn Donor-Advised Grts, 4668
Trinity Fnd Grants, 4669
Trinity Fnd Grants, 4670
Trinity Trust Comm Response Grants, 4671
Trinity Trust Summer Youth Mini Grants, 4672
Trull Fnd Grants, 4673
TSA Advanced Surveillance Grants, 4674
TSYSF Individual Scholarships, 4675
TSYSF Team Grants, 4676
Tulane University Comm Service Scholars, 4677
Tull Charitable Fnd Grants, 4679
Turner B. Bunn, Jr. & Catherine E. Bunn Grants, 4680
Turner Fnd Grants, 4681
Turner Voices Corporate Contributions, 4682
TWS Fnd Grants, 4683
U.S. Bank Fnd Grants, 4686
US Dept of Educ 21st Century Learning Centers, 4687
US Dept of Educ Cntrs for Independent Lvng, 4688
US Dept of Educ Child Care Access Means Parents in School Grants, 4689
US Dept of Educ Disability and Rehabilitation Research and Related Projects, 4690
US Dept of Educ Early Reading First Grants, 4691
US Dept of Educ Innovative Strategies in Comm Colleges for Working Adults and Displaced Workers Grants, 4692
US Dept of Educ Migrant and Seasonal Farmworkers Grants, 4693
US Dept of Educ Parent Info & Trng, 4695
US Dept of Educ Pgms for Native Hawaiians, 4696
US Dept of Educ Rehab Trng--Rehabilitation Continuing Educ Programs --Institute on Rehabilitation Issues, 4700
US Dept of Educ Special Education--National Activities--Parent Information Centers, 4701

US Dept of Educ Voc Rehab Svcs Projects for American Indians with Disabilities Grts, 4702
U.S. Lacrosse Emerging Groups Grants, 4703
U.S. Lacrosse Equipment Grants, 4704
UniBank 911 Emergency Personnel Educ Fund, 4707
Union Bank, N.A. Corporate Sponsorships and Donations, 4708
Union Bank, N.A. Fnd Grants, 4709
Union Benevolent Association Grants, 4710
Union County Comm Fnd Grants, 4711
Union County Fnd Grants, 4712
Union Labor Health Fnd Comm Grts, 4713
Union Pacific Fdn Comm & Civic Grts, 4714
Union Pacific Fdn Health & Human Svcs Grts, 4715
Union Square Arts Award, 4716
Union Square Award for Social Justice, 4717
Union Square Awards Grants, 4718
United Methodist Committee on Relief Hunger and Poverty Grants, 4720
United Methodist Hlth Mnstry Fund Grts, 4722
United Methodist Women Brighter Future for Children and Youth Grants, 4723
United Technologies Corporation Grants, 4725
Unity Fnd Of LaPorte County Grants, 4726
UPS Corporate Giving Grants, 4727
UPS Fnd Comm Safety Grants, 4728
UPS Fnd Diversity Grants, 4729
UPS Fdn Enviro Sustainability Grts, 4731
UPS Fdn Nonprofit Effectiveness Grts, 4732
Ursula Thrush Peace Seed Grants, 4733
USAA – Ann Hoyt / Jim Easton JOAD Grants, 4734
USAID/Cambodia Maternal and Child Health, Tuberculosis, HIV/AIDS. and Malaria Grants, 4736
USAID Accelerating Progress Against Tuberculosis in Kenya Grants, 4737
USAID African Institutions Innovation Mechanism Grants, 4738
USAID Albania Critical Economic Growth Areas Grants, 4740
USAID Bengal Tiger Csrvtn Actvty Grts, 4741
USAID Call for Public-Private Alliance Proposals in Serbia, 4742
USAID Civic Participation Grants, 4743
USAID Civil Society Sustainability Project Grants in Bosnia and Herzegovina, 4744
USAID Comm Infrastructure Dev Grants, 4745
USAID Comm Livelihoods in Yemen Grant, 4746
USAID Comprehensive District-Based Support for Better HIV/TB Patient Outcomes Grants, 4747
USAID Dev Assistance Fund Grants, 4748
USAID Economic Prospectsfor Armenia-Turkey Normalization Grants, 4750
USAID Family Health Plus Project Grants, 4751
USAID Food Security, Nutrition, Biodiversity and Conservation Grants, 4752
USAID Global Dev Alliance Grants, 4753
USAID Grant for Operationalizing a Neighborhood Approach to Reduce Urban Disaster Risk in Latin America and the Caribbean, 4754
USAID Grants for Building Disaster-Resilient Communities in Southern Africa, 4755
USAID HIV Prevention with Key Populations - Mali Grants, 4757
USAID Implementation Science for Strengthening Use of Evidence in Family Planning/Reproductive Health Programming Grants, 4758
USAID India-Africa Agriculture Innovation Bridge Grants, 4760
USAID India Partnership Grants, 4761
USAID Integration of Care within the Health System to Support Better Patient Outcomes Grants, 4762
USAID Int'l Emergency Food Assistance Grants, 4763
USAID Int'l Food Relief Partnership Grants, 4764
USAID Knowledge for Health II Grants, 4765
USAID Leadership Initiative for Good Governance in Africa Grants, 4766
USAID Malawi Local Capacity Dev Grants, 4767
USAID Media and Elections Rwanda Grants, 4768
USAID Mekong Partnership for the Environment Project Grants, 4769

Community Development

USAID National Governance Project Grant, 4770
USAID NGO Health Service Delivery Grants, 4771
USAID Pakistan Private Investment Grants, 4772
USAID Palestinian Comm Astnc Grts, 4773
USAID Palestinian Comm Infrastructure Grants, 4774
USAID Rapid Response for Sudan Grants, 4776
USAID Rapid Response to Pakistanis Affected by Disasters - Phase Two Grants, 4777
USAID Reading Enhancement for Dev Grants, 4778
USAID Resilience and Economic Growth in the Sahel - Enhanced Resilience Grants, 4779
USAID Service Delivery & Support for Families Caring for Orphans & Vulnerable Children Grants, 4781
USAID Strengthening Democratic Local Governance in South Sudan Grants, 4782
USAID Strengthening Free and Independent Media in South Sudan Grants, 4783
USAID Strengthening RMNCH Through Indian Health Professional Associations and Scaling Up Uptake Grants, 4784
USAID Systems Strengthening for Better HIV/TB Patient Outcomes Grants, 4785
USAID Unsolicited Proposal Grants, 4786
USAID Workforce Dev in Mexico Grants, 4787
US Airways Comm Contributions, 4788
US Airways Comm Fnd Grants, 4789
US Airways Educ Fnd Grants, 4790
USA Volleyball Fnd Educational Grants, 4791
USBC Annual Zeb Scholarship, 4792
USBC Earl Anthony Memorial Scholarships, 4793
USCM HIV/AIDS Prevention Grants, 4794
US CRDF Science and Tech Entrepreneurship Program Business Partnership Grant - Armenia, 4795
US CRDF STEP Business Partnership Grant Competition Ukraine, 4796
USDA 1890 Land Grant Colleges and Universities Initiative Grants, 4797
USDA Child and Adult Care Food Program, 4800
USDA Comm Facility Grants, 4801
USDA Comm Food Projects Competitive Grants, 4802
USDA Cooperative Extension Educ Grants, 4803
USDA Delta Health Care Services Grants, 4804
USDA Denali Comm High Energy Cost Grants, 4805
USDA Distance Lrng & Telemedicine Grts, 4806
USDA Emergency Comm Water Assistance, 4807
USDA Farmers Market Promotion Grants, 4808
USDA Farm Labor Housing Grants, 4809
USDA High Energy Cost Grants, 4812
USDA Household Water Well System Grants, 4814
USDA Housing Application Packaging Grants, 4815
USDA Housing Preservation Grants, 4816
USDA Indiv Water & Waste Water Grts, 4817
USDA Multi-Family Housing Preservation and Revitalization Grants, 4819
USDA PreDev Planning Grants, 4821
USDA Public Telev Digital Transition Grts, 4822
USDA Rural Business Enterprise Grants, 4823
USDA Rural Business Opportunity Grants, 4824
USDA Rural Comm Dev Initiative Grants, 4825
USDA Rural Cooperative Dev Grants, 4826
USDA Rural Economic Dev Grants, 4827
USDA Rural Energy for America - Energy Audit & Renewable Energy Dev Assistance Grts, 4828
USDA Rural Energy for America - Feasibility Study Grants, 4829
USDA Rural Energy for America - Renewable Energy System and Energy Efficiency Improvement Guaranteed Grants, 4830
USDA Rural Housing Repair and Rehabi Grants, 4831
USDA Rural Microentrepreneur Astnc Grts, 4832
USDA Rural Utilities Service Weather Radio Transmitter Grants, 4833
USDA Section 306C Water and Waste Disposal Grants to Alleviate Health Risks, 4834
USDA Section 306D Water and Waste System Grants for Alaskan Villages, 4835
USDA Self-Help Tech Assistance Grants, 4836
USDA Socially-Disadvantaged Producer Grants, 4837
USDA Solid Waste Management Grants, 4838
USDA State Bulk Fuel Revolving Fund Grants, 4840
USDA Value-Added Producer Grants, 4843
USDA Water and Waste Disposal Grants, 4844
USDC/NOAA American Rivers Comm-Based Restoration Program River Grants, 4845
USDC Advanced Manufacturing Jobs and Innovation Accelerator Challenge Grants, 4848
USDC Business Center - American Indian and Alaska Native Grants, 4849
USDC i6 Challenge Grants, 4851
USDC Low-Power Television and Translator Upgrade Grants, 4852
USDC Planning and Local Tech Assistance, 4854
USDC Public Works and Economic Adjustment Assistance Grants, 4856
USDC State Broadband Initiative Grants, 4857
USDC Strong Cities, Strong Communities Visioning Challenge Grants, 4858
USDC Supplemental Appropriations Disaster Relief Opportunity Grants, 4859
USDC Tech Opportunities Pgm Grts, 4860
USDC University Center Economic Dev Program Competition, 4861
USDD Cultural Resources Program Assistance Announcement Grants, 4862
USDJ Edward Byrne Memorial Justice Grants, 4863
USFA Equipment Subsidy Grants, 4867
US Soccer Fdn Annual Pgm & Field Grts, 4870
US Soccer Fnd Planning Grants, 4871
USTA Althea Gibson Leadership Awards, 4872
USTA CTA and NJTL Comm Tennis Dev Workshop Scholarships, 4873
USTA Excellence Grants, 4874
USTA Junior Team Tennis Stipends, 4875
USTA Multicultural Excellence Grants, 4876
USTA Multicultural Individual Player Grant for National Competition and Training, 4877
USTA NJTL Arthur Ashe Essay & Art Cnst, 4878
USTA NJTL Tennis and Leadership Camp Scholarships, 4879
USTA Okechi Womeodu Scholar Athlete Grts, 4880
USTA Player Dev Grants, 4881
USTA Pro Circuit Comm Involvement Grants, 4882
USTA Public Facility Assistance Grants, 4883
USTA Recreational Tennis Grants, 4884
USTA Serves College Educ Scholarships, 4885
USTA Serves College Textbook Scholarships, 4886
USTA Serves Dwight F. Davis Scholarships, 4887
USTA Serves Dwight Mosley Scholarships, 4888
USTA Serves Eve Kraft Scholarships, 4889
USTA Serves Marian Wood Baird Scholarship, 4890
USTA Serves Player Incentive Awards, 4891
USTA Tennis Block Party Grants, 4892
V.V. Cooke Fnd Grants, 4896
Valentine Fnd Grants, 4897
Valerie Adams Mem Char Trust Grts, 4898
Vancouver Fnd Disability Supports for Employment Grants, 4899
Vancouver Fnd Grants and Comm Initiatives, 4900
Vancouver Sun Children's Fund Grants, 4901
Vanderburgh Comm Fnd Grants, 4902
Vanderburgh Comm Fdn Women's Fund, 4903
Vanguard Public Fnd Grant Funds, 4904
Van Kampen Boyer Molinari Char Fdn Grts, 4905
Van Kampen Fnd Grants, 4906
Vectren Fnd Grants, 4907
Verizon Fnd Connecticut Grants, 4908
Verizon Fnd Delaware Grants, 4909
Verizon Fnd Grants, 4911
Verizon Fnd Great Lakes Region Grants, 4912
Verizon Fnd Health Care and Accessibility Grants, 4913
Verizon Fnd Internet Safety Grants, 4914
Verizon Fnd Maryland Grants, 4917
Verizon Fnd New York Grants, 4919
Verizon Fnd NE Region Grants, 4920
Verizon Fnd Pennsylvania Grants, 4921
Verizon Fnd South Carolina Lit & Internet Safety Grants, 4922
Verizon Fnd SE Region Grants, 4923
Verizon Fnd Vermont Grants, 4924
Verizon Fnd Virginia Grants, 4925
Verizon Fnd West Virginia Grants, 4926
Verizon Wireless Hopeline Grants, 4927
Vermillion Cty Comm Fdn Grts, 4928
Vermont Comm Fnd Grants, 4929
Vernon K. Krieble Fnd Grants, 4930
Viacom Fnd Grants (Formerly CBS Fnd), 4932
Victor E. Speas Fnd Grants, 4933
Victoria S. and Bradley L. Geist Fnd Capacity Building Grants, 4934
Victoria S. and Bradley L. Geist Fnd Enhancement Grants, 4935
Victoria S. and Bradley L. Geist Fnd Grants Supporting Foster Care and Their Caregivers, 4936
Victoria S. and Bradley L. Geist Fnd Grants Supporting Transitioning Foster Youth, 4937
Vigneron Grants, 4938
Virginia Commission for the Arts Local Government Challenge Grants, 4943
Virginia Comsn for the Arts Proj Grts, 4944
Virginia Fnd for Humanities Discretionary Grants, 4946
Virginia Fdn for the Humanities Open Grants, 4947
Virginia W. Kettering Fnd Grants, 4950
Visiting Nurse Fnd Grants, 4951
Volvo Adventure Environmental Awards, 4952
VSA/Metlife Connect All Grants, 4953
VSA Int'l Art Program for Children with Disabilities Grants, 4955
Vulcan Materials Company Fnd Grants, 4956
W.C. Griffith Fnd Grants, 4957
WK Kellogg Fdn Healthy Kids Grants, 4961
WK Kellogg Fdn Racial Equity Grants, 4962
WK Kellogg Fdn Secure Families Grants, 4963
WM Keck Fdn Southern California Grts, 4964
W.P. and Bulah Luse Fnd Grants, 4965
W Paul & Lucille Caudill Little Fdn Grts, 4966
W Waldo & Jenny Lynn M Bradley Fdn Grts, 4967
Wabash River Enhancement Corporation Agricultural Cost-Share Grants, 4968
Wabash River Enhancement Corp Urban, 4969
Wabash River Heritage Corridor Fund Grants, 4970
Wabash Valley Comm Fnd Grants, 4971
Waitt Family Fnd Grants, 4973
Wallace Alexander Gerbode Fnd Grants, 4974
Wallace Fnd Grants, 4976
Wallace Global Fund Grants, 4977
Walmart Fnd Facility Giving Grants, 4978
Walmart Fnd National Giving Grants, 4979
Walmart Fnd State Giving Grants, 4980
Walt Disney Company Fnd Grants, 4981
Walter and Elise Haas Fund Grants, 4982
Walter L. Gross III Family Fnd Grants, 4983
Walton Family Fdn Home Region Grts, 4984
Warren County Comm Fnd Grants, 4985
Warren Cty Comm Fdn Mini-Grants, 4986
Warrick Cty Comm Fdn Grants, 4987
Washington Area Fuel Fund Grants, 4988
Washington Area Women's Fnd African American Women's Giving Circle Grants, 4989
Washington Area Women's Fnd Early Care and Educ Funders Collaborative Grants, 4990
Washington Area Women's Fnd Financial Educ and Wealth Creation Fund Grants, 4991
Washington Area Women's Fdn Jobs Fund Grts, 4992
Washington Area Women's Fnd Ldrsp Awds, 4993
Washington Area Women's Fnd Open Door Capacity Fund Grants, 4994
Washington Area Women's Fnd Rainmakers Giving Circle Grants, 4995
Washington Area Women's Fnd Strategic Opportunity and Partnership Fund Grants, 4996
Washington Cty Comm Fdn Grts, 4997
Washington Cty Comm Fdn Youth Grts, 4998
Washington Gas Char Gvg Contributions, 5000
Waste Management Charitable Giving Grants, 5001
Water and Land Stewardship Fund Grants, 5002
Wayne and Gladys Valley Fnd Grants, 5003
Wayne County Fnd - Vigran Family Fnd Grants, 5004
Wayne County Fnd Grants, 5005
Wayne Cty Fdn Women's Fund Grts, 5006
WCI Childcare Capacity Grants, 5007

PROGRAM TYPE INDEX

WCI Comm Leadership Fellowships, 5008
WCI Comm Mobilization Grants, 5009
WCI Family Econ Success Local Impact Grts, 5010
WCI Family Econ Success Regionwide Grts, 5011
WCI Leadership Dev Grants, 5012
Weatherwax Fnd Grants, 5014
Weaver Fnd Grants, 5015
Weaver Popcorn Fnd Grants, 5016
Weingart Fnd Grants, 5018
Welborn Baptist Fnd Faith-Based Grants, 5019
Welborn Baptist Fnd Gen Opportunity Grants, 5020
Welborn Baptist Fnd Improvements to Comm Health Status Grants, 5021
Wells County Fnd Grants, 5022
Wells Fargo Housing Fnd Grants, 5023
Western Indiana Comm Fdn Grts, 5024
Western New York Fnd Grants, 5025
Western Pennsylvania Environmental Awards, 5026
West Hawai'i Fund for Nonprofit Orgs, 5027
Westinghouse Charitable Giving Grants, 5028
West Virginia Commission on the Arts Accessibility Services Grants, 5029
West Virginia Commission on the Arts Artist Visit Grants, 5030
West Virginia Commission on the Arts Challenge America Partnership Grants, 5031
West Virginia Commission on the Arts Comm Connections Grants, 5032
West Virginia Commission on the Arts Cultural Facilities and Capital Resources Grants, 5033
West Virginia Commission on the Arts Fast Track ADA and Emergency Grants, 5034
West Virginia Commission on the Arts Initiative/Opportunity Grants, 5035
West Virginia Commission on the Arts Long-Range Planning Grants, 5036
West Virginia Commission on the Arts Major Institutions Support Grants, 5038
West Virginia Commission on the Arts Media Arts Grants, 5039
West Virginia Commission on the Arts Mid-Size Institutions Support Grants, 5040
West Virginia Commission on the Arts Peer Assistance Network Grants, 5042
West Virginia Commission on the Arts Presenting Artists Grants, 5044
West Virginia Commission on the Arts Re-Granting Grants, 5046
West Virginia Commission on the Arts Staffing Support Grants, 5049
West Virginia Comm on the Arts Visual Grants, 5051
WestWind Fnd Environment Grants, 5052
Weyerhaeuser Company Fnd Grants, 5053
Weyerhaeuser Family Fnd Environment, Conservation and Preservation Grants, 5054
Whatcom Comm Fnd Grants, 5055
Whirlpool Fnd Grants, 5056
White County Comm Fnd Grants, 5057
Whitehorse Fnd Grants, 5058
Whiting Fnd Grants, 5059
Whitley Cty Comm Fdn Grts, 5060
Whitney Fnd Grants, 5061
WHO Fnd Education/Lit Grants, 5062
WHO Fnd General Grants, 5063
Widgeon Point Charitable Fnd Grants, 5064
Wieboldt Fnd Grants, 5065
Wilbur & Patsy Bradley Family Fdn Grts, 5066
Wilburforce Fnd Grants, 5067
WILD Fnd Grants, 5068
Wild Rivers Comm Fnd Holiday Partnerships, 5069
Wild Rivers Comm Fnd Summer Youth Grants, 5070
Willary Fnd Grants, 5071
William A. Badger Fnd Grants, 5072
William A. Miller Fnd Grants, 5073
William B. Dietrich Fnd Grants, 5075
William B. Stokely Jr. Fnd Grants, 5076
William Blair and Company Fnd Grants, 5078
William C. Kenney Watershed Protection Fnd Ecosystem Grants, 5079
William G & Helen C Hoffman Fnd Grants, 5080

William G. Baker, Jr. Grants, 5081
William G. Gilmore Fnd Grants, 5082
William G. McGowan Charitable Fund Grants, 5084
William G Selby & Marie Selby Fdn Grts, 5085
William J. and Dorothy K. O'Neill Fnd Grants, 5087
William J. Brace Charitable Trust, 5088
William L. and Victorine Q. Adams Fnd Grants, 5089
William M. Weaver Fnd Grants, 5091
William Robert Baird Charitable Trust Grants, 5093
William S. Abell Fnd Grants, 5094
Williams Companies Fnd Grants, 5095
William T. Grant Youth Service Impr Grants, 5096
William T. Sloper Trust for Andres J. Sloper Musical Fund Grants, 5097
Wilson-Wood Fnd Grants, 5098
Windward Youth Leadership Fund Grants, 5100
Winston-Salem Fdn Competitive Grts, 5102
Winston-Salem Fdn Elkin/Tri-County Grants, 5103
Winston-Salem Fdn Stokes County Grants, 5104
Winthrop Rockefeller Fnd Grants, 5105
Wisconsin Energy Fnd Grants, 5106
Wisconsin Humanities Council Mini-Grants for Scholarly Research, 5108
Wolfe Associates Grants, 5110
Women's Fdn Greater Kansas City Grts, 5111
Women's Funding Alliance Grants, 5112
Wood-Claeyssens Fnd Grants, 5113
Woods Charitable Fund Grants, 5114
Woods Fund of Chicago Grants, 5115
WSF Rusty Kanokogi Fund for the Advancement of U.S. Judo Grants, 5118
Xcel Energy Fnd Grants, 5121
Xerox Fnd Grants, 5122
Yampa Valley Comm Fnd Erickson Business Week Scholarships, 5123
Yawkey Fnd Grants, 5125
Yellow Corporate Fnd Grants, 5126
Young Family Fnd Grants, 5127
Youth As Resources Grants, 5130
Youth as Resources Mini-Grants, 5131
Youth Philanthropy Project, 5132
YSA ABC Summer of Service Awards, 5133
YSA Global Yth Svc Day Lead Agency Grts, 5135
YSA MLK Day Lead Organizer Grants, 5136
YSA National Child Awareness Month Youth Ambassador Grants, 5137
YSA NEA Youth Leaders for Lit Grants, 5138
YSA Sodexo Lead Organizer Grants, 5140
YSA State Farm Good Neighbor YOUth In The Driver Seat Grants, 5141
YSA UnitedHealth HEROES Service-Learning Grants, 5142
Z. Smith Reynolds Fnd Economic Dev Grants, 5144
Z. Smith Reynolds Fnd Democracy and Civic Engagement Grants, 5145

Consulting/Visiting Personnel

AAAS Science and Tech Policy Fellowships: Energy, Environment, and Agriculture, 52
AAP Leonard P. Rome Comm Access to Child Health Visiting Professorships, 67
Abbott Fund Access to Health Care Grants, 80
Abbott Fund Global AIDS Care Grants, 82
Able To Serve Grants, 102
Alabama State Council on the Arts Comm Arts Tech Assistance Grants, 240
Alabama State Council on Arts Partnership Grants, 242
Alabama State Council on the Arts Tech Assistance Grants for Individuals, 249
Alabama State Council on the Arts Tech Assistance Grants for Organizations, 250
ALA Maureen Hayes Author/Illustrator Award, 299
ALFJ Astraea U.S. and Int'l Movement Fund, 361
Applied Materials Corp Philanthropy Pgm, 515
Arizona Comsn on the Arts Educ Projects Grts, 536
Arizona Comm on Arts Folklorist Residencies, 537
Arizona Commission on the Arts Individual Artist Residencies, 538
Arizona Commission on the Arts Visual/Media Arts Organizations Grants, 539

Arts Council of Winston-Salem and Forsyth County Organizational Support Grants, 577
Assurant Health Fnd Grants, 596
Atkinson Fnd Comm Grants, 606
Avon Products Fnd Grants, 625
Ball Brothers Fnd Rapid Grants, 639
Baltimore Comm Fnd Arts and Culture Grants, 641
Bay and Paul Fnds Grants, 693
BCBSM Fdn Proposal Dev Awds, 709
Beckley Area Fnd Grants, 716
Bill Hannon Fnd Grants, 771
Bodenwein Public Benevolent Fdn Grants, 806
British Columbia Arts Council Educ Grants, 842
California Arts Council Public Value Grants, 895
California Arts Council Statewide Ntwks Grts, 897
Chesapeake Bay Trust Capacity Bldg Grts, 1068
City of Oakland Cultural Arts Dept Grts, 1142
Clarence E Heller Charitable Fdn Grants, 1150
Claude Pepper Fnd Grants, 1160
Claude Worthington Benedum Fdn Grants, 1161
Columbus Fnd Small Grants, 1232
Columbus Fnd Traditional Grants, 1233
Comm Fdn for Grtr Buffalo Grants, 1247
Comm Fdn for Monterey Cty Grants, 1255
Comm Fdn for Muskegon Cty Grants, 1256
Comm Fdn for Southern Arizona Grants, 1261
Comm Fdn in Jacksonville Art Ventures Small Arts Orgs Professional Assistance Grts, 1262
Comm Fdn of E Ctrl Illinois Grts, 1278
Comm Fnd of Greater Fort Wayne - Cmty Endwt & Clarke Endwt Grants, 1285
Comm Fnd of St. Joseph County ArtsEverywhere Grants, 1313
Comm Fnd Silicon Valley Grants, 1331
ConAgra Foods Fnd Nourish Our Comm Grants, 1343
Connecticut Comm Fnd Grants, 1350
D. W. McMillan Fnd Grants, 1426
Dade Comm Fnd AIDS Partnership Grants, 1428
Delaware Comm Fnd-Youth Philanthropy Board for Kent County, 1483
Drs. Bruce and Lee Fnd Grants, 1607
East Tennessee Fnd Grants, 1646
Eddie C. and Sylvia Brown Family Fnd Grants, 1653
Edina Realty Fnd Grants, 1656
Eileen Fisher Women-Owned Business Grants, 1677
Eisner Fnd Grants, 1678
Emily Davie and Joseph S. Kornfeld Fnd Grants, 1697
Ewing Marion Kauffman Fnd Grants, 1777
FAR Fund Grants, 1787
Florida BRAIVE Fund of Dade Comm Fnd, 1846
Florida Div of Cultural Affairs Dance Grts, 1850
Florida Division of Cultural Affairs Underserved Cultural Comm Dev Grants, 1864
Foellinger Fnd Grants, 1877
Frances L & Edwin L Cummings Mem Fund, 1919
Fremont Area Cmty Fdn Amazing X Grants, 1953
Fremont Area Comm Fnd Grants, 1955
Fund for the City of New York Grants, 1978
GMFUS Black Sea Trust Regional Corp Grants, 2065
GNOF Jefferson Comm Grants, 2085
GNOF Plaquemines Comm Grants, 2091
GNOF St. Bernard Comm Grants, 2092
Goldseker Fnd Comm Grants, 2101
Goldseker Fnd Non-Profit Management Assistance Grants, 2103
Grand Rapids Comm Fnd Ionia County Youth Fund Grants, 2120
Gulf Coast Fnd of Comm Operating Grants, 2176
Gulf Coast Fnd of Comm Grants, 2177
Hartford Fdn Implementation Sppt Grts, 2251
Hartford Fdn Nonprofit Support Grants, 2252
Helen Steiner Rice Fnd Grants, 2299
Historic Landmarks Fnd of Indiana Preservation Grants, 2337
Historic Landmarks Legal Defense Grants, 2338
Hogg Fnd for Mental Health Grants, 2343
HRSA Nurse Education, Practice, Quality and Retention Grants, 2381
Huntington Arts Council Arts-in-Educ Programs, 2400
Hyde Family Fnds Grants, 2414

1054 / Consulting/Visiting Personnel

Illinois Arts Council Educ Residency Grants, 2463
Indiana Arts Commission American Masterpieces Grants, 2530
Indiana Arts Commission Statewide Arts Service Organization Grants, 2533
Indianapolis Preservation Grants, 2543
Indiana Preservation Grants, 2544
Iowa Arts Council Artists in Schools/Communities Residency Grants, 2571
James & Abigail Campbell Fam Fdn Grts, 2620
James R. Thorpe Fnd Grants, 2636
Jennings County Comm Fdn Grts, 2664
Jessie Ball Dupont Fund Grants, 2671
Joel L. Fleishman Civil Society Fellowships, 2683
John G. Martin Fnd Grants, 2696
Kansas Arts Commission Artist Fellowships, 2776
Lafayette - West Lafayette Convention and Visitors Bureau Tourist Promotion Grants, 2849
LaGrange Independent Fnd for Endowments, 2851
Leo Niessen Jr., Charitable Trust Grants, 2885
MacArthur Fnd Chicago Arts and Culture Int'l Connections Grants, 2962
Massachusetts Fnd for Humanities Project Grants, 3060
Melville Charitable Trust Grants, 3115
Meyer Fnd Mgmt Assistance Grts, 3144
Montgomery Cty Comm Fdn Grants, 3213
National Endowment for Democracy Reagan-Fascell Democracy Fellowships, 3252
NEH Preservation Assistance Grants for Smaller Institutions, 3293
NEH Preservation Microfilming of Brittle Books and Serials Grants, 3294
Nellie Mae Educ Fnd State Level Systems Change Grants, 3299
Nevada Arts Council Jackpot Grants, 3312
Nevada Arts Council Professional Dev Grants, 3314
NFF Comm Assistance Grants, 3343
NHSCA Artist Residencies in Schools Grants, 3423
NHSCA General Project Grants, 3427
NHSCA Operating Grants, 3428
Noble County Comm Fnd Grants, 3456
North Carolina Arts Council Arts in Educ Artist Residencies Grants, 3468
North Carolina Arts Council Arts in Educ Initiatives Grants, 3469
North Carolina Arts Council Arts in Educ Rural Dev Grants, 3470
North Carolina Arts Council Folklife Grants, 3476
North Carolina Arts Council Outreach Grants, 3479
North Carolina Arts Council Res Center Grants, 3481
North Carolina Arts Council Tech Assistance, 3482
North Carolina Arts Council Touring/Presenting Grants, 3483
North Carolina Arts Council Visual Arts Program Support Grants, 3484
North Carolina Comm Fnd Grants, 3489
North Dakota Council on the Arts Comm Access Grants, 3494
NYCT Workforce Dev Grants, 3560
NYHC Speakers in the Humanities Grants, 3569
NYSCA Architecture, Planning, and Design: Design and Planning Studies Grants, 3572
NYSCA Architecture, Planning, and Design: Project Support Grants, 3576
NYSCA Arts Education: Comm-based Learning Grants, 3577
NYSCA Arts Education: K-12 In-School Grants, 3580
NYSCA Arts Educ: Svcs to the Field Grts, 3582
NYSCA Dance: Commissions Grants, 3583
NYSCA Dance: Long-Term Residency in New York State Grants, 3586
NYSCA Electr Media & Film Workspace Grants, 3593
NYSCA Folk Arts: Presentation Grants, 3596
NYSCA Folk Arts: Regional and County Folk Arts Grants, 3597
NYSCA Lit: Public Programs, 3600
NYSCA Museum: Project Support Grants, 3604
NYSCA Music: Cmy Music Schools Grts, 3605
NYSCA Special Arts Services: Instruction and Training Grants, 3616

NYSCA Visual Arts: Svcs to the Field Grts, 3630
Ohio Arts Council Artist Express Grants, 3643
Ohio Arts Council Artist in Residence Grants for Artists, 3644
Ohio Arts Council Artist in Residence Grants for Sponsors, 3645
Ohio Arts Council Int'l Partnership Grts, 3653
OneFamily Fnd Grants, 3673
Ordean Fnd Grants, 3691
Packard Fnd Organizational Effectiveness and Philanthropy Grants, 3730
Patrick and Anna M. Cudahy Fund Grants, 3751
PCA-PCD Organizational Short-Term Professional Dev and Consulting Grants, 3769
PCA Arts in Educ Residencies, 3772
PCA Arts Organizations and Grants for Crafts, 3778
PCA Arts Organizations & Grants for Visual Arts, 3785
PCA Entry Track Arts Organizations and Arts Grants for Crafts, 3790
PCA Entry Track Arts Organizations and Arts Grants for Visual Arts, 3799
PCA Mgmt/Techn Assistance Grts, 3800
PCA Pennsylvania Partners in the Arts Project Stream Grants, 3802
PennPAT Artist Tech Assistance Grants, 3811
Pew Charitable Trusts Arts and Culture Grants, 3857
Pike County Comm Fnd Grants, 3888
Pinellas County Grants, 3891
Pittsburgh Fdn Comm Fund Grts, 3910
PMP Professional Dev Grants, 3919
Poets & Writers Readings/Workshops Grants, 3927
Price Gilbert, Jr. Charitable Fund Grants, 3953
Prudential Fnd Educ Grants, 3977
Puerto Rico Comm Fnd Grants, 3986
Rhode Island Fnd Grants, 4073
Robert Sterling Clark Arts & Culture Grants, 4122
Rochester Area Comm Fnd Grants, 4127
Ronald McDonald House Charities Grants, 4149
Rose Communities and Environment Northern California Environmental Grassroots Grants, 4158
Ross Fnd Grants, 4164
RRF Accessible Faith Grants, 4169
RWJF Local Funding Partnerships Grants, 4186
Samuel S. Johnson Fnd Grants, 4239
Seabury Fnd Grants, 4316
Shell Oil Company Fnd Grants, 4343
Sport Manitoba Athlete Skill Dev Clinics Grants, 4453
Sport Manitoba Coaches/Officials Travel Assistance Grants, 4455
TAC Arts Access Grant, 4549
TAC Arts Access Tech Assistance Grants, 4550
TAC Arts Build Communities Grants, 4551
TAC Arts Educ Mini Grants, 4553
TAC Arts Projects Grants, 4554
TAC Rural Arts Project Support Grants, 4555
TAC Tech Assistance Grants, 4556
Tanner Humanities Cntr Rsch Fellowships, 4559
Telluride Fnd Comm Grants, 4573
Telluride Fdn Tech Assistance Grts, 4575
Temple Univ George D McDowell Fellowship, 4577
Texas Cmsn on the Arts Arts Respond Prj Grts, 4581
Texas Comm on Arts Cultural Connections Grant, 4591
Tides Fdn Calif Wildlands Grassroots Fund, 4630
USDA Self-Help Tech Assistance Grants, 4836
USDC Market Dev Cooperator Grants, 4853
Virginia Comsn for the Arts Proj Grts, 4944
Virginia Fnd for Humanities Resid Fellowships, 4948
West Virginia Commission on the Arts Long-Range Planning Grants, 5036
West Virginia Commission on the Arts Long-Term Artist Residencies, 5037
West Virginia Commission on the Arts Peer Assistance Network Grants, 5042
West Virginia Commission on the Arts Short-Term Artist Residencies, 5047

Cultural Outreach

3M Company Arts and Culture Grants, 12
3M Fnd Comm Giving Grants, 15
A.C. Ratshesky Fnd Grants, 39

A.J. Fletcher Fnd Grants, 41
A.O. Smith Comm Grants, 46
Aaron Copland Fund for Music Recording, 71
Aaron Fnd Grants, 73
Abbot & Dorothy H Stevens Fdn Grants, 79
Abbott Fund Comm Grants, 81
Abell-Hanger Fnd Grants, 91
Abell Fnd Arts and Culture Grants, 92
ABIG Fnd Grants, 99
Abington Fnd Grants, 100
ABS Fnd Grants, 107
Achelis Fnd Grants, 127
Ackerman Fnd Grants, 129
Acuity Charitable Fnd Grants, 140
Adams-Mastrovich Family Fnd Grants, 146
Adams Cty Comm Fdn of Indiana Grts, 148
Adams Fnd Grants, 155
Adelaide Breed Bayrd Fnd Grants, 161
Adolph Coors Fnd Grants, 171
Advanced Micro Dvcs Comm Affairs Grts, 172
AEC Trust Grants, 175
Aetna Fdn Diversity Grants in Connecticut, 182
AFG Industries Grants, 191
African American Fund of New Jersey Grants, 192
A Friends' Fnd Trust Grants, 194
Agape Fnd for Nonviolent Social Change Board of Trustees Grants, 197
Agway Fnd Grants, 205
Ahmanson Fnd Grants, 207
Air Products and Chemicals Grants, 216
Akonadi Fnd Anti-Racism Grants, 217
Akzo Nobel Chemicals Grants, 219
Alabama Humanities Fnd Mini Grants, 231
Alabama Humanities Fnd Planning Grants, 232
Alabama State Council on the Arts Comm Arts Collaborative Ventures Grants, 236
Alabama State Council on the Arts Comm Arts Operating Support Grants, 237
Alabama State Council on the Arts Comm Arts Presenting Grants, 238
Alabama State Council on the Arts Comm Planning & Design Grants, 241
Alabama State Council on the Arts Multi-Discipline and Festival Grants, 243
ALA Carnegie Corporation of New York/New York Times I Love My Librarian Award, 254
ALA Coretta Scott King Book Donation Grant, 261
ALA Dartmouth Medal, 262
Aladdin Industries Fnd Grants, 263
ALA Diversity and Outreach Fair, 267
ALA Loleta D. Fyan Grant, 295
Alaska State Council on the Arts Comm Grants, 327
Alaska State Council on the Arts Operating Support Grants, 328
ALA Writers Live at the Library Grants, 336
Albert and Bessie Mae Kronkosky Charitable Fnd Grants, 339
Albert and Margaret Alkek Fnd Grants, 340
Albert B Cuppage Charitable Fdn Grts, 341
Albert E. and Birdie W. Einstein Fund Grants, 342
Alberto Culver Corporate Contributions Grants, 343
Albert Pick Jr. Fund Grants, 344
Albertson's Charitable Giving Grants, 345
Albuquerque Comm Fnd Grants, 348
Alcatel-Lucent Technologies Fnd Grants, 349
Alexander & Baldwin Fnd Hawaiian and Pacific Island Grants, 352
Alexander & Baldwin Fdn Mainland Grants, 353
Alex Stern Family Fnd Grants, 360
ALFJ Astraea U.S. and Int'l Movement Fund, 361
ALFJ Astraea U.S. General Fund, 362
Alfred P Sloan Fdn Civic Initiatives Grts, 368
Allegheny Fnd Grants, 376
Allen Hilles Fund Grants, 378
Allen P & Josephine B Green Fdn Grts, 380
Alliant Energy Fnd Comm Grants, 384
Allstate Corp Hometown Commitment Grants, 387
Allstate Tolerance, Inclusion, & Diversity Grants, 391
Alticor Corporation Comm Contributions Grants, 396
Altman Fnd Health Care Grants, 397

PROGRAM TYPE INDEX

Cultural Outreach / 1055

Altria Group Arts and Culture Grants, 399
Alvin & Fanny Blaustein Thalheimer Fdn Grts, 403
ALZA Corporate Contributions Grants, 405
Amador Comm Fnd Grants, 408
Ambrose and Ida Fredrickson Fnd Grants, 414
Ambrose Monell Fnd Grants, 415
Ameren Corporation Comm Grants, 418
American-Scandinavian Fnd Public Project Grants, 419
American Express Historic Preservation Grants, 431
American for the Arts Emergency Relief Fund, 435
American Savings Fnd Grants, 445
Amerigroup Fnd Grants, 452
AmerUs Group Charitable Fnd, 455
Amgen Fnd Grants, 456
Amon G. Carter Fnd Grants, 458
Anderson Fnd Grants, 460
Andy Warhol Fdn for the Visual Arts Grts, 464
Anheuser-Busch Fnd Grants, 470
ANLAF Int'l Fund for Sexual Minorities Grts, 471
Anne L. and George H. Clapp Charitable and Educational Trust Grants, 476
Annenberg Fnd Grants, 477
Anne Thorne Weaver Family Fnd Grants, 478
Annie Sinclair Knudsen Memorial Fund/Kaua'i Comm Grants, 482
Ann L. and Carol Green Rhodes Grants, 483
Ann Peppers Fnd Grants, 484
Anschutz Family Fnd Grants, 486
AON Fnd Grants, 491
APAP Cultural Exchange Grants, 492
Appalachian Regional Commission Tourist Grants, 511
Applied Biosystems Grants, 514
Applied Materials Corp Philanthropy Pgm, 515
Aratani Fnd Grants, 523
Arcadia Fnd Grants, 525
Archer Daniels Midland Fnd Grants, 527
Arcus Fnd Fund Grants, 529
Arcus Fnd National Fund Grants, 531
Argyros Fnd Grants, 532
Arie and Ida Crown Memorial Grants, 533
Arizona Cardinals Grants, 534
Arizona Comsn on the Arts Educ Projects Grts, 536
Arizona Commission on the Arts Visual/Media Arts Organizations Grants, 539
Arizona Comm Fnd Grants, 540
Arizona Public Service Corp Gvg Pgm Grts, 545
Arizona Republic Newspaper Corp Contribs, 547
Arizona State Library LSTA Learning Grants, 550
Arkansas Arts Cncl Collab Proj Support, 555
Arkansas Arts Council Expansion Arts Grants, 556
Arkansas Comm Fnd Grants, 561
Armstrong McDonald Fnd Grants, 565
ARS Fnd Grants, 568
Arthur Ashley Williams Fnd Grants, 572
Arthur F & Alice E Adams Charitable Fdn Grts, 574
Arts and Science Council Grants, 576
Arts Council of Winston-Salem and Forsyth County Organizational Support Grants, 577
Arts Midwest Performing Arts Grants, 579
ArtsWave Impact Grants, 580
ArtsWave Project Grants, 581
ArvinMeritor Fdn Arts & Culture Grts, 582
ArvinMeritor Grants, 585
Ashland Corporate Contributions Grants, 587
Assisi Fnd of Memphis General Grants, 594
Assisi Fnd of Memphis Mini Grants, 595
Assurant Health Fnd Grants, 596
AT&T Fnd Civic and Comm Service Grants, 599
Atherton Family Fnd Grants, 604
Athwin Fnd Grants, 605
Atlanta Fnd Grants, 608
Auburn Fnd Grants, 611
Audrey and Sydney Irmas Charitable Fnd Grants, 612
Aurora Fnd Grants, 613
Austin Comm Fnd Grants, 616
Autauga Area Comm Fnd Grants, 618
Autzen Fnd Grants, 622
Avery Dennison Fnd Grants, 623
Avista Fnd Grants, 624
Avon Products Fnd Grants, 625

AXA Fnd Scholarships, 629
Ayres Fnd Grants, 630
Babcock Charitable Trust Grants, 632
Back Home Again Fnd Grants, 633
Bacon Family Fnd Grants, 634
Bailey Fnd Grants, 635
Ball Brothers Fnd General Grants, 637
Baltimore Comm Fnd Arts and Culture Grants, 641
Banfi Vintners Fnd Grants, 653
Bank of America Charitable Fnd Matching Gifts, 658
Bank of America Charitable Fnd Volunteer Grants, 660
Bank of America Corporation Sponsorships, 661
Barberton Comm Fnd Grants, 666
Barker Welfare Fnd Grants, 669
Barnes Group Fnd Grants, 672
Barra Fnd Comm Fund Grants, 673
Barra Fnd Project Grants, 674
Barrasso Usdin Kupperman Freeman and Sarver LLC Corporate Grants, 675
Barr Fnd Grants (Massachusetts), 676
Barr Fund Grants, 678
Batchelor Fnd Grants, 679
Baton Rouge Area Fnd Grants, 682
Battle Creek Comm Fnd Grants, 684
Batts Fnd Grants, 687
Baxter Int'l Corporate Giving Grants, 689
Baxter Int'l Fnd Grants, 691
Bay and Paul Fnds, Inc Grants, 692
Bay and Paul Fnds Grants, 693
Bay Area Comm Fnd Grants, 694
BCBSNC Fnd Grants, 712
Bechtel Group Fnd Building Positive Comm Relationships Grants, 715
Beckley Area Fnd Grants, 716
Beerman Fnd Grants, 717
Beim Fnd Grants, 718
Belk Fnd Grants, 721
Bemis Company Fnd Grants, 723
Beneficia Fnd Grants, 727
Benton County Fnd Grants, 731
Berks County Comm Fnd Grants, 734
Bernard & Audre Rapoport Arts & Culture Grants, 735
Bernard Osher Fnd Grants, 742
Berrien Comm Fnd Grants, 744
Besser Fnd Grants, 748
Beverley Taylor Sorenson Art Wks for Kids Grts, 757
Bill and Melinda Gates Ag Dev Grants, 765
Bill and Melinda Gates Fnd Emergency Response Grants, 766
Bill and Melinda Gates Fnd Financial Services for the Poor Grants, 767
Bill and Melinda Gates Fnd Policy and Advocacy Grants, 769
Biogen Corporate Giving Grants, 773
Blackford Cty Comm Fdn Grts, 780
Black Hills Corporation Grants, 781
Blade Fnd Grants, 783
Blanche and Irving Laurie Fnd Grants, 784
Blanche & Julian Robertson Family Fdn Grants, 785
Blandin Fnd Itasca County Area Vitality Grants, 789
Bloomington Area Arts Council Grants, 791
Blue Cross Blue Shield of Minnesota Fdn-Healthy Equity: Public Libraries for Health Grts, 797
Blue Cross Blue Shield of Minnesota Fnd - Healthy Neighborhoods: Connect for Health Challenge Grants, 798
Blue Grass Comm Fnd Grants, 799
Blue Mountain Comm Fnd Grants, 800
Blum-Kovler Fnd Grants, 803
Blumenthal Fnd Grants, 804
Bodenwein Public Benevolent Fdn Grants, 806
Bodman Fnd Grants, 807
Boeing Company Contributions Grants, 809
Boettcher Fnd Grants, 810
Bonfils-Stanton Fnd Grants, 814
Booth-Bricker Fund Grants, 815
Booth Ferris Fnd Grants, 816
Boston Fnd Grants, 819
Boston Fnd Initiative to Strengthen Arts and Cultural Service Organizations, 820

Boston Globe Fnd Grants, 821
Boston Jewish Cmnty Women's Fund Grts, 822
Boulder County Arts Alliance Neodata Endowment Grants, 823
Bradley-Turner Fnd Grants, 828
Brico Fund Grants, 835
Bridgestone/Firestone Trust Fund Grants, 836
Bristol-Myers Squibb Fnd Comm Grants, 840
British Columbia Arts Council Educ Grants, 842
Brooklyn Comm Fnd Comm Arts for All Grants, 849
Brooklyn Comm Fnd Educ and Youth Achievement Grants, 851
Brown Fnd Grants, 854
Buhl Fnd - Frick Educational Fund, 859
Bunbury Company Grants, 863
Burlington Industries Fnd Grants, 865
Burlington Northern Santa Fe Fdn Grants, 866
Business Bank of Nevada Comm Grants, 879
Bydale Fnd Grants, 882
Caesars Fnd Grants, 891
Caleb C. and Julia W. Dula Educational and Charitable Fnd Grants, 893
California Arts Council Public Value Grants, 895
California Arts Council State-Local Partnership Grants, 896
California Arts Council Statewide Ntwks Grts, 897
California Arts Council Tech Assistance Grts, 898
California Comm Fnd Art Grants, 900
Cambridge Comm Fnd Grants, 913
Campbell Hoffman Fnd Grants, 915
Campbell Soup Fnd Grants, 916
Cape Branch Fnd Grants, 919
Carl & Eloise Pohlad Family Fdn Grants, 927
Carl B. and Florence E. King Fnd Grants, 928
Carl C. Icahn Fnd Grants, 929
Carl Gellert and Celia Berta Gellert Fdn Grts, 930
Carl M. Freeman Fnd FACES Grants, 932
Carl M. Freeman Fnd Grants, 933
Carnegie Corporation of New York Grants, 940
Carolyn Fnd Grants, 942
Carpenter Fnd Grants, 943
Carrie Estelle Doheny Fnd Grants, 945
Carroll County Comm Fnd Grants, 947
CCH California Story Fund Grants, 965
CCH Documentary California Reads Grants, 968
CCH Documentary Project Production Grants, 969
CCH Documentary Public Engagement Grants, 970
CCH Documentary Research and Dev Grants, 971
CDECD Arts Catalyze Placemaking in Every Comm Grants, 977
CDECD Arts Catalyze Placemaking Leadership Grants, 978
CDECD Arts Catalyze Placemaking Sustaining Relevance Grants, 979
CDECD Tourism Product Dev Grants, 984
Cemala Fnd Grants, 988
Central Carolina Comm Impact Grants, 994
Central Okanagan Fnd Grants, 997
Cessna Fnd Grants, 1000
CFFVR Chilton Area Comm Fnd Grants, 1006
CFFVR Clintonville Area Fnd Grants, 1008
CFFVR Fox Valley Comm Arts Grants, 1011
CFFVR Jewelers Mutual Char Gvg Grts, 1014
CFFVR Project Grants, 1017
CFFVR Shawano Area Comm Fnd Grants, 1021
Chamberlain Fnd Grants, 1027
Champlin Fnds Grants, 1029
Chapman Family Charitable Trust Grants, 1034
Charles H. Dater Fnd Grants, 1042
Charles H. Hall Fnd, 1044
Charles H. Price II Family Fnd Grants, 1046
Charles Lafitte Fnd Grants, 1049
Charles M. Bair Family Trust Grants, 1051
Chas Parker Trust for Public Music Fund Grts, 1053
Charlotte County Comm Fnd Grts, 1056
Charlotte Martin Fnd Youth Grants, 1057
Chatlos Fnd Grants, 1061
Chesapeake Corporation Fnd Grants, 1076
Chicago Board of Trade Fnd Grants, 1079
Chicago CityArts Grants, 1080

Cultural Outreach

Chicago Comm Arts Assistance Grants, 1081
Chicago Comm Trust Arts and Culture Grants: SMART Growth, 1083
Chicago Comm Trust Arts and Culture Grants: Supporting Diverse Arts Productions and Fostering Art in Every Comm, 1084
Chicago Cultural Outreach Grants, 1095
Chicago Neighborhood Arts Grants, 1097
Chicago Sun Times Charity Trust Grants, 1098
Chicago Title & Trust Co Fdn Grants, 1099
Chicago Tribune Fnd Civic Grants, 1100
Chicago Tribune Grants for Cultural Organizations, 1101
Chiles Fnd Grants, 1108
Christy-Houston Fnd Grants, 1115
CICF City of Noblesville Comm Grant, 1118
CICF Clare Noyes Grant, 1119
CICF Efroymson Grants, 1120
CICF Indianapolis Fdn Comm Grants, 1123
CICF Legacy Fund Grants, 1126
CIGNA Fnd Grants, 1130
Cinergy Fnd Grants, 1133
Cingular Wireless Charitable Contributions, 1134
Circle K Corporation Contributions Grants, 1136
Citigroup Fnd Grants, 1139
Citizens Bank Mid-Atlantic Char Fdn Grts, 1140
Claneil Fnd Grants, 1145
Clarcor Fnd Grants, 1148
Claremont Comm Fnd Grants, 1149
Clarence E Heller Charitable Fdn Grants, 1150
Clark-Winchcole Fdn Grants, 1152
Clark Charitable Trust Grants, 1155
Cleveland Browns Fnd Grants, 1166
Clipper Ship Fnd Grants, 1175
Clowes Fund Grants, 1177
CNA Fnd Grants, 1179
CNL Corporate Giving Arts & Culture Grants, 1190
Coastal Bend Comm Fnd Grants, 1192
Coastal Comm Fdn of SC Grants, 1193
Cobb Family Fnd Grants, 1194
Coca-Cola Fnd Grants, 1195
Cockrell Fnd Grants, 1196
Collins Fnd Grants, 1209
Colonel Stanley R. McNeil Fnd Grants, 1210
Colorado Springs Cmty Trust Fund Grants, 1215
Columbus Fnd Competitive Grants, 1220
Columbus Fnd John W. and Edna McManus Shepard Fund Grants, 1223
Columbus Fnd Siemer Family Grants, 1231
Columbus Fnd Small Grants, 1232
Comcast Fnd Grants, 1235
Comer Fnd Grants, 1236
Comerica Charitable Fnd Grants, 1237
Commonwealth Edison Grants, 1240
Comm Fnd Alliance City of Evansville Endowment Fund Grants, 1246
Comm Fdn for Monterey Cty Grants, 1255
Comm Fdn for Muskegon Cty Grants, 1256
Comm Fdn for NE Michigan Grants, 1257
Comm Fdn for San Benito County Grants, 1258
Comm Fnd for SE Michigan Grants, 1259
Comm Fdn for Southern Arizona Grants, 1261
Comm Fnd of Bartholomew County Heritage Fund Grants, 1267
Comm Fnd of Bloomington and Monroe County Grants, 1271
Comm Fnd of Broward Grants, 1275
Comm Fdn of Central Illinois Grants, 1276
Comm Fdn of E Ctrl Illinois Grts, 1278
Comm Fdn of Grant Cty Grants, 1279
Comm Fdn of Grtr Birmingham Grants, 1280
Comm Fnd of Greater Chattanooga Grants, 1281
Comm Fnd of Greater Flint Grants, 1282
Comm Fnd of Greater Fort Wayne - Cmty Endwt & Clarke Endwt Grants, 1285
Comm Fnd of Grtr Fort Wayne - John S & James L Knight Fdn Donor-Advised Grants, 1287
Comm Fnd of Greater Greensboro Grants, 1288
Comm Fnd of Greater Tampa Grts, 1292
Comm Fnd of Greenville-Greenville Women Giving Grants, 1293
Comm Fnd of Greenville Hollingsworth Funds Program/Project Grants, 1296
Comm Fdn of Howard County Grts, 1297
Comm Fdn of Jackson County Grts, 1298
Comm Fnd of Louisville Grants, 1299
Comm Fdn of Mdl Tennessee Grants, 1300
Comm Fnd of Mt Vernon & Knox County Grants, 1301
Comm Fnd of Muncie & Delaware County Grant, 1302
Comm Fnd of Muncie and Delaware County Maxon Grants, 1303
Comm Fdn of Riverside County Grants, 1304
Comm Fdn of Santa Cruz County Grants, 1305
Comm Fdn of Sarasota County Grts, 1306
Comm Fdn of Shreveport-Bossier Grts, 1307
Comm Fdn of S Alabama Grants, 1308
Comm Fdn of SE Connecticut Grants, 1309
Comm Fnd of South Puget Sound Grants, 1311
Comm Fnd of the Eastern Shore Needs Grants, 1317
Comm Fnd of the Verdugos Educational Endowment Fund Grants, 1321
Comm Fnd of the Verdugos Grants, 1322
Comm Fnd of Western North Carolina Grants, 1327
Comm Fnd Partnerships - Martin County Grants, 1329
Comm Fnd Silicon Valley Advancing Arts Grants, 1330
Comm Fnd Silicon Valley Grants, 1331
Comm Impact Fund, 1332
Compton Fnd Grants, 1338
ConAgra Foods Fnd Comm Impact Grants, 1342
Con Edison Corp Giving Arts & Culture Grants, 1344
Connecticut Commission on the Arts Art in Public Spaces, 1349
Connecticut Comm Fnd Grants, 1350
Connelly Fnd Grants, 1353
ConocoPhillips Fnd Grants, 1354
ConocoPhillips Grants, 1355
Conseil des arts de Montreal Touring Grants, 1358
CONSOL Coal Group Grants, 1360
Constantin Fnd Grants, 1362
Constellation Energy Corporate Grants, 1364
Consumers Energy Fnd, 1365
Cooke Fnd Grants, 1368
Cooper Fnd Grants, 1369
Cooper Industries Fnd Grants, 1370
Cord Fnd Grants, 1372
Cornerstone Fdn of NE Wisconsin Grants, 1375
Corning Fnd Cultural Grants, 1376
Coughlin-Saunders Fnd Grants, 1377
Covenant Educational Fnd Grants, 1383
Covenant Fdn of New York Signature Grts, 1386
Cowles Charitable Trust Grants, 1392
Cranston Fnd Grants, 1395
Creative Work Fund Grants, 1396
Crescent Porter Hale Fnd Grants, 1398
Crossroads Fund Seed Grants, 1400
Crystelle Waggoner Charitable Trust Grants, 1405
CSRA Comm Fnd Grants, 1407
CSX Corporate Contributions Grants, 1408
Cudd Fnd Grants, 1410
Cullen Fnd Grants, 1411
Cultural Society of Filipino Americans Grants, 1412
Cumberland Comm Fnd Grants, 1413
Cumberland Comm Fnd Summer Kids Grants, 1414
CUNA Mutual Group Fnd, 1416
Cyrus Eaton Fnd Grants, 1423
D.F. Halton Fnd Grants, 1424
Dade Comm Fnd GLBT Comm Projects Grants, 1429
Dade Comm Fnd Grants, 1430
Dairy Queen Corporate Contributions Grants, 1433
Dale and Edna Walsh Grants, 1435
Dallas Fnd Grants, 1436
Dance Advance Grants, 1441
Darden Restaurants Fnd Grants, 1446
Davenport-Hatch Fnd Grants, 1448
David & Barbara B. Hirschhorn Fdn Grt, 1450
David Bohnett Fnd Grants, 1451
Daviess County Comm Arts & Culture Grants, 1455
Davis Family Fnd Grants, 1462
Dayton Fnd Grants, 1463
Dayton Power and Light Fnd Grants, 1464
Daywood Fnd Grants, 1465

DB Americas Fnd Grants, 1466
Deborah Munroe Noonan Mem Fund Grts, 1475
DeKalb County Comm Fnd - Lit Grant, 1480
Delaware Comm Fnd-Youth Philanthropy Board for Kent County, 1483
Delaware Comm Fnd Fund For Women Grants, 1484
Delaware Comm Fnd Next Generation Grants, 1485
Delaware Comm Fdn Youth Philanthropy Board for New Castle County Grts, 1486
Delaware Division of the Arts Comm-Based Organizations Opportunity Grants, 1487
Delaware Division of the Arts Opportunity Grants-- Arts Organizations, 1488
Delaware Division of the Arts Opportunity Grants- Artists, 1489
Delonne Anderson Family Fnd, 1492
Delta Air Lines Fdn Arts & Culture Grts, 1493
Deluxe Corporation Fnd Grants, 1496
DeMatteis Family Fnd Grants, 1497
Denver Broncos Charities Fund Grants, 1501
Denver Fnd Comm Grants, 1502
Dermody Properties Fnd Grants, 1517
DeRoy Testamentary Fnd Grants, 1518
District of Columbia Commission on the Arts-Arts Educ Teacher Mini-Grants, 1549
Dole Food Company Charitable Contributions, 1564
Dolfinger-McMahon Fnd Grants, 1565
Donald & Sylvia Robinson Family Fdn Grts, 1573
Donald W Reynolds Fdn Spcl Projects Grts, 1577
Doris Duke Charitable Fnd Arts Grants, 1584
Dorot Fnd Grants, 1586
Dorothy Rider Pool Health Care Grants, 1589
Dorrance Family Fnd Grants, 1590
Dorr Fnd Grants, 1591
Dr. P. Phillips Fnd Grants, 1601
Dr. Scholl Fnd Grants, 1602
Draper Richards Kaplan Fnd Grants, 1603
Drs. Bruce and Lee Fnd Grants, 1607
DTE Energy Fnd Cultural Grants, 1610
DTE Energy Fnd Diversity Grants, 1611
Duluth-Superior Area Comm Fdn Grts, 1620
Dunspaugh-Dalton Fnd Grants, 1623
DuPage Comm Fnd Grants, 1624
Durfee Fnd Sabbatical Grants, 1625
Dyer-Ives Fnd Small Grants, 1629
E.L. Wiegand Fnd Grants, 1639
E Rhodes & Leona B Carpenter Fdn Grts, 1640
Eastman Chemical Co Fdn Grants, 1643
East Tennessee Fnd Grants, 1646
Eaton Charitable Fund Grants, 1647
Eberly Fnd Grants, 1649
Eddie C. and Sylvia Brown Family Fnd Grants, 1653
Eden Hall Fnd Grants, 1655
Edina Realty Fnd Grants, 1656
Edith and Francis Mulhall Achilles Grants, 1657
Edward Bangs Kelley & Elza Kelley Fdn Grts, 1665
Edward S. Moore Fnd Grants, 1668
Edwin S. Webster Fnd Grants, 1671
Edwin W & Catherine M Davis Fdn Grants, 1672
Edyth Bush Charitable Fnd Grants, 1673
Eisner Fnd Grants, 1678
Elizabeth Morse Genius Char Trust Grants, 1682
Elkhart Cty Comm Fdn Grants, 1684
Elmer L & Eleanor J Andersen Fdn Grnts, 1687
El Paso Comm Fnd Grants, 1688
El Pomar Fnd Awards and Grants, 1690
Elsie H. Wilcox Fnd Grants, 1691
EMC Corporation Grants, 1693
Emerson Charitable Trust Grants, 1694
Emily Davie and Joseph S. Kornfeld Fnd Grants, 1697
Emily Hall Tremaine Fnd Grants, 1698
Emma A. Sheafer Charitable Trust Grants, 1699
Emma B. Howe Memorial Fnd Grants, 1700
Emy-Lou Biedenharn Fnd Grants, 1703
Ensign-Bickford Fnd Grants, 1709
Ensworth Charitable Fnd Grants, 1710
Entergy Charitable Fnd Low-Income Initiatives and Solutions Grants, 1711
Entergy Corporation Micro Grants, 1712
Entergy Corp Open Grants for Arts and Culture, 1713

PROGRAM TYPE INDEX

Cultural Outreach

EQT Fnd Art and Culture Grants, 1743
EQT Fnd Comm Grants, 1744
Erie Comm Fnd Grants, 1750
Essex County Comm Fnd Discretionary Grants, 1752
Essex County Comm Fnd Merrimack Valley General Fund Grants, 1756
Esther M. and Freeman E. Everett Charitable Fnd Grants, 1757
Ethel and Raymond F. Rice Fnd Grants, 1758
Ethel Sergeant Clark Smith Fnd Grants, 1761
Eugene M. Lang Fnd Grants, 1764
Eulalie Bloedel Schneider Fnd Grants, 1767
Evan Frankel Fnd Grants, 1770
Evanston Comm Fnd Grants, 1771
F.M. Kirby Fnd Grants, 1780
F.R. Bigelow Fnd Grants, 1781
Fallon OrNda Comm Health Fund Grants, 1783
Fam Lit & HI Pizza Hut Lit Fund, 1785
FAR Fund Grants, 1787
Fargo-Moorhead Area Fnd Grants, 1788
Farmers Insurance Corporate Giving Grants, 1791
Faye McBeath Fnd Grants, 1794
FEDCO Charitable Fdn Educ Grts, 1798
Federal Express Corporate Contributions, 1799
Fel-Pro Mecklenburger Fnd Grants, 1800
Ferree Fnd Grants, 1804
Field Fnd of Illinois Grants, 1806
Fieldstone Fnd Grants, 1808
Fifth Third Bank Corporate Giving, 1809
First People's Fund Comm Spirit Awards, 1825
Fishman Family Fnd Grants, 1835
Flinn Fnd Grants, 1842
Florida BRAIVE Fund of Dade Comm Fnd, 1846
Florida Division of Cultural Affairs Comm Theatre Grants, 1847
Florida Division of Cultural Affairs Culture Builds Florida Expansion Funding, 1848
Florida Division of Cultural Affairs Culture Builds Florida Seed Funding, 1849
Florida Div of Cultural Affairs Dance Grts, 1850
Florida Div of Cultural Affairs Folk Arts Grts, 1853
Florida Division of Cultural Affairs General Program Support Grants, 1854
Florida Division of Cultural Affairs Lit Grants, 1855
Florida Div of Cultural Affairs Media Arts Grants, 1856
Florida Division of Cultural Affairs Multidisciplinary Grants, 1857
Florida Div of Cultural Affairs Museum Grts, 1858
Florida Div of Cultural Affairs Music Grts, 1859
Florida Div of Cultural Afrs Presenter Grts, 1860
Florida Division of Cultural Affairs Professional Theatre Grants, 1861
Florida Division of Cultural Affairs Specific Cultural Project Grants, 1862
Florida Division of Cultural Affairs State Touring Grants, 1863
Florida Division of Cultural Affairs Underserved Cultural Comm Dev Grants, 1864
Florida Div of Cultural Affairs Visual Arts Grants, 1865
Florida Humanities Council Major Grants, 1868
Florida Humanities Council Mini Grants, 1869
Florida Humanities Council Partnership Grants, 1870
Floyd A. and Kathleen C. Cailloux Fnd Grants, 1874
Fluor Fnd Grants, 1875
Foellinger Fnd Grants, 1877
Fondren Fnd Grants, 1878
Ford Fnd Diversity Fellowships, 1883
Ford Motor Company Fund Grants, 1885
Forrest C. Lattner Fnd Grants, 1887
Foster Fnd Grants, 1888
Fdn for Enhancing Communities Grts, 1893
Fnd for the Carolinas Grants, 1896
Fnd for the Mid South Comm Dev Grants, 1897
Fnd NW Grants, 1906
France-Merrick Fnds Grants, 1915
Francis Beidler Fnd Grants, 1921
Francis L. Abreu Charitable Trust Grants, 1922
Francis T & Louise T Nichols Fdn Grts, 1923
Frank and Lydia Bergen Fnd Grants, 1925
Frank M. Tait Fnd Grants, 1932
Frank Stanley Beveridge Fnd Grants, 1936
Fred Baldwin Memorial Fnd Grants, 1941
Fred C & Mary R Koch Fnd Grants, 1943
Fred L. Emerson Fnd Grants, 1949
Freeman Fnd Grants, 1952
Fremont Area Cmty Fdn Amazing X Grants, 1953
Fremont Area Comm Fnd Elderly Needs Grants, 1954
Fremont Area Comm Fnd Grants, 1955
Fremont Area Comm Fnd Summer Youth Grants, 1956
Fulbright Binational Business Grants in Mexico, 1969
Fulbright Business Grants in Spain, 1970
Fulbright Grad Degree Pgm Grants in Mexico, 1971
G.N. Wilcox Trust Grants, 1982
Gannett Fdn Comm Action Grants, 1984
Gateway Fnd Grants, 1992
Gaylord & Dorothy Donnelley Fdn Grants, 1993
Gebbie Fnd Grants, 1995
GenCorp Fnd Grants, 1998
Gene Haas Fnd, 1999
General Dynamics Corporation Grants, 2001
General Mills Fnd Grants, 2003
General Motors Fnd Grants, 2004
George A & Grace L Long Fdn Grts, 2008
George and Ruth Bradford Fnd Grants, 2010
George A Ohl Jr. Fnd Grants, 2012
George B. Storer Fnd Grants, 2014
George Family Fnd Grants, 2017
George Fnd Grants, 2018
George Frederick Jewett Fnd Grants, 2019
George Gund Fnd Grants, 2020
George H.C. Ensworth Grants, 2022
George I. Alden Trust Grants, 2023
George J. and Effie L. Seay Fnd Grants, 2024
George Kress Fnd Grants, 2025
George S & Dolores Dore Eccles Fdn Grants, 2027
Georgia-Pacific Fnd Educ Grants, 2031
Georgia Council for the Arts Partner Grants for Organizations, 2035
Georgia Council for the Arts Partner Grants for Service Organizations, 2036
Georgia Council for the Arts Project Grants, 2037
Georgia Power Fnd Grants, 2039
Geraldine R. Dodge Fnd Arts Grants, 2040
Gertrude & William C Wardlaw Fund Grts, 2045
Giant Eagle Fnd Grants, 2049
Giant Food Charitable Grants, 2050
Gibson Fnd Grants, 2052
Gil and Dody Weaver Fnd Grants, 2053
Gill Fnd Gay & Lesbian Fund, 2054
GlaxoSmithKline Corporate Grants, 2060
GMFUS Urban & Regnl Policy Fwsps, 2067
GNOF Exxon-Mobil Grants, 2074
GNOF IMPACT Grants for Arts and Culture, 2078
GNOF Norco Comm Grants, 2089
Goizueta Fnd Grants, 2096
Golden Rule Fnd Grants, 2098
Golden State Warriors Fnd Grants, 2099
Goodrich Corporation Fnd Grants, 2104
Good Works Fnd Grants, 2105
Goodyear Tire Grants, 2106
Grable Fnd Grants, 2108
Grace and Franklin Bernsen Fnd Grants, 2109
Grand Circle Fnd Associates Grants, 2112
Grand Rapids Area Comm Fdn Grts, 2114
Grand Rapids Area Comm Fnd Nashwauk Area Endowment Fund Grants, 2115
Grand Rapids Area Comm Fnd Wyoming Youth Fund Grants, 2117
Grand Rapids Comm Fdn Ionia Cty Grts, 2119
Grand Rapids Comm Fnd Ionia County Youth Fund Grants, 2120
Grand Rapids Comm Fnd Lowell Area Grants, 2121
Greater Cincinnati Fnd Priority and Small Projects/Capacity-Building Grants, 2132
Greater Des Moines Fnd Grants, 2134
Grtr Green Bay Comm Fdn Grts, 2135
Greater Kanawha Valley Fnd Grants, 2136
Greater Milwaukee Fnd Grants, 2137
Greater Saint Louis Comm Fdn Grants, 2138
Greater Tacoma Comm Fdn Grts, 2139
Greater Worcester Comm Discretionary Grants, 2140
Greater Worcester Comm Fnd Jeppson Memorial Fund for Brookfield Grants, 2141
Greater Worcester Comm Fnd Youth for Comm Improvement Grants, 2144
Green Bay Packers Fnd Grants, 2148
Green Diamond Charitable Contributions, 2149
Greenfield Fnd of Florida Grants, 2151
Green Fnd Arts Grants, 2152
Greenwall Fdn Arts & Humanities Grts, 2157
Group 70 Fnd Fund, 2167
Grundy Fnd Grants, 2169
Guido A & Elizabeth H Binda Fdn Grants, 2172
GUITS Library Acquisitions Grants, 2173
Gulf Coast Comm Fnd Grants, 2174
Guy I. Bromley Trust Grants, 2180
H & R Fnd Grants, 2181
HA & Mary K Chapman Char Trust Grts, 2182
H.B. Fuller Company Fnd Grants, 2183
H.J. Heinz Company Fnd Grants, 2184
H. Leslie Hoffman & Elaine S. Hoffman Grants, 2185
HAF Arts and Culture: Lynne and Bob Wells Grant for Performing Artists, 2190
HAF Arts & Culture: Project Grts to Artists, 2191
HAF Comm Grants, 2193
HAF Comm Partnerships with Native Artists, 2194
HAF Native Cultures Fund Grants, 2201
HAF Southern Humboldt Grants, 2204
Hahl Proctor Charitable Trust Grants, 2208
Hall Family Fnd Grants, 2210
Halliburton Fnd Grants, 2211
Hallmark Corporate Fnd Grants, 2212
Hamilton Family Fnd Grants, 2213
Hampton Roads Comm Fnd Nonprofit Facilities Improvement Grants, 2218
Harley Davidson Fnd Grants, 2224
Harold Alfond Fnd Grants, 2225
Harold & Arlene Schnitzer CARE Fdn Grts, 2226
Harold K. L. Castle Fnd Grants, 2228
Harold R. Bechtel Charitable Remainder Uni-Trust Grants, 2229
Harold Simmons Fnd Grants, 2230
Harrison Cty Comm Fdn Grts, 2233
Harrison County Comm Fnd Signature Grants, 2234
Harry Bramhall Gilbert Char Trust Grts, 2238
Harry W. Bass, Jr. Fnd Grants, 2246
Hartford Fnd Regular Grants, 2253
Hawaiian Electric Industries Charitable Grants, 2259
Hawaii Comm Fnd Reverend Takie Okumura Family Grants, 2264
Hawaii Comm Fnd West Hawaii Fund Grants, 2266
HCA Fnd Grants, 2274
Hearst Fnds Culture Grants, 2284
Heartland Arts Fund, 2286
Heineman Fnd for Research, Education, Charitable and Scientific Purposes, 2290
Heinz Endowments Grants, 2291
Helena Rubinstein Fnd Grants, 2292
Helen Bader Fnd Grants, 2293
Helen Gertrude Sparks Charitable Trust Grants, 2294
Helen Irwin Littauer Educational Trust Grants, 2295
Helen K & Arthur E Johnson Fdn Grts, 2296
Helen Pumphrey Denit Charitable Trust Grants, 2297
Helen V. Brach Fnd Grants, 2300
Henrietta Tower Wurts Memorial Fnd Grants, 2304
Henry & Ruth Blaustein Rosenberg Fdn Grants, 2306
Henry E. Niles Fnd Grants, 2309
Henry M. Jackson Fnd Grants, 2311
Herbert A & Adrian W Woods Fdn Grts, 2313
Herbert H & Grace A Dow Fdn Grants, 2315
Herman Abbott Family Fnd Grants, 2316
Herman Goldman Fnd Grants, 2317
Hershey Company Grants, 2318
Highmark Corporate Giving Grants, 2319
Hill Crest Fnd Grants, 2324
Hill Fnd Grants, 2326
Hillman Fnd Grants, 2327
Hillsdale County Comm General Adult Grants, 2328
Hillsdale Fund Grants, 2329
Hilton Head Island Fnd Grants, 2330

Hoblitzelle Fnd Grants, 2341
Hoglund Fnd Grants, 2344
Holland/Zeeland Comm Fdn Grts, 2345
Homer Fnd Grants, 2352
Honda of America Manufacturing Fnd Grants, 2354
Honor the Earth Grants, 2361
Horace A Kimball & S Ella Kimball Fdn Grts, 2362
Horace Moses Charitable Fnd Grants, 2363
Horizon Fnd for New Jersey Grants, 2364
Horizon Fnd Grants, 2365
Horizons Comm Issues Grants, 2366
Houston Endowment Grants, 2373
Howard and Bush Fnd Grants, 2374
Howard County Comm Fdn Grts, 2375
Hudson Webber Fnd Grants, 2383
Huffy Fnd Grants, 2384
Hugh J. Andersen Fnd Grants, 2385
Huie-Dellmon Trust Grants, 2386
Humana Fnd Grants, 2388
Huntington Arts Council Arts-in-Educ Programs, 2400
Huntington National Bank Comm Affairs Grants, 2409
Hut Fnd Grants, 2411
Hutton Fnd Grants, 2412
Hyams Fnd Grants, 2413
Hyde Family Fnds Grants, 2414
I.A. O'Shaughnessy Fnd Grants, 2416
IBM Arts and Culture Grants, 2424
ICC Faculty Fellowships, 2428
Idaho Comm Eastern Region Competitive Grants, 2432
Idaho Power Co Corp Contributions, 2433
IFP New York State Council on the Arts Electronic Media & Film Pgm Distrib Grts, 2451
IIE David L. Boren Fellowships, 2454
IIE Freeman Fnd Indonesia Internships, 2456
Illinois Arts Council Educ Residency Grants, 2463
Illinois Arts Cncl Comm Arts Access Grts, 2466
Illinois Arts Council Ethnic and Folk Arts Master Apprentice Grants, 2468
Illinois Arts Council Multidisciplinary Grants, 2473
Illinois Arts Cncl Prtnrs in Excellence Grts, 2475
Illinois Arts Council Presenters Dev Grants, 2476
Illinois Arts Council Vis Arts Pgm Grts, 2478
Illinois Humanities Council Comm Project Grant, 2510
IMLS 21st Cent Museum Pros Grts, 2512
IMLS American Heritage Preservation Grants, 2513
IMLS Grants to State Library Adm Agencies, 2514
IMLS National Leadership Grants, 2515
IMLS Partnership for a Nation of Learners Comm Collaboration Grants, 2520
Impact 100 Grants, 2522
Inasmuch Fnd Grants, 2523
Independence Comm Fnd Education, Culture & Arts Grant, 2526
Indiana Arts Commission American Masterpieces Grants, 2530
Indiana Arts Commission Multi-regional Major Arts Institutions Grants, 2532
Indiana Humanities Council Initiative Grants, 2539
Infinity Fnd Grants, 2553
ING Fnd Grants, 2555
Intergrys Corporation Grants, 2565
Iowa Arts Council Artists in Schools/Communities Residency Grants, 2571
IRC Comm Collaboratives for Refugee Women and Youth Grants, 2573
IREX Egypt Media Dev Grants, 2575
IREX Small Grant Fund for Civil Society Projects in Africa and Asia, 2581
IREX Small Grant Fund for Media Projects in Africa and Asia, 2582
Irving S. Gilmore Fnd Grants, 2584
Irvin Stern Fnd Grants, 2585
J.B. Reynolds Fnd Grants, 2592
J. Bulow Campbell Fnd Grants, 2593
J.C. Penney Company Grants, 2594
J. Edwin Treakle Fnd Grants, 2596
J.L. Bedsole Fnd Grants, 2600
J.M. Long Fnd Grants, 2603
J. Mack Robinson Fnd Grants, 2604
J. Walton Bissell Fnd Grants, 2608

J. Willard Marriott, Jr. Fnd Grants, 2610
Jackson Cty Comm Fdn Unrestricted Grts, 2611
Jackson Fnd Grants, 2613
Jacob G. Schmidlapp Trust Grants, 2616
Jacobs Family Fnd Spirit of the Diamond Grants, 2618
Jacobs Family Fdn Vlg Neighborhoods Grants, 2619
James & Abigail Campbell Fam Fdn Grts, 2620
James F & Marion L Miller Fdn Grts, 2622
James Ford Bell Fnd Grants, 2623
James G.K. McClure Educational Grants, 2624
James Graham Brown Fdn Qlty of Life Grts, 2625
James Irvine Fnd Creative Connections Grants, 2628
James J & Angelia M Harris Fdn Grts, 2630
James L & Mary Jane Bowman Char Trust, 2632
James M. Collins Fnd Grants, 2633
James M. Cox Fnd of Georgia Grants, 2634
James R. Thorpe Fnd Grants, 2636
James S. Copley Fnd Grants, 2637
Jane's Trust Grants, 2639
Jane Bradley Pettit Fnd Arts and Culture Grants, 2641
Janus Fnd Grants, 2647
Japan Fnd Center for Global Partnership Grants, 2649
Japan Fnd Los Angeles Mini-Grants for Japanese Arts & Culture, 2651
Japan Fnd New York Small Arts & Culture Grants, 2652
Jaqua Fnd Grants, 2653
Jay & Rose Phillips Fam Fdn Grts, 2656
Jayne and Leonard Abess Fnd Grants, 2657
Jean and Louis Dreyfus Fnd Grants, 2658
JELD-WEN Fnd Grants, 2661
Jennings County Comm Fnd Women's Giving Circle Grant, 2665
Jerome Fnd Grants, 2667
Jerome Fnd Travel and Study Grants, 2668
Jessie B. Cox Charitable Trust Grants, 2670
Jessie Ball Dupont Fund Grants, 2671
Jewish Women's Fnd of New York Grants, 2677
Jim Moran Fnd Grants, 2680
John Ben Snow Memorial Trust Grants, 2687
John Deere Fnd Grants, 2692
John I. Smith Charities Grants, 2700
John J. Leidy Fnd Grants, 2701
John P. Murphy Fnd Grants, 2708
John R. Oishei Fnd Grants, 2709
Johns Manville Fund Grants, 2716
John W & Anna H Hanes Fdn Grants, 2728
John W. Speas and Effie E. Speas Memorial Trust Grants, 2732
Joseph Drown Fnd Grants, 2735
Joseph H & Florence A Roblee Fdn Grants, 2736
Joyce Awards, 2746
Joyce Fnd Culture Grants, 2747
JP Morgan Chase Arts and Culture Grants, 2752
Judith and Jean Pape Adams Charitable Fnd Tulsa Area Grants, 2755
Kahuku Comm Fund, 2762
Kalamazoo Comm Fnd Economic and Comm Dev Grants, 2765
Kalamazoo Comm Fnd Good Neighbor Grants, 2768
Kalamazoo Comm Fnd John E. Fetzer Institute Fund Grants, 2770
Kalamazoo Comm Fdn Mini-Grts, 2772
Kansas Arts Commission American Masterpieces Kansas Grants, 2775
Kansas Arts Commission Artist Fellowships, 2776
Kansas Arts Comsn Arts-in-Educ Grts, 2779
Kansas Arts Commission Arts on Tour Grants, 2780
Kansas Arts Commission Visual Arts Grants, 2783
Katharine Matthies Fnd Grants, 2788
Kelvin and Eleanor Smith Fnd Grants, 2796
Kenneth T & Eileen L Norris Fdn Grants, 2802
Kent D. Steadley and Mary L. Steadley Grants, 2804
Kentucky Arts Cncl Access Astnce Grts, 2805
Kentucky Arts Council Al Smith Fellowship, 2806
Kentucky Arts Council Emerging Artist Award, 2807
Kentucky Arts Council Folk and Traditional Arts Apprenticeship Grant, 2808
Kentucky Arts Cncl Poetry Out Loud Grts, 2810
Kentucky Arts Council Teaching Together Grants, 2811
Kettering Family Fnd Grants, 2817

KeyBank Fnd Grants, 2820
KeySpan Fnd Grants, 2821
Knight Fdn Donor Advised Fund Grts, 2828
Kohler Fnd Grants, 2833
Koret Fnd Grants, 2837
Kovler Family Fnd Grants, 2840
Kroger Fnd Diversity Grants, 2842
L. W. Pierce Family Fnd Grants, 2846
Laclede Gas Charitable Trust Grants, 2848
Laidlaw Fnd Multi-Year Grants, 2852
Laidlaw Fnd Youth Organizaing Grants, 2854
Laila Twigg-Smith Art Scholarship, 2855
Lana'i Comm Benefit Fund, 2857
Land O'Lakes Fdn California Region Grts, 2858
Laura Jane Musser Intrcltrl Harmony Grts, 2862
Laurel Fnd Grants, 2867
Lee and Ramona Bass Fnd Grants, 2871
Leeway Fnd Art and Change Grants, 2872
Leeway Fnd Transformation Award, 2873
Legler Benbough Fnd Grants, 2877
Leicester Savings Bank Fund, 2879
Leo Goodwin Fnd Grants, 2882
Leon and Thea Koerner Fnd Grants, 2883
Leo Niessen Jr., Charitable Trust Grants, 2885
Lettie Pate Evans Fnd Grants, 2887
Lewis H. Humphreys Charitable Trust Grants, 2889
Liberty Bank Fnd Grants, 2890
Libra Fnd Grants, 2899
Lied Fnd Trust Grants, 2900
Lillian S. Wells Fnd Grants, 2901
Lincoln Financial Group Fnd Grants, 2906
Lindbergh Grants, 2907
Lisa and Douglas Goldman Fund Grants, 2910
Lotus 88 Fnd for Women and Children, 2921
Louie M & Betty M Phillips Fdn Grants, 2923
Louis and Elizabeth Nave Flarsheim Charitable Fnd Grants, 2924
Louis Calder Fnd Grants, 2925
Lubrizol Corporation Comm Grants, 2932
Lubrizol Fnd Grants, 2933
Lucy Downing Nisbet Charitable Fund Grants, 2935
Ludwick Family Fnd Grants, 2938
Lynde and Harry Bradley Fnd Grants, 2947
Lyndhurst Fnd Grants, 2949
M. Bastian Family Fnd Grants, 2951
M.J. Murdock Charitable Trust General Grants, 2954
Mabel F. Hoffman Charitable Trust Grants, 2957
Mabel Louise Riley Fnd Family Strengthening Small Grants, 2958
Mabel Louise Riley Fnd Grants, 2959
Mabel Y. Hughes Charitable Trust Grants, 2960
MacArthur Fnd Policy Research Grants, 2964
Macquarie Bank Fnd Grants, 2966
Madison County Comm Fnd General Grants, 2973
Maine Comm Fnd Charity Grants, 2977
Maine Comm Fnd Expansion Arts Grants, 2981
Maine Comm Fdn Peaks Island Grts, 2984
Maine Comm Fnd Rines/Thompson Grants, 2987
Maine Comm Fnd Vincent B. and Barbara G. Welch Grants, 2990
Manitoba Arts Council Literary Arts Publishers Project Grants, 2996
Marcia and Otto Koehler Fnd Grants, 3000
Margaret & James A Elkins Jr Fdn Grts, 3003
Margaret T. Morris Fnd Grants, 3005
Marin Comm Fnd Social Justice and Interfaith Understanding Grants, 3012
Marion Gardner Jackson Char Trust Grts, 3017
Marion I & Henry J Knott Fdn Discret Grants, 3018
Marion I & Henry J Knott Fdn Std Grants, 3019
MARPAT Fnd Grants, 3023
Mars Fnd Grants, 3025
Marsh Corporate Grants, 3027
Mary D. & Walter F Frear Eleemosynary Trust, 3035
Mary Duke Biddle Fnd Grants, 3036
Mary K. Chapman Fnd Grants, 3042
Mary Owen Borden Fnd Grants, 3046
Massachusetts Cultural Council Adams Grants, 3052
Massachusetts Cultural Council Cultural Investment Portfolio, 3056

PROGRAM TYPE INDEX

Cultural Outreach / 1059

Massachusetts Cultural Council Local Cultural Council Grants, 3057
Massachusetts Cultural Council Traditional Arts Apprenticeships, 3058
Massachusetts Fnd for Humanities Project Grants, 3060
Maurice Amado Fnd Grants, 3063
Maurice J. Masserini Charitable Trust Grants, 3064
Max A. Adler Charitable Fnd Grants, 3065
Maximilian E & Marion O Hoffman Fdn, 3067
Maxon Charitable Fnd Grants, 3068
McCune Charitable Fnd Grants, 3077
McCune Fnd Humananities Grants, 3079
McGraw-Hill Companies Comm Grants, 3081
McInerny Fnd Grants, 3083
McKesson Fnd Grants, 3084
McLean Contributionship Grants, 3088
Mead Johnson Nutritionals Evansville-Area Organizations Grants, 3103
Meadows Fnd Grants, 3104
MeadWestvaco Sustainable Communities Grants, 3105
Mead Witter Fnd Grants, 3106
Medtronic Fnd Comm Link Arts, Civic, and Culture Grants, 3109
Medtronic Fnd CommLink Health Grants, 3111
Memorial Fnd for Children Grants, 3116
Mercedes-Benz USA Corporate Contributions, 3118
Mericos Fnd Grants, 3121
Meriden Fnd Grants, 3122
Mertz Gilmore Fnd NYC Dance Grants, 3127
Meyer and Stephanie Eglin Fnd Grants, 3139
Meyer Memorial Trust Grassroots Grants, 3147
Meyer Memorial Trust Responsive Grants, 3148
Meyer Memorial Trust Special Grants, 3149
MGN Family Fnd Grants, 3154
Miami County Comm Fnd - Operation Round Up Grants, 3156
Microsoft Comty Affairs Puget Sound Grts, 3163
Microsoft Software Donation Grants, 3164
Mid Atlantic Arts American Masterpieces Grants, 3169
Mid Atlantic Arts Fdn ArtsConnect Grts, 3170
Mid Atlantic Arts Fnd Folk Arts Outreach Project Grants, 3171
Miguel Aleman Fnd Grants, 3175
Millipore Fnd Grants, 3182
Mimi and Peter Haas Fund Grants, 3185
Minnesota State Arts Board Cultural Comm Partnership Grants, 3188
Mockingbird Fnd Grants, 3196
Monfort Family Fnd Grants, 3203
Monsanto Access to the Arts Grants, 3204
Montana Arts Cncl Cltrl & Aesthetic Proj Grts, 3209
Montana Comm Fnd Grants, 3211
Morris & Gwendolyn Cafritz Fdn Grants, 3218
Motorola Fnd Grants, 3221
Mr. and Mrs. William Foulds Family Fnd Grants, 3222
NAR HOPE Awards for Minority Owners, 3238
Nathan Cummings Fnd Grants, 3246
Nathaniel & Elizabeth P Stevens Fdn Grants, 3247
National Endowment for the Arts - National Partnership Agreement Grants, 3256
National Endowment for Arts Our Town Grants, 3257
National Endowment for the Arts - State Partnership Agreement Grants, 3259
National Endowment for the Arts Artist Communities Grants, 3260
National Endowment for the Arts Dance Grants, 3262
National Endowment for the Arts Local Arts Agencies Grants, 3263
National Endowment for Arts Media Grants, 3264
National Endowment for Arts Museum Grants, 3265
National Endowment for the Arts Music Grants, 3266
National Endowment for the Arts Opera Grants, 3267
National Endowment for the Arts Presenting Grants, 3268
National Endowment for the Arts Theater and Musical Theater Grants, 3269
Natonal Endowment for the Arts Research Grants, 3286
Nevada Arts Council Circuit Rider Grants, 3308
Nevada Arts Cncl Folklife Apprenticeship Grts, 3309
Nevada Arts Cncl Folklife Opportunities Grts, 3310
Nevada Arts Council Jackpot Grants, 3312

Nevada Arts Council Learning Grants, 3313
Nevada Arts Council Professional Dev Grants, 3314
Nevada Arts Council Residency Express Grants, 3315
New Earth Fnd Grants, 3317
Newfoundland and Labrador Arts Council Comm Arts Grants, 3318
Newfoundland and Labrador Arts Council Professional Artists Travel Fund, 3320
Newfoundland and Labrador Arts Council Professional Festivals Grants, 3321
Newfoundland and Labrador Arts Council Professional Project Grants, 3322
Newfoundland and Labrador Arts Council Sustaining Grants, 3323
Newfoundland and Labrador Arts Council Visiting Artists Grants, 3324
New York Fnd Grants, 3338
New York Life Fnd Grants, 3341
NFL Charities NFL Player Fnd Grants, 3347
NHSCA Conservation License Plate Grants, 3425
NHSCA Youth Arts Project Grants: For Extended Arts Learning, 3430
NIAF Italian Culture and Heritage Grants, 3432
Nicholas H Noyes Jr Mem Fdn Grants, 3434
Nissan Fnd Grants, 3444
Nissan Neighbors Grants, 3445
NJSCA Arts Project Support, 3446
NJSCA Folk Arts Apprenticeships, 3448
NJSCA General Program Support Grants, 3449
NJSCA Projects Serving Artists Grants, 3450
Noble County Comm Fnd Celebrate Diversity Project Grants, 3455
Noble County Comm Fnd Grants, 3456
Norcliffe Fnd Grants, 3459
Nord Family Fnd Grants, 3461
Nordson Corporation Fnd Grants, 3462
Norfolk Southern Fnd Grants, 3463
Norman Fnd Grants, 3464
North Carolina Arts Council Folklife Grants, 3476
North Carolina Arts Council New Realities Grant, 3478
North Carolina Arts Council Outreach Grants, 3479
North Carolina Arts Council Tech Assistance, 3482
North Carolina Arts Council Touring/Presenting Grants, 3483
North Carolina Arts Council Visual Arts Program Support Grants, 3484
North Carolina Comm Fnd Grants, 3489
North Dakota Comm Fnd Grants, 3493
North Dakota Council on the Arts Comm Access Grants, 3494
North Dakota Council on the Arts Institutional Support Grants, 3496
Northern Chautauqua Comm Fnd Comm Grants, 3499
Northern Trust Company Charitable Trust and Corporate Giving Program, 3504
North Georgia Comm Fnd Grants, 3505
NW Mutual Fnd Grants, 3509
Norwin S & Elizabeth N Bean Fdn Grts, 3515
Nuffield Fnd Africa Grants, 3532
Nu Skin Force for Good Fnd Grants, 3536
NYCT Fund for New Citizens Grants, 3547
NYCT Human Justice Grants, 3552
NYCT Hunger and Homelessnes Grants, 3553
NYFA Building Up Infrastructure Levels for Dance Grants, 3563
NYSCA Architecture, Planning, and Design: General Program Support Grants, 3574
NYSCA Architecture, Planning, and Design: Project Support Grants, 3576
NYSCA Arts Education: General Operating Support Grants, 3578
NYSCA Arts Education: General Program Support Grants, 3579
NYSCA Arts Education: K-12 In-School Grants, 3580
NYSCA Arts Education: Local Capacity Building Grants, 3581
NYSCA Dance: Commissions Grants, 3583
NYSCA Dance: Long-Term Residency in New York State Grants, 3586
NYSCA Dance: Services to the Field Grants, 3587

NYSCA Electronic Media and Film: Film Festivals Grants, 3588
NYSCA Electronic Media and Film: General Exhibition Grants, 3589
NYSCA Electronic Media and Film: General Operating Support, 3590
NYSCA Electronic Media and Film: General Program Support, 3591
NYSCA Electronic Media and Film: Screenings Grants, 3592
NYSCA Electronic Media and Film: Workspace Grants, 3593
NYSCA Folk Arts: Exhibitions Grants, 3594
NYSCA Folk Arts: Gen Pgm Support Grts, 3595
NYSCA Folk Arts: Presentation Grants, 3596
NYSCA Folk Arts: Regional and County Folk Arts Grants, 3597
NYSCA Lit: General Operating Support Grants, 3598
NYSCA Lit: General Program Support Grants, 3599
NYSCA Lit: Public Programs, 3600
NYSCA Lit: Svcs to the Field Grts, 3601
NYSCA Museum: General Operating Support, 3602
NYSCA Museum: Gen Pgm Support Grts, 3603
NYSCA Museum: Project Support Grants, 3604
NYSCA Music: Cmy Music Schools Grts, 3605
NYSCA Music: Gen Operating Support Grts, 3606
NYSCA Music: Gen Pgm Support Grts, 3607
NYSCA Music: New Music Facilities, 3608
NYSCA Presenting: General Operating Support, 3609
NYSCA Presenting: General Program Support, 3610
NYSCA Presenting: Presenting Grants, 3611
NYSCA Presenting: Svcs to the Field Grts, 3612
NYSCA Special Art Services: Project Support, 3613
NYSCA Special Arts Services: General Operating Support Grants, 3614
NYSCA Special Arts Services: General Program Support Grants, 3615
NYSCA Special Arts Services: Instruction and Training Grants, 3616
NYSCA Special Arts Services: Professional Performances Grants, 3617
NYSCA State and Local Partnerships: General Operating Support Grants, 3619
NYSCA State and Local Partnerships: General Program Support Grants, 3620
NYSCA State and Local Partnerships: Services to the Field Grants, 3621
NYSCA State and Local Partnerships: Workshops Grants, 3622
NYSCA Theatre: Gen Operating Support Grts, 3623
NYSCA Theatre: Gen Pgm Support Grts, 3624
NYSCA Theatre: Pro Performances Grts, 3625
NYSCA Theatre: Services to the Field Grants, 3626
NYSCA Visual Arts: Exhibitions and Installations Grants, 3627
NYSCA Visual Arts: General Operating Support Grants, 3628
NYSCA Visual Arts: General Program Support, 3629
NYSCA Visual Arts: Wrkspc Facilities Grts, 3631
Ogden Codman Trust Grants, 3641
Ohio Arts Council Artist Express Grants, 3643
Ohio Arts Council Arts Access Grants, 3647
Ohio Arts Council Arts Innovation Pgm Grts, 3649
Ohio River Border Initiative Grants, 3661
Oleonda Jameson Trust Grants, 3667
Olive B. Cole Fnd Grants, 3670
Ontario Arts Cncl Aboriginal Arts Project Grts, 3675
Ontario Arts Council Artists in the Comm/Workplace Grants, 3676
Ontario Arts Council Integrated Arts Grants, 3678
Ontario Arts Council Orchestras Grants, 3679
Ontario Arts Cncl Presenter/Producer Grts, 3680
Ontario Arts Council Theatre Creators' Grants, 3681
Ontario Arts Council Travel Assistance Grants, 3682
Oppenstein Brothers Fnd Grants, 3685
Orange County Comm Fnd Grants, 3687
Orange County Comm Fnd Grants, 3688
Ordean Fnd Grants, 3691
Otto Bremer Fnd Grants, 3713
Owens Corning Fnd Grants, 3717

Cultural Outreach

PACCAR Fnd Grants, 3719
Pacific Life Fnd Grants, 3726
Packard Fnd Local Grants, 3729
Palm Beach and Martin Counties Grants, 3733
Parker Fnd (California) Grants, 3736
Parkersburg Area Comm Fdn Action Grts, 3738
Patrick and Aimee Butler Family Fnd Comm Arts and Humanities Grants, 3747
Patrick and Anna M. Cudahy Fund Grants, 3751
Paul and Edith Babson Fnd Grants, 3755
Paul and Mary Haas Fnd Contributions and Student Scholarships, 3756
Paul E & Klare N Reinhold Fdn Grts, 3758
Paul G. Allen Family Fnd Grants, 3759
Paul Green Fnd Playwrights Fellowship, 3762
PCA-PCD Organizational Short-Term Professional Dev and Consulting Grants, 3769
PCA Art Organizations and Art Grants for Presenting Organizations, 3771
PCA Arts in Educ Residencies, 3772
PCA Arts Management Internship, 3773
PCA Arts Organizations and Grants for Music, 3774
PCA Arts Organizations and Arts Grants for Arts Educ Organizations, 3776
PCA Arts Organizations and Grants for Crafts, 3778
PCA Arts Organizations and Arts Grants for Lit, 3781
PCA Arts Organizations & Grants for Local Arts, 3782
PCA Arts Organizations and Grants for Theatre, 3783
PCA Arts Organizations and Arts Grants for Traditional and Folk Arts, 3784
PCA Arts Organizations & Grants for Visual Arts, 3785
PCA Busing Grants, 3786
PCA Entry Track Arts Organizations and Arts Grants for Art Museums, 3787
PCA Entry Track Arts Orgs & Arts Pgms Grts for Arts Educ Orgs, 3788
PCA Entry Track Arts Organizations and Arts Grants for Crafts, 3790
PCA Entry Track Arts Organizations and Arts Grants for Lit, 3793
PCA Entry Track Arts Organizations and Arts Grants for Local Arts, 3794
PCA Entry Track Arts Organizations and Arts Grants for Music, 3795
PCA Entry Track Arts Organizations and Arts Grants for Presenting Organizations, 3796
PCA Entry Track Arts Organizations and Arts Grants for Theatre, 3797
PCA Entry Track Arts Orgs & Arts Pgms Grts for Traditional & Folk Arts, 3798
PCA Entry Track Arts Organizations and Arts Grants for Visual Arts, 3799
PCA Mgmt/Techn Assistance Grts, 3800
PCA Pennsylvania Partners in the Arts Program Stream Grants, 3801
PCA Pennsylvania Partners in the Arts Project Stream Grants, 3802
PCA Strategies for Success Grts-Adv Level, 3804
PCA Strategies for Success Grants - Basic Level, 3805
PCA Strategies for Success Grts-Intrmd Lvl, 3806
PDF Comm Organizing Grants, 3807
PennPAT Artist Tech Assistance Grants, 3811
PennPAT Fee-Support Grants for Presenters, 3812
PennPAT New Directions Grants for Presenters, 3813
PennPAT Presenter Travel Grants, 3814
PennPAT Strategic Opportunity Grants, 3815
Peoples Bancorp Fnd Grants, 3817
Percy B. Ferebee Endowment Grants, 3820
Perkins Charitable Fnd Grants, 3823
Peter Kiewit Fnd General Grants, 3845
Peter Kiewit Fnd Small Grants, 3847
Peter Norton Family Fnd Grants, 3849
Pew Charitable Trusts Arts and Culture Grants, 3857
Peyton Anderson Fnd Grants, 3862
PGE Fnd Grants, 3869
Phelps County Comm Fnd Grants, 3870
Philadelphia Fdn Org'l Effectiveness Grts, 3872
Philanthrofund Fnd Grants, 3874
Phil Hardin Fnd Grants, 3875
Philip L. Graham Fund Grants, 3876

Phoenix Coyotes Charities Grants, 3879
Phoenix Neighborhood Block Watch Grants, 3880
Phoenix Suns Charities Grants, 3881
Piedmont Natural Gas Corporate and Charitable Contributions, 3883
Pier 1 Imports Grants, 3887
Pinnacle Entertainment Fnd Grants, 3893
Piper Trust Arts and Culture Grants, 3900
Piper Trust Reglious Organizations Grants, 3905
Pittsburgh Fdn Comm Fund Grts, 3910
Plum Creek Fnd Grants, 3917
PMI Fnd Grants, 3918
PMP Professional Dev Grants, 3919
PNC Charitable Trust and Fnd Grants, 3921
PNC Ecnomic Dev Grants, 3922
PNM Reduce Your Use Grants, 3926
Polk Bros. Fnd Grants, 3929
Pollock Fnd Grants, 3930
Porter County Comm Fnd Grants, 3931
Portland Fnd Grants, 3936
Portland General Electric Fnd Grants, 3937
Posey Comm Fdn Women's Fund Grts, 3938
Powell Fnd Grants, 3942
PPG Industries Fnd Grants, 3943
Price Chopper's Golub Fnd Grants, 3950
Price Gilbert, Jr. Charitable Fund Grants, 3953
Priddy Fnd Grants, 3957
Pride Fnd Grants, 3958
Prince Charitable Trusts Chicago Grants, 3959
Prince Char Trusts Dist of Columbia Grts, 3960
Prince Charitable Trusts Rhode Island Grants, 3961
Principal Financial Group Fnd Grants, 3966
Procter and Gamble Fund Grants, 3967
Progress Energy Corp Contributions Grts, 3968
Prudential Fnd Arts and Culture Grants, 3975
Puerto Rico Comm Fnd Grants, 3986
Putnam Cty Comm Fdn Grts, 3990
Putnam Fnd Grants, 3991
Qualcomm Grants, 3993
R.C. Baker Fnd Grants, 3999
Rajiv Gandhi Fnd Grants, 4011
Ralph M. Parsons Fnd Grants, 4013
Ralphs Food 4 Less Fnd Grants, 4014
Rasmuson Fdn Creative Ventures Grts, 4021
Rasmuson Fdn Individual Artists Awds, 4022
Rasmuson Organizational Advancement Grants, 4023
Rathmann Family Fnd Grants, 4026
RBC Dain Rauscher Fnd Grants, 4031
RCF General Comm Grants, 4032
Regence Fdn Access to Health Care Grts, 4039
Reinberger Fnd Grants, 4052
Reynolds American Fnd Grants, 4068
Rhode Island Fnd Grants, 4073
Rice Fnd Grants, 4074
Richard & Caroline T Gwathmey Mem Tr Grts, 4075
Richard and Rhoda Goldman Fund Grants, 4077
Richard & Susan Smith Family Fdn Grts, 4078
Richard H. Driehaus Fnd Grants, 4084
Richard H. Driehaus Fnd MacArthur Fund for Arts and Culture, 4085
Richard H. Driehaus Fnd Small Theater and Dance Grants, 4086
Richard King Mellon Fnd Grants, 4087
Rich Fnd Grants, 4090
Richland County Bank Grants, 4091
Riley Fnd Grants, 4094
Ripley County Comm Fnd Grants, 4095
Ripley County Comm Fnd Small Project Grants, 4096
RISCA Project Grants for Organizations, Individuals and Education, 4100
Robert and Helen Haddad Fnd Grants, 4103
Robert B McMillen Fnd Grants, 4106
Robert F Stoico/FIRSTFED Char Fdn Grts, 4112
Robert G. Cabell III and Maude Morgan Cabell Fnd Grants, 4113
Robert Lee Blaffer Fnd Grants, 4115
Robert R. Meyer Fnd Grants, 4121
Robert Sterling Clark Arts & Culture Grants, 4122
Robert W. Woodruff Fnd Grants, 4124
Rochester Area Comm Fnd Grants, 4127

Rochester Area Fnd Grants, 4128
Rockefeller Brothers Fund Charles E. Culpeper Arts and Culture Grants in New York City, 4129
Rockefeller Brothers Democratic Practice Grants, 4131
Rockefeller Bros Fund Peace & Security Grts, 4133
Rockefeller Brothers Fund Pivotal Places Grants: Serbia, Montenegro, and Kosova, 4135
Rockefeller Brothers Sustainable Dev Grants, 4136
Rockefeller Fnd Grants, 4138
Rockefeller Fnd Partnerships Affirming Comm Transformation Grants, 4139
Rockwell Int'l Corporate Trust Grants, 4141
Roger L. and Agnes C. Dell Charitable Grants, 4143
Rohm and Haas Company Grants, 4145
Rollin M. Gerstacker Fnd Grants, 4146
Ronald McDonald House Charities Grants, 4149
Rose Hills Fnd Grants, 4162
Roy & Christine Sturgis Charitable Trust Grts, 4166
Ruth and Vernon Taylor Fnd Grants, 4177
Ruth Mott Fnd Grants, 4180
Ryder System Charitable Fnd Grants, 4191
S. D. Bechtel, Jr. Fnd / Stephen Bechtel Fund Environmental Educ Grants, 4192
S. Mark Taper Fnd Grants, 4201
S. Spencer Scott Fund Grants, 4202
Safeco Insurance Comm Grants, 4203
Sage Fnd Grants, 4204
Saginaw Comm Fdn Discretionary Grts, 4205
Saginaw Comm Fnd YWCA Fund for Women and Girls Grants, 4207
Saigh Fnd Grants, 4210
Saint Paul Companies Fnd Grants, 4217
Saint Paul Fnd Grants, 4219
Salem Fnd Charitable Trust Grants, 4223
Salisbury Comm Fnd Grants, 4224
Samuel N. and Mary Castle Fnd Grants, 4236
Samuel Rubin Fnd Grants, 4237
Samuel S. Fels Fund Grants, 4238
Samuel S. Johnson Fnd Grants, 4239
San Antonio Area Fnd Grants, 4240
San Diego Fnd Arts & Culture Grants, 4243
San Diego Fnd for Change Grants, 4247
San Diego Women's Fnd Grants, 4252
San Francisco Fnd FAITHS Arts and Culture Mini Grants, 4268
San Juan Island Comm Fnd Grants, 4283
Santa Barbara Fnd Towbes Fund for the Performing Arts Grants, 4288
Santa Fe Comm Fnd Seasonal Grants-Fall Cycle, 4290
Sarah Scaife Fnd Grants, 4295
Sara Lee Fnd Grants, 4296
Sarkeys Fnd Grants, 4297
Sartain Lanier Family Fnd Grants, 4298
Schering-Plough Fdn Comm Initvs Grts, 4303
Scherman Fnd Grants, 4305
Schlessman Family Fnd Grants, 4307
Schramm Fnd Grants, 4310
Scott B & Annie P Appleby Char Trust Grts, 4313
Scott County Comm Fnd Grants, 4314
Seagate Tech Corp Capacity to Care Grants, 4317
Seattle Fnd Arts and Culture Grants, 4320
Sensient Technologies Fnd Grants, 4337
Shopko Fdn Comm Charitable Grts, 4346
Shopko Fnd Green Bay Area Comm Grants, 4347
Siebert Lutheran Fnd Grants, 4351
Simmons Fnd Grants, 4360
Sioux Falls Area Comm Fnd Comm Fund Grants, 4364
Sioux Falls Area Comm Fnd Field-of-Interest and Donor-Advised Grants, 4365
Sioux Falls Area Comm Fnd Spot Grants, 4366
Siragusa Fnd Arts & Culture Grants, 4367
Skoll Fdn Awds for Social Entrepreneurship, 4383
SOCFOC Catholic Ministries Grants, 4392
Social Justice Fund NW Economic Justice Giving Project Grants, 4395
Social Justice Fund NW General Grants, 4397
Social Justice Fund NW Montana Giving Project, 4399
Sonoco Fnd Grants, 4403
Sonora Area Fnd Competitive Grants, 4404
Sony Corp of America Corp Philant Grants, 4405

PROGRAM TYPE INDEX   Curriculum Development/Teacher Training / 1061

Sorenson Legacy Fnd Grants, 4407
Sosland Fnd Grants, 4408
Southbury Comm Trust Fund, 4409
South Carolina Arts Comsn Accessibility Grts, 4410
South Carolina Arts Commission Cultural Tourism Initiative Grants, 4419
South Carolina Arts Comm Cultural Visions Grants, 4420
Southwest Florida Comm Competitive Grants, 4442
Spencer Cty Comm Fdn Grants, 4451
Sprague Fnd Grants, 4461
Sprint Fnd Grants, 4463
Square D Fnd Grants, 4464
Stackpole-Hall Fnd Grants, 4472
Starr Fnd Grants, 4483
State Street Fnd Grants, 4495
Steelcase Fnd Grants, 4497
Sterling-Turner Charitable Fnd Grants, 4499
Steve Young Family Fnd Grants, 4503
Stewart Huston Charitable Trust Grants, 4505
Stinson Fnd Grants, 4506
Stockton Rush Bartol Fnd Grants, 4508
Stowe Family Fnd Grants, 4510
Strake Fnd Grants, 4511
Stranahan Fnd Grants, 4512
Subaru of Indiana Automotive Fdn Grts, 4519
Sulzberger Fnd Grants, 4522
Summit Fnd Grants, 4524
Sunbeam Products Grants, 4526
Susan Mott Webb Charitable Trust Grants, 4536
T.L.L. Temple Fnd Grants, 4546
T. Rowe Price Associates Fnd Grants, 4548
TAC Arts Access Grant, 4549
TAC Arts Build Communities Grants, 4551
TAC Arts Educ Comm-Learning Grts, 4552
TAC Arts Educ Mini Grants, 4553
TAC Arts Projects Grants, 4554
TAC Rural Arts Project Support Grants, 4555
TAC Touring Arts and Access Touring Grants, 4557
Talbert and Leota Abrams Fnd, 4558
Tanner Humanities Cntr Rsch Fellowships, 4559
Target Corporation Local Store Grants, 4561
Target Fnd Grants, 4562
Tauck Family Fnd Grants, 4563
TCF Bank Fnd Grants, 4565
Teaching Tolerance Grants, 4567
TE Fnd Grants, 4572
Telluride Fdn Emergency/Out of Cycle Grts, 4574
Temple-Inland Fnd Grants, 4576
Tension Envelope Fnd Grants, 4578
Texas Comsn on the Arts Arts in Educ Team Building/Texas Music Project Grants, 4580
Texas Cmsn on the Arts Arts Respond Prj Grts, 4581
Texas Comm on Arts Cultural Connections Grant, 4591
Texas Instruments Corp Arts & Culture Grts, 4596
Textron Corporate Contributions Grants, 4601
Thelma Braun and Bocklett Family Fnd Grants, 4603
Third Millennium Fnd Grants, 4607
Thomas B & Elizabeth M Sheridan Fdn Grts, 4614
Thomas C. Ackerman Fnd Grants, 4615
Thomas J. Long Fnd Comm Grants, 4618
Thomas Sill Fnd Grants, 4619
Thomas W. Briggs Fnd Grants, 4621
Thompson Charitable Fnd Grants, 4622
Thornton Fnd Grants, 4624
Tides Fnd Grants, 4632
Tom's of Maine Grants, 4640
Topeka Comm Fnd Grants, 4644
Toro Fnd Grants, 4647
Tourism Cares Worldwide Grants, 4649
Toyota Motor Mfg of Mississippi Grts, 4655
Toyota Motor Manufacturing of Texas Grants, 4656
Toyota Motor Manuf of West Virginia Grants, 4657
Toyota Motor Sales, USA Grants, 4659
Triangle Comm Fdn Comm Grts, 4667
Triangle Comm Fdn Donor-Advised Grts, 4668
Trull Fnd Grants, 4673
Tull Charitable Fnd Grants, 4679
Turner Voices Corporate Contributions, 4682
TWS Fnd Grants, 4683
U.S. Bank Fnd Grants, 4686

Union Bank, N.A. Corporate Sponsorships and Donations, 4708
Union Bank, N.A. Fnd Grants, 4709
Union County Fnd Grants, 4712
Union Pacific Fdn Comm & Civic Grts, 4714
Union Square Arts Award, 4716
Union Square Awards Grants, 4718
United Technologies Corporation Grants, 4725
UPS Corporate Giving Grants, 4727
USDD Cultural Resources Program Assistance Announcement Grants, 4862
Valerie Adams Mem Char Trust Grts, 4898
Vancouver Fnd Grants and Comm Initiatives, 4900
Vanderburgh Comm Fdn Women's Fund, 4903
Vanguard Public Fnd Grant Funds, 4904
Viacom Fnd Grants (Formerly CBS Fnd), 4932
Vigneron Grants, 4938
Virginia Commission for the Arts Artists in Educ Residency Grants, 4941
Virginia Comsn for the Arts Proj Grts, 4944
Virginia Commission for Arts Touring Assistance, 4945
Virginia Fnd for Humanities Discretionary Grants, 4946
Virginia Fdn for the Humanities Open Grants, 4947
Virginia W. Kettering Fnd Grants, 4950
VSA/Volkswagen Grp of America Exhib Awds, 4954
VSA Int'l Art Program for Children with Disabilities Grants, 4955
W.C. Griffith Fnd Grants, 4957
WM Keck Fdn Southern California Grts, 4964
W Paul & Lucille Caudill Little Fdn Grts, 4966
Wabash Valley Comm Fnd Grants, 4971
Waitt Family Fnd Grants, 4973
Wallace Alexander Gerbode Fnd Grants, 4974
Wallace Alexander Gerbode Fdn Spcl Awd Grts, 4975
Wallace Fnd Grants, 4976
Walt Disney Company Fnd Grants, 4981
Walter and Elise Haas Fund Grants, 4982
Walter L. Gross III Family Fnd Grants, 4983
Washington Cty Comm Fdn Grts, 4997
Washington Cty Comm Fdn Youth Grts, 4998
Wayne County Fnd - Vigran Family Fnd Grants, 5004
Wayne County Fnd Grants, 5005
Weatherwax Fnd Grants, 5014
Weingart Fnd Grants, 5018
Western Indiana Comm Fdn Grts, 5024
Western New York Fnd Grants, 5025
Westinghouse Charitable Giving Grants, 5028
West Virginia Commission on the Arts Accessibility Services Grants, 5029
West Virginia Commission on the Arts Artist Visit Grants, 5030
West Virginia Commission on the Arts Challenge America Partnership Grants, 5031
West Virginia Commission on the Arts Comm Connections Grants, 5032
West Virginia Commission on the Arts Cultural Facilities and Capital Resources Grants, 5033
West Virginia Commission on the Arts Fast Track ADA and Emergency Grants, 5034
West Virginia Commission on the Arts Initiative/Opportunity Grants, 5035
West Virginia Commission on the Arts Long-Range Planning Grants, 5036
West Virginia Commission on the Arts Major Institutions Support Grants, 5038
West Virginia Comm on the Arts Media Grants, 5039
West Virginia Commission on the Arts Mid-Size Institutions Support Grants, 5040
West Virginia Commission on the Arts Peer Assistance Network Grants, 5042
West Virginia Commission on the Arts Presenting Artists Grants, 5044
West Virginia Commission on the Arts Professional Dev for Artists Grants, 5045
West Virginia Commission on the Arts Re-Granting Grants, 5046
West Virginia Commission on the Arts Special Projects Grants, 5048
West Virginia Commission on the Arts Staffing Support Grants, 5049

West Virginia Commission on the Arts Travel and Training Grants, 5050
West Virginia Commission on the Arts Visual Arts Grants, 5051
Weyerhaeuser Company Fnd Grants, 5053
Whatcom Comm Fnd Grants, 5055
Whirlpool Fnd Grants, 5056
White County Comm Fnd Grants, 5057
Whiting Fnd Grants, 5059
Whitney Fnd Grants, 5061
Widgeon Point Charitable Fnd Grants, 5064
Wilbur & Patsy Bradley Family Fdn Grts, 5066
WILD Fnd Grants, 5068
Willary Fnd Grants, 5071
William B. Dietrich Fnd Grants, 5075
William B. Stokely Jr. Fnd Grants, 5076
William Bingham Fnd Grants, 5077
William Blair and Company Fnd Grants, 5078
William G. Baker, Jr. Grants, 5081
William G. Gilmore Fnd Grants, 5082
William J. and Dorothy K. O'Neill Fnd Grants, 5087
William L. and Victorine Q. Adams Fnd Grants, 5089
Williams Companies Fnd Grants, 5095
Windgate Charitable Fnd Grants, 5099
Winston-Salem Fdn Competitive Grts, 5102
Winston-Salem Fdn Stokes County Grants, 5104
Winthrop Rockefeller Fnd Grants, 5105
Wisconsin Energy Fnd Grants, 5106
Wisconsin Humanities Council Major Grants, 5107
Wisconsin Humanities Council Mini-Grants for Scholarly Research, 5108
Wolfe Associates Grants, 5110
Wood-Claeyssens Fnd Grants, 5113
Woods Charitable Fund Grants, 5114
Woods Fund of Chicago Grants, 5115
Xcel Energy Fnd Grants, 5121
Xerox Fnd Grants, 5122
Yellow Corporate Fnd Grants, 5126
Young Family Fnd Grants , 5127

Curriculum Development/Teacher Training
3M Fnd Comm Giving Grants, 15
A.J. Muste Memorial Institute Counter Recruitment Fund Grants, 43
AAAAI RSLAAIS Leadership Award, 49
Abbott Fund Science Educ Grants, 83
Abell Fnd Workforce Dev Grants, 97
Abington Fnd Grants, 100
Advanced Micro Dvcs Comm Affairs Grts, 172
A Fund for Women Grants, 195
Agere Corporate and Comm Involvement Grants, 199
Ahearn Family Fnd Grants, 206
Air Force Association Junior ROTC Grants, 215
Alabama State Council on the Arts in Educ Partnership Grants, 242
Albertson's Charitable Giving Grants, 345
Alliant Energy Fnd Comm Grants, 384
ALZA Corporate Contributions Grants, 405
AMD Corporate Contributions Grants, 416
American Electric Power Grants, 428
American Foodservice Charitable Trust Grants, 433
Amerigroup Fnd Grants, 452
Amgen Fnd Grants, 456
Anderson Fnd Grants, 460
Angels Baseball Fnd Grants, 465
Annenberg Fnd Grants, 477
Appalachian Regional Commission Telecommunications Grants, 510
Aratani Fnd Grants, 523
Arcus Fnd National Fund Grants, 531
Arizona Comsn on the Arts Educ Projects Grts, 536
Arizona Comm on Arts Folklorist Residencies, 537
Arkansas Arts Council AIE Arts Curriculum Project Grants, 552
Arkema Fnd Science Teachers Program, 563
Autauga Area Comm Fnd Grants, 618
AutoNation Corporate Giving Grants, 620
Ayres Fnd Grants, 630
Babcock Charitable Trust Grants, 632
Ball Brothers Fnd General Grants, 637

Curriculum Development/Teacher Training

Bank of America Charitable Fnd Educ and Workforce Dev Grants, 657
Barra Fnd Comm Fund Grants, 673
Battle Creek Comm Fdn Mini-Grants, 685
Baxter Int'l Corporate Giving Grants, 689
Bayer Fnd Grants, 696
Benton Comm Fnd Grants, 730
Benwood Fnd Focus Area Grants, 733
Best Buy Children's Fnd @15 Teach Awards, 751
Better World Books LEAP Grants for Libraries, 755
Beverley Taylor Sorenson Art Wks for Kids Grts, 757
Blanche & Julian Robertson Family Fdn Grants, 785
Blue River Comm Fnd Grants, 801
Boeing Company Contributions Grants, 809
Bonfils-Stanton Fnd Grants, 814
Bowling Green Comm Fnd Grants, 824
British Columbia Arts Council Educ Grants, 842
Brown County Comm Fnd Grants, 853
Cabot Corporation Fnd Grants, 887
California Arts Council Statewide Ntwks Grts, 897
Cambridge Comm Fnd Grants, 913
Carl M. Freeman Fnd Grants, 933
Carnahan-Jackson Fnd Grants, 939
Carnegie Corporation of New York Grants, 940
Caroline Lawson Ivey Memorial Fdn Grts, 941
Carolyn Fnd Grants, 942
Carrie Estelle Doheny Fnd Grants, 945
CenterPointEnergy Minnegasco Grants, 993
CFFVR Alcoholism and Drug Abuse Grants, 1001
CFFVR Clintonville Area Fnd Grants, 1008
Chapman Charitable Fnd Grants, 1033
Charity Incorporated Grants, 1035
Charles H. Price II Family Fnd Grants, 1046
Charles Hayden Fnd Grants, 1048
Charles Stewart Mott Fnd Grants, 1055
Chefs Move to Schools Grants, 1066
Chesapeake Bay Trust Capacity Bldg Grts, 1068
Chesapeake Bay Environmental Educ Grants, 1069
Chicago Comty Trust Educ Grts Priority 2, 1085
Chiron Fnd Comm Grants, 1111
Christensen Fund Regional Grants, 1112
Circle K Corporation Contributions Grants, 1136
Civic Educ Consortium Grants, 1144
Clarence E Heller Charitable Fdn Grants, 1150
Clark County Comm Fnd Grants, 1156
Clinton County Comm Fnd Grants, 1174
CNL Corporate Giving Entrepreneurship & Leadership Grants, 1191
Coca-Cola Fnd Grants, 1195
Coleman Fnd Entrepreneurship Educ Grants, 1201
Columbus Fnd Dorothy E. Ann Fund (D.E.A.F.) Traditional Grants, 1221
Columbus Fnd Siemer Family Grants, 1231
Comm Fnd Alliance City of Evansville Endowment Fund Grants, 1246
Comm Fnd of Bartholomew County Heritage Fund Grants, 1267
Comm Fdn of Boone County Grants, 1274
Comm Fdn of Grtr Birmingham Grants, 1280
Comm Fnd of the Verdugos Educational Endowment Fund Grants, 1321
Comm Fdn of Wabash Cty Grants, 1326
Comprehensive Health Educ Fdn Grts, 1337
ConocoPhillips Fnd Grants, 1354
Cooper Fnd Grants, 1369
Corina Higginson Trust Grants, 1373
Crail-Johnson Fnd Grants, 1393
CTCNet/Youth Visions for Stronger Neighborhoods Grants, 1409
Cudd Fnd Grants, 1410
DB Americas Fnd Grants, 1466
Dean Foods Comm Involvement Grants, 1469
Delonne Anderson Family Fnd, 1492
Dept of Ed Alaska Native Ed Pgms, 1506
District of Columbia Commission on the Arts-Arts Educ Teacher Mini-Grants, 1549
Dollar General Adult Lit Grants, 1568
Dollar General Family Lit Grants, 1569
Dollar General Youth Lit Grants, 1570
Dorr Fnd Grants, 1591

Dubois County Comm Fnd Grants, 1615
Dunn Fnd K-12 Grants, 1622
Dyson Fnd Mid-Hudson Philanthropy Grants, 1633
eBay Fnd Comm Grants, 1648
Eddie C. and Sylvia Brown Family Fnd Grants, 1653
EDS Tech Grants, 1662
Edward W & Stella C Van Houten Mem Fund, 1670
Effie and Wofford Cain Fnd Grants, 1674
Elizabeth Carse Fnd Grants, 1681
Ellen Abbott Gilman Trust Grants, 1685
Emily Davie and Joseph S. Kornfeld Fnd Grants, 1697
EPA Environmental Educ Grants, 1729
Eugene McDermott Fnd Grants, 1765
Fam Lit & HI Pizza Hut Lit Fund, 1785
Faye McBeath Fnd Grants, 1794
Field Fnd of Illinois Grants, 1806
FirstEnergy Math, Science, & Tech Educ Grants, 1820
Fleishhacker Fnd Educ Grants, 1838
Ford Motor Company Fund Grants, 1885
Fnd for a Drug-Free Wrld Clsrm Tools, 1890
Fnd for the Mid South Comm Dev Grants, 1897
Fnd for the Mid South Educ Grts, 1898
Frank and Lydia Bergen Fnd Grants, 1925
Frank Stanley Beveridge Fnd Grants, 1936
FRED Tech Grants for Rural Schools, 1951
Fremont Area Comm Fnd Grants, 1955
Fuller Fnd Grants, 1974
GEF Green Thumb Challenge, 1996
GenCorp Fnd Grants, 1998
George A. Hormel Testamentary Trust Grants, 2009
Gheens Fnd Grants, 2048
Gibson Fnd Grants, 2052
Ginger and Barry Ackerley Fnd Grants, 2055
GNOF Exxon-Mobil Grants, 2074
GNOF IMPACT Grants for Education, 2079
GNOF IMPACT Kahn-Oppenheim Trst Grts, 2084
Goodrich Corporation Fnd Grants, 2104
Grable Fnd Grants, 2108
Grand Rapids Area Comm Fdn Grts, 2114
Grand Rapids Area Comm Fnd Nashwauk Area Endowment Fund Grants, 2115
Grand Victoria Fnd Illinois Core Grants, 2126
Greater Worcester Comm Fnd Jeppson Memorial Fund for Brookfield Grants, 2141
Green Fnd Educ Grants, 2153
GreenWorks! Butterfly Garden Grants, 2159
GreenWorks! Grants, 2160
Guido A & Elizabeth H Binda Fdn Grants, 2172
HAF Native Cultures Fund Grants, 2201
Harrison County Comm Fnd Signature Grants, 2234
Heineman Fnd for Research, Education, Charitable and Scientific Purposes, 2290
Hillsdale County Comm General Adult Grants, 2328
Hilton Hotels Corporate Giving, 2331
Hoglund Fnd Grants, 2344
Honda of America Manufacturing Fnd Grants, 2354
Hormel Fnd Grants, 2369
Huntington Arts Council Arts-in-Educ Programs, 2400
Huntington County Comm Fnd - Make a Difference Grants, 2406
ICC Scholarship of Engagement Faculty Grants, 2430
Illinois DCEO Eliminate the Digital Divide, 2489
Illinois DNR Biodiversity Field Trip Grants, 2496
Illinois DNR Schlyd Habitat Action Grts, 2500
Illinois DNR Wildlife Preservation Fund Small Project Grants, 2506
Indiana Rural Capacity Grants , 2547
Iowa Arts Council Artists in Schools/Communities Residency Grants, 2571
J.C. Penney Company Grants, 2594
J. Edwin Treakle Fnd Grants, 2596
James & Abigail Campbell Fam Fdn Grts, 2620
James R. Dougherty Jr. Fnd Grants, 2635
Janus Fnd Grants, 2647
Jennings County Comm Fdn Grts, 2664
Jessie Ball Dupont Fund Grants, 2671
Jewish Women's Fdn of New York Grants, 2677
Joe W & Dorothy Dorsett Brown Fdn Grants, 2684
John Jewett & Helen Chandler Garland Fdn, 2702
John M. Weaver Fnd Grants, 2705

John P. McGovern Fnd Grants, 2707
John W. Speas and Effie E. Speas Memorial Trust Grants, 2732
Joseph Alexander Fnd Grants, 2734
Joseph H & Florence A Roblee Fdn Grants, 2736
Josephine Goodyear Fnd Grants, 2738
Josiah W & Bessie H Kline Fdn Grants, 2742
Kansas Arts Comsn Arts-in-Educ Grts, 2779
Ka Papa O Kakuhihewa Fund, 2785
Katherine Baxter Memorial Fnd Grants, 2789
LaGrange Independent Fnd for Endowments, 2851
Laurel Fnd Grants, 2867
Leave No Trace Master Educator Scholarships, 2870
Lotus 88 Fnd for Women and Children, 2921
Louis and Elizabeth Nave Flarsheim Charitable Fnd Grants, 2924
Louis Calder Fnd Grants, 2925
Louis R. Cappelli Fnd Grants, 2926
Lowe's Outdoor Classroom Grants, 2928
Lubbock Area Fnd Grants, 2931
M3C Fellowships, 2955
Massachusetts Cultural Council Local Cultural Council Grants, 3057
Massachusetts Fnd for Humanities Project Grants, 3060
McColl Fnd Grants, 3074
Mead Johnson Nutritionals Evansville-Area Organizations Grants, 3103
Meadows Fnd Grants, 3104
Melinda Gray Ardia Environmental Fnd Grants, 3114
Meyer Fnd Educ Grants, 3142
Meyer Memorial Trust Responsive Grants, 3148
Meyer Memorial Trust Special Grants, 3149
Mid-Iowa Health Fdn Comty Response Grts, 3168
Mimi and Peter Haas Fund Grants, 3185
Mockingbird Fnd Grants, 3196
Montgomery Cty Comm Fdn Grants, 3213
NACC William Diaz Fellowships, 3236
National Inclusion Grants, 3278
Nellie Mae Educ Fnd State Level Systems Change Grants, 3299
New Earth Fnd Grants, 3317
New Jersey Office of Faith Based Initiatives Creating Wealth Through Asset Building Grants, 3331
New Jersey Office of Faith Based Initiatives English as a Second Language Grants, 3332
New York Life Fnd Grants, 3341
NGA Youth Garden Grants, 3409
NHSCA Youth Arts Project Grants: For Extended Arts Learning, 3430
Nicor Corporate Contributions, 3435
North Carolina Arts Council Arts in Educ Artist Residencies Grants, 3468
North Carolina Arts Council Arts in Educ Initiatives Grants, 3469
North Carolina Arts Council Arts in Educ Rural Dev Grants, 3470
Northern Chautauqua Comm Fnd Comm Grants, 3499
NRA Fnd Grants, 3517
NYSCA Arts Education: Comm-based Learning Grants, 3577
NYSCA Arts Education: K-12 In-School Grants, 3580
NYSCA Arts Education: Local Capacity Building Grants , 3581
NYSCA Arts Educ: Svcs to the Field Grts, 3582
NYSCA Music: Cmy Music Schools Grts, 3605
NYSCA Special Arts Services: Instruction and Training Grants, 3616
Ohio Arts Council Arts Partnership Grants, 3650
Ohio County Comm Board of Directors Grants, 3656
OJJDP National Mentoring Grants, 3664
Oppenstein Brothers Fnd Grants, 3685
PacifiCare Fnd Grants, 3725
Pacific Rainbow Fnd Grants, 3728
Paul and Mary Haas Fnd Contributions and Student Scholarships, 3756
Pew Charitable Trusts Children & Youth Grts, 3858
Pew Char Trusts Spcl Civic Project Grts, 3859
Phelps County Comm Fnd Grants, 3870
Piedmont Natural Gas Fnd Environmental Stewardship and Energy Sustainability Grant, 3884

PROGRAM TYPE INDEX

Demonstration Grants / 1063

Piper Trust Educ Grants, 3902
PNC Fnd Grow Up Great Grants, 3924
Polk Bros. Fnd Grants, 3929
Procter and Gamble Fund Grants, 3967
Public Educ Power Grants, 3981
Randall L. Tobias Fnd Grants, 4017
Rathmann Family Fnd Grants, 4026
Reynolds and Reynolds Co Fdn Grants, 4070
Richard & Susan Smith Family Fdn Grts, 4078
Richard Davoud Donchian Fnd Grants, 4080
Richland County Bank Grants, 4091
Ripley County Comm Fnd Small Project Grants, 4096
Robert Lee Blaffer Fnd Grants, 4115
Robert R. Meyer Fnd Grants, 4121
S. D. Bechtel, Jr. Fnd / Stephen Bechtel Fund Environmental Educ Grants, 4192
Saint Paul Companies Fnd Grants, 4217
Samuel S. Fels Fund Grants, 4238
San Diego Women's Fnd Grants, 4252
SAS Institute Comm Relations Donations, 4300
Schlessman Family Fnd Grants, 4307
Seabury Fnd Grants, 4316
Seattle Fnd Arts and Culture Grants, 4320
Seattle Fnd Educ Grants, 4326
Seattle Fnd Health and Wellness Grants, 4328
Shell Oil Company Fnd Grants, 4343
Sidgmore Family Fnd Grants, 4348
Sonora Area Fnd Competitive Grants, 4404
Sony Corp of America Corp Philant Grants, 4405
Sorenson Legacy Fnd Grants, 4407
Southern Minnesota Initiative Fnd Youth Explorer Grants, 4436
South Madison Comm Fnd Grants, 4440
Sprint Fnd Grants, 4463
Staples Fnd for Learning Grants, 4475
State Justice Institute Curriculum Adaptation and Training Grants, 4488
State Justice Institute Partner Grants, 4489
State Justice Institute Strategic Initiative Grants, 4492
Strowd Roses Grants, 4515
Summit Fnd Grants, 4524
Sun Academic Excellence Grants, 4525
TAC Arts Educ Mini Grants, 4553
Teaching Tolerance Grants, 4567
Texas Comm on the Arts Educ Project 1 Grants, 4579
Thomas Sill Fnd Grants, 4619
Toyota Motor Mfg of Alabama Grts, 4652
Toyota Motor Manufacturing of Indiana Grants, 4653
Toyota Motor Mfg of Mississippi Grts, 4655
Toyota Motor Manufacturing of Texas Grants, 4656
Toyota Motor Manuf of West Virginia Grants, 4657
Toyota Motor Sales, USA Grants, 4659
Toyota Tech Center Grants, 4660
Toyota USA Fnd Safety Grants, 4662
US Dept of Educ Native Hawaiian Educ Grts, 4694
US Dept of Educ Pgms for Native Hawaiians, 4696
Union Bank, N.A. Fnd Grants, 4709
Union County Comm Fnd Grants, 4711
UPS Fnd Economic and Global Lit Grants, 4730
USAID In-Support for Teacher Educ Program (In-STEP) Grants, 4759
USAID Public-Private Alliance Proposals in Burma, Thailand, and Vietnam, 4775
USDA Native American Indian Utilities Grants, 4820
USGA Fdn for the Good of the Game Grts, 4868
Vancouver Fnd Grants and Comm Initiatives, 4900
Vectren Fnd Grants, 4907
Verizon Fnd Grants, 4911
Verizon Fnd Maine Grants, 4916
Verizon Fnd Maryland Grants, 4917
Verizon Fnd Vermont Grants, 4924
Verizon Fnd Virginia Grants, 4925
Viacom Fnd Grants (Formerly CBS Fnd), 4932
Virginia Commission for the Arts Artists in Educ Residency Grants, 4941
Virginia Fnd for Humanities Discretionary Grants, 4946
Virginia Fdn for the Humanities Open Grants, 4947
WH & Mary Ellen Cobb Char Trust Grts, 4959
Weatherwax Fnd Grants, 5014
Weaver Popcorn Fnd Grants, 5016

Weingart Fnd Grants, 5018
Wells Fargo Housing Fnd Grants, 5023
Western Indiana Comm Fdn Grts, 5024
Weyerhaeuser Company Fnd Grants, 5053
William T. Grant Fnd Youth Service Improvement Grants, 5096
Winston-Salem Fdn Elkin/Tri-County Grants, 5103
Winston-Salem Fdn Stokes County Grants, 5104
Winthrop Rockefeller Fnd Grants, 5105
Xerox Fnd Grants, 5122
Young Family Fnd Grants, 5127
YSA State Farm Good Neighbor YOUth In The Driver Seat Grants, 5141
YSA UnitedHealth HEROES Service-Learning Grants, 5142

Demonstration Grants
AAA Fnd for Traffic Safety Grants, 50
ACF Native American Social and Economic Dev Strategies Grants, 123
ACTION Council of Monterey County Grants, 134
Aetna Fnd Racial and Ethnic Health Care Equity Grants, 186
American Chemical Scty Corp Assocs Seed Grts, 425
American Legacy Fdn Small Innovative Grants, 442
ANLAF Int'l Fund for Sexual Minorities Grts, 471
Arizona Commission on the Arts Visual/Media Arts Organizations Grants, 539
Bank of America Charitable Fnd Matching Gifts, 658
Barra Fnd Project Grants, 674
Berks County Comm Fnd Grants, 734
Bikes Belong Grants, 763
Blue Cross Blue Shield of Minnesota Healthy Equity: Impact Assessment Demonstration Project Grants, 795
Bullitt Fnd Grants, 862
Burton D. Morgan Adult Entrepreneurship Grants, 868
Burton D Morgan Fdn Hudson Comty Grts, 869
Caesars Fnd Grants, 891
Campbell Hoffman Fnd Grants, 915
Carlisle Fnd Grants, 931
Cause Populi Worthy Cause Grants, 958
Charles Hayden Fnd Grants, 1048
Charles Stewart Mott Fdn Anti-Poverty Grts, 1054
Charles Stewart Mott Fnd Grants, 1055
Chesapeake Bay Trust Restoration Grants, 1075
Chicago Comm Trust Preventing and Eliminating Hunger Grants, 1092
Cigna Civic Affairs Sponsorships, 1129
Circle K Corporation Contributions Grants, 1136
CNCS AmeriCorps State and National Planning Grants, 1183
CNCS School Turnaround AmeriCorps Grants, 1186
CNCS Social Innovation Grants, 1189
Colorado Bioscience Discovery Eval Grts, 1211
Columbus Fnd Competitive Grants, 1220
Comm Fnd of Greater Fort Wayne - Cmty Endwt & Clarke Endwt Grants, 1285
Comm Fdn of S Alabama Grants, 1308
Comm Fnd of Western North Carolina Grants, 1327
Con Edison Corp Gvg Comm Grts, 1346
Denver Fnd Comm Grants, 1502
Dept of Ed Alaska Native Ed Pgms, 1506
DHHS Adolescent Family Life Demo Projects, 1524
DHHS Emergency Medical Svcs for Children, 1531
DHHS Spcl Pgms for the Aging Trng, Rsch, and Discretionary Projects and Pgms Grts, 1538
DHHS Welfare Reform Research, Evaluations, and National Studies Grants, 1540
Dolfinger-McMahon Fnd Grants, 1565
Dyson Fnd Mid-Hudson Valley Project Grants, 1636
EPA Environmental Educ Grants, 1729
EPA Hazardous Waste Manag Grants for Tribes, 1733
EPA Tribal Solid Waste Management Assistance, 1741
Evelyn and Walter Haas, Jr. Fund Immigrant Rights Grants, 1773
Florida Humanities Cncl Civic Reflection Grts, 1867
G.A. Ackermann Grants, 1981
GNOF Metropolitan Opportunities Grants, 2087
Great Lakes Protection Fund Grants, 2147
Harold R. Bechtel Charitable Grants, 2229

Health Fnd of Grtr Cincinnati Grts, 2281
Henry J. Kaiser Family Fnd Grants, 2310
Hydrogen Student Design Contest, 2415
Illinois DCEO Coal Demonstration Grants, 2485
Illinois DCEO Emerging Technological Enterprises Grants, 2490
Illinois DCEO Employer Trng Investment Pgm Grts - Competitive Component, 2491
Illinois DCEO Employer Trng Investment Pgm Grts - Incentive Component, 2492
Illinois DCEO Employer Trng Investment Pgm Multi-Company Trng Grts, 2493
Illinois DCEO Employer Trng Investment Pgm Single Company Trng Grts, 2494
Illinois DCEO Large Business Dev Grants, 2495
IMLS 21st Cent Museum Pros Grts, 2512
IMLS Grants to State Library Adm Agencies, 2514
IMLS National Leadership Grants, 2515
Indiana Rural Capacity Grants, 2547
Ittleson Fnd AIDS Grants, 2589
Ittleson Fnd Mental Health Grants, 2590
Jenifer Altman Fnd Grants, 2662
JohnS & JamesL Knight Fdn Communities Grts, 2711
Johnson Controls Fdn Civic Activities Grts, 2720
Kalamazoo Economic and Comm Dev Grants, 2765
Kansas Arts Comsn Arts-in-Educ Grts, 2779
Laidlaw Fnd Youh Organizing Catalyst Grants, 2853
Laidlaw Fnd Youth Organizaing Grants, 2854
Laura Jane Musser Intrcltrl Harmony Grts, 2862
Liberty Hill Fdn Enviro Justice Fund Grts, 2891
Merck Family Fund Youth Transforming Urban Communities Grants, 3120
Mt. Sinai Health Care Fnd Health of the Jewish Comm Grants, 3226
Mt. Sinai Health Care Fnd Health Policy Grants, 3228
New Hampshire Charitable Fnd Grants, 3325
NFF Mid-Capacity Assistance Grants, 3345
NFWF/Exxon Save the Tiger Fund Grants, 3354
NFWF Chesapeake Bay Conservation Innovation Grants, 3363
NFWF Chesapeake Bay Tgtd Watershed Grts, 3365
NFWF Pulling Together Initiative Grants, 3387
NFWF Shell Marine Habitat Grants, 3391
NFWF Wildlife Links Grants, 3400
Nike and Ashoka GameChangers: Change the Game for Women in Sport, 3439
Northern Chautauqua Comm Fnd Comm Grants, 3499
Patrick and Aimee Butler Family Comm Philanthropy & the Non-Profit Management Grants, 3750
Pinkerton Fnd Grants, 3892
Pittsburgh Fdn Comm Fund Grts, 3910
Plough Fnd Grants, 3915
Principal Financial Group Fnd Grants, 3966
Prudential Fdn Econ Dev Grants, 3976
RESIST Accessibility Grants, 4054
Retirement Rsch Fdn Accessible Faith Grants, 4066
Robert Sterling Clark Fnd Government Accountability Grants, 4123
RRF General Grants, 4170
RWJF New Jersey Health Initiatives Grants, 4187
Saint Luke's Health Initiatives Grants, 4216
SAMHSA Campus Suicide Prevention Grants, 4229
San Diego Fnd Arts & Culture Grants, 4243
Sapelo Fnd Social Justice Grants, 4294
Seattle Fnd Benjamin N. Phillips Grants, 4322
Self Fnd Grants, 4335
Siragusa Fnd Human Services Grants, 4369
Sonora Area Fnd Competitive Grants, 4404
State Justice Institute Partner Grants, 4489
State Justice Institute Project Grants, 4490
State Justice Institute Strategic Initiative Grants, 4492
Stuart Fnd Grants, 4516
Taylor S. Abernathy and Patti Harding Abernathy Charitable Trust Grants, 4564
Thompson Fnd Grants, 4623
Union Bank, N.A. Fnd Grants, 4709
Union Square Award for Social Justice, 4717
Unity Fnd Of LaPorte County Grants, 4726
UPS Fdn Nonprofit Effectiveness Grts, 4732
USAID Family Health Plus Project Grants, 4751

1064 / Demonstration Grants

USAID Reading Enhancement for Advancing Dev Grants, 4778
USAID Resilience and Economic Growth in the Sahel - Enhanced Resilience Grants, 4779
USAID Strengthening Free and Independent Media in South Sudan Grants, 4783
USAID Workforce Dev in Mexico Grants, 4787
USDC Advanced Manufacturing Jobs and Innovation Accelerator Challenge Grants, 4848
USDC Business Center - American Indian and Alaska Native Grants, 4849
USDC i6 Challenge Grants, 4851
USDC Strong Cities, Strong Communities Visioning Challenge Grants, 4858
USDC Tech Opportunities Pgm Grts, 4860
Virginia Comsn for the Arts Proj Grts, 4944
Washington Area Women's Fdn Jobs Fund Grts, 4992
Whitehorse Fnd Grants, 5058
Xerox Fnd Grants, 5122

Development (Institutional/Departmental)
A.J. Fletcher Fnd Grants, 41
A.J. Muste Memorial Institute Int'l Nonviolence Training Fund Grants, 45
AACC Building Better Communities Through Regional Economic Dev Partnerships, 54
AACC Plus 50 Initiative Grants, 55
Abbey Charitable Trust Grants, 78
Able Trust Voc Rehab Grants for Agencies, 103
ACF Assets for Indep Demo Grants, 114
ACF Native American Social and Economic Dev Strategies Grants, 123
ACTION Council of Monterey County Grants, 134
Acuity Charitable Fnd Grants, 140
AEGON Transamerica Fdn Civic Grants, 177
Aetna Fnd Racial and Ethnic Health Care Equity Grants, 186
Agape Fnd for Nonviolent Social Change Board of Trustees Grants, 197
Agape Fnd for Nonviolent Social Change Prizes, 198
Alaska Conservation Fnd Operating Grants, 323
Alaska State Council on the Arts Comm Grants, 327
Albuquerque Comm Fnd Grants, 348
Alfred & Tillie Shemanski Testamentary Grants, 363
Alvin & Fanny Blaustein Thalheimer Fdn Grts, 403
American Chemical Society Award for Team Innovation, 423
American Chemical Society Chemical Tech Partnership Mini Grants, 424
American Chemical Scty Corp Assocs Seed Grts, 425
American Express Charitable Fund Grants, 429
Amerigroup Fnd Grants, 452
AMERIND Comm Service Project Grants, 453
Anheuser-Busch Fnd Grants, 470
Ann & Robert H Lurie Family Fdn Grants, 473
Ann Arbor Area Comm Fnd Grants, 474
APAP Cultural Exchange Grants, 492
Appalachian Regional Commission Comm Infrastructure Grants, 502
Appalachian Regional Commission Export and Trade Dev Grants, 506
AptarGroup Fnd Grants, 519
Arizona Republic Newspaper Corp Contribs, 547
ArtsWave Impact Grants, 580
ArtsWave Project Grants, 581
Assisi Fnd of Memphis General Grants, 594
Assisi Fnd of Memphis Mini Grants, 595
Athwin Fnd Grants, 605
Atlanta Falcons Youth Fnd Grants, 607
Baltimore Comm Fnd Neighborhood Grants, 646
Bank of America Charitable Fnd Volunteer Grants, 660
Baxter Int'l Fnd Grants, 691
BCBSM Fdn Proposal Dev Awds, 709
BCBSNC Fnd Grants, 712
Best Buy Children's Fnd @15 Comm Grants, 749
Best Buy Children's Fnd National Grants, 752
Best Buy Children's Fnd Twin Cities Minnesota Capital Grants, 753
Bill and Melinda Gates Fnd Financial Services for the Poor Grants, 767

Bill and Melinda Gates Fnd Policy and Advocacy Grants, 769
Blandin Fdn Expand Opportunity Grants, 787
Blue Cross Blue Shield of Minnesota Fnd - Healthy Children: Growing Up Healthy Grants, 794
Blumenthal Fnd Grants, 804
Bohemian Fnd Pharos Fund Grants, 811
Bonfils-Stanton Fnd Grants, 814
Booth Ferris Fnd Grants, 816
Boston Fnd Initiative to Strengthen Arts and Cultural Service Organizations, 820
Boulder County Arts Alliance Neodata Endowment Grants, 823
Boyd Gaming Corporation Contributions, 825
Brainerd Fnd Grants, 831
Brooklyn Comm Fnd Comm Dev Grants, 850
Burlington Industries Fnd Grants, 865
Bush Fnd Arts & Humanities Cap Projects Grants, 872
Bush Fdn Health & Human Svcs Grts, 875
Bush Fnd Regional Arts Dev Program II Grants, 878
C.F. Adams Charitable Trust Grants, 884
California Endowment Innovative Ideas Challenge Grants, 904
Cambridge Comm Fnd Grants, 913
Caring Fnd Grants, 926
Carl C. Icahn Fnd Grants, 929
Carl M. Freeman Fnd Grants, 933
Carnegie Corporation of New York Grants, 940
Carolyn Fnd Grants, 942
Cartis Creative Services Grants, 948
Cash 4 Clubs Sports Grants, 951
CCCF Alpha Fund Grants, 959
CCH California Story Fund Grants, 965
CCH Documentary California Reads Grants, 968
CCH Documentary Public Engagement Grants, 970
CCH Documentary Research and Dev Grants, 971
CE and S Fnd Grants, 985
Center on Philanthropy and Civil Society's Emerging Leaders Int'l Fellows Program, 992
CFFVR Clintonville Area Fnd Grants, 1008
Changemakers Comm-Based Grants, 1030
Charity Incorporated Grants, 1035
Charles M. Bair Family Trust Grants, 1051
Charlotte County Comm Fdn Grts, 1056
CHCF Grants, 1063
Chesapeake Bay Trust Capacity Bldg Grts, 1068
ChevronTexaco Contributions Program, 1078
Chicago Comm Trust Arts and Culture Grants: SMART Growth, 1083
Chicago Comty Trust Educ Grts Priority 2, 1085
Chicago Comm Trust Fellowships, 1086
Chicago Comm Trust Housing Grants: Advancing Affordable Rental Housing, 1088
Chicago Comm Trust Housing Grants: Preventing and Ending Homelessness, 1090
Chicago Comm Trust Poverty Alleviation Grants, 1091
Chicago Comm Pub Safety & Justice Grants, 1093
Children Affected by AIDS Fnd Camp Network Grants, 1106
Cincinnati Bell Fnd Grants, 1131
Cincinnati Milacron Fnd Grants, 1132
Circle K Corporation Contributions Grants, 1136
CLIF Bar Family Fnd Grants, 1173
Clowes Fund Grants, 1177
CNCS AmeriCorps Indian Tribes Plng Grts, 1180
CNCS AmeriCorps NCCC Project Grants, 1181
CNCS AmeriCorps State and National Grants, 1182
CNCS Social Innovation Grants, 1189
Colorado Trust Partnerships for Health Init, 1217
Comm Dev Financial Inst Bank Enterprise Awards, 1244
Comm Fnd for Greater New Haven Responsive New Grants, 1251
Comm Fdn in Jacksonville Art Ventures Small Arts Orgs Professional Assistance Grts, 1262
Comm Fnd of Broward Grants, 1275
Comm Fnd of Collier County Capacity Building Grants, 1277
Comm Fnd of Santa Cruz County Grants, 1305
Comm Fnd of St. Joseph County ArtsEverywhere Grants, 1313

PROGRAM TYPE INDEX

Comm Fnd of St. Joseph County Special Project Challenge Grants, 1314
Comm Tech Fdn of California Building Communities Through Tech Grants, 1336
Council on Fnds Emerging Philanthropic Leaders Fellowships, 1378
Crossroads Fund Seed Grants, 1400
CSL Behring Local Empowerment for Advocacy Dev Grants, 1406
Dallas Women's Fnd Grants, 1438
Dance Advance Grants, 1441
Daphne Seybolt Culpeper Mem Fdn Grts, 1445
Dave Thomas Fnd for Adoption Grants, 1449
Deborah Munroe Noonan Mem Fund Grts, 1475
Delaware Division of the Arts Opportunity Grants-- Arts Organizations, 1488
Dept of Ed Even Start Grants, 1508
DHHS ARRA Strengthening Communities Fund - Nonprofit Capacity Building Grants, 1527
DHHS ARRA Strengthening Communities Fund - State, Local, and Tribal Government Capacity Building Grants, 1528
DHHS Comm Svcs Blk Grant Trng & Techn Assistance, 1529
DHS ARRA Fire Station Const Grants, 1542
DHS ARRA Port Security Grants, 1543
DHS ARRA Transit Security Grants, 1544
DHS FY 2009 Transit Security Grants, 1545
DOJ Gang-Free Schools and Communities Intervention Grants, 1557
DOJ Internet Crimes against Children Task Force Grants, 1558
Do Something Plum Youth Grants, 1593
Dubois County Comm Fnd Grants, 1615
Duluth-Superior Area Comm Fdn Grts, 1620
Dwight Stuart Youth Fnd Capacity-Building Initiative Grants, 1627
Dyer-Ives Fnd Small Grants, 1629
Dynegy Fnd Grants, 1630
Dyson Fnd Management Assistance Mini-Grants, 1632
Edna McConnell Clark Fnd Grants, 1659
Edward Bangs Kelley & Elza Kelley Fdn Grts, 1665
Eileen Fisher Activating Leadership Grants for Women and Girls, 1676
Emerson Kampen Fnd Grants, 1696
Energy Fnd Transportation Grants, 1708
Eulalie Bloedel Schneider Fnd Grants, 1767
Evelyn and Walter Haas, Jr. Fund Immigrant Rights Grants, 1773
F.R. Bigelow Fnd Grants, 1781
FAR Fund Grants, 1787
Farmers Insurance Corporate Giving Grants, 1791
Feldman Fnd Grants, 1801
FEMA Assistance to Firefighters Grants, 1802
Fidelity Fnd Grants, 1805
Fifth Third Bank Corporate Giving, 1809
Fifth Third Fnd Grants, 1810
Finish Line Youth Fnd Legacy Grants, 1814
Fisa Fnd Grants, 1826
Florida Division of Cultural Affairs Endowment Grants, 1851
Florida Div of Cultural Affairs Folk Arts Grts, 1853
Florida Division of Cultural Affairs General Program Support Grants, 1854
Florida Division of Cultural Affairs Professional Theatre Grants, 1861
Florida Division of Cultural Affairs Underserved Cultural Comm Dev Grants, 1864
Florida Humanities Council Partnership Grants, 1870
Florida Sports Fnd Junior Golf Grants, 1872
Florida Sports Fnd Major and Regional Grants, 1873
Fnd for the Carolinas Grants, 1896
Fnd for the Mid South Comm Dev Grants, 1897
Fnd for the Mid South Educ Grts, 1898
FRED Tech Grants for Rural Schools, 1951
Frist Fnd Grants, 1964
Fund for the City of New York Grants, 1978
Funding Exchange Martin-Baro Fund Grants, 1979
George B. Page Fnd Grants, 2013
George I. Alden Trust Grants, 2023

PROGRAM TYPE INDEX

Development (Institutional/Departmental) / 1065

Georgia Council for the Arts Partner Grants for Organizations, 2035
Ginger and Barry Ackerley Fnd Grants, 2055
Ginn Fnd Grants, 2056
GNOF Bayou Communities Grants, 2069
GNOF Comm Revitalization Grants, 2071
GNOF Metropolitan Opportunities Grants, 2087
GNOF New Orleans Works Grants, 2088
GNOF Organizational Effectiveness Grants, 2090
GNOF Stand Up For Our Children Grants, 2093
Goldseker Fdn Comm Affairs Grants, 2100
Goldseker Fnd Comm Grants, 2101
Goldseker Fnd Human Services Grants, 2102
Goldseker Fnd Non-Profit Management Assistance Grants, 2103
Grand Rapids Comm Fnd Grants, 2118
Grand Rapids Comm Fnd Lowell Area Grants, 2121
Grand Victoria Fnd Illinois Core Grants, 2126
Greater Cincinnati Fnd Priority and Small Projects/Capacity-Building Grants, 2132
Grtr Columbus Arts Council Operating Grts, 2133
Greater Saint Louis Comm Fnd Grants, 2138
Greygates Fnd Grants, 2164
Grover Hermann Fnd Grants, 2168
Gulf Coast Comm Capacity Building Grants, 2175
HAF Techn Assistance Pgm Grts, 2206
Harry A & Margaret D Towsley Fdn Grts, 2236
Harry Kramer Grants, 2242
Harvest Fnd Grants, 2254
Hawaii Comm Fnd Capacity Building Grants, 2260
Hawaii Comm Fnd Organizational Capacity Building Grants, 2263
Health Fnd of South Florida Responsive Grants, 2283
Hilton Head Island Fnd Grants, 2330
Hoffberger Fnd Grants, 2342
Homer A Scott & Mildred S Scott Fdn Grants, 2350
Honor the Earth Grants, 2361
Hudson Webber Fnd Grants, 2383
Hyams Fnd Grants, 2413
Ian Hague Perl 6 Dev Grants, 2421
ICC Listening to Communities Grants, 2429
ICC Scholarship of Engagement Faculty Grants, 2430
IDPH Hosptial Capital Investment Grants, 2441
Illinois Arts Council Arts Service Organizations Grants, 2464
Illinois Arts Council Dance Grants, 2467
Illinois Arts Council Ethnic and Folk Arts Grants, 2469
Illinois Arts Council Lit Pgm Grts, 2470
Illinois Humanities Council Comm General Support Grants, 2509
Indiana 21st Century Research & Tech Awards, 2528
Indiana Arts Commission Cap Bldg Grts, 2531
Indiana Arts Commission Statewide Arts Service Organization Grants, 2533
Indianapolis Preservation Grants, 2543
Indiana Preservation Grants, 2544
Indiana Reg'l Econ Dev Partnership Grts, 2546
Information Soc Innovation Fund Grts, 2554
Intergrys Corporation Grants, 2565
IREX Kosovo Civil Soc Project Grts, 2576
ISI William E Simon Fwsps for Noble Purpose, 2588
J.M. Kaplan Fund Migrations Grants, 2602
Jackson Fnd Grants, 2613
James Ford Bell Fnd Grants, 2623
Janus Fnd Grants, 2647
Jay & Rose Phillips Fam Fdn Grts, 2656
Jessie Ball Dupont Fund Grants, 2671
Joan Bentinck-Smith Charitable Fdn Grts, 2682
John D. and Catherine T. MacArthur Fnd Global Challenges Grants, 2690
John J. Leidy Fnd Grants, 2701
John Merck Fund Grants, 2706
Johnson Controls Fnd Arts and Culture Grants, 2719
Johnson Scholarship Fnd Grants, 2726
John W & Anna H Hanes Fdn Grants, 2728
John W. Speas and Effie E. Speas Grants, 2732
Jovid Fnd Grants, 2745
Kalamazoo Comm Fnd Capacity Building Grants, 2764
Kalamazoo Comm Fnd Economic and Comm Dev Grants, 2765

Kaneta Fnd Grants, 2774
Kenneth A. Scott Charitable Trust Grants, 2801
Kiki Madazine Grow Strong Girls through Leadership Grants, 2822
Leighton Award for Nonprofit Excellence, 2880
Lettie Pate Whitehead Fnd Grants, 2888
Long Island Comm Fnd Grants, 2920
Lotus 88 Fnd for Women and Children, 2921
Louis and Elizabeth Nave Flarsheim Charitable Fnd Grants, 2924
Lucy Gooding Charitable Fdn Trust Grts, 2937
M3C Fellowships, 2955
Marion I & Henry J Knott Fdn Discret Grants, 3018
Marion I & Henry J Knott Fdn Std Grants, 3019
Mary's Pence Ministry Grants, 3029
Mary E. Babcock Fnd, 3038
Mary Reynolds Babcock Fnd Grants, 3047
Maurice J. Masserini Charitable Trust Grants, 3064
May & Stanley Smith Char Trust Grants, 3069
Maytree Fdn Assisting Local Leaders w/ Immigrant Employment Strategies Grts, 3070
Mertz Gilmore Fnd NYC Communities Grants, 3126
Mertz Gilmore Fnd NYC Dance Grants, 3127
Meyer Fnd Benevon Grants, 3140
Meyer Fnd Educ Grants, 3142
Meyer Fnd Healthy Communities Grts, 3143
Meyer Fnd Mgmt Assistance Grts, 3144
Meyer Fdn Strong Nonprofit Sector Grts, 3145
MFRI Operation Diploma Grants for Student Veterans Organizations, 3151
Michael Reese Health Trust Core Grants, 3159
Mid-Iowa Health Fdn Comty Response Grts, 3168
Middlesex Savings Charitable Fnd Capacity Building Grants, 3172
Mitsubishi Electric America Fnd Grants, 3190
MMS & Alliance Char Fdn Grts for Comm Action and Care for the Medically Uninsured, 3194
MMS and Alliance Charitable Fnd Int'l Health Studies Grants, 3195
Montana Arts Cncl Cltrl & Aesthetic Proj Grts, 3209
Mt. Sinai Health Care Fnd Health of the Jewish Comm Grants, 3226
Mt. Sinai Health Care Fnd Health of the Urban Comm Grants, 3227
Mt. Sinai Health Care Fnd Health Policy Grants, 3228
National Housing Endowment Challenge/Build/Grow Grant, 3277
NEH Preservation Assistance Grants for Smaller Institutions, 3293
New Hampshire Charitable Fnd Grants, 3325
New York Fnd Grants, 3338
NFF Comm Assistance Grants, 3343
NFWF National Wildlife Refuge Friends Group Grants, 3379
NHLBI Ruth L. Kirschstein National Research Service Award Short-Term Institutional Research Training Grants, 3422
NJSCA Financial and Institutional Stabilization Grants, 3447
Noble County Comm Fnd Grants, 3456
Norcross Wildlife Fnd Grants, 3460
Norman Fnd Grants, 3464
North Carolina Arts Council Outreach Grants, 3479
North Carolina Arts Council Tech Assistance, 3482
North Carolina BioTech Center Reg Dev Grants, 3488
North Dakota Council on the Arts Comm Access Grants, 3494
North Dakota Council on the Arts Institutional Support Grants, 3496
North Georgia Comm Fnd Grants, 3505
NW Fund for the Environment Grants, 3510
NSF Atmospheric Sciences Mid-Size Infrastructure Opportunity Grants, 3521
NSF CISE Computing Rsch Infrastructure, 3526
NSS Fnd Hunting Heritage Partnership Grants, 3530
NWHF Partners Investing in Nursing's Future, 3539
NYFA Building Up Infrastructure Levels for Dance Grants, 3563
NYSCA Architecture, Planning, and Design: Design and Planning Studies Grants, 3572

NYSCA Architecture, Planning, and Design: Independent Project Grants, 3575
NYSCA Arts Education: General Support Grants, 3579
NYSCA Dance: Gen Pgm Support Grts, 3585
NYSCA Dance: Services to the Field Grants, 3587
NYSCA Folk Arts: Exhibitions Grants, 3594
NYSCA Museum: General Operating Support, 3602
NYSCA Museum: Gen Pgm Support Grts, 3603
NYSCA Music: Gen Pgm Support Grts, 3607
NYSCA State and Local Partnerships: Administrative Salary Support Grants, 3618
NYSCA State and Local Partnerships: General Program Support Grants, 3620
NYSCA State and Local Partnerships: Services to the Field Grants, 3621
Ohio Arts Council Arts Partnership Grants, 3650
Ohio Arts Council Capacity Building Grants for Organizations and Communities, 3652
Ontario Arts Cncl Presenter/Producer Grts, 3680
Open Meadows Fnd Grants, 3683
Otto Bremer Fnd Grants, 3713
Overbrook Fnd Grants, 3715
Pajaro Valley Comm Health Health Trust Insurance/Coverage & Educ on Using the System Grants, 3731
Pajaro Valley Comm Health Trust Diabetes and Contributing Factors Grants, 3732
PCA-PCD Organizational Short-Term Professional Dev and Consulting Grants, 3769
PCA Arts Management Internship, 3773
PCA Mgmt/Techn Assistance Grts, 3800
PCA Strategies for Success Grts-Adv Level, 3804
PCA Strategies for Success Grants - Basic Level, 3805
PCA Strategies for Success Grts-Intrmd Lvl, 3806
Perkin Fund Grants, 3821
Peter and Elizabeth C. Tower Fnd Annual Intellectual Disabilities Grants, 3834
Peter and Elizabeth C. Tower Fnd Annual Mental Health Grants, 3835
Peter and Elizabeth C. Tower Fnd Mental Health Reference and Resource Materials Mini-Grants, 3837
Peter and Elizabeth C. Tower Fnd Organizational Scholarships, 3838
Peter and Elizabeth C. Tower Fnd Phase II Tech Initiative Grants, 3839
Peter and Elizabeth C. Tower Fnd Phase I Tech Initiative Grants, 3840
Philadelphia Fdn Org'l Effectiveness Grts, 3872
Philanthrofund Fnd Grants, 3874
PIP Communities for Public Educ Reform Grants, 3898
Piper Trust Educ Grants, 3902
Piper Trust Healthcare & Med Rsch Grts, 3903
Piper Trust Older Adults Grants, 3904
Piper Trust Reglious Organizations Grants, 3905
Pittsburgh Fdn Comm Fund Grts, 3910
Porter County Comm Fnd Grants, 3931
Price Chopper's Golub Fnd Grants, 3950
Priddy Fnd Organizational Dev Grants, 3956
Prince Charitable Trusts Chicago Grants, 3959
Prince Char Trusts Dist of Columbia Grts, 3960
Princeton Area Comm Fnd Fund for Women and Girls Grants, 3962
Quality Health Fnd Grants, 3994
R.E.B. Awards for Distinguished Educational Leadership, 4000
Regional Arts and Cultural Council General Support Grants, 4045
Regional Arts and Cultural Council Professional Dev Grants, 4047
RESIST General Support Grants, 4058
RESIST Multi-Year Grants, 4063
Rhode Island Fnd Grants, 4073
Richard Davoud Donchian Fnd Grants, 4080
Rockwell Int'l Corporate Trust Grants, 4141
Rohm and Haas Company Grants, 4145
Ruth Mott Fnd Grants, 4180
RWJF Partners Investing in Nursing's Future, 4188
RWJF Vulnerable Populations Portfolio Grants, 4190
S.E.VEN Fund Annual Grants, 4195
Saginaw Comm Fdn Discretionary Grts, 4205
Saint Luke's Health Initiatives Grants, 4216

Saint Paul Fdn Mgmt Improvement Fund Grts, 4221
Santa Barbara Fdn Monthly Express Grts, 4284
Santa Barbara Strategy Capital Support, 4285
Santa Barbara Strategy Core Support Grants, 4286
Santa Barbara Fnd Strategy Grants - Innovation, 4287
Santa Barbara Fnd Towbes Fund for the Performing Arts Grants, 4288
Santa Fe Comm Fdn root2fruit Santa Fe, 4289
Santa Fe Comm Fnd Seasonal Grants-Spring, 4291
Sapelo Fnd Social Justice Grants, 4294
Sartain Lanier Family Fnd Grants, 4298
Schering-Plough Fnd Health Grants, 4304
Scherman Fnd Grants, 4305
Seattle Fnd Health and Wellness Grants, 4328
Sensient Technologies Fnd Grants, 4337
Sierra Health Fnd Responsive Grants, 4353
Sioux Falls Area Comm Fnd Comm Fund Grants, 4364
Sioux Falls Area Comm Fnd Spot Grants, 4366
Sister Fund Grants for Women's Organizations, 4371
Sisters of Charity Fnd of Canton Grants, 4372
Sisters of Mercy of North Carolina Fdn Grts, 4375
Sisters of St Joseph Healthcare Fnd Grts, 4377
Skillman Fnd Good Schools Grants, 4382
Social Justice Fund NW Criminal Justice Giving Project Grants, 4394
Solo Cup Fnd Grants, 4401
Sonora Area Fnd Competitive Grants, 4404
Sosland Fnd Grants, 4408
South Carolina Arts Commission Annual Operating Support for Organizations Grants, 4414
South Carolina Arts Commission Arts and Economic Impact Study Assistance Grants, 4416
South Carolina Arts Commission Cultural Tourism Initiative Grants, 4419
South Carolina Arts Commission Cultural Visions Grants, 4420
South Carolina Arts Commission Incentive Grants for Employer Sponsored Benefits, 4422
South Carolina Arts Commission Leadership and Organizational Dev Grants, 4423
South Carolina Arts Commission Long Term Operating Support for Organizations Grants, 4424
Southwest Florida Arts & Attractions Grants, 4441
Sport Manitoba Bingo Allocations Grants, 4454
Sport Manitoba Sport Special Initiatives Grants, 4459
Sprague Fnd Grants, 4461
Stark Comm Fnd Grants, 4477
Starr Fnd Grants, 4483
Stewart Huston Charitable Trust Grants, 4505
Strowd Roses Grants, 4515
Sunflower Fnd Bridge Grants, 4528
Susan Mott Webb Charitable Trust Grants, 4536
SVP Early Childhood Dev and Parenting Grants, 4538
SVP Environment Grants, 4539
T. James Kavanagh Fnd Grants, 4545
T. Rowe Price Associates Fnd Grants, 4548
TAC Arts Access Tech Assistance Grants, 4550
TAC Tech Assistance Grants, 4556
Taproot Fnd Capacity-Building Service Grants, 4560
Tech Enhancement Certification for Hoosiers, 4571
Telluride Fdn Tech Assistance Grts, 4575
Texas Comsn on the Arts Create-3 Pgm Grts, 4585
Texas Instruments Corp Arts & Culture Grts, 4596
Third Sector New England Inclusion Grants, 4608
Third Wave Fnd Lela Breitbart Grants, 4609
Third Wave Fnd Organizing and Advocacy Grants, 4610
Third Wave Fnd Reproductive Health and Justice Grants, 4611
Thomas B & Elizabeth M Sheridan Fdn Grts, 4614
Threshold Fnd Thriving Resilient Communities Funding Circle, 4628
TJX Fnd Grants, 4637
Trull Fnd Grants, 4673
TSA Advanced Surveillance Grants, 4674
TWS Fnd Grants, 4683
US Dept of Educ 21st Cent Cmty Lrng Cnts, 4687
US Dept of Educ Disability and Rehabilitation Research and Related Projects, 4690
US Dept of Educ Innovative Strategies in Comm Clgs for Wkg Adults & Displaced Wrks Grts, 4692
US Dept of Educ Native Hawaiian Educ Grts, 4694
US Dept of Educ Parent Info & Trng, 4695
US Dept of Educ Pgms for Native Hawaiians, 4696
US Dept of Educ Promoting Postbac Opportunities for Hispanic Americans Grts, 4697
US Dept of Educ Rehabilitation Research Training Centers, 4699
US Dept of Educ Rehab Trng--Rehabilitation Continuing Educ Programs --Institute on Rehabilitation Issues, 4700
US Dept of Educ Voc Rehab Svcs Projects for American Indians with Disabilities Grts, 4702
Union Bank, N.A. Fnd Grants, 4709
USAID Call for Public-Private Alliance Proposals in Serbia, 4742
USAID Pakistan Private Investment Grants, 4772
US CRDF Science and Tech Entrepreneurship Program Business Partnership Grant - Armenia, 4795
US CRDF STEP Business Partnership Grant Competition Ukraine, 4796
USDA Hispanic-Serving Institutions Grants, 4813
USDC Market Dev Cooperator Grants, 4853
USFA Dev Grants, 4866
USFA Equipment Subsidy Grants, 4867
US Soccer Fnd Planning Grants, 4871
USTA Excellence Grants, 4874
USTA Player Dev Grants, 4881
USTA Recreational Tennis Grants, 4884
Vancouver Fnd Disability Supports for Employment Grants, 4899
Vancouver Fnd Grants and Comm Initiatives, 4900
Verizon Fnd New Jersey Check into Lit Grants, 4918
Verizon Fnd SE Region Grants, 4923
Victoria S. and Bradley L. Geist Fnd Capacity Building Grants, 4934
Visiting Nurse Fnd Grants, 4951
Waitt Family Fnd Grants, 4973
Wallace Fnd Grants, 4976
Wallace Global Fund Grants, 4977
Weatherwax Fnd Grants, 5014
Wieboldt Fnd Grants, 5065
Wilburforce Fnd Grants, 5067
William C. Kenney Watershed Protection Fnd Ecosystem Grants, 5079
William J. and Dorothy K. O'Neill Fnd Grants, 5087
William Robert Baird Charitable Trust Grants, 5093
William T. Grant Fnd Youth Service Improvement Grants, 5096
WSF Travel and Training Fund Grants, 5119
Youth Philanthropy Project, 5132

Dissertation/Thesis Research Support
Dale and Edna Walsh Fnd Grants, 1435
Nestle Fnd Training Grant, 3301
NHLBI Ruth L Kirschstein Nat'l Rsch Svc Awds for Indiv Predoc Fellowships to Promote Diversity in Health-Related Research, 3419
Tanner Humanities Cntr Rsch Fellowships, 4559
Temple Univ George D McDowell Fellowship, 4577

Educational Programs
1st Source Fnd Grants, 3
2 Depot Square Ipswich Charitable Fnd Grants, 4
3 Dog Garage Museum Tours, 8
3M Company Arts and Culture Grants, 12
3M Company Environmental Giving Grants, 13
3M Company Health and Human Services Grants, 14
3M Fnd Comm Giving Grants, 15
4imprint One by One Charitable Giving, 16
4S Ranch~Del Sur Comm Fdn Grts, 17
21st Century ILGWU Heritage Fund Grants, 20
21st Century Threshold Project Gifts, 21
49ers Fnd Grants, 23
200 Club of Mercer County Grants, 30
360 Degrees of Giving Grants, 32
786 Fnd Grants, 33
1104 Fnd Grants, 34
1675 Fnd Grants, 35
A.C. Ratshesky Fnd Grants, 39
A.J. Fletcher Fnd Grants, 41

A.J. Muste Memorial Institute Counter Recruitment Fund Grants, 43
A.O. Smith Comm Grants, 46
AAAAI RSLAAIS Leadership Award, 49
AAA Fnd for Traffic Safety Grants, 50
AAAS Science and Tech Policy Fellowships: Energy, Environment, and Agriculture, 52
AAAS Science and Tech Policy Fellowships: Health, Educ and Human Services, 53
AACC Building Better Communities Through Regional Economic Dev Partnerships, 54
AACC Project Reach Grants, 56
AACC Service Learning Mini-Grants, 57
AAF Accent on Architecture Comm Grants, 58
AAF Richard Riley Award, 59
AAP Resident Initiative Fund Grants, 69
Aaron Fnd Grants, 73
AAUW Comm Action Grants, 75
AAUW Int'l Project Grants, 76
Abbey Charitable Trust Grants, 78
Abbot & Dorothy H Stevens Fdn Grants, 79
Abbott Fund Access to Health Care Grants, 80
Abbott Fund Comm Grants, 81
Abbott Fund Global AIDS Care Grants, 82
Abbott Fund Science Educ Grants, 83
Abel & Sophia Sheng Charitable Fdn Grts, 86
Abelard Fnd East Grants, 87
Abeles Fnd Grants, 89
Abel Fnd Grants, 90
Abell-Hanger Fnd Grants, 91
Abell Fnd Arts and Culture Grants, 92
Abell Fnd Conservation and Environment Grants, 94
Abell Fnd Workforce Dev Grants, 97
Abernethy Family Fnd Grants, 98
ABIG Fnd Grants, 99
Abington Fnd Grants, 100
Able To Serve Grants, 102
Abney Fnd Grants, 105
ABS Fnd Grants, 107
Abundance Fnd Int'l Grants, 108
Abundance Fdn Local Comm Grts, 109
ACE Charitable Fnd Grants, 111
ACF Assets for Indep Demo Grants, 114
ACF Assets for Independence Individual Dev Account Grants, 115
ACF Comm-Based Abstinence Educ Grants, 116
ACF Ethnic Comm Self-Help Grants, 118
ACF Fnd Grants, 119
ACF Head Start and Early Head Start Grants, 120
ACF Native American Environmental Regulatory Enhancement Grants, 122
ACF Native American Social and Economic Dev Strategies Grants, 123
ACF Supplemental Services for Recently Arrived Refugees Grants, 125
A Charitable Fnd Grants, 126
Achelis Fnd Grants, 127
Ackerman Fnd Grants, 129
ACMP Fnd Comm Music Grants, 130
ACS Award for Encouraging Disadvantaged Students into Careers in the Chemical Sciences, 132
ACS Award for Encouraging Women into Careers in the Chemical Sciences, 133
ACTION Council of Monterey County Grants, 134
Actors Fund Soc Svcs & Financial Assistance, 139
Acuity Charitable Fnd Grants, 140
Adam Richter Charitable Trust Grants, 145
Adams-Mastrovich Family Fnd Grants, 146
Adams and Reese LLP Corporate Giving Grants, 147
Adams Cty Comm Fdn of Indiana Grts, 148
Adams County Comm Fnd of Pennsylvania Grants, 149
Adams Family Fnd I Grants, 150
Adams Family Fnd of Ohio Grants, 151
Adams Fnd Grants, 154
Adams Fnd Grants, 153
Adams Fnd Grants, 155
ADEC Agricultural Telecommunications Grants, 159
Adelaide Breed Bayrd Fnd Grants, 161
Adelaide Dawson Lynch Trust Grants, 163
Adler-Clark Electric Comm Commitment Grants, 164

PROGRAM TYPE INDEX

Educational Programs / 1067

Administaff Comm Affairs Grants, 165
Administration on Aging Senior Medicare Patrol Project Grants, 166
Adobe Art and Culture Grants, 167
Adobe Comm Investment Grants, 168
Adobe Youth Voices Grants, 170
Adolph Coors Fnd Grants, 171
Advanced Micro Dvcs Comm Affairs Grts, 172
Advocate Safehouse Project Grants, 174
AEC Trust Grants, 175
AEGON Transamerica Fdn Civic Grants, 177
AEGON Transamerica Health and Welfare Grants, 179
AEP Corporate Giving Grants, 180
Aetna Fdn Educ Grts in Connecticut, 183
Aetna Fnd Summer Academic Enrichment Grants, 189
AFG Industries Grants, 191
African American Fund of New Jersey Grants, 192
A Friends' Fnd Trust Grants, 194
A Fund for Women Grants, 195
Agere Corporate and Comm Involvement Grants, 199
Agnes B. Hunt Trust Grants, 202
Agnes M. Lindsay Trust Grants, 203
A Good Neighbor Fnd Grants, 204
Agway Fnd Grants, 205
Ahearn Family Fnd Grants, 206
Ahmanson Fnd Grants, 207
AHS Fnd Grants, 208
Aid for Starving Children African American Independence Single Mother's Grants, 210
Air Force Assoc Civil Air Patrol Unit Grts, 214
Air Force Association Junior ROTC Grants, 215
Air Products and Chemicals Grants, 216
Akonadi Fnd Anti-Racism Grants, 217
Akzo Nobel Chemicals Grants, 219
ALA Baker and Taylor Summer Reading Grants, 230
Alabama State Council on the Arts Comm Arts Collaborative Ventures Grants, 236
Alabama State Council on the Arts in Educ Partnership Grants, 242
Alabama State Council on the Arts Operating Support Grants, 244
Alabama State Council Arts Presenting Grants, 245
Alabama State Council on the Arts Program Dev Grants, 246
ALA Distinguished School Admin Award, 266
ALA Diversity and Outreach Fair, 267
ALA Gale Cengage Learning Award for Excellence in Reference and Adult Library Services, 281
ALA Loleta D. Fyan Grant, 295
Alaska Airlines Corporate Giving Grants, 320
Alaska Airlines Fnd Grants, 321
Alaska Conservation Fnd Awards, 322
ALA Ulrich's Serials Librarianship Award, 334
ALA Writers Live at the Library Grants, 336
Alberta Law Fnd Grants, 338
Albert and Margaret Alkek Fnd Grants, 340
Albert B Cuppage Charitable Fdn Grts, 341
Albert E. and Birdie W. Einstein Fund Grants, 342
Alberto Culver Corporate Contributions Grants, 343
Albert Pick Jr. Fund Grants, 344
Albertson's Charitable Giving Grants, 345
Albert W. Cherne Fnd Grants, 346
Albert W. Rice Charitable Fnd Grants, 347
Albuquerque Comm Fnd Grants, 348
Alcatel-Lucent Technologies Fnd Grants, 349
Alcoa Fnd Grants, 350
Alcon Fnd Grants, 351
Alexander & Baldwin Fnd Hawaiian and Pacific Island Grants, 352
Alexander & Baldwin Fdn Mainland Grants, 353
Alexander and Margaret Stewart Trust Grants, 354
Alexander Eastman Fnd Grants, 355
Alexander H. Bright Charitable Trust Grants, 358
Alex Stern Family Fnd Grants, 360
ALFJ Astraea U.S. General Fund, 362
Alfred & Tillie Shemanski Testamentary Grants, 363
Alfred Bersted Fnd Grants, 364
Alfred E. Chase Charitable Fnd Grants, 366
Alfred J Mcallister and Dorothy N Mcallister Fnd Grants, 367

Alfred P Sloan Fdn Civic Initiatives Grts, 368
Allan C. and Leila J. Garden Fnd Grants, 374
Allegan County Comm Fnd Grants, 375
Allegheny Fnd Grants, 376
Allegheny Technologies Charitable Trust, 377
Allen Hilles Fund Grants, 378
Allen Lane Fnd Grants, 379
Allen P & Josephine B Green Fdn Grts, 380
All for the Earth Fnd Grants, 381
Alliance Healthcare Fnd Grants, 383
Alliant Energy Fnd Comm Grants, 384
Allstate Corporate Giving Grants, 386
Allstate Corp Hometown Commitment Grants, 387
Allstate Fdn Economic Empowerment Grants, 389
Allstate Fnd Safe and Vital Communities Grants, 390
Allstate Tolerance, Inclusion, & Diversity Grants, 391
Allyn Fnd Grants, 392
Alpha Kappa Alpha Educational Advancement Fnd Comm Assistance Awards, 393
Alticor Corporation Comm Contributions Grants, 396
Altman Fnd Health Care Grants, 397
Altria Group Arts and Culture Grants, 399
Altria Group Positive Youth Dev Grts, 401
Alvin & Fanny Blaustein Thalheimer Fdn Grts, 403
Alvin and Lucy Owsley Fnd Grants, 404
ALZA Corporate Contributions Grants, 405
AMA-MSS Chapter Involvement Grants, 406
Amador Comm Fnd Grants, 408
AMA Fdn Fund for Better Health Grts, 409
Ambrose and Ida Fredrickson Fnd Grants, 414
Ambrose Monell Fnd Grants, 415
AMD Corporate Contributions Grants, 416
Amelia Sillman Rockwell and Carlos Perry Rockwell Charities Fund Grants, 417
Ameren Corporation Comm Grants, 418
American-Scandinavian Fnd Public Project Grants, 419
American Chemical Society Chemical Tech Partnership Mini Grants, 424
American Chemical Scty Corp Assocs Seed Grts, 425
American College of Bankruptcy Grants, 426
American Electric Power Grants, 428
American Express Charitable Fund Grants, 429
American Express Historic Preservation Grants, 431
American Express Leaders for Tomorrow Grants, 432
American Foodservice Charitable Trust Grants, 433
American Gas Fnd Grants, 437
American Honda Fnd Grants, 439
American Jewish World Service Grants, 441
American Psychiatric Fnd Helping Hands Grants, 443
American Savings Fnd Grants, 445
American Society for Yad Vashem Grants, 447
Amerigroup Fnd Grants, 452
AMERIND Poster Contest, 454
AmerUs Group Charitable Fnd, 455
AMI Semiconductors Corporate Grants, 457
Andersen Corporate Fnd, 459
Anderson Fnd Grants, 460
Andre Agassi Charitable Fnd Grants, 461
Andrew Family Fnd Grants, 462
Andy Warhol Fnd for the Visual Arts Grts, 464
Angels Baseball Fnd Grants, 465
Angels On Track Fnd Grants, 468
Angels Wings Fnd Int'l Grants, 469
Anheuser-Busch Fnd Grants, 470
ANLAF Int'l Fund for Sexual Minorities Grts, 471
Anna Fitch Ardenghi Trust Grants, 472
Ann & Robert H Lurie Family Fdn Grants, 473
Ann Arbor Area Comm Fnd Grants, 474
Anne J. Caudal Fnd Grants, 475
Anne L. and George H. Clapp Charitable and Educational Trust Grants, 476
Annenberg Fnd Grants, 477
Annie's Cases for Causes Product Donations, 479
Annie's Grants for Gardens, 480
Annie E. Casey Fnd Grants, 481
Annie Sinclair Knudsen Memorial Fund/Kaua'i Comm Grants, 482
Ann L. and Carol Green Rhodes Grants, 483
Annunziata Sanguinetti Fnd Grants, 485
Anschutz Family Fnd Grants, 486

Anthem Blue Cross and Blue Shield Grants, 488
Anthony R. Abraham Fnd Grants, 489
Antone & Edene Vidinha Char Trust Grts, 490
AON Fnd Grants, 491
Appalachian Ministries Grants, 499
Appalachian Regional Commission Business Dev Revolving Loan Fund Grants, 501
Appalachian Regional Commission Educ and Training Grants, 504
Appalachian Regional Commission Health Care Grants, 507
Appalachian Regional Commission Leadership Dev and Capacity Building Grants, 509
Appalachian Regional Commission Telecommunications Grants, 510
Appalachian Regional Commission Tourist Grants, 511
Applied Biosystems Grants, 514
Applied Materials Corp Philanthropy Pgm, 515
APSAA Fnd Grants, 516
APS Fnd Grants, 518
Aquila Corporate Grants, 521
Aragona Family Fnd Grants, 522
Aratani Fnd Grants, 523
Arbor Day Fnd Grants, 524
Arcadia Fnd Grants, 525
Archer Daniels Midland Fnd Grants, 527
ARCO Fnd Educ Grants, 528
Arcus Fnd Fund Grants, 529
Arcus Fnd Gay and Lesbian Fund Grants, 530
Arcus Fnd National Fund Grants, 531
Arie and Ida Crown Memorial Grants, 533
Arizona Cardinals Grants, 534
Arizona Comsn on the Arts Educ Projects Grts, 536
Arizona Comm Fnd Grants, 540
Arizona Diamondbacks Charities Grants, 542
Arizona Fnd for Women Deborah Carstens Grants, 543
Arizona Fnd for Women General Grants, 544
Arizona Public Service Corp Gvg Pgm Grts, 545
Arizona Republic Fnd Grants, 546
Arizona Republic Newspaper Corp Contribs, 547
Arizona State Library LSTA Collections Grants, 548
Arizona State Library LSTA Comm Grants, 549
Arizona State Library LSTA Learning Grants, 550
Arkansas Arts Council AIE After School/Summer Residency Grants, 551
Arkansas Arts Council AIE Arts Curriculum Project Grants, 552
Arkansas Arts Council AIE In-School Residency, 553
Arkansas Arts Council AIE Mini Grants, 554
Arkansas Arts Council Sally A. Williams Artist Fund Grants, 558
Arkansas Comm Fnd Arkansas Black Hall of Fame Grants, 559
Arkansas Comm Fnd Giving Tree Grants, 560
Arkansas Comm Fnd Grants, 561
Arkell Hall Fnd Grants, 562
Arkema Fnd Science Teachers Program, 563
Arlington Comm Fnd Grants, 564
Armstrong McDonald Fnd Grants, 565
A Rocha USA Grants, 566
Arronson Fnd Grants, 567
ARS Fnd Grants, 568
ARTBA Transportation Dev Fnd Grants, 569
Arthur and Rochelle Belfer Fnd Grants, 570
Arthur and Sara Jo Kobacker, Alfred and Ida Kobacker Fnd Grants, 571
Arthur Ashley Williams Fnd Grants, 572
Arthur B. Schultz Fnd Grants, 573
Arthur F & Alice E Adams Charitable Fdn Grts, 574
Arts Fnd, 578
Arts Midwest Performing Arts Grants, 579
ArvinMeritor Fdn Arts & Culture Grts, 582
ArvinMeritor Fnd Civic Grants, 583
ArvinMeritor Grants, 585
Ashland Corporate Contributions Grants, 587
Asian American Institute Impact Fellowships, 588
Aspen Comm Fnd Grants, 592
Assisi Fnd of Memphis General Grants, 594
Assisi Fnd of Memphis Mini Grants, 595
Assurant Health Fnd Grants, 596

Educational Programs

As You Sow, 598
AT&T Fnd Civic and Comm Service Grants, 599
ATA Local Comm Relations Grants, 600
ATF Gang Resistance Educ and Training Program Cooperative Agreements, 603
Atherton Family Fnd Grants, 604
Athwin Fnd Grants, 605
Atkinson Fnd Comm Grants, 606
Atlanta Falcons Youth Fnd Grants, 607
Atlanta Fnd Grants, 608
Atlanta Women's Fnd Grants, 609
Atran Fnd Grants, 610
Auburn Fnd Grants, 611
Audrey and Sydney Irmas Charitable Fnd Grants, 612
Aurora Fnd Grants, 613
Austin-Bailey Health and Wellness Fnd Grants, 614
Austin Comm Fnd Grants, 616
Austin S. Nelson Fnd Grants, 617
Autauga Area Comm Fnd Grants, 618
Autodesk Comm Relations Grants, 619
AutoNation Corporate Giving Grants, 620
AutoZone Comm Relations Grants, 621
Autzen Fnd Grants, 622
Avery Dennison Fnd Grants, 623
Avista Fnd Grants, 624
AWDF Main Grants, 627
AWDF Solidarity Fund Grants, 628
Ayres Fnd Grants, 630
Babcock Charitable Trust Grants, 632
Back Home Again Fnd Grants, 633
Bacon Family Fnd Grants, 634
Bailey Fnd Grants, 635
Balfe Family Fnd Grants, 636
Ball Brothers Fnd General Grants, 637
Ball Brothers Fnd Organizational Effectiveness/Executive Mentoring Grants, 638
Baltimore Comm Fnd Arts and Culture Grants, 641
Baltimore Comm Fnd Children's Fresh Air Society Fund Grants, 642
Baltimore Comm Fnd Environment Path Grants, 643
Baltimore Comm Fnd Human Services Grants, 644
Baltimore Comm Fnd Neighborhood Grants , 646
Baltimore Comm Fnd Youth Path Grants, 649
BancorpSouth Fnd Grants, 651
Banfield Charitable Trust Grants, 652
Banfi Vintners Fnd Grants, 653
Bank of America Charitable Fnd Educ and Workforce Dev Grants, 657
Bank of America Charitable Fnd Matching Gifts, 658
Bank of America Charitable Fnd Student Leaders Grants, 659
Bank of America Charitable Fnd Volunteer Grants, 660
Bank of America Corporation Sponsorships, 661
Banrock Station Wines Wetlands Cons Grants, 662
Baptist Comm Ministries Grants, 664
Barberton Comm Fnd Grants, 666
Baring Fnd Grants, 667
Barker Fnd Grants, 668
Barker Welfare Fnd Grants, 669
Barnes and Noble Local Sponsorships and Charitable Donations, 670
Barnes and Noble National Sponsorships and Charitable Donations, 671
Barnes Group Fnd Grants, 672
Barra Fnd Comm Fund Grants, 673
Barra Fnd Project Grants, 674
Barr Fnd Grants (Massachusetts), 676
Barr Fnd Grants , 677
Barr Fund Grants, 678
Batchelor Fnd Grants, 679
Baton Rouge Area Fdn Credit Bureau Grts, 680
Baton Rouge Area Every Kid a King Grants, 681
Baton Rouge Area Fnd Grants, 682
Batters Up USA Equipment Grants, 683
Battle Creek Comm Fnd Grants, 684
Battle Creek Comm Fdn Mini-Grants, 685
Batts Fnd Grants, 687
Baughman Fnd Grants, 688
Baxter Int'l Corporate Giving Grants, 689
Baxter Int'l Fnd Grants, 691

Bay and Paul Fnds, Inc Grants, 692
Bay and Paul Fnds Grants, 693
Bay Area Comm Fnd Grants, 694
Bayer Advanced Grow Together with Roses School Garden Awards, 695
Bayer Fnd Grants, 696
BBF Florida Family Lit Initiative Grants, 697
BBF Maine Family Lit Initiative Planning Grants, 699
BBF Maryland Family Lit Planning Grants, 701
BBF National Grants for Family Lit, 702
BBVA Compass Fnd Charitable Grants, 703
BCBSM Building Healthy Communities Engaging Elementary Schools & Comm Partners, 704
BCBSM Fnd Student Award Program, 710
BCBSNC Fnd Grants, 712
Beazley Fnd Grants, 714
Bechtel Group Fnd Building Positive Comm Relationships Grants, 715
Beckley Area Fnd Grants, 716
Beerman Fnd Grants, 717
Beirne Carter Fnd Grants, 719
Belk Fnd Grants, 721
Bemis Company Fnd Grants, 723
Ben B. Cheney Fnd Grants, 725
Bender Fnd Grants, 726
Bennett Family Fnd of Texas Grants, 728
Benton Comm Fnd - The Cookie Jar Grant, 729
Benton Comm Fnd Grants, 730
Benton County Fnd Grants, 731
Benwood Fnd Focus Area Grants, 733
Berks County Comm Fnd Grants, 734
Bernard and Audre Rapoport Fnd Democracy and Civic Participation Grants, 737
Bernard F & Alva B Gimbel Fdn Grts, 740
Bernard Osher Fnd Grants, 742
Berrien Comm Fnd Grants, 744
Bert W. Martin Fnd Grants, 747
Besser Fnd Grants, 748
Best Buy Children's Fnd @15 Comm Grants, 749
Best Buy Children's Fdn @15 Teach Awards, 751
Best Buy Children's Fnd Twin Cities Minnesota Capital Grants, 753
Better Way Fnd Grants, 754
Better World Books LEAP Grants for Libraries, 755
Better World Bks LEAP Grts for Nonprofits, 756
Beverley Taylor Sorenson Art Wks for Kids Grts, 757
Bicknell Fund Grants, 759
Bikes Belong Fnd Paul David Clark Bicycling Safety Grants, 760
Bill and Katie Weaver Charitable Trust Grants, 764
Bill and Melinda Gates Ag Dev Grants, 765
Bill and Melinda Gates Fnd Policy and Advocacy Grants, 769
Bill and Melinda Gates Fnd Water, Sanitation and Hygiene Grants, 770
Bill Hannon Fnd Grants, 771
Biogen Corporate Giving Grants, 773
BJ's Charitable Fnd Grants, 777
Blackford County Comm Fnd - WOW Grants, 779
Blackford Cty Comm Fdn Grts, 780
Black Hills Corporation Grants, 781
Black River Falls Area Fnd Grants, 782
Blade Fnd Grants, 783
Blanche and Irving Laurie Fnd Grants, 784
Blanche & Julian Robertson Family Fdn Grants, 785
Blanche M. Walsh Charity Trust Grants, 786
Blandin Fdn Expand Opportunity Grants, 787
Blandin Fnd Invest Early Grants, 788
Bloomington Area Arts Council Grants, 791
Blue Cross Blue Shield of Minnesota Fnd Health Equity: Bldg Health Equity Together Grts, 793
Blue Cross Blue Shield of Minnesota Healthy Equity: Impact Assessment Demonstration Project Grants, 795
Blue Cross Blue Shield of Minnesota Fnd Healthy Equity: Health Impact Assessment Grts, 796
Blue Cross Blue Shield of Minnesota Fdn-Healthy Equity: Public Libraries for Health Grts, 797
Blue Mountain Comm Fnd Grants, 800
Blue River Comm Fnd Grants, 801
Blue Shield of California Grants, 802

Blum-Kovler Fnd Grants, 803
Blumenthal Fnd Grants, 804
BoatUS Fnd Grassroots Grants, 805
Bodenwein Public Benevolent Fdn Grants, 806
Bodman Fnd Grants, 807
Boeckmann Charitable Fnd Grants, 808
Boeing Company Contributions Grants, 809
Boettcher Fnd Grants, 810
Bohemian Fnd Pharos Fund Grants, 811
Bollinger Fnd Grants, 812
Booth-Bricker Fund Grants, 815
Booth Ferris Fnd Grants, 816
Bosque Fnd Grants, 818
Boston Fnd Grants, 819
Boston Globe Fnd Grants, 821
Boston Jewish Cmnty Women's Fund Grts, 822
Boulder County Arts Alliance Neodata Endowment Grants, 823
Bowling Green Comm Fnd Grants, 824
Boyd Gaming Corporation Contributions, 825
Brad Brock Family Fnd Grants, 827
Bradley-Turner Fnd Grants, 828
Bradley Family Fnd (California) Grants, 829
Bradley Family Fdn Grants, 830
Brian G. Dyson Fnd Grants, 834
Bridgestone/Firestone Trust Fund Grants, 836
Bright Family Fnd Grants, 837
Bright Promises Fnd Grants, 838
Bristol-Myers Squibb Fnd Comm Grants, 840
Brookdale Fdn Relatives as Parents Grts, 846
Brooklyn Benevolent Society Grants, 847
Brooklyn Comm Fnd Comm Arts for All Grants, 849
Brooklyn Comm Fnd Comm Dev Grants, 850
Brooklyn Comm Fnd Educ and Youth Achievement Grants, 851
Brooklyn Comm Fnd Green Communities Grants, 852
Brown County Comm Fnd Grants, 853
Brown Fnd Grants, 854
Brown Rudnick Relationship Grants, 855
Brunswick Fnd Dollars for Doers Grants, 856
Brunswick Fnd Grants, 857
Bryan Adams Fnd Grants, 858
Buhl Fnd - Frick Educational Fund, 859
Build-A-Bear Workshop Bear Hugs Fnd Lit and Educ Grants, 860
Build-A-Bear Workshop Fnd Grants, 861
Bullitt Fnd Grants, 862
Bunbury Company Grants, 863
Burlington Industries Fnd Grants, 865
Burlington Northern Santa Fe Fdn Grants, 866
Burton D. Morgan Adult Entrepreneurship Grants, 868
Burton D Morgan Fdn Hudson Comty Grts, 869
Burton D Morgan Youth Entrepreneurship Grants, 870
Burton G. Bettingen Grants, 871
Bush Fdn Health & Human Svcs Grts, 875
Business Bank of Nevada Comm Grants, 879
Business Wire Lit Initiative, 880
Bydale Fnd Grants, 882
Byerly Fnd Grants, 883
Cable Positive's Tony Cox Comm Fund, 886
Caddock Fnd Grants, 888
Cadence Design Systems Grants, 889
Caesars Fnd Grants, 891
California Arts Council Public Value Grants, 895
California Arts Council Statewide Ntwks Grts, 897
California Coastal Art and Poetry Contest, 899
California Comm Fnd Art Grants, 900
California Endowment Innovative Ideas Challenge Grants, 904
California Fertilizer Fnd School Garden Grants, 905
Callaway Fnd Grants, 909
Callaway Golf Company Fnd Grants, 910
Cambridge Comm Fnd Grants, 913
Camp-Younts Fnd Grants, 914
Campbell Soup Fnd Grants, 916
Canadian Optometric Ed Trust Fund Grants, 918
Cape Branch Fnd Grants, 919
Capital City Bank Group Fnd Grants, 920
Capital Region Comm Fnd Grants, 921
Captain Planet Fnd Grants, 922

PROGRAM TYPE INDEX

Educational Programs / 1069

Cardinal Health Fnd Grants, 923
CarEth Fnd Grants, 924
Cargill Citizenship Fund-Corp Gvg Grants, 925
Caring Fnd Grants, 926
Carl & Eloise Pohlad Family Fdn Grants, 927
Carl B. and Florence E. King Fnd Grants, 928
Carl C. Icahn Fnd Grants, 929
Carl M. Freeman Fnd FACES Grants, 932
Carl M. Freeman Fnd Grants, 933
Carl R. Hendrickson Family Fnd Grants, 935
Carls Fnd Grants, 937
Carnegie Corporation of New York Grants, 940
Caroline Lawson Ivey Memorial Fdn Grts, 941
Carolyn Fnd Grants, 942
Carpenter Fnd Grants, 943
Carrie E. and Lena V. Glenn Fnd Grants, 944
Carrie Estelle Doheny Fnd Grants, 945
Carrier Corporation Contributions Grants, 946
Carroll County Comm Fnd Grants, 947
Carylon Fnd Grants, 949
Cass County Comm Fnd Grants, 952
Caterpillar Fnd Grants, 954
Catherine Manley Gaylord Fnd Grants, 956
CCF Comm Priorities Fund, 961
CCFF Comm Grant, 962
CCHD Comm Dev Grants, 966
CDC School Health Programs to Prevent the Spread of HIV Cooperative Agreements, 975
CDECD Arts Catalyze Placemaking in Every Comm Grants, 977
CDECD Arts Catalyze Placemaking Leadership Grants, 978
CDECD Arts Catalyze Placemaking Sustaining Relevance Grants, 979
CE and S Fnd Grants, 985
Ceil & Michael E. Pulitzer Fnd Grants, 987
Cemala Fnd Grants, 988
Center for the Study of Philanthropy Fellowships, 989
Center for the Study of Philanthropy Senior Int'l Fellowships, 990
Center on Philanthropy and Civil Society's Emerging Leaders Int'l Fellows Program, 992
Central Carolina Comm Impact Grants, 994
Central Minnesota Comm Fnd Grants, 995
Central Okanagan Fnd Grants, 997
CenturyLink Clarke M Williams Fdn Grts, 998
Cessna Fnd Grants, 1000
CFFVR Alcoholism and Drug Abuse Grants, 1001
CFFVR Basic Needs Gvg Partnership Grts, 1002
CFFVR Chilton Area Comm Fnd Grants, 1006
CFFVR Clintonville Area Fnd Grants, 1007
CFFVR Clintonville Area Fnd Grants, 1008
CFFVR Doug & Carla Salmon Fdn Grts, 1009
CFFVR Environmental Stewardship Grants, 1010
CFFVR Frank C. Shattuck Comm Grants, 1012
CFFVR Jewelers Mutual Char Gvg Grts, 1014
CFFVR Mielke Family Fnd Grants, 1015
CFFVR Myra M. & Robert L. Vandehey Grants, 1016
CFFVR Project Grants, 1017
CFFVR Robert and Patricia Endries Family Fnd Grants, 1018
CFFVR SAC Dev Disabilities Grts, 1019
CFFVR Schmidt Family G4 Grants, 1020
CFFVR Shawano Area Comm Fnd Grants, 1021
CFFVR Waupaca Area Comm Fnd Grants, 1023
CFFVR Wisconsin Daughters and Sons Grants, 1024
CFFVR Women's Fund for the Fox Valley Region Grants, 1025
Chamberlain Fnd Grants, 1027
Champ-A Champion Fur Kids Grants, 1028
Champlin Fnds Grants, 1029
Chapman Charitable Fnd Grants, 1033
Chapman Family Charitable Trust Grants, 1034
Charity Incorporated Grants, 1035
CharityWorks Grants, 1036
Charles A. Frueauff Fnd Grants, 1037
Charles & Lynn Schusterman Fam Fdn Grants, 1038
Charles Delmar Fnd Grants, 1039
Charles F. Bacon Trust Grants, 1040
Charles H. Dater Fnd Grants, 1042

Charles H. Hall Fnd, 1044
Charles H. Pearson Fnd Grants, 1045
Charles H. Price II Family Fnd Grants, 1046
Charles H. Revson Fnd Grants, 1047
Charles Hayden Fnd Grants, 1048
Charles Lafitte Fnd Grants, 1049
Charles M & Mary D Grant Fdn Grants, 1050
Charles M. Bair Family Trust Grants, 1051
Charles Nelson Robinson Fund Grants, 1052
Charles Stewart Mott Fdn Anti-Poverty Grts, 1054
Charles Stewart Mott Fnd Grants, 1055
Charlotte County Comm Fnd Grts, 1056
Charlotte Martin Fnd Youth Grants, 1057
Chase Paymentech Corporate Giving Grants, 1059
Chatham Athletic Fnd Grants, 1060
Chatlos Fnd Grants, 1061
Chefs Move to Schools Grants, 1066
Chesapeake Bay Trust Capacity Bldg Grts, 1068
Chesapeake Bay Environmental Educ Grants, 1069
Chesapeake Bay Trust Mini Grants, 1072
Chesapeake Bay Trust Outreach and Comm Engagement Grants, 1073
Chesapeake Corporation Fnd Grants, 1076
Chevron Hawaii Educ Fund, 1077
ChevronTexaco Contributions Program, 1078
Chicago Board of Trade Fnd Grants, 1079
Chicago Comm Trust Arts & Culture Grts: Improving Access to Arts Lrng Opportunities, 1082
Chicago Comty Trust Educ Grts Priority 2, 1085
Chicago Comm Trust Health Grants, 1087
Chicago Comm Trust Workforce Grants, 1094
Chicago Cultural Outreach Grants, 1095
Chicago Fnd for Women Grants, 1096
Chicago Neighborhood Arts Grants, 1097
Chicago Title & Trust Co Fdn Grants, 1099
Chicago Tribune Fnd Grants for Cultural Organizations, 1101
Child's Dream Grants, 1104
Chiles Fnd Grants, 1108
Chiquita Brands Int'l Grants, 1110
Chiron Fnd Comm Grants, 1111
Christensen Fund Regional Grants, 1112
Christine and Katharina Pauly Charitable Grants, 1114
Christy-Houston Fnd Grants, 1115
Chula Vista Charitable Fnd Grants, 1116
CICF Clare Noyes Grant, 1119
CICF Efroymson Grants, 1120
CICF Indianapolis Fdn Comm Grants, 1123
CICF Jn Harrison Brown & Robert Burse Grt, 1125
CICF Legacy Fund Grants, 1126
CICF Senior Grants, 1127
CICF Summer Youth Grants, 1128
Cigna Civic Affairs Sponsorships, 1129
CIGNA Fnd Grants, 1130
Cincinnati Bell Fnd Grants, 1131
Cincinnati Milacron Fnd Grants, 1132
Cingular Wireless Charitable Contributions, 1134
CIRCLE Civic Educ at the High School Level Research Grants, 1135
Circle K Corporation Contributions Grants, 1136
CIT Corporate Giving Grants, 1138
Citigroup Fnd Grants, 1139
Citizens Bank Mid-Atlantic Char Fdn Grts, 1140
City of Oakland Cultural Arts Dept Grts, 1142
Civic Educ Consortium Grants, 1144
Claneil Fnd Grants, 1145
Clara Blackford Smith and W. Aubrey Smith Charitable Fnd Grants, 1147
Clarcor Fnd Grants, 1148
Clarence E Heller Charitable Fdn Grants, 1150
Clarence T.C. Ching Fnd Grants, 1151
Clark-Winchcole Fnd Grants, 1152
Clark and Carolyn Adams Fnd Grants, 1153
Clark Charitable Trust Grants, 1155
Clark County Comm Fnd Grants, 1156
Clark Fnd Grants, 1157
Claude Bennett Family Fnd Grants, 1159
Claude Pepper Fnd Grants, 1160
Claude Worthington Benedum Fdn Grants, 1161
Clay Fnd Grants, 1162

Cleveland-Cliffs Fnd Grants, 1165
Cleveland Browns Fnd Grants, 1166
Cleveland Fnd Comm Responsive Grants, 1168
Cleveland Fnd Fenn Educational Fund Grants, 1169
Cleveland Fdn Lake-Geauga Fund Grts, 1170
Cleveland H. Dodge Fnd Grants, 1172
Clinton County Comm Fnd Grants, 1174
Clorox Company Fnd Grants, 1176
Clowes Fund Grants, 1177
CMA Fnd Grants, 1178
CNA Fnd Grants, 1179
CNCS AmeriCorps Indian Tribes Plng Grts, 1180
CNCS AmeriCorps NCCC Project Grants, 1181
CNCS AmeriCorps State and National Grants, 1182
CNCS School Turnaround AmeriCorps Grants, 1186
CNCS Senior Corps Retired and Senior Volunteer Grants, 1188
CNL Corporate Giving Entrepreneurship & Leadership Grants, 1191
Coastal Bend Comm Fnd Grants, 1192
Coastal Comm Fdn of SC Grants, 1193
Cobb Family Fnd Grants, 1194
Coca-Cola Fnd Grants, 1195
Cockrell Fnd Grants, 1196
Coeta and Donald Barker Fnd Grants, 1197
Cogswell Benevolent Trust Grants, 1198
Coleman Fnd Entrepreneurship Educ Grants, 1201
Colgate-Palmolive Company Grants, 1202
Colin Higgins Fnd Grants, 1204
Collins C. Diboll Private Fnd Grants, 1208
Collins Fnd Grants, 1209
Colonel Stanley R. McNeil Fnd Grants, 1210
Colorado Clean Enrg Fd Solar Innovation Grts, 1212
Colorado Interstate Gas Grants, 1213
Colorado Springs Cmty Trust Fund Grants, 1215
Columbia Gas of Virginia Grants, 1218
Columbus Fnd Competitive Grants, 1220
Columbus Fnd Dorothy E. Ann Fund (D.E.A.F.) Traditional Grants, 1221
Columbus Fnd J. Floyd Dixon Grants, 1222
Columbus Fnd Mary Eleanor Morris Fund Grants, 1225
Columbus Fdn Neighborhood Partnership Grts, 1226
Columbus Fnd Paul G. Duke Grants, 1227
Columbus Fnd Scotts Miracle-Gro Comm Garden Academy Fund Grants, 1230
Columbus Fnd Siemer Family Grants, 1231
Columbus Fnd Small Grants, 1232
Columbus Fnd Traditional Grants, 1233
Comcast Fnd Grants, 1235
Comer Fnd Grants, 1236
Comerica Charitable Fnd Grants, 1237
Commission on Religion in Appalachia Grants, 1238
Commonweal Fnd Comm Assistance Grants, 1239
Commonwealth Edison Grants, 1240
Comm Fnd AIDS Endwt Awds, 1245
Comm Fnd Alliance City of Evansville Endowment Fund Grants, 1246
Comm Fdn for Grtr Buffalo Grants, 1247
Comm Fnd for Greater New Haven Quinnipiac River Fund Grants, 1250
Comm Fnd for Greater New Haven Women & Girls Grants, 1254
Comm Fdn for Monterey Cty Grants, 1255
Comm Fdn for Muskegon Cty Grants, 1256
Comm Fnd for NE Michigan Grants, 1257
Comm Fnd for San Benito County Grants, 1258
Comm Fnd for Southern Arizona Grants, 1261
Comm Fnd of Abilene Humane Treatment of Animals Grants, 1266
Comm Fnd of Bartholomew County Heritage Fund Grants, 1267
Comm Fnd of Bloomington and Monroe County Grants, 1271
Comm Fnd of Boone County - Adult Lit Grants, 1272
Comm Fnd of Boone County - Women's Grants, 1273
Comm Fdn of Boone County Grants, 1274
Comm Fnd of Broward Grants, 1275
Comm Fdn of Central Illinois Grants, 1276
Comm Fdn of E Ctrl Illinois Grts, 1278
Comm Fdn of Grant Cty Grants, 1279

Educational Programs

Comm Fdn of Grtr Birmingham Grants, 1280
Comm Fdn of Greater Flint Grants, 1282
Comm Fnd of Greater Fort Wayne - Cmty Endwt & Clarke Endwt Grants, 1285
Comm Fnd of Greater Fort Wayne Edna Grants, 1286
Comm Fdn of Grtr Fort Wayne - John S & James L Knight Fdn Donor-Advised Grts, 1287
Comm Fdn of Grtr New Britain Grts, 1291
Comm Fdn of Greater Tampa Grts, 1292
Comm Fnd of Greenville Women Giving Grants, 1293
Comm Fnd of Greenville Hollingsworth Funds Program/Project Grants, 1296
Comm Fdn of Howard County Grts, 1297
Comm Fdn of Jackson County Grts, 1298
Comm Fdn of Mdl Tennessee Grants, 1300
Comm Fnd of Mt Vernon & Knox County Grants, 1301
Comm Fnd of Muncie & Delaware County Grant, 1302
Comm Fnd of Muncie and Delaware County Maxon Grants, 1303
Comm Fdn of Riverside County Grts, 1304
Comm Fdn of Santa Cruz County Grants, 1305
Comm Fdn of Sarasota County Grts, 1306
Comm Fdn of Shreveport-Bossier Grts, 1307
Comm Fdn of S Alabama Grants, 1308
Comm Fdn of SE Connecticut Grants, 1309
Comm Fdn of Southern Indiana Grts, 1310
Comm Fdn of South Puget Sound Grants, 1311
Comm Fnd of St. Joseph County African American Comm Grants, 1312
Comm Fnd of St. Joseph County ArtsEverywhere Grants, 1313
Comm Fnd of St. Joseph County Special Project Challenge Grants, 1314
Comm Fnd of Switzerland County Grants, 1315
Comm Fnd of Tampa Bay Grants, 1316
Comm Fnd of the Verdugos Educational Endowment Fund Grants, 1321
Comm Fnd of the Verdugos Grants, 1322
Comm Fnd Of The Virgin Islands Anderson Family Teacher Grants, 1323
Comm Fnd of the Virgin Isl Kimelman Grants, 1324
Comm Fnd Of The Virgin Islands Mini Grants, 1325
Comm Fnd of Western North Carolina Grants, 1327
Comm Fnd Partners Lawrence County Grants, 1328
Comm Fnd Partnerships - Martin County Grants, 1329
Comm Fnd Silicon Valley Grants, 1331
Comm Impact Fund, 1332
Comm Memorial Fnd Grants, 1334
Comm Partners on Waste Educ and Reduction, 1335
Comm Tech Fdn of California Building Communities Through Tech Grants, 1336
Comprehensive Health Educ Fdn Grts, 1337
Compton Fnd Int'l Fellowships, 1339
Compton Fnd Mentor Fellowships, 1340
Computer Associates Comm Grants, 1341
ConAgra Foods Fnd Comm Impact Grants, 1342
ConAgra Foods Fnd Nourish Our Comm Grants, 1343
Con Edison Corp Giving Arts & Culture Grants, 1344
Con Edison Corporate Giving Civic Grants, 1345
Con Edison Corp Gvg Environmental Grts, 1347
Cone Health Fnd Grants, 1348
Connecticut Comm Fnd Grants, 1350
Connecticut Light & Power Corp Contribs, 1352
Connelly Fnd Grants, 1353
ConocoPhillips Fnd Grants, 1354
ConocoPhillips Grants, 1355
Conservation, Food, and Health Fnd Grants for Developing Countries, 1359
Constantin Fnd Grants, 1362
Constellation Energy Corp EcoStar Grts, 1363
Constellation Energy Corporate Grants, 1364
Consumers Energy Fnd, 1365
Cooper Fnd Grants, 1369
Cooper Industries Fnd Grants, 1370
Coors Brewing Corporate Contributions Grants, 1371
Corina Higginson Trust Grants, 1373
Cornell Lab of Ornithology Mini-Grants, 1374
Cornerstone Fnd of NE Wisconsin Grants, 1375
Corning Fnd Cultural Grants, 1376
Coughlin-Saunders Fnd Grants, 1377

Countess Moira Charitable Fnd Grants, 1381
Covenant Fdn of New York Ignition Grts, 1385
Covenant Fdn of New York Signature Grts, 1386
Covidien Partnership for Neighborhood Wellness Grants, 1391
Cowles Charitable Trust Grants, 1392
Crail-Johnson Fnd Grants, 1393
Cralle Fnd Grants, 1394
Cranston Fnd Grants, 1395
Credit Suisse First Boston Fnd Grants, 1397
Crescent Porter Hale Fnd Grants, 1398
Crown Point Comm Fnd Grants, 1402
Cruise Industry Charitable Fnd Grants, 1404
Crystelle Waggoner Charitable Trust Grants, 1405
CSRA Comm Fnd Grants, 1407
CSX Corporate Contributions Grants, 1408
Cudd Fnd Grants, 1410
Cullen Fnd Grants, 1411
Cultural Society of Filipino Americans Grants, 1412
Cumberland Comm Fnd Grants, 1413
Cumberland Comm Fnd Summer Kids Grants, 1414
Cummins Fnd Grants, 1415
CUNA Mutual Group Fnd, 1416
Curtis and Edith Munson Fnd Grants, 1418
Curtis Fnd Grants, 1419
CVS All Kids Can Grants, 1420
CVS Caremark Charitable Trust Grants, 1421
CVS Comm Grants, 1422
Cyrus Eaton Fnd Grants, 1423
D.F. Halton Fnd Grants, 1424
DV & Ida J McEachern Char Trust Grts, 1425
Dade Comm Fnd AIDS Partnership Grants, 1428
Dade Comm Fnd GLBT Comm Projects Grants, 1429
Dade Comm Fnd Grants, 1430
Dairy Queen Corporate Contributions Grants, 1433
Daisy Marquis Jones Fnd Grants, 1434
Dale and Edna Walsh Fnd Grants, 1435
Dallas Fnd Grants, 1436
Dallas Mavericks Fnd Grants, 1437
Dallas Women's Fnd Grants, 1438
Dammann Fund Grants, 1439
Daniels Fund Grants, 1443
Dan Murphy Fnd Grants, 1444
Daphne Seybolt Culpeper Mem Fdn Grts, 1445
Darden Restaurants Fnd Grants, 1446
Davenport-Hatch Fnd Grants, 1448
David & Barbara B. Hirschhorn Fdn Grt, 1450
David Robinson Fnd Grants, 1454
Davis Family Fnd Grants, 1462
Dayton Fnd Grants, 1463
Dayton Power and Light Fnd Grants, 1464
Daywood Fnd Grants, 1465
DB Americas Fnd Grants, 1466
Deaconess Comm Fnd Grants, 1467
Dean Foods Comm Involvement Grants, 1469
Dearborn Comm Fnd City of Aurora Grants, 1470
Dearborn Comm Fnd County Progress Grants, 1473
Dearborn Comm Fnd Sprint Educational Excellence Grants, 1474
Deborah Munroe Noonan Mem Fund Grts, 1475
DeKalb County Comm Fnd - Lit Grants, 1480
DeKalb County Comm Fdn Grts, 1481
Dekko Fnd Grants, 1482
Delaware Comm Fnd-Youth Philanthropy Board for Kent County, 1483
Dell Fnd Open Grants, 1490
Delonne Anderson Family Fnd, 1492
Delta Air Lines Fdn Arts & Culture Grts, 1493
Delta Air Lines Fnd Cmty Enrichment Grants, 1494
Deluxe Corporation Fnd Grants, 1496
DeMatteis Family Fnd Grants, 1497
Dennis & Phyllis Washington Fdn Grants, 1498
DENSO North America Fnd Grants, 1499
Denver Broncos Charities Fund Grants, 1501
Denver Fdn Social Venture Partners Grts, 1503
Dept of Ed Alaska Native Ed Pgms, 1506
Dept of Ed Child Care Access Means Parents in School Grants, 1507
Dept of Ed Even Start Grants, 1508
Dept of Ed Magnet Schools Assistance Grants, 1509

Dept of Ed Parental Infor & Resource Cntrs, 1510
Dept of Ed Recreational Services for Individuals with Disabilities, 1512
Dept of Ed Safe and Drug-Free Schools and Communities State Grants, 1513
Dept of Ed Upward Bound Program, 1514
Dermody Properties Fnd Grants, 1517
DeRoy Testamentary Fnd Grants, 1518
Detroit Lions Charities Grants, 1520
Deuce McAllister Catch 22 Fnd Grants, 1521
DHHS American Recovery and Reinvestment Act of 2009 Head Start Expansion, 1526
DHHS ARRA Strengthening Communities Fund - Nonprofit Capacity Building Grants, 1527
DHHS Comm Svcs Grant Trng & Tech Assistance Pgm: Capacity-Bldg for Ongoing CSBG Pgm, 1529
Diageo Fnd Grants, 1546
Dining for Women Grants, 1548
District of Columbia Commission on the Arts-Arts Educ Teacher Mini-Grants, 1549
Diversity Leadership Academy Grants, 1550
DOJ Comm-Based Delinquency Prev Grants, 1556
DOJ Juvenile Mentoring Pgm Grts, 1560
Dole Food Company Charitable Contributions, 1564
Dolfinger-McMahon Fnd Grants, 1565
Dollar General Adult Lit Grants, 1568
Dollar General Family Lit Grants, 1569
Dollar General Youth Lit Grants, 1570
DOL Youthbuild Grants, 1571
Donaldson Fnd Grants, 1574
Donald W. Reynolds Fnd Children's Discovery Initiative Grants, 1576
Donnie Avery Catches for Kids Fnd, 1578
Dora Roberts Fnd Grants, 1579
Doree Taylor Charitable Fnd, 1580
Do Right Fnd Grants, 1581
Doris and Victor Day Fnd Grants, 1582
Doris Duke Charitable Fnd Child Abuse Prevention Grants, 1585
Dorot Fnd Grants, 1586
Dorothea Haus Ross Fnd Grants, 1587
Dorothy Rider Pool Health Care Grants, 1589
Dorrance Family Fnd Grants, 1590
Dorr Fnd Grants, 1591
Do Something BR!CK Awards, 1592
Douty Fnd Grants, 1595
Dow Chemical Company Grants, 1596
Dow Corning Corporate Contributions Grants, 1597
DPA Promoting Policy Change Advocacy Grts, 1598
Dr. and Mrs. Paul Pierce Memorial Fnd Grants, 1599
Dr. P. Phillips Fnd Grants, 1601
Draper Richards Kaplan Fnd Grants, 1603
Dream Weaver Fnd, 1604
Dresher Fnd Grants, 1605
Dreyer's Fnd Large Grants, 1606
Drs. Bruce and Lee Fnd Grants, 1607
Drug Free Communities Support Program, 1608
DTE Energy Fdn Comm Dev Grants, 1609
DTE Energy Fnd Diversity Grants, 1611
DTE Energy Fnd Environmental Grts, 1612
DTE Energy Health & Human Services Grants, 1613
DTE Energy Fnd Leadership Grants, 1614
Dubois County Comm Fnd Grants, 1615
Duke Endowment Child Care Grants, 1617
Duke Energy Fdn Econ Dev Grants, 1619
Duluth-Superior Area Comm Fnd Grts, 1620
Duneland Health Council Incorporated Grants, 1621
Dunn Fnd K-12 Grants, 1622
Dunspaugh-Dalton Fnd Grants, 1623
DuPage Comm Fnd Grants, 1624
Durfee Fnd Sabbatical Grants, 1625
Dwight Stuart Youth Fnd Grants, 1628
Dyer-Ives Fnd Small Grants, 1629
Dynegy Fnd Grants, 1630
Dyson Fnd Mid-Hudson Philanthropy Grants, 1633
Dyson Fnd Mid-Hudson Valley Project Grants, 1636
E.J. Grassmann Trust Grants, 1638
E.L. Wiegand Fnd Grants, 1639
E Rhodes & Leona B Carpenter Fdn Grts, 1640
Eastman Chemical Co Fdn Grants, 1643

PROGRAM TYPE INDEX

Educational Programs / 1071

Easton Fnds Archery Facility Grants, 1644
East Tennessee Fnd Grants, 1646
Eaton Charitable Fund Grants, 1647
eBay Fnd Comm Grants, 1648
Eberly Fnd Grants, 1649
Eddie C. and Sylvia Brown Family Fnd Grants, 1653
Eddy Knight Family Fnd Grants, 1654
Eden Hall Fnd Grants, 1655
Edina Realty Fnd Grants, 1656
Edith and Francis Mulhall Achilles Grants, 1657
Edna McConnell Clark Fnd Grants, 1659
EDS Fnd Grants, 1661
EDS Tech Grants, 1662
Edward and Helen Bartlett Fnd Grants, 1664
Edward Bangs Kelley & Elza Kelley Fdn Grts, 1665
Edward R. Godfrey Fnd Grants, 1667
Edward S. Moore Fnd Grants, 1668
Edward W & Stella C Van Houten Mem Fund, 1670
Edwin S. Webster Fnd Grants, 1671
Edwin W & Catherine M Davis Fdn Grants, 1672
Edyth Bush Charitable Fnd Grants, 1673
Effie and Wofford Cain Fnd Grants, 1674
EIF Comm Grants, 1675
Eileen Fisher Activating Leadership Grants for Women and Girls, 1676
Eisner Fnd Grants, 1678
Elizabeth & Avola W Callaway Fdn Grants, 1680
Elizabeth Carse Fnd Grants, 1681
Elizabeth Morse Genius Char Trust Grants, 1682
Elkhart Cty Comm Fdn Grants, 1684
Ellen Abbott Gilman Trust Grants, 1685
Elliot Fnd Inc Grants, 1686
Elmer L & Eleanor J Andersen Fdn Grnts, 1687
El Paso Comm Fnd Grants, 1688
El Paso Corporate Fnd Grants, 1689
El Pomar Fnd Awards and Grants, 1690
Elsie H. Wilcox Fnd Grants, 1691
Elsie Lee Garthwaite Memorial Fdn Grts, 1692
EMC Corporation Grants, 1693
Emerson Charitable Trust Grants, 1694
Emerson Kampen Fnd Grants, 1696
Emily Davie and Joseph S. Kornfeld Fnd Grants, 1697
Emily Hall Tremaine Fnd Grants, 1698
Emma B. Howe Memorial Fnd Grants, 1700
Emma G. Harris Fnd Grants, 1701
Energy Fnd Climate Grants, 1706
Ensign-Bickford Fnd Grants, 1709
Ensworth Charitable Fnd Grants, 1710
Entergy Charitable Fnd Low-Income Initiatives and Solutions Grants, 1711
Entergy Corporation Micro Grants, 1712
Entergy Corp Open Grants for Arts and Culture, 1713
Entergy Corporation Open Grants for Comm Improvement & Enrichment, 1714
Entergy Corp Open Grants for Healthy Families, 1715
Enterprise Rent-A-Car Fnd Grants, 1721
EPA Air Pollution Control Pgm Support Grts, 1722
EPA Brownfields Environmental Workforce Dev and Job Training Grants, 1726
EPA Children's Health Protection Grants, 1728
EPA Environmental Educ Grants, 1729
EPA Environmental Justice Small Grants, 1731
EPA Hazardous Waste Manag Grants for Tribes, 1733
EPA Pestwise Registration Improvement Act Partnership Grants, 1734
EPA Regional Agricultural IPM Grants, 1735
EPA Source Reduction Assistance Grants, 1737
EQT Fnd Art and Culture Grants, 1743
EQT Fnd Educ Grants, 1745
EREF Solid Waste Research Grants, 1747
EREF Sustainability Research Grants, 1748
EREF Unsolicited Proposal Grants, 1749
Erie Comm Fnd Grants, 1750
Essex County Comm Fnd Discretionary Grants, 1752
Essex County Comm Fnd First Jobs Grant, 1754
Essex County Comm Fnd Greater Lawrence Summer Fund Grants, 1755
Essex County Comm Fnd Merrimack Valley General Fund Grants, 1756
Esther M. and Freeman E. Everett Grants, 1757

Ethel and Raymond F. Rice Fnd Grants, 1758
Ethel S. Abbott Charitable Fnd Grants, 1760
Ethel Sergeant Clark Smith Fnd Grants, 1761
Eugene B. Casey Fnd Grants, 1762
Eugene G. & Margaret M. Blackford Grants, 1763
Eugene M. Lang Fnd Grants, 1764
Eugene McDermott Fnd Grants, 1765
Eulalie Bloedel Schneider Fnd Grants, 1767
Eva L & Joseph M Bruening Fdn Grants, 1768
Evan and Susan Bayh Fnd Grants, 1769
Evan Frankel Fnd Grants, 1770
Evanston Comm Fnd Grants, 1771
Evelyn and Walter Haas, Jr. Fund Gay and Lesbian Rights Grants, 1772
Evelyn and Walter Haas, Jr. Fund Immigrant Rights Grants, 1773
Evelyn and Walter Haas, Jr. Fund Nonprofit Leadership Grants, 1774
Ewing Marion Kauffman Fnd Grants, 1777
ExxonMobil Fnd Women's Economic Opp Grants, 1778
Ezra M. Cutting Trust Grants, 1779
F.M. Kirby Fnd Grants, 1780
F.R. Bigelow Fnd Grants, 1781
Fairfield County Comm Fdn Grts, 1782
Families Count: The National Honors Program, 1784
Fam Lit & HI Pizza Hut Lit Fund, 1785
FAR Fund Grants, 1787
Fargo-Moorhead Area Fnd Grants, 1788
Farmers Insurance Corporate Giving Grants, 1791
FAS Project Schools Grants, 1792
Faye McBeath Fnd Grants, 1794
Fayette County Fnd Grants, 1795
FEDCO Charitable Fdn Educ Grts, 1798
Federal Express Corporate Contributions, 1799
Fel-Pro Mecklenburger Fnd Grants, 1800
Feldman Fnd Grants, 1801
FEMA Assistance to Firefighters Grants, 1802
Ferree Fnd Grants, 1804
Fidelity Fnd Grants, 1805
Field Fnd of Illinois Grants, 1806
Fields Pond Fnd Grants, 1807
Fieldstone Fnd Grants, 1808
Fifth Third Bank Corporate Giving, 1809
Fifth Third Fnd Grants, 1810
Financial Capability Innovation Fund II Grants, 1811
FINRA Investor Educ Fnd Financial Educ in Your Comm Grants, 1815
FINRA Smart Investing@Your Library Grants, 1816
Firelight Fnd Grants, 1817
FirstEnergy Fnd Comm Grants, 1819
FirstEnergy Math, Science, & Tech Educ Grants, 1820
First Lady's Family Lit Initiative for Texas Family Lit Trailblazer Grants, 1821
First Lady's Family Lit Initiative for Texas Implementation Grants, 1823
First Lady's Family Lit Initiative for Texas Planning Grants, 1824
First People's Fund Comm Spirit Awards, 1825
Fisher Fnd Grants, 1831
Fishman Family Fnd Grants, 1835
Fitzpatrick and Francis Family Business Continuity Fnd Grants, 1837
Fleishhacker Fnd Educ Grants, 1838
Fleishhacker Fdn Small Grants in the Arts, 1839
Fleishhacker Fnd Special Arts Grants, 1840
Flinn Fnd Scholarships, 1843
Florian O. Bartlett Trust Grants, 1845
Florida BRAIVE Fund of Dade Comm Fnd, 1846
Florida Division of Cultural Affairs Culture Builds Florida Expansion Funding, 1848
Florida Division of Cultural Affairs Culture Builds Florida Seed Funding, 1849
Florida Div of Cultural Affairs Dance Grts, 1850
Florida Div of Cultural Affairs Folk Arts Grts, 1853
Florida Div of Cultural Affairs Media Arts Grants, 1856
Florida Div of Cultural Affairs Museum Grts, 1858
Florida Div of Cultural Affairs Music Grts, 1859
Florida Div of Cultural Afrs Presenter Grts, 1860
Florida Division of Cultural Affairs Specific Cultural Project Grants, 1862

Florida Division of Cultural Affairs State Touring Grants, 1863
Florida Div of Cultural Affairs Visual Arts Grants, 1865
Florida High School/High Tech Project Grants, 1866
Florida Humanities Council Major Grants, 1868
Florida Humanities Council Mini Grants, 1869
Florida Humanities Council Partnership Grants, 1870
Florida Sea Turtle Grants, 1871
Florida Sports Fnd Junior Golf Grants, 1872
Floyd A. and Kathleen C. Cailloux Fnd Grants, 1874
Fluor Fnd Grants, 1875
FMC Fnd Grants, 1876
Foellinger Fnd Grants, 1877
Fondren Fnd Grants, 1878
Ford Fnd Diversity Fellowships, 1883
Ford Motor Company Fund Grants, 1885
Forrest C. Lattner Fnd Grants, 1887
Foster Fnd Grants, 1888
Fnd for a Drug-Free Wrld Clsrm Tools, 1890
Fnd for a Healthy Kentucky Grants, 1891
Fdn for Enhancing Communities Grts, 1893
Fnd for Health Enhancement Grants, 1894
Fnd for Seacoast Health Grants, 1895
Fnd for the Mid South Comm Dev Grants, 1897
Fnd for the Mid South Educ Grts, 1898
Fnd for Mid South Health & Wellness Grants, 1899
Fnd for the MidSouth Wlth Bldg Grts, 1900
Fnd for Young Ausies Indigenous Small Grants, 1901
Fnd for Young Australians Spark Fund Grants, 1902
Fnd for Young Australians Youth Change Makers Grants, 1904
Fnd for Young Ausies Youth Led Futures Grants, 1905
Fnd NW Grants, 1906
Fnds of East Chicago Health Grants, 1910
Fnds of East Chicago Youth Dev Grants, 1912
Fourjay Fnd Grants, 1913
France-Merrick Fnds Grants, 1915
Frances & Benjamin Benenson Fdn Grts, 1916
Frances and John L. Loeb Family Fund Grants, 1917
Frances C & William P Smallwood Fdn Grts, 1918
Frances L & Edwin L Cummings Mem Fund, 1919
Frances W. Emerson Fnd Grants, 1920
Francis Beidler Fnd Grants, 1921
Francis L. Abreu Charitable Trust Grants, 1922
Francis T & Louise T Nichols Fdn Grts, 1923
Frank and Lydia Bergen Grants, 1925
Frank B. Hazard General Charity Fund Grants, 1926
Frank E. and Seba B. Payne Fnd Grants, 1927
Frank G & Freida K Brotz Fam Fdn Grts, 1928
Franklin County Comm Fdn Grts, 1929
Franklin H. Wells and Ruth L. Wells Fnd Grants, 1930
Frank Loomis Palmer Fund Grants, 1931
Frank Reed and Margaret Jane Peters Memorial Fund I Grants, 1933
Frank Reed and Margaret Jane Peters Memorial Fund II Grants, 1934
Frank Stanley Beveridge Fnd Grants, 1936
Frank W & Carl S Adams Mem Fund Grts, 1937
Fraser-Parker Fnd Grants, 1938
Fred & Gretel Biel Charitable Trust Grants, 1939
Fred and Sherry Abernethy Fnd Grants, 1940
Fred Baldwin Memorial Fnd Grants, 1941
Fred C & Katherine B Andersen Fdn Grts, 1942
Fred C & Mary R Koch Fnd Grants, 1943
Freddie Mac Fnd Grants, 1944
FRED Educational Ethyl Grants, 1945
Frederick McDonald Trust Grants, 1946
Frederick W. Marzahl Grants, 1948
Fred L. Emerson Fnd Grants, 1949
Fred Meyer Fnd Grants, 1950
FRED Tech Grants for Rural Schools, 1951
Fremont Area Cmty Fdn Amazing X Grants, 1953
Fremont Area Comm Fnd Elderly Needs Grants, 1954
Fremont Area Comm Fnd Grants, 1955
Fremont Area Comm Fnd Summer Youth Grants, 1956
Fritz B. Burns Fnd Grants, 1965
Frost Fnd Grants, 1966
Fruit Tree 101, 1967
Fulbright/Garcia Robles Grants, 1968
Fulbright Binational Business Grants in Mexico, 1969

1072 / Educational Programs — PROGRAM TYPE INDEX

Fulbright Business Grants in Spain, 1970
Fulbright Grad Degree Pgm Grants in Mexico, 1971
Fulbright Public Policy Grants in Mexico, 1972
Fuller Fnd Grants, 1974
Fulton County Comm Fnd Grants, 1975
Funding Exchange Martin-Baro Fund Grants, 1979
G.A. Ackermann Grants, 1981
G.N. Wilcox Trust Grants, 1982
Gamble Fnd Grants, 1983
Gannett Fdn Comm Action Grants, 1984
Gardiner Howland Shaw Fnd Grants, 1986
Gardiner Savings Institution Charitable Grants, 1987
Garland & Agnes Taylor Gray Fdn Grts, 1988
Gates Family Parks, Conservation & Rec Grants, 1991
Gateway Fnd Grants, 1992
Gebbie Fnd Grants, 1995
GEF Green Thumb Challenge, 1996
GEICO Public Service Awards, 1997
GenCorp Fnd Grants, 1998
Gene Haas Fnd, 1999
Genentech Corporate Charitable Contributions, 2000
General Dynamics Corporation Grants, 2001
General Mills Fnd Celebrating Communities of Color Grants, 2002
General Mills Fnd Grants, 2003
General Motors Fnd Grants, 2004
George A & Grace L Long Fdn Grts, 2008
George A. Hormel Testamentary Trust Grants, 2009
George and Ruth Bradford Fnd Grants, 2010
George A Ohl Jr. Fnd Grants, 2012
George B. Storer Fnd Grants, 2014
George F. Baker Trust Grants, 2016
George Family Fnd Grants, 2017
George Fnd Grants, 2018
George Frederick Jewett Fnd Grants, 2019
George Gund Fnd Grants, 2020
George H & Jane A Mifflin Mem Fund Grts, 2021
George H.C. Ensworth Grants, 2022
George I. Alden Trust Grants, 2023
George J. and Effie L. Seay Fnd Grants, 2024
George Kress Fnd Grants, 2025
George P. Davenport Trust Fund Grants, 2026
George S & Dolores Dore Eccles Fdn Grants, 2027
George W. Brackenridge Fnd Grants, 2028
George W Codrington Charitable Fdn Grts, 2029
George W. Wells Fnd Grants, 2030
Georgia-Pacific Fdn Entrepreneurship Grts, 2033
Georgia-Pacific Fdn Environment Grts, 2034
Georgia Council for the Arts Partner Grants for Service Organizations, 2036
Georgia Council for the Arts Project Grants, 2037
Georgiana Goddard Eaton Mem Fund Grts, 2038
Georgia Power Fnd Grants, 2039
Geraldine R. Dodge Fnd Arts Grants, 2040
Geraldine R. Dodge Fnd Environment Grants, 2041
Geraldine R. Dodge Fnd Media Grants, 2042
Gertrude & William C Wardlaw Fund Grts, 2045
Gertrude E Skelly Charitable Fdn Grts, 2046
Gheens Fnd Grants, 2048
Giant Eagle Fnd Grants, 2049
Gibson County Comm Fnd Women's Fund, 2051
Gibson Fnd Grants, 2052
Gil and Dody Weaver Fnd Grants, 2053
Gill Fnd Gay & Lesbian Fund, 2054
Ginger and Barry Ackerley Fnd Grants, 2055
Ginn Fnd Grants, 2056
Giving Sum Annual Grant, 2058
Gladys Brooks Fnd Grants, 2059
GlaxoSmithKline Corporate Grants, 2060
Glazer Family Fnd Grants, 2062
Gleitsman Fnd Activist Awards, 2063
GNOF Cox Charities of New Orleans Grants, 2072
GNOF Environmental Fund Grants, 2073
GNOF Exxon-Mobil Grants, 2074
GNOF Gert Comm Fund Grants, 2076
GNOF Gulf Coast Oil Spill Grants, 2077
GNOF IMPACT Grants for Arts and Culture, 2078
GNOF IMPACT Grants for Education, 2079
GNOF IMPACT Grants for Health and Human Services, 2080

GNOF IMPACT Grts for Youth Dev't, 2081
GNOF IMPACT Kahn-Oppenheim Trst Grts, 2084
GNOF Jefferson Comm Grants, 2085
GNOF New Orleans Works Grants, 2088
GNOF Norco Grants, 2089
GNOF Organizational Effectiveness Grants, 2090
GNOF Plaquemines Comm Grants, 2091
GNOF Stand Up For Our Children Grants, 2093
Go Daddy Cares Charitable Contributions, 2094
Godfrey Fnd Grants, 2095
Goizueta Fnd Grants, 2096
Golden LEAF Fnd Grants, 2097
Golden Rule Fnd Grants, 2098
Golden State Warriors Fnd Grants, 2099
Goodrich Corporation Fnd Grants, 2104
Good Works Fnd Grants, 2105
Goodyear Tire Grants, 2106
Grable Fnd Grants, 2108
Grace and Franklin Bernsen Fnd Grants, 2109
Grace Bersted Fnd Grants, 2110
Graco Fnd Grants, 2111
Grand Haven Area Comm Fdn Grants, 2113
Grand Rapids Area Comm Fdn Grts, 2114
Grand Rapids Area Comm Fnd Nashwauk Area Endowment Fund Grants, 2115
Grand Rapids Area Comm Fnd Wyoming Grants, 2116
Grand Rapids Area Comm Fnd Wyoming Youth Fund Grants, 2117
Grand Rapids Comm Fnd Grants, 2118
Grand Rapids Comm Fdn Ionia Cty Grts, 2119
Grand Rapids Comm Fnd Ionia County Youth Grants, 2120
Grand Rapids Comm Fnd Lowell Area Grants, 2121
Grand Rapids Comm Fnd SE Ottawa Grants, 2122
Grand Rapids Comm Fnd SE Ottawa Youth Fund Grants, 2123
Grand Rapids Comm Fdn Sparta Grts, 2124
Grand Rapids Comm Fnd Sparta Youth Grants, 2125
Grand Victoria Fnd Illinois Core Grants, 2126
Great-West Life Grants, 2130
Greater Cincinnati Fnd Priority and Small Projects/Capacity-Building Grants, 2132
Grtr Green Bay Comm Fnd Grts, 2135
Greater Kanawha Valley Fnd Grants, 2136
Greater Milwaukee Fnd Grants, 2137
Greater Saint Louis Comm Fdn Grants, 2138
Greater Tacoma Comm Fdn Grts, 2139
Greater Worcester Comm Discretionary Grants, 2140
Greater Worcester Comm Fnd Jeppson Memorial Fund for Brookfield Grants, 2141
Greater Worcester Comm Fnd Mini-Grants, 2142
Green Bay Packers Fnd Grants, 2148
Green Diamond Charitable Contributions, 2149
Greene County Fnd Grants, 2150
Greenfield Fnd of Florida Grants, 2151
Green Fnd Educ Grants, 2153
Greenspun Family Fnd Grants, 2156
Greenwall Fdn Arts & Humanities Grts, 2157
GreenWorks! Butterfly Garden Grants, 2159
GreenWorks! Grants, 2160
Gregory C. Carr Fnd Grants, 2161
Grotto Fnd Project Grants, 2166
Group 70 Fnd Fund, 2167
Grundy Fnd Grants, 2169
GTECH After School Advantage Grants, 2170
GTECH Comm Involvement Grants, 2171
Guido A & Elizabeth H Binda Fdn Grants, 2172
GUITS Library Acquisitions Grants, 2173
Gulf Coast Comm Fnd Grants, 2174
Gulf Coast Fnd of Comm Operating Grants, 2176
Gulf Coast Fnd of Comm Grants, 2177
Gumdrop Books Librarian Scholarships, 2179
Guy I. Bromley Trust Grants, 2180
H & R Fnd Grants, 2181
HA & Mary K Chapman Char Trust Grts, 2182
H.B. Fuller Company Fnd Grants, 2183
H.J. Heinz Company Fnd Grants, 2184
H. Leslie Hoffman & Elaine S. Hoffman Grants, 2185
H. Reimers Bechtel Charitable Grants, 2186
Hackett Fnd Grants, 2188
Haddad Fnd Grants, 2189

HAF Comm Grants, 2193
HAF Comm Partnerships with Native Artists, 2194
HAF Educ Grants, 2196
HAF Native Cultures Fund Grants, 2201
HAF Southern Humboldt Grants, 2204
HAF Summer Youth Funding Prtnrsp Grts, 2205
Hagedorn Fund Grants, 2207
Hahl Proctor Charitable Trust Grants, 2208
Hall-Perrine Fnd Grants, 2209
Halliburton Fnd Grants, 2211
Hallmark Corporate Fnd Grants, 2212
Hamilton Family Fnd Grants, 2213
Hampton Roads Comm Fnd Nonprofit Facilities Improvement Grants, 2218
Hancock County Fnd - Field of Interest Grants, 2219
Hannaford Charitable Fnd Grants, 2222
Harbus Fnd Grants, 2223
Harley Davidson Fnd Grants, 2224
Harold Alfond Fnd Grants, 2225
Harold & Arlene Schnitzer CARE Fdn Grts, 2226
Harold Brooks Fnd Grants, 2227
Harold K. L. Castle Fnd Grants, 2228
Harold R. Bechtel Charitable Grants, 2229
Harris and Eliza Kempner Fund Grants, 2231
Harrison Cty Comm Fdn Grts, 2233
Harrison County Comm Fnd Signature Grants, 2234
Harris Teeter Corporate Contributions Grants, 2235
Harry B. and Jane H. Brock Fnd Grants, 2237
Harry Bramhall Gilbert Char Trust Grts, 2238
Harry C. Trexler Trust Grants, 2239
Harry Chapin Fnd Grants, 2240
Harry S. Black and Allon Fuller Fund Grants, 2243
Harry S. Truman Scholarships, 2244
Harry Sudakoff Fnd Grants, 2245
Harry W. Bass, Jr. Fnd Grants, 2246
Hartford Courant Fnd Grants, 2248
Hartford Fnd Regular Grants, 2253
Harvest Fnd Grants, 2254
Harvey Randall Wickes Fnd Grants, 2255
Hasbro Children's Fund, 2256
Hatton W. Sumners Fnd for the Study and Teaching of Self Government Grants, 2257
Hawai'i Children's Trust Fund Comm Awareness Events Grants, 2258
Hawaiian Electric Industries Charitable Grants, 2259
Hawaii Comm Fnd Reverend Takie Okumura Family Grants, 2264
Hawaii Comm Fnd West Hawaii Fund Grants, 2266
Hazen Fnd Public Educ Grants, 2269
HBF Pathways Out of Poverty Grants, 2273
HCA Fnd Grants, 2274
Head Start Replacement Grantee: Colorado, 2275
Head Start Replacement Grantee: Florida, 2276
Head Start Rplcmt Grantee: West Virginia, 2277
Healthcare Fnd of New Jersey Grants, 2280
Health Fnd of Grtr Cincinnati Grts, 2281
Health Fnd of South Florida Responsive Grants, 2283
Hearst Fnds Culture Grants, 2284
Hearst Fnds Social Service Grants, 2285
Heartland Arts Fund, 2286
Hedco Fnd Grants, 2287
Heifer Educational Fund Grants for Principals, 2288
Heifer Educational Fund Grants for Teachers, 2289
Heineman Fnd for Research, Education, Charitable and Scientific Purposes, 2290
Heinz Endowments Grants, 2291
Helena Rubinstein Fnd Grants, 2292
Helen Bader Fnd Grants, 2293
Helen Gertrude Sparks Charitable Trust Grants, 2294
Helen Irwin Littauer Educational Trust Grants, 2295
Helen K & Arthur E Johnson Fdn Grts, 2296
Helen Pumphrey Denit Charitable Trust Grants, 2297
Helen S. Boylan Fnd Grants, 2298
Helen Steiner Rice Fnd Grants, 2299
Helen V. Brach Fnd Grants, 2300
Hendricks Cty Comm Fdn Grts, 2302
Henrietta Tower Wurts Memorial Fnd Grants, 2304
Henry & Ruth Blaustein Rosenberg Fdn Grants, 2306
Henry County Comm Fnd - TASC Youth Grants, 2307
Henry E. Niles Fnd Grants, 2309

Henry M. Jackson Fnd Grants, 2311
Henry W. Bull Fnd Grants, 2312
Herbert A & Adrian W Woods Fdn Grts, 2313
Herbert B. Jones Fnd Grants, 2314
Herbert H & Grace A Dow Fdn Grants, 2315
Hershey Company Grants, 2318
Highmark Corporate Giving Grants, 2319
High Meadow Fnd Grants, 2321
Hilda and Preston Davis Fnd Grants, 2322
Hill Crest Fnd Grants, 2324
Hillcrest Fnd Grants, 2325
Hillman Fnd Grants, 2327
Hillsdale County Comm General Adult Grants, 2328
Hillsdale Fund Grants, 2329
Hilton Head Island Fnd Grants, 2330
Hilton Hotels Corporate Giving, 2331
Hirtzel Memorial Fnd Grants, 2332
Historic Landmarks Fnd of Indiana Historic Preservation Educ Grants, 2334
Hoblitzelle Fnd Grants, 2341
Hoffberger Fnd Grants, 2342
Hogg Fnd for Mental Health Grants, 2343
Hoglund Fnd Grants, 2344
Holland/Zeeland Comm Fdn Grts, 2345
Hollie and Anna Oakley Fnd Grants, 2346
HomeBanc Fnd Grants, 2347
Home Building Industry Disaster Relief Fund, 2348
Homer A Scott & Mildred S Scott Fdn Grants, 2350
Homer Fnd Grants, 2352
Honda of America Manufacturing Fnd Grants, 2354
Honeywell Corp Leadership Challenge Academy, 2359
Horace A Kimball & S Ella Kimball Fdn Grts, 2362
Horace Moses Charitable Fnd Grants, 2363
Horizon Fnd Grants, 2365
Household Int'l Corp Giving Grants, 2372
Houston Endowment Grants, 2373
Howard and Bush Fnd Grants, 2374
Howard County Comm Fdn Grts, 2375
Howard H. Callaway Fnd Grants, 2376
Howe Fnd of North Carolina Grants, 2377
HRF Hudson River Improvement Grants, 2378
HRSA Nurse Education, Practice, Quality and Retention Grants, 2381
Huber Fnd Grants, 2382
Hudson Webber Fnd Grants, 2383
Hugh J. Andersen Fnd Grants, 2385
Huie-Dellmon Trust Grants, 2386
Humana Fnd Grants, 2388
Humanitas Fnd Grants, 2390
Hundred Club of Denver Grants, 2394
Hundred Club of Durango Grants, 2395
Huntington Arts Council Arts-in-Educ Programs, 2400
Huntington Clinical Fnd Grants, 2404
Huntington County Comm Hiner Family Grant, 2405
Huntington County Comm Fnd - Make a Difference Grants, 2406
Huntington Fnd Grants, 2408
Huntington National Bank Comm Affairs Grants, 2409
Hutchinson Comm Fnd Grants, 2410
Hut Fnd Grants, 2411
Hutton Fnd Grants, 2412
Hyams Fnd Grants, 2413
Hyde Family Fnds Grants, 2414
Hydrogen Student Design Contest, 2415
I.A. O'Shaughnessy Fnd Grants, 2416
IAFF Harvard Univ Trade Union Scholarships, 2417
IAFF Labour College of Canada Residential Scholarship, 2418
IAFF National Labor College Scholarships, 2419
IAFF W. H. McClennan Scholarship, 2420
IBM Adult Trng & Workforce Dev Grts, 2423
IBM Arts and Culture Grants, 2424
ICC Comm Service Mini-Grant , 2426
ICC Day of Service Action Grants, 2427
ICC Faculty Fellowships, 2428
ICC Listening to Communities Grants, 2429
ICC Scholarship of Engagement Faculty Grants, 2430
Ida Alice Ryan Charitable Trust Grants, 2431
Idaho Comm Eastern Region Competitive Grants, 2432
Idaho Power Co Corp Contributions, 2433

IIE David L. Boren Fellowships, 2454
IIE Freeman Fnd Indonesia Internships, 2456
IIE New Leaders Group Award for Mutual Understanding, 2460
IIE Toyota Int'l Teacher Professional Dev Grants, 2461
Illinois Arts Council Educ Residency Grants, 2463
Illinois Arts Council Service Organizations Grant, 2464
Illinois Arts Council Ethnic and Folk Arts Master Apprentice Grants, 2468
Illinois Arts Council Ethnic and Folk Arts Grants, 2469
Illinois Clean Energy Comm Fnd K-12 Wind Schools Pilot Grants, 2480
Illinois DCEO Eliminate the Digital Divide, 2489
Illinois DNR Biodiversity Field Trip Grants, 2496
Illinois DNR Schlyd Habitat Action Grts, 2500
Illinois DNR Wildlife Preservation Fund Large Project Grants, 2505
Illinois DNR Wildlife Preservation Fund Small Project Grants, 2506
Illinois DNR Youth Recreation Corps Grants, 2508
Illinois Humanities Council Comm Project Grant, 2510
Illinois Tool Works Fnd Grants, 2511
IMLS American Heritage Preservation Grants, 2513
IMLS National Leadership Grants , 2515
IMLS Partnership for a Nation of Learners Comm Collaboration Grants, 2520
Impact 100 Grants, 2522
Inasmuch Fnd Grants, 2523
Independence Comm Fnd Quality of Life Grant, 2525
Independence Comm Fnd Education, Culture & Arts Grant, 2526
Indiana AIDS Fund Grants, 2529
Indiana Arts Commission American Masterpieces Grants, 2530
Indiana Arts Commission Multi-regional Major Arts Institutions Grants, 2532
Indiana Humanities Council Initiative Grants, 2539
Indianapolis Power & Light Company Grants, 2540
Indiana Reg'l Econ Dev Partnership Grts, 2546
Indiana Rural Capacity Grants , 2547
Indiana SBIR/STTR Commercialization Enhancement Program , 2548
Indiana Space Grant Consortium Grants for Informal Educ Partnerships, 2549
Indiana Space Grant Consortium Workforce Dev Grants, 2550
Indiana Workforce Acceleration Grants, 2552
Infinity Fnd Grants, 2553
ING Fnd Grants, 2555
Intel Comm Grants, 2562
Intel Finance Internships, 2563
Intel Int'l Comm Grants, 2564
Int'l Association of Emergency Man Scholarships, 2566
Int'l Paper Co Fnd Grants, 2568
Int'l Paper Environmental Awards, 2569
Iowa Arts Council Artists in Schools/Communities Residency Grants, 2571
IRA Pearson Fdn-IRA-Rotary Lit Awds, 2572
IRC Comm Collaboratives for Refugee Women and Youth Grants, 2573
Ireland Family Fnd Grants, 2574
IREX Small Grant Fund for Civil Society Projects in Africa and Asia, 2581
IREX Small Grant Fund for Media Projects in Africa and Asia, 2582
IREX Yemen Women's Leadership Grants, 2583
Irving S. Gilmore Fnd Grants, 2584
Irvin Stern Fnd Grants, 2585
Isabel Allende Fnd Esperanza Grants, 2586
ISA John Z. Duling Grants, 2587
Ittleson Fnd AIDS Grants, 2589
Ittleson Fnd Mental Health Grants, 2590
J.B. Reynolds Fnd Grants, 2592
J. Bulow Campbell Fnd Grants, 2593
J.C. Penney Company Grants, 2594
J.E. and L.E. Mabee Fnd Grants, 2595
J. Edwin Treakle Fnd Grants, 2596
J. F. Maddox Fnd Grants, 2597
J. Jill Compassion Fund Grants, 2598
J. Knox Gholston Fnd Grants, 2599

J.L. Bedsole Fnd Grants, 2600
J.M. Long Fnd Grants, 2603
J. Mack Robinson Fnd Grants, 2604
J. Marion Sims Fnd Teachers' Pet Grant, 2605
J. Walton Bissell Fnd Grants, 2608
J Willard & Alice S Marriott Fdn Grts, 2609
J. Willard Marriott, Jr. Fnd Grants, 2610
Jackson Cty Comm Fdn Unrestricted Grts, 2611
Jackson Fnd Grants, 2613
Jacob and Hilda Blaustein Fnd Grants, 2615
Jacob G. Schmidlapp Trust Grants, 2616
Jacobs Family Fdn Vlg Neighborhoods Grants, 2619
James & Abigail Campbell Fam Fdn Grts, 2620
James A. and Faith Knight Fnd Grants, 2621
James F & Marion L Miller Fdn Grts, 2622
James Ford Bell Fnd Grants, 2623
James Graham Brown Fdn Qlty of Life Grts, 2625
James H. Cummings Fnd Grants, 2626
James J & Angelia M Harris Fdn Grts, 2630
James J. McCann Charitable Trust and McCann Fnd, Inc Grants, 2631
James L & Mary Jane Bowman Char Trust, 2632
James M. Collins Fnd Grants, 2633
James M. Cox Fnd of Georgia Grants, 2634
James R. Thorpe Fnd Grants, 2636
James S. Copley Fnd Grants, 2637
Jane's Trust Grants, 2639
Jane and Jack Fitzpatrick Fund Grants, 2640
Jane Bradley Pettit Comm & Social Dev Grants, 2642
Janesville Fnd Grants, 2644
Janirve Fnd Grants, 2645
Janus Fnd Grants, 2647
Japan Fnd Center for Global Partnership Grants, 2649
Japan Fnd Los Angeles Mini-Grants for Japanese Arts & Culture, 2651
Japan Fnd New York Small Arts & Culture Grants, 2652
Jaqua Fnd Grants, 2653
Jaquelin Hume Fnd Grants, 2654
Jasper Fnd Grants, 2655
Jay & Rose Phillips Fam Fdn Grts, 2656
Jayne and Leonard Abess Fnd Grants, 2657
Jean and Louis Dreyfus Fnd Grants, 2658
Jeffris Wood Fnd Grants, 2660
JELD-WEN Fnd Grants, 2661
Jenkins Fnd: Improving the Health of Greater Richmond Grants, 2663
Jennings County Comm Fdn Grts, 2664
Jennings County Comm Fnd Women's Giving Circle Grant, 2665
Jerome Fnd Travel and Study Grants, 2668
Jessie B. Cox Charitable Trust Grants, 2670
Jessie Ball Dupont Fund Grants, 2671
Jewish Comm Fnd of Los Angeles Israel Grants, 2674
Jewish Women's Fdn of New York Grants, 2677
Jim Blevins Fnd Grants, 2678
Jim Moran Fnd Grants, 2680
JM Fnd Grants, 2681
Joan Bentinck-Smith Charitable Fdn Grts, 2682
Joe W & Dorothy Dorsett Brown Fdn Grants, 2684
John Clarke Trust Grants, 2689
John Deere Fnd Grants, 2692
John Edward Fowler Mem Fnd Grants, 2693
John F. Kennedy Center for the Performing Arts National Rosemary Kennedy Internship, 2694
John G. Duncan Trust Grants, 2695
John H. and Wilhelmina D. Harland Charitable Fnd Grants, 2698
John I. Smith Charities Grants, 2700
John J. Leidy Fnd Grants, 2701
John Jewett & Helen Chandler Garland Fdn, 2702
John Lord Knight Fnd Grants, 2703
John M. Ross Fnd Grants, 2704
John M. Weaver Fnd Grants, 2705
John Merck Fund Grants, 2706
John P. McGovern Fnd Grants, 2707
John P. Murphy Fnd Grants, 2708
John R. Oishei Fnd Grants, 2709
John S & James L Knight Fdn Dnr Adv Fd Grts, 2712
Johns Manville Fund Grants, 2716
Johnson & Johnson Corp Contribs Grants, 2718

Johnson Controls Fnd Arts and Culture Grants, 2719
Johnson Controls Fdn Civic Activities Grts, 2720
Johnson Controls Fnd Health and Social Services Grants, 2722
Johnson Fnd Wingspread Conference Support, 2725
Johnson Scholarship Fnd Grants, 2726
John W. Alden Trust Grants, 2727
John W & Anna H Hanes Fdn Grants, 2728
John W. Anderson Fnd Grants, 2729
John W. Speas and Effie E. Speas Grants, 2732
Joseph Alexander Fnd Grants, 2734
Joseph Drown Fnd Grants, 2735
Joseph H & Florence A Roblee Fdn Grants, 2736
Josephine G. Russell Trust Grants, 2737
Josephine Goodyear Fnd Grants, 2738
Josephine S. Gumbiner Fnd Grants, 2739
Joseph S. Stackpole Charitable Trust Grants, 2741
Josiah W & Bessie H Kline Fdn Grants, 2742
Joukowsky Family Fnd Grants, 2743
Journal Gazette Fnd Grants, 2744
Jovid Fnd Grants, 2745
JP Morgan Chase Arts and Culture Grants, 2752
Judge Isaac Anderson, Jr. Scholarship, 2754
Judith and Jean Pape Adams Charitable Fnd Tulsa Area Grants, 2755
K. M. Hunter Charitable Social Welfare Grants, 2757
Kahuku Comm Fund, 2762
Kaiser Permanente Cares for Communities Grts, 2763
Kalamazoo Comm Fnd Good Neighbor Grants, 2768
Kalamazoo Comm Fnd John E. Fetzer Institute Fund Grants, 2770
Kalamazoo Comm LBGT Equality Fund Grants, 2771
Kalamazoo Comm Fdn Mini-Grts, 2772
Kalamazoo Comm Fnd Youth Dev Grants, 2773
Kaneta Fnd Grants, 2774
Kansas Arts Commission American Masterpieces Kansas Grants, 2775
Kansas Arts Comsn Arts-in-Educ Grts, 2779
Kansas Arts Commission Partnership Agreement Grants, 2782
Ka Papa O Kakuhihewa Fund, 2785
Katharine Matthies Fnd Grants, 2788
Katherine Baxter Memorial Fnd Grants, 2789
Kathryne Beynon Fnd Grants, 2791
Katrine Menzing Deakins Char Trust Grts, 2793
Kelvin and Eleanor Smith Fnd Grants, 2796
Kendrick Fnd Grants, 2797
Kennedy Center HSC Fnd Internship, 2799
Kennedy Center Summer HSC Fnd Internship, 2800
Kenneth A. Scott Charitable Trust Grants, 2801
Kenneth T & Eileen L Norris Fdn Grants, 2802
Kent D. Steadley and Mary L. Steadley Grants, 2804
Kentucky Arts Cncl Access Astnce Grts, 2805
Kessler Fdn Comm Employment Grts, 2814
Kessler Fdn Signature Employment Grts, 2816
Kettering Family Fnd Grants, 2817
Kevin P & Sydney B Knight Family Fdn Grts, 2819
KeySpan Fnd Grants, 2821
Kiki Madazine Grow Strong Girls through Leadership Grants, 2822
Kimberly-Clark Comm Grants, 2824
Kiplinger Program in Public Affairs Journalism Fellowships, 2826
Knight Fdn Donor Advised Fund Grts, 2828
Knight Fnd Grants - Georgia, 2829
Knox County Comm Fnd Grants, 2831
Kohl's Cares Scholarships, 2832
Kohler Fnd Grants, 2833
Komen Grtr NYC Clin Rsch Enrollment Grts, 2834
Komen Grtr NYC Comty Breast Health Grts, 2835
Koret Fnd Grants, 2837
Kosciusko Cty Comm Fdn Grts, 2838
Kovler Family Fnd Grants, 2840
Kroger Fnd Diversity Grants, 2842
Kuki'o Comm Fund, 2845
L. W. Pierce Family Fnd Grants, 2846
Laclede Gas Charitable Trust Grants, 2848
LaGrange Cty Comm Fnd Grts, 2850
LaGrange Independent Fnd for Endowments, 2851
Laidlaw Fnd Youth Organizaing Grants, 2854

Laila Twigg-Smith Art Scholarship, 2855
Lana'i Comm Benefit Fund, 2857
Land O'Lakes Fdn California Region Grts, 2858
Lands' End Corporate Giving Program, 2861
Laura Jane Musser Intrcltrl Harmony Grts, 2862
Laura Jane Musser Rural Arts Grants, 2863
Laura Jane Musser Rural Initiative Grants, 2864
Laura L. Adams Fnd Grants, 2865
Laura Moore Cunningham Fnd Grants, 2866
Lawrence J. and Anne Rubenstein Charitable Fnd Grants, 2868
Leave No Trace Master Educator Scholarships, 2870
Lee and Ramona Bass Fnd Grants, 2871
Legacy Partners in Environmental Educ Grts, 2875
Legacy Partners in Environmental Ed Grants, 2876
LEGO Children's Fund Grants, 2878
Leicester Savings Bank Fund, 2879
Leo Goodwin Fnd Grants, 2882
Leon and Thea Koerner Fnd Grants, 2883
Leonard L & Bertha U Abess Fdn Grts, 2884
Leo Niessen Jr., Charitable Trust Grants, 2885
Lettie Pate Evans Fnd Grants, 2887
Lewis H. Humphreys Charitable Trust Grants, 2889
Liberty Bank Fnd Grants, 2890
Liberty Hill Fund for New Los Angeles Grants, 2892
Liberty Hill Fdn Queer Youth Fund Grts, 2895
Liberty Hill Fnd Special Opportunity Grants, 2897
Libra Fnd Grants, 2899
Lied Fnd Trust Grants, 2900
Lily Palmer Fry Memorial Trust Grants, 2905
Lincoln Financial Group Fnd Grants, 2906
Linden Fnd Grants, 2908
Lisa and Douglas Goldman Fund Grants, 2910
LISC Financial Opportunity Center Social Innovation Fund Grants, 2911
Liz Claiborne Fnd Grants, 2915
Lloyd G. Balfour Fnd Attleboro-Specific Charities Grants, 2916
Local Initiatives Support Corporation Grants, 2917
Long Island Comm Fnd Grants, 2920
Lotus 88 Fnd for Women and Children, 2921
Louetta M. Cowden Fnd Grants, 2922
Louie M & Betty M Phillips Fdn Grants, 2923
Louis and Elizabeth Nave Flarsheim Charitable Fnd Grants, 2924
Louis Calder Fnd Grants, 2925
Louis R. Cappelli Fnd Grants, 2926
Lowe's Charitable and Educational Fnd Grants, 2927
Lowe's Outdoor Classroom Grants, 2928
Lowe Fnd Grants, 2929
Lubbock Area Fnd Grants, 2931
Lubrizol Corporation Comm Grants, 2932
Lubrizol Fnd Grants, 2933
Lucile Horton Howe & Mitchell B. Howe Grants, 2934
Lucy Downing Nisbet Charitable Fund Grants, 2935
Lucy Gooding Charitable Fnd Trust, 2936
Lucy Gooding Charitable Fdn Trust Grts, 2937
Luella Kemper Trust Grants, 2939
Lumpkin Family Healthy Environments Grants, 2941
Lumpkin Family Fnd Lively Arts and Dynamic Learning Communities Grants, 2943
Lumpkin Family Fnd Strong Leadership Grants, 2944
Luther I. Replogle Fnd Grants, 2945
Lydia deForest Charitable Trust Grants, 2946
Lynde and Harry Bradley Fnd Grants, 2947
Lyndhurst Fnd Grants, 2949
M.B. and Edna Zale Fnd Grants, 2950
M. Bastian Family Fnd Grants, 2951
M.E. Raker Fnd Grants, 2953
M.J. Murdock Charitable Trust General Grants, 2954
M3C Fellowships, 2955
Mabel A. Horne Trust Grants, 2956
Mabel F. Hoffman Charitable Trust Grants, 2957
Mabel Louise Riley Fnd Grants, 2959
Mabel Y. Hughes Charitable Trust Grants, 2960
MacDonald-Peterson Fnd Grants, 2965
Macquarie Bank Fnd Grants, 2966
Maddie's Fund Cmty Shelter Data Grts, 2968
Madison Comm Fnd Altrusa Int'l Grants, 2970
Madison Comm Fnd Grants, 2971

Madison County Comm Fnd General Grants, 2973
Maine Comm Belvedere Animal Welfare Grants, 2975
Maine State Troopers Fnd Grants, 2991
Maine Women's Fund Econ Security Grts, 2992
Maine Women's Fund Girls' Grntmkg Init, 2993
Marcia and Otto Koehler Fnd Grants, 3000
Mardag Fnd Grants, 3001
Margaret Abell Powell Fund Grants, 3002
Margaret & James A Elkins Jr Fdn Grts, 3003
Margaret L. Wendt Fnd Grants, 3004
Margaret T. Morris Fnd Grants, 3005
Marie C. and Joseph C. Wilson Rochester Grants, 3006
Marie H. Bechtel Charitable Remainder Grants, 3007
Marin Comm Ending Cycle of Poverty Grants, 3011
Marin Comm Fnd Social Justice and Interfaith Understanding Grants, 3012
Marion Gardner Jackson Char Trust Grts, 3017
Marion I & Henry J Knott Fdn Discret Grants, 3018
Marion I & Henry J Knott Fdn Std Grants, 3019
Marjorie Moore Charitable Fnd Grants, 3021
MARPAT Fnd Grants, 3023
Mars Fnd Grants, 3025
Marshall Cty Comm Fnd Grts, 3026
Marsh Corporate Grants, 3027
Mary's Pence Study Grants, 3030
Mary Black Fnd Active Living Grants, 3031
Mary Black Fdn Comm Health Grts, 3032
Mary Black Fdn Early Childhood Dev Grants, 3033
Mary C. & Perry F. Spencer Fnd Grants, 3034
Mary D. & Walter F Frear Eleemosynary Trust, 3035
Mary E. Babcock Fnd, 3038
Mary E. Ober Fnd Grants, 3039
Mary Jennings Sport Camp Scholarship, 3041
Mary K. Chapman Fnd Grants, 3042
Mary Owen Borden Fnd Grants, 3046
Mary S & David C Corbin Fdn Grants, 3048
Mary Wilmer Covey Charitable Trust Grants, 3049
Massachusetts Bar Fnd Legal Intern Fellowships, 3051
Massachusetts Cultural Council Adams Grants, 3052
Massachusetts Cultural Council Local Cultural Council Grants, 3057
Massachusetts Fnd for the Humanities Cultural Economic Dev Grants, 3059
Massachusetts Fnd for Humanities Project Grants, 3060
Mathile Family Fnd Grants, 3062
Maurice Amado Fnd Grants, 3063
Maurice J. Masserini Charitable Trust Grants, 3064
Maximilian E & Marion O Hoffman Fdn, 3067
Maxon Charitable Fnd Grants, 3068
May & Stanley Smith Char Trust Grants, 3069
McCallum Family Fnd Grants, 3072
McCarthy Family Fnd Grants, 3073
McColl Fnd Grants, 3074
McCombs Fnd Grants, 3075
McConnell Fnd Grants, 3076
McCune Charitable Fnd Grants, 3077
McCune Fnd Civic Grants, 3078
McCune Fnd Humananities Grants, 3079
McGraw-Hill Companies Comm Grants, 3081
McGregor Fund Grants, 3082
McInerny Fnd Grants, 3083
McKesson Fnd Grants, 3084
McLean Contributionship Grants, 3088
McLean Fnd Grants, 3089
McMillen Fnd Grants, 3090
MDARD AgD Value Added/Regional Food Systems Grants, 3091
MDEQ Clean Diesel Grants, 3096
MDEQ Local Water Qlty Monitoring Grants, 3100
Mead Johnson Nutritionals Evansville-Area Organizations Grants, 3103
Meadows Fnd Grants, 3104
Mead Witter Fnd Grants, 3106
MedImmune Charitable Grants, 3108
Medtronic Fnd Comm Link Arts, Civic, and Culture Grants, 3109
Medtronic Fnd CommLink Educ Grants, 3110
Medtronic Fnd CommLink Health Grants, 3111
Medtronic Fnd Patient Link Grants, 3113
Melinda Gray Ardia Environmental Fnd Grants, 3114

PROGRAM TYPE INDEX

Educational Programs / 1075

Melville Charitable Trust Grants, 3115
Memorial Fnd for Children Grants, 3116
Mercedes-Benz USA Corporate Contributions, 3118
Merck Family Fund Youth Transforming Urban Communities Grants, 3120
Mericos Fnd Grants, 3121
Meriden Fnd Grants, 3122
Merkel Family Fnd Grants, 3123
Merkel Fnd Grants, 3124
MetLife Fnd Empowering Older Adults Grants, 3130
MetLife Fdn Preparing Young People Grts, 3131
Metro Health Fnd Grants, 3133
MetroWest Health Fnd Grants to Reduce the Incidence of High Risk Behaviors Among Adolescents, 3136
Metzger-Price Fund Grants, 3137
Meyer Fnd Economic Security Grants, 3141
Meyer Fnd Educ Grants, 3142
Meyer Fdn Healthy Communities Grts, 3143
Meyer Fdn Strong Nonprofit Sector Grts, 3145
Meyer Memorial Trust Grassroots Grants, 3147
Meyer Memorial Trust Responsive Grants, 3148
Meyer Memorial Trust Special Grants, 3149
MFRI Operation Diploma Grants for Higher Educ Institutions, 3150
MFRI Operation Diploma Grants for Student Veterans Organizations, 3151
MFRI Operation Diploma Small Grants for Indiana Family Readiness Groups, 3152
MGM Resorts Fnd Comm Grants, 3153
MGN Family Fnd Grants, 3154
Miami County Operation Round Up Grants, 3156
Miami County Comm Fnd Grants, 3157
Michael and Susan Dell Fnd Grants, 3158
Micron Tech Fdn Comm Grts, 3161
Microsoft Comty Affairs Puget Sound Grts, 3163
Microsoft Software Donation Grants, 3164
Middlesex Savings Charitable Fnd Educational Opportunities Grants, 3174
Miguel Aleman Fnd Grants, 3175
Mildred V. Horn Fnd Grants, 3176
Military Ex-Prisoners of War Fdn Grts, 3177
Milken Family Fnd Grants, 3178
Miller Brewing Corporate Contributions Grants, 3180
Miller Fnd Grants, 3181
Millipore Fnd Grants, 3182
Milton and Sally Avery Arts Fnd Grants, 3183
Mimi and Peter Haas Fund Grants, 3185
Minneapolis Fnd Comm Grants, 3186
Minnesota Small Cities Dev Grants, 3187
Mitsubishi Electric America Fnd Grants, 3190
Mix It Up Grants, 3191
MMS & Alliance Char Fdn Grts for Comm Action and Care for the Medically Uninsured, 3194
Mockingbird Fnd Grants, 3196
Moline Fnd Comm Grants, 3202
Montana Comm Fnd Grants, 3211
Montana Comm Fdn Women's Grts, 3212
Montgomery Cty Comm Fdn Grants, 3213
MONY Fnd Grants, 3214
Moody Fnd Grants, 3215
Moran Family Fnd Grants, 3216
Morris & Gwendolyn Cafritz Fdn Grants, 3218
Motorola Fnd Grants, 3221
Mr. and Mrs. William Foulds Family Fnd Grants, 3222
Ms Fdn for Women Bldg Democracy Grts, 3223
Ms Fdn for Women Ending Violence Grts, 3224
Ms. Fnd for Women Health Grants, 3225
Mt. Sinai Health Care Fnd Health of the Urban Comm Grants, 3227
Musgrave Fnd Grants, 3231
NACC David Stevenson Fellowships, 3235
NACC William Diaz Fellowships, 3236
NAGC Masters and Specialists Award, 3237
NAR HOPE Awards for Minority Owners, 3238
Natalie W. Furniss Charitable Trust Grants, 3244
Nathan B & Florence R Burt Fdn Grts, 3245
Nathan Cummings Fnd Grants, 3246
Nathaniel & Elizabeth P Stevens Fdn Grants, 3247
National 4-H Afterschool Training Grants, 3248
National Book Scholarship Fund, 3249

National Center for Responsible Gaming Conference Scholarships, 3250
National Endowment for the Arts - Grants for Arts Projects: Challenge America Fast-Track, 3254
Nat'l Endowment for the Arts Big Read, 3261
National Endowment for the Arts Local Arts Agencies Grants, 3263
National Endowment for Arts Media Grants, 3264
National Endowment for Arts Museum Grants, 3265
National Endowment for the Arts Music Grants, 3266
National Endowment for the Arts Opera Grants, 3267
National Endowment for Arts Presenting Grants, 3268
National Endowment for the Arts Theater and Musical Theater Grants, 3269
National Geographic Young Explorers Grants, 3275
National Home Library Fnd Grants, 3276
National Housing Endowment Challenge/Build/Grow Grant, 3277
National Inclusion Grants, 3278
NCFL/Better World Bks Libs & Families Awd, 3288
Needmor Fund Grants, 3289
Nehemiah Comm Fnd Grants, 3290
NEH Family and Youth Programs in American History Grants, 3291
NEH Interpreting America's Historic Places, 3292
NEH Preservation Assistance Grants for Smaller Institutions, 3293
NASE Fdn Future Entrepreneur Schlrsp, 3296
Nellie Mae Educ Fnd District Change Grants, 3297
Nellie Mae Educ Public Understanding Grants, 3298
Nellie Mae Educ Fnd State Level Systems Change Grants, 3299
Nevada Arts Council Learning Grants, 3313
Nevada Arts Council Residency Express Grants, 3315
Nevada Comm Fnd Grants, 3316
New Earth Fnd Grants, 3317
New Hampshire Charitable Fnd Grants, 3325
New Jersey Center for Hispanic Policy, Research and Dev Entrepreneurship Grants, 3326
New Jersey Cntr for Hispanic Policy, Rsch & Dev Governor's Hispanic Fwsps, 3327
New Jersey Center for Hispanic Policy, Research and Dev Immigration Integration Grants, 3328
New Jersey Center for Hispanic Policy, Research and Dev Innovative Initiatives Grants, 3329
New Jersey Center for Hispanic Policy, Research and Dev Workforce Grants, 3330
New Jersey Office of Faith Based Initiatives Creating Wealth Through Asset Building Grants, 3331
New Jersey Office of Faith Based Initiatives English as a Second Language Grants, 3332
New Jersey Office of Faith Based Initiatives Service to Seniors Grants, 3333
New Voices J-Lab Journalism Grants, 3337
New York Life Fnd Grants, 3341
NFL Charities NFL Player Fnd Grants, 3347
NFL Charities Pro Bowl Comm Grants in Hawaii, 3348
NFWF/Exxon Save the Tiger Fund Grants, 3354
NFWF Alaska Fish and Wildlife Fund Grants, 3356
NFWF Columbia River Estuarine Coastal Fund Grants, 3367
NFWF Five-Star Restoration Challenge Grants, 3373
NFWF Freshwater Fish Conservation Grants, 3374
NFWF Marine & Coastal Conservation Grants, 3377
NFWF National Whale Conservation Fund, 3378
NFWF Nature of Learning Grants, 3381
NFWF Pacific Grassroots Salmonid Init Grts, 3384
NFWF Pulling Together Initiative Grants, 3387
NFWF Seafarer's Environmental Educ Grants, 3390
NFWF Southern Company Power of Flight Bird Conservation Grants, 3393
NFWF Wildlife & Habitat Conservation Grants, 3399
NFWF Wildlife Links Grants, 3400
NGA 'Remember Me' Rose Schl Garden Awds, 3401
NGA Hansen's Natural and Native School Garden Grants, 3402
NGA Healthy Sprouts Awards, 3403
NGA Hooked on Hydroponics Awards, 3405
NGA Mantis Award, 3406
NGA Midwest School Garden Grants, 3407

NGA Wuzzleburg Preschool Garden Awards, 3408
NGA Youth Garden Grants, 3409
NHLBI Investigator Initiated Multi-Site Clinical Trials, 3413
NHSCA Artist Residencies in Schools Grants, 3423
NHSCA Arts in Health Care Project Grants, 3424
NHSCA Conservation License Plate Grants, 3425
NHSCA Youth Arts Project Grants: For Extended Arts Learning, 3430
NIAF Italian Culture and Heritage Grants, 3432
Nicholas H Noyes Jr Mem Fdn Grants, 3434
Nicor Corporate Contributions, 3435
NIEHS Hazardous Materials Worker Health and Safety Training Grants, 3438
Nike and Ashoka GameChangers: Change the Game for Women in Sport, 3439
Nike Bowerman Track Renovation Grants, 3440
Nike Fnd Grants, 3441
Nike Giving - Cash and Product Grants, 3442
Nissan Neighbors Grants, 3445
NJSCA Arts Project Support, 3446
NJSCA Folk Arts Apprenticeships, 3448
NJSCA General Program Support Grants, 3449
NJSCA Projects Serving Artists Grants, 3450
NNEDVF/Altria Doors of Hope Program, 3452
NOAA Undersea Rsch Pgm Project Grts, 3454
Noble County Comm Fnd Celebrate Diversity Project Grants, 3455
Noble County Comm Fnd Grants, 3456
Nonprofit Management Fund Grants, 3458
Norcliffe Fnd Grants, 3459
Nord Family Fnd Grants, 3461
Nordson Corporation Fnd Grants, 3462
Norfolk Southern Fnd Grants, 3463
Norman Fnd Grants, 3464
North Carolina Arts Council Arts in Educ Artist Residencies, 3468
North Carolina Arts Council Arts in Educ Grants, 3469
North Carolina Arts Council Arts in Educ Rural Dev Grants, 3470
North Carolina Arts Council Comm Public Art and Design Dev Grants, 3472
North Carolina Arts Council Comm Public Art and Design Implementation Grants, 3473
North Carolina BioTech Center Event Sponsorship Grants, 3485
North Carolina Comm Fnd Grants, 3489
North Carolina GlaxoSmithKline Fdn Grts, 3490
North Central Health Services Grants, 3492
North Central Health Services Grants, 3491
North Dakota Comm Fnd Grants, 3493
NE Utilities Fnd Grants, 3498
Northern Chautauqua Comm Fnd Comm Grants, 3499
Northern Chautauqua Cmty Fdn DFT Communications Cmy Betterment Grts, 3500
Northern Chautauqua Environmental Grants, 3501
Northern Chautauqua Comm Fdn Lake Shore Svgs & Loan Comnty Reinvestment Grts, 3502
Northern New York Comm Fdn Grts, 3503
Northern Trust Company Charitable Trust and Corporate Giving Program, 3504
North Georgia Comm Fnd Grants, 3505
Northrop Grumman Corporation Grants, 3507
NW Mutual Fnd Grants, 3509
NW Minnesota Fnd Women's Fund Grants, 3512
NW Minnesota Fnd Women's Fund Scholarships, 3513
Norton Fnd Grants, 3514
Norwin S & Elizabeth N Bean Fdn Grts, 3515
Notsew Orm Sands Fnd Grants, 3516
NRA Fnd Grants, 3517
NSF Atmospheric Sciences Mid-Size Infrastructure Opportunity Grants, 3521
NSF CISE Computing Rsch Infrastructure, 3526
NSF Communicating Rsch to Public Audiences, 3527
NSTA Distinguished Informal Science Award, 3531
Nuffield Fnd Africa Grants, 3532
NYCT AIDS/HIV Grants, 3542
NYCT Civic Affairs Grants, 3545
NYCT Comm Dev Grants, 3546
NYCT Fund for New Citizens Grants, 3547

Educational Programs / PROGRAM TYPE INDEX

NYCT Girls and Young Women Grants, 3548
NYCT Hunger and Homelessnes Grants, 3553
NYCT New York City Environment Grants, 3556
NYCT Social Services and Welfare Grants, 3557
NYCT Substance Abuse Grants, 3558
NYCT Workforce Dev Grants, 3560
NYCT Youth Dev Grants, 3561
NYFA Artists in the School Planning Grants, 3562
NYSCA Architecture, Planning, and Design: General Program Support Grants, 3574
NYSCA Architecture, Planning, and Design: Project Support Grants, 3576
NYSCA Arts Education: Comm-based Learning Grants, 3577
NYSCA Arts Education: General Operating Support Grants, 3578
NYSCA Arts Education: General Program Support Grants, 3579
NYSCA Arts Education: K-12 In-School Grants, 3580
NYSCA Arts Education: Local Capacity Building Grants, 3581
NYSCA Arts Educ: Svcs to the Field Grts, 3582
NYSCA Dance: Gen Operating Support Grts, 3584
NYSCA Dance: Gen Pgm Support Grts, 3585
NYSCA Dance: Long-Term Residency in New York State Grants, 3586
NYSCA Electronic Media and Film: General Program Support, 3591
NYSCA Electronic Media and Film: Workspace Grants, 3593
NYSCA Folk Arts: Gen Pgm Support Grts, 3595
NYSCA Folk Arts: Presentation Grants, 3596
NYSCA Folk Arts: Regional and County Folk Arts Grants, 3597
NYSCA Lit: Public Programs, 3600
NYSCA Museum: General Operating Support, 3602
NYSCA Museum: Gen Pgm Support Grts, 3603
NYSCA Museum: Project Support Grants, 3604
NYSCA Music: Cmy Music Schools Grts, 3605
NYSCA Music: Gen Operating Support Grts, 3606
NYSCA Music: Gen Pgm Support Grts, 3607
NYSCA Music: New Music Facilities, 3608
NYSCA Special Arts Services: General Operating Support Grants, 3614
NYSCA Special Arts Services: General Program Support Grants, 3615
NYSCA Special Arts Services: Instruction and Training Grants, 3616
NYSCA State and Local Partnerships: Workshops Grants, 3622
NYSCA Theatre: Pro Performances Grts, 3625
Oak Fnd Child Abuse Grants, 3632
Ober Kaler Comm Grants, 3635
OceanFirst Fnd Grants, 3636
Oceanside Charitable Fnd Grants, 3637
Office Depot Fdn Caring is Sharing Grts, 3639
Ohio Arts Council Artist Express Grants, 3643
Ohio Arts Council Arts Partnership Grants, 3650
Ohio Arts Council Int'l Partnership Grts, 3653
Ohio Arts Council Sustainability Pgm Grts, 3654
Ohio County Comm Board of Directors Grants, 3656
Ohio County Comm Fnd Grants, 3658
Ohio Cty Comm Fdn Junior Grts, 3659
Ohio Cty Comm Fdn Mini-Grants, 3660
OJJDP National Mentoring Grants, 3664
OJJDP Tribal Juvenile Accountability Discretionary Grants, 3665
Oklahoma City Comm Pgms & Grts, 3666
Oleonda Jameson Trust Grants, 3667
Olga Sipolin Children's Fund Grants, 3668
Olin Corporation Charitable Trust Grants, 3669
Olive B. Cole Fnd Grants, 3670
Onan Family Fnd Grants, 3672
OneFamily Fnd Grants, 3673
Ontario Arts Council Compass Grants, 3677
Oppenstein Brothers Fnd Grants, 3685
Oracle Corporate Contributions Grants, 3686
Orange County Comm Fnd Grants, 3687
Orange County Comm Fnd Grants, 3688
Ordean Fnd Grants, 3691

Oscar Rennebohm Fnd Grants, 3694
OSF-Baltimore Comm Fellowships, 3695
OSF-Baltimore Crim & Juv Justice Grts, 3696
OSF-Baltimore Educ and Youth Dev Grants, 3697
OSF-Baltimore Tackling Drug Adctn Grts, 3698
OSF Advancing the Rights and Integration of Roma Grants, 3699
OSF Burma Project/SE Asia Init Grts, 3702
OSF Cmpgn for Blk Male Achievement Grts, 3703
OSF European Commission Internships for Young Roma Graduates, 3707
OSI After Prison Initiative Grants, 3710
OSI Sentencing and Incarceration Alternatives Project Grants, 3711
Otto Bremer Fnd Grants, 3713
Owen County Comm Fnd Grants, 3716
Owens Corning Fnd Grants, 3717
Owens Fnd Grants, 3718
PACCAR Fnd Grants, 3719
Pacers Fnd Be Drug-Free Grants, 3720
Pacers Fnd Be Educated Grants, 3721
Pacers Fnd Be Healthy and Fit Grants, 3722
Pacers Fnd Be Tolerant Grants, 3723
Pacers Fnd Indiana Fever's Be Younique Grants, 3724
PacifiCare Fnd Grants, 3725
Pacific Life Fnd Grants, 3726
PacifiCorp Fnd for Learning Grants, 3727
Pacific Rainbow Fnd Grants, 3728
Packard Fnd Local Grants, 3729
Palm Beach and Martin Counties Grants, 3733
Parkersburg Area Comm Fdn Action Grts, 3738
Park Fnd Grants, 3739
PAS Internship, 3742
Paso del Norte Health Fnd Grants, 3743
Pathways to Nature Conservation Fund Grants, 3745
Patricia Price Peterson Fnd Grants, 3746
Patrick and Aimee Butler Family Fnd Comm Arts and Humanities Grants, 3747
Patrick and Anna M. Cudahy Fund Grants, 3751
Patrick John Bennett, Jr. Memorial Fnd Grants, 3752
Paul & Daisy Soros Fwsps for New Americans, 3754
Paul and Edith Babson Fnd Grants, 3755
Paul and Mary Haas Fnd Contributions and Student Scholarships, 3756
Paul E & Klare N Reinhold Fdn Grts, 3758
Paul G. Allen Family Fnd Grants, 3759
Paul Ogle Fnd Grants, 3764
PCA Arts in Educ Residencies, 3772
PCA Arts Organizations and Arts Grants for Art Museums, 3775
PCA Arts Organizations and Arts Grants for Arts Educ Organizations, 3776
PCA Arts Organizations and Grants for Crafts, 3778
PCA Arts Organizations & Grants for Visual Arts, 3785
PCA Entry Track Arts Organizations and Arts Grants for Art Museums, 3787
PCA Entry Track Arts Orgs & Arts Pgms Grts for Arts Educ Orgs, 3788
PCA Entry Track Arts Organizations and Arts Grants for Crafts, 3790
PCA Entry Track Arts Organizations and Arts Grants for Visual Arts, 3799
PCA Pennsylvania Partners in Arts Stream Grant, 3801
PCA Pennsylvania Partners in the Arts Project Stream Grants, 3802
PDF Comm Organizing Grants, 3807
PDF Fiscal Sponsorship Grant, 3808
Peacock Fnd Grants, 3809
Pentair Fnd Educ and Comm Grants, 3816
Peoples Bancorp Fnd Grants, 3817
PeopleSoft Comm Relations Grants, 3818
PepsiCo Fnd Grants, 3819
Percy B. Ferebee Endowment Grants, 3820
Perkins Charitable Fnd Grants, 3823
Perpetual Trust for Charitable Giving Grants, 3826
Perry County Comm Fnd Grants, 3827
Pet Care Trust Fish in the Classroom Grant, 3828
Petco Fnd 4 Rs Project Support Grants, 3830
Peter and Elizabeth C. Tower Fnd Annual Intellectual Disabilities Grants, 3834

Peter and Elizabeth C. Tower Fnd Annual Mental Health Grants, 3835
Peter and Elizabeth C. Tower Fnd Learning Disability Grants, 3836
Peter and Elizabeth C. Tower Fnd Mental Health Reference and Resource Materials Mini-Grants, 3837
Peter and Elizabeth C. Tower Fnd Organizational Scholarships, 3838
Peter and Elizabeth C. Tower Fnd Phase II Tech Initiative Grants, 3839
Peter and Elizabeth C. Tower Fnd Phase I Tech Initiative Grants, 3840
Peter and Elizabeth C. Tower Fnd Social and Emotional Preschool Curriculum Grants, 3841
Peter & Elizabeth Tower Substance Abuse Grants, 3842
Peter and Georgia Angelos Fnd Grants, 3843
Peter Kiewit Fnd General Grants, 3845
Peter Kiewit Fnd Small Grants, 3847
Peter M. Putnam Fnd Grants, 3848
Peter Norton Family Fnd Grants, 3849
PetSmart Charities Conf Sponsorship Grts, 3851
PetSmart Charities Free-Roaming Cat Spay-Neuter Grants, 3852
PetSmart Charities Grts for Canadian Agncs, 3853
PetSmart Charities Model Volunteering Grants, 3854
PetSmart Charities Spay/Neuter Clinic Equipment Grant, 3855
PetSmart Charities Tgtd Spay/Neuter Grts, 3856
Pew Charitable Trusts Arts and Culture Grants, 3857
Pew Charitable Trusts Children & Youth Grts, 3858
Pew Char Trusts Spcl Civic Project Grts, 3859
PeyBack Fnd Grants, 3861
Peyton Anderson Fnd Grants, 3862
Pfizer Healthcare Charitable Contributions, 3863
Pfizer Medical Educ Track One Grants, 3864
PG&E Bright Ideas Grants, 3866
PG&E Comm Vitality Grants, 3868
PGE Fnd Grants, 3869
Phelps County Comm Fnd Grants, 3870
Philadelphia Fdn Org'l Effectiveness Grts, 3872
Philadelphia Fdn YOUTHadelphia Grts, 3873
Philanthrofund Fnd Grants, 3874
Phil Hardin Fnd Grants, 3875
Philip L. Graham Fund Grants, 3876
Phoenix Coyotes Charities Grants, 3879
Phoenix Neighborhood Block Watch Grants, 3880
Phoenix Suns Charities Grants, 3881
Piedmont Health Fnd Grants, 3882
Piedmont Natural Gas Corporate and Charitable Contributions, 3883
Piedmont Natural Gas Fnd Environmental Stewardship and Energy Sustainability Grant, 3884
Pier 1 Imports Grants, 3887
Pike County Comm Fnd Grants, 3888
Pinellas County Grants, 3891
Pinnacle Entertainment Fnd Grants, 3893
Pinnacle Fnd Grants, 3894
Pioneer Hi-Bred Comm Grants, 3895
PIP Communities for Public Educ Reform Grants, 3898
Piper Trust Arts and Culture Grants, 3900
Piper Trust Children Grants, 3901
Piper Trust Educ Grants, 3902
Piper Trust Older Adults Grants, 3904
Piper Trust Reglous Organizations Grants, 3905
PIP Four Freedoms Fund Grants, 3906
PIP Fulfilling the Dream Fund, 3907
PIP Racial Justice Collaborative Grants, 3908
PIP U.S. Human Rights Fund Grants, 3909
Pittsburgh Fdn Comm Fund Grts, 3910
Planet Dog Fnd Grants, 3911
Playboy Fnd Grants, 3913
Playboy Social Change Documentary Film Grants, 3914
Plough Fnd Grants, 3915
Plum Creek Fnd Grants, 3917
PMI Fnd Grants, 3918
PNC Charitable Trust and Fnd Grants, 3921
PNC Fnd Grow Up Great Grants, 3924
PNM Reduce Your Use Grants, 3926
Poets & Writers Readings/Workshops Grants, 3927
Pohlad Family Fnd, 3928

PROGRAM TYPE INDEX

Educational Programs / 1077

Polk Bros. Fnd Grants, 3929
Pollock Fnd Grants, 3930
Porter County Comm Fnd Grants, 3931
Porter County Health and Wellness Grant, 3933
Porter County Women's Grant, 3934
Portland Fdn - Women's Giving Circle Grt, 3935
Portland Fnd Grants, 3936
Portland General Electric Fnd Grants, 3937
Posey Comm Fdn Women's Fund Grts, 3938
Posey County Comm Fnd Grants, 3939
Pott Fnd Grants, 3940
Powell Family Fnd Grants, 3941
Powell Fnd Grants, 3942
PPG Industries Fnd Grants, 3943
Praxair Fnd Grants, 3944
Premera Blue Cross CARES Grants, 3945
Presbyterian Health Fnd Bridge, Seed and Equipment Grants, 3947
Price Chopper's Golub Fnd Grants, 3950
Price Family Charitable Fund Grants, 3952
Price Gilbert, Jr. Charitable Fund Grants, 3953
Priddy Fnd Grants, 3957
Pride Fnd Grants, 3958
Prince Charitable Trusts Chicago Grants, 3959
Prince Char Trusts Dist of Columbia Grts, 3960
Prince Charitable Trusts Rhode Island Grants, 3961
Princeton Comm Fnd Greater Mercer Grants, 3963
Princeton Area Comm Fnd Thomas George Artists Fund Grants, 3965
Principal Financial Group Fnd Grants, 3966
Procter and Gamble Fund Grants, 3967
Progress Energy Corp Contributions Grts, 3968
Project AWARE Fnd Grants, 3971
Project Orange Thumb Grants, 3972
Proteus Fund Grants, 3973
Prudential Fnd Educ Grants, 3977
PSEG Corporate Contributions Grants, 3979
PSEG Environmental Educ Grants, 3980
Public Educ Power Grants, 3981
Public Safety Fnd of America Grants, 3983
Publix Super Markets Charities Local Grants, 3985
Puerto Rico Comm Fnd Grants, 3986
Pulaski County Comm Fnd Grants, 3988
Pulte Homes Corporate Contributions, 3989
Putnam Cty Comm Fdn Grts, 3990
Quaker Oats Company Kids Care Clubs Grants, 3992
Qualcomm Grants, 3993
Quality Health Fnd Grants, 3994
Quantum Fnd Grants, 3996
Questar Corporate Contributions Grants, 3997
QuikTrip Corporate Contributions Grants, 3998
R.C. Baker Fnd Grants, 3999
R.E.B. Awards for Distinguished Educational Leadership, 4000
R.J. McElroy Trust Grants, 4001
R.S. Gernon Trust Grants, 4002
Rachel Alexandra Girls Grants, 4003
Rainbow Fund Grants, 4009
Rainbow Media Holdings Corp Gvg Prgm Grts, 4010
Rajiv Gandhi Fnd Grants, 4011
Ralphs Food 4 Less Fnd Grants, 4014
Raskob Fdn for Catholic Activities Grts, 4019
Rathmann Family Fnd Grants, 4026
Ray Fnd Grants, 4027
Raymond John Wean Fnd Grants, 4028
Ray Solem Fnd Grants to Help Immigrants Learn English in Innovative Ways, 4029
Raytheon Grants, 4030
RBC Dain Rauscher Fnd Grants, 4031
RCF General Comm Grants, 4032
RCF Individual Assistance Grants, 4033
RCF Summertime Kids Grants, 4034
RCF The Women's Fund Grants, 4035
Red Robin Fnd U-ACT Grants, 4038
Regence Fnd Health Care Comm Awareness and Engagement Grants, 4040
Regence Fdn Improving End-of-Life Grts, 4042
Regents Professional Opportunity Scholarships, 4044
Reinberger Fnd Grants, 4052
Retirement Research Fdn Gen Pgm Grts, 4067

Reynolds American Fnd Grants, 4068
Reynolds & Reynolds Assoc Fdn Grants, 4069
Reynolds and Reynolds Co Fdn Grants, 4070
RGK Fnd Grants, 4072
Rhode Island Fnd Grants, 4073
Rice Fnd Grants, 4074
Richard & Caroline T Gwathmey Mem Tr Grts, 4075
Richard & Susan Smith Family Fdn Grts, 4078
Richard D. Bass Fnd Grants, 4079
Richard Davoud Donchian Fnd Grants, 4080
Richard F. and Janice F. Weaver Educational Trust Grants, 4082
Richard King Mellon Fnd Grants, 4087
Rich Fnd Grants, 4090
Richland County Bank Grants, 4091
Richmond Eye and Ear Fund Grants, 4092
Riley Fnd Grants, 4094
Ripley County Comm Fnd Grants, 4095
Ripley County Comm Fnd Small Project Grants, 4096
RISCA Project Grants for Organizations, Individuals and Education, 4100
Roberta Leventhal Sudakoff Fnd Grants, 4102
Robert and Helen Haddad Fnd Grants, 4103
Robert and Joan Dircks Fnd Grants, 4104
Robert and Polly Dunn Fnd Grants, 4105
Robert Bowne Fnd Fellowships, 4107
Robert E & Evelyn McKee Fdn Grants, 4110
Robert G. Cabell III and Maude Morgan Cabell Fnd Grants, 4113
Robert Lee Blaffer Fnd Grants, 4115
Robert M. Hearin Fnd Grants, 4116
Robert P & Clara I Milton Fund for Sr Housing, 4117
Robert R. McCormick Tribune Comm Grants, 4119
Robert R. McCormick Tribune Veterans Grants, 4120
Robert R. Meyer Fnd Grants, 4121
Robert Sterling Clark Arts & Culture Grants, 4122
Robert Sterling Clark Fnd Government Accountability Grants, 4123
Robert W. Woodruff Fnd Grants, 4124
Robins Fnd Grants, 4126
Rochester Area Comm Fnd Grants, 4127
Rochester Area Fnd Grants, 4128
Rockefeller Brothers Democratic Practice Grants, 4131
Rockefeller Brothers Sustainable Dev Grants, 4136
Rockefeller Fnd Partnerships Affirming Comm Transformation Grants, 4139
Rockwell Fund, Inc. Grants, 4140
Roger L. and Agnes C. Dell Charitable Grants, 4143
Rohm and Haas Company Grants, 4145
Rollins-Luetkemeyer Fnd Grants, 4147
Romic Environmental's Charitable Contributions, 4148
Ronald McDonald House Charities Grants, 4149
Roney-Fitzpatrick Fnd Grants, 4150
Rose Comm Fnd Child and Family Dev Grants, 4153
Rose Comm Fdn Jewish Life Grts, 4155
Rose Communities and Environment Northern California Environmental Grassroots Grants, 4158
Rose Hills Fnd Grants, 4162
Ross Fnd Grants, 4164
Royal Caribbean Cruises Ocean Fund, 4165
Roy & Christine Sturgis Charitable Trust Grts, 4166
RR Donnelley Comm Grants, 4168
RRF General Grants, 4170
Rush County Comm Fnd Grants, 4174
Russell Berrie Fnd Grants, 4175
Ruth Anderson Fnd Grants, 4176
Ruth and Vernon Taylor Fnd Grants, 4177
Ruth Eleanor Bamberger and John Ernest Bamberger Memorial Fnd Grants, 4178
Ruth H & Warren A Ellsworth Fdn Grts, 4179
Rutter's Children's Charities Grants, 4181
RWJF Jobs to Careers: Promoting Work-Based Learning for Quality Care, 4185
RWJF Partners Investing in Nursing's Future, 4188
Ryder System Charitable Fnd Grants, 4191
S. D. Bechtel, Jr. Fnd / Stephen Bechtel Fund Environmental Educ Grants, 4192
S.H. Cowell Fnd Grants, 4199
S. Mark Taper Fnd Grants, 4201
S. Spencer Scott Fund Grants, 4202

Safeco Insurance Comm Grants, 4203
Sage Fnd Grants, 4204
Saginaw Comm Fdn Discretionary Grts, 4205
Saigh Fnd Grants, 4210
Saint Paul Companies Fnd Grants, 4217
Saint Paul Fnd Grants, 4219
Salem Fnd Charitable Trust Grants, 4223
Salisbury Comm Fnd Grants, 4224
Salmon Fnd Grants, 4225
Samuel Huntington Public Service Award, 4232
Samueli Fnd Youth Services Grants, 4234
Samuel N. and Mary Castle Fnd Grants, 4236
Samuel S. Fels Fund Grants, 4238
Samuel S. Johnson Fnd Grants, 4239
San Antonio Area Fnd Grants, 4240
San Diego Fnd for Change Grants, 4247
San Diego HIV Funding Collaborative Grants, 4251
San Diego Women's Fnd Grants, 4252
SanDisk Corp Comm Sharing Pgm, 4253
Sandy Hill Fnd Grants, 4257
San Francisco Fnd Comm Health Grants, 4263
San Francisco Fnd Koshland Program Arts and Culture Mini-Grants, 4280
San Juan Island Comm Fnd Grants, 4283
Santa Barbara Fnd Towbes Fund for the Performing Arts Grants, 4288
Santa Fe Comm Fnd Seasonal Grants-Fall Cycle, 4290
Santa Fe Comm Fnd Seasonal Grants-Spring, 4291
Sapelo Fnd Environmental Protection Grts, 4293
Sarah Scaife Fnd Grants, 4295
Sara Lee Fnd Grants, 4296
Sarkeys Fnd Grants, 4297
Sartain Lanier Family Fnd Grants, 4298
SAS Institute Comm Relations Donations, 4300
Saucony Run for Good Fnd Grants, 4301
Schering-Plough Fnd Health Grants, 4304
Schlessman Family Fnd Grants, 4307
Scholastic Book Grants, 4308
Schramm Fnd Grants, 4310
Schumann Fund for New Jersey Grants, 4311
Scott B & Annie P Appleby Char Trust Grts, 4313
Scott County Comm Fnd Grants, 4314
Scotts Company Give Back to Grow Awards, 4315
Seabury Fnd Grants, 4316
Seagate Tech Corp Capacity to Care Grants, 4317
Seattle Fnd Annual Neighborhoods Grants, 4319
Seattle Fnd Arts and Culture Grants, 4320
Seattle Fnd Benjamin N. Phillips Grants, 4322
Seattle Fdn C Keith Birkenfeld Mem Tr Grts, 4323
Seattle Fnd Economy Grants, 4325
Seattle Fnd Educ Grants, 4326
Seattle Fnd Environment Grants, 4327
Seattle Fnd Neighbor to Neighbor Small Grts, 4330
Seaver Institute Grants, 4331
Selby and Richard McRae Fnd Grants, 4334
Self Fnd Grants, 4335
Seneca Foods Fnd Grants, 4336
Sensient Technologies Fnd Grants, 4337
Shastri Indo-Canadian Institute Action Research Project Grants, 4341
Shaw's Supermarkets Donations, 4342
Shell Oil Company Fnd Grants, 4343
Sheltering Arms Fund Grants, 4344
Shopko Fdn Comm Charitable Grts, 4346
Shopko Fnd Green Bay Area Comm Grants, 4347
Sidgmore Family Fnd Grants, 4348
Sidney Stern Memorial Trust Grants, 4349
Sid W. Richardson Fnd Grants, 4350
Siebert Lutheran Fnd Grants, 4351
Sierra Fund Grants, 4352
Sierra Health Fnd Responsive Grants, 4353
Silicon Valley Comm Fnd Educ Grants, 4356
Simmons Fnd Grants, 4360
Simpson Lumber Charitable Contributions, 4362
Singing for Change Fnd Grants, 4363
Sioux Falls Area Comm Fnd Comm Fund Grants, 4364
Sioux Falls Area Comm Fnd Field-of-Interest and Donor-Advised Grants, 4365
Sioux Falls Area Comm Fnd Spot Grants, 4366
Siragusa Fnd Arts & Culture Grants, 4367

Educational Programs — Program Type Index

Siragusa Fnd Human Services Grants, 4369
Sir Dorabji Tata Trust Grants for NGOs or Voluntary Organizations, 4370
Sister Fund Grants for Women's Organizations, 4371
Sisters of Charity Fnd of Canton Grants, 4372
Sisters of Charity Cleveland Reducing Health & Educational Disparities Grants, 4374
Sisters of Mercy of North Carolina Fdn Grts, 4375
Sisters of St Joseph Healthcare Fdn Grts, 4377
Skaggs Fnd Grants, 4378
Skillman Fnd Comm Connections Small Grants, 4379
Skillman Fdn Good Opportunities Grts, 4381
Skillman Fnd Good Schools Grants, 4382
Skoll Fdn Awds for Social Entrepreneurship, 4383
Slow Food in Schools Micro-Grants, 4384
Snee Reinhardt Charitable Fnd Grants, 4387
SOBP A.E. Bennett Research Award, 4388
Sobrato Family Fnd Grants, 4389
Sobrato Family Fdn Meeting Space Grts, 4390
Sobrato Family Fnd Office Space Grants, 4391
Social Justice Fund NW Criminal Justice Grants, 4394
Social Justice Fund NW Economic Justice Giving Project Grants, 4395
Social Justice Fund NW Environmental Justice Giving Project Grants, 4396
Social Justice Fund NW General Grants, 4397
Social Justice Fund NW LGBTQ Giving Grants, 4398
Social Justice Fund NW Montana Giving Grants, 4399
Sodexo Fdn STOP Hunger Scholarships, 4400
Solutia Fund Grants, 4402
Sonoco Fnd Grants, 4403
Sonora Area Fnd Competitive Grants, 4404
Sony Corp of America Corp Philant Grants, 4405
Sorenson Legacy Fnd Grants, 4407
Sosland Fnd Grants, 4408
Southbury Comm Trust Fund, 4409
South Carolina Arts Commission AIE Residency Plus Individual Site Grants, 4411
South Carolina Arts Commission AIE Residency Plus Multi-Site Grants, 4412
South Carolina Arts Commission American Masterpieces in South Carolina Grants, 4413
South Carolina Arts Commission Annual Operating Support for Organizations Grants, 4414
South Carolina Arts Commission Arts in Educ After School Arts Initiative Grants, 4418
South Carolina Arts Commission Long Term Operating Support for Organizations Grants, 4424
Southern Calif Edison Environmental Grts, 4429
Southern California Edison Public Safety and Preparedness Grants, 4430
Southern Minnesota Initiative BookStart Grants, 4432
Southern Minnesota Fnd Home Visiting Grants, 4434
Southern Minnesota Initiative Fnd Youth Explorer Grants, 4436
South Madison Comm Fnd Grants, 4440
Southwest Florida Comm Competitive Grants, 4442
Southwest Florida Comm Fnd Undergraduate and Graduate Scholarships, 4444
Southwire Company Grants, 4447
Special Olympics Project UNIFY Grants, 4449
Speer Trust Grants, 4450
Spencer Cty Comm Fnd Grants, 4451
Sport Manitoba Athlete/Team Travel Assistance Grants, 4452
Sport Manitoba Athlete Skill Dev Clinics Grants, 4453
Sport Manitoba Bingo Allocations Grants, 4454
Sport Manitoba Coaches/Officials Travel Assistance Grants, 4455
Sport Manitoba Hosting Regional Championships Grants, 4456
Sport Manitoba Intro of a New Sport Grts, 4457
Sport Manitoba Sport Special Initiatives Grants, 4459
Springs Close Fnd Grants, 4462
Sprint Fnd Grants, 4463
Square D Fnd Grants, 4464
St. Joseph Comm Health Cath Kasper Award, 4468
St. Louis-Jefferson Solid Waste Management Waste Reduction and Recycling Grants, 4470
Stackpole-Hall Fnd Grants, 4472

Stanley Smith Horticultural Trust Grants, 4474
Staples Fnd for Learning Grants, 4475
Stark Comm Fdn Women's Fund Grants, 4481
State Farm Companies Safe Neighbors Grants, 4484
State Farm Companies Strong Neighborhoods, 4485
State Farm Fnd Grants, 4486
State Farm Project Ignition Grants, 4487
State Justice Institute Curriculum Adaptation and Training Grants, 4488
State Justice Institute Project Grants, 4490
State Justice Institute Scholarships, 4491
State Justice Institute Strategic Initiative Grants, 4492
State Street Fnd Grants, 4495
Staunton Farm Fnd Grants, 4496
Steelcase Fnd Grants, 4497
Steele-Reese Fnd Grants, 4498
Sterling-Turner Charitable Fnd Grants, 4499
Steuben County Comm Fnd Grants, 4501
Steven B. Achelis Fnd Grants, 4502
Steve Young Family Fnd Grants, 4503
Stewart Huston Charitable Trust Grants, 4505
Stinson Fnd Grants, 4506
Stocker Fnd Grants, 4507
Stockton Rush Bartol Fnd Grants, 4508
Stowe Family Fnd Grants, 4510
Strake Fnd Grants, 4511
Stranahan Fnd Grants, 4512
Strengthening Families - Strengthening Communities Grants, 4513
Strolling of the Heifers Schlrsps for Farmers, 4514
Strowd Roses Grants, 4515
Stuart Fnd Grants, 4516
Subaru Adopt a School Garden Grants, 4517
Subaru of America Fnd Grants, 4518
Subaru of Indiana Automotive Fdn Grts, 4519
Sulzberger Fnd Grants, 4522
Summit Fnd Grants, 4524
Sun Academic Excellence Grants, 4525
Sunbeam Products Grants, 4526
Sunderland Fnd Grants, 4527
Sunny and Abe Rosenberg Fnd Grants, 4529
Sunoco Fnd Grants, 4530
Susan Mott Webb Charitable Trust Grants, 4536
Susan Vaughan Fnd Grants, 4537
SVP Early Childhood Dev and Parenting Grants, 4538
Symantec Comm Relations and Corporate Philanthropy Grants, 4544
T. James Kavanagh Fnd Grants, 4545
T.L.L. Temple Fnd Grants, 4546
T. Rowe Price Associates Fnd Grants, 4548
TAC Arts Educ Comm-Learning Grts, 4552
TAC Arts Educ Mini Grants, 4553
Talbert and Leota Abrams Fnd, 4558
Tanner Humanities Cntr Rsch Fellowships, 4559
Taproot Fnd Capacity-Building Service Grants, 4560
Target Corporation Local Store Grants, 4561
Tauck Family Fnd Grants, 4563
Taylor S. Abernathy and Patti Harding Abernathy Charitable Trust Grants, 4564
TCF Bank Fnd Grants, 4565
TD4HIM Fnd Grants, 4566
Teaching Tolerance Grants, 4567
Teagle Fnd Grants, 4569
Tech Enhancement Certification for Hoosiers, 4571
TE Fnd Grants, 4572
Telluride Fnd Comm Grants, 4573
Telluride Fdn Emergency/Out of Cycle Grts, 4574
Telluride Fdn Tech Assistance Grts, 4575
Temple-Inland Fnd Grants, 4576
Temple Univ George D McDowell Fellowship, 4577
Tension Envelope Fnd Grants, 4578
Texas Comm on the Arts Educ Project 1 Grants, 4579
Texas Comsn on the Arts Arts in Educ Team Building/Texas Music Project Grants, 4580
Texas Cmsn on the Arts Arts Respond Prj Grts, 4581
Texas Comsn on the Arts Young Masters Grants, 4594
Textron Corporate Contributions Grants, 4601
Thelma Braun and Bocklett Family Fnd Grants, 4603
Theodore Edson Parker Fnd Grants, 4605
Third Millennium Fnd Grants, 4607

Thomas & Dorothy Leavey Fdn Grants, 4612
Thomas Austin Finch, Sr. Fnd Grants, 4613
Thomas B & Elizabeth M Sheridan Fdn Grts, 4614
Thomas C. Ackerman Fnd Grants, 4615
Thomas J. Atkins Memorial Trust Fund Grants, 4617
Thomas J. Long Fnd Comm Grants, 4618
Thomas Sill Fnd Grants, 4619
Thomas Thompson Trust Grants, 4620
Thomas W. Briggs Fnd Grants, 4621
Thompson Charitable Fnd Grants, 4622
Thompson Fnd Grants, 4623
Thornton Fnd Grants, 4624
Threshold Fnd Election Integrity Grants, 4625
Threshold Fdn Justice & Democracy Grts, 4626
Thrivent Financial for Lutherans Fdn Grts, 4629
Tifa Fnd Grants, 4633
Tiger Woods Fnd Grants, 4634
Time Warner Diverse Voices in the Arts Grants, 4635
Time Warner Yth Media & Creative Arts Grts, 4636
TJX Fnd Grants, 4637
Toby Wells Fnd Grants, 4638
Todd Brock Family Fnd Grants, 4639
Tom's of Maine Grants, 4640
Topeka Comm Fnd Grants, 4644
Topeka West Rotary Youth Enrichment Grants, 4645
Toro Fnd Grants, 4647
Toyota Motor Engineering & Manufacturing North America Grants, 4651
Toyota Motor Mfg of Alabama Grts, 4652
Toyota Motor Manufacturing of Indiana Grants, 4653
Toyota Motor Mfg of Kentucky Grts, 4654
Toyota Motor Mfg of Mississippi Grts, 4655
Toyota Motor Manufacturing of Texas Grants, 4656
Toyota Motor Manuf of West Virginia Grants, 4657
Toyota Motor North America of NY Grts, 4658
Toyota Motor Sales, USA Grants, 4659
Toyota Tech Center Grants, 4660
Toyota USA Fnd Safety Grants, 4662
TRDRP Participatory Research Awards, 4663
Tri-State Comm Twenty-first Century Endowment Fund Grants, 4666
Triangle Comm Fdn Donor-Advised Grts, 4668
Trinity Fnd Grants, 4669
Trull Fnd Grants, 4673
Tulane University Comm Service Scholars, 4677
Tulane University Public Service Fellows, 4678
Tull Charitable Fnd Grants, 4679
Turner B. Bunn, Jr. & Catherine E. Bunn Grants, 4680
Turner Fnd Grants, 4681
Turner Voices Corporate Contributions, 4682
TWS Fnd Grants, 4683
U.S. Bank Fnd Grants, 4686
US Dept of Educ 21st Century Comm Learning Centers, 4687
US Dept of Educ Cntrs for Independent Lvng, 4688
US Dept of Educ Child Care Access Means Parents in School Grants, 4689
US Dept of Educ Disability and Rehabilitation Research and Related Projects, 4690
US Dept of Educ Early Reading First Grants, 4691
US Dept of Educ Innovative Strategies in Comm Colleges for Working Adults and Displaced Workers Grants, 4692
US Dept of Educ Migrant and Seasonal Farmworkers Grants, 4693
US Dept of Educ Native Hawaiian Educ Grts, 4694
US Dept of Educ Parent Info & Trng, 4695
US Dept of Educ Pgms for Native Hawaiians, 4696
US Dept of Educ Promoting Postbac Opportunities for Hispanic Americans Grts, 4697
US Dept of Educ Rehabilitation Engineering Research Centers Grants, 4698
US Dept of Educ Rehab Research Training Centers, 4699
US Dept of Educ Rehabilitation Continuing Educ Programs --Institute on Rehabilitation Issues, 4700
US Dept of Educ Special Education--National Activities--Parent Information Centers, 4701
US Dept of Educ Voc Rehab Svcs Projects for American Indians with Disabilities Grts, 4702
UniBank 911 Emergency Personnel Educ Fund, 4707

PROGRAM TYPE INDEX

Educational Programs / 1079

Union Bank, N.A. Corporate Sponsorships and Donations, 4708
Union Bank, N.A. Fnd Grants, 4709
Union Benevolent Association Grants, 4710
Union County Comm Fnd Grants, 4711
Union County Fnd Grants, 4712
Union Square Arts Award, 4716
Union Square Award for Social Justice, 4717
United Methodist Committee on Relief Global AIDS Fund Grants, 4719
United Methodist Hlth Mnstry Fund Grts, 4722
United States Institute of Peace - National Peace Essay Contest for High School Students, 4724
United Technologies Corporation Grants, 4725
Unity Fnd Of LaPorte County Grants, 4726
UPS Corporate Giving Grants, 4727
UPS Fnd Comm Safety Grants, 4728
UPS Fnd Economic and Global Lit Grants, 4730
UPS Fdn Enviro Sustainability Grts, 4731
Ursula Thrush Peace Seed Grants, 4733
USAA – Ann Hoyt / Jim Easton JOAD Grants, 4734
USAID/Cambodia Maternal and Child Health, Tuberculosis, HIV/AIDS. and Malaria Grants, 4736
USAID African Institutions Innovation Mechanism Grants, 4738
USAID Civil Society Sustainability Project Grants in Bosnia and Herzegovina, 4744
USAID Dev Assistance Fund Grants, 4748
USAID Economic Prospectsfor Armenia-Turkey Normalization Grants, 4750
USAID Family Health Plus Project Grants, 4751
USAID Global Dev Alliance Grants, 4753
USAID HIV Prevention with Key Populations - Mali Grants, 4757
USAID Implementation Science for Strengthening Use of Evidence in Family Planning/Reproductive Health Programming Grants, 4758
USAID In-Support for Teacher Educ Program (In-STEP) Grants, 4759
USAID India-Africa Agriculture Innovation Bridge Grants, 4760
USAID India Partnership Grants, 4761
USAID Malawi Local Capacity Dev Grants, 4767
USAID Media and Elections Program in Rwanda Grants, 4768
USAID NGO Health Service Delivery Grants, 4771
USAID Palestinian Comm Astnc Grts, 4773
USAID Public-Private Alliance Proposals in Burma, Thailand, and Vietnam, 4775
USAID Reading Enhancement for Advancing Dev Grants, 4778
USAID Scholarships for Youth and Teachers, 4780
USAID Service Delivery & Support for Families Caring for Orphans & Vulnerable Children Grants, 4781
USAID Strengthening RMNCH Through Indian Health Professional Associations and Scaling Up Uptake Grants, 4784
USAID Unsolicited Proposal Grants, 4786
USAID Workforce Dev in Mexico Grants, 4787
US Airways Comm Contributions, 4788
US Airways Comm Fnd Grants, 4789
US Airways Educ Fnd Grants, 4790
USA Volleyball Fnd Educational Grants, 4791
USBC Earl Anthony Memorial Scholarships, 4793
USDA 1890 Land Grant Colleges and Universities Initiative Grants, 4797
USDA Agricultural and Rural Economic Grants, 4798
USDA Delta Health Care Services Grants, 4804
USDA Distance Lrng & Telemedicine Grts, 4806
USDA Hispanic-Serving Institutions Grants, 4813
USDA Housing Application Packaging Grants, 4815
USDA Rural Business Enterprise Grants, 4823
USDA Rural Microentrepreneur Astnc Grts, 4832
USDA Value-Added Producer Grants, 4843
USDC Advanced Manufacturing Jobs and Innovation Accelerator Challenge Grants, 4848
USDC i6 Challenge Grants, 4851
USDC State Broadband Initiative Grants, 4857
USDC Tech Opportunities Pgm Grts, 4860
USFA Dev Grants, 4866

USFA Equipment Subsidy Grants, 4867
USGA Fdn for the Good of the Game Grts, 4868
USG Fnd Grants, 4869
US Soccer Fdn Annual Pgm & Field Grts, 4870
US Soccer Fnd Planning Grants, 4871
USTA Okechi Womeodu Scholar Athlete Grts, 4880
USTA Public Facility Assistance Grants, 4883
USTA Serves College Educ Scholarships, 4885
USTA Serves College Textbook Scholarships, 4886
USTA Serves Dwight F. Davis Scholarships, 4887
USTA Serves Dwight Mosley Scholarships, 4888
USTA Serves Eve Kraft Scholarships, 4889
USTA Serves Marian Wood Baird Scholarship, 4890
USTA Tennis Block Party Grants, 4892
V.V. Cooke Fnd Grants, 4896
Valerie Adams Mem Char Trust Grts, 4898
Vancouver Fnd Grants and Comm Initiatives, 4900
Vanderburgh Comm Fnd Grants, 4902
Vanderburgh Comm Fdn Women's Fund, 4903
Van Kampen Boyer Molinari Char Fdn Grts, 4905
Vectren Fnd Grants, 4907
Verizon Fnd Connecticut Grants, 4908
Verizon Fnd Delaware Grants, 4909
Verizon Fnd Domestic Violence Prevention, 4910
Verizon Fnd Grants, 4911
Verizon Fnd Great Lakes Region Grants, 4912
Verizon Fnd Internet Safety Grants, 4914
Verizon Fnd Lit Grants, 4915
Verizon Fnd Maine Grants, 4916
Verizon Fnd Maryland Grants, 4917
Verizon Fnd New Jersey Check into Lit Grants, 4918
Verizon Fnd New York Grants, 4919
Verizon Fnd NE Region Grants, 4920
Verizon Fnd Pennsylvania Grants, 4921
Verizon Fnd SE Region Grants, 4923
Verizon Fnd Vermont Grants, 4924
Verizon Fnd Virginia Grants, 4925
Vermont Comm Fnd Grants, 4929
Viacom Fnd Grants (Formerly CBS Fnd), 4932
Victor E. Speas Fnd Grants, 4933
Vigneron Grants, 4938
Viking Children's Fund Grants, 4939
Virginia Commission for the Arts Artists in Educ Residency Grants, 4941
Virginia Comsn for the Arts Proj Grts, 4944
Virginia Fnd for Humanities Discretionary Grants, 4946
Virginia Fdn for the Humanities Open Grants, 4947
Virginia Fnd for the Humanities Fellowships, 4948
Virginia Historical Society Rsch Fwsps, 4949
Virginia W. Kettering Fnd Grants, 4950
Visiting Nurse Fnd Grants, 4951
Volvo Adventure Environmental Awards, 4952
VSA/Metlife Connect All Grants, 4953
VSA/Volkswagen Grp of America Exhib Awds, 4954
VSA Int'l Art Program for Children with Disabilities Grants, 4955
Vulcan Materials Company Fnd Grants, 4956
W.C. Griffith Fnd Grants, 4957
WH & Mary Ellen Cobb Char Trust Grts, 4959
WK Kellogg Fdn Healthy Kids Grants, 4961
WK Kellogg Fdn Racial Equity Grants, 4962
WK Kellogg Fdn Secure Families Grants, 4963
WM Keck Fdn Southern California Grts, 4964
W.P. and Bulah Luse Fnd Grants, 4965
W Paul & Lucille Caudill Little Fdn Grants, 4966
Wabash River Heritage Corridor Fund Grants, 4970
Wabash Valley Comm Fnd Grants, 4971
Wallace Fnd Grants, 4976
Walmart Fnd Facility Giving Grants, 4978
Walmart Fnd National Giving Grants, 4979
Walmart Fnd State Giving Grants, 4980
Walt Disney Company Fnd Grants, 4981
Walter and Elise Haas Fund Grants, 4982
Walter L. Gross III Family Fnd Grants, 4983
Walton Family Fdn Home Region Grts, 4984
Warrick Cty Comm Fnd Grants, 4987
Washington Area Women's Fnd African American Women's Giving Circle Grants, 4989
Washington Area Women's Fnd Early Care and Educ Funders Collaborative Grants, 4990

Washington Area Women's Fnd Financial Educ and Wealth Creation Fund Grants, 4991
Washington Area Women's Fnd Open Door Capacity Fund Grants, 4994
Washington Area Women's Fnd Rainmakers Giving Circle Grants, 4995
Washington Cty Comm Fdn Grts, 4997
Washington Cty Comm Fdn Youth Grts, 4998
Washington Gas Char Gvg Contributions, 5000
Waste Management Charitable Giving Grants, 5001
Water and Land Stewardship Fund Grants, 5002
Wayne and Gladys Valley Fnd Grants, 5003
Wayne County Fnd - Vigran Family Fnd Grants, 5004
Wayne County Fnd Grants, 5005
WCI Comm Leadership Fellowships, 5008
Weatherwax Fnd Grants, 5014
Weaver Fnd Grants, 5015
Weaver Popcorn Fnd Grants, 5016
Weingart Fnd Grants, 5018
Welborn Baptist Fnd Gen Opportunity Grants, 5020
Wells County Fnd Grants, 5022
Western Indiana Comm Fdn Grts, 5024
Western New York Fnd Grants, 5025
Western Pennsylvania Environmental Awards, 5026
Westinghouse Charitable Giving Grants, 5028
West Virginia Commission on Arts Visit Grants, 5030
West Virginia Commission on the Arts Long-Term Artist Residencies, 5037
West Virginia Commission on the Arts Special Projects Grants, 5048
Weyerhaeuser Company Fnd Grants, 5053
Weyerhaeuser Family Fnd Environment, Conservation and Preservation Grants, 5054
White County Comm Fnd Grants, 5057
Whitney Fnd Grants, 5061
WHO Fnd Education/Lit Grants, 5062
WHO Fnd General Grants, 5063
Widgeon Point Charitable Fnd Grants, 5064
Wieboldt Fnd Grants, 5065
Wilbur & Patsy Bradley Family Fdn Grts, 5066
WILD Fnd Grants, 5068
Willary Fnd Grants, 5071
William A. Badger Fnd Grants, 5072
William B. Stokely Jr. Fnd Grants, 5076
William Bingham Fnd Grants, 5077
William Blair and Company Fnd Grants, 5078
William G & Helen C Hoffman Fdn Grants, 5080
William G. Baker, Jr. Grants, 5081
William G. Gilmore Fnd Grants, 5082
William G. McGowan Charitable Fund Grants, 5084
William G Selby & Marie Selby Fdn Grts, 5085
William H. Hannon Fnd Grants, 5086
William J. and Dorothy K. O'Neill Fnd Grants, 5087
William J. Brace Charitable Trust, 5088
William L. and Victorine Q. Adams Fnd Grants, 5089
William M. Cage Library Trust Grants, 5090
William McCaskey Chapman and Adaline Dinsmore Chapman Fnd Grants, 5092
William T. Grant Youth Service Grants, 5096
Wilson-Wood Fnd Grants, 5098
Windgate Charitable Fnd Grants, 5099
Windward Youth Leadership Fund Grants, 5100
Winifred & Harry B. Allen Fnd Grants, 5101
Winston-Salem Fdn Competitive Grts, 5102
Winston-Salem Fdn Elkin/Tri-County Grants, 5103
Winston-Salem Fdn Stokes County Grants, 5104
Winthrop Rockefeller Fnd Grants, 5105
Wisconsin Energy Fnd Grants, 5106
Wolf Aviation Fund Grants, 5109
Wolfe Associates Grants, 5110
Women's Fdn Greater Kansas City Grts, 5111
Women's Funding Alliance Grants, 5112
Wood-Claeyssens Fnd Grants, 5113
Woods Charitable Fund Grants, 5114
Woodward Fund Grants, 5116
World Bank JJ/WBGSP Partners Programs, 5117
Xcel Energy Fnd Grants, 5121
Xerox Fnd Grants, 5122
Yampa Valley Comm Fnd Erickson Business Week Scholarships, 5123

1080 / Educational Programs

Yampa Valley Comm Fnd Grants, 5124
Yawkey Fnd Grants, 5125
Yellow Corporate Fnd Grants, 5126
Young Family Fnd Grants, 5127
Youth Action Net Fellowships, 5128
Youth As Resources Grants, 5130
Youth Philanthropy Project, 5132
YSA ABC Summer of Service Awards, 5133
YSA Get Ur Good On Grants, 5134
YSA MLK Day Lead Organizer Grants, 5136
YSA National Child Awareness Month Youth Ambassador Grants, 5137
YSA NEA Youth Leaders for Lit Grants, 5138
YSA Sodexo Lead Organizer Grants, 5140
YSA State Farm Good Neighbor YOUth In The Driver Seat Grants, 5141
YSA UnitedHealth HEROES Service-Learning, 5142
Z. Smith Reynolds Fnd Democracy and Civic Engagement Grants, 5145

Emergency Programs

2 Life 18 Fnd Grants, 5
Able Trust Vocational Rehabilitation Grants for Individuals, 104
Abundance Fnd Int'l Grants, 108
ACF ACYF Runaway and Homeless Youth Basic Center Grants, 112
ACFEF Disaster Relief Fund Member Assistance, 117
Actors Fund Dancers' Resource, 137
Actors Fund Soc Svcs & Financial Assistance, 139
Acushnet Fnd Grants, 143
Adams Family Fnd of Tennessee Grants, 152
Adelaide Breed Bayrd Fnd Grants, 161
Adelaide Dawson Lynch Trust Grants, 163
Adler-Clark Electric Comm Commitment Grants, 164
AEGON Transamerica Fdn Disaster Rlf Grts, 178
AEGON Transamerica Health and Welfare Grants, 179
AGMA Relief Fund Grants, 201
Ahearn Family Fnd Grants, 206
Aid for Starving Children African American Independence Single Mother's Grants, 210
Aid for Starving Children Emergency Assistance Fund Grants, 211
Aid for Starving Children Int'l Grants, 212
AIG Disaster Relief Fund Grants, 213
Alcatel-Lucent Technologies Fnd Grants, 349
Alex Stern Family Fnd Grants, 360
Allan C. and Leila J. Garden Fnd Grants, 374
Alvah H & Wyline P Chapman Fdn Grts, 402
American Express Charitable Fund Grants, 429
American Express Fnd Comm Service Grants, 430
American Foodservice Charitable Trust Grants, 433
American for the Arts Emergency Relief Fund, 435
Amon G. Carter Fnd Grants, 458
Anheuser-Busch Fnd Grants, 470
Applied Materials Corp Philanthropy Pgm, 515
Arizona Fnd for Women General Grants, 544
Arizona Republic Fnd Grants, 546
Auburn Fnd Grants, 611
Austin S. Nelson Fnd Grants, 617
Avon Products Fnd Grants, 625
Banfield Charitable Trust Grants, 652
Bank of America Critical Needs Grants, 656
Bank of America Charitable Fnd Matching Gifts, 658
Bank of America Charitable Fnd Volunteer Grants, 660
Baton Rouge Area Every Kid a King Grants, 681
Baxter Int'l Corporate Giving Grants, 689
Bill and Melinda Gates Fnd Emergency Response Grants, 766
Blanche & Julian Robertson Family Fnd Grants, 785
Blowitz-Ridgeway Fnd Grants, 792
Blum-Kovler Fnd Grants, 803
Blumenthal Fnd Grants, 804
Boeing Company Contributions Grants, 809
Borkee-Hagley Fnd Grants, 817
Brooklyn Comty Fdn Caring Neighbors Grts, 848
Caesar Puff Fnd Grants, 890
Callaway Golf Company Fnd Grants, 910
Campbell Soup Fnd Grants, 916
Cargill Citizenship Fund-Corp Gvg Grants, 925

Carl R. Hendrickson Family Fnd Grants, 935
Carpenter Fnd Grants, 943
CDC Fdn Emergency Response Fund Grts, 972
CDC Fnd Global Disaster Response Fund Grants, 973
CE and S Fnd Grants, 985
Cemala Fnd Grants, 988
Central Okanagan Fnd Grants, 997
Charles H. Hall Fnd, 1044
Charles Nelson Robinson Fund Grants, 1052
Chicago Comm Trust Housing Grants: Preventing and Ending Homelessness, 1090
Children Affected by AIDS Fnd Family Assistance Emergency Fund Grants, 1107
Clara Blackford Smith and W. Aubrey Smith Charitable Fnd Grants, 1147
CNCS AmeriCorps Indian Tribes Plng Grts, 1180
CNCS AmeriCorps NCCC Project Grants, 1181
CNCS AmeriCorps State and National Grants, 1182
CNCS AmeriCorps VISTA Project Grants, 1184
Coastal Comm Fdn of SC Grants, 1193
Coca-Cola Fnd Grants, 1195
Cockrell Fnd Grants, 1196
Communities Fnd of Texas Grants, 1243
Comm Fdn for Monterey Cty Grants, 1255
Comm Fdn for Muskegon Cty Grants, 1256
Comm Fdn of Grtr Birmingham Grants, 1280
Comm Fnd of Greater Fort Wayne - Cmty Endwt & Clarke Endwt Grants, 1285
Comm Fnd of Mt Vernon & Knox County Grants, 1301
Comm Fdn of SE Connecticut Grants, 1309
Computer Associates Comm Grants, 1341
Connelly Fnd Grants, 1353
Cord Fnd Grants, 1372
Cornerstone Fdn of NE Wisconsin Grants, 1375
Coughlin-Saunders Fnd Grants, 1377
Covidien Medical Product Donations, 1390
Cruise Industry Charitable Fnd Grants, 1404
Cudd Fnd Grants, 1410
Cullen Fnd Grants, 1411
Dana Corporation Fnd Grants, 1440
Daywood Fnd Grants, 1465
DB Americas Fnd Grants, 1466
Dearborn Comm Fnd City of Aurora Grants, 1470
DeKalb County Immediate Response Grant, 1479
Dermody Properties Fdn Capstone Awd, 1516
DFN Hurricane Katrina and Disability Rapid Response Grants, 1522
Diageo Fnd Grants, 1546
DIFFA/Chicago Grants, 1547
Dining for Women Grants, 1548
Dollar Energy Fund Grants, 1567
Dominion Fnd Human Needs Grants, 1572
Donald & Sylvia Robinson Family Fdn Grants, 1573
Donnie Avery Catches for Kids Fnd, 1578
Doree Taylor Charitable Fnd, 1580
Doris and Victor Day Fnd Grants, 1582
Dr. and Mrs. Paul Pierce Memorial Fnd Grants, 1599
Drs. Bruce and Lee Fnd Grants, 1607
Dyson Fnd Emergency Fund Grants, 1631
Edward & Ellen Roche Relief Fdn Grants, 1663
Edyth Bush Charitable Fnd Grants, 1673
Emma J. Adams Grants, 1702
Erie Comm Fnd Grants, 1750
Essex County Comm Fnd Emergency Grants, 1753
Ethel Frends Fnd Grants, 1759
FAR Fund Grants, 1787
Farm Aid Grants, 1790
Fifth Third Bank Corporate Giving, 1809
Finish Line Youth Fnd Founder's Grants, 1812
Flextronics Fnd Disaster Relief Grants, 1841
Florida Division of Cultural Affairs Comm Theatre Grants, 1847
Florida Sea Turtle Grants, 1871
Ford Family Fdn Grts-Critical Needs, 1879
Fnds of E Chgo Fin Independence Grts, 1909
Fnds of E Chgo Public Sfty Grts, 1911
Frank B. Hazard General Charity Fund Grants, 1926
Franklin H. Wells and Ruth L. Wells Fnd Grants, 1930
Frank Stanley Beveridge Fnd Grants, 1936
Fred L. Emerson Fnd Grants, 1949

PROGRAM TYPE INDEX

Fremont Area Comm Fnd Grants, 1955
Gene Haas Fnd, 1999
George B. Page Fnd Grants, 2013
George H.C. Ensworth Grants, 2022
Georgia-Pacific Fnd Enrichment Grants, 2032
Gill Fnd Gay & Lesbian Fund, 2054
GNOF Albert N & Hattie M McClure Grts, 2068
GNOF Bayou Communities Grants, 2069
GNOF Gulf Coast Oil Spill Grants, 2077
GNOF IMPACT Grants for Health and Human Services, 2080
GNOF IMPACT Harold W. Newman, Jr. Charitable Trust Grants, 2083
GNOF Maison Hospitaliere Grants, 2086
GNOF Plaquemines Comm Grants, 2091
Grace Bersted Fnd Grants, 2110
Green Fnd Human Services Grants, 2154
Green Fnd Special Project Grants, 2155
Gulf Coast Comm Fnd Grants, 2174
Gulf Coast Fdn of Comm Operating Grts, 2176
Gulf Coast Fdn of Comm Grants, 2177
H.J. Heinz Company Fnd Grants, 2184
Hahl Proctor Charitable Trust Grants, 2208
Hall Family Fnd Grants, 2210
Harold & Arlene Schnitzer CARE Fdn Grts, 2226
Harold Brooks Fnd Grants, 2227
Harrison County Comm Fnd Signature Grants, 2234
Haymarket Urgent Response Grants, 2268
Hearst Fnds Social Service Grants, 2285
Helen V. Brach Fnd Grants, 2300
Henrietta Tower Wurts Memorial Fnd Grants, 2304
Herbert A & Adrian W Woods Fdn Grts, 2313
High Meadow Fnd Grants, 2321
Hillcrest Fnd Grants, 2325
Hoglund Fnd Grants, 2344
Home Building Industry Disaster Relief Fund, 2348
Homer Fnd Grants, 2352
Honeywell Corp Family Safety & Security Grts, 2356
Honeywell Corp Humanitarian Relief Grts, 2358
Horace Moses Charitable Fnd Grants, 2363
Humana Fnd Grants, 2388
Hundred Club of Colorado Springs Grants, 2391
IAFF Labour College of Canada Residential Scholarship, 2418
IAFF National Labor College Scholarships, 2419
IAFF W. H. McClennan Scholarship, 2420
IDPH Local Health Dept Public Health Emergency Response Grants, 2442
Illinois DNR Volunteer Fire Assistance Grants, 2504
Indiana AIDS Fund Grants, 2529
J. Jill Compassion Fund Grants, 2598
James & Abigail Campbell Fam Fdn Grts, 2620
James Graham Brown Fdn Qlty of Life Grts, 2625
James R. Thorpe Fnd Grants, 2636
Jane's Trust Grants, 2639
Jim Blevins Fnd Grants, 2678
John Deere Fnd Grants, 2692
John G. Duncan Trust Grants, 2695
John I. Smith Charities Grants, 2700
John Jewett & Helen Chandler Garland Fdn, 2702
John P. McGovern Fnd Grants, 2707
Johns Manville Fund Grants, 2716
John W & Anna H Hanes Fdn Grants, 2728
John W. Boynton Fund Grants, 2730
John W. Speas and Effie E. Speas Grants, 2732
Josephine G. Russell Trust Grants, 2737
Joseph S. Stackpole Charitable Trust Grants, 2741
Josiah W & Bessie H Kline Fdn Grants, 2742
Judith Clark-Morrill Fnd Grants, 2756
Kalamazoo Individuals and Families Grants, 2769
Kessler Fdn Hurricane Sandy Emergency Grts, 2815
Kroger Fdn Grassroots Comty Support Grants, 2843
Lena Benas Grants, 2881
Louis and Elizabeth Nave Flarsheim Grants, 2924
Lucy Downing Nisbet Charitable Fund Grants, 2935
Lydia deForest Charitable Trust Grants, 2946
Marion and Miriam Rose Fund Grants, 3015
Marion I & Henry J Knott Fdn Discret Grants, 3018
Marion Isabell Coe Fund Grants, 3020
Marriott Int'l Corporate Giving Grts, 3024

PROGRAM TYPE INDEX

McCune Fnd Human Services Grants, 3080
Merkel Fnd Grants, 3124
Mertz Gilmore Fnd NYC Communities Grants, 3126
Meyer Fnd Economic Security Grants, 3141
Meyer Fdn Healthy Communities Grts, 3143
Meyer Memorial Trust Emergency Grants, 3146
Middlesex Savings Charitable Comm Dev Grants, 3173
Modest Needs Bridge Grants, 3197
Modest Needs Hurcn Sandy Rlf Grts: Phs 2, 3198
Modest Needs New Employment Grants, 3199
Modest Needs Self-Sufficiency Grants, 3201
Montana Comm Fnd Big Sky LIFT Grants, 3210
Morris & Gwendolyn Cafritz Fdn Grants, 3218
Nathaniel & Elizabeth P Stevens Fdn Grants, 3247
Nationwide Insurance Fnd Grants, 3285
New Jersey Office of Faith Based Initiatives Service to Seniors Grants, 3333
Nordson Corporation Fnd Grants, 3462
NW Airlines KidCares Medical Travel Assistance, 3508
NW Mutual Fnd Grants, 3509
Oak Fdn Housing & Homelessness Grts, 3633
Office Depot Fnd Disaster Relief Grants, 3640
Oleonda Jameson Trust Grants, 3667
Olga Sipolin Children's Fund Grants, 3668
Oppenstein Brothers Fnd Grants, 3685
Packard Fnd Local Grants, 3729
Patrick and Aimee Butler Family Fnd Comm Human Services Grants, 3749
Perkins-Ponder Fnd Grants, 3822
PG&E Comm Vitality Grants, 3868
Piedmont Natural Gas Fnd Health and Human Services Grants, 3885
Pinkerton Fnd Grants, 3892
PMI Fnd Grants, 3918
Pohlad Family Fnd, 3928
Porter County Emergency Grants, 3932
Prince Char Trusts Dist of Columbia Grts, 3960
Public Welfare Fnd Grants, 3984
Puerto Rico Comm Fnd Grants, 3986
R.S. Gernon Trust Grants, 4002
RCF Individual Assistance Grants, 4033
Reinberger Fnd Grants, 4052
RESIST Emergency Grants, 4056
Rhode Island Fnd Grants, 4073
Richard and Rhoda Goldman Fund Grants, 4077
Robert R. Meyer Fnd Grants, 4121
Ross Fnd Grants, 4164
S. Livingston Mather Charitable Trust Grants, 4200
Safeco Insurance Comm Grants, 4203
SAG Motion Pic Plyrs Welfare Fund Grts, 4209
Saint Paul Fdn Comm Sharing Fund Grts, 4218
Salt River Health and Human Services Grants, 4228
Samuel S. Johnson Fnd Grants, 4239
Sands Fnd Crisis Fund Grants, 4254
San Francisco Fnd Disability Rights Advocate Fund Emergency Grants, 4265
Santa Fe Comm Special & Urgent Needs Grants, 4292
Sapelo Fnd Social Justice Grants, 4294
Seattle Fnd Basic Needs Grants, 4321
Seattle Fdn C Keith Birkenfeld Mem Tr Grts, 4323
Seattle Fnd Health and Wellness Grants, 4328
Seneca Foods Fnd Grants, 4336
Silicon Valley Comm Economic Security Grants, 4355
Sioux Falls Area Comm Fnd Comm Fund Grants, 4364
Sioux Falls Area Comm Fnd Field-of-Interest and Donor-Advised Grants, 4365
Sioux Falls Area Comm Fnd Spot Grants, 4366
Siragusa Fnd Human Services Grants, 4369
Sisters of Charity Fnd of Cleveland Good Samaritan Grants, 4373
Sobrato Family Fnd Grants, 4389
Sobrato Family Fdn Meeting Space Grts, 4390
Sobrato Family Fnd Office Space Grants, 4391
Sony Corp of America Corp Philant Grants, 4405
Southern Calif Edison Civic Affairs Grts, 4428
Southern California Edison Public Safety and Preparedness Grants, 4430
Southwest Florida Good Samaritan Grants, 4443
Sunoco Fnd Grants, 4530
Swindells Charitable Fnd, 4542

Sylvia Adams Charitable Trust Grants, 4543
Telluride Fdn Emergency/Out of Cycle Grts, 4574
Texas Cmsn on the Arts Arts Respond Prj Grts, 4581
Textron Corporate Contributions Grants, 4601
TJX Fnd Grants, 4637
Todd Brock Family Fnd Grants, 4639
Trinity Trust Comm Response Grants, 4671
UNESCO World Heritage Fund Grants, 4706
Union Bank, N.A. Corporate Sponsorships, 4708
Union Bank, N.A. Fnd Grants, 4709
Union Pacific Fdn Health & Human Svcs Grts, 4715
USAID Haiti Disaster Risk Reduction Capacity Building Grants, 4756
USAID Int'l Emergency Food Assistance Grants, 4763
USAID Rapid Response for Sudan Grants, 4776
USDA Child and Adult Care Food Program, 4800
USDA Emergency Comm Water Assistance, 4807
USDC Disaster Relief Opportunity Grants, 4850
USDC Supplemental Appropriations Disaster Relief Opportunity Grants, 4859
VHA Health Fnd Grants, 4931
Victor E. Speas Fnd Grants, 4933
WH & Mary Ellen Cobb Char Trust Grts, 4959
Washington Area Fuel Fund Grants, 4988
Washington Gas Char Gvg Contributions, 5000
Welborn Baptist Fnd Improvements to Comm Health Status Grants, 5021
William & Flora Hewlett Environmental Grants, 5074
William B. Stokely Jr. Fnd Grants, 5076

Endowments
Achelis Fnd Grants, 127
Adams Fnd Grants, 155
AHS Fnd Grants, 208
Alfred & Tillie Shemanski Testamentary Grants, 363
Alvah H & Wyline P Chapman Fdn Grts, 402
Blanche and Irving Laurie Fnd Grants, 784
Blandin Fnd Itasca County Area Vitality Grants, 789
Blum-Kovler Fnd Grants, 803
Blumenthal Fnd Grants, 804
Bodman Fnd Grants, 807
Bradley Family Fdn Grants, 830
Caesars Fnd Grants, 891
Countess Moira Charitable Fnd Grants, 1381
Cralle Fnd Grants, 1394
Doug and Carla Salmon Fnd Grants, 1594
Florida Div of Cultural Affairs Endowments, 1851
Gertrude M. Conduff Fnd Grants, 2047
GNOF Freeman Challenge Grants, 2075
Grover Hermann Fnd Grants, 2168
Hearst Fnds Culture Grants, 2284
J. Knox Gholston Fnd Grants, 2599
J.W. Kieckhefer Fnd Grants, 2607
Jane and Jack Fitzpatrick Fund Grants, 2640
Johnson Scholarship Fnd Grants, 2726
Kovler Family Fnd Grants, 2840
Lied Fnd Trust Grants, 2900
Margaret T. Morris Fnd Grants, 3005
McLean Contributionship Grants, 3088
Morris K. Udall and Stewart L. Udall Fnd Native American Congressional Internships, 3220
Norcliffe Fnd Grants, 3459
Paso del Norte Health Fnd Grants, 3743
Perkin Fund Grants, 3821
PMI Fnd Grants, 3918
Prudential Fnd Arts and Culture Grants, 3975
RCF The Women's Fund Grants, 4035
Reinberger Fnd Grants, 4052
Robert R. Meyer Fnd Grants, 4121
Roy & Christine Sturgis Charitable Trust Grts, 4166
Saigh Fnd Grants, 4210
Santa Barbara Fdn Monthly Express Grts, 4284
Sony Corp of America Corp Philant Grants, 4405
Textron Corporate Contributions Grants, 4601
Union Bank, N.A. Fnd Grants, 4709
W.P. and Bulah Luse Fnd Grants, 4965
William Blair and Company Fnd Grants, 5078

Environmental Programs
3 Rivers Wet Weather Demonstration Grants, 9
3M Company Environmental Giving Grants, 13
3M Fnd Comm Giving Grants, 15
1675 Fnd Grants, 35
1772 Fnd Fellowships, 36
AAAS Science and Tech Policy Fellowships: Energy, Environment, and Agriculture, 52
AAAS Science and Tech Policy Fellowships: Health, Educ and Human Services, 53
Abbot & Dorothy H Stevens Fdn Grants, 79
Abbott Fund Comm Grants, 81
Abelard Fnd East Grants, 87
Abelard Fnd West Grants, 88
Abel Fnd Grants, 90
Abell-Hanger Fnd Grants, 91
Abell Fnd Conservation and Environment Grants, 94
Access Fund Climbing Preservation Grants, 110
ACE Charitable Fnd Grants, 111
ACF Native American Environmental Regulatory Enhancement Grants, 122
ACF Native American Social and Economic Dev Strategies Grants, 123
A Charitable Fnd Grants, 126
Achelis Fnd Grants, 127
Acorn Fnd Grants, 131
ACTION Council of Monterey County Grants, 134
Adams Fnd Grants, 154
Administaff Comm Affairs Grants, 165
Adobe Comm Investment Grants, 168
AEP Corporate Giving Grants, 180
Agape Fnd for Nonviolent Social Change Board of Trustees Grants, 197
Aid for Starving Children Int'l Grants, 212
Air Products and Chemicals Grants, 216
Akonadi Fnd Anti-Racism Grants, 217
Alabama Power Plant a Tree Grants, 234
Alaska Airlines Corporate Giving Grants, 320
Alaska Airlines Fnd Grants, 321
Alaska Conservation Fnd Awards, 322
Alaska Conservation Fnd Operating Grants, 323
Alaska Conservation Fnd Opportunity Grants, 324
Alaska Conservation Fnd Rapid Response Grants, 325
Alaska Conservation Fnd Watchable Wildlife Conservation Trust Grants, 326
Albert and Bessie Mae Kronkosky Grants, 339
Alberto Culver Corporate Contributions Grants, 343
Albert Pick Jr. Fund Grants, 344
Albuquerque Comm Fnd Grants, 348
Alcoa Fnd Grants, 350
Alexander & Baldwin Fnd Hawaiian and Pacific Island Grants, 352
Alexander & Baldwin Fdn Mainland Grants, 353
Alexander H. Bright Charitable Trust Grants, 358
Alfred J Mcallister & Dorothy N Mcallister Grants, 367
Alfred P Sloan Fdn Civic Initiatives Grts, 368
Alfred P Sloan Fdn Selected Nat'l Issues Grts, 370
Allegan County Comm Fnd Grants, 375
Allen P & Josephine B Green Fdn Grts, 380
All for the Earth Fnd Grants, 381
Alliance for Comm Trees Home Depot Fnd NeighborWoods Grants, 382
Alliant Energy Fnd Comm Grants, 384
Allstate Corporate Giving Grants, 386
Allstate Corp Hometown Commitment Grants, 387
Alpine Winter Fnd Grants, 394
ALSAM Fnd Grants, 395
Altria Group Environment Grants, 400
Amador Comm Fnd Grants, 408
Ambrose and Ida Fredrickson Fnd Grants, 414
Ameren Corporation Comm Grants, 418
Americana Fnd Grants, 422
American Electric Power Grants, 428
American Express Historic Preservation Grants, 431
American Forests Global ReLeaf Grants, 434
American Gas Fnd Grants, 437
American Hiking Society National Trails Grants, 438
American Honda Fnd Grants, 439
American Rivers Comm-Based Restoration Program River Grants, 444

Environmental Programs

America the Beautiful Fund Operation Green Plant Grants, 451
AmerUs Group Charitable Fnd, 455
Amgen Fnd Grants, 456
Anderson Fnd Grants, 460
Andrew Family Fnd Grants, 462
Angels Baseball Fnd Grants, 465
Anheuser-Busch Fnd Grants, 470
Ann Arbor Area Comm Fnd Grants, 474
Anne L. and George H. Clapp Charitable and Educational Trust Grants, 476
Annie's Cases for Causes Product Donations, 479
Annie's Grants for Gardens, 480
Annie Sinclair Knudsen Memorial Fund/Kaua'i Comm Grants, 482
Ann L. and Carol Green Rhodes Grants, 483
Appalachian Reg'l Commission Energy Grts, 505
Applied Biosystems Grants, 514
APS Fnd Grants, 518
Arbor Day Fnd Grants, 524
Arcadia Fnd Grants, 525
Archer Daniels Midland Fnd Grants, 527
Arcus Fnd Fund Grants, 529
Arizona Public Service Corp Gvg Pgm Grts, 545
Arkansas Comm Fnd Grants, 561
A Rocha USA Grants, 566
Arthur Ashley Williams Fnd Grants, 572
Arthur B. Schultz Fnd Grants, 573
Ashland Corporate Contributions Grants, 587
As You Sow, 598
AT&T Fnd Civic and Comm Service Grants, 599
Atherton Family Fnd Grants, 604
Athwin Fnd Grants, 605
Atkinson Fnd Comm Grants, 606
Austin Comm Fnd Grants, 616
Autauga Area Comm Fnd Grants, 618
Autodesk Comm Relations Grants, 619
Autzen Fnd Grants, 622
Azadoutioun Fnd Grants, 631
Babcock Charitable Trust Grants, 632
Bacon Family Fnd Grants, 634
Baltimore Comm Fnd Children's Fresh Air Society Fund Grants, 642
Baltimore Comm Fnd Environment Path Grants, 643
Banfi Vintners Fnd Grants, 653
Bank of America Charitable Fnd Matching Gifts, 658
Bank of America Charitable Fnd Volunteer Grants, 660
Banrock Station Wines Wetlands Cons Grants, 662
Barker Welfare Fnd Grants, 669
Barra Fnd Comm Fund Grants, 673
Barrasso Usdin Kupperman Freeman and Sarver LLC Corporate Grants, 675
Barr Fnd Grants (Massachusetts), 676
Batchelor Fnd Grants, 679
Baton Rouge Area Fnd Grants, 682
Battle Creek Comm Fdn Mini-Grants, 685
Baxter Int'l Corporate Giving Grants, 689
Bay and Paul Fnds, Inc Grants, 692
Bay and Paul Fnds Grants, 693
Beazley Fnd Grants, 714
Beim Fnd Grants, 718
Beirne Carter Fnd Grants, 719
Beldon Fund Grants, 720
Belk Fnd Grants, 721
Bella Vista Fnd Grants, 722
Ben & Jerry's Fnd Grants, 724
Bender Fnd Grants, 726
Beneficia Fnd Grants, 727
Bennett Family Fnd of Texas Grants, 728
Benton Comm Fnd Grants, 730
Benton County Fnd Grants, 731
Benwood Fnd Focus Area Grants, 733
Berks County Comm Fnd Grants, 734
Bernard F & Alva B Gimbel Fdn Grts, 740
Bikes Belong Fnd REI Grants, 761
Bikes Belong Fnd Research Grants, 762
Bikes Belong Grants, 763
Bill & Melinda Gates Ag Dev Grants, 765
Bill & Melinda Gates Emergency Response Grants, 766
Bill & Melinda Gates Policy and Advocacy Grants, 769
Black Hills Corporation Grants, 781
Blanche & Julian Robertson Family Fdn Grants, 785
Blue Mountain Comm Fnd Grants, 800
Blue River Comm Fnd Grants, 801
Blum-Kovler Fnd Grants, 803
Blumenthal Fnd Grants, 804
Bodenwein Public Benevolent Fdn Grants, 806
Bodman Fnd Grants, 807
Boeing Company Contributions Grants, 809
Booth Ferris Fnd Grants, 816
Boston Fnd Grants, 819
Boston Globe Fnd Grants, 821
Bowling Green Comm Fnd Grants, 824
Boyd Gaming Corporation Contributions, 825
BP Conservation Programme Future Conservationist Awards, 826
Brainerd Fnd Grants, 831
Brian G. Dyson Fnd Grants, 834
Bridgestone/Firestone Trust Fund Grants, 836
Brooklyn Comm Fnd Green Communities Grants, 852
Brown County Comm Fnd Grants, 853
Brunswick Fnd Dollars for Doers Grants, 856
Brunswick Fnd Grants, 857
Build-A-Bear Workshop Fnd Grants, 861
Bullitt Fnd Grants, 862
Bunbury Company Grants, 863
Burlington Northern Santa Fe Fdn Grants, 866
Burning Fnd Grants, 867
Burton D Morgan Fdn Hudson Comty Grts, 869
Burton G. Bettingen Grants, 871
Bush Fnd Ecological Health Grants, 874
Cabot Corporation Fnd Grants, 887
California Coastal Art and Poetry Contest, 899
California Fertilizer Fnd School Garden Grants, 905
Calif Green Trees for The Golden State Grt, 906
California State Parks Restor & Cleanup Grants, 908
Callaway Fnd Grants, 909
Cambridge Comm Fnd Grants, 913
Cape Branch Fnd Grants, 919
Capital Region Comm Fnd Grants, 921
Captain Planet Fnd Grants, 922
Cargill Citizenship Fund-Corp Gvg Grants, 925
Carl & Eloise Pohlad Family Fdn Grants, 927
Carl C. Icahn Fnd Grants, 929
Carl M. Freeman Fnd FACES Grants, 932
Carl M. Freeman Fnd Grants, 933
Carls Fnd Grants, 937
Carolyn Fnd Grants, 942
Carpenter Fnd Grants, 943
Carrie E. and Lena V. Glenn Fnd Grants, 944
Carrier Corporation Contributions Grants, 946
Cass County Comm Fnd Grants, 952
CE and S Fnd Grants, 985
CenterPointEnergy Minnegasco Grants, 993
Central Okanagan Fnd Grants, 997
Cessna Fnd Grants, 1000
CFFVR Environmental Stewardship Grants, 1010
CFFVR Project Grants, 1017
CFFVR Shawano Area Comm Fnd Grants, 1021
Champlin Fnds Grants, 1029
Chapman Charitable Fnd Grants, 1033
Charles Delmar Fnd Grants, 1039
Charles G. Koch Charitable Fnd Grants, 1041
Charles H. Hall Fnd, 1044
Charles M & Mary D Grant Fdn Grants, 1050
Charles Stewart Mott Fnd Grants, 1055
Charlotte County Comm Fdn Grts, 1056
CHC Fnd Grants, 1065
Chesapeake Bay Trust Capacity Bldg Grts, 1068
Chesapeake Bay Environmental Educ Grants, 1069
Chesapeake Bay Trust Fisheries and Headwaters Grants, 1070
Chesapeake Bay Trust Forestry Mini Grants, 1071
Chesapeake Bay Trust Mini Grants, 1072
Chesapeake Bay Trust Outreach and Comm Engagement Grants, 1073
Chesapeake Bay Trust Pioneer Grants, 1074
Chesapeake Bay Trust Restoration Grants, 1075
Chevron Hawaii Educ Fund, 1077
Chicago Board of Trade Fnd Grants, 1079
Chingos Fnd Grants, 1109
Chiquita Brands Int'l Grants, 1110
Christensen Fund Regional Grants, 1112
Chula Vista Charitable Fnd Grants, 1116
CICF Efroymson Grants, 1120
CICF Indianapolis Fdn Comm Grants, 1123
Cinergy Fnd Grants, 1133
Circle K Corporation Contributions Grants, 1136
Citigroup Fnd Grants, 1139
Citizens Bank Mid-Atlantic Char Fdn Grts, 1140
Clarence E Heller Charitable Fdn Grants, 1150
Clark Charitable Trust Grants, 1155
Clark County Comm Fnd Grants, 1156
Clark Fnd Grants, 1157
Claude Worthington Benedum Fdn Grants, 1161
Clayton Baker Trust Grants, 1163
Cleveland-Cliffs Fnd Grants, 1165
CLIF Bar Family Fnd Grants, 1173
Clinton County Comm Fnd Grants, 1174
CNCS AmeriCorps Indian Tribes Plng Grts, 1180
CNCS AmeriCorps NCCC Project Grants, 1181
CNCS AmeriCorps State and National Grants, 1182
CNCS AmeriCorps VISTA Project Grants, 1184
CNCS Senior Corps Retired and Senior Volunteer Grants, 1188
Coastal Comm Fdn of SC Grants, 1193
Coca-Cola Fnd Grants, 1195
Coeta and Donald Barker Fnd Grants, 1197
Collective Brands Fnd Grants, 1206
Collins Fnd Grants, 1209
Colorado Bioscience Discovery Eval Grts, 1211
Colorado Clean Enrg Fd Solar Innovation Grts, 1212
Colorado Interstate Gas Grants, 1213
Colorado Renewables in Performance Contracting Grants, 1214
Columbia Gas of Virginia Grants, 1218
Columbus Fnd Competitive Grants, 1220
Columbus Fnd Joseph A. Jeffrey Endowment Fund Grants, 1224
Columbus Fnd Mary Eleanor Morris Fund Grants, 1225
Columbus Fnd Scotts Miracle-Gro Comm Garden Academy Fund Grants, 1230
Columbus Fnd Small Grants, 1232
Comm Fnd Alliance City of Evansville Endowment Fund Grants, 1246
Comm Fdn for Grtr Buffalo Grants, 1247
Comm Fnd for Greater New Haven Quinnipiac River Fund Grants, 1250
Comm Fdn for Monterey Cty Grants, 1255
Comm Fdn for Muskegon Cty Grants, 1256
Comm Fdn for NE Michigan Grants, 1257
Comm Fnd for San Benito County Grants, 1258
Comm Fnd of Bartholomew County Heritage Fund Grants, 1267
Comm Fdn of Boone County Grants, 1274
Comm Fdn of E Ctrl Illinois Grts, 1278
Comm Fnd of Grtr Birmingham Grants, 1280
Comm Fnd of Greater Chattanooga Grants, 1281
Comm Fnd of Greater Flint Grants, 1282
Comm Fnd of Greater Greensboro Grants, 1288
Comm Fnd of Greater Tampa Grts, 1292
Comm Fnd of Greenville Women Giving Grants, 1293
Comm Fnd of Louisville Grants, 1299
Comm Fnd of Mdl Tennessee Grants, 1300
Comm Fnd of Mt Vernon & Knox County Grants, 1301
Comm Fnd of Muncie & Delaware County Grant, 1302
Comm Fnd of Muncie and Delaware County Maxon Grants, 1303
Comm Fnd of Santa Cruz County Grants, 1305
Comm Fdn of Sarasota County Grts, 1306
Comm Fdn of S Alabama Grants, 1308
Comm Fdn of SE Connecticut Grants, 1309
Comm Fdn of Southern Indiana Grts, 1310
Comm Fnd of South Puget Sound Grants, 1311
Comm Fnd of Switzerland County Grants, 1315
Comm Fnd of Tampa Bay Grants, 1316
Comm Fnd of the Eastern Shore Needs Grants, 1317
Comm Fnd of the Verdugos Grants, 1322
Comm Fnd of Western North Carolina Grants, 1327
Comm Fnd Silicon Valley Grants, 1331
Comm Partners on Waste Educ and Reduction, 1335

PROGRAM TYPE INDEX   Environmental Programs / 1083

Compton Fnd Grants, 1338
Con Edison Corp Gvg Environmental Grts, 1347
Connecticut Comm Fnd Grants, 1350
Connecticut Light & Power Corp Contribs, 1352
ConocoPhillips Fnd Grants, 1354
ConocoPhillips Grants, 1355
Conservation, Food, and Health Fnd Grants for Developing Countries, 1359
Constellation Energy Corp EcoStar Grts, 1363
Constellation Energy Corporate Grants, 1364
Cooke Fnd Grants, 1368
Cooper Fnd Grants, 1369
Cooper Industries Fnd Grants, 1370
Coors Brewing Corporate Contributions Grants, 1371
Corina Higginson Trust Grants, 1373
Cornell Lab of Ornithology Mini-Grants, 1374
Cowles Charitable Trust Grants, 1392
Cranston Fnd Grants, 1395
Cruise Industry Charitable Fnd Grants, 1404
Crystelle Waggoner Charitable Trust Grants, 1405
CSRA Comm Fnd Grants, 1407
CSX Corporate Contributions Grants, 1408
Cudd Fnd Grants, 1410
Cumberland Comm Fnd Grants, 1413
Curtis and Edith Munson Fnd Grants, 1418
Cyrus Eaton Fnd Grants, 1423
Dade Comm Fnd Grants, 1430
DaimlerChrysler Corporation Fund Grants, 1432
Dana Corporation Fnd Grants, 1440
Darden Restaurants Fnd Grants, 1446
David Bohnett Fnd Grants, 1451
David Robinson Fnd Grants, 1454
Daviess County Comm Fnd Environment Grants, 1456
Davis Conservation Fnd Grants, 1461
Dayton Fnd Grants, 1463
Dean Foods Comm Involvement Grants, 1469
Dearborn Comm Fnd County Progress Grants, 1473
DeKalb County Comm Fdn Grts, 1481
Diageo Fnd Grants, 1546
DOE Initial H-Prize Competition for Breakthrough Advances in Materials for Hydrogen Storage, 1551
DogTime Annual Grant, 1552
Dole Food Company Charitable Contributions, 1564
Dolfinger-McMahon Fnd Grants, 1565
Doree Taylor Charitable Fnd, 1580
Dorot Fnd Grants, 1586
Do Something BR!CK Awards, 1592
Dow Chemical Company Grants, 1596
Dr. Scholl Fnd Grants, 1602
Draper Richards Kaplan Fnd Grants, 1603
Drs. Bruce and Lee Fnd Grants, 1607
DTE Energy Fdn Environmental Grts, 1612
Dubois County Comm Fnd Grants, 1615
Duluth-Superior Area Comm Fnd Grts, 1620
Dyer-Ives Fnd Small Grants, 1629
Dyson Fnd Mid-Hudson Valley Project Grants, 1636
E.J. Grassmann Trust Grants, 1638
Earth Island Brower Youth Awards, 1641
Earth Island Comm Wetland Restoration Grants, 1642
eBay Fnd Comm Grants, 1648
Edna Wardlaw Charitable Trust Grants, 1660
Edward and Helen Bartlett Fnd Grants, 1664
Edward Bangs Kelley & Elza Kelley Fdn Grts, 1665
Edward R. Godfrey Fnd Grants, 1667
Edwin W & Catherine M Davis Fdn Grants, 1672
EIF Comm Grants, 1675
Elliot Fnd Inc Grants, 1686
Elmer L & Eleanor J Andersen Fdn Grnts, 1687
El Paso Comm Fnd Grants, 1688
El Pomar Fnd Awards and Grants, 1690
Emily Hall Tremaine Fnd Grants, 1698
Energy Fnd Buildings Grants, 1705
Energy Fnd Climate Grants, 1706
Energy Fnd Power Grants, 1707
Energy Fnd Transportation Grants, 1708
Enterprise Comm Partners Green Grants, 1716
Enterprise Comm Partners Pre-Dev Grants, 1718
EPA Air Pollution Control Pgm Support Grts, 1722
EPA Brownfields Area-Wide Planning Grants, 1723
EPA Brownfields Assessment Pilot Grants, 1724

EPA Brownfields Cleanup Grants, 1725
EPA Brownfields Environmental Workforce Dev and Job Training Grants, 1726
EPA Brownfields Training, Research, and Tech Assistance Grants, 1727
EPA Children's Health Protection Grants, 1728
EPA Environmental Educ Grants, 1729
EPA Environmental Justice Collaborative Problem-Solving Cooperative Agreements Program, 1730
EPA Environmental Justice Small Grants, 1731
EPA Environmental Justice Small Grants, 1732
EPA Hazardous Waste Manag Grants for Tribes, 1733
EPA Pestwise Registration Improvement Act Partnership Grants, 1734
EPA Regional Agricultural IPM Grants, 1735
EPA Sr Environmental Employment Gras, 1736
EPA Source Reduction Assistance Grants, 1737
EPA State Indoor Radon Grants, 1738
EPA State Senior Envir Employment Grants, 1739
EPA Surveys, Studies, Research, Investigations, Demonstrations, and Special Purpose Activities Relating to the Clean Air Act, 1740
EPA Tribal Solid Waste Management Assistance Grants, 1741
EPA Tribal Support for the National Environmental Information Exchange Network, 1742
EQT Fnd Environment Grants, 1746
EREF Solid Waste Research Grants, 1747
EREF Sustainability Research Grants, 1748
EREF Unsolicited Proposal Grants, 1749
Erie Comm Fnd Grants, 1750
ESRI Conservation Grants, 1751
Essex County Comm Fnd Discretionary Grants, 1752
Esther M. and Freeman E. Everett Grants, 1757
Eugene B. Casey Fnd Grants, 1762
Eulalie Bloedel Schneider Fnd Grants, 1767
Evan Frankel Fnd Grants, 1770
Ewing Halsell Fnd Grants, 1776
Fairfield County Comm Fnd Grts, 1782
Fargo-Moorhead Area Fnd Grants, 1788
FEDCO Charitable Fdn Educ Grts, 1798
Ferree Fnd Grants, 1804
Fields Pond Fnd Grants, 1807
FirstEnergy Fnd Comm Grants, 1819
FishAmerica Fdn Chesapeake Bay Grts, 1827
FishAmerica Fnd Conservation Grants, 1828
FishAmerica Fnd Marine and Anadromous Fish Habitat Restoration Grants, 1829
FishAmerica Fnd Research Grants, 1830
Fisheries and Habitat Partnership Grants, 1834
Florida Sea Turtle Grants, 1871
Ford Fdn Peace & Social Justice Grts, 1884
Forest Fnd Grants, 1886
Forrest C. Lattner Fnd Grants, 1887
Fnd for Appalachian Ohio Access to Environmental Educ Mini-Grants, 1892
Fnd for the Mid South Comm Dev Grants, 1897
Fnds of East Chicago Comm Economic Grants, 1907
Frances and John L. Loeb Family Fund Grants, 1917
Francis T & Louise T Nichols Fdn Grts, 1923
Franklin County Comm Fnd Grts, 1929
Frank Stanley Beveridge Fnd Grants, 1936
Fraser-Parker Fnd Grants, 1938
Fred Baldwin Memorial Fnd Grants, 1941
Frederick W. Marzahl Grants, 1948
Freeman Fnd Grants, 1952
Fremont Area Comm Fnd Grants, 1955
Freshwater Future Advocate Mentor Program, 1957
Freshwater Future Climate Grants, 1958
Freshwater Future Healing Our Waters Grants, 1959
Freshwater Future Insight Services Grants, 1960
Freshwater Future Project Grants, 1961
Freshwater Future Special Opportunity Grants, 1962
Frey Fnd Grants, 1963
Frost Fnd Grants, 1966
Fruit Tree 101, 1967
Fuller Fnd Grants, 1974
Fulton County Comm Fnd Grants, 1975
G.N. Wilcox Trust Grants, 1982
Gamble Fnd Grants, 1983

Gannett Fdn Comm Action Grants, 1984
Garden Crusader Award, 1985
Gates Family Fnd Parks, Conservation & Recreation Grants, 1991
Gaylord & Dorothy Donnelley Fdn Grants, 1993
Gebbie Fnd Grants, 1995
GEF Green Thumb Challenge, 1996
Gene Haas Fnd, 1999
General Motors Fnd Grants, 2004
George and Ruth Bradford Fnd Grants, 2010
George A Ohl Jr. Fnd Grants, 2012
George B. Storer Fnd Grants, 2014
George Frederick Jewett Fnd Grants, 2019
George Gund Fnd Grants, 2020
George H & Jane A Mifflin Mem Fund Grts, 2021
George H.C. Ensworth Grants, 2022
George S & Dolores Dore Eccles Fdn Grants, 2027
Georgia-Pacific Fdn Environment Grts, 2034
Georgia Power Fnd Grants, 2039
Geraldine R. Dodge Fnd Environment Grants, 2041
Giving Sum Annual Grant, 2058
GNOF Bayou Communities Grants, 2069
GNOF Coastal 5 + 1 Grants, 2070
GNOF Environmental Fund Grants, 2073
GNOF Exxon-Mobil Grants, 2074
GNOF Gert Comm Fund Grants, 2076
GNOF Gulf Coast Oil Spill Grants, 2077
GNOF Norco Comm Grants, 2089
GNOF Plaquemines Comm Grants, 2091
Goldseker Fnd Comm Grants, 2101
Goodrich Corporation Fnd Grants, 2104
Good Works Fnd Grants, 2105
Grace and Franklin Bernsen Fnd Grants, 2109
Grand Haven Area Comm Fdn Grants, 2113
Grand Rapids Area Comm Fnd Nashwauk Area Endowment Fund Grants, 2115
Grand Rapids Area Comm Fnd Wyoming Grants, 2116
Grand Rapids Comm Fnd Grants, 2118
Grand Rapids Comm Fdn Ionia Cty Grts, 2119
Grand Rapids Comm Fnd Lowell Area Grants, 2121
Grand Rapids Comm Fnd SE Ottawa Grants, 2122
Grand Rapids Comm Fnd Sparta Grts, 2124
Grand Victoria Fnd Illinois Core Grants, 2126
Grassroots Exchange Fund Grants, 2128
Greater Cincinnati Fnd Priority and Small Projects/Capacity-Building Grants, 2132
Grtr Green Bay Comm Fdn Grts, 2135
Greater Milwaukee Fnd Grants, 2137
Greater Saint Louis Comm Fdn Grants, 2138
Greater Tacoma Comm Fdn Grts, 2139
Greater Worcester Comm Discretionary Grants, 2140
Greater Worcester Comm Fnd Youth for Comm Improvement Grants, 2144
Great Lakes Fishery Trust Access Grants, 2145
Great Lakes Fishery Trust Habitat Protection and Restoration Grants, 2146
Great Lakes Protection Fund Grants, 2147
Green Diamond Charitable Contributions, 2149
Green Fnd Special Project Grants, 2155
GreenWorks! Grants, 2160
Greygates Fnd Grants, 2164
Group 70 Fnd Fund, 2167
Grundy Fnd Grants, 2169
HA & Mary K Chapman Char Trust Grts, 2182
H. Reimers Bechtel Charitable Remainder Uni-Trust Grants, 2186
HAF Co-op Comm Fund Grants, 2192
HAF Natural Environment Grants, 2202
HAF Southern Humboldt Grants, 2204
Hampton Roads Comm Fnd Nonprofit Facilities Improvement Grants, 2218
Hannaford Charitable Fnd Grants, 2222
Harold K. L. Castle Fnd Grants, 2228
Harrison Cty Comm Fdn Grts, 2233
Harrison County Comm Fnd Signature Grants, 2234
Harry A & Margaret D Towsley Fdn Grts, 2236
Harry C. Trexler Trust Grants, 2239
Harry Chapin Fnd Grants, 2240
Hawaiian Electric Industries Charitable Grants, 2259
Hawaii Comm Fnd Geographic-Specific Grants, 2261

Environmental Programs / PROGRAM TYPE INDEX

Hawaii Comm Fnd West Hawaii Fund Grants, 2266
Heifer Educational Fund Grants for Principals, 2288
Heifer Educational Fund Grants for Teachers, 2289
Heineman Fnd for Research, Education, Charitable and Scientific Purposes, 2290
Heinz Endowments Grants, 2291
Helen S. Boylan Fnd Grants, 2298
Hendricks Cty Comm Fdn Grts, 2302
Henry J. Kaiser Family Fnd Grants, 2310
Henry M. Jackson Fnd Grants, 2311
Herbert A & Adrian W Woods Fdn Grts, 2313
Hershey Company Grants, 2318
High Meadow Fnd Grants, 2321
Hillman Fnd Grants, 2327
Hillsdale County Comm General Adult Grants, 2328
Hilton Head Island Fnd Grants, 2330
Hoblitzelle Fnd Grants, 2341
Holland/Zeeland Comm Fdn Grts, 2345
Homer Fnd Grants, 2352
Hometown Indiana Grants, 2353
Honda of America Manufacturing Fnd Grants, 2354
Honeybee Health Improvement Project Grants, 2355
Honeywell Corp Sustainable Opportunities, 2360
Honor the Earth Grants, 2361
Horace A Kimball & S Ella Kimball Fdn Grts, 2362
Horizon Fnd Grants, 2365
Household Int'l Corp Giving Grants, 2372
Houston Endowment Grants, 2373
HRF Hudson River Improvement Grants, 2378
HRF New York City Environmental Grants for Newton Creek, 2379
HRF Tibor T. Polgar Fellowships, 2380
Huntington County Comm Fnd - Make a Difference Grants, 2406
Idaho Power Co Corp Contributions, 2433
IDEM Section 205(j) Water Quality Management Planning Grants, 2434
IDEM Section 319(h) Nonpoint Source Grants, 2435
IIE David L. Boren Fellowships, 2454
Illinois Clean Energy Comm Efficiency Grants, 2479
Illinois Clean Energy Comm Fnd K-12 Wind Schools Pilot Grants, 2480
Illinois Clean Energy Comm Fnd Renewable Energy Grants, 2481
Illinois Clean Energy Comm Fnd Solar Thermal Installation Grants, 2482
Illinois DCEO Coal Competitiveness Grants, 2484
Illinois DCEO Coal Demonstration Grants, 2485
Illinois DCEO Coal Dev Grants, 2486
Illinois DCEO Coal Revival Grants, 2487
Illinois DNR Biodiversity Field Trip Grants, 2496
Illinois DNR Habitat Fund Grants, 2497
Illinois DNR Migratory Waterfowl Stamp Grants, 2498
Illinois DNR Park and Recreational Facility Construction Grants, 2499
Illinois DNR Schlyd Habitat Action Grts, 2500
Illinois DNR State Furbearer Fund Grants, 2501
Illinois DNR State Pheasant Fund Grants, 2502
Illinois DNR Urban & Cmty Forestry Grts, 2503
Illinois DNR Wildlife Preservation Fund Large Project Grants, 2505
Illinois DNR Wildlife Preservation Fund Small Project Grants, 2506
Illinois DNR Wildlife Preservation Maintenance of Wildlife Rehabilitation Facilities Grants, 2507
Illinois DNR Youth Recreation Corps Grants, 2508
IMLS 21st Cent Museum Pros Grts, 2512
Impact 100 Grants, 2522
Inasmuch Fnd Grants, 2523
Indiana Boating Infrastructure Grants (BIG P), 2534
Indiana Clean Vessel Act Grants, 2535
Indiana Corn Marketing Council Retailer Grant for Tank Cleaning, 2536
Indiana Historic Preservation Fund Grants, 2537
Indiana Household Hazardous Waste Grants, 2538
Indianapolis Power & Light Company Grants, 2540
Indianapolis Power & Light Company Environmentalist of the Year Award, 2541
Indianapolis Power & Light Company Golden Eagle Environmental Grants, 2542
Indiana Recycling Grants, 2545
Initiative Fnd Healthy Lakes & Rivers Partnerships, 2558
Intel Comm Grants, 2562
Intel Int'l Comm Grants, 2564
Int'l Paper Co Fnd Grants, 2568
Int'l Paper Environmental Awards, 2569
ISA John Z. Duling Grants, 2587
J.C. Penney Company Grants, 2594
J.M. Kaplan Fund City Life Grants, 2601
J.W. Kieckhefer Fnd Grants, 2607
Jackson Cty Comm Fdn Unrestricted Grts, 2611
Jacobs Family Fnd Spirit of the Diamond Grants, 2618
Jacobs Family Fdn Vlg Neighborhoods Grants, 2619
James & Abigail Campbell Fam Fdn Grts, 2620
James Ford Bell Fnd Grants, 2623
James M. Cox Fnd of Georgia Grants, 2634
James S. Copley Fnd Grants, 2637
Jane's Trust Grants, 2639
Janirve Fnd Grants, 2645
Jasper Fnd Grants, 2655
Jeffris Wood Fnd Grants, 2660
Jenifer Altman Fnd Grants, 2662
Jennings County Comm Fdn Grts, 2664
Jennings County Women's Giving Circle Grant, 2665
Jessie B. Cox Charitable Trust Grants, 2670
Jessie Smith Noyes Fnd Grants, 2672
John D. and Catherine T. MacArthur Fnd Global Challenges Grants, 2690
John Deere Fnd Grants, 2692
John S & James L Knight Fdn Dnr Adv Fd Grts, 2712
John W & Anna H Hanes Fdn Grants, 2728
Joyce Fnd Environment Grants, 2750
Kalamazoo Comm Environment Fund Grants, 2766
Ka Papa O Kakuhihewa Fund, 2785
Katie's Krops Grants, 2792
KEEN Effect Grants, 2795
Kelvin and Eleanor Smith Fnd Grants, 2796
Kettering Family Fnd Grants, 2817
Kettering Fund Grants, 2818
KeySpan Fnd Grants, 2821
Kirkpatrick Fnd Grants, 2827
Knox County Comm Fnd Grants, 2831
Kosciusko Cty Comm Fdn Grts, 2838
LaGrange Cty Comm Fdn Grts, 2850
LaGrange Independent Fund for Endowments, 2851
Laidlaw Fnd Youth Orgaizaing Grants, 2854
Lands' End Corporate Giving Program, 2861
Laura Jane Musser Rural Initiative Grants, 2864
Laurel Fnd Grants, 2867
Leave No Trace Master Educator Scholarships, 2870
Legacy Partners in Environmental Educ Grts, 2875
Legacy Partners in Environmental Ed Grants, 2876
Letha E. House Fnd Grants, 2886
Libra Fnd Grants, 2899
Lily Palmer Fry Memorial Trust Grants, 2905
Lincoln Financial Group Fnd Grants, 2906
Lindbergh Grants, 2907
Lisa and Douglas Goldman Fund Grants, 2910
LISC Financial Opportunity Center Social Innovation Fund Grants, 2911
Liz Claiborne & Art Ortenberg Fdn Grts, 2914
Local Initiatives Support Corporation Grants, 2917
Long Island Comm Fnd Grants, 2920
Lotus 88 Fnd for Women and Children, 2921
Louis Calder Fnd Grants, 2925
Lubrizol Fnd Grants, 2933
Lucy Downing Nisbet Charitable Fund Grants, 2935
Lumpkin Family Healthy Environments Grants, 2941
Lynde and Harry Bradley Fnd Grants, 2947
Lyndhurst Fnd Grants, 2949
M.E. Raker Fnd Grants, 2953
MacArthur Conservation & Sustainable Grants, 2963
Macquarie Bank Fnd Grants, 2966
Madison Comm Fnd Grants, 2971
Maine Comm Fnd Land Conservation Grants, 2983
Margaret & James A Elkins Jr Fdn Grts, 3003
Margaret L. Wendt Fnd Grants, 3004
Margaret T. Morris Fnd Grants, 3005
Marie C. and Joseph C. Wilson Fnd Rochester Small Grants, 3006
Marie H. Bechtel Charitable Remainder Grants, 3007
Marjorie Moore Charitable Fnd Grants, 3021
MARPAT Fnd Grants, 3023
Marriott Int'l Corporate Giving Grts, 3024
Mars Fnd Grants, 3025
Marshall Cty Comm Fdn Grts, 3026
Mary C. & Perry F. Spencer Fnd Grants, 3034
Mary K. Chapman Fnd Grants, 3042
Mary Owen Borden Fnd Grants, 3046
Max and Anna Levinson Fnd Grants, 3066
Maxon Charitable Fnd Grants, 3068
McConnell Fnd Grants, 3076
McCune Charitable Fnd Grants, 3077
McInerny Fnd Grants, 3083
McKesson Fnd Grants, 3084
McLean Contributionship Grants, 3088
MDEQ Beach Monitoring - Inland Lakes, 3094
MDEQ Brownfield ReDev & Site Reclamation, 3095
MDEQ Clean Diesel Grants, 3096
MDEQ Coastal Management Planning and Construction Grants, 3097
MDEQ Comm Pollution Prevention (P2) Grants: Household Drug Collections, 3098
MDEQ Great Lakes Areas of Concern Land Acquisition Grants, 3099
MDEQ Local Water Qlty Monitoring Grants, 3100
MDEQ Wellhead Protection Grants, 3101
Mead Johnson Nutritionals Evansville-Area Organizations Grants, 3103
MeadWestvaco Sustainable Communities Grants, 3105
Mead Witter Fnd Grants, 3106
Melinda Gray Ardia Environmental Fnd Grants, 3114
Mertz Gilmore Climate Change Solutions Grants, 3125
Meyer Memorial Trust Grassroots Grants, 3147
Meyer Memorial Trust Responsive Grants, 3148
Meyer Memorial Trust Special Grants, 3149
Miami County Comm Fnd - Operation Round Up Grants, 3156
Microsoft Comty Affairs Puget Sound Grts, 3163
Miguel Aleman Fnd Grants, 3175
Mimi and Peter Haas Fund Grants, 3185
Montgomery Cty Comm Fdn Grants, 3213
Morris & Gwendolyn Cafritz Fdn Grants, 3218
Motorola Fnd Grants, 3221
Natalie W. Furniss Charitable Trust Grants, 3244
Nathan Cummings Fnd Grants, 3246
National Endowment for Democracy Fellows, 3253
National Environmental Educ Fnd - Dept of Defense Legacy Award, 3270
National Environmental Educ Every Day Grants, 3271
National Geographic Soc All Roads Seed Grts, 3272
National Geographic Society Conservation Grants, 3273
National Geographic Society Genographic Legacy Fund Grants, 3274
National Geographic Young Explorers Grants, 3275
National Wetlands Awards, 3282
Nature Hills Nursery Green America Awards, 3287
NASE Fdn Future Entrepreneur Schlrsp, 3296
New Earth Fnd Grants, 3317
NFF Collaboration Support Grants, 3342
NFF Comm Assistance Grants, 3343
NFF Matching Grants, 3344
NFF Mid-Capacity Assistance Grants, 3345
NFF Wilderness Stewardship Grants, 3346
NFWF/Exxon Save the Tiger Fund Grants, 3354
NFWF Acres for America Grants, 3355
NFWF Alaska Fish and Wildlife Fund Grants, 3356
NFWF Aleutian Islands Risk Assessment Grants, 3357
NFWF Bird Conservation Initiative Grants, 3358
NFWF Bring Back the Natives Grants, 3359
NFWF Bronx Rvr Watershed Init Grts, 3360
NFWF Budweiser Conservationist of the Yr Awd, 3361
NFWF California Cstl Restor Fund Grts, 3362
NFWF Chesapeake Bay Conservation Grants, 3363
NFWF Chesapeake Bay Stewardship Fund Small Watershed Grants, 3364
NFWF Chesapeake Bay Tgtd Watershed Grts, 3365
NFWF Columbia Basin Water Trans Grants, 3366
NFWF Columbia River Estuarine Coastal Fund Grants, 3367

PROGRAM TYPE INDEX

Environmental Programs / 1085

NFWF Comm Salmon Fund Partnerships, 3368
NFWF ConocoPhillips SPIRIT of Conservation Migratory Bird Grants, 3369
NFWF Coral Reef Conservation Project Grants, 3370
NFWF Delaware Estuary Watershed Grants, 3371
NFWF Dissolved Oxygen Environmental Benefit Fund Grants, 3372
NFWF Five-Star Restoration Challenge Grants, 3373
NFWF Freshwater Fish Conservation Grants, 3374
NFWF King County Comm Salmon Grants, 3375
NFWF Long Island Sound Futures Fund Grants, 3376
NFWF Marine & Coastal Conservation Grants, 3377
NFWF National Whale Conservation Fund, 3378
NFWF National Wildlife Refuge Friends Group Grants, 3379
NFWF Native Plant Conserv Init Grts, 3380
NFWF Nature of Learning Grants, 3381
NFWF One Fly Conserv Partnership Grts, 3382
NFWF Oregon Governor's Fund for the Environment Grants, 3383
NFWF Pacific Grassroots Salmonid Init Grts, 3384
NFWF Pierce County Comm Salmon Grants, 3385
NFWF Pioneers in Conservation Grants, 3386
NFWF Pulling Together Initiative Grants, 3387
NFWF Radical Salmon Design Contest, 3388
NFWF Salmon Recovery Funding Board Comm Salmon Fund Grants, 3389
NFWF Seafarer's Environmental Educ Grants, 3390
NFWF Shell Marine Habitat Grants, 3391
NFWF Southern Co Longleaf Legacy Grts, 3392
NFWF Southern Company Power of Flight Bird Conservation Grants, 3393
NFWF Southern Co Power of Flight Grts, 3394
NFWF State Comprehensive Wildlife Conservation Support Grants, 3395
NFWF Sustain Our Great Lakes Grants, 3396
NFWF Tampa Bay Environmental Fund Grts, 3397
NFWF Upper Mississippi River Watershed Fund Grants, 3398
NFWF Wildlife and Habitat Conservation Initiative Grants, 3399
NFWF Wildlife Links Grants, 3400
NGA 'Remember Me' Rose Schl Garden Awds, 3401
NGA Hansen's Natural and Native School Garden Grants, 3402
NGA Heinz Wholesome Memories Intergenerational Garden Awards, 3404
NGA Hooked on Hydroponics Awards, 3405
NGA Mantis Award, 3406
NGA Midwest School Garden Grants, 3407
NGA Wuzzleburg Preschool Garden Awards, 3408
NHSCA Conservation License Plate Grants, 3425
Nicor Corporate Contributions, 3435
NIEHS Hazardous Materials Worker Health and Safety Training Grants, 3438
Nike Fnd Grants, 3441
Nina Mason Pulliam Charitable Trust Grants, 3443
Nissan Fnd Grants, 3444
Nissan Neighbors Grants, 3445
NOAA Projects to Improve or Amend Coral Reef Fishery Management Plans, 3453
NOAA Undersea Rsch Pgm Project Grts, 3454
Norcliffe Fnd Grants, 3459
Norcross Wildlife Fnd Grants, 3460
Norfolk Southern Fnd Grants, 3463
Norman Fnd Grants, 3464
North American Wetlands Conserv Grts, 3465
North Carolina Comm Fnd Grants, 3489
North Dakota Comm Fnd Grants, 3493
NE Utilities Fnd Grants, 3498
Northern Chautauqua Comm Fnd Comm Grants, 3499
Northern Chautauqua Comm Fnd Environmental Grants, 3501
North Georgia Comm Fnd Grants, 3505
Northrop Grumman Corporation Grants, 3507
NW Fund for the Environment Grants, 3510
Norwin S & Elizabeth N Bean Fnd Grts, 3515
NRA Fnd Grants, 3517
NSF Atmospheric Sciences Mid-Size Infrastructure Opportunity Grants, 3521

Nu Skin Force for Good Fnd Grants, 3536
NYCT New York City Environment Grants, 3556
Ogden Codman Trust Grants, 3641
Ohio County Comm Board of Directors Grants, 3656
Ohio County Comm Fnd Grants, 3658
Olin Corporation Charitable Trust Grants, 3669
Open Spaces Sacred Places National Awards, 3684
Oppenstein Brothers Fnd Grants, 3685
Oracle Corporate Contributions Grants, 3686
Orange County Comm Fnd Grants, 3687
Orchard Fnd Grants, 3690
Oscar Rennebohm Fnd Grants, 3694
Ottinger Fnd Grants, 3712
Otto Bremer Fnd Grants, 3713
Overbrook Fnd Grants, 3715
Owen County Comm Fnd Grants, 3716
Pacific Life Fnd Grants, 3726
PacifiCorp Fnd for Learning Grants, 3727
Packard Fnd Local Grants, 3729
Palm Beach and Martin Counties Grants, 3733
Parker Fnd (California) Grants, 3736
Park Fnd Grants, 3739
Pathways to Nature Conservation Fund Grants, 3745
Patricia Price Peterson Fnd Grants, 3746
Patrick and Aimee Butler Family Fnd Comm Arts and Humanities Grants, 3747
Patrick and Aimee Butler Family Fnd Comm Environment Grants, 3748
Patrick and Anna M. Cudahy Fund Grants, 3751
Paul and Edith Babson Fnd Grants, 3755
Paul G. Allen Family Fnd Grants, 3759
Peacock Fnd Grants, 3809
PepsiCo Fnd Grants, 3819
Perkins Charitable Fnd Grants, 3823
Perry County Comm Fnd Grants, 3827
Peter Kiewit Fnd Neighborhood Grants, 3846
PG&E Bright Ideas Grants, 3866
PG&E Comm Investment Grants, 3867
PG&E Comm Vitality Grants, 3868
PGE Fnd Grants, 3869
Piedmont Natural Gas Corporate and Charitable Contributions, 3883
Piedmont Natural Gas Fnd Environmental Stewardship and Energy Sustainability Grant, 3884
Pike County Comm Fnd Grants, 3888
Pinellas County Grants, 3891
Pioneer Hi-Bred Comm Grants, 3895
PIP Racial Justice Collaborative Grants, 3908
Pittsburgh Fdn Comm Fund Grts, 3910
Plum Creek Fnd Grants, 3917
PNC Fnd Green Building Grants, 3923
PNM Power Up Grants, 3925
PNM Reduce Your Use Grants, 3926
Porter County Comm Fnd Grants, 3931
Posey County Comm Fnd Grants, 3939
Powell Fnd Grants, 3942
Praxair Fnd Grants, 3944
Premera Blue Cross CARES Grants, 3945
Prince Charitable Trusts Chicago Grants, 3959
Prince Char Trusts Dist of Columbia Grts, 3960
Prince Charitable Trusts Rhode Island Grants, 3961
Princeton Comm Fnd Greater Mercer Grants, 3963
Principal Financial Group Fnd Grants, 3966
Procter and Gamble Fund Grants, 3967
Progress Energy Corp Contributions Grts, 3968
Progress Energy Fnd Environmental Stewardship Grants, 3970
Project AWARE Fnd Grants, 3971
Project Orange Thumb Grants, 3972
PSEG Corporate Contributions Grants, 3979
PSEG Environmental Educ Grants, 3980
Public Welfare Fnd Grants, 3984
Pulaski County Comm Fnd Grants, 3988
Pulte Homes Corporate Contributions, 3989
Putnam Cty Comm Fnd Grts, 3990
Putnam Fnd Grants, 3991
Rajiv Gandhi Fnd Grants, 4011
Rathmann Family Fnd Grants, 4026
RCF General Comm Grants, 4032
REI Conservation & Outdoor Recreation Grts, 4051

Rhode Island Fnd Grants, 4073
Rice Fnd Grants, 4074
Richard and Rhoda Goldman Fund Grants, 4077
Richard King Mellon Fnd Grants, 4087
Richland County Bank Grants, 4091
Riley Fnd Grants, 4094
Ripley County Comm Fnd Grants, 4095
Ripley County Comm Fnd Small Project Grants, 4096
Roberta Leventhal Sudakoff Fnd Grants, 4102
Robert R. Meyer Fnd Grants, 4121
Robert W. Woodruff Fnd Grants, 4124
Rochester Area Comm Fnd Grants, 4127
Rockefeller Brothers Fund Cross-Programmatic Initiative: Energy Grants, 4130
Rockefeller Brothers Fund Pivotal Places Grants: New York City, 4134
Rockefeller Brothers Sustainable Dev Grants, 4136
Rockefeller Family Fund Grants, 4137
Rohm and Haas Company Grants, 4145
Ronald McDonald House Charities Grants, 4149
Rose Fdn for Communities & the Environment Consumer Privacy Rights Grts, 4156
Rose Fdn For Communities & the Environment Kern Cty Air Pollution Mitigation Grts, 4157
Rose Communities and Environment Northern California Environmental Grassroots Grants, 4158
Rose Fnd For Communities and the Environment SE Madera County Responsible Growth Grants, 4159
Rose Fnd For Communities and the Environment Watershed Protection Grants, 4160
Ross Fnd Grants, 4164
Royal Caribbean Cruises Ocean Fund, 4165
Ruth Anderson Fnd Grants, 4176
Ruth and Vernon Taylor Fnd Grants, 4177
Ruth Eleanor Bamberger and John Ernest Bamberger Memorial Fnd Grants, 4178
Rutter's Children's Charities Grants, 4181
S. Livingston Mather Charitable Trust Grants, 4200
S. Mark Taper Fnd Grants, 4201
Saginaw Comm Fdn Discretionary Grts, 4205
Salisbury Comm Fnd Grants, 4224
Salt River Project Environmental Qlty Grts, 4227
Samuel S. Johnson Fnd Grants, 4239
San Diego Fdn Environment Blasker Grts, 4245
San Diego Fnd Environment Comm Grants, 4246
San Diego Fnd for Change Grants, 4247
SanDisk Corp Comm Sharing Pgm, 4253
San Francisco Fnd Environment Grants, 4266
San Juan Island Comm Fnd Grants, 4283
Santa Fe Comm Fnd Seasonal Grants-Spring, 4291
Sapelo Fdn Environmental Protection Grts, 4293
Sartain Lanier Family Fnd Grants, 4298
Schering-Plough Fdn Comm Initvs Grts, 4303
Scherman Fnd Grants, 4305
Schumann Fund for New Jersey Grants, 4311
Scott County Comm Fnd Grants, 4314
Scotts Company Give Back to Grow Awards, 4315
Seabury Fnd Grants, 4316
Seagate Tech Corp Capacity to Care Grants, 4317
Seattle Fnd Environment Grants, 4327
SeaWorld & Busch Gardens Conservation Grants, 4332
SEJ Annual Awds for Rptg on the Environment, 4333
Shared Earth Fnd Grants, 4339
Shaw's Supermarkets Donations, 4342
Shell Oil Company Fnd Grants, 4343
Sierra Fnd Grants, 4352
Singing for Change Fnd Grants, 4363
Sioux Falls Area Comm Fnd Comm Fund Grants, 4364
Sioux Falls Area Comm Fnd Field-of-Interest and Donor-Advised Grants, 4365
Sioux Falls Area Comm Fnd Spot Grants, 4366
Siragusa Fnd Arts & Culture Grants, 4367
Sir Dorabji Tata Trust Grants for NGOs or Voluntary Organizations, 4370
Skaggs Fnd Grants, 4378
Skoll Fdn Awds for Social Entrepreneurship, 4383
Snee Reinhardt Charitable Fnd Grants, 4387
Social Justice Fund NW Environmental Justice Giving Project Grants, 4396
Social Justice Fund NW LGBTQ Giving Grants, 4398

1086 / Environmental Programs

Sonora Area Fnd Competitive Grants, 4404
Sony Corp of America Corp Philant Grants, 4405
Sorenson Legacy Fnd Grants, 4407
Southbury Comm Trust Fund, 4409
Southern Calif Edison Environmental Grts, 4429
Southwest Florida Comm Competitive Grants, 4442
Spencer Cty Comm Fdn Grants, 4451
Springs Close Fnd Grants, 4462
St. Louis-Jefferson Solid Waste Management Waste Reduction and Recycling Grants, 4470
Stackpole-Hall Fnd Grants, 4472
Stanley Smith Horticultural Trust Grants, 4474
Steelcase Fnd Grants, 4497
Steuben County Comm Fdn Grants, 4501
Stonyfield Farm Profits for the Planet Grants, 4509
Stowe Family Fnd Grants, 4510
Strolling of the Heifers Schlrsps for Farmers, 4514
Strowd Roses Grants, 4515
Subaru Adopt a School Garden Grants, 4517
Sulzberger Fnd Grants, 4522
Summit Fnd Grants, 4524
Sunbeam Products Grants, 4526
Sunderland Fnd Grants, 4527
Sunoco Fnd Grants, 4530
Surdna Fdn Sustainable Environments Grants, 4533
Susan Mott Webb Charitable Trust Grants, 4536
Susan Vaughan Fnd Grants, 4537
SVP Environment Grants, 4539
Sweet Water Trust Grants, 4541
T.L.L. Temple Fnd Grants, 4546
Taproot Fnd Capacity-Building Service Grants, 4560
Telluride Fnd Comm Grants, 4573
Telluride Fdn Tech Assistance Grts, 4575
Texas Cmsn on the Arts Arts Respond Prj Grts, 4581
Theodore Edson Parker Fnd Grants, 4605
Thomas J. Long Fnd Comm Grants, 4618
Thomas Sill Fnd Grants, 4619
Thompson Charitable Fnd Grants, 4622
Threshold Fdn Sustainable Planet Grts, 4627
Threshold Fnd Thriving Resilient Communities Funding Circle, 4628
Tides Fdn Calif Wildlands Grassroots Fund, 4630
Tides Fnd Grants, 4632
Tom's of Maine Grants, 4640
Topeka Comm Trust Grants, 4644
Toro Fnd Grants, 4647
Tourism Cares Worldwide Grants, 4649
Town Creek Fnd Grants, 4650
Toyota Motor Engineering & Manufacturing North America Grants, 4651
Toyota Motor Mfg of Alabama Grts, 4652
Toyota Motor Manufacturing of Indiana Grants, 4653
Toyota Motor Mfg of Kentucky Grts, 4654
Toyota Motor Mfg of Mississippi Grts, 4655
Toyota Motor Manufacturing of Texas Grants, 4656
Toyota Motor Manuf of West Virginia Grants, 4657
Toyota Motor North America of NY Grts, 4658
Toyota Motor Sales, USA Grants, 4659
Toyota Tech Center Grants, 4660
Toyota USA Fnd Environmental Grants, 4661
Triangle Comm Fdn Donor-Advised Grts, 4668
Trinity Fnd Grants, 4669
Trull Fnd Grants, 4673
Turner Fnd Grants, 4681
Union Bank, N.A. Corporate Sponsorships, 4708
Union Bank, N.A. Fnd Grants, 4709
Union Benevolent Association Grants, 4710
Union Pacific Fdn Comm & Civic Grts, 4714
United Technologies Corporation Grants, 4725
Unity Fnd Of LaPorte County Grants, 4726
UPS Fdn Enviro Sustainability Grts, 4731
USAID African Institutions Innovation Mechanism Grants, 4738
USAID Bengal Tiger Csrvtn Actvty Grts, 4741
USAID Food Security, Nutrition, Biodiversity and Conservation Grants, 4752
USAID Grants for Building Disaster-Resilient Communities in Southern Africa, 4755
USAID Haiti Disaster Risk Reduction Capacity Building Grants, 4756

USAID India-Africa Ag Innovation Bridge Grant, 4760
USAID Mekong Partnership for the Environment Project Grants, 4769
USAID Rapid Response for Sudan Grants, 4776
USAID Rapid Response to Pakistanis Affected by Disasters - Phase Two Grants, 4777
USAID Strengthening Democratic Local Governance in South Sudan Grants, 4782
USDA Bioenergy Program for Advanced Biofuel Payments to Advanced Biofuel Producers, 4799
USDA Denali Comm High Energy Cost Grants, 4805
USDA Farmers Market Promotion Grants, 4808
USDA Federal-State Mktg Imprvmt Grts, 4810
USDA High Energy Cost Grants, 4812
USDA Indiv Water & Waste Water Grts, 4817
USDA PreDev Planning Grants, 4821
USDA Rural Business Enterprise Grants, 4823
USDA Rural Energy for America - Energy Audit & Renewable Energy Dev Assistance Grts, 4828
USDA Rural Energy for America Feasibility Grant, 4829
USDA Rural Energy for America - Renewable Energy System and Energy Efficiency Improvement Guaranteed Grants, 4830
USDA Rural Housing Repair and Rehabilitation Grants, 4831
USDA Section 306C Water and Waste Disposal Grants to Alleviate Health Risks, 4834
USDA Section 306D Water and Waste System Grants for Alaskan Villages, 4835
USDA Socially-Disadvantaged Producer Grants, 4837
USDA Tech Assistance and Training Grants for Rural Waste Systems, 4842
USDA Value-Added Producer Grants, 4843
USDC/NOAA American Rivers Comm-Based Restoration Program River Grants, 4845
USDC/NOAA Nat Marine Aquaculture Grants, 4846
USDC/NOAA Open Rivers Initiative Grants, 4847
Vancouver Fnd Grants and Comm Initiatives, 4900
Vanderburgh Comm Fnd Grants, 4902
Vanderburgh Comm Fdn Women's Fund, 4903
Vermont Comm Fnd Grants, 4929
Virginia W. Kettering Fnd Grants, 4950
Volvo Adventure Environmental Awards, 4952
Vulcan Materials Company Fnd Grants, 4956
W.C. Griffith Fnd Grants, 4957
Wabash River Enhancement Corporation Agricultural Cost-Share Grants, 4968
Wabash River Enhancement Corp Urban, 4969
Wabash River Heritage Corridor Fund Grants, 4970
Wallace Alexander Gerbode Fnd Grants, 4974
Wallace Global Fund Grants, 4977
Walmart Fnd Facility Giving Grants, 4978
Walmart Fnd National Giving Grants, 4979
Walmart Fnd State Giving Grants, 4980
Walter L. Gross III Family Fnd Grants, 4983
Warrick Cty Comm Fdn Grants, 4987
Washington Cty Comm Fdn Grts, 4997
Washington Cty Comm Fdn Youth Grts, 4998
Washington Gas Char Gvg Contributions, 5000
Waste Management Charitable Giving Grants, 5001
Water and Land Stewardship Fund Grants, 5002
Weaver Fnd Grants, 5015
Wells County Fnd Grants, 5022
Western Indiana Comm Fnd Grts, 5024
Western Pennsylvania Environmental Awards, 5026
Westinghouse Charitable Giving Grants, 5028
WestWind Fnd Environment Grants, 5052
Weyerhaeuser Company Fnd Grants, 5053
Weyerhaeuser Family Fnd Environment, Conservation and Preservation Grants, 5054
Whatcom Comm Fnd Grants, 5055
Whirlpool Fnd Grants, 5056
White County Comm Fnd Grants, 5057
Widgeon Point Charitable Fnd Grants, 5064
Wilburforce Fnd Grants, 5067
WILD Fnd Grants, 5068
William B. Stokely Jr. Fnd Grants, 5076
William C. Kenney Watershed Protection Fnd Ecosystem Grants, 5079
William G & Helen C Hoffman Fnd Grants, 5080

PROGRAM TYPE INDEX

Windward Youth Leadership Fund Grants, 5100
Winifred & Harry B. Allen Fnd Grants, 5101
Winston-Salem Fdn Stokes County Grants, 5104
Wisconsin Energy Fnd Grants, 5106
Xerox Fnd Grants, 5122
Yampa Valley Comm Fnd Grants, 5124

Exchange Programs

Laura Jane Musser Intrcltrl Harmony Grts, 2862
MacArthur Fnd Chicago Arts and Culture Int'l Connections Grants, 2962

Exhibitions, Collections, Performances, Video/Film Production

3M Fnd Comm Giving Grants, 15
18th Street Arts Complex Residency Grants, 19
A.C. Ratshesky Fnd Grants, 39
AAF Accent on Architecture Comm Grants, 58
Aaron Fnd Grants, 73
Abell-Hanger Fnd Grants, 91
Abell Fnd Arts and Culture Grants, 92
ACMP Fnd Comm Music Grants, 130
Adobe Youth Voices Grants, 170
Aetna Fnd Arts Grants in Connecticut, 181
Agape Fnd for Nonviolent Social Change Grants, 197
Air Force Association Junior ROTC Grants, 215
Akron Comm Fnd Arts & Culture Grants, 218
ALA Baker and Taylor Entertainment Audio Music/Video Product Award, 229
Alabama State Council on the Arts Collaborative Ventures Grants, 235
Alabama State Council on the Arts Comm Presenting Grants, 238
Alabama State Council on the Arts Comm Arts Program Dev Grants, 239
Alabama State Council on the Arts Multi-Discipline and Festival Grants, 243
Alabama State Council Arts Presenting Grants, 245
Alabama State Council on the Arts Dev Grants, 246
Alabama State Council on the Arts Projects of Individual Artists Grants, 248
Alaska Airlines Fnd Grants, 321
ALA Writers Live at the Library Grants, 336
Albert E. and Birdie W. Einstein Fund Grants, 342
Alcatel-Lucent Technologies Fnd Grants, 349
Altria Group Arts and Culture Grants, 399
American Express Charitable Fund Grants, 429
American for the Arts Emergency Relief Fund, 435
Amon G. Carter Fnd Grants, 458
Anna Fitch Ardenghi Trust Grants, 472
Anne J. Caudal Fnd Grants, 475
Ann L. and Carol Green Rhodes Grants, 483
APAP Cultural Exchange Grants, 492
Arthur Ashley Williams Fnd Grants, 572
Artist Trust GAP Grants, 575
Arts Council of Winston-Salem and Forsyth County Organizational Support Grants, 577
ArtsWave Impact Grants, 580
Atlanta Women's Fnd Grants, 609
Autauga Area Comm Fnd Grants, 618
Bacon Family Fnd Grants, 634
Bank of America Charitable Fnd Matching Gifts, 658
Benton Comm Fnd Grants, 730
Blanche & Julian Robertson Family Fdn Grants, 785
Bloomington Area Arts Council Grants, 791
Blue Mountain Comm Fnd Grants, 800
Blue River Comm Fnd Grants, 801
BoatUS Fnd Grassroots Grants, 805
Boeing Company Contributions Grants, 809
Bonfils-Stanton Fnd Grants, 814
Boston Fnd Initiative to Strengthen Arts and Cultural Service Organizations, 820
Bunbury Company Grants, 863
Burton D Morgan Fdn Hudson Comty Grts, 869
Bush Fnd Arts & Humanities Grants: Short-Term Organizational Support, 873
Bush Fnd Regional Arts Dev Program II Grants, 878
Cable Positive's Tony Cox Comm Fund, 886
Caesars Fnd Grants, 891
California Arts Council Statewide Ntwks Grts, 897
Captain Planet Fnd Grants, 922

PROGRAM TYPE INDEX

Exhibitions, Collections, Performances, Video/Film Production / 1087

Carl M. Freeman Fnd FACES Grants, 932
Carl M. Freeman Fnd Grants, 933
CCH California Story Fund Grants, 965
CCH Documentary Project Production Grants, 969
CDECD Arts Catalyze Placemaking in Every Comm Grants, 977
CDECD Arts Catalyze Placemaking Leadership Grants, 978
CDECD Arts Catalyze Placemaking Sustaining Relevance Grants, 979
CFFVR Fox Valley Comm Arts Grants, 1011
CFFVR Project Grants, 1017
Charles M. Bair Family Trust Grants, 1051
Chicago CityArts Grants, 1080
Chicago Comm Trust Arts and Culture Grants: Supporting Diverse Arts Productions and Fostering Art in Every Comm, 1084
Chicago Cultural Outreach Grants, 1095
Chicago Neighborhood Arts Grants, 1097
CICF Clare Noyes Grant, 1119
Citigroup Fnd Grants, 1139
City of Oakland Cultural Arts Dept Grts, 1142
CNL Corporate Giving Arts & Culture Grants, 1190
Coca-Cola Fnd Grants, 1195
Collins Fnd Grants, 1209
Columbus Fnd Small Grants, 1232
Comm Fdn for Muskegon Cty Grants, 1256
Comm Fdn of Riverside County Grts, 1304
Comm Fdn of SE Connecticut Grants, 1309
Comm Fnd of St. Joseph County ArtsEverywhere Grants, 1313
Comm Fnd of Western North Carolina Grants, 1327
Comm Fnd Partnerships - Martin County Grants, 1329
Conseil des arts de Montreal Diversity Award, 1357
Constance Saltonstall Fdn for the Arts Grts, 1361
Cowles Charitable Trust Grants, 1392
Cralle Fnd Grants, 1394
Crystelle Waggoner Charitable Trust Grants, 1405
CSRA Comm Fnd Grants, 1407
Cumberland Comm Fnd Summer Kids Grants, 1414
D.F. Halton Fnd Grants, 1424
Dance Advance Grants, 1441
Dayton Fnd Grants, 1463
Delaware Division of the Arts Comm-Based Organizations Opportunity Grants, 1487
Deluxe Corporation Fnd Grants, 1496
DENSO North America Fnd Grants, 1499
District of Columbia Commission on the Arts-Arts Educ Teacher Mini-Grants, 1549
Donald & Sylvia Robinson Family Fdn Grts, 1573
Donald W Reynolds Fdn Spcl Projects Grts, 1577
Dorrance Family Fnd Grants, 1590
Drs. Bruce and Lee Fnd Grants, 1607
Dwight Stuart Youth Fnd Grants, 1628
Eddie C. and Sylvia Brown Family Fnd Grants, 1653
Edward R. Godfrey Fnd Grants, 1667
Edyth Bush Charitable Fnd Grants, 1673
Elmer L & Eleanor J Andersen Fdn Grnts, 1687
EMC Corporation Grants, 1693
Ensworth Charitable Fnd Grants, 1710
Fifth Third Fnd Grants, 1810
Fleishhacker Fdn Small Grants in the Arts, 1839
Fleishhacker Fnd Special Arts Grants, 1840
Flinn Fnd Grants, 1842
Florida Division of Cultural Affairs Comm Theatre Grants, 1847
Florida Division of Cultural Affairs Culture Builds Florida Expansion Funding, 1848
Florida Division of Cultural Affairs Culture Builds Florida Seed Funding, 1849
Florida Div of Cultural Affairs Folk Arts Grts, 1853
Florida Division of Cultural Affairs General Program Support Grants, 1854
Florida Division of Cultural Affairs Lit Grants, 1855
Florida Div of Cultural Affairs Media Arts Grants, 1856
Florida Division of Cultural Affairs Multidisciplinary Grants, 1857
Florida Div of Cultural Affairs Museum Grts, 1858
Florida Div of Cultural Affairs Music Grts, 1859
Florida Div of Cultural Afrs Presenter Grts, 1860

Florida Division of Cultural Affairs State Touring Grants, 1863
Florida Div of Cultural Affairs Visual Arts Grants, 1865
Florida Humanities Council Major Grants, 1868
Florida Humanities Council Mini Grants, 1869
Florida Humanities Council Partnership Grants, 1870
Foster Fnd Grants, 1888
Frank and Lydia Bergen Fnd Grants, 1925
Frank Loomis Palmer Fund Grants, 1931
George A Ohl Jr. Fnd Grants, 2012
George B. Storer Fnd Grants, 2014
George S & Dolores Dore Eccles Fdn Grants, 2027
Georgia-Pacific Fnd Educ Grants, 2031
Georgia Council for the Arts Partner Grants for Organizations, 2035
Georgia Council for the Arts Partner Grants for Service Organizations, 2036
Geraldine R. Dodge Fnd Arts Grants, 2040
Gil and Dody Weaver Fnd Grants, 2053
GNOF Exxon-Mobil Grants, 2074
GNOF IMPACT Grants for Arts and Culture, 2078
Goodrich Corporation Fnd Grants, 2104
Grand Rapids Area Comm Fdn Grts, 2114
Greater Worcester Comm Fnd Jeppson Memorial Fund for Brookfield Grants, 2141
Greater Worcester Comm Fnd Mini-Grants, 2142
Greater Worcester Comm Fnd Youth for Comm Improvement Grants, 2144
Greenfield Fnd of Florida Grants, 2151
Green Fnd Arts Grants, 2152
HAF Arts and Culture: Lynne and Bob Wells Grant for Performing Artists, 2190
HAF Arts & Culture: Project Grts to Artists, 2191
HAF Comm Partnerships with Native Artists, 2194
HAF Natural Environment Grants, 2202
Hahl Proctor Charitable Trust Grants, 2208
Harold R. Bechtel Charitable Remainder Uni-Trust Grants, 2229
Health Fnd of Grtr Indianapolis Grts, 2282
Hearst Fnds Culture Grants, 2284
Heartland Arts Fund, 2286
Heifer Educational Fund Grants for Principals, 2288
Helen Gertrude Sparks Charitable Trust Grants, 2294
Helen Pumphrey Denit Charitable Trust Grants, 2297
Honda of America Manufacturing Fnd Grants, 2354
Horace Moses Charitable Fnd Grants, 2363
Horizons Comm Issues Grants, 2366
Huntington Arts Council JP Morgan Chase Artist Reach Out Grants, 2402
IFP Chicago Production Fund In-Kind Grant, 2446
IFP Minnesota Fresh Filmmakers Produc Grts, 2447
IFP Minnesota McKnight Filmmaking Fwsps, 2448
IFP Minnesota McKnight Screenwriters Fwsps, 2449
IFP Minnesota TV Grants, 2450
IFP New York State Council on the Arts Electronic Media & Film Pgm Distrib Grts, 2451
Illinois Arts Council Artstour Grants, 2465
Illinois Arts Cncl Comm Arts Access Grts, 2466
Illinois Arts Council Music Grants, 2474
Illinois Arts Council Vis Arts Pgm Grts, 2478
Illinois Humanities Council Comm Project Grant, 2510
Indiana Arts Commission American Masterpieces Grants, 2530
Indiana Arts Commission Multi-regional Major Arts Institutions Grants, 2532
Iowa Arts Council Artists in Schools/Communities Residency Grants, 2571
IREX Egypt Media Dev Grants, 2575
IREX MENA Media TV Produc Fund Grts, 2577
James F & Marion L Miller Fdn Grts, 2622
James Irvine Fnd Creative Connections Grants, 2628
Janus Fnd Grants, 2647
Japan Fnd Los Angeles Mini-Grants for Japanese Arts & Culture, 2651
Japan Fnd New York Small Arts & Culture Grants, 2652
Jaqua Fnd Grants, 2653
Jean and Price Daniel Fnd Grants, 2659
Jerome Fnd Grants, 2667
Jerome Fnd Travel and Study Grants, 2668
Jewish Women's Fdn of New York Grants, 2677

John Reynolds and Eleanor B. Allen Charitable Fnd Grants, 2710
JohnS & JamesL Knight Fdn Communities Grts, 2711
John W. Speas and Effie E. Speas Grants, 2732
Joyce Awards, 2746
Joyce Fnd Culture Grants, 2747
JP Morgan Chase Arts and Culture Grants, 2752
Judith and Jean Pape Adams Charitable Fnd Tulsa Area Grants, 2755
Kansas Arts Commission American Masterpieces Kansas Grants, 2775
Kansas Arts Commission Arts-in-Communities Project Grants, 2777
Kansas Arts Commission Arts-in-Communities Project Mini-Grants, 2778
Kansas Arts Commission Arts on Tour Grants, 2780
Kansas Arts Commission Visual Arts Grants, 2783
Ka Papa O Kakuhihewa Fund, 2785
Kentucky Arts Cncl Access Astnce Grts, 2805
Kentucky Arts Cncl Poetry Out Loud Grts, 2810
KeyBank Fnd Grants, 2820
Kiplinger Program in Public Affairs Journalism Fellowships, 2826
Leeway Fnd Transformation Award, 2873
Leo Goodwin Fnd Grants, 2882
Libra Fnd Grants, 2899
Louis and Elizabeth Nave Flarsheim Grants, 2924
MacArthur Fnd Chicago Arts and Culture Int'l Connections Grants, 2962
MacDonald-Peterson Fnd Grants, 2965
Margaret Abell Powell Fund Grants, 3002
Margaret L. Wendt Fnd Grants, 3004
Marietta McNeill Morgan and Samuel Tate Morgan, Jr. Trust Grants, 3008
Marie Walsh Sharpe Art Fnd Grants, 3009
MARPAT Fnd Grants, 3023
Mary Duke Biddle Fnd Grants, 3036
Massachusetts Cultural Council Local Cultural Council Grants, 3057
Massachusetts Fnd for the Humanities Cultural Economic Dev Grants, 3059
Massachusetts Fnd for Humanities Project Grants, 3060
McCombs Fnd Grants, 3075
MDARD County Fairs Cap Imprvmt Grts, 3092
Meriden Fnd Grants, 3122
Mertz Gilmore Fnd NYC Dance Grants, 3127
Meyer and Stephanie Eglin Fnd Grants, 3139
Mid Atlantic Arts American Masterpieces Grants, 3169
Mid Atlantic Arts Fdn ArtsConnect Grts, 3170
Mid Atlantic Arts Fnd Folk Arts Outreach Grants, 3171
Milton and Sally Avery Arts Fnd Grants, 3183
Minnesota State Arts Board Cultural Comm Partnership Grants, 3188
Mr. and Mrs. William Foulds Family Fnd Grants, 3222
National Endowment for the Arts Dance Grants, 3262
National Endowment for the Arts Local Arts Agencies Grants, 3263
National Endowment for Arts Media Grants, 3264
National Endowment for Arts Museum Grants, 3265
National Endowment for the Arts Opera Grants, 3267
National Endowment for Arts Presenting Grants, 3268
National Geographic Soc All Roads Seed Grts, 3272
Nevada Arts Council Jackpot Grants, 3312
Nevada Arts Council Residency Express Grants, 3315
Newfoundland and Labrador Arts Council Comm Arts Grants, 3318
Newfoundland and Labrador Arts Council Labrador Cultural Travel Grants, 3319
New Voices J-Lab Journalism Grants, 3337
NHSCA General Project Grants, 3427
NIAF Italian Culture and Heritage Grants, 3432
Nicor Corporate Contributions, 3435
NJSCA Arts Project Support, 3446
NJSCA General Program Support Grants, 3449
NJSCA Projects Serving Artists Grants, 3450
Norcliffe Fnd Grants, 3459
North Carolina Arts Council Arts and Audiences Grants, 3466
North Carolina Arts Council Arts in Educ Initiatives Grants, 3469

North Carolina Arts Council Comm Public Art and Design Dev Grants, 3472
North Carolina Arts Council Comm Public Art and Design Implementation Grants, 3473
North Dakota Council on the Arts Presenter Support Grants, 3497
NYFA Building Up Infrastructure Levels for Dance Grants, 3563
NYSCA Architecture, Planning, and Design: Capital Fixtures and Equipment Purchase Grants, 3570
NYSCA Architecture, Planning, and Design: General Operating Support Grants, 3573
NYSCA Architecture, Planning, and Design: General Program Support Grants, 3574
NYSCA Architecture, Planning, and Design: Project Support Grants, 3576
NYSCA Arts Education: General Operating Support Grants, 3578
NYSCA Arts Education: General Program Support Grants, 3579
NYSCA Arts Education: K-12 In-School Grants, 3580
NYSCA Dance: Commissions Grants, 3583
NYSCA Dance: Gen Pgm Support Grts, 3585
NYSCA Dance: Long-Term Residency in New York State Grants, 3586
NYSCA Electronic Media and Film: Film Festivals Grants, 3588
NYSCA Electronic Media and Film: General Exhibition Grants, 3589
NYSCA Electronic Media and Film: General Operating Support, 3590
NYSCA Electronic Media and Film: General Program Support, 3591
NYSCA Electronic Media and Film: Screenings Grants, 3592
NYSCA Electronic Media and Film: Workspace Grants, 3593
NYSCA Folk Arts: Exhibitions Grants, 3594
NYSCA Folk Arts: Gen Pgm Support Grts, 3595
NYSCA Folk Arts: Presentation Grants, 3596
NYSCA Folk Arts: Regional and County Folk Arts Grants, 3597
NYSCA Lit: Public Programs, 3600
NYSCA Lit: Svcs to the Field Grts, 3601
NYSCA Museum: Gen Pgm Support Grts, 3603
NYSCA Museum: Project Support Grants, 3604
NYSCA Music: Gen Operating Support Grts, 3606
NYSCA Music: Gen Pgm Support Grts, 3607
NYSCA Music: New Music Facilities, 3608
NYSCA Presenting: General Operating Support, 3609
NYSCA Presenting: General Program Support, 3610
NYSCA Presenting: Presenting Grants, 3611
NYSCA Presenting: Svcs to the Field Grts, 3612
NYSCA Special Art Services: Project Support, 3613
NYSCA Special Arts Services: General Operating Support Grants, 3614
NYSCA Special Arts Services: General Program Support Grants, 3615
NYSCA Special Arts Services: Instruction and Training Grants, 3616
NYSCA Special Arts Services: Professional Performances Grants, 3617
NYSCA State and Local Partnerships: General Operating Support Grants, 3619
NYSCA Theatre: Gen Operating Support Grts, 3623
NYSCA Theatre: Gen Pgm Support Grts, 3624
NYSCA Theatre: Pro Performances Grts, 3625
NYSCA Theatre: Services to the Field Grants, 3626
NYSCA Visual Arts: Exhibitions and Installations Grants, 3627
NYSCA Visual Arts: General Operating Support Grants, 3628
NYSCA Visual Arts: General Program Support, 3629
NYSCA Visual Arts: Wrkspc Facilities Grts, 3631
ODKF Athletic Grants, 3638
Ohio Arts Council Artist in Residence Grants for Sponsors, 3645
Ohio Arts Council Artists with Disabilities Access Grants, 3646
Ohio Arts Council Arts Access Grants, 3647
Ohio Arts Council Arts Indiv Excellence Awds, 3648
Ohio Arts Council Arts Innovation Pgm Grts, 3649
Ohio Arts Council Arts Partnership Grants, 3650
Ohio Arts Council Building Cultural Diversity Initiative Grants, 3651
Ohio Arts Council Int'l Partnership Grts, 3653
Ohio Arts Council Sustainability Pgm Grts, 3654
Ohio River Border Initiative Grants, 3661
Ontario Arts Cncl Aboriginal Arts Project Grts, 3675
Ontario Arts Council Integrated Arts Grants, 3678
Ontario Arts Council Theatre Creators' Grants, 3681
Oppenstein Brothers Fnd Grants, 3685
ORBI Artist Fast Track Grants, 3689
OSF Documentary Photography Project Audience Engagement Grant, 3706
Palm Beach and Martin Counties Grants, 3733
Parker Fnd (California) Grants, 3736
Paul G. Allen Family Fnd Grants, 3759
Paul Green Fnd Playwrights Fellowship, 3762
PCA Art Organizations and Art Grants for Presenting Organizations, 3771
PCA Arts Organizations and Grants for Music, 3774
PCA Arts Organizations and Arts Grants for Art Museums, 3775
PCA Arts Organizations and Grants for Crafts, 3778
PCA Arts Organizations & Grants for Dance, 3779
PCA Arts Organizations and Arts Grants for Film and Electronic Media, 3780
PCA Arts Organizations and Arts Grants for Lit, 3781
PCA Arts Organizations & Grants for Local Arts, 3782
PCA Arts Organizations and Grants for Theatre, 3783
PCA Arts Organizations & Grants for Visual Arts, 3785
PCA Busing Grants, 3786
PCA Entry Track Arts Organizations and Arts Grants for Art Museums, 3787
PCA Entry Track Arts Organizations and Arts Grants for Crafts, 3790
PCA Entry Track Arts Organizations and Arts Grants for Dance, 3791
PCA Entry Track Arts Orgs & Arts Pgms Grts for Film & Electronic Media, 3792
PCA Entry Track Arts Organizations and Arts Grants for Lit, 3793
PCA Entry Track Arts Organizations and Arts Grants for Local Arts, 3794
PCA Entry Track Arts Organizations and Arts Grants for Music, 3795
PCA Entry Track Arts Organizations and Arts Grants for Presenting Organizations, 3796
PCA Entry Track Arts Organizations and Arts Grants for Theatre, 3797
PCA Entry Track Arts Organizations and Arts Grants for Visual Arts, 3799
PCA Pennsylvania Partners in the Arts Program Stream Grants, 3801
PCA Pennsylvania Partners in the Arts Project Stream Grants, 3802
PCA Strategies for Success Grts-Adv Level, 3804
PCA Strategies for Success Grants - Basic Level, 3805
PCA Strategies for Success Grts-Intrmd Lvl, 3806
PennPAT Artist Tech Assistance Grants, 3811
PennPAT Fee-Support Grants for Presenters, 3812
PennPAT New Directions Grants for Presenters, 3813
PennPAT Presenter Travel Grants, 3814
PennPAT Strategic Opportunity Grants, 3815
Peter Norton Family Fnd Grants, 3849
Pew Charitable Trusts Arts and Culture Grants, 3857
Pew Fellowships in the Arts, 3860
Piedmont Natural Gas Corporate and Charitable Contributions, 3883
Pi Lambda Theta Anna Tracey Mem Awd, 3889
Playboy Social Change Documentary Film Grants, 3914
PMP Professional Dev Grants, 3919
Pollock Fnd Grants, 3930
Price Chopper's Golub Fnd Grants, 3950
Price Family Charitable Fund Grants, 3952
Princeton Area Comm Fnd Thomas George Artists Fund Grants, 3965
Progress Energy Fnd Economic Vitality Grants, 3969
Rasmuson Fdn Creative Ventures Grts, 4021
Regional Arts and Cultural Council Opportunity Grants, 4046
Regional Arts & Cultural Council Project Grts, 4048
Reinberger Fnd Grants, 4052
Reynolds American Fnd Grants, 4068
Richard & Caroline T Gwathmey Mem Tr Grts, 4075
Richard and Rhoda Goldman Fund Grants, 4077
Richard D. Bass Fnd Grants, 4079
Richard Florsheim Art Fund Grants, 4083
Richard H. Driehaus Fnd Grants, 4084
RISCA Project Grants for Organizations, Individuals and Education, 4100
Robert F Stoico/FIRSTFED Char Fdn Grts, 4112
Robert R. Meyer Fnd Grants, 4121
Rockefeller Brothers Fund Charles E. Culpeper Arts and Culture Grants in New York City, 4129
Rohm and Haas Company Grants, 4145
Royal Caribbean Cruises Ocean Fund, 4165
Ruth Mott Fnd Grants, 4180
Safeco Insurance Comm Grants, 4203
San Diego Fnd for Change Grants, 4247
San Francisco Faith Arts and Culture Grants, 4267
San Francisco Fnd FAITHS Arts and Culture Mini Grants, 4268
San Francisco Fnd James D. Phelan Award in Film, Video, and Digital Media, 4278
Santa Barbara Fnd Towbes Fund for the Performing Arts Grants, 4288
Santa Fe Comm Fnd Seasonal Grants-Fall Cycle, 4290
Schurz Communications Fnd Grants, 4312
Scott B & Annie P Appleby Char Trust Grts, 4313
Seattle Arts and Culture Grants, 4320
Silicon Valley Comm Fnd Donor Circle for the Arts Grants, 4354
Sioux Falls Area Comm Fnd Comm Fund Grants, 4364
Sioux Falls Area Comm Fnd Spot Grants, 4366
Snee Reinhardt Charitable Fnd Grants, 4387
Sony Corp of America Corp Philant Grants, 4405
Southbury Comm Trust Fund, 4409
South Carolina Arts Comsn Accessibility Grts, 4410
South Carolina Arts Commission American Masterpieces in South Carolina Grants, 4413
South Carolina Arts Commission Annual Operating Support for Organizations Grants, 4414
South Carolina Arts Commission Arts Facility Projects Grants, 4417
South Carolina Arts Commission Cultural Tourism Initiative Grants, 4419
South Carolina Arts Commission Folklife & Traditional Arts Grants, 4421
South Carolina Arts Commission Long Term Operating Support for Organizations Grants, 4424
South Carolina Arts Commission Statewide Arts Participation Initiative Grants, 4425
Stewart Huston Charitable Trust Grants, 4505
Suffolk County Office of Film and Cultural Affairs Cultural Arts Grants, 4521
TAC Arts Access Grant, 4549
TAC Arts Build Communities Grants, 4551
TAC Arts Projects Grants, 4554
TAC Rural Arts Project Support Grants, 4555
TAC Touring Arts and Arts Access Touring Arts Grants, 4557
Target Fnd Grants, 4562
Taylor S. Abernathy and Patti Harding Abernathy Charitable Trust Grants, 4564
TCF Bank Fnd Grants, 4565
Texas Comsn on the Arts Cultural Connections-Performance Support Grants, 4588
Texas Comsn on the Arts Cultural Connections-Visual & Media Arts Touring Exhibits Grants, 4589
Texas Filmmakers Production Grants, 4595
Texas Instruments Fnd Arts and Culture Grants, 4599
Thomas J. Long Fnd Comm Grants, 4618
Thornton Fnd Grants, 4624
Toro Fnd Grants, 4647
Union Bank, N.A. Fnd Grants, 4709
United Technologies Corporation Grants, 4725
USDD Cultural Resources Program Assistance Announcement Grants, 4862

PROGRAM TYPE INDEX

Virginia Commission for the Arts Artists in Educ Residency Grants, 4941
Virginia Commission for the Arts General Operating Grants, 4942
Virginia Comsn for the Arts Proj Grts, 4944
Virginia Fnd for Humanities Discretionary Grants, 4946
Virginia Fdn for the Humanities Open Grants, 4947
VSA Int'l Art Program for Children with Disabilities Grants, 4955
W.C. Griffith Fnd Grants, 4957
WM Keck Fdn Southern California Grts, 4964
W Paul & Lucille Caudill Little Fdn Grts, 4966
Wabash River Heritage Corridor Fund Grants, 4970
Wabash Valley Comm Fnd Grants, 4971
Walter L. Gross III Family Fnd Grants, 4983
West Virginia Commission on the Arts Media Arts Grants, 5039
West Virginia Commission on the Arts Mid-Size Institutions Support Grants, 5040
West Virginia Comsn on the Arts Mini Grts, 5041
West Virginia Commission on the Arts Performing Arts Grants, 5043
West Virginia Commission on the Arts Presenting Artists Grants, 5044
West Virginia Commission on the Arts Visual Arts Grants, 5051
William T. Sloper Trust for Andres J. Sloper Musical Fund Grants, 5097
Winston-Salem Fdn Competitive Grts, 5102
Wisconsin Humanities Council Mini-Grants for Scholarly Research, 5108
Yellow Corporate Fnd Grants, 5126
Zellerbach Family Fnd Comm Arts Grants, 5150

Faculty/Professional Development
Able Trust Vocational Rehabilitation Grants for Individuals, 104
ALA ALSC Distinguished Service Award, 223
ALA Carnegie Corporation of New York/New York Times I Love My Librarian Award, 254
ALA DEMCO New Leaders Travel Grants, 264
ALA Distinguished School Admin Award, 266
ALA Diversity Research Grant, 268
ALA First Step Award/Wiley Prof Dev Grant, 279
ALA HW Wilson Library Staff Dev Grt, 283
ALA Melvil Dewey Medal, 301
ALA Pat Carterette Prof Dev Grt, 306
ALA Supporting Diversity Stipend, 333
American Chemical Society Chemical Tech Partnership Mini Grants, 424
Amerigroup Fnd Grants, 452
AMI Semiconductors Corporate Grants, 457
Amon G. Carter Fnd Grants, 458
Anheuser-Busch Fnd Grants, 470
Annenberg Fnd Grants, 477
Arizona Comsn on the Arts Educ Projects Grts, 536
Arkansas Arts Council Sally A. Williams Artist Fund Grants, 558
Assisi Fnd of Memphis General Grants, 594
Assisi Fnd of Memphis Mini Grants, 595
ATF Gang Resistance Educ and Training Program Cooperative Agreements, 603
Ball Brothers Fnd General Grants, 637
Ball Brothers Fnd Rapid Grants, 639
Baxter Int'l Fnd Grants, 691
Boeing Company Contributions Grants, 809
Booth Ferris Fnd Grants, 816
Boyd Gaming Corporation Contributions, 825
Brookdale Fnd Leadership in Aging Fellowships, 844
Buhl Fnd - Frick Educational Fund, 859
Bush Fnd Medical Fellowships, 877
Cabot Corporation Fnd Grants, 887
Canada-U.S. Fulbright Mid-Career Prof Grants, 917
Canadian Optometric Ed Trust Fund Grts, 918
Carl B. and Florence E. King Fnd Grants, 928
Carl M. Freeman Fnd Grants, 933
Carpenter Fnd Grants, 943
Carrie Estelle Doheny Fnd Grants, 945
Carrier Corporation Contributions Grants, 946
CFFVR Basic Needs Gvg Partnership Grts, 1002

CFFVR Environmental Stewardship Grants, 1010
CFFVR Mielke Family Fnd Grants, 1015
Charlotte County Comm Fdn Grts, 1056
Chesapeake Bay Trust Capacity Bldg Grts, 1068
Chesapeake Bay Environmental Educ Grants, 1069
ChevronTexaco Contributions Program, 1078
Chicago Comty Trust Educ Grts Priority 2, 1085
Chiron Fnd Comm Grants, 1111
Christensen Fund Regional Grants, 1112
CIRCLE Civic Educ at the High School Level Research Grants, 1135
Clarence E Heller Charitable Fdn Grants, 1150
Claude Worthington Benedum Fdn Grants, 1161
Cleveland-Cliffs Fnd Grants, 1165
Cockrell Fnd Grants, 1196
Columbus Fnd Competitive Grants, 1220
Comm Fnd for Greater New Haven Neighborhood Small Grants, 1249
Comm Fnd for Greater New Haven Valley Neighborhood Grants, 1253
Comm Fdn for Muskegon Cty Grants, 1256
Comm Fdn in Jacksonville Art Ventures Small Arts Orgs Professional Assistance Grts, 1262
Comm Fdn of Grtr Birmingham Grants, 1280
Comm Fdn of Grtr New Britain Grts, 1291
Comm Fnd of St. Joseph County African American Comm Grants, 1312
Comm Fnd of St. Joseph County ArtsEverywhere Grants, 1313
Comm Fnd of the Verdugos Educational Endowment Fund Grants, 1321
ConAgra Foods Fnd Nourish Our Comm Grants, 1343
Constellation Energy Corporate Grants, 1364
Cowles Charitable Trust Grants, 1392
Cumberland Comm Fnd Summer Kids Grants, 1414
Dave Thomas Fnd for Adoption Grants, 1449
Denton A. Cooley Fnd Grants, 1500
District of Columbia Commission on the Arts-Arts Educ Teacher Mini-Grants, 1549
Dresher Fnd Grants, 1605
Drs. Bruce and Lee Fnd Grants, 1607
Dubois County Comm Fnd Grants, 1615
Dunspaugh-Dalton Fnd Grants, 1623
Dwight Stuart Youth Fnd Capacity-Building Initiative Grants, 1627
Dyson Fnd Management Assistance Program Mini-Grants, 1632
Eaton Charitable Fund Grants, 1647
Eberly Fnd Grants, 1649
EDS Tech Grants, 1662
Edward W & Stella C Van Houten Mem Fund, 1670
Edwin S. Webster Fnd Grants, 1671
Effie and Wofford Cain Fnd Grants, 1674
El Paso Comm Fnd Grants, 1688
Emily Davie and Joseph S. Kornfeld Fnd Grants, 1697
EPA Environmental Educ Grants, 1729
Eugene M. Lang Fnd Grants, 1764
Eugene McDermott Fnd Grants, 1765
FAR Fund Grants, 1787
Fargo-Moorhead Area Fnd Woman's Fund Grants, 1789
Faye McBeath Fnd Grants, 1794
FEMA Staffing for Adequate Fire and Emergency Response Grants, 1803
Florida Division of Cultural Affairs Culture Builds Florida Expansion Funding, 1848
Florida Division of Cultural Affairs Culture Builds Florida Seed Funding, 1849
Frances L & Edwin L Cummings Mem Fund, 1919
Frank and Lydia Bergen Fnd Grants, 1925
Fremont Area Cmty Fdn Amazing X Grants, 1953
Fremont Area Comm Fnd Grants, 1955
Fritz B. Burns Fnd Grants, 1965
George A Ohl Jr. Fnd Grants, 2012
George Fnd Grants, 2018
George Kress Fnd Grants, 2025
George S & Dolores Dore Eccles Fdn Grants, 2027
GNOF IMPACT Grts for Youth Dev't, 2081
Goldseker Fnd Non-Profit Management Assistance Grants, 2103
Grand Victoria Fnd Illinois Core Grants, 2126

GreenWorks! Butterfly Garden Grants, 2159
GreenWorks! Grants, 2160
Gumdrop Books Librarian Scholarships, 2179
HAF Techn Assistance Pgm Grts, 2206
Harry A & Margaret D Towsley Fnd Grts, 2236
Hartford Aging and Health Program Awards, 2247
Hartford Fdn Nonprofit Support Grants, 2252
Health Fnd of Grtr Indianapolis Grts, 2282
Hill Crest Fnd Grants, 2324
Hillman Fnd Grants, 2327
Humanitas Fnd Grants, 2390
Huntington Arts Council Arts-in-Educ Programs, 2400
ICC Scholarship of Engagement Faculty Grants, 2430
IMLS Native American Library Services Grants, 2517
IMLS Native American Library Services Enhancement Grants, 2518
IMLS Native Hawaiian Library Services Grants, 2519
Independence Blue Cross Charitable Medical Care Grants, 2524
Indiana Arts Commission Statewide Arts Service Organization Grants, 2533
J.M. Long Fnd Grants, 2603
Jacob and Hilda Blaustein Fnd Grants, 2615
James Irvine Fnd Leadership Awards, 2629
James R. Dougherty Jr. Fnd Grants, 2635
Jerome Fnd Grants, 2667
Jerome Fnd Travel and Study Grants, 2668
Jessie Ball Dupont Fund Grants, 2671
John P. McGovern Fnd Grants, 2707
John S Dunn Research Fdn Grants & Chairs, 2715
Johnson & Johnson Corp Contribs Grants, 2718
Joseph Alexander Fnd Grants, 2734
Kansas Arts Commission Partnership Agreement Grants, 2782
Kennedy Center HSC Fnd Internship, 2799
Kennedy Center Summer HSC Fnd Internship, 2800
Kenneth T & Eileen L Norris Fdn Grants, 2802
Kosciusko Cty Comm Fdn Grts, 2838
Leave No Trace Master Educator Scholarships, 2870
Lowe Fnd Grants, 2929
Lynde and Harry Bradley Fnd Grants, 2947
M.B. and Edna Zale Fnd Grants, 2950
Manitoba Arts Council Spcl Opps Grts, 2997
Margaret & James A Elkins Jr Fdn Grts, 3003
Mary Kay Ash Charitable Fnd Grants, 3043
Massachusetts Fnd for Humanities Project Grants, 3060
Meadows Fnd Grants, 3104
Mead Witter Fnd Grants, 3106
Meyer Fdn Strong Nonprofit Sector Grts, 3145
Micron Tech Fdn Comm Grts, 3161
MMS and Alliance Charitable Fnd Int'l Health Studies Grants, 3195
NACC David Stevenson Fellowships, 3235
NACC William Diaz Fellowships, 3236
NASE Succeed Scholarships, 3243
Nevada Arts Council Jackpot Grants, 3312
New Earth Fnd Grants, 3317
NFF Comm Assistance Grants, 3343
NHLBI Ruth L Kirschstein Nat'l Rsch Svc Awds for Indiv Predoc Fellowships to Promote Diversity in Health-Related Research, 3419
NHLBI Ruth L. Kirschstein National Research Service Awards for Individual Senior Fellows, 3421
Nicor Corporate Contributions, 3435
Noble County Comm Fnd Grants, 3456
North Carolina Arts Council Arts in Educ Artist Residencies Grants, 3468
North Carolina Arts Council Regional Grants, 3480
North Carolina BioTech Center Reg Dev Grants, 3488
North Carolina GlaxoSmithKline Fdn Grts, 3490
Northern Chautauqua Comm Fnd Comm Grants, 3499
NRA Fnd Grants, 3517
NSTA Distinguished Informal Science Award, 3531
NYSCA Arts Education: Local Capacity Building Grants , 3581
NYSCA Dance: Commissions Grants, 3583
NYSCA Dance: Gen Pgm Support Grts, 3585
NYSCA Dance: Services to the Field Grants, 3587
NYSCA Electronic Media and Film: General Operating Support, 3590

NYSCA Electronic Media and Film: Workspace Grants, 3593
NYSCA Folk Arts: Gen Pgm Support Grts, 3595
NYSCA Lit: Svcs to the Field Grts, 3601
NYSCA Presenting: Svcs to the Field Grts, 3612
NYSCA Special Arts Services: General Operating Support Grants, 3614
NYSCA Special Arts Services: General Program Support Grants, 3615
NYSCA Special Arts Services: Instruction and Training Grants, 3616
NYSCA State and Local Partnerships: Services to the Field Grants, 3621
NYSCA State and Local Partnerships: Workshops Grants, 3622
NYSCA Theatre: Gen Pgm Support Grts, 3624
NYSCA Theatre: Pro Performances Grts, 3625
NYSCA Theatre: Services to the Field Grants, 3626
Ohio Arts Council Capacity Building Grants for Organizations and Communities, 3652
Ontario Arts Council Artists in the Comm/Workplace Grants, 3676
Ontario Arts Council Compass Grants, 3677
Park Fnd Grants, 3739
PCA-PCD Professional Dev for Individual Artists Grants, 3770
PCA Arts in Educ Residencies, 3772
PCA Arts Organizations & Grants for Visual Arts, 3785
PCA Entry Track Arts Organizations and Arts Grants for Crafts, 3790
PCA Entry Track Arts Organizations and Arts Grants for Visual Arts, 3799
PCA Pennsylvania Partners in the Arts Project Stream Grants, 3802
PCA Professional Dev Grants, 3803
Philadelphia Fdn Org'l Effectiveness Grts, 3872
Phi Upsilon Omicron Florence Fallgatter Distinguished Service Award, 3877
Phi Upsilon Omicron Frances Morton Holbrook Alumni Award, 3878
PMP Professional Dev Grants, 3919
Presbyterian Health Fnd Bridge, Seed and Equipment Grants, 3947
Price Gilbert, Jr. Charitable Fund Grants, 3953
Prince Char Trusts Dist of Columbia Grts, 3960
Public Educ Power Grants, 3981
Puerto Rico Comm Fnd Grants, 3986
Pulaski County Comm Fnd Grants, 3988
Pulte Homes Corporate Contributions, 3989
R.E.B. Awards for Distinguished Educational Leadership, 4000
Rasmuson Fnd Sabbatical Grants, 4024
Regional Arts and Cultural Council Professional Dev Grants, 4047
Rhode Island Fnd Grants, 4073
RISCA Professional Arts Dev Grants, 4099
RISCA Project Grants for Organizations, Individuals and Education, 4100
Robert M. Hearin Fnd Grants, 4116
Robert P & Clara I Milton Fund for Sr Housing, 4117
Rohm and Haas Company Grants, 4145
Ronald McDonald House Charities Grants, 4149
Roney-Fitzpatrick Fnd Grants, 4150
RRF General Grants, 4170
San Antonio Area Fnd Grants, 4240
Sarkeys Fnd Grants, 4297
SAS Institute Comm Relations Donations, 4300
Schering-Plough Fnd Health Grants, 4304
Skaggs Fnd Grants, 4378
SOBP A.E. Bennett Research Award, 4388
Sonora Area Fnd Competitive Grants, 4404
South Carolina Arts Commission Leadership and Organizational Dev Grants, 4423
South Carolina Arts Commission Subgrants, 4426
Sport Manitoba Women to Watch Grants, 4460
Sprint Fnd Grants, 4463
Square D Fnd Grants, 4464
St. Joseph Comm Health Cath Kasper Award, 4468
St. Joseph Comm Health Fnd Improving Healthcare Access Grants, 4469

Stark Comm Fnd Neighborhood Comm and Economic Dev Tech Assistance Grants, 4478
State Justice Institute Project Grants, 4490
Steele-Reese Fnd Grants, 4498
Stettinius Fund for Nonprofit Ldrsp Awds, 4500
Subaru of America Fnd Grants, 4518
TAC Arts Educ Comm-Learning Grts, 4552
TAC Arts Projects Grants, 4554
TAC Rural Arts Project Support Grants, 4555
Texas Comsn on the Arts Create-1 Pgm Grts, 4583
Tourism Cares Professional Dev Scholarships, 4648
US Dept of Educ Native Hawaiian Educ Grts, 4694
Union County Comm Fnd Grants, 4711
USDA Hispanic-Serving Institutions Grants, 4813
USDA Rural Business Opportunity Grants, 4824
V.V. Cooke Fnd Grants, 4896
Vancouver Fnd Grants and Comm Initiatives, 4900
Virginia Fnd for the Humanities Residential Fellowships, 4948
Wallace Global Fund Grants, 4977
Wayne and Gladys Valley Fnd Grants, 5003
Weingart Fnd Grants, 5018
West Virginia Commission on the Arts Professional Dev for Artists Grants, 5045
WILD Fnd Grants, 5068
William T. Grant Fnd Youth Service Improvement Grants, 5096
Xerox Fnd Grants, 5122
Youth Philanthropy Project, 5132

Fellowships
3M Fnd Comm Giving Grants, 15
AAAS Science and Tech Policy Fellowships: Energy, Environment, and Agriculture, 52
AAAS Science and Tech Policy Fellowships: Health, Educ and Human Services, 53
Abbott Fund Science Educ Grants, 83
Abell-Hanger Fnd Grants, 91
Abney Fnd Grants, 105
Acumen East Africa Fellowship, 141
Acumen Global Fellowships, 142
Alliant Energy Fnd Comm Grants, 384
Andy Warhol Fdn for the Visual Arts Grts, 464
Applied Materials Corp Philanthropy Pgm, 515
APSA Minority Fellowships, 517
Aratani Fnd Grants, 523
Arie and Ida Crown Memorial Grants, 533
Arthur and Rochelle Belfer Fnd Grants, 570
Arts and Science Council Grants, 576
Asian American Institute Impact Fellowships, 588
ASM Congressional Science Fellowships, 589
Ball Brothers Fnd General Grants, 637
Boeing Company Contributions Grants, 809
Brookdale Fnd Leadership in Aging Fellowships, 844
Bush Fnd Leadership Fellowships, 876
Cabot Corporation Fnd Grants, 887
Caddock Fnd Grants, 888
Caesars Fnd Grants, 891
Carrier Corporation Contributions Grants, 946
Carroll County Comm Fnd Grants, 947
Cemala Fnd Grants, 988
Center for the Study of Philanthropy Fellowships, 989
Center for the Study of Philanthropy Senior Int'l Fellowships, 990
Chapin Hall Int'l Fellowships in Children's Policy, 1032
Charles & Lynn Schusterman Fam Fdn Grants, 1038
Charles H. Revson Fnd Grants, 1047
Chicago Comm Trust Fellowships, 1086
Christensen Fund Regional Grants, 1112
CIGNA Fnd Grants, 1130
Coastal Bend Comm Fnd Grants, 1192
Coca-Cola Fnd Grants, 1195
Commonwealth Fund Australian-American Health Policy Fellowships, 1241
Commonwealth Fund Harkness Fellowships in Health Care Policy and Practice, 1242
Comm Fdn for NE Michigan Grants, 1257
Comm Fdn for Southern Arizona Grants, 1261
Comm Tech Fdn of California Building Communities Through Tech Grants, 1336

Compton Fnd Int'l Fellowships, 1339
Compton Fnd Mentor Fellowships, 1340
Council on Fnds Emerging Philanthropic Leaders Fellowships, 1378
DOJ National Inst of Justice Visiting Fellowships, 1561
Dorot Fnd Grants, 1586
Durfee Fnd Stanton Fellowship, 1626
Echoing Green Fellowships, 1650
Edward W & Stella C Van Houten Mem Fund, 1670
Edwin S. Webster Fnd Grants, 1671
Edwin W & Catherine M Davis Fdn Grants, 1672
Effie and Wofford Cain Fnd Grants, 1674
Enterprise Comm Partners Rose Architectural Fellowships, 1719
Enterprise Comm Partners Terwilliger Fellowship, 1720
Eugene M. Lang Fnd Grants, 1764
Evan Frankel Fnd Grants, 1770
Ford Fnd Diversity Fellowships, 1883
Ford Fdn Peace & Social Justice Grts, 1884
Fritz B. Burns Fnd Grants, 1965
Germanistic Society of America Fellowships, 2043
Gertrude E Skelly Charitable Fdn Grts, 2046
GMFUS Marshall Memorial Fellowships, 2066
HA & Mary K Chapman Char Trust Grts, 2182
H. Schaffer Fnd Grants, 2187
Hirtzel Memorial Fnd Grants, 2332
HRF Tibor T. Polgar Fellowships, 2380
ICC Faculty Fellowships, 2428
IFP Minnesota McKnight Filmmaking Fwsps, 2448
IFP Minnesota McKnight Screenwriters Fwsps, 2449
IIE David L. Boren Fellowships, 2454
IIE Leonora Lindsley Memorial Fellowships, 2458
Institute for Agriculture and Trade Policy Food and Society Fellowships, 2561
Iowa Arts Council Artists in Schools/Communities Residency Grants, 2571
ISI William E Simon Fwsps for Noble Purpose, 2588
Japan Fnd Center for Global Partnership Grants, 2649
Jerome Fnd Grants, 2667
Joel L. Fleishman Civil Society Fellowships, 2683
John Deere Fnd Grants, 2692
Johnson & Johnson Corp Contribs Grants, 2718
Kansas Health Fnd Recognition Grants, 2784
Kentucky Arts Council Al Smith Fellowship, 2806
Kiplinger Program in Public Affairs Journalism Fellowships, 2826
Lloyd G. Balfour Fnd Attleboro-Specific Charities Grants, 2916
Lubrizol Fnd Grants, 2933
Luther I. Replogle Fnd Grants, 2945
Lynde and Harry Bradley Fnd Grants, 2947
M3C Fellowships, 2955
Mary Duke Biddle Fnd Grants, 3036
Mary K. Chapman Fnd Grants, 3042
Massachusetts Bar Fnd Legal Intern Fellowships, 3051
MedImmune Charitable Grants, 3108
Mericos Fnd Grants, 3121
Microsoft Comty Affairs Puget Sound Grts, 3163
Morris & Gwendolyn Cafritz Fdn Grants, 3218
Morris K. Udall and Stewart L. Udall Fnd Dissertation Fellowships, 3219
NACC David Stevenson Fellowships, 3235
NACC William Diaz Fellowships, 3236
National Endowment for Democracy Reagan-Fascell Democracy Fellowships, 3252
National Endowment for Democracy Visiting Fellows Program, 3253
National Urban Fellows Program, 3281
Nation Institute Robert Masur Fellowship in Civil Liberties, 3284
New Hampshire Charitable Fnd Grants, 3325
NHLBI Ruth L Kirschstein Nat'l Rsch Svc Awds for Indiv Predoc Fellowships to Promote Diversity in Health-Related Research, 3419
NHLBI Ruth L. Kirschstein National Research Service Awards for Individual Predoctoral MD/PhD Fellows and Other Dual Degree Fellows, 3420
NHLBI Ruth L. Kirschstein National Research Service Awards for Individual Senior Fellows, 3421
Norcliffe Fnd Grants, 3459

PROGRAM TYPE INDEX

North Dakota Council on the Arts Individual Artist Fellowships, 3495
NYFA Deutsche Bank Americas Fellowship, 3564
NYFA Gregory Millard Fellowships, 3565
NYSCA Music: Cmy Music Schools Grts, 3605
Oklahoma City Comm Pgms & Grts, 3666
Olin Corporation Charitable Trust Grants, 3669
OSF-Baltimore Comm Fellowships, 3695
OSF Civil Service Awards, 3705
Park Fnd Grants, 3739
Patrick and Anna M. Cudahy Fund Grants, 3751
Paul & Daisy Soros Fwsps for New Americans, 3754
Paul Green Fnd Playwrights Fellowship, 3762
PCA Arts Organizations and Grants for Crafts, 3778
Pew Fellowships in the Arts, 3860
Phil Hardin Fnd Grants, 3875
Price Family Charitable Fund Grants, 3952
R.C. Baker Fnd Grants, 3999
Radcliffe Inst Indiv Residential Fellowships, 4004
Rajiv Gandhi Fnd Grants, 4011
Ralph M. Parsons Fnd Grants, 4013
RAND Corporation Graduate Student Summer Associateships, 4018
Rasmuson Fdn Individual Artists Awds, 4022
Rathmann Family Fnd Grants, 4026
Rhode Island Fnd Grants, 4073
RISCA Design Innovation Grant, 4097
Rockefeller Bros Fund Fwsp in Nonprofit Law, 4132
RWJF Health Policy Fellowships, 4184
San Francisco Fnd Fund for Artists Arts Teacher Fellowships, 4269
San Francisco Fnd Fund Shenson Performing Arts Fellowships, 4275
San Francisco Fnd John Gutmann Photography Fellowship Award, 4279
San Francisco Fdn Multicultural Fwsp, 4281
San Francisco Fnd Murphy and Cadogan Fellowships in the Fine Arts, 4282
Sarah Scaife Fnd Grants, 4295
Shell Oil Company Fnd Grants, 4343
Siragusa Fnd Health Services & Medical Research Grants, 4368
South Carolina Arts Comsn Artists Fwsps, 4415
SSHRC Therese F. Casgrain Fellowship, 4466
SSRC-Van Alen Fellowships, 4467
Supreme Ct Fellows Commission Fwsps, 4532
Tanner Humanities Cntr Rsch Fellowships, 4559
Temple Univ George D McDowell Fellowship, 4577
Tulane University Public Service Fellows, 4678
Virginia Fnd for the Humanities Residential Fellowships, 4948
Virginia Historical Society Rsch Fwsps, 4949
Vulcan Materials Company Fnd Grants, 4956
Walt Disney Company Fnd Grants, 4981
Weyerhaeuser Company Fnd Grants, 5053
Xerox Fnd Grants, 5122
Youth Action Net Fellowships, 5128

General Operating Support
1st Source Fnd Grants, 3
2COBS Private Charitable Fnd Grants, 6
41 Washington Street Fnd Grants, 22
100 Angels Charitable Fnd Grants, 24
100 Women in Hedge Funds Fnd Grants, 28
118 Fnd Grants, 29
786 Fnd Grants, 33
1104 Fnd Grants, 34
2701 Fnd Grants, 37
A.C. Ratshesky Fnd Grants, 39
A.V. Hunter Trust Grants, 47
A/H Fnd Grants, 48
Abbot & Dorothy H Stevens Fdn Grants, 79
Abbott Fund Access to Health Care Grants, 80
Abbott Fund Comm Grants, 81
Abbott Fund Global AIDS Care Grants, 82
Abbott Fund Science Educ Grants, 83
Abel & Sophia Sheng Charitable Fdn Grts, 86
Abelard Fnd East Grants, 87
Abelard Fnd West Grants, 88
Abeles Fnd Grants, 89

Abel Fnd Grants, 90
Abell-Hanger Fnd Grants, 91
Abell Fnd Arts and Culture Grants, 92
Abell Fdn Comm Dev Grts, 93
Abell Fnd Conservation and Environment Grants, 94
Abell Fdn Criminal Justice & Addictions Grts, 95
Abell Fdn Health & Human Svcs Grts, 96
Abernethy Family Fnd Grants, 98
Able To Serve Grants, 102
Aboudane Family Fnd Grants, 106
Abundance Fnd Int'l Grants, 108
ACF ACYF Runaway and Homeless Youth Basic Center Grants, 112
ACF Mentoring Children of Prisoners Grants, 121
ACF Preferred Communities Grants, 124
ACF Supplemental Services for Recently Arrived Refugees Grants, 125
A Charitable Fnd Grants, 126
Achelis Fnd Grants, 127
Ackerman Fnd Grants, 129
Actors Fund Soc Svcs & Financial Assistance, 139
Acuity Charitable Fnd Grants, 140
Adam Reineman Charitable Trust Grants, 144
Adam Richter Charitable Trust Grants, 145
Adams-Mastrovich Family Fnd Grants, 146
Adams and Reese LLP Corporate Giving Grants, 147
Adams County Comm Fnd of Pennsylvania Grants, 149
Adams Family Fnd I Grants, 150
Adams Family Fnd of Ohio Grants, 151
Adams Family Fnd of Tennessee Grants, 152
Adams Fnd Grants, 155
Adam Shikiar Fnd Grants, 156
Adolph Coors Fnd Grants, 171
AEC Trust Grants, 175
AEGON Transamerica Fdn Arts & Culture Grts, 176
AEGON Transamerica Fdn Civic Grants, 177
AEGON Transamerica Fdn Health and Welfare Grants, 179
Aetna Fnd Strengthening Neighborhhods Grants in Connecticut, 188
AFG Industries Grants, 191
African American Fund of New Jersey Grants, 192
AHS Fnd Grants, 208
Air Products and Chemicals Grants, 216
Akonadi Fnd Anti-Racism Grants, 217
Alabama Power Fnd Grants, 233
Alabama State Council on the Arts Comm Arts Operating Support Grants, 237
Alabama State Council on the Arts Operating Support Grants, 244
Alabama State Council on the Arts Program Dev Grants, 246
Aladdin Industries Fnd Grants, 263
Alaska Airlines Corporate Giving Grants, 320
Alaska Conservation Fnd Operating Grants, 323
Alaska State Council on the Arts Operating Support Grants, 328
Alberta Law Fnd Grants, 338
Albert and Bessie Mae Kronkosky Charitable Fnd Grants, 339
Alberto Culver Corporate Contributions Grants, 343
Albert Pick Jr. Fund Grants, 344
Albertson's Charitable Giving Grants, 345
Albert W. Cherne Fnd Grants, 346
Albert W. Rice Charitable Fnd Grants, 347
Albuquerque Comm Fnd Grants, 348
Alcatel-Lucent Technologies Fnd Grants, 349
Alcoa Fnd Grants, 350
Alcon Fnd Grants, 351
Alexander & Baldwin Fnd Hawaiian and Pacific Island Grants, 352
Alexander & Baldwin Fdn Mainland Grants, 353
Alexander H. Bright Charitable Trust Grants, 358
Alex Brown & Sons Charitable Fdn Grants, 359
Alex Stern Family Fnd Grants, 360
ALFJ Astraea U.S. and Int'l Movement Fund, 361
Alfred & Tillie Shemanski Testamentary Grants, 363
Alfred Bersted Fnd Grants, 364
Alfred C & Ersa S Arbogast Fdn Grants, 365
Alfred E. Chase Charitable Fnd Grants, 366

Alfred P Sloan Fdn Civic Initiatives Grts, 368
A Little Hope Grants, 373
Allegheny Fnd Grants, 376
Allegheny Technologies Charitable Trust, 377
Allen Hilles Fund Grants, 378
Alliant Energy Fnd Comm Grants, 384
Alpine Winter Fnd Grants, 394
Altria Group Arts and Culture Grants, 399
Alvah H & Wyline P Chapman Fdn Grts, 402
Alvin & Fanny Blaustein Thalheimer Fdn Grts, 403
Amador Comm Fnd Grants, 408
AMA Fnd Healthy Communities/Healthy America Grants, 410
Amelia Sillman Rockwell and Carlos Perry Rockwell Charities Fund Grants, 417
Ameren Corporation Comm Grants, 418
Americana Fnd Grants, 422
American Chemical Scty Corp Assocs Seed Grts, 425
American Express Charitable Fund Grants, 429
American Express Fnd Comm Service Grants, 430
American Express Historic Preservation Grants, 431
American Foodservice Charitable Trust Grants, 433
American Fnd Grants, 436
American Schlafhorst Fnd Grants, 446
Amerigroup Fnd Grants, 452
AMERIND Comm Service Project Grants, 453
AmerUs Group Charitable Fnd, 455
Amgen Fnd Grants, 456
AMI Semiconductors Corporate Grants, 457
Amon G. Carter Fnd Grants, 458
Andersen Corporate Fnd, 459
Anderson Fnd Grants, 460
Andre Agassi Charitable Fnd Grants, 461
Andrew Family Fnd Grants, 462
Anheuser-Busch Fnd Grants, 470
ANLAF Int'l Fund for Sexual Minorities Grts, 471
Anne J. Caudal Fnd Grants, 475
Anne L. and George H. Clapp Charitable and Educational Trust Grants, 476
Anne Thorne Weaver Family Fnd Grants, 478
Ann L. and Carol Green Rhodes Grants, 483
Ann Peppers Fnd Grants, 484
Anschutz Family Fnd Grants, 486
Anthony R. Abraham Fnd Grants, 489
Antone & Edene Vidinha Char Trust Grts, 490
Appalachian Comm Fund Gen Fund Grts, 493
Appalachian Regional Commission Distressed Counties Grants, 503
Appalachian Regional Commission Export and Trade Dev Grants, 506
Aragona Family Fnd Grants, 522
Aratani Fnd Grants, 523
Arbor Day Fnd Grants, 524
Arcadia Fnd Grants, 525
Arca Fnd Grants, 526
ARCO Fnd Educ Grants, 528
Arcus Fnd Fund Grants, 529
Arie and Ida Crown Memorial Grants, 533
Arizona Comm Fnd Grants, 540
Arizona Diamondbacks Charities Grants, 542
Arizona Public Service Corp Gvg Pgm Grts, 545
Arizona Republic Fnd Grants, 546
Arizona Republic Newspaper Corp Contribs, 547
Arkansas Arts Council Expansion Arts Grants, 556
Arkansas Arts Council Gen Op Support, 557
Arkell Hall Fnd Grants, 562
Arlington Comm Fnd Grants, 564
Armstrong McDonald Fnd Grants, 565
Arronson Fnd Grants, 567
ARS Fnd Grants, 568
Arthur and Rochelle Belfer Fnd Grants, 570
Arthur F & Alice E Adams Charitable Fdn Grts, 574
Artist Trust GAP Grants, 575
Arts Council of Winston-Salem and Forsyth County Organizational Support Grants, 577
ArvinMeritor Fdn Arts & Culture Grts, 582
Aspen Comm Fnd Grants, 592
Atherton Family Fnd Grants, 604
Athwin Fnd Grants, 605
Atkinson Fnd Comm Grants, 606

Atlanta Fnd Grants, 608
Atlanta Women's Fnd Grants, 609
Atran Fnd Grants, 610
Auburn Fnd Grants, 611
Audrey and Sydney Irmas Charitable Fnd Grants, 612
Austin S. Nelson Fnd Grants, 617
Autauga Area Comm Fnd Grants, 618
AutoNation Corporate Giving Grants, 620
Avon Products Fnd Grants, 625
AWDF Main Grants, 627
Ayres Fnd Grants, 630
Azadoutioun Fnd Grants, 631
Babcock Charitable Trust Grants, 632
Back Home Again Fnd Grants, 633
Bacon Family Fnd Grants, 634
Bailey Fnd Grants, 635
Balfe Family Fnd Grants, 636
Ball Brothers Fnd General Grants, 637
Ball Brothers Fnd Rapid Grants, 639
Baltimore Comm Fnd Arts and Culture Grants, 641
BancorpSouth Fnd Grants, 651
Banfi Vintners Fnd Grants, 653
BankAtlantic Fnd Grants, 654
Bank of America Charitable Fnd Matching Gifts, 658
Bank of America Charitable Fnd Volunteer Grants, 660
Bank of America Corporation Sponsorships, 661
Baptist-Trinity Lutheran Legacy Fdn Grants, 663
Barbara Meyer Elsner Fnd Grants, 665
Barker Fnd Grants, 668
Barker Welfare Fnd Grants, 669
Barrasso Usdin Kupperman Freeman and Sarver LLC Corporate Grants, 675
Barr Fund Grants, 678
Batchelor Fnd Grants, 679
Batts Fnd Grants, 687
Baughman Fnd Grants, 688
Baxter Int'l Corporate Giving Grants, 689
Baxter Int'l Fnd Grants, 691
Bay and Paul Fnds, Inc Grants, 692
Bay and Paul Fnds Grants, 693
BBF Florida Family Lit Initiative Grants, 697
Beazley Fnd Grants, 714
Bechtel Group Fnd Building Positive Comm Relationships Grants, 715
Beerman Fnd Grants, 717
Beim Fnd Grants, 718
Beldon Fund Grants, 720
Belk Fnd Grants, 721
Bemis Company Fnd Grants, 723
Ben & Jerry's Fnd Grants, 724
Bender Fnd Grants, 726
Beneficia Fnd Grants, 727
Bennett Family Fnd of Texas Grants, 728
Berks County Comm Fnd Grants, 734
Bernard F. Reynolds Charitable Trust Grants, 741
Bernard Osher Fnd Grants, 742
Berrien Comm Fnd Grants, 744
Bertha Russ Lytel Fnd Grants, 745
Besser Fnd Grants, 748
Bicknell Fund Grants, 759
Bill and Katie Weaver Charitable Trust Grants, 764
Bill and Melinda Gates Ag Dev Grants, 765
Bill and Melinda Gates Fnd Emergency Response Grants, 766
Bill and Melinda Gates Fnd Water, Sanitation and Hygiene Grants, 770
Bitha Godfrey & Maude J. Thomas Charitable Fnd Grants, 776
Blanche and Irving Laurie Fnd Grants, 784
Blanche & Julian Robertson Family Fnd Grants, 785
Blandin Fdn Expand Opportunity Grants, 787
Blandin Fnd Itasca County Area Vitality Grants, 789
Blandin Fnd Rural Comm Leadership Grants, 790
Blowitz-Ridgeway Fnd Grants, 792
Blue Cross Blue Shield of Minnesota Fdn-Healthy Equity: Public Libraries for Health Grts, 797
Blue Mountain Comm Fnd Grants, 800
Blum-Kovler Fnd Grants, 803
Blumenthal Fnd Grants, 804
Bodman Fnd Grants, 807

Boeckmann Charitable Fnd Grants, 808
Boeing Company Contributions Grants, 809
Boettcher Fnd Grants, 810
Bohemian Fnd Pharos Fund Grants, 811
Bonfils-Stanton Fnd Grants, 814
Booth Ferris Fnd Grants, 816
Borkee-Hagley Fnd Grants, 817
Boston Fnd Grants, 819
Boston Fnd Initiative to Strengthen Arts and Cultural Service Organizations, 820
Boston Globe Fnd Grants, 821
Boulder County Arts Alliance Neodata Endowment Grants, 823
Boyd Gaming Corporation Contributions, 825
Bradley-Turner Fnd Grants, 828
Brainerd Fnd Grants, 831
Brett Family Fnd Grants, 833
Brico Fund Grants, 835
Bright Family Fnd Grants, 837
Bright Promises Fnd Grants, 838
Brookdale Fdn National Group Respite Grts, 845
Brooklyn Benevolent Society Grants, 847
Brooklyn Comty Fnd Caring Neighbors Grts, 848
Brooklyn Comm Fnd Comm Arts for All Grants, 849
Brooklyn Comm Fnd Comm Dev Grants, 850
Brooklyn Comm Fnd Educ and Youth Achievement Grants, 851
Brooklyn Comm Fnd Green Communities Grants, 852
Brown Fnd Grants, 854
Brunswick Fnd Dollars for Doers Grants, 856
Brunswick Fnd Grants, 857
Build-A-Bear Workshop Bear Hugs Fnd Lit and Educ Grants, 860
Build-A-Bear Workshop Fnd Grants, 861
Bullitt Fnd Grants, 862
Bunbury Company Grants, 863
Burlington Northern Santa Fe Fnd Grants, 866
Burton D. Morgan Adult Entrepreneurship Grants, 868
Burton G. Bettinger Grants, 871
Bush Fnd Arts & Humanities Grants: Short-Term Organizational Support, 873
Bush Fnd Ecological Health Grants, 874
Bush Fdn Health & Human Svcs Grts, 875
Bush Fnd Regional Arts Dev Program II Grants, 878
Butler Mfg Co Fnd Grants, 881
Bydale Fnd Grants, 882
C.F. Adams Charitable Trust Grants, 884
Cabot Corporation Fnd Grants, 887
Caddock Fnd Grants, 888
Caesar Puff Fnd Grants, 890
Caesars Fnd Grants, 891
Cailloux Fnd Grants, 892
Caleb C. and Julia W. Dula Educational and Charitable Fnd Grants, 893
California Arts Council State-Local Partnership Grants, 896
California Comm Fnd Health Care Grants, 901
Callaway Fnd Grants, 909
Callaway Golf Company Fnd Grants, 910
Cambridge Comm Fnd Grants, 913
Camp-Younts Fnd Grants, 914
Campbell Hoffman Fnd Grants, 915
Campbell Soup Fnd Grants, 916
Cape Branch Fnd Grants, 919
CarEth Fnd Grants, 924
Cargill Citizenship Fund-Corp Gvg Grants, 925
Caring Fnd Grants, 926
Carl & Eloise Pohlad Family Fdn Grants, 927
Carl C. Icahn Fnd Grants, 929
Carl Gellert and Celia Berta Gellert Fdn Grts, 930
Carl M. Freeman Fnd FACES Grants, 932
Carl M. Freeman Fnd Grants, 933
Carl R. Hendrickson Family Fnd Grants, 935
Carl W. and Carrie Mae Joslyn Trust Grants, 938
Carnahan-Jackson Fnd Grants, 939
Carnegie Corporation of New York Grants, 940
Carolyn Fnd Grants, 942
Carpenter Fnd Grants, 943
Carrie E. and Lena V. Glenn Fnd Grants, 944
Carrie Estelle Doheny Fnd Grants, 945

Carrier Corporation Contributions Grants, 946
Carylon Fnd Grants, 949
Castle and Cooke California Corp Giving, 953
Caterpillar Fnd Grants, 954
Catherine Manley Gaylord Fnd Grants, 956
CCHD Economic Dev Grants, 967
CDECD Arts Catalyze Placemaking in Every Comm Grants, 977
CDECD Arts Catalyze Placemaking Leadership Grants, 978
CDECD Arts Catalyze Placemaking Sustaining Relevance Grants, 979
CE and S Fnd Grants, 985
Cemala Fnd Grants, 988
Central New York Comm Fdn Grants, 996
CFFVR Alcoholism and Drug Abuse Grants, 1001
CFFVR Basic Needs Gvg Partnership Grts, 1002
CFFVR Bridge Grants, 1003
CFFVR Capital Credit Union Charitable Giving Grants, 1005
CFFVR Clintonville Area Fnd Grants, 1007
CFFVR Clintonville Area Fnd Grants, 1008
CFFVR Environmental Stewardship Grants, 1010
CFFVR Frank C. Shattuck Comm Grants, 1012
CFFVR SAC Dev Disabilities Grts, 1019
CFFVR Schmidt Family G4 Grants, 1020
CFFVR Shawano Area Comm Fnd Grants, 1021
CFFVR Wisconsin Daughters and Sons Grants, 1024
CFFVR Women's Fund for the Fox Valley Region Grants, 1025
Chamberlain Fnd Grants, 1027
Champ-A Champion Fur Kids Grants, 1028
Chapman Charitable Fnd Grants, 1033
Charity Incorporated Grants, 1035
Charles A. Frueauff Fnd Grants, 1037
Charles & Lynn Schusterman Fam Fdn Grants, 1038
Charles Delmar Fnd Grants, 1039
Charles G. Koch Charitable Fnd Grants, 1041
Charles H. Farnsworth Trust Grants, 1043
Charles H. Pearson Fnd Grants, 1045
Charles M & Mary D Grant Fdn Grants, 1050
Charles M. Bair Family Trust Grants, 1051
Charles Nelson Robinson Fund Grants, 1052
Charles Stewart Mott Fdn Anti-Poverty Grts, 1054
Charles Stewart Mott Fnd Grants, 1055
Charlotte County Comm Fnd Grts, 1056
Chatlos Fnd Grants, 1061
Chautauqua Region Comm Fdn Grts, 1062
CHC Fnd Grants, 1065
Chemtura Corporation Contributions Grants, 1067
Chesapeake Bay Environmental Educ Grants, 1069
Chesapeake Bay Trust Outreach and Comm Engagement Grants, 1073
Chicago Board of Trade Fnd Grants, 1079
Chicago CityArts Grants, 1080
Chicago Comm Trust Workforce Grants, 1094
Chicago Neighborhood Arts Grants, 1097
Chicago Sun Times Charity Trust Grants, 1098
Chicago Title & Trust Co Fdn Grants, 1099
Chicago Tribune Fnd Civic Grants, 1100
Chicago Tribune Fnd Grants for Cultural Organizations, 1101
Chiles Fnd Grants, 1108
Chingos Fnd Grants, 1109
Christensen Fund Regional Grants, 1112
Christine and Katharina Pauly Charitable Grants, 1114
CICF Indianapolis Fdn Comm Grants, 1123
CICF Jn Harrison Brown & Robert Burse Grt, 1125
CICF Senior Grants, 1127
CIGNA Fnd Grants, 1130
Cincinnati Bell Fnd Grants, 1131
Cincinnati Milacron Fnd Grants, 1132
Circle K Corporation Contributions Grants, 1136
Citigroup Fnd Grants, 1139
Citizens Savings Fnd Grants, 1141
City of Oakland Cultural Arts Dept Grts, 1142
Claneil Fnd Grants, 1145
Clara Blackford Smith and W. Aubrey Smith Charitable Fnd Grants, 1147
Clarcor Fnd Grants, 1148

PROGRAM TYPE INDEX

General Operating Support

Clarence E Heller Charitable Fdn Grants, 1150
Clarence T.C. Ching Fnd Grants, 1151
Clark-Winchcole Fnd Grants, 1152
Clark and Carolyn Adams Fnd Grants, 1153
Clark and Ruby Baker Fnd Grants, 1154
Clark Charitable Trust Grants, 1155
Clark Fnd Grants, 1157
Claude A. and Blanche McCubbin Abbott Charitable Trust Grants, 1158
Claude Bennett Family Fnd Grants, 1159
Claude Worthington Benedum Fdn Grants, 1161
Clayton Baker Trust Grants, 1163
Cleveland-Cliffs Fnd Grants, 1165
Clowes Fund Grants, 1177
CMA Fnd Grants, 1178
CNA Fnd Grants, 1179
CNCS Foster Grandparent Projects Grants, 1185
CNCS Senior Companion Grants, 1187
CNCS Senior Corps Retired and Senior Volunteer Grants, 1188
Coastal Bend Comm Fnd Grants, 1192
Coastal Comm Fdn of SC Grants, 1193
Cobb Family Fnd Grants, 1194
Coca-Cola Fnd Grants, 1195
Coeta and Donald Barker Fnd Grants, 1197
Coleman Fnd Cancer Care Grants, 1199
Coleman Fnd Deval Disabilities Grants, 1200
Colgate-Palmolive Company Grants, 1202
Colin Higgins Fnd Grants, 1204
Collins C. Diboll Private Fnd Grants, 1208
Collins Fnd Grants, 1209
Colonel Stanley R. McNeil Fnd Grants, 1210
Colorado Interstate Gas Grants, 1213
Colorado Springs Cmty Trust Fund Grants, 1215
Colorado Trust Grants, 1216
Columbus Fnd Dorothy E. Ann Fund (D.E.A.F.) Traditional Grants, 1221
Columbus Fnd John W. and Edna McManus Shepard Fund Grants, 1223
Columbus Fnd Mary Eleanor Morris Fund Grants, 1225
Columbus Fnd Traditional Grants, 1233
Comer Fnd Grants, 1236
Commission on Religion in Appalachia Grants, 1238
Comm Fdn for Grtr Buffalo Grants, 1247
Comm Fnd for Greater New Haven $5,000 and Under Grants, 1248
Comm Fnd for Greater New Haven Quinnipiac River Fund Grants, 1250
Comm Fnd for Greater New Haven Responsive New Grants, 1251
Comm Fnd for Greater New Haven Women & Girls Grants, 1254
Comm Fdn for Monterey Cty Grants, 1255
Comm Fdn for Southern Arizona Grants, 1261
Comm Fnd of Bartholomew County Heritage Fund Grants, 1267
Comm Fdn of Central Illinois Grants, 1276
Comm Fnd of Collier County Capacity Building Grants, 1277
Comm Fdn of Grant Cty Grants, 1279
Comm Fdn of Grtr Birmingham Grants, 1280
Comm Fdn of Greater Flint Grants, 1282
Comm Fnd of Greater Greensboro Grants, 1288
Comm Fnd of Greenville Hollingsworth Funds Program/Project Grants, 1296
Comm Fnd of Louisville Grants, 1299
Comm Fnd of Muncie & Delaware County Grant, 1302
Comm Fdn of S Alabama Grants, 1308
Comm Fnd of South Puget Sound Grants, 1311
Comm Fnd of St. Joseph County ArtsEverywhere Grants, 1313
Comm Fnd of St. Joseph County Special Project Challenge Grants, 1314
Comm Fnd of Switzerland County Grants, 1315
Comm Fnd of the Ozarks Grants, 1320
Comm Fnd of the Verdugos Educational Endowment Fund Grants, 1321
Comm Fnd of the Verdugos Grants, 1322
Comm Fnd of the Virgin Isl Kimelman Grants, 1324
Comm Fnd of Wabash Cty Grants, 1326

Comm Fnd Silicon Valley Advancing Arts Grants, 1330
Comm Fnd Silicon Valley Grants, 1331
Comm Memorial Fnd Grants, 1334
Comprehensive Health Educ Fdn Grts, 1337
Compton Fnd Grants, 1338
ConAgra Foods Fnd Comm Impact Grants, 1342
ConAgra Foods Fnd Nourish Our Comm Grants, 1343
Con Edison Corp Giving Arts & Culture Grants, 1344
Connelly Fnd Grants, 1353
ConocoPhillips Fnd Grants, 1354
ConocoPhillips Grants, 1355
Constellation Energy Corp EcoStar Grts, 1363
Constellation Energy Corporate Grants, 1364
Consumers Energy Fnd, 1365
Conwood Charitable Trust Grants, 1366
Cooke Fnd Grants, 1368
Cooper Fnd Grants, 1369
Cooper Industries Fnd Grants, 1370
Cord Fnd Grants, 1372
Corina Higginson Trust Grants, 1373
Cornerstone Fdn of NE Wisconsin Grants, 1375
Coughlin-Saunders Fnd Grants, 1377
Countess Moira Charitable Fnd Grants, 1381
Covenant Mountain Ministries Grants, 1387
Cowles Charitable Trust Grants, 1392
Crail-Johnson Fnd Grants, 1393
Cralle Fnd Grants, 1394
Cranston Fnd Grants, 1395
Crescent Porter Hale Fnd Grants, 1398
Crestlea Fnd Grants, 1399
Crossroads Fund Seed Grants, 1400
Crowell Trust Grants, 1401
Cullen Fnd Grants, 1411
Cummins Fnd Grants, 1415
D.F. Halton Fnd Grants, 1424
D. W. McMillan Fnd Grants, 1426
Dade Comm Fnd AIDS Partnership Grants, 1428
Dade Comm Fnd Grants, 1430
Dade Comm Fdn Safe Passage Grts, 1431
DaimlerChrysler Corporation Fund Grants, 1432
Dale and Edna Walsh Fnd Grants, 1435
Dallas Women's Fnd Grants, 1438
Dana Corporation Fnd Grants, 1440
Danellie Fnd Grants, 1442
Dan Murphy Fnd Grants, 1444
Daphne Seybolt Culpeper Mem Fdn Grts, 1445
Dave Coy Fnd Grants, 1447
David & Barbara B. Hirschhorn Fdn Grt, 1450
David Bohnett Fnd Grants, 1451
David Geffen Fnd Grants, 1452
Dayton Fnd Grants, 1463
Dayton Power and Light Fnd Grants, 1464
Daywood Fnd Grants, 1465
Deaconess Comm Fnd Grants, 1467
Deborah Munroe Noonan Mem Fund Grts, 1475
DeKalb County Comm Fdn Grts, 1481
Delaware Division of the Arts Opportunity Grants-- Arts Organizations, 1488
Denton A. Cooley Fnd Grants, 1500
DeRoy Testamentary Fnd Grants, 1518
DHHS American Recovery and Reinvestment Act of 2009 Head Start Expansion, 1526
DHHS ARRA Strengthening Communities Fund - Nonprofit Capacity Building Grants, 1527
DHHS ARRA Strengthening Communities Fund - State, Local, and Tribal Government Capacity Building Grants, 1528
DHHS Comm Svcs Grant Trng & Tech Assistance Pgm: Capacity-Bldg for Ongoing CSBG Pgm, 1529
DHL Charitable Shipment Support, 1541
DHS ARRA Fire Station Const Grants , 1542
DHS ARRA Port Security Grants, 1543
DHS ARRA Transit Security Grants , 1544
Dining for Women Grants, 1548
DogTime Tech Grant, 1553
Dolan Fnd Grants, 1563
Donald & Sylvia Robinson Family Fdn Grts, 1573
Dora Roberts Fnd Grants, 1579
Doree Taylor Charitable Fnd, 1580
Do Right Fnd Grants, 1581

Doris and Victor Day Fnd Grants, 1582
Doris Duke Charitable Fnd Child Abuse Prevention Grants, 1585
Dorothy G Griffin Char Fdn Grts, 1588
Dorrance Family Fnd Grants, 1590
Dorr Fnd Grants, 1591
Do Something Plum Youth Grants, 1593
Doug and Carla Salmon Fnd Grants, 1594
Douty Fnd Grants, 1595
DPA Promoting Policy Change Advocacy Grts, 1598
Dream Weaver Fnd, 1604
Dresher Fnd Grants, 1605
Dreyer's Fnd Large Grants, 1606
Drug Free Communities Support Program, 1608
DTE Energy Fdn Comm Dev Grants, 1609
DTE Energy Fnd Cultural Grants, 1610
DTE Energy Health & Human Services Grants, 1613
DTE Energy Fnd Leadership Grants, 1614
Dubois County Comm Fnd Grants, 1615
Duchossois Family Fnd Grants, 1616
Duke Energy Fdn Comm Vitality Grants, 1618
Duke Energy Fnd Econ Dev Grants, 1619
Duluth-Superior Area Comm Fdn Grts, 1620
Dunspaugh-Dalton Fnd Grants, 1623
Dwight Stuart Youth Fnd Grants, 1628
Dyson Fnd Mid-Hudson Valley General Operating Support Grants, 1635
East Tennessee Fnd Grants, 1646
Eaton Charitable Fund Grants, 1647
eBay Fnd Comm Grants, 1648
Ed and Carole Abel Fnd Grants, 1652
Eddy Knight Family Fnd Grants, 1654
Edina Realty Fnd Grants, 1656
Edna Wardlaw Charitable Trust Grants, 1660
Edward & Ellen Roche Relief Fdn Grants, 1663
Edward N. and Della L. Thome Memorial Fnd Direct Services Grants, 1666
Edward R. Godfrey Fnd Grants, 1667
Edward S. Moore Fnd Grants, 1668
Edwards Memorial Trust Grants, 1669
Edward W & Stella C Van Houten Mem Fund, 1670
Edwin S. Webster Fnd Grants, 1671
Edwin W & Catherine M Davis Fdn Grants, 1672
Effie and Wofford Cain Fnd Grants, 1674
Eileen Fisher Activating Leadership Grants for Women and Girls, 1676
Eileen Fisher Women-Owned Business Grants, 1677
Eisner Fnd Grants, 1678
Elizabeth & Avola W Callaway Fdn Grants, 1680
Elizabeth Morse Genius Char Trust Grants, 1682
Ellen Abbott Gilman Trust Grants, 1685
Elliot Fnd Inc Grants, 1686
Elmer L & Eleanor J Andersen Fdn Grnts, 1687
El Paso Comm Fnd Grants, 1688
El Pomar Fnd Awards and Grants, 1690
Elsie H. Wilcox Fnd Grants, 1691
Elsie Lee Garthwaite Memorial Fdn Grts, 1692
Emerson Charitable Trust Grants, 1694
Emerson Electric Co Contributions Grts, 1695
Emily Hall Tremaine Fnd Grants, 1698
Emma B. Howe Memorial Fnd Grants, 1700
Emy-Lou Biedenharn Fnd Grants, 1703
Enterprise Rent-A-Car Fnd Grants, 1721
Essex County Comm Fnd Discretionary Grants, 1752
Esther M. and Freeman E. Everett Charitable Fnd Grants, 1757
Ethel and Raymond F. Rice Fnd Grants, 1758
Ethel Frends Fnd Grants, 1759
Ethel S. Abbott Charitable Fnd Grants, 1760
Ethel Sergeant Clark Smith Fnd Grants, 1761
Eugene B. Casey Fnd Grants, 1762
Eugene M. Lang Fnd Grants, 1764
Eugene McDermott Fnd Grants, 1765
Eulalie Bloedel Schneider Fnd Grants, 1767
Evan Frankel Fnd Grants, 1770
Evelyn and Walter Haas, Jr. Fund Gay and Lesbian Rights Grants, 1772
Evelyn & Walter Haas, Jr. Immigrant Rights Grant, 1773
Evelyn and Walter Haas, Jr. Fund Nonprofit Leadership Grants, 1774

Ewing Marion Kauffman Fnd Grants, 1777
Fairfield County Comm Fdn Grts, 1782
Fallon OrNda Comm Health Fund Grants, 1783
Fan Fox & Leslie R Samuels Fdn Grants, 1786
FAR Fund Grants, 1787
Faye McBeath Fnd Grants, 1794
Fel-Pro Mecklenburger Fnd Grants, 1800
Feldman Fnd Grants, 1801
FEMA Assistance to Firefighters Grants, 1802
Ferree Fnd Grants, 1804
Field Fnd of Illinois Grants, 1806
Fieldstone Fnd Grants, 1808
Fifth Third Bank Corporate Giving, 1809
Finish Line Youth Fnd Founder's Grants, 1812
FirstEnergy Fnd Comm Grants, 1819
Fisa Fnd Grants, 1826
Fisher Fnd Grants, 1831
Fleishhacker Fdn Small Grants in the Arts, 1839
Fleishhacker Fnd Special Arts Grants, 1840
Florian O. Bartlett Trust Grants, 1845
Florida BRAIVE Fund of Dade Comm Fnd, 1846
Florida Division of Cultural Affairs Endowment Grants, 1851
Florida Division of Cultural Affairs General Program Support Grants, 1854
Florida Division of Cultural Affairs Multidisciplinary Grants, 1857
Florida Division of Cultural Affairs Professional Theatre Grants, 1861
Florida Division of Cultural Affairs Specific Cultural Project Grants, 1862
Florida Division of Cultural Affairs Underserved Cultural Comm Dev Grants, 1864
Florida Sports Fnd Major and Regional Grants, 1873
Fluor Fnd Grants, 1875
FMC Fnd Grants, 1876
Foellinger Fnd Grants, 1877
Fondren Fnd Grants, 1878
Ford Family Fnd Grants - Tech Assistance, 1882
Ford Motor Company Fund Grants, 1885
Forest Fnd Grants, 1886
Foster Fnd Grants, 1888
Fnd NW Grants, 1906
Fourjay Fnd Grants, 1913
Frances & Benjamin Benenson Fdn Grts, 1916
Frances W. Emerson Fnd Grants, 1920
Francis Beidler Fnd Grants, 1921
Francis L. Abreu Charitable Trust Grants, 1922
Francis T & Louise T Nichols Fdn Grts, 1923
Frank & Larue Reynolds Char Trust Grts, 1924
Frank and Lydia Bergen Fnd Grants, 1925
Frank B. Hazard General Charity Fund Grants, 1926
Frank E. and Seba B. Payne Fnd Grants, 1927
Frank G & Freida K Brotz Fam Fdn Grts, 1928
Franklin County Comm Fdn Grts, 1929
Frank Reed and Margaret Jane Peters Memorial Fund I Grants, 1933
Frank Reed and Margaret Jane Peters Memorial Fund II Grants, 1934
Frank Stanley Beveridge Fnd Grants, 1936
Frank W & Carl S Adams Mem Fund Grts, 1937
Fraser-Parker Fnd Grants, 1938
Fred & Gretel Biel Charitable Trust Grants, 1939
Fred C & Katherine B Andersen Fdn Grts, 1942
Fred C & Mary R Koch Fnd Grants, 1943
Freddie Mac Fnd Grants, 1944
Frederick McDonald Trust Grants, 1946
Frederick S. Upton Fnd Grants, 1947
Fred Meyer Fnd Grants, 1950
Fremont Area Cmty Fdn Amazing X Grants, 1953
Fremont Area Comm Fnd Elderly Needs Grants, 1954
Fremont Area Comm Fnd Grants, 1955
Fremont Area Comm Fnd Summer Youth Grants, 1956
Frist Fnd Grants, 1964
Frost Fnd Grants, 1966
Fuller E. Callaway Fnd Grants, 1973
Fuller Fnd Grants, 1974
Fund for the City of New York Grants, 1978
G.N. Wilcox Trust Grants, 1982
Gamble Fnd Grants, 1983

Gardiner Howland Shaw Fnd Grants, 1986
Gaylord & Dorothy Donnelley Fdn Grants, 1993
Gebbie Fnd Grants, 1995
GenCorp Fnd Grants, 1998
Gene Haas Fnd, 1999
Genentech Corporate Charitable Contributions, 2000
General Dynamics Corporation Grants, 2001
General Mills Fnd Grants, 2003
General Motors Fnd Grants, 2004
General Service Fnd Colorado Grants, 2005
George and Ruth Bradford Fnd Grants, 2010
George and Sarah Buchanan Fnd Grants, 2011
George A Ohl Jr. Fnd Grants, 2012
George B. Page Fnd Grants, 2013
George B. Storer Fnd Grants, 2014
George E. Hatcher, Jr. and Ann Williams Hatcher Fnd Grants, 2015
George F. Baker Trust Grants, 2016
George Fnd Grants, 2018
George Frederick Jewett Fnd Grants, 2019
George Gund Fnd Grants, 2020
George H & Jane A Mifflin Mem Fund Grts, 2021
George P. Davenport Trust Fund Grants, 2026
George S & Dolores Dore Eccles Fdn Grants, 2027
George W Codrington Charitable Fdn Grts, 2029
George W. Wells Fnd Grants, 2030
Georgia-Pacific Fdn Entrepreneurship Grts, 2033
Georgia Council for the Arts Partner Grants for Organizations, 2035
Georgia Council for the Arts Partner Grants for Service Organizations, 2036
Georgiana Goddard Eaton Mem Fund Grts, 2038
Geraldine R. Dodge Fnd Arts Grants, 2040
Geraldine R. Dodge Fnd Environment Grants, 2041
Geraldine R. Dodge Fnd Media Grants, 2042
German Protestant Orphan Asylum Fnd Grants, 2044
Gertrude & William C Wardlaw Fund Grts, 2045
Gheens Fnd Grants, 2048
Gibson Fnd Grants, 2052
Gil and Dody Weaver Fnd Grants, 2053
Ginger and Barry Ackerley Fnd Grants, 2055
Ginn Fnd Grants, 2056
Girl's Best Friend Fnd Grants, 2057
GNOF Bayou Communities Grants, 2069
GNOF Environmental Fund Grants, 2073
GNOF IMPACT Grants for Arts and Culture, 2078
GNOF IMPACT Grants for Education, 2079
GNOF IMPACT Grants for Health and Human Services, 2080
GNOF IMPACT Grts for Youth Dev't, 2081
GNOF IMPACT Harold W. Newman, Jr. Charitable Trust Grants, 2083
GNOF Maison Hospitaliere Grants, 2086
GNOF Metropolitan Opportunities Grants, 2087
GNOF Plaquemines Comm Grants, 2091
Godfrey Fnd Grants, 2095
Golden Rule Fnd Grants, 2098
Goldseker Fdn Comm Affairs Grants, 2100
Goldseker Fnd Human Services Grants, 2102
Goodrich Corporation Fnd Grants, 2104
Good Works Fnd Grants, 2105
Google Grants Beta, 2107
Grace and Franklin Bernsen Fnd Grants, 2109
Grace Bersted Fnd Grants, 2110
Grand Rapids Area Comm Fdn Grts, 2114
Grand Rapids Area Comm Fnd Nashwauk Area Endowment Fund Grants, 2115
Grand Victoria Fnd Illinois Core Grants, 2126
Grtr Columbus Arts Council Operating Grts, 2133
Greater Saint Louis Comm Fdn Grants, 2138
Greater Tacoma Comm Fdn Grts, 2139
Greater Worcester Comm Fnd Jeppson Memorial Fund for Brookfield Grants, 2141
Greene County Fnd Grants, 2150
Greenspun Family Fnd Grants, 2156
Greenwall Fdn Arts & Humanities Grts, 2157
Gregory Family Fdn Grts (Massachusetts), 2162
Gregory L Gibson Char Fdn Grts, 2163
Greygates Fnd Grants, 2164
Griffin Fnd Grants, 2165

Grotto Fnd Project Grants, 2166
Grover Hermann Fnd Grants, 2168
Grundy Fnd Grants, 2169
Gulf Coast Fnd of Comm Operating Grants, 2176
Guy I. Bromley Trust Grants, 2180
H & R Fnd Grants, 2181
HA & Mary K Chapman Char Trust Grts, 2182
H.J. Heinz Company Fnd Grants, 2184
H. Leslie Hoffman & Elaine S. Hoffman Grants, 2185
H. Schaffer Fnd Grants, 2187
Hagedorn Fund Grants, 2207
Hahl Proctor Charitable Trust Grants, 2208
Hall Family Fnd Grants, 2210
Halliburton Fnd Grants, 2211
Hallmark Corporate Fnd Grants, 2212
Hamilton Family Fnd Grants, 2213
Handsel Fnd Grants, 2221
Harold & Arlene Schnitzer CARE Fdn Grts, 2226
Harold Simmons Fnd Grants, 2230
Harris and Eliza Kempner Fund Grants, 2231
Harry B. and Jane H. Brock Fnd Grants, 2237
Harry Bramhall Gilbert Char Trust Grts, 2238
Harry C. Trexler Trust Grants, 2239
Harry Edison Fnd, 2241
Harry S. Black and Allon Fuller Fund Grants, 2243
Harry W. Bass, Jr. Fnd Grants, 2246
Hartford Aging and Health Program Awards, 2247
Hartford Fnd Regular Grants, 2253
Harvest Fnd Grants, 2254
Haymarket People's Fund Sustaining Grants, 2267
HCA Fnd Grants, 2274
Head Start Replacement Grantee: Colorado, 2275
Head Start Replacement Grantee: Florida, 2276
Head Start Rplcmt Grantee: West Virginia, 2277
Health Fnd of Grtr Indianapolis Grts, 2282
Health Fnd of South Florida Responsive Grants, 2283
Hearst Fnds Culture Grants, 2284
Hearst Fnds Social Service Grants, 2285
Heinz Endowments Grants, 2291
Helena Rubinstein Fnd Grants, 2292
Helen Bader Fnd Grants, 2293
Helen K & Arthur E Johnson Fdn Grts, 2296
Helen Pumphrey Denit Charitable Trust Grants, 2297
Helen S. Boylan Fnd Grants, 2298
Helen Steiner Rice Fnd Grants, 2299
Helen V. Brach Fnd Grants, 2300
Henrietta Tower Wurts Memorial Fnd Grants, 2304
Henry A. and Mary J. MacDonald Fnd, 2305
Henry & Ruth Blaustein Rosenberg Fdn Grants, 2306
Henry J. Kaiser Family Fnd Grants, 2310
Henry W. Bull Fnd Grants, 2312
Herbert A & Adrian W Woods Fdn Grts, 2313
Herbert H & Grace A Dow Fdn Grants, 2315
Herman Abbott Family Fnd Grants, 2316
Herman Goldman Fnd Grants, 2317
High Meadow Fnd Grants, 2321
Hillman Fnd Grants, 2327
Hilton Hotels Corporate Giving, 2331
Hirtzel Memorial Fnd Grants, 2332
Historic Landmarks Legal Defense Grants, 2338
Hoglund Fnd Grants, 2344
Hollie and Anna Oakley Fnd Grants, 2346
Honor the Earth Grants, 2361
Horace A Kimball & S Ella Kimball Fdn Grts, 2362
Horace Moses Charitable Fnd Grants, 2363
Horizon Fnd for New Jersey Grants, 2364
Horizons Comm Issues Grants, 2366
Hormel Family Fdn Business Plan Awd, 2367
Hormel Foods Charitable Trust Grants, 2368
Hormel Fnd Grants, 2369
Household Int'l Corp Giving Grants, 2372
Howard County Comm Fdn Grts, 2375
Howard H. Callaway Fnd Grants, 2376
Howe Fnd of North Carolina Grants, 2377
Huber Fnd Grants, 2382
Hudson Webber Fnd Grants, 2383
Huffy Fnd Grants, 2384
Hugh J. Andersen Fnd Grants, 2385
Huie-Dellmon Trust Grants, 2386
Hulman & Company Fnd Grants, 2387

PROGRAM TYPE INDEX

General Operating Support / 1095

Humane Society of the United States Foreclosure Pets Grants, 2389
Humanitas Fnd Grants, 2390
Huntington Arts Council JP Morgan Chase Organization/Stabilization Regrants, 2403
Huntington Clinical Fnd Grants, 2404
Huntington Fnd Grants, 2408
Hyams Fnd Grants, 2413
Hyde Family Fnds Grants, 2414
I.A. O'Shaughnessy Fnd Grants, 2416
Ian Hague Perl 6 Dev Grants, 2421
Idaho Power Co Corp Contributions, 2433
IDEM Section 205(j) Water Quality Management Planning Grants, 2434
IDEM Section 319(h) Nonpoint Source Grants, 2435
IEDC Industrial Dev Grant Fund, 2443
Illinois Arts Council Local Arts Agencies Grants, 2471
Illinois Arts Council Multidisciplinary Grants, 2473
Illinois Arts Council Music Grants, 2474
Illinois Arts Cncl Prtnrs in Excellence Grts, 2475
Illinois Arts Council Theater Grants, 2477
Illinois DCEO Comm Dev Assistance Pgm for Economic Dev (CDAP-ED) Grants, 2488
Illinois Humanities Council Comm General Support Grants, 2509
Illinois Tool Works Fnd Grants, 2511
Independence Blue Cross Charitable Medical Care Grants, 2524
Independence Comm Fnd Quality of Life Grant, 2525
Independence Comm Fnd Education, Culture & Arts Grant, 2526
Independence Comm Fnd Neighborhood Renewal Grants, 2527
Indiana 21st Century Research & Tech Awards, 2528
Indiana Arts Commission Cap Bldg Grts, 2531
Indiana Arts Commission Statewide Arts Service Organization Grants, 2533
Indiana Household Hazardous Waste Grants, 2538
Indiana Recycling Grants, 2545
Indiana Rural Capacity Grants, 2547
Indiana SBIR/STTR Commercialization Enhancement Program, 2548
Indiana Waste Tire Fund Pgm Grts, 2551
Intergrys Corporation Grants, 2565
IREX Kosovo Civil Soc Project Grts, 2576
IREX MENA Media TV Produc Fund Grts, 2577
Irving S. Gilmore Fnd Grants, 2584
Irvin Stern Fnd Grants, 2585
Ittleson Fnd Mental Health Grants, 2590
J.B. Reynolds Fnd Grants, 2592
J. F. Maddox Fnd Grants, 2597
J. Spencer Barnes Memorial Fnd Grants, 2606
J.W. Kieckhefer Fnd Grants, 2607
J. Walton Bissell Fnd Grants, 2608
J Willard & Alice S Marriott Fdn Grts, 2609
Jackson Fnd Grants, 2613
Jacob and Hilda Blaustein Fnd Grants, 2615
Jacobs Family Fnd Spirit of the Diamond Grants, 2618
Jacobs Family Fdn Vlg Neighborhoods Grants, 2619
James & Abigail Campbell Fam Fdn Grts, 2620
James A. and Faith Knight Fnd Grants, 2621
James Ford Bell Fnd Grants, 2623
James Irvine Fnd Creative Connections Grants, 2628
James Irvine Fnd Leadership Awards, 2629
James L & Mary Jane Bowman Char Trust, 2632
James R. Dougherty Jr. Fnd Grants, 2635
James R. Thorpe Fnd Grants, 2636
Jane's Trust Grants, 2639
Jane and Jack Fitzpatrick Fund Grants, 2640
Jane Bradley Pettit Fnd Arts and Culture Grants, 2641
Jane Bradley Pettit Comm & Social Dev Grants, 2642
Jaquelin Hume Fnd Grants, 2654
Jayne and Leonard Abess Fnd Grants, 2657
Jean and Louis Dreyfus Fnd Grants, 2658
Jean and Price Daniel Fnd Grants, 2659
Jeffris Wood Fnd Grants, 2660
JELD-WEN Fnd Grants, 2661
Jenkins Fnd: Improving the Health of Greater Richmond Grants, 2663
Jerome Fnd Grants, 2667

Jerry L & Barbara J Burris Fdn Grts, 2669
Jessie Ball Dupont Fund Grants, 2671
Jessie Smith Noyes Fnd Grants, 2672
Jewish Fund Grants, 2675
Jim Moran Fnd Grants, 2680
Joan Bentinck-Smith Charitable Fdn Grts, 2682
Joe W & Dorothy Dorsett Brown Fdn Grants, 2684
John and Margaret Post Fnd Grants, 2686
John D & Katherine A Johnston Fdn Grants, 2691
John Deere Fnd Grants, 2692
John Edward Fowler Mem Fdn Grants, 2693
John H. and Wilhelmina D. Harland Charitable Fnd Grants, 2698
John I. Smith Charities Grants, 2700
John J. Leidy Fnd Grants, 2701
John Jewett & Helen Chandler Garland Fdn, 2702
John M. Ross Fnd Grants, 2704
John M. Weaver Fnd Grants, 2705
John P. McGovern Fnd Grants, 2707
Johns Manville Fund Grants, 2716
Johnson & Johnson Corp Contribs Grants, 2718
Johnson Controls Fdn Civic Activities Grts, 2720
Johnson Controls Health & Social Services Grant, 2722
John W. Anderson Fnd Grants, 2729
John W. Boynton Fund Grants, 2730
John W. Speas and Effie E. Speas Grants, 2732
Joseph Alexander Fnd Grants, 2734
Joseph Drown Fnd Grants, 2735
Joseph H & Florence A Roblee Fdn Grants, 2736
Josephine G. Russell Trust Grants, 2737
Josephine S. Gumbiner Fnd Grants, 2739
Joseph S. Stackpole Charitable Trust Grants, 2741
Journal Gazette Fnd Grants, 2744
Joyce Fnd Democracy Grants, 2748
Joyce Fdn Gun Violence Prevention Grts, 2751
JP Morgan Chase Arts and Culture Grants, 2752
Judith and Jean Pape Adams Charitable Fnd Tulsa Area Grants, 2755
K. M. Hunter Charitable Social Welfare Grants, 2757
K.S. Adams Fnd Grants, 2758
K21 Health Fdn Cancer Care Fund Grts, 2759
Kaneta Fnd Grants, 2774
Kansas Arts Commission Operational Support for Arts and Cultural Organizations, 2781
Kansas Health Fnd Recognition Grants, 2784
Kate B. Reynolds Charitable Health Care Grants, 2786
Kate B. Reynolds Charitable Trust Poor and Needy Grants, 2787
Katharine Matthies Fnd Grants, 2788
Katherine Baxter Memorial Fnd Grants, 2789
Kathryne Beynon Fnd Grants, 2791
Kawabe Grants, 2794
Kelvin and Eleanor Smith Fnd Grants, 2796
Kenneth T & Eileen L Norris Fdn Grants, 2802
Kenny's Kids Grants, 2803
Kentucky Arts Council Partnership Grants, 2809
Kessler Fdn Comm Employment Grts, 2814
Kirkpatrick Fnd Grants, 2827
Knight Fnd Grants - Georgia, 2829
Knight Fnd Grants - Montana, 2830
Koret Fnd Grants, 2837
Kovler Family Fnd Grants, 2840
Kroger Fnd Diversity Grants, 2842
Kroger Fdn Grassroots Comty Support Grants, 2843
Kroger Fnd Hunger Relief Grants, 2844
L. W. Pierce Family Fnd Grants, 2846
Laclede Gas Charitable Trust Grants, 2848
Laura L. Adams Fnd Grants, 2865
Laurel Fnd Grants, 2867
Lawrence J. and Anne Rubenstein Charitable Fnd Grants, 2868
Leicester Savings Bank Fund, 2879
Lena Benas Grants, 2881
Leonard L & Bertha U Abess Fdn Grts, 2884
Leo Niessen Jr., Charitable Trust Grants, 2885
Lewis H. Humphreys Charitable Trust Grants, 2889
Lillian S. Wells Fnd Grants, 2901
Lilly Endowment Giving Indiana Funds for Tomorrow Grants, 2903
Liz Claiborne Fnd Grants, 2915

Lloyd G. Balfour Fnd Attleboro-Specific Charities Grants, 2916
Lotus 88 Fnd for Women and Children, 2921
Louie M & Betty M Phillips Fdn Grants, 2923
Louis and Elizabeth Nave Flarsheim Charitable Fnd Grants, 2924
Louis Calder Fnd Grants, 2925
Lowe Fnd Grants, 2929
Lowell Berry Fnd Grants, 2930
Lubbock Area Fnd Grants, 2931
Lubrizol Corporation Comm Grants, 2932
Lubrizol Fnd Grants, 2933
Lucile Horton Howe & Mitchell B. Howe Grants, 2934
Lucy Downing Nisbet Charitable Fund Grants, 2935
Lucy Gooding Charitable Fnd Trust, 2936
Lumpkin Family Fdn Healthy People Grts, 2942
Luther I. Replogle Fnd Grants, 2945
Lydia deForest Charitable Trust Grants, 2946
Lynde and Harry Bradley Fnd Grants, 2947
Lyndhurst Fnd Grants, 2949
M.B. and Edna Zale Fnd Grants, 2950
M. Bastian Family Fnd Grants, 2951
M.E. Raker Fnd Grants, 2953
Mabel Y. Hughes Charitable Trust Grants, 2960
MacArthur Fnd Chicago Arts and Culture General Operations Grants, 2961
MacDonald-Peterson Fnd Grants, 2965
Macquarie Bank Fnd Grants, 2966
Madison County Comm Fnd General Grants, 2973
Maine Women's Fund Econ Security Grts, 2992
Mann T. Lowry Fnd Grants, 2998
Marathon Petroleum Corporation Grants, 2999
Marcia and Otto Koehler Fnd Grants, 3000
Mardag Fnd Grants, 3001
Margaret Abell Powell Fund Grants, 3002
Margaret T. Morris Fnd Grants, 3005
Marie C. and Joseph C. Wilson Fnd Rochester Small Grants, 3006
Marin Comm Fnd Social Justice and Interfaith Understanding Grants, 3012
Marin Comm Fnd Successful Aging Grants, 3014
Marion and Miriam Rose Fund Grants, 3015
Marion Gardner Jackson Char Trust Grts, 3017
Marion I & Henry J Knott Fdn Discret Grants, 3018
Marion I & Henry J Knott Fdn Std Grants, 3019
Marjorie Moore Charitable Fnd Grants, 3021
Mars Fnd Grants, 3025
Marsh Corporate Grants, 3027
Mary's Pence Ministry Grants, 3029
Mary Black Fnd Active Living Grants, 3031
Mary D. & Walter F Frear Eleemosynary Trust, 3035
Mary K. Chapman Fnd Grants, 3042
Mary Owen Borden Fnd Grants, 3046
Mary Reynolds Babcock Fnd Grants, 3047
Massachusetts Cultural Council Cultural Investment Portfolio, 3056
Mathile Family Fnd Grants, 3062
Maurice J. Masserini Charitable Trust Grants, 3064
Max A. Adler Charitable Fnd Grants, 3065
Max and Anna Levinson Fnd Grants, 3066
Maxon Charitable Fnd Grants, 3068
May & Stanley Smith Char Trust Grants, 3069
Maytree Fdn Assisting Local Leaders w/ Immigrant Employment Strategies Grts, 3070
McCarthy Family Fnd Grants, 3073
McColl Fnd Grants, 3074
McCune Charitable Fnd Grants, 3077
McCune Fnd Human Services Grants, 3080
McGregor Fund Grants, 3082
McInerny Fnd Grants, 3083
McKesson Fnd Grants, 3084
MeadWestvaco Sustainable Communities Grants, 3105
Mead Witter Fnd Grants, 3106
Melville Charitable Trust Grants, 3115
Memorial Fnd for Children Grants, 3116
Memorial Fnd Grants, 3117
Merck Family Fund Urban Farming and Youth Leadership Grants, 3119
Merck Family Fund Youth Transforming Urban Communities Grants, 3120

Mericos Fnd Grants, 3121
Meriden Fnd Grants, 3122
Merkel Fnd Grants, 3124
Mervin Bovaird Fnd Grants, 3128
Metro Health Fnd Grants, 3133
Metzger-Price Fund Grants, 3137
Meyer & Pepa Gold Family Fnd Grants, 3138
Meyer Fnd Economic Security Grants, 3141
Meyer Fnd Educ Grants, 3142
Meyer Fdn Healthy Communities Grts, 3143
Meyer Fdn Strong Nonprofit Sector Grts, 3145
Meyer Memorial Trust Grassroots Grants, 3147
Meyer Memorial Trust Responsive Grants, 3148
Meyer Memorial Trust Special Grants, 3149
MGN Family Fnd Grants, 3154
Michael Reese Health Trust Core Grants, 3159
Michael Reese Health Trust Responsive Grants, 3160
Microsoft Comty Affairs Puget Sound Grts, 3163
Mildred V. Horn Fnd Grants, 3176
Miller, Canfield, Paddock and Stone, P.L.C. Corporate Giving Grants, 3179
Miller Brewing Corporate Contributions Grants, 3180
Millipore Fnd Grants, 3182
Mimi and Peter Haas Fund Grants, 3185
Minneapolis Fnd Comm Grants, 3186
Mitsubishi Electric America Fnd Grants, 3190
Modest Needs Non-Profit Grants, 3200
Monfort Family Fnd Grants, 3203
Montana Arts Cncl Cltrl & Aesthetic Proj Grts, 3209
Montana Comm Fnd Grants, 3211
Montgomery Cty Comm Fdn Grants, 3213
MONY Fnd Grants, 3214
Morris & Gwendolyn Cafritz Fdn Grants, 3218
Motorola Fnd Grants, 3221
Mt. Sinai Health Care Fnd Health of the Urban Comm Grants, 3227
Musgrave Fnd Grants, 3231
Natalie W. Furniss Charitable Trust Grants, 3244
Nathaniel & Elizabeth P Stevens Fdn Grants, 3247
Nationwide Insurance Fnd Grants, 3285
Needmor Fund Grants, 3289
Nellie Mae Educ Fnd District Change Grants, 3297
Nellie Mae Educ Fnd State Level Systems Change Grants, 3299
Nevada Arts Council Professional Dev Grants, 3314
New Earth Fnd Grants, 3317
Newfoundland and Labrador Arts Council Professional Project Grants, 3322
Newfoundland and Labrador Arts Council Sustaining Grants, 3323
Newman W. Benson Fnd Grants, 3334
New York Fnd Grants, 3338
New York Life Fnd Grants, 3341
NFF Comm Assistance Grants, 3343
NHSCA Cultural Facilities Grants: Barrier Free Access for All, 3426
NHSCA Operating Grants, 3428
Nicholas H Noyes Jr Mem Fdn Grants, 3434
Nicor Corporate Contributions, 3435
Nina Mason Pulliam Charitable Trust Grants, 3443
NNEDVF/Altria Doors of Hope Program, 3452
Noble County Comm Fnd Grants, 3456
Norcliffe Fnd Grants, 3459
Nordson Corporation Fnd Grants, 3462
Norfolk Southern Fnd Grants, 3463
Norman Fnd Grants, 3464
North Carolina Arts Council Folklife Grants, 3476
North Carolina Arts Council Gen Support Grants, 3477
North Carolina Arts Council Outreach Grants, 3479
North Carolina Arts Council Tech Assistance, 3482
North Carolina Arts Council Visual Arts Program Support Grants, 3484
North Carolina GlaxoSmithKline Fdn Grts, 3490
North Dakota Council on the Arts Comm Access Grants, 3494
North Dakota Council on the Arts Institutional Support Grants, 3496
North Dakota Council on the Arts Presenter Support Grants, 3497
Northern Chautauqua Comm Fnd Comm Suants, 3499
Northern Trust Company Charitable Trust and Corporate Giving Program, 3504
NW Mutual Fnd Grants, 3509
NW Fund for the Environment Grants, 3510
Norton Fnd Grants, 3514
Norwin S & Elizabeth N Bean Fdn Grts, 3515
NYCT AIDS/HIV Grants, 3542
NYCT Girls and Young Women Grants, 3548
NYCT Health Svcs, Systems & Policies Grts, 3550
NYFA Artists in the School Planning Grants, 3562
NYFA Building Up Infrastructure Levels for Dance Grants, 3563
NYSCA Architecture, Planning, and Design: General Operating Support Grants, 3573
NYSCA Architecture, Planning, and Design: Independent Project Grants, 3575
NYSCA Arts Education: General Operating Support Grants, 3578
NYSCA Arts Education: Local Capacity Building Grants, 3581
NYSCA Dance: Gen Operating Support Grts, 3584
NYSCA Electronic Media and Film: General Operating Support, 3590
NYSCA Lit: General Operating Support Grants, 3598
NYSCA Museum: General Operating Support, 3602
NYSCA Music: Gen Operating Support Grts, 3606
NYSCA Presenting: General Operating Support, 3609
NYSCA State and Local Partnerships: General Operating Support Grants, 3619
NYSCA Theatre: Gen Operating Support Grts, 3623
Ohio Arts Council Arts Indiv Excellence Awds, 3648
Ohio Arts Council Sustainability Pgm Grts, 3654
Oklahoma City Comm Pgms & Grts, 3666
Olin Corporation Charitable Trust Grants, 3669
Olive B. Cole Fnd Grants, 3670
Olive Smith Browning Charitable Trust Grants, 3671
OneFamily Fnd Grants, 3673
Ontario Arts Council Orchestras Grants, 3679
Oppenstein Brothers Fnd Grants, 3685
ORBI Artist Fast Track Grants, 3689
Orchard Fnd Grants, 3690
Ordean Fnd Grants, 3691
Oregon Youth Soccer Fnd Grants, 3692
Ottinger Fnd Grants, 3712
Otto Bremer Fnd Grants, 3713
Overbrook Fnd Grants, 3715
Owen County Comm Fnd Grants, 3716
Owens Fnd Grants, 3718
Pacers Fnd Be Drug-Free Grants, 3720
Pacers Fnd Be Educated Grants, 3721
Pacers Fnd Be Healthy and Fit Grants, 3722
Pacers Fnd Be Tolerant Grants, 3723
Pacers Fnd Indiana Fever's Be Younique Grants, 3724
PacifiCare Fnd Grants, 3725
Pacific Life Fnd Grants, 3726
Packard Fnd Local Grants, 3729
Pajaro Valley Comm Health Health Trust Insurance/Coverage & Educ on Using the System Grants, 3731
Pajaro Valley Comm Health Trust Diabetes and Contributing Factors Grants, 3732
Parker Fnd (California) Grants, 3736
Park Fnd Grants, 3739
Partnership Enhancement Pgm Grts, 3740
Patricia Price Peterson Fnd Grants, 3746
Patrick and Aimee Butler Family Fnd Comm Arts and Humanities Grants, 3747
Patrick and Aimee Butler Family Fnd Comm Environment Grants, 3748
Patrick and Aimee Butler Family Fnd Comm Human Services Grants, 3749
Patrick and Aimee Butler Family Comm Philanthropy & the Non-Profit Management Grants, 3750
Patrick and Anna M. Cudahy Fund Grants, 3751
Patrick John Bennett, Jr. Memorial Fnd Grants, 3752
Paul and Edith Babson Fnd Grants, 3755
Paul and Mary Haas Fnd Contributions and Student Scholarships, 3756
Paul E & Klare N Reinhold Fdn Grts, 3758
Pauline E. Fitzpatrick Charitable Trust, 3763
Paul Rapoport Fnd Grants, 3765
PCA Arts Organizations and Arts Grants for Art Museums, 3775
PCA Entry Track Arts Organizations and Arts Grants for Art Museums, 3787
PDF Comm Organizing Grants, 3807
Pentair Fnd Educ and Comm Grants, 3816
Percy B. Ferebee Endowment Grants, 3820
Perkin Fund Grants, 3821
Perl 6 Microgrants, 3824
Perl Fnd Grants, 3825
Perpetual Trust for Charitable Giving Grants, 3826
Peter Kiewit Fnd General Grants, 3845
Peter Kiewit Fnd Small Grants, 3847
Peter Norton Family Fnd Grants, 3849
Phelps County Comm Fnd Grants, 3870
Philadelphia Fdn Org'l Effectiveness Grts, 3872
Philanthrofund Fnd Grants, 3874
Phil Hardin Fnd Grants, 3875
Phoenix Suns Charities Grants, 3881
Piedmont Health Fnd Grants, 3882
Piedmont Natural Gas Fnd Health and Human Services Grants, 3885
Pinellas County Grants, 3891
Pinkerton Fnd Grants, 3892
Pinnacle Entertainment Fnd Grants, 3893
Pioneer Hi-Bred Comm Grants, 3895
PIP American Dream Fund Grants, 3897
Piper Jaffray Fdn Communities Giving Grts, 3899
Piper Trust Arts and Culture Grants, 3900
Piper Trust Children Grants, 3901
Piper Trust Educ Grants, 3902
Playboy Fnd Grants, 3913
PMI Fnd Grants, 3918
Pollock Fnd Grants, 3930
Porter County Health and Wellness Grant, 3933
Powell Family Fnd Grants, 3941
Powell Fnd Grants, 3942
PPG Industries Fnd Grants, 3943
Price Chopper's Golub Fnd Grants, 3950
Price Family Charitable Fund Grants, 3952
Price Gilbert, Jr. Charitable Fund Grants, 3953
Priddy Fnd Operating Grants, 3955
Prince Charitable Trusts Chicago Grants, 3959
Prince Char Trusts Dist of Columbia Grts, 3960
Prince Charitable Trusts Rhode Island Grants, 3961
Principal Financial Group Fnd Grants, 3966
Procter and Gamble Fund Grants, 3967
Proteus Fund Grants, 3973
Prudential Fnd Arts and Culture Grants, 3975
Prudential Fdn Econ Dev Grants, 3976
Prudential Fnd Educ Grants, 3977
Public Welfare Fnd Grants, 3984
Publix Super Markets Charities Local Grants, 3985
Puerto Rico Comm Fnd Grants, 3986
Putnam Cty Comm Fdn Grts, 3990
Putnam Fnd Grants, 3991
R.C. Baker Fnd Grants, 3999
RadioShack StreetSentz Comm Grts, 4005
Ralph and Virginia Mullin Fnd Grants, 4012
Ralph M. Parsons Fnd Grants, 4013
Ralphs Food 4 Less Fnd Grants, 4014
Raskob Fdn for Catholic Activities Grts, 4019
Rathmann Family Fnd Grants, 4026
RBC Dain Rauscher Fnd Grants, 4031
RCF General Comm Grants, 4032
Regional Arts & Cultural Council Support Grants, 4045
Reinberger Fnd Grants, 4052
RESIST Arthur Raymond Cohen Grants, 4055
RESIST Freda Friedman Salzman Grants, 4057
RESIST General Support Grants, 4058
RESIST Hell Yes! Award, 4059
RESIST Ken Hale Tribute Grants, 4060
RESIST Leslie D'Cora Holmes Grants, 4061
RESIST Mike Riegle Tribute Grants, 4062
RESIST Multi-Year Grants, 4063
RESIST Sharon Kurtz Grants, 4064
Reynolds Family Fnd Grants, 4071
Rhode Island Fnd Grants, 4073
Rice Fnd Grants, 4074
Richard and Helen DeVos Fnd Grants, 4076

PROGRAM TYPE INDEX

Richard and Rhoda Goldman Fund Grants, 4077
Richard & Susan Smith Family Fdn Grts, 4078
Richard D. Bass Fnd Grants, 4079
Richard E. Griffin Family Fnd Grants, 4081
Richard F. and Janice F. Weaver Educational Trust Grants, 4082
Richard H. Driehaus Fnd Grants, 4084
Richard H. Driehaus Fnd MacArthur Fund for Arts and Culture, 4085
Richard H. Driehaus Fnd Small Theater and Dance Grants, 4086
Richard King Mellon Fnd Grants, 4087
Rich Fnd Grants, 4090
Richland County Bank Grants, 4091
Righteous Persons Fnd Grants, 4093
Riley Fnd Grants, 4094
Ripley County Comm Fnd Grants, 4095
Robert and Helen Haddad Fnd Grants, 4103
Robert and Polly Dunn Fnd Grants, 4105
Robert B McMillen Fnd Grants, 4106
Robert G. Cabell III and Maude Morgan Cabell Fnd Grants, 4113
Robert Lee Adams Fnd Grants, 4114
Robert Lee Blaffer Fnd Grants, 4115
Robert R. McCormick Tribune Veterans Grants, 4120
Robert R. Meyer Fnd Grants, 4121
Robin Hood Fnd Grants, 4125
Robins Fnd Grants, 4126
Rochester Area Comm Fnd Grants, 4127
Rockefeller Brothers Fund Charles E. Culpeper Arts and Culture Grants in New York City, 4129
Rockefeller Brothers Fund Cross-Programmatic Initiative: Energy Grants, 4130
Rockefeller Brothers Democratic Practice Grants, 4131
Rockefeller Brothers Fund Pivotal Places Grants: New York City, 4134
Rockefeller Brothers Sustainable Dev Grants, 4136
Rockwell Int'l Corporate Trust Grants, 4141
Roger L. and Agnes C. Dell Charitable Grants, 4143
Rogers Family Fnd Grants, 4144
Rollins-Luetkemeyer Fnd Grants, 4147
Roney-Fitzpatrick Fnd Grants, 4150
Rose Fdn For Communities & the Environment Consumer Privacy Rights Grts, 4156
Rose Communities and Environment Northern California Environmental Grassroots Grants, 4158
Rose Fnd For Communities and the Environment SE Madera County Responsible Growth Grants, 4159
Rose Hills Fnd Grants, 4162
Ross Fnd Grants, 4164
Roy & Christine Sturgis Charitable Trust Grts, 4166
RRF General Grants, 4170
Rucker & Margaret Agee Fund Grants, 4171
Rucker-Donnell Fnd Grants, 4172
Russell Berrie Fnd Grants, 4175
Ruth Anderson Fnd Grants, 4176
Ruth and Vernon Taylor Fnd Grants, 4177
Ruth Eleanor Bamberger and John Ernest Bamberger Memorial Fnd Grants, 4178
Ruth H & Warren A Ellsworth Fdn Grts, 4179
Ruth Mott Fnd Grants, 4180
RWJF Partners Investing in Nursing's Future, 4188
Ryder System Charitable Fnd Grants, 4191
S. D. Bechtel, Jr. Fnd / Stephen Bechtel Fund Environmental Educ Grants, 4192
S.H. Cowell Fnd Grants, 4199
S. Livingston Mather Charitable Trust Grants, 4200
S. Mark Taper Fnd Grants, 4201
Sage Fnd Grants, 4204
Saint Louis Rams Fdn Comm Donations, 4214
Saint Paul Companies Fnd Grants, 4217
Salem Fnd Charitable Trust Grants, 4223
Salmon Fnd Grants, 4225
Samuel Rubin Fnd Grants, 4237
Samuel S. Fels Fund Grants, 4238
Samuel S. Johnson Fnd Grants, 4239
San Antonio Area Fnd Grants, 4240
San Diego Fnd Arts & Culture Grants, 4243
San Diego Fnd Civil Society Grants, 4244
San Diego Fnd Environment Comm Grants, 4246

San Diego Fnd Science & Tech Blasker Grants, 4250
San Diego HIV Funding Collaborative Grants, 4251
San Diego Women's Fnd Grants, 4252
Sands Memorial Fnd Grants, 4256
San Francisco Fnd Comm Health Grants, 4263
Santa Barbara Strategy Core Support Grants, 4286
Santa Barbara Fnd Towbes Fund for the Performing Arts Grants, 4288
Santa Fe Comm Fdn root2fruit Santa Fe, 4289
Santa Fe Comm Fnd Seasonal Grants-Fall Cycle, 4290
Santa Fe Comm Fnd Seasonal Grants-Spring, 4291
Santa Fe Comm Special & Urgent Needs Grants, 4292
Sapelo Fdn Environmental Protection Grts, 4293
Sapelo Fnd Social Justice Grants, 4294
Sarah Scaife Fnd Grants, 4295
Sara Lee Fnd Grants, 4296
Sartain Lanier Family Fnd Grants, 4298
Schering-Plough Fdn Comm Initvs Grts, 4303
Schering-Plough Fnd Health Grants, 4304
Scherman Fnd Grants, 4305
Scheumann Fnd Grants, 4306
Schlessman Family Fnd Grants, 4307
Schramm Fnd Grants, 4310
Schumann Fund for New Jersey Grants, 4311
Schurz Communications Fnd Grants, 4312
Scott B & Annie P Appleby Char Trust Grts, 4313
Seattle Fnd Annual Neighborhoods Grants, 4319
Seattle Fnd Arts and Culture Grants, 4320
Seattle Fnd Basic Needs Grants, 4321
Seattle Fnd Benjamin N. Phillips Grants, 4322
Seattle Fnd Economy Grants, 4325
Seattle Fnd Environment Grants, 4327
Seattle Fnd Health and Wellness Grants, 4328
Seattle Fnd Medical Funds Grants, 4329
Seattle Fdn Neighbor to Neighbor Small Grts, 4330
Selby and Richard McRae Fnd Grants, 4334
Seneca Foods Fnd Grants, 4336
Sensient Technologies Fnd Grants, 4337
Seybert Inst for Poor Boys & Girls Grts, 4338
Shared Earth Fnd Grants, 4339
Sheltering Arms Fund Grants, 4344
Shirley W. & William L. Griffin Grants, 4345
Sidgmore Family Fnd Grants, 4348
Sidney Stern Memorial Trust Grants, 4349
Sid W. Richardson Fnd Grants, 4350
Siebert Lutheran Fnd Grants, 4351
Simmons Fnd Grants, 4360
Sioux Falls Area Comm Fnd Comm Fund Grants, 4364
Sioux Falls Area Comm Fnd Spot Grants, 4366
Siragusa Fnd Human Services Grants, 4369
Sister Fund Grants for Women's Organizations, 4371
Sisters of Charity Fnd of Canton Grants, 4372
Sisters of Charity Fnd of Cleveland Good Samaritan Grants, 4373
Sisters of Charity Cleveland Reducing Health & Educational Disparities Grants, 4374
Sisters of Mercy of North Carolina Fdn Grts, 4375
Sisters of St Joseph Healthcare Fdn Grts, 4377
Skaggs Fnd Grants, 4378
Skillman Fdn Good Neighborhoods Grts, 4380
Skillman Fnd Good Schools Grants, 4382
Skoll Fdn Awds for Social Entrepreneurship, 4383
SOCFOC Catholic Ministries Grants, 4392
Social Justice Fund NW Economic Justice Giving Project Grants, 4395
Social Justice Fund NW Environmental Justice Giving Project Grants, 4396
Social Justice Fund NW General Grants, 4397
Social Justice Fund NW Montana Giving Project Grants, 4399
Solo Cup Fnd Grants, 4401
Sonoco Fnd Grants, 4403
Sony Corp of America Corp Philant Grants, 4405
Sophia Romero Trust Grants, 4406
Sorenson Legacy Fnd Grants, 4407
Sosland Fnd Grants, 4408
South Carolina Arts Commission Annual Operating Support for Organizations Grants, 4414
South Carolina Arts Commission Incentive Grants for Employer Sponsored Benefits, 4422

General Operating Support / 1097

South Carolina Arts Commission Leadership and Organizational Dev Grants, 4423
South Carolina Arts Commission Long Term Operating Support for Organizations Grants, 4424
Southwest Florida Comm Fnd Arts & Attractions Grants, 4441
Southwest Gas Corporation Fnd Grants, 4445
Sport Manitoba KidSport Athlete Grants, 4458
Sport Manitoba Women to Watch Grants, 4460
Sprague Fnd Grants, 4461
Sprint Fnd Grants, 4463
Square D Fnd Grants, 4464
St. Joseph Comm Health Fnd Improving Healthcare Access Grants, 4469
St. Louis-Jefferson Solid Waste Management Waste Reduction and Recycling Grants, 4470
Stackner Family Fnd Grants, 4471
Stan and Sandy Checketts Fnd, 4473
Stanley Smith Horticultural Trust Grants, 4474
Staples Fnd for Learning Grants, 4475
Starr Fnd Grants, 4483
State Farm Companies Safe Neighbors Grants, 4484
State Farm Companies Strong Neighborhoods, 4485
State Strategies Fund Grants, 4494
State Street Fnd Grants, 4495
Staunton Farm Fnd Grants, 4496
Steelcase Fnd Grants, 4497
Steele-Reese Fnd Grants, 4498
Sterling-Turner Charitable Fnd Grants, 4499
Stewart Huston Charitable Trust Grants, 4505
Stowe Family Fnd Grants, 4510
Strake Fnd Grants, 4511
Stranahan Fnd Grants, 4512
Strengthening Families - Strengthening Communities Grants, 4513
Strowd Roses Grants, 4515
Stuart Fnd Grants, 4516
Sulzberger Fnd Grants, 4522
Surdna Fdn Sustainable Environments Grants, 4533
Susan Mott Webb Charitable Trust Grants, 4536
Susan Vaughan Fnd Grants, 4537
SVP Early Childhood Dev and Parenting Grants, 4538
Swaim-Gause-Rucker Fnd Grants, 4540
Swindells Charitable Fnd, 4542
T. James Kavanagh Fnd Grants, 4545
T Raymond Gregory Family Fdn Grts, 4547
T. Rowe Price Associates Fnd Grants, 4548
TAC Arts Projects Grants, 4554
TAC Rural Arts Project Support Grants, 4555
Target Fnd Grants, 4562
TD4HIM Fnd Grants, 4566
TE Fnd Grants, 4572
Telluride Fnd Comm Grants, 4573
Telluride Fdn Emergency/Out of Cycle Grts, 4574
Temple-Inland Fnd Grants, 4576
Texas Cmsn on the Arts Arts Respond Prj Grts, 4581
Texas C'msn on Arts County Expansion Grants, 4582
Texas Comsn on the Arts Create-4 Pgm Grts, 4586
Texas Comsn on the Arts Create-5 Pgm Grts, 4587
Texas Comsn on the Arts GPA1, 4592
Textron Corporate Contributions Grants, 4601
Thelma Doelger Charitable Trust Grants, 4604
Third Wave Fnd Lela Breitbart Grants, 4609
Third Wave Fnd Organizing and Advocacy Grants, 4610
Third Wave Fnd Reproductive Health and Justice Grants, 4611
Thomas & Dorothy Leavey Fdn Grants, 4612
Thomas Austin Finch, Sr. Fnd Grants, 4613
Thomas C. Ackerman Fnd Grants, 4615
Thomas Sill Fnd Grants, 4619
Thomas Thompson Trust Grants, 4620
Thomas W. Briggs Fnd Grants, 4621
Thompson Charitable Fnd Grants, 4622
Thompson Fnd Grants, 4623
Thornton Fnd Grants, 4624
Tides Fnd Grants, 4632
Todd Brock Family Fnd Grants, 4639
Topeka Comm Fnd Grants, 4644
Town Creek Fnd Grants, 4650
Toyota Motor North America of NY Grts, 4658

Triangle Comm Fdn Donor-Advised Grts, 4668
Trinity Fnd Grants, 4669
TSA Advanced Surveillance Grants, 4674
TSYSF Team Grants, 4676
TWS Fnd Grants, 4683
U.S. Bank Fnd Grants, 4686
US Dept of Educ Child Care Access Means Parents in School Grants, 4689
US Dept of Educ Early Reading First Grants, 4691
Union Bank, N.A. Fnd Grants, 4709
Union Pacific Fdn Comm & Civic Grts, 4714
Union Pacific Fdn Health & Human Svcs Grts, 4715
Union Square Arts Award, 4716
Union Square Award for Social Justice, 4717
Union Square Awards Grants, 4718
United Technologies Corporation Grants, 4725
UPS Fdn Nonprofit Effectiveness Grts, 4732
USTA Tennis Block Party Grants, 4892
V.V. Cooke Fnd Grants, 4896
Valentine Fnd Grants, 4897
Valerie Adams Mem Char Trust Grts, 4898
Vancouver Fnd Disability Supports for Employment Grants, 4899
Vanguard Public Fnd Grant Funds, 4904
Viacom Fnd Grants (Formerly CBS Fnd), 4932
Victor E. Speas Fnd Grants, 4933
Victoria & Bradley L. Geist Enhancement Grants, 4935
Vigneron Grants, 4938
Virginia Commission for the Arts General Operating Grants, 4942
Virginia Comsn for the Arts Proj Grts, 4944
Visiting Nurse Fnd Grants, 4951
Vulcan Materials Company Fnd Grants, 4956
W. C. Griffith Fnd Grants, 4958
W Waldo & Jenny Lynn M Bradley Fdn Grts, 4967
Wallace Global Fund Grants, 4977
Walt Disney Company Fnd Grants, 4981
Walter and Elise Haas Fund Grants, 4982
Walter L. Gross III Family Fnd Grants, 4983
Wayne and Gladys Valley Fnd Grants, 5003
Wayne County Fnd - Vigran Family Fnd Grants, 5004
Weatherwax Fnd Grants, 5014
Weaver Fnd Grants, 5015
Weaver Popcorn Fnd Grants, 5016
West Virginia Commission on the Arts Major Institutions Support Grants, 5038
Weyerhaeuser Company Fnd Grants, 5053
Whirlpool Fnd Grants, 5056
Whitehorse Fnd Grants, 5058
Widgeon Point Charitable Fnd Grants, 5064
Wieboldt Fnd Grants, 5065
Wilbur & Patsy Bradley Family Fdn Grts, 5066
WILD Fnd Grants, 5068
William A. Badger Fnd Grants, 5072
William Blair and Company Fnd Grants, 5078
William C. Kenney Watershed Protection Fnd Ecosystem Grants, 5079
William G & Helen C Hoffman Fdn Grants, 5080
William G. Gilmore Fnd Grants, 5082
William G. McGowan Charitable Fund Grants, 5084
William J. Brace Charitable Trust, 5088
William L. and Victorine Q. Adams Fnd Grants, 5089
William M. Weaver Fnd Grants, 5091
William McCaskey Chapman and Adaline Dinsmore Chapman Fnd Grants, 5092
William Robert Baird Charitable Trust Grants, 5093
Wilson-Wood Fnd Grants, 5098
Windward Youth Leadership Fund Grants, 5100
Winifred & Harry B. Allen Fnd Grants, 5101
Wolfe Associates Grants, 5110
Women's Funding Alliance Grants, 5112
Woods Fund of Chicago Grants, 5115
Xerox Fnd Grants, 5122
Yampa Valley Comm Fnd Grants, 5124
Yellow Corporate Fnd Grants, 5126
Young Family Fnd Grants, 5127
Youth Philanthropy Project, 5132
YSA Global Yth Svc Day Lead Agency Grts, 5135
YSA National Child Awareness Month Youth Ambassador Grants, 5137
Z. Smith Reynolds Fnd Economic Dev Grants, 5144
Z. Smith Reynolds Fnd Democracy and Civic Engagement Grants, 5145

Graduate Assistantships
Abbott Fund Science Educ Grants, 83
Vancouver Fnd Grants and Comm Initiatives, 4900
Xerox Fnd Grants, 5122

Grants to Individuals
1st Source Fnd Ernestine M. Raclin Comm Leadership Award, 2
ACFEF Disaster Relief Fund Member Assistance, 117
A Charitable Fnd Grants, 126
Adams Family Fnd of Tennessee Grants, 152
Adams Rotary Memorial Fund A Grants, 157
Aid for Starving Children Emergency Assistance Fund Grants, 211
AIG Disaster Relief Fund Grants, 213
ALA ProQuest Documents to the People Award, 311
ALA Supporting Diversity Stipend, 333
ASTA Academic Scholarships, 597
Bank of America Critical Needs Grants, 656
Bingham McHale LLP Pro Bono Services, 772
Chicago Comm Arts Assistance Grants, 1081
Clara Abbott Fnd Need-Based Grants, 1146
Dollar Energy Fund Grants, 1567
Durfee Fnd Stanton Fellowship, 1626
Emma J. Adams Grants, 1702
Fitzpatrick, Cella, Harper & Scinto Pro Bono, 1836
HAF Arts and Culture: Lynne and Bob Wells Grant for Performing Artists, 2190
HAF Arts & Culture: Project Grts to Artists, 2191
HAF Kayla Wood Girls Grants, 2199
Kalamazoo Comm Fnd Individuals and Families Grants, 2769
Katie's Krops Grants, 2792
Kentucky Arts Council Al Smith Fellowship, 2806
Kentucky Arts Council Folk and Traditional Arts Apprenticeship Grant, 2808
Maine Comm Fnd Gracie Grants, 2982
Marin Comm Fnd Stinson Bolinas Comm Grants, 3013
Minnesota State Arts Board Cultural Comm Partnership Grants, 3188
MMS and Alliance Charitable Fnd Int'l Health Studies Grants, 3195
Modest Needs Bridge Grants, 3197
Modest Needs Hurcn Sandy Rlf Grts: Phs 2, 3198
Modest Needs New Employment Grants, 3199
Modest Needs Self-Sufficiency Grants, 3201
Montana Arts Cncl Cltrl & Aesthetic Proj Grts, 3209
Montana Comm Fnd Big Sky LIFT Grants, 3210
NAA Fdn Diversity PowerMind Fwsps, 3232
NAA Fnd Minority Fellowships, 3233
NAA Fnd Teacher Fellowships, 3234
NASE Succeed Scholarships, 3243
National Endowment for the Arts Local Arts Agencies Grants, 3263
Nevada Arts Council Professional Dev Grants, 3314
Newfoundland and Labrador Arts Council Labrador Cultural Travel Grants, 3319
NJSCA Folk Arts Apprenticeships, 3448
NYFA Strategic Opportunity Stipends, 3566
Ohio Arts Council Artist Express Grants, 3643
Paul Green Fnd Efforts to Abolish the Death Penalty in North Carolina Grants, 3760
PCA-PCD Professional Dev for Individual Artists Grants, 3770
PCA Arts Management Internship, 3773
PCA Pennsylvania Partners in the Arts Project Stream Grants, 3802
PCA Professional Dev Grants, 3803
PennPAT Artist Tech Assistance Grants, 3811
PennPAT Strategic Opportunity Grants, 3815
Phi Upsilon Omicron Florence Fallgatter Distinguished Service Award, 3877
Phi Upsilon Omicron Frances Morton Holbrook Alumni Award, 3878
Ploughshares Fund Grants, 3916
Quaker Oats Company Kids Care Clubs Grants, 3992
Rasmuson Fdn Individual Artists Awds, 4022
RISCA Design Innovation Grant, 4097
RISCA Professional Arts Dev Grants, 4099
RISCA Project Grants for Organizations, Individuals and Education, 4100
Sands Fnd Crisis Fund Grants, 4254
Southern Calif Edison Civic Affairs Grts, 4428
Stan and Sandy Checketts Fnd, 4473
Tourism Cares Professional Dev Scholarships, 4648
TSYSF Individual Scholarships, 4675
USDA Farm Labor Housing Grants, 4809
USDA Indiv Water & Waste Water Grts, 4817
USDA Rural Energy for America - Feasibility Study Grants, 4829
USDA Rural Energy for America - Renewable Energy System and Energy Efficiency Improvement Guaranteed Grants, 4830
USDA Rural Microentrepreneur Astnc Grts, 4832
Washington Area Fuel Fund Grants, 4988
WCI Comm Leadership Fellowships, 5008
West Virginia Commission on the Arts Professional Dev for Artists Grants, 5045
West Virginia Commission on the Arts Travel and Training Grants, 5050
Willary Fnd Grants, 5071
WSF Travel and Training Fund Grants, 5119

International Exchange Programs
APAP Cultural Exchange Grants, 492
Aratani Fnd Grants, 523
Coca-Cola Fnd Grants, 1195
Fnd for Young Ausies Indigenous Small Grants, 1901
Japan Fnd Center for Global Partnership Grants, 2649
MARPAT Fnd Grants, 3023
NHLBI Investigator Initiated Multi-Site Clinical Trials, 3413
Nuffield Fnd Open Door Grants, 3534
Summit Fnd Grants, 4524
UNCFSP TIEAD Internship, 4705
USAID Scholarships for Youth and Teachers, 4780

International Grants
A.J. Muste Memorial Institute General Grants, 44
A.J. Muste Memorial Institute Int'l Nonviolence Training Fund Grants, 45
AAAAI RSLAAIS Leadership Award, 49
AAUW Int'l Project Grants, 76
Abbott Fund Global AIDS Care Grants, 82
Abundance Fnd Int'l Grants, 108
A Charitable Fnd Grants, 126
Acorn Fnd Grants, 131
ADC Fnd Tech Access Grants, 158
ADEC Agricultural Telecommunications Grants, 159
Aid for Starving Children Int'l Grants, 212
AIG Disaster Relief Fund Grants, 213
Air Products and Chemicals Grants, 216
ALA ALTAFF/GALE Outstanding Trustee Conference Grant, 224
ALA Bogle Pratt Int'l Library Travel Fund Grant, 251
ALA Carnegie-Whitney Awards, 253
ALA Margaret Mann Citation, 297
Alberta Law Fnd Grants, 338
Alcoa Fnd Grants, 350
Allen Lane Fnd Grants, 379
Amarillo Area/Harrington Fnds Grants, 412
Ambrose Monell Fnd Grants, 415
AMD Corporate Contributions Grants, 416
American Express Historic Preservation Grants, 431
American Jewish World Service Grants, 441
American Society for Yad Vashem Grants, 447
Amgen Fnd Grants, 456
Andy Warhol Fdn for the Visual Arts Grts, 464
Angels Wings Fnd Int'l Grants, 469
ANLAF Int'l Fund for Sexual Minorities Grts, 471
AON Fnd Grants, 491
APAP Cultural Exchange Grants, 492
Arca Fnd Grants, 526
Archer Daniels Midland Fnd Grants, 527
Arronson Fnd Grants, 567
Arthur B. Schultz Fnd Grants, 573

PROGRAM TYPE INDEX

International Grants / 1099

Atran Fnd Grants, 610
Avon Products Fnd Grants, 625
AWDF Main Grants, 627
AWDF Solidarity Fund Grants, 628
Azadoutioun Fnd Grants, 631
Banfi Vintners Fnd Grants, 653
Bank of America Charitable Fnd Matching Gifts, 658
Baring Fnd Grants, 667
Baxter Int'l Corporate Giving Grants, 689
Baxter Int'l Fnd Grants, 691
Bay and Paul Fnds, Inc Grants, 692
Besser Fnd Grants, 748
Best Buy Children's Fnd @15 Scholarship, 750
Bill & Melinda Gates Ag Dev Grants, 765
Bill & Melinda Gates Emergency Response Grants, 766
Bill & Melinda Gates Policy and Advocacy Grants, 769
Bill and Melinda Gates Fnd Water, Sanitation and Hygiene Grants, 770
Boeckmann Charitable Fnd Grants, 808
Boston Jewish Cmnty Women's Fund Grts, 822
BP Conservation Programme Future Conservationist Awards, 826
Brainerd Fnd Grants, 831
Burden Trust Grants, 864
Bydale Fnd Grants, 882
Cabot Corporation Fnd Grants, 887
Caddock Fnd Grants, 888
Caesars Fnd Grants, 891
Canada-U.S. Fulbright Mid-Career Professional Grants, 917
Canadian Optometric Ed Trust Fund Grts, 918
Cargill Citizenship Fund-Corp Gvg Grants, 925
Carnegie Corporation of New York Grants, 940
Carylon Fnd Grants, 949
Caterpillar Fnd Grants, 954
CDC Fnd Global Disaster Response Fund Grants, 973
CE and S Fnd Grants, 985
Center for the Study of Philanthropy Fellowships, 989
Center for the Study of Philanthropy Senior Int'l Fellowships, 990
Center on Philanthropy and Civil Society's Emerging Leaders Int'l Fellows Program, 992
Central Okanagan Fnd Grants, 997
Changemakers Innovation Awards, 1031
Chapin Hall Int'l Fellowships in Children's Policy Research, 1032
Charles Delmar Fnd Grants, 1039
Charles H. Revson Fnd Grants, 1047
Charles Stewart Mott Fnd Grants, 1055
Chase Paymentech Corporate Giving Grants, 1059
Chatlos Fnd Grants, 1061
Chesapeake Corporation Fnd Grants, 1076
ChevronTexaco Contributions Program, 1078
Child's Dream Grants, 1104
Chiles Fnd Grants, 1108
Chiquita Brands Int'l Grants, 1110
Christensen Fund Regional Grants, 1112
CIGNA Fnd Grants, 1130
Citigroup Fnd Grants, 1139
Coca-Cola Fnd Grants, 1195
Collective Brands Fnd Payless Gives Shoes 4 Kids Grants, 1207
Columbus Jewish Fnd Grants, 1234
Commonwealth Fund Harkness Fellowships in Health Care Policy and Practice, 1242
Compton Fnd Grants, 1338
Computer Associates Comm Grants, 1341
ConocoPhillips Fnd Grants, 1354
ConocoPhillips Grants, 1355
Conrad N. Hilton Humanitarian Prize, 1356
Conservation, Food, and Health Fnd Grants for Developing Countries, 1359
Cooper Industries Fnd Grants, 1370
Cultural Society of Filipino Americans Grants, 1412
Cummins Fnd Grants, 1415
DAAD Research Grants for Doctoral Candidates and Young Academics and Scientists, 1427
Dale and Edna Walsh Fnd Grants, 1435
Danellie Fnd Grants, 1442
Dave Thomas Fnd for Adoption Grants, 1449

DENSO North America Fnd Grants, 1499
Diageo Fnd Grants, 1546
Dorot Fnd Grants, 1586
Dow Chemical Company Grants, 1596
eBay Fnd Comm Grants, 1648
Echoing Green Fellowships, 1650
EDS Tech Grants, 1662
ESRI Conservation Grants, 1751
ExxonMobil Fnd Women's Economic Opp Grants, 1778
Federal Express Corporate Contributions, 1799
Feldman Fnd Grants, 1801
Firelight Fnd Grants, 1817
Fishman Family Fnd Grants, 1835
Fluor Fnd Grants, 1875
FMC Fnd Grants, 1876
Ford Fdn Peace & Social Justice Grts, 1884
Fnd for Young Ausies Indigenous Small Grants, 1901
Fnd for Young Australians Spark Fund Grants, 1902
Fnd for Young Ausies Youth Led Futures Grants, 1905
Frances & Benjamin Benenson Fdn Grts, 1916
Fulbright/Garcia Robles Grants, 1968
Fulbright Binational Business Grants in Mexico, 1969
Fulbright Business Grants in Spain, 1970
Fulbright Grad Degree Pgm Grants in Mexico, 1971
Fulbright Public Policy Grants in Mexico, 1972
Funding Exchange Martin-Baro Fund Grants, 1979
Germanistic Society of America Fellowships, 2043
GMFUS Black Sea Trust for Reg'l Corp Grts, 2065
GMFUS Urban & Regnl Policy Fwsps, 2067
Greater Saint Louis Comm Fdn Grants, 2138
Gregory C. Carr Fnd Grants, 2161
Greygates Fnd Grants, 2164
H.B. Fuller Company Fnd Grants, 2183
H.J. Heinz Company Fnd Grants, 2184
Harold Simmons Fnd Grants, 2230
Harry S. Truman Scholarships, 2244
Health Canada National Seniors Indep Grants, 2278
Helen Bader Fnd Grants, 2293
Henry J. Kaiser Family Fnd Grants, 2310
Hershey Company Grants, 2318
Hoffberger Fnd Grants, 2342
Horowitz Fnd for Social Policy Grants, 2370
Horowitz Fdn for Social Policy Spcl Awds, 2371
Hydrogen Student Design Contest, 2415
IAFF Labour College of Canada Residential Scholarship, 2418
IEDC Int'l Trade Show Assistance Pgm, 2444
IIE David L. Boren Fellowships, 2454
Information Soc Innovation Fund Grts, 2554
Int'l Human Rights Funders Grants, 2567
IRA Pearson Fdn-IRA-Rotary Lit Awds, 2572
IREX Egypt Media Dev Grants, 2575
IREX Kosovo Civil Soc Project Grts, 2576
IREX MENA Media TV Produc Fund Grts, 2577
IREX Moldova Citizen Participation Grants, 2578
IREX Project Smile Grants, 2579
IREX Russia Civil Society Support Pgm Grts, 2580
IREX Small Grant Fund for Civil Society Projects in Africa and Asia, 2581
IREX Small Grant Fund for Media Projects in Africa and Asia, 2582
IREX Yemen Women's Leadership Grants, 2583
Isabel Allende Fnd Esperanza Grants, 2586
Jacob and Hilda Blaustein Fnd Grants, 2615
James H. Cummings Fnd Grants, 2626
Japan-US Comm Educ and Exchange Grants, 2648
Japan Fnd Center for Global Partnership Grants, 2649
Japan Fnd Center for Global Partnership Institutional Grants, 2650
Jenifer Altman Fnd Grants, 2662
Jewish Women's Fdn of New York Grants, 2677
Joel L. Fleishman Civil Society Fellowships, 2683
John D. and Catherine T. MacArthur Fnd Global Challenges Grants, 2690
John Deere Fnd Grants, 2692
Johns Manville Fund Grants, 2716
Johnson & Johnson Comm Health Care Grants, 2717
Johnson & Johnson Corp Contribs Grants, 2718
King Baudouin Int'l Dev Prize, 2825
Lindbergh Grants, 2907

Ludwick Family Fnd Grants, 2938
MacArthur Fnd Chicago Arts and Culture Int'l Connections Grants, 2962
MacArthur Fnd Conservation and Sustainable Dev Grants, 2963
Mary's Pence Ministry Grants, 3029
Mary's Pence Study Grants, 3030
Mary Kay Ash Charitable Fnd Grants, 3043
May & Stanley Smith Char Trust Grants, 3069
Miguel Aleman Fnd Grants, 3175
Millipore Fnd Grants, 3182
MMS and Alliance Charitable Fnd Int'l Health Studies Grants, 3195
Motorola Fnd Grants, 3221
National Endowment for Democracy Reagan-Fascell Democracy Fellowships, 3252
National Geographic Soc All Roads Seed Grts, 3272
National Geographic Society Conservation Trust Grants, 3273
National Geographic Society Genographic Legacy Fund Grants, 3274
National Geographic Young Explorers Grants, 3275
National Lottery Comm Fund Grants, 3279
Nestle Fnd Training Grant, 3301
NFWF/Exxon Save the Tiger Fund Grants, 3354
NFWF Coral Reef Conservation Project Grants, 3370
NIAF Anthony Campitelli Endwd Fund Grts, 3431
Nike and Ashoka GameChangers: Change the Game for Women in Sport, 3439
Nike Bowerman Track Renovation Grants, 3440
Nike Giving - Cash and Product Grants, 3442
Norman Fnd Grants, 3464
Notsew Orm Sands Fnd Grants, 3516
NSERC Brockhouse Canada Prize for Interdisciplinary Research in Science and Engineering Grant, 3518
Nuffield Fdn Children and Families Grants, 3533
Nuffield Fnd Small Grants, 3535
Oak Fnd Child Abuse Grants, 3632
Ohio Arts Council Int'l Partnership Grts, 3653
Olin Corporation Charitable Trust Grants, 3669
Ontario Arts Council Artists in the Comm/Workplace Grants, 3676
OSF Advancing the Rights and Integration of Roma Grants, 3699
OSF Affordable Access to Digital Communications Initiative, 3700
OSF Arab Regional Office Grants, 3701
OSF Central Eurasia Project Grants, 3704
OSF European Commission Internships for Young Roma Graduates, 3707
OSF Human Rights and Governance Grants, 3708
OSF Mental Health Initiative Grants, 3709
Overbrook Fnd Grants, 3715
Patricia Price Peterson Fnd Grants, 3746
Patrick and Anna M. Cudahy Fund Grants, 3751
Paul Balint Charitable Trust Grants, 3757
PDF Comm Organizing Grants, 3807
PDF Fiscal Sponsorship Grant, 3808
Pentair Fnd Educ and Comm Grts, 3816
PepsiCo Fnd Grants, 3819
Petra Fnd Fellows Awards, 3850
Pfizer Healthcare Charitable Contributions, 3863
Pfizer Medical Educ Track One Grants, 3864
Pfizer Special Events Grants, 3865
Ploughshares Fund Grants, 3916
Project Orange Thumb Grants, 3972
Public Welfare Fnd Grants, 3984
Radcliffe Inst Indiv Residential Fellowships, 4004
Rajiv Gandhi Fnd Grants, 4011
Raskob Fdn for Catholic Activities Grts, 4019
Regional Fund for Digital Innovation in Latin America and the Caribbean Grants, 4049
Richard and Rhoda Goldman Fund Grants, 4077
Robert F. Kennedy Human Rights Award, 4111
Rockefeller Brothers Fund Cross-Programmatic Initiative: Energy Grants, 4130
Rockefeller Brothers Democratic Practice Grants, 4131
Rockefeller Bros Fund Peace & Security Grts, 4133
Rockefeller Brothers Fund Pivotal Places Grants: Serbia, Montenegro, and Kosova, 4135

1100 / International Grants

Rockefeller Brothers Sustainable Dev Grants, 4136
Rockefeller Fnd Grants, 4138
Rohm and Haas Company Grants, 4145
Ronald McDonald House Charities Grants, 4149
Russell Berrie Fnd Grants, 4175
S.E.VEN Fund $50k VINE Project Prizes, 4193
S.E.VEN Fund Open Enterprise Solutions to Poverty RFP Grants, 4197
S.E.VEN Fund WHY Prize, 4198
Samuel Huntington Public Service Award, 4232
Samueli Fnd Human Security Grants, 4233
Samuel Rubin Fnd Grants, 4237
SanDisk Corp Comm Sharing Pgm, 4253
Seagate Tech Corp Capacity to Care Grants, 4317
Shared Earth Fnd Grants, 4339
Shastri Indo-Canadian Institute Action Research Project Grants, 4341
Sir Dorabji Tata Trust Grants for NGOs or Voluntary Organizations, 4370
Sister Fund Grants for Women's Organizations, 4371
Skoll Fnd Awds for Social Entrepreneurship, 4383
SSHRC Therese F. Casgrain Fellowship, 4466
Stanley Smith Horticultural Trust Grants, 4474
Starr Fnd Grants, 4483
State Street Fnd Grants, 4495
Steelcase Fnd Grants, 4497
Sweet Water Trust Grants, 4541
Sylvia Adams Charitable Trust Grants, 4543
TechFnd TechGrants, 4570
TE Fnd Grants, 4572
Texas Instruments Corporation Civic and Business Grants, 4597
Third Millennium Fnd Grants, 4607
Tifa Fnd Grants, 4633
Topeka Comm Fnd Building Families Grants, 4643
Tourism Cares Worldwide Grants, 4649
Trull Fnd Grants, 4673
UNESCO World Heritage Fund Grants, 4706
United Methodist Committee on Relief Hunger and Poverty Grants, 4720
United Technologies Corporation Grants, 4725
UPS Fnd Economic and Global Lit Grants, 4730
USAID Accelerating Progress Against Tuberculosis in Kenya Grants, 4737
USAID African Institutions Innovation Mechanism Grants, 4738
USAID Albania Critical Economic Growth Areas Grants, 4740
USAID Call for Public-Private Alliance Proposals in Serbia, 4742
USAID Civic Participation Grants, 4743
USAID Comm Infrastructure Dev Grants, 4745
USAID Comprehensive District-Based Support for Better HIV/TB Patient Outcomes Grants, 4747
USAID Dev Assistance Fund Grants, 4748
USAID Dev Innov Ventures Grts, 4749
USAID Economic Prospectsfor Armenia-Turkey Normalization Grants, 4750
USAID Family Health Plus Project Grants, 4751
USAID Food Security, Nutrition, Biodiversity and Conservation Grants, 4752
USAID Grant for Operationalizing a Neighborhood Approach to Reduce Urban Disaster Risk in Latin America and the Caribbean, 4754
USAID Haiti Disaster Risk Reduction Capacity Building Grants, 4756
USAID HIV Prevention with Key Populations - Mali Grants, 4757
USAID Implementation Science for Strengthening Use of Evidence in Family Planning/Reproductive Health Programming Grants, 4758
USAID India Partnership Grants, 4761
USAID Integration of Care and Support within the Health System to Support Better Patient Outcomes Grants, 4762
USAID Int'l Emergency Food Assistance Grants, 4763
USAID Knowledge for Health II Grants, 4765
USAID Leadership Initiative for Good Governance in Africa Grants, 4766
USAID Malawi Local Capacity Dev Grants, 4767
USAID Mekong Partnership for the Environment Project Grants, 4769
USAID Pakistan Private Investment Grants, 4772
USAID Palestinian Comm Astnc Grts, 4773
USAID Palestinian Comm Infrastructure Grants, 4774
USAID Public-Private Alliance Proposals in Burma, Thailand, and Vietnam, 4775
USAID Rapid Response for Sudan Grants, 4776
USAID Rapid Response to Pakistanis Affected by Disasters - Phase Two Grants, 4777
USAID Reading Enhancement for Advancing Dev Grants, 4778
USAID Strengthening Democratic Local Governance in South Sudan Grants, 4782
USAID Strengthening RMNCH Through Indian Health Professional Associations and Scaling Up Uptake Grants, 4784
USAID Unsolicited Proposal Grants, 4786
USAID Workforce Dev in Mexico Grants, 4787
US CRDF Science and Tech Entrepreneurship Program Business Partnership Grant - Armenia, 4795
USDA Foreign Market Dev Grants, 4811
USDA Market Access Grants, 4818
USDC Market Dev Cooperator Grants, 4853
Virginia Fnd for the Humanities Residential Fellowships, 4948
Volvo Adventure Environmental Awards, 4952
WK Kellogg Fnd Healthy Kids Grants, 4961
Wallace Global Fund Grants, 4977
WILD Fnd Grants, 5068
World Bank JJ/WBGSP Partners Programs, 5117
Xerox Fnd Grants, 5122
Yves Rocher Fnd Women of the Earth Awards, 5143

Job Training/Adult Vocational Programs

3M Fnd Comm Giving Grants, 15
A.C. Ratshesky Fnd Grants, 39
Abell Fnd Workforce Dev Grants, 97
Able Trust Voc Rehab Grants for Agencies, 103
Able Trust Vocational Rehabilitation Grants for Individuals, 104
ACE Charitable Fnd Grants, 111
ACF Native American Social and Economic Dev Strategies Grants, 123
ACF Supplemental Services for Recently Arrived Refugees Grants, 125
Achelis Fnd Grants, 127
Actors Fund Soc Svcs & Financial Assistance, 139
Adolph Coors Fnd Grants, 171
A Fund for Women Grants, 195
Alaska Airlines Fnd Grants, 321
Alcoa Fnd Grants, 350
Allen Lane Fnd Grants, 379
Allstate Corporate Giving Grants, 386
Allstate Fnd Safe and Vital Communities Grants, 390
AMD Corporate Contributions Grants, 416
Anderson Fnd Grants, 460
Anschutz Family Fnd Grants, 486
Appalachian Regional Commission Telecommunications Grants, 510
ARCO Fnd Educ Grants, 528
Arizona Fnd for Women Deborah G. Carstens Fund Grants, 543
Arizona Republic Newspaper Corp Contribs, 547
Ashland Corporate Contributions Grants, 587
Assisi Fnd of Memphis General Grants, 594
Assisi Fnd of Memphis Mini Grants, 595
Assurant Health Fnd Grants, 596
ASTA Academic Scholarships, 597
AT&T Fnd Civic and Comm Service Grants, 599
Atkinson Fnd Comm Grants, 606
Autauga Area Comm Fnd Grants, 618
Avista Fnd Grants, 624
Baltimore Comm Fnd Human Services Grants, 644
Bank of America Charitable Fnd Educ and Workforce Dev Grants, 657
Bank of America Charitable Fnd Student Leaders Grants, 659
BBF Maine Family Lit Initiative Planning Grants, 699
BBVA Compass Fnd Charitable Grants, 703

Benton Comm Fnd Grants, 730
Berks County Comm Fnd Grants, 734
Bernard F & Alva B Gimbel Fdn Grts, 740
Blue River Comm Fnd Grants, 801
Bodman Fnd Grants, 807
Boeing Company Contributions Grants, 809
Boston Fnd Grants, 819
Boston Jewish Cmnty Women's Fund Grts, 822
Bridgestone/Firestone Trust Fund Grants, 836
Brooklyn Comty Fdn Caring Neighbors Grts, 848
Brooklyn Comm Fnd Comm Dev Grants, 850
Brooklyn Comm Fnd Educ and Youth Achievement Grants, 851
Brooklyn Comm Fnd Green Communities Grants, 852
Brown County Comm Fnd Grants, 853
Burlington Industries Fnd Grants, 865
Burton D Morgan Youth Entrepreneurship Grants, 870
Bush Fnd Health & Human Svcs Grts, 875
Butler Mfg Co Fnd Grants, 881
Cargill Citizenship Fund-Corp Gvg Grants, 925
Carl M. Freeman Fnd Grants, 933
Carrie Estelle Doheny Fnd Grants, 945
CCHD Comm Dev Grants, 966
CCHD Economic Dev Grants, 967
CenturyLink Clarke M Williams Fdn Grts, 998
Ceres Fnd Grants, 999
CFFVR Jewelers Mutual Char Gvg Grts, 1014
CFFVR Schmidt Family G4 Grants, 1020
Charles Stewart Mott Fdn Anti-Poverty Grts, 1054
Charlotte County Comm Fnd Grts, 1056
Chicago Comm Trust Workforce Grants, 1094
Chicago Title & Trust Co Fdn Grants, 1099
Chiron Fnd Comm Grants, 1111
CICF Efroymson Grants, 1120
Citizens Bank Mid-Atlantic Char Fdn Grts, 1140
Clark Fnd Grants, 1157
Clay Fnd Grants, 1162
Cleveland Browns Fnd Grants, 1166
Cleveland Fnd Fenn Educational Fund Grants, 1169
CNA Fnd Grants, 1179
Comer Fnd Grants, 1236
Comm Fnd of Bartholomew County Heritage Fund Grants, 1267
Comm Fnd of Broward Grants, 1275
Comm Fnd of Louisville Grants, 1299
Comm Fdn of Mdl Tennessee Grants, 1300
Comm Fnd of Muncie and Delaware County Maxon Grants, 1303
Connecticut Light & Power Corp Contribs, 1352
Constellation Energy Corporate Grants, 1364
Coors Brewing Corporate Contributions Grants, 1371
Cruise Industry Charitable Fnd Grants, 1404
DaimlerChrysler Corporation Fund Grants, 1432
Dallas Women's Fnd Grants, 1438
Darden Restaurants Fnd Grants, 1446
DB Americas Fnd Grants, 1466
Deluxe Corporation Fnd Grants, 1496
Denver Fnd Comm Grants, 1502
Dept of Ed Projects with Industry Grants, 1511
Dept of Ed Recreational Services for Individuals with Disabilities, 1512
Diageo Fnd Grants, 1546
DOL Homeless Veterans Reintegration Grants, 1566
DOL Youthbuild Grants, 1571
Duke Energy Fnd Econ Dev Grants, 1619
Dynegy Fnd Grants, 1630
Dyson Fnd Emergency Fund Grants, 1631
eBay Fnd Comm Grants, 1648
Edward & Ellen Roche Relief Fdn Grants, 1663
Emma G. Harris Fnd Grants, 1701
Essex County Comm Fnd First Jobs Grant, 1754
Eulalie Bloedel Schneider Fnd Grants, 1767
Evelyn and Walter Haas, Jr. Fund Immigrant Rights Grants, 1773
ExxonMobil Fnd Women's Economic Opportunity Grants, 1778
Faye McBeath Fnd Grants, 1794
Fel-Pro Mecklenburger Fnd Grants, 1800
FEMA Assistance to Firefighters Grants, 1802
Field Fnd of Illinois Grants, 1806

PROGRAM TYPE INDEX

Fisher Fnd Grants, 1831
Fitzpatrick and Francis Family Business Continuity Fnd Grants, 1837
Ford Motor Company Fund Grants, 1885
Fnd for the Carolinas Grants, 1896
Frances L & Edwin L Cummings Mem Fund, 1919
Gannett Fdn Comm Action Grants, 1984
Gardiner Howland Shaw Fnd Grants, 1986
General Service Fnd Colorado Grants, 2005
George Family Fnd Grants, 2017
George Gund Fnd Grants, 2020
Georgia-Pacific Fdn Entrepreneurship Grts, 2033
Gertrude M. Conduff Fnd Grants, 2047
GNOF Metropolitan Opportunities Grants, 2087
GNOF New Orleans Works Grants, 2088
Go Daddy Cares Charitable Contributions, 2094
Golden LEAF Fnd Grants, 2097
Grand Rapids Area Comm Fnd Wyoming Youth Fund Grants, 2117
Grand Victoria Fnd Illinois Core Grants, 2126
Greater Milwaukee Fnd Grants, 2137
HAF Comm Grants, 2193
Hallmark Corporate Fnd Grants, 2212
Hampton Roads Comm Fnd Health and Human Service Grants, 2216
Harry S. Black and Allon Fuller Fund Grants, 2243
Hartford Fdn Nonprofit Support Grants, 2252
Harvest Fnd Grants, 2254
HBF Pathways Out of Poverty Grants, 2273
Hearst Fnds Social Service Grants, 2285
Helen Bader Fnd Grants, 2293
Helen V. Brach Fnd Grants, 2300
Henry & Ruth Blaustein Rosenberg Fdn Grants, 2306
Highmark Corporate Giving Grants, 2319
Hoffberger Fnd Grants, 2342
Household Int'l Corp Giving Grants, 2372
Hudson Webber Fnd Grants, 2383
Humanitas Fnd Grants, 2390
Hutchinson Comm Fnd Grants, 2410
Hyams Fnd Grants, 2413
IBM Adult Trng & Workforce Dev Grts, 2423
IEDC Skills Enhancement Fund , 2445
Illinois DCEO Employer Trng Investment Pgm Grts - Competitive Component, 2491
Illinois DCEO Employer Trng Investment Pgm Grts - Incentive Component, 2492
Illinois DCEO Employer Trng Investment Pgm Multi-Company Trng Grts, 2493
Illinois DCEO Employer Trng Investment Pgm Single Company Trng Grts, 2494
Illinois DCEO Large Business Dev Grants, 2495
Independence Comm Fnd Education, Culture & Arts Grant, 2526
Independence Comm Fnd Neighborhood Renewal Grants, 2527
Indiana Reg'l Econ Dev Partnership Grts, 2546
Indiana Space Grant Consortium Workforce Dev Grants, 2550
Indiana Workforce Acceleration Grants, 2552
Intel Comm Grants, 2562
Int'l Paper Co Fnd Grants, 2568
Irvin Stern Fnd Grants, 2585
Isabel Allende Fnd Esperanza Grants, 2586
J. Jill Compassion Fund Grants, 2598
Jacobs Family Fdn Vlg Neighborhoods Grants, 2619
Jane Bradley Pettit Comm & Social Dev Grants, 2642
JM Fnd Grants, 2681
John Edward Fowler Mem Fdn Grants, 2693
John F. Kennedy Center for the Performing Arts National Rosemary Kennedy Internship, 2694
John Merck Fund Grants, 2706
Johnson & Johnson Corp Contribs Grants, 2718
Jovid Fnd Grants, 2745
JP Morgan Chase Comm Dev Grts, 2753
K. M. Hunter Charitable Social Welfare Grants, 2757
Katharine Matthies Fnd Grants, 2788
Kennedy Center HSC Fnd Internship, 2799
Kennedy Center Summer HSC Fnd Internship, 2800
Kessler Fdn Comm Employment Grts, 2814
Kessler Fdn Signature Employment Grts, 2816

Kimball Int'l-Habig Fdn Grts, 2823
Liberty Bank Fnd Grants, 2890
Linden Fnd Grants, 2908
Liz Claiborne Fnd Grants, 2915
Luther I. Replogle Fnd Grants, 2945
M.B. and Edna Zale Fnd Grants, 2950
Mabel Louise Riley Fnd Family Strengthening Small Grants, 2958
MARPAT Fnd Grants, 3023
Marriott Int'l Corporate Giving Grts, 3024
May & Stanley Smith Char Trust Grants, 3069
McCune Charitable Fnd Grants, 3077
McGregor Fund Grants, 3082
Meyer Fnd Economic Security Grants, 3141
Microsoft Comty Affairs Puget Sound Grts, 3163
Middlesex Savings Charitable Fnd Educational Opportunities Grants, 3174
Miller Fnd Grants, 3181
Minnesota Small Cities Dev Grants, 3187
Montgomery Cty Comm Fdn Grants, 3213
Morris & Gwendolyn Cafritz Fdn Grants, 3218
NASE Succeed Scholarships, 3243
National Housing Endowment Challenge/Build/Grow Grant, 3277
Nehemiah Comm Fnd Grants, 3290
New Jersey Center for Hispanic Policy, Research and Dev Workforce Grants, 3330
New Mexico Women's Fnd Grants, 3335
Nike Fnd Grants, 3441
Nissan Fnd Grants, 3444
NNEDVF/Altria Doors of Hope Program, 3452
Norcliffe Fnd Grants, 3459
Norman Fnd Grants, 3464
NE Utilities Fnd Grants, 3498
Northern Trust Company Charitable Trust and Corporate Giving Program, 3504
Norton Fnd Grants, 3514
NYCT Comm Dev Grants, 3546
OceanFirst Fnd Grants, 3636
Ohio Arts Council Artists with Disabilities Access Grants, 3646
OneFamily Fnd Grants, 3673
Oppenstein Brothers Fnd Grants, 3685
ORBI Artist Fast Track Grants, 3689
PacifiCare Fnd Grants, 3725
Palm Beach and Martin Counties Grants, 3733
Patrick and Anna M. Cudahy Fund Grants, 3751
Paul and Mary Haas Fnd Contributions and Student Scholarships, 3756
Pentair Fnd Educ and Comm Grants, 3816
Perry County Comm Fnd Grants, 3827
PG&E Comm Vitality Grants, 3868
PGE Fnd Grants, 3869
Piedmont Natural Gas Corporate and Charitable Contributions, 3883
Piedmont Natural Gas Fnd Workforce Dev Grant, 3886
Piper Jaffray Fdn Communities Giving Grts, 3899
Polk Bros. Fnd Grants, 3929
Portland General Electric Fnd Grants, 3937
Price Chopper's Golub Fnd Grants, 3950
Principal Financial Group Fnd Grants, 3966
Prudential Fdn Econ Dev Grants, 3976
Public Welfare Fnd Grants, 3984
Pulaski County Comm Fnd Grants, 3988
Reinberger Fnd Grants, 4052
Reynolds American Fnd Grants, 4068
Richard King Mellon Fnd Grants, 4087
Robert P & Clara I Milton Fund for Sr Housing, 4117
Robert R. McCormick Tribune Veterans Grants, 4120
Rockefeller Fnd Grants, 4138
Rockwell Fund, Inc. Grants, 4140
RWJF Jobs to Careers: Promoting Work-Based Learning for Quality Care, 4185
S. Mark Taper Fnd Grants, 4201
SAG Motion Pic Plyrs Welfare Fund Grts, 4209
Salmon Fnd Grants, 4225
Samuel S. Johnson Fnd Grants, 4239
Santa Fe Comm Fnd Seasonal Grants-Spring, 4291
Seneca Foods Fnd Grants, 4336
Sid W. Richardson Fnd Grants, 4350

Land Acquisition / 1101

Sierra Health Fnd Responsive Grants, 4353
Sioux Falls Area Comm Fnd Comm Fund Grants, 4364
Sioux Falls Area Comm Fnd Spot Grants, 4366
Sobrato Family Fnd Grants, 4389
Sobrato Family Fdn Meeting Space Grts, 4390
Sobrato Family Fnd Office Space Grants, 4391
Sorenson Legacy Fnd Grants, 4407
Speer Trust Grants, 4450
SSA Work Incentives Planning and Assistance, 4465
Stackpole-Hall Fnd Grants, 4472
Starr Fnd Grants, 4483
State Street Fnd Grants, 4495
Strake Fnd Grants, 4511
Strolling of the Heifers Schlrsps for Farmers, 4514
Taproot Fnd Capacity-Building Service Grants, 4560
Tech Enhancement Certification for Hoosiers , 4571
Textron Corporate Contributions Grants, 4601
Thomas Sill Fnd Grants, 4619
Topfer Family Fnd Grants, 4646
Toyota Motor Mfg of Mississippi Grts, 4655
Toyota Motor Manuf of West Virginia Grants, 4657
Tri-State Comm Twenty-first Century Endowment Fund Grants, 4666
U.S. Bank Fnd Grants, 4686
US Dept of Educ Innovative Strategies in Comm Colleges for Working Adults and Displaced Workers Grants, 4692
US Dept of Educ Migrant and Seasonal Farmworkers Grants, 4693
US Dept of Educ Parent Info & Trng, 4695
US Dept of Educ Rehabilitation Research Training Centers , 4699
US Dept of Educ Voc Rehab Svcs Projects for American Indians with Disabilities Grts, 4702
Union Bank, N.A. Fnd Grants, 4709
UPS Fnd Economic and Global Lit Grants, 4730
USAID Call for Public-Private Alliance Proposals in Serbia, 4742
USAID Comm Livelihoods in Yemen Grant, 4746
USAID Economic Prospectsfor Armenia-Turkey Normalization Grants, 4750
USAID Workforce Dev in Mexico Grants, 4787
USDA Rural Business Enterprise Grants, 4823
USDA Rural Business Opportunity Grants, 4824
USDC Advanced Manufacturing Jobs and Innovation Accelerator Challenge Grants, 4848
USDC Business Center - American Indian and Alaska Native Grants, 4849
USDC i6 Challenge Grants, 4851
USDC Public Works and Economic Adjustment Assistance Grants, 4856
Vanderburgh Comm Fdn Women's Fund, 4903
Vectren Fnd Grants, 4907
Verizon Fnd Connecticut Grants, 4908
Verizon Fnd Great Lakes Region Grants, 4912
Verizon Fnd Lit Grants, 4915
Verizon Fnd Maryland Grants, 4917
Verizon Fnd New York Grants, 4919
Verizon Fnd Pennsylvania Grants, 4921
Verizon Fnd SE Region Grants, 4923
Verizon Fnd West Virginia Grants, 4926
Waitt Family Fnd Grants, 4973
Whirlpool Fnd Grants, 5056
Wieboldt Fnd Grants, 5065
WILD Fnd Grants, 5068
Women's Funding Alliance Grants, 5112
Xerox Fnd Grants, 5122

Land Acquisition
Appalachian Regional Commission Transportation and Highways Grants, 512
Duke Energy Fdn Comm Vitality Grants, 1618
Enterprise Comm Partners Rose Architectural Fellowships, 1719
G.A. Ackermann Grants, 1981
Georgia-Pacific Fnd Enrichment Grants, 2032
GNOF Environmental Fund Grants, 2073
GNOF Metropolitan Opportunities Grants, 2087
Harrison County Comm Fnd Signature Grants, 2234
HRF Hudson River Improvement Grants, 2378

1102 / Land Acquisition

Illinois DCEO Comm Dev Assistance Pgm for Economic Dev (CDAP-ED) Grants, 2488
Illinois DCEO Emerging Technological Enterprises Grants, 2490
Illinois DNR Park and Recreational Facility Construction Grants, 2499
Jane and Jack Fitzpatrick Fund Grants, 2640
Janson Fnd Grants, 2646
Massachusetts Cultural Council Cultural Facilities Capital Grants, 3053
Massachusetts Cultural Council Cultural Facilities Systems Replacement Plan Grants Grants, 3055
MDEQ Great Lakes Areas of Concern Land Acquisition Grants, 3099
Norcliffe Fnd Grants, 3459
North Central Health Services Grants, 3491
PNM Power Up Grants, 3925
Priddy Fnd Capital Grants, 3954
Robert R. Meyer Fnd Grants, 4121
Santa Barbara Strategy Capital Support, 4285
Seattle Fdn C Keith Birkenfeld Mem Tr Grts, 4323
USDA 1890 Land Grant Colleges and Universities Initiative Grants, 4797
Van Kampen Boyer Molinari Char Fnd Grts, 4905

Matching/Challenge Funds
3M Fnd Comm Giving Grants, 15
21st Century Threshold Project Gifts, 21
1772 Fnd Fellowships, 36
A.O. Smith Comm Grants, 46
AACC Service Learning Mini-Grants, 57
AAF Accent on Architecture Comm Grants, 58
Abbot & Dorothy H Stevens Fdn Grants, 79
Abbott Fund Global AIDS Care Grants, 82
Abell-Hanger Fnd Grants, 91
Able To Play Challenge Grants, 101
Access Fund Climbing Preservation Grants, 110
ACE Charitable Fnd Grants, 111
ACF Assets for Indep Demo Grants, 114
ACF Assets for Independence Individual Dev Account Grants, 115
ACF Head Start and Early Head Start Grants, 120
ACF Native American Environmental Regulatory Enhancement Grants, 122
ACF Native American Social and Economic Dev Strategies Grants, 123
ACTION Council of Monterey County Grants, 134
AEC Trust Grants, 175
AEGON Transamerica Fdn Arts & Culture Grts, 176
AEGON Transamerica Fdn Civic Grants, 177
AEGON Transamerica Fdn Disaster Rlf Grts, 178
AEP Corporate Giving Grants, 180
Aetna Fdn Diversity Grants in Connecticut, 182
African American Heritage Grants, 193
Agere Corporate and Comm Involvement Grants, 199
Agnes M. Lindsay Trust Grants, 203
Ahmanson Fnd Grants, 207
Air Products and Chemicals Grants, 216
Alabama Humanities Fnd Mini Grants, 231
Alabama Humanities Fnd Planning Grants, 232
Alabama Power Fnd Grants, 233
Alabama State Council on the Arts Comm Arts Presenting Grants, 238
Alabama State Council on the Arts Comm Arts Program Dev Grants, 239
Alabama State Council on the Arts Projects of Individual Artists Grants, 248
Alaska State Council on the Arts Comm Grants, 327
Alaska State Council on the Arts Operating Support Grants, 328
Albert and Bessie Mae Kronkosky Charitable Fnd Grants, 339
Alberto Culver Corporate Contributions Grants, 343
Albertson's Charitable Giving Grants, 345
Alcoa Fnd Grants, 350
Alex Stern Family Fnd Grants, 360
Alice Tweed Tuohy Fnd Grants, 372
Allegan County Comm Fnd Grants, 375
Allegheny Technologies Charitable Trust, 377
Allen P & Josephine B Green Fnd Grts, 380

Alliant Energy Fnd Hometown Challenge Grants, 385
Allstate Corporate Giving Grants, 386
Allstate Corp Hometown Commitment Grants, 387
Allstate Fnd Safe and Vital Communities Grants, 390
Allyn Fnd Grants, 392
Amarillo Area/Harrington Fnds Grants, 412
Americana Fnd Grants, 422
AMI Semiconductors Corporate Grants, 457
Amon G. Carter Fnd Grants, 458
Angels On Track Fnd Grants, 468
Anheuser-Busch Fnd Grants, 470
Ann Arbor Area Comm Fnd Grants, 474
Anne L. and George H. Clapp Charitable and Educational Trust Grants, 476
Ann Peppers Fnd Grants, 484
Appalachian Regional Commission Asset-Based Dev Project Grants, 500
Appalachian Regional Commission Business Dev Revolving Loan Fund Grants, 501
Appalachian Regional Commission Comm Infrastructure Grants, 502
Appalachian Regional Commission Distressed Counties Grants, 503
Appalachian Regional Commission Educ and Training Grants, 504
Appalachian Reg'l Commission Energy Grts, 505
Appalachian Regional Commission Export and Trade Dev Grants, 506
Appalachian Regional Commission Health Care Grants, 507
Appalachian Regional Commission Leadership Dev and Capacity Building Grants, 509
Appalachian Regional Commission Telecommunications Grants, 510
Appalachian Regional Commission Tourist Grants, 511
ARCO Fnd Educ Grants, 528
Arie and Ida Crown Memorial Grants, 533
Arizona Commission on the Arts Visual/Media Arts Organizations Grants, 539
Arizona Comm Fnd Grants, 540
Arizona Public Service Corp Gvg Pgm Grts, 545
Arkansas Arts Council AIE After School/Summer Residency Grants, 551
Arkansas Arts Council AIE Arts Curriculum Project Grants, 552
Arkansas Arts Council AIE In-School Residency Grants, 553
Arkansas Arts Council AIE Mini Grants, 554
Arkansas Arts Cncl Collab Proj Support, 555
Arkansas Arts Council Expansion Arts Grants, 556
Arkell Hall Fnd Grants, 562
Arthur Ashley Williams Fnd Grants, 572
Ashland Corporate Contributions Grants, 587
Aspen Comm Fnd Grants, 592
Assisi Fdn of Memphis Capital Project Grants, 593
Assurant Health Fnd Grants, 596
Atherton Family Fnd Grants, 604
Atran Fnd Grants, 610
Austin Comm Fnd Grants, 616
AutoNation Corporate Giving Grants, 620
AutoZone Comm Relations Grants, 621
Autzen Fnd Grants, 622
Avon Products Fnd Grants, 625
Ayres Fnd Grants, 630
Bailey Fnd Grants, 635
Ball Brothers Fnd General Grants, 637
Baltimore Comm Fnd Arts and Culture Grants, 641
Bank of America Charitable Fnd Matching Gifts, 658
Barker Welfare Fnd Grants, 669
Barra Fnd Project Grants, 674
Batchelor Fnd Grants, 679
Baton Rouge Area Fnd Grants, 682
Battle Creek Comm Fnd Grants, 684
Batts Fnd Grants, 687
Baxter Int'l Corporate Giving Grants, 689
Baxter Int'l Fnd Grants, 691
Bay and Paul Fnds, Inc Grants, 692
Bay and Paul Fnds, Inc Grants, 693
BCBSM Fnd Comm Health Matching Grants, 707
Beckley Area Fnd Grants, 716

PROGRAM TYPE INDEX

Bemis Company Fnd Grants, 723
Bender Fnd Grants, 726
Benton Comm Fnd Grants, 730
Bertha Russ Lytel Fnd Grants, 745
Besser Fnd Grants, 748
Bikes Belong Grants, 763
Blanche & Julian Robertson Family Fdn Grants, 785
Blandin Fnd Itasca County Area Vitality Grants, 789
Blue Cross Blue Shield of Minnesota Fdn Healthy Equity: Health Impact Assessment Grts, 796
Blue Grass Comm Fnd Grants, 799
Blue River Comm Fnd Grants, 801
Blumenthal Fnd Grants, 804
Bodenwein Public Benevolent Fdn Grants, 806
Boeing Company Contributions Grants, 809
Boettcher Fnd Grants, 810
Booth Ferris Fnd Grants, 816
Boston Fnd Grants, 819
Bradley Family Fnd (California) Grants, 829
Brainerd Fnd Grants, 831
Brico Fund Grants, 835
Bridgestone/Firestone Trust Fund Grants, 836
British Columbia Arts Council Educ Grants, 842
Brookdale Fnd Relatives as Parents Grts, 846
Brown Fnd Grants, 854
Brunswick Fnd Dollars for Doers Grants, 856
Brunswick Fnd Grants, 857
Bullitt Fnd Grants, 862
Bunbury Company Grants, 863
Burlington Industries Fnd Grants, 865
Burlington Northern Santa Fe Fdn Grants, 866
Burton G. Bettingen Grants, 871
Bush Fnd Arts & Humanities Cap Projects Grants, 872
Butler Mfg Co Fnd Grants, 881
Bydale Fnd Grants, 882
Cabot Corporation Fnd Grants, 887
Cadence Design Systems Grants, 889
Cailloux Fnd Grants, 892
California Arts Council Statewide Ntwks Grts, 897
California Comm Fnd Neighborhood Revitalization Grants, 903
Calif Green Trees for The Golden State Grt, 906
Callaway Fnd Grants, 909
Callaway Golf Company Fnd Grants, 910
Campbell Soup Fnd Grants, 916
Captain Planet Fnd Grants, 922
Cardinal Health Fnd Grants, 923
CarEth Fnd Grants, 924
Cargill Citizenship Fund-Corp Gvg Grants, 925
Carl & Eloise Pohlad Family Fdn Grants, 927
Carl C. Icahn Fnd Grants, 929
Carlisle Fnd Grants, 931
Carl M. Freeman Fnd Grants, 933
Carlos and Marguerite Mason Trust Grants, 934
Carnahan-Jackson Fnd Grants, 939
Carpenter Fnd Grants, 943
Carrie E. and Lena V. Glenn Fnd Grants, 944
Carrie Estelle Doheny Fnd Grants, 945
Cass County Comm Fnd Grants, 952
Caterpillar Fnd Grants, 954
Cause Populi Worthy Cause Grants, 958
CCH California Story Fund Grants, 965
CCHD Comm Dev Grants, 966
CDECD Arts Catalyze Placemaking in Every Comm Grants, 977
CDECD Arts Catalyze Placemaking Leadership Grants, 978
CDECD Arts Catalyze Placemaking Sustaining Relevance Grants, 979
CDECD Endangered Properties Grants, 980
CDECD Historic Preservation Survey and Planning Grants, 982
CDECD Historic Restoration Grants, 983
CDECD Tourism Product Dev Grants, 984
Cemala Fnd Grants, 988
Central Carolina Comm Impact Grants, 994
Central New York Comm Fdn Grants, 996
CenturyLink Clarke M Williams Fdn Grts, 998
Cessna Fnd Grants, 1000
CFFVR Clintonville Area Fnd Grants, 1008

PROGRAM TYPE INDEX

Matching/Challenge Funds / 1103

CFFVR Fox Valley Comm Arts Grants, 1011
CFFVR Robert and Patricia Endries Family Fnd Grants, 1018
CFFVR Women's Fund for the Fox Valley Region Grants, 1025
Charity Incorporated Grants, 1035
Charles A. Frueauff Fnd Grants, 1037
Charles & Lynn Schusterman Fam Fdn Grants, 1038
Charles H. Revson Fnd Grants, 1047
Charles Hayden Fnd Grants, 1048
Charles Stewart Mott Fdn Anti-Poverty Grts, 1054
Chatlos Fnd Grants, 1061
CHCF Local Coverage Expansion Initiative, 1064
CHC Fnd Grants, 1065
Chemtura Corporation Contributions Grants, 1067
Chesapeake Bay Trust Mini Grants, 1072
Chesapeake Corporation Fnd Grants, 1076
Chicago Title & Trust Co Fdn Grants, 1099
Chicago Tribune Fnd Civic Grants, 1100
Chicago Tribune Fnd Grants for Cultural Organizations, 1101
Christensen Fund Regional Grants, 1112
Christy-Houston Fnd Grants, 1115
CICF City of Noblesville Comm Grant, 1118
CIGNA Fnd Grants, 1130
Cincinnati Bell Fnd Grants, 1131
Circle K Corporation Contributions Grants, 1136
Claneil Fnd Grants, 1145
Clark Charitable Trust Grants, 1155
Claude Worthington Benedum Fdn Grants, 1161
Clay Fnd Grants, 1162
Cleveland-Cliffs Fnd Grants, 1165
Cleveland Fnd Capital Grants, 1167
Cleveland Fnd Neighborhood Connections Grants, 1171
Cleveland H. Dodge Fnd Grants, 1172
Clowes Fund Grants, 1177
CNA Fnd Grants, 1179
CNCS AmeriCorps Indian Tribes Plng Grts, 1180
CNCS AmeriCorps State and National Grants, 1182
CNCS AmeriCorps State and National Planning Grants, 1183
CNCS Foster Grandparent Projects Grants, 1185
CNCS Senior Companion Grants, 1187
CNCS Senior Corps Retired and Senior Volunteer Grants, 1188
CNCS Social Innovation Grants, 1189
Coca-Cola Fnd Grants, 1195
Cockrell Fnd Grants, 1196
Colgate-Palmolive Company Grants, 1202
Collins Fnd Grants, 1209
Colonel Stanley R. McNeil Fnd Grants, 1210
Colorado Renewables in Performance Contracting Grants, 1214
Columbus Fnd Competitive Grants, 1220
Columbus Fnd Paul G. Duke Grants, 1227
Communities Fnd of Texas Grants, 1243
Comm Dev Financial Institution Bank Enterprise Awards, 1244
Comm Fdn for Grtr Buffalo Grants, 1247
Comm Fdn for Monterey Cty Grants, 1255
Comm Fdn for Muskegon Cty Grants, 1256
Comm Fdn for NE Michigan Grants, 1257
Comm Fdn for Southern Arizona Grants, 1261
Comm Fdn of Abilene Comm Grts, 1264
Comm Fdn of Bartholomew County Heritage Fund Grants, 1267
Comm Fdn of Boone County Grants, 1274
Comm Fdn of Collier County Capacity Building Grants, 1277
Comm Fdn of Grtr Birmingham Grants, 1280
Comm Fdn of Greater Fort Wayne - Cmty Endwt & Clarke Endwt Grants, 1285
Comm Fdn of Grtr Lafayette Grts, 1289
Comm Fdn of Greater Tampa Grts, 1292
Comm Fnd of Greenville-Greenville Women Giving Grants, 1293
Comm Fnd of Greenville Enrichment Grants, 1294
Comm Fnd of Louisville Grants, 1299
Comm Fnd of Mt Vernon & Knox County Grants, 1301
Comm Fnd of Muncie & Delaware County Grant, 1302

Comm Fdn of Riverside County Grts, 1304
Comm Fdn of Sarasota County Grts, 1306
Comm Fdn of Shreveport-Bossier Grts, 1307
Comm Fdn of S Alabama Grants, 1308
Comm Fnd of South Puget Sound Grants, 1311
Comm Fnd of St. Joseph County African American Comm Grants, 1312
Comm Fnd of St. Joseph County ArtsEverywhere Grants, 1313
Comm Fnd of St. Joseph County Special Project Challenge Grants, 1314
Comm Fnd of the Ozarks Grants, 1320
Comm Fnd of the Verdugos Educational Endowment Fund Grants, 1321
Comm Fnd of Wabash Cty Grants, 1326
Comm Fnd Silicon Valley Grants, 1331
Comm Tech Fdn of California Building Communities Through Tech Grants, 1336
Connecticut Commission on the Arts Art in Public Spaces, 1349
Connecticut Comm Fnd Grants, 1350
Connelly Fnd Grants, 1353
ConocoPhillips Fnd Grants, 1354
ConocoPhillips Grants, 1355
Constantin Fnd Grants, 1362
Constellation Energy Corporate Grants, 1364
Cooke Fnd Grants, 1368
Cooper Fnd Grants, 1369
Cooper Industries Fnd Grants, 1370
Cord Fnd Grants, 1372
Corina Higginson Trust Grants, 1373
Cornerstone Fdn of NE Wisconsin Grants, 1375
Corning Fnd Cultural Grants, 1376
Cowles Charitable Trust Grants, 1392
Cralle Fnd Grants, 1394
Cranston Fnd Grants, 1395
Crescent Porter Hale Fnd Grants, 1398
Crowell Trust Grants, 1401
CSRA Comm Fnd Grants, 1407
Cumberland Comm Fnd Grants, 1413
Cummins Fnd Grants, 1415
Curtis and Edith Munson Fnd Grants, 1418
DaimlerChrysler Corporation Fund Grants, 1432
Dale and Edna Walsh Fnd Grants, 1435
Dallas Fnd Grants, 1436
Dana Corporation Fnd Grants, 1440
Daniels Fund Grants, 1443
Daphne Seybolt Culpeper Mem Fdn Grts, 1445
Dave Coy Fnd Grants, 1447
Dave Thomas Fnd for Adoption Grants, 1449
Daywood Fnd Grants, 1465
Decatur County Comm Fnd Large Project Grants, 1476
Dekko Fnd Grants, 1482
Delaware Division of the Arts Opportunity Grants--Arts Organizations, 1488
Deluxe Corporation Fnd Grants, 1496
DHHS Adolescent Family Life Demo Projects, 1524
DHHS ARRA Strengthening Communities Fund - Nonprofit Capacity Building Grants, 1527
DHHS ARRA Strengthening Communities Fund - State, Local, and Tribal Government Capacity Building Grants, 1528
DHHS Comm Svcs Grant Trng & Tech Assistance Pgm: Capacity-Bldg for Ongoing CSBG Pgm, 1529
DHHS Healthy Tomorrows Pshp for Children, 1534
DOI Urban Park and Rec Recovery Grants, 1554
DOJ Comm-Based Delinquency Prev Grants, 1556
Dolan Fnd Grants, 1563
DOL Youthbuild Grants, 1571
Dorothea Haus Ross Fnd Grants, 1587
Dr. John T. Macdonald Fnd Grants, 1600
Dr. P. Phillips Fnd Grants, 1601
Drs. Bruce and Lee Fnd Grants, 1607
Drug Free Communities Support Program, 1608
Duchossois Family Fnd Grants, 1616
Duke Energy Fdn Econ Dev Grants, 1619
Duluth-Superior Area Comm Fdn Grts, 1620
Dunspaugh-Dalton Fnd Grants, 1623
DuPage Comm Fnd Grants, 1624
Dynegy Fnd Grants, 1630

Dyson Fnd Mid-Hudson Valley Project Grants, 1636
East Tennessee Fnd Grants, 1646
Eaton Charitable Fund Grants, 1647
Eberly Fnd Grants, 1649
Eckerd Family Fnd Grants, 1651
Edward Bangs Kelley & Elza Kelley Fdn Grts, 1665
Edward S. Moore Fnd Grants, 1668
Edward W & Stella C Van Houten Mem Fund, 1670
Edwin S. Webster Fnd Grants, 1671
Edyth Bush Charitable Fnd Grants, 1673
Effie and Wofford Cain Fnd Grants, 1674
Eisner Fnd Grants, 1678
Elizabeth Morse Genius Char Trust Grants, 1682
Elkhart Cty Comm Fdn Grants, 1684
El Paso Comm Fnd Grants, 1688
Emerson Charitable Trust Grants, 1694
Emily Davie and Joseph S. Kornfeld Fnd Grants, 1697
Emma A. Sheafer Charitable Trust Grants, 1699
Ensign-Bickford Fnd Grants, 1709
Enterprise Comm Partners Green Grants, 1716
Enterprise Comm Partners Pre-Dev Grants, 1718
EPA Environmental Educ Grants, 1729
Erie Comm Fnd Grants, 1750
Eugene McDermott Fnd Grants, 1765
Evan Frankel Fnd Grants, 1770
Evelyn and Walter Haas, Jr. Fund Gay and Lesbian Rights Grants, 1772
Evelyn and Walter Haas, Jr. Fund Immigrant Rights Grants, 1773
Ewing Halsell Fnd Grants, 1776
F.R. Bigelow Fnd Grants, 1781
Fairfield County Comm Fdn Grts, 1782
Fargo-Moorhead Area Fnd Woman's Fund Grants, 1789
Farmers Insurance Corporate Giving Grants, 1791
Fayette County Fnd Grants, 1795
Federal Express Corporate Contributions, 1799
Fidelity Fnd Grants, 1805
Field Fnd of Illinois Grants, 1806
Fields Pond Fnd Grants, 1807
Fieldstone Fnd Grants, 1808
FirstEnergy Fnd Comm Grants, 1819
First Lady's Fam Lit Init for Texas Grants, 1822
Fisheries and Habitat Partnership Grants, 1834
Florida Division of Cultural Affairs Comm Theatre Grants, 1847
Florida Division of Cultural Affairs Culture Builds Florida Expansion Funding, 1848
Florida Division of Cultural Affairs Culture Builds Florida Seed Funding, 1849
Florida Div of Cultural Affairs Dance Grts, 1850
Florida Division of Cultural Affairs Endowment Grants, 1851
Florida Div of Cultural Affrs Facilities Grts, 1852
Florida Div of Cultural Affairs Folk Arts Grts, 1853
Florida Division of Cultural Affairs General Program Support Grants, 1854
Florida Division of Cultural Affairs Lit Grants, 1855
Florida Division of Cultural Affairs Media Arts Grants, 1856
Florida Division of Cultural Affairs Multidisciplinary Grants, 1857
Florida Div of Cultural Affairs Museum Grts, 1858
Florida Div of Cultural Affairs Music Grts, 1859
Florida Div of Cultural Afrs Presenter Grts, 1860
Florida Division of Cultural Affairs Professional Theatre Grants, 1861
Florida Division of Cultural Affairs Specific Cultural Project Grants, 1862
Florida Division of Cultural Affairs Underserved Cultural Comm Dev Grants, 1864
Florida Div of Cultural Affairs Visual Arts Grants, 1865
Florida Humanities Council Partnership Grants, 1870
Florida Sports Fnd Junior Golf Grants, 1872
Fluor Fnd Grants, 1875
FMC Fnd Grants, 1876
Foellinger Fnd Grants, 1877
Ford Family Grants Public Convening Spaces, 1881
Forest Fnd Grants, 1886
Foster Fnd Grants, 1888
Fnd for Seacoast Health Grants, 1895
Fnd for the Carolinas Grants, 1896

1104 / Matching/Challenge Funds PROGRAM TYPE INDEX

Fnd NW Grants, 1906
Frances L & Edwin L Cummings Mem Fund, 1919
Francis L. Abreu Charitable Trust Grants, 1922
Franklin County Comm Fdn Grts, 1929
Frank M. Tait Fnd Grants, 1932
FRED Educational Ethyl Grants, 1945
Fred L. Emerson Fnd Grants, 1949
Fremont Area Comm Fnd Grants, 1955
Freshwater Future Insight Services Grants, 1960
Frey Fnd Grants, 1963
Fuller E. Callaway Fnd Grants, 1973
Fuller Fnd Grants, 1974
G.N. Wilcox Trust Grants, 1982
Gebbie Fnd Grants, 1995
GenCorp Fnd Grants, 1998
Gene Haas Fnd, 1999
Genentech Corporate Charitable Contributions, 2000
General Mills Fnd Grants, 2003
George B. Storer Fnd Grants, 2014
George F. Baker Trust Grants, 2016
George Fnd Grants, 2018
George Frederick Jewett Fnd Grants, 2019
George Gund Fnd Grants, 2020
George H & Jane A Mifflin Mem Fund Grts, 2021
George I. Alden Trust Grants, 2023
George P. Davenport Trust Fund Grants, 2026
George S & Dolores Dore Eccles Fdn Grants, 2027
Georgia-Pacific Fdn Entrepreneurship Grts, 2033
Georgia Council for the Arts Partner Grants for Service Organizations, 2036
Georgia Council for the Arts Project Grants, 2037
Georgia Power Fnd Grants, 2039
German Protestant Orphan Asylum Fnd Grants, 2044
Gertrude E Skelly Charitable Fdn Grts, 2046
Ginger and Barry Ackerley Fnd Grants, 2055
GNOF Freeman Challenge Grants, 2075
Goldseker Fnd Non-Profit Management Assistance Grants, 2103
Goodrich Corporation Fnd Grants, 2104
Grace and Franklin Bernsen Fnd Grants, 2109
Graco Fnd Grants, 2111
Grand Haven Area Comm Fdn Grants, 2113
Grand Rapids Area Comm Fdn Grts, 2114
Grand Rapids Area Comm Fnd Nashwauk Area Endowment Fund Grants, 2115
Grand Rapids Area Comm Fnd Wyoming Grants, 2116
Grand Rapids Comm Fnd Grants, 2118
Grand Rapids Comm Fdn Ionia Cty Grts, 2119
Grand Rapids Comm Fnd SE Ottawa Grants, 2122
Grand Rapids Comm Fdn Sparta Grts, 2124
Grand Victoria Fnd Illinois Core Grants, 2126
Great-West Life Grants, 2130
Greater Cincinnati Fnd Priority and Small Projects/Capacity-Building Grants, 2132
Greater Worcester Comm Discretionary Grants, 2140
GreenWorks! Butterfly Garden Grants, 2159
GreenWorks! Grants, 2160
Gulf Coast Comm Fnd Grants, 2174
H & R Fnd Grants, 2181
HA & Mary K Chapman Char Trust Grts, 2182
Halliburton Fnd Grants, 2211
Harold & Arlene Schnitzer CARE Fdn Grts, 2226
Harold K. L. Castle Fnd Grants, 2228
Harris and Eliza Kempner Fund Grants, 2231
Harry A & Margaret D Towsley Fdn Grts, 2236
Harry C. Trexler Trust Grants, 2239
Hartford Courant Fnd Grants, 2248
Hartford Fnd Regular Grants, 2253
Harvey Randall Wickes Fnd Grants, 2255
Hatton W. Sumners Fnd for the Study and Teaching of Self Government Grants, 2257
Hawai'i Children's Trust Fund Comm Awareness Events Grants, 2258
HCA Fnd Grants, 2274
Health Fnd of Grtr Indianapolis Grts, 2282
Hedco Fnd Grants, 2287
Henry W. Bull Fnd Grants, 2312
Herbert A & Adrian W Woods Fdn Grants, 2313
Herbert H & Grace A Dow Fdn Grants, 2315
High Meadow Fnd Grants, 2321

Hill Crest Fnd Grants, 2324
Hillcrest Fnd Grants, 2325
Hill Fnd Grants, 2326
Historic Landmarks Fnd of Indiana African American Heritage Grants, 2333
Historic Landmarks Fnd of Indiana Legal Defense Grants, 2335
Historic Landmarks Fnd of Indiana Preservation Grants, 2337
Historic Landmarks Legal Defense Grants, 2338
Holland/Zeeland Comm Fdn Grts, 2345
Homer A Scott & Mildred S Scott Fdn Grants, 2350
Hometown Indiana Grants, 2353
Honda of America Manufacturing Fnd Grants, 2354
Horace A Kimball & S Ella Kimball Fdn Grts, 2362
Horizon Fnd Grants, 2365
Hormel Foods Charitable Trust Grants, 2368
Household Int'l Corp Giving Grants, 2372
Howard and Bush Fnd Grants, 2374
Huffy Fnd Grants, 2384
Hugh J. Andersen Fnd Grants, 2385
Huie-Dellmon Trust Grants, 2386
Humana Fnd Grants, 2388
Humanitas Fnd Grants, 2390
Hundred Club of Palm Springs Grants, 2397
Huntington Arts Council Decentralization Comm Arts Grants, 2401
Hutton Fnd Grants, 2412
Hyde Family Fnds Grants, 2414
ICC Comm Service Mini-Grant, 2426
ICC Day of Service Action Grants, 2427
ICC Faculty Fellowships, 2428
ICC Listening to Communities Grants, 2429
ICC Scholarship of Engagement Faculty Grants, 2430
Idaho Power Co Corp Contributions, 2433
IDEM Section 319(h) Nonpoint Source Grants, 2435
IDOT Economic Dev Pgm Grts, 2436
IEDC Industrial Dev Grant Fund, 2443
Illinois DCEO Coal Competitiveness Grants, 2484
Illinois DCEO Coal Demonstration Grants, 2485
Illinois DCEO Coal Dev Grants, 2486
Illinois DCEO Emerging Technological Enterprises Grants, 2490
Illinois DNR Habitat Fund Grants, 2497
Illinois DNR Urban & Cmty Forestry Grts, 2503
Illinois DNR Volunteer Fire Assistance Grants, 2504
Illinois Tool Works Fnd Grants, 2511
IMLS 21st Cent Museum Pros Grts, 2512
IMLS National Leadership Grants, 2515
Indiana 21st Century Research & Tech Awards, 2528
Indiana Arts Commission American Masterpieces Grants, 2530
Indiana Arts Commission Cap Bldg Grts, 2531
Indiana Arts Commission Multi-regional Major Arts Institutions Grants, 2532
Indiana Arts Commission Statewide Arts Service Organization Grants, 2533
Indiana Boating Infrastructure Grants (BIG P), 2534
Indiana Clean Vessel Act Grants, 2535
Indiana Historic Preservation Fund Grants, 2537
Indiana Household Hazardous Waste Grants, 2538
Indianapolis Preservation Grants, 2543
Indiana Preservation Grants, 2544
Indiana Recycling Grants, 2545
Indiana Reg'l Econ Dev Partnership Grts, 2546
Indiana Space Grant Consortium Grants for Informal Educ Partnerships, 2549
Indiana Waste Tire Fund Pgm Grts, 2551
ING Fnd Grants, 2555
Intergrys Corporation Grants, 2565
Int'l Paper Co Fnd Grants, 2568
Iowa Arts Council Artists in Schools/Communities Residency Grants, 2571
J. Bulow Campbell Fnd Grants, 2593
J. F. Maddox Fnd Grants, 2597
J.W. Kieckhefer Fnd Grants, 2607
Jackson Fnd Grants, 2613
James H. Cummings Fnd Grants, 2626
James J & Angelia M Harris Fdn Grts, 2630
James R. Dougherty Jr. Fnd Grants, 2635

James R. Thorpe Fnd Grants, 2636
James S. Copley Fnd Grants, 2637
Jane's Trust Grants, 2639
Janus Fnd Grants, 2647
Jean and Louis Dreyfus Fnd Grants, 2658
JELD-WEN Fnd Grants, 2661
Jennings County Comm Fdn Grts, 2664
Jessie Ball Dupont Fund Grants, 2671
JM Fnd Grants, 2681
John Ben Snow Memorial Trust Grants, 2687
John Deere Fnd Grants, 2692
John G. Martin Fnd Grants, 2696
John Jewett & Helen Chandler Garland Fdn, 2702
John P. McGovern Fnd Grants, 2707
John R. Oishei Fnd Grants, 2709
Johnson Controls Fnd Educ and Arts Matching Gift Grants, 2721
John W. Alden Trust Grants, 2727
John W & Anna H Hanes Fdn Grants, 2728
Joseph Drown Fnd Grants, 2735
Josephine Goodyear Fnd Grants, 2738
Josiah W & Bessie H Kline Fdn Grants, 2742
KaBOOM-CA Playground Challenge Grants, 2761
Kalamazoo Comm Fnd Economic and Comm Dev Grants, 2765
Kansas Arts Commission American Masterpieces Kansas Grants, 2775
Kansas Arts Commission Artist Fellowships, 2776
Kansas Arts Commission Arts-in-Communities Project Grants, 2777
Kansas Arts Commission Arts-in-Communities Project Mini-Grants, 2778
Kansas Arts Comsn Arts-in-Educ Grts, 2779
Kansas Arts Commission Arts on Tour Grants, 2780
Kansas Arts Commission Operational Support for Arts and Cultural Organizations, 2781
Kansas Arts Commission Partnership Agreement Grants, 2782
Kenneth T & Eileen L Norris Fdn Grants, 2802
Kentucky Arts Cncl Access Astnce Grts, 2805
Kentucky Arts Council Teaching Together Grants, 2811
KeySpan Fnd Grants, 2821
Kiki Madazine Grow Strong Girls through Leadership Grants, 2822
Lafayette - West Lafayette Convention and Visitors Bureau Tourist Promotion Grants, 2849
Laura Jane Musser Rural Initiative Grants, 2864
Laurel Fnd Grants, 2867
LEGO Children's Fund Grants, 2878
Leicester Savings Bank Fund, 2879
Leighton Award for Nonprofit Excellence, 2880
Liberty Hill Fnd Special Opportunity Grants, 2897
Lied Fnd Trust Grants, 2900
Lillian S. Wells Fnd Grants, 2901
Lilly Endowment Giving Indiana Funds for Tomorrow Grants, 2903
Liz Claiborne Fnd Grants, 2915
Lloyd G. Balfour Fnd Attleboro-Specific Charities Grants, 2916
Lotus 88 Fnd for Women and Children, 2921
Louis Calder Fnd Grants, 2925
Lubbock Area Fnd Grants, 2931
Lubrizol Corporation Comm Grants, 2932
Lubrizol Fnd Grants, 2933
Lucy Downing Nisbet Charitable Fund Grants, 2935
Lumpkin Family Fdn Healthy People Grts, 2942
Lynde and Harry Bradley Fnd Grants, 2947
Lyndhurst Fnd Grants, 2949
M.D. Anderson Fnd Grants, 2952
M.E. Raker Fnd Grants, 2953
Mabel Louise Riley Fnd Grants, 2959
Maine Comm Fnd Ram Island Conservation Challenge Grants, 2986
Mardag Fnd Grants, 3001
Margaret & James A Elkins Jr Fdn Grts, 3003
Margaret T. Morris Fnd Grants, 3005
Marietta McNeill Morgan and Samuel Tate Morgan, Jr. Trust Grants, 3008
Mary D. & Walter F Frear Eleemosynary Trust, 3035
Mary Duke Biddle Fnd Grants, 3036

PROGRAM TYPE INDEX

Matching/Challenge Funds / 1105

Mary K. Chapman Fnd Grants, 3042
Mary Owen Borden Fnd Grants, 3046
Mary S & David C Corbin Fdn Grants, 3048
Mathile Family Fnd Grants, 3062
Maurice J. Masserini Charitable Trust Grants, 3064
McCarthy Family Fnd Grants, 3073
McConnell Fnd Grants, 3076
McCune Charitable Fnd Grants, 3077
McGraw-Hill Companies Comm Grants, 3081
McGregor Fund Grants, 3082
McKesson Fnd Grants, 3084
McMillen Fnd Grants, 3090
MDARD AgD Value Added/Regional Food Systems Grants, 3091
MDARD County Fairs Cap Imprvmt Grts, 3092
MDARD Spclty Crop Block Grant-Farm Bill, 3093
MDEQ Beach Monitoring - Inland Lakes, 3094
MDEQ Clean Diesel Grants, 3096
MDEQ Coastal Management Planning and Construction Grants, 3097
MDEQ Comm Pollution Prevention (P2) Grants: Household Drug Collections, 3098
MDEQ Local Water Qlty Monitoring Grants, 3100
Mead Witter Fnd Grants, 3106
Medtronic Fnd Patient Link Grants, 3113
Melville Charitable Trust Grants, 3115
Mercedes-Benz USA Corporate Contributions, 3118
Mericos Fnd Grants, 3121
Mertz Gilmore Climate Change Solutions Grants, 3125
Mertz Gilmore Fnd NYC Communities Grants, 3126
Mertz Gilmore Fnd NYC Dance Grants, 3127
Mervin Bovaird Fnd Grants, 3128
Metro Health Fnd Grants, 3133
MetroWest Health Fnd Capital Grants for Health-Related Facilities, 3134
Meyer Fnd Mgmt Assistance Grts, 3144
Meyer Memorial Trust Grassroots Grants, 3147
Meyer Memorial Trust Responsive Grants, 3148
Meyer Memorial Trust Special Grants, 3149
Microsoft Comty Affairs Puget Sound Grts, 3163
Millipore Fnd Grants, 3182
Mimi and Peter Haas Fund Grants, 3185
Montana Arts Cncl Cltrl & Aesthetic Proj Grts, 3209
MONY Fnd Grants, 3214
Morris & Gwendolyn Cafritz Fdn Grants, 3218
Motorola Fnd Grants, 3221
Musgrave Fnd Grants, 3231
National Endowment for the Arts - National Partnership Agreement Grants, 3256
National Endowment for the Arts - State Partnership Agreement Grants, 3259
National Endowment for the Arts Artist Communities Grants, 3260
National Endowment for the Arts Dance Grants, 3262
National Endowment for Arts Media Grants, 3264
National Endowment for Arts Museum Grants, 3265
National Endowment for the Arts Music Grants, 3266
National Endowment for the Arts Opera Grants, 3267
National Endowment for Arts Presenting Grants, 3268
National Endowment for the Arts Theater and Musical Theater Grants, 3269
National Home Library Fnd Grants, 3276
NEH Family and Youth Programs in American History Grants, 3291
NEH Preservation Assistance Grants for Smaller Institutions, 3293
NEH Preservation Microfilming of Brittle Books and Serials Grants, 3294
NASE Fdn Future Entrepreneur Schlrsp, 3296
Nevada Arts Council Circuit Rider Grants, 3308
Nevada Arts Cncl Folklife Apprenticeship Grts, 3309
Nevada Arts Council Jackpot Grants, 3312
Nevada Arts Council Learning Grants, 3313
New York Landmarks Cons Sacred Sites Grants, 3340
New York Life Fnd Grants, 3341
NFF Matching Grants, 3344
NFF Wilderness Stewardship Grants, 3346
NFL Club Matching Youth Football Field/Stadium Grants, 3349
NFL Grassroots Field Grants, 3350

NFWF Alaska Fish and Wildlife Fund Grants, 3356
NFWF ConocoPhillips SPIRIT of Conservation Migratory Bird Grants, 3369
NFWF Coral Reef Conservation Project Grants, 3370
NFWF Pulling Together Initiative Grants, 3387
NHSCA Artist Residencies in Schools Grants, 3423
NHSCA Arts in Health Care Project Grants, 3424
NHSCA Conservation License Plate Grants, 3425
NHSCA Cultural Facilities Grants: Barrier Free Access for All, 3426
NHSCA General Project Grants, 3427
NHSCA Operating Grants, 3428
NHSCA Youth Arts Project Grants: For Extended Arts Learning, 3430
Nike Bowerman Track Renovation Grants, 3440
Nina Mason Pulliam Charitable Trust Grants, 3443
NJSCA Arts Project Support, 3446
NJSCA General Program Support Grants, 3449
NJSCA Projects Serving Artists Grants, 3450
Noble County Comm Fnd Celebrate Diversity Project Grants, 3455
Noble County Comm Fnd Grants, 3456
Nonprofit Management Fund Grants, 3458
Norcliffe Fnd Grants, 3459
Nordson Corporation Fnd Grants, 3462
Norfolk Southern Fnd Grants, 3463
North American Wetlands Conserv Grts, 3465
North Carolina Arts Council Arts and Audiences Grants, 3466
North Carolina Arts Council Arts in Educ Artist Residencies Grants, 3468
North Carolina Arts Council Arts in Educ Initiatives Grants, 3469
North Carolina Arts Council Arts in Educ Rural Dev Grants, 3470
North Carolina Arts Council Comm Public Art and Design Dev Grants, 3472
North Carolina Arts Council Comm Public Art and Design Implementation Grants, 3473
North Carolina Arts Cncl Facility Dsgn Grts, 3474
North Carolina Arts Council Folklife Grants, 3476
North Carolina Arts Council General Support, 3477
North Carolina Arts Council New Realities Grant, 3478
North Carolina Arts Council Outreach Grants, 3479
North Carolina Arts Council Regional Artist Project Grants, 3480
North Carolina Arts Council Tech Assistance, 3482
North Carolina Arts Council Touring/Presenting Grants, 3483
North Carolina Arts Council Visual Arts Program Support Grants, 3484
North Central Health Services Grants, 3491
Northern Chautauqua Comm Fnd Comm Grants, 3499
NW Mutual Fnd Grants, 3509
NWHF Partners Investing in Nursing's Future, 3539
NYFA Artists in the School Planning Grants, 3562
NYSCA Dance: Gen Operating Support Grts, 3584
Ohio Arts Council Artist in Residence Grants for Sponsors, 3645
Ohio Arts Council Arts Access Grants, 3647
Ohio Arts Council Arts Partnership Grants, 3650
Ohio Arts Council Building Cultural Diversity Initiative Grants, 3651
Ohio Arts Council Int'l Partnership Grts, 3653
Ohio Arts Council Sustainability Pgm Grts, 3654
Oklahoma City Comm Pgms & Grts, 3666
Oppenstein Brothers Fnd Grants, 3685
Ordean Fnd Grants, 3691
Otto Bremer Fnd Grants, 3713
Pacers Fnd Be Drug-Free Grants, 3720
Pacers Fnd Be Educated Grants, 3721
Pacers Fnd Be Healthy and Fit Grants, 3722
Pacers Fnd Be Tolerant Grants, 3723
Pacers Fnd Indiana Fever's Be Younique Grants, 3724
Parkersburg Area Comm Fdn Action Grts, 3738
Park Fnd Grants, 3739
Partnership Enhancement Pgm Grts, 3740
Pasadena Fnd Average Grants, 3741
Pathways to Nature Conservation Fund Grants, 3745
Patron Saints Fnd Grants, 3753

Paul and Mary Haas Fnd Contributions and Student Scholarships, 3756
Paul E & Klare N Reinhold Fdn Grts, 3758
Paul Rapoport Fnd Grants, 3765
PCA Art Organizations and Art Grants for Presenting Organizations, 3771
PCA Arts in Educ Residencies, 3772
PCA Arts Organizations and Grants for Music, 3774
PCA Arts Organizations and Arts Grants for Art Museums, 3775
PCA Arts Organizations and Arts Grants for Arts Educ Organizations, 3776
PCA Arts Organizations and Arts Grants for Arts Service Organizations, 3777
PCA Arts Organizations and Grants for Crafts, 3778
PCA Arts Organizations & Grants for Dance, 3779
PCA Arts Organizations and Arts Grants for Film and Electronic Media, 3780
PCA Arts Organizations and Arts Grants for Lit, 3781
PCA Arts Organizations & Grants for Local Arts, 3782
PCA Arts Organizations and Grants for Theatre, 3783
PCA Arts Organizations and Arts Grants for Traditional and Folk Arts, 3784
PCA Entry Track Arts Organizations and Arts Grants for Art Museums, 3787
PCA Entry Track Arts Orgs & Arts Pgms Grts for Arts Educ Orgs, 3788
PCA Entry Track Arts Orgs & Arts Pgms Grts for Arts Svc Orgs, 3789
PCA Entry Track Arts Organizations and Arts Grants for Crafts, 3790
PCA Entry Track Arts Organizations and Arts Grants for Dance, 3791
PCA Entry Track Arts Orgs & Arts Pgms Grts for Film & Electronic Media, 3792
PCA Entry Track Arts Organizations and Arts Grants for Lit, 3793
PCA Entry Track Arts Organizations and Arts Grants for Local Arts, 3794
PCA Entry Track Arts Organizations and Arts Grants for Music, 3795
PCA Entry Track Arts Organizations and Arts Grants for Presenting Organizations, 3796
PCA Entry Track Arts Organizations and Arts Grants for Theatre, 3797
PCA Entry Track Arts Orgs & Arts Pgms Grts for Traditional & Folk Arts, 3798
PCA Pennsylvania Partners in the Arts Project Stream Grants, 3802
PCA Strategies for Success Grts-Adv Level, 3804
PCA Strategies for Success Grts-Intrmd Lvl, 3806
Pegasus Fnd Grants, 3810
PennPAT Artist Tech Assistance Grants, 3811
PennPAT Strategic Opportunity Grants, 3815
Perkin Fnd Grants, 3821
Peter Kiewit Fnd General Grants, 3845
Peter Kiewit Fnd Small Grants, 3847
Peter M. Putnam Fnd Grants, 3848
PeyBack Fnd Grants, 3861
Phelps County Comm Fnd Grants, 3870
Philadelphia Fdn Org'l Effectiveness Grts, 3872
Phil Hardin Fnd Grants, 3875
Phoenix Suns Charities Grants, 3881
Piedmont Natural Gas Corporate and Charitable Contributions, 3883
Pinkerton Fnd Grants, 3892
Piper Jaffray Fdn Communities Giving Grts, 3899
Playboy Fnd Grants, 3913
Plough Fnd Grants, 3915
PMI Fnd Grants, 3918
Poets & Writers Readings/Workshops Grants, 3927
Porter County Comm Fnd Grants, 3931
Portland Fnd Grants, 3936
Praxair Fnd Grants, 3944
President's Student Service Scholarships, 3949
Price Chopper's Golub Fnd Grants, 3950
Principal Financial Group Fnd Grants, 3966
Prudential Fnd Educ Grants, 3977
Public Welfare Fnd Grants, 3984
Puerto Rico Comm Fnd Grants, 3986

Matching/Challenge Funds

Pulaski County Comm Fnd Grants, 3988
Putnam Cty Comm Fdn Grts, 3990
Quantum Fnd Grants, 3996
R.C. Baker Fnd Grants, 3999
Ralph M. Parsons Fnd Grants, 4013
Raskob Fdn for Catholic Activities Grts, 4019
Rasmuson Fdn Creative Ventures Grts, 4021
Rathmann Family Fnd Grants, 4026
RBC Dain Rauscher Fnd Grants, 4031
RCF General Comm Grants, 4032
RCF Individual Assistance Grants, 4033
Reinberger Fnd Grants, 4052
Rhode Island Fnd Grants, 4073
Richard & Caroline T Gwathmey Mem Tr Grts, 4075
Richard and Helen DeVos Fnd Grants, 4076
Richard H. Driehaus Fnd Grants, 4084
Richard H. Driehaus Fnd MacArthur Fund for Arts and Culture, 4085
Richard King Mellon Fnd Grants, 4087
Righteous Persons Fnd Grants, 4093
Ripley County Comm Fnd Grants, 4095
RISCA Professional Arts Dev Grants, 4099
RISCA Project Grants for Organizations, Individuals and Education, 4100
Robert G. Cabell III & Maude Cabell Fnd Grants, 4113
Robert W. Woodruff Fnd Grants, 4124
Rochester Area Fnd Grants, 4128
Rockwell Int'l Corporate Trust Grants, 4141
Rohm and Haas Company Grants, 4145
Rollins-Luetkemeyer Fnd Grants, 4147
Ronald McDonald House Charities Grants, 4149
Rose Comm Fnd Aging Grants, 4152
Rose Comm Fnd Child and Family Dev Grants, 4153
Rose Hills Fnd Grants, 4162
Ross Fnd Grants, 4164
Roy & Christine Sturgis Charitable Trust Grts, 4166
RRF Accessible Faith Grants, 4169
RRF General Grants, 4170
Rush County Comm Fnd Grants, 4174
Ruth Anderson Fnd Grants, 4176
RWJF Local Funding Partnerships Grants, 4186
RWJF Partners Investing in Nursing's Future, 4188
Ryder System Charitable Fnd Grants, 4191
S.E.VEN Fund WHY Prize, 4198
S. Mark Taper Fnd Grants, 4201
Sage Fnd Grants, 4204
Saint Paul Fnd Grants, 4219
Saint Paul Fdn Mgmt Improvement Fund Grts, 4221
Samuel S. Fels Fund Grants, 4238
Samuel S. Johnson Fnd Grants, 4239
San Diego Women's Fnd Grants, 4252
San Francisco Fnd Fund For Artists Matching Commissions Grants, 4274
San Juan Island Comm Fnd Grants, 4283
Santa Barbara Fdn Monthly Express Grts, 4284
Sarah Scaife Fnd Grants, 4295
Sara Lee Fnd Grants, 4296
Sarkeys Fnd Grants, 4297
Schering-Plough Fnd Health Grants, 4304
Scherman Fnd Grants, 4305
Schlessman Family Fnd Grants, 4307
Schramm Fnd Grants, 4310
Scott County Comm Fnd Grants, 4314
Self Fnd Grants, 4335
Shell Oil Company Fnd Grants, 4343
Sid W. Richardson Fnd Grants, 4350
Sister Fund Grants for Women's Organizations, 4371
Sisters of Charity Fnd of Canton Grants, 4372
Sisters of St Joseph Healthcare Fdn Grts, 4377
Skaggs Fnd Grants, 4378
Sonoco Fnd Grants, 4403
Sony Corp of America Corp Philant Grants, 4405
Sosland Fnd Grants, 4408
South Carolina Arts Comsn Accessibility Grts, 4410
South Carolina Arts Commission AIE Residency Plus Individual Site Grants, 4411
South Carolina Arts Commission AIE Residency Plus Multi-Site Grants, 4412
South Carolina Arts Commission American Masterpieces in South Carolina Grants, 4413
South Carolina Arts Commission Annual Operating Support for Organizations Grants, 4414
South Carolina Arts Commission Arts and Economic Impact Study Assistance Grants, 4416
South Carolina Arts Commission Arts Facility Projects Grants, 4417
South Carolina Arts Commission Arts in Educ After School Arts Initiative Grants, 4418
South Carolina Arts Commission Cultural Tourism Initiative Grants, 4419
South Carolina Arts Comm Cultural Visions Grants, 4420
South Carolina Arts Commission Folklife & Traditional Arts Grants, 4421
South Carolina Arts Commission Incentive Grants for Employer Sponsored Benefits, 4422
South Carolina Arts Commission Leadership and Organizational Dev Grants, 4423
South Carolina Arts Commission Long Term Operating Support for Organizations Grants, 4424
South Carolina Arts Commission Statewide Arts Participation Initiative Grants, 4425
South Carolina Arts Commission Subgrants, 4426
South Madison Comm Fnd Grants, 4440
Southwest Florida Comm Competitive Grants, 4442
Sport Manitoba Athlete Skill Dev Clinics Grants, 4453
Sport Manitoba Hosting Regional Championships Grants, 4456
Sport Manitoba Intro of a New Sport Grts, 4457
Sport Manitoba Sport Special Initiatives Grants, 4459
Sport Manitoba Women to Watch Grants, 4460
Sprague Fnd Grants, 4461
Sprint Fnd Grants, 4463
Square D Fnd Grants, 4464
SSA Work Incentives Planning and Assistance, 4465
St. Joseph Comm Health Fnd Improving Healthcare Access Grants, 4469
Stackpole-Hall Fnd Grants, 4472
State Justice Institute Curriculum Adaptation and Training Grants, 4488
State Justice Institute Partner Grants, 4489
State Justice Institute Project Grants, 4490
State Justice Inst Tech Assistance Grts, 4493
Steelcase Fnd Grants, 4497
Steele-Reese Fnd Grants, 4498
Steuben County Comm Fdn Grants, 4501
Stewart Huston Charitable Trust Grants, 4505
Strake Fnd Grants, 4511
Strowd Roses Grants, 4515
Summit Fnd Grants, 4524
Sunderland Fnd Grants, 4527
Surdna Fdn Sustainable Environments Grants, 4533
Susan Vaughan Fnd Grants, 4537
T. Rowe Price Associates Fnd Grants, 4548
TAC Arts Access Grant, 4549
TAC Arts Build Communities Grants, 4551
TAC Arts Projects Grants, 4554
TAC Rural Arts Project Support Grants, 4555
TAC Touring Arts and Arts Access Touring Arts Grants, 4557
TCF Bank Fnd Grants, 4565
TE Fnd Grants, 4572
Telluride Fnd Comm Grants, 4573
Temple-Inland Fnd Grants, 4576
Texas Comsn on the Arts Arts in Educ Team Building/Texas Music Project Grants, 4580
Texas Cmsn on the Arts Arts Respond Prj Grts, 4581
Texas Comsn on the Arts County Arts Expansion Program, 4582
Texas Comsn on the Arts Create-1 Pgm Grts, 4583
Texas Comsn on the Arts Create-3 Pgm Grts, 4585
Texas Comsn on the Arts Cultural Connections-Performance Support Grants, 4588
Texas Comsn on the Arts Cultural Connections-Visual & Media Arts Touring Exhibits Grants, 4589
Texas Comsn on the Arts Cultural Connections Consultant/Simply Solutions Grants, 4590
Texas Comm on Arts Cultural Connections Grant, 4591
Texas Comsn on the Arts GPA1, 4592
Texas Comsn on the Arts Special Opps Grants, 4593
Textron Corporate Contributions Grants, 4601
Theodore Edson Parker Fnd Grants, 4605
Thomas Austin Finch, Sr. Fnd Grants, 4613
Thomas B & Elizabeth M Sheridan Fdn Grts, 4614
Thomas C. Ackerman Fnd Grants, 4615
Topeka Comm Fnd Building Families Grants, 4643
Topeka Comm Fnd Grants, 4644
Tourism Cares Worldwide Grants, 4649
Town Creek Fnd Grants, 4650
Toyota Motor Manuf of West Virginia Grants, 4657
Toyota Motor North America of NY Grts, 4658
Trinity Trust Comm Response Grants, 4671
Trull Fnd Grants, 4673
Turner Voices Corporate Contributions, 4682
US Dept of Educ Migrant and Seasonal Farmworkers Grants, 4693
UNCFSP TIEAD Internship, 4705
Union Bank, N.A. Fnd Grants, 4709
Union County Fnd Grants, 4712
Union Pacific Fdn Comm & Civic Grts, 4714
Union Pacific Fdn Health & Human Svcs Grts, 4715
United Technologies Corporation Grants, 4725
UPS Fnd Economic and Global Lit Grants, 4730
USDA Denali Comm High Energy Cost Grants, 4805
USDA High Energy Cost Grants, 4812
USDA Rural Cooperative Dev Grants, 4826
USDA Rural Energy for America - Energy Audit & Renewable Energy Dev Assistance Grts, 4828
USDA Rural Energy for America - Renewable Energy System and Energy Efficiency Improvement Guaranteed Grants, 4830
USDC i6 Challenge Grants, 4851
USDC Market Dev Cooperator Grants, 4853
USDC Public Works and Economic Adjustment Assistance Grants, 4856
USDC Tech Opportunities Pgm Grts, 4860
USTA Public Facility Assistance Grants, 4883
Verizon Fnd Grants, 4911
Verizon Fnd Virginia Grants, 4925
Viacom Fnd Grants (Formerly CBS Fnd), 4932
Victor E. Speas Fnd Grants, 4933
Virginia Commission for the Arts Artists in Educ Residency Grants, 4941
Virginia Commission for the Arts Local Government Challenge Grants, 4943
Virginia Fnd for Humanities Discretionary Grants, 4946
Virginia Fdn for the Humanities Open Grants, 4947
Vulcan Materials Company Fnd Grants, 4956
Wabash River Heritage Corridor Fund Grants, 4970
Wabash Valley Comm Fnd Grants, 4971
Walt Disney Company Fnd Grants, 4981
Walter and Elise Haas Fund Grants, 4982
Washington Cty Comm Fdn Grts, 4997
Washington Cty Comm Fdn Youth Grts, 4998
Wayne and Gladys Valley Fnd Grants, 5003
Weatherwax Fnd Grants, 5014
Weingart Fnd Grants, 5018
West Virginia Comsn on the Arts Mini Grts, 5041
Weyerhaeuser Company Fnd Grants, 5053
Whirlpool Fnd Grants, 5056
Wilburforce Fnd Grants, 5067
William G. McGowan Charitable Fund Grants, 5084
William G Selby & Marie Selby Fdn Grts, 5085
William J. and Dorothy K. O'Neill Fnd Grants, 5087
William McCaskey Chapman and Adaline Dinsmore Chapman Fnd Grants, 5092
William Robert Baird Charitable Trust Grants, 5093
Williams Companies Fnd Grants, 5095
Windgate Charitable Fnd Grants, 5099
Winston-Salem Fdn Competitive Grts, 5102
Winthrop Rockefeller Fnd Grants, 5105
Xerox Fnd Grants, 5122
Yellow Corporate Fnd Grants, 5126
Z. Smith Reynolds Fnd Economic Dev Grants, 5144
Z. Smith Reynolds Fnd Democracy and Civic Engagement Grants, 5145

Materials/Equipment Acquisition (Computers, Books, Videos, etc.)
4imprint One by One Charitable Giving, 16
100 Club of Arizona Sfty Enhncmt Stipends, 26

PROGRAM TYPE INDEX Materials/Equioment Acquisition (Computers, Books, Videos, etc.) / 1107

A.C. Ratshesky Fnd Grants, 39
A.J. Fletcher Fnd Grants, 41
Abbey Charitable Trust Grants, 78
Abbot & Dorothy H Stevens Fdn Grants, 79
Abell-Hanger Fnd Grants, 91
Abington Fnd Grants, 100
Able To Play Challenge Grants, 101
Able To Serve Grants, 102
Able Trust Voc Rehab Grants for Agencies, 103
Able Trust Vocational Rehabilitation Grants for Individuals, 104
ACFEF Disaster Relief Fund Member Assistance, 117
Achelis Fnd Grants, 127
Actors Fund Funeral and Burial Assistance, 138
Acushnet Fnd Grants, 143
Adams County Comm Fnd of Pennsylvania Grants, 149
ADC Fnd Tech Access Grants, 158
Adelaide Breed Bayrd Fnd Grants, 161
Administaff Comm Affairs Grants, 165
Adobe Youth Voices Grants, 170
AEC Trust Grants, 175
AEP Corporate Giving Grants, 180
Agnes M. Lindsay Trust Grants, 203
Ahearn Family Fnd Grants, 206
Ahmanson Fnd Grants, 207
Air Force Association Junior ROTC Grants, 215
Air Products and Chemicals Grants, 216
Akzo Nobel Chemicals Grants, 219
ALA ALSC Bookapalooza Grants, 222
ALA Atlas Systems Mentoring Award, 227
ALA Baker and Taylor Entertainment Audio Music/Video Product Award, 229
Alabama State Council on the Arts Program Dev Grants, 246
Alabama State Council on the Arts Tech Assistance Grants for Individuals, 249
Alabama State Council on the Arts Tech Assistance Grants for Organizations, 250
ALA BWI Collection Dev Grant, 252
ALA Citizens-Save-Libraries Grants, 257
ALA Coretta Scott King Book Donation Grant, 261
ALA Esther J. Piercy Award, 275
ALA Gale Cengage Learning Award for Excellence in Reference and Adult Library Services, 281
ALA Great Books Giveaway Competition, 282
ALA Romance Writers of America Lib Grt, 314
Albert W. Rice Charitable Fnd Grants, 347
Alexander and Margaret Stewart Trust Grants, 354
Alex Brown & Sons Charitable Fdn Grants, 359
Alex Stern Family Fnd Grants, 360
ALFJ Astraea U.S. and Int'l Movement Fund, 361
Alice Tweed Tuohy Fnd Grants, 372
Allegan County Comm Fnd Grants, 375
Allegheny Technologies Charitable Trust, 377
Allen P & Josephine B Green Fdn Grts, 380
Alliance for Comm Trees Home Depot Fnd NeighborWoods Grants, 382
Alliant Energy Fnd Comm Grants, 384
Allyn Fnd Grants, 392
Amber Grants, 413
Amelia Sillman Rockwell and Carlos Perry Rockwell Charities Fund Grants, 417
Ameren Corporation Comm Grants, 418
American Academy of Dermatology Shade Structure Grants, 420
American Forests Global ReLeaf Grants, 434
American Savings Fnd Grants, 445
American Schlafhorst Grants, 446
America the Beautiful Fund Operation Green Plant Grants, 451
Amgen Fnd Grants, 456
Amon G. Carter Fnd Grants, 458
Anheuser-Busch Fnd Grants, 470
Ann Arbor Area Comm Fnd Grants, 474
Annie's Cases for Causes Product Donations, 479
Annunziata Sanguinetti Fnd Grants, 485
Antone & Edene Vidinha Char Trust Grts, 490
Apple Worldwide Developers Conference Student Scholarships, 513
Applied Materials Corp Philanthropy Pgm, 515

Arbor Day Fnd Grants, 524
Arcadia Fnd Grants, 525
ARCO Fnd Educ Grants, 528
Arcus Fnd Fund Grants, 529
Arie and Ida Crown Memorial Grants, 533
Arizona Comm Fnd Grants, 540
Arizona Republic Newspaper Corp Contribs, 547
Arizona State Library LSTA Collections Grants, 548
Arizona State Library LSTA Learning Grants, 550
Arkell Hall Fnd Grants, 562
Armstrong McDonald Fnd Grants, 565
Arthur B. Schultz Fnd Grants, 573
Artist Trust GAP Grants, 575
ArvinMeritor Fdn Arts & Culture Grts, 582
Aspen Comm Fnd Grants, 592
Assisi Fdn of Memphis Capital Project Grants, 593
Assisi Fnd of Memphis General Grants, 594
Assisi Fnd of Memphis Mini Grants, 595
ASTA Academic Scholarships, 597
AT&T Fnd Civic and Comm Service Grants, 599
Atherton Family Fnd Grants, 604
Atlanta Fnd Grants, 608
Atlanta Women's Fnd Grants, 609
Auburn Fnd Grants, 611
Aurora Fnd Grants, 613
Autauga Area Comm Fnd Grants, 618
AutoNation Corporate Giving Grants, 620
Back Home Again Fnd Grants, 633
Bailey Fnd Grants, 635
Ball Brothers Fnd Rapid Grants, 639
Bally's Total Fitness Equipment Grants, 640
Baltimore Comm Fnd Arts and Culture Grants, 641
Barker Welfare Fnd Grants, 669
Barnes Group Fnd Grants, 672
Barrasso Usdin Kupperman Freeman and Sarver LLC Corporate Grants, 675
Baton Rouge Area Fnd Credit Bureau Grts, 680
Batters Up USA Equipment Grants, 683
Battle Creek Comm Fnd Grants, 684
Battle Creek Comm Fdn Mini-Grants, 685
Bayer Advanced Grow Together with Roses School Garden Awards, 695
BCBSM Fdn Proposal Dev Awds, 709
BCBSNC Fnd Grants, 712
Beazley Fnd Grants, 714
Beckley Area Fnd Grants, 716
Beim Fnd Grants, 718
Ben B. Cheney Fnd Grants, 725
Benton Comm Fnd Grants, 730
Best Buy Children's Fdn @15 Teach Awards, 751
Better World Books LEAP Grants for Libraries, 755
Better World Bks LEAP Grts for Nonprofits, 756
Bicknell Fund Grants, 759
Bill and Melinda Gates Ag Dev Grants, 765
Bill and Melinda Gates Fnd Financial Services for the Poor Grants, 767
Bill & Melinda Gates Fdn Library Grts, 768
BJ's Wholesale Clubs Local Charitable Giving, 778
Blanche and Irving Laurie Fnd Grants, 784
Blanche & Julian Robertson Family Fdn Grants, 785
Blandin Fdn Expand Opportunity Grants, 787
Blue Cross Blue Shield of Minnesota Fdn-Healthy Equity: Public Libraries for Health Grts, 797
Blue Grass Comm Fnd Grants, 799
Blue River Comm Fnd Grants, 801
Blumenthal Fnd Grants, 804
Bodenwein Public Benevolent Fdn Grants, 806
Bodman Fnd Grants, 807
Boeing Company Contributions Grants, 809
Boettcher Fnd Grants, 810
Bohemian Fnd Pharos Fund Grants, 811
Bollinger Fnd Grants, 812
Booth-Bricker Fund Grants, 815
Booth Ferris Fnd Grants, 816
Borkee-Hagley Fnd Grants, 817
Bosque Fnd Grants, 818
Boston Globe Fnd Grants, 821
Boulder County Arts Alliance Neodata Endowment Grants, 823
Bowling Green Comm Fnd Grants, 824

Brainerd Fnd Grants, 831
Brooklyn Comm Fnd Comm Arts for All Grants, 849
Brooklyn Comm Fnd Comm Dev Grants, 850
Brooklyn Comm Fnd Educ and Youth Achievement Grants, 851
Brooklyn Comm Fnd Green Communities Grants, 852
Brown County Comm Fnd Grants, 853
Brunswick Fnd Dollars for Doers Grants, 856
Buhl Fnd - Frick Educational Fund, 859
Bush Fnd Arts & Humanities Cap Projects Grants, 872
Bush Fnd Ecological Health Grants, 874
Butler Mfg Co Fnd Grants, 881
Cabot Corporation Fnd Grants, 887
Caesar Puff Fnd Grants, 890
Caesars Fnd Grants, 891
Cailloux Fnd Grants, 892
California Endowment Innovative Ideas Challenge Grants, 904
Callaway Fnd Grants, 909
Callaway Golf Company Fnd Grants, 910
Cambridge Comm Fnd Grants, 913
Campbell Hoffman Fnd Grants, 915
Campbell Soup Fnd Grants, 916
Capital Region Comm Fnd Grants, 921
Cargill Citizenship Fund-Corp Gvg Grants, 925
Carl Gellert and Celia Berta Gellert Fdn Grts, 930
Carl M. Freeman Fnd FACES Grants, 932
Carl M. Freeman Fnd Grants, 933
Carlos and Marguerite Mason Trust Grants, 934
Carls Fnd Grants, 937
Carl W. and Carrie Mae Joslyn Trust Grants, 938
Carnahan-Jackson Fnd Grants, 939
Carpenter Fnd Grants, 943
Carrie E. and Lena V. Glenn Fnd Grants, 944
Carrie Estelle Doheny Fnd Grants, 945
Cartis Creative Services Grants, 948
Cash 4 Clubs Sports Grants, 951
Catherine Manley Gaylord Fnd Grants, 956
CCH Documentary California Reads Grants, 968
CCH Documentary Public Engagement Grants, 970
CCH Documentary Research and Dev Grants, 971
CDECD Historic Preserv Enhancement Grts, 981
CE and S Fnd Grants, 985
Cemala Fnd Grants, 988
Central Carolina Comm Impact Grants, 994
Central Minnesota Comm Fdn Grants, 995
Central New York Comm Fdn Grants, 996
Central Okanagan Fnd Grants, 997
Cessna Fnd Grants, 1000
CFFVR Alcoholism and Drug Abuse Grants, 1001
CFFVR Basic Needs Gvg Partnership Grts, 1002
CFFVR Capital Credit Union Charitable Giving Grants, 1005
CFFVR Clintonville Area Fnd Grants, 1007
CFFVR Clintonville Area Fnd Grants, 1008
CFFVR Environmental Stewardship Grants, 1010
CFFVR Mielke Family Fnd Grants, 1015
CFFVR Shawano Area Comm Fnd Grants, 1021
Chamberlain Fnd Grants, 1027
Champ-A Champion Fur Kids Grants, 1028
Champlin Fnds Grants, 1029
Charles A. Frueauff Fnd Grants, 1037
Charles H. Dater Fnd Grants, 1042
Charles H. Farnsworth Trust Grants, 1043
Charles H. Pearson Fnd Grants, 1045
Charles Hayden Fnd Grants, 1048
Chatham Athletic Fnd Grants, 1060
Chatlos Fnd Grants, 1061
Chautauqua Region Comm Fdn Grts, 1062
Chefs Move to Schools Grants, 1066
Chesapeake Bay Environmental Educ Grants, 1069
Chesapeake Bay Fisheries and Headwaters Grants, 1070
Chesapeake Bay Trust Mini Grants, 1072
Chesapeake Bay Trust Outreach and Comm Engagement Grants, 1073
Chevron Hawaii Educ Fund, 1077
Chicago Comm Trust Poverty Alleviation Grants, 1091
Children Affected by AIDS Fnd Family Assistance Emergency Fund Grants, 1107
Chiles Fnd Grants, 1108

Materials/Equipment Acquisition (Computers, Books, Videos, etc.)

Christy-Houston Fnd Grants, 1115
CICF Indianapolis Fdn Comm Grants, 1123
Cincinnati Bell Fnd Grants, 1131
Cisco Systems Fnd San Jose Comm Grants, 1137
Citigroup Fnd Grants, 1139
Citizens Savings Fnd Grants, 1141
Claneil Fnd Grants, 1145
Clara Blackford Smith and W. Aubrey Smith Charitable Fnd Grants, 1147
Claremont Comm Fnd Grants, 1149
Clarence T.C. Ching Fnd Grants, 1151
Clark Charitable Trust Grants, 1155
Clark County Comm Fnd Grants, 1156
Clark Fnd Grants, 1157
Claude Worthington Benedum Fdn Grants, 1161
Cleveland Fnd Capital Grants, 1167
Cleveland H. Dodge Fnd Grants, 1172
CNA Fnd Grants, 1179
CNCS Foster Grandparent Projects Grants, 1185
CNCS Senior Companion Grants, 1187
CNCS Senior Corps Retired and Senior Volunteer Grants, 1188
Coastal Bend Comm Fnd Grants, 1192
Coeta and Donald Barker Fnd Grants, 1197
Collins Fnd Grants, 1209
Colorado Interstate Gas Grants, 1213
Colorado Springs Cmty Trust Fund Grants, 1215
Columbus Fnd Dorothy E. Ann Fund (D.E.A.F.) Traditional Grants, 1221
Columbus Fnd Small Grants, 1232
Comcast Fnd Grants, 1235
Comerica Charitable Fnd Grants, 1237
Communities Fnd of Texas Grants, 1243
Comm Fdn for Grtr Buffalo Grants, 1247
Comm Fnd for Greater New Haven Quinnipiac River Fund Grants, 1250
Comm Fnd for Greater New Haven Women & Girls Grants, 1254
Comm Fnd for Monterey Cty Grants, 1255
Comm Fnd for Muskegon Cty Grants, 1256
Comm Fnd for Southern Arizona Grants, 1261
Comm Fdn in Jacksonville Art Ventures Small Arts Orgs Professional Assistance Grts, 1262
Comm Fnd in Jacksonville Senior Roundtable Aging Adults Grants, 1263
Comm Fdn of Abilene Comm Grts, 1264
Comm Fdn of Abilene Future Fund Grants, 1265
Comm Fnd of Bartholomew County Heritage Fund Grants, 1267
Comm Fnd of Bloomington and Monroe County Grants, 1271
Comm Fdn of Boone County Grants, 1274
Comm Fdn of Broward Grants, 1275
Comm Fdn of Central Illinois Grants, 1276
Comm Fdn of Collier County Capacity Building Grants, 1277
Comm Fdn of E Ctrl Illinois Grts, 1278
Comm Fdn of Grtr Birmingham Grants, 1280
Comm Fnd of Greater Fort Wayne - Cmty Endwt & Clarke Endwt Grants, 1285
Comm Fnd of Greater Tampa Grts, 1292
Comm Fnd of Greenville-Greenville Women Giving Grants, 1293
Comm Fnd of Greenville Hollingsworth Funds Capital Projects Grants, 1295
Comm Fnd of Louisville Grants, 1299
Comm Fnd of Mt Vernon & Knox County Grants, 1301
Comm Fnd of Muncie & Delaware County Grant, 1302
Comm Fdn of Riverside County Grts, 1304
Comm Fdn of Sarasota County Grts, 1306
Comm Fdn of Shreveport-Bossier Grts, 1307
Comm Fdn of SE Connecticut Grants, 1309
Comm Fdn of Southern Indiana Grts, 1310
Comm Fnd of South Puget Sound Grants, 1311
Comm Fnd of the Verdugos Educational Endowment Fund Grants, 1321
Comm Fnd of the Verdugos Grants, 1322
Comm Fnd of the Virgin Isl Kimelman Grants, 1324
Comm Fdn of Wabash Cty Grants, 1326
Comm Partners on Waste Educ and Reduction, 1335

Computer Associates Comm Grants, 1341
ConAgra Foods Fnd Comm Impact Grants, 1342
ConAgra Foods Fnd Nourish Our Comm Grants, 1343
Connecticut Comm Fnd Grants, 1350
Connelly Fnd Grants, 1353
ConocoPhillips Fnd Grants, 1354
Constantin Fnd Grants, 1362
Constellation Energy Corp EcoStar Grts, 1363
Constellation Energy Corporate Grants, 1364
Consumers Energy Fnd, 1365
Coors Brewing Corporate Contributions Grants, 1371
Cord Fnd Grants, 1372
Corina Higginson Trust Grants, 1373
Cornerstone Fdn of NE Wisconsin Grants, 1375
Coughlin-Saunders Fnd Grants, 1377
Cowles Charitable Trust Grants, 1392
Crail-Johnson Fnd Grants, 1393
Cralle Fnd Grants, 1394
Crestlea Fnd Grants, 1399
Crossroads Fund Seed Grants, 1400
Crowell Trust Grants, 1401
CSRA Comm Fnd Grants, 1407
Cudd Fnd Grants, 1410
Cullen Fnd Grants, 1411
Cumberland Comm Fnd Summer Kids Grants, 1414
DV & Ida J McEachern Char Trust Grts, 1425
Dade Comm Fnd AIDS Partnership Grants, 1428
Dade Comm Fnd GLBT Comm Projects Grants, 1429
DaimlerChrysler Corporation Fund Grants, 1432
Daisy Marquis Jones Fnd Grants, 1434
Dallas Fnd Grants, 1436
Dallas Women's Fnd Grants, 1438
Dana Corporation Fnd Grants, 1440
Daphne Seybolt Culpeper Mem Fdn Grts, 1445
Dave Coy Fnd Grants, 1447
Dayton Fnd Grants, 1463
Daywood Fnd Grants, 1465
Deaconess Comm Fnd Grants, 1467
Deborah Munroe Noonan Mem Fund Grts, 1475
Dekko Fnd Grants, 1482
Delaware Comm Fdn Youth Philanthropy Board for New Castle County Grts, 1486
Deluxe Corporation Fnd Grants, 1496
DeMatteis Family Fnd Grants, 1497
DENSO North America Fnd Grants, 1499
Denver Fnd Comm Grants, 1502
DFN Hurricane Katrina and Disability Rapid Response Grants, 1522
DHS ARRA Transit Security Grants, 1544
DHS FY 2009 Transit Security Grants, 1545
DogTime Annual Grant, 1552
DogTime Tech Grant, 1553
DOJ Gang-Free Schools and Communities Intervention Grants, 1557
Dolan Fnd Grants, 1563
Dollar General Adult Lit Grants, 1568
Dollar General Family Lit Grants, 1569
Doree Taylor Charitable Fnd, 1580
Doris and Victor Day Fnd Grants, 1582
Doris Day Animal Fnd Grants, 1583
Dorothea Haus Ross Fnd Grants, 1587
Dr. P. Phillips Fnd Grants, 1601
Dreyer's Fnd Large Grants, 1606
Drs. Bruce and Lee Fnd Grants, 1607
Dubois County Comm Fnd Grants, 1615
Dunn Fnd K-12 Grants, 1622
Dwight Stuart Youth Fnd Capacity-Building Initiative Grants, 1627
E.J. Grassmann Trust Grants, 1638
E.L. Wiegand Fnd Grants, 1639
E Rhodes & Leona B Carpenter Fdn Grts, 1640
Eastman Chemical Co Fdn Grants, 1643
East Tennessee Fnd Grants, 1646
Eckerd Family Fnd Grants, 1651
EDS Fnd Grants, 1661
EDS Tech Grants, 1662
Edward N. and Della L. Thorne Memorial Fnd Direct Services Grants, 1666
Edward S. Moore Fnd Grants, 1668
Edwards Memorial Trust Grants, 1669

Edward W & Stella C Van Houten Mem Fund, 1670
Edwin S. Webster Fnd Grants, 1671
Edyth Bush Charitable Fnd Grants, 1673
Effie and Wofford Cain Fnd Grants, 1674
Eisner Fnd Grants, 1678
El Paso Comm Fnd Grants, 1688
El Pomar Fnd Awards and Grants, 1690
Elsie H. Wilcox Fnd Grants, 1691
Ensign-Bickford Fnd Grants, 1709
Erie Comm Fnd Grants, 1750
ESRI Conservation Grants, 1751
Ethel and Raymond F. Rice Fnd Grants, 1758
Ethel Frends Fnd Grants, 1759
Eugene B. Casey Fnd Grants, 1762
Eugene McDermott Fnd Grants, 1765
Eva L & Joseph M Bruening Fdn Grants, 1768
Evelyn and Walter Haas, Jr. Fund Immigrant Rights Grants, 1773
Ewing Halsell Fnd Grants, 1776
F.M. Kirby Fnd Grants, 1780
Fairfield County Comm Fdn Grts, 1782
Families Count: The National Honors Program, 1784
Fan Fox & Leslie R Samuels Fdn Grants, 1786
Faye McBeath Fnd Grants, 1794
FEMA Assistance to Firefighters Grants, 1802
Field Fnd of Illinois Grants, 1806
Fifth Third Bank Corporate Giving, 1809
Finish Line Youth Fnd Founder's Grants, 1812
Fireman's Fund Ins Co Heritage Grts, 1818
FirstEnergy Fnd Comm Grants, 1819
Fisa Fnd Grants, 1826
FishAmerica Fnd Conservation Grants, 1828
Flextronics Fnd Disaster Relief Grants, 1841
Florida Sea Turtle Grants, 1871
Florida Sports Fnd Junior Golf Grants, 1872
FMC Fnd Grants, 1876
Foellinger Fnd Grants, 1877
Ford Motor Company Fund Grants, 1885
Fnd for a Drug-Free Wrld Clsrm Tools, 1890
Fdn for Enhancing Communities Grts, 1893
Fnd for Seacoast Health Grants, 1895
Fnd for the Carolinas Grants, 1896
Fnd for Mid South Health & Wellness Grants, 1899
Frances C & William P Smallwood Fdn Grts, 1918
Francis L. Abreu Charitable Trust Grants, 1922
Frank and Lydia Bergen Fnd Grants, 1925
Frank E. and Seba B. Payne Fnd Grants, 1927
Frank G & Freida K Brotz Fam Fdn Grts, 1928
Frank Reed and Margaret Jane Peters Memorial Fund I Grants, 1933
Frank Reed and Margaret Jane Peters Memorial Fund II Grants, 1934
Frank Stanley Beveridge Fnd Grants, 1936
Fred C & Katherine B Andersen Fdn Grts, 1942
FRED Educational Ethyl Grants, 1945
Frederick McDonald Trust Grants, 1946
FRED Tech Grants for Rural Schools, 1951
Freeman Fnd Grants, 1952
Fremont Area Cmty Fdn Amazing X Grants, 1953
Fremont Area Comm Fnd Elderly Needs Grants, 1954
Fremont Area Comm Fnd Grants, 1955
Fremont Area Comm Fnd Summer Youth Grants, 1956
Frey Fnd Grants, 1963
Frist Fnd Grants, 1964
Fritz B. Burns Fnd Grants, 1965
Fruit Tree 101, 1967
Fuller E. Callaway Fnd Grants, 1973
G.N. Wilcox Trust Grants, 1982
Gamble Fnd Grants, 1983
Gateway Fnd Grants, 1992
Gebbie Fnd Grants, 1995
GEF Green Thumb Challenge, 1996
General Dynamics Corporation Grants, 2001
General Motors Fnd Grants, 2004
George A. Hormel Testamentary Trust Grants, 2009
George A Ohl Jr. Fnd Grants, 2012
George Fnd Grants, 2018
George Frederick Jewett Fnd Grants, 2019
George I. Alden Trust Grants, 2023
George Kress Fnd Grants, 2025

PROGRAM TYPE INDEX   Materials/Equioment Acquisition (Computers, Books, Videos, etc.) / 1109

George W Codrington Charitable Fdn Grts, 2029
George W. Wells Fnd Grants, 2030
Georgia-Pacific Fdn Entrepreneurship Grts, 2033
Georgia Council for the Arts Partner Grants for Organizations, 2035
Georgia Council for the Arts Partner Grants for Service Organizations, 2036
Gil and Dody Weaver Fnd Grants, 2053
Ginger and Barry Ackerley Fnd Grants, 2055
Gladys Brooks Fnd Grants, 2059
GNOF Albert N & Hattie M McClure Grts, 2068
Go Daddy Cares Charitable Contributions, 2094
Goldseker Fdn Comm Affairs Grants, 2100
Goldseker Fnd Human Services Grants, 2102
Grace and Franklin Bernsen Fnd Grants, 2109
Graco Fnd Grants, 2111
Grand Rapids Area Comm Fnd Wyoming Grants, 2116
Grand Rapids Area Comm Fnd Wyoming Youth Fund Grants, 2117
Grand Rapids Comm Fnd Grants, 2118
Grand Rapids Comm Fdn Ionia Cty Grts, 2119
Grand Rapids Comm Fnd Lowell Area Grants, 2121
Grand Rapids Comm Fnd SE Ottawa Grants, 2122
Grand Rapids Comm Fnd SE Ottawa Youth Fund Grants, 2123
Grand Rapids Comm Fdn Sparta Grts, 2124
Grand Rapids Comm Fnd Sparta Youth Grants, 2125
Greater Saint Louis Comm Fdn Grants, 2138
Greater Tacoma Comm Fdn Grts, 2139
Greater Worcester Comm Fnd Jeppson Memorial Fund for Brookfield Grants, 2141
Green Bay Packers Fnd Grants, 2148
Greygates Fnd Grants, 2164
Grover Hermann Fnd Grants, 2168
Grundy Fnd Grants, 2169
GTECH After School Advantage Grants, 2170
GUITS Library Acquisitions Grants, 2173
H & R Fnd Grants, 2181
HA & Mary K Chapman Char Trust Grts, 2182
Hackett Fnd Grants, 2188
Harold & Arlene Schnitzer CARE Fdn Grts, 2226
Harris and Eliza Kempner Fund Grants, 2231
Harris Graduate School of Public Policy Studies Research Dev Grants, 2232
Harrison Cty Comm Fdn Grts, 2233
Harrison County Comm Fnd Signature Grants, 2234
Harry C. Trexler Trust Grants, 2239
Harry W. Bass, Jr. Fnd Grants, 2246
Hartford Fdn Implementation Sppt Grts, 2251
Hartford Fdn Nonprofit Support Grants, 2252
Hartford Fnd Regular Grants, 2253
Harvest Fnd Grants, 2254
HCA Fnd Grants, 2274
Head Start Rplcmt Grantee: West Virginia, 2277
Health Fnd of Grtr Indianapolis Grts, 2282
Hearst Fnds Social Service Grants, 2285
Helen Bader Fnd Grants, 2293
Helen Irwin Littauer Educational Trust Grants, 2295
Helen Pumphrey Denit Charitable Trust Grants, 2297
Helen S. Boylan Fnd Grants, 2298
Helen V. Brach Fnd Grants, 2300
Henrietta Tower Wurts Memorial Fnd Grants, 2304
Henry E. Niles Fnd Grants, 2309
Henry W. Bull Fnd Grants, 2312
Highmark Physician eHealth Collab Grts, 2320
High Meadow Fnd Grants, 2321
Hillcrest Fnd Grants, 2325
Hill Crest Fnd Grants, 2324
Hill Fnd Grants, 2326
Hillman Fnd Grants, 2327
Hilton Hotels Corporate Giving, 2331
Hirtzel Memorial Fnd Grants, 2332
Hoffberger Fnd Grants, 2342
Homer Fnd Grants, 2352
Honor the Earth Grants, 2361
Horace Moses Charitable Fnd Grants, 2363
Hormel Fnd Grants, 2369
Household Int'l Corp Giving Grts, 2372
Howard and Bush Fnd Grants, 2374
HRF Hudson River Improvement Grants, 2378

Hudson Webber Fnd Grants, 2383
Huie-Dellmon Trust Grants, 2386
Huntington Arts Council Arts-in-Educ Programs, 2400
Huntington Clinical Fnd Grants, 2404
Hyams Fnd Grants, 2413
I.A. O'Shaughnessy Fnd Grants, 2416
ICC Day of Service Action Grants, 2427
ICC Listening to Communities Grants, 2429
Idaho Power Co Corp Contributions, 2433
IDPH Hosptial Capital Investment Grants, 2441
IDPH Local Health Dept Public Health Emergency Response Grants, 2442
IFP Chicago Production Fund In-Kind Grant, 2446
Illinois Arts Council Presenters Dev Grants, 2476
Illinois DCEO Comm Dev Assistance Pgm for Economic Dev (CDAP-ED) Grants, 2488
Illinois DCEO Eliminate the Digital Divide, 2489
Illinois DCEO Emerging Technological Enterprises Grants, 2490
IMLS American Heritage Preservation Grants, 2513
IMLS Grants to State Library Adm Agencies, 2514
IMLS Native American Library Services Grants, 2517
IMLS Native American Library Services Enhancement Grants, 2518
Independence Blue Cross Charitable Medical Care Grants, 2524
Independence Comm Fnd Education, Culture & Arts Grant, 2526
Indiana Clean Vessel Act Grants, 2535
Irvin Stern Fnd Grants, 2585
J.B. Reynolds Fnd Grants, 2592
J. Edwin Treakle Fnd Grants, 2596
J. F. Maddox Fnd Grants, 2597
J. Knox Gholston Fnd Grants, 2599
J.M. Long Fnd Grants, 2603
J.W. Kieckhefer Fnd Grants, 2607
Jackson Fnd Grants, 2613
Jacob and Hilda Blaustein Fnd Grants, 2615
Jacob G. Schmidlapp Trust Grants, 2616
Jacobs Family Fnd Spirit of the Diamond Grants, 2618
James & Abigail Campbell Fam Fdn Grts, 2620
James Graham Brown Fdn Qlty of Life Grts, 2625
James Hervey Johnson Charitable Educational Trust Grants, 2627
James J. McCann Charitable Trust and McCann Fnd, Inc Grants, 2631
James L & Mary Jane Bowman Char Trust, 2632
James R. Thorpe Fnd Grants, 2636
James S. Copley Fnd Grants, 2637
Jane and Jack Fitzpatrick Fund Grants, 2640
Janesville Fnd Grants, 2644
Janirve Fnd Grants, 2645
Janson Fnd Grants, 2646
Jaquelin Hume Fnd Grants, 2654
Jay & Rose Phillips Fam Fdn Grts, 2656
JELD-WEN Fnd Grants, 2661
Jenkins Fnd: Improving the Health of Greater Richmond Grants, 2663
Jennings County Comm Fdn Grts, 2664
Jessie Ball Dupont Fund Grants, 2671
John Ben Snow Memorial Trust Grants, 2687
John D & Katherine A Johnston Fdn Grants, 2691
John G. Duncan Trust Grants, 2695
John H. and Wilhelmina D. Harland Charitable Fnd Grants, 2698
John J. Leidy Fnd Grants, 2701
John Jewett & Helen Chandler Garland Fdn, 2702
John M. Weaver Fnd Grants, 2705
John P. Murphy Fnd Grants, 2708
John S & James L Knight Fdn Dnr Adv Fd Grts, 2712
John S Dunn Research Fdn Grants & Chairs, 2715
John W & Anna H Hanes Fdn Grants, 2728
John W. Speas and Effie E. Speas Memorial Trust Grants, 2732
Joseph Alexander Fnd Grants, 2734
Joseph H & Florence A Roblee Fdn Grants, 2736
Josephine Goodyear Fnd Grants, 2738
Josiah W & Bessie H Kline Fdn Grants, 2742
JP Morgan Chase Arts and Culture Grants, 2752
KaBOOM-CA Playground Challenge Grants, 2761

Katharine Matthies Fnd Grants, 2788
Katherine John Murphy Fnd Grants, 2790
Katie's Krops Grants, 2792
Kawabe Grants, 2794
Kelvin and Eleanor Smith Fnd Grants, 2796
Kenneth A. Scott Charitable Trust Grants, 2801
Kenneth T & Eileen L Norris Fdn Grants, 2802
Kessler Fdn Hurricane Sandy Emergency Grts, 2815
Kiki Madazine Grow Strong Girls through Leadership Grants, 2822
Koret Fnd Grants, 2837
LA84 Fnd Grants, 2847
LaGrange Independent Fnd for Endowments, 2851
Lana'i Comm Benefit Fund, 2857
Lawrence J. and Anne Rubenstein Charitable Fnd Grants, 2868
Leicester Savings Bank Fund, 2879
Lettie Pate Evans Fnd Grants, 2887
Lewis H. Humphreys Charitable Trust Grants, 2889
Lied Fnd Trust Grants, 2900
Linford & Mildred White Char Fund Grts, 2909
Lotus 88 Fnd for Women and Children, 2921
Louie M & Betty M Phillips Fdn Grants, 2923
Louis and Elizabeth Nave Flarsheim Charitable Fnd Grants, 2924
Louis Calder Fnd Grants, 2925
Lubbock Area Fnd Grants, 2931
Lubrizol Corporation Comm Grants, 2932
Lubrizol Fnd Grants, 2933
Lucy Downing Nisbet Charitable Fund Grants, 2935
Lucy Gooding Charitable Fnd Trust, 2936
Lucy Gooding Charitable Fdn Trust Grts, 2937
Ludwick Family Fnd Grants, 2938
Lumpkin Family Fdn Healthy People Grts, 2942
Lydia deForest Charitable Trust Grants, 2946
Lynde and Harry Bradley Fnd Grants, 2947
M.D. Anderson Fnd Grants, 2952
M.J. Murdock Charitable Trust General Grants, 2954
Mabel A. Horne Trust Grants, 2956
Mabel Louise Riley Fnd Grants, 2959
Mabel Y. Hughes Charitable Trust Grants, 2960
Macquarie Bank Fnd Grants, 2966
Marcia and Otto Koehler Fnd Grants, 3000
Mardag Fnd Grants, 3001
Margaret & James A Elkins Jr Fdn Grts, 3003
Margaret L. Wendt Fnd Grants, 3004
Marie C. and Joseph C. Wilson Fnd Rochester Small Grants, 3006
Marin Comm Fnd Social Justice and Interfaith Understanding Grants, 3012
Marion Gardner Jackson Char Trust Grts, 3017
Marion I & Henry J Knott Fdn Discret Grants, 3018
Marion I & Henry J Knott Fdn Std Grants, 3019
Mars Fnd Grants, 3025
Mary Black Fnd Active Living Grants, 3031
Mary D. & Walter F Frear Eleemosynary Trust, 3035
Mary K. Chapman Fnd Grants, 3042
Mary Owen Borden Fnd Grants, 3046
Mary S & David C Corbin Fdn Grants, 3048
Massachusetts Cultural Council Traditional Arts Apprenticeships, 3058
Maurice J. Masserini Charitable Trust Grants, 3064
Max A. Adler Charitable Fnd Grants, 3065
Max and Anna Levinson Fnd Grants, 3066
Maxon Charitable Fnd Grants, 3068
May & Stanley Smith Char Trust Grants, 3069
McConnell Fnd Grants, 3076
McCune Charitable Fnd Grants, 3077
McGregor Fund Grants, 3082
McInerny Fnd Grants, 3083
McKesson Fnd Grants, 3084
McLean Contributionship Grants, 3088
MDARD AgD Value Added/Regional Food Systems Grants, 3091
MDARD County Fairs Cap Imprvmt Grts, 3092
Meacham Fnd Memorial Grants, 3102
Meadows Fnd Grants, 3104
Mead Witter Fnd Grants, 3106
Melville Charitable Trust Grants, 3115
Memorial Fnd Grants, 3117

Materials/Equipment Acquisition (Computers, Books, Videos, etc.)

Mericos Fnd Grants, 3121
Meriden Fnd Grants, 3122
Metro Health Fnd Grants, 3133
MetroWest Health Fnd Capital Grants for Health-Related Facilities, 3134
Meyer Fnd Educ Grants, 3142
Meyer Memorial Trust Grassroots Grants, 3147
Meyer Memorial Trust Responsive Grants, 3148
Meyer Memorial Trust Special Grants, 3149
MFRI Operation Diploma Grants for Student Veterans Organizations, 3151
MFRI Operation Diploma Small Grants for Indiana Family Readiness Groups, 3152
MGN Family Fnd Grants, 3154
Michael and Susan Dell Fnd Grants, 3158
Microsoft Authorized Refurbisher Donations, 3162
Microsoft Comty Affairs Puget Sound Grts, 3163
Microsoft Software Donation Grants, 3164
Microsoft Unlimited Potential - Comm Tech Skills Grants, 3165
Mimi and Peter Haas Fund Grants, 3185
Minneapolis Fnd Comm Grants, 3186
MLB Tomorrow Fund Grants, 3193
Mockingbird Fnd Grants, 3196
Modest Needs Non-Profit Grants, 3200
Montgomery Cty Comm Fdn Grants, 3213
Moran Family Fnd Grants, 3216
Morris & Gwendolyn Cafritz Fdn Grants, 3218
Musgrave Fnd Grants, 3231
Natalie W. Furniss Charitable Trust Grants, 3244
National Home Library Fnd Grants, 3276
Nature Hills Nursery Green America Awards, 3287
NCFL/Better World Bks Libs & Families Awd, 3288
NEH Preservation Grants for Smaller Institutions, 3293
NEH Preservation Microfilming of Brittle Books and Serials Grants, 3294
Nellie Mae Educ Fnd State Level Systems Change Grants, 3299
New Earth Fnd Grants, 3317
NFF Comm Assistance Grants, 3343
NFL Grassroots Field Grants, 3350
NGA Hansen's Natural and Native School Garden Grants, 3402
NGA Healthy Sprouts Awards, 3403
NGA Heinz Wholesome Memories Intergenerational Garden Awards, 3404
NGA Hooked on Hydroponics Awards, 3405
NGA Mantis Award, 3406
NGA Midwest School Garden Grants, 3407
NGA Wuzzleburg Preschool Garden Awards, 3408
NGA Youth Garden Grants, 3409
Nicor Corporate Contributions, 3435
Nike and Ashoka GameChangers: Change the Game for Women in Sport, 3439
Nike Bowerman Track Renovation Grants, 3440
Nike Giving - Cash and Product Grants, 3442
Noble County Comm Fnd Celebrate Diversity Project Grants, 3455
Noble County Comm Fnd Grants, 3456
Norcliffe Fnd Grants, 3459
Norcross Wildlife Fnd Grants, 3460
Nordson Corporation Fnd Grants, 3462
Norfolk Southern Fnd Grants, 3463
North Carolina Arts Council Arts in Educ Initiatives Grants, 3469
North Carolina Arts Council Folklife Documentary Project Grants, 3475
North Carolina Arts Council Touring/Presenting Grants, 3483
North Central Health Services Grants, 3492
Northern Chautauqua Comm Fnd Comm Grants, 3499
Northern Trust Company Charitable Trust and Corporate Giving Program, 3504
Norton Fnd Grants, 3514
Norwin S & Elizabeth N Bean Fdn Grts, 3515
NSF Atmospheric Sciences Mid-Size Infrastructure Opportunity Grants, 3521
NYCT Tech Assistance Grants, 3559
NYSCA Architecture, Planning, and Design: Capital Fixtures and Equipment Purchase Grants, 3570
NYSCA Architecture, Planning, and Design: Capital Project Grants, 3571
NYSCA Arts Education: K-12 In-School Grants, 3580
NYSCA Electronic Media and Film: General Exhibition Grants, 3589
NYSCA Electronic Media and Film: Workspace Grants, 3593
NYSCA Music: New Music Facilities, 3608
NYSCA Visual Arts: Wrkspc Facilities Grts, 3631
Office Depot Fdn Caring is Sharing Grts, 3639
Ohio Arts Council Artists with Disabilities Access Grants, 3646
Ohio Arts Council Arts Partnership Grants, 3650
Ohio County Comm Fnd Board of Directors Grants, 3656
Ohio Valley Fnd Grants, 3662
OJJDP Tribal Juvenile Accountability Discretionary Grants, 3665
Oklahoma City Comm Pgms & Grts, 3666
Oleonda Jameson Trust Grants, 3667
Olga Sipolin Children's Fund Grants, 3668
Olin Corporation Charitable Trust Grants, 3669
OneFamily Fnd Grants, 3673
Open Spaces Sacred Places National Awards, 3684
Oppenstein Brothers Fnd Grants, 3685
Oregon Youth Soccer Fnd Grants, 3692
Oscar Rennebohm Fnd Grants, 3694
Owens Fnd Grants, 3718
Parker Fnd (California) Grants, 3736
Parkersburg Area Comm Fdn Action Grts, 3738
Pasadena Fnd Average Grants, 3741
Patricia Price Peterson Fnd Grants, 3746
Patrick and Anna M. Cudahy Fund Grants, 3751
Patron Saints Fnd Grants, 3753
Paul and Mary Haas Fnd Contributions and Student Scholarships, 3756
Paul E & Klare N Reinhold Fdn Grts, 3758
Paul Ogle Fnd Grants, 3764
Perpetual Trust for Charitable Giving Grants, 3826
Petco Fnd Product Support Grants, 3832
Peter and Elizabeth C. Tower Fnd Phase II Tech Initiative Grants, 3839
Peter and Elizabeth C. Tower Fnd Social and Emotional Preschool Curriculum Grants, 3841
Peter Kiewit Fnd General Grants, 3845
Peter Kiewit Fnd Small Grants, 3847
Peter Norton Family Fnd Grants, 3849
Pew Charitable Trusts Children & Youth Grts, 3858
Pfizer Special Events Grants, 3865
Phelps County Comm Fnd Grants, 3870
Phil Hardin Fnd Grants, 3875
Philip L. Graham Fund Grants, 3876
Pinellas County Grants, 3891
Pioneer Hi-Bred Comm Grants, 3895
Piper Trust Arts and Culture Grants, 3900
Piper Trust Children Grants, 3901
Piper Trust Educ Grants, 3902
Piper Trust Healthcare & Med Rsch Grts, 3903
Piper Trust Older Adults Grants, 3904
Piper Trust Reglious Organizations Grants, 3905
Pittsburgh Fdn Comm Fund Grts, 3910
Plum Creek Fnd Grants, 3917
PNC Fnd Grow Up Great Grants, 3924
PNM Power Up Grants, 3925
Porter County Comm Fnd Grants, 3931
Portland General Electric Fnd Grants, 3937
Posey Comm Fdn Women's Fund Grts, 3938
Powell Family Fnd Grants, 3941
PPG Industries Fnd Grants, 3943
Praxair Fnd Grants, 3944
Presbyterian Health Fnd Bridge, Seed and Equipment Grants, 3947
Price Family Charitable Fund Grants, 3952
Price Gilbert, Jr. Charitable Fund Grants, 3953
Priddy Fnd Capital Grants, 3954
Prince Charitable Trusts Chicago Grants, 3959
Prince Char Trusts Dist of Columbia Grts, 3960
Prince Charitable Trusts Rhode Island Grants, 3961
Principal Financial Group Fnd Grants, 3966
Project Orange Thumb Grants, 3972
Prudential Fnd Educ Grants, 3977
Public Safety Fnd of America Grants, 3983
Puerto Rico Comm Fnd Grants, 3986
R.C. Baker Fnd Grants, 3999
Ralph M. Parsons Fnd Grants, 4013
Raskob Fdn for Catholic Activities Grts, 4019
Rasmuson Fnd Capital Grants, 4020
Rathmann Family Fnd Grants, 4026
RCF General Comm Grants, 4032
RealNetworks Fnd Grants, 4037
REI Conservation & Outdoor Recreation Grts, 4051
Reinberger Fnd Grants, 4052
RESIST General Support Grants, 4058
RESIST Multi-Year Grants, 4063
Rhode Island Fnd Grants, 4073
Richard & Susan Smith Family Fdn Grts, 4078
Rich Fnd Grants, 4090
Ripley County Comm Fnd Grants, 4095
Ripley County Comm Fnd Small Project Grants, 4096
Robert G. Cabell III and Maude Morgan Cabell Fnd Grants, 4113
Robert M. Hearin Fnd Grants, 4116
Robert R. Meyer Fnd Grants, 4121
Robert W. Woodruff Fnd Grants, 4124
Robins Fnd Grants, 4126
Rochester Area Comm Fnd Grants, 4127
Rochester Area Fnd Grants, 4128
Ronald McDonald House Charities Grants, 4149
Ross Fnd Grants, 4164
Roy & Christine Sturgis Charitable Trust Grts, 4166
RRF Accessible Faith Grants, 4169
Rush County Comm Fnd Grants, 4174
Russell Berrie Fnd Grants, 4175
Ruth Eleanor Bamberger and John Ernest Bamberger Memorial Fnd Grants, 4178
Ruth H & Warren A Ellsworth Fnd Grts, 4179
RWJF Partners Investing in Nursing's Future, 4188
Ryder System Charitable Fnd Grants, 4191
Sage Fnd Grants, 4204
Saginaw Comm Fdn Discretionary Grts, 4205
Saint Luke's Health Initiatives Grants, 4216
Saint Paul Companies Fnd Grants, 4217
Samuel S. Johnson Fnd Grants, 4239
San Antonio Area Fnd Grants, 4240
Sands Memorial Fnd Grants, 4256
San Juan Island Comm Fnd Grants, 4283
Santa Barbara Strategy Capital Support, 4285
Santa Barbara Strategy Core Support Grants, 4286
Santa Fe Comm Fdn root2fruit Santa Fe, 4289
Santa Fe Comm Fnd Seasonal Grants-Fall Cycle, 4290
Santa Fe Comm Fnd Seasonal Grants-Spring, 4291
Sarah Scaife Fnd Grants, 4295
Sarkeys Fnd Grants, 4297
SAS Institute Comm Relations Donations, 4300
SCBWI Don Freeman Memorial Grant, 4302
Schering-Plough Fnd Health Grants, 4304
Schlessman Family Fnd Grants, 4307
Schramm Fnd Grants, 4310
Seabury Fnd Grants, 4316
Seattle Fnd Arts and Culture Grants, 4320
Seattle Fdn C Keith Birkenfeld Mem Tr Grts, 4323
Seattle Fnd Medical Funds Grants, 4329
Sensient Technologies Fnd Grants, 4337
Sheltering Arms Fund Grants, 4344
Shopko Fnd Green Bay Area Comm Grants, 4347
Sidney Stern Memorial Trust Grants, 4349
Sid W. Richardson Fnd Grants, 4350
Siebert Lutheran Fnd Grants, 4351
Sierra Health Fnd Responsive Grants, 4353
Simmons Fnd Grants, 4360
Sioux Falls Area Comm Fnd Comm Fund Grants, 4364
Sioux Falls Area Comm Fnd Spot Grants, 4366
Sisters of Mercy of North Carolina Fdn Grts, 4375
Sisters of St Joseph Healthcare Fdn Grts, 4377
Skaggs Fnd Grants, 4378
Slow Food in Schools Micro-Grants, 4384
SOBP A.E. Bennett Research Award, 4388
SOCFOC Catholic Ministries Grants, 4392
Solo Cup Fnd Grants, 4401
Sonora Area Fnd Competitive Grants, 4404
Sony Corp of America Corp Philant Grants, 4405

PROGRAM TYPE INDEX

Sorenson Legacy Fnd Grants, 4407
Sosland Fnd Grants, 4408
South Carolina Arts Commission Folklife & Traditional Arts Grants, 4421
Southwest Florida Comm Fnd Arts & Attractions Grants, 4441
Spartan Fnd Grants, 4448
Sport Manitoba Bingo Allocations Grants, 4454
Sport Manitoba Women to Watch Grants, 4460
Square D Fnd Grants, 4464
St. Joseph Comm Health Cath Kasper Award, 4468
St. Joseph Comm Health Fnd Improving Healthcare Access Grants, 4469
St. Louis-Jefferson Solid Waste Management Waste Reduction and Recycling Grants, 4470
Stackner Family Fnd Grants, 4471
Stackpole-Hall Fnd Grants, 4472
Stanley Smith Horticultural Trust Grants, 4474
Starr Fnd Grants, 4483
Steele-Reese Fnd Grants, 4498
Sterling-Turner Charitable Fnd Grants, 4499
Stewart Huston Charitable Trust Grants, 4505
Stocker Fnd Grants, 4507
Strake Fnd Grants, 4511
Strengthening Families - Strengthening Communities Grants, 4513
Strowd Roses Grants, 4515
Subaru Adopt a School Garden Grants, 4517
Subaru of Indiana Automotive Fdn Grts, 4519
Summit Fnd Grants, 4524
Sun Academic Excellence Grants, 4525
Sunderland Fnd Grants, 4527
Sunoco Fnd Grants, 4530
Susan Mott Webb Charitable Trust Grants, 4536
SVP Early Childhood Dev and Parenting Grants, 4538
T. James Kavanagh Fnd Grants, 4545
T.L.L. Temple Fnd Grants, 4546
TAC Arts Projects Grants, 4554
TAC Rural Arts Project Support Grants, 4555
Target Fnd Grants, 4562
TechFnd TechGrants, 4570
TE Fnd Grants, 4572
Telluride Fnd Comm Grants, 4573
Texas Filmmakers Production Grants, 4595
Texas Instruments Corp Arts & Culture Grts, 4596
Textron Corporate Contributions Grants, 4601
Theodore Edson Parker Fnd Grants, 4605
Thomas Austin Finch, Sr. Fnd Grants, 4613
Thomas B & Elizabeth M Sheridan Fdn Grts, 4614
Thomas J. Long Fnd Comm Grants, 4618
Thomas Sill Fnd Grants, 4619
Thomas Thompson Trust Grants, 4620
Tides Fdn Calif Wildlands Grassroots Fund, 4630
Time Warner Diverse Voices in the Arts Initiative Grants, 4635
Time Warner Yth Media & Creative Arts Grts, 4636
TJX Fnd Grants, 4637
Toyota Motor Engineering & Manufacturing North America Grants, 4651
Toyota Motor Mfg of Alabama Grts, 4652
Toyota Motor Manuf of West Virginia Grants, 4657
Toyota Motor Sales, USA Grants, 4659
Tri-County Electric People Fund Grants, 4665
Tri-State Comm Twenty-first Century Endowment Fund Grants, 4666
Trull Fnd Grants, 4673
TSA Advanced Surveillance Grants, 4674
TSYSF Individual Scholarships, 4675
TSYSF Team Grants, 4676
U.S. Bank Fnd Grants, 4686
US Dept of Educ Promoting Postbac Opportunities for Hispanic Americans Grts, 4697
US Dept of Educ Rehabilitation Engineering Research Centers Grants, 4698
U.S. Lacrosse Emerging Groups Grants, 4703
U.S. Lacrosse Equipment Grants, 4704
Union Bank, N.A. Fnd Grants, 4709
Union Pacific Fdn Comm & Civic Grts, 4714
United Technologies Corporation Grants, 4725
UPS Fnd Economic and Global Lit Grants, 4730

USAA – Ann Hoyt / Jim Easton JOAD Grants, 4734
USA Football Equipment Grants, 4735
US Airways Comm Fnd Grants, 4789
USDA 1890 Land Grant Colleges and Universities Initiative Grants, 4797
USDA Hispanic-Serving Institutions Grants, 4813
USFA Dev Grants, 4866
USFA Equipment Subsidy Grants, 4867
USGA Fdn for the Good of the Game Grts, 4868
USTA Recreational Tennis Grants, 4884
USTA Serves College Textbook Scholarships, 4886
V.V. Cooke Fnd Grants, 4896
Vancouver Fnd Grants and Comm Initiatives, 4900
Van Kampen Boyer Molinari Char Fdn Grts, 4905
Vectren Fnd Grants, 4907
Verizon Fnd Domestic Violence Prevention, 4910
Verizon Fnd Health Care and Accessibility Grants, 4913
Verizon Fnd Maine Grants, 4916
Verizon Fnd SE Region Grants, 4923
Vermillion Cty Comm Fnd Grts, 4928
Victor E. Speas Fnd Grants, 4933
Vigneron Grants, 4938
Virginia Comsn for the Arts Proj Grts, 4944
Visiting Nurse Fnd Grants, 4951
WM Keck Fdn Southern California Grts, 4964
Waitt Family Fnd Grants, 4973
Walter and Elise Haas Fund Grants, 4982
Walter L. Gross III Family Fnd Grants, 4983
Wayne County Fnd Grants, 5005
Weatherwax Fnd Grants, 5014
Wege Fnd Grants, 5017
Weingart Fnd Grants, 5018
Wells Fargo Housing Fnd Grants, 5023
Western Indiana Comm Fdn Grts, 5024
West Virginia Commission on the Arts Professional Dev for Artists Grants, 5045
Weyerhaeuser Company Fnd Grants, 5053
Whirlpool Fnd Grants, 5056
Widgeon Point Charitable Fnd Grants, 5064
Wilbur & Patsy Bradley Family Fdn Grts, 5066
William G & Helen C Hoffman Fdn Grants, 5080
William G. Gilmore Fnd Grants, 5082
William G. McGowan Charitable Fund Grants, 5084
William G Selby & Marie Selby Fdn Grts, 5085
William M. Cage Library Trust Grants, 5090
Wilson-Wood Fnd Grants, 5098
Windward Youth Leadership Fund Grants, 5100
Woodward Fund Grants, 5116

Preservation/Restoration
1772 Fnd Fellowships, 36
Abell-Hanger Fnd Grants, 91
Aetna Fnd Strengthening Neighborhhods Grants in Connecticut, 188
African American Heritage Grants, 193
Ahearn Family Fnd Grants, 206
AHS Fnd Grants, 208
Akron Comm Fnd Arts & Culture Grants, 218
Albuquerque Comm Fnd Grants, 348
Alliance for Comm Trees Home Depot Fnd NeighborWoods Grants, 382
Ambrose and Ida Fredrickson Fnd Grants, 414
American Express Historic Preservation Grants, 431
American Society for Yad Vashem Grants, 447
Anderson Fnd Grants, 460
Andy Warhol Fdn for the Visual Arts Grts, 464
Anne J. Caudal Fnd Grants, 475
Anne L. and George H. Clapp Charitable and Educational Trust Grants, 476
Annenberg Fnd Grants, 477
Anschutz Family Fnd Grants, 486
Arts Fnd, 578
Ashland Corporate Contributions Grants, 587
Baltimore Comm Fnd Neighborhood Grants , 646
Baltimore Comm Fnd Neighborhoods Path Grants, 647
Bank of America Charitable Fnd Matching Gifts, 658
Barker Welfare Fnd Grants, 669
Batchelor Fnd Grants, 679
Battle Creek Comm Fnd Neighborhood Grants, 686
Bay and Paul Fnds, Inc Grants, 692

Preservation/Restoration / 1111

Blue Mountain Comm Fnd Grants, 800
Blue River Comm Fnd Grants, 801
Booth-Bricker Fund Grants, 815
California Comm Fnd Neighborhood Revitalization Grants, 903
Callaway Fnd Grants, 909
Carl M. Freeman Fnd Grants, 933
CDECD Endangered Properties Grants, 980
CDECD Historic Preserv Enhancement Grts, 981
CDECD Historic Preservation Survey and Planning Grants, 982
CDECD Historic Restoration Grants, 983
Cessna Fnd Grants, 1000
CFFVR Environmental Stewardship Grants, 1010
Champlin Fnds Grants, 1029
Charlotte County Comm Fdn Grts, 1056
Chesapeake Bay Environmental Educ Grants, 1069
Chesapeake Bay Trust Forestry Mini Grants, 1071
Chesapeake Bay Trust Mini Grants, 1072
Chesapeake Bay Trust Pioneer Grants, 1074
Chula Vista Charitable Fnd Grants, 1116
CICF Efroymson Grants, 1120
Circle K Corporation Contributions Grants, 1136
Clarence E Heller Charitable Fdn Grants, 1150
CLIF Bar Family Fnd Grants, 1173
Columbus Fnd Joseph A. Jeffrey Endowment Fund Grants, 1224
Columbus Fnd Small Grants, 1232
Comm Fnd Alliance City of Evansville Endowment Fund Grants, 1246
Comm Fdn for Grtr Buffalo Grants, 1247
Comm Fnd for Greater New Haven Quinnipiac River Fund Grants, 1250
Comm Fnd for Monterey Cty Grants, 1255
Comm Fdn of Greater Tampa Grts, 1292
Comm Fdn of Mdl Tennessee Grants, 1300
Comm Fnd of Western North Carolina Grants, 1327
Comm Fnd Partnerships - Martin County Grants, 1329
ConocoPhillips Fnd Grants, 1354
Consumers Energy Fnd, 1365
Cudd Fnd Grants, 1410
D.F. Halton Fnd Grants, 1424
Dearborn Comm Fnd City of Aurora Grants, 1470
Denver Fnd Strengthening Neighborhoods Grants, 1504
Donald W. Reynolds Fnd Children's Discovery Initiative Grants, 1576
E Rhodes & Leona B Carpenter Fdn Grts, 1640
Earth Island Institute Brower Youth Awards, 1641
Edwin S. Webster Fnd Grants, 1671
El Pomar Fnd Awards and Grants, 1690
Fargo-Moorhead Area Fnd Grants, 1788
Ferree Fnd Grants, 1804
Fifth Third Bank Corporate Giving, 1809
FishAmerica Fdn Chesapeake Bay Grts, 1827
FishAmerica Fnd Conservation Grants, 1828
Fisheries and Habitat Partnership Grants, 1834
Florida Humanities Council Major Grants, 1868
Florida Sea Turtle Grants, 1871
Forrest C. Lattner Fnd Grants, 1887
Fnd for the Carolinas Grants, 1896
France-Merrick Fnds Grants, 1915
Garland & Agnes Taylor Gray Fdn Grts, 1988
George Kress Fnd Grants, 2025
GNOF Coastal 5 + 1 Grants, 2070
GNOF Comm Revitalization Grants, 2071
GNOF Environmental Fund Grants, 2073
GNOF Exxon-Mobil Grants, 2074
GNOF Gert Comm Fund Grants, 2076
GNOF Jefferson Comm Grants, 2085
GNOF Metropolitan Opportunities Grants, 2087
Goldseker Fnd Comm Grants, 2101
Grand Victoria Fnd Illinois Core Grants, 2126
Grtr Green Bay Comm Fdn Grts, 2135
Greater Milwaukee Fnd Grants, 2137
Greater Tacoma Comm Fdn Grts, 2139
Green Diamond Charitable Contributions, 2149
Green Fnd Special Project Grants, 2155
HAF Native Cultures Fund Grants, 2201
Harold R. Bechtel Charitable Remainder Uni-Trust Grants, 2229

1112 / Preservation/Restoration

Harrison Cty Comm Fnd Grts, 2233
Harrison County Comm Fnd Signature Grants, 2234
Hawaii Comm Fnd Geographic-Specific Grants, 2261
High Meadow Fnd Grants, 2321
Hillcrest Fnd Grants, 2325
Historic Landmarks Fnd of Indiana African American Heritage Grants, 2333
Historic Landmarks Fnd of Indiana Historic Preservation Educ Grants, 2334
Historic Landmarks Fnd of Indiana Legal Defense Grants, 2335
Historic Landmarks Fnd of Indiana Marion County Historic Preservation Funds, 2336
Historic Landmarks Fnd of Indiana Preservation Grants, 2337
Historic Landmarks Legal Defense Grants, 2338
Hoblitzelle Fnd Grants, 2341
Holland/Zeeland Comm Fdn Grts, 2345
Homer C. and Martha W. Gutchess Fnd Grants, 2351
Hometown Indiana Grants, 2353
Horizon Fnd Grants, 2365
HRF Hudson River Improvement Grants, 2378
Huntington County Comm Fnd - Make a Difference Grants, 2406
Hyams Fnd Grants, 2413
IMLS 21st Cent Museum Pros Grts, 2512
IMLS Grants to State Library Adm Agencies, 2514
IMLS National Leadership Grants , 2515
Independence Comm Fnd Neighborhood Renewal Grants, 2527
Indiana Historic Preservation Fund Grants, 2537
Indianapolis Preservation Grants, 2543
Indiana Preservation Grants, 2544
J.M. Kaplan Fund City Life Grants, 2601
J.W. Kieckhefer Fnd Grants, 2607
Jane and Jack Fitzpatrick Fund Grants, 2640
Jean and Price Daniel Fnd Grants, 2659
Jennings County Comm Fdn Grts, 2664
John Ben Snow Memorial Trust Grants, 2687
John J. Leidy Fnd Grants, 2701
John W & Anna H Hanes Fdn Grants, 2728
Joyce Fnd Environment Grants, 2750
Knox County Comm Fnd Grants, 2831
Laura Jane Musser Rural Initiative Grants, 2864
Letha E. House Fnd Grants, 2886
Lily Auchincloss Fnd Grants, 2904
Lotus 88 Fnd for Women and Children, 2921
Luther I. Replogle Fnd Grants, 2945
M.E. Raker Fnd Grants, 2953
Marcia and Otto Koehler Fnd Grants, 3000
Margaret & James A Elkins Jr Fdn Grts, 3003
Margaret L. Wendt Fnd Grants, 3004
Marion Cty Historic Preservn Fund Grts, 3016
MARPAT Fnd Grants, 3023
Mars Fnd Grants, 3025
Mary Black Fnd Active Living Grants, 3031
McCombs Fnd Grants, 3075
McCune Charitable Fnd Grants, 3077
McLean Contributionship Grants, 3088
MDEQ Brownfield ReDev and Site Reclamation Grants, 3095
Mildred V. Horn Fnd Grants, 3176
MLB Tomorrow Fund Grants, 3193
Montana Arts Cncl Cltrl & Aesthetic Proj Grts, 3209
National Endowment for Arts Museum Grants, 3265
National Endowment for Arts Presenting Grants, 3268
National Geographic Soc All Roads Seed Grts, 3272
National Geographic Society Conservation Trust Grants, 3273
National Geographic Young Explorers Grants, 3275
National Trust for Historic Preservation Diversity Scholarship, 3280
NEH Preservation Assistance Grants for Smaller Institutions, 3293
NEH Preservation Microfilming of Brittle Books and Serials Grants, 3294
New York Landmarks Conservancy City Ventures Grants, 3339
NFF Wilderness Stewardship Grants, 3346
NIAF Anthony Campitelli Endwd Fund Grts, 3431

NIAF Italian Culture and Heritage Grants, 3432
Nina Mason Pulliam Charitable Trust Grants, 3443
Norcliffe Fnd Grants, 3459
Norfolk Southern Fnd Grants, 3463
North Carolina Comm Fnd Grants, 3489
Northern Chautauqua Cmty Fdn DFT Communications Cmy Betterment Grts, 3500
Northern Chautauqua Comm Fdn Lake Shore Svgs & Loan Comnty Reinvestment Grts, 3502
NYCT Historic Preservation Grants, 3551
NYCT Neighborhood Revitalization Grants, 3555
NYCT New York City Environment Grants, 3556
NYSCA Architecture, Planning, and Design: Capital Fixtures and Equipment Purchase Grants, 3570
NYSCA Architecture, Planning, and Design: Capital Project Grants, 3571
NYSCA Architecture, Planning, and Design: Design and Planning Studies Grants, 3572
NYSCA Architecture, Planning, and Design: General Operating Support Grants, 3573
NYSCA Architecture, Planning, and Design: Independent Project Grants, 3575
NYSCA Architecture, Planning, and Design: Project Support Grants, 3576
NYSCA Arts Education: General Program Support Grants, 3579
NYSCA Electronic Media and Film: General Program Support, 3591
NYSCA Electronic Media and Film: Screenings Grants, 3592
NYSCA Folk Arts: Exhibitions Grants, 3594
NYSCA Folk Arts: Gen Pgm Support Grts, 3595
NYSCA Folk Arts: Presentation Grants, 3596
NYSCA Folk Arts: Regional and County Folk Arts Grants, 3597
NYSCA Lit: General Program Support Grants, 3599
NYSCA Museum: General Operating Support, 3602
NYSCA Museum: Gen Pgm Support Grts, 3603
NYSCA Museum: Project Support Grants, 3604
NYSCA Special Art Services: Project Support, 3613
NYSCA Special Arts Services: General Operating Support Grants, 3614
NYSCA Special Arts Services: General Program Support Grants, 3615
NYSCA Special Arts Services: Instruction and Training Grants, 3616
Ogden Codman Trust Grants, 3641
PacifiCorp Fnd for Learning Grants, 3727
Palm Beach and Martin Counties Grants, 3733
Parkersburg Area Comm Fdn Action Grts, 3738
Pasadena Fnd Average Grants, 3741
Perkins Charitable Fnd Grants, 3823
Pew Charitable Trusts Arts and Culture Grants, 3857
Posey County Comm Fnd Grants, 3939
Preservation Maryland Heritage Fund Grants, 3948
Prince Charitable Trusts Chicago Grants, 3959
Prince Char Trusts Dist of Columbia Grts, 3960
Putnam Cty Comm Fdn Grts, 3990
Rhode Island Fnd Grants, 4073
Richard & Caroline T Gwathmey Mem Tr Grts, 4075
Ripley County Comm Fnd Grants, 4095
Ripley County Comm Fnd Small Project Grants, 4096
Robert G. Cabell III & Maude Cabell Grants, 4113
Robert R. Meyer Fnd Grants, 4121
Rockefeller Brothers Fund Charles E. Culpeper Arts and Culture Grants in New York City, 4129
Rockefeller Brothers Fund Cross-Programmatic Initiative: Energy Grants, 4130
Rockefeller Brothers Fund Pivotal Places Grants: New York City, 4134
Rollins-Luetkemeyer Fnd Grants, 4147
Rose Communities and Environment Northern California Environmental Grassroots Grants, 4158
Ross Fnd Grants, 4164
Saginaw Comm Fnd Discretionary Grts, 4205
Saint Paul Fdn Lowertown Future Fund Grts, 4220
Salem Fnd Charitable Trust Grants, 4223
Salisbury Comm Fnd Grants, 4224
Schering-Plough Fdn Comm Initvs Grts, 4303
Sioux Falls Area Comm Fnd Comm Fund Grants, 4364

PROGRAM TYPE INDEX

Sioux Falls Area Comm Fnd Spot Grants, 4366
Skillman Fdn Good Neighborhoods Grts, 4380
South Carolina Arts Commission Folklife & Traditional Arts Grants, 4421
Southern Calif Edison Environmental Grts, 4429
Southwest Florida Comm Competitive Grants, 4442
Spencer Cty Comm Fdn Grants, 4451
State Farm Companies Strong Neighborhoods, 4485
Stewart Huston Charitable Trust Grants, 4505
Strake Fnd Grants, 4511
Taylor S. Abernathy and Patti Harding Abernathy Charitable Trust Grants, 4564
Textron Corporate Contributions Grants, 4601
Thomas Austin Finch, Sr. Fnd Grants, 4613
Tourism Cares Worldwide Grants, 4649
Toyota Motor Mfg of Mississippi Grts, 4655
Tri-State Comm Fnd Twenty-first Century Endowment Fund Grants, 4666
Trull Fnd Grants, 4673
Turner Fnd Grants, 4681
Union Bank, N.A. Fnd Grants, 4709
USDC/NOAA American Rivers Comm-Based Restoration Program River Grants, 4845
USDC/NOAA Open Rivers Initiative Grants, 4847
Vanderburgh Comm Fdn Women's Fund, 4903
Vermont Comm Fnd Grants, 4929
Virginia Comsn for the Arts Proj Grts, 4944
Virginia Fnd for Humanities Discretionary Grants, 4946
Virginia Fdn for the Humanities Open Grants, 4947
Wabash River Enhancement Corporation Agricultural Cost-Share Grants, 4968
Wabash River Enhancement Corp Urban, 4969
Wabash River Heritage Corridor Fund Grants, 4970
Washington Cty Comm Fdn Grts, 4997
Washington Cty Comm Fdn Youth Grts, 4998
Western Indiana Comm Fnd Grants, 5024
Widgeon Point Charitable Fnd Grants, 5064
WILD Fnd Grants, 5068
Winston-Salem Fdn Stokes County Grants, 5104

Professorships
Patricia Price Peterson Fnd Grants, 3746
Roy & Christine Sturgis Charitable Trust Grts, 4166

Publishing/Editing/Translating
AEC Trust Grants, 175
Akron Comm Fnd Arts & Culture Grants, 218
ALA Carnegie-Whitney Awards, 253
ALA Dartmouth Medal, 262
Albuquerque Comm Fnd Grants, 348
Alfred P Sloan Fdn Civic Initiatives Grts, 368
Anderson Fnd Grants, 460
Andy Warhol Fdn for the Visual Arts Grts, 464
Ann Arbor Area Comm Fnd Grants, 474
Arizona Comm Fnd Grants, 540
Atran Fnd Grants, 610
Ball Brothers Fnd General Grants, 637
Battle Creek Comm Fnd Grants, 684
Bay and Paul Fnds, Inc Grants, 692
Bodenwein Public Benevolent Fdn Grants, 806
CAA Millard Meiss Publication Fund Grants, 885
Carl Gellert and Celia Berta Gellert Fdn Grts, 930
Charles & Lynn Schusterman Fam Fdn Grants, 1038
Chatlos Fnd Grants, 1061
Chautauqua Region Comm Fdn Grts, 1062
Chesapeake Bay Trust Outreach and Comm Engagement Grants, 1073
Claremont Comm Fnd Grants, 1149
Clarence E Heller Charitable Fdn Grants, 1150
Coastal Comm Fdn of SC Grants, 1193
Columbus Fnd Competitive Grants, 1220
Comm Fdn for Muskegon Cty Grants, 1256
Comm Fdn for NE Michigan Grants, 1257
Comm Fdn for Southern Arizona Grants, 1261
Comm Fdn of E Ctrl Illinois Grts, 1278
Comm Fdn of Grtr Birmingham Grants, 1280
Comm Fdn of Louisville Grants, 1299
Comm Fdn of SE Connecticut Grants, 1309
Comm Fdn of the Verdugos Educational Endowment Fund Grants, 1321

PROGRAM TYPE INDEX

Religious Programs / 1113

Connecticut Comm Fnd Grants, 1350
Conservation, Food, and Health Fnd Grants for Developing Countries, 1359
Corina Higginson Trust Grants, 1373
Cummins Fnd Grants, 1415
Dolfinger-McMahon Fnd Grants, 1565
Dyson Fnd Mid-Hudson Valley Project Grants, 1636
East Tennessee Fnd Grants, 1646
Elmer L & Eleanor J Andersen Fdn Grnts, 1687
Ensign-Bickford Fnd Grants, 1709
Ewing Halsell Fnd Grants, 1776
Ford Fdn Peace & Social Justice Grts, 1884
Fdn for Enhancing Communities Grts, 1893
Frank Stanley Beveridge Fnd Grants, 1936
General Motors Fnd Grants, 2004
George A Ohl Jr. Fnd Grants, 2012
George Gund Fnd Grants, 2020
Grable Fnd Grants, 2108
H. Reimers Bechtel Charitable Remainder Uni-Trust Grants, 2186
Hartford Aging and Health Program Awards, 2247
Helen V. Brach Fnd Grants, 2300
Henry M. Jackson Fnd Grants, 2311
Hill Crest Fnd Grants, 2324
Huber Fnd Grants, 2382
Ian Hague Perl 6 Dev Grants, 2421
Illinois Arts Council Lit Pgm Grts, 2470
Illinois Arts Council Media Arts Pgm Grts, 2472
J.B. Reynolds Fnd Grants, 2592
J.W. Kieckhefer Fnd Grants, 2607
James J. McCann Charitable Trust and McCann Fnd, Inc Grants, 2631
Japan Fnd Center for Global Partnership Grants, 2649
Jaquelin Hume Fnd Grants, 2654
Jerome Fnd Grants, 2667
Jessie Ball Dupont Fund Grants, 2671
Jewish Women's Fdn of New York Grants, 2677
JM Fnd Grants, 2681
John P. McGovern Fnd Grants, 2707
Josephine G. Russell Trust Grants, 2737
Koret Fnd Grants, 2837
Laurel Fnd Grants, 2867
Lubbock Area Fnd Grants, 2931
Lynde and Harry Bradley Fnd Grants, 2947
Manitoba Arts Council Literary Arts Publishers Project Grants, 2996
Max and Anna Levinson Fnd Grants, 3066
McLean Contributionship Grants, 3088
Melville Charitable Trust Grants, 3115
National Endowment for the Arts Music Grants, 3266
Norcliffe Fnd Grants, 3459
North Carolina Arts Council Folklife Grants, 3476
North Dakota Council on the Arts Comm Access Grants, 3494
North Dakota Council on the Arts Institutional Support Grants, 3496
NYSCA Electronic Media and Film: General Program Support, 3591
NYSCA Lit: General Operating Support Grants, 3598
NYSCA Lit: General Program Support Grants, 3599
NYSCA Visual Arts: Svcs to the Field Grts, 3630
Ohio Arts Council Arts Indiv Excellence Awds, 3648
Ohio County Comm Board of Directors Grants, 3656
Olin Corporation Charitable Trust Grants, 3669
Overbrook Fnd Grants, 3715
Paul Rapoport Fnd Grants, 3765
PCA Arts Organizations and Arts Grants for Lit, 3781
PCA Arts Organizations & Grants for Visual Arts, 3785
PCA Entry Track Arts Organizations and Arts Grants for Lit, 3793
PCA Entry Track Arts Organizations and Arts Grants for Visual Arts, 3799
Perl 6 Microgrants, 3824
Perl Fnd Grants, 3825
Phelps County Comm Fnd Grants, 3870
Phil Hardin Fnd Grants, 3875
Playboy Fnd Grants, 3913
Puerto Rico Comm Fnd Grants, 3986
Reinberger Fnd Grants, 4052
Rochester Area Comm Fnd Grants, 4127

Ross Fnd Grants, 4164
S.E.VEN Fund 'In The River They Swim' Essay Competition, 4194
S.E.VEN Fund Mini-Grants, 4196
S.E.VEN Fund Open Enterprise Solutions to Poverty RFP Grants, 4197
S.E.VEN Fund WHY Prize, 4198
Sarah Scaife Fnd Grants, 4295
SCBWI Don Freeman Memorial Grant, 4302
Shell Oil Company Fnd Grants, 4343
Sid W. Richardson Fnd Grants, 4350
South Madison Comm Fnd Grants, 4440
Stanley Smith Horticultural Trust Grants, 4474
Susan Mott Webb Charitable Trust Grants, 4536
TAC Arts Access Grant, 4549
TAC Arts Build Communities Grants, 4551
TAC Arts Projects Grants, 4554
TAC Rural Arts Project Support Grants, 4555
Textron Corporate Contributions Grants, 4601
Time Warner Yth Media & Creative Arts Grts, 4636
USAID Strengthening Free and Independent Media in South Sudan Grants, 4783
USDA Agricultural and Rural Economic Research Grants, 4798
Virginia Fnd for Humanities Discretionary Grants, 4946
Virginia Fdn for the Humanities Open Grants, 4947
Virginia Fnd for the Humanities Residential Fellowships, 4948
Wayne County Fnd Grants, 5005
Weyerhaeuser Company Fnd Grants, 5053
WILD Fnd Grants, 5068

Religious Programs
100 Mile Man Fnd Grants, 27
1104 Fnd Grants, 34
A.C. Ratshesky Fnd Grants, 39
A.H.K. Fnd Grants, 40
A.J. Fletcher Fnd Grants, 41
A/H Fnd Grants, 48
Aaron Catzen Fnd Grants, 70
Aaron Fnd Grants, 73
ABC Charities Grants, 85
Abel Fnd Grants, 90
Abell-Hanger Fnd Grants, 91
Able To Serve Grants, 102
Aboudane Family Fnd Grants, 106
Achelis Fnd Grants, 127
Adams-Mastrovich Family Fnd Grants, 146
Adams Family Fnd of Ohio Grants, 151
Adelaide Christian Home For Children Grants, 162
Adelaide Dawson Lynch Trust Grants, 163
AEGON Transamerica Fdn Disaster Rlf Grts, 178
Aetna Fnd Regional Health Grants, 187
A Friends' Fnd Trust Grants, 194
Ahmanson Fnd Grants, 207
AHS Fnd Grants, 208
Alabama Humanities Fnd Mini Grants, 231
Alabama Humanities Fnd Planning Grants, 232
Alabama Power Fnd Grants, 233
Alavi Fnd Grants, 335
Albert and Bessie Mae Kronkosky Charitable Fnd Grants, 339
Albert and Margaret Alkek Fnd Grants, 340
Albert B Cuppage Charitable Fdn Grts, 341
Albertson's Charitable Giving Grants, 345
Albuquerque Comm Fnd Grants, 348
Alcoa Fnd Grants, 350
Alfred & Tillie Shemanski Testamentary Grants, 363
Allen Hilles Fund Grants, 378
Allyn Fnd Grants, 392
Alpha Kappa Alpha Educational Advancement Fnd Comm Assistance Awards, 393
ALSAM Fnd Grants, 395
Alvin & Fanny Blaustein Thalheimer Fdn Grts, 403
Alvin and Lucy Owsley Fnd Grants, 404
Ambrose Monell Fnd Grants, 415
Ameren Corporation Comm Grants, 418
American Academy of Religion Reg Dev Grants, 421
American Express Charitable Fund Grants, 429
American Foodservice Charitable Trust Grants, 433

American Jewish World Service Grants, 441
American Savings Fnd Grants, 445
Amerigroup Fnd Grants, 452
AmerUs Group Charitable Fnd, 455
Amon G. Carter Fnd Grants, 458
Anderson Fnd Grants, 460
Andre Agassi Charitable Fnd Grants, 461
Anheuser-Busch Fnd Grants, 470
Ann Arbor Area Comm Fnd Grants, 474
Anne Thorne Weaver Family Fnd Grants, 478
Anschutz Family Fnd Grants, 486
Ansell, Zaro, Grimm & Aaron Fdn Grts, 487
Anthony R. Abraham Fnd Grants, 489
Antone & Edene Vidinha Char Trust Grts, 490
Appalachian Ministries Grants, 499
Applied Materials Corp Philanthropy Pgm, 515
Aquila Corporate Grants, 521
Aragona Family Fnd Grants, 522
Aratani Fnd Grants, 523
Arcadia Fnd Grants, 525
Archer Daniels Midland Fnd Grants, 527
Argyros Fnd Grants, 532
Arie and Ida Crown Memorial Grants, 533
Arizona Comm Fnd Grants, 540
Arkansas Comm Fnd Grants, 561
Arkell Hall Fnd Grants, 562
Arlington Comm Fnd Grants, 564
Armstrong McDonald Fnd Grants, 565
A Rocha USA Grants, 566
Arronson Fnd Grants, 567
Arthur and Rochelle Belfer Fnd Grants, 570
Arthur Ashley Williams Fnd Grants, 572
ArvinMeritor Grants, 585
Ashland Corporate Contributions Grants, 587
Assisi Fnd of Memphis General Grants, 594
Assisi Fnd of Memphis Mini Grants, 595
Atherton Family Fnd Grants, 604
Athwin Fnd Grants, 605
Atkinson Fnd Comm Grants, 606
Atran Fnd Grants, 610
Audrey and Sydney Irmas Charitable Fnd Grants, 612
Ayres Fnd Grants, 630
Babcock Charitable Trust Grants, 632
Bacon Family Fnd Grants, 634
Bailey Fnd Grants, 635
Banfi Vintners Fnd Grants, 653
Baptist Comm Ministries Grants, 664
Barra Fnd Project Grants, 674
Barr Fund Grants, 678
Baton Rouge Area Every Kid a King Grants, 681
Baton Rouge Area Fnd Grants, 682
Bay and Paul Fnds, Inc Grants, 692
Bay and Paul Fnds Grants, 693
BCBS of Massachusetts Fnd Grants, 713
Beazley Fnd Grants, 714
Beerman Fnd Grants, 717
Beim Fnd Grants, 718
Beldon Fund Grants, 720
Belk Fnd Grants, 721
Bender Fnd Grants, 726
Benton County Fnd Grants, 731
Bernard F. Reynolds Charitable Trust Grants, 741
Besser Fnd Grants, 748
Bill and Katie Weaver Charitable Trust Grants, 764
Bill Hannon Fnd Grants, 771
Biogen Corporate Giving Grants, 773
Bishop Robert Paddock Trust Grants, 775
Blanche and Irving Laurie Fnd Grants, 784
Blanche M. Walsh Charity Trust Grants, 786
Blowitz-Ridgeway Fnd Grants, 792
Blue Cross Blue Shield of Minnesota Healthy Neighborhoods: Connect for Challenge Grants, 798
Blue Shield of California Grants, 802
Blum-Kovler Fnd Grants, 803
Blumenthal Fnd Grants, 804
Bodenwein Public Benevolent Fdn Grants, 806
Bodman Fnd Grants, 807
Boeckmann Charitable Fnd Grants, 808
Boettcher Fnd Grants, 810
Bohemian Fnd Pharos Fund Grants, 811

Religious Programs

Bolthouse Fnd Grants, 813
Booth-Bricker Fund Grants, 815
Booth Ferris Fnd Grants, 816
Borkee-Hagley Fnd Grants, 817
Boston Fnd Grants, 819
Boston Jewish Cmnty Women's Fund Grts, 822
Brad Brock Family Fnd Grants, 827
Bradley-Turner Fnd Grants, 828
Bradley Family Fnd (California) Grants, 829
Bradley Family Fdn Grants, 830
Brainerd Fnd Grants, 831
Bright Family Fnd Grants, 837
Bright Promises Fnd Grants, 838
Brooklyn Benevolent Society Grants, 847
Brunswick Fnd Grants, 857
Buhl Fnd - Frick Educational Fund, 859
Burden Trust Grants, 864
Burton G. Bettengen Grants, 871
Cabot Corporation Fnd Grants, 887
Caddock Fnd Grants, 888
Caesar Puff Fnd Grants, 890
Caleb C. and Julia W. Dula Educational and Charitable Fnd Grants, 893
Callaway Fnd Grants, 909
Callaway Golf Company Fnd Grants, 910
Cambridge Comm Fnd Grants, 913
Camp-Younts Fnd Grants, 914
Campbell Hoffman Fnd Grants, 915
Cargill Citizenship Fund-Corp Gvg Grants, 925
Carl C. Icahn Fnd Grants, 929
Carl Gellert and Celia Berta Gellert Fdn Grts, 930
Carl R. Hendrickson Family Fnd Grants, 935
Carnahan-Jackson Fnd Grants, 939
Carolyn Fnd Grants, 942
Carrie E. and Lena V. Glenn Fnd Grants, 944
Carrie Estelle Doheny Fnd Grants, 945
Carylon Fnd Grants, 949
Caterpillar Fnd Grants, 954
Catherine Kennedy Home Fnd Grants, 955
Catherine Manley Gaylord Fnd Grants, 956
CCCF Alpha Fund Grants, 959
CCCF Dora Maclellan Brown Christian Priority Grants, 960
CCF Comm Priorities Fund, 961
CCHD Comm Dev Grants, 966
CCHD Economic Dev Grants, 967
CE and S Fnd Grants, 985
Center for Venture Philanthropy, 991
CenterPointEnergy Minnegasco Grants, 993
Central Minnesota Comm Fnd Grants, 995
Central New York Comm Fnd Grants, 996
Central Okanagan Fnd Grants, 997
CenturyLink Clarke M Williams Fdn Grts, 998
CFFVR Alcoholism and Drug Abuse Grants, 1001
CFFVR Basic Needs Gvg Partnership Grts, 1002
CFFVR Capital Credit Union Charitable Giving Grants, 1005
CFFVR Myra M. & Robert L. Vandehey Grants, 1016
CFFVR Robert and Patricia Endries Family Fnd Grants, 1018
Chamberlain Fnd Grants, 1027
Champlin Fnds Grants, 1029
Chapman Charitable Fnd Grants, 1033
Chapman Family Charitable Trust Grants, 1034
Charity Incorporated Grants, 1035
Charles & Lynn Schusterman Fam Fdn Grants, 1038
Charles Delmar Fnd Grants, 1039
Charles H. Hall Fnd, 1044
Charles H. Revson Fnd Grants, 1047
Charles Hayden Fnd Grants, 1048
Charles Nelson Robinson Fund Grants, 1052
Chas Parker Trust for Public Music Fund Grts, 1053
Charles Stewart Mott Fnd Grants, 1055
Chatlos Fnd Grants, 1061
Chautauqua Region Comm Fdn Grts, 1062
Chicago Sun Times Charity Trust Grants, 1098
Chiles Fnd Grants, 1108
Cincinnati Milacron Fnd Grants, 1132
CIT Corporate Giving Grants, 1138
Citigroup Fnd Grants, 1139

Citizens Bank Mid-Atlantic Char Fdn Grts, 1140
Clark-Winchcole Fnd Grants, 1152
Clark and Carolyn Adams Fnd Grants, 1153
Clark and Ruby Baker Fnd Grants, 1154
Claude A. and Blanche McCubbin Abbott Charitable Trust Grants, 1158
Claude Worthington Benedum Fnd Grants, 1161
Cleveland-Cliffs Fnd Grants, 1165
Cleveland Browns Fnd Grants, 1166
Clowes Fund Grants, 1177
CNA Fnd Grants, 1179
CNCS AmeriCorps NCCC Project Grants, 1181
CNCS Foster Grandparent Projects Grants, 1185
CNCS Senior Companion Grants, 1187
Coastal Comm Fdn of SC Grants, 1193
Cobb Family Fnd Grants, 1194
Cockrell Fnd Grants, 1196
Coeta and Donald Barker Fnd Grants, 1197
Cogswell Benevolent Trust Grants, 1198
Colin Higgins Fnd Grants, 1204
Collins C. Diboll Private Fnd Grants, 1208
Collins Fnd Grants, 1209
Columbus Fnd Competitive Grants, 1220
Columbus Jewish Fnd Grants, 1234
Commission on Religion in Appalachia Grants, 1238
Communities Fnd of Texas Grants, 1243
Comm Fdn for Grtr Buffalo Grants, 1247
Comm Fdn for Monterey Cty Grants, 1255
Comm Fdn for Muskegon Cty Grants, 1256
Comm Fnd of Bartholomew County Women's Giving Circle, 1269
Comm Fdn of Central Illinois Grants, 1276
Comm Fdn of E Ctrl Illinois Grts, 1278
Comm Fnd of Greater Flint Grants, 1282
Comm Fnd of Greater Fort Wayne - Cmty Endwt & Clarke Endwt Grants, 1285
Comm Fnd of Greenville Hollingsworth Funds Program/Project Grants, 1296
Comm Fdn of Mdl Tennessee Grants, 1300
Comm Fnd of Mt Vernon & Knox County Grants, 1301
Connecticut Health Fnd Health Initiative Grants, 1351
Connelly Fnd Grants, 1353
ConocoPhillips Fnd Grants, 1354
Cooke-Hay Fnd Grants, 1367
Cord Fnd Grants, 1372
Coughlin-Saunders Fnd Grants, 1377
Covenant Fnd of Atlanta Grants, 1384
Covenant Fdn of New York Ignition Grts, 1385
Covenant Fdn of New York Signature Grts, 1386
Covenant Mountain Ministries Grants, 1387
Covidien Partnership for Neighborhood Wellness Grants, 1391
Crescent Porter Hale Fnd Grants, 1398
Crowell Trust Grants, 1401
CSRA Comm Fnd Grants, 1407
Cumberland Comm Fnd Summer Kids Grants, 1414
CUNA Mutual Group Fnd, 1416
Dade Comm Fnd Grants, 1430
DaimlerChrysler Corporation Fund Grants, 1432
Danellie Fnd Grants, 1442
Dan Murphy Fnd Grants, 1444
Dave Coy Fnd Grants, 1447
Davenport-Hatch Fnd Grants, 1448
Dave Thomas Fnd for Adoption Grants, 1449
David & Barbara B. Hirschhorn Fdn Grt, 1450
David Geffen Fnd Grants, 1452
David Robinson Fnd Grants, 1454
Daywood Fnd Grants, 1465
Delonne Anderson Family Fnd, 1492
Dennis & Phyllis Washington Fdn Grants, 1498
DHL Charitable Shipment Support, 1541
Diversity Leadership Academy Grants, 1550
Donald & Sylvia Robinson Family Fdn Grts, 1573
Dora Roberts Fnd Grants, 1579
Doris Duke Charitable Fnd Child Abuse Prevention Grants, 1585
Dorot Fnd Grants, 1586
Dorrance Family Fnd Grants, 1590
Douty Fnd Grants, 1595
Dr. Scholl Fnd Grants, 1602

Dresher Fnd Grants, 1605
Dyson Fnd Emergency Fund Grants, 1631
Dyson Fnd Mid-Hudson Valley Faith-Based Organization Grants, 1634
E Rhodes & Leona B Carpenter Fdn Grts, 1640
eBay Fnd Comm Grants, 1648
Ed and Carole Abel Fnd Grants, 1652
Eden Hall Fnd Grants, 1655
Edward S. Moore Fnd Grants, 1668
Edwin W & Catherine M Davis Fdn Grants, 1672
Edyth Bush Charitable Fnd Grants, 1673
Effie and Wofford Cain Fnd Grants, 1674
Elden and Mary Lee Gutwein Family Fnd Grants, 1679
Elizabeth & Avola W Callaway Fdn Grants, 1680
Elliot Fnd Inc Grants, 1686
El Pomar Fnd Awards and Grants, 1690
Elsie H. Wilcox Fnd Grants, 1691
Emerson Kampen Fnd Grants, 1696
Emily Davie and Joseph S. Kornfeld Fnd Grants, 1697
Emma J. Adams Grants, 1702
Energy Fnd Buildings Grants, 1705
Ensworth Charitable Fnd Grants, 1710
Entergy Corporation Micro Grants, 1712
Essex County Comm Fnd Discretionary Grants, 1752
Eugene B. Casey Fnd Grants, 1762
Evan Frankel Fnd Grants, 1770
F.M. Kirby Fnd Grants, 1780
Feldman Fnd Grants, 1801
Fieldstone Fnd Grants, 1808
FirstEnergy Fnd Comm Grants, 1819
Fishman Family Fnd Grants, 1835
Floyd A. and Kathleen C. Cailloux Fnd Grants, 1874
Forest Fnd Grants, 1886
Fnd for a Healthy Kentucky Grants, 1891
Fnd for the Carolinas Grants, 1896
Fnd NW Grants, 1906
Frances & Benjamin Benenson Fdn Grts, 1916
Francis Beidler Fnd Grants, 1921
Frank B. Hazard General Charity Fund Grants, 1926
Frank G & Freida K Brotz Fam Fdn Grts, 1928
Franklin County Comm Fdn Grts, 1929
Frank M. Tait Fnd Grants, 1932
Frank Reed and Margaret Jane Peters Memorial Fund II Grants, 1934
Frank Stanley Beveridge Fnd Grants, 1936
Fred and Sherry Abernethy Fnd Grants, 1940
Frederick S. Upton Fnd Grants, 1947
Fred L. Emerson Fnd Grants, 1949
Frist Fnd Grants, 1964
Fritz B. Burns Fnd Grants, 1965
Fuller E. Callaway Fnd Grants, 1973
Furth Family Fnd Grants, 1980
G.A. Ackermann Grants, 1981
G.N. Wilcox Trust Grants, 1982
Gannett Fdn Comm Action Grants, 1984
George and Sarah Buchanan Fnd Grants, 2011
George E. Hatcher, Jr. and Ann Williams Hatcher Fnd Grants, 2015
George Family Fnd Grants, 2017
George Frederick Jewett Fnd Grants, 2019
George H.C. Ensworth Grants, 2022
George I. Alden Trust Grants, 2023
George Kress Fnd Grants, 2025
George P. Davenport Trust Fund Grants, 2026
George W. Brackenridge Fnd Grants, 2028
Gertrude E Skelly Charitable Fdn Grts, 2046
Gertrude M. Conduff Fnd Grants, 2047
Gheens Fnd Grants, 2048
Giant Eagle Fnd Grants, 2049
Giant Food Charitable Grants, 2050
Ginn Fnd Grants, 2056
Girl's Best Friend Fnd Grants, 2057
Golden LEAF Fnd Grants, 2097
Golden State Warriors Fnd Grants, 2099
Grace and Franklin Bernsen Fnd Grants, 2109
Granger Fnd Grants, 2127
Great-West Life Grants, 2130
Greater Cincinnati Fnd Priority and Small Projects/Capacity-Building Grants, 2132
Greater Saint Louis Comm Fdn Grants, 2138

PROGRAM TYPE INDEX

Religious Programs / 1115

Greater Tacoma Comm Fdn Grts, 2139
Greater Worcester Comm Discretionary Grants, 2140
Greater Worcester Comm Fnd Ministries Grants, 2143
Green Bay Packers Fnd Grants, 2148
Greenspun Family Fnd Grants, 2156
Guido A & Elizabeth H Binda Fdn Grants, 2172
H. Leslie Hoffman & Elaine S. Hoffman Grants, 2185
H. Reimers Bechtel Charitable Remainder Uni-Trust Grants, 2186
H. Schaffer Fnd Grants, 2187
Hackett Fnd Grants, 2188
HAF Hansen Family Trust Christian Endowment Fund Grants, 2197
Hagedorn Fund Grants, 2207
Hahl Proctor Charitable Trust Grants, 2208
Harold & Arlene Schnitzer CARE Fdn Grants, 2226
Harold Simmons Fnd Grants, 2230
Harrison Cty Comm Fdn Grts, 2233
Harrison County Comm Fnd Signature Grants, 2234
Harry Kramer Grants, 2242
Harry W. Bass, Jr. Fnd Grants, 2246
Harvey Randall Wickes Fnd Grants, 2255
Hawai'i Children's Trust Fund Comm Awareness Events Grants, 2258
Hawaii Comm Fnd Reverend Takie Okumura Family Grants, 2264
HBF Pathways Out of Poverty Grants, 2273
HCA Fnd Grants, 2274
Healthcare Fdn for Orange Cty Grts, 2279
Healthcare Fnd of New Jersey Grants, 2280
Helen Bader Fnd Grants, 2293
Helen Steiner Rice Fnd Grants, 2299
Helen V. Brach Fnd Grants, 2300
Henrietta Lange Burk Fund Grants, 2303
Henry E. Niles Fnd Grants, 2309
Henry W. Bull Fnd Grants, 2312
Herbert A & Adrian W Woods Fdn Grts, 2313
Herbert H & Grace A Dow Fdn Grants, 2315
Herman Abbott Family Fnd Grants, 2316
Highmark Corporate Giving Grants, 2319
Hilda and Preston Davis Fnd Grants, 2322
Hilfiger Family Fnd Grants, 2323
Hillsdale Fund Grants, 2329
Hoffberger Fnd Grants, 2342
Hollie and Anna Oakley Fnd Grants, 2346
Honeywell Corp Family Safety & Security Grts, 2356
Household Int'l Corp Giving Grants, 2372
Howe Fnd of North Carolina Grants, 2377
Huffy Fnd Grants, 2384
Huie-Dellmon Trust Grants, 2386
Humanitas Fnd Grants, 2390
Huntington Fnd Grants, 2408
I.A. O'Shaughnessy Fnd Grants, 2416
Ida Alice Ryan Charitable Trust Grants, 2431
Infinity Fnd Grants, 2553
ING Fnd Grants, 2555
Intergrys Corporation Grants, 2565
Irvin Stern Fnd Grants, 2585
J. Bulow Campbell Fnd Grants, 2593
J.C. Penney Company Grants, 2594
J.E. and L.E. Mabee Fnd Grants, 2595
J. Mack Robinson Fnd Grants, 2604
Jacob and Hilda Blaustein Fnd Grants, 2615
James Hervey Johnson Charitable Educational Trust Grants, 2627
James J & Angelia M Harris Fdn Grts, 2630
James J. McCann Charitable Trust and McCann Fnd, Inc Grants, 2631
James L & Mary Jane Bowman Char Trust, 2632
James M. Collins Fnd Grants, 2633
Janus Fnd Grants, 2647
Jayne and Leonard Abess Fnd Grants, 2657
Jean and Price Daniel Fnd Grants, 2659
Jeffris Wood Fnd Grants, 2660
Jenifer Altman Fnd Grants, 2662
Jessie Ball Dupont Fund Grants, 2671
Jewish Comm Fnd of Los Angeles Cutting Edge Grants, 2673
Jewish Comm Fnd of Los Angeles Israel Grants, 2674
Jewish Fund Grants, 2675

Jewish Funds for Justice Grants, 2676
Jewish Women's Fnd of New York Grants, 2677
Jim Blevins Fnd Grants, 2678
Joe W & Dorothy Dorsett Brown Fdn Grants, 2684
John & Elizabeth Whiteley Fdn Grts, 2685
John C. Lasko Fnd Trust Grants, 2688
John Clarke Trust Grants, 2689
John Edward Fowler Mem Fdn Grants, 2693
John G. Duncan Trust Grants, 2695
John H. and Wilhelmina D. Harland Charitable Fnd Grants, 2698
John I. Smith Charities Grants, 2700
John M. Weaver Fnd Grants, 2705
John P. Murphy Fnd Grants, 2708
JohnS & JamesL Knight Fdn Communities Grts, 2711
Johns Manville Fund Grants, 2716
Johnson Scholarship Fnd Grants, 2726
Joseph Alexander Fnd Grants, 2734
Joseph H & Florence A Roblee Fdn Grants, 2736
Judith Clark-Morrill Fnd Grants, 2756
Kaiser Permanente Cares for Communities Grts, 2763
Kaneta Fnd Grants, 2774
Katharine Matthies Fnd Grants, 2788
Kawabe Grants, 2794
Ken W. Davis Fnd Grants, 2813
Kevin P & Sydney B Knight Family Fdn Grts, 2819
Kimball Int'l-Habig Fdn Grts, 2823
Kimberly-Clark Comm Grants, 2824
Knight Fnd Grants - Georgia, 2829
Koret Fnd Grants, 2837
Kovler Family Fnd Grants, 2840
Kroger Fnd Diversity Grants, 2842
Kroger Fdn Grassroots Comty Support Grants, 2843
Kroger Fnd Hunger Relief Grants, 2844
Lands' End Corporate Giving Program, 2861
Laura Jane Musser Intrcltrl Harmony Grts, 2862
Leonard L & Bertha U Abess Fdn Grts, 2884
Leo Niessen Jr., Charitable Trust Grants, 2885
Lettie Pate Whitehead Fnd Grants, 2888
Liberty Bank Fnd Grants, 2890
Libra Fnd Grants, 2899
Lilly Endowment Clergy Renewal Program for Indiana Congregations, 2902
Lotus 88 Fnd for Women and Children, 2921
Louis Calder Fnd Grants, 2925
Lowell Berry Fnd Grants, 2930
Lubbock Area Fnd Grants, 2931
Lucile Horton Howe & Mitchell B. Howe Grants, 2934
Lumpkin Family Fdn Healthy People Grts, 2942
Lumpkin Family Fnd Strong Leadership Grants, 2944
Lydia deForest Charitable Trust Grants, 2946
Lynde and Harry Bradley Fnd Grants, 2947
M. Bastian Family Fnd Grants, 2951
M.J. Murdock Charitable Trust General Grants, 2954
Mardag Fnd Grants, 3001
Margaret & James A Elkins Jr Fdn Grts, 3003
Margaret L. Wendt Fnd Grants, 3004
Marin Comm Fnd Social Justice and Interfaith Understanding Grants, 3012
Marion Gardner Jackson Char Trust Grts, 3017
Marion I & Henry J Knott Fdn Discret Grants, 3018
Marion I & Henry J Knott Fdn Std Grants, 3019
Mary's Pence Ministry Grants, 3029
Mary's Pence Study Grants, 3030
Mary Black Fnd Active Living Grants, 3031
Mary C. & Perry F. Spencer Fnd Grants, 3034
Mary D. & Walter F Frear Eleemosynary Trust, 3035
Mary Duke Biddle Fnd Grants, 3036
Mary E. and Michael Blevins Charitable Grants, 3037
Mary E. Ober Fnd Grants, 3039
Mathile Family Fnd Grants, 3062
Maurice Amado Fnd Grants, 3063
Maurice J. Masserini Charitable Trust Grants, 3064
Max A. Adler Charitable Fnd Grants, 3065
Max and Anna Levinson Fnd Grants, 3066
Maxon Charitable Fnd Grants, 3068
McCallum Family Fnd Grants, 3072
McCune Fnd Humanities Grants, 3079
McCune Fnd Human Services Grants, 3080
McKesson Fnd Grants, 3084

Mead Johnson Nutritionals Evansville-Area Organizations Grants, 3103
Mead Witter Fnd Grants, 3106
Medtronic Fnd CommLink Health Grants, 3111
Memorial Fnd Grants, 3117
Meriden Fnd Grants, 3122
Merkel Family Fnd Grants, 3123
Merkel Fnd Grants, 3124
Mertz Gilmore Fnd NYC Dance Grants, 3127
Mervin Bovaird Fnd Grants, 3128
Meyer and Stephanie Eglin Fnd Grants, 3139
MGN Family Fnd Grants, 3154
Michael and Susan Dell Fnd Grants, 3158
Michael Reese Health Trust Core Grants, 3159
Michael Reese Health Trust Responsive Grants, 3160
Missouri United Methodist Fnd Ministry Grants, 3189
Mitsubishi Electric America Fnd Grants, 3190
Moody Fnd Grants, 3215
Moran Family Fnd Grants, 3216
Morris & Gwendolyn Cafritz Fdn Grants, 3218
Motorola Fnd Grants, 3221
Mr. and Mrs. William Foulds Family Fnd Grants, 3222
Mt. Sinai Health Care Fnd Health of the Jewish Comm Grants, 3226
Mt. Sinai Health Care Fnd Health of the Urban Comm Grants, 3227
Musgrave Fnd Grants, 3231
Nathan Cummings Fnd Grants, 3246
Nathaniel & Elizabeth P Stevens Fdn Grants, 3247
Needmor Fund Grants, 3289
Nehemiah Comm Fnd Grants, 3290
Nellie Mae Educ Fnd State Level Systems Change Grants, 3299
Nell Warren Elkin and William Simpson Elkin Fnd Grants, 3300
New Hampshire Charitable Fnd Grants, 3325
New Jersey Office of Faith Based Initiatives Service to Seniors Grants, 3333
Newman W. Benson Fnd Grants, 3334
NIAF Anthony Campitelli Endwd Fund Grts, 3431
Nina Mason Pulliam Charitable Trust Grants, 3443
Norcliffe Fnd Grants, 3459
North Carolina Arts Council Arts in Educ Rural Dev Grants, 3470
North Carolina Comm Fnd Grants, 3489
North Georgia Comm Fnd Grants, 3505
NYCT Social Services and Welfare Grants, 3557
Onan Family Fnd Grants, 3672
Oppenstein Brothers Fnd Grants, 3685
Otto Bremer Fnd Grants, 3713
Overbrook Fnd Grants, 3715
PacifiCare Fnd Grants, 3725
PacifiCorp Fnd for Learning Grants, 3727
Palm Beach and Martin Counties Grants, 3733
Patrick and Anna M. Cudahy Fund Grants, 3751
Paul and Mary Haas Fnd Contributions and Student Scholarships, 3756
Paul Balint Charitable Trust Grants, 3757
Paul E & Klare N Reinhold Fdn Grts, 3758
Pauline E. Fitzpatrick Charitable Trust, 3763
Perkins-Ponder Fnd Grants, 3822
Perkins Charitable Fnd Grants, 3823
Perpetual Trust for Charitable Giving Grants, 3826
Peter and Georgia Angelos Fnd Grants, 3843
PG&E Comm Vitality Grants, 3868
PGE Fnd Grants, 3869
Phelps County Comm Fnd Grants, 3870
Philadelphia Fdn Org'l Effectiveness Grts, 3872
Phoenix Neighborhood Block Watch Grants, 3880
Pinkerton Fnd Grants, 3892
Piper Trust Reglious Organizations Grants, 3905
Pittsburgh Fdn Comm Fund Grts, 3910
Polk Bros. Fnd Grants, 3929
Pollock Fnd Grants, 3930
Powell Fnd Grants, 3942
Premera Blue Cross CARES Grants, 3945
Presbyterian Church USA Sam and Helen R. Walton Award, 3946
Priddy Fnd Organizational Dev Grants, 3956
Priddy Fnd Grants, 3957

1116 / Religious Programs

Procter and Gamble Fund Grants, 3967
Public Safety Fnd of America Grants, 3983
Public Welfare Fnd Grants, 3984
Putnam Fnd Grants, 3991
Quality Health Fnd Grants, 3994
R.C. Baker Fnd Grants, 3999
Rainbow Endowment Grants, 4007
Raskob Fdn for Catholic Activities Grts, 4019
Rathmann Family Fnd Grants, 4026
Retirement Rsch Fdn Accessible Faith Grants, 4066
RGK Fnd Grants, 4072
Richard & Caroline T Gwathmey Mem Tr Grts, 4075
Richard and Helen DeVos Fnd Grants, 4076
Richard and Rhoda Goldman Fund Grants, 4077
Richard D. Bass Fnd Grants, 4079
Richard King Mellon Fnd Grants, 4087
Righteous Persons Fnd Grants, 4093
Robert and Helen Haddad Fnd Grants, 4103
Robert E & Evelyn McKee Fdn Grants, 4110
Robert G. Cabell III and Maude Morgan Cabell Fnd Grants, 4113
Robert R. McCormick Tribune Comm Grants, 4119
Robert W. Woodruff Fnd Grants, 4124
Robins Fnd Grants, 4126
Rockwell Int'l Corporate Trust Grants, 4141
Rollin M. Gerstacker Fnd Grants, 4146
Rollins-Luetkemeyer Fnd Grants, 4147
Ronald McDonald House Charities Grants, 4149
Rose Comm Fnd Aging Grants, 4152
Rose Comm Fdn Jewish Life Grts, 4155
RRF Accessible Faith Grants, 4169
Russell Berrie Fnd Grants, 4175
RWJF Local Funding Partnerships Grants, 4186
S.H. Cowell Fnd Grants, 4199
S. Spencer Scott Fund Grants, 4202
Sage Fnd Grants, 4204
Saint Luke's Fnd Grants, 4215
Saint Paul Fnd Grants, 4219
Salisbury Comm Fnd Grants, 4224
San Antonio Area Fnd Grants, 4240
San Diego Fnd for Change Grants, 4247
Sandy Hill Fnd Grants, 4257
San Francisco Faith Arts and Culture Grants, 4267
Sara Lee Fnd Grants, 4296
Schlessman Family Fnd Grants, 4307
Scott B & Annie P Appleby Char Trust Grts, 4313
Seagate Tech Corp Capacity to Care Grants, 4317
Shirley W. & William L. Griffin Grants, 4345
Sidney Stern Memorial Trust Grants, 4349
Siebert Lutheran Fnd Grants, 4351
Sierra Health Fnd Responsive Grants, 4353
Sioux Falls Area Comm Fnd Comm Fund Grants, 4364
Sioux Falls Area Comm Fnd Field-of-Interest and Donor-Advised Grants, 4365
Sioux Falls Area Comm Fnd Spot Grants, 4366
Siragusa Fnd Human Services Grants, 4369
Sister Fund Grants for Women's Organizations, 4371
Sisters of Charity Fnd of Canton Grants, 4372
Sisters of Charity Fnd of Cleveland Good Samaritan Grants, 4373
Sisters of Charity Cleveland Reducing Health & Educational Disparities Grants, 4374
Sisters of Saint Joseph Charitable Fund Grants, 4376
Sisters of St Joseph Healthcare Fdn Grts, 4377
Skoll Fnd Awds for Social Entrepreneurship, 4383
SOCFOC Catholic Ministries Grants, 4392
SOCFOC Comm Collaborations Grants, 4393
Solo Cup Fnd Grants, 4401
Sorenson Legacy Fnd Grants, 4407
Sosland Fnd Grants, 4408
Southwire Company Grants, 4447
Speer Trust Grants, 4450
Square D Fnd Grants, 4464
St. Joseph Comm Health Fnd Improving Healthcare Access Grants, 4469
Stan and Sandy Checketts Fnd, 4473
State Strategies Fund Grants, 4494
Stewart Huston Charitable Trust Grants, 4505
Stowe Family Fnd Grants, 4510
Strake Fnd Grants, 4511

Strowd Roses Grants, 4515
Sunderland Fnd Grants, 4527
Sunny and Abe Rosenberg Fnd Grants, 4529
Susan Mott Webb Charitable Trust Grants, 4536
SVP Early Childhood Dev and Parenting Grants, 4538
SVP Environment Grants, 4539
Symantec Comm Relations and Corporate Philanthropy Grants, 4544
T. James Kavanagh Fnd Grants, 4545
T.L.L. Temple Fnd Grants, 4546
Talbert and Leota Abrams Fnd, 4558
Tanner Humanities Cntr Rsch Fellowships, 4559
Target Fnd Grants, 4562
Temple-Inland Fnd Grants, 4576
Tension Envelope Fnd Grants, 4578
Thomas & Dorothy Leavey Fnd Grants, 4612
Thomas Austin Finch, Sr. Fnd Grants, 4613
Thomas C. Ackerman Fnd Grants, 4615
Thompson Charitable Fnd Grants, 4622
Thrivent Financial for Lutherans Fnd Grts, 4629
Todd Brock Family Fnd Grants, 4639
Topeka Comm Fnd Building Families Grants, 4643
Topeka West Rotary Youth Enrichment Grants, 4645
Triangle Comm Fdn Donor-Advised Grts, 4668
Trull Fnd Grants, 4673
Turner B. Bunn, Jr. & Catherine E. Bunn Grants, 4680
Tyler Aaron Bookman Memorial Grants, 4684
United Methodist Committee on Relief Global AIDS Fund Grants, 4719
United Methodist Committee on Relief Hunger and Poverty Grants, 4720
United Methodist Child Mental Health Grants, 4721
United Methodist Hlth Mnstry Fund Grts, 4722
UUA Holmes-Weatherly Award, 4894
UUA Skinner Sermon Award, 4895
V.V. Cooke Fnd Grants, 4896
Vancouver Fnd Grants and Comm Initiatives, 4900
Vanderburgh Comm Fdn Women's Fund, 4903
Van Kampen Fnd Grants, 4906
Victoria S. and Bradley L. Geist Fnd Grants Supporting Foster Care and Their Caregivers, 4936
Victoria S. and Bradley L. Geist Fnd Grants Supporting Transitioning Foster Youth, 4937
W.C. Griffith Fnd Grants, 4957
WK Kellogg Fdn Secure Families Grants, 4963
W.P. and Bulah Luse Fnd Grants, 4965
W Waldo & Jenny Lynn M Bradley Fdn Grts, 4967
Walter L. Gross III Family Fnd Grants, 4983
Washington Area Fuel Fund Grants, 4988
Washington Gas Char Gvg Contributions, 5000
Waste Management Charitable Giving Grants, 5001
Wayne and Gladys Valley Fnd Grants, 5003
Welborn Baptist Fnd Faith-Based Grants, 5019
Weyerhaeuser Company Fnd Grants, 5053
Widgeon Point Charitable Fnd Grants, 5064
Wilbur & Patsy Bradley Family Fdn Grts, 5066
William G & Helen C Hoffman Fdn Grants, 5080
William H. Hannon Fnd Grants, 5086
William M. Weaver Fnd Grants, 5091
William S. Abell Fnd Grants, 5094
Windgate Charitable Fnd Grants, 5099
Wisconsin Humanities Council Major Grants, 5107
Woodward Fund Grants, 5116
Xcel Energy Fnd Grants, 5121
Young Family Fnd Grants, 5127

Scholarships

A.O. Smith Comm Grants, 46
Abbot & Dorothy H Stevens Fdn Grants, 79
Abbott Fund Science Educ Grants, 83
Abell-Hanger Fnd Grants, 91
Achelis Fnd Grants, 127
Acushnet Fnd Grants, 143
Adams Cty Comm Fdn of Indiana Grts, 148
Adams County Comm Fnd of Pennsylvania Grants, 149
AEGON Transamerica Fdn Arts & Culture Grts, 176
AEP Corporate Giving Grants, 180
Agape Fnd for Nonviolent Social Change Board of Trustees Grants, 197
Agnes M. Lindsay Trust Grants, 203

PROGRAM TYPE INDEX

Ahmanson Fnd Grants, 207
Akron Comm Fnd Arts & Culture Grants, 218
Alabama Power Fnd Grants, 233
Aladdin Industries Fnd Grants, 263
ALA e-Learning Scholarships, 270
ALA Robert L. Oakley Memorial Scholarship, 313
Alavi Fnd Grants, 335
Albert and Margaret Alkek Fnd Grants, 340
Albert B Cuppage Charitable Fdn Grts, 341
Albuquerque Comm Fnd Grants, 348
Alcatel-Lucent Technologies Fnd Grants, 349
Alcoa Fnd Grants, 350
Alex Brown & Sons Charitable Fdn Grants, 359
Alex Stern Family Fnd Grants, 360
Alfred & Tillie Shemanski Testamentary Grants, 363
Alice Tweed Tuohy Fnd Grants, 372
Allyn Fnd Grants, 392
Alpine Winter Fnd Grants, 394
ALSAM Fnd Grants, 395
ALZA Corporate Contributions Grants, 405
American Council of the Blind Scholarships, 427
American Foodservice Charitable Trust Grants, 433
American Savings Fnd Grants, 445
American Schlafhorst Fnd Grants, 446
AMI Semiconductors Corporate Grants, 457
Andre Agassi Charitable Fnd Grants, 461
Andrew Family Fnd Grants, 462
Angels Baseball Fnd Grants, 465
Angels Wings Fnd Int'l Grants, 469
Anheuser-Busch Fnd Grants, 470
ANLAF Int'l Fund for Sexual Minorities Grts, 471
Ann Arbor Area Comm Fnd Grants, 474
Ann Peppers Fnd Grants, 484
Antone & Edene Vidinha Char Trust Grts, 490
Appalachian Ministries Grants, 499
Apple Worldwide Developers Conference Student Scholarships, 513
Applied Materials Corp Philanthropy Pgm, 515
Aratani Fnd Grants, 523
Arcadia Fnd Grants, 525
Archer Daniels Midland Fnd Grants, 527
ARCO Fnd Educ Grants, 528
Argyros Fnd Grants, 532
Arie and Ida Crown Memorial Grants, 533
Arizona Comm Fnd Grants, 540
Arizona Comm Fnd Scholarships, 541
Arizona Republic Newspaper Corp Contribs, 547
Arkansas Comm Fnd Grants, 561
Arkell Hall Fnd Grants, 562
Arlington Comm Fnd Grants, 564
Arronson Fnd Grants, 567
Assurant Health Fnd Grants, 596
ASTA Academic Scholarships, 597
Atherton Family Fnd Grants, 604
Atkinson Fnd Comm Grants, 606
Atran Fnd Grants, 610
AutoNation Corporate Giving Grants, 620
Avista Fnd Grants, 624
Avon Products Fnd Grants, 625
AXA Fnd Scholarships, 629
Bailey Fnd Grants, 635
Barberton Comm Fnd Grants, 666
Battle Creek Comm Fnd Grants, 684
Batts Fnd Grants, 687
Bay Area Comm Fnd Grants, 694
Beazley Fnd Grants, 714
Beckley Area Fnd Grants, 716
Bemis Company Fnd Grants, 723
Ben B. Cheney Fnd Grants, 725
Bender Fnd Grants, 726
Berks County Comm Fnd Grants, 734
Bernard and Audre Rapoport Fnd University of Texas at Austin Scholarships, 739
Bertha Russ Lytel Fnd Grants, 745
Besser Fnd Grants, 748
Best Buy Children's Fnd @15 Scholarship, 750
Bill Hannon Fnd Grants, 771
Blade Fnd Grants, 783
Blanche and Irving Laurie Fnd Grants, 784
Blue Grass Comm Fnd Grants, 799

PROGRAM TYPE INDEX

Scholarships / 1117

Blue Mountain Comm Fnd Grants, 800
Bodenwein Public Benevolent Fdn Grants, 806
Bodman Fnd Grants, 807
Boeing Company Contributions Grants, 809
Bollinger Fnd Grants, 812
Bowling Green Comm Fnd Grants, 824
Bread and Roses Comm Fund Grants, 832
Bright Family Fnd Grants, 837
Brunswick Fnd Grants, 857
Burlington Northern Santa Fe Fdn Grants, 866
Butler Mfg Co Fnd Grants, 881
Cabot Corporation Fnd Grants, 887
Cambridge Comm Fnd Grants, 913
Campbell Soup Fnd Grants, 916
Cape Branch Fnd Grants, 919
Cargill Citizenship Fund-Corp Gvg Grants, 925
Carl & Eloise Pohlad Family Fdn Grants, 927
Carl Gellert and Celia Berta Gellert Fdn Grts, 930
Carnahan-Jackson Fnd Grants, 939
Carolyn Fnd Grants, 942
Carpenter Fnd Grants, 943
Carrie Estelle Doheny Fnd Grants, 945
Carrier Corporation Contributions Grants, 946
Carroll County Comm Fnd Grants, 947
Catherine Manley Gaylord Fnd Grants, 956
CE and S Fnd Grants, 985
Cemala Fnd Grants, 988
CenterPointEnergy Minnegasco Grants, 993
Central Carolina Comm Impact Grants, 994
Central Minnesota Comm Fdn Grants, 995
Central New York Comm Fdn Grants, 996
Central Okanagan Fnd Grants, 997
Cessna Fnd Grants, 1000
CFFVR Doug & Carla Salmon Fdn Grts, 1009
CFFVR Shawano Area Comm Fnd Grants, 1021
CFFVR Women's Fund for the Fox Valley Region Grants, 1025
Champlin Fnds Grants, 1029
Charles A. Frueauff Fnd Grants, 1037
Charles & Lynn Schusterman Fam Fdn Grants, 1038
Charles Delmar Fnd Grants, 1039
Charles G. Koch Charitable Fnd Grants, 1041
Charles H. Price II Family Fnd Grants, 1046
Charlotte R. Schmidlapp Fund Grants, 1058
Chatlos Fnd Grants, 1061
Chautauqua Region Comm Fdn Grts, 1062
Chesapeake Corporation Fnd Grants, 1076
Chicago White Metal Charitable Fdn Grants, 1102
Chick and Sophie Major Memorial Duck Calling Contest Scholarships, 1103
Chiles Fnd Grants, 1108
Christensen Fund Regional Grants, 1112
Christy-Houston Fnd Grants, 1115
CIGNA Fnd Grants, 1130
Citizens Savings Fnd Grants, 1141
Claneil Fnd Grants, 1145
Clarence E Heller Charitable Fdn Grants, 1150
Clarence T.C. Ching Fnd Grants, 1151
Clark-Winchcole Fnd Grants, 1152
Clark Charitable Trust Grants, 1155
Clark Fnd Grants, 1157
Claude Pepper Fnd Grants, 1160
Cleveland-Cliffs Fnd Grants, 1165
Coastal Bend Comm Fnd Grants, 1192
Coastal Comm Fdn of SC Grants, 1193
Coeta and Donald Barker Fnd Grants, 1197
Colgate-Palmolive Company Grants, 1202
Colin Higgins Fnd Grants, 1204
Collins Fnd Grants, 1209
Colorado Interstate Gas Grants, 1213
Columbus Fnd Competitive Grants, 1220
Columbus Fnd Dorothy E. Ann Fund (D.E.A.F.) Traditional Grants, 1221
Comerica Charitable Fnd Grants, 1237
Comm Fdn for Grtr Buffalo Grants, 1247
Comm Fdn for Muskegon Cty Grants, 1256
Comm Fdn for NE Michigan Grants, 1257
Comm Fdn for Southern Arizona Grants, 1261
Comm Fnd of Bloomington and Monroe County Grants, 1271

Comm Fdn of E Ctrl Illinois Grts, 1278
Comm Fdn of Greater Flint Grants, 1282
Comm Fnd of Greater Fort Wayne - Cmty Endwt & Clarke Endwt Grants, 1285
Comm Fdn of Greater Greensboro Grants, 1288
Comm Fdn of Grtr New Britain Grts, 1291
Comm Fdn of Louisville Grants, 1299
Comm Fnd of Mt Vernon & Knox County Grants, 1301
Comm Fdn of Riverside County Grts, 1304
Comm Fdn of Sarasota County Grts, 1306
Comm Fdn of Shreveport-Bossier Grts, 1307
Comm Fdn of S Alabama Grants, 1308
Comm Fnd of South Puget Sound Grants, 1311
Comm Fnd of the Ozarks Grants, 1320
Comm Fnd of the Verdugos Grants, 1322
Comm Fnd of Wabash Cty Grants, 1326
Comm Fnd of Western North Carolina Grants, 1327
Comm Fnd Silicon Valley Grants, 1331
Compton Fnd Grants, 1338
Connecticut Comm Fnd Grants, 1350
Connecticut Health Fnd Health Initiative Grants, 1351
ConocoPhillips Grants, 1355
Constellation Energy Corporate Grants, 1364
Conwood Charitable Trust Grants, 1366
Cooper Fnd Grants, 1369
Cooper Industries Fnd Grants, 1370
Cord Fnd Grants, 1372
Coughlin-Saunders Fnd Grants, 1377
Cralle Fnd Grants, 1394
Cranston Fnd Grants, 1395
Crescent Porter Hale Fnd Grants, 1398
Crowell Trust Grants, 1401
Crown Point Comm Fdn Scholarships, 1403
Cruise Industry Charitable Fnd Grants, 1404
CSRA Comm Fnd Grants, 1407
Cudd Fnd Grants, 1410
Cultural Society of Filipino Americans Grants, 1412
Cummins Fnd Grants, 1415
D.F. Halton Fnd Grants, 1424
DaimlerChrysler Corporation Fund Grants, 1432
Danellie Fnd Grants, 1442
Daphne Seybolt Culpeper Mem Fdn Grants, 1445
Dell Scholars Program Scholarships, 1491
Delonne Anderson Family Fnd, 1492
Dennis & Phyllis Washington Fdn Grants, 1498
DENSO North America Fnd Grants, 1499
DeRoy Testamentary Fnd Grants, 1518
Doris and Victor Day Fnd Grants, 1582
Do Something BR!CK Awards, 1592
Dresher Fnd Grants, 1605
DuPage Comm Fnd Grants, 1624
Dyson Fnd Mid-Hudson Philanthropy Grants, 1633
East Tennessee Fnd Grants, 1646
eBay Fnd Comm Grants, 1648
Eden Hall Fnd Grants, 1655
Edna Haddad Welfare Trust Fund Scholarships, 1658
Edward Bangs Kelley & Elza Kelley Fdn Grts, 1665
Edward S. Moore Fnd Grants, 1668
Edward W & Stella C Van Houten Mem Fund, 1670
Edwin S. Webster Fnd Grants, 1671
Edwin W & Catherine M Davis Fdn Grants, 1672
Effie and Wofford Cain Fnd Grants, 1674
El Paso Comm Fnd Grants, 1688
Elsie H. Wilcox Fnd Grants, 1691
Emerson Charitable Trust Grants, 1694
Emerson Electric Co Contributions Grts, 1695
Ensign-Bickford Fnd Grants, 1709
Enterprise Rent-A-Car Fnd Grants, 1721
Erie Comm Fnd Grants, 1750
Ethel and Raymond F. Rice Fnd Grants, 1758
Eugene B. Casey Fnd Grants, 1762
Eugene M. Lang Fnd Grants, 1764
Eugene McDermott Fnd Grants, 1765
Evan and Susan Bayh Fnd Grants, 1769
Evan Frankel Fnd Grants, 1770
Fairfield County Comm Fnd Grts, 1782
Fargo-Moorhead Area Fnd Woman's Fund Grants, 1789
Feldman Fnd Grants, 1801
Finish Line Youth Fnd Grants, 1813
Fishman Family Fnd Grants, 1835

Flinn Fnd Grants, 1842
Flinn Fnd Scholarships, 1843
Fluor Fnd Grants, 1875
FMC Fnd Grants, 1876
Fnd for Seacoast Health Grants, 1895
Fnd for the Carolinas Grants, 1896
Frances and John L. Loeb Family Fund Grants, 1917
Frank and Lydia Bergen Fnd Grants, 1925
Fred C & Mary R Koch Fnd Grants, 1943
Fred L. Emerson Fnd Grants, 1949
Fremont Area Comm Fnd Grants, 1955
Fritz B. Burns Fnd Grants, 1965
Fuller E. Callaway Fnd Grants, 1973
G.N. Wilcox Trust Grants, 1982
Gene Haas Fnd, 1999
George A. Hormel Testamentary Trust Grants, 2009
George and Ruth Bradford Fnd Grants, 2010
George Family Fnd Grants, 2017
George Fnd Grants, 2018
George H & Jane A Mifflin Mem Fund Grts, 2021
George I. Alden Trust Grants, 2023
George S & Dolores Dore Eccles Fdn Grants, 2027
George W. Brackenridge Fnd Grants, 2028
Georgia-Pacific Fdn Entrepreneurship Grts, 2033
Gertrude E Skelly Charitable Fdn Grts, 2046
Giant Eagle Fnd Grants, 2049
Gladys Brooks Fnd Grants, 2059
Goizueta Fnd Grants, 2096
Golden Rule Fnd Grants, 2098
Graco Fnd Grants, 2111
Grand Haven Area Comm Fdn Grants, 2113
Grand Victoria Fnd Illinois Core Grants, 2126
Greater Saint Louis Comm Fdn Grants, 2138
Greater Worcester Comm Discretionary Grants, 2140
Green Bay Packers Fnd Grants, 2148
Griffin Fnd Grants, 2165
Grover Hermann Fnd Grants, 2168
Guido A & Elizabeth H Binda Fdn Grants, 2172
Gulf Coast Comm Fnd Grants, 2174
Gulf Coast Fdn of Comm Scholarships, 2178
Gumdrop Books Librarian Scholarships, 2179
H & R Fnd Grants, 2181
H. Schaffer Fnd Grants, 2187
Harold & Arlene Schnitzer CARE Fdn Grts, 2226
Harrison Cty Comm Fdn Grts, 2233
Harry Bramhall Gilbert Char Trust Grts, 2238
Harry Kramer Grants, 2242
Harry S. Truman Scholarships, 2244
Helena Rubinstein Fnd Grants, 2292
Helen Bader Fnd Grants, 2293
Helen Irwin Littauer Educational Trust Grants, 2295
Helen V. Brach Fnd Grants, 2300
High Meadow Fnd Grants, 2321
Hill Fnd Grants, 2326
Hillsdale County Comm General Adult Grants, 2328
Hilton Hotels Corporate Giving, 2331
Hirtzel Memorial Fnd Grants, 2332
HomeBanc Fnd Grants, 2347
Homer A Scott & Mildred S Scott Fdn Grants, 2350
Homer Fnd Grants, 2352
Hormel Foods Charitable Trust Grants, 2368
Hormel Fnd Grants, 2369
Houston Endowment Grants, 2373
Huie-Dellmon Trust Grants, 2386
Humana Fnd Grants, 2388
Hundred Club of Connecticut Grants, 2392
Hundred Club of Pueblo Grants, 2398
Huntington Arts Council Arts-in-Educ Programs, 2400
IAFF Harvard Univ Trade Union Scholarships, 2417
IAFF Labour College of Canada Residential Scholarship, 2418
IAFF National Labor College Scholarships, 2419
IAFF W. H. McClennan Scholarship, 2420
IIE Adell and Hancock Scholarships, 2452
IIE AmCham U.S. Studies Scholarship, 2453
IIE Eurobank EFG Scholarships, 2455
IIE Nancy Petry Scholarship, 2459
IIE Western Union Family Scholarships, 2462
Illinois Tool Works Fnd Grants, 2511
Indiana Workforce Acceleration Grants, 2552

Scholarships

Intel Int'l Comm Grants, 2564
Int'l Association of Emergency Man Scholarships, 2566
Isabel Allende Fnd Esperanza Grants, 2586
J.C. Penney Company Grants, 2594
J.E. and L.E. Mabee Fnd Grants, 2595
J.L. Bedsole Fnd Grants, 2600
J Willard & Alice S Marriott Fdn Grts, 2609
J. Willard Marriott, Jr. Fnd Grants, 2610
Jacob and Hilda Blaustein Fnd Grants, 2615
James & Abigail Campbell Fam Fdn Grts, 2620
James G.K. McClure Educational and Dev Fund Grants, 2624
James J & Angelia M Harris Fdn Grts, 2630
James J. McCann Charitable Trust and McCann Fnd, Inc Grants, 2631
James R. Dougherty Jr. Fnd Grants, 2635
James R. Thorpe Fnd Grants, 2636
James S. Copley Fnd Grants, 2637
Janus Fnd Grants, 2647
JELD-WEN Fnd Grants, 2661
Jerry L & Barbara J Burris Fdn Grts, 2669
Jim Blevins Fnd Scholarships, 2679
Joe W & Dorothy Dorsett Brown Fdn Grants, 2684
John & Elizabeth Whiteley Fdn Grts, 2685
John Ben Snow Memorial Trust Grants, 2687
John Deere Fnd Grants, 2692
John H. and Wilhelmina D. Harland Charitable Fnd Grants, 2698
John I. Smith Charities Grants, 2700
John J. Leidy Fnd Grants, 2701
John Jewett & Helen Chandler Garland Fdn, 2702
John M. Ross Fnd Grants, 2704
John P. McGovern Fnd Grants, 2707
Johns Manville Fund Grants, 2716
John W. Anderson Fnd Grants, 2729
Joseph Alexander Fnd Grants, 2734
Joseph Drown Fnd Grants, 2735
Josephine G. Russell Trust Grants, 2737
Josiah W & Bessie H Kline Fdn Grants, 2742
Judge Isaac Anderson, Jr. Scholarship, 2754
Kaiser Permanente Cares for Communities Grts, 2763
Kathryne Beynon Fnd Grants, 2791
Kawabe Grants, 2794
Kenneth T & Eileen L Norris Fdn Grants, 2802
Kettering Fund Grants, 2818
Kohl's Cares Scholarships, 2832
Laila Twigg-Smith Art Scholarship, 2855
Laura L. Adams Fnd Grants, 2865
Lawrence J. and Anne Rubenstein Charitable Fnd Grants, 2868
Leave No Trace Master Educator Scholarships, 2870
Leo Goodwin Fnd Grants, 2882
Lettie Pate Whitehead Fnd Grants, 2888
Lillian S. Wells Fnd Grants, 2901
Lincoln Financial Group Fnd Grants, 2906
Louis Calder Fnd Grants, 2925
Lowe's Charitable and Educational Fnd Grants, 2927
Lowell Berry Fnd Grants, 2930
Lubbock Area Fnd Grants, 2931
Lubrizol Fnd Grants, 2933
Lynde and Harry Bradley Fnd Grants, 2947
M. Bastian Family Fnd Grants, 2951
Marathon Petroleum Corporation Grants, 2999
Margaret T. Morris Fnd Grants, 3005
Mars Fnd Grants, 3025
Mary's Pence Study Grants, 3030
Mary D. & Walter F Frear Eleemosynary Trust, 3035
Mary Duke Biddle Fnd Grants, 3036
Mary Jennings Sport Camp Scholarship, 3041
Mary M. Aaron Memorial Trust Scholarships, 3045
Maxon Charitable Fnd Grants, 3068
McCune Charitable Fnd Grants, 3077
McGraw-Hill Companies Comm Grants, 3081
McInerny Fnd Grants, 3083
McKesson Fnd Grants, 3084
Mead Witter Fnd Grants, 3106
Meriden Fnd Grants, 3122
Mervin Bovaird Fnd Grants, 3128
Metro Health Fnd Grants, 3133
MGN Family Fnd Grants, 3154

Miami County Comm Fnd Grants, 3157
Military Ex-Prisoners of War Fdn Grts, 3177
Miller Brewing Corporate Contributions Grants, 3180
MONY Fnd Grants, 3214
Morgan Babcock Scholarships, 3217
Morris & Gwendolyn Cafritz Fdn Grants, 3218
Morris K. Udall and Stewart L. Udall Fnd Native American Congressional Internships, 3220
Musgrave Fnd Grants, 3231
NAGC Masters and Specialists Award, 3237
NASE Fdn Future Entrepreneur Schlrsp, 3241
NASE Succeed Scholarships, 3243
National Book Scholarship Fund, 3249
New Hampshire Charitable Fnd Grants, 3325
New York Life Fnd Grants, 3341
Nicholas H Noyes Jr Mem Fdn Grants, 3434
Norcliffe Fnd Grants, 3459
Nordson Corporation Fnd Grants, 3462
Norfolk Southern Fnd Grants, 3463
North Carolina Comm Fnd Grants, 3489
North Carolina GlaxoSmithKline Fnd Grts, 3490
North Georgia Comm Fnd Grants, 3505
NW Mutual Fnd Grants, 3509
NW Minnesota Fnd Women's Fund Scholarships, 3513
Norton Fnd Grants, 3514
Oklahoma City Comm Fnd Pgms & Grts, 3666
Oleonda Jameson Trust Grants, 3667
Olin Corporation Charitable Trust Grants, 3669
Ordean Fnd Grants, 3691
Park Fnd Grants, 3739
PAS PASIC Scholarships, 3744
Patricia Price Peterson Fnd Grants, 3746
Patrick and Anna M. Cudahy Fund Grants, 3751
Patrick John Bennett, Jr. Memorial Fnd Grants, 3752
Paul & Daisy Soros Fwsps for New Americans, 3754
Paul and Mary Haas Fnd Contributions and Student Scholarships, 3756
Paul Stock Fnd Grants, 3766
Percy B. Ferebee Endowment Grants, 3820
Peter and Elizabeth C. Tower Fnd Organizational Scholarships, 3838
Peter Kiewit Fnd General Grants, 3845
Peter Kiewit Fnd Small Grants, 3847
Peyton Anderson Fnd Grants, 3862
PG&E Comm Vitality Grants, 3868
PGE Fnd Grants, 3869
Phelps County Comm Fnd Grants, 3870
Phil Hardin Fnd Grants, 3875
Piper Jaffray Fdn Communities Giving Grts, 3899
Portland General Electric Fnd Grants, 3937
Pott Fnd Grants, 3940
PPG Industries Fnd Grants, 3943
President's Student Service Scholarships, 3949
Price Chopper's Golub Fnd Grants, 3950
Price Chopper's Golub Fnd Two-Year Health Care Scholarship, 3951
Price Family Charitable Fund Grants, 3952
Principal Financial Group Fnd Grants, 3966
Prudential Fnd Educ Grants, 3977
Pulte Homes Corporate Contributions, 3989
Putnam Cty Comm Fdn Grts, 3990
R.C. Baker Fnd Grants, 3999
Rajiv Gandhi Fnd Grants, 4011
Ralph M. Parsons Fnd Grants, 4013
Randall L. Tobias Fnd Grants, 4017
Rathmann Family Fnd Grants, 4026
Regents Professional Opportunity Scholarships, 4044
Reinberger Fnd Grants, 4052
Rhode Island Fnd Grants, 4073
Richland County Bank Grants, 4091
Robert and Polly Dunn Fnd Grants, 4105
Robert E & Evelyn McKee Fdn Grants, 4110
Robert M. Hearin Fnd Grants, 4116
Robert R. Meyer Fnd Grants, 4121
Rockwell Int'l Corporate Trust Grants, 4141
Roger L. and Agnes C. Dell Charitable Grants, 4143
Ronald McDonald House Charities Grants, 4149
Ruth Eleanor Bamberger and John Ernest Bamberger Memorial Fnd Grants, 4178
Ryder System Charitable Fnd Grants, 4191

S. Livingston Mather Charitable Trust Grants, 4200
S. Mark Taper Fnd Grants, 4201
Sage Fnd Grants, 4204
Saint George's Society of NY Scholarships, 4213
Saint Paul Companies Fnd Grants, 4217
Samuel Huntington Public Service Award, 4232
Samuel S. Johnson Fnd Grants, 4239
San Antonio Area Fnd Grants, 4240
San Juan Island Comm Fnd Grants, 4283
Sara Lee Fnd Grants, 4296
Sartain Lanier Family Fnd Grants, 4298
Schering-Plough Fnd Health Grants, 4304
Schramm Fnd Grants, 4310
Scott B & Annie P Appleby Char Trust Grts, 4313
Seabury Fnd Grants, 4316
Seattle Fdn Doyne M Green Scholarships, 4324
Selby and Richard McRae Fnd Grants, 4334
Seneca Foods Fnd Grants, 4336
Shell Oil Company Fnd Grants, 4343
Simmons Fnd Grants, 4360
Sisters of Charity Fnd of Cleveland Good Samaritan Grants, 4373
Sodexo Fdn STOP Hunger Scholarships, 4400
Solo Cup Fnd Grants, 4401
Sony Corp of America Corp Philant Grants, 4405
Southwest Florida Comm Fnd Undergraduate and Graduate Scholarships, 4444
Sprint Fnd Grants, 4463
Square D Fnd Grants, 4464
Stackpole-Hall Fnd Grants, 4472
Starr Fnd Grants, 4483
State Justice Institute Scholarships, 4491
Steele-Reese Fnd Grants, 4498
Strake Fnd Grants, 4511
Stranahan Fnd Grants, 4512
Strolling of the Heifers Schlrsps for Farmers, 4514
Strowd Roses Grants, 4515
Sulzberger Fnd Grants, 4522
Summit Fnd Grants, 4524
T. James Kavanagh Fnd Grants, 4545
T. Rowe Price Associates Fnd Grants, 4548
Target Corporation Local Store Grants, 4561
Telluride Fnd Comm Grants, 4573
Temple-Inland Fnd Grants, 4576
Third Wave Fnd Reproductive Health and Justice Grants, 4611
Thomas & Dorothy Leavey Fdn Grants, 4612
Thomas Austin Finch, Sr. Fnd Grants, 4613
Thomas B & Elizabeth M Sheridan Fdn Grts, 4614
Thomas C. Ackerman Fnd Grants, 4615
Thompson Charitable Fnd Grants, 4622
Thompson Fnd Grants, 4623
Tiger Woods Fnd Grants, 4634
Tourism Cares Professional Dev Scholarships, 4648
Trinity Fnd Grants, 4669
Trull Fnd Grants, 4673
TSYSF Individual Scholarships, 4675
Tulane University Comm Service Scholars, 4677
Tull Charitable Fnd Grants, 4679
TWS Fnd Grants, 4683
U.S. Army ROTC Scholarships, 4685
Union Bank, N.A. Fnd Grants, 4709
Union Pacific Fdn Comm & Civic Grts, 4714
United States Institute of Peace - National Peace Essay Contest for High School Students, 4724
USAID Scholarships for Youth and Teachers, 4780
US Airways Educ Fnd Grants, 4790
USBC Annual Zeb Scholarship, 4792
USBC Earl Anthony Memorial Scholarships, 4793
USTA CTA and NJTL Comm Tennis Dev Workshop Scholarships, 4873
USTA NJTL Tennis and Leadership Camp Scholarships, 4879
USTA Recreational Tennis Grants, 4884
USTA Serves College Educ Scholarships, 4885
USTA Serves College Textbook Scholarships, 4886
USTA Serves Dwight F. Davis Scholarships, 4887
USTA Serves Dwight Mosley Scholarships, 4888
USTA Serves Eve Kraft Scholarships, 4889
USTA Serves Marian Wood Baird Scholarship, 4890

PROGRAM TYPE INDEX

USTA Serves Player Incentive Awards, 4891
Verizon Fnd Grants, 4911
Viacom Fnd Grants (Formerly CBS Fnd), 4932
Vulcan Materials Company Fnd Grants, 4956
W.P. and Bulah Luse Fnd Grants, 4965
Walt Disney Company Fnd Grants, 4981
Wayne and Gladys Valley Fnd Grants, 5003
Wayne County Fnd Grants, 5005
Weatherwax Fnd Grants, 5014
Whirlpool Fnd Grants, 5056
William Blair and Company Fnd Grants, 5078
William G & Helen C Hoffman Fdn Grants, 5080
William G. Gilmore Fnd Grants, 5082
William G. McGowan Charitable Fund Grants, 5084
William G Selby & Marie Selby Fdn Grts, 5085
William McCaskey Chapman and Adaline Dinsmore Chapman Fnd Grants, 5092
Williams Companies Fnd Grants, 5095
Winston-Salem Fdn Competitive Grts, 5102
Wolfe Associates Grants, 5110
Women's Funding Alliance Grants, 5112
World Bank JJ/WBGSP Partners Programs, 5117
Xcel Energy Fnd Grants, 5121
Xerox Fnd Grants, 5122
Yampa Valley Comm Fnd Grants, 5124
Young Family Fnd Grants, 5127

Seed Grants

3 Roots Fnd Grants, 10
3M Company Health and Human Services Grants, 14
100 Mile Man Fnd Grants, 27
100 Women in Hedge Funds Fnd Grants, 28
A.C. Ratshesky Fnd Grants, 39
A.V. Hunter Trust Grants, 47
AAAAI RSLAAIS Leadership Award, 49
AACC Plus 50 Initiative Grants, 55
AAUW Comm Action Grants, 75
Abbot & Dorothy H Stevens Fdn Grants, 79
Abbott Fund Comm Grants, 81
Abelard Fnd East Grants, 87
Abelard Fnd West Grants, 88
Abell-Hanger Fnd Grants, 91
Achelis Fnd Grants, 127
ACTION Council of Monterey County Grants, 134
Acushnet Fnd Grants, 143
Adams County Comm Fnd of Pennsylvania Grants, 149
Adams Fnd Grants, 155
Adelaide Breed Bayrd Fnd Grants, 161
Adolph Coors Fnd Grants, 171
A Friends' Fnd Trust Grants, 194
Agape Fnd for Nonviolent Social Change Alice Hamburg Emergency Grants, 196
Agape Fnd for Nonviolent Social Change Board of Trustees Grants, 197
A Glimmer of Hope Fnd Grants, 200
Agnes M. Lindsay Trust Grants, 203
Ahmanson Fnd Grants, 207
Air Products and Chemicals Grants, 216
Alabama Power Fnd Grants, 233
Aladdin Industries Fnd Grants, 263
Albert and Bessie Mae Kronkosky Charitable Fnd Grants, 339
Alberto Culver Corporate Contributions Grants, 343
Albuquerque Comm Fnd Grants, 348
Alcoa Fnd Grants, 350
Alcon Fnd Grants, 351
Alexander and Margaret Stewart Trust Grants, 354
Alfred & Tillie Shemanski Testamentary Grants, 363
Allegheny Fnd Grants, 376
Allen Hilles Fund Grants, 378
Allen P & Josephine B Green Fdn Grts, 380
Alliance Healthcare Fnd Grants, 383
Alliant Energy Fnd Comm Grants, 384
Allstate Corporate Giving Grants, 386
Allstate Corp Hometown Commitment Grants, 387
Allyn Fnd Grants, 392
Amador Comm Fnd Grants, 408
AMA Fdn Fund for Better Health Grts, 409
Amber Grants, 413
Ameren Corporation Comm Grants, 418
American Chemical Scty Corp Assocs Seed Grts, 425
American Express Historic Preservation Grants, 431
American Schlafhorst Fnd Grants, 446
Amon G. Carter Fnd Grants, 458
Anderson Fnd Grants, 460
Angels Baseball Fnd Grants, 465
Anna Fitch Ardenghi Trust Grants, 472
Ann Arbor Area Comm Fnd Grants, 474
Annenberg Fnd Grants, 477
Anschutz Family Fnd Grants, 486
Appalachian Regional Commission Asset-Based Dev Project Grants, 500
Applied Materials Corp Philanthropy Pgm, 515
Aratani Fnd Grants, 523
ARCO Fnd Educ Grants, 528
Arizona Comm Fnd Grants, 540
Arizona Fnd for Women General Grants, 544
Arkansas Comm Fnd Grants, 561
Arkell Hall Fnd Grants, 562
Arlington Comm Fnd Grants, 564
Arronson Fnd Grants, 567
Arthur Ashley Williams Fnd Grants, 572
Aspen Comm Fnd Grants, 592
AT&T Fnd Civic and Comm Service Grants, 599
Atherton Family Fnd Grants, 604
Atkinson Fnd Comm Grants, 606
Atlanta Fnd Grants, 608
Atran Fnd Grants, 610
Austin Comm Fnd Grants, 616
Austin S. Nelson Fnd Grants, 617
Autauga Area Comm Fnd Grants, 618
Autzen Fnd Grants, 622
Ayres Fnd Grants, 630
Babcock Charitable Trust Grants, 632
Bacon Family Fnd Grants, 634
Ball Brothers Fnd General Grants, 637
Ball Brothers Fnd Rapid Grants, 639
Baltimore Comm Fnd Neighborhood Grants, 646
BankAtlantic Fnd Grants, 654
Bank of America Comm Dev Grants, 655
Bank of America Charitable Fnd Matching Gifts, 658
Bank of America Charitable Fnd Volunteer Grants, 660
Barker Welfare Fnd Grants, 669
Barra Fnd Comm Fund Grants, 673
Barra Fnd Project Grants, 674
Baton Rouge Area Fnd Grants, 682
Battle Creek Comm Fnd Grants, 684
Baxter Int'l Corporate Giving Grants, 689
Baxter Int'l Fnd Grants, 691
Bay and Paul Fnds, Inc Grants, 692
Bay and Paul Fnds Grants, 693
Beckley Area Fnd Grants, 716
Beim Fnd Grants, 718
Beldon Fund Grants, 720
Bender Fnd Grants, 726
Berks County Comm Fnd Grants, 734
Bertha Russ Lytel Fnd Grants, 745
Better Way Fnd Grants, 754
Bikes Belong Grants, 763
Bill and Melinda Gates Ag Dev Grants, 765
Bishop Robert Paddock Trust Grants, 775
Blandin Fdn Expand Opportunity Grants, 787
Blue Grass Comm Fnd Grants, 799
Blue Mountain Comm Fnd Grants, 800
Blue River Comm Fnd Grants, 801
Blumenthal Fnd Grants, 804
Bodenwein Public Benevolent Fdn Grants, 806
Bodman Fnd Grants, 807
Boeing Company Contributions Grants, 809
Boettcher Fnd Grants, 810
Booth Ferris Fnd Grants, 816
Boston Fnd Grants, 819
Boston Globe Fnd Grants, 821
Brainerd Fnd Grants, 831
Brico Fund Grants, 835
Bristol-Myers Squibb Fnd Comm Grants, 840
Brookdale Fdn National Group Respite Grts, 845
Brookdale Fdn Relatives as Parents Grts, 846
Brunswick Fnd Dollars for Doers Grants, 856
Buhl Fnd - Frick Educational Fund, 859
Bullitt Fnd Grants, 862
Bush Fnd Regional Arts Dev Program II Grants, 878
Butler Mfg Co Fnd Grants, 881
Bydale Fnd Grants, 882
Cabot Corporation Fnd Grants, 887
Caesar Puff Fnd Grants, 890
Caesars Fnd Grants, 891
California Arts Council Statewide Ntwks Grts, 897
California Comm Fnd Human Dev Grants, 902
Cambridge Comm Fnd Grants, 913
Campbell Soup Fnd Grants, 916
Capital Region Comm Fnd Grants, 921
Captain Planet Fnd Grants, 922
Carlisle Fnd Grants, 931
Carl M. Freeman Fnd Grants, 933
Carlos and Marguerite Mason Trust Grants, 934
Carls Fnd Grants, 937
Carnahan-Jackson Fnd Grants, 939
Carpenter Fnd Grants, 943
Carrie E. and Lena V. Glenn Fnd Grants, 944
Carrie Estelle Doheny Fnd Grants, 945
CCHD Comm Dev Grants, 966
Cemala Fnd Grants, 988
Central Carolina Comm Impact Grants, 994
Central Minnesota Comm Fdn Grants, 995
Central New York Comm Fdn Grants, 996
Central Okanagan Fnd Grants, 997
CenturyLink Clarke M Williams Fdn Grts, 998
CFFVR Alcoholism and Drug Abuse Grants, 1001
CFFVR Clintonville Area Fnd Grants, 1008
CFFVR Clintonville Area Fnd Grants, 1007
CFFVR Mielke Family Fnd Grants, 1015
CFFVR Schmidt Family G4 Grants, 1020
CFFVR Women's Fund for the Fox Valley Region Grants, 1025
Chapman Charitable Fnd Grants, 1033
Charity Incorporated Grants, 1035
Charles & Lynn Schusterman Fam Fdn Grants, 1038
Charles Delmar Fnd Grants, 1039
Charles G. Koch Charitable Fnd Grants, 1041
Charles H. Farnsworth Trust Grants, 1043
Charles Stewart Mott Fdn Anti-Poverty Grts, 1054
Charlotte County Comm Fnd Grts, 1056
Chautauqua Region Comm Fdn Grts, 1062
Chesapeake Bay Trust Mini Grants, 1072
Chicago Sun Times Charity Trust Grants, 1098
Christensen Fund Regional Grants, 1112
Cigna Civic Affairs Sponsorships, 1129
Cincinnati Milacron Fnd Grants, 1132
Circle K Corporation Contributions Grants, 1136
Civic Educ Consortium Grants, 1144
Claneil Fnd Grants, 1145
Clarence E Heller Charitable Fdn Grants, 1150
Clark County Comm Fnd Grants, 1156
Clark Fnd Grants, 1157
Claude Worthington Benedum Fdn Grants, 1161
Clay Fnd Grants, 1162
Clayton Baker Trust Grants, 1163
Clowes Fund Grants, 1177
CNCS AmeriCorps State and National Grants, 1182
Coastal Bend Comm Fnd Grants, 1192
Coastal Comm Fdn of SC Grants, 1193
Collins C. Diboll Private Fnd Grants, 1208
Colonel Stanley R. McNeil Fnd Grants, 1210
Colorado Springs Cmty Trust Fund Grants, 1215
Columbus Fnd Competitive Grants, 1220
Columbus Fnd Traditional Grants, 1233
Columbus Jewish Fnd Grants, 1234
Communities Fnd of Texas Grants, 1243
Comm Fnd Alliance City of Evansville Endowment Fund Grants, 1246
Comm Fnd for Grtr Buffalo Grants, 1247
Comm Fnd for Monterey Cty Grants, 1255
Comm Fnd for Muskegon Cty Grants, 1256
Comm Fnd for NE Michigan Grants, 1257
Comm Fnd for Southern Arizona Grants, 1261
Comm Fnd of Bartholomew County Heritage Fund Grants, 1267
Comm Fnd of Bloomington and Monroe County Grants, 1271

Comm Fdn of Boone County Grants, 1274
Comm Fdn of Central Illinois Grants, 1276
Comm Fdn of Grtr Birmingham Grants, 1280
Comm Fdn of Greater Flint Grants, 1282
Comm Fdn of Greater Fort Wayne - Cmty Endwt & Clarke Endwt Grants, 1285
Comm Fdn of Greater Greensboro Grants, 1288
Comm Fdn of Greater Memphis Grts, 1290
Comm Fdn of Howard County Grts, 1297
Comm Fdn of Louisville Grants, 1299
Comm Fdn of Mdl Tennessee Grants, 1300
Comm Fnd of Mt Vernon & Knox County Grants, 1301
Comm Fdn of Muncie & Delaware County Grant, 1302
Comm Fdn of Sarasota County Grts, 1306
Comm Fdn of Shreveport-Bossier Grts, 1307
Comm Fdn of S Alabama Grants, 1308
Comm Fdn of SE Connecticut Grants, 1309
Comm Fdn of Tampa Bay Grants, 1316
Comm Fdn of the Eastern Shore Needs Grants, 1317
Comm Fdn of the Eastern Shore Youth Grants, 1319
Comm Fdn of the Ozarks Grants, 1320
Comm Fdn of Wabash Cty Grants, 1326
Comm Fdn of Western North Carolina Grants, 1327
Comm Fnd Silicon Valley Grants, 1331
Comm Memorial Fnd Grants, 1334
Con Edison Corp Giving Arts & Culture Grants, 1344
Connecticut Comm Fnd Grants, 1350
Conservation, Food, and Health Fnd Grants for Developing Countries, 1359
Cooke Fnd Grants, 1368
Cooper Industries Fnd Grants, 1370
Corina Higginson Trust Grants, 1373
Countess Moira Charitable Fnd Grants, 1381
Covenant Fdn of New York Ignition Grts, 1385
Covenant Fdn of New York Signature Grts, 1386
Cowles Charitable Trust Grants, 1392
Cralle Fnd Grants, 1394
Crossroads Fund Seed Grants, 1400
CSRA Comm Fnd Grants, 1407
Cummins Fnd Grants, 1415
Curtis and Edith Munson Fnd Grants, 1418
Dana Corporation Fnd Grants, 1440
Davenport-Hatch Fnd Grants, 1448
Dave Thomas Fnd for Adoption Grants, 1449
David Bohnett Fnd Grants, 1451
Daywood Fnd Grants, 1465
Deaconess Fnd Advocacy Grants, 1468
Dearborn Comm Fnd City of Aurora Grants, 1470
Decatur County Comm Fnd Large Project Grants, 1476
Dekko Fnd Grants, 1482
Dermody Properties Fnd Grants, 1517
Dolfinger-McMahon Fnd Grants, 1565
Doris and Victor Day Fnd Grants, 1582
Doris Duke Charitable Fnd Arts Grants, 1584
Dorothea Haus Ross Fnd Grants, 1587
Dorr Fnd Grants, 1591
Dr. John T. Macdonald Fnd Grants, 1600
Drs. Bruce and Lee Fnd Grants, 1607
Dwight Stuart Youth Fnd Capacity-Building Initiative Grants, 1627
Dyson Fnd Mid-Hudson Valley Project Grants, 1636
East Tennessee Fnd Grants, 1646
Echoing Green Fellowships, 1650
Eckerd Family Fnd Grants, 1651
Eddie C. and Sylvia Brown Family Fnd Grants, 1653
Edward Bangs Kelley & Elza Kelley Fdn Grts, 1665
Edward S. Moore Fnd Grants, 1668
Edyth Bush Charitable Fnd Grants, 1673
Effie and Wofford Cain Fnd Grants, 1674
Eileen Fisher Activating Leadership Grants for Women and Girls, 1676
Eileen Fisher Women-Owned Business Grants, 1677
Eisner Fnd Grants, 1678
Elizabeth Morse Genius Char Trust Grants, 1682
Elmer L & Eleanor J Andersen Fdn Grnts, 1687
El Paso Comm Fnd Grants, 1688
El Pomar Fnd Awards and Grants, 1690
Emerson Kampen Fnd Grants, 1696
Emily Davie and Joseph S. Kornfeld Fnd Grants, 1697
Emma B. Howe Memorial Fnd Grants, 1700

Ensign-Bickford Fnd Grants, 1709
Erie Comm Fnd Grants, 1750
Essex County Comm Fnd Discretionary Grants, 1752
Eugene M. Lang Fnd Grants, 1764
Eugene McDermott Fnd Grants, 1765
Eva L & Joseph M Bruening Fdn Grants, 1768
Evan and Susan Bayh Fnd Grants, 1769
Evanston Comm Fnd Grants, 1771
Evelyn and Walter Haas, Jr. Fund Immigrant Rights Grants, 1773
Evelyn and Walter Haas, Jr. Fund Nonprofit Leadership Grants, 1774
Ewing Halsell Fnd Grants, 1776
Ewing Marion Kauffman Fnd Grants, 1777
F.M. Kirby Fnd Grants, 1780
F.R. Bigelow Fnd Grants, 1781
Fargo-Moorhead Area Fnd Grants, 1788
Federal Express Corporate Contributions, 1799
Fel-Pro Mecklenburger Fnd Grants, 1800
Field Fnd of Illinois Grants, 1806
Fifth Third Bank Corporate Giving, 1809
FINRA Investor Educ Fnd Financial Educ in Your Comm Grants, 1815
Fireman's Fund Ins Co Heritage Grts, 1818
Flinn Fnd Grants, 1842
Florida Division of Cultural Affairs Endowment Grants, 1851
Foellinger Fnd Grants, 1877
Fondren Fnd Grants, 1878
Fdn for Enhancing Communities Grts, 1893
Fnd for Seacoast Health Grants, 1895
Fnd for the Carolinas Grants, 1896
Fnd NW Grants, 1906
Frances L & Edwin L Cummings Mem Fund, 1919
Francis Beidler Fnd Grants, 1921
Francis L. Abreu Charitable Trust Grants, 1922
Franklin H. Wells and Ruth L. Wells Grants, 1930
Frank M. Tait Fnd Grants, 1932
Frank Stanley Beveridge Fnd Grants, 1936
Fremont Area Comm Fnd Grants, 1955
Frey Fnd Grants, 1963
Fulton County Comm Fnd Grants, 1975
Furth Family Fnd Grants, 1980
G.N. Wilcox Trust Grants, 1982
Gardiner Howland Shaw Fnd Grants, 1986
Gates Fnd Children, Youth & Family Grants, 1989
Gebbie Fnd Grants, 1995
Gene Haas Fnd, 1999
General Motors Fnd Grants, 2004
George B. Page Fnd Grants, 2013
George Fnd Grants, 2018
George Frederick Jewett Fnd Grants, 2019
George Gund Fnd Grants, 2020
George P. Davenport Trust Fund Grants, 2026
George W. Wells Fnd Grants, 2030
Georgiana Goddard Eaton Mem Fund Grts, 2038
German Protestant Orphan Asylum Fnd Grants, 2044
Gil and Dody Weaver Fnd Grants, 2053
Girl's Best Friend Fnd Grants, 2057
GlaxoSmithKline Corporate Grants, 2060
GNOF Exxon-Mobil Grants, 2074
GNOF Norco Comm Grants, 2089
Grand Haven Area Comm Fdn Grants, 2113
Grand Rapids Area Comm Fnd Wyoming Grants, 2116
Grand Rapids Comm Fnd Grants, 2118
Grand Rapids Comm Fdn Ionia Cty Grts, 2119
Grand Rapids Comm Fnd SE Ottawa Grants, 2122
Grand Rapids Comm Fdn Sparta Grts, 2124
Greater Saint Louis Comm Fdn Grants, 2138
Greater Tacoma Comm Fdn Grts, 2139
Greater Worcester Comm Discretionary Grants, 2140
Green Fnd Human Services Grants, 2154
GreenWorks! Butterfly Garden Grants, 2159
Grover Hermann Fnd Grants, 2168
Guido A & Elizabeth H Binda Fdn Grants, 2172
Gulf Coast Fnd of Comm Grants, 2177
H.J. Heinz Company Fnd Grants, 2184
H. Schaffer Fnd Grants, 2187
Harold K. L. Castle Fnd Grants, 2228
Harold Simmons Fnd Grants, 2230

Harris and Eliza Kempner Fund Grants, 2231
Harry A & Margaret D Towsley Fdn Grts, 2236
Harry Edison Fnd, 2241
Harry Kramer Grants, 2242
Hartford Courant Fnd Grants, 2248
Hartford Fnd Regular Grants, 2253
Harvey Randall Wickes Fnd Grants, 2255
Hasbro Children's Fund, 2256
Haymarket People's Fund Sustaining Grants, 2267
Haymarket Urgent Response Grants, 2268
Health Fnd of Grtr Indianapolis Grts, 2282
Heineman Fnd for Research, Education, Charitable and Scientific Purposes, 2290
Helen S. Boylan Fnd Grants, 2298
Helen Steiner Rice Fnd Grants, 2299
Henrietta Tower Wurts Memorial Fnd Grants, 2304
Henry M. Jackson Fnd Grants, 2311
Herbert H & Grace A Dow Fdn Grants, 2315
Herman Goldman Fnd Grants, 2317
Hill Crest Fnd Grants, 2324
Hilton Head Island Fnd Grants, 2330
Holland/Zeeland Comm Fdn Grts, 2345
Honeywell Corp Housing & Shelter Grts, 2357
Honeywell Corp Sustainable Opportunities, 2360
Honor the Earth Grants, 2361
Horace A Kimball & S Ella Kimball Fdn Grts, 2362
Howard and Bush Fnd Grants, 2374
Huber Fnd Grants, 2382
Huffy Fnd Grants, 2384
Humanitas Fnd Grants, 2390
Hyams Fnd Grants, 2413
Hyde Family Fnds Grants, 2414
IBM Comm Dev Grants, 2425
Idaho Comm Eastern Region Competitive Grants, 2432
Illinois DCEO Emerging Technological Enterprises Grants, 2490
Illinois Tool Works Fnd Grants, 2511
Impact 100 Grants, 2522
Independence Comm Fnd Neighborhood Renewal Grants, 2527
Indiana 21st Century Research & Tech Awards, 2528
Indiana Recycling Grants, 2545
Indiana Reg'l Econ Dev Partnership Grts, 2546
Information Soc Innovation Fund Grts, 2554
Int'l Paper Co Fnd Grants, 2568
ISA John Z. Duling Grants, 2587
Ittleson Fnd AIDS Grants, 2589
Ittleson Fnd Mental Health Grants, 2590
J. Edwin Treakle Fnd Grants, 2596
J. F. Maddox Fnd Grants, 2597
J. Spencer Barnes Memorial Fnd Grants, 2606
J. Walton Bissell Fnd Grants, 2608
Jackson Cty Comm Fdn Unrestricted Grts, 2611
Jacob G. Schmidlapp Trust Grants, 2616
Jacobs Family Fdn Vlg Neighborhoods Grants, 2619
James Ford Bell Fnd Grants, 2623
James H. Cummings Fnd Grants, 2626
James J & Angelia M Harris Fdn Grts, 2630
James J. McCann Charitable Trust and McCann Fnd, Inc Grants, 2631
James L & Mary Jane Bowman Char Trust, 2632
James R. Dougherty Jr. Fnd Grants, 2635
Janesville Fnd Grants, 2644
JELD-WEN Fnd Grants, 2661
Jessie Ball Dupont Fund Grants, 2671
Jewish Fund Grants, 2675
JM Fnd Grants, 2681
John Ben Snow Memorial Trust Grants, 2687
John Deere Fnd Grants, 2692
John G. Duncan Trust Grants, 2695
John Merck Fund Grants, 2706
John P. Murphy Fnd Grants, 2708
Johns Manville Fund Grants, 2716
Johnson Cty Comm Fdn Grts, 2723
John W. Alden Trust Grants, 2727
John W & Anna H Hanes Fdn Grants, 2728
Joseph Drown Fnd Grants, 2735
Josephine Goodyear Fnd Grants, 2738
Joseph P. Kennedy Jr. Fnd Grants, 2740
Judith Clark-Morrill Fnd Grants, 2756

PROGRAM TYPE INDEX

Seed Grants / 1121

Kalamazoo Comm Fnd Capacity Building Grants, 2764
Kalamazoo Comm LBGT Equality Fund Grants, 2771
Kalamazoo Comm Fnd Youth Dev Grants, 2773
Kate B. Reynolds Charitable Health Care Grants, 2786
Kate B. Reynolds Charitable Trust Poor and Needy Grants, 2787
Katharine Matthies Fnd Grants, 2788
Katherine John Murphy Fnd Grants, 2790
Kenny's Kids Grants, 2803
Kettering Fund Grants, 2818
Komen Greater NYC Small Grants, 2836
Koret Fnd Grants, 2837
Kosciusko Cty Comm Fdn Grts, 2838
Kroger Fnd Diversity Grants, 2842
Kroger Fdn Grassroots Comty Support Grants, 2843
Kroger Fnd Hunger Relief Grants, 2844
Lettie Pate Evans Fnd Grants, 2887
Liberty Hill Fdn Fund for Change Grts, 2893
Liberty Hill Fnd Seed Fund Grants, 2896
Lied Fnd Trust Grants, 2900
LISC NFL Grassroots Grants, 2913
Lloyd G. Balfour Fnd Attleboro-Specific Charities Grants, 2916
Lubbock Area Fnd Grants, 2931
Lubrizol Corporation Comm Grants, 2932
Lucy Gooding Charitable Fnd Trust, 2936
Lyndhurst Fnd Grants, 2949
M.B. and Edna Zale Fnd Grants, 2950
M.D. Anderson Fnd Grants, 2952
Mabel Louise Riley Fnd Grants, 2959
Mabel Y. Hughes Charitable Trust Grants, 2960
Macquarie Bank Fnd Grants, 2966
Maine Women's Fund Econ Security Grts, 2992
Marathon Petroleum Corporation Grants, 2999
Mardag Fnd Grants, 3001
Marie C. and Joseph C. Wilson Fnd Rochester Small Grants, 3006
Mary D. & Walter F Frear Eleemosynary Trust, 3035
Mary Duke Biddle Fnd Grants, 3036
Mary E. Babcock Fnd, 3038
Mary Owen Borden Fnd Grants, 3046
Mary Reynolds Babcock Fnd Grants, 3047
Max and Anna Levinson Fnd Grants, 3066
Maytree Fdn Assisting Local Leaders w/ Immigrant Employment Strategies Grts, 3070
Maytree Fdn Refugee & Immigrant Grants, 3071
McCarthy Family Fnd Grants, 3073
McConnell Fnd Grants, 3076
McCune Charitable Fnd Grants, 3077
McCune Fnd Human Services Grants, 3080
McGregor Fund Grants, 3082
McInerny Fnd Grants, 3083
McKesson Fnd Grants, 3084
McLean Contributionship Grants, 3088
Meadows Fnd Grants, 3104
MeadWestvaco Sustainable Communities Grants, 3105
Mead Witter Fnd Grants, 3106
Melville Charitable Trust Grants, 3115
Memorial Fnd for Children Grants, 3116
Memorial Fnd Grants, 3117
Merck Family Fund Urban Farming and Youth Leadership Grants, 3119
Merck Family Fund Youth Transforming Urban Communities Grants, 3120
MetLife Building Livable Communities Grants, 3129
Metro Health Fnd Grants, 3133
Meyer Memorial Trust Grassroots Grants, 3147
Meyer Memorial Trust Responsive Grants, 3148
Meyer Memorial Trust Special Grants, 3149
Modest Needs Non-Profit Grants, 3200
Morris & Gwendolyn Cafritz Fdn Grants, 3218
MTV Think Venturer Comnty Svc Grts, 3229
NASE Growth Grants, 3242
National Geographic Society Genographic Legacy Fund Grants, 3274
Needmor Fund Grants, 3289
Nellie Mae Educ Fnd District Change Grants, 3297
Nellie Mae Educ Fnd State Level Systems Change Grants, 3299
New Hampshire Charitable Fnd Grants, 3325

New York Fnd Grants, 3338
NFF Comm Assistance Grants, 3343
NFL Club Matching Youth Football Field/Stadium Grants, 3349
NFL High School Coach of the Week Grant, 3351
NFL High Schl Football Coach of the Yr Awd, 3352
NFL Player Youth Football Camp Grants, 3353
NFWF National Wildlife Refuge Friends Group Grants, 3379
NFWF Nature of Learning Grants, 3381
NGA Heinz Wholesome Memories Intergenerational Garden Awards, 3404
NGA Youth Garden Grants, 3409
Nina Mason Pulliam Charitable Trust Grants, 3443
Noble County Comm Fnd Grants, 3456
Norcliffe Fnd Grants, 3459
Nordson Corporation Fnd Grants, 3462
Norfolk Southern Fnd Grants, 3463
North Carolina GlaxoSmithKline Fdn Grts, 3490
North Dakota Council on the Arts Comm Access Grants, 3494
Northern Chautauqua Comm Fnd Comm Grants, 3499
Northern Chautauqua Cmty Fdn DFT Communications Cmy Betterment Grts, 3500
Northern New York Comm Fdn Grts, 3503
North Georgia Comm Fnd Grants, 3505
NW Minnesota Fnd Women's Fund Grants, 3512
Norton Fnd Grants, 3514
Notsew Orm Sands Fnd Grants, 3516
NWHF Health Advocacy Small Grants, 3537
NYHC Major and Mini Grants, 3567
Oak Fnd Child Abuse Grants, 3632
Ohio Cty Comm Fdn Junior Grts, 3659
Olin Corporation Charitable Trust Grants, 3669
Open Meadows Fnd Grants, 3683
Oppenstein Brothers Fnd Grants, 3685
Orchard Fnd Grants, 3690
PacifiCare Fnd Grants, 3725
Palm Beach and Martin Counties Grants, 3733
Park Fnd Grants, 3739
Patricia Price Peterson Fnd Grants, 3746
Patrick and Aimee Butler Family Fnd Comm Human Services Grants, 3749
Patrick and Anna M. Cudahy Fund Grants, 3751
Patron Saints Fnd Grants, 3753
Paul and Mary Haas Fnd Contributions and Student Scholarships, 3756
Paul E & Klare N Reinhold Fdn Grts, 3758
Paul Green Fnd Human Rights Project Grants, 3761
Pauline E. Fitzpatrick Charitable Trust, 3763
Paul Rapoport Fnd Grants, 3765
PDF Comm Organizing Grants, 3807
Peter Kiewit Fnd General Grants, 3845
Peter Kiewit Fnd Small Grants, 3847
Peter Norton Family Fnd Grants, 3849
Pew Char Trusts Spcl Civic Project Grts, 3859
Peyton Anderson Fnd Grants, 3862
Phelps County Comm Fnd Grants, 3870
Philadelphia Fdn Org'l Effectiveness Grts, 3872
Phil Hardin Fnd Grants, 3875
Philip L. Graham Fund Grants, 3876
Piedmont Health Fnd Grants, 3882
Pinkerton Fnd Grants, 3892
Pinnacle Entertainment Fnd Grants, 3893
Pioneer Hi-Bred Comm Grants, 3895
Playboy Fnd Grants, 3913
Plough Fnd Grants, 3915
PNC Fnd Grow Up Great Grants, 3924
Portland Fnd Grants, 3936
Price Chopper's Golub Fnd Grants, 3950
Priddy Fnd Organizational Dev Grants, 3956
Principal Financial Group Fnd Grants, 3966
Proteus Fund Grants, 3973
Prudential Fdn Econ Dev Grants, 3976
Prudential Fnd Educ Grants, 3977
Public Welfare Fnd Grants, 3984
Quantum Fnd Grants, 3996
R.J. McElroy Trust Grants, 4001
Ralph and Virginia Mullin Fnd Grants, 4012
Ralph M. Parsons Fnd Grants, 4013

Raskob Fdn for Catholic Activities Grts, 4019
Rathmann Family Fnd Grants, 4026
RBC Dain Rauscher Fnd Grants, 4031
RCF General Comm Grants, 4032
RESIST Accessibility Grants, 4054
Rhode Island Fnd Grants, 4073
Richard and Helen DeVos Fnd Grants, 4076
Richard and Rhoda Goldman Fund Grants, 4077
Richard & Susan Smith Family Fdn Grts, 4078
Richard H. Driehaus Fnd Grants, 4084
Richard King Mellon Fnd Grants, 4087
Richland County Bank Grants, 4091
Righteous Persons Fnd Grants, 4093
Ripley County Comm Fnd Grants, 4095
Ripley County Comm Fnd Small Project Grants, 4096
RISCA Design Innovation Grant, 4097
Robert Lee Blaffer Fnd Grants, 4115
Robert R. Meyer Fnd Grants, 4121
Robert Sterling Clark Fnd Government Accountability Grants, 4123
Robin Hood Fnd Grants, 4125
Rochester Area Comm Fnd Grants, 4127
Rockefeller Brothers Fund Charles E. Culpeper Arts and Culture Grants in New York City, 4129
Rohm and Haas Company Grants, 4145
Ronald McDonald House Charities Grants, 4149
Ross Fnd Grants, 4164
Roy & Christine Sturgis Charitable Trust Grts, 4166
Ruth Anderson Fnd Grants, 4176
Ruth H & Warren A Ellsworth Fdn Grts, 4179
Rutter's Children's Charities Grants, 4181
S.E.VEN Fund Mini-Grants, 4196
S. Livingston Mather Charitable Trust Grants, 4200
S. Mark Taper Fnd Grants, 4201
S. Spencer Scott Fund Grants, 4202
Saigh Fnd Grants, 4210
Saint Paul Companies Fnd Grants, 4217
Salem Fnd Charitable Trust Grants, 4223
Samuel Rubin Fnd Grants, 4237
Samuel S. Johnson Fnd Grants, 4239
San Antonio Area Fnd Grants, 4240
San Diego County Bar Fnd Grants, 4241
San Diego Fnd Environment Comm Grants, 4246
San Diego Women's Fnd Grants, 4252
Sands Memorial Fnd Grants, 4256
San Francisco Fnd Comm Health Grants, 4263
Santa Barbara Fdn Monthly Express Grts, 4284
Sapelo Fdn Environmental Protection Grts, 4293
Sarah Scaife Fnd Grants, 4295
Sartain Lanier Family Fnd Grants, 4298
Schering-Plough Fnd Health Grants, 4304
Scherman Fnd Grants, 4305
Schumann Fund for New Jersey Grants, 4311
Scott County Comm Fnd Grants, 4314
Seabury Fnd Grants, 4316
Seattle Fnd Health and Wellness Grants, 4328
Seaver Institute Grants, 4331
Sensient Technologies Fnd Grants, 4337
Sidney Stern Memorial Trust Grants, 4349
Sid W. Richardson Fnd Grants, 4350
Siebert Lutheran Fnd Grants, 4351
Sioux Falls Area Comm Fnd Comm Fund Grants, 4364
Sioux Falls Area Comm Fnd Spot Grants, 4366
Sister Fund Grants for Women's Organizations, 4371
Sisters of Mercy of North Carolina Fdn Grts, 4375
Sisters of St Joseph Healthcare Fdn Grts, 4377
Skillman Fnd Comm Connections Small Grants, 4379
Smith Richardson Fdn Direct Service Grts, 4385
SOBP A.E. Bennett Research Award, 4388
Sonora Area Fnd Competitive Grants, 4404
Sony Corp of America Corp Philant Grants, 4405
Sosland Fnd Grants, 4408
Southern Calif Edison Environmental Grts, 4429
St. Joseph Comm Health Fnd Improving Healthcare Access Grants, 4469
Stackpole-Hall Fnd Grants, 4472
Stark Comm Fnd Grants, 4477
Stewart Huston Charitable Trust Grants, 4505
Stranahan Fnd Grants, 4512
Strowd Roses Grants, 4515

1122 / Seed Grants

Stuart Fnd Grants, 4516
Summit Fnd Grants, 4524
Sunoco Fnd Grants, 4530
SVP Early Childhood Dev and Parenting Grants, 4538
Taylor S. Abernathy and Patti Harding Abernathy Charitable Trust Grants, 4564
Telluride Fnd Comm Grants, 4573
Textron Corporate Contributions Grants, 4601
Thomas Austin Finch, Sr. Fnd Grants, 4613
Thomas B & Elizabeth M Sheridan Fdn Grts, 4614
Thomas C. Ackerman Fnd Grants, 4615
Thompson Fnd Grants, 4623
Time Warner Diverse Voices in the Arts Initiative Grants, 4635
Todd Brock Family Fnd Grants, 4639
Topeka Comm Fnd Grants, 4644
Town Creek Fnd Grants, 4650
Toyota Motor Engineering & Manufacturing North America Grants, 4651
Toyota Motor Mfg of Alabama Grts, 4652
Toyota Motor Manufacturing of Indiana Grants, 4653
Toyota Motor Mfg of Kentucky Grts, 4654
Toyota Motor Mfg of Mississippi Grts, 4655
Toyota Motor Manufacturing of Texas Grants, 4656
Toyota Motor Manuf of West Virginia Grants, 4657
Toyota Motor North America of NY Grts, 4658
Toyota Tech Center Grants, 4660
Toyota USA Fnd Environmental Grants, 4661
Toyota USA Fnd Safety Grants, 4662
Tri-State Comm Twenty-first Century Endowment Fund Grants, 4666
U.S. Lacrosse Emerging Groups Grants, 4703
Union County Comm Fnd Grants, 4711
Union County Fnd Grants, 4712
Unity Fnd Of LaPorte County Grants, 4726
USA Football Equipment Grants, 4735
USAID Media and Elections Program in Rwanda Grants, 4768
USAID Pakistan Private Investment Grants, 4772
USAID Resilience and Economic Growth in the Sahel - Enhanced Resilience Grants, 4779
USDA Rural Business Enterprise Grants, 4823
USFA Dev Grants, 4866
USTA Junior Team Tennis Stipends, 4875
Vanguard Public Fnd Grant Funds, 4904
Van Kampen Boyer Molinari Char Fdn Grts, 4905
Verizon Fnd Vermont Grants, 4924
Victor E. Speas Fnd Grants, 4933
Virginia Comsn for the Arts Proj Grts, 4944
Virginia W. Kettering Fnd Grants, 4950
Vulcan Materials Company Fnd Grants, 4956
WK Kellogg Fdn Secure Families Grants, 4963
WM Keck Fdn Southern California Grts, 4964
Wabash Valley Comm Fnd Grants, 4971
Walter and Elise Haas Fund Grants, 4982
Washington Area Women's Fdn Jobs Fund Grts, 4992
Washington Area Women's Fnd Strategic Opportunity and Partnership Fund Grants, 4996
Wayne County Fnd Grants, 5005
Wayne Cty Fdn Women's Fund Grts, 5006
Weingart Fnd Grants, 5018
Weyerhaeuser Company Fnd Grants, 5053
William G. McGowan Charitable Fund Grants, 5084
William J. and Dorothy K. O'Neill Fnd Grants, 5087
William Robert Baird Charitable Trust Grants, 5093
Windgate Charitable Fnd Grants, 5099
Windward Youth Leadership Fund Grants, 5100
Winston-Salem Fnd Competitive Grts, 5102
YSA Get Ur Good On Grants, 5134
YSA Radio Disney's Hero for Change Award, 5139
Z. Smith Reynolds Fnd Economic Dev Grants, 5144
Z. Smith Reynolds Fnd Democracy and Civic Engagement Grants, 5145

Service Delivery Programs
1st and 10 Fnd Grants, 1
1st Source Fnd Grants, 3
2 Depot Square Ipswich Charitable Fnd Grants, 4
2 Life 18 Fnd Grants, 5
2COBS Private Charitable Fnd Grants, 6

3M Company Health and Human Services Grants, 14
3M Fnd Comm Giving Grants, 15
4imprint One by One Charitable Giving, 16
49ers Fnd Grants, 23
100 Club of Arizona Benefit Grants, 25
100 Club of Arizona Sfty Enhncmt Stipends, 26
118 Fnd Grants, 29
786 Fnd Grants, 33
1104 Fnd Grants, 34
2701 Fnd Grants, 37
A & B Family Fnd Grants, 38
A.C. Ratshesky Fnd Grants, 39
A.H.K. Fnd Grants, 40
A.J. Muste Memorial Institute Int'l Nonviolence Training Fund Grants, 45
A.O. Smith Comm Grants, 46
A.V. Hunter Trust Grants, 47
AACC Project Reach Grants, 56
AAP Comm Access To Child Health Advocacy Training Grants, 62
AAP Access To Child Health Implementation, 63
AAP Access to Child Health Planning Grants, 64
AAP Access To Child Health Residency Training Grants, 65
AAP Access To Child Health Resident Grants, 66
AAP Leonard P. Rome Comm Access to Child Health Visiting Professorships, 67
AAP Resident Initiative Fund Grants, 69
Aaron Catzen Fnd Grants, 70
Aaron Fnd Grants, 72
Aaron Fnd Grants, 73
ABA Labor Lawyer Student Writing Contest, 77
Abbot & Dorothy H Stevens Fdn Grants, 79
Abbott Fund Access to Health Care Grants, 80
Abbott Fund Comm Grants, 81
Abbott Fund Global AIDS Care Grants, 82
Abbott Fund Science Educ Grants, 83
ABC Charities Grants, 85
Abel & Sophia Sheng Charitable Fdn Grts, 86
Abelard Fnd East Grants, 87
Abelard Fnd West Grants, 88
Abel Fnd Grants, 90
Abell-Hanger Fnd Grants, 91
Abell Fdn Comm Dev Grts, 93
Abell Fdn Criminal Justice & Addictions Grts, 95
Abell Fdn Health & Human Svcs Grts, 96
Abernethy Family Fnd Grants, 98
ABIG Fnd Grants, 99
Abington Fnd Grants, 100
Able To Serve Grants, 102
Able Trust Voc Rehab Grants for Agencies, 103
Able Trust Vocational Rehabilitation Grants for Individuals, 104
Aboudane Family Fnd Grants, 106
ABS Fnd Grants, 107
ACE Charitable Fnd Grants, 111
ACF ACYF Runaway and Homeless Youth Basic Center Grants, 112
ACF Adoption Opportunities Project Grants, 113
ACF Assets for Indep Demo Grants, 114
ACF Assets for Independence Individual Dev Account Grants, 115
ACF Comm-Based Abstinence Educ Grants, 116
ACF Ethnic Comm Self-Help Grants, 118
ACF Fnd Grants, 119
ACF Head Start and Early Head Start Grants, 120
ACF Mentoring Children of Prisoners Grants, 121
ACF Native American Social and Economic Dev Strategies Grants, 123
ACF Preferred Communities Grants, 124
ACF Supplemental Services for Recently Arrived Refugees Grants, 125
A Charitable Fnd Grants, 126
Achelis Fnd Grants, 127
A Child Waits Fnd Grants, 128
ACTION Council of Monterey County Grants, 134
Active Awareness Fund Grants, 136
Acushnet Fnd Grants, 143
Adam Reineman Charitable Trust Grants, 144
Adam Richter Charitable Trust Grants, 145

Adams Cty Comm Fdn of Indiana Grts, 148
Adams County Comm Fnd of Pennsylvania Grants, 149
Adams Family Fnd of Tennessee Grants, 152
Adams Rotary Memorial Fund A Grants, 157
Adelaide Breed Bayrd Fnd Grants, 161
Adelaide Christian Home For Children Grants, 162
Adelaide Dawson Lynch Trust Grants, 163
Adler-Clark Electric Comm Commitment Grants, 164
Administaff Comm Affairs Grants, 165
Administration on Aging Senior Medicare Patrol Project Grants, 166
Adobe Comm Investment Grants, 168
Adobe Hunger and Homelessness Grants, 169
Advanced Micro Dvcs Comm Affairs Grts, 172
Advancing Colorado's Mental Health Care Project Grants, 173
Advocate Safehouse Project Grants, 174
AEC Trust Grants, 175
AEGON Transamerica Fdn Civic Grants, 177
AEGON Transamerica Fdn Health and Welfare Grants, 179
AEP Corporate Giving Grants, 180
Aetna Fnd Health Grants in Connecticut, 184
Aetna Fnd Obesity Grants, 185
Aetna Fnd Racial and Ethnic Health Care Equity Grants, 186
Aetna Fnd Regional Health Grants, 187
AFG Industries Grants, 191
African American Fund of New Jersey Grants, 192
A Friends' Fnd Trust Grants, 194
A Fund for Women Grants, 195
Agape Fnd for Nonviolent Social Change Alice Hamburg Emergency Grants, 196
Agape Fnd for Nonviolent Social Change Board of Trustees Grants, 197
Agere Corporate and Comm Involvement Grants, 199
Agnes B. Hunt Trust Grants, 202
Agnes M. Lindsay Trust Grants, 203
A Good Neighbor Fnd Grants, 204
Agway Fnd Grants, 205
Ahmanson Fnd Grants, 207
AHS Fnd Grants, 208
Aid for Starving Children African American Independence Single Mother's Grants, 210
Air Products and Chemicals Grants, 216
Akzo Nobel Chemicals Grants, 219
Alabama Humanities Fnd Mini Grants, 231
Aladdin Industries Fnd Grants, 263
Alaska Airlines Corporate Giving Grants, 320
Alaska Airlines Fnd Grants, 321
Alberta Law Fnd Grants, 338
Albert and Bessie Mae Kronkosky Charitable Fnd Grants, 339
Albert and Margaret Alkek Fnd Grants, 340
Albert B Cuppage Charitable Fdn Grts, 341
Albert E. and Birdie W. Einstein Fund Grants, 342
Alberto Culver Corporate Contributions Grants, 343
Albert Pick Jr. Fund Grants, 344
Albertson's Charitable Giving Grants, 345
Albert W. Cherne Fnd Grants, 346
Albert W. Rice Charitable Fnd Grants, 347
Albuquerque Comm Fnd Grants, 348
Alcatel-Lucent Technologies Fnd Grants, 349
Alcoa Fnd Grants, 350
Alexander & Baldwin Fnd Hawaiian and Pacific Island Grants, 352
Alexander & Baldwin Fdn Mainland Grants, 353
Alexander and Margaret Stewart Trust Grants, 354
Alexander Eastman Fnd Grants, 355
Alexander Fnd Emergency Grants, 356
Alexander Fnd Holiday Grants, 357
Alexander H. Bright Charitable Trust Grants, 358
Alex Stern Family Fnd Grants, 360
Alfred & Tillie Shemanski Testamentary Grants, 363
Alfred C & Ersa S Arbogast Fdn Grts, 365
Alfred E. Chase Charitable Fnd Grants, 366
Alfred J Mcallister and Dorothy N Mcallister Fnd Grants, 367
Alfred P Sloan Fdn Selected Nat'l Issues Grts, 370
Alice C. A. Sibley Fund Grants, 371

PROGRAM TYPE INDEX

Service Delivery Programs / 1123

Allan C. and Leila J. Garden Fnd Grants, 374
Allegan County Comm Fnd Grants, 375
Allegheny Technologies Charitable Trust, 377
Allen Hilles Fund Grants, 378
Allen Lane Fnd Grants, 379
Allen P & Josephine B Green Fdn Grts, 380
All for the Earth Fnd Grants, 381
Alliance for Comm Trees Home Depot Fnd NeighborWoods Grants, 382
Alliance Healthcare Fnd Grants, 383
Alliant Energy Fnd Comm Grants, 384
Alliant Energy Fnd Hometown Challenge Grants, 385
Allstate Corporate Giving Grants, 386
Allstate Corp Hometown Commitment Grants, 387
Allstate Fnd Safe and Vital Communities Grants, 390
Allyn Fnd Grants, 392
Alpha Kappa Alpha Educational Advancement Fnd Comm Assistance Awards, 393
ALSAM Fnd Grants, 395
Alticor Corporation Comm Contributions Grants, 396
Altman Fnd Strengthening Communities Grants, 398
Altria Group Positive Youth Dev Grts, 401
Alvin & Fanny Blaustein Thalheimer Fdn Grts, 403
Alvin and Lucy Owsley Fnd Grants, 404
ALZA Corporate Contributions Grants, 405
Amador Comm Fnd Grants, 408
AMA Fdn Fund for Better Health Grts, 409
AMA Fnd Healthy Communities/Healthy America Grants, 410
Amarillo Area/Harrington Fnds Grants, 412
Ambrose and Ida Fredrickson Fnd Grants, 414
Ambrose Monell Fnd Grants, 415
AMD Corporate Contributions Grants, 416
Amelia Sillman Rockwell and Carlos Perry Rockwell Charities Fund Grants, 417
American Chemical Scty Corp Assocs Seed Grts, 425
American Electric Power Grants, 428
American Express Charitable Fund Grants, 429
American Express Fnd Comm Service Grants, 430
American Forests Global ReLeaf Grants, 434
American Honda Fnd Grants, 439
American Jewish World Service Grants, 441
American Psychiatric Fnd Helping Hands Grants, 443
American Savings Fnd Grants, 445
America the Beautiful Fund Operation Green Plant Grants, 451
Amerigroup Fnd Grants, 452
AmerUs Group Charitable Fnd, 455
Amgen Fnd Grants, 456
AMI Semiconductors Corporate Grants, 457
Anderson Fnd Grants, 460
Andre Agassi Charitable Fnd Grants, 461
Angels Baseball Fnd Grants, 465
Angels for Kids Fnd Grants, 466
Angels in Motion Fnd Grants, 467
Angels Wings Fnd Int'l Grants, 469
Anheuser-Busch Fnd Grants, 470
Anna Fitch Ardenghi Trust Grants, 472
Ann & Robert H Lurie Family Fdn Grants, 473
Ann Arbor Area Comm Fnd Grants, 474
Anne J. Caudal Fnd Grants, 475
Anne L. and George H. Clapp Charitable and Educational Trust Grants, 476
Anne Thorne Weaver Family Fnd Grants, 478
Annie's Cases for Causes Product Donations, 479
Annie's Grants for Gardens, 480
Annie E. Casey Fnd Grants, 481
Annie Sinclair Knudsen Memorial Fund/Kaua'i Comm Grants, 482
Ann L. and Carol Green Rhodes Grants, 483
Ann Peppers Fnd Grants, 484
Annunziata Sanguinetti Fnd Grants, 485
Ansell, Zaro, Grimm & Aaron Fdn Grts, 487
Anthem Blue Cross and Blue Shield Grants, 488
Anthony R. Abraham Fnd Grants, 489
AON Fnd Grants, 491
Appalachian Comm Fund Special Opportunities Grants, 497
Appalachian Regional Commission Distressed Counties Grants, 503

Appalachian Regional Commission Health Care Grants, 507
Applied Biosystems Grants, 514
APSAA Fnd Grants, 516
APS Fnd Grants, 518
A Quiet Place Grants, 520
Aquila Corporate Grants, 521
Aratani Fnd Grants, 523
Arcadia Fnd Grants, 525
Archer Daniels Midland Fnd Grants, 527
ARCO Fnd Educ Grants, 528
Arcus Fnd Gay and Lesbian Fund Grants, 530
Arcus Fnd National Fund Grants, 531
Argyros Fnd Grants, 532
Arie and Ida Crown Memorial Grants, 533
Arizona Cardinals Grants, 534
Arizona Comm Fnd Grants, 540
Arizona Diamondbacks Charities Grants, 542
Arizona Fnd for Women Deborah G. Carstens Fund Grants, 543
Arizona Fnd for Women General Grants, 544
Arizona Republic Fnd Grants, 546
Arizona Republic Newspaper Corp Contribs, 547
Arkansas Comm Fnd Arkansas Black Hall of Fame Grants, 559
Arkansas Comm Fnd Giving Tree Grants, 560
Arkansas Comm Fnd Grants, 561
Arkell Hall Fnd Grants, 562
Arlington Comm Fnd Grants, 564
Armstrong McDonald Fnd Grants, 565
Aronson Fnd Grants, 567
ARS Fnd Grants, 568
Arthur and Rochelle Belfer Fnd Grants, 570
Arthur Ashley Williams Fnd Grants, 572
ArvinMeritor Fdn Arts & Culture Grts, 582
ArvinMeritor Fdn Human Svcs Grts, 584
ArvinMeritor Grants, 585
Ashland Corporate Contributions Grants, 587
Asian American Institute Impact Fellowships, 588
Aspen Comm Fnd Grants, 592
Assisi Fnd of Memphis General Grants, 594
Assisi Fnd of Memphis Mini Grants, 595
AT&T Fnd Civic and Comm Service Grants, 599
Atherton Family Fnd Grants, 604
Athwin Fnd Grants, 605
Atkinson Fnd Comm Grants, 606
Atlanta Fnd Grants, 608
Atlanta Women's Fnd Grants, 609
Atran Fnd Grants, 610
Auburn Fnd Grants, 611
Audrey and Sydney Irmas Charitable Fnd Grants, 612
Austin-Bailey Health and Wellness Fnd Grants, 614
Austin Comm Fnd Grants, 616
Austin S. Nelson Fnd Grants, 617
Autauga Area Comm Fnd Grants, 618
Autodesk Comm Relations Grants, 619
AutoZone Comm Relations Grants, 621
Autzen Fnd Grants, 622
Avery Dennison Fnd Grants, 623
Avon Products Fnd Grants, 625
AWDF Main Grants, 627
AXA Fnd Scholarships, 629
Ayres Fnd Grants, 630
Azadoutioun Fnd Grants, 631
Babcock Charitable Trust Grants, 632
Back Home Again Fnd Grants, 633
Bailey Fnd Grants, 635
Balfe Family Fnd Grants, 636
Ball Brothers Fnd General Grants, 637
Baltimore Comm Fnd Human Services Grants, 644
Baltimore Comm Fnd Kelly People's Emergency Fund Grants, 645
Banfi Vintners Fnd Grants, 653
Bank of America Critical Needs Grants, 656
Bank of America Charitable Fnd Matching Gifts, 658
Baptist-Trinity Lutheran Legacy Fnd Grants, 663
Baptist Comm Ministries Grants, 664
Barberton Comm Fnd Grants, 666
Baring Fnd Grants, 667
Barker Fnd Grants, 668

Barker Welfare Fnd Grants, 669
Barnes and Noble National Sponsorships and Charitable Donations, 671
Barra Fnd Comm Fund Grants, 673
Barra Fnd Project Grants, 674
Barr Fnd Grants , 677
Barr Fund Grants, 678
Batchelor Fnd Grants, 679
Baton Rouge Area Every Kid a King Grants, 681
Baton Rouge Area Fnd Grants, 682
Batters Up USA Equipment Grants, 683
Battle Creek Comm Fnd Grants, 684
Battle Creek Comm Fdn Mini-Grants, 685
Baxter Int'l Corporate Giving Grants, 689
Baxter Int'l Fnd Grants, 691
Bayer Advanced Grow Together with Roses School Garden Awards, 695
BBVA Compass Fnd Charitable Grants, 703
BCBSM Fnd Comm Health Matching Grants, 707
BCBSM Fdn Proposal Dev Awds, 709
BCBSNC Fnd Fit Together Grants, 711
BCBSNC Fnd Grants, 712
BCBS of Massachusetts Fnd Grants, 713
Beazley Fnd Grants, 714
Beckley Area Fnd Grants, 716
Beerman Fnd Grants, 717
Beim Fnd Grants, 718
Belk Fnd Grants, 721
Bemis Company Fnd Grants, 723
Ben & Jerry's Fnd Grants, 724
Ben B. Cheney Fnd Grants, 725
Bender Fnd Grants, 726
Benton Comm Fnd Grants, 730
Benton County Fnd Grants, 731
Benwood Fnd Comm Grants, 732
Benwood Fnd Focus Area Grants, 733
Berks County Comm Fnd Grants, 734
Bernard F & Alva B Gimbel Fdn Grts, 740
Bernard F. Reynolds Charitable Trust Grants, 741
Bernice Barbour Fnd Grants, 743
Bertha Wolf-Rosenthal Comm Service Stipend, 746
Besser Fnd Grants, 748
Better Way Fnd Grants, 754
Better World Books LEAP Grants for Libraries, 755
BHHS Legacy Fnd Grants, 758
Bicknell Fund Grants, 759
Bikes Belong Grants, 763
Bill and Katie Weaver Charitable Trust Grants, 764
Bill and Melinda Gates Ag Dev Grants, 765
Bill Hannon Fnd Grants, 771
Biogen Corporate Giving Grants, 773
Birmingham Fnd Grants, 774
Bitha Godfrey & Maude J. Thomas Charitable Fnd Grants, 776
BJ's Charitable Fnd Grants, 777
BJ's Wholesale Clubs Local Charitable Giving, 778
Black River Falls Area Fnd Grants, 782
Blade Fnd Grants, 783
Blanche and Irving Laurie Fnd Grants, 784
Blanche M. Walsh Charity Trust Grants, 786
Blandin Fdn Expand Opportunity Grants, 787
Blandin Fnd Invest Early Grants, 788
Blandin Fnd Itasca County Area Vitality Grants, 789
Blowitz-Ridgeway Fnd Grants, 792
Blue Cross Blue Shield of Minnesota Fdn Health Equity: Bldg Health Equity Together Grts, 793
Blue Cross Blue Shield of Minnesota Fnd - Healthy Children: Growing Up Healthy Grants, 794
Blue Grass Comm Fnd Grants, 799
Blue Mountain Comm Fnd Grants, 800
Blue River Comm Fnd Grants, 801
Blue Shield of California Grants, 802
Blum-Kovler Fnd Grants, 803
Blumenthal Fnd Grants, 804
BoatUS Fnd Grassroots Grants, 805
Bodenwein Public Benevolent Fdn Grants, 806
Bodman Fnd Grants, 807
Boeckmann Charitable Fnd Grants, 808
Boettcher Fnd Grants, 810
Bohemian Fnd Pharos Fund Grants, 811

1124 / Service Delivery Programs

PROGRAM TYPE INDEX

Booth-Bricker Fund Grants, 815
Booth Ferris Fnd Grants, 816
Boston Fnd Grants, 819
Boston Globe Fnd Grants, 821
Boston Jewish Cmnty Women's Fund Grts, 822
Bowling Green Comm Fnd Grants, 824
Brad Brock Family Fnd Grants, 827
Bradley-Turner Fnd Grants, 828
Brett Family Fnd Grants, 833
Brian G. Dyson Fnd Grants, 834
Bridgestone/Firestone Trust Fund Grants, 836
Bright Family Fnd Grants, 837
Bright Promises Fnd Grants, 838
Bristol-Myers Squibb Fnd Comm Grants, 840
Bristol-Myers Squibb Patient Assistance Grants, 841
Brookdale Fnd Leadership in Aging Fellowships, 844
Brookdale Fdn Relatives as Parents Grts, 846
Brooklyn Benevolent Society Grants, 847
Brown County Comm Fnd Grants, 853
Brown Fnd Grants, 854
Brunswick Fnd Dollars for Doers Grants, 856
Build-A-Bear Workshop Bear Hugs Fnd Lit and Educ Grants, 860
Build-A-Bear Workshop Fnd Grants, 861
Burden Trust Grants, 864
Burlington Northern Santa Fe Fdn Grants, 866
Burning Fnd Grants, 867
Burton D Morgan Fdn Hudson Comty Grts, 869
Burton G. Bettingen Grants, 871
Bush Fnd Arts & Humanities Cap Projects Grants, 872
Bush Fdn Health & Human Svcs Grts, 875
Business Bank of Nevada Comm Grants, 879
Cable Positive's Tony Cox Comm Fund, 886
Caddock Fnd Grants, 888
Caesar Puff Fnd Grants, 890
Caesars Fnd Grants, 891
Caleb C. and Julia W. Dula Educational and Charitable Fnd Grants, 893
California Comm Fnd Health Care Grants, 901
California Comm Fnd Human Dev Grants, 902
California Endowment Innovative Ideas Challenge Grants, 904
California Pizza Kitchen Fnd Grants, 907
Callaway Golf Company Fnd Grants, 910
Callaway Golf Company Fnd Violence Prevention Grants, 911
Cambridge Comm Fnd Grants, 913
Camp-Younts Fnd Grants, 914
Campbell Hoffman Fnd Grants, 915
Canadian Optometric Ed Trust Fund Grts, 918
Capital City Bank Group Fnd Grants, 920
Cardinal Health Fnd Grants, 923
Cargill Citizenship Fund-Corp Gvg Grants, 925
Carl & Eloise Pohlad Family Fdn Grants, 927
Carl C. Icahn Fnd Grants, 929
Carlisle Fnd Grants, 931
Carl M. Freeman Fnd FACES Grants, 932
Carl M. Freeman Fnd Grants, 933
Carlos and Marguerite Mason Trust Grants, 934
Carl R. Hendrickson Family Fnd Grants, 935
Carlsbad Charitable Fnd Grants, 936
Carl W. and Carrie Mae Joslyn Trust Grants, 938
Carnahan-Jackson Fnd Grants, 939
Carolyn Fnd Grants, 942
Carpenter Fnd Grants, 943
Carrie Estelle Doheny Fnd Grants, 945
Cartis Creative Services Grants, 948
Cass County Comm Fnd Grants, 952
Caterpillar Fnd Grants, 954
Catherine Kennedy Home Fnd Grants, 955
CCF Comm Priorities Fund, 961
CCHD Comm Dev Grants, 966
CCHD Economic Dev Grants, 967
CE and S Fnd Grants, 985
Cemala Fnd Grants, 988
CenterPointEnergy Minnegasco Grants, 993
Central Carolina Comm Impact Grants, 994
Central New York Comm Fdn Grants, 996
Ceres Fnd Grants, 999
Cessna Fnd Grants, 1000

CFFVR Basic Needs Gvg Partnership Grts, 1002
CFFVR Capacity Building Grants, 1004
CFFVR Project Grants, 1017
CFFVR Shawano Area Comm Fnd Grants, 1021
CFFVR Waupaca Area Comm Fnd Grants, 1023
CFNCR Starbucks Memorial Fund, 1026
Champ-A Champion Fur Kids Grants, 1028
Champlin Fnds Grants, 1029
Chapman Charitable Fnd Grants, 1033
Chapman Family Charitable Trust Grants, 1034
Charity Incorporated Grants, 1035
CharityWorks Grants, 1036
Charles A. Frueauff Fnd Grants, 1037
Charles F. Bacon Trust Grants, 1040
Charles G. Koch Charitable Fnd Grants, 1041
Charles H. Dater Fnd Grants, 1042
Charles H. Farnsworth Trust Grants, 1043
Charles H. Hall Fnd, 1044
Charles H. Pearson Fnd Grants, 1045
Charles Lafitte Fnd Grants, 1049
Charles M & Mary D Grant Fdn Grants, 1050
Charles M. Bair Family Trust Grants, 1051
Charles Nelson Robinson Fund Grants, 1052
Charles Stewart Mott Fnd Grants, 1055
Charlotte County Comm Fnd Grts, 1056
Charlotte Martin Fnd Youth Grants, 1057
Charlotte R. Schmidlapp Fund Grants, 1058
Chase Paymentech Corporate Giving Grants, 1059
Chatham Athletic Fnd Grants, 1060
Chatlos Fnd Grants, 1061
CHCF Grants, 1063
CHCF Local Coverage Expansion Initiative, 1064
CHC Fnd Grants, 1065
Chesapeake Corporation Fnd Grants, 1076
ChevronTexaco Contributions Program, 1078
Chicago Comm Trust Arts & Culture Grts: Improving Access to Arts Lrng Opportunities, 1082
Chicago Comm Trust Arts and Culture Grants: SMART Growth, 1083
Chicago Comm Trust Fellowships, 1086
Chicago Comm Trust Health Grants, 1087
Chicago Comm Trust Housing Grants: Advancing Affordable Rental Housing, 1088
Chicago Comm Trust Hsg Grants: Preserving Hm Ownership & Preventing Foreclosure, 1089
Chicago Comm Trust Housing Grants: Preventing and Ending Homelessness, 1090
Chicago Comm Trust Poverty Alleviation Grants, 1091
Chicago Comm Trust Preventing and Eliminating Hunger Grants, 1092
Chicago Comm Pub Safety & Justice Grants, 1093
Chicago Comm Trust Workforce Grants, 1094
Chicago Fnd for Women Grants, 1096
Chicago Sun Times Charity Trust Grants, 1098
Chicago Title & Trust Co Fdn Grants, 1099
Chicago White Metal Charitable Fdn Grants, 1102
Child's Dream Grants, 1104
Child Care Center Enhancement Grants, 1105
Children Affected by AIDS Fnd Camp Network Grants, 1106
Children Affected by AIDS Fnd Family Assistance Emergency Fund Grants, 1107
Chiron Fnd Comm Grants, 1111
Christine and Katharina Pauly Charitable Grants, 1114
Christy-Houston Fnd Grants, 1115
Chula Vista Charitable Fnd Grants, 1116
CICF City of Noblesville Comm Grant, 1118
CICF Indianapolis Fdn Comm Grants, 1123
CICF Jn Harrison Brown & Robert Burse Grt, 1125
CICF Legacy Fund Grants, 1126
Cigna Civic Affairs Sponsorships, 1129
CIGNA Fnd Grants, 1130
Cinergy Fnd Grants, 1133
Cingular Wireless Charitable Contributions, 1134
Circle K Corporation Contributions Grants, 1136
CIT Corporate Giving Grants, 1138
Citigroup Fnd Grants, 1139
Citizens Bank Mid-Atlantic Char Fdn Grts, 1140
Claneil Fnd Grants, 1145
Clara Abbott Fnd Need-Based Grants, 1146

Clara Blackford Smith and W. Aubrey Smith Charitable Fnd Grants, 1147
Clarcor Fnd Grants, 1148
Claremont Comm Fnd Grants, 1149
Clarence E Heller Charitable Fdn Grants, 1150
Clark-Winchcole Fnd Grants, 1152
Clark and Ruby Baker Fnd Grants, 1154
Clark County Comm Fnd Grants, 1156
Clark Fnd Grants, 1157
Claude A. and Blanche McCubbin Abbott Charitable Trust Grants, 1158
Claude Bennett Family Fnd Grants, 1159
Claude Worthington Benedum Fdn Grants, 1161
Clay Fnd Grants, 1162
Clayton Baker Trust Grants, 1163
Cleo Fnd Grants, 1164
Cleveland-Cliffs Fnd Grants, 1165
Cleveland Browns Fnd Grants, 1166
Cleveland Fnd Capital Grants, 1167
Cleveland Fnd Comm Responsive Grants, 1168
Cleveland Fnd Fenn Educational Fund Grants, 1169
Cleveland Fdn Lake-Geauga Fund Grts, 1170
Cleveland Fnd Neighborhood Connections Grants, 1171
Cleveland H. Dodge Fnd Grants, 1172
CLIF Bar Family Fnd Grants, 1173
Clinton County Comm Fnd Grants, 1174
Clipper Ship Fnd Grants, 1175
Clowes Fund Grants, 1177
CMA Fnd Grants, 1178
CNA Fnd Grants, 1179
CNCS AmeriCorps Indian Tribes Plng Grts, 1180
CNCS AmeriCorps NCCC Project Grants, 1181
CNCS AmeriCorps State and National Grants, 1182
CNCS AmeriCorps State & Nat Planning Grants, 1183
CNCS Foster Grandparent Projects Grants, 1185
CNCS Senior Companion Grants, 1187
CNCS Senior Corps Retired and Senior Volunteer Grants, 1188
CNCS Social Innovation Grants, 1189
Coastal Bend Comm Fnd Grants, 1192
Coastal Comm Fdn of SC Grants, 1193
Cockrell Fnd Grants, 1196
Cogswell Benevolent Trust Grants, 1198
Coleman Fnd Deval Disabilities Grants, 1200
Coleman Fnd Entrepreneurship Educ Grants, 1201
Colgate-Palmolive Company Grants, 1202
Colin Higgins Fnd Grants, 1204
Collins Fnd Grants, 1209
Colonel Stanley R. McNeil Fnd Grants, 1210
Colorado Clean Enrg Fd Solar Innovation Grts, 1212
Colorado Interstate Gas Grants, 1213
Colorado Renewables in Performance Contracting Grants, 1214
Colorado Springs Cmty Trust Fund Grants, 1215
Colorado Trust Partnerships for Health Init, 1217
Columbia Gas of Virginia Grants, 1218
Columbus Fnd Allen Eiry Fund Grants, 1219
Columbus Fnd Competitive Grants, 1220
Columbus Fnd Dorothy E. Ann Fund (D.E.A.F.) Traditional Grants, 1221
Columbus Fnd J. Floyd Dixon Grants, 1222
Columbus Fnd John W. and Edna McManus Shepard Fund Grants, 1223
Columbus Fnd Mary Eleanor Morris Fund Grants, 1225
Columbus Fdn Neighborhood Partnership Grts, 1226
Columbus Fnd Paul G. Duke Grants, 1227
Columbus Fnd R. Alvin Stevenson Fund Grants, 1228
Columbus Fnd Robert E. and Genevieve B. Schaefer Fund Grants, 1229
Columbus Fnd Siemer Family Grants, 1231
Columbus Fnd Traditional Grants, 1233
Comcast Fnd Grants, 1235
Comer Fnd Grants, 1236
Comerica Charitable Fnd Grants, 1237
Commission on Religion in Appalachia Grants, 1238
Commonweal Fnd Comm Assistance Grants, 1239
Commonwealth Edison Grants, 1240
Comm Fnd AIDS Endwt Awds, 1245
Comm Fnd Alliance City of Evansville Endowment Fund Grants, 1246

PROGRAM TYPE INDEX

Service Delivery Programs / 1125

Comm Fdn for Monterey Cty Grants, 1255
Comm Fdn for Muskegon Cty Grants, 1256
Comm Fdn for NE Michigan Grants, 1257
Comm Fdn for Southern Arizona Grants, 1261
Comm Fdn in Jacksonville Art Ventures Small Arts Orgs Professional Assistance Grts, 1262
Comm Fnd in Jacksonville Senior Roundtable Aging Adults Grants, 1263
Comm Fnd of Bartholomew Cnty Heritage Grants, 1267
Comm Fnd of Bloomington and Monroe County Grants, 1271
Comm Fdn of Boone County Grants, 1274
Comm Fnd of Broward Grants, 1275
Comm Fdn of Central Illinois Grants, 1276
Comm Fdn of E Ctrl Illinois Grts, 1278
Comm Fdn of Grtr Birmingham Grants, 1280
Comm Fdn of Greater Flint Grants, 1282
Comm Fdn of Greater Fort Wayne - Cmty Endwt & Clarke Endwt Grants, 1285
Comm Fnd of Greater Fort Wayne Edna Grants, 1286
Comm Fdn of Greater Greensboro Grants, 1288
Comm Fdn of Greater Tampa Grts, 1292
Comm Fnd of Greenville Hollingsworth Funds Program/Project Grants, 1296
Comm Fdn of Mdl Tennessee Grants, 1300
Comm Fnd of Mt Vernon & Knox County Grants, 1301
Comm Fnd of Muncie & Delaware County Grant, 1302
Comm Fnd of Muncie and Delaware County Maxon Grants, 1303
Comm Fdn of Riverside County Grts, 1304
Comm Fnd of Santa Cruz County Grants, 1305
Comm Fdn of Sarasota County Grts, 1306
Comm Fdn of Shreveport-Bossier Grts, 1307
Comm Fnd of SE Connecticut Grants, 1309
Comm Fnd of South Puget Sound Grants, 1311
Comm Fnd of St. Joseph County African American Comm Grants, 1312
Comm Fnd of St. Joseph County ArtsEverywhere Grants, 1313
Comm Fnd of St. Joseph County Special Project Challenge Grants, 1314
Comm Fnd of the Verdugos Grants, 1322
Comm Fnd of Western North Carolina Grants, 1327
Comm Fnd Partners Lawrence County Grants, 1328
Comm Fnd Partnerships - Martin County Grants, 1329
Comm Fnd Silicon Valley Grants, 1331
Comm Impact Fund, 1332
Comm in the Connecting AAPIs To Advocate and Lead Grants, 1333
Comm Memorial Fnd Grants, 1334
Comm Partners on Waste Educ and Reduction, 1335
Comm Tech Fdn of California Building Communities Through Tech Grants, 1336
Comprehensive Health Educ Fdn Grts, 1337
Compton Fnd Grants, 1338
Computer Associates Comm Grants, 1341
Cone Health Fnd Grants, 1348
Connecticut Comm Fnd Grants, 1350
Connecticut Health Fnd Health Initiative Grants, 1351
Connecticut Light & Power Corp Contribs, 1352
Connelly Fnd Grants, 1353
ConocoPhillips Fnd Grants, 1354
Conservation, Food, and Health Fnd Grants for Developing Countries, 1359
Constantin Fnd Grants, 1362
Consumers Energy Fnd, 1365
Cooke-Hay Fnd Grants, 1367
Cooke Fnd Grants, 1368
Cooper Fnd Grants, 1369
Cooper Industries Fnd Grants, 1370
Coors Brewing Corporate Contributions Grants, 1371
Corina Higginson Trust Grants, 1373
Cornerstone Fdn of NE Wisconsin Grants, 1375
Countess Moira Charitable Fnd Grants, 1381
Covenant Educational Fnd Grants, 1383
Covenant Fnd of Atlanta Grants, 1384
Covenant Mountain Ministries Grants, 1387
Covenant to Care for Children Critical Goods, 1388
Covenant to Care for Children Enrichment Fund Grants, 1389

Covidien Medical Product Donations, 1390
Covidien Partnership for Neighborhood Wellness Grants, 1391
Cowles Charitable Trust Grants, 1392
Crail-Johnson Fnd Grants, 1393
Cralle Fnd Grants, 1394
Cranston Fnd Grants, 1395
Credit Suisse First Boston Fnd Grants, 1397
Crescent Porter Hale Fnd Grants, 1398
Crossroads Fund Seed Grants, 1400
Cruise Industry Charitable Fnd Grants, 1404
Crystelle Waggoner Charitable Trust Grants, 1405
CSL Behring Local Empowerment for Advocacy Dev Grants, 1406
CSRA Comm Fnd Grants, 1407
CSX Corporate Contributions Grants, 1408
Cudd Fnd Grants, 1410
Cullen Fnd Grants, 1411
Cultural Society of Filipino Americans Grants, 1412
CUNA Mutual Group Fnd, 1416
CVS All Kids Can Grants, 1420
CVS Caremark Charitable Trust Grants, 1421
CVS Comm Grants, 1422
Cyrus Eaton Fnd Grants, 1423
D.F. Halton Fnd Grants, 1424
DV & Ida J McEachern Char Trust Grts, 1425
DaimlerChrysler Corporation Fund Grants, 1432
Dairy Queen Corporate Contributions Grants, 1433
Dallas Fnd Grants, 1436
Dallas Mavericks Fnd Grants, 1437
Dammann Fnd Grants, 1439
Daniels Fund Grants, 1443
Dan Murphy Fnd Grants, 1444
Daphne Seybolt Culpeper Mem Fdn Grts, 1445
Darden Restaurants Fnd Grants, 1446
Dave Coy Fnd Grants, 1447
Davenport-Hatch Fnd Grants, 1448
Dave Thomas Fnd for Adoption Grants, 1449
David Geffen Fnd Grants, 1452
David N. Lane Trust Grants for Aged and Indigent Women, 1453
David Robinson Fnd Grants, 1454
Daviess County Comm Fnd Health Grants, 1457
Daviess County Comm Human Services Grants, 1458
Dayton Power and Light Fnd Grants, 1464
Daywood Fnd Grants, 1465
Deaconess Comm Fnd Grants, 1467
Deaconess Fnd Advocacy Grants, 1468
Dean Foods Comm Involvement Grants, 1469
Dekko Fnd Grants, 1482
Dell Fnd Open Grants, 1490
Delta Air Lines Fdn Cmty Enrichment Grants, 1494
Deluxe Corporation Fnd Grants, 1496
DeMatteis Family Fnd Grants, 1497
Dennis & Phyllis Washington Fdn Grants, 1498
DENSO North America Fnd Grants, 1499
Denver Broncos Charities Fund Grants, 1501
Denver Fnd Comm Grants, 1502
Dept of Ed Projects with Industry Grants, 1511
Dermody Properties Fdn Capstone Awd, 1516
DeRoy Testamentary Fnd Grants, 1518
Detlef Schrempf Fnd Grants, 1519
Detroit Lions Charities Grants, 1520
Deuce McAllister Catch 22 Fnd Grants, 1521
DFN Hurricane Katrina and Disability Rapid Response Grants, 1522
DHHS Abandoned Infants Assistance Grants, 1523
DHHS Adolescent Family Life Demo Projects, 1524
DHHS AIDS Project Grants, 1525
DHHS ARRA Strengthening Communities Fund - Nonprofit Capacity Building Grants, 1527
DHHS ARRA Strengthening Communities Fund - State, Local, and Tribal Government Capacity Building Grants, 1528
DHHS Comm Svcs Grant Trng & Tech Assistance Pgm: Capacity-Bldg for Ongoing CSBG Pgm, 1529
DHHS Comprehensive Comm Mental Health Services Grants for Children with Serious Emotional Disturbances, 1530
DHHS Maternal & Child Health Projects Grts, 1536

DHS ARRA Fire Station Const Grants, 1542
DHS ARRA Port Security Grants, 1543
DHS ARRA Transit Security Grants, 1544
DHS FY 2009 Transit Security Grants, 1545
Diageo Fnd Grants, 1546
DIFFA/Chicago Grants, 1547
Dining for Women Grants, 1548
DogTime Annual Grant, 1552
DogTime Tech Grant, 1553
DOJ Children's Justice Act Partnership for Indian Communities, 1555
DOJ Gang-Free Schools and Communities Intervention Grants, 1557
Dolan Fnd Grants, 1563
Dole Food Company Charitable Contributions, 1564
Dolfinger-McMahon Fnd Grants, 1565
Dollar Energy Fund Grants, 1567
Dollar General Adult Lit Grants, 1568
Dollar General Family Lit Grants, 1569
DOL Youthbuild Grants, 1571
Dominion Fnd Human Needs Grants, 1572
Donald & Sylvia Robinson Family Fdn Grts, 1573
Donaldson Fnd Grants, 1574
Donald W. Reynolds Fnd Charitable Food Distribution Grants, 1575
Donnie Avery Catches for Kids Fnd, 1578
Dora Roberts Fnd Grants, 1579
Doree Taylor Charitable Fnd, 1580
Doris and Victor Day Fnd Grants, 1582
Doris Day Animal Fnd Grants, 1583
Doris Duke Charitable Fnd Child Abuse Prevention Grants, 1585
Dorothy Rider Pool Health Care Grants, 1589
Dorrance Family Fnd Grants, 1590
Do Something BR!CK Awards, 1592
Do Something Plum Youth Grants, 1593
Douty Fnd Grants, 1595
Dr. and Mrs. Paul Pierce Memorial Fnd Grants, 1599
Dr. John T. Macdonald Fnd Grants, 1600
Dr. P. Phillips Fnd Grants, 1601
Dr. Scholl Fnd Grants, 1602
Draper Richards Kaplan Fnd Grants, 1603
Drs. Bruce and Lee Fnd Grants, 1607
Drug Free Communities Support Program, 1608
DTE Energy Fdn Comm Dev Grants, 1609
DTE Energy Health & Human Services Grants, 1613
Duke Endowment Child Care Grants, 1617
Duke Energy Fdn Comm Vitality Grants, 1618
Duluth-Superior Area Comm Fdn Grts, 1620
Dunspaugh-Dalton Fnd Grants, 1623
DuPage Comm Fnd Grants, 1624
Dwight Stuart Youth Fnd Capacity-Building Initiative Grants, 1627
Dwight Stuart Youth Fnd Grants, 1628
Dyer-Ives Fnd Small Grants, 1629
Dyson Fnd Mid-Hudson Valley Faith-Based Organization Grants, 1634
E.J. Grassmann Trust Grants, 1638
E Rhodes & Leona B Carpenter Fdn Grts, 1640
Eastman Chemical Co Fdn Grants, 1643
Easton Fnds Archery Facility Grants, 1644
Eckerd Family Fnd Grants, 1651
Ed and Carole Abel Fnd Grants, 1652
Eddie C. and Sylvia Brown Family Fnd Grants, 1653
Eden Hall Fnd Grants, 1655
Edina Realty Fnd Grants, 1656
Edna McConnell Clark Fnd Grants, 1659
Edna Wardlaw Charitable Trust Grants, 1660
EDS Fnd Grants, 1661
Edward & Ellen Roche Relief Fdn Grants, 1663
Edward and Helen Bartlett Fnd Grants, 1664
Edward Bangs Kelley & Elza Kelley Fdn Grts, 1665
Edward N. and Della L. Thome Memorial Fnd Direct Services Grants, 1666
Edward S. Moore Fnd Grants, 1668
Edwards Memorial Trust Grants, 1669
Edwin W & Catherine M Davis Fdn Grants, 1672
Edyth Bush Charitable Fnd Grants, 1673
Effie and Wofford Cain Fnd Grants, 1674
EIF Comm Grants, 1675

Eileen Fisher Activating Leadership Grants for Women and Girls, 1676
Eisner Fnd Grants, 1678
Elden and Mary Lee Gutwein Family Fnd Grants, 1679
Elizabeth Carse Fnd Grants, 1681
Elizabeth Morse Genius Char Trust Grants, 1682
Elkhart Cty Comm Fdn Grants, 1684
Ellen Abbott Gilman Trust Grants, 1685
Elmer L & Eleanor J Andersen Fdn Grnts, 1687
El Paso Comm Fnd Grants, 1688
El Pomar Fnd Awards and Grants, 1690
Elsie H. Wilcox Fnd Grants, 1691
EMC Corporation Grants, 1693
Emerson Charitable Trust Grants, 1694
Emily Davie and Joseph S. Kornfeld Fnd Grants, 1697
Emily Hall Tremaine Fnd Grants, 1698
Emma B. Howe Memorial Fnd Grants, 1700
Emma J. Adams Grants, 1702
Emy-Lou Biedenharn Fnd Grants, 1703
Ensign-Bickford Fnd Grants, 1709
Entergy Charitable Fnd Low-Income Initiatives and Solutions Grants, 1711
Entergy Corporation Micro Grants, 1712
Entergy Corporation Open Grants for Comm Improvement & Enrichment, 1714
Entergy Corp Open Grants for Healthy Families, 1715
Enterprise Comm Partners MetLife Fnd Awards for Excellence in Affordable Housing, 1717
Enterprise Rent-A-Car Fnd Grants, 1721
EPA Children's Health Protection Grants, 1728
EPA Hazardous Waste Manag Grants for Tribes, 1733
EPA Tribal Solid Waste Management Assistance Grants, 1741
EQT Fnd Educ Grants, 1745
Erie Comm Fnd Grants, 1750
Essex County Comm Fnd Discretionary Grants, 1752
Essex County Comm Fnd Merrimack Valley General Fund Grants, 1756
Ethel and Raymond F. Rice Fnd Grants, 1758
Ethel S. Abbott Charitable Fnd Grants, 1760
Ethel Sergeant Clark Smith Fnd Grants, 1761
Eugene G. & Margaret M. Blackford Grants, 1763
Eugene M. Lang Fnd Grants, 1764
Eva L & Joseph M Bruening Fdn Grants, 1768
Evan and Susan Bayh Fnd Grants, 1769
Evanston Comm Fnd Grants, 1771
Evelyn and Walter Haas, Jr. Fund Immigrant Rights Grants, 1773
Ewa Beach Comm Trust Fund, 1775
F.M. Kirby Fnd Grants, 1780
F.R. Bigelow Fnd Grants, 1781
Fairfield County Comm Fdn Grts, 1782
Fallon OrNda Comm Health Fund Grants, 1783
Families Count: The National Honors Program, 1784
Fam Lit & HI Pizza Hut Lit Fund, 1785
Fan Fox & Leslie R Samuels Fdn Grants, 1786
Fargo-Moorhead Area Fnd Grants, 1788
Farm Aid Grants, 1790
Farmers Insurance Corporate Giving Grants, 1791
Fassino Fnd Grants, 1793
Faye McBeath Fnd Grants, 1794
FCD Child Dev Grants, 1796
FCYO Youth Organizing Grants, 1797
Federal Express Corporate Contributions, 1799
Fel-Pro Mecklenburger Fnd Grants, 1800
Feldman Fnd Grants, 1801
FEMA Assistance to Firefighters Grants, 1802
FEMA Staffing for Adequate Fire and Emergency Response Grants, 1803
Ferree Fnd Grants, 1804
Fidelity Fnd Grants, 1805
Field Fnd of Illinois Grants, 1806
Fieldstone Fnd Grants, 1808
Fifth Third Bank Corporate Giving, 1809
Fifth Third Fnd Grants, 1810
Financial Capability Innovation Fund II Grants, 1811
Finish Line Youth Fnd Founder's Grants, 1812
Finish Line Youth Fnd Grants, 1813
Finish Line Youth Fnd Legacy Grants, 1814
Firelight Fnd Grants, 1817

FirstEnergy Fnd Comm Grants, 1819
Fisher Fnd Grants, 1831
Fitzpatrick, Cella, Harper & Scinto Pro Bono, 1836
Flextronics Fnd Disaster Relief Grants, 1841
Flinn Fnd Grants, 1842
Florence Hunt Maxwell Fnd Grants, 1844
Florida Div of Cultural Affrs Facilities Grts, 1852
Florida Humanities Cncl Civic Reflection Grts, 1867
Florida Humanities Council Major Grants, 1868
Florida Humanities Council Mini Grants, 1869
Florida Sports Fnd Junior Golf Grants, 1872
Floyd A. and Kathleen C. Cailloux Fnd Grants, 1874
Foellinger Fnd Grants, 1877
Fondren Fnd Grants, 1878
Ford Fdn Peace & Social Justice Grts, 1884
Ford Motor Company Fund Grants, 1885
Forest Fnd Grants, 1886
Forrest C. Lattner Fnd Grants, 1887
Fnd for a Drug-Free Wrld Clsrm Tools, 1890
Fnd for a Healthy Kentucky Grants, 1891
Fdn for Enhancing Communities Grts, 1893
Fnd for Health Enhancement Grants, 1894
Fnd for Seacoast Health Grants, 1895
Fnd for the Carolinas Grants, 1896
Fnd for the Mid South Comm Dev Grants, 1897
Fnd for the Mid South Educ Grts, 1898
Fnd for Mid South Health & Wellness Grants, 1899
Fnd for the MidSouth Wlth Bldg Grts, 1900
Fnd for Young Ausies Indigenous Small Grants, 1901
Fnd for Young Australians Spark Fund Grants, 1902
Fnd for Young Australians Youth Change Makers Grants, 1904
Fnd for Young Ausies Youth Led Futures Grants, 1905
Fnd NW Grants, 1906
Fnds of East Chicago Health Grants, 1910
Fnds of E Chgo Public Sfty Grts, 1911
Fourjay Fnd Grants, 1913
Four Times Fnd Grants, 1914
France-Merrick Fnds Grants, 1915
Frances & Benjamin Benenson Fdn Grts, 1916
Frances and John L. Loeb Family Fund Grants, 1917
Frances C & William P Smallwood Fdn Grts, 1918
Frances L & Edwin L Cummings Mem Fund, 1919
Francis Beidler Fnd Grants, 1921
Francis L. Abreu Charitable Trust Grants, 1922
Francis T & Louise T Nichols Fnd Grts, 1923
Frank & Larue Reynolds Char Trust Grts, 1924
Frank B. Hazard General Charity Fund Grants, 1926
Frank E. and Seba B. Payne Fnd Grants, 1927
Frank G & Freida K Brotz Fam Fdn Grts, 1928
Franklin H. Wells and Ruth L. Wells Fnd Grants, 1930
Frank Reed and Margaret Jane Peters Memorial Fund I Grants, 1933
Frank Reed and Margaret Jane Peters Memorial Fund II Grants, 1934
Frank Stanley Beveridge Fnd Grants, 1936
Frank W & Carl S Adams Mem Fund Grts, 1937
Fraser-Parker Fnd Grants, 1938
Fred & Gretel Biel Charitable Trust Grants, 1939
Fred and Sherry Abernethy Fnd Grants, 1940
Fred Baldwin Memorial Fnd Grants, 1941
Fred C & Mary R Koch Fnd Grants, 1943
Freddie Mac Fnd Grants, 1944
Frederick McDonald Trust Grants, 1946
Fred L. Emerson Fnd Grants, 1949
Fred Meyer Fnd Grants, 1950
Fremont Area Cmty Fdn Amazing X Grants, 1953
Fremont Area Comm Fnd Grants, 1955
Frey Fnd Grants, 1963
Frist Fnd Grants, 1964
Frost Fnd Grants, 1966
Fuller E. Callaway Fnd Grants, 1973
Fund for the City of New York Grants, 1978
Furth Family Fnd Grants, 1980
G.A. Ackermann Grants, 1981
G.N. Wilcox Trust Grants, 1982
Gannett Fdn Comm Action Grants, 1984
Gardiner Howland Shaw Fnd Grants, 1986
Gardiner Savings Institution Charitable Grants, 1987
Garland & Agnes Taylor Gray Fdn Grts, 1988

Gateway Fnd Grants, 1992
Gaylord & Dorothy Donnelley Fdn Grants, 1993
GCI Corporate Contributions Grants, 1994
Gebbie Fnd Grants, 1995
GEF Green Thumb Challenge, 1996
GEICO Public Service Awards, 1997
GenCorp Fnd Grants, 1998
Gene Haas Fnd, 1999
Genentech Corporate Charitable Contributions, 2000
General Dynamics Corporation Grants, 2001
General Mills Fnd Grants, 2003
George A & Grace L Long Fdn Grts, 2008
George A. Hormel Testamentary Trust Grants, 2009
George and Ruth Bradford Fnd Grants, 2010
George B. Storer Fnd Grants, 2014
George E. Hatcher, Jr. and Ann Williams Hatcher Fnd Grants, 2015
George F. Baker Trust Grants, 2016
George Family Fnd Grants, 2017
George Fnd Grants, 2018
George Frederick Jewett Fnd Grants, 2019
George Gund Fnd Grants, 2020
George H & Jane A Mifflin Mem Fund Grts, 2021
George H.C. Ensworth Grants, 2022
George J. and Effie L. Seay Fnd Grants, 2024
George Kress Fnd Grants, 2025
George P. Davenport Trust Fund Grants, 2026
George W Codrington Charitable Fdn Grts, 2029
George W. Wells Fnd Grants, 2030
Georgia-Pacific Fnd Enrichment Grants, 2032
Georgiana Goddard Eaton Mem Fund Grts, 2038
Georgia Power Fnd Grants, 2039
German Protestant Orphan Asylum Fnd Grants, 2044
Gertrude M. Conduff Fnd Grants, 2047
Gheens Fnd Grants, 2048
Giant Food Charitable Grants, 2050
Gibson County Comm Fnd Women's Fund, 2051
Gibson Fnd Grants, 2052
Gil and Dody Weaver Fnd Grants, 2053
Gill Fnd Gay & Lesbian Fund, 2054
Ginn Fnd Grants, 2056
Giving Sum Annual Grant, 2058
GlaxoSmithKline Corporate Grants, 2060
Glazer Family Fnd Grants, 2062
GNOF Albert N & Hattie M McClure Grts, 2068
GNOF Bayou Communities Grants, 2069
GNOF Exxon-Mobil Grants, 2074
GNOF Gert Comm Fund Grants, 2076
GNOF Gulf Coast Oil Spill Grants, 2077
GNOF IMPACT Grants for Health and Human Services, 2080
GNOF IMPACT Grts for Youth Dev't, 2081
GNOF IMPACT Gulf States Eye Surg Fund, 2082
GNOF IMPACT Harold W. Newman, Jr. Charitable Trust Grants, 2083
GNOF Maison Hospitaliere Grants, 2086
GNOF Norco Comm Grants, 2089
GNOF Organizational Effectiveness Grants, 2090
GNOF Plaquemines Comm Grants, 2091
GNOF Stand Up For Our Children Grants, 2093
Go Daddy Cares Charitable Contributions, 2094
Godfrey Fnd Grants, 2095
Goizueta Fnd Grants, 2096
Golden Rule Fnd Grants, 2098
Golden State Warriors Fnd Grants, 2099
Goldseker Fdn Comm Affairs Grants, 2100
Goldseker Fnd Comm Grants, 2101
Goldseker Fnd Human Services Grants, 2102
Goldseker Fnd Non-Profit Management Assistance Grants, 2103
Goodrich Corporation Fnd Grants, 2104
Good Works Fnd Grants, 2105
Goodyear Tire Grants, 2106
Grable Fnd Grants, 2108
Grace and Franklin Bernsen Fnd Grants, 2109
Grace Bersted Fnd Grants, 2110
Graco Fnd Grants, 2111
Grand Rapids Area Comm Fdn Grts, 2114
Grand Rapids Area Comm Fnd Nashwauk Area Endowment Fund Grants, 2115

PROGRAM TYPE INDEX

Grand Rapids Comm Fnd Grants, 2118
Grand Rapids Comm Fnd Lowell Area Grants, 2121
Granger Fnd Grants, 2127
Great-West Life Grants, 2130
Great Clips Corporate Giving, 2131
Greater Cincinnati Fnd Priority and Small Projects/Capacity-Building Grants, 2132
Greater Des Moines Fnd Grants, 2134
Grtr Green Bay Comm Fdn Grts, 2135
Greater Kanawha Valley Fnd Grants, 2136
Greater Milwaukee Fnd Grants, 2137
Greater Saint Louis Comm Fdn Grants, 2138
Greater Tacoma Comm Fdn Grts, 2139
Greater Worcester Comm Discretionary Grants, 2140
Greater Worcester Comm Fnd Ministries Grants, 2143
Greater Worcester Comm Fnd Youth for Comm Improvement Grants, 2144
Green Bay Packers Fnd Grants, 2148
Green Diamond Charitable Contributions, 2149
Green Fnd Human Services Grants, 2154
Greenspun Family Fnd Grants, 2156
Greenwall Fnd Bioethics Grants, 2158
GreenWorks! Butterfly Garden Grants, 2159
GreenWorks! Grants, 2160
Griffin Fnd Grants, 2165
Grotto Fnd Project Grants, 2166
Grundy Fnd Grants, 2169
GTECH After School Advantage Grants, 2170
GTECH Comm Involvement Grants, 2171
Guido A & Elizabeth H Binda Fdn Grants, 2172
Gulf Coast Comm Fnd Grants, 2174
Gulf Coast Fnd of Comm Grants, 2177
Gumdrop Books Librarian Scholarships, 2179
Guy I. Bromley Trust Grants, 2180
H & R Fnd Grants, 2181
HA & Mary K Chapman Char Trust Grts, 2182
H.B. Fuller Company Fnd Grants, 2183
H.J. Heinz Company Fnd Grants, 2184
H. Leslie Hoffman & Elaine S. Hoffman Grants, 2185
H. Reimers Bechtel Charitable Remainder Uni-Trust Grants, 2186
H. Schaffer Fnd Grants, 2187
Hackett Fnd Grants, 2188
Haddad Fnd Grants, 2189
HAF Comm Grants, 2193
HAF Mada Huggins Caldwell Fund Grants, 2200
HAF Native Cultures Fund Grants, 2201
HAF Senior Opportunities Grants, 2203
HAF Southern Humboldt Grants, 2204
Hagedorn Fund Grants, 2207
Hahl Proctor Charitable Trust Grants, 2208
Hall-Perrine Fnd Grants, 2209
Hall Family Fnd Grants, 2210
Halliburton Fnd Grants, 2211
Hallmark Corporate Fnd Grants, 2212
Hamilton Family Fnd Grants, 2213
Hampton Roads Comm Fnd Health and Human Service Grants, 2216
Hampton Roads Comm Fnd Nonprofit Facilities Improvement Grants, 2218
Hancock County Fnd - Field of Interest Grants, 2219
Hannaford Charitable Fnd Grants, 2222
Harley Davidson Fnd Grants, 2224
Harold Alfond Fnd Grants, 2225
Harold & Arlene Schnitzer CARE Fdn Grts, 2226
Harold Brooks Fnd Grants, 2227
Harold K. L. Castle Fnd Grants, 2228
Harold R. Bechtel Charitable Remainder Uni-Trust Grants, 2229
Harold Simmons Fnd Grants, 2230
Harrison Cty Comm Fdn Grts, 2233
Harrison County Comm Fnd Signature Grants, 2234
Harris Teeter Corporate Contributions Grants, 2235
Harry Chapin Fnd Grants, 2240
Harry Sudakoff Fnd Grants, 2245
Harry W. Bass, Jr. Fnd Grants, 2246
Hartford Aging and Health Program Awards, 2247
Hartford Fnd Regular Grants, 2253
Harvest Fnd Grants, 2254
Harvey Randall Wickes Fnd Grants, 2255

Hasbro Children's Fund, 2256
Hawai'i Children's Trust Fund Comm Awareness Events Grants, 2258
Hawaiian Electric Industries Charitable Grants, 2259
Hawaii Comm Fnd Geographic-Specific Grants, 2261
Hawaii Comm Fnd Human Services Grants, 2262
Hawaii Comm Fnd Reverend Takie Okumura Family Grants, 2264
Hawaii Comm Fnd West Hawaii Fund Grants, 2266
Hazen Fnd Public Educ Grants, 2269
Hazen Fnd Youth Organizing Grants, 2270
HCA Fnd Grants, 2274
Health Canada National Seniors Indep Grants, 2278
Healthcare Fdn for Orange Cty Grts, 2279
Healthcare Fnd of New Jersey Grants, 2280
Health Fnd of Grtr Cincinnati Grts, 2281
Health Fnd of Grtr Indianapolis Grts, 2282
Health Fnd of South Florida Responsive Grants, 2283
Hearst Fnds Social Service Grants, 2285
Heinz Endowments Grants, 2291
Helena Rubinstein Fnd Grants, 2292
Helen Bader Fnd Grants, 2293
Helen Gertrude Sparks Charitable Trust Grants, 2294
Helen Irwin Littauer Educational Trust Grants, 2295
Helen K & Arthur E Johnson Fdn Grts, 2296
Helen Pumphrey Denit Charitable Trust Grants, 2297
Helen Steiner Rice Fnd Grants, 2299
Helen V. Brach Fnd Grants, 2300
Help America Fnd Grants, 2301
Henrietta Lange Burk Fund Grants, 2303
Henry & Ruth Blaustein Rosenberg Fdn Grants, 2306
Henry E. Niles Fnd Grants, 2309
Henry J. Kaiser Family Fnd Grants, 2310
Herbert A & Adrian W Woods Fdn Grts, 2313
Herbert H & Grace A Dow Fdn Grants, 2315
Herman Goldman Fnd Grants, 2317
Hershey Company Grants, 2318
Highmark Corporate Giving Grants, 2319
Hilda and Preston Davis Fnd Grants, 2322
Hilfiger Family Fnd Grants, 2323
Hill Crest Fnd Grants, 2324
Hillcrest Fnd Grants, 2325
Hill Fnd Grants, 2326
Hillman Fnd Grants, 2327
Hillsdale County Comm General Adult Grants, 2328
Hillsdale Fund Grants, 2329
Hilton Head Island Fnd Grants, 2330
Hirtzel Memorial Fnd Grants, 2332
Hitachi Fnd Yoshiyama Awards, 2340
Hoblitzelle Fnd Grants, 2341
Hoffberger Fnd Grants, 2342
Hogg Fnd for Mental Health Grants, 2343
Hoglund Fnd Grants, 2344
Holland/Zeeland Comm Fdn Grants, 2345
HomeBanc Fnd Grants, 2347
Home Building Industry Disaster Relief Fund, 2348
Homer Fnd Grants, 2352
Honda of America Manufacturing Fnd Grants, 2354
Honeywell Corp Housing & Shelter Grts, 2357
Horace Moses Charitable Fnd Grants, 2363
Horizon Fnd for New Jersey Grants, 2364
Horizon Fnd Grants, 2365
Horizons Comm Issues Grants, 2366
Household Int'l Corp Giving Grants, 2372
Houston Endowment Grants, 2373
Howard and Bush Fnd Grants, 2374
Howard County Comm Fdn Grts, 2375
Huber Fnd Grants, 2382
Hudson Webber Fnd Grants, 2383
Huffy Fnd Grants, 2384
Hugh J. Andersen Fnd Grants, 2385
Huie-Dellmon Trust Grants, 2386
Humana Fnd Grants, 2388
Humane Society of the United States Foreclosure Pets Grants, 2389
Humanitas Fnd Grants, 2390
Hundred Club of Colorado Springs Grants, 2391
Hundred Club of Connecticut Grants, 2392
Hundred Club of Contra Costa County Survivor Benefits Grants, 2393

Service Delivery Programs / 1127

Hundred Club of Denver Grants, 2394
Hundred Club of Durango Grants, 2395
Hundred Club of Los Angeles Grants, 2396
Hundred Club of Palm Springs Grants, 2397
Hundred Club of Pueblo Grants, 2398
Hundred Club of Santa Clara County Grants, 2399
Huntington County Comm Fnd - Make a Difference Grants, 2406
Huntington Fnd Grants, 2408
Huntington National Bank Comm Affairs Grants, 2409
Hutchinson Comm Fnd Grants, 2410
Hut Fnd Grants, 2411
Hutton Fnd Grants, 2412
Hyams Fnd Grants, 2413
I.A. O'Shaughnessy Fnd Grants, 2416
IAFF Harvard Univ Trade Union Scholarships, 2417
IAFF Labour College of Canada Residential Scholarship, 2418
IAFF W. H. McClennan Scholarship, 2420
Ian Hague Perl 6 Dev Grants, 2421
IBCAT Screening Mammography Grants, 2422
ICC Comm Service Mini-Grant, 2426
ICC Day of Service Action Grants, 2427
ICC Faculty Fellowships, 2428
ICC Listening to Communities Grants, 2429
ICC Scholarship of Engagement Faculty Grants, 2430
Ida Alice Ryan Charitable Trust Grants, 2431
Idaho Comm Eastern Region Competitive Grants, 2432
Idaho Power Co Corp Contributions, 2433
IDEM Section 205(j) Water Quality Management Planning Grants, 2434
IDEM Section 319(h) Nonpoint Source Grants, 2435
IDPH Emergency Med Svcs Astnc Fund Grts, 2440
IDPH Hosptial Capital Investment Grants, 2441
IDPH Local Health Dept Public Health Emergency Response Grants, 2442
IEDC Industrial Dev Grant Fund, 2443
Illinois DCEO Business Dev Public Infrastructure Grants, 2483
Illinois Humanities Council Comm Project Grant, 2510
Illinois Tool Works Fnd Grants, 2511
IMLS Native American Library Services Grants, 2517
IMLS Native American Library Services Enhancement Grants, 2518
IMLS Native Hawaiian Library Services Grants, 2519
Inasmuch Fnd Grants, 2523
Independence Blue Cross Charitable Medical Care Grants, 2524
Independence Comm Fnd Quality of Life Grant, 2525
Independence Comm Fnd Neighborhood Renewal Grants, 2527
Indiana AIDS Fund Grants, 2529
Indiana Arts Commission American Masterpieces Grants, 2530
Indiana Arts Commission Multi-regional Major Arts Institutions Grants, 2532
Indiana Boating Infrastructure Grants (BIG P), 2534
Indiana Household Hazardous Waste Grants, 2538
Indiana Recycling Grants, 2545
Indiana Reg'l Econ Dev Partnership Grts, 2546
Indiana Rural Capacity Grants, 2547
Indiana Waste Tire Fund Pgm Grts, 2551
ING Fnd Grants, 2555
Intel Comm Grants, 2562
Intel Int'l Comm Grants, 2564
Intergrys Corporation Grants, 2565
Int'l Human Rights Funders Grants, 2567
Int'l Paper Co Fnd Grants, 2568
IREX Egypt Media Dev Grants, 2575
IREX Moldova Citizen Participation Grants, 2578
IREX Russia Civil Society Support Grants, 2580
IREX Small Grant Fund for Civil Society Projects in Africa and Asia, 2581
IREX Small Grant Fund for Media Projects in Africa and Asia, 2582
Irving S. Gilmore Fnd Grants, 2584
Irvin Stern Fnd Grants, 2585
Isabel Allende Fnd Esperanza Grants, 2586
ISI William E Simon Fwsps for Noble Purpose, 2588
Ittleson Fnd AIDS Grants, 2589

Ittleson Fnd Mental Health Grants, 2590
J.B. Reynolds Fnd Grants, 2592
J. Bulow Campbell Fnd Grants, 2593
J.C. Penney Company Grants, 2594
J.E. and L.E. Mabee Fnd Grants, 2595
J. Edwin Treakle Fnd Grants, 2596
J. Jill Compassion Fund Grants, 2598
J.L. Bedsole Fnd Grants, 2600
J.M. Long Fnd Grants, 2603
J.W. Kieckhefer Fnd Grants, 2607
J. Walton Bissell Fnd Grants, 2608
J Willard & Alice S Marriott Fdn Grts, 2609
Jackson Cty Comm Fdn Unrestricted Grts, 2611
Jackson Fnd Grants, 2613
Jacksonville Jaguars Fnd Grants, 2614
Jacob and Hilda Blaustein Fnd Grants, 2615
Jacob G. Schmidlapp Trust Grants, 2616
Jacobs Family Fdn Vlg Neighborhoods Grants, 2619
James & Abigail Campbell Fam Fdn Grts, 2620
James A. and Faith Knight Fnd Grants, 2621
James Ford Bell Fnd Grants, 2623
James J. McCann Charitable Trust and McCann Fnd, Inc Grants, 2631
James L & Mary Jane Bowman Char Trust, 2632
James M. Collins Fnd Grants, 2633
James M. Cox Fnd of Georgia Grants, 2634
James R. Thorpe Fnd Grants, 2636
James S. Copley Fnd Grants, 2637
Jane's Trust Grants, 2639
Jane Bradley Pettit Comm & Social Dev Grants, 2642
Jay & Rose Phillips Fam Fdn Grts, 2656
Jean and Louis Dreyfus Fnd Grants, 2658
Jeffris Wood Fnd Grants, 2660
JELD-WEN Fnd Grants, 2661
Jenkins Fnd: Improving the Health of Greater Richmond Grants, 2663
Jennings County Comm Fnd Women's Giving Circle Grant, 2665
Jerome & Mildred Paddock Fdn Grts, 2666
Jessie Ball Dupont Fund Grants, 2671
Jewish Fund Grants, 2675
Jewish Funds for Justice Grants, 2676
Jewish Women's Fdn of New York Grants, 2677
Jim Blevins Fnd Grants, 2678
Jim Moran Fnd Grants, 2680
JM Fnd Grants, 2681
Joan Bentinck-Smith Charitable Fdn Grts, 2682
Joe W & Dorothy Dorsett Brown Fdn Grants, 2684
John Clarke Trust Grants, 2689
John D & Katherine A Johnston Fdn Grants, 2691
John Deere Fnd Grants, 2692
John Edward Fowler Mem Fdn Grants, 2693
John Gogian Family Fnd Grants, 2697
John J. Leidy Fnd Grants, 2701
John Lord Knight Fnd Grants, 2703
John M. Weaver Fnd Grants, 2705
John Merck Fund Grants, 2706
John P. Murphy Fnd Grants, 2708
John R. Oishei Fnd Grants, 2709
John S & James L Knight Fdn Dnr Adv Fd Grts, 2712
Johns Manville Fund Grants, 2716
Johnson & Johnson Comm Health Care Grants, 2717
Johnson & Johnson Corp Contribs Grants, 2718
Johnson Controls Fnd Health and Social Services Grants, 2722
John W & Anna H Hanes Fdn Grants, 2728
John W. Gardner Leadership Award, 2731
John W. Speas and Effie E. Speas Grants, 2732
Join Hands Day Excellence Awards, 2733
Joseph H & Florence A Roblee Fdn Grants, 2736
Josephine Goodyear Fnd Grants, 2738
Josephine S. Gumbiner Fnd Grants, 2739
Joseph P. Kennedy Jr. Fnd Grants, 2740
Joseph S. Stackpole Charitable Trust Grants, 2741
Josiah W & Bessie H Kline Fdn Grants, 2742
Joyce Fnd Democracy Grants, 2748
Joyce Fdn Gun Violence Prevention Grts, 2751
JP Morgan Chase Comm Dev Grts, 2753
Judith and Jean Pape Adams Charitable Fnd Tulsa Area Grants, 2755

Judith Clark-Morrill Fnd Grants, 2756
K. M. Hunter Charitable Social Welfare Grants, 2757
Kahuku Comm Fund, 2762
Kaiser Permanente Cares for Communities Grts, 2763
Kalamazoo Comm Fnd Economic and Comm Dev Grants, 2765
Kalamazoo Comm Fnd Individuals and Families Grants, 2769
Kalamazoo Comm Fdn Mini-Grts, 2772
Kaneta Fnd Grants, 2774
Kansas Health Fnd Recognition Grants, 2784
Kate B. Reynolds Charitable Health Care Grants, 2786
Kate B. Reynolds Charitable Trust Poor and Needy Grants, 2787
Katharine Matthies Fnd Grants, 2788
Kathryne Beynon Fnd Grants, 2791
Katrine Menzing Deakins Char Trust Grts, 2793
Kawabe Grants, 2794
KEEN Effect Grants, 2795
Kelvin and Eleanor Smith Fnd Grants, 2796
Kendrick Fnd Grants, 2797
Kenneth A. Scott Charitable Trust Grants, 2801
Kenneth T & Eileen L Norris Fdn Grants, 2802
Kenny's Kids Grants, 2803
Kent D. Steadley and Mary L. Steadley Grants, 2804
Ken W. Davis Fnd Grants, 2813
Kessler Fdn Comm Employment Grts, 2814
Kessler Fdn Hurricane Sandy Emergency Grts, 2815
Kessler Fdn Signature Employment Grts, 2816
Kettering Family Fnd Grants, 2817
Kettering Fund Grants, 2818
KeyBank Fnd Grants, 2820
KeySpan Fnd Grants, 2821
Kimball Int'l-Habig Fdn Grts, 2823
Kimberly-Clark Comm Grants, 2824
Knight Fdn Donor Advised Fund Grts, 2828
Knight Fnd Grants - Montana, 2830
Koret Fnd Grants, 2837
Kovler Family Fnd Grants, 2840
Kroger Fnd Hunger Relief Grants, 2844
Kuki'o Comm Fund, 2845
L. W. Pierce Family Fnd Grants, 2846
Laclede Gas Charitable Trust Grants, 2848
LaGrange Cty Comm Fdn Grts, 2850
LaGrange Independent Fnd for Endowments, 2851
Lana'i Comm Benefit Fund, 2857
Lands' End Corporate Giving Program, 2861
Laura Jane Musser Intrcltrl Harmony Grts, 2862
Laurel Fnd Grants, 2867
Leadership IS Award, 2869
Leave No Trace Master Educator Scholarships, 2870
LEGO Children's Fund Grants, 2878
Leicester Savings Bank Fund, 2879
Leo Goodwin Fnd Grants, 2882
Leon and Thea Koerner Fnd Grants, 2883
Leo Niessen Jr., Charitable Trust Grants, 2885
Lettie Pate Evans Fnd Grants, 2887
Lettie Pate Whitehead Fnd Grants, 2888
Liberty Bank Fnd Grants, 2890
Liberty Hill Fdn Enviro Justice Fund Grts, 2891
Liberty Hill Fund for New Los Angeles Grants, 2892
Liberty Hill Fnd Lesbian & Gay Grants, 2894
Liberty Hill Fdn Queer Youth Fund Grts, 2895
Liberty Hill Fnd Seed Fund Grants, 2896
Liberty Hill Fnd Special Opportunity Grants, 2897
Libra Fnd Grants, 2899
Lied Fnd Trust Grants, 2900
Lincoln Financial Group Fnd Grants, 2906
Linden Fnd Grants, 2908
LISC Financial Opportunity Center Social Innovation Fund Grants, 2911
Local Initiatives Support Corporation Grants, 2917
Louetta M. Cowden Grants, 2922
Louie M & Betty M Phillips Fdn Grants, 2923
Louis and Elizabeth Nave Flarsheim Charitable Fnd Grants, 2924
Louis Calder Fnd Grants, 2925
Louis R. Cappelli Fnd Grants, 2926
Lowe's Charitable and Educational Fnd Grants, 2927
Lowe Fnd Grants, 2929

Lowell Berry Fnd Grants, 2930
Lubbock Area Fnd Grants, 2931
Lubrizol Corporation Comm Grants, 2932
Lucile Horton Howe & Mitchell B. Howe Grants, 2934
Lucy Gooding Charitable Fnd Trust, 2936
Ludwick Family Fnd Grants, 2938
Luella Kemper Trust Grants, 2939
Lumpkin Family Fnd Strong Leadership Grants, 2944
Luther I. Replogle Fnd Grants, 2945
Lydia deForest Charitable Trust Grants, 2946
Lynde and Harry Bradley Fnd Grants, 2947
M.B. and Edna Zale Fnd Grants, 2950
M. Bastian Family Fnd Grants, 2951
M.E. Raker Fnd Grants, 2953
M3C Fellowships, 2955
Mabel A. Horne Trust Grants, 2956
Mabel Louise Riley Fnd Grants, 2959
Mabel Y. Hughes Charitable Trust Grants, 2960
Macquarie Bank Fnd Grants, 2966
Madison Comm Fnd Grants, 2971
Maine State Troopers Fnd Grants, 2991
Marathon Petroleum Corporation Grants, 2999
Marcia and Otto Koehler Fnd Grants, 3000
Margaret & James A Elkins Jr Fdn Grts, 3003
Margaret L. Wendt Fnd Grants, 3004
Margaret T. Morris Fnd Grants, 3005
Marie C. and Joseph C. Wilson Fnd Rochester Small Grants, 3006
Marie H. Bechtel Charitable Remainder Uni-Trust Grants, 3007
Marion and Miriam Rose Fund Grants, 3015
Marion Gardner Jackson Char Trust Grts, 3017
Marion I & Henry J Knott Fdn Discret Grants, 3018
Marion I & Henry J Knott Fdn Std Grants, 3019
Marion Isabell Coe Fund Grants, 3020
Mark Wahlberg Youth Fnd Grants, 3022
MARPAT Fnd Grants, 3023
Mars Fnd Grants, 3025
Marshall Cty Comm Fdn Grts, 3026
Marsh Corporate Grants, 3027
Martin C. Kauffman 100 Club of Alameda County Survivor Benefits Grants, 3028
Mary's Pence Ministry Grants, 3029
Mary's Pence Study Grants, 3030
Mary Black Fnd Active Living Grants, 3031
Mary Black Fdn Comm Health Grts, 3032
Mary Black Fdn Early Childhood Dev Grants, 3033
Mary E. and Michael Blevins Charitable Grants, 3037
Mary E. Babcock Fnd, 3038
Mary E. Ober Fnd Grants, 3039
Mary K. Chapman Fnd Grants, 3042
Mary Kay Fnd Domestic Violence Shelter Grants, 3044
Mary Owen Borden Fnd Grants, 3046
Mary S & David C Corbin Fdn Grants, 3048
Mary Wilmer Covey Charitable Trust Grants, 3049
Massachusetts Bar Fnd IOLTA Grants, 3050
Massachusetts Bar Fnd Legal Intern Fellowships, 3051
Massachusetts Fnd for the Humanities Cultural Economic Dev Grants, 3059
Massage Therapy Fnd Comm Service Grants, 3061
Mathile Family Fnd Grants, 3062
Maurice J. Masserini Charitable Trust Grants, 3064
Maximilian E & Marion O Hoffman Fdn, 3067
Maytree Fdn Refugee & Immigrant Grants, 3071
McCallum Family Fnd Grants, 3072
McCarthy Family Fnd Grants, 3073
McCombs Fnd Grants, 3075
McConnell Fnd Grants, 3076
McCune Charitable Fnd Grants, 3077
McCune Fnd Human Services Grants, 3080
McGraw-Hill Companies Comm Grants, 3081
McGregor Fund Grants, 3082
McInerny Fnd Grants, 3083
McKnight Fnd Multiservice Grants, 3085
McKnight Fnd Virginia McKnight Binger Awards in Human Service, 3087
McLean Contributionship Grants, 3088
McLean Fnd Grants, 3089
MDEQ Beach Monitoring - Inland Lakes, 3094
MDEQ Clean Diesel Grants, 3096

PROGRAM TYPE INDEX

MDEQ Coastal Management Planning and Construction Grants, 3097
MDEQ Comm Pollution Prevention (P2) Grants: Household Drug Collections, 3098
MDEQ Local Water Qlty Monitoring Grants, 3100
Meacham Fnd Memorial Grants, 3102
Mead Johnson Nutritionals Evansville-Area Organizations Grants, 3103
Meadows Fnd Grants, 3104
MeadWestvaco Sustainable Communities Grants, 3105
Mead Witter Fnd Grants, 3106
MedImmune Charitable Grants, 3108
Medtronic Fnd CommLink Health Grants, 3111
Medtronic Fnd Comm Human Services Grants, 3112
Medtronic Fnd Patient Link Grants, 3113
Memorial Fnd Grants, 3117
Mercedes-Benz USA Corporate Contributions, 3118
Mericos Fnd Grants, 3121
Meriden Fnd Grants, 3122
Mertz Gilmore Climate Change Solutions Grants, 3125
Mertz Gilmore Fnd NYC Communities Grants, 3126
Mertz Gilmore Fnd NYC Dance Grants, 3127
Mervin Bovaird Fnd Grants, 3128
Metro Health Fnd Grants, 3133
MetroWest Health Fnd Capital Grants for Health-Related Facilities, 3134
MetroWest Health Fnd Grants--Healthy Aging, 3135
MetroWest Health Fnd Grants to Reduce the Incidence of High Risk Behaviors Among Adolescents, 3136
Metzger-Price Fund Grants, 3137
Meyer Fnd Economic Security Grants, 3141
Meyer Fdn Healthy Communities Grts, 3143
Meyer Fdn Strong Nonprofit Sector Grts, 3145
Meyer Memorial Trust Grassroots Grants, 3147
Meyer Memorial Trust Responsive Grants, 3148
Meyer Memorial Trust Special Grants, 3149
MFRI Operation Diploma Grants for Higher Educ Institutions, 3150
MFRI Operation Diploma Grants for Student Veterans Organizations, 3151
MFRI Operation Diploma Small Grants for Indiana Family Readiness Groups, 3152
MGM Resorts Fnd Comm Grants, 3153
MGN Family Fnd Grants, 3154
Michael Reese Health Trust Core Grants, 3159
Michael Reese Health Trust Responsive Grants, 3160
Microsoft Comty Affairs Puget Sound Grts, 3163
Mid-Iowa Health Fdn Comty Response Grts, 3168
Middlesex Savings Charitable Fnd Capacity Building Grants, 3172
Middlesex Savings Charitable Comm Dev Grants, 3173
Miguel Aleman Fnd Grants, 3175
Miller, Canfield, Paddock and Stone, P.L.C. Corporate Giving Grants, 3179
Miller Brewing Corporate Contributions Grants, 3180
Miller Fnd Grants, 3181
Millipore Fnd Grants, 3182
Milton Hicks Wood and Helen Gibbs Wood Charitable Trust Grants, 3184
Mimi and Peter Haas Fund Grants, 3185
Minneapolis Fnd Comm Grants, 3186
Minnesota Small Cities Dev Grants, 3187
Mix It Up Grants, 3191
MMS & Alliance Char Fdn Grts for Comm Action and Care for the Medically Uninsured, 3194
MMS and Alliance Charitable Fnd Int'l Health Studies Grants, 3195
Modest Needs Non-Profit Grants, 3200
Moline Fnd Comm Grants, 3202
Monsanto Int'l Grants, 3207
Montana Arts Cncl Cltrl & Aesthetic Proj Grts, 3209
Montana Comm Fnd Grants, 3211
Montana Comm Fdn Women's Grts, 3212
Montgomery Cty Comm Fdn Grants, 3213
MONY Fnd Grants, 3214
Moody Fnd Grants, 3215
Moran Family Fnd Grants, 3216
Morris & Gwendolyn Cafritz Fdn Grants, 3218
Motorola Fnd Grants, 3221
Ms Fdn for Women Ending Violence Grts, 3224

Ms. Fnd for Women Health Grants, 3225
Mt. Sinai Health Care Fnd Health of the Jewish Comm Grants, 3226
Mt. Sinai Health Care Fnd Health of the Urban Comm Grants, 3227
Mt. Sinai Health Care Fnd Health Policy Grants, 3228
MTV Think Venturer Comnty Svc Grts, 3229
Musgrave Fnd Grants, 3231
Nathan B & Florence R Burt Fdn Grts, 3245
Nathan Cummings Fnd Grants, 3246
Nathaniel & Elizabeth P Stevens Fdn Grants, 3247
National Book Scholarship Fund, 3249
National Inclusion Grants, 3278
Nationwide Insurance Fnd Grants, 3285
Nature Hills Nursery Green America Awards, 3287
Needmor Fnd Grants, 3289
NEH Preservation Assistance Grants for Smaller Institutions, 3293
NASE Fdn Future Entrepreneur Schlrsp, 3296
Nell Warren Elkin and William Simpson Elkin Fnd Grants, 3300
Nestle Purina PetCare Educational Grants, 3302
Nestle Purina PetCare Emergency Response and Disaster Relief Grants, 3303
Nestle Purina PetCare Pet Related Grants, 3304
Nestle Purina PetCare Support Dog and Police K-9 Organization Grants, 3305
Nestle Purina PetCare Youth Grants, 3306
New Earth Fnd Grants, 3317
New Jersey Center for Hispanic Policy, Research and Dev Immigration Integration Grants, 3328
New Jersey Center for Hispanic Policy, Research and Dev Innovative Initiatives Grants, 3329
New Jersey Office of Faith Based Initiatives Service to Seniors Grants, 3333
Newman W. Benson Fnd Grants, 3334
NGA 'Remember Me' Rose Schl Garden Awds, 3401
NGA Healthy Sprouts Awards, 3403
NGA Hooked on Hydroponics Awards, 3405
NGA Mantis Award, 3406
NGA Youth Garden Grants, 3409
NHLBI Bioengineering and Obesity Grants, 3411
NHLBI Investigator Initiated Multi-Site Clinical Trials, 3413
NHLBI Lymphatics in Health and Disease in the Digestive, Urinary, Cardiovascular and Pulmonary Systems, 3415
NHSCA Arts in Health Care Project Grants, 3424
Nicholas H Noyes Jr Mem Fdn Grants, 3434
Nicor Corporate Contributions, 3435
Nicor Gas Sharing Grants, 3436
Nike and Ashoka GameChangers: Change the Game for Women in Sport, 3439
Nike Bowerman Track Renovation Grants, 3440
Nike Fnd Grants, 3441
Nike Giving - Cash and Product Grants, 3442
Nina Mason Pulliam Charitable Trust Grants, 3443
Norcliffe Fnd Grants, 3459
Norcross Wildlife Fnd Grants, 3460
Nord Family Fnd Grants, 3461
Nordson Corporation Fnd Grants, 3462
North Carolina Comm Fnd Grants, 3489
North Carolina GlaxoSmithKline Fdn Grts, 3490
North Central Health Services Grants, 3491
Northern Chautauqua Comm Fnd Comm Grants, 3499
Northern New York Comm Fdn Grts, 3503
Northern Trust Company Charitable Trust and Corporate Giving Program, 3504
North Georgia Comm Fnd Grants, 3505
Northland Fnd Grants, 3506
NW Mutual Fnd Grants, 3509
NW Minnesota Fnd Women's Fund Grants, 3512
Norton Fnd Grants, 3514
Norwin S & Elizabeth N Bean Fdn Grts, 3515
NSF CISE Computing Rsch Infrastructure, 3526
NSF Communicating Rsch to Public Audiences, 3527
NWHF Physical Activity and Nutrition Grants, 3540
NYCT AIDS/HIV Grants, 3542
NYCT Blindness and Visual Disabilities Grants, 3543
NYCT Children & Youth w/ Disabilities Grts, 3544

NYCT Comm Dev Grants, 3546
NYCT Fund for New Citizens Grants, 3547
NYCT Girls and Young Women Grants, 3548
NYCT Grants for the Elderly, 3549
NYCT Health Svcs, Systems & Policies Grts, 3550
NYCT Hunger and Homelessnes Grants, 3553
NYCT Mental Health and Retardation Grants, 3554
NYCT Social Services and Welfare Grants, 3557
NYCT Substance Abuse Grants, 3558
NYCT Tech Assistance Grants, 3559
NYCT Youth Dev Grants, 3561
NYSCA Dance: Services to the Field Grants, 3587
NYSCA State and Local Partnerships: Services to the Field Grants, 3621
Oak Fnd Child Abuse Grants, 3632
Oak Fdn Housing & Homelessness Grts, 3633
Oakland Fund for Children and Youth Grants, 3634
OceanFirst Fnd Grants, 3636
Ogden Codman Trust Grants, 3641
Ohio Artists on Tour Fee Support Requests, 3642
Ohio Arts Council Artist in Residence Grants, 3644
Ohio Arts Council Arts Access Grants, 3647
Ohio Arts Council Arts Innovation Pgm Grts, 3649
Ohio Arts Council Arts Partnership Grants, 3650
Ohio Arts Council Int'l Partnership Grts, 3653
Ohio Arts Council Sustainability Pgm Grts, 3654
Ohio County Comm Board of Directors Grants, 3656
Ohio County Comm Fnd Grants, 3658
Ohio Cty Comm Fdn Junior Grts, 3659
Ohio River Border Initiative Grants, 3661
Ohio Valley Fnd Grants, 3662
Oklahoma City Comm Pgms & Grts, 3666
Oleonda Jameson Trust Grants, 3667
Olga Sipolin Children's Fund Grants, 3668
Olin Corporation Charitable Trust Grants, 3669
Olive B. Cole Fnd Grants, 3670
Onan Family Fnd Grants, 3672
OneFamily Fnd Grants, 3673
OneStar Fnd AmeriCorps Grants, 3674
Open Meadows Fnd Grants, 3683
Oppenstein Brothers Fnd Grants, 3685
Orange County Comm Fnd Grants, 3687
Orange County Comm Fnd Grants, 3688
Ordean Fnd Grants, 3691
Oscar Rennebohm Fnd Grants, 3694
OSF-Baltimore Comm Fellowships, 3695
OSF-Baltimore Crim & Juv Justice Grts, 3696
OSF-Baltimore Tackling Drug Adctn Grts, 3698
OSF Cmpgn for Blk Male Achievement Grts, 3703
OSF Mental Health Initiative Grants, 3709
OSI After Prison Initiative Grants, 3710
OSI Sentencing and Incarceration Alternatives Project Grants, 3711
Otto Bremer Fnd Grants, 3713
OUT Fund for Lesbian & Gay Liberation Grts, 3714
Overbrook Fnd Grants, 3715
Owens Fnd Grants, 3718
PACCAR Fnd Grants, 3719
Pacers Fnd Be Drug-Free Grants, 3720
Pacers Fnd Be Educated Grants, 3721
Pacers Fnd Be Healthy and Fit Grants, 3722
Pacers Fnd Be Tolerant Grants, 3723
Pacers Fnd Indiana Fever's Be Younique Grants, 3724
PacifiCare Fnd Grants, 3725
Pacific Life Fnd Grants, 3726
PacifiCorp Fnd for Learning Grants, 3727
Packard Fnd Local Grants, 3729
Pajaro Valley Comm Health Health Trust Insurance/Coverage & Educ on Using the System Grants, 3731
Pajaro Valley Comm Health Trust Diabetes and Contributing Factors Grants, 3732
Palm Beach and Martin Counties Grants, 3733
Parker Fnd (California) Grants, 3736
Parkersburg Area Comm Fdn Action Grts, 3738
Park Fnd Grants, 3739
Pasadena Fnd Average Grants, 3741
Paso del Norte Health Fnd Grants, 3743
Patricia Price Peterson Fnd Grants, 3746
Patrick and Aimee Butler Family Fnd Comm Human Services Grants, 3749

1130 / Service Delivery Programs

PROGRAM TYPE INDEX

Patrick and Anna M. Cudahy Fund Grants, 3751
Patron Saints Fnd Grants, 3753
Paul and Edith Babson Fnd Grants, 3755
Paul and Mary Haas Fnd Contributions and Student Scholarships, 3756
Paul Balint Charitable Trust Grants, 3757
Paul G. Allen Family Fnd Grants, 3759
Paul Rapoport Fnd Grants, 3765
Paul V. Sherlock Center on Disabilities Access for All Abilities Mini Grants, 3767
Pay It Forward Fnd Mini Grants, 3768
PCA Arts Organizations and Arts Grants for Arts Service Organizations, 3777
PCA Arts Organizations & Grants for Local Arts, 3782
PCA Busing Grants, 3786
PCA Entry Track Arts Orgs & Arts Pgms Grts for Arts Svc Orgs, 3789
PCA Entry Track Arts Organizations and Arts Grants for Local Arts, 3794
PCA Entry Track Arts Orgs & Arts Pgms Grts for Traditional & Folk Arts, 3798
PCA Pennsylvania Partners in the Arts Program Stream Grants, 3801
PCA Pennsylvania Partners in the Arts Project Stream Grants, 3802
PDF Fiscal Sponsorship Grant, 3808
Pegasus Fnd Grants, 3810
Peoples Bancorp Fnd Grants, 3817
Percy B. Ferebee Endowment Grants, 3820
Perkins-Ponder Fnd Grants, 3822
Perpetual Trust for Charitable Giving Grants, 3826
Peter and Elizabeth C. Tower Fnd Annual Intellectual Disabilities Grants, 3834
Peter and Elizabeth C. Tower Fnd Annual Mental Health Grants, 3835
Peter and Elizabeth C. Tower Fnd Learning Disability Grants, 3836
Peter and Elizabeth C. Tower Fnd Mental Health Reference and Resource Materials Mini-Grants, 3837
Peter and Elizabeth C. Tower Fnd Phase II Tech Initiative Grants, 3839
Peter and Elizabeth C. Tower Fnd Phase I Tech Initiative Grants, 3840
Peter and Elizabeth C. Tower Fnd Social and Emotional Preschool Curriculum Grants, 3841
Peter & Elizabeth Tower Fnd Substance Abuse Grants, 3842
Peter Kiewit Fnd General Grants, 3845
Peter Kiewit Fnd Small Grants, 3847
Peter Norton Family Fnd Grants, 3849
Pew Charitable Trusts Children & Youth Grts, 3858
PeyBack Fnd Grants, 3861
Peyton Anderson Fnd Grants, 3862
Pfizer Healthcare Charitable Contributions, 3863
Pfizer Medical Educ Track One Grants, 3864
PG&E Comm Vitality Grants, 3868
Phelps County Comm Fnd Grants, 3870
Philadelphia Fdn Org'l Effectiveness Grts, 3872
Philanthrofund Grants, 3874
Philip L. Graham Fund Grants, 3876
Phoenix Coyotes Charities Grants, 3879
Phoenix Neighborhood Block Watch Grants, 3880
Phoenix Suns Charities Grants, 3881
Piedmont Health Fnd Grants, 3882
Piedmont Natural Gas Corporate and Charitable Contributions, 3883
Piedmont Natural Gas Fnd Health and Human Services Grants, 3885
Pinellas County Grants, 3891
Pinkerton Fnd Grants, 3892
Pinnacle Fnd Grants, 3894
Pioneer Hi-Bred Comm Grants, 3895
Piper Jaffray Fdn Communities Giving Grts, 3899
Piper Trust Arts and Culture Grants, 3900
Piper Trust Children Grants, 3901
Piper Trust Educ Grants, 3902
Piper Trust Healthcare & Med Rsch Grts, 3903
Piper Trust Older Adults Grants, 3904
Piper Trust Reglous Organizations Grants, 3905
PIP Four Freedoms Fund Grants, 3906
PIP Fulfilling the Dream Fund, 3907

PIP Racial Justice Collaborative Grants, 3908
Pittsburgh Fdn Comm Fund Grts, 3910
Plough Fnd Grants, 3915
Ploughshares Fund Grants, 3916
Plum Creek Fnd Grants, 3917
PMI Fnd Grants, 3918
PNC Ecnomic Dev Grants, 3922
PNM Power Up Grants, 3925
PNM Reduce Your Use Grants, 3926
Poets & Writers Readings/Workshops Grants, 3927
Polk Bros. Fnd Grants, 3929
Pollock Fnd Grants, 3930
Portland Fnd Grants, 3936
Portland General Electric Fnd Grants, 3937
Posey County Comm Fnd Grants, 3939
PPG Industries Fnd Grants, 3943
Premera Blue Cross CARES Grants, 3945
Price Chopper's Golub Fnd Grants, 3950
Priddy Fnd Grants, 3957
Prince Charitable Trusts Chicago Grants, 3959
Prince Char Trusts Dist of Columbia Grts, 3960
Princeton Comm Fnd Greater Mercer Grants, 3963
Principal Financial Group Fnd Grants, 3966
Procter and Gamble Fund Grants, 3967
Progress Energy Corp Contributions Grts, 3968
Project Orange Thumb Grants, 3972
PSEG Corporate Contributions Grants, 3979
PSEG Environmental Educ Grants, 3980
Public Educ Power Grants, 3981
Public Interest Law Fdn Comm Grts, 3982
Public Safety Fnd of America Grants, 3983
Public Welfare Fnd Grants, 3984
Publix Super Markets Charities Local Grants, 3985
Puerto Rico Comm Fnd Grants, 3986
Pulte Homes Corporate Contributions, 3989
Putnam Cty Comm Fdn Grts, 3990
Qualcomm Grants, 3993
Quality Health Fnd Grants, 3994
Quantum Corporation Snap Server Grants, 3995
Quantum Fnd Grants, 3996
Questar Corporate Contributions Grants, 3997
QuikTrip Corporate Contributions Grants, 3998
R.C. Baker Fnd Grants, 3999
R.S. Gernon Trust Grants, 4002
RadioShack StreetSentz Comm Grts, 4005
Rainbow Families Fnd Grants, 4008
Rainbow Fund Grants, 4009
Ralph and Virginia Mullin Fnd Grants, 4012
Ralph M. Parsons Fnd Grants, 4013
Ralphs Food 4 Less Fnd Grants, 4014
Rancho Bernardo Comm Fdn Grts, 4015
RAND Corporation Graduate Student Summer Associateships, 4018
Raskob Fdn for Catholic Activities Grts, 4019
Rasmuson Fnd Special Project Grants, 4025
Rathmann Family Fnd Grants, 4026
Raymond John Wean Fnd Grants, 4028
Ray Solem Fnd Grants to Help Immigrants Learn English in Innovative Ways, 4029
RBC Dain Rauscher Fnd Grants, 4031
RCF General Comm Grants, 4032
RCF Individual Assistance Grants, 4033
Reader's Digest Partners for Sight Fdn Grts, 4036
Regence Fdn Access to Health Care Grts, 4039
Regence Fnd Health Care Comm Awareness and Engagement Grants, 4040
Regence Fnd Health Care Connections Grants, 4041
Regence Fdn Improving End-of-Life Grts, 4042
Regence Fdn Tools & Tech Grts, 4043
Rehab Therapy Fnd Grants, 4050
REI Conservation & Outdoor Recreation Grts, 4051
Reinberger Fnd Grants, 4052
Reynolds American Fnd Grants, 4068
Reynolds & Reynolds Assoc Fdn Grants, 4069
RGK Fnd Grants, 4072
Rhode Island Fnd Grants, 4073
Rice Fnd Grants, 4074
Richard and Helen DeVos Fnd Grants, 4076
Richard and Rhoda Goldman Fund Grants, 4077
Richard & Susan Smith Family Fdn Grts, 4078

Richard Davoud Donchian Fnd Grants, 4080
Richard King Mellon Fnd Grants, 4087
Rich Fnd Grants, 4090
Richland County Bank Grants, 4091
Richmond Eye and Ear Fund Grants, 4092
Riley Fnd Grants, 4094
Robert and Helen Haddad Fnd Grants, 4103
Robert and Joan Dircks Fnd Grants, 4104
Robert and Polly Dunn Fnd Grants, 4105
Robert E & Evelyn McKee Fdn Grants, 4110
Robert G. Cabell III and Maude Morgan Cabell Fnd Grants, 4113
Robert Lee Adams Fnd Grants, 4114
Robert Lee Blaffer Fnd Grants, 4115
Robert P & Clara I Milton Fund for Sr Housing, 4117
Robert R. McCormick Tribune Comm Grants, 4119
Robert R. McCormick Tribune Veterans Grants, 4120
Robert R. Meyer Fnd Grants, 4121
Robert W. Woodruff Fnd Grants, 4124
Robin Hood Fnd Grants, 4125
Robins Fnd Grants, 4126
Rochester Area Comm Fnd Grants, 4127
Rochester Area Fnd Grants, 4128
Rockefeller Brothers Fund Pivotal Places Grants: New York City, 4134
Rockefeller Fnd Grants, 4138
Rockwell Int'l Corporate Trust Grants, 4141
Rohm and Haas Company Grants, 4145
Rollin M. Gerstacker Fnd Grants, 4146
Rollins-Luetkemeyer Fnd Grants, 4147
Ronald McDonald House Charities Grants, 4149
Rosalynn Carter Institute Georgia Caregiver of the Year Awards, 4151
Rose Comm Fnd Aging Grants, 4152
Rose Comm Fnd Child and Family Dev Grants, 4153
Rose Comm Fnd Health Grants, 4154
ROSE Fund Grants, 4161
Rose Hills Fnd Grants, 4162
Rosie's For All Kids Fnd Grants, 4163
Roy & Christine Sturgis Charitable Trust Grts, 4166
RRF General Grants, 4170
Russell Berrie Fnd Grants, 4175
Ruth Anderson Fnd Grants, 4176
Ruth and Vernon Taylor Fnd Grants, 4177
Ruth Eleanor Bamberger and John Ernest Bamberger Memorial Fnd Grants, 4178
Ruth H & Warren A Ellsworth Fdn Grts, 4179
Ruth Mott Fnd Grants, 4180
Rutter's Children's Charities Grants, 4181
RWJF Comm Health Leaders Awards, 4183
RWJF Jobs to Careers: Promoting Work-Based Learning for Quality Care, 4185
RWJF Local Funding Partnerships Grants, 4186
RWJF New Jersey Health Initiatives Grants, 4187
RWJF Pioneer Portfolio Grants, 4189
RWJF Vulnerable Populations Portfolio Grants, 4190
Ryder System Charitable Fnd Grants, 4191
S.E.VEN Fund Annual Grants, 4195
S. Mark Taper Fnd Grants, 4201
Safeco Insurance Comm Grants, 4203
Sage Fnd Grants, 4204
Saigh Fnd Grants, 4210
Sailors' Snug Harbor of Boston Elder Grants, 4211
Saint Louis Rams Fdn Comm Donations, 4214
Saint Luke's Fnd Grants, 4215
Saint Luke's Health Initiatives Grants, 4216
Saint Paul Fnd Grants, 4219
Salem Fnd Charitable Trust Grants, 4223
Salisbury Comm Fnd Grants, 4224
Salmon Fnd Grants, 4225
SAMHSA Campus Suicide Prevention Grants, 4229
Samueli Fnd Human Security Grants, 4233
Samuel S. Fels Fund Grants, 4238
Samuel S. Johnson Fnd Grants, 4239
San Antonio Area Fnd Grants, 4240
San Diego County Bar Fnd Grants, 4241
San Diego Fnd for Change Grants, 4247
San Diego Fnd Health & Human Services Grants, 4248
San Diego Fnd Paradise Valley Hospital Comm Fund Grants, 4249

PROGRAM TYPE INDEX

Service Delivery Programs

San Diego HIV Funding Collaborative Grants, 4251
San Diego Women's Fnd Grants, 4252
Sands Fnd Grants, 4255
San Francisco Fnd Comm Health Grants, 4263
San Francisco Fnd Disability Rights Advocate Fund Emergency Grants, 4265
San Juan Island Comm Fnd Grants, 4283
Santa Barbara Fdn Monthly Express Grts, 4284
Santa Barbara Strategy Capital Support, 4285
Santa Barbara Strategy Core Support Grants, 4286
Santa Barbara Fnd Strategy Grants - Innovation, 4287
Santa Barbara Fnd Towbes Fund for the Performing Arts Grants, 4288
Santa Fe Comm Fdn root2fruit Santa Fe, 4289
Santa Fe Comm Fnd Seasonal Grants-Fall Cycle, 4290
Santa Fe Comm Fnd Seasonal Grants-Spring, 4291
Santa Fe Comm Special & Urgent Needs Grants, 4292
Sapelo Fnd Social Justice Grants, 4294
Sara Lee Fnd Grants, 4296
Sarkeys Fnd Grants, 4297
Sartain Lanier Family Fnd Grants, 4298
Saucony Run for Good Fnd Grants, 4301
Schering-Plough Fdn Comm Initvs Grts, 4303
Schering-Plough Fnd Health Grants, 4304
Scherman Fnd Grants, 4305
Schlessman Family Fnd Grants, 4307
Scholastic Welch's Harvest Grants, 4309
Schramm Fnd Grants, 4310
Schumann Fund for New Jersey Grants, 4311
Scott B & Annie P Appleby Char Trust Grts, 4313
Seagate Tech Corp Capacity to Care Grants, 4317
Search Dog Fnd Rescue Dog Assistance, 4318
Seattle Fnd Arts and Culture Grants, 4320
Seattle Fnd Basic Needs Grants, 4321
Seattle Fnd Benjamin N. Phillips Grants, 4322
Seattle Fdn C Keith Birkenfeld Mem Tr Grts, 4323
Seaver Institute Grants, 4331
Self Fnd Grants, 4335
Sensient Technologies Fnd Grants, 4337
Seybert Inst for Poor Boys & Girls Grts, 4338
Share Our Strength Grants, 4340
Shaw's Supermarkets Donations, 4342
Shell Oil Company Fnd Grants, 4343
Sheltering Arms Fund Grants, 4344
Shopko Fdn Comm Charitable Grts, 4346
Shopko Fnd Green Bay Area Comm Grants, 4347
Sidgmore Family Fnd Grants, 4348
Sidney Stern Memorial Trust Grants, 4349
Sid W. Richardson Fnd Grants, 4350
Siebert Lutheran Fnd Grants, 4351
Sierra Health Fnd Responsive Grants, 4353
Simmons Fnd Grants, 4360
Simpson Lumber Charitable Contributions, 4362
Singing for Change Fnd Grants, 4363
Sioux Falls Area Comm Fnd Comm Fund Grants, 4364
Sioux Falls Area Comm Fnd Field-of-Interest and Donor-Advised Grants, 4365
Sioux Falls Area Comm Fnd Spot Grants, 4366
Siragusa Fnd Arts & Culture Grants, 4367
Sir Dorabji Tata Trust Grants for NGOs or Voluntary Organizations, 4370
Sisters of Charity Fnd of Canton Grants, 4372
Sisters of Charity Fnd of Cleveland Good Samaritan Grants, 4373
Sisters of Mercy of North Carolina Fdn Grts, 4375
Sisters of Saint Joseph Charitable Fund Grants, 4376
Sisters of St Joseph Healthcare Fdn Grts, 4377
Slow Food in Schools Micro-Grants, 4384
Smith Richardson Fdn Direct Service Grts, 4385
Sobrato Family Fnd Grants, 4389
Sobrato Family Fdn Meeting Space Grts, 4390
Sobrato Family Fnd Office Space Grants, 4391
Sodexo Fnd STOP Hunger Scholarships, 4400
Solo Cup Fnd Grants, 4401
Solutia Fund Grants, 4402
Sonoco Fnd Grants, 4403
Sonora Area Fnd Competitive Grants, 4404
Sony Corp of America Corp Philant Grants, 4405
Sophia Romero Trust Grants, 4406
Sorenson Legacy Fnd Grants, 4407

Sosland Fnd Grants, 4408
Southbury Comm Trust Fund, 4409
South Carolina Arts Comsn Accessibility Grts, 4410
South Carolina Arts Commission AIE Residency Plus Individual Site Grants, 4411
South Carolina Arts Commission AIE Residency Plus Multi-Site Grants, 4412
South Carolina Arts Commission American Masterpieces in South Carolina Grants, 4413
South Carolina Arts Commission Annual Operating Support for Organizations Grants, 4414
South Carolina Arts Commission Arts and Economic Impact Study Assistance Grants, 4416
South Carolina Arts Commission Arts Facility Projects Grants, 4417
South Carolina Arts Commission Arts in Educ After School Arts Initiative Grants, 4418
South Carolina Arts Commission Cultural Tourism Initiative Grants, 4419
South Carolina Arts Commission Cultural Visions Grants, 4420
South Carolina Arts Commission Folklife & Traditional Arts Grants, 4421
South Carolina Arts Commission Incentive Grants for Employer Sponsored Benefits, 4422
South Carolina Arts Commission Leadership and Organizational Dev Grants, 4423
South Carolina Arts Commission Long Term Operating Support for Organizations Grants, 4424
South Carolina Arts Commission Statewide Arts Participation Initiative Grants, 4425
South Carolina Arts Commission Subgrants, 4426
South Carolina Arts Commission Traditional Arts Apprenticeship Grants, 4427
Southern Minnesota Initiative BookStart Grants, 4432
Southern Minnesota Initiative Fnd Comm Growth Initiative Grants, 4433
Southern Minnesota Initiative Incentive Grants, 4435
Southwest Florida Comm Competitive Grants, 4442
Southwest Florida Good Samaritan Grants, 4443
Southwire Company Grants, 4447
Special Olympics Project UNIFY Grants, 4449
Speer Trust Grants, 4450
Sport Manitoba Athlete/Team Travel Assistance Grants, 4452
Sport Manitoba Athlete Skill Dev Clinics Grants, 4453
Sport Manitoba Bingo Allocations Grants, 4454
Sport Manitoba Coaches/Officials Travel Assistance Grants, 4455
Sport Manitoba Intro of a New Sport Grts, 4457
Sport Manitoba KidSport Athlete Grants, 4458
Sport Manitoba Sport Special Initiatives Grants, 4459
Sprint Fnd Grants, 4463
Square D Fnd Grants, 4464
SSA Work Incentives Planning and Assistance, 4465
Stackner Family Fnd Grants, 4471
Stackpole-Hall Fnd Grants, 4472
Stan and Sandy Checketts Fnd, 4473
Staples Fnd for Learning Grants, 4475
Starbucks Fdn Shared Planet Youth Action, 4476
Starr Fnd Grants, 4483
State Farm Fnd Grants, 4486
State Farm Project Ignition Grants, 4487
State Street Fnd Grants, 4495
Staunton Farm Fnd Grants, 4496
Steelcase Fnd Grants, 4497
Steele-Reese Fnd Grants, 4498
Sterling-Turner Charitable Fnd Grants, 4499
Steven B. Achelis Fnd Grants, 4502
Stewart Huston Charitable Trust Grants, 4505
Stocker Fnd Grants, 4507
Stowe Family Fnd Grants, 4510
Strake Fnd Grants, 4511
Stranahan Fnd Grants, 4512
Strengthening Families - Strengthening Communities Grants, 4513
Stuart Fnd Grants, 4516
Subaru of Indiana Automotive Fdn Grts, 4519
Sulzberger Fnd Grants, 4522
Summit Fnd Grants, 4524

Sunbeam Products Grants, 4526
Sunflower Fnd Bridge Grants, 4528
Sunny and Abe Rosenberg Fnd Grants, 4529
Sunoco Fnd Grants, 4530
SVP Early Childhood Dev and Parenting Grants, 4538
Swindells Charitable Fnd, 4542
Sylvia Adams Charitable Trust Grants, 4543
Symantec Comm Relations and Corporate Philanthropy Grants, 4544
T.L.L. Temple Fnd Grants, 4546
T. Rowe Price Associates Fnd Grants, 4548
Taproot Fnd Capacity-Building Service Grants, 4560
Target Corporation Local Store Grants, 4561
Target Fnd Grants, 4562
Tauck Family Fnd Grants, 4563
Taylor S. Abernathy and Patti Harding Abernathy Charitable Trust Grants, 4564
TCF Bank Fnd Grants, 4565
TD4HIM Fnd Grants, 4566
Teaching Tolerance Grants, 4567
Teaching Tolerance Mix-it-Up Grants, 4568
TE Fnd Grants, 4572
Telluride Fdn Emergency/Out of Cycle Grts, 4574
Telluride Fdn Tech Assistance Grts, 4575
Temple-Inland Fnd Grants, 4576
Tension Envelope Fnd Grants, 4578
Textron Corporate Contributions Grants, 4601
Thelma Doelger Charitable Trust Grants, 4604
Theodore Edson Parker Fnd Grants, 4605
Thomas C. Ackerman Fnd Grants, 4615
Thomas J. Atkins Memorial Trust Fund Grants, 4617
Thomas J. Long Fnd Comm Grants, 4618
Thomas Sill Fnd Grants, 4619
Thomas Thompson Trust Grants, 4620
Thomas W. Briggs Fnd Grants, 4621
Thompson Charitable Fnd Grants, 4622
Thompson Fnd Grants, 4623
Tifa Fnd Grants, 4633
TJX Fnd Grants, 4637
Todd Brock Family Fnd Grants, 4639
Tom's of Maine Grants, 4640
Topeka Comm Boss Hawg's Charitable Giving, 4642
Topeka Comm Fnd Building Families Grants, 4643
Topeka Comm Fnd Grants, 4644
Topfer Family Fnd Grants, 4646
Toro Fnd Grants, 4647
Toyota Motor Engineering & Manufacturing North America Grants, 4651
Toyota Motor Mfg of Alabama Grts, 4652
Toyota Motor Manufacturing of Indiana Grants, 4653
Toyota Motor Mfg of Kentucky Grts, 4654
Toyota Motor Mfg of Mississippi Grts, 4655
Toyota Motor Manufacturing of Texas Grants, 4656
Toyota Motor Manuf of West Virginia Grants, 4657
Toyota Motor North America of NY Grts, 4658
Toyota Motor Sales, USA Grants, 4659
Toyota Tech Center Grants, 4660
Tri-County Electric People Fund Grants, 4665
Tri-State Comm Twenty-first Century Endowment Fund Grants, 4666
Triangle Comm Fdn Donor-Advised Grts, 4668
Trinity Trust Summer Youth Mini Grants, 4672
Trull Fnd Grants, 4673
TSA Advanced Surveillance Grants, 4674
TSYSF Team Grants, 4676
Tull Charitable Fnd Grants, 4679
Turner Voices Corporate Contributions, 4682
TWS Fnd Grants, 4683
U.S. Bank Fnd Grants, 4686
US Dept of Educ 21st Century Comm Learning Centers, 4687
US Dept of Educ Cntrs for Independent Lvng, 4688
US Dept of Educ Child Care Access Means Parents in School Grants, 4689
US Dept of Educ Disability and Rehabilitation Research and Related Projects, 4690
US Dept of Educ Early Reading First Grants, 4691
US Dept of Educ Innovative Strategies in Comm Colleges for Working Adults and Displaced Workers Grants, 4692

US Dept of Educ Migrant and Seasonal Farmworkers Grants, 4693
US Dept of Educ Native Hawaiian Educ Grts, 4694
US Dept of Educ Parent Info & Trng, 4695
US Dept of Educ Pgms for Native Hawaiians, 4696
US Dept of Educ Rehabilitation Engineering Research Centers Grants, 4698
US Dept of Educ Rehabilitation Research Training Centers , 4699
US Dept of Educ Rehab Trng--Rehabilitation Continuing Educ Programs --Institute on Rehabilitation Issues , 4700
US Dept of Educ Special Education--National Activities--Parent Information Centers, 4701
US Dept of Educ Voc Rehab Svcs Projects for American Indians with Disabilities Grts, 4702
Union Bank, N.A. Corporate Sponsorships and Donations, 4708
Union Bank, N.A. Fnd Grants, 4709
Union Benevolent Association Grants, 4710
Union Labor Health Fnd Comm Grts, 4713
Union Pacific Fnd Comm & Civic Grts, 4714
Union Pacific Fnd Health & Human Svcs Grts, 4715
Union Square Award for Social Justice, 4717
United Methodist Committee on Relief Global AIDS Fund Grants, 4719
United Methodist Committee on Relief Hunger and Poverty Grants, 4720
United Methodist Child Mental Health Grants, 4721
United Methodist Women Brighter Future for Children and Youth Grants, 4723
United Technologies Corporation Grants, 4725
UPS Fnd Comm Safety Grants, 4728
USAA – Ann Hoyt / Jim Easton JOAD Grants, 4734
USAID/Cambodia Maternal and Child Health, Tuberculosis, HIV/AIDS. and Malaria Grants, 4736
USAID Comm Infrastructure Dev Grants, 4745
USAID Integration of Care and Support within the Health System to Support Better Patient Outcomes Grants, 4762
USAID Int'l Food Relief Partnership Grants, 4764
USAID NGO Health Service Delivery Grants, 4771
USAID Strengthening RMNCH Through Indian Health Professional Associations and Scaling Up Uptake Grants, 4784
US Airways Comm Contributions, 4788
US Airways Comm Fnd Grants, 4789
US Airways Educ Fnd Grants, 4790
US CRDF STEP Business Partnership Grant Competition Ukraine, 4796
USDA Delta Health Care Services Grants, 4804
USDA Distance Lrng & Telemedicine Grts, 4806
USDC Tech Opportunities Pgm Grts, 4860
USDJ Edward Byrne Memorial Justice Assistance Grants, 4863
USDJ Nat Criminal History Improvement Grants, 4864
USDJ NICS Act Record Improvement Grants, 4865
USFA Dev Grants, 4866
USFA Equipment Subsidy Grants, 4867
US Soccer Fdn Annual Pgm & Field Grts, 4870
US Soccer Fnd Planning Grants, 4871
USTA CTA and NJTL Comm Tennis Dev Workshop Scholarships, 4873
USTA Junior Team Tennis Stipends, 4875
USTA Multicultural Excellence Grants, 4876
USTA Player Dev Grants, 4881
USTA Pro Circuit Comm Involvement Grants, 4882
USTA Public Facility Assistance Grants, 4883
USTA Recreational Tennis Grants, 4884
USTA Tennis Block Party Grants, 4892
Vancouver Fnd Grants and Comm Initiatives, 4900
Vanderburgh Comm Fnd Women's Fund, 4903
Vectren Fnd Grants, 4907
Verizon Fnd Domestic Violence Prevention, 4910
Verizon Fnd Health Care and Accessibility Grants, 4913
Verizon Fnd New York Grants, 4919
Verizon Fnd NE Region Grants, 4920
Verizon Fnd Virginia Grants, 4925
VHA Health Fnd Grants, 4931
Victor E. Speas Fnd Grants, 4933
Victoria S. and Bradley L. Geist Fnd Grants Supporting Foster Care and Their Caregivers, 4936
Victoria S. and Bradley L. Geist Fnd Grants Supporting Transitioning Foster Youth, 4937
Vigneron Grants, 4938
Viking Children's Fund Grants, 4939
Virginia W. Kettering Fnd Grants, 4950
Visiting Nurse Fnd Grants, 4951
Vulcan Materials Company Fnd Grants, 4956
W.C. Griffith Fnd Grants, 4957
WH & Mary Ellen Cobb Char Trust Grts, 4959
WK Kellogg Fdn Healthy Kids Grants, 4961
WK Kellogg Fdn Racial Equity Grants, 4962
WM Keck Fdn Southern California Grts, 4964
W.P. and Bulah Luse Fnd Grants, 4965
Waitt Family Fnd Grants, 4973
Wallace Fnd Grants, 4976
Walt Disney Company Fnd Grants, 4981
Walter and Elise Haas Fund Grants, 4982
Walter L. Gross III Family Fnd Grants, 4983
Washington Area Fuel Fund Grants, 4988
Washington Families Fund Grants, 4999
Washington Gas Char Gvg Contributions, 5000
Wayne and Gladys Valley Fnd Grants, 5003
Wayne County Fnd Grants, 5005
Weaver Popcorn Fnd Grants, 5016
Weingart Fnd Grants, 5018
Welborn Baptist Fnd Gen Opportunity Grants, 5020
Welborn Baptist Fnd Improvements to Comm Health Status Grants, 5021
Wells Fargo Housing Fnd Grants, 5023
Western Indiana Comm Fdn Grts, 5024
Westinghouse Charitable Giving Grants, 5028
Weyerhaeuser Company Fnd Grants, 5053
Whirlpool Fnd Grants, 5056
Whitehorse Fnd Grants, 5058
Whiting Fnd Grants, 5059
WHO Fnd Education/Lit Grants, 5062
WHO Fnd General Grants, 5063
Widgeon Point Charitable Fnd Grants, 5064
Willary Fnd Grants, 5071
William B. Stokely Jr. Fnd Grants, 5076
William Blair and Company Fnd Grants, 5078
William G. Kelley Fnd Grants, 5083
William G. McGowan Charitable Fund Grants, 5084
William G Selby & Marie Selby Fdn Grts, 5085
William J. and Dorothy K. O'Neill Fnd Grants, 5087
William M. Weaver Fnd Grants, 5091
William Robert Baird Charitable Trust Grants, 5093
William S. Abell Fnd Grants, 5094
Williams Companies Fnd Grants, 5095
William T. Grant Fnd Youth Service Improvement Grants , 5096
Wilson-Wood Fnd Grants, 5098
Windward Youth Leadership Fund Grants, 5100
Winston-Salem Fdn Competitive Grts, 5102
Winston-Salem Fdn Elkin/Tri-County Grants, 5103
Winston-Salem Fdn Stokes County Grants, 5104
Winthrop Rockefeller Fnd Grants, 5105
Wolfe Associates Grants, 5110
Women's Funding Alliance Grants, 5112
Woods Charitable Fund Grants, 5114
Woods Fund of Chicago Grants, 5115
Woodward Fund Grants, 5116
Xerox Fnd Grants, 5122
Yellow Corporate Fnd Grants, 5126
Young Family Fnd Grants , 5127
Youth as Resources Mini-Grants, 5131
Youth Philanthropy Project, 5132
YSA ABC Summer of Service Awards, 5133
YSA Get Ur Good On Grants, 5134
YSA Global Yth Svc Day Lead Agency Grts, 5135
YSA MLK Day Lead Organizer Grants, 5136
YSA NEA Youth Leaders for Lit Grants, 5138
YSA Radio Disney's Hero for Change Award, 5139
YSA State Farm Good Neighbor YOUth In The Driver Seat Grants, 5141
YSA UnitedHealth HEROES Service-Learning Grants, 5142
Yves Rocher Fdn Women of the Earth Awards, 5143

Symposiums, Conferences, Workshops, Seminars
AAP Comm Access To Child Health Advocacy Training Grants, 62
Agape Fnd for Nonviolent Social Change Board of Trustees Grants, 197
Air Force Association Junior ROTC Grants, 215
ALA ALSC Bookapalooza Grants, 222
ALA ALTAFF/GALE Outstanding Trustee Conference Grant, 224
Alabama Humanities Fnd Planning Grants, 232
ALA Bogle Pratt Int'l Library Travel Fund Grant, 251
ALA NMRT Professional Dev Grant, 305
ALA Pat Carterette Prof Dev Grt, 306
ALA Romance Writers of America Lib Grt, 314
Alaska Airlines Fnd Grants, 321
ALA Supporting Diversity Stipend, 333
ALA Writers Live at the Library Grants, 336
ALA Young Adult Lit Symposium Stipend, 337
Alcoa Fnd Grants, 350
ALFJ Astraea U.S. and Int'l Movement Fund, 361
Alfred P Sloan Fdn Civic Initiatives Grts, 368
Allen P & Josephine B Green Fdn Grts, 380
ALZA Corporate Contributions Grants, 405
AMA-MSS Chapter Involvement Grants, 406
AMA Fnd Jack B. McConnell, MD Awards for Excellence in Volunteerism, 411
Ambrose Monell Fnd Grants, 415
Ameren Corporation Comm Grants, 418
American Academy of Religion Reg Dev Grants, 421
Americana Fnd Grants, 422
American Express Leaders for Tomorrow Grants, 432
AMI Semiconductors Corporate Grants, 457
ANLAF Int'l Fund for Sexual Minorities Grts, 471
Ann Arbor Area Comm Fnd Grants, 474
Apple Worldwide Developers Conference Student Scholarships, 513
Aratani Fnd Grants, 523
Archer Daniels Midland Fnd Grants, 527
Arizona Comm on Arts Folklorist Residencies, 537
Arizona Commission on the Arts Visual/Media Arts Organizations Grants, 539
Arizona Public Service Corp Gvg Pgm Grts, 545
Arkansas Arts Council AIE Mini Grants, 554
Arkansas Arts Council Sally A. Williams Artist Fund Grants, 558
ARTBA Transportation Dev Fnd Grants, 569
Arts Midwest Performing Arts Grants, 579
Asian American Institute Comm Impact Fellowships, 588
Atlanta Women's Fnd Grants, 609
Atran Fnd Grants, 610
AWDF Solidarity Fund Grants, 628
Ball Brothers Fnd General Grants, 637
Battle Creek Comm Fnd Grants, 684
Bay and Paul Fnds Grants, 693
Berks County Comm Fnd Grants, 734
Blanche & Julian Robertson Family Fdn Grants, 785
Blue Cross Blue Shield of Minnesota Fdn Healthy Equity: Health Impact Assessment Grts, 796
Blue Cross Blue Shield of Minnesota Fdn-Healthy Equity: Public Libraries for Health Grts, 797
Blue Cross Blue Shield of Minnesota Fnd - Healthy Neighborhoods: Connect for Health Challenge Grants, 798
Blumenthal Fnd Grants, 804
BoatUS Fnd Grassroots Grants, 805
Bodenwein Public Benevolent Fdn Grants, 806
Boeing Company Contributions Grants, 809
Brainerd Fnd Grants, 831
British Columbia Arts Council Educ Grants, 842
Bullitt Fnd Grants, 862
Bydale Fnd Grants, 882
Caddock Fnd Grants, 888
California Arts Council Statewide Ntwks Grts, 897
Carl M. Freeman Fnd Grants, 933
Cash 4 Clubs Sports Grants, 951
Catherine Manley Gaylord Fnd Grants, 956
CDECD Arts Catalyze Placemaking in Every Comm Grants, 977
CDECD Arts Catalyze Placemaking Leadership Grants, 978

PROGRAM TYPE INDEX

Symposiums, Conferences, Workshops, Seminars / 1133

CDECD Arts Catalyze Placemaking Sustaining Relevance Grants, 979
Central Minnesota Comm Fnd Grants, 995
CFFVR Alcoholism and Drug Abuse Grants, 1001
CFFVR Environmental Stewardship Grants, 1010
CFFVR Mielke Family Fnd Grants, 1015
Charles Delmar Fnd Grants, 1039
Charles G. Koch Charitable Fnd Grants, 1041
Charles Lafitte Fnd Grants, 1049
Charles Stewart Mott Fdn Anti-Poverty Grts, 1054
Charles Stewart Mott Fnd Grants, 1055
Chautauqua Region Comm Fdn Grts, 1062
Chesapeake Bay Trust Capacity Bldg Grts, 1068
Chesapeake Bay Trust Outreach and Engagement Grants, 1073
CIGNA Fnd Grants, 1130
City of Oakland Cultural Arts Dept Grts, 1142
Claude Worthington Benedum Fdn Grants, 1161
Cleveland-Cliffs Fnd Grants, 1165
Comm Fdn for Grtr Buffalo Grants, 1247
Comm Fdn for Muskegon Cty Grants, 1256
Comm Fdn for NE Michigan Grants, 1257
Comm Fnd of Greater Fort Wayne - Barbara Burt Leadership Dev Grants, 1283
Comm Fnd of Greater Fort Wayne - Collaborative Efforts Grants, 1284
Comm Fdn of Grtr Fort Wayne - John S & James L Knight Fdn Donor-Advised Grts, 1287
Comm Fnd of Louisville Grants, 1299
Comm Fdn of Muncie & Delaware County Grant, 1302
Comm Fdn of SE Connecticut Grants, 1309
Comm Fnd of St. Joseph County ArtsEverywhere Grants, 1313
Comm Fnd of Western North Carolina Grants, 1327
Comm in the Connecting AAPIs To Advocate and Lead Grants, 1333
Connecticut Comm Fnd Grants, 1350
ConocoPhillips Grants, 1355
Constellation Energy Corp EcoStar Grts, 1363
Corina Higginson Trust Grants, 1373
Covidien Partners for Neighborhood Wellness, 1391
Cummins Fnd Grants, 1415
Dallas Women's Fnd Grants, 1438
Dave Thomas Fnd for Adoption Grants, 1449
DeKalb County Comm Fnd - Lit Grant, 1480
Delaware Division of the Arts Opportunity Grants--Arts Organizations, 1488
Denver Fnd Comm Grants, 1502
Dept of Ed Parental Infor & Resource Cntrs, 1510
District of Columbia Commission on the Arts-Arts Educ Teacher Mini-Grants, 1549
Dolfinger-McMahon Fnd Grants, 1565
Dubois County Comm Fnd Grants, 1615
Dynegy Fnd Grants, 1630
Dyson Fnd Mid-Hudson Valley Project Grants, 1636
Eileen Fisher Women-Owned Business Grants, 1677
Ensign-Bickford Fnd Grants, 1709
Eugene M. Lang Fnd Grants, 1764
Evanston Comm Fnd Grants, 1771
Ewing Marion Kauffman Fnd Grants, 1777
Fam Lit & HI Pizza Hut Lit Fund, 1785
Faye McBeath Fnd Grants, 1794
Fayette County Fnd Grants, 1795
FINRA Smart Investing@Your Library Grants, 1816
Fleishhacker Fnd Educ Grants, 1838
Florida Humanities Cncl Civic Reflection Grts, 1867
Florida Humanities Council Major Grants, 1868
Florida Humanities Council Mini Grants, 1869
Florida Humanities Council Partnership Grants, 1870
Florida Sports Fnd Junior Golf Grants, 1872
Foellinger Fnd Grants, 1877
Ford Fdn Peace & Social Justice Grts, 1884
Frances C & William P Smallwood Fdn Grts, 1918
Frank and Lydia Bergen Fnd Grants, 1925
Fremont Area Comm Fnd Grants, 1955
Fulton County Comm Fnd Grants, 1975
George Gund Fnd Grants, 2020
George J. and Effie L. Seay Fnd Grants, 2024
Georgia Council for the Arts Partner Grants for Organizations, 2035

Gill Fnd Gay & Lesbian Fund, 2054
GMFUS Black Sea Trust Regional Corp Grants, 2065
GMFUS Urban & Regnl Policy Fwsps, 2067
GNOF Environmental Fund Grants, 2073
GNOF IMPACT Grts for Youth Dev't, 2081
GNOF Organizational Effectiveness Grants, 2090
Greater Saint Louis Comm Fdn Grants, 2138
Greater Worcester Comm Fnd Jeppson Memorial Fund for Brookfield Grants, 2141
Greater Worcester Comm Fnd Mini-Grants, 2142
HAF Comm Grants, 2193
HAF Southern Humboldt Grants, 2204
Halliburton Fnd Grants, 2211
Hartford Aging and Health Program Awards, 2247
Hartford Fdn Nonprofit Support Grants, 2252
Hatton W. Sumners Fnd for the Study and Teaching of Self Government Grants, 2257
Hawai'i Children's Trust Fund Comm Awareness Events Grants, 2258
Haymarket People's Fund Sustaining Grants, 2267
Haymarket Urgent Response Grants, 2268
Health Fnd of Grtr Indianapolis Grts, 2282
Helen Bader Fnd Grants, 2293
Historic Landmarks Fnd of Indiana Historic Preservation Educ Grants, 2334
Honeywell Corporation Leadership Challenge Academy, 2359
Honor the Earth Grants, 2361
Humanitas Fnd Grants, 2390
Hydrogen Student Design Contest, 2415
ICC Listening to Communities Grants, 2429
IEDC Int'l Trade Show Assistance Pgm, 2444
Illinois Arts Council Lit Pgm Grts, 2470
Illinois Arts Council Media Arts Pgm Grts, 2472
Indiana Arts Commission American Masterpieces Grants, 2530
Indiana Arts Commission Statewide Arts Service Organization Grants, 2533
Indiana Rural Capacity Grants , 2547
Internet Society Fellowships, 2570
J.W. Kieckhefer Fnd Grants, 2607
Jacobs Family Fdn Vlg Neighborhoods Grants, 2619
James J. McCann Charitable Trust and McCann Fnd, Inc Grants, 2631
Japan Fnd Center for Global Partnership Grants, 2649
Japan Fnd Los Angeles Mini-Grants for Japanese Arts & Culture, 2651
Japan Fnd New York Small Arts & Culture Grants, 2652
Jewish Women's Fnd of New York Grants, 2677
John D. and Catherine T. MacArthur Fnd Global Challenges Grants, 2690
John P. McGovern Fnd Grants, 2707
Johnson Fnd Wingspread Conference Support, 2725
John W. Speas and Effie E. Speas Memorial Trust Grants, 2732
Joseph Alexander Fnd Grants, 2734
Kaiser Permanente Cares for Communities Grts, 2763
Ka Papa O Kakuhihewa Fund, 2785
Kentucky Arts Cncl Access Astnce Grts, 2805
Kiki Madazine Grow Strong Girls through Leadership Grants, 2822
Komen Greater NYC Small Grants, 2836
Koret Fnd Grants, 2837
Laurel Fnd Grants, 2867
LEGO Children's Fund Grants, 2878
Lillian S. Wells Fnd Grants, 2901
Louis and Elizabeth Nave Flarsheim Grants, 2924
Louis Calder Fnd Grants, 2925
Lowell Berry Fnd Grants, 2930
Lynde and Harry Bradley Fnd Grants, 2947
MacArthur Fnd Conservation and Sustainable Dev Grants, 2963
Marie C. and Joseph C. Wilson Fnd Rochester Small Grants, 3006
Mary Black Fnd Active Living Grants, 3031
Mary D. & Walter F Frear Eleemosynary Trust, 3035
Mary Duke Biddle Fnd Grants, 3036
Mary Jennings Sport Camp Scholarship, 3041
Massachusetts Fnd for the Humanities Cultural Economic Dev Grants, 3059

Massachusetts Fnd for Humanities Project Grants, 3060
Maurice Amado Fnd Grants, 3063
Max and Anna Levinson Fnd Grants, 3066
McCune Charitable Fnd Grants, 3077
McLean Contributionship Grants, 3088
Melville Charitable Trust Grants, 3115
Mertz Gilmore Fnd NYC Dance Grants, 3127
Meyer Fnd Benevon Grants, 3140
MFRI Operation Diploma Grants for Student Veterans Organizations, 3151
MFRI Operation Diploma Small Grants for Indiana Family Readiness Groups, 3152
MGN Family Fnd Grants, 3154
Mitsubishi Electric America Fnd Grants, 3190
NACC David Stevenson Fellowships, 3235
NACC William Diaz Fellowships, 3236
NASE Succeed Scholarships, 3243
National Center for Responsible Gaming Conference Scholarships, 3250
National Endowment for the Arts - National Partnership Agreement Grants, 3256
National Endowment for the Arts - Regional Partnership Agreement Grants, 3258
National Endowment for the Arts Artist Communities Grants, 3260
National Endowment for the Arts Dance Grants, 3262
National Endowment for the Arts Local Arts Agencies Grants, 3263
National Endowment for the Arts Music Grants, 3266
National Endowment for Arts Presenting Grants, 3268
National Endowment for the Arts Theater and Musical Theater Grants, 3269
Nellie Mae Educ Fnd District Change Grants, 3297
Nellie Mae Educ Fnd State Level Systems Change Grants, 3299
Nevada Arts Council Jackpot Grants, 3312
NFWF State Comprehensive Wildlife Conservation Support Grants, 3395
NIAF Italian Culture and Heritage Grants, 3432
NICHD Academic-Comm Partnership Conference Series Grants, 3433
Noble County Comm Fnd Grants, 3456
Nonprofit Management Fund Grants, 3458
Norcliffe Fnd Grants, 3459
North Carolina Arts Council Arts in Educ Artist Residencies Grants, 3468
North Carolina Arts Council Folklife Grants, 3476
North Carolina BioTech Center Event Sponsorship Grants, 3485
North Carolina BioTech Center Meeting Grants, 3486
North Carolina BioTech Center Multidisciplinary Research Grants, 3487
North Carolina Comm Fnd Grants, 3489
North Carolina GlaxoSmithKline Fdn Grts, 3490
North Dakota Council on the Arts Comm Access Grants, 3494
North Dakota Council on the Arts Institutional Support Grants, 3496
NW Fund for the Environment Grants, 3510
NSF Communicating Rsch to Public Audiences, 3527
NYSCA Architecture, Planning, and Design: Project Support Grants, 3576
NYSCA Arts Education: Comm-based Learning Grants, 3577
NYSCA Electronic Media and Film: Workspace Grants, 3593
NYSCA Lit: Public Programs, 3600
NYSCA Presenting: Svcs to the Field Grts, 3612
NYSCA Special Arts Services: General Program Support Grants, 3615
NYSCA State and Local Partnerships: Workshops Grants, 3622
NYSCA Theatre: Services to the Field Grants, 3626
NYSCA Visual Arts: Svcs to the Field Grts, 3630
Olin Corporation Charitable Trust Grants, 3669
Oppenstein Brothers Fnd Grants, 3685
ORBI Artist Fast Track Grants, 3689
OSF Advancing the Rights and Integration of Roma Grants, 3699
Overbrook Fnd Grants, 3715

Symposiums, Conferences, Workshops, Seminars

Palm Beach and Martin Counties Grants, 3733
PAS PASIC Scholarships, 3744
Paul Rapoport Fnd Grants, 3765
PCA-PCD Professional Dev for Artists Grants, 3770
PCA Arts in Educ Residencies, 3772
PCA Arts Organizations and Arts Grants for Arts Educ Organizations, 3776
PCA Entry Track Arts Orgs & Arts Pgms Grts for Arts Educ Orgs, 3788
PCA Entry Track Arts Organizations and Arts Grants for Crafts, 3790
PCA Professional Dev Grants, 3803
PennPAT Artist Tech Assistance Grants, 3811
Peter and Elizabeth C. Tower Fnd Organizational Scholarships, 3838
PetSmart Charities Conf Sponsorship Grts, 3851
Pew Charitable Trusts Arts and Culture Grants, 3857
Pfizer Medical Educ Track One Grants, 3864
Phil Hardin Fnd Grants, 3875
Pinellas County Grants, 3891
Pioneer Hi-Bred Confs & Mtgs Grts, 3896
PMP Professional Dev Grants, 3919
Poets & Writers Readings/Workshops Grants, 3927
Principal Financial Group Fnd Grants, 3966
Prudential Fnd Educ Grants, 3977
Public Educ Power Grants, 3981
Puerto Rico Comm Fnd Grants, 3986
Quantum Corporation Snap Server Grants, 3995
Raskob Fdn for Catholic Activities Grts, 4019
Rathmann Family Fnd Grants, 4026
RGK Fnd Grants, 4072
Rhode Island Fnd Grants, 4073
Rochester Area Comm Fnd Grants, 4127
Rochester Area Fnd Grants, 4128
Rockefeller Brothers Democratic Practice Grants, 4131
Rockefeller Brothers Sustainable Dev Grants, 4136
Rockwell Int'l Corporate Trust Grants, 4141
Rose Comm Fnd Aging Grants, 4152
RWJF Local Funding Partnerships Grants, 4186
RWJF Partners Investing in Nursing's Future, 4188
San Antonio Area Fnd Grants, 4240
Sarah Scaife Fnd Grants, 4295
SAS Institute Comm Relations Donations, 4300
Saucony Run for Good Fnd Grants, 4301
Sid W. Richardson Fnd Grants, 4350
SOBP A.E. Bennett Research Award, 4388
Social Justice Fund NW Criminal Justice Grants, 4394
South Carolina Arts Commission Folklife & Traditional Arts Grants, 4421
South Carolina Arts Commission Leadership and Organizational Dev Grants, 4423
South Madison Comm Fnd Grants, 4440
Sport Manitoba Athlete Skill Dev Clinics Grants, 4453
Sport Manitoba Hosting Regional Championships Grants, 4456
Stark Comm Fnd Neighborhood Comm and Economic Dev Tech Assistance Grants, 4478
Strowd Roses Grants, 4515
Summit Fnd Grants, 4524
TAC Arts Access Grant, 4549
TAC Arts Build Communities Grants, 4551
TAC Arts Projects Grants, 4554
TAC Rural Arts Project Support Grants, 4555
Taylor S. Abernathy and Patti Harding Abernathy Charitable Trust Grants, 4564
Telluride Fnd Comm Grants, 4573
Texas Comm on Arts Cultural Connections Grant, 4591
Textron Corporate Contributions Grants, 4601
Tourism Cares Professional Dev Scholarships, 4648
US Soccer Fdn Annual Pgm & Field Grts, 4870
USTA NJTL Arthur Ashe Essay & Art Cnst, 4878
Wayne County Fnd Grants, 5005
WCI Leadership Dev Grants, 5012
Weatherwax Fnd Grants, 5014
Weyerhaeuser Company Fnd Grants, 5053
YSA National Child Awareness Month Youth Ambassador Grants, 5137
Z. Smith Reynolds Fnd Economic Dev Grants, 5144
Z. Smith Reynolds Fnd Democracy and Civic Engagement Grants, 5145

Technical Assistance

A.C. Ratshesky Fnd Grants, 39
AAAS Science and Tech Policy Fellowships: Health, Educ and Human Services, 53
Abbot & Dorothy H Stevens Fdn Grants, 79
Abbott Fund Access to Health Care Grants, 80
Abbott Fund Global AIDS Care Grants, 82
Able To Play Challenge Grants, 101
Actors Fund Dancers' Resource, 137
Actors Fund Funeral and Burial Assistance, 138
AEC Trust Grants, 175
African American Fund of New Jersey Grants, 192
AGMA Relief Fund Grants, 201
Ahearn Family Fnd Grants, 206
Alabama State Council on the Arts Comm Arts Tech Assistance Grants, 240
Alabama State Council on the Arts Project Assistance Grants, 247
Alabama State Council on the Arts Tech Assistance Grants for Individuals, 249
Alabama State Council on the Arts Tech Assistance Grants for Organizations, 250
ALA Citizens-Save-Libraries Grants, 257
Albert Pick Jr. Fund Grants, 344
Albuquerque Comm Fnd Grants, 348
Alex Stern Family Fnd Grants, 360
ALFJ Astraea U.S. and Int'l Movement Fund, 361
Allstate Corporate Giving Grants, 386
Altman Fnd Health Care Grants, 397
Amador Comm Fnd Grants, 408
Americana Fnd Grants, 422
American Express Charitable Fund Grants, 429
Anderson Fnd Grants, 460
Anschutz Family Fnd Grants, 486
Appalachian Comm Fund Special Opps Grants, 497
Appalachian Comm Fund Tech Assistance Grants, 498
Appalachian Regional Commission Asset-Based Dev Project Grants, 500
Appalachian Reg'l Commission Housing Grts, 508
Appalachian Regional Commission Leadership Dev and Capacity Building Grants, 509
Appalachian Regional Commission Telecommunications Grants, 510
Appalachian Regional Commission Transportation and Highways Grants, 512
ARCO Fnd Educ Grants, 528
Arie and Ida Crown Memorial Grants, 533
Arizona Comm Fnd Grants, 540
Arizona Fnd for Women Deborah G. Carstens Fund Grants, 543
Arizona Republic Newspaper Corp Contribs, 547
Arkansas Arts Council AIE Arts Curriculum Project Grants, 552
Arkansas Arts Cncl Collab Proj Support, 555
Arkansas Arts Council Expansion Arts Grants, 556
Arkansas Comm Fnd Giving Tree Grants, 560
Arlington Comm Fnd Grants, 564
ARTBA Transportation Dev Fnd Grants, 569
ArvinMeritor Fnd Civic Grants, 583
Aspen Comm Fnd Grants, 592
Assisi Fnd of Memphis General Grants, 594
Assisi Fnd of Memphis Mini Grants, 595
Atkinson Fnd Comm Grants, 606
Autauga Area Comm Fnd Grants, 618
AutoNation Corporate Giving Grants, 620
Avon Products Fnd Grants, 625
Ball Brothers Fnd General Grants, 637
Baltimore Comm Fnd Transportation Path Grants, 648
Battle Creek Comm Fnd Mini-Grants, 685
Baxter Int'l Corporate Giving Grants, 689
Bay and Paul Fnds Grants, 693
BCBSM Fdn Proposal Dev Awds, 709
BCBSNC Fnd Fit Together Grants, 711
BCBS of Massachusetts Fnd Grants, 713
Beldon Fund Grants, 720
Best Buy Children's Fnd @15 Teach Awards, 751
Best Buy Children's Fnd National Grants, 752
Bill and Melinda Gates Ag Dev Grants, 765
Bill and Melinda Gates Fnd Financial Services for the Poor Grants, 767

Bill & Melinda Gates Fdn Library Grts, 768
Blanche & Julian Robertson Family Fdn Grants, 785
Blandin Fdn Expand Opportunity Grants, 787
Blue Cross Blue Shield of Minnesota Fdn Healthy Equity: Health Impact Assessment Grts, 796
Blue River Comm Fnd Grants, 801
Boeing Company Contributions Grants, 809
Bohemian Fnd Pharos Fund Grants, 811
Boston Fnd Grants, 819
Boston Globe Fnd Grants, 821
Boulder County Arts Alliance Neodata Endowment Grants, 823
Bowling Green Comm Fnd Grants, 824
Brainerd Fnd Grants, 831
Brookdale Fnd Relatives as Parents Grts, 846
Bullitt Fnd Grants, 862
Burlington Industries Fnd Grants, 865
Bush Fnd Regional Arts Dev Program II Grants, 878
Caesars Fnd Grants, 891
Cailloux Fnd Grants, 892
California Arts Council Arts and Accessibility Tech Assistance Grants, 894
California Arts Council Tech Assistance Grts, 898
California Comm Fnd Art Grants, 900
Cambridge Comm Fnd Grants, 913
Carl M. Freeman Fnd Grants, 933
Carpenter Fnd Grants, 943
Cash 4 Clubs Sports Grants, 951
Cass County Comm Fnd Grants, 952
Cause Populi Worthy Cause Grants, 958
CDC School Health Programs to Prevent the Spread of HIV Cooperative Agreements, 975
Central Minnesota Comm Fnd Grants, 995
Central New York Comm Fnd Grants, 996
CenturyLink Clarke M Williams Fdn Grts, 998
CFFVR Basic Needs Gvg Partnership Grts, 1002
CFFVR Environmental Stewardship Grants, 1010
Charles & Lynn Schusterman Fam Fdn Grants, 1038
Charles H. Farnsworth Trust Grants, 1043
Charles Hayden Fnd Grants, 1048
Charles Stewart Mott Fdn Anti-Poverty Grts, 1054
Charles Stewart Mott Fnd Grants, 1055
CHCF Local Coverage Expansion Initiative, 1064
Chefs Move to Schools Grants, 1066
Chesapeake Bay Trust Capacity Bldg Grts, 1068
Chesapeake Bay Trust Pioneer Grants, 1074
Chicago Comm Trust Arts & Culture Grts: Improving Access to Arts Lrng Opportunities, 1082
Chicago Comm Trust Hsg Grants: Preserving Hm Ownership & Preventing Foreclosure, 1089
Circle K Corporation Contributions Grants, 1136
Claneil Fnd Grants, 1145
Clarence E Heller Charitable Fdn Grants, 1150
Clark Fnd Grants, 1157
Cleveland Fnd Neighborhood Connections Grants, 1171
Clipper Ship Fnd Grants, 1175
CNCS Foster Grandparent Projects Grants, 1185
CNCS School Turnaround AmeriCorps Grants, 1186
CNCS Senior Companion Grants, 1187
CNCS Senior Corps Retired and Senior Volunteer Grants, 1188
Coastal Comm Fdn of SC Grants, 1193
Colorado Trust Partnerships for Health Init, 1217
Columbus Fnd Competitive Grants, 1220
Columbus Fnd Traditional Grants, 1233
Comm Dev Financial Institution Bank Enterprise Awards, 1244
Comm Fnd Alliance City of Evansville Endowment Fund Grants, 1246
Comm Fdn for Grtr Buffalo Grants, 1247
Comm Fnd for Greater New Haven Neighborhood Small Grants, 1249
Comm Fnd for Greater New Haven Quinnipiac River Fund Grants, 1250
Comm Fnd for Greater New Haven Responsive New Grants, 1251
Comm Fnd for Greater New Haven Valley Neighborhood Grants, 1253
Comm Fnd for Greater New Haven Women & Girls Grants, 1254

PROGRAM TYPE INDEX

Technical Training / 1135

Comm Fdn for Monterey Cty Grants, 1255
Comm Fdn for NE Michigan Grants, 1257
Comm Fdn for Southern Arizona Grants, 1261
Comm Fdn in Jacksonville Art Ventures Small Arts Orgs Professional Assistance Grts, 1262
Comm Fdn of Boone County Grants, 1274
Comm Fdn of Greater Flint Grants, 1282
Comm Fnd of Greater Fort Wayne - Cmty Endwt & Clarke Endwt Grants, 1285
Comm Fnd of Muncie & Delaware County Grant, 1302
Comm Fdn of Santa Cruz County Grants, 1305
Comm Fdn of SE Connecticut Grants, 1309
Comm Fdn of the Ozarks Grants, 1320
Comm Fdn of Wabash Cty Grants, 1326
Comm Fnd of Western North Carolina Grants, 1327
Comm Fnd Silicon Valley Advancing Arts Grants, 1330
Comm Fnd Silicon Valley Grants, 1331
Comm in the Connecting AAPIs To Advocate and Lead Grants, 1333
Comm Partners on Waste Educ and Reduction, 1335
Connecticut Comm Fnd Grants, 1350
ConocoPhillips Fnd Grants, 1354
Conservation, Food, and Health Fnd Grants for Developing Countries, 1359
Consumers Energy Fnd, 1365
Cooke Fnd Grants, 1368
Crail-Johnson Fnd Grants, 1393
Cummins Fnd Grants, 1415
Daisy Marquis Jones Fnd Grants, 1434
Dallas Women's Fnd Grants, 1438
Dave Coy Fnd Grants, 1447
Dave Thomas Fnd for Adoption Grants, 1449
Deborah Munroe Noonan Mem Fund Grts, 1475
Dekko Fnd Grants, 1482
Denver Fdn Tech Assistance Grts, 1505
Dept of Ed Magnet Schools Assistance Grants, 1509
DHHS ARRA Strengthening Communities Fund - Nonprofit Capacity Building Grants, 1527
DHHS ARRA Strengthening Communities Fund - State, Local, and Tribal Government Capacity Building Grants, 1528
DHHS Comm Svcs Grant Trng & Tech Assistance Pgm: Capacity-Bldg for Ongoing CSBG Pgm, 1529
DHHS Maternal & Child Health Projects Grts, 1536
DHHS Tech and Non-Financial Assistance to Health Centers, 1539
DogTime Annual Grant, 1552
DogTime Tech Grant, 1553
Dorothea Haus Ross Fnd Grants, 1587
DTE Energy Fdn Comm Dev Grants, 1609
Duluth-Superior Area Comm Fdn Grts, 1620
Dyson Fnd Mid-Hudson Valley Project Grants, 1636
East Tennessee Fnd Grants, 1646
Echoing Green Fellowships, 1650
Edina Realty Fnd Grants, 1656
Edna McConnell Clark Fnd Grants, 1659
Edward Bangs Kelley & Elza Kelley Fdn Grts, 1665
Edyth Bush Charitable Fnd Grants, 1673
Eileen Fisher Women-Owned Business Grants, 1677
Elizabeth Morse Genius Char Trust Grants, 1682
Elkhart Cty Comm Fdn Grants, 1684
Elmer L & Eleanor J Andersen Fdn Grnts, 1687
El Paso Comm Fnd Grants, 1688
Elsie Lee Garthwaite Memorial Fdn Grts, 1692
Entergy Charitable Fnd Low-Income Initiatives and Solutions Grants, 1711
Enterprise Comm Partners Green Grants, 1716
EPA Air Pollution Control Pgm Support Grts, 1722
EPA Brownfields Area-Wide Planning Grants, 1723
EPA Brownfields Training, Research, and Tech Assistance Grants, 1727
EPA Environmental Justice Small Grants, 1732
EPA Surveys, Studies, Research, Investigations, Demonstrations, and Special Purpose Activities Relating to the Clean Air Act, 1740
Eulalie Bloedel Schneider Fnd Grants, 1767
Evelyn and Walter Haas, Jr. Fund Nonprofit Leadership Grants, 1774
Ewing Halsell Fnd Grants, 1776
Ewing Marion Kauffman Fnd Grants, 1777

Fairfield County Comm Fdn Grts, 1782
Fan Fox & Leslie R Samuels Fdn Grants, 1786
Fargo-Moorhead Area Fnd Grants, 1788
Farm Aid Grants, 1790
Faye McBeath Fnd Grants, 1794
Fidelity Fnd Grants, 1805
Field Fnd of Illinois Grants, 1806
Financial Capability Innovation Fund II Grants, 1811
FINRA Smart Investing@Your Library Grants, 1816
First Lady's Fam Lit Init for Texas Grants, 1822
Florida BRAIVE Fund of Dade Comm Fnd, 1846
Florida Division of Cultural Affairs Comm Theatre Grants, 1847
Florida Div of Cultural Affairs Dance Grts, 1850
Florida Div of Cultural Affairs Folk Arts Grts, 1853
Florida Division of Cultural Affairs General Program Support Grants, 1854
Florida Division of Cultural Affairs Lit Grants, 1855
Florida Div of Cultural Affairs Media Arts Grants, 1856
Florida Division of Cultural Affairs Multidisciplinary Grants, 1857
Florida Div of Cultural Affairs Museum Grts, 1858
Florida Div of Cultural Affairs Music Grts, 1859
Florida Div of Cultural Afrs Presenter Grts, 1860
Florida Division of Cultural Affairs Specific Cultural Project Grants, 1862
Florida Division of Cultural Affairs Underserved Cultural Comm Dev Grants, 1864
Florida Div of Cultural Affairs Visual Arts Grants, 1865
Fluor Fnd Grants, 1875
Ford Family Fnd Grants - Tech Assistance, 1882
Fnd for a Drug-Free Wrld Clsrm Tools, 1890
Frances L & Edwin L Cummings Mem Fund, 1919
Frank Stanley Beveridge Fnd Grants, 1936
Frederick McDonald Trust Grants, 1946
Fremont Area Comm Fnd Grants, 1955
Freshwater Future Healing Our Waters Grants, 1959
Frey Fnd Grants, 1963
Fund for Southern Communities Grants, 1977
Gardiner Howland Shaw Fnd Grants, 1986
Gateway Fnd Grants, 1992
Gaylord & Dorothy Donnelley Fdn Grants, 1993
Gene Haas Fnd, 1999
General Motors Fnd Grants, 2004
George Frederick Jewett Fnd Grants, 2019
Georgia Council for the Arts Partner Grants for Organizations, 2035
Georgia Council for the Arts Partner Grants for Service Organizations, 2036
Girl's Best Friend Fnd Grants, 2057
GNOF Comm Revitalization Grants, 2071
GNOF IMPACT Grts for Youth Dev't, 2081
GNOF Organizational Effectiveness Grants, 2090
Goldseker Fnd Comm Grants, 2101
Goldseker Fnd Non-Profit Management Assistance Grants, 2103
Grand Rapids Area Comm Fnd Wyoming Youth Fund Grants, 2117
Grand Rapids Comm Fnd Ionia County Youth Fund Grants, 2120
Grand Victoria Fnd Illinois Core Grants, 2126
Greater Tacoma Comm Fdn Grts, 2139
Greater Worcester Comm Discretionary Grants, 2140
GTECH After School Advantage Grants, 2170
Gulf Coast Comm Fnd Grants, 2174
Gulf Coast Comm Capacity Building Grants, 2175
Gulf Coast Fnd of Comm Operating Grants, 2176
Gulf Coast Fnd of Comm Grants, 2177
H.J. Heinz Company Fnd Grants, 2184
HAF Techn Assistance Pgm Grts, 2206
Hall Family Fnd Grants, 2210
Hartford Fnd Evaluation Grants, 2250
Hartford Fdn Implementation Sppt Grts, 2251
Hartford Fdn Nonprofit Support Grants, 2252
Hawaii Comm Fnd Capacity Building Grants, 2260
Hawaii Comm Fnd Organizational Capacity Building Grants, 2263
Hawaii Comm Fnd Social Change Grants, 2265
Health Fnd of Grtr Indianapolis Grts, 2282
Heifer Educational Fund Grants for Teachers, 2289

Hill Crest Fnd Grants, 2324
Historic Landmarks Fnd of Indiana Legal Defense Grants, 2335
Hoffberger Fnd Grants, 2342
Honeywell Corp Sustainable Opportunities, 2360
Honor the Earth Grants, 2361
Household Int'l Corp Giving Grants, 2372
Hyams Fnd Grants, 2413
Hyde Family Fnds Grants, 2414
Ian Hague Perl 6 Dev Grants, 2421
IBM Comm Dev Grants, 2425
Illinois Arts Council Arts Service Organizations Grants, 2464
Illinois Arts Cncl Comm Arts Access Grts, 2466
Illinois DCEO Eliminate the Digital Divide, 2489
Illinois DCEO Emerging Technological Enterprises Grants, 2490
Illinois DCEO Employer Trng Investment Pgm Grts - Competitive Component, 2491
Illinois DCEO Employer Trng Investment Pgm Grts - Incentive Component, 2492
Illinois DCEO Employer Trng Investment Pgm Multi-Company Trng Grts, 2493
Illinois DCEO Employer Trng Investment Pgm Single Company Trng Grts, 2494
Illinois DCEO Large Business Dev Grants, 2495
Illinois Humanities Council Comm Project Grant, 2510
Independence Comm Fnd Neighborhood Renewal Grants, 2527
Indiana Arts Commission Statewide Arts Service Organization Grants, 2533
IYI Responsible Fatherhood Grants, 2591
Jacob G. Schmidlapp Trust Grants, 2616
Jacobs Family Fdn Vlg Neighborhoods Grants, 2619
James R. Dougherty Jr. Fnd Grants, 2635
Jane and Jack Fitzpatrick Fund Grants, 2640
Jewish Funds for Justice Grants, 2676
JM Fnd Grants, 2681
Joseph H & Florence A Roblee Fdn Grants, 2736
Josephine Goodyear Fnd Grants, 2738
KaBOOM-CA Playground Challenge Grants, 2761
Kalamazoo Comm Fnd Economic and Comm Dev Grants, 2765
Kansas Health Fnd Recognition Grants, 2784
Katie's Krops Grants, 2792
L. W. Pierce Family Fnd Grants, 2846
Lewis H. Humphreys Charitable Trust Grants, 2889
Liberty Hill Fdn Fund for Change Grts, 2893
Lilly Endowment Giving Indiana Funds for Tomorrow Grants, 2903
Linford & Mildred White Char Fund Grts, 2909
Louetta M. Cowden Fnd Grants, 2922
Lubrizol Corporation Comm Grants, 2932
MacArthur Fnd Chicago Arts and Culture Int'l Connections Grants, 2962
Mary Reynolds Babcock Fnd Grants, 3047
Massachusetts Cultural Council Cultural Facilities Feasibility and Tech Assistance Grants, 3054
Massachusetts Cultural Council Cultural Investment Portfolio, 3056
McCune Charitable Fnd Grants, 3077
MDARD AgD Value Added/Regional Food Systems Grants, 3091
Melville Charitable Trust Grants, 3115
Mertz Gilmore Fnd NYC Communities Grants, 3126
Mertz Gilmore Fnd NYC Dance Grants, 3127
MGN Family Fnd Grants, 3154
Michael Reese Health Trust Core Grants, 3159
Mimi and Peter Haas Fund Grants, 3185
Minneapolis Fnd Comm Grants, 3186
Modest Needs Non-Profit Grants, 3200
Montgomery Cty Comm Fdn Grants, 3213
Motorola Fnd Grants, 3221
Ms. Fnd for Women Health Grants, 3225
Mt. Sinai Health Care Fnd Health Policy Grants, 3228
National Book Scholarship Fund, 3249
National Endowment for the Arts Dance Grants, 3262
National Endowment for the Arts Local Arts Agencies Grants, 3263
National Endowment for Arts Media Grants, 3264

Technical Training

National Endowment for Arts Museum Grants, 3265
National Endowment for the Arts Music Grants, 3266
National Endowment for the Arts Opera Grants, 3267
National Endowment for Arts Presenting Grants, 3268
National Endowment for the Arts Theater and Musical Theater Grants, 3269
Needmor Fund Grants, 3289
Nevada Arts Council Circuit Rider Grants, 3308
Nevada Arts Council Professional Dev Grants, 3314
New Earth Fnd Grants, 3317
New Hampshire Charitable Fnd Grants, 3325
New York Fnd Grants, 3338
New York Landmarks Conservancy City Ventures Grants, 3339
NFF Comm Assistance Grants, 3343
NFF Mid-Capacity Assistance Grants, 3345
NFL Grassroots Field Grants, 3350
NFL Player Youth Football Camp Grants, 3353
NGA Midwest School Garden Grants, 3407
NHSCA Operating Grants, 3428
Nonprofit Management Fund Grants, 3458
Norcliffe Fnd Grants, 3459
Nordson Corporation Fnd Grants, 3462
North Carolina Arts Council Arts in Educ Artist Residencies Grants, 3468
North Carolina Arts Council Outreach Grants, 3479
North Carolina Arts Council Tech Assistance, 3482
NW Minnesota Fnd Asset Building Grants, 3511
NWHF Health Advocacy Small Grants, 3537
NWHF Physical Activity and Nutrition Grants, 3540
NYCT New York City Environment Grants, 3556
NYCT Tech Assistance Grants, 3559
NYFA Artists in the School Planning Grants, 3562
NYSCA Architecture, Planning, and Design: Capital Project Grants, 3571
NYSCA Architecture, Planning, and Design: Independent Project Grants, 3575
NYSCA Dance: Services to the Field Grants, 3587
NYSCA Electronic Media and Film: Workspace Grants, 3593
NYSCA Lit: General Operating Support Grants, 3598
NYSCA Lit: Svcs to the Field Grts, 3601
NYSCA Music: New Music Facilities, 3608
NYSCA State and Local Partnerships: Services to the Field Grants, 3621
NYSCA Visual Arts: Wrkspc Facilities Grts, 3631
Ohio County Comm Board of Directors Grants, 3656
Ohio River Border Initiative Grants, 3661
OJJDP Tribal Juvenile Accountability Discretionary Grants, 3665
OneFamily Fnd Grants, 3673
Ontario Arts Council Compass Grants, 3677
OSF Affordable Access to Digital Communications Initiative, 3700
OSF Mental Health Initiative Grants, 3709
Packard Fnd Organizational Effectiveness and Philanthropy Grants, 3730
Paso del Norte Health Fnd Grants, 3743
Paul Rapoport Fnd Grants, 3765
PCA-PCD Organizational Short-Term Professional Dev and Consulting Grants, 3769
PCA Mgmt/Techn Assistance Grts, 3800
PDF Comm Organizing Grants, 3807
PennPAT Artist Tech Assistance Grants, 3811
Perl 6 Microgrants, 3824
Perl Fnd Grants, 3825
Petco Fnd 4 Rs Project Support Grants, 3830
Peter and Elizabeth C. Tower Fnd Phase II Tech Initiative Grants, 3839
Peter and Elizabeth C. Tower Fnd Phase I Tech Initiative Grants, 3840
Peter and Elizabeth C. Tower Fnd Social and Emotional Preschool Curriculum Grants, 3841
Peter Norton Family Fnd Grants, 3849
Pew Charitable Trusts Arts and Culture Grants, 3857
Philadelphia Fdn Org'l Effectiveness Grts, 3872
Pinkerton Fnd Grants, 3892
PIP American Dream Fund Grants, 3897
PIP Racial Justice Collaborative Grants, 3908
PMP Professional Dev Grants, 3919

Price Gilbert, Jr. Charitable Fund Grants, 3953
Proteus Fund Grants, 3973
Prudential Fnd Arts and Culture Grants, 3975
Prudential Fdn Econ Dev Grants, 3976
Prudential Fnd Educ Grants, 3977
Public Safety Fnd of America Grants, 3983
Puerto Rico Comm Fnd Grants, 3986
Putnam Cty Comm Fdn Grts, 3990
Rainbow Fund Grants, 4009
RESIST Tech Assistance Grants, 4065
Reynolds and Reynolds Co Fdn Grants, 4070
Rhode Island Fnd Grants, 4073
Rich Fnd Grants, 4090
Robert Sterling Clark Arts & Culture Grants, 4122
Rochester Area Comm Fnd Grants, 4127
Rockefeller Brothers Fund Cross-Programmatic Initiative: Energy Grants, 4130
Rose Fdn For Communities & the Environment Consumer Privacy Rights Grts, 4156
Rose Communities and Environment Northern California Environmental Grassroots Grants, 4158
SAG Motion Pic Plyrs Welfare Fund Grts, 4209
Saint Paul Fdn Mgmt Improvement Fund Grts, 4221
Saint Paul Fnd SpectrumTrust Grants, 4222
San Diego Fnd Environment Comm Grants, 4246
San Diego Fnd for Change Grants, 4247
Santa Barbara Fdn Monthly Express Grts, 4284
Santa Fe Comm Fdn root2fruit Santa Fe, 4289
Sapelo Fdn Environmental Protection Grts, 4293
Scherman Fnd Grants, 4305
Seabury Fnd Grants, 4316
Seattle Fnd Arts and Culture Grants, 4320
Seattle Fnd Economy Grants, 4325
Seattle Fnd Educ Grants, 4326
Seattle Fnd Health and Wellness Grants, 4328
Seattle Fnd Medical Funds Grants, 4329
Seattle Fdn Neighbor to Neighbor Small Grts, 4330
Sister Fund Grants for Women's Organizations, 4371
Skaggs Fnd Grants, 4378
Skillman Fdn Good Opportunities Grts, 4381
Social Justice Fund NW Criminal Justice Giving Project Grants, 4394
Solo Cup Fnd Grants, 4401
Sosland Fnd Grants, 4408
South Carolina Arts Commission Traditional Arts Apprenticeship Grants, 4427
Southern Poverty Law Center Strategic Litigation Grants, 4439
South Madison Comm Fnd Grants, 4440
St. Joseph Comm Health Cath Kasper Award, 4468
St. Joseph Comm Health Fnd Improving Healthcare Access Grants, 4469
Stark Comm Fnd Neighborhood Comm and Economic Dev Tech Assistance Grants, 4478
State Farm Fnd Grants, 4486
State Justice Institute Partner Grants, 4489
State Justice Institute Strategic Initiative Grants, 4492
State Justice Inst Tech Assistance Grts, 4493
State Street Fnd Grants, 4495
Stewart Huston Charitable Trust Grants, 4505
Stuart Fnd Grants, 4516
Surdna Fdn Sustainable Environments Grants, 4533
Susan Mott Webb Charitable Trust Grants, 4536
SVP Early Childhood Dev and Parenting Grants, 4538
TAC Arts Access Tech Assistance Grants, 4550
TAC Arts Projects Grants, 4554
TAC Rural Arts Project Support Grants, 4555
TAC Tech Assistance Grants, 4556
Taylor S. Abernathy and Patti Harding Abernathy Charitable Trust Grants, 4564
TechFnd TechGrants, 4570
Telluride Fnd Comm Grants, 4573
Telluride Fdn Emergency/Out of Cycle Grts, 4574
Telluride Fdn Tech Assistance Grts, 4575
Texas Comm on Arts Cultural Connections Grant, 4591
Textron Corporate Contributions Grants, 4601
Theodore Edson Parker Fnd Grants, 4605
Tides Fnd Grants, 4632
Time Warner Diverse Voices in the Arts Initiative Grants, 4635

Time Warner Yth Media & Creative Arts Grts, 4636
Tony Hawk Fnd Grants, 4641
Toyota Motor Manuf of West Virginia Grants, 4657
Toyota Motor North America of NY Grts, 4658
Toyota Motor Sales, USA Grants, 4659
Tri-State Comm Twenty-first Century Endowment Fund Grants, 4666
US Dept of Educ Parent Info & Trng, 4695
US Dept of Educ Rehab Trng--Rehabilitation Continuing Educ Programs --Institute on Rehabilitation Issues , 4700
UNESCO World Heritage Fund Grants, 4706
Union Bank, N.A. Fnd Grants, 4709
Union Pacific Fdn Health & Human Svcs Grts, 4715
Union Square Award for Social Justice, 4717
UPS Fnd Diversity Grants, 4729
USA Football Equipment Grants, 4735
USAID Call for Public-Private Alliance Proposals in Serbia, 4742
USAID Implementation Science for Strengthening Use of Evidence in Family Planning/Reproductive Health Programming Grants, 4758
USAID Leadership Initiative for Good Governance in Africa Grants, 4766
USAID Unsolicited Proposal Grants, 4786
USAID Workforce Dev in Mexico Grants, 4787
USDA 1890 Land Grant Colleges and Universities Initiative Grants, 4797
USDA Agricultural & Economic Research Grants, 4798
USDA Comm Facility Grants, 4801
USDA Emergency Comm Water Assistance, 4807
USDA Foreign Market Dev Grants, 4811
USDA Housing Application Packaging Grants, 4815
USDA Market Access Grants, 4818
USDA Rural Business Enterprise Grants, 4823
USDA Rural Business Opportunity Grants, 4824
USDA Rural Comm Dev Initiative Grants, 4825
USDA Rural Cooperative Dev Grants, 4826
USDA Rural Economic Dev Grants, 4827
USDA Rural Energy for America - Energy Audit & Renewable Energy Dev Assistance Grts, 4828
USDA Rural Microentrepreneur Astnc Grts, 4832
USDA Section 306D Water and Waste System Grants for Alaskan Villages, 4835
USDA Self-Help Tech Assistance Grants, 4836
USDA Tech & Supervisory Astnc Grts, 4841
USDA Tech Assistance and Training Grants for Rural Waste Systems, 4842
USDA Value-Added Producer Grants, 4843
USDC Advanced Manufacturing Jobs and Innovation Accelerator Challenge Grants, 4848
USDC Business Center - American Indian and Alaska Native Grants, 4849
USDC i6 Challenge Grants, 4851
USDC Low-Power Television and Translator Upgrade Grants, 4852
USDC State Broadband Initiative Grants, 4857
USDC University Center Economic Dev Program Competition, 4861
USDJ Edward Byrne Memorial Justice Assistance Grants, 4863
USDJ Nat Criminal History Improvement Grants, 4864
USDJ NICS Act Record Improvement Grants, 4865
US Soccer Fnd Planning Grants, 4871
USTA Public Facility Assistance Grants, 4883
Vancouver Fnd Grants and Comm Initiatives, 4900
Vanguard Public Fnd Grant Funds, 4904
Verizon Fnd Vermont Grants, 4924
Virginia Commission for the Arts Artists in Educ Residency Grants, 4941
Virginia Comsn for the Arts Proj Grts, 4944
WM Keck Fdn Southern California Grts, 4964
Washington Area Women's Fnd African American Women's Giving Circle Grants, 4989
Washington Area Women's Fnd Early Care and Educ Funders Collaborative Grants, 4990
Washington Area Women's Fnd Open Door Capacity Fund Grants, 4994
Washington Area Women's Fnd Rainmakers Giving Circle Grants, 4995

PROGRAM TYPE INDEX

Weatherwax Fnd Grants, 5014
Western Indiana Comm Fdn Grts, 5024
Weyerhaeuser Company Fnd Grants, 5053
Whitehorse Fnd Grants, 5058
Wieboldt Fnd Grants, 5065
WILD Fnd Grants, 5068
William C. Kenney Watershed Protection Fnd Ecosystem Grants, 5079
William G. Gilmore Fnd Grants, 5082
Xerox Fnd Grants, 5122
YSA ABC Summer of Service Awards, 5133
YSA Global Yth Svc Day Lead Agency Grts, 5135
YSA MLK Day Lead Organizer Grants, 5136
YSA National Child Awareness Month Youth Ambassador Grants, 5137
Z. Smith Reynolds Fnd Economic Dev Grants, 5144
Z. Smith Reynolds Fnd Democracy and Civic Engagement Grants, 5145

Training Programs/Internships
360 Degrees of Giving Grants, 32
AACC Service Learning Mini-Grants, 57
AAP Comm Access To Child Health Advocacy Training Grants, 62
AAP Comm Access To Child Health Residency Training Grants, 65
AAUW Comm Action Grants, 75
Abbey Charitable Trust Grants, 78
ACF Native American Social and Economic Dev Strategies Grants, 123
Achelis Fnd Grants, 127
Adolph Coors Fnd Grants, 171
Alabama State Council on the Arts Project Assistance Grants, 247
ALA Info Today Library of the Future Awd, 287
AMD Corporate Contributions Grants, 416
Anschutz Family Fnd Grants, 486
Applied Materials Corp Philanthropy Pgm, 515
Arcus Fnd Fund Grants, 529
ARTBA Transportation Dev Fnd Grants, 569
ASTA Academic Scholarships, 597
Bank of America Charitable Fnd Educ and Workforce Dev Grants, 657
Bank of America Charitable Fnd Student Leaders Grants, 659
Baxter Int'l Corporate Giving Grants, 689
Blowitz-Ridgeway Fnd Grants, 792
Bodman Fnd Grants, 807
Buhl Fnd - Frick Educational Fund, 859
California Arts Council Public Value Grants, 895
Carrie Estelle Doheny Fnd Grants, 945
Carrier Corporation Contributions Grants, 946
Cash 4 Clubs Sports Grants, 951
CE and S Fnd Grants, 985
CenterPointEnergy Minnegasco Grants, 993
Central New York Comm Fdn Grants, 996
Charles A. Frueauff Fnd Grants, 1037
Charles Delmar Fnd Grants, 1039
Charles H. Revson Fnd Grants, 1047
Charles Stewart Mott Fdn Anti-Poverty Grts, 1054
ChevronTexaco Contributions Program, 1078
Chicago Comty Trust Educ Grts Priority 2, 1085
Chicago Comm Trust Workforce Grants, 1094
Circle K Corporation Contributions Grants, 1136
Cleveland Fnd Fenn Educational Fund Grants, 1169
CNCS AmeriCorps State and National Planning Grants, 1183
CNCS Social Innovation Grants, 1189
Collins Fnd Grants, 1209
Columbus Fnd Competitive Grants, 1220
Comm Fdn for Grtr Buffalo Grants, 1247
Conservation, Food, and Health Fnd Grants for Developing Countries, 1359
Corina Higginson Trust Grants, 1373
Cruise Industry Charitable Fnd Grants, 1404
Dept of Ed Projects with Industry Grants, 1511
DHHS Adolescent Family Life Demo Projects, 1524
DHHS Emerging Leaders Program Internships, 1532
DHHS Spcl Pgms for the Aging Trng, Rsch, and Discretionary Projects and Pgms Grts, 1538

DHHS Tech and Non-Financial Assistance to Health Centers, 1539
District of Columbia Commission on the Arts-Arts Educ Teacher Mini-Grants, 1549
DOJ Comm-Based Delinquency Prev Grants, 1556
DOJ Gang-Free Schools and Communities Intervention Grants, 1557
Donald W. Reynolds Fnd Children's Discovery Initiative Grants, 1576
Dr. John T. Macdonald Fnd Grants, 1600
Duke Energy Fdn Econ Dev Grants, 1619
Dwight Stuart Youth Fnd Grants, 1628
E.L. Wiegand Fnd Grants, 1639
Edward S. Moore Fnd Grants, 1668
Edwin S. Webster Fnd Grants, 1671
Effie and Wofford Cain Fnd Grants, 1674
Emma G. Harris Fnd Grants, 1701
Ensign-Bickford Fnd Grants, 1709
Enterprise Comm Partners Rose Architectural Fellowships, 1719
EPA Environmental Educ Grants, 1729
Essex County Comm Fnd First Jobs Grant, 1754
Essex County Comm Fnd Merrimack Valley General Fund Grants, 1756
Eugene M. Lang Fnd Grants, 1764
Eulalie Bloedel Schneider Fnd Grants, 1767
F.R. Bigelow Fnd Grants, 1781
Farm Aid Grants, 1790
Faye McBeath Fnd Grants, 1794
FCD Child Dev Grants, 1796
FEMA Assistance to Firefighters Grants, 1802
Ford Fdn Peace & Social Justice Grts, 1884
Fnd for Seacoast Health Grants, 1895
Fnd for the Mid South Comm Dev Grants, 1897
Frederick W. Marzahl Grants, 1948
Fred L. Emerson Fnd Grants, 1949
Frist Fnd Grants, 1964
George Family Fnd Grants, 2017
George Gund Fnd Grants, 2020
GNOF Gulf Coast Oil Spill Grants, 2077
GNOF Metropolitan Opportunities Grants, 2087
GNOF New Orleans Works Grants, 2088
Golden LEAF Fnd Grants, 2097
Green Bay Packers Fnd Grants, 2148
HAF Comm Grants, 2193
Hartford Fdn Nonprofit Support Grants, 2252
Hatton W. Sumners Fnd for the Study and Teaching of Self Government Grants, 2257
Hawai'i Children's Trust Fund Comm Awareness Events Grants, 2258
Hearst Fnds Social Service Grants, 2285
Helen Bader Fnd Grants, 2293
Helen Irwin Littauer Educational Trust Grants, 2295
Hogg Fnd for Mental Health Grants, 2343
Holland/Zeeland Comm Fdn Grts, 2345
Huntington Arts Council Arts-in-Educ Programs, 2400
IEDC Skills Enhancement Fund, 2445
IIE Freeman Fnd Indonesia Internships, 2456
Illinois Arts Council Media Arts Pgm Grts, 2472
Illinois Arts Cncl Prtnrs in Excellence Grts, 2475
Independence Comm Fnd Neighborhood Renewal Grants, 2527
Indiana Arts Commission Statewide Arts Service Organization Grants, 2533
Indiana Rural Capacity Grants, 2547
Intel Finance Internships, 2563
Intel Int'l Comm Grants, 2564
IREX Egypt Media Dev Grants, 2575
IREX Small Grant Fund for Media Projects in Africa and Asia, 2582
JM Fnd Grants, 2681
John F. Kennedy Center for the Performing Arts National Rosemary Kennedy Internship, 2694
John Merck Fund Grants, 2706
Johnson & Johnson Corp Contribs Grants, 2718
JP Morgan Chase Comm Dev Grts, 2753
Kalamazoo Comm Fdn Mini-Grts, 2772
Kennedy Center Experiential Educ Internship, 2798
Kennedy Center HSC Fnd Internship, 2799
Kennedy Center Summer HSC Fnd Internship, 2800

Kessler Fdn Comm Employment Grts, 2814
Kessler Fdn Signature Employment Grts, 2816
Linden Fnd Grants, 2908
Lynde and Harry Bradley Fnd Grants, 2947
Macquarie Bank Fnd Grants, 2966
Maine Comm Belvedere Animal Welfare Grants, 2975
Maine Women's Fund Econ Security Grts, 2992
Marin Comm Fnd Social Justice and Interfaith Understanding Grants, 3012
Mary's Pence Study Grants, 3030
Mary Jennings Sport Camp Scholarship, 3041
Massachusetts Bar Fnd Legal Intern Fellowships, 3051
May & Stanley Smith Char Trust Grants, 3069
Maytree Fdn Assisting Local Leaders w/ Immigrant Employment Strategies Grts, 3070
McLean Contributionship Grants, 3088
MDARD AgD Value Added/Regional Food Systems Grants, 3091
Meadows Fnd Grants, 3104
Meyer Fnd Economic Security Grants, 3141
Meyer Fnd Educ Grants, 3142
Middlesex Savings Charitable Fnd Educational Opportunities Grants, 3174
Mitsubishi Electric America Fnd Grants, 3190
Montgomery Cty Comm Fdn Grants, 3213
Morris K. Udall and Stewart L. Udall Fnd Native American Congressional Internships, 3220
Murphy Institute Judith Kelleher Schafer Summer Internship Grants, 3230
NAA Fdn Diversity PowerMind Fwsps, 3232
NAA Fnd Minority Fellowships, 3233
NASE Succeed Scholarships, 3243
National Book Scholarship Fund, 3249
National Endowment for the Arts Dance Grants, 3262
NEH Preservation Microfilming of Brittle Books and Serials Grants, 3294
Nellie Mae Educ Fnd State Level Systems Change Grants, 3299
Nevada Arts Cncl Folklife Opportunities Grts, 3310
Nevada Arts Council Professional Dev Grants, 3314
New Hampshire Charitable Fnd Grants, 3325
New Jersey Cntr for Hispanic Policy, Rsch & Dev Governor's Hispanic Fwsps, 3327
NFF Comm Assistance Grants, 3343
NFWF Chesapeake Bay Conservation Innovation Grants, 3363
NFWF Chesapeake Bay Stewardship Fund Small Watershed Grants, 3364
NFWF Chesapeake Bay Tgtd Watershed Grts, 3365
NHLBI Ruth L. Kirschstein National Research Service Award Short-Term Institutional Research Training Grants, 3422
NHSCA Traditional Arts Apprenticeships, 3429
NJSCA Folk Arts Apprenticeships, 3448
NNEDVF/Altria Doors of Hope Program, 3452
North Carolina Arts Council Arts Folklife Internship, 3467
North Carolina Arts Council Comm Arts Administration Internship, 3471
NRA Fnd Grants, 3517
NYSCA Electronic Media and Film: Workspace Grants, 3593
Ohio Arts Council Traditional Arts Apprenticeship Grants, 3655
Ohio County Comm Fnd Conference Grants, 3657
Olin Corporation Charitable Trust Grants, 3669
OSF European Commission Internships for Young Roma Graduates, 3707
Otto Bremer Fnd Grants, 3713
PAS Internship, 3742
PCA Arts Management Internship, 3773
PCA Arts Organizations and Grants for Crafts, 3778
PCA Entry Track Arts Organizations and Arts Grants for Crafts, 3790
Peter Kiewit Fnd General Grants, 3845
Peter Kiewit Fnd Small Grants, 3847
Pfizer Medical Educ Track One Grants, 3864
Piedmont Natural Gas Fnd Workforce Dev Grant, 3886
Pinkerton Fnd Grants, 3892
PPG Industries Fnd Grants, 3943

1138 / Training Programs/Internships

Principal Financial Group Fnd Grants, 3966
Prudential Fnd Educ Grants, 3977
Ralph M. Parsons Fnd Grants, 4013
RAND Corporation Graduate Student Summer Associateships, 4018
Raskob Fdn for Catholic Activities Grts, 4019
Rathmann Family Fnd Grants, 4026
RISCA Folk Arts Apprenticeships, 4098
Rockefeller Brothers Democratic Practice Grants, 4131
Rockefeller Brothers Sustainable Dev Grants, 4136
Rose Comm Fnd Child and Family Dev Grants, 4153
Ruth Eleanor Bamberger and John Ernest Bamberger Memorial Fnd Grants, 4178
Saint Luke's Health Initiatives Grants, 4216
Salmon Fnd Grants, 4225
Samuel S. Fels Fund Grants, 4238
Santa Fe Comm Fnd Seasonal Grants-Spring, 4291
Sidgmore Family Fnd Grants, 4348
Sierra Health Fnd Responsive Grants, 4353
Sioux Falls Area Comm Fnd Comm Fund Grants, 4364
Sioux Falls Area Comm Fnd Spot Grants, 4366
Skaggs Fnd Grants, 4378
Sony Corp of America Corp Philant Grants, 4405
Sorenson Legacy Fnd Grants, 4407
South Carolina Arts Commission Traditional Arts Apprenticeship Grants, 4427
Southern New England Folk and Traditional Arts Apprenticeship Grants, 4438
Sport Manitoba Athlete Skill Dev Clinics Grants, 4453
SSRC-Van Alen Fellowships, 4467
Strowd Roses Grants, 4515
Stuart Fnd Grants, 4516
Susan Mott Webb Charitable Trust Grants, 4536
TAC Arts Access Grant, 4549
TAC Arts Projects Grants, 4554
TAC Rural Arts Project Support Grants, 4555
TechFnd TechGrants, 4570
Tech Enhancement Certification for Hoosiers, 4571
TE Fnd Grants, 4572
Texas Comsn on the Arts Create-1 Pgm Grts, 4583
Textron Corporate Contributions Grants, 4601
TSA Advanced Surveillance Grants, 4674
UNCFSP TIEAD Internship, 4705
UniBank 911 Emergency Personnel Educ Fund, 4707
Union Bank, N.A. Fnd Grants, 4709
UPS Fdn Nonprofit Effectiveness Grts, 4732
USAID Global Dev Alliance Grants, 4753
US Airways Educ Fnd Grants, 4790
USDC i6 Challenge Grants, 4851
USDC Postsecondary Grants Internships, 4855
US Soccer Fdn Annual Pgm & Field Grts, 4870
Vancouver Fnd Disability Supports for Employment Grants, 4899
Vectren Fnd Grants, 4907
Verizon Fnd Connecticut Grants, 4908
Verizon Fnd New Jersey Check into Lit Grants, 4918
Verizon Fnd New York Grants, 4919
WCI Comm Leadership Fellowships, 5008
WCI Leadership Dev Grants, 5012
Weingart Fnd Grants, 5018
West Virginia Commission on the Arts Professional Dev for Artists Grants, 5045
Wilburforce Fnd Grants, 5067
World Bank JJ/WBGSP Partners Programs, 5117
Xerox Fnd Grants, 5122

Travel Grants
AAP Anne E. Dyson Child Advocacy Awards, 61
AAP Program Delegate Awards, 68
Air Force Association Junior ROTC Grants, 215
ALA Adelaide Del Frate Conference Sponsorship Award, 220
ALA ALTAFF/GALE Outstanding Trustee Conference Grant, 224
ALA Atlas Systems Mentoring Award, 227
ALA Baker and Taylor Conference Grants, 228
ALA Bogle Pratt Int'l Library Travel Fund Grant, 251
ALA Carnegie Corporation of New York/New York Times I Love My Librarian Award, 254
ALA DEMCO New Leaders Travel Grants, 264

ALA Diversity Research Grant, 268
ALA EBSCO Midwinter Meeting Sponsorship, 274
ALA First Step Award/Wiley Prof Dev Grant, 279
ALA Jan Merrill-Oldham Professional Dev Grant, 291
ALA Maureen Hayes Author/Illustrator Award, 299
ALA Morningstar Pub Librarian Support Awd, 302
ALA NewsBank/Rdx Catharine J Reynolds Awd, 304
ALA NMRT Professional Dev Grant, 305
ALA Penguin Young Readers Group Award, 308
ALA Romance Writers of America Lib Grt, 314
ALA Routledge Distance Learning Librarianship Conference Sponsorship Award, 315
ALA Supporting Diversity Stipend, 333
ALFJ Astraea U.S. and Int'l Movement Fund, 361
AMA Fnd Jack B. McConnell, MD Awards for Excellence in Volunteerism, 411
Amarillo Area/Harrington Fnds Grants, 412
APAP Cultural Exchange Grants, 492
Arkansas Arts Council Sally A. Williams Artist Fund Grants, 558
Artist Trust GAP Grants, 575
Arts Midwest Performing Arts Grants, 579
Ball Brothers Fnd Rapid Grants, 639
Bush Fnd Medical Fellowships, 877
Carl M. Freeman Fnd Grants, 933
CCF Grassroots Exchange Fund Grants, 963
Colin Higgins Fnd Courage Awards, 1203
DAAD Research Grants for Doctoral Candidates and Young Academics and Scientists, 1427
Decatur County Comm Fnd Large Project Grants, 1476
Dorot Fnd Grants, 1586
Fisher House Fnd Hero Miles Program, 1832
Florida Division of Cultural Affairs State Touring Grants, 1863
Fulton County Comm Fnd Grants, 1975
Germanistic Society of America Fellowships, 2043
GNOF Organizational Effectiveness Grants, 2090
Great Lakes Protection Fund Grants, 2147
Harris Graduate School of Public Policy Studies Research Dev Grants, 2232
Hydrogen Student Design Contest, 2415
IIE Japan-U.S. Teacher Exchange for Educ for Sustainable Dev, 2457
Illinois DNR Biodiversity Field Trip Grants, 2496
Internet Society Fellowships, 2570
Japan Fnd Center for Global Partnership Grants, 2649
Jerome Fnd Travel and Study Grants, 2668
Kalamazoo Comm Fdn Mini-Grts, 2772
Kentucky Arts Council TranspARTation Grant, 2812
Komen Greater NYC Small Grants, 2836
LaGrange Independent Fnd for Endowments, 2851
Meyer Fnd Benevon Grants, 3140
MFRI Operation Diploma Grants for Student Veterans Organizations, 3151
MFRI Operation Diploma Small Grants for Indiana Family Readiness Groups, 3152
MMS and Alliance Charitable Fnd Int'l Health Studies Grants, 3195
NAA Fnd Teacher Fellowships, 3234
NACC David Stevenson Fellowships, 3235
NACC William Diaz Fellowships, 3236
National Center for Responsible Gaming Conference Scholarships, 3250
Nat'l Cntr for Responsible Gaming Travel Grts, 3251
National Endowment for Democracy Reagan-Fascell Democracy Fellowships, 3252
Nevada Arts Council Jackpot Grants, 3312
Newfoundland and Labrador Arts Council Comm Arts Grants, 3318
Newfoundland and Labrador Arts Council Labrador Cultural Travel Grants, 3319
Newfoundland and Labrador Arts Council Professional Artists Travel Fund, 3320
Newfoundland and Labrador Arts Council Professional Festivals Grants, 3321
Newfoundland and Labrador Arts Council Professional Project Grants, 3322
Newfoundland and Labrador Arts Council Visiting Artists Grants, 3324
NHSCA Operating Grants, 3428

PROGRAM TYPE INDEX

North Carolina Arts Council Folklife Documentary Project Grants, 3475
North Carolina Arts Council General Support, 3477
North Carolina Arts Council Outreach Grants, 3479
North Carolina Arts Council Res Center Grants, 3481
North Carolina Arts Council Touring/Presenting Grants, 3483
NW Airlines KidCares Medical Travel Assistance, 3508
NYSCA Visual Arts: Svcs to the Field Grts, 3630
Ohio County Comm Fnd Conference Grants, 3657
Ontario Arts Council Travel Assistance Grants, 3682
PAS PASIC Scholarships, 3744
PCA-PCD Professional Dev for Individual Artists Grants, 3770
PCA Busing Grants, 3786
PCA Professional Dev Grants, 3803
PennPAT Artist Tech Assistance Grants, 3811
PennPAT Presenter Travel Grants, 3814
PennPAT Strategic Opportunity Grants, 3815
Phi Upsilon Omicron Florence Fallgatter Distinguished Service Award, 3877
Phi Upsilon Omicron Frances Morton Holbrook Alumni Award, 3878
Pinellas County Grants, 3891
Pioneer Hi-Bred Confs & Mtgs Grts, 3896
PSEG Environmental Educ Grants, 3980
Shastri Indo-Canadian Institute Action Research Project Grants, 4341
Sport Manitoba Athlete/Team Travel Assistance Grants, 4452
Sport Manitoba Coaches/Officials Travel Assistance Grants, 4455
Sport Manitoba Women to Watch Grants, 4460
Stark Comm Fnd Neighborhood Comm and Economic Dev Tech Assistance Grants, 4478
Texas Comm on Arts Cultural Connections Grant, 4591
Tides Fdn Calif Wildlands Grassroots Fund, 4630
TSYSF Team Grants, 4676
US Airways Comm Contributions, 4788
USTA CTA and NJTL Comm Tennis Dev Workshop Scholarships, 4873
USTA NJTL Arthur Ashe Essay & Art Cnst, 4878
USTA NJTL Tennis and Leadership Camp Scholarships, 4879
Virginia Historical Society Rsch Fwsps, 4949
West Virginia Commission on the Arts Travel and Training Grants, 5050
Youth Philanthropy Project, 5132
YSA Global Yth Svc Day Lead Agency Grts, 5135
YSA National Child Awareness Month Youth Ambassador Grants, 5137

Vocational Education
Achelis Fnd Grants, 127
Adolph Coors Fnd Grants, 171
Alliant Energy Fnd Comm Grants, 384
AMD Corporate Contributions Grants, 416
Arizona Fnd for Women Deborah G. Carstens Fund Grants, 543
ArvinMeritor Grants, 585
ASTA Academic Scholarships, 597
AutoZone Comm Relations Grants, 621
Bodman Fnd Grants, 807
Bush Fdn Health & Human Svcs Grts, 875
Carl M. Freeman Fnd Grants, 933
Carrier Corporation Contributions Grants, 946
CenterPointEnergy Minnegasco Grants, 993
Charlotte County Comm Fdn Grts, 1056
Chicago Comm Trust Workforce Grants, 1094
CICF Efroymson Grants, 1120
Cisco Systems Fnd San Jose Comm Grants, 1137
Claude Pepper Fnd Grants, 1160
Cleveland Browns Fnd Grants, 1166
CNA Fnd Grants, 1179
CNCS AmeriCorps State and National Grants, 1182
Connecticut Light & Power Corp Contribs, 1352
ConocoPhillips Fnd Grants, 1354
Consumers Energy Fnd, 1365
Crail-Johnson Fnd Grants, 1393
D.F. Halton Fnd Grants, 1424

PROGRAM TYPE INDEX

Vocational Education / 1139

Danellie Fnd Grants, 1442
Dept of Educ Workplace & Comm Transition Trng for Incarcerated Youth Offenders, 1515
DHHS ARRA Strengthening Communities Fund - Nonprofit Capacity Building Grants, 1527
Diageo Fnd Grants, 1546
DOL Youthbuild Grants, 1571
Duke Energy Fdn Econ Dev Grants, 1619
Dynegy Fnd Grants, 1630
Elizabeth Morse Genius Char Trust Grants, 1682
Emma G. Harris Fnd Grants, 1701
Eulalie Bloedel Schneider Fnd Grants, 1767
Fnds of E Chgo Fin Independence Grts, 1909
Frank Reed and Margaret Jane Peters Memorial Fund II Grants, 1934
Gamble Fnd Grants, 1983
George W. Wells Fnd Grants, 2030
GNOF Gulf Coast Oil Spill Grants, 2077
GNOF Metropolitan Opportunities Grants, 2087
GNOF New Orleans Works Grants, 2088
Golden LEAF Fnd Grants, 2097
Goodrich Corporation Fnd Grants, 2104
Grand Rapids Area Comm Fnd Wyoming Youth Fund Grants, 2117
Grand Victoria Fnd Illinois Core Grants, 2126
HAF Comm Grants, 2193
Harvest Fnd Grants, 2254
HBF Pathways Out of Poverty Grants, 2273
Hearst Fnds Social Service Grants, 2285
Illinois Tool Works Fnd Grants, 2511
Indiana Reg'l Econ Dev Partnership Grts, 2546
Intel Comm Grants, 2562
IREX Egypt Media Dev Grants, 2575
IREX Small Grant Fund for Media Projects in Africa and Asia, 2582
Irvin Stern Fnd Grants, 2585
Jane Bradley Pettit Comm & Social Dev Grants, 2642
Janus Fnd Grants, 2647
John Gogian Family Fnd Grants, 2697
John Merck Fund Grants, 2706
Johnson Scholarship Fnd Grants, 2726
JP Morgan Chase Comm Dev Grts, 2753
Kessler Fdn Comm Employment Grts, 2814
Kessler Fdn Signature Employment Grts, 2816
Leo Goodwin Fnd Grants, 2882
Mabel Louise Riley Fnd Grants, 2959
May & Stanley Smith Char Trust Grants, 3069
Meyer Fnd Economic Security Grants, 3141
Meyer Fnd Educ Grants, 3142
Middlesex Savings Charitable Fnd Educational Opportunities Grants, 3174
National Housing Endowment Challenge/Build/Grow Grant, 3277
NYCT Hunger and Homelessnes Grants, 3553
NYCT Workforce Dev Grants, 3560
Oppenstein Brothers Fnd Grants, 3685
Pentair Fnd Educ and Comm Grants, 3816
PG&E Comm Vitality Grants, 3868
Piedmont Natural Gas Fnd Workforce Dev Grant, 3886
Prudential Fdn Econ Dev Grants, 3976
Reinberger Fnd Grants, 4052
Robert R. McCormick Tribune Veterans Grants, 4120
Robert R. Meyer Fnd Grants, 4121
RWJF Jobs to Careers: Promoting Work-Based Learning for Quality Care, 4185
Samuel S. Johnson Fnd Grants, 4239
Seabury Fnd Grants, 4316
Skillman Fnd Good Schools Grants, 4382
Staples Fnd for Learning Grants, 4475
Textron Corporate Contributions Grants, 4601
Thomas Sill Fnd Grants, 4619
Tourism Cares Professional Dev Scholarships, 4648
TWS Fnd Grants, 4683
US Dept of Educ Innovative Strategies in Comm Colleges for Working Adults and Displaced Workers Grants, 4692
US Dept of Educ Migrant and Seasonal Farmworkers Grants, 4693
US Dept of Educ Parent Info & Trng, 4695
US Dept of Educ Rehabilitation Research Training Centers , 4699
US Dept of Educ Voc Rehab Svcs Projects for American Indians with Disabilities Grts, 4702
Union Bank, N.A. Fnd Grants, 4709
Vancouver Fnd Disability Supports for Employment Grants, 4899
Vancouver Fnd Grants and Comm Initiatives, 4900
Vectren Fnd Grants, 4907
Verizon Fnd Connecticut Grants, 4908
Verizon Fnd Pennsylvania Grants, 4921
Verizon Fnd West Virginia Grants, 4926
Wells Fargo Housing Fnd Grants, 5023
WILD Fnd Grants, 5068
Xcel Energy Fnd Grants, 5121
Xerox Fnd Grants, 5122

Geographic Index

Note: This index lists grants for which applicants must be residents of or located in a specific geographic area. Numbers refer to entry numbers.

United States

Alabama
2 Life 18 Fndn Grants, 5
3M Company Arts and Culture Grants, 12
3M Company Environmental Giving Grants, 13
3M Company Health and Human Services Grants, 14
3M Fndn Community Giving Grants, 15
ABC Charities Grants, 85
Abelard Fndn East Grants, 87
Adams and Reese LLP Corporate Giving Grants, 147
Adams Fndn Grants, 153
Alabama Humanities Fndn Mini Grants, 231
Alabama Humanities Planning/Consultant Grants, 232
Alabama Power Fndn Grants, 233
Alabama Power Plant a Tree Grants, 234
Alabama State Council on the Arts Collaborative Ventures Grants, 235
Alabama State Council on the Arts Community Arts Collaborative Ventures Grants, 236
Alabama State Council on the Arts Community Arts Operating Support Grants, 237
Alabama State Council on the Arts Community Arts Presenting Grants, 238
Alabama State Council on the Arts Community Arts Program Development Grants, 239
Alabama State Council on the Arts Community Arts Technical Assistance Grants, 240
Alabama State Council on the Arts Community Planning & Design Grants, 241
Alabama State Council on the Arts in Education Partnership Grants, 242
Alabama State Council on the Arts Multi-Discipline and Festival Grants, 243
Alabama State Council on the Arts Operating Support Grants, 244
Alabama State Council on Arts Presenting Grants, 245
Alabama State Council on the Arts Program Development Grants, 246
Alabama State Council on the Arts Project Assistance Grants, 247
Alabama State Council on the Arts Projects of Individual Artists Grants, 248
Alabama State Council on the Arts Technical Assistance Grants for Individuals, 249
Alabama State Council on the Arts Technical Assistance Grants for Organizations, 250
Appalachian Regional Comm Asset-Based Development Project Grants, 500
Appalachian Regional Comm Business Development Revolving Loan Fund Grants, 501
Appalachian Regional Comm Community Infrastructure Grants, 502
Appalachian Regional Comm Distressed Counties Grants, 503
Appalachian Regional Comm Education and Training Grants, 504
Appalachian Regional Comm Energy Grants, 505
Appalachian Regional Comm Export and Trade Development Grants, 506
Appalachian Regional Comm Health Care Grants, 507
Appalachian Reg Comm Housing Grants, 508
Appalachian Regional Comm Leadership Development and Capacity Building Grants, 509
Appalachian Regional Comm Telecommunications Grants, 510
Appalachian Regional Comm Tourist Development Grants, 511
Appalachian Regional Comm Transportation and Highways Grants, 512
Arkema Fndn Science Teachers Program, 563
Assisi Fndn of Memphis Mini Grants, 595
Autauga Area Community Fndn Grants, 618
BBVA Compass Fndn Charitable Grants, 703
Belk Fndn Grants, 721
Boeing Company Contributions Grants, 809
Bridgestone/Firestone Trust Fund Grants, 836
Brunswick Fndn Dollars for Doers Grants, 856
Brunswick Fndn Grants, 857
Capital City Bank Group Fndn Grants, 920
Caring Fndn Grants, 926
Caroline Lawson Ivey Fndn Grants, 941
Carrier Corporation Contributions Grants, 946
CenturyLink Clarke M. Williams Grants, 998
Charles A. Frueauff Fndn Grants, 1037
Charles M. and Mary D. Grant Found Grants, 1050
Cingular Wireless Charitable Contributions, 1134
Circle K Corporation Contributions Grants, 1136
Cleveland-Cliffs Fndn Grants, 1165
Comcast Fndn Grants, 1235
Community Fndn of Greater Birmingham Grants, 1280
Community Fndn of S Alabama Grants, 1308
Cooper Industries Fndn Grants, 1370
CSX Corporate Contributions Grants, 1408
D. W. McMillan Fndn Grants, 1426
Dean Foods Community Involvement Grants, 1469
Dekko Fndn Grants, 1482
DHHS Healthy Tomorrows for Children, 1534
Dollar General Adult Literacy Grants, 1568
Dollar General Family Literacy Grants, 1569
Dollar General Youth Literacy Grants, 1570
El Paso Corporate Fndn Grants, 1689
Gannett Fndn Community Action Grants, 1984
GenCorp Fndn Grants, 1998
Georgia-Pacific Fndn Education Grants, 2031
Georgia-Pacific Fndn Enrichment Grants, 2032
Georgia-Pacific Entrepreneurship Grants, 2033
Georgia-Pacific Fndn Environment Grants, 2034
Gumdrop Books Librarian Scholarships, 2179
Harley Davidson Fndn Grants, 2224
Harry B. and Jane H. Brock Fndn Grants, 2237
Hill Crest Fndn Grants, 2324
J. Bulow Campbell Fndn Grants, 2593
J.L. Bedsole Fndn Grants, 2600
Johnson & Johnson Comm Health Care Grants, 2717
Kimberly-Clark Community Grants, 2824
Legacy Partners in Environmental Educ Grants, 2875
Legacy Partners in Environmental Ed Grants, 2876
Lettie Pate Whitehead Fndn Grants, 2888
Mary E. and Michael Blevins Charitable Grants, 3037
Mary Reynolds Babcock Fndn Grants, 3047
MeadWestvaco Sustainable Communities Grants, 3105
Mercedes-Benz USA Corporate Contributions, 3118
NFWF So Company Power of Flight Grants, 3394
Norfolk Southern Fndn Grants, 3463
Paul Green Fndn Playwrights Fellowship, 3762
Plum Creek Fndn Grants, 3917
Publix Super Markets Charities Local Grants, 3985
Robert R. Meyer Fndn Grants, 4121
Rucker & Margaret Agee Fund Grants, 4171
Salmon Fndn Grants, 4225
Solutia Fund Grants, 4402
Southwire Company Grants, 4447
Steelcase Fndn Grants, 4497
Sunoco Fndn Grants, 4530
Susan Mott Webb Charitable Trust Grants, 4536
TAC Arts Access Technical Assistance Grants, 4550
TAC Arts Educ Community-Learning Grants, 4552
TAC Arts Education Mini Grants, 4553
TAC Arts Projects Grants, 4554
TAC Rural Arts Project Support Grants, 4555
TAC Technical Assistance Grants, 4556
TAC Touring Arts and Access Grants, 4557
Toyota Motor Manufacturing of Alabama Grants, 4652
USDA Delta Health Care Services Grants, 4804
Verizon Fndn Southeast Region Grants, 4923
Vulcan Materials Company Fndn Grants, 4956
Wells Fargo Housing Fndn Grants, 5023
Weyerhaeuser Company Fndn Grants, 5053
Williams Companies Fndn Grants, 5095
Woodward Fund Grants, 5116

Alaska
3M Company Arts and Culture Grants, 12
3M Company Environmental Giving Grants, 13
3M Company Health and Human Services Grants, 14
3M Fndn Community Giving Grants, 15
ACF Native American Social and Economic Development Strategies Grants, 123
Alaska Airlines Corporate Giving Grants, 320
Alaska Airlines Fndn Grants, 321
Alaska Conservation Fndn Operating Support Grants, 323
Alaska Conservation Found Opportunity Grants, 324
Alaska Conservation Fndn Rapid Response Grants, 325
Alaska Conservation Fndn Watchable Wildlife Conservation Trust Grants, 326
Alaska State Council on the Arts Community Arts Development Grants, 327
Alaska State Council on the Arts Operating Grants, 328
ARCO Fndn Education Grants, 528
Brainerd Fndn Grants, 831
Bullitt Fndn Grants, 862
Charlotte Martin Fndn Youth Grants, 1057
ConocoPhillips Fndn Grants, 1354
ConocoPhillips Grants, 1355
DOJ Rural Domestic Violence and Child Victimization Enforcement Grants, 1562
Fluor Fndn Grants, 1875
Foster Fndn Grants, 1888
Fred Meyer Fndn Grants, 1950
GCI Corporate Contributions Grants, 1994
Homer Fndn Grants, 2352
KeyBank Fndn Grants, 2820
M.J. Murdock Charitable Trust General Grants, 2954
Paul G. Allen Family Fndn Grants, 3759
Premera Blue Cross CARES Grants, 3945
Pride Fndn Grants, 3958
Rasmuson Capital Grants, 4020
Rasmuson Creative Ventures Grants, 4021
Rasmuson Individual Artists Awards, 4022
Rasmuson Organizational Advancement Grants, 4023
Rasmuson Sabbatical Grants, 4024
Rasmuson Special Project Grants, 4025
REI Conservation and Outdoor Rec Grants, 4051
Robert B McMillen Fndn Grants, 4106
Skaggs Fndn Grants, 4378
USDA Denali Comm High Energy Grants, 4805
USDA Section 306D Water and Waste System Grants for Alaskan Villages, 4835
Wells Fargo Housing Fndn Grants, 5023
Wilburforce Fndn Grants, 5067
William C. Kenney Watershed Protection Fndn Ecosystem Grants, 5079

American Samoa
Bank of America Charitable Matching Gifts, 658
Bank of America Charitable Volunteer Grants, 660
EPA Environmental Justice Small Grants, 1731
EPA Pestwise Registration Improvement Act Partnership Grants, 1734
EPA Regional Agricultural IPM Grants, 1735
EPA Source Reduction Assistance Grants, 1737
EPA State Indoor Radon Grants, 1738
EPA Tribal Support for the National Environmental Information Exchange Network, 1742
NHLBI Ancillary Studies in Clinical Trials, 3410
NHLBI Bioengineering and Obesity Grants, 3411
NHLBI Career Transition Awards, 3412
NHLBI Ruth L. Kirschstein National Research Service Awards for Individual Senior Fellows, 3421
USDA Farmers Market Promotion Grants, 4808
USDA Farm Labor Housing Grants, 4809
USDA Technical Assistance and Training Grants for Rural Waste Systems, 4842
USDC Public Works and Economic Adjustment Assistance Grants, 4856

Arizona
100 Club of Arizona Benefit Grants, 25
100 Club of Arizona Safety Enhancement Stipends, 26
Abbott Fund Access to Health Care Grants, 80
Abbott Fund Community Grants, 81
Abbott Fund Global AIDS Care Grants, 82

Alabama

Abbott Fund Science Education Grants, 83
ABC Charities Grants, 85
Abelard Fndn West Grants, 88
ACE Charitable Fndn Grants, 111
Aetna Fndn Regional Health Grants, 187
Albertson's Charitable Giving Grants, 345
American Express Charitable Fund Grants, 429
APS Fndn Grants, 518
ARCO Fndn Education Grants, 528
Arizona Cardinals Grants, 534
Arizona Comm on Arts After-School Residencies, 535
Arizona Comm on Arts Education Projects Grants, 536
Arizona Comm on Arts Folklorist Residencies, 537
Arizona Comm on Arts Individual Residencies, 538
Arizona Comm on Arts Visual/Media Arts Organizations Grants, 539
Arizona Community Fndn Grants, 540
Arizona Community Fndn Scholarships, 541
Arizona Diamondbacks Charities Grants, 542
Arizona Fndn for Women Deborah G. Carstens Fund Grants, 543
Arizona Fndn for Women General Grants, 544
Arizona Public Service Corporate Giving Grants, 545
Arizona Republic Fndn Grants, 546
Arizona Republic Newspaper Corporate Contributions Grants, 547
Arizona State Library LSTA Collections Grants, 548
Arizona State Library LSTA Community Grants, 549
Arizona State Library LSTA Learning Grants, 550
BBVA Compass Fndn Charitable Grants, 703
Bechtel Group Fndn Building Positive Community Relationships Grants, 715
Bert W. Martin Fndn Grants, 747
BHHS Legacy Fndn Grants, 758
Boeing Company Contributions Grants, 809
Brunswick Fndn Dollars for Doers Grants, 856
Brunswick Fndn Grants, 857
Caesars Fndn Grants, 891
Carrier Corporation Contributions Grants, 946
Castle and Cooke California Corp Givorateing, 953
CenturyLink Clarke M. Williams Grants, 998
Charlotte Martin Fndn Youth Grants, 1057
Chase Paymentech Corporate Giving Grants, 1059
Circle K Corporation Contributions Grants, 1136
Comcast Fndn Grants, 1235
Comerica Charitable Fndn Grants, 1237
Community Fndn for So Arizona Grants, 1261
ConAgra Foods Community Impact Grants, 1342
ConAgra Foods Nourish Our Comm Grants, 1343
Deluxe Corporation Fndn Grants, 1496
DOJ Rural Domestic Violence and Child Victimization Enforcement Grants, 1562
Dollar General Adult Literacy Grants, 1568
Dollar General Family Literacy Grants, 1569
Dollar General Youth Literacy Grants, 1570
Dorrance Family Fndn Grants, 1590
E.L. Wiegand Fndn Grants, 1639
Flinn Fndn Grantss, 1842
Flinn Fndn Scholarships, 1843
FMC Fndn Grants, 1876
Gannett Fndn Community Action Grants, 1984
General Mills Fndn Grants, 2003
Go Daddy Cares Charitable Contributions, 2094
GTECH Community Involvement Grants, 2171
Gumdrop Books Librarian Scholarships, 2179
Halliburton Fndn Grants, 2211
Humana Fndn Grants, 2388
Intel Community Grants, 2562
JP Morgan Chase Arts and Culture Grants, 2752
JP Morgan Chase Community Devel Grants, 2753
Kevin P. and Sydney B. Knight Family Grants, 2819
Margaret T. Morris Fndn Grants, 3005
Medtronic Community Link Arts, Civic, and Culture Grants, 3109
Medtronic CommunityLink Education Grants, 3110
Medtronic CommunityLink Health Grants, 3111
Medtronic Comm Link Human Services Grants, 3112
Motorola Fndn Grants, 3221
Nationwide Insurance Fndn Grants, 3285
Needmor Fund Grants, 3289
Nestle Purina PetCare Educational Grants, 3302
Nestle Purina PetCare Pet Related Grants, 3304
Nestle Purina PetCare Support Dog and Police K-9 Organization Grants, 3305
Nestle Purina PetCare Youth Grants, 3306
Nina Mason Pulliam Charitable Trust Grants, 3443
PacifiCare Fndn Grants, 3725
Phoenix Coyotes Charities Grants, 3879
Phoenix Neighborhood Block Watch Grants, 3880
Phoenix Suns Charities Grants, 3881
Piper Jaffray Fndn Communities Giving, 3899
Piper Trust Arts and Culture Grants, 3900
Piper Trust Children Grants, 3901
Piper Trust Education Grants, 3902
Piper Trust Healthcare and Med Research Grants, 3903
Piper Trust Older Adults Grants, 3904
Piper Trust Reglous Organizations Grants, 3905
Poets & Writers Readings/Workshops Grants, 3927
Prudential Fndn Arts and Culture Grants, 3975
Prudential Fndn Economic Devel Grants, 3976
Prudential Fndn Education Grants, 3977
QuikTrip Corporate Contributions Grants, 3998
RBC Dain Rauscher Fndn Grants, 4031
REI Conservation and Outdoor Rec Grants, 4051
Saint Luke's Health Initiatives Grants, 4216
Salt River Project Civic Leadership Grants, 4226
Salt River Project Environmental Quality Grants, 4227
Salt River Health and Human Services Grants, 4228
Southwest Gas Corporation Fndn Grants, 4445
Stocker Fndn Grants, 4507
Texas Instruments Arts and Culture Grants, 4596
Texas Instruments Civic and Business Grants, 4597
Texas Instruments Fndn Arts and Culture Grants, 4599
Toyota Technical Center Grants, 4660
U.S. Bank Fndn Grants, 4686
Union Pacific Community and Civic Grants, 4714
Union Pacific Fndn Health and Human Services Grants, 4715
US Airways Community Contributions, 4788
US Airways Community Fndn Grants, 4789
US Airways Education Fndn Grants, 4790
USDA Individual Water and Waste Water Grants, 4817
VSA/Metlife Connect All Grants, 4953
Vulcan Materials Company Fndn Grants, 4956
Wells Fargo Housing Fndn Grants, 5023
Weyerhaeuser Company Fndn Grants, 5053
Wilburforce Fndn Grants, 5067
William C. Kenney Watershed Protection Fndn Ecosystem Grants, 5079

Arkansas

3M Company Arts and Culture Grants, 12
3M Company Environmental Giving Grants, 13
3M Company Health and Human Services Grants, 14
3M Fndn Community Giving Grants, 15
Abelard Fndn East Grants, 87
ACE Charitable Fndn Grants, 111
AEGON Transamerica Arts & Culture Grants, 176
AEGON Transamerica Fndn Civic and Community Grants, 177
AEGON Transamerica Fndn Health and Welfare Grants, 179
AEP Corporate Giving Grants, 180
Albertson's Charitable Giving Grants, 345
American Electric Power Grants, 428
Archer Daniels Midland Grants, 527
Arkansas Arts Council AIE After School/Summer Residency Grants, 551
Arkansas Arts Council AIE Arts Curriculum Project Grants, 552
Arkansas Arts Council AIE In-School Residency Grants, 553
Arkansas Arts Council AIE Mini Grants, 554
Arkansas Arts Council Collaborative Support, 555
Arkansas Arts Council Expansion Arts Grants, 556
Arkansas Arts Council General Operating Support, 557
Arkansas Arts Council Sally A. Williams Artist Fund Grants, 558
Arkansas Community Fndn Arkansas Black Hall of Fame Grants, 559
Arkansas Community Fndn Giving Tree, 560
Arkansas Community Fndn Grants, 561
Assisi Found of Memphis Capital Project Grants, 593
Assisi Fndn of Memphis General Grants, 594
BancorpSouth Fndn Grants, 651
Belk Fndn Grants, 721
Bitha Godfrey & Maude J. Thomas Charitable Fndn Grants, 776
Bridgestone/Firestone Trust Fund Grants, 836
Carl B. and Florence E. King Fndn Grants, 928
CenturyLink Clarke M. Williams Grants, 998
Charles A. Frueauff Fndn Grants, 1037
Cingular Wireless Charitable Contributions, 1134
Circle K Corporation Contributions Grants, 1136
Comcast Fndn Grants, 1235
ConAgra Foods Community Impact Grants, 1342
ConAgra Foods Nourish Our Comm Grants, 1343
DOJ Rural Domestic Violence and Child Victimization Enforcement Grants, 1562
Dollar General Adult Literacy Grants, 1568
Dollar General Family Literacy Grants, 1569
Dollar General Youth Literacy Grants, 1570
Donald W. Reynolds Fndn Charitable Food Distribution Grants, 1575
Donald W. Reynolds Fndn Children's Discovery Initiative Grants, 1576
Eaton Charitable Fund Grants, 1647
Entergy Charitable Fndn Low-Income Initiatives and Solutions Grants, 1711
Entergy Corporation Micro Grants, 1712
Entergy Corp Grants for Arts and Culture, 1713
Entergy Corporation Open Grants for Community Improvement & Enrichment, 1714
Entergy Corp Grants for Healthy Families, 1715
Fndn for the Mid South Community Development Grants, 1897
Fndn for the Mid South Education Grants, 1898
Fndn for Mid South Health & Wellness Grants, 1899
Fndn for Mid So Wealth Building Grants, 1900
Gannett Fndn Community Action Grants, 1984
GenCorp Fndn Grants, 1998
General Mills Fndn Grants, 2003
Georgia-Pacific Fndn Education Grants, 2031
Georgia-Pacific Fndn Enrichment Grants, 2032
Georgia-Pacific Entrepreneurship Grants, 2033
Georgia-Pacific Fndn Environment Grants, 2034
Hatton W. Sumners Fndn for the Study and Teaching of Self Government Grants, 2257
J.E. and L.E. Mabee Fndn Grants, 2595
Johnson & Johnson Comm Health Care Grants, 2717
Kimberly-Clark Community Grants, 2824
Land O'Lakes Fndn Community Grants, 2859
Land O'Lakes Fndn Dollars for Doers, 2860
Marion and Miriam Rose Fund Grants, 3015
Mary E. and Michael Blevins Charitable Grants, 3037
Mary Reynolds Babcock Fndn Grants, 3047
MeadWestvaco Sustainable Communities Grants, 3105
Mid-America Arts Alliance Community Engagement with Touring Artists Grants, 3166
Mid-America Arts Alliance Reg Touring Grants, 3167
Piper Jaffray Fndn Communities Giving, 3899
Plum Creek Fndn Grants, 3917
Ross Fndn Grants, 4164
Roy and Christine Sturgis Trust Grants, 4166
Southwire Company Grants, 4447
Sunderland Fndn Grants, 4527
T.L.L. Temple Fndn Grants, 4546
TAC Arts Access Technical Assistance Grants, 4550
TAC Arts Educ Community-Learning Grants, 4552
TAC Arts Education Mini Grants, 4553
TAC Arts Projects Grants, 4554
TAC Rural Arts Project Support Grants, 4555
TAC Technical Assistance Grants, 4556
TAC Touring Arts and Access Grants, 4557
Trinity Fndn Grants, 4669
U.S. Bank Fndn Grants, 4686
Union Pacific Community and Civic Grants, 4714
Union Pacific Fndn Health and Human Services Grants, 4715
USDA Delta Health Care Services Grants, 4804

GEOGRAPHIC INDEX

Vulcan Materials Company Fndn Grants, 4956
Walton Family Fndn Home Region Grants, 4984
Wells Fargo Housing Fndn Grants, 5023
Weyerhaeuser Company Fndn Grants, 5053
Winthrop Rockefeller Fndn Grants, 5105

California

3M Company Arts and Culture Grants, 12
3M Company Environmental Giving Grants, 13
3M Company Health and Human Services Grants, 14
3M Fndn Community Giving Grants, 15
4S Ranch~Del Sur Community Fndn Grants, 17
18th Street Arts Complex Residency Grants, 19
49ers Fndn Grants, 23
A.H.K. Fndn Grants, 40
A/H Fndn Grants, 48
Aaron Fndn Grants, 72
Abbott Fund Access to Health Care Grants, 80
Abbott Fund Community Grants, 81
Abbott Fund Global AIDS Care Grants, 82
Abbott Fund Science Education Grants, 83
Abelard Fndn West Grants, 88
ABS Fndn Grants, 107
Abundance Fndn Local Community Grants, 109
ACE Charitable Fndn Grants, 111
A Charitable Fndn Grants, 126
ACTION Council of Monterey County Grants, 134
Adam Richter Charitable Trust Grants, 145
Adams-Mastrovich Family Fndn Grants, 146
Adelaide Christian Home For Children Grants, 162
Adobe Art and Culture Grants, 167
Adobe Community Investment Grants, 168
Adobe Hunger and Homelessness Grants, 169
Advanced Micro Devices Comm Affairs Grants, 172
AEGON Transamerica Arts & Culture Grants, 176
AEGON Transamerica Fndn Civic and Community Grants, 177
AEGON Transamerica Fndn Health and Welfare Grants, 179
Aetna Fndn Regional Health Grants, 187
Agape Fndn for Nonviolent Social Change Board of Trustees Grants, 197
Agape Fndn for Nonviolent Social Change Peace Prizes, 198
Ahmanson Fndn Grants, 207
AHS Fndn Grants, 208
Akonadi Fndn Anti-Racism Grants, 217
Albertson's Charitable Giving Grants, 345
Alice Tweed Tuohy Fndn Grants, 372
Alliance Healthcare Fndn Grants, 383
Alpine Winter Fndn Grants, 394
ALZA Corporate Contributions Grants, 405
Amador Community Fndn Grants, 408
American Express Charitable Fund Grants, 429
American Rivers Community-Based Restoration Program River Grants, 444
Angels Baseball Fndn Grants, 465
Anheuser-Busch Fndn Grants, 470
Ann Peppers Fndn Grants, 484
Annunziata Sanguinetti Fndn Grants, 485
Aratani Fndn Grants, 523
Archer Daniels Midland Fndn Grants, 527
ARCO Fndn Education Grants, 528
Argyros Fndn Grants, 532
Atkinson Fndn Community Grants, 606
Audrey and Sydney Irmas Charitable Fndn Grants, 612
Avista Fndn Grants, 624
Bayer Fndn Grants, 696
BBVA Compass Fndn Charitable Grants, 703
Bechtel Group Fndn Building Positive Community Relationships Grants, 715
Bella Vista Fndn Grants, 722
Ben B. Cheney Fndn Grants, 725
Bernard Osher Fndn Grants, 742
Bertha Russ Lytel Fndn Grants, 745
Bertha Wolf-Rosenthal Fndn for Community Service Stipend, 746
Better Way Fndn Grants, 754
Bill Hannon Fndn Grants, 771
Biogen Corporate Giving Grants, 773

Blue Shield of California Grants, 802
Boeckmann Charitable Fndn Grants, 808
Boeing Company Contributions Grants, 809
Bright Family Fndn Grants, 837
Burton G. Bettingen Grants, 871
Cadence Design Systems Grants, 889
Caesars Fndn Grants, 891
California Arts Council Arts and Accessibility Tech Assistance Grants, 894
California Arts Creating Public Value Grants, 895
California Arts Council State-Local Partnership Grants, 896
California Arts Council State Networks Grants, 897
California Arts Council Tech Assistance Grants, 898
California Coastal Art and Poetry Contest, 899
California Community Fndn Art Grants, 900
California Community Fndn Health Care Grants, 901
California Community Fndn Human Development Grants, 902
California Community Fndn Neighborhood Revitalization Grants, 903
California Endowment Innovative Ideas Challenge Grants, 904
California Fertilizer Fndn School Garden Grants, 905
California Green Trees for Golden State Grant, 906
California State Parks Restore and Cleanup Grants, 908
Callaway Golf Company Fndn Grants, 910
CarEth Fndn Grants, 924
Carl Gellert and Celia Berta Gellert Fndn Grants, 930
Carlsbad Charitable Fndn Grants, 936
Castle and Cooke California Corp Givorateing, 953
CCF Social and Economic Justice Fund Grants, 964
CCH California Story Fund Grants, 965
CCH Documentary California Reads Grants, 968
CCH Documentary Project Production Grants, 969
CCH Documentary Public Engagement Grants, 970
CCH Documentary Project Research and Development Grants, 971
Ceil & Michael E. Pulitzer Fndn Grants, 987
Center for Venture Philanthropy, 991
CenturyLink Clarke M. Williams Grants, 998
Ceres Fndn Grants, 999
Chapman Charitable Fndn Grants, 1033
Charles H. Price II Family Fndn Grants, 1046
CHCF Grants, 1063
Chiles Fndn Grants, 1108
Chiron Fndn Community Grants, 1111
Chula Vista Charitable Fndn Grants, 1116
Cingular Wireless Charitable Contributions, 1134
Circle K Corporation Contributions Grants, 1136
Cisco Systems Fndn San Jose Community Grants, 1137
Claremont Community Fndn Grants, 1149
Clarence E. Heller Charitable Fndn Grants, 1150
Cleo Fndn Grants, 1164
Clorox Company Fndn Grants, 1176
Coeta and Donald Barker Fndn Grants, 1197
Comcast Fndn Grants, 1235
Comerica Charitable Fndn Grants, 1237
Community Found for Monterey County Grants, 1255
Community Found for San Benito County Grants, 1258
Community Found of Riverside County Grants, 1304
Community Found of Santa Cruz County Grants, 1305
Community Fndn of the Verdugos Educational Endowment Fund Grants, 1321
Community Fndn of the Verdugos Grants, 1322
Community Fndn Silicon Valley Advancing the Arts Initiative, 1330
Community Fndn Silicon Valley Grants, 1331
Community Tech Fndn of California Building Communities Through Technology Grants, 1336
ConAgra Foods Community Impact Grants, 1342
ConAgra Foods Nourish Our Comm Grants, 1343
Con Edison Corporate Environmental Grants, 1347
ConocoPhillips Fndn Grants, 1354
ConocoPhillips Grants, 1355
Crail-Johnson Fndn Grants, 1393
Creative Work Fund Grants, 1396
Credit Suisse First Boston Fndn Grants, 1397
Crescent Porter Hale Fndn Grants, 1398
Dan Murphy Fndn Grants, 1444

California / 1143

Darden Restaurants Fndn Grants, 1446
David Geffen Fndn Grants, 1452
Dean Foods Community Involvement Grants, 1469
Deluxe Corporation Fndn Grants, 1496
Dunspaugh-Dalton Fndn Grants, 1623
Durfee Fndn Sabbatical Grants, 1625
Durfee Fndn Stanton Fellowship, 1626
Dwight Stuart Youth Fndn Capacity-Building Initiative Grants, 1627
Dwight Stuart Youth Fndn Grants, 1628
E.L. Wiegand Fndn Grants, 1639
Earth Island Institute Community Wetland Restoration Grants, 1642
eBay Fndn Community Grants, 1648
EDS Fndn Grants, 1661
EDS Technology Grants, 1662
Edward R. Godfrey Fndn Grants, 1667
EIF Community Grants, 1675
Eisner Fndn Grants, 1678
Ethel Frends Fndn Grants, 1759
Evelyn and Walter Haas, Jr. Fund Immigrant Rights Grants, 1773
Evelyn and Walter Haas, Jr. Fund Nonprofit Leadership Grants, 1774
FEDCO Charitable Found Education Grants, 1798
Fieldstone Fndn Grants, 1808
Fitzpatrick, Cella, Harper & Scinto Pro Bono, 1836
Fleishhacker Fndn Education Grants, 1838
Fleishhacker Found Small Grants in the Arts, 1839
Fleishhacker Fndn Special Arts Grants, 1840
Fluor Fndn Grants, 1875
FMC Fndn Grants, 1876
Ford Family Fndn Grants - Critical Needs, 1879
Ford Family Fndn Grants - Positive Youth Development, 1880
Ford Family Grants Public Convening Spaces, 1881
Ford Family Fndn Tech Assistance Grants, 1882
Fritz B. Burns Fndn Grants, 1965
Furth Family Fndn Grants, 1980
Gamble Fndn Grants, 1983
Gannett Fndn Community Action Grants, 1984
GenCorp Fndn Grants, 1998
Gene Haas Fndn, 1999
Genentech Corporate Charitable Contributions, 2000
General Mills Fndn Grants, 2003
George and Ruth Bradford Fndn Grants, 2010
George B. Page Fndn Grants, 2013
George Frederick Jewett Fndn Grants, 2019
Georgia-Pacific Fndn Education Grants, 2031
Georgia-Pacific Fndn Enrichment Grants, 2032
Georgia-Pacific Fndn Entrepreneurship Grants, 2033
Georgia-Pacific Fndn Environment Grants, 2034
Gil and Dody Weaver Fndn Grants, 2053
Go Daddy Cares Charitable Contributions, 2094
Golden State Warriors Fndn Grants, 2099
Good Works Fndn Grants, 2105
Green Diamond Charitable Contributions, 2149
Grover Hermann Fndn Grants, 2168
GTECH Community Involvement Grants, 2171
H.B. Fuller Company Fndn Grants, 2183
H. Leslie Hoffman and Elaine S. Hoffman Fndn Grants, 2185
HAF Arts and Culture: Lynne and Bob Wells Grant for Performing Artists, 2190
HAF Arts and Culture: Project Grants to Artists, 2191
HAF Co-op Community Fund Grants, 2192
HAF Community Grants, 2193
HAF Community Partnerships with Native Artists Grants, 2194
HAF Companion Animal Welfare and Rescue, 2195
HAF Education Grants, 2196
HAF Hansen Family Trust Christian Endowment Fund Grants, 2197
HAF Justin Keele Make a Difference Award, 2198
HAF Kayla Wood Girls Memorial Fund Grants, 2199
HAF Mada Huggins Caldwell Fund Grants, 2200
HAF Native Cultures Fund Grants, 2201
HAF Natural Environment Grants, 2202
HAF Senior Opportunities Grants, 2203
HAF Southern Humboldt Grants, 2204

HAF Summer Youth Partnership Grants, 2205
HAF Technical Assistance Program Grants, 2206
Hazen Fndn Public Education Grants, 2269
Healthcare Found for Orange County Grants, 2279
Hedco Fndn Grants, 2287
Hilda and Preston Davis Fndn Grants, 2322
Hilton Hotels Corporate Giving Grants, 2331
Horizons Community Issues Grants, 2366
Hormel Foods Charitable Trust Grants, 2368
Huffy Fndn Grants, 2384
Hundred Club of Contra Costa County Survivor Benefits Grants, 2393
Hundred Club of Los Angeles Grants, 2396
Hundred Club of Palm Springs Grants, 2397
Hundred Club of Santa Clara County Grants, 2399
Hut Fndn Grants, 2411
Hutton Fndn Grants, 2412
IIE Western Union Family Scholarships, 2462
Intel Community Grants, 2562
Ireland Family Fndn Grants, 2574
Isabel Allende Fndn Esperanza Grants, 2586
J.M. Long Fndn Grants, 2603
Jacobs Family Fndn Jabara Learning Opportunities Grants, 2617
Jacobs Family Spirit of the Diamond Grants, 2618
Jacobs Family Village Neighborhoods Grants, 2619
James Irvine Found Creative Connections Grants, 2628
James Irvine Fndn Leadership Awards, 2629
James S. Copley Fndn Grants, 2637
Jewish Community Fndn of Los Angeles Cutting Edge Grants, 2673
Jewish Community Fndn of LA Israel Grants, 2674
John Gogian Family Fndn Grants, 2697
John Jewett and Helen Chandler Garland Grants, 2702
John M. Weaver Fndn Grants, 2705
John S. and James L. Knight Fndn Communities Grants, 2711
Johnson & Johnson Comm Health Care Grants, 2717
Joseph Drown Fndn Grants, 2735
Josephine S. Gumbiner Fndn Grants, 2739
JP Morgan Chase Arts and Culture Grants, 2752
JP Morgan Chase Community Devel Grants, 2753
Katherine Baxter Memorial Fndn Grants, 2789
Kathryne Beynon Fndn Grants, 2791
Kenneth T. and Eileen L. Norris Found Grants, 2802
Kimball Int'l-Habig Fndn Grants, 2823
Kimberly-Clark Community Grants, 2824
LA84 Fndn Grants, 2847
Land O'Lakes Fndn California Grants, 2858
Land O'Lakes Fndn Community Grants, 2859
Land O'Lakes Fndn Dollars for Doers, 2860
Legler Benbough Fndn Grants, 2877
Liberty Hill Environmental Justice Fund Grants, 2891
Liberty Hill Fndn for a New L.A. Grants, 2892
Liberty Hill Fndn Fund for Change Grants, 2893
Liberty Hill Fndn Lesbian & Gay Community Fund Grants, 2894
Liberty Hill Fndn Seed Fund Grants, 2896
Liberty Hill Special Opportunity Fund Grants, 2897
LISC Financial Opportunity Center Social Innovation Fund Grants, 2911
Liz Claiborne Fndn Grants, 2915
Lockheed Martin Philanthropic Grants, 2918
Lowell Berry Fndn Grants, 2930
Lucile Horton Howe and Mitchell B. Howe Fndn Grants, 2934
Lumpkin Family Strong Community Leadership Grants, 2944
Marin Community Affordable Housing Grants, 3010
Marin Community Fndn Ending the Cycle of Poverty Grants, 3011
Marin Community Fndn Social Justice and Interfaith Understanding Grants, 3012
Marin Community Fndn Stinson Bolinas Community Grants, 3013
Marin Community Successful Aging Grants, 3014
Martin C. Kauffman 100 Club of Alameda County Survivor Benefits Grants, 3028
Mary M. Aaron Memorial Trust Scholarships, 3045
Maurice J. Masserini Charitable Trust Grants, 3064

McCarthy Family Fndn Grants, 3073
McConnell Fndn Grants, 3076
McLean Fndn Grants, 3089
MeadWestvaco Sustainable Communities Grants, 3105
Medtronic Comm Arts, Civic, and Culture Grants, 3109
Medtronic CommunityLink Education Grants, 3110
Medtronic CommunityLink Health Grants, 3111
Medtronic Comm Link Human Services Grants, 3112
Mercedes-Benz USA Corporate Contributions, 3118
Mericos Fndn Grants, 3121
Miller Brewing Corporate Contributions Grants, 3180
Mimi and Peter Haas Fund Grants, 3185
Mizuho USA Fndn Grants, 3192
Motorola Fndn Grants, 3221
Nationwide Insurance Fndn Grants, 3285
Needmor Fund Grants, 3289
Nehemiah Community Fndn Grants, 3290
Nestle Purina PetCare Educational Grants, 3302
Nestle Purina PetCare Pet Related Grants, 3304
Nestle Purina PetCare Support Dog and Police K-9 Organization Grants, 3305
Nestle Purina PetCare Youth Grants, 3306
NGA Hansen's Natural and Native School Garden Grants, 3402
Nissan Fndn Grants, 3444
Nissan Neighbors Grants, 3445
Nordson Corporation Fndn Grants, 3462
Oakland Fund for Children and Youth Grants, 3634
Oceanside Charitable Fndn Grants, 3637
Orange County Community Fndn Grants, 3688
PacifiCare Fndn Grants, 3725
PacifiCorp Fndn for Learning Grants, 3727
Packard Fndn Local Grants, 3729
Pajaro Valley Community Health Insurance/Coverage & Education on Using the System Grants, 3731
Pajaro Valley Community Health Trust Diabetes and Contributing Factors Grants, 3732
Parker Fndn (California) Grants, 3736
Pasadena Fndn Average Grants, 3741
Patricia Price Peterson Fndn Grants, 3746
Patron Saints Grants, 3753
Peter Kiewit Fndn General Grants, 3845
Peter Kiewit Fndn Small Grants, 3847
Peter Norton Family Fndn Grants, 3849
PG&E Bright Ideas Grants, 3866
PG&E Community Investment Grants, 3867
PG&E Community Vitality Grants, 3868
Piper Jaffray Fndn Communities Giving, 3899
Poets & Writers Readings/Workshops Grants, 3927
Price Family Charitable Fund Grants, 3952
Princeton Area Community Fndn Rebecca Annitto Service Opps for Students Award, 3964
Prudential Fndn Arts and Culture Grants, 3975
Prudential Fndn Economic Devel Grants, 3976
Prudential Fndn Education Grants, 3977
Qualcomm Grants, 3993
Quantum Corporation Snap Server Grants, 3995
Ralph M. Parsons Fndn Grants, 4013
Ralphs Food 4 Less Fndn Grants, 4014
Rancho Bernardo Community Found Grants, 4015
Rancho Santa Fe Fndn Grants, 4016
Rathmann Family Fndn Grants, 4026
RBC Dain Rauscher Fndn Grants, 4031
RealNetworks Fndn Grants, 4037
REI Conservation and Outdoor Rec Grants, 4051
Reynolds Family Fndn Grants, 4071
Richard and Rhoda Goldman Fund Grants, 4077
Robert Lee Adams Fndn Grants, 4114
Robert R. McCormick Tribune Comm Grants, 4119
Romic Environmental's Charitable Contributions, 4148
Rose Found For Communities and the Environment Consumer Privacy Grants, 4156
Rose Found for Communities and Environment Kern County Air Pollution Mitigation Grants, 4157
Rose Fndn For Communities and the Environment Northern California Environmental Grassroots Grants, 4158
Rose Fndn For Communities and the Environment Southeast Madera County Responsible Growth Grants, 4159

Rose Fndn For Communities and the Environment Watershed Protection Grants, 4160
Rose Hills Fndn Grants, 4162
Ryder System Charitable Fndn Grants, 4191
S. D. Bechtel, Jr. Fndn / Stephen Bechtel Fund Environmental Education Grants, 4192
S.H. Cowell Fndn Grants, 4199
S. Mark Taper Fndn Grants, 4201
Safeco Insurance Community Grants, 4203
Salmon Fndn Grants, 4225
San Diego County Bar Fndn Grants, 4241
San Diego After-the-Fires Grants, 4242
San Diego Arts & Culture Grants, 4243
San Diego Civil Society Grants, 4244
San Diego Environment Blasker Grants, 4245
San Diego Environment Community Grants, 4246
San Diego Health & Human Services Grants, 4248
San Diego Paradise Valley Hospital Comm Grants, 4249
San Diego Science & Technology Blasker Grants, 4250
San Diego HIV Funding Collaborative Grants, 4251
San Diego Women's Fndn Grants, 4252
San Francisco Art Awards James Duval Phelan Literary Award, 4258
San Francisco Art Awards Joseph Henry Jackson Literary Award, 4259
San Francisco Art Awards Mary Tanenbaum Literary Award, 4260
San Francisco Bay Area Documentary Grants, 4261
San Francisco Community Development Grants, 4262
San Francisco Community Health Grants, 4263
San Francisco Community Leadership Awards, 4264
San Francisco Disability Rights Advocate Fund Emergency Grants, 4265
San Francisco Environment Grants, 4266
San Francisco Faith Program and Arts and Culture Program, 4267
San Francisco FAITHS Arts and Culture Grants, 4268
San Francisco Fund for Artists Arts Teacher Fellowships, 4269
San Francisco Fund For Artists Award For Choreographers, 4270
San Francisco Fund for Artists Award for Composers and Music Ensembles, 4271
San Francisco Fund For Artists Award For Playwrights and Theatre Ensembles, 4272
San Francisco Fund for Artists Award for Visual and Media Artists, 4273
San Francisco Fund For Artists Matching Comms Grants, 4274
San Francisco Fund Shenson Performing Arts Fellowships, 4275
San Francisco James D. Phelan Art Award in Photography, 4276
San Francisco James D. Phelan Art Award in Printmaking, 4277
San Francisco James D. Phelan Award in Film, Video, and Digital Media, 4278
San Francisco John Gutmann Photography Fellowship Award, 4279
San Francisco Koshland Program Arts and Culture Mini-Grants, 4280
San Francisco Found Multicultural Fellowship, 4281
San Francisco Murphy and Cadogan Fellowships in the Fine Arts, 4282
Santa Barbara Found Monthly Express Grants, 4284
Santa Barbara Strategy Grants - Capital Support, 4285
Santa Barbara Strategy Grants - Core Support, 4286
Santa Barbara Fndn Strategy Grants - Innovation, 4287
Santa Barbara Fndn Towbes Fund for the Performing Arts Grants, 4288
Seagate Tech Corp Capacity to Care Grants, 4317
Shopko Fndn Community Grants, 4346
Sidney Stern Memorial Trust Grants, 4349
Sierra Health Fndn Responsive Grants, 4353
Silicon Valley Community Fndn Donor Circle for the Arts Grants, 4354
Silicon Valley Community Fndn Economic Security Grants, 4355
Silicon Valley Community Education Grants, 4356

GEOGRAPHIC INDEX

Silicon Valley Community Fndn Elizabeth Anabo BRICC Awards, 4357
Silicon Valley Community Fndn Immigrant Integration Grants, 4358
Silicon Valley Community Fndn Regional Planning Grants, 4359
Sisters of St. Joseph Healthcare Found Grants, 4377
Sobrato Family Fndn Grants, 4389
Sobrato Family Found Meeting Space Grants, 4390
Sobrato Family Fndn Office Space Grants, 4391
Solutia Fund Grants, 4402
Sonora Area Fndn Competitive Grants, 4404
Southern California Edison Civic Affairs Grants, 4428
Southern California Edison Environmental Grants, 4429
Southern California Edison Public Safety and Preparedness Grants, 4430
Southwest Gas Corporation Fndn Grants, 4445
State Street Fndn Grants, 4495
Steelcase Fndn Grants, 4497
Stocker Fndn Grants, 4507
Stuart Fndn Grants, 4516
Symantec Community Relations and Corporate Philanthropy Grants, 4544
Taproot Fndn Capacity-Building Grants, 4560
TE Fndn Grants, 4572
Tension Envelope Fndn Grants, 4578
Texas Instruments Arts and Culture Grants, 4596
Texas Instruments Civic and Business Grants, 4597
Texas Instruments Fndn Arts and Culture Grants, 4599
Thelma Doelger Charitable Trust Grants, 4604
Thomas and Dorothy Leavey Fndn Grants, 4612
Thomas C. Ackerman Fndn Grants, 4615
Thomas J. Long Fndn Community Grants, 4618
Thornton Fndn Grants, 4624
Tides California Wildlands Grassroots Fund, 4630
Tiger Woods Fndn Grants, 4634
Toby Wells Fndn Grants, 4638
Toro Fndn Grants, 4647
Toyota Motor Sales, USA Grants, 4659
Toyota Technical Center Grants, 4660
TRDRP Participatory Awards: CARA/SARA, 4663
TRDRP Research Grants, 4664
Trinity Trust Community Response Grants, 4671
Trinity Trust Summer Youth Mini Grants, 4672
Turner Voices Corporate Contributions, 4682
U.S. Bank Fndn Grants, 4686
Union Bank, N.A. Corporate Sponsorships and Donations, 4708
Union Bank, N.A. Fndn Grants, 4709
Union Labor Health Found Community Grants, 4713
Union Pacific Community and Civic Grants, 4714
Union Pacific Fndn Health and Human Services Grants, 4715
USDA Individual Water and Waste Water Grants, 4817
Vanguard Public Fndn Grant Funds, 4904
VSA/Metlife Connect All Grants, 4953
Vulcan Materials Company Fndn Grants, 4956
W.M. Keck Fndn So California Grants, 4964
Waitt Family Fndn Grants, 4973
Wallace Alexander Gerbode Fndn Grants, 4974
Wallace Alexander Gerbode Fndn Special Award Grants, 4975
Walt Disney Company Fndn Grants, 4981
Walter and Elise Haas Fund Grants, 4982
Wayne and Gladys Valley Fndn Grants, 5003
Weingart Fndn Grants, 5018
Wells Fargo Housing Fndn Grants, 5023
Weyerhaeuser Company Fndn Grants, 5053
Wild Rivers Community Fndn Holiday Partnership Grants, 5069
Wild Rivers Community Fndn Summer Youth Mini Grants, 5070
William C. Kenney Watershed Protection Fndn Ecosystem Grants, 5079
William G. Gilmore Fndn Grants, 5082
William G. McGowan Charitable Fund Grants, 5084
William H. Hannon Fndn Grants, 5086
William McCaskey Chapman and Adaline Dinsmore Chapman Fndn Grants, 5092
Winifred & Harry B. Allen Fndn Grants, 5101
Wood-Claeyssens Fndn Grants, 5113
Zellerbach Family Fndn Community Arts Grants, 5150
Zellerbach Family Fndn Grants, 5151

Colorado

A.H.K. Fndn Grants, 40
A.V. Hunter Trust Grants, 47
Abelard Fndn West Grants, 88
ABS Fndn Grants, 107
ACE Charitable Fndn Grants, 111
Action for Affordable Housing Grants, 135
Advancing Colorado's Mental Health Care Grants, 173
Advocate Safehouse Project Grants, 174
AEC Trust Grants, 175
Albertson's Charitable Giving Grants, 345
Alexander Fndn Emergency Grants, 356
Alexander Fndn Holiday Grants, 357
Anheuser-Busch Fndn Grants, 470
Anschutz Family Fndn Grants, 486
Anthem Blue Cross and Blue Shield Grants, 488
Aquila Corporate Grants, 521
ARCO Fndn Education Grants, 528
Aspen Community Fndn Grants, 592
Bacon Family Fndn Grants, 634
Baughman Fndn Grants, 688
BBVA Compass Fndn Charitable Grants, 703
Beim Fndn Grants, 718
Bill and Katie Weaver Charitable Trust Grants, 764
Boeing Company Contributions Grants, 809
Boettcher Fndn Grants, 810
Bohemian Fndn Pharos Fund Grants, 811
Bonfils-Stanton Fndn Grants, 814
Boulder County Arts Alliance Neodata Grants, 823
Brett Family Fndn Grants, 833
Bridgestone/Firestone Trust Fund Grants, 836
Carl W. and Carrie Mae Joslyn Trust Grants, 938
CenturyLink Clarke M. Williams Grants, 998
Chamberlain Fndn Grants, 1027
Charles A. Frueauff Fndn Grants, 1037
Circle K Corporation Contributions Grants, 1136
Colorado Bioscience Discovery Evaluation Grants, 1211
Colorado Clean Energy Solar Innovation Grants, 1212
Colorado Interstate Gas Grants, 1213
Colorado Renewables in Performance Contracting Grants, 1214
Colorado Springs Community Trust Fund Grants, 1215
Colorado Trust Grants, 1216
Colorado Trust Partnerships for Health Initiative, 1217
Comcast Fndn Grants, 1235
ConAgra Foods Community Impact Grants, 1342
ConAgra Foods Nourish Our Comm Grants, 1343
Cooke-Hay Fndn Grants, 1367
Coors Brewing Corporate Contributions Grants, 1371
D.F. Halton Fndn Grants, 1424
Daniels Fund Grants, 1443
Dean Foods Community Involvement Grants, 1469
Deluxe Corporation Fndn Grants, 1496
Denver Broncos Charities Fund Grants, 1501
Denver Community Grants, 1502
Denver Social Venture Partners Grants, 1503
Denver Strengthening Neighborhoods Grants, 1504
Denver Technical Assistance Grants, 1505
DOJ Rural Domestic Violence and Child Victimization Enforcement Grants, 1562
Dollar General Adult Literacy Grants, 1568
Dollar General Family Literacy Grants, 1569
Dollar General Youth Literacy Grants, 1570
Eaton Charitable Fund Grants, 1647
Ed and Carole Abel Fndn Grants, 1652
EDS Fndn Grants, 1661
EDS Technology Grants, 1662
El Paso Corporate Fndn Grants, 1689
El Pomar Fndn Awards and Grants, 1690
Esther M. and Freeman E. Everett Grants, 1757
Gannett Fndn Community Action Grants, 1984
Gates Family Children, Youth & Family Grants, 1989
Gates Family Fndn Community Development & Revitalization Grants, 1990
Gates Family Fndn Parks, Conservation & Recreation Grants, 1991
General Service Fndn Colorado Grants, 2005
Gill Fndn - Gay and Lesbian Fund Grants, 2054
Go Daddy Cares Charitable Contributions, 2094
Griffin Fndn Grants, 2165
GTECH Community Involvement Grants, 2171
Gumdrop Books Librarian Scholarships, 2179
Head Start Replacement Grantee: Colorado, 2275
Helen K. and Arthur E. Johnson Grants, 2296
Hill Fndn Grants, 2326
Humana Fndn Grants, 2388
Hundred Club of Colorado Springs Grants, 2391
Hundred Club of Denver Grants, 2394
Hundred Club of Durango Grants, 2395
Hundred Club of Pueblo Grants, 2398
IIE Nancy Petry Scholarship, 2459
IIE Western Union Family Scholarships, 2462
Inasmuch Fndn Grants, 2523
Intel Community Grants, 2562
John G. Duncan Trust Grants, 2695
John S. and James L. Knight Fndn Communities Grants, 2711
Johns Manville Fund Grants, 2716
JP Morgan Chase Arts and Culture Grants, 2752
JP Morgan Chase Community Devel Grants, 2753
KeyBank Fndn Grants, 2820
Laura Jane Musser Intercultural Harmony Grants, 2862
Laura Jane Musser Rural Arts Grants, 2863
Laura Jane Musser Rural Initiative Grants, 2864
Lockheed Martin Philanthropic Grants, 2918
Mabel Y. Hughes Charitable Trust Grants, 2960
Medtronic Community Link Arts, Civic, and Culture Grants, 3109
Medtronic CommunityLink Education Grants, 3110
Medtronic CommunityLink Health Grants, 3111
Medtronic Comm Link Human Services Grants, 3112
Monfort Family Fndn Grants, 3203
Nathan B. and Florence R. Burt Grants, 3245
Nationwide Insurance Fndn Grants, 3285
Needmor Fund Grants, 3289
Nestle Purina PetCare Educational Grants, 3302
Nestle Purina PetCare Pet Related Grants, 3304
Nestle Purina PetCare Support Dog and Police K-9 Organization Grants, 3305
Nestle Purina PetCare Youth Grants, 3306
PacifiCare Fndn Grants, 3725
Packard Fndn Local Grants, 3729
PeyBack Fndn Grants, 3861
Piper Jaffray Fndn Communities Giving, 3899
Qualcomm Grants, 3993
Questar Corporate Contributions Grants, 3997
REI Conservation and Outdoor Rec Grants, 4051
Robert R. McCormick Tribune Fndn Community Grants, 4119
Rose Community Fndn Aging Grants, 4152
Rose Community Fndn Child and Family Development Grants, 4153
Rose Community Fndn Health Grants, 4154
Rose Community Fndn Jewish Life Grants, 4155
Ruth and Vernon Taylor Fndn Grants, 4177
Safeco Insurance Community Grants, 4203
Salmon Fndn Grants, 4225
Schlessman Family Fndn Grants, 4307
Schramm Fndn Grants, 4310
Seagate Tech Corp Capacity to Care Grants, 4317
Subaru of America Fndn Grants, 4518
Summit Fndn Grants, 4524
TCF Bank Fndn Grants, 4565
Telluride Fndn Community Grants, 4573
Telluride Found Emergency/Out of Cycle Grants, 4574
Telluride Fndn Tech Assistance Grants, 4575
U.S. Bank Fndn Grants, 4686
Union Pacific Community and Civic Grants, 4714
Union Pacific Fndn Health and Human Services Grants, 4715
VSA/Metlife Connect All Grants, 4953
Wells Fargo Housing Fndn Grants, 5023
Weyerhaeuser Company Fndn Grants, 5053
William C. Kenney Watershed Protection Fndn Ecosystem Grants, 5079
William G. Gilmore Fndn Grants, 5082

1146 / Colorado

Yampa Valley Community Fndn Erickson Business Week Scholarships, 5123
Yampa Valley Community Fndn Grants, 5124

Connecticut

3M Company Arts and Culture Grants, 12
3M Company Environmental Giving Grants, 13
3M Company Health and Human Services Grants, 14
3M Fndn Community Giving Grants, 15
1772 Fndn Fellowships, 36
Aaron Fndn Grants, 73
Abelard Fndn East Grants, 87
ACE Charitable Fndn Grants, 111
Aetna Fndn Arts Grants in Connecticut, 181
Aetna Fndn Diversity Grants in Connecticut, 182
Aetna Fndn Educ Grants in Connecticut, 183
Aetna Fndn Health Grants in Connecticut, 184
Aetna Fndn Regional Health Grants, 187
Aetna Fndn Strengthening Neighborhhods Grants in Connecticut, 188
Aetna Fndn Summer Academic Grants, 189
Agway Fndn Grants, 205
Ahearn Family Fndn Grants, 206
Alexander H. Bright Charitable Trust Grants, 358
American Rivers Community-Based Restoration Program River Grants, 444
American Savings Fndn Grants, 445
Anna Fitch Ardenghi Trust Grants, 472
Anthem Blue Cross and Blue Shield Grants, 488
ARS Fndn Grants, 568
Barnes Group Fndn Grants, 672
Bay and Paul Fndns, Inc Grants, 692
Bayer Fndn Grants, 696
BJ's Charitable Fndn Grants, 777
BJ's Wholesale Clubs Local Charitable Giving, 778
Bodenwein Public Benevolent Fndn Grants, 806
Bridgestone/Firestone Trust Fund Grants, 836
Bristol-Myers Squibb Fndn Community Initiatives Grants, 840
Brown Rudnick Charitable Relationship Grants, 855
Brunswick Fndn Dollars for Doers Grants, 856
Brunswick Fndn Grants, 857
Campbell Soup Fndn Grants, 916
Carlisle Fndn Grants, 931
Carolyn Fndn Grants, 942
Carrier Corporation Contributions Grants, 946
CDECD Arts Catalyze Placemaking in Every Community Grants, 977
CDECD Arts Catalyze Placemaking Leadership Grants, 978
CDECD Arts Catalyze Placemaking Sustaining Relevance Grants, 979
CDECD Endangered Properties Grants, 980
CDECD Historic Preservation Grants, 981
CDECD Historic Preservation Survey and Planning Grants, 982
CDECD Historic Restoration Grants, 983
CDECD Tourism Product Development Grants, 984
CenturyLink Clarke M. Williams Grants, 998
Ceres Fndn Grants, 999
Charles A. Frueauff Fndn Grants, 1037
Charles Nelson Robinson Fund Grants, 1052
Charles Parker Trust for Public Music Grants, 1053
Chemtura Corporation Contributions Grants, 1067
Cingular Wireless Charitable Contributions, 1134
Clowes Fund Grants, 1177
Comcast Fndn Grants, 1235
Community Fndn for Greater New Haven $5,000 and Under Grants, 1248
Community Fndn for Greater New Haven Neighborhood Small Grants, 1249
Community Fndn for Greater New Haven Quinnipiac River Fund Grants, 1250
Community Fndn for Greater New Haven Responsive New Grants, 1251
Community Fndn for Greater New Haven Sponsorship Grants, 1252
Community Fndn for Greater New Haven Valley Neighborhood Grants, 1253

Community Fndn for Greater New Haven Women & Girls Grants, 1254
Community Found of Greater New Britain Grants, 1291
Community Fndn of SE Connecticut Grants, 1309
ConAgra Foods Nourish Our Comm Grants, 1343
Connecticut Comm on the Arts in Public Spaces, 1349
Connecticut Community Fndn Grants, 1350
Connecticut Health Fndn Initiative Grants, 1351
Connecticut Light and Power CorpContributions, 1352
Countess Moira Charitable Fndn Grants, 1381
Covenant to Care for Children Critical Grants, 1388
Covenant to Care for Children Enrichment Fund Grants, 1389
CSX Corporate Contributions Grants, 1408
Dammann Fund Grants, 1439
Daphne Seybolt Culpeper Fndn Grants, 1445
David N. Lane Trust Grants for Aged and Indigent Women, 1453
Davis Conservation Fndn Grants, 1461
Dean Foods Community Involvement Grants, 1469
Dominion Fndn Human Needs Grants, 1572
Dorr Fndn Grants, 1591
Edna McConnell Clark Fndn Grants, 1659
Edward S. Moore Fndn Grants, 1668
Elizabeth Carse Fndn Grants, 1681
Ensign-Bickford Fndn Grants, 1709
Ensworth Charitable Fndn Grants, 1710
Eugene G. & Margaret M. Blackford Grants, 1763
Fairfield County Community Fndn Grants, 1782
Fields Pond Fndn Grants, 1807
Fisher Fndn Grants, 1831
Frank Loomis Palmer Fund Grants, 1931
Frederick W. Marzahl Memorial Fund Grants, 1948
George A. and Grace L. Long Found Grants, 2008
George F. Baker Trust Grants, 2016
George H.C. Ensworth Memorial Fund Grants, 2022
George I. Alden Trust Grants, 2023
Gladys Brooks Fndn Grants, 2059
Gregory Family Fndn Grants, 2162
Hallmark Corporate Fndn Grants, 2212
Hartford Courant Fndn Grants, 2248
Hartford Found Application Planning Grants, 2249
Hartford Fndn Evaluation Grants, 2250
Hartford Fndn Implementation Support, 2251
Hartford Fndn Nonprofit Support Grants, 2252
Hartford Fndn Regular Grants, 2253
Haymarket People's Fund Sustaining Grants, 2267
Haymarket Urgent Response Grants, 2268
Hilda and Preston Davis Fndn Grants, 2322
Horizon Fndn Grants, 2365
Hundred Club of Connecticut Grants, 2392
J. Walton Bissell Fndn Grants, 2608
Jessie B. Cox Charitable Trust Grants, 2670
John G. Martin Fndn Grants, 2696
Joseph S. Stackpole Charitable Trust Grants, 2741
Joukowsky Family Fndn Grants, 2743
JP Morgan Chase Arts and Culture Grants, 2752
JP Morgan Chase Community Devel Grants, 2753
Katharine Matthies Fndn Grants, 2788
KeySpan Fndn Grants, 2821
Kimberly-Clark Community Grants, 2824
Lena Benas Memorial Fund Grants, 2881
Liberty Bank Fndn Grants, 2890
Lily Palmer Fry Memorial Trust Grants, 2905
Lincoln Financial Group Fndn Grants, 2906
Linford and Mildred White Charitable Grants, 2909
Lumpkin Family Strong Community Leadership Grants, 2944
Mabel F. Hoffman Charitable Trust Grants, 2957
Marion Isabell Coe Fund Grants, 3020
Marjorie Moore Charitable Fndn Grants, 3021
Maximilian E. and Marion O. Hoffman Grants, 3067
Meriden Fndn Grants, 3122
Modest Needs Hurricane Sandy Relief Grants, 3198
Mr. and Mrs. William Foulds Family Grants, 3222
Nellie Mae Education Fndn District-Level Change Grants, 3297
Norfolk Southern Fndn Grants, 3463
Northeast Utilities Fndn Grants, 3498
Olga Sipolin Children's Fund Grants, 3668

GEOGRAPHIC INDEX

Orchard Fndn Grants, 3690
Pauline E. Fitzpatrick Charitable Trust, 3763
Perkin Fund Grants, 3821
Price Chopper's Golub Fndn Grants, 3950
Price Chopper's Golub Fndn Two-Year Health Care Scholarship, 3951
Prudential Fndn Arts and Culture Grants, 3975
Prudential Fndn Economic Devel Grants, 3976
Prudential Fndn Education Grants, 3977
R.S. Gernon Trust Grants, 4002
Rainbow Media Holdings Corporate Giving, 4010
REI Conservation and Outdoor Rec Grants, 4051
Richard Davoud Donchian Fndn Grants, 4080
Robert and Joan Dircks Fndn Grants, 4104
S. Spencer Scott Fund Grants, 4202
Safeco Insurance Community Grants, 4203
Salmon Fndn Grants, 4225
Shaw's Supermarkets Donations, 4342
Smith Richardson Found Direct Service Grants, 4385
Southbury Community Trust Fund, 4409
Southern New England Folk and Traditional Arts Apprenticeship Grants, 4438
State Street Fndn Grants, 4495
Stocker Fndn Grants, 4507
Sunoco Fndn Grants, 4530
Sweet Water Trust Grants, 4541
Swindells Charitable Fndn, 4542
Tauck Family Fndn Grants, 4563
Thomas J. Atkins Memorial Trust Fund Grants, 4617
TWS Fndn Grants, 4683
Verizon Fndn Connecticut Grants, 4908
VSA/Metlife Connect All Grants, 4953
Wells Fargo Housing Fndn Grants, 5023
Widgeon Point Charitable Fndn Grants, 5064
William T. Grant Fndn Youth Service Improvement Grants, 5096
William T. Sloper Trust for Andres J. Sloper Musical Fund Grants, 5097
Yawkey Fndn Grants, 5125

Delaware

Abelard Fndn East Grants, 87
ACE Charitable Fndn Grants, 111
Albertson's Charitable Giving Grants, 345
Allen Hilles Fund Grants, 378
American Rivers Community-Based Restoration Program River Grants, 444
Amerigroup Fndn Grants, 452
BJ's Charitable Fndn Grants, 777
BJ's Wholesale Clubs Local Charitable Giving, 778
Borkee-Hagley Fndn Grants, 817
Carl M. Freeman Fndn FACES Grants, 932
Carl M. Freeman Fndn Grants, 933
Ceres Fndn Grants, 999
Charles A. Frueauff Fndn Grants, 1037
Chesapeake Bay Fisheries and Headwaters Grants, 1070
Comcast Fndn Grants, 1235
Crestlea Fndn Grants, 1399
CSX Corporate Contributions Grants, 1408
Delaware Community Fndn-Youth Philanthropy Board for Kent County, 1483
Delaware Community Fund For Women Grants, 1484
Delaware Community Next Generation Grants, 1485
Delaware Community Fndn Youth Philanthropy Board for New Castle County Grants, 1486
Delaware Division of the Arts Community-Based Organizations Opportunity Grants, 1487
Delaware Division of the Arts Opportunity Grants--Arts Organizations, 1488
Delaware Division of the Arts Opportunity Grants-Artists, 1489
DHHS Healthy Tomorrows for Children, 1534
Dollar General Adult Literacy Grants, 1568
Dollar General Family Literacy Grants, 1569
Dollar General Youth Literacy Grants, 1570
FMC Fndn Grants, 1876
Gannett Fndn Community Action Grants, 1984
Giant Food Charitable Grants, 2050
Gladys Brooks Fndn Grants, 2059
Hilda and Preston Davis Fndn Grants, 2322

GEOGRAPHIC INDEX

JP Morgan Chase Arts and Culture Grants, 2752
JP Morgan Chase Community Devel Grants, 2753
Merck Family Fund Urban Farming and Youth Leadership Grants, 3119
Mid Atlantic Arts Fndn American Masterpieces Grants, 3169
Mid Atlantic Arts Found ArtsConnect Grants, 3170
Mid Atlantic Arts Fndn Folk Arts Outreach Project Grants, 3171
NFWF Chesapeake Bay Conservation Innovation Grants, 3363
NFWF Chesapeake Bay Targeted Grants, 3365
NFWF Delaware Estuary Watershed Grants, 3371
Norfolk Southern Fndn Grants, 3463
PennPAT Fee-Support Grants for Presenters, 3812
PennPAT New Directions Grants for Presenters, 3813
PNC Ecnomic Development Grants, 3922
PNC Fndn Green Building Grants, 3923
PNC Fndn Grow Up Great Grants, 3924
Principal Financial Group Fndn Grants, 3966
PSEG Environmental Education Grants, 3980
Richard Davoud Donchian Fndn Grants, 4080
Speer Trust Grants, 4450
Sunoco Fndn Grants, 4530
Verizon Fndn Delaware Grants, 4909
Wells Fargo Housing Fndn Grants, 5023

District of Columbia
Abelard Fndn East Grants, 87
ACE Charitable Fndn Grants, 111
Adams and Reese LLP Corporate Giving Grants, 147
Aetna Fndn Regional Health Grants, 187
Alexander and Margaret Stewart Trust Grants, 354
Altria Group Arts and Culture Grants, 399
American Express Charitable Fund Grants, 429
American Rivers Community-Based Restoration Program River Grants, 444
Amerigroup Fndn Grants, 452
Aratani Fndn Grants, 523
Bank of America Charitable Matching Gifts, 658
Bank of America Charitable Volunteer Grants, 660
Bender Fndn Grants, 726
Bill and Katie Weaver Charitable Trust Grants, 764
Blum-Kovler Fndn Grants, 803
Boeing Company Contributions Grants, 809
Brookdale Fndn Relatives as Parents Grants, 846
CarEth Fndn Grants, 924
Case Fndn Grants, 950
CenturyLink Clarke M. Williams Grants, 998
Ceres Fndn Grants, 999
CFNCR Starbucks Memorial Fund, 1026
CharityWorks Grants, 1036
Charles A. Frueauff Fndn Grants, 1037
Charles Delmar Fndn Grants, 1039
Chesapeake Bay Trust Fisheries and Headwaters Grants, 1070
Cingular Wireless Charitable Contributions, 1134
Clark-Winchcole Fndn Grants, 1152
Comcast Fndn Grants, 1235
Commonweal Community Assistance Grants, 1239
ConAgra Foods Community Impact Grants, 1342
ConAgra Foods Nourish Our Comm Grants, 1343
Corina Higginson Trust Grants, 1373
District of Columbia Comm on the Arts-Arts Education Teacher Mini-Grants, 1549
E.L. Wiegand Fndn Grants, 1639
EPA Environmental Justice Small Grants, 1731
EPA Pestwise Registration Improvement Act Partnership Grants, 1734
EPA Regional Agricultural IPM Grants, 1735
EPA Source Reduction Assistance Grants, 1737
EPA State Indoor Radon Grants, 1738
EPA Tribal Support for the National Environmental Information Exchange Network, 1742
Eugene B. Casey Fndn Grants, 1762
Fitzpatrick, Cella, Harper & Scinto Pro Bono, 1836
Freddie Mac Fndn Grants, 1944
Gannett Fndn Community Action Grants, 1984
Giant Food Charitable Grants, 2050
Ginn Fndn Grants, 2056

HBF Pathways Out of Poverty Grants, 2273
Hilda and Preston Davis Fndn Grants, 2322
IIE Western Union Family Scholarships, 2462
J. Willard and Alice S. Marriott Grants, 2609
J. Willard Marriott, Jr. Fndn Grants, 2610
John Edward Fowler Memorial Found Grants, 2693
Jovid Fndn Grants, 2745
Kennedy Center HSC Fndn Internship, 2799
Kennedy Center Summer HSC Internship, 2800
Luther I. Replogle Fndn Grants, 2945
Margaret Abell Powell Fund Grants, 3002
MARPAT Fndn Grants, 3023
MeadWestvaco Sustainable Communities Grants, 3105
Meyer Fndn Benevon Grants, 3140
Meyer Fndn Education Grants, 3142
Meyer Fndn Management Assistance, 3144
Mid Atlantic Arts Fndn American Masterpieces Grants, 3169
Mid Atlantic Arts Found ArtsConnect Grants, 3170
Mid Atlantic Arts Fndn Folk Arts Outreach Project Grants, 3171
Moran Family Fndn Grants, 3216
Morris and Gwendolyn Cafritz Found Grants, 3218
NFWF Chesapeake Bay Conservation Innovation Grants, 3363
NFWF Chesapeake Bay Targeted Grants, 3365
Norfolk Southern Fndn Grants, 3463
Ober Kaler Community Grants, 3635
PennPAT Fee-Support Grants for Presenters, 3812
PennPAT New Directions Grants for Presenters, 3813
Philip L. Graham Fund Grants, 3876
PNC Charitable Trust and Fndn Grants, 3921
PNC Ecnomic Development Grants, 3922
PNC Fndn Green Building Grants, 3923
Poets & Writers Readings/Workshops Grants, 3927
Prince Charitable District of Columbia Grants, 3960
Quality Health Fndn Grants, 3994
REI Conservation and Outdoor Rec Grants, 4051
Richard Davoud Donchian Fndn Grants, 4080
Robert G. Cabell III and Maude Morgan Cabell Fndn Grants, 4113
Robert R. McCormick Tribune Fndn Community Grants, 4119
Salmon Fndn Grants, 4225
Solutia Fund Grants, 4402
Sunoco Fndn Grants, 4530
Thomas B. and Elizabeth M. Sheridan Grants, 4614
Tiger Woods Fndn Grants, 4634
Turner Voices Corporate Contributions, 4682
U.S. Department of Education Rehabilitation Training--Rehabilitation Continuing Education Programs--Institute on Rehabilitation Issues, 4700
US Airways Community Contributions, 4788
US Airways Education Fndn Grants, 4790
Washington Area Fuel Fund Grants, 4988
Washington Area Women's Fndn African American Women's Giving Circle Grants, 4989
Washington Area Women's Fndn Early Care and Education Funders Collaborative Grants, 4990
Washington Area Women's Fndn Financial Education and Wealth Creation Fund Grants, 4991
Washington Area Women's Fndn Jobs Grants, 4992
Washington Area Women's Leadership Awards, 4993
Washington Area Women's Fndn Open Door Capacity Fund Grants, 4994
Washington Area Women's Fndn Rainmakers Giving Circle Grants, 4995
Washington Area Women's Fndn Strategic Opportunity and Partnership Fund Grants, 4996
Washington Gas Charitable Contributions, 5000
Wells Fargo Housing Fndn Grants, 5023
Weyerhaeuser Company Fndn Grants, 5053
William G. McGowan Charitable Fund Grants, 5084
William J. and Dorothy K. O'Neill Grants, 5087
William S. Abell Fndn Grants, 5094
Winifred & Harry B. Allen Fndn Grants, 5101

Florida
1st and 10 Fndn Grants, 1
2 Life 18 Fndn Grants, 5

Florida / 1147

100 Angels Charitable Fndn Grants, 24
2701 Fndn Grants, 37
ABC Charities Grants, 85
Abelard Fndn East Grants, 87
Abernethy Family Fndn Grants, 98
ABIG Fndn Grants, 99
Able Trust Vocational Rehabilitation Grants for Agencies, 103
Able Trust Voc Rehab Grants for Individuals, 104
ACE Charitable Fndn Grants, 111
Adams and Reese LLP Corporate Giving Grants, 147
AEC Trust Grants, 175
AEGON Transamerica Arts & Culture Grants, 176
AEGON Transamerica Fndn Civic and Community Grants, 177
AEGON Transamerica Fndn Health and Welfare Grants, 179
Aetna Fndn Regional Health Grants, 187
A Friends' Fndn Trust Grants, 194
Albert E. and Birdie W. Einstein Fund Grants, 342
Albertson's Charitable Giving Grants, 345
Alvah H. and Wyline P. Chapman Found Grants, 402
American Express Charitable Fund Grants, 429
Amerigroup Fndn Grants, 452
Angels for Kids Fndn Grants, 466
Anheuser-Busch Fndn Grants, 470
A Quiet Place Grants, 520
Aratani Fndn Grants, 523
Babcock Charitable Trust Grants, 632
BankAtlantic Fndn Grants, 654
Batchelor Fndn Grants, 679
BBF Florida Family Literacy Initiative Grants, 697
BBVA Compass Fndn Charitable Grants, 703
Beldon Fund Grants, 720
Belk Fndn Grants, 721
Bert W. Martin Fndn Grants, 747
BJ's Charitable Fndn Grants, 777
BJ's Wholesale Clubs Local Charitable Giving, 778
Boeing Company Contributions Grants, 809
Bridgestone/Firestone Trust Fund Grants, 836
Brunswick Fndn Dollars for Doers Grants, 856
Brunswick Fndn Grants, 857
Camp-Younts Fndn Grants, 914
Campbell Soup Fndn Grants, 916
Capital City Bank Group Fndn Grants, 920
Castle and Cooke California Corp Givorateing, 953
CenturyLink Clarke M. Williams Grants, 998
Ceres Fndn Grants, 999
Charles A. Frueauff Fndn Grants, 1037
Charles M. and Mary D. Grant Found Grants, 1050
Charlotte County Community Fndn Grants, 1056
Chase Paymentech Corporate Giving Grants, 1059
Chingos Fndn Grants, 1109
Cingular Wireless Charitable Contributions, 1134
Circle K Corporation Contributions Grants, 1136
Clark and Carolyn Adams Fndn Grants, 1153
Claude A. and Blanche McCubbin Abbott Charitable Trust Grants, 1158
CNL Corporate Giving Arts & Culture Grants, 1190
CNL Corporate Giving Entrepreneurship & Leadership Grants, 1191
Cobb Family Fndn Grants, 1194
Comcast Fndn Grants, 1235
Comerica Charitable Fndn Grants, 1237
Community Fndn in Jacksonville Art Ventures Small Arts Organizations Professional Grants, 1262
Community Fndn in Jacksonville Senior Roundtable Aging Adults Grants, 1263
Community Fndn of Broward Grants, 1275
Community Fndn of Collier County Capacity Building Grants, 1277
Community Found of Greater Tampa Grants, 1292
Community Found of Sarasota County Grants, 1306
Community Fndn of Tampa Bay Grants, 1316
ConAgra Foods Community Impact Grants, 1342
ConAgra Foods Nourish Our Comm Grants, 1343
Cooke-Hay Fndn Grants, 1367
Cowles Charitable Trust Grants, 1392
Credit Suisse First Boston Fndn Grants, 1397
CSX Corporate Contributions Grants, 1408

1148 / Florida

D. W. McMillan Fndn Grants, 1426
Dade Community Fndn Community AIDS Partnership Grants, 1428
Dade Community Fndn GLBT Community Projects Grants, 1429
Dade Community Fndn Grants, 1430
Dade Community Found Safe Passage Grants, 1431
Daphne Seybolt Culpeper Fndn Grants, 1445
Darden Restaurants Fndn Grants, 1446
Dean Foods Community Involvement Grants, 1469
Dekko Fndn Grants, 1482
DHHS Healthy Tomorrows for Children, 1534
Dollar General Adult Literacy Grants, 1568
Dollar General Family Literacy Grants, 1569
Dollar General Youth Literacy Grants, 1570
Dr. John T. Macdonald Fndn Grants, 1600
Dr. P. Phillips Fndn Grants, 1601
Dream Weaver Fndn, 1604
Dunspaugh-Dalton Fndn Grants, 1623
Eaton Charitable Fund Grants, 1647
Edward R. Godfrey Fndn Grants, 1667
Edyth Bush Charitable Fndn Grants, 1673
Fifth Third Bank Corporate Giving, 1809
Fifth Third Fndn Grants, 1810
Florida BRAIVE Fund of Dade Community Fndn Grants, 1846
Florida Division of Cultural Affairs Community Theatre Grants, 1847
Florida Division of Cultural Affairs Culture Builds Florida Expansion Funding, 1848
Florida Division of Cultural Affairs Culture Builds Florida Seed Funding, 1849
Florida Division of Cultural Affairs Dance Grants, 1850
Florida Division of Cultural Affairs Endowment Grants, 1851
Florida Div of Cultural Affairs Facilities Grants, 1852
Florida Div of Cultural Affairs Folk Arts Grants, 1853
Florida Division of Cultural Affairs General Program Support Grants, 1854
Florida Div of Cultural Affairs Literature Grants, 1855
Florida Div of Cultural Affairs Media Arts Grants, 1856
Florida Division of Cultural Affairs Multidisciplinary Grants, 1857
Florida Div of Cultural Affairs Museum Grants, 1858
Florida Division of Cultural Affairs Music Grants, 1859
Florida Div of Cultural Affairs Presenter Grants, 1860
Florida Division of Cultural Affairs Professional Theatre Grants, 1861
Florida Division of Cultural Affairs Specific Cultural Project Grants, 1862
Florida Division of Cultural Affairs State Touring Grants, 1863
Florida Division of Cultural Affairs Underserved Cultural Community Development Grants, 1864
Florida Div of Cultural Affairs Visual Arts Grants, 1865
Florida High School/High Tech Project Grants, 1866
Florida Humanities Cou Civic Reflection Grants, 1867
Florida Humanities Council Major Grants, 1868
Florida Humanities Council Mini Grants, 1869
Florida Humanities Council Partnership Grants, 1870
Florida Sea Turtle Grants, 1871
Florida Sports Fndn Junior Golf Grants, 1872
Florida Sports Found Major and Regional Grants, 1873
FMC Fndn Grants, 1876
Forrest C. Lattner Fndn Grants, 1887
Frances C. and William P. Smallwood Grants, 1918
Gannett Fndn Community Action Grants, 1984
George F. Baker Trust Grants, 2016
Georgia-Pacific Fndn Education Grants, 2031
Georgia-Pacific Fndn Enrichment Grants, 2032
Georgia-Pacific Entrepreneurship Grants, 2033
Georgia-Pacific Fndn Environment Grants, 2034
Gladys Brooks Fndn Grants, 2059
Glazer Family Fndn Grants, 2062
Greenfield Fndn of Florida Grants, 2151
GTECH Community Involvement Grants, 2171
Gulf Coast Fndn of Community Capacity Building Grants, 2175
Gulf Coast Fndn of Comm Operating Grants, 2176
Gulf Coast Fndn of Community Grants, 2177

Gulf Coast Found of Community Scholarships, 2178
H.B. Fuller Company Fndn Grants, 2183
Harold Alfond Fndn Grants, 2225
Harry Sudakoff Fndn Grants, 2245
Hazen Fndn Public Education Grants, 2269
Head Start Replacement Grantee: Florida, 2276
Health Fndn of S Florida Responsive Grants, 2283
Hollie and Anna Oakley Fndn Grants, 2346
HomeBanc Fndn Grants, 2347
Humana Fndn Grants, 2388
IIE Western Union Family Scholarships, 2462
J. Bulow Campbell Fndn Grants, 2593
Jacksonville Jaguars Fndn Grants, 2614
Jane's Trust Grants, 2639
Jerry L. and Barbara J. Burris Fndn Grants, 2669
Jim Moran Fndn Grants, 2680
John Lord Knight Fndn Grants, 2703
John Reynolds and Eleanor B. Allen Charitable Fndn Grants, 2710
John S. & James L. Knight Communities Grants, 2711
Johnson & Johnson Comm Health Care Grants, 2717
Joseph H. and Florence A. Roblee Found Grants, 2736
JP Morgan Chase Arts and Culture Grants, 2752
JP Morgan Chase Community Devel Grants, 2753
Judge Isaac Anderson, Jr. Scholarship, 2754
Kimball Int'l-Habig Fndn Grants, 2823
Knight Fndn Grants - Georgia, 2829
L. W. Pierce Family Fndn Grants, 2846
Leo Goodwin Fndn Grants, 2882
Leonard L. and Bertha U. Abess Grants, 2884
Lettie Pate Whitehead Fndn Grants, 2888
Lillian S. Wells Fndn Grants, 2901
Lockheed Martin Philanthropic Grants, 2918
Lucy Gooding Charitable Fndn Trust, 2936
Lucy Gooding Charitable Fndn Grants, 2937
Luther I. Replogle Fndn Grants, 2945
M.B. and Edna Zale Fndn Grants, 2950
McLean Contributionship Grants, 3088
MeadWestvaco Sustainable Communities Grants, 3105
Medtronic Community Link Arts, Civic, and Culture Grants, 3109
Medtronic CommunityLink Education Grants, 3110
Medtronic CommunityLink Health Grants, 3111
Medtronic Comm Link Human Services Grants, 3112
Mercedes-Benz USA Corporate Contributions, 3118
Motorola Fndn Grants, 3221
Nationwide Insurance Fndn Grants, 3285
NFWF So Company Power of Flight Grants, 3394
NFWF Tampa Bay Environmental Fund Grants, 3397
Norfolk Southern Fndn Grants, 3463
Palm Beach and Martin Counties Grants, 3733
Paul E. and Klare N. Reinhold Fndn Grants, 3758
Paul Green Fndn Playwrights Fellowship, 3762
Peacock Fndn Grants, 3809
Pinellas County Grants, 3891
Plum Creek Fndn Grants, 3917
PNC Ecnomic Development Grants, 3922
PNC Fndn Green Building Grants, 3923
Progress Energy Corporate Contributions Grants, 3968
Progress Energy Economic Vitality Grants, 3969
Progress Energy Fndn Environmental Stewardship Grants, 3970
Prudential Fndn Arts and Culture Grants, 3975
Prudential Fndn Economic Devel Grants, 3976
Prudential Fndn Education Grants, 3977
Public Education Power Grants, 3981
Publix Super Markets Charities Local Grants, 3985
Quantum Fndn Grants, 3996
Rainbow Fund Grants, 4009
Richard and Helen DeVos Fndn Grants, 4076
Richard Davoud Donchian Fndn Grants, 4080
Roberta Leventhal Sudakoff Fndn Grants, 4102
Robert R. McCormick Tribune Fndn Community Grants, 4119
RRF General Grants, 4170
Ruth Anderson Fndn Grants, 4176
Ryder System Charitable Fndn Grants, 4191
Safeco Insurance Community Grants, 4203
Solutia Fund Grants, 4402

GEOGRAPHIC INDEX

Southwest Florida Community Fndn Arts & Attractions Grants, 4441
Southwest Florida Community Fndn Competitive Grants, 4442
Southwest Florida Community Fndn Good Samaritan Grants, 4443
Southwest Florida Community Fndn Undergraduate and Graduate Scholarships, 4444
State Street Fndn Grants, 4495
Sunoco Fndn Grants, 4530
Symantec Community Relations and Corporate Philanthropy Grants, 4544
Tiger Woods Fndn Grants, 4634
Turner Voices Corporate Contributions, 4682
VSA/Metlife Connect All Grants, 4953
Vulcan Materials Company Fndn Grants, 4956
Walt Disney Company Fndn Grants, 4981
Wells Fargo Housing Fndn Grants, 5023
William G. Selby and Marie Selby Grants, 5085
William J. and Dorothy K. O'Neill Grants, 5087
Wilson-Wood Fndn Grants, 5098
Woodward Fund Grants, 5116

Georgia

3M Company Arts and Culture Grants, 12
3M Company Environmental Giving Grants, 13
3M Company Health and Human Services Grants, 14
3M Fndn Community Giving Grants, 15
Abelard Fndn East Grants, 87
ABS Fndn Grants, 107
ACE Charitable Fndn Grants, 111
ADC Fndn Technology Access Grants, 158
AEC Trust Grants, 175
AEGON Transamerica Arts & Culture Grants, 176
AEGON Transamerica Fndn Civic and Community Grants, 177
AEGON Transamerica Fndn Health and Welfare Grants, 179
Aetna Fndn Regional Health Grants, 187
Agnes B. Hunt Trust Grants, 202
Albertson's Charitable Giving Grants, 345
Allan C. and Leila J. Garden Fndn Grants, 374
American Express Charitable Fund Grants, 429
American Foodservice Charitable Trust Grants, 433
Amerigroup Fndn Grants, 452
Anheuser-Busch Fndn Grants, 470
Appalachian Regional Comm Asset-Based Development Project Grants, 500
Appalachian Regional Comm Business Development Revolving Loan Fund Grants, 501
Appalachian Regional Comm Community Infrastructure Grants, 502
Appalachian Regional Comm Distressed Counties Grants, 503
Appalachian Regional Comm Education and Training Grants, 504
Appalachian Regional Comm Energy Grants, 505
Appalachian Regional Comm Export and Trade Development Grants, 506
Appalachian Regional Comm Health Care Grants, 507
Appalachian Reg Comm Housing Grants, 508
Appalachian Regional Comm Leadership Development and Capacity Building Grants, 509
Appalachian Regional Comm Telecommunications Grants, 510
Appalachian Regional Comm Tourist Development Grants, 511
Appalachian Regional Comm Transportation and Highways Grants, 512
Archer Daniels Midland Fndn Grants, 527
Atlanta Falcons Youth Fndn Grants, 607
Atlanta Fndn Grants, 608
Atlanta Women's Fndn Grants, 609
Bayer Fndn Grants, 696
BBVA Compass Fndn Charitable Grants, 703
Belk Fndn Grants, 721
BJ's Charitable Fndn Grants, 777
BJ's Wholesale Clubs Local Charitable Giving, 778
Boeing Company Contributions Grants, 809
Bradley-Turner Fndn Grants, 828

GEOGRAPHIC INDEX

Brian G. Dyson Fndn Grants, 834
Brunswick Fndn Dollars for Doers Grants, 856
Brunswick Fndn Grants, 857
Cabot Corporation Fndn Grants, 887
Callaway Fndn Grants, 909
Camp-Younts Fndn Grants, 914
Capital City Bank Group Fndn Grants, 920
Carlos and Marguerite Mason Trust Grants, 934
Caroline Lawson Ivey Fndn Grants, 941
Carrier Corporation Contributions Grants, 946
CCCF Dora Maclellan Brown Christian Priority Grants, 960
CenturyLink Clarke M. Williams Grants, 998
Ceres Fndn Grants, 999
Charles A. Frueauff Fndn Grants, 1037
Charles M. and Mary D. Grant Found Grants, 1050
Chemtura Corporation Contributions Grants, 1067
Cingular Wireless Charitable Contributions, 1134
Circle K Corporation Contributions Grants, 1136
Clark and Ruby Baker Fndn Grants, 1154
Comcast Fndn Grants, 1235
ConAgra Foods Community Impact Grants, 1342
ConAgra Foods Nourish Our Comm Grants, 1343
Cooper Industries Fndn Grants, 1370
Covenant Fndn of Atlanta Grants, 1384
Credit Suisse First Boston Fndn Grants, 1397
CSRA Community Fndn Grants, 1407
CSX Corporate Contributions Grants, 1408
Darden Restaurants Fndn Grants, 1446
Dean Foods Community Involvement Grants, 1469
Deluxe Corporation Fndn Grants, 1496
Dermody Properties Fndn Grants, 1517
DHHS Healthy Tomorrows for Children, 1534
Dollar General Adult Literacy Grants, 1568
Dollar General Family Literacy Grants, 1569
Dollar General Youth Literacy Grants, 1570
Dream Weaver Fndn, 1604
E.J. Grassmann Trust Grants, 1638
Eaton Charitable Fund Grants, 1647
EDS Fndn Grants, 1661
EDS Technology Grants, 1662
Elizabeth & Avola W. Callaway Grants, 1680
Florence Hunt Maxwell Fndn Grants, 1844
Forrest C. Lattner Fndn Grants, 1887
Francis L. Abreu Charitable Trust Grants, 1922
Fuller E. Callaway Fndn Grants, 1973
Fund for Southern Communities Grants, 1977
Gannett Fndn Community Action Grants, 1984
General Mills Fndn Grants, 2003
George E. Hatcher, Jr. and Ann Williams Hatcher Fndn Grants, 2015
Georgia-Pacific Fndn Education Grants, 2031
Georgia-Pacific Fndn Enrichment Grants, 2032
Georgia-Pacific Entrepreneurship Grants, 2033
Georgia-Pacific Fndn Environment Grants, 2034
Georgia Council for the Arts Partner Grants for Organizations, 2035
Georgia Council for the Arts Partner Grants for Service Organizations, 2036
Georgia Council for the Arts Project Grants, 2037
Georgia Power Fndn Grants, 2039
Gertrude and William C. Wardlaw Fund Grants, 2045
Goizueta Fndn Grants, 2096
GTECH Community Involvement Grants, 2171
H.B. Fuller Company Fndn Grants, 2183
Hallmark Corporate Fndn Grants, 2212
HomeBanc Fndn Grants, 2347
Hormel Foods Charitable Trust Grants, 2368
Howard H. Callaway Fndn Grants, 2376
Humana Fndn Grants, 2388
Ida Alice Ryan Charitable Trust Grants, 2431
J. Bulow Campbell Fndn Grants, 2593
J. Knox Gholston Fndn Grants, 2599
J. Mack Robinson Fndn Grants, 2604
James J. and Angelia M. Harris Grants, 2630
Jim Blevins Fndn Scholarships, 2679
John Deere Fndn Grants, 2692
John H. and Wilhelmina D. Harland Grants, 2698
John S. and James L. Knight Fndn Communities Grants, 2711

Katherine John Murphy Fndn Grants, 2790
Kimberly-Clark Community Grants, 2824
Knight Fndn Grants - Georgia, 2829
Lettie Pate Evans Fndn Grants, 2887
Lettie Pate Whitehead Fndn Grants, 2888
Lockheed Martin Philanthropic Grants, 2918
Mary E. and Michael Blevins Charitable Grants, 3037
Mary Reynolds Babcock Fndn Grants, 3047
Mary Wilmer Covey Charitable Trust Grants, 3049
MeadWestvaco Sustainable Communities Grants, 3105
Motorola Fndn Grants, 3221
Nationwide Insurance Fndn Grants, 3285
Nestle Purina PetCare Educational Grants, 3302
Nestle Purina PetCare Pet Related Grants, 3304
Nestle Purina PetCare Support Dog and Police K-9 Organization Grants, 3305
Nestle Purina PetCare Youth Grants, 3306
NFWF So Company Power of Flight Grants, 3394
Nissan Fndn Grants, 3444
Nordson Corporation Fndn Grants, 3462
Norfolk Southern Fndn Grants, 3463
North Georgia Community Fndn Grants, 3505
OSF Civil Service Awards, 3705
Paul Green Fndn Playwrights Fellowship, 3762
Perkins-Ponder Fndn Grants, 3822
Peyton Anderson Fndn Grants, 3862
Plum Creek Fndn Grants, 3917
Poets & Writers Readings/Workshops Grants, 3927
Price Gilbert, Jr. Charitable Fund Grants, 3953
Prudential Fndn Arts and Culture Grants, 3975
Prudential Fndn Economic Devel Grants, 3976
Prudential Fndn Education Grants, 3977
Publix Super Markets Charities Local Grants, 3985
Qualcomm Grants, 3993
QuikTrip Corporate Contributions Grants, 3998
Rainbow Fund Grants, 4009
REI Conservation and Outdoor Rec Grants, 4051
Rich Fndn Grants, 4090
Robert and Polly Dunn Fndn Grants, 4105
Robert W. Woodruff Fndn Grants, 4124
Rosalynn Carter Institute Georgia Caregiver of the Year Awards, 4151
Ryder System Charitable Fndn Grants, 4191
Safeco Insurance Community Grants, 4203
Sapelo Found Environmental Protection Grants, 4293
Sapelo Fndn Social Justice Grants, 4294
Sartain Lanier Family Fndn Grants, 4298
Solutia Fund Grants, 4402
Southwire Company Grants, 4447
State Street Fndn Grants, 4495
Steele-Reese Fndn Grants, 4498
Stewart Huston Charitable Trust Grants, 4505
Subaru of America Fndn Grants, 4518
Sunoco Fndn Grants, 4530
Suntrust Bank Atlanta Fndn Grants, 4531
TAC Arts Access Technical Assistance Grants, 4550
TAC Arts Educ Community-Learning Grants, 4552
TAC Arts Education Mini Grants, 4553
TAC Arts Projects Grants, 4554
TAC Rural Arts Project Support Grants, 4555
TAC Technical Assistance Grants, 4556
TAC Touring Arts and Access Grants, 4557
Textron Corporate Contributions Grants, 4601
Tull Charitable Fndn Grants, 4679
Turner Voices Corporate Contributions, 4682
Verizon Fndn Southeast Region Grants, 4923
VSA/Metlife Connect All Grants, 4953
Vulcan Materials Company Fndn Grants, 4956
W. Waldo and Jenny Lynn M. Bradley Grants, 4967
Wells Fargo Housing Fndn Grants, 5023
Weyerhaeuser Company Fndn Grants, 5053
Winifred & Harry B. Allen Fndn Grants, 5101
Woodward Fund Grants, 5116

Guam

Bank of America Fndn Matching Gifts, 658
Bank of America Charitable Volunteer Grants, 660
EPA Environmental Justice Small Grants, 1731
EPA Pestwise Registration Improvement Act Partnership Grants, 1734

EPA Source Reduction Assistance Grants, 1737
EPA State Indoor Radon Grants, 1738
EPA Tribal Support for the National Environmental Information Exchange Network, 1742
Gannett Fndn Community Action Grants, 1984
NHLBI Ancillary Studies in Clinical Trials, 3410
NHLBI Bioengineering and Obesity Grants, 3411
NHLBI Career Transition Awards, 3412
NHLBI Lymphatics in Health and Disease Digestive, Cardiovascular and Pulmonary Systems, 3414
NHLBI Lymphatics in Health and Disease in the Digestive, Urinary, Cardiovascular and Pulmonary Systems, 3415
NHLBI Research on the Role of Cardiomyocyte Mitochondria in Heart Disease, 3417
NHLBI Ruth L. Kirschstein National Research Service Awards for Individual Postdoctoral Fellows, 3418
NHLBI Ruth L. Kirschstein National Research Service Awards for Individual Senior Fellows, 3421
NHLBI Ruth L. Kirschstein National Research Service Award Short-Term Institutional Research Training Grants, 3422
USDA Farmers Market Promotion Grants, 4808
USDA Farm Labor Housing Grants, 4809
USDC Public Works and Economic Adjustment Assistance Grants, 4856

Hawaii

3M Company Arts and Culture Grants, 12
3M Company Environmental Giving Grants, 13
3M Company Health and Human Services Grants, 14
3M Fndn Community Giving Grants, 15
ABS Fndn Grants, 107
ACE Charitable Fndn Grants, 111
A Charitable Fndn Grants, 126
AHS Fndn Grants, 208
Alexander & Baldwin Fndn Hawaiian and Pacific Island Grants, 352
Annie Sinclair Knudsen Memorial Fund/Kaua'i Community Grants, 482
Antone & Edene Vidinha Charitable Trust Grants, 490
Atherton Family Fndn Grants, 604
Boeing Company Contributions Grants, 809
Boyd Gaming Corporation Contributions Program, 825
Chevron Hawaii Education Fund, 1077
Clarence T.C. Ching Fndn Grants, 1151
Cooke Fndn Grants, 1368
Dean Foods Community Involvement Grants, 1469
DHHS Healthy Tomorrows for Children, 1534
Elsie H. Wilcox Fndn Grants, 1691
Ewa Beach Community Trust Fund, 1775
Family Literacy and Hawaii Pizza Hut Literacy, 1785
Fred Baldwin Memorial Fndn Grants, 1941
G.N. Wilcox Trust Grants, 1982
Gannett Fndn Community Action Grants, 1984
Group 70 Fndn Fund, 2167
Harold K. L. Castle Fndn Grants, 2228
Hawai'i Children's Trust Fund Community Awareness Events Grants, 2258
Hawaiian Electric Industries Charitable Grants, 2259
Hawaii Community Fndn Community Capacity Building Grants, 2260
Hawaii Community Fndn Geographic-Specific Fund Grants, 2261
Hawaii Community Human Services Grants, 2262
Hawaii Community Fndn Organizational Capacity Building Grants, 2263
Hawaii Community Fndn Reverend Takie Okumura Family Grants, 2264
Hawaii Community Social Change Grants, 2265
Hawaii Community West Hawaii Fund Grants, 2266
Hershey Company Grants, 2318
IMLS Native Hawaiian Library Services Grants, 2519
J.M. Long Fndn Grants, 2603
James & Abigail Campbell Family Grants, 2620
John M. Ross Fndn Grants, 2704
Kahuku Community Fund, 2762
Kaneta Fndn Grants, 2774
Ka Papa O Kakuhihewa Fund, 2785
Kuki'o Community Fund, 2845

1150 / Hawaii

Laila Twigg-Smith Art Scholarship, 2855
Lana'i Community Benefit Fund, 2857
Laura Jane Musser Intercultural Harmony Grants, 2862
Laura Jane Musser Rural Arts Grants, 2863
Laura Jane Musser Rural Initiative Grants, 2864
Mary D. and Walter F. Frear Eleemosynary Trust Grants, 3035
McInerny Fndn Grants, 3083
NFL Charities Pro Bowl Community Grants in Hawaii, 3348
ODKF Athletic Grants, 3638
Pacific Rainbow Fndn Grants, 3728
Samuel N. and Mary Castle Fndn Grants, 4236
Victoria S. and Bradley L. Geist Fndn Capacity Building Grants, 4934
Victoria S. and Bradley L. Geist Fndn Enhancement Grants, 4935
Victoria S. and Bradley L. Geist Fndn Grants Supporting Foster Care and Their Caregivers, 4936
Victoria S. and Bradley L. Geist Fndn Grants Supporting Transitioning Foster Youth, 4937
Wallace Alexander Gerbode Fndn Grants, 4974
West Hawai'i Fund for Nonprofit Organizations, 5027
William J. and Dorothy K. O'Neill Grants, 5087
Windward Youth Leadership Fund Grants, 5100

Idaho

Abelard Fndn West Grants, 88
Albertson's Charitable Giving Grants, 345
American Rivers Community-Based Restoration Program River Grants, 444
Avista Fndn Grants, 624
Brainerd Fndn Grants, 831
Bullitt Fndn Grants, 862
CenturyLink Clarke M. Williams Grants, 998
Charlotte Martin Fndn Youth Grants, 1057
CHC Fndn Grants, 1065
Comcast Fndn Grants, 1235
ConAgra Foods Community Impact Grants, 1342
ConAgra Foods Nourish Our Comm Grants, 1343
Dean Foods Community Involvement Grants, 1469
Dell Fndn Open Grants, 1490
Detlef Schrempf Fndn Grants, 1519
DHHS Healthy Tomorrows for Children, 1534
DOJ Rural Domestic Violence and Child Victimization Enforcement Grants, 1562
E.L. Wiegand Fndn Grants, 1639
Foster Fndn Grants, 1888
Fndn Northwest Grants, 1906
Fred Meyer Fndn Grants, 1950
Idaho Community Fndn Eastern Region Competitive Grants, 2432
Idaho Power Company Corporate Contributions, 2433
KeyBank Fndn Grants, 2820
Kimball Int'l-Habig Fndn Grants, 2823
Kimberly-Clark Community Grants, 2824
Land O'Lakes Fndn Community Grants, 2859
Land O'Lakes Fndn Dollars for Doers, 2860
Laura Moore Cunningham Fndn Grants, 2866
M.J. Murdock Charitable Trust General Grants, 2954
Micron Tech Fndn Community Grants, 3161
NFWF Columbia Basin Water Transactions Grants, 3366
NFWF Columbia River Estuarine Coastal Fund Grants, 3367
NFWF One Fly Conservation Partnerships, 3382
NWHF Health Advocacy Small Grants, 3537
Olive Smith Browning Charitable Trust Grants, 3671
PacifiCorp Fndn for Learning Grants, 3727
Paul G. Allen Family Fndn Grants, 3759
Peter M. Putnam Fndn Grants, 3848
Piper Jaffray Fndn Communities Giving, 3899
Plum Creek Fndn Grants, 3917
Pride Fndn Grants, 3958
Regence Access to Health Care Grants, 4039
Regence Health Care Community Awareness and Engagement Grants, 4040
Regence Health Care Connections Grants, 4041
Regence Improving End-of-Life Grants, 4042
Regence Tools and Technology Grants, 4043
REI Conservation and Outdoor Rec Grants, 4051

Shopko Fndn Community Grants, 4346
Social Justice Fund Northwest Criminal Justice Giving Project Grants, 4394
Social Justice Fund Northwest Economic Justice Project Grants, 4395
Social Justice Fund Northwest Environmental Justice Giving Project Grants, 4396
Social Justice Fund Northwest General Grants, 4397
Social Justice Fund Northwest LGBTQ Grants, 4398
Steele-Reese Fndn Grants, 4498
Sunderland Fndn Grants, 4527
SVP Environment Grants, 4539
U.S. Bank Fndn Grants, 4686
Union Pacific Community and Civic Grants, 4714
Union Pacific Fndn Health and Human Services Grants, 4715
Wells Fargo Housing Fndn Grants, 5023
Weyerhaeuser Company Fndn Grants, 5053
William C. Kenney Watershed Protection Fndn Ecosystem Grants, 5079

Illinois

3M Company Arts and Culture Grants, 12
3M Company Environmental Giving Grants, 13
3M Company Health and Human Services Grants, 14
3M Fndn Community Giving Grants, 15
A & B Family Fndn Grants, 38
A.H.K. Fndn Grants, 40
Abbott Fund Access to Health Care Grants, 80
Abbott Fund Community Grants, 81
Abbott Fund Global AIDS Care Grants, 82
Abbott Fund Science Education Grants, 83
Abelard Fndn East Grants, 87
ACE Charitable Fndn Grants, 111
Aetna Fndn Regional Health Grants, 187
Albert Pick Jr. Fund Grants, 344
Albertson's Charitable Giving Grants, 345
Alfred Bersted Fndn Grants, 364
Alliant Energy Fndn Community Grants, 384
Alliant Energy Fndn Hometown Challenge Grants, 385
Allstate Corp Hometown Commitment Grants, 387
Ameren Corporation Community Grants, 418
American Express Charitable Fund Grants, 429
Anderson Fndn Grants, 460
Andrew Family Fndn Grants, 462
Ann and Robert H. Lurie Fndn Grants, 473
AptarGroup Fndn Grants, 519
Archer Daniels Midland Fndn Grants, 527
Arie and Ida Crown Memorial Grants, 533
Arts Midwest Performing Arts Grants, 579
Asian American Institute Impact Fellowships, 588
Aurora Fndn Grants, 613
Barr Fund Grants, 678
Baxter Int'l Fndn Grants, 691
Blowitz-Ridgeway Fndn Grants, 792
Blum-Kovler Fndn Grants, 803
Boeing Company Contributions Grants, 809
Boyd Gaming Corporation Contributions Program, 825
Bridgestone/Firestone Trust Fund Grants, 836
Bright Promises Fndn Grants, 838
Brunswick Fndn Dollars for Doers Grants, 856
Brunswick Fndn Grants, 857
Cabot Corporation Fndn Grants, 887
Caesars Fndn Grants, 891
Campbell Soup Fndn Grants, 916
Carl R. Hendrickson Family Fndn Grants, 935
Carrier Corporation Contributions Grants, 946
CenturyLink Clarke M. Williams Grants, 998
Charles A. Frueauff Fndn Grants, 1037
Chemtura Corporation Contributions Grants, 1067
Chicago Board of Trade Fndn Grants, 1079
Chicago CityArts Grants, 1080
Chicago Community Arts Assistance Grants, 1081
Chicago Community Trust Arts and Culture Grants: Improving Access to Arts Learning Opps, 1082
Chicago Community Trust Arts and Culture Grants: SMART Growth, 1083
Chicago Community Trust Arts and Culture Grants: Supporting Diverse Arts Productions and Fostering Art in Every Community, 1084

Chicago Community Trust Education Grants, 1085
Chicago Community Trust Fellowships, 1086
Chicago Community Trust Health Grants, 1087
Chicago Community Trust Housing Grants: Advancing Affordable Rental Housing, 1088
Chicago Community Trust Housing Grants: Preserving Home Ownership and Preventing Foreclosure, 1089
Chicago Community Trust Housing Grants: Preventing and Ending Homelessness, 1090
Chicago Community Poverty Alleviation Grants, 1091
Chicago Community Trust Preventing and Eliminating Hunger Grants, 1092
Chicago Community Trust Public Safety and Justice Grants, 1093
Chicago Community Trust Workforce Grants, 1094
Chicago Cultural Outreach Grants, 1095
Chicago Fndn for Women Grants, 1096
Chicago Neighborhood Arts Grants, 1097
Chicago Sun Times Charity Trust Grants, 1098
Chicago Title and Trust Fndn Grants, 1099
Chicago Tribune Fndn Civic Grants, 1100
Chicago Tribune Fndn Grants for Cultural Organizations, 1101
Chicago White Metal Charitable Grants, 1102
Cingular Wireless Charitable Contributions, 1134
Circle K Corporation Contributions Grants, 1136
Citizens Savings Fndn Grants, 1141
Clarcor Fndn Grants, 1148
Coleman Cancer Care Grants, 1199
Coleman Developmental Disabilities Grants, 1200
Coleman Entrepreneurship Education Grants, 1201
Colonel Stanley R. McNeil Fndn Grants, 1210
Comcast Fndn Grants, 1235
Comer Fndn Grants, 1236
Commonwealth Edison Grants, 1240
Community Found of Central Illinois Grants, 1276
Community Found of E Central Illinois Grants, 1278
Community Memorial Fndn Grants, 1334
ConAgra Foods Community Impact Grants, 1342
ConAgra Foods Nourish Our Comm Grants, 1343
ConocoPhillips Fndn Grants, 1354
ConocoPhillips Grants, 1355
Cooper Industries Fndn Grants, 1370
Credit Suisse First Boston Fndn Grants, 1397
Crossroads Fund Seed Grants, 1400
CSX Corporate Contributions Grants, 1408
Darden Restaurants Fndn Grants, 1446
Deaconess Fndn Advocacy Grants, 1468
Dean Foods Community Involvement Grants, 1469
Deluxe Corporation Fndn Grants, 1496
Dermody Properties Fndn Grants, 1517
DIFFA/Chicago Grants, 1547
Dollar General Adult Literacy Grants, 1568
Dollar General Family Literacy Grants, 1569
Dollar General Youth Literacy Grants, 1570
Dominion Fndn Human Needs Grants, 1572
Donaldson Fndn Grants, 1574
Doris and Victor Day Fndn Grants, 1582
Duchossois Family Fndn Grants, 1616
DuPage Community Fndn Grants, 1624
EDS Fndn Grants, 1661
EDS Technology Grants, 1662
Elizabeth Morse Genius Charitable Trust Grants, 1682
Emerson Kampen Fndn Grants, 1696
Evanston Community Fndn Grants, 1771
Fel-Pro Mecklenburger Fndn Grants, 1800
Field Fndn of Illinois Grants, 1806
Fifth Third Bank Corporate Giving, 1809
Fifth Third Fndn Grants, 1810
FMC Fndn Grants, 1876
Fndn for Health Enhancement Grants, 1894
Francis Beidler Fndn Grants, 1921
Frank E. and Seba B. Payne Fndn Grants, 1927
G.A. Ackermann Memorial Fund Grants, 1981
Gaylord and Dorothy Donnelley Found Grants, 1993
General Mills Fndn Grants, 2003
Georgia-Pacific Fndn Education Grants, 2031
Georgia-Pacific Fndn Enrichment Grants, 2032
Georgia-Pacific Entrepreneurship Grants, 2033
Georgia-Pacific Fndn Environment Grants, 2034

GEOGRAPHIC INDEX

Indiana / 1151

Ginn Fndn Grants, 2056
Girl's Best Friend Fndn Grants, 2057
Gladys Brooks Fndn Grants, 2059
Grace Bersted Fndn Grants, 2110
Grand Victoria Fndn Illinois Core Grants, 2126
Greater Saint Louis Community Found Grants, 2138
Great Lakes Fishery Trust Access Grants, 2145
Great Lakes Fishery Trust Habitat Protection and Restoration Grants, 2146
Grover Hermann Fndn Grants, 2168
GTECH Community Involvement Grants, 2171
Gumdrop Books Librarian Scholarships, 2179
H.B. Fuller Company Fndn Grants, 2183
H. Reimers Bechtel Charitable Remainder Uni-Trust Grants, 2186
Hallmark Corporate Fndn Grants, 2212
Harry S. Black and Allon Fuller Fund Grants, 2243
Heartland Arts Fund, 2286
Henrietta Lange Burk Fund Grants, 2303
Hershey Company Grants, 2318
Hollie and Anna Oakley Fndn Grants, 2346
Hormel Foods Charitable Trust Grants, 2368
Humana Fndn Grants, 2388
I.A. O'Shaughnessy Fndn Grants, 2416
IDOT Economic Development Program Grants, 2436
IDOT Rail Freight Program Loans and Grants, 2437
IDOT Truck Access Route Program Grants, 2438
IDPH Carolyn Adams Ticket for the Cure Community Grants, 2439
IDPH Emergency Medical Services Assistance Fund Grants, 2440
IDPH Hosptial Capital Investment Grants, 2441
IDPH Local Health Department Public Health Emergency Response Grants, 2442
IFP Chicago Production Fund In-Kind Grant, 2446
IIE Western Union Family Scholarships, 2462
Illinois Arts Council Arts-in-Education Residency Grants, 2463
Illinois Arts Council Arts Service Organizations Grants, 2464
Illinois Arts Council Artstour Grants, 2465
Illinois Arts Council Community Access Grants, 2466
Illinois Arts Council Dance Grants, 2467
Illinois Arts Council Ethnic and Folk Arts Master Apprentice Grants, 2468
Illinois Arts Council Ethnic and Folk Grants, 2469
Illinois Arts Council Literature Grants, 2470
Illinois Arts Council Local Arts Agencies Grants, 2471
Illinois Arts Council Media Arts Grants, 2472
Illinois Arts Council Multidisciplinary Grants, 2473
Illinois Arts Council Music Grants, 2474
Illinois Arts Council Partners in Excellence Grants, 2475
Illinois Arts Council Presenters Grants, 2476
Illinois Arts Council Theater Grants, 2477
Illinois Arts Council Visual Arts Grants, 2478
Illinois Clean Energy Community Fndn Energy Efficiency Grants, 2479
Illinois Clean Energy Community Fndn K-12 Wind Schools Pilot Grants, 2480
Illinois Clean Energy Community Fndn Renewable Energy Grants, 2481
Illinois Clean Energy Community Fndn Solar Thermal Installation Grants, 2482
Illinois DCEO Business Development Public Infrastructure Program Grants, 2483
Illinois DCEO Coal Competitiveness Grants, 2484
Illinois DCEO Coal Demonstration Grants, 2485
Illinois DCEO Coal Development Grants, 2486
Illinois DCEO Coal Revival Grants, 2487
Illinois DCEO Community Development Assistance Program for Economic Development Grants, 2488
Illinois DCEO Eliminate Digital Divide Grants, 2489
Illinois DCEO Emerging Technological Enterprises Grants, 2490
Illinois DCEO Employer Training Investment Program Grants - Competitive Component, 2491
Illinois DCEO Employer Training Investment Program Grants - Incentive Component, 2492
Illinois DCEO Employer Training Investment Program Multi-Company Training Grants, 2493

Illinois DCEO Employer Training Investment Program Single Company Training Grants, 2494
Illinois DNR Biodiversity Field Trip Grants, 2496
Illinois DNR Habitat Fund Grants, 2497
Illinois DNR Migratory Waterfowl Stamp Fund Grants, 2498
Illinois DNR Park and Recreational Facility Construction Grants, 2499
Illinois DNR Schoolyard Habitat Action Grants, 2500
Illinois DNR State Furbearer Fund Grants, 2501
Illinois DNR State Pheasant Fund Grants, 2502
Illinois DNR Urban and Comm Forestry Grants, 2503
Illinois DNR Volunteer Fire Assistance Grants, 2504
Illinois DNR Wildlife Preservation Fund Large Project Grants, 2505
Illinois DNR Wildlife Preservation Fund Small Project Grants, 2506
Illinois DNR Wildlife Preservation Maintenance of Wildlife Rehabilitation Facilities Grants, 2507
Illinois DNR Youth Recreation Corps Grants, 2508
Illinois Humanities Council Community General Support Grants, 2509
Illinois Humanities Council Community Project Grants, 2510
Intergrys Corporation Grants, 2565
James S. Copley Fndn Grants, 2637
John Deere Fndn Grants, 2692
Joseph H. and Florence A. Roblee Found Grants, 2736
Joyce Fndn Culture Grants, 2747
Joyce Fndn Democracy Grants, 2748
Joyce Fndn Employment Grants, 2749
JP Morgan Chase Arts and Culture Grants, 2752
JP Morgan Chase Community Devel Grants, 2753
Kenny's Kids Grants, 2803
Kovler Family Fndn Grants, 2840
Land O'Lakes Fndn Community Grants, 2859
Land O'Lakes Fndn Dollars for Doers, 2860
Lillian S. Wells Fndn Grants, 2901
Lincoln Financial Group Fndn Grants, 2906
LISC Financial Opportunity Center Social Innovation Fund Grants, 2911
Lumpkin Family Healthy Environments Grants, 2941
Lumpkin Family Lively Arts and Dynamic Learning Communities Grants, 2943
Lumpkin Family Strong Community Leadership Grants, 2944
Luther I. Replogle Fndn Grants, 2945
M3C Fellowships, 2955
MacArthur Fndn Chicago Arts and Culture General Operations Grants, 2961
MacArthur Fndn Chicago Arts and Culture Int'l Connections Grants, 2962
MacArthur Fndn Policy Research Grants, 2964
Marathon Petroleum Corporation Grants, 2999
Marion Gardner Jackson Charitable Trust Grants, 3017
MeadWestvaco Sustainable Communities Grants, 3105
Mercedes-Benz USA Corporate Contributions, 3118
Michael Reese Health Trust Core Grants, 3159
Michael Reese Health Trust Responsive Grants, 3160
Mildred V. Horn Fndn Grants, 3176
Moline Fndn Community Grants, 3202
Monsanto America's Farmers Grow Rural Education Grants, 3205
Motorola Fndn Grants, 3221
NGA Midwest School Garden Grants, 3407
Nicor Corporate Contributions, 3435
Nicor Gas Sharing Grants, 3436
Norfolk Southern Fndn Grants, 3463
Northern Trust Company Charitable Trust and Corporate Giving Program, 3504
Owens Fndn Grants, 3718
Patrick and Anna M. Cudahy Fund Grants, 3751
Piper Jaffray Fndn Communities Giving, 3899
PNC Econmic Development Grants, 3922
PNC Fndn Green Building Grants, 3923
Poets & Writers Readings/Workshops Grants, 3927
Polk Bros. Fndn Grants, 3929
Prince Charitable Trusts Chicago Grants, 3959
Prudential Fndn Arts and Culture Grants, 3975
Prudential Fndn Education Grants, 3977

RBC Dain Rauscher Fndn Grants, 4031
REI Conservation and Outdoor Rec Grants, 4051
Retirement Research Accessible Faith Grants, 4066
Rice Fndn Grants, 4074
Richard H. Driehaus Fndn Grants, 4084
Richard H. Driehaus Fndn MacArthur Fund for Arts and Culture, 4085
Richard H. Driehaus Fndn Small Theater and Dance Grants, 4086
Robert R. McCormick Tribune Civics Grants, 4118
Robert R. McCormick Tribune Fndn Community Grants, 4119
Robert R. McCormick Tribune Veterans Initiative Grants, 4120
Roy J. Carver Charitable Trust Youth Grants, 4167
RR Donnelley Community Grants, 4168
RRF Accessible Faith Grants, 4169
RRF General Grants, 4170
Ruth and Vernon Taylor Fndn Grants, 4177
Safeco Insurance Community Grants, 4203
Sara Lee Fndn Grants, 4296
Seabury Fndn Grants, 4316
Shopko Fndn Community Grants, 4346
Siragusa Fndn Arts & Culture Grants, 4367
Siragusa Fndn Health Services & Medical Research Grants, 4368
Siragusa Fndn Human Services Grants, 4369
Solo Cup Fndn Grants, 4401
Solutia Fund Grants, 4402
Southwire Company Grants, 4447
Square D Fndn Grants, 4464
State Street Fndn Grants, 4495
Subaru of America Fndn Grants, 4518
TCF Bank Fndn Grants, 4565
Texas Instruments Arts and Culture Grants, 4596
Texas Instruments Civic and Business Grants, 4597
Texas Instruments Fndn Arts and Culture Grants, 4599
Textron Corporate Contributions Grants, 4601
Topfer Family Fndn Grants, 4646
Toyota Motor Manufacturing of Indiana Grants, 4653
Turner Voices Corporate Contributions, 4682
U.S. Bank Fndn Grants, 4686
Union Pacific Community and Civic Grants, 4714
USDA Delta Health Care Services Grants, 4804
Verizon Fndn Great Lakes Region Grants, 4912
Visiting Nurse Fndn Grants, 4951
Vulcan Materials Company Fndn Grants, 4956
Welborn Baptist Fndn Faith-Based Grants, 5019
Welborn Baptist Fndn Improvements to Community Health Status Grants, 5021
Wells Fargo Housing Fndn Grants, 5023
Weyerhaeuser Company Fndn Grants, 5053
Wieboldt Fndn Grants, 5065
William Blair and Company Fndn Grants, 5078
William G. McGowan Charitable Fund Grants, 5084
Woods Fund of Chicago Grants, 5115

Indiana
1st Source Fndn Ernestine M. Raclin Community Leadership Award, 2
1st Source Fndn Grants, 3
3M Company Arts and Culture Grants, 12
3M Company Environmental Giving Grants, 13
3M Company Health and Human Services Grants, 14
3M Fndn Community Giving Grants, 15
ABC Charities Grants, 85
Abelard Fndn East Grants, 87
ACE Charitable Fndn Grants, 111
Adams County Comm Fndn of Indiana Grants, 148
Adams Rotary Memorial Fund A Grants, 157
AEP Corporate Giving Grants, 180
African American Heritage Grants, 193
Albertson's Charitable Giving Grants, 345
Alfred J Mcallister and Dorothy N Mcallister Fndn Grants, 367
Allstate Corp Hometown Commitment Grants, 387
American Electric Power Grants, 428
AmerUs Group Charitable Fndn, 455
Anderson Fndn Grants, 460
Anthem Blue Cross and Blue Shield Grants, 488

Indiana

Archer Daniels Midland Fndn Grants, 527
Arts Midwest Performing Arts Grants, 579
Ayres Fndn Grants, 630
Back Home Again Fndn Grants, 633
Ball Brothers Fndn General Grants, 637
Ball Brothers Fndn Organizational Effectiveness/ Executive Mentoring Grants, 638
Ball Brothers Fndn Rapid Grants, 639
Barker Welfare Fndn Grants, 669
Bayer Fndn Grants, 696
Benton Community Fndn Cookie Jar Grant, 729
Benton Community Fndn Grants, 730
Better Way Fndn Grants, 754
Bingham McHale LLP Pro Bono Services, 772
Blackford County Community WOW Grants, 779
Blackford County Community Fndn Grants, 780
Bloomington Area Arts Council Grants, 791
Blue River Community Fndn Grants, 801
Boyd Gaming Corporation Contributions Program, 825
Bridgestone/Firestone Trust Fund Grants, 836
Brown County Community Fndn Grants, 853
Brunswick Fndn Dollars for Doers Grants, 856
Brunswick Fndn Grants, 857
Caesars Fndn Grants, 891
Carrier Corporation Contributions Grants, 946
Carroll County Community Fndn Grants, 947
Cass County Community Fndn Grants, 952
CenturyLink Clarke M. Williams Grants, 998
Charles A. Frueauff Fndn Grants, 1037
Charles H. Dater Fndn Grants, 1042
Chemtura Corporation Contributions Grants, 1067
Christian Science Society of Boonville Trust, 1113
CICF Christmas Fund, 1117
CICF City of Noblesville Community Grant, 1118
CICF Clare Noyes Grant, 1119
CICF Efroymson Grants, 1120
CICF F.R. Hensel Grant for Fine Arts, Music, and Education, 1121
CICF Howard Intermill and Marion Intermill Fenstermaker Grants, 1122
CICF Indianapolis Fndn Comm Grants, 1123
CICF Proctor Grant for Aged Men and Women, 1124
CICF John H Brown and Robert Burse Grant, 1125
CICF Legacy Fund Grants, 1126
CICF Senior Grants, 1127
CICF Summer Youth Grants, 1128
Cinergy Fndn Grants, 1133
Cingular Wireless Charitable Contributions, 1134
Circle K Corporation Contributions Grants, 1136
Citizens Savings Fndn Grants, 1141
Clinton County Community Fndn Grants, 1174
Clowes Fund Grants, 1177
Coleman Cancer Care Grants, 1199
Coleman Developmental Disabilities Grants, 1200
Coleman Entrepreneurship Education Grants, 1201
Comcast Fndn Grants, 1235
Community Fndn Alliance City of Evansville Endowment Fund Grants, 1246
Community Fndn of Bartholomew County Heritage Fund Grants, 1267
Community Fndn of Bartholomew County James A. Henderson Award for Fundraising, 1268
Community Fndn of Bartholomew County Women's Giving Circle, 1269
Community Fndn of Bloomington and Monroe County Precision Health Network Grants, 1270
Community Fndn of Bloomington and Monroe County Grants, 1271
Community Fndn of Boone County - Adult Literacy Initiative Grants, 1272
Community Fndn of Boone Cnty Women's Grants, 1273
Community Fndn of Boone County Grants, 1274
Community Fndn of Grant County Grants, 1279
Community Fndn of Greater Fort Wayne - Barbara Burt Leadership Development Grants, 1283
Community Fndn of Greater Fort Wayne - Collaborative Efforts Grants, 1284
Community Fndn of Greater Fort Wayne - Community Endowment and Clarke Endowment Grants, 1285
Community Fndn of Greater Fort Wayne - Edna Fndn Grants, 1286
Community Fndn of Greater Fort Wayne - John S. and James L. Knight Fndn Donor-Advised Grants, 1287
Community Found Of Greater Lafayette Grants, 1289
Community Found of Howard County Grants, 1297
Community Found of Jackson County Grants, 1298
Community Fndn of Muncie and Delaware County Grants, 1302
Community Fndn of Muncie and Delaware County Maxon Grants, 1303
Community Found of Southern Indiana Grants, 1310
Community Fndn of St. Joseph County African American Community Grants, 1312
Community Fndn of St. Joseph County ArtsEverywhere Grants, 1313
Community Fndn of St. Joseph County Special Project Challenge Grants, 1314
Community Found of Switzerland County Grants, 1315
Community Found of Wabash County Grants, 1326
Community Fndn Partnerships - Lawrence County Grants, 1328
Community Fndn Partnerships - Martin County Grants, 1329
ConAgra Foods Community Impact Grants, 1342
ConAgra Foods Nourish Our Comm Grants, 1343
Crossroads Fund Seed Grants, 1400
Crown Point Community Fndn Grants, 1402
Crown Point Community Found Scholarships, 1403
CSX Corporate Contributions Grants, 1408
Cummins Fndn Grants, 1415
Daviess County Community Fndn Arts and Culture Grants, 1455
Daviess County Community Fndn Environment Grants, 1456
Daviess County Community Fndn Health Grants, 1457
Daviess County Community Fndn Human Services Grants, 1458
Daviess County Community Fndn Rec Grants, 1459
Daviess County Community Fndn Youth Development Grants, 1460
Dean Foods Community Involvement Grants, 1469
Dearborn Community Fndn Aurora Grants, 1470
Dearborn Community Fndn City of Lawrenceburg Community Grants, 1471
Dearborn Community Fndn City of Lawrenceburg Youth Grants, 1472
Dearborn Community County Progress Grants, 1473
Dearborn Community Fndn Sprint Educational Excellence Grants, 1474
Decatur County Community Fndn Large Project Grants, 1476
Decatur County Community Fndn Small Project Grants, 1477
DeKalb County Community Fndn - Garrett Hospital Aid Fndn Grants, 1478
DeKalb County Community Fndn - Immediate Response Grant, 1479
DeKalb County Community Fndn Lit Grant, 1480
DeKalb County Community Fndn Grants, 1481
Dekko Fndn Grants, 1482
Deluxe Corporation Fndn Grants, 1496
DHHS Healthy Tomorrows for Children, 1534
Dollar General Adult Literacy Grants, 1568
Dollar General Family Literacy Grants, 1569
Dollar General Youth Literacy Grants, 1570
Dominion Fndn Human Needs Grants, 1572
Donaldson Fndn Grants, 1574
Dow Corning Corporate Contributions Grants, 1597
Dubois County Community Fndn Grants, 1615
Duke Energy Community Vitality Grants, 1618
Duke Energy Economic Dev Grants, 1619
Duneland Health Council Incorporated Grants, 1621
Elkhart County Community Fndn Fund for Elkhart County, 1683
Elkhart County Community Fndn Grants, 1684
Elliot Fndn Inc Grants, 1686
Emerson Kampen Fndn Grants, 1696
Evan and Susan Bayh Fndn Grants, 1769
Fayette County Fndn Grants, 1795
Fifth Third Bank Corporate Giving, 1809
Fifth Third Fndn Grants, 1810
Foellinger Fndn Grants, 1877
Fndns of East Chicago Community Economic Development Grants, 1907
Fndns of East Chicago Family Support, 1908
Fndns of East Chicago Financial Indep Grants, 1909
Fndns of East Chicago Health Grants, 1910
Fndns of E Chicago Public Safety Grants, 1911
Fndns of East Chicago Youth Devel Grants, 1912
Franklin County Community Fndn Grants, 1929
Fulton County Community Fndn Grants, 1975
Fulton County Community Fndn Women's Giving Circle Grants, 1976
Gannett Fndn Community Action Grants, 1984
Gaylord and Dorothy Donnelley Found Grants, 1993
General Mills Fndn Grants, 2003
Georgia-Pacific Fndn Education Grants, 2031
Georgia-Pacific Fndn Enrichment Grants, 2032
Georgia-Pacific Entrepreneurship Grants, 2033
Georgia-Pacific Fndn Environment Grants, 2034
Gibson County Community Fndn Women's Fund, 2051
Giving Sum Annual Grant, 2058
Gladys Brooks Fndn Grants, 2059
Greater Cincinnati Fndn Priority and Small Projects/ Capacity-Building Grants, 2132
Great Lakes Fishery Trust Access Grants, 2145
Great Lakes Fishery Trust Habitat Protection and Restoration Grants, 2146
Greene County Fndn Grants, 2150
Gregory L. Gibson Charitable Fndn Grants, 2163
GTECH Community Involvement Grants, 2171
H.B. Fuller Company Fndn Grants, 2183
Hancock County Community Fndn - Field of Interest Grants, 2219
Hancock County Community Fndn - Programming Mini-Grants, 2220
Harrison County Community Fndn Grants, 2233
Harrison County Community Signature Grants, 2234
Health Fndn of Greater Cincinnati Grants, 2281
Health Fndn of Greater Indianapolis Grants, 2282
Heartland Arts Fund, 2286
Hendricks County Community Fndn Grants, 2302
Henry County Community Fndn - TASC Youth Grants, 2307
Henry County Community Fndn Grants, 2308
Historic Landmarks Fndn of Indiana African American Heritage Grants, 2333
Historic Landmarks Fndn of Indiana Historic Preservation Education Grants, 2334
Historic Landmarks Fndn of Indiana Legal Defense Grants, 2335
Historic Landmarks Fndn of Indiana Marion County Historic Preservation Funds, 2336
Historic Landmarks Fndn of Indiana Preservation Grants, 2337
Historic Landmarks Legal Defense Grants, 2338
Hollie and Anna Oakley Fndn Grants, 2346
Hometown Indiana Grants, 2353
Hulman & Company Fndn Grants, 2387
Humana Fndn Grants, 2388
Huntington County Community Fndn - Hiner Family Grant, 2405
Huntington County Community Fndn - Make a Difference Grants, 2406
Huntington County Community Fndn - Stephanie Pyle Grant, 2407
Huntington National Bank Community Grants, 2409
IBCAT Screening Mammography Grants, 2422
ICC Community Service Mini-Grant, 2426
ICC Day of Service Action Grants, 2427
ICC Faculty Fellowships, 2428
ICC Listening to Communities Grants, 2429
ICC Scholarship of Engagement Faculty Grants, 2430
IDEM Section 205(j) Water Quality Management Planning Grants, 2434
IDEM Section 319(h) Nonpoint Source Grants, 2435
IEDC Industrial Development Grant Fund, 2443
IEDC Int'l Trade Show Assistance Program, 2444
IEDC Skills Enhancement Fund, 2445

GEOGRAPHIC INDEX

IFP Chicago Production Fund In-Kind Grant, 2446
Impact 100 Grants, 2522
Indiana 21st Century Research and Technology Fund Awards, 2528
Indiana AIDS Fund Grants, 2529
Indiana Arts Comm American Masterpieces Grants, 2530
Indiana Arts Comm Capacity Building Grants, 2531
Indiana Arts Comm Multi-regional Major Arts Institutions Grants, 2532
Indiana Arts Comm Statewide Arts Service Organization Grants, 2533
Indiana Boating Infrastructure Grants (BIG P), 2534
Indiana Clean Vessel Act Grants, 2535
Indiana Corn Marketing Council Retailer Grant for Tank Cleaning, 2536
Indiana Historic Preservation Fund Grants, 2537
Indiana Household Hazardous Waste Grants, 2538
Indiana Humanities Council Initiative Grants, 2539
Indianapolis Power & Light Company Community Grants, 2540
Indianapolis Power & Light Company Environmentalist of the Year Award, 2541
Indianapolis Power & Light Company Golden Eagle Environmental Grants, 2542
Indianapolis Preservation Grants, 2543
Indiana Preservation Grants, 2544
Indiana Recycling Grants, 2545
Indiana Regional Economic Development Partnership Grants, 2546
Indiana Rural Capacity Grants, 2547
Indiana SBIR/STTR Commercialization Enhancement Program, 2548
Indiana Space Grant Consortium Grants for Informal Education Partnerships, 2549
Indiana Space Grant Consortium Workforce Development Grants, 2550
Indiana Waste Tire Fund Grants, 2551
Indiana Workforce Acceleration Grants, 2552
IYI Responsible Fatherhood Grants, 2591
Jacob G. Schmidlapp Trust Grants, 2616
Jasper Fndn Grants, 2655
Jennings County Community Fndn Grants, 2664
Jennings County Community Fndn Women's Giving Circle Grant, 2665
Jerry L. and Barbara J. Burris Fndn Grants, 2669
John S. and James L. Knight Fndn Communities Grants, 2711
John S. and James L. Knight Fndn Grants, 2713
Johnson County Community Fndn Grants, 2723
Johnson County Community Fndn Youth Philanthropy Initiative Grants, 2724
John W. Anderson Fndn Grants, 2729
Journal Gazette Fndn Grants, 2744
Joyce Fndn Employment Grants, 2749
JP Morgan Chase Arts and Culture Grants, 2752
JP Morgan Chase Community Devel Grants, 2753
Judith Clark-Morrill Fndn Grants, 2756
K21 Health Fndn Cancer Care Grants, 2759
K21 Health Fndn Grants, 2760
Kendrick Fndn Grants, 2797
KeyBank Fndn Grants, 2820
Kimball Int'l-Habig Fndn Grants, 2823
Knox County Community Fndn Grants, 2831
Kosciusko County Comm Fndn Grants, 2838
Kosciusko County Community Fndn REMC Operation Round Up Grants, 2839
Lafayette - West Lafayette Convention and Visitors Bureau Tourist Promotion Grants, 2849
LaGrange County Comm Fndn Grants, 2850
LaGrange Independent Found for Endowments, 2851
Lake County Community Fund Grants, 2856
Land O'Lakes Fndn Community Grants, 2859
Land O'Lakes Fndn Dollars for Doers, 2860
Legacy Fndn College Readiness Grant, 2874
Leighton Award for Nonprofit Excellence, 2880
Lilly Endowment Clergy Renewal Program for Indiana Congregations, 2902
Lilly Endowment Giving Indiana Funds for Tomorrow Grants, 2903
Lincoln Financial Group Fndn Grants, 2906

LISC Financial Opportunity Center Social Innovation Fund Grants, 2911
Lumpkin Family Strong Community Leadership Grants, 2944
M.E. Raker Fndn Grants, 2953
M3C Fellowships, 2955
Madison County Community Fndn - City of Anderson Quality of Life Grant, 2972
Madison County Community General Grants, 2973
Marathon Petroleum Corporation Grants, 2999
Marion County Historic Preservation Grants, 3016
Marshall County Community Fndn Grants, 3026
Marsh Corporate Grants, 3027
Mary C. & Perry F. Spencer Fndn Grants, 3034
Mary Jane Luick Trust Grants, 3040
Maxon Charitable Fndn Grants, 3068
McMillen Fndn Grants, 3090
Mead Johnson Nutritionals Evansville-Area Organizations Grants, 3103
Medtronic Community Link Arts, Civic, and Culture Grants, 3109
Medtronic CommunityLink Health Grants, 3111
Medtronic Comm Link Human Services Grants, 3112
MFRI Operation Diploma Grants for Higher Education Institutions, 3150
MFRI Operation Diploma Grants for Student Veterans Organizations, 3151
MFRI Operation Diploma Small Grants for Indiana Family Readiness Groups, 3152
Miami County Community Fndn - Boomerang Sisterhood Grant, 3155
Miami County Community Fndn - Operation Round Up Grants, 3156
Miami County Community Fndn Grants, 3157
Mildred V. Horn Fndn Grants, 3176
Montgomery County Comm Fndn Grants, 3213
Newton County Community Fndn Grants, 3336
NGA Midwest School Garden Grants, 3407
Nicholas H. Noyes Jr. Memorial Grants, 3434
Nina Mason Pulliam Charitable Trust Grants, 3443
Noble County Community Fndn Celebrate Diversity Project Grants, 3455
Noble County Community Fndn Grants, 3456
Norfolk Southern Fndn Grants, 3463
North Central Health Services Grants, 3492
North Central Health Services Grants, 3491
Ohio County Community Fndn Board of Directors Grants, 3656
Ohio County Community Fndn Conference/Training Grants, 3657
Ohio County Community Fndn Grants, 3658
Ohio County Comm Fndn Junior Grants, 3659
Ohio County Comm Fndn Mini-Grants, 3660
Olive B. Cole Fndn Grants, 3670
Orange County Community Fndn Grants, 3687
Owen County Community Fndn Grants, 3716
Parke County Community Fndn Grants, 3735
Paul Ogle Fndn Grants, 3764
Perry County Community Fndn Grants, 3827
PeyBack Fndn Grants, 3861
Pike County Community Fndn Grants, 3888
Pi Lambda Theta Anna Tracey Memorial Award, 3889
Pi Lambda Theta Lillian and Henry Barry Award in Human Relations, 3890
PNC Charitable Trust and Fndn Grants, 3921
PNC Ecnomic Development Grants, 3922
PNC Fndn Green Building Grants, 3923
PNC Fndn Grow Up Great Grants, 3924
Porter County Community Fndn Grants, 3931
Porter County Emergency Grants, 3932
Porter County Health and Wellness Grant, 3933
Porter County Women's Grant, 3934
Portland Found Women's Giving Circle Grant, 3935
Portland Fndn Grants, 3936
Posey Community Fndn Women's Grants, 3938
Posey County Community Fndn Grants, 3939
Pulaski County Community Fndn Grants, 3988
Putnam County Community Fndn Grants, 3990
Randall L. Tobias Fndn Grants, 4017
Richard M. Fairbanks Fndn Grants, 4088

Ripley County Community Fndn Grants, 4095
Ripley County Community Fndn Small Grants, 4096
Robert and Helen Haddad Fndn Grants, 4103
Robert Lee Blaffer Fndn Grants, 4115
Robert & Clara Milton Fund for Senior Housing, 4117
RRF General Grants, 4170
Rush County Community Fndn Grants, 4174
Safeco Insurance Community Grants, 4203
Scheumann Fndn Grants, 4306
Schurz Communications Fndn Grants, 4312
Scott County Community Fndn Grants, 4314
Sensient Technologies Fndn Grants, 4337
Shopko Fndn Community Grants, 4346
South Madison Community Fndn Grants, 4440
Spencer County Community Fndn Grants, 4451
Square D Fndn Grants, 4464
St. Joseph Community Health Fndn Catherine Kasper Award, 4468
St. Joseph Community Health Fndn Improving Healthcare Access Grants, 4469
Starke County Community Fndn Grants, 4482
Steuben County Community Fndn Grants, 4501
Subaru of Indiana Automotive Fndn Grants, 4519
Sunoco Fndn Grants, 4530
TCF Bank Fndn Grants, 4565
Tech Enhancement Certification for Hoosiers, 4571
Thomas D. McGrain Cedar Glade Grants, 4616
Toyota Motor Engineering & Manufacturing North America Grants, 4651
Toyota Motor Manufacturing of Indiana Grants, 4653
Union County Fndn Grants, 4712
Unity Fndn Of LaPorte County Grants, 4726
Vanderburgh Community Fndn Grants, 4902
Vanderburgh Community Women's Fund, 4903
Vectren Fndn Grants, 4907
Verizon Fndn Great Lakes Region Grants, 4912
Vermillion County Community Grants, 4928
Vulcan Materials Company Fndn Grants, 4956
W. C. Griffith Fndn Grants, 4958
Wabash River Enhancement Corporation Agricultural Cost-Share Grants, 4968
Wabash River Heritage Corridor Fund Grants, 4970
Wabash Valley Community Fndn Grants, 4971
Wabash Valley Human Services Grants, 4972
Warren County Community Fndn Grants, 4985
Warren County Community Mini-Grants, 4986
Warrick County Community Fndn Grants, 4987
Washington County Community Grants, 4997
Washington County Comm Fndn Youth Grants, 4998
Wayne County Fndn Vigran Family Fndn Grants, 5004
Wayne County Fndn Grants, 5005
Wayne County Fndn Women's Grants, 5006
Weaver Popcorn Fndn Grants, 5016
Welborn Baptist Fndn Faith-Based Grants, 5019
Welborn Baptist Fndn Improvements to Community Health Status Grants, 5021
Wells County Fndn Grants, 5022
Wells Fargo Housing Fndn Grants, 5023
Western Indiana Community Fndn Grants, 5024
White County Community Fndn Grants, 5057
Whitley County Community Fndn Grants, 5060
William A. Miller Fndn Grants, 5073

Iowa
3M Company Arts and Culture Grants, 12
3M Company Environmental Giving Grants, 13
3M Company Health and Human Services Grants, 14
3M Fndn Community Giving Grants, 15
AEGON Transamerica Arts & Culture Grants, 176
AEGON Transamerica Fndn Civic and Community Grants, 177
AEGON Transamerica Fndn Health and Welfare Grants, 179
Albertson's Charitable Giving Grants, 345
Alliant Energy Fndn Community Grants, 384
Alliant Energy Fndn Hometown Challenge Grants, 385
AmerUs Group Charitable Fndn, 455
Andersen Corporate Fndn, 459
Anne Thorne Weaver Family Fndn Grants, 478
Aquila Corporate Grants, 521

Iowa

Archer Daniels Midland Fndn Grants, 527
Arts Fndn, 578
Arts Midwest Performing Arts Grants, 579
Bridgestone/Firestone Trust Fund Grants, 836
Caesars Fndn Grants, 891
CenturyLink Clarke M. Williams Grants, 998
Circle K Corporation Contributions Grants, 1136
Coleman Cancer Care Grants, 1199
Coleman Developmental Disabilities Grants, 1200
Coleman Entrepreneurship Education Grants, 1201
ConAgra Foods Community Impact Grants, 1342
ConAgra Foods Nourish Our Comm Grants, 1343
Courage Center Judd Jacobson Memorial Award, 1382
Cummins Fndn Grants, 1415
CUNA Mutual Group Fndn, 1416
CUNA Mutual Group Fndn Grants, 1417
Dekko Fndn Grants, 1482
DHHS Healthy Tomorrows for Children, 1534
DOJ Rural Domestic Violence and Child Victimization Enforcement Grants, 1562
Dollar General Adult Literacy Grants, 1568
Dollar General Family Literacy Grants, 1569
Dollar General Youth Literacy Grants, 1570
Donaldson Fndn Grants, 1574
Doris and Victor Day Fndn Grants, 1582
Gannett Fndn Community Action Grants, 1984
General Mills Fndn Grants, 2003
Georgia-Pacific Fndn Education Grants, 2031
Georgia-Pacific Fndn Enrichment Grants, 2032
Georgia-Pacific Entrepreneurship Grants, 2033
Georgia-Pacific Fndn Environment Grants, 2034
Go Daddy Cares Charitable Contributions, 2094
Greater Des Moines Fndn Grants, 2134
Great Lakes Fishery Trust Access Grants, 2145
Great Lakes Fishery Trust Habitat Protection and Restoration Grants, 2146
H. Reimers Bechtel Charitable Remainder Uni-Trust Grants, 2186
Hall-Perrine Fndn Grants, 2209
Harold R. Bechtel Charitable Remainder Uni-Trust Grants, 2229
Heartland Arts Fund, 2286
Hormel Foods Charitable Trust Grants, 2368
IFP Chicago Production Fund In-Kind Grant, 2446
Iowa Arts Council Artists in Schools/Communities Residency Grants, 2571
John Deere Fndn Grants, 2692
Land O'Lakes Fndn Community Grants, 2859
Land O'Lakes Fndn Dollars for Doers, 2860
Lied Fndn Trust Grants, 2900
M3C Fellowships, 2955
Marie H. Bechtel Charitable Grants, 3007
Mid-Iowa Health Community Response Grants, 3168
Moline Fndn Community Grants, 3202
Nationwide Insurance Fndn Grants, 3285
Nestle Purina PetCare Educational Grants, 3302
Nestle Purina PetCare Pet Related Grants, 3304
Nestle Purina PetCare Support Dog and Police K-9 Organization Grants, 3305
Nestle Purina PetCare Youth Grants, 3306
NGA Midwest School Garden Grants, 3407
Norfolk Southern Fndn Grants, 3463
Peter Kiewit Fndn General Grants, 3845
Peter Kiewit Fndn Small Grants, 3847
Philanthrofund Fndn Grants, 3874
Piper Jaffray Fndn Communities Giving, 3899
Principal Financial Group Fndn Grants, 3966
Prudential Fndn Arts and Culture Grants, 3975
Prudential Fndn Economic Devel Grants, 3976
Prudential Fndn Education Grants, 3977
QuikTrip Corporate Contributions Grants, 3998
R.J. McElroy Trust Grants, 4001
RBC Dain Rauscher Fndn Grants, 4031
Roy J. Carver Charitable Trust Youth Grants, 4167
RRF General Grants, 4170
Shopko Fndn Community Grants, 4346
Square D Fndn Grants, 4464
Sunderland Fndn Grants, 4527
Tension Envelope Fndn Grants, 4578
Trinity Fndn Grants, 4670
U.S. Bank Fndn Grants, 4686
Union Pacific Community and Civic Grants, 4714
Union Pacific Fndn Health and Human Services Grants, 4715
Viking Children's Fund Grants, 4939
Vulcan Materials Company Fndn Grants, 4956
Waitt Family Fndn Grants, 4973
Wells Fargo Housing Fndn Grants, 5023

Kansas

360 Degrees of Giving Grants, 32
Abbott Fund Access to Health Care Grants, 80
Abbott Fund Community Grants, 81
Abbott Fund Global AIDS Care Grants, 82
Abbott Fund Science Education Grants, 83
Abelard Fndn West Grants, 88
ACE Charitable Fndn Grants, 111
Albertson's Charitable Giving Grants, 345
Aquila Corporate Grants, 521
Archer Daniels Midland Fndn Grants, 527
Baughman Fndn Grants, 688
Bayer Fndn Grants, 696
Boeing Company Contributions Grants, 809
CenturyLink Clarke M. Williams Grants, 998
Charles A. Frueauff Fndn Grants, 1037
Comcast Fndn Grants, 1235
Deluxe Corporation Fndn Grants, 1496
DHHS Healthy Tomorrows for Children, 1534
DOJ Rural Domestic Violence and Child Victimization Enforcement Grants, 1562
Dollar General Adult Literacy Grants, 1568
Dollar General Family Literacy Grants, 1569
Dollar General Youth Literacy Grants, 1570
Eaton Charitable Fund Grants, 1647
Ethel and Raymond F. Rice Fndn Grants, 1758
Forrest C. Lattner Fndn Grants, 1887
GTECH Community Involvement Grants, 2171
H & R Fndn Grants, 2181
Hallmark Corporate Fndn Grants, 2212
Hatton W. Sumners Fndn for the Study and Teaching of Self Government Grants, 2257
Hormel Foods Charitable Trust Grants, 2368
Humana Fndn Grants, 2388
Hutchinson Community Fndn Grants, 2410
I.A. O'Shaughnessy Fndn Grants, 2416
IFP Chicago Production Fund In-Kind Grant, 2446
J.E. and L.E. Mabee Fndn Grants, 2595
John Deere Fndn Grants, 2692
John S. and James L. Knight Fndn Communities Grants, 2711
Kansas Arts Comm American Masterpieces Kansas Grants, 2775
Kansas Arts Comm Artist Fellowships, 2776
Kansas Arts Comm Arts-in-Communities Project Grants, 2777
Kansas Arts Comm Arts-in-Communities Project Mini-Grants, 2778
Kansas Arts Comm Arts-in-Education Grants, 2779
Kansas Arts Comm Arts on Tour Grants, 2780
Kansas Arts Comm Operational Support for Arts and Cultural Organizations, 2781
Kansas Arts Comm Partnership Grants, 2782
Kansas Arts Comm Visual Arts Grants, 2783
Kansas Health Fndn Recognition Grants, 2784
Land O'Lakes Fndn Community Grants, 2859
Land O'Lakes Fndn Dollars for Doers, 2860
Lewis H. Humphreys Charitable Trust Grants, 2889
Lied Fndn Trust Grants, 2900
M3C Fellowships, 2955
MeadWestvaco Sustainable Communities Grants, 3105
Mid-America Arts Alliance Community Engagement with Touring Artists Grants, 3166
Mid-America Arts Alliance Reg Touring Grants, 3167
NGA Midwest School Garden Grants, 3407
Piper Jaffray Fndn Communities Giving, 3899
QuikTrip Corporate Contributions Grants, 3998
Rachel Alexandra Girls Grants, 4003
RBC Dain Rauscher Fndn Grants, 4031
Shopko Fndn Community Grants, 4346
Sosland Fndn Grants, 4408
Sunderland Fndn Grants, 4527
Sunflower Fndn Bridge Grants, 4528
Taylor S. Abernathy and Patti Harding Abernathy Charitable Trust Grants, 4564
Tension Envelope Fndn Grants, 4578
Textron Corporate Contributions Grants, 4601
Topeka Community Fndn Boss Hawg's Charitable Giving Grants, 4642
Topeka Community Building Families Grants, 4643
Topeka Community Fndn Grants, 4644
Topeka West Rotary Youth Enrichment Grants, 4645
U.S. Bank Fndn Grants, 4686
Union Pacific Community and Civic Grants, 4714
Union Pacific Fndn Health and Human Services Grants, 4715
United Methodist Child Mental Health Grants, 4721
United Methodist Health Ministry Fund Grants, 4722
Vulcan Materials Company Fndn Grants, 4956
Wells Fargo Housing Fndn Grants, 5023

Kentucky

3M Company Arts and Culture Grants, 12
3M Company Environmental Giving Grants, 13
3M Company Health and Human Services Grants, 14
3M Fndn Community Giving Grants, 15
Abelard Fndn East Grants, 87
AEP Corporate Giving Grants, 180
A Good Neighbor Fndn Grants, 204
American Electric Power Grants, 428
Anthem Blue Cross and Blue Shield Grants, 488
Appalachian Community Fund General Grants, 493
Appalachian Community Fund GLBTQ Initiative Grants, 494
Appalachian Community Media Justice Grants, 495
Appalachian Community Fund Seize the Moment Grants, 496
Appalachian Community Fund Special Opportunities Grants, 497
Appalachian Community Fund Technical Assistance Grants, 498
Appalachian Regional Comm Asset-Based Development Project Grants, 500
Appalachian Regional Comm Business Development Revolving Loan Fund Grants, 501
Appalachian Regional Comm Community Infrastructure Grants, 502
Appalachian Regional Comm Distressed Counties Grants, 503
Appalachian Regional Comm Education and Training Grants, 504
Appalachian Regional Comm Energy Grants, 505
Appalachian Regional Comm Export and Trade Development Grants, 506
Appalachian Regional Comm Health Care Grants, 507
Appalachian Reg Comm Housing Grants, 508
Appalachian Regional Comm Leadership Development and Capacity Building Grants, 509
Appalachian Regional Comm Telecommunications Grants, 510
Appalachian Regional Comm Tourist Development Grants, 511
Appalachian Regional Comm Transportation and Highways Grants, 512
Archer Daniels Midland Fndn Grants, 527
Arkema Fndn Science Teachers Program, 563
Ashland Corporate Contributions Grants, 587
Belk Fndn Grants, 721
Blue Grass Community Fndn Grants, 799
Bridgestone/Firestone Trust Fund Grants, 836
Brunswick Fndn Dollars for Doers Grants, 856
Brunswick Fndn Grants, 857
Charles A. Frueauff Fndn Grants, 1037
Charles H. Dater Fndn Grants, 1042
Charles M. and Mary D. Grant Found Grants, 1050
Cincinnati Bell Fndn Grants, 1131
Cinergy Fndn Grants, 1133
Cingular Wireless Charitable Contributions, 1134
Circle K Corporation Contributions Grants, 1136
Clarcor Fndn Grants, 1148
Clark County Community Fndn Grants, 1156

GEOGRAPHIC INDEX

Maine / 1155

Comcast Fndn Grants, 1235
Community Fndn of Louisville Grants, 1299
Cralle Fndn Grants, 1394
CSX Corporate Contributions Grants, 1408
Dean Foods Community Involvement Grants, 1469
Dollar General Adult Literacy Grants, 1568
Dollar General Family Literacy Grants, 1569
Dollar General Youth Literacy Grants, 1570
Donaldson Fndn Grants, 1574
Dow Corning Corporate Contributions Grants, 1597
Duke Energy Community Vitality Grants, 1618
Duke Energy Economic Development Grants, 1619
Eaton Charitable Fund Grants, 1647
EQT Fndn Art and Culture Grants, 1743
EQT Fndn Community Grants, 1744
EQT Fndn Education Grants, 1745
EQT Fndn Environment Grants, 1746
Fifth Third Bank Corporate Giving, 1809
Fifth Third Fndn Grants, 1810
Fndn for a Healthy Kentucky Grants, 1891
Gannett Fndn Community Action Grants, 1984
Georgia-Pacific Fndn Education Grants, 2031
Georgia-Pacific Fndn Enrichment Grants, 2032
Georgia-Pacific Entrepreneurship Grants, 2033
Georgia-Pacific Fndn Environment Grants, 2034
Gheens Fndn Grants, 2048
Greater Cincinnati Fndn Priority and Small Projects/ Capacity-Building Grants, 2132
GTECH Community Involvement Grants, 2171
H.B. Fuller Company Fndn Grants, 2183
Health Fndn of Greater Cincinnati Grants, 2281
Humana Fndn Grants, 2388
Huntington National Bank Comm Grants, 2409
IFP Chicago Production Fund In-Kind Grant, 2446
Impact 100 Grants, 2522
Jacob G. Schmidlapp Trust Grants, 2616
James Graham Brown Quality of Life Grants, 2625
John S. and James L. Knight Fndn Communities Grants, 2711
John S. and James L. Knight Fndn Donor Advised Fund Grants, 2712
JP Morgan Chase Arts and Culture Grants, 2752
JP Morgan Chase Community Devel Grants, 2753
Kentucky Arts Council Access Assistance Grants, 2805
Kentucky Arts Council Al Smith Individual Fellowship, 2806
Kentucky Arts Council Emerging Artist Award, 2807
Kentucky Arts Council Folk and Traditional Arts Apprenticeship Grant, 2808
Kentucky Arts Council Partnership Grants, 2809
Kentucky Arts Council Poetry Out Loud Grants, 2810
Kentucky Arts Council Teaching Together Grants, 2811
Kentucky Arts Council TranspARTation Grant, 2812
KeyBank Fndn Grants, 2820
Kimball Int'l-Habig Fndn Grants, 2823
Kimberly-Clark Community Grants, 2824
LISC Financial Opportunity Center Social Innovation Fund Grants, 2911
M3C Fellowships, 2955
Marathon Petroleum Corporation Grants, 2999
Mary E. and Michael Blevins Charitable Grants, 3037
Mary Reynolds Babcock Fndn Grants, 3047
Mildred V. Horn Fndn Grants, 3176
Norfolk Southern Fndn Grants, 3463
Norton Fndn Grants, 3514
Paul Green Fndn Playwrights Fellowship, 3762
Paul Ogle Fndn Grants, 3764
Peoples Bancorp Fndn Grants, 3817
Piper Jaffray Fndn Communities Giving, 3899
PNC Charitable Trust and Fndn Grants, 3921
PNC Fndn Grow Up Great Grants, 3924
Rainbow Fund Grants, 4009
Richard F. and Janice F. Weaver Educational Trust Grants, 4082
RRF General Grants, 4170
Shopko Fndn Community Grants, 4346
Southwire Company Grants, 4447
Square D Fndn Grants, 4464
Steele-Reese Fndn Grants, 4498
Sunoco Fndn Grants, 4530

TAC Arts Access Technical Assistance Grants, 4550
TAC Arts Educ Community-Learning Grants, 4552
TAC Arts Education Mini Grants, 4553
TAC Arts Projects Grants, 4554
TAC Rural Arts Project Support Grants, 4555
TAC Technical Assistance Grants, 4556
TAC Touring Arts and Access Grants, 4557
Thompson Charitable Fndn Grants, 4622
Toyota Motor Engineering & Manufacturing North America Grants, 4651
Toyota Motor Manufacturing of Indiana Grants, 4653
Toyota Motor Manufacturing of Kentucky Grants, 4654
Tri-State Community Twenty-first Century Endowment Fund Grants, 4666
U.S. Bank Fndn Grants, 4686
USDA Delta Health Care Services Grants, 4804
V.V. Cooke Fndn Grants, 4896
Verizon Fndn Southeast Region Grants, 4923
Vulcan Materials Company Fndn Grants, 4956
W. Paul and Lucille Caudill Little Grants, 4966
Walter L. Gross III Family Fndn Grants, 4983
Welborn Baptist Fndn Faith-Based Grants, 5019
Welborn Baptist Fndn Improvements to Community Health Status Grants, 5021
Weyerhaeuser Company Fndn Grants, 5053

Louisiana
2 Life 18 Fndn Grants, 5
Abelard Fndn East Grants, 87
ACE Charitable Fndn Grants, 111
Adams and Reese LLP Corporate Giving Grants, 147
AEP Corporate Giving Grants, 180
Albertson's Charitable Giving Grants, 345
American Electric Power Grants, 428
Baptist Community Ministries Grants, 664
Barrasso Usdin Kupperman Freeman and Sarver LLC Corporate Grants, 675
Baton Rouge Fndn Credit Bureau Grants, 680
Baton Rouge Area Fndn Every Kid a King Fund Grants, 681
Baton Rouge Area Fndn Grants, 682
Belk Fndn Grants, 721
Booth-Bricker Fund Grants, 815
Boyd Gaming Corporation Contributions Program, 825
Bridgestone/Firestone Trust Fund Grants, 836
Brunswick Fndn Dollars for Doers Grants, 856
Brunswick Fndn Grants, 857
Cabot Corporation Fndn Grants, 887
Caesars Fndn Grants, 891
CenturyLink Clarke M. Williams Grants, 998
Charles A. Frueauff Fndn Grants, 1037
Cingular Wireless Charitable Contributions, 1134
Collins C. Diboll Private Fndn Grants, 1208
Comcast Fndn Grants, 1235
Community Found of Shreveport-Bossier Grants, 1307
ConAgra Foods Community Impact Grants, 1342
ConAgra Foods Nourish Our Comm Grants, 1343
ConocoPhillips Fndn Grants, 1354
ConocoPhillips Grants, 1355
Coughlin-Saunders Fndn Grants, 1377
CSX Corporate Contributions Grants, 1408
Cudd Fndn Grants, 1410
Dean Foods Community Involvement Grants, 1469
Deuce McAllister Catch 22 Fndn Grants, 1521
DHHS Healthy Tomorrows for Children, 1534
Dollar Energy Fund Grants, 1567
Dollar General Adult Literacy Grants, 1568
Dollar General Family Literacy Grants, 1569
Dollar General Youth Literacy Grants, 1570
Eaton Charitable Fund Grants, 1647
Eddy Knight Family Fndn Grants, 1654
Emy-Lou Biedenharn Fndn Grants, 1703
Entergy Charitable Fndn Low-Income Initiatives and Solutions Grants, 1711
Entergy Corporation Micro Grants, 1712
Entergy Corp Grants for Arts and Culture, 1713
Entergy Corporation Open Grants for Community Improvement & Enrichment, 1714
Entergy Corp Grants for Healthy Families, 1715
FAR Fund Grants, 1787

Fluor Fndn Grants, 1875
FMC Fndn Grants, 1876
Fndn for the Mid South Community Development Grants, 1897
Fndn for the Mid South Education Grants, 1898
Fndn for Mid South Health & Wellness Grants, 1899
Fndn for Mid So Wealth Building Grants, 1900
Frost Fndn Grants, 1966
Gannett Fndn Community Action Grants, 1984
Georgia-Pacific Fndn Education Grants, 2031
Georgia-Pacific Fndn Enrichment Grants, 2032
Georgia-Pacific Entrepreneurship Grants, 2033
Georgia-Pacific Fndn Environment Grants, 2034
German Protestant Orphan Asylum Fndn Grants, 2044
Gheens Fndn Grants, 2048
Gil and Dody Weaver Fndn Grants, 2053
Gladys Brooks Fndn Grants, 2059
GNOF Albert N. & Hattie M. McClure Grants, 2068
GNOF Bayou Communities Grants, 2069
GNOF Cox Charities of New Orleans Grants, 2072
GNOF Exxon-Mobil Grants, 2074
GNOF Freeman Challenge Grants, 2075
GNOF Gulf Coast Oil Spill Grants, 2077
GNOF Jefferson Community Grants, 2085
GNOF Norco Community Grants, 2089
GNOF Organizational Effectiveness Grants and Workshops, 2090
GNOF Plaquemines Community Grants, 2091
GNOF St. Bernard Community Grants, 2092
GNOF Stand Up For Our Children Grants, 2093
Hatton W. Sumners Fndn for the Study and Teaching of Self Government Grants, 2257
Hazen Fndn Public Education Grants, 2269
Huie-Dellmon Trust Grants, 2386
Humana Fndn Grants, 2388
Joe W. and Dorothy Dorsett Brown Grants, 2684
John Deere Fndn Grants, 2692
JP Morgan Chase Arts and Culture Grants, 2752
JP Morgan Chase Community Devel Grants, 2753
Lettie Pate Whitehead Fndn Grants, 2888
Lockheed Martin Philanthropic Grants, 2918
Marathon Petroleum Corporation Grants, 2999
Mary Reynolds Babcock Fndn Grants, 3047
MeadWestvaco Sustainable Communities Grants, 3105
Murphy Institute Judith Kelleher Schafer Summer Internship Grants, 3230
Norfolk Southern Fndn Grants, 3463
PeyBack Fndn Grants, 3861
Pinnacle Entertainment Fndn Grants, 3893
Plum Creek Fndn Grants, 3917
Poets & Writers Readings/Workshops Grants, 3927
Prudential Fndn Economic Devel Grants, 3976
Prudential Fndn Education Grants, 3977
RBC Dain Rauscher Fndn Grants, 4031
Textron Corporate Contributions Grants, 4601
Tulane University Community Service Scholars, 4677
Tulane University Public Service Fellows, 4678
Turner Voices Corporate Contributions, 4682
Union Pacific Community and Civic Grants, 4714
Union Pacific Fndn Health and Human Services Grants, 4715
USDA Delta Health Care Services Grants, 4804
Vulcan Materials Company Fndn Grants, 4956
Weyerhaeuser Company Fndn Grants, 5053
William Robert Baird Charitable Trust Grants, 5093
Williams Companies Fndn Grants, 5095

Maine
1772 Fndn Fellowships, 36
Abelard Fndn East Grants, 87
Aetna Fndn Regional Health Grants, 187
Agnes M. Lindsay Trust Grants, 203
Agway Fndn Grants, 205
Albertson's Charitable Giving Grants, 345
Alexander H. Bright Charitable Trust Grants, 358
American Rivers Community-Based Restoration Program River Grants, 444
Anthem Blue Cross and Blue Shield Grants, 488
Barnes Group Fndn Grants, 672
Bay and Paul Fndns, Inc Grants, 692

1156 / Maine

BBF Maine Family Literacy Initiative Implementation Grants, 698
BBF Maine Family Literacy Planning Grants, 699
Beim Fndn Grants, 718
Bernard Osher Fndn Grants, 742
BJ's Charitable Fndn Grants, 777
BJ's Wholesale Clubs Local Charitable Giving, 778
C.F. Adams Charitable Trust Grants, 884
Carlisle Fndn Grants, 931
Ceres Fndn Grants, 999
Charles A. Frueauff Fndn Grants, 1037
Clowes Fund Grants, 1177
Comcast Fndn Grants, 1235
ConAgra Foods Nourish Our Comm Grants, 1343
Davis Conservation Fndn Grants, 1461
Davis Family Fndn Grants, 1462
Dean Foods Community Involvement Grants, 1469
DHHS Healthy Tomorrows for Children, 1534
DOJ Rural Domestic Violence and Child Victimization Enforcement Grants, 1562
Doree Taylor Charitable Fndn, 1580
Dorr Fndn Grants, 1591
Eaton Charitable Fund Grants, 1647
Edna McConnell Clark Fndn Grants, 1659
Fields Pond Fndn Grants, 1807
FMC Fndn Grants, 1876
Fndn for Seacoast Health Grants, 1895
Frances W. Emerson Fndn Grants, 1920
Francis T. & Louise T. Nichols Grants, 1923
Gannett Fndn Community Action Grants, 1984
Gardiner Savings Institution Fndn Grants, 1987
George I. Alden Trust Grants, 2023
George P. Davenport Trust Fund Grants, 2026
Gladys Brooks Fndn Grants, 2059
Hannaford Charitable Fndn Grants, 2222
Harold Alfond Fndn Grants, 2225
Haymarket People's Fund Sustaining Grants, 2267
Haymarket Urgent Response Grants, 2268
Horizon Fndn Grants, 2365
Jane's Trust Grants, 2639
Jessie B. Cox Charitable Trust Grants, 2670
Joukowsky Family Fndn Grants, 2743
KeyBank Fndn Grants, 2820
KeySpan Fndn Grants, 2821
Libra Fndn Future Grants, 2898
Libra Fndn Grants, 2899
Maine Community Found Baldwin Area Grants, 2974
Maine Community Fndn Belvedere Animal Welfare Grants, 2975
Maine Community Fndn Belvedere Historic Preservation Grants, 2976
Maine Community Fndn Charity Grants, 2977
Maine Community Building Grants, 2978
Maine Community Fndn Edward H. Daveis Benevolent Grants, 2979
Maine Community Fndn Equity Grants, 2980
Maine Community Found Expansion Arts Grants, 2981
Maine Community Fndn Gracie Grants, 2982
Maine Community Fndn Maine Land Conservation Grants, 2983
Maine Community Found Peaks Island Grants, 2984
Maine Community Fndn People of Color Grants, 2985
Maine Community Fndn Ram Island Conservation Challenge Grants, 2986
Maine Community Rines/Thompson Grants, 2987
Maine Community Fndn Rose and Samuel Rudman Library Grants, 2988
Maine Community Fndn Steeples Grants, 2989
Maine Community Fndn Vincent B. and Barbara G. Welch Grants, 2990
Maine State Troopers Fndn Grants, 2991
Maine Women's Fund Economic Security Grants, 2992
Maine Women's Fund Girls' Grantmaking, 2993
Merck Family Fund Urban Farming and Youth Leadership Grants, 3119
Norfolk Southern Fndn Grants, 3463
Orchard Fndn Grants, 3690
Plum Creek Fndn Grants, 3917
Richard Davoud Donchian Fndn Grants, 4080
Robert and Joan Dircks Fndn Grants, 4104
S. Spencer Scott Fund Grants, 4202
Shaw's Supermarkets Donations, 4342
Simmons Fndn Grants, 4360
Stowe Family Fndn Grants, 4510
Sunoco Fndn Grants, 4530
Sweet Water Trust Grants, 4541
Verizon Fndn Maine Grants, 4916
Verizon Wireless Hopeline Grants, 4927
Yawkey Fndn Grants, 5125

Marshall Islands

Bank of America Charitable Matching Gifts, 658
Bank of America Charitable Volunteer Grants, 660
EPA Environmental Justice Small Grants, 1731
EPA Pestwise Registration Improvement Act Partnership Grants, 1734
EPA Regional Agricultural IPM Grants, 1735
EPA Source Reduction Assistance Grants, 1737
EPA State Indoor Radon Grants, 1738
EPA Tribal Support for the National Environmental Information Exchange Network, 1742
NHLBI Ancillary Studies in Clinical Trials, 3410
NHLBI Bioengineering and Obesity Grants, 3411
NHLBI Career Transition Awards, 3412
NHLBI Lymphatics in Health and Disease in the Digestive, Cardiovascular and Pulmonary, 3414
NHLBI Lymphatics in Health and Disease in the Digestive, Urinary, Cardiovascular and Pulmonary Systems, 3415
NHLBI Research on the Role of Cardiomyocyte Mitochondria in Heart Disease: An Integrated Approach, 3417
NHLBI Ruth L. Kirschstein National Research Service Awards for Individual Postdoctoral Fellows, 3418
NHLBI Ruth L. Kirschstein National Research Service Awards for Individual Senior Fellows, 3421
NHLBI Ruth L. Kirschstein National Research Service Award Short-Term Institutional Research Training Grants, 3422
USDA Farmers Market Promotion Grants, 4808
USDC Public Works and Economic Adjustment Assistance Grants, 4856

Maryland

21st Century Threshold Project Gifts, 21
Aaron Catzen Fndn Grants, 70
Abelard Fndn East Grants, 87
Abell Fndn Arts and Culture Grants, 92
Abell Fndn Community Development Grants, 93
Abell Fndn Conservation and Environment Grants, 94
Abell Fndn Criminal Justice and Addictions Grants, 95
Abell Found Health and Human Services Grants, 96
Abell Fndn Workforce Development Grants, 97
ACE Charitable Fndn Grants, 111
AEGON Transamerica Arts & Culture Grants, 176
AEGON Transamerica Fndn Civic and Community Grants, 177
AEGON Transamerica Fndn Health and Welfare Grants, 179
Aetna Fndn Regional Health Grants, 187
Albertson's Charitable Giving Grants, 345
Alex Brown and Sons Charitable Grants, 359
Alvin and Fanny Blaustein Thalheimer Grants, 403
American Rivers Community-Based Restoration Program River Grants, 444
Appalachian Regional Comm Asset-Based Development Project Grants, 500
Appalachian Regional Comm Business Development Revolving Loan Fund Grants, 501
Appalachian Regional Comm Community Infrastructure Grants, 502
Appalachian Regional Comm Distressed Counties Grants, 503
Appalachian Regional Comm Education and Training Grants, 504
Appalachian Regional Comm Energy Grants, 505
Appalachian Regional Comm Export and Trade Development Grants, 506
Appalachian Regional Comm Health Care Grants, 507
Appalachian Reg Comm Housing Grants, 508

GEOGRAPHIC INDEX

Appalachian Regional Comm Leadership Development and Capacity Building Grants, 509
Appalachian Regional Comm Telecommunications Grants, 510
Appalachian Regional Comm Tourist Development Grants, 511
Appalachian Regional Comm Transportation and Highways Grants, 512
Baltimore Community Fndn Arts and Culture Path Grants, 641
Baltimore Community Fndn Children's Fresh Air Society Fund Grants, 642
Baltimore Community Fndn Environment Grants, 643
Baltimore Community Fndn Human Services Path Grants, 644
Baltimore Community Fndn Kelly People's Emergency Fund Grants, 645
Baltimore Community Neighborhood Grants, 646
Baltimore Community Fndn Neighborhoods Path Grants, 647
Baltimore Community Fndn Transportation Path Grants, 648
Baltimore Community Found Youth Path Grants, 649
Baltimore Women's Giving Circle Grants, 650
BBF Maryland Family Literacy Initiative Implementation Grants, 700
BBF Maryland Family Literacy Initiative Planning Grants, 701
Bechtel Group Fndn Building Positive Community Relationships Grants, 715
Belk Fndn Grants, 721
Bender Fndn Grants, 726
BJ's Charitable Fndn Grants, 777
BJ's Wholesale Clubs Local Charitable Giving, 778
Boeing Company Contributions Grants, 809
Brunswick Fndn Dollars for Doers Grants, 856
Brunswick Fndn Grants, 857
Carl M. Freeman Fndn FACES Grants, 932
Carl M. Freeman Fndn Grants, 933
CenturyLink Clarke M. Williams Grants, 998
Ceres Fndn Grants, 999
CFNCR Starbucks Memorial Fund, 1026
Charles A. Frueauff Fndn Grants, 1037
Charles Delmar Fndn Grants, 1039
Chase Paymentech Corporate Giving Grants, 1059
Chesapeake Bay Trust Capacity Building Grants, 1068
Chesapeake Bay Trust Environmental Education Grants, 1069
Chesapeake Bay Trust Fisheries and Headwaters Grants, 1070
Chesapeake Bay Trust Forestry Mini Grants, 1071
Chesapeake Bay Trust Mini Grants, 1072
Chesapeake Bay Trust Outreach and Community Engagement Grants, 1073
Chesapeake Bay Trust Pioneer Grants, 1074
Chesapeake Bay Trust Restoration Grants, 1075
Cingular Wireless Charitable Contributions, 1134
Claude A. and Blanche McCubbin Abbott Charitable Trust Grants, 1158
Clayton Baker Trust Grants, 1163
Comcast Fndn Grants, 1235
Commonweal Community Assistance Grants, 1239
Community Fndn of the Eastern Shore Community Needs Grants, 1317
Community Fndn of the Eastern Shore Field of Interest Grants, 1318
Community Fndn of the Eastern Shore Youth Fndn Grants, 1319
Corina Higginson Trust Grants, 1373
Credit Suisse First Boston Fndn Grants, 1397
CSX Corporate Contributions Grants, 1408
Danellie Fndn Grants, 1442
Dean Foods Community Involvement Grants, 1469
DHHS Healthy Tomorrows for Children, 1534
Dollar Energy Fund Grants, 1567
Dollar General Adult Literacy Grants, 1568
Dollar General Family Literacy Grants, 1569
Dollar General Youth Literacy Grants, 1570
Dominion Fndn Human Needs Grants, 1572
Dresher Fndn Grants, 1605

GEOGRAPHIC INDEX

Eaton Charitable Fund Grants, 1647
Eddie C. and Sylvia Brown Family Grants, 1653
Edward N. and Della L. Thome Memorial Fndn Direct Services Grants, 1666
Eugene B. Casey Fndn Grants, 1762
FirstEnergy Fndn Math, Science, and Technology Education Grants, 1820
FishAmerica Fndn Chesapeake Bay Grants, 1827
FMC Fndn Grants, 1876
France-Merrick Fndns Grants, 1915
Freddie Mac Fndn Grants, 1944
Gannett Fndn Community Action Grants, 1984
General Mills Fndn Grants, 2003
Giant Food Charitable Grants, 2050
Gladys Brooks Fndn Grants, 2059
Goldseker Fndn Comm Affairs Grants, 2100
Goldseker Fndn Community Grants, 2101
Goldseker Fndn Human Services Grants, 2102
Goldseker Fndn Non-Profit Management Assistance Grants, 2103
HBF Pathways Out of Poverty Grants, 2273
Helen Pumphrey Denit Charitable Trust Grants, 2297
Henry and Ruth Blaustein Rosenberg Grants, 2306
Hilda and Preston Davis Fndn Grants, 2322
Hoffberger Fndn Grants, 2342
Howard County Community Fndn Grants, 2375
J. Willard and Alice S. Marriott Grants, 2609
J. Willard Marriott, Jr. Fndn Grants, 2610
Jacob and Hilda Blaustein Fndn Grants, 2615
John Edward Fowler Memorial Found Grants, 2693
John J. Leidy Fndn Grants, 2701
Kennedy Center HSC Fndn Internship, 2799
Kennedy Center Summer HSC Internship, 2800
Lockheed Martin Philanthropic Grants, 2918
Margaret Abell Powell Fund Grants, 3002
Marion I. and Henry J. Knott Fndn Discretionary Grants, 3018
Marion I. and Henry J. Knott Standard Grants, 3019
MARPAT Fndn Grants, 3023
Mercedes-Benz USA Corporate Contributions, 3118
Merck Family Fund Urban Farming and Youth Leadership Grants, 3119
Meyer Fndn Benevon Grants, 3140
Meyer Fndn Education Grants, 3142
Meyer Fndn Management Assistance, 3144
Mid Atlantic Arts Fndn American Masterpieces Grants, 3169
Mid Atlantic Arts Found ArtsConnect Grants, 3170
Mid Atlantic Arts Fndn Folk Arts Outreach Project Grants, 3171
Morris and Gwendolyn Cafritz Found Grants, 3218
Nationwide Insurance Fndn Grants, 3285
NFWF Chesapeake Bay Conservation Innovation Grants, 3363
NFWF Chesapeake Bay Targeted Grants, 3365
Norfolk Southern Fndn Grants, 3463
Ober Kaler Community Grants, 3635
OSF-Baltimore Criminal & Juvenile Justice Grants, 3696
OSF-Baltimore Education and Youth Development Grants, 3697
OSF-Baltimore Tackling Drug Addiction Grants, 3698
Patrick John Bennett, Jr. Memorial Grants, 3752
PennPAT Fee-Support Grants for Presenters, 3812
PennPAT New Directions Grants for Presenters, 3813
Peter and Georgia Angelos Fndn Grants, 3843
Philip L. Graham Fund Grants, 3876
PNC Charitable Trust and Fndn Grants, 3921
PNC Ecnomic Development Grants, 3922
PNC Fndn Green Building Grants, 3923
PNC Fndn Grow Up Great Grants, 3924
Preservation Maryland Heritage Fund Grants, 3948
Quality Health Fndn Grants, 3994
Rathmann Family Fndn Grants, 4026
REI Conservation and Outdoor Rec Grants, 4051
Richard Davoud Donchian Fndn Grants, 4080
Robert G. Cabell III and Maude Morgan Cabell Fndn Grants, 4113
Rollins-Luetkemeyer Fndn Grants, 4147
S. Spencer Scott Fund Grants, 4202
Salmon Fndn Grants, 4225
Speer Trust Grants, 4450
Sunoco Fndn Grants, 4530
T. Rowe Price Associates Fndn Grants, 4548
Texas Instruments Arts and Culture Grants, 4596
Texas Instruments Civic and Business Grants, 4597
Texas Instruments Fndn Arts and Culture Grants, 4599
Textron Corporate Contributions Grants, 4601
Thomas B. and Elizabeth M. Sheridan Grants, 4614
Tiger Woods Fndn Grants, 4634
Verizon Fndn Maryland Grants, 4917
VSA/Metlife Connect All Grants, 4953
Vulcan Materials Company Fndn Grants, 4956
Washington Area Fuel Fund Grants, 4988
Washington Gas Charitable Contributions, 5000
Wells Fargo Housing Fndn Grants, 5023
Weyerhaeuser Company Fndn Grants, 5053
William G. Baker, Jr. Memorial Fund Grants, 5081
William J. and Dorothy K. O'Neill Grants, 5087
William L. and Victorine Q. Adams Grants, 5089
William S. Abell Fndn Grants, 5094
Youth As Resources Grants, 5130

Massachusetts

2 Depot Square Ipswich Charitable Grants, 4
3 B's Fndn Grants, 7
3M Company Arts and Culture Grants, 12
3M Company Environmental Giving Grants, 13
3M Company Health and Human Services Grants, 14
3M Fndn Community Giving Grants, 15
1675 Fndn Grants, 35
1772 Fndn Fellowships, 36
A.C. Ratshesky Fndn Grants, 39
Aaron Fndn Grants, 73
Abbot and Dorothy H. Stevens Fndn Grants, 79
Abbott Fund Access to Health Care Grants, 80
Abbott Fund Community Grants, 81
Abbott Fund Global AIDS Care Grants, 82
Abbott Fund Science Education Grants, 83
Abel and Sophia Sheng Charitable Grants, 86
Abelard Fndn East Grants, 87
ACE Charitable Fndn Grants, 111
Acushnet Fndn Grants, 143
Adams Fndn Grants, 154
Adelaide Breed Bayrd Fndn Grants, 161
AEC Trust Grants, 175
Agnes M. Lindsay Trust Grants, 203
Agway Fndn Grants, 205
Albertson's Charitable Giving Grants, 345
Albert W. Rice Charitable Fndn Grants, 347
Alexander H. Bright Charitable Trust Grants, 358
Alfred E. Chase Charitable Fndn Grants, 366
Alice C. A. Sibley Fund Grants, 371
Amelia Sillman Rockwell and Carlos Perry Rockwell Charities Fund Grants, 417
American Express Charitable Fund Grants, 429
American Rivers Community-Based Restoration Program River Grants, 444
AmerUs Group Charitable Fndn, 455
Archer Daniels Midland Fndn Grants, 527
Auburn Fndn Grants, 611
Banfi Vintners Fndn Grants, 653
Barnes Group Fndn Grants, 672
Barr Fndn Grants (Massachusetts), 676
Bay and Paul Fndns, Inc Grants, 692
Bayer Fndn Grants, 696
BCBS of Massachusetts Fndn Grants, 713
Biogen Corporate Giving Grants, 773
BJ's Charitable Fndn Grants, 777
BJ's Wholesale Clubs Local Charitable Giving, 778
Boston Fndn Grants, 819
Boston Fndn Initiative to Strengthen Arts and Cultural Service Organizations, 820
Boston Globe Fndn Grants, 821
Boston Jewish Community Women's Fund Grants, 822
Bristol-Myers Squibb Fndn Community Initiatives Grants, 840
Brown Rudnick Charitable Relationship Grants, 855
C.F. Adams Charitable Trust Grants, 884
Cabot Corporation Fndn Grants, 887
Cambridge Community Fndn Grants, 913
Carlisle Fndn Grants, 931
Ceres Fndn Grants, 999
Charles A. Frueauff Fndn Grants, 1037
Charles F. Bacon Trust Grants, 1040
Charles H. Farnsworth Trust Grants, 1043
Charles H. Hall Fndn, 1044
Charles H. Pearson Fndn Grants, 1045
Charles Hayden Fndn Grants, 1048
Cisco Systems Fndn San Jose Community Grants, 1137
Clipper Ship Fndn Grants, 1175
Clowes Fund Grants, 1177
Comcast Fndn Grants, 1235
ConAgra Foods Community Impact Grants, 1342
ConAgra Foods Nourish Our Comm Grants, 1343
Cranston Fndn Grants, 1395
Credit Suisse First Boston Fndn Grants, 1397
CSX Corporate Contributions Grants, 1408
Davis Conservation Fndn Grants, 1461
Dean Foods Community Involvement Grants, 1469
Deborah Munroe Noonan Memorial Fund Grants, 1475
Deluxe Corporation Fndn Grants, 1496
DHHS Healthy Tomorrows for Children, 1534
Dominion Fndn Human Needs Grants, 1572
Dorr Fndn Grants, 1591
Edna McConnell Clark Fndn Grants, 1659
Edward Bangs Kelley and Elza Kelley Grants, 1665
Edwin S. Webster Fndn Grants, 1671
Ellen Abbott Gilman Trust Grants, 1685
Entergy Charitable Fndn Low-Income Initiatives and Solutions Grants, 1711
Entergy Corporation Micro Grants, 1712
Entergy Corp Grants for Arts and Culture, 1713
Entergy Corporation Open Grants for Community Improvement & Enrichment, 1714
Entergy Corp Grants for Healthy Families, 1715
Essex County Community Fndn Discretionary Fund Grants, 1752
Essex County Community Fndn Emergency Fund Grants, 1753
Essex County Community Fndn First Jobs Grant, 1754
Essex County Community Fndn Greater Lawrence Summer Fund Grants, 1755
Essex County Community Fndn Merrimack Valley General Fund Grants, 1756
Ezra M. Cutting Trust Grants, 1779
Fallon OrNda Community Health Fund Grants, 1783
Fassino Fndn Grants, 1793
Fields Pond Fndn Grants, 1807
Florian O. Bartlett Trust Grants, 1845
Frances W. Emerson Fndn Grants, 1920
Frank Reed and Margaret Jane Peters Memorial Fund I Grants, 1933
Frank Reed and Margaret Jane Peters Memorial Fund II Grants, 1934
Frank Stanley Beveridge Fndn Grants, 1936
Frank W. and Carl S. Adams Memorial Grants, 1937
Fuller Fndn Grants, 1974
Gardiner Howland Shaw Fndn Grants, 1986
General Mills Fndn Grants, 2003
George F. Baker Trust Grants, 2016
George H. and Jane A. Mifflin Memorial Grants, 2021
George I. Alden Trust Grants, 2023
George W. Wells Fndn Grants, 2030
Georgia-Pacific Fndn Education Grants, 2031
Georgia-Pacific Fndn Enrichment Grants, 2032
Georgia-Pacific Entrepreneurship Grants, 2033
Georgia-Pacific Fndn Environment Grants, 2034
Georgiana Goddard Eaton Memorial Grants, 2038
Gladys Brooks Fndn Grants, 2059
Grand Circle Fndn Associates Grants, 2112
Greater Worcester Community Fndn Discretionary Grants, 2140
Greater Worcester Community Fndn Jeppson Memorial Fund for Brookfield Grants, 2141
Greater Worcester Community Mini-Grants, 2142
Greater Worcester Community Fndn Ministries Grants, 2143
Greater Worcester Community Fndn Youth for Community Improvement Grants, 2144
Gregory C. Carr Fndn Grants, 2161

Massachusetts

Hannaford Charitable Fndn Grants, 2222
Harbus Fndn Grants, 2223
Harold Brooks Fndn Grants, 2227
Hasbro Children's Fund, 2256
Haymarket People's Fund Sustaining Grants, 2267
Haymarket Urgent Response Grants, 2268
High Meadow Fndn Grants, 2321
Hilda and Preston Davis Fndn Grants, 2322
Horace Moses Charitable Fndn Grants, 2363
Horizon Fndn Grants, 2365
Hyams Fndn Grants, 2413
IAFF Harvard University Trade Union Scholars, 2417
Intel Community Grants, 2562
Jane's Trust Grants, 2639
Jane and Jack Fitzpatrick Fund Grants, 2640
Jessie B. Cox Charitable Trust Grants, 2670
Joan Bentinck-Smith Charitable Grants, 2682
Johnson & Johnson Comm Health Care Grants, 2717
John W. Alden Trust Grants, 2727
John W. Boynton Fund Grants, 2730
Josephine G. Russell Trust Grants, 2737
Joukowsky Family Fndn Grants, 2743
KeySpan Fndn Grants, 2821
Lawrence J. and Anne Rubenstein Charitable Fndn Grants, 2868
Leicester Savings Bank Fund, 2879
Linden Fndn Grants, 2908
Lloyd G. Balfour Fndn Attleboro-Specific Charities Grants, 2916
Mabel A. Horne Trust Grants, 2956
Mabel Louise Riley Fndn Family Strengthening Small Grants, 2958
Mabel Louise Riley Fndn Grants, 2959
Massachusetts Bar IOLTA Grants, 3050
Massachusetts Bar Legal Intern Fellowships, 3051
Massachusetts Cultural Adams Arts Grants, 3052
Massachusetts Cultural Council Cultural Facilities Capital Grants, 3053
Massachusetts Cultural Council Cultural Facilities Feasibility and Technical Assistance Grants, 3054
Massachusetts Cultural Council Cultural Facilities Systems Replacement Plan Grants Grants, 3055
Massachusetts Cultural Council Cultural Investment Portfolio, 3056
Massachusetts Cultural Council Local Cultural Council Grants, 3057
Massachusetts Cultural Council Traditional Arts Apprenticeships, 3058
Massachusetts Fndn for the Humanities Cultural Economic Development Grants, 3059
Massachusetts Fndn for Humanities Project Grants, 3060
McCallum Family Fndn Grants, 3072
Medtronic Community Link Arts, Civic, and Culture Grants, 3109
Medtronic CommunityLink Education Grants, 3110
Medtronic CommunityLink Health Grants, 3111
Medtronic Comm Link Human Services Grants, 3112
Merck Family Fund Urban Farming and Youth Leadership Grants, 3119
MetroWest Health Fndn Capital Grants for Health-Related Facilities, 3134
MetroWest Health Fndn Grants--Healthy Aging, 3135
MetroWest Health Fndn Grants to Reduce the Incidence of High Risk Behaviors Among Adolescents, 3136
Middlesex Savings Charitable Fndn Capacity Building Grants, 3172
Middlesex Savings Charitable Fndn Community Development Grants, 3173
Middlesex Savings Charitable Fndn Educational Opportunities Grants, 3174
MMS and Alliance Charitable Fndn Grants for Community Action and Care for the Medically Uninsured, 3194
MMS and Alliance Charitable Fndn Int'l Health Studies Grants, 3195
Morgan Babcock Scholarships, 3217
Motorola Fndn Grants, 3221
Nathaniel and Elizabeth P. Stevens Grants, 3247

Nellie Mae Education Fndn District-Level Change Grants, 3297
Nordson Corporation Fndn Grants, 3462
Norfolk Southern Fndn Grants, 3463
Northeast Utilities Fndn Grants, 3498
Orchard Fndn Grants, 3690
Paul and Edith Babson Fndn Grants, 3755
Perkin Fund Grants, 3821
Perpetual Trust for Charitable Giving Grants, 3826
Peter and Elizabeth C. Tower Fndn Annual Intellectual Disabilities Grants, 3834
Peter and Elizabeth C. Tower Fndn Annual Mental Health Grants, 3835
Peter and Elizabeth C. Tower Fndn Learning Disability Grants, 3836
Peter and Elizabeth C. Tower Fndn Mental Health Reference and Resource Materials Grants, 3837
Peter and Elizabeth C. Tower Fndn Organizational Scholarships, 3838
Peter and Elizabeth C. Tower Fndn Phase II Technology Initiative Grants, 3839
Peter and Elizabeth C. Tower Fndn Phase I Technology Initiative Grants, 3840
Peter and Elizabeth C. Tower Fndn Social and Emotional Preschool Curriculum Grants, 3841
Peter and Elizabeth C. Tower Fndn Substance Abuse Grants, 3842
Price Chopper's Golub Fndn Grants, 3950
Price Chopper's Golub Fndn Two-Year Health Care Scholarship, 3951
REI Conservation and Outdoor Rec Grants, 4051
Richard and Susan Smith Family Grants, 4078
Robert and Joan Dircks Fndn Grants, 4104
Robert F. Stoico / FIRSTFED Charitable Fndn Grants, 4112
Rogers Family Fndn Grants, 4144
Ruth H. and Warren A. Ellsworth Grants, 4179
S. Spencer Scott Fund Grants, 4202
Sailors' Snug Harbor of Boston Elder Grants, 4211
Sailors' Snug Harbor of Boston Fishing Communities Initiative Grants, 4212
Seagate Technology Corporation Capacity to Care Grants, 4317
Shaw's Supermarkets Donations, 4342
Solutia Fund Grants, 4402
Sophia Romero Trust Grants, 4406
Southern New England Folk and Traditional Arts Apprenticeship Grants, 4438
Sprague Fndn Grants, 4461
State Street Fndn Grants, 4495
Sunoco Fndn Grants, 4530
Sweet Water Trust Grants, 4541
TE Fndn Grants, 4572
Texas Instruments Arts and Culture Grants, 4596
Texas Instruments Civic and Business Grants, 4597
Texas Instruments Fndn Arts and Culture Grants, 4599
Textron Corporate Contributions Grants, 4601
Theodore Edson Parker Fndn Grants, 4605
Third Sector New England Inclusion Grants, 4608
Turner Voices Corporate Contributions, 4682
UniBank 911 Emergency Personnel Education, 4707
US Airways Community Contributions, 4788
US Airways Education Fndn Grants, 4790
Verizon Fndn Northeast Region Grants, 4920
VSA/Metlife Connect All Grants, 4953
Water and Land Stewardship Fund Grants, 5002
William G. Kelley Fndn Grants, 5083
Winifred & Harry B. Allen Fndn Grants, 5101
Yawkey Fndn Grants, 5125

Michigan

3M Company Arts and Culture Grants, 12
3M Company Environmental Giving Grants, 13
3M Company Health and Human Services Grants, 14
3M Fndn Community Giving Grants, 15
41 Washington Street Fndn Grants, 22
Abbott Fund Access to Health Care Grants, 80
Abbott Fund Community Grants, 81
Abbott Fund Global AIDS Care Grants, 82
Abbott Fund Science Education Grants, 83

Abelard Fndn East Grants, 87
ACE Charitable Fndn Grants, 111
AEP Corporate Giving Grants, 180
Albertson's Charitable Giving Grants, 345
Allegan County Community Fndn Grants, 375
Americana Fndn Grants, 422
American Electric Power Grants, 428
Anderson Fndn Grants, 460
Angels in Motion Fndn Grants, 467
Ann and Robert H. Lurie Fndn Grants, 473
Ann Arbor Area Community Fndn Grants, 474
Archer Daniels Midland Fndn Grants, 527
Arcus Fndn Fund Grants, 529
Arcus Fndn Gay and Lesbian Fund Grants, 530
Arkema Fndn Science Teachers Program, 563
Arts Midwest Performing Arts Grants, 579
Battle Creek Community Fndn Grants, 684
Battle Creek Community Fndn Mini-Grants, 685
Battle Creek Community Neighborhood Grants, 686
Batts Fndn Grants, 687
Bay Area Community Fndn Grants, 694
BCBSM Building Healthy Communities Engaging Elementary Schools and Community Partners Grants, 704
BCBSM Children Angel Awards, 705
BCBSM Corporate Contributions Grants, 706
BCBSM Community Health Matching Grants, 707
BCBSM Investigator Initiated Research Grants, 708
BCBSM Found Proposal Development Awards, 709
BCBSM Fndn Student Award Program, 710
Beldon Fndn Grants, 720
Berrien Community Fndn Grants, 744
Besser Fndn Grants, 748
Bridgestone/Firestone Trust Fund Grants, 836
Brunswick Fndn Dollars for Doers Grants, 856
Brunswick Fndn Grants, 857
Campbell Soup Fndn Grants, 916
Capital Region Community Fndn Grants, 921
Carls Fndn Grants, 937
Carrier Corporation Contributions Grants, 946
CenturyLink Clarke M. Williams Grants, 998
Cincinnati Milacron Fndn Grants, 1132
Cingular Wireless Charitable Contributions, 1134
Circle K Corporation Contributions Grants, 1136
Cleveland-Cliffs Fndn Grants, 1165
Coleman Cancer Care Grants, 1199
Coleman Developmental Disabilities Grants, 1200
Coleman Entrepreneurship Education Grants, 1201
Comcast Fndn Grants, 1235
Comerica Charitable Fndn Grants, 1237
Community Found for Muskegon County Grants, 1256
Community Fndn for NE Michigan Grants, 1257
Community Fndn for SE Michigan Grants, 1259
Community Fndn for SE Michigan HOPE Fund Grants, 1260
Community Fndn of Greater Flint Grants, 1282
ConAgra Foods Community Impact Grants, 1342
ConAgra Foods Nourish Our Comm Grants, 1343
Consumers Energy Fndn, 1365
CSX Corporate Contributions Grants, 1408
Darden Restaurants Fndn Grants, 1446
Dean Foods Community Involvement Grants, 1469
DeRoy Testamentary Fndn Grants, 1518
Detroit Lions Charities Grants, 1520
Dollar General Adult Literacy Grants, 1568
Dollar General Family Literacy Grants, 1569
Dollar General Youth Literacy Grants, 1570
Dow Corning Corporate Contributions Grants, 1597
DTE Energy Community Development Grants, 1609
DTE Energy Fndn Cultural Grants, 1610
DTE Energy Fndn Diversity Grants, 1611
DTE Energy Fndn Environmental Grants, 1612
DTE Energy Fndn Health and Human Services Grants, 1613
DTE Energy Fndn Leadership Grants, 1614
Eaton Charitable Fund Grants, 1647
EDS Fndn Grants, 1661
EDS Technology Grants, 1662
Edward N. and Della L. Thome Memorial Fndn Direct Services Grants, 1666

GEOGRAPHIC INDEX

Entergy Charitable Fndn Low-Income Initiatives and Solutions Grants, 1711
Entergy Corporation Micro Grants, 1712
Entergy Corp Grants for Arts and Culture, 1713
Entergy Corporation Open Grants for Community Improvement & Enrichment, 1714
Entergy Corp Grants for Healthy Families, 1715
Fifth Third Bank Corporate Giving, 1809
Fifth Third Fndn Grants, 1810
Frederick S. Upton Fndn Grants, 1947
Fremont Area Community Amazing X Grants, 1953
Fremont Area Community Elderly Needs Grants, 1954
Fremont Area Community Fndn Grants, 1955
Fremont Area Community Fndn Summer Youth Grants, 1956
Frey Fndn Grants, 1963
Gannett Fndn Community Action Grants, 1984
General Mills Fndn Grants, 2003
Georgia-Pacific Fndn Education Grants, 2031
Georgia-Pacific Fndn Enrichment Grants, 2032
Georgia-Pacific Entrepreneurship Grants, 2033
Georgia-Pacific Fndn Environment Grants, 2034
Grand Haven Community Fndn Grants, 2113
Grand Rapids Area Community Fndn Wyoming Youth Fund Grants, 2117
Grand Rapids Community Fndn Grants, 2118
Grand Rapids Community Ionia County Grants, 2119
Grand Rapids Community Fndn Ionia County Youth Fund Grants, 2120
Grand Rapids Community Fndn Lowell Area Fund Grants, 2121
Grand Rapids Community Fndn Southeast Ottawa Grants, 2122
Grand Rapids Community Fndn Southeast Ottawa Youth Fund Grants, 2123
Grand Rapids Community Sparta Grants, 2124
Grand Rapids Community Fndn Sparta Youth Fund Grants, 2125
Granger Fndn Grants, 2127
Great Lakes Fishery Trust Access Grants, 2145
Great Lakes Fishery Trust Habitat Protection and Restoration Grants, 2146
Guido A. and Elizabeth H. Binda Grants, 2172
H.B. Fuller Company Fndn Grants, 2183
Harry A. and Margaret D. Towsley Grants, 2236
Harvey Randall Wickes Fndn Grants, 2255
Heartland Arts Fund, 2286
Herbert H. and Grace A. Dow Grants, 2315
Hillsdale County Community General Adult Fndn Grants, 2328
Holland/Zeeland Community Grants, 2345
Hudson Webber Fndn Grants, 2383
Humana Fndn Grants, 2388
Huntington National Bank Comm Grants, 2409
IFP Chicago Production Fund In-Kind Grant, 2446
Intergrys Corporation Grants, 2565
Irving S. Gilmore Fndn Grants, 2584
J. Spencer Barnes Memorial Fndn Grants, 2606
Jackson County Community Unrestricted Grants, 2611
Jackson County Community Fndn Youth Advisory Committee Grants, 2612
Jacob G. Schmidlapp Trust Grants, 2616
James A. and Faith Knight Fndn Grants, 2621
Jewish Fund Grants, 2675
John and Elizabeth Whiteley Fndn Grants, 2685
Joyce Fndn Democracy Grants, 2748
JP Morgan Chase Arts and Culture Grants, 2752
JP Morgan Chase Community Devel Grants, 2753
Kalamazoo Community Fndn Capacity Building Grants, 2764
Kalamazoo Community Fndn Economic and Community Development Grants, 2765
Kalamazoo Community Fndn Environment Fund Grants, 2766
Kalamazoo Community Fndn Front Porch Grants, 2767
Kalamazoo Community Good Neighbor Grants, 2768
Kalamazoo Community Fndn Individuals and Families Grants, 2769
Kalamazoo Community Fndn John E. Fetzer Institute Fund Grants, 2770

Kalamazoo Community Fndn LBGT Equality Fund Grants, 2771
Kalamazoo Community Fndn Mini-Grants, 2772
Kalamazoo Community Fndn Youth Development Grants, 2773
KeyBank Fndn Grants, 2820
Kimberly-Clark Community Grants, 2824
Land O'Lakes Fndn Community Grants, 2859
Land O'Lakes Fndn Dollars for Doers, 2860
Laura Jane Musser Intercultural Harmony Grants, 2862
Laura Jane Musser Rural Arts Grants, 2863
Laura Jane Musser Rural Initiative Grants, 2864
LISC Financial Opportunity Center Social Innovation Fund Grants, 2911
M3C Fellowships, 2955
Marathon Petroleum Corporation Grants, 2999
McGregor Fund Grants, 3082
MDARD AgD Value Added/Regional Food Systems Grants, 3091
MDARD County Fairs Cap Improvement Grants, 3092
MDARD Specialty Crop Block Grants-Farm Bill, 3093
MDEQ Beach Monitoring Grants - Inland Lakes, 3094
MDEQ Brownfield Redevelopment and Site Reclamation Grants, 3095
MDEQ Clean Diesel Grants, 3096
MDEQ Coastal Management Planning and Construction Grants, 3097
MDEQ Community Pollution Prevention (P2) Grants: Household Drug Collections, 3098
MDEQ Great Lakes Areas of Concern Land Acquisition Grants, 3099
MDEQ Local Water Quality Monitoring Grants, 3100
MDEQ Wellhead Protection Grants, 3101
Metro Health Fndn Grants, 3133
MGM Resorts Fndn Community Grants, 3153
Miller, Canfield, Paddock and Stone, P.L.C. Corporate Giving Grants, 3179
Miller Fndn Grants, 3181
NGA Midwest School Garden Grants, 3407
Nissan Fndn Grants, 3444
Nissan Neighbors Grants, 3445
Norfolk Southern Fndn Grants, 3463
PNC Ecnomic Development Grants, 3922
PNC Fndn Green Building Grants, 3923
Poets & Writers Readings/Workshops Grants, 3927
REI Conservation and Outdoor Rec Grants, 4051
Richard and Helen DeVos Fndn Grants, 4076
Rollin M. Gerstacker Fndn Grants, 4146
Saginaw Community Fndn Grants, 4205
Saginaw Community Fndn Senior Citizen Enrichment Fund, 4206
Saginaw Community Fndn YWCA Fund for Women and Girls Grants, 4207
Saginaw County Community Fndn Youth FORCE Grants, 4208
Shopko Fndn Community Grants, 4346
Skillman Community Connections Small Grants, 4379
Skillman Fndn Good Neighborhoods Grants, 4380
Skillman Fndn Good Opportunities Grants, 4381
Skillman Fndn Good Schools Grants, 4382
Solutia Fund Grants, 4402
Steelcase Fndn Grants, 4497
Sunoco Fndn Grants, 4530
Talbert and Leota Abrams Fndn, 4558
TCF Bank Fndn Grants, 4565
TE Fndn Grants, 4572
Thompson Fndn Grants, 4623
Toyota Technical Center Grants, 4660
Tri-County Electric People Fund Grants, 4665
Turner Voices Corporate Contributions, 4682
Verizon Fndn Great Lakes Region Grants, 4912
VSA/Metlife Connect All Grants, 4953
Weatherwax Fndn Grants, 5014
Wege Fndn Grants, 5017
Wells Fargo Housing Fndn Grants, 5023
Weyerhaeuser Company Fndn Grants, 5053
Whiting Fndn Grants, 5059
Wisconsin Energy Fndn Grants, 5106

Minnesota
3M Company Arts and Culture Grants, 12
3M Company Environmental Giving Grants, 13
3M Company Health and Human Services Grants, 14
3M Fndn Community Giving Grants, 15
Abelard Fndn East Grants, 87
ACE Charitable Fndn Grants, 111
ADC Fndn Technology Access Grants, 158
AHS Fndn Grants, 208
Albert B. Cuppage Charitable Fndn Grants, 341
Albertson's Charitable Giving Grants, 345
Albert W. Cherne Fndn Grants, 346
Alex Stern Family Fndn Grants, 360
Alliant Energy Fndn Community Grants, 384
Alliant Energy Fndn Hometown Challenge Grants, 385
Andersen Corporate Fndn, 459
Archer Daniels Midland Fndn Grants, 527
Arkema Fndn Science Teachers Program, 563
Arts Midwest Performing Arts Grants, 579
Athwin Fndn Grants, 605
Beim Fndn Grants, 718
Beldon Fund Grants, 720
Best Buy Children's Fndn Twin Cities Minnesota Capital Grants, 753
Better Way Fndn Grants, 754
Blandin Fndn Expand Opportunity Grants, 787
Blandin Fndn Invest Early Grants, 788
Blandin Fndn Itasca County Area Vitality Grants, 789
Blandin Fndn Rural Comm Leadership Grants, 790
Blue Cross Blue Shield of Minnesota Fndn Building Health Equity Together Grants, 793
Blue Cross Blue Shield of Minnesota Fndn - Healthy Children: Growing Up Healthy Grants, 794
Blue Cross Blue Shield of Minnesota Healthy Equity: Public Libraries for Health Grants, 797
Blue Cross Blue Shield of Minnesota Fndn - Healthy Neighborhoods: Connect for Health Challenge Grants, 798
Bridgestone/Firestone Trust Fund Grants, 836
Brunswick Fndn Dollars for Doers Grants, 856
Brunswick Fndn Grants, 857
Bush Fndn Arts & Humanities Grants: Capital Projects, 872
Bush Fndn Arts & Humanities Grants: Short-Term Organizational Support, 873
Bush Fndn Ecological Health Grants, 874
Bush Found Health & Human Services Grants, 875
Bush Fndn Leadership Fellowships, 876
Bush Fndn Medical Fellowships, 877
Bush Fndn Regional Arts Dev Grants, 878
Carl and Eloise Pohlad Family Fndn Grants, 927
Carolyn Fndn Grants, 942
CCF Community Priorities Fund, 961
CenterPointEnergy Minnegasco Grants, 993
Central Minnesota Community Found Grants, 995
CenturyLink Clarke M. Williams Grants, 998
Charity Incorporated Grants, 1035
Cleveland-Cliffs Fndn Grants, 1165
Comcast Fndn Grants, 1235
Community POWER (Partners On Waste Education and Reduction), 1335
ConAgra Foods Community Impact Grants, 1342
ConAgra Foods Nourish Our Comm Grants, 1343
Courage Center Judd Jacobson Memorial Award, 1382
Cummins Fndn Grants, 1415
Dairy Queen Corporate Contributions Grants, 1433
Dean Foods Community Involvement Grants, 1469
Dekko Fndn Grants, 1482
Deluxe Corporation Fndn Grants, 1496
Dollar General Adult Literacy Grants, 1568
Dollar General Family Literacy Grants, 1569
Dollar General Youth Literacy Grants, 1570
Donaldson Fndn Grants, 1574
Duluth-Superior Area Community Grants, 1620
Eaton Charitable Fund Grants, 1647
Edina Realty Fndn Grants, 1656
Edwards Memorial Trust Grants, 1669
Elmer L. and Eleanor J. Andersen Grants, 1687
Emma B. Howe Memorial Fndn Grants, 1700
F.R. Bigelow Fndn Grants, 1781

1160 / Minnesota

Fargo-Moorhead Area Fndn Grants, 1788
Fargo-Moorhead Area Fndn Woman's Grants, 1789
Four Times Fndn Grants, 1914
Gannett Fndn Community Action Grants, 1984
General Mills Fndn Celebrating Communities of Color Grants, 2002
General Mills Fndn Grants, 2003
George A. Hormel Testamentary Trust Grants, 2009
George Family Fndn Grants, 2017
Ginn Fndn Grants, 2056
Graco Fndn Grants, 2111
Grand Rapids Area Community Grants, 2114
Grand Rapids Area Community Fndn Nashwauk Area Endowment Fund Grants, 2115
Grotto Fndn Project Grants, 2166
GTECH Community Involvement Grants, 2171
H.B. Fuller Company Fndn Grants, 2183
Heartland Arts Fund, 2286
Hormel Foods Charitable Trust Grants, 2368
Hormel Fndn Grants, 2369
Hugh J. Andersen Fndn Grants, 2385
I.A. O'Shaughnessy Fndn Grants, 2416
IFP Minnesota Filmmakers Production Grants, 2447
IFP Minnesota McKnight Film Fellowships, 2448
IFP Minnesota McKnight Screen Fellowships, 2449
IFP Minnesota TV Grants, 2450
Initiaive Fndn Inside-Out Grants, 2556
Initiative Fndn Healthy Communities Partnership Grants, 2557
Initiative Fndn Healthy Lakes and Rivers Partnership Grants, 2558
Initiative Fndn Innovation Fund Grants, 2559
Initiative Fndn Minnesota Early Childhood Initiative Grants, 2560
Intergrys Corporation Grants, 2565
James Ford Bell Fndn Grants, 2623
James R. Thorpe Fndn Grants, 2636
Jay and Rose Phillips Family Fndn Grants, 2656
Jerome Fndn Grants, 2667
Jerome Fndn Travel and Study Grants, 2668
John S. and James L. Knight Fndn Communities Grants, 2711
Joyce Fndn Democracy Grants, 2748
Joyce Fndn Employment Grants, 2749
Land O'Lakes Fndn Community Grants, 2859
Land O'Lakes Fndn Dollars for Doers, 2860
Laura Jane Musser Intercultural Harmony Grants, 2862
Laura Jane Musser Rural Arts Grants, 2863
Laura Jane Musser Rural Initiative Grants, 2864
LISC Financial Opportunity Center Social Innovation Fund Grants, 2911
Lockheed Martin Philanthropic Grants, 2918
Luther I. Replogle Fndn Grants, 2945
M3C Fellowships, 2955
Mardag Fndn Grants, 3001
McKnight Fndn Multiservice Grants, 3085
McKnight Fndn Region & Communities Grants, 3086
McKnight Fndn Virginia McKnight Binger Awards in Human Service, 3087
MeadWestvaco Sustainable Communities Grants, 3105
Medtronic Community Link Arts, Civic, and Culture Grants, 3109
Medtronic CommunityLink Education Grants, 3110
Medtronic CommunityLink Health Grants, 3111
Medtronic Comm Link Human Services Grants, 3112
Minneapolis Fndn Community Grants, 3186
Minnesota Small Cities Development Grants, 3187
Minnesota State Arts Board Cultural Community Partnership Grants, 3188
Monsanto America's Farmers Grow Rural Education Grants, 3205
NGA Midwest School Garden Grants, 3407
Northland Fndn Grants, 3506
Northwest Minnesota Asset Building Grants, 3511
Northwest Minnesota Women's Fund Grants, 3512
Northwest Minnesota Fndn Women's Fund Scholarships, 3513
Onan Family Fndn Grants, 3672
Ordean Fndn Grants, 3691
Otto Bremer Fndn Grants, 3713
Patrick and Aimee Butler Family Fndn Community Arts and Humanities Grants, 3747
Patrick and Aimee Butler Family Fndn Community Environment Grants, 3748
Patrick and Aimee Butler Family Fndn Community Human Services Grants, 3749
Patrick and Aimee Butler Family Fndn Community Philanthropy & the Non-Profit Management Grants, 3750
Philanthrofund Fndn Grants, 3874
Piper Jaffray Fndn Communities Giving, 3899
Pohlad Family Fndn, 3928
Prudential Fndn Arts and Culture Grants, 3975
Prudential Fndn Economic Devel Grants, 3976
Prudential Fndn Education Grants, 3977
Rathmann Family Fndn Grants, 4026
RBC Dain Rauscher Fndn Grants, 4031
REI Conservation and Outdoor Rec Grants, 4051
Rochester Area Fndn Grants, 4128
Roger L. and Agnes C. Dell Charitable Grants, 4143
Saint Paul Companies Fndn Grants, 4217
Saint Paul Fndn Community Sharing Grants, 4218
Saint Paul Fndn Grants, 4219
Saint Paul Fndn Lowertown Future Grants, 4220
Saint Paul Fndn Management Improvement Fund Grants, 4221
Saint Paul Fndn SpectrumTrust Grants, 4222
Seagate Technology Corporation Capacity to Care Grants, 4317
Shopko Fndn Community Grants, 4346
Southern Minnesota Initiative Fndn AmeriCorps Leap Grants, 4431
Southern Minnesota Initiative BookStart Grants, 4432
Southern Minnesota Initiative Fndn Community Growth Initiative Grants, 4433
Southern Minnesota Initiative Fndn Home Visiting Grants, 4434
Southern Minnesota Fndn Incentive Grants, 4435
Southern Minnesota Initiative Fndn Youth Explorer Grants, 4436
Southern Minnesota Initiative Fund Grants, 4437
Southwest Initiative Fndn Grants, 4446
Symantec Community Relations and Corporate Philanthropy Grants, 4544
Target Fndn Grants, 4562
TCF Bank Fndn Grants, 4565
Tension Envelope Fndn Grants, 4578
Toro Fndn Grants, 4647
U.S. Bank Fndn Grants, 4686
Union Pacific Community and Civic Grants, 4714
Union Pacific Fndn Health and Human Services Grants, 4715
Viking Children's Fund Grants, 4939
VSA/Metlife Connect All Grants, 4953
WCI Childcare Capacity Grants, 5007
WCI Community Leadership Fellowships, 5008
WCI Community Mobilization Grants, 5009
WCI Family Economic Success Local Grants, 5010
WCI Family Economic Success Regional Grants, 5011
WCI Leadership Development Grants, 5012
WCI Minnesota Beautiful Grants, 5013
Wells Fargo Housing Fndn Grants, 5023
Weyerhaeuser Company Fndn Grants, 5053
Whitney Fndn Grants, 5061

Mississippi

2 Life 18 Fndn Grants, 5
Abelard Fndn East Grants, 87
Adams and Reese LLP Corporate Giving Grants, 147
Albertson's Charitable Giving Grants, 345
Appalachian Regional Comm Asset-Based Development Project Grants, 500
Appalachian Regional Comm Business Development Revolving Loan Fund Grants, 501
Appalachian Regional Comm Community Infrastructure Grants, 502
Appalachian Regional Comm Distressed Counties Grants, 503
Appalachian Regional Comm Education and Training Grants, 504
Appalachian Regional Comm Energy Grants, 505
Appalachian Regional Comm Export and Trade Development Grants, 506
Appalachian Regional Comm Health Care Grants, 507
Appalachian Regional Comm Leadership Development and Capacity Building Grants, 509
Appalachian Regional Comm Telecommunications Grants, 510
Appalachian Regional Comm Tourist Development Grants, 511
Appalachian Regional Comm Transportation and Highways Grants, 512
Archer Daniels Midland Fndn Grants, 527
Assisi Found of Memphis Capital Project Grants, 593
Assisi Fndn of Memphis General Grants, 594
Assisi Fndn of Memphis Mini Grants, 595
BancorpSouth Fndn Grants, 651
Belk Fndn Grants, 721
Boyd Gaming Corporation Contributions Program, 825
Bridgestone/Firestone Trust Fund Grants, 836
Brunswick Fndn Dollars for Doers Grants, 856
Brunswick Fndn Grants, 857
Caesars Fndn Grants, 891
Charles A. Frueauff Fndn Grants, 1037
Charles M. and Mary D. Grant Found Grants, 1050
Cingular Wireless Charitable Contributions, 1134
Circle K Corporation Contributions Grants, 1136
Comcast Fndn Grants, 1235
Comm on Religion in Appalachia Grants, 1238
ConAgra Foods Community Impact Grants, 1342
ConAgra Foods Nourish Our Comm Grants, 1343
CSX Corporate Contributions Grants, 1408
Deuce McAllister Catch 22 Fndn Grants, 1521
DHHS Healthy Tomorrows for Children, 1534
Dollar General Adult Literacy Grants, 1568
Dollar General Family Literacy Grants, 1569
Dollar General Youth Literacy Grants, 1570
Entergy Charitable Fndn Low-Income Initiatives and Solutions Grants, 1711
Entergy Corporation Micro Grants, 1712
Entergy Corp Grants for Arts and Culture, 1713
Entergy Corporation Open Grants for Community Improvement & Enrichment, 1714
Entergy Corp Grants for Healthy Families, 1715
Fndn for the Mid South Community Development Grants, 1897
Fndn for the Mid South Education Grants, 1898
Fndn for Mid South Health & Wellness Grants, 1899
Fndn for Mid So Wealth Building Grants, 1900
Gannett Fndn Community Action Grants, 1984
Georgia-Pacific Fndn Education Grants, 2031
Georgia-Pacific Fndn Enrichment Grants, 2032
Georgia-Pacific Entrepreneurship Grants, 2033
Georgia-Pacific Fndn Environment Grants, 2034
Gil and Dody Weaver Fndn Grants, 2053
Gulf Coast Community Fndn Grants, 2174
Hazen Fndn Public Education Grants, 2269
Joe W. and Dorothy Dorsett Brown Grants, 2684
John S. and James L. Knight Fndn Communities Grants, 2711
Kimberly-Clark Community Grants, 2824
Land O'Lakes Fndn Community Grants, 2859
Land O'Lakes Fndn Dollars for Doers, 2860
Lettie Pate Whitehead Fndn Grants, 2888
Lockheed Martin Philanthropic Grants, 2918
Mary Reynolds Babcock Fndn Grants, 3047
MGM Resorts Fndn Community Grants, 3153
NFWF So Company Power of Flight Grants, 3394
Nissan Fndn Grants, 3444
Nissan Neighbors Grants, 3445
Norfolk Southern Fndn Grants, 3463
Paul Green Fndn Playwrights Fellowship, 3762
Plum Creek Fndn Grants, 3917
Rainbow Fund Grants, 4009
Riley Fndn Grants, 4094
Robert M. Hearin Fndn Grants, 4116
Selby and Richard McRae Fndn Grants, 4334
Southwire Company Grants, 4447
TAC Arts Access Technical Assistance Grants, 4550
TAC Arts Educ Community-Learning Grants, 4552

GEOGRAPHIC INDEX

TAC Arts Education Mini Grants, 4553
TAC Arts Projects Grants, 4554
TAC Rural Arts Project Support Grants, 4555
TAC Technical Assistance Grants, 4556
TAC Touring Arts and Access Grants, 4557
Toro Fndn Grants, 4647
USDA Delta Health Care Services Grants, 4804
Vulcan Materials Company Fndn Grants, 4956
Walton Family Fndn Home Region Grants, 4984
Wells Fargo Housing Fndn Grants, 5023
Weyerhaeuser Company Fndn Grants, 5053
William Robert Baird Charitable Trust Grants, 5093

Missouri
3M Company Arts and Culture Grants, 12
3M Company Environmental Giving Grants, 13
3M Company Health and Human Services Grants, 14
3M Fndn Community Giving Grants, 15
360 Degrees of Giving Grants, 32
Abelard Fndn East Grants, 87
ACF Fndn Grants, 119
Albertson's Charitable Giving Grants, 345
Allen P. and Josephine B. Green Found Grants, 380
Ameren Corporation Community Grants, 418
Anheuser-Busch Fndn Grants, 470
Anthem Blue Cross and Blue Shield Grants, 488
Aquila Corporate Grants, 521
Archer Daniels Midland Fndn Grants, 527
Baptist-Trinity Lutheran Legacy Grants, 663
Boeing Company Contributions Grants, 809
Butler Manufacturing Company Grants, 881
Caesars Fndn Grants, 891
Catherine Manley Gaylord Fndn Grants, 956
Ceil & Michael E. Pulitzer Fndn Grants, 987
CenturyLink Clarke M. Williams Grants, 998
Charles A. Frueauff Fndn Grants, 1037
Charles H. Price II Family Fndn Grants, 1046
Christine and Katharina Pauly Charitable Grants, 1114
Cingular Wireless Charitable Contributions, 1134
Comcast Fndn Grants, 1235
Community Fndn of the Ozarks Grants, 1320
ConAgra Foods Community Impact Grants, 1342
ConAgra Foods Nourish Our Comm Grants, 1343
Cooper Industries Fndn Grants, 1370
Deaconess Fndn Advocacy Grants, 1468
Deluxe Corporation Fndn Grants, 1496
DHHS Healthy Tomorrows for Children, 1534
Dollar General Adult Literacy Grants, 1568
Dollar General Family Literacy Grants, 1569
Dollar General Youth Literacy Grants, 1570
Donaldson Fndn Grants, 1574
Donnie Avery Catches for Kids Fndn, 1578
Ed and Carole Abel Fndn Grants, 1652
Edna Haddad Welfare Trust Fund Scholarships, 1658
FMC Fndn Grants, 1876
Frank & Larue Reynolds Charitable Trust Grants, 1924
Gannett Fndn Community Action Grants, 1984
Gateway Fndn Grants, 1992
General Mills Fndn Grants, 2003
Greater Saint Louis Community Found Grants, 2138
GTECH Community Involvement Grants, 2171
H & R Fndn Grants, 2181
Hall Family Fndn Grants, 2210
Hallmark Corporate Fndn Grants, 2212
Harley Davidson Fndn Grants, 2224
Harry Edison Fndn, 2241
Hatton W. Sumners Fndn for the Study and Teaching of Self Government Grants, 2257
Helen S. Boylan Fndn Grants, 2298
Herbert A. and Adrian W. Woods Grants, 2313
IFP Chicago Production Fund In-Kind Grant, 2446
J.B. Reynolds Fndn Grants, 2592
J.E. and L.E. Mabee Fndn Grants, 2595
John Deere Fndn Grants, 2692
John W. Speas and Effie E. Speas Memorial Trust Grants, 2732
Joseph H. and Florence A. Roblee Found Grants, 2736
Kent D. Steadley and Mary L. Steadley Memorial Trust, 2804
Laclede Gas Charitable Trust Grants, 2848

Land O'Lakes Fndn Community Grants, 2859
Land O'Lakes Fndn Dollars for Doers, 2860
Louetta M. Cowden Fndn Grants, 2922
Louis and Elizabeth Nave Flarsheim Charitable Fndn Grants, 2924
Lumpkin Family Strong Community Leadership Grants, 2944
M3C Fellowships, 2955
Mary E. and Michael Blevins Charitable Grants, 3037
Mid-America Arts Alliance Community Engagement with Touring Artists Grants, 3166
Mid-America Arts Alliance Reg Touring Grants, 3167
Mildred V. Horn Fndn Grants, 3176
Missouri United Methodist Ministry Grants, 3189
Monsanto Access to the Arts Grants, 3204
Monsanto Civic Partnership Grants, 3206
Monsanto Kids Garden Fresh Grants, 3208
Musgrave Fndn Grants, 3231
Nestle Purina PetCare Educational Grants, 3302
Nestle Purina PetCare Pet Related Grants, 3304
Nestle Purina PetCare Support Dog and Police K-9 Organization Grants, 3305
Nestle Purina PetCare Youth Grants, 3306
NGA Midwest School Garden Grants, 3407
Norfolk Southern Fndn Grants, 3463
Oppenstein Brothers Fndn Grants, 3685
Piper Jaffray Fndn Communities Giving, 3899
PNC Ecnomic Development Grants, 3922
PNC Fndn Green Building Grants, 3923
Pott Fndn Grants, 3940
Powell Family Fndn Grants, 3941
QuikTrip Corporate Contributions Grants, 3998
Rachel Alexandra Girls Grants, 4003
REI Conservation and Outdoor Rec Grants, 4051
RRF General Grants, 4170
Ryder System Charitable Fndn Grants, 4191
Safeco Insurance Community Grants, 4203
Saigh Fndn Grants, 4210
Saint Louis Rams Found Community Donations, 4214
Sensient Technologies Fndn Grants, 4337
Shopko Fndn Community Grants, 4346
Solutia Fund Grants, 4402
Sosland Fndn Grants, 4408
St. Louis-Jefferson Solid Waste Management Waste Reduction and Recycling Grants, 4470
State Street Fndn Grants, 4495
Sunderland Fndn Grants, 4527
TAC Arts Access Technical Assistance Grants, 4550
TAC Arts Educ Community-Learning Grants, 4552
TAC Arts Education Mini Grants, 4553
TAC Arts Projects Grants, 4554
TAC Rural Arts Project Support Grants, 4555
TAC Technical Assistance Grants, 4556
TAC Touring Arts and Access Grants, 4557
Taylor S. Abernathy and Patti Harding Abernathy Charitable Trust Grants, 4564
Tension Envelope Fndn Grants, 4578
U.S. Bank Fndn Grants, 4686
Union Pacific Community and Civic Grants, 4714
Union Pacific Fndn Health and Human Services Grants, 4715
USDA Delta Health Care Services Grants, 4804
Victor E. Speas Fndn Grants, 4933
VSA/Mctlife Connect All Grants, 4953
Vulcan Materials Company Fndn Grants, 4956
Weyerhaeuser Company Fndn Grants, 5053
Wilbur and Patsy Bradley Family Grants, 5066
William G. McGowan Charitable Fund Grants, 5084
William J. Brace Charitable Trust, 5088
Women's Fndn Greater Kansas City Grants, 5111
Yellow Corporate Fndn Grants, 5126

Montana
Abelard Fndn West Grants, 88
Albertson's Charitable Giving Grants, 345
Archer Daniels Midland Fndn Grants, 527
Avista Fndn Grants, 624
Brainerd Fndn Grants, 831
Bullitt Fndn Grants, 862
CenturyLink Clarke M. Williams Grants, 998

Charles M. Bair Family Trust Grants, 1051
Charlotte Martin Fndn Youth Grants, 1057
ConocoPhillips Fndn Grants, 1354
ConocoPhillips Grants, 1355
Dean Foods Community Involvement Grants, 1469
Dennis and Phyllis Washington Grants, 1498
DHHS Healthy Tomorrows for Children, 1534
DOJ Rural Domestic Violence and Child Victimization Enforcement Grants, 1562
Foster Fndn Grants, 1888
Four Times Fndn Grants, 1914
Gannett Fndn Community Action Grants, 1984
General Mills Fndn Grants, 2003
Homer A. Scott and Mildred S. Scott Grants, 2350
Knight Fndn Grants - Montana, 2830
Liz Claiborne and Art Ortenberg Grants, 2914
M.J. Murdock Charitable Trust General Grants, 2954
Montana Arts Council Cultural and Aesthetic Project Grants, 3209
Montana Community Big Sky LIFT Grants, 3210
Montana Community Fndn Grants, 3211
Montana Community Found Women's Grants, 3212
NFWF Columbia Basin Water Transactions Grants, 3366
NFWF Columbia River Estuarine Coastal Fund Grants, 3367
NFWF One Fly Conservation Partnerships, 3382
Paul G. Allen Family Fndn Grants, 3759
Piper Jaffray Fndn Communities Giving, 3899
Plum Creek Fndn Grants, 3917
Pride Fndn Grants, 3958
RBC Dain Rauscher Fndn Grants, 4031
REI Conservation and Outdoor Rec Grants, 4051
Ruth and Vernon Taylor Fndn Grants, 4177
Sands Memorial Fndn Grants, 4256
Shopko Fndn Community Grants, 4346
Social Justice Fund Northwest Criminal Justice Giving Project Grants, 4394
Social Justice Fund Northwest Economic Justice Giving Project Grants, 4395
Social Justice Fund Northwest Environmental Justice Giving Project Grants, 4396
Social Justice Fund Northwest General Grants, 4397
Social Justice Fund Northwest LGBTQ Giving Project Grants, 4398
Social Justice Fund Northwest Montana Giving Project Grants, 4399
Steele-Reese Fndn Grants, 4498
Sunderland Fndn Grants, 4527
U.S. Bank Fndn Grants, 4686
Union Pacific Community and Civic Grants, 4714
Union Pacific Fndn Health and Human Services Grants, 4715
Wells Fargo Housing Fndn Grants, 5023
William C. Kenney Watershed Protection Fndn Ecosystem Grants, 5079

Nebraska
3M Company Arts and Culture Grants, 12
3M Company Environmental Giving Grants, 13
3M Company Health and Human Services Grants, 14
3M Fndn Community Giving Grants, 15
Abelard Fndn West Grants, 88
Abel Fndn Grants, 90
ADC Fndn Technology Access Grants, 158
Albertson's Charitable Giving Grants, 345
Anne Thorne Weaver Family Fndn Grants, 478
Aquila Corporate Grants, 521
Archer Daniels Midland Fndn Grants, 527
Brunswick Fndn Dollars for Doers Grants, 856
Brunswick Fndn Grants, 857
CenturyLink Clarke M. Williams Grants, 998
Charles A. Frueauff Fndn Grants, 1037
Clarcor Fndn Grants, 1148
Cooper Fndn Grants, 1369
Dean Foods Community Involvement Grants, 1469
DOJ Rural Domestic Violence and Child Victimization Enforcement Grants, 1562
Dollar General Adult Literacy Grants, 1568
Dollar General Family Literacy Grants, 1569
Dollar General Youth Literacy Grants, 1570

1162 / Nebraska

Ethel S. Abbott Charitable Fndn Grants, 1760
GTECH Community Involvement Grants, 2171
Hatton W. Sumners Fndn for the Study and Teaching of Self Government Grants, 2257
Hormel Family Fndn Business Plan Award, 2367
Hormel Foods Charitable Trust Grants, 2368
IFP Chicago Production Fund In-Kind Grant, 2446
Land O'Lakes Fndn Community Grants, 2859
Land O'Lakes Fndn Dollars for Doers, 2860
Lied Fndn Trust Grants, 2900
Lincoln Financial Group Fndn Grants, 2906
Mid-America Arts Alliance Community Engagement with Touring Artists Grants, 3166
Mid-America Arts Alliance Reg Touring Grants, 3167
Nationwide Insurance Fndn Grants, 3285
Nestle Purina PetCare Educational Grants, 3302
Nestle Purina PetCare Pet Related Grants, 3304
Nestle Purina PetCare Support Dog and Police K-9 Organization Grants, 3305
Nestle Purina PetCare Youth Grants, 3306
NGA Midwest School Garden Grants, 3407
Peter Kiewit Fndn General Grants, 3845
Peter Kiewit Fndn Neighborhood Grants, 3846
Peter Kiewit Fndn Small Grants, 3847
Phelps County Community Fndn Grants, 3870
Piper Jaffray Fndn Communities Giving, 3899
Principal Financial Group Fndn Grants, 3966
QuikTrip Corporate Contributions Grants, 3998
RBC Dain Rauscher Fndn Grants, 4031
Shopko Fndn Community Grants, 4346
Square D Fndn Grants, 4464
Sunderland Fndn Grants, 4527
Toro Fndn Grants, 4647
U.S. Bank Fndn Grants, 4686
Union Pacific Community and Civic Grants, 4714
Union Pacific Fndn Health and Human Services Grants, 4715
Waitt Family Fndn Grants, 4973
Wells Fargo Housing Fndn Grants, 5023
Woods Charitable Fund Grants, 5114

Nevada

Abelard Fndn West Grants, 88
ACE Charitable Fndn Grants, 111
Albertson's Charitable Giving Grants, 345
Amerigroup Fndn Grants, 452
Andre Agassi Charitable Fndn Grants, 461
Anthem Blue Cross and Blue Shield Grants, 488
ARCO Fndn Education Grants, 528
Boeing Company Contributions Grants, 809
Boyd Gaming Corporation Contributions Program, 825
Bridgestone/Firestone Trust Fund Grants, 836
Business Bank of Nevada Community Grants, 879
Caesars Fndn Grants, 891
Carrier Corporation Contributions Grants, 946
Circle K Corporation Contributions Grants, 1136
Cord Fndn Grants, 1372
Dean Foods Community Involvement Grants, 1469
Dermody Properties Fndn Capstone Award, 1516
Dermody Properties Fndn Grants, 1517
DHHS Healthy Tomorrows for Children, 1534
DOJ Rural Domestic Violence and Child Victimization Enforcement Grants, 1562
Donald W. Reynolds Fndn Charitable Food Distribution Grants, 1575
Donald W. Reynolds Fndn Children's Discovery Initiative Grants, 1576
E.L. Wiegand Fndn Grants, 1639
Frances C. and William P. Smallwood Grants, 1918
Gannett Fndn Community Action Grants, 1984
Greenspun Family Fndn Grants, 2156
Lied Fndn Trust Grants, 2900
MeadWestvaco Sustainable Communities Grants, 3105
MGM Resorts Fndn Community Grants, 3153
Nevada Arts Council Circuit Rider Grants, 3308
Nevada Arts Council Folklife Apprenticeships, 3309
Nevada Arts Council Folklife Opps Grants, 3310
Nevada Arts Council Heritage Awards, 3311
Nevada Arts Council Jackpot Grants, 3312
Nevada Arts Council Learning Grants, 3313
Nevada Arts Council Professional Development Grants, 3314
Nevada Arts Council Residency Express Grants, 3315
Nevada Community Fndn Grants, 3316
PacifiCare Fndn Grants, 3725
Pinnacle Entertainment Fndn Grants, 3893
Piper Jaffray Fndn Communities Giving, 3899
REI Conservation and Outdoor Rec Grants, 4051
RR Donnelley Community Grants, 4168
Sands Fndn Crisis Fund Grants, 4254
Sands Fndn Grants, 4255
Sierra Fund Grants, 4352
Southwest Gas Corporation Fndn Grants, 4445
Tiger Woods Fndn Grants, 4634
U.S. Bank Fndn Grants, 4686
Union Pacific Community and Civic Grants, 4714
Union Pacific Fndn Health and Human Services Grants, 4715
US Airways Community Contributions, 4788
US Airways Education Fndn Grants, 4790
Wells Fargo Housing Fndn Grants, 5023
Wilburforce Fndn Grants, 5067
William C. Kenney Watershed Protection Fndn Ecosystem Grants, 5079

New Hampshire

Abelard Fndn East Grants, 87
Agnes M. Lindsay Trust Grants, 203
Agway Fndn Grants, 205
Albertson's Charitable Giving Grants, 345
Alexander Eastman Fndn Grants, 355
Alexander H. Bright Charitable Trust Grants, 358
American Rivers Community-Based Restoration Program River Grants, 444
Anheuser-Busch Fndn Grants, 470
Anthem Blue Cross and Blue Shield Grants, 488
Barker Fndn Grants, 668
Barnes Group Fndn Grants, 672
Bay and Paul Fndns, Inc Grants, 692
BJ's Charitable Fndn Grants, 777
BJ's Wholesale Clubs Local Charitable Giving, 778
Carlisle Fndn Grants, 931
Ceres Fndn Grants, 999
Charles A. Frueauff Fndn Grants, 1037
Chase Paymentech Corporate Giving Grants, 1059
Clowes Fund Grants, 1177
Cogswell Benevolent Trust Grants, 1198
Comcast Fndn Grants, 1235
ConAgra Foods Nourish Our Comm Grants, 1343
Davis Conservation Fndn Grants, 1461
DHHS Healthy Tomorrows for Children, 1534
Dorr Fndn Grants, 1591
Edna McConnell Clark Fndn Grants, 1659
Entergy Charitable Fndn Low-Income Initiatives and Solutions Grants, 1711
Entergy Corporation Micro Grants, 1712
Entergy Corp Grants for Arts and Culture, 1713
Entergy Corporation Open Grants for Community Improvement & Enrichment, 1714
Entergy Corp Grants for Healthy Families, 1715
Fields Pond Fndn Grants, 1807
Fndn for Seacoast Health Grants, 1895
Fuller Fndn Grants, 1974
George I. Alden Trust Grants, 2023
Gladys Brooks Fndn Grants, 2059
GTECH Community Involvement Grants, 2171
Hannaford Charitable Fndn Grants, 2222
Haymarket People's Fund Sustaining Grants, 2267
Haymarket Urgent Response Grants, 2268
Hilda and Preston Davis Fndn Grants, 2322
J. Willard Marriott, Jr. Fndn Grants, 2610
Jane's Trust Grants, 2639
Jessie B. Cox Charitable Trust Grants, 2670
Joukowsky Family Fndn Grants, 2743
KeySpan Fndn Grants, 2821
Lincoln Financial Group Fndn Grants, 2906
Linden Fndn Grants, 2908
McLean Contributionship Grants, 3088
Merck Family Fund Urban Farming and Youth Leadership Grants, 3119

GEOGRAPHIC INDEX

New Hampshire Charitable Fndn Grants, 3325
NHSCA Artist Residencies in Schools Grants, 3423
NHSCA Arts in Health Care Project Grants, 3424
NHSCA Conservation License Plate Grants, 3425
NHSCA Cultural Facilities Grants: Barrier Free Access for All, 3426
NHSCA General Project Grants, 3427
NHSCA Operating Grants, 3428
NHSCA Traditional Arts Apprenticeships, 3429
NHSCA Youth Arts Project Grants: For Extended Arts Learning, 3430
Norfolk Southern Fndn Grants, 3463
Northeast Utilities Fndn Grants, 3498
Norwin S. and Elizabeth N. Bean Grants, 3515
Oleonda Jameson Trust Grants, 3667
Orchard Fndn Grants, 3690
Price Chopper's Golub Fndn Grants, 3950
Price Chopper's Golub Fndn Two-Year Health Care Scholarship, 3951
Putnam Fndn Grants, 3991
Robert and Joan Dircks Fndn Grants, 4104
Rogers Family Fndn Grants, 4144
S. Spencer Scott Fund Grants, 4202
Salmon Fndn Grants, 4225
Shaw's Supermarkets Donations, 4342
State Street Fndn Grants, 4495
Sunoco Fndn Grants, 4530
Sweet Water Trust Grants, 4541
Texas Instruments Arts and Culture Grants, 4596
Texas Instruments Civic and Business Grants, 4597
Texas Instruments Fndn Arts and Culture Grants, 4599
Verizon Wireless Hopeline Grants, 4927
Weyerhaeuser Company Fndn Grants, 5053
Yawkey Fndn Grants, 5125

New Jersey

3M Company Arts and Culture Grants, 12
3M Company Environmental Giving Grants, 13
3M Company Health and Human Services Grants, 14
200 Club of Mercer County Grants, 30
1772 Fndn Fellowships, 36
Abbott Fund Access to Health Care Grants, 80
Abbott Fund Community Grants, 81
Abbott Fund Global AIDS Care Grants, 82
Abbott Fund Science Education Grants, 83
Abelard Fndn East Grants, 87
ACE Charitable Fndn Grants, 111
Aetna Fndn Regional Health Grants, 187
African American Fund of New Jersey Grants, 192
AHS Fndn Grants, 208
Albertson's Charitable Giving Grants, 345
Ambrose and Ida Fredrickson Fndn Grants, 414
American Rivers Community-Based Restoration Program River Grants, 444
Anheuser-Busch Fndn Grants, 470
Ansell, Zaro, Grimm & Aaron Fndn Grants, 487
Archer Daniels Midland Fndn Grants, 527
Arkema Fndn Science Teachers Program, 563
Bay and Paul Fndns, Inc Grants, 692
Bayer Fndn Grants, 696
BJ's Charitable Fndn Grants, 777
BJ's Wholesale Clubs Local Charitable Giving, 778
Blanche and Irving Laurie Fndn Grants, 784
Bodman Fndn Grants, 807
Boyd Gaming Corporation Contributions Program, 825
Bread and Roses Community Fund Grants and Scholarships, 832
Bristol-Myers Squibb Fndn Community Initiatives Grants, 840
Bunbury Company Grants, 863
Caesars Fndn Grants, 891
Campbell Soup Fndn Grants, 916
Cape Branch Fndn Grants, 919
Carl C. Icahn Fndn Grants, 929
CenturyLink Clarke M. Williams Grants, 998
Charles A. Frueauff Fndn Grants, 1037
Chatham Athletic Fndn Grants, 1060
Comcast Fndn Grants, 1235
ConocoPhillips Fndn Grants, 1354
ConocoPhillips Grants, 1355

GEOGRAPHIC INDEX

Countess Moira Charitable Fndn Grants, 1381
CSX Corporate Contributions Grants, 1408
Danellie Fndn Grants, 1442
Dean Foods Community Involvement Grants, 1469
Deluxe Corporation Fndn Grants, 1496
DHHS Healthy Tomorrows for Children, 1534
Dollar General Adult Literacy Grants, 1568
Dollar General Family Literacy Grants, 1569
Dollar General Youth Literacy Grants, 1570
E.J. Grassmann Trust Grants, 1638
Eaton Charitable Fund Grants, 1647
Edward W. and Stella C. Van Houten Memorial Fund Grants, 1670
Emerson Kampen Fndn Grants, 1696
F.M. Kirby Fndn Grants, 1780
FirstEnergy Fndn Community Grants, 1819
FirstEnergy Fndn Math, Science, and Technology Education Grants, 1820
Fluor Fndn Grants, 1875
FMC Fndn Grants, 1876
Frances L. and Edwin L. Cummings Memorial Fund Grants, 1919
Frank S. Flowers Fndn Grants, 1935
Gannett Fndn Community Action Grants, 1984
General Mills Fndn Grants, 2003
George A Ohl Jr. Fndn Grants, 2012
George I. Alden Trust Grants, 2023
Georgia-Pacific Fndn Education Grants, 2031
Georgia-Pacific Fndn Enrichment Grants, 2032
Georgia-Pacific Entrepreneurship Grants, 2033
Georgia-Pacific Fndn Environment Grants, 2034
Geraldine R. Dodge Fndn Arts Grants, 2040
Geraldine R. Dodge Found Environment Grants, 2041
Geraldine R. Dodge Fndn Media Grants, 2042
Gladys Brooks Fndn Grants, 2059
GTECH Community Involvement Grants, 2171
Hackett Fndn Grants, 2188
Healthcare Fndn of New Jersey Grants, 2280
Hilda and Preston Davis Fndn Grants, 2322
Horizon Fndn for New Jersey Grants, 2364
Horizon Fndn Grants, 2365
Independence Community Fndn Community Quality of Life Grant, 2525
Independence Community Fndn Education, Culture & Arts Grant, 2526
Independence Community Fndn Neighborhood Renewal Grants, 2527
John and Margaret Post Fndn Grants, 2686
Johnson & Johnson Comm Health Care Grants, 2717
Joukowsky Family Fndn Grants, 2743
JP Morgan Chase Arts and Culture Grants, 2752
JP Morgan Chase Community Devel Grants, 2753
Kessler Found Community Employment Grants, 2814
Kessler Hurricane Sandy Emergency Grants, 2815
Liz Claiborne Fndn Grants, 2915
Lockheed Martin Philanthropic Grants, 2918
Lydia deForest Charitable Trust Grants, 2946
Mary Owen Borden Fndn Grants, 3046
MeadWestvaco Sustainable Communities Grants, 3105
Mercedes-Benz USA Corporate Contributions, 3118
Merck Family Fund Urban Farming and Youth Leadership Grants, 3119
Meyer and Pepa Gold Family Fndn Grants, 3138
Mid Atlantic Arts Fndn American Masterpieces Grants, 3169
Mid Atlantic Arts Found ArtsConnect Grants, 3170
Mid Atlantic Arts Fndn Folk Arts Outreach Project Grants, 3171
Modest Needs Hurricane Sandy Relief Grants, 3198
Motorola Fndn Grants, 3221
Natalie W. Furniss Charitable Trust Grants, 3244
New Jersey Center for Hispanic Policy, Research and Development Entrepreneurship Grants, 3326
New Jersey Center for Hispanic Policy, Research and Development Governor's Fellowships, 3327
New Jersey Center for Hispanic Policy, Research and Development Immigration Integration Grants, 3328
New Jersey Center for Hispanic Policy, Research and Development Innovative Initiatives Grants, 3329
New Jersey Center for Hispanic Policy, Research and Development Workforce Grants, 3330
New Jersey Office of Faith Based Initiatives Creating Wealth Through Asset Building Grants, 3331
New Jersey Office of Faith Based Initiatives English as a Second Language Grants, 3332
New Jersey Office of Faith Based Initiatives Service to Seniors Grants, 3333
NFWF Delaware Estuary Watershed Grants, 3371
NJSCA Arts Project Support, 3446
NJSCA Financial and Institutional Stabilization Grants, 3447
NJSCA Folk Arts Apprenticeships, 3448
NJSCA General Program Support Grants, 3449
NJSCA Projects Serving Artists Grants, 3450
Norfolk Southern Fndn Grants, 3463
OceanFirst Fndn Grants, 3636
PennPAT Fee-Support Grants for Presenters, 3812
PennPAT New Directions Grants for Presenters, 3813
PNC Charitable Trust and Fndn Grants, 3921
PNC Ecnomic Development Grants, 3922
PNC Fndn Green Building Grants, 3923
PNC Fndn Grow Up Great Grants, 3924
Princeton Area Community Fndn Fund for Women and Girls Grants, 3962
Princeton Area Community Fndn Greater Mercer Grants, 3963
Princeton Area Community Fndn Thomas George Artists Fund Grants, 3965
Prudential Fndn Arts and Culture Grants, 3975
Prudential Fndn Economic Devel Grants, 3976
Prudential Fndn Education Grants, 3977
PSEG Corporate Contributions Grants, 3979
PSEG Environmental Education Grants, 3980
Qualcomm Grants, 3993
Rainbow Academy Fndn Grants, 4006
Rainbow Media Holdings Corporate Giving, 4010
REI Conservation and Outdoor Rec Grants, 4051
Richard Davoud Donchian Fndn Grants, 4080
Russell Berrie Fndn Grants, 4175
Ruth and Vernon Taylor Fndn Grants, 4177
RWJF New Jersey Health Initiatives Grants, 4187
Schumann Fund for New Jersey Grants, 4311
State Street Fndn Grants, 4495
Subaru Adopt a School Garden Grants, 4517
Subaru of America Fndn Grants, 4518
Sunoco Fndn Grants, 4530
Tyler Aaron Bookman Memorial Grants, 4684
Verizon New Jersey Check into Literacy Grants, 4918
Verizon Wireless Hopeline Grants, 4927
Wells Fargo Housing Fndn Grants, 5023
Weyerhaeuser Company Fndn Grants, 5053
Williams Companies Fndn Grants, 5095
William T. Grant Fndn Youth Service Improvement Grants, 5096

New Mexico
Abeles Fndn Grants, 89
ADC Fndn Technology Access Grants, 158
Albertson's Charitable Giving Grants, 345
Albuquerque Community Fndn Grants, 348
Amerigroup Fndn Grants, 452
BBVA Compass Fndn Charitable Grants, 703
Beim Fndn Grants, 718
Boeing Company Contributions Grants, 809
Cabot Corporation Fndn Grants, 887
CenturyLink Clarke M. Williams Grants, 998
Charles A. Frueauff Fndn Grants, 1037
Circle K Corporation Contributions Grants, 1136
Comcast Fndn Grants, 1235
ConAgra Foods Community Impact Grants, 1342
ConAgra Foods Nourish Our Comm Grants, 1343
Cudd Fndn Grants, 1410
Daniels Fund Grants, 1443
Dean Foods Community Involvement Grants, 1469
DOJ Rural Domestic Violence and Child Victimization Enforcement Grants, 1562
Dollar General Adult Literacy Grants, 1568
Dollar General Family Literacy Grants, 1569
Dollar General Youth Literacy Grants, 1570
Four Times Fndn Grants, 1914
Frost Fndn Grants, 1966
GenCorp Fndn Grants, 1998
General Mills Fndn Grants, 2003
Gil and Dody Weaver Fndn Grants, 2053
GTECH Community Involvement Grants, 2171
Hatton W. Sumners Fndn for the Study and Teaching of Self Government Grants, 2257
Intel Community Grants, 2562
J.E. and L.E. Mabee Fndn Grants, 2595
J. F. Maddox Fndn Grants, 2597
Lockheed Martin Philanthropic Grants, 2918
Lumpkin Family Strong Community Leadership Grants, 2944
McCune Charitable Fndn Grants, 3077
Needmor Fund Grants, 3289
New Mexico Women's Fndn Grants, 3335
PNM Power Up Grants, 3925
PNM Reduce Your Use Grants, 3926
REI Conservation and Outdoor Rec Grants, 4051
Santa Fe Community root2fruit Santa Fe, 4289
Santa Fe Community Seasonal Grants-Fall Cycle, 4290
Santa Fe Community Fndn Seasonal Grants-Spring Cycle, 4291
Santa Fe Community Fndn Special and Urgent Needs Grants, 4292
Stocker Fndn Grants, 4507
U.S. Bank Fndn Grants, 4686
Union Pacific Community and Civic Grants, 4714
Union Pacific Fndn Health and Human Services Grants, 4715
USDA Individual Water and Waste Water Grants, 4817
Vulcan Materials Company Fndn Grants, 4956
Wells Fargo Housing Fndn Grants, 5023
Weyerhaeuser Company Fndn Grants, 5053
Wilburforce Fndn Grants, 5067
William C. Kenney Watershed Protection Fndn Ecosystem Grants, 5079

New York
3M Company Arts and Culture Grants, 12
3M Company Environmental Giving Grants, 13
3M Company Health and Human Services Grants, 14
3M Fndn Community Giving Grants, 15
21st Century ILGWU Heritage Fund Grants, 20
100 Mile Man Fndn Grants, 27
100 Women in Hedge Funds Fndn Grants, 28
300th Quincy Block Association Grants, 31
1772 Fndn Fellowships, 36
Abbott Fund Access to Health Care Grants, 80
Abbott Fund Community Grants, 81
Abbott Fund Global AIDS Care Grants, 82
Abbott Fund Science Education Grants, 83
Abel and Sophia Sheng Charitable Grants, 86
Abelard Fndn East Grants, 87
ACE Charitable Fndn Grants, 111
A Charitable Fndn Grants, 126
Achelis Fndn Grants, 127
Adams Fndn Grants, 155
Adam Shikiar Fndn Grants, 156
AEGON Transamerica Arts & Culture Grants, 176
AEGON Transamerica Fndn Civic and Community Grants, 177
AEGON Transamerica Fndn Health and Welfare Grants, 179
Aetna Fndn Regional Health Grants, 187
Alfred P. Sloan Fndn Civic Initiatives, 368
Alfred P. Sloan Fndn Public Service Awards, 369
Allyn Fndn Grants, 392
Altman Fndn Health Care Grants, 397
Altman Fndn Strengthening Communities Grants, 398
American Express Charitable Fund Grants, 429
American Rivers Community-Based Restoration Program River Grants, 444
Amerigroup Fndn Grants, 452
AmerUs Group Charitable Fndn, 455
Anheuser-Busch Fndn Grants, 470
Appalachian Regional Comm Asset-Based Development Project Grants, 500
Appalachian Regional Comm Business Development Revolving Loan Fund Grants, 501

1164 / New York

Appalachian Regional Comm Community Infrastructure Grants, 502
Appalachian Regional Comm Distressed Counties Grants, 503
Appalachian Regional Comm Education and Training Grants, 504
Appalachian Regional Comm Energy Grants, 505
Appalachian Regional Comm Export and Trade Development Grants, 506
Appalachian Regional Comm Health Care Grants, 507
Appalachian Reg Comm Housing Grants, 508
Appalachian Regional Comm Leadership Development and Capacity Building Grants, 509
Appalachian Regional Comm Telecommunications Grants, 510
Appalachian Regional Comm Tourist Development Grants, 511
Appalachian Regional Comm Transportation and Highways Grants, 512
Aratani Fndn Grants, 523
Archer Daniels Midland Fndn Grants, 527
Arkell Hall Fndn Grants, 562
Arkema Fndn Science Teachers Program, 563
ARS Fndn Grants, 568
Arthur and Rochelle Belfer Fndn Grants, 570
AXA Fndn Scholarships, 629
Banfi Vintners Fndn Grants, 653
Barker Welfare Fndn Grants, 669
Bay and Paul Fndns, Inc Grants, 692
Bayer Fndn Grants, 696
Bernard F. and Alva B. Gimbel Fndn Grants, 740
BJ's Charitable Fndn Grants, 777
BJ's Wholesale Clubs Local Charitable Giving, 778
Bodman Fndn Grants, 807
Booth Ferris Fndn Grants, 816
Bristol-Myers Squibb Fndn Community Initiatives Grants, 840
Brooklyn Benevolent Society Grants, 847
Brooklyn Community Caring Neighbors Grants, 848
Brooklyn Community Fndn Community Arts for All Grants, 849
Brooklyn Community Fndn Community Development Grants, 850
Brooklyn Community Fndn Education and Youth Achievement Grants, 851
Brooklyn Community Fndn Green Communities Grants, 852
Brown Rudnick Charitable Relationship Grants, 855
Business Wire Literacy Initiative, 880
CarEth Fndn Grants, 924
Carl C. Icahn Fndn Grants, 929
Carnahan-Jackson Fndn Grants, 939
Carrier Corporation Contributions Grants, 946
Ceil & Michael E. Pulitzer Fndn Grants, 987
Central New York Community Fndn Grants, 996
CenturyLink Clarke M. Williams Grants, 998
Ceres Fndn Grants, 999
Chapman Family Charitable Trust Grants, 1034
Charles A. Frueauff Fndn Grants, 1037
Charles Hayden Fndn Grants, 1048
Chautauqua Region Community Found Grants, 1062
Chesapeake Bay Trust Fisheries and Headwaters Grants, 1070
Cingular Wireless Charitable Contributions, 1134
Cisco Systems Fndn San Jose Community Grants, 1137
Clark Fndn Grants, 1157
Community Found for Greater Buffalo Grants, 1247
Con Edison Corporate Giving Arts and Culture Grants, 1344
Con Edison Corporate Giving Civic Grants, 1345
Con Edison Corporate Community Grants, 1346
Constance Saltonstall Found for the Arts Grants, 1361
Cooper Industries Fndn Grants, 1370
Countess Moira Charitable Fndn Grants, 1381
Cowles Charitable Trust Grants, 1392
Cranston Fndn Grants, 1395
Credit Suisse First Boston Fndn Grants, 1397
CSX Corporate Contributions Grants, 1408
Cummins Fndn Grants, 1415
Daisy Marquis Jones Fndn Grants, 1434

Dammann Fund Grants, 1439
Davenport-Hatch Fndn Grants, 1448
David Geffen Fndn Grants, 1452
Dean Foods Community Involvement Grants, 1469
Deluxe Corporation Fndn Grants, 1496
DeMatteis Family Fndn Grants, 1497
Dolan Fndn Grants, 1563
Dollar General Adult Literacy Grants, 1568
Dollar General Family Literacy Grants, 1569
Dollar General Youth Literacy Grants, 1570
Dorothy G. Griffin Charitable Found Grants, 1588
Dorr Fndn Grants, 1591
Dyson Fndn Emergency Fund Grants, 1631
Dyson Fndn Management Assistance Program Mini-Grants, 1632
Dyson Found Mid-Hudson Philanthropy Grants, 1633
Dyson Fndn Mid-Hudson Valley Faith-Based Organization Grants, 1634
Dyson Fndn Mid-Hudson Valley General Operating Support Grants, 1635
Dyson Fndn Mid-Hudson Valley Project Support Grants, 1636
Dyson Fndn Nonprofit Strategic Restructuring Initiative Grants, 1637
E.L. Wiegand Fndn Grants, 1639
Eaton Charitable Fund Grants, 1647
Edith and Francis Mulhall Achilles Grants, 1657
Edward and Ellen Roche Relief Fndn Grants, 1663
Edward S. Moore Fndn Grants, 1668
Emma A. Sheafer Charitable Trust Grants, 1699
Emma J. Adams Memorial Fund Grants, 1702
Entergy Charitable Fndn Low-Income Initiatives and Solutions Grants, 1711
Entergy Corporation Micro Grants, 1712
Entergy Corp Grants for Arts and Culture, 1713
Entergy Corporation Open Grants for Community Improvement & Enrichment, 1714
Entergy Corp Grants for Healthy Families, 1715
Eugene M. Lang Fndn Grants, 1764
Fan Fox and Leslie R. Samuels Fndn Grants, 1786
Feldman Fndn Grants, 1801
Fields Pond Fndn Grants, 1807
Fitzpatrick, Cella, Harper & Scinto Pro Bono, 1836
Fluor Fndn Grants, 1875
FMC Fndn Grants, 1876
Frances L. and Edwin L. Cummings Memorial Fund Grants, 1919
Frederick McDonald Trust Grants, 1946
Fred L. Emerson Fndn Grants, 1949
Fund for the City of New York Grants, 1978
G.A. Ackermann Memorial Fund Grants, 1981
Gannett Fndn Community Action Grants, 1984
Gebbie Fndn Grants, 1995
General Mills Fndn Grants, 2003
George F. Baker Trust Grants, 2016
George I. Alden Trust Grants, 2023
Georgia-Pacific Fndn Education Grants, 2031
Georgia-Pacific Fndn Enrichment Grants, 2032
Georgia-Pacific Entrepreneurship Grants, 2033
Georgia-Pacific Fndn Environment Grants, 2034
Gladys Brooks Fndn Grants, 2059
Greenwall Fndn Arts and Humanities Grants, 2157
GTECH Community Involvement Grants, 2171
Gumdrop Books Librarian Scholarships, 2179
H. Schaffer Fndn Grants, 2187
Hackett Fndn Grants, 2188
Hagedorn Fund Grants, 2207
Hannaford Charitable Fndn Grants, 2222
Harry S. Black and Allon Fuller Fund Grants, 2243
Hazen Fndn Public Education Grants, 2269
Helena Rubinstein Fndn Grants, 2292
Herman Goldman Fndn Grants, 2317
Hilda and Preston Davis Fndn Grants, 2322
Hilfiger Family Fndn Grants, 2323
Hirtzel Memorial Fndn Grants, 2332
Homer C. and Martha W. Gutchess Fndn Grants, 2351
Howard and Bush Fndn Grants, 2374
HRF Hudson River Improvement Grants, 2378
HRF New York City Environmental Grants for Newton Creek, 2379

Huntington Arts Council Arts-in-Education, 2400
Huntington Arts Council Decentralization Community Arts Grants, 2401
Huntington Arts Council JP Morgan Chase Artist Reach Out Grants, 2402
Huntington Arts Council JP Morgan Chase Organization/Stabilization Regrants, 2403
IFP New York State Council on the Arts Electronic Media and Film Program Distribution Grants, 2451
IIE Western Union Family Scholarships, 2462
Independence Community Fndn Community Quality of Life Grant, 2525
Independence Community Fndn Education, Culture & Arts Grant, 2526
Independence Community Fndn Neighborhood Renewal Grants, 2527
J.M. Kaplan Fund City Life Grants, 2601
James H. Cummings Fndn Grants, 2626
James J. McCann Charitable Trust and McCann Fndn, Inc Grants, 2631
Jean and Louis Dreyfus Fndn Grants, 2658
Jerome Fndn Grants, 2667
Jewish Women's Fndn of New York Grants, 2677
John R. Oishei Fndn Grants, 2709
Joseph Alexander Fndn Grants, 2734
Josephine Goodyear Fndn Grants, 2738
Joukowsky Family Fndn Grants, 2743
JP Morgan Chase Arts and Culture Grants, 2752
JP Morgan Chase Community Devel Grants, 2753
KeyBank Fndn Grants, 2820
KeySpan Fndn Grants, 2821
Komen Greater NYC Clinical Research Enrollment Grants, 2834
Komen Greater NYC Community Breast Health Grants, 2835
Komen Greater NYC Small Grants, 2836
Laura L. Adams Fndn Grants, 2865
Lily Auchincloss Fndn Grants, 2904
Lily Palmer Fry Memorial Trust Grants, 2905
Liz Claiborne Fndn Grants, 2915
Lockheed Martin Philanthropic Grants, 2918
Long Island Community Fndn Grants, 2920
Louis R. Cappelli Fndn Grants, 2926
Lumpkin Family Strong Community Leadership Grants, 2944
M.B. and Edna Zale Fndn Grants, 2950
Margaret L. Wendt Fndn Grants, 3004
Marie C. and Joseph C. Wilson Fndn Rochester Small Grants, 3006
Mary Duke Biddle Fndn Grants, 3036
Max A. Adler Charitable Fndn Grants, 3065
MeadWestvaco Sustainable Communities Grants, 3105
Merck Family Fund Urban Farming and Youth Leadership Grants, 3119
Mertz Gilmore NYC Communities Grants, 3126
Mertz Gilmore Fndn NYC Dance Grants, 3127
Metzger-Price Fund Grants, 3137
Meyer and Pepa Gold Family Fndn Grants, 3138
Mid Atlantic Arts Fndn American Masterpieces Grants, 3169
Mid Atlantic Arts Found ArtsConnect Grants, 3170
Mid Atlantic Arts Fndn Folk Arts Outreach Project Grants, 3171
Milton and Sally Avery Arts Fndn Grants, 3183
Mizuho USA Fndn Grants, 3192
Modest Needs Hurricane Sandy Relief Grants, 3198
Nationwide Insurance Fndn Grants, 3285
Nestle Purina PetCare Educational Grants, 3302
Nestle Purina PetCare Pet Related Grants, 3304
Nestle Purina PetCare Support Dog and Police K-9 Organization Grants, 3305
Nestle Purina PetCare Youth Grants, 3306
New York Fndn Grants, 3338
New York Landmarks Conservancy City Ventures Grants, 3339
New York Landmarks Conservancy Sacred Sites Grants, 3340
NFWF Bronx River Watershed Initiative Grants, 3360
NFWF Chesapeake Bay Conservation Innovation Grants, 3363

NFWF Chesapeake Bay Targeted Grants, 3365
Nissan Fndn Grants, 3444
Norfolk Southern Fndn Grants, 3463
Northern Chautauqua Community Fndn Community Grants, 3499
Northern Chautauqua Fndn Communications Community Betterment Grants, 3500
Northern Chautauqua Community Fndn Environmental Grants, 3501
Northern Chautauqua Community Fndn Lake Shore Savings and Loan Community Reinvestment Grants, 3502
Northern New York Community Found Grants, 3503
NYCH Together Grants, 3541
NYCT AIDS/HIV Grants, 3542
NYCT Blindness and Visual Disabilities Grants, 3543
NYCT Children & Youth with Disabilities Grants, 3544
NYCT Civic Affairs Grants, 3545
NYCT Community Development Grants, 3546
NYCT Fund for New Citizens Grants, 3547
NYCT Girls and Young Women Grants, 3548
NYCT Grants for the Elderly, 3549
NYCT Health Services and Policies Grants, 3550
NYCT Historic Preservation Grants, 3551
NYCT Human Justice Grants, 3552
NYCT Hunger and Homelessnes Grants, 3553
NYCT Mental Health and Retardation Grants, 3554
NYCT Neighborhood Revitalization Grants, 3555
NYCT New York City Environment Grants, 3556
NYCT Social Services and Welfare Grants, 3557
NYCT Substance Abuse Grants, 3558
NYCT Technical Assistance Grants, 3559
NYCT Workforce Development Grants, 3560
NYCT Youth Development Grants, 3561
NYFA Artists in the School Community Planning Grants, 3562
NYFA Building Up Infrastructure Levels for Dance Grants, 3563
NYFA Deutsche Bank Americas Fellowship, 3564
NYFA Gregory Millard Fellowships, 3565
NYFA Strategic Opportunity Stipends, 3566
NYHC Major and Mini Grants, 3567
NYHC Reading and Discussion Grants, 3568
NYHC Speakers in the Humanities Grants, 3569
NYSCA Architecture, Planning, and Design: Capital Fixtures and Equipment Purchase Grants, 3570
NYSCA Architecture, Planning, and Design: Capital Project Grants, 3571
NYSCA Architecture, Planning, and Design: Design and Planning Studies Grants, 3572
NYSCA Architecture, Planning, and Design: General Operating Support Grants, 3573
NYSCA Architecture, Planning, and Design: General Program Support Grants, 3574
NYSCA Architecture, Planning, and Design: Independent Project Grants, 3575
NYSCA Architecture, Planning, and Design: Project Support Grants, 3576
NYSCA Arts Education: Community-based Learning Grants, 3577
NYSCA Arts Education: General Operating Support Grants, 3578
NYSCA Arts Education: General Program Support Grants, 3579
NYSCA Arts Education: K-12 In-School Programs Grants, 3580
NYSCA Arts Education: Local Capacity Building Grants, 3581
NYSCA Arts Educ: Services to the Field Grants, 3582
NYSCA Dance: Comms Grants, 3583
NYSCA Dance: General Operating Grants, 3584
NYSCA Dance: General Support Grants, 3585
NYSCA Dance: Long-Term Residency in New York State Grants, 3586
NYSCA Dance: Services to the Field Grants, 3587
NYSCA Electronic Media and Film: Film Festivals Grants, 3588
NYSCA Electronic Media and Film: General Exhibition Grants, 3589

NYSCA Electronic Media and Film: General Operating Support, 3590
NYSCA Electronic Media and Film: General Program Support, 3591
NYSCA Electronic Media and Film: Screenings Grants, 3592
NYSCA Electronic Media and Film: Workspace Grants, 3593
NYSCA Folk Arts: Exhibitions Grants, 3594
NYSCA Folk Arts: General Support Grants, 3595
NYSCA Folk Arts: Presentation Grants, 3596
NYSCA Folk Arts: Regional and County Folk Arts Programs Grants, 3597
NYSCA Literature: General Operating Support Grants, 3598
NYSCA Literature: General Support Grants, 3599
NYSCA Literature: Public Programs, 3600
NYSCA Literature: Services to the Field Grants, 3601
NYSCA Museum: Operating Support Grants, 3602
NYSCA Museum: Program Support Grants, 3603
NYSCA Museum: Project Support Grants, 3604
NYSCA Music: Community Schools Grants, 3605
NYSCA Music: Operating Support Grants, 3606
NYSCA Music: Program Support Grants, 3607
NYSCA Music: New Music Facilities, 3608
NYSCA Presenting: General Operating Support Grants, 3609
NYSCA Presenting: General Program Support, 3610
NYSCA Presenting: Presenting Grants, 3611
NYSCA Presenting: Services to the Field Grants, 3612
NYSCA Special Art Services: Project Grants, 3613
NYSCA Special Arts Services: General Operating Support Grants, 3614
NYSCA Special Arts Services: General Program Support Grants, 3615
NYSCA Special Arts Services: Instruction and Training Grants, 3616
NYSCA Special Arts Services: Professional Performances Grants, 3617
NYSCA State and Local Partnerships: Administrative Salary Support Grants, 3618
NYSCA State and Local Partnerships: General Operating Support Grants, 3619
NYSCA State and Local Partnerships: General Program Support Grants, 3620
NYSCA State and Local Partnerships: Services to the Field Grants, 3621
NYSCA State and Local Partnerships: Workshops Grants, 3622
NYSCA Theatre: Operating Support Grants, 3623
NYSCA Theatre: Program Support Grants, 3624
NYSCA Theatre: Profess Performances Grants, 3625
NYSCA Theatre: Services to the Field Grants, 3626
NYSCA Visual Arts: Exhibitions and Installations Grants, 3627
NYSCA Visual Arts: General Operating Support Grants, 3628
NYSCA Visual Arts: General Support Grants, 3629
NYSCA Visual Arts: Services to the Field Grants, 3630
NYSCA Visual Arts: Workspace Facilities Grants, 3631
Orchard Fndn Grants, 3690
Paul Rapoport Fndn Grants, 3765
PennPAT Fee-Support Grants for Presenters, 3812
PennPAT New Directions Grants for Presenters, 3813
Perkin Fund Grants, 3821
Peter and Elizabeth C. Tower Fndn Annual Intellectual Disabilities Grants, 3834
Peter and Elizabeth C. Tower Fndn Annual Mental Health Grants, 3835
Peter and Elizabeth C. Tower Fndn Learning Disability Grants, 3836
Peter and Elizabeth C. Tower Mental Health Reference and Resource Materials Mini-Grants, 3837
Peter and Elizabeth C. Tower Fndn Organizational Scholarships, 3838
Peter and Elizabeth C. Tower Fndn Phase II Technology Initiative Grants, 3839
Peter and Elizabeth C. Tower Fndn Phase I Technology Initiative Grants, 3840

Peter and Elizabeth C. Tower Fndn Social and Emotional Preschool Curriculum Grants, 3841
Peter and Elizabeth C. Tower Fndn Substance Abuse Grants, 3842
Poets & Writers Readings/Workshops Grants, 3927
Price Chopper's Golub Fndn Grants, 3950
Price Chopper's Golub Fndn Two-Year Health Care Scholarship, 3951
Prudential Fndn Arts and Culture Grants, 3975
Prudential Fndn Economic Devel Grants, 3976
Prudential Fndn Education Grants, 3977
Rainbow Media Holdings LLC Corporate Giving Grants, 4010
Regents Professional Opportunity Scholarships, 4044
Richard Davoud Donchian Fndn Grants, 4080
Robert Bowne Fndn Fellowships, 4107
Robert Bowne Fndn Literacy Grants, 4108
Robert Bowne Found Youth-Centered Grants, 4109
Robert R. McCormick Tribune Fndn Community Grants, 4119
Robert Sterling Clark Arts and Culture Grants, 4122
Robert Sterling Clark Fndn Government Accountability Grants, 4123
Robin Hood Fndn Grants, 4125
Rochester Area Community Fndn Grants, 4127
Rockefeller Brothers Fund Charles E. Culpeper Arts and Culture Grants in New York City, 4129
Rockefeller Brothers Fund Pivotal Places Grants: New York City, 4134
RR Donnelley Community Grants, 4168
Russell Berrie Fndn Grants, 4175
Ruth and Vernon Taylor Fndn Grants, 4177
S. Spencer Scott Fund Grants, 4202
Safeco Insurance Community Grants, 4203
SAG Motion Picture Players Welfare Grants, 4209
Saint George's Society of New York Scholarships, 4213
Sandy Hill Fndn Grants, 4257
Scherman Fndn Grants, 4305
Shirley W. & William L. Griffin Charitable Fndn Grants, 4345
Solutia Fund Grants, 4402
Sprague Fndn Grants, 4461
State Street Fndn Grants, 4495
Stowe Family Fndn Grants, 4510
Suffolk County Office of Film and Cultural Affairs Cultural Arts Grants, 4521
Sunny and Abe Rosenberg Fndn Grants, 4529
Sunoco Fndn Grants, 4530
Sweet Water Trust Grants, 4541
Taproot Fndn Capacity-Building Grants, 4560
Textron Corporate Contributions Grants, 4601
Thomas Thompson Trust Grants, 4620
Time Warner Youth and Creative Arts Grants, 4636
Turner Voices Corporate Contributions, 4682
TWS Fndn Grants, 4683
Union Square Arts Award, 4716
Union Square Award for Social Justice, 4717
Union Square Awards Grants, 4718
US Airways Community Contributions, 4788
US Airways Education Fndn Grants, 4790
Verizon Fndn New York Grants, 4919
Verizon Wireless Hopeline Grants, 4927
Walt Disney Company Fndn Grants, 4981
Wells Fargo Housing Fndn Grants, 5023
Western New York Fndn Grants, 5025
Widgeon Point Charitable Fndn Grants, 5064
William G. McGowan Charitable Fund Grants, 5084
William J. and Dorothy K. O'Neill Grants, 5087
William T. Grant Fndn Youth Service Improvement Grants, 5096
Winifred & Harry B. Allen Fndn Grants, 5101

North Carolina
A.J. Fletcher Fndn Grants, 41
Abbott Fund Access to Health Care Grants, 80
Abbott Fund Community Grants, 81
Abbott Fund Global AIDS Care Grants, 82
Abbott Fund Science Education Grants, 83
Abelard Fndn East Grants, 87
Able To Serve Grants, 102

North Carolina

ACE Charitable Fndn Grants, 111
Aetna Fndn Regional Health Grants, 187
American Express Charitable Fund Grants, 429
American Schlafhorst Fndn Grants, 446
Appalachian Regional Comm Asset-Based Development Project Grants, 500
Appalachian Regional Comm Business Development Revolving Loan Fund Grants, 501
Appalachian Regional Comm Community Infrastructure Grants, 502
Appalachian Regional Comm Distressed Counties Grants, 503
Appalachian Regional Comm Education and Training Grants, 504
Appalachian Regional Comm Energy Grants, 505
Appalachian Regional Comm Export and Trade Development Grants, 506
Appalachian Regional Comm Health Care Grants, 507
Appalachian Reg Comm Housing Grants, 508
Appalachian Regional Comm Leadership Development and Capacity Building Grants, 509
Appalachian Regional Comm Telecommunications Grants, 510
Appalachian Regional Comm Tourist Development Grants, 511
Appalachian Regional Comm Transportation and Highways Grants, 512
Archer Daniels Midland Fndn Grants, 527
Arts and Science Council Grants, 576
Arts Council of Winston-Salem and Forsyth County Organizational Support Grants, 577
Bayer Fndn Grants, 696
BCBSNC Fndn Fit Together Grants, 711
BCBSNC Fndn Grants, 712
Beldon Fund Grants, 720
Belk Fndn Grants, 721
Biogen Corporate Giving Grants, 773
BJ's Charitable Fndn Grants, 777
BJ's Wholesale Clubs Local Charitable Giving, 778
Blanche and Julian Robertson Family Fndn Grants, 785
Blumenthal Fndn Grants, 804
Bridgestone/Firestone Trust Fund Grants, 836
Brunswick Fndn Dollars for Doers Grants, 856
Brunswick Fndn Grants, 857
Burlington Industries Fndn Grants, 865
Caesars Fndn Grants, 891
Camp-Younts Fndn Grants, 914
Campbell Soup Fndn Grants, 916
CarEth Fndn Grants, 924
Carrie E. and Lena V. Glenn Fndn Grants, 944
Carrier Corporation Contributions Grants, 946
Catherine Kennedy Home Fndn Grants, 955
Cemala Fndn Grants, 988
CenturyLink Clarke M. Williams Grants, 998
Ceres Fndn Grants, 999
Charles A. Frueauff Fndn Grants, 1037
Charles M. and Mary D. Grant Found Grants, 1050
Cingular Wireless Charitable Contributions, 1134
Circle K Corporation Contributions Grants, 1136
Cisco Systems San Jose Community Grants, 1137
Clarcor Fndn Grants, 1148
Community Found of Greater Greensboro Grants, 1288
Community Fndn of W North Carolina Grants, 1327
ConAgra Foods Community Impact Grants, 1342
ConAgra Foods Nourish Our Comm Grants, 1343
Cone Health Fndn Grants, 1348
Cooke-Hay Fndn Grants, 1367
Cooper Industries Fndn Grants, 1370
Covenant Educational Fndn Grants, 1383
CSX Corporate Contributions Grants, 1408
Cumberland Community Fndn Grants, 1413
Cumberland Community Fndn Summertime Kids Grants, 1414
Cummins Fndn Grants, 1415
D.F. Halton Fndn Grants, 1424
Dean Foods Community Involvement Grants, 1469
Deluxe Corporation Fndn Grants, 1496
DHHS Healthy Tomorrows for Children, 1534
Dollar General Adult Literacy Grants, 1568
Dollar General Family Literacy Grants, 1569

Dollar General Youth Literacy Grants, 1570
Dominion Fndn Human Needs Grants, 1572
Dow Corning Corporate Contributions Grants, 1597
Duke Endowment Child Care Grants, 1617
Duke Energy Community Vitality Grants, 1618
Duke Energy Economic Development Grants, 1619
Dunspaugh-Dalton Fndn Grants, 1623
Eaton Charitable Fund Grants, 1647
Edith and Francis Mulhall Achilles Memorial Fund Grants, 1657
F.M. Kirby Fndn Grants, 1780
Fluor Fndn Grants, 1875
FMC Fndn Grants, 1876
Fndn for the Carolinas Grants, 1896
Fred and Sherry Abernethy Fndn Grants, 1940
Fund for Southern Communities Grants, 1977
Gannett Fndn Community Action Grants, 1984
Georgia-Pacific Fndn Education Grants, 2031
Georgia-Pacific Fndn Enrichment Grants, 2032
Georgia-Pacific Entrepreneurship Grants, 2033
Georgia-Pacific Fndn Environment Grants, 2034
Golden LEAF Fndn Grants, 2097
Gumdrop Books Librarian Scholarships, 2179
Hillsdale Fund Grants, 2329
Howe Fndn of North Carolina Grants, 2377
Ireland Family Fndn Grants, 2574
J. Bulow Campbell Fndn Grants, 2593
James G.K. McClure Educational and Development Fund Grants, 2624
James H. Cummings Fndn Grants, 2626
James J. and Angelia M. Harris Grants, 2630
Janirve Fndn Grants, 2645
John Deere Fndn Grants, 2692
John H. Wellons Fndn Grants, 2699
John S. and James L. Knight Fndn Communities Grants, 2711
John W. and Anna H. Hanes Fndn Grants, 2728
Kate B. Reynolds Charitable Health Care Grants, 2786
Kate B. Reynolds Charitable Trust Poor and Needy Grants, 2787
Kimberly-Clark Community Grants, 2824
Lettie Pate Whitehead Fndn Grants, 2888
Lincoln Financial Group Fndn Grants, 2906
Mary Duke Biddle Fndn Grants, 3036
Mary E. and Michael Blevins Charitable Grants, 3037
Mary Reynolds Babcock Fndn Grants, 3047
McColl Fndn Grants, 3074
MeadWestvaco Sustainable Communities Grants, 3105
Nationwide Insurance Fndn Grants, 3285
Norfolk Southern Fndn Grants, 3463
North Carolina Arts Council Arts and Audiences Grants, 3466
North Carolina Arts Council Folklife Internship, 3467
North Carolina Arts Council Arts in Education Artist Residencies Grants, 3468
North Carolina Arts Council Arts in Education Initiatives Grants, 3469
North Carolina Arts Council Arts in Education Rural Development Grants, 3470
North Carolina Arts Council Community Arts Administration Internship, 3471
North Carolina Arts Council Community Public Art and Design Development Grants, 3472
North Carolina Arts Council Community Public Art and Design Implementation Grants, 3473
North Carolina Arts Facility Design Grants, 3474
North Carolina Arts Council Folklife Documentary Project Grants, 3475
North Carolina Arts Folklife Public Grants, 3476
North Carolina Arts General Support Grants, 3477
North Carolina Arts New Realities Grants, 3478
North Carolina Arts Council Outreach Grants, 3479
North Carolina Arts Council Regional Artist Project Grants, 3480
North Carolina Arts Residency Center Grants, 3481
North Carolina Arts Council Technical Assistance Grants, 3482
North Carolina Arts Council Touring/Presenting Grants, 3483

North Carolina Arts Council Visual Arts Program Support Grants, 3484
North Carolina Biotechnology Center Event Sponsorship Grants, 3485
North Carolina Biotech Center Meeting Grants, 3486
North Carolina Biotechnology Center Multidisciplinary Research Grants, 3487
North Carolina Biotechnology Center Regional Development Grants, 3488
North Carolina Community Fndn Grants, 3489
North Carolina GlaxoSmithKline Grants, 3490
Paul Green Fndn Efforts to Abolish the Death Penalty in North Carolina Grants, 3760
Paul Green Fndn Human Rights Grants, 3761
Paul Green Fndn Playwrights Fellowship, 3762
Percy B. Ferebee Endowment Grants, 3820
Piedmont Natural Gas Corporate and Charitable Contributions, 3883
Piedmont Natural Gas Fndn Environmental Stewardship and Energy Sustainability Grant, 3884
Piedmont Natural Gas Fndn Health and Human Services Grants, 3885
Piedmont Natural Gas Fndn Workforce Development Grant, 3886
Plum Creek Fndn Grants, 3917
Progress Energy Corporate Contributions Grants, 3968
Progress Energy Economic Vitality Grants, 3969
Progress Energy Fndn Environmental Stewardship Grants, 3970
Qualcomm Grants, 3993
Rehab Therapy Fndn Grants, 4050
REI Conservation and Outdoor Rec Grants, 4051
Richard Davoud Donchian Fndn Grants, 4080
Salisbury Community Fndn Grants, 4224
Samuel L. Phillips Family Fndn Grants, 4235
SAS Institute Community Relations Donations, 4300
Simple Advise Education Center Grants, 4361
Sisters of Mercy of North Carolina Grants, 4375
Smith Richardson Found Direct Service Grants, 4385
Square D Fndn Grants, 4464
Steele-Reese Fndn Grants, 4498
Strowd Roses Grants, 4515
Sunoco Fndn Grants, 4530
TAC Arts Access Technical Assistance Grants, 4550
TAC Arts Educ Community-Learning Grants, 4552
TAC Arts Education Mini Grants, 4553
TAC Arts Projects Grants, 4554
TAC Rural Arts Project Support Grants, 4555
TAC Technical Assistance Grants, 4556
TAC Touring Arts and Access Grants, 4557
TE Fndn Grants, 4572
Tension Envelope Fndn Grants, 4578
Textron Corporate Contributions Grants, 4601
Thomas Austin Finch, Sr. Fndn Grants, 4613
Triangle Community Fndn Grants, 4667
Triangle Community Donor-Advised Grants, 4668
Turner B. Bunn, Jr. and Catherine E. Bunn Fndn Grants, 4680
Tyler Aaron Bookman Memorial Fndn Grants, 4684
Union County Community Fndn Grants, 4711
US Airways Community Contributions, 4788
US Airways Community Fndn Grants, 4789
US Airways Education Fndn Grants, 4790
Verizon Fndn Southeast Region Grants, 4923
VSA/Metlife Connect All Grants, 4953
Vulcan Materials Company Fndn Grants, 4956
W. Waldo and Jenny Lynn M. Bradley Grants, 4967
Weaver Fndn Grants, 5015
Wells Fargo Housing Fndn Grants, 5023
Weyerhaeuser Company Fndn Grants, 5053
Williams Companies Fndn Grants, 5095
Winston-Salem Fndn Competitive Grants, 5102
Winston-Salem Found Elkin/Tri-County Grants, 5103
Winston-Salem Found Stokes County Grants, 5104
Woodward Fund Grants, 5116
Z. Smith Reynolds Fndn Community Economic Development Grants, 5144
Z. Smith Reynolds Fndn Democracy and Civic Engagement Grants, 5145

GEOGRAPHIC INDEX

Z. Smith Reynolds Fndn Nancy Susan Reynolds Awards, 5146
Z. Smith Reynolds Fndn Sabbatical Grants, 5147

North Dakota
Abelard Fndn West Grants, 88
Albertson's Charitable Giving Grants, 345
Alex Stern Family Fndn Grants, 360
Archer Daniels Midland Fndn Grants, 527
Arts Midwest Performing Arts Grants, 579
Bush Fndn Arts & Humanities Grants: Capital Projects, 872
Bush Fndn Arts & Humanities Grants: Short-Term Organizational Support, 873
Bush Fndn Ecological Health Grants, 874
Bush Found Health & Human Services Grants, 875
Bush Fndn Medical Fellowships, 877
Bush Found Regional Arts Development Grants, 878
CenturyLink Clarke M. Williams Grants, 998
Courage Center Judd Jacobson Memorial Award, 1382
Dean Foods Community Involvement Grants, 1469
DHHS Healthy Tomorrows for Children, 1534
DOJ Rural Domestic Violence and Child Victimization Enforcement Grants, 1562
Fargo-Moorhead Area Fndn Grants, 1788
Fargo-Moorhead Area Woman's Fund Grants, 1789
Heartland Arts Fund, 2286
Land O'Lakes Fndn Community Grants, 2859
Land O'Lakes Fndn Dollars for Doers, 2860
NGA Midwest School Garden Grants, 3407
North Dakota Community Fndn Grants, 3493
North Dakota Council on the Arts Community Access Grants, 3494
North Dakota Council on the Arts Individual Artist Fellowships, 3495
North Dakota Council on the Arts Institutional Support Grants, 3496
North Dakota Council on the Arts Presenter Support Grants, 3497
Otto Bremer Fndn Grants, 3713
Philanthrofund Fndn Grants, 3874
Piper Jaffray Fndn Communities Giving, 3899
RBC Dain Rauscher Fndn Grants, 4031
Shopko Fndn Community Grants, 4346
U.S. Bank Fndn Grants, 4686
Viking Children's Fund Grants, 4939
Wells Fargo Housing Fndn Grants, 5023

Northern Mariana Islands
Bank of America Charitable Matching Gifts, 658
Bank of America Charitable Volunteer Grants, 660
EPA Environmental Justice Small Grants, 1731
EPA Pestwise Registration Improvement Act Partnership Grants, 1734
EPA Regional Agricultural IPM Grants, 1735
EPA State Indoor Radon Grants, 1738
EPA Tribal Support for the National Environmental Information Exchange Network, 1742
NHLBI Ancillary Studies in Clinical Trials, 3410
NHLBI Bioengineering and Obesity Grants, 3411
NHLBI Career Transition Awards, 3412
NHLBI Lymphatics Disease in the Digestive, Cardiovascular and Pulmonary Systems, 3414
NHLBI Lymphatics in Health and Disease in the Digestive, Urinary, Cardiovascular and Pulmonary Systems, 3415
NHLBI Research on the Role of Cardiomyocyte Mitochondria in Heart Disease: An Integrated Approach, 3417
NHLBI Ruth L. Kirschstein National Research Service Awards for Individual Postdoctoral Fellows, 3418
NHLBI Ruth L. Kirschstein National Research Service Awards for Individual Senior Fellows, 3421
NHLBI Ruth L. Kirschstein National Research Service Award Short-Term Institutional Research Training Grants, 3422
USDA Farmers Market Promotion Grants, 4808
USDC Public Works and Economic Adjustment Assistance Grants, 4856

Ohio
3M Company Arts and Culture Grants, 12
3M Company Environmental Giving Grants, 13
3M Company Health and Human Services Grants, 14
3M Fndn Community Giving Grants, 15
Abbott Fund Access to Health Care Grants, 80
Abbott Fund Community Grants, 81
Abbott Fund Global AIDS Care Grants, 82
Abbott Fund Science Education Grants, 83
ABC Charities Grants, 85
Abelard Fndn East Grants, 87
Abington Fndn Grants, 100
ACE Charitable Fndn Grants, 111
Adams Family Fndn of Ohio Grants, 151
AEP Corporate Giving Grants, 180
Aetna Fndn Regional Health Grants, 187
A Good Neighbor Fndn Grants, 204
AHS Fndn Grants, 208
Akron Community Found Arts & Culture Grants, 218
American Electric Power Grants, 428
Amerigroup Fndn Grants, 452
Anderson Fndn Grants, 460
Angels On Track Fndn Grants, 468
Anheuser-Busch Fndn Grants, 470
Anthem Blue Cross and Blue Shield Grants, 488
Appalachian Regional Comm Asset-Based Development Project Grants, 500
Appalachian Regional Comm Business Development Revolving Loan Fund Grants, 501
Appalachian Regional Comm Community Infrastructure Grants, 502
Appalachian Regional Comm Distressed Counties Grants, 503
Appalachian Regional Comm Education and Training Grants, 504
Appalachian Regional Comm Energy Grants, 505
Appalachian Regional Comm Export and Trade Development Grants, 506
Appalachian Regional Comm Health Care Grants, 507
Appalachian Reg Comm Housing Grants, 508
Appalachian Regional Comm Leadership Development and Capacity Building Grants, 509
Appalachian Regional Comm Telecommunications Grants, 510
Appalachian Regional Comm Tourist Development Grants, 511
Appalachian Regional Comm Transportation and Highways Grants, 512
Archer Daniels Midland Fndn Grants, 527
Arthur and Sara Jo Kobacker, Alfred and Ida Kobacker Fndn Grants, 571
Arts Midwest Performing Arts Grants, 579
ArtsWave Impact Grants, 580
ArtsWave Project Grants, 581
Ashland Corporate Contributions Grants, 587
Austin-Bailey Health and Wellness Grants, 614
Barberton Community Fndn Grants, 666
Bayer Fndn Grants, 696
Beerman Fndn Grants, 717
Bicknell Fund Grants, 759
BJ's Charitable Fndn Grants, 777
BJ's Wholesale Clubs Local Charitable Giving, 778
Blade Fndn Grants, 783
Boeing Company Contributions Grants, 809
Bowling Green Community Fndn Grants, 824
Bridgestone/Firestone Trust Fund Grants, 836
Burton D. Morgan Fndn Adult Entrepreneurship Grants, 868
Burton D. Morgan Hudson Community Grants, 869
Burton D. Morgan Fndn Youth Entrepreneurship Grants, 870
Caesar Puff Fndn Grants, 890
Campbell Soup Fndn Grants, 916
CenturyLink Clarke M. Williams Grants, 998
Charles H. Dater Fndn Grants, 1042
Charlotte R. Schmidlapp Fund Grants, 1058
Chase Paymentech Corporate Giving Grants, 1059
Cincinnati Bell Fndn Grants, 1131
Cincinnati Milacron Fndn Grants, 1132
Cinergy Fndn Grants, 1133
Cingular Wireless Charitable Contributions, 1134
Circle K Corporation Contributions Grants, 1136
Clarcor Fndn Grants, 1148
Cleveland-Cliffs Fndn Grants, 1165
Cleveland Browns Fndn Grants, 1166
Cleveland Capital Grants, 1167
Cleveland Comm Responsive Grants, 1168
Cleveland Fenn Educational Grants, 1169
Cleveland Lake-Geauga Fund Grants, 1170
Cleveland Neighborhood Connections Grants, 1171
CMA Fndn Grants, 1178
Coleman Cancer Care Grants, 1199
Coleman Developmental Disabilities Grants, 1200
Coleman Entrepreneurship Education Grants, 1201
Columbus Allen Eiry Fund Grants, 1219
Columbus Competitive Grants, 1220
Columbus Dorothy E. Ann Traditional Grants, 1221
Columbus J. Floyd Dixon Memorial Fund Grants, 1222
Columbus John W. and Edna McManus Shepard Fund Grants, 1223
Columbus Joseph A. Jeffrey Endowment Grants, 1224
Columbus Mary Eleanor Morris Fund Grants, 1225
Columbus Neighborhood Partnership Grants, 1226
Columbus Paul G. Duke Grants, 1227
Columbus R. Alvin Stevenson Fund Grants, 1228
Columbus Robert E. and Genevieve B. Schaefer Fund Grants, 1229
Columbus Scotts Miracle-Gro Community Garden Academy Fund Grants, 1230
Columbus Small Grants, 1232
Columbus Traditional Grants, 1233
Comcast Fndn Grants, 1235
Community Fndn of Mount Vernon and Knox County Grants, 1301
ConAgra Foods Community Impact Grants, 1342
ConAgra Foods Nourish Our Comm Grants, 1343
CSX Corporate Contributions Grants, 1408
Cummins Fndn Grants, 1415
Cyrus Eaton Fndn Grants, 1423
Darden Restaurants Fndn Grants, 1446
Dayton Fndn Grants, 1463
Dayton Power and Light Fndn Grants, 1464
Deaconess Community Fndn Grants, 1467
Dean Foods Community Involvement Grants, 1469
Deluxe Corporation Fndn Grants, 1496
Dollar Energy Fund Grants, 1567
Dollar General Adult Literacy Grants, 1568
Dollar General Family Literacy Grants, 1569
Dollar General Youth Literacy Grants, 1570
Dominion Fndn Human Needs Grants, 1572
Duke Energy Community Vitality Grants, 1618
Duke Energy Economic Development Grants, 1619
Eaton Charitable Fund Grants, 1647
Eva L. and Joseph M. Bruening Grants, 1768
Fifth Third Bank Corporate Giving, 1809
Fifth Third Fndn Grants, 1810
FirstEnergy Fndn Community Grants, 1819
FirstEnergy Fndn Math, Science, and Technology Education Grants, 1820
Fndn for Appalachian Ohio Access to Environmental Education Mini-Grants, 1892
Frank M. Tait Fndn Grants, 1932
Gannett Fndn Community Action Grants, 1984
General Mills Fndn Grants, 2003
George W. Codrington Charitable Grants, 2029
Georgia-Pacific Fndn Education Grants, 2031
Georgia-Pacific Fndn Enrichment Grants, 2032
Georgia-Pacific Entrepreneurship Grants, 2033
Georgia-Pacific Fndn Environment Grants, 2034
Giant Eagle Fndn Grants, 2049
Ginn Fndn Grants, 2056
Gladys Brooks Fndn Grants, 2059
Graco Fndn Grants, 2111
Greater Cincinnati Fndn Priority and Small Projects/Capacity-Building Grants, 2132
Greater Columbus Arts Operating Grants, 2133
Great Lakes Fishery Trust Access Grants, 2145
Great Lakes Fishery Trust Habitat Protection and Restoration Grants, 2146
H.B. Fuller Company Fndn Grants, 2183

1168 / Ohio

Health Fndn of Greater Cincinnati Grants, 2281
Heartland Arts Fund, 2286
Helen Steiner Rice Fndn Grants, 2299
Honda of America Manufacturing Grants, 2354
Huffy Fndn Grants, 2384
Humana Fndn Grants, 2388
Huntington National Bank Comm Grants, 2409
IFP Chicago Production Fund In-Kind Grant, 2446
Impact 100 Grants, 2522
Jacob G. Schmidlapp Trust Grants, 2616
James S. Copley Fndn Grants, 2637
John Lord Knight Fndn Grants, 2703
John P. Murphy Fndn Grants, 2708
John S. and James L. Knight Fndn Communities Grants, 2711
Johnson & Johnson Comm Health Care Grants, 2717
Joyce Fndn Democracy Grants, 2748
JP Morgan Chase Arts and Culture Grants, 2752
JP Morgan Chase Community Devel Grants, 2753
Kelvin and Eleanor Smith Fndn Grants, 2796
Kettering Fund Grants, 2818
KeyBank Fndn Grants, 2820
Kimberly-Clark Community Grants, 2824
Land O'Lakes Fndn Community Grants, 2859
Land O'Lakes Fndn Dollars for Doers, 2860
Laura Jane Musser Intercultural Harmony Grants, 2862
Laura Jane Musser Rural Arts Grants, 2863
Laura Jane Musser Rural Initiative Grants, 2864
Letha E. House Fndn Grants, 2886
LISC Financial Opportunity Center Social Innovation Fund Grants, 2911
Lockheed Martin Philanthropic Grants, 2918
Lubrizol Corporation Community Grants, 2932
Lubrizol Fndn Grants, 2933
M3C Fellowships, 2955
Marathon Petroleum Corporation Grants, 2999
Marsh Corporate Grants, 3027
Mary E. Babcock Fndn, 3038
Mary S. and David C. Corbin Fndn Grants, 3048
Mathile Family Fndn Grants, 3062
MeadWestvaco Sustainable Communities Grants, 3105
Mildred V. Horn Fndn Grants, 3176
Moran Family Fndn Grants, 3216
Mt. Sinai Health Care Fndn Health of the Jewish Community Grants, 3226
Mt. Sinai Health Care Fndn Health of the Urban Community Grants, 3227
Mt. Sinai Health Care Health Policy Grants, 3228
Nationwide Insurance Fndn Grants, 3285
Nestle Purina PetCare Educational Grants, 3302
Nestle Purina PetCare Pet Related Grants, 3304
Nestle Purina PetCare Support Dog and Police K-9 Organization Grants, 3305
Nestle Purina PetCare Youth Grants, 3306
NGA Midwest School Garden Grants, 3407
Nord Family Fndn Grants, 3461
Nordson Corporation Fndn Grants, 3462
Norfolk Southern Fndn Grants, 3463
Ohio Artists on Tour Fee Support Requests, 3642
Ohio Arts Council Artist Express Grants, 3643
Ohio Arts Council Artist in Residence Grants for Artists, 3644
Ohio Arts Council Artist in Residence Grants for Sponsors, 3645
Ohio Arts Council Artists with Disabilities Access Grants, 3646
Ohio Arts Council Arts Access Grants, 3647
Ohio Arts Council Individual Excellence Awards, 3648
Ohio Arts Council Arts Innovation Grants, 3649
Ohio Arts Council Arts Partnership Grants, 3650
Ohio Arts Council Building Cultural Diversity Initiative Grants, 3651
Ohio Arts Council Capacity Building Grants for Organizations and Communities, 3652
Ohio Arts Council Int'l Partnership Grants, 3653
Ohio Arts Council Sustainability Grants, 3654
Ohio Arts Council Traditional Arts Apprenticeship Grants, 3655
Ohio River Border Initiative Grants, 3661
Ohio Valley Fndn Grants, 3662
ORBI Artist Fast Track Grants, 3689
Parkersburg Area Community Action Grants, 3738
PennPAT Fee-Support Grants for Presenters, 3812
PennPAT New Directions Grants for Presenters, 3813
Peoples Bancorp Fndn Grants, 3817
Piper Jaffray Fndn Communities Giving, 3899
PNC Charitable Trust and Fndn Grants, 3921
PNC Ecnomic Development Grants, 3922
PNC Fndn Green Building Grants, 3923
PNC Fndn Grow Up Great Grants, 3924
Raymond John Wean Fndn Grants, 4028
RCF General Community Grants, 4032
RCF Individual Assistance Grants, 4033
RCF Summertime Kids Grants, 4034
RCF The Women's Fund Grants, 4035
Reinberger Fndn Grants, 4052
Reynolds and Reynolds Fndn Grants, 4069
Reynolds and Reynolds Company Grants, 4070
Rollin M. Gerstacker Fndn Grants, 4146
Ryder System Charitable Fndn Grants, 4191
S. Livingston Mather Charitable Trust Grants, 4200
Safeco Insurance Community Grants, 4203
Saint Luke's Fndn Grants, 4215
Shopko Fndn Community Grants, 4346
Sisters of Charity Fndn of Canton Grants, 4372
Sisters of Charity Fndn of Cleveland Good Samaritan Grants, 4373
Sisters of Charity Fndn of Cleveland Reducing Health and Educational Disparities in the Central Neighborhood Grants, 4374
Sisters of Saint Joseph Charitable Fund Grants, 4376
SOCFOC Catholic Ministries Grants, 4392
SOCFOC Community Collaborations Grants, 4393
Solutia Fund Grants, 4402
Stark Community Fndn Grants, 4477
Stark Community Fndn Neighborhood Community and Economic Development Technical Assistance Grants, 4478
Stark Community Fndn Neighborhood Partnership Grants, 4479
Stark Community SummerTime Kid Grants, 4480
Stark Community Fndn Women's Grants, 4481
Stocker Fndn Grants, 4507
Sunoco Fndn Grants, 4530
T. Raymond Gregory Family Fndn Grants, 4547
Toyota Motor Engineering & Manufacturing North America Grants, 4651
Tri-State Community Twenty-first Century Endowment Fund Grants, 4666
Turner Fndn Grants, 4681
U.S. Bank Fndn Grants, 4686
Verizon Fndn Great Lakes Region Grants, 4912
Virginia W. Kettering Fndn Grants, 4950
Walter L. Gross III Family Fndn Grants, 4983
Wells Fargo Housing Fndn Grants, 5023
Weyerhaeuser Company Fndn Grants, 5053
William J. and Dorothy K. O'Neill Grants, 5087
Wolfe Associates Grants, 5110

Oklahoma

Abelard Fndn West Grants, 88
AEP Corporate Giving Grants, 180
Albertson's Charitable Giving Grants, 345
American Electric Power Grants, 428
Archer Daniels Midland Fndn Grants, 527
Baughman Fndn Grants, 688
Boeing Company Contributions Grants, 809
Brunswick Fndn Dollars for Doers Grants, 856
Brunswick Fndn Grants, 857
Cable Positive's Tony Cox Community Grants, 886
Charles A. Frueauff Fndn Grants, 1037
Circle K Corporation Contributions Grants, 1136
Clarcor Fndn Grants, 1148
ConocoPhillips Fndn Grants, 1354
ConocoPhillips Grants, 1355
Darden Restaurants Fndn Grants, 1446
Dean Foods Community Involvement Grants, 1469
DOJ Rural Domestic Violence and Child Victimization Enforcement Grants, 1562
Dollar General Adult Literacy Grants, 1568
Dollar General Family Literacy Grants, 1569
Dollar General Youth Literacy Grants, 1570
Donald W. Reynolds Fndn Charitable Food Distribution Grants, 1575
Donald W. Reynolds Fndn Children's Discovery Initiative Grants, 1576
Ed and Carole Abel Fndn Grants, 1652
Edward and Helen Bartlett Fndn Grants, 1664
General Mills Fndn Grants, 2003
Georgia-Pacific Fndn Education Grants, 2031
Georgia-Pacific Fndn Enrichment Grants, 2032
Georgia-Pacific Entrepreneurship Grants, 2033
Georgia-Pacific Fndn Environment Grants, 2034
Gil and Dody Weaver Fndn Grants, 2053
Grace and Franklin Bernsen Fndn Grants, 2109
GTECH Community Involvement Grants, 2171
H.A. and Mary K. Chapman Charitable Grants, 2182
Hatton W. Sumners Fndn for the Study and Teaching of Self Government Grants, 2257
Inasmuch Fndn Grants, 2523
J.E. and L.E. Mabee Fndn Grants, 2595
JP Morgan Chase Arts and Culture Grants, 2752
JP Morgan Chase Community Devel Grants, 2753
Judith and Jean Pape Adams Charitable Fndn Tulsa Area Grants, 2755
K.S. Adams Fndn Grants, 2758
Kimberly-Clark Community Grants, 2824
Kirkpatrick Fndn Grants, 2827
Mary K. Chapman Fndn Grants, 3042
Merkel Family Fndn Grants, 3123
Mervin Bovaird Fndn Grants, 3128
Mid-America Arts Alliance Community Engagement with Touring Artists Grants, 3166
Mid-America Arts Alliance Reg Touring Grants, 3167
Nestle Purina PetCare Educational Grants, 3302
Nestle Purina PetCare Pet Related Grants, 3304
Nestle Purina PetCare Support Dog and Police K-9 Organization Grants, 3305
Nestle Purina PetCare Youth Grants, 3306
Oklahoma City Community Grants, 3666
PACCAR Fndn Grants, 3719
PacifiCare Fndn Grants, 3725
Plum Creek Fndn Grants, 3917
Presbyterian Health Fndn Bridge, Seed and Equipment Grants, 3947
Priddy Fndn Capital Grants, 3954
Priddy Fndn Operating Grants, 3955
Priddy Fndn Organizational Development Grants, 3956
Priddy Fndn Grants, 3957
Questar Corporate Contributions Grants, 3997
QuikTrip Corporate Contributions Grants, 3998
RBC Dain Rauscher Fndn Grants, 4031
Sarkeys Fndn Grants, 4297
Seagate Technology Corporation Capacity to Care Grants, 4317
Union Pacific Community and Civic Grants, 4714
Union Pacific Fndn Health and Human Services Grants, 4715
VSA/Metlife Connect All Grants, 4953
Weyerhaeuser Company Fndn Grants, 5053

Oregon

Abelard Fndn West Grants, 88
ACE Charitable Fndn Grants, 111
Albertson's Charitable Giving Grants, 345
American Rivers Community-Based Restoration Program River Grants, 444
Aratani Fndn Grants, 523
Autzen Fndn Grants, 622
Avista Fndn Grants, 624
Bella Vista Fndn Grants, 722
Ben B. Cheney Fndn Grants, 725
Benton County Fndn Grants, 731
Blue Mountain Community Fndn Grants, 800
Boeing Company Contributions Grants, 809
Brainerd Fndn Grants, 831
Brunswick Fndn Dollars for Doers Grants, 856
Brunswick Fndn Grants, 857
Bullitt Fndn Grants, 862
Burning Fndn Grants, 867

GEOGRAPHIC INDEX

Pennsylvania / 1169

Cable Positive's Tony Cox Community Grants, 886
Carpenter Fndn Grants, 943
Ceres Fndn Grants, 999
Charlotte Martin Fndn Youth Grants, 1057
Chiles Fndn Grants, 1108
Circle K Corporation Contributions Grants, 1136
Coeta and Donald Barker Fndn Grants, 1197
Collins Fndn Grants, 1209
Comcast Fndn Grants, 1235
ConAgra Foods Community Impact Grants, 1342
ConAgra Foods Nourish Our Comm Grants, 1343
Dell Fndn Open Grants, 1490
Detlef Schrempf Fndn Grants, 1519
DOJ Rural Domestic Violence and Child Victimization Enforcement Grants, 1562
E.L. Wiegand Fndn Grants, 1639
Ford Family Fndn Grants - Critical Needs, 1879
Ford Family Fndn Grants - Positive Youth Development, 1880
Ford Family Grants Public Convening Spaces, 1881
Ford Family Fndn Tech Assistance Grants, 1882
Foster Fndn Grants, 1888
Fred Meyer Fndn Grants, 1950
Gannett Fndn Community Action Grants, 1984
Georgia-Pacific Fndn Education Grants, 2031
Georgia-Pacific Fndn Enrichment Grants, 2032
Georgia-Pacific Entrepreneurship Grants, 2033
Georgia-Pacific Fndn Environment Grants, 2034
GTECH Community Involvement Grants, 2171
Harold and Arlene Schnitzer CARE Grants, 2226
Idaho Power Company Corporate Contributions, 2433
Intel Community Grants, 2562
Jackson Fndn Grants, 2613
James F. and Marion L. Miller Fndn Grants, 2622
KeyBank Fndn Grants, 2820
Land O'Lakes Fndn Community Grants, 2859
Land O'Lakes Fndn Dollars for Doers, 2860
M.B. and Edna Zale Fndn Grants, 2950
M.J. Murdock Charitable Trust General Grants, 2954
Meyer Memorial Trust Emergency Grants, 3146
Meyer Memorial Trust Grassroots Grants, 3147
Meyer Memorial Trust Responsive Grants, 3148
Meyer Memorial Trust Special Grants, 3149
NFWF Columbia Basin Water Transactions Program Grants, 3366
NFWF Columbia River Estuarine Coastal Fund Grants, 3367
NFWF Oregon Governor's Fund for the Environment Grants, 3383
NWHF Health Advocacy Small Grants, 3537
NWHF Kaiser Permanente Community Grants, 3538
NWHF Physical Activity and Nutrition Grants, 3540
Oregon Youth Soccer Fndn Grants, 3692
PacifiCare Fndn Grants, 3725
PacifiCorp Fndn for Learning Grants, 3727
Paul G. Allen Family Fndn Grants, 3759
Peter M. Putnam Fndn Grants, 3848
PGE Fndn Grants, 3869
Piper Jaffray Fndn Communities Giving, 3899
Plum Creek Fndn Grants, 3917
Portland General Electric Fndn Grants, 3937
Pride Fndn Grants, 3958
RBC Dain Rauscher Fndn Grants, 4031
Regence Access to Health Care Grants, 4039
Regence Health Care Community Awareness and Engagement Grants, 4040
Regence Health Care Connections Grants, 4041
Regence Improving End-of-Life Grants, 4042
Regence Tools and Technology Grants, 4043
Regional Arts and Cultural Council General Support Grants, 4045
Regional Arts and Cultural Council Opportunity Grants, 4046
Regional Arts and Cultural Council Professional Development Grants, 4047
Regional Arts & Cultural Council Project Grants, 4048
REI Conservation and Outdoor Rec Grants, 4051
Safeco Insurance Community Grants, 4203
Salem Fndn Charitable Trust Grants, 4223
Samuel S. Johnson Fndn Grants, 4239

Shopko Fndn Community Grants, 4346
Social Justice Fund Northwest Criminal Justice Giving Project Grants, 4394
Social Justice Fund Northwest Economic Justice Giving Project Grants, 4395
Social Justice Fund Northwest Environmental Justice Giving Project Grants, 4396
Social Justice Fund Northwest General Grants, 4397
Social Justice Fund Northwest LGBTQ Giving Project Grants, 4398
Sunderland Fndn Grants, 4527
SVP Environment Grants, 4539
U.S. Bank Fndn Grants, 4686
Union Bank, N.A. Corporate Sponsorships and Donations, 4708
Union Bank, N.A. Fndn Grants, 4709
Union Pacific Community and Civic Grants, 4714
Union Pacific Fndn Health and Human Services Grants, 4715
VSA/Metlife Connect All Grants, 4953
Wells Fargo Housing Fndn Grants, 5023
Weyerhaeuser Company Fndn Grants, 5053
Wilburforce Fndn Grants, 5067
William C. Kenney Watershed Protection Fndn Ecosystem Grants, 5079
William G. Gilmore Fndn Grants, 5082

Pennsylvania

3 Rivers Wet Weather Demonstration Program (3RWW) Grants, 9
1675 Fndn Grants, 35
Abelard Fndn East Grants, 87
ACE Charitable Fndn Grants, 111
Adam Reineman Charitable Trust Grants, 144
Adams County Community Fndn of Pennsylvania Grants, 149
Adams Fndn Grants, 155
AEGON Transamerica Arts & Culture Grants, 176
AEGON Transamerica Fndn Civic and Community Grants, 177
AEGON Transamerica Fndn Health and Welfare Grants, 179
Aetna Fndn Regional Health Grants, 187
Agere Corp and Community Involvement Grants, 199
Albertson's Charitable Giving Grants, 345
Allegheny Fndn Grants, 376
Allegheny Technologies Charitable Trust, 377
Allen Hilles Fund Grants, 378
American Express Charitable Fund Grants, 429
American Foodservice Charitable Trust Grants, 433
American Rivers Community-Based Restoration Program River Grants, 444
Anne L. and George H. Clapp Charitable and Educational Trust Grants, 476
Appalachian Regional Comm Asset-Based Development Project Grants, 500
Appalachian Regional Comm Business Development Revolving Loan Fund Grants, 501
Appalachian Regional Comm Community Infrastructure Grants, 502
Appalachian Regional Comm Distressed Counties Grants, 503
Appalachian Regional Comm Education and Training Grants, 504
Appalachian Regional Comm Energy Grants, 505
Appalachian Regional Comm Export and Trade Development Grants, 506
Appalachian Regional Comm Health Care Grants, 507
Appalachian Reg Comm Housing Grants, 508
Appalachian Regional Comm Leadership Development and Capacity Building Grants, 509
Appalachian Regional Comm Telecommunications Grants, 510
Appalachian Regional Comm Tourist Development Grants, 511
Appalachian Regional Comm Transportation and Highways Grants, 512
Arcadia Fndn Grants, 525
Archer Daniels Midland Fndn Grants, 527
Arkema Fndn Science Teachers Program, 563

Arronson Fndn Grants, 567
Babcock Charitable Trust Grants, 632
Barra Fndn Community Fund Grants, 673
Barra Fndn Project Grants, 674
Bayer Fndn Grants, 696
Berks County Community Fndn Grants, 734
Birmingham Fndn Grants, 774
BJ's Charitable Fndn Grants, 777
BJ's Wholesale Clubs Local Charitable Giving, 778
Boeing Company Contributions Grants, 809
Bread and Roses Community Fund Grants and Scholarships, 832
Bridgestone/Firestone Trust Fund Grants, 836
Buhl Fndn - Frick Educational Fund, 859
Cable Positive's Tony Cox Community Grants, 886
Cabot Corporation Fndn Grants, 887
Caesar Puff Fndn Grants, 890
Caesars Fndn Grants, 891
Campbell Soup Fndn Grants, 916
CenturyLink Clarke M. Williams Grants, 998
Charles A. Frueauff Fndn Grants, 1037
Chemtura Corporation Contributions Grants, 1067
Chesapeake Bay Trust Fisheries and Headwaters Grants, 1070
Child Care Center Enhancement Grants, 1105
Chiron Fndn Community Grants, 1111
Cingular Wireless Charitable Contributions, 1134
Circle K Corporation Contributions Grants, 1136
Claneil Fndn Grants, 1145
Clarcor Fndn Grants, 1148
Claude Worthington Benedum Grants, 1161
Comcast Fndn Grants, 1235
ConAgra Foods Community Impact Grants, 1342
ConAgra Foods Nourish Our Comm Grants, 1343
Connelly Fndn Grants, 1353
ConocoPhillips Fndn Grants, 1354
ConocoPhillips Grants, 1355
Credit Suisse First Boston Fndn Grants, 1397
CSX Corporate Contributions Grants, 1408
Dance Advance Grants, 1441
Dean Foods Community Involvement Grants, 1469
Deluxe Corporation Fndn Grants, 1496
Dermody Properties Fndn Grants, 1517
Dolfinger-McMahon Fndn Grants, 1565
Dollar Energy Fund Grants, 1567
Dollar General Adult Literacy Grants, 1568
Dollar General Family Literacy Grants, 1569
Dollar General Youth Literacy Grants, 1570
Dominion Fndn Human Needs Grants, 1572
Donald and Sylvia Robinson Family Fndn Grants, 1573
Dorothy Rider Pool Health Care Grants, 1589
Douty Fndn Grants, 1595
Eastman Chemical Company Fndn Grants, 1643
Eaton Charitable Fund Grants, 1647
Eberly Fndn Grants, 1649
Eden Hall Fndn Grants, 1655
Elsie Lee Garthwaite Memorial Grants, 1692
EQT Fndn Art and Culture Grants, 1743
EQT Fndn Community Grants, 1744
EQT Fndn Education Grants, 1745
EQT Fndn Environment Grants, 1746
Erie Community Fndn Grants, 1750
Ethel Sergeant Clark Smith Fndn Grants, 1761
Eugene M. Lang Fndn Grants, 1764
F.M. Kirby Fndn Grants, 1780
Ferree Fndn Grants, 1804
FirstEnergy Fndn Community Grants, 1819
FirstEnergy Fndn Math, Science, and Technology Education Grants, 1820
Fisa Fndn Grants, 1826
Fluor Fndn Grants, 1875
FMC Fndn Grants, 1876
Fndn for Enhancing Communities Grants, 1893
Fourjay Fndn Grants, 1913
Frank E. and Seba B. Payne Fndn Grants, 1927
Franklin H. Wells and Ruth L. Wells Grants, 1930
Frank S. Flowers Fndn Grants, 1935
General Mills Fndn Grants, 2003
George I. Alden Trust Grants, 2023
Georgia-Pacific Fndn Education Grants, 2031

1170 / Pennsylvania

Georgia-Pacific Fndn Enrichment Grants, 2032
Georgia-Pacific Entrepreneurship Grants, 2033
Georgia-Pacific Fndn Environment Grants, 2034
Giant Eagle Fndn Grants, 2049
Gladys Brooks Fndn Grants, 2059
GlaxoSmithKline Corporate Grants, 2060
GlaxoSmithKline Fndn IMPACT Awards, 2061
Grable Fndn Grants, 2108
Grundy Fndn Grants, 2169
Gumdrop Books Librarian Scholarships, 2179
Hackett Fndn Grants, 2188
Hamilton Family Fndn Grants, 2213
Harley Davidson Fndn Grants, 2224
Harry C. Trexler Trust Grants, 2239
Heinz Endowments Grants, 2291
Henrietta Tower Wurts Memorial Grants, 2304
Hershey Company Grants, 2318
Highmark Corporate Giving Grants, 2319
Highmark Physician eHealth Grants, 2320
Hilda and Preston Davis Fndn Grants, 2322
Hillman Fndn Grants, 2327
Hirtzel Memorial Fndn Grants, 2332
Huffy Fndn Grants, 2384
Independence Blue Cross Charitable Medical Care Grants, 2524
John S. and James L. Knight Fndn Communities Grants, 2711
Josiah W. and Bessie H. Kline Fndn Grants, 2742
Joukowsky Family Fndn Grants, 2743
Kimberly-Clark Community Grants, 2824
L. W. Pierce Family Fndn Grants, 2846
Land O'Lakes Fndn Community Grants, 2859
Land O'Lakes Fndn Dollars for Doers, 2860
Laurel Fndn Grants, 2867
Lawrence J. and Anne Rubenstein Charitable Fndn Grants, 2868
Leeway Fndn Art and Change Grants, 2872
Leeway Fndn Transformation Award, 2873
Leo Niessen Jr., Charitable Trust Grants, 2885
Lincoln Financial Group Fndn Grants, 2906
Lockheed Martin Philanthropic Grants, 2918
McLean Contributionship Grants, 3088
Merck Family Fund Urban Farming and Youth Leadership Grants, 3119
Meyer and Stephanie Eglin Fndn Grants, 3139
Mid Atlantic Arts Fndn American Masterpieces Grants, 3169
Mid Atlantic Arts Found ArtsConnect Grants, 3170
Mid Atlantic Arts Fndn Folk Arts Outreach Project Grants, 3171
Motorola Fndn Grants, 3221
Nationwide Insurance Fndn Grants, 3285
Nestle Purina PetCare Educational Grants, 3302
Nestle Purina PetCare Pet Related Grants, 3304
Nestle Purina PetCare Support Dog and Police K-9 Organization Grants, 3305
Nestle Purina PetCare Youth Grants, 3306
NFWF Chesapeake Bay Conservation Innovation Grants, 3363
NFWF Chesapeake Bay Targeted Grants, 3365
NFWF Delaware Estuary Watershed Grants, 3371
Norfolk Southern Fndn Grants, 3463
Patrick John Bennett, Jr. Memorial Grants, 3752
PCA-PCD Organizational Short-Term Professional Development and Consulting Grants, 3769
PCA-PCD Professional Development for Individual Artists Grants, 3770
PCA Art Organizations and Art Programs Grants for Presenting Organizations, 3771
PCA Arts in Education Residencies, 3772
PCA Arts Management Internship, 3773
PCA Arts Organizations Grants for Music, 3774
PCA Arts Organizations and Arts Programs Grants for Art Museums, 3775
PCA Arts Organizations and Arts Programs Grants for Arts Education Organizations, 3776
PCA Arts Organizations and Arts Programs Grants for Arts Service Organizations, 3777
PCA Arts Organizations and Arts Programs Grants for Crafts, 3778
PCA Arts Organizations and Arts Programs Grants for Dance, 3779
PCA Arts Organizations and Arts Programs Grants for Film and Electronic Media, 3780
PCA Arts Organizations and Arts Programs Grants for Literature, 3781
PCA Arts Organizations and Arts Programs Grants for Local Arts, 3782
PCA Arts Organizations and Arts Programs Grants for Theatre, 3783
PCA Arts Organizations and Arts Programs Grants for Traditional and Folk Arts, 3784
PCA Arts Organizations and Arts Programs Grants for Visual Arts, 3785
PCA Busing Grants, 3786
PCA Entry Track Arts Organizations and Arts Programs Grants for Art Museums, 3787
PCA Entry Track Arts Organizations and Arts Grants for Arts Education Organizations, 3788
PCA Entry Track Arts Organizations and Arts Grants for Arts Service Organizations, 3789
PCA Entry Track Arts Organizations and Arts Programs Grants for Crafts, 3790
PCA Entry Track Arts Organizations and Arts Programs Grants for Dance, 3791
PCA Entry Track Arts Organizations and Arts Grants for Film and Electronic Media, 3792
PCA Entry Track Arts Organizations and Arts Programs Grants for Literature, 3793
PCA Entry Track Arts Organizations and Arts Programs Grants for Local Arts, 3794
PCA Entry Track Arts Organizations and Arts Programs Grants for Music, 3795
PCA Entry Track Arts Organizations and Arts Programs Grants for Presenting Organizations, 3796
PCA Entry Track Arts Organizations and Arts Programs Grants for Theatre, 3797
PCA Entry Track Arts Organizations and Arts Grants for Traditional and Folk Arts, 3798
PCA Entry Track Arts Organizations and Arts Programs Grants for Visual Arts, 3799
PCA Management/Technical Assistance Grants, 3800
PCA Pennsylvania Partners in the Arts Program Stream Grants, 3801
PCA Pennsylvania Partners in the Arts Project Stream Grants, 3802
PCA Professional Development Grants, 3803
PCA Strategies for Success Grants - Advanced, 3804
PCA Strategies for Success Grants - Basic, 3805
PCA Strategies for Success Grants - Intermediate, 3806
PennPAT Artist Technical Assistance Grants, 3811
PennPAT Fee-Support Grants for Presenters, 3812
PennPAT New Directions Grants for Presenters, 3813
PennPAT Strategic Opportunity Grants, 3815
Pew Fellowships in the Arts, 3860
Philadelphia Fndn Organizational Effectiveness Grants, 3872
Philadelphia Fndn YOUTHadelphia Grants, 3873
Pittsburgh Fndn Community Fund Grants, 3910
Plum Creek Fndn Grants, 3917
PMP Professional Development Grants, 3919
PMP Project Grants, 3920
PNC Charitable Trust and Fndn Grants, 3921
PNC Ecnomic Development Grants, 3922
PNC Fndn Green Building Grants, 3923
PNC Fndn Grow Up Great Grants, 3924
PPG Industries Fndn Grants, 3943
Price Chopper's Golub Fndn Grants, 3950
Price Chopper's Golub Fndn Two-Year Health Care Scholarship, 3951
Prudential Fndn Arts and Culture Grants, 3975
Prudential Fndn Economic Devel Grants, 3976
Prudential Fndn Education Grants, 3977
Rathmann Family Fndn Grants, 4026
Raymond John Wean Fndn Grants, 4028
REI Conservation and Outdoor Rec Grants, 4051
Richard King Mellon Fndn Grants, 4087
Ruth and Vernon Taylor Fndn Grants, 4177
Rutter's Children's Charities Grants, 4181
S. Spencer Scott Fund Grants, 4202

GEOGRAPHIC INDEX

Salmon Fndn Grants, 4225
Samuel S. Fels Fund Grants, 4238
Sands Fndn Crisis Fund Grants, 4254
Sands Fndn Grants, 4255
Seybert Institution for Poor Boys and Girls Grants, 4338
Stackpole-Hall Fndn Grants, 4472
Staunton Farm Fndn Grants, 4496
Stewart Huston Charitable Trust Grants, 4505
Stockton Rush Bartol Fndn Grants, 4508
Stowe Family Fndn Grants, 4510
Sunoco Fndn Grants, 4530
TE Fndn Grants, 4572
Textron Corporate Contributions Grants, 4601
Tiger Woods Fndn Grants, 4634
Tyler Aaron Bookman Memorial Trust Grants, 4684
Union Benevolent Association Grants, 4710
US Airways Community Contributions, 4788
US Airways Community Fndn Grants, 4789
US Airways Education Fndn Grants, 4790
Verizon Fndn Pennsylvania Grants, 4921
VSA/Metlife Connect All Grants, 4953
Vulcan Materials Company Fndn Grants, 4956
Wells Fargo Housing Fndn Grants, 5023
Western Pennsylvania Environmental Awards, 5026
Weyerhaeuser Company Fndn Grants, 5053
Willary Fndn Grants, 5071
William G. McGowan Charitable Fund Grants, 5084
Williams Companies Fndn Grants, 5095

Puerto Rico

Abbott Fund Access to Health Care Grants, 80
Abbott Fund Community Grants, 81
Abbott Fund Global AIDS Care Grants, 82
Abbott Fund Science Education Grants, 83
ACE Charitable Fndn Grants, 111
Archer Daniels Midland Fndn Grants, 527
Bank of America Charitable Matching Gifts, 658
Bank of America Charitable Volunteer Grants, 660
Best Buy Children's Fndn @15 Scholarship, 750
Brookdale Fndn Relatives as Parents Grants, 846
Case Fndn Grants, 950
EPA Environmental Justice Small Grants, 1731
EPA Pestwise Registration Improvement Act Partnership Grants, 1734
EPA Regional Agricultural IPM Grants, 1735
EPA Source Reduction Assistance Grants, 1737
EPA State Indoor Radon Grants, 1738
Medtronic CommunityLink Education Grants, 3110
Medtronic CommunityLink Health Grants, 3111
NHLBI Ancillary Studies in Clinical Trials, 3410
NHLBI Bioengineering and Obesity Grants, 3411
NHLBI Career Transition Awards, 3412
NHLBI Lymphatics Disease in the Digestive, Cardiovascular and Pulmonary Systems, 3414
NHLBI Lymphatics in Health and Disease in the Digestive, Urinary, Cardiovascular and Pulmonary Systems, 3415
NHLBI Research on the Role of Cardiomyocyte Mitochondria in Heart Disease: An Integrated Approach, 3417
NHLBI Ruth L. Kirschstein National Research Service Awards for Individual Postdoctoral Fellows, 3418
NHLBI Ruth L. Kirschstein National Research Service Awards for Individual Senior Fellows, 3421
NHLBI Ruth L. Kirschstein National Research Service Award Short-Term Institutional Research Training Grants, 3422
PDF Community Organizing Grants, 3807
PDF Fiscal Sponsorship Grant, 3808
Puerto Rico Community Fndn Grants, 3986
U.S. Department of Education Rehabilitation Training--Rehabilitation Continuing Education Programs--Institute on Rehabilitation Issues, 4700
USDA Farmers Market Promotion Grants, 4808
USDA Farm Labor Housing Grants, 4809
USDA Technical Assistance and Training Grants for Rural Waste Systems, 4842
USDC Public Works and Economic Adjustment Assistance Grants, 4856

GEOGRAPHIC INDEX

Rhode Island
1772 Fndn Fellowships, 36
Aaron Fndn Grants, 73
Abel and Sophia Sheng Charitable Grants, 86
Abelard Fndn East Grants, 87
Adelaide Dawson Lynch Trust Grants, 163
Agway Fndn Grants, 205
Alexander H. Bright Charitable Trust Grants, 358
American Rivers Community-Based Restoration Program River Grants, 444
Aratani Fndn Grants, 523
Barnes Group Fndn Grants, 672
Bay and Paul Fndns, Inc Grants, 692
BJ's Charitable Fndn Grants, 777
BJ's Wholesale Clubs Local Charitable Giving, 778
Brown Rudnick Charitable Relationship Grants, 855
Cable Positive's Tony Cox Community Grants, 886
Carlisle Fndn Grants, 931
Ceres Fndn Grants, 999
Champlin Fndns Grants, 1029
Charles A. Frueauff Fndn Grants, 1037
Citizens Bank Mid-Atlantic Charitable Grants, 1140
Clowes Fund Grants, 1177
ConAgra Foods Nourish Our Comm Grants, 1343
Cranston Fndn Grants, 1395
Davis Conservation Fndn Grants, 1461
Dominion Fndn Human Needs Grants, 1572
Dora Roberts Fndn Grants, 1579
Edna McConnell Clark Fndn Grants, 1659
Emma G. Harris Fndn Grants, 1701
Fields Pond Fndn Grants, 1807
Forrest C. Lattner Fndn Grants, 1887
Frank B. Hazard General Charity Fund Grants, 1926
George I. Alden Trust Grants, 2023
Gladys Brooks Fndn Grants, 2059
Hasbro Children's Fund, 2256
Haymarket People's Fund Sustaining Grants, 2267
Haymarket Urgent Response Grants, 2268
Hilda and Preston Davis Fndn Grants, 2322
Horace A. Kimball and S. Ella Kimball Grants, 2362
Jessie B. Cox Charitable Trust Grants, 2670
John Clarke Trust Grants, 2689
John D. and Katherine A. Johnston Grants, 2691
Joukowsky Family Fndn Grants, 2743
KeySpan Fndn Grants, 2821
LISC Financial Opportunity Center Social Innovation Fund Grants, 2911
Merck Family Fund Urban Farming and Youth Leadership Grants, 3119
Nellie Mae Education Fndn District-Level Change Grants, 3297
Nordson Corporation Fndn Grants, 3462
Norfolk Southern Fndn Grants, 3463
Orchard Fndn Grants, 3690
Paul V. Sherlock Center on Disabilities Access for All Abilities Mini Grants, 3767
Prince Charitable Trusts Rhode Island Grants, 3961
REI Conservation and Outdoor Rec Grants, 4051
Rhode Island Fndn Grants, 4073
RISCA Design Innovation Grant, 4097
RISCA Folk Arts Apprenticeships, 4098
RISCA Professional Arts Development Grants, 4099
RISCA Project Grants for Organizations, Individuals and Education, 4100
Robert and Joan Dircks Fndn Grants, 4104
Robert F. Stoico / FIRSTFED Charitable Fndn Grants, 4112
S. Spencer Scott Fund Grants, 4202
Shaw's Supermarkets Donations, 4342
Southern New England Folk and Traditional Arts Apprenticeship Grants, 4438
Sunoco Fndn Grants, 4530
Sweet Water Trust Grants, 4541
Textron Corporate Contributions Grants, 4601
TWS Fndn Grants, 4683
Verizon Fndn Northeast Region Grants, 4920
Verizon Wireless Hopeline Grants, 4927
Vigneron Memorial Fund Grants, 4938
VSA/Metlife Connect All Grants, 4953
Yawkey Fndn Grants, 5125

South Carolina
3M Company Arts and Culture Grants, 12
3M Company Environmental Giving Grants, 13
3M Company Health and Human Services Grants, 14
3M Fndn Community Giving Grants, 15
Abelard Fndn East Grants, 87
Abney Fndn Grants, 105
ACE Charitable Fndn Grants, 111
Amerigroup Fndn Grants, 452
Appalachian Regional Comm Asset-Based Development Project Grants, 500
Appalachian Regional Comm Business Development Revolving Loan Fund Grants, 501
Appalachian Regional Comm Community Infrastructure Grants, 502
Appalachian Regional Comm Distressed Counties Grants, 503
Appalachian Regional Comm Education and Training Grants, 504
Appalachian Regional Comm Energy Grants, 505
Appalachian Regional Comm Export and Trade Development Grants, 506
Appalachian Regional Comm Health Care Grants, 507
Appalachian Reg Comm Housing Grants, 508
Appalachian Regional Comm Leadership Development and Capacity Building Grants, 509
Appalachian Regional Comm Telecommunications Grants, 510
Appalachian Regional Comm Tourist Development Grants, 511
Appalachian Regional Comm Transportation and Highways Grants, 512
Archer Daniels Midland Fndn Grants, 527
Bailey Fndn Grants, 635
Belk Fndn Grants, 721
BJ's Charitable Fndn Grants, 777
BJ's Wholesale Clubs Local Charitable Giving, 778
Boeing Company Contributions Grants, 809
Bradley Family Fndn Grants, 830
Bridgestone/Firestone Trust Fund Grants, 836
Brunswick Fndn Dollars for Doers Grants, 856
Brunswick Fndn Grants, 857
Burlington Industries Fndn Grants, 865
Byerly Fndn Grants, 883
Cable Positive's Tony Cox Community Grants, 886
Campbell Soup Fndn Grants, 916
Carrier Corporation Contributions Grants, 946
Central Carolina Community Fndn Community Impact Grants, 994
Ceres Fndn Grants, 999
Chapman Family Charitable Trust Grants, 1034
Charles A. Frueauff Fndn Grants, 1037
Charles M. and Mary D. Grant Found Grants, 1050
Cingular Wireless Charitable Contributions, 1134
Circle K Corporation Contributions Grants, 1136
Coastal Community Fndn of S Carolina Grants, 1193
Comcast Fndn Grants, 1235
Community Fndn of Greenville-Greenville Women Giving Grants, 1293
Community Fndn of Greenville Community Enrichment Grants, 1294
Community Fndn of Greenville Hollingsworth Funds Capital Projects Grants, 1295
Community Fndn of Greenville Hollingsworth Funds Program/Project Grants, 1296
ConAgra Foods Community Impact Grants, 1342
ConAgra Foods Nourish Our Comm Grants, 1343
Cooper Industries Fndn Grants, 1370
CSX Corporate Contributions Grants, 1408
Cummins Fndn Grants, 1415
Dean Foods Community Involvement Grants, 1469
DHHS Healthy Tomorrows for Children, 1534
Dollar General Adult Literacy Grants, 1568
Dollar General Family Literacy Grants, 1569
Dollar General Youth Literacy Grants, 1570
Drs. Bruce and Lee Fndn Grants, 1607
Duke Endowment Child Care Grants, 1617
Duke Energy Community Vitality Grants, 1618
Duke Energy Economic Development Grants, 1619
Eastman Chemical Company Fndn Grants, 1643

Eaton Charitable Fund Grants, 1647
Fluor Fndn Grants, 1875
Fndn for the Carolinas Grants, 1896
Fund for Southern Communities Grants, 1977
Gannett Fndn Community Action Grants, 1984
Gaylord and Dorothy Donnelley Found Grants, 1993
Georgia-Pacific Fndn Education Grants, 2031
Georgia-Pacific Fndn Enrichment Grants, 2032
Georgia-Pacific Entrepreneurship Grants, 2033
Georgia-Pacific Fndn Environment Grants, 2034
Gumdrop Books Librarian Scholarships, 2179
Hilton Head Island Fndn Grants, 2330
J. Bulow Campbell Fndn Grants, 2593
J. Marion Sims Fndn Teachers' Pet Grant, 2605
John I. Smith Charities Grants, 2700
John S. and James L. Knight Fndn Communities Grants, 2711
Kimberly-Clark Community Grants, 2824
Knight Fndn Donor Advised Fund Grants, 2828
Lettie Pate Whitehead Fndn Grants, 2888
Lockheed Martin Philanthropic Grants, 2918
Mary Black Fndn Active Living Grants, 3031
Mary Black Found Community Health Grants, 3032
Mary Black Fndn Early Childhood Development Grants, 3033
Mary E. and Michael Blevins Charitable Grants, 3037
Mary Reynolds Babcock Fndn Grants, 3047
MeadWestvaco Sustainable Communities Grants, 3105
Norfolk Southern Fndn Grants, 3463
Paul Green Fndn Playwrights Fellowship, 3762
Piedmont Health Fndn Grants, 3882
Piedmont Natural Gas Corporate and Charitable Contributions, 3883
Piedmont Natural Gas Fndn Environmental Stewardship and Energy Sustainability Grant, 3884
Piedmont Natural Gas Fndn Health and Human Services Grants, 3885
Piedmont Natural Gas Fndn Workforce Development Grant, 3886
Plum Creek Fndn Grants, 3917
Progress Energy Corporate Contributions Grants, 3968
Progress Energy Fndn Environmental Stewardship Grants, 3970
Publix Super Markets Charities Local Grants, 3985
Richard Davoud Donchian Fndn Grants, 4080
Self Fndn Grants, 4335
Solutia Fund Grants, 4402
Sonoco Fndn Grants, 4403
South Carolina Arts Comm Accessibility Grants, 4410
South Carolina Arts Comm AIE Residency Plus Individual Site Grants, 4411
South Carolina Arts Comm AIE Residency Plus Multi-Site Grants, 4412
South Carolina Arts Comm American Masterpieces in South Carolina Grants, 4413
South Carolina Arts Comm Annual Operating Support for Organizations Grants, 4414
South Carolina Arts Comm Fellowships, 4415
South Carolina Arts Comm Arts and Economic Impact Study Assistance Grants, 4416
South Carolina Arts Comm Arts Facility Projects Grants, 4417
South Carolina Arts Comm Arts in Education After School Arts Initiative Grants, 4418
South Carolina Arts Comm Cultural Tourism Initiative Grants, 4419
South Carolina Arts Cultural Visions Grants, 4420
South Carolina Arts Comm Folklife & Traditional Arts Grants, 4421
South Carolina Arts Comm Incentive Grants for Employer Sponsored Benefits, 4422
South Carolina Arts Comm Leadership and Organizational Development Grants, 4423
South Carolina Arts Comm Long Term Operating Support for Organizations Grants, 4424
South Carolina Arts Comm Statewide Arts Participation Initiative Grants, 4425
South Carolina Arts Commi Subgranting Grants, 4426
South Carolina Arts Comm Traditional Arts Apprenticeship Grants, 4427

1172 / South Carolina

Springs Close Fndn Grants, 4462
Sunoco Fndn Grants, 4530
TE Fndn Grants, 4572
Verizon Fndn South Carolina Literacy & Internet Safety Grants, 4922
Verizon Fndn Southeast Region Grants, 4923
Vulcan Materials Company Fndn Grants, 4956
Wells Fargo Housing Fndn Grants, 5023
Weyerhaeuser Company Fndn Grants, 5053
Williams Companies Fndn Grants, 5095
Woodward Fund Grants, 5116
Yawkey Fndn Grants, 5125

South Dakota

3M Company Arts and Culture Grants, 12
3M Company Environmental Giving Grants, 13
3M Company Health and Human Services Grants, 14
3M Fndn Community Giving Grants, 15
Abelard Fndn West Grants, 88
Adams-Mastrovich Family Fndn Grants, 146
Albertson's Charitable Giving Grants, 345
Arts Midwest Performing Arts Grants, 579
Black Hills Corporation Grants, 781
Bush Fndn Arts & Humanities Grants: Capital Projects, 872
Bush Fndn Arts & Humanities Grants: Short-Term Organizational Support, 873
Bush Fndn Ecological Health Grants, 874
Bush Found Health & Human Services Grants, 875
Bush Fndn Medical Fellowships, 877
Bush Fndn Regional Arts Development Program II (RADP II) Grants, 878
Cable Positive's Tony Cox Community Grants, 886
CenturyLink Clarke M. Williams Grants, 998
Charles A. Frueauff Fndn Grants, 1037
Courage Center Judd Jacobson Memorial Award, 1382
Dean Foods Community Involvement Grants, 1469
DOJ Rural Domestic Violence and Child Victimization Enforcement Grants, 1562
Dollar General Adult Literacy Grants, 1568
Dollar General Family Literacy Grants, 1569
Dollar General Youth Literacy Grants, 1570
Four Times Fndn Grants, 1914
Gannett Fndn Community Action Grants, 1984
Graco Fndn Grants, 2111
GTECH Community Involvement Grants, 2171
Heartland Arts Fund, 2286
John S. and James L. Knight Fndn Communities Grants, 2711
Land O'Lakes Fndn Community Grants, 2859
Land O'Lakes Fndn Dollars for Doers, 2860
NGA Midwest School Garden Grants, 3407
Philanthrofund Fndn Grants, 3874
Piper Jaffray Fndn Communities Giving, 3899
RBC Dain Rauscher Fndn Grants, 4031
Shopko Fndn Community Grants, 4346
Sioux Falls Area Community Fndn Community Fund Grants (Unrestricted), 4364
Sioux Falls Area Community Fndn Field-of-Interest and Donor-Advised Grants, 4365
Sioux Falls Area Fndn Spot Grants, 4366
U.S. Bank Fndn Grants, 4686
Viking Children's Fund Grants, 4939
Waitt Family Fndn Grants, 4973
Wells Fargo Housing Fndn Grants, 5023

Tennessee

1st and 10 Fndn Grants, 1
ABC Charities Grants, 85
Abelard Fndn East Grants, 87
Adams and Reese LLP Corporate Giving Grants, 147
Adams Family Fndn I Grants, 150
Adams Family Fndn of Tennessee Grants, 152
AEP Corporate Giving Grants, 180
Aetna Fndn Regional Health Grants, 187
AFG Industries Grants, 191
Aladdin Industries Fndn Grants, 263
Albertson's Charitable Giving Grants, 345
American Electric Power Grants, 428
Amerigroup Fndn Grants, 452
Appalachian Community Fund General Grants, 493
Appalachian Community Fund GLBTQ Initiative Grants, 494
Appalachian Community Media Justice Grants, 495
Appalachian Community Fund Seize the Moment Grants, 496
Appalachian Community Fund Special Opportunities Grants, 497
Appalachian Community Fund Technical Assistance Grants, 498
Appalachian Regional Comm Asset-Based Development Project Grants, 500
Appalachian Regional Comm Business Development Revolving Loan Fund Grants, 501
Appalachian Regional Comm Community Infrastructure Grants, 502
Appalachian Regional Comm Distressed Counties Grants, 503
Appalachian Regional Comm Education and Training Grants, 504
Appalachian Regional Comm Energy Grants, 505
Appalachian Regional Comm Export and Trade Development Grants, 506
Appalachian Regional Comm Health Care Grants, 507
Appalachian Reg Comm Housing Grants, 508
Appalachian Regional Comm Leadership Development and Capacity Building Grants, 509
Appalachian Regional Comm Telecommunications Grants, 510
Appalachian Regional Comm Tourist Development Grants, 511
Appalachian Regional Comm Transportation and Highways Grants, 512
Archer Daniels Midland Fndn Grants, 527
Arkema Fndn Science Teachers Program, 563
Assisi Found of Memphis Capital Project Grants, 593
Assisi Fndn of Memphis General Grants, 594
Assisi Fndn of Memphis Mini Grants, 595
BancorpSouth Fndn Grants, 651
Bechtel Group Fndn Building Positive Community Relationships Grants, 715
Belk Fndn Grants, 721
Benwood Fndn Community Grants, 732
Benwood Fndn Focus Area Grants, 733
Bridgestone/Firestone Trust Fund Grants, 836
Brunswick Fndn Dollars for Doers Grants, 856
Brunswick Fndn Grants, 857
Cable Positive's Tony Cox Community Grants, 886
Carrier Corporation Contributions Grants, 946
CCCF Alpha Fund Grants, 959
CCCF Dora Maclellan Brown Christian Priority Grants, 960
CenturyLink Clarke M. Williams Grants, 998
Charles A. Frueauff Fndn Grants, 1037
Charles M. and Mary D. Grant Found Grants, 1050
Christy-Houston Fndn Grants, 1115
Cingular Wireless Charitable Contributions, 1134
Circle K Corporation Contributions Grants, 1136
Comcast Fndn Grants, 1235
Community of Greater Chattanooga Grants, 1281
Community Found of Greater Memphis Grants, 1290
Community Found of Middle Tennessee Grants, 1300
ConAgra Foods Community Impact Grants, 1342
ConAgra Foods Nourish Our Comm Grants, 1343
Conwood Charitable Trust Grants, 1366
Coors Brewing Corporate Contributions Grants, 1371
CSX Corporate Contributions Grants, 1408
Cummins Fndn Grants, 1415
Dean Foods Community Involvement Grants, 1469
Dell Fndn Open Grants, 1490
Dollar Energy Fund Grants, 1567
Dollar General Adult Literacy Grants, 1568
Dollar General Family Literacy Grants, 1569
Dollar General Youth Literacy Grants, 1570
Eastman Chemical Company Fndn Grants, 1643
East Tennessee Affordable Housing Trust Fund, 1645
East Tennessee Fndn Grants, 1646
Fifth Third Bank Corporate Giving, 1809
Fifth Third Fndn Grants, 1810
Fluor Fndn Grants, 1875
FMC Fndn Grants, 1876
Frist Fndn Grants, 1964
Gannett Fndn Community Action Grants, 1984
GenCorp Fndn Grants, 1998
General Mills Fndn Grants, 2003
Georgia-Pacific Fndn Education Grants, 2031
Georgia-Pacific Fndn Enrichment Grants, 2032
Georgia-Pacific Entrepreneurship Grants, 2033
Georgia-Pacific Fndn Environment Grants, 2034
Gladys Brooks Fndn Grants, 2059
GTECH Community Involvement Grants, 2171
Gumdrop Books Librarian Scholarships, 2179
HCA Fndn Grants, 2274
Hershey Company Grants, 2318
Hilton Hotels Corporate Giving Grants, 2331
Humana Fndn Grants, 2388
Hyde Family Fndns Grants, 2414
J. Bulow Campbell Fndn Grants, 2593
Jim Blevins Fndn Grants, 2678
Jim Blevins Fndn Scholarships, 2679
John Deere Fndn Grants, 2692
Johns Manville Fund Grants, 2716
Kimberly-Clark Community Grants, 2824
Lettie Pate Whitehead Fndn Grants, 2888
Louie M. and Betty M. Phillips Grants, 2923
Mary E. and Michael Blevins Charitable Grants, 3037
Mary Reynolds Babcock Fndn Grants, 3047
Medtronic Community Link Arts, Civic, and Culture Grants, 3109
Medtronic CommunityLink Education Grants, 3110
Medtronic CommunityLink Health Grants, 3111
Medtronic Comm Link Human Services Grants, 3112
Memorial Fndn Grants, 3117
Mildred V. Horn Fndn Grants, 3176
National Trust for Historic Preservation Diversity Scholarship, 3280
Nationwide Insurance Fndn Grants, 3285
Nissan Fndn Grants, 3444
Nissan Neighbors Grants, 3445
Norfolk Southern Fndn Grants, 3463
Paul Green Fndn Playwrights Fellowship, 3762
PeyBack Fndn Grants, 3861
Piedmont Natural Gas Corporate and Charitable Contributions, 3883
Piedmont Natural Gas Fndn Environmental Stewardship and Energy Sustainability Grant, 3884
Piedmont Natural Gas Fndn Health and Human Services Grants, 3885
Piedmont Natural Gas Fndn Workforce Development Grant, 3886
Piper Jaffray Fndn Communities Giving, 3899
Plough Fndn Grants, 3915
Publix Super Markets Charities Local Grants, 3985
REI Conservation and Outdoor Rec Grants, 4051
Rucker-Donnell Fndn Grants, 4172
Safeco Insurance Community Grants, 4203
Salmon Fndn Grants, 4225
Solutia Fund Grants, 4402
Square D Fndn Grants, 4464
Sunoco Fndn Grants, 4530
TAC Arts Access Grant, 4549
TAC Arts Access Technical Assistance Grants, 4550
TAC Arts Build Communities Grants, 4551
TAC Arts Educ Community-Learning Grants, 4552
TAC Arts Education Mini Grants, 4553
TAC Arts Projects Grants, 4554
TAC Rural Arts Project Support Grants, 4555
TAC Technical Assistance Grants, 4556
TAC Touring Arts and Access Grants, 4557
Tension Envelope Fndn Grants, 4578
Thomas W. Briggs Fndn Grants, 4621
Thompson Charitable Fndn Grants, 4622
U.S. Bank Fndn Grants, 4686
Union Pacific Community and Civic Grants, 4714
Union Pacific Fndn Health and Human Services Grants, 4715
USDA Delta Health Care Services Grants, 4804
VSA/Metlife Connect All Grants, 4953
Vulcan Materials Company Fndn Grants, 4956
Wells Fargo Housing Fndn Grants, 5023

GEOGRAPHIC INDEX

Texas / 1173

William B. Stokely Jr. Fndn Grants, 5076
Woodward Fund Grants, 5116

Texas
2 Life 18 Fndn Grants, 5
3 Roots Fndn Grants, 10
3M Company Arts and Culture Grants, 12
3M Company Environmental Giving Grants, 13
3M Company Health and Human Services Grants, 14
3M Fndn Community Giving Grants, 15
Abbott Fund Access to Health Care Grants, 80
Abbott Fund Community Grants, 81
Abbott Fund Global AIDS Care Grants, 82
Abbott Fund Science Education Grants, 83
ABC Charities Grants, 85
Abell-Hanger Fndn Grants, 91
ACE Charitable Fndn Grants, 111
Adams and Reese LLP Corporate Giving Grants, 147
Advanced Micro Devices Comm Affairs Grants, 172
AEGON Transamerica Arts & Culture Grants, 176
AEGON Transamerica Fndn Civic and Community Grants, 177
AEGON Transamerica Fndn Health and Welfare Grants, 179
AEP Corporate Giving Grants, 180
Aetna Fndn Regional Health Grants, 187
A Glimmer of Hope Fndn Grants, 200
Albert and Bessie Mae Kronkosky Charitable Fndn Grants, 339
Albert and Margaret Alkek Fndn Grants, 340
Albertson's Charitable Giving Grants, 345
Alvin and Lucy Owsley Fndn Grants, 404
Amarillo Area/Harrington Fndns Grants, 412
American Electric Power Grants, 428
American Express Charitable Fund Grants, 429
American Foodservice Charitable Trust Grants, 433
Amerigroup Fndn Grants, 452
Anheuser-Busch Fndn Grants, 470
Ann L. and Carol Green Rhodes Charitable Trust Grants, 483
Aragona Family Fndn Grants, 522
Archer Daniels Midland Fndn Grants, 527
ARCO Fndn Education Grants, 528
Arkema Fndn Science Teachers Program, 563
Austin Community Fndn Grants, 616
Bayer Fndn Grants, 696
BBVA Compass Fndn Charitable Grants, 703
Bechtel Group Fndn Building Positive Community Relationships Grants, 715
Belk Fndn Grants, 721
Bennett Family Fndn of Texas Grants, 728
Bill and Katie Weaver Charitable Trust Grants, 764
Boeing Company Contributions Grants, 809
Bosque Fndn Grants, 818
Brad Brock Family Fndn Grants, 827
Bridgestone/Firestone Trust Fund Grants, 836
Brown Fndn Grants, 854
Brunswick Fndn Dollars for Doers Grants, 856
Brunswick Fndn Grants, 857
Cable Positive's Tony Cox Community Grants, 886
Cabot Corporation Fndn Grants, 887
Campbell Soup Fndn Grants, 916
Carl B. and Florence E. King Fndn Grants, 928
Carrier Corporation Contributions Grants, 946
Cartis Creative Services Grants, 948
CenturyLink Clarke M. Williams Grants, 998
Charles A. Frueauff Fndn Grants, 1037
Chase Paymentech Corporate Giving Grants, 1059
Cingular Wireless Charitable Contributions, 1134
Circle K Corporation Contributions Grants, 1136
Clara Blackford Smith and W. Aubrey Smith Charitable Fndn Grants, 1147
Coastal Bend Community Fndn Grants, 1192
Cockrell Fndn Grants, 1196
Comcast Fndn Grants, 1235
Comerica Charitable Fndn Grants, 1237
Communities Fndn of Texas Grants, 1243
Community Fndn of Abilene Community Grants, 1264
Community Found of Abilene Future Grants, 1265

Community Fndn of Abilene Humane Treatment of Animals Grants, 1266
ConAgra Foods Community Impact Grants, 1342
ConAgra Foods Nourish Our Comm Grants, 1343
ConocoPhillips Fndn Grants, 1354
ConocoPhillips Grants, 1355
Constantin Fndn Grants, 1362
Cooper Industries Fndn Grants, 1370
Credit Suisse First Boston Fndn Grants, 1397
Crystelle Waggoner Charitable Trust Grants, 1405
Cullen Fndn Grants, 1411
Cummins Fndn Grants, 1415
Curtis Fndn Grants, 1419
Dallas Fndn Grants, 1436
Dallas Mavericks Fndn Grants, 1437
Dallas Women's Fndn Grants, 1438
Darden Restaurants Fndn Grants, 1446
Dave Coy Fndn Grants, 1447
David Robinson Fndn Grants, 1454
Dean Foods Community Involvement Grants, 1469
Dell Fndn Open Grants, 1490
Deluxe Corporation Fndn Grants, 1496
Denton A. Cooley Fndn Grants, 1500
DHHS Healthy Tomorrows for Children, 1534
Dollar Energy Fund Grants, 1567
Dollar General Adult Literacy Grants, 1568
Dollar General Family Literacy Grants, 1569
Dollar General Youth Literacy Grants, 1570
Dominion Fndn Human Needs Grants, 1572
Dr. and Mrs. Paul Pierce Memorial Grants, 1599
Eastman Chemical Company Fndn Grants, 1643
Eaton Charitable Fund Grants, 1647
EDS Fndn Grants, 1661
EDS Technology Grants, 1662
Edward R. Godfrey Fndn Grants, 1667
Effie and Wofford Cain Fndn Grants, 1674
El Paso Community Fndn Grants, 1688
El Paso Corporate Fndn Grants, 1689
Entergy Charitable Fndn Low-Income Initiatives and Solutions Grants, 1711
Entergy Corporation Micro Grants, 1712
Entergy Corp Grants for Arts and Culture, 1713
Entergy Corporation Open Grants for Community Improvement & Enrichment, 1714
Entergy Corp Grants for Healthy Families, 1715
Eugene McDermott Fndn Grants, 1765
Eugene Straus Charitable Trust, 1766
Ewing Halsell Fndn Grants, 1776
Feldman Fndn Grants, 1801
First Lady's Family Literacy Initiative for Texas Family Literacy Trailblazer Grants, 1821
First Lady's Family Literacy for Texas Grants, 1822
First Lady's Family Literacy Initiative for Texas Implementation Grants, 1823
First Lady's Family Literacy Initiative for Texas Planning Grants, 1824
Fluor Fndn Grants, 1875
FMC Fndn Grants, 1876
Fondren Fndn Grants, 1878
Forrest C. Lattner Fndn Grants, 1887
Frances C. and William P. Smallwood Grants, 1918
George Fndn Grants, 2018
George W. Brackenridge Fndn Grants, 2028
Georgia-Pacific Fndn Education Grants, 2031
Georgia-Pacific Fndn Enrichment Grants, 2032
Georgia-Pacific Fndn Entrepreneurship Grants, 2033
Georgia-Pacific Fndn Environment Grants, 2034
Gil and Dody Weaver Fndn Grants, 2053
GTECH Community Involvement Grants, 2171
H.B. Fuller Company Fndn Grants, 2183
Hahl Proctor Charitable Trust Grants, 2208
Halliburton Fndn Grants, 2211
Hallmark Corporate Fndn Grants, 2212
Harold Simmons Fndn Grants, 2230
Harris and Eliza Kempner Fund Grants, 2231
Harry W. Bass, Jr. Fndn Grants, 2246
Hatton W. Sumners Fndn for the Study and Teaching of Self Government Grants, 2257
Helen Gertrude Sparks Charitable Trust Grants, 2294
Helen S. Boylan Fndn Grants, 2298

Hillcrest Fndn Grants, 2325
Hoblitzelle Fndn Grants, 2341
Hogg Fndn for Mental Health Grants, 2343
Hoglund Fndn Grants, 2344
Houston Endowment Grants, 2373
Humana Fndn Grants, 2388
I.A. O'Shaughnessy Fndn Grants, 2416
Intel Community Grants, 2562
J.E. and L.E. Mabee Fndn Grants, 2595
James M. Collins Fndn Grants, 2633
James R. Dougherty Jr. Fndn Grants, 2635
Jean and Price Daniel Fndn Grants, 2659
John P. McGovern Fndn Grants, 2707
John S. Dunn Research Fndn Grants, 2715
JP Morgan Chase Arts and Culture Grants, 2752
JP Morgan Chase Community Devel Grants, 2753
Katrine Menzing Deakins Charitable Grants, 2793
Ken W. Davis Fndn Grants, 2813
Kimberly-Clark Community Grants, 2824
Land O'Lakes Fndn Community Grants, 2859
Land O'Lakes Fndn Dollars for Doers, 2860
LISC Financial Opportunity Center Social Innovation Fund Grants, 2911
Lockheed Martin Philanthropic Grants, 2918
Lowe Fndn Grants, 2929
Lubbock Area Fndn Grants, 2931
Lubrizol Fndn Grants, 2933
Luella Kemper Trust Grants, 2939
M.B. and Edna Zale Fndn Grants, 2950
M.D. Anderson Fndn Grants, 2952
MacDonald-Peterson Fndn Grants, 2965
Marathon Petroleum Corporation Grants, 2999
Marcia and Otto Koehler Fndn Grants, 3000
Margaret and James A. Elkins Jr. Grants, 3003
McCombs Fndn Grants, 3075
Meadows Fndn Grants, 3104
MeadWestvaco Sustainable Communities Grants, 3105
Medtronic Community Link Arts, Civic, and Culture Grants, 3109
Medtronic CommunityLink Education Grants, 3110
Medtronic CommunityLink Health Grants, 3111
Medtronic Comm Link Human Services Grants, 3112
Mercedes-Benz USA Corporate Contributions, 3118
Michael and Susan Dell Fndn Grants, 3158
Mid-America Arts Alliance Community Engagement with Touring Artists Grants, 3166
Mid-America Arts Alliance Reg Touring Grants, 3167
Milton Hicks Wood and Helen Gibbs Wood Charitable Trust Grants, 3184
Moody Fndn Grants, 3215
Motorola Fndn Grants, 3221
Nationwide Insurance Fndn Grants, 3285
Nissan Fndn Grants, 3444
Nissan Neighbors Grants, 3445
Norfolk Southern Fndn Grants, 3463
PACCAR Fndn Grants, 3719
PacifiCare Fndn Grants, 3725
Paso del Norte Health Fndn Grants, 3743
Paul and Mary Haas Fndn Contributions and Student Scholarships, 3756
Pier 1 Imports Grants, 3887
Plum Creek Fndn Grants, 3917
Poets & Writers Readings/Workshops Grants, 3927
Pollock Fndn Grants, 3930
Powell Fndn Grants, 3942
Priddy Fndn Capital Grants, 3954
Priddy Fndn Operating Grants, 3955
Priddy Fndn Organizational Development Grants, 3956
Priddy Fndn Grants, 3957
Prudential Fndn Arts and Culture Grants, 3975
Prudential Fndn Economic Devel Grants, 3976
Prudential Fndn Education Grants, 3977
Qualcomm Grants, 3993
QuikTrip Corporate Contributions Grants, 3998
Rainbow Fund Grants, 4009
RBC Dain Rauscher Fndn Grants, 4031
REI Conservation and Outdoor Rec Grants, 4051
Robert E. and Evelyn McKee Fndn Grants, 4110
Rockwell Fund, Inc. Grants, 4140
Roy and Christine Sturgis Trust Grants, 4166

Texas

Ruth and Vernon Taylor Fndn Grants, 4177
Ryder System Charitable Fndn Grants, 4191
Safeco Insurance Community Grants, 4203
San Antonio Area Fndn Grants, 4240
Sid W. Richardson Fndn Grants, 4350
Solutia Fund Grants, 4402
Southwire Company Grants, 4447
Square D Fndn Grants, 4464
Steele-Reese Fndn Grants, 4498
Sterling-Turner Charitable Fndn Grants, 4499
Stinson Fndn Grants, 4506
Susan Vaughan Fndn Grants, 4537
Swaim-Gause-Rucker Fndn Grants, 4540
T.L.L. Temple Fndn Grants, 4546
TE Fndn Grants, 4572
Tension Envelope Fndn Grants, 4578
Texas Comm on the Arts Arts Education Project 1 Grants, 4579
Texas Comm on the Arts Arts in Education Team Building/Texas Music Project Grants, 4580
Texas Comm on the Arts Respond Grants, 4581
Texas Comm on the Arts County Arts Expansion Program, 4582
Texas Comm on the Arts Create-1 Grants, 4583
Texas Comm on the Arts Create-2 Grants, 4584
Texas Comm on the Arts Create-3 Grants, 4585
Texas Comm on the Arts Create-4 Grants, 4586
Texas Comm on the Arts Create-5 Grants, 4587
Texas Comm on the Arts Cultural Connections-Performance Support Grants, 4588
Texas Comm on the Arts Cultural Connections-Visual & Media Arts Touring Exhibits Grants, 4589
Texas Comm On The Arts Cultural Connections Consultant/Simply Solutions Grants, 4590
Texas Comm on Arts Cultural Connections Grants, 4591
Texas Comm On The Arts GPA1, 4592
Texas Comm on the Arts Special Opportunities Grants, 4593
Texas Comm on the Arts Young Masters Grants, 4594
Texas Filmmakers Production Grants, 4595
Texas Instruments Arts and Culture Grants, 4596
Texas Instruments Civic and Business Grants, 4597
Texas Instru Health and Human Services Grants, 4598
Texas Instruments Fndn Arts and Culture Grants, 4599
Texas Instruments Community Services Grants, 4600
Textron Corporate Contributions Grants, 4601
Thelma Braun and Bocklett Fndn Grants, 4603
Tiger Woods Fndn Grants, 4634
Todd Brock Family Fndn Grants, 4639
Topfer Family Fndn Grants, 4646
Toro Fndn Grants, 4647
Toyota Motor Manufacturing of Texas Grants, 4656
Turner Voices Corporate Contributions, 4682
TWS Fndn Grants, 4683
Union Pacific Community and Civic Grants, 4714
Union Pacific Fndn Health and Human Services Grants, 4715
USDA Individual Water and Waste Water Grants, 4817
VSA/Metlife Connect All Grants, 4953
Vulcan Materials Company Fndn Grants, 4956
W.H. and Mary Ellen Cobb Charitable Grants, 4959
W.P. and Bulah Luse Fndn Grants, 4965
Wells Fargo Housing Fndn Grants, 5023
Weyerhaeuser Company Fndn Grants, 5053
William J. and Dorothy K. O'Neill Grants, 5087
William M. Weaver Fndn Grants, 5091
Williams Companies Fndn Grants, 5095
Young Family Fndn Grants, 5127

US Virgin Islands

Bank of America Charitable Matching Gifts, 658
Bank of America Charitable Volunteer Grants, 660
Community Fndn Of The Virgin Islands Anderson Family Teacher Grants, 1323
Community Fndn Of The Virgin Islands Kimelman Grants, 1324
Community Fndn Of The Virgin Islands Grants, 1325
EPA Environmental Justice Small Grants, 1731
EPA Pestwise Registration Improvement Act Partnership Grants, 1734
EPA Regional Agricultural IPM Grants, 1735
EPA Source Reduction Assistance Grants, 1737
EPA State Indoor Radon Grants, 1738
EPA Tribal Support for the National Environmental Information Exchange Network, 1742
Mid Atlantic Arts Fndn American Masterpieces Grants, 3169
Mid Atlantic Arts Found ArtsConnect Grants, 3170
Mid Atlantic Arts Fndn Folk Arts Outreach Project Grants, 3171
NHLBI Ancillary Studies in Clinical Trials, 3410
NHLBI Bioengineering and Obesity Grants, 3411
NHLBI Career Transition Awards, 3412
NHLBI Lymphatics Disease in the Digestive, Cardiovascular and Pulmonary Systems, 3414
NHLBI Lymphatics in Health and Disease in the Digestive, Urinary, Cardiovascular and Pulmonary Systems, 3415
NHLBI Research on the Role of Cardiomyocyte Mitochondria in Heart Disease: An Integrated Approach, 3417
NHLBI Ruth L. Kirschstein National Research Service Awards for Individual Postdoctoral Fellows, 3418
NHLBI Ruth L. Kirschstein National Research Service Awards for Individual Senior Fellows, 3421
NHLBI Ruth L. Kirschstein National Research Service Award Short-Term Institutional Research Training Grants, 3422
PDF Fiscal Sponsorship Grant, 3808
PennPAT Fee-Support Grants for Presenters, 3812
PennPAT New Directions Grants for Presenters, 3813
U.S. Department of Education Rehabilitation Training--Rehabilitation Continuing Education Programs--Institute on Rehabilitation Issues, 4700
USDA Farmers Market Promotion Grants, 4808
USDA Farm Labor Housing Grants, 4809
USDA Technical Assistance and Training Grants for Rural Waste Systems, 4842
USDC Public Works and Economic Adjustment Assistance Grants, 4856

Utah

3M Company Arts and Culture Grants, 12
3M Company Environmental Giving Grants, 13
3M Company Health and Human Services Grants, 14
3M Fndn Community Giving Grants, 15
Abbott Fund Access to Health Care Grants, 80
Abbott Fund Community Grants, 81
Abbott Fund Global AIDS Care Grants, 82
Abbott Fund Science Education Grants, 83
Abelard Fndn West Grants, 88
Albertson's Charitable Giving Grants, 345
American Express Charitable Fund Grants, 429
Beverley Taylor Sorenson Art for Kids Grants, 757
Boeing Company Contributions Grants, 809
Bridgestone/Firestone Trust Fund Grants, 836
Cable Positive's Tony Cox Community Grants, 886
Campbell Soup Fndn Grants, 916
CenturyLink Clarke M. Williams Grants, 998
Comcast Fndn Grants, 1235
Daniels Fund Grants, 1443
Dean Foods Community Involvement Grants, 1469
Delonne Anderson Family Fndn, 1492
Deluxe Corporation Fndn Grants, 1496
DOJ Rural Domestic Violence and Child Victimization Enforcement Grants, 1562
Dollar General Adult Literacy Grants, 1568
Dollar General Family Literacy Grants, 1569
Dollar General Youth Literacy Grants, 1570
E.L. Wiegand Fndn Grants, 1639
eBay Fndn Community Grants, 1648
Fieldstone Fndn Grants, 1808
Gannett Fndn Community Action Grants, 1984
GenCorp Fndn Grants, 1998
George S. and Dolores Dore Eccles Grants, 2027
Humana Fndn Grants, 2388
Intel Community Grants, 2562
JP Morgan Chase Arts and Culture Grants, 2752
JP Morgan Chase Community Devel Grants, 2753
KeyBank Fndn Grants, 2820
Kimberly-Clark Community Grants, 2824
PacifiCorp Fndn for Learning Grants, 3727
Piper Jaffray Fndn Communities Giving, 3899
Questar Corporate Contributions Grants, 3997
RBC Dain Rauscher Fndn Grants, 4031
Regence Access to Health Care Grants, 4039
Regence Health Care Community Awareness and Engagement Grants, 4040
Regence Health Care Connections Grants, 4041
Regence Improving End-of-Life Grants, 4042
Regence Tools and Technology Grants, 4043
REI Conservation and Outdoor Rec Grants, 4051
Ruth Eleanor Bamberger and John Ernest Bamberger Memorial Fndn Grants, 4178
Shopko Fndn Community Grants, 4346
Southwire Company Grants, 4447
Stan and Sandy Checketts Fndn, 4473
Sunderland Fndn Grants, 4527
U.S. Bank Fndn Grants, 4686
Union Pacific Community and Civic Grants, 4714
Union Pacific Fndn Health and Human Services Grants, 4715
Wells Fargo Housing Fndn Grants, 5023
Weyerhaeuser Company Fndn Grants, 5053
Wilburforce Fndn Grants, 5067
William C. Kenney Watershed Protection Fndn Ecosystem Grants, 5079

Vermont

Abelard Fndn East Grants, 87
Agnes M. Lindsay Trust Grants, 203
Agway Fndn Grants, 205
Albertson's Charitable Giving Grants, 345
Alexander H. Bright Charitable Trust Grants, 358
American Rivers Community-Based Restoration Program River Grants, 444
Barnes Group Fndn Grants, 672
Bay and Paul Fndns, Inc Grants, 692
Cable Positive's Tony Cox Community Grants, 886
Carlisle Fndn Grants, 931
Ceres Fndn Grants, 999
Charles A. Frueauff Fndn Grants, 1037
Clowes Fund Grants, 1177
Comcast Fndn Grants, 1235
ConAgra Foods Nourish Our Comm Grants, 1343
Davis Conservation Fndn Grants, 1461
DOJ Rural Domestic Violence and Child Victimization Enforcement Grants, 1562
Dollar General Adult Literacy Grants, 1568
Dollar General Family Literacy Grants, 1569
Dollar General Youth Literacy Grants, 1570
Dorr Fndn Grants, 1591
Edna McConnell Clark Fndn Grants, 1659
Entergy Corporation Micro Grants, 1712
Entergy Corp Grants for Arts and Culture, 1713
Entergy Corporation Open Grants for Community Improvement & Enrichment, 1714
Entergy Corp Grants for Healthy Families, 1715
Fields Pond Fndn Grants, 1807
Gannett Fndn Community Action Grants, 1984
George I. Alden Trust Grants, 2023
Gladys Brooks Fndn Grants, 2059
Hannaford Charitable Fndn Grants, 2222
Haymarket People's Fund Sustaining Grants, 2267
Haymarket Urgent Response Grants, 2268
Heifer Educational Fund Grants for Principals, 2288
Heifer Educational Fund Grants for Teachers, 2289
Hilda and Preston Davis Fndn Grants, 2322
Jane's Trust Grants, 2639
Jessie B. Cox Charitable Trust Grants, 2670
Joukowsky Family Fndn Grants, 2743
KeyBank Fndn Grants, 2820
KeySpan Fndn Grants, 2821
Lucy Downing Nisbet Charitable Fund Grants, 2935
Merck Family Fund Urban Farming and Youth Leadership Grants, 3119
Norfolk Southern Fndn Grants, 3463
Orchard Fndn Grants, 3690
Price Chopper's Golub Fndn Grants, 3950

GEOGRAPHIC INDEX

Price Chopper's Golub Fndn Two-Year Health Care Scholarship, 3951
Richard Davoud Donchian Fndn Grants, 4080
Robert and Joan Dircks Fndn Grants, 4104
S. Spencer Scott Fund Grants, 4202
Shaw's Supermarkets Donations, 4342
Strolling of the Heifers Scholarships for Farmers, 4514
Sunoco Fndn Grants, 4530
Sweet Water Trust Grants, 4541
Thomas Thompson Trust Grants, 4620
Verizon Fndn Vermont Grants, 4924
Verizon Wireless Hopeline Grants, 4927
Vermont Community Fndn Grants, 4929
Yawkey Fndn Grants, 5125

Virginia

Abbott Fund Access to Health Care Grants, 80
Abbott Fund Community Grants, 81
Abbott Fund Global AIDS Care Grants, 82
Abbott Fund Science Education Grants, 83
Abelard Fndn East Grants, 87
ACE Charitable Fndn Grants, 111
AEP Corporate Giving Grants, 180
Aetna Fndn Regional Health Grants, 187
Altria Group Arts and Culture Grants, 399
American Electric Power Grants, 428
American Rivers Community-Based Restoration Program River Grants, 444
Amerigroup Fndn Grants, 452
Andersen Corporate Fndn, 459
Anheuser-Busch Fndn Grants, 470
Anthem Blue Cross and Blue Shield Grants, 488
Appalachian Community Fund General Grants, 493
Appalachian Community Fund GLBTQ Initiative Grants, 494
Appalachian Community Media Justice Grants, 495
Appalachian Community Fund Seize the Moment Grants, 496
Appalachian Community Fund Special Opportunities Grants, 497
Appalachian Community Fund Technical Assistance Grants, 498
Appalachian Regional Comm Asset-Based Development Project Grants, 500
Appalachian Regional Comm Business Development Revolving Loan Fund Grants, 501
Appalachian Regional Comm Community Infrastructure Grants, 502
Appalachian Regional Comm Distressed Counties Grants, 503
Appalachian Regional Comm Education and Training Grants, 504
Appalachian Regional Comm Energy Grants, 505
Appalachian Regional Comm Export and Trade Development Grants, 506
Appalachian Regional Comm Health Care Grants, 507
Appalachian Reg Comm Housing Grants, 508
Appalachian Regional Comm Leadership Development and Capacity Building Grants, 509
Appalachian Regional Comm Telecommunications Grants, 510
Appalachian Regional Comm Tourist Development Grants, 511
Appalachian Regional Comm Transportation and Highways Grants, 512
Arlington Community Fndn Grants, 564
Beazley Fndn Grants, 714
Bechtel Group Fndn Building Positive Community Relationships Grants, 715
Beirne Carter Fndn Grants, 719
Belk Fndn Grants, 721
BJ's Charitable Fndn Grants, 777
BJ's Wholesale Clubs Local Charitable Giving, 778
Burlington Industries Fndn Grants, 865
Cable Positive's Tony Cox Community Grants, 886
Camp-Younts Fndn Grants, 914
Campbell Hoffman Fndn Grants, 915
CenturyLink Clarke M. Williams Grants, 998
Ceres Fndn Grants, 999
CFNCR Starbucks Memorial Fund, 1026

Charles A. Frueauff Fndn Grants, 1037
Charles Delmar Fndn Grants, 1039
Charles M. and Mary D. Grant Found Grants, 1050
Chesapeake Bay Trust Fisheries and Headwaters Grants, 1070
Columbia Gas of Virginia Grants, 1218
Comcast Fndn Grants, 1235
Commonweal Fndn Community Grants, 1239
Community Fndn AIDS Awards, 1245
Coors Brewing Corporate Contributions Grants, 1371
Corina Higginson Trust Grants, 1373
CSX Corporate Contributions Grants, 1408
Dammann Fund Grants, 1439
Dean Foods Community Involvement Grants, 1469
Dollar Energy Fund Grants, 1567
Dollar General Adult Literacy Grants, 1568
Dollar General Family Literacy Grants, 1569
Dollar General Youth Literacy Grants, 1570
Dominion Fndn Human Needs Grants, 1572
EDS Fndn Grants, 1661
EDS Technology Grants, 1662
Fluor Fndn Grants, 1875
Freddie Mac Fndn Grants, 1944
Gannett Fndn Community Action Grants, 1984
Garland and Agnes Taylor Gray Grants, 1988
GenCorp Fndn Grants, 1998
George and Sarah Buchanan Fndn Grants, 2011
George J. and Effie L. Seay Fndn Grants, 2024
Georgia-Pacific Fndn Education Grants, 2031
Georgia-Pacific Fndn Enrichment Grants, 2032
Georgia-Pacific Fndn Entrepreneurship Grants, 2033
Georgia-Pacific Fndn Environment Grants, 2034
Gertrude M. Conduff Fndn Grants, 2047
Giant Food Charitable Grants, 2050
Gumdrop Books Librarian Scholarships, 2179
Hampton Roads Community Beach Fund Grants, 2214
Hampton Roads Community Fndn Community Leadership Partners Grants, 2215
Hampton Roads Community Fndn Health and Human Service Grants, 2216
Hampton Roads Community Fndn Horticulture Education Grants, 2217
Hampton Roads Community Fndn Nonprofit Facilities Improvement Grants, 2218
Harry Bramhall Gilbert Charitable Trust Grants, 2238
Harvest Fndn Grants, 2254
HBF Pathways Out of Poverty Grants, 2273
Hershey Company Grants, 2318
Hilda and Preston Davis Fndn Grants, 2322
Hut Fndn Grants, 2411
J. Edwin Treakle Fndn Grants, 2596
J. Willard and Alice S. Marriott Grants, 2609
James L. and Mary Jane Bowman Charitable Trust Grants, 2632
Jenkins Fndn: Improving the Health of Greater Richmond Grants, 2663
John Edward Fowler Memorial Found Grants, 2693
Kennedy Center HSC Fndn Internship, 2799
Kennedy Center Summer HSC Internship, 2800
Lettie Pate Evans Fndn Grants, 2887
Lettie Pate Whitehead Fndn Grants, 2888
Lockheed Martin Philanthropic Grants, 2918
Mann T. Lowry Fndn Grants, 2998
Margaret Abell Powell Fund Grants, 3002
Marietta McNeill Morgan and Samuel Tate Morgan, Jr. Trust Grants, 3008
MARPAT Fndn Grants, 3023
Mary E. and Michael Blevins Charitable Grants, 3037
Mary Reynolds Babcock Fndn Grants, 3047
Mary Wilmer Covey Charitable Trust Grants, 3049
MeadWestvaco Sustainable Communities Grants, 3105
Memorial Fndn for Children Grants, 3116
Meyer Fndn Benevon Grants, 3140
Meyer Fndn Education Grants, 3142
Meyer Fndn Management Assistance, 3144
Micron Tech Fndn Community Grants, 3161
Mid Atlantic Arts Fndn American Masterpieces Grants, 3169
Mid Atlantic Arts Found ArtsConnect Grants, 3170

Mid Atlantic Arts Fndn Folk Arts Outreach Project Grants, 3171
Mildred V. Horn Fndn Grants, 3176
Moran Family Fndn Grants, 3216
Morris and Gwendolyn Cafritz Found Grants, 3218
Nationwide Insurance Fndn Grants, 3285
Nestle Purina PetCare Educational Grants, 3302
Nestle Purina PetCare Pet Related Grants, 3304
Nestle Purina PetCare Support Dog and Police K-9 Organization Grants, 3305
Nestle Purina PetCare Youth Grants, 3306
NFWF Chesapeake Bay Conservation Innovation Grants, 3363
NFWF Chesapeake Bay Targeted Grants, 3365
Norfolk Southern Fndn Grants, 3463
Paul Green Fndn Playwrights Fellowship, 3762
PennPAT Fee-Support Grants for Presenters, 3812
PennPAT New Directions Grants for Presenters, 3813
Philip L. Graham Fund Grants, 3876
Plum Creek Fndn Grants, 3917
R.E.B. Awards for Distinguished Educational Leadership, 4000
REI Conservation and Outdoor Rec Grants, 4051
Richard and Caroline T. Gwathmey Memorial Trust Grants, 4075
Richard Davoud Donchian Fndn Grants, 4080
Richmond Eye and Ear Fund Grants, 4092
Robert G. Cabell III and Maude Morgan Cabell Fndn Grants, 4113
Robins Fndn Grants, 4126
Safeco Insurance Community Grants, 4203
Salmon Fndn Grants, 4225
Sheltering Arms Fund Grants, 4344
Solutia Fund Grants, 4402
Stettinius Fund for Nonprofit Leadership Awards, 4500
Strengthening Families - Strengthening Communities Grants, 4513
Sunoco Fndn Grants, 4530
Symantec Community Relations and Corporate Philanthropy Grants, 4544
TAC Arts Access Technical Assistance Grants, 4550
TAC Arts Educ Community-Learning Grants, 4552
TAC Arts Education Mini Grants, 4553
TAC Arts Projects Grants, 4554
TAC Rural Arts Project Support Grants, 4555
TAC Technical Assistance Grants, 4556
TAC Touring Arts and Access Grants, 4557
TE Fndn Grants, 4572
Thomas B. and Elizabeth M. Sheridan Grants, 4614
Thompson Charitable Fndn Grants, 4622
Tiger Woods Fndn Grants, 4634
Verizon Fndn Virginia Grants, 4925
Virginia Comm for the Arts Artists in Education Residency Grants, 4941
Virginia Comm for Arts Gen Operating Grants, 4942
Virginia Comm for the Arts Local Government Challenge Grants, 4943
Virginia Comm for the Arts Project Grants, 4944
Virginia Comm for the Arts Touring Assistance Grants, 4945
Virginia Historical Society Research Fellowships, 4949
Vulcan Materials Company Fndn Grants, 4956
Washington Area Fuel Fund Grants, 4988
Washington Gas Charitable Contributions, 5000
Wells Fargo Housing Fndn Grants, 5023
Weyerhaeuser Company Fndn Grants, 5053
William G. McGowan Charitable Fund Grants, 5084
William J. and Dorothy K. O'Neill Grants, 5087
William M. Cage Library Trust Grants, 5090
Williams Companies Fndn Grants, 5095
Youth Philanthropy Project, 5132

Washington

Abelard Fndn West Grants, 88
ACE Charitable Fndn Grants, 111
Adobe Art and Culture Grants, 167
Adobe Community Investment Grants, 168
Adobe Hunger and Homelessness Grants, 169
Aetna Fndn Regional Health Grants, 187
Alaska Airlines Corporate Giving Grants, 320

1176 / Vermont

Alaska Airlines Fndn Grants, 321
Albertson's Charitable Giving Grants, 345
Alfred and Tillie Shemanski Testamentary Trust Grants, 363
American Rivers Community-Based Restoration Program River Grants, 444
Aratani Fndn Grants, 523
Archer Daniels Midland Fndn Grants, 527
ARCO Fndn Education Grants, 528
Artist Trust GAP Grants, 575
Autzen Fndn Grants, 622
Avista Fndn Grants, 624
Bechtel Group Fndn Building Positive Community Relationships Grants, 715
Ben B. Cheney Fndn Grants, 725
Better Way Fndn Grants, 754
Blue Mountain Community Fndn Grants, 800
Boeing Company Contributions Grants, 809
Brainerd Fndn Grants, 831
Brunswick Fndn Dollars for Doers Grants, 856
Brunswick Fndn Grants, 857
Bullitt Fndn Grants, 862
Burning Fndn Grants, 867
Cable Positive's Tony Cox Community Grants, 886
Campbell Soup Fndn Grants, 916
CenturyLink Clarke M. Williams Grants, 998
Ceres Fndn Grants, 999
Charlotte Martin Fndn Youth Grants, 1057
Chiron Fndn Community Grants, 1111
Cingular Wireless Charitable Contributions, 1134
Circle K Corporation Contributions Grants, 1136
Clowes Fund Grants, 1177
Comcast Fndn Grants, 1235
Community Found of South Puget Sound Grants, 1311
Comprehensive Health Education Grants, 1337
ConAgra Foods Community Impact Grants, 1342
ConAgra Foods Nourish Our Comm Grants, 1343
ConocoPhillips Fndn Grants, 1354
D.V. and Ida J. McEachern Charitable Grants, 1425
Detlef Schrempf Fndn Grants, 1519
E.L. Wiegand Fndn Grants, 1639
Edwin W. and Catherine M. Davis Grants, 1672
Fluor Fndn Grants, 1875
Forest Fndn Grants, 1886
Foster Fndn Grants, 1888
Fndn Northwest Grants, 1906
Fred & Gretel Biel Charitable Trust Grants, 1939
Fred Meyer Fndn Grants, 1950
GenCorp Fndn Grants, 1998
George Frederick Jewett Fndn Grants, 2019
Georgia-Pacific Fndn Education Grants, 2031
Georgia-Pacific Fndn Enrichment Grants, 2032
Georgia-Pacific Entrepreneurship Grants, 2033
Georgia-Pacific Fndn Environment Grants, 2034
Ginger and Barry Ackerley Fndn Grants, 2055
Greater Tacoma Community Fndn Grants, 2139
Green Diamond Charitable Contributions, 2149
GTECH Community Involvement Grants, 2171
H.B. Fuller Company Fndn Grants, 2183
Harold and Arlene Schnitzer CARE Grants, 2226
Hasbro Children's Fund, 2256
Herbert B. Jones Fndn Grants, 2314
Intel Community Grants, 2562
Janson Fndn Grants, 2646
Jeffris Wood Fndn Grants, 2660
Kawabe Memorial Fund Grants, 2794
KeyBank Fndn Grants, 2820
Kimberly-Clark Community Grants, 2824
Land O'Lakes Fndn Community Grants, 2859
Land O'Lakes Fndn Dollars for Doers Grants, 2860
M.J. Murdock Charitable Trust General Grants, 2954
Medtronic Community Link Arts, Civic, and Culture Grants, 3109
Medtronic CommunityLink Education Grants, 3110
Medtronic CommunityLink Health Grants, 3111
Medtronic Comm Link Human Services Grants, 3112
Meyer Memorial Trust Emergency Grants, 3146
Meyer Memorial Trust Grassroots Grants, 3147
Meyer Memorial Trust Responsive Grants, 3148
Meyer Memorial Trust Special Grants, 3149
Microsoft Comm Affairs Puget Sound Grants, 3163
NFWF Columbia Basin Water Transactions Program Grants, 3366
NFWF Columbia River Estuarine Coastal Fund Grants, 3367
NFWF Community Salmon Fund Partnerships, 3368
NFWF King County Community Salmon Fund Grants, 3375
NFWF Pierce County Community Salmon Fund Grants, 3385
NFWF Radical Salmon Design Contest, 3388
NFWF Salmon Recovery Funding Board Community Salmon Fund Grants, 3389
Norcliffe Fndn Grants, 3459
Northwest Fund for the Environment Grants, 3510
NWHF Health Advocacy Small Grants, 3537
NWHF Kaiser Permanente Community Grants, 3538
NWHF Physical Activity and Nutrition Grants, 3540
OneFamily Fndn Grants, 3673
PACCAR Fndn Grants, 3719
PacifiCare Fndn Grants, 3725
PacifiCorp Fndn for Learning Grants, 3727
Paul G. Allen Family Fndn Grants, 3759
Peter M. Putnam Fndn Grants, 3848
Piper Jaffray Fndn Communities Giving, 3899
Plum Creek Fndn Grants, 3917
PNC Fndn Grow Up Great Grants, 3924
Poets & Writers Readings/Workshops Grants, 3927
Premera Blue Cross CARES Grants, 3945
Pride Fndn Grants, 3958
Principal Financial Group Fndn Grants, 3966
Rathmann Family Fndn Grants, 4026
RBC Dain Rauscher Fndn Grants, 4031
Regence Access to Health Care Grants, 4039
Regence Health Care Community Awareness and Engagement Grants, 4040
Regence Health Care Connections Grants, 4041
Regence Improving End-of-Life Grants, 4042
Regence Tools and Technology Grants, 4043
REI Conservation and Outdoor Rec Grants, 4051
Robert B McMillen Fndn Grants, 4106
Safeco Insurance Community Grants, 4203
Samuel S. Johnson Fndn Grants, 4239
San Juan Island Community Fndn Grants, 4283
Seattle Fndn Annual Neighborhoods and Communities Grants, 4319
Seattle Fndn Arts and Culture Grants, 4320
Seattle Fndn Basic Needs Grants, 4321
Seattle Fndn Benjamin N. Phillips Memorial Fund Grants, 4322
Seattle Fndn C. Keith Birkenfeld Memorial Trust Grants, 4323
Seattle Fndn Doyne M. Green Scholarships, 4324
Seattle Fndn Economy Grants, 4325
Seattle Fndn Education Grants, 4326
Seattle Fndn Environment Grants, 4327
Seattle Fndn Health and Wellness Grants, 4328
Seattle Fndn Medical Funds Grants, 4329
Seattle Fndn Neighbor to Neighbor Small Grants, 4330
Shopko Fndn Community Grants, 4346
Simpson Lumber Charitable Contributions, 4362
Social Justice Fund Northwest Criminal Justice Giving Project Grants, 4394
Social Justice Fund Northwest Economic Justice Giving Project Grants, 4395
Social Justice Fund Northwest Environmental Justice Giving Project Grants, 4396
Social Justice Fund Northwest General Grants, 4397
Social Justice Fund Northwest LGBTQ Giving Project Grants, 4398
Solutia Fund Grants, 4402
Stocker Fndn Grants, 4507
Stuart Fndn Grants, 4516
Sunderland Fndn Grants, 4527
SVP Early Childhood Development and Parenting Grants, 4538
SVP Environment Grants, 4539
U.S. Bank Fndn Grants, 4686
Union Bank, N.A. Corporate Sponsorships and Donations, 4708
Union Bank, N.A. Fndn Grants, 4709
Union Pacific Community and Civic Grants, 4714
Union Pacific Fndn Health and Human Services Grants, 4715
VSA/Metlife Connect All Grants, 4953
Wells Fargo Housing Fndn Grants, 5023
Weyerhaeuser Company Fndn Grants, 5053
Whatcom Community Fndn Grants, 5055
Whitehorse Fndn Grants, 5058
Wilburforce Fndn Grants, 5067
William C. Kenney Watershed Protection Fndn Ecosystem Grants, 5079
Women's Funding Alliance Grants, 5112

West Virginia

1st and 10 Fndn Grants, 1
Abelard Fndn East Grants, 87
AEP Corporate Giving Grants, 180
American Electric Power Grants, 428
Appalachian Community Fund General Grants, 493
Appalachian Community Fund GLBTQ Initiative Grants, 494
Appalachian Community Media Justice Grants, 495
Appalachian Community Fund Seize the Moment Grants, 496
Appalachian Community Fund Special Opportunities Grants, 497
Appalachian Community Fund Technical Assistance Grants, 498
Appalachian Regional Comm Asset-Based Development Project Grants, 500
Appalachian Regional Comm Business Development Revolving Loan Fund Grants, 501
Appalachian Regional Comm Community Infrastructure Grants, 502
Appalachian Regional Comm Distressed Counties Grants, 503
Appalachian Regional Comm Education and Training Grants, 504
Appalachian Regional Comm Energy Grants, 505
Appalachian Regional Comm Export and Trade Development Grants, 506
Appalachian Regional Comm Health Care Grants, 507
Appalachian Reg Comm Housing Grants, 508
Appalachian Regional Comm Leadership Development and Capacity Building Grants, 509
Appalachian Regional Comm Telecommunications Grants, 510
Appalachian Regional Comm Tourist Development Grants, 511
Appalachian Regional Comm Transportation and Highways Grants, 512
Ashland Corporate Contributions Grants, 587
Bayer Fndn Grants, 696
Beckley Area Fndn Grants, 716
Belk Fndn Grants, 721
Cable Positive's Tony Cox Community Grants, 886
Cabot Corporation Fndn Grants, 887
Caesar Puff Fndn Grants, 890
Carl M. Freeman Fndn FACES Grants, 932
Carl M. Freeman Fndn Grants, 933
Ceres Fndn Grants, 999
Charles A. Frueauff Fndn Grants, 1037
Charles Delmar Fndn Grants, 1039
Charles M. and Mary D. Grant Found Grants, 1050
Chesapeake Bay Trust Fisheries and Headwaters Grants, 1070
Claude Worthington Benedum Fndn Grants, 1161
Clay Fndn Grants, 1162
Cleveland-Cliffs Fndn Grants, 1165
Comcast Fndn Grants, 1235
Covenant Mountain Ministries Grants, 1387
CSX Corporate Contributions Grants, 1408
Daywood Fndn Grants, 1465
DHHS Healthy Tomorrows for Children, 1534
Dollar Energy Fund Grants, 1567
Dollar General Adult Literacy Grants, 1568
Dollar General Family Literacy Grants, 1569
Dollar General Youth Literacy Grants, 1570
Dominion Fndn Human Needs Grants, 1572

GEOGRAPHIC INDEX

EQT Fndn Art and Culture Grants, 1743
EQT Fndn Community Grants, 1744
EQT Fndn Education Grants, 1745
EQT Fndn Environment Grants, 1746
Fifth Third Bank Corporate Giving, 1809
Fifth Third Fndn Grants, 1810
FirstEnergy Fndn Math, Science, and Technology Education Grants, 1820
FMC Fndn Grants, 1876
Georgia-Pacific Fndn Education Grants, 2031
Georgia-Pacific Fndn Enrichment Grants, 2032
Georgia-Pacific Entrepreneurship Grants, 2033
Georgia-Pacific Fndn Environment Grants, 2034
Greater Kanawha Valley Fndn Grants, 2136
Haddad Fndn Grants, 2189
Head Start Replacement Grantee: West Virginia, 2277
Hilda and Preston Davis Fndn Grants, 2322
Huntington Clinical Fndn Grants, 2404
Huntington Fndn Grants, 2408
Huntington National Bank Comm Grants, 2409
JP Morgan Chase Arts and Culture Grants, 2752
JP Morgan Chase Community Devel Grants, 2753
Marathon Petroleum Corporation Grants, 2999
Mary E. and Michael Blevins Charitable Grants, 3037
Mary Reynolds Babcock Fndn Grants, 3047
MeadWestvaco Sustainable Communities Grants, 3105
Mid Atlantic Arts Fndn American Masterpieces Grants, 3169
Mid Atlantic Arts Found ArtsConnect Grants, 3170
Mid Atlantic Arts Fndn Folk Arts Outreach Project Grants, 3171
Mildred V. Horn Fndn Grants, 3176
Nestle Purina PetCare Educational Grants, 3302
Nestle Purina PetCare Pet Related Grants, 3304
Nestle Purina PetCare Support Dog and Police K-9 Organization Grants, 3305
Nestle Purina PetCare Youth Grants, 3306
NFWF Chesapeake Bay Conservation Innovation Grants, 3363
NFWF Chesapeake Bay Targeted Grants, 3365
Norfolk Southern Fndn Grants, 3463
ORBI Artist Fast Track Grants, 3689
Parkersburg Area Community Action Grants, 3738
Paul Green Fndn Playwrights Fellowship, 3762
PennPAT Fee-Support Grants for Presenters, 3812
PennPAT New Directions Grants for Presenters, 3813
Peoples Bancorp Fndn Grants, 3817
Plum Creek Fndn Grants, 3917
Sisters of Saint Joseph Charitable Fund Grants, 4376
Spartan Fndn Grants, 4448
Sunoco Fndn Grants, 4530
Toyota Motor of West Virginia Grants, 4657
Tri-State Community Twenty-first Century Endowment Fund Grants, 4666
Verizon Fndn West Virginia Grants, 4926
West Virginia Comm on the Arts Accessibility Services Grants, 5029
West Virginia Comm on the Arts Visit Grants, 5030
West Virginia Comm on the Arts Challenge America Partnership Grants, 5031
West Virginia Comm on the Arts Community Connections Grants, 5032
West Virginia Comm on the Arts Cultural Facilities and Capital Resources Grants, 5033
West Virginia Comm on the Arts Fast Track ADA and Emergency Grants, 5034
West Virginia Comm on the Arts Initiative/Opportunity Grants, 5035
West Virginia Comm on the Arts Long-Range Planning Grants, 5036
West Virginia Comm on the Arts Long-Term Artist Residencies, 5037
West Virginia Comm on the Arts Major Institutions Support Grants, 5038
West Virginia Comm on the Arts Media Grants, 5039
West Virginia Comm on the Arts Mid-Size Institutions Support Grants, 5040
West Virginia Comm on the Arts Mini Grants, 5041
West Virginia Comm on the Arts Peer Assistance Network Grants, 5042
West Virginia Comm on the Arts Performing Arts Grants, 5043
West Virginia Comm on the Arts Presenting Artists Grants, 5044
West Virginia Comm on the Arts Professional Development for Artists Grants, 5045
West Virginia Comm on the Arts Grants, 5046
West Virginia Comm on the Arts Short-Term Artist Residencies, 5047
West Virginia Comm on the Arts Special Projects Grants, 5048
West Virginia Comm on the Arts Staffing Support Grants, 5049
West Virginia Comm on the Arts Travel and Training Grants, 5050
West Virginia Comm on the Arts Visual Grants, 5051
Weyerhaeuser Company Fndn Grants, 5053

Wisconsin

3M Company Arts and Culture Grants, 12
3M Company Environmental Giving Grants, 13
3M Company Health and Human Services Grants, 14
3M Fndn Community Giving Grants, 15
786 Fndn Grants, 33
Abelard Fndn East Grants, 87
Acuity Charitable Fndn Grants, 140
Adler-Clark Electric Community Commitment Fndn Grants, 164
A Fund for Women Grants, 195
Albertson's Charitable Giving Grants, 345
Alliant Energy Fndn Community Grants, 384
Alliant Energy Fndn Hometown Challenge Grants, 385
Andersen Corporate Fndn, 459
Anthem Blue Cross and Blue Shield Grants, 488
Archer Daniels Midland Fndn Grants, 527
Arts Midwest Performing Arts Grants, 579
Assurant Health Fndn Grants, 596
Athwin Fndn Grants, 605
Barbara Meyer Elsner Fndn Grants, 665
Beldon Fund Grants, 720
Black River Falls Area Fndn Grants, 782
Brico Fund Grants, 835
Bridgestone/Firestone Trust Fund Grants, 836
Brunswick Fndn Dollars for Doers Grants, 856
Brunswick Fndn Grants, 857
Bush Fndn Arts & Humanities Grants: Short-Term Organizational Support, 873
Cable Positive's Tony Cox Community Grants, 886
Campbell Soup Fndn Grants, 916
CenturyLink Clarke M. Williams Grants, 998
CFFVR Alcoholism and Drug Abuse Grants, 1001
CFFVR Basic Needs Giving Partnership Grants, 1002
CFFVR Bridge Grants, 1003
CFFVR Capacity Building Grants, 1004
CFFVR Capital Credit Union Charitable Giving Grants, 1005
CFFVR Chilton Area Community Grants, 1006
CFFVR Clintonville Area Fndn Grants, 1008
CFFVR Clintonville Area Fndn Grants, 1007
CFFVR Doug and Carla Salmon Grants, 1009
CFFVR Environmental Stewardship Grants, 1010
CFFVR Fox Valley Community Arts Grants, 1011
CFFVR Frank C. Shattuck Community Grants, 1012
CFFVR Infant Welfare Circle of Kings Daughters Grants, 1013
CFFVR Jewelers Mutual Charitable Giving, 1014
CFFVR Mielke Family Fndn Grants, 1015
CFFVR Myra M. and Robert L. Vandehey Fndn Grants, 1016
CFFVR Project Grants, 1017
CFFVR Robert and Patricia Endries Family Fndn Grants, 1018
CFFVR SAC Developmental Disabilities Grants, 1019
CFFVR Schmidt Family G4 Grants, 1020
CFFVR Shawano Area Community Fndn Grants, 1021
CFFVR Sikora Family Memorial Grants, 1022
CFFVR Waupaca Area Community Fndn Grants, 1023
CFFVR Wisconsin King's Daughters/Sons Grants, 1024
CFFVR Women's Fund for the Fox Valley Region Grants, 1025
Coleman Cancer Care Grants, 1199
Coleman Developmental Disabilities Grants, 1200
Coleman Entrepreneurship Education Grants, 1201
Comcast Fndn Grants, 1235
ConAgra Foods Community Impact Grants, 1342
ConAgra Foods Nourish Our Comm Grants, 1343
Cooper Industries Fndn Grants, 1370
Cornerstone Fndn of NE Wisconsin Grants, 1375
Courage Center Judd Jacobson Memorial Award, 1382
Cummins Fndn Grants, 1415
CUNA Mutual Group Fndn Grants, 1417
Dean Foods Community Involvement Grants, 1469
DHHS Healthy Tomorrows for Children, 1534
Dollar General Adult Literacy Grants, 1568
Dollar General Family Literacy Grants, 1569
Dollar General Youth Literacy Grants, 1570
Donaldson Fndn Grants, 1574
Doug and Carla Salmon Fndn Grants, 1594
Duluth-Superior Area Comm Fndn Grants, 1620
Eaton Charitable Fund Grants, 1647
Esther M. and Freeman E. Everett Grants, 1757
Faye McBeath Fndn Grants, 1794
Frank G. and Freida K. Brotz Family Grants, 1928
Gannett Fndn Community Action Grants, 1984
Gaylord and Dorothy Donnelley Found Grants, 1993
General Mills Fndn Grants, 2003
George Kress Fndn Grants, 2025
Georgia-Pacific Fndn Education Grants, 2031
Georgia-Pacific Fndn Enrichment Grants, 2032
Georgia-Pacific Entrepreneurship Grants, 2033
Georgia-Pacific Fndn Environment Grants, 2034
Godfrey Fndn Grants, 2095
Greater Green Bay Comm Fndn Grants, 2135
Greater Milwaukee Fndn Grants, 2137
Great Lakes Fishery Trust Access Grants, 2145
Great Lakes Fishery Trust Habitat Protection and Restoration Grants, 2146
Green Bay Packers Fndn Grants, 2148
GTECH Community Involvement Grants, 2171
Harley Davidson Fndn Grants, 2224
Heartland Arts Fund, 2286
Hormel Foods Charitable Trust Grants, 2368
Huffy Fndn Grants, 2384
Hugh J. Andersen Fndn Grants, 2385
Humana Fndn Grants, 2388
IFP Chicago Production Fund In-Kind Grant, 2446
IFP Minnesota Fresh Film Production Grants, 2447
Intergrys Corporation Grants, 2565
Jane Bradley Pettit Fndn Arts and Culture Grants, 2641
Jane Bradley Pettit Fndn Community and Social Development Grants, 2642
Jane Bradley Pettit Fndn Health Grants, 2643
Janesville Fndn Grants, 2644
John Deere Fndn Grants, 2692
Joyce Fndn Democracy Grants, 2748
JP Morgan Chase Arts and Culture Grants, 2752
JP Morgan Chase Community Devel Grants, 2753
Kimberly-Clark Community Grants, 2824
Kohler Fndn Grants, 2833
Land O'Lakes Fndn Community Grants, 2859
Land O'Lakes Fndn Dollars for Doers, 2860
Lands' End Corporate Giving Program, 2861
Lumpkin Family Strong Community Leadership Grants, 2944
M3C Fellowships, 2955
Madison Community Fndn Altrusa Int'l of Madison Grants, 2970
Madison Community Fndn Grants, 2971
Mead Witter Fndn Grants, 3106
Merkel Fndn Grants, 3124
Nationwide Insurance Fndn Grants, 3285
Nestle Purina PetCare Educational Grants, 3302
Nestle Purina PetCare Pet Related Grants, 3304
Nestle Purina PetCare Support Dog and Police K-9 Organization Grants, 3305
Nestle Purina PetCare Youth Grants, 3306
NGA Midwest School Garden Grants, 3407
Nonprofit Management Fund Grants, 3458
Norfolk Southern Fndn Grants, 3463
Northwestern Mutual Fndn Grants, 3509

1178 / Wisconsin

Oscar Rennebohm Fndn Grants, 3694
Otto Bremer Fndn Grants, 3713
Patrick and Anna M. Cudahy Fund Grants, 3751
Pentair Fndn Educ and Community Grants, 3816
Philanthrofund Fndn Grants, 3874
Piper Jaffray Fndn Communities Giving, 3899
Plum Creek Fndn Grants, 3917
PNC Ecnomic Development Grants, 3922
PNC Fndn Green Building Grants, 3923
REI Conservation and Outdoor Rec Grants, 4051
Richland County Bank Grants, 4091
RRF General Grants, 4170
Sensient Technologies Fndn Grants, 4337
Shopko Fndn Community Grants, 4346
Shopko Fndn Green Bay Area Community Grants, 4347
Siebert Lutheran Fndn Grants, 4351
SOBP A.E. Bennett Research Award, 4388
Square D Fndn Grants, 4464
Stackner Family Fndn Grants, 4471
TCF Bank Fndn Grants, 4565
Toro Fndn Grants, 4647
U.S. Bank Fndn Grants, 4686
Union Pacific Community and Civic Grants, 4714
Union Pacific Fndn Health and Human Services Grants, 4715
Verizon Fndn Great Lakes Region Grants, 4912
Viking Children's Fund Grants, 4939
Vulcan Materials Company Fndn Grants, 4956
Wells Fargo Housing Fndn Grants, 5023
Weyerhaeuser Company Fndn Grants, 5053
Wisconsin Energy Fndn Grants, 5106
Wisconsin Humanities Council Major Grants, 5107
Wisconsin Humanities Council Mini-Grants for Scholarly Research, 5108

Wyoming
Abelard Fndn West Grants, 88
Albertson's Charitable Giving Grants, 345
Cable Positive's Tony Cox Community Grants, 886
CenturyLink Clarke M. Williams Grants, 998
Daniels Fund Grants, 1443
DHHS Healthy Tomorrows for Children, 1534
DOJ Rural Domestic Violence and Child Victimization Enforcement Grants, 1562
FMC Fndn Grants, 1876
Griffin Fndn Grants, 2165
Hill Fndn Grants, 2326
Homer A. Scott and Mildred S. Scott Grants, 2350
Laura Jane Musser Intercultural Harmony Grants, 2862
Laura Jane Musser Rural Arts Grants, 2863
Laura Jane Musser Rural Initiative Grants, 2864
Needmor Fund Grants, 3289
NFWF One Fly Conservation Partnerships, 3382
PacifiCorp Fndn for Learning Grants, 3727
Paul Stock Fndn Grants, 3766
Peter Kiewit Fndn General Grants, 3845
Peter Kiewit Fndn Small Grants, 3847
Piper Jaffray Fndn Communities Giving, 3899
Questar Corporate Contributions Grants, 3997
RBC Dain Rauscher Fndn Grants, 4031
Ruth and Vernon Taylor Fndn Grants, 4177
Shopko Fndn Community Grants, 4346
Social Justice Fund Northwest Criminal Justice Giving Project Grants, 4394
Social Justice Fund Northwest Economic Justice Giving Project Grants, 4395
Social Justice Fund Northwest Environmental Justice Giving Project Grants, 4396
Social Justice Fund Northwest General Grants, 4397
Social Justice Fund Northwest LGBTQ Giving Project Grants, 4398
Steele-Reese Fndn Grants, 4498
U.S. Bank Fndn Grants, 4686
Union Pacific Community and Civic Grants, 4714
Union Pacific Fndn Health and Human Services Grants, 4715
Wells Fargo Housing Fndn Grants, 5023
William C. Kenney Watershed Protection Fndn Ecosystem Grants, 5079

Canada
4imprint One by One Charitable Giving, 16
A. J. Macdonald Fndn for Animal Welfare, 42
Abbott Fund Community Grants, 81
Abbott Fund Science Education Grants, 83
Adobe Art and Culture Grants, 167
Adobe Community Investment Grants, 168
Adobe Hunger and Homelessness Grants, 169
ALA Margaret Mann Citation, 297
Alaska Airlines Corporate Giving Grants, 320
Alberta Law Fndn Grants, 338
Andersen Corporate Fndn, 459
ATA Local Community Relations Grants, 600
ATA Political Engagement Grant, 601
ATA School-Community Relations Awards, 602
Austin S. Nelson Fndn Grants, 617
Bank of America Charitable Matching Gifts, 658
Bank of America Charitable Volunteer Grants, 660
Bechtel Group Fndn Building Positive Community Relationships Grants, 715
Boeing Company Contributions Grants, 809
Brainerd Fndn Grants, 831
British Columbia Arts Council Artists in Education Grants, 842
Build-A-Bear Workshop Bear Hugs Fndn Literacy and Education Grants, 860
Bullitt Fndn Grants, 862
Cabot Corporation Fndn Grants, 887
Canada-U.S. Fulbright Mid-Career Professional Grants, 917
Canadian Optometric Education Trust Grants, 918
Central Okanagan Fndn Grants, 997
Champ-A Champion Fur Kids Grants, 1028
Chase Paymentech Corporate Giving Grants, 1059
Computer Associates Community Grants, 1341
Conseil des arts de Montreal Diversity Award, 1357
Conseil des arts de Montreal Touring Grants, 1358
Dave Thomas Fndn for Adoption Grants, 1449
Do Something Plum Youth Grants, 1593
DPA Promoting Policy Change Grants, 1598
Fitzpatrick and Francis Family Business Continuity Fndn Grants, 1837
Fluor Fndn Grants, 1875
FMC Fndn Grants, 1876
Fred C. and Mary R. Koch Fndn Grants, 1943
Gloria Barron Prize for Young Heroes, 2064
Health Canada National Seniors Grants, 2278
Honeywell Corp Housing and Shelter Grants, 2357
Honor the Earth Grants, 2361
IAFF Labour College of Canada Residential Scholarship, 2418
IAFF National Labor College Scholarships, 2419
James H. Cummings Fndn Grants, 2626
John Deere Fndn Grants, 2692
Johns Manville Fund Grants, 2716
Johnson Scholarship Fndn Grants, 2726
K. M. Hunter Charitable Fndn Social Welfare Grants, 2757
KaBOOM-CA Playground Challenge Grants, 2761
Laidlaw Fndn Multi-Year Grants, 2852
Laidlaw Fndn Youh Organizing Grants, 2853
Laidlaw Fndn Youth Organizaing Initiatives Grants, 2854
Leon and Thea Koerner Fndn Grants, 2883
Lockheed Martin Philanthropic Grants, 2918
Manitoba Arts Council Artist in Community Residency Grants, 2994
Manitoba Arts Council Community Connections and Access Grants, 2995
Manitoba Arts Council Literary Arts Publishers Project Grants, 2996
Manitoba Arts Council Special Opps Grants, 2997
Mary's Pence Ministry Grants, 3029
Mary's Pence Study Grants, 3030
May and Stanley Smith Charitable Trust Grants, 3069
Maytree Fndn Assisting Local Leaders with Immigrant Employment Strategies Grants, 3070
Maytree Refugee and Immigrant Grants, 3071
Medtronic CommunityLink Education Grants, 3110
Medtronic CommunityLink Health Grants, 3111

GEOGRAPHIC INDEX

Medtronic Patient Link Grants, 3113
MLB Tomorrow Fund Grants, 3193
Nelda C. and H.J. Lutcher Stark Grants, 3296
Newfoundland and Labrador Arts Council Community Arts Grants, 3318
Newfoundland and Labrador Arts Council Labrador Cultural Travel Grants, 3319
Newfoundland and Labrador Arts Council Professional Artists Travel Fund, 3320
Newfoundland and Labrador Arts Council Professional Festivals Grants, 3321
Newfoundland and Labrador Arts Council Professional Project Grants, 3322
Newfoundland and Labrador Arts Council Sustaining Grants, 3323
Newfoundland and Labrador Arts Council Visiting Artists Grants, 3324
NSERC Brockhouse Canada Prize for Interdisciplinary Research in Science and Engineering Grant, 3518
NSERC Michael Smith Awards, 3519
Oak Fndn Child Abuse Grants, 3632
Ontario Arts Council Aboriginal Arts Grants, 3675
Ontario Arts Council Artists in the Community/Workplace Grants, 3676
Ontario Arts Council Compass Grants, 3677
Ontario Arts Council Integrated Arts Grants, 3678
Ontario Arts Council Orchestras Grants, 3679
Ontario Arts Presenter/Producer Grants, 3680
Ontario Arts Theatre Creators' Reserve Grants, 3681
Ontario Arts Council Travel Assistance Grants, 3682
PACCAR Fndn Grants, 3719
Peter F. Drucker Award for Canadian Nonprofit Innovation, 3844
PetSmart Charities Grants for Canada Agencies, 3853
Project Orange Thumb Grants, 3972
Shastri Indo-Canadian Institute Action Research Project Grants, 4341
Sport Manitoba Athlete/Team Travel Assistance Grants, 4452
Sport Manitoba Athlete Skill Development Clinics Grants, 4453
Sport Manitoba Bingo Allocations Grants, 4454
Sport Manitoba Coaches/Officials Travel Assistance Grants, 4455
Sport Manitoba Hosting Regional Championships Grants, 4456
Sport Manitoba Intro of a New Sport Grants, 4457
Sport Manitoba KidSport Athlete Grants, 4458
Sport Manitoba Sport Special Initiatives Grants, 4459
Sport Manitoba Women to Watch Grants, 4460
SSHRC Therese F. Casgrain Fellowship, 4466
Steelcase Fndn Grants, 4497
Sweet Water Trust Grants, 4541
Texas Instruments Arts and Culture Grants, 4596
Texas Instruments Civic and Business Grants, 4597
Texas Instruments Fndn Arts and Culture Grants, 4599
Thomas Sill Fndn Grants, 4619
Vancouver Fndn Disability Supports for Employment Grants, 4899
Vancouver Fndn Grants and Community Initiatives Program, 4900
Vancouver Sun Children's Fund Grants, 4901
Virginia Fndn for Humanities Open Grants, 4947
Wilburforce Fndn Grants, 5067
William and Flora Hewlett Fndn Environmental Grants, 5074
William C. Kenney Watershed Protection Fndn Ecosystem Grants, 5079
YSA Global Youth Service Day Agency Grants, 5135

Other Foreign Countries

All Countries
AAUW Int'l Project Grants, 76
Acumen Global Fellowships, 142
AEGON Transamerica Disaster Relief Grants, 178
AIG Disaster Relief Fund Grants, 213
ALA Carnegie-Whitney Awards, 253
ALA May Hill Arbuthnot Honor Lecture Award, 300

GEOGRAPHIC INDEX

Alcatel-Lucent Technologies Fndn Grants, 349
ALFJ Astraea U.S. and Int'l Movement Fund, 361
American Express Community Service Grants, 430
American Express Historic Preservation Grants, 431
American Express Leaders for Tomorrow Grants, 432
ASME Charles T. Main Awards, 590
AWDF Main Grants, 627
AWDF Solidarity Fund Grants, 628
Baxter Int'l Corporate Giving Grants, 689
Baxter Int'l Fndn Foster G. McGaw Prize, 690
Baxter Int'l Fndn Grants, 691
Better World Books LEAP Grants for Libraries, 755
Better World Books LEAP Grants for Nonprofits, 756
Bill and Melinda Gates Fndn Agricultural Development Grants, 765
Bill and Melinda Gates Fndn Emergency Response Grants, 766
Bill and Melinda Gates Fndn Financial Services for the Poor Grants, 767
Bill and Melinda Gates Fndn Policy and Advocacy Grants, 769
Bill and Melinda Gates Fndn Water, Sanitation and Hygiene Grants, 770
Bryan Adams Fndn Grants, 858
CAA Millard Meiss Publication Fund Grants, 885
Cause Populi Worthy Cause Grants, 958
CDC Fndn Global Disaster Response Grants, 973
Changemakers Innovation Awards, 1031
Conservation, Food, and Health Fndn Grants for Developing Countries, 1359
Covidien Medical Product Donations, 1390
Delta Air Lines Prize for Global Understanding, 1495
Edward and Ellen Roche Relief Grants, 1663
ExxonMobil Fndn Women's Economic Opportunity Grants, 1778
Greygates Fndn Grants, 2164
Helen Bader Fndn Grants, 2293
Honeywell Corp Humanitarian Relief Grants, 2358
IIE Adell and Hancock Scholarships, 2452
IIE New Leaders Group Award for Mutual Understanding, 2460
IRA Pearson Fndn-IRA-Rotary Lit Awards, 2572
John C. Lasko Fndn Trust Grants, 2688
KEEN Effect Grants, 2795
MacArthur Fndn Chicago Arts and Culture Int'l Connections Grants, 2962
Macquarie Bank Fndn Grants, 2966
MeadWestvaco Sustainable Communities Grants, 3105
Monsanto Int'l Grants, 3207
National Endowment for the Arts - National Arts and Humanities Youth Program Awards, 3255
Nestle Fndn Training Grant, 3301
NHLBI Ancillary Studies in Clinical Trials, 3410
NHLBI Investigator Initiated Multi-Site Clinical Trials, 3413
NHLBI Lymphatics Disease in the Digestive, Cardiovascular and Pulmonary Systems, 3414
NHLBI Lymphatics in Health and Disease in the Digestive, Urinary, Cardiovascular and Pulmonary Systems, 3415
NHLBI Research on the Role of Cardiomyocyte Mitochondria in Heart Disease: An Integrated Approach, 3417
NHLBI Ruth L. Kirschstein National Research Service Awards for Individual Postdoctoral Fellows, 3418
Office Depot Fndn Disaster Relief Grants, 3640
OSF Affordable Access to Digital Communications Initiative, 3700
OSF Documentary Photography Project Audience Engagement Grant, 3706
PepsiCo Fndn Grants, 3819
Pfizer Healthcare Charitable Contributions, 3863
Pfizer Medical Education Track One Grants, 3864
Pfizer Special Events Grants, 3865
Phi Kappa Phi Scholar Award, 3871
Ploughshares Fund Grants, 3916
Radcliffe Institute Indivi Residential Fellowships, 4004
Raskob Fndn for Catholic Activities Grants, 4019
Stanley Smith Horticultural Trust Grants, 4474
Tourism Cares Worldwide Grants, 4649

UNESCO World Heritage Fund Grants, 4706
United Methodist Committee on Relief Hunger and Poverty Grants, 4720
United Technologies Corporation Grants, 4725
USAID/Cambodia Maternal and Child Health, Tuberculosis, HIV/AIDS. and Malaria Grants, 4736
USAID Community Livelihoods Project in Yemen Grant, 4746
USAID Development Innovation Ventures Grants, 4749
USAID Economic Prospectsfor Armenia-Turkey Normalization Grants, 4750
USAID Food Security, Nutrition, Biodiversity and Conservation Grants, 4752
USAID Global Development Alliance Grants, 4753
USAID Haiti Disaster Risk Reduction Capacity Building Grants, 4756
USAID India Partnership Grants, 4761
USAID Knowledge for Health II Grants, 4765
USAID Leadership Initiative for Good Governance in Africa Grants, 4766
USAID Media and Elections Program in Rwanda Grants, 4768
USAID National Governance Project Grant, 4770
USAID Pakistan Private Investment Grants, 4772
USAID Public-Private Alliance Proposals in Burma, Thailand, and Vietnam, 4775
USAID Rapid Response for Sudan Grants, 4776
USAID Rapid Response to Pakistanis Affected by Disasters - Phase Two Grants, 4777
USAID Resilience and Economic Growth in the Sahel - Enhanced Resilience Grants, 4779
USAID Strengthening Democratic Local Governance in South Sudan Grants, 4782
USAID Strengthening Free and Independent Media in South Sudan Grants, 4783
USAID Unsolicited Proposal Grants, 4786
Virginia Fndn for the Humanities Residential Fellowships, 4948
Volvo Adventure Environmental Awards, 4952
VSA Int'l Art Program for Children with Disabilities Grants, 4955
WWF Int'l Smart Gear Competition, 5120
Zonta Int'l Fndn Young Women in Public Affairs Award, 5153

Abkhazia
H.B. Fuller Company Fndn Grants, 2183
Nike Fndn Grants, 3441

Afghanistan
H.B. Fuller Company Fndn Grants, 2183
Nike Fndn Grants, 3441

Albania
Advanced Micro Devices Comm Affairs Grants, 172
Cargill Citizenship Corporate Giving Grants, 925
Charles Delmar Fndn Grants, 1039
Fluor Fndn Grants, 1875
Fulbright Business Grants in Spain, 1970
OSF Advancing the Rights and Integration of Roma Grants, 3699
OSF European Comm Internships for Young Roma Graduates, 3707
OSF Mental Health Initiative Grants, 3709
Sir Dorabji Tata Trust Grants for NGOs or Voluntary Organizations, 4370
USAID Albania Critical Economic Growth Areas Grants, 4740

Algeria
Aid for Starving Children Int'l Grants, 212
Cargill Citizenship Corporate Giving Grants, 925
Gregory C. Carr Fndn Grants, 2161
IREX Small Grant Fund for Civil Society Projects in Africa and Asia, 2581
IREX Small Grant Fund for Media Projects in Africa and Asia, 2582
Liz Claiborne and Art Ortenberg Grants, 2914
Murphy Institute Judith Kelleher Schafer Summer Internship Grants, 3230

Nike Fndn Grants, 3441
Nuffield Fndn Africa Grants, 3532
OSF Arab Regional Office Grants, 3701

Andorra
Advanced Micro Devices Comm Affairs Grants, 172
Cargill Citizenship Corporate Giving Grants, 925
Charles Delmar Fndn Grants, 1039
Fluor Fndn Grants, 1875
Fulbright Business Grants in Spain, 1970
Sir Dorabji Tata Trust Grants for NGOs or Voluntary Organizations, 4370

Angola
Aid for Starving Children Int'l Grants, 212
Cargill Citizenship Corporate Giving Grants, 925
Gregory C. Carr Fndn Grants, 2161
IREX Small Grant Fund for Civil Society Projects in Africa and Asia, 2581
IREX Small Grant Fund for Media Projects in Africa and Asia, 2582
Liz Claiborne and Art Ortenberg Grants, 2914
Murphy Institute Judith Kelleher Schafer Summer Internship Grants, 3230
Nike Fndn Grants, 3441
Nuffield Fndn Africa Grants, 3532
USAID Malawi Local Capacity Development Initiative Grants, 4767

Antigua & Barbuda
Atkinson Fndn Community Grants, 606
Liz Claiborne and Art Ortenberg Grants, 2914
Mary's Pence Ministry Grants, 3029
Mary's Pence Study Grants, 3030
Regional Fund for Digital Innovation in Latin America and the Caribbean Grants, 4049

Argentina
Charles Delmar Fndn Grants, 1039
Katherine John Murphy Fndn Grants, 2790
Mary's Pence Ministry Grants, 3029
Mary's Pence Study Grants, 3030
Regional Fund for Digital Innovation in Latin America and the Caribbean Grants, 4049
Turner Voices Corporate Contributions, 4682

Armenia
Advanced Micro Devices Comm Affairs Grants, 172
Cargill Citizenship Corporate Giving Grants, 925
Charles Delmar Fndn Grants, 1039
Fluor Fndn Grants, 1875
Fulbright Business Grants in Spain, 1970
GMFUS Black Sea Trust for Regional Corporation Grants, 2065
H.B. Fuller Company Fndn Grants, 2183
Nike Fndn Grants, 3441
Sir Dorabji Tata Trust Grants for NGOs or Voluntary Organizations, 4370

Australia
Adelaide Benevolent Society Grants, 160
Bechtel Group Fndn Building Positive Community Relationships Grants, 715
Boeing Company Contributions Grants, 809
Computer Associates Community Grants, 1341
Fluor Fndn Grants, 1875
Fndn for Young Australians Indigenous Grants, 1901
Fndn for Young Australians Spark Fund Grants, 1902
Fndn for Young Ausies Your Eyes Only Awards, 1903
Fndn for Young Australians Youth Change Makers Grants, 1904
Fndn for Young Ausies Youth Led Futures Grants, 1905
May and Stanley Smith Charitable Trust Grants, 3069
PACCAR Fndn Grants, 3719
Project Orange Thumb Grants, 3972
Texas Instruments Arts and Culture Grants, 4596
Texas Instruments Civic and Business Grants, 4597
Texas Instruments Fndn Arts and Culture Grants, 4599
Turner Voices Corporate Contributions, 4682

Austria
Advanced Micro Devices Comm Affairs Grants, 172
Cargill Citizenship Corporate Giving Grants, 925
Charles Delmar Fndn Grants, 1039
Fluor Fndn Grants, 1875
Fulbright Business Grants in Spain, 1970
OSF Human Rights and Governance Grants, 3708
Sir Dorabji Tata Trust Grants for NGOs or Voluntary Organizations, 4370
Texas Instruments Arts and Culture Grants, 4596
Texas Instruments Civic and Business Grants, 4597
Texas Instruments Fndn Arts and Culture Grants, 4599

Azerbaijan
Advanced Micro Devices Comm Affairs Grants, 172
Cargill Citizenship Corporate Giving Grants, 925
Charles Delmar Fndn Grants, 1039
Fluor Fndn Grants, 1875
Fulbright Business Grants in Spain, 1970
GMFUS Black Sea Trust for Regional Corporation Grants, 2065
H.B. Fuller Company Fndn Grants, 2183
Nike Fndn Grants, 3441
Sir Dorabji Tata Trust Grants for NGOs or Voluntary Organizations, 4370

Bahamas
Atkinson Fndn Community Grants, 606
Liz Claiborne and Art Ortenberg Grants, 2914
Mary's Pence Ministry Grants, 3029
Mary's Pence Study Grants, 3030
May and Stanley Smith Charitable Trust Grants, 3069
Regional Fund for Digital Innovation in Latin America and the Caribbean Grants, 4049

Bahrain
H.B. Fuller Company Fndn Grants, 2183
Nike Fndn Grants, 3441
OSF Arab Regional Office Grants, 3701

Bangladesh
H.B. Fuller Company Fndn Grants, 2183
Nike Fndn Grants, 3441
USAID Bengal Tiger Conservation Grants, 4741

Barbados
Atkinson Fndn Community Grants, 606
Liz Claiborne and Art Ortenberg Grants, 2914
Mary's Pence Ministry Grants, 3029
Mary's Pence Study Grants, 3030
Regional Fund for Digital Innovation in Latin America and the Caribbean Grants, 4049

Belarus
Advanced Micro Devices Comm Affairs Grants, 172
Cargill Citizenship Corporate Giving Grants, 925
Charles Delmar Fndn Grants, 1039
Fluor Fndn Grants, 1875
Fulbright Business Grants in Spain, 1970
John Deere Fndn Grants, 2692
OSF Human Rights and Governance Grants, 3708
Sir Dorabji Tata Trust Grants for NGOs or Voluntary Organizations, 4370

Belgium
Advanced Micro Devices Comm Affairs Grants, 172
Cabot Corporation Fndn Grants, 887
Cargill Citizenship Corporate Giving Grants, 925
Charles Delmar Fndn Grants, 1039
Fluor Fndn Grants, 1875
Fulbright Business Grants in Spain, 1970
Lubrizol Corporation Community Grants, 2932
Medtronic Patient Link Grants, 3113
Sir Dorabji Tata Trust Grants for NGOs or Voluntary Organizations, 4370
Texas Instruments Arts and Culture Grants, 4596
Texas Instruments Civic and Business Grants, 4597
Texas Instruments Fndn Arts and Culture Grants, 4599

Belize
Atkinson Fndn Community Grants, 606
Liz Claiborne and Art Ortenberg Grants, 2914
Mary's Pence Ministry Grants, 3029
Mary's Pence Study Grants, 3030
Patricia Price Peterson Fndn Grants, 3746
Regional Fund for Digital Innovation in Latin America and the Caribbean Grants, 4049

Benin
Aid for Starving Children Int'l Grants, 212
Cargill Citizenship Corporate Giving Grants, 925
Gregory C. Carr Fndn Grants, 2161
IREX Small Grant Fund for Civil Society Projects in Africa and Asia, 2581
IREX Small Grant Fund for Media Projects in Africa and Asia, 2582
Liz Claiborne and Art Ortenberg Grants, 2914
Murphy Institute Judith Kelleher Schafer Summer Internship Grants, 3230
Nike Fndn Grants, 3441
Nuffield Fndn Africa Grants, 3532

Bhutan
H.B. Fuller Company Fndn Grants, 2183
Nike Fndn Grants, 3441

Bolivia
Charles Delmar Fndn Grants, 1039
Katherine John Murphy Fndn Grants, 2790
Mary's Pence Ministry Grants, 3029
Mary's Pence Study Grants, 3030
Regional Fund for Digital Innovation in Latin America and the Caribbean Grants, 4049

Bosnia & Herzegovina
Advanced Micro Devices Comm Affairs Grants, 172
Cargill Citizenship Corporate Giving Grants, 925
Charles Delmar Fndn Grants, 1039
Fluor Fndn Grants, 1875
Fulbright Business Grants in Spain, 1970
OSF Advancing the Rights and Integration of Roma Grants, 3699
OSF European Comm Internships for Young Roma Graduates, 3707
OSF Mental Health Initiative Grants, 3709
Sir Dorabji Tata Trust Grants for NGOs or Voluntary Organizations, 4370
USAID Civil Society Sustainability Project Grants in Bosnia and Herzegovina, 4744

Botswana
Aid for Starving Children Int'l Grants, 212
Bill and Melinda Gates Library Grants, 768
Cargill Citizenship Corporate Giving Grants, 925
Gregory C. Carr Fndn Grants, 2161
IREX Small Grant Fund for Civil Society Projects in Africa and Asia, 2581
IREX Small Grant Fund for Media Projects in Africa and Asia, 2582
Liz Claiborne and Art Ortenberg Grants, 2914
Murphy Institute Judith Kelleher Schafer Summer Internship Grants, 3230
Nike Fndn Grants, 3441
Nuffield Fndn Africa Grants, 3532
USAID Malawi Local Capacity Development Initiative Grants, 4767

Brazil
Abbott Fund Community Grants, 81
Abbott Fund Science Education Grants, 83
Avery Dennison Fndn Grants, 623
Bechtel Group Fndn Building Positive Community Relationships Grants, 715
Charles Delmar Fndn Grants, 1039
Cummins Fndn Grants, 1415
Hershey Company Grants, 2318
John Deere Fndn Grants, 2692
Katherine John Murphy Fndn Grants, 2790
Mary's Pence Ministry Grants, 3029
Mary's Pence Study Grants, 3030
Nike Fndn Grants, 3441
Oak Fndn Child Abuse Grants, 3632
Regional Fund for Digital Innovation in Latin America and the Caribbean Grants, 4049
Texas Instruments Arts and Culture Grants, 4596
Texas Instruments Civic and Business Grants, 4597
Texas Instruments Fndn Arts and Culture Grants, 4599
Turner Voices Corporate Contributions, 4682

British Indian Ocean Territory
H.B. Fuller Company Fndn Grants, 2183
Nike Fndn Grants, 3441

Brunei
H.B. Fuller Company Fndn Grants, 2183
Nike Fndn Grants, 3441

Bulgaria
Advanced Micro Devices Comm Affairs Grants, 172
Bill and Melinda Gates Library Grants, 768
Cargill Citizenship Corporate Giving Grants, 925
Charles Delmar Fndn Grants, 1039
Fluor Fndn Grants, 1875
Fulbright Business Grants in Spain, 1970
GMFUS Black Sea Trust for Regional Corporation Grants, 2065
Oak Fndn Child Abuse Grants, 3632
OSF Advancing the Rights and Integration of Roma Grants, 3699
OSF Mental Health Initiative Grants, 3709
Sir Dorabji Tata Trust Grants for NGOs or Voluntary Organizations, 4370

Burkina Faso
Aid for Starving Children Int'l Grants, 212
Cargill Citizenship Corporate Giving Grants, 925
Gregory C. Carr Fndn Grants, 2161
IREX Small Grant Fund for Civil Society Projects in Africa and Asia, 2581
IREX Small Grant Fund for Media Projects in Africa and Asia, 2582
Liz Claiborne and Art Ortenberg Grants, 2914
Murphy Institute Judith Kelleher Schafer Summer Internship Grants, 3230
Nike Fndn Grants, 3441
Nuffield Fndn Africa Grants, 3532

Burma
H.B. Fuller Company Fndn Grants, 2183
Nike Fndn Grants, 3441
OSF Burma Project/Southeast Asia Grants, 3702

Burundi
Acumen East Africa Fellowship, 141
Aid for Starving Children Int'l Grants, 212
Cargill Citizenship Corporate Giving Grants, 925
Gregory C. Carr Fndn Grants, 2161
IREX Small Grant Fund for Civil Society Projects in Africa and Asia, 2581
IREX Small Grant Fund for Media Projects in Africa and Asia, 2582
Liz Claiborne and Art Ortenberg Grants, 2914
Murphy Institute Judith Kelleher Schafer Summer Internship Grants, 3230
Nike Fndn Grants, 3441
Nuffield Fndn Africa Grants, 3532
USAID African Institutions Innovation Mechanism Grants, 4739
USAID African Institutions Innovation Mechanism Grants, 4738

Cambodia
H.B. Fuller Company Fndn Grants, 2183
Nike Fndn Grants, 3441
OSF Burma Project/Southeast Asia Grants, 3702
USAID NGO Health Service Delivery Grants, 4771

Cameroon
Aid for Starving Children Int'l Grants, 212

GEOGRAPHIC INDEX

Cargill Citizenship Corporate Giving Grants, 925
Gregory C. Carr Fndn Grants, 2161
IREX Small Grant Fund for Civil Society Projects in Africa and Asia, 2581
IREX Small Grant Fund for Media Projects in Africa and Asia, 2582
Liz Claiborne and Art Ortenberg Grants, 2914
Murphy Institute Judith Kelleher Schafer Summer Internship Grants, 3230
Nike Fndn Grants, 3441
Nuffield Fndn Africa Grants, 3532

Cape Verde
Aid for Starving Children Int'l Grants, 212
Cargill Citizenship Corporate Giving Grants, 925
Gregory C. Carr Fndn Grants, 2161
IREX Small Grant Fund for Civil Society Projects in Africa and Asia, 2581
IREX Small Grant Fund for Media Projects in Africa and Asia, 2582
Liz Claiborne and Art Ortenberg Grants, 2914
Murphy Institute Judith Kelleher Schafer Summer Internship Grants, 3230
Nike Fndn Grants, 3441
Nuffield Fndn Africa Grants, 3532

Caribbean
Fluor Fndn Grants, 1875
PDF Fiscal Sponsorship Grant, 3808
Regional Fund for Digital Innovation in Latin America and the Caribbean Grants, 4049

Central African Republic
Aid for Starving Children Int'l Grants, 212
Cargill Citizenship Corporate Giving Grants, 925
Gregory C. Carr Fndn Grants, 2161
IREX Small Grant Fund for Civil Society Projects in Africa and Asia, 2581
IREX Small Grant Fund for Media Projects in Africa and Asia, 2582
Liz Claiborne and Art Ortenberg Grants, 2914
Murphy Institute Judith Kelleher Schafer Summer Internship Grants, 3230
Nike Fndn Grants, 3441
Nuffield Fndn Africa Grants, 3532

Chad
Aid for Starving Children Int'l Grants, 212
Cargill Citizenship Corporate Giving Grants, 925
Gregory C. Carr Fndn Grants, 2161
IREX Small Grant Fund for Civil Society Projects in Africa and Asia, 2581
IREX Small Grant Fund for Media Projects in Africa and Asia, 2582
Liz Claiborne and Art Ortenberg Grants, 2914
Murphy Institute Judith Kelleher Schafer Summer Internship Grants, 3230
Nike Fndn Grants, 3441
Nuffield Fndn Africa Grants, 3532

Chile
Bill and Melinda Gates Library Grants, 768
Charles Delmar Fndn Grants, 1039
Katherine John Murphy Fndn Grants, 2790
Mary's Pence Ministry Grants, 3029
Mary's Pence Study Grants, 3030
Regional Fund for Digital Innovation in Latin America and the Caribbean Grants, 4049
Turner Voices Corporate Contributions, 4682

China
Avery Dennison Fndn Grants, 623
Bechtel Group Fndn Building Positive Community Relationships Grants, 715
Cabot Corporation Fndn Grants, 887
Fluor Fndn Grants, 1875
H.B. Fuller Company Fndn Grants, 2183
Hershey Company Grants, 2318
Intel Int'l Community Grants, 2564
Kimball Int'l-Habig Fndn Grants, 2823

Nike Fndn Grants, 3441
Seagate Technology Corp Capacity to Care Grants, 4317
Texas Instruments Arts and Culture Grants, 4596
Texas Instruments Civic and Business Grants, 4597
Texas Instruments Fndn Arts and Culture Grants, 4599
Turner Voices Corporate Contributions, 4682

Christmas Island
H.B. Fuller Company Fndn Grants, 2183
Nike Fndn Grants, 3441

Cocos
H.B. Fuller Company Fndn Grants, 2183
Nike Fndn Grants, 3441

Colombia
Charles Delmar Fndn Grants, 1039
Katherine John Murphy Fndn Grants, 2790
Mary's Pence Ministry Grants, 3029
Mary's Pence Study Grants, 3030
Regional Fund for Digital Innovation in Latin America and the Caribbean Grants, 4049
Turner Voices Corporate Contributions, 4682

Comoros
Aid for Starving Children Int'l Grants, 212
Cargill Citizenship Corporate Giving Grants, 925
Gregory C. Carr Fndn Grants, 2161
IREX Small Grant Fund for Civil Society Projects in Africa and Asia, 2581
IREX Small Grant Fund for Media Projects in Africa and Asia, 2582
Liz Claiborne and Art Ortenberg Grants, 2914
Murphy Institute Judith Kelleher Schafer Summer Internship Grants, 3230
Nike Fndn Grants, 3441
Nuffield Fndn Africa Grants, 3532
OSF Arab Regional Office Grants, 3701

Congo
Aid for Starving Children Int'l Grants, 212
Cargill Citizenship Corporate Giving Grants, 925
Gregory C. Carr Fndn Grants, 2161
IREX Small Grant Fund for Civil Society Projects in Africa and Asia, 2581
IREX Small Grant Fund for Media Projects in Africa and Asia, 2582
Liz Claiborne and Art Ortenberg Grants, 2914
Murphy Institute Judith Kelleher Schafer Summer Internship Grants, 3230
Nike Fndn Grants, 3441
Nuffield Fndn Africa Grants, 3532

Congo, Democratic Republic of
Aid for Starving Children Int'l Grants, 212
Cargill Citizenship Corporate Giving Grants, 925
Gregory C. Carr Fndn Grants, 2161
IREX Small Grant Fund for Civil Society Projects in Africa and Asia, 2581
IREX Small Grant Fund for Media Projects in Africa and Asia, 2582
Liz Claiborne and Art Ortenberg Grants, 2914
Murphy Institute Judith Kelleher Schafer Summer Internship Grants, 3230
Nike Fndn Grants, 3441
Nuffield Fndn Africa Grants, 3532
USAID African Institutions Innovation Mechanism Grants, 4739
USAID African Institutions Innovation Mechanism Grants, 4738

Costa Rica
Atkinson Fndn Community Grants, 606
Katherine John Murphy Fndn Grants, 2790
Liz Claiborne and Art Ortenberg Grants, 2914
Mary's Pence Ministry Grants, 3029
Mary's Pence Study Grants, 3030
Patricia Price Peterson Fndn Grants, 3746
Regional Fund for Digital Innovation in Latin America and the Caribbean Grants, 4049

Cote d' Ivoire (Ivory Coast)
Aid for Starving Children Int'l Grants, 212
Cargill Citizenship Corporate Giving Grants, 925
Gregory C. Carr Fndn Grants, 2161
IREX Small Grant Fund for Civil Society Projects in Africa and Asia, 2581
IREX Small Grant Fund for Media Projects in Africa and Asia, 2582
Liz Claiborne and Art Ortenberg Grants, 2914
Murphy Institute Judith Kelleher Schafer Summer Internship Grants, 3230
Nike Fndn Grants, 3441
Nuffield Fndn Africa Grants, 3532

Croatia
Advanced Micro Devices Comm Affairs Grants, 172
Cargill Citizenship Corporate Giving Grants, 925
Charles Delmar Fndn Grants, 1039
Fluor Fndn Grants, 1875
Fulbright Business Grants in Spain, 1970
OSF Advancing the Rights and Integration of Roma Grants, 3699
OSF European Comm Internships for Young Roma Graduates, 3707
OSF Mental Health Initiative Grants, 3709
Sir Dorabji Tata Trust Grants for NGOs or Voluntary Organizations, 4370

Cuba
Atkinson Fndn Community Grants, 606
Katherine John Murphy Fndn Grants, 2790
Liz Claiborne and Art Ortenberg Grants, 2914
Mary's Pence Ministry Grants, 3029
Mary's Pence Study Grants, 3030
Patricia Price Peterson Fndn Grants, 3746
Regional Fund for Digital Innovation in Latin America and the Caribbean Grants, 4049
Turner Voices Corporate Contributions, 4682

Cyprus
Advanced Micro Devices Comm Affairs Grants, 172
Cargill Citizenship Corporate Giving Grants, 925
Charles Delmar Fndn Grants, 1039
Fluor Fndn Grants, 1875
Fulbright Business Grants in Spain, 1970
H.B. Fuller Company Fndn Grants, 2183
Nike Fndn Grants, 3441
Sir Dorabji Tata Trust Grants for NGOs or Voluntary Organizations, 4370

Czech Republic
Advanced Micro Devices Comm Affairs Grants, 172
Cargill Citizenship Corporate Giving Grants, 925
Charles Delmar Fndn Grants, 1039
Fluor Fndn Grants, 1875
Fulbright Business Grants in Spain, 1970
OSF Advancing the Rights and Integration of Roma Grants, 3699
OSF Human Rights and Governance Grants, 3708
OSF Mental Health Initiative Grants, 3709
Sir Dorabji Tata Trust Grants for NGOs or Voluntary Organizations, 4370
Texas Instruments Arts and Culture Grants, 4596
Texas Instruments Civic and Business Grants, 4597
Texas Instruments Fndn Arts and Culture Grants, 4599

Denmark
Advanced Micro Devices Comm Affairs Grants, 172
Cargill Citizenship Corporate Giving Grants, 925
Charles Delmar Fndn Grants, 1039
Fluor Fndn Grants, 1875
Fulbright Business Grants in Spain, 1970
Medtronic Patient Link Grants, 3113
Sir Dorabji Tata Trust Grants for NGOs or Voluntary Organizations, 4370
Texas Instruments Arts and Culture Grants, 4596
Texas Instruments Civic and Business Grants, 4597
Texas Instruments Fndn Arts and Culture Grants, 4599
Turner Voices Corporate Contributions, 4682

Djibouti
Acumen East Africa Fellowship, 141
Aid for Starving Children Int'l Grants, 212
Cargill Citizenship Corporate Giving Grants, 925
Gregory C. Carr Fndn Grants, 2161
IREX Small Grant Fund for Civil Society Projects in Africa and Asia, 2581
IREX Small Grant Fund for Media Projects in Africa and Asia, 2582
Liz Claiborne and Art Ortenberg Grants, 2914
Murphy Institute Judith Kelleher Schafer Summer Internship Grants, 3230
Nike Fndn Grants, 3441
Nuffield Fndn Africa Grants, 3532
OSF Arab Regional Office Grants, 3701
USAID African Institutions Innovation Mechanism Grants, 4739
USAID African Institutions Innovation Mechanism Grants, 4738

Dominica
Atkinson Fndn Community Grants, 606
Liz Claiborne and Art Ortenberg Grants, 2914
Mary's Pence Ministry Grants, 3029

Dominican Republic
Atkinson Fndn Community Grants, 606
Katherine John Murphy Fndn Grants, 2790
Liz Claiborne and Art Ortenberg Grants, 2914
Mary's Pence Ministry Grants, 3029

East Timor
OSF Burma Project/Southeast Asia Grants, 3702

Ecuador
Charles Delmar Fndn Grants, 1039
Katherine John Murphy Fndn Grants, 2790
Mary's Pence Ministry Grants, 3029
Mary's Pence Study Grants, 3030
Regional Fund for Digital Innovation in Latin America and the Caribbean Grants, 4049

Egypt
Aid for Starving Children Int'l Grants, 212
Cargill Citizenship Corporate Giving Grants, 925
Gregory C. Carr Fndn Grants, 2161
IREX Small Grant Fund for Civil Society Projects in Africa and Asia, 2581
IREX Small Grant Fund for Media Projects in Africa and Asia, 2582
Liz Claiborne and Art Ortenberg Grants, 2914
Murphy Institute Judith Kelleher Schafer Summer Internship Grants, 3230
Nike Fndn Grants, 3441
Nuffield Fndn Africa Grants, 3532
OSF Arab Regional Office Grants, 3701
Turner Voices Corporate Contributions, 4682

El Salvador
Atkinson Fndn Community Grants, 606
Katherine John Murphy Fndn Grants, 2790
Liz Claiborne and Art Ortenberg Grants, 2914
Mary's Pence Ministry Grants, 3029
Patricia Price Peterson Fndn Grants, 3746

Equatorial Guinea
Aid for Starving Children Int'l Grants, 212
Cargill Citizenship Corporate Giving Grants, 925
Gregory C. Carr Fndn Grants, 2161
IREX Small Grant Fund for Civil Society Projects in Africa and Asia, 2581
IREX Small Grant Fund for Media Projects in Africa and Asia, 2582
Liz Claiborne and Art Ortenberg Grants, 2914
Murphy Institute Judith Kelleher Schafer Summer Internship Grants, 3230
Nike Fndn Grants, 3441
Nuffield Fndn Africa Grants, 3532

Eritrea
Acumen East Africa Fellowship, 141
Aid for Starving Children Int'l Grants, 212
Cargill Citizenship Corporate Giving Grants, 925
Gregory C. Carr Fndn Grants, 2161
IREX Small Grant Fund for Civil Society Projects in Africa and Asia, 2581
IREX Small Grant Fund for Media Projects in Africa and Asia, 2582
Liz Claiborne and Art Ortenberg Grants, 2914
Murphy Institute Judith Kelleher Schafer Summer Internship Grants, 3230
Nike Fndn Grants, 3441
Nuffield Fndn Africa Grants, 3532

Estonia
Advanced Micro Devices Comm Affairs Grants, 172
Cargill Citizenship Corporate Giving Grants, 925
Charles Delmar Fndn Grants, 1039
Fluor Fndn Grants, 1875
Fulbright Business Grants in Spain, 1970
John Deere Fndn Grants, 2692
OSF Human Rights and Governance Grants, 3708
OSF Mental Health Initiative Grants, 3709
Sir Dorabji Tata Trust Grants for NGOs or Voluntary Organizations, 4370

Ethiopia
Acumen East Africa Fellowship, 141
Aid for Starving Children Int'l Grants, 212
Cargill Citizenship Corporate Giving Grants, 925
Firelight Fndn Grants, 1817
Gregory C. Carr Fndn Grants, 2161
IREX Small Grant Fund for Civil Society Projects in Africa and Asia, 2581
IREX Small Grant Fund for Media Projects in Africa and Asia, 2582
Liz Claiborne and Art Ortenberg Grants, 2914
Murphy Institute Judith Kelleher Schafer Summer Internship Grants, 3230
Nike Fndn Grants, 3441
Nuffield Fndn Africa Grants, 3532
Oak Fndn Child Abuse Grants, 3632
USAID African Institutions Innovation Mechanism Grants, 4739
USAID African Institutions Innovation Mechanism Grants, 4738

Finland
Advanced Micro Devices Comm Affairs Grants, 172
Cargill Citizenship Corporate Giving Grants, 925
Charles Delmar Fndn Grants, 1039
Fluor Fndn Grants, 1875
Fulbright Business Grants in Spain, 1970
Medtronic Patient Link Grants, 3113
Sir Dorabji Tata Trust Grants for NGOs or Voluntary Organizations, 4370
Texas Instruments Arts and Culture Grants, 4596
Texas Instruments Civic and Business Grants, 4597
Texas Instruments Fndn Arts and Culture Grants, 4599

France
Advanced Micro Devices Comm Affairs Grants, 172
Cargill Citizenship Corporate Giving Grants, 925
Charles Delmar Fndn Grants, 1039
Fluor Fndn Grants, 1875
Fulbright Business Grants in Spain, 1970
IIE Leonora Lindsley Memorial Fellowships, 2458
Medtronic Patient Link Grants, 3113
OSF Advancing the Rights and Integration of Roma Grants, 3699
Sir Dorabji Tata Trust Grants for NGOs or Voluntary Organizations, 4370
Texas Instruments Arts and Culture Grants, 4596
Texas Instruments Civic and Business Grants, 4597
Texas Instruments Arts and Culture Grants, 4599
Turner Voices Corporate Contributions, 4682

Gabon
Aid for Starving Children Int'l Grants, 212
Cargill Citizenship Corporate Giving Grants, 925
Gregory C. Carr Fndn Grants, 2161
IREX Small Grant Fund for Civil Society Projects in Africa and Asia, 2581
IREX Small Grant Fund for Media Projects in Africa and Asia, 2582
Liz Claiborne and Art Ortenberg Grants, 2914
Murphy Institute Judith Kelleher Schafer Summer Internship Grants, 3230
Nike Fndn Grants, 3441
Nuffield Fndn Africa Grants, 3532

Gambia
Aid for Starving Children Int'l Grants, 212
Cargill Citizenship Corporate Giving Grants, 925
Gregory C. Carr Fndn Grants, 2161
IREX Small Grant Fund for Civil Society Projects in Africa and Asia, 2581
IREX Small Grant Fund for Media Projects in Africa and Asia, 2582
Liz Claiborne and Art Ortenberg Grants, 2914
Murphy Institute Judith Kelleher Schafer Summer Internship Grants, 3230
Nike Fndn Grants, 3441
Nuffield Fndn Africa Grants, 3532

Georgia
Advanced Micro Devices Comm Affairs Grants, 172
Cargill Citizenship Corporate Giving Grants, 925
Charles Delmar Fndn Grants, 1039
Fluor Fndn Grants, 1875
Fulbright Business Grants in Spain, 1970
H.B. Fuller Company Fndn Grants, 2183
Nike Fndn Grants, 3441
Sir Dorabji Tata Trust Grants for NGOs or Voluntary Organizations, 4370

Germany
Abbott Fund Community Grants, 81
Abbott Fund Science Education Grants, 83
ADC Fndn Technology Access Grants, 158
Advanced Micro Devices Comm Affairs Grants, 172
Cargill Citizenship Corporate Giving Grants, 925
Charles Delmar Fndn Grants, 1039
Chiles Fndn Grants, 1108
Fluor Fndn Grants, 1875
Fulbright Business Grants in Spain, 1970
Medtronic Patient Link Grants, 3113
OSF Human Rights and Governance Grants, 3708
OSF Mental Health Initiative Grants, 3709
Sir Dorabji Tata Trust Grants for NGOs or Voluntary Organizations, 4370
Texas Instruments Arts and Culture Grants, 4596
Texas Instruments Civic and Business Grants, 4597
Texas Instruments Arts and Culture Grants, 4599
Textron Corporate Contributions Grants, 4601
Turner Voices Corporate Contributions, 4682

Ghana
Aid for Starving Children Int'l Grants, 212
Cargill Citizenship Corporate Giving Grants, 925
Gregory C. Carr Fndn Grants, 2161
IREX Small Grant Fund for Civil Society Projects in Africa and Asia, 2581
IREX Small Grant Fund for Media Projects in Africa and Asia, 2582
Liz Claiborne and Art Ortenberg Grants, 2914
Murphy Institute Judith Kelleher Schafer Summer Internship Grants, 3230
Nike Fndn Grants, 3441
Nuffield Fndn Africa Grants, 3532

Great Britain
Abbott Fund Community Grants, 81
Abbott Fund Science Education Grants, 83
Medtronic Patient Link Grants, 3113
Textron Corporate Contributions Grants, 4601

GEOGRAPHIC INDEX

Greece
Advanced Micro Devices Comm Affairs Grants, 172
Cargill Citizenship Corporate Giving Grants, 925
Charles Delmar Fndn Grants, 1039
Fluor Fndn Grants, 1875
Fulbright Business Grants in Spain, 1970
Sir Dorabji Tata Trust Grants for NGOs or Voluntary Organizations, 4370

Grenada
Atkinson Fndn Community Grants, 606
Liz Claiborne and Art Ortenberg Grants, 2914
Mary's Pence Ministry Grants, 3029

Guatemala
Atkinson Fndn Community Grants, 606
Katherine John Murphy Fndn Grants, 2790
Liz Claiborne and Art Ortenberg Grants, 2914
Mary's Pence Ministry Grants, 3029
Patricia Price Peterson Fndn Grants, 3746

Guinea
Aid for Starving Children Int'l Grants, 212
Cargill Citizenship Corporate Giving Grants, 925
Gregory C. Carr Fndn Grants, 2161
IREX Small Grant Fund for Civil Society Projects in Africa and Asia, 2581
IREX Small Grant Fund for Media Projects in Africa and Asia, 2582
Liz Claiborne and Art Ortenberg Grants, 2914
Murphy Institute Judith Kelleher Schafer Summer Internship Grants, 3230
Nike Fndn Grants, 3441
Nuffield Fndn Africa Grants, 3532

Guinea-Bissau
Aid for Starving Children Int'l Grants, 212
Cargill Citizenship Corporate Giving Grants, 925
Gregory C. Carr Fndn Grants, 2161
IREX Small Grant Fund for Civil Society Projects in Africa and Asia, 2581
IREX Small Grant Fund for Media Projects in Africa and Asia, 2582
Liz Claiborne and Art Ortenberg Grants, 2914
Murphy Institute Judith Kelleher Schafer Summer Internship Grants, 3230
Nike Fndn Grants, 3441
Nuffield Fndn Africa Grants, 3532

Guyana
Charles Delmar Fndn Grants, 1039
Mary's Pence Ministry Grants, 3029
Mary's Pence Study Grants, 3030
Regional Fund for Digital Innovation in Latin America and the Caribbean Grants, 4049

Haiti
Abundance Fndn Int'l Grants, 108
Atkinson Fndn Community Grants, 606
Katherine John Murphy Fndn Grants, 2790
Liz Claiborne and Art Ortenberg Grants, 2914
Mary's Pence Ministry Grants, 3029
PDF Community Organizing Grants, 3807
PDF Fiscal Sponsorship Grant, 3808

Honduras
Atkinson Fndn Community Grants, 606
Katherine John Murphy Fndn Grants, 2790
Liz Claiborne and Art Ortenberg Grants, 2914
Mary's Pence Ministry Grants, 3029
Patricia Price Peterson Fndn Grants, 3746

Hong Kong
H.B. Fuller Company Fndn Grants, 2183
IIE AmCham Charitable Fndn U.S. Studies Scholarship, 2453
Lubrizol Corporation Community Grants, 2932
May and Stanley Smith Charitable Trust Grants, 3069
Nike Fndn Grants, 3441
Turner Voices Corporate Contributions, 4682

Hungary
Advanced Micro Devices Comm Affairs Grants, 172
Cargill Citizenship Corporate Giving Grants, 925
Charles Delmar Fndn Grants, 1039
Fluor Fndn Grants, 1875
Fulbright Business Grants in Spain, 1970
OSF Advancing the Rights and Integration of Roma Grants, 3699
OSF Human Rights and Governance Grants, 3708
OSF Mental Health Initiative Grants, 3709
Sir Dorabji Tata Trust Grants for NGOs or Voluntary Organizations, 4370
Texas Instruments Arts and Culture Grants, 4596
Texas Instruments Civic and Business Grants, 4597
Texas Instruments Fndn Arts and Culture Grants, 4599
Turner Voices Corporate Contributions, 4682

Iceland
Advanced Micro Devices Comm Affairs Grants, 172
Cargill Citizenship Corporate Giving Grants, 925
Charles Delmar Fndn Grants, 1039
Fluor Fndn Grants, 1875
Fulbright Business Grants in Spain, 1970
Medtronic Patient Link Grants, 3113
Sir Dorabji Tata Trust Grants for NGOs or Voluntary Organizations, 4370
Turner Voices Corporate Contributions, 4682

India
ADC Fndn Technology Access Grants, 158
H.B. Fuller Company Fndn Grants, 2183
Michael and Susan Dell Fndn Grants, 3158
Nike Fndn Grants, 3441
Oak Found Housing and Homelessness Grants, 3633
Prudential Spirit of Community Awards, 3978
Shastri Indo-Canadian Institute Action Research Project Grants, 4341
Texas Instruments Arts and Culture Grants, 4596
Texas Instruments Civic and Business Grants, 4597
Texas Instruments Arts and Culture Grants, 4599
Turner Voices Corporate Contributions, 4682
USAID India-Africa Ag Innovation Bridge Grants, 4760
USAID Strengthening RMNCH Through Indian Health Professional Associations and Scaling Up Uptake Grants, 4784

Indonesia
H.B. Fuller Company Fndn Grants, 2183
IIE Freeman Fndn Indonesia Internships, 2456
Nike Fndn Grants, 3441
Turner Voices Corporate Contributions, 4682

Iran
H.B. Fuller Company Fndn Grants, 2183
Nike Fndn Grants, 3441

Iraq
H.B. Fuller Company Fndn Grants, 2183
Nike Fndn Grants, 3441
OSF Arab Regional Office Grants, 3701

Ireland
Abbott Fund Community Grants, 81
Abbott Fund Science Education Grants, 83
Advanced Micro Devices Comm Affairs Grants, 172
Cargill Citizenship Corporate Giving Grants, 925
Charles Delmar Fndn Grants, 1039
Fluor Fndn Grants, 1875
Fulbright Business Grants in Spain, 1970
Medtronic CommunityLink Education Grants, 3110
Medtronic CommunityLink Health Grants, 3111
Medtronic Patient Link Grants, 3113
Prudential Spirit of Community Awards, 3978
Seagate Technology Corporation Capacity to Care Grants, 4317
Sir Dorabji Tata Trust Grants for NGOs or Voluntary Organizations, 4370
Texas Instruments Arts and Culture Grants, 4596
Texas Instruments Civic and Business Grants, 4597
Texas Instruments Fndn Arts and Culture Grants, 4599

Israel
American Society for Yad Vashem Grants, 447
Boston Jewish Community Women's Grants, 822
David Geffen Fndn Grants, 1452
H.B. Fuller Company Fndn Grants, 2183
Harry Kramer Memorial Fund Grants, 2242
Intel Int'l Community Grants, 2564
Koret Fndn Grants, 2837
Nike Fndn Grants, 3441
Russell Berrie Fndn Grants, 4175
Texas Instruments Arts and Culture Grants, 4596
Texas Instruments Civic and Business Grants, 4597
Texas Instruments Fndn Arts and Culture Grants, 4599
Turner Voices Corporate Contributions, 4682
USAID Civic Participation Grants, 4743
USAID Palestinian Community Assistance, 4773

Italy
Abbott Fund Community Grants, 81
Abbott Fund Science Education Grants, 83
Advanced Micro Devices Comm Affairs Grants, 172
Cargill Citizenship Corporate Giving Grants, 925
Charles Delmar Fndn Grants, 1039
Fluor Fndn Grants, 1875
Fulbright Business Grants in Spain, 1970
Medtronic Patient Link Grants, 3113
Micron Tech Fndn Community Grants, 3161
NIAF Anthony Campitelli Endowed Grants, 3431
OSF Advancing the Rights and Integration of Roma Grants, 3699
Sir Dorabji Tata Trust Grants for NGOs or Voluntary Organizations, 4370
Texas Instruments Arts and Culture Grants, 4596
Texas Instruments Civic and Business Grants, 4597
Texas Instruments Fndn Arts and Culture Grants, 4599
Turner Voices Corporate Contributions, 4682

Jamaica
Atkinson Fndn Community Grants, 606
Liz Claiborne and Art Ortenberg Grants, 2914
Mary's Pence Ministry Grants, 3029
Patricia Price Peterson Fndn Grants, 3746

Japan
Abbott Fund Community Grants, 81
Abbott Fund Science Education Grants, 83
Bechtel Group Fndn Building Positive Community Relationships Grants, 715
Cummins Fndn Grants, 1415
Fluor Fndn Grants, 1875
H.B. Fuller Company Fndn Grants, 2183
Medtronic CommunityLink Education Grants, 3110
Medtronic CommunityLink Health Grants, 3111
Medtronic Patient Link Grants, 3113
Micron Tech Fndn Community Grants, 3161
Nike Fndn Grants, 3441
Prudential Spirit of Community Awards, 3978
Texas Instruments Arts and Culture Grants, 4596
Texas Instruments Civic and Business Grants, 4597
Texas Instruments Fndn Arts and Culture Grants, 4599
Turner Voices Corporate Contributions, 4682

Jordan
H.B. Fuller Company Fndn Grants, 2183
Nike Fndn Grants, 3441
OSF Arab Regional Office Grants, 3701

Kazakhstan
H.B. Fuller Company Fndn Grants, 2183
Nike Fndn Grants, 3441
OSF Central Eurasia Project Grants, 3704

Kenya
Acumen East Africa Fellowship, 141
Aid for Starving Children Int'l Grants, 212
Cargill Citizenship Corporate Giving Grants, 925
Firelight Fndn Grants, 1817
Gregory C. Carr Fndn Grants, 2161
IREX Small Grant Fund for Civil Society Projects in Africa and Asia, 2581

1184 / Kenya

IREX Small Grant Fund for Media Projects in Africa and Asia, 2582
Liz Claiborne and Art Ortenberg Grants, 2914
Murphy Institute Judith Kelleher Schafer Summer Internship Grants, 3230
Nike Fndn Grants, 3441
Nuffield Fndn Africa Grants, 3532
USAID Accelerating Progress Against Tuberculosis in Kenya Grants, 4737
USAID African Institutions Innovation Mechanism Grants, 4738
USAID African Institutions Innovation Mechanism Grants, 4739
USAID Malawi Local Capacity Development Initiative Grants, 4767

Korea
Texas Instruments Arts and Culture Grants, 4596
Texas Instruments Civic and Business Grants, 4597
Texas Instruments Fndn Arts and Culture Grants, 4599
Turner Voices Corporate Contributions, 4682

Kosovo
Advanced Micro Devices Comm Affairs Grants, 172
Cargill Citizenship Corporate Giving Grants, 925
Charles Delmar Fndn Grants, 1039
Fluor Fndn Grants, 1875
Fulbright Business Grants in Spain, 1970
OSF Advancing the Rights and Integration of Roma Grants, 3699
OSF European Comm Internships for Young Roma Graduates, 3707
OSF Mental Health Initiative Grants, 3709
Sir Dorabji Tata Trust Grants for NGOs or Voluntary Organizations, 4370

Kuwait
H.B. Fuller Company Fndn Grants, 2183
Nike Fndn Grants, 3441
OSF Arab Regional Office Grants, 3701

Kyrgyzstan
H.B. Fuller Company Fndn Grants, 2183
Nike Fndn Grants, 3441
OSF Central Eurasia Project Grants, 3704

Laos
H.B. Fuller Company Fndn Grants, 2183
Nike Fndn Grants, 3441
OSF Burma Project/Southeast Asia Grants, 3702

Latvia
Advanced Micro Devices Comm Affairs Grants, 172
Bill and Melinda Gates Library Grants, 768
Cargill Citizenship Corporate Giving Grants, 925
Charles Delmar Fndn Grants, 1039
Fluor Fndn Grants, 1875
Fulbright Business Grants in Spain, 1970
John Deere Fndn Grants, 2692
Oak Fndn Child Abuse Grants, 3632
OSF Human Rights and Governance Grants, 3708
OSF Mental Health Initiative Grants, 3709
Sir Dorabji Tata Trust Grants for NGOs or Voluntary Organizations, 4370

Lebanon
H.B. Fuller Company Fndn Grants, 2183
Nike Fndn Grants, 3441
OSF Arab Regional Office Grants, 3701
Turner Voices Corporate Contributions, 4682

Lesotho
Aid for Starving Children Int'l Grants, 212
Cargill Citizenship Corporate Giving Grants, 925
Firelight Fndn Grants, 1817
Gregory C. Carr Fndn Grants, 2161
IREX Small Grant Fund for Civil Society Projects in Africa and Asia, 2581
IREX Small Grant Fund for Media Projects in Africa and Asia, 2582

Liz Claiborne and Art Ortenberg Grants, 2914
Murphy Institute Judith Kelleher Schafer Summer Internship Grants, 3230
Nike Fndn Grants, 3441
Nuffield Fndn Africa Grants, 3532

Liberia
Aid for Starving Children Int'l Grants, 212
Cargill Citizenship Corporate Giving Grants, 925
Gregory C. Carr Fndn Grants, 2161
IREX Small Grant Fund for Civil Society Projects in Africa and Asia, 2581
IREX Small Grant Fund for Media Projects in Africa and Asia, 2582
Liz Claiborne and Art Ortenberg Grants, 2914
Murphy Institute Judith Kelleher Schafer Summer Internship Grants, 3230
Nike Fndn Grants, 3441
Nuffield Fndn Africa Grants, 3532

Libya
Aid for Starving Children Int'l Grants, 212
Cargill Citizenship Corporate Giving Grants, 925
Gregory C. Carr Fndn Grants, 2161
IREX Small Grant Fund for Civil Society Projects in Africa and Asia, 2581
IREX Small Grant Fund for Media Projects in Africa and Asia, 2582
Liz Claiborne and Art Ortenberg Grants, 2914
Murphy Institute Judith Kelleher Schafer Summer Internship Grants, 3230
Nike Fndn Grants, 3441
Nuffield Fndn Africa Grants, 3532
OSF Arab Regional Office Grants, 3701

Liechtenstein
Advanced Micro Devices Comm Affairs Grants, 172
Cargill Citizenship Corporate Giving Grants, 925
Charles Delmar Fndn Grants, 1039
Fluor Fndn Grants, 1875
Fulbright Business Grants in Spain, 1970
OSF Human Rights and Governance Grants, 3708
Sir Dorabji Tata Trust Grants for NGOs or Voluntary Organizations, 4370

Lithuania
Advanced Micro Devices Comm Affairs Grants, 172
Bill and Melinda Gates Library Grants, 768
Cargill Citizenship Corporate Giving Grants, 925
Charles Delmar Fndn Grants, 1039
Fluor Fndn Grants, 1875
Fulbright Business Grants in Spain, 1970
John Deere Fndn Grants, 2692
Medtronic Patient Link Grants, 3113
OSF Human Rights and Governance Grants, 3708
OSF Mental Health Initiative Grants, 3709
Sir Dorabji Tata Trust Grants for NGOs or Voluntary Organizations, 4370

Luxembourg
Advanced Micro Devices Comm Affairs Grants, 172
Cargill Citizenship Corporate Giving Grants, 925
Charles Delmar Fndn Grants, 1039
Fluor Fndn Grants, 1875
Fulbright Business Grants in Spain, 1970
Medtronic Patient Link Grants, 3113
Sir Dorabji Tata Trust Grants for NGOs or Voluntary Organizations, 4370

Macau
H.B. Fuller Company Fndn Grants, 2183
Nike Fndn Grants, 3441
Sands Fndn Crisis Fund Grants, 4254
Sands Fndn Grants, 4255

Macedonia
Advanced Micro Devices Comm Affairs Grants, 172
Cargill Citizenship Corporate Giving Grants, 925
Charles Delmar Fndn Grants, 1039
Fluor Fndn Grants, 1875

GEOGRAPHIC INDEX

Fulbright Business Grants in Spain, 1970
OSF Advancing the Rights and Integration of Roma Grants, 3699
OSF European Comm Internships for Young Roma Graduates, 3707
OSF Mental Health Initiative Grants, 3709
Sir Dorabji Tata Trust Grants for NGOs or Voluntary Organizations, 4370

Madagascar
Aid for Starving Children Int'l Grants, 212
Cargill Citizenship Corporate Giving Grants, 925
Gregory C. Carr Fndn Grants, 2161
IREX Small Grant Fund for Civil Society Projects in Africa and Asia, 2581
IREX Small Grant Fund for Media Projects in Africa and Asia, 2582
Liz Claiborne and Art Ortenberg Grants, 2914
Murphy Institute Judith Kelleher Schafer Summer Internship Grants, 3230
Nike Fndn Grants, 3441
Nuffield Fndn Africa Grants, 3532

Malawi
Aid for Starving Children Int'l Grants, 212
Cargill Citizenship Corporate Giving Grants, 925
Firelight Fndn Grants, 1817
Gregory C. Carr Fndn Grants, 2161
IREX Small Grant Fund for Civil Society Projects in Africa and Asia, 2581
IREX Small Grant Fund for Media Projects in Africa and Asia, 2582
Liz Claiborne and Art Ortenberg Grants, 2914
Murphy Institute Judith Kelleher Schafer Summer Internship Grants, 3230
Nike Fndn Grants, 3441
Nuffield Fndn Africa Grants, 3532
USAID Malawi Local Capacity Development Initiative Grants, 4767

Malaysia
H.B. Fuller Company Fndn Grants, 2183
Nike Fndn Grants, 3441
OSF Burma Project/Southeast Asia Grants, 3702
Seagate Technology Corporation Capacity to Care Grants, 4317
Texas Instruments Arts and Culture Grants, 4596
Texas Instruments Civic and Business Grants, 4597
Texas Instruments Arts and Culture Grants, 4599

Maldives
H.B. Fuller Company Fndn Grants, 2183
Nike Fndn Grants, 3441

Mali
Aid for Starving Children Int'l Grants, 212
Cargill Citizenship Corporate Giving Grants, 925
Gregory C. Carr Fndn Grants, 2161
IREX Small Grant Fund for Civil Society Projects in Africa and Asia, 2581
IREX Small Grant Fund for Media Projects in Africa and Asia, 2582
Liz Claiborne and Art Ortenberg Grants, 2914
Murphy Institute Judith Kelleher Schafer Summer Internship Grants, 3230
Nike Fndn Grants, 3441
Nuffield Fndn Africa Grants, 3532
USAID HIV Prevention with Key Populations - Mali Grants, 4757

Malta
Advanced Micro Devices Comm Affairs Grants, 172
Cargill Citizenship Corporate Giving Grants, 925
Charles Delmar Fndn Grants, 1039
Fluor Fndn Grants, 1875
Fulbright Business Grants in Spain, 1970
Sir Dorabji Tata Trust Grants for NGOs or Voluntary Organizations, 4370

GEOGRAPHIC INDEX

Mauritania
Aid for Starving Children Int'l Grants, 212
Cargill Citizenship Corporate Giving Grants, 925
Gregory C. Carr Fndn Grants, 2161
IREX Small Grant Fund for Civil Society Projects in Africa and Asia, 2581
IREX Small Grant Fund for Media Projects in Africa and Asia, 2582
Liz Claiborne and Art Ortenberg Grants, 2914
Murphy Institute Judith Kelleher Schafer Summer Internship Grants, 3230
Nike Fndn Grants, 3441
Nuffield Fndn Africa Grants, 3532
OSF Arab Regional Office Grants, 3701

Mauritius
Aid for Starving Children Int'l Grants, 212
Cargill Citizenship Corporate Giving Grants, 925
Gregory C. Carr Fndn Grants, 2161
IREX Small Grant Fund for Civil Society Projects in Africa and Asia, 2581
IREX Small Grant Fund for Media Projects in Africa and Asia, 2582
Liz Claiborne and Art Ortenberg Grants, 2914
Murphy Institute Judith Kelleher Schafer Summer Internship Grants, 3230
Nike Fndn Grants, 3441
Nuffield Fndn Africa Grants, 3532

Mexico
ADC Fndn Technology Access Grants, 158
Alaska Airlines Corporate Giving Grants, 320
Atkinson Fndn Community Grants, 606
Bill and Melinda Gates Library Grants, 768
Cummins Fndn Grants, 1415
Fluor Fndn Grants, 1875
Fulbright Binational Business Grants in Mexico, 1969
General Service Fndn Human Rights and Economic Justice Grants, 2006
Hershey Company Grants, 2318
Honeywell Corp Housing and Shelter Grants, 2357
KaBOOM-CA Playground Challenge Grants, 2761
Katherine John Murphy Fndn Grants, 2790
Kimball Int'l-Habig Fndn Grants, 2823
Liz Claiborne and Art Ortenberg Grants, 2914
Mary's Pence Ministry Grants, 3029
Oak Fndn Child Abuse Grants, 3632
PACCAR Fndn Grants, 3719
Paso del Norte Health Fndn Grants, 3743
Patricia Price Peterson Fndn Grants, 3746
PDF Community Organizing Grants, 3807
PDF Fiscal Sponsorship Grant, 3808
Seagate Technology Corporation Capacity to Care Grants, 4317
Steelcase Fndn Grants, 4497
Texas Instruments Arts and Culture Grants, 4596
Texas Instruments Civic and Business Grants, 4597
Texas Instruments Fndn Arts and Culture Grants, 4599
Turner Voices Corporate Contributions, 4682
USAID Scholarships for Youth and Teachers, 4780

Micronesia
USDA Farmers Market Promotion Grants, 4808
USDC Public Works and Economic Adjustment Assistance Grants, 4856

Moldova
Advanced Micro Devices Comm Affairs Grants, 172
Cargill Citizenship Corporate Giving Grants, 925
Charles Delmar Fndn Grants, 1039
Fluor Fndn Grants, 1875
Fulbright Business Grants in Spain, 1970
GMFUS Black Sea Trust for Regional Corporation Grants, 2065
John Deere Fndn Grants, 2692
Oak Fndn Child Abuse Grants, 3632
OSF Advancing the Rights and Integration of Roma Grants, 3699
OSF Civil Service Awards, 3705
OSF Human Rights and Governance Grants, 3708

Sir Dorabji Tata Trust Grants for NGOs or Voluntary Organizations, 4370

Monaco
Advanced Micro Devices Comm Affairs Grants, 172
Cargill Citizenship Corporate Giving Grants, 925
Charles Delmar Fndn Grants, 1039
Fluor Fndn Grants, 1875
Fulbright Business Grants in Spain, 1970
Sir Dorabji Tata Trust Grants for NGOs or Voluntary Organizations, 4370

Mongolia
H.B. Fuller Company Fndn Grants, 2183
Nike Fndn Grants, 3441
OSF Human Rights and Governance Grants, 3708

Montenegro
Advanced Micro Devices Comm Affairs Grants, 172
Cargill Citizenship Corporate Giving Grants, 925
Charles Delmar Fndn Grants, 1039
Fluor Fndn Grants, 1875
Fulbright Business Grants in Spain, 1970
OSF Advancing the Rights and Integration of Roma Grants, 3699
OSF European Comm Internships for Young Roma Graduates, 3707
OSF Mental Health Initiative Grants, 3709
Sir Dorabji Tata Trust Grants for NGOs or Voluntary Organizations, 4370

Morocco
Aid for Starving Children Int'l Grants, 212
Cargill Citizenship Corporate Giving Grants, 925
Gregory C. Carr Fndn Grants, 2161
IREX Small Grant Fund for Civil Society Projects in Africa and Asia, 2581
IREX Small Grant Fund for Media Projects in Africa and Asia, 2582
Liz Claiborne and Art Ortenberg Grants, 2914
Murphy Institute Judith Kelleher Schafer Summer Internship Grants, 3230
Nike Fndn Grants, 3441
Nuffield Fndn Africa Grants, 3532
OSF Arab Regional Office Grants, 3701

Mozambique
Aid for Starving Children Int'l Grants, 212
Cargill Citizenship Corporate Giving Grants, 925
Gregory C. Carr Fndn Grants, 2161
IREX Small Grant Fund for Civil Society Projects in Africa and Asia, 2581
IREX Grant Media Projects in Africa and Asia, 2582
Liz Claiborne and Art Ortenberg Grants, 2914
Murphy Institute Judith Kelleher Schafer Summer Internship Grants, 3230
Nike Fndn Grants, 3441
Nuffield Fndn Africa Grants, 3532

Nagorno-Karabakh
H.B. Fuller Company Fndn Grants, 2183
Nike Fndn Grants, 3441

Namibia
Aid for Starving Children Int'l Grants, 212
Cargill Citizenship Corporate Giving Grants, 925
Gregory C. Carr Fndn Grants, 2161
IREX Small Grant Fund for Civil Society Projects in Africa and Asia, 2581
IREX Small Grant Fund for Media Projects in Africa and Asia, 2582
Liz Claiborne and Art Ortenberg Grants, 2914
Murphy Institute Judith Kelleher Schafer Summer Internship Grants, 3230
Nike Fndn Grants, 3441
Nuffield Fndn Africa Grants, 3532
USAID Malawi Local Capacity Development Initiative Grants, 4767

Nepal
H.B. Fuller Company Fndn Grants, 2183
Nike Fndn Grants, 3441

Netherlands
Abbott Fund Community Grants, 81
Abbott Fund Science Education Grants, 83
Medtronic CommunityLink Education Grants, 3110
Medtronic CommunityLink Health Grants, 3111
Medtronic Patient Link Grants, 3113
Oak Fndn Child Abuse Grants, 3632
PACCAR Fndn Grants, 3719
Texas Instruments Arts and Culture Grants, 4596
Texas Instruments Civic and Business Grants, 4597
Texas Instruments Fndn Arts and Culture Grants, 4599

New Zealand
Fluor Fndn Grants, 1875
Project Orange Thumb Grants, 3972

Nicaragua
Atkinson Fndn Community Grants, 606
Katherine John Murphy Fndn Grants, 2790
Liz Claiborne and Art Ortenberg Grants, 2914
Mary's Pence Ministry Grants, 3029
Patricia Price Peterson Fndn Grants, 3746

Niger
Aid for Starving Children Int'l Grants, 212
Cargill Citizenship Corporate Giving Grants, 925
Gregory C. Carr Fndn Grants, 2161
IREX Small Grant Fund for Civil Society Projects in Africa and Asia, 2581
IREX Small Grant Fund for Media Projects in Africa and Asia, 2582
Liz Claiborne and Art Ortenberg Grants, 2914
Murphy Institute Judith Kelleher Schafer Summer Internship Grants, 3230
Nike Fndn Grants, 3441
Nuffield Fndn Africa Grants, 3532

Nigeria
Aid for Starving Children Int'l Grants, 212
Cargill Citizenship Corporate Giving Grants, 925
Gregory C. Carr Fndn Grants, 2161
IREX Small Grant Fund for Civil Society Projects in Africa and Asia, 2581
IREX Small Grant Fund for Media Projects in Africa and Asia, 2582
Liz Claiborne and Art Ortenberg Grants, 2914
Murphy Institute Judith Kelleher Schafer Summer Internship Grants, 3230
Nike Fndn Grants, 3441
Nuffield Fndn Africa Grants, 3532
USAID Family Health Plus Project Grants, 4751

North Korea
H.B. Fuller Company Fndn Grants, 2183
Nike Fndn Grants, 3441

Northern Cyprus
H.B. Fuller Company Fndn Grants, 2183
Nike Fndn Grants, 3441

Norway
Advanced Micro Devices Comm Affairs Grants, 172
Cargill Citizenship Corporate Giving Grants, 925
Charles Delmar Fndn Grants, 1039
Fluor Fndn Grants, 1875
Fulbright Business Grants in Spain, 1970
Medtronic Patient Link Grants, 3113
Sir Dorabji Tata Trust Grants for NGOs or Voluntary Organizations, 4370
Texas Instruments Arts and Culture Grants, 4596
Texas Instruments Civic and Business Grants, 4597
Texas Instruments Fndn Arts and Culture Grants, 4599
Turner Voices Corporate Contributions, 4682

Oman
H.B. Fuller Company Fndn Grants, 2183

Nike Fndn Grants, 3441
OSF Arab Regional Office Grants, 3701

Pakistan
H.B. Fuller Company Fndn Grants, 2183
Nike Fndn Grants, 3441
Turner Voices Corporate Contributions, 4682

Palau
USDC Public Works and Economic Adjustment Assistance Grants, 4856

Palestinian Authority
H.B. Fuller Company Fndn Grants, 2183
Nike Fndn Grants, 3441

Palestinian Territory
OSF Arab Regional Office Grants, 3701

Panama
Katherine John Murphy Fndn Grants, 2790
Patricia Price Peterson Fndn Grants, 3746
Turner Voices Corporate Contributions, 4682

Paraguay
Charles Delmar Fndn Grants, 1039
Katherine John Murphy Fndn Grants, 2790
Mary's Pence Ministry Grants, 3029
Mary's Pence Study Grants, 3030
Regional Fund for Digital Innovation in Latin America and the Caribbean Grants, 4049

Peru
Bechtel Group Fndn Building Positive Community Relationships Grants, 715
Charles Delmar Fndn Grants, 1039
Fluor Fndn Grants, 1875
Katherine John Murphy Fndn Grants, 2790
Mary's Pence Ministry Grants, 3029
Mary's Pence Study Grants, 3030
Regional Fund for Digital Innovation in Latin America and the Caribbean Grants, 4049
USAID Development Assistance Fund Grants, 4748

Philippines
Bechtel Group Fndn Building Positive Community Relationships Grants, 715
Fluor Fndn Grants, 1875
H.B. Fuller Company Fndn Grants, 2183
Intel Int'l Community Grants, 2564
Nike Fndn Grants, 3441
OSF Burma Project/Southeast Asia Grants, 3702
Texas Instruments Arts and Culture Grants, 4596
Texas Instruments Civic and Business Grants, 4597
Texas Instruments Fndn Arts and Culture Grants, 4599

Poland
Advanced Micro Devices Comm Affairs Grants, 172
Bechtel Group Fndn Building Positive Community Relationships Grants, 715
Bill and Melinda Gates Library Grants, 768
Cargill Citizenship Corporate Giving Grants, 925
Charles Delmar Fndn Grants, 1039
Fluor Fndn Grants, 1875
Fluor Fndn Grants, 1875
Fulbright Business Grants in Spain, 1970
Kimball Int'l-Habig Fndn Grants, 2823
Medtronic Patient Link Grants, 3113
OSF Human Rights and Governance Grants, 3708
OSF Mental Health Initiative Grants, 3709
Sir Dorabji Tata Trust Grants for NGOs or Voluntary Organizations, 4370
Texas Instruments Arts and Culture Grants, 4596
Texas Instruments Civic and Business Grants, 4597
Texas Instruments Fndn Arts and Culture Grants, 4599
Turner Voices Corporate Contributions, 4682

Portugal
Advanced Micro Devices Comm Affairs Grants, 172
Cargill Citizenship Corporate Giving Grants, 925
Charles Delmar Fndn Grants, 1039
Fluor Fndn Grants, 1875
Fulbright Business Grants in Spain, 1970
Medtronic Patient Link Grants, 3113
Sir Dorabji Tata Trust Grants for NGOs or Voluntary Organizations, 4370
Texas Instruments Arts and Culture Grants, 4596
Texas Instruments Civic and Business Grants, 4597
Texas Instruments Fndn Arts and Culture Grants, 4599

Qatar
H.B. Fuller Company Fndn Grants, 2183
Nike Fndn Grants, 3441
OSF Arab Regional Office Grants, 3701

Romania
Advanced Micro Devices Comm Affairs Grants, 172
Bill and Melinda Gates Library Grants, 768
Cargill Citizenship Corporate Giving Grants, 925
Charles Delmar Fndn Grants, 1039
Fluor Fndn Grants, 1875
Fulbright Business Grants in Spain, 1970
GMFUS Black Sea Trust for Regional Corporation Grants, 2065
OSF Advancing the Rights and Integration of Roma Grants, 3699
OSF Mental Health Initiative Grants, 3709
Sir Dorabji Tata Trust Grants for NGOs or Voluntary Organizations, 4370
Texas Instruments Arts and Culture Grants, 4596
Texas Instruments Civic and Business Grants, 4597
Texas Instruments Arts and Culture Grants, 4599
Turner Voices Corporate Contributions, 4682

Russia
Advanced Micro Devices Comm Affairs Grants, 172
Bechtel Group Fndn Building Positive Community Relationships Grants, 715
Cargill Citizenship Corporate Giving Grants, 925
Charles Delmar Fndn Grants, 1039
Fluor Fndn Grants, 1875
Fluor Fndn Grants, 1875
Fulbright Business Grants in Spain, 1970
GMFUS Black Sea Trust for Regional Corporation Grants, 2065
H.B. Fuller Company Fndn Grants, 2183
Intel Int'l Community Grants, 2564
IREX Russia Civil Society Support Grants, 2580
Nike Fndn Grants, 3441
OSF Human Rights and Governance Grants, 3708
OSF Mental Health Initiative Grants, 3709
Sir Dorabji Tata Trust Grants for NGOs or Voluntary Organizations, 4370
Turner Voices Corporate Contributions, 4682

Russian Federation
Texas Instruments Arts and Culture Grants, 4596
Texas Instruments Civic and Business Grants, 4597
Texas Instruments Fndn Arts and Culture Grants, 4599

Rwanda
Acumen East Africa Fellowship, 141
Aid for Starving Children Int'l Grants, 212
Cargill Citizenship Corporate Giving Grants, 925
Firelight Fndn Grants, 1817
Gregory C. Carr Fndn Grants, 2161
IREX Small Grant Fund for Civil Society Projects in Africa and Asia, 2581
IREX Small Grant Fund for Media Projects in Africa and Asia, 2582
Liz Claiborne and Art Ortenberg Grants, 2914
Murphy Institute Judith Kelleher Schafer Summer Internship Grants, 3230
Nike Fndn Grants, 3441
Nuffield Fndn Africa Grants, 3532
USAID African Institutions Innovation Mechanism Grants, 4739
USAID African Institutions Innovation Mechanism Grants, 4738

San Marino
Advanced Micro Devices Comm Affairs Grants, 172
Cargill Citizenship Corporate Giving Grants, 925
Charles Delmar Fndn Grants, 1039
Fluor Fndn Grants, 1875
Fulbright Business Grants in Spain, 1970
Sir Dorabji Tata Trust Grants for NGOs or Voluntary Organizations, 4370

Sao Tome & Principe
Aid for Starving Children Int'l Grants, 212
Cargill Citizenship Corporate Giving Grants, 925
Gregory C. Carr Fndn Grants, 2161
IREX Small Grant Fund for Civil Society Projects in Africa and Asia, 2581
IREX Small Grant Fund for Media Projects in Africa and Asia, 2582
Liz Claiborne and Art Ortenberg Grants, 2914
Murphy Institute Judith Kelleher Schafer Summer Internship Grants, 3230
Nike Fndn Grants, 3441
Nuffield Fndn Africa Grants, 3532

Saudi Arabia
H.B. Fuller Company Fndn Grants, 2183
Nike Fndn Grants, 3441
OSF Arab Regional Office Grants, 3701

Senegal
Aid for Starving Children Int'l Grants, 212
Cargill Citizenship Corporate Giving Grants, 925
Gregory C. Carr Fndn Grants, 2161
IREX Small Grant Fund for Civil Society Projects in Africa and Asia, 2581
IREX Small Grant Fund for Media Projects in Africa and Asia, 2582
Liz Claiborne and Art Ortenberg Grants, 2914
Murphy Institute Judith Kelleher Schafer Summer Internship Grants, 3230
Nike Fndn Grants, 3441
Nuffield Fndn Africa Grants, 3532

Serbia
Advanced Micro Devices Comm Affairs Grants, 172
Cargill Citizenship Corporate Giving Grants, 925
Charles Delmar Fndn Grants, 1039
Fluor Fndn Grants, 1875
Fulbright Business Grants in Spain, 1970
IIE Eurobank EFG Scholarships, 2455
OSF Advancing the Rights and Integration of Roma Grants, 3699
OSF European Comm Internships for Young Roma Graduates, 3707
OSF Mental Health Initiative Grants, 3709
Sir Dorabji Tata Trust Grants for NGOs or Voluntary Organizations, 4370
USAID Call for Public-Private Alliance Proposals in Serbia, 4742

Seychelles
Aid for Starving Children Int'l Grants, 212
Cargill Citizenship Corporate Giving Grants, 925
Gregory C. Carr Fndn Grants, 2161
IREX Small Grant Fund for Civil Society Projects in Africa and Asia, 2581
IREX Small Grant Fund for Media Projects in Africa and Asia, 2582
Liz Claiborne and Art Ortenberg Grants, 2914
Murphy Institute Judith Kelleher Schafer Summer Internship Grants, 3230
Nike Fndn Grants, 3441
Nuffield Fndn Africa Grants, 3532

Sierra Leone
Aid for Starving Children Int'l Grants, 212
Cargill Citizenship Corporate Giving Grants, 925
Gregory C. Carr Fndn Grants, 2161
IREX Small Grant Fund for Civil Society Projects in Africa and Asia, 2581

GEOGRAPHIC INDEX

IREX Small Grant Fund for Media Projects in Africa and Asia, 2582
Liz Claiborne and Art Ortenberg Grants, 2914
Murphy Institute Judith Kelleher Schafer Summer Internship Grants, 3230
Nike Fndn Grants, 3441
Nuffield Fndn Africa Grants, 3532

Singapore
H.B. Fuller Company Fndn Grants, 2183
Micron Tech Fndn Community Grants, 3161
Nike Fndn Grants, 3441
OSF Burma Project/Southeast Asia Grants, 3702
Sands Fndn Crisis Fund Grants, 4254
Sands Fndn Grants, 4255
Seagate Technology Corporation Capacity to Care Grants, 4317
Texas Instruments Arts and Culture Grants, 4596
Texas Instruments Civic and Business Grants, 4597
Texas Instruments Fndn Arts and Culture Grants, 4599
Turner Voices Corporate Contributions, 4682

Slovakia
Advanced Micro Devices Comm Affairs Grants, 172
Cargill Citizenship Corporate Giving Grants, 925
Charles Delmar Fndn Grants, 1039
Fluor Fndn Grants, 1875
Fulbright Business Grants in Spain, 1970
OSF Advancing the Rights and Integration of Roma Grants, 3699
OSF Human Rights and Governance Grants, 3708
OSF Mental Health Initiative Grants, 3709
Sir Dorabji Tata Trust Grants for NGOs or Voluntary Organizations, 4370

Slovenia
Advanced Micro Devices Comm Affairs Grants, 172
Cargill Citizenship Corporate Giving Grants, 925
Charles Delmar Fndn Grants, 1039
Fluor Fndn Grants, 1875
Fulbright Business Grants in Spain, 1970
OSF Human Rights and Governance Grants, 3708
OSF Mental Health Initiative Grants, 3709
Sir Dorabji Tata Trust Grants for NGOs or Voluntary Organizations, 4370

Somalia
Acumen East Africa Fellowship, 141
Aid for Starving Children Int'l Grants, 212
Cargill Citizenship Corporate Giving Grants, 925
Gregory C. Carr Fndn Grants, 2161
IREX Small Grant Fund for Civil Society Projects in Africa and Asia, 2581
IREX Small Grant Fund for Media Projects in Africa and Asia, 2582
Liz Claiborne and Art Ortenberg Grants, 2914
Murphy Institute Judith Kelleher Schafer Summer Internship Grants, 3230
Nike Fndn Grants, 3441
Nuffield Fndn Africa Grants, 3532
OSF Arab Regional Office Grants, 3701
USAID African Institutions Innovation Mechanism Grants, 4739

South Africa
Aid for Starving Children Int'l Grants, 212
Cargill Citizenship Corporate Giving Grants, 925
Firelight Fndn Grants, 1817
Gregory C. Carr Fndn Grants, 2161
IREX Small Grant Fund for Civil Society Projects in Africa and Asia, 2581
IREX Small Grant Fund for Media Projects in Africa and Asia, 2582
Liz Claiborne and Art Ortenberg Grants, 2914
Michael and Susan Dell Fndn Grants, 3158
Murphy Institute Judith Kelleher Schafer Summer Internship Grants, 3230
Nike Fndn Grants, 3441
Nuffield Fndn Africa Grants, 3532
Oak Fndn Child Abuse Grants, 3632

Turner Voices Corporate Contributions, 4682
USAID Comprehensive District-Based Support for Better HIV/TB Patient Outcomes Grants, 4747
USAID Integration of Care and Support within the Health System to Support Better Patient Outcomes Grants, 4762
USAID Malawi Local Capacity Development Initiative Grants, 4767
USAID Service Delivery and Support for Families Caring For Orphans and Vulnerable Children Grants, 4781
USAID Systems Strengthening for Better HIV/TB Patient Outcomes Grants, 4785

South Korea
H.B. Fuller Company Fndn Grants, 2183
Nike Fndn Grants, 3441
Prudential Spirit of Community Awards, 3978

South Ossetia
H.B. Fuller Company Fndn Grants, 2183
Nike Fndn Grants, 3441

Spain
Advanced Micro Devices Comm Affairs Grants, 172
Cargill Citizenship Corporate Giving Grants, 925
Charles Delmar Fndn Grants, 1039
Fluor Fndn Grants, 1875
Fulbright Business Grants in Spain, 1970
Medtronic Patient Link Grants, 3113
OSF Advancing the Rights and Integration of Roma Grants, 3699
Sir Dorabji Tata Trust Grants for NGOs or Voluntary Organizations, 4370
Texas Instruments Arts and Culture Grants, 4596
Texas Instruments Civic and Business Grants, 4597
Texas Instruments Fndn Arts and Culture Grants, 4599
Turner Voices Corporate Contributions, 4682

Sri Lanka
H.B. Fuller Company Fndn Grants, 2183
Nike Fndn Grants, 3441

Sudan
Acumen East Africa Fellowship, 141
Aid for Starving Children Int'l Grants, 212
Cargill Citizenship Corporate Giving Grants, 925
Gregory C. Carr Fndn Grants, 2161
IREX Small Grant Fund for Civil Society Projects in Africa and Asia, 2581
IREX Small Grant Fund for Media Projects in Africa and Asia, 2582
Liz Claiborne and Art Ortenberg Grants, 2914
Murphy Institute Judith Kelleher Schafer Summer Internship Grants, 3230
Nike Fndn Grants, 3441
Nuffield Fndn Africa Grants, 3532
OSF Arab Regional Office Grants, 3701
USAID African Institutions Innovation Mechanism Grants, 4739
USAID African Institutions Innovation Mechanism Grants, 4738

Swaziland
Aid for Starving Children Int'l Grants, 212
Cargill Citizenship Corporate Giving Grants, 925
Gregory C. Carr Fndn Grants, 2161
IREX Small Grant Fund for Civil Society Projects in Africa and Asia, 2581
IREX Small Grant Fund for Media Projects in Africa and Asia, 2582
Liz Claiborne and Art Ortenberg Grants, 2914
Murphy Institute Judith Kelleher Schafer Summer Internship Grants, 3230
Nike Fndn Grants, 3441
Nuffield Fndn Africa Grants, 3532

Sweden
Advanced Micro Devices Comm Affairs Grants, 172
Cargill Citizenship Corporate Giving Grants, 925

Charles Delmar Fndn Grants, 1039
Fluor Fndn Grants, 1875
Fulbright Business Grants in Spain, 1970
Medtronic Patient Link Grants, 3113
Sir Dorabji Tata Trust Grants for NGOs or Voluntary Organizations, 4370
Texas Instruments Arts and Culture Grants, 4596
Texas Instruments Civic and Business Grants, 4597
Texas Instruments Fndn Arts and Culture Grants, 4599
Turner Voices Corporate Contributions, 4682

Switzerland
Advanced Micro Devices Comm Affairs Grants, 172
Cabot Corporation Fndn Grants, 887
Cargill Citizenship Corporate Giving Grants, 925
Charles Delmar Fndn Grants, 1039
Fluor Fndn Grants, 1875
Fulbright Business Grants in Spain, 1970
Medtronic CommunityLink Health Grants, 3111
Medtronic Patient Link Grants, 3113
Oak Fndn Child Abuse Grants, 3632
OSF Human Rights and Governance Grants, 3708
Sir Dorabji Tata Trust Grants for NGOs or Voluntary Organizations, 4370
Texas Instruments Arts and Culture Grants, 4596
Texas Instruments Civic and Business Grants, 4597
Texas Instruments Fndn Arts and Culture Grants, 4599

Syria
H.B. Fuller Company Fndn Grants, 2183
Nike Fndn Grants, 3441
OSF Arab Regional Office Grants, 3701

Taiwan
H.B. Fuller Company Fndn Grants, 2183
Nike Fndn Grants, 3441
Prudential Spirit of Community Awards, 3978
Texas Instruments Arts and Culture Grants, 4596
Texas Instruments Civic and Business Grants, 4597
Texas Instruments Fndn Arts and Culture Grants, 4599
Turner Voices Corporate Contributions, 4682

Tajikistan
H.B. Fuller Company Fndn Grants, 2183
Nike Fndn Grants, 3441
OSF Central Eurasia Project Grants, 3704

Tanzania
Acumen East Africa Fellowship, 141
Better Way Fndn Grants, 754
Firelight Fndn Grants, 1817
Oak Fndn Child Abuse Grants, 3632
USAID African Institutions Innovation Mechanism Grants, 4739
USAID African Institutions Innovation Mechanism Grants, 4738
USAID Malawi Local Capacity Development Initiative Grants, 4767

Thailand
H.B. Fuller Company Fndn Grants, 2183
Nike Fndn Grants, 3441
OSF Burma Project/Southeast Asia Grants, 3702
Seagate Technology Corporation Capacity to Care Grants, 4317
Texas Instruments Arts and Culture Grants, 4596
Texas Instruments Civic and Business Grants, 4597
Texas Instruments Fndn Arts and Culture Grants, 4599
Turner Voices Corporate Contributions, 4682

The Netherlands
Advanced Micro Devices Comm Affairs Grants, 172
Cargill Citizenship Corporate Giving Grants, 925
Charles Delmar Fndn Grants, 1039
Fluor Fndn Grants, 1875
Fulbright Business Grants in Spain, 1970
Medtronic Patient Link Grants, 3113
Sir Dorabji Tata Trust Grants for NGOs or Voluntary Organizations, 4370

Timor-Lester
H.B. Fuller Company Fndn Grants, 2183
Nike Fndn Grants, 3441
OSF Burma Project/Southeast Asia Grants, 3702

Tunisia
OSF Arab Regional Office Grants, 3701

Turkey
Advanced Micro Devices Comm Affairs Grants, 172
Cargill Citizenship Corporate Giving Grants, 925
Charles Delmar Fndn Grants, 1039
Fluor Fndn Grants, 1875
Fulbright Business Grants in Spain, 1970
GMFUS Black Sea Trust for Regional Corporation Grants, 2065
H.B. Fuller Company Fndn Grants, 2183
Nike Fndn Grants, 3441
Sir Dorabji Tata Trust Grants for NGOs or Voluntary Organizations, 4370
Texas Instruments Arts and Culture Grants, 4596
Texas Instruments Civic and Business Grants, 4597
Texas Instruments Fndn Arts and Culture Grants, 4599
Turner Voices Corporate Contributions, 4682

Turkmenistan
H.B. Fuller Company Fndn Grants, 2183
Nike Fndn Grants, 3441
OSF Central Eurasia Project Grants, 3704

Uganda
Acumen East Africa Fellowship, 141
Firelight Fndn Grants, 1817
Oak Fndn Child Abuse Grants, 3632
USAID African Institutions Innovation Mechanism Grants, 4739
USAID African Institutions Innovation Mechanism Grants, 4738

Ukraine
Advanced Micro Devices Comm Affairs Grants, 172
Bill and Melinda Gates Library Grants, 768
Cargill Citizenship Corporate Giving Grants, 925
Charles Delmar Fndn Grants, 1039
Fluor Fndn Grants, 1875
Fulbright Business Grants in Spain, 1970
GMFUS Black Sea Trust for Regional Corporation Grants, 2065
John Deere Fndn Grants, 2692
OSF Human Rights and Governance Grants, 3708
Sir Dorabji Tata Trust Grants for NGOs or Voluntary Organizations, 4370
US CRDF Science and Technology Entrepreneurship Business Partnership Grant Competition, 4795
US CRDF STEP Business Partnership Grant Competition Ukraine, 4796

United Arab Emirates
H.B. Fuller Company Fndn Grants, 2183
Nike Fndn Grants, 3441
OSF Arab Regional Office Grants, 3701
Turner Voices Corporate Contributions, 4682

United Kingdom
Abbey Charitable Trust Grants, 78
ADC Fndn Technology Access Grants, 158
Advanced Micro Devices Comm Affairs Grants, 172
Allen Lane Fndn Grants, 379
Bank of America Charitable Matching Gifts, 658
Bank of America Charitable Volunteer Grants, 660
Baring Fndn Grants, 667
Bechtel Group Fndn Building Positive Community Relationships Grants, 715
Cabot Corporation Fndn Grants, 887
Cargill Citizenship Corporate Giving Grants, 925
Cash 4 Clubs Sports Grants, 951
Charles Delmar Fndn Grants, 1039
Commonwealth Fund Harkness Fellowships in Health Care Policy and Practice, 1242
Computer Associates Community Grants, 1341
Cooper Industries Fndn Grants, 1370
Fluor Fndn Grants, 1875
Fulbright Business Grants in Spain, 1970
Gannett Found Community Action Grants, 1984
Lincoln Financial Group Fndn Grants, 2906
May and Stanley Smith Charitable Trust Grants, 3069
Medtronic Patient Link Grants, 3113
Nuffield Fndn Africa Grants, 3532
Nuffield Found Children and Families Grants, 3533
Nuffield Fndn Open Door Grants, 3534
Nuffield Fndn Small Grants, 3535
Oak Fndn Child Abuse Grants, 3632
Oak Housing and Homelessness Grants, 3633
PACCAR Fndn Grants, 3719
Saint Paul Companies Fndn Grants, 4217
Sir Dorabji Tata Trust Grants for NGOs or Voluntary Organizations, 4370
Sylvia Adams Charitable Trust Grants, 4543
Turner Voices Corporate Contributions, 4682

Uruguay
Katherine John Murphy Fndn Grants, 2790

Uzbekistan
H.B. Fuller Company Fndn Grants, 2183
Nike Fndn Grants, 3441
OSF Central Eurasia Project Grants, 3704

Vatican City
Advanced Micro Devices Comm Affairs Grants, 172
Cargill Citizenship Corporate Giving Grants, 925
Charles Delmar Fndn Grants, 1039
Fluor Fndn Grants, 1875
Fulbright Business Grants in Spain, 1970
Medtronic Patient Link Grants, 3113
Sir Dorabji Tata Trust Grants for NGOs or Voluntary Organizations, 4370

Venezuela
Fluor Fndn Grants, 1875
Katherine John Murphy Fndn Grants, 2790

Vietnam
Bill and Melinda Gates Library Grants, 768
H.B. Fuller Company Fndn Grants, 2183
Nike Fndn Grants, 3441
OSF Burma Project/Southeast Asia Grants, 3702
Texas Instruments Arts and Culture Grants, 4596
Texas Instruments Civic and Business Grants, 4597
Texas Instruments Fndn Arts and Culture Grants, 4599

Yemen
H.B. Fuller Company Fndn Grants, 2183
Nike Fndn Grants, 3441
OSF Arab Regional Office Grants, 3701

Zambia
Firelight Fndn Grants, 1817

Zimbabwe
Firelight Fndn Grants, 1817

Printed in the USA
CPSIA information can be obtained
at www.ICGtesting.com
LVHW081308271023
762324LV00012B/215